PUBLIC LIBRARY CORE COLLECTION: NONFICTION

CORE COLLECTION SERIES

**FORMERLY
STANDARD CATALOG SERIES**

SHAUNA GRIFFIN, MLIS, GENERAL EDITOR

**CHILDREN'S CORE COLLECTION
FICTION CORE COLLECTION
GRAPHIC NOVELS CORE COLLECTION
MIDDLE AND JUNIOR HIGH CORE COLLECTION
PUBLIC LIBRARY CORE COLLECTION: NONFICTION
SENIOR HIGH CORE COLLECTION
YOUNG ADULT FICTION CORE COLLECTION**

PUBLIC LIBRARY CORE COLLECTION: NONFICTION

Twentieth Edition

Volume 2

EDITED BY
KENDAL SPIRES

H. W. Wilson
A Division of EBSCO Information Services, Inc.
Ipswich, Massachusetts
2025

GREY HOUSE PUBLISHING

Cover: iStock

Copyright © 2025 by H. W. Wilson, A Division of EBSCO Information Services, Inc. All rights reserved. No part of this work may be used or reproduced in any manner whatsoever or transmitted in any form or by any means, electronic or mechanical, including photocopy, recording, or any information storage and retrieval system, without written permission from the copyright owner. For permissions requests, contact proprietarypublishing@ebsco.com.

ISBN 979-8-89179-060-5

The Dewey Decimal Classification is © 2003-2017 OCLC Online Computer Library Center, Inc. Used with Permission. DDC, Dewey, Dewey Decimal Classification and WebDewey are registered trademarks/service marks of OCLC Online Computer Library Center, Inc.

Public Library Core Collection: Nonfiction, Twentieth Edition, published by Grey House Publishing, Inc., Amenia, NY, under exclusive license from EBSCO Information Services, Inc.

CONTENTS

Preface vii
Purpose and Organization xi
Acknowledgments... xv
Volume 1. Essential and Recommended Titles 1
Volume 2. Author, Title, Series, and Subject Index 1553

PREFACE

PUBLIC LIBRARY CORE COLLECTION: NONFICTION is a curated list of nonfiction titles for adults that may be used to develop a collection serving general readers in public libraries of all sizes. It also includes professional materials for librarians, including titles focusing on collection development, readers' advisory, reference, and managing a public library.

This Core Collection is an abridgment of the database available from EBSCO Information Services, which has an additional two recommendation levels, Lexile measures, book reviews and articles, and expanded metadata. It is updated weekly. Contact your EBSCO or NoveList sales rep for a free trial, or visit https://www.ebscohost.com/novelist/our-products/core-collections for more information. EBSCO also invites feedback from Core Collections customers at novelist@ebsco.com.

What's in this Edition?

This edition continues to emphasize equity, diversity, and inclusion, representing and reflecting a varied community in which many voices can be heard. Significant weeding is undertaken to ensure that older, outdated books are removed in favor of more relevant recommendations.

With more than 11,000 nonfiction titles appropriate to general adult readers as well as a selection of professional materials of use to librarians and library administrators, this 20th edition contains both new titles that reflect new topics of interest or new interpretations of traditional knowledge as well as older titles—sometimes in updated versions—that remain the best in their field.

As always, a star (★) at the start of an entry indicates that a book is an *Essential* title, our highest recommendation level. These titles are the essential books in a given category or on a given subject; while there are often a number of recommended titles, this designation helps users who want only a small selection. Non-starred entries represent *Recommended* titles, which provide a fuller list of recommended books. This is reflected in both the Classified section and, for the first time, in the Index as well.

History

The first of several installments of the "Standard Catalog" for the general library was published in 1918. It was called STANDARD CATALOG: SOCIOLOGY SECTION. Additional installments were issued over the next fourteen years, covering Biography; Fiction; Fine Arts; History and Travel; Science and Useful Arts; Literature and Philology; and Philosophy, Religion, and General Works. Finally, a fully integrated first edition of the STANDARD CATALOG FOR PUBLIC LIBRARIES was assembled and published in 1934. The contents were displayed in classified order, according to the Dewey Decimal Classification. The name was changed to PUBLIC LIBRARY CATALOG with the publication of the fifth edition in 1969, and then to PUBLIC LIBRARY CORE COLLECTION: NONFICTION with the thirteenth edition in 2008.

The collection subsequently evolved, along with other Core Collections, into an online resource called WilsonWeb. EBSCO Information Services acquired H.W. Wilson in 2011, and the collections became EBSCO*host* databases in 2012. In 2020, the readers' advisory experts at NoveList applied their expertise: while Core Collections continues to provide impartial collection development guidance by experts in their fields, this marriage of

PUBLIC LIBRARY CORE COLLECTION: NONFICTION
Twentieth Edition

readers advisory and collection development expertise strengthened the application of genre and subject headings, expanded awards content, and improved search and browse capabilities in the online Core Collections databases.

Scope

PUBLIC LIBRARY CORE COLLECTION: NONFICTION is a guide to nonfiction books published in the United States or published in other countries and distributed in the United States. It excludes non-print materials; periodicals; non-English items (with the exception of dictionaries); and works of an ephemeral nature. Original paperback materials are included. Multiple subjects provide access points via the subject index.

The Core Collection is intended to serve the needs of public and undergraduate libraries and stands as a basic or "opening day" collection. The newer titles help in identifying areas in a collection that can be updated or strengthened, while the retention of useful material from the previous edition enables the librarian to make informed decisions about weeding a collection. With its classified arrangement, complete bibliographical data, and descriptive and evaluative annotations, the Core Collection provides useful information for the acquisitions librarian, the reference librarian, and the cataloger.

Although a Fiction Section was issued in 1923, followed by supplements in 1928 and 1931, fiction was omitted from the first edition of the complete Catalog in 1934. A new expanded edition of the Fiction Section was published as FICTION CATALOG in 1942. In its preface, that Catalog was referred to as a "companion volume to the Standard Catalog for Public Libraries." This complementary relationship has continued to the present: PUBLIC LIBRARY COLRE COLLECTION: NONFICTION has always listed works of literary criticism and literary history, as well as books about literary technique.

Books are listed with an ISBN—most frequently for a hardcover edition published in the United States, or published in Canada or the United Kingdom and distributed in the U.S. Out-of-print titles are retained in the belief that good books are not obsolete simply because they happen to go out of print.

The Database

This Core Collection is derived from the database available from EBSCO Information Services. Metadata for the titles in this volume is provided by the metadata librarians at NoveList, who manage and apply a controlled vocabulary that adapts as terms come in and out of style, or as events require new ones. There are additional, browsable access points, plus full-text book reviews and articles, full-color cover art, Lexile measures, and all of the *Supplemental* book recommendations and *Weeded* titles. It is updated weekly. For more information or for a free trial, contact your EBSCO or NoveList sales rep, or visit https://www.ebscohost.com/novelist/our-products/core-collections. EBSCO also invites feedback from Core Collections customers at novelist@ebsco.com.

In 2017, EBSCO renamed the PUBLIC LIBRARY CORE COLLECTION: NONFICTION database. Now called NONFICTION CORE COLLECTION, it is in line with the other database names, is less cumbersome, and signifies its applicability to general readers in libraries of all types. Although the title of this edition is different from the database from which it is derived, it contains the same content, and is not a separate set of book recommendations.

PREFACE

Preparation

Books included in Core Collections are selected by experienced librarians representing public library systems, school libraries, and academic libraries across the United States and Canada, as well as NoveList staff. These librarians also act as advisors on library policy, trends, and special projects. The names of participating librarians and their affiliations are listed in the Acknowledgements.

Core Collections Products

For recommendations for children's books, librarians are encouraged to investigate the following databases and their associated print versions:

CHILDREN'S CORE COLLECTION
MIDDLE AND JUNIOR HIGH CORE COLLECTION
SENIOR HIGH CORE COLLECTION

For young adult fiction specifically, consult the YOUNG ADULT FICTION CORE COLLECTION, available only in print.

For adult nonfiction for the general reader, try the database NONFICTION CORE COLLECTION or the associated print volume PUBLIC LIBRARY CORE COLLECTION: NONFICTION. For fiction, please use FICTION CORE COLLECTION, either as a database or the associated print version.

For Graphic Novels for all ages, try the GRAPHIC NOVELS CORE COLLECTION in print or database form, which includes both fiction and nonfiction recommendations.

In 2023, the CORE COLLECTION EN ESPAÑOL was launched, which includes titles for a Spanish-speaking audience at all levels, available only as a database.

PURPOSE AND ORGANIZATION

PURPOSE

CORE COLLECTIONS is designed to serve a number of purposes:

As an aid in purchasing. Core Collections is designed to assist in the selection and ordering of titles. Summaries and evaluative excerpts are provided for each title along with information regarding the publisher, ISBN, page count, and publication year. In evaluating the suitability of a work, each library will want to consider the needs of the unique patron base it serves.

As an aid in verification of information. For this purpose, bibliographical information is provided in the list of works. Entries also include recommended subject headings based on NoveList's proprietary subject vocabulary. Notes may describe editions available and other content; for the most up-to-date metadata, please consult the EBSCO*host* database.

As an aid in curriculum or programming support. The classified approach, subject indexing, annotations, and evaluative excerpts are helpful in identifying materials appropriate for classroom support, for book discussions, and other programming.

As an aid in collection maintenance. Information about titles available on a subject facilitates decisions to rebind, replace, or discard items. If a book has been demoted to the Supplemental or Weeded recommendation levels and therefore no longer appears in the print abridgement of the database, that demotion is not intended as a sign that the book is no longer valuable or that it should necessarily be weeded from your library's collection.

As an aid in professional development or instruction. The Core Collection is useful in courses or professional training that deal with collection development and readers' advisory; it may also be used in course that deal with literature and book selection, especially in the creation of bibliographies and reading lists.

As an aid to readers' advisory. Every title in this Core Collection is a recommended work and can be given with confidence to a user who expresses a need based on topic, genre, etc. Readers' advisory and user service are further aided by series and awards information, by the descriptive summaries and evaluative excerpts from trusted review sources, and by the subject headings in the Title and Subject Index applied by professional metadata librarians at NoveList.

ORGANIZATION

This Core Collection consists of two parts: a list of Essential and Recommended Titles, found in Volume 1, and a Title, Author, Series, and Subject Index, found in Volume 2.

Volume 1. Essential and Recommended Titles

The list of Essential and Recommended Titles is arranged and classified according to the Dewey Decimal Classification in numerical order from 000 to 999. The exception is individual biographies, which are classed at 92 and

PUBLIC LIBRARY CORE COLLECTION: NONFICTION
Twentieth Edition

close out the collection. These will have a subject heading B and are organized by author. Locate biographies by subject by using the Author, Title, Series, and Subject Index.

An Outline of Classification, which serves as a table for contents for the list of Essential and Recommended Titles, is reproduced following this section. It should be noted that many topics can be classified in more than one discipline. If a particular title is not found where it might be expected, the Index should be consulted to determine if it is classified elsewhere.

Within classes, works are arranged alphabetically under main entry, first by author, then by title.

Each listing consists of a bibliographic description, suggested subject headings derived from NoveList, series and awards information where relevant, a suggested classification number from the *Abridged Dewey Decimal Classification and Relative Index*, a brief description of the contents of the book, and where possible an evaluative excerpt from a notable source. The following is an example of a typical entry and a description of its components.

> **Roach, Mary**
> ★ *Stiff: The Curious Lives of Human Cadavers*. Mary Roach.
> W.W. Norton & Co., 2003. 303 p. : Illustration
> ISBN 0393050939
> Grades: 11 12 Adult   **611**
>   1. Human experimentation in medicine 2. Dead 3. Human dissection 4. Medical research 5. Forensic sciences 6. Forensic scientists 7. Forensic medicine 8. Cannibalism 9. Transplantation of organs, tissues, etc. 10. True Crime—Forensic sciences 11. Science Writing—Biology 12. Adult books for young adults 13. Nonfiction that reads like fiction
>   LC 2002152908
> Alex Award, 2004 ; Booklist Editors' Choice: Adult Books for Young Adults, 2003 ; Garden State Teen Book Award (New Jersey), Nonfiction, 2006 ; School Library Journal Best Books: Best Adult Books 4 Teens, 2003 ; YALSA Best Books for Young Adults, 2004.
>   A look inside the world of forensics examines the use of human cadavers in a wide range of endeavors, including research into new surgical procedures, space exploration, and a Tennessee human decay research facility.
>   "Roach writes in an insouciant style and displays her metier in tangents about bizarre incidents in pathological history. Death may have the last laugh, but, in the meantime, Roach finds merriment in the macabre." —*Booklist*
>   Includes bibliographical references (p.[295]-303).

The name of the author, Mary Roach, is given in conformity with Library of Congress Authorities. The star at the start of the title indicates that this is an Essential title. The title of the book is Stiff: The Curious Lives of Human Cadavers. The book was published by W.W. Norton & Co. in 2003. It has 303 pages, and illustrations. If it were part of a series, the series name would follow this information.

PURPOSE AND ORGANIZATION

An ISBN (International Standard Book Number) is included to facilitate ordering; however, there will often be many editions and formats of a given title; due to space constraints these ISBNs are not provided in the print edition, though many can be found in the corresponding database.

This book is recommended for older teens (11th and 12th graders) and adutls, At the end of the last line of type in the body entry is 611 in boldface type. This is the classification number or category derived from the fifteenth edition of the *Abridged Dewey Decimal Classification*.

The numbered terms "1. Human experimentation in medicine. 2. Dead. 3. Human dissection. 4. Medical research." are recommended subject headings for this book.

The Library of Congress control number is provided when available.

Any awards the book has won, or notable lists the book has landed on, follows. In this case, the Alex Award, the Garden State Awards, and several lists. These are followed by a brief summary and an evaluative excerpt from a critical reviewing source, in this case Booklist. Such summaries and excerpts are useful in evaluating books for selection and in determining which of several books on the same subject is best suited for the individual reader or purchasing library.

Notes are also made to describe special features, such as a bibliography, if applicable. or to describe series order and companion volumes, editions available, awards, and publication history.

Volume 2. Author, Title, Series, and Subject Index

The Index is a single alphabetical list of all the books entered in the Core Collection. Each book is entered under author, title, series, and subject. The classification number, displayed in boldface type, is the key to the location of the main entry for the book in the list of Essential and Recommended titles. Biographies will have the subject indicator B.

The following are examples of index entries for the book cited above:

Author	**Roach, Mary** ★ *Stiff*	611
Title	★ *Stiff*. Roach, Mary	611
Subject	**HUMAN EXPERIMENTATION IN MEDICINE** Roach, Mary. ★ *Stiff*	611

ACKNOWLEDGMENTS

H.W. Wilson, NoveList, and EBSCO Information Services express special gratitude to the following librarians who advised on editorial matters and assisted in the selection and weeding of titles for this Core Collection.

Steven Ashley
Librarian
Carrboro, North Carolina

Manda Carr
Librarian
Troy Public Library
Troy, MI

Cassidy Charles
Legislative Data Analysis Librarian
Library of Congress
Washington, DC

Laura Cohen
Readers & Information Services Librarian
Vernon Area Public Library District
Lincolnshire, IL

Heather Cover
Special Projects Librarian
Homewood Public Library
Homewood, AL

Andrienne Cruz
Librarian
Azusa City Library
Azusa, CA

Gail de Vos
Storyteller & Adjunct Instructor, SLIS
University of Alberta, Edmonton
Canada

Brian Flota
Humanities Librarian
James Madison University
Harrisonburg, VA

Francisca Goldsmith
Library and Media Consultant
Worcester, MA

Patrick Holt
Graphic Designer and Former Librarian
Durham, NC

Malia Jackson
Freelance librarian
Bloomington, IN

Jane Jorgenson
Library Supervisor
Madison Public LIbrary
Madison, WI

Angela Leeper
Director, Curricular Materials Center
University of Richmond
Richmond, Virginia

Marcela Peres
Director
Lewiston Public Library
Lewiston, Maine

Stephanie Sendaula
Programming & Outreach Specialist
LibraryLinkNJ
Ewing, NJ

Sara Shiver McBride
Librarian
Richland Library
Columbia, SC

Jennie Stevens
Teen Librarian
Naperville Public Library
Naperville, IL

Sarah Bean Thompson
Youth Services Manager
Springfield-Green County
Springfield, Missouri

PUBLIC LIBRARY CORE COLLECTION: NONFICTION
Twentieth Edition

Rebecca Vargha
Head Librarian
School of Information and Library Science
UNC-Chapel Hill
Chapel Hill, NC

Basia Wilson
Poet & NoveList Advisor
Collingswood, New Jersey

AUTHOR, TITLE, SERIES, AND SUBJECT INDEX

This index to the books in the Classified List of Works includes author, title, series, and subject entries all arranged in one alphabet. The number or symbol in at the end of each entry refers to the Dewey Decimal Classification or to the Biography (B) section where the main entry for the book will be found.

★*1,000 Books to Read*. Mustich, James	028
1-2-3 Magic. Phelan, Thomas W.	649
21. Santiago, Wilfred	741.5
★*21 Lessons for the 21st Century*. Harari, Yuval N.	909.82
★*21st Century Monetary Policy*. Bernanke, Ben	332.1
24. Mays, Willie	B
24 Hours in Charlottesville. Neus, Nora	973.933
24/6. Shlain, Tiffany	158.1
25 Great Sentences and How They Got That Way. Woods, Geraldine	808
26 Marathons. Keflezighi, Meb	B
27 Essential Principles of Story. Rubin, Daniel Joshua	808.02
3 Kings. Greenburg, Zack O'Malley	782.421649
3 Shades of Blue. Kaplan, James	920
30 Animals That Made Us Smarter. Aryee, Patrick	590
The 30 Day Sobriety Solution. Canfield, Jack	616.89
32 Yolks. Ripert, Eric	B
33 Revolutions per Minute. Lynskey, Dorian	782.42
The 34-Ton Bat. Rushin, Steve	796.357
350+ Crochet Tips, Techniques, and Trade Secrets. Eaton, Jan	746.432
★*The 36-Hour Day*. Mace, Nancy L.	616.8
37 Words. Boschert, Sherry	344.73
The 37th Parallel. Mezrich, Ben	001.942
★*38 Nooses*. Berg, Scott W.	973.7
The 272. Swarns, Rachel L.	975.2
40 Million Slaves. Rhoden, William C.	796
41. Bush, George W.	B
438 Days. Franklin, Jonathan	910.91
4th and Goal Every Day. Savage, Phil	796.332
4TH CENTURY	
Wills, Garry. *Saint Augustine*	B
The 5 Principles of Parenting. Pressman, Aliza	649.1
50 CENT (MUSICIAN)	
Jackson, Curtis. *Hustle Harder, Hustle Smarter*	B
50 Children. Pressman, Steven	940.53
50 Great American Places. Glass, Brent D	973
50 Inventions That Shaped the Modern Economy. Harford, Tim	609
50 Knitted Wraps and Shawls. Noldeke, Marisa	746.43
500 Crochet Stitches. Knight, Erika	746.43
52 Small Changes for the Mind. Blumenthal, Brett	616.89
52 Ways to Walk. Streets, Annabel	796.51
6 Spices 60 Dishes. Kahate, Ruta	641.595
60 Songs That Explain the '90s. Harvilla, Rob	782.42164
6TH CENTURY	
Puhak, Shelley. *The Dark Queens*	944
★*The 7 Habits of Highly Effective People*. Covey, Stephen R.	158
750 Knitting Stitches. Knight, Erika	746.43
8 Billion and Counting. Sciubba, Jennifer Dabbs	304.6
81 Days Below Zero. Murphy, Brian	940.54
85 Years of the Oscar. Osborne, Robert	791.43079
The 8th Habit. Covey, Stephen R.	158
The 9-11 Report. Jacobson, Sidney	741.5
99. Gretzky, Wayne	B
99 Poems. Gioia, Dana	811
★*The 99% Invisible City*. Mars, Roman	720
999. Macadam, Heather Dune	940.53
9TH CENTURY	
Winder, Simon. *Lotharingia*	944
100 Amazing Facts About the Negro. Gates, Henry Louis	973
★*100 Days of Real Food*. Leake, Lisa	641.5
100 Days of Real Food on a Budget. Leake, Lisa	641.5
100 Flowers to Knit & Crochet. Stanfield, Lesley	746.43
100 Morning Treats. Kieffer, Sarah	641.5
★*100 Places to See After You Die*. Jennings, Ken	202
★*100 Plants to Feed the Birds*. Erickson, Laura	635

100 Suns. Light, Michael	779
1000 Words. Attenberg, Jami	808.02
1000 Years of Joys and Sorrows. Ai, Weiwei	709.2
101 Asian Dishes You Need to Cook Before You Die. Tila, Jet	641.595
101 Magic Tricks. Miles, Bryan	793.8
101 Top Tips from Professional Manga Artists. Leong, Sonia	741.5
102 Minutes. Dwyer, Jim	974.7
10TH CENTURY	
Hansen, Valerie. *The Year 1000*	909
10 Granny Squares, 30 Blankets. Hubert, Margaret	746.43
10 Keys to Happier Living. King, Vanessa	158
★*10% Happier*. Harris, Dan	158.1
10% Human. Collen, Alanna	612.3
11TH CENTURY	
Morris, Marc. *The Norman Conquest*	942.02
12 Strong. Stanton, Doug	958.104
12TH CENTURY	
Asbridge, Thomas S. *The Greatest Knight*	942.03
13 Things Mentally Strong Parents Don't Do. Morin, Amy	649
13 Things Mentally Strong Women Don't Do. Morin, Amy	158.1
13th Balloon. Bibbins, Mark	813
13TH CENTURY	
Bergreen, Laurence. *Marco Polo*	B
Morris, Marc. *A Great and Terrible King*	B
Morris, Marc. *King John*	942.033
140 Days to Hiroshima. Barrett, David Dean	940.54
1453. Crowley, Roger	949.61
★*1491*. Mann, Charles C.	970.01
14TH CENTURY	
Harrington, Joel F. *Dangerous Mystic*	B
Jones, Michael K. *The Black Prince*	B
Kelly, John. *The Great Mortality*	614.5
Tuchman, Barbara W. ★*A Distant Mirror*	944
150 Glimpses of the Beatles. Brown, Craig	920
150+ Screen-Free Activities for Kids. Citro, Asia	796.5
15TH CENTURY	
Barker, Juliet R. V. *Agincourt*	944
Benner, Erica. *Be Like the Fox*	B
Borman, Tracy. *The Private Lives of the Tudors*	920
Castor, Helen. *Joan of Arc*	B
Downey, Kirstin. *Isabella*	B
Felder, Deborah G. *The American Women's Almanac*	305.40973
Greenblatt, Stephen. ★*The Swerve*	940.2
Gristwood, Sarah. *Blood Sisters*	942.04092
Gristwood, Sarah. *The Tudors in Love*	941.05
Hibbert, Christopher. *The Borgias and Their Enemies*	920
Jager, Eric. *Blood Royal*	944.026
Jones, Dan. ★*The Wars of the Roses*	942.04
King, Ross. *Brunelleschi's Dome*	726.6
King, Ross. ★*Leonardo and the Last Supper*	759.5
Man, John. *Ninja*	355.5
Meyer, G. J. *The Borgias*	920
Mikhail, Alan. *God's Shadow*	B
Penn, Thomas. *The Brothers York*	942.04
Shaw, Bernard. *Saint Joan*	822
Spoto, Donald. *Joan*	B
Strathern, Paul. *The Borgias*	945.06
Tallis, Nicola. *Uncrowned Queen*	B
Weir, Alison. *The Wars of the Roses*	942.04
Wilson-Lee, Edward. ★*The Catalogue of Shipwrecked Books*	B
1690S	
Schiff, Stacy. *The Witches*	345
16TH CENTURY	
Alexander, Amir R. *Infinitesimal*	511
Bakewell, Sarah. *How to Live—Or—A Life of Montaigne*	B

PUBLIC LIBRARY CORE COLLECTION: NONFICTION
Twentieth Edition

Benner, Erica. *Be Like the Fox*	B
Bergreen, Laurence. *In Search of a Kingdom*	B
Bergreen, Laurence. *Over the Edge of the World*	B
Borman, Tracy. *Elizabeth's Women*	B
Borman, Tracy. *The Private Lives of the Tudors*	920
Borman, Tracy. *Thomas Cromwell*	B
Bradford, Sarah. *Lucrezia Borgia*	B
Bremer, Francis J. *John Winthrop*	B
Bryson, Bill. *Shakespeare*	B
Cervantes, Fernando. *Conquistadores*	970.01
Fauber, L. S. *Heaven on Earth*	B
Felder, Deborah G. *The American Women's Almanac*	305.40973
Fraser, Antonia. *Mary, Queen of Scots*	B
Fraser, Antonia. ★*The Wives of Henry VIII*	942.05
Goldstone, Nancy Bazelon. *The Rival Queens*	944
Goodman, Ruth. *How to Be a Tudor*	942.05
Goodman, Ruth. *How to Behave Badly in Elizabethan England*	942.05
Graham-Dixon, Andrew. *Caravaggio*	B
Greenblatt, Stephen. ★*The Swerve*	940.2
Greenblatt, Stephen. ★*Will in the World*	B
Gristwood, Sarah. *The Tudors in Love*	941.05
Guy, John. *Hunting the Falcon*	B
Hale, Sheila. *Titian*	B
Harrington, Joel F. *The Faithful Executioner*	B
Heaney, Christopher. *Cradle of Gold*	B
Horn, James P. P. *A Kingdom Strange*	975.6
King, Ross. *Michelangelo & the Pope's Ceiling*	759.5
Lawler, Andrew. *The Secret Token*	975.6
Lockley, Thomas. *African Samurai*	B
MacCulloch, Diarmaid. *The Reformation*	270.6
Metaxas, Eric. *Martin Luther*	B
Meyer, G. J. *The Tudors*	920
Mikhail, Alan. *God's Shadow*	B
Mortimer, Ian. *The Time Traveler's Guide to Elizabethan England*	942.05
Nicholl, Charles. *The Reckoning*	B
Nuttall, A. D. *Shakespeare the Thinker*	822.33
Oberman, Heiko Augustinus. *Luther*	B
Paranque, Estelle. *Blood, Fire & Gold*	920
Pettegree, Andrew. *The Book in the Renaissance*	070.5
Porter, Linda. *Katherine the Queen*	B
Restall, Matthew. *When Montezuma Met Cortes*	972
Ronald, Susan. *The Pirate Queen*	B
Rounding, Virginia. *The Burning Time*	272
Russell, Gareth. *Young and Damned and Fair*	B
Sobel, Dava. *A More Perfect Heaven*	520.9
Starkey, David. *Six Wives*	942.05
Strathern, Paul. *The Borgias*	945.06
Tallis, Nicola. *Crown of Blood*	B
Thomas, Hugh. *Rivers of Gold*	980
Unger, Miles. ★*Michelangelo*	B
Weir, Alison. *Henry VIII*	B
Weir, Alison. *The Lady in the Tower*	B
Weir, Alison. *The Life of Elizabeth I*	B
Weir, Alison. *The Lost Tudor Princess*	B
Weir, Alison. *Mary, Queen of Scots, and the Murder of Lord Darnley*	941.105
Weir, Alison. *The Six Wives of Henry VIII*	942.05
Wilson, Derek. *Out of the Storm*	B
Winkler, Elizabeth. *Shakespeare Was a Woman & Other Heresies*	822.33
17 Carnations. Morton, Andrew	941.084

1700S (DECADE)
Brooks, James. *Mesa of Sorrows*	979.1004

1770S
Ketchum, Richard M. *Saratoga*	973.3
Maier, Pauline. *American Scripture*	973.3
McCullough, David G. ★*1776*	973.3
Norton, Mary Beth. *1774*	973.3
Philbrick, Nathaniel. ★*Bunker Hill*	973.3
Rakove, Jack N. *Revolutionaries*	973.3
1774. Norton, Mary Beth	973.3
1775. Phillips, Kevin	973.3
★*1776*. McCullough, David G.	973.3

1780S
Broadwater, Jeff. ★*George Mason*	B
Ellis, Joseph J. ★*His Excellency*	B
Ellis, Joseph J. *The Quartet*	342.7302
Gordon-Reed, Annette. ★*Most Blessed of the Patriarchs*	973.4
Groom, Winston. *The Patriots*	920
Isaacson, Walter. ★*Benjamin Franklin*	B

Larson, Edward J. *The Return of George Washington*	B
Maier, Pauline. *American Scripture*	973.3
Middlekauff, Robert. *The Glorious Cause*	973.3
Philbrick, Nathaniel. ★*Bunker Hill*	973.3

1790S
Bell, Madison Smartt. *Toussaint Louverture*	B

17TH CENTURY
Ackroyd, Peter. *Rebellion*	941.06
Ackroyd, Peter. *Revolution*	941.07
Alexander, Amir R. *Infinitesimal*	511
Blom, Onno. *Young Rembrandt*	B
Bremer, Francis J. *John Winthrop*	B
Bunker, Nick. ★*Making Haste from Babylon*	974.4
Cohen, Eliot A. *Conquered into Liberty*	355.009747
Collins, Paul. *The Book of William*	016.8223
DeJean, Joan E. *The Essence of Style*	391
DeJean, Joan E. *How Paris Became Paris*	944
Descartes, Rene. ★*Descartes*	194
Dolnick, Edward. *Seeds of Life*	612.6
Felder, Deborah G. *The American Women's Almanac*	305.40973
Fischer, David Hackett. *Champlain's Dream*	B
Fraser, Antonia. *Faith and Treason*	942.06
Fraser, Antonia. *Love and Louis XIV*	B
Geck, Martin. ★*Johann Sebastian Bach*	780.92
Goldstone, Nancy Bazelon. *Daughters of the Winter Queen*	920
Graham-Dixon, Andrew. *Caravaggio*	B
Grayling, A. C. *The Age of Genius*	940.2
Greenblatt, Stephen. ★*The Swerve*	940.2
Gristwood, Sarah. *The Tudors in Love*	941.05
Horn, James P. P. *Land as God Made It*	975.5
Johnson, Steven. *Enemy of All Mankind*	910.4
Juana Ines de la Cruz, Sister. *Selected Works*	861
Kaufmann, Miranda. *Black Tudors*	941
Kritzler, Ed. *Jewish Pirates of the Caribbean*	972.9
Lepore, Jill. *The Name of War*	973.2
Mansel, Philip. *King of the World*	B
Mortimer, Ian. *The Time Traveler's Guide to Restoration Britain*	941.06
Murphy, Andrew R. *William Penn*	B
Pepys, Samuel. *The Diary of Samuel Pepys*	B
Pestana, Carla Gardina. *The World of Plymouth Plantation*	974.4
Philbrick, Nathaniel. ★*Mayflower*	973.2
Price, David A. ★*Love and Hate in Jamestown*	975.5
Schama, Simon. *The Embarrassment of Riches*	949.2
Schiff, Stacy. *The Witches*	345
Schultz, Eric B. *King Philip's War*	973.2
Shapiro, James. *The Year of Lear*	822.33
Smith, Emma. *This Is Shakespeare*	822.33
Snyder, Laura J. *Eye of the Beholder*	920
Stuart, Andrea. *Sugar in the Blood*	338.1
Thomson, Keith. *Born to Be Hanged*	910.4
Tomalin, Claire. *Samuel Pepys*	B
Whittock, Martyn. *Mayflower Lives*	974.4
Woolley, Benjamin. *The King's Assassin*	B
★*18 Tiny Deaths*. Goldfarb, Bruce	B

1800S (DECADE)
Bell, Madison Smartt. *Toussaint Louverture*	B
Kilmeade, Brian. ★*Thomas Jefferson and the Tripoli Pirates*	973.4
Sedgwick, John. *War of Two*	973.4

1810S
Snow, Peter. *When Britain Burned the White House*	975.3
Taylor, Alan. *The Civil War of 1812*	973.5
Taylor, Alan. ★*The Internal Enemy*	975.5
Wills, Garry. *James Madison*	B

1820S
Mazower, Mark. *The Greek Revolution*	949.5

1830S
Saunt, Claudio. *Unworthy Republic*	323.1197

1840S
Broyles, Michael. ★*Revolutions in American Music*	780.9
Carlsen, William. *Jungle of Stone*	B
Collins, Gail. *William Henry Harrison*	B
Crouch, Gregory. *The Bonanza King*	B
Crutchfield, James A. *Revolt at Taos*	972
Eisler, Benita. ★*Chopin's Funeral*	B
Puleo, Stephen. *Voyage of Mercy*	363.8

1852-1912
Keene, Donald. *Emperor of Japan*	952.03

1554

AUTHOR, TITLE, SERIES AND SUBJECT INDEX

1860S
Ayers, Edward L. ★*The Thin Light of Freedom*	975.5
Berg, Scott W. ★*38 Nooses*	973.7
Brands, H. W. ★*The Zealot and the Emancipator*	920
Burlingame, Michael. *Abraham Lincoln*	B
Egerton, Douglas R. *Thunder at the Gates*	973.7
Foner, Eric. *The Fiery Trial*	973.7092
Foner, Eric. ★*Reconstruction*	973.8
Foote, Shelby. *The Civil War*	973.7
Goodheart, Adam. *1861*	973.7
Goodwin, Doris Kearns. ★*Team of Rivals*	B
Groom, Winston. *Shiloh, 1862*	973.7
Horwitz, Tony. ★*Midnight Rising*	973.7
Keegan, John. *The American Civil War*	973.7
Langguth, A. J. *After Lincoln*	973.8
Levine, Bruce C. *Thaddeus Stevens*	B
Manning, Chandra. *Troubled Refuge*	973.7
McPherson, James M. *Battle Cry of Freedom*	973.7
McPherson, James M. *Drawn with the Sword*	973.7
McPherson, James M. *For Cause and Comrades*	973.7
Meltzer, Brad. *The Lincoln Conspiracy*	973.7092
Meyer, Eugene L. *Five for Freedom*	973.7
Reynolds, David S. *John Brown, Abolitionist*	B
Reynolds, David S. *Mightier Than the Sword*	813
Sandburg, Carl. *Abraham Lincoln*	B
Sears, Stephen W. *Gettysburg*	973.7
Stahr, Walter. *Seward*	B
Stiles, T. J. *Jesse James*	B
Widmer, Edward L. *Lincoln on the Verge*	B
Williams, David. *Bitterly Divided*	973.7
Willis, Deborah. *Envisioning Emancipation*	973.7
1861. Goodheart, Adam	

1870S
Ayers, Edward L. ★*The Thin Light of Freedom*	975.5
Connell, Evan S. *Son of the Morning Star*	973.8
Crosby, Molly Caldwell. *The American Plague*	614.5
De Waal, Edmund. *The Hare with Amber Eyes*	B
Foner, Eric. ★*Reconstruction*	973.8
Langguth, A. J. *After Lincoln*	973.8
Levine, Bruce C. *Thaddeus Stevens*	B
Mort, T. A. *Thieves' Road*	978.3
Philbrick, Nathaniel. ★*The Last Stand*	973.8
Sharfstein, Daniel J. ★*Thunder in the Mountains*	979.5
Sides, Hampton. ★*In the Kingdom of Ice*	910.4

1880S
Cornwell, Patricia Daniels. *Ripper*	364.152
Roker, Al. *Ruthless Tide*	974.8

1890S
Herlihy, David V. *The Lost Cyclist*	B
Larson, Erik. ★*The Devil in the White City*	364.15
Macy, Beth. ★*Truevine*	B
Okrent, Daniel. *The Guarded Gate*	344.73
Robertson, Cara. *The Trial of Lizzie Borden*	345.744
Sancton, Julian. *Madhouse at the End of the Earth*	919.8904

18TH CENTURY
Ackroyd, Peter. *Revolution*	941.07
Adams, John. *My Dearest Friend*	973.4
Alexander, Caroline. *The Bounty*	996.1
Allgor, Catherine. *A Perfect Union*	B
Avlon, John P. *Washington's Farewell*	973.4
Beeman, Richard R. *Our Lives, Our Fortunes and Our Sacred Honor*	973.3
Beeman, Richard R. ★*Plain, Honest Men*	342.7302
Bobrick, Benson. *Angel in the Whirlwind*	973.3
Boles, John B. *Jefferson*	B
Bordewich, Fergus M. *Washington*	975.3
Boswell, James. ★*The Life of Samuel Johnson*	B
Brady, Patricia. *Martha Washington*	B
Brands, H. W. *The First American*	B
Broadwater, Jeff. ★*George Mason*	B
Broadwater, Jeff. *James Madison*	B
Broers, Michael. *Napoleon*	B
Broers, Michael. *Napoleon*	B
Brooks, James. *Mesa of Sorrows*	979.1004
Bunker, Nick. *Young Benjamin Franklin*	B
Burke, Edmund. *Reflections on the Revolution in France*	944.04
Burns, Eric. *Infamous Scribblers*	071
Burstein, Andrew. *Madison and Jefferson*	973.4
Calloway, Colin G. *The Indian World of George Washington*	323.1197
Carretta, Vincent. *Equiano, the African*	B
Cheney, Lynne V. *The Virginia Dynasty*	B
Chernow, Ron. ★*Alexander Hamilton*	B
Chernow, Ron. *Washington*	B
Coe, Alexis. ★*You Never Forget Your First*	B
Cohen, Eliot A. *Conquered into Liberty*	355.009747
Coleridge, Samuel Taylor. *The Complete Poems*	821
Cox, Anna-Lisa. *The Bone and Sinew of the Land*	977
Cozzens, Peter. *Tecumseh and the Prophet*	920
Curran, Andrew S. *Diderot and the Art of Thinking Freely*	194
Dalrymple, William. ★*The Anarchy*	954.03
Dalrymple, William. *White Mughals*	954
Damrosch, Leopold. *The Club*	920
Darnton, Robert. *The Revolutionary Temper*	944
Davidson, Ian. *The French Revolution*	944.04
Dolin, Eric Jay. ★*Rebels at Sea*	973.3
Dolnick, Edward. *Seeds of Life*	612.6
Drury, Bob. *Blood and Treasure*	B
Drury, Bob. *Valley Forge*	973.3
Dunbar, Erica Armstrong. ★*Never Caught*	B
Eckert, Allan W. *A Sorrow in Our Heart*	B
Ellis, Joseph J. *American Creation*	973.3
Ellis, Joseph J. ★*American Dialogue*	973.3
Ellis, Joseph J. *The Cause*	973.3
Ellis, Joseph J. *First Family*	973.4
Ellis, Joseph J. *Founding Brothers*	973.4
Ellis, Joseph J. ★*His Excellency*	B
Ellis, Joseph J. ★*Revolutionary Summer*	973.3
Eustace, Nicole. ★*Covered with Night*	364.152
Felder, Deborah G. *The American Women's Almanac*	305.40973
Feldman, Noah. *The Broken Constitution*	973.7
Feldman, Noah. *The Three Lives of James Madison*	B
Ferling, John E. *Winning Independence*	973.3
Ferreiro, Larrie D. *Brothers at Arms*	327.73
Fischer, David Hackett. *Paul Revere's Ride*	973.3
Fischer, David Hackett. *Washington's Crossing*	973.3
Flexner, James Thomas. *George Washington and the New Nation, 1783-1793*	973.4
Flexner, James Thomas. *George Washington*	B
Ford, Lacy K. *Deliver Us from Evil*	973.7
Foreman, Amanda. *Georgiana, Duchess of Devonshire*	B
Franklin, Benjamin. ★*Autobiography, Poor Richard, and Later Writings*	973.2
Franklin, Benjamin. *The Compleated Autobiography*	B
Fraser, Antonia. *Love and Louis XIV*	B
Fraser, Antonia. *Marie Antoinette*	B
Gay, Peter. *The Enlightenment*	190
Gay, Peter. *The Enlightenment*	190
Geck, Martin. ★*Johann Sebastian Bach*	780.92
Goldstone, Nancy Bazelon. *In the Shadow of the Empress*	920
Gordon, Charlotte. *Romantic Outlaws*	920
Gordon-Reed, Annette. ★*Most Blessed of the Patriarchs*	973.4
Grann, David. ★*The Wager*	910.91
Grant, James. ★*John Adams*	B
Greenblatt, Stephen. ★*The Swerve*	940.2
Hall, Rebecca. ★*Wake*	741.5
Harris, Ellen T. *George Frideric Handel*	B
Harris, J. William. *The Hanging of Thomas Jeremiah*	B
Hochschild, Adam. *Bury the Chains*	326
Hogeland, William. *Declaration*	973.3
Holmes, Richard. *The Age of Wonder*	509
Holton, Woody. *Abigail Adams*	B
Horn, Jonathan. *Washington's End*	B
Hughes, Robert. *The Fatal Shore*	994
Hughes, Robert. *Goya*	B
Hyde, Anne Farrar. ★*Born of Lakes and Plains*	978
Isaacson, Walter. ★*Benjamin Franklin*	B
Isenberg, Nancy. *The Problem of Democracy*	973.4
Jeffers, Honorée Fanonne. *The Age of Phillis*	811
Jefferson, Thomas. *Writings*	973.3
Johnson, Paul. *George Washington*	B
Johnson, Paul. *Napoleon*	B
Kars, Marjoleine. *Blood on the River*	306.3
Kearse, Bettye. *The Other Madisons*	920
Keneally, Thomas. *A Commonwealth of Thieves*	994
Kilmeade, Brian. ★*George Washington's Secret Six*	973.4
Klarman, Michael J. *The Framers' Coup*	342.7302
Kluger, Richard. *Indelible Ink*	B

PUBLIC LIBRARY CORE COLLECTION: NONFICTION
Twentieth Edition

Korda, Michael. *Clouds of Glory*	B
Lahn, Bussho. *Singing and Dancing Are the Voice of the Law*	294.3
Larson, Edward J. *The Return of George Washington*	B
Lepore, Jill. *Book of Ages*	B
Lepore, Jill. *New York Burning*	974.7
Lever, Evelyne. *Marie Antoinette*	B
Maier, Pauline. *American Scripture*	973.3
Maier, Pauline. *Ratification*	342.7302
Massie, Robert K. *Catherine the Great*	B
McCullough, David G. ★*John Adams*	B
McCullough, David G. *The Pioneers*	920
McGrath, Tim. *James Monroe*	B
Meltzer, Brad. ★*The First Conspiracy*	973.4
Meyerson, Michael. *Liberty's Blueprint*	342.7302
Miller, Marla. *Betsy Ross and the Making of America*	B
Moore, Peter. *Life, Liberty, and the Pursuit of Happiness*	199
Moore, Susanna. *Paradise of the Pacific*	996.9
Morison, Samuel Eliot. *John Paul Jones*	B
Nicolson, Adam. *The Making of Poetry*	821.709
O'Donnell, Patrick K. *The Indispensables*	973.3
Paine, Thomas. ★*Rights of Man*	320.5
Pearson, Roger. *Voltaire Almighty*	B
Philbrick, Nathaniel. *Travels with George*	973.4
Philbrick, Nathaniel. ★*Valiant Ambition*	B
Phillips, Kevin. *1775*	973.3
Pressly, Paul M. *On the Rim of the Caribbean*	975.8
Purnell, Carolyn. *The Sensational Past*	152.109
Rakove, Jack N. *Revolutionaries*	973.3
Randall, Willard Sterne. *The Founders' Fortunes*	973.3
Randall, Willard Sterne. *George Washington*	B
Raphael, Ray. *Constitutional Myths*	342.7302
Raphael, Ray. *Mr. President*	352.230973
Reiss, Tom. *The Black Count*	B
Roberts, Andrew. ★*Napoleon*	B
Roberts, Cokie. *Founding Mothers*	920
Roberts, Cokie. *Ladies of Liberty*	920
Roberts, Jason. ★*Every Living Thing*	578
Robertson, Ritchie. *The Enlightenment*	190
Rosen, Charles. *The Classical Style*	780.9
Rosen, Jeffrey. *The Pursuit of Happiness*	973.3
Rousseau, Jean-Jacques. *Confessions*	B
Safranski, Rudiger. *Goethe*	B
Sankovitch, Nina. *American Rebels*	920
Satia, Priya. *Empire of Guns*	330.941
Schama, Simon. *Citizens*	944.04
Simon, James F. *What Kind of Nation*	342.73
Sobel, Dava. *Longitude*	526
Staiti, Paul J. *Of Arms and Artists*	B
Stark, Peter. *Young Washington*	B
Stewart, David O. *George Washington*	973.4
Stewart, David O. *Madison's Gift*	B
Swafford, Jan. *Mozart*	B
Taylor, Alan. *American Republics*	973.3
Taylor, Alan. *American Revolutions*	973.3
Taylor, Alan. *The Divided Ground*	974.7
Taylor, Stephen. *Commander*	B
Unger, Harlow G. *American Tempest*	973.3
Unger, Harlow G. *The Last Founding Father*	B
Waldstreicher, David. *The Odyssey of Phillis Wheatley*	B
Weintraub, Stanley. *Iron Tears*	973.3
Weisman, Steven R. *The Chosen Wars*	296.0973
Wiencek, Henry. *Master of the Mountain*	973.4
Wills, Garry. *James Madison*	B
Wise, Steven M. *Though the Heavens May Fall*	342.42
Wulf, Andrea. *The Brother Gardeners*	920
Wulf, Andrea. *Magnificent Rebels*	830.9
Zambone, Albert Louis. *Daniel Morgan*	B
Zamoyski, Adam. *Napoleon*	B

1900S (DECADE)

Bruner, Robert F. ★*The Panic of 1907, 2nd Ed.*	330.973
Creighton, Margaret S. *The Electrifying Fall of Rainbow City*	607
Goodwin, Doris Kearns. ★*The Bully Pulpit*	973.91
Hartman, Darrell. *Battle of Ink and Ice*	998
Morris, Edmund. ★*The Rise of Theodore Roosevelt*	B
Morris, Edmund. ★*Theodore Rex*	973.911
Okrent, Daniel. *The Guarded Gate*	344.73
Randall, David K. *The King and Queen of Malibu*	B
Rapp, David. *Tinker to Evers to Chance*	796.357

Rilke, Rainer Maria. ★*Letters to a Young Poet*	831
Roe, Sue. *In Montmartre*	920
Winchester, Simon. *A Crack in the Edge of the World*	979.4

1910S

Akcam, Taner. *A Shameful Act*	956.6
Alexander, Caroline. *The Endurance*	919.8
Anderson, Scott. *Lawrence in Arabia*	B
Balakian, Peter. *The Burning Tigris*	956.6
Barry, John M. ★*The Great Influenza*	614.5
Bascomb, Neal. *The Escape Artists*	940.4
Beevor, Antony. *Russia*	947.084
Berg, A. Scott. ★*Wilson*	B
Brands, H. W. *Woodrow Wilson*	B
Butler, Daniel Allen. *"Unsinkable"*	910
Cooper, John Milton. *Woodrow Wilson*	B
Davenport, Matthew J. *First Over There*	940.4
Figes, Orlando. *A People's Tragedy*	947.08
Gildea, William. *The Longest Fight*	B
Hastings, Max. *Catastrophe 1914*	940.3
Heaney, Christopher. *Cradle of Gold*	B
Herman, Arthur. *1917*	940.3
Hochschild, Adam. *American Midnight*	973.91
Hochschild, Adam. *King Leopold's Ghost*	967.51
Keegan, John. *The First World War*	940.3
King, Greg. *The Assassination of the Archduke*	B
King, Ross. ★*Mad Enchantment*	759.4
Kinzer, Stephen. ★*The True Flag*	327.73
Larson, Erik. ★*Dead Wake*	940.4
Lehr, Dick. ★*The Birth of a Nation*	305.800973
Lloyd, Nick. *The Western Front*	940.4
Lowenstein, Roger. *America's Bank*	332.1
Mackeen, Dawn Anahid. *The Hundred-Year Walk*	956.6
MacMillan, Margaret. *Paris 1919*	940.3
Massie, Robert K. *Castles of Steel*	940.4
McNamara, Kevin J. *Dreams of a Great Small Nation*	355.009437
Morris, Edmund. ★*Colonel Roosevelt*	B
Morris, Edmund. ★*Theodore Rex*	973.911
Neu, Charles E. *Colonel House*	B
Okrent, Daniel. *The Guarded Gate*	344.73
Phillips, Patrick. *Blood at the Root*	305.8
Pipes, Richard. *A Concise History of the Russian Revolution*	947.084
Rogan, Eugene L. *The Fall of the Ottomans*	940.3
Scotti, R. A. *Vanished Smile*	759.5
Spinney, Laura. ★*Pale Rider*	614.5
Strang, Dean A. *Worse Than the Devil*	345.775
Tuchman, Barbara W. ★*The Guns of August*	940.4
Von Drehle, Dave. ★*Triangle*	974.7
1912. Turney, Chris	998
1917. Herman, Arthur	940.3
1919. Ewing, Eve L.	811

1920S

Abbott, Karen. *American Rose*	B
Allen, Frederick Lewis. *Only Yesterday*	973.9
Barry, John M. *Rising Tide*	977
Beevor, Antony. *Russia*	947.084
Berg, A. Scott. ★*Wilson*	B
Blum, Deborah. *The Poisoner's Handbook*	614
Boyle, Kevin. *Arc of Justice*	345.73
Brands, H. W. *Woodrow Wilson*	B
Broyles, Michael. ★*Revolutions in American Music*	780.9
Bryson, Bill. *One Summer*	973.91
Cooper, John Milton. *Woodrow Wilson*	B
Davis, Wade. *Into the Silence*	B
Egan, Timothy. ★*A Fever in the Heartland*	322.4
Eilenberger, Wolfram. *Time of the Magicians*	920
Ellsworth, Scott. *The Ground Breaking*	976.6
Figes, Orlando. *A People's Tragedy*	947.08
Gage, Beverly. *The Day Wall Street Exploded*	974.7
Grann, David. ★*Killers of the Flower Moon*	976.6004
Hett, Benjamin Carter. *The Death of Democracy*	943.085
Hochschild, Adam. *American Midnight*	973.91
Jaher, David. *The Witch of Lime Street*	B
Jobb, Dean. *A Gentleman and a Thief*	364.16
Kennedy, David M. ★*Freedom from Fear*	973.91
King, David. *The Trial of Adolf Hitler*	345.43
King, Greg. *Nothing but the Night*	364.152
Kotkin, Stephen. *Stalin*	B
McCracken, Patti. *The Angel Makers*	364.152

AUTHOR, TITLE, SERIES AND SUBJECT INDEX

Miller, Donald L. *Supreme City*	974.7
Montillo, Roseanne. *Fire on the Track*	B
Morris, Edmund. ★*Colonel Roosevelt*	B
Mortimer, Gavin. *The Great Swim*	B
Morton, Andrew. *Wallis in Love*	B
Neu, Charles E. *Colonel House*	B
Niven, Jennifer. *Ada Blackjack*	B
Okrent, Daniel. *The Guarded Gate*	344.73
Okrent, Daniel. *Last Call*	363.4
Pipes, Richard. *A Concise History of the Russian Revolution*	947.084
Roth, Joseph. *What I Saw*	943
Shlaes, Amity. *Coolidge*	B
Shlaes, Amity. *The Forgotten Man*	973.91
Smilios, Maria. ★*The Black Angels*	610.73
Smith, Douglas. *The Russian Job*	947.084
Spinney, Laura. ★*Pale Rider*	614.5
Swift, Earl. *Hell Put to Shame*	364.15
Terkel, Studs. ★*Hard Times*	973.91
Ullrich, Volker. *Germany 1923*	943.085
Weiss, Elaine F. *The Woman's Hour*	324.6
Willetts, Paul. *King Con*	B
Zminda, Don. *Double Plays and Double Crosses*	796.357

1930S

Alinder, Mary Street. *Group F.64*	770.92
Allen, Frederick Lewis. *Only Yesterday*	973.9
Allport, Alan. *Britain at Bay*	940.53
Applebaum, Anne. ★*Red Famine*	947.708
Atria, Travis. *Better Days Will Come Again*	B
Brown, Daniel James. ★*The Boys in the Boat*	797.12
Bryson, Bill. *One Summer*	973.91
Burns, Cherie. *The Great Hurricane—1938*	974.7
Cadbury, Deborah. *Princes at War*	920
Cadbury, Deborah. *The School That Escaped from the Nazis*	940.53
Caesar, Ed. *The Moth and the Mountain*	B
Carter, Stephen L. *Invisible*	B
Chang, Iris. ★*The Rape of Nanking*	951.04
Checkoway, Julie. *The Three-Year Swim Club*	797.2
Cornwell, John. *Hitler's Pope*	B
Croke, Vicki. *The Lady and the Panda*	599.789
De Courcy, Anne. *Chanel's Riviera*	944.9
Egan, Timothy. *The Worst Hard Time*	978
Eig, Jonathan. *Get Capone*	364.1
Ellsworth, Scott. *The World Beneath Their Feet*	796.522
Evans, Richard J. *The Third Reich at War*	940.53
Fisher, Marshall Jon. *A Terrible Splendor*	796.342
Friedlander, Saul. *Nazi Germany and the Jews*	940.53
Golay, Michael. *America 1933*	B
Gup, Ted. *A Secret Gift*	977.1
Hillenbrand, Laura. ★*Seabiscuit*	798.4
Hochschild, Adam. *Spain in Our Hearts*	946.081
Holland, James. *The Rise of Germany, 1939-1941; Vol. 1*	940.54
Hughes, Langston. ★*I Wonder as I Wander*	B
Katznelson, Ira. *Fear Itself*	973.917
Kennedy, David M. ★*Freedom from Fear*	973.91
Klemperer, Victor. *I Will Bear Witness*	B
Kotkin, Stephen. *Stalin*	B
Krimstein, Ken. *When I Grow Up*	741.5
Larson, Erik. *In the Garden of Beasts*	B
Lewis, Damien. *The Dog Who Could Fly*	940.54
Mitter, Rana. *Forgotten Ally*	951.04
Morrison, Melanie. *Murder on Shades Mountain*	345.761
Mortimer, Gavin. *The Great Swim*	B
Phillips, Adrian. *Fighting Churchill, Appeasing Hitler*	327.41043
Preston, Paul. *The Spanish Holocaust*	946.081
Quinn, Susan. *Eleanor and Hick*	B
Rees, Laurence. *Auschwitz*	940.53
Rosenzweig, Laura B. *Hollywood's Spies*	791.43
Roth, Joseph. *What I Saw*	943
Schwartz, A. Brad. ★*Broadcast Hysteria*	791.44
Sevigny, Melissa L. ★*Brave the Wild River*	580.9
Shlaes, Amity. *The Forgotten Man*	973.91
Stahr, Celia. *Frida in America*	B
Stashower, Daniel. *American Demon*	364.152
Stout, David. *The Kidnap Years*	364.15
Taylor, Fred. *1939*	940.53
Terkel, Studs. ★*Hard Times*	973.91
Thomas, Gordon. *Defying Hitler*	920
1939. Taylor, Fred	940.53

1940S

Aleksievich, Svetlana. ★*The Unwomanly Face of War*	940.53
Allport, Alan. *Britain at Bay*	940.53
Ambrose, Stephen E. *Citizen Soldiers*	940.54
Ambrose, Stephen E. *D-Day, June 6, 1944*	940.54
Ambrose, Stephen E. *The Victors*	940.54
Ambrose, Stephen E. *The Wild Blue*	940.54
Anthony, Carl Sferrazza. *Camera Girl*	B
Atkinson, Rick. *An Army at Dawn*	940.54
Atkinson, Rick. *The Day of Battle*	940.54
Atkinson, Rick. *The Guns at Last Light*	940.54
Baime, A. J. *The Accidental President*	B
Bass, Gary Jonathan. ★*Judgment at Tokyo*	952.04
Beevor, Antony. *Ardennes 1944*	940.54
Beevor, Antony. *D-Day*	940.54
Beevor, Antony. *The Second World War*	940.54
Beevor, Antony. *Stalingrad*	940.54
Berr, Helene. *The Journal of Helene Berr*	B
Beschloss, Michael R. *The Conquerors*	940.53
Borneman, Walter R. *The Admirals*	B
Bradley, James. *Flags of Our Fathers*	940.54
Brown, Claude. *Manchild in the Promised Land*	B
Cannell, Michael T. *A Brotherhood Betrayed*	B
Chiger, Krystyna. *The Girl in the Green Sweater*	B
Childers, Thomas. *The Third Reich*	943.086
Churchill, Winston. *The Grand Alliance*	940.53
Churchill, Winston. *Their Finest Hour*	940.53
Churchill, Winston. *Triumph and Tragedy*	940.53
Conant, Jennet. *The Lotus Eaters*	940.54
Cooke, Alistair. *The American Home Front, 1941-1942*	940.53
Cornwell, John. *Hitler's Pope*	B
Dallek, Robert. *Harry S. Truman*	B
Dickson, Paul. *The Rise of the G.I. Army 1940-1941*	940.54
Dower, John W. *Embracing Defeat*	952.04
Edmonds, David. *Wittgenstein's Poker*	192
Edsel, Robert M. *The Monuments Men*	940.53
Epplin, Luke. *Our Team*	796.357
Evans, Richard J. *The Third Reich at War*	940.53
Fishman, David E. *The Book Smugglers*	940.53
Frank, Jeffrey. *The Trials of Harry S. Truman*	973.918
Friedman, Matti. *Spies of No Country*	327.12
Fullilove, Michael. *Rendezvous with Destiny*	973.917092
Gergel, Richard. *Unexampled Courage*	323.1196
Giangreco, D. M. *Hell to Pay*	940.54
Gillette, Michael L. *Lady Bird Johnson*	B
Hajari, Nisid. *Midnight's Furies*	954.04
Halberstam, David. *Summer of '49*	796.357
Halberstam, David. *The Teammates*	B
Hampton, Dan. *Chasing the Demon*	629.132
Hampton, Dan. *Operation Vengeance*	940.54
Harris, Mark. ★*Five Came Back*	791.4302
Hastings, Max. *Armageddon*	940.54
Hastings, Max. *Inferno*	940.54
Hastings, Max. *Operation Chastise*	940.54
Hastings, Max. *Overlord*	940.54
Hemming, Henry. *Agents of Influence*	940.54
Henderson, Bruce B. *Sons and Soldiers*	940.53
Hersey, John. ★*Hiroshima*	940.54
Highsmith, Patricia. ★*Patricia Highsmith's Diaries and Notebooks*	818
Holland, James. *Battle of Britain*	940.54
Holland, James. *The Rise of Germany, 1939-1941; Vol. 1*	940.54
Holland, James. *Sicily '43*	940.54
Hornfischer, James D. *Neptune's Inferno*	940.54
Humbert, Agnes. *Resistance*	B
Isserman, Maurice. *The Winter Army*	940.54
Karski, Jan. *Story of a Secret State*	940.53
Katznelson, Ira. *Fear Itself*	973.917
Kennedy, David M. ★*Freedom from Fear*	973.91
Kershaw, Alex. *The Few*	940.54
King, David. *Death in the City of Light*	364.152
Klemperer, Victor. *I Will Bear Witness*	B
Korda, Michael. *With Wings Like Eagles*	940.54
Kurtz-Phelan, Daniel. *The China Mission*	951.04
Lambert, Raymond. *Every Man a Hero*	B
Lowry, Beverly. *Deer Creek Drive*	364.152
Macadam, Heather Dune. *999*	940.53
Macintyre, Ben. *Agent Zigzag*	B
Macintyre, Ben. ★*Operation Mincemeat*	940.54

PUBLIC LIBRARY CORE COLLECTION: NONFICTION
Twentieth Edition

Makos, Adam. ★*A Higher Call*	940.54
McCarten, Anthony. *Darkest Hour*	941.084
McCullough, David G. *Truman*	B
Mitter, Rana. *Forgotten Ally*	951.04
Moorehead, Caroline. *A Train in Winter*	940.53
Moorhouse, Roger. *Berlin at War*	943
Moynahan, Brian. *Leningrad*	780.92
Norman, Michael. *Tears in the Darkness*	940.54
Oshinsky, David M. ★*Polio*	614.5
Oz, Amos. *A Tale of Love and Darkness*	B
Pellegrino, Charles R. *To Hell and Back*	940.54
Plokhy, Serhii. *Yalta*	940.53
Prange, Gordon W. *At Dawn We Slept*	940.54
Preston, Diana. *Eight Days at Yalta*	940.53
Purnell, Sonia. *Clementine*	B
Rajchman, Chil. *The Last Jew of Treblinka*	940.53
Rees, Laurence. *Auschwitz*	940.53
Reid, Anna. *Leningrad*	940.54
Reid, David. *The Brazen Age*	974.7
Rosbottom, Ronald C. *When Paris Went Dark*	944.0816
Russell, Jan Jarboe. *The Train to Crystal City*	940.53
Sakamoto, Pamela Rotner. *Midnight in Broad Daylight*	940.53
Sands, Philippe. *East West Street*	345
Scott, James. *Rampage*	940.54
Scott, James. *Target Tokyo*	940.54
Simon, Marie. *Underground in Berlin*	B
Southard, Susan. *Nagasaki*	940.54
Sullivan, James. *Unsinkable*	940.54
Symonds, Craig L. *The Battle of Midway*	940.54
Thomas, Gordon. *Defying Hitler*	920
Tobin, James. *Ernie Pyle's War*	B
Toll, Ian W. *The Conquering Tide*	940.54
Toll, Ian W. *Pacific Crucible*	940.54
Toll, Ian W. *Twilight of the Gods*	940.54
Twomey, Steve. *Countdown to Pearl Harbor*	940.54
Ullrich, Volker. ★*Eight Days in May*	943.086
Weinman, Sarah. *The Real Lolita*	362.88092
Winik, Jay. *1944*	940.53
Zuckoff, Mitchell. *Frozen in Time*	998.2
1944. Winik, Jay	940.53
1948. Morris, Benny	956.04

1950S

Abrahamian, Ervand. *The Coup*	955.05
Anthony, Carl Sferrazza. *Camera Girl*	B
Baier, Bret. *Three Days in January*	B
Brady, James. *The Coldest War*	B
Branch, Taylor. *Parting the Waters*	973
Brown, Claude. *Manchild in the Promised Land*	B
Broyles, Michael. ★*Revolutions in American Music*	780.9
Bryson, Bill. *The Life and Times of the Thunderbolt Kid*	B
Capote, Truman. ★*In Cold Blood*	364.1
Carlson, Peter. *K Blows Top*	947.085
Child, Julia. ★*My Life in France*	B
Cumings, Bruce. *The Korean War*	951.904
Dallek, Robert. *Harry S. Truman*	B
Dillard, Annie. *An American Childhood*	B
Dittrich, Luke. ★*Patient H.M.*	616.85
Eichar, Donnie. *Dead Mountain*	914
Evans, Martin. *Algeria*	965
Faust, Drew Gilpin. *Necessary Trouble*	B
Fessler, Ann. *The Girls Who Went Away*	362.82
Frankel, Glenn. *High Noon*	791.43
Frost, Mark. *The Match*	796.352
Gates, Henry Louis. *Colored People*	B
George-Warren, Holly. ★*Janis*	B
Gillette, Michael L. *Lady Bird Johnson*	B
Goodman, Matthew. *The City Game*	796.323
Gordin, Michael D. *Red Cloud at Dawn*	355.02
Halberstam, David. ★*The Children*	323.1
Halberstam, David. *The Coldest Winter*	951.904
Halberstam, David. *The Fifties*	973.92
Highsmith, Patricia. ★*Patricia Highsmith's Diaries and Notebooks*	818
Hirsch, Foster. ★*Hollywood and the Movies of the Fifties*	791.43
Hitchcock, William I. *The Age of Eisenhower*	973.921092
Johnson, Paul. *Eisenhower*	B
Joseph, Peniel E. *The Sword and the Shield*	B
Kerouac, Jack. *Book of Sketches, 1952-57*	818
King, Gilbert. *Beneath a Ruthless Sun*	B
Lauterbach, Preston. *Bluff City*	B
Letts, Elizabeth. ★*The Ride of Her Life*	B
Lewis, John. *Walking with the Wind*	B
Lowe, George. *Letters from Everest*	796.522
MacLean, Harry N. *Starkweather*	364.152
Maddox, Brenda. *Rosalind Franklin*	B
Margolick, David. *Elizabeth and Hazel*	379.2
Martin, Rachel Louise. *A Most Tolerant Little Town*	379.2
McCullough, David G. *Truman*	B
Michener, James A. *The Bridge at Andau*	943.9
Montillo, Roseanne. *Deliberate Cruelty*	364.152
Moore, Susanna. *Miss Aluminum*	813
Ngugi wa Thiong'o. *In the House of the Interpreter*	B
Oliphant, Thomas. ★*The Road to Camelot*	973.922092
Olsen, Craig. *P.S. Burn This Letter Please*	306.76
Oshinsky, David M. ★*Polio*	614.5
Oz, Amos. *A Tale of Love and Darkness*	B
Peiffer, Prudence. *The Slip*	709.73
Poole, W. Scott. *Vampira*	B
Reid, Joy-Ann Lomena. ★*Medgar and Myrlie*	920
Sacco, Joe. *Footnotes in Gaza*	741.5
Sallah, Michael. *The Yankee Comandante*	972.91
Satrapi, Marjane. *Chicken with Plums*	741.5
Sides, Hampton. *On Desperate Ground*	951.904
Simon, James F. *Eisenhower vs. Warren*	347.73
Thomas, Evan. *Ike's Bluff*	973.921092
Von Tunzelmann, Alex. *Blood and Sand*	909.82
Winder, Elizabeth. *Pain, Parties, Work*	B

1960S

Abrams, Dan. *Kennedy's Avenger*	973.922
Achebe, Chinua. *There Was a Country*	B
Austerlitz, Saul. *Just a Shot Away*	781.66078
B., David. *Epileptic*	741.5
Baier, Bret. *Three Days in January*	B
Baker, Deborah. *The Convert*	B
Baldwin, James. ★*Collected Essays*	814
Belkin, Lisa. *Genealogy of a Murder*	362.88
Bernstein, Carl. ★*Chasing History*	B
Bingham, Clara. *Witness to the Revolution*	303.48
Boot, Max. ★*The Road Not Taken*	B
Bowden, Mark. ★*Hue 1968*	959.704
Boyle, Kevin. *The Shattering*	973.923
Bradley, Mark A. *Blood Runs Coal*	B
Branch, Taylor. ★*At Canaan's Edge*	323.1196
Branch, Taylor. *Parting the Waters*	973
Branch, Taylor. ★*Pillar of Fire*	323.1
Branigan, Tania. *Red Memory*	951.05
Brinkley, Alan. *John F. Kennedy*	B
Brokaw, Tom. *The Fall of Richard Nixon*	B
Caro, Robert A. ★*The Passage of Power*	B
Clarke, Thurston. *JFK's Last Hundred Days*	B
Clarke, Thurston. *The Last Campaign*	B
Cleveland, Pat. *Walking with the Muses*	B
Cohen, Andrew. *Two Days in June*	973.922
Coleman, David G. *The Fourteenth Day*	973.922092
Colt, George Howe. *The Game*	796.332
Connolly, Ray. *Being John Lennon*	B
Cooke, Julia. *Come Fly the World*	387.7
Dallek, Robert. *Let Every Nation Know*	B
Dallek, Robert. *An Unfinished Life*	B
Dobbs, Michael. *King Richard*	973.924
Doherty, Maggie. *The Equivalents*	920
Donovan, Jim. ★*Shoot for the Moon*	629.45
Eire, Carlos M. N. *Learning to Die in Miami*	B
Euchner, Charles C. *Nobody Turn Me Around*	975.3
Evans, Martin. *Algeria*	965
Faust, Drew Gilpin. *Necessary Trouble*	B
Feldstein, Mark Avrom. *Poisoning the Press*	973.924092
Fessler, Ann. *The Girls Who Went Away*	362.82
Fishman, Charles. ★*One Giant Leap*	629.45
FitzGerald, Frances. *Fire in the Lake*	959.704
Frankel, Glenn. *Shooting Midnight Cowboy*	791.43
Garrett, Kent. *The Last Negroes at Harvard*	920
Gates, Henry Louis. *Colored People*	B
George-Warren, Holly. ★*Janis*	B
Goodwin, Doris Kearns. ★*An Unfinished Love Story*	B
Graff, Garrett M. *Watergate*	973.924
Halberstam, David. *The Best and the Brightest*	973.92

AUTHOR, TITLE, SERIES AND SUBJECT INDEX

Halberstam, David. ★*The Children*	323.1
Harris, Mark. *Pictures at a Revolution*	791.43
Hastings, Max. *The Abyss*	972.9106
Hawley, Sam. *Speed Duel*	796.72
Hill, Clint. *Mrs. Kennedy and Me*	973.922092
Johnson, Lyndon B. *Taking Charge*	973.923
Johnson, Paul. *Eisenhower*	B
Jones, Chip. *The Organ Thieves*	617.4
Jones, Doug. *Bending Toward Justice*	323.1196
Joseph, Peniel E. *The Sword and the Shield*	B
Kamp, David. *Sunny Days*	791.4502
King, Martin Luther. *Why We Can't Wait*	305.8
Kix, Paul. ★*You Have to Be Prepared to Die Before You Can Begin to Live*	976.1
Kluger, Jeffrey. ★*Apollo 8*	629.45
Kot, Greg. *I'll Take You There*	B
Kotz, Nick. *Judgment Days*	323
Kurlansky, Mark. *1968*	909.82
Lang, Michael. *The Road to Woodstock*	781.66
Lattin, Don. *The Harvard Psychedelic Club*	973.922092
Lauterbach, Preston. *Bluff City*	B
Leaming, Barbara. *Mrs. Kennedy*	B
Lee, Heath Hardage. ★*The League of Wives*	959.704
Lewis, John. ★*March; Book Three*	741.5
Lewis, John. ★*March; Book Two*	741.5
Lewis, John. *Walking with the Wind*	B
Maddow, Rachel. *Bag Man*	B
Mahoney, Richard D. *Sons & Brothers*	920
Maier, Thomas. *Mafia Spies*	364.1060973
Manzione, Gianmarc. *Pin Action*	B
Maraniss, David. *They Marched into Sunlight*	959.704
McCartney, Paul. ★*1964*	782.42166
McKeen, William. *Everybody Had an Ocean*	781.6609
McKeon, Kathy. *Jackie's Girl*	B
McNamara, Robert S. *In Retrospect*	959.704
McShane Wulfhart, Nell. *The Great Stewardess Rebellion*	331.4
McWhorter, Diane. *Carry Me Home*	976.1
Merriman, Helena. ★*Tunnel 29*	943
Minutaglio, Bill. *Dallas 1963*	973.922092
Minutaglio, Bill. *The Most Dangerous Man in America*	B
Moore, Harold G. *We Were Soldiers Once—And Young*	959.704
Moore, Susanna. *Miss Aluminum*	813
Morley, Jefferson. *Scorpions' Dance*	973.924
Nelson, Craig. *Rocket Men*	629.45
O'Neill, Tom. ★*Chaos*	364.152
Oliphant, Thomas. ★*The Road to Camelot*	973.922092
Olsen, Craig. *P.S. Burn This Letter Please*	306.76
Olson, Lynne. ★*Empress of the Nile*	B
Oren, Michael B. *Six Days of War*	956.04
Peiffer, Prudence. *The Slip*	709.73
Perlstein, Rick. ★*Nixonland*	973.924
Posner, Gerald L. *Case Closed*	364.1
Rasenberger, Jim. *The Brilliant Disaster*	972.9106
Reid, Joy-Ann Lomena. ★*Medgar and Myrlie*	920
Reid, Stuart A. *The Lumumba Plot*	967.51
Reston, James. *The Conviction of Richard Nixon*	973.924092
Richardson, Lance. *House of Nutter*	B
Risen, Clay. *The Bill of the Century*	342.7308
Rosenfeld, Seth. *Subversives*	378.1
Santopietro, Tom. *The Sound of Music Story*	791.43
Savage, Jon. ★*1966*	781.6609
Schultz, Kevin Michael. *Buckley and Mailer*	920
Sheehan, Neil. *A Bright Shining Lie*	959.704
Sherman, Casey. *Above and Beyond*	973.922092
Shultz, Richard H. *The Secret War Against Hanoi*	959.704
Sides, Hampton. *Hellhound on His Trail*	364.152
Simon, James F. *Eisenhower vs. Warren*	347.73
Smith, Patti. ★*Just Kids*	B
Sorensen, Theodore C. *Counselor*	B
Stanton, Doug. *The Odyssey of Echo Company*	959.704
Stein, Judith E. *Eye of the Sixties*	B
Steinbeck, John. *Travels with Charley*	B
Swanson, James L. *End of Days*	973.922092
Sweig, Julia. *Lady Bird Johnson*	B
Szerlip, Barbara. *The Man Who Designed the Future*	B
Talty, Stephan. *The Good Assassin*	364.15
Theoharis, Jeanne. *The Rebellious Life of Mrs. Rosa Parks*	B
Thomas, Evan. *Being Nixon*	B
Thompson, Hunter S. ★*Fear and Loathing in America*	B
Thomson, Graeme. *George Harrison*	B
Van Meter, Matthew. *Deep Delta Justice*	345.763
Voloj, Julian. *Ghetto Brother*	741.5
Wadman, Meredith. *The Vaccine Race*	614.5
Wald, Elijah. *Dylan Goes Electric!*	782.42164
Waters, Alice. *Coming to My Senses*	B
Weiner, Tim. *One Man Against the World*	B
Whitaker, Mark. ★*Saying It Loud*	973.923
White, Adam. ★*Motown*	781.644
Wilkie, Curtis. *When Evil Lived in Laurel*	305.8
Winder, Elizabeth. *Parachute Women*	782.42164
Wolfe, Tom. ★*The Right Stuff*	629.4
Woods, Randall Bennett. *Prisoners of Hope*	973.923
Yang, Jisheng. *The World Turned Upside Down*	951.05
Young, Rob. *Electric Eden*	781.62
Yousse, Bower. *Freddie Steinmark*	796.332
Zeitz, Joshua. *Building the Great Society*	973.923
★*1964*. McCartney, Paul	782.42166
★*1966*. Savage, Jon	781.6609
1968. Kurlansky, Mark	909.82

1970S

Alexie, Sherman. *You Don't Have to Say You Love Me*	818
B., David. *Epileptic*	741.5
Bernstein, Carl. ★*All the President's Men*	364.1
Bingham, Clara. *Witness to the Revolution*	303.48
Bird, Kai. *The Outlier*	973.926
Bowden, Mark. *Guests of the Ayatollah*	955.05
Branigan, Tania. *Red Memory*	951.05
Brokaw, Tom. *The Fall of Richard Nixon*	B
Brokhausen, Nick. *Whispers in the Tall Grass*	959.704
Broome, Brian. ★*Punch Me up to the Gods*	B
Bui, Thi. ★*The Best We Could Do*	741.5
Burke, Monte. *Lords of the Fly*	799.124
Burrough, Bryan. *Days of Rage*	303.48
Carney, Scott. *The Vortex*	954.92
Carter, Jimmy. *A Full Life*	B
Carter, Jimmy. *Keeping Faith*	B
Carter, Jimmy. *White House Diary*	973.926
Cleveland, Pat. *Walking with the Muses*	B
Coll, Steve. ★*Ghost Wars*	958.104
Cook, Kevin. *Ten Innings at Wrigley*	796.357
Cooke, Julia. *Come Fly the World*	387.7
Cunningham, Benjamin. *The Liar*	327.1273
De Vise, Daniel. ★*The Blues Brothers*	791.43
Derf. *Kent State*	741.5
Dobbs, Michael. *King Richard*	973.924
Eizenstat, Stuart. ★*President Carter*	B
Feifer, Gregory. *The Great Gamble*	958.104
Feinstein, Michael. *The Gershwins and Me*	782.42164
Feldstein, Mark Avrom. *Poisoning the Press*	973.924092
Fieseler, Robert W. *Tinderbox*	364.152
FitzGerald, Frances. *Fire in the Lake*	959.704
Follett, Ken. *On Wings of Eagles*	955
Forman, James. *Locking up Our Own*	364.973
Fuller, Alexandra. *Don't Let's Go to the Dogs Tonight*	B
Givhan, Robin. *The Battle of Versailles*	746.9
Graff, Garrett M. *Watergate*	973.924
Green, Robin. *The Only Girl*	070.92
Guillermoprieto, Alma. *Dancing with Cuba*	972.9106
Guinn, Jeff. *The Road to Jonestown*	289.9
Halberstam, David. *The Best and the Brightest*	973.92
Harry, Debbie. *Face It*	B
Hazzard, Kevin M. *American Sirens*	362.18
Heller, Jason. *Strange Stars*	781.6609
Hendricks, Steve. *The Unquiet Grave*	323.1197
Hermes, Will. *Love Goes to Buildings on Fire*	781.64
Indyk, Martin. *Master of the Game*	327.73
Kanigel, Robert. *Eyes on the Street*	B
Kaufmann, Uri R. *Eighteen Days of October*	956.04
Keefe, Patrick Radden. ★*Say Nothing*	364.152
King, David. *Six Days in August*	364.15
Lattin, Don. *The Harvard Psychedelic Club*	973.922092
Lee, Heath Hardage. ★*The League of Wives*	959.704
Levin, Josh. *The Queen*	364.16
Levy, Shawn. ★*In on the Joke*	792.7
Maddow, Rachel. *Bag Man*	B
Manzione, Gianmarc. *Pin Action*	B

PUBLIC LIBRARY CORE COLLECTION: NONFICTION
Twentieth Edition

McCallum, Jack. *Golden Days*	796.323
McShane Wulfhart, Nell. *The Great Stewardess Rebellion*	331.4
Mendez, Antonio J. *Argo*	955.05
Minutaglio, Bill. *The Most Dangerous Man in America*	B
Moore, Susanna. *Miss Aluminum*	813
Morley, Jefferson. *Scorpions' Dance*	973.924
O'Brien, Keith. *Paradise Falls*	363.738
Parini, Jay. *Borges and Me*	813
Parrado, Nando. ★*Miracle in the Andes*	982
Perlstein, Rick. *The Invisible Bridge*	973.924
Perlstein, Rick. ★*Reaganland*	973.926
Phillips-Fein, Kim. *Fear City*	330.9747
Prose, Francine. *1974*	B
Read, Piers Paul. ★*Alive*	982
Reston, James. *The Conviction of Richard Nixon*	973.924092
Reynolds, Simon. *Shock and Awe*	781.6609
Riedel, Michael. *Razzle Dazzle*	792.09
Rumsfeld, Donald. *When the Center Held*	973.925092
Rush, Chris. *The Light Years*	B
Schulman, Bruce J. *The Seventies*	973.92
Smith, Richard Norton. *An Ordinary Man*	B
Stanley, Bob. ★*The Story of the Bee Gees*	782.42164
Tarantino, Quentin. *Cinema Speculation*	791.43
Theroux, Paul. *The Great Railway Bazaar*	915
Thomas, Evan. *Being Nixon*	B
Thompson, Heather Ann. *Blood in the Water*	365
Ung, Loung. *First They Killed My Father*	959.604
Vickers, Michael G. *By All Means Available*	355
Voloj, Julian. *Ghetto Brother*	741.5
Waters, Alice. *Coming to My Senses*	B
Weiner, Tim. *One Man Against the World*	B
Williams, Mary. *The Lost Daughter*	B
Winder, Elizabeth. *Parachute Women*	782.42164
Woodward, Bob. *The Final Days*	B
Yang, Jisheng. *The World Turned Upside Down*	951.05
Young, Rob. *Electric Eden*	781.62
1974. Prose, Francine	B

1980S

Alexie, Sherman. *You Don't Have to Say You Love Me*	818
Ambinder, Marc. *The Brink*	355.5
Baker, Peter. *The Man Who Ran Washington*	B
Berendt, John. *Midnight in the Garden of Good and Evil*	975.8
Bird, Kai. *The Outlier*	973.926
Bowden, Mark. *Guests of the Ayatollah*	955.05
Brands, H. W. *Reagan*	B
Broome, Brian. ★*Punch Me up to the Gods*	B
Brown, Tina. *The Vanity Fair Diaries*	B
Burke, Monte. *Lords of the Fly*	799.124
Carter, Jimmy. *A Full Life*	B
Carter, Jimmy. *Keeping Faith*	B
Carter, Jimmy. *White House Diary*	973.926
Coffey, Wayne R. ★*The Boys of Winter*	796.962
Coll, Steve. ★*Ghost Wars*	958.104
De Semlyen, Nick. *Wild and Crazy Guys*	920
De Vise, Daniel. ★*The Blues Brothers*	791.43
Deng, Alephonsion. *They Poured Fire on Us from the Sky*	B
Douglas, John E. *When a Killer Calls*	364.152
Eizenstat, Stuart. ★*President Carter*	B
Fairbanks, Amanda M. *The Lost Boys of Montauk*	910.91
Feifer, Gregory. *The Great Gamble*	958.104
France, David. *How to Survive a Plague*	362.196
Friedman, Thomas L. ★*From Beirut to Jerusalem*	956.04
Golinkin, Lev. *A Backpack, a Bear, and Eight Crates of Vodka*	B
Gooch, Brad. *Radiant*	B
Gordon, Kim. *Girl in a Band*	B
Greenman, Ben. *Dig If You Will the Picture*	B
Grossman, David. *The Yellow Wind*	956.95
Gulman, Gary. *Misfit*	B
Halberstam, David. *The Amateurs*	B
Higginbotham, Adam. ★*Midnight in Chernobyl*	363.17
Kenda, Joe. *Killer Triggers*	364.152
Lanegan, Mark. *Sing Backwards and Weep*	B
Longo, Matthew. *The Picnic*	947.084
Mann, Jim. *The Rebellion of Ronald Reagan*	973.927092
Mar, Alex. *Seventy Times Seven*	362.88
McGough, Matthew. *The Lazarus Files*	364.152
McGrath, Tom. *Triumph of the Yuppies*	305.242
Mealer, Bryan. *The Kings of Big Spring*	B
Mike D. *Beastie Boys Book*	782.42164
Mohan, Rohini. *The Seasons of Trouble*	954.9303
Moss, Gabrielle. *Paperback Crush*	813.009
Navarro, Joe. *Three Minutes to Doomsday*	B
Pearlman, Jeff. *Football for a Buck*	796.332
Perlstein, Rick. ★*Reaganland*	973.926
Ramsey, Donovan X. ★*When Crack Was King*	362.29
Reagan, Ronald. *The Reagan Diaries*	B
Remnick, David. *Lenin's Tomb*	947.085
Riedel, Michael. *Razzle Dazzle*	792.09
Rosen, Charles. *Sugar*	B
Satrapi, Marjane. ★*The Complete Persepolis*	741.5
Sattouf, Riad. *The Arab of the Future 2*	741.5
Sebestyen, Victor. *Revolution 1989*	947.085
Spitz, Bob. ★*Reagan*	B
Taubman, William. *Gorbachev*	B
Taylor, Fred. *The Berlin Wall*	943
Tumulty, Karen. *The Triumph of Nancy Reagan*	B
Vickers, Michael G. *By All Means Available*	355
Weingarten, Gene. ★*One Day*	973
Wertheim, L. Jon. *Glory Days*	796.09

1990S

Abdurraqib, Hanif. ★*There's Always This Year*	796.323
Beah, Ishmael. ★*A Long Way Gone*	B
Berendt, John. *The City of Falling Angels*	945
Blair, Tony. *A Journey*	B
Bowden, Mark. *Black Hawk Down*	967.7305
Branch, Taylor. *The Clinton Tapes*	973.929
Bukreev, Anatolii Nikolaevich. *The Climb*	796.52
Carriere, Alice. *Everything/Nothing/Someone*	B
Clinton, Bill. *My Life*	B
Coll, Steve. ★*Ghost Wars*	958.104
Corrigan, Kelly. *Glitter and Glue*	B
Crowe, Lauren Goldstein. *The Towering World of Jimmy Choo*	391.4
Deng, Alephonsion. *They Poured Fire on Us from the Sky*	B
Fernando, S. H., Jr. *From the Streets of Shaolin*	782.421
France, David. *How to Survive a Plague*	362.196
Friedman, Matti. *Pumpkinflowers*	B
Friedman, Thomas L. ★*From Beirut to Jerusalem*	956.04
Ganz, John. *When the Clock Broke*	320.52
Green, Elon. *Last Call*	363.15
Harris, Blake J. *Console Wars*	338.7
Harvilla, Rob. *60 Songs That Explain the '90s*	782.42164
Hemon, Aleksandar. *My Parents*	814
Higginbotham, Adam. ★*Midnight in Chernobyl*	363.17
Hsu, Hua. ★*Stay True*	B
Junger, Sebastian. *The Perfect Storm*	974.4
Kenda, Joe. *Killer Triggers*	364.152
Klosterman, Chuck. ★*The Nineties*	306.0973
Kornacki, Steve. *The Red and the Blue*	306.20973
Lanegan, Mark. *Sing Backwards and Weep*	B
Maass, Peter. *Love Thy Neighbor*	949.702
Marshall, Greg. *Leg*	B
Moby. *Porcelain*	B
Mohan, Rohini. *The Seasons of Trouble*	954.9303
Moss, Gabrielle. *Paperback Crush*	813.009
Murakami, Haruki. *Underground*	364.15
Pearlman, Jeff. ★*Three-Ring Circus*	796.323
Rakoff, Joanna Smith. *My Salinger Year*	B
Ramsey, Donovan X. ★*When Crack Was King*	362.29
Remnick, David. *Lenin's Tomb*	947.085
Riedel, Michael. *Singular Sensation*	792
Sebestyen, Victor. *Revolution 1989*	947.085
Singh, Simon. *Fermat's Enigma*	512
Taubman, William. *Gorbachev*	B
Worley, Jennifer. *Neon Girls*	792.7
Yang, Jeff. ★*Rise*	973
The 1997 Masters. Woods, Tiger	B

19TH CENTURY

Achorn, Edward. *The Lincoln Miracle*	973.6
Ackmann, Martha. ★*These Fevered Days*	B
Ackroyd, Peter. *Revolution*	941.07
Allgor, Catherine. *A Perfect Union*	B
Aly, Gotz. *Europe Against the Jews*	305.892
Ambrose, Stephen E. *Nothing Like It in the World*	385
Ambrose, Stephen E. ★*Undaunted Courage*	917.804
Arana, Marie. *Bolivar*	B
Ash, Stephen V. *Firebrand of Liberty*	973.7

AUTHOR, TITLE, SERIES AND SUBJECT INDEX

Auster, Paul. *Burning Boy*	B
Ayers, Edward L. *American Visions*	973.5
Ball, Edward. *Life of a Klansman*	305.8009763
Barnes, Julian. *Keeping an Eye Open*	709.04
Barnes, Julian. *The Man in the Red Coat*	B
Baron, David. *American Eclipse*	523.7
Barra, Allen. *Inventing Wyatt Earp*	B
Barry, John M. *Rising Tide*	977
Bartlett, Rosamund. ★*Tolstoy*	B
Basbanes, Nicholas A. ★*Cross of Snow*	B
Bate, Jonathan. *Radical Wordsworth*	B
Baudelaire, Charles. *Les Fleurs Du Mal*	841
Baudelaire, Charles. *Poems*	841
Beam, Alex. *American Crucifixion*	B
Beeman, Richard R. *Our Lives, Our Fortunes and Our Sacred Honor*	973.3
Begley, Adam. *The Great Nadar*	B
Bell, Julian. *Van Gogh*	B
Bellos, David. *The Novel of the Century*	843
Berg, Scott W. ★*38 Nooses*	973.7
Berger, William. *Puccini Without Excuses*	782.1
Berger, William. *Verdi with a Vengeance*	B
Binyon, T. J. *Pushkin*	B
Black Elk. *Black Elk Speaks*	B
Blackmon, Douglas A. *Slavery by Another Name*	305.896
Blight, David W. ★*Frederick Douglass*	B
Blight, David W. *A Slave No More*	B
Blum, Deborah. *Ghost Hunters*	133.9
Blumenthal, Sidney. ★*All the Powers of Earth*	B
Blumenthal, Sidney. *A Self-Made Man*	B
Blumenthal, Sidney. *Wrestling with His Angel*	B
Boessenecker, John. *Gentleman Bandit*	B
Boles, John B. *Jefferson*	B
Boorstin, Daniel J. *The Americans*	973
Bordewich, Fergus M. *America's Great Debate*	973.6
Bordewich, Fergus M. *Bound for Canaan*	973.7
Bordewich, Fergus M. *Congress at War*	324.2734
Bordewich, Fergus M. *Klan War*	973.8
Borges, Jorge Luis. ★*Selected Poems*	861
Borneman, Walter R. *Polk*	B
Bostridge, Mark. *Florence Nightingale*	B
Brands, H. W. *The Age of Gold*	979.4
Brands, H. W. ★*Andrew Jackson, His Life and Times*	B
Brands, H. W. *The First American*	B
Brands, H. W. ★*Heirs of the Founders*	973.5
Brands, H. W. ★*The Man Who Saved the Union*	B
Brands, H. W. ★*The Zealot and the Emancipator*	920
Brandt, Anthony. *The Man Who Ate His Boots*	910.91
Brewster, Todd. *Lincoln's Gamble*	973.7
Broadwater, Jeff. ★*George Mason*	B
Broadwater, Jeff. *James Madison*	B
Broers, Michael. *Napoleon*	B
Broers, Michael. *Napoleon*	944.05
Broers, Michael. *Napoleon*	B
Brown, Daniel James. *The Indifferent Stars Above*	B
Brown, Dee. *The American West*	978
Brown, Dee. ★*Bury My Heart at Wounded Knee*	978
Brown, Jasmine. *Twice as Hard*	610.92
Brown, Terence. *The Life of W.B. Yeats*	B
Browne, E. J. *Charles Darwin*	B
Browne, E. J. *Charles Darwin*	B
Browning, Robert. ★*Robert Browning's Poetry*	821
Bunting, Josiah. *Ulysses S. Grant*	B
Burlingame, Michael. *Abraham Lincoln*	B
Burlingame, Michael. *The Black Man's President*	973.7
Burns, Mike. *The Only One Living to Tell*	305.897
Burrough, Bryan. *Forget the Alamo*	976.043
Burstein, Andrew. *Madison and Jefferson*	973.4
Buruma, Ian. *Inventing Japan, 1853-1964*	952.03
Byrne, Eugene. *Darwin*	741.5
Campbell, Olivia. *Women in White Coats*	610.92
Cannato, Vincent. *American Passage*	325.73
Carretta, Vincent. *Equiano, the African*	B
Carwardine, Richard. *Lincoln*	B
Castner, Brian. *Stampede*	971.9
Chang, Gordon H. *Ghosts of Gold Mountain*	331.6
Chang, Jung. *Empress Dowager Cixi*	B
Chasteen, John Charles. *Americanos*	980
Cheever, Susan. *American Bloomsbury*	920
Cheney, Lynne V. *James Madison*	B
Cheney, Lynne V. *The Virginia Dynasty*	B
Chernaik, Judith. *Schumann*	B
Chernow, Ron. ★*Grant*	978.1
Clavin, Thomas. *Dodge City*	B
Clavin, Thomas. *Wild Bill*	B
Clinton, Catherine. *Harriet Tubman*	B
Colaiaco, James A. *Frederick Douglass and the Fourth of July*	973.7
Coleridge, Samuel Taylor. *The Complete Poems*	821
Collins, Gail. *William Henry Harrison*	B
Conaway, James. *America's Library*	027.5
Connell, Evan S. *Son of the Morning Star*	973.8
Cook, Jane Hampton. *American Phoenix*	973.5
Cornwell, Bernard. *Waterloo*	940.2
Cornwell, Patricia Daniels. *Ripper*	364.152
Cox, Anna-Lisa. *The Bone and Sinew of the Land*	977
Cozzens, Peter. *A Brutal Reckoning*	973.5
Cozzens, Peter. *The Earth Is Weeping*	978
Craig, William. *Yankee Come Home*	972.9107
Craughwell, Thomas J. *Stealing Lincoln's Body*	973.7092
Crosby, Molly Caldwell. *The American Plague*	614.5
Cross, William R. *Winslow Homer*	759.13
Crutchfield, James A. *Revolt at Taos*	972
Dalrymple, William. *The Return of a King*	958.1
Dana, Richard Henry. *Two Years Before the Mast*	910.4
Darwin, Charles. ★*The Voyage of the Beagle*	508
Dawidziak, Mark. *A Mystery of Mysteries*	B
De Courcy, Anne. *The Husband Hunters*	920
Delbanco, Andrew. *The War Before the War*	973.7
Dilbeck, D. H. *Frederick Douglass*	B
Dinesen, Isak. *Out of Africa*	967.62
Dolnick, Edward. *Seeds of Life*	612.6
Donald, David Herbert. *Lincoln*	B
Donovan, Jim. *The Blood of Heroes*	976.4
Donovan, Jim. *A Terrible Glory*	973.8
Douglass, Frederick. ★*Frederick Douglass*	973.8
Douglass, Frederick. *My Bondage and My Freedom*	B
Douglass, Frederick. *The Portable Frederick Douglass*	973.8
Dray, Philip. *Capitol Men*	973.8
Drury, Bob. *The Heart of Everything That Is*	B
Duggan, Christopher. *The Force of Destiny*	945
Dunbar, Erica Armstrong. ★*She Came to Slay*	B
Durkin, Hannah. ★*The Survivors of the Clotilda*	306.362
Eckert, Allan W. *A Sorrow in Our Heart*	B
Egan, Timothy. ★*Short Nights of the Shadow Catcher*	770.92
Egerton, Douglas R. *Thunder at the Gates*	973.7
Eisler, Benita. *The Red Man's Bones*	B
Ellis, Joseph J. *American Creation*	973.3
Ellis, Joseph J. *American Sphinx*	973.4
Ellis, Joseph J. *The Cause*	973.3
Ellmann, Richard. *Oscar Wilde*	B
Essinger, James. *Ada's Algorithm*	B
Evans, Richard J. *The Pursuit of Power*	940.2
Feder, Rachel. *The Darcy Myth*	823
Felder, Deborah G. *The American Women's Almanac*	305.40973
Feldman, Noah. *The Broken Constitution*	973.7
Fields-Black, Edda L. *Combee*	973.7
Figes, Orlando. *The Crimean War*	947
Figes, Orlando. *The Europeans*	920
Finkelman, Paul. *Millard Fillmore*	B
Fitzharris, Lindsey. *The Butchering Art*	B
Flanders, Judith. *The Victorian City*	942.1
Foner, Eric. *The Fiery Trial*	973.7092
Foner, Eric. *Forever Free*	973.8
Foner, Eric. ★*Gateway to Freedom*	973.7
Foner, Eric. ★*Reconstruction*	973.8
Ford, Lacy K. *Deliver Us from Evil*	973.7
Fox, Margalit. *The Talented Mrs. Mandelbaum*	364.1
Frank, Joseph. ★*Dostoevsky*	B
Franklin, Benjamin. ★*Autobiography, Poor Richard, and Later Writings*	973.2
Franklin, Benjamin. *The Compleated Autobiography*	B
Freeberg, Ernest. *A Traitor to His Species*	B
Freeman, Douglas Southall. *Lee*	B
Frey, Julia Bloch. *Toulouse-Lautrec*	B
Gallagher, Winifred. *New Women in the Old West*	978.02
Garcia Lorca, Federico. *Collected Poems*	861
Garcia Lorca, Federico. *Poet in New York*	861

PUBLIC LIBRARY CORE COLLECTION: NONFICTION
Twentieth Edition

Gardner, Mark L. *The Earth Is All That Lasts*	978.004
Gaskell, Elizabeth Cleghorn. *The Life of Charlotte Bronte*	B
Gates, Henry Louis. ★*Stony the Road*	973
Genovese, Eugene D. *Roll, Jordan, Roll*	975
Gerdts, William H. *American Impressionism*	759.13
Gienapp, William E. *Abraham Lincoln and Civil War America*	B
Ginzberg, Lori D. *Elizabeth Cady Stanton*	B
Goldstone, Lawrence. *On Account of Race*	342.7308
Gompertz, Will. *What Are You Looking At?*	709
Goodheart, Adam. *1861*	973.7
Goodman, Ruth. *How to Be a Victorian*	941.08
Goodwin, Doris Kearns. ★*Team of Rivals*	B
Gordon, Andrew. *A Modern History of Japan*	952
Gordon, Charlotte. *Romantic Outlaws*	920
Gordon-Reed, Annette. *Andrew Johnson*	B
Gordon-Reed, Annette. ★*The Hemingses of Monticello*	920
Grant, James. ★*John Adams*	B
Grant, Ulysses S. ★*The Annotated Memoirs of Ulysses S. Grant*	B
Gray, Charlotte. ★*Reluctant Genius*	920
Greenberg, Amy S. *Lady First*	B
Greenidge, Kerri. *Black Radical*	B
Guelzo, Allen C. *Lincoln and Douglas*	973.6
Gutzman, Kevin R. C. *The Jeffersonians*	973.5
Gwynne, S. C. *Empire of the Summer Moon*	B
Haag, Pamela. ★*The Gunning of America*	338.4
Hahn, Steven. *A Nation Under Our Feet*	975
Hallman, J. C. *Say Anarcha*	618.1
Hamlin, Kimberly A. *Free Thinker*	B
Hardy, Thomas. *The Collected Letters of Thomas Hardy*	823
Harlan, Elizabeth. *George Sand*	B
Harlan, Louis R. *Booker T. Washington*	B
Harlan, Louis R. *Booker T. Washington*	B
Harman, Claire. *Charlotte Bronte*	B
Harman, Claire. *Murder by the Book*	364.152
Harris, J. William. *The Hanging of Thomas Jeremiah*	B
Harvey, Eleanor Jones. *The Civil War and American Art*	740.9
Herbert, Zbigniew. *The Collected Poems, 1956-1998*	891.8
Herlihy, David V. *The Lost Cyclist*	B
Hiltzik, Michael A. *Iron Empires*	385.0973
Hitchens, Christopher. *Thomas Jefferson*	B
Hochschild, Adam. *Bury the Chains*	326
Hochschild, Adam. *King Leopold's Ghost*	967.51
Hogeland, William. *Declaration*	973.3
Holifield, E. Brooks. *Theology in America*	230
Holway, Tatiana M. *The Flower of Empire*	727
Holzer, Harold. *Brought Forth on This Continent*	973.7
Holzer, Harold. *A Just and Generous Nation*	973.7092
Holzer, Harold. *Monument Man*	B
Horwitz, Tony. ★*Midnight Rising*	973.7
Howe, Daniel Walker. *What Hath God Wrought*	973.5
Hoyer, Katja. *Blood and Iron*	943.08
Hughes, Robert. *The Fatal Shore*	994
Hughes, Robert. *Goya*	B
Humez, Jean McMahon. *Harriet Tubman*	B
Hutton, Paul Andrew. *The Apache Wars*	979
Hutton, Ronald. *The Triumph of the Moon*	133.4
Huxley, Elspeth Joscelin Grant. *The Flame Trees of Thika*	B
Hyde, Anne Farrar. ★*Born of Lakes and Plains*	978
Inskeep, Steve. *Imperfect Union*	B
Inskeep, Steve. *Jacksonland*	973.56
Isaacson, Walter. ★*Benjamin Franklin*	B
Isenberg, Nancy. *The Problem of Democracy*	973.4
Jackson, Joe. *Black Elk*	978.004
Jacobs, Harriet. ★*Incidents in the Life of a Slave Girl*	B
James, Henry. *Literary Criticism; Vol. 1*	809
Jeal, Tim. *Explorers of the Nile*	920
Jefferson, Thomas. *Writings*	973.3
Johnson, Paul. *Napoleon*	B
Johnson, Steven. *The Ghost Map*	614.5
Johnson, Victoria. ★*American Eden*	580.973
Johnson, Walter. *Soul by Soul*	976.3
Jones, Jacqueline. *Saving Savannah*	975.8
Kaplan, Fred. *John Quincy Adams*	B
Kaplan, Fred. *Lincoln and the Abolitionists*	973.7092
Karnow, Stanley. *Vietnam, a History*	959.704
Kaufman, Jonathan. *The Last Kings of Shanghai*	951
Kaufman, Kenn. *The Birds That Audubon Missed*	598
Kavanagh, Julie. *The Irish Assassins*	941.5
Kearse, Bettye. *The Other Madisons*	920
Keegan, John. *The American Civil War*	973.7
Kelly, John. *The Graves Are Walking*	941.5081
Keneally, Thomas. *A Commonwealth of Thieves*	994
Kennedy, Michael. *Richard Strauss*	B
Kertzer, David I. *The Pope Who Would Be King*	282.092
Kiernan, Denise. *The Last Castle*	975.6
Kildea, Paul Francis. *Chopin's Piano*	B
Kilmeade, Brian. ★*Andrew Jackson and the Miracle of New Orleans*	973.5
King, Greg. *Twilight of Empire*	943.6
King, Ross. *The Judgment of Paris*	759.4
Koch, Bea. *Mad and Bad*	920
Korda, Michael. *Clouds of Glory*	B
Kytle, Ethan J. *Denmark Vesey's Garden*	975.7
Lance, Rachel. *In the Waves*	973.7
Lane, Charles. *The Day Freedom Died*	976.3
Lane, Charles. *Freedom's Detective*	B
Langguth, A. J. *After Lincoln*	973.8
Larson, Erik. ★*The Devil in the White City*	364.15
Larson, Kate Clifford. *Bound for the Promised Land*	B
Laskin, David. *The Children's Blizzard*	977
Leerhsen, Charles. ★*Butch Cassidy*	B
Lemann, Nicholas. *Redemption*	975
Levine, Bruce C. *The Fall of the House of Dixie*	973.7
Levine, Bruce C. *Thaddeus Stevens*	B
Levine, Robert S. ★*The Failed Promise*	973.8
Lewis, David L. ★*W.E.B. Du Bois*	B
Lincoln, Abraham. *Speeches and Writings, 1832-1858*	973.5
Lincoln, Abraham. *Speeches and Writings, 1859-1865*	973.6
Lineberry, Cate. *Be Free or Die*	B
Lowenstein, Roger. *Ways and Means*	973.7
Lucey, Donna M. *Sargent's Women*	920
Luxenberg, Steve. ★*Separate*	342.7308
MacColl, Gail. *To Marry an English Lord*	974.7
Maier, Pauline. *American Scripture*	973.3
Masur, Kate. *Until Justice Be Done*	323.1196
May, Gary. *John Tyler*	B
May, Gregory. *A Madman's Will*	973.5
Mazower, Mark. *The Greek Revolution*	949.5
McCalman, Iain. *Darwin's Armada*	576.8
McClain, James. *Japan*	952.03
McCullough, David G. *The Greater Journey*	920
McCullough, David G. ★*John Adams*	B
McCullough, David G. *The Path Between the Seas*	972.87
McGrath, Tim. *James Monroe*	B
McLoughlin, William Gerald. *After the Trail of Tears*	973
McMurtry, Larry. *Crazy Horse*	B
McPherson, James M. ★*Abraham Lincoln*	B
McPherson, James M. *For Cause and Comrades*	973.7
McPherson, James M. ★*Tried by War*	973.7
Meacham, Jon. ★*American Lion*	B
Meacham, Jon. ★*And There Was Light*	B
Meacham, Jon. ★*Thomas Jefferson*	B
Meltzer, Brad. *The Lincoln Conspiracy*	973.7092
Merchant, Brian. *Blood in the Machine*	303.48
Merry, Robert W. *A Country of Vast Designs*	B
Merry, Robert W. *President McKinley*	B
Meyer, Eugene L. *Five for Freedom*	973.7
Miles, Tiya. ★*Night Flyer*	B
Millard, Candice. *Destiny of the Republic*	973.8
Millard, Candice. ★*Hero of the Empire*	968.04
Miller, Char. *Gifford Pinchot and the Making of Modern Environmentalism*	B
Miller, Lucasta. ★*Keats*	821
Miller, Scott. *The President and the Assassin*	973.8
Mirski, Sean A. *We May Dominate the World*	973.91
Mitchell, Elizabeth. *Lincoln's Lie*	973.7092
Montillo, Roseanne. *The Lady and Her Monsters*	823
Moore, Kate. ★*The Woman They Could Not Silence*	B
Mordden, Ethan. *Ziegfeld*	B
Morgan-Owens, Jessie. *Girl in Black and White*	B
Morris, Edmund. ★*The Rise of Theodore Roosevelt*	B
Morrison, Robert. *The Regency Years*	941.07
Morrison, Toni. ★*The Origin of Others*	809
Mort, T. A. *Thieves' Road*	978.3
Naifeh, Steven W. *Van Gogh*	B
Nasaw, David. *The Chief*	B
Nathans, Sydney. *To Free a Family*	B
Nelson, Megan Kate. *The Three-Cornered War*	978

AUTHOR, TITLE, SERIES AND SUBJECT INDEX

Nimura, Janice P. *Daughters of the Samurai*	920
Nimura, Janice P. ★*The Doctors Blackwell*	610.92
Norgren, Jill. *Belva Lockwood*	B
Norrell, Robert J. *Up from History*	B
Northup, Solomon. *Twelve Years a Slave*	B
O'Keeffe, Paul. *Waterloo*	940.2
O'Sullivan, Emer. *The Fall of the House of Wilde*	B
Ogilvie, Sarah. *The Dictionary People*	423
Oller, John. *American Queen*	B
Paine, Thomas. ★*Rights of Man*	320.5
Painter, Nell Irvin. ★*Sojourner Truth*	B
Parks, Tim. *The Hero's Way*	945
Paul, Joel R. *Indivisible*	973.5
Philbrick, Nathaniel. ★*The Last Stand*	973.8
Phillips, Kevin. *1775*	973.3
Platt, Stephen R. *Autumn in the Heavenly Kingdom*	951
Platt, Stephen R. *Imperial Twilight*	951
Postel, Charles. *Equality*	305.50973
Powers, Thomas. *The Killing of Crazy Horse*	B
Pryor, Elizabeth Brown. *Six Encounters with Lincoln*	973.7092
Puleo, Stephen. *Voyage of Mercy*	363.8
Raban, Jonathan. *Bad Land*	978
Rae, Noel. ★*The Great Stain*	306.3
Raines, Ben. *The Last Slave Ship*	306.362
Rakove, Jack N. *Revolutionaries*	973.3
Rasenberger, Jim. *Revolver*	B
Rasmussen, Daniel. *American Uprising*	976.3
Rathbone, John Paul. *The Sugar King of Havana*	B
Rediker, Marcus. *The Amistad Rebellion*	326.0973
Reese, William J. *Testing Wars in the Public Schools*	371.260973
Reid, David. *The Brazen Age*	974.7
Reynolds, David S. ★*Abe*	B
Reynolds, David S. *John Brown, Abolitionist*	B
Rhoden, William C. *$40 Million Slaves*	796
Richardson, Edmund. *The King's Shadow*	958.1
Richardson, Heather Cox. ★*How the South Won the Civil War*	306.20973
Richardson, Robert D. *Emerson*	814
Richardson, Robert D. *William James*	B
Robb, Graham. *The Discovery of France*	944
Roberts, Andrew. ★*Napoleon*	B
Roberts, Cokie. *Founding Mothers*	920
Roberts, Cokie. *Ladies of Liberty*	920
Roberts, David. *Once They Moved Like the Wind*	B
Roberts, Jason. *A Sense of the World*	B
Roe, Sue. *The Private Lives of the Impressionists*	920
Roker, Al. *Ruthless Tide*	974.8
Rothman, Joshua D. *The Ledger and the Chain*	306.362
Rubenhold, Hallie. ★*The Five*	362.88
Sachs, Harvey. *The Ninth*	784.2
Safranski, Rudiger. *Goethe*	B
Sampson, Fiona. *In Search of Mary Shelley*	B
Sancton, Julian. *Madhouse at the End of the Earth*	919.8904
Sandburg, Carl. *Abraham Lincoln*	B
Saunt, Claudio. *Unworthy Republic*	323.1197
Schindler, Meriel. *The Lost Cafe Schindler*	943.64
Sedgwick, John. *War of Two*	973.4
Seiple, Samantha. *Louisa on the Front Lines*	B
Senik, Troy. *A Man of Iron*	B
Servadio, Gaia. *Rossini*	B
Sharfstein, Daniel J. ★*Thunder in the Mountains*	979.5
Shelden, Michael. *Mark Twain*	B
Sides, Hampton. *Blood and Thunder*	978
Sides, Hampton. ★*In the Kingdom of Ice*	910.4
Simon, James F. *What Kind of Nation*	342.73
Sims, Michael. *Arthur and Sherlock*	B
Sinha, Manisha. ★*The Rise and Fall of the Second American Republic*	973.8
Skal, David J. *Something in the Blood*	823
Smith, Helmut Walser. *Germany, a Nation in Its Time*	943
Smith, Patricia. *Unshuttered*	811
Snodgrass, Mary Ellen. *The Underground Railroad*	973.7
Snow, Peter. *When Britain Burned the White House*	975.3
Snyder, Christina. *Great Crossings*	976.9
Sohn, Amy. *The Man Who Hated Women*	363.28
Spence, Jonathan D. *God's Chinese Son*	951
Stahr, Walter. *Seward*	B
Stanley, Amy. *Stranger in the Shogun's City*	B
Stark, Peter. *Astoria*	979.5
Stauffer, John. *Picturing Fredrick Douglass*	B
Steinberg, Jonathan. *Bismarck*	B
Stewart, David O. *George Washington*	973.4
Stiles, T. J. *Custer's Trials*	B
Stiles, T. J. ★*The First Tycoon*	B
Sturgis, Matthew. *Oscar Wilde*	B
Swafford, Jan. *Johannes Brahms*	B
Swarns, Rachel L. *The 272*	975.2
Symonds, Craig L. *Lincoln and His Admirals*	B
Tabor, Nick. *Africatown*	976.1
Tallis, Frank. ★*Mortal Secrets*	B
Taylor, Alan. *American Civil Wars*	973.7
Taylor, Alan. *American Republics*	973.3
Taylor, Alan. *The Civil War of 1812*	973.5
Taylor, Alan. *The Divided Ground*	974.7
Taylor, Stephen. *Commander*	B
Tefertiller, Casey. *Wyatt Earp*	B
Tennyson, Alfred. *Poems*	821
Thomas, Louisa. *Louisa*	B
Thoreau, Henry David. *The Maine Woods*	917
Thoreau, Henry David. ★*Walden, Or, Life in the Woods*	813
Tobin, Jacqueline. *From Midnight to Dawn*	973.7
Tobin, Jacqueline. *Hidden in Plain View*	973.7
Todd, Kim. *Sensational*	920
Tomalin, Claire. *Thomas Hardy*	B
Traub, James. *John Quincy Adams*	B
Tresch, John. *The Reason for the Darkness of the Night*	B
Trubert-Tollu, Chantal. ★*The House of Worth 1858-1954*	746.92
Tuccille, Jerome. *The Roughest Riders*	973.8
Twain, Mark. *Autobiography of Mark Twain*	B
Twain, Mark. ★*Autobiography of Mark Twain*	B
Twain, Mark. ★*Autobiography of Mark Twain*	B
Ujifusa, Steven. *Barons of the Sea*	387.5
Unger, Harlow G. *The Last Founding Father*	B
Utley, Robert M. ★*Geronimo*	B
Utley, Robert M. *Sitting Bull*	B
Von Drehle, Dave. ★*Triangle*	974.7
Walker, Ronald W. ★*Massacre at Mountain Meadows*	979.2
Walls, Laura Dassow. ★*Henry David Thoreau*	B
Ward, Geoffrey C. *A Disposition to Be Rich*	B
Ward, Geoffrey C. *The West*	978
Washington, Booker T. ★*Up from Slavery*	B
Wasik, Bill. ★*Our Kindred Creatures*	179
Wayne, Tiffany K. *Critical Companion to Ralph Waldo Emerson*	814
Weisman, Steven R. *The Chosen Wars*	296.0973
Wert, Jeffry D. *Cavalryman of the Lost Cause*	B
Wert, Jeffry D. *Custer*	B
White, Gayle Jessup. *Reclamation*	B
White, Ronald C. *A. Lincoln*	B
White, Ronald C. ★*American Ulysses*	B
White, Ronald C. *Lincoln in Private*	B
White, Shane. *Prince of Darkness*	B
Whitman, Walt. ★*Leaves of Grass*	811
Whitman, Walt. ★*Poetry and Prose*	811
Whyte, Kenneth. *The Uncrowned King*	B
Wickenden, Dorothy. *The Agitators*	920
Widmer, Edward L. *Lincoln on the Verge*	B
Widmer, Edward L. *Martin Van Buren*	B
Wilkerson, Isabel. ★*The Warmth of Other Suns*	304.80973
Wilkinson, Toby A. H. *A World Beneath the Sands*	932
Williams, David. *Bitterly Divided*	973.7
Williams, Kidada E. *I Saw Death Coming*	973.8
Willis, Deborah. ★*The Black Civil War Soldier*	973.7
Willis, Deborah. *Envisioning Emancipation*	973.7
Willis, Deborah. *Reflections in Black*	770
Wills, Garry. *James Madison*	B
Wills, Garry. *Lincoln at Gettysburg*	973.7
Wilson, A. N. *The Mystery of Charles Dickens*	823
Wilson, Robert. *Barnum*	B
Wilson, Robert. *Mathew Brady*	B
Winchester, Simon. *The Map That Changed the World*	B
Winchester, Simon. *The Professor and the Madman*	423
Wineapple, Brenda. *Ecstatic Nation*	973.6
Wineapple, Brenda. *The Impeachers*	973.8
Winik, Jay. *April 1865*	973.7
Wojczuk, Tana. *Lady Romeo*	B
Wood, Gordon S. *Empire of Liberty*	973.4
Woodward, C. Vann. *The Strange Career of Jim Crow*	305.896
Wright, Jennifer Ashley. ★*Madame Restell*	B

PUBLIC LIBRARY CORE COLLECTION: NONFICTION
Twentieth Edition

Wulf, Andrea. *Magnificent Rebels*	830.9
Young, Kevin. *Ardency*	811
Zamoyski, Adam. *Napoleon*	B
Zucchino, David. *Wilmington's Lie*	305.8009756
2,100 Asanas. Lacerda, Daniel	613.7
2.00 A Day. Edin, Kathryn	339.4
★*200+ Original and Adapted Story Program Activities*. Reid, Rob	027.62

2000S (DECADE)

Ackerman, Spencer. *Reign of Terror*	973.931
Atwood, Margaret. *Burning Questions*	814
Balz, Daniel J. *The Battle for America, 2008*	973.932
Blair, Tony. *A Journey*	B
Bush, George W. *Decision Points*	B
Chandrasekaran, Rajiv. *Imperial Life in the Emerald City*	956.7044
Clinton, Hillary Rodham. *Living History*	B
Coates, Ta-Nehisi. ★*We Were Eight Years in Power*	305.896
Coll, Steve. ★*The Achilles Trap*	956.7044
Coll, Steve. *Directorate S*	958.104
D'Antonio, Michael. *The Hunting of Hillary*	B
Deng, Alephonsion. *They Poured Fire on Us from the Sky*	B
Ditum, Sarah. *Toxic*	920.72
Dorey-Stein, Beck. *From the Corner of the Oval*	B
Draper, Robert. *To Start a War*	956.7044
Klay, Phil. *Uncertain Ground*	359.9
Kranish, Michael. *Trump Revealed*	B
Kushner, Jacob. *Look Away*	305.9
Litt, David. *Thanks, Obama*	B
Martin, Brett. *Difficult Men*	791.4509
Mayer, Jane. ★*Dark Money*	973.932
Mohan, Rohini. *The Seasons of Trouble*	954.9303
Obama, Barack. ★*The Audacity of Hope*	B
Obama, Barack. ★*A Promised Land*	B
Obama, Michelle. ★*Becoming*	B
Packer, George. *The Assassins' Gate*	956.7044
Paulson, Henry M. *On the Brink*	330.973
Pearlman, Jeff. ★*Three-Ring Circus*	796.323
Remnick, David. *The Bridge*	B
Rhodes, Benjamin J. *The World as It Is*	973.932
Rice, Condoleezza. *No Higher Honor*	B
Riedel, Michael. *Singular Sensation*	792
Smith, Jean Edward. *Bush*	973.931
Soufan, Ali H. *The Black Banners Declassified*	363.325
Vonnegut, Kurt. ★*A Man Without a Country*	818
Wilson, Rick. *Running Against the Devil*	973.933
Yang, Jeff. ★*Rise*	973

2010S

Abouzeid, Rania. *No Turning Back*	956.9104
Abrams, Stacey. *Our Time Is Now*	324.60973
Ackerman, Spencer. *Reign of Terror*	973.931
Ahmad, Aeham. *The Pianist from Syria*	B
Atwood, Margaret. *Burning Questions*	814
Azad. *Long Shot*	B
Baker, Peter. *The Divider*	973.933
Berman, Geoffrey. *Holding the Line*	345.73
Bryant, Howard. *Full Dissidence*	306.20973
Carpenter, Amanda B. *Gaslighting America*	973.933
Clinton, Hillary Rodham. *What Happened*	328.73
D'Antonio, Michael. *The Hunting of Hillary*	B
Dagher, Sam. *Assad or We Burn the Country*	956.9104
Di Giovanni, Janine. *The Morning They Came for Us*	956.9104
Dorey-Stein, Beck. *From the Corner of the Oval*	B
Faleiro, Sonia. *The Good Girls*	364.152
Fenton, Justin. *We Own This City*	364.1
Finkel, David. *An American Dreamer*	975.8
Frum, David. *Trumpocracy*	973.933
Gessen, Masha. *Surviving Autocracy*	973.933
Hasen, Richard L. *Election Meltdown*	324.973
Hoffman, Carl. *Liar's Circus*	973.933
Johnston, David Cay. *It's Even Worse Than You Think*	973.933
Karl, Jonathan. *Front Row at the Trump Show*	973.933
Kirshner, Jodie Adams. ★*Broke*	336.3
Klay, Phil. *Uncertain Ground*	359.9
Kranish, Michael. *Trump Revealed*	B
Kurtz, Howard. *Media Madness*	973.933
Lemmon, Gayle Tzemach. *The Daughters of Kobani*	956.9104
Leonnig, Carol. *I Alone Can Fix It*	973.933
Levin, Daniel. *Proof of Life*	956.9104
Litt, David. *Thanks, Obama*	B
Mahtani, Shibani. *Among the Braves*	951.25
Malek, Alia. *The Home That Was Our Country*	B
Martin, Brett. *Difficult Men*	791.4509
Martini, Adrienne. *Somebody's Gotta Do It*	B
Mayer, Jane. ★*Dark Money*	973.932
Moore, Wes. ★*Five Days*	363.32
Obama, Barack. ★*A Promised Land*	B
Obama, Michelle. ★*Becoming*	B
Pearlman, Wendy. *We Crossed a Bridge and It Trembled*	956.9104
Petri, Alexandra. *Nothing Is Wrong and Here Is Why*	973.933
Preston, Richard. *Crisis in the Red Zone*	614.5
Reichl, Ruth. *My Kitchen Year*	641.5
Rezaian, Jason. *Prisoner*	B
Rhodes, Benjamin J. *The World as It Is*	973.932
Russell, Rupert. *Price Wars*	332.64
Samer. *The Raqqa Diaries*	956.9104
Schmidt, Michael S. ★*Donald Trump v. The United States*	973.933
Sullivan, Kevin. *Trump on Trial*	342.73
Thomson, Mike. *Syria's Secret Library*	956.9104
Toobin, Jeffrey. *True Crimes and Misdemeanors*	973.933
Trump, Mary L. *Too Much and Never Enough*	B
Vaillant, John. ★*Fire Weather*	363.37
Ward, Clarissa. *On All Fronts*	B
Warrick, Joby. *Red Line*	956.9104
Wilson, Rick. *Running Against the Devil*	973.933
Wolff, Michael. *Landslide*	973.933
Woodward, Bob. *Fear*	973.933
Yang, Jeff. ★*Rise*	973
★*2020*. Klinenberg, Eric	306

2020S

Abouzeid, Rania. *No Turning Back*	956.9104
Abrams, Stacey. *Our Time Is Now*	324.60973
Adichie, Chimamanda Ngozi. *Notes on Grief*	155.9
Ahmad, Aeham. *The Pianist from Syria*	B
Atwood, Margaret. *Burning Questions*	814
Azad. *Long Shot*	B
Baker, Peter. *The Divider*	973.933
Berman, Geoffrey. *Holding the Line*	345.73
Bryant, Howard. *Full Dissidence*	306.20973
Carpenter, Amanda B. *Gaslighting America*	973.933
Clinton, Hillary Rodham. *What Happened*	328.73
Dagher, Sam. *Assad or We Burn the Country*	956.9104
Di Giovanni, Janine. *The Morning They Came for Us*	956.9104
Finkel, David. *An American Dreamer*	975.8
Frum, David. *Trumpocracy*	973.933
Gessen, Masha. *Surviving Autocracy*	973.933
Hasen, Richard L. *Election Meltdown*	324.973
Hoffman, Carl. *Liar's Circus*	973.933
Johnston, David Cay. *It's Even Worse Than You Think*	973.933
Karl, Jonathan. *Front Row at the Trump Show*	973.933
Kelley, Margot Anne. *A Gardener at the End of the World*	615.8
Klay, Phil. *Uncertain Ground*	359.9
Kurtz, Howard. *Media Madness*	973.933
Lemmon, Gayle Tzemach. *The Daughters of Kobani*	956.9104
Leonnig, Carol. *I Alone Can Fix It*	973.933
Levin, Daniel. *Proof of Life*	956.9104
Malek, Alia. *The Home That Was Our Country*	B
Martini, Adrienne. *Somebody's Gotta Do It*	B
Pearlman, Wendy. *We Crossed a Bridge and It Trembled*	956.9104
Petri, Alexandra. *Nothing Is Wrong and Here Is Why*	973.933
Reilly, Ryan J. ★*Sedition Hunters*	364.1
Renkl, Margaret. *The Comfort of Crows*	814.6
Samer. *The Raqqa Diaries*	956.9104
Schmidt, Michael S. ★*Donald Trump v. The United States*	973.933
Sullivan, Kevin. *Trump on Trial*	342.73
Thomson, Mike. *Syria's Secret Library*	956.9104
Toobin, Jeffrey. *True Crimes and Misdemeanors*	973.933
Trump, Mary L. *Too Much and Never Enough*	B
Ward, Clarissa. *On All Fronts*	B
Warrick, Joby. *Red Line*	956.9104
Wilson, Rick. *Running Against the Devil*	973.933
Wolff, Michael. *Landslide*	973.933
Woodward, Bob. *Fear*	973.933
Woodward, Bob. *Peril*	973.933

20TH CENTURY

Abbott, Karen. *American Rose*	B
Abrahamian, Ervand. *The Coup*	955.05
Abrams, Dan. *Kennedy's Avenger*	973.922

1564

AUTHOR, TITLE, SERIES AND SUBJECT INDEX

Abrams, Dan. *Theodore Roosevelt for the Defense*	345.73
Abuelaish, Izzeldin. *I Shall Not Hate*	B
Achebe, Chinua. *The Education of a British-Protected Child*	B
Achebe, Chinua. *There Was a Country*	B
Ackerman, Diane. ★*The Zookeeper's Wife*	940.53
Ackmann, Martha. *The Mercury 13*	920
Ackroyd, Peter. *Innovation*	942.082
Adams, John. *Hallelujah Junction*	B
Adams, Michael Henry. *Style and Grace*	747
Agee, James. ★*Cotton Tenants*	976.1
Ahamed, Liaquat. *Lords of Finance*	920
Akcam, Taner. *A Shameful Act*	956.6
Akhmatova, Anna Andreevna. *Poems*	891.71
Albertine, Viv. *Clothes, Clothes, Clothes. Music, Music, Music*	B
Albright, Madeleine Korbel. *Prague Winter*	943.71
Aleksievich, Svetlana. *Last Witnesses*	940.53
Aleksievich, Svetlana. ★*The Unwomanly Face of War*	940.53
Alexander, Caroline. *The Endurance*	919.8
Allen, Frederick Lewis. *Only Yesterday*	973.9
Allende, Isabel. *My Invented Country*	B
Allende, Isabel. ★*Paula*	B
Allende, Isabel. *The Sum of Our Days*	B
Allport, Alan. *Britain at Bay*	940.53
Alt, Matt. *Pure Invention*	306.0952
Alter, Jonathan. *His Very Best*	B
Aly, Gotz. *Europe Against the Jews*	305.892
Ambrose, Stephen E. *Citizen Soldiers*	940.54
Ambrose, Stephen E. *D-Day, June 6, 1944*	940.54
Ambrose, Stephen E. *The Victors*	940.54
Amis, Martin. *Koba the Dread*	947.084
Anderson, Jon Lee. *Che Guevara*	B
Anderson, Lars. *Carlisle vs. Army*	796.332
Andrews, Becca. ★*No Choice*	362.1988
Angelou, Maya. ★*I Know Why the Caged Bird Sings*	B
Angelou, Maya. *A Song Flung up to Heaven*	B
Anolik, Lili. *Hollywood's Eve*	747
Anthony, Carl Sferrazza. *Nellie Taft*	B
Applebaum, Anne. ★*Gulag*	365
Applebaum, Anne. *Iron Curtain*	947
Appy, Christian G. *American Reckoning*	959.704
Arana, Marie. *American Chica*	B
Arendt, Hannah. *The Origins of Totalitarianism*	320.53
Armstrong, Jennifer Keishin. *Seinfeldia*	791.45
Armstrong, Jennifer Keishin. *Sex and the City and Us*	791.45
Armstrong, Jennifer Keishin. *When Women Invented Television*	791.45
Arnold, James R. *Jungle of Snakes*	355.02
Asbrink, Elisabeth. *And in the Vienna Woods the Trees Remain*	B
Ashbery, John. *John Ashbery*	811
Ashbery, John. *Selected Poems*	811
Ashon, Will. *Chamber Music*	782.421649
Atkinson, Rick. *An Army at Dawn*	940.54
Atkinson, Rick. *The Day of Battle*	940.54
Atria, Travis. *Better Days Will Come Again*	B
Attwell, David. *J. M. Coetzee and the Life of Writing*	823
Auden, W. H. *Collected Poems*	811
Auden, W. H. *Selected Poems*	821
Austerlitz, Saul. *Just a Shot Away*	781.66078
Bacon, John U. *The Great Halifax Explosion*	971.6
Baier, Bret. *Three Days in January*	B
Baime, A. J. *The Accidental President*	B
Baime, A. J. *White Lies*	B
Bair, Deirdre. *Al Capone*	B
Baker, Peter. *The Man Who Ran Washington*	B
Balakian, Peter. *The Burning Tigris*	956.6
Baldwin, James. ★*Notes of a Native Son*	305.8
Balf, Todd. *Major*	B
Ball, Lucille. *Love, Lucy*	B
Barker, Nigel. *Models of Influence*	746.92092
Barnes, Julian. *Keeping an Eye Open*	709.04
Barnes, Julian. *The Man in the Red Coat*	B
Barnitz, Jacqueline. *Twentieth-Century Art of Latin America*	709.8
Barr, James. *A Line in the Sand*	956
Barr, James. *Lords of the Desert*	956
Barra, Allen. ★*The Last Coach*	B
Barra, Allen. ★*Yogi Berra*	B
Barrett, David Dean. *140 Days to Hiroshima*	940.54
Barry, John M. ★*The Great Influenza*	614.5
Barry, John M. *Rising Tide*	977
Basinger, Jeanine. *The Star Machine*	384
Bass, Gary Jonathan. ★*Judgment at Tokyo*	952.04
Bass, Rick. *Why I Came West*	333.78
Baum, Dan. *Nine Lives*	B
Beckett, Samuel. *The Letters of Samuel Beckett*	848
Beevor, Antony. *Russia*	947.084
Beevor, Antony. *The Second World War*	940.54
Bell, Madison Smartt. *Child of Light*	B
Berfield, Susan. *The Hour of Fate*	973.91
Berg, A. Scott. *Kate Remembered*	B
Berg, A. Scott. ★*Wilson*	B
Berg, Raffi. *Red Sea Spies*	327.125694
Berkow, Ira. *How Life Imitates Sports*	070.4
Bernstein, Burton. ★*Leonard Bernstein*	B
Bernstein, Carl. ★*All the President's Men*	364.1
Bhattacharya, Ananyo. *The Man from the Future*	B
Bigsby, Christopher William Edgar. *Arthur Miller*	B
Bilger, Burkhard. *Fatherland*	B
Bird, Kai. *American Prometheus*	B
Bird, Kai. *The Outlier*	973.926
Birdsall, John. *The Man Who Ate Too Much*	B
Bix, Herbert P. *Hirohito and the Making of Modern Japan*	B
Bjork, Daniel W. *B.F. Skinner*	B
Blackmon, Douglas A. *Slavery by Another Name*	305.896
Blum, Deborah. *The Poisoner's Handbook*	614
Blume, Lesley M. M. *Fallout*	940.54
Bogosian, Eric. *Operation Nemesis*	956.62
Bogus, Carl T. *Buckley*	B
Bond, Julian. ★*Julian Bond's Time to Teach*	323.0975
Borneman, Walter R. *The Admirals*	B
Bowker, Gordon. ★*James Joyce*	B
Boyd, Herb. *We Shall Overcome*	323.1196
Boylan, Jennifer Finney. *Good Boy*	B
Boyle, Kevin. *Arc of Justice*	345.73
Boyle, Kevin. *The Shattering*	973.923
Bradbury, Dominic. *The Iconic Interior*	747
Bradley, James. *Flyboys*	940.54
Bram, Christopher. *Eminent Outlaws*	920
Branch, Taylor. ★*At Canaan's Edge*	323.1196
Branch, Taylor. *The Clinton Tapes*	973.929
Branch, Taylor. ★*Pillar of Fire*	323.1
Brands, H. W. *Reagan*	B
Brands, H. W. *Traitor to His Class*	B
Brands, H. W. *Woodrow Wilson*	B
Brazile, Donna. *For Colored Girls Who Have Considered Politics*	328.73
Breihan, Tom. ★*The Number Ones*	782.42164
Brewer, John. *The American Leonardo*	759.5
Briggs, Julia. *Virginia Woolf*	823
Brill, Steven. *Tailspin*	306.0973
Brinkley, Alan. *John F. Kennedy*	B
Brinkley, Alan. ★*The Publisher*	B
Brokaw, Tom. *The Fall of Richard Nixon*	B
Brooks, Mel. ★*All About Me!*	B
Brookwood, Marilyn. *The Orphans of Davenport*	305.231
Broven, John. *Record Makers and Breakers*	B
Brown, Carolyn. *Chance and Circumstance*	B
Brown, Daniel James. ★*The Boys in the Boat*	797.12
Brown, Daniel James. ★*Facing the Mountain*	940.54
Brown, David S. *Paradise Lost*	813
Brown, Jasmine. *Twice as Hard*	610.92
Brown, Terence. *The Life of W.B. Yeats*	B
Brown, Tina. ★*The Palace Papers*	920
Bruner, Robert F. ★*The Panic of 1907, 2nd Ed.*	330.973
Bruning, John R. *The Race of Aces*	940.54
Bryant, Howard. *The Last Hero*	B
Bryson, Bill. *The Life and Times of the Thunderbolt Kid*	B
Bryson, Bill. *Notes from a Small Island*	914
Bryson, Bill. *One Summer*	973.91
Bryson, Bill. ★*A Walk in the Woods*	917
Buckland, Gail. *Who Shot Rock & Roll*	779
Budiansky, Stephen. *Oliver Wendell Holmes*	B
Bui, Thi. ★*The Best We Could Do*	741.5
Burger, Ariel. *Witness*	848
Burnham, Margaret A. ★*By Hands Now Known*	342.73
Burns, Cherie. *The Great Hurricane—1938*	974.7
Bush, George. *All the Best, George Bush*	973.928
Bush, George W. *41*	B
Butler, Isaac. *The Method*	792.02

PUBLIC LIBRARY CORE COLLECTION: NONFICTION
Twentieth Edition

Byrne, Paula. *Kick*	B
Cadbury, Deborah. *Princes at War*	920
Cadbury, Deborah. *The School That Escaped from the Nazis*	940.53
Caddick-Adams, Peter. *Sand and Steel*	940.54
Caldwell, Christopher. *The Age of Entitlement*	305.240973
Campbell, Hayley. *The Art of Neil Gaiman*	B
Campbell-Kelly, Martin. *From Airline Reservations to Sonic the Hedgehog*	338.4
Cannato, Vincent. *American Passage*	325.73
Cannell, Michael T. *A Brotherhood Betrayed*	B
Capote, Truman. ★*In Cold Blood*	364.1
Capote, Truman. ★*Portraits and Observations*	814
Capote, Truman. *Too Brief a Treat*	B
Capozzola, Christopher. *Bound by War*	355
Capparell, Stephanie. *The Real Pepsi Challenge*	338.7
Carlin, John. *Playing the Enemy*	968.06
Carlin, Peter Ames. *Bruce*	B
Caro, Robert A. ★*The Passage of Power*	B
Caro, Robert A. *The Power Broker*	B
Carroll, Rory. *There Will Be Fire*	363.325
Carter, David. *Stonewall*	306.76
Carter, Jimmy. *A Full Life*	B
Carter, Jimmy. *An Hour Before Daylight*	B
Carter, Jimmy. *Palestine*	956.04
Carter, Jimmy. *Sharing Good Times*	973.926
Carter, Jimmy. *White House Diary*	973.926
Case, Anne. *Deaths of Despair and the Future of Capitalism*	362.28
Castro, Fidel. *Fidel Castro*	B
Cather, Willa. *The Selected Letters of Willa Cather*	B
Century, Douglas. *Barney Ross*	B
Cep, Casey N. ★*Furious Hours*	364.152
Cercas, Javier. *Lord of All the Dead*	868
Chabon, Michael. *Manhood for Amateurs*	B
Chang, Jung. *Big Sister, Little Sister, Red Sister*	B
Chang, Jung. *Mao*	B
Chuck D. *Chuck D Presents This Day in Rap and Hip-Hop History*	782.421649
Churchill, Winston. *The Grand Alliance*	940.53
Churchill, Winston. *Their Finest Hour*	940.53
Churchill, Winston. *Triumph and Tragedy*	940.53
Churchwell, Sarah Bartlett. *Behold, America*	973.9
Cisneros, Sandra. *A House of My Own*	B
Clark, Taylor. *Starbucked*	338
Clarke, Thurston. *JFK's Last Hundred Days*	B
Clavin, Thomas. *The DiMaggios*	920
Cleaver, Eldridge. *Soul on Ice*	B
Cleveland, Pat. *Walking with the Muses*	B
Clifton, Lucille. *Mercy*	811
Clinton, Bill. *My Life*	B
Clinton, Hillary Rodham. *Living History*	B
Coates, Ta-Nehisi. *The Beautiful Struggle*	B
Coffin, Judith G. *Sex, Love, and Letters*	848
Cohen, Andrew. *Two Days in June*	973.922
Cohen, Deborah. *Last Call at the Hotel Imperial*	070.92
Cohen, Lizabeth. *A Consumers' Republic*	339.4
Coll, Steve. *The Bin Ladens*	920
Collins, Larry. *O Jerusalem!*	956
Colt, George Howe. *The Game*	796.332
Coltman, Leycester. *The Real Fidel Castro*	B
Common. *One Day It'll All Make Sense*	B
Conant, Jennet. *The Lotus Eaters*	940.54
Conant, Jennet. *Man of the Hour*	B
Conaway, James. *America's Library*	027.5
Connolly, Ray. *Being John Lennon*	B
Conradi, Peter J. *Iris*	B
Conroy, Pat. *My Losing Season*	B
Conway, Edmund. *The Summit*	337.09
Cook, Blanche Wiesen. *Eleanor Roosevelt; Volume 2*	B
Cook, Blanche Wiesen. ★*Eleanor Roosevelt; Volume 3*	B
Cook, Kevin. *Ten Innings at Wrigley*	796.357
Cooper, Andrew Scott. *The Fall of Heaven*	B
Cooper, Helene. *Madame President*	966.62
Cooper, John Milton. *Woodrow Wilson*	B
Copeland, B. Jack. *Turing*	B
Cordery, Stacy A. *Alice*	B
Cornwell, John. *Hitler's Pope*	B
Cox, Caroline. *The World Atlas of Street Fashion*	391.009
Crasnianski, Tania. *The Children of Nazis*	943.086
Crawford, Bill. ★*All American*	B
Creamer, Robert W. *Stengel*	796.357
Creighton, Margaret S. *The Electrifying Fall of Rainbow City*	607
Crespino, Joseph. *Atticus Finch*	B
Crouch, Stanley. *Kansas City Lightning*	B
Crowe, Lauren Goldstein. *The Towering World of Jimmy Choo*	391.4
Crowther, Gail. *Three-Martini Afternoons at the Ritz*	920
Cumings, Bruce. *The Korean War*	951.904
Cummings, E. E. ★*Complete Poems, 1904-1962*	811
Curtis, William J. R. *Modern Architecture Since 1900*	724
Cusk, Rachel. *Aftermath*	B
Dallek, Robert. ★*Franklin D. Roosevelt*	B
Dallek, Robert. *Harry S. Truman*	B
Dallek, Robert. *Let Every Nation Know*	B
Dallek, Robert. *Nixon and Kissinger*	B
Dallek, Robert. *An Unfinished Life*	B
Daniels, Roger. *Prisoners Without Trial*	940.53
Danticat, Edwidge. ★*Brother, I'm Dying*	B
Daunton, M. J. ★*The Economic Government of the World*	337
Davenport, Matthew J. *The Longest Minute*	979.4
Davis, Jack E. *An Everglades Providence*	B
Davis, Michael. *Street Gang*	791.43
Day, Timothy. ★*A Century of Recorded Music*	780
Day-Lewis, Cecil. *The Complete Poems of C. Day Lewis*	821
De Courcy, Anne. *Chanel's Riviera*	944.9
De Courcy, Anne. *The Husband Hunters*	920
De Long, J. Bradford. *Slouching Towards Utopia*	330.9
Dean, John W. *The Nixon Defense*	973.924092
Dearborn, Mary V. *Ernest Hemingway*	B
Delmont, Matthew F. *Half American*	940.54
Demick, Barbara. ★*Nothing to Envy*	920
Denevi, Timothy. *Freak Kingdom*	B
Deng, Alephonsion. *They Poured Fire on Us from the Sky*	B
Dennison, Matthew. *Behind the Mask*	B
DePalma, Anthony. *The Cubans*	920
Derf. *Kent State*	741.5
Dery, Mark. *Born to Be Posthumous*	B
Dickerman, Leah. *Dada*	709
Dickinson, Bruce. *What Does This Button Do?*	B
Dickson, Paul. *The Rise of the G.I. Army 1940-1941*	940.54
Didion, Joan. ★*The Year of Magical Thinking*	B
Dillard, Annie. *An American Childhood*	B
Dillard, Annie. *The Writing Life*	B
Dinesen, Isak. *Out of Africa*	967.62
Dobbs, Michael. *King Richard*	973.924
Doggett, Peter. *Electric Shock*	781.64
Doggett, Peter. *You Never Give Me Your Money*	B
Doherty, Maggie. *The Equivalents*	920
Donald, Aida DiPace. *Citizen Soldier*	B
Donner, Rebecca. *All the Frequent Troubles of Our Days*	943
Dower, John W. *Cultures of War*	355.00973
Dower, John W. *Embracing Defeat*	952.04
Drape, Joe. *Black Maestro*	B
DuBois, Ellen Carol. *Suffrage*	324.6
Dubus, Andre. *Townie*	B
Duggan, Christopher. *The Force of Destiny*	945
Duiker, William J. *Ho Chi Minh*	B
Duncan, Robert. *Selected Poems*	811
Dunn, Stephen. *New & Selected Poems*	811
Dylan, Bob. ★*The Philosophy of Modern Song*	782.42
Dyson, Freeman J. *Maker of Patterns*	B
Eade, Philip. *Evelyn Waugh*	B
Ebert, Roger. *Life Itself*	B
Ebert, Roger. *Scorsese by Ebert*	B
Eder, Mari K. *The Girls Who Stepped Out of Line*	920
Edsel, Robert M. *The Monuments Men*	940.53
Edwards, Anne. *Matriarch*	B
Edwards, Bob. *Edward R. Murrow and the Birth of Broadcast Journalism*	B
Egan, Timothy. ★*The Big Burn*	973.911
Egan, Timothy. ★*Short Nights of the Shadow Catcher*	770.92
Egan, Timothy. *The Worst Hard Time*	978
Ehrenreich, Barbara. *Had I Known*	814
Ehrenreich, Barbara. ★*Nickel and Dimed*	B
Ehrlich, Gretel. *This Cold Heaven*	998.2
Ehrlich, Gretel. *Unsolaced*	B
Eichar, Donnie. *Dead Mountain*	914
Eig, Jonathan. ★*King*	B
Einstein, Albert. ★*A Stubbornly Persistent Illusion*	530.092

AUTHOR, TITLE, SERIES AND SUBJECT INDEX

Eisen, Norman L. *The Last Palace*	920
Eisner, Peter. *The Pope's Last Crusade*	282.092
Eizenstat, Stuart. ★*President Carter*	B
Eliot, T. S. ★*Complete Poems and Plays.*	810
Elkins, Caroline. *Legacy of Violence*	909
Elledge, Scott. *E.B. White*	B
Ellison, Ralph. *The Selected Letters of Ralph Ellison*	813
Ellsworth, Scott. *The Ground Breaking*	976.6
English, Charlie. *The Gallery of Miracles and Madness*	709.04
Englund, Peter. *The Beauty and the Sorrow*	940.309
Erdrich, Louise. *Books and Islands in Ojibwe Country*	977
Ernaux, Annie. ★*The Years*	B
Essin, Christin. *Stage Designers in Early Twentieth-Century America*	792.02
Euchner, Charles C. *Nobody Turn Me Around*	975.3
Evans, R. Tripp. *Grant Wood*	B
Evans, Richard J. *The Third Reich in Power, 1933-1939*	943.086
Evaristo, Bernardine. *Manifesto*	B
Ewing, Eve L. *1919*	811
Eyman, Scott. *Cary Grant*	B
Eyman, Scott. *Hank and Jim*	920
Eyman, Scott. *John Wayne*	B
Fadiman, Anne. *The Spirit Catches You and You Fall Down*	306.4
Farley, Audrey Clare. *The Unfit Heiress*	B
Farrell, John A. *Clarence Darrow*	B
Farrell, John A. ★*Richard Nixon*	B
Farrell, John A. *Ted Kennedy*	B
Faust, Drew Gilpin. *Necessary Trouble*	B
Feigel, Lara. *The Bitter Taste of Victory*	320.943
Feinstein, Adam. *Pablo Neruda*	B
Feinstein, Michael. *The Gershwins and Me*	782.42164
Felder, Deborah G. *The American Women's Almanac*	305.40973
Feldstein, Mark Avrom. *Poisoning the Press*	973.924092
Ferguson, Niall. *Kissinger*	973.924
Ferlinghetti, Lawrence. *These Are My Rivers*	811
Fernando, S. H., Jr. *From the Streets of Shaolin*	782.421
Fessler, Pam. *Carville's Cure*	362.19699
Feynman, Richard P. ★*The Meaning of It All*	500
Figes, Orlando. ★*The Whisperers*	306.850947
Finn, Peter. *The Zhivago Affair*	891.73
Fishman, Charles. ★*One Giant Leap*	629.45
Fishman, David E. *The Book Smugglers*	940.53
Fisk, Robert. *The Great War for Civilisation*	956.04
FitzGerald, Michael C. ★*Picasso and American Art*	709.73
Follett, Ken. *On Wings of Eagles*	955
Fox, Margalit. *The Confidence Men*	940.4
Francis. *Life*	B
Frank, Barney. *Frank*	B
Frank, Jeffrey. *The Trials of Harry S. Truman*	973.918
Frank, Michael. ★*One Hundred Saturdays*	B
Franklin, Ruth. *Shirley Jackson*	B
Franklin, Sara B. ★*The Editor*	B
Fraser, Caroline. ★*Prairie Fires*	B
Fraser, Steve. *The Age of Acquiescence*	973.91
Freedman, Samuel G. *Jew vs. Jew*	296
French, Patrick. *The World Is What It Is*	B
Friedman, Matti. *Spies of No Country*	327.12
Friedman, Thomas L. ★*From Beirut to Jerusalem*	956.04
Friedwald, Will. ★*Sinatra! the Song Is You*	782.42164
Fritzsche, Peter. *Life and Death in the Third Reich*	943.086
Frost, Mark. *The Match*	796.352
Fullilove, Michael. *Rendezvous with Destiny*	973.917092
Gabler, Neal. ★*Against the Wind*	B
Gabler, Neal. *Catching the Wind*	B
Gabriel, Mary. *Ninth Street Women*	920
Gage, Beverly. *The Day Wall Street Exploded*	974.7
Gage, Beverly. *G-Man*	B
Galeano, Eduardo. *Soccer in Sun and Shadow*	796.334
Gallagher, Winifred. *New Women in the Old West*	978.02
Ganz, Nicholas. ★*Graffiti World*	751.7
Garcia Marquez, Gabriel. *Living to Tell the Tale*	B
Garelick, Rhonda K. *Mademoiselle*	B
Garrett, Kent. *The Last Negroes at Harvard*	920
Gary, Amy. *In the Great Green Room*	813
Gaskell, Elizabeth Cleghorn. *The Life of Charlotte Bronte*	B
Gates, Henry Louis. *The Future of the Race*	305.896
Gates, Henry Louis. ★*Stony the Road*	973
Gates, Robert Michael. ★*Exercise of Power*	973.929
Gatrell, Peter. *The Unsettling of Europe*	304.8
Gavin, James. ★*Stormy Weather*	782.42164
Gefter, Philip. *What Becomes a Legend Most*	B
Gehrig, Lou. *The Lost Memoir*	B
Gehring, Wes D. *James Dean*	B
Gentile, Olivia. *Life List*	598.072
Gessen, Masha. *Never Remember*	365
Ghez, Didier. *The Hidden Art of Disney's Golden Age*	741.5
Gibson, Larry S. *Young Thurgood*	B
Giddings, Paula. *Ida*	B
Giddins, Gary. *Bing Crosby*	B
Giddins, Gary. *Bing Crosby*	B
Gidla, Sujatha. *Ants Among Elephants*	305.5
Gilbert, Martin. *The Second World War*	940.53
Gilbert, Sandra M. ★*Still Mad*	810.9
Gill, Anton. *Art Lover*	B
Gill, Jonathan. *Harlem*	974.7
Gillette, Michael L. *Lady Bird Johnson*	B
Gilliam, Dorothy Butler. *Trailblazer*	B
Ginsberg, Allen. ★*Howl*	811.54
Girzone, Joseph F. *Never Alone*	248.4
Givhan, Robin. *The Battle of Versailles*	746.9
Glenconner, Anne. ★*Lady in Waiting*	B
Glendinning, Victoria. *Leonard Woolf*	B
Goldberger, Paul. *Building Art*	B
Goldblatt, David. *The Games*	796.4809
Goldsmith, Martin. *The Inextinguishable Symphony*	B
Goldstone, Lawrence. *Drive!*	338.4
Goldstone, Lawrence. *On Account of Race*	342.7308
Gompertz, Will. *What Are You Looking At?*	709
Gooch, Brad. ★*Flannery*	B
Goodman, Matthew. *The City Game*	796.323
Goodman, Simon. *The Orpheus Clock*	940.53
Goodwin, Doris Kearns. ★*The Bully Pulpit*	973.91
Goodwin, Doris Kearns. *No Ordinary Time*	920
Gopnik, Blake. ★*Warhol*	B
Gorbachev, Mikhail. *On My Country and the World*	947.085
Gordin, Michael D. *Red Cloud at Dawn*	355.02
Gordis, Daniel. *Israel*	956.9405
Gordon, Edmund. *The Invention of Angela Carter*	B
Gordon, Linda. *Dorothea Lange*	B
Gordon, Lyndall. ★*T.S. Eliot*	B
Gordon, Meryl. *Bunny Mellon*	B
Gordon, Robert J. ★*The Rise and Fall of American Growth*	339.4
Gottlieb, Robert. *George Balanchine*	B
Graetz, Michael J. *The Burger Court and the Rise of the Judicial Right*	347.73
Graff, Garrett M. *Watergate*	973.924
Graham, Jorie. *The Dream of the Unified Field*	811
Grandmaster Flash. *The Adventures of Grandmaster Flash*	B
Grant, Gail Milissa. *At the Elbows of My Elders*	B
Gray, Charlotte. ★*Reluctant Genius*	920
Grayling, A. C. *Among the Dead Cities*	940.54
Green, Robin. *The Only Girl*	070.92
Greene, Graham. *Graham Greene*	823
Greenidge, Kerri. *Black Radical*	B
Greenman, Ben. *Dig If You Will the Picture*	B
Groom, Winston. *The Aviators*	920
Groom, Winston. *The Generals*	920
Grumbach, Didier. *History of International Fashion*	746.9
Guarnere, William. *Brothers in Battle, Best of Friends*	B
Guevara, Che. *Diary of a Combatant*	972.91063
Guha, Ramachandra. *Gandhi Before India*	B
Guha, Ramachandra. *Gandhi*	B
Guha, Ramachandra. *India After Gandhi*	954.04
Guillermoprieto, Alma. *Dancing with Cuba*	972.9106
Guinn, Jeff. ★*Manson*	B
Guinn, Jeff. ★*War on the Border*	972.08
Gunn, Thom. ★*The Letters of Thom Gunn*	821
Gup, Ted. *A Secret Gift*	977.1
Gwynne, S. C. *His Majesty's Airship*	363.12
Hafner, Katie. *A Romance on Three Legs*	786.2092
Hager, Jenna Bush. *Sisters First*	B
Hahn, Steven. *A Nation Under Our Feet*	975
Hajari, Nisid. *Midnight's Furies*	954.04
Halberstam, David. ★*The Children*	323.1
Halberstam, David. *The Coldest Winter*	951.904
Halberstam, David. *The Fifties*	973.92
Haley, James L. *Captive Paradise*	996.9

PUBLIC LIBRARY CORE COLLECTION: NONFICTION
Twentieth Edition

Hall, Alvin D. *Driving the Green Book*	917.304
Hamlin, Kimberly A. *Free Thinker*	B
Hammer, Langdon. *James Merrill*	B
Harding, Thomas. *The House by the Lake*	943
Hardman, Robert. *Queen of Our Times*	B
Hardman, Robert. *Queen of the World*	B
Hardy, Thomas. *The Collected Letters of Thomas Hardy*	823
Harlan, Louis R. *Booker T. Washington*	B
Harris, Mark. *Pictures at a Revolution*	791.43
Hastings, Max. *Inferno*	940.54
Hastings, Max. *Operation Chastise*	940.54
Hastings, Max. *Overlord*	940.54
Hastings, Max. *Retribution*	940.54
Hastings, Selina. *The Secret Lives of Somerset Maugham*	B
Hatzfeld, Jean. *Machete Season*	967.57104
Hayek, Friedrich A. von. *The Road to Serfdom*	330.1
Hayes, Peter. *Why?*	940.53
Haygood, Wil. *Showdown*	B
Hazzard, Kevin M. *American Sirens*	362.18
Healy, Thomas. *The Great Dissent*	342.7308
Heat Moon, William Least. *Blue Highways*	917.304
Hechinger, John. ★*True Gentlemen*	371.85
Hedges, Chris. *Days of Destruction, Days of Revolt*	741.5
Hedges, Chris. *War Is a Force That Gives Us Meaning*	355.02
Heller, Jason. *Strange Stars*	781.6609
Helm, Sarah. *A Life in Secrets*	B
Hemingway, Ernest. *Dear Papa*	813
Henderson, Bruce B. *Sons and Soldiers*	940.53
Hendrickson, Paul. *The Living and the Dead*	959.704
Henry, John. *Great White Fleet*	387.243
Hepworth, David. *Uncommon People*	B
Herbert, Brian. *Dreamer of Dune*	B
Herman, Arthur. ★*Douglas Macarthur*	B
Herman, Arthur. *Freedom's Forge*	940.53
Hermes, Will. *Love Goes to Buildings on Fire*	781.64
Hernandez, Kelly Lytle. ★*Bad Mexicans*	972
Herrera, Hayden. *Listening to Stone*	B
Herriot, James. *All Things Wise and Wonderful*	B
Hester, Diarmuid. *Nothing Ever Just Disappears*	306.76
Heyman, Stephen. *The Planter of Modern Life*	B
Hiaasen, Carl. *The Downhill Lie*	B
Hickam, Homer H. ★*Rocket Boys*	B
Higginbotham, Adam. ★*Challenger*	629.45
Highsmith, Patricia. ★*Patricia Highsmith's Diaries and Notebooks*	818
Hilfiger, Tommy. *American Dreamer*	B
Hill, Clint. *Five Days in November*	973.922092
Hill, Clint. *Five Presidents*	B
Hill, David. *The Vapors*	976.7
Hill, Geoffrey. *Selected Poems*	821
Hillenbrand, Laura. ★*Unbroken*	B
Hiltzik, Michael A. *Iron Empires*	385.0973
Hindley, Meredith. *Destination Casablanca*	940.54
Hirono, Mazie. *Heart of Fire*	B
Hirsch, Foster. ★*Hollywood and the Movies of the Fifties*	791.43
Hirsch, James S. *Riot and Remembrance*	976.6
Hirshman, Linda R. *Reckoning*	305.420973
Hirshman, Linda R. *Sisters in Law*	347.73
Hitchcock, William I. *The Age of Eisenhower*	973.921092
Hitler, Adolf. *Mein Kampf*	B
Hoagland, Tony. *Priest Turned Therapist Treats Fear of God*	811
Hochschild, Adam. *American Midnight*	973.91
Hochschild, Adam. *Rebel Cinderella*	B
Hochschild, Adam. *The Unquiet Ghost*	947.084
Hoffman, Bruce. *Anonymous Soldiers*	956.94
Hoffman, David E. *Give Me Liberty*	B
Hogan, Linda. *The Woman Who Watches Over the World*	B
Holland, James. *Big Week*	940.54
Holland, James. *Brothers in Arms*	940.54
Holland, James. *Normandy '44*	940.54
Hollis, B. Dylan. ★*Baking Yesteryear*	641.81
Hollis, Matthew. *The Waste Land*	821
Honey, Michael K. *To the Promised Land*	323
Hornbacher, Marya. *Wasted*	B
Hornfischer, James D. *Neptune's Inferno*	940.54
Hornfischer, James D. *Who Can Hold the Sea*	359.00973
Hotta, Eri. *Japan 1941*	940.54
Howard, Johnette. *The Rivals*	B
Howe, Sean. *Marvel Comics*	741.5
Howell, Georgina. *Gertrude Bell*	B
Hoyer, Katja. *Blood and Iron*	943.08
Huang, Yunte. *Daughter of the Dragon*	B
Huffman, Alan. *Here I Am*	B
Hughes, Langston. ★*I Wonder as I Wander*	B
Humphreys, Richard. *Under Pressure*	B
Hunter-Gault, Charlayne. ★*My People*	305.48
Hurston, Zora Neale. *Dust Tracks on a Road*	B
Hurston, Zora Neale. ★*You Don't Know Us Negroes and Other Essays*	814
Hurston, Zora Neale. *Zora Neale Hurston*	B
Hutton, Robin L. *Sgt. Reckless*	951.904
Hutton, Ronald. *The Triumph of the Moon*	133.4
Huxley, Elspeth Joscelin Grant. *The Flame Trees of Thika*	B
Huxtable, Ada Louise. *On Architecture*	724
Iandoli, Kathy. *Baby Girl*	B
Indyk, Martin. *Master of the Game*	327.73
Isaacson, Walter. ★*Steve Jobs*	B
Isserman, Maurice. *The Winter Army*	940.54
Jackson, Angela. *A Surprised Queenhood in the New Black Sun*	B
Jackson, Julian. *De Gaulle*	B
Jackson, Lawrence Patrick. *Chester B. Himes*	B
Jackson, Shirley. ★*The Letters of Shirley Jackson*	813
Jackson, Troy. *Becoming King*	B
Jacobs, Alexandra. *Still Here*	B
Jacobsen, Annie. ★*Operation Paperclip*	940.54
Jadhav, Narendra. *Untouchables*	305.5
Jaher, David. *The Witch of Lime Street*	B
Jahner, Harald. ★*Aftermath*	943.087
Jarrell, Randall. ★*The Complete Poems*	811
Jayapal, Pramila. *Use the Power You Have*	B
Jerkins, Morgan. *Wandering in Strange Lands*	305.896
Johnson, George. *Miss Leavitt's Stars*	522
Johnson, Graham. *Poulenc*	B
Johnson, Joyce. *The Voice Is All*	B
Johnson, Kirk W. *The Fishermen and the Dragon*	976.4
Johnson, Lyndon B. *Taking Charge*	973.923
Johnson, Paul. *Churchill*	B
Johnson, Paul. *Eisenhower*	B
Jones, Brian Jay. ★*Becoming Dr. Seuss*	B
Jones, Gerard. *Men of Tomorrow*	741.5
Jordan, Jonathan W. *Brothers, Rivals, Victors*	940.54
Joseph, Peniel E. *The Sword and the Shield*	B
Joseph, Peniel E. *Waiting 'Til the Midnight Hour*	323.1196
Judt, Tony. *Postwar*	940.55
Junger, Sebastian. *Fire*	909.82
Kahn, Ashley. *The House That Trane Built*	781.6509
Kaiser, Menachem. *Plunder*	940.53
Kaku, Michio. ★*Hyperspace*	530.1
Kamp, David. *Sunny Days*	791.4502
Kan, Karoline. *Under Red Skies*	B
Kandel, Eric R. *The Age of Insight*	154.2
Kandel, Eric R. *In Search of Memory*	B
Kanigel, Robert. *Eyes on the Street*	B
Kanigel, Robert. *The Man Who Knew Infinity*	B
Kapilow, Robert. ★*Listening for America*	782.42164
Kaplan, James. *3 Shades of Blue*	920
Karnow, Stanley. *Vietnam, a History*	959.704
Kashner, Sam. *Furious Love*	B
Katznelson, Ira. *Fear Itself*	973.917
Kaufman, Jonathan. *The Last Kings of Shanghai*	951
Kaufmann, Uri R. *Eighteen Days of October*	956.04
Kavanagh, Julie. *Nureyev*	B
Keefe, Patrick Radden. ★*Say Nothing*	364.152
Keegan, John. *The First World War*	940.3
Keith, Philip A. *All Blood Runs Red*	B
Kempner, Joanna. *Psychedelic Outlaws*	615.7
Kempowski, Walter. *Swansong 1945*	940.54
Kenneally, Christine. *Ghosts of the Orphanage*	362.73
Kennedy, Kostya. *True*	B
Kerouac, Jack. *Selected Letters, 1940-1956*	813
Kershaw, Alex. *Avenue of Spies*	940.53
Kershaw, Alex. *The Few*	940.54
Kershaw, Ian. *The Global Age*	940.55
Khan, Yasmin Sabina. *Enlightening the World*	974.7
Khlevniuk, Oleg V. *Stalin*	B
Kindsvatter, Peter S. *American Soldiers*	355
King, Charles. *Midnight at the Pera Palace*	949.61
King, Coretta Scott. ★*My Life, My Love, My Legacy*	B

AUTHOR, TITLE, SERIES AND SUBJECT INDEX

King, David. *The Trial of Adolf Hitler*	345.43
King, Greg. *Twilight of Empire*	943.6
King, Martin Luther. *The Autobiography of Martin Luther King, Jr.*	B
King, Stephen. *On Writing*	B
Kingston, Maxine Hong. *The Woman Warrior*	B
Kinzer, Stephen. ★*The True Flag*	327.73
Kirsch, Adam. *The Blessing and the Curse*	809
Kix, Paul. *The Saboteur*	940.53
Klosterman, Chuck. ★*The Nineties*	306.0973
Knight, Sam. *The Premonitions Bureau*	133.8
Koppel, Lily. *The Astronaut Wives Club*	920
Korda, Michael. *With Wings Like Eagles*	940.54
Kornacki, Steve. *The Red and the Blue*	306.20973
Kotkin, Stephen. *Stalin*	B
Kotkin, Stephen. *Stalin*	B
Kotz, Nick. *Judgment Days*	323
Kozol, Jonathan. *Letters to a Young Teacher*	371.1
Kraus, Dita. *A Delayed Life*	B
Kriegel, Mark. *Pistol*	B
Krist, Gary. *Empire of Sin*	976.3
Krist, Gary. *The White Cascade*	979.7
Krug, Nora. ★*Belonging*	741.5
Kundera, Milan. *Encounter*	809
Kupperman, Michael. *All the Answers*	741.5
Kurlansky, Mark. *1968*	909.82
Kurtz, Glenn. *Three Minutes in Poland*	947.7
Lambert, Raymond. *Every Man a Hero*	B
Lamott, Anne. ★*Dusk, Night, Dawn*	B
Lang, Michael. *The Road to Woodstock*	781.66
Larkin, Philip. *The Complete Poems*	821
Larman, Alexander. *The Windsors at War*	940.53
Larson, Edward J. *An Empire of Ice*	919.8
Larson, Erik. ★*Dead Wake*	940.4
Larson, Erik. ★*The Splendid and the Vile*	940.54
Lasch, Christopher. ★*The Revolt of the Elites*	306
Lawrence, T. E. *Seven Pillars of Wisdom*	940.4
Leader, Zachary. *The Life of Saul Bellow*	B
Leaming, Barbara. *Jacqueline Bouvier Kennedy Onassis*	B
Leaming, Barbara. *Kick Kennedy*	B
Leaming, Barbara. *Mrs. Kennedy*	B
Lear, Linda J. *Beatrix Potter*	B
Leavitt, David. *The Man Who Knew Too Much*	B
Leavy, Jane. *The Big Fella*	B
Leavy, Jane. *The Last Boy*	B
Leavy, Jane. *Sandy Koufax*	B
LeBor, Adam. *City of Oranges*	956.94
Lehr, Dick. ★*The Birth of a Nation*	305.800973
Lemann, Nicholas. *Transaction Man*	330.973
Leonhardt, David. ★*Ours Was the Shining Future*	330.973
Lepore, Jill. ★*The Secret History of Wonder Woman*	741.5
Lessig, Lawrence. *Remix*	346.7304
Lessing, Doris May. *Under My Skin*	823
Levi, Primo. ★*The Drowned and the Saved*	940.53
Levi, Primo. *The Periodic Table*	858
Levi, Primo. *The Reawakening*	B
Levy, Shawn. ★*In on the Joke*	792.7
Lewis, C. S. ★*The Screwtape Letters*	248.4
Lewis, Damien. *Churchill's Hellraisers*	940.54
Lewis, Damien. *The Dog Who Could Fly*	940.54
Lewis, David L. ★*W.E.B. Du Bois*	B
Lewis, John. ★*March; Book One*	741.5
Lewis, John. ★*March; Book Three*	741.5
Lewis, John. ★*March; Book Two*	741.5
Lewis, John. ★*Run; Book One*	741.5
Lewis, Robin Coste. *To the Realization of Perfect Helplessness*	811
Li, Zhuqing. *Daughters of the Flower Fragrant Garden*	951.04
Liao, Yiwu. *Bullets and Opium*	951.05
Lightman, Alan P. *The Discoveries*	509
Lim, Louisa. *The People's Republic of Amnesia*	951.05
Lisle, John. *The Dirty Tricks Department*	940.54
Lively, Penelope. *Life in the Garden*	B
Loftis, Larry. *Code Name*	B
Logevall, Fredrik. ★*JFK*	B
Longworth, Karina. *Seduction*	920
Louvin, Charlie. *Satan Is Real*	B
Louvish, Simon. *Monkey Business*	
Lovell, Julia. *Maoism*	335.43
Lovell, Mary S. *The Sisters*	920.72

Lowe, Keith. *Savage Continent*	940.55
Lowit, Roxanne. *Yves Saint Laurent*	746.9
Lucey, Donna M. *Sargent's Women*	920
Lukacs, John. *Five Days in London, May 1940*	940.53
Lunenfeld, Peter. *City at the Edge of Forever*	979.4
Lynn, Loretta. *Still Woman Enough*	B
Lynskey, Dorian. *33 Revolutions per Minute*	782.42
Lynskey, Dorian. *The Ministry of Truth*	823
MacGillis, Alec. *Fulfillment*	381
Macintyre, Ben. ★*Agent Sonya*	B
Macintyre, Ben. *Agent Zigzag*	B
Macintyre, Ben. *Double Cross*	940.54
Macintyre, Ben. ★*Operation Mincemeat*	940.54
Macintyre, Ben. *A Spy Among Friends*	B
Mackeen, Dawn Anahid. *The Hundred-Year Walk*	956.6
MacMillan, Margaret. *Paris 1919*	940.3
Madigan, Tim. *The Burning*	976.6
Mahon, Maureen. ★*Black Diamond Queens*	782.421
Maier, Thomas. *Mafia Spies*	364.1060973
Malala, Justice. *The Plot to Save South Africa*	968.07
Malhotra, Aanchal. *Remnants of Partition*	954.04
Mamet, David. *True and False*	792
Manchester, William. *Goodbye, Darkness*	B
Manchester, William. *The Last Lion, Winston Spencer Churchill.*	B
Manchester, William. *The Last Lion, Winston Spencer Churchill.*	B
Manchester, William. *The Last Lion, Winston Spencer Churchill.*	B
Mandela, Nelson. *Dare Not Linger*	B
Mandela, Nelson. *In His Own Words*	B
Mandela, Nelson. ★*Long Walk to Freedom*	B
Mandela, Nelson. *Mandela*	B
Mandela, Nelson. *The Prison Letters of Nelson Mandela*	968.06092
Mandery, Evan J. *A Wild Justice*	345.73
Mann, Jim. *The Rebellion of Ronald Reagan*	973.927092
Mann, William J. *The Contender*	B
Mann, William J. *Hello, Gorgeous*	B
Mann, William J. *The Wars of the Roosevelts*	B
Marable, Manning. ★*Malcolm X*	B
Maraniss, Andrew. *Strong Inside*	B
Maraniss, David. *Clemente*	B
Marnham, Patrick. *Dreaming with His Eyes Open*	B
Martin, Gerald. ★*Gabriel Garcia Marquez*	B
Marton, Kati. *The Great Escape*	920
Marton, Kati. *Hidden Power*	B
Massie, Robert K. *Castles of Steel*	940.4
Matisse, Henri. *Henri Matisse*	709.2
Matteson, John. *Eden's Outcasts*	920
Matthews, Christopher. *Bobby Kennedy*	B
Matthews, Christopher. *Kennedy & Nixon*	973.922
Mays, Willie. *24*	B
Mazower, Mark. *Hitler's Empire*	940.53
Mazzeo, Tilar J. *Irena's Children*	B
McBride, James. *Kill 'Em and Leave*	B
McCarten, Anthony. *Darkest Hour*	941.084
McCormick, Mack. *Biography of a Phantom*	782.421643
McCourt, Frank. *'Tis*	B
McCourt, Malachy. *Singing My Him Song*	B
McCubbin, Lisa. *Betty Ford*	B
McCullough, David G. *Truman*	B
McCullough, David G. ★*The Wright Brothers*	B
McGilligan, Patrick. *Funny Man*	B
McGilligan, Patrick. *Oscar Micheaux*	B
McKay, Sinclair. *Berlin*	943
McKean, David. *Watching Darkness Fall*	940.53
McKeen, William. *Everybody Had an Ocean*	781.6609
McManus, John C. *Fire and Fortitude*	940.54
McManus, John C. *Island Infernos*	940.54
McMeekin, Sean. *July 1914*	940.3
McMeekin, Sean. *Stalin's War*	940.53
McPhee, John. *Tabula Rasa; V.1*	818
McWhorter, Diane. *Carry Me Home*	976.1
Meacham, Jon. ★*Destiny and Power*	B
Meacham, Jon. *Franklin and Winston*	940.53
Medvedev, Roy Aleksandrovich. *Let History Judge*	947.084
Menand, Louis. *The Free World*	306.0973
Merridale, Catherine. *Ivan's War*	940.54
Messud, Claire. *Kant's Little Prussian Head and Other Reasons Why I Write*	B
Michaelis, David. ★*Eleanor*	973.917

PUBLIC LIBRARY CORE COLLECTION: NONFICTION
Twentieth Edition

Mieville, China. *October*	947.084
Milford, Nancy. *Savage Beauty*	B
Millay, Edna St. Vincent. *Collected Poems*	811
Miller, Char. *Gifford Pinchot and the Making of Modern Environmentalism*	B
Miller, Donald L. *Supreme City*	974.7
Milosz, Czeslaw. *Milosz's ABC's*	891.8
Milton, Giles. *Checkmate in Berlin*	943
Minutaglio, Bill. *Dallas 1963*	973.922092
Mirski, Sean A. *We May Dominate the World*	973.91
Mitford, Jessica. ★*The American Way of Death Revisited*	338.4
Montillo, Roseanne. *Deliberate Cruelty*	364.152
Moody, Anthony David. *Ezra Pound*	B
Moore, Charles. *Margaret Thatcher*	941.085
Moore, Harold G. *We Are Soldiers Still*	959.704
Moore, Kate. *The Radium Girls*	363.17
Moore, Marianne. *The Selected Letters of Marianne Moore*	B
Moore, Wendy. *No Man's Land*	940.4
Moore, Wes. *The Other Wes Moore*	B
Moorehead, Caroline. *A House in the Mountains*	940.53
Moorhouse, Roger. *Berlin at War*	943
Mordden, Ethan. *Ziegfeld*	B
Morley, Jefferson. *Scorpions' Dance*	973.924
Morris, Benny. *1948*	956.04
Morris, Benny. *Righteous Victims*	956
Morris, Desmond. *The Lives of the Surrealists*	B
Morris, Edmund. *Colonel Roosevelt*	B
Morris, Edmund. ★*The Rise of Theodore Roosevelt*	B
Morris, Edmund. ★*Theodore Rex*	973.911
Morrison, Melanie. *Murder on Shades Mountain*	345.761
Morton, Andrew. *Wallis in Love*	B
Moser, Benjamin. *Why This World*	B
Moss, Gabrielle. *Paperback Crush*	813.009
Mowat, Farley. *Born Naked*	B
Muhammad, Khalil Gibran. *The Condemnation of Blackness*	364.2
Nagorski, Andrew. *Saving Freud*	940.53
Nasaw, David. *The Chief*	B
Nasaw, David. *The Last Million*	940.53
Nasr, Seyyed Vali Reza. *The Shia Revival*	297.8
Nelson, Craig. *Pearl Harbor*	940.54
Nelson, Craig. ★*V Is for Victory*	973.917
Nelson, Willie. *It's a Long Story*	B
Nemat, Marina. *Prisoner of Tehran*	B
Nemiroff, Robert. *To Be Young, Gifted, and Black*	B
Neruda, Pablo. *All the Odes*	861
Neruda, Pablo. *Then Come Back*	861
Neruda, Pablo. *World's End*	861
Neu, Charles E. *Colonel House*	B
Nevala-Lee, Alec. *Astounding*	809.3
Nez, Chester. *Code Talker*	B
Ngugi wa Thiong'o. *In the House of the Interpreter*	B
Nicolson, Juliet. *The Great Silence*	941.083
Niven, Penelope. *Thornton Wilder*	B
Noor. *Leap of Faith*	B
Norman, Elizabeth M. *We Band of Angels*	940.54
Norman, Philip. *George Harrison*	B
Norman, Philip. *John Lennon*	B
Norrell, Robert J. *Up from History*	B
Norris, Robert S. *Racing for the Bomb*	B
Nourse, Victoria F. *In Reckless Hands*	344.7304
Nusbaum, Eric. *Stealing Home*	796.357
Nusseibeh, Sari. *Once Upon a Country*	B
O'Brien, Keith. *Paradise Falls*	363.738
O'Brien, Phillips Payson. *The Second Most Powerful Man in the World*	B
O'Connor, Garry. *Universal Father*	B
O'Hara, Maryanne. *Little Matches*	B
O'Toole, Fintan. ★*We Don't Know Ourselves*	941.7
O'Toole, Patricia. *The Moralist*	B
Oelhafen, Ingrid von. *Hitler's Stolen Children*	B
Ohler, Norman. *The Bohemians*	940.53
Okrent, Daniel. *Last Call*	363.4
Oliphant, Thomas. ★*The Road to Camelot*	973.922092
Oliver, Mary. *New and Selected Poems,; Vol. 1*	811
Oller, John. *White Shoe*	346.73
Ollivier, Bernard. *Out of Istanbul*	B
Olson, Lynne. *Those Angry Days*	940.53
Onassis, Jacqueline Kennedy. *Historic Conversations on Life with John F. Kennedy*	B
Oren, Michael B. *Six Days of War*	956.04
Ostertag, Bob. *People's Movements, People's Press*	071
Ours, Dorothy. *Man O' War*	798.400929
Packer, George. *Our Man*	B
Packer, George. ★*The Unwinding*	973.924
Page, Susan. ★*The Matriarch*	B
Pakula, Hannah. *The Last Empress*	B
Palahniuk, Chuck. *Consider This*	B
Pan, Philip P. *Out of Mao's Shadow*	306.20951
Pantsov, Alexander. *Mao*	B
Parini, Jay. *Borges and Me*	813
Parini, Jay. *Robert Frost*	B
Parkin, Simon. *The Island of Extraordinary Captives*	940.53
Parton, Dolly. ★*Behind the Seams*	B
Pasternak, Judy. *Yellow Dirt*	979.1004
Patton, George S. *War as I Knew It*	B
Pawel, Miriam. *The Crusades of Cesar Chavez*	B
Paxson, Margaret. *The Plateau*	362.87
Payne, Les. ★*The Dead Are Arising*	B
Peiffer, Prudence. *The Slip*	709.73
Pellegrino, Charles R. *To Hell and Back*	940.54
Perlstein, Rick. *The Invisible Bridge*	973.924
Perlstein, Rick. ★*Nixonland*	973.924
Perlstein, Rick. ★*Reaganland*	973.926
Perry, Imani. *May We Forever Stand*	782.25
Perry, Mark. *The Most Dangerous Man in America*	B
Persico, Joseph E. *Franklin and Lucy*	973.917092
Person, Charles. *Buses Are a Comin'*	B
Peters, Charles. *Lyndon B. Johnson*	B
Petraeus, David Howell. *Conflict*	355
Petropoulos, Jonathan. *The Faustian Bargain*	709
Petrushevskaia, Liudmila. *The Girl from the Metropol Hotel*	B
Peyser, Marc N. *Hissing Cousins*	B
Pham, Andrew X. ★*The Eaves of Heaven*	B
Phillips, Julie. *James Tiptree, Jr.*	B
Phillips-Fein, Kim. *Fear City*	330.9747
Pinckney, Darryl. *Come Back in September*	B
Pipher, Mary Bray. *The Middle of Everywhere*	305.9
Pitzer, Andrea. *The Secret History of Vladimir Nabokov*	813
Plokhy, Serhii. ★*Nuclear Folly*	972.9106
Plokhy, Serhii. *Yalta*	940.53
Pontzen, Andrew. *The Universe in a Box*	523.1
Popoff, Alexandra. *Vasily Grossman and the Soviet Century*	B
Posnanski, Joe. ★*The Life and Afterlife of Harry Houdini*	793.8
Posnanski, Joe. *The Soul of Baseball*	796.357
Posner, Gerald L. *Case Closed*	364.1
Posner, Gerald L. *God's Bankers*	364.16
Povey, Glenn. *Echoes*	782.42166
Prager, Joshua. *The Family Roe*	342.7308
Preston, Diana. *Before the Fallout*	303.48
Preston, Diana. *Eight Days at Yalta*	940.53
Preston, Paul. *A People Betrayed*	946
Price, David A. *Geniuses at War*	940.54
Prothero, Stephen R. *God the Bestseller*	070.5
Prud'homme, Alex. *The French Chef in America*	B
Purdum, Todd S. *An Idea Whose Time Has Come*	342.7308
Purdum, Todd S. *Something Wonderful*	B
Purnell, Sonia. *Clementine*	B
Questlove. ★*Hip-Hop Is History*	782.421649
Raban, Jonathan. *Bad Land*	978
Radzinskii, Edvard. *Stalin*	947.084
Raffel, Dawn. *The Strange Case of Dr. Couney*	B
Rampersad, Arnold. *The Life of Langston Hughes*	B
Rampersad, Arnold. ★*The Life of Langston Hughes*	B
Rampersad, Arnold. ★*Ralph Ellison*	B
Ramsey, Donovan X. ★*When Crack Was King*	362.29
Randall, David K. *Black Death at the Golden Gate*	616.9
Rappaport, Helen. *After the Romanovs*	944
Rappaport, Helen. *The Romanov Sisters*	920
Rappleye, Charles. *Herbert Hoover in the White House*	B
Rawlence, Ben. *City of Thorns*	967.7305
Reagan, Ronald. *The Reagan Diaries*	B
Reagan, Ronald. *Reagan*	B
Reed, Julia. *Dispatches from the Gilded Age*	B
Rees, Laurence. *Hitler and Stàlin*	940.53
Rehak, Melanie. *Girl Sleuth*	813
Reid, David. *The Brazen Age*	974.7
Reid, Joy-Ann Lomena. ★*Medgar and Myrlie*	920
Rembert, Winfred. *Chasing Me to My Grave*	B

AUTHOR, TITLE, SERIES AND SUBJECT INDEX

Remnick, David. *Lenin's Tomb*	947.085
Renehan, Edward. *Commodore*	B
Reston, James. *The Conviction of Richard Nixon*	973.924092
Reynolds, Simon. *Shock and Awe*	781.6609
Rhoden, William C. *$40 Million Slaves*	796
Rhodes, Richard. *Scientist*	B
Ribowsky, Mark. *Howard Cosell*	070.449796
Ribowsky, Mark. *Signed, Sealed, and Delivered*	B
Ribowsky, Mark. *The Supremes*	B
Rich, Adrienne. *Collected Early Poems, 1950-1970*	811
Ricks, Thomas E. ★*The Generals*	B
Riedel, Michael. *Singular Sensation*	792
Rilke, Rainer Maria. ★*Letters to a Young Poet*	831
Rinehart, Lorissa. *First to the Front*	B
Risen, Clay. *The Bill of the Century*	342.7308
Risen, James. ★*The Last Honest Man*	973.92
Robb, Graham. *The Discovery of France*	944
Robb, John. *Punk Rock*	781.6609
Roberts, Andrew. ★*Churchill*	B
Robertson, Robbie. ★*Testimony*	B
Robinson, Ray. *Iron Horse*	B
Roe, Sue. *In Montmartre*	920
Roethke, Theodore. *The Collected Poems of Theodore Roethke*	811
Rogan, Eugene L. *The Fall of the Ottomans*	940.3
Roll, David L. *George Marshall*	B
Rosbottom, Ronald C. *When Paris Went Dark*	944.0816
Rosenberg, Rosalind. ★*Jane Crow*	B
Rosenblitt, J. Alison. *The Beauty of Living*	B
Rosenzweig, Laura B. *Hollywood's Spies*	791.43
Rosnay, Tatiana de. *Manderley Forever*	B
Roth, Joseph. *What I Saw*	943
Rothstein, Richard. ★*The Color of Law*	305.800973
Roundtree, Dovey Johnson. ★*Mighty Justice*	B
Rudd, Mark. *Underground*	378.1
Rumsfeld, Donald. *When the Center Held*	973.925092
Runstedtler, Theresa. *Black Ball*	796.323
Russell, Jan Jarboe. *The Train to Crystal City*	940.53
Ryback, Timothy W. *Takeover*	943.086
Rynecki, Elizabeth. *Chasing Portraits*	B
Sacco, Joe. *Footnotes in Gaza*	741.5
Salisbury, Katie Gee. ★*Not Your China Doll*	B
Salle, David. *How to See*	709.04
Sands, Philippe. *The Ratline*	B
Sanneh, Kelefa. ★*Major Labels*	781.64
Santana, Carlos. *The Universal Tone*	B
Sarotte, M. E. *The Collapse*	943.087
Satow, Julie. *When Women Ran Fifth Avenue*	381.141
Satrapi, Marjane. *Chicken with Plums*	741.5
Satrapi, Marjane. ★*The Complete Persepolis*	741.5
Satrapi, Marjane. *Embroideries*	741.5
Sattouf, Riad. *The Arab of the Future*	741.5
Schaap, Jeremy. *Cinderella Man*	B
Schell, Orville. *Wealth and Power*	920
Schiavi, Michael R. *Celluloid Activist*	B
Schindler, Meriel. *The Lost Cafe Schindler*	943.64
Schlesinger, Arthur M. *Journals, 1952-2000*	973.91092
Schlesinger, Arthur M. *A Life in the Twentieth Century*	B
Schloss, Edith. *The Loft Generation*	700.9
Schulman, Bruce J. *The Seventies*	973.92
Schultz, Kevin Michael. *Buckley and Mailer*	920
Schumacher, Michael. *Will Eisner*	741.5
Schwartz, A. Brad. ★*Broadcast Hysteria*	791.44
Schwarz, Geraldine. *Those Who Forget*	940.53
Scott, James. *Black Snow*	940.54
Sebag-Montefiore, Simon. *Stalin*	B
Sebag-Montefiore, Simon. *Young Stalin*	B
Sebba, Anne. *Ethel Rosenberg*	B
Sedgewick, Augustine. *Coffeeland*	338.4
Seidelman, Susan. *Desperately Seeking Something*	B
Seierstad, Asne. *Angel of Grozny*	947.086
Self, Robert O. *All in the Family*	320.50973
Service, Robert. *The End of the Cold War 1985-1991*	909.82
Sevigny, Melissa L. ★*Brave the Wild River*	580.9
Shafrir, Doree. *Thanks for Waiting*	B
Shapiro, James. ★*The Playbook*	792
Shapland, Jenn. *My Autobiography of Carson McCullers*	B
Shawcross, William. *The Queen Mother*	B
Sheinkin, Steve. *Bomb*	623.4
Sherman, Casey. *Above and Beyond*	973.922092
Sherwin, Martin J. *Gambling with Armageddon*	972.9106
Shesol, Jeff. *Supreme Power*	347.73
Shetterly, Margot Lee. ★*Hidden Figures*	510.92
Shlaes, Amity. *Coolidge*	B
Shlaes, Amity. *The Forgotten Man*	973.91
Sides, Hampton. ★*Ghost Soldiers*	940.54
Sides, Hampton. *Hellhound on His Trail*	364.152
Simon, James F. *FDR and Chief Justice Hughes*	973.917092
Sinha, Manisha. ★*The Rise and Fall of the Second American Republic*	973.8
Sisman, Adam. *The Professor and the Parson*	364.16
Slawenski, Kenneth. ★*Salinger*	B
Slezkine, Yuri. *The House of Government*	947.084
Smiley, Jane. *Thirteen Ways of Looking at the Novel*	
Smilios, Maria. ★*The Black Angels*	610.73
Smith, David James. *Young Mandela*	B
Smith, Helmut Walser. *Germany, a Nation in Its Time*	943
Smith, Jean Edward. *FDR*	B
Smith, Jim B. *The Last Mission*	940.54
Smith, Patti. ★*Year of the Monkey*	B
Smith, Richard Norton. *On His Own Terms*	973.925092
Smith, Richard Norton. *An Ordinary Man*	B
Smith, Sally Bedell. *Elizabeth the Queen*	B
Smith, Sally Bedell. *Prince Charles*	B
Sohn, Amy. *The Man Who Hated Women*	363.28
Solnit, Rebecca. *Orwell's Roses*	B
Solomon, Deborah. *Jackson Pollock*	B
Sorensen, Theodore C. *Counselor*	B
Sorin, Gretchen Sullivan. *Driving While Black*	323.1196
Spence, Jonathan D. *The Search for Modern China*	951
Spiegelman, Art. *Co-Mix*	741.5
Spiegelman, Art. *Metamaus*	B
Spitz, Bob. ★*The Beatles*	B
Spitz, Bob. ★*Reagan*	B
Spoto, Donald. *High Society*	B
Springsteen, Bruce. ★*Born to Run*	B
Spurling, Hilary. *Anthony Powell*	B
Spurling, Hilary. *Matisse the Master*	B
Standiford, Les. *Bringing Adam Home*	364.15
Stanley, Brian. *Christianity in the Twentieth Century*	270.8
Stanley, Paul. *Backstage Pass*	B
Stanley, Paul. *Face the Music*	B
Stanton, Doug. *The Odyssey of Echo Company*	959.704
Stargardt, Nicholas. *The German War*	940.53
Steil, Benn. *The Battle of Bretton Woods*	339.5
Steil, Benn. ★*The Marshall Plan*	338.91
Stein, Jean. *West of Eden*	979.4
Steinbeck, John. *Travels with Charley*	B
Steinberg, Jonny. *A Man of Good Hope*	B
Stephanopoulos, George. ★*The Situation Room*	973.09
Stevens, Dana. *Camera Man*	791.4302
Stevens, Wallace. *Collected Poetry and Prose*	811
Stone, Dan. ★*The Holocaust*	940.53
Stone, Robert. *Chasing the Moon*	629.45
Stout, David. *The Kidnap Years*	364.15
Strang, Dean A. *Worse Than the Devil*	345.775
Strauss, Gwen. *The Nine*	940.53
Stuart, Amanda Mackenzie. *Empress of Fashion*	B
Sullivan, Patricia. *Lift Every Voice*	973
Sullivan, Rosemary. *Stalin's Daughter*	B
Suny, Ronald Grigor. *Stalin*	B
Susanka, Sarah. *Creating the Not so Big House*	728
Swanson, James L. *End of Days*	973.922092
Sweig, Julia. *Lady Bird Johnson*	B
Swift, Earl. *Across the Airless Wilds*	629.45
Symonds, Craig L. *World War II at Sea*	940.54
Taffa, Deborah Jackson. ★*Whiskey Tender*	B
Taing, Mae Bunseng. *Under the Naga Tail*	B
Tallent, Elizabeth. *Scratched*	B
Tallis, Frank. ★*Mortal Secrets*	B
Talty, Stephan. *Agent Garbo*	940.5
Talty, Stephan. *Saving Bravo*	959.704
Taraborrelli, J. Randy. ★*Jackie*	B
Taraborrelli, J. Randy. ★*The Secret Life of Marilyn Monroe*	B
Taubman, William. *Khrushchev*	B
Taylor, D. J. *Orwell*	B
Taylor, Fred. *1939*	940.53
Taylor, Fred. *The Berlin Wall*	943

1571

PUBLIC LIBRARY CORE COLLECTION: NONFICTION
Twentieth Edition

Taylor, Jay. *The Generalissimo*	B
Taylor, Nick. *American Made*	331.13
Teachout, Terry. ★*All in the Dances*	B
Telushkin, Joseph. *Rebbe*	296.833
Thant Myint-U. *The Hidden History of Burma*	959.105
Theoharis, Jeanne. *A More Beautiful and Terrible History*	323.1196
Theroux, Paul. *The Great Railway Bazaar*	915
Theroux, Paul. *Riding the Iron Rooster*	915
Thomas, Dylan. *A Child's Christmas in Wales*	B
Thomas, Dylan. *The Poems of Dylan Thomas*	821
Thomas, Evan. *Being Nixon*	B
Thomas, Evan. ★*First*	B
Thomas, Evan. *Ike's Bluff*	973.921092
Thomas, Evan. *Sea of Thunder*	940.54
Thompson, Hunter S. ★*Fear and Loathing in America*	B
Thompson, Juan F. *Stories I Tell Myself*	B
Thompson, Nicholas. *The Hawk and the Dove*	973.92
Thomson, Graeme. *George Harrison*	B
Thomson, Jennifer. *Josephine Tey*	823
Thwaite, Ann. *Goodbye Christopher Robin*	B
Todd, Olivier. *Albert Camus*	B
Tolinski, Brad. *Light and Shade*	B
Tomalin, Claire. *Thomas Hardy*	B
Toobin, Jeffrey. *The Nine*	347.73
Trahair, R. C. S. *Encyclopedia of Cold War Espionage, Spies, and Secret Operations 3rd Ed.*	327.12
Travisano, Thomas J. *Love Unknown*	B
Tremlett, Giles. *Ghosts of Spain*	946.08
Trentmann, Frank. *Out of the Darkness*	943.08
Trethewey, Natasha D. ★*Memorial Drive*	B
Treuer, David. ★*The Heartbeat of Wounded Knee*	970.004
Trimborn, Jurgen. *Leni Riefenstahl*	B
Trofimov, Yaroslav. *The Siege of Mecca*	953.805
Trubert-Tollu, Chantal. ★*The House of Worth 1858-1954*	746.92
Tsu, Jing. *Kingdom of Characters*	495.111
Tubbs, Anna Malaika. *The Three Mothers*	306.874
Tuchman, Barbara W. *The Proud Tower*	909.82
Tuchman, Barbara W. *Stilwell and the American Experience in China, 1911-45*	B
Tucker, Todd. *The Great Starvation Experiment*	174.2
Turbow, Jason. *They Bled Blue*	796.357
Twitty, Michael. ★*The Cooking Gene*	641.59
Tye, Larry. ★*Demagogue*	B
Tye, Larry. ★*The Jazzmen*	781.6509
Tye, Larry. *Satchel*	B
Tyson, Timothy B. *Blood Done Sign My Name*	975.6
Tyson, Timothy B. *The Blood of Emmett Till*	364.1
Ung, Loung. *Lucky Child*	B
Updegrove, Mark K. *The Last Republicans*	973.928
Updike, John. *Always Looking*	700
Urofsky, Melvin I. *Louis D. Brandeis*	B
Urwand, Ben. *The Collaboration*	791.430973
Vogel, Ezra F. *Deng XIaoping and the Transformation of China*	B
Vogel, Steve. *Betrayal in Berlin*	327.1273043
Von Drehle, Dave. ★*Triangle*	974.7
Von Drehle, David. ★*The Book of Charlie*	B
Von Tunzelmann, Alex. *Blood and Sand*	909.82
Vonnegut, Kurt. *Kurt Vonnegut*	813
Vonnegut, Kurt. ★*A Man Without a Country*	818
Wagamese, Richard. *One Native Life*	B
Wald, Elijah. *Dylan Goes Electric!*	782.42164
Walker, Alice. *Gathering Blossoms Under Fire*	B
Walker, Hunter. *The Truce*	324.2736
Walker, Stephen. *Beyond*	629.45
Wallace, Chris. *Countdown 1945*	940.54
Wallace, Christopher. *Twentieth-Century Man*	B
Wallach, Janet. *Desert Queen*	B
Ward, Geoffrey C. *The Roosevelts*	B
Ward, Geoffrey C. ★*The Vietnam War*	959.704
Ward, Gerald W. R. *Chihuly*	709
Warren, Rosanna. *Max Jacob*	B
Wasson, Sam. *Fifth Avenue, 5 A.M.*	791.43
Wasson, Sam. ★*Improv Nation*	792.02
Watson, Bruce. *Freedom Summer*	323.1196
Watts, Steven. *The People's Tycoon*	B
Watts, Steven. *Self-Help Messiah*	B
Weiner, Tim. *Legacy of Ashes*	327.1273009
Weiner, Tim. *One Man Against the World*	B
Weldon, Glen. ★*The Caped Crusade*	741.5
Weller, Sam. *The Bradbury Chronicles*	B
Welty, Eudora. *One Writer's Beginnings*	B
Wertheim, L. Jon. *Glory Days*	796.09
Westad, Odd Arne. *The Cold War*	909.825
Whipple, Chris. *The Gatekeepers*	973.92092
Whitaker, Mark. ★*Saying It Loud*	973.923
Whitaker, Mark. *Smoketown*	305.896
White, Richard. *Who Killed Jane Stanford?*	364.152
Whyte, Kenneth. *Hoover*	B
Whyte, Kenneth. *The Uncrowned King*	B
Wiederhorn, Jon. *Louder Than Hell*	781.6609
Wiesel, Elie. *All Rivers Run to the Sea*	B
Wilkerson, Isabel. ★*The Warmth of Other Suns*	304.80973
Wilkinson, Alec. *The Protest Singer*	B
Williams, Juan. *Eyes on the Prize*	323.4
Williams, William Carlos. *Paterson*	811
Williamson, Edwin. *Borges*	B
Willis, Deborah. *Reflections in Black*	770
Willner, Nina. *Forty Autumns*	B
Wills, Clair. ★*Missing Persons*	929.2
Wilson, A. N. *C.S. Lewis*	823
Wilson, August. *Fences*	812
Wilson, Victoria. *A Life of Barbara Stanwyck*	B
Winchester, Simon. *A Crack in the Edge of the World*	979.4
Winder, Elizabeth. *Pain, Parties, Work*	B
Wolfe, Tom. ★*The Right Stuff*	629.4
Wolff, Daniel J. *Grown-Up Anger*	920
Wolff, Tobias. *This Boy's Life*	B
Womack, Kenneth. *All Things Must Pass Away*	781.66
Wong, Carmen Rita. *Why Didn't You Tell Me?*	B
Wood, James. *How Fiction Works*	808.3
Woodress, James Leslie. *Willa Cather*	B
Woods, Randall Bennett. *Prisoners of Hope*	973.923
Woodward, Bob. *The Final Days*	B
Woodward, Bob. *Shadow*	973.92
Woodward, C. Vann. *The Strange Career of Jim Crow*	305.896
Woodward, Kenneth L. *Making Saints*	235.24
Woolf, Virginia. *Moments of Being*	B
Worsley, Lucy. ★*Agatha Christie*	B
Wright, C. D. *One with Others*	811
Wright, Lawrence. *Going Clear*	299
Wright, Lawrence. ★*The Looming Tower*	973.931
Wright, Richard. ★*Black Boy*	B
Wukovits, John F. *Lost at Sea*	940.54
Xue, XInran. *The Book of Secrets*	951.05
Yang, Jeff. ★*Rise*	973
Yang, Jia Lynn. ★*One Mighty and Irresistible Tide*	325.73
Yang, Jisheng. *The World Turned Upside Down*	951.05
Yeebo, Yepoka. *Anansi's Gold*	364.16
Yellin, Emily. *Our Mothers' War*	940.53
Yergin, Daniel. ★*The Prize*	338.2
Yergin, Daniel. *The Quest*	333.79
Young, Rob. *Electric Eden*	781.62
Ypi, Lea. ★*Free*	B
Zapruder, Alexandra. *Twenty-Six Seconds*	973.922092
Zeitz, Joshua. *Building the Great Society*	973.923
Zelizer, Julian E. *Burning Down the House*	328.73
Zenith, Richard. *Pessoa*	B
Zia, Helen. *Last Boat Out of Shanghai*	951.04
Zimmerman, Paul. *Dr. Z*	B
Zminda, Don. *Double Plays and Double Crosses*	796.357

21ST CENTURY

Ackerman, Spencer. *Reign of Terror*	973.931
Alberta, Tim. *American Carnage*	324.2734
Albright, Madeleine Korbel. *Hell and Other Destinations*	B
Alexander, Elizabeth. ★*The Trayvon Generation*	305.896
Alexander, Kwame. *Light for the World to See*	811.6
Alkon, Amy. *Good Manners for Nice People*	395
Allen, Jonathan. *Lucky*	324.973
Allen, Jonathan. *Shattered*	324.973
Andrews, Becca. ★*No Choice*	362.1988
Applebaum, Anne. *Twilight of Democracy*	321.9
Armstrong, Karen. *Muhammad*	B
Armstrong, Karen. *The Spiral Staircase*	B
Asghar, Fatimah. *If They Come for Us*	811
Atwood, Margaret. *Burning Questions*	814
Auletta, Ken. *Media Man*	B

AUTHOR, TITLE, SERIES AND SUBJECT INDEX

Bade, Rachael. ★*Unchecked*	342.73
Bailey, Issac J. *Why Didn't We Riot?*	305.800973
Baker, Peter. *The Divider*	973.933
Baker, Peter. *The Man Who Ran Washington*	B
Balz, Daniel J. *The Battle for America, 2008*	973.932
Bauer, Shane. *American Prison*	365
Baum, Dan. *Nine Lives*	B
Bayoumi, Moustafa. *How Does It Feel to Be a Problem?*	305.892
Beavan, Colin. *No Impact Man*	B
Bender, Michael C. *"Frankly, We Did Win This Election"*	973.933
Berkow, Ira. *How Life Imitates Sports*	070.4
Bernard, Emily. *Black Is the Body*	305.48
Bhutto, Benazir. *Reconciliation*	297.2
Bialosky, Jill. *Poetry Will Save Your Life*	B
Bilal, Wafaa. *Shoot an Iraqi*	B
Bomey, Nathan. *Detroit Resurrected*	977.4
Bowden, Mark. *The Steal*	973.933
Boykin, Keith. *Race Against Time*	305.8
Bradbury, Dominic. *The Iconic Interior*	747
Branch, Taylor. *The Clinton Tapes*	973.929
Brazile, Donna. *For Colored Girls Who Have Considered Politics*	328.73
Breihan, Tom. ★*The Number Ones*	782.42164
Brenner, Marie. *The Desperate Hours*	362.1962
Brill, Steven. *Class Warfare*	371.010973
Brill, Steven. *Tailspin*	306.0973
Brinkley, Douglas. *The Great Deluge*	976.3
Brown, Mick. ★*Tearing Down the Wall of Sound*	B
Brown, Molly McCully. *Places I've Taken My Body*	B
Brown, Tina. ★*The Palace Papers*	920
Bryson, Bill. *The Road to Little Dribbling*	914
Buckland, Gail. *Who Shot Rock & Roll*	779
Bush, George W. *41*	B
Bush, George W. *Decision Points*	B
Butler, Paul. *Chokehold*	363.2
Caldwell, Christopher. *The Age of Entitlement*	305.240973
Carcaterra, Lorenzo. *Three Dreamers*	B
Carpenter, Amanda B. *Gaslighting America*	973.933
Carruthers, Charlene A. *Unapologetic*	305.48
Carter, Jimmy. *Palestine*	956.04
Cenziper, Debbie. ★*Love Wins*	346.7301
Chait, Jonathan. *Audacity*	973.932
Chandrasekaran, Rajiv. *Imperial Life in the Emerald City*	956.7044
Chertoff, Michael. *Exploding Data*	343.7309
Chinen, Nate. *Playing Changes*	781.6509
Chittister, Joan. *Following the Path*	248.4
Chivers, C. J. *The Fighters*	920
Chozick, Amy. *Chasing Hillary*	B
Clark, Taylor. *Starbucked*	338
Clinton, Bill. *My Life*	B
Clinton, Hillary Rodham. *Living History*	B
Coker, Margaret. *The Spymaster of Baghdad*	956.7044
Coll, Steve. *Private Empire*	338.7
Common. *One Day It'll All Make Sense*	B
Copaken, Deborah. *Ladyparts*	B
Cottom, Tressie McMillan. *Thick*	301
Cox, Caroline. *The World Atlas of Street Fashion*	391.009
Coyle, Marcia. *The Roberts Court*	347.73
Currie, Elliott. *A Peculiar Indifference*	305.800973
D'Antonio, Michael. *The Hunting of Hillary*	B
Daniels, Stormy. *Full Disclosure*	B
Danler, Stephanie. *Stray*	B
Daunton, M. J. ★*The Economic Government of the World*	337
Davidson, Adam. *The Passion Economy*	330.9
Davis, Michael. *Street Gang*	791.43
Dayen, David. *Chain of Title*	330.973
Delisle, Guy. *Pyongyang*	741.5
Deng, Alephonsion. *They Poured Fire on Us from the Sky*	B
DePalma, Anthony. *The Cubans*	920
DeParle, Jason. ★*A Good Provider Is One Who Leaves*	305.899
Di Giovanni, Janine. *The Morning They Came for Us*	956.9104
Diamond, Jared M. *Swing Kings*	796.357
Diaz, Natalie. ★*Postcolonial Love Poem*	811
Doggett, Peter. *Electric Shock*	781.64
Dorey-Stein, Beck. *From the Corner of the Oval*	B
Dower, John W. *Cultures of War*	355.00973
Draper, Robert. *To Start a War*	956.7044
Du Mez, Kristin Kobes. *Jesus and John Wayne*	277.308
Duggan, Christopher. *The Force of Destiny*	945
Dunmore, Helen. *Inside the Wave*	821
Dwyer, Jim. *102 Minutes*	974.7
Dyson, Michael Eric. *Come Hell or High Water*	976.3
Ebert, Roger. *Life Itself*	B
Eggers, Dave. *Zeitoun*	305.892
Ehrenreich, Barbara. *Had I Known*	814
Ellis, Joseph J. ★*American Dialogue*	973.3
Ellis, Richard. *Tuna*	333.95
Ellsworth, Scott. *The Ground Breaking*	976.6
Emanuel, Rahm. *The Nation City*	352.23
Engel, Richard. *And Then All Hell Broke Loose*	956.05
Eyre, Eric. *Death in Mud Lick*	362.29
Faizullah, Tarfia. *Registers of Illuminated Villages*	811
Farmer, John J. *The Ground Truth*	973.931
Farrell, John A. *Ted Kennedy*	B
Felder, Deborah G. *The American Women's Almanac*	305.40973
Finkel, David. *The Good Soldiers*	956.7044
Finkel, David. *Thank You for Your Service*	920
Fisk, Robert. *The Great War for Civilisation*	956.04
Forsythe, Kelly. *Perennial*	811
Francis. *Life*	B
Frederick, Jim. *Black Hearts*	956.7044
Friedman, George. *Flashpoints*	940.56
Gabler, Neal. *Catching the Wind*	B
Gates, Robert Michael. ★*Exercise of Power*	973.929
Gerth, Karl. *As China Goes, so Goes the World*	339.4
Gessen, Masha. *Never Remember*	365
Gessen, Masha. *Surviving Autocracy*	973.933
Ghobash, Omar Saif. *Letters to a Young Muslim*	297.09
Gilbert, Sandra M. ★*Still Mad*	810.9
Giovanni, Nikki. *A Good Cry*	811
Giridharadas, Anand. ★*The Persuaders*	320.973
Goldberg, Emma. *Life on the Line*	362.1962
Goldblatt, David. ★*The Age of Football*	796.334
Golembesky, Michael. *Level Zero Heroes*	958.104
Goudeau, Jessica. ★*After the Last Border*	362.83
Graff, Garrett M. ★*The Only Plane in the Sky*	973.931
Graham, Jorie. *Fast*	811
Grandmaster Flash. *The Adventures of Grandmaster Flash*	B
Greene, Andy. *The Office*	791.45
Grieve, Paul. *A Brief Guide to Islam*	297
Harari, Yuval N. ★*21 Lessons for the 21st Century*	909.82
Hardman, Robert. *Queen of Our Times*	B
Hardman, Robert. *Queen of the World*	B
Hawes, Jennifer. *Grace Will Lead Us Home*	364.152
Hayes, Christopher. *A Colony in a Nation*	364.3
Hayes, Terrance. ★*American Sonnets for My Past and Future Assassin*	811
Hayes, Terrance. *How to Be Drawn*	811
Hayes, Terrance. ★*Lighthead*	811
Hennessey, Susan. *Unmaking the Presidency*	973.933
Hessler, Peter. *The Buried*	962.05
Hewitt, Ben. ★*The Town That Food Saved*	338.1
Hiaasen, Carl. *The Downhill Lie*	B
Hill, Geoffrey. *Selected Poems*	821
Hirono, Mazie. *Heart of Fire*	B
Hirshman, Linda R. *Reckoning*	305.420973
Hitchens, Christopher. *Hitch-22*	920
Hoffman, Carl. *Liar's Circus*	973.933
Hoffman, Liz. *Crash Landing*	330
Hope, Bradley. *Blood and Oil*	B
Hubbard, Ben (Journalist). *Mbs*	B
Huffman, Alan. *Here I Am*	B
Hunter-Gault, Charlayne. ★*My People*	305.48
Issenberg, Sasha. ★*The Engagement*	346.7301
Jacobson, Sidney. *The 9-11 Report*	741.5
Jarrett, Valerie. *Finding My Voice*	B
Jayapal, Pramila. *Use the Power You Have*	B
Johnson, Lizzie. ★*Paradise*	363.37
Johnston, David Cay. *The Big Cheat*	973.933
Jones, Brenda. *Alexandria Ocasio-Cortez*	B
Jones, Brenda. *Maxine Waters*	B
Jones, Gerard. *Men of Tomorrow*	741.5
Jordan, Mary. *The Art of Her Deal*	B
Kamenetz, Anya. *The Stolen Year*	306.43
Karl, Jonathan. *Betrayal*	973.933
Karl, Jonathan. *Front Row at the Trump Show*	973.933
Kasischke, Laura. *Space, in Chains*	811
Keene, John. ★*Punks*	811

PUBLIC LIBRARY CORE COLLECTION: NONFICTION
Twentieth Edition

Keinan, Tal. *God Is in the Crowd*	305.892
Kempner, Joanna. *Psychedelic Outlaws*	615.7
Kershaw, Ian. *The Global Age*	940.55
Klay, Phil. *Uncertain Ground*	359.9
Klein, Ezra. ★*Why We're Polarized*	306.0973
Klinenberg, Eric. ★*2020*	306
Klosterman, Chuck. *But What If We're Wrong*	909.83
Kornacki, Steve. *The Red and the Blue*	306.20973
Kozol, Jonathan. *Fire in the Ashes*	362.77
Kristof, Nicholas D. ★*Tightrope*	306.0973
Krugman, Paul R. *Arguing with Zombies*	330.973
Kurutz, Steven. *American Flannel*	338.4
Lalami, Laila. *Conditional Citizens*	323.60973
Langewiesche, William. *The Atomic Bazaar*	355.02
Lebron, Christopher J. *The Making of Black Lives Matter*	305.896
Lehr, Dick. *White Hot Hate*	363.325
Lemmon, Gayle Tzemach. *The Daughters of Kobani*	956.9104
Leonhardt, David. ★*Ours Was the Shining Future*	330.973
Leonnig, Carol. *I Alone Can Fix It*	973.933
Lessig, Lawrence. *Remix*	346.7304
Lewis, Michael. *The Big Short*	330.973
Lewis, Michael. ★*The Premonition*	614.5
Li, Yiyun. *Dear Friend, from My Life I Write to You in Your Life*	B
Limon, Ada. *Bright Dead Things*	811
Limon, Ada. ★*The Carrying*	811
Linden, Eugene. *Fire and Flood*	304.2
Lithwick, Dahlia. *Lady Justice*	345.73
Litt, David. *Thanks, Obama*	B
Lorenz, Taylor. ★*Extremely Online*	302.23
Lowery, Wesley. ★*American Whitelash*	305.8
Loyn, David. *The Long War*	958.104
Lynskey, Dorian. *33 Revolutions per Minute*	782.42
Manson, Mark. *Everything Is F*cked*	152.4
Margonelli, Lisa. *Oil on the Brain*	338.2
Markovits, Daniel. *The Meritocracy Trap*	305.5
Martin, Jonathan. *This Will Not Pass*	973.933
Marton, Kati. ★*The Chancellor*	B
Mayer, Jane. *The Dark Side*	973.931
McAlevey, Jane. *A Collective Bargain*	331.890973
McCraw, David Edward. *Truth in Our Times*	342.7308
McKay, Sinclair. *Berlin*	943
McKibben, Bill. *Falter*	909.83
McLaren, Brian D. *Life After Doom*	200.1
McLean, Bethany. *All the Devils Are Here*	330.973
McMillan, Tracie. *The American Way of Eating*	338.4
Merchant, Brian. *Blood in the Machine*	303.48
Messud, Claire. *Kant's Little Prussian Head and Other Reasons Why I Write*	B
Miranda, Lin-Manuel. *Hamilton*	782.1
Mogelson, Luke. *The Storm Is Here*	973.933
Monforton, Celeste. *On the Job*	331.1
Mooney, Paul. *Black Is the New White*	792.7
Moore, Michael Scott. *The Desert and the Sea*	364.15
Moran, Caitlin. *How to Be a Woman*	B
Moran, Caitlin. *More Than a Woman*	B
Morgan, Wesley. *The Hardest Place*	958.104
Murakami, Haruki. *What I Talk About When I Talk About Running*	B
Navai, Ramita. *City of Lies*	955
Neiwert, David A. ★*The Age of Insurrection*	303.48
Neufeld, Josh. *A.D.*	741.5
Neus, Nora. *24 Hours in Charlottesville*	973.933
Nixon, John. *Debriefing the President*	956.7044
Nussbaum, Martha Craven. *The Monarchy of Fear*	306.20973
O'Connor, Garry. *Universal Father*	B
O'Neil, Cathy. *Weapons of Math Destruction*	005.7
O'Toole, Fintan. ★*We Don't Know Ourselves*	941.7
Obama, Barack. ★*A Promised Land*	B
Obama, Michelle. ★*Becoming*	B
Oppenheimer, Mark. *Squirrel Hill*	364.152
Osnos, Evan. *Age of Ambition*	951.06
Osnos, Evan. *Wildland*	973.93
Otfinoski, Steven. *Latinos in the Arts*	700.89
Pablo Cruz, Rosayra. *The Book of Rosy*	B
Packer, George. *Last Best Hope*	973.93
Packer, George. ★*The Unwinding*	973.924
Page, Susan. ★*The Matriarch*	B
Pan, Philip P. *Out of Mao's Shadow*	306.20951
Parry, Richard Lloyd. *Ghosts of the Tsunami*	952.05
Parton, Dolly. ★*Behind the Seams*	B
Perry, Imani. ★*South to America*	917
Pilling, David. *Bending Adversity*	952.0512
Pipher, Mary Bray. *The Middle of Everywhere*	305.9
Plokhy, Serhii. ★*The Russo-Ukrainian War*	947.7
Poniewozik, James. *Audience of One*	324.7
Pontzen, Andrew. *The Universe in a Box*	523.1
Posner, Gerald L. *God's Bankers*	364.16
Povey, Glenn. *Echoes*	782.42166
Prothero, Stephen R. *God Is Not One*	200
Questlove. ★*Hip-Hop Is History*	782.421649
Raddatz, Martha. *The Long Road Home*	B
Rakoff, Joanna Smith. *My Salinger Year*	200
Reichl, Ruth. *My Kitchen Year*	641.5
Reid, T. R. *A Fine Mess*	336.200973
Rhodes, Benjamin J. *The World as It Is*	973.932
Ribowsky, Mark. *Signed, Sealed, and Delivered*	B
Ricks, Thomas E. *Fiasco*	956.7044
Rivlin, Gary. *Broke, USA*	339.4
Rothkopf, David J. *American Resistance*	973.933
Rothschild, Mike. *The Storm Is Upon Us*	973.933
Roy, Arundhati. *Walking with the Comrades*	954
Salle, David. *How to See*	709.04
Samuels, Robert. ★*His Name Is George Floyd*	B
Sandel, Michael J. *Justice*	172
Sanneh, Kelefa. ★*Major Labels*	781.64
Scahill, Jeremy. *Dirty Wars*	355.00973
Schell, Orville. *Wealth and Power*	920
Schlesinger, Arthur M. *Journals, 1952-2000*	973.91092
Schmidt, Michael S. ★*Donald Trump v. The United States*	973.933
Schumacher, Michael. *Will Eisner*	741.5
Schwartz, Nelson. *The Velvet Rope Economy*	339.2
Scott-Clark, Cathy. *The Forever Prisoner*	364.6
Seierstad, Asne. *Angel of Grozny*	947.086
Seierstad, Asne. *A Hundred and One Days*	956.70443
Self, Robert O. *All in the Family*	320.50973
Sharma, Ruchir. *The Rise and Fall of Nations*	330.9
Shteyngart, Gary. ★*Little Failure*	B
Shuster, Simon. ★*The Showman*	B
Signer, Michael. *Cry Havoc*	305.800973
Slevin, Peter. *Michelle Obama*	B
Smith, Jean Edward. *Bush*	973.931
Smith, Sally Bedell. *Elizabeth the Queen*	B
Soboroff, Jacob. ★*Separated*	325.73
Sommer, Will. ★*Trust the Plan*	973.933
Sorkin, Andrew Ross. *Too Big to Fail*	330.973
Souza, Pete. *Obama*	973.932
Souza, Pete. *The West Wing and Beyond*	917.53
Stanton, Doug. *12 Strong*	958.104
Steinhauer, Jennifer. *The Firsts*	320.082
Stephanopoulos, George. ★*The Situation Room*	973.09
Stiglitz, Joseph E. *The Price of Inequality*	305.50973
Strayed, Cheryl. ★*Wild*	B
Sullivan, Kevin. *Trump on Trial*	342.73
Sundeen, Mark. *The Unsettlers*	640
Taibbi, Matt. *I Can't Breathe*	363.2
Taub, Jennifer. *Big Dirty Money*	364.16
Taylor, Barbara Brown. *Holy Envy*	B
Taylor, Justin. *Riding with the Ghost*	B
Thomas, Elizabeth Marshall. *Growing Old*	305.26
Thomas, R. Eric. *Here for It*	B
Thompson, Jamie. *Standoff*	364.152
Tickle, Phyllis. *The Great Emergence*	270.8
Tinsley, Omise'eke Natasha. *Beyonce in Formation*	782.42164
Tolentino, Jia. ★*Trick Mirror*	973.93
Toobin, Jeffrey. *The Nine*	347.73
Toobin, Jeffrey. *True Crimes and Misdemeanors*	973.933
Trentmann, Frank. *Out of the Darkness*	943.08
Trump, Mary L. *Too Much and Never Enough*	B
Tudor, Daniel. *North Korea Confidential*	951.93
Updegrove, Mark K. *The Last Republicans*	973.928
Vaughan, Liam. *Flash Crash*	B
Verini, James. *They Will Have to Die Now*	956.7044
Vladeck, Stephen I. *The Shadow Docket*	347.73
Volpe, Joseph. *The Toughest Show on Earth*	B
Vonnegut, Kurt. *Kurt Vonnegut*	813
Wald, Elijah. *How the Beatles Destroyed Rock 'N' Roll*	781.64
Walker, Hunter. *The Truce*	324.2736

AUTHOR, TITLE, SERIES AND SUBJECT INDEX

Wallace, Chris. *Countdown Bin Laden*	958.104
Ward, Gerald W. R. *Chihuly*	709
Warrick, Joby. *Black Flags*	956.9104
Weissmann, Andrew. ★*Where Law Ends*	324.7
Wertheim, L. Jon. *Blood in the Cage*	796.815
Wessel, David. *In Fed We Trust*	332.1
Westhoff, Ben. *Dirty South*	782.421649
Whipple, Chris. *The Fight of His Life*	973.934
Whitlock, Craig. ★*Fat Leonard*	364.16
Wickersham, Seth. ★*It's Better to Be Feared*	796.332
Wilkinson, Alec. *The Protest Singer*	B
Wilson, Rick. *Running Against the Devil*	973.933
Wise, Tim J. *Dispatches from the Race War*	305.8
Wolff, Michael. *Fire and Fury*	973.933
Wolff, Michael. *Landslide*	973.933
Wong, Chun Han. *Party of One*	951.06
Wood, Graeme. *The Way of the Strangers*	363.325
Woodward, Bob. *Fear*	973.933
Woodward, Bob. *Peril*	973.933
Woodward, Bob. *Shadow*	973.92
Worth, Robert Forsyth. ★*A Rage for Order*	909
Wright, Evan. *Generation Kill*	956.7044
XIe, Jenny. *Eye Level*	811
Xuecun, Murong. *Deadly Quiet City*	614.5
Yang, Jeff. ★*Rise*	973
Zelizer, Julian E. *Burning Down the House*	328.73

A

★*An A-Z of Pasta*. Roddy, Rachel	641.82
A. Lincoln. White, Ronald C.	B
A.D. Neufeld, Josh	741.5
AALIYAH, 1979-2001	
Iandoli, Kathy. *Baby Girl*	B
AARON, HANK, 1934-2021	
Bryant, Howard. *The Last Hero*	B
The Abacus and the Cross. Brown, Nancy Marie	B
★*Abandoned*. Kim, Anne	305.2350973
ABANDONED ANIMALS	
Novello, Carol. *Mutual Rescue*	636.088
ABANDONED CATS	
Myron, Vicki. ★*Dewey*	636.80092
ABANDONED CHILDREN	
Calcaterra, Regina. *Etched in Sand*	B
Henderson, Rob Kim. *Troubled*	B
ABANDONED DOGS	
Achterberg, Cara Sue. *Another Good Dog*	636.7
Bragg, Rick. *The Speckled Beauty*	636.7
Abandoned in Hell. Albracht, William	959.704
ABANDONMENT (PSYCHOLOGY)	
Ford, Ashley C. ★*Somebody's Daughter*	B
Hamilton, Lisa M. *The Hungry Season*	B
Miller, Michelle. *Belonging*	B
Owusu, Nadia. *Aftershocks*	B
Prickett, Pamela J. ★*The Unclaimed*	363.7
Seierstad, Asne. *Angel of Grozny*	947.086
ABARCA, LYDIA	
Valby, Karen. *The Swans of Harlem*	792.8
Abbondio, Sarah	
Mini Amigurumi Animals	746.43
Abbot, Sebastian	
The Away Game	796.334
ABBOTT, BERENICE, 1898-1991	
Van Haaften, Julia. ★*Berenice Abbott*	B
Abbott, Karen	
American Rose	
Liar, Temptress, Soldier, Spy	920
Abdelmahmoud, Elamin	
Son of Elsewhere	B
ABDELMAHMOUD, ELAMIN	
Abdelmahmoud, Elamin. *Son of Elsewhere*	B
Abdul Rauf, Feisal	
Moving the Mountain	297
Abdul-Ahad, Ghaith	
A Stranger in Your Own City	956.7044

ABDUL-AHAD, GHAITH	
Abdul-Ahad, Ghaith. *A Stranger in Your Own City*	956.7044
Abdul-Jabbar, Kareem	
Coach Wooden and Me	B
ABDUL-JABBAR, KAREEM, 1947-	
Abdul-Jabbar, Kareem. *Coach Wooden and Me'*	B
Abdulali, Sohaila	
What We Talk About When We Talk About Rape	364.15
ABDULLAHI, ASAD	
Steinberg, Jonny. *A Man of Good Hope*	B
Abdurraqib, Hanif	
A Fortune for Your Disaster	811
Go Ahead in the Rain	782.421649
★*A Little Devil in America*	791.089
★*There's Always This Year*	796.323
ABDURRAQIB, HANIF, 1983-	
Abdurraqib, Hanif. *Go Ahead in the Rain*	782.421649
Abdurraqib, Hanif. ★*There's Always This Year*	796.323
★*Abe*. Reynolds, David S.	B
Abel, Jessica	
Drawing Words, Writing Pictures	741.5
Mastering Comics	741.5
ABERNATHY, RALPH, 1926-1990	
Kix, Paul. ★*You Have to Be Prepared to Die Before You Can Begin to Live*	976.1
Abigail Adams. Adams, Abigail	973.4
Abigail Adams. Holton, Woody	
ABILITY	
Chittister, Joan. *Following the Path*	248.4
Epstein, David J. ★*Range*	153.9
Ericsson, K. Anders. *Peak*	153.9
Friedman, Rachel. ★*And Then We Grew Up*	305.24
Grant, Adam M. *Hidden Potential*	153.8
Hansen, Morten T. *Great at Work*	650.1
Markovits, Daniel. *The Meritocracy Trap*	305.5
White, Richard Antoine. *I'm Possible*	B
Young, Scott H. *Get Better at Anything*	650.1
ABLEISM	
Blake, Melissa. *Beautiful People*	362.4
Hardwick, Lamar. *How Ableism Fuels Racism*	261.8
Heumann, Judith E. *Being Heumann*	B
Lehrer, Riva. *Golem Girl*	B
Leland, Andrew. ★*The Country of the Blind*	B
Mattlin, Ben. *Disability Pride*	323.3
Ndopu, Eddie. *Sipping Dom Pérignon Through a Straw*	B
Sjunneson, Elsa. *Being Seen*	362.4
Taussig, Rebekah. *Sitting Pretty*	B
Wong, Alice. ★*Year of the Tiger*	B
Abolition. Davis, Angela Y.	364.6
ABOLITIONISTS	
Ayers, Edward L. *American Visions*	973.5
Blight, David W. ★*Frederick Douglass*	B
Bordewich, Fergus M. *Bound for Canaan*	973.7
Brands, H. W. ★*The Zealot and the Emancipator*	920
Burlingame, Michael. *The Black Man's President*	973.7
Davis, Angela Y. *Abolition*	364.6
Delbanco, Andrew. *The War Before the War*	973.7
Dilbeck, D. H. *Frederick Douglass*	B
Douglass, Frederick. *My Bondage and My Freedom*	B
Douglass, Frederick. *Narrative of the Life of Frederick Douglass, an American Slave*	B
Foner, Eric. *The Fiery Trial*	973.7092
Foner, Eric. ★*Gateway to Freedom*	973.7
Greenidge, Kerri. ★*The Grimkes*	973.5
Grinspan, Jon. *Wide Awake*	973.7
Hochschild, Adam. *Bury the Chains*	326
Horwitz, Tony. ★*Midnight Rising*	973.7
Kaplan, Fred. *Lincoln and the Abolitionists*	973.7092
Levine, Bruce C. *Thaddeus Stevens*	B
Meyer, Eugene L. *Five for Freedom*	973.7
Miles, Tiya. ★*Night Flyer*	B
Morgan-Owens, Jessie. *Girl in Black and White*	B
Oakes, James. *Freedom National*	973.7
Painter, Nell Irvin. ★*Sojourner Truth*	B
Reynolds, David S. *John Brown, Abolitionist*	B
Shane, Scott. ★*Flee North*	973.7
Sinha, Manisha. *The Slave's Cause*	326
Snodgrass, Mary Ellen. *The Underground Railroad*	973.7

PUBLIC LIBRARY CORE COLLECTION: NONFICTION
Twentieth Edition

Stauffer, John. *Picturing Fredrick Douglass* — B
Taylor, Alan. *American Civil Wars* — 973.7
Abominable Science! Loxton, Daniel — 001.944
ABORTION
    Andrews, Becca. ★*No Choice* — 362.1988
    Blair, Gabrielle Stanley. ★*Ejaculate Responsibly* — 362.1988
    Foster, Diana Greene. *The Turnaway Study* — 362.1988
    Kolbert, Kathryn. *Controlling Women* — 362.1988
    Luthra, Shefali. ★*Undue Burden* — 362.1988
    Matthews, Hannah. *You or Someone You Love* — 362.1988
    Peters, Rebecca Todd. *Trust Women* — 362.1988
    Prager, Joshua. *The Family Roe* — 342.7308
    Rankin, Lauren. *Bodies on the Line* — 362.1988
    Sanger, Carol. *About Abortion* — 179.7
    Shah, Meera. *You're the Only One I've Told* — 362.1988
    Stone, Geoffrey R. ★*Sex and the Constitution* — 345.7302
    Waldman, Michael. *The Supermajority* — 347.73
    Wright, Jennifer Ashley. ★*Madame Restell* — B
ABORTION CLINICS AND REFERRAL SERVICES
    Rankin, Lauren. *Bodies on the Line* — 362.1988
    Shah, Meera. *You're the Only One I've Told* — 362.1988
ABORTION POLICY
    Luthra, Shefali. ★*Undue Burden* — 362.1988
    Matthews, Hannah. *You or Someone You Love* — 362.1988
ABORTION PROVIDERS
    Matthews, Hannah. *You or Someone You Love* — 362.1988
    Shah, Meera. *You're the Only One I've Told* — 362.1988
    Wright, Jennifer Ashley. ★*Madame Restell* — B
Abou El Fadl, Khaled
    The Great Theft — 297.09
About A Mountain. D'Agata, John — 979.3
About Abortion. Sanger, Carol — 179.7
About My Mother. Rowe, Peggy — B
Abouzeid, Rania
    No Turning Back — 956.9104
ABOUZEID, RANIA
    Abouzeid, Rania. *No Turning Back* — 956.9104
Above and Beyond. Sherman, Casey — 973.922092
★*Above Ground*. Smith, Clint — 811
Above The River. Wright, James Arlington — 811
Abraham Lincoln. Burlingame, Michael — B
★*Abraham Lincoln*. McPherson, James M. — B
Abraham Lincoln. Sandburg, Carl — B
Abraham Lincoln and Civil War America. Gienapp, William E. — B
Abrahamian, Ervand
    The Coup — 955.05
ABRAHAMS, JIM, 1944-
    Zucker, David. *Surely You Can't Be Serious* — 791.43
Abramovic, Marina
    Walk Through Walls — B
ABRAMOVIC, MARINA
    Abramovic, Marina. *Walk Through Walls* — B
Abrams, Dan
    Kennedy's Avenger — 973.922
    Theodore Roosevelt for the Defense — 345.73
ABRAMS, J., 1886-1953
    Healy, Thomas. *The Great Dissent* — 342.7308
Abrams, Jonathan P. D.
    Boys Among Men — 796.323
    ★*The Come Up* — 782.421649
Abrams, Stacey
    Lead from the Outside — B
    Level Up — 658.4
    Our Time Is Now — 324.60973
ABRAMS, STACEY
    Abrams, Stacey. *Lead from the Outside* — B
    Abrams, Stacey. *Our Time Is Now* — 324.60973
Abramson, John
    Sickening — 338.4
Abrev, Ileana
    The Little Big Book of White Spells — 133.4
Abril, Andy
    Mayo Clinic Guide to Fibromyalgia — 616.7
ABSENCE AND PRESUMPTION OF DEATH
    Fischer, Paul. *The Man Who Invented Motion Pictures* — 791.43
ABSENT-MINDEDNESS
    Schacter, Daniel L. *The Seven Sins of Memory* — 153.1

ABSENTEE VOTING
    Abrams, Stacey. *Our Time Is Now* — 324.60973
    Hasen, Richard L. *Election Meltdown* — 324.973
    Wehle, Kim. *What You Need to Know About Voting and Why* — 324.60973
★*Absolutely on Music*. Murakami, Haruki — 784.2
ABSTRACT EXPRESSIONISM
    Albers, Patricia. *Joan Mitchell* — B
    Gabriel, Mary. *Ninth Street Women* — 920
    Knausgaard, Karl Ove. *So Much Longing in so Little Space* — 759.81
    Livingston, Jane. *The Paintings of Joan Mitchell* — 759.13
    Schloss, Edith. *The Loft Generation* — 700.9
    Solomon, Deborah. *Jackson Pollock* — B
ABSTRACT EXPRESSIONISTS
    Albers, Patricia. *Joan Mitchell* — B
    Solomon, Deborah. *Jackson Pollock* — B
Abu Sayf, Atif
    The Drone Eats with Me — B
ABU SAYF, ATIF
    Abu Sayf, Atif. *The Drone Eats with Me* — B
Abuelaish, Izzeldin
    I Shall Not Hate — B
ABUELAISH, IZZELDIN
    Abuelaish, Izzeldin. *I Shall Not Hate* — B
Abuelita Faith. Armas, Kat — 248.8
The Abundance. Dillard, Annie — 814
ABUREDWAN, RAMZI
    Tolan, Sandy. *Children of the Stone* — 780
ABUSE OF ADMINISTRATIVE POWER
    Sullivan, Kevin. *Trump on Trial* — 342.73
ABUSED WOMEN
    Bravo, Reah. ★*Complicit* — 331.4
    Butcher, Amy. *Mothertrucker* — B
    Cooper, Alex. *Saving Alex* — B
    Gaye, Jan. *After the Dance* — B
    Hill, Anita. ★*Believing* — 305.42
    Horton, Michelle. *Dear Sister* — B
    James, Victoria. *Wine Girl* — B
    Jang, Lucia. *Stars Between the Sun and Moon* — 365.45092
    Kruzan, Sara. *I Cried to Dream Again* — B
    Means, Brittany. *Hell If We Don't Change Our Ways* — B
    Selvaratnam, Tanya. *Assume Nothing* — B
    Snyder, Rachel Louise. *No Visible Bruises* — 362.82
    Sundberg, Kelly. *Goodbye, Sweet Girl* — B
    Suvari, Mena. *The Great Peace* — B
    West, Cait. ★*Rift* — B
ABUSIVE MEN
    Berman, Sarah. *Don't Call It a Cult* — 361.4
    Gupta, Prachi. ★*They Called Us Exceptional* — B
    Kizzia, Tom. *Pilgrim's Wilderness* — B
    Selvaratnam, Tanya. *Assume Nothing* — B
    Sundberg, Kelly. *Goodbye, Sweet Girl* — B
    Tran, Phuc. ★*Sigh, Gone* — B
    V. *The Apology* — 818
The Abyss. Hastings, Max — 972.9106
ACADEMIC LIBRARIES
    Turnbow, Dominique. ★*Demystifying Online Instruction in Libraries* — 028.7
ACADEMIC RIVALRY
    Massing, Michael. *Fatal Discord* — 920
ACADEMY AWARD FILM NOMINEES
    Henson, Taraji P. *Around the Way Girl* — B
    Huston, Anjelica. *Watch Me* — B
ACADEMY AWARDS (FILMS)
    Hirsch, Paul. *A Long Time Ago in a Cutting Room Far, Far Away* — B
    Schulman, Michael. ★*Oscar Wars* — 791.43
Acceptance. Nietfeld, Emi — B
ACCEPTANCE AND COMMITMENT THERAPY
    Boone, Matthew S. *Stop Avoiding Stuff* — 152.4
    McKay, Matthew. *Self-Esteem* — 155.2
Accepted. Patterson, Pat — B
Access to Asia. Schweitzer, Sharon — 395.5
The Accessible Home. Pierce, D. — 728
Accessory to War. Tyson, Neil deGrasse — 355.001
ACCIDENT VICTIMS
    Butcher, Barbara. *What the Dead Know* — 614
    Williams, Jay. *Life Is Not an Accident* — B
Accidental Astronomy. Lintott, Chris — 520
ACCIDENTAL DEATH
    Greene, Jayson. *Once More We Saw Stars* — 155.9

AUTHOR, TITLE, SERIES AND SUBJECT INDEX

Singer, Jessie. *There Are No Accidents*	363.1
The *Accidental* President. Baime, A. J.	B
Accidental Presidents. Cohen, Jared	973.09
Accidental Saints. Bolz-Weber, Nadia	284.1
The *Accidental* Veterinarian. Schott, Philipp	B
ACCIDENTS	
Black Thought. *The Upcycled Self*	B
Cassidy, Cody. *And Then You're Dead*	612
Gwynne, S. C. *His Majesty's Airship*	363.12
Higginbotham, Adam. ★*Midnight in Chernobyl*	363.17
O'Farrell, Maggie. *I Am, I Am, I Am*	B
Rieder, Travis. *In Pain*	362.29
Robison, Peter. ★*Flying Blind*	338.7
Roripaugh, Lee Ann. *Tsunami vs. the Fukushima 50*	811
Singer, Jessie. *There Are No Accidents*	363.1
Slade, Rachel. *Into the Raging Sea*	910.91
ACCOUNTING	
Siegel, Joel G. *Accounting Handbook.*	657
Accounting Handbook. Siegel, Joel G.	657
ACCULTURATION	
Bui, Thi. ★*The Best We Could Do*	741.5
Kohli, Sahaj Kaur. ★*But What Will People Say?*	616.89
Moore, Susanna. *Paradise of the Pacific*	996.9
Acedia & Me. Norris, Kathleen	248.8
Acemoglu, Daron	
The Narrow Corridor	320.01
Power and Progress	303.48
Achebe, Chinua	
The Education of a British-Protected Child	B
There Was a Country	B
ACHEBE, CHINUA	
Achebe, Chinua. *The Education of a British-Protected Child*	B
Achebe, Chinua. *There Was a Country*	B
Acheson. Chase, James	B
ACHESON, DEAN, 1893-1971	
Chase, James. *Acheson*	B
Acheson, Hugh	
The Chef and the Slow Cooker	641.5
ACHIEVEMENT MOTIVATION	
Alter, Adam L. *Anatomy of a Breakthrough*	158.1
Chittister, Joan. *Following the Path*	248.4
Epstein, David J. ★*Range*	153.9
Gladwell, Malcolm. *Outliers*	302
Grant, Adam M. *Hidden Potential*	153.8
Shankar, Shalini. *Beeline*	155.4
Toussaint, Alex. ★*Activate Your Greatness*	158.1
ACHILLES (GREEK MYTHOLOGY)	
Alexander, Caroline. *The War That Killed Achilles*	883
Homer. *The Iliad*	883
Homer. *The Iliad*	883
Homer. *Iliad*	883
Homer. ★*The Iliad*	883
★The *Achilles* Trap. Coll, Steve	956.7044
Achorn, Edward	
The Lincoln Miracle	973.6
Achterberg, Cara Sue	
Another Good Dog	636.7
ACHTERBERG, CARA SUE	
Achterberg, Cara Sue. *Another Good Dog*	636.7
Ackerman, Diane	
The Human Age	304.2
A Natural History of the Senses	152.1
★*The Zookeeper's Wife*	940.53
Ackerman, Elliot	
The Fifth Act	958.104
Places and Names	B
ACKERMAN, ELLIOT	
Ackerman, Elliot. *The Fifth Act*	958.104
Ackerman, Elliot. *Places and Names*	B
Ackerman, Jennifer	
The Bird Way	598.15
★*What an Owl Knows*	598.9
Ackerman, Spencer	
Reign of Terror	973.931
Ackerman-Leist, Philip	
Rebuilding the Foodshed	338.1
Ackmann, Martha	
The Mercury 13	920

★*These Fevered Days*	B
Ackroyd, Peter	
Charlie Chaplin	B
The Death of King Arthur	823
Foundation	942
Innovation	942.082
London	942.1
Rebellion	941.06
Revolution	941.07
Tudors	942.05
Acocella, Joan Ross	
★*The Bloodied Nightgown*	814
ACQUAINTANCE RAPE	
Grigoriadis, Vanessa. *Blurred Lines*	371.7
Krakauer, Jon. *Missoula*	362.883
Vanasco, Jeannie. *Things We Didn't Talk About When I Was a Girl*	B
ACROBATICS	
Wall, Duncan. *The Ordinary Acrobat*	B
ACROBATS	
Wall, Duncan. *The Ordinary Acrobat*	B
Across The Airless Wilds. Swift, Earl	629.45
ACRYLIC PAINTING	
Kloosterboer, Lorena. *Painting in Acrylics*	751.42
Act Like You Got Some Sense. Foxx, Jamie	B
Act Natural. Traig, Jennifer	306.874
Act of Congress. Kaiser, Robert G.	346.73
ACTING	
Adler, Stella. *Stella Adler*	792
Butler, Isaac. *The Method*	792.02
Cohen, Robert. *Acting Power*	792.02
Common. *One Day It'll All Make Sense*	B
Cumming, Alan. *Baggage*	B
Dench, Judi. *Shakespeare*	792
Dromgoole, Dominic. *Hamlet Globe to Globe*	792.9
Eyman, Scott. *Cary Grant*	B
Felton, Tom. ★*Beyond the Wand*	B
Fischer, Jenna. *The Actor's Life*	792.02
Gless, Sharon. *Apparently There Were Complaints*	B
Hagen, Uta. ★*Respect for Acting*	792.02
Lahti, Christine. *True Stories from an Unreliable Eyewitness*	B
Liu, Simu. ★*We Were Dreamers*	B
Mamet, David. *True and False*	792
Mann, William J. *The Contender*	B
Margulies, Julianna. *Sunshine Girl*	B
Martin, Steve. *Number One Is Walking*	B
Mills, Hayley. *Forever Young*	B
Newman, Paul. *The Extraordinary Life of an Ordinary Man*	B
Perry, Matthew. *Friends, Lovers, and the Big Terrible Thing*	B
Philipps, Busy. *This Will Only Hurt a Little*	B
Posey, Parker. *You're on an Airplane*	B
Powell, Michael. *The Acting Bible*	792.02
Rannells, Andrew. *Too Much Is Not Enough*	792.02
Rowe, Mickey. *Fearlessly Different*	B
Salisbury, Katie Gee. ★*Not Your China Doll*	B
Shatner, William. *Boldly Go*	B
Shatner, William. *Live Long And—*	B
Smith, Jada Pinkett. *Worthy*	B
Trejo, Danny. *Trejo*	B
Tyson, Cicely. ★*Just as I Am*	B
Washington, Kerry. *Thicker Than Water*	B
Winkler, Henry. ★*Being Henry*	B
Wu, Constance. *Making a Scene*	B
The *Acting* Bible. Powell, Michael	792.02
Acting Power. Cohen, Robert	792.02
ACTIONS AND DEFENSES	
Abrams, Dan. *Theodore Roosevelt for the Defense*	345.73
★*Activate* Your Greatness. Toussaint, Alex	158.1
ACTIVE LEARNING	
Cleaver, Samantha. *Raising an Active Reader*	372.4
ACTIVITY PROGRAMS IN EDUCATION	
Alvarez, Celine. *The Natural Laws of Children*	372.21
Del Negro, Janice. *Folktales Aloud*	027.62
Ghoting, Saroj Nadkarni. *Step into Storytime*	027.62
Maddigan, Beth. *Community Library Programs That Work*	021.2
Maxwell, Lucas. *Podcasting with Youth*	006.7
Phoenix, Jack. *Maximizing the Impact of Comics in Your Library*	026
Reid, Rob. ★*200+ Original and Adapted Story Program Activities*	027.62
The *Actor's* Life. Fischer, Jenna	792.02

PUBLIC LIBRARY CORE COLLECTION: NONFICTION
Twentieth Edition

An Actor's Work. Stanislavsky, Konstantin	792.02	Huang, Yunte. *Daughter of the Dragon*		B
ACTORS AND ACTRESSES		Hussey, Olivia. *The Girl on the Balcony*		B
Ackroyd, Peter. *Charlie Chaplin*	B	Huston, Anjelica. *Watch Me*		B
Ahdoot, Dan. *Undercooked*	647.95	Iandoli, Kathy. *Baby Girl*		B
Andrews, Julie. *Home Work*	B	Imperioli, Michael. *Woke up This Morning*		791.45
Andrews, Julie. *Home*	B	Isen, Tajja. *Some of My Best Friends*		305.8
Arkin, Alan. *An Improvised Life*	B	Itzkoff, Dave. ★*Robin*		B
Armstrong, Jennifer Keishin. *When Women Invented Television*	791.45	Jacobs, Alexandra. *Still Here*		B
Austerlitz, Saul. *Kind of a Big Deal*	791.43	Jobrani, Maziyar. *I'm Not a Terrorist, but I've Played One on TV*		B
Bacall, Lauren. *By Myself and Then Some*	B	Kaling, Mindy. *Why Not Me?*		B
Ball, Lucille. *Love, Lucy*	B	Kanfer, Stefan. *Tough Without a Gun*		B
Basinger, Jeanine. *Hollywood*	791.43	Kashner, Sam. *Furious Love*		B
Basinger, Jeanine. *The Star Machine*	384	Katz, Evan Ross. *Into Every Generation a Slayer Is Born*		791.45
Beauvais, Garcelle. *Love Me as I Am*	B	Keaton, Diane. ★*Brother & Sister*		B
Berg, A. Scott. *Kate Remembered*	B	Kelly, Minka. ★*Tell Me Everything*		B
Bertinelli, Valerie. *Enough Already*	B	Kemper, Ellie. *My Squirrel Days*		B
Biskind, Peter. *Star*	B	Kenny, Glenn. *Made Men*		791.43
Blair, Selma. *Mean Baby*	B	Kenny, Glenn. *The World Is Yours*		791.43
Blais, Madeleine. *Queen of the Court*	B	Lahti, Christine. *True Stories from an Unreliable Eyewitness*		B
Bogle, Donald. *Bright Boulevards, Bold Dreams*	791.43	Lane, Christina. *Phantom Lady*		B
Branum, Guy. *My Life as a Goddess*	B	Lane, Stewart F. *Black Broadway*		792.089
Brooks, Mel. ★*All About Me!*	B	Leamer, Laurence. *Hitchcock's Blondes*		791.43
Brower, Kate Andersen. *Elizabeth Taylor*	B	Levy, Shawn. ★*The Castle on Sunset*		647.95
Burrows, James. ★*Directed by James Burrows*	791.4502	Lewis, Jenifer. *Walking in My Joy*		B
Caine, Michael. *Blowing the Bloody Doors Off*	B	Lifford, Tina. *The Little Book of Big Lies*		155.2
Callow, Simon. ★*Orson Welles*	B	Liu, Simu. ★*We Were Dreamers*		B
Carlin, Kelly. *A Carlin Home Companion*	B	Longworth, Karina. *Seduction*		B
Carr, C. *Candy Darling*	B	Louvish, Simon. *Monkey Business*		B
Casillo, Charles. *Marilyn Monroe*	B	Mamet, David. *True and False*		792
Chan, Jackie. *Never Grow Up*	B	Mann, William J. *Bogie & Bacall*		920
Coel, Michaela. ★*Misfits*	158.2	Mann, William J. *The Contender*		B
Cumming, Alan. *Baggage*	B	Mann, William J. *Hello, Gorgeous*		B
Curtis, James. *Buster Keaton*	B	Mann, William J. *Kate*		B
Curtis, James. *Spencer Tracy*	B	Margulies, Julianna. *Sunshine Girl*		B
Daniels, Stormy. *Full Disclosure*	B	Martin, Brett. *Difficult Men*		791.4509
Davis, Geena. *Dying of Politeness*	B	Martin, Steve. *Number One Is Walking*		B
Davis, Viola. ★*Finding Me*	B	McCabe, John. *Cagney*		B
De Semlyen, Nick. *Wild and Crazy Guys*	920	McConaughey, Matthew. *Greenlights*		B
Dench, Judi. *Shakespeare*	792	McCourt, Malachy. *A Monk Swimming*		B
DiMarco, Nyle. ★*Deaf Utopia*	B	McCourt, Malachy. *Singing My Him Song*		B
Driver, Minnie. *Managing Expectations*	B	McGilligan, Patrick. *Funny Man*		B
Dunne, Griffin. ★*The Friday Afternoon Club*	B	McGowan, Rose. *Brave*		B
Elwes, Cary. *As You Wish*	791.43	Merritt, Tyler. *I Take My Coffee Black*		791.4302
Evaristo, Bernardine. *Manifesto*	B	Meslow, Scott. *From Hollywood with Love*		791.43
Eyman, Scott. *Cary Grant*	B	Mills, Hayley. *Forever Young*		B
Eyman, Scott. *Charlie Chaplin vs. America*	B	Min, Anchee. *Red Azalea*		B
Eyman, Scott. *Hank and Jim*	920	Mulgrew, Kate. *Born with Teeth*		791.45028
Eyman, Scott. *John Wayne*	B	Newman, Paul. *The Extraordinary Life of an Ordinary Man*		B
Felton, Tom. ★*Beyond the Wand*	B	Nolte, Nick. *Rebel*		B
Field, Sally. *In Pieces*	B	O'Connor, Garry. *Ian McKellen*		B
Fischer, Jenna. *The Office BFFs*	791.45	Odenkirk, Bob. *Comedy Comedy Comedy Drama*		B
Fischer, Paul. *A Kim Jong-Il Production*	791.43	Offerman, Nick. *The Greatest Love Story Ever Told*		B
Fisher, Todd. *My Girls*	B	Offerman, Nick. *Where the Deer and the Antelope Play*		973.93
Foster, Sutton. *Hooked*	B	Orji, Yvonne. *Bamboozled by Jesus*		B
Fox, Julia. *Down the Drain*	B	Page, Elliot. *Pageboy*		B
Fox, Michael J. *No Time Like the Future*	B	Parke, Henry C. *The Greatest Westerns Ever Made and the People Who Made Them*		791.43
Foxx, Jamie. *Act Like You Got Some Sense*	B	Peisner, David. *Homey Don't Play That!*		791.45
Frankel, Glenn. *Shooting Midnight Cowboy*	791.43	Penn, Kal. *You Can't Be Serious*		B
Gavin, James. ★*Stormy Weather*	782.42164	Perry, Matthew. *Friends, Lovers, and the Big Terrible Thing*		B
Gehring, Wes D. *James Dean*	B	Philipps, Busy. *This Will Only Hurt a Little*		B
Giddins, Gary. *Bing Crosby*	B	Plummer, Christopher. *In Spite of Myself*		B
Giddins, Gary. *Bing Crosby*	B	Poehler, Amy. *Yes Please*		B
Gless, Sharon. *Apparently There Were Complaints*	B	Poitier, Sidney. *The Measure of a Man*		B
Goessel, Tracey. *The First King of Hollywood*	B	Polly, Matthew. ★*Bruce Lee*		B
Goldberg, Whoopi. *Bits and Pieces*	B	Porter, Billy. ★*Unprotected*		B
Goudsouzian, Aram. *Sidney Poitier*	B	Posey, Parker. *You're on an Airplane*		B
Greene, Andy. *The Office*	791.45	Rannells, Andrew. *Too Much Is Not Enough*		792.02
Greenfield, Robert. *True West*	B	Rannells, Andrew. *Uncle of the Year*		B
Grey, Jennifer. *Out of the Corner*	B	Ratajkowski, Emily. ★*My Body*		B
Grey, Joel. *Master of Ceremonies*	B	Retta. *So Close to Being the Sh*t, Y'all Don't Even Know*		B
Haddish, Tiffany. *The Last Black Unicorn*	B	Rhodes, Richard. *Hedy's Folly*		B
Harden, Marcia Gay. *The Seasons of My Mother*	B	Riedel, Michael. *Singular Sensation*		792
Harris, Mark. *Mike Nichols*	B	Riley, Kathleen. *The Astaires*		B
Harris, Neil Patrick. *Neil Patrick Harris*	B	Ripa, Kelly. *Live Wire*		B
Henson, Taraji P. *Around the Way Girl*	B	Robeson, Paul. *The Undiscovered Paul Robeson*		B
Heughan, Sam. *Waypoints*	B	Robinson, Staci. ★*Tupac Shakur*		B
Hilton, Paris. *Paris*	B	Rogen, Seth. ★*Yearbook*		B
Howard, Ron. ★*The Boys*	B			

AUTHOR, TITLE, SERIES AND SUBJECT INDEX

Rowe, Mickey. *Fearlessly Different*	B
Salisbury, Katie Gee. ★*Not Your China Doll*	B
Saul, Scott. ★*Becoming Richard Pryor*	B
Scheer, Paul. *Joyful Recollections of Trauma*	B
Selleck, Tom. *You Never Know*	B
Sestero, Greg. *The Disaster Artist*	791.43
Shannon, Molly. ★*Hello, Molly!*	B
Shatner, William. *Boldly Go*	B
Shatner, William. *Live Long And—*	B
Shearer, Stephen Michael. *Beautiful*	B
Shelton, Ron. *The Church of Baseball*	791.43
Shields, Aomawa L. *Life on Other Planets*	B
Short, Martin. *I Must Say*	B
Silver, Alain. ★*From the Moment They Met It Was Murder*	791.43
Sinise, Gary. *Grateful American*	B
Slate, Jenny. *Little Weirds*	B
Smith, Jada Pinkett. *Worthy*	B
Smith, Starr. *Jimmy Stewart*	B
Smith, Will. ★*Will*	B
Spitz, Bob. ★*Reagan*	B
Spoto, Donald. *High Society*	B
Stamos, John. *If You Would Have Told Me*	B
Stevens, Dana. *Camera Man*	791.4302
Stewart, Patrick. ★*Making It So*	B
Stone, Sharon. *The Beauty of Living Twice*	B
Streisand, Barbra. ★*My Name Is Barbra*	B
Suvari, Mena. *The Great Peace*	B
Tamblyn, Amber. ★*Era of Ignition*	B
Taraborrelli, J. Randy. ★*The Secret Life of Marilyn Monroe*	B
Thompson, Kenan. *When I Was Your Age*	B
Thomson, David. *Bette Davis*	B
Thomson, David. *The Big Screen*	791.430973
Thomson, David. *Ingrid Bergman*	B
Thomson, David. *The New Biographical Dictionary of Film*	791.4302
Tietjen, Jill S. *Hollywood, Her Story*	791.43
Trejo, Danny. *Trejo*	B
Tucci, Stanley. ★*Taste*	B
Turan, Kenneth. ★*Free for All*	B
Turan, Kenneth. *Not to Be Missed*	791.43
Tyson, Cicely. ★*Just as I Am*	B
Union, Gabrielle. *We're Going to Need More Wine*	B
Union, Gabrielle. *You Got Anything Stronger?*	B
Van Zandt, Steve. *Unrequited Infatuations*	B
Ward, Maitland. *Rated X*	B
Washington, Kerry. *Thicker Than Water*	B
Wasson, Sam. *The Big Goodbye*	791.43
Watts, Jill. *Hattie McDaniel*	B
Weller, Sheila. *Carrie Fisher*	B
Williams, Billy Dee. ★*What Have We Here*	B
Williams, Michael Kenneth. *Scenes from My Life*	B
Wilson, Rebel. *Rebel Rising*	B
Wilson, Victoria. *A Life of Barbara Stanwyck*	B
Winder, Elizabeth. *Parachute Women*	782.42164
Winkler, Henry. ★*Being Henry*	B
Wojczuk, Tana. *Lady Romeo*	B
Wong, Ali. ★*Dear Girls*	B
Wu, Constance. *Making a Scene*	B
Yang, Jeff. *The Golden Screen*	791.43
Zucker, David. *Surely You Can't Be Serious*	791.43
Zweibel, Alan. *Laugh Lines*	B
Zwick, Edward. ★*Hits, Flops, and Other Illusions*	B
Ad Infinitum. Ostler, Nicholas	470
Ada Blackjack. Niven, Jennifer	B
Ada's Algorithm. Essinger, James	B
ADAM (BIBLICAL FIGURE)	
Feiler, Bruce. *The First Love Story*	222
Greenblatt, Stephen. *The Rise and Fall of Adam and Eve*	233
Adam Smith. Norman, Jesse	B
Adam, David	
The Man Who Couldn't Stop	616.85
ADAM, DAVID, 1972-	
Adam, David. *The Man Who Couldn't Stop*	616.85
ADAMS FAMILY	
Sankovitch, Nina. *American Rebels*	920
Traub, James. *John Quincy Adams*	B
Adams, Abigail	
Abigail Adams	973.4

ADAMS, ABIGAIL, 1744-1818	
Adams, Abigail. *Abigail Adams*	973.4
Adams, John. *My Dearest Friend*	973.4
Ellis, Joseph J. *First Family*	973.4
Holton, Woody. *Abigail Adams*	B
Sankovitch, Nina. *American Rebels*	920
ADAMS, ANSEL, 1902-1984	
Alinder, Mary Street. *Ansel Adams*	B
Galassi, Peter. *Ansel Adams in Yosemite Valley*	770.92
Szarkowski, John. *Ansel Adams at 100*	B
ADAMS, HARRIET STRATEMEYER	
Rehak, Melanie. *Girl Sleuth*	813
Adams, Jarrett	
Redeeming Justice	340.092
ADAMS, JARRETT	
Adams, Jarrett. *Redeeming Justice*	340.092
Adams, Jocelyn Delk	
Everyday Grand	641.5975
Grandbaby Cakes	641.86
Adams, John	
Hallelujah Junction	B
My Dearest Friend	973.4
ADAMS, JOHN QUINCY, 1767-1848	
Cook, Jane Hampton. *American Phoenix*	973.5
Isenberg, Nancy. *The Problem of Democracy*	973.4
Kaplan, Fred. *John Quincy Adams*	B
Kaplan, Fred. *Lincoln and the Abolitionists*	973.7092
Thomas, Louisa. *Louisa*	B
Traub, James. *John Quincy Adams*	B
ADAMS, JOHN, 1735-1826	
Adams, John. *My Dearest Friend*	973.4
Brands, H. W. ★*Founding Partisans*	973.3
Ellis, Joseph J. *First Family*	973.4
Grant, James. ★*John Adams*	B
Groom, Winston. *The Patriots*	920
Holton, Woody. *Abigail Adams*	B
Isenberg, Nancy. *The Problem of Democracy*	973.4
McCullough, David G. ★*John Adams*	B
Ricks, Thomas E. ★*First Principles*	973.09
Sankovitch, Nina. *American Rebels*	920
Wood, Gordon S. *Friends Divided*	920
ADAMS, JOHN, 1947-	
Adams, John. *Hallelujah Junction*	B
Adams, Laurie	
★*Italian Renaissance Art*	709.45
Adams, Liza	
Needle Felting	746
ADAMS, LOUISA CATHERINE, 1775-1852	
Cook, Jane Hampton. *American Phoenix*	973.5
Thomas, Louisa. *Louisa*	B
Adams, Mark	
Tip of the Iceberg	917.9804
Turn Right at Machu Picchu	985
ADAMS, MARK, 1967-	
Adams, Mark. *Tip of the Iceberg*	917.9804
Adams, Mark. *Turn Right at Machu Picchu*	985
Adams, Michael Henry	
Style and Grace	747
Adams, Simon	
Journey	910.9
ADAPTABILITY	
Davies, Richard. *Extreme Economies*	306.3
Fagan, Brian M. *Climate Chaos*	304.2
Hastings, Reed. *No Rules Rules*	384.55
Levine, Madeline. ★*Ready or Not*	649
McCarthy, Catherine. *Raising a Kid Who Can*	649
Sonenshein, Scott. *Stretch*	153.3
ADAPTATION	
Anthony, Leslie. *The Aliens Among Us*	578.6
Attenborough, David. *Life in the Undergrowth*	592
Bohannon, Cat. ★*Eve*	613
Brown, Sarah L. *The Hidden Language of Cats*	636.8
Catania, Kenneth. *Great Adaptations*	576.8
Eagleman, David. *Livewired*	612.8
Hanson, Thor. *Hurricane Lizards and Plastic Squid*	577.2
Losos, Jonathan B. *Improbable Destinies*	576.8
Schilthuizen, Menno. *Darwin Comes to Town*	577.5
Wohlleben, Peter. *The Secret Wisdom of Nature*	508

PUBLIC LIBRARY CORE COLLECTION: NONFICTION
Twentieth Edition

Adarme, Adrianna
  The Year of Cozy — 641.3
Adayfi, Mansoor
  Don't Forget Us Here — B
ADAYFI, MANSOOR
  Adayfi, Mansoor. *Don't Forget Us Here* — B
Add A Pinch Cookbook. Stone, Robyn — 641.5975
Addario, Lynsey
  It's What I Do — B
  Of Love & War — 779
ADDARIO, LYNSEY
  Addario, Lynsey. *It's What I Do* — B
  Addario, Lynsey. *Of Love & War* — 779
ADDICTION
  Akbar, Kaveh. *Pilgrim Bell* — 811
  Aron, Nina Renata. *Good Morning, Destroyer of Men's Souls* — B
  Blair, Selma. *Mean Baby* — B
  Broome, Brian. ★*Punch Me up to the Gods* — B
  Buhle, Kathleen. *If We Break* — B
  Carr, David. *The Night of the Gun* — B
  Chapin, Sasha. *All the Wrong Moves* — 794.1092
  Chapman, Rex. ★*It's Hard for Me to Live with Me* — B
  Cross, Charles R. *Here We Are Now* — 782.42166
  Dakwar, Elias. *The Captive Imagination* — 616.85
  Danler, Stephanie. *Stray* — B
  Dresner, Amy. *My Fair Junkie* — B
  Elliott, Andrea. ★*Invisible Child* — 362.7
  Elwood, Phil. *All the Worst Humans* — 659.2
  Eyre, Eric. *Death in Mud Lick* — 362.29
  Fisher, Carl Erik. ★*The Urge* — 362.29
  Franklin, Ruth. *Shirley Jackson* — B
  Gerard, Sarah. *Sunshine State* — 814
  Hardin, Lara Love. ★*The Many Lives of Mama Love* — B
  Higham, Scott. *American Cartel* — 338.4
  Hughes, Evan. *The Hard Sell* — 338.4
  Jamison, Leslie. ★*The Recovering* — B
  John, Elton. ★*Me* — B
  Johnston, Ann Dowsett. *Drink* — 362.292
  Jollett, Mikel. ★*Hollywood Park* — B
  Kalb, Claudia. *Andy Warhol Was a Hoarder* — 920
  Kelly, Minka. ★*Tell Me Everything* — B
  Kennedy, Patrick J. ★*Profiles in Mental Health Courage* — 362.29
  Lanegan, Mark. *Sing Backwards and Weep* — B
  Leach, Samantha. ★*The Elissas* — 362.73
  Lecrae. ★*I Am Restored* — B
  Lembke, Anna. *Dopamine Nation* — 152.4
  McCurdy, Jennette. ★*I'm Glad My Mom Died* — B
  Moss, Michael. ★*Hooked* — 613.2
  Moss, Michael. *Salt, Sugar, Fat* — 613.2
  Nietfeld, Emi. *Acceptance* — B
  Oluseyi, Hakeem M. *A Quantum Life* — B
  Parks, Casey. *Diary of a Misfit* — B
  Perry, Matthew. *Friends, Lovers, and the Big Terrible Thing* — B
  Phillips, Adam. *On Giving up* — 158.2
  Posner, Gerald L. ★*Pharma* — 338.4
  Price, Margo. *Maybe We'll Make It* — B
  Sabathia, CC. *Till the End* — 796.357
  Smith, Freda Love. *I Quit Everything* — B
  Streep, Abe. *Brothers on Three* — 306.85
  Trejo, Danny. *Trejo* — B
  Wagamese, Richard. *For Joshua* — B
  Way, Niobe. *Rebels with a Cause* — 649
  Williams, Michael Kenneth. *Scenes from My Life* — B
  Williams, Zach. *Rescue Story* — B
ADDICTION AND CREATIVITY
  Jamison, Leslie. ★*The Recovering* — B
The Addiction Inoculation. Lahey, Jessica — 649
ADDICTS
  Barnett, Erica C. *Quitter* — B
  Bond, Melissa. *Blood Orange Night* — 616.8
  Fisher, Carl Erik. ★*The Urge* — 362.29
  Perry, Matthew. *Friends, Lovers, and the Big Terrible Thing* — B
ADDIMANDO, NIKKI
  Horton, Michelle. *Dear Sister* — B
Adding Layers. Doughty, Kathy — 746.46
Addis, Ferdinand
  The Eternal City — 945.6

Addison, Corban
  Wastelands — 346.73
The Address Book. Mask, Deirdre — 388.1
ADENAUER, KONRAD, 1876-1967
  Kissinger, Henry. *Leadership* — 303.3
ADHD Does Not Exist. Saul, Richard — 618.92
ADHD Nation. Schwarz, Alan — 618.92
Adichie, Chimamanda Ngozi
  Dear Ijeawele — 649
  Notes on Grief — 155.9
  We Should All Be Feminists — 305.42
ADICHIE, CHIMAMANDA NGOZI, 1977-
  Adichie, Chimamanda Ngozi. *Notes on Grief* — 155.9
ADJUSTMENT
  Cacciatore, Joanne. *Bearing the Unbearable* — 155.9
  Gallego, Ruben. *They Called Us* — 956.7044
  Goldsmith, Marshall. *Triggers* — 155.2
  Kesling, Ben. *Bravo Company* — 958.104
  Kushner, Harold S. *Overcoming Life's Disappointments* — 296.7
  Lieberman, David J. *Never Get Angry Again* — 152.4
  Mariani, Mike. ★*What Doesn't Kill Us Makes Us* — 155.9
  Rehm, Diane. *On My Own* — B
  Smith, Freda Love. *I Quit Everything* — B
  Winn, Raynor. *The Wild Silence* — B
ADLER, ALFRED, 1870-1937
  Kishimi, Ichiro. *The Courage to Be Disliked* — 158
Adler, Kevin F.
  When We Walk By — 362.5
Adler, Margot
  Drawing Down the Moon — 299
Adler, Mortimer Jerome
  Aristotle for Everybody — 185
Adler, Stella
  Stella Adler — 792
Adler, Tamar
  An Everlasting Meal — 641.5
ADMINISTRATIVE AGENCIES
  Reynolds, Nicholas E. *Need to Know* — 940.54
  Risen, James. ★*The Last Honest Man* — 973.92
An Admirable Point. Hazrat, Florence — 411
The Admirals. Borneman, Walter R. — B
ADMIRALS
  Bergreen, Laurence. *In Search of a Kingdom* — B
  Borneman, Walter R. *The Admirals* — B
  Hampton, Dan. *Operation Vengeance* — 940.54
  McRaven, William H. *Sea Stories* — B
  Morison, Samuel Eliot. *John Paul Jones* — B
  O'Brien, Phillips Payson. *The Second Most Powerful Man in the World* — B
  Thomas, Evan. ★*John Paul Jones* — B
Admissions. Marsh, Henry — B
Admit One. Collins, Martha — 811
Admony, Einat
  Shuk — 641.595
ADOLESCENCE
  Brown, Emma. *To Raise a Boy* — 649
  Damour, Lisa. *Untangled* — 305.235
  Fagell, Phyllis L. ★*Middle School Matters* — 373.236
  Goodan, Chelsey. *Underestimated* — 305.235
  Hobbs, Jeff. *Show Them You're Good* — 373
  Krimstein, Ken. *When I Grow Up* — 741.5
  Mead, Margaret. *Coming of Age in Samoa* — 306
  Siegel, Daniel J. *Brainstorm* — 155.5
ADOLESCENT PSYCHOLOGY
  Apter, T. E. *The Teen Interpreter* — 306.874
  Damour, Lisa. *Untangled* — 305.235
  Galinsky, Ellen. ★*The Breakthrough Years* — 649
ADOPTED CHILDREN
  Austin, Nefertiti. *Motherhood so White* — B
  Brierley, Saroo. *A Long Way Home* — B
  Carroll, Rebecca. *Surviving the White Gaze* — B
  Chung, Nicole. ★*A Living Remedy* — B
  Glaser, Gabrielle. *American Baby* — B
  Guida-Richards, Melissa. *What White Parents Should Know About Transracial Adoption* — 362.734
  Harrison, Valerie I. *Do Right by Me* — 649
  Hayasaki, Erika. *Somewhere Sisters* — 362.7
  Oelhafen, Ingrid von. *Hitler's Stolen Children* — B

AUTHOR, TITLE, SERIES AND SUBJECT INDEX

ADOPTED DOGS
   Bragg, Rick. *The Speckled Beauty* — 636.7
ADOPTED TEENAGERS
   Williams, Mary. *The Lost Daughter* — B
ADOPTEES
   Bee, Vanessa A. *Home Bound* — B
   Chung, Nicole. *All You Can Ever Know* — B
   Masters, Oksana. *The Hard Parts* — B
ADOPTION
   Albom, Mitch. *Finding Chika* — B
   Asgarian, Roxanna. *We Were Once a Family* — 364.152
   Austin, Nefertiti. *Motherhood so White* — B
   Cobbs-Leonard, Tasha. *Do It Anyway* — 241
   Daley, Mark. *Safe* — B
   Doyne, Maggie. *Between the Mountain and the Sky* — B
   Fessler, Ann. *The Girls Who Went Away* — 362.82
   Glaser, Gabrielle. *American Baby* — B
   Harrison, Valerie I. *Do Right by Me* — 649
   Mehra, Nishta. *Brown, White, Black* — 305.800973
   Moody, Anne. *The Children Money Can Buy* — 362.73
   Mulgrew, Kate. *Born with Teeth* — 791.45028
   Nutt, Amy Ellis. *Becoming Nicole* — 920
   Sisson, Gretchen E. ★*Relinquished* — 362.734
ADOPTION AGENCIES
   Glaser, Gabrielle. *American Baby* — B
ADOPTION REUNIONS
   Chung, Nicole. *All You Can Ever Know* — B
ADOPTIVE FAMILIES
   Moody, Anne. *The Children Money Can Buy* — 362.73
ADOPTIVE MOTHERS
   Austin, Nefertiti. *Motherhood so White* — B
ADOPTIVE PARENTS
   Chung, Nicole. ★*A Living Remedy* — B
   Guida-Richards, Melissa. *What White Parents Should Know About Transracial Adoption* — 362.734
   Harrison, Valerie I. *Do Right by Me* — 649
ADULT BOOKS FOR YOUNG ADULTS
   Ackerman, Diane. ★*The Zookeeper's Wife* — 940.53
   Ackmann, Martha. *The Mercury 13* — 920
   Adichie, Chimamanda Ngozi. *We Should All Be Feminists* — 305.42
   AL Samawi, Mohammed. *The Fox Hunt* — 953
   Alexander, Caroline. *The Bounty* — 996.1
   Alexander, Caroline. *The Endurance* — 919.8
   Alexie, Sherman. *You Don't Have to Say You Love Me* — 818
   Allende, Isabel. *My Invented Country* — B
   Almond, Steve. ★*Candyfreak* — 338.4
   Alvarez, Julia. *The Woman I Kept to Myself* — 811
   Alvarez, Noe. *Spirit Run* — 796.42
   Ambrose, Stephen E. *Nothing Like It in the World* — 385
   Ambrose, Stephen E. ★*Undaunted Courage* — 917.804
   Ambrose, Stephen E. *The Victors* — 940.54
   Anderson, Lars. *Carlisle vs. Army* — 796.332
   Angelou, Maya. *Letter to My Daughter* — 814
   Angelou, Maya. *A Song Flung up to Heaven* — B
   Anthony, Leslie. *The Aliens Among Us* — 578.6
   Aptowicz, Cristin O'Keefe. *Dr. Mutter's Marvels* — B
   Arana, Marie. *American Chica* — B
   Armstrong, Karen. ★*Islam* — 297
   Armstrong, Karen. *The Spiral Staircase* — B
   Asim, Jabari. *We Can't Breathe* — 305.896
   Attenborough, David. *Life in the Undergrowth* — 592
   B., David. *Epileptic* — 741.5
   Bailey, Elisabeth. *The Sound of a Wild Snail Eating* — 594
   Bailey, Lily. *Because We Are Bad* — B
   Balf, Todd. *Major* — B
   Ball, Edward. *Slaves in the Family* — 975.7
   Barnes, Cinelle. *Monsoon Mansion* — B
   Barra, Allen. ★*Yogi Berra* — B
   Barrow, John D. *The Infinite Book* — 111
   Barry, John M. ★*The Great Influenza* — 614.5
   Bass, Amy. *One Goal* — 796.334
   Bass, Rick. *Why I Came West* — 333.78
   Bass, William M. *Death's Acre* — 614
   Bauer, Shane. *American Prison* — 365
   Baur, Gene. *Farm Sanctuary* — 179
   Bayoumi, Moustafa. *How Does It Feel to Be a Problem?* — 305.892
   Beah, Ishmael. ★*A Long Way Gone* — B
   Bechdel, Alison. ★*Fun Home* — 741.5

Bell, Darrin. ★*The Talk* — 741.5
Belliveau, Denis. *In the Footsteps of Marco Polo* — 915
Berg, Mary. *The Diary of Mary Berg* — B
Berg, Ryan. *No House to Call My Home* — B
Bergner, Daniel. ★*Sing for Your Life* — B
Bernstein, Burton. ★*Leonard Bernstein* — B
Berr, Helene. *The Journal of Helene Berr* — B
Berry, Mary Frances. *My Face Is Black Is True* — B
Bialosky, Jill. *Poetry Will Save Your Life* — B
Bilal, Wafaa. *Shoot an Iraqi* — B
Bilott, Robert. *Exposure* — 344.04
Bingham, Clara. *Witness to the Revolution* — 303.48
Black, Dustin Lance. *Mama's Boy* — B
Blakeslee, Nate. *American Wolf* — 599.773
Blanco, Richard. *The Prince of Los Cocuyos* — B
Blight, David W. *A Slave No More* — B
Blount, Roy. *Robert E. Lee* — B
Blum, Deborah. *Ghost Hunters* — 133.9
Blumenthal, Eileen. *Puppetry* — 791.5
Bodanis, David. *Electric Universe* — 537
Bogira, Steve. *Courtroom 302* — 345.773
Boo, Katherine. ★*Behind the Beautiful Forevers* — 305.5
Bostridge, Mark. *Florence Nightingale* — B
Bradburd, Rus. *All the Dreams We've Dreamed* — 796.323
Bradley, James. *Flags of Our Fathers* — 940.54
Bradshaw, John. ★*Cat Sense* — 636.8
Brady, James. *The Coldest War* — B
Braitman, Laurel. *Animal Madness* — 591.5
Brand, Christo. *Mandela* — B
Brands, H. W. ★*Andrew Jackson, His Life and Times* — B
Brands, H. W. *Dreams of El Dorado* — 978
Brands, H. W. *Traitor to His Class* — B
Brenner, Joel Glenn. *The Emperors of Chocolate* — 338.7
Brickell, Francesca Cartier. *The Cartiers* — B
Brier, Bob. *The Murder of Tutankhamen* — B
Brooks, Maegan Parker. *Fannie Lou Hamer* — B
Brosh, Allie. ★*Solutions and Other Problems* — 741.5
Brown, Austin Channing. ★*I'm Still Here* — B
Brown, Mick. ★*Tearing Down the Wall of Sound* — B
Bruchac, Joseph. *Our Stories Remember* — 973.04
Brusatte, Stephen. ★*The Rise and Fall of the Dinosaurs* — 567.9
Bryson, Bill. *The Life and Times of the Thunderbolt Kid* — B
Bryson, Bill. *Shakespeare* — B
Bryson, Bill. ★*A Short History of Nearly Everything* — 500
Bryson, Bill. ★*A Walk in the Woods* — 917
Buford, Kate. *Native American Son* — B
Bui, Thi. ★*The Best We Could Do* — 741.5
Bullock, Darryl W. *David Bowie Made Me Gay* — 780
Bunting, Josiah. *Ulysses S. Grant* — B
Burkett, Elinor. *Golda* — B
Burns, Eric. *Infamous Scribblers* — 071
Byrne, Eugene. *Darwin* — 741.5
Cahalan, Susannah. *Brain on Fire* — 616.8
Cahill, Thomas. *Sailing the Wine-Dark Sea* — 909
Callahan, David. *The Cheating Culture* — 174
Campbell, Deborah. *A Disappearance in Damascus* — 365
Capote, Truman. ★*In Cold Blood* — 364.1
Caputo, Philip. *A Rumor of War* — 959.704
Carballo, David M. *America* — 912
Carlin, John. *Playing the Enemy* — 968.06
Carlin, Peter Ames. *Bruce* — B
Carlo, Philip. *Gaspipe* — B
Carr, David. *The Night of the Gun* — B
Carson, Anne. *Autobiography of Red* — 811
Carter, Jimmy. *An Hour Before Daylight* — B
Carter, Jimmy. *Palestine* — 956.04
Carwardine, Richard. *Lincoln* — B
Cassidy, Cody. *And Then You're Dead* — 612
Chandler, Adam. *Drive-Thru Dreams* — 647.95
Chang, Iris. ★*The Rape of Nanking* — 951.04
Chang, Jeff. *Can't Stop, Won't Stop* — 306.4
Chang, Leslie T. *Factory Girls* — 331.4
Checkoway, Julie. *The Three-Year Swim Club* — 797.2
Chemaly, Soraya L. *Rage Becomes Her* — 155.3
Chiger, Krystyna. *The Girl in the Green Sweater* — B
Child, Julia. ★*My Life in France* — B
Chown, Marcus. *Infinity in the Palm of Your Hand* — 523.1
Chung, Nicole. *All You Can Ever Know* — B

PUBLIC LIBRARY CORE COLLECTION: NONFICTION
Twentieth Edition

Cisneros, Sandra. *A House of My Own*	B
Clarke, Gemma. *Soccerwomen*	796.334
Clinton, Catherine. *Harriet Tubman*	B
Coates, Ta-Nehisi. ★*Between the World and Me*	305.800973
Coffey, Wayne R. ★*The Boys of Winter*	796.962
Coleman, Rick. ★*Blue Monday*	B
Collins, Gail. *When Everything Changed*	305.40973
Collins, Paul. *The Book of William*	016.8223
Colton, Larry. *Counting Coup*	796.323
Conroy, Pat. *My Losing Season*	B
Cooke, Mervyn. *The Chronicle of Jazz*	781.6509
Cooney, Kara. *When Women Ruled the World*	920
Cooper, Alex. *Saving Alex*	B
Cooper, Brittney C. *Eloquent Rage*	B
Cooper, Helene. *The House at Sugar Beach*	921
Copeland, Misty. ★*Life in Motion*	B
Costello, Elvis. *Unfaithful Music & Disappearing Ink*	B
Cott, Jonathan. *There's a Mystery There*	813
Couch, Dick. *The Warrior Elite*	359.9
Cousteau, Jacques Yves. *The Human, the Orchid, and the Octopus*	B
Covey, Stephen R. ★*The 7 Habits of Highly Effective People*	158
Cox, Lynne. *Swimming to Antarctica*	B
Crawford, Bill. ★*All American*	B
Croke, Vicki. *The Lady and the Panda*	599.789
Cronkite, Walter. *A Reporter's Life*	B
Cross, Charles R. *Room Full of Mirrors*	B
Cullen, David. *Parkland*	371.7
Czerski, Helen. *Storm in a Teacup*	530
Dallek, Robert. *Harry S. Truman*	B
Dallek, Robert. *Let Every Nation Know*	B
Danticat, Edwidge. ★*Brother, I'm Dying*	B
Davis, Joshua. *Spare Parts*	629.8
Davis, Michael. *Street Gang*	791.43
De Courcy, Anne. *Chanel's Riviera*	944.9
Dean, Cornelia. *Against the Tide*	333.91
DeJean, Joan E. *The Essence of Style*	391
Delisle, Guy. *Pyongyang*	741.5
Deng, Alephonsion. *They Poured Fire on Us from the Sky*	B
Dennis, Felix. *How to Get Rich*	B
Dennis, Jerry. *The Living Great Lakes*	977
Dennison, Matthew. *The Man in the Willows*	B
Derf. *Kent State*	741.5
Diamond, Jared M. *Collapse*	304.2
Diamond, Jared M. *Guns, Germs, and Steel*	303.4
Diaz, Jaquira. *Ordinary Girls*	818
Didion, Joan. ★*The Year of Magical Thinking*	B
Dolnick, Edward. *The Rescue Artist*	364.16
Doughty, Caitlin. *From Here to Eternity*	393
Doughty, Caitlin. *Will My Cat Eat My Eyeballs?*	306.9
Dray, Philip. *Capitol Men*	973.8
Dubus, Andre. *Townie*	B
Dunbar, Erica Armstrong. ★*Never Caught*	B
Dunbar, Erica Armstrong. ★*She Came to Slay*	B
Durrani, Matin. *Furry Logic*	591.5
Dwork, Deborah. ★*Holocaust*	940
Dwyer, Jim. *102 Minutes*	974.7
Eberhardt, Jennifer L. ★*Biased*	303.3
Egan, Timothy. *The Worst Hard Time*	978
Ehrenreich, Barbara. ★*Nickel and Dimed*	B
Ehrlich, Gretel. *This Cold Heaven*	998.2
Eisner, Will. ★*Comics and Sequential Art*	741.5
Ellis, Joseph J. *Founding Brothers*	973.4
Ellis, Joseph J. ★*His Excellency*	B
Ellis, Richard. ★*The Empty Ocean*	577.7
Ellis, Richard. *Tuna*	333.95
Epstein, Franci. *Franci's War*	B
Erdman, Sarah. *Nine Hills to Nambonkaha*	966.68
Evans, Claire Lisa. *Broad Band*	920
Everitt, Anthony. *Cicero*	B
Ewing, Eve L. *Ghosts in the Schoolyard*	370.89
Fagone, Jason. *The Woman Who Smashed Codes*	B
Fasulo, Linda M. *An Insider's Guide to the Un, 4th Ed.*	341.23
Faust, Drew Gilpin. *This Republic of Suffering*	973.7
Feinstein, John. ★*Last Dance*	796.323
Felisbret, Eric. *Graffiti New York*	751.7
Fernandez-Armesto, Felipe. ★*Amerigo*	B
Fessler, Ann. *The Girls Who Went Away*	362.82
Finch, Christopher. *The Art of Walt Disney*	791.43092
Finkel, David. *The Good Soldiers*	956.7044
Finkel, Michael. *The Stranger in the Woods*	B
Fischer, David Hackett. *Champlain's Dream*	B
Fischer, David Hackett. *Washington's Crossing*	973.3
Fleming, Melissa. *A Hope More Powerful Than the Sea*	956.9104
Foer, Jonathan Safran. *Eating Animals*	641.3
Foner, Eric. *Forever Free*	973.8
Ford, Tanisha C. *Dressed in Dreams*	391
Fox, Amaryllis. *Life Undercover*	B
Franklin, Benjamin. *The Compleated Autobiography*	B
Franklin, Missy. *Relentless Spirit*	B
Fraser, Caroline. ★*Prairie Fires*	B
French, Patrick. *The World Is What It Is*	B
Frenkel, Francoise. *A Bookshop in Berlin*	B
Friedman, Rachel. ★*And Then We Grew Up*	305.24
Fuller, Alexandra. *Don't Let's Go to the Dogs Tonight*	B
Fuller, Alexandra. *Leaving Before the Rains Come*	B
Funk, Mason. *The Book of Pride*	920
Ganz, Nicholas. ★*Graffiti World*	751.7
Garcia Marquez, Gabriel. *Living to Tell the Tale*	B
Gardner, Mark L. *Rough Riders*	973.911
Gates, Henry Louis. *In Search of Our Roots*	973
Gehring, Wes D. *James Dean*	B
Gerald, Casey. *There Will Be No Miracles Here*	B
Giddings, Paula. *Ida*	B
Gienapp, William E. *Abraham Lincoln and Civil War America*	B
Gioia, Ted. *The History of Jazz*	781.6509
Girma, Haben. *Haben*	B
Glass, Philip. *Words Without Music*	B
Goldstein, Jacob. *Money*	332.4
Goldstein, Nancy. *Jackie Ormes*	B
Gooch, Brad. ★*Flannery*	B
Goodall, Jane. ★*Beyond Innocence*	B
Goodall, Jane. ★*The Ten Trusts*	333.95
Gordon-Reed, Annette. ★*The Hemingses of Monticello*	920
Graham, Ashley. *A New Model*	B
Grande, Reyna. ★*The Distance Between Us*	973
Grandin, Temple. ★*Animals in Translation*	591.5
Grandmaster Flash. *The Adventures of Grandmaster Flash*	B
Grann, David. ★*Killers of the Flower Moon*	976.6004
Grant, Gail Milissa. *At the Elbows of My Elders*	B
Gray, Charlotte. ★*Reluctant Genius*	920
Gray, Michael. *Hand Me My Travelin' Shoes*	B
Grayling, A. C. *Among the Dead Cities*	940.54
Greek, C. Ray. *Sacred Cows and Golden Geese*	179
Greenberg, Paul. *Four Fish*	333.95
Greenburg, Zack O'Malley. *3 Kings*	782.421649
Greene, B. *The Fabric of the Cosmos*	523.1
Grogan, John. ★*Marley & Me*	636.752
Gross, Edward. *The Fifty Year Mission*	791.45
Guelzo, Allen C. *Lincoln and Douglas*	973.6
Guibert, Emmanuel. *Alan's War*	741.5
Guibert, Emmanuel. *The Photographer*	741.5
Hafner, Katie. *A Romance on Three Legs*	786.2092
Halberstam, David. ★*The Children*	323.1
Hamilton, Gabrielle. *Blood, Bones, and Butter*	B
Hamilton, Lisa M. *Deeply Rooted*	338.10973
Hample, Zack. *The Baseball*	796.357
Hanna-Attisha, Mona. *What the Eyes Don't See*	615.9
Hari, Daoud. *The Translator*	B
Harjo, Joy. *Crazy Brave*	B
Harris, David. *The Genius*	B
Harryhausen, Ray. *The Art of Ray Harryhausen*	778
Hart, Hannah. *Buffering*	B
Hart, Kevin. *I Can't Make This Up*	B
Hass, Robert. *Summer Snow*	811.6
Hastings, Max. *Retribution*	940.54
Hastings, Max. *Warriors*	355
Hawes, Jennifer. *Grace Will Lead Us Home*	364.152
Hawking, Stephen. ★*A Briefer History of Time*	523.1
Hawking, Stephen. ★*The Universe in a Nutshell*	530.12
Hazleton, Lesley. *After the Prophet*	297.8
Heacox, Kim. ★*John Muir and the Ice That Started a Fire*	333.7209798
Heat Moon, William Least. *Roads to Quoz*	917.3
Hegar, Mary Jennings. *Shoot Like a Girl*	B
Helm, Sarah. *A Life in Secrets*	B
Henig, Robin Marantz. *The Monk in the Garden*	B
Hennessey, Jonathan. *The United States Constitution*	741.5

AUTHOR, TITLE, SERIES AND SUBJECT INDEX

Hensley, William L. Iggiagruk. *Fifty Miles from Tomorrow*	B
Henson, Taraji P. *Around the Way Girl*	B
Herbert, Brian. *Dreamer of Dune*	B
Herman, Eleanor. *The Royal Art of Poison*	364.152
Hernandez, Daisy. *A Cup of Water Under My Bed*	B
Herriot, James. *Every Living Thing*	B
Hewitt, Ben. ★*The Town That Food Saved*	338.1
Hewitt, Catherine. *Renoir's Dancer*	B
Hilfiger, Tommy. *American Dreamer*	B
Hillenbrand, Laura. ★*Seabiscuit*	798.4
Hillenbrand, Laura. ★*Unbroken*	B
Hilsum, Lindsey. *In Extremis*	371.7
Hirsch, Jennifer S. *Sexual Citizens*	371.7
Hirshman, Linda R. *Reckoning*	305.420973
Hirsi Ali, Ayaan. ★*Infidel*	B
Hitchens, Christopher. *Thomas Jefferson*	B
Hoare, Philip. *The Whale*	599.5
Hobbs, Jeff. ★*The Short and Tragic Life of Robert Peace*	B
Hogan, Linda. *The Woman Who Watches Over the World*	B
Holden, Wendy. ★*Born Survivors*	940.53
Holt, Nathalia. ★*Rise of the Rocket Girls*	629.4
Hornbacher, Marya. *Wasted*	B
Horne, Jed. *Breach of Faith*	976.3
Horwitz, Tony. *Confederates in the Attic*	973.7
Horwitz, Tony. ★*A Voyage Long and Strange*	970.01
Howard, Johnette. *The Rivals*	B
Huang, Eddie. *Fresh off the Boat*	B
Hughes, Robert. *Rome*	945.6
Humbert, Agnes. *Resistance*	B
Iandoli, Kathy. *God Save the Queens*	782.421649
Iftin, Abdi Nor. *Call Me American*	305.893
Iversen, Kristen. *Full Body Burden*	363.17
Iyer, Pico. *The Open Road*	B
Jacob, Mira. *Good Talk*	741.5
Jacobson, Sidney. *The 9-11 Report*	741.5
Jadhav, Narendra. *Untouchables*	305.5
Jahren, Hope. ★*Lab Girl*	B
Jameson, A. D. *I Find Your Lack of Faith Disturbing*	791.43
Jauhar, Sandeep. *Heart*	612.1
Jefferson, Margo. *Negroland*	305.896
Jenkins, Peter. *Looking for Alaska*	979.8
Jewel. *Never Broken*	782.42164
Johnson, Mindy. *Ink & Paint*	B
Johnson, Paul. ★*Art*	709
Jones, Brian Jay. *George Lucas*	B
Jones, Saeed. *How We Fight for Our Lives*	B
Junger, Sebastian. *Fire*	909.82
Junger, Sebastian. *The Perfect Storm*	974.4
Junger, Sebastian. *War*	958.104
Kamkwamba, William. ★*The Boy Who Harnessed the Wind*	B
Kaplan, Janice. *The Genius of Women*	920
Karbo, Karen. *In Praise of Difficult Women*	920
Katin, Miriam. *We Are on Our Own*	741.5
Kaur, Rupi. *The Sun and Her Flowers*	811.6
Kean, Sam. *The Disappearing Spoon*	546
Kerouac, Jack. *Book of Sketches, 1952-57*	818
Kershaw, Ian. *Hitler*	B
King, Coretta Scott. ★*My Life, My Love, My Legacy*	B
King, Stephen. *On Writing*	B
Kingsolver, Barbara. ★*Animal, Vegetable, Miracle*	641
Kobabe, Maia. *Gender Queer*	741.5
Koch, Bea. *Mad and Bad*	920
Koh, EJ. *The Magical Language of Others*	813
Kozol, Jonathan. *Letters to a Young Teacher*	371.1
Krakauer, Jon. *Into the Wild*	917.9804
Krakauer, Jon. ★*Into Thin Air*	796.52
Krakauer, Jon. *Missoula*	362.883
Kramer, Clara. *Clara's War*	B
Kugel, Seth. *Rediscovering Travel*	306.4
Kurlansky, Mark. *The Eastern Stars*	796.357
Kurlansky, Mark. *Salt*	553.6
Lamb, Christina. *House of Stone*	968.91
Lang, Michael. *The Road to Woodstock*	781.66
Lansky, Aaron. *Outwitting History*	002
Larson, Erik. ★*The Devil in the White City*	364.15
Larson, Kate Clifford. *Bound for the Promised Land*	B
Laskin, David. *The Children's Blizzard*	977
Launius, Roger D. *The Smithsonian History of Space Exploration*	629.4

Laymon, Kiese. ★*Heavy*	B
Leavitt, David. *The Man Who Knew Too Much*	B
Lemmon, Gayle Tzemach. *The Dressmaker of Khair Khana*	B
Lewis, Damien. *The Dog Who Could Fly*	940.54
Lewis, John. ★*March; Book One*	741.5
Lewis, John. ★*March; Book Three*	741.5
Lewis, John. ★*March; Book Two*	741.5
Lewis, John. ★*Run; Book One*	741.5
Lewis, John. *Walking with the Wind*	B
Lewis, Michael. *The Blind Side*	B
Lewis, Michael. ★*Moneyball*	796.357
Lifford, Tina. *The Little Book of Big Lies*	155.2
Light, Michael. *100 Suns*	779
Lightman, Alan P. *The Discoveries*	509
Lipstadt, Deborah E. *History on Trial*	940.53
Lockley, Thomas. *African Samurai*	B
Longman, Jere. *Among the Heroes*	974.8
Louv, Richard. *Our Wild Calling*	615.8
Lucas, Jack. *Indestructible*	B
Lynas, Mark. *Six Degrees*	551.6
Maathai, Wangari. *Unbowed*	B
Macdougall, J. D. *Frozen Earth*	551.7
MacMullan, Jackie. ★*Basketball*	796.323
MacNeal, David. *Bugged*	595.7
Macy, Beth. ★*Dopesick*	362.29
Madden, T Kira. *Long Live the Tribe of Fatherless Girls*	814
Maddox, Brenda. *Rosalind Franklin*	B
Madigan, Tim. *The Burning*	976.6
Malek, Alia. *The Home That Was Our Country*	B
Malinowski, Erik. *Betaball*	796.323
Mandela, Nelson. *In His Own Words*	B
Mankoff, Robert. *How About Never—Is Never Good for You?*	741.5
Mann, Charles C. ★*1491*	970.01
Mann, Sally. ★*Hold Still*	B
Maraniss, Andrew. *Strong Inside*	B
Maraniss, David. *Clemente*	B
Maraniss, David. *They Marched into Sunlight*	959.704
Mardini, Yusra. *Butterfly*	B
Margonelli, Lisa. *Oil on the Brain*	338.2
Markham, Lauren. ★*The Far Away Brothers*	920
Marsalis, Wynton. *Moving to Higher Ground*	781.65
Masters, Oksana. *The Hard Parts*	B
Mazower, Mark. *The Balkans*	949.6
McCloud, Scott. *Making Comics*	741.5
McCloud, Scott. ★*Understanding Comics*	741.5
McCourt, Frank. *Teacher Man*	B
McCullough, David G. ★*1776*	973.3
McCurdy, Jennette. ★*I'm Glad My Mom Died*	B
McDougall, Christopher. *Running with Sherman*	636.1
McNamara, Michelle. *I'll Be Gone in the Dark*	364.152
McPhee, John. *Uncommon Carriers*	388
McPherson, James M. ★*Abraham Lincoln*	B
McPherson, James M. *For Cause and Comrades*	973.7
McPherson, James M. *Hallowed Ground*	973.7
McPherson, James M. ★*Tried by War*	973.7
Meacham, Jon. ★*American Lion*	B
Mekhennet, Souad. *I Was Told to Come Alone*	363.3250956
Melvin, Leland. *Chasing Space*	B
Mike D. *Beastie Boys Book*	782.42164
Miller, Char. *Gifford Pinchot and the Making of Modern Environmentalism*	B
Miller, Marla. *Betsy Ross and the Making of America*	B
Mills, Dan. *Sniper One*	956.7044
Miranda, Lin-Manuel. *Gmorning, Gnight!*	811
Miranda, Lin-Manuel. *Hamilton*	782.1
Mizrahi, Isaac. *I.M.*	B
Mizuki, Shigeru. *Showa 1926-1939*	741.5
Mock, Janet. *Surpassing Certainty*	B
Montgomery, Sy. *The Good Good Pig*	636.4
Montillo, Roseanne. *Fire on the Track*	B
Mooallem, Jon. *Wild Ones*	333.95
Moore, Marcus J. *The Butterfly Effect*	B
Mordden, Ethan. *Ziegfeld*	B
Morris, Bonnie J. ★*The Feminist Revolution*	305.4209
Morris, Edmund. *Beethoven*	B
Mortimer, Gavin. *The Great Swim*	B
Moss, Gabrielle. *Paperback Crush*	813.009
Murakami, Haruki. *What I Talk About When I Talk About Running*	B
Murray, Liz. *Breaking Night*	B

PUBLIC LIBRARY CORE COLLECTION: NONFICTION
Twentieth Edition

Myron, Vicki. ★Dewey	636.80092
Nafisi, Azar. ★Reading Lolita in Tehran	B
Nafisi, Azar. Things I've Been Silent About	B
Nelson, Craig. Rocket Men	629.45
Nestor, James. Deep	797.2
Ngugi wa Thiong'o. In the House of the Interpreter	B
Nimura, Janice P. Daughters of the Samurai	920
Niven, Jennifer. Ada Blackjack	B
Noah, Trevor. Born a Crime	B
Nordberg, Jenny. The Underground Girls of Kabul	305.3
Nordgren, Tyler E. Sun, Moon, Earth	523.7
Nordhaus, Hannah. The Beekeeper's Lament	638
Norgren, Jill. Belva Lockwood	B
Norrell, Robert J. Up from History	B
Norwich, John Julius. A Short History of Byzantium	949.5
Nourse, Victoria F. In Reckless Hands	344.7304
O'Brady, Colin. ★The Impossible First	919.8904
O'Kane, Bernard. Treasures of Islam	709.1
O'Meara, Mallory. The Lady from the Black Lagoon	921
O'Neil, Dennis. The DC Comics Guide to Writing Comics	808
O'Toole, Jennifer Cook. Autism in Heels	B
Ollestad, Norman. Crazy for the Storm	B
Oluo, Ijeoma. So You Want to Talk About Race	305.800973
Onwuachi, Kwame. ★Notes from a Young Black Chef	641.59
Orenstein, Ronald I. Ivory, Horn and Blood	333.95
Orlean, Susan. Rin Tin Tin	636.737
Oshinsky, David M. ★Polio	614.5
Ottaviani, Jim. Hawking	741.5
Packer, George. The Assassins' Gate	956.7044
Paglia, Camille. ★Break, Blow, Burn	821.009
Pan, Philip P. Out of Mao's Shadow	306.20951
Parkin, Simon. A Game of Birds and Wolves	940.54
Parrado, Nando. Miracle in the Andes	982
Parrish, Thomas D. The Submarine	359.9
Passarlay, Gulwali. The Lightless Sky	B
Patchett, Ann. Truth & Beauty	B
Pavlychenko, Liudmyla Mykhailivna. Lady Death	B
Paxton, Robert O. The Anatomy of Fascism	320.53
Pearson, Roger. Voltaire Almighty	B
Petersen, Anne Helen. Can't Even	305.242
Peterson, Dale. The Moral Lives of Animals	156
Petrushevskaia, Liudmila. The Girl from the Metropol Hotel	B
Philbrick, Nathaniel. ★Mayflower	973.2
Pipes, Richard. Communism	335.43
Pipher, Mary Bray. The Middle of Everywhere	305.9
Pittman, Craig. Cat Tale	599.75
Plummer, Christopher. In Spite of Myself	B
Pollan, Michael. The Omnivore's Dilemma	394.1
Posnanski, Joe. The Soul of Baseball	796.357
Powell, Michael. ★Canyon Dreams	796.323
Pratchett, Terry. A Slip of the Keyboard	824
Press, Joy. Stealing the Show	791.45
Preston, Diana. Before the Fallout	303.48
Preston, Richard. The Hot Zone	614.5
Preston, Richard. The Wild Trees	585
Price, David A. ★Love and Hate in Jamestown	975.5
Pringle, Heather Anne. The Mummy Congress	393
Prior-Palmer, Lara. Rough Magic	798.4
Pullman, Philip. ★Fairy Tales from the Brothers Grimm	398.2
Purdum, Todd S. An Idea Whose Time Has Come	342.7308
Pyenson, Nick. Spying on Whales	599.5
Quin, Tegan. ★High School	B
Quinn, Zoe. Crash Override	794.8
Raddatz, Martha. The Long Road Home	B
Raffel, Dawn. The Strange Case of Dr. Couney	B
Rakoff, Joanna Smith. My Salinger Year	B
Ralston, Aron. Between a Rock and a Hard Place	796.522
Ramos, Jorge. Stranger	325.73
Ratliff, Ben. The Jazz Ear	781.6509
Rawlence, Ben. City of Thorns	967.7305
Read, Piers Paul. ★Alive	982
Redniss, Lauren. ★Oak Flat	970.5
Rehak, Melanie. Girl Sleuth	813
Rhoden, William C. $40 Million Slaves	796
Ribowsky, Mark. The Supremes	B
Richards, Cecile. Make Trouble	B
Rioux, Anne Boyd. Meg, Jo, Beth, Amy	813
Rippon, Adam. Beautiful on the Outside	B
Roach, Mary. ★Grunt	355
Roach, Mary. Packing for Mars	571.0919
Roach, Mary. ★Spook	129
Roach, Mary. ★Stiff	611
Roberts, Cokie. Founding Mothers	920
Roberts, Jason. A Sense of the World	B
Ronson, Jon. So You've Been Publicly Shamed	152.4
Rose, Sarah. D-Day Girls	940.53
Rosenbloom, Joseph. Redemption	B
Rybczynski, Witold. The Look of Architecture	721
Safina, Carl. ★Becoming Wild	591.7
Safina, Carl. Beyond Words	591.56
Saini, Angela. Inferior	305.4
Samuelsson, Marcus. Yes, Chef	B
Sanchez, Aaron. Where I Come From	641.5092
Sands, Philippe. East West Street	345
Sarsour, Linda. We Are Not Here to Be Bystanders	B
Satow, Julie. The Plaza	917.47
Satrapi, Marjane. ★The Complete Persepolis	741.5
Sawchik, Travis. Big Data Baseball	796.357
Scheeres, Julia. Jesus Land	B
Schumacher, Michael. Will Eisner	741.5
Schutt, Bill. Cannibalism	394
Searcey, Dionne. In Pursuit of Disobedient Women	B
Seierstad, Asne. Angel of Grozny	947.086
Seierstad, Asne. The Bookseller of Kabul	958.1
Seierstad, Asne. A Hundred and One Days	956.70443
Seife, Charles. Proofiness	510
Seiple, Samantha. Louisa on the Front Lines	B
Sepinwall, Alan. ★TV (the Book)	791.45
Severin, Timothy. In Search of Robinson Crusoe	996.1
Shachtman, Tom. ★Rumspringa	305.235
Shahani, Aarti Namdev. Here We Are	B
Shales, Tom. Live from New York	791.45
Sharapova, Maria. Unstoppable	B
Sharpton, Al. Rise Up	973.933
Sherr, Lynn. Sally Ride	B
Shetterly, Margot Lee. ★Hidden Figures	510.92
Showalter, Elaine. ★A Jury of Her Peers	810.9
Sibley, David. The Sibley Guide to Birds	598.097
Sides, Hampton. ★Ghost Soldiers	940.54
Simmons, Bill. The Book of Basketball	796.323
Simon, Matt. The Wasp That Brainwashed the Caterpillar	578.4
Singh, Simon. Fermat's Enigma	512
Slawenski, Kenneth. ★Salinger	B
Smith, Bren. Eat Like a Fish	338.3
Smith, David James. Young Mandela	B
Smith, Mychal Denzel. Invisible Man, Got the Whole World Watching	305.242
Smith, Patti. ★M Train	B
Smith, Richard MacLean. Unexplained	130
Sobel, Dava. Longitude	526
Sobel, Dava. A More Perfect Heaven	520.9
Sotomayor, Sonia. ★My Beloved World	B
Southon, Emma. Agrippina	B
Spiegelman, Nadja. ★I'm Supposed to Protect You from All This	741.5
Spoto, Donald. Joan	B
St. John, Warren. Outcasts United	B
Standage, Tom. An Edible History of Humanity	394.1
Stanley, Paul. Face the Music	B
Stanton, Doug. In Harm's Way	940.54
Starkey, David. Six Wives	942.05
Steinhauer, Jennifer. The Firsts	320.082
Stewart, Rory. The Prince of the Marshes	956.7044
Stone, Robert. Chasing the Moon	629.45
Strayed, Cheryl. ★Wild	B
Strickland, Carol. The Annotated Mona Lisa	709
Stuart, Colin. How to Live in Space	629.45
Switek, Brian. Skeleton Keys	611
Symonds, Craig L. Lincoln and His Admirals	B
Takaki, Ronald T. Double Victory	940.53
Tamblyn, Amber. ★Era of Ignition	B
Tammet, Daniel. Born on a Blue Day	B
Taylor, Alan. The Divided Ground	974.7
Terkel, Studs. Hope Dies Last	920
Thomas, Etan. We Matter	796.08
Thomas, Evan. ★Robert Kennedy	B
Thorpe, Helen. The Newcomers	373.18

1584

AUTHOR, TITLE, SERIES AND SUBJECT INDEX

Tietjen, Jill S. *Hollywood, Her Story*	791.43
Tobia, Jacob. *Sissy*	305.30973
Tobin, Jacqueline. *From Midnight to Dawn*	973.7
Tolan, Sandy. ★*The Lemon Tree*	B
Toler, Pamela D. *Women Warriors*	355.0092
Tolokonnikova, Nadezhda. *Rules for Rulebreakers*	782.42166
Traister, Rebecca. *Good and Mad*	305.420973
Tran, Phuc. ★*Sigh, Gone*	B
Tucker, Todd. *The Great Starvation Experiment*	174.2
Turow, Scott. ★*Ultimate Punishment*	345.73
Tutu, Desmond. *The Book of Forgiving*	179
Tutu, Desmond. *Made for Goodness*	170
Tyson, Neil deGrasse. ★*Astrophysics for People in a Hurry*	523.01
Tyson, Neil deGrasse. *Letters from an Astrophysicist*	520.92
Tyson, Neil deGrasse. *Welcome to the Universe*	523.1
Ung, Loung. *First They Killed My Father*	959.604
Ung, Loung. *Lucky Child*	B
Urrea, Luis Alberto. *The Devil's Highway*	304.8
Vanasco, Jeannie. *Things We Didn't Talk About When I Was a Girl*	B
Vargas, Jose Antonio. *Dear America*	B
Vella, Christina. *George Washington Carver*	B
Voloj, Julian. *Ghetto Brother*	741.5
Von Drehle, Dave. ★*Triangle*	974.7
Vowell, Sarah. *Assassination Vacation*	B
Waal, F. B. M. de. ★*Mama's Last Hug*	599.885
Wald, Elijah. ★*Escaping the Delta*	B
Waldbauer, Gilbert. *What Good Are Bugs?*	595.717
Walder, Tracy. *The Unexpected Spy*	B
Waldman, Jonathan. *Sam*	629.8
Waldman, Steven. *Sacred Liberty*	341.4
Walls, Jeannette. ★*The Glass Castle*	B
Ward, Geoffrey C. *Jazz*	781.6509
Ward, Geoffrey C. ★*The Vietnam War*	959.704
Ward, Jesmyn. ★*The Fire This Time*	305.896
Ward, Peter Douglas. *Life as We Do Not Know It*	576.839
Wariner, Ruth. *The Sound of Gravel*	B
Warren, Louis S. *Buffalo Bill's America*	B
Waterman, Jonathan. *National Geographic Atlas of the National Parks*	917.304
Weatherford, J. McIver. ★*Genghis Khan and the Making of the Modern World*	B
Weiner, Mark Stuart. *Black Trials*	342.7308
Weingarten, Gene. ★*One Day*	973
Weir, Alison. *The Life of Elizabeth I*	B
Weldon, Glen. ★*The Caped Crusade*	741.5
Weller, Sam. *The Bradbury Chronicles*	B
Welteroth, Elaine. *More Than Enough*	B
Wert, Jeffry D. *Cavalryman of the Lost Cause*	B
West, Lindy. *Shrill*	818
Westhoff, Ben. *Original Gangstas*	782.421649
Westover, Tara. ★*Educated*	B
Wheelan, Charles J. *Naked Economics*	330
White, Ronald C. *A. Lincoln*	B
Whyte, Kenneth. *The Uncrowned King*	B
Wides-Munoz, Laura. *The Making of a Dream*	920
Widmer, Edward L. *Martin Van Buren*	B
Wilder, Laura Ingalls. *Pioneer Girl*	B
Wilder, Laura Ingalls. *The Selected Letters of Laura Ingalls Wilder*	B
Williams, Juan. *Eyes on the Prize*	323.4
Willner, Nina. *Forty Autumns*	B
Wills, Garry. *James Madison*	B
Wilson, Edward O. ★*Letters to a Young Scientist*	570.92
Wilson, Edward O. *A Window on Eternity*	333.95
Winchester, Simon. *The Professor and the Madman*	423
Winroth, Anders. *The Age of the Vikings*	948
Winters, Kathleen C. *Amelia Earhart*	B
Winters, Richard D. *Beyond Band of Brothers*	B
Wong, Ali. ★*Dear Girls*	B
Woodford, Chris. *Atoms Under the Floorboards*	500
Worster, Donald. *A Passion for Nature the Life of John Muir*	B
Wright, Evan. *Generation Kill*	956.7044
Wright, Richard. ★*Black Boy*	B
Wullschlager, Jackie. ★*Chagall*	B
Yellin, Emily. *Our Mothers' War*	940.53
Young, Kevin. *Ardency*	811
Zamora, Javier. ★*Solito*	B
Zuckoff, Mitchell. *Frozen in Time*	998.2
Zwonitzer, Mark. *Will You Miss Me When I'm Gone?*	920

ADULT CHILD ABUSE VICTIMS	
Bass, Ellen. ★*The Courage to Heal*	616.85
Bonner, Betsy. *The Book of Atlantis Black*	364.152
Burke Harris, Nadine. *The Deepest Well*	618.92
Butler, Marcia. *The Skin Above My Knee*	B
Fleming, Brandon P. *Miseducated*	B
Harjo, Joy. *Crazy Brave*	B
Harjo, Joy. ★*Poet Warrior*	B
Marzano-Lesnevich, Alexandria. *The Fact of a Body*	364.152
Shorter, Frank. *My Marathon*	796.42
Sullivan, Randall. *Graveyard of the Pacific*	979.7
Wagamese, Richard. *One Native Life*	B
ADULT CHILD SEXUAL ABUSE VICTIMS	
Krouse, Erika. ★*Tell Me Everything*	363.25
Lecrae. ★*I Am Restored*	B
Mills, Stephen Tukel. *Chosen*	B
V. *The Apology*	818
Vasquez-Lavado, Silvia. *In the Shadow of the Mountain*	B
Wariner, Ruth. *The Sound of Gravel*	B
ADULT CHILDREN	
Hibbs, B. Janet. *You're Not Done Yet*	649
Lythcott-Haims, Julie. *Your Turn*	305.24
ADULT CHILDREN LIVING WITH PARENTS	
McConville, Mark. *Failure to Launch*	155.6
ADULT CHILDREN OF ALCOHOLICS	
Szczeszak-Brewer, Agata. *The Hunger Book*	B
ADULT CHILDREN OF DIVORCED PARENTS	
Burton, Susan. *Empty*	B
ADULT CHILDREN OF DRUG ABUSERS	
Madden, T Kira. *Long Live the Tribe of Fatherless Girls*	814
ADULT CHILDREN OF DYSFUNCTIONAL FAMILIES	
Calhoun, Ada. *Also a Poet*	B
ADULT CHILDREN OF PEOPLE WITH ALZHEIMER'S DISEASE	
Kozol, Jonathan. *The Theft of Memory*	B
ADULT CHILDREN OF SUICIDE VICTIMS	
Sullivan, Rosemary. *Stalin's Daughter*	B
ADULT EDUCATION	
Rose, Mike. *Back to School*	374
ADULT LEARNERS	
Painter, Nell Irvin. *Old in Art School*	B
Rose, Mike. *Back to School*	374
ADULTHOOD	
Alderton, Dolly. *Everything I Know About Love*	B
Birbiglia, Mike. *The New One*	B
Byas, Taylor. *I Done Clicked My Heels Three Times*	811
Damour, Lisa. *Untangled*	305.235
Friedman, Rachel. ★*And Then We Grew Up*	305.24
Georges, Gigi. *Downeast*	974.1
Jenkins, Jedidiah. *To Shake the Sleeping Self*	B
Kim, Anne. ★*Abandoned*	305.2350973
Lythcott-Haims, Julie. *Your Turn*	305.24
McConville, Mark. *Failure to Launch*	155.6
Means, Brittany. *Hell If We Don't Change Our Ways*	B
Ng, Fae Myenne. *Orphan Bachelors*	B
Rannells, Andrew. *Uncle of the Year*	B
Sanchez, Erika L. *Crying in the Bathroom*	B
Watkins, D. *Black Boy Smile*	B
Adunis	
Concerto Al-Quds	892.7
***Advanced** Chain Maille Jewelry Workshop*. Karon, Karen	745.594
***Advanced** Parenting*. Fradin, Kelly	649
***Advancing** The Story*. Wenger, Debora Halpern	070.1
ADVENTURE	
Ballard, Robert D. *Into the Deep*	551.46092
Bowden, Mark. *Black Hawk Down*	967.7305
Bukreev, Anatolii Nikolaevich. *The Climb*	796.52
Ellsworth, Scott. *The World Beneath Their Feet*	796.522
Grylls, Bear. *Never Give Up*	B
Harrison, Jim. *The Search for the Genuine*	814
Krakauer, Jon. *Into the Wild*	917.9804
Krakauer, Jon. ★*Into Thin Air*	796.52
Levy, Buddy. *Labyrinth of Ice*	910.91
Pennington, Emily. *Feral*	B
ADVENTURE FILMS	
Hendrix, Grady. *These Fists Break Bricks*	791
★*The **Adventure** of English*. Bragg, Melvyn	420
ADVENTURE TRAVEL	
Jenkins, Peter. *Looking for Alaska*	979.8

PUBLIC LIBRARY CORE COLLECTION: NONFICTION
Twentieth Edition

Jenkins, Peter. *A Walk Across America* — 917.304
ADVENTURE WRITING — ADVENTURE TRAVEL
Caesar, Ed. *The Moth and the Mountain* — B
Clark, Doug Bock. *The Last Whalers* — 639.2
Clark, Liz. *Swell* — B
Cordes, Kelly. *The Tower* — 796.522
Finnegan, William. *Barbarian Days* — B
Harrison, Jim. *The Search for the Genuine* — 814
Kirkby, Bruce. *Blue Sky Kingdom* — 954.96
Michaud-Skog, Summer. *Fat Girls Hiking* — 796.51
O'Brien, Vanessa. *To the Greatest Heights* — B
Roberts, Jason. *A Sense of the World* — B
Strøksnes, Morten Andreas. *Shark Drunk* — 338.3
Synnott, Mark. *The Third Pole* — 796.522
ADVENTURE WRITING — EXPLORATION
Ballard, Robert D. *Into the Deep* — 551.46092
Bellows, Amanda Brickell. *The Explorers* — 910.92
Bergreen, Laurence. *Over the Edge of the World* — B
Carlsen, William. *Jungle of Stone* — B
Conefrey, Mick. *The Ghosts of K2* — 796.522
Ellsworth, Scott. *The World Beneath Their Feet* — 796.522
Fiennes, Ranulph. *Shackleton* — B
Goodheart, Adam. *The Last Island* — 954
Hartman, Darrell. *Battle of Ink and Ice* — 998
Hunt, Will. *Underground* — 624.1
Jeal, Tim. *Explorers of the Nile* — 920
Kurson, Robert. *Pirate Hunters* — 910.91
Larson, Edward J. *An Empire of Ice* — 919.8
Levy, Buddy. *Labyrinth of Ice* — 910.91
Lowe, George. *Letters from Everest* — 796.522
Mearns, David L. *The Shipwreck Hunter* — 910.452
Millard, Candice. *River of Doubt* — 918.1
Millard, Candice. ★*River of the Gods* — 916.204
O'Brady, Colin. ★*The Impossible First* — 919.8904
Preston, Douglas J. ★*The Lost City of the Monkey God* — 972.85
Richardson, Edmund. *The King's Shadow* — 958.1
Ross, John F. *The Promise of the Grand Canyon* — 917.91
Sancton, Julian. *Madhouse at the End of the Earth* — 919.8904
Sides, Hampton. ★*The Wide Wide Sea* — 910.92
Tabor, James M. *Blind Descent* — 796.52
Welky, David. ★*A Wretched and Precarious Situation* — 910.911
ADVENTURE WRITING — GENERAL
Alexander, Caroline. *The Bounty* — 996.1
Barbarisi, Daniel. *Chasing the Thrill* — 796.1
Diamond, Cheryl. *Nowhere Girl* — B
Junger, Sebastian. *Fire* — 909.82
ADVENTURE WRITING — NATURAL DISASTER
Aktipis, Athena. ★*A Field Guide to the Apocalypse* — 155.2
Bukreev, Anatolii Nikolaevich. *The Climb* — 796.52
Burns, Cherie. *The Great Hurricane—1938* — 974.7
Junger, Sebastian. *The Perfect Storm* — 974.4
Slade, Rachel. *Into the Raging Sea* — 910.91
ADVENTURE WRITING — SURVIVAL
Alexander, Caroline. *The Endurance* — 919.8
Bowden, Mark. *Black Hawk Down* — 967.7305
Finkel, Michael. *The Stranger in the Woods* — B
Grylls, Bear. *Never Give Up* — B
Gutman, Matt. *The Boys in the Cave* — 796.52
Hall, Andy. *Denali's Howl* — 796.522
Krakauer, Jon. *Into the Wild* — 917.9804
Krakauer, Jon. ★*Into Thin Air* — 796.52
Lineberry, Cate. *The Secret Rescue* — 940.54
Messenger, Alex. *The Twenty-Ninth Day* — B
Murphy, Brian. *81 Days Below Zero* — 940.54
Niven, Jennifer. *Ada Blackjack* — B
Ollestad, Norman. *Crazy for the Storm* — B
Parrado, Nando. ★*Miracle in the Andes* — 982
Ralston, Aron. *Between a Rock and a Hard Place* — 796.522
Read, Piers Paul. ★*Alive* — 982
Reel, Monte. *The Last of the Tribe* — 981
Ripley, Amanda. *The Unthinkable* — 155.9
Roberts, David. *Alone on the Ice* — 919.8904
Sancton, Julian. *Madhouse at the End of the Earth* — 919.8904
Sides, Hampton. ★*In the Kingdom of Ice* — 910.4
Sprinkle, Timothy. *Lost and Stranded* — 613.6
Zuckoff, Mitchell. *Frozen in Time* — 998.2
Zuckoff, Mitchell. *Lost in Shangri-La* — 940.54
The Adventurer's Son. Dial, Roman — 917.286

ADVENTURERS
Ballard, Robert D. *Into the Deep* — 551.46092
Belliveau, Denis. *In the Footsteps of Marco Polo* — 915
Bellows, Amanda Brickell. *The Explorers* — 910.92
Caesar, Ed. *The Moth and the Mountain* — B
Dial, Roman. *The Adventurer's Son* — 917.286
Fox, Porter. *The Last Winter* — 363.738
Grann, David. *The White Darkness* — B
Groom, Winston. *The Aviators* — 920
Homer. *The Odyssey* — 883
Homer. *Odyssey* — 883
Homer. ★*The Odyssey* — 883
Krakauer, Jon. *Into the Wild* — 917.9804
Kugel, Seth. *Rediscovering Travel* — 306.4
Roberts, David. *Limits of the Known* — B
Virgil. ★*The Aeneid* — 873
Wilkinson, Toby A. H. *A World Beneath the Sands* — 932
Adventures in Slow Cooking. DiGregorio, Sarah — 641.5
Adventures in the Screen Trade. Goldman, William — 384
Adventures of a Young Naturalist. Attenborough, David — B
The Adventures of Grandmaster Flash. Grandmaster Flash — B
ADVERTISING
Auletta, Ken. *Frenemies* — 659.1
Haag, Pamela. ★*The Gunning of America* — 338.4
Linn, Susan. *Who's Raising the Kids?* — 649
Windhorst, Brian. *Lebron, Inc.* — B
Wu, Tim. *The Attention Merchants* — 659.1
ADVERTISING AGENCIES
Auletta, Ken. *Frenemies* — 659.1
ADVICE
Adichie, Chimamanda Ngozi. *Dear Ijeawele* — 649
Ashley, Maurice. *Move by Move* — 158
Backman, Fredrik. *Things My Son Needs to Know About the World* — B
Baskette, Molly Phinney. *How to Begin When Your World Is Ending* — 248.8
Boa, Kenneth D. *Recalibrate Your Life* — 248.8
Bradbury, Ray. ★*Remembrance* — 813
Brem, Rachel. *No Longer Radical* — 616.99
Brown, Theresa. *Healing* — 616.99
Coel, Michaela. ★*Misfits* — 158.2
Febos, Melissa. ★*Body Work* — 808.06
Gay, Roxane. ★*Opinions* — 814
Ghobash, Omar Saif. *Letters to a Young Muslim* — 297.09
Godin, Seth. *The Practice* — 153.3
Griffin, Susan. *Out of Silence, Sound. Out of Nothing, Something* — 808.02
Guthrie, Savannah. *Mostly What God Does* — 248.4
Hakkakiyan, Ruya. *A Beginner's Guide to America* — 646.7
Kelly, Kevin. ★*Excellent Advice for Living* — 158.1
King, Charles Monroe. *A Journal for Jordan* — 956.7044
Lima, Jamie Kern. *Believe It* — B
Lythcott-Haims, Julie. *Your Turn* — 305.24
Malone, Sharon. *Grown Woman Talk* — 362.1
Mattel, Trixie. *Working Girls* — 650.1
Odenkirk, Bob. *Comedy Comedy Comedy Drama* — B
Palahniuk, Chuck. *Consider This* — B
Posey, Parker. *You're on an Airplane* — B
Psaki, Jen. *Say More* — B
Rubin, Rick. ★*The Creative Act* — 153.3
Vanek Smith, Stacey. *Machiavelli for Women* — 650.1
Von Drehle, David. ★*The Book of Charlie* — B
Wilson, Edward O. ★*Letters to a Young Scientist* — 570.92
ADVICE COLUMNISTS
Dickinson, Amy. *Strangers Tend to Tell Me Things* — B
Goldstein, Meredith. *Can't Help Myself* — B
Havrilesky, Heather. *Foreverland* — 306.81
Lavery, Daniel M. *Dear Prudence* — 170
ADVICE COLUMNS
Lavery, Daniel M. *Dear Prudence* — 170
Advice Not Given. Epstein, Mark — 294.3
ADVOCACY FOR PEOPLE WITH DISABILITIES
Blake, Melissa. *Beautiful People* — 362.4
Mattlin, Ben. *Disability Pride* — 323.3
AEGEAN SEA REGION
Cline, Eric H. *After 1177 B.C.* — 937
AENEAS (LEGENDARY CHARACTER)
Virgil. ★*The Aeneid* — 873
Virgil. *The Aeneid* — 873
★*The Aeneid*. Virgil — 873
The Aeneid. Virgil — 873

AUTHOR, TITLE, SERIES AND SUBJECT INDEX

AERIAL BOMBING
    Ambrose, Stephen E. *The Wild Blue*   940.54
    Frank, Richard B. *Downfall*   940.54
    Gladwell, Malcolm. ★*The Bomber Mafia*   940.54
    Hastings, Max. *Operation Chastise*   940.54
    Hersey, John. ★*Hiroshima*   940.54
    Larson, Erik. ★*The Splendid and the Vile*   940.54
    Makos, Adam. ★*A Higher Call*   940.54
    McKay, Sinclair. *The Fire and the Darkness*   940.54
    Scott, James. *Black Snow*   940.54
    Scott, James. *Target Tokyo*   940.54
AERIAL OPERATIONS
    Alexander, Caroline. *Skies of Thunder*   940.54
    Ambrose, Stephen E. *The Wild Blue*   940.54
    Bruning, John R. *Indestructible*   B
    Bruning, John R. *The Race of Aces*   940.54
    Drury, Bob. *Lucky 666*   B
    Erwin, Jon. *Beyond Valor*   B
    Graff, Garrett M. ★*When the Sea Came Alive*   940.54
    Grayling, A. C. *Among the Dead Cities*   940.54
    Hamilton-Paterson, James. *Marked for Death*   358.400941
    Hampton, Dan. *Operation Vengeance*   940.54
    Hastings, Max. *Operation Pedestal*   940.54
    Hynes, Samuel. *The Unsubstantial Air*   940.4
    Kershaw, Alex. *The Few*   940.54
    Korda, Michael. *With Wings Like Eagles*   940.54
    Makos, Adam. ★*A Higher Call*   940.54
    Maurer, Kevin. *Damn Lucky*   940.54
    McKay, Sinclair. *The Fire and the Darkness*   940.54
    Murphy, Brian. *81 Days Below Zero*   940.54
    Scott, James. *Target Tokyo*   940.54
    Smith, Jim B. *The Last Mission*   940.54
    Snyder, Steve. *Shot Down*   940.54
    Wallace, Chris. *Countdown 1945*   940.54
    Winters, Richard D. *Beyond Band of Brothers*   B
    Zuckoff, Mitchell. *Frozen in Time*   998.2
    Zuckoff, Mitchell. *Lost in Shangri-La*   940.54
AERIAL PHOTOGRAPHY
    Begley, Adam. *The Great Nadar*   B
AERONAUTICAL ENGINEERS
    Guthrie, Julian. *How to Make a Spaceship*   629.47
    Hampton, Dan. *Chasing the Demon*   629.132
    Mulley, Clare. *The Women Who Flew for Hitler*   920
AEROSPACE ENGINEERS
    Davenport, Christian. *The Space Barons*   920
    Hickam, Homer H. ★*Rocket Boys*   B
AEROSPACE INDUSTRY AND TRADE
    Berger, Eric. *Liftoff*   B
    Davenport, Christian. *The Space Barons*   920
Aeschylus
    The Oresteia   882
AESCHYLUS
    Aeschylus. *The Oresteia*   882
AESTHETICS
    Bethencourt, Kahran. *Glory*   779.2
    Eco, Umberto. *History of Beauty*   111
    Eco, Umberto. *On Ugliness*   111
    Finkel, Michael. *The Art Thief*   364.1628
    Kundera, Milan. *Encounter*   809
    Rowland, Ingrid D. *The Collector of Lives*   B
    Whitefield-Madrano, Autumn. *Face Value*   111
AESTHETICS, JAPANESE
    Keene, Donald. *The Pleasures of Japanese Literature*   895.6
AFFIRMATIONS
    Gawain, Shakti. ★*Creative Visualization*   153.3
    Osteen, Joel. *The Power of I Am*   248.4
AFFIRMATIVE ACTION
    Greene, Jamal. *How Rights Went Wrong*   342.7308
    Urofsky, Melvin I. *The Affirmative Action Puzzle*   331.13
AFFIRMATIVE ACTION IN EDUCATION
    Garrett, Kent. *The Last Negroes at Harvard*   920
    Urofsky, Melvin I. *The Affirmative Action Puzzle*   331.13
The Affirmative Action Puzzle. Urofsky, Melvin I.   331.13
An Affirming Flame. Cohen, Roger   071
AFGHAN PEOPLE
    Ghafari, Zarifa. *Zarifa*   B
    Zuckoff, Mitchell. *The Secret Gate*   958.104

AFGHAN WAR VETERANS
    Chesney, Will. *No Ordinary Dog*   958.104
    Edstrom, Erik. *Un-American*   B
    Kander, Jason. *Invisible Storm*   B
AFGHAN WAR, 2001-2021
    Ackerman, Elliot. *The Fifth Act*   958.104
    Ackerman, Elliot. *Places and Names*   B
    Brennan, Thomas J. *Shooting Ghosts*   B
    Carpenter, Kyle. *You Are Worth It*   B
    Chesney, Will. *No Ordinary Dog*   958.104
    Chivers, C. J. *The Fighters*   920
    Edstrom, Erik. *Un-American*   B
    Golembesky, Michael. *Level Zero Heroes*   958.104
    Gopal, Anand. *No Good Men Among the Living*   920
    Hegar, Mary Jennings. *Shoot Like a Girl*   B
    Hennessey, Patrick. *The Junior Officers' Reading Club*   B
    Junger, Sebastian. *War*   958.104
    Kesling, Ben. *Bravo Company*   958.104
    Lemmon, Gayle Tzemach. *Ashley's War*   B
    Loyn, David. *The Long War*   958.104
    Luttrell, Marcus. *Lone Survivor*   958.104
    Meyer, Dakota. *Into the Fire*   958.104
    Morgan, Wesley. *The Hardest Place*   958.104
    O'Neill, Robert. *The Operator*   B
    Owen, Mark. *No Easy Day*   B
    Poole, Robert M. *Section 60*   975.5
    Romesha, Clinton. *Red Platoon*   958.104
    Stanton, Doug. *12 Strong*   958.104
    Van Agtmael, Peter. *Look at the USA*   070
    Whitlock, Craig. *The Afghanistan Papers*   958.104
    Wise, Beau. *Three Wise Men*   958.104
    Zuckoff, Mitchell. *The Secret Gate*   958.104
AFGHANISTAN
    Ackerman, Elliot. *The Fifth Act*   958.104
    Ackerman, Elliot. *Places and Names*   B
    Addario, Lynsey. *Of Love & War*   779
    Ansary, Mir Tamim. *Games Without Rules*   958.1
    Badkhen, Anna. *The World Is a Carpet*   305.409581
    Coll, Steve. *Directorate S*   958.104
    Coll, Steve. ★*Ghost Wars*   958.104
    Dalrymple, William. *The Return of a King*   958.1
    Edstrom, Erik. *Un-American*   B
    Feifer, Gregory. *The Great Gamble*   958.104
    Fritz, Ian. *What the Taliban Told Me*   B
    Ghafari, Zarifa. *Zarifa*   B
    Golembesky, Michael. *Level Zero Heroes*   958.104
    Gopal, Anand. *No Good Men Among the Living*   920
    Grossi, Craig. *Craig & Fred*   B
    Guibert, Emmanuel. *The Photographer*   741.5
    Junger, Sebastian. *War*   958.104
    Loyn, David. *In Afghanistan*   958.1
    Loyn, David. *The Long War*   958.104
    Luttrell, Marcus. *Lone Survivor*   958.104
    Meyer, Dakota. *Into the Fire*   958.104
    Morgan, Wesley. *The Hardest Place*   958.104
    Nordberg, Jenny. *The Underground Girls of Kabul*   305.3
    O'Neill, Robert. *The Operator*   B
    Owen, Mark. *No Easy Day*   B
    Passarlay, Gulwali. *The Lightless Sky*   B
    Qadiri, Humayra. *Dancing in the Mosque*   B
    Rahmani, Niloofar. *Open Skies*   B
    Rashid, Ahmed. *Taliban*   958.104
    Richardson, Edmund. *The King's Shadow*   958.1
    Romesha, Clinton. *Red Platoon*   958.104
    Stanton, Doug. *12 Strong*   958.104
    Van Agtmael, Peter. *Look at the USA*   070
    Vickers, Michael G. *By All Means Available*   355
    Whitlock, Craig. *The Afghanistan Papers*   958.104
    Zuckoff, Mitchell. *The Secret Gate*   958.104
The Afghanistan Papers. Whitlock, Craig   958.104
Afremow, James A.
    The Champion's Mind   796.01
AFRICA
    Addario, Lynsey. *Of Love & War*   779
    Burgis, Tom. *The Looting Machine*   338.2
    Churchill, Winston. *The Grand Alliance*   940.53
    Cliff, Nigel. *Holy War*   909
    Ehrlich, Gretel. *Unsolaced*   B

PUBLIC LIBRARY CORE COLLECTION: NONFICTION
Twentieth Edition

Erdman, Sarah. *Nine Hills to Nambonkaha*	966.68
Evans, Martin. *Algeria*	965
Faloyin, Dipo. ★*Africa Is Not a Country*	960.33
Farmer, Paul. *Fevers, Feuds, and Diamonds*	614.5
Gates, Henry Louis. *In Search of Our Roots*	973
Hochschild, Adam. *King Leopold's Ghost*	967.51
Johanson, Donald C. *Lucy*	569
Kamkwamba, William. ★*The Boy Who Harnessed the Wind*	B
Meredith, Martin. *The Fortunes of Africa*	960
Owens, Delia. *The Eye of the Elephant*	639.9
Preston, Richard. *Crisis in the Red Zone*	614.5
Preston, Richard. *The Hot Zone*	614.5
Soyinka, Wole. *Of Africa*	960
Tesfamariam, Rahiel. ★*Imagine Freedom*	305.896
Tjipombo, Tupa. *I Am Not Your Slave*	B
Umar, Ousman. *North to Paradise*	B
Wainaina, Binyavanga. ★*How to Write About Africa*	814
★*Africa Is Not a Country*. Faloyin, Dipo	960.33

AFRICAN AMERICAN ABOLITIONISTS
Blight, David W. ★*Frederick Douglass*	B
Colaiaco, James A. *Frederick Douglass and the Fourth of July*	973.7
Dilbeck, D. H. *Frederick Douglass*	B
Douglass, Frederick. *My Bondage and My Freedom*	B
Douglass, Frederick. *Narrative of the Life of Frederick Douglass, an American Slave*	B
Douglass, Frederick. *The Portable Frederick Douglass*	973.8
Meyer, Eugene L. *Five for Freedom*	973.7
Painter, Nell Irvin. ★*Sojourner Truth*	B
Shane, Scott. ★*Flee North*	973.7
Stauffer, John. *Picturing Fredrick Douglass*	B

AFRICAN AMERICAN AGRICULTURISTS
Vella, Christina. *George Washington Carver*	B
An *African* American and Latinx History of the United States. Ortiz, Paul	305.8

AFRICAN AMERICAN ART
Farrington, Lisa E. *Creating Their Own Image*	704
Griffin, Farah Jasmine. *Read Until You Understand*	810.9
Patton, Sharon F. *African-American Art*	704.03
Stanislaus, Grace C. *Instill & Inspire*	704.03

AFRICAN AMERICAN ARTISTS
Griffin, Farah Jasmine. *Read Until You Understand*	810.9
Rembert, Winfred. *Chasing Me to My Grave*	B

AFRICAN AMERICAN ASTRONAUTS
Bagby, Meredith E. *The New Guys*	305
Melvin, Leland. *Chasing Space*	B
Paul, Richard. *We Could Not Fail*	920

AFRICAN AMERICAN ATHLETES
Haygood, Wil. ★*Sweet Thunder*	B
Kram, Mark. *Smokin' Joe*	B
Perkins, Kendrick. *The Education of Kendrick Perkins*	B
Rhoden, William C. *$40 Million Slaves*	796
Thomas, Etan. *We Matter*	796.08
Tyson, Mike. *Iron Ambition*	B
Whitaker, Mark. *Smoketown*	305.896
Williams, Jay. *Life Is Not an Accident*	B

AFRICAN AMERICAN AUTHORS
Abdurraqib, Hanif. ★*A Little Devil in America*	791.089
Abdurraqib, Hanif. ★*There's Always This Year*	796.323
Angelou, Maya. ★*I Know Why the Caged Bird Sings*	B
Angelou, Maya. ★*A Song Flung up to Heaven*	B
Bader, Philip. *African-American Writers*	810.9
Broome, Brian. ★*Punch Me up to the Gods*	B
Carter, Stephen L. *Invisible*	B
Cleaver, Eldridge. *Soul on Ice*	B
Coates, Ta-Nehisi. *The Beautiful Struggle*	B
Cole, Teju. *Blind Spot*	770
Ellison, Ralph. *The Selected Letters of Ralph Ellison*	813
Griffin, Farah Jasmine. *Read Until You Understand*	810.9
Hall, Alvin D. *Driving the Green Book*	917.304
Hughes, Langston. ★*I Wonder as I Wander*	B
Hurston, Zora Neale. *Dust Tracks on a Road*	B
Hurston, Zora Neale. *Zora Neale Hurston*	B
Jackson, Lawrence Patrick. *Chester B. Himes*	B
Jones, Saeed. *How We Fight for Our Lives*	B
Jones, Sharon L. *Critical Companion to Zora Neale Hurston*	813
Kenan, Randall. *Black Folk Could Fly*	813
McGilligan, Patrick. *Oscar Micheaux*	B
Mullen, Bill. ★*James Baldwin*	B
Rampersad, Arnold. ★*Ralph Ellison*	B

Shakur, Prince. *When They Tell You to Be Good*	B
Watkins, D. *Black Boy Smile*	B
Wright, Richard. ★*Black Boy*	B
Young, Kevin. *Stones*	811
Young, R. J. *Requiem for the Massacre*	305.8

AFRICAN AMERICAN BALLET DANCERS
Copeland, Misty. ★*Life in Motion*	B
Valby, Karen. *The Swans of Harlem*	792.8

AFRICAN AMERICAN BAPTISTS
Eig, Jonathan. ★*King*	B

AFRICAN AMERICAN BASEBALL PLAYERS
Bryant, Howard. *The Last Hero*	B
Epplin, Luke. *Our Team*	796.357
Hirsch, James S. *Willie Mays*	B
Kennedy, Kostya. *True*	B
Ortiz, David. *Papi*	B
Perron, Cam. ★*Comeback Season*	796.357
Posnanski, Joe. *The Soul of Baseball*	796.357
Rapoport, Ron. *Let's Play Two*	B
Robinson, Jackie. *I Never Had It Made*	B
Ruck, Rob. *Raceball*	796.357
Snyder, Brad. *A Well-Paid Slave*	B
Tye, Larry. *Satchel*	B

AFRICAN AMERICAN BASKETBALL PLAYERS
Baylor, Elgin. *Hang Time*	B
Bella, Timothy. *Barkley*	B
Benedict, Jeff. *Lebron*	B
Bradburd, Rus. *All the Dreams We've Dreamed*	796.323
Bryant, Kobe. *The Mamba Mentality*	B
Iguodala, Andre. *The Sixth Man*	B
Maraniss, Andrew. *Strong Inside*	B
Oakley, Charles. *The Last Enforcer*	B
Perkins, Kendrick. *The Education of Kendrick Perkins*	B
Pippen, Scottie. *Unguarded*	B
Runstedtler, Theresa. *Black Ball*	796.323
Sielski, Mike. *The Rise*	B

AFRICAN AMERICAN BOXERS
Eig, Jonathan. ★*Ali*	B
Gildea, William. *The Longest Fight*	B
Kram, Mark. *Smokin' Joe*	B
Montville, Leigh. *Sting Like a Bee*	B
Roberts, Randy. *Joe Louis*	B
Stratton, W. K. *Floyd Patterson*	B
Tyson, Mike. *Iron Ambition*	B
Ward, Geoffrey C. *Unforgivable Blackness*	B

AFRICAN AMERICAN BROTHERS
Jackson family. *The Jacksons*	782.421644
Scheeres, Julia. *Jesus Land*	B

AFRICAN AMERICAN BUSINESSPEOPLE
Bundles, A'Lelia. *On Her Own Ground*	B
Chatelain, Marcia. ★*Franchise*	339
Greenburg, Zack O'Malley. *3 Kings*	782.421649
Jackson, Curtis. *Hustle Harder, Hustle Smarter*	B
Miller, Klancy. ★*For the Culture*	641.59
Saint John, Bozoma. *The Urgent Life*	B
Washington, Booker T. ★*Up from Slavery*	B
White, Shane. *Prince of Darkness*	B

AFRICAN AMERICAN CARTOONISTS
Goldstein, Nancy. *Jackie Ormes*	B

AFRICAN AMERICAN CELEBRITIES
Mooney, Paul. *Black Is the New White*	792.7
Porter, Billy. ★*Unprotected*	B

AFRICAN AMERICAN CHILDREN
Asgarian, Roxanna. *We Were Once a Family*	364.152
Bell, Darrin. ★*The Talk*	741.5
Bethencourt, Kahran. *Glory*	779.2
Browne, Mahogany L. ★*Black Girl Magic*	811.6
Elliott, Andrea. ★*Invisible Child*	362.7
Finney, Nikky. *Love Child's Hotbed of Occasional Poetry*	811
Harrison, Valerie I. *Do Right by Me*	649
Henning, Kristin. *The Rage of Innocence*	364.36
Hill, DaMaris B. *Breath Better Spent*	811
Love, Bettina L. *Punished for Dreaming*	371.829
Macy, Beth. ★*Truevine*	B
Mans, Jasmine. *Black Girl, Call Home*	811
Mar, Alex. *Seventy Times Seven*	362.88
Porter, Billy. ★*Unprotected*	B

AUTHOR, TITLE, SERIES AND SUBJECT INDEX

Tatum, Beverly Daniel. ★ *"Why Are All the Black Kids Sitting Together in the Cafeteria?"* — 305.800973
Watkins, D. *Black Boy Smile* — B

AFRICAN AMERICAN CHURCHES
Gates, Henry Louis. ★ *The Black Church* — 277

AFRICAN AMERICAN CIVIL RIGHTS
Alexander, Kwame. *Light for the World to See* — 811.6
Anderson, Carol. ★ *White Rage* — 305.800973
Baldwin, James. *I Am Not Your Negro* — 323.1196
Baldwin, James. ★ *Notes of a Native Son* — 305.8
Branch, Taylor. *Parting the Waters* — 973
Branch, Taylor. ★ *Pillar of Fire* — 323.1
Carruthers, Charlene A. *Unapologetic* — 305.48
Chatelain, Marcia. ★ *Franchise* — 339
Chemerinsky, Erwin. *Presumed Guilty* — 344.7305
Cummings, Elijah. ★ *We're Better Than This* — B
Delmont, Matthew F. *Half American* — 940.54
Dyson, Michael Eric. *Come Hell or High Water* — 976.3
Gergel, Richard. *Unexampled Courage* — 323.1196
Gibson, Larry S. *Young Thurgood* — B
Hinton, Elizabeth Kai. ★ *America on Fire* — 305.800973
Hunter-Gault, Charlayne. ★ *My People* — 305.48
Jackson, Kellie Carter. *We Refuse* — 323.1196
Jones, Doug. *Bending Toward Justice* — 323.1196
Joseph, Peniel E. *Waiting 'Til the Midnight Hour* — 323.1196
King, Gilbert. ★ *Devil in the Grove* — 305.896
King, Martin Luther. *A Testament of Hope* — 323.1
King, Martin Luther. *Why We Can't Wait* — 305.8
Levine, Robert S. ★ *The Failed Promise* — 973.8
Levingston, Steven. *Kennedy and King* — 920
Lewis, John. ★*March; Book One* — 741.5
Lewis, John. ★*March; Book Three* — 741.5
Lewis, John. ★*March; Book Two* — 741.5
Lewis, John. ★*Run; Book One* — 741.5
Lewis, John. *Walking with the Wind* — B
Manning, Chandra. *Troubled Refuge* — 973.7
Meacham, Jon. *His Truth Is Marching On* — B
Moore, Wes. ★ *Five Days* — 363.32
Morrison, Melanie. *Murder on Shades Mountain* — 345.761
Payne, Les. ★ *The Dead Are Arising* — B
Plant, Deborah G. *Of Greed and Glory* — 326
Reid, Joy-Ann Lomena. ★ *Medgar and Myrlie* — 920
Rembert, Winfred. *Chasing Me to My Grave* — B
Samuels, Robert. ★ *His Name Is George Floyd* — B
Sharpton, Al. *Rise Up* — 973.933
Spofford, Tim. *What the Children Told Us* — 150.92
Theoharis, Jeanne. *The Rebellious Life of Mrs. Rosa Parks* — B
Walker, Vanessa Siddle. *The Lost Education of Horace Tate* — 370.92
Zucchino, David. *Wilmington's Lie* — 305.8009756

AFRICAN AMERICAN CIVIL RIGHTS WORKERS
Arsenault, Raymond. *John Lewis* — B
Canellos, Peter S. *The Great Dissenter* — B
Eig, Jonathan. ★*King* — B
Gilliam, Dorothy Butler. *Trailblazer* — B
Greenidge, Kerri. *Black Radical* — B
Hayes, Elaine M. ★ *Queen of Bebop* — B
Jackson, Troy. *Becoming King* — B
King, Martin Luther. *The Autobiography of Martin Luther King, Jr.* — B
Lauterbach, Preston. *Bluff City* — B
Lewis, David L. ★ *W.E.B. Du Bois* — B
Lewis, John. *Walking with the Wind* — B
Marable, Manning. ★*Malcolm X* — B
Meacham, Jon. *His Truth Is Marching On* — B
Payne, Les. ★ *The Dead Are Arising* — B
Person, Charles. *Buses Are a Comin'* — B
Reid, Joy-Ann Lomena. ★ *Medgar and Myrlie* — 920
Rosenberg, Rosalind. ★ *Jane Crow* — B
Rosenbloom, Joseph. *Redemption* — B
Sides, Hampton. *Hellhound on His Trail* — 364.152
Sokol, Jason. *The Heavens Might Crack* — 323.092
Swift, Earl. *Hell Put to Shame* — 364.15
Wexler, Stuart. *Killing King* — 323.092
Wilkie, Curtis. *When Evil Lived in Laurel* — 305.8

AFRICAN AMERICAN CLERGY
Curry, Michael B. *Love Is the Way* — 241
Newman, Richard S. *Freedom's Prophet* — B

AFRICAN AMERICAN CLERGYWOMEN
Bailey, Jennifer. *To My Beloveds* — 261.8

AFRICAN AMERICAN COLLEGE STUDENTS
Garrett, Kent. *The Last Negroes at Harvard* — 920
Hobbs, Jeff. ★*The Short and Tragic Life of Robert Peace* — B

AFRICAN AMERICAN COLLEGE TEACHERS
Ford, Tanisha C. *Dressed in Dreams* — 391
Griffin, Farah Jasmine. *Read Until You Understand* — 810.9
Wilderson, Frank B. *Afropessimism* — B

AFRICAN AMERICAN COMEDIANS
Brunson, Quinta. *She Memes Well* — B
Foxx, Jamie. *Act Like You Got Some Sense* — B
Haddish, Tiffany. *The Last Black Unicorn* — B
Mooney, Paul. *Black Is the New White* — 792.7
Orji, Yvonne. *Bamboozled by Jesus* — B
Peisner, David. *Homey Don't Play That!* — 791.45
Saul, Scott. ★*Becoming Richard Pryor* — B
Thompson, Kenan. *When I Was Your Age* — B

AFRICAN AMERICAN COMMUNITIES
Ewing, Eve L. *1919* — 811
Gates, Henry Louis. *The Black Box* — 908
Leovy, Jill. *Ghettoside* — 364.152
Lewis, Robin Coste. *To the Realization of Perfect Helplessness* — 811

AFRICAN AMERICAN COMMUNITY LIFE
Lewis, Robin Coste. *To the Realization of Perfect Helplessness* — 811

AFRICAN AMERICAN COOKS
Deetz, Kelley Fanto. *Bound to the Fire* — 641.59
Onwuachi, Kwame. ★*Notes from a Young Black Chef* — 641.59
Raiford, Matthew. *Bress 'N' Nyam* — 641.59
Samuelsson, Marcus. ★ *The Rise* — 641.59
Tipton-Martin, Toni. *The Jemima Code* — 641.59
Tipton-Martin, Toni. ★*Jubilee* — 641.59

AFRICAN AMERICAN DANCERS
Copeland, Misty. *The Wind at My Back* — B
Williams, Michael Kenneth. *Scenes from My Life* — B

AFRICAN AMERICAN DEFENDANTS
Adams, Jarrett. *Redeeming Justice* — 340.092
Van Meter, Matthew. *Deep Delta Justice* — 345.763

AFRICAN AMERICAN DISC JOCKEYS
Grandmaster Flash. *The Adventures of Grandmaster Flash* — B

AFRICAN AMERICAN EDUCATORS
Harlan, Louis R. *Booker T. Washington* — B
Norrell, Robert J. *Up from History* — B

AFRICAN AMERICAN ENGINEERS
Paul, Richard. *We Could Not Fail* — 920

AFRICAN AMERICAN ENTERTAINERS
Lane, Stewart F. *Black Broadway* — 792.089
Lewis, Damien. *Agent Josephine* — B

AFRICAN AMERICAN ENTREPRENEURS
Greenburg, Zack O'Malley. *3 Kings* — 782.421649
Kenner, Rob. *The Marathon Don't Stop* — B

AFRICAN AMERICAN EXECUTIVES
Capparell, Stephanie. *The Real Pepsi Challenge* — 338.7

AFRICAN AMERICAN FAMILIES
Alexander, Kwame. *Why Fathers Cry at Night* — B
Asgarian, Roxanna. *We Were Once a Family* — 364.152
Broom, Sarah M. *The Yellow House* — B
Carter, Stephen L. *Invisible* — B
Ford, Ashley C. ★ *Somebody's Daughter* — B
Franklin, John Hope. *In Search of the Promised Land* — 929
Goldberg, Whoopi. *Bits and Pieces* — B
Gordon-Reed, Annette. ★*The Hemingses of Monticello* — 920
Grant, Gail Milissa. *At the Elbows of My Elders* — B
Hansberry, Lorraine. ★ *A Raisin in the Sun* — 812
Harriot, Michael. ★*Black AF History* — 973
Harris, Taylor. *This Boy We Made* — B
Holley, Santi Elijah. *An Amerikan Family* — 920
Jackson family. *The Jacksons* — 782.421644
Jackson, Mitchell S. *Survival Math* — B
Kearse, Bettye. *The Other Madisons* — 920
Kendi, Ibram X. ★*How to Raise an Antiracist* — 649
Lauterbach, Preston. *Beale Street Dynasty* — 976.8
Laymon, Kiese. *How to Slowly Kill Yourself and Others in America* — 814.6
Luckerson, Victor. *Built from the Fire* — 976.6
McCaulley, Esau. *How Far to the Promised Land* — B
Pardlo, Gregory. *Air Traffic* — B
Perry, Imani. ★*South to America* — 917
Pryce, Jessica. ★*Broken* — 362.7
Raiford, Matthew. *Bress 'N' Nyam* — 641.59
Rice, Condoleezza. *Extraordinary, Ordinary People* — B

PUBLIC LIBRARY CORE COLLECTION: NONFICTION
Twentieth Edition

Roberts, Dorothy E. *Torn Apart*	362.7
Ruffin, Amber. ★*The World Record Book of Racist Stories*	305.896
Samuels, Robert. ★*His Name Is George Floyd*	B
Savage, Jodi M. *The Death of a Jaybird*	B
Smith, Tracy K. ★*To Free the Captives*	818
Tubbs, Anna Malaika. *The Three Mothers*	306.874
White, Gayle Jessup. *Reclamation*	B

AFRICAN AMERICAN FARMERS

Baszile, Natalie. *We Are Each Other's Harvest*	630.89
Miller, Klancy. ★*For the Culture*	641.59
Raiford, Matthew. *Bress 'N' Nyam*	641.59

AFRICAN AMERICAN FASHION DESIGNERS

Day, Daniel R. *Dapper Dan*	B

AFRICAN AMERICAN FASHION MODELS

Givhan, Robin. *The Battle of Versailles*	746.9

AFRICAN AMERICAN FEMINISM

Briggs, Lyvonne. ★*Sensual Faith*	204
Jackson, Jenn M. ★*Black Women Taught Us*	305.48
Tinsley, Omise'eke Natasha. *Beyonce in Formation*	782.42164

AFRICAN AMERICAN FICTION

Hansberry, Lorraine. ★*A Raisin in the Sun*	812

AFRICAN AMERICAN FILM PRODUCERS AND DIRECTORS

McGilligan, Patrick. *Oscar Micheaux*	B

AFRICAN AMERICAN FOOTBALL PLAYERS

Melvin, Leland. *Chasing Space*	B
Pearlman, Jeff. *Sweetness*	B

AFRICAN AMERICAN GANGS

Brown, Claude. *Manchild in the Promised Land*	B

AFRICAN AMERICAN GAY MEN

Arceneaux, Michael. *I Finally Bought Some Jordans*	306.76
Broome, Brian. ★*Punch Me up to the Gods*	B
Duberman, Martin B. *Hold Tight Gently*	920
Gerald, Casey. *There Will Be No Miracles Here*	B
Mullen, Bill. ★*James Baldwin*	B
Porter, Billy. ★*Unprotected*	B
Shakur, Prince. *When They Tell You to Be Good*	B
Thomas, R. Eric. ★*Congratulations, the Best Is Over!*	B
Thomas, R. Eric. *Here for It*	B

AFRICAN AMERICAN HISTORY

Baker, Calvin. *A More Perfect Reunion*	305.800973
Ball, Edward. *Slaves in the Family*	975.7
Berlin, Ira. *The Making of African America*	973
Berry, Daina Ramey. ★*A Black Women's History of the United States*	305.48
Blackmon, Douglas A. *Slavery by Another Name*	305.896
Bond, Julian. ★*Julian Bond's Time to Teach*	323.0975
Boyd, Herb. *We Shall Overcome*	323.1196
Boyle, Kevin. *Arc of Justice*	345.73
Branch, Taylor. ★*At Canaan's Edge*	323.1196
Brazile, Donna. *For Colored Girls Who Have Considered Politics*	328.73
Colaiaco, James A. *Frederick Douglass and the Fourth of July*	973.7
Cox, Anna-Lisa. *The Bone and Sinew of the Land*	977
Crump, Benjamin. *Open Season*	364
Davis, Thomas J. *History of African Americans*	973
Douglass, Frederick. ★*Frederick Douglass*	973.8
Douglass, Frederick. *The Portable Frederick Douglass*	973.8
Dunbar, Erica Armstrong. ★*Never Caught*	B
Egerton, Douglas R. *Thunder at the Gates*	973.7
Ellison, Ralph. ★*The Collected Essays of Ralph Ellison*	814
Else, Jon. *True South*	305.800973
Euchner, Charles C. *Nobody Turn Me Around*	975.3
Finney, Nikky. *Love Child's Hotbed of Occasional Poetry*	811
Fischer, David Hackett. ★*African Founders*	973
Foner, Eric. ★*Gateway to Freedom*	973.7
Foner, Eric. ★*Reconstruction*	973.8
Ford, Tanisha C. *Dressed in Dreams*	391
Ford, Tanisha C. *Our Secret Society*	B
Franklin, John Hope. ★*From Slavery to Freedom*	973
Gates, Henry Louis. *100 Amazing Facts About the Negro*	973
Gates, Henry Louis. *The Black Box*	908
Gates, Henry Louis. ★*Life Upon These Shores*	973
Gates, Henry Louis. ★*Stony the Road*	973
Gill, Jonathan. *Harlem*	974.7
Goldstone, Lawrence. *On Account of Race*	342.7308
Grant, Gail Milissa. *At the Elbows of My Elders*	B
Greenidge, Kerri. *Black Radical*	B
Gregory, Dick. *Defining Moments in Black History*	973
Halberstam, David. ★*The Children*	323.1
Hall, Alvin D. *Driving the Green Book*	917.304

Harriot, Michael. ★*Black AF History*	973
Harris, M. A. *The Black Book*	920
Hirsch, James S. *Riot and Remembrance*	976.6
Hurston, Zora Neale. ★*Barracoon*	B
Jackson, Jenn M. ★*Black Women Taught Us*	305.48
Jackson, Troy. *Becoming King*	B
Jones, Jacqueline. *Saving Savannah*	975.8
Kennedy, Kostya. *True*	B
King, Coretta Scott. ★*My Life, My Love, My Legacy*	B
King, Martin Luther. *The Autobiography of Martin Luther King, Jr.*	B
Kotz, Nick. *Judgment Days*	323
Langguth, A. J. *After Lincoln*	973.8
Lemann, Nicholas. *Redemption*	975
Lepore, Jill. *New York Burning*	974.7
Levine, Bruce C. *Thaddeus Stevens*	B
Lewis, David L. ★*W.E.B. Du Bois*	B
Lomax, Alan. ★*The Land Where the Blues Began*	781.643
Lusane, Clarence. *The Black History of the White House*	975.3
Luxenberg, Steve. ★*Separate*	342.7308
Madigan, Tim. *The Burning*	976.6
Masur, Kate. *Until Justice Be Done*	323.1196
McGill, Joseph. *Sleeping with the Ancestors*	306.362
McWhorter, Diane. *Carry Me Home*	976.1
Ortiz, Paul. *An African American and Latinx History of the United States*	305.8
Person, Charles. *Buses Are a Comin'*	B
Pinn, Anthony B. *The Black Practice of Disbelief*	211
Plant, Deborah G. *Of Greed and Glory*	326
Proenza-Coles, Christina. *American Founders*	973
Rae, Noel. ★*The Great Stain*	306.3
Raines, Ben. *The Last Slave Ship*	306.362
Risen, Clay. *The Bill of the Century*	342.7308
Smith, Tracy K. ★*To Free the Captives*	818
Sullivan, Patricia. *Lift Every Voice*	973
Theoharis, Jeanne. *A More Beautiful and Terrible History*	323.1196
Tubbs, Anna Malaika. *The Three Mothers*	306.874
Twitty, Michael. ★*Koshersoul*	641.5
Tye, Larry. ★*The Jazzmen*	781.6509
Van Meter, Matthew. *Deep Delta Justice*	345.763
Ward, Andrew. ★*The Slaves' War*	973.7
Watson, Bruce. *Freedom Summer*	323.1196
Weiner, Mark Stuart. *Black Trials*	342.7308
Whitaker, Mark. *Saying It Loud*	973.923
Wilkerson, Isabel. ★*The Warmth of Other Suns*	304.80973
Wilkins, Robert L. *Long Road to Hard Truth*	069
Williams, Juan. *Eyes on the Prize*	323.4
Williams, Juan. *I'll Find a Way or Make One*	378.73
Williams, Juan. *This Far by Faith*	200
Willis, Deborah. *Envisioning Emancipation*	973.7
Wilson, August. *Fences*	812
Woodward, C. Vann. *The Strange Career of Jim Crow*	305.896
Young, R. J. *Requiem for the Massacre*	305.8

AFRICAN AMERICAN INTELLECTUALS

Bell-Scott, Patricia. *The Firebrand and the First Lady*	920
Gates, Henry Louis. *The Future of the Race*	305.896
Lewis, David L. ★*W.E.B. Du Bois*	B
Painter, Nell Irvin. *Old in Art School*	B
Stewart, Jeffrey C. ★*The New Negro*	191
Wilderson, Frank B. *Afropessimism*	B

AFRICAN AMERICAN JAZZ MUSICIANS

Armstrong, Louis. *Louis Armstrong, in His Own Words*	B
Brothers, Thomas David. ★*Louis Armstrong, Master of Modernism*	B
Chinen, Nate. *Playing Changes*	781.6509
Kaplan, James. *3 Shades of Blue*	920
Teachout, Terry. *Duke*	B
Teachout, Terry. *Pops*	B
Tye, Larry. ★*The Jazzmen*	781.6509
Ward, Geoffrey C. *Jazz*	781.6509

AFRICAN AMERICAN JOCKEYS

Drape, Joe. *Black Maestro*	B

AFRICAN AMERICAN JOURNALISTS

Cardwell, Diane. *Rockaway*	B
Greenidge, Kerri. *Black Radical*	B

AFRICAN AMERICAN JUDGES

Brown-Nagin, Tomiko. *Civil Rights Queen*	B
Forman, James. *Locking up Our Own*	364.973
Gibson, Larry S. *Young Thurgood*	B
Haygood, Wil. *Showdown*	B

AUTHOR, TITLE, SERIES AND SUBJECT INDEX

Robin, Corey. *The Enigma of Clarence Thomas*	347.73
Starks, Glenn L. *Thurgood Marshall*	B
Williams, Juan. *Thurgood Marshall*	B

AFRICAN AMERICAN LAWYERS

Adams, Jarrett. *Redeeming Justice*	340.092
Crump, Benjamin. *Open Season*	364
Jackson, Bruce. *Never Far from Home*	B
Obama, Michelle. ★*Becoming*	B
Rosen, Richard A. *Julius Chambers*	B
Rosenberg, Rosalind. ★*Jane Crow*	B

AFRICAN AMERICAN LEADERSHIP

Gates, Henry Louis. *The Future of the Race*	305.896
Sanders, Chad. *Black Magic*	305.896

AFRICAN AMERICAN LEGISLATORS

Abrams, Stacey. *Lead from the Outside*	B
Arsenault, Raymond. *John Lewis*	B
Cummings, Elijah. ★*We're Better Than This*	B
Dray, Philip. *Capitol Men*	973.8
Katz, David. *Barack Before Obama*	B
Lewis, John. ★*Run; Book One*	741.5
Lewis, John. *Walking with the Wind*	B
Lineberry, Cate. *Be Free or Die*	B
Obama, Barack. ★*The Audacity of Hope*	B
Obama, Barack. ★*Dreams from My Father*	B
Sellers, Bakari. *My Vanishing Country*	B

AFRICAN AMERICAN LESBIANS

Carruthers, Charlene A. *Unapologetic*	305.48

AFRICAN AMERICAN MAYORS

Tubbs, Michael. *The Deeper the Roots*	B

AFRICAN AMERICAN MEN

Anthony, Carmelo. *Where Tomorrows Aren't Promised*	B
Arceneaux, Michael. *I Finally Bought Some Jordans*	306.76
Ashley, Maurice. *Move by Move*	158
Babb, Valerie Melissa. *The Book of James*	B
Baime, A. J. *White Lies*	B
Bamberger, Michael. *The Second Life of Tiger Woods*	B
Barron, Justine. *They Killed Freddie Gray*	363.32
Bell, Darrin. ★*The Talk*	741.5
Benedict, Jeff. ★*Tiger Woods*	B
Bergner, Daniel. ★*Sing for Your Life*	B
Black Thought. *The Upcycled Self*	B
Brown, Claude. *Manchild in the Promised Land*	B
Butler, Paul. *Chokehold*	363.2
Clemmons, Francois S. *Officer Clemmons*	B
Coates, Ta-Nehisi. ★*Between the World and Me*	305.800973
Conyers, Jonathan. *I Wasn't Supposed to Be Here*	B
Cooper, Christian. *Better Living Through Birding*	B
Dennis, David J., Jr. *The Movement Made Us*	B
Dunn, Harry. *Standing My Ground*	B
Eig, Jonathan. ★*King*	B
Fleming, Brandon P. *Miseducated*	B
Garrett, Kent. *The Last Negroes at Harvard*	920
Grandmaster Flash. *The Adventures of Grandmaster Flash*	B
Harlan, Louis R. *Booker T. Washington*	B
Hart, Kevin. *I Can't Make This Up*	B
Hobbs, Jeff. ★*The Short and Tragic Life of Robert Peace*	920
Ice-T. *Split Decision*	B
Jackson, Ted. ★*You Ought to Do a Story About Me*	B
Jawando, Will. ★*My Seven Black Fathers*	B
Keith, Philip A. *All Blood Runs Red*	B
Kweli, Talib. *Vibrate Higher*	B
Laymon, Kiese. *How to Slowly Kill Yourself and Others in America*	814.6
Leovy, Jill. *Ghettoside*	364.152
Lineberry, Cate. *Be Free or Die*	B
Makos, Adam. *Devotion*	920
Manuel, Ian. *My Time Will Come*	B
McBride, James. *The Color of Water*	B
McPhee, John. *Levels of the Game*	796.34
Merritt, Tyler. *I Take My Coffee Black*	791.4302
Moore, Marcus J. *The Butterfly Effect*	B
Moore, Wes. *The Work*	B
Norrell, Robert J. *Up from History*	B
Oluseyi, Hakeem M. *A Quantum Life*	B
Ross, Dax-Devlon. *Letters to My White Male Friends*	305.8
Samuels, Robert. ★*His Name Is George Floyd*	B
Shane, Scott. ★*Flee North*	973.7
Sheff, David. *The Buddhist on Death Row*	B
Smith, Kenny. *Talk of Champions*	B
Smith, Mychal Denzel. *Invisible Man, Got the Whole World Watching*	305.242
Smith, Will. ★*Will*	B
Taibbi, Matt. *I Can't Breathe*	363.2
Thomas, Franklin A. *An Unplanned Life*	B
Vella, Christina. *George Washington Carver*	B
Ward, Jesmyn. ★*Men We Reaped*	B
Williams, Billy Dee. ★*What Have We Here*	B
Wilson, August. *King Hedley II*	812
Wilson, Chris. *The Master Plan*	B

AFRICAN AMERICAN MILLIONAIRES

White, Shane. *Prince of Darkness*	B

AFRICAN AMERICAN MOTHERS

Tubbs, Anna Malaika. *The Three Mothers*	306.874

AFRICAN AMERICAN MUSIC

Ferris, William R. *Give My Poor Heart Ease*	781.643
Komunyakaa, Yusef. ★*Everyday Mojo Songs of Earth*	811
Marovich, Robert M. *A City Called Heaven*	782.25
McNally, Dennis. *On Highway 61*	781.64
Powers, Ann. *Good Booty*	781.64
Ribowsky, Mark. *The Supremes*	B
White, Adam. ★*Motown*	781.644

AFRICAN AMERICAN MUSICIANS

Ashon, Will. *Chamber Music*	782.421649
Bego, Mark. *Aretha Franklin*	B
Friedwald, Will. *Straighten up and Fly Right*	782.42164
Gray, Michael. *Hand Me My Travelin' Shoes*	B
Greenman, Ben. *Dig If You Will the Picture*	B
Iandoli, Kathy. *Baby Girl*	B
Marovich, Robert M. *A City Called Heaven*	782.25
McBride, James. *Kill 'Em and Leave*	B
McCormick, Mack. *Biography of a Phantom*	782.421643
Moore, Marcus J. *The Butterfly Effect*	B
Murray, Charles Shaar. *Crosstown Traffic*	B
Norman, Philip. ★*Wild Thing*	B
Robinson, Staci. ★*Tupac Shakur*	B
Stone, Sly. *Thank You (Falettinme Be Mice Elf Agin)*	B
White, Richard Antoine. *I'm Possible*	B
Wood, Damon. *Working for the Man, Playing in the Band*	782.42164

AFRICAN AMERICAN NEIGHBORHOODS

Chatelain, Marcia. ★*Franchise*	339
Ellsworth, Scott. *The Ground Breaking*	976.6
Ewing, Eve L. *Ghosts in the Schoolyard*	370.89
Hansberry, Lorraine. ★*A Raisin in the Sun*	812
Jackson, Mitchell S. *Survival Math*	B
Luckerson, Victor. *Built from the Fire*	976.6
Samaha, Albert. *Never Ran, Never Will*	920
Wilson, August. *Two Trains Running*	812

AFRICAN AMERICAN NURSES

Smilios, Maria. ★*The Black Angels*	610.73

AFRICAN AMERICAN PAINTERS

Rembert, Winfred. *Chasing Me to My Grave*	B

AFRICAN AMERICAN PARENT AND CHILD

Kendi, Ibram X. ★*How to Raise an Antiracist*	649

AFRICAN AMERICAN PARENTS

Austin, Nefertiti. *Motherhood so White*	B

AFRICAN AMERICAN PHOTOGRAPHERS

Lauterbach, Preston. *Bluff City*	B
Willis, Deborah. *Reflections in Black*	770

AFRICAN AMERICAN PHYSICIANS

Brown, Jasmine. *Twice as Hard*	610.92

AFRICAN AMERICAN PILOTS

Keith, Philip A. *All Blood Runs Red*	B

AFRICAN AMERICAN PLAYWRIGHTS

Hartigan, Patti. *August Wilson*	B
Nemiroff, Robert. *To Be Young, Gifted, and Black*	B
Perry, Imani. *Looking for Lorraine*	B
Shields, Charles J. *Lorraine Hansberry*	B

AFRICAN AMERICAN POETRY

Alexander, Elizabeth. *Crave Radiance*	811
Alexander, Will. *Refractive Africa*	811
Angelou, Maya. *The Complete Poetry*	811
Baraka, Amiri. *S O S*	811
Betts, Reginald Dwayne. *Felon*	811
Brooks, Gwendolyn. ★*The Essential Gwendolyn Brooks*	811
Brooks, Gwendolyn. *In Montgomery, and Other Poems*	811
Browne, Mahogany L. ★*Black Girl Magic*	811.6
Dove, Rita. *Playlist for the Apocalypse*	811

PUBLIC LIBRARY CORE COLLECTION: NONFICTION
Twentieth Edition

Dove, Rita. ★*Selected Poems*	811
Dove, Rita. *Sonata Mulattica*	811
Ellis, Thomas Sayers. *Skin, Inc.*	811
Ferlinghetti, Lawrence. *These Are My Rivers*	811
Giovanni, Nikki. ★*The Collected Poetry of Nikki Giovanni, 1968-1998*	811
Giovanni, Nikki. *A Good Cry*	811
Girmay, Aracelis. *The Black Maria*	811
Hacker, Marilyn. *Selected Poems, 1965-1990*	811
Hayden, Robert. *Collected Poems*	811
Hayes, Terrance. *How to Be Drawn*	811
Hayes, Terrance. ★*Lighthead*	811
Hayes, Terrance. *So to Speak*	811
Hughes, Langston. ★*Selected Poems of Langston Hughes*	811
Jackson, Major. *Razzle Dazzle*	811
Johnson, James Weldon. *Complete Poems*	811
Jones, Saeed. *Prelude to Bruise*	811
Keene, John. ★*Punks*	811
Komunyakaa, Yusef. *Warhorses*	811
Lewis, Robin Coste. *To the Realization of Perfect Helplessness*	811
Mackey, Nathaniel. *Splay Anthem*	811
Pardlo, Gregory. *Spectral Evidence*	811
Parker, Morgan. *There Are More Beautiful Things Than Beyonce*	811
Reed, Justin Phillip. *Indecency*	811
Shockley, Evie. *The New Black*	811
Shockley, Evie. *Semiautomatic*	811
Shockley, Evie. *Suddenly We*	811
Smith, Clint. ★*Above Ground*	811
Smith, Patricia. ★*Incendiary Art*	811.54
Smith, Patricia. *Shoulda Been Jimi Savannah*	811
Smith, Tracy K. *Duende*	811
Smith, Tracy K. ★*Life on Mars*	811
Walker, Alice. *Hard Times Require Furious Dancing*	811
Wheatley, Phillis. *The Poems of Phillis Wheatley*	811
Wicker, Marcus. *Silencer*	811
Young, Kevin. *Book of Hours*	811

AFRICAN AMERICAN POETS

Clifton, Lucille. *Mercy*	811
Hartigan, Patti. *August Wilson*	B
Hughes, Langston. ★*I Wonder as I Wander*	B
Jackson, Angela. *A Surprised Queenhood in the New Black Sun*	B
Mouton, Deborah D. E. E. P. *Black Chameleon*	B
Phillips, Carl. ★*Then the War*	811
Rampersad, Arnold. *The Life of Langston Hughes*	B
Rampersad, Arnold. ★*The Life of Langston Hughes*	B
Waldstreicher, David. *The Odyssey of Phillis Wheatley*	B

AFRICAN AMERICAN POLICE

Forman, James. *Locking up Our Own*	364.973
Horace, Matthew. *The Black and the Blue*	B

AFRICAN AMERICAN POLITICAL ACTIVISTS

Holley, Santi Elijah. *An Amerikan Family*	920
Robeson, Paul. *The Undiscovered Paul Robeson*	B
Shakur, Prince. *When They Tell You to Be Good*	B
Sharpton, Al. *Rise Up*	973.933
Whitaker, Mark. ★*Saying It Loud*	973.923
Wilderson, Frank B. *Afropessimism*	B

AFRICAN AMERICAN POLITICIANS

Arsenault, Raymond. *John Lewis*	B
Brazile, Donna. *For Colored Girls Who Have Considered Politics*	328.73
Cummings, Elijah. ★*We're Better Than This*	B
Dray, Philip. *Capitol Men*	973.8
Forman, James. *Locking up Our Own*	364.973
Lewis, John. *Carry On*	328.73
Meacham, Jon. *His Truth Is Marching On*	B
Obama, Barack. ★*A Promised Land*	B
Remnick, David. *The Bridge*	B
Sharpton, Al. *Rise Up*	973.933
Tubbs, Michael. *The Deeper the Roots*	B

AFRICAN AMERICAN PRESIDENTIAL CANDIDATES

Katz, David. *Barack Before Obama*	B

AFRICAN AMERICAN PRISONERS

Alexander, Michelle. *The New Jim Crow*	364.973
Blackmon, Douglas A. *Slavery by Another Name*	305.896
Hale, Grace Elizabeth. *In the Pines*	364.13
Moore, Wes. *The Other Wes Moore*	B
Rembert, Winfred. *Chasing Me to My Grave*	B
Woodfox, Albert. *Solitary*	B
Zerwick, Phoebe. *Beyond Innocence*	347

AFRICAN AMERICAN PSYCHOLOGISTS

Spofford, Tim. *What the Children Told Us*	150.92

AFRICAN AMERICAN QUILTS

Tobin, Jacqueline. *Hidden in Plain View*	973.7

AFRICAN AMERICAN RADICALS

Greenidge, Kerri. *Black Radical*	B

AFRICAN AMERICAN RAP MUSICIANS

Ghostface Killah. *Rise of a Killah*	B
Grandmaster Flash. *The Adventures of Grandmaster Flash*	B
Hope, Clover. *The Motherlode*	920

AFRICAN AMERICAN REVOLUTIONARIES

Holley, Santi Elijah. *An Amerikan Family*	920

AFRICAN AMERICAN ROCK MUSICIANS

Greenman, Ben. *Dig If You Will the Picture*	B
Mahon, Maureen. ★*Black Diamond Queens*	782.421
Murray, Charles Shaar. *Crosstown Traffic*	B

AFRICAN AMERICAN SCHOLARS

Gates, Henry Louis. *Colored People*	B

AFRICAN AMERICAN SCIENTISTS

Alexander, Stephon. *Fear of a Black Universe*	523.1
Graham, Jasmin. *Sharks Don't Sink*	597.3
Vella, Christina. *George Washington Carver*	B

AFRICAN AMERICAN SHARECROPPERS

Simmons, Ruth. ★*Up Home*	B

AFRICAN AMERICAN SINGERS

Alexander, Paul. *Bitter Crop*	B
Belafonte, Harry. ★*My Song*	782.42164
Bogle, Donald. *Heat Wave*	782.42164
Cohodas, Nadine. *Princess Noire*	782.42164
Gaye, Jan. *After the Dance*	B
Keiler, Allan. *Marian Anderson*	B
Neville, Aaron. *Tell It Like It Is*	B
Ribowsky, Mark. *Signed, Sealed, and Delivered*	B
Robeson, Paul. *The Undiscovered Paul Robeson*	B
Smith, Danyel. *Shine Bright*	782.42164
Stone, Sly. *Thank You (Falettinme Be Mice Elf Agin)*	B

AFRICAN AMERICAN SINGLE MOTHERS

Austin, Nefertiti. *Motherhood so White*	B

AFRICAN AMERICAN SISTERS

Delany, Sarah Louise. *Having Our Say*	B

AFRICAN AMERICAN SOCIAL ADVOCATES

Adams, Jarrett. *Redeeming Justice*	340.092
Burke, Tarana. ★*Unbound*	B
Theoharis, Jeanne. *The Rebellious Life of Mrs. Rosa Parks*	B

AFRICAN AMERICAN SOLDIERS

Ash, Stephen V. *Firebrand of Liberty*	973.7
Blight, David W. *A Slave No More*	B
Delmont, Matthew F. *Half American*	940.54
Egerton, Douglas R. *Thunder at the Gates*	973.7
Foner, Eric. *Forever Free*	973.8
Hervieux, Linda. *Forgotten*	940.54
Manning, Chandra. *Troubled Refuge*	973.7
O'Donnell, Patrick K. *The Indispensables*	973.3
Taylor, Alan. ★*The Internal Enemy*	975.5
Tuccille, Jerome. *The Roughest Riders*	973.8
Ward, Andrew. ★*The Slaves' War*	973.7
Willis, Deborah. ★*The Black Civil War Soldier*	973.7

AFRICAN AMERICAN STUDENTS

Halberstam, David. ★*The Children*	323.1
Margolick, David. *Elizabeth and Hazel*	379.2
Martin, Rachel Louise. *A Most Tolerant Little Town*	379.2

AFRICAN AMERICAN TEACHERS

Walker, Vanessa Siddle. *The Lost Education of Horace Tate*	370.92

AFRICAN AMERICAN TEENAGERS

Brown, Claude. *Manchild in the Promised Land*	B
Browne, Mahogany L. ★*Black Girl Magic*	811.6
Ford, Ashley C. ★*Somebody's Daughter*	B
Moore, Wes. *The Other Wes Moore*	B
Samaha, Albert. *Never Ran, Never Will*	920
Tatum, Beverly Daniel. ★*"Why Are All the Black Kids Sitting Together in the Cafeteria?"*	305.800973
Williams, Mary. *The Lost Daughter*	B

AFRICAN AMERICAN TENNIS PLAYERS

McPhee, John. *Levels of the Game*	796.34

AFRICAN AMERICAN UNIVERSITIES AND COLLEGES

Harris, Adam. ★*The State Must Provide*	379.2
Williams, Juan. *I'll Find a Way or Make One*	378.73

AUTHOR, TITLE, SERIES AND SUBJECT INDEX

AFRICAN AMERICAN WOMEN
Alexander, Paul. *Bitter Crop* — B
Alvis-Walker, Marcie. *Everybody Come Alive* — B
Bailey, Jennifer. *To My Beloveds* — 261.8
Barnett, Brittany K. ★*A Knock at Midnight* — B
Beauvais, Garcelle. *Love Me as I Am* — B
Bernard, Emily. *Black Is the Body* — 305.48
Berry, Daina Ramey. ★*A Black Women's History of the United States* — 305.48
Blay, Zeba. *Carefree Black Girls* — 305.48
Bogle, Donald. *Heat Wave* — 782.42164
Bowen, Sesali. *Bad Fat Black Girl* — 305.42
Bradford, Joy Harden. *Sisterhood Heals* — 158.2
Brazile, Donna. *For Colored Girls Who Have Considered Politics* — 328.73
Briggs, Lyvonne. ★*Sensual Faith* — 204
Browne, Mahogany L. ★*Black Girl Magic* — 811.6
Brunson, Quinta. *She Memes Well* — B
Burke, Tarana. ★*Unbound* — B
Busby, Jill Louise. *Unfollow Me* — 305.08
Byas, Taylor. *I Done Clicked My Heels Three Times* — 811
Carruthers, Charlene A. *Unapologetic* — 305.48
Carter, Ruth E. ★*The Art of Ruth E. Carter* — 746.9
Cleveland, Pat. *Walking with the Muses* — B
Clifton, Lucille. *How to Carry Water* — 811
Clinton, Catherine. *Harriet Tubman* — B
Cobbs-Leonard, Tasha. *Do It Anyway* — 241
Davis, Viola. ★*Finding Me* — B
Delany, Sarah Louise. *Having Our Say* — B
Derricotte, Toi. *I* — 811
DuBois, Ellen Carol. *Suffrage* — 324.6
Dunbar, Erica Armstrong. ★*She Came to Slay* — B
Dungy, Camille T. *Soil* — 635.0978
Emberton, Carole. *To Walk About in Freedom* — 306.3
Fabre, Cin. *Wolf Hustle* — 332.6
Felix, Camonghne. *Dyscalculia* — B
Fields-Black, Edda L. *Combee* — 973.7
Finney, Nikky. *Love Child's Hotbed of Occasional Poetry* — 811
Ford, Ashley C. ★*Somebody's Daughter* — B
Ford, Tanisha C. *Dressed in Dreams* — 391
Ford, Tanisha C. *Our Secret Society* — B
Fumudoh, Ziwe. ★*Black Friend* — 814
Gavin, James. ★*Stormy Weather* — 782.42164
Giddings, Paula. *Ida* — B
Gilliam, Dorothy Butler. *Trailblazer* — B
Giovanni, Nikki. *Quilting the Black-Eyed Pea* — 811
Goldberg, Whoopi. *Bits and Pieces* — B
Griffin, Farah Jasmine. ★*In Search of a Beautiful Freedom* — 814
Haddish, Tiffany. *The Last Black Unicorn* — B
Hall, Rebecca. ★*Wake* — 741.5
Harris, Taylor. *This Boy We Made* — B
Hecimovich, Gregg A. ★*The Life and Times of Hannah Crafts* — B
Henny, Ally. *I Won't Shut Up* — 305.896
Henson, Taraji P. *Around the Way Girl* — B
Hill, DaMaris B. *Breath Better Spent* — 811
Hill, Jemele. *Uphill* — B
hooks, bell. *Remembered Rapture* — 808
hooks, bell. *Wounds of Passion* — B
Hubbard, Shanita. ★*Ride-Or-Die* — 305.48
Humez, Jean McMahon. *Harriet Tubman* — B
Hurston, Zora Neale. *Dust Tracks on a Road* — B
Iandoli, Kathy. *Baby Girl* — B
Irby, Samantha. ★*Quietly Hostile* — 814
Irby, Samantha. *We Are Never Meeting in Real Life* — 814
Jackson, Angela. *A Surprised Queenhood in the New Black Sun* — B
Jackson, Jenn M. ★*Black Women Taught Us* — 305.48
Jacobs, Harriet. ★*Incidents in the Life of a Slave Girl* — B
Jacobs, Sally H. *Althea* — B
Jarrett, Valerie. *Finding My Voice* — B
Jefferson, Margo. *Negroland* — 305.896
Johnson, Katherine G. *My Remarkable Journey* — B
Johnson, Stephanie. *Tanquerey* — B
Jones, Brenda. *Maxine Waters* — B
King, Chrissy. *The Body Liberation Project* — 306.4
King, Coretta Scott. ★*My Life, My Love, My Legacy* — B
Larson, Kate Clifford. *Bound for the Promised Land* — B
Levin, Josh. *The Queen* — 364.16
Lewis, Damien. *Agent Josephine* — B
Lorde, Audre. ★*The Selected Works of Audre Lorde* — 814
Lorde, Audre. *Sister Outsider* — 814
Mahon, Maureen. ★*Black Diamond Queens* — 782.421
Malone, Sharon. *Grown Woman Talk* — 362.1
Mans, Jasmine. *Black Girl, Call Home* — 811
Marshall, Cynthia. *You've Been Chosen* — B
Miles, Tiya. ★*Night Flyer* — B
Miles, Tiya. ★*Wild Girls* — 304.2
Mock, Janet. *Surpassing Certainty* — B
Morris, James McGrath. *Eye on the Struggle* — B
Mouton, Deborah D. E. E. P. *Black Chameleon* — B
Muhammad, Ibtihaj. *Proud* — B
Nathans, Sydney. *To Free a Family* — B
Obama, Michelle. ★*Becoming* — B
Obama, Michelle. ★*The Light We Carry* — B
Parker, Morgan. ★*You Get What You Pay For* — 305.896
Perkins, Nichole. *Sometimes I Trip on How Happy We Could Be* — B
Perry, Imani. *Looking for Lorraine* — B
Perry, Imani. ★*South to America* — 917
Petrosino, Kiki. *White Blood* — 811
Prescod, Danielle. *Token Black Girl* — B
Raboteau, Emily. *Lessons for Survival* — 814
Rice, Condoleezza. *Extraordinary, Ordinary People* — B
Rice, Condoleezza. *No Higher Honor* — B
Robinson, Phoebe. *Please Don't Sit on My Bed in Your Outside Clothes* — 818
Robinson, Phoebe. *You Can't Touch My Hair and Other Things I Still Have to Explain* — 792.7
Roundtree, Dovey Johnson. ★*Mighty Justice* — B
Ruffin, Amber. *You'll Never Believe What Happened to Lacey* — 305.896
Savage, Jodi M. *The Death of a Jaybird* — B
Shange, Ntozake. ★*Sing a Black Girl's Song* — 818
Shetterly, Margot Lee. ★*Hidden Figures* — 510.92
Shields, Aomawa L. *Life on Other Planets* — B
Shields, Charles J. *Lorraine Hansberry* — B
Simmons, Ruth. ★*Up Home* — B
Skloot, Rebecca. ★*The Immortal Life of Henrietta Lacks* — B
Slevin, Peter. *Michelle Obama* — B
Smilios, Maria. ★*The Black Angels* — 610.73
Smith, Jada Pinkett. *Worthy* — B
Strings, Sabrina. *The End of Love* — 155.3
Taylor, Goldie. *The Love You Save* — B
Tinsley, Omise'eke Natasha. *Beyonce in Formation* — 782.42164
Trice, Dawn Turner. ★*Three Girls from Bronzeville* — 977.311
Tubbs, Anna Malaika. *The Three Mothers* — 306.874
Tyson, Cicely. ★*Just as I Am* — B
Union, Gabrielle. *We're Going to Need More Wine* — B
Valby, Karen. *The Swans of Harlem* — 792.8
Verdelle, A. J. *Miss Chloe* — B
Washington, Kerry. *Thicker Than Water* — B
Watts, Jill. *Hattie McDaniel* — B
White, Gayle Jessup. *Reclamation* — B
Wilkinson, Crystal. *Praisesong for the Kitchen Ghosts* — 641.5975
Williams, Bari A. *Seen yet Unseen* — 338.4
Willis, Raquel. *The Risk It Takes to Bloom* — B
Wilson, A'ja. ★*Dear Black Girls* — 158.1
Wilson, Jessica. *It's Always Been Ours* — 613
Wynn-Grant, Rae. *Wild Life* — B
Zack, Ian. *Odetta* — B

AFRICAN AMERICAN WOMEN ABOLITIONISTS
Dunbar, Erica Armstrong. ★*She Came to Slay* — B

AFRICAN AMERICAN WOMEN ARTISTS
Farrington, Lisa E. *Creating Their Own Image* — 704
Painter, Nell Irvin. *Old in Art School* — B

AFRICAN AMERICAN WOMEN AUTHORS
Angelou, Maya. ★*I Know Why the Caged Bird Sings* — B
Angelou, Maya. *A Song Flung up to Heaven* — B
Broom, Sarah M. *The Yellow House* — B
Carroll, Rebecca. *Surviving the White Gaze* — B
Hecimovich, Gregg A. ★*The Life and Times of Hannah Crafts* — B
Henderson, Danielle. ★*The Ugly Cry* — B
Hurston, Zora Neale. *Zora Neale Hurston* — B
Ikpi, Bassey. *I'm Telling the Truth, but I'm Lying* — 814
Jeffers, Honorée Fanonne. *The Age of Phillis* — 811
Jerkins, Morgan. *Wandering in Strange Lands* — 305.896
Perkins, Nichole. *Sometimes I Trip on How Happy We Could Be* — B
Smith, Tracy K. ★*To Free the Captives* — 818
Verdelle, A. J. *Miss Chloe* — B
Walker, Alice. *Gathering Blossoms Under Fire* — B
Ward, Jesmyn. ★*Men We Reaped* — B
Wilkinson, Crystal. *Praisesong for the Kitchen Ghosts* — 641.5975

PUBLIC LIBRARY CORE COLLECTION: NONFICTION
Twentieth Edition

AFRICAN AMERICAN WOMEN CABINET OFFICERS
  Rice, Condoleezza. *Extraordinary, Ordinary People* — B
  Rice, Condoleezza. *No Higher Honor* — B

AFRICAN AMERICAN WOMEN CIVIL RIGHTS WORKERS
  Bell-Scott, Patricia. *The Firebrand and the First Lady* — 920
  Blain, Keisha N. *Until I Am Free* — B
  Brooks, Maegan Parker. *Fannie Lou Hamer* — B
  Giddings, Paula. *Ida* — B
  Perry, Imani. *Looking for Lorraine* — B
  Shields, Charles J. *Lorraine Hansberry* — B
  Theoharis, Jeanne. *The Rebellious Life of Mrs. Rosa Parks* — B

AFRICAN AMERICAN WOMEN COLLEGE TEACHERS
  Cottom, Tressie McMillan. *Thick* — 301

AFRICAN AMERICAN WOMEN COOKS
  Tipton-Martin, Toni. *The Jemima Code* — 641.59

AFRICAN AMERICAN WOMEN DANCERS
  Lewis, Damien. *Agent Josephine* — B

AFRICAN AMERICAN WOMEN DEFENSE ATTORNEYS
  Barnett, Brittany K. ★*A Knock at Midnight* — B

AFRICAN AMERICAN WOMEN EXECUTIVES
  Bundles, A'Lelia. *On Her Own Ground* — B

AFRICAN AMERICAN WOMEN JOURNALISTS
  Gilliam, Dorothy Butler. *Trailblazer* — B
  Welteroth, Elaine. *More Than Enough* — B

AFRICAN AMERICAN WOMEN LAWYERS
  Carter, Stephen L. *Invisible* — B
  Jarrett, Valerie. *Finding My Voice* — B
  Obama, Michelle. ★*Becoming* — B

AFRICAN AMERICAN WOMEN LEGISLATORS
  Andrews-Dyer, Helena. *Reclaiming Her Time* — B
  Jones, Brenda. *Maxine Waters* — B

AFRICAN AMERICAN WOMEN MUSICIANS
  Bego, Mark. *Aretha Franklin* — B
  Smith, Danyel. *Shine Bright* — 782.42164
  Turner, Tina. ★*Happiness Becomes You* — 158.1

AFRICAN AMERICAN WOMEN PHYSICIANS
  Brown, Jasmine. *Twice as Hard* — 610.92
  Harper, Michele. *The Beauty in Breaking* — B
  Malone, Sharon. *Grown Woman Talk* — 362.1

AFRICAN AMERICAN WOMEN POETS
  Giovanni, Nikki. ★*The Collected Poetry of Nikki Giovanni, 1968-1998* — 811
  Ikpi, Bassey. *I'm Telling the Truth, but I'm Lying* — 814
  Jackson, Angela. *A Surprised Queenhood in the New Black Sun* — B
  Waldstreicher, David. *The Odyssey of Phillis Wheatley* — B

AFRICAN AMERICAN WOMEN POLITICAL ACTIVISTS
  Berry, Mary Frances. *My Face Is Black Is True* — B
  Jackson, Jenn M. ★*Black Women Taught Us* — 305.48
  Painter, Nell Irvin. ★*Sojourner Truth* — B

AFRICAN AMERICAN WOMEN POLITICIANS
  Abrams, Stacey. *Lead from the Outside* — B
  Andrews-Dyer, Helena. *Reclaiming Her Time* — B
  Brazile, Donna. *For Colored Girls Who Have Considered Politics* — 328.73
  Jones, Brenda. *Maxine Waters* — B
  Rice, Condoleezza. *Extraordinary, Ordinary People* — B
  Rice, Condoleezza. *No Higher Honor* — B

AFRICAN AMERICAN WOMEN SINGERS
  Gavin, James. ★*Stormy Weather* — 782.42164
  Hope, Clover. *The Motherlode* — 920
  Keiler, Allan. *Marian Anderson* — B
  Ribowsky, Mark. *The Supremes* — B
  Tinsley, Omise'eke Natasha. *Beyonce in Formation* — 782.42164
  Williams, Michelle. *Checking In* — B
  Zack, Ian. *Odetta* — B

AFRICAN AMERICAN WOMEN SOCIAL REFORMERS
  Edelman, Marian Wright. *Lanterns* — 362.7
  Giddings, Paula. *Ida* — B
  Larson, Kate Clifford. *Walk with Me* — B

AFRICAN AMERICAN WORLD WAR II VETERANS
  Gergel, Richard. *Unexampled Courage* — 323.1196

AFRICAN AMERICAN YOUNG MEN
  Coates, Ta-Nehisi. *The Beautiful Struggle* — B
  Henning, Kristin. *The Rage of Innocence* — 364.36

AFRICAN AMERICAN-OWNED BUSINESSES
  Chatelain, Marcia. ★*Franchise* — 339
  Luckerson, Victor. *Built from the Fire* — 976.6
  Miller, Klancy. ★*For the Culture* — 641.59

AFRICAN AMERICANS
  Abdurraqib, Hanif. *A Fortune for Your Disaster* — 811

Adams, Michael Henry. *Style and Grace* — 747
Alexander, Elizabeth. ★*The Trayvon Generation* — 305.896
Alexander, Kwame. *Light for the World to See* — 811.6
Alexander, Michelle. *The New Jim Crow* — 364.973
Alvis-Walker, Marcie. *Everybody Come Alive* — B
Anderson, Carol. ★*One Person, No Vote* — 324.6
Arceneaux, Michael. *I Finally Bought Some Jordans* — 306.76
Armstrong, Jennifer Keishin. *When Women Invented Television* — 791.45
Asim, Jabari. *We Can't Breathe* — 305.896
Bader, Philip. *African-American Writers* — 810.9
Bailey, Issac J. *Why Didn't We Riot?* — 305.800973
Baldwin, James. ★*The Fire Next Time* — 305.896
Baldwin, James. ★*Notes of a Native Son* — 305.8
Baszile, Natalie. *We Are Each Other's Harvest* — 630.89
Bella, Timothy. *Barkley* — B
Bellows, Amanda Brickell. *The Explorers* — 910.92
Benedict, Jeff. *Lebron* — B
Berlin, Ira. *The Making of African America* — 973
Bernard, Emily. *Black Is the Body* — 305.48
Berry, Mary Frances. *My Face Is Black Is True* — B
Bethencourt, Kahran. *Glory* — 779.2
Betts, Reginald Dwayne. ★*Redaction* — 704.9
Blackmon, Douglas A. *Slavery by Another Name* — 305.896
Blain, Keisha N. *Until I Am Free* — B
Blay, Zeba. *Carefree Black Girls* — 305.48
Blight, David W. ★*Frederick Douglass* — B
Blight, David W. *A Slave No More* — B
Blount, Tommye. *Fantasia for the Man in Blue* — 811
Blum, Edward J. *The Color of Christ* — 232
Bogle, Donald. *Bright Boulevards, Bold Dreams* — 791.43
Boyd, Herb. *Black Detroit* — 977.4
Boykin, Keith. *Race Against Time* — 305.8
Boykin, Keith. ★*Why Does Everything Have to Be About Race?* — 305.8
Boyle, Kevin. *Arc of Justice* — 345.73
Brazile, Donna. *For Colored Girls Who Have Considered Politics* — 328.73
Brooks, Gwendolyn. *In Montgomery, and Other Poems* — 811
Brooks, Maegan Parker. *Fannie Lou Hamer* — B
Broom, Sarah M. *The Yellow House* — B
Brown, Austin Channing. ★*I'm Still Here* — B
Brown, Claude. *Manchild in the Promised Land* — B
Brown, Jericho. ★*The Tradition* — 811
Bundles, A'Lelia. *On Her Own Ground* — B
Canellos, Peter S. *The Great Dissenter* — B
Carroll, Rebecca. *Surviving the White Gaze* — B
Carter, Ruth E. ★*The Art of Ruth E. Carter* — 746.9
Clark, Tiana. *I Can't Talk About the Trees Without the Blood* — 811
Cleaver, Eldridge. *Soul on Ice* — B
Coates, Laura Gayle. *Just Pursuit* — 345.73
Coates, Ta-Nehisi. *The Beautiful Struggle* — B
Coates, Ta-Nehisi. ★*Between the World and Me* — 305.800973
Collins-Dexter, Brandi. *Black Skinhead* — 324.2734
Cottom, Tressie McMillan. *Thick* — 301
Cox, Anna-Lisa. *The Bone and Sinew of the Land* — 977
Cross, Tiffany D. ★*Say It Louder!* — 324.6
Crump, Benjamin. *Open Season* — 364
Currie, Elliott. *A Peculiar Indifference* — 305.800973
Davis, Thomas J. *History of African Americans* — 973
Deetz, Kelley Fanto. *Bound to the Fire* — 641.59
Delany, Sarah Louise. *Having Our Say* — B
Du Bois, W. E. B. *The Oxford W.E.B. Du Bois Reader* — 305.896
Du Bois, W. E. B. ★*The Souls of Black Folk* — 973
Du Bois, W. E. B. ★*Writings* — 973
Dungy, Camille T. *Soil* — 635.0978
Durkin, Hannah. ★*The Survivors of the Clotilda* — 306.362
Dyson, Michael Eric. *The Black Presidency* — 305.800973
Dyson, Michael Eric. *Come Hell or High Water* — 976.3
Dyson, Michael Eric. *Long Time Coming* — 305.800973
Dyson, Michael Eric. *Tears We Cannot Stop* — 305.800973
Dyson, Michael Eric. *What Truth Sounds Like* — 305.800973
Eig, Jonathan. ★*King* — B
Ellison, Ralph. ★*The Collected Essays of Ralph Ellison* — 814
Ellsworth, Scott. *The Ground Breaking* — 976.6
Evans, William. *Black Nerd Problems* — 814.6
Evanzz, Karl. *The Messenger* — B
Ewing, Eve L. *Ghosts in the Schoolyard* — 370.89
Fabre, Cin. *Wolf Hustle* — 332.6
Fenn, Lisa. *Carry On* — B
Ferris, William R. *Give My Poor Heart Ease* — 781.643

AUTHOR, TITLE, SERIES AND SUBJECT INDEX

Fischer, David Hackett. ★*African Founders*	973
Fisher, Thomas. ★*The Emergency*	362.1089
Flitter, Emily. *The White Wall*	332.0973
Foner, Eric. ★*Reconstruction*	973.8
Ford, Tanisha C. *Dressed in Dreams*	391
Foxx, Jamie. *Act Like You Got Some Sense*	B
Franklin, John Hope. *In Search of the Promised Land*	929
Gaddy, K. R. ★*Well of Souls*	787
Garrett, Kent. *The Last Negroes at Harvard*	920
Garrow, David J. *Rising Star*	B
Garza, Alicia. *The Purpose of Power*	303.48
Gates, Henry Louis. *And Still I Rise*	305.896
Gates, Henry Louis. *The Black Box*	908
Gates, Henry Louis. ★*The Black Church*	277
Gates, Henry Louis. *Colored People*	B
Gates, Henry Louis. *The Future of the Race*	305.896
Gates, Henry Louis. *In Search of Our Roots*	973
Gates, Henry Louis. ★*Life Upon These Shores*	973
Gates, Henry Louis. ★*Stony the Road*	973
Gayle, Caleb. *We Refuse to Forget*	975.004
Geter, Hafizah. *Un-American*	811
Giovanni, Nikki. *Make Me Rain*	811
Givens, Jarvis R. ★*School Clothes*	371.829
Glaude, Eddie S. *Begin Again*	305.800973
Goldstein, Nancy. *Jackie Ormes*	B
Goldstone, Lawrence. *On Account of Race*	342.7308
Gordon-Reed, Annette. *Andrew Johnson*	B
Gordon-Reed, Annette. ★*The Hemingses of Monticello*	920
Goudsouzian, Aram. *Sidney Poitier*	B
Grant, Gail Milissa. *At the Elbows of My Elders*	B
Greenburg, Zack O'Malley. *3 Kings*	782.421649
Greenidge, Kerri. *Black Radical*	B
Gregory, Dick. *Defining Moments in Black History*	973
Griffin, Chante. *Loving Your Black Neighbor as Yourself*	261
Griffin, Farah Jasmine. ★*In Search of a Beautiful Freedom*	814
Griffin, Farah Jasmine. *Read Until You Understand*	810.9
Haddish, Tiffany. *The Last Black Unicorn*	B
Hahn, Steven. *A Nation Under Our Feet*	975
Hansberry, Lorraine. ★*A Raisin in the Sun*	812
Harig, Bob. *Drive*	796.352
Harlan, Louis R. *Booker T. Washington*	B
Harlan, Louis R. *Booker T. Washington*	B
Harriot, Michael. ★*Black AF History*	973
Hartigan, Patti. *August Wilson*	B
Hayes, Terrance. *So to Speak*	811
Hays, Jeanine. *Remix*	747
Hazzard, Kevin M. *American Sirens*	362.18
Honey, Michael K. *To the Promised Land*	323
hooks, bell. *Remembered Rapture*	808
hooks, bell. *Wounds of Passion*	B
Hunter-Gault, Charlayne. ★*My People*	305.48
Hurston, Zora Neale. *Dust Tracks on a Road*	B
Hurston, Zora Neale. ★*You Don't Know Us Negroes and Other Essays*	814
Hylton, Antonia. *Madness*	362.2
Jackson, Mitchell S. *Survival Math*	B
Jacoby, Karl. *The Strange Career of William Ellis*	B
Jawando, Will. ★*My Seven Black Fathers*	B
Jefferson, Margo. *Negroland*	305.896
Jerkins, Morgan. *Wandering in Strange Lands*	305.896
Johnson, James Weldon. *Complete Poems*	811
Johnson, Katherine G. *My Remarkable Journey*	B
Johnson, Theodore R. *When the Stars Begin to Fall*	305.800973
Johnson, Walter. *Soul by Soul*	976.3
Jones, Chip. *The Organ Thieves*	617.4
Jones, Saeed. *Alive at the End of the World*	811
Jones, Saeed. *How We Fight for Our Lives*	B
Joseph, Peniel E. *The Sword and the Shield*	B
Joseph, Peniel E. *Waiting 'Til the Midnight Hour*	323.1196
Kaplan, Fred. *Lincoln and the Abolitionists*	973.7092
Keene, John. ★*Punks*	811
Kelley, Blair Murphy. *Black Folk*	331.6
Kennedy, Kostya. *True*	B
King, Martin Luther. *The Autobiography of Martin Luther King, Jr.*	B
Kix, Paul. ★*You Have to Be Prepared to Die Before You Can Begin to Live*	976.1
Kotz, Nick. *Judgment Days*	323
Kranish, Michael. *The World's Fastest Man*	B
Lane, Charles. *Freedom's Detective*	B
Lane, Stewart F. *Black Broadway*	792.089
Laymon, Kiese. ★*Heavy*	B
Lebron, Christopher J. *The Making of Black Lives Matter*	305.896
Lecrae. ★*I Am Restored*	B
Lemon, Don. *This Is the Fire*	305.896
Levinsohn, Florence Hamlish. *Looking for Farrakhan*	B
Levy, Aidan. *Saxophone Colossus*	B
Lewis, David L. ★*W.E.B. Du Bois*	B
Lewis, Jenifer. *Walking in My Joy*	B
Lewis, Robin Coste. *To the Realization of Perfect Helplessness*	811
Lifford, Tina. *The Little Book of Big Lies*	155.2
Lineberry, Cate. *Be Free or Die*	B
Lomax, Alan. ★*The Land Where the Blues Began*	781.643
Lowery, Wesley. ★*American Whitelash*	305.8
Luckerson, Victor. *Built from the Fire*	976.6
Lusane, Clarence. *The Black History of the White House*	975.3
Malcolm X. ★*The Autobiography of Malcolm X*	B
Mallory, Tamika D. *State of Emergency*	305.896
Marable, Manning. ★*Malcolm X*	B
Maraniss, David. ★*Barack Obama*	B
Marovich, Robert M. *A City Called Heaven*	782.25
Masur, Kate. *Until Justice Be Done*	323.1196
May, Gregory. *A Madman's Will*	973.5
Mays, Kyle. ★*An Afro-Indigenous History of the United States*	973
McCalman, George. *Illustrated Black History*	920
McCauley, Esau. *How Far to the Promised Land*	B
McNally, Dennis. *On Highway 61*	781.64
McWhorter, John H. *Talking Back, Talking Black*	427
Meckler, Laura. ★*Dream Town*	305.8
Merritt, Tyler. *I Take My Coffee Black*	791.4302
Miles, Tiya. ★*Night Flyer*	B
Montero, David. ★*The Stolen Wealth of Slavery*	381
Moore, Marcus J. *The Butterfly Effect*	B
Mouton, Deborah D. E. E. P. *Black Chameleon*	B
Muhammad, Khalil Gibran. *The Condemnation of Blackness*	364.2
Nemiroff, Robert. *To Be Young, Gifted, and Black*	B
Norrell, Robert J. *Up from History*	B
Northup, Solomon. *Twelve Years a Slave*	B
Obama, Barack. ★*Dreams from My Father*	B
Oluo, Ijeoma. ★*So You Want to Talk About Race*	305.800973
Pardlo, Gregory. *Spectral Evidence*	811
Parker, Morgan. *Magical Negro*	811
Parker, Morgan. ★*You Get What You Pay For*	305.896
Payne, Les. ★*The Dead Are Arising*	B
Peisner, David. *Homey Don't Play That!*	791.45
Penniman, Leah. ★*Black Earth Wisdom*	333.72
Perry, Bruce. *Malcolm*	B
Perry, Imani. *May We Forever Stand*	782.25
Pinckney, Darryl. *Busted in New York and Other Essays*	305.800973
Pinn, Anthony B. *The Black Practice of Disbelief*	211
Plant, Deborah G. *Of Greed and Glory*	326
Poitier, Sidney. *The Measure of a Man*	B
Raboteau, Emily. *Lessons for Survival*	814
Ramsey, Donovan X. ★*When Crack Was King*	362.29
Rankine, Claudia. ★*Citizen*	814
Rankine, Claudia. ★*Just Us*	305.896
Rankine, Claudia. *The White Card*	812
Rasmussen, Daniel. *American Uprising*	976.3
Ribowsky, Mark. *The Supremes*	B
Rice, Condoleezza. *Extraordinary, Ordinary People*	B
Risen, Clay. *The Bill of the Century*	342.7308
Robeson, Paul. *Here I Stand*	B
Robeson, Paul. *The Undiscovered Paul Robeson*	B
Robinson, Jackie. *I Never Had It Made*	B
Robinson, Staci. ★*Tupac Shakur*	B
Rose, Tricia. ★*Metaracism*	305.8
Rosen, Richard A. *Julius Chambers*	B
Rosenberg, Rosalind. ★*Jane Crow*	B
Rothstein, Richard. ★*The Color of Law*	305.800973
Ruffin, Amber. ★*The World Record Book of Racist Stories*	305.896
RuPaul. ★*The House of Hidden Meanings*	B
Sanders, Chad. *Black Magic*	305.896
Saul, Scott. ★*Becoming Richard Pryor*	B
Savage, Jodi M. *The Death of a Jaybird*	B
Sharma, Nina. *The Way You Make Me Feel*	B
Sharpe, Christina Elizabeth. *Ordinary Notes*	305.896
Shockley, Evie. *Suddenly We*	811
Simon, James F. *Eisenhower vs. Warren*	347.73

1595

PUBLIC LIBRARY CORE COLLECTION: NONFICTION
Twentieth Edition

Sinha, Manisha. *The Slave's Cause*	326
Smith, Clint. ★*How the Word Is Passed*	973
Smith, Danez. ★*Don't Call Us Dead*	811.6
Smith, Danez. ★*Homie*	811
Smith, Mychal Denzel. *Invisible Man, Got the Whole World Watching*	305.242
Smith, Patricia. ★*Incendiary Art*	811.54
Smith, Patricia. *Unshuttered*	811
Smith, Tracy K. ★*To Free the Captives*	818
Snyder, Christina. *Great Crossings*	976.9
Sorin, Gretchen Sullivan. *Driving While Black*	323.1196
Starks, Glenn L. *Thurgood Marshall*	B
Stewart, Jeffrey C. ★*The New Negro*	191
Swift, Earl. *Hell Put to Shame*	364.15
Tabor, Nick. *Africatown*	976.1
Taibbi, Matt. *I Can't Breathe*	363.2
Talley, Andre Leon. *The Chiffon Trenches*	B
Tatum, Beverly Daniel. ★*"Why Are All the Black Kids Sitting Together in the Cafeteria?"*	305.800973
Terry, Bryant. *Black Food*	394.1
Tesfamariam, Rahiel. ★*Imagine Freedom*	305.896
Thomas, Etan. *We Matter*	796.08
Thomas, Franklin A. *An Unplanned Life*	B
Thompson, Kenan. *When I Was Your Age*	B
Thompson-Hernandez, Walter. *The Compton Cowboys*	920
Tipton-Martin, Toni. ★*Jubilee*	641.59
Tipton-Martin, Toni. *Juke Joints, Jazz Clubs & Juice*	641.87
Tobin, Jacqueline. *From Midnight to Dawn*	973.7
Trethewey, Natasha D. ★*Monument*	811
Tye, Larry. ★*The Jazzmen*	781.6509
Tyson, Cicely. ★*Just as I Am*	B
Tyson, Timothy B. *Blood Done Sign My Name*	975.6
Tyson, Timothy B. *The Blood of Emmett Till*	364.1
Union, Gabrielle. *You Got Anything Stronger?*	B
Villarosa, Linda. ★*Under the Skin*	362.1089
Walker-Hill, Helen. *From Spirituals to Symphonies*	780
Wallace, Carvell. *Another Word for Love*	B
Ward, Andrew. ★*The Slaves' War*	973.7
Ward, Jesmyn. ★*The Fire This Time*	305.896
Ward, Jesmyn. ★*Men We Reaped*	B
Washington, Booker T. ★*Up from Slavery*	B
Watson, Bruce. *Freedom Summer*	323.1196
Watts, Jill. *Hattie McDaniel*	B
Weiner, Mark Stuart. *Black Trials*	342.7308
West, Cornel. *Black Prophetic Fire*	920
Whitaker, Mark. *Smoketown*	305.896
White, Shane. *Prince of Darkness*	B
Wilder, Craig Steven. *Ebony and Ivy*	379.2
Wilderson, Frank B. *Afropessimism*	B
Wilkerson, Isabel. ★*The Warmth of Other Suns*	304.80973
Wilkins, Robert L. *Long Road to Hard Truth*	069
Williams, Juan. *I'll Find a Way or Make One*	378.73
Williams, Juan. *This Far by Faith*	200
Williams, Kidada E. *I Saw Death Coming*	973.8
Williams, Michael Kenneth. *Scenes from My Life*	B
Willis, Deborah. ★*The Black Civil War Soldier*	973.7
Willis, Raquel. *The Risk It Takes to Bloom*	B
Wills, Shomari. *Black Fortunes*	920
Wilson, August. *The Piano Lesson*	812
Wilson, August. *Two Trains Running*	812
Wingfield, Adia Harvey. *Gray Areas*	331.6
Winters, Mary-Frances. *Black Fatigue*	305.896
Wise, Tim J. *Dispatches from the Race War*	305.8
Woodward, C. Vann. *The Strange Career of Jim Crow*	305.896
Wright, Richard. ★*Black Boy*	B
Young, Damon. ★*What Doesn't Kill You Makes You Blacker*	B
Young, Kevin. *Brown*	811

AFRICAN AMERICANS AND SPORTS
Iguodala, Andre. *The Sixth Man*	B

AFRICAN AMERICANS IN ART
Willis, Deborah. *Reflections in Black*	770

AFRICAN AMERICANS IN FILMS
Bogle, Donald. *Bright Boulevards, Bold Dreams*	791.43
Carter, Ruth E. ★*The Art of Ruth E. Carter*	746.9
Haygood, Wil. ★*Colorization*	791.43

AFRICAN AMERICANS IN LITERATURE
Bader, Philip. *African-American Writers*	810.9
Gorra, Michael Edward. *The Saddest Words*	813
hooks, bell. *Remembered Rapture*	808
Jones, Sharon L. *Critical Companion to Zora Neale Hurston*	813
Morrison, Toni. *Playing in the Dark*	810.9
Thursby, Jacqueline S. *Critical Companion to Maya Angelou*	818

AFRICAN AMERICANS IN MASS MEDIA
Babb, Valerie Melissa. *The Book of James*	B
Bailey, Issac J. *Why Didn't We Riot?*	305.800973

AFRICAN AMERICANS IN POPULAR CULTURE
Evans, William. *Black Nerd Problems*	814.6
Marovich, Robert M. *A City Called Heaven*	782.25

AFRICAN AMERICANS IN TELEVISION
Peisner, David. *Homey Don't Play That!*	791.45

AFRICAN AMERICANS IN THE PERFORMING ARTS
Abdurraqib, Hanif. ★*A Little Devil in America*	791.089
Lane, Stewart F. *Black Broadway*	792.089
McGilligan, Patrick. *Oscar Micheaux*	B

AFRICAN CIVILIZATION
French, Howard W. *Born in Blackness*	960
Meredith, Martin. *The Fortunes of Africa*	960
Soyinka, Wole. *Of Africa*	960

AFRICAN DIASPORA
Alexander, Will. *Refractive Africa*	811
Bailey, Desiree C. *What Noise Against the Cane*	811
French, Howard W. *Born in Blackness*	960
Gray, Jon. *Ghetto Gastro Black Power Kitchen*	641.5
Harris, Jessica B. *High on the Hog*	641.59
Moore, Wayetu. *The Dragons, the Giant, the Women*	B
Reed, Justin Phillip. *The Malevolent Volume*	811
Samuelsson, Marcus. ★*The Rise*	641.59
Shockley, Evie. *Suddenly We*	811

AFRICAN ELEPHANT
Orenstein, Ronald I. *Ivory, Horn and Blood*	333.95
Wood, Levison. *The Last Giants*	599.67

★*African Founders*. Fischer, David Hackett	973

AFRICAN HISTORY
Achebe, Chinua. *There Was a Country*	B
Anderson, David. *Histories of the Hanged*	967.62
Beah, Ishmael. ★*A Long Way Gone*	B
Carlin, John. *Playing the Enemy*	968.06
Cooper, Helene. *The House at Sugar Beach*	921
Cooper, Helene. *Madame President*	966.62
French, Howard W. *Born in Blackness*	960
Fuller, Alexandra. *Don't Let's Go to the Dogs Tonight*	B
Guha, Ramachandra. *Gandhi Before India*	B
Hammer, Joshua. *The Bad-Ass Librarians of Timbuktu*	025.8
Hatzfeld, Jean. *Blood Papa*	967.5710431
Hatzfeld, Jean. *Machete Season*	967.57104
Hochschild, Adam. *King Leopold's Ghost*	967.51
Huffman, Alan. *Here I Am*	B
Kars, Marjoleine. *Blood on the River*	306.3
Lamb, Christina. *House of Stone*	968.91
Ngugi wa Thiong'o. *In the House of the Interpreter*	B
Prendergast, John. *Congo Stories*	967.5103
Reid, Stuart A. *The Lumumba Plot*	967.51
Soyinka, Wole. *Of Africa*	960
Wainaina, Binyavanga. *One Day I Will Write About This Place*	B
Wilkinson, Toby A. H. *The Nile*	962
Yeebo, Yepoka. *Anansi's Gold*	364.16

AFRICAN PEOPLE
Bethencourt, Kahran. *Glory*	779.2
Kaufmann, Miranda. *Black Tudors*	941
Yeebo, Yepoka. *Anansi's Gold*	364.16

AFRICAN PEOPLE IN FOREIGN COUNTRIES
Fischer, David Hackett. ★*African Founders*	973
Kaufmann, Miranda. *Black Tudors*	941
Lockley, Thomas. *African Samurai*	B
Moore, Wayetu. *The Dragons, the Giant, the Women*	B

AFRICAN PEOPLE IN THE UNITED STATES
Fischer, David Hackett. ★*African Founders*	973
Moore, Wayetu. *The Dragons, the Giant, the Women*	B

African Samurai. Lockley, Thomas	B
African-American Art. Patton, Sharon F.	704.03
African-American Writers. Bader, Philip	810.9
Africana. Umah-Shaylor, Lerato	641.596
Africatown. Tabor, Nick	976.1
★*An Afro-Indigenous History of the United States*. Mays, Kyle	973
Afro-Vegan. Terry, Bryant	641.59

AUTHOR, TITLE, SERIES AND SUBJECT INDEX

AFROFUTURISM
   Carter, Ruth E. ★ *The Art of Ruth E. Carter* — 746.9
Afropessimism. Wilderson, Frank B. — B
After. Hirshfield, Jane — 811
After 1177 B.C. Cline, Eric H. — 937
After Camelot. Taraborrelli, J. Randy — B
After Lincoln. Langguth, A. J. — 973.8
After The Dance. Gaye, Jan — B
★ *After The Last Border*. Goudeau, Jessica — 362.83
After The Prophet. Hazleton, Lesley — 297.8
After The Romanovs. Rappaport, Helen — 944
After The Trail of Tears. McLoughlin, William Gerald — 973
The Aftergrief. Edelman, Hope — 155.9
Afterland. Vang, Mai Der — 811
Aftermath. Cusk, Rachel — B
★ *Aftermath*. Jahner, Harald — 943.087
Aftershocks. Owusu, Nadia — B
Against All Odds. Kershaw, Alex — 940.54
Against Memoir. Tea, Michelle — B
Against The Tide. Dean, Cornelia — 333.91
★ *Against The Wind*. Gabler, Neal — B
Against White Feminism. Zakaria, Rafia — 305.42
AGAMEMNON (GREEK MYTHOLOGY)
   Aeschylus. *The Oresteia* — 882
   Homer. ★ *The Iliad* — 883
Agarwal, Pragya
   Sway — 177
Agassi, Andre
   Open — B
AGASSI, ANDRE, 1970-
   Agassi, Andre. *Open* — B
★ *Agatha Christie*. Worsley, Lucy — B
The Age of Acquiescence. Fraser, Steve — 973.91
Age of Ambition. Osnos, Evan — 951.06
Age of Anger. Mishra, Pankaj — 909.8
The Age of Bowie. Morley, Paul — B
The Age of Deer. Howsare, Erika — 599.65
The Age of Eisenhower. Hitchcock, William I. — 973.921092
The Age of Entitlement. Caldwell, Christopher — 305.240973
AGE OF EXPLORATION (1419-1610)
   Benner, Erica. *Be Like the Fox* — B
   Bradford, Sarah. *Lucrezia Borgia* — B
   Dodds Pennock, Caroline. ★ *On Savage Shores* — 970.004
   Downey, Kirstin. *Isabella* — B
   Hibbert, Christopher. *The Borgias and Their Enemies* — 920
   King, Ross. *Michelangelo & the Pope's Ceiling* — 759.5
   Lockley, Thomas. *African Samurai* — B
   Meyer, G. J. *The Borgias* — 920
   Nuland, Sherwin B. *Leonardo Da Vinci* — B
   Strathern, Paul. *The Borgias* — 945.06
   Thomas, Hugh. *Rivers of Gold* — 980
★ *The Age of Football*. Goldblatt, David — 796.334
The Age of Genius. Grayling, A. C. — 940.2
The Age of Gold. Brands, H. W. — 979.4
The Age of Insight. Kandel, Eric R. — 154.2
★ *The Age of Insurrection*. Neiwert, David A. — 303.48
★ *The Age of Magical Overthinking*. Montell, Amanda — 153.4
★ *The Age of Movies*. Kael, Pauline — 791.43
The Age of Phillis. Jeffers, Honorée Fanonne — 811
Age of Revolutions. Zakaria, Fareed — 303.6
The Age of Sustainable Development. Sachs, Jeffrey — 338.9
The Age of the Vikings. Winroth, Anders — 948
The Age of Wonder. Holmes, Richard — 509
Agee, James
   ★ *Cotton Tenants* — 976.1
   Let Us Now Praise Famous Men — 976.1
AGEE, JAMES, 1909-1955
   Agee, James. *Let Us Now Praise Famous Men* — 976.1
AGEISM
   Applewhite, Ashton. *This Chair Rocks* — 155.67
   Painter, Nell Irvin. *Old in Art School* — B
Ageless Soul. Moore, Thomas — 155.67
Agent Garbo. Talty, Stephan — 940.5
Agent Josephine. Lewis, Damien — B
AGENT ORANGE
   Black, George. ★ *The Long Reckoning* — 959.704
★ *Agent Sonya*. Macintyre, Ben — B
Agent Zigzag. Macintyre, Ben — B

Agents of Grace. Darling, Daniel — 158.2
Agents of Influence. Hemming, Henry — 940.54
Ages of American Capitalism. Levy, Jonathan — 330.12
AGGRESSION (INTERNATIONAL RELATIONS)
   Harding, Luke. *Invasion* — 947.7
   McKean, David. *Watching Darkness Fall* — 940.53
   Miller, Christopher. *The War Came to Us* — 947.7
   Phillips, Adrian. *Fighting Churchill, Appeasing Hitler* — 327.41043
AGGRESSIVENESS
   Asbridge, Thomas S. ★ *The Crusades* — 909.07
   Bazelon, Emily. *Sticks and Stones* — 302.34
AGGRESSIVENESS IN CHILDREN
   Simmons, Rachel. *Odd Girl Out* — 302.5
Agincourt. Barker, Juliet R. V. — 944
AGINCOURT, BATTLE OF, 1415
   Barker, Juliet R. V. *Agincourt* — 944
AGING
   Albright, Madeleine Korbel. *Hell and Other Destinations* — B
   Applewhite, Ashton. *This Chair Rocks* — 155.67
   Aronson, Louise. *Elderhood* — 362.60973
   Attia, Peter. ★ *Outlive* — 612.6
   Bercovici, Jeff. *Play On* — 613.7
   Berg, Elizabeth. *I'll Be Seeing You* — 306.874
   Boa, Kenneth D. *Recalibrate Your Life* — 248.8
   Bruni, Frank. *The Beauty of Dusk* — B
   Cameron, Julia. *It's Never Too Late to Begin Again* — 155.67
   Chast, Roz. ★ *Can't We Talk About Something More Pleasant?* — 741.5
   Chittister, Joan. *The Gift of Years* — 200
   Conley, Chip. ★ *Learning to Love Midlife* — 646.7
   Cooper, Anderson. *The Rainbow Comes and Goes* — B
   Day, John D. *The Longevity Plan* — 612.6
   Delany, Sarah Louise. *Having Our Say* — B
   Doust, Kelly. *The Power Age* — 305.244
   Dunn, Jancee. *Hot and Bothered* — 618.1
   Ehrenreich, Barbara. *Natural Causes* — 613.2
   Ellis, Helen. *Bring Your Baggage and Don't Pack Light* — 814
   Esmonde-White, Miranda. *Aging Backwards* — 613.7
   Esty, Katharaine C. *Eightysomethings* — 612.6
   Evaristo, Bernardine. *Manifesto* — B
   Foreman, Tom. *My Year of Running Dangerously* — B
   Gawande, Atul. ★ *Being Mortal* — 362.17
   Giovanni, Nikki. *Make Me Rain* — 811
   Gluck, Louise. *Winter Recipes from the Collective* — 811
   Grass, Gunter. *Of All That Ends* — 838
   Green, Stefanie. *This Is Assisted Dying* — 616.02
   Gupta, Sanjay. ★ *Keep Sharp* — 153.4
   Hagerty, Barbara Bradley. *Life Reimagined* — 155.6
   Hecht, M. E. *Two Old Broads* — 613
   Klein, Jessi. *I'll Show Myself Out* — B
   Lahti, Christine. *True Stories from an Unreliable Eyewitness* — B
   Le Guin, Ursula K. *No Time to Spare* — 814
   Le Guin, Ursula K. *So Far so Good* — 811
   Levy, Deborah. ★ *Real Estate* — B
   Lippman, Laura. *My Life as a Villainess* — B
   Lively, Penelope. *Life in the Garden* — B
   Loh, Sandra Tsing. *The Madwoman and the Roomba* — B
   Malone, Sharon. *Grown Woman Talk* — 362.1
   Manly, Carla Marie. *Aging Joyfully* — 305.26
   Max, D. T. *Finale* — 782.1
   Moore, Thomas. *Ageless Soul* — 155.67
   Moran, Caitlin. *More Than a Woman* — B
   Morton, Brian. *Tasha* — B
   Nevins, Sheila. *You Don't Look Your Age* — B
   Notaro, Laurie. *Excuse Me While I Disappear* — B
   Ondaatje, Michael. *A Year of Last Things* — 811
   Orenstein, Peggy. *Unraveling* — B
   Pipher, Mary Bray. *Women Rowing North* — 305.26
   Porizkova, Paulina. *No Filter* — B
   Sinclair, David A. *Lifespan* — 570
   Smith, Patti. ★ *Year of the Monkey* — B
   Thomas, Elizabeth Marshall. *Growing Old* — 305.26
   Warraich, Haider. *Modern Death* — 179.7
   Waters, John. *Mr. Know-It-All* — 814
   Yalom, Irvin D. *Staring at the Sun* — 155.9
Aging Backwards. Esmonde-White, Miranda — 613.7
Aging Joyfully. Manly, Carla Marie — 305.26
AGING PARENTS
   Chast, Roz. ★ *Can't We Talk About Something More Pleasant?* — 741.5

PUBLIC LIBRARY CORE COLLECTION: NONFICTION
Twentieth Edition

The Agitators. Wickenden, Dorothy — 920
AGNEW, SPIRO T., 1918-1996
   Maddow, Rachel. *Bag Man* — B
Agnostic. Hazleton, Lesley — 211
AGNOSTICISM
   Hazleton, Lesley. *Agnostic* — 211
   Zuckerman, Phil. *Living the Secular Life* — 211
AGNOSTICS
   Hazleton, Lesley. *Agnostic* — 211
Agrawal, Roma
   Nuts and Bolts — 609
AGRIBUSINESS
   Addison, Corban. *Wastelands* — 346.73
   Bittman, Mark. *Animal, Vegetable, Junk* — 394.1
   Cullen, Art. *Storm Lake* — 071.7
   Freeman, Andrea. ★*Ruin Their Crops on the Ground* — 338.1
   Genoways, Ted. *The Chain* — 338.7
   Hamilton, Lisa M. *Deeply Rooted* — 338.10973
   Hvistendahl, Mara. ★*The Scientist and the Spy* — 364.16
   Sorvino, Chloe. *Raw Deal* — 338.1
AGRICULTURAL CHEMICALS INDUSTRY AND TRADE
   Elmore, Bartow J. *Seed Money* — 338.7
AGRICULTURAL LABORERS
   Swift, Earl. *Hell Put to Shame* — 364.15
AGRICULTURAL PESTS
   Lavoipierre, Frederique. *Garden Allies* — 635
AGRICULTURAL POLICY
   Bittman, Mark. *A Bone to Pick* — 338.10973
   Dikotter, Frank. *Mao's Great Famine* — 951.05
AGRICULTURAL POLLUTION
   Addison, Corban. *Wastelands* — 346.73
AGRICULTURAL PRODUCTS
   Zuckerman, Jocelyn C. *Planet Palm* — 633.8
AGRICULTURAL RESEARCH
   Vella, Christina. *George Washington Carver* — B
AGRICULTURAL TECHNOLOGY
   Bittman, Mark. *Animal, Vegetable, Junk* — 394.1
   Hvistendahl, Mara. ★*The Scientist and the Spy* — 364.16
   Zimberoff, Larissa. *Technically Food* — 613.2
AGRICULTURE
   Ackerman-Leist, Philip. *Rebuilding the Foodshed* — 338.1
   Barber, Dan. *The Third Plate* — 641.3
   Baszile, Natalie. *We Are Each Other's Harvest* — 630.89
   Berry, Wendell. *The Art of Loading Brush* — 338.10973
   Berry, Wendell. ★*The World-Ending Fire* — 818
   Bittman, Mark. *Animal, Vegetable, Junk* — 394.1
   Ditmore, Melissa Hope. ★*Unbroken Chains* — 306.74
   Elmore, Bartow J. *Seed Money* — 338.7
   Friedman, Andrew. *The Dish* — 647.95
   Genoways, Ted. *This Blessed Earth* — 630.9
   Hamilton, Lisa M. *Deeply Rooted* — 338.10973
   Hamilton, Lisa M. *The Hungry Season* — B
   Hesiod. *Works and Days and Theogony* — 881
   Heyman, Stephen. *The Planter of Modern Life* — B
   Kingsolver, Barbara. ★*Animal, Vegetable, Miracle* — 641
   Logsdon, Gene. *Letter to a Young Farmer* — 338.10973
   Monbiot, George. ★*Regenesis* — 338.1
   Penniman, Leah. ★*Black Earth Wisdom* — 333.72
   Standage, Tom. *An Edible History of Humanity* — 394.1
   Stone, Daniel. *The Food Explorer* — B
   Stuart, Andrea. *Sugar in the Blood* — 338.1
AGRICULTURISTS
   Vella, Christina. *George Washington Carver* — B
Agrippina. Southon, Emma — B
AGRIPPINA, MINOR, 15-59
   Southon, Emma. *Agrippina* — B
Aguon, Julian
   No Country for Eight-Spot Butterflies — 305.89
Ahamed, Liaquat
   Lords of Finance — 920
Ahdoot, Dan
   Undercooked — 647.95
AHDOOT, DAN
   Ahdoot, Dan. *Undercooked* — 647.95
Ahead of All Parting. Rilke, Rainer Maria — 831
Ahead of the Curve. Kenny, Brian — 796.357
Ahmad, Aeham
   The Pianist from Syria — B

AHMAD, AEHAM, 1988-
   Ahmad, Aeham. *The Pianist from Syria* — B
Ahmed, Azam
   Fear Is Just a Word — 364.152
Ahmed, Sara
   The Feminist Killjoy Handbook — 305.42
Ahuvia, Aaron
   ★*The Things We Love* — 790.1
AI 2041. Lee, Kai-Fu — 006.3
Ai Weiwei. Ai, Weiwei — 709.51
Ai, Weiwei
   1000 Years of Joys and Sorrows — 709.2
   Ai Weiwei — 709.51
   Zodiac — 741.5
AI, WEIWEI
   Ai, Weiwei. *1000 Years of Joys and Sorrows* — 709.2
   Ai, Weiwei. *Ai Weiwei* — 709.51
   Ai, Weiwei. *Zodiac* — 741.5
AIDID, MOHAMMED FARAH, 1934-1996
   Bowden, Mark. *Black Hawk Down* — 967.7305
AIDS (DISEASE)
   Bibbins, Mark. *13th Balloon* — 813
   Duberman, Martin B. *Hold Tight Gently* — 920
   France, David. *How to Survive a Plague* — 362.196
   Holt, Nathalia. *Cured* — 614.5
   Keene, John. ★*Punks* — 811
   Kushner, Tony. *Angels in America* — 812
   Quammen, David. ★*Spillover* — 614.4
   Shilts, Randy. ★*And the Band Played On* — 362.196
AIDS ACTIVISTS
   Bono. ★*Surrender* — B
   Duberman, Martin B. *Hold Tight Gently* — 920
   France, David. *How to Survive a Plague* — 362.196
Aimless Love. Collins, Billy — 811
AINSWORTH, WILLIAM HARRISON, 1805-1882
   Harman, Claire. *Murder by the Book* — 364.152
AIR
   Kean, Sam. *Caesar's Last Breath* — 551.51
AIR BATTLES
   Wheelan, Joseph. *Midnight in the Pacific* — 940.54
AIR DEFENSES
   Scott, James. *Target Tokyo* — 940.54
AIR POLLUTION
   Arsenault, Kerri. *Mill Town* — B
   Hendrickson, Debra. ★*The Air They Breathe* — 363.7
   MacPhail, Theresa. *Allergic* — 616.97
AIR POWER
   Holland, James. *Big Week* — 940.54
AIR QUALITY
   Hendrickson, Debra. ★*The Air They Breathe* — 363.7
AIR SHOWS
   O'Brien, Keith. *Fly Girls* — 920
★*The Air They Breathe.* Hendrickson, Debra — 363.7
Air Traffic. Pardlo, Gregory — B
AIR TRAVEL
   Gwynne, S. C. *His Majesty's Airship* — 363.12
   Hodgman, John. *Medallion Status* — B
   Rose, Alexander. *Empires of the Sky* — 920
AIR WARFARE
   Ambrose, Stephen E. *The Wild Blue* — 940.54
   Frank, Richard B. *Downfall* — 940.54
   Hastings, Max. *Operation Chastise* — 940.54
   Hillenbrand, Laura. ★*Unbroken* — B
   Holland, James. *Big Week* — 940.54
   Kershaw, Alex. *The Few* — 940.54
   Makos, Adam. ★*A Higher Call* — 940.54
   Miller, Donald L. ★*Masters of the Air* — 940.54
   Simms, Brendan. *The Silver Waterfall* — 940.54
   Smith, Starr. *Jimmy Stewart* — B
AIRBORNE TROOPS
   Ambrose, Stephen E. ★*Band of Brothers* — 920
   Beevor, Antony. *The Battle of Arnhem* — 940.54
AIRCRAFT CARRIERS
   Fabey, Michael. *Heavy Metal* — 338.4
AIRCRAFT INDUSTRY AND TRADE
   Robison, Peter. ★*Flying Blind* — 338.7
AIRLINERS
   Robison, Peter. ★*Flying Blind* — 338.7

AUTHOR, TITLE, SERIES AND SUBJECT INDEX

AIRLINES
    Cooke, Julia. *Come Fly the World* — 387.7
    McShane Wulfhart, Nell. *The Great Stewardess Rebellion* — 331.4
AIRMEN
    Bascomb, Neal. *The Escape Artists* — 940.4
    Hastings, Max. *Operation Chastise* — 940.54
AIRPLANE ACCIDENT SURVIVORS
    Ollestad, Norman. *Crazy for the Storm* — B
AIRPLANE ACCIDENT VICTIMS
    Longman, Jere. *Among the Heroes* — 974.8
    Ollestad, Norman. *Crazy for the Storm* — B
    Parrado, Nando. ★*Miracle in the Andes* — 982
AIRPLANE ACCIDENTS
    Erwin, Jon. *Beyond Valor* — B
    Lineberry, Cate. *The Secret Rescue* — 940.54
    Murphy, Brian. *81 Days Below Zero* — 940.54
    Ollestad, Norman. *Crazy for the Storm* — B
    Parrado, Nando. ★*Miracle in the Andes* — 982
    Read, Piers Paul. ★*Alive* — 982
    Robison, Peter. ★*Flying Blind* — 338.7
    Wukovits, John F. *Lost at Sea* — 940.54
    Zuckoff, Mitchell. *Frozen in Time* — 998.2
    Zuckoff, Mitchell. *Lost in Shangri-La* — 940.54
AIRPLANE RACING
    O'Brien, Keith. *Fly Girls* — 920
AIRPLANES
    Caesar, Ed. *The Moth and the Mountain* — B
    McCullough, David G. ★*The Wright Brothers* — B
    Rose, Alexander. *Empires of the Sky* — 920
AIRSHIPS
    Gwynne, S. C. *His Majesty's Airship* — 363.12
    Preston, Diana. *A Higher Form of Killing* — 940.4
    Rose, Alexander. *Empires of the Sky* — 920
Airton, Lee
    ★*Gender* — 305.3
AISHAH, CA. 614-678
    Hazleton, Lesley. *After the Prophet* — 297.8
Aitken-Smith, Trent
    The Tattoo Dictionary — 391.6
AJAK, BENJAMIN
    Deng, Alephonsion. *They Poured Fire on Us from the Sky* — B
Akbar, Kaveh
    Calling a Wolf a Wolf — 811
    Pilgrim Bell — 811
Akcam, Taner
    A Shameful Act — 956.6
AKHENATEN, KING OF EGYPT
    Darnell, John Coleman. *Egypt's Golden Couple* — 932
Akhmatova, Anna Andreevna
    ★*The Complete Poems of Anna Akhmatova* — 891.71
    Poems — 891.71
AKHMATOVA, ANNA ANDREEVNA, 1889-1966
    Akhmatova, Anna Andreevna. *Poems* — 891.71
Akins, Damon B.
    ★*We Are the Land* — 978
Akiyama, Lance
    Duct Tape Engineer — 745.5
    Rubber Band Engineer — 745.57
Aktipis, Athena
    ★*A Field Guide to the Apocalypse* — 155.2
Akyol, Mustafa
    The Islamic Jesus — 297.2
    ★*Reopening Muslim Minds* — 297.09
Al Capone. Bair, Deirdre
AL SA'UD, HOUSE OF
    Hope, Bradley. *Blood and Oil* — B
    Hubbard, Ben (Journalist). *Mbs* — B
AL SA'UD, MUHAMMAD BIN SALMAN BIN ABD AL-AZIZ, CROWN PRINCE OF SAUDI ARABIA, 1985-
    Hope, Bradley. *Blood and Oil* — B
AL Samawi, Mohammed
    The Fox Hunt — 953
AL SAMAWI, MOHAMMED, 1986-
    AL Samawi, Mohammed. *The Fox Hunt* — 953
Al-Khalili, Jim
    The House of Wisdom — 509
Al-Maria, Sophia
    The Girl Who Fell to Earth — B

ALABAMA
    Agee, James. *Let Us Now Praise Famous Men* — 976.1
    Archibald, John. *Shaking the Gates of Hell* — B
    Bragg, Rick. *The Speckled Beauty* — 636.7
    Cep, Casey N. ★*Furious Hours* — 364.152
    Durkin, Hannah. ★*The Survivors of the Clotilda* — 306.362
    Hinton, Anthony Ray. *The Sun Does Shine* — B
    Inskeep, Steve. *Jacksonland* — 973.56
    Jackson, Troy. *Becoming King* — B
    Jones, Doug. *Bending Toward Justice* — 323.1196
    Lewis, John. ★*March; Book One* — 741.5
    McCaulley, Esau. *How Far to the Promised Land* — B
    McWhorter, Diane. *Carry Me Home* — 976.1
    Mitchell, Jerry. ★*Race Against Time* — 364.152
    Morrison, Melanie. *Murder on Shades Mountain* — 345.761
    Raines, Ben. *The Last Slave Ship* — 306.362
    Raines, Howell. *Silent Cavalry* — 973.7
    Reverby, Susan M. *Examining Tuskegee* — 174.2
    Savage, Phil. *4th and Goal Every Day* — 796.332
    Stevenson, Bryan. *Just Mercy* — B
    Tabor, Nick. *Africatown* — 976.1
Alabaster, Carol
    Developing an Outstanding Core Collection — 025.2
Aladdin. Seale, Yasmine — 398.2
ALADDIN (LEGENDARY CHARACTER)
    Seale, Yasmine. *Aladdin* — 398.2
Alan's War. Guibert, Emmanuel — 741.5
ALANBROOKE, VISCOUNT, 1883-1963
    Roberts, Andrew. *Masters and Commanders* — 940.5322
Alaska. Borneman, Walter R. — 979.8
ALASKA
    Adams, Mark. *Tip of the Iceberg* — 917.9804
    Borneman, Walter R. *Alaska* — 979.8
    Butcher, Amy. *Mothertrucker* — B
    Coffin, Jaed. *Roughhouse Friday* — B
    Hall, Andy. *Denali's Howl* — 796.522
    Heacox, Kim. ★*John Muir and the Ice That Started a Fire* — 333.7209798
    Heacox, Kim. *Rhythm of the Wild* — 979.8
    Hensley, William L. Iggiagruk. *Fifty Miles from Tomorrow* — 979.8
    Jenkins, Peter. *Looking for Alaska* — 979.8
    Jewel. *Never Broken* — 782.42164
    Kizzia, Tom. *Pilgrim's Wilderness* — B
    Krakauer, Jon. *Into the Wild* — 917.9804
    Malarkey, Tucker. *Stronghold* — 639.2
    Murphy, Brian. *81 Days Below Zero* — 940.54
    Pace, Kristin Knight. *This Much Country* — B
    Rinella, Steven. *American Buffalo* — 599.64
    Sardy, Marin. *The Edge of Every Day* — B
    Van Hemert, Caroline. *The Sun Is a Compass* — 979.8
    Wohlforth, Charles P. *The Fate of Nature* — 304.209798
ALBANIA
    Ypi, Lea. ★*Free* — B
Albee, Edward
    ★*Who's Afraid of Virginia Woolf?* — 812
Albers, Patricia
    Joan Mitchell — B
Albert Camus. Todd, Olivier — B
Albert, Daniel M.
    Are We There Yet? — 303.48
ALBERT, PRINCE CONSORT, CONSORT OF VICTORIA, QUEEN OF GREAT BRITAIN, 1819-1861
    Gill, Gillian. *We Two* — 941.081
ALBERTA
    Vaillant, John. ★*Fire Weather* — 363.37
Alberta, Tim
    American Carnage — 324.2734
    The Kingdom, the Power, and the Glory — 270.8
Albertine, Viv
    Clothes, Clothes, Clothes. Music, Music, Music — B
ALBERTINE, VIV, 1954-
    Albertine, Viv. *Clothes, Clothes, Clothes. Music, Music, Music* — B
ALBINISM
    Macy, Beth. ★*Trueview* — B
    Talusan, Meredith. *Fairest* — 305.30973
Albom, Mitch
    Finding Chika — B
    Tuesdays with Morrie — B

PUBLIC LIBRARY CORE COLLECTION: NONFICTION
Twentieth Edition

ALBOM, MITCH, 1958-
   Albom, Mitch. *Finding Chika* — B
Albracht, William
   Abandoned in Hell — 959.704
ALBRACHT, WILLIAM
   Albracht, William. *Abandoned in Hell* — 959.704
Albright, Madeleine Korbel
   Hell and Other Destinations — B
   Prague Winter — 943.71
ALBRIGHT, MADELEINE KORBEL 1937-2022
   Albright, Madeleine Korbel. *Hell and Other Destinations* — B
   Albright, Madeleine Korbel. *Prague Winter* — 943.71
Albright, Mary Beth
   ★*Eat & Flourish* — 612.3
ALCHEMY
   Harkness, Deborah E. *The World of All Souls* — 813
ALCOHOL
   Johnston, Ann Dowsett. *Drink* — 362.292
   O'Meara, Mallory. *Girly Drinks* — 641.2
   Okrent, Daniel. *Last Call* — 363.4
ALCOHOLIC AUTHORS
   Jamison, Leslie. ★*The Recovering* — B
ALCOHOLIC BEVERAGES
   Cheever, Susan. *Drinking in America* — 394.1
   English, Camper. *Doctors and Distillers* — 615.7
   O'Meara, Mallory. *Girly Drinks* — 641.2
   Rogers, Adam. *Proof* — 663
   Tipton-Martin, Toni. *Juke Joints, Jazz Clubs & Juice* — 641.87
ALCOHOLIC FATHERS
   Crowell, Rodney. *Chinaberry Sidewalks* — B
ALCOHOLIC MEN
   Hillenbrand, Laura. ★*Unbroken* — B
   Madden, T Kira. *Long Live the Tribe of Fatherless Girls* — 814
   Metatawabin, Edmund. *Up Ghost River* — B
   Stump, Al. *Cobb* — B
ALCOHOLIC MOTHERS
   Crais, Clifton C. *History Lessons* — B
   Geller, Danielle. *Dog Flowers* — B
ALCOHOLIC WOMEN
   Barnett, Erica C. *Quitter* — B
   Butcher, Barbara. *What the Dead Know* — 614
   Dresner, Amy. *My Fair Junkie* — B
   Hamill, Kirkland. *Filthy Beasts* — B
   Jacobs, Alexandra. *Still Here* — B
   Johnston, Ann Dowsett. *Drink* — 362.292
   Mann, William J. *Kate* — B
   Whitaker, Holly. ★*Quit Like a Woman* — 616.86
   Wilder-Taylor, Stefanie. ★*Drunk-Ish* — B
ALCOHOLICS
   Akbar, Kaveh. *Calling a Wolf a Wolf* — 811
   Canfield, Jack. *The 30 Day Sobriety Solution* — 616.89
   Fisher, Carl Erik. ★*The Urge* — 362.29
   Keaton, Diane. ★*Brother & Sister* — B
   Wilder-Taylor, Stefanie. ★*Drunk-Ish* — B
ALCOHOLISM
   Akbar, Kaveh. *Calling a Wolf a Wolf* — 811
   Barnett, Erica C. *Quitter* — B
   Biden, Robert Hunter. *Beautiful Things* — B
   Blair, Selma. *Mean Baby* — B
   Byas, Taylor. *I Done Clicked My Heels Three Times* — 811
   Canfield, Jack. *The 30 Day Sobriety Solution* — 616.89
   Case, Anne. *Deaths of Despair and the Future of Capitalism* — 362.28
   Curtis, James. *Spencer Tracy* — B
   Dearborn, Mary V. *Carson McCullers* — B
   Ebert, Roger. *Life Itself* — B
   Gless, Sharon. *Apparently There Were Complaints* — B
   Jamison, Leslie. ★*The Recovering* — B
   McCourt, Malachy. *A Monk Swimming* — B
   McCourt, Malachy. *Singing My Him Song* — B
   Sabathia, CC. *Till the End* — 796.357
   Smith, Freda Love. *I Quit Everything* — B
   Vasquez-Lavado, Silvia. *In the Shadow of the Mountain* — B
   Whitaker, Holly. ★*Quit Like a Woman* — 616.86
   Wilder-Taylor, Stefanie. ★*Drunk-Ish* — B
ALCOHOLISM TREATMENT CENTERS AND CLINICS
   Barnett, Erica C. *Quitter* — B
ALCOTT, LOUISA MAY, 1832-1888
   Matteson, John. *Eden's Outcasts* — 920

   Rioux, Anne Boyd. *Meg, Jo, Beth, Amy* — 813
   Seiple, Samantha. *Louisa on the Front Lines* — B
Alda, Alan
   If I Understood You, Would I Have This Look on My Face? — 153.6
Alden, Ginger
   Elvis and Ginger — B
ALDEN, GINGER
   Alden, Ginger. *Elvis and Ginger* — B
Alderfer, Jonathan K.
   National Geographic Birding Essentials — 598.072
Alderton, Dolly
   Everything I Know About Love — B
ALDERTON, DOLLY
   Alderton, Dolly. *Everything I Know About Love* — B
Aldrin, Buzz
   Mission to Mars — 523.43
   No Dream Is Too High — B
ALDRIN, BUZZ
   Aldrin, Buzz. *No Dream Is Too High* — B
Aleixandre, Vicente
   A Longing for the Light — 861
ALEIXANDRE, VICENTE, 1898-1984
   Aleixandre, Vicente. *A Longing for the Light* — 861
Alekhina, Mariija
   Riot Days — B
ALEKHINA, MARIIJA, 1988-
   Alekhina, Mariija. *Riot Days* — B
Aleksievich, Svetlana
   Last Witnesses — 940.53
   ★*Secondhand Time* — 947.086
   ★*The Unwomanly Face of War* — 940.53
★*Alexander* Hamilton. Chernow, Ron — B
Alexander The Great. Everitt, Anthony — B
ALEXANDER VI, POPE, 1431-1503
   Bradford, Sarah. *Lucrezia Borgia* — B
   Strathern, Paul. *The Borgias* — 945.06
Alexander, Amir R.
   Infinitesimal — 511
Alexander, Brian
   ★*The Hospital* — 362.10973
Alexander, Caroline
   The Bounty — 996.1
   The Endurance — 919.8
   Skies of Thunder — 940.54
   The War That Killed Achilles — 883
Alexander, Elizabeth
   Crave Radiance — 811
   ★*The Trayvon Generation* — 305.896
Alexander, Jane
   Wild Things, Wild Places — 333.95
ALEXANDER, JANE, 1939-
   Alexander, Jane. *Wild Things, Wild Places* — 333.95
Alexander, Kwame
   Light for the World to See — 811.6
   Why Fathers Cry at Night — B
ALEXANDER, KWAME
   Alexander, Kwame. *Why Fathers Cry at Night* — B
Alexander, Larry
   Biggest Brother — B
Alexander, Lissa
   Oh, Scrap! — 746.46
Alexander, Michelle
   The New Jim Crow — 364.973
Alexander, Paul
   Bitter Crop — B
Alexander, Rosemary
   ★*The Essential Garden Design Workbook* — 712
Alexander, Stephon
   Fear of a Black Universe — 523.1
ALEXANDER, STEPHON
   Alexander, Stephon. *Fear of a Black Universe* — 523.1
ALEXANDER, THE GREAT, 356-323 B.C.E
   Everitt, Anthony. *Alexander the Great* — B
Alexander, Will
   Refractive Africa — 811
Alexandra Petri's US History. Petri, Alexandra — 817

AUTHOR, TITLE, SERIES AND SUBJECT INDEX

ALEXANDRA, EMPRESS, CONSORT OF NICHOLAS II, EMPEROR OF RUSSIA, 1872-1918
   Massie, Robert K. *Nicholas and Alexandra* — B
   Massie, Robert K. *The Romanovs* — 947
   Rappaport, Helen. *The Romanov Sisters* — 920
Alexandria Ocasio-Cortez. Jones, Brenda — B
Alexie, Sherman
   You Don't Have to Say You Love Me — 818
ALEXIE, SHERMAN, 1966-
   Alexie, Sherman. *You Don't Have to Say You Love Me* — 818
ALEXIUS I COMNENUS, EMPEROR OF THE EAST, 1048-1118
   Frankopan, Peter. *The First Crusade* — 956
★*Alfie and Me.* Safina, Carl — 598.9
Alford, Henry
   And Then We Danced — 792.8
ALFORD, HENRY, 1962-
   Alford, Henry. *And Then We Danced* — 792.8
Alford, Terry
   Fortune's Fool — B
Algeria. Evans, Martin — 965
ALGERIA
   Evans, Martin. *Algeria* — 965
   Shatz, Adam. *The Rebel's Clinic* — 965
ALGERIAN PEOPLE
   Shatz, Adam. *The Rebel's Clinic* — 965
   Todd, Olivier. *Albert Camus* — B
ALGORITHMS
   Chayka, Kyle. *Filterworld* — 306
   DiResta, Renee. *Invisible Rulers* — 320
   Essinger, James. *Ada's Algorithm* — B
   Fortnow, Lance. *The Golden Ticket* — 511.3
   Algorithms to Live By. Christian, Brian — 153.4
★*Ali.* Eig, Jonathan — B
ALI IBN ABI TALIB, CALIPH, CA. 600-661
   Hazleton, Lesley. *After the Prophet* — 297.8
Ali, Fatima
   ★*Savor* — B
ALI, FATIMA, -2019
   Ali, Fatima. ★*Savor* — B
Ali, Laila
   Food for Life — 641.5
ALI, MUHAMMAD, 1942-2016
   Eig, Jonathan. ★*Ali* — B
   Montville, Leigh. *Sting Like a Bee* — B
   Roberts, Randy. *Blood Brothers* — 920
ALI, TAHA MUHAMMAD
   Hoffman, Adina. ★*My Happiness Bears No Relation to Happiness* — B
Ali, Wajahat
   Go Back to Where You Came From — B
ALI, WAJAHAT
   Ali, Wajahat. *Go Back to Where You Came From* — B
Ali-Karamali, Sumbul
   Demystifying Shariah — 340.5
Alice. Cordery, Stacy A. — B
Alice Neel. Hoban, Phoebe — B
Alice's Piano. Mueller, Melissa — B
Alicia, Anna
   Bags — 646.4
ALIEN (HACKER)
   Smith, Jeremy N. *Breaking and Entering* — B
★*Alien Earths.* Kaltenegger, Lisa — 523.2
The Alien Perspective. Whitehouse, David — 523.1
ALIEN PLANTS
   Stone, Daniel. *The Food Explorer* — B
Alien Worlds. Nicholls, Steve — 595.7
ALIENATION
   Bitsui, Sherwin. *Dissolve* — 811
   Geter, Hafizah. *Un-American* — 811
   Gottlieb, Lori. ★*Maybe You Should Talk to Someone* — B
   Gupta, Prachi. ★*They Called Us Exceptional* — B
   Henning, Kristin. *The Rage of Innocence* — 364.36
   Miller, Kei. *Things I Have Withheld* — 814
   Parker, Morgan. ★*You Get What You Pay For* — 305.896
   Roberts, Matthias. *Holy Runaways* — 262
   Satrapi, Marjane. ★*The Complete Persepolis* — 741.5
   Seuss, Diane. ★*Frank* — 811
   Ward, Jon. *Testimony* — 277.308
   Way, Niobe. *Rebels with a Cause* — 649

ALIENS
   Kershenbaum, Arik. *The Zoologist's Guide to the Galaxy* — 576.8
   Loeb, Abraham. *Extraterrestrial* — 576.8
   Prothero, Donald R. *UFOs, Chemtrails, and Aliens* — 001.94
   Scoles, Sarah. *They Are Already Here* — 001.942
   Summers, Michael E. *Exoplanets* — 523.2
   Ward, Peter Douglas. *Life as We Do Not Know It* — 576.839
The Aliens Among Us. Anthony, Leslie — 578.6
Alikhani, Nasim
   Sofreh — 641.595
Alinder, Mary Street
   Ansel Adams — B
   Group F.64 — 770.92
Alinizhad, Masih
   The Wind in My Hair — B
ALINIZHAD, MASIH, 1976-
   Alinizhad, Masih. *The Wind in My Hair* — B
Alison Glass Applique. Glass, Alison — 746.44
★*Alive.* Read, Piers Paul — 982
Alive At the End of the World. Jones, Saeed — 811
ALKHANSHALI, MOKHTAR
   Eggers, Dave. *The Monk of Mokha* — B
Alkon, Amy
   Good Manners for Nice People — 395
All About Cake. Tosi, Christina — 641.86
All About Cookies. Tosi, Christina — 641.86
★*All About Me!* Brooks, Mel — B
★*All American.* Crawford, Bill — B
All Blood Runs Red. Keith, Philip A. — B
★*All Creatures Great and Small.* Herriot, James — B
All creatures great and small [Series]. Herriot, James — B
All Down Darkness Wide. Hewitt, Sean — B
All Fishermen Are Liars. Gierach, John — 799.12
All Governments Lie. MacPherson, Myra — B
All Hell Breaking Loose. Klare, Michael T. — 355.20973
★*All In.* King, Billie Jean — B
★*All in Her Head.* Comen, Elizabeth — 613
All in Her Head. Pratt, Misty — 616.89
★*All in the Dances.* Teachout, Terry — B
All in the Family. Self, Robert O. — 320.50973
★*All Is Change.* Sutin, Lawrence — 294.309
All Joy and No Fun. Senior, Jennifer — 306.874
All My Knotted-Up Life. Moore, Beth — B
All of It Singing. Gregg, Linda — 811.54
★*All of the Marvels.* Wolk, Douglas — 741.5
All of Us. Carver, Raymond — 811
All Points Patchwork. Gilleland, Diane — 746.46
All Rivers Run to the Sea. Wiesel, Elie — B
All That Happiness Is. Gopnik, Adam — 158.1
All That Moves Us. Wellons, Jay — 617.4
All That You Leave Behind. Carr, Erin Lee — B
All The Answers. Kupperman, Michael — 741.5
All The Best, George Bush. Bush, George — 973.928
All The Colors Came Out. Fagan, Kate — B
All The Devils Are Here. McLean, Bethany — 330.973
All The Dreams We've Dreamed. Bradburd, Rus — 796.323
All The Flowers Kneeling. Tran, Paul — 811
All The Frequent Troubles of Our Days. Donner, Rebecca — 943
★*All The Knowledge in the World.* Garfield, Simon — 030.9
All The Kremlin's Men. Zygar, Mikhail — 947.086
All The Lives We Ever Lived. Smyth, Katharine — B
All The Living and the Dead. Campbell, Hayley — 363.7
All The Odes. Neruda, Pablo — 861
★*All The Powers of Earth.* Blumenthal, Sidney — B
★*All The President's Men.* Bernstein, Carl — 364.1
★*All The Shah's Men.* Kinzer, Stephen — 955.05
All The Songs. Guesdon, Jean-Michel — 782.42166
All The Stops. Whitney, Craig R. — 786.5
All The Time in the World. Jenkins, Jessica Kerwin — 390
★*All The Way.* Namath, Joe Willie — B
All The Worst Humans. Elwood, Phil — 659.2
All The Wrong Moves. Chapin, Sasha — 794.1092
★*All Things Are Too Small.* Rothfeld, Becca — 814
All Things Must Pass Away. Womack, Kenneth — 781.66
All Things Wise and Wonderful. Herriot, James — B
All You Can Ever Know. Chung, Nicole — B
Allen, Arthur
   ★*The Fantastic Laboratory of Dr. Weigl* — 614.5

PUBLIC LIBRARY CORE COLLECTION: NONFICTION
Twentieth Edition

Allen, Brigette
   Living Without Plastic — 640
Allen, Cory
   Now Is the Way — 158.1
Allen, David
   ★*Getting Things Done* — 646.7
Allen, Frederick Lewis
   Only Yesterday — 973.9
Allen, Jonathan
   Lucky — 324.973
   Shattered — 324.973
ALLEN, MARK, 1958-
   Fitzgerald, Matt. *Iron War* — 796.42
Allen, Marshall
   ★*Never Pay the First Bill* — 610.28
ALLEN, RICHARD, 1760-1831
   Newman, Richard S. *Freedom's Prophet* — B
ALLENDE FAMILY
   Allende, Isabel. ★*Paula* — B
Allende, Isabel
   My Invented Country — B
   ★*Paula* — B
   The Sum of Our Days — B
ALLENDE, ISABEL
   Allende, Isabel. *My Invented Country* — B
   Allende, Isabel. ★*Paula* — B
   Allende, Isabel. *The Sum of Our Days* — B
ALLERGENS
   MacPhail, Theresa. *Allergic* — 616.97
Allergic. MacPhail, Theresa — 616.97
ALLERGIC REACTION
   MacPhail, Theresa. *Allergic* — 616.97
ALLERGY
   MacPhail, Theresa. *Allergic* — 616.97
The Allergy Book. Sears, Robert W. — 618.92
Allert, Tilman
   Heil Hitler — 395.4
Allgor, Catherine
   A Perfect Union — B
ALLIANCES
   Broers, Michael. *Napoleon* — 944.05
   Capozzola, Christopher. *Bound by War* — 355
   Charter, David. *Royal Audience* — 941.085
   Cozzens, Peter. *Tecumseh and the Prophet* — 920
   Dugard, Martin. *Taking Berlin* — 940.54
   Ferling, John E. *Winning Independence* — 973.3
   Ferreiro, Larrie D. *Brothers at Arms* — 327.73
   Hanna-Attisha, Mona. *What the Eyes Don't See* — 615.9
   Katz, Catherine Grace. *The Daughters of Yalta* — 920
   Roll, David L. *Ascent to Power* — 973.918
   Silverman, David J. ★*This Land Is Their Land* — 974.4
   Stanley, Matthew. *Einstein's War* — 530
Allibhoy, Omar
   Spanish Made Simple — 641.594
The Allies. Groom, Winston — 940.5309
ALLIGATORS
   Renner, Rebecca. ★*Gator Country* — 364.16
ALLILUEVA, SVETLANA, 1926-2011
   Sullivan, Rosemary. *Stalin's Daughter* — B
Allitt, Patrick
   The Conservatives — 320.520973
Allmen, Tara
   Menopause Confidential — 618.1
Allport, Alan
   Britain at Bay — 940.53
Allred, Alexandra Powe
   When Women Stood — 796.082
The Allure of Battle. Nolan, Cathal J. — 355.409
ALLUSIONS
   Brewer, Ebenezer Cobham. ★*Brewer's Dictionary of Phrase & Fable* — 423
ALMANACS
   Felder, Deborah G. *The American Women's Almanac* — 305.40973
   Keffer, Ken. *Earth Almanac* — 508
Almond, Steve
   ★*Candyfreak* — 338.4
   Rock and Roll Will Save Your Life — 781.6
ALMOND, STEVE
   Almond, Steve. ★*Candyfreak* — 338.4

Almost Everything. Lamott, Anne — 170
The Almost Nearly Perfect People. Booth, Michael — 948.071
An Almost Perfect Christmas. Stibbe, Nina — 394.2663
Almost President. Farris, Scott — 324.973
Almost There. DiFelice, Bekah — 248.8
Aloha Kitchen. Kysar, Alana — 641.59969
Alone. Korda, Michael — 940.54
Alone on the Ice. Roberts, David — 919.8904
Alone on the Wall. Honnold, Alex — B
Alpha. Philipps, David — 956.7044
ALPHABET
   Rosen, Michael. *Alphabetical* — 421
Alphabetical. Rosen, Michael — 421
Alphabetical Diaries. Heti, Sheila — 818
ALPHABETS
   Rodriguez, Dina. *The Big Awesome Book of Hand & Chalk Lettering* — 745.6
   ★*Already Toast*. Washington, Kate — 649.8
Also A Poet. Calhoun, Ada — B
Alt, Matt
   Pure Invention — 306.0952
Alter, Adam L.
   Anatomy of a Breakthrough — 158.1
Alter, Jonathan
   His Very Best — B
ALTERED STATES OF CONSCIOUSNESS
   Pollan, Michael. *How to Change Your Mind* — 615.7
ALTERMAN, IRA
   Alterman, Sara Faith. *Let's Never Talk About This Again* — 616.8
Alterman, Sara Faith
   Let's Never Talk About This Again — 616.8
The Alternative. Romeo, Nick — 174
ALTERNATIVE COMICS
   Inman, Matthew. *The Terrible and Wonderful Reasons Why I Run Long Distances* — 741.5
ALTERNATIVE ENERGY DEVELOPMENT
   Scheyder, Ernest. *The War Below* — 333.7
ALTERNATIVE FUELS
   Higgins, Tim. *Power Play* — 338.7
ALTERNATIVE LIFESTYLES
   Cohen, Rhaina. ★*The Other Significant Others* — 177
   McGrath, Ben. *Riverman* — 797.122
   Rawles, James Wesley. *Tools for Survival* — 613.6
   Sundeen, Mark. *The Unsettlers* — 640
ALTERNATIVE MEDICINE
   B., David. *Epileptic* — 741.5
   Beres, Derek. *Conspirituality* — 001.9
   Harrison, Christy. *The Wellness Trap* — 613
   Hongoltz-Hetling, Matthew. *If It Sounds Like a Quack* — 615.8
   Hotz, Julia. ★*The Connection Cure* — 610
   Marchant, Jo. *Cure* — 616.89
   Nigg, Joel T. *Getting Ahead of ADHD* — 618.92
   Ryckman, Pamela. *Candace Pert* — B
   Servan-Schreiber, David. *Anticancer* — 616.99
   Taylor, Madisyn. *Unmedicated* — 615.8
   Waldman, Ayelet. *A Really Good Day* — B
   Weil, Andrew. *Mind Over Meds* — 362.29
ALTERNATIVE ROCK MUSIC
   Cross, Charles R. *Here We Are Now* — 782.42166
   Gordon, Kim. *Girl in a Band* — B
   Hyden, Steven. *Long Road* — 782.42166
   Mehr, Bob. *Trouble Boys* — 920
   Moore, Thurston. *Sonic Life* — B
   Schemel, Patty. *Hit so Hard* — B
ALTERNATIVE ROCK MUSICIANS
   Cross, Charles R. *Here We Are Now* — 782.42166
   Gordon, Kim. *Girl in a Band* — B
   Moore, Thurston. *Sonic Life* — B
   Schemel, Patty. *Hit so Hard* — B
   Tweedy, Jeff. *Let's Go (so We Can Get Back)* — B
ALTERNATIVE SCHOOLS
   Kuo, Michelle. *Reading with Patrick* — B
ALTERNATIVES TO IMPRISONMENT
   Davis, Angela Y. *Abolition* — 364.6
Althea. Jacobs, Sally H. — B
Altmann, Tanya Remer
   What to Feed Your Baby — 649
ALTRUISM
   Grant, Adam M. *Give and Take* — 158.2

AUTHOR, TITLE, SERIES AND SUBJECT INDEX

Keltner, Dacher. *Born to Be Good*	155.2
Lapierre, Dominique. *The City of Joy*	954
Moore, Wes. *The Work*	B
Paxson, Margaret. *The Plateau*	362.87
Solnit, Rebecca. *A Paradise Built in Hell*	303.48
Yunus, Muhammad. *A World of Three Zeros*	330

ALVARENGA, SALVADOR, APPROXIMATELY 1977
Franklin, Jonathan. *438 Days*	910.91

Alvarez, Celine
The Natural Laws of Children	372.21

Alvarez, Julia
The Woman I Kept to Myself	811

Alvarez, Noe
Spirit Run	796.42

ALVAREZ, NOE
Alvarez, Noe. *Spirit Run*	796.42

Alvarez, Walter
A Most Improbable Journey	550

Alvis-Walker, Marcie
Everybody Come Alive	B

ALVIS-WALKER, MARCIE
Alvis-Walker, Marcie. *Everybody Come Alive*	B

Always Hungry?. Ludwig, David — 613.2
Always Looking. Updike, John — 700

Aly, Gotz
Europe Against the Jews	305.892

Alyan, Hala
The Moon That Turns You Back	811

ALZHEIMER'S DISEASE
Alterman, Sara Faith. *Let's Never Talk About This Again*	616.8
Bloom, Amy. *In Love*	B
Cornelius, Maria M. *The Final Season*	B
Coste, Joanne Koenig. *Learning to Speak Alzheimer's*	362.1
Davis, Patti. *Floating in the Deep End*	616.8
Harden, Marcia Gay. *The Seasons of My Mother*	B
Karlawish, Jason. ★*The Problem of Alzheimer's*	616.8
Kiper, Dasha. ★*Travelers to Unimaginable Lands*	616.8
Kozol, Jonathan. *The Theft of Memory*	B
Kupperman, Michael. *All the Answers*	741.5
Mace, Nancy L. ★*The 36-Hour Day*	616.8
Mitchell, Wendy. *Somebody I Used to Know*	B
Powell, Tia. *Dementia Reimagined*	616.8
Pratchett, Terry. *A Slip of the Keyboard*	824

Am I Alone Here?. Orner, Peter — 814
Am I Dying?! Kelly, Christopher R. — 362.1
Ama. Centeno, Josef — 641.5979

Amanat, Abbas
Iran	955

Amano, Hugh
Let's Make Dumplings!	741.5

Amar, Akhil Reed
★*America's Constitution*	342.7302
The Constitution Today	342.73
The Words That Made Us	342.7302

AMATEUR DETECTIVES
Lankford, Andrea. *Trail of the Lost*	363.2

AMATEUR FILMS
Kurtz, Glenn. *Three Minutes in Poland*	947.7
Zapruder, Alexandra. *Twenty-Six Seconds*	973.922092

AMATEUR MUSICIANS
Rusbridger, Alan. ★*Play It Again*	B

The Amateurs. Halberstam, David — B
The Amazing Story of Quantum Mechanics. Kakalios, James — 530.12

AMAZON RIVER
Grann, David. *The Lost City of Z*	918.1

AMAZON RIVER REGION
Wallace, Scott. *The Unconquered*	981

AMAZON VALLEY
Davis, Wade. *One River*	581.6
Millard, Candice. *River of Doubt*	918.1

AMBASSADORS
Eisen, Norman L. *The Last Palace*	920
Ghobash, Omar Saif. *Letters to a Young Muslim*	297.09
Kemper, Steve. *Our Man in Tokyo*	952.03
McKean, David. *Watching Darkness Fall*	940.53
Nasaw, David. ★*The Patriarch*	B
Packer, George. *Our Man*	B
Thompson, Nicholas. *The Hawk and the Dove*	973.92
Yovanovitch, Marie. *Lessons from the Edge*	973.933

Ambinder, Marc
The Brink	355.5

AMBITION
Asher, Zain E. *Where the Children Take Us*	942.1
Baker, Peter. *The Man Who Ran Washington*	B
Bernstein, Andrea. *American Oligarchs*	920
Blumenthal, Sidney. ★*All the Powers of Earth*	B
Blumenthal, Sidney. *A Self-Made Man*	B
Blumenthal, Sidney. *Wrestling with His Angel*	B
Bunker, Nick. *Young Benjamin Franklin*	B
Clark, Lloyd. *The Commanders*	940.53
Davidson, Adam. *The Passion Economy*	330.9
Davis, Seth. *Wooden*	B
Davis, Viola. ★*Finding Me*	B
Driver, Minnie. *Managing Expectations*	B
Ferguson, Jane. *No Ordinary Assignment*	B
Fox, Margalit. *The Talented Mrs. Mandelbaum*	364.1
Gabriel, Mary. *Madonna*	B
Gardner, Chris. ★*Permission to Dream*	158.1
Gelwicks, Andrew. *The Queer Advantage*	920
Georges, Gigi. *Downeast*	974.1
Gillard, Julia. ★*Women and Leadership*	158
Goldstone, Nancy Bazelon. *The Rival Queens*	944
Greenberg, Amy S. *Lady First*	B
Guelzo, Allen C. *Robert E. Lee*	B
Hallman, J. C. *Say Anarcha*	618.1
Harris, Mark. *Mike Nichols*	B
Harss, Marina. *The Boy from Kyiv*	B
Heughan, Sam. *Waypoints*	B
Hill, Jemele. *Uphill*	B
Holiday, Ryan. *Ego Is the Enemy*	158.1
Hope, Bradley. *Blood and Oil*	B
Hubbard, Ben (Journalist). *Mbs*	B
Jahren, Hope. ★*Lab Girl*	B
James, Victoria. *Wine Girl*	B
Jordan, Mary. *The Art of Her Deal*	B
Krimstein, Ken. *When I Grow Up*	741.5
Landdeck, Katherine Sharp. *The Women with Silver Wings*	920
Lozada, Carlos. *The Washington Book*	320
Manchester, William. *The Last Lion, Winston Spencer Churchill*	B
Mann, William J. *The Wars of the Roosevelts*	B
McGilligan, Patrick. *Young Orson*	B
Meacham, Jon. ★*Thomas Jefferson*	B
Miller, Donald L. *Supreme City*	974.7
Norgren, Jill. *Belva Lockwood*	B
Oller, John. *American Queen*	B
Packer, George. *Our Man*	B
Page, Susan. ★*The Rulebreaker*	B
Pak, Jung H. *Becoming Kim Jong Un*	B
Porter, Billy. ★*Unprotected*	B
Price, Margo. *Maybe We'll Make It*	B
Rannells, Andrew. *Too Much Is Not Enough*	792.02
Rannells, Andrew. *Uncle of the Year*	B
Risen, James. ★*The Last Honest Man*	973.92
Simmons, Ruth. ★*Up Home*	B
Southon, Emma. *Agrippina*	B
Stanley, Paul. *Face the Music*	B
Stark, Peter. *Astoria*	979.5
Strathern, Paul. *The Borgias*	945.06
Sun, Carrie. *Private Equity*	B
Thompson, Wright. *The Cost of These Dreams*	B
Ward, Maitland. *Rated X*	B
White, Richard Antoine. *I'm Possible*	B
Windhorst, Brian. *Lebron, Inc.*	B

Ambition and Desire. Williams, Kate — B

AMBITION IN CHILDREN
Hobbs, Jeff. *Show Them You're Good*	373

AMBIVALENCE
Berg, Anastasia. ★*What Are Children For?*	306.87

Amboy. Cailan, Alvin — 641.595

Ambrose, Stephen E.
★*Band of Brothers*	920
Citizen Soldiers	940.54
D-Day, June 6, 1944	940.54
Nothing Like It in the World	385
★*Undaunted Courage*	917.804
The Victors	940.54

PUBLIC LIBRARY CORE COLLECTION: NONFICTION
Twentieth Edition

    The Wild Blue   940.54
Ambroz, David
    A Place Called Home   B
AMBROZ, DAVID
    Ambroz, David. *A Place Called Home*   B
AMBULANCE SERVICE
    Hazzard, Kevin M. *American Sirens*   362.18
AMBUSHES AND SURPRISES
    Maraniss, David. *They Marched into Sunlight*   959.704
Amelia Earhart. Winters, Kathleen C.   B
★*The Amen Effect.* Brous, Sharon   296.3
Amer, Lindz
    Rainbow Parenting   649
America. Carballo, David M.   912
America. Langholtz, Gabrielle   641.5973
America 1933. Golay, Michael   B
America and Iran. Ghazvinian, John   327
America for Americans. Lee, Erika   305.800973
America in the King years [Series]. Branch, Taylor   973
★*America on Fire*. Hinton, Elizabeth Kai   305.800973
America The Philosophical. Romano, Carlin   191
America's Bank. Lowenstein, Roger   332.1
★*America's Constitution*. Amar, Akhil Reed   342.7302
America's Game. Rice, Jerry   796.332
America's Great Debate. Bordewich, Fergus M.   973.6
America's Great Hiking Trails. Berger, Karen   796.510973
America's Library. Conaway, James   027.5
America's Most Haunted Hotels. Whitmer, Jamie Davis   133.1
America's Musical Life. Crawford, Richard   780
America's Other Audubon. Kiser, Joy M.   B
America's Pastor. Wacker, Grant   B
America's Reluctant Prince. Gillon, Steven M.   B
America's War for the Greater Middle East. Bacevich, Andrew J.   956.05
American Baby. Glaser, Gabrielle   B
The American Bible. Prothero, Stephen R.   973
AMERICAN BISON
    Duncan, Dayton. *Blood Memory*   599.64
    Rinella, Steven. *American Buffalo*   599.64
American Bloomsbury. Cheever, Susan   920
American Buffalo. Rinella, Steven   599.64
★*American Cake*. Byrn, Anne   641.86
American Carnage. Alberta, Tim   324.2734
American Cartel. Higham, Scott   338.4
American Catch. Greenberg, Paul   333.95
American Chica. Arana, Marie   B
An American Childhood. Dillard, Annie   B
The American Civil War. Keegan, John   973.7
AMERICAN CIVIL WAR ERA (1861-1865)
    Abbott, Karen. *Liar, Temptress, Soldier, Spy*   920
    Ash, Stephen V. *Firebrand of Liberty*   973.7
    Avlon, John P. *Lincoln and the Fight for Peace*   973.7
    Ayers, Edward L. ★*The Thin Light of Freedom*   975.5
    Blanton, DeAnne. *They Fought Like Demons*   973.7
    Blight, David W. *A Slave No More*   B
    Blount, Roy. *Robert E. Lee*   B
    Bordewich, Fergus M. *America's Great Debate*   973.6
    Bordewich, Fergus M. *Congress at War*   324.2734
    Brands, H. W. ★*The Zealot and the Emancipator*   920
    Brewster, Todd. *Lincoln's Gamble*   973.7
    Burlingame, Michael. *Abraham Lincoln*   B
    Carwardine, Richard. *Lincoln*   B
    Chernow, Ron. ★*Grant*   B
    Cwiklik, Robert. *Sheridan's Secret Mission*   973.8
    Davis, William C. *Crucible of Command*   920
    Delbanco, Andrew. *The War Before the War*   973.7
    Donald, David Herbert. *Lincoln*   B
    Egan, Timothy. ★*The Immortal Irishman*   B
    Egerton, Douglas R. *Thunder at the Gates*   973.7
    Faust, Drew Gilpin. *Mothers of Invention*   973.7
    Faust, Drew Gilpin. *This Republic of Suffering*   973.7
    Fields-Black, Edda L. *Combee*   973.7
    Finkelman, Paul. *Millard Fillmore*   B
    Foner, Eric. *The Fiery Trial*   973.7092
    Foner, Eric. *Forever Free*   973.8
    Foner, Eric. *The Second Founding*   342.73
    Foote, Shelby. *The Civil War*   973.7
    Gienapp, William E. *Abraham Lincoln and Civil War America*   B
    Goodheart, Adam. *1861*   973.7
    Goodwin, Doris Kearns. ★*Team of Rivals*   B
    Gorra, Michael Edward. *The Saddest Words*   813
    Grant, Ulysses S. ★*The Annotated Memoirs of Ulysses S. Grant*   B
    Grinspan, Jon. *Wide Awake*   973.7
    Groom, Winston. *Shiloh, 1862*   973.7
    Guelzo, Allen C. *Gettysburg*   973.7
    Gwynne, S. C. *Hymns of the Republic*   973.7
    Gwynne, S. C. *Rebel Yell*   B
    Harvey, Eleanor Jones. *The Civil War and American Art*   740.9
    Holzer, Harold. *A Just and Generous Nation*   973.7092
    Horwitz, Tony. *Confederates in the Attic*   973.7
    Jones, Jacqueline. *Saving Savannah*   975.8
    Keegan, John. *The American Civil War*   973.7
    Korda, Michael. *Clouds of Glory*   B
    Lance, Rachel. *In the Waves*   973.7
    Larson, Erik. ★*The Demon of Unrest*   973.7
    Levine, Bruce C. *The Fall of the House of Dixie*   973.7
    Levine, Bruce C. *Thaddeus Stevens*   B
    Levine, Robert S. ★*The Failed Promise*   973.8
    Lincoln, Abraham. *Speeches and Writings, 1859-1865*   973.6
    Lineberry, Cate. *Be Free or Die*   B
    Lowenstein, Roger. *Ways and Means*   973.7
    Manning, Chandra. *Troubled Refuge*   973.7
    Marvel, William. *Lincoln's Autocrat*   B
    Masur, Louis P. *The Civil War*   973.7
    McDonough, James L. *William Tecumseh Sherman*   B
    McMurtry, Larry. *Custer*
    McPherson, James M. *Battle Cry of Freedom*   973.7
    McPherson, James M. *Drawn with the Sword*   973.7
    McPherson, James M. *For Cause and Comrades*   973.7
    McPherson, James M. *Hallowed Ground*   973.7
    McPherson, James M. ★*Tried by War*   973.7
    Meltzer, Brad. *The Lincoln Conspiracy*   973.7092
    Melville, Herman. *Complete Poems*   811
    Miller, Donald L. *Vicksburg*   973.7
    Mitchell, Elizabeth. *Lincoln's Lie*   973.7092
    Nelson, Megan Kate. *The Three-Cornered War*   978
    O'Donnell, Patrick K. *The Unvanquished*   973.7
    Oakes, James. *Freedom National*   973.7
    Postel, Charles. *Equality*   305.50973
    Pryor, Elizabeth Brown. *Six Encounters with Lincoln*   973.7092
    Raines, Howell. *Silent Cavalry*   973.7
    Reynolds, David S. ★*Abe*   B
    Reynolds, David S. *Mightier Than the Sword*   813
    Richards, Leonard L. *Who Freed the Slaves?*   342.7308
    Richardson, Heather Cox. ★*How the South Won the Civil War*   306.20973
    Roberts, Cokie. *Capital Dames*   920
    Sandburg, Carl. *Abraham Lincoln*   B
    Sears, Stephen W. ★*Chancellorsville*   973.7
    Sears, Stephen W. *Gettysburg*   973.7
    Sears, Stephen W. ★*Landscape Turned Red*   973.7
    Sears, Stephen W. *Lincoln's Lieutenants*   920
    Seidule, Ty. *Robert E. Lee and Me*   973.7
    Seiple, Samantha. *Louisa on the Front Lines*   B
    Stahr, Walter. *Seward*   B
    Stahr, Walter. ★*Stanton*   B
    Stiles, T. J. *Custer's Trials*   B
    Stiles, T. J. *Jesse James*   B
    Symonds, Craig L. *Lincoln and His Admirals*   B
    Taylor, Alan. *American Civil Wars*   973.7
    Toler, Pamela D. *Heroines of Mercy Street*   973.7
    Varon, Elizabeth R. *Longstreet*   B
    Waller, Douglas C. *Lincoln's Spies*   973.7
    Ward, Andrew. ★*The Slaves' War*   973.7
    Ward, Geoffrey C. *The Civil War*   973.7
    Wert, Jeffry D. *Cavalryman of the Lost Cause*   B
    Wheelan, Joseph. ★*Terrible Swift Sword*   B
    White, Ronald C. *A. Lincoln*   B
    White, Ronald C. ★*American Ulysses*   B
    Wickenden, Dorothy. *The Agitators*   920
    Williams, David. *Bitterly Divided*   973.7
    Willis, Deborah. ★*The Black Civil War Soldier*   973.7
    Willis, Deborah. *Envisioning Emancipation*   973.7
    Wills, Garry. *Lincoln at Gettysburg*   973.7
    Wilson, Robert. *Mathew Brady*   B
    Wineapple, Brenda. *Ecstatic Nation*   973.6
    Winik, Jay. *April 1865*   973.7
    Witt, John Fabian. *Lincoln's Code*   343.73

AUTHOR, TITLE, SERIES AND SUBJECT INDEX

American Civil Wars. Taylor, Alan	973.7
★*American* Cookie. Byrn, Anne	641.86
American Creation. Ellis, Joseph J.	973.3
American Crucifixion. Beam, Alex	B
★*American* Dance. Fuhrer, Margaret	792.809
American Demon. Stashower, Daniel	364.152
★*American* Dialogue. Ellis, Joseph J.	973.3
AMERICAN DREAM	
Brands, H. W. *Dreams of El Dorado*	978
Campoverdi, Alejandra. *First Gen*	B
Churchwell, Sarah Bartlett. *Behold, America*	973.9
Gerald, Casey. *There Will Be No Miracles Here*	B
Goudeau, Jessica. ★*After the Last Border*	362.83
Herold, Benjamin. *Disillusioned*	307.76
Hinojosa, Maria. *Once I Was You*	B
Johnson, Theodore R. *When the Stars Begin to Fall*	305.800973
Lemann, Nicholas. *Transaction Man*	330.973
Leonhardt, David. ★*Ours Was the Shining Future*	330.973
Liu, Simu. ★*We Were Dreamers*	B
Luiselli, Valeria. *Tell Me How It Ends*	305.23086
McCullough, David G. ★*The American Spirit*	973
Moore, Peter. *Life, Liberty, and the Pursuit of Happiness*	199
Nietfeld, Emi. *Acceptance*	B
Osnos, Evan. *Wildland*	973.93
Putnam, Robert D. *Our Kids*	305.5
Quart, Alissa. *Bootstrapped*	305.5
Rubenstein, David M. *The American Experiment*	973
Shahani, Aarti Namdev. *Here We Are*	B
Shih, David. *Chinese Prodigal*	B
Smith, Mychal Denzel. *Stakes Is High*	973.933
Tesfamariam, Rahiel. ★*Imagine Freedom*	305.896
An *American* Dreamer. Finkel, David	975.8
American Dreamer. Hilfiger, Tommy	B
American Eclipse. Baron, David	523.7
★*American* Eden. Johnson, Victoria	580.973
American Empire Project [Series]. Gopal, Anand	920
American Epic. Wald, Elijah	781.64
The *American* Experiment. Rubenstein, David M.	973
American Flannel. Kurutz, Steven	338.4
American Founders. Proenza-Coles, Christina	973
American Girls. Roy, Jessica	305.48
American Ground. Langewiesche, William	974.7
American Grown. Obama, Michelle	635.09
American Gun. McWhirter, Cameron	683.4
The *American* Heritage Dictionary of Idioms. Ammer, Christine	423
The *American* Home Front, 1941-1942. Cooke, Alistair	940.53
American Hoodie. Slade, Rachel	338.4
American Huckster. Papenfuss, Mary	B
American Impressionism. Gerdts, William H.	759.13
American Injustice. Rudolf, David S.	345.73
★*American* Judaism. Sarna, Jonathan D.	296
American Kleptocracy. Michel, Casey	364.16
The *American* Leonardo. Brewer, John	759.5
★*American* Lion. Meacham, Jon	B
AMERICAN LITERATURE	
Bader, Philip. *African-American Writers*	810.9
Brown, David S. *Paradise Lost*	813
Franklin, Sara B. ★*The Editor*	B
Gilbert, Sandra M. ★*Still Mad*	810.9
Griffin, Farah Jasmine. *Read Until You Understand*	810.9
Hart, James David. *The Oxford Companion to American Literature*	810.9
Martinez Wood, Jamie. *Latino Writers and Journalists*	B
Rioux, Anne Boyd. *Meg, Jo, Beth, Amy*	813
Row, Jess. *White Flights*	813
Showalter, Elaine. ★*A Jury of Her Peers*	810.9
American Made. Taylor, Nick	331.13
American Melancholy. Oates, Joyce Carol	811
American Midnight. Hochschild, Adam	973.91
The *American* Military. Glatthaar, Joseph T.	355.00973
American Mirror. Solomon, Deborah	B
★*American* Moonshot. Brinkley, Douglas	629.40973
American Mother. McCann, Colum	956.9104
American Oligarchs. Bernstein, Andrea	920
American Originality. Gluck, Louise	814
American Overdose. McGreal, Chris	362.29
AMERICAN PARTICIPATION IN WARS	
Brown, Daniel James. ★*Facing the Mountain*	940.54
Carroll, Andrew. *My Fellow Soldiers*	940.4
Delmont, Matthew F. *Half American*	940.54
Hervieux, Linda. *Forgotten*	940.54
Hogan, William R. *Task Force Hogan*	940.54
Tuccille, Jerome. *The Roughest Riders*	973.8
American Passage. Cannato, Vincent	325.73
AMERICAN PEOPLE	
Ahdoot, Dan. *Undercooked*	647.95
Alexander, Kwame. *Why Fathers Cry at Night*	B
Alexander, Paul. *Bitter Crop*	B
Andrews, Lena S. ★*Valiant Women*	940.53
Arana, Marie. ★*Latinoland*	973
Arsenault, Raymond. *John Lewis*	B
Ashley, Maurice. *Move by Move*	158
Babb, Valerie Melissa. *The Book of James*	B
Baier, Bret. *To Rescue the Constitution*	973.4
Bell, Darrin. ★*The Talk*	741.5
Bellows, Amanda Brickell. *The Explorers*	910.92
Bergstein, Rachelle. *The Genius of Judy*	813
Bertch, Jane. *The French Ingredient*	B
Black Thought. *The Upcycled Self*	B
Blair, Gabrielle Stanley. ★*Ejaculate Responsibly*	362.1988
Blake, Melissa. *Beautiful People*	362.4
Bradbury, Ray. ★*Remembrance*	813
Braitman, Laurel. *What Looks Like Bravery*	B
Brown, Daniel James. ★*The Boys in the Boat*	797.12
Bunting, Josiah. ★*The Making of a Leader*	B
Butcher, Barbara. *What the Dead Know*	614
Campoverdi, Alejandra. *First Gen*	B
Carr, Caleb. *My Beloved Monster*	B
Cecchi-Azzolina, Michael. *Your Table Is Ready*	647.95
Chapman, Rex. ★*It's Hard for Me to Live with Me*	B
Cheney, Liz. *Oath and Honor*	328.73
Chin, Curtis. *Everything I Learned, I Learned in a Chinese Restaurant*	B
Chrisinger, David. *The Soldier's Truth*	940.54
Chung, Nicole. ★*A Living Remedy*	B
Cobbs-Leonard, Tasha. *Do It Anyway*	241
Cohen, Jared. *Life After Power*	973.09
Conyers, Jonathan. *I Wasn't Supposed to Be Here*	B
Cooper, Christian. *Better Living Through Birding*	B
Cooper, Sean Patrick. *The Shooter at Midnight*	363.25
Crosley, Sloane. *Grief Is for People*	B
Daley, Mark. *Safe*	B
Daugherty, Tracy. *Larry McMurtry*	B
Dearborn, Mary V. *Carson McCullers*	B
Drabkin, Ronald. *Beverly Hills Spy*	940.54
Dubus, Andre. *Ghost Dogs*	814
Duggar, Jill. *Counting the Cost*	B
Dunn, Harry. *Standing My Ground*	B
Dunne, Griffin. ★*The Friday Afternoon Club*	B
Ellis, Joseph J. *American Creation*	973.3
Elwood, Phil. *All the Worst Humans*	659.2
Etheridge, Melissa. *Talking to My Angels*	B
Eyman, Scott. *Charlie Chaplin vs. America*	B
Fall, Jeremy. *Falling Upwards*	158.1
Finkel, David. *An American Dreamer*	975.8
Flannery, Kate. *Strip Tees*	338.4
Fleshman, Lauren. ★*Good for a Girl*	B
Foer, Franklin. ★*The Last Politician*	973.934
Ford, Christine Blasey. *One Way Back*	B
Ford, Tanisha C. *Our Secret Society*	B
Fox, Julia. *Down the Drain*	B
Fumudoh, Ziwe. ★*Black Friend*	814
Gabriel, Mary. *Madonna*	B
Gage, Beverly. *G-Man*	B
Gaines, Joanna. *The Stories We Tell*	B
Garner, Dwight. *The Upstairs Delicatessen*	B
Gooch, Brad. *Radiant*	B
Gorrindo, Simone. ★*The Wives*	B
Greenidge, Kerri. ★*The Grimkes*	973.5
Grush, Loren. ★*The Six*	629.4
Gulman, Gary. *Misfit*	B
Gupta, Prachi. ★*They Called Us Exceptional*	B
Gutzman, Kevin R. C. *The Jeffersonians*	973.5
Hahn, Emanuel. *Koreatown Dreaming*	979.4
Hallman, J. C. *Say Anarcha*	618.1
Hamilton, Lisa M. *The Hungry Season*	B
Handler, Daniel. ★*And Then? and Then? What Else?*	813
Hanna, Kathleen. *Rebel Girl*	B

PUBLIC LIBRARY CORE COLLECTION: NONFICTION
Twentieth Edition

Hansberry, Lorraine. ★*A Raisin in the Sun*	812
Harry. ★*Spare*	B
Harss, Marina. *The Boy from Kyiv*	B
Heat Moon, William Least. *Roads to Quoz*	917.3
Henderson, Rob Kim. *Troubled*	B
Hermes, Will. *Lou Reed*	B
Hobbs, Jeff. *Children of the State*	364.36
Hoja, Gulchehra. *A Stone Is Most Precious Where It Belongs*	B
Holley, Santi Elijah. *An Amerikan Family*	920
Horton, Michelle. *Dear Sister*	B
Hulls, Tessa. ★*Feeding Ghosts*	741.5
Isaacson, Walter. ★*Elon Musk*	B
Jacobs, Sally H. *Althea*	B
Jun, Tasha. ★*Tell Me the Dream Again*	248
Kemper, Steve. *Our Man in Tokyo*	952.03
Kerouac, Jack. *Book of Sketches, 1952-57*	818
Kershaw, Alex. *The Few*	940.54
Kissinger, Meg. *While You Were Out*	362.2
Kristof, Nicholas D. ★*Chasing Hope*	B
Lauretta, D. S. *The Asteroid Hunter*	523.44
Leon, Donna. *My Venice and Other Essays*	945
Lewis, Robin Coste. *To the Realization of Perfect Helplessness*	811
Li, Fei-Fei. *The Worlds I See*	B
Mann, William J. *Bogie & Bacall*	920
Marshall, Greg. *Leg*	B
Masters, Oksana. *The Hard Parts*	B
Mattlin, Ben. *Disability Pride*	323.3
Max, D. T. *Finale*	782.1
McCormick, Mack. *Biography of a Phantom*	782.421643
McDonald, Greg (Producer). *Elvis and the Colonel*	920
McDonald, Michael. ★*What a Fool Believes*	B
McMillan, Tracie. ★*The White Bonus*	305.8
McNeur, Catherine. *Mischievous Creatures*	920
McPhee, John. *The Ransom of Russian Art*	709
Means, Brittany. *Hell If We Don't Change Our Ways*	B
Miles, Tiya. ★*Wild Girls*	304.2
Mojica Rodriguez, Prisca Dorcas. *For Brown Girls with Sharp Edges and Tender Hearts*	305.48
Monroe, Jana. *Hearts of Darkness*	363.25
Moore, Beth. *All My Knotted-Up Life*	B
Moore, Thurston. *Sonic Life*	B
Morgenson, Gretchen. *These Are the Plunderers*	332.6
Myers, Leah. *Thinning Blood*	B
Nathan, Joan. ★*My Life in Recipes*	641.5
Neiman, Garrett. *Rich White Men*	305.5
Nezhukumatathil, Aimee. *Bite by Bite*	641.3
Ng, Fae Myenne. *Orphan Bachelors*	B
Nguyen, Bich Minh. *Owner of a Lonely Heart*	B
Nguyen, Viet Thanh. ★*A Man of Two Faces*	B
Norris, Michele. ★*Our Hidden Conversations*	305
Norton, Hughes. ★*Rainmaker*	796.352
O'Brien, Keith. *Charlie Hustle*	796.357
Obama, Michelle. ★*The Light We Carry*	B
Osnos, Evan. *Wildland*	973.93
Page, Elliot. *Pageboy*	B
Pepin, Jacques. *Art of the Chicken*	641.665
Pittard, Hannah. *We Are Too Many*	B
Platt, Stephen R. *Autumn in the Heavenly Kingdom*	951
Popkin, Jim. *Code Name Blue Wren*	327.12
Psaki, Jen. *Say More*	B
Quinones, John. ★*One Year in Uvalde*	371.7
Raban, Jonathan. *Father and Son*	B
Raymond, Edwin. *An Inconvenient Cop*	363.2
Regan, Iliana. *Fieldwork*	B
Renkl, Margaret. *The Comfort of Crows*	814.6
Ressa, Maria. ★*How to Stand up to a Dictator*	070.92
Risen, James. ★*The Last Honest Man*	973.92
Robinson, Staci. ★*Tupac Shakur*	B
Roll, David L. *Ascent to Power*	973.918
Roy, Jessica. *American Girls*	305.48
Royster, Francesca T. *Choosing Family*	B
Ruffin, Amber. ★*The World Record Book of Racist Stories*	305.8
Salama, Jordan. ★*Stranger in the Desert*	982
Satow, Julie. *When Women Ran Fifth Avenue*	381.141
Schneider, Amy. *In the Form of a Question*	B
Selleck, Tom. *You Never Know*	B
Shane, Scott. ★*Flee North*	973.7
Shapiro, Ari. ★*The Best Strangers in the World*	B
Simmons, Ruth. ★*Up Home*	B
Singer, Matt. *Opposable Thumbs*	791.43
Sisson, Gretchen E. ★*Relinquished*	362.734
Smith, Freda Love. *I Quit Everything*	B
Smith, Jada Pinkett. *Worthy*	B
Smith, Richard Norton. *An Ordinary Man*	B
Smith, Tracy K. ★*To Free the Captives*	818
So, Anthony Veasna. ★*Songs on Endless Repeat*	814
Sokolik, Vicki. ★*If You See Them*	362.5
Sole-Smith, Virginia. ★*Fat Talk*	649.1
Spears, Britney. *The Woman in Me*	B
Stamos, John. *If You Would Have Told Me*	B
Stone, Sly. *Thank You (Falettinme Be Mice Elf Agin)*	B
Streisand, Barbra. ★*My Name Is Barbra*	B
Sun, Carrie. *Private Equity*	B
Taraborrelli, J. Randy. ★*Jackie*	B
Tate, Christie. *B.F.F.*	B
Tocqueville, Alexis de. ★*Democracy in America*	320.973
Toobin, Jeffrey. *Homegrown*	363.325
Valby, Karen. *The Swans of Harlem*	792.8
Velour, Sasha. ★*The Big Reveal*	792.7
Wallace, Carvell. *Another Word for Love*	B
Ward, Jon. *Testimony*	277.308
Washington, Kerry. *Thicker Than Water*	B
Watts, Reggie. *Great Falls, MT*	B
Weigel, Alicia Roth. *Inverse Cowgirl*	B
White, Ralph. *Getting Out of Saigon*	959.704
White, Ronald C. *On Great Fields*	B
Williams, Billy Dee. ★*What Have We Here*	B
Williams, Marlena. *Night Mother*	791.43
Wilson, A'ja. ★*Dear Black Girls*	158.1
Winkler, Henry. ★*Being Henry*	B
Wynn-Grant, Rae. *Wild Life*	B
Zwick, Edward. ★*Hits, Flops, and Other Illusions*	B
AMERICAN PEOPLE IN AFRICA	
Hessler, Peter. *The Buried*	962.05
Theroux, Paul. *The Last Train to Zona Verde*	916
AMERICAN PEOPLE IN ASIA	
Ansary, Mir Tamim. *Games Without Rules*	958.1
Bruning, John R. *Indestructible*	B
Capozzola, Christopher. *Bound by War*	355
Junger, Sebastian. *War*	958.104
Loyn, David. *In Afghanistan*	958.1
Meyer, Dakota. *Into the Fire*	958.104
Theroux, Paul. *The Great Railway Bazaar*	915
Theroux, Paul. *Riding the Iron Rooster*	915
AMERICAN PEOPLE IN AUSTRALIA	
Corrigan, Kelly. *Glitter and Glue*	B
AMERICAN PEOPLE IN CUBA	
Kurlansky, Mark. *Havana*	972.91
AMERICAN PEOPLE IN ENGLAND	
Byrne, Paula. *Kick*	B
Crawford, Robert. *Eliot After the Waste Land*	B
Leaming, Barbara. *Kick Kennedy*	B
AMERICAN PEOPLE IN EUROPE	
Callow, Simon. ★*Orson Welles*	B
Donner, Rebecca. *All the Frequent Troubles of Our Days*	943
Hochschild, Adam. *Spain in Our Hearts*	946.081
Larson, Erik. *In the Garden of Beasts*	B
Parini, Jay. *Borges and Me*	813
AMERICAN PEOPLE IN FOREIGN COUNTRIES	
Collins, Lauren. *When in French*	B
Kershaw, Alex. *The Few*	940.54
Leon, Donna. *My Venice and Other Essays*	945
Loyn, David. *In Afghanistan*	958.1
McPhee, John. *The Ransom of Russian Art*	709
Pressman, Steven. *50 Children*	940.53
AMERICAN PEOPLE IN FRANCE	
Bard, Elizabeth. *Lunch in Paris*	B
Bard, Elizabeth. *Picnic in Provence*	B
Buford, Bill. ★*Dirt*	B
Child, Julia. ★*My Life in France*	B
Kershaw, Alex. *Avenue of Spies*	940.53
McCullough, David G. *The Greater Journey*	920
Ronald, Susan. *A Dangerous Woman*	B
Sciolino, Elaine. *The Only Street in Paris*	944
Verant, Samantha. *Seven Letters from Paris*	B

AUTHOR, TITLE, SERIES AND SUBJECT INDEX

AMERICAN PEOPLE IN GREAT BRITAIN
   Bryson, Bill. *The Road to Little Dribbling*   914
   De Courcy, Anne. *The Husband Hunters*   920
AMERICAN PEOPLE IN INDIA
   Guha, Ramachandra. *Rebels Against the Raj*   954.03
AMERICAN PEOPLE IN IRELAND
   McCourt, Frank. ★*Angela's Ashes*   929
AMERICAN PEOPLE IN ITALY
   Mayes, Frances. *Bella Tuscany*   945
   Mayes, Frances. *See You in the Piazza*   914.5
   Mayes, Frances. *Under the Tuscan Sun*   945
   Wilson, Katherine. *Only in Naples*   B
AMERICAN PEOPLE IN MEXICO
   Wariner, Ruth. *The Sound of Gravel*   B
AMERICAN PEOPLE IN SOUTHWEST ASIA AND NORTH AFRICA (MIDDLE EAST)
   Bowden, Mark. *Guests of the Ayatollah*   955.05
   Follett, Ken. *On Wings of Eagles*   955
   Housden, Roger. *Saved by Beauty*   955
   Packer, George. *The Assassins' Gate*   956.7044
   Raddatz, Martha. *The Long Road Home*   B
American Pharoah. Drape, Joe   798.40092
AMERICAN PHAROAH (HORSE)
   Drape, Joe. *American Pharoah*   798.40092
American Philosophy. Kaag, John J.   191
American Phoenix. Cook, Jane Hampton   973.5
American Photographs. Evans, Walker   779
The American Plague. Crosby, Molly Caldwell   614.5
AMERICAN POETRY
   Akbar, Kaveh. *Calling a Wolf a Wolf*   811
   Alexander, Elizabeth. *Crave Radiance*   811
   Angelou, Maya. *The Complete Poetry*   811
   Armantrout, Rae. *Versed*   811
   Asghar, Fatimah. *If They Come for Us*   811
   Ashbery, John. *Commotion of the Birds*   811
   Ashbery, John. *John Ashbery*   811
   Ashbery, John. *Notes from the Air*   811
   Ashbery, John. *Selected Poems*   811
   Baca, Jimmy Santiago. *Selected Poems*   811
   Bang, Mary Jo. *The Bride of E*   811
   Bang, Mary Jo. *A Doll for Throwing*   811
   Bang, Mary Jo. *Elegy*   811
   Baraka, Amiri. *S O S*   811
   Berry, Wendell. *New Collected Poems*   811
   Berry, Wendell. *A Timbered Choir*   811
   Berryman, John. *Collected Poems, 1937-1971*   811
   Bialosky, Jill. *Poetry Will Save Your Life*   B
   Bidart, Frank. ★*Half-Light*   811
   Bishop, Elizabeth. ★*Poems*   811
   Blount, Tommye. *Fantasia for the Man in Blue*   811
   Boruch, Marianne. *Eventually One Dreams the Real Thing*   811
   Borzutzky, Daniel. *Lake Michigan*   811
   Borzutzky, Daniel. *The Performance of Becoming Human*   811
   Brock-Broido, Lucie. *Stay, Illusion*   811
   Brooks, Gwendolyn. ★*The Essential Gwendolyn Brooks*   811
   Brooks, Gwendolyn. *In Montgomery, and Other Poems*   811
   Brown, Molly McCully. *The Virginia State Colony for Epileptics and Feebleminded*   811
   Carver, Raymond. *All of Us*   811
   Carver, Raymond. *A New Path to the Waterfall*   811
   Charles, Jos. *Feeld*   811
   Collins, Billy. *Aimless Love*   811
   Collins, Billy. *Sailing Alone Around the Room*   811
   Collins, Billy. *The Trouble with Poetry and Other Poems*   811
   Collins, Martha. *Admit One*   811
   Cummings, E. E. ★*Complete Poems, 1904-1962*   811
   Diaz, Natalie. ★*Postcolonial Love Poem*   811
   Dickinson, Emily. ★*The Complete Poems.*   811.4
   Dickinson, Emily. *Dickinson*   811
   Doty, Mark. *Deep Lane*   811
   Doty, Mark. *Fire to Fire*   811
   Dove, Rita. ★*Selected Poems*   811
   Dove, Rita. *Sonata Mulattica*   811
   Duncan, Robert. *Selected Poems*   811
   Dunn, Stephen. *Local Visitations*   811
   Dunn, Stephen. *New & Selected Poems*   811
   Eliot, T. S. ★*Complete Poems and Plays.*   810
   Ellis, Thomas Sayers. *Skin, Inc.*   811

Faizullah, Tarfia. *Registers of Illuminated Villages*   811
Ferlinghetti, Lawrence. *These Are My Rivers*   811
Flynn, Nick. *The Captain Asks for a Show of Hands*   811
Forche, Carolyn. *Blue Hour*   811
Forsythe, Kelly. *Perennial*   811
Gallagher, Tess. *Dear Ghosts*   811
Gay, Ross. ★*Catalog of Unabashed Gratitude*   811
Gilbert, Jack. *Collected Poems*   811
Ginsberg, Allen. ★*Howl*   811.54
Gioia, Dana. *99 Poems*   811
Giovanni, Nikki. ★*The Collected Poetry of Nikki Giovanni, 1968-1998*   811
Giovanni, Nikki. *A Good Cry*   811
Girmay, Aracelis. *The Black Maria*   811
Gluck, Louise. *Averno*   811
Gluck, Louise. ★*Poems 1962-2012*   811
Graham, Jorie. *The Dream of the Unified Field*   811
Graham, Jorie. *Fast*   811
Graham, Jorie. *From the New World*   811
Graham, Jorie. *Overlord*   811
Gregg, Linda. *All of It Singing*   811.54
Hacker, Marilyn. *A Stranger's Mirror*   811
Hall, Donald. *The Back Chamber*   811
Hall, Donald. *The Selected Poems of Donald Hall.*   811
Hall, Donald. *White Apples and the Taste of Stone*   811
Harjo, Joy. *A Map to the Next World*   811
Harrison, Jim. *Songs of Unreason*   811
Harrison, Leslie. *The Book of Endings*   811
Hass, Robert. *The Apple Trees at Olema*   811
Hayden, Robert. *Collected Poems*   811
Hayes, Terrance. ★*American Sonnets for My Past and Future Assassin*   811
Hayes, Terrance. *How to Be Drawn*   811
Hayes, Terrance. ★*Lighthead*   811
Hirsch, Edward. *Gabriel*   811
Hirsch, Edward. *The Living Fire*   811
Hirsch, Edward. *Special Orders*   811
Hirsch, Edward. *Stranger by Night*   811
Hirshfield, Jane. *After*   811
Hirshfield, Jane. *The Beauty*   811
Hoagland, Tony. *Priest Turned Therapist Treats Fear of God*   811
Hoagland, Tony. *Unincorporated Persons in the Late Honda Dynasty*   811
Howe, Fanny. *Second Childhood*   811
Hughes, Langston. ★*Selected Poems of Langston Hughes*   811
Hutchinson, Ishion. *House of Lords and Commons*   811
Jarrell, Randall. ★*The Complete Poems*   811
Jeffers, Robinson. *The Selected Poetry of Robinson Jeffers*   811
Johnson, James Weldon. *Complete Poems*   811
Jones, Saeed. *Prelude to Bruise*   811
Karr, Mary. *Tropic of Squalor*   811
Kasischke, Laura. *Space, in Chains*   811
Keene, John. ★*Punks*   811
Kendall, Tim. *The Art of Robert Frost*   811
Kerouac, Jack. *Book of Blues*   811
Kerouac, Jack. *Scattered Poems*   811
Kinnell, Galway. *Collected Poems*   811
Kinnell, Galway. *A New Selected Poems*   811
Kinnell, Galway. *Strong Is Your Hold*   811
Komunyakaa, Yusef. *Warhorses*   811
Kooser, Ted. *Delights & Shadows*   811
Kunitz, Stanley. ★*The Collected Poems*   811
Levine, Philip. *The Simple Truth*   811
Limon, Ada. *Bright Dead Things*   811
Limon, Ada. ★*The Carrying*   811
Lowell, Amy. *Selected Poems*   821
Lowell, Robert. *Collected Poems*   811
Mackey, Nathaniel. *Splay Anthem*   811
McCrae, Shane. *In the Language of My Captor*   811
Merwin, W. S. *The Shadow of Sirius*   811
Millay, Edna St. Vincent. *Collected Poems*   811
Millay, Edna St. Vincent. *Selected Poems*   811
Moore, Marianne. *New Collected Poems*   811
Myles, Eileen. *I Must Be Living Twice*   811.54
Nezhukumatathil, Aimee. *Oceanic*   811
Nguyen, Diana Khoi. *Ghost of*   811
Nguyen, Hieu Minh. *Not Here*   811
Notley, Alice. *Certain Magical Acts*   811
O'Hara, Frank. *Lunch Poems.*   811
Oliver, Mary. ★*Devotions*   811
Oliver, Mary. *Dream Work*   811

PUBLIC LIBRARY CORE COLLECTION: NONFICTION
Twentieth Edition

Oliver, Mary. *New and Selected Poems,; Vol. 1*		811
Oliver, Mary. *A Poetry Handbook*		808.1
Oliver, Mary. *A Thousand Mornings*		811
Padgett, Ron. *Collected Poems*		811
Parker, Morgan. *There Are More Beautiful Things Than Beyonce*		811
Perillo, Lucia. *On the Spectrum of Possible Deaths*		811
Perillo, Lucia. *Time Will Clean the Carcass Bones*		811
Pico, Tommy. *Feed*		811
Pico, Tommy. *Junk*		811
Pico, Tommy. *Nature Poem*		811
Pinsky, Robert. *The Figured Wheel*		811
Plath, Sylvia. ★*Ariel*		811
Plath, Sylvia. ★*The Collected Poems*		811
Pound, Ezra. ★*Poems and Translations*		811
Powell, D. A. *Useless Landscape*		811
Rasmussen, Matt. *Black Aperture*		811
Reed, Ishmael. *New and Collected Poems, 1964-2007*		811
Reed, Justin Phillip. *Indecency*		811
Rich, Adrienne. *Collected Early Poems, 1950-1970*		811
Rich, Adrienne. *Collected Poems*		811
Rich, Adrienne. *Later Poems*		811
Rich, Adrienne. *The School Among the Ruins*		811
Ritvo, Max. *Four Reincarnations*		811
Roethke, Theodore. *The Collected Poems of Theodore Roethke*		811
Rogers, Pattiann. *Quickening Fields*		811
Ruefle, Mary. *Selected Poems*		811
Rukeyser, Muriel. *Selected Poems*		811
Ryan, Kay. *The Best of It*		811
Salter, Mary Jo. *The Surveyors*		811
Sandburg, Carl. ★*The Complete Poems of Carl Sandburg*		811
Sato, Hiroaki. *On Haiku*		809.1
Schuyler, James. *Collected Poems*		811
Seidel, Frederick. ★*Frederick Seidel Selected Poems*		811
Seuss, Diane. ★*Frank*		811
Seuss, Diane. *Still Life with Two Dead Peacocks and a Girl*		811.6
Sexton, Anne. *Selected Poems of Anne Sexton*		811
Shapiro, Karl. *Selected Poems*		811
Sharif, Solmaz. *Look*		811
Shockley, Evie. *The New Black*		811
Shockley, Evie. *Semiautomatic*		811
Simic, Charles. *Come Closer and Listen*		811
Simic, Charles. *The Lunatic*		811
Simic, Charles. *New and Selected Poems*		811
Simic, Charles. *The Voice at 3*		811
Smith, Patricia. *Blood Dazzler*		811
Smith, Patricia. *Incendiary Art*		811.54
Smith, Patricia. *Shoulda Been Jimi Savannah*		811
Smith, Tracy K. *Duende*		811
Smith, Tracy K. ★*Life on Mars*		811
Snyder, Gary. *No Nature*		811
Som, Brandon. *Tripas*		811
Spicer, Jack. *My Vocabulary Did This to Me*		811
Stanford, Frank. *What About This*		811
Stevens, Wallace. *Collected Poetry and Prose*		811
Swenson, May. *Collected Poems*		811
Tapahonso, Luci. *A Radiant Curve*		811
Trethewey, Natasha D. ★*Native Guard*		811
Valentine, Jean. *Door in the Mountain*		811
Vang, Mai Der. *Afterland*		811
Waldrop, Keith. *Transcendental Studies*		811
Walker, Alice. *Hard Times Require Furious Dancing*		811
Wheatley, Phillis. *The Poems of Phillis Wheatley*		811
Whitman, Walt. ★*Leaves of Grass*		811
Whitman, Walt. ★*Poetry and Prose*		811
Whitman, Walt. ★*Selected Poems*		811
Wicker, Marcus. *Silencer*		811
Wilbur, Richard. *Anterooms*		811
Wilbur, Richard. ★*Collected Poems, 1943-2004*		811
Williams, C. K. *Falling Ill*		811
Williams, William Carlos. *Paterson*		811
Wright, C. D. *One with Others*		811
Wright, James Arlington. *Above the River*		811
XIe, Jenny. *Eye Level*		811
Youn, Monica. *Blackacre*		811.6
Young, Kevin. *Book of Hours*		811
Zapruder, Matthew. *Come on All You Ghosts*		811
American poets continuum series [Series]. Nye, Naomi Shihab		811
American poets project [Series]. Brooks, Gwendolyn		811

American *Poison*. Porter, Eduardo		305.800973
American *Predator*. Callahan, Maureen		364.152
American Presidents series (Times Books) [Series]. Brinkley, Alan		B
American presidents series (Times Books) [Series]. Wills, Garry		B
American *Prison*. Bauer, Shane		365
American *Prometheus*. Bird, Kai		B
American *Queen*. Oller, John		B
American *Quilts*. Shaw, Robert		746.46
American *Radical*. Elnoury, Tamer		B
American *Rebels*. Sankovitch, Nina		920
American *Reckoning*. Appy, Christian G.		959.704
American *Republics*. Taylor, Alan		973.3
American *Resistance*. Rothkopf, David J.		973.933
AMERICAN REVOLUTION, 1775-1783		
Adams, John. *My Dearest Friend*		973.4
Atkinson, Rick. ★*The British Are Coming*		973.3
Beeman, Richard R. *Our Lives, Our Fortunes and Our Sacred Honor*		973.3
Bobrick, Benson. *Angel in the Whirlwind*		973.3
Boles, John B. *Jefferson*		B
Brands, H. W. ★*Our First Civil War*		973.3
Broadwater, Jeff. ★*George Mason*		B
Calloway, Colin G. *The Indian World of George Washington*		323.1197
Crawford, Alan Pell. *This Fierce People*		975
Daughan, George C. *Revolution on the Hudson*		974.7
Dolin, Eric Jay. ★*Rebels at Sea*		973.3
Drury, Bob. *Valley Forge*		973.3
Ellis, Joseph J. *American Creation*		973.3
Ellis, Joseph J. *The Cause*		973.3
Ellis, Joseph J. ★*His Excellency*		B
Ellis, Joseph J. *The Quartet*		342.7302
Ellis, Joseph J. ★*Revolutionary Summer*		973.3
Ferling, John E. *Winning Independence*		973.3
Ferreiro, Larrie D. *Brothers at Arms*		327.73
Fischer, David Hackett. *Paul Revere's Ride*		973.3
Fischer, David Hackett. *Washington's Crossing*		973.3
Gaines, James R. *For Liberty and Glory*		B
Hogeland, William. *Declaration*		973.3
Holton, Woody. *Liberty Is Sweet*		973.3
Hoock, Holger. *Scars of Independence*		973.3
Johnson, Paul. *George Washington*		B
Ketchum, Richard M. *Saratoga*		973.3
Kilmeade, Brian. ★*George Washington's Secret Six*		973.4
Maier, Pauline. *American Scripture*		973.3
McCraw, Thomas K. ★*The Founders and Finance*		330.973
McCullough, David G. ★*1776*		973.3
McKean, David. *Suspected of Independence*		B
Middlekauff, Robert. *The Glorious Cause*		973.3
Miller, Marla. *Betsy Ross and the Making of America*		B
Morison, Samuel Eliot. *John Paul Jones*		B
O'Connell, Robert L. *Revolutionary*		
O'Donnell, Patrick K. *The Indispensables*		973.3
Philbrick, Nathaniel. ★*Bunker Hill*		973.3
Philbrick, Nathaniel. ★*In the Hurricane's Eye*		973.3
Philbrick, Nathaniel. ★*Valiant Ambition*		B
Phillips, Kevin. *1775*		973.3
Rakove, Jack N. *Revolutionaries*		973.3
Raphael, Ray. *A People's History of the American Revolution*		973.3
Roberts, Cokie. *Founding Mothers*		920
Sankovitch, Nina. *American Rebels*		920
Staiti, Paul J. *Of Arms and Artists*		B
Taylor, Alan. *American Revolutions*		973.3
Taylor, Alan. *The Divided Ground*		974.7
Thomas, Evan. ★*John Paul Jones*		B
Thompson, Bob. *Revolutionary Roads*		973.3
Unger, Harlow G. *American Tempest*		973.3
Unger, Harlow G. *First Founding Father*		B
Weintraub, Stanley. *Iron Tears*		973.3
Zambone, Albert Louis. *Daniel Morgan*		B
American *Revolutions*. Taylor, Alan		973.3
American *Rose*. Abbott, Karen		B
American *Rule*. Sexton, Jared Yates		973
American *Saint*. Barthel, Joan		B
American *Scripture*. Maier, Pauline		973.3
★***American*** *Sherlock*. Dawson, Kate Winkler		B
American *Shield*. Gonell, Aquilino		B
An ***American*** *Sickness*. Rosenthal, Elisabeth		362.10973
AMERICAN SIGN LANGUAGE		
Fouts, Roger. *Next of Kin*		156

AUTHOR, TITLE, SERIES AND SUBJECT INDEX

Tennant, Richard A. *The American Sign Language Handshape Dictionary*   419
The American Sign Language Handshape Dictionary. Tennant, Richard A.   419
American Sirens. Hazzard, Kevin M.   362.18
American Soldiers. Kindsvatter, Peter S.   355
The American Songbag. Sandburg, Carl   782.42162
★*American Sonnets for My Past and Future Assassin*. Hayes, Terrance   811
American Sphinx. Ellis, Joseph J.   973.4
American Spirit. Kyle, Taya   B
★*The American Spirit*. McCullough, David G.   973
The American Story. Rubenstein, David M.   973.07202
An American Sunrise. Harjo, Joy   811
★*American Tapestry*. Swarns, Rachel L.   B
American Tempest. Unger, Harlow G.   973.3
★*American Ulysses*. White, Ronald C.   B
American Uprising. Rasmussen, Daniel   976.3
American Veda. Goldberg, Philip   294.509
American Visions. Ayers, Edward L.   973.5
American Visions. Hughes, Robert   709
★*The American Way of Death Revisited*. Mitford, Jessica   338.4
The American Way of Eating. McMillan, Tracie   338.4
The American West. Brown, Dee   978
AMERICAN WESTWARD EXPANSION (1803-1899)
   Baron, David. *American Eclipse*   523.7
   Boessenecker, John. *Gentleman Bandit*   B
   Brands, H. W. *Dreams of El Dorado*   978
   Clavin, Thomas. *Dodge City*   978.1
   Clavin, Thomas. *Wild Bill*   B
   Cozzens, Peter. *The Earth Is Weeping*   978
   Crouch, Gregory. *The Bonanza King*   B
   Duncan, Dayton. *Blood Memory*   599.64
   Gallagher, Winifred. *New Women in the Old West*   978.02
   Hickman, Katie. *Brave Hearted*   978
   Inskeep, Steve. *Imperfect Union*   B
   Ross, John F. *The Promise of the Grand Canyon*   917.91
   Snyder, Christina. *Great Crossings*   976.9
   Wallis, Michael. *The Best Land Under Heaven*   978
American Whiskey, Bourbon, & Rye. Risen, Clay   641.2
★*American Whitelash*. Lowery, Wesley   305.8
AMERICAN WIT AND HUMOR
   Robinson, Phoebe. *Please Don't Sit on My Bed in Your Outside Clothes*   818
   Trillin, Calvin. *The Lede*   071
American Witness. Smith, R. J.   B
American Wolf. Blakeslee, Nate   599.773
★*American Woman*. Rogers, Katie   973.09
The American Women's Almanac. Felder, Deborah G   305.40973
American Workers, American Unions, 4th Ed. Zieger, Robert H.   331.88
American Zion. Park, Benjamin E.   289.3
AMERICANA
   Manseau, Peter. *Objects of Devotion*   277
   Solomon, Deborah. *American Mirror*   B
AMERICANISMS
   Ammer, Christine. *The American Heritage Dictionary of Idioms*   423
   Bailey, Richard W. *Speaking American*   427
AMERICANIZATION
   Arce, Julissa. *You Sound Like a White Girl*   303.48
   Boorstin, Daniel J. *The Americans*   973
   Pipher, Mary Bray. *The Middle of Everywhere*   305.9
   Thorpe, Helen. *The Newcomers*   373.18
Americanos. Chasteen, John Charles   980
The Americans. Boorstin, Daniel J.   973
The Americans. Boorstin, Daniel J.   973
★*Amerigo*. Fernandez-Armesto, Felipe   B
An Amerikan Family. Holley, Santi Elijah   920
AMES, ADELBERT, 1835-1933
   Lemann, Nicholas. *Redemption*   975
AMES, ALDRICH HAZEN, 1941-
   Macintyre, Ben. ★*The Spy and the Traitor*   B
Amichai, Yehuda
   Open Closed Open   892.4
AMICHAI, YEHUDA
   Amichai, Yehuda. *Open Closed Open*   892.4
AMIGURUMI
   Abbondio, Sarah. *Mini Amigurumi Animals*   746.43
   Bergstrom, Lauren. *Cute & Cuddly Crochet*   746.43
   Bergstrom, Lauren. *Mini Crochet Creatures*   746.43
   Green-Hite, Vincent. *Knot Bad Amigurumi*   746.43

AMIR, YIGAL
   Ephron, Dan. *Killing a King*   956.9405
Amis, Martin
   Koba the Dread   947.084
   The Rub of Time   824
AMISH
   Kraybill, Donald B. ★*On the Backroad to Heaven*   289.7
   Mackall, Joe. *Plain Secrets*   289.7
   Scott, Chris. *Homage*   641.5
   Shachtman, Tom. ★*Rumspringa*   305.235
The Amistad Rebellion. Rediker, Marcus   326.0973
Ammer, Christine
   The American Heritage Dictionary of Idioms   423
Ammu. Khan, Asma   641.595
AMNESIA
   Crais, Clifton C. *History Lessons*   B
   Dittrich, Luke. ★*Patient H.M.*   616.85
   Eichenwald, Kurt. *A Mind Unraveled*   B
Among The Braves. Mahtani, Shibani   951.25
Among The Bros. Marshall, McMillan   362.29
Among The Dead Cities. Grayling, A. C.   940.54
Among The Heroes. Longman, Jere   974.8
Amore, Anthony M.
   The Art of the Con   702.8
Amos, Tori
   Resistance   B
AMOS, TORI, 1963-
   Amos, Tori. *Resistance*   B
AMPHIBIANS
   McGinnis, Samuel M. ★*Peterson Field Guide to Western Reptiles and Amphibians*   597.9
★*Amphibious Soul*. Foster, Craig   155.9
AMPHIBIOUS WARFARE
   Kershaw, Alex. *The First Wave*   940.54
   Lance, Rachel. *Chamber Divers*   940.54
   McManus, John C. *Island Infernos*   940.54
★*The Ams Weather Book*. Williams, Jack   551.5
Amsterdam. Shorto, Russell   949.2
AMSTERDAM, NETHERLANDS
   Frank, Anne. ★*The Diary of a Young Girl*   940.53
   Frank, Anne. *The Diary of Anne Frank*   B
   Gies, Miep. ★*Anne Frank Remembered*   B
   Iperen, Roxane van. *The Sisters of Auschwitz*   940.53
   Jacobson, Sidney. *Anne Frank*   741.5
   Pick-Goslar, Hannah Elizabeth. ★*My Friend Anne Frank*   B
   Shorto, Russell. *Amsterdam*   949.2
   Van Wijk-Voskuijl, Joop. *The Last Secret of the Secret Annex*   940.53
AMUNDSEN, ROALD, 1872-1928
   Sancton, Julian. *Madhouse at the End of the Earth*   919.8904
AMUSEMENT PARKS
   Snow, Richard. *Disney's Land*   791.06
AMUSEMENTS
   Alt, Matt. *Pure Invention*   306.0952
   Ho, Oliver. *The Ultimate Book of Family Card Games*   795.4
   Iggulden, Conn. *The Double Dangerous Book for Boys*   031.02
   Johnson, Steven. *Wonderland*   790.1
   Owen, Oscar. *Mind-Blowing Magic Tricks for Everyone*   793.8
Amusing Ourselves to Death. Postman, Neil   302.2
AMYOTROPHIC LATERAL SCLEROSIS
   Fitzmaurice, Simon. *It's Not yet Dark*   616.8
   Hawking, Stephen. *My Brief History*   B
ANABAPTISTS
   Kraybill, Donald B. *Concise Encyclopedia of Amish, Brethren, Hutterites, and Mennonites*   289.7
ANALGESICS
   Lalkhen, Abdul-Ghaaliq. *An Anatomy of Pain*   616
   Quinones, Sam. *Dreamland*   362.29
Anand, Anita
   The Patient Assassin   B
Anansi's Gold. Yeebo, Yepoka   364.16
Ananthaswamy, Anil
   Through Two Doors at Once   530.12
ANARCHISM
   Avrich, Paul. *Sasha and Emma*   920
   Butterworth, Alex. *The World That Never Was*   335
   Miller, Scott. *The President and the Assassin*   973.8
ANARCHISTS
   Avrich, Paul. *Sasha and Emma*   920

PUBLIC LIBRARY CORE COLLECTION: NONFICTION
Twentieth Edition

Butterworth, Alex. *The World That Never Was*	335
Johnson, Steven. *The Infernal Machine*	335
Strang, Dean A. *Worse Than the Devil*	345.775
★*The Anarchy*. Dalrymple, William	954.03

ANASAZI CULTURE
Childs, Craig. *House of Rain*	978.9

ANASTASIA NIKOLAEVNA, GRAND DUCHESS, DAUGHTER OF NICHOLAS II, EMPEROR OF RUSSIA, 1901-1918
Massie, Robert K. *The Romanovs*	947
Rappaport, Helen. *The Romanov Sisters*	920

ANATOMY
Bohannon, Cat. ★*Eve*	613
Enright, Lynn. *Vagina*	612.6
Gross, Rachel E. *Vagina Obscura*	618.1
Gunter, Jen. *The Vagina Bible*	612.6
Hale, Robert Beverly. *Anatomy Lessons from the Great Masters*	743.4
Lester, Toby. *Da Vinci's Ghost*	741.092
Loomis, Andrew. *Figure Drawing for All It's Worth*	743.4
Schutt, Bill. *Pump*	612.1
Winslow, Valerie L. *Classic Human Anatomy*	743.4
Anatomy Lessons from the Great Masters. Hale, Robert Beverly	743.4
Anatomy of a Breakthrough. Alter, Adam L.	158.1
The *Anatomy* of Fascism. Paxton, Robert O.	320.53
An *Anatomy* of Pain. Lalkhen, Abdul-Ghaaliq	616

Anbinder, Tyler
★*City of Dreams*	974.7
★*The Ancestor's Tale*. Dawkins, Richard	576.8

ANCESTORS
Jacobs, A. J. *It's All Relative*	929.1
Jerkins, Morgan. *Wandering in Strange Lands*	305.896
LaPointe, Sasha taqwseblu. *Thunder Song*	814
Swarns, Rachel L. ★*American Tapestry*	B
The *Anchor* Bible reference library [Series]. Schiffman, Lawrence H.	296.1

ANCHORAGE, ALASKA
Sardy, Marin. *The Edge of Every Day*	B

ANCIENT AEGEAN CIVILIZATIONS (3000-1000 B.C.E.)
Homer. *The Iliad*	883
Homer. ★*The Iliad*	883
Homer. *The Odyssey*	883
Homer. *The Odyssey*	883
Homer. *Odyssey*	883
Homer. ★*The Odyssey*	883

ANCIENT ART
Beard, Mary. ★*How Do We Look*	704.9
Robins, Gay. *The Art of Ancient Egypt*	709
Ancient Bones. Bohme, Madelaine	599.93

ANCIENT CITIES AND TOWNS
Beard, Mary. *The Fires of Vesuvius*	937
Hessler, Peter. *The Buried*	962.05
Kriwaczek, Paul. *Babylon*	935

ANCIENT EGYPT
Beard, Mary. ★*How Do We Look*	704.9
Brier, Bob. *The Murder of Tutankhamen*	B
Cooney, Kara. *When Women Ruled the World*	920
Darnell, John Coleman. *Egypt's Golden Couple*	932
Goldsworthy, Adrian Keith. *Antony and Cleopatra*	937
Mertz, Barbara. *Temples, Tombs, & Hieroglyphs*	932
Romer, John. *A History of Ancient Egypt*	932
Schiff, Stacy. ★*Cleopatra*	B
Shaw, Ian. *The Princeton Dictionary of Ancient Egypt*	932
Wilkinson, Toby A. H. ★*The Rise and Fall of Ancient Egypt*	932

ANCIENT EGYPT (3100 B.C.E.-640 C.E.)
Brier, Bob. *The Murder of Tutankhamen*	B
Cooney, Kara. *When Women Ruled the World*	920
Darnell, John Coleman. *Egypt's Golden Couple*	932
Goldsworthy, Adrian Keith. *Antony and Cleopatra*	937
Mertz, Barbara. *Temples, Tombs, & Hieroglyphs*	932
Romer, John. *A History of Ancient Egypt*	932
Schiff, Stacy. ★*Cleopatra*	B
Shaw, Ian. *The Princeton Dictionary of Ancient Egypt*	932
Wilkinson, Toby A. H. *The Nile*	962
Wilkinson, Toby A. H. ★*The Rise and Fall of Ancient Egypt*	932

ANCIENT GEOGRAPHY
Childs, Craig. *Atlas of a Lost World*	551.7

ANCIENT GREECE
Alexander, Caroline. *The War That Killed Achilles*	883
Beard, Mary. ★*How Do We Look*	704.9
Cahill, Thomas. *Sailing the Wine-Dark Sea*	909
Everitt, Anthony. *Alexander the Great*	B
Everitt, Anthony. *The Rise of Athens*	938
Fox, Margalit. *The Riddle of the Labyrinth*	920
Herodotus. *The Histories*	938
Homer. ★*The Iliad*	883
Homer. *The Odyssey*	883
Homer. ★*The Odyssey*	883
Hughes, Bettany. ★*The Hemlock Cup*	B
Johnson, Paul. *Socrates*	183
Kagan, Donald. *The Peloponnesian War*	938
Kagan, Donald. *Thucydides*	938
Kawa, Abraham. *Democracy*	741.5
Nicolson, Adam. *How to Be*	180
Roberts, Jennifer Tolbert. *The Plague of War*	938

ANCIENT GREECE (800 B.C.E.-640 C.E.)
Cahill, Thomas. *Sailing the Wine-Dark Sea*	909
Everitt, Anthony. *Alexander the Great*	B
Everitt, Anthony. *The Rise of Athens*	938
Hanson, Victor Davis. *The Father of Us All*	355.0209
Herodotus. *The Histories*	938
Johnson, Paul. *Socrates*	183
Kagan, Donald. *The Peloponnesian War*	938
Kagan, Donald. *Thucydides*	938
Nicolson, Adam. *How to Be*	180
Ricks, Thomas E. ★*First Principles*	973.09
Roberts, Jennifer Tolbert. *The Plague of War*	938

ANCIENT HISTORY
Armstrong, Karen. ★*The Great Transformation*	200.9
Beard, Mary. ★*S.P.Q.R.*	937
Brown, Peter. *Through the Eye of a Needle*	270.2
Everitt, Anthony. *Hadrian and the Triumph of Rome*	B
Everitt, Anthony. *The Rise of Rome*	937
Goldsworthy, Adrian Keith. *Augustus*	B
Goldsworthy, Adrian Keith. *Pax Romana*	937
Hanson, Victor Davis. *The Father of Us All*	355.0209
Herodotus. *The Histories*	938
Kagan, Donald. *Thucydides*	938
MacGregor, Neil. *A History of the World in 100 Objects*	930.1
Romer, John. *A History of Ancient Egypt*	932
Southon, Emma. *Agrippina*	B
Strauss, Barry S. *The Death of Caesar*	937
Suetonius. ★*The Twelve Caesars*	B
Wilkinson, Toby A. H. ★*The Rise and Fall of Ancient Egypt*	932

ANCIENT MILITARY HISTORY
Cotterell, Arthur. *Chariot*	357
Roberts, Jennifer Tolbert. *The Plague of War*	938

ANCIENT PHILOSOPHERS
Hughes, Bettany. ★*The Hemlock Cup*	B
Johnson, Paul. *Socrates*	183
Nicolson, Adam. *How to Be*	180

ANCIENT ROME
Addis, Ferdinand. *The Eternal City*	945.6
Beard, Mary. ★*Emperor of Rome*	937
Beard, Mary. *The Fires of Vesuvius*	937
Beard, Mary. ★*S.P.Q.R.*	937
Brown, Peter. *Through the Eye of a Needle*	270.2
Brownworth, Lars. *Lost to the West*	949.5
Catullus, Gaius Valerius. *The Poems of Catullus*	874
Cicero, Marcus Tullius. ★*The Republic*	320.1
Everitt, Anthony. *Cicero*	B
Everitt, Anthony. *Hadrian and the Triumph of Rome*	B
Everitt, Anthony. *The Rise of Rome*	937
Gibbon, Edward. ★*The Decline and Fall of the Roman Empire*	937
Goldsworthy, Adrian Keith. *Antony and Cleopatra*	937
Goldsworthy, Adrian Keith. *Augustus*	B
Goldsworthy, Adrian Keith. ★*Caesar*	B
Goldsworthy, Adrian Keith. *Pax Romana*	937
Harper, Kyle. *The Fate of Rome*	937
Horace. *Odes and Epodes*	874
Hughes, Robert. *Rome*	945.6
Hunt, Patrick. *Hannibal*	B
McGregor, James H. *Rome from the Ground up*	711
O'Connell, Robert L. *The Ghosts of Cannae*	937
Ricks, Thomas E. ★*First Principles*	973.09
Southon, Emma. *Agrippina*	B
Strauss, Barry S. *The Death of Caesar*	937
Strauss, Barry S. *Ten Caesars*	937
Strauss, Barry S. ★*The War That Made the Roman Empire*	937

AUTHOR, TITLE, SERIES AND SUBJECT INDEX

Suetonius. ★*The Twelve Caesars*	B
Virgil. ★*The Aeneid*	873
Wickham, Chris. *The Inheritance of Rome*	940.1
Woolf, Greg. *Rome*	937
ANCIENT SCIENCE	
Al-Khalili, Jim. *The House of Wisdom*	509
Weinberg, Steven. *To Explain the World*	509
And How Are You, Dr. Sacks?. Weschler, Lawrence	B
And in the Vienna Woods the Trees Remain. Asbrink, Elisabeth	B
And Still I Rise. Gates, Henry Louis	305.896
★*And The Band Played On*. Shilts, Randy	362.196
And The Prophet Said. Gibran, Kahlil	811
And The Sea Is Never Full. Wiesel, Elie	B
And Then All Hell Broke Loose. Engel, Richard	956.05
And Then We Danced. Alford, Henry	792.8
★*And Then We Grew Up*. Friedman, Rachel	305.24
★*And Then We Rise*. Common	613
And Then You're Dead. Cassidy, Cody	612
★*And Then? and Then? What Else?*. Handler, Daniel	813
★*And There Was Light*. Meacham, Jon	B
ANDAMAN AND NICOBAR ISLANDS (INDIA)	
Goodheart, Adam. *The Last Island*	954
Anders, Charlie Jane	
★*Never Say You Can't Survive*	808.02
ANDERS, CHARLIE JANE	
Anders, Charlie Jane. ★*Never Say You Can't Survive*	808.02
Andersen, Christopher P.	
The Good Son	B
Andersen, Jens	
Astrid Lindgren	B
Andersen, Kurt	
★*Fantasyland*	973
Anderson, Amelia	
Library Programming for Autistic Children and Teens	027.6
Anderson, Carol	
★*One Person, No Vote*	324.6
★*The Second*	344.7305
★*White Rage*	305.800973
Anderson, Christopher	
The Numbers Game	796.334
Anderson, David	
Histories of the Hanged	967.62
ANDERSON, ELIZABETH GARRETT, 1836-1917	
Campbell, Olivia. *Women in White Coats*	610.92
Anderson, Fred	
The Dominion of War	973
ANDERSON, JACK, 1922-2005	
Feldstein, Mark Avrom. *Poisoning the Press*	973.924092
Anderson, Jimmeka	
Power Lines	020
Anderson, Jon Lee	
Che Guevara	B
Anderson, Lars	
Carlisle vs. Army	796.332
ANDERSON, MARIAN, 1897-1993	
Keiler, Allan. *Marian Anderson*	B
ANDERSON, OSBORNE P. (OSBORNE PERRY), 1830-1872	
Meyer, Eugene L. *Five for Freedom*	973.7
Anderson, Pam	
How to Cook Without a Book	641.5
ANDERSON, PETER STICKNEY	
Green, Elon. *Last Call*	363.15
Anderson, Sam	
Boom Town	976.6
Anderson, Sarah	
The Spinner's Book of Yarn Designs	746.1
Anderson, Scott	
Lawrence in Arabia	B
★*The Quiet Americans*	327.12
ANDERSON, THOMAS CHARLES, 1858-1931	
Krist, Gary. *Empire of Sin*	976.3
ANDES	
Parrado, Nando. ★*Miracle in the Andes*	982
Read, Piers Paul. ★*Alive*	982
ANDES REGION	
Parrado, Nando. ★*Miracle in the Andes*	982
Read, Piers Paul. ★*Alive*	982
Salama, Jordan. ★*Stranger in the Desert*	982

ANDRE, CHRISTOPHE	
Delisle, Guy. *Hostage*	741.5
Andrea Dworkin. Duberman, Martin B.	B
Andres, Jose	
Vegetables Unleashed	641.5
Andrew Carnegie. Nasaw, David	B
★*Andrew Jackson and the Miracle of New Orleans*. Kilmeade, Brian	973.5
★*Andrew Jackson, His Life and Times*. Brands, H. W.	B
Andrew Johnson. Gordon-Reed, Annette	B
Andrew, Christopher M.	
The Secret World	327.1209
Andrews, Becca	
★*No Choice*	362.1988
Andrews, Colman	
The Country Cooking of Ireland	641.594
Andrews, Julie	
Home Work	B
Home	B
ANDREWS, JULIE	
Andrews, Julie. *Home Work*	B
Andrews, Julie. *Home*	B
Santopietro, Tom. *The Sound of Music Story*	791.43
Andrews, Lena S.	
★*Valiant Women*	940.53
Andrews-Dyer, Helena	
Reclaiming Her Time	B
Andy Warhol Was a Hoarder. Kalb, Claudia	920
Ang, Tom	
Digital Photographer's Handbook	771
Digital Photography Masterclass	770
Photography	770.9
The Angel and the Assassin. Nakazawa, Donna Jackson	612.8
Angel in the Whirlwind. Bobrick, Benson	973.3
The Angel Makers. McCracken, Patti	364.152
Angel of Grozny. Seierstad, Asne	947.086
Angel on My Shoulder. Cole, Natalie	B
★*Angela's Ashes*. McCourt, Frank	929
Angelou, Maya	
The Complete Poetry	811
Great Food, All Day Long	641.5973
Hallelujah! the Welcome Table	641.5973
★*I Know Why the Caged Bird Sings*	B
Letter to My Daughter	814
A Song Flung up to Heaven	B
Wouldn't Take Nothing for My Journey Now	814
ANGELOU, MAYA	
Angelou, Maya. *Hallelujah! the Welcome Table*	641.5973
Angelou, Maya. ★*I Know Why the Caged Bird Sings*	B
Angelou, Maya. *Letter to My Daughter*	814
Angelou, Maya. *A Song Flung up to Heaven*	B
Thursby, Jacqueline S. *Critical Companion to Maya Angelou*	818
ANGELS	
Bartlett, Sarah. *A Brief History of Angels and Demons*	202
Kushner, Tony. *Angels in America*	812
Angels in America. Kushner, Tony	812
ANGER	
Boland, Eavan. *The Historians*	821
Boyer, Anne. *The Undying*	B
Brown, Jericho. ★*The Tradition*	811
Chemaly, Soraya L. *Rage Becomes Her*	155.3
Coffin, Jaed. *Roughhouse Friday*	B
Dubin, Minna. ★*Mom Rage*	306.874
Eltahawy, Mona. *The Seven Necessary Sins for Women and Girls*	305.42
Gunst, Kathy. *Rage Baking*	641.86
Gupta, Shalene. *The Cycle*	618.1
Kubler-Ross, Elisabeth. *Life Lessons*	170
Lerner, Harriet Goldhor. ★*The Dance of Anger*	152.4
Lieberman, David J. *Never Get Angry Again*	152.4
Owens, Lama Rod. *Love and Rage*	152.4
Spiegelman, Art. *In the Shadow of No Towers*	741.5
Traister, Rebecca. *Good and Mad*	305.420973
Wolff, Daniel J. *Grown-Up Anger*	920
ANGLETON, JAMES, 1917-1987	
Macintyre, Ben. *A Spy Among Friends*	B
ANGLICANS	
Wilson, A. N. *C.S. Lewis*	823
ANGLO-SAXON PERIOD (449-1066)	
Ackroyd, Peter. *The Death of King Arthur*	823

PUBLIC LIBRARY CORE COLLECTION: NONFICTION
Twentieth Edition

    Morris, Marc. ★*The Anglo-Saxons*   942.01
    Morris, Marc. *The Norman Conquest*   942.02
★*The Anglo-Saxons*. Morris, Marc   942.01
ANGLO-SAXONS
    Morris, Marc. ★*The Anglo-Saxons*   942.01
Angyal, Chloe
    Turning Pointe   792.8
ANIMAL ADAPTATION
    Brand, Adele. *The Hidden World of the Fox*   599.775
    Catania, Kenneth. *Great Adaptations*   576.8
    Simon, Matt. *The Wasp That Brainwashed the Caterpillar*   578.4
ANIMAL ANATOMY
    Catania, Kenneth. *Great Adaptations*   576.8
ANIMAL ATTACKS
    Messenger, Alex. *The Twenty-Ninth Day*   B
ANIMAL BEHAVIOR
    Ackerman, Jennifer. *The Bird Way*   598.15
    Aryee, Patrick. *30 Animals That Made Us Smarter*   590
    Balcombe, Jonathan P. *What a Fish Knows*   597.15
    Birkhead, T. R. *Bird Sense*   598
    Bradshaw, John. ★*Cat Sense*   636.8
    Bradshaw, John. ★*Dog Sense*   636.7
    Braitman, Laurel. *Animal Madness*   591.5
    Brown, Sarah L. *The Hidden Language of Cats*   636.8
    Catania, Kenneth. *Great Adaptations*   576.8
    Cheshire, James. *Where the Animals Go*   591.47
    Cooke, Lucy. *Bitch*   591.56
    Cooke, Lucy. *The Truth About Animals*   590.2
    Darlington, Miriam. *Otter Country*   599.769
    Durrani, Matin. *Furry Logic*   591.5
    Fossey, Dian. ★*Gorillas in the Mist*   599.884
    Fouts, Roger. *Next of Kin*   156
    Goodall, Jane. ★*In the Shadow of Man*   599.8
    Grandin, Temple. ★*Animals in Translation*   591.5
    Grandin, Temple. ★*Animals Make Us Human*   636.08
    Higgins, Jackie. *Sentient*   573.8
    Holldobler, Bert. *The Superorganism*   595.7
    Horowitz, Alexandra. ★*Being a Dog*   636.7
    Horowitz, Alexandra. ★*Inside of a Dog*   636.7
    Horowitz, Alexandra. ★*The Year of the Puppy*   636.7
    Jones, Darryl N. *The Birds at My Table*   598.072
    Keim, Brandon. *Meet the Neighbors*   591.5
    Losos, Jonathan B. *The Cat's Meow*   636.8
    Martin, Wednesday. *Primates of Park Avenue*   974.7
    McIntyre, Rick. *The Reign of Wolf 21*   599.773
    Miller, Pat. ★*The Power of Positive Dog Training*   636.7
    Mustill, Tom. *How to Speak Whale*   591.59
    Nichols, Kerry. *Puppy Brain*   636.7
    Nicolson, Adam. *Life Between the Tides*   577.69
    Peterson, Dale. *The Moral Lives of Animals*   156
    Pryor, Karen. ★*Don't Shoot the Dog*   153.8
    Roach, Mary. ★*Fuzz*   591.5
    Roman, Joe. *Eat, Poop, Die*   577
    Safina, Carl. *Beyond Words*   591.56
    Scheel, David. *Many Things Under a Rock*   594
    Schotz, Susanne. *The Secret Language of Cats*   636.8
    Schutt, Bill. *Cannibalism*   394
    Skaife, Christopher. *The Ravenmaster*   B
    Skomal, Gregory. *Chasing Shadows*   597.3
    Suddendorf, Thomas. *The Gap*   156
    Toomey, David. *Kingdom of Play*   591.56
    Waal, F. B. M. de. *Bonobo*   599.88
    Waal, F. B. M. de. ★*Mama's Last Hug*   599.885
    Waal, F. B. M. de. *Our Inner Ape*   156
    Waldbauer, Gilbert. *What Good Are Bugs?*   595.717
    Ward, Ashley. *The Social Lives of Animals*   591.7
    Weitzman, Gary. *National Geographic Complete Guide to Pet Health, Behavior, and Happiness*   636.088
    Wilson, Edward O. *Genesis*   591.5
    Wood, Levison. *The Last Giants*   599.67
    Wynne, Clive D. L. ★*Dog Is Love*   636.7
    Yong, Ed. *An Immense World*   591.5
ANIMAL BIOGRAPHIES
    Bragg, Rick. *The Speckled Beauty*   636.7
    Hillenbrand, Laura. ★*Seabiscuit*   798.4
    Orlean, Susan. *Rin Tin Tin*   636.737
ANIMAL COMMUNICATION
    Ackerman, Jennifer. ★*What an Owl Knows*   598.9

    Balcombe, Jonathan P. *What a Fish Knows*   597.15
    Fouts, Roger. *Next of Kin*   156
    Keim, Brandon. *Meet the Neighbors*   591.5
    Mustill, Tom. *How to Speak Whale*   591.59
    Schotz, Susanne. *The Secret Language of Cats*   636.8
    Stewart, Tracey. *Do Unto Animals*   590
    Ward, Ashley. *The Social Lives of Animals*   591.7
ANIMAL CONTROL (PUBLIC HEALTH)
    Randall, David K. *Black Death at the Golden Gate*   616.9
ANIMAL CULTURE
    Foer, Jonathan Safran. ★*We Are the Weather*   636
ANIMAL DEFENSES
    Emlen, Douglas John. *Animal Weapons*   591.47
ANIMAL DROPPINGS
    Roman, Joe. *Eat, Poop, Die*   577
ANIMAL ECOLOGY
    Nicholls, Steve. *Alien Worlds*   595.7
ANIMAL EXPERIMENTATION
    Greek, C. Ray. *Sacred Cows and Golden Geese*   179
ANIMAL FOOD HABITS
    Schutt, Bill. *Cannibalism*   394
ANIMAL GROUPS
    Ward, Ashley. *The Social Lives of Animals*   591.7
ANIMAL HABITATIONS
    Anthony, Leslie. *The Aliens Among Us*   578.6
    Keim, Brandon. *Meet the Neighbors*   591.5
    Losos, Jonathan B. *The Cat's Meow*   636.8
    Stewart, Tracey. *Do Unto Animals*   590
ANIMAL INDUSTRY AND TRADE
    Baur, Gene. *Farm Sanctuary*   179
    Faruqi, Sonia. *Project Animal Farm*   338.1
ANIMAL INTELLIGENCE
    Ackerman, Jennifer. *The Bird Way*   598.15
    Balcombe, Jonathan P. *What a Fish Knows*   597.15
    Bradshaw, John. ★*Cat Sense*   636.8
    Bradshaw, John. ★*Dog Sense*   636.7
    Keim, Brandon. *Meet the Neighbors*   591.5
    Neiwert, David A. *Of Orcas and Men*   599.53
    Safina, Carl. *Beyond Words*   591.56
    Skaife, Christopher. *The Ravenmaster*   B
★*Animal Liberation*. Singer, Peter   179
ANIMAL LIFE CYCLES
    Connell, John. *The Farmer's Son*   630.9
    Tougias, Robert. *Birder on Berry Lane*   598.072
Animal Madness. Braitman, Laurel   591.5
ANIMAL MIGRATION
    Goldfarb, Ben. *Crossings*   333.77
    Hanson, Thor. *Hurricane Lizards and Plastic Squid*   577.2
    Van Hemert, Caroline. *The Sun Is a Compass*   979.8
    Weidensaul, Scott. *A World on the Wing*   598.156
ANIMAL MORPHOLOGY
    MacPhee, R. D. E. *End of the Megafauna*   591.4
ANIMAL PHYSIOLOGY
    Higgins, Jackie. *Sentient*   573.8
ANIMAL POPULATIONS
    Preston, Christopher J. *Tenacious Beasts*   591.68
ANIMAL RESCUE
    Carr, Caleb. *My Beloved Monster*   B
    McDougall, Christopher. *Running with Sherman*   636.1
    Montgomery, Sy. ★*Of Time and Turtles*   597.92
    Novello, Carol. *Mutual Rescue*   636.088
    Sutherland, Amy. *Rescuing Penny Jane*   636.7
ANIMAL RIGHTS
    Alexander, Jane. *Wild Things, Wild Places*   333.95
    Beers, Diane L. ★*For the Prevention of Cruelty*   179
    Freeberg, Ernest. *A Traitor to His Species*   B
    Goodall, Jane. ★*The Ten Trusts*   333.95
    Greek, C. Ray. *Sacred Cows and Golden Geese*   179
    Keim, Brandon. *Meet the Neighbors*   591.5
    Kurlansky, Mark. *Milk!*   637
    Singer, Peter. ★*Animal Liberation*   179
    Wasik, Bill. ★*Our Kindred Creatures*   179
    Woolfson, Esther. *Between Light and Storm*   599.93
ANIMAL RIGHTS ADVOCATES
    Beers, Diane L. ★*For the Prevention of Cruelty*   179
    Freeberg, Ernest. *A Traitor to His Species*   B
ANIMAL RIGHTS MOVEMENT
    Beers, Diane L. ★*For the Prevention of Cruelty*   179

AUTHOR, TITLE, SERIES AND SUBJECT INDEX

ANIMAL SHELTER WORKERS
   Sutherland, Amy. *Rescuing Penny Jane* — 636.7
ANIMAL SHELTERS
   Montgomery, Sy. ★*Of Time and Turtles* — 597.92
   Novello, Carol. *Mutual Rescue* — 636.088
   Sutherland, Amy. *Rescuing Penny Jane* — 636.7
ANIMAL SOCIETIES
   Holldobler, Bert. *The Superorganism* — 595.7
   Safina, Carl. ★*Becoming Wild* — 591.7
ANIMAL SOUNDS
   Schotz, Susanne. *The Secret Language of Cats* — 636.8
ANIMAL TRACKS
   Murie, Olaus J. ★*A Field Guide to Animal Tracks* — 599
ANIMAL TRAINING
   Pryor, Karen. ★*Don't Shoot the Dog* — 153.8
ANIMAL WASTE
   Addison, Corban. *Wastelands* — 346.73
Animal Weapons. Emlen, Douglas John — 591.47
ANIMAL WEAPONS
   Emlen, Douglas John. *Animal Weapons* — 591.47
ANIMAL WELFARE
   Achterberg, Cara Sue. *Another Good Dog* — 636.7
   Alexander, Jane. *Wild Things, Wild Places* — 333.95
   Baur, Gene. *Farm Sanctuary* — 179
   Beers, Diane L. ★*For the Prevention of Cruelty* — 179
   Danforth, Adam. *Butchering Poultry, Rabbit, Lamb, Goat, and Pork* — 664
   Faruqi, Sonia. *Project Animal Farm* — 338.1
   Foer, Jonathan Safran. *Eating Animals* — 641.3
   Freeberg, Ernest. *A Traitor to His Species* — B
   Goodall, Jane. ★*The Ten Trusts* — 333.95
   Grandin, Temple. ★*Animals Make Us Human* — 636.08
   Horowitz, Alexandra. *Our Dogs, Ourselves* — 636.7
   McDougall, Christopher. *Running with Sherman* — 636.1
   Montgomery, Sy. ★*Of Time and Turtles* — 597.92
   Novello, Carol. *Mutual Rescue* — 636.088
   Pratchett, Terry. *A Slip of the Keyboard* — 824
   Singer, Peter. ★*Animal Liberation* — 179
   Sorvino, Chloe. *Raw Deal* — 338.1
   Sutherland, Amy. *Rescuing Penny Jane* — 636.7
   Wasik, Bill. ★*Our Kindred Creatures* — 179
   Williams, Wyatt. *Springer Mountain* — 394.1
Animal, Vegetable, Junk. Bittman, Mark — 394.1
★*Animal, Vegetable, Miracle*. Kingsolver, Barbara — 641
ANIMALS
   Aryee, Patrick. *30 Animals That Made Us Smarter* — 590
   Brookshire, Bethany. *Pests* — 590
   Cheshire, James. *Where the Animals Go* — 591.47
   Cooke, Lucy. *Bitch* — 591.56
   Cooke, Lucy. *The Truth About Animals* — 590.2
   Dickie, Gloria. *Eight Bears* — 599.78
   Emlen, Douglas John. *Animal Weapons* — 591.47
   Fincham-Gray, Suzanne. *My Patients and Other Animals* — B
   Grandin, Temple. ★*Animals in Translation* — 591.5
   Greek, C. Ray. *Sacred Cows and Golden Geese* — 179
   Heinrich, Bernd. *A Naturalist at Large* — 508
   Herriot, James. ★*All Creatures Great and Small* — B
   Herriot, James. *All Things Wise and Wonderful* — B
   Herriot, James. *Every Living Thing* — B
   Herriot, James. *James Herriot's Animal Stories* — B
   Kaufman, Kenn. *The Birds That Audubon Missed* — 598
   Kisor, Henry. *Traveling with Service Animals* — 362.4
   Kumar, Priyanka. *Conversations with Birds* — 598
   Louv, Richard. *Our Wild Calling* — 615.8
   Montgomery, Sy. *How to Be a Good Creature* — 590
   Mooallem, Jon. *Wild Ones* — 333.95
   Murie, Olaus J. ★*A Field Guide to Animal Tracks* — 599
   Nezhukumatathil, Aimee. *World of Wonders* — 590
   Orlean, Susan. *On Animals* — 590
   Roman, Joe. *Eat, Poop, Die* — 577
   Rutherford, Adam. *Humanimal* — 599.93
   Safina, Carl. ★*Becoming Wild* — 591.7
   Schott, Philipp. *The Accidental Veterinarian* — B
   Toomey, David. *Kingdom of Play* — 591.56
   Turvey, Samuel. ★*The Tomb of the Mili Mongga* — 398.24
   Wasik, Bill. ★*Our Kindred Creatures* — 179
   Welz, Adam. *The End of Eden* — 577.2
   Williams, Wyatt. *Springer Mountain* — 394.1
   Wintz, Jack. *Will I See My Dog in Heaven?* — 231.7

   Wohlleben, Peter. *The Secret Wisdom of Nature* — 508
   Woolfson, Esther. *Between Light and Storm* — 599.93
ANIMALS AND CIVILIZATION
   Brookshire, Bethany. *Pests* — 590
   Roach, Mary. ★*Fuzz* — 591.5
ANIMALS AND HISTORY
   Brookshire, Bethany. *Pests* — 590
ANIMALS AS CARRIERS OF DISEASE
   Wasik, Bill. *Rabid* — 614.5
ANIMALS IN ART
   Hayakawa, Hiroshi. *Kirigami Menagerie* — 736.98
   Higuchi, Yumiko. *Embroidered Animals* — 746.44
   Rott, Ira. *Crochet Animal Rugs* — 746.7
★*Animals in Translation*. Grandin, Temple — 591.5
ANIMALS IN WAR
   Chesney, Will. *No Ordinary Dog* — 958.104
   Lewis, Damien. *The Dog Who Could Fly* — 940.54
★*Animals Make Us Human*. Grandin, Temple — 636.08
ANIMALS WITH DISABILITIES
   Kugler, Rob. *A Dog Named Beautiful* — B
ANIMATED FILM INDUSTRY AND TRADE
   Holt, Nathalia. *The Queens of Animation* — 920
   Isen, Tajja. *Some of My Best Friends* — 305.8
ANIMATED FILMS
   Alt, Matt. *Pure Invention* — 306.0952
   Cavalier, Stephen. *The World History of Animation* — 791.43
   Clements, Jonathan. *The Anime Encyclopedia* — 791.43
   Ghez, Didier. *The Hidden Art of Disney's Golden Age* — 741.5
   Holt, Nathalia. *The Queens of Animation* — 920
   Johnson, Mindy. *Ink & Paint* — B
   Lenburg, Jeff. *The Encyclopedia of Animated Cartoons* — 791.43
ANIMATION (CINEMATOGRAPHY)
   Cavalier, Stephen. *The World History of Animation* — 791.43
   Finch, Christopher. *The Art of Walt Disney* — 791.43092
   Ghez, Didier. *The Hidden Art of Disney's Golden Age* — 741.5
   Johnson, Mindy. *Ink & Paint* — B
   Williams, Richard. *The Animator's Survival Kit* — 778
The Animator's Survival Kit. Williams, Richard — 778
ANIMATORS
   Cavalier, Stephen. *The World History of Animation* — 791.43
   Delisle, Guy. *Pyongyang* — 741.5
   Finch, Christopher. *The Art of Walt Disney* — 791.43092
   Gabler, Neal. *Walt Disney* — B
   Ghez, Didier. *The Hidden Art of Disney's Golden Age* — 741.5
   Harryhausen, Ray. *The Art of Ray Harryhausen* — 778
The Anime Encyclopedia. Clements, Jonathan — 791.43
Anna. Odell, Amy — B
Anne Boleyn and Elizabeth I. Borman, Tracy — 920
ANNE BOLEYN, QUEEN, CONSORT OF HENRY VIII, KING OF ENGLAND, 1507-1536
   Bordo, Susan. *The Creation of Anne Boleyn* — 942.05
   Borman, Tracy. *Anne Boleyn and Elizabeth I* — 920
   Fraser, Antonia. ★*The Wives of Henry VIII* — 942.05
   Guy, John. *Hunting the Falcon* — B
   Starkey, David. *Six Wives* — 942.05
   Weir, Alison. *The Lady in the Tower* — B
Anne Frank. Jacobson, Sidney — 741.5
Anne Frank. Muller, Melissa — B
★*Anne Frank Remembered*. Gies, Miep — B
ANNE, OF CLEVES, QUEEN, CONSORT OF HENRY VIII, KING OF ENGLAND, 1515-1557
   Fraser, Antonia. ★*The Wives of Henry VIII* — 942.05
   Starkey, David. *Six Wives* — 942.05
ANNE, QUEEN OF GREAT BRITAIN, 1665-1714
   Ackroyd, Peter. *Revolution* — 941.07
ANNE, QUEEN, CONSORT OF RICHARD II, KING OF ENGLAND, 1366-1394
   Weir, Alison. *Queens of the Age of Chivalry* — 920
ANNE, QUEEN, CONSORT OF RICHARD III, KING OF ENGLAND, 1456-1485
   Gristwood, Sarah. *Blood Sisters* — 942.04092
ANNIGONI, TONY
   McCumber, David. *Playing off the Rail* — B
★*The Annotated Memoirs of Ulysses S. Grant*. Grant, Ulysses S. — B
The Annotated Mona Lisa. Strickland, Carol — 709
Anolik, Lili
   Hollywood's Eve — B

PUBLIC LIBRARY CORE COLLECTION: NONFICTION
Twentieth Edition

ANONYMOUS LETTERS
   Shane, Scott. ★*Flee North* — 973.7
ANONYMOUS PEOPLE
   Goldblatt, Duchess. *Becoming Duchess Goldblatt* — B
Anonymous Soldiers. Hoffman, Bruce — 956.94
ANONYMS AND PSEUDONYMS
   Goldblatt, Duchess. *Becoming Duchess Goldblatt* — B
   Zenith, Richard. *Pessoa* — B
ANOREXIA NERVOSA
   Burton, Susan. *Empty* — B
   Clein, Emmeline. ★*Dead Weight* — 616.85
   Freeman, Hadley. *Good Girls* — 616.85
   Hornbacher, Marya. *Wasted* — B
Another Good Dog. Achterberg, Cara Sue — 636.7
Another Word for Love. Wallace, Carvell — B
Ansary, Mir Tamim
   Games Without Rules — 958.1
Ansel Adams. Alinder, Mary Street — B
Ansel Adams at 100. Szarkowski, John — B
Ansel Adams in Yosemite Valley. Galassi, Peter — 770.92
ANSON, COLIN EDWARD, 1922-2016
   Garrett, Leah. *X Troop* — 940.54
The Answer Is .. Trebek, Alex — 791.4502
Answering The Call. Jones, Nathaniel R. — B
ANTARCTICA
   Alexander, Caroline. *The Endurance* — 919.8
   Anthony, Jason C. *Hoosh* — 394.1
   Bound, Mensun. *The Ship Beneath the Ice* — 919.8904
   Fiennes, Ranulph. *Shackleton* — B
   Grann, David. *The White Darkness* — B
   Larson, Edward J. *An Empire of Ice* — 919.8
   O'Brady, Colin. ★*The Impossible First* — 919.8904
   Roberts, David. *Alone on the Ice* — 919.8904
   Sancton, Julian. *Madhouse at the End of the Earth* — 919.8904
   Turney, Chris. *1912* — 998
   Wood, Gillen D'Arcy. *Land of Wondrous Cold* — 919.89
ANTARCTICA HISTORY
   Anthony, Jason C. *Hoosh* — 394.1
ANTEBELLUM AMERICA (1820-1861)
   Grinspan, Jon. *Wide Awake* — 973.7
   Hahn, Steven. *A Nation Under Our Feet* — 975
   Kytle, Ethan J. *Denmark Vesey's Garden* — 975.7
   May, Gregory. *A Madman's Will* — 973.5
   Reynolds, David S. ★*Abe* — B
   Shane, Scott. ★*Flee North* — 973.7
   Taylor, Alan. *American Republics* — 973.3
   Woo, Ilyon. ★*Master Slave Husband Wife* — 920
   Wood, Gordon S. *Empire of Liberty* — 973.4
Anterooms. Wilbur, Richard — 811
ANTHEMS
   Clague, Mark. *O Say Can You Hear?* — 782.42
ANTHOLOGIES
   Acocella, Joan Ross. ★*The Bloodied Nightgown* — 814
   Ellison, Ralph. ★*The Collected Essays of Ralph Ellison* — 814
   Ephron, Nora. *The Most of Nora Ephron* — 814
   Gates, Henry Louis. *The Black Box* — 908
   Gibran, Kahlil. *And the Prophet Said* — 811
   Gibran, Kahlil. *The Prophet* — 811
   Graff, Garrett M. ★*When the Sea Came Alive* — 940.54
   Gregory, Dick. ★*The Essential Dick Gregory* — 818
   Hochschild, Adam. *Lessons from a Dark Time* — 909.82
   Jackson, Major. *Razzle Dazzle* — 811
   Lavery, Daniel M. *Dear Prudence* — 170
   Norris, Michele. ★*Our Hidden Conversations* — 305
   Parker, James. ★*Get Me Through the Next Five Minutes* — 158.1
   Romeo, Nick. *The Alternative* — 174
   Schonwerth, Franz Xaver von. *The Turnip Princess* — 398.2
   Sedaris, David. *Theft by Finding* — B
   Shange, Ntozake. ★*Sing a Black Girl's Song* — 818
   Spiegelman, Art. *Co-Mix* — 741.5
   Tuama, Padraig O. ★*Poetry Unbound* — 808.1
   Wainaina, Binyavanga. *How to Write About Africa* — 814
   Ward, Jesmyn. ★*The Fire This Time* — 305.896
Anthony Powell. Spurling, Hilary — B
Anthony, Carl Sferrazza
   Camera Girl — B
   Nellie Taft — B

Anthony, Carmelo
   Where Tomorrows Aren't Promised — B
ANTHONY, CARMELO, 1984-
   Anthony, Carmelo. *Where Tomorrows Aren't Promised* — B
Anthony, Jason C.
   Hoosh — 394.1
Anthony, Leslie
   The Aliens Among Us — 578.6
Anthony, Michael
   V Is for Vegetables — 641.6
ANTHROPOLOGISTS
   De Leon, Jason. ★*Soldiers and Kings* — 364.1
   Hagerty, Alexa. ★*Still Life with Bones* — 599.9
   King, Charles. ★*Gods of the Upper Air* — 920
   Paxson, Margaret. *The Plateau* — 362.87
   Szwed, John F. *Cosmic Scholar* — B
ANTHROPOLOGY
   Bohannon, Cat. ★*Eve* — 613
   Childs, Craig. *Atlas of a Lost World* — 551.7
   D'Agata, John. *About a Mountain* — 979.3
   Foster, Charles. *Being a Human* — 155.7
   Garfinkel, Yosef. *In the Footsteps of King David* — 933
   Howsare, Erika. *The Age of Deer* — 599.65
   Hughes, Bettany. *Istanbul* — 949.61
   Krause, Johannes. *A Short History of Humanity* — 599.9
   Kuper, Adam. *The Museum of Other People* — 305.8
   Lopez, Barry Holstun. *Horizon* — B
   Mann, Charles C. ★*1491* — 970.01
   Puglionesi, Alicia. *In Whose Ruins* — 973
   Raff, Jennifer. *Origin* — 576.5
   Scott, Andy. *One Kiss or Two?* — 395.4
   Turvey, Samuel. ★*The Tomb of the Mili Mongga* — 398.24
ANTI-APARTHEID ACTIVISTS
   Mandela, Nelson. *Conversations with Myself* — B
   Mandela, Nelson. *Dare Not Linger* — B
   Mandela, Nelson. ★*Long Walk to Freedom* — B
   Mandela, Nelson. *Mandela* — B
   Mandela, Nelson. *The Prison Letters of Nelson Mandela* — 968.06092
ANTI-APARTHEID MOVEMENTS
   Smith, David James. *Young Mandela* — B
   Steinberg, Jonny. *Winnie and Nelson* — 920
ANTI-COMMUNISM
   Gage, Beverly. *G-Man* — B
   McCullough, David G. *Truman* — B
   Roll, David L. *Ascent to Power* — 973.918
   Shapiro, James. ★*The Playbook* — 792
   Warren, James A. *Year of the Hawk* — 959.704
ANTI-COMMUNIST MOVEMENTS
   Conant, Jennet. *The Lotus Eaters* — 940.54
   Thompson, Nicholas. *The Hawk and the Dove* — 973.92
   Tye, Larry. ★*Demagogue* — B
ANTI-ENVIRONMENTALISM
   Linden, Eugene. *Fire and Flood* — 304.2
ANTI-FASCISM
   Bailey, Catherine. *A Castle in Wartime* — 943.086
   Kushner, Jacob. *Look Away* — 305.9
   Ricks, Thomas E. *Churchill and Orwell* — 920
   Watling, Sarah. *Tomorrow Perhaps the Future* — 946.081
ANTI-IMPERIALIST MOVEMENTS
   Ortiz, Paul. *An African American and Latinx History of the United States* — 305.8
ANTI-NAZI MOVEMENT
   Allen, Arthur. ★*The Fantastic Laboratory of Dr. Weigl* — 614.5
   Bailey, Catherine. *A Castle in Wartime* — 943.086
   Donner, Rebecca. *All the Frequent Troubles of Our Days* — 943
   Dumbach, Annette E. *Sophie Scholl and the White Rose* — 943.086
   Hurowitz, Richard. *In the Garden of the Righteous* — 940.53
   Marsh, Charles. *Strange Glory* — B
   Matzen, Robert. *Dutch Girl* — B
   Mazzeo, Tilar J. *Sisters in Resistance* — 945.091
   Moorehead, Caroline. *A House in the Mountains* — 940.53
   Moorehead, Caroline. *Village of Secrets* — 944
   Ohler, Norman. *The Bohemians* — 940.53
   Pomerantsev, Peter. ★*How to Win an Information War* — 940.53
   Rosenberg, Justus. *The Art of Resistance* — B
   Rosenzweig, Laura B. *Hollywood's Spies* — 791.43
   Strauss, Gwen. *The Nine* — 940.53
   Thomas, Gordon. *Defying Hitler* — 920

AUTHOR, TITLE, SERIES AND SUBJECT INDEX

Todd, Olivier. *Albert Camus*	B
Van De Perre, Selma. *My Name Is Selma*	940.53

ANTI-NAZIS

Thomas, Gordon. *Defying Hitler*	920
Anti-Racist Ally. Williams, Sophie	305.8

ANTI-SLAVERY MOVEMENTS

Blight, David W. ★*Frederick Douglass*	B
Bordewich, Fergus M. *Bound for Canaan*	973.7
Burlingame, Michael. *The Black Man's President*	973.7
Burrough, Bryan. *Forget the Alamo*	976.043
Colaiaco, James A. *Frederick Douglass and the Fourth of July*	973.7
Dilbeck, D. H. *Frederick Douglass*	B
Douglass, Frederick. ★*Frederick Douglass*	973.8
Douglass, Frederick. *The Portable Frederick Douglass*	973.8
Foner, Eric. ★*Gateway to Freedom*	973.7
Freeman, Joanne B. *The Field of Blood*	973.7
Greenidge, Kerri. ★*The Grimkes*	973.5
Grinspan, Jon. *Wide Awake*	973.7
Hochschild, Adam. *Bury the Chains*	326
Horwitz, Tony. ★*Midnight Rising*	973.7
Inskeep, Steve. *Imperfect Union*	B
Miles, Tiya. ★*Night Flyer*	B
Morgan-Owens, Jessie. *Girl in Black and White*	B
Painter, Nell Irvin. ★*Sojourner Truth*	B
Rediker, Marcus. *The Amistad Rebellion*	326.0973
Reynolds, David S. *John Brown, Abolitionist*	B
Shane, Scott. ★*Flee North*	973.7
Snodgrass, Mary Ellen. *The Underground Railroad*	973.7
Stauffer, John. *Picturing Fredrick Douglass*	B
Wickenden, Dorothy. *The Agitators*	920
Wineapple, Brenda. *Ecstatic Nation*	973.6
Young, Kevin. *Ardency*	811

ANTI-VACCINATION MOVEMENT

Deer, Brian. *The Doctor Who Fooled the World*	610.92
Hotez, Peter J. *Preventing the Next Pandemic*	362.1969
Kinch, Michael S. *Between Hope and Fear*	614.4
McNeil, Donald G. ★*The Wisdom of Plagues*	614.4

ANTIBIOTICS

Blaser, Martin J. *Missing Microbes*	615.7
Zaman, Muhammad H. *Biography of Resistance*	616.9
Anticancer. Servan-Schreiber, David	616.99

ANTIDEPRESSANTS

Kramer, Peter D. ★*Ordinarily Well*	615.7
Riley, Alex. ★*A Cure for Darkness*	616.85

ANTIETAM, BATTLE OF, MD., 1862

Sears, Stephen W. ★*Landscape Turned Red*	973.7

ANTIFEMINISM

Bates, Laura. *Men Who Hate Women*	305.3
Darby, Seyward. ★*Sisters in Hate*	305.800973

ANTIHEROES AND ANTIHEROINES

Harman, Claire. *Murder by the Book*	364.152
Martin, Brett. *Difficult Men*	791.4509

ANTIPOVERTY PROGRAMS

Kim, Anne. ★*Poverty for Profit*	302.5
Woods, Randall Bennett. *Prisoners of Hope*	973.923

ANTIQUARIAN BOOKSELLERS

Darkshire, Oliver. *Once Upon a Tome*	B

ANTIQUE DEALERS

Raab, Nathan. *The Hunt for History*	790.1

ANTIQUE THEFTS

Fishman, David E. *The Book Smugglers*	940.53

ANTIQUITIES

Beard, Mary. ★*How Do We Look*	704.9
Berlo, Janet Catherine. ★*Native North American Art*	704.03
Bingham, Hiram. ★*Lost City of the Incas*	985
Brown, Nancy Marie. *Ivory Vikings*	736
Childs, Craig. *Atlas of a Lost World*	551.7
Childs, Craig. *House of Rain*	978.9
Coe, Michael D. *The Maya*	972
Darnell, John Coleman. *Egypt's Golden Couple*	932
Fox, Margalit. *The Riddle of the Labyrinth*	920
Hessler, Peter. *The Buried*	962.05
Krause, Johannes. *A Short History of Humanity*	599.9
Lance, Rachel. *In the Waves*	973.7
MacGregor, Neil. *A History of the World in 100 Objects*	930.1
Maiklem, Lara. *Mudlark*	B
Mann, Charles C. ★*1491*	970.01
Olson, Lynne. ★*Empress of the Nile*	B
Parker Pearson, Michael. *Stonehenge*	936.2
Price, Neil S. ★*Children of Ash and Elm*	948
Richardson, Edmund. *The King's Shadow*	958.1
Shaw, Ian. *The Princeton Dictionary of Ancient Egypt*	932
Treister, Kenneth. *Easter Island's Silent Sentinels*	996.18
Wilkinson, Toby A. H. *A World Beneath the Sands*	932

ANTIQUITIES, PREHISTORIC

Langlands, Alex. *Craeft*	306.4
MacGregor, Neil. *A History of the World in 100 Objects*	930.1

ANTIRACISM

Asika, Uju. *Bringing up Race*	155.4
Baxley, Traci. *Social Justice Parenting*	649
Bell, W. Kamau. ★*Do the Work!*	305.8
Bond, Julian. ★*Julian Bond's Time to Teach*	323.0975
Boykin, Keith. ★*Why Does Everything Have to Be About Race?*	305.8
Cargle, Rachel Elizabeth. *A Renaissance of Our Own*	B
Hamad, Ruby. *White Tears/Brown Scars*	305.8
Hawthorne, Britt. ★*Raising Antiracist Children*	649
Jackson, Regina. *White Women*	305.8
Kendi, Ibram X. ★*How to Be an Antiracist*	305.8
Kendi, Ibram X. ★*Stamped from the Beginning*	305.8
Neus, Nora. *24 Hours in Charlottesville*	973.933
Oluo, Ijeoma. ★*Be a Revolution*	305.8
Phillips, Collette A. M. *The Includers*	658.4
Purnell, Derecka. *Becoming Abolitionists*	363.20973
Ricketts, Rachel. ★*Do Better*	305.800973
Ross, Dax-Devlon. *Letters to My White Male Friends*	305.8
Whitaker, Mark. ★*Saying It Loud*	973.923
Williams, Sophie. *Anti-Racist Ally*	305.8

ANTIRACIST ACTION

Sharpton, Al. *Rise Up*	973.933

ANTIRACIST LITERATURE

Alexander, Kwame. *Light for the World to See*	811.6
Alexander, Michelle. *The New Jim Crow*	364.973
Anderson, Carol. ★*White Rage*	305.800973
Archibald, John. *Shaking the Gates of Hell*	B
Asika, Uju. *Bringing up Race*	155.4
Baldwin, James. ★*Collected Essays*	814
Baldwin, James. ★*The Fire Next Time*	305.896
Baxley, Traci. *Social Justice Parenting*	649
Bayoumi, Moustafa. *How Does It Feel to Be a Problem?*	305.892
Bell, Darrin. ★*The Talk*	741.5
Bell, W. Kamau. ★*Do the Work!*	305.8
Berman, Ari. *Give Us the Ballot*	324.6
Bernard, Emily. *Black Is the Body*	305.48
Bond, Julian. ★*Julian Bond's Time to Teach*	323.0975
Boykin, Keith. *Race Against Time*	305.8
Boykin, Keith. ★*Why Does Everything Have to Be About Race?*	305.8
Brennan, Chad. *Faithful Antiracism*	277.308
Brown, Austin Channing. ★*I'm Still Here*	B
Busby, Jill Louise. *Unfollow Me*	305.08
Carter, Stephen L. *Invisible*	B
Castillo, Elaine. ★*How to Read Now*	418
Coates, Ta-Nehisi. ★*Between the World and Me*	305.800973
Cooper, Brittney C. *Eloquent Rage*	B
Currie, Elliott. *A Peculiar Indifference*	305.800973
DiAngelo, Robin J. *White Fragility*	305.8
Dunbar-Ortiz, Roxanne. ★*An Indigenous Peoples' History of the United States*	970.004
Dyson, Michael Eric. *Long Time Coming*	305.800973
Dyson, Michael Eric. *Tears We Cannot Stop*	305.800973
Eberhardt, Jennifer L. ★*Biased*	303.3
Eddo-Lodge, Reni. *Why I'm No Longer Talking to White People About Race*	305.8
Espada, Martin. ★*Floaters*	811
Fersko, Diana. ★*We Need to Talk About Antisemitism*	305.892
Forman, James. *Locking up Our Own*	364.973
Francois, Willie Dwayne. *Silencing White Noise*	277
Franklin, John Hope. ★*From Slavery to Freedom*	973
Garza, Alicia. *The Purpose of Power*	303.48
Gates, Henry Louis. ★*The Black Church*	277
Gates, Henry Louis. *The Future of the Race*	305.896
Gilliard, Dominique Dubois. *Rethinking Incarceration*	261.8
Glaude, Eddie S. *Begin Again*	305.800973
Griffin, Farah Jasmine. *Read Until You Understand*	810.9
Hall, Rebecca. ★*Wake*	741.5
Hamad, Ruby. *White Tears/Brown Scars*	305.8
Hawthorne, Britt. ★*Raising Antiracist Children*	649

PUBLIC LIBRARY CORE COLLECTION: NONFICTION
Twentieth Edition

Headlee, Celeste Anne. *Speaking of Race*	305.8
Henny, Ally. *I Won't Shut Up*	305.896
Horace, Matthew. *The Black and the Blue*	305.896
Hurston, Zora Neale. ★*Barracoon*	B
Imani, Blair. *Read This to Get Smarter*	303.3
Jackson, Regina. *White Women*	305.8
Johnson, Theodore R. *When the Stars Begin to Fall*	305.800973
Jones, Saeed. *How We Fight for Our Lives*	B
Kendall, Mikki. *Hood Feminism*	305.420973
Kendi, Ibram X. ★*How to Be an Antiracist*	305.8
Kendi, Ibram X. ★*How to Raise an Antiracist*	649
Kendi, Ibram X. ★*Stamped from the Beginning*	305.8
Laymon, Kiese. ★*Heavy*	B
Lebron, Christopher J. *The Making of Black Lives Matter*	305.896
Lemon, Don. *This Is the Fire*	305.896
Lewis, John. ★*March; Book One*	741.5
Lewis, John. ★*March; Book Three*	741.5
Lewis, John. ★*March; Book Two*	741.5
Lewis, John. ★*Run; Book One*	741.5
Lewis, John. *Walking with the Wind*	B
Livingston, Robert W. *The Conversation*	305.8
Lorde, Audre. *Sister Outsider*	814
Lowery, Wesley. ★*American Whitelash*	305.8
Luckerson, Victor. *Built from the Fire*	976.6
Mallory, Tamika D. *State of Emergency*	305.896
Mandela, Nelson. ★*Long Walk to Freedom*	B
Muhammad, Khalil Gibran. *The Condemnation of Blackness*	364.2
Mukantabana, Yseult P. ★*Real Friends Talk About Race*	305.8
Noah, Trevor. *Born a Crime*	B
Obama, Barack. ★*Dreams from My Father*	B
Oluo, Ijeoma. ★*Be a Revolution*	305.8
Oluo, Ijeoma. ★*So You Want to Talk About Race*	305.800973
Onwuachi, Kwame. ★*Notes from a Young Black Chef*	641.59
Ortiz, Paul. *An African American and Latinx History of the United States*	305.8
Person, Charles. *Buses Are a Comin'*	B
Phillips, Collette A. M. *The Includers*	658.4
Picower, Bree. *Reading, Writing, and Racism*	371.829
Prescod, Danielle. *Token Black Girl*	B
Ramesh, Jaya. *Parenting at the Intersections*	649
Rankine, Claudia. ★*Citizen*	814
Ricketts, Rachel. ★*Do Better*	305.800973
Roberts-Miller, Patricia. *Speaking of Race*	305.8
Robinson, Phoebe. *You Can't Touch My Hair and Other Things I Still Have to Explain*	792.7
Ross, Dax-Devlon. *Letters to My White Male Friends*	305.8
Rothstein, Richard. ★*The Color of Law*	305.800973
Rubinstein, Julian. ★*The Holly*	364.106
Ruffin, Amber. ★*The World Record Book of Racist Stories*	305.896
Ruffin, Amber. *You'll Never Believe What Happened to Lacey*	305.896
Saad, Layla F. ★*Me and White Supremacy*	305.809
Stevenson, Bryan. *Just Mercy*	B
Tatum, Beverly Daniel. ★*"Why Are All the Black Kids Sitting Together in the Cafeteria?"*	305.800973
Tobar, Hector. ★*Our Migrant Souls*	305.868
Tran, Phuc. ★*Sigh, Gone*	B
Villarosa, Linda. ★*Under the Skin*	362.1089
Whitaker, Mark. ★*Saying It Loud*	973.923
Wiesel, Elie. ★*Night*	B
Williams, Sophie. *Anti-Racist Ally*	305.8
Winters, Mary-Frances. *Black Fatigue*	305.896
Wise, Tim J. *Dispatches from the Race War*	305.8
Yoshino, Kenji. *Say the Right Thing*	305.3
Young, Damon. ★*What Doesn't Kill You Makes You Blacker*	B

ANTISEMITES

Tye, Larry. ★*Demagogue*	B
Watts, Steven. *The People's Tycoon*	B

ANTISEMITISM

Aly, Gotz. *Europe Against the Jews*	305.892
Arendt, Hannah. *The Origins of Totalitarianism*	320.53
Asbrink, Elisabeth. *And in the Vienna Woods the Trees Remain*	B
Cornwell, John. *Hitler's Pope*	B
Dwork, Deborah. ★*Holocaust*	940
Fersko, Diana. ★*We Need to Talk About Antisemitism*	305.892
Frank, Michael. *One Hundred Saturdays*	B
Freeman, Hadley. *House of Glass*	B
Friedman, Tova. ★*The Daughter of Auschwitz*	B
Gill, Anton. *Art Lover*	B
Goldhagen, Daniel Jonah. *Hitler's Willing Executioners*	940.53
Hayes, Peter. *Why?*	940.53
Horn, Dara. ★*People Love Dead Jews*	909
Kershaw, Ian. *Hitler*	B
Kershaw, Ian. *Hitler*	B
Kramer, Clara. *Clara's War*	B
Longerich, Peter. *Goebbels*	B
Longerich, Peter. *Hitler*	B
Lowe, Keith. *Savage Continent*	940.55
Maddow, Rachel. ★*Prequel*	320.53
Mazower, Mark. *Hitler's Empire*	940.53
McDonough, Frank. *The Hitler Years*	943.086
Morris, Marc. *A Great and Terrible King*	B
O'Donnell, Svenja. *Inge's War*	943.086
Okrent, Daniel. *The Guarded Gate*	344.73
Oppenheimer, Mark. *Squirrel Hill*	364.152
Oz, Amos. *A Tale of Love and Darkness*	B
Pick-Goslar, Hannah Elizabeth. ★*My Friend Anne Frank*	B
Pressman, Steven. *50 Children*	940.53
Ross, Steven Joseph. *Hitler in Los Angeles*	979.4
Rydell, Anders. *The Book Thieves*	027
Sattouf, Riad. *The Arab of the Future 2*	741.5
Schindler, Meriel. *The Lost Cafe Schindler*	943.64
Spiegel, Renia. *Renia's Diary*	B
Urwand, Ben. *The Collaboration*	791.430973

ANTISEMITISM IN CHRISTIANITY

Carroll, James. *Constantine's Sword*	261
Pagels, Elaine H. *The Origin of Satan*	235

ANTISEMITISM IN THE CATHOLIC CHURCH

Wills, Garry. *The Future of the Catholic Church with Pope Francis*	282.09

ANTISOCIAL PERSONALITY DISORDERS

Gagne, Patric. *Sociopath*	B
Ronson, Jon. ★*The Psychopath Test*	616.85

ANTITERRORIST POLICY

Bergen, Peter L. *The Longest War*	909.83
Bergen, Peter L. *The Rise and Fall of Osama Bin Laden*	958.104
Brooks, Rosa. *How Everything Became War and the Military Became Everything*	355
Mayer, Jane. *The Dark Side*	973.931
Scahill, Jeremy. *Dirty Wars*	355.00973
Soufan, Ali H. *The Black Banners Declassified*	363.325
Warrick, Joby. *Red Line*	956.9104
Wright, Lawrence. ★*The Looming Tower*	973.931

ANTITERRORISTS

Elnoury, Tamer. *American Radical*	B
Fox, Amaryllis. *Life Undercover*	B
Verini, James. *They Will Have to Die Now*	956.7044
Wallace, Chris. *Countdown Bin Laden*	958.104
★*Antitrust*. Klobuchar, Amy	343.73

ANTITRUST LAW

Berfield, Susan. *The Hour of Fate*	973.91
Dayen, David. *Monopolized*	338.8
Klobuchar, Amy. ★*Antitrust*	343.73
Teachout, Zephyr. *Break 'Em Up*	338.8

ANTITRUST LAW AND COMPETITION

Klobuchar, Amy. ★*Antitrust*	343.73
Antoni. Porowski, Antoni	641.5

ANTONIUS, MARCUS, 83-30 B.C.E

Goldsworthy, Adrian Keith. *Antony and Cleopatra*	937
Strauss, Barry S. ★*The War That Made the Roman Empire*	937
Antony and Cleopatra. Goldsworthy, Adrian Keith	937

ANTS

Wilson, Edward O. *Tales from the Ant World*	595.79
Ants Among Elephants. Gidla, Sujatha	305.5

ANXIETY

Baskette, Molly Phinney. *How to Begin When Your World Is Ending*	248.8
Boone, Matthew S. *Stop Avoiding Stuff*	152.4
Boyes, Alice. *The Anxiety Toolkit*	616.85
Breggin, Peter Roger. *Guilt, Shame, and Anxiety*	152.4
Brown, Brene. *Braving the Wilderness*	305.8
Calhoun, Ada. *Why We Can't Sleep*	305.244
Davis, KC. ★*How to Keep House While Drowning*	648
Fall, Jeremy. *Falling Upwards*	158.1
Franklin, Ruth. *Shirley Jackson*	B
Galanti, Regine. ★*Parenting Anxious Kids*	155.4
Gardner, Dan. *The Science of Fear*	152.4
Haidt, Jonathan. ★*The Anxious Generation*	305.23
Haig, Matt. *Notes on a Nervous Planet*	616.89

AUTHOR, TITLE, SERIES AND SUBJECT INDEX

Harris, Taylor. *This Boy We Made*	B
Harvey, Samantha. *The Shapeless Unease*	B
Lamott, Anne. *Almost Everything*	170
Lancaster, Jen. *Welcome to the United States of Anxiety*	155.4
Lawson, Jenny. ★*Broken*	B
Lawson, Jenny. *Furiously Happy*	B
Millet, Lydia. *We Loved It All*	813
Petersen, Andrea. *On Edge*	616.85
Philpott, Mary Laura. *Bomb Shelter*	B
Pritchett, Georgia. *My Mess Is a Bit of a Life*	B
Rannells, Andrew. *Uncle of the Year*	B
Raskin, Allison. *Overthinking About You*	646.7
Rauch, Jonathan. *The Happiness Curve*	155.6
Sehee, Baek. *I Want to Die but I Want to Eat Tteokbokki*	B
Stahl, Jerry. *Nein, Nein, Nein!*	
Stern, Amanda. *Little Panic*	616.8522
Tillich, Paul. ★*The Courage to Be*	179
Tweedy, Jeff. *Let's Go (so We Can Get Back)*	B
Wilson, Sarah. *First, We Make the Beast Beautiful*	616.85
Wray, Britt. *Generation Dread*	155.9

ANXIETY DISORDERS
Crampton, Caroline. *A Body Made of Glass*	616.85
Ikpi, Bassey. *I'm Telling the Truth, but I'm Lying*	814
Petersen, Andrea. *On Edge*	616.85
Stern, Amanda. *Little Panic*	616.8522
Taylor, Madisyn. *Unmedicated*	615.8

ANXIETY IN CHILDREN
Galanti, Regine. ★*Parenting Anxious Kids*	155.4
Hobbs, Jeff. *Show Them You're Good*	373
Pentland, Jenny. *This Will Be Funny Later*	B
The Anxiety Toolkit. Boyes, Alice	616.85
★*The Anxious Generation*. Haidt, Jonathan	305.23
Any Person Is the Only Self. Gabbert, Elisa	814
Anything Goes. Mordden, Ethan	782.1
Anything's Pastable. Pashman, Dan	641.82

APACHE (NORTH AMERICAN PEOPLE)
Brands, H. W. *The Last Campaign*	973.8
Hutton, Paul Andrew. *The Apache Wars*	979
Nelson, Megan Kate. *The Three-Cornered War*	978
Redniss, Lauren. ★*Oak Flat*	970.5
Roberts, David. *Once They Moved Like the Wind*	B
Utley, Robert M. ★*Geronimo*	B

APACHE KID, APPROXIMATELY 1860-
Hutton, Paul Andrew. *The Apache Wars*	979
The Apache Wars. Hutton, Paul Andrew	979

APARTHEID
Malala, Justice. *The Plot to Save South Africa*	968.07
Smith, David James. *Young Mandela*	B
Steinberg, Jonny. *Winnie and Nelson*	920

APARTMENT DWELLERS
Slezkine, Yuri. *The House of Government*	947.084

APARTMENTS
Podemski, Max. *A Paradise of Small Houses*	363.5

APATHY
Norris, Kathleen. *Acedia & Me*	248.8

APES
Fossey, Dian. ★*Gorillas in the Mist*	599.884

Apfelbaum, Chanie
★*Totally Kosher*	641.5

APHRODITE (GREEK DEITY)
Hughes, Bettany. *Venus and Aphrodite*	292

APOCALYPTIC LITERATURE
Newitz, Annalee. *Scatter, Adapt, and Remember*	576.8

APOCRYPHAL BOOKS (NEW TESTAMENT)
Pagels, Elaine H. ★*The Gnostic Gospels*	273

APOLLO 11 (SPACECRAFT)
Aldrin, Buzz. *No Dream Is Too High*	B
Donovan, Jim. ★*Shoot for the Moon*	629.45
★*Apollo 8*. Kluger, Jeffrey	629.45

APOLLO 8 (SPACECRAFT)
Kluger, Jeffrey. ★*Apollo 8*	629.45
Kurson, Robert. ★*Rocket Men*	629.45
★*Apollo's Angels*. Homans, Jennifer	792.8
Apollo's Arrow. Christakis, Nicholas A.	362.1962
Apollo's Legacy. Launius, Roger D.	629.45

APOLOGIZING
Howes, Molly. *A Good Apology*	158.2
Ingall, Marjorie. *Sorry, Sorry, Sorry*	158.2
Shapiro, Susan. *The Forgiveness Tour*	158.2
V. *The Apology*	818
The Apology. V	818

APPALACHIAN REGION
Eisenberg, Emma Copley. ★*The Third Rainbow Girl*	364.152
Leamer, Laurence. *The Price of Justice*	346.7302
Maher, Kris. *Desperate*	344
Wilkinson, Crystal. *Praisesong for the Kitchen Ghosts*	641.5975

APPALACHIAN REGION, SOUTHERN
Dissen, William Stark. *Thoughtful Cooking*	641.5975
Kingsolver, Barbara. ★*Animal, Vegetable, Miracle*	641
Spira, Timothy P. *Waterfalls and Wildflowers in the Southern Appalachians*	796.5109756

APPALACHIAN TRAIL
Bryson, Bill. ★*A Walk in the Woods*	917
Davis, Jennifer Pharr. *Called Again*	B

APPALACHIANS (PEOPLE)
Wilkinson, Crystal. *Praisesong for the Kitchen Ghosts*	641.5975
Apparently There Were Complaints. Gless, Sharon	B
The Apparitionists. Manseau, Peter	B

APPARITIONS
Manseau, Peter. *The Apparitionists*	B
An Appeal to the World. Dalai Lama	170

APPEARANCES
Smil, Vaclav. *Size*	153.7
Appeasement. Bouverie, Tim	327.41043

Appelman, J. Reuben
While Idaho Slept	364.152

APPETITE
Tandoh, Ruby. ★*Eat Up*	641.3
An Appetite for Wonder. Dawkins, Richard	B
★*Appetites*. Bourdain, Anthony	641.5

APPETIZERS
Lanza, Fabrizia. *The Food of Sicily*	641.594
Mullen, Marissa. *That Cheese Plate Wants to Party*	641.6
The Apple Trees at Olema. Hass, Robert	811

Applebaum, Allison
Stand by Me	649.8

Applebaum, Anne
★*Gulag*	365
Iron Curtain	947
★*Red Famine*	947.708
Twilight of Democracy	321.9

Appleman, Deborah
Literature and the New Culture Wars	807
Apples to Cider. White, April	663

Applewhite, Ashton
This Chair Rocks	155.67

APPLIED MATHEMATICS
Brooks, Michael. *The Art of More*	510.9

APPLIED PSYCHOLOGY
Hammond, Claudia. *Mind Over Money*	332.401
Zimbardo, Philip G. *The Lucifer Effect*	155.9

APPLIQUE
Glass, Alison. *Alison Glass Applique*.	746.44

APPOMATTOX CAMPAIGN, 1865
Winik, Jay. *April 1865*	973.7

APPORTIONMENT (ELECTION LAW)
Seabrook, Nicholas R. *One Person, One Vote*	328.3
Smith, J. Douglas. *On Democracy's Doorstep*	342.73
The Apprentice. Pepin, Jacques	B

APPRENTICESHIP
Pinckney, Darryl. *Come Back in September*	B
Approaching The Buddhist Path. Dalai Lama	294.3

Appy, Christian G.
American Reckoning	959.704
April 1865. Winik, Jay	973.7

Apter, T. E.
The Teen Interpreter	306.874

Aptowicz, Cristin O'Keefe
Dr. Mutter's Marvels	B

AQUACULTURE
Smith, Bren. *Eat Like a Fish*	338.3

AQUATIC ANIMALS
Kingdon, Amorina. ★*Sing Like Fish*	591.77

AQUATIC BIOLOGY
Kingdon, Amorina. ★*Sing Like Fish*	591.77

PUBLIC LIBRARY CORE COLLECTION: NONFICTION
Twentieth Edition

AQUATIC ECOLOGY
   Kingdon, Amorina. ★*Sing Like Fish* — 591.77
AQUI, 1962-
   Lamb, Christina. *House of Stone* — 968.91
Aquino, Lucia
   Leonardo Da Vinci — 709.2
ARAB AMERICANS
   Al-Maria, Sophia. *The Girl Who Fell to Earth* — B
   Bayoumi, Moustafa. *How Does It Feel to Be a Problem?* — 305.892
   Mufleh, Luma. ★*Learning America* — 371.826
   Shanahan, Charif. *Trace Evidence* — 811
ARAB COUNTRIES
   Barr, James. *Lords of the Desert* — 956
   Friedman, Thomas L. ★*From Beirut to Jerusalem* — 956.04
   Morris, Benny. *1948* — 956.04
   Seale, Yasmine. *Aladdin* — 398.2
   Worth, Robert Forsyth. ★*A Rage for Order* — 909
   Zoepf, Katherine. *Excellent Daughters* — 305.42
   The Arab of the Future. Sattouf, Riad — 741.5
   The Arab of the Future 2. Sattouf, Riad — 741.5
ARAB PEOPLE
   Hoffman, Adina. ★*My Happiness Bears No Relation to Happiness* — B
   Kershner, Isabel. *The Land of Hope and Fear* — 956.9405
   Lawrence, T. E. *Seven Pillars of Wisdom* — 940.4
   LeBor, Adam. *City of Oranges* — 956.94
   Salama, Jordan. ★*Stranger in the Desert* — 982
ARAB SPRING, 2010-2012
   Dagher, Sam. *Assad or We Burn the Country* — 956.9104
   Di Giovanni, Janine. *The Morning They Came for Us* — 956.9104
   Hessler, Peter. *The Buried* — 962.05
   Malek, Alia. *The Home That Was Our Country* — B
   Rusbridger, Alan. ★*Play It Again* — B
   Worth, Robert Forsyth. ★*A Rage for Order* — 909
ARAB-ISRAELI CONFLICT
   Abu Sayf, Atif. *The Drone Eats with Me* — B
   Abuelaish, Izzeldin. *I Shall Not Hate* — B
   Ahmad, Aeham. *The Pianist from Syria* — B
   Bennis, Phyllis. *Understanding the Palestinian-Israeli Conflict* — 956.9405
   Carter, Jimmy. *Palestine* — 956.04
   Di Cintio, Marcello. *Pay No Heed to the Rockets* — 956.9405
   Ehrenreich, Ben. *The Way to the Spring* — 956.95
   Friedman, Matti. *Pumpkinflowers* — B
   Friedman, Thomas L. ★*From Beirut to Jerusalem* — 956.04
   Goodman, Micah. *Catch-67* — 956.04
   Gordis, Daniel. *Israel* — 956.9405
   Grossman, David. *The Yellow Wind* — 956.95
   Halevi, Yossi Klein. ★*Letters to My Palestinian Neighbor* — 956.94054
   Indyk, Martin. *Master of the Game* — 327.73
   Khalidi, Rashid. ★*The Hundred Years' War on Palestine* — 956.9405
   Kimmerling, Baruch. *The Palestinian People* — 956.94
   Mead, Walter Russell. *The Arc of a Covenant* — 327.73
   Mitchell, George J. *A Path to Peace* — 956.9405
   Morris, Benny. *1948* — 956.04
   Morris, Benny. *Righteous Victims* — 956
   Noor. *Leap of Faith* — B
   Nusseibeh, Sari. *Once Upon a Country* — B
   Nye, Naomi Shihab. *The Tiny Journalist* — 811
   Pappe, Ilan. *The Biggest Prison on Earth* — 956.9405
   Petraeus, David Howell. *Conflict* — 355
   Qashu, Sayed. *Native* — 892.4
   Sacco, Joe. *Footnotes in Gaza* — 741.5
   Sefarad, Mikhael. *The Wall and the Gate* — 341.48
   Shavit, Ari. *My Promised Land* — 956.05
   Shehadeh, Raja. ★*We Could Have Been Friends, My Father and I* — B
   Shehadeh, Raja. *Where the Line Is Drawn* — 956.9405
   Shlaim, Avi. *The Iron Wall* — 956.04
   Sokatch, Daniel. *Can We Talk About Israel?* — 956.9405
   Tamimi, Ahed. ★*They Called Me a Lioness* — B
   Tolan, Sandy. ★*The Lemon Tree* — B
   Von Tunzelmann, Alex. *Blood and Sand* — 909.82
   Wright, Lawrence. *Thirteen Days in September* — 956.04
ARAB-ISRAELI RELATIONS
   Halevi, Yossi Klein. ★*Letters to My Palestinian Neighbor* — 956.94054
   Indyk, Martin. *Master of the Game* — 327.73
   Kaufmann, Uri R. *Eighteen Days of October* — 956.04
   Khalidi, Rashid. ★*The Hundred Years' War on Palestine* — 956.9405
   Morris, Benny. *Righteous Victims* — 956
   Oren, Michael B. *Six Days of War* — 956.04

   Sacco, Joe. *Footnotes in Gaza* — 741.5
   Shavit, Ari. *My Promised Land* — 956.05
   Thrall, Nathan. ★*A Day in the Life of Abed Salama* — 956.05
Arabesque. Roden, Claudia — 641.59
ARABIAN PENINSULA
   AL Samawi, Mohammed. *The Fox Hunt* — 953
   Lawrence, T. E. *Seven Pillars of Wisdom* — 940.4
ARABIC LANGUAGE
   Mackintosh-Smith, Tim. *Arabs* — 909.04
Arabiyya. Assil, Reem — 641.595
Arabs. Mackintosh-Smith, Tim — 909.04
Arana, Marie
   American Chica — B
   Bolivar — B
   ★*Latinoland* — 973
ARANA, MARIE
   Arana, Marie. *American Chica* — B
ARAPAHO (NORTH AMERICAN PEOPLE)
   Connell, Evan S. *Son of the Morning Star* — 973.8
The Arbornaut. Lowman, Margaret — 581.7
ARBUS, DIANE, 1923-1971
   Lubow, Arthur. *Diane Arbus* — B
The Arc of a Covenant. Mead, Walter Russell — 327.73
Arc of Justice. Boyle, Kevin — 345.73
Arcadia. Stoppard, Tom — 822
Arce, Julissa
   You Sound Like a White Girl — 303.48
Arceneaux, Michael
   I Finally Bought Some Jordans — 306.76
ARCHAEOASTRONOMY
   Nordgren, Tyler E. *Sun, Moon, Earth* — 523.7
ARCHAEOLOGICAL EXPEDITIONS
   Bound, Mensun. *The Ship Beneath the Ice* — 919.8904
   Carlsen, William. *Jungle of Stone* — B
   Ceram, C. W. *Gods, Graves & Scholars* — 930.1
ARCHAEOLOGICAL SITES
   Ceram, C. W. *Gods, Graves & Scholars* — 930.1
   Roberts, David. *The Bears Ears* — 979.2
ARCHAEOLOGISTS
   Ceram, C. W. *Gods, Graves & Scholars* — 930.1
   Olson, Lynne. ★*Empress of the Nile* — B
   Richardson, Edmund. *The King's Shadow* — 958.1
   Wilkinson, Toby A. H. *A World Beneath the Sands* — 932
ARCHAEOLOGY
   Ceram, C. W. *Gods, Graves & Scholars* — 930.1
   Childs, Craig. *Atlas of a Lost World* — 551.7
   Cline, Eric H. *After 1177 B.C.* — 937
   Dolnick, Edward. *The Writing of the Gods* — 493
   Fagan, Brian M. *Fishing* — 338.3
   Fox, Margalit. *The Riddle of the Labyrinth* — 920
   Garfinkel, Yosef. *In the Footsteps of King David* — 933
   Judah, Hettie. *Lapidarium* — 553.8
   Krause, Johannes. *A Short History of Humanity* — 599.9
   Mann, Charles C. ★*1491* — 970.01
   Parker Pearson, Michael. *Stonehenge* — 936.2
   Pattison, Kermit. *Fossil Men* — 569.9
   Preston, Douglas J. *The Lost Tomb* — 930.1
   Pryor, Francis. ★*Stonehenge* — 936.2
   Robb, Graham. *The Debatable Land* — 941.3
   Tigay, Chanan. *The Lost Book of Moses* — 098
ARCHAEOLOGY AND HISTORY
   Lawler, Andrew. *The Secret Token* — 975.6
ARCHES
   Blockley, David. *Bridges* — 725
ARCHETYPE (PSYCHOLOGY)
   Bly, Robert. *More Than True* — 398.2
   Campbell, Joseph. *The Masks of God* — 201.3
   Grossman, Pam. *Waking the Witch* — 133.4
   Tatar, Maria. *The Heroine with 1001 Faces* — 809
Archibald, John
   Shaking the Gates of Hell — B
ARCHIBALD, JOHN, 1963-
   Archibald, John. *Shaking the Gates of Hell* — B
ARCHITECTS
   Cornille, Didier. *Who Built That?* — 720
   Howard, Hugh. *Architects of an American Landscape* — 712.092
   Huxtable, Ada Louise. ★*Frank Lloyd Wright* — B
   King, Ross. *Brunelleschi's Dome* — 726.6

AUTHOR, TITLE, SERIES AND SUBJECT INDEX

Larson, Erik. ★*The Devil in the White City*	364.15
Secrest, Meryle. *Frank Lloyd Wright*	B
Speer, Albert. *Inside the Third Reich*	B
Van Hensbergen, Gijs. *The Sagrada Familia*	726.5
Architects of an American Landscape. Howard, Hugh	712.092

ARCHITECTURAL CRITICISM
Glancey, Jonathan. *The Story of Architecture*	720
Huxtable, Ada Louise. *On Architecture*	724

ARCHITECTURAL DESIGN
Goldhagen, Sarah Williams. *Welcome to Your World*	720.1
Rybczynski, Witold. *The Look of Architecture*	721

ARCHITECTURAL PHOTOGRAPHY
Glancey, Jonathan. *The Story of Architecture*	720

ARCHITECTURE
Bauermeister, Erica. *House Lessons*	B
Beard, Mary. ★*How Do We Look*	704.9
Blockley, David. *Bridges*	725
Ching, Francis D. K. ★*A Global History of Architecture*	720.9
Cornille, Didier. *Who Built That?*	720
Finkelstein, Elizabeth. *Cheap Old Houses*	643
Glancey, Jonathan. *The Story of Architecture*	720
Goldhagen, Sarah Williams. *Welcome to Your World*	720.1
Hollis, Edward. *The Secret Lives of Buildings*	720.9
Hughes, Robert. *Barcelona*	946
Huxtable, Ada Louise. *On Architecture*	724
Kiernan, Denise. *The Last Castle*	975.6
Lester, Toby. *Da Vinci's Ghost*	741.092
Lunenfeld, Peter. *City at the Edge of Forever*	979.4
McGregor, James H. *Rome from the Ground up*	711
Norwich, John Julius. *A History of Venice*	945
Podemski, Max. *A Paradise of Small Houses*	363.5
Russell, Gareth. ★*The Palace*	942.1
Rybczynski, Witold. *The Look of Architecture*	721
Satow, Julie. *The Plaza*	917.47
Susanka, Sarah. *Creating the Not so Big House*	728
Van Hensbergen, Gijs. *The Sagrada Familia*	726.5
Watkin, David. *A History of Western Architecture*	720

ARCHITECTURE AND HISTORY
Hollis, Edward. *The Secret Lives of Buildings*	720.9

ARCHITECTURE AND RELIGION
King, Ross. *Brunelleschi's Dome*	726.6

ARCHITECTURE AND SOCIETY
Hollis, Edward. *The Secret Lives of Buildings*	720.9
Huxtable, Ada Louise. *On Architecture*	724
Pamuk, Orhan. *Istanbul*	949.61
Russell, Gareth. ★*The Palace*	942.1
Rybczynski, Witold. *Mysteries of the Mall*	720
Snow, Richard. *Disney's Land*	791.06
Watkin, David. *A History of Western Architecture*	720

ARCHITECTURE, AMERICAN
Goldberger, Paul. *Building Art*	B
Satow, Julie. *The Plaza*	917.47
Secrest, Meryle. *Frank Lloyd Wright*	B
Snow, Richard. *Disney's Land*	791.06

ARCHITECTURE, BRITISH
Morris, Marc. *Castles*	728.81

ARCHITECTURE, DOMESTIC
Adams, Michael Henry. *Style and Grace*	747
Bradbury, Dominic. *Mountain Modern*	728
Bryson, Bill. ★*At Home*	643
Hirsch, William J. *Designing Your Perfect House*	728
Howard, Hugh. *Architects of an American Landscape*	712.092
Koones, Sheri. *Prefabulous Small Houses*	728
McAlester, Virginia. *A Field Guide to American Houses*	728
Susanka, Sarah. *Creating the Not so Big House*	728
Susanka, Sarah. *Not so Big Solutions for Your Home*	728
Versaci, Russell. *Creating a New Old House*	728
Wilhide, Elizabeth. *Scandinavian Home*	728

ARCHITECTURE, GREEK
Everitt, Anthony. *The Rise of Athens*	938

ARCHITECTURE, ISLAMIC
O'Kane, Bernard. *Treasures of Islam*	709.1

ARCHITECTURE, ITALIAN
Madden, Thomas F. *Venice*	945

ARCHITECTURE, MODERN
Curtis, William J. R. *Modern Architecture Since 1900*	724
Wilhide, Elizabeth. *Scandinavian Home*	728

ARCHITECTURE, RENAISSANCE (EUROPE)
King, Ross. *Brunelleschi's Dome*	726.6

ARCHIVES
Connelly, Matthew James. *The Declassification Engine*	352.3
Finkelstein, Daniel. *Two Roads Home*	920
Goodwin, Doris Kearns. ★*An Unfinished Love Story*	B
Thenell, Jan. *The Library's Crisis Communications Planner*	021.7
Wilson-Lee, Edward. ★*The Catalogue of Shipwrecked Books*	B

ARCHIVISTS
Crowley, Bill. *Defending Professionalism*	020.92

ARCTIC OCEAN
Geroux, William. *The Ghost Ships of Archangel*	940.54
Sides, Hampton. ★*In the Kingdom of Ice*	910.4

ARCTIC REGIONS
Brandt, Anthony. *The Man Who Ate His Boots*	910.91
Ehrlich, Gretel. *Unsolaced*	B
Hartman, Darrell. *Battle of Ink and Ice*	998
Levy, Buddy. *Labyrinth of Ice*	910.91
Niven, Jennifer. *Ada Blackjack*	B
O'Brady, Colin. ★*The Impossible First*	919.8904
Van Hemert, Caroline. *The Sun Is a Compass*	979.8
Watson, Paul. *Ice Ghosts*	917
Welky, David. ★*A Wretched and Precarious Situation*	910.911
Zuckoff, Mitchell. *Frozen in Time*	998.2
Ardency. Young, Kevin	811
Ardennes 1944. Beevor, Antony	940.54

ARDENNES, BATTLE OF THE, 1944-1945
Beevor, Antony. *Ardennes 1944*	940.54
Ardor. Calasso, Roberto	294.5
Are Numbers Real?. Clegg, Brian	510
Are We There Yet?. Albert, Daniel M.	303.48

Arefi, Yossy
Snacking Cakes	641.86
The Arena. Kohan, Rafi	796.06

Arendt, Hannah
The Origins of Totalitarianism	320.53
Aretha Franklin. Bego, Mark	B

ARGENTINA
Cordes, Kelly. *The Tower*	796.522
Hagerty, Alexa. ★*Still Life with Bones*	599.9
Salama, Jordan. ★*Stranger in the Desert*	982
Williamson, Edwin. *Borges*	B

ARGENTINE PEOPLE
Francis. *Life*	B
Salama, Jordan. ★*Stranger in the Desert*	982
Argo. Mendez, Antonio J.	955.05
★*The Argonauts*. Nelson, Maggie	B
Arguing for a Better World. Shahvisi, Arianne	170
Arguing with Zombies. Krugman, Paul R.	330.973

ARGUMENTATION
Boykin, Keith. ★*Why Does Everything Have to Be About Race?*	305.8
Hayhoe, Katharine. *Saving Us*	304.2
McLaren, Brian D. *Do I Stay Christian?*	270.8
Novella, Steven. *The Skeptics' Guide to the Universe*	500
Seo, Bo. *Good Arguments*	808.53
Shahvisi, Arianne. *Arguing for a Better World*	170
The Argumentative Indian. Sen, Amartya	954
Arias. Olds, Sharon	811

ARID REGIONS
Owens, Jay. *Dust*	551.51
★*Ariel*. Plath, Sylvia	811

Ariely, Dan
Dollars and Sense	332.024
The Honest Truth About Dishonesty	177
Predictably Irrational	153.8

ARIKARA (NORTH AMERICAN PEOPLE)
Murdoch, Sierra Crane. ★*Yellow Bird*	364.152

Ariosto, Lodovico
Orlando Furioso =	851

ARISTOCRACY
Aristotle. ★*Politics, 2nd Ed*	320
Byrne, Paula. *Kick*	B
De Courcy, Anne. *The Husband Hunters*	920
Dennison, Matthew. *Behind the Mask*	B
Figes, Orlando. ★*The Story of Russia*	947
Kix, Paul. *The Saboteur*	940.53
Leaming, Barbara. *Kick Kennedy*	B
MacColl, Gail. *To Marry an English Lord*	974.7

PUBLIC LIBRARY CORE COLLECTION: NONFICTION
Twentieth Edition

Manchester, William. *The Last Lion, Winston Spencer Churchill.* — B
Mansel, Philip. *King of the World* — B
Millard, Candice. ★*River of the Gods* — 916.204
Rappaport, Helen. *After the Romanovs* — 944
Reiss, Tom. *The Black Count* — B
Ronald, Susan. *Hitler's Aristocrats* — 940.53
Smith, Douglas. *Rasputin* — B
Aristotle
  ★*The Basic Works of Aristotle* — 185
  ★*Nicomachean Ethics* — 171
  ★*Politics* — 320
  ★*Politics, 2nd Ed* — 320
ARISTOTLE
  Adler, Mortimer Jerome. *Aristotle for Everybody* — 185
  Shields, Christopher John. *Aristotle* — 185
Aristotle. Shields, Christopher John — 185
Aristotle for Everybody. Adler, Mortimer Jerome — 185
ARITHMETIC
  Clegg, Brian. *Are Numbers Real?* — 510
ARIZONA
  Brooks, James. *Mesa of Sorrows* — 979.1004
  Powell, Michael. ★*Canyon Dreams* — 796.323
  Redniss, Lauren. ★*Oak Flat* — 970.5
  Ronstadt, Linda. *Feels Like Home* — B
  Taffa, Deborah Jackson. ★*Whiskey Tender* — B
  Tefertiller, Casey. *Wyatt Earp* — B
ARKANSAS
  Clinton, Bill. *My Life* — B
  Ford, Richard. *Between Them* — B
  Hill, David. *The Vapors* — 976.7
  Roy, Jessica. *American Girls* — 305.48
  Wise, Beau. *Three Wise Men* — 958.104
Arkin, Alan
  An Improvised Life — B
ARKIN, ALAN
  Arkin, Alan. *An Improvised Life* — B
ARLINGTON, VIRGINIA
  Cotton, Tom. *Sacred Duty* — 355.6
  McElya, Micki. *The Politics of Mourning* — 975.5
  Poole, Robert M. *Section 60* — 975.5
The Arm. Passan, Jeff — 796.3576
ARM
  Passan, Jeff. *The Arm* — 796.3576
Arm Knitting. Bassetti, Amanda — 746.43
★*Armageddon.* Ehrman, Bart D. — 236
Armageddon. Hastings, Max — 940.54
ARMAGEDDON (CHRISTIAN THEOLOGY)
  Ehrman, Bart D. ★*Armageddon* — 236
Armantrout, Rae
  Versed — 811
  Wobble — 811
Armas, Kat
  Abuelita Faith — 248.8
ARMED FORCES
  Atkinson, Rick. *An Army at Dawn* — 940.54
  Atkinson, Rick. *The Day of Battle* — 940.54
  Brady, James. *The Coldest War* — B
  Brooks, Rosa. *How Everything Became War and the Military Became Everything* — 355
  Chivers, C. J. *The Fighters* — 920
  Couch, Dick. *The Warrior Elite* — 359.9
  Delmont, Matthew F. *Half American* — 940.54
  Evans, Richard J. *The Third Reich at War* — 940.53
  Giangreco, D. M. *Hell to Pay* — 940.54
  Glatthaar, Joseph T. *The American Military* — 355.00973
  Graff, Garrett M. *Raven Rock* — 363.350973
  Holland, James. *Battle of Britain* — 940.54
  Jacobsen, Annie. *Phenomena* — 133.8
  Katz, Catherine Grace. *The Daughters of Yalta* — 920
  Klare, Michael T. *All Hell Breaking Loose* — 355.20973
  Klay, Phil. *Uncertain Ground* — 359.9
  Loyn, David. *In Afghanistan* — 958.1
  Mills, Dan. *Sniper One* — 956.7044
  O'Connell, Robert L. *The Ghosts of Cannae* — 937
  Paradis, Michel. *The Light of Battle* — 940.54
  Patterson, James. *Walk in My Combat Boots* — 920
  Ricks, Thomas E. *Fiasco* — 956.7044
  Stanton, Doug. *12 Strong* — 958.104

ARMED FORCES AND POLITICS
  Preston, Paul. *The Spanish Holocaust* — 946.081
ARMENIAN GENOCIDE SURVIVORS
  Mackeen, Dawn Anahid. *The Hundred-Year Walk* — 956.6
ARMENIAN GENOCIDE, 1915-1923
  Akcam, Taner. *A Shameful Act* — 956.6
  Balakian, Peter. *The Burning Tigris* — 956.6
  Bogosian, Eric. *Operation Nemesis* — 956.62
  Mackeen, Dawn Anahid. *The Hundred-Year Walk* — 956.6
ARMENIAN PEOPLE
  Balakian, Peter. *The Burning Tigris* — 956.6
  Mackeen, Dawn Anahid. *The Hundred-Year Walk* — 956.6
Arment, Ainsley
  The Wild + Free Family — 649
ARMFIELD, JOHN, 1797-1871
  Rothman, Joshua D. *The Ledger and the Chain* — 306.362
ARMIES
  Atkinson, Rick. ★*The British Are Coming* — 973.3
  Dalrymple, William. ★*The Anarchy* — 954.03
  Dickson, Paul. *The Rise of the G.I. Army 1940-1941* — 940.54
  Dugard, Martin. *Taking Berlin* — 940.54
  Harding, Luke. *Invasion* — 947.7
  Jones, Dan. *The Templars* — 271
  Kneale, Matthew. *Rome* — 945.6
  Sears, Stephen W. *Lincoln's Lieutenants* — 920
Armitage, David
  Civil Wars — 355.02
ARMS RACE
  Gordin, Michael D. *Red Cloud at Dawn* — 355.02
  Sherwin, Martin J. *Gambling with Armageddon* — 972.91006
  Westad, Odd Arne. *The Cold War* — 909.825
Armstrong, Jennifer Keishin
  Seinfeldia — 791.45
  Sex and the City and Us — 791.45
  When Women Invented Television — 791.45
Armstrong, Karen
  The Battle for God — 200
  The Bible — 220.09
  Buddha — B
  The Case for God — 211
  Fields of Blood — 201
  ★*The Great Transformation* — 200.9
  A History of God — 202
  ★*Islam* — 297
  Jerusalem — 956.94
  The Lost Art of Scripture — 208
  Muhammad — B
  ★*A Short History of Myth* — 201
  The Spiral Staircase — B
  Twelve Steps to a Compassionate Life — 177
ARMSTRONG, KAREN, 1944-
  Armstrong, Karen. *The Spiral Staircase* — B
ARMSTRONG, LANCE
  Hamilton, Tyler. *The Secret Race* — 796.62
Armstrong, Louis
  Louis Armstrong, in His Own Words — B
ARMSTRONG, LOUIS, 1901-1971
  Armstrong, Louis. *Louis Armstrong, in His Own Words* — B
  Brothers, Thomas David. ★*Louis Armstrong, Master of Modernism* — B
  Teachout, Terry. *Pops* — B
  Tye, Larry. ★*The Jazzmen* — 781.6509
ARMSTRONG, NEIL, 1930-2012
  Barbree, Jay. *Neil Armstrong* — B
An Army At Dawn. Atkinson, Rick — 940.54
Army of Evil. Weale, Adrian — 940.54
ARMY SPOUSES
  Gorrindo, Simone. ★*The Wives* — B
Arnason, H. Harvard
  ★*History of Modern Art* — 709.04
ARNAZ, DESI, 1917-1986
  Ball, Lucille. *Love, Lucy* — B
ARNHEM, BATTLE OF, 1944
  Beevor, Antony. *The Battle of Arnhem* — 940.54
Arnie. Callahan, Tom — B
ARNOLD, BENEDICT, 1741-1801
  Philbrick, Nathaniel. ★*Valiant Ambition* — B
Arnold, James R.
  Jungle of Snakes — 355.02

AUTHOR, TITLE, SERIES AND SUBJECT INDEX

Arnold, Jeremy
  Turner Classic Movies — 791.43
Arnsdorf, Isaac
  ★*Finish What We Started* — 320.52
AROMATHERAPY
  Keville, Kathi. *The Aromatherapy Garden* — 635.9
The Aromatherapy Garden. Keville, Kathi — 635.9
Aron, Jules
  Vegan Cheese — 641.5
Aron, Nina Renata
  Good Morning, Destroyer of Men's Souls — B
ARON, NINA RENATA
  Aron, Nina Renata. *Good Morning, Destroyer of Men's Souls* — B
Aronson, Joseph
  The Encyclopedia of Furniture — 749
Aronson, Louise
  Elderhood — 362.60973
ARONSON, SAM
  Zuckoff, Mitchell. *The Secret Gate* — 958.104
Around My French Table. Greenspan, Dorie — 641.594
Around The Corner Crochet Borders. Eckman, Edie — 746.43
Around The Way Girl. Henson, Taraji P. — B
Around The World in 80 Books. Damrosch, David — 809
Around The World in 80 Plants. Drori, Jonathan — 581.63
Around The World in 80 Trees. Drori, Jonathan — 582.16
★*Around The World in Eighty Games*. Du Sautoy, Marcus — 790.1
ARRANGED MARRIAGE
  Cadbury, Deborah. *Queen Victoria's Matchmaking* — 941.081
  Hamilton, Lisa M. *The Hungry Season* — B
  Satrapi, Marjane. *Embroideries* — 741.5
ARREST
  Eggers, Dave. *Zeitoun* — 305.892
  Eig, Jonathan. *Get Capone* — 364.1
Arrington, Leonard J.
  Brigham Young — B
Arsenault, Kerri
  Mill Town — B
ARSENAULT, KERRI
  Arsenault, Kerri. *Mill Town* — B
Arsenault, Raymond
  John Lewis — B
ARSENIC
  McCracken, Patti. *The Angel Makers* — 364.152
ARSON
  Berendt, John. *The City of Falling Angels* — 945
  Fieseler, Robert W. *Tinderbox* — 364.152
  Orlean, Susan. ★*The Library Book* — 027.4
ARSON INVESTIGATION
  Berendt, John. *The City of Falling Angels* — 945
  Orlean, Susan. ★*The Library Book* — 027.4
Art. Cumming, Robert — 700
★*Art*. Johnson, Paul — 709
ART
  Baker, Nicholson. *Finding a Likeness* — B
  Barnes, Julian. *The Man in the Red Coat* — B
  Beard, Mary. ★*How Do We Look* — 704.9
  Bosker, Bianca. *Get the Picture* — 701
  Cohen-Solal, Annie. *Mark Rothko* — 759.13
  Congdon, Lisa. *Art Inc.* — 702
  Cross, William R. *Winslow Homer* — 759.13
  Cumming, Robert. *Art* — 700
  Dasal, Jennifer. *Artcurious* — 709
  Dederer, Claire. ★*Monsters* — 700.1
  Eco, Umberto. *History of Beauty* — 111
  Eco, Umberto. *On Ugliness* — 111
  English, Charlie. *The Gallery of Miracles and Madness* — 709.04
  Garfield, Simon. *In Miniature* — 745.5928
  Gopnik, Adam. *The Real Work* — 153.9
  Grandin, Temple. ★*Visual Thinking* — 152.14
  Griffel, Lois. *Painting the Impressionist Landscape* — 751.45
  Griffin, Farah Jasmine. ★*In Search of a Beautiful Freedom* — 814
  Hardwick, Elizabeth. *The Dolphin Letters, 1970-1979* — 811
  Hough, Stephen. *Rough Ideas* — 786.2092
  Hughes, Robert. *American Visions* — 709
  King, Ross. ★*Leonardo and the Last Supper* — 759.5
  Kline, Fred R. *Leonardo's Holy Child* — 741.09
  Knausgaard, Karl Ove. *So Much Longing in so Little Space* — 759.81
  Kundera, Milan. *Encounter* — 809
  Lynes, Barbara Buhler. *Georgia O'Keeffe Museum Collections* — 759.13
  Magsamen, Susan. *Your Brain on Art* — 111
  Messud, Claire. *Kant's Little Prussian Head and Other Reasons Why I Write* — B
  Moss, Adam. ★*The Work of Art* — 701
  Nelson, Maggie. ★*Like Love* — 814
  Nguyen, Viet Thanh. *Nothing Ever Dies* — 959.704
  Nuland, Sherwin B. *Leonardo Da Vinci* — B
  Painter, Nell Irvin. ★*I Just Keep Talking* — 814
  Pardlo, Gregory. *Spectral Evidence* — 811
  Parker, Meghan. *Teaching Artfully* — 741.5
  Patchett, Ann. ★*These Precious Days* — 814
  Peiffer, Prudence. *The Slip* — 709.73
  Petropoulos, Jonathan. *The Faustian Bargain* — 709
  Pham, Larissa. *Pop Song* — 709.2
  Prideaux, Sue. *Edvard Munch* — B
  Raboteau, Emily. *Lessons for Survival* — 814
  Rady, Martyn C. *The Middle Kingdoms* — 943
  Rothfeld, Becca. ★*All Things Are Too Small* — 814
  Rovelli, Carlo. *There Are Places in the World Where Rules Are Less Important Than Kindness* — 500
  Rushdie, Salman. ★*Knife* — B
  Rynecki, Elizabeth. *Chasing Portraits* — B
  Sabatini Sloan, Aisha. *Dreaming of Ramadi in Detroit* — 814
  Scotti, R. A. *Vanished Smile* — 759.5
  Self, Caroline. *Chinese Brush Painting* — 751.4
  Seuss, Diane. *Still Life with Two Dead Peacocks and a Girl* — 811.6
  Shaw, Jennifer Laurie. *Exist Otherwise* — 709.2
  Shnayerson, Michael. *Boom* — 701
  Small, Zachary. ★*Token Supremacy* — 332.4
  Snyder, Laura J. *Eye of the Beholder* — 920
  Stanislaus, Grace C. *Instill & Inspire* — 704.03
  Strickland, Carol. *The Annotated Mona Lisa* — 709
  Taplin, Jonathan. *Move Fast and Break Things* — 330.9
  Tetro, Tony. *Con/Artist* — B
  Thurman, Judith. ★*A Left-Handed Woman* — 814
  Trimborn, Jurgen. *Leni Riefenstahl* — B
  Urwand, Ben. *The Collaboration* — 791.430973
  Ustvedt, Oystein. *Edvard Munch* — 759.81
  Warren, Rosanna. *Max Jacob* — B
  Wu, Simon. *Dancing on My Own* — 700.1
  Wullschlager, Jackie. ★*Chagall* — B
  Zambreno, Kate. *The Light Room* — B
ART AND CULTURE
  Figes, Orlando. *The Europeans* — 920
ART AND HISTORY
  Staiti, Paul J. *Of Arms and Artists* — B
ART AND MENTAL ILLNESS
  English, Charlie. *The Gallery of Miracles and Madness* — 709.04
ART AND MUSIC
  Ross, Alex. *Wagnerism* — B
ART AND MUSIC — ARTS AND CRAFTS — DRAWING AND PAINTING
  Abel, Jessica. *Drawing Words, Writing Pictures* — 741.5
  Abel, Jessica. *Mastering Comics* — 741.5
  Lee, Stan. *Stan Lee's How to Draw Comics* — 741.5
  O'Neil, Dennis. *The DC Comics Guide to Writing Comics* — 808
  Self, Caroline. *Chinese Brush Painting* — 751.4
ART AND MUSIC — MUSIC
  Patrick, James. *Robert Johnson* — B
ART AND MUSIC — TELEVISION AND RADIO
  Page, Susan. ★*The Rulebreaker* — B
ART AND MUSIC — VISUAL ARTS
  Bang, Molly. ★*Picture This* — 741.6
  Ganz, Nicholas. ★*Graffiti World* — 751.7
ART AND MUSIC — VISUAL ARTS — ARCHITECTURE
  Cornille, Didier. *Who Built That?* — 720
ART AND MUSIC — VISUAL ARTS — CARTOONING AND ANIMATION
  Abel, Jessica. *Drawing Words, Writing Pictures* — 741.5
  Abel, Jessica. *Mastering Comics* — 741.5
  Lee, Stan. *Stan Lee's How to Draw Comics* — 741.5
  O'Neil, Dennis. *The DC Comics Guide to Writing Comics* — 808
ART AND MYTHOLOGY
  Hughes, Bettany. *Venus and Aphrodite* — 292
ART AND PHILOSOPHY
  Eco, Umberto. *History of Beauty* — 111
  Eco, Umberto. *On Ugliness* — 111
ART AND POLITICS
  Ai, Weiwei. *Zodiac* — 741.5

PUBLIC LIBRARY CORE COLLECTION: NONFICTION
Twentieth Edition

English, Charlie. *The Gallery of Miracles and Madness* — 709.04
Goodman, Elyssa. *Glitter and Concrete* — 792.7
Pitzer, Andrea. *The Secret History of Vladimir Nabokov* — 813
Staiti, Paul J. *Of Arms and Artists* — B
Tolokonnikova, Nadezhda. *Rules for Rulebreakers* — 782.42166

ART AND RELIGION
Beard, Mary. ★*How Do We Look* — 704.9
Greenblatt, Stephen. *The Rise and Fall of Adam and Eve* — 233
Wiman, Christian. *He Held Radical Light* — 814
The Art and Science of Connection. Killam, Kasley — 302

ART AND SOCIETY
Bosker, Bianca. *Get the Picture* — 701
Dasal, Jennifer. *Artcurious* — 709
English, Charlie. *The Gallery of Miracles and Madness* — 709.04
Harvey, Eleanor Jones. *The Civil War and American Art* — 740.9
King, Ross. ★*Leonardo and the Last Supper* — 759.5
Laing, Olivia. ★*The Lonely City* — 700.1
Menand, Louis. *The Free World* — 306.0973
Morrison, Toni. ★*The Source of Self-Regard* — 814
Pamuk, Orhan. *Istanbul* — 949.61
Schloss, Edith. *The Loft Generation* — 700.9
Shnayerson, Michael. *Boom* — 701
Stein, Judith E. *Eye of the Sixties* — B
Strathern, Paul. *The Florentines* — 945
Wu, Simon. *Dancing on My Own* — 700.1

ART AND TECHNOLOGY
Fleming, Renee. ★*Music and Mind* — 615.8

ART AND WAR
Edsel, Robert M. *The Monuments Men* — 940.53
Goodman, Simon. *The Orpheus Clock* — 940.53
Nguyen, Viet Thanh. *Nothing Ever Dies* — 959.704
Thomson, David. *The Fatal Alliance* — 791.43

ART APPRECIATION
Barnes, Julian. *Keeping an Eye Open* — 709.04
Bosker, Bianca. *Get the Picture* — 701
Ganz, Nicholas. ★*Graffiti World* — 751.7
Hall, James. *The Self-Portrait* — 704.9
Hecht, Jennifer Michael. ★*The Wonder Paradox* — 808.1
Hoving, Thomas. *Art for Dummies* — 709
Salle, David. *How to See* — 709.04
Strickland, Carol. *The Annotated Mona Lisa* — 709
Updike, John. *Always Looking* — 700

ART AS AN INVESTMENT
Shnayerson, Michael. *Boom* — 701

ART AUCTIONS
Small, Zachary. ★*Token Supremacy* — 332.4
Art Beyond the West. Kampen-O'Riley, Michael — 709

ART CENTERS
Meier, Richard. *Building the Getty* — 727

ART COLLECTORS AND COLLECTING
Bosker, Bianca. *Get the Picture* — 701
De Waal, Edmund. *The Hare with Amber Eyes* — B
Gill, Anton. *Art Lover* — B
Hoffman, Carl. ★*Savage Harvest* — 995.1
Kline, Fred R. *Leonardo's Holy Child* — 741.09
Shnayerson, Michael. *Boom* — 701

ART CRITICISM
Barnes, Julian. *Keeping an Eye Open* — 709.04
Harvey, Eleanor Jones. *The Civil War and American Art* — 740.9
Knausgaard, Karl Ove. *So Much Longing in so Little Space* — 759.81
Tomlinson, Janis A. ★*Goya* — B
Updike, John. *Always Looking* — 700

ART CRITICS
Calhoun, Ada. *Also a Poet* — B
Schloss, Edith. *The Loft Generation* — 700.9

ART CURATORS
Obrist, Hans-Ulrich. *Ways of Curating* — 707.5

ART DEALERS
Barbarisi, Daniel. *Chasing the Thrill* — 796.1
Hook, Philip. *Rogues' Gallery* — 709.2
Shnayerson, Michael. *Boom* — 701
Stein, Judith E. *Eye of the Sixties* — B

ART EXHIBITIONS
Harvey, Eleanor Jones. *The Civil War and American Art* — 740.9
Szarkowski, John. *Ansel Adams at 100* — B
Art for Dummies. Hoving, Thomas — 709

ART FORGERIES
Amore, Anthony M. *The Art of the Con* — 702.8
Brewer, John. *The American Leonardo* — 759.5
Tetro, Tony. *Con/Artist* — B

ART FORGERS
Tetro, Tony. *Con/Artist* — B

ART GALLERIES, COMMERCIAL
Bosker, Bianca. *Get the Picture* — 701
Shnayerson, Michael. *Boom* — 701

ART HISTORIANS
Stourton, James. *Kenneth Clark* — B

ART HISTORY
Baker, Nicholson. *Finding a Likeness* — B
Dasal, Jennifer. *Artcurious* — 709
De Hamel, Christopher. *The Manuscripts Club* — 091
Gombrich, E. H. ★*The Story of Art* — 709
Gompertz, Will. *What Are You Looking At?* — 709
Holladay, Wilhelmina Cole. *A Museum of Their Own* — 704
James, Jamie. *The Glamour of Strangeness* — 700.1
Janson, H. W. ★*Janson's History of Art* — 709
Johnson, Paul. ★*Art* — 709
Kampen-O'Riley, Michael. *Art Beyond the West* — 709
Kandel, Eric R. *The Age of Insight* — 154.2
King, Ross. *Florence* — 759.5
King, Ross. ★*Mad Enchantment* — 759.4
Knausgaard, Karl Ove. *So Much Longing in so Little Space* — 759.81
Norwich, John Julius. *A History of Venice* — 945
Quinn, Bridget. *Broad Strokes* — 920
Rowland, Ingrid D. *The Collector of Lives* — B
Schama, Simon. *The Power of Art* — 709
Staiti, Paul J. *Of Arms and Artists* — B
Strickland, Carol. *The Annotated Mona Lisa* — 709
Tetro, Tony. *Con/Artist* — B
Art Inc. Congdon, Lisa — 702
Art Lover. Gill, Anton — B
Art Makers [Series]. Frazer, Amy L. — 746.44

ART MOVEMENTS
Wulf, Andrea. *Magnificent Rebels* — 830.9

ART MUSEUMS
Bosker, Bianca. *Get the Picture* — 701
Finkel, Michael. *The Art Thief* — 364.1628
Obrist, Hans-Ulrich. *Ways of Curating* — 707.5
The Art of Ancient Egypt. Robins, Gay — 709
★*The Art of Asking.* Palmer, Amanda — 782.42164
The Art of Choosing. Iyengar, Sheena — 153.8
The Art of Comic Book Writing. Kneece, Mark — 741.5
The Art of Conversation. Blyth, Catherine — 395.5
The Art of Death. Danticat, Edwidge — 809
The Art of Drag. Hall, Jake — 792.8
The Art of Dying Well. Butler, Katy — 616.02
The Art of French Pastry. Pfeiffer, Jacquy — 641.86
★*The Art of Happy Moving.* Wenzke, Ali — 648
The Art of Harvey Kurtzman. Kitchen, Denis — 741.5
The Art of Her Deal. Jordan, Mary — B
The Art of Invisibility. Mitnick, Kevin D. — 005.8
The Art of Living. Nhat Hanh — 294.3
The Art of Loading Brush. Berry, Wendell — 338.10973
★*The Art of Losing.* Young, Kevin — 811
The Art of Making Memories. Wiking, Meik — 153.1
The Art of Memoir. Karr, Mary — B
The Art of Metal Clay. Haab, Sherri — 739.27
The Art of More. Brooks, Michael — 510.9
The Art of Neil Gaiman. Campbell, Hayley — B
The Art of Quilling Paper Jewelry. Martin, Ann — 745.54
The Art of Raising a Puppy. Monks of New Skete — 636.7
The Art of Ray Harryhausen. Harryhausen, Ray — 778
The Art of Reading. Young, Damon — 028.9
The Art of Resistance. Rosenberg, Justus — B
The Art of Rivalry. Smee, Sebastian — 700.92
The Art of Robert Frost. Kendall, Tim — 811
★*The Art of Ruth E. Carter.* Carter, Ruth E. — 746.9
The Art of Simple Food. Waters, Alice — 641.5
The Art of Simple Living. Masuno, Shunmy — 294.3
★*The Art of Tapestry Weaving.* Mezoff, Rebecca — 746.7
The Art of Teaching. Parini, Jay — 378.1
Art of the Chicken. Pepin, Jacques — 641.665
The Art of the Con. Amore, Anthony M. — 702.8
★*Art of the Pie.* McDermott, Kate — 641.86
The Art of the Start 2.0. Kawasaki, Guy — 658.1
The Art of Thinking Clearly. Dobelli, Rolf — 153.4

AUTHOR, TITLE, SERIES AND SUBJECT INDEX

The Art of Tinkering. Wilkinson, Karen	500
The Art of Walt Disney. Finch, Christopher	791.43092
ART PATRONAGE	
De Waal, Edmund. *The Hare with Amber Eyes*	B
Gill, Anton. *Art Lover*	B
Tomlinson, Janis A. ★*Goya*	B
ART PATRONS	
De Waal, Edmund. *The Hare with Amber Eyes*	B
Gill, Anton. *Art Lover*	B
Strathern, Paul. *The Medici*	945.5
ART SCHOOLS	
Painter, Nell Irvin. *Old in Art School*	B
ART STUDENTS	
Painter, Nell Irvin. *Old in Art School*	B
ART TEACHERS	
Parker, Meghan. *Teaching Artfully*	741.5
ART TECHNIQUE	
Barnes, Julian. *Keeping an Eye Open*	709.04
Doh, Jenny. *Creative Lettering*	745.6
Flor, Martina. *The Golden Secrets of Lettering*	745.6
Glynn, Kathy. *Hand Lettering Step by Step*	745.6
Rodriguez, Dina. *The Big Awesome Book of Hand & Chalk Lettering*	745.6
Shepherd, Margaret. *Learn Calligraphy*	745.6
ART THEFTS	
Amore, Anthony M. *The Art of the Con*	702.8
Dolnick, Edward. *The Rescue Artist*	364.16
Edsel, Robert M. *The Monuments Men*	940.53
Finkel, Michael. *The Art Thief*	364.1628
Fishman, David E. *The Book Smugglers*	940.53
Goodman, Simon. *The Orpheus Clock*	940.53
Scotti, R. A. *Vanished Smile*	759.5
ART THERAPY	
Fleming, Renee. ★*Music and Mind*	615.8
The Art Thief. Finkel, Michael	364.1628
ART TREASURES IN WAR	
Edsel, Robert M. *The Monuments Men*	940.53
Fishman, David E. *The Book Smugglers*	940.53
Goodman, Simon. *The Orpheus Clock*	940.53
Petropoulos, Jonathan. *The Faustian Bargain*	709
ART, AMERICAN	
FitzGerald, Michael C. ★*Picasso and American Art*	709.73
Harvey, Eleanor Jones. *The Civil War and American Art*	740.9
Hughes, Robert. *American Visions*	709
Updike, John. *Always Looking*	700
ART, CHINESE	
Tregear, Mary. *Chinese Art*	709.51
ART, EGYPTIAN	
Robins, Gay. *The Art of Ancient Egypt*	709
ART, EUROPEAN	
King, Ross. *Florence*	759.5
ART, GREEK	
Boardman, John. ★*Greek Art*	709
ART, INDIGENOUS	
Berlo, Janet Catherine. ★*Native North American Art*	704.03
ART, ISLAMIC	
Husain, Ed. ★*The House of Islam*	297
Khalili, Nasser D. *Islamic Art and Culture*	709.1
O'Kane, Bernard. *Treasures of Islam*	709.1
ART, ITALIAN	
Adams, Laurie. ★*Italian Renaissance Art*	709.45
Hale, Sheila. *Titian*	B
Hirst, Michael. *Michelangelo.*	B
Strathern, Paul. *The Borgias*	945.06
Strathern, Paul. *The Medici*	945.5
ART, LATIN AMERICAN	
Barnitz, Jacqueline. *Twentieth-Century Art of Latin America*	709.8
ART, RENAISSANCE (EUROPE)	
Adams, Laurie. ★*Italian Renaissance Art*	709.45
Hale, Sheila. *Titian*	B
Hales, Dianne R. *Mona Lisa*	B
Madden, Thomas F. *Venice*	945
Artcurious. Dasal, Jennifer	709
The Artful Parent. Van't Hul, Jean	745.5083
The Artful Year. Van't Hul, Jean	745.594
Artfully Embroidered. Shimoda, Naoko	746.44
ARTHRITIS	
Fishman, Loren. *Yoga for Arthritis*	616.7
Arthur and Sherlock. Sims, Michael	B
Arthur Miller. Bigsby, Christopher William Edgar	B
Arthur, Alua	
★*Briefly Perfectly Human*	306.9
ARTHUR, ALUA	
Arthur, Alua. ★*Briefly Perfectly Human*	306.9
ARTHUR, CHESTER ALAN, 1829-1886	
Cohen, Jared. *Accidental Presidents*	973.09
ARTHUR, KING	
Ackroyd, Peter. *The Death of King Arthur*	823
ARTHURIAN LEGENDS	
Ackroyd, Peter. *The Death of King Arthur*	823
Malory, Thomas. *Le Morte Darthur, Or, the Hoole Book of Kyng Arthur and of His Noble Knyghtes of the Rounde Table*	823
ARTIFICIAL HEART	
Swartz, Mimi. *Ticker*	617.4
ARTIFICIAL INTELLIGENCE	
Copeland, B. Jack. *Turing*	B
Hill, Kashmir. ★*Your Face Belongs to Us*	006.2
Kaku, Michio. ★*The Future of Humanity*	629.45
Kasparov, G. K. *Deep Thinking*	006.3
Leavitt, David. *The Man Who Knew Too Much*	B
Lee, Kai-Fu. *AI 2041*	006.3
Li, Fei-Fei. *The Worlds I See*	B
Malone, Thomas W. *Superminds*	005.7
McKibben, Bill. *Falter*	909.83
Merchant, Brian. *Blood in the Machine*	303.48
Molnar, Petra. *The Walls Have Eyes*	363.28
Murgia, Madhumita. *Code Dependent*	303.48
Mustill, Tom. *How to Speak Whale*	591.59
O'Gieblyn, Meghan. *God, Human, Animal, Machine*	814
Russell, Stuart J. *Human Compatible*	006.301
Scharre, Paul. *Four Battlegrounds*	006.3
Scott, Kevin. *Reprogramming the American Dream*	338
Suleyman, Mustafa. *The Coming Wave*	303.48
Tegmark, Max. *Life 3.0*	006.301
ARTIFICIAL SATELLITES	
Vance, Ashlee. *When the Heavens Went on Sale*	621.43
ARTISANS	
Falick, Melanie. *Making a Life*	745.5
Langlands, Alex. *Craeft*	306.4
Miller, Marla. *Betsy Ross and the Making of America*	B
ARTISANSHIP	
Gorges, Eric. *A Craftsman's Legacy*	745.5
The Artist as Critic. Wilde, Oscar	809
The Artist's Compass. Moore, Rachel	791
The Artist's Complete Guide to Figure Drawing. Ryder, Anthony	743.4
The Artist's Library. Damon-Moore, Laura C.	021.2
ARTISTIC COLLABORATION	
Browne, David. *Crosby, Stills, Nash and Young*	920
ARTISTIC PHOTOGRAPHY	
Bethencourt, Kahran. *Glory*	779.2
Brandow, Todd. *Edward Steichen*	770.92
Campany, David. *The Open Road*	770
Evans, Walker. *American Photographs*	779
Fagans, Michael. *iPhone Photography for Everybody*	770
McCurry, Steve. *The Iconic Photographs*	779.092
Peterson, Bryan. *Learning to See Creatively*	770
Smith, Joel. *Edward Steichen*	779
Stanton, Brandon. *Humans*	779
Szarkowski, John. *Ansel Adams at 100*	B
ARTISTIC RIVALRY	
King, Ross. *Michelangelo & the Pope's Ceiling*	759.5
Womack, Kenneth. *All Things Must Pass Away*	781.66
ARTISTS	
Acocella, Joan Ross. ★*The Bloodied Nightgown*	814
Ai, Weiwei. *1000 Years of Joys and Sorrows*	709.2
Ai, Weiwei. *Zodiac*	741.5
Alinder, Mary Street. *Group F.64*	770.92
B., David. *Epileptic*	741.5
Bair, Deirdre. *Saul Steinberg*	B
Begley, Adam. *The Great Nadar*	B
Bilal, Wafaa. *Shoot an Iraqi*	B
Bosker, Bianca. *Get the Picture*	701
Carter, Alice A. *The Red Rose Girls*	B
Cohen-Solal, Annie. *Mark Rothko*	759.13
Congdon, Lisa. *Art Inc.*	702
Cross, William R. *Winslow Homer*	759.13
Damrosch, Leopold. *The Club*	920

PUBLIC LIBRARY CORE COLLECTION: NONFICTION
Twentieth Edition

Dasal, Jennifer. *Artcurious*	709
Dederer, Claire. ★*Monsters*	700.1
Dery, Mark. *Born to Be Posthumous*	B
Eisler, Benita. *The Red Man's Bones*	B
English, Charlie. *The Gallery of Miracles and Madness*	709.04
Feaver, William. ★*The Lives of Lucian Freud*	B
Fischer, Paul. *The Man Who Invented Motion Pictures*	791.43
Frey, Julia Bloch. *Toulouse-Lautrec*	B
Gefter, Philip. *What Becomes a Legend Most*	B
Gooch, Brad. *Radiant*	B
Gopnik, Blake. ★*Warhol*	B
Graham-Dixon, Andrew. *Caravaggio*	B
Hale, Sheila. *Titian*	B
Hall, James. *The Self-Portrait*	704.9
Herrera, Hayden. *Listening to Stone*	B
Hester, Diarmuid. *Nothing Ever Just Disappears*	306.76
Hirst, Michael. *Michelangelo.*	B
Hoban, Phoebe. *Alice Neel*	B
Holzer, Harold. *Monument Man*	B
Hughes, Robert. *Goya*	B
Isaacson, Walter. ★*Leonardo Da Vinci*	B
James, Jamie. *The Glamour of Strangeness*	700.1
Johnson, Paul. ★*Art*	709
Kamensky, Jane. *A Revolution in Color*	759.13
King, Ross. ★*Leonardo and the Last Supper*	759.5
King, Ross. ★*Mad Enchantment*	759.4
King, Ross. *Michelangelo & the Pope's Ceiling*	759.5
Knausgaard, Karl Ove. *So Much Longing in so Little Space*	759.81
Laing, Olivia. ★*The Lonely City*	700.1
Leal, Brigitte. *The Ultimate Picasso*	B
Levin, Gail. *Edward Hopper*	759.13
Lozano, Luis-Martín. *Frida Kahlo*	759.972
Lucey, Donna M. *Sargent's Women*	920
Madden, Thomas F. *Venice*	945
McCullough, David G. *The Greater Journey*	920
Moss, Adam. ★*The Work of Art*	701
Moyle, Franny. *Turner*	B
Naifeh, Steven W. *Van Gogh*	B
Norwick, Kenneth P. *The Legal Guide for Writers, Artists and Other Creative People*	346.04
Nuland, Sherwin B. *Leonardo Da Vinci*	B
Painter, Nell Irvin. *Old in Art School*	B
Peiffer, Prudence. *The Slip*	709.73
Perl, Jed. *Calder*	B
Perl, Jed. ★*Calder*	B
Popova, Maria. *Figuring*	920
Prideaux, Sue. *Edvard Munch*	B
Rankine, Claudia. *The White Card*	812
Robinson, Roxana. *Georgia O'Keeffe*	B
Roe, Sue. *In Montmartre*	920
Roe, Sue. *The Private Lives of the Impressionists*	920
Roiphe, Katie. *The Violet Hour*	809
Rowland, Ingrid D. *The Collector of Lives*	B
Rush, Chris. *The Light Years*	B
Schama, Simon. *The Power of Art*	709
Schloss, Edith. *The Loft Generation*	700.9
Shaw, Jennifer Laurie. *Exist Otherwise*	709.2
Smee, Sebastian. *The Art of Rivalry*	700.92
Smith, Patti. ★*Just Kids*	B
Solomon, Deborah. *Jackson Pollock*	B
Spurling, Hilary. *Matisse the Master*	B
Stahr, Celia. *Frida in America*	B
Stevens, Norma. *Avedon*	B
Strathern, Paul. *The Medici*	945.5
Sykes, Christopher Simon. *David Hockney*	B
Sykes, Christopher Simon. *David Hockney*	B
Szwed, John F. *Cosmic Scholar*	B
Unger, Miles. ★*Michelangelo*	B
Unger, Miles. *Picasso and the Painting That Shocked the World*	759.4
Updike, John. *Always Looking*	700
Ustvedt, Oystein. *Edvard Munch*	759.81
Warren, Rosanna. *Max Jacob*	B
Waters, John. *Role Models*	B
Winder, Elizabeth. *Parachute Women*	782.42164
Wullschlager, Jackie. ★*Chagall*	B

ARTISTS' BOOKS
Rivers, Charlotte. *Little Book of Book Making*	686

ARTISTS' MODELS
Hales, Dianne R. *Mona Lisa*	B
Hewitt, Catherine. *Renoir's Dancer*	B

ARTISTS' STUDIOS
Carter, Alice A. *The Red Rose Girls*	B
Muller, Kristin. *The Potter's Studio Handbook*	738.1
Peiffer, Prudence. *The Slip*	709.73

ARTS
Damon-Moore, Laura C. *The Artist's Library*	021.2
Dederer, Claire. ★*Monsters*	700.1
Friedman, Rachel. ★*And Then We Grew Up*	305.24
Ghosh, Amitav. *The Great Derangement*	809
Hughes, Robert. *Barcelona*	946
Morris, Desmond. *The Lives of the Surrealists*	B
Morrison, Robert. *The Regency Years*	941.07

ARTS AND CRAFTS MOVEMENT
Miller, Judith. *Miller's Arts & Crafts*	745.409034

ARTS AND ENTERTAINMENT — ANTIQUES AND COLLECTIBLES
Aronson, Joseph. *The Encyclopedia of Furniture*	749
Lee, Vinny. *Kitchenalia*	747.7
Manseau, Peter. *Objects of Devotion*	277
Miller, Judith. *Furniture*	749
Pourny, Christophe. ★*The Furniture Bible*	684.1
Wong, Stephen. *Game Worn*	796.357
Wong, Stephen. *Smithsonian Baseball*	796.357

ARTS AND ENTERTAINMENT — ARCHITECTURE
Bauermeister, Erica. *House Lessons*	B
Blockley, David. *Bridges*	725
Bradbury, Dominic. *The Iconic Interior*	747
Bradbury, Dominic. *Mountain Modern*	728
Brenwall, Cynthia S. *The Central Park*	974.7
Ching, Francis D. K. ★*A Global History of Architecture*	720.9
Curtis, William J. R. *Modern Architecture Since 1900*	724
DeJean, Joan E. *How Paris Became Paris*	944
Finkelstein, Elizabeth. *Cheap Old Houses*	643
Glancey, Jonathan. *The Story of Architecture*	720
Goldberger, Paul. *Ballpark*	796.357
Goldberger, Paul. *Building Art*	B
Goldhagen, Sarah Williams. *Welcome to Your World*	720.1
Gura, Judith. *The Guide to Period Styles for Interiors*	747
Hirsch, William J. *Designing Your Perfect House*	728
Hollis, Edward. *The Secret Lives of Buildings*	720.9
Holzer, Harold. *Monument Man*	B
Howard, Hugh. *Architects of an American Landscape*	712.092
Hughes, Robert. *Barcelona*	946
Huxtable, Ada Louise. ★*Frank Lloyd Wright*	B
Huxtable, Ada Louise. *On Architecture*	724
Jordan, Wendy Adler. *Universal Design for the Home*	728
Khan, Yasmin Sabina. *Enlightening the World*	974.7
Kiernan, Denise. *The Last Castle*	975.6
King, Ross. *Brunelleschi's Dome*	726.6
Koones, Sheri. *Prefabulous Small Houses*	728
McAlester, Virginia. *A Field Guide to American Houses*	728
Meier, Richard. *Building the Getty*	727
Morris, Marc. *Castles*	728.81
Podemski, Max. *A Paradise of Small Houses*	363.5
Russell, Gareth. ★*The Palace*	942.1
Rybczynski, Witold. *The Look of Architecture*	721
Rybczynski, Witold. *Mysteries of the Mall*	720
Satow, Julie. *The Plaza*	917.47
Secrest, Meryle. *Frank Lloyd Wright*	B
Smith, Michael S. *Designing History*	975.3
Snow, Richard. *Disney's Land*	791.06
Storrer, William Allin. *The Frank Lloyd Wright Companion*	720.92
Thorstensen, Ole. *Making Things Right*	690
Treister, Kenneth. *Easter Island's Silent Sentinels*	996.18
Tychonievich, Joseph. *Rock Gardening*	635.9
Van Doren, Adam. *The House Tells the Story*	728
Van Hensbergen, Gijs. *The Sagrada Familia*	726.5
Versaci, Russell. *Creating a New Old House*	728
Watkin, David. *A History of Western Architecture*	720

ARTS AND ENTERTAINMENT — COMEDY
Ackroyd, Peter. *Charlie Chaplin*	B
Ball, Lucille. *Love, Lucy*	B
Branum, Guy. *My Life as a Goddess*	B
Brunson, Quinta. *She Memes Well*	B
Courogen, Carrie. ★*Miss May Does Not Exist*	B
Fox, Jesse David. *Comedy Book*	792.7

AUTHOR, TITLE, SERIES AND SUBJECT INDEX

Gold, Judy. *Yes I Can Say That*	792.7
Haddish, Tiffany. *The Last Black Unicorn*	B
Hart, Kevin. *I Can't Make This Up*	B
Itzkoff, Dave. ★*Robin*	B
Jennings, Ken. *Planet Funny*	809.7
Kaling, Mindy. *Why Not Me?*	B
Key, Keegan-Michael. ★*The History of Sketch Comedy*	792.2
Levy, Shawn. ★*In on the Joke*	792.7
Louvish, Simon. *Monkey Business*	B
Meslow, Scott. *From Hollywood with Love*	791.43
Mooney, Paul. *Black Is the New White*	792.7
Myers, Paul. *The Kids in the Hall*	920
Nesteroff, Kliph. *The Comedians*	792.7
Nesteroff, Kliph. *We Had a Little Real Estate Problem*	970.004
Odenkirk, Bob. *Comedy Comedy Comedy Drama*	B
Orji, Yvonne. *Bamboozled by Jesus*	B
Pellegrino, Danny. *How Do I Un-Remember This?*	B
Rainbow, Randy. *Playing with Myself*	B
Rosenfield, Stephen. *Mastering Stand-Up*	792.7
Saul, Scott. ★*Becoming Richard Pryor*	B
Scheer, Paul. *Joyful Recollections of Trauma*	B
Seinfeld, Jerry. *Is This Anything?*	818
Shales, Tom. *Live from New York*	791.45
Shannon, Molly. ★*Hello, Molly!*	B
Smith, Chris. *The Daily Show (the Book)*	791.45
Thompson, Kenan. *When I Was Your Age*	B
Wasson, Sam. ★*Improv Nation*	792.02
Watts, Reggie. *Great Falls, MT*	B
Zoglin, Richard. *Hope*	B
Zucker, David. *Surely You Can't Be Serious*	791.43
Zweibel, Alan. *Laugh Lines*	B

ARTS AND ENTERTAINMENT — COMICS, CARTOONS, AND ANIMATION

Brunetti, Ivan. *Cartooning*	741.5
Cavalier, Stephen. *The World History of Animation*	791.43
Clements, Jonathan. *The Anime Encyclopedia*	791.43
DePastino, Todd. *Bill Mauldin*	B
Eisner, Will. ★*Comics and Sequential Art*	741.5
Finch, Christopher. *The Art of Walt Disney*	791.43092
Fingeroth, Danny. *A Marvelous Life*	741.5
Gabler, Neal. *Walt Disney*	B
Ghez, Didier. *The Hidden Art of Disney's Golden Age*	741.5
Gitlin, Marty. *A Celebration of Animation*	741.5
Goldstein, Nancy. *Jackie Ormes*	B
Holt, Nathalia. *The Queens of Animation*	920
Johnson, Mindy. *Ink & Paint*	B
Jones, Gerard. *Men of Tomorrow*	741.5
Kitchen, Denis. *The Art of Harvey Kurtzman*	741.5
Lenburg, Jeff. *The Encyclopedia of Animated Cartoons*	791.43
Leong, Sonia. *101 Top Tips from Professional Manga Artists*	741.5
Lepore, Jill. ★*The Secret History of Wonder Woman*	741.5
Mankoff, Robert. *How About Never—Is Never Good for You?*	741.5
McCloud, Scott. *Making Comics*	741.5
McCloud, Scott. *Reinventing Comics*	741.5
McCloud, Scott. ★*Understanding Comics*	741.5
Michaelis, David. *Schulz and Peanuts*	B
Riesman, Abraham. *True Believer*	741.5
Schumacher, Michael. *Will Eisner*	741.5
Sipress, David. *What's so Funny?*	B
Spiegelman, Art. *Co-Mix*	741.5
Tomine, Adrian. *The Loneliness of the Long-Distance Cartoonist*	741.5
Williams, Richard. *The Animator's Survival Kit*	778
Wolk, Douglas. *All of the Marvels*	741.5
Wood, Lawrence. *Your Caption Has Been Selected*	741.5

ARTS AND ENTERTAINMENT — CRAFTS AND HOBBIES

Adarme, Adrianna. *The Year of Cozy*	641.3
Akiyama, Lance. *Duct Tape Engineer*	745.5
Akiyama, Lance. *Rubber Band Engineer*	745.57
Baldwin, Debra Lee. *Succulents Simplified*	635.9
Benzakein, Erin. *Floret Farm's Cut Flower Garden*	635.9
Blumenthal, Eileen. *Puppetry*	791.5
Bried, Erin. *How to Sew a Button*	640
Chapin, Kari. ★*The Handmade Marketplace*	745.5
Chezar, Ariella. ★*Seasonal Flower Arranging*	635.9
Corwin, Lena. *Printing by Hand*	745.5
Cylinder, Carly. *The Flower Chef*	745.92
Damon-Moore, Laura C. *The Artist's Library*	021.2
Doh, Jenny. *Creative Lettering*	745.6
Doorley, Rachelle. *Tinkerlab*	600
Falick, Melanie. *Making a Life*	745.5
Frisoni, Christine-Lea. *The Big Book of a Miniature House*	745.592
Godas, Maru. *Organic Beauty*	646.7
Gorges, Eric. *A Craftsman's Legacy*	745.5
Harampolis, Alethea. *The Flower Recipe Book*	745.92
Hingley, Brian D. *Furniture Repair & Restoration*	684.1
Irish, Lora S. *Basket Essentials*	746.412
Joyce, Anna. *Stamp Stencil Paint*	745.7
Katz, Emily. *Modern Macrame*	746.42
Kistler, Vivian Carli. *The Complete Photo Guide to Framing and Displaying Artwork*	749
Kneece, Mark. *The Art of Comic Book Writing*	741.5
Langlands, Alex. *Craeft*	306.4
Larson, Elsie. *A Beautiful Mess Happy Handmade Home*	745
Logan, M. David. *Mat, Mount, and Frame It Yourself*	749
Minter, Laura. *Mini Makers*	745.5
Neuburger, Emily K. *Show Me a Story*	745.5083
Oppenheimer, Betty. *The Candlemaker's Companion*	745.593
Orenstein, Peggy. *Unraveling*	B
Pester, Sophie. *Supercraft*	745.5
Pigza, Jessica. *Bibliocraft*	745.5
Preszler, Trent. *Little and Often*	B
Rich, Chris. *Stained Glass Basics*	748.5
Rivers, Charlotte. *Little Book of Book Making*	686
Rodabaugh, Katrina. *The Paper Playhouse*	745.5
Rodriguez, Dina. *The Big Awesome Book of Hand & Chalk Lettering*	745.6
Sloan, Annie. *Color Recipes for Painted Furniture and More*	745.7
Smith, Sally J. *Fairy Houses*	745.592
Stevenson, Christine Kellmann. *Creative Stained Glass*	748.50282
Swearington, Jen. *Printing on Fabric*	746.6
Tobin, Jacqueline. *Hidden in Plain View*	973.7
Van't Hul, Jean. *The Artful Year*	745.594
Vanderpoel, John Henry. *The Human Figure*	743
Wilkinson, Karen. *The Art of Tinkering*	500
Zedenius, Fanny. *Macrame*	746.42

ARTS AND ENTERTAINMENT — CRAFTS AND HOBBIES — CERAMICS

Brody, Mark. *Mosaic Garden Projects*	712
Burnett, Jason Bige. *Graphic Clay*	738.1
Haab, Sherri. *The Art of Metal Clay*	739.27
Heaser, Sue. *The Polymer Clay Techniques Book*	731.4
Muller, Kristin. *The Potter's Studio Handbook*	738.1
Nelson, Glenn C. *Ceramics*	738
Stone, Francesca. *Easy Homemade Pottery*	738.1
Taylor, Brian J. *Glaze*	738.1

ARTS AND ENTERTAINMENT — CRAFTS AND HOBBIES — FOLKCRAFTS

Lapierre, Corinne. *Folk Embroidered Felt Birds*	746.0463

ARTS AND ENTERTAINMENT — CRAFTS AND HOBBIES — GARDEN AND NATURE

Alexander, Rosemary. ★*The Essential Garden Design Workbook*	712
Baldwin, Debra Lee. *Succulents Simplified*	635.9
Bellamy, Andrea. *Small-Space Vegetable Gardens*	635
Belsinger, Susan. *Grow Your Own Herbs*	635
Benzakein, Erin. *Floret Farm's Cut Flower Garden*	635.9
Benzakein, Erin. *Floret Farm's Discovering Dahlias*	635.9
Black, Scott Hoffman. *Gardening for Butterflies*	638
Bohl, Loree. *Fearless Gardening*	712
Bohmig, Franz. ★*The Month-By-Month Gardening Guide*	635
Bradley, Steve. *Pruning Simplified*	631.5
Branhagen, Alan. *Native Plants of the Midwest*	635.9
Brody, Mark. *Mosaic Garden Projects*	712
Brown, Kendall H. *Quiet Beauty*	712.09
Buchanan, Rita. *Taylor's Master Guide to Landscaping*	712
Carey, Jenny Rose. *The Ultimate Flower Gardener's Guide*	635.9
Chesshire, Charles. *Japanese Gardening*	712
Cowden, Meg McAndrews. ★*Plant Grow Harvest Repeat*	635.9
Crary, Calvert. *The Encyclopedia of Cut Flowers*	745.92
Darke, Rick. *The Living Landscape*	712
Deardorff, David C. *What's Wrong with My Houseplant?*	635.9
Druse, Kenneth. *The New Shade Garden*	635.9
Durber, Sarah. *Make Your Own Indoor Garden*	635
Foley, Caroline. *Topiary, Knots and Parterres*	715
Frey, Kate. *The Bee-Friendly Garden*	595.79
Frey, Kate. *Ground Rules*	635
Gough, Robert E. *The Complete Guide to Saving Seeds*	631.5
Greayer, Rochelle. *Cultivating Garden Style*	712
Halleck, Leslie F. *Plant Parenting*	631.5

PUBLIC LIBRARY CORE COLLECTION: NONFICTION
Twentieth Edition

Hay Hinsdale, Emily L. *What Is My Plant Telling Me?*	635.9
Hayward, Gordon. *Stone in the Garden*	717
Helm, Ben. *The Water Gardener's Bible*	635.9
Holmes, Kier. *The Garden Refresh*	635
Holmes, Roger. *Midwest Home Landscaping*	712
Howcroft, Heidi. *Garden Design*	712
Iannotti, Marie. *The Beginner's Guide to Growing Heirloom Vegetables*	635
Jabbour, Niki. ★*Groundbreaking Food Gardens*	635
Jabbour, Niki. *Growing Under Cover*	635
Jabbour, Niki. *Niki Jabbour's Veggie Garden Remix*	635
Johnsen, Jan. ★*Gardentopia*	635.9
Keville, Kathi. *The Aromatherapy Garden*	635.9
Lavelle, Christine. *How to Create a Wildlife Garden*	635
LeHoullier, Craig. *Epic Tomatoes*	635
Loades, Greg. *The Modern Cottage Garden*	635
Mansfield, Stephen. *Japanese Stone Gardens*	712
Martin, Tovah. ★*The Indestructible Houseplant*	635.9
Martin, Tovah. *The New Terrarium*	635.9
Martin, Tovah. *The Unexpected Houseplant*	635.9
McIndoe, Andrew. *The Creative Shrub Garden*	635.9
McLeary, Susan. *Flowers for All*	745.92
Moss, Charlotte. *Garden Inspirations*	747
Murphy, Emily. *Grow Now*	635
Offolter, Enid. *Welcome to the Jungle*	635.9
Ondra, Nancy J. *Container Theme Gardens*	635.9
Pember, Mat. *DIY Garden Projects*	712
Pleasant, Barbara. *The Complete Compost Gardening Guide*	631.8
Pleasant, Barbara. *The Complete Houseplant Survival Manual*	635.9
Pleasant, Barbara. *Homegrown Pantry*	635
Pleasant, Barbara. ★*Starter Vegetable Gardens*	635
Ralph, Ann. *Grow a Little Fruit Tree*	634
Schwartz, Bobbie. *Garden Renovation*	635
Silver, Johanna. ★*The Bold Dry Garden*	635.9
Smith, Edward C. *The Vegetable Gardener's Bible*	635
Smith, Edward C. *The Vegetable Gardener's Container Bible*	635
Smith, Nathan. *Color Concrete Garden Projects*	721
Smith, Sally J. *Fairy Houses*	745.592
Stearns, Jen. *The Inspired Houseplant*	635.9
Stewart, Martha. ★*Martha's Flowers*	635.9
Tallamy, Douglas W. ★*Nature's Best Hope*	635.9
Tophill, Frances. ★*Container Gardener's Handbook*	635.9
Tychonievich, Joseph. *Rock Gardening*	635.9
Underwood, Kiana. *Color Me Floral*	745.92
Walliser, Jessica. ★*Attracting Beneficial Bugs to Your Garden*	635
Walliser, Jessica. *Plant Partners*	635
Whitman, John. *Fresh from the Garden*	635.9
Williams, Bunny. *On Garden Style*	712
Woods, Christopher. *Gardenlust*	635.022
Ziegler, Lisa Mason. *Vegetables Love Flowers*	635

ARTS AND ENTERTAINMENT — CRAFTS AND HOBBIES — JEWELRY AND BEADWORK

Bluhm, Lisa. *Creative Soldered Jewelry & Accessories*	745.594
Codina, Carles. *The Complete Book of Jewelry Making*	739.27
Combs, Rebecca Ann. *Kumihimo*	745.594
Crowther, Janet. *Make a Statement*	745.594
DeCoster, Marcia. ★*Marcia Decoster's Beaded Opulence*	739.27
Geary, Theresa Flores. *The Illustrated Bead Bible*	745.594
Gedeon, Jade. *Beautiful Bracelets by Hand*	745.594
Haab, Sherri. *The Art of Metal Clay*	739.27
Karon, Karen. *Advanced Chain Maille Jewelry Workshop*	745.594
Katz, Amy. *Seed Bead Chic*	745.594
Legenhausen, Courtney. *Fashion Jewelry*	745.594
Martin, Ann. *The Art of Quilling Paper Jewelry*	745.54
McGrath, Jinks. *The Complete Jewelry Making Course*	739.27028
Michaels, Chris Franchetti. *Teach Yourself Visually Jewelry Making & Beading*	739.27
Pavelka, Lisa. *The Complete Book of Polymer Clay*	738.1
Wiseman, Jill. *Jill Wiseman's Beautiful Beaded Ropes*	745.594
Young, Anastasia. *The Workbench Guide to Jewelry Techniques*	739.27

ARTS AND ENTERTAINMENT — CRAFTS AND HOBBIES — PAPERCRAFTS

Baard, Nellianna van den. *Better Living Through Origami*	736.982
Cetti, Livia. *The Exquisite Book of Paper Flowers*	745.594
Descamps, Ghylenn. *Beginner's Guide to Kirigami*	745.54
Hayakawa, Hiroshi. *Kirigami Menagerie*	736.98
Martin, Ann. *The Art of Quilling Paper Jewelry*	745.54
Morin, John. *Inspired Origami*	736.982
Thuss, Rebecca. *Paper to Petal*	745.54
Turner, Tiffanie. *The Fine Art of Paper Flowers*	745.92
Watanabe, Judi. *The Complete Photo Guide to Cardmaking*	745.594
Yamazaki, Hiromi. *Japanese Paper Flowers*	745.594

ARTS AND ENTERTAINMENT — CRAFTS AND HOBBIES — SEASONAL

Brown, Stephen. *Glitterville's Handmade Christmas*	B
Cupp, Lundy. *Realistic Pumpkin Carving*	745.5941646
Pester, Sophie. *Homemade Holiday*	745.594
Rosenstrach, Jenny. *How to Celebrate Everything*	641.5
Samuell, Kristine. *A Year of Gingerbread Houses*	745.5

ARTS AND ENTERTAINMENT — CRAFTS AND HOBBIES — TEXTILES AND NEEDLEWORK

Abbondio, Sarah. *Mini Amigurumi Animals*	746.43
Adams, Liza. *Needle Felting*	746
Alexander, Lissa. *Oh, Scrap!*	746.46
Alicia, Anna. *Bags*	646.4
Anderson, Sarah. *The Spinner's Book of Yarn Designs*	746.1
Atherley, Kate. *The Knitter's Dictionary*	746.43
Baca, Salena. *Oversize Fashion Crochet*	746.43
Bassetti, Amanda. *Arm Knitting*	746.43
Belyea, Patricia. *East-Meets-West Quilts*	746.46
Bergstrom, Lauren. *Cute & Cuddly Crochet*	746.43
Bergstrom, Lauren. *Mini Crochet Creatures*	746.43
Bernard, Wendy. *Up, Down, All-Around Stitch Dictionary*	746.43
Bestor, Leslie Ann. *Cast On, Bind Off*	746.432
Beyer, Jinny. *A Quilter's Album of Patchwork Patterns*	746.46
Bliss, Debbie. ★*The Knitter's Book of Knowledge*	746.43
Boggs, Jacey. *Spin Art*	746.1
Brandvig, Jera. *Quilt As-You-Go Made Vintage*	746.46
Brasfield, Hope. *Satisfying Stitches*	746.44
Budd, Ann. *The Knitter's Handy Book of Top-Down Sweaters*	746.43
Budd, Ann. *New Directions in Sock Knitting*	746.43
Budd, Ann. *Sock Knitting Master Class*	746.43
Callahan, Gail. *Hand Dyeing Yarn and Fleece*	746.6
Chachula, Robyn. *Unexpected Afghans*	746.43
Chanin, Natalie. ★*The Geometry of Hand-Sewing*	746.44
Chapman, Baylor. ★*Decorating with Plants*	635.9
Christensen, Jo Ippolito. ★*The Needlepoint Book*	746.44
Conahan, Gillian. *The Hero's Closet*	646.2
Corkhill, Betsan. *Crochet Therapy*	746.43
Corwin, Lena. *Lena Corwin's Made by Hand*	746.6
Cox, Shelley. *Bead Embroidery*	746.5
Crowfoot, Jane. *Ultimate Crochet Bible*	746.43
Daly, Fiona. *Weaving on a Little Loom*	746.1
Dassau, Jennifer. *Knitting Short Rows*	746.43
Dixon, Anne. *The Handweaver's Pattern Directory*	746.1
Dixon, Anne. *The Weaver's Inkle Pattern Directory*	746.1
Doughty, Kathy. *Adding Layers*	746.46
Duerr, Sasha. *Natural Color*	746.6
Durant, Judith. *Cable Left, Cable Right*	746.43
Durant, Judith. *Increase, Decrease*	746.43
Eaton, Jan. *350+ Crochet Tips, Techniques, and Trade Secrets*	746.432
Eaton, Jan. *Mary Thomas's Dictionary of Embroidery Stitches.*	746.44
Eckman, Edie. *Around the Corner Crochet Borders*	746.43
Eckman, Edie. *Beyond the Square Crochet Motifs*	746.43
Eckman, Edie. *Connect the Shapes Crochet Motifs*	746.43
Eckman, Edie. *The Crochet Answer Book*	746.43
Edwards, Zoe. *Mend It, Wear It, Love It!*	646
Epstein, Nicky. *Nicky Epstein, the Essential Edgings Collection*	746.43
Faerm, Steven. *Fashion Design Course*	746.9
Frazer, Amy L. *Empowered Embroidery*	746.44
Galbraith, Melissa. *How to Embroider Texture and Pattern*	746.44
Ganderton, Lucinda. ★*Embroidery*	746.44
Gaughan, Norah. *Norah Gaughan's Knitted Cable Sourcebook*	746.43
Gering, Jacquie. *Quilting Modern*	746.46
Gering, Jacquie. *Walk*	746.46
Gethin, Rosanna Clare. *Sew Luxe Leather*	745.53
Gilchrist, Abby. *Modern Fabric*	746.092
Gilleland, Diane. *All Points Patchwork*	746.46
Glass, Alison. *Alison Glass Applique*	746.44
Goertzen, Vanessa. ★*Charm School*	746.46
Goldsmith, Becky. *The Ultimate Thread Guide*	677
Goldsworthy, Lynne. *Quick & Easy Quilts*	746.46
Green-Hite, Vincent. *Knot Bad Amigurumi*	746.43
Grisham, Candyce Copp. *Dresden Quilt Blocks Reimagined*	746.46
Gullberg, Maria. *Tapestry Crochet and More*	746.43
Hartman, Elizabeth. *Modern Patchwork*	746.46
Hatchard, Gurinder Kaur. *Hooked on Shakespeare*	746.43

AUTHOR, TITLE, SERIES AND SUBJECT INDEX

Herbertson, Angie. *Sewing Face Masks, Scrub Caps, Arm Slings, and More*	646.4
Herzog, Amy. *Knit Wear Love*	746.43
Herzog, Amy. *You Can Knit That*	746.432
Hewett, Jen. *Print, Pattern, Sew*	646.4
Hiatt, June. *The Principles of Knitting*	746.43
Higuchi, Yumiko. *Embroidered Animals*	746.44
Hubert, Margaret. *10 Granny Squares, 30 Blankets*	746.43
Hubert, Margaret. *The Complete Photo Guide to Crochet*	746.43
Hubert, Margaret. *The Granny Square Book*	746.43
Huff, Mary Scott. *The Mitten Handbook*	746.43
Hunter, Bonnie K. *String Frenzy*	746.46
Impelen, Helgrid van. *Big Knits Big Needles*	746.43
Ishida, Sanae. *Sewing Happiness*	646.2
Ishida, Sanae. *Sewing Love*	646
Jarchow, Deborah. *The Weaving Explorer*	746.1
Joyce, Anna. *Hand Dyed*	746.6
Kartus, Lisa. *Knit Fix*	746.43
Knight, Erika. *500 Crochet Stitches*	746.43
Knight, Erika. *750 Knitting Stitches*	746.43
Lapierre, Corinne. *Folk Embroidered Felt Birds*	746.0463
Leapman, Melissa. *Mastering Color Knitting*	746.43
Lindsay, Virginia Keleher. *Sewing to Sell*	746
Lowry, Melissa. *Vibrant Punch Needle Decor*	746.44
Ludwig, Frauke. *Essential Knit Sweaters*	746.43
Maxwell, Sarah. *Fearless with Fabric*	746.46
Melville, Sally. *Knitting Pattern Essentials*	746.43
Mezoff, Rebecca. ★*The Art of Tapestry Weaving*	746.7
Misumi, Noriko. *Mending with Love*	646.6
Mitchell, Syne. *Inventive Weaving on a Little Loom*	746.1
Montenegro, Sonya. *Mending Life*	646
Mornu, Nathalie. *Embroider Your Life*	746.44
Mullett-Bowlsby, Shannon. ★*Complete Crochet Course*	746.43
Murphy, Marilyn. *Woven to Wear*	746.1
Newton, Deborah. *Finishing School*	746.43
Nicholas, Kristin. *Crafting a Patterned Home*	745.5
Nico, Brooke. *More Lovely Knitted Lace*	746.43
Noldeke, Marisa. *50 Knitted Wraps and Shawls*	746.43
Nyberg, Amanda Jean. *No Scrap Left Behind*	746.46
Ohrenstein, Dora. *The Crocheter's Skill-Building Workshop*	746.43
Parkes, Clara. *The Knitter's Book of Yarn*	677
Patrick, Jane. *The Weaver's Idea Book*	746.1
Phelps, Isela. *Loom Knitting Primer*	746.43
Quindt, Svetlana. *The Costume Making Guide*	646.4
Radcliffe, Margaret. *Circular Knitting Workshop*	746.43
Radcliffe, Margaret. *The Knitting Answer Book*	746.43
Radcliffe, Margaret. *The Knowledgeable Knitter*	746.43
Redford, Catherine. *Modern Machine Quilting*	746.46
Righetti, Maggie. *Crocheting in Plain English*	746.43
Righetti, Maggie. *Knitting in Plain English*	746.432
Ringquist, Rebecca. ★*Rebecca Ringquist's Embroidery Workshops*	746.44
Robson, Deborah. *The Field Guide to Fleece*	677
Rosenthal, Maxine. *One-Block Wonders of the World*	746.46
Rott, Ira. *Crochet Animal Rugs*	746.7
Shaw, Robert. *American Quilts*	746.46
Shida, Hitomi. *Japanese Knitting Stitch Bible*	746.43
Shimoda, Naoko. *Artfully Embroidered*	746.44
Spainhower, Courtney. *Elemental Knits*	746.43
Square, Vicki. *The Knitter's Companion*	746.432
Stanfield, Lesley. *100 Flowers to Knit & Crochet*	746.43
Stocker, Blair. *Wise Craft Quilts*	746.46
Stoller, Debbie. *Stitch 'N Bitch Superstar Knitting*	746.43
Stoller, Debbie. ★*Stitch 'N Bitch*	746.43
Storey, Martin. *Easy Fair Isle Knitting*	746.43
Susa, Sachiko. *Sweet & Simple Needle Felted Animals*	746
Talley, Safiyyah. *Knit 2 Socks in 1*	746.43
Todhunter, Tracey. *Crochet, Learn It. Love It.*	746.43
Tomasson, Dara. *Walk, Jog, Run*	746.46
Turner, Sharon. *Teach Yourself Visually Knitting*	746.43
Walters, Angela. *Free-Motion Meandering*	746.46
Watson, Sarah. *Pen to Thread*	746.44
Weil, Anne. *Knitting Without Needles*	746.43
Werker, Kim P. *Teach Yourself Visually Crochet*	746.43
Wolfe, Victoria Findlay. *Modern Quilt Magic*	746.46
Wood, Jennifer. *Refined Knits*	746.43
Wood, Sherri. *The Improv Handbook for Modern Quilters*	746.46
Yaker, Rebecca. *Little One-Yard Wonders*	646.2
Yang, April. *DIY Thrift Flip*	646.2
Zimmermann, Elizabeth. ★*Knitting Without Tears*	746.4

ARTS AND ENTERTAINMENT — CRAFTS AND HOBBIES — WOODWORKING

Barker, Margaret A. *Audubon Birdhouse Book*	728
Barn the Spoon. *Woodcraft*	684
Christiana, Asa. *Build Stuff with Wood*	684
Horwood, Roger. *Woodworker's Handbook*	684
Jones, Andrew. *Stickmaking Handbook*	736
Pourny, Christophe. ★*The Furniture Bible*	684.1

ARTS AND ENTERTAINMENT — DANCE

Alford, Henry. *And Then We Danced*	792.8
Brown, Carolyn. *Chance and Circumstance*	B
Copeland, Misty. ★*Ballerina Body*	792.8
Copeland, Misty. ★*Life in Motion*	B
Copeland, Misty. *The Wind at My Back*	B
Duncan, Isadora. *My Life*	B
Flaherty, Meghan. *Tango Lessons*	793.3
Fuhrer, Margaret. ★*American Dance*	792.809
Gottlieb, Robert. *George Balanchine*	B
Guillermoprieto, Alma. *Dancing with Cuba*	972.9106
Hallberg, David. *A Body of Work*	B
Harss, Marina. *The Boy from Kyiv*	B
Homans, Jennifer. ★*Apollo's Angels*	792.8
Jacobs, Laura. ★*Celestial Bodies*	792.8
Kavanagh, Julie. *Nureyev*	B
Kessler, Lauren. *Raising the Barre*	792.8
Minden, Eliza Gaynor. *The Ballet Companion*	792.8
Morris, Mark. *Out Loud*	B
Morrison, Simon Alexander. *Bolshoi Confidential*	792.8
Riley, Kathleen. *The Astaires*	B
Robb, Alice. ★*Don't Think, Dear*	792.8
Teachout, Terry. ★*All in the Dances*	B
Valby, Karen. *The Swans of Harlem*	792.8

ARTS AND ENTERTAINMENT — FASHION

Alicia, Anna. *Bags*	646.4
Bari, Shahidha K. *Dressed*	391
Barker, Nigel. *Models of Influence*	746.92092
Bowles, Hamish. *Vogue & the Metropolitan Museum of Art Costume Institute*	746.9
Brickell, Francesca Cartier. *The Cartiers*	B
Brown, Tina. *The Vanity Fair Diaries*	B
Carter, Ruth E. ★*The Art of Ruth E. Carter*	746.9
Cleveland, Pat. *Walking with the Muses*	B
Cline, Elizabeth L. *The Conscious Closet*	646
Crowe, Lauren Goldstein. *The Towering World of Jimmy Choo*	391.4
Cunningham, William J. ★*Fashion Climbing*	B
Day, Daniel R. *Dapper Dan*	B
De Courcy, Anne. *Chanel's Riviera*	944.9
Dirix, Emmanuelle. *Dressing the Decades*	746.92
Edwards, Lydia. *How to Read a Dress*	391
Enninful, Edward. *A Visible Man*	B
Faerm, Steven. *Fashion Design Course*	746.9
Flannery, Kate. *Strip Tees*	338.4
Ford, Tanisha C. *Dressed in Dreams*	391
Fox, Julia. *Down the Drain*	B
Garelick, Rhonda K. *Mademoiselle*	B
Givhan, Robin. *The Battle of Versailles*	746.9
Greenfield, Martin. ★*Measure of a Man*	B
Grumbach, Didier. *History of International Fashion*	746.9
Hardy, Alyssa. *Worn Out*	338.4
Hilfiger, Tommy. *American Dreamer*	B
Holmes, Elizabeth. *HRH*	941.085
Karen, Dawnn. *Dress Your Best Life*	646
Leventon, Melissa. *What People Wore When*	391.009
Lowit, Roxanne. *Yves Saint Laurent*	746.9
Meder, Danielle. *Draw Fashion Now*	741.6
Mizrahi, Isaac. *I.M.*	B
Quindt, Svetlana. *The Costume Making Guide*	646.4
Richardson, Lance. *House of Nutter*	B
Satow, Julie. *When Women Ran Fifth Avenue*	381.141
Shida, Hitomi. *Japanese Knitting Stitch Bible*	746.43
Stuart, Amanda Mackenzie. *Empress of Fashion*	B
Talley, Andre Leon. *The Chiffon Trenches*	B
Tanov, Erica. *Design by Nature*	747
Thanhauser, Sofi. *Worn*	391
Thomas, Dana. *Gods and Kings*	920
Tonti, Lucianne. *Sundressed*	746.9
Trubert-Tollu, Chantal. ★*The House of Worth 1858-1954*	746.92

PUBLIC LIBRARY CORE COLLECTION: NONFICTION
Twentieth Edition

Von Furstenberg, Diane. *The Woman I Wanted to Be* — B
Wicker, Alden. ★*To Dye For* — 746

ARTS AND ENTERTAINMENT — GENERAL

Abdurraqib, Hanif. ★*A Little Devil in America* — 791.089
Adler, Stella. *Stella Adler* — 792
Aitken-Smith, Trent. *The Tattoo Dictionary* — 391.6
Arnold, Jeremy. *Turner Classic Movies* — 791.43
Baker, Nicholson. *The World on Sunday* — 071
Baraka, Sho. *He Saw That It Was Good* — 261.5
Bellos, David. *Who Owns This Sentence?* — 346.73
Black, Alexandra. *Design* — 745.4
Bloom, Harold. *Genius* — 153.9
Bordo, Susan. *The Creation of Anne Boleyn* — 942.05
Bosker, Bianca. *Get the Picture* — 701
Cameron, Julia. ★*The Listening Path* — 153.6
Carlin, Kelly. *A Carlin Home Companion* — B
Carter, Alice A. *The Red Rose Girls* — B
Chayka, Kyle. *The Longing for Less* — 179.9
Cohen, Robert. *Acting Power* — 792.02
Corwin, Lena. *Lena Corwin's Made by Hand* — 746.6
Crumb, R. *R. Crumb* — 741.6
Dederer, Claire. ★*Monsters* — 700.1
Dench, Judi. *Shakespeare* — 792
Diaconis, Persi. *Magical Mathematics* — 793.8
DiMarco, Nyle. ★*Deaf Utopia* — B
Doherty, Maggie. *The Equivalents* — 920
Eco, Umberto. *History of Beauty* — 111
Eco, Umberto. *On Ugliness* — 111
Farrington, Lisa E. *Creating Their Own Image* — 704
Figes, Orlando. *The Europeans* — 920
Fischer, Bobby. ★*Bobby Fischer Teaches Chess* — 794.1
Fischer, Jenna. *The Actor's Life* — 792.02
Friedman, Rachel. ★*And Then We Grew Up* — 305.24
Garfield, Simon. *In Miniature* — 745.5928
Gay, Roxane. *Bad Feminist* — 814
Gerber, Robin. *Barbie and Ruth* — B
Gladstone, Brooke. *The Influencing Machine* — 741.5
Godin, Seth. *The Practice* — 153.3
Gombrich, E. H. ★*The Story of Art* — 709
Gopnik, Adam. *All That Happiness Is* — 158.1
Gopnik, Adam. *The Real Work* — 153.9
Griffin, Farah Jasmine. *Read Until You Understand* — 810.9
Grove, Kirsten. *Simply Styling* — 747
Hagen, Uta. ★*Respect for Acting* — 792.02
Hellmuth, Phil. *Play Poker Like the Pros* — 795.41
Hook, Philip. *Rogues' Gallery* — 709.2
Hughes, Robert. *American Visions* — 709
Isen, Tajja. *Some of My Best Friends* — 305.8
Jenkins, Jessica Kerwin. *All the Time in the World* — 390
Johnson, Stephanie. *Tanqueray* — B
Johnson, Steven. *Wonderland* — 790.1
Kundera, Milan. *Encounter* — 809
Laing, Olivia. ★*The Lonely City* — 700.1
Lanzmann, Claude. *The Patagonian Hare* — B
Lessig, Lawrence. *Remix* — 346.7304
Levy, Reynold. *They Told Me Not to Take That Job* — 792.09
Levy, Shawn. ★*The Castle on Sunset* — 647.95
Linklater, Kristin. *Freeing the Natural Voice* — 808.5
Magsamen, Susan. *Your Brain on Art* — 111
Mann, William J. *Hello, Gorgeous* — B
Mazzeo, Tilar J. *The Secret of Chanel No. 5* — 338.7
McCullough, David G. *The Greater Journey* — 920
McGonigal, Jane. *Super Better* — 794.8
Mifflin, Margot. *Looking for Miss America* — 791.6
Miles, Bryan. *101 Magic Tricks* — 793.8
Miller, Megan. ★*The Ultimate Unofficial Encyclopedia for Minecrafters* — 794.8
Moore, Rachel. *The Artist's Compass* — 791
Moore, Sonia. *The Stanislavski System* — 792
Morrison, Robert. *The Regency Years* — 941.07
Moss, Adam. ★*The Work of Art* — 701
Nelson, Maggie. ★*Like Love* — 814
O'Kane, Bernard. *Treasures of Islam* — 709.1
Owen, Oscar. *Mind-Blowing Magic Tricks for Everyone* — 793.8
Parker, James. *Get Me Through the Next Five Minutes* — 158.1
Parkin, Simon. *An Illustrated History of 151 Video Games* — 794.8
Patterson, James. *What Really Happens in Vegas* — 920
Phillips, Maya. *Nerd* — 302.23

Poirier, Agnes. *Left Bank* — 944
Porter, Billy. ★*Unprotected* — B
Powell, Michael. *The Acting Bible* — 792.02
Rees, Darrel. *How to Be an Illustrator* — 741.6
Rendgen, Sandra. *Understanding the World* — 741.6
Rodriguez, Dina. *The Big Awesome Book of Hand & Chalk Lettering* — 745.6
Rogers, Adam. *Full Spectrum* — 152.14
Rosenfield, Stephen. *Mastering Stand-Up* — 792.7
Rowe, Mickey. *Fearlessly Different* — B
Rubin, Rick. ★*The Creative Act* — 153.3
Sabatini Sloan, Aisha. *Dreaming of Ramadi in Detroit* — 814
Small, Zachary. ★*Token Supremacy* — 332.4
Standiford, Les. ★*Battle for the Big Top* — 791.3
Stanislavsky, Konstantin. *An Actor's Work* — 792.02
Stein, Jean. *West of Eden* — 979.4
Strickland, Carol. *The Annotated Mona Lisa* — 709
Szwed, John F. *Cosmic Scholar* — B
Velour, Sasha. ★*The Big Reveal* — 792.7
Wall, Duncan. *The Ordinary Acrobat* — B
Wu, Simon. *Dancing on My Own* — 700.1

ARTS AND ENTERTAINMENT — MOVIES AND TELEVISION

Ackroyd, Peter. *Charlie Chaplin* — B
Andrews, Julie. *Home Work* — B
Andrews, Julie. *Home* — B
Arkin, Alan. *An Improvised Life* — B
Armstrong, Jennifer Keishin. *Seinfeldia* — 791.45
Armstrong, Jennifer Keishin. *Sex and the City and Us* — 791.45
Armstrong, Jennifer Keishin. *When Women Invented Television* — 791.45
Arnold, Jeremy. *Turner Classic Movies* — 791.43
Auletta, Ken. *Media Man* — B
Ausaja, S. M. M. *Bollywood* — 791.43
Austerlitz, Saul. *Kind of a Big Deal* — 791.43
Austerlitz, Saul. *Money for Nothing* — 780.26
Bacall, Lauren. *By Myself and Then Some* — B
Ball, Lucille. *Love, Lucy* — B
Basinger, Jeanine. *Hollywood* — 791.43
Basinger, Jeanine. *The Star Machine* — 384
Beauvais, Garcelle. *Love Me as I Am* — B
Benson, Michael. *Space Odyssey* — 791.43
Berg, A. Scott. *Kate Remembered* — B
Bertinelli, Valerie. *Enough Already* — B
Bingen, Steven. *Easy Rider* — 791.4372
Biskind, Peter. *Pandora's Box* — 791.45
Biskind, Peter. *Star* — B
Blair, Selma. *Mean Baby* — B
Bogle, Donald. *Bright Boulevards, Bold Dreams* — 791.45
Britt, Ryan. *Phasers on Stun!* — 791.45
Britt, Ryan. ★*The Spice Must Flow* — 813
Brooks, Mel. ★*All About Me!* — B
Brower, Kate Andersen. *Elizabeth Taylor* — B
Bruck, Connie. *When Hollywood Had a King* — B
Buck, Joe. *Lucky Bastard* — B
Burnett, Carol. *In Such Good Company* — 791.45
Burrows, James. ★*Directed by James Burrows* — 791.4502
Butler, Isaac. *The Method* — 792.02
Caine, Michael. *Blowing the Bloody Doors Off* — B
Callow, Simon. ★*Orson Welles* — B
Carle-Sanders, Theresa. *Outlander Kitchen* — 641.5
Carlson, Erin. *I'll Have What She's Having* — 791.43
Carter, Ash. *Life Isn't Everything* — B
Carter, Ruth E. ★*The Art of Ruth E. Carter* — 746.9
Chan, Jackie. *Never Grow up* — B
Clements, Jonathan. *The Anime Encyclopedia* — 791.43
Clemmons, Francois S. *Officer Clemmons* — B
Coppola, Francis Ford. *Live Cinema and Its Techniques* — 791.4302
Couric, Katie. *Going There* — B
Courogen, Carrie. ★*Miss May Does Not Exist* — B
Curtis, James. *Buster Keaton* — B
Curtis, James. *Spencer Tracy* — B
Davis, Geena. *Dying of Politeness* — B
Davis, Michael. *Street Gang* — 791.43
Davis, Viola. ★*Finding Me* — B
De Semlyen, Nick. *Wild and Crazy Guys* — 920
De Vise, Daniel. ★*The Blues Brothers* — 791.43
Decherney, Peter. *Hollywood's Copyright Wars* — 346.7304
Dixon, Wheeler W. *A Short History of Film* — 791.43
Driver, Minnie. *Managing Expectations* — B
Duggar, Jill. *Counting the Cost* — B

AUTHOR, TITLE, SERIES AND SUBJECT INDEX

Ebert, Roger. *Scorsese by Ebert* — B
Edwards, Bob. *Edward R. Murrow and the Birth of Broadcast Journalism* — B
Else, Jon. *True South* — 305.800973
Elwes, Cary. *As You Wish* — 791.43
Eyman, Scott. *Cary Grant* — B
Eyman, Scott. *Charlie Chaplin vs. America* — B
Eyman, Scott. *Empire of Dreams* — B
Eyman, Scott. *Hank and Jim* — 920
Eyman, Scott. *John Wayne* — B
Fager, Jeffrey. *Fifty Years of 60 Minutes* — 070.1
Felton, Tom. ★*Beyond the Wand* — B
Field, Sally. *In Pieces* — B
Fischer, Jenna. *The Office BFFs* — 791.45
Fischer, Paul. *The Man Who Invented Motion Pictures* — 791.43
Fisher, Todd. *My Girls* — B
Foster, Sutton. *Hooked* — B
Fournier-Lanzoni, Remi. *French Cinema, 2nd Ed.* — 791.43
Fox, Julia. *Down the Drain* — B
Frankel, Glenn. *High Noon* — 791.43
Frankel, Glenn. *Shooting Midnight Cowboy* — 791.43
Gehring, Wes D. *James Dean* — B
Gleiberman, Owen. *Movie Freak* — B
Gless, Sharon. *Apparently There Were Complaints* — B
Goetz, Kevin. *Audienceology* — 791.43
Goldman, William. *Adventures in the Screen Trade* — 384
Goudsouzian, Aram. *Sidney Poitier* — B
Greene, Andy. *The Office* — 791.45
Grey, Jennifer. *Out of the Corner* — B
Gross, Edward. *The Fifty Year Mission* — 791.45
Grylls, Bear. *Never Give Up* — B
Haddish, Tiffany. *The Last Black Unicorn* — B
Harris, Mark. ★*Five Came Back* — 791.4302
Harris, Mark. *Mike Nichols* — B
Harris, Mark. *Pictures at a Revolution* — 791.43
Harryhausen, Ray. *The Art of Ray Harryhausen* — 778
Haskell, Molly. *Steven Spielberg* — B
Hayes, Dade. *Binge Times* — 384.55
Haygood, Wil. ★*Colorization* — 791.43
Hendrix, Grady. *These Fists Break Bricks* — 791
Henson, Taraji P. *Around the Way Girl* — B
Herzog, Werner. ★*Every Man for Himself and God Against All* — B
Heughan, Sam. *Waypoints* — B
Hirsch, Foster. ★*Hollywood and the Movies of the Fifties* — 791.43
Hirsch, Paul. *A Long Time Ago in a Cutting Room Far, Far Away* — B
Holt, Nathalia. *The Queens of Animation* — 920
Howard, Ron. ★*The Boys* — B
Huang, Yunte. *Daughter of the Dragon* — B
Hussey, Olivia. *The Girl on the Balcony* — B
Huston, Anjelica. *Watch Me* — B
Imperioli, Michael. *Woke up This Morning* — 791.45
Jameson, A. D. *I Find Your Lack of Faith Disturbing* — 791.43
Kael, Pauline. ★*The Age of Movies* — 791.43
Kamp, David. *Sunny Days* — 791.4502
Kanfer, Stefan. *Tough Without a Gun* — B
Karp, Josh. *Orson Welles's Last Movie* — 791.43
Katz, Evan Ross. *Into Every Generation a Slayer Is Born* — 791.45
Kaufman, Amy. *Bachelor Nation* — 791.45
Kemper, Ellie. *My Squirrel Days* — B
Kenny, Glenn. *Made Men* — 791.43
Kenny, Glenn. *The World Is Yours* — 791.43
Key, Keegan-Michael. ★*The History of Sketch Comedy* — 792.2
King, Maxwell. *The Good Neighbor* — B
Klastorin, Michael. *Close Encounters of the Third Kind* — 791.43
Kolker, Robert Phillip. *Kubrick* — B
Kurosawa, Akira. *Something Like an Autobiography* — B
Lane, Christina. *Phantom Lady* — B
Leamer, Laurence. *Hitchcock's Blondes* — 791.43
Lear, Norman. *Even This I Get to Experience* — B
Lebo, Harlan. ★*Citizen Kane* — 791.43
Lewis, Jenifer. *Walking in My Joy* — B
Liu, Simu. ★*We Were Dreamers* — B
Longworth, Karina. *Seduction* — B
Lumet, Sidney. *Making Movies* — 791.43
Lynch, David. *Room to Dream* — B
Maguire, James. *Impresario* — B
Mamet, David. *True and False* — 792
Mann, William J. *Bogie & Bacall* — 920
Mann, William J. *The Contender* — B

Mann, William J. *Kate* — B
Margulies, Julianna. *Sunshine Girl* — B
Martin, Brett. *Difficult Men* — 791.4509
Martin, Steve. *Number One Is Walking* — B
Mattel, Trixie. *Working Girls* — 650.1
McCabe, John. *Cagney* — B
McConaughey, Matthew. *Greenlights* — B
McGilligan, Patrick. *Funny Man* — B
McGilligan, Patrick. *Oscar Micheaux* — B
McGilligan, Patrick. *Young Orson* — B
McKee, Robert. *Dialogue* — 809
Meslow, Scott. *From Hollywood with Love* — 791.43
Milch, David. *Life's Work* — B
Mills, Hayley. *Forever Young* — B
Mulgrew, Kate. *Born with Teeth* — 791.45028
Myers, Paul. *The Kids in the Hall* — 920
Nashawaty, Chris. *Caddyshack* — 791.43
Nawaz, Zarqa. *Laughing All the Way to the Mosque* — 791.45028
Newman, Paul. *The Extraordinary Life of an Ordinary Man* — B
Nussbaum, Emily. *Cue the Sun!* — 791.45
Nussbaum, Emily. *I Like to Watch* — 791.45
O'Connor, Garry. *Ian McKellen* — B
O'Meara, Mallory. *The Lady from the Black Lagoon* — 921
Odenkirk, Bob. *Comedy Comedy Comedy Drama* — B
Orji, Yvonne. *Bamboozled by Jesus* — B
Orlean, Susan. *Rin Tin Tin* — 636.737
Osborne, Robert. *85 Years of the Oscar* — 791.43079
Page, Elliot. *Pageboy* — B
Parke, Henry C. *The Greatest Westerns Ever Made and the People Who Made Them* — 791.43
Peiffer, Prudence. *The Slip* — 709.73
Peisner, David. *Homey Don't Play That!* — 791.45
Penn, Kal. *You Can't Be Serious* — B
Perry, Matthew. *Friends, Lovers, and the Big Terrible Thing* — B
Philipps, Busy. *This Will Only Hurt a Little* — B
Pincus, Edward. *The Filmmaker's Handbook* — 777
Plummer, Christopher. *In Spite of Myself* — B
Poehler, Amy. *Yes Please* — B
Poitier, Sidney. *The Measure of a Man* — B
Polly, Matthew. ★*Bruce Lee* — B
Posey, Parker. *You're on an Airplane* — B
Postman, Neil. *Amusing Ourselves to Death* — 302.2
Press, Joy. *Stealing the Show* — 791.45
Rannells, Andrew. *Too Much Is Not Enough* — 792.02
Reiss, Mike. *Springfield Confidential* — 791.45
Rhodes, Richard. *Hedy's Folly* — B
Ribowsky, Mark. *Howard Cosell* — 070.449796
Riley, Kathleen. *The Astaires* — B
Rinzler, J. W. *The Making of Aliens* — 791.4372
Ripa, Kelly. *Live Wire* — B
Robinson, Joanna. ★*McU* — 791.43
Rogen, Seth. ★*Yearbook* — B
Rosenbaum, Jonathan. ★*Essential Cinema* — 791.43
RuPaul. ★*The House of Hidden Meanings* — B
Ryan, Maureen. *Burn It Down* — 791.43
Salisbury, Katie Gee. ★*Not Your China Doll* — B
Santopietro, Tom. *The Sound of Music Story* — 791.43
Schechter, Harold. ★*Ripped from the Headlines!* — 791.43
Schickel, Richard. *Keepers* — 791.430973
Schneider, Amy. *In the Form of a Question* — B
Schulman, Michael. ★*Oscar Wars* — 791.43
Schwartzel, Erich. *Red Carpet* — 791.43
Seal, Mark. ★*Leave the Gun, Take the Cannoli* — 791.43
Seidelman, Susan. *Desperately Seeking Something* — B
Seitz, Matt Zoller. *The Sopranos Sessions* — 791.45
Selleck, Tom. *You Never Know* — B
Sepinwall, Alan. ★*TV (the Book)* — 791.45
Sestero, Greg. *The Disaster Artist* — 791.43
Shales, Tom. *Live from New York* — 791.45
Shatner, William. *Boldly Go* — B
Shatner, William. *Live Long And—* — B
Shearer, Stephen Michael. *Beautiful* — B
Shelton, Ron. *The Church of Baseball* — 791.43
Shepard, Jim. *The Tunnel at the End of the Light* — 791.43
Shone, Tom. *The Nolan Variations* — 791.4302
Short, Martin. *I Must Say* — B
Silver, Alain. ★*From the Moment They Met It Was Murder* — 791.43
Singer, Matt. *Opposable Thumbs* — 791.43

1629

PUBLIC LIBRARY CORE COLLECTION: NONFICTION
Twentieth Edition

Smith, Chris. *The Daily Show (the Book)*	791.45
Smith, Jada Pinkett. *Worthy*	B
Smith, Starr. *Jimmy Stewart*	B
Smith, Will. ★*Will*	B
Spiegel, Maura. *Sidney Lumet*	B
Spoto, Donald. *The Dark Side of Genius*	B
Spoto, Donald. *High Society*	B
Stamos, John. *If You Would Have Told Me*	B
Stelter, Brian. *Top of the Morning*	791.456
Stevens, Dana. *Camera Man*	791.4302
Stevens, George, Jr. *Conversations at the American Film Institute with the Great Moviemakers*	791.4302
Stewart, Patrick. ★*Making It So*	B
Stone, Sharon. *The Beauty of Living Twice*	B
Stratton, W. K. *The Wild Bunch*	791.43
Suvari, Mena. *The Great Peace*	B
Taraborrelli, J. Randy. ★*The Secret Life of Marilyn Monroe*	B
Tarantino, Quentin. *Cinema Speculation*	791.43
Thomson, David. *Bette Davis*	B
Thomson, David. *The Big Screen*	791.430973
Thomson, David. *The Fatal Alliance*	791.43
Thomson, David. ★*How to Watch a Movie*	791.43
Thomson, David. *Ingrid Bergman*	B
Tietjen, Jill S. *Hollywood, Her Story*	791.43
Trebek, Alex. *The Answer Is ...*	791.4502
Trejo, Danny. *Trejo*	B
Trimborn, Jurgen. *Leni Riefenstahl*	B
Turan, Kenneth. *Not to Be Missed*	791.43
Tyson, Cicely. ★*Just as I Am*	B
Union, Gabrielle. *We're Going to Need More Wine*	B
Union, Gabrielle. *You Got Anything Stronger?*	B
Urwand, Ben. *The Collaboration*	791.430973
Vick, Tom. *Asian Cinema*	791.43
Vogler, Christopher. ★*The Writer's Journey*	808.2
Ward, Maitland. *Rated X*	B
Washington, Kerry. *Thicker Than Water*	B
Wasson, Sam. *The Big Goodbye*	791.43
Wasson, Sam. ★*Improv Nation*	792.02
Waters, John. *Mr. Know-It-All*	814
Waters, John. *Role Models*	B
Watts, Jill. *Hattie McDaniel*	B
Waxman, Sharon. *Rebels on the Backlot*	791.4302
Weismann, Brad. *Lost in the Dark*	791.43
Weller, Sheila. *Carrie Fisher*	B
Wilkman, Jon. *Screening Reality*	070.1
Williams, Billy Dee. ★*What Have We Here*	B
Williams, Michael Kenneth. *Scenes from My Life*	B
Wilson, Rebel. *Rebel Rising*	B
Wilson, Victoria. *A Life of Barbara Stanwyck*	B
Winkler, Henry. ★*Being Henry*	B
Wu, Constance. *Making a Scene*	B
Yang, Jeff. *The Golden Screen*	791.43
Yomota, Inuhiko. *What Is Japanese Cinema?*	791.43
Zucker, David. *Surely You Can't Be Serious*	791.43
Zweibel, Alan. *Laugh Lines*	B
Zwick, Edward. ★*Hits, Flops, and Other Illusions*	B

ARTS AND ENTERTAINMENT — MUSEUMS AND COLLECTIONS

Ai, Weiwei. *Ai Weiwei*	709.51
Berenbaum, Michael. *The World Must Know*	940.53
Cogeval, Guy. *Edouard Vuillard*	759.4
Dickerman, Leah. *Dada*	709
FitzGerald, Michael C. ★*Picasso and American Art*	709.73
Gill, Anton. *Art Lover*	B
Holladay, Wilhelmina Cole. *A Museum of Their Own*	704
Jenkins, Jessica D. *Exploring Women's Suffrage Through 50 Historic Treasures*	324.6
Katsushika, Hokusai. *Hokusai*	769.92
Kuper, Adam. *The Museum of Other People*	305.8
Leibovitz, Annie. *A Photographer's Life, 1990-2005*	779
Levin, Gail. *Edward Hopper*	759.13
Livingston, Jane. *The Paintings of Joan Mitchell*	759.13
Lynes, Barbara Buhler. *Georgia O'Keeffe Museum Collections*	759.13
Matisse, Henri. *Henri Matisse*	709.2
Obrist, Hans-Ulrich. *Ways of Curating*	707.5
Shackelford, George T. M. *Monet*	759.4
Stanislaus, Grace C. *Instill & Inspire*	704.03
Stourton, James. *Kenneth Clark*	B
Willis, Deborah. *Reflections in Black*	770

ARTS AND ENTERTAINMENT — MUSIC

Adams, John. *Hallelujah Junction*	B
Austerlitz, Saul. *Money for Nothing*	780.26
Belafonte, Harry. ★*My Song*	782.42164
Bogle, Donald. *Heat Wave*	782.42164
Boilen, Bob. *Your Song Changed My Life*	780.92
Brown, Mick. ★*Tearing Down the Wall of Sound*	B
Broyles, Michael. ★*Revolutions in American Music*	780.9
Bullock, Darryl W. *David Bowie Made Me Gay*	780
Burton-Hill, Clemency. ★*Year of Wonder*	780.9
Calamar, Gary. *Record Store Days*	780.26
Carlile, Brandi. *Broken Horses*	B
Chappell, Jon. ★*Guitar All-In-One for Dummies*	787.87
Clague, Mark. *O Say Can You Hear?*	782.42
Cohodas, Nadine. *Princess Noire*	782.42164
Craine, Debra. *The Oxford Dictionary of Dance*	792.8
Crawford, Richard. *America's Musical Life*	780
Day, Timothy. ★*A Century of Recorded Music*	780
DeRogatis, Jim. *Soulless*	B
DiFranco, Ani. *No Walls and the Recurring Dream*	782.42164
Doggett, Peter. *Electric Shock*	781.64
Dolby, Thomas. *The Speed of Sound*	B
Dylan, Bob. ★*The Philosophy of Modern Song*	782.42
Feinstein, Michael. *The Gershwins and Me*	782.42164
Garnice, Michael. *The Ultimate Guide to Great Reggae*	781.646
Gasser, Nolan. *Why You Like It*	781.1
Gavin, James. ★*Stormy Weather*	782.42164
Gioia, Ted. *Music*	780.9
Grant, Colin. *The Natural Mystics*	B
Guralnick, Peter. ★*Sam Phillips*	B
Harvilla, Rob. *60 Songs That Explain the '90s*	782.42164
Hermes, Will. *Love Goes to Buildings on Fire*	781.64
Houghton, Mick. *Becoming Elektra*	781.64
Hyland, William G. *George Gershwin*	B
Isacoff, Stuart. *Musical Revolutions*	780.9
Kapilow, Robert. ★*Listening for America*	782.42164
Koenig, Joan. *The Musical Child*	780.71
Larson, Kay. *Where the Heart Beats*	700.1
Lehman, David. *A Fine Romance*	781.64
Lynskey, Dorian. *33 Revolutions per Minute*	782.42
Mason, Nick. *Inside Out*	B
Matos, Michaelangelo. *The Underground Is Massive*	781.648
Max, D. T. *Finale*	782.1
McNally, Dennis. *On Highway 61*	781.64
Meacham, Jon. *Songs of America*	782.42
Milner, Greg. *Perfecting Sound Forever*	781.49
Moby. *Porcelain*	B
Moby. *Then It Fell Apart*	B
Momus. *Niche*	B
Murakami, Haruki. ★*Absolutely on Music*	784.2
Newkey-Burden, Chas. *Taylor Swift*	B
Philip, Robert. *The Classical Music Lover's Companion to Orchestral Music*	784.2
Piston, Walter. *Orchestration*	781.63
Porter, Cecelia Hopkins. *Five Lives in Music*	B
Powers, Ann. *Good Booty*	781.64
Questlove. *Music Is History*	782.42164
Rapkin, Mickey. *Pitch Perfect*	782.5
Remnick, David. *Holding the Note*	781.64
Rodgers, Mary. *Shy*	B
Rogers, Susan E. ★*This Is What It Sounds Like*	781.1
Sachs, Harvey. *Ten Masterpieces of Music*	780.9
Sandburg, Carl. *The American Songbag*	782.42162
Sanneh, Kelefa. ★*Major Labels*	781.64
Seeger, Pete. *How to Play the 5-String Banjo*	787
Simmons, Sylvie. *I'm Your Man*	B
Smith, Danyel. *Shine Bright*	782.42164
Smith, Patti. *Collected Lyrics*	782
Smith, Patti. ★*Just Kids*	B
Smith, Patti. ★*Year of the Monkey*	B
Sondheim, Stephen. *Look, I Made a Hat*	782.1
Spera, Keith. *Groove Interrupted*	B
Spitzer, Michael. *The Musical Human*	780.9
Stanley, Bob. *Let's Do It*	781.64
Stempel, Larry. ★*Showtime*	792.609
Taupin, Bernie. *Scattershot*	B
Tweedy, Jeff. *How to Write One Song*	782.42
Waksman, Steve. *This Ain't the Summer of Love*	781.66

AUTHOR, TITLE, SERIES AND SUBJECT INDEX

Wald, Elijah. *American Epic*	781.64
Walker-Hill, Helen. *From Spirituals to Symphonies*	780
Warner, Daniel. *Live Wires*	786.7
Watts, Reggie. *Great Falls, MT*	B
Wenner, Jann. *Like a Rolling Stone*	B
White, Adam. ★*Motown*	781.644
Williams, Zach. *Rescue Story*	B

ARTS AND ENTERTAINMENT — MUSIC — CHRISTIAN AND GOSPEL

Gioia, Ted. *Work Songs*	782.42
Kot, Greg. *I'll Take You There*	B
Marovich, Robert M. *A City Called Heaven*	782.25

ARTS AND ENTERTAINMENT — MUSIC — CLASSICAL

Bergner, Daniel. ★*Sing for Your Life*	B
Berlin, Edward A. *King of Ragtime*	B
Bernstein, Burton. ★*Leonard Bernstein*	B
Bostridge, Ian. *Schubert's Winter Journey*	782.4
Burton-Hill, Clemency. ★*Year of Wonder*	780.9
Chernaik, Judith. *Schumann*	B
Eisler, Benita. ★*Chopin's Funeral*	B
Gardiner, John Eliot. *Bach*	B
Geck, Martin. ★*Johann Sebastian Bach*	780.92
Glass, Philip. *Words Without Music*	B
Gutman, Robert W. *Mozart*	B
Hamilton-Paterson, James. ★*Beethoven's Eroica*	784.18
Harris, Ellen T. *George Frideric Handel*	B
Haupt, Lyanda Lynn. *Mozart's Starling*	B
Hoffman, Miles. *The NPR Classical Music Companion*	780.3
Horowitz, Joseph. ★*Classical Music in America*	781.6
Hough, Stephen. *Rough Ideas*	786.2092
Johnson, Graham. *Poulenc*	B
Kennedy, Michael. *Richard Strauss*	B
Kennicott, Philip. *Counterpoint*	B
Kildea, Paul Francis. *Chopin's Piano*	B
Lockwood, Lewis. *Beethoven*	B
Mauceri, John. *For the Love of Music*	781.1
Mauceri, John. *Maestros and Their Music*	781.45
Morris, Edmund. *Beethoven*	B
Mueller, Melissa. *Alice's Piano*	B
Philip, Robert. *The Classical Music Lover's Companion to Orchestral Music*	784.2
Pollack, Howard. ★*George Gershwin*	B
Rosen, Charles. *The Classical Style*	780.9
Rusbridger, Alan. ★*Play It Again*	B
Sachs, Harvey. *The Ninth*	784.2
Servadio, Gaia. *Rossini*	B
Steinberg, Michael. *The Symphony*	784.2
Suchet, John. *Mozart*	B
Suchet, John. *Verdi*	782.1092
Swafford, Jan. ★*Beethoven*	B
Swafford, Jan. *Charles Ives*	B
Swafford, Jan. *Johannes Brahms*	B
Swafford, Jan. *Mozart*	B
Tunstall, Tricia. *Changing Lives*	780.71
Walsh, Stephen. ★*Debussy*	B
Warsaw-Fan Rauch, Arianna. ★*Declassified*	781.1
White, Richard Antoine. *I'm Possible*	B
Wolff, Christoph. *Johann Sebastian Bach*	B

ARTS AND ENTERTAINMENT — MUSIC — COUNTRY

Cash, Rosanne. ★*Composed*	B
Crowell, Rodney. *Chinaberry Sidewalks*	B
Duncan, Dayton. ★*Country Music*	781.642
Eliot, Marc. *The Hag*	B
Hemphill, Paul. *Lovesick Blues*	B
Hilburn, Robert. ★*Johnny Cash*	B
Lambert, Miranda. *Y'all Eat Yet?*	641.5976
Louvin, Charlie. *Satan Is Real*	920
Lynn, Loretta. ★*Me & Patsy Kickin' up Dust*	B
Lynn, Loretta. *Still Woman Enough*	B
McDonough, Jimmy. *Tammy Wynette*	B
Moss, Marissa R. *Her Country*	781.642
Nelson, Willie. *It's a Long Story*	B
Parton, Dolly. ★*Behind the Seams*	B
Parton, Dolly. ★*Dolly Parton, Songteller*	B
Price, Margo. *Maybe We'll Make It*	B
Russell, Tony. *Country Music Originals*	B
Travis, Randy. *Forever and Ever, Amen*	B
Williams, Lucinda. *Don't Tell Anybody the Secrets I Told You*	B
Zwonitzer, Mark. *Will You Miss Me When I'm Gone?*	920

ARTS AND ENTERTAINMENT — MUSIC — DISCO

Stanley, Bob. ★*The Story of the Bee Gees*	782.42164

ARTS AND ENTERTAINMENT — MUSIC — FOLK

Dunaway, David King. ★*How Can I Keep from Singing?*	B
Dylan, Bob. *Chronicles; Volume 1*	B
Gioia, Ted. *Work Songs*	782.42
Lang, Michael. *The Road to Woodstock*	781.66
Polenberg, Richard. *Hear My Sad Story*	782.42162
Powers, Ann. ★*Traveling*	B
Sandburg, Carl. *The American Songbag*	782.42162
Santopietro, Tom. *The Sound of Music Story*	791.43
Strom, Yale. *The Book of Klezmer*	781.62
Thomas, Richard F. ★*Why Bob Dylan Matters*	782.42164
Wilkinson, Alec. *The Protest Singer*	B
Yaffe, David. *Reckless Daughter*	782.42164
Young, Rob. *Electric Eden*	781.62
Zack, Ian. *Odetta*	B

ARTS AND ENTERTAINMENT — MUSIC — INSTRUMENTS

Gaddy, K. R. ★*Well of Souls*	787
Hafner, Katie. *A Romance on Three Legs*	786.2092
Port, Ian S. *The Birth of Loud*	787.87
White, Richard Antoine. *I'm Possible*	B
Whitney, Craig R. *All the Stops*	786.5

ARTS AND ENTERTAINMENT — MUSIC — JAZZ AND THE BLUES

Alexander, Paul. *Bitter Crop*	B
Armstrong, Louis. *Louis Armstrong, in His Own Words*	B
Basie, Count. *Good Morning Blues*	B
Brothers, Thomas David. ★*Louis Armstrong, Master of Modernism*	B
Chinen, Nate. *Playing Changes*	781.6509
Cole, Natalie. *Angel on My Shoulder*	B
Cooke, Mervyn. *The Chronicle of Jazz*	781.6509
Crouch, Stanley. *Kansas City Lightning*	B
Dance, Stanley. ★*The World of Earl Hines*	B
DeVeaux, Scott Knowles. *Jazz*	781.65
Dregni, Michael. *Django*	B
Ferris, William R. *Give My Poor Heart Ease*	781.643
Friedwald, Will. *The Great Jazz and Pop Vocal Albums*	016.78
Friedwald, Will. ★*Sinatra! the Song Is You*	782.42164
Friedwald, Will. *Straighten up and Fly Right*	782.42164
Gabbard, Krin. *Better Git It in Your Soul*	B
Giddins, Gary. *Bing Crosby*	B
Giddins, Gary. *Bing Crosby*	B
Giddins, Gary. *Weather Bird*	781.6509
Gioia, Ted. *The History of Jazz*	781.6509
Gioia, Ted. *Work Songs*	782.42
Gray, Michael. *Hand Me My Travelin' Shoes*	B
Jones, Booker T. *Time Is Tight*	B
Kahn, Ashley. *The House That Trane Built*	781.6509
Kaplan, James. *3 Shades of Blue*	920
Kaplan, James. *Sinatra*	782.42164
King, B. B. ★*Blues All Around Me*	B
Lees, Gene. *You Can't Steal a Gift*	B
Levy, Aidan. *Saxophone Colossus*	B
Lomax, Alan. ★*The Land Where the Blues Began*	781.643
Marsalis, Wynton. *Moving to Higher Ground*	781.65
McBride, James. *Kill 'Em and Leave*	B
McBrien, William. *Cole Porter*	B
McCormick, Mack. *Biography of a Phantom*	782.421643
Morgenstern, Dan. *Living with Jazz*	781.65
Morton, Brian. ★*The Penguin Jazz Guide*	016
Myers, Marc. *Why Jazz Happened*	781.65
Oppedisano, Tony. *Sinatra and Me*	B
Ratliff, Ben. *The Jazz Ear*	781.6509
Ribowsky, Mark. *Dreams to Remember*	B
Sandke, Randy. *Where the Dark and the Light Folks Meet*	781.6509
Teachout, Terry. *Duke*	B
Teachout, Terry. *Pops*	B
Threadgill, Henry. *Easily Slip into Another World*	B
Torgoff, Martin. *Bop Apocalypse*	781.65
Tye, Larry. ★*The Jazzmen*	781.6509
Wald, Elijah. ★*Escaping the Delta*	B
Ward, Geoffrey C. *Jazz*	781.6509
Wolfe, Charles K. ★*The Life and Legend of Leadbelly*	B
Wood, Damon. *Working for the Man, Playing in the Band*	782.42164

ARTS AND ENTERTAINMENT — MUSIC — OPERA

Berger, William. *Puccini Without Excuses*	782.1
Berger, William. *Verdi with a Vengeance*	B
Gay, John. *The Beggar's Opera*	782.1

PUBLIC LIBRARY CORE COLLECTION: NONFICTION
Twentieth Edition

Keiler, Allan. *Marian Anderson*	B
Rose, Michael. *The Birth of an Opera*	782.1
Ross, Alex. *Wagnerism*	B

ARTS AND ENTERTAINMENT — MUSIC — POP

Breihan, Tom. ★*The Number Ones*	782.42164
Friedwald, Will. *The Great Jazz and Pop Vocal Albums*	016.78
Gabriel, Mary. *Madonna*	B
Greenman, Ben. *Dig If You Will the Picture*	B
Hay, Matt. *Soundtrack of Silence*	B
Jefferson, Margo. *On Michael Jackson*	B
John, Elton. ★*Me*	B
McCartney, Paul. ★*1964*	782.42166
Sloan, Nate. *Switched on Pop*	781.64
Spears, Britney. *The Woman in Me*	B
Stanley, Bob. *Let's Do It*	781.64
Vogel, Joseph. *Man in the Music*	B
Wald, Elijah. *How the Beatles Destroyed Rock 'N' Roll*	781.64

ARTS AND ENTERTAINMENT — MUSIC — RAP AND R&B

Abdurraqib, Hanif. *Go Ahead in the Rain*	782.421649
Abrams, Jonathan P. D. ★*The Come Up*	782.421649
Ashon, Will. *Chamber Music*	782.421649
Bego, Mark. *Aretha Franklin*	B
Black Thought. *The Upcycled Self*	B
Chang, Jeff. *Can't Stop, Won't Stop*	306.4
Charnas, Dan. *The Big Payback*	306.4
Chuck D. *Chuck D Presents This Day in Rap and Hip-Hop History*	782.421649
Dyson, Michael Eric. *Holler If You Hear Me*	B
Edwards, Paul. *The Concise Guide to Hip-Hop Music*	782.421649
Fernando, S. H., Jr. *From the Streets of Shaolin*	782.421
Ghostface Killah. *Rise of a Killah*	B
Grandmaster Flash. *The Adventures of Grandmaster Flash*	B
Greenburg, Zack O'Malley. *3 Kings*	782.421649
Hope, Clover. *The Motherlode*	920
Iandoli, Kathy. *Baby Girl*	B
Iandoli, Kathy. *God Save the Queens*	782.421649
Jackson family. *The Jacksons*	782.421644
Kenner, Rob. *The Marathon Don't Stop*	B
Kweli, Talib. *Vibrate Higher*	B
Mike D. *Beastie Boys Book*	782.42164
Moore, Marcus J. *The Butterfly Effect*	B
Neville, Aaron. *Tell It Like It Is*	B
Prince. *The Beautiful Ones*	B
Questlove. ★*Hip-Hop Is History*	782.421649
Questlove. *Mo' Meta Blues*	782.42164
Ribowsky, Mark. *Signed, Sealed, and Delivered*	B
Ribowsky, Mark. *The Supremes*	B
Robinson, Staci. ★*Tupac Shakur*	B
Simmons, Nadirah. ★*First Things First*	782.42164
Stone, Sly. *Thank You (Falettinme Be Mice Elf Agin)*	B
Westhoff, Ben. *Dirty South*	782.421649
Westhoff, Ben. *Original Gangstas*	782.421649

ARTS AND ENTERTAINMENT — MUSIC — ROCK

Albertine, Viv. *Clothes, Clothes, Clothes. Music, Music, Music*	B
Alden, Ginger. *Elvis and Ginger*	B
Almond, Steve. *Rock and Roll Will Save Your Life*	781.6
Bono. ★*Surrender*	B
Broven, John. *Record Makers and Breakers*	B
Brown, Craig. *150 Glimpses of the Beatles*	920
Browne, David. *Crosby, Stills, Nash and Young*	920
Browne, David. *So Many Roads*	B
Buckland, Gail. *Who Shot Rock & Roll*	779
Carlin, Peter Ames. *Bruce*	B
Clapton, Eric. *Clapton*	B
Cohen, Rich. *The Sun and the Moon and the Rolling Stones*	782.42166
Coleman, Rick. ★*Blue Monday*	B
Connolly, Ray. *Being John Lennon*	B
Costello, Elvis. *Unfaithful Music & Disappearing Ink*	B
Cross, Charles R. *Here We Are Now*	782.42164
Cross, Charles R. *Room Full of Mirrors*	B
Davidson, Mark A. ★*Bob Dylan*	B
Davis, Stephen. *Gold Dust Woman*	B
DeCurtis, Anthony. *Lou Reed*	B
Dickinson, Bruce. *What Does This Button Do?*	B
Doggett, Peter. *You Never Give Me Your Money*	B
Etheridge, Melissa. *Talking to My Angels*	B
Fogerty, John. *Fortunate Son*	B
Garcia, Mayte. *The Most Beautiful*	920
Garfunkel, Art. *What Is It All but Luminous*	782.42164
George-Warren, Holly. ★*Janis*	B
Gordon, Kim. *Girl in a Band*	B
Greenman, Ben. *Dig If You Will the Picture*	B
Guesdon, Jean-Michel. *All the Songs*	782.42166
Hagan, Joe. *Sticky Fingers*	B
Hanna, Kathleen. *Rebel Girl*	B
Harry, Debbie. *Face It*	B
Heller, Jason. *Strange Stars*	781.6609
Hepworth, David. *Uncommon People*	B
Hermes, Will. *Lou Reed*	B
Hopkins, Jerry. *No One Here Gets Out Alive*	B
Hopper, Jessica. *The First Collection of Criticism by a Living Female Rock Critic*	781.66
Hyden, Steven. *Long Road*	782.42166
Hyden, Steven. *Twilight of the Gods*	781.6609
Jarnow, Jesse. *Big Day Coming*	B
Johnson, Brian. *The Lives of Brian*	B
Jollett, Mikel. ★*Hollywood Park*	B
Jones, Dylan. *David Bowie*	B
Kaye, Lenny. ★*Lightning Striking*	781.66
Kozinn, Allan. *The McCartney Legacy*	B
Lanegan, Mark. *Sing Backwards and Weep*	B
Lang, Michael. *The Road to Woodstock*	781.66
Mahon, Maureen. ★*Black Diamond Queens*	782.421
Margotin, Philippe. *The Rolling Stones*	782.42166
McCartney, Paul. *The Lyrics*	782.42166
McDonald, Greg (Producer). *Elvis and the Colonel*	920
McDonald, Michael. ★*What a Fool Believes*	B
McKeen, William. *Everybody Had an Ocean*	781.6609
Mehr, Bob. *Trouble Boys*	920
Moore, Thurston. *Sonic Life*	B
Morley, Paul. *The Age of Bowie*	B
Murray, Charles Shaar. *Crosstown Traffic*	B
Norman, Philip. *George Harrison*	B
Norman, Philip. *John Lennon*	B
Norman, Philip. ★*Wild Thing*	B
O'Connor, Sinead. ★*Rememberings*	B
Osbourne, Ozzy. *I Am Ozzy*	B
Perry, Joe. *Rocks*	B
Phair, Liz. *Horror Stories*	B
Povey, Glenn. *Echoes*	782.42166
Prince. *The Beautiful Ones*	B
Reynolds, Simon. *Shock and Awe*	781.6609
Richards, Keith. *Life*	B
Robb, John. *Punk Rock*	781.6609
Robertson, Robbie. ★*Testimony*	B
Santana, Carlos. *The Universal Tone*	B
Schemel, Patty. *Hit so Hard*	B
Smith, Patti. ★*M Train*	B
Spitz, Bob. ★*The Beatles*	B
Spitz, Bob. *Led Zeppelin*	782.42166
Springsteen, Bruce. ★*Born to Run*	B
Stanley, Paul. *Backstage Pass*	B
Stanley, Paul. *Face the Music*	B
Thomas, Richard F. ★*Why Bob Dylan Matters*	782.42164
Thomson, Graeme. *George Harrison*	B
Tolinski, Brad. *Light and Shade*	B
Turner, Tina. ★*Happiness Becomes You*	158.1
Tweedy, Jeff. *Let's Go (so We Can Get Back)*	B
Wald, Elijah. *Dylan Goes Electric!*	782.42164
Wald, Elijah. *How the Beatles Destroyed Rock 'N' Roll*	781.64
White, Charles. *The Life and Times of Little Richard*	B
White, Ryan. *Jimmy Buffett*	782.42164
Wiederhorn, Jon. *Louder Than Hell*	781.6609
Winder, Elizabeth. *Parachute Women*	782.42164
Womack, Kenneth. *All Things Must Pass Away*	781.66
Young, Neil. *Waging Heavy Peace*	B
Zanes, Warren. *Deliver Me from Nowhere*	782.42164
Zanes, Warren. *Petty*	B

ARTS AND ENTERTAINMENT — PAINTING, DRAWING, AND SCULPTURE

Adams, Laurie. ★*Italian Renaissance Art*	709.45
Ai, Weiwei. *Ai Weiwei*	709.51
Ai, Weiwei. *Zodiac*	741.5
Albers, Patricia. *Joan Mitchell*	B
Amore, Anthony M. *The Art of the Con*	702.8
Aquino, Lucia. *Leonardo Da Vinci*	709.2

AUTHOR, TITLE, SERIES AND SUBJECT INDEX

Arnason, H. Harvard. ★*History of Modern Art*	709.04
Baker, Nicholson. *Finding a Likeness*	B
Barnes, Julian. *Keeping an Eye Open*	709.04
Barnitz, Jacqueline. *Twentieth-Century Art of Latin America*	709.8
Beard, Mary. ★*How Do We Look*	704.9
Bell, Julian. *Van Gogh*	B
Berlo, Janet Catherine. ★*Native North American Art*	704.03
Bilal, Wafaa. *Shoot an Iraqi*	B
Birch, Helen. *Freehand*	741.2
Blom, Onno. *Young Rembrandt*	B
Bosker, Bianca. *Get the Picture*	701
Bradley, Barbara. *Drawing People*	743.4
Brehm, Matthew T. *Drawing Perspective*	742
Brenwall, Cynthia S. *The Central Park*	974.7
Brewer, John. *The American Leonardo*	759.5
Chelsea, David. *Perspective in Action*	741.5
Clements, Jonathan. *The Anime Encyclopedia*	791.43
Cohen-Solal, Annie. *Mark Rothko*	759.13
Crilley, Mark. *The Realism Challenge*	751.4
Cross, William R. *Winslow Homer*	759.13
Cumming, Laura. ★*The Vanishing Velazquez*	759.6
Dasal, Jennifer. *Artcurious*	709
De Reyna, Rudy. *How to Draw What You See*	741.2
Dery, Mark. *Born to Be Posthumous*	B
Dolnick, Edward. *The Rescue Artist*	364.16
Eagle, Ellen. *Pastel Painting Atelier*	741.2
Edsel, Robert M. *The Monuments Men*	940.53
Edwards, Betty. *Color*	752
Edwards, Betty. *Drawing on the Right Side of the Brain*	741.2
English, Charlie. *The Gallery of Miracles and Madness*	709.04
Feaver, William. ★*The Lives of Lucian Freud*	B
Felisbret, Eric. *Graffiti New York*	751.7
Finkel, Michael. *The Art Thief*	364.1628
FitzGerald, Michael C. ★*Picasso and American Art*	709.73
Flor, Martina. *The Golden Secrets of Lettering*	745.6
Frey, Julia Bloch. *Toulouse-Lautrec*	B
Gerdts, William H. *American Impressionism*	759.13
Glynn, Kathy. *Hand Lettering Step by Step*	745.6
Gohr, Siegfried. ★*Magritte*	759.9493
Gompertz, Will. *What Are You Looking At?*	709
Goodman, Simon. *The Orpheus Clock*	940.53
Gopnik, Blake. ★*Warhol*	B
Graham-Dixon, Andrew. *Caravaggio*	B
Griffel, Lois. *Painting the Impressionist Landscape*	751.45
Hale, Robert Beverly. *Anatomy Lessons from the Great Masters*	743.4
Hale, Sheila. *Titian*	B
Hall, James. *The Self-Portrait*	704.9
Hand, Diana. *Draw Horses in 15 Minutes*	743.6
Harmon, Katharine A. *The Map as Art*	760
Hart, Christopher. *Cartooning for the Beginner*	741.5
Hart, Christopher. *Human Anatomy Made Amazingly Easy*	743.4
Harvey, Eleanor Jones. *The Civil War and American Art*	740.9
Herdrich, Stephanie L. ★*Sargent*	759.13
Herrera, Hayden. *Frida*	B
Herrera, Hayden. *Listening to Stone*	B
Hesse, Maria. ★*Frida Kahlo*	B
Hoban, Phoebe. *Alice Neel*	B
Holzer, Harold. *Monument Man*	B
Hughes, Robert. *Goya*	B
Huston, Steve. *Figure Drawing for Artists*	743.4
Isaacson, Walter. ★*Leonardo Da Vinci*	B
James, Jamie. *The Glamour of Strangeness*	700.1
Johnson, Paul. ★*Art*	709
Jung, Kwan. *Chinese Brush Painting*	751.4
Kahlo, Frida. *The Diary of Frida Kahlo*	B
Kampen-O'Riley, Michael. *Art Beyond the West*	709
Kandel, Eric R. *The Age of Insight*	154.2
Katsushika, Hokusai. *Hokusai*	769.92
Kelder, Diane. *The Great Book of French Impressionism*	759.4
Kersey, Geoff. *Painting Successful Watercolours from Photographs*	751.42
King, Ross. *Florence*	759.5
King, Ross. *The Judgment of Paris*	759.4
King, Ross. *Leonardo and the Last Supper*	759.5
King, Ross. ★*Mad Enchantment*	759.4
King, Ross. *Michelangelo & the Pope's Ceiling*	759.5
Klastorin, Michael. *Close Encounters of the Third Kind*	791.43
Kline, Fred R. *Leonardo's Holy Child*	741.09
Kloosterboer, Lorena. *Painting in Acrylics*	751.42
Knausgaard, Karl Ove. *So Much Longing in so Little Space*	759.81
Leal, Brigitte. *The Ultimate Picasso*	B
Levin, Gail. *Edward Hopper*	759.13
Livingston, Jane. *The Paintings of Joan Mitchell*	759.13
Loomis, Andrew. *Figure Drawing for All It's Worth*	743.4
Lozano, Luis-Martin. *Frida Kahlo*	759.972
Lucey, Donna M. *Sargent's Women*	920
Lynes, Barbara Buhler. *Georgia O'Keeffe Museum Collections*	759.13
Marcus, Leonard S. ★*Pictured Worlds*	741.6
Marine, Carol. *Daily Painting*	751.4
Marnham, Patrick. *Dreaming with His Eyes Open*	B
Matisse, Henri. *Henri Matisse*	709.2
McKinley, Richard. *Pastel Pointers*	741.2
McPhee, John. *The Ransom of Russian Art*	709
Meder, Danielle. *Draw Fashion Now*	741.6
Micklewright, Keith. *Drawing*	741.2
Miller, Judith. *Miller's Arts & Crafts*	745.409034
Morris, Desmond. *The Lives of the Surrealists*	B
Moyle, Franny. *Turner*	B
O'Connor, Birgit. *Watercolor Essentials*	751.42
Obrist, Hans-Ulrich. *Ways of Curating*	707.5
Ogura, Yoshiko. *The Complete Guide to Drawing for Beginners*	740
Owen, Imogen. *Modern Calligraphy Workshop*	745.6
Painter, Nell Irvin. *Old in Art School*	B
Parkin, Simon. *An Illustrated History of 151 Video Games*	794.8
Parks, Carrie. *Secrets to Drawing Realistic Faces*	743.4
Peiffer, Prudence. *The Slip*	709.73
Perl, Jed. *Calder*	B
Perl, Jed. ★*Calder*	B
Price, Maggie. *Painting with Pastels*	741.2
Prideaux, Sue. *Edvard Munch*	B
Prose, Francine. *Caravaggio*	759.5
Robinson, Mario Andres. *Lessons in Realistic Watercolor*	751.42
Robinson, Roxana. *Georgia O'Keeffe*	B
Rodriguez, Dina. *The Big Awesome Book of Hand & Chalk Lettering*	745.6
Roe, Sue. *In Montmartre*	920
Roe, Sue. *The Private Lives of the Impressionists*	920
Rothko, Mark. *Rothko*	759.13
Ryder, Anthony. *The Artist's Complete Guide to Figure Drawing*	743.4
Salle, David. *How to See*	709.04
Schama, Simon. *The Power of Art*	709
Scheinberger, Felix. *Dare to Sketch*	741.2
Scotti, R. A. *Vanished Smile*	759.5
Secrest, Meryle. *Modigliani*	B
Sewell, Darrel. *Thomas Eakins*	759.13
Shackelford, George T. M. *Monet*	759.4
Shaw, Jennifer Laurie. *Exist Otherwise*	709.2
Shepherd, Margaret. *Learn Calligraphy*	745.6
Shnayerson, Michael. *Boom*	701
Smee, Sebastian. *The Art of Rivalry*	700.92
Solomon, Deborah. *American Mirror*	B
Solomon, Deborah. *Jackson Pollock*	B
Spurling, Hilary. *Matisse the Master*	B
Stahr, Celia. *Frida in America*	B
Staiti, Paul J. *Of Arms and Artists*	B
Stanislaus, Grace C. *Instill & Inspire*	704.03
Stein, Judith E. *Eye of the Sixties*	B
Sykes, Christopher Simon. *David Hockney*	B
Sykes, Christopher Simon. *David Hockney*	B
Tetro, Tony. *Con/Artist*	B
Thorpe, Molly Suber. *Modern Calligraphy*	745.6
Tomlinson, Janis A. ★*Goya*	B
Unger, Miles. *Picasso and the Painting That Shocked the World*	759.4
Updike, John. *Always Looking*	700
Ustvedt, Oystein. *Edvard Munch*	759.81
Ward, Gerald W. R. *Chihuly*	709
Ward, Ossian. *Look Again*	750.1
Warren, Rosanna. *Max Jacob*	B
Whistler, Catherine. *Venice and Drawing, 1500-1800*	741.09
Willenbrink, Mark. *Drawing for the Absolute Beginner*	741.2
Winslow, Valerie L. *Classic Human Anatomy*	743.4
Wullschlager, Jackie. ★*Chagall*	B
Zickefoose, Julie. *Baby Birds*	751.42

ARTS AND ENTERTAINMENT — PHOTOGRAPHY

Alinder, Mary Street. *Group F.64*	770.92
Ang, Tom. *Digital Photographer's Handbook*	771
Ang, Tom. *Digital Photography Masterclass*	770
Ang, Tom. *Photography*	770.9

PUBLIC LIBRARY CORE COLLECTION: NONFICTION
Twentieth Edition

Arnold, Jeremy. *Turner Classic Movies*	791.43
Barker, Nigel. *Models of Influence*	746.92092
Begley, Adam. *The Great Nadar*	B
Bowles, Hamish. *Vogue & the Metropolitan Museum of Art Costume Institute*	746.9
Brandow, Todd. *Edward Steichen*	770.92
Buckland, Gail. *Who Shot Sports*	779
Buell, Hal. *Moments*	070.4
Burke, Carolyn. *Lee Miller*	B
Company, David. *The Open Road*	770
Chace, Teri Dunn. *Seeing Seeds*	581.4
Cole, Teju. *Blind Spot*	770
Cox, Caroline. *The World Atlas of Street Fashion*	391.009
Curtis, Edward S. *Edward S. Curtis*	770.92
Evans, Walker. *American Photographs*	779
Fagans, Michael. *iPhone Photography for Everybody*	770
Fischer, Paul. *The Man Who Invented Motion Pictures*	791.43
Fordham, Demetrius. ★*If You're Bored with Your Camera Read This Book*	770.23
Freeman, Michael. *The Photographer's Mind*	770
Friedman, Elias Weiss. *The Dogist*	779
Galassi, Peter. *Ansel Adams in Yosemite Valley*	770.92
Gatcum, Chris. ★*The Beginner's Photography Guide*	770
Gefter, Philip. *What Becomes a Legend Most*	B
Gordon, Linda. *Dorothea Lange*	B
Gruen, Bob. *Right Place, Right Time*	B
Gulbrandsen, Don. *Edward Sheriff Curtis*	970.004
Hahn, Emanuel. *Koreatown Dreaming*	979.4
Heacox, Kim. *National Geographic the National Parks*	363.6
Horenstein, Henry. *Digital Photography*	770
Huffman, Alan. *Here I Am*	B
Lee, Corky. ★*Corky Lee's Asian America*	770
Leibovitz, Annie. *Women*	779
Lubow, Arthur. *Diane Arbus*	B
Manseau, Peter. *The Apparitionists*	B
Marks, Ann. *Vivian Maier Developed*	778.9
McCurry, Steve. *The Iconic Photographs*	779.092
Menuez, Doug. *Fearless Genius*	979.4
Morris, Errol. *Believing Is Seeing*	770.9
Peterson, Bryan. *Learning to See Creatively*	770
Peterson, Bryan. *Understanding Exposure*	771
Rinehart, Lorissa. *First to the Front*	B
Sartore, Joel. ★*The Photo Ark*	779
Shahidi, Afshin. *Prince*	B
Smith, Joel. *Edward Steichen*	779
Smith, R. J. *American Witness*	B
Souza, Pete. *Obama*	973.932
Souza, Pete. *Shade*	973.932
Stevens, Norma. *Avedon*	B
Szarkowski, John. *Ansel Adams at 100*	B
Taylor, David. *Digital Photography Complete Course*	770
Van Agtmael, Peter. *Look at the USA*	070
Van Haaften, Julia. ★*Berenice Abbott*	B
Watkins, Carleton E. *Carleton Watkins*	778.9
Welty, Eudora. *One Time, One Place*	976.2
Willis, Deborah. *Reflections in Black*	770
Wilson, Robert. *Mathew Brady*	B
Wong, Stephen. *Smithsonian Baseball*	796.357
Woods, Christopher. *Gardenlust*	635.022

ARTS AND ENTERTAINMENT — RADIO

Dunning, John. *On the Air*	791.44
Duran, Elvis. *Where Do I Begin?*	B
Napoli, Lisa. *Susan, Linda, Nina & Cokie*	920
Schwartz, A. Brad. ★*Broadcast Hysteria*	791.44

ARTS AND ENTERTAINMENT — THEATER

Bacall, Lauren. *By Myself and Then Some*	B
Bigsby, Christopher William Edgar. *Arthur Miller*	B
Bloom, Ken. *Broadway Musicals*	792.6
Blumenthal, Eileen. *Puppetry*	791.5
Brockett, Oscar G. *History of the Theatre*	792
Bryson, Bill. *Shakespeare*	B
Butler, Isaac. *The Method*	792.02
Butler, Isaac. *The World Only Spins Forward*	812
Dromgoole, Dominic. *Hamlet Globe to Globe*	792.9
Essin, Christin. *Stage Designers in Early Twentieth-Century America*	792.02
Gillette, J. Michael. *Designing with Light*	792
Gillette, J. Michael. *Theatrical Design and Production*	792.02
Greenblatt, Stephen. ★*Will in the World*	B
Greenfield, Robert. *True West*	B
Grey, Joel. *Master of Ceremonies*	B
Hall, Jake. *The Art of Drag*	792.8
Hartigan, Patti. *August Wilson*	B
Hischak, Thomas S. *The Oxford Companion to the American Musical*	782.1
Hudes, Quiara Alegria. ★*My Broken Language*	B
Hytner, Nicholas. *Balancing Acts*	B
Jacobs, Alexandra. *Still Here*	B
Kapilow, Robert. ★*Listening for America*	782.42164
Karim-Cooper, Farah. ★*The Great White Bard*	822.33
Lane, Stewart F. *Black Broadway*	792.089
Lloyd Webber, Andrew. *Unmasked*	B
Maslon, Laurence. ★*Broadway*	782.1
Merritt, Tyler. *I Take My Coffee Black*	791.4302
Miranda, Lin-Manuel. *Hamilton*	782.1
Mordden, Ethan. *Anything Goes*	782.1
Mordden, Ethan. *Ziegfeld*	B
Niven, Penelope. *Thornton Wilder*	B
Norwich, John Julius. *Shakespeare's Kings*	822.33
O'Brien, Jack. *Jack Be Nimble*	B
O'Connor, Garry. *Ian McKellen*	B
Ottemiller, John H. *Ottemiller's Index to Plays in Collections*	016
Perry, Imani. *Looking for Lorraine*	B
Posnanski, Joe. ★*The Life and Afterlife of Harry Houdini*	793.8
Purdum, Todd S. *Something Wonderful*	B
Quindt, Svetlana. *The Costume Making Guide*	646.4
Rannells, Andrew. *Too Much Is Not Enough*	792.02
Rannells, Andrew. *Uncle of the Year*	B
Riedel, Michael. *Razzle Dazzle*	792.09
Riedel, Michael. *Singular Sensation*	792
Rodgers, Mary. *Shy*	B
Sartre, Jean-Paul. ★*No Exit, and Three Other Plays*	842
Shaffer, Peter. ★*Equus*	822
Shapiro, James. ★*The Playbook*	792
Shapiro, James. *Shakespeare in a Divided America*	822.33
Shields, Charles J. *Lorraine Hansberry*	B
Smith, Emma. *This Is Shakespeare*	822.33
Stanislavsky, Konstantin. *An Actor's Work*	792.02
Turan, Kenneth. ★*Free for All*	B
Viertel, Jack. *The Secret Life of the American Musical*	792.609
Volpe, Joseph. *The Toughest Show on Earth*	B
Warren, Louis S. *Buffalo Bill's America*	B
Wasson, Sam. ★*Improv Nation*	792.02
Williams, Tennessee. *Plays, 1937-1955*	812
Williams, Tennessee. *Plays, 1957-1980*	812
Wojczuk, Tana. *Lady Romeo*	B
Zemeckis, Leslie Harter. *Behind the Burly Q*	792.7

ARTS AND ENTERTAINMENT — THEATER — PLAYS

Albee, Edward. ★*Who's Afraid of Virginia Woolf?*	812
Auburn, David. *Proof*	812
Bolt, Robert. *A Man for All Seasons*	822
Camus, Albert. *Caligula & Three Other Plays*	842
Chekhov, Anton Pavlovich. *The Complete Plays*	891.72
Coward, Noel. *Three Plays*	822
Edson, Margaret. *Wit*	812
Fugard, Athol. ★*"master Harold"—And the Boys*	822
Gibson, William. ★*The Miracle Worker*	812
Goodrich, Frances. *The Diary of Anne Frank*	812
Kushner, Tony. *Angels in America*	812
Marlowe, Christopher. *The Complete Plays*	822
Nemiroff, Robert. *To Be Young, Gifted, and Black*	B
Osborne, John. *Look Back in Anger*	822
Rankine, Claudia. *The White Card*	812
Rose, Reginald. *Twelve Angry Men*	812
Shaffer, Peter. *Peter Shaffer's Amadeus*	822
Shakespeare, William. ★*The Complete Works*	822.33
Shanley, John Patrick. *Doubt*	812
Shaw, Bernard. *Heartbreak House*	822
Shaw, Bernard. *Man and Superman*	822
Shaw, Bernard. ★*Pygmalion*	822
Sheridan, Richard Brinsley. *The School for Scandal and Other Plays*	822
Stoppard, Tom. *Arcadia*	822
Stoppard, Tom. *The Invention of Love*	822
Stoppard, Tom. ★*Rosencrantz & Guildenstern Are Dead*	822
Thomas, Dylan. *Under Milk Wood*	822.91
Wilde, Oscar. ★*The Importance of Being Earnest and Other Plays*	822
Wilder, Thornton. *Our Town*	812
Wilder, Thornton. *Thornton Wilder*	812

AUTHOR, TITLE, SERIES AND SUBJECT INDEX

Williams, Tennessee. *Plays, 1937-1955*	812
Williams, Tennessee. *Plays, 1957-1980*	812
Williams, Tennessee. ★*A Streetcar Named Desire*	812
Wilson, August. *Fences*	812
Wilson, August. *King Hedley II*	812
Wilson, August. *Ma Rainey's Black Bottom*	812
Wilson, August. *The Piano Lesson*	812
Wilson, August. *Two Trains Running*	812

ARTS AND ENTERTAINMENT — WRITING AND PUBLISHING

Achebe, Chinua. *The Education of a British-Protected Child*	B
Ackmann, Martha. ★*These Fevered Days*	B
Adams, Abigail. *Abigail Adams*	973.4
Aeschylus. *The Oresteia*	882
Allende, Isabel. *My Invented Country*	B
Allende, Isabel. *The Sum of Our Days*	B
Anders, Charlie Jane. ★*Never Say You Can't Survive*	808.02
Angelou, Maya. *I Know Why the Caged Bird Sings*	B
Angelou, Maya. *Letter to My Daughter*	814
Angelou, Maya. *A Song Flung up to Heaven*	B
Anolik, Lili. *Hollywood's Eve*	B
Anthony, Carl Sferrazza. *Camera Girl*	B
Appleman, Deborah. *Literature and the New Culture Wars*	807
Aristotle. ★*The Basic Works of Aristotle*	185
Attenberg, Jami. *1000 Words*	808.02
Atwood, Margaret. *Burning Questions*	814
Atwood, Margaret. *In Other Worlds*	813
Auster, Paul. *Burning Boy*	B
Bailey, Richard W. *Speaking American*	427
Barker, Elspeth. ★*Notes from the Henhouse*	828
Baron, Dennis E. *What's Your Pronoun?*	425.55
Baron, Martin. ★*Collision of Power*	070.4
Bartlett, Rosamund. ★*Tolstoy*	B
Basbanes, Nicholas A. ★*Cross of Snow*	B
Basbanes, Nicholas A. *Every Book Its Reader*	028
Bass, Rick. *The Traveling Feast*	B
Bass, Rick. *Why I Came West*	333.78
Bate, Jonathan. *Radical Wordsworth*	B
Batuman, Elif. *The Possessed*	891.7
Beckett, Samuel. *The Letters of Samuel Beckett*	848
Bell, Madison Smartt. *Child of Light*	B
Bellos, David. *The Novel of the Century*	843
Bernstein, Carl. ★*Chasing History*	B
Berry, Wendell. *Imagination in Place*	814
Binyon, T. J. *Pushkin*	B
Blaisdell, Robert. *Creating Anna Karenina*	891.7
Bloom, Harold. *Shakespeare*	822.33
Bloom, Harold. *The Western Canon*	809
Bly, Robert. *More Than True*	398.2
Borges, Jorge Luis. *Selected Non-Fictions*	864
Boswell, James. ★*The Life of Samuel Johnson*	B
Bowker, Gordon. ★*James Joyce*	B
Bradbury, Ray. ★*Remembrance*	813
Bragg, Melvyn. *The Adventure of English*	420
Bram, Christopher. *Eminent Outlaws*	920
Brandreth, Gyles Daubeney. *Have You Eaten Grandma?*	428
Briggs, Julia. *Virginia Woolf*	823
Briggs, Kate. *This Little Art*	418
Brinkley, Alan. ★*The Publisher*	B
Brown, Noah. *Reading Together*	028.5
Brown, Terence. *The Life of W.B. Yeats*	B
Bryson, Bill. *The Life and Times of the Thunderbolt Kid*	B
Bryson, Bill. *Shakespeare*	B
Burns, Eric. *Infamous Scribblers*	071
Burt, Stephanie. *Don't Read Poetry*	811
Calhoun, Ada. *Also a Poet*	B
Calvino, Italo. *Collection of Sand*	854
Camus, Albert. *Resistance, Rebellion, and Death*	844
Capote, Truman. ★*Portraits and Observations*	814
Capote, Truman. *Too Brief a Treat*	B
Caro, Robert A. ★*Working*	B
Castleman, Michael. *The Untold Story of Books*	381
Cather, Willa. *The Selected Letters of Willa Cather*	B
Chabon, Michael. *Bookends*	818
Chabon, Michael. *Manhood for Amateurs*	B
Chabon, Michael. *Maps and Legends*	801
Cheever, Susan. *American Bloomsbury*	920
Clark, Heather. ★*Red Comet*	B
Cleage, Pearl. *Things I Should Have Told My Daughter*	B

Clifton, Lucille. *Mercy*	811
Coetzee, J. M. *Late Essays, 2006-2017*	824
Coffin, Judith G. *Sex, Love, and Letters*	848
Cohen, Deborah. *Last Call at the Hotel Imperial*	070.92
Collins, Max Allan. *Spillane*	B
Collins, Paul. *The Book of William*	016.8223
Conradi, Peter J. *Iris*	B
Conroy, Pat. *My Losing Season*	B
Corbett, Emily. *In Transition*	809
Cott, Jonathan. *There's a Mystery There*	813
Crase, Douglas. *On Autumn Lake*	809
Crawford, Robert. *Eliot After the Waste Land*	B
Crespino, Joseph. *Atticus Finch*	B
Cronkite, Walter. *Cronkite's War*	070.4
Cronkite, Walter. *A Reporter's Life*	B
Crowther, Gail. *Three-Martini Afternoons at the Ritz*	920
Crystal, David. ★*How Language Works*	410
Crystal, David. *Spell It Out*	421
Crystal, David. ★*The Stories of English*	427
Crystal, David. *The Story of English in 100 Words*	422
Curzan, Anne. ★*Says Who?*	428
Cusk, Rachel. *Coventry*	814
Dante Alighieri. *Inferno*	851
Danticat, Edwidge. *The Art of Death*	809
Darkshire, Oliver. *Once Upon a Tome*	B
Davis, Margaret Leslie. *The Lost Gutenberg*	093
Dawidziak, Mark. *A Mystery of Mysteries*	B
Dearborn, Mary V. *Carson McCullers*	B
Dearborn, Mary V. *Ernest Hemingway*	B
Dennison, Matthew. *The Man in the Willows*	B
Dery, Mark. *Born to Be Posthumous*	B
Deutsch, Babette. *Poetry Handbook*	808.1
Deutscher, Guy. ★*Through the Language Glass*	410
Di Cintio, Marcello. *Pay No Heed to the Rockets*	956.9405
Didion, Joan. ★*Let Me Tell You What I Mean*	814
Dillard, Annie. *The Writing Life*	B
Dochartaigh, Kerri ni. *Cacophony of Bone*	B
Doty, Cate. *Mergers and Acquisitions*	395.2
Doty, Mark. *What Is the Grass*	811
Douglass, Frederick. *The Portable Frederick Douglass*	973.8
Dreyer, Benjamin. *Dreyer's English*	808.02
Du Bois, W. E. B. *The Oxford W.E.B. Du Bois Reader*	305.896
Du Bois, W. E. B. ★*Writings*	973
Duberman, Martin B. *Andrea Dworkin*	B
Dubus, Andre. *Townie*	B
Duncan, Dennis. *Index, a History of The*	025.3
Elledge, Scott. *E.B. White*	B
Ellison, Ralph. *The Selected Letters of Ralph Ellison*	813
Ellmann, Richard. *Oscar Wilde*	B
Emerson, Ralph Waldo. ★*Collected Poems and Translations*	811
Emezi, Akwaeke. ★*Dear Senthuran*	B
Ephron, Nora. *The Most of Nora Ephron*	814
Febos, Melissa. ★*Body Work*	808.06
Fehrman, Craig. *Author in Chief*	920
Feinstein, Adam. *Pablo Neruda*	B
Feldstein, Mark Avrom. *Poisoning the Press*	973.924092
Ferguson, Jane. *No Ordinary Assignment*	B
Ferrante, Elena. *In the Margins*	809
Ferrara, Silvia. *The Greatest Invention*	411
Finn, Peter. *The Zhivago Affair*	891.73
Fishman, Stephen. ★*The Copyright Handbook, 15th Ed.*	346.7304
Frank, Joseph. ★*Dostoevsky*	B
Franklin, Ruth. *Shirley Jackson*	B
Franklin, Sara B. ★*The Editor*	B
Franzen, Jonathan. *Farther Away*	814
French, Patrick. *The World Is What It Is*	B
Funder, Anna. *Wifedom*	B
Gaiman, Neil. *The View from the Cheap Seats*	824
Garcia Marquez, Gabriel. *Living to Tell the Tale*	B
Garfield, Simon. ★*All the Knowledge in the World*	030.9
Garner, Dwight. *The Upstairs Delicatessen*	B
Gary, Amy. *In the Great Green Room*	813
Gaskell, Elizabeth Cleghorn. *The Life of Charlotte Bronte*	B
Gay, Roxane. ★*Opinions*	814
Ghosh, Amitav. *The Great Derangement*	809
Ginsberg, Allen. *Best Minds of My Generation*	810.9
Gluck, Louise. *American Originality*	814
Gooch, Brad. ★*Flannery*	B

1635

PUBLIC LIBRARY CORE COLLECTION: NONFICTION
Twentieth Edition

Gordon, Charlotte. *Romantic Outlaws*	920
Gordon, Edmund. *The Invention of Angela Carter*	B
Gordon, Lyndall. ★*T.S. Eliot*	B
Gorra, Michael Edward. *The Saddest Words*	813
Grande, Reyna. ★*The Distance Between Us*	973
Grant, Ulysses S. *Memoirs and Selected Letters*	B
Grass, Gunter. *Of All That Ends*	838
Greenblatt, Stephen. ★*Will in the World*	B
Griffin, Susan. *Out of Silence, Sound. Out of Nothing, Something*	808.02
Gunn, Thom. ★*The Letters of Thom Gunn*	821
Gurdon, Meghan Cox. *The Enchanted Hour*	372.4
Handler, Daniel. ★*And Then? and Then? What Else?*	813
Hardwick, Elizabeth. *The Dolphin Letters, 1970-1979*	811
Hardy, Thomas. *The Collected Letters of Thomas Hardy*	823
Harjo, Joy. *Catching the Light*	818
Harjo, Joy. *Crazy Brave*	B
Harjo, Joy. ★*Poet Warrior*	B
Harkness, Deborah E. *The World of All Souls*	813
Harlan, Elizabeth. *George Sand*	B
Hartman, Darrell. *Battle of Ink and Ice*	998
Hastings, Selina. *The Secret Lives of Somerset Maugham*	B
Hazrat, Florence. *An Admirable Point*	411
Heller, Jason. *Strange Stars*	781.6609
Hemingway, Ernest. *Dear Papa*	813
Hemon, Aleksandar. *My Parents*	814
Herbert, Brian. *Dreamer of Dune*	B
Hersh, Seymour M. *Reporter*	B
Heti, Sheila. *Alphabetical Diaries*	818
Heughan, Sam. *Waypoints*	B
Highsmith, Patricia. ★*Patricia Highsmith's Diaries and Notebooks*	818
Hill, Jemele. *Uphill*	B
Hirsch, Edward. *How to Read a Poem*	808.1
Hitchens, Christopher. *Hitch-22*	920
Hitchings, Henry. *The Language Wars*	420.9
Hoffman, Adina. ★*My Happiness Bears No Relation to Happiness*	B
Hogan, Linda. *The Woman Who Watches Over the World*	B
Hollis, Matthew. *The Waste Land*	821
hooks, bell. *Remembered Rapture*	808
hooks, bell. *Wounds of Passion*	B
Houston, Keith. *The Book*	002.09
Houston, Keith. *Shady Characters*	411
Howe, Sean. *Marvel Comics*	741.5
Hughes, Langston. ★*I Wonder as I Wander*	B
Hurston, Zora Neale. *Dust Tracks on a Road*	B
Hurston, Zora Neale. ★*You Don't Know Us Negroes and Other Essays*	814
Hurston, Zora Neale. *Zora Neale Hurston*	B
Huxley, Aldous. ★*Brave New World Revisited*	823
Jackson, Angela. *A Surprised Queenhood in the New Black Sun*	B
Jackson, Shirley. ★*The Letters of Shirley Jackson*	813
James, P. D. *Talking About Detective Fiction*	823
Jamison, Leslie. ★*Make It Scream, Make It Burn*	814
Jones, Brian Jay. ★*Becoming Dr. Seuss*	B
Jones, Sharon L. *Critical Companion to Zora Neale Hurston*	813
Kakutani, Michiko. *Ex Libris*	028
Kant, Immanuel. ★*Basic Writings of Kant*	193
Kaplan, Alice Yaeger. *Looking for the Stranger*	B
Karim-Cooper, Farah. ★*The Great White Bard*	822.33
Karr, Mary. *The Art of Memoir*	B
Kelly, Helena. *Jane Austen, the Secret Radical*	823
Kenan, Randall. *Black Folk Could Fly*	813
Kerouac, Jack. *Selected Letters, 1940-1956*	813
Kerouac, Jack. ★*Some of the Dharma*	294.3
Kidder, Tracy. *Good Prose*	808.02
King, Stephen. *On Writing*	B
Konnikova, Maria. *Mastermind*	153.4
Korda, Michael. *Muse of Fire*	940.4
Kristof, Nicholas D. ★*Chasing Hope*	B
Kroeger, Brooke. *Undaunted*	070.4
Kroger, Lisa. *Monster, She Wrote*	920
LaFollette, Marcel C. *Writing for Their Lives*	071.3
Lahiri, Jhumpa. *Translating Myself and Others*	418
Laing, Olivia. *The Garden Against Time*	635
Lamott, Anne. *Bird by Bird*	808
Lansky, Aaron. *Outwitting History*	002
Larimer, Kevin. *The Poets & Writers Complete Guide to Being a Writer*	808
Le Guin, Ursula K. ★*Ursula K. Le Guin*	B
Le Guin, Ursula K. *Words Are My Matter*	818
Leader, Zachary. *The Life of Saul Bellow*	B
Lear, Linda J. *Beatrix Potter*	B
Lee, Marshall. *Bookmaking*	686
Leithauser, Brad. *Rhyme's Rooms*	808.1
Lepore, Jill. ★*The Deadline*	814
Lessing, Doris May. *Under My Skin*	823
Levy, Deborah. ★*Real Estate*	B
Lewis, John. *Carry On*	328.73
Lincoln, Abraham. *Speeches and Writings, 1832-1858*	973.5
Lynskey, Dorian. *The Ministry of Truth*	823
Madison, James. ★*The Constitutional Convention*	342.7302
Malcolm, Janet. *Reading Chekhov*	891.72
Manguel, Alberto. *The Dictionary of Imaginary Places*	809
Manguel, Alberto. *Homer's the Iliad and the Odyssey*	883
Mantel, Hilary. *Mantel Pieces*	824.914
Marcus, Leonard S. ★*Pictured Worlds*	741.6
Martin, Gerald. ★*Gabriel Garcia Marquez*	B
Matteson, John. *Eden's Outcasts*	920
McCann, Colum. *Letters to a Young Writer*	808.02
McCourt, Frank. *'Tis*	B
McCraw, David Edward. *Truth in Our Times*	342.7308
McCrum, Robert. ★*The Story of English*	420
McDermott, Alice. *What About the Baby?*	814
McIlwaine, Catherine. *Tolkien*	002.09
McPhee, John. *Tabula Rasa; V.1*	818
Mead, Rebecca. *My Life in Middlemarch*	823
Messud, Claire. *Kant's Little Prussian Head and Other Reasons Why I Write*	B
Milford, Nancy. *Savage Beauty*	B
Miller, Adrienne. *In the Land of Men*	070.5
Miraldi, Robert. *Seymour Hersh*	B
Montillo, Roseanne. *The Lady and Her Monsters*	823
Moody, Anthony David. *Ezra Pound*	B
Moore, Lorrie. *See What Can Be Done*	801
Moore, Marianne. *The Selected Letters of Marianne Moore*	B
Morris, James McGrath. *Pulitzer*	B
Morris, Jan. *A Writer's House in Wales*	942.9
Morrison, Toni. *Playing in the Dark*	810.9
Morrison, Toni. ★*The Source of Self-Regard*	814
Moser, Benjamin. ★*Sontag*	B
Moser, Benjamin. *Why This World*	B
Moss, Gabrielle. *Paperback Crush*	813.009
Mullen, Bill. ★*James Baldwin*	B
Murakami, Haruki. ★*Novelist as a Vocation*	895.64
Mustich, James. ★*1,000 Books to Read*	028
Nadeau, Jean-Benoit. ★*The Story of French*	440
Nadeau, Jean-Benoit. ★*The Story of Spanish*	460
Nafisi, Azar. ★*Reading Lolita in Tehran*	B
Nafisi, Azar. *The Republic of Imagination*	B
Nagourney, Adam. *The Times*	071
Nevala-Lee, Alec. *Astounding*	809.3
Nicolson, Adam. *The Making of Poetry*	821.709
Nicolson, Adam. *Why Homer Matters*	883
Nietzsche, Friedrich Wilhelm. ★*Basic Writings of Nietzsche*	193
Niven, Penelope. *Thornton Wilder*	B
Norris, Mary. *Between You and Me*	428.2
Norwich, John Julius. *Shakespeare's Kings*	822.33
Nuttall, Jennifer Anne. ★*Mother Tongue*	422
Odell, Amy. *Anna*	B
Ogilvie, Sarah. *The Dictionary People*	423
Okorafor, Nnedi. *Broken Places & Outer Spaces*	153.3
Oliver, Mary. ★*Upstream*	814
Orner, Peter. *Am I Alone Here?*	814
Orwell, George. *Diaries*	828
Ostertag, Bob. *People's Movements, People's Press*	071
Oyler, Lauren. *No Judgment*	814
Oz, Amos. *A Tale of Love and Darkness*	B
Ozick, Cynthia. *Critics, Monsters, Fanatics, and Other Literary Essays*	801
Palahniuk, Chuck. *Consider This*	B
Parini, Jay. *Borges and Me*	813
Parini, Jay. *Robert Frost*	B
Patchett, Ann. ★*These Precious Days*	814
Patterson, James. *James Patterson by James Patterson*	B
Paul, Pamela. ★*How to Raise a Reader*	649
Percy, Benjamin. *Thrill Me*	808.3
Pettegree, Andrew. *The Book in the Renaissance*	070.5
Phillips, Julie. *James Tiptree, Jr.*	B
Pinckney, Darryl. *Come Back in September*	B
Plath, Sylvia. *The Letters of Sylvia Plath*	811.54

1636

AUTHOR, TITLE, SERIES AND SUBJECT INDEX

Plath, Sylvia. *The Letters of Sylvia Plath*	811.54
Poe, Edgar Allan. *Essays and Reviews*	809
Poe, Edgar Allan. ★*Poetry and Tales*	818
Popoff, Alexandra. *Vasily Grossman and the Soviet Century*	B
Prose, Francine. *What to Read and Why*	028
Prothero, Stephen R. *God the Bestseller*	070.5
Proulx, Annie. *Bird Cloud*	B
Puchner, Martin. *The Written World*	809
Rakoff, Joanna Smith. *My Salinger Year*	B
Rampersad, Arnold. *The Life of Langston Hughes*	B
Rampersad, Arnold. ★*The Life of Langston Hughes*	B
Rampersad, Arnold. ★*Ralph Ellison*	B
Reed, Julia. *Dispatches from the Gilded Age*	B
Reed, Shannon. *Why We Read*	028
Rehak, Melanie. *Girl Sleuth*	813
Reynolds, David S. *Mightier Than the Sword*	813
Richardson, Robert D. *Emerson*	814
Rilke, Rainer Maria. ★*Letters to a Young Poet*	831
Rioux, Anne Boyd. *Meg, Jo, Beth, Amy*	813
Roberts, Steven V. *Cokie*	B
Rosenblitt, J. Alison. *The Beauty of Living*	B
Rosnay, Tatiana de. *Manderley Forever*	B
Row, Jess. *White Flights*	813
Rubin, Daniel Joshua. *27 Essential Principles of Story*	808.02
Ruhl, Sarah. *Letters from Max*	811
Rushdie, Salman. *Languages of Truth*	824
Russo, Richard. *The Destiny Thief*	814
Salesses, Matthew. ★*Craft in the Real World*	808.3
Salter, James. *Don't Save Anything*	818
Sante, Lucy. *I Heard Her Call My Name*	B
Sato, Hiroaki. *On Haiku*	809.1
Saunders, George. ★*A Swim in a Pond in the Rain*	891.7
Scalzi, John. *Don't Live for Your Obituary*	808.02
Schultz, Philip. *Comforts of the Abyss*	801
Sepetys, Ruta. ★*You*	808.02
Severin, Timothy. *In Search of Robinson Crusoe*	996.1
Shakespeare, Nicholas. *Ian Fleming*	B
Shange, Ntozake. ★*Sing a Black Girl's Song*	818
Shapiro, Ari. ★*The Best Strangers in the World*	B
Shapiro, James. *Contested Will*	822.33
Shapiro, James. *Shakespeare in a Divided America*	822.33
Shattuck, Roger. *Proust's Way*	843
Shaw, Bernard. *Major Barbara*	822
Shaw, Bernard. *Saint Joan*	822
Shelden, Michael. *Mark Twain*	B
Showalter, Elaine. ★*A Jury of Her Peers*	810.9
Simpson, J. A. *The Word Detective*	B
Sims, Michael. *Arthur and Sherlock*	B
Slawenski, Kenneth. ★*Salinger*	B
Smiley, Jane. *Thirteen Ways of Looking at the Novel*	B
Smith, Adam. ★*The Wealth of Nations*	330.15
Smith, Emma. *Portable Magic*	002
Smith, Patti. ★*A Book of Days*	779
Smyth, Adam. *The Book-Makers*	686.2
So, Anthony Veasna. ★*Songs on Endless Repeat*	814
Sol, Adam. *How a Poem Moves*	808.1
Solnit, Rebecca. *The Faraway Nearby*	814
Solnit, Rebecca. *Orwell's Roses*	B
Souder, William. *Mad at the World*	813
Spence, Annie. *Dear Fahrenheit 451*	028.9
Spurling, Hilary. *Anthony Powell*	B
Stein, Gertrude. *Writings, 1932-1946*	818
Sturgis, Matthew. *Oscar Wilde*	B
Styron, William. *My Generation*	814
Sullivan, Margaret. *Newsroom Confidential*	070.92
Tatar, Maria. *The Heroine with 1001 Faces*	809
Taylor, D. J. *Orwell*	B
Thompson, Hunter S. *Fear and Loathing at Rolling Stone*	070.1
Thompson, Hunter S. ★*Fear and Loathing in America*	B
Thoreau, Henry David. ★*Collected Essays and Poems*	818
Todd, Kim. *Sensational*	920
Todd, Olivier. *Albert Camus*	B
Tomalin, Claire. *Samuel Pepys*	B
Tomalin, Claire. *Thomas Hardy*	B
Tran, Phuc. ★*Sigh, Gone*	B
Tresch, John. *The Reason for the Darkness of the Night*	B
Trillin, Calvin. *The Lede*	071
Tsu, Jing. *Kingdom of Characters*	495.111
Tur, Katy. *Rough Draft*	B
Twain, Mark. *Autobiography of Mark Twain*	B
Twain, Mark. *Autobiography of Mark Twain*	B
Twain, Mark. ★*Autobiography of Mark Twain*	B
Tweedy, Jeff. *How to Write One Song*	782.42
Vargas Llosa, Mario. *The Call of the Tribe*	868
Vargas Llosa, Mario. *Conversation at Princeton*	868
Vonnegut, Kurt. *Kurt Vonnegut*	813
Vonnegut, Kurt. ★*A Man Without a Country*	818
Wagamese, Richard. *One Native Life*	B
Waldstreicher, David. *The Odyssey of Phillis Wheatley*	B
Walker, Alice. *Gathering Blossoms Under Fire*	B
Wallace, David Foster. *Consider the Lobster*	814
Warren, Rosanna. *Max Jacob*	B
Wassef, Nadia. *Shelf Life*	B
Watson, Cecelia. *Semicolon*	428.2
Watts, Steven. *Self-Help Messiah*	B
Weller, Sam. *The Bradbury Chronicles*	B
Wellman, Victoria. *Before You Say Anything*	808.5
Welty, Eudora. *One Writer's Beginnings*	B
Wenner, Jann. *Like a Rolling Stone*	B
Whitman, Walt. ★*Poetry and Prose*	811
Wiesel, Elie. *All Rivers Run to the Sea*	B
Wiesel, Elie. *And the Sea Is Never Full*	B
Wilder, Laura Ingalls. *The Selected Letters of Laura Ingalls Wilder*	B
Williamson, Edwin. *Borges*	B
Wilson, A. N. *C.S. Lewis*	823
Wilson, A. N. *The Mystery of Charles Dickens*	823
Wilson-Lee, Edward. ★*The Catalogue of Shipwrecked Books*	B
Wiman, Christian. *He Held Radical Light*	814
Wiman, Christian. *Zero at the Bone*	818
Winder, Elizabeth. *Pain, Parties, Work*	B
Winkler, Elizabeth. *Shakespeare Was a Woman & Other Heresies*	822.33
Wood, James. *How Fiction Works*	808.3
Wood, Lawrence. *Your Caption Has Been Selected*	741.5
Woods, Geraldine. *25 Great Sentences and How They Got That Way*	808
Woolf, Virginia. *The London Scene*	942.1
Woolf, Virginia. *Moments of Being*	B
Worsley, Lucy. ★*Agatha Christie*	B
Yager, Jan. *How to Self Publish Your Book*	070.5
Young, Damon. *The Art of Reading*	028.9
Zenith, Richard. *Pessoa*	B

ARTS AND ENTERTAINMENT — WRITING AND PUBLISHING — LITERARY CRITICISM

Acocella, Joan Ross. ★*The Bloodied Nightgown*	814
Akhmatova, Anna Andreevna. ★*The Complete Poems of Anna Akhmatova*	891.71
Alexander, Caroline. *The War That Killed Achilles*	883
Amis, Martin. *The Rub of Time*	824
Andersen, Jens. *Astrid Lindgren*	B
Atwood, Margaret. *In Other Worlds*	813
Baez, Fernando. *Universal History of the Destruction of Books*	098
Bass, Rick. *The Traveling Feast*	B
Batuman, Elif. *The Possessed*	891.7
Bellos, David. *The Novel of the Century*	843
Bergstein, Rachelle. *The Genius of Judy*	813
Bernard, Emily. *Black Is the Body*	305.48
Bigsby, Christopher William Edgar. *Arthur Miller*	B
Blake, William. ★*The Complete Poetry and Prose of William Blake*	821
Bloom, Harold. *Lear*	822.33
Bly, Robert. *More Than True*	398.2
Boswell, James. ★*The Life of Samuel Johnson*	B
Bram, Christopher. *Eminent Outlaws*	920
Braudy, Leo. *Haunted*	398.45
Briggs, Julia. *Virginia Woolf*	823
Briggs, Kate. *This Little Art*	418
Britt, Ryan. ★*The Spice Must Flow*	813
Browning, Robert. ★*Robert Browning's Poetry*	821
Burke, Edmund. *Reflections on the Revolution in France*	944.04
Burt, Stephanie. *Don't Read Poetry*	811
Calvino, Italo. *Collection of Sand*	854
Catullus, Gaius Valerius. *The Poems of Catullus*	874
Chabon, Michael. *Bookends*	818
Chaucer, Geoffrey. ★*The Complete Poetry and Prose of Geoffrey Chaucer*	821
Cheever, Susan. *American Bloomsbury*	920
Chekhov, Anton Pavlovich. *Chekhov*	891.72
Cott, Jonathan. *There's a Mystery There*	813

PUBLIC LIBRARY CORE COLLECTION: NONFICTION
Twentieth Edition

Crase, Douglas. *On Autumn Lake*	809
Crespino, Joseph. *Atticus Finch*	B
Damrosch, David. *Around the World in 80 Books*	809
Damrosch, Leopold. *The Club*	920
Daugherty, Tracy. *Larry McMurtry*	B
Dennison, Matthew. *The Man in the Willows*	B
Dickinson, Emily. *Dickinson*	811
Ellison, Ralph. *The Selected Letters of Ralph Ellison*	813
Feder, Rachel. *The Darcy Myth*	823
Foster, Thomas C. *How to Read Poetry Like a Professor*	808.1
Frank, Joseph. ★*Dostoevsky*	B
Fraser, Caroline. ★*Prairie Fires*	B
Gabbert, Elisa. *Any Person Is the Only Self*	814
Ghosh, Amitav. *The Great Derangement*	809
Gilbert, Sandra M. ★*Still Mad*	810.9
Gillespie, Carmen. *Critical Companion to Toni Morrison*	813
Ginsberg, Allen. *Best Minds of My Generation*	810.9
Gordon, Edmund. *The Invention of Angela Carter*	B
Griffin, Farah Jasmine. ★*In Search of a Beautiful Freedom*	814
Hardy, Thomas. *The Collected Letters of Thomas Hardy*	823
Hardy, Thomas. *Thomas Hardy*	821
Harman, Claire. *Charlotte Bronte*	B
Hart, James David. *The Oxford Companion to American Literature*	810.9
Heaney, Seamus. *Opened Ground*	821
Hecht, Jennifer Michael. ★*The Wonder Paradox*	808.1
Heller, Jason. *Strange Stars*	781.6609
Hirsch, Edward. *Poet's Choice*	808.81
Hirsch, Edward. *A Poet's Glossary*	808.1
Hoffman, Adina. ★*My Happiness Bears No Relation to Happiness*	B
Horace. *Odes and Epodes*	874
Ignatieff, Michael. *On Consolation*	152.4
James, Henry. *Literary Criticism; Vol. 1*	809
Jameson, A. D. *I Find Your Lack of Faith Disturbing*	791.43
Jenkyns, Richard. *Classical Literature*	880.09
Kalder, Daniel. *The Infernal Library*	321.9
Kandel, Eric R. *The Age of Insight*	154.2
Kaplan, Alice Yaeger. *Looking for the Stranger*	B
Keene, Donald. *The Pleasures of Japanese Literature*	895.6
Kelly, Helena. *Jane Austen, the Secret Radical*	823
Kendall, Tim. *The Art of Robert Frost*	811
Kenner, Hugh. *The Pound Era*	811
Kroger, Lisa. *Monster, She Wrote*	920
Kundera, Milan. ★*The Curtain*	801
Kundera, Milan. *Encounter*	809
Lahiri, Jhumpa. *Translating Myself and Others*	418
Le Guin, Ursula K. *Ursula K. Le Guin*	B
Le Guin, Ursula K. *Words Are My Matter*	818
Leader, Zachary. *The Life of Saul Bellow*	B
Leithauser, Brad. *Rhyme's Rooms*	808.1
Lynskey, Dorian. *The Ministry of Truth*	823
Malory, Thomas. *Le Morte Darthur, Or, the Hoole Book of Kyng Arthur and of His Noble Knyghtes of the Rounde Table*	823
Miller, Lucasta. ★*Keats*	821
Montillo, Roseanne. *The Lady and Her Monsters*	823
Moody, Anthony David. *Ezra Pound*	B
Moore, Lorrie. *See What Can Be Done*	801
Morrison, Toni. ★*The Origin of Others*	809
Moss, Gabrielle. *Paperback Crush*	813.009
Nafisi, Azar. *Read Dangerously*	809
Nevala-Lee, Alec. *Astounding*	809.3
Nicolson, Adam. *Why Homer Matters*	883
Nuttall, A. D. *Shakespeare the Thinker*	822.33
Oliver, Mary. *A Poetry Handbook*	808.1
Orner, Peter. *Am I Alone Here?*	814
Orr, David. *You, Too, Could Write a Poem*	808.1
Orr, Gregory. *A Primer for Poets & Readers of Poetry*	808.1
Pepys, Samuel. *The Diary of Samuel Pepys*	B
Pettegree, Andrew. *The Book in the Renaissance*	070.5
Philbrick, Nathaniel. *Why Read Moby-Dick?*	813
Pinsky, Robert. *The Sounds of Poetry*	808.5
Pitzer, Andrea. *The Secret History of Vladimir Nabokov*	813
Poe, Edgar Allan. *Complete Poems*	810
Prose, Francine. *What to Read and Why*	028
Puchner, Martin. *The Written World*	809
Reid, David. *The Brazen Age*	974.7
Rioux, Anne Boyd. *Meg, Jo, Beth, Amy*	813
Roiphe, Katie. *The Violet Hour*	809
Row, Jess. *White Flights*	813
Ruden, Sarah. *The Face of Water*	220.5
Salter, James. *Don't Save Anything*	818
Sampson, Fiona. *In Search of Mary Shelley*	B
Schwalbe, Will. ★*The End of Your Life Book Club*	B
Shakespeare, William. ★*The Complete Works*	822.33
Shapiro, James. *Contested Will*	822.33
Shapiro, James. *The Year of Lear*	822.33
Showalter, Elaine. ★*A Jury of Her Peers*	810.9
Skal, David J. *Something in the Blood*	823
Smith, Patti. ★*M Train*	B
Smith, Patti. ★*Year of the Monkey*	B
Smyth, Katharine. *All the Lives We Ever Lived*	B
Sol, Adam. *How a Poem Moves*	808.1
Spence, Annie. *Dear Fahrenheit 451*	028.9
Stein, Gertrude. *Writings, 1903-1932*	818
Teicher, Craig Morgan. *We Begin in Gladness*	808.1
Thursby, Jacqueline S. *Critical Companion to Maya Angelou*	818
Tolentino, Jia. ★*Trick Mirror*	973.93
Town, Caren J. *LGBTQ Young Adult Fiction*	813.009
Travisano, Thomas J. *Love Unknown*	B
Twain, Mark. ★*Autobiography of Mark Twain*	B
Viertel, Jack. *The Secret Life of the American Musical*	792.609
Villon, Francois. *The Poems of Francois Villon*	841
Walls, Laura Dassow. ★*Henry David Thoreau*	B
Watling, Sarah. *Tomorrow Perhaps the Future*	946.081
Wayne, Tiffany K. *Critical Companion to Ralph Waldo Emerson*	814
Weldon, Glen. ★*The Caped Crusade*	741.5
Wilde, Oscar. *The Artist as Critic*	809
Wilder, Laura Ingalls. *The Selected Letters of Laura Ingalls Wilder*	B
Woodress, James Leslie. *Willa Cather*	B
Woolf, Virginia. *The Virginia Woolf Reader*	823
Young, Kevin. *Bunk*	177

ARTS CAMPS
Friedman, Rachel. ★*And Then We Grew Up*	305.24

Aryee, Patrick
30 Animals That Made Us Smarter	590
As China Goes, so Goes the World. Gerth, Karl	339.4
★*As Long as You Need.* Park, J. S.	248.8
As You Wish. Elwes, Cary	791.43

Asbridge, Thomas S.
★*The Crusades*	909.07
The Greatest Knight	942.03

Asbrink, Elisabeth
And in the Vienna Woods the Trees Remain	B
Ascent to Power. Roll, David L.	973.918

ASCETICISM
Krakauer, Jon. *Into the Wild*	917.9804

Aschwanden, Christie
Good to Go	617.1
Asd, The Complete Autism Spectrum Disorder Health & Diet Guide. Smith, R. Garth	616.85

ASEXUALITY
Dery, Mark. *Born to Be Posthumous*	B
Kobabe, Maia. *Gender Queer*	741.5

Asgarian, Roxanna
We Were Once a Family	364.152

Asghar, Fatimah
If They Come for Us	811

Ash, Lamorna
Dark, Salt, Clear	942.3

ASH, LAMORNA
Ash, Lamorna. *Dark, Salt, Clear*	942.3

Ash, Stephen V.
Firebrand of Liberty	973.7

Ashbery, John
Commotion of the Birds	811
John Ashbery	811
Notes from the Air	811
Selected Poems	811

ASHBERY, JOHN, 1927-2017
Roffman, Karin. *The Songs We Know Best*	B

ASHE, ARTHUR
McPhee, John. *Levels of the Game*	796.34

Asher, Zain E.
Where the Children Take Us	942.1

ASHEVILLE, NORTH CAROLINA
Dissen, William Stark. *Thoughtful Cooking*	641.5975
Ashley's War. Lemmon, Gayle Tzemach	B

AUTHOR, TITLE, SERIES AND SUBJECT INDEX

ASHLEY, JAMES MITCHELL, 1824-1896
   Richards, Leonard L. *Who Freed the Slaves?* — 342.7308
Ashley, Maurice
   Move by Move — 158
ASHLEY, MAURICE
   Ashley, Maurice. *Move by Move* — 158
Ashon, Will
   Chamber Music — 782.421649
ASHRAMS
   Gilbert, Elizabeth. *Eat, Pray, Love* — B
Ashton, Dianne
   Hanukkah in America — 296.4
Ashton, Jennifer
   The New Normal — 613
ASIA
   Belliveau, Denis. *In the Footsteps of Marco Polo* — 915
   Bergreen, Laurence. *Marco Polo* — B
   Bhutto, Benazir. *Reconciliation* — 297.2
   Choy, Catherine Ceniza. ★*Asian American Histories of the United States* — 973
   Frankopan, Peter. *The Silk Roads* — 909
   Hansen, Valerie. *The Year 1000* — 909
   Lee, Sung-Yoon. *The Sister* — 951.93
   Mishra, Pankaj. *From the Ruins of Empire* — 950.4
   Ollivier, Bernard. *Out of Istanbul* — B
   Samatar, Sofia. *The White Mosque* — B
   Schwartzel, Erich. *Red Carpet* — 791.43
   Schweitzer, Sharon. *Access to Asia* — 395.5
   Theroux, Paul. *The Great Railway Bazaar* — 915
   Vick, Tom. *Asian Cinema* — 791.43
ASIAN AMERICAN CHILDREN
   Hobbs, Jeff. *Show Them You're Good* — 373
★*Asian American Histories of the United States*. Choy, Catherine Ceniza — 973
ASIAN AMERICAN MEN
   Bamberger, Michael. *The Second Life of Tiger Woods* — B
   Benedict, Jeff. ★*Tiger Woods* — B
ASIAN AMERICAN WOMEN
   Gupta, Prachi. ★*They Called Us Exceptional* — B
   Hong, Cathy Park. *Minor Feelings* — 305.48
   Lee, Julia Sun-Joo. *Biting the Hand* — B
   Li, Fei-Fei. *The Worlds I See* — B
   Li, Yiyun. *Dear Friend, from My Life I Write to You in Your Life* — B
   Wang, Connie. *Oh My Mother!* — B
   Wong, Ali. ★*Dear Girls* — B
   Wong, Alice. ★*Year of the Tiger* — B
   Wu, Constance. *Making a Scene* — B
ASIAN AMERICANS
   Choy, Catherine Ceniza. ★*Asian American Histories of the United States* — 973
   Han, Chenxing. *Be the Refuge* — 294.3
   Hong, Cathy Park. *Minor Feelings* — 305.48
   Johnson, Kirk W. *The Fishermen and the Dragon* — 976.4
   Koh, EJ. *The Magical Language of Others* — 813
   Lee, Corky. ★*Corky Lee's Asian America* — 770
   Lee, Erika. *The Making of Asian America* — 973
   Lee, Julia Sun-Joo. *Biting the Hand* — B
   So, Anthony Veasna. ★*Songs on Endless Repeat* — 814
   Talusan, Meredith. *Fairest* — 305.30973
   Tran, Paul. *All the Flowers Kneeling* — 811
   Wang, Connie. *Oh My Mother!* — B
   Wong, Alice. ★*Year of the Tiger* — B
   Woo, Ronnie. *Did You Eat Yet?* — 641.595
   Yang, Jeff. *The Golden Screen* — 791.43
   Yang, Jeff. ★*Rise* — 973
Asian Cinema. Vick, Tom — 791.43
ASIAN HISTORY
   Ansary, Mir Tamim. *Games Without Rules* — 958.1
   Black, George. ★*The Long Reckoning* — 959.704
   Bowden, Mark. ★*Hue 1968* — 959.704
   Bruning, John R. *Indestructible* — B
   Bui, Thi. ★*The Best We Could Do* — 741.5
   Coll, Steve. ★*Ghost Wars* — 958.104
   Dalrymple, William. *The Return of a King* — 958.1
   Edstrom, Erik. *Un-American* — B
   Feifer, Gregory. *The Great Gamble* — 958.104
   Frankopan, Peter. *The Silk Roads* — 909
   Guibert, Emmanuel. *The Photographer* — 741.5
   Hajari, Nisid. *Midnight's Furies* — 954.04
   Jeppesen, Travis. *See You Again in Pyongyang* — 951.93
   Karnow, Stanley. *Vietnam, a History* — 959.704

   Kelly, John. *The Great Mortality* — 614.5
   Lee, Erika. *The Making of Asian America* — 973
   Lim, Louisa. *Indelible City* — 951.25
   Loyn, David. *In Afghanistan* — 958.1
   Loyn, David. *The Long War* — 958.104
   Malhotra, Aanchal. *Remnants of Partition* — 954.04
   Marozzi, Justin. *Tamerlane* — 950.2
   Meyer, Dakota. *Into the Fire* — 958.104
   Mohan, Rohini. *The Seasons of Trouble* — 954.9303
   Morgan, Wesley. *The Hardest Place* — 958.104
   Oberdorfer, Don. *The Two Koreas 3rd Ed.* — 951.904
   Pak, Jung H. *Becoming Kim Jong Un* — B
   Pakula, Hannah. *The Last Empress* — B
   Pham, Andrew X. ★*The Eaves of Heaven* — B
   Richardson, Edmund. *The King's Shadow* — 958.1
   Samaha, Albert. *Concepcion* — 929
   Sides, Hampton. *On Desperate Ground* — 951.904
   Stanton, Doug. *The Odyssey of Echo Company* — 959.704
   Taing, Mae Bunseng. *Under the Naga Tail* — B
   Taylor, Jay. *The Generalissimo* — B
   Thant Myint-U. *The Hidden History of Burma* — 959.105
   Vickers, Michael G. *By All Means Available* — 355
   Walsh, Declan. *The Nine Lives of Pakistan* — 954.91
   Ward, Geoffrey C. ★*The Vietnam War* — 959.704
   Whitlock, Craig. *The Afghanistan Papers* — 958.104
ASIAN PEOPLE
   Lee, Erika. *The Making of Asian America* — 973
Asika, Uju
   Bringing up Race — 155.4
Asim, Jabari
   We Can't Breathe — 305.896
ASIMOV, ISAAC, 1920-1992
   Nevala-Lee, Alec. *Astounding* — 809.3
Ask. Stryker, Kitty — 302
Ask A Manager. Green, Alison — 650.1
Ask Me About My Uterus. Norman, Abby — 618.1
Askwith, Richard
   Unbreakable — B
Aslan, Reza
   God — 211
   ★*No God but God* — 297
Asprey, Dave
   Game Changers — 158.1
Assad or We Burn the Country. Dagher, Sam — 956.9104
ASSAD, BASHAR, 1965-
   Abouzeid, Rania. *No Turning Back* — 956.9104
   Dagher, Sam. *Assad or We Burn the Country* — 956.9104
ASSAD, HAFEZ, 1930-2000
   Sattouf, Riad. *The Arab of the Future 2* — 741.5
   Sattouf, Riad. *The Arab of the Future* — 741.5
Assael, Shaun
   The Murder of Sonny Liston — B
ASSASSINATION
   Abrams, Dan. *Kennedy's Avenger* — 973.922
   Beam, Alex. *American Crucifixion* — B
   Bergen, Peter L. *The Rise and Fall of Osama Bin Laden* — 958.104
   Caruana Galizia, Paul. ★*A Death in Malta* — 364.15
   Ephron, Dan. *Killing a King* — 956.9405
   Hampton, Dan. *Operation Vengeance* — 940.54
   Hill, Clint. *Five Days in November* — 973.922092
   Hubbard, Ben (Journalist). *Mbs* — B
   Igort. *The Ukrainian and Russian Notebooks* — 741.5
   Jacobsen, Annie. *Surprise, Kill, Vanish* — 327.1273
   Jager, Eric. *Blood Royal* — 944.026
   Johnson, Steven. *The Infernal Machine* — 335
   Kavanagh, Julie. *The Irish Assassins* — 941.5
   Kean, Sam. *The Bastard Brigade* — 355.8
   King, Greg. *The Assassination of the Archduke* — B
   Lane, Charles. *Freedom's Detective* — B
   Malala, Justice. *The Plot to Save South Africa* — 968.07
   Man, John. *Ninja* — 355.5
   Meltzer, Brad. ★*The First Conspiracy* — 973.4
   Millard, Candice. *Destiny of the Republic* — 973.8
   Miller, Scott. *The President and the Assassin* — 973.8
   Minutaglio, Bill. *Dallas 1963* — 973.922092
   Posner, Gerald L. *Case Closed* — 364.1
   Rappaport, Helen. *The Race to Save the Romanovs* — 947.08
   Reid, Stuart A. *The Lumumba Plot* — 967.51

Risen, James. ★*The Last Honest Man* — 973.92
Scahill, Jeremy. *Dirty Wars* — 355.00973
Sides, Hampton. *Hellhound on His Trail* — 364.152
Southon, Emma. *Agrippina* — B
Strauss, Barry S. *The Death of Caesar* — 937
Swanson, James L. *End of Days* — 973.922092
Talty, Stephan. *The Good Assassin* — 364.15
Vowell, Sarah. *Assassination Vacation* — B
Wallace, Chris. *Countdown Bin Laden* — 958.104
Woolley, Benjamin. *The King's Assassin* — B
The Assassination of the Archduke. King, Greg

ASSASSINATION PLOTS
Bogosian, Eric. *Operation Nemesis* — 956.62
Meltzer, Brad. ★*The First Conspiracy* — 973.4
Meltzer, Brad. *The Lincoln Conspiracy* — 973.7092
Woolley, Benjamin. *The King's Assassin* — B
Assassination Vacation. Vowell, Sarah

ASSASSINS
Abrams, Dan. *Kennedy's Avenger* — 973.922
Bogosian, Eric. *Operation Nemesis* — 956.62
Cannell, Michael T. *A Brotherhood Betrayed* — B
Friedman, Matti. *Spies of No Country* — 327.12
Garrison, Jessica. *The Devil's Harvest* — B
Maier, Thomas. *Mafia Spies* — 364.1060973
Sherman, Casey. *Hunting Whitey* — B
Vowell, Sarah. *Assassination Vacation*
The Assassins' Gate. Packer, George — 956.7044

ASSAULT AND BATTERY
Glass, Sara. *Kissing Girls on Shabbat* — B
Rose, Jacqueline. *On Violence and on Violence Against Women* — 362.88

ASSAULT WEAPONS
McWhirter, Cameron. *American Gun* — 683.4

ASSERTIVENESS
Patrick, Vanessa M. *The Power of Saying No* — 158.1
Vanek Smith, Stacey. *Machiavelli for Women* — 650.1
Assessing Service Quality. Hernon, Peter — 025.5
The Asshole Survival Guide. Sutton, Robert I. — 650.1

Assil, Reem
Arabiyya — 641.595

ASSIMILATION (SOCIOLOGY)
Arce, Julissa. *You Sound Like a White Girl* — 303.48
DeParle, Jason. ★*A Good Provider Is One Who Leaves* — 305.899
Eire, Carlos M. N. *Learning to Die in Miami* — B
Hsu, Hua. ★*Stay True* — B
Khakpour, Porochista. *Brown Album* — 304.8
Nayeri, Dina. ★*The Ungrateful Refugee* — 362.87
Pipher, Mary Bray. *The Middle of Everywhere* — 305.9
Taffa, Deborah Jackson. ★*Whiskey Tender* — B
Tran, Phuc. ★*Sigh, Gone* — B
Treuer, David. ★*The Heartbeat of Wounded Knee* — 970.004

ASSISI, ITALY
Martin, Valerie. *Salvation* — B

ASSISTED SUICIDE
Engelhart, Katie. *The Inevitable* — 179.7
Hannig, Anita. *The Day I Die* — 364.152
Rehm, Diane. ★*When My Time Comes* — 179.7
Wanzer, Sidney H. ★*To Die Well* — 179.7
Assume Nothing. Selvaratnam, Tanya — B

ASTAIRE, ADELE
Riley, Kathleen. *The Astaires* — B

ASTAIRE, FRED, 1899-1987
Riley, Kathleen. *The Astaires* — B
The Astaires. Riley, Kathleen

ASTELL, MARY, 1666-1731
Penaluna, Regan. ★*How to Think Like a Woman* — 190.82
The Asteroid Hunter. Lauretta, D. S. — 523.44

ASTEROIDS
Black, Riley. *The Last Days of the Dinosaurs* — 576.8
Lauretta, D. S. *The Asteroid Hunter* — 523.44

ASTOR, JOHN JACOB, 1763-1848
Pyle, Robert Michael. *Nature Matrix* — 508
Stark, Peter. *Astoria* — 979.5
Astoria. Stark, Peter — 979.5
Astounding. Nevala-Lee, Alec — 809.3

ASTRAL PROJECTION
Roach, Mary. ★*Spook* — 129
Astrid Lindgren. Andersen, Jens — B
Astroball. Reiter, Ben — 796.357

ASTROLOGERS
Brooks, Michael. *The Quantum Astrologer's Handbook* — B

ASTROLOGY
Brown, Maressa. *Raising Baby by the Stars* — 133.5
Crawford, Saffi. *The Power of Birthdays, Stars & Numbers* — 133.5
Goldschneider, Gary. ★*The Secret Language of Birthdays* — 133.5
Goodman, Linda. *Linda Goodman's Star Signs* — 133.5
Goodman, Linda. *Linda Goodman's Sun Signs* — 133.5
Miller, Susan. *Planets and Possibilities* — 133.5
Snodgrass, Mary Ellen. *Signs of the Zodiac* — 133.5
The Astronaut Wives Club. Koppel, Lily — 920

ASTRONAUTICS
Ackmann, Martha. *The Mercury 13* — 920
Bell, Jim. *The Interstellar Age* — 919
Koppel, Lily. *The Astronaut Wives Club* — 920
Launius, Roger D. *The Smithsonian History of Space Exploration* — 629.4
Nelson, Craig. *Rocket Men* — 629.45
Roach, Mary. *Packing for Mars* — 571.0919
Sheehan, Neil. *A Fiery Peace in a Cold War* — B
Shesol, Jeff. *Mercury Rising* — 629.45
Tyson, Neil deGrasse. *Space Chronicles* — 629.40973
Virts, Terry. *How to Astronaut* — 629.45
Walker, Stephen. *Beyond* — 629.45
Wohlforth, Charles P. *Beyond Earth* — 629.45
Wolfe, Tom. ★*The Right Stuff* — 629.4

ASTRONAUTS
Aldrin, Buzz. *No Dream Is Too High* — B
Bagby, Meredith E. *The New Guys* — 305
Barbree, Jay. *Neil Armstrong* — B
Brinkley, Douglas. ★*American Moonshot* — 629.40973
Cook, Kevin. *The Burning Blue* — 629.45
Donovan, Jim. ★*Shoot for the Moon* — 629.45
Higginbotham, Adam. ★*Challenger* — 629.45
Jones, Tom. *Space Shuttle Stories* — 629.44
Kelly, Scott. ★*Endurance* — B
Kluger, Jeffrey. ★*Apollo 8* — 629.45
Koppel, Lily. *The Astronaut Wives Club* — 920
Kurson, Robert. ★*Rocket Men* — 629.45
Leinbach, Michael D. *Bringing Columbia Home* — 363.12
Melvin, Leland. *Chasing Space* — B
Nelson, Craig. *Rocket Men* — 629.45
Sherr, Lynn. *Sally Ride* — B
Swift, Earl. *Across the Airless Wilds* — 629.45
Virts, Terry. *How to Astronaut* — 629.45
Walker, Stephen. *Beyond* — 629.45
Wolfe, Tom. ★*The Right Stuff* — 629.4

ASTRONOMERS
Baron, David. *American Eclipse* — 523.7
Cervini, Eric. *The Deviant's War* — B
Fauber, L. S. *Heaven on Earth* — B
Fletcher, Seth. *Einstein's Shadow* — 523.8
Lauretta, D. S. *The Asteroid Hunter* — 523.44
Levesque, Emily. *The Last Stargazers* — 520
Lintott, Chris. *Accidental Astronomy* — 520
Loeb, Abraham. *Extraterrestrial* — 576.8
Shields, Aomawa L. *Life on Other Planets* — B
Sobel, Dava. *A More Perfect Heaven* — 520.9

ASTRONOMICAL DISCOVERIES
Johnson, Sarah Stewart. *The Sirens of Mars* — 576.8
Tyson, Neil deGrasse. *To Infinity and Beyond* — 520

ASTRONOMICAL OBSERVATORIES
Levesque, Emily. *The Last Stargazers* — 520
Tucker, Wallace H. *Chandra's Cosmos* — 523.1

ASTRONOMY
Baron, David. *American Eclipse* — 523.7
Boyle, Rebecca. *Our Moon* — 523.3
Christian, Carol. *A Question and Answer Guide to Astronomy* — 520
Cliff, Harry. *How to Make an Apple Pie from Scratch* — 523.01
Cox, Brian. *Universal* — 523.1
Fauber, L. S. *Heaven on Earth* — B
Hawking, Stephen. ★*Black Holes and Baby Universes and Other Essays* — 530.1
Hawking, Stephen. *A Brief History of Time* — 523.1
Hawking, Stephen. ★*A Briefer History of Time* — 523.1
Johnson, George. *Miss Leavitt's Stars* — 522
Johnson, Sarah Stewart. *The Sirens of Mars* — 576.8
Levesque, Emily. *The Last Stargazers* — 520
Levin, Janna. *Black Hole Blues* — 539.7

AUTHOR, TITLE, SERIES AND SUBJECT INDEX

Lintott, Chris. *Accidental Astronomy*	520
Loeb, Abraham. *Extraterrestrial*	576.8
Marchant, Jo. *The Human Cosmos*	523.1
McTier, Moiya. *The Milky Way*	523.1
Nordgren, Tyler E. *Sun, Moon, Earth*	523.7
Plait, Philip C. *Under Alien Skies*	520
Pontzen, Andrew. *The Universe in a Box*	523.1
Ridpath, Ian. *Stars & Planets*	520
Sagan, Carl. *Cosmos*	520
Sanders, Ella Frances. *Eating the Sun*	520
Shields, Aomawa L. *Life on Other Planets*	B
Shore, Linda. *The Total Skywatcher's Manual*	523
Sobel, Dava. *A More Perfect Heaven*	520.9
Tegmark, Max. *Our Mathematical Universe*	523.1
Tirion, Wil. *The Cambridge Star Atlas*	523.8
Tonelli, Guido. *Genesis*	523.1
Trefil, James. *Space Atlas*	520
Tucker, Wallace H. *Chandra's Cosmos*	523.1
Tyson, Neil deGrasse. *Cosmic Queries*	523.1
Tyson, Neil deGrasse. *Letters from an Astrophysicist*	520.92
Tyson, Neil deGrasse. *To Infinity and Beyond*	520
Tyson, Neil deGrasse. *Welcome to the Universe*	523.1
Ward, Peter Douglas. *Life as We Do Not Know It*	576.839
ASTROPHYSICISTS	
Mlodinow, Leonard. *Stephen Hawking*	B
Oluseyi, Hakeem M. *A Quantum Life*	B
Prescod-Weinstein, Chanda. *The Disordered Cosmos*	523.01
Seager, Sara. *The Smallest Lights in the Universe*	B
Tyson, Neil deGrasse. *Letters from an Astrophysicist*	520.92
ASTROPHYSICS	
Cham, Jorge. *Frequently Asked Questions About the Universe*	523.1
Cox, Brian. *Universal*	523.1
Fletcher, Seth. *Einstein's Shadow*	523.8
Hawking, Stephen. *The Nature of Space and Time*	530.1
Kaku, Michio. ★*The Future of Humanity*	629.45
Lintott, Chris. *Accidental Astronomy*	520
Loeb, Abraham. *Extraterrestrial*	576.8
Mack, Katie. *The End of Everything*	523.1
Oluseyi, Hakeem M. *A Quantum Life*	B
Pontzen, Andrew. *The Universe in a Box*	523.1
Prescod-Weinstein, Chanda. *The Disordered Cosmos*	523.01
Randall, Lisa. *Dark Matter and the Dinosaurs*	523.1
Sanders, Ella Frances. *Eating the Sun*	520
Smil, Vaclav. *Size*	153.7
Tyson, Neil deGrasse. *Accessory to War*	355.001
Tyson, Neil deGrasse. ★*Astrophysics for People in a Hurry*	523.01
Tyson, Neil deGrasse. *Cosmic Queries*	523.1
Tyson, Neil deGrasse. *Letters from an Astrophysicist*	520.92
Tyson, Neil deGrasse. *Starry Messenger*	901
Tyson, Neil deGrasse. *To Infinity and Beyond*	520
Tyson, Neil deGrasse. *Welcome to the Universe*	523.1
★*Astrophysics for People in a Hurry*. Tyson, Neil deGrasse	523.01
Asylum. Okporo, Edafe	B
ASYLUM, RIGHT OF	
Paxson, Margaret. *The Plateau*	362.87
★*At Canaan's Edge*. Branch, Taylor	323.1196
At Dawn We Slept. Prange, Gordon W.	940.54
★*At Day's Close*. Ekirch, A. Roger	306.4
★*At Home*. Bryson, Bill	643
At Home in the Kitchen. Kinch, David	641.5973
At Home with Nature. Gidding, John	635.9
At My Table. Lawson, Nigella	641.59
At The Elbows of My Elders. Grant, Gail Milissa	B
★*At The Existentialist Cafe*. Bakewell, Sarah	920
At The Hands of Persons Unknown. Dray, Philip	364.1
At The Same Time. Sontag, Susan	814
AT-RISK YOUTH	
Ice-T. *Split Decision*	920
Kim, Anne. ★*Abandoned*	305.2350973
Leach, Samantha. ★*The Elissas*	362.73
Sweeney, Jennifer. *Literacy*	027.62
ATHEISM	
Bignon, Guillaume. *Confessions of a French Atheist*	239
Dawkins, Richard. *An Appetite for Wonder*	B
De Botton, Alain. *Religion for Atheists*	200
Gay, Peter. *A Godless Jew*	150.19
Hitchens, Christopher. *The Four Horsemen*	211
Minois, Georges. *The Atheist's Bible*	200
Zuckerman, Phil. *Living the Secular Life*	211
The Atheist's Bible. Minois, Georges	200
ATHEISTS	
Bignon, Guillaume. *Confessions of a French Atheist*	239
De Botton, Alain. *Religion for Atheists*	200
ATHENS, ANCIENT GREECE	
Kagan, Donald. *The Peloponnesian War*	938
Kagan, Donald. *Thucydides*	938
Roberts, Jennifer Tolbert. *The Plague of War*	938
Stone, I. F. *The Trial of Socrates*	183
ATHENS, GREECE	
Everitt, Anthony. *The Rise of Athens*	938
Hughes, Bettany. ★*The Hemlock Cup*	B
Atherley, Kate	
The Knitter's Dictionary	746.43
The Athlete's Guide to Recovery. Rountree, Sage	617.1
ATHLETES	
Aschwanden, Christie. *Good to Go*	617.1
Bamberger, Michael. *The Second Life of Tiger Woods*	B
Barnes, Katie. ★*Fair Play*	796.082
Benedict, Jeff. ★*Tiger Woods*	B
Bercovici, Jeff. *Play On*	613.7
Berkow, Ira. *How Life Imitates Sports*	070.4
Brown, Daniel James. ★*The Boys in the Boat*	797.12
Buford, Kate. *Native American Son*	B
Butler, Brin-Jonathan. *The Domino Diaries*	796.83
Clarey, Christopher. ★*The Master*	B
Cox, Lynne. *Swimming to Antarctica*	B
Crawford, Bill. ★*All American*	B
Crouse, Karen. *Norwich*	796
Gessner, David. *Ultimate Glory*	796.2
Halberstam, David. *The Amateurs*	B
Hamilton, Tyler. *The Secret Race*	796.62
Kohan, Rafi. ★*Trash Talk*	179
Maraniss, David. *Clemente*	B
Maraniss, David. ★*Path Lit by Lightning*	B
McDougall, Christopher. ★*Born to Run*	796.42
Moore, Colten. *Catching the Sky*	B
Norton, Hughes. ★*Rainmaker*	796.352
Parry, John Weston. *The Burden of Sports*	796.01
Pesca, Mike. *Upon Further Review*	796
Polly, Matthew. ★*Bruce Lee*	B
Ravin, Idan. *The Hoops Whisperer*	796.323
Rivera, Mariano. *The Closer*	B
Rotella, Robert J. *How Champions Think*	796.01
Rountree, Sage. *The Athlete's Guide to Recovery*	617.1
Santiago, Wilfred. *"21"*	741.5
Thomas, Etan. *We Matter*	796.08
Thompson, Wright. *The Cost of These Dreams*	B
Walker, Sam. *The Captain Class*	796.07
Wertheim, L. Jon. *This Is Your Brain on Sports*	796.01
Zimmerman, Paul. *Dr. Z*	B
ATHLETES WITH DISABILITIES	
Shriver, Timothy P. *Fully Alive*	796.087
ATHLETIC ABILITY	
Montgomery, Patrick. *Baseball's Great Expectations*	796.357
ATHLETIC COACHES	
Abdul-Jabbar, Kareem. *Coach Wooden and Me*	B
Davis, Seth. *Getting to Us*	796.07
Davis, Seth. *Wooden*	B
O'Connor, Ian. *Coach K*	B
Thompson, Wright. *The Cost of These Dreams*	B
ATHLETIC SHOES	
Knight, Philip H. *Shoe Dog*	B
ATKINS, VERA, 1908-2000	
Helm, Sarah. *A Life in Secrets*	B
Atkinson, Rick	
An Army at Dawn	940.54
★*The British Are Coming*	973.3
The Day of Battle	940.54
The Guns at Last Light	940.54
ATLANTA, GEORGIA	
Trethewey, Natasha D. ★*Memorial Drive*	B
Williams, Patricia. *Rabbit*	B
Atlantic. Winchester, Simon	551.46
ATLANTIC CITY, NEW JERSEY	
Wong, Jane. ★*Meet Me Tonight in Atlantic City*	B

PUBLIC LIBRARY CORE COLLECTION: NONFICTION
Twentieth Edition

ATLANTIC COAST (UNITED STATES)
   Messineo, Janet. *Casting into the Light* — 799.1
ATLANTIC OCEAN
   Berlin, Ira. *The Making of African America* — 973
   Carson, Rachel. *Under the Sea Wind* — 578.77
   Churchill, Winston. *The Grand Alliance* — 940.53
   Diaz, Von. ★*Islas* — 641.59
   Dimbleby, Jonathan. *The Battle of the Atlantic* — 940.54
   Dolin, Eric Jay. *Black Flags, Blue Waters* — 973.2
   Dolin, Eric Jay. *A Furious Sky* — 363.34
   Junger, Sebastian. *The Perfect Storm* — 974.4
   Slade, Rachel. *Into the Raging Sea* — 910.91
   Winchester, Simon. *Atlantic* — 551.46
Atlas Obscura. Foer, Joshua — 910.41
★*Atlas Obscura 2nd Ed.* Foer, Joshua — 910.41
Atlas of a Lost World. Childs, Craig — 551.7
Atlas of Islamic History. Sluglett, Peter — 912.19
An Atlas of Natural Beauty. Taillac, Victoire de — 646.7
ATLASES
   Carballo, David M. *America* — 912
   Hayes, Derek. *Historical Atlas of the United States* — 911
   Sluglett, Peter. *Atlas of Islamic History* — 912.19
   Tirion, Wil. *The Cambridge Star Atlas* — 523.8
Atleework, Kendra
   Miracle Country — 979.4
ATLEEWORK, KENDRA, 1989-
   Atleework, Kendra. *Miracle Country* — 979.4
ATMOSPHERE
   Kean, Sam. *Caesar's Last Breath* — 551.51
Atomic Adventures. Mahaffey, James A. — 333.792
The Atomic Bazaar. Langewiesche, William — 355.02
ATOMIC BOMB
   Barrett, David Dean. *140 Days to Hiroshima* — 940.54
   Bascomb, Neal. *The Winter Fortress* — 940.54
   Bird, Kai. *American Prometheus* — B
   Blume, Lesley M. M. *Fallout* — 940.54
   Conant, Jennet. *Man of the Hour* — B
   Ham, Paul. *Hiroshima Nagasaki* — 940.54
   Hersey, John. ★*Hiroshima* — 940.54
   Kaplan, Fred M. *The Bomb* — 355.8
   Kean, Sam. *The Bastard Brigade* — 355.8
   Kiernan, Denise. *The Girls of Atomic City* — 976.8
   Kunetka, James W. *The General and the Genius* — 355.8
   Pellegrino, Charles R. *To Hell and Back* — 940.54
   Preston, Diana. *Before the Fallout* — 303.48
   Sakamoto, Pamela Rotner. *Midnight in Broad Daylight* — 940.54
   Sheinkin, Steve. *Bomb* — 623.4
   Smith, Jim B. *The Last Mission* — 940.54
   Southard, Susan. *Nagasaki* — 940.54
   Toll, Ian W. *Twilight of the Gods* — 940.54
   Wallace, Chris. *Countdown 1945* — 940.54
★*Atomic Habits*. Clear, James — 155.24
ATOMIC THEORY
   Kaku, Michio. *Quantum Supremacy* — 006.3
   Mahaffey, James A. *Atomic Adventures* — 333.792
ATOMS
   Feynman, Richard P. ★*Six Easy Pieces* — 530
   Gray, Theodore W. ★*The Elements* — 546
   Levitt, Dan. *What's Gotten into You* — 539.7
   Mahaffey, James A. *Atomic Adventures* — 333.792
Atoms Under the Floorboards. Woodford, Chris — 500
ATONEMENT
   Ruttenberg, Danya. *On Repentance and Repair* — 202
Atria, Travis
   Better Days Will Come Again — B
ATROCITIES
   Anand, Anita. *The Patient Assassin* — B
   Applebaum, Anne. ★*Red Famine* — 947.708
   Bass, Gary Jonathan. ★*Judgment at Tokyo* — 952.04
   Bradley, James. *Flyboys* — 940.54
   Carney, Scott. *The Vortex* — 954.92
   Cervantes, Fernando. *Conquistadores* — 970.01
   Childers, Thomas. *The Third Reich* — 943.086
   Deng, Alephonsion. *They Poured Fire on Us from the Sky* — B
   Fair, Eric. *Consequence* — B
   Frederick, Jim. *Black Hearts* — 956.7044
   Gross, Jan Tomasz. *Neighbors* — 940.53
   Ham, Paul. *Hiroshima Nagasaki* — 940.54
   Hastings, Max. ★*Vietnam* — 959.704
   Hatzfeld, Jean. *Blood Papa* — 967.5710431
   Hatzfeld, Jean. *Machete Season* — 967.57104
   Hoock, Holger. *Scars of Independence* — 973.3
   Igort. *The Ukrainian and Russian Notebooks* — 741.5
   Macadam, Heather Dune. *999* — 940.53
   Mackeen, Dawn Anahid. *The Hundred-Year Walk* — 956.6
   Marwell, David G. *Mengele* — B
   Montero, David. ★*The Stolen Wealth of Slavery* — 381
   Norman, Michael. *Tears in the Darkness* — 940.54
   Pick-Goslar, Hannah Elizabeth. ★*My Friend Anne Frank* — B
   Rees, Laurence. *Auschwitz* — 940.53
   Rogoyska, Jane. *Surviving Katyn* — 940.54
   Rohde, David. *Endgame* — 949.703
   Samer. *The Raqqa Diaries* — 956.9104
   Sands, Philippe. *The Ratline* — B
   Satter, David. *The Less You Know, the Better You Sleep* — 947.086
   Scott, James. *Rampage* — 940.54
   Sides, Hampton. ★*Ghost Soldiers* — 940.54
   Snyder, Timothy. ★*Bloodlands* — 940.54
   Stangneth, Bettina. *Eichmann Before Jerusalem* — B
   Stern, Jessica. *My War Criminal* — 341.6
   Taing, Mae Bunseng. *Under the Naga Tail* — B
   Ung, Loung. *First They Killed My Father* — 959.604
   Ung, Loung. *Lucky Child* — B
   V. ★*Reckoning* — 814
   Wachsmann, Nikolaus. *Kl* — 940.53
   Warrick, Joby. *Red Line* — 956.9104
ATTACHMENT BEHAVIOR
   Marriott, Sue. *Secure Relating* — 158.1
Attas, Amy
   Pets and the City — B
ATTAS, AMY
   Attas, Amy. *Pets and the City* — B
ATTEMPTED ASSASSINATION
   Carroll, Rory. *There Will Be Fire* — 363.325
   Maier, Thomas. *Mafia Spies* — 364.1060973
   Meltzer, Brad. *The Lincoln Conspiracy* — 973.7092
   Widmer, Edward L. *Lincoln on the Verge* — B
ATTEMPTED MURDER
   Hale, Kathleen. ★*Slenderman* — 364.152
   Rubin, Kathy Kleiner. *A Light in the Dark* — 364.152
   Rushdie, Salman. ★*Knife* — B
Attenberg, Jami
   1000 Words — 808.02
Attenborough, David
   Adventures of a Young Naturalist — B
   Life in the Undergrowth — 592
   The Life of Birds — 598.15
   A Life on Our Planet — 508
ATTENBOROUGH, DAVID, 1926-
   Attenborough, David. *Adventures of a Young Naturalist* — B
   Attenborough, David. *A Life on Our Planet* — 508
ATTENTION
   Cameron, Julia. ★*The Listening Path* — 153.6
   Crawford, Matthew B. *The World Beyond Your Head* — 155.2
   Goleman, Daniel. *Focus* — 153.7
The Attention Merchants. Wu, Tim — 659.1
ATTENTION-DEFICIT HYPERACTIVITY DISORDER
   Barkley, Russell A. *Taking Charge of ADHD* — 618.92
   Davis, KC. ★*How to Keep House While Drowning* — 648
   Flink, David. *Thinking Differently* — 371.9
   Gadsby, Hannah. ★*Ten Steps to Nanette* — B
   Milliken, Kirsten. *PLAYDHD* — 616.85
   Nigg, Joel T. *Getting Ahead of ADHD* — 618.92
   Saline, Sharon. *What Your ADHD Child Wishes You Knew* — 618.92
   Saul, Richard. *ADHD Does Not Exist* — 618.92
   Schwarz, Alan. *ADHD Nation* — 618.92
Attia, Peter
   ★*Outlive* — 612.6
Atticus Finch. Crespino, Joseph — B
ATTITUDE
   Currid-Halkett, Elizabeth. *The Overlooked Americans* — 307.76
   Hendricks, Gay. *Conscious Luck* — 158.1
   Hessler, Peter. *Other Rivers* — 378.1
   Pinker, Steven. ★*Enlightenment Now* — 303.44
   Visser, Margaret. *The Gift of Thanks* — 394

AUTHOR, TITLE, SERIES AND SUBJECT INDEX

ATTITUDE CHANGE
    Hamilton, Denise. ★*Indivisible* — 658.3
    Roberts, Randy. *Blood Brothers* — 920
ATTORNEYS GENERAL
    Selvaratnam, Tanya. *Assume Nothing* — B
★*Attracting Beneficial Bugs to Your Garden*. Walliser, Jessica — 635
Attwell, David
    J. M. Coetzee and the Life of Writing — 823
Atwood, Margaret
    Burning Questions — 814
    Dearly — 811
    In Other Worlds — 813
ATWOOD, MARGARET, 1939-
    Atwood, Margaret. *In Other Worlds* — 813
Au-Yeung, Angel
    Wonder Boy — B
Auburn, David
    Proof — 812
AUCHINCLOSS, JANET LEE, 1907-1989
    Taraborrelli, J. Randy. *Jackie, Janet & Lee* — 920
Audacity. Chait, Jonathan — 973.932
★*The Audacity of Hope*. Obama, Barack — B
Auden, W. H.
    Collected Poems — 811
    Selected Poems — 821
AUDIBERT-BOULLOCHE, CHRISTIANE
    Kaiser, Charles. *The Cost of Courage* — B
Audience of One. Poniewozik, James — 324.7
Audienceology. Goetz, Kevin — 791.43
AUDITIONS
    Rannells, Andrew. *Too Much Is Not Enough* — 792.02
Audubon Birdhouse Book. Barker, Margaret A. — 728
Audubon North American Birdfeeder Guide. Burton, Robert — 598
The *Audubon* Society field guide series [Series]. Meinkoth, Norman August — 592
★The *Audubon* Society Field Guide to North American Fossils. Thompson, Ida — 560
★The *Audubon* Society Field Guide to North American Insects and Spiders. Milne, Lorus Johnson — 595.7097
The *Audubon* Society Field Guide to North American Mushrooms. Lincoff, Gary — 579.6
The *Audubon* Society Field Guide to North American Seashells. Rehder, Harald Alfred — 594
The *Audubon* Society Field Guide to North American Seashore Creatures. Meinkoth, Norman August — 592
The *Audubon* Society Field Guide to North American Trees. Little, Elbert L. — 582.16097

AUDUBON, JOHN JAMES, 1785-1851
    Kaufman, Kenn. *The Birds That Audubon Missed* — 598
Auerbach, Annie
    Flex — 331.25
August Wilson. Hartigan, Patti — B
Augustine
    Concerning the City of God Against the Pagans — 239
    Confessions — B
AUGUSTINE, SAINT, BISHOP OF HIPPO
    Augustine. *Confessions* — B
    Wills, Garry. *Saint Augustine* — B
Augustus. Goldsworthy, Adrian Keith — B
AUGUSTUS, EMPEROR OF ROME, 63 B.C.E.-14 C.E
    Goldsworthy, Adrian Keith. *Augustus* — B
    Strauss, Barry S. ★*The War That Made the Roman Empire* — 937
Auletta, Ken
    Frenemies — 659.1
    Googled — 338.7
    ★*Hollywood Ending* — 791.43
    Media Man — B
AUNG SAN SUU KYI
    Thant Myint-U. *The Hidden History of Burma* — 959.105
Ausaja, S. M. M.
    Bollywood — 791.43
Auschwitz. Rees, Laurence — 940.53
Austen, Ben
    Correction — 364.6
AUSTEN, JANE, 1775-1817
    Feder, Rachel. *The Darcy Myth* — 823
    Kelly, Helena. *Jane Austen, the Secret Radical* — 823
Auster, Paul
    Bloodbath Nation — 363.33
    Burning Boy — B
Austerlitz, Saul
    Just a Shot Away — 781.66078
    Kind of a Big Deal — 791.43
    Money for Nothing — 780.26
Austin, Nefertiti
    Motherhood so White — B
AUSTIN, NEFERTITI
    Austin, Nefertiti. *Motherhood so White* — B
AUSTIN, TEXAS
    Goudeau, Jessica. ★*After the Last Border* — 362.83
AUSTRALIA
    Bryson, Bill. *In a Sunburned Country* — 919
    Corrigan, Kelly. *Glitter and Glue* — B
    Hughes, Robert. *The Fatal Shore* — 994
    Keneally, Thomas. *A Commonwealth of Thieves* — 994
AUSTRALIAN HISTORY
    Hughes, Robert. *The Fatal Shore* — 994
    Keneally, Thomas. *A Commonwealth of Thieves* — 994
    Preston, Diana. *Paradise in Chains* — 996.18
AUSTRALIAN LITERATURE
    Baird, Julia. ★*Victoria the Queen* — B
    Burke, Carolyn. *Lee Miller* — B
    Doust, Kelly. *The Power Age* — 305.244
    Finkel, Elizabeth. *The Genome Generation* — 599.93
    Flannery, Tim F. *Europe* — 508.4
    Fullilove, Michael. *Rendezvous with Destiny* — 973.917092
    Grose, Peter. *A Good Place to Hide* — 940.53
    Ham, Paul. *Hiroshima Nagasaki* — 940.54
    Hughes, Robert. *The Fatal Shore* — 994
    Jones, Darryl N. *The Birds at My Table* — 598.072
    Keneally, Thomas. *A Commonwealth of Thieves* — 994
    McCalman, Iain. *Darwin's Armada* — 576.8
    Mearns, David L. *The Shipwreck Hunter* — 910.452
    Olds, Sally. ★*People Who Lunch* — 824
    Richardson, Lance. *House of Nutter* — B
    Seo, Bo. *Good Arguments* — 808.53
    Smee, Sebastian. *The Art of Rivalry* — 700.92
    Taylor, Cory. *Dying* — B
    Turney, Chris. *1912* — 998
    White, Shane. *Prince of Darkness* — B
    Wilson, Sarah. *First, We Make the Beast Beautiful* — 616.85
    Young, Damon. *The Art of Reading* — 028.9
    Zhu, Mimi. *Be Not Afraid of Love* — 152.4
AUSTRALOPITHECUS AFARENSIS
    Johanson, Donald C. *Lucy* — 569
AUSTRIA
    Golinkin, Lev. *A Backpack, a Bear, and Eight Crates of Vodka* — B
    King, Greg. *The Assassination of the Archduke* — B
    King, Greg. *Twilight of Empire* — 943.6
    Lichtblau, Eric. *Return to the Reich* — B
    Pressman, Steven. *50 Children* — 940.53
    Schindler, Meriel. *The Lost Cafe Schindler* — 943.64
    Swafford, Jan. ★*Beethoven* — B
Authentic Mexican. Bayless, Rick — 641.5972
★*The Authentic Ukrainian Kitchen*. Klopotenko, Yevhen — 641.594
AUTHENTICITY (PHILOSOPHY)
    Bly, Robert. *Collected Poems* — 811
    Fox, Dan. *Pretentiousness* — 700
Author in Chief. Fehrman, Craig — 920
AUTHORITARIANISM
    Ackerman, Spencer. *Reign of Terror* — 973.931
    Applebaum, Anne. *Twilight of Democracy* — 321.9
    Evangelista, Patricia. ★*Some People Need Killing* — 364.4
    Frum, David. *Trumpocracy* — 973.933
    Hubbard, Ben (Journalist). *Mbs* — B
    Neiwert, David A. ★*The Age of Insurrection* — 303.48
    Osnos, Evan. *Age of Ambition* — 951.06
    Ressa, Maria. ★*How to Stand up to a Dictator* — 070.92
    Richardson, Heather Cox. *Democracy Awakening* — 320.473
    Stevens, Stuart. *The Conspiracy to End America* — 324.2734
    Strittmatter, Kai. *We Have Been Harmonized* — 323.44
    Taing, Mae Bunseng. *Under the Naga Tail* — B
    Wolf, Martin. ★*The Crisis of Democratic Capitalism* — 330.12
AUTHORITY
    Lewis, James R. *Legitimating New Religions* — 200
★*The Authority of the Court and the Peril of Politics*. Breyer, Stephen G. — 347.73

PUBLIC LIBRARY CORE COLLECTION: NONFICTION
Twentieth Edition

AUTHORS

Acocella, Joan Ross. ★*The Bloodied Nightgown*	814
Alexander, Kwame. *Why Fathers Cry at Night*	B
Allende, Isabel. *My Invented Country*	B
Allende, Isabel. ★*Paula*	B
Allende, Isabel. *The Sum of Our Days*	B
Alterman, Sara Faith. *Let's Never Talk About This Again*	616.8
Baker, Nicholson. *Finding a Likeness*	B
Bartlett, Rosamund. ★*Tolstoy*	B
Bellos, David. *The Novel of the Century*	843
Bennett, Jackie. *The Writer's Garden*	920
Bragg, Rick. *The Speckled Beauty*	636.7
Broome, Brian. ★*Punch Me up to the Gods*	B
Caro, Robert A. ★*Working*	B
Chabon, Michael. *Maps and Legends*	801
Chee, Alexander. *How to Write an Autobiographical Novel*	B
Coetzee, J. M. *Late Essays, 2006-2017*	824
Cole, Teju. *Blind Spot*	770
Collins, Max Allan. *Spillane*	B
Corbett, Emily. *In Transition*	809
Cott, Jonathan. *There's a Mystery There*	813
Coyne, Tom. *A Course Called Scotland*	796.352
Damrosch, David. *Around the World in 80 Books*	809
Damrosch, Leopold. *The Club*	920
Danticat, Edwidge. *The Art of Death*	809
Dawidziak, Mark. *A Mystery of Mysteries*	B
Delorme, Geoffroy. *Deer Man*	599.65
Dery, Mark. *Born to Be Posthumous*	B
Di Cintio, Marcello. *Pay No Heed to the Rockets*	956.9405
Fehrman, Craig. *Author in Chief*	920
Feinstein, Adam. *Pablo Neruda*	B
Figes, Orlando. *The Europeans*	920
Frampton, Saul. *When I Am Playing with My Cat, How Do I Know She Is Not Playing with Me?*	844
Gaiman, Neil. *The View from the Cheap Seats*	824
Gomez, Edgar. *High-Risk Homosexual*	B
Gopnik, Adam. *All That Happiness Is*	158.1
Greenfield, Robert. *True West*	B
Handler, Daniel. ★*And Then? and Then? What Else?*	813
Hardwick, Elizabeth. *The Dolphin Letters, 1970-1979*	811
Harrison, Jim. *The Search for the Genuine*	814
Havrilesky, Heather. *What If This Were Enough?*	152.4
Herzog, Werner. ★*Every Man for Himself and God Against All*	B
Hessler, Peter. *Other Rivers*	378.1
Hester, Diarmuid. *Nothing Ever Just Disappears*	306.76
Heughan, Sam. *Waypoints*	B
Jackson, Lawrence Patrick. *Chester B. Himes*	B
Jackson, Mitchell S. *Survival Math*	B
Karr, Mary. *The Art of Memoir*	B
Kendi, Ibram X. ★*How to Raise an Antiracist*	649
Knausgaard, Karl Ove. *So Much Longing in so Little Space*	759.81
Knausgaard, Karl Ove. *Spring*	B
Lamott, Anne. *Bird by Bird*	808
Larimer, Kevin. *The Poets & Writers Complete Guide to Being a Writer*	808
Laughlin, James. *The Luck of Friendship*	B
Le Guin, Ursula K. *So Far so Good*	811
Lear, Linda J. *Beatrix Potter*	B
Mahjoub, Jamal. *A Line in the River*	962.404
Marshall, Greg. *Leg*	B
Martin, Gerald. ★*Gabriel Garcia Marquez*	B
McCann, Colum. *Letters to a Young Writer*	808.02
McCourt, Frank. *'Tis*	B
McDermott, Alice. *What About the Baby?*	814
McIlwaine, Catherine. *Tolkien*	002.09
Miller, Kei. *Things I Have Withheld*	814
Montillo, Roseanne. *Deliberate Cruelty*	364.152
Moore, Lorrie. *See What Can Be Done*	801
Moss, Adam. ★*The Work of Art*	701
Murakami, Haruki. ★*Absolutely on Music*	784.2
Murakami, Haruki. ★*Novelist as a Vocation*	895.64
Ngugi wa Thiong'o. *In the House of the Interpreter*	B
Norwick, Kenneth P. *The Legal Guide for Writers, Artists and Other Creative People*	346.04
Ondaatje, Michael. *A Year of Last Things*	811
Orwell, George. *Diaries*	828
Palahniuk, Chuck. *Consider This*	B
Palmer, Amanda. ★*The Art of Asking*	782.42164
Parini, Jay. *Borges and Me*	813
Percy, Benjamin. *Thrill Me*	808.3
Popova, Maria. *Figuring*	920
Prose, Francine. *1974*	B
Prose, Francine. *What to Read and Why*	028
Raban, Jonathan. *Father and Son*	B
Rilke, Rainer Maria. ★*Letters to a Young Poet*	831
Robb, Graham. *France*	944
Robinson, Kim Stanley. *The High Sierra*	917.94
Roiphe, Katie. *The Violet Hour*	809
Rosnay, Tatiana de. *Manderley Forever*	B
Rushdie, Salman. ★*Knife*	B
Rushdie, Salman. *Languages of Truth*	824
Russo, Richard. *The Destiny Thief*	814
Sacks, Oliver. *Gratitude*	306.9
Salama, Jordan. ★*Stranger in the Desert*	982
Scalzi, John. *Don't Live for Your Obituary*	808.02
Sedaris, David. ★*A Carnival of Snackery*	818
Sedaris, David. ★*Happy-Go-Lucky*	814
Shehadeh, Raja. *Where the Line Is Drawn*	956.9405
Smith, Patti. ★*M Train*	B
Twain, Mark. *Autobiography of Mark Twain*	B
Twain, Mark. ★*Autobiography of Mark Twain*	B
Twain, Mark. ★*Autobiography of Mark Twain*	B
Vargas Llosa, Mario. *The Call of the Tribe*	868
Verdelle, A. J. *Miss Chloe*	B
Wainaina, Binyavanga. *One Day I Will Write About This Place*	B
Wang, Connie. *Oh My Mother!*	B
Weiner, Eric. *Ben & Me*	B
Weinman, Sarah. *The Real Lolita*	362.88092
Wilder, Laura Ingalls. *The Selected Letters of Laura Ingalls Wilder*	B
Wilson, A. N. *The Mystery of Charles Dickens*	823
Woolever, Laurie. *Bourdain*	B
Worsley, Lucy. ★*Agatha Christie*	B
Wulf, Andrea. *Magnificent Rebels*	830.9
Yancey, Philip. ★*Where the Light Fell*	B
Zhu, Mimi. *Be Not Afraid of Love*	152.4
Zimmerman, Paul. *Dr. Z*	B

AUTHORS AND EDITORS

Miller, Adrienne. *In the Land of Men*	070.5

AUTHORS AND READERS

Chabon, Michael. *Maps and Legends*	801
Coffin, Judith G. *Sex, Love, and Letters*	848

AUTHORS' SPOUSES

Funder, Anna. *Wifedom*	B

AUTHORS, AMERICAN

Abbott, Karen. *American Rose*	B
Angelou, Maya. ★*I Know Why the Caged Bird Sings*	B
Angelou, Maya. *A Song Flung up to Heaven*	B
Auster, Paul. *Burning Boy*	B
Bader, Philip. *African-American Writers*	810.9
Baker, Nicholson. *Baseless*	358
Bass, Rick. *The Traveling Feast*	B
Bass, Rick. *Why I Came West*	333.78
Beavan, Colin. *No Impact Man*	B
Bell, Madison Smartt. *Child of Light*	B
Berry, Wendell. ★*The World-Ending Fire*	818
Boylan, Jennifer Finney. *Good Boy*	B
Bradbury, Ray. ★*Remembrance*	813
Bram, Christopher. *Eminent Outlaws*	920
Brown, David S. *Paradise Lost*	813
Bryson, Bill. *The Life and Times of the Thunderbolt Kid*	B
Burroughs, Augusten. *Toil & Trouble*	B
Capote, Truman. ★*Portraits and Observations*	814
Capote, Truman. *Too Brief a Treat*	B
Carcaterra, Lorenzo. *Three Dreamers*	B
Caro, Robert A. ★*Working*	B
Cather, Willa. *The Selected Letters of Willa Cather*	B
Chabon, Michael. *Manhood for Amateurs*	B
Cheever, Susan. *American Bloomsbury*	920
Cisneros, Sandra. *A House of My Own*	B
Clark, Heather. ★*Red Comet*	B
Conroy, Pat. *My Losing Season*	B
Copaken, Deborah. *Ladyparts*	B
Crespino, Joseph. *Atticus Finch*	B
Danler, Stephanie. *Stray*	B
Danticat, Edwidge. ★*Brother, I'm Dying*	B
Daugherty, Tracy. *Larry McMurtry*	B
Daugherty, Tracy. *The Last Love Song*	B

AUTHOR, TITLE, SERIES AND SUBJECT INDEX

Davis, Jack E. *An Everglades Providence*	B
Dawidziak, Mark. *A Mystery of Mysteries*	B
Dearborn, Mary V. *Ernest Hemingway*	B
Didion, Joan. ★*The Year of Magical Thinking*	B
Dillard, Annie. *An American Childhood*	B
Dillard, Annie. *The Writing Life*	B
Dubus, Andre. *Townie*	B
Ehrlich, Gretel. *Unsolaced*	B
Elledge, Scott. *E.B. White*	B
Ellison, Ralph. *The Selected Letters of Ralph Ellison*	813
Erdrich, Louise. *Books and Islands in Ojibwe Country*	977
Franklin, Ruth. *Shirley Jackson*	B
Fraser, Caroline. ★*Prairie Fires*	B
Gary, Amy. *In the Great Green Room*	813
Ginsberg, Allen. *Best Minds of My Generation*	810.9
Greenfield, Robert. *True West*	B
Hart, James David. *The Oxford Companion to American Literature*	810.9
Hemingway, Ernest. *Dear Papa*	813
Herbert, Brian. *Dreamer of Dune*	B
Heyman, Stephen. *The Planter of Modern Life*	B
Hitchens, Christopher. *Hitch-22*	920
Hitchens, Christopher. *Mortality*	304.6
Hodgman, John. *Medallion Status*	B
Hogan, Linda. *The Woman Who Watches Over the World*	B
Hood, Ann. *Kitchen Yarns*	641.5
Hughes, Langston. ★*I Wonder as I Wander*	B
Hurston, Zora Neale. *Dust Tracks on a Road*	B
Hurston, Zora Neale. *Zora Neale Hurston*	B
Jackson, Shirley. ★*The Letters of Shirley Jackson*	813
Johnson, Joyce. *The Voice Is All*	B
Jones, Brian Jay. ★*Becoming Dr. Seuss*	B
Kerouac, Jack. *Selected Letters, 1940-1956*	813
Kessler, Lauren. *Raising the Barre*	792.8
King, Stephen. *On Writing*	B
Kingston, Maxine Hong. *The Woman Warrior*	B
Lamott, Anne. ★*Dusk, Night, Dawn*	B
Lamott, Anne. ★*Somehow*	814
Le Guin, Ursula K. *Ursula K. Le Guin*	B
Leader, Zachary. *The Life of Saul Bellow*	B
Li, Yiyun. *Dear Friend, from My Life I Write to You in Your Life*	B
Lopez, Barry Holstun. *Horizon*	B
Manchester, William. *Goodbye, Darkness*	B
Matar, Hisham. *The Return*	B
Matteson, John. *Eden's Outcasts*	920
McCullough, David G. *The Greater Journey*	920
Merton, Thomas. ★*The Seven Storey Mountain*	B
Messud, Claire. *Kant's Little Prussian Head and Other Reasons Why I Write*	B
Millet, Lydia. *We Loved It All*	813
Moore, Susanna. *Miss Aluminum*	813
Mullen, Bill. ★*James Baldwin*	B
Nevala-Lee, Alec. *Astounding*	809.3
Niven, Penelope. *Thornton Wilder*	B
O'Hara, Maryanne. *Little Matches*	B
Orner, Peter. *Am I Alone Here?*	814
Palahniuk, Chuck. *Consider This*	B
Patchett, Ann. *This Is the Story of a Happy Marriage*	B
Patterson, James. *James Patterson by James Patterson*	B
Phillips, Julie. *James Tiptree, Jr.*	B
Pinckney, Darryl. *Come Back in September*	B
Pitzer, Andrea. *The Secret History of Vladimir Nabokov*	813
Rakoff, Joanna Smith. *My Salinger Year*	B
Rampersad, Arnold. ★*Ralph Ellison*	B
Richardson, Robert D. *Emerson*	814
Rosenblatt, J. Alison. *The Beauty of Living*	B
Schlesinger, Arthur M. *Journals, 1952-2000*	973.91092
Schultz, Kevin Michael. *Buckley and Mailer*	920
Schultz, Philip. *Comforts of the Abyss*	801
Shapland, Jenn. *My Autobiography of Carson McCullers*	B
Shelden, Michael. *Mark Twain*	B
Shteyngart, Gary. ★*Little Failure*	B
Slawenski, Kenneth. ★*Salinger*	B
Slouka, Mark. *Nobody's Son*	B
Smiley, Jane. *Thirteen Ways of Looking at the Novel*	B
Smith, Lee. *Dimestore*	975.5
Souder, William. *Mad at the World*	813
Steinbeck, John. *Travels with Charley*	B
Strayed, Cheryl. ★*Wild*	B
Styron, William. *My Generation*	814
Tan, Amy. ★*Where the Past Begins*	B
Taylor, Justin. *Riding with the Ghost*	B
Tea, Michelle. *Against Memoir*	B
Theroux, Paul. *The Great Railway Bazaar*	915
Theroux, Paul. *Riding the Iron Rooster*	915
Thomas, R. Eric. ★*Congratulations, the Best Is Over!*	B
Thomas, R. Eric. *Here for It*	B
Thompson, Juan F. *Stories I Tell Myself*	B
Thoreau, Henry David. *The Maine Woods*	917
Thoreau, Henry David. ★*Walden, Or, Life in the Woods*	813
Tresch, John. *The Reason for the Darkness of the Night*	B
Twain, Mark. *Autobiography of Mark Twain*	B
Twain, Mark. ★*Autobiography of Mark Twain*	B
Twain, Mark. ★*Autobiography of Mark Twain*	B
Vonnegut, Kurt. *Kurt Vonnegut*	813
Vonnegut, Kurt. ★*A Man Without a Country*	818
Walker, Alice. *Gathering Blossoms Under Fire*	B
Walls, Laura Dassow. ★*Henry David Thoreau*	B
Watts, Steven. *Self-Help Messiah*	B
Wayne, Tiffany K. *Critical Companion to Ralph Waldo Emerson*	814
Weller, Sam. *The Bradbury Chronicles*	B
Welty, Eudora. *One Writer's Beginnings*	B
Wilder, Laura Ingalls. *Pioneer Girl*	B
Wolff, Tobias. *This Boy's Life*	B
Wong, Carmen Rita. *Why Didn't You Tell Me?*	B
Woodress, James Leslie. *Willa Cather*	B
Wright, Lawrence. *Going Clear*	299
Wright, Richard. ★*Black Boy*	B

AUTHORS, ARGENTINE

Parini, Jay. *Borges and Me*	813
Williamson, Edwin. *Borges*	B

AUTHORS, AUSTRALIAN

Attwell, David. *J. M. Coetzee and the Life of Writing*	823

AUTHORS, BRAZILIAN

Moser, Benjamin. *Why This World*	B

AUTHORS, BRITISH

Dennison, Matthew. *The Man in the Willows*	B
Rosnay, Tatiana de. *Manderley Forever*	B
Rushdie, Salman. *Joseph Anton*	B
Tomalin, Claire. *Samuel Pepys*	B

AUTHORS, CANADIAN

Mowat, Farley. *Born Naked*	B
Wagamese, Richard. *One Native Life*	B

AUTHORS, CHINESE

Guo, Xiaolu. *Nine Continents*	B

AUTHORS, COLOMBIAN

Garcia Marquez, Gabriel. *Living to Tell the Tale*	B
Garcia, Rodrigo. *A Farewell to Gabo and Mercedes*	B
Martin, Gerald. ★*Gabriel Garcia Marquez*	B

AUTHORS, DANISH

Dinesen, Isak. *Out of Africa*	967.62

AUTHORS, ENGLISH

Boswell, James. ★*The Life of Samuel Johnson*	B
Bryson, Bill. *Shakespeare*	B
Campbell, Hayley. *The Art of Neil Gaiman*	B
Conradi, Peter J. *Iris*	B
Cusk, Rachel. *Aftermath*	B
Dennison, Matthew. *Behind the Mask*	B
Eade, Philip. *Evelyn Waugh*	B
Gaskell, Elizabeth Cleghorn. *The Life of Charlotte Bronte*	B
Glendinning, Victoria. *Leonard Woolf*	B
Gordon, Charlotte. *Romantic Outlaws*	920
Gordon, Edmund. *The Invention of Angela Carter*	B
Greene, Graham. *Graham Greene*	823
Hardy, Thomas. *The Collected Letters of Thomas Hardy*	823
Harman, Claire. *Charlotte Bronte*	B
Hastings, Selina. *The Secret Lives of Somerset Maugham*	B
Huxley, Elspeth Joscelin Grant. *The Flame Trees of Thika*	B
Le Carre, John. *The Pigeon Tunnel*	B
Lear, Linda J. *Beatrix Potter*	B
Lessing, Doris May. *Under My Skin*	823
Lively, Penelope. *Life in the Garden*	B
Lynskey, Dorian. *The Ministry of Truth*	823
McIlwaine, Catherine. *Tolkien*	002.09
Ricks, Thomas E. *Churchill and Orwell*	920
Shakespeare, Nicholas. *Ian Fleming*	B
Skal, David J. *Something in the Blood*	823

PUBLIC LIBRARY CORE COLLECTION: NONFICTION
Twentieth Edition

Solnit, Rebecca. *Orwell's Roses*	B
Spurling, Hilary. *Anthony Powell*	B
Taylor, D. J. *Orwell*	B
Thwaite, Ann. *Goodbye Christopher Robin*	B
Tomalin, Claire. *Thomas Hardy*	B
Wilson, A. N. *C.S. Lewis*	823
Wilson, A. N. *The Mystery of Charles Dickens*	823
Woolf, Virginia. *Moments of Being*	B

AUTHORS, FRENCH
Bakewell, Sarah. *How to Live—Or—A Life of Montaigne*	B
Beckett, Samuel. *The Letters of Samuel Beckett*	848
Burger, Ariel. *Witness*	848
Ernaux, Annie. ★*The Years*	B
Harlan, Elizabeth. *George Sand*	B
Kaplan, Alice Yaeger. *Looking for the Stranger*	B
Ollivier, Bernard. *Out of Istanbul*	B
Pearson, Roger. *Voltaire Almighty*	B
Rousseau, Jean-Jacques. *Confessions*	B
Todd, Olivier. *Albert Camus*	B
Wiesel, Elie. *All Rivers Run to the Sea*	B

AUTHORS, GERMAN
Rilke, Rainer Maria. ★*Letters to a Young Poet*	831
Safranski, Rudiger. *Goethe*	B

AUTHORS, IRISH
Banville, John. *Time Pieces*	914.1
Beckett, Samuel. *The Letters of Samuel Beckett*	848
Bowker, Gordon. ★*James Joyce*	B
Dochartaigh, Kerri ni. *Cacophony of Bone*	B
Ellmann, Richard. *Oscar Wilde*	B
O'Farrell, Maggie. *I Am, I Am, I Am*	B
O'Sullivan, Emer. *The Fall of the House of Wilde*	B
Phelan, Tom. *We Were Rich and We Didn't Know It*	B
Sturgis, Matthew. *Oscar Wilde*	B
Toibin, Colm. *Mad, Bad, Dangerous to Know*	920

AUTHORS, ISRAELI
Oz, Amos. *A Tale of Love and Darkness*	B

AUTHORS, ITALIAN
Benner, Erica. *Be Like the Fox*	B
Levi, Primo. ★*The Drowned and the Saved*	940.53
Levi, Primo. *The Reawakening*	B

AUTHORS, JAPANESE
Murakami, Haruki. *What I Talk About When I Talk About Running*	B

AUTHORS, JEWISH
Wiesel, Elie. *All Rivers Run to the Sea*	B
Wiesel, Elie. *And the Sea Is Never Full*	B

AUTHORS, NIGERIAN
Achebe, Chinua. *The Education of a British-Protected Child*	B
Achebe, Chinua. *There Was a Country*	B
Emezi, Akwaeke. ★*Dear Senthuran*	B

AUTHORS, NORWEGIAN
Grue, Jan. *I Live a Life Like Yours*	B

AUTHORS, POLISH
Milosz, Czeslaw. ★*Milosz's ABC's*	891.8

AUTHORS, RUSSIAN
Bartlett, Rosamund. ★*Tolstoy*	B
Batuman, Elif. *The Possessed*	891.7
Blaisdell, Robert. *Creating Anna Karenina*	891.7
Finn, Peter. *The Zhivago Affair*	891.73
Frank, Joseph. ★*Dostoevsky*	B
Petrushevskaia, Liudmila. *The Girl from the Metropol Hotel*	B
Pitzer, Andrea. *The Secret History of Vladimir Nabokov*	813
Popoff, Alexandra. *Vasily Grossman and the Soviet Century*	B

AUTHORS, SCOTTISH
Barker, Elspeth. ★*Notes from the Henhouse*	828
Sims, Michael. *Arthur and Sherlock*	B
Thomson, Jennifer. *Josephine Tey*	823

AUTHORS, SOUTH AFRICAN
Attwell, David. *J. M. Coetzee and the Life of Writing*	823

AUTHORS, SWEDISH
Andersen, Jens. *Astrid Lindgren*	B
Backman, Fredrik. *Things My Son Needs to Know About the World*	B
Mankell, Henning. *Quicksand*	B

AUTHORS, TRINIDADIAN
French, Patrick. *The World Is What It Is*	B
Autism Adulthood. Senator, Susan	616.85
Autism in Heels. O'Toole, Jennifer Cook	B

AUTISM SPECTRUM DISORDERS
Anderson, Amelia. *Library Programming for Autistic Children and Teens*	027.6
Donvan, John. *In a Different Key*	616.85
Fleming, Jory. *How to Be Human*	616.85
Freeman, Hadley. *Good Girls*	616.85
Goh, Suzanne. *Magnificent Minds*	618.92
Grandin, Temple. ★*Animals in Translation*	591.5
Grandin, Temple. *Navigating Autism*	618.92
Hafner, Katie. *A Romance on Three Legs*	786.2092
James, Laura E. *Odd Girl Out*	B
McAnulty, Dara. *Diary of a Young Naturalist*	508.092
Moorer, Allison. *I Dream He Talks to Me*	782.42164
O'Toole, Jennifer Cook. *Autism in Heels*	B
Prizant, Barry M. ★*Uniquely Human*	618.92
Robison, John Elder. *Look Me in the Eye*	B
Rodgers, Jodi. ★*How to Find a Four-Leaf Clover*	616.85
Rogers-Whitehead, Carrie. ★*Serving Teens and Adults on the Autism Spectrum*	027.6
Ruthsatz, Joanne. *The Prodigy's Cousin*	155.45
Senator, Susan. *Autism Adulthood*	616.85
Smith, R. Garth. *Asd, the Complete Autism Spectrum Disorder Health & Diet Guide*	616.85
Tammet, Daniel. *Born on a Blue Day*	B

AUTISTIC CHILDREN
Anderson, Amelia. *Library Programming for Autistic Children and Teens*	027.6
Goh, Suzanne. *Magnificent Minds*	618.92
Grandin, Temple. *Navigating Autism*	618.92
Kirkby, Bruce. *Blue Sky Kingdom*	954.96
Moorer, Allison. *I Dream He Talks to Me*	782.42164
Prizant, Barry M. ★*Uniquely Human*	618.92
Rowe, Mickey. *Fearlessly Different*	B
Ruthsatz, Joanne. *The Prodigy's Cousin*	155.45

AUTISTIC PEOPLE
Anderson, Amelia. *Library Programming for Autistic Children and Teens*	027.6
Donvan, John. *In a Different Key*	616.85
Fleming, Jory. *How to Be Human*	616.85
Grandin, Temple. ★*Animals in Translation*	591.5
James, Laura E. *Odd Girl Out*	B
O'Toole, Jennifer Cook. *Autism in Heels*	B
Ramesh, Jaya. *Parenting at the Intersections*	649
Robison, John Elder. *Look Me in the Eye*	B
Rodgers, Jodi. ★*How to Find a Four-Leaf Clover*	616.85
Rogers-Whitehead, Carrie. ★*Serving Teens and Adults on the Autism Spectrum*	027.6
Rowe, Mickey. *Fearlessly Different*	B
Senator, Susan. *Autism Adulthood*	616.85
Tammet, Daniel. *Born on a Blue Day*	B

AUTISTIC TEENAGERS
Anderson, Amelia. *Library Programming for Autistic Children and Teens*	027.6
McAnulty, Dara. *Diary of a Young Naturalist*	508.092
Rogers-Whitehead, Carrie. ★*Serving Teens and Adults on the Autism Spectrum*	027.6

AUTISTIC WOMEN
Gadsby, Hannah. ★*Ten Steps to Nanette*	B
James, Laura E. *Odd Girl Out*	B
Legler, Casey. ★*Godspeed*	B
Nerenberg, Jenara. *Divergent Mind*	616.89
O'Toole, Jennifer Cook. *Autism in Heels*	B
Seager, Sara. *The Smallest Lights in the Universe*	B

AUTOBIOGRAPHICAL COMICS
Ai, Weiwei. *Zodiac*	741.5
B., David. *Epileptic*	741.5
Beaton, Kate. ★*Ducks*	741.5
Bechdel, Alison. ★*Fun Home*	741.5
Bechdel, Alison. ★*The Secret to Superhuman Strength*	741.5
Bell, Darrin. ★*The Talk*	741.5
Brosh, Allie. ★*Hyperbole and a Half*	741.5
Brosh, Allie. ★*Solutions and Other Problems*	741.5
Bui, Thi. ★*The Best We Could Do*	741.5
Chast, Roz. ★*Can't We Talk About Something More Pleasant?*	741.5
Findakly, Brigitte. *Poppies of Iraq*	741.5
Guibert, Emmanuel. *The Photographer*	741.5
Hall, Rebecca. ★*Wake*	741.5
Hulls, Tessa. ★*Feeding Ghosts*	741.5

AUTHOR, TITLE, SERIES AND SUBJECT INDEX

Jacob, Mira. *Good Talk*	741.5
Katin, Miriam. *We Are on Our Own*	741.5
Kobabe, Maia. *Gender Queer*	741.5
Krug, Nora. ★*Belonging*	741.5
Lewis, John. ★*March; Book One*	741.5
Lewis, John. ★*March; Book Three*	741.5
Lewis, John. ★*March; Book Two*	741.5
Lewis, John. ★*Run; Book One*	741.5
Martin, Steve. *Number One Is Walking*	B
Mizuki, Shigeru. *Showa 1926-1939*	741.5
Radtke, Kristen. *Seek You*	741.5
Satrapi, Marjane. ★*The Complete Persepolis*	741.5
Sattouf, Riad. *The Arab of the Future 2*	741.5
Sattouf, Riad. *The Arab of the Future*	741.5
Tomine, Adrian. *The Loneliness of the Long-Distance Cartoonist*	741.5

AUTOBIOGRAPHICAL FICTION

Kerouac, Jack. *Book of Sketches, 1952-57*	818

AUTOBIOGRAPHIES AND MEMOIRS

Abdelmahmoud, Elamin. *Son of Elsewhere*	B
Abdul-Jabbar, Kareem. *Coach Wooden and Me*	B
Abdurraqib, Hanif. ★*A Little Devil in America*	791.089
Abouzeid, Rania. *No Turning Back*	956.9104
Abramovic, Marina. *Walk Through Walls*	B
Abu Sayf, Atif. *The Drone Eats with Me*	B
Abuelaish, Izzeldin. *I Shall Not Hate*	B
Achebe, Chinua. *The Education of a British-Protected Child*	B
Achebe, Chinua. *There Was a Country*	B
Achterberg, Cara Sue. *Another Good Dog*	636.7
Ackerman, Elliot. *Places and Names*	B
Adam, David. *The Man Who Couldn't Stop*	616.85
Adams, Jarrett. *Redeeming Justice*	340.092
Adams, John. *Hallelujah Junction*	B
Adams, Mark. *Tip of the Iceberg*	917.9804
Adayfi, Mansoor. *Don't Forget Us Here*	B
Addario, Lynsey. *It's What I Do*	779
Addario, Lynsey. *Of Love & War*	B
Adichie, Chimamanda Ngozi. *Notes on Grief*	155.9
Agassi, Andre. *Open*	B
Aguon, Julian. *No Country for Eight-Spot Butterflies*	305.89
Ahdoot, Dan. *Undercooked*	647.95
Ahmad, Aeham. *The Pianist from Syria*	B
Ai, Weiwei. *1000 Years of Joys and Sorrows*	709.2
AL Samawi, Mohammed. *The Fox Hunt*	953
Al-Maria, Sophia. *The Girl Who Fell to Earth*	B
Albertine, Viv. *Clothes, Clothes, Clothes. Music, Music, Music*	B
Albom, Mitch. *Tuesdays with Morrie*	B
Albracht, William. *Abandoned in Hell*	959.704
Albright, Madeleine Korbel. *Hell and Other Destinations*	B
Albright, Madeleine Korbel. *Prague Winter*	943.71
Alderton, Dolly. *Everything I Know About Love*	B
Aldrin, Buzz. *No Dream Is Too High*	B
Alekhina, Mariija. *Riot Days*	B
Alexander, Jane. *Wild Things, Wild Places*	333.95
Alexander, Kwame. *Why Fathers Cry at Night*	B
Alexie, Sherman. *You Don't Have to Say You Love Me*	818
Alford, Henry. *And Then We Danced*	792.8
Ali, Fatima. ★*Savor*	B
Ali, Wajahat. *Go Back to Where You Came From*	B
Alinizhad, Masih. *The Wind in My Hair*	B
Allende, Isabel. *My Invented Country*	B
Allende, Isabel. ★*Paula*	B
Allende, Isabel. *The Sum of Our Days*	B
Almond, Steve. *Rock and Roll Will Save Your Life*	781.6
Alterman, Sara Faith. *Let's Never Talk About This Again*	616.8
Alvarez, Noe. *Spirit Run*	796.42
Ambroz, David. *A Place Called Home*	B
Amos, Tori. *Resistance*	B
Andrews, Julie. *Home Work*	B
Andrews, Julie. *Home*	B
Angelou, Maya. ★*I Know Why the Caged Bird Sings*	B
Angelou, Maya. *A Song Flung up to Heaven*	B
Anthony, Carmelo. *Where Tomorrows Aren't Promised*	B
Arana, Marie. *American Chica*	B
Archibald, John. *Shaking the Gates of Hell*	B
Arkin, Alan. *An Improvised Life*	B
Armstrong, Karen. *The Spiral Staircase*	B
Aron, Nina Renata. *Good Morning, Destroyer of Men's Souls*	B
Arsenault, Kerri. *Mill Town*	B
Arthur, Alua. ★*Briefly Perfectly Human*	306.9
Ashley, Maurice. *Move by Move*	158
Atleework, Kendra. *Miracle Country*	979.4
Attenborough, David. *Adventures of a Young Naturalist*	B
Augustine. *Confessions*	B
Austin, Nefertiti. *Motherhood so White*	B
Auvinen, Karen. *Rough Beauty*	B
B., David. *Epileptic*	741.5
Bacall, Lauren. *By Myself and Then Some*	B
Bailey, Elisabeth. *The Sound of a Wild Snail Eating*	594
Bailey, Jennifer. *To My Beloveds*	261.8
Bailey, Lily. *Because We Are Bad*	B
Baime, A. J. *White Lies*	B
Baker, Billy. *We Need to Hang Out*	177
Baker, Nicholson. *Finding a Likeness*	B
Baker, Nicholson. *Substitute*	371.14
Ball, Edward. *Life of a Klansman*	305.8009763
Ball, Lucille. *Love, Lucy*	B
Ballard, Robert D. *Into the Deep*	551.46092
Bamford, Maria. *Sure, I'll Join Your Cult*	B
Banville, John. *Time Pieces*	914.1
Barbarisi, Daniel. *Dueling with Kings*	793.93
Bard, Elizabeth. *Lunch in Paris*	B
Barkan, Ady. *Eyes to the Wind*	B
Barker, Elspeth. ★*Notes from the Henhouse*	828
Barlow, John Perry. *Mother American Night*	782.42164
Barnes, Cinelle. *Monsoon Mansion*	B
Barnett, Brittany K. ★*A Knock at Midnight*	B
Barnett, Erica C. *Quitter*	B
Basie, Count. *Good Morning Blues*	B
Bass, Rick. *The Traveling Feast*	B
Bass, Rick. *Why I Came West*	333.78
Bastianich, Lidia. *My American Dream*	B
Bauermeister, Erica. *House Lessons*	B
Baylor, Elgin. *Hang Time*	B
Beah, Ishmael. ★*A Long Way Gone*	B
Beauvais, Garcelle. *Love Me as I Am*	B
Beavan, Colin. *No Impact Man*	B
Bechdel, Alison. ★*Fun Home*	741.5
Bee, Vanessa A. *Home Bound*	B
Belafonte, Harry. ★*My Song*	782.42164
Belcher, Chris. *Pretty Baby*	B
Belcourt, Billy-Ray. ★*A History of My Brief Body*	B
Bell, Laura. *Claiming Ground*	B
Benjamin, A. K. *Let Me Not Be Mad*	612.8
Bennett, Michael. *Things That Make White People Uncomfortable*	305.896
Bennetts, Leslie. *Last Girl Before Freeway*	B
Berg, Elizabeth. *I'll Be Seeing You*	306.874
Berg, Ryan. *No House to Call My Home*	B
Berger, Lynn. *Second Thoughts*	306.85
Berlin, Lucia. ★*Welcome Home*	B
Berman, Geoffrey. *Holding the Line*	345.73
Bernard, Emily. *Black Is the Body*	305.48
Bernstein, Carl. ★*Chasing History*	B
Bertch, Jane. *The French Ingredient*	B
Bertinelli, Valerie. *Enough Already*	B
Betz-Hamilton, Axton. *The Less People Know About Us*	364.16
Bialosky, Jill. *Poetry Will Save Your Life*	B
Biden Owens, Valerie. *Growing up Biden*	B
Biden, Jill. *Where the Light Enters*	B
Biden, Joseph R. *Promise Me, Dad*	B
Biden, Robert Hunter. *Beautiful Things*	B
Bignon, Guillaume. *Confessions of a French Atheist*	239
Bilal, Wafaa. *Shoot an Iraqi*	B
Bilger, Burkhard. *Fatherland*	B
Billings, J. Todd. *Rejoicing in Lament*	248.8
Bilton, Chrysta. *Normal Family*	B
Black Elk. *Black Elk Speaks*	B
Black Thought. *The Upcycled Self*	B
Black, Dustin Lance. *Mama's Boy*	B
Black, Michael Ian. *A Better Man*	305.31
Blackstock, Uche. *Legacy*	610.92
Blair, Selma. *Mean Baby*	B
Blair, Tony. *A Journey*	B
Blake, Melissa. *Beautiful People*	362.4
Blakinger, Keri. *Corrections in Ink*	B
Blanco, Richard. *The Prince of Los Cocuyos*	B
Blau, Magda Hellinger. *The Nazis Knew My Name*	940.53

PUBLIC LIBRARY CORE COLLECTION: NONFICTION
Twentieth Edition

Bloom, Amy. *In Love*	B
Boeheim, Jim. *Bleeding Orange*	B
Bolz-Weber, Nadia. *Accidental Saints*	284.1
Bond, Melissa. *Blood Orange Night*	616.8
Bonner, Betsy. *The Book of Atlantis Black*	364.152
Bono. ★*Surrender*	B
Bosker, Bianca. *Cork Dork*	641.2
Bossiere, Zoe. *Cactus Country*	306
Bourdain, Anthony. ★*Kitchen Confidential*	B
Bourdain, Anthony. *Medium Raw*	B
Bowdler, Michelle. ★*Is Rape a Crime?*	B
Bowler, Kate. *No Cure for Being Human*	B
Boylan, Jennifer Finney. *Good Boy*	B
Brady, James. *The Coldest War*	B
Bragg, Rick. ★*The Best Cook in the World*	641.5975
Bragg, Rick. *The Speckled Beauty*	636.7
Braitman, Laurel. *What Looks Like Bravery*	B
Branum, Guy. *My Life as a Goddess*	B
Brazile, Donna. *For Colored Girls Who Have Considered Politics*	328.73
Brennan, Thomas J. *Shooting Ghosts*	B
Brierley, Saroo. *A Long Way Home*	B
Briggs, Kate. *This Little Art*	418
Brina, Elizabeth Miki. *Speak, Okinawa*	305.48
Brokaw, Tom. *The Fall of Richard Nixon*	B
Brokhausen, Nick. *Whispers in the Tall Grass*	959.704
Brooks, Mel. ★*All About Me!*	B
Broom, Sarah M. *The Yellow House*	B
Broome, Brian. ★*Punch Me up to the Gods*	B
Brosh, Allie. ★*Hyperbole and a Half*	741.5
Brosh, Allie. ★*Solutions and Other Problems*	741.5
Brown, Austin Channing. ★*I'm Still Here*	B
Brown, Carolyn. *Chance and Circumstance*	B
Brown, Claude. *Manchild in the Promised Land*	B
Brown, Molly McCully. *Places I've Taken My Body*	B
Brown, Robert J. *You Can't Go Wrong Doing Right*	B
Brown, Theresa. *Healing*	616.99
Bruni, Frank. *The Beauty of Dusk*	B
Bryant, Kobe. *The Mamba Mentality*	B
Bryson, Bill. *The Life and Times of the Thunderbolt Kid*	B
Buck, Joe. *Lucky Bastard*	B
Buford, Bill. ★*Dirt*	B
Buhle, Kathleen. *If We Break*	B
Bunnell, David. *Good Friday on the Rez*	B
Burcaw, Shane. ★*Laughing at My Nightmare*	B
Burger, Ariel. *Witness*	848
Burgess, Ann Wolbert. *A Killer by Design*	364.3
Burgin, R. V. *Islands of the Damned*	B
Burnett, Carol. *In Such Good Company*	791.45
Burns, Mike. *The Only One Living to Tell*	305.897
Burns, William J. *The Back Channel*	B
Burroughs, Augusten. ★*Toil & Trouble*	B
Burrows, James. ★*Directed by James Burrows*	791.4502
Burton, Susan. *Becoming Ms. Burton*	B
Burton, Susan. *Empty*	B
Bush, George W. *Decision Points*	B
Butcher, Amy. *Mothertrucker*	B
Butcher, Barbara. *What the Dead Know*	614
Butler, Brin-Jonathan. *The Domino Diaries*	796.83
Butler, Marcia. *The Skin Above My Knee*	B
Buttigieg, Pete. *Shortest Way Home*	B
Cacioppo, Stephanie. *Wired for Love*	616.8
Cahalan, Susannah. *Brain on Fire*	616.8
Caine, Michael. *Blowing the Bloody Doors Off*	B
Calcaterra, Regina. *Etched in Sand*	B
Caldwell, Gail. *Let's Take the Long Way Home*	B
Calhoun, Ada. *Also a Poet*	B
Campbell, Deborah. *A Disappearance in Damascus*	365
Campoverdi, Alejandra. *First Gen*	B
Cantu, Francisco. *The Line Becomes a River*	B
Caputo, Philip. *A Rumor of War*	959.704
Carcaterra, Lorenzo. *Three Dreamers*	B
Cardwell, Diane. *Rockaway*	B
Cargle, Rachel Elizabeth. *A Renaissance of Our Own*	B
Carlin, Kelly. *A Carlin Home Companion*	B
Carlo, Philip. *Gaspipe*	B
Caro, Robert A. ★*Working*	B
Carpenter, Kyle. *You Are Worth It*	B
Carr, Caleb. *My Beloved Monster*	B
Carr, David. *The Night of the Gun*	B
Carr, Erin Lee. *All That You Leave Behind*	B
Carriere, Alice. *Everything/Nothing/Someone*	B
Carroll, Rebecca. *Surviving the White Gaze*	B
Carruthers, Charlene A. *Unapologetic*	305.48
Carter, Jimmy. *A Full Life*	B
Carter, Jimmy. *An Hour Before Daylight*	B
Carter, Jimmy. *Keeping Faith*	B
Carter, Jimmy. *Sharing Good Times*	973.926
Carter, Jimmy. *White House Diary*	973.926
Carter, Ruth E. ★*The Art of Ruth E. Carter*	746.9
Case, Molly. *How to Treat People*	616.1
Cash, Rosanne. ★*Composed*	B
Castner, Brian. *The Long Walk*	B
Castro, Fidel. *Fidel Castro*	B
Cayton-Holland, Adam. *Tragedy Plus Time*	B
Cecchi-Azzolina, Michael. *Your Table Is Ready*	647.95
Cercas, Javier. *Lord of All the Dead*	868
Chabon, Michael. *Manhood for Amateurs*	B
Chabon, Michael. *Pops*	306.874
Chan, Jackie. *Never Grow Up*	B
Chang, David. ★*Eat a Peach*	641.5
Chapin, Sasha. *All the Wrong Moves*	794.1092
Chapman, Rex. ★*It's Hard for Me to Live with Me*	B
Chast, Roz. ★*Can't We Talk About Something More Pleasant?*	741.5
Chee, Alexander. *How to Write an Autobiographical Novel*	B
Chen, Da. *Colors of the Mountain*	951.05
Cheney, Liz. *Oath and Honor*	328.73
Cheng, Nien. *Life and Death in Shanghai*	B
Chesney, Will. *No Ordinary Dog*	958.104
Cheung, Karen. *The Impossible City*	951.25
Chiger, Krystyna. *The Girl in the Green Sweater*	B
Child, Julia. ★*My Life in France*	B
Chin, Curtis. *Everything I Learned, I Learned in a Chinese Restaurant*	B
Chisholm, Edward. *A Waiter in Paris*	B
Chittister, Joan. *Following the Path*	248.4
Chow, Kat. *Seeing Ghosts*	B
Christie, Chris. *Let Me Finish*	B
Chu, Jeff. *Does Jesus Really Love Me?*	261.8
Chu, Lenora. *Little Soldiers*	370
Chude-Sokei, Louis Onuorah. *Floating in a Most Peculiar Way*	979.4
Chung, Nicole. *All You Can Ever Know*	B
Chung, Nicole. ★*A Living Remedy*	B
Chung, Vinh. *Where the Wind Leads*	B
Cisneros, Sandra. *A House of My Own*	B
Clapton, Eric. *Clapton*	B
Clark, John Lee. *Touch the Future*	B
Clark, Liz. *Swell*	B
Clarke, Rachel. *Dear Life*	B
Cleage, Pearl. *Things I Should Have Told My Daughter*	B
Cleaver, Eldridge. *Soul on Ice*	B
Clemmons, Francois S. *Officer Clemmons*	B
Cleveland, Pat. *Walking with the Muses*	B
Clinton, Bill. *My Life*	B
Clinton, Hillary Rodham. *Living History*	B
Coates, Ta-Nehisi. *The Beautiful Struggle*	B
Coates, Ta-Nehisi. ★*Between the World and Me*	305.800973
Cobbs-Leonard, Tasha. *Do It Anyway*	241
Coffin, Jaed. *Roughhouse Friday*	B
Coldstream, Catherine. ★*Cloistered*	B
Cole, Natalie. *Angel on My Shoulder*	B
Collins, Lauren. *When in French*	B
Colwell, Rita R. *A Lab of One's Own*	B
Common. *One Day It'll All Make Sense*	B
Conaboy, Kelly. *The Particulars of Peter*	636.7
Connell, John. *The Farmer's Son*	630.9
Conroy, Pat. *My Losing Season*	B
Conyers, Jonathan. *I Wasn't Supposed to Be Here*	B
Coombes, Joshua. *Do Something for Nothing*	362.5
Cooper, Alex. *Saving Alex*	B
Cooper, Brittney C. *Eloquent Rage*	B
Cooper, Christian. *Better Living Through Birding*	B
Cooper, Helene. *The House at Sugar Beach*	921
Copeland, Misty. ★*Life in Motion*	B
Copeland, Misty. *The Wind at My Back*	B
Corrigan, Kelly. *Glitter and Glue*	B
Corrigan, Kelly. *Tell Me More*	153.6
Costello, Elvis. *Unfaithful Music & Disappearing Ink*	B

AUTHOR, TITLE, SERIES AND SUBJECT INDEX

Couric, Katie. *Going There*	B
Cox, Lynne. *Swimming to Antarctica*	B
Crabapple, Molly. *Drawing Blood*	B
Crais, Clifton C. *History Lessons*	B
Crampton, Caroline. *A Body Made of Glass*	616.85
Crawford, Lacy. *Notes on a Silencing*	B
Crawford, Robert. *Eliot After the Waste Land*	B
Cregan, Mary. *The Scar*	616.85
Croke, Ken. *Riding with Evil*	364.106
Cronkite, Walter. *A Reporter's Life*	B
Crosley, Sloane. *Grief Is for People*	B
Crosley, Sloane. *I Was Told There'd Be Cake*	814
Crosley, Sloane. ★*Look Alive Out There*	814
Crowell, Rodney. *Chinaberry Sidewalks*	B
Crump, Benjamin. *Open Season*	364
Cumming, Alan. *Baggage*	B
Cummings, Elijah. ★*We're Better Than This*	B
Cunningham, William J. ★*Fashion Climbing*	B
Curtis, James. *Buster Keaton*	B
Dalai Lama. *Freedom in Exile*	B
Daley, Mark. *Safe*	B
Daley, Tom. *Coming up for Air*	B
Dana, Richard Henry. *Two Years Before the Mast*	910.4
Daniels, Stormy. *Full Disclosure*	B
Danler, Stephanie. *Stray*	B
Danticat, Edwidge. *The Art of Death*	809
Danticat, Edwidge. ★*Brother, I'm Dying*	B
Darkshire, Oliver. *Once Upon a Tome*	B
Darling, Ron. *The Complete Game*	B
Darlington, Miriam. *Otter Country*	599.769
Davis, Geena. *Dying of Politeness*	B
Davis, Jennifer Pharr. *Called Again*	B
Davis, Jennifer Pharr. *The Pursuit of Endurance*	796.51
Davis, Viola. ★*Finding Me*	B
Dawkins, Richard. *An Appetite for Wonder*	B
Dawkins, Richard. *Brief Candle in the Dark*	B
Day, Daniel R. *Dapper Dan*	B
Day, John D. *The Longevity Plan*	612.6
Debreczeni, Jozsef. *Cold Crematorium*	940.53
Delaney, Rob. ★*A Heart That Works*	B
Delany, Sarah Louise. *Having Our Say*	B
Delisle, Guy. *Pyongyang*	741.5
Delorme, Geoffroy. *Deer Man*	599.65
Dench, Judi. *Shakespeare*	792
Dennis, David J., Jr. *The Movement Made Us*	B
Dennis, Felix. *How to Get Rich*	B
Deraniyagala, Sonali. *Wave*	B
Devantez, Chelsea. ★*I Shouldn't Be Telling You This*	B
Dial, Roman. *The Adventurer's Son*	917.286
Diamant, Anita. *Pitching My Tent*	296.7
Diamond, Cheryl. *Nowhere Girl*	B
Diaz, Jaquira. *Ordinary Girls*	818
Dickinson, Bruce. *What Does This Button Do?*	B
Didion, Joan. *Where I Was from*	979.4
Didion, Joan. ★*The Year of Magical Thinking*	B
Dietrich, Sean. *You Are My Sunshine*	B
DiFelice, Bekah. *Almost There*	248.8
DiFranco, Ani. *No Walls and the Recurring Dream*	782.42164
DiGiulian, Sasha. *Take the Lead*	B
Dillard, Annie. *An American Childhood*	B
DiMarco, Nyle. ★*Deaf Utopia*	B
Dinesen, Isak. *Out of Africa*	967.62
Dochartaigh, Kerri ní. *Cacophony of Bone*	B
Dogon, Mondiant. *Those We Throw Away Are Diamonds*	B
Dolby, Thomas. *The Speed of Sound*	B
Dorey-Stein, Beck. *From the Corner of the Oval*	B
Doty, Cate. *Mergers and Acquisitions*	395.2
Doughty, Caitlin. *Smoke Gets in Your Eyes*	B
Douglass, Frederick. *My Bondage and My Freedom*	B
Downs, Paul. *Boss Life*	338.7
Doyle, Glennon. *Untamed*	B
Doyne, Maggie. *Between the Mountain and the Sky*	B
Dresner, Amy. *My Fair Junkie*	B
Driver, Minnie. *Managing Expectations*	B
Dubus, Andre. *Townie*	B
Duckworth, Tammy. *Every Day Is a Gift*	B
Dufu, Tiffany. *Drop the Ball*	650.1
Duncan, Isadora. *My Life*	B
Dungy, Camille T. *Soil*	635.0978
Dunn, Harry. *Standing My Ground*	B
Dunne, Griffin. ★*The Friday Afternoon Club*	B
Duran, Elvis. *Where Do I Begin?*	B
Dutta, Sunil. *Stealing Green Mangoes*	973
Dykstra, Lenny. *House of Nails*	B
Dylan, Bob. *Chronicles; Volume 1*	B
Dyson, Freeman J. *Maker of Patterns*	B
Ebersol, Dick. *From Saturday Night to Sunday Night*	B
Ebert, Roger. *Life Itself*	B
Eddy, Mary Baker. ★*Mary Baker Eddy*	289.5
Edelman, Marian Wright. *Lanterns*	362.7
Edmundson, Mark. *Why Football Matters*	B
Edstrom, Erik. *Un-American*	B
Egan, Kerry. *On Living*	170
Eger, Edith Eva. *The Choice*	B
Eggers, Dave. *Zeitoun*	305.892
Ehrlich, Gretel. *Unsolaced*	B
Eichenwald, Kurt. *A Mind Unraveled*	B
Eire, Carlos M. N. *Learning to Die in Miami*	B
Eisen, Max. *By Chance Alone*	940.5318
Eisenberg, Emma Copley. ★*The Third Rainbow Girl*	364.152
Ellis, Helen. *Southern Lady Code*	814
Elnoury, Tamer. *American Radical*	B
Else, Jon. *True South*	305.800973
Elwes, Cary. *As You Wish*	791.43
Elwood, Phil. *All the Worst Humans*	659.2
Emezi, Akwaeke. ★*Dear Senthuran*	B
Engel, Richard. *And Then All Hell Broke Loose*	956.05
Engle, Charlie. *Running Man*	B
Enninful, Edward. *A Visible Man*	B
Ephron, Delia. *Left on Tenth*	B
Ephron, Nora. *The Most of Nora Ephron*	814
Epstein, Mark. *Advice Not Given*	294.3
Erdman, Sarah. *Nine Hills to Nambonkaha*	966.68
Ernaux, Annie. ★*The Years*	B
Eruzione, Mike. *The Making of a Miracle*	B
Ervin, Kristine S. *Rabbit Heart*	364.152
Eteraz, Ali. *Children of Dust*	B
Etheridge, Melissa. *Talking to My Angels*	B
Evaristo, Bernardine. *Manifesto*	B
Fabes, Stephen. *Signs of Life*	B
Fabre, Cin. *Wolf Hustle*	332.6
Fagan, Kate. *All the Colors Came Out*	B
Fair, Eric. *Consequence*	B
Faliveno, Melissa. *Tomboyland*	B
Fall, Jeremy. *Falling Upwards*	158.1
Faludi, Susan. *In the Darkroom*	B
Fauci, Anthony S. *Expect the Unexpected*	610.92
Faust, Drew Gilpin. *Necessary Trouble*	B
Favro, Terri. *Generation Robot*	006.3
Febos, Melissa. *Girlhood*	818
Feige, David. *Indefensible*	B
Feinstein, Michael. *The Gershwins and Me*	782.42164
Feldman, Deborah. *Exodus*	B
Feldman, Deborah. *Unorthodox*	B
Felix, Camonghne. *Dyscalculia*	B
Felton, Tom. ★*Beyond the Wand*	B
Fenn, Lisa. *Carry On*	B
Fennelly, Beth Ann. *Heating & Cooling*	B
Ferguson, Jane. *No Ordinary Assignment*	B
Field, Sally. *In Pieces*	B
Fincham-Gray, Suzanne. *My Patients and Other Animals*	B
Findakly, Brigitte. *Poppies of Iraq*	741.5
Finn, Adharanand. *The Rise of the Ultra Runners*	B
Finnegan, William. *Barbarian Days*	B
Fisher, Thomas. ★*The Emergency*	362.1089
Fisher, Todd. *My Girls*	B
Fishman, Boris. *Savage Feast*	B
Fitzgerald, Isaac. *Dirtbag, Massachusetts*	B
Fitzmaurice, Simon. *It's Not yet Dark*	616.8
Flaherty, Meghan. *Tango Lessons*	793.3
Flannery, Kate. *Strip Tees*	338.4
Fleming, Brandon P. *Miseducated*	B
Fleming, Jory. *How to Be Human*	616.85
Fleshman, Lauren. ★*Good for a Girl*	B
Foer, Esther Safran. *I Want You to Know We're Still Here*	B
Fogerty, John. *Fortunate Son*	B

PUBLIC LIBRARY CORE COLLECTION: NONFICTION
Twentieth Edition

Foles, Nick. *Believe It*	B
Foo, Stephanie. ★*What My Bones Know*	B
Forche, Carolyn. *What You Have Heard Is True*	B
Ford, Ashley C. ★*Somebody's Daughter*	B
Ford, Christine Blasey. *One Way Back*	B
Ford, Elizabeth. *Sometimes Amazing Things Happen*	B
Ford, Richard. *Between Them*	B
Ford, Tanisha C. *Dressed in Dreams*	391
Foreman, Tom. *My Year of Running Dangerously*	B
Foster, Craig. ★*Amphibious Soul*	155.9
Foster, Sutton. *Hooked*	B
Fowlds, Grant. *Saving the Last Rhinos*	599.66
Fox, Amaryllis. *Life Undercover*	B
Fox, Julia. *Down the Drain*	B
Fox, Michael J. *No Time Like the Future*	B
Foxx, Jamie. *Act Like You Got Some Sense*	B
Frangello, Gina. *Blow Your House Down*	813
Frank, Anne. ★*The Diary of a Young Girl*	940.53
Frank, Anne. *The Diary of Anne Frank*	B
Frank, Barney. *Frank*	B
Franklin, Benjamin. ★*The Autobiography of Benjamin Franklin*	B
Franklin, Missy. *Relentless Spirit*	B
Freeman, Hadley. *Good Girls*	616.85
Freeman, Scott. *Saving Tarboo Creek*	333.72
Freitas, Donna. *Consent*	364.158092
Fremont, Helen. *The Escape Artist*	B
Frenkel, Francoise. *A Bookshop in Berlin*	B
Friedman, Matti. *Pumpkinflowers*	B
Friedman, Rachel. *And Then We Grew Up*	305.24
Friedman, Tova. ★*The Daughter of Auschwitz*	B
Fritz, Ian. *What the Taliban Told Me*	B
Fuller, Alexandra. *Don't Let's Go to the Dogs Tonight*	B
Fuller, Alexandra. *Leaving Before the Rains Come*	B
Fumudoh, Ziwe. ★*Black Friend*	814
Gadsby, Hannah. ★*Ten Steps to Nanette*	B
Gaffigan, Jeannie. *When Life Gives You Pears*	B
Gaffigan, Jim. *Dad Is Fat*	814
Gaffney, Ginger. *Half Broke*	B
Gaiman, Neil. *The View from the Cheap Seats*	824
Gaines, Joanna. *The Stories We Tell*	B
Gallego, Ruben. *They Called Us*	956.7044
Gandhi. *An Autobiography*	B
Garcia Marquez, Gabriel. *Living to Tell the Tale*	B
Garcia, Angela. ★*The Way That Leads Among the Lost*	362.29
Garcia, Mayte. *The Most Beautiful*	920
Garcia, Rodrigo. *A Farewell to Gabo and Mercedes*	B
Gardner, Chris. ★*Permission to Dream*	158.1
Garfunkel, Art. *What Is It All but Luminous*	782.42164
Garner, Dwight. *The Upstairs Delicatessen*	B
Garrett, Kent. *The Last Negroes at Harvard*	920
Garza, Alicia. *The Purpose of Power*	303.48
Gates, Henry Louis. *Colored People*	B
Gay, Ross. *The Book of (more) Delights*	814
Gay, Ross. *Inciting Joy*	814
Gaye, Jan. *After the Dance*	B
Gehrig, Lou. *The Lost Memoir*	B
Geller, Danielle. *Dog Flowers*	B
Gerald, Casey. *There Will Be No Miracles Here*	B
Gerard, Sarah. *Sunshine State*	814
Gerson, Merissa Nathan. *Forget Prayers, Bring Cake*	155.9
Gessner, David. *Ultimate Glory*	796.2
Ghafari, Zarifa. *Zarifa*	B
Ghostface Killah. *Rise of a Killah*	B
Gidla, Sujatha. *Ants Among Elephants*	305.5
Gies, Miep. ★*Anne Frank Remembered*	B
Gilbert, Elizabeth. *Eat, Pray, Love*	B
Gilder, Ginny. *Course Correction*	797.12
Gildiner, Catherine. *Good Morning, Monster*	616.89
Gilliam, Dorothy Butler. *Trailblazer*	B
Ginsburg, Ruth Bader. ★*My Own Words*	347.73
Girma, Haben. *Haben*	B
Glass, Philip. *Words Without Music*	B
Glass, Sara. *Kissing Girls on Shabbat*	B
Gleiberman, Owen. *Movie Freak*	B
Glenconner, Anne. ★*Lady in Waiting*	B
Gless, Sharon. *Apparently There Were Complaints*	B
Godwin, Gail. *Getting to Know Death*	B
Goetsch, Diana. *This Body I Wore*	B
Goldberg, Carrie. *Nobody's Victim*	345.73
Goldberg, Whoopi. *Bits and Pieces*	B
Goldblatt, Duchess. *Becoming Duchess Goldblatt*	B
Goldstein, Meredith. *Can't Help Myself*	B
Golembesky, Michael. *Level Zero Heroes*	958.104
Golinkin, Lev. *A Backpack, a Bear, and Eight Crates of Vodka*	B
Gomez, Edgar. *High-Risk Homosexual*	B
Gonell, Aquilino. *American Shield*	B
Goodall, Jane. ★*Beyond Innocence*	B
Goodman, Simon. *The Orpheus Clock*	940.53
Goodwin, Doris Kearns. ★*An Unfinished Love Story*	B
Gordon, Kim. *Girl in a Band*	B
Gorrindo, Simone. ★*The Wives*	B
Gotch, Jen. *The Upside of Being Down*	B
Gottlieb, Lori. ★*Maybe You Should Talk to Someone*	B
Gracie, Rickson. *Breathe*	B
Graham, Ashley. *A New Model*	B
Graham, Jasmin. *Sharks Don't Sink*	597.3
Granata, Vince. *Everything Is Fine*	B
Grande, Reyna. ★*The Distance Between Us*	973
Grandmaster Flash. *The Adventures of Grandmaster Flash*	B
Grant, Gail Milissa. *At the Elbows of My Elders*	B
Grant, Ulysses S. ★*The Annotated Memoirs of Ulysses S. Grant*	B
Grant, Will. *The Last Ride of the Pony Express*	917.804
Grathwohl, Marya. *This Wheel of Rocks*	271
Green, Kristen. *Something Must Be Done About Prince Edward County*	379.2
Green, Robin. *The Only Girl*	070.92
Green, Stefanie. *This Is Assisted Dying*	616.02
Greene, Jayson. *Once More We Saw Stars*	155.9
Greenfield, Martin. ★*Measure of a Man*	B
Gregory, Dick. ★*The Essential Dick Gregory*	818
Gregory, Rebekah. *Taking My Life Back*	B
Greitens, Eric. *Resilience*	155.2
Gretzky, Wayne. *99*	B
Grey, Jennifer. *Out of the Corner*	B
Grey, Joel. *Master of Ceremonies*	B
Grossi, Craig. *Craig & Fred*	B
Grue, Jan. *I Live a Life Like Yours*	B
Gruen, Bob. *Right Place, Right Time*	779.2
Grylls, Bear. *Never Give Up*	B
Gucci, Patricia. *In the Name of Gucci*	B
Guevara, Che. *Diary of a Combatant*	972.91063
Guibert, Emmanuel. *The Photographer*	741.5
Guillermoprieto, Alma. *Dancing with Cuba*	972.9106
Gulman, Gary. *Misfit*	B
Guo, Xlaolu. *Nine Continents*	B
Gupta, Prachi. ★*They Called Us Exceptional*	B
Gutman, Matt. ★*No Time to Panic*	616.85
H, Lamya. ★*Hijab Butch Blues*	B
Haddish, Tiffany. *The Last Black Unicorn*	B
Haffner, Sebastian. *Defying Hitler*	943.085
Hagberg, Eva. *How to Be Loved*	616.7
Haig, Matt. *Notes on a Nervous Planet*	616.89
Haitiwaji, Gulbahar. *How I Survived a Chinese "Reeducation" Camp*	305.8
Hall, Sands. ★*Flunk, Start*	B
Hallberg, David. *A Body of Work*	B
Halpern, Sue. *A Dog Walks into a Nursing Home*	B
Hamill, Kirkland. *Filthy Beasts*	B
Hamilton, Gabrielle. *Blood, Bones, and Butter*	B
Hamilton, Tyler. *The Secret Race*	796.62
Handler, Daniel. ★*And Then? and Then? What Else?*	813
Hanna, Kathleen. *Rebel Girl*	B
Hanna-Attisha, Mona. *What the Eyes Don't See*	615.9
Harden, Marcia Gay. *The Seasons of My Mother*	B
Hardin, Lara Love. ★*The Many Lives of Mama Love*	B
Hardy, Jason Matthew. ★*The Second Chance Club*	364.6
Hari, Daoud. *The Translator*	B
Harjo, Joy. *Crazy Brave*	B
Harjo, Joy. ★*Poet Warrior*	B
Harper, Michele. *The Beauty in Breaking*	B
Harpham, Heather Elise. *Happiness*	B
Harris, Dan. ★*10% Happier*	158.1
Harris, Kate. *Lands of Lost Borders*	915.804
Harris, Neil Patrick. *Neil Patrick Harris*	B
Harris, Taylor. *This Boy We Made*	B
Harrison, Scott. *Thirst*	B
Harry. ★*Spare*	B
Harry, Debbie. *Face It*	B

1650

AUTHOR, TITLE, SERIES AND SUBJECT INDEX

Harryhausen, Ray. *The Art of Ray Harryhausen*	778
Hart, Hannah. *Buffering*	B
Hart, Kevin. *I Can't Make This Up*	B
Hartke, Austen. *Transforming*	277
Harvey, Samantha. *The Shapeless Unease*	B
Haupt, Lyanda Lynn. *Mozart's Starling*	B
Hauser, CJ. *The Crane Wife*	B
Havrilesky, Heather. *Foreverland*	306.81
Hawking, Stephen. *My Brief History*	B
Hay, Matt. *Soundtrack of Silence*	B
Hazzard, Kevin. *A Thousand Naked Strangers*	B
Hegar, Mary Jennings. *Shoot Like a Girl*	B
Heinrich, Bernd. *A Naturalist at Large*	508
Heminsley, Alexandra. *Running Like a Girl*	B
Hemon, Aleksandar. *My Parents*	814
Hempel, Jessi. *The Family Outing*	B
Henderson, Artis. *Unremarried Widow*	B
Henderson, Danielle. ★*The Ugly Cry*	B
Henderson, Rob Kim. *Troubled*	B
Hendrickson, John. *Life on Delay*	B
Hennessey, Patrick. *The Junior Officers' Reading Club*	B
Hensley, William L. Iggiagruk. *Fifty Miles from Tomorrow*	B
Henson, Taraji P. *Around the Way Girl*	B
Hernandez Castillo, Marcelo. *Children of the Land*	B
Hernandez, Daisy. *A Cup of Water Under My Bed*	B
Hernandez, Keith. *I'm Keith Hernandez*	B
Herriot, James. ★*All Creatures Great and Small*	B
Herriot, James. *All Things Wise and Wonderful*	B
Herriot, James. *Every Living Thing*	B
Herriot, James. *James Herriot's Animal Stories*	B
Herriot, James. *James Herriot's Cat Stories*	636.8
Herriot, James. *James Herriot's Dog Stories*	636.7
Herriot, James. *James Herriot's Favorite Dog Stories*	636.7
Hersh, Seymour M. *Reporter*	B
Herzog, Werner. ★*Every Man for Himself and God Against All*	B
Heti, Sheila. *Alphabetical Diaries*	818
Heughan, Sam. *Waypoints*	B
Heumann, Judith E. *Being Heumann*	B
Hewitt, Sean. *All Down Darkness Wide*	B
Hiaasen, Carl. *The Downhill Lie*	B
Hickam, Homer H. ★*Rocket Boys*	B
Hilfiger, Tommy. *American Dreamer*	B
Hill, Clint. *Five Days in November*	973.922092
Hill, Clint. *Five Presidents*	B
Hill, Clint. *Mrs. Kennedy and Me*	973.922092
Hill, Clint. *My Travels with Mrs. Kennedy*	B
Hill, Fiona. *There Is Nothing for You Here*	327.2
Hill, Jemele. *Uphill*	B
Hill, Katie. *She Will Rise*	305.42
Hilton, Paris. *Paris*	B
Hinojosa, Maria. *Once I Was You*	B
Hinton, Anthony Ray. *The Sun Does Shine*	B
Hirono, Mazie. *Heart of Fire*	B
Hirsch, Paul. *A Long Time Ago in a Cutting Room Far, Far Away*	B
Hirsi Ali, Ayaan. ★*Infidel*	B
Hitchens, Christopher. *Hitch-22*	920
Hitchens, Christopher. *Mortality*	304.6
Hitler, Adolf. *Mein Kampf*	B
Hodgman, John. *Medallion Status*	B
Hodgman, John. *Vacationland*	B
Hoja, Gulchehra. *A Stone Is Most Precious Where It Belongs*	B
Holes, Paul. *Unmasked*	363.25
Holloway, Kris. *Monique and the Mango Rains*	B
Hong, Cathy Park. *Minor Feelings*	305.48
Honnold, Alex. *Alone on the Wall*	B
Hood, Ann. *Kitchen Yarns*	641.5
hooks, bell. *Wounds of Passion*	B
Hopwood, Shon. *Law Man*	B
Horace, Matthew. *The Black and the Blue*	B
Hornbacher, Marya. *Wasted*	B
Horton, Michelle. *Dear Sister*	B
Hough, Lauren. *Leaving Isn't the Hardest Thing*	B
Howe, Ben Ryder. *My Korean Deli*	B
Hsu, Hua. ★*Stay True*	B
Huang, Eddie. *Fresh off the Boat*	B
Hudes, Quiara Alegría. ★*My Broken Language*	B
Hughes, Langston. ★*I Wonder as I Wander*	B
Hurston, Zora Neale. *Dust Tracks on a Road*	B
Hussey, Olivia. *The Girl on the Balcony*	B
Huston, Anjelica. *Watch Me*	B
Hutchinson, Cassidy. *Enough*	B
Huxley, Elspeth Joscelin Grant. *The Flame Trees of Thika*	B
Hytner, Nicholas. *Balancing Acts*	B
Iftin, Abdi Nor. *Call Me American*	305.893
Iguodala, Andre. *The Sixth Man*	B
Ikpi, Bassey. *I'm Telling the Truth, but I'm Lying*	814
Ingrassia, Lawrence. *A Fatal Inheritance*	616.99
Irby, Samantha. ★*Quietly Hostile*	814
Irby, Samantha. *We Are Never Meeting in Real Life*	814
Irving, Apricot Anderson. *The Gospel of Trees*	B
Ishikawa, Masaji. ★*A River in Darkness*	B
Iversen, Kristen. *Full Body Burden*	363.17
Izgil, Tahir Hamut. *Waiting to Be Arrested at Night*	B
Izzard, Eddie. *Believe Me*	B
Jackson, Bruce. *Never Far from Home*	B
Jackson, Curtis. *Hustle Harder, Hustle Smarter*	B
Jackson, Mitchell S. *Survival Math*	B
Jacob, Mira. *Good Talk*	741.5
Jacobs, A. J. *The Puzzler*	793.73
Jacobs, A. J. ★*The Year of Living Constitutionally*	342.73
Jacobs, Harriet. *Incidents in the Life of a Slave Girl*	B
Jadhav, Narendra. *Untouchables*	305.5
Jahren, Hope. ★*Lab Girl*	B
Jaku, Eddie. ★*The Happiest Man on Earth*	B
James, Laura E. *Odd Girl Out*	B
James, Victoria. *Wine Girl*	B
Jamison, Leslie. *The Empathy Exams*	813
Jamison, Leslie. ★*The Recovering*	B
Jang, Jin-Sung. *Dear Leader*	B
Jang, Lucia. *Stars Between the Sun and Moon*	365.45092
Jaouad, Suleika. *Between Two Kingdoms*	B
Jarrett, Valerie. *Finding My Voice*	B
Jauhar, Sandeep. *Heart*	612.1
Jawando, Will. ★*My Seven Black Fathers*	B
Jayapal, Pramila. *Use the Power You Have*	B
Jefferson, Margo. *Negroland*	305.896
Jenkins, Jedidiah. *To Shake the Sleeping Self*	B
Jeppesen, Travis. *See You Again in Pyongyang*	951.93
Jerkins, Morgan. *Wandering in Strange Lands*	305.896
Jeter, Derek. *Jeter Unfiltered*	B
Jewel. *Never Broken*	782.42164
Jobrani, Maziyar. *I'm Not a Terrorist, but I've Played One on TV*	B
John, Elton. ★*Me*	B
Johnson, Brian. *The Lives of Brian*	B
Johnson, Katherine G. *My Remarkable Journey*	B
Johnson, Stephanie. *Tanqueray*	B
Johnston, Ann Dowsett. *Drink*	362.292
Jollett, Mikel. ★*Hollywood Park*	B
Jones, Booker T. *Time Is Tight*	B
Jones, Chloe Cooper. ★*Easy Beauty*	B
Jones, Faith. *Sex Cult Nun*	B
Jones, Lucy. ★*Matrescence*	306.874
Jones, Nathaniel R. *Answering the Call*	B
Jones, Saeed. *How We Fight for Our Lives*	B
Joyce, Russell W. *His Face Like Mine*	248
Juan, Li. *Winter Pasture*	951.06
Jun, Tasha. ★*Tell Me the Dream Again*	248
Kaag, John J. *American Philosophy*	191
Kaag, John J. *Hiking with Nietzsche*	193
Kaiser, Menachem. *Plunder*	940.53
Kakutani, Michiko. *Ex Libris*	028
Kalanithi, Paul. ★*When Breath Becomes Air*	B
Kalb, Bess. ★*Nobody Will Tell You This but Me*	306.874
Kaling, Mindy. *Why Not Me?*	B
Kamkwamba, William. ★*The Boy Who Harnessed the Wind*	B
Kan, Karoline. *Under Red Skies*	B
Kandel, Eric R. *In Search of Memory*	B
Kander, Jason. *Invisible Storm*	B
Kang, Mia. *Knockout*	B
Kariko, Katalin. *Breaking Through*	B
Karski, Jan. *Story of a Secret State*	940.53
Katin, Miriam. *We Are on Our Own*	741.5
Keaton, Diane. ★*Brother & Sister*	B
Keeling, Ida. *Can't Nothing Bring Me Down*	B
Keenan, Cody. *Grace*	973.932
Keflezighi, Meb. *26 Marathons*	B

1651

PUBLIC LIBRARY CORE COLLECTION: NONFICTION
Twentieth Edition

Keizer, Garret. *Getting Schooled*	373.1102
Keller, Helen. ★*The Story of My Life*	B
Kelley, Margot Anne. *A Gardener at the End of the World*	615.8
Kelly, Minka. ★*Tell Me Everything*	B
Kelly, Scott. ★*Endurance*	B
Kemper, Ellie. *My Squirrel Days*	B
Kenda, Joe. *Killer Triggers*	364.152
Kendi, Ibram X. ★*How to Be an Antiracist*	305.8
Kennicott, Philip. *Counterpoint*	B
Kerry, John. *Every Day Is Extra*	B
Kessler, Lauren. *Raising the Barre*	792.8
Key, Keegan-Michael. ★*The History of Sketch Comedy*	792.2
Khalaf, Farida. *The Girl Who Escaped Isis*	B
Khar, Erin. *Strung Out*	B
Kidder, Tracy. ★*Rough Sleepers*	362.5
Kim, Suki. *Without You, There Is No Us*	B
King, B. B. ★*Blues All Around Me*	B
King, Billie Jean. ★*All In*	B
King, Charles Monroe. *A Journal for Jordan*	956.7044
King, Chrissy. *The Body Liberation Project*	306.4
King, Coretta Scott. ★*My Life, My Love, My Legacy*	B
King, Greg. *The Ghost Forest*	333.75
King, Martin Luther. *The Autobiography of Martin Luther King, Jr.*	B
King, Stephen. *On Writing*	B
Kingsolver, Barbara. ★*Animal, Vegetable, Miracle*	641
Kingston, Genevieve. *Did I Ever Tell You?*	B
Kingston, Maxine Hong. *The Woman Warrior*	B
Kirkby, Bruce. *Blue Sky Kingdom*	954.96
Kirschbaum, Erik. *Soccer Without Borders*	B
Kissinger, Meg. *While You Were Out*	362.2
Klagsbrun, Francine. *Lioness*	B
Klein, Jessi. *I'll Show Myself Out*	B
Knausgaard, Karl Ove. *Spring*	B
Knight, Philip H. *Shoe Dog*	B
Kobabe, Maia. *Gender Queer*	741.5
Koh, EJ. *The Magical Language of Others*	813
Kois, Dan. *How to Be a Family*	910.4
Konnikova, Maria. *The Biggest Bluff*	795.412
Kouchner, Camille. *The Familia Grande*	B
Kozol, Jonathan. *The Theft of Memory*	B
Kramer, Clara. *Clara's War*	B
Kraus, Dita. *A Delayed Life*	B
Kristof, Nicholas D. ★*Chasing Hope*	B
Krouse, Erika. ★*Tell Me Everything*	363.25
Krug, Nora. ★*Belonging*	741.5
Kruzan, Sara. *I Cried to Dream Again*	B
Kugler, Rob. *A Dog Named Beautiful*	B
Kumar, Priyanka. *Conversations with Birds*	598
Kuo, Michelle. *Reading with Patrick*	B
Kurosawa, Akira. *Something Like an Autobiography*	B
Kurtz, Glenn. *Three Minutes in Poland*	947.7
Kweli, Talib. *Vibrate Higher*	B
Lahiri, Jhumpa. *In Other Words*	B
Lahiri, Jhumpa. *Translating Myself and Others*	418
Lahti, Christine. *True Stories from an Unreliable Eyewitness*	B
Laing, Olivia. ★*The Lonely City*	700.1
Lake, Dianne. *Member of the Family*	364.152
Lakshmi, Padma. *Love, Loss, and What We Ate*	791.4502
Lalami, Laila. *Conditional Citizens*	323.60973
Lamb, Christina. *House of Stone*	968.91
Lambert, Raymond. *Every Man a Hero*	B
Lamott, Anne. *Almost Everything*	170
Lamott, Anne. ★*Dusk, Night, Dawn*	B
Lamott, Anne. *Small Victories*	248
Lance, Rachel. *In the Waves*	973.7
Land, Stephanie. *Maid*	B
Lanegan, Mark. *Sing Backwards and Weep*	B
Lang, Maya. *What We Carry*	B
Lang, Michael. *The Road to Woodstock*	781.66
Lanzmann, Claude. *The Patagonian Hare*	B
Laughlin, James. *The Luck of Friendship*	B
Lavery, Daniel M. *Something That May Shock and Discredit You*	814
Lawrence, T. E. *Seven Pillars of Wisdom*	940.4
Lawson, Jenny. ★*Broken*	B
Lawson, Jenny. *Furiously Happy*	B
Lawton, Georgina. *Raceless*	B
Laymon, Kiese. ★*Heavy*	B
Le Carre, John. *The Pigeon Tunnel*	B
Lear, Norman. *Even This I Get to Experience*	B
Lecrae. ★*I Am Restored*	B
LeDuff, Charlie. *Detroit*	977.4
Lee, Julia Sun-Joo. *Biting the Hand*	B
LeFavour, Cree. *Lights On, Rats Out*	616.85
Legler, Casey. ★*Godspeed*	B
Leland, Andrew. ★*The Country of the Blind*	B
Lemay, Mimi. *What We Will Become*	306.874
Leng'ete, Nice. *The Girls in the Wild Fig Tree*	B
Leon, Donna. *My Venice and Other Essays*	945
Lessing, Doris May. *Under My Skin*	823
Levesque, Emily. *The Last Stargazers*	520
Levi, Primo. *The Periodic Table*	858
Levi, Primo. *The Reawakening*	B
Levin, Daniel. *Proof of Life*	956.9104
Levin, Daniel Barban. *Slonim Woods 9*	B
Levy, Deborah. *The Cost of Living*	B
Levy, Deborah. ★*Real Estate*	B
Levy, Deborah. ★*Things I Don't Want to Know*	B
Levy, Reynold. *They Told Me Not to Take That Job*	792.09
Lewis, Damien. *The Dog Who Could Fly*	940.54
Lewis, Jenifer. *Walking in My Joy*	B
Lewis, John. ★*March; Book One*	741.5
Lewis, John. ★*March; Book Three*	741.5
Lewis, John. ★*March; Book Two*	741.5
Lewis, John. ★*Run; Book One*	741.5
Lewis, Oscar. *The Children of Sanchez*	306.85
Li, Fei-Fei. *The Worlds I See*	B
Li, Yiyun. *Dear Friend, from My Life I Write to You in Your Life*	B
Lieu, Susan. ★*The Manicurist's Daughter*	B
Lifford, Tina. *The Little Book of Big Lies*	155.2
Lima, Jamie Kern. *Believe It*	B
Lin, Amy. *Here After*	B
Lin, Jami Nakamura. *The Night Parade*	B
Lippman, Laura. *My Life as a Villainess*	B
Lipska, Barbara K. *The Neuroscientist Who Lost Her Mind*	B
Litt, David, *Thanks, Obama*	B
Liu, Simu. ★*We Were Dreamers*	B
Lively, Penelope. *Life in the Garden*	B
Lloyd Webber, Andrew. *Unmasked*	B
Lloyd, Carli. *When Nobody Was Watching*	B
Locke, Tembi. ★*From Scratch*	B
Lockwood, Patricia. *Priestdaddy*	B
Loh, Sandra Tsing. *The Madwoman and the Roomba*	B
Louvin, Charlie. *Satan Is Real*	920
Lovato, Roberto. *Unforgetting*	B
Lowe, George. *Letters from Everest*	796.522
Lowman, Margaret. *The Arbornaut*	581.7
Lowman, Margaret. *Life in the Treetops*	B
Lundquist, Verne. *Play by Play*	B
Luttrell, Marcus. *Lone Survivor*	958.104
Luttrell, Marcus. *Service*	956.7044
Lynch, David. *Room to Dream*	B
Lynn, Loretta. ★*Me & Patsy Kickin' up Dust*	B
Lynn, Loretta. *Still Woman Enough*	B
Maathai, Wangari. *Unbowed*	B
Machado, Carmen Maria. ★*In the Dream House*	B
Madden, T Kira. *Long Live the Tribe of Fatherless Girls*	814
Magdalena, Carlos. *The Plant Messiah*	333.95
Mahjoub, Jamal. *A Line in the River*	962.404
Maiklem, Lara. *Mudlark*	B
Mailhot, Terese Marie. *Heart Berries*	B
Maisel, Ivan. *I Keep Trying to Catch His Eye*	B
Malcolm X. ★*The Autobiography of Malcolm X*	B
Malek, Alia. *The Home That Was Our Country*	B
Malone, Jo. *Jo Malone*	B
Manchester, William. *Goodbye, Darkness*	B
Mandel, Sarah. *Little Earthquakes*	B
Mandela, Nelson. *Dare Not Linger*	B
Mandela, Nelson. *In His Own Words*	B
Mandela, Nelson. ★*Long Walk to Freedom*	B
Mandela, Nelson. *Mandela*	B
Mankell, Henning. *Quicksand*	B
Mankoff, Robert. *How About Never—Is Never Good for You?*	741.5
Mann, Sally. ★*Hold Still*	B
Mann, William J. *The Wars of the Roosevelts*	B
Manning, Chelsea. *Readme.Txt*	B
Mantel, Hilary. *Mantel Pieces*	824.914

AUTHOR, TITLE, SERIES AND SUBJECT INDEX

Manuel, Ian. *My Time Will Come*	B
Marcum, Diana. *The Fallen Stones*	B
Mardini, Yusra. *Butterfly*	B
Markham, Beryl. *West with the Night*	B
Marsh, Henry. *Admissions*	B
Marsh, Henry. ★*Do No Harm*	B
Marshall, Cynthia. *You've Been Chosen*	B
Marshall, Greg. *Leg*	B
Martin, Clancy W. *How Not to Kill Yourself*	362.28
Martin, Manjula. *The Last Fire Season*	B
Martin, Steve. *Number One Is Walking*	B
Martin, Wednesday. *Primates of Park Avenue*	974.7
Martini, Adrienne. *Somebody's Gotta Do It*	B
Marzano-Lesnevich, Alexandria. *The Fact of a Body*	364.152
Masters, Oksana. *The Hard Parts*	B
Matar, Hisham. *The Return*	B
Maupin, Armistead. *Logical Family*	B
May, Katherine. *Enchantment*	158.1
May, Katherine. *Wintering*	155.9
May, Meredith. *The Honey Bus*	B
Mayes, Frances. *Bella Tuscany*	945
Mayes, Frances. *Under the Tuscan Sun*	945
Mayle, Peter. *My Twenty-Five Years in Provence*	944.9
Mays, Willie. *24*	B
McAnulty, Dara. *Diary of a Young Naturalist*	508.092
McCammon, Sarah. ★*The Exvangelicals*	277.308
McCann, Colum. *American Mother*	956.9104
McCauley, Esau. *How Far to the Promised Land*	B
McClelland, Mac. *Irritable Hearts*	B
McCloskey, Jim. *When Truth Is All You Have*	B
McColl, Sarah. *Joy Enough*	B
McConaughey, Matthew. *Greenlights*	B
McCourt, Frank. ★*Angela's Ashes*	929
McCourt, Frank. *Teacher Man*	B
McCourt, Frank. *'Tis*	B
McCourt, Malachy. *A Monk Swimming*	B
McCourt, Malachy. *Singing My Him Song*	B
McCraw, David Edward. *Truth in Our Times*	342.7308
McCurdy, Jennette. ★*I'm Glad My Mom Died*	B
McDonald, Michael. ★*What a Fool Believes*	B
McDougall, Christopher. *Running with Sherman*	636.1
McGarrahan, Ellen. *Two Truths and a Lie*	364.152
McGowan, Rose. *Brave*	B
McInerny, Nora. *The Hot Young Widows Club*	155.9
McKeon, Kathy. *Jackie's Girl*	B
McMillan, Tracie. ★*The White Bonus*	305.8
McRaven, William H. *Sea Stories*	B
Mead, Rebecca. *My Life in Middlemarch*	823
Means, Brittany. *Hell If We Don't Change Our Ways*	B
Mehra, Nishta. *Brown, White, Black*	305.800973
Mekhennet, Souad. *I Was Told to Come Alone*	363.3250956
Meltzer, Marisa. *This Is Big*	613.25
Melville, Wilma. ★*Hero Dogs*	636.7
Melvin, Leland. *Chasing Space*	B
Merritt, Tyler. *I Take My Coffee Black*	791.4302
Merton, Thomas. ★*The Seven Storey Mountain*	B
Messenger, Alex. *The Twenty-Ninth Day*	B
Messineo, Janet. *Casting into the Light*	799.1
Messud, Claire. *Kant's Little Prussian Head and Other Reasons Why I Write*	B
Metatawabin, Edmund. *Up Ghost River*	B
Meyer, Dakota. *Into the Fire*	958.104
Mezrich, Joshua D. *When Death Becomes Life*	617.9
Milch, David. *Life's Work*	B
Miller, Adrienne. *In the Land of Men*	070.5
Miller, Chanel. *Know My Name*	B
Miller, Kei. *Things I Have Withheld*	814
Miller, Lulu. *Why Fish Don't Exist*	B
Miller, Michelle. *Belonging*	B
Mills, Dan. *Sniper One*	956.7044
Mills, Hayley. *Forever Young*	B
Mills, Stephen Tukel. *Chosen*	B
Min, Anchee. *Red Azalea*	B
Mitchell, Jerry. ★*Race Against Time*	364.152
Mitchell, Wendy. *Somebody I Used to Know*	B
Mizrahi, Isaac. *I.M.*	B
Mizuki, Shigeru. *Showa 1926-1939*	741.5
Mlodinow, Leonard. *Stephen Hawking*	B
Moby. *Porcelain*	B
Moby. *Then It Fell Apart*	B
Mock, Janet. *Surpassing Certainty*	B
Moe, John. *The Hilarious World of Depression*	616.85
Moghul, Haroon. *How to Be a Muslim*	B
Momus. *Niche*	B
Monroe, Jana. *Hearts of Darkness*	363.25
Montgomery, Sy. *The Good Good Pig*	636.4
Montgomery, Sy. *How to Be a Good Creature*	590
Montville, Leigh. *Tall Men, Short Shorts*	796.323
Mooney, Paul. *Black Is the New White*	792.7
Moore, Beth. *All My Knotted-Up Life*	B
Moore, Colten. *Catching the Sky*	B
Moore, Michael Scott. *The Desert and the Sea*	364.15
Moore, Susanna. *Miss Aluminum*	813
Moore, Thurston. *Sonic Life*	B
Moore, Wayetu. *The Dragons, the Giant, the Women*	B
Moore, Wes. *The Other Wes Moore*	B
Moore, Wes. *The Work*	B
Moorer, Allison. *I Dream He Talks to Me*	782.42164
Moran, Caitlin. *How to Be a Woman*	B
Moran, Caitlin. *More Than a Woman*	B
Moran, Rachel. *Paid For*	306.74082
Morgan, Abi. *This Is Not a Pity Memoir*	B
Morris, David J. *The Evil Hours*	616.85
Morris, Jan. *A Writer's House in Wales*	942.9
Morris, Mark. *Out Loud*	B
Mortimer, Frank. *Bee People and the Bugs They Love*	B
Morton, Brian. *Tasha*	B
Morton, Michael. *Getting Life*	B
Mouton, Deborah D. E. E. P. *Black Chameleon*	B
Movsesian, Sona. *The World's Worst Assistant*	791.4302
Mowat, Farley. *Born Naked*	B
Muhammad, Ibtihaj. *Proud*	B
Muir, John. *Nature Writings*	B
Mulgrew, Kate. *Born with Teeth*	791.45028
Murad, Nadia. ★*The Last Girl*	B
Murakami, Haruki. ★*Absolutely on Music*	784.2
Murakami, Haruki. ★*Novelist as a Vocation*	895.64
Murakami, Haruki. *What I Talk About When I Talk About Running*	B
Murray, Liz. *Breaking Night*	B
Myers, Leah. *Thinning Blood*	B
Nadella, Satya. *Hit Refresh*	B
Nafisi, Azar. *The Republic of Imagination*	B
Nafisi, Azar. *Things I've Been Silent About*	B
Nakazawa, Donna Jackson. *The Angel and the Assassin*	612.8
Namath, Joe Willie. ★*All the Way*	B
Narayan, Shoba. *The Milk Lady of Bangalore*	390
Nathan, Joan. ★*My Life in Recipes*	641.5
Navarro, Joe. *Three Minutes to Doomsday*	B
Nawaz, Zarqa. *Laughing All the Way to the Mosque*	791.45028
Nayeri, Dina. ★*The Ungrateful Refugee*	362.87
Ndopu, Eddie. *Sipping Dom Pérignon Through a Straw*	B
Nelson, Maggie. ★*The Argonauts*	B
Nelson, Willie. *It's a Long Story*	B
Nemat, Marina. *Prisoner of Tehran*	B
Nesmith, Michael. *Infinite Tuesday*	B
Neumann, Ariana. *When Time Stopped*	B
Neville, Aaron. *Tell It Like It Is*	B
Nevins, Sheila. *You Don't Look Your Age*	B
Newman, Magdalena. *Normal*	611
Nezhukumatathil, Aimee. *Bite by Bite*	641.3
Ng, Fae Myenne. *Orphan Bachelors*	B
Ngugi wa Thiong'o. *In the House of the Interpreter*	B
Nguyen, Viet Thanh. ★*A Man of Two Faces*	B
Nietfeld, Emi. *Acceptance*	B
Nir, Sarah Maslin. *Horse Crazy*	B
Noah, Trevor. *Born a Crime*	B
Nolte, Nick. *Rebel*	B
Noor. *Leap of Faith*	B
Nooyi, Indra. ★*My Life in Full*	B
Nordland, Rod. *Waiting for the Monsoon*	B
Norman, Abby. *Ask Me About My Uterus*	618.1
Norris, Mary. *Between You and Me*	428.2
Northup, Solomon. *Twelve Years a Slave*	B
Norton, Peter. ★*Rainmaker*	796.352
Notaro, Laurie. *Excuse Me While I Disappear*	B
Nunn, Emily. *The Comfort Food Diaries*	641.5973

PUBLIC LIBRARY CORE COLLECTION: NONFICTION
Twentieth Edition

Nyad, Diana. *Find a Way*	B
Nyamayaro, Elizabeth. *I Am a Girl from Africa*	B
Nye, Bill. *Everything All at Once*	153.4
O'Brady, Colin. ★*The Impossible First*	919.8904
O'Brien, Jack. *Jack Be Nimble*	B
O'Brien, Vanessa. *To the Greatest Heights*	B
O'Connor, Sinead. ★*Rememberings*	B
O'Farrell, Maggie. *I Am, I Am, I Am*	B
O'Gieblyn, Meghan. *God, Human, Animal, Machine*	814
O'Hara, Maryanne. *Little Matches*	B
O'Neill, Robert. *The Operator*	B
O'Reilly, Seamas. ★*Did Ye Hear Mammy Died?*	B
O'Toole, Jennifer Cook. *Autism in Heels*	B
Oakley, Charles. *The Last Enforcer*	B
Obama, Barack. ★*Dreams from My Father*	B
Obama, Barack. *A Promised Land*	B
Obama, Michelle. ★*Becoming*	B
Obrist, Hans-Ulrich. *Ways of Curating*	707.5
Odenkirk, Bob. *Comedy Comedy Comedy Drama*	B
Oelhafen, Ingrid von. *Hitler's Stolen Children*	B
Offerman, Nick. *The Greatest Love Story Ever Told*	B
Okorafor, Nnedi. *Broken Places & Outer Spaces*	153.3
Okporo, Edafe. *Asylum*	B
Oliva, Alejandra. *Rivermouth*	305.9
Ollivier, Bernard. *Out of Istanbul*	B
Oluseyi, Hakeem M. *A Quantum Life*	B
Onassis, Jacqueline Kennedy. *Historic Conversations on Life with John F. Kennedy*	B
Onwuachi, Kwame. ★*Notes from a Young Black Chef*	641.59
Orenstein, Peggy. *Unraveling*	B
Orji, Yvonne. *Bamboozled by Jesus*	B
Orner, Peter. *Am I Alone Here?*	814
Ortiz, David. *Papi*	B
Osbourne, Ozzy. *I Am Ozzy*	B
Owen, Mark. *No Easy Day*	B
Owen, Mark. *No Hero*	B
Owens, Delia. *The Eye of the Elephant*	639.9
Owusu, Nadia. *Aftershocks*	B
Oz, Amos. *A Tale of Love and Darkness*	B
Pace, Kristin Knight. *This Much Country*	B
Page, Elliot. *Pageboy*	B
Pagels, Elaine H. ★*Why Religion?*	B
Painter, Nell Irvin. *Old in Art School*	B
Palahniuk, Chuck. *Consider This*	B
Palmer, Amanda. ★*The Art of Asking*	782.42164
Palmer, Arnold. *A Golfer's Life*	B
Pamuk, Orhan. *Istanbul*	949.61
Panagore, Peter Baldwin. *Heaven Is Beautiful*	B
Paperny, Anna Mehler. *Hello I Want to Die Please Fix Me*	362.2
Parcells, Bill. *Parcells*	B
Pardlo, Gregory. *Air Traffic*	B
Parini, Jay. *The Art of Teaching*	378.1
Parini, Jay. *Borges and Me*	813
Parker, Lara. *Vagina Problems*	618.1
Parker, Morgan. ★*You Get What You Pay For*	305.896
Parks, Casey. *Diary of a Misfit*	B
Parton, Dolly. ★*Behind the Seams*	B
Parton, Dolly. ★*Dolly Parton, Songteller*	B
Passarlay, Gulwali. *The Lightless Sky*	B
Pataki, Allison. *Beauty in the Broken Places*	B
Patchett, Ann. *This Is the Story of a Happy Marriage*	B
Patchett, Ann. *Truth & Beauty*	B
Patterson, James. *James Patterson by James Patterson*	B
Patterson, Pat. *Accepted*	B
Patton, George S. *War as I Knew It*	B
Paulsen, Gary. *Winterdance*	B
Pavlychenko, Liudmyla Mykhailivna. *Lady Death*	B
Paxson, Margaret. *The Plateau*	362.87
Peer, Basharat. *Curfewed Night*	B
Pellegrino, Danny. *How Do I Un-Remember This?*	B
Penn, Kal. *You Can't Be Serious*	B
Pennington, Emily. *Feral*	B
Pentland, Jenny. *This Will Be Funny Later*	B
Pepin, Jacques. *The Apprentice*	B
Perkins, Kendrick. *The Education of Kendrick Perkins*	B
Perkins, Nichole. *Sometimes I Trip on How Happy We Could Be*	B
Perron, Cam. ★*Comeback Season*	796.357
Perry, Joe. *Rocks*	B
Perry, Matthew. *Friends, Lovers, and the Big Terrible Thing*	B
Person, Charles. *Buses Are a Comin'*	B
Petersen, Andrea. *On Edge*	616.85
Peterson, Marlon. *Bird Uncaged*	B
Petrushevskaia, Liudmila. *The Girl from the Metropol Hotel*	B
Pfeifer, Joseph. *Ordinary Heroes*	973.931
Phair, Liz. *Horror Stories*	B
Pham, Larissa. *Pop Song*	709.2
Phelan, Tom. *We Were Rich and We Didn't Know It*	B
Philipps, Busy. *This Will Only Hurt a Little*	B
Philpott, Mary Laura. *Bomb Shelter*	B
Pick-Goslar, Hannah Elizabeth. ★*My Friend Anne Frank*	B
Pinckney, Darryl. *Come Back in September*	B
Pipher, Mary Bray. *A Life in Light*	B
Pippen, Scottie. *Unguarded*	B
Pittard, Hannah. *We Are Too Many*	B
Pivnik, Sam. *Survivor*	940.5318
Plummer, Christopher. *In Spite of Myself*	B
Poehler, Amy. *Yes Please*	B
Pogrebin, Abigail. *My Jewish Year*	296.4
Poitier, Sidney. *The Measure of a Man*	B
Porizkova, Paulina. *No Filter*	B
Porter, Billy. ★*Unprotected*	B
Posey, Parker. *You're on an Airplane*	B
Possanza, Amelia. *Lesbian Love Story*	B
Potts, Monica. *The Forgotten Girls*	B
Powell, Julie. *Julie and Julia*	641.5
Power, Carla. *If the Oceans Were Ink*	B
Power, Marianne. *Help Me!*	158.1
Pratchett, Terry. *A Slip of the Keyboard*	824
Prejean, Helen. *River of Fire*	B
Prescod, Danielle. *Token Black Girl*	B
Preston, Douglas J. ★*The Lost City of the Monkey God*	972.85
Preston, Katherine. *Out with It*	B
Preszler, Trent. *Little and Often*	B
Price, Margo. *Maybe We'll Make It*	B
Prince. *The Beautiful Ones*	B
Prior-Palmer, Lara. *Rough Magic*	798.4
Pritchett, Georgia. *My Mess Is a Bit of a Life*	B
Prose, Francine. *1974*	B
Proulx, Annie. *Bird Cloud*	B
Psaki, Jen. *Say More*	B
Qadiri, Humayra. *Dancing in the Mosque*	B
Qashu, Sayed. *Native*	892.4
Qu, Anna. *Made in China*	B
Quave, Cassandra Leah. *The Plant Hunter*	581.6
Questlove. *Mo' Meta Blues*	782.42164
Quin, Tegan. ★*High School*	B
Quindlen, Anna. ★*Nanaville*	B
Quinn, Tallu Schuyler. *What We Wish Were True*	B
Raban, Jonathan. *Father and Son*	B
Raboteau, Emily. *Lessons for Survival*	814
Rademacher, Tom. *It Won't Be Easy*	B
Radtke, Kristen. *Seek You*	741.5
Rahmani, Niloofar. *Open Skies*	B
Rainbow, Randy. *Playing with Myself*	B
Rakoff, Joanna Smith. *My Salinger Year*	B
Rallo, Eli. *I Didn't Know I Needed This*	306.73
Ramey, Sarah. *The Lady's Handbook for Her Mysterious Illness*	B
Ramos, Jorge. *Stranger*	325.73
Ramsey, Franchesca. *Well, That Escalated Quickly*	B
Rannells, Andrew. *Too Much Is Not Enough*	792.02
Rannells, Andrew. *Uncle of the Year*	B
Rao, Cheeni. *In Hanuman's Hands*	B
Rapinoe, Megan. *One Life*	B
Rapping, Jonathan. *Gideon's Promise*	345.73
Raskin, Allison. *Overthinking About You*	646.7
Ravin, Idan. *The Hoops Whisperer*	796.323
Raymond, Edwin. *An Inconvenient Cop*	363.2
Reang, Putsata. *Ma and Me*	B
Rear, Rachel. *Catch the Sparrow*	364.152
Rebanks, James. *The Shepherd's Life*	942.7
Reed, Shannon. *Why We Read*	028
Regan, Iliana. *Fieldwork*	B
Rehm, Diane. *On My Own*	B
Rehman, Sabeeha. *Threading My Prayer Rug*	305.8
Reichl, Ruth. *Comfort Me with Apples*	B
Reichl, Ruth. *Garlic and Sapphires*	B

AUTHOR, TITLE, SERIES AND SUBJECT INDEX

Reichl, Ruth. *My Kitchen Year*	641.5
Reichl, Ruth. ★*Save Me the Plums*	B
Rembert, Winfred. *Chasing Me to My Grave*	B
Renkl, Margaret. *The Comfort of Crows*	814.6
Retta. *So Close to Being the Sh*t, Y'all Don't Even Know*	B
Reynolds, Debbie. *Make 'Em Laugh*	B
Rezaian, Jason. *Prisoner*	B
Rhodes, Benjamin J. *The World as It Is*	973.932
Rhodes, James. *Instrumental*	B
Ricanati, Elizabeth. *Braided*	B
Rice, Condoleezza. *Extraordinary, Ordinary People*	B
Rice, Condoleezza. *No Higher Honor*	B
Richards, Cecile. *Make Trouble*	B
Richards, Keith. *Life*	B
Rieder, Travis. *In Pain*	362.29
Riess, Jana. *Flunking Sainthood*	248.4
Riggs, Nina. *The Bright Hour*	B
Rigsby, Cody. ★*XOXO, Cody*	B
Rinder, Mike. ★*A Billion Years*	B
Ripa, Kelly. *Live Wire*	B
Ripert, Eric. *32 Yolks*	B
Rippon, Adam. *Beautiful on the Outside*	B
Risner, Vaneetha Rendall. *Walking Through Fire*	B
Rivera, Mariano. *The Closer*	B
Roach, Margaret. ★*A Way to Garden*	635
Robb, Alice. ★*Don't Think, Dear*	792.8
Roberts, David. *Limits of the Known*	B
Robertson, Robbie. ★*Testimony*	B
Robinson, Jackie. *I Never Had It Made*	B
Robinson, Phoebe. *Please Don't Sit on My Bed in Your Outside Clothes*	818
Robinson, Phoebe. *You Can't Touch My Hair and Other Things I Still Have to Explain*	792.7
Robison, John Elder. *Look Me in the Eye*	B
Rodgers, Mary. *Shy*	B
Rogen, Seth. ★*Yearbook*	B
Rogers, Robbie. *Coming Out to Play*	B
Roig-Debellis, Kaitlin. *Choosing Hope*	371.7
Rojas Contreras, Ingrid. ★*The Man Who Could Move Clouds*	B
Ronstadt, Linda. *Feels Like Home*	B
Rosen, Jonathan. ★*The Best Minds*	616.89
Rosenberg, Justus. *The Art of Resistance*	B
Rosenthal, Jason. *My Wife Said You May Want to Marry Me*	B
Roundtree, Dovey Johnson. ★*Mighty Justice*	B
Rowe, Mickey. *Fearlessly Different*	B
Rowe, Peggy. *About My Mother*	B
Royster, Francesca T. *Choosing Family*	B
Rubin, Kathy Kleiner. *A Light in the Dark*	364.152
Rudd, Mark. *Underground*	378.1
Ruhl, Sarah. *Smile*	B
RuPaul. ★*The House of Hidden Meanings*	B
Rusbridger, Alan. ★*Play It Again*	B
Rush, Chris. *The Light Years*	B
Rushdie, Salman. *Joseph Anton*	B
Rushdie, Salman. ★*Knife*	B
Russert, Luke. *Look for Me There*	B
Sabathia, CC. *Till the End*	796.357
Sacks, Oliver. *On the Move*	B
Saint John, Bozoma. *The Urgent Life*	B
Salaam, Yusef. *Better, Not Bitter*	B
Salama, Jordan. ★*Stranger in the Desert*	982
Sale, Anna. ★*Let's Talk About Hard Things*	153.6
Samaha, Albert. *Concepcion*	929
Samatar, Sofia. *The White Mosque*	B
Samer. *The Raqqa Diaries*	956.9104
Samuelsson, Marcus. *Yes, Chef*	B
Sanchez, Aaron. *Where I Come From*	641.5092
Sanchez, Erika L. *Crying in the Bathroom*	B
Santana, Carlos. *The Universal Tone*	B
Sante, Lucy. *I Heard Her Call My Name*	B
Sardy, Marin. *The Edge of Every Day*	B
Sarsour, Linda. *We Are Not Here to Be Bystanders*	B
Sartre, Jean-Paul. *We Have Only This Life to Live*	848
Sasakamoose, Fred. *Call Me Indian*	B
Satrapi, Marjane. ★*The Complete Persepolis*	741.5
Saunders, John. *Playing Hurt*	B
Savage, Jodi M. *The Death of a Jaybird*	B
Scheer, Paul. *Joyful Recollections of Trauma*	B
Scheeres, Julia. *Jesus Land*	B
Scheier, Liz. *Never Simple*	B
Schemel, Patty. *Hit so Hard*	B
Schindler, Meriel. *The Lost Cafe Schindler*	943.64
Schlesinger, Arthur M. *A Life in the Twentieth Century*	B
Schneider, Amy. *In the Form of a Question*	B
Schott, Philipp. *The Accidental Veterinarian*	B
Schreiber, Flora Rheta. *Sybil*	616.85
Schulz, Kathryn. ★*Lost & Found*	B
Schwalbe, Will. ★*The End of Your Life Book Club*	B
Schwalbe, Will. *We Should Not Be Friends*	B
Schwarz, Geraldine. *Those Who Forget*	940.53
Sciolino, Elaine. *The Seine*	944
Scottoline, Lisa. *I See Life Through Rose-Colored Glasses*	813
Scovell, Nell. *Just the Funny Parts*	B
Seager, Sara. *The Smallest Lights in the Universe*	B
Searcey, Dionne. *In Pursuit of Disobedient Women*	B
Sedaris, David. ★*The Best of Me*	818
Sedaris, David. *Calypso*	814
Segura, Tom. ★*I'd Like to Play Alone, Please*	B
Sehee, Baek. *I Want to Die but I Want to Eat Tteokbokki*	B
Seidelman, Susan. *Desperately Seeking Something*	B
Seinfeld, Jerry. *Is This Anything?*	818
Selleck, Tom. *You Never Know*	B
Sellers, Bakari. *My Vanishing Country*	B
Selvaratnam, Tanya. *Assume Nothing*	B
Semenya, Caster. *The Race to Be Myself*	B
Sen, Amartya. *Home in the World*	B
Senator, Susan. *Autism Adulthood*	616.85
Sentilles, Sarah. *Stranger Care*	B
Sestero, Greg. *The Disaster Artist*	791.43
Shafrir, Doree. *Thanks for Waiting*	B
Shahani, Aarti Namdev. *Here We Are*	B
Shakur, Prince. *When They Tell You to Be Good*	B
Shannon, Molly. ★*Hello, Molly!*	B
Shapiro, Ari. ★*The Best Strangers in the World*	B
Shapiro, Dani. ★*Inheritance*	B
Shapland, Jenn. *My Autobiography of Carson McCullers*	B
Sharapova, Maria. *Unstoppable*	B
Sharma, Nina. *The Way You Make Me Feel*	B
Shatner, William. *Boldly Go*	B
Shatner, William. *Live Long And—*	B
Shattuck, Ben. *Six Walks*	B
Sheehan, Jason. *Cooking Dirty*	B
Shehadeh, Raja. ★*We Could Have Been Friends, My Father and I*	B
Sherman, Anna. *The Bells of Old Tokyo*	952
Shields, Aomawa L. *Life on Other Planets*	B
Shih, David. *Chinese Prodigal*	B
Short, Martin. *I Must Say*	B
Shorter, Frank. *My Marathon*	796.42
Shraya, Vivek. *I'm Afraid of Men*	813
Shriver, Timothy P. *Fully Alive*	796.087
Shteyngart, Gary. ★*Little Failure*	B
Simard, S. *Finding the Mother Tree*	582.16
Simmons, Ruth. ★*Up Home*	B
Simon, Carly. ★*Boys in the Trees*	782.42164
Simon, Marie. *Underground in Berlin*	B
Simpson, J. A. *The Word Detective*	B
Sinclair, Safiya. ★*How to Say Babylon*	B
Singh, Julietta. *The Breaks*	B
Sinise, Gary. *Grateful American*	B
Sipress, David. *What's so Funny?*	B
Sjunneson, Elsa. *Being Seen*	362.4
Skaife, Christopher. *The Ravenmaster*	B
Skelton, Marc. *Pounding the Rock*	796.323
Slahi, Mohamedou Ould. *The Mauritanian*	958.104
Slate, Jenny. *Little Weirds*	B
Slouka, Mark. *Nobody's Son*	B
Smarsh, Sarah. ★*Heartland*	B
Smith, Bren. *Eat Like a Fish*	338.3
Smith, Carol. *Crossing the River*	B
Smith, Danyel. *Shine Bright*	782.42164
Smith, Freda Love. *I Quit Everything*	B
Smith, Jada Pinkett. *Worthy*	B
Smith, Kenny. *Talk of Champions*	B
Smith, Lee. *Dimestore*	975.5
Smith, Maggie. ★*You Could Make This Place Beautiful*	B
Smith, Mychal Denzel. *Invisible Man, Got the Whole World Watching*	305.242

PUBLIC LIBRARY CORE COLLECTION: NONFICTION
Twentieth Edition

Smith, Patti. ★*Just Kids*	B
Smith, Patti. ★*Year of the Monkey*	B
Smith, Tracy K. ★*To Free the Captives*	818
Smith, Will. ★*Will*	B
Smyth, Katharine. *All the Lives We Ever Lived*	B
Snyder, Rachel Louise. *Women We Buried, Women We Burned*	B
Sokolik, Vicki. ★*If You See Them*	362.5
Solnit, Rebecca. ★*Recollections of My Nonexistence*	B
Solomonov, Michael. *Zahav*	641.595
Soloway, Jill. *She Wants It*	B
Sone, Monica Itoi. *Nisei Daughter*	979.7
Sorensen, Theodore C. *Counselor*	B
Sotomayor, Sonia. ★*My Beloved World*	B
Spears, Britney. *The Woman in Me*	B
Speer, Albert. *Inside the Third Reich*	B
Spiegelman, Art. ★*Maus*	741.5
Spiegelman, Art. *Metamaus*	B
Spiegelman, Nadja. ★*I'm Supposed to Protect You from All This*	741.5
Springsteen, Bruce. ★*Born to Run*	B
Spurrier, Steve. *Head Ball Coach*	B
Stamos, John. *If You Would Have Told Me*	B
Standefer, Katherine E. *Lightning Flowers*	B
Staniforth, Nate. *Here Is Real Magic*	B
Stanley, Paul. *Backstage Pass*	B
Stanley, Paul. *Face the Music*	B
Stern, Adam. *Committed*	616.89
Stern, Amanda. *Little Panic*	616.8522
Stevens, John Paul. *The Making of a Justice*	B
Stevenson, Bryan. *Just Mercy*	B
Stewart, Patrick. ★*Making It So*	B
Stewart, Rory. *The Prince of the Marshes*	956.7044
Stone, Alex. *Fooling Houdini*	B
Stone, Lillian. ★*Everybody's Favorite*	814.6
Stone, Sharon. *The Beauty of Living Twice*	B
Stone, Sly. *Thank You (Falettinme Be Mice Elf Agin)*	B
Strayed, Cheryl. ★*Wild*	B
Streisand, Barbra. ★*My Name Is Barbra*	B
Stuart, Amanda Mackenzie. *Empress of Fashion*	B
Styron, William. *My Generation*	814
Sullivan, Margaret. *Newsroom Confidential*	070.92
Sullivan, Randall. *Graveyard of the Pacific*	979.7
Summitt, Pat Head. *Sum It Up*	B
Sun, Carrie. *Private Equity*	B
Sundberg, Kelly. *Goodbye, Sweet Girl*	B
Sutherland, Amy. *Rescuing Penny Jane*	636.7
Suvari, Mena. *The Great Peace*	B
Swisher, Kara. *Burn Book*	303.48
Swofford, Anthony. *Jarhead*	956.7044
Szczeszak-Brewer, Agata. *The Hunger Book*	B
Taing, Mae Bunseng. *Under the Naga Tail*	B
Tallent, Elizabeth. *Scratched*	B
Talley, Andre Leon. *The Chiffon Trenches*	B
Talusan, Meredith. *Fairest*	305.30973
Tamblyn, Amber. ★*Era of Ignition*	B
Tamimi, Ahed. ★*They Called Me a Lioness*	B
Tammet, Daniel. *Born on a Blue Day*	B
Tan, Amy. ★*Where the Past Begins*	B
Tanais. *In Sensorium*	B
Tate, Christie. *B.F.F.*	B
Tate, Christie. ★*Group*	B
Taupin, Bernie. *Scattershot*	B
Taussig, Rebekah. *Sitting Pretty*	B
Taylor, Barbara Brown. *Holy Envy*	B
Taylor, Cory. *Dying*	B
Taylor, Goldie. *The Love You Save*	B
Taylor, Jill Bolte. *My Stroke of Insight*	362.19681
Taylor, Justin. *Riding with the Ghost*	B
Teege, Jennifer. *My Grandfather Would Have Shot Me*	929.2
Teffi, N. A. *Memories*	B
Tegmark, Max. *Our Mathematical Universe*	523.1
Teigen, Chrissy. *Cravings*	641.5
Tenzin Priyadarshi. *Running Toward Mystery*	B
Tester, Jon. *Grounded*	B
Tetro, Tony. *Con/Artist*	B
Thi, Kim Phuc Phan. *Fire Road*	B
Thomas, Dylan. *A Child's Christmas in Wales*	B
Thomas, Elizabeth Marshall. *Growing Old*	305.26
Thomas, Franklin A. *An Unplanned Life*	B
Thomas, Joseph Earl. *Sink*	B
Thomas, R. Eric. *Here for It*	B
Thompson, J. M. *Running Is a Kind of Dreaming*	B
Thorp, Edward O. *A Man for All Markets*	B
Threadgill, Henry. *Easily Slip into Another World*	B
Tjipombo, Tupa. *I Am Not Your Slave*	B
Tobia, Jacob. *Sissy*	305.30973
Tolokonnikova, Nadezhda. *Rules for Rulebreakers*	782.42166
Tometich, Annabelle. *The Mango Tree*	B
Tomine, Adrian. *The Loneliness of the Long-Distance Cartoonist*	741.5
Tomlinson, Tommy. *The Elephant in the Room*	B
Toorpakai, Maria. *A Different Kind of Daughter*	B
Torre, Joe. *The Yankee Years*	B
Totenberg, Nina. ★*Dinners with Ruth*	B
Toussaint, Alex. ★*Activate Your Greatness*	158.1
Tran, Ly. *House of Sticks*	B
Tran, Phuc. ★*Sigh, Gone*	B
Travis, Randy. *Forever and Ever, Amen*	B
Trebek, Alex. *The Answer Is ...*	791.4502
Trebincevic, Kenan. *The Bosnia List*	B
Trejo, Danny. *Trejo*	B
Trethewey, Natasha D. ★*Memorial Drive*	B
Trice, Dawn Turner. *Three Girls from Bronzeville*	977.311
Tubbs, Michael. *The Deeper the Roots*	B
Tucci, Stanley. ★*Taste*	B
Tur, Katy. *Rough Draft*	B
Turner, Tina. ★*Happiness Becomes You*	158.1
Twain, Mark. *Autobiography of Mark Twain*	B
Twain, Mark. ★*Autobiography of Mark Twain*	B
Twain, Mark. ★*Autobiography of Mark Twain*	B
Tweedy, Jeff. *Let's Go (so We Can Get Back)*	B
Tworkov, Helen. *Lotus Girl*	B
Tye, Larry. *Satchel*	B
Tyson, Cicely. ★*Just as I Am*	B
Tyson, Mike. *Iron Ambition*	B
Tyson, Timothy B. *Blood Done Sign My Name*	975.6
Ulander, Perry A. *Walking Point*	B
Ullman, Ellen. *Life in Code*	B
Umar, Ousman. *North to Paradise*	B
Ung, Loung. *First They Killed My Father*	959.604
Ung, Loung. *Lucky Child*	B
Union, Gabrielle. *We're Going to Need More Wine*	B
Union, Gabrielle. *You Got Anything Stronger?*	B
V. *The Apology*	818
Van De Perre, Selma. *My Name Is Selma*	940.53
Van Es, Bart. *The Cut Out Girl*	B
Van Hemert, Caroline. *The Sun Is a Compass*	979.8
Van Zandt, Steve. *Unrequited Infatuations*	B
Vanasco, Jeannie. *Things We Didn't Talk About When I Was a Girl*	B
Vance, J. D. *Hillbilly Elegy*	B
Vargas Llosa, Mario. *The Call of the Tribe*	868
Vargas, Jose Antonio. *Dear America*	B
Vasquez-Lavado, Silvia. *In the Shadow of the Mountain*	B
Velshi, Ali. *Small Acts of Courage*	B
Verant, Samantha. *Seven Letters from Paris*	B
Verdelle, A. J. *Miss Chloe*	B
Vickers, Michael G. *By All Means Available*	355
Villarreal, Vanessa Anglica. *Magical/Realism*	814
Volpe, Joseph. *The Toughest Show on Earth*	B
Von Furstenberg, Diane. *The Woman I Wanted to Be*	B
Vonnegut, Kurt. ★*A Man Without a Country*	818
Wade, Becky. *Run the World*	796.42
Wagamese, Richard. *For Joshua*	B
Wagamese, Richard. *One Native Life*	B
Wagner, Alex. *Futureface*	B
Wainaina, Binyavanga. *One Day I Will Write About This Place*	B
Walder, Tracy. *The Unexpected Spy*	B
Waldman, Ayelet. *A Really Good Day*	B
Walker, Alice. *The Cushion in the Road*	814
Wall, Duncan. *The Ordinary Acrobat*	B
Wallace, Carvell. *Another Word for Love*	B
Walls, Jeannette. ★*The Glass Castle*	B
Walters, Billy. *Gambler*	796.092
Walton, Bill. *Back from the Dead*	B
Wambach, Abby. *Forward*	B
Wang, Connie. *Oh My Mother!*	B
Wang, Qian Julie. ★*Beautiful Country*	B
Ward, Clarissa. *On All Fronts*	B

AUTHOR, TITLE, SERIES AND SUBJECT INDEX

Ward, Jesmyn. ★*Men We Reaped*	B
Ward, Jon. *Testimony*	277.308
Ward, Maitland. *Rated X*	B
Wariner, Ruth. *The Sound of Gravel*	B
Warraich, Haider. *The Song of Our Scars*	616
Warren, W. Lee. *No Place to Hide*	B
Warsaw-Fan Rauch, Arianna. ★*Declassified*	781.1
Washington, Booker T. ★*Up from Slavery*	B
Washington, Kate. ★*Already Toast*	649.8
Washington, Kerry. *Thicker Than Water*	B
Wassef, Nadia. *Shelf Life*	B
Waters, Alice. *Coming to My Senses*	B
Waters, John. *Mr. Know-It-All*	814
Watkins, D. *Black Boy Smile*	B
Watts, Reggie. *Great Falls, MT*	B
Webb, Kinari. *Guardians of the Trees*	B
Weigel, Alicia Roth. *Inverse Cowgirl*	B
Weiner, Eric. *Ben & Me*	B
Weisman, Eliot. *The Way It Was*	782.42164
Weiss, Helga. *Helga's Diary*	B
Wellman, Victoria. *Before You Say Anything*	808.5
Wellons, Jay. *All That Moves Us*	617.4
Welteroth, Elaine. *More Than Enough*	B
Welty, Eudora. *One Writer's Beginnings*	B
Wenner, Jann. *Like a Rolling Stone*	B
Wertheim, L. Jon. *Blood in the Cage*	796.815
Weschler, Lawrence. *And How Are You, Dr. Sacks?*	B
West, Cait. ★*Rift*	B
West, Jerry. *West by West*	B
Westheimer, Ruth. *The Doctor Is In*	B
Westover, Tara. ★*Educated*	B
Wetherall, Tyler. *No Way Home*	B
Whippman, Ruth. ★*Boymom*	305.23
Whitaker, Holly. ★*Quit Like a Woman*	616.86
White, Gayle Jessup. *Reclamation*	B
White, Neil. *In the Sanctuary of Outcasts*	B
White, Ralph. *Getting Out of Saigon*	959.704
White, Richard Antoine. *I'm Possible*	B
Whitney, Emerson. *Heaven*	B
Widder, Edith. *Below the Edge of Darkness*	551.46092
Wiener, Anna. ★*Uncanny Valley*	B
Wiesel, Elie. *All Rivers Run to the Sea*	B
Wiesel, Elie. *And the Sea Is Never Full*	B
Wiesel, Elie. ★*Night*	B
Wiesenthal, Simon. ★*The Sunflower*	179.7
Wilder, Laura Ingalls. *Pioneer Girl*	B
Wilder-Taylor, Stefanie. ★*Drunk-Ish*	B
Wilderson, Frank B. *Afropessimism*	B
Wilkinson, Crystal. *Praisesong for the Kitchen Ghosts*	641.5975
Williams, Bari A. *Seen yet Unseen*	338.4
Williams, Billy Dee. ★*What Have We Here*	B
Williams, Florence. *Heartbreak*	306.7
Williams, Jay. *Life Is Not an Accident*	B
Williams, Lucinda. *Don't Tell Anybody the Secrets I Told You*	B
Williams, Marlena. *Night Mother*	791.43
Williams, Mary. *The Lost Daughter*	B
Williams, Michael Kenneth. *Scenes from My Life*	B
Williams, Michelle. *Checking In*	B
Williams, Patricia. *Rabbit*	B
Williams, Richard. *Black and White*	B
Williams, Zach. *Rescue Story*	B
Willis, Raquel. *The Risk It Takes to Bloom*	B
Willner, Nina. *Forty Autumns*	B
Wills, Clair. ★*Missing Persons*	929.2
Wilson, A'ja. ★*Dear Black Girls*	158.1
Wilson, Brian. *I Am Brian Wilson*	B
Wilson, Chris. *The Master Plan*	B
Wilson, Katherine. *Only in Naples*	B
Wilson, Rebel. *Rebel Rising*	B
Wiman, Christian. *He Held Radical Light*	814
Wiman, Christian. *Zero at the Bone*	818
Windsor, Edie. *A Wild and Precious Life*	B
Winkler, Henry. ★*Being Henry*	B
Winn, Raynor. ★*The Salt Path*	B
Winn, Raynor. *The Wild Silence*	B
Winter, Molly Roden. *More*	B
Winters, Richard D. *Beyond Band of Brothers*	B
Wise, Beau. *Three Wise Men*	958.104
Wizenberg, Molly. *Fixed Stars*	B
Wolf, Brandon J. *A Place for Us*	B
Wolff, Tobias. *This Boy's Life*	B
Wong, Ali. ★*Dear Girls*	B
Wong, Alice. ★*Year of the Tiger*	B
Wong, Carmen Rita. *Why Didn't You Tell Me?*	B
Wong, Jane. ★*Meet Me Tonight in Atlantic City*	B
Wood, Damon. *Working for the Man, Playing in the Band*	782.42164
Woodfox, Albert. *Solitary*	B
Woods, Tiger. *The 1997 Masters*	B
Woolf, Virginia. *Moments of Being*	B
Worley, Jennifer. *Neon Girls*	792.7
Wright, Lawrence. *God Save Texas*	917.64
Wright, Richard. ★*Black Boy*	B
Wu, Constance. *Making a Scene*	B
Wynn-Grant, Rae. *Wild Life*	B
Yancey, Philip. ★*Where the Light Fell*	B
Yip-Williams, Julie. ★*The Unwinding of the Miracle*	973
Young, Damon. ★*What Doesn't Kill You Makes You Blacker*	B
Young, Daniella Mestyanek. *Uncultured*	B
Young, Neil. *Waging Heavy Peace*	B
Young, Steve. *QB*	B
Yousafzai, Malala. *I Am Malala*	B
Yousafzai, Ziauddin. *Let Her Fly*	B
Yovanovitch, Marie. *Lessons from the Edge*	973.933
Ypi, Lea. ★*Free*	B
Zambreno, Kate. *The Light Room*	B
Zamora, Javier. ★*Solito*	B
Zara, Christopher. *Uneducated*	B
Zauner, Michelle. ★*Crying in H Mart*	B
Zhu, Mimi. *Be Not Afraid of Love*	152.4
Zimmerman, Paul. *Dr. Z*	B
Zweibel, Alan. *Laugh Lines*	B
Zwick, Edward. ★*Hits, Flops, and Other Illusions*	B
An *Autobiography*. Gandhi	

AUTOBIOGRAPHY

Febos, Melissa. ★*Body Work*	808.06
Fehrman, Craig. *Author in Chief*	920
Karr, Mary. *The Art of Memoir*	B
Piercy, Marge. *So You Want to Write*	808.3
★*The Autobiography of Benjamin Franklin*. Franklin, Benjamin	B
★*The Autobiography of Malcolm X*. Malcolm X	B
Autobiography of Mark Twain. Twain, Mark	B
★*Autobiography of Mark Twain*. Twain, Mark	B
★*Autobiography of Mark Twain*. Twain, Mark	B
The Autobiography of Martin Luther King, Jr. King, Martin Luther	B
Autobiography of Red. Carson, Anne	811
★*Autobiography, Poor Richard, and Later Writings*. Franklin, Benjamin	973.2

AUTOIMMUNE DISEASES

Cahalan, Susannah. *Brain on Fire*	616.8
Myers, Amy. *The Autoimmune Solution Cookbook*	641.5
Myers, Amy. ★*The Autoimmune Solution*	616.97
Nakazawa, Donna Jackson. *The Angel and the Assassin*	612.8
O'Rourke, Meghan. ★*The Invisible Kingdom*	616
Richtel, Matt. ★*An Elegant Defense*	616.07
★*The Autoimmune Solution*. Myers, Amy	616.97
The Autoimmune Solution Cookbook. Myers, Amy	641.5

AUTOMATION

Merchant, Brian. *Blood in the Machine*	303.48
Russell, Stuart J. *Human Compatible*	006.301
Tegmark, Max. *Life 3.0*	006.301

AUTOMOBILE DESIGNERS

Baime, A. J. ★*Go Like Hell*	796.7209
Brinkley, Douglas. *Wheels for the World*	B
Watts, Steven. *The People's Tycoon*	B

AUTOMOBILE DRIVING

Albert, Daniel M. *Are We There Yet?*	303.48

AUTOMOBILE FACTORIES

Goldstein, Amy. *Janesville*	330.9775

AUTOMOBILE INDUSTRY AND TRADE

Albert, Daniel M. *Are We There Yet?*	303.48
Brinkley, Douglas. *Wheels for the World*	B
DeBord, Matthew. *Return to Glory*	338.4
Ewing, Jack. *Faster, Higher, Farther*	338.7
Goldstein, Amy. *Janesville*	330.9775
Goldstone, Lawrence. *Drive!*	338.4
Higgins, Tim. *Power Play*	338.7
Parissien, Steven. *The Life of the Automobile*	629.222

PUBLIC LIBRARY CORE COLLECTION: NONFICTION
Twentieth Edition

Vlasic, Bill. *Once Upon a Car*	338.4
Watts, Steven. *The People's Tycoon*	B
AUTOMOBILE PARKING	
Grabar, Henry. *Paved Paradise*	388.474
AUTOMOBILE PURCHASING	
Milchtein, Chaya M. ★*Mechanic Shop Femme's Guide to Car Ownership*	629.222
AUTOMOBILE RACING	
Bascomb, Neal. *Faster*	796.7209
DeBord, Matthew. *Return to Glory*	338.4
AUTOMOBILE RACING DRIVERS	
Bascomb, Neal. *Faster*	796.7209
Busbee, Jay. *Earnhardt Nation*	B
AUTOMOBILE TRAVEL	
Bunnell, David. *Good Friday on the Rez*	B
Heat Moon, William Least. *Blue Highways*	917.304
Lee, Edward. *Buttermilk Graffiti*	641.59
Sorin, Gretchen Sullivan. *Driving While Black*	323.1196
Steinbeck, John. *Travels with Charley*	B
Wexler, Jay. *Holy Hullabaloos*	342.7308
AUTOMOBILES	
Albert, Daniel M. *Are We There Yet?*	303.48
Baime, A. J. ★*Go Like Hell*	796.7209
Goldstein, Amy. *Janesville*	330.9775
Goldstone, Lawrence. *Drive!*	338.4
Heat Moon, William Least. *Blue Highways*	917.304
Higgins, Tim. *Power Play*	338.7
Milchtein, Chaya M. ★*Mechanic Shop Femme's Guide to Car Ownership*	629.222
Parissien, Steven. *The Life of the Automobile*	629.222
Schwartz, Samuel I. *No One at the Wheel*	629.2
Standage, Tom. *A Brief History of Motion*	388
Vlasic, Bill. *Once Upon a Car*	338.4
AUTOMOBILES, RACING	
DeBord, Matthew. *Return to Glory*	338.4
Hawley, Sam. *Speed Duel*	796.72
AUTONOMOUS VEHICLES	
Albert, Daniel M. *Are We There Yet?*	303.48
Schwartz, Samuel I. *No One at the Wheel*	629.2
AUTONOMY	
Durvasula, Ramani. ★*It's Not You*	155.2
AUTOPSY	
Di Maio, Vincent J. M. *Morgue*	B
Autumn in the Heavenly Kingdom. Platt, Stephen R.	951
Autumn of the Black Snake. Hogeland, William	970.004
Auvinen, Karen	
Rough Beauty	B
AUVINEN, KAREN	
Auvinen, Karen. *Rough Beauty*	B
AVALANCHES	
Krist, Gary. *The White Cascade*	979.7
AVANT-GARDE (AESTHETICS)	
Brown, Carolyn. *Chance and Circumstance*	B
Dery, Mark. *Born to Be Posthumous*	B
FitzGerald, Michael C. ★*Picasso and American Art*	709.73
Gabriel, Mary. *Ninth Street Women*	920
Lynch, David. *Room to Dream*	B
Shaw, Jennifer Laurie. *Exist Otherwise*	709.2
Warren, Rosanna. *Max Jacob*	B
AVATARS (RELIGION)	
Reed, Justin Phillip. *The Malevolent Volume*	811
Avedon. Stevens, Norma	B
AVEDON, RICHARD	
Gefter, Philip. *What Becomes a Legend Most*	B
Stevens, Norma. *Avedon*	B
Avenue of Spies. Kershaw, Alex	940.53
Averno. Gluck, Louise	811
AVERY, JOHN, ACTIVE 1695	
Johnson, Steven. *Enemy of All Mankind*	910.4
AVIAN INFLUENZA	
Quammen, David. ★*Spillover*	614.4
AVIATION	
Bell, Jim. *The Interstellar Age*	919
Hazelgrove, William Elliott. *Wright Brothers, Wrong Story*	920
McCullough, David G. ★*The Wright Brothers*	B
O'Brien, Keith. *Fly Girls*	920
AVIATION HISTORY	
Aldrin, Buzz. *No Dream Is Too High*	B
Barbree, Jay. *Neil Armstrong*	B
Bruning, John R. *The Race of Aces*	940.54
Groom, Winston. *The Aviators*	920
Hampton, Dan. *Chasing the Demon*	629.132
Hastings, Max. *Operation Chastise*	940.54
Holmes, Richard. *Falling Upwards*	387.7
Hynes, Samuel. *The Unsubstantial Air*	940.4
Launius, Roger D. *Apollo's Legacy*	629.45
Leinbach, Michael D. *Bringing Columbia Home*	363.12
McCullough, David G. ★*The Wright Brothers*	B
Rose, Alexander. *Empires of the Sky*	920
Sheehan, Neil. *A Fiery Peace in a Cold War*	B
Stone, Robert. *Chasing the Moon*	629.45
Teitel, Amy Shira. *Fighting for Space*	920
Walker, Stephen. *Beyond*	629.45
The Aviators. Groom, Winston	920
Aviv, Rachel	
★*Strangers to Ourselves*	616.89
AVIV, RACHEL	
Aviv, Rachel. ★*Strangers to Ourselves*	616.89
Avlon, John P.	
Lincoln and the Fight for Peace	973.7
Washington's Farewell	973.4
AVOIDANCE (PSYCHOLOGY)	
Boone, Matthew S. *Stop Avoiding Stuff*	152.4
Avrich, Paul	
Sasha and Emma	920
Awakening. Vogelstein, Rachel B.	305.42
Aware. Siegel, Daniel J.	158.1
AWARENESS	
Corbett, Emily. *In Transition*	809
Fersko, Diana. ★*We Need to Talk About Antisemitism*	305.892
Havrilesky, Heather. *What If This Were Enough?*	152.4
Nhat Hanh. *The Art of Living*	294.3
Rubin, Gretchen Craft. ★*Life in Five Senses*	152.1
The Away Game. Abbot, Sebastian	796.334
★*Awe.* Keltner, Dacher	152.4
Axelrod, Matt	
Your Guide to the Jewish Holidays	296.4
AYATOLLAHS	
Rushdie, Salman. *Joseph Anton*	B
Ayers, Edward L.	
American Visions	973.5
★*The Thin Light of Freedom*	975.5
AYKROYD, DAN, 1952-	
De Semlyen, Nick. *Wild and Crazy Guys*	920
De Vise, Daniel. ★*The Blues Brothers*	791.43
Aykroyd, Peter	
A History of Ghosts	133.1
AYSE GULBAHAR HATUN, CONSORT OF BAYEZID II, SULTAN OF THE TURKS, -1505	
Mikhail, Alan. *God's Shadow*	B
Ayubi, Durkhanai	
Parwana	641.595
Azad	
Long Shot	B
AZAD, 1983-	
Azad. *Long Shot*	B
AZTEC (MEXICAN PEOPLE)	
Cervantes, Fernando. *Conquistadores*	970.01
Restall, Matthew. *When Montezuma Met Cortes*	972
Townsend, Richard F. *The Aztecs*	972
The Aztecs. Townsend, Richard F.	972

B

B-17 BOMBER	
Drury, Bob. *Lucky 666*	B
Snyder, Steve. *Shot Down*	940.54
B-24 BOMBER	
Ambrose, Stephen E. *The Wild Blue*	940.54
Murphy, Brian. *81 Days Below Zero*	940.54
B-29 BOMBER	
Erwin, Jon. *Beyond Valor*	B
Frank, Richard B. *Downfall*	940.54
Scott, James. *Black Snow*	940.54
Smith, Jim B. *The Last Mission*	940.54

AUTHOR, TITLE, SERIES AND SUBJECT INDEX

B., David
  Epileptic   741.5
***B.F.** Skinner*. Bjork, Daniel W.   B
B.F.F. Tate, Christie   B
Baard, Nellianna van den
  Better Living Through Origami   736.982
BABAUTA, JEFF
  Renner, Rebecca. ★*Gator Country*   364.16
Babb, Valerie Melissa
  The Book of James   B
BABBAGE, CHARLES, 1791-1871
  Essinger, James. *Ada's Algorithm*   B
Babe. Creamer, Robert W.   B
BABIES
  Altmann, Tanya Remer. *What to Feed Your Baby*   649
  Brown, Maressa. *Raising Baby by the Stars*   133.5
  Ezzo, Gary. *On Becoming Baby Wise*   649
  Klass, Perri. *A Good Time to Be Born*   362.19892
  Knausgaard, Karl Ove. *Spring*   B
  Knoll, Debra J. *Engaging Babies in the Library*   027.62
  Kurcinka, Mary Sheedy. *Raising Your Spirited Baby*   306.874
  Murkoff, Heidi Eisenberg. *What to Expect the First Year*   305.232
  Porto, Anthony. *The Pediatrician's Guide to Feeding Babies & Toddlers*   618.92
  Pulde, Alona. *Forks Over Knives Family*   641.5
  Sentilles, Sarah. *Stranger Care*   B
BABITZ, EVE
  Anolik, Lili. *Hollywood's Eve*   B
***Baby** Birds*. Zickefoose, Julie   751.42
*The **Baby** Book*. Bhattacharya, Shaoni   649.1
BABY BOOM GENERATION
  Germer, Fawn. *Coming Back*   650.14
BABY CARE
  Bhattacharya, Shaoni. *The Baby Book*   649.1
  Bryson, Tina Payne. *The Bottom Line for Baby*   618.92
  Haelle, Tara. *The Informed Parent*   649
  Murkoff, Heidi Eisenberg. *What to Expect the First Year*   305.232
  Trubo, Richard. *Caring for Your Baby and Young Child*   618.92
BABY FOODS
  Helwig, Jenna. *Baby-Led Feeding*   641.3
  Pulde, Alona. *Forks Over Knives Family*   641.5
***Baby** Girl*. Iandoli, Kathy   B
BABY PSYCHOLOGY
  Bryson, Tina Payne. *The Bottom Line for Baby*   618.92
  Kurcinka, Mary Sheedy. *Raising Your Spirited Baby*   306.874
***Baby**, Unplugged*. Brickman, Sophie   306.874
***Baby-**Led Feeding*. Helwig, Jenna   641.3
Babylon. Kriwaczek, Paul   935
BABYLONIA
  Kriwaczek, Paul. *Babylon*   935
Baca, Jimmy Santiago
  Selected Poems   811
Baca, Salena
  Oversize Fashion Crochet   746.43
Bacall, Lauren
  By Myself and Then Some   B
BACALL, LAUREN, 1924-2014
  Bacall, Lauren. *By Myself and Then Some*   B
  Mann, William J. *Bogie & Bacall*   920
Bacevich, Andrew J.
  America's War for the Greater Middle East   956.05
Bach. Gardiner, John Eliot   B
BACH, JOHANN SEBASTIAN, 1685-1750
  Gardiner, John Eliot. *Bach*   B
  Geck, Martin. ★*Johann Sebastian Bach*   780.92
  Kennicott, Philip. *Counterpoint*   B
  Wolff, Christoph. *Johann Sebastian Bach*   B
BACH, MARIA, 1896-1978
  Porter, Cecelia Hopkins. *Five Lives in Music*   B
***Bachelor** Nation*. Kaufman, Amy   791.45
*The **Back** Chamber*. Hall, Donald   811
*The **Back** Channel*. Burns, William J.   B
***Back** from the Dead*. Walton, Bill   B
***Back** in the Day Bakery, Made with Love*. Day, Cheryl   641.81
★*The **Back** Roads to March*. Feinstein, John   796.323
***Back** to School*. Rose, Mike   374
Backman, Fredrik
  Things My Son Needs to Know About the World   B

BACKMAN, FREDRIK, 1981-
  Backman, Fredrik. *Things My Son Needs to Know About the World*   B
*A **Backpack**, A Bear, and Eight Crates of Vodka*. Golinkin, Lev   B
*The **Backpacker's** Handbook*. Townsend, Chris   796.51
BACKPACKING
  Townsend, Chris. *The Backpacker's Handbook*   796.51
***Backstage** Pass*. Stanley, Paul   B
BACKYARD ANIMALS
  Renkl, Margaret. *The Comfort of Crows*   814.6
*The **Backyard** Beekeeper*. Flottum, Kim   638
★*The **Backyard** Bird Chronicles*. Tan, Amy   598
BACKYARD BIRDS
  Renkl, Margaret. *The Comfort of Crows*   814.6
Backyard Series [Series]. Muller, Kristin   738.1
BACKYARDS
  Tougias, Robert. *Birder on Berry Lane*   598.072
BACON, FRANCIS, 1909-1992
  Smee, Sebastian. *The Art of Rivalry*   700.92
Bacon, John U.
  The Great Halifax Explosion   971.6
BACTERIA
  Collen, Alanna. *10% Human*   612.3
  Finlay, B. Brett. *Let Them Eat Dirt*   616.9
  Ireland, Tom. *The Good Virus*   579.2
BACTERIOLOGY
  Ireland, Tom. *The Good Virus*   579.2
★***Bad** Blood*. Carreyrou, John   338.7
***Bad** Fat Black Girl*. Bowen, Sesali   305.42
***Bad** Feminist*. Gay, Roxane   814
***Bad** Indians*. Miranda, Deborah A.   305.8009794
***Bad** Land*. Raban, Jonathan   978
BAD LUCK
  Montgomery, Patrick. *Baseball's Great Expectations*   796.357
★***Bad** Mexicans*. Hernandez, Kelly Lytle   972
***Bad** Paper*. Halpern, Jake   332.7
***Bad** Science*. Goldacre, Ben   500
*The **Bad-Ass** Librarians of Timbuktu*. Hammer, Joshua   025.8
***Badass** Vegan*. Lewis, John   641.5
Bade, Rachael
  ★*Unchecked*   342.73
Bader, Philip
  African-American Writers   810.9
Badkhen, Anna
  The World Is a Carpet   305.409581
BAEK, HONGYONG, 1912-2012
  Lee, Helie. *In the Absence of Sun*   B
Baer, Daniel Brooks
  The Four Tests   320.973
Baer, Kate
  What Kind of Woman   811
BAER, MAX, 1909-1959
  Schaap, Jeremy. *Cinderella Man*   B
Baez, Fernando
  Universal History of the Destruction of Books   098
***Bag** Man*. Maddow, Rachel   B
Bagby, Meredith E.
  The New Guys   305
BAGELS
  Barrow, Cathy. *Bagels, Schmears, and a Nice Piece of Fish*   641.81
***Bagels**, Schmears, and a Nice Piece of Fish*. Barrow, Cathy   641.81
Baggage. Cumming, Alan   B
BAGHDAD, IRAQ
  Abdul-Ahad, Ghaith. *A Stranger in Your Own City*   956.7044
  Newton, Michael A. *Enemy of the State*   345.567
Bags. Alicia, Anna   646.4
Bahcall, Safi
  Loonshots   658.4
Baier, Bret
  Three Days in January   B
  To Rescue the Constitution   973.4
Bailey, Catherine
  A Castle in Wartime   943.086
Bailey, Desiree C.
  What Noise Against the Cane   811
Bailey, Elisabeth
  The Sound of a Wild Snail Eating   594
BAILEY, ELISABETH
  Bailey, Elisabeth. *The Sound of a Wild Snail Eating*   594

PUBLIC LIBRARY CORE COLLECTION: NONFICTION
Twentieth Edition

Bailey, Issac J.
   Why Didn't We Riot?   305.800973
BAILEY, JAMES, 1847-1906
   Standiford, Les. ★*Battle for the Big Top*   791.3
Bailey, Jennifer
   To My Beloveds   261.8
BAILEY, JENNIFER
   Bailey, Jennifer. *To My Beloveds*   261.8
Bailey, Lily
   Because We Are Bad   B
BAILEY, LILY
   Bailey, Lily. *Because We Are Bad*   B
Bailey, Richard W.
   Speaking American   427
BAILOUTS (GOVERNMENT POLICY)
   Hoffman, Liz. *Crash Landing*   330
   Jacoby, Melissa B. ★*Unjust Debts*   346.73
Baime, A. J.
   The Accidental President   B
   ★*Go Like Hell*   796.7209
   White Lies   B
Bain, Ken
   What the Best College Students Do   378.1
Bainbridge, David A
   Gardening with Less Water   635.9
Bair, Deirdre
   Al Capone   B
   Saul Steinberg   B
Baird, Julia
   ★*Victoria the Queen*   B
BAISSAC, LISE DE, 1905-2004
   Rose, Sarah. *D-Day Girls*   940.53
★*Bake*. Hollywood, Paul   641.81
★*Bake from Scratch; Volume Two*. Hoffman, Brian Hart   641.81
Bake Smart. Seneviratne, Samantha   641.81
BAKED PRODUCTS
   Hazan, Jack. *Mind Over Batter*   641.81
   Kieffer, Sarah. *100 Morning Treats*   641.5
   Kulaga, Agatha. *Ovenly*   641.81
   McDowell, Erin Jeanne. ★*The Book on Pie*   641.86
   Wade, Greg. ★*Bread Head*   664
   Weller, Melissa. *A Good Bake*   641.86
Baker, Billy
   We Need to Hang Out   177
BAKER, BILLY (JOURNALIST)
   Baker, Billy. *We Need to Hang Out*   177
Baker, Calvin
   A More Perfect Reunion   305.800973
Baker, Deborah
   The Convert   B
BAKER, ELLA, 1903-1986
   West, Cornel. *Black Prophetic Fire*   920
BAKER, JAMES ADDISON, 1930-
   Baker, Peter. *The Man Who Ran Washington*   B
Baker, James W.
   Thanksgiving   394.2649
BAKER, JOSEPHINE, 1906-1975
   Lewis, Damien. *Agent Josephine*   B
BAKER, LA FAYETTE C. (LA FAYETTE CURRY), 1826-1868
   Waller, Douglas C. *Lincoln's Spies*   973.7
Baker, Nicholson
   Baseless   358
   Finding a Likeness   B
   Substitute   371.14
   The World on Sunday   071
BAKER, NICHOLSON, 1957-
   Baker, Nicholson. *Baseless*   358
   Baker, Nicholson. *Finding a Likeness*   B
   Baker, Nicholson. *Substitute*   371.14
Baker, Peter
   The Divider   973.933
   The Man Who Ran Washington   B
Bakerita. Conners, Rachel   641.81
Bakewell, Sarah
   ★*At the Existentialist Cafe*   920
   How to Live—Or—A Life of Montaigne   B
Baking. Greenspan, Dorie   641.8

BAKING
   Adams, Jocelyn Delk. *Grandbaby Cakes*   641.86
   Arefi, Yossy. *Snacking Cakes*   641.86
   Behan, Ren. ★*The Sweet Polish Kitchen*   641.594
   Beranbaum, Rose Levy. ★*The Baking Bible*   641.81
   Beranbaum, Rose Levy. ★*The Cookie Bible*   641.86
   Beranbaum, Rose Levy. ★*Rose's Baking Basics*   641.81
   Bittman, Mark. ★*How to Bake Everything*   641.81
   Byrn, Anne. *A New Take on Cake*   641.86
   Chang, Joanne. *Pastry Love*   641.86
   Cho, Kristina. *Mooncakes + Milk Bread*   641.595
   Conners, Rachel. *Bakerita*   641.81
   Day, Cheryl. *Back in the Day Bakery, Made with Love*   641.81
   Day, Cheryl. *Cheryl Day's Treasury of Southern Baking*   641.81
   Emberling, Amy. *Zingerman's Bakehouse*   641.81
   Forkish, Ken. *Evolutions in Bread*   664
   Francois, Zoe. *Zoe Bakes Cakes*   641.86
   Goldman, Duff. *Duff Bakes*   641.81
   Greenspan, Dorie. *Baking Chez Moi*   641.86
   Greenspan, Dorie. ★*Baking with Dorie*   641.81
   Greenspan, Dorie. *Baking with Julia*   641.8
   Greenspan, Dorie. *Baking*   641.8
   Greenspan, Dorie. ★*Dorie's Cookies*   641.86
   Gunst, Kathy. *Rage Baking*   641.86
   Guy, Jerrelle. *Black Girl Baking*   641.59
   Hazan, Jack. *Mind Over Batter*   641.81
   Heatter, Maida. ★*Happiness Is Baking*   641.86
   Hoffman, Brian Hart. ★*Bake from Scratch; Volume Two*   641.81
   Hollis, B. Dylan. ★*Baking Yesteryear*   641.81
   Hollywood, Paul. ★*Bake*   641.81
   Hussain, Nadiya. ★*Nadiya Bakes*   641.81
   Hussain, Nadiya. ★*Nadiya's Everyday Baking*   641.5
   Jade, Holly. *The Essential Book of Vegan Bakes*   641.5
   Kartes, Danielle. *Butter, Flour, Sugar, Joy*   641.86
   Keller, Thomas. *Bouchon Bakery*   641.594
   Kieffer, Sarah. *100 Morning Treats*   641.5
   Kieffer, Sarah. ★*Baking for the Holidays*   641.5
   Lahey, Jim. *The Sullivan Street Bakery Cookbook*   641.81
   Larsen, Jeffrey. *Gluten-Free Baking at Home*   641.5
   Lloyd, Bobbie. *The Magnolia Bakery Handbook*   641.86
   Lomas, Vallery. ★*Life Is What You Bake It*   641.81
   McDermott, Kate. ★*Art of the Pie*   641.86
   McDowell, Erin Jeanne. ★*The Book on Pie*   641.86
   McDowell, Erin Jeanne. *The Fearless Baker*   641.81
   Mubarak, Heather. *Stuffed*   641.86
   Nederlanden, Elisabet der. ★*Holiday Cookies*   641.86
   Nelson, Candace. *The Sprinkles Baking Book*   641.81
   Pansino, Rosanna. *Baking All Year Round*   641.86
   Parks, Stella. ★*Bravetart*   641.86
   Poliafito, Renato. ★*Dolci!*   641.81
   Ricanati, Elizabeth. *Braided*   B
   Roman, Alison. *Sweet Enough*   641.86
   Saltz, Joanna. ★*Delish Insane Sweets*   641.81
   Seneviratne, Samantha. *Bake Smart*   641.81
   Sever, Shauna. ★*Midwest Made*   641.5977
   Sheehan, Jessie. ★*Snackable Bakes*   641.7
   Silverton, Nancy. ★*The Cookie That Changed My Life*   641.81
   Stewart, Martha. ★*Martha Stewart's Baking Handbook*   641.8
   Stewart, Martha. *Martha Stewart's Cake Perfection*   641.86
   Tosi, Christina. *All About Cookies*   641.86
   Wade, Greg. ★*Bread Head*   664
   Weiss, Luisa. *Classic German Baking*   641.594
   Weller, Melissa. *A Good Bake*   641.86
   Wright, Caroline. *Cake Magic!*   641.86
Baking All Year Round. Pansino, Rosanna   641.86
★*The Baking Bible*. Beranbaum, Rose Levy   641.81
Baking Chez Moi. Greenspan, Dorie   641.86
★*Baking for the Holidays*. Kieffer, Sarah   641.5
★*Baking with Dorie*. Greenspan, Dorie   641.81
Baking with Julia. Greenspan, Dorie   641.8
★*Baking Yesteryear*. Hollis, B. Dylan   641.81
Bakke, Gretchen Anna
   The Grid   333.793
Balakian, Peter
   The Burning Tigris   956.6
Balakrishnan, Chris
   How to Win Friends and Influence Fungi   502

AUTHOR, TITLE, SERIES AND SUBJECT INDEX

BALANCE
    Lembke, Anna. *Dopamine Nation*   152.4
BALANCE OF POWER
    Kennedy, Paul M. *The Rise and Fall of the Great Powers*   909.82
    Von Tunzelmann, Alex. *Blood and Sand*   909.82
BALANCHINE, GEORGE
    Gottlieb, Robert. *George Balanchine*   B
    Teachout, Terry. ★*All in the Dances*   B
Balancing Acts. Hytner, Nicholas   B
Balcombe, Jonathan P.
    Super Fly   595.77
    What a Fish Knows   597.15
The Bald Eagle. Davis, Jack E.   598.9
BALD EAGLE
    Davis, Jack E. *The Bald Eagle*   598.9
BALD EAGLE (SYMBOL)
    Davis, Jack E. *The Bald Eagle*   598.9
Bald Is Better with Earrings. Hutton, Andrea   362.19699
Baldick, Chris
    ★*The Oxford Dictionary of Literary Terms*   803
Baldwin, Debra Lee
    Succulents Simplified   635.9
BALDWIN, EMMA BERDIS JONES, -1999
    Tubbs, Anna Malaika. *The Three Mothers*   306.874
Baldwin, James
    ★*Collected Essays*   814
    ★*The Fire Next Time*   305.896
    I Am Not Your Negro   323.1196
    ★*Notes of a Native Son*   305.8
BALDWIN, JAMES, 1924-1987
    Baldwin, James. ★*Notes of a Native Son*   305.8
    Dyson, Michael Eric. *What Truth Sounds Like*   305.800973
    Glaude, Eddie S. *Begin Again*   305.800973
    Mullen, Bill. ★*James Baldwin*   B
    Tubbs, Anna Malaika. *The Three Mothers*   306.874
Balf, Todd
    Major   B
BALFOUR DECLARATION
    Barr, James. *A Line in the Sand*   956
BALI (ISLAND)
    Gilbert, Elizabeth. *Eat, Pray, Love*   B
BALKAN PENINSULA
    Kassabova, Kapka. *Border*   949.9
    Mazower, Mark. *The Balkans*   949.6
The Balkans. Mazower, Mark   949.6
Balko, Radley
    ★*The Cadaver King and the Country Dentist*   614
BALL FAMILY
    Ball, Edward. *Slaves in the Family*   975.7
BALL GAMES
    Barry, Dan. *Bottom of the 33rd*   796.357
    Gingrich, Dayne. *Pickleball Mindset*   796.34
    Parker, Vergil R. *Pickleball 101*   796.34
Ball, Edward
    Life of a Klansman   305.8009763
    Slaves in the Family   975.7
Ball, Lucille
    Love, Lucy   B
BALL, LUCILLE, 1911-1989
    Ball, Lucille. *Love, Lucy*   B
Ball, Molly
    ★*Pelosi*   B
Ball, Philip
    Patterns in Nature   500.201
BALLARD, RICE C. (RICE CARTER), -1860
    Rothman, Joshua D. *The Ledger and the Chain*   306.362
Ballard, Robert D.
    Into the Deep   551.46092
BALLARD, ROBERT D.
    Ballard, Robert D. *Into the Deep*   551.46092
★*Ballerina Body*. Copeland, Misty   792.8
BALLET
    Angyal, Chloe. *Turning Pointe*   792.8
    Copeland, Misty. ★*Life in Motion*   B
    Copeland, Misty. *The Wind at My Back*   B
    Craine, Debra. *The Oxford Dictionary of Dance*   792.8
    Hallberg, David. *A Body of Work*   B
    Harss, Marina. *The Boy from Kyiv*   B

    Homans, Jennifer. ★*Apollo's Angels*   792.8
    Jacobs, Laura. ★*Celestial Bodies*   792.8
    Kavanagh, Julie. *Nureyev*   B
    Robb, Alice. ★*Don't Think, Dear*   792.8
    Valby, Karen. *The Swans of Harlem*   792.8
The Ballet Companion. Minden, Eliza Gaynor   792.8
BALLET DANCERS
    Copeland, Misty. ★*Ballerina Body*   792.8
    Copeland, Misty. ★*Life in Motion*   B
    Copeland, Misty. *The Wind at My Back*   B
    Gottlieb, Robert. *George Balanchine*   B
    Hallberg, David. *A Body of Work*   B
    Harss, Marina. *The Boy from Kyiv*   B
    Homans, Jennifer. ★*Apollo's Angels*   792.8
    Kavanagh, Julie. *Nureyev*   B
    Kessler, Lauren. *Raising the Barre*   792.8
    Matzen, Robert. *Dutch Girl*   B
    Morrison, Simon Alexander. *Bolshoi Confidential*   792.8
    Teachout, Terry. ★*All in the Dances*   B
BALLETS
    Morrison, Simon Alexander. *Bolshoi Confidential*   792.8
BALLISTIC MISSILES
    Coleman, David G. *The Fourteenth Day*   973.922092
    Hastings, Max. *The Abyss*   972.9106
    Sherman, Casey. *Above and Beyond*   973.922092
    Sorensen, Theodore C. *Counselor*   B
BALLOONING
    Begley, Adam. *The Great Nadar*   B
    Holmes, Richard. *Falling Upwards*   387.7
BALLOONISTS
    Holmes, Richard. *Falling Upwards*   387.7
BALLOONS (AERONAUTICS)
    Begley, Adam. *The Great Nadar*   B
    Holmes, Richard. *Falling Upwards*   387.7
Ballpark. Goldberger, Paul   796.357
BALLS (PARTIES)
    Bowles, Hamish. *Vogue & the Metropolitan Museum of Art Costume Institute*   746.9
BALTIMORE, MARYLAND
    Anthony, Carmelo. *Where Tomorrows Aren't Promised*   B
    Bowden, Mark. *Life Sentence*   364.106
    Coates, Ta-Nehisi. *The Beautiful Struggle*   B
    Meltzer, Brad. *The Lincoln Conspiracy*   973.7092
    Moore, Wes. ★*Five Days*   363.32
    Moore, Wes. *The Other Wes Moore*   B
    Rudacille, Deborah. *Roots of Steel*   338.4
    Shane, Scott. ★*Flee North*   973.7
    Thomas, R. Eric. ★*Congratulations, the Best Is Over!*   B
    Watkins, D. *Black Boy Smile*   B
Balz, Daniel J.
    The Battle for America, 2008   973.932
BAMBERGER, LOUIS, 1855-1944
    Forgosh, Linda B. *Louis Bamberger*   B
Bamberger, Michael
    The Second Life of Tiger Woods   B
Bamboozled by Jesus. Orji, Yvonne   B
Bambrick, Yvonne
    The Urban Cycling Survival Guide   796.6
Bamford, Maria
    Sure, I'll Join Your Cult   B
BAMFORD, MARIA, 1970-
    Bamford, Maria. *Sure, I'll Join Your Cult*   B
★*Band of Brothers*. Ambrose, Stephen E.   920
BANDS (MUSIC)
    Abdurraqib, Hanif. *Go Ahead in the Rain*   782.421649
    Black Thought. *The Upcycled Self*   B
    Brown, Craig. *150 Glimpses of the Beatles*   920
    Carlin, Peter Ames. *Bruce*   B
    Jackson family. *The Jacksons*   782.421644
    Jarnow, Jesse. *Big Day Coming*   B
    Kaye, Lenny. ★*Lightning Striking*   781.66
    McCartney, Paul. ★*1964*   782.42166
    Richards, Keith. *Life*   B
    Spitz, Bob. ★*The Beatles*   B
Bang, Mary Jo
    The Bride of E   811
    A Doll for Throwing   811
    Elegy   811

PUBLIC LIBRARY CORE COLLECTION: NONFICTION
Twentieth Edition

Bang, Molly
   ★*Picture This*   741.6
BANGLADESH
   Carney, Scott. *The Vortex*   954.92
BANGLADESHI AMERICANS
   Tanais. *In Sensorium*   B
BANGLADESHI PEOPLE
   Craig, Mya-Rose. *Birdgirl*   B
BANIER, FRANCOIS-MARIE
   Sancton, Thomas. *The Bettencourt Affair*   B
BANJO
   Gaddy, K. R. ★*Well of Souls*   787
   Seeger, Pete. *How to Play the 5-String Banjo*   787
BANK EMPLOYEES
   White, Ralph. *Getting Out of Saigon*   959.704
BANK FAILURES
   Bruner, Robert F. ★*The Panic of 1907, 2nd Ed.*   330.973
   Grind, Kirsten. *The Lost Bank*   332.3
   Sorkin, Andrew Ross. *Too Big to Fail*   330.973
BANK REGULATION
   Servon, Lisa J. *The Unbanking of America*   332.10973
BANK ROBBERIES
   Hopwood, Shon. *Law Man*   B
   King, David. *Six Days in August*   364.15
   Kushner, Jacob. *Look Away*   305.9
   Leerhsen, Charles. ★*Butch Cassidy*   B
   O'Connell, Mark. *A Thread of Violence*   364.152
BANK ROBBERS
   King, David. *Six Days in August*   364.15
BANKERS
   Ahamed, Liaquat. *Lords of Finance*   920
   Cannadine, David. ★*Mellon*   B
   Chernow, Ron. *The Warburgs*   B
   De Waal, Edmund. *The Hare with Amber Eyes*   B
   Moore, Wes. *The Work*   B
   White, Ralph. *Getting Out of Saigon*   959.704
BANKING CORRUPTION
   Enrich, David. *Dark Towers*   332.1
   Hudson, Michael W. *The Monster*   332.63
BANKMAN-FRIED, SAM
   Lewis, Michael. ★*Going Infinite*   305.5
BANKRUPTCY
   Bomey, Nathan. *Detroit Resurrected*   977.4
   Jacoby, Melissa B. ★*Unjust Debts*   346.73
   Kirshner, Jodie Adams. ★*Broke*   336.3
   Lewis, Michael. ★*Going Infinite*   305.5
   Nelson, Willie. *It's a Long Story*   B
   O'Neill, Cara. *Chapter 13 Bankruptcy, 17th Ed.*   346.7307
BANKS AND BANKING
   Ahamed, Liaquat. *Lords of Finance*   920
   Bruner, Robert F. ★*The Panic of 1907, 2nd Ed.*   330.973
   Dayen, David. *Chain of Title*   330.973
   Enrich, David. *Dark Towers*   332.1
   Flitter, Emily. *The White Wall*   332.0973
   Goldstein, Jacob. *Money*   332.4
   Grind, Kirsten. *The Lost Bank*   332.3
   Howard, Timothy. *The Mortgage Wars*   332.7
   Karabell, Zachary. *Inside Money*   332.1
   Lanchester, John. *How to Speak Money*   330.1
   Lowenstein, Roger. *America's Bank*   332.1
   McCraw, Thomas K. ★*The Founders and Finance*   330.973
   Montero, David. ★*The Stolen Wealth of Slavery*   381
   Perino, Michael A. *The Hellhound of Wall Street*   330.973
   Posner, Gerald L. *God's Bankers*   364.16
   Schulman, Daniel. *The Money Kings*   332.0973
   Servon, Lisa J. *The Unbanking of America*   332.10973
   Sowell, Thomas. *Basic Economics*   330
   Wessel, David. *In Fed We Trust*   332.1
   Wheelan, Charles J. *Naked Economics*   330
BANKS, ERNIE, 1931-2015
   Rapoport, Ron. *Let's Play Two*   B
BANNED BOOKS
   Appleman, Deborah. *Literature and the New Culture Wars*   807
   Baez, Fernando. *Universal History of the Destruction of Books*   098
   Bergstein, Rachelle. *The Genius of Judy*   813
   Berkshire, Jennifer. *The Education Wars*   371.01
   Finn, Peter. *The Zhivago Affair*   891.73
   LaRue, James. ★*On Censorship*   025.2

   Nafisi, Azar. ★*Reading Lolita in Tehran*   B
Banville, John
   Time Pieces   914.1
BANVILLE, JOHN
   Banville, John. *Time Pieces*   914.1
BAPTISTS
   Barry, John M. *Roger Williams and the Creation of the American Soul*   974.5
   Carter, Jimmy. *Sources of Strength*   248.4
   Jackson, Troy. *Becoming King*   B
   King, Coretta Scott. ★*My Life, My Love, My Legacy*   B
   King, Martin Luther. *The Autobiography of Martin Luther King, Jr.*   B
   Sharpton, Al. *Rise Up*   973.933
Bar Chef. Rollich, Christiaan   641.87
Barack Before Obama. Katz, David   B
★*Barack Obama.* Maraniss, David   B
Baraka, Amiri
   S O S   811
Baraka, Sho
   He Saw That It Was Good   261.5
BARAKA, SHO
   Baraka, Sho. *He Saw That It Was Good*   261.5
BARBADOS
   Stuart, Andrea. *Sugar in the Blood*   338.1
Barbarian Days. Finnegan, William   B
Barbarisi, Daniel
   Chasing the Thrill   796.1
   Dueling with Kings   793.93
BARBARISI, DANIEL
   Barbarisi, Daniel. *Chasing the Thrill*   796.1
   Barbarisi, Daniel. *Dueling with Kings*   793.93
BARBECUE COOKING
   Bittman, Mark. ★*How to Grill Everything*   641.7
BARBECUING
   Bittman, Mark. ★*How to Grill Everything*   641.7
   Franklin, Aaron. *Franklin Barbecue*   641.7
   Goldwyn, Meathead. ★*Meathead*   641.7
   Kim, Bill. *Korean BBQ*   641.595
   Martin, Pat. *Life of Fire*   641.5
   Moore, Matt. *Serial Griller*   641.7
   Perry Lang, Adam. *Serious Barbecue*   641.5
   Purviance, Jamie. *Weber's Greatest Hits*   641.5
   Purviance, Jamie. *Weber's Ultimate Grilling*   641.5
   Raichlen, Steven. *How to Grill Vegetables*   641.6
   Rapoport, Adam. *The Grilling Book*   641.7
   Scott, Rodney. ★*Rodney Scott's World of BBQ*   641.7
   Symon, Michael. *Michael Symon's Playing with Fire*   641.7
Barber, Dan
   The Third Plate   641.3
Barber, William J.
   We Are Called to Be a Movement   261.8
Barbie and Ruth. Gerber, Robin   B
BARBIE DOLLS
   Gerber, Robin. *Barbie and Ruth*   B
   Lobel, Orly. *You Don't Own Me*   346.7304
Barbree, Jay
   Neil Armstrong   B
Barcelona. Hughes, Robert   946
BARCELONA, SPAIN
   Hughes, Robert. *Barcelona*   946
   Van Hensbergen, Gijs. *The Sagrada Familia*   726.5
BARCHA, MERCEDES
   Garcia, Rodrigo. *A Farewell to Gabo and Mercedes*   B
Bard, Elizabeth
   Lunch in Paris   B
   Picnic in Provence   B
BARD, ELIZABETH
   Bard, Elizabeth. *Lunch in Paris*   B
   Bard, Elizabeth. *Picnic in Provence*   B
Bardenwerper, William
   The Prisoner in His Palace   956.7044
Barefoot Contessa at Home. Garten, Ina   641.5
Barefoot Contessa Family Style. Garten, Ina   641.5
★*Barefoot Contessa, How Easy Is That?.* Garten, Ina   641.5
Barefoot in Paris. Garten, Ina   641.594
BARGES
   McPhee, John. *Uncommon Carriers*   388
Bargh, John A
   Before You Know It   154.2

AUTHOR, TITLE, SERIES AND SUBJECT INDEX

Bari, Shahidha K.
   Dressed — 391
Barkan, Ady
   Eyes to the Wind — B
BARKAN, ADY
   Barkan, Ady. *Eyes to the Wind* — B
Barker, Elspeth
   ★*Notes from the Henhouse* — 828
BARKER, ELSPETH
   Barker, Elspeth. ★*Notes from the Henhouse* — 828
Barker, Juliet R. V.
   Agincourt — 944
Barker, Margaret A.
   Audubon Birdhouse Book — 728
Barker, Nigel
   Models of Influence — 746.92092
***Barkley*.** Bella, Timothy — B
BARKLEY, CHARLES, 1963-
   Bella, Timothy. *Barkley* — B
Barkley, Russell A.
   Taking Charge of ADHD — 618.92
Barlow, John Perry
   Mother American Night — 782.42164
BARLOW, JOHN PERRY, 1947-2018
   Barlow, John Perry. *Mother American Night* — 782.42164
Barn the Spoon
   Woodcraft — 684
Barnes, Cinelle
   Monsoon Mansion — B
BARNES, CINELLE
   Barnes, Cinelle. *Monsoon Mansion* — B
Barnes, Julian
   Keeping an Eye Open — 709.04
   The Man in the Red Coat — B
Barnes, Katie
   ★*Fair Play* — 796.082
Barnes, Simon
   The Meaning of Birds — 598
Barnett, Brittany K.
   ★*A Knock at Midnight* — B
BARNETT, BRITTANY K.
   Barnett, Brittany K. ★*A Knock at Midnight* — B
Barnett, Cynthia
   Rain — 551.57
   ★*The Sound of the Sea* — 591.47
Barnett, Erica C.
   Quitter — B
BARNETT, ERICA C.
   Barnett, Erica C. *Quitter* — B
***Barney Ross*.** Century, Douglas — B
Barnitz, Jacqueline
   Twentieth-Century Art of Latin America — 709.8
***Barnum*.** Wilson, Robert — B
BARNUM, P. T. (PHINEAS TAYLOR), 1810-1891
   Standiford, Les. ★*Battle for the Big Top* — 791.3
   Wilson, Robert. *Barnum* — B
Baron, David
   American Eclipse — 523.7
Baron, Dennis E.
   What's Your Pronoun? — 425.55
Baron, Martin
   ★*Collision of Power* — 070.4
BARON, MARTIN, 1954-
   Baron, Martin. ★*Collision of Power* — 070.4
Barons of the Sea. Ujifusa, Steven — 387.5
Barot, Rick
   The Galleons — 811
Barr, James
   A Line in the Sand — 956
   Lords of the Desert — 956
Barr, John
   Start by Believing — 364.15
Barr, Luke
   Ritz & Escoffier — 920
Barr, Patricia
   Ultimate Star Wars — 791.43
Barra, Allen
   Inventing Wyatt Earp — B

   ★*The Last Coach* — B
   ★*Yogi Berra* — B
★*Barracoon*. Hurston, Zora Neale — B
Barrett, David Dean
   140 Days to Hiroshima — 940.54
Barrett, Duncan
   GI Brides — 920
Barrett, Lisa Feldman
   ★*How Emotions Are Made* — 152.4
Barrett, Pearl
   Trim Healthy Mama Trim Healthy Table — 613.2
Barrett, William
   Irrational Man — 142
BARRIER-FREE DESIGN
   Clark, John Lee. *Touch the Future* — B
   Jordan, Wendy Adler. *Universal Design for the Home* — 728
   Pierce, D. *The Accessible Home* — 728
   Taussig, Rebekah. *Sitting Pretty* — B
Barron, David J.
   Waging War — 342.73
Barron, James
   The One-Cent Magenta — 769.569
Barron, Justine
   They Killed Freddie Gray — 363.32
Barrow, Cathy
   Bagels, Schmears, and a Nice Piece of Fish — 641.81
   ★*Pie Squared* — 641.86
BARROW, CLYDE, 1909-1934
   Boessenecker, John. *Texas Ranger* — B
   Guinn, Jeff. *Go Down Together* — B
Barrow, John D.
   The Infinite Book — 111
Barrow, Mark V.
   Nature's Ghosts — 333.95
Barry, Dan
   Bottom of the 33rd — 796.357
Barry, Harry
   Emotional Healing — 158.1
Barry, John M.
   ★*The Great Influenza* — 614.5
   Rising Tide — 977
   Roger Williams and the Creation of the American Soul — 974.5
BARS (DRINKING ESTABLISHMENTS)
   Martin, Justin. *Rebel Souls* — 920
Barsh, Joanna
   Grow Wherever You Work — 658.4
BARTENDING
   Rollich, Christiaan. *Bar Chef* — 641.87
Barthel, Joan
   American Saint — B
BARTHOLDI, FREDERIC AUGUSTE, 1834-1904
   Khan, Yasmin Sabina. *Enlightening the World* — 974.7
Bartlett's Familiar Quotations, 19th Ed. Bartlett, John — 808.88
Bartlett, John
   Bartlett's Familiar Quotations, 19th Ed. — 808.88
Bartlett, Rosamund
   ★*Tolstoy* — B
Bartlett, Sarah
   A Brief History of Angels and Demons — 202
Bartlett, Wendy K.
   Floating Collections — 025.2
BARTON, CLARA, 1821-1912
   Gwynne, S. C. *Hymns of the Republic* — 973.7
Barton, John
   A History of the Bible — 220.09
Barzun, Jacques
   From Dawn to Decadence — 940.2
Basbanes, Nicholas A.
   ★*Cross of Snow* — B
   Every Book Its Reader — 028
   On Paper — 676
Bascomb, Neal
   The Escape Artists — 940.4
   Faster — 796.7209
   Hunting Eichmann — 943.086
   The Winter Fortress — 940.54
The **Baseball**. Hample, Zack — 796.357

PUBLIC LIBRARY CORE COLLECTION: NONFICTION
Twentieth Edition

BASEBALL
    Barra, Allen. ★*Yogi Berra* — B
    Barry, Dan. *Bottom of the 33rd* — 796.357
    Bradlee, Ben. *The Kid* — B
    Brown, Tim. ★*The Tao of the Backup Catcher* — 796.357
    Bryant, Howard. *Rickey* — B
    Clavin, Thomas. *The DiMaggios* — 920
    Darling, Ron. *The Complete Game* — B
    Diamond, Jared M. *Swing Kings* — 796.357
    Eisenberg, John. *The Streak* — 796.357
    Feinstein, John. *Where Nobody Knows Your Name* — 796.357
    Formosa, Dan. *Baseball Field Guide* — 796.357
    Gehrig, Lou. *The Lost Memoir* — B
    Halberstam, David. *Summer of '49* — 796.357
    Halberstam, David. *The Teammates* — B
    Hample, Zack. *The Baseball* — 796.357
    Hernandez, Keith. *I'm Keith Hernandez* — B
    Hirsch, James S. *Willie Mays* — B
    Jamieson, David. *Mint Condition* — 796.357
    Jeter, Derek. *Jeter Unfiltered* — B
    Kenny, Brian. *Ahead of the Curve* — 796.357
    Knight, Molly. *The Best Team Money Can Buy* — 796.357
    Kurkjian, Tim. *I'm Fascinated by Sacrifice Flies* — 796.357
    Kurlansky, Mark. *The Eastern Stars* — 796.357
    Law, Keith. *The Inside Game* — 796.35764
    Lewis, Michael. ★*Moneyball* — 796.357
    Lindbergh, Ben. *The Only Rule Is That It Has to Work* — 796.357
    Maraniss, David. *Clemente* — B
    Mays, Willie. *24* — B
    Megdal, Howard. *The Baseball Talmud* — 796.357
    Montgomery, Patrick. *Baseball's Great Expectations* — 796.357
    Neyer, Rob. *Power Ball* — 796.357
    Ortiz, David. *Papi* — B
    Pappu, Sridhar. *The Year of the Pitcher* — 920
    Passan, Jeff. *The Arm* — 796.3576
    Perron, Cam. ★*Comeback Season* — 796.357
    Pessah, Jon. *The Game* — 796.357
    Peta, Joe. *Trading Bases* — 796.357
    Posnanski, Joe. ★*Why We Love Baseball* — 796.357
    Rapoport, Ron. *Let's Play Two* — B
    Reiter, Ben. *Astroball* — 796.357
    Ripken, Bill. *State of Play* — 796.357
    Rivera, Mariano. *The Closer* — B
    Ruck, Rob. *Raceball* — 796.357
    Sabathia, CC. *Till the End* — 796.357
    Sawchik, Travis. *Big Data Baseball* — 796.357
    Shelton, Ron. *The Church of Baseball* — 791.43
    Svrluga, Barry. *The Grind* — 796.357
    Torre, Joe. *The Yankee Years* — B
    Turbow, Jason. *The Baseball Codes* — 796.357
    Wong, Stephen. *Game Worn* — 796.357
    Wong, Stephen. *Smithsonian Baseball* — 796.357
    Zminda, Don. *Double Plays and Double Crosses* — 796.357
    The Baseball 100. Posnanski, Joe — 796.357

BASEBALL BATS
    Diamond, Jared M. *Swing Kings* — 796.357

BASEBALL BETTING
    O'Brien, Keith. *Charlie Hustle* — 796.357
    Zminda, Don. *Double Plays and Double Crosses* — 796.357

BASEBALL CARDS
    Jamieson, David. *Mint Condition* — 796.357

BASEBALL COACHES
    Barra, Allen. ★*Yogi Berra* — B
    The Baseball Codes. Turbow, Jason — 796.357

BASEBALL FANS
    Cohen, Rich. *The Chicago Cubs* — 796.357
    Hample, Zack. *The Baseball* — 796.357
    Perron, Cam. ★*Comeback Season* — 796.357
    Simon, Scott. *My Cubs* — 796.357
    Baseball Field Guide. Formosa, Dan — 796.357

BASEBALL FIELDS
    Goldberger, Paul. *Ballpark* — 796.357
    Nusbaum, Eric. *Stealing Home* — 796.357
    Stout, Glenn. *Fenway 1912* — 796.357

BASEBALL HALL OF FAME MEMBERS
    Eisenberg, John. *The Streak* — 796.357
    Kepner, Tyler. *K* — 796.357
    Leavy, Jane. *The Big Fella* — B

    Leavy, Jane. *The Last Boy* — B
    Robinson, Ray. *Iron Horse* — B

BASEBALL HISTORY
    Barry, Dan. *Bottom of the 33rd* — 796.357
    Bryant, Howard. *The Last Hero* — B
    Cook, Kevin. *Ten Innings at Wrigley* — 796.357
    Creamer, Robert W. *Stengel* — 796.357
    Epplin, Luke. *Our Team* — 796.357
    Goldberger, Paul. *Ballpark* — 796.357
    Hample, Zack. *The Baseball* — 796.357
    Kennedy, Kostya. *True* — B
    Kepner, Tyler. *K* — 796.357
    Law, Keith. *Smart Baseball* — 796.357
    Leavy, Jane. *The Big Fella* — B
    Leavy, Jane. *The Last Boy* — B
    Montgomery, Patrick. *Baseball's Great Expectations* — 796.357
    Nusbaum, Eric. *Stealing Home* — 796.357
    Pennington, Bill. *Billy Martin* — B
    Perron, Cam. ★*Comeback Season* — 796.357
    Posnanski, Joe. *The Baseball 100* — 796.357
    Posnanski, Joe. *The Soul of Baseball* — 796.357
    Rapp, David. *Tinker to Evers to Chance* — 796.357
    Ruck, Rob. *Raceball* — 796.357
    Rushin, Steve. *The 34-Ton Bat* — 796.357
    Tye, Larry. *Satchel* — B

BASEBALL MANAGERS
    O'Brien, Keith. *Charlie Hustle* — 796.357
    Torre, Joe. *The Yankee Years* — B
    Turbow, Jason. *They Bled Blue* — 796.357

BASEBALL PLAYERS
    Barra, Allen. ★*Yogi Berra* — B
    Bradlee, Ben. *The Kid* — B
    Brown, Tim. ★*The Tao of the Backup Catcher* — 796.357
    Bryant, Howard. *The Last Hero* — B
    Bryant, Howard. *Rickey* — B
    Clavin, Thomas. *The DiMaggios* — 920
    Cook, Kevin. *Ten Innings at Wrigley* — 796.357
    Cramer, Richard Ben. *Joe DiMaggio* — B
    Crawford, Bill. ★*All American* — B
    Creamer, Robert W. *Babe* — B
    Creamer, Robert W. *Stengel* — 796.357
    Darling, Ron. *The Complete Game* — B
    Diamond, Jared M. *Swing Kings* — 796.357
    Eisenberg, John. *The Streak* — 796.357
    Epplin, Luke. *Our Team* — 796.357
    Feinstein, John. *Where Nobody Knows Your Name* — 796.357
    Gehrig, Lou. *The Lost Memoir* — B
    Halberstam, David. *The Teammates* — B
    Hernandez, Keith. *I'm Keith Hernandez* — B
    Hirsch, James S. *Willie Mays* — B
    Jeter, Derek. *Jeter Unfiltered* — B
    Kennedy, Kostya. *True* — B
    Kepner, Tyler. *K* — 796.357
    Kornhauser, Jacob. *The Cup of Coffee Club* — 796.357
    Kurlansky, Mark. *The Eastern Stars* — 796.357
    Law, Keith. *The Inside Game* — 796.35764
    Law, Keith. *Smart Baseball* — 796.357
    Leavy, Jane. *The Big Fella* — B
    Leavy, Jane. *The Last Boy* — B
    Leavy, Jane. *Sandy Koufax* — B
    Lewis, Michael. ★*Moneyball* — 796.357
    Maraniss, David. *Clemente* — B
    Mays, Willie. *24* — B
    Megdal, Howard. *The Baseball Talmud* — 796.357
    Montgomery, Patrick. *Baseball's Great Expectations* — 796.357
    O'Brien, Keith. *Charlie Hustle* — 796.357
    Ortiz, David. *Papi* — B
    Pappu, Sridhar. *The Year of the Pitcher* — 920
    Passan, Jeff. *The Arm* — 796.3576
    Pearlman, Jeff. *The Last Folk Hero* — B
    Pennington, Bill. *Billy Martin* — B
    Pessah, Jon. *The Game* — 796.357
    Pessah, Jon. *Yogi* — B
    Posnanski, Joe. *The Baseball 100* — 796.357
    Posnanski, Joe. ★*Why We Love Baseball* — 796.357
    Rapoport, Ron. *Let's Play Two* — B
    Rapp, David. *Tinker to Evers to Chance* — 796.357
    Rivera, Mariano. *The Closer* — B

AUTHOR, TITLE, SERIES AND SUBJECT INDEX

Robinson, Jackie. *I Never Had It Made*	B
Robinson, Ray. *Iron Horse*	B
Rushin, Steve. *The 34-Ton Bat*	796.357
Sabathia, CC. *Till the End*	796.357
Santiago, Wilfred. *"21"*	741.5
Sawchik, Travis. *Big Data Baseball*	796.357
Snyder, Brad. *A Well-Paid Slave*	B
Stump, Al. *Cobb*	B
Svrluga, Barry. *The Grind*	796.357
Turbow, Jason. *The Baseball Codes*	796.357
Turbow, Jason. *They Bled Blue*	796.357
Tye, Larry. *Satchel*	B
The Baseball Talmud. Megdal, Howard	796.357
BASEBALL TEAM OWNERS	
Pessah, Jon. *The Game*	796.357
BASEBALL TEAMS	
Clavin, Thomas. *The DiMaggios*	920
Cohen, Rich. *The Chicago Cubs*	796.357
Cook, Kevin. *Ten Innings at Wrigley*	796.357
Epplin, Luke. *Our Team*	796.357
Halberstam, David. *Summer of '49*	796.357
Knight, Molly. *The Best Team Money Can Buy*	796.357
Law, Keith. *The Inside Game*	796.35764
Law, Keith. *Smart Baseball*	796.357
Neyer, Rob. *Power Ball*	796.357
Posnanski, Joe. ★*Why We Love Baseball*	796.357
Reiter, Ben. *Astroball*	796.357
Sawchik, Travis. *Big Data Baseball*	796.357
Simon, Scott. *My Cubs*	796.357
Torre, Joe. *The Yankee Years*	B
Turbow, Jason. *The Baseball Codes*	796.357
Baseball's Great Expectations. Montgomery, Patrick	796.357
BASEBALLS	
Hample, Zack. *The Baseball*	796.357
Kepner, Tyler. *K*	796.357
Baseless. Baker, Nicholson	358
The Basic Beliefs of Judaism. Epstein, Lawrence J.	296.3
Basic Economics. Sowell, Thomas	330
★*The Basic Works of Aristotle*. Aristotle	185
Basic Writings. Heidegger, Martin	193
★*The Basic Writings of C.G. Jung*. Jung, C. G.	150.19
★*Basic Writings of Kant*. Kant, Immanuel	193
★*Basic Writings of Nietzsche*. Nietzsche, Friedrich Wilhelm	193
★*The Basic Writings of Sigmund Freud*. Freud, Sigmund	150.19
Basie, Count	
Good Morning Blues	B
BASIE, COUNT, 1904-1984	
Basie, Count. *Good Morning Blues*	B
Tye, Larry. ★*The Jazzmen*	781.6509
Basinger, Jeanine	
Hollywood	791.43
The Star Machine	384
Basket Essentials. Irish, Lora S.	746.412
BASKET MAKING	
Irish, Lora S. *Basket Essentials*	746.412
★*Basketball*. MacMullan, Jackie	796.323
BASKETBALL	
Abdurraqib, Hanif. ★*There's Always This Year*	796.323
Anderson, Sam. *Boom Town*	976.6
Babb, Valerie Melissa. *The Book of James*	B
Bella, Timothy. *Barkley*	B
Benedict, Jeff. *Lebron*	B
Bradburd, Rus. *All the Dreams We've Dreamed*	796.323
Bryant, Kobe. *The Mamba Mentality*	B
Colton, Larry. *Counting Coup*	796.323
Davis, Seth. *Wooden*	B
Dohrmann, George. ★*Play Their Hearts Out*	796.323
Fagan, Kate. *All the Colors Came Out*	B
Feinstein, John. *A March to Madness*	796.323
Fury, Shawn. *Rise and Fire*	796.323
Glockner, Andy. *Chasing Perfection*	796.323
Goodman, Matthew. *The City Game*	796.323
Iguodala, Andre. *The Sixth Man*	B
Kriegel, Mark. *Pistol*	B
Lunardi, Joe. ★*Bracketology*	796.323
MacMullan, Jackie. ★*Basketball*	796.323
Malinowski, Erik. *Betaball*	796.323
Maraniss, Andrew. *Strong Inside*	B

McCallum, Jack. *Golden Days*	796.323
O'Connor, Ian. *Coach K*	B
Oakley, Charles. *The Last Enforcer*	B
Perkins, Kendrick. *The Education of Kendrick Perkins*	B
Pippen, Scottie. *Unguarded*	B
Powell, Michael. ★*Canyon Dreams*	796.323
Ravin, Idan. *The Hoops Whisperer*	796.323
Runstedtler, Theresa. *Black Ball*	796.323
Serrano, Shea. *Basketball (and Other Things)*	796.323
Sielski, Mike. *The Rise*	B
Simmons, Bill. *The Book of Basketball*	796.323
Skelton, Marc. *Pounding the Rock*	796.323
Smith, Kenny. *Talk of Champions*	B
Smith, Sam. *Hard Labor*	796.323
Streep, Abe. *Brothers on Three*	306.85
Sullivan, Matt. *Can't Knock the Hustle*	796.323
West, Jerry. *West by West*	B
Windhorst, Brian. *Lebron, Inc.*	B
Basketball (and Other Things). Serrano, Shea	796.323
BASKETBALL COACHES	
Abdul-Jabbar, Kareem. *Coach Wooden and Me*	B
Boeheim, Jim. *Bleeding Orange*	B
Bradburd, Rus. *All the Dreams We've Dreamed*	796.323
Cornelius, Maria M. *The Final Season*	B
Dohrmann, George. ★*Play Their Hearts Out*	796.323
Feinstein, John. ★*The Legends Club*	B
Feinstein, John. *A March to Madness*	796.323
MacMullan, Jackie. ★*Basketball*	796.323
Pearlman, Jeff. ★*Three-Ring Circus*	796.323
Skelton, Marc. *Pounding the Rock*	796.323
West, Jerry. *West by West*	B
BASKETBALL COACHING	
Boeheim, Jim. *Bleeding Orange*	B
Davis, Seth. *Wooden*	B
BASKETBALL FANS	
Abdurraqib, Hanif. ★*There's Always This Year*	796.323
Serrano, Shea. *Basketball (and Other Things)*	796.323
BASKETBALL FOR CHILDREN	
Blais, Madeleine. *In These Girls, Hope Is a Muscle*	796.323
BASKETBALL FOR WOMEN	
Colton, Larry. *Counting Coup*	796.323
Summitt, Pat Head. *Sum It Up*	B
BASKETBALL HISTORY	
Feinstein, John. ★*Last Dance*	796.323
Fury, Shawn. *Rise and Fire*	796.323
Lunardi, Joe. ★*Bracketology*	796.323
McCallum, Jack. *Dream Team*	796.323
Montville, Leigh. *Tall Men, Short Shorts*	796.323
Rosen, Charles. *Sugar*	B
Runstedtler, Theresa. *Black Ball*	796.323
BASKETBALL PLAYERS	
Abdurraqib, Hanif. ★*There's Always This Year*	796.323
Abrams, Jonathan P. D. *Boys Among Men*	796.323
Babb, Valerie Melissa. *The Book of James*	B
Baylor, Elgin. *Hang Time*	B
Benedict, Jeff. *Lebron*	B
Bryant, Kobe. *The Mamba Mentality*	B
Chapman, Rex. ★*It's Hard for Me to Live with Me*	B
Conroy, Pat. *My Losing Season*	B
Dohrmann, George. ★*Play Their Hearts Out*	796.323
Fagan, Kate. *All the Colors Came Out*	B
Fury, Shawn. *Rise and Fire*	796.323
Kriegel, Mark. *Pistol*	B
MacMullan, Jackie. ★*Basketball*	796.323
McCallum, Jack. *Dream Team*	796.323
Oakley, Charles. *The Last Enforcer*	B
Pearlman, Jeff. ★*Three-Ring Circus*	796.323
Perkins, Kendrick. *The Education of Kendrick Perkins*	B
Rosen, Charles. *Sugar*	B
Sielski, Mike. *The Rise*	B
Streep, Abe. *Brothers on Three*	306.85
Sullivan, Matt. *Can't Knock the Hustle*	796.323
Walton, Bill. *Back from the Dead*	B
Weitzman, Yaron. *Tanking to the Top*	796.323
West, Jerry. *West by West*	B
Williams, Jay. *Life Is Not an Accident*	B
Windhorst, Brian. *Lebron, Inc.*	B

BASKETBALL TEAM OWNERS
Smith, Sam. *Hard Labor* — 796.323
BASKETBALL TEAMS
Davis, Seth. *Wooden* — B
Feinstein, John. ★*The Back Roads to March* — 796.323
Feinstein, John. ★*Last Dance* — 796.323
Feinstein, John. ★*The Legends Club* — 796.323
Feinstein, John. *A March to Madness* — 796.323
Glockner, Andy. *Chasing Perfection* — 796.323
Goodman, Matthew. *The City Game* — 796.323
Iguodala, Andre. *The Sixth Man* — B
Lunardi, Joe. ★*Bracketology* — 796.323
Malinowski, Erik. *Betaball* — 796.323
McCallum, Jack. *Dream Team* — 796.323
McCallum, Jack. *Golden Days* — 796.323
Montville, Leigh. *Tall Men, Short Shorts* — 796.323
Pearlman, Jeff. ★*Three-Ring Circus* — 796.323
Streep, Abe. *Brothers on Three* — 306.85
BASKETBALL TOURNAMENTS
Feinstein, John. ★*Last Dance* — 796.323
Lunardi, Joe. ★*Bracketology* — 796.323
BASKETS
Irish, Lora S. *Basket Essentials* — 746.412
Baskette, Molly Phinney
How to Begin When Your World Is Ending — 248.8
BASKETTE, MOLLY PHINNEY, 1970-
Baskette, Molly Phinney. *How to Begin When Your World Is Ending* — 248.8
The *Basque* History of the World. Kurlansky, Mark — 946
BASQUE PROVINCES
Kurlansky, Mark. *The Basque History of the World* — 946
BASQUES
Kurlansky, Mark. *The Basque History of the World* — 946
BASS PLAYERS
Gabbard, Krin. *Better Git It in Your Soul* — B
Bass, Amy
One Goal — 796.334
Bass, Diana Butler
Grateful — 241
Bass, Ellen
★*The Courage to Heal* — 616.85
Bass, Gary Jonathan
Freedom's Battle — 341.5
★*Judgment at Tokyo* — 952.04
Bass, Rick
The Traveling Feast — B
Why I Came West — 333.78
BASS, RICK, 1958-
Bass, Rick. *The Traveling Feast* — B
Bass, Rick. *Why I Came West* — 333.78
Bass, William M.
Death's Acre — 614
Bassetti, Amanda
Arm Knitting — 746.43
The *Bastard* Brigade. Kean, Sam — 355.8
Bastianich, Lidia
Felidia — 641.594
Lidia Cooks from the Heart of Italy — 641.594
★*Lidia's a Pot, a Pan, and a Bowl* — 641.82
Lidia's Commonsense Italian Cooking — 641.594
Lidia's Family Table — 641.594
Lidia's Favorite Recipes — 641.594
★*Lidia's from Our Family Table to Yours* — 641.594
Lidia's Mastering the Art of Italian Cuisine — 641.594
Lidia's — 641.594
My American Dream — B
BASTIANICH, LIDIA
Bastianich, Lidia. *My American Dream* — B
Baszile, Natalie
We Are Each Other's Harvest — 630.89
BATAAN DEATH MARCH, 1942
Norman, Michael. *Tears in the Darkness* — 940.54
Batali, Mario
Mario Batali Big American Cookbook — 641.5973
Batalion, Judith
The Light of Days — 940.53
Batch Cocktails. Hoffman, Maggie — 641.87
Bate, Jonathan
Radical Wordsworth — B

Bates, Laura
Men Who Hate Women — 305.3
BATES, LAURA, 1986-
Bates, Laura. *Men Who Hate Women* — 305.3
***Bathed* in Prayer**. Karon, Jan — 242
BATHROOMS
Bryson, Bill. ★*At Home* — 643
Gold, Jamie. *Taunton's New Bathroom Idea Book* — 747.7
BATMAN (FICTITIOUS CHARACTER)
Weldon, Glen. ★*The Caped Crusade* — 741.5
BATMANGLIJ, NAJMIEH, 1947-
Sen, Mayukh. *Taste Makers* — 641.5092
Bats. Taylor, Marianne — 599.4
BATS
Taylor, Marianne. *Bats* — 599.4
BATTERS (BASEBALL)
Cramer, Richard Ben. *Joe DiMaggio* — B
Kepner, Tyler. *K* — 796.357
Ortiz, David. *Papi* — B
Batterson, Mark
Please, Sorry, Thanks — 179
BATTING (BASEBALL)
Bradlee, Ben. *The Kid* — B
BATTLE CASUALTIES
Carpenter, Kyle. *You Are Worth It* — B
Stephenson, Michael. *The Last Full Measure* — 305.9
Battle Cry of Freedom. McPherson, James M. — 973.7
The *Battle* for America, 2008. Balz, Daniel J. — 973.932
The *Battle* for God. Armstrong, Karen — 200
★*Battle* for the Big Top. Standiford, Les — 791.3
BATTLE HISTORY
Atkinson, Rick. *The Guns at Last Light* — 940.54
Caddick-Adams, Peter. *Sand and Steel* — 940.54
Guelzo, Allen C. *Gettysburg* — 973.7
Holland, James. *Normandy '44* — 940.54
Philbrick, Nathaniel. ★*Bunker Hill* — 973.3
The *Battle* of Arnhem. Beevor, Antony — 940.54
The *Battle* of Bretton Woods. Steil, Benn — 339.5
Battle of Britain. Holland, James — 940.54
Battle of Ink and Ice. Hartman, Darrell — 998
The *Battle* of Midway. Symonds, Craig L. — 940.54
The *Battle* of the Atlantic. Dimbleby, Jonathan — 940.54
The *Battle* of Versailles. Givhan, Robin — 746.9
BATTLES
Ackroyd, Peter. *Innovation* — 942.082
Ambrose, Stephen E. *Citizen Soldiers* — 940.54
Ambrose, Stephen E. *D-Day, June 6, 1944* — 940.54
Atkinson, Rick. *The Day of Battle* — 940.54
Barker, Juliet R. V. *Agincourt* — 944
Beevor, Antony. *Ardennes 1944* — 940.54
Beevor, Antony. *D-Day* — 940.54
Berg, Scott W. ★*38 Nooses* — 973.7
Brands, H. W. *The Last Campaign* — 973.8
Brown, Dee. ★*Bury My Heart at Wounded Knee* — 978
Burrough, Bryan. *Forget the Alamo* — 976.043
Chrisinger, David. *The Soldier's Truth* — 940.54
Clark, Lloyd. *The Commanders* — 940.53
Crawford, Alan Pell. *This Fierce People* — 975
Donovan, Jim. *The Blood of Heroes* — 976.4
Dugard, Martin. *Taking Berlin* — 940.54
Dugard, Martin. *Taking Paris* — 940.54
Ellis, Joseph J. ★*Revolutionary Summer* — 973.3
Englund, Peter. *November 1942* — 940.53
Finkel, David. *The Good Soldiers* — 956.7044
Fischer, David Hackett. *Washington's Crossing* — 973.3
Frank, Richard B. *Tower of Skulls* — 940.54
Gallego, Ruben. *They Called Us* — 956.7044
Graff, Garrett M. ★*When the Sea Came Alive* — 940.54
Groom, Winston. *Shiloh, 1862* — 973.7
Guinn, Jeff. ★*War on the Border* — 972.08
Gwynne, S. C. *Empire of the Summer Moon* — B
Hanson, Victor Davis. *The Second World Wars* — 940.54
Hindley, Meredith. *Destination Casablanca* — 940.54
Holland, James. *Battle of Britain* — 940.54
Holland, James. *Brothers in Arms* — 940.54
Holland, James. ★*Burma '44* — 940.54
Holland, James. *The Savage Storm* — 940.53
Hutton, Paul Andrew. *The Apache Wars* — 979

AUTHOR, TITLE, SERIES AND SUBJECT INDEX

Isserman, Maurice. *The Winter Army*	940.54
Junger, Sebastian. *War*	958.104
Kilmeade, Brian. ★*Andrew Jackson and the Miracle of New Orleans*	973.5
Kneale, Matthew. *Rome*	945.6
Korda, Michael. *With Wings Like Eagles*	940.54
Luttrell, Marcus. *Lone Survivor*	958.104
MacGregor, Iain. *The Lighthouse of Stalingrad*	940.54
McPherson, James M. *Hallowed Ground*	973.7
Meyer, Dakota. *Into the Fire*	958.104
Milton, Giles. *Soldier, Sailor, Frogman, Spy, Airman, Gangster, Kill or Die*	940.54
Moore, Harold G. *We Were Soldiers Once—And Young*	959.704
Morris, Marc. *The Norman Conquest*	942.02
Nolan, Cathal J. *The Allure of Battle*	355.409
Norwich, John Julius. *A History of France*	944
Patton, George S. *War as I Knew It*	B
Philbrick, Nathaniel. ★*The Last Stand*	973.8
Romesha, Clinton. *Red Platoon*	958.104
Symonds, Craig L. *The Battle of Midway*	940.54
Toll, Ian W. *The Conquering Tide*	940.54
Utley, Robert M. ★*Geronimo*	B
Warren, James A. *Year of the Hawk*	959.704
Wheelan, Joseph. *Midnight in the Pacific*	940.54
Woolf, Greg. *Rome*	937

Batuman, Elif
The Possessed	891.7

Baudelaire, Charles
Les Fleurs Du Mal	841
Poems	841

BAUDELAIRE, CHARLES, 1821-1867
Baudelaire, Charles. *Poems*	841

Bauer, Shane
American Prison	365

Bauer, Susan Wise
Rethinking School	371.19

Bauermeister, Erica
House Lessons	B

BAUERMEISTER, ERICA
Bauermeister, Erica. *House Lessons*	B

Baum, Dan
Nine Lives	B

BAUM, HERBERT, 1912-1942
Thomas, Gordon. *Defying Hitler*	920

Baur, Gene
Farm Sanctuary	179

Bawer, Bruce
The Victims' Revolution	320.973

BAXLEY FAMILY
Kolata, Gina Bari. *Mercies in Disguise*	616

BAXLEY, AMANDA
Kolata, Gina Bari. *Mercies in Disguise*	616

Baxley, Traci
Social Justice Parenting	649

BAY OF PIGS INVASION, 1961
Rasenberger, Jim. *The Brilliant Disaster*	972.9106
Sorensen, Theodore C. *Counselor*	B

Bayless, Rick
Authentic Mexican	641.5972
★*Fiesta at Rick's*	641.5972
Mexican Everyday	641.5972
★*More Mexican Everyday*	641.5972
Rick Bayless Mexico One Plate at a Time	641.5972

Baylor, Elgin
Hang Time	B

BAYLOR, ELGIN
Baylor, Elgin. *Hang Time*	B

Bayoumi, Moustafa
How Does It Feel to Be a Problem?	305.892

Baz, Molly
Cook This Book	641.5

Bazelon, Emily
★*Charged*	345.73
Sticks and Stones	302.34

★*Be A Revolution*. Oluo, Ijeoma	305.8
Be Free or Die. Lineberry, Cate	B
Be Like the Fox. Benner, Erica	
Be Not Afraid of Love. Zhu, Mimi	152.4
Be Recorder. Gimenez Smith, Carmen	811
Be The Refuge. Han, Chenxing	294.3
Be Water, My Friend. Lee, Shannon	796.8
★*Be With*. Gander, Forrest	811
Bead Embroidery. Cox, Shelley	746.5

BEADWORK
Combs, Rebecca Ann. *Kumihimo*	745.594
DeCoster, Marcia. ★*Marcia Decoster's Beaded Opulence*	739.27
Geary, Theresa Flores. *The Illustrated Bead Bible*	745.594
Katz, Amy. *Seed Bead Chic*	745.594
Michaels, Chris Franchetti. *Teach Yourself Visually Jewelry Making & Beading*	739.27
Wiseman, Jill. *Jill Wiseman's Beautiful Beaded Ropes*	745.594

Beah, Ishmael
★*A Long Way Gone*	B

BEAH, ISHMAEL, 1980-
Beah, Ishmael. ★*A Long Way Gone*	B

Beaks, Bones, and Bird Songs. Lederer, Roger J.	598
Beale Street Dynasty. Lauterbach, Preston	976.8

Beam, Alex
American Crucifixion	B

Bean by Bean. Dragonwagon, Crescent	641.6

BEANS
Dragonwagon, Crescent. *Bean by Bean*	641.6
Frank, Lois Ellen. *Seed to Plate, Soil to Sky*	641.5

BEARD, JAMES, 1903-1985
Birdsall, John. *The Man Who Ate Too Much*	B

Beard, Mary
★*Emperor of Rome*	937
The Fires of Vesuvius	937
★*How Do We Look*	704.9
★*S.P.Q.R.*	937
★*Women & Power*	305.409

BEARD, PETER HILL, 1938-2020
Wallace, Christopher. *Twentieth-Century Man*	B

Bearing The Unbearable. Cacciatore, Joanne	155.9

BEARS
Dickie, Gloria. *Eight Bears*	599.78
The Bears Ears. Roberts, David	979.2

BEARS EARS NATIONAL MONUMENT (UTAH)
Roberts, David. *The Bears Ears*	979.2
Williams, Terry Tempest. *Erosion*	814

Beastie Boys Book. Mike D.	782.42164

BEAT AUTHORS
Johnson, Joyce. *The Voice Is All*	B
Kerouac, Jack. *Book of Sketches, 1952-57*	818

BEAT CULTURE
Johnson, Joyce. *The Voice Is All*	B
Kerouac, Jack. *Book of Sketches, 1952-57*	818
Martin, Justin. *Rebel Souls*	920
Torgoff, Martin. *Bop Apocalypse*	781.65

BEAT GENERATION
Ginsberg, Allen. *Best Minds of My Generation*	810.9
Ginsberg, Allen. ★*Howl*	811.54
Kerouac, Jack. *Selected Letters, 1940-1956*	813
Szwed, John F. *Cosmic Scholar*	B

BEAT POETS
Ginsberg, Allen. *Best Minds of My Generation*	810.9
Johnson, Joyce. *The Voice Is All*	B

BEATITUDES
Fusco, Daniel. *Crazy Happy*	248.4
★*The Beatles*. Spitz, Bob	B

Beaton, Kate
★*Ducks*	741.5

Beatrix Potter. Lear, Linda J.	B

Beattie, Melody
Codependent No More	616.86

BEATTY, WARREN, 1937-
Biskind, Peter. *Star*	B

Beaty, Katelyn
Celebrities for Jesus	261

BEAUFORT, MARGARET, COUNTESS OF RICHMOND AND DERBY, 1443-1509
Gristwood, Sarah. *Blood Sisters*	942.04092
Jones, Dan. ★*The Wars of the Roses*	942.04
Tallis, Nicola. *Uncrowned Queen*	B

Beautiful. Shearer, Stephen Michael	B
Beautiful Bracelets by Hand. Gedeon, Jade	745.594
★*Beautiful Country*. Wang, Qian Julie	B

A Beautiful Mess Happy Handmade Home. Larson, Elsie — 745
Beautiful on the Outside. Rippon, Adam — B
The Beautiful Ones. Prince — B
Beautiful People. Blake, Melissa — 362.4
Beautiful People Don't Just Happen. Sauls, Scott — 248.8
The Beautiful Struggle. Coates, Ta-Nehisi — B
Beautiful Things. Biden, Robert Hunter — B
★*Beautifully Organized.* Boyd, Nikki — 648
The Beauty. Hirshfield, Jane — 811

BEAUTY
- Bethencourt, Kahran. *Glory* — 779.2
- Cottom, Tressie McMillan. *Thick* — 301
- Jones, Chloe Cooper. ★*Easy Beauty* — B
- Kneeland, Jessi. *Body Neutral* — 306.4
- Komunyakaa, Yusef. ★*Everyday Mojo Songs of Earth* — 811
- Limon, Ada. ★*The Hurting Kind* — 811
- Malone, Jo. *Jo Malone* — B
- Otto, Mary. *Teeth* — 617
- Pardlo, Gregory. *Spectral Evidence* — 811
- Vince, Gaia. *Transcendence* — 599.93
- Whitefield-Madrano, Autumn. *Face Value* — 111
- Yong, Sable. *Die Hot with a Vengeance* — 646.7

The Beauty and the Sorrow. Englund, Peter — 940.309

BEAUTY CARE
- Godas, Maru. *Organic Beauty* — 646.7
- Hamblin, James. *Clean* — 613
- Hankir, Zahra. *Eyeliner* — 391.6
- Hu, Elise. *Flawless* — 646.7
- Whitefield-Madrano, Autumn. *Face Value* — 111
- Yong, Sable. *Die Hot with a Vengeance* — 646.7

BEAUTY CONTEST INDUSTRY AND TRADE
- Mifflin, Margot. *Looking for Miss America* — 791.6

BEAUTY CONTESTANTS
- Mifflin, Margot. *Looking for Miss America* — 791.6

BEAUTY CONTESTS
- Mifflin, Margot. *Looking for Miss America* — 791.6

The Beauty in Breaking. Harper, Michele — B

BEAUTY IN NATURE
- Diaz, Natalie. ★*Postcolonial Love Poem* — 811
- Macfarlane, Robert. *The Lost Spells* — 811
- Nicolson, Adam. *Life Between the Tides* — 577.69
- Wohlleben, Peter. *Forest Walking* — 582.16
- Wohlleben, Peter. *The Hidden Life of Trees* — 582.16

Beauty in the Broken Places. Pataki, Allison — B
The Beauty of Dirty Skin. Bowe, Whitney — 646.7
The Beauty of Dusk. Bruni, Frank — B
The Beauty of Living. Rosenblitt, J. Alison — B
The Beauty of Living Twice. Stone, Sharon — B
The Beauty of the Husband. Carson, Anne — 811
The Beauty of What Remains. Leder, Steven Z. — 306.9

BEAUTY PRODUCTS
- Godas, Maru. *Organic Beauty* — 646.7
- Hankir, Zahra. *Eyeliner* — 391.6

Beauvais, Garcelle
  Love Me as I Am — B
Beauvoir, Simone de
  ★*The Second Sex* — 305.4

BEAUVOIR, SIMONE DE, 1908-1986
- Coffin, Judith G. *Sex, Love, and Letters* — 848

Beavan, Colin
  No Impact Man — B

BEAVAN, COLIN
- Beavan, Colin. *No Impact Man* — B

BEAVER LODGES
- Goldfarb, Ben. *Eager* — 333.95

BEAVERS
- Goldfarb, Ben. *Eager* — 333.95

BEBOP MUSIC
- Hayes, Elaine M. ★*Queen of Bebop* — B

Because of Sex. Thomas, Gillian — 344.7301
Because We Are Bad. Bailey, Lily — B

Bechdel, Alison
  ★*Fun Home* — 741.5
  ★*The Secret to Superhuman Strength* — 741.5

BECHDEL, ALISON, 1960-
- Bechdel, Alison. ★*Fun Home* — 741.5
- Bechdel, Alison. ★*The Secret to Superhuman Strength* — 741.5

BECHTEL FAMILY
- Denton, Sally. *The Profiteers* — B

BECHTEL, WARREN A., 1872-1933
- Denton, Sally. *The Profiteers* — B

Beck, Amanda Martinez
  More of You — 613
Beck, Martha Nibley
  The Way of Integrity — 158.1
Becker, Adam
  What Is Real? — 920
Becker, Elizabeth
  Overbooked — 338.4
Becker, Ernest
  ★*The Denial of Death* — 128
Becker, Holly
  Decorate — 747
Becker, Jo
  ★*Forcing the Spring* — 346.79401
Becker, Joshua
  The Minimalist Home — 241
  The More of Less — 241
Beckert, Sven
  Empire of Cotton — 338.4
Beckett, Samuel
  Collected Poems in English and French — 841
  The Letters of Samuel Beckett — 848

BECKETT, SAMUEL, 1906-1989
- Beckett, Samuel. *The Letters of Samuel Beckett* — 848

BECKWITH, JAMES, 1832-1912
- Lane, Charles. *The Day Freedom Died* — 976.3

★*Becoming.* Obama, Michelle — B
Becoming Abolitionists. Purnell, Derecka — 363.20973
★*Becoming Dr. Seuss.* Jones, Brian Jay — B
Becoming Duchess Goldblatt. Goldblatt, Duchess — B
★*Becoming Earth.* Jabr, Ferris — 570.1
Becoming Elektra. Houghton, Mick — 781.64
★*Becoming Elisabeth Elliot.* Vaughn, Ellen Santilli — B
Becoming Hitler. Weber, Thomas — B
★*Becoming Jewish.* Reuben, Steven Carr — 296.7
Becoming Justice Blackmun. Greenhouse, Linda — B
Becoming Kim Jong Un. Pak, Jung H. — B
Becoming King. Jackson, Troy — B
Becoming Ms. Burton. Burton, Susan — B
Becoming Nicole. Nutt, Amy Ellis — 920
★*Becoming Richard Pryor.* Saul, Scott — B
Becoming Steve Jobs. Schlender, Brent — B
★*Becoming Wild.* Safina, Carl — 591.7
★*Becoming Wise.* Tippett, Krista — 158.1

BEDOUINS
- Lawrence, T. E. *Seven Pillars of Wisdom* — 940.4

Bee People and the Bugs They Love. Mortimer, Frank — B

BEE PRODUCTS
- Nordhaus, Hannah. *The Beekeeper's Lament* — 638

Bee, Vanessa A.
  Home Bound — B

BEE, VANESSA A., 1988-
- Bee, Vanessa A. *Home Bound* — B

The Bee-Friendly Garden. Frey, Kate — 595.79
The Beekeeper. Mikhaiil, Dunya — 956.7044
The Beekeeper's Lament. Nordhaus, Hannah — 638

BEEKEEPERS
- Mikhaiil, Dunya. *The Beekeeper* — 956.7044
- Mortimer, Frank. *Bee People and the Bugs They Love* — B

BEEKEEPING
- Flottum, Kim. *The Backyard Beekeeper* — 638
- May, Meredith. *The Honey Bus* — B
- Mortimer, Frank. *Bee People and the Bugs They Love* — B
- Nordhaus, Hannah. *The Beekeeper's Lament* — 638
- Wilson, Joseph S. *The Bees in Your Backyard* — 595.79

Beeline. Shankar, Shalini — 155.4

Beeman, Richard R.
  Our Lives, Our Fortunes and Our Sacred Honor — 973.3
  ★*Plain, Honest Men* — 342.7302

BEER
- Hoalst-Pullen, Nancy. *National Geographic Atlas of Beer* — 663
- Knoedelseder, William. *Bitter Brew* — 338.7

Beers, Diane L.
  ★*For the Prevention of Cruelty* — 179

AUTHOR, TITLE, SERIES AND SUBJECT INDEX

BEES
    Frey, Kate. *The Bee-Friendly Garden* — 595.79
    May, Meredith. *The Honey Bus* — B
    Mortimer, Frank. *Bee People and the Bugs They Love* — B
    Nordhaus, Hannah. *The Beekeeper's Lament* — 638
    Wilson, Joseph S. *The Bees in Your Backyard* — 595.79
The **Bees** *in Your Backyard.* Wilson, Joseph S. — 595.79
Beethoven. Lockwood, Lewis — B
Beethoven. Morris, Edmund — B
Beethoven. Suchet, John — B
★**Beethoven**. Swafford, Jan — B
★**Beethoven's** *Eroica.* Hamilton-Paterson, James — 784.18
BEETHOVEN, LUDWIG VAN, 1770-1827
    Hamilton-Paterson, James. ★*Beethoven's Eroica* — 784.18
    Lockwood, Lewis. *Beethoven* — B
    Morris, Edmund. *Beethoven* — B
    Rosen, Charles. *The Classical Style* — 780.9
    Sachs, Harvey. *The Ninth* — 784.2
    Suchet, John. *Beethoven* — B
    Swafford, Jan. ★*Beethoven* — B
Beevor, Antony
    Ardennes 1944 — 940.54
    The Battle of Arnhem — 940.54
    D-Day — 940.54
    The Fall of Berlin, 1945 — 940.54
    Russia — 947.084
    The Second World War — 940.54
    Stalingrad — 940.54
Before Amen. Lucado, Max — 248.3
Before It's Gone. Vigliotti, Jonathan — 577
Before The Fallout. Preston, Diana — 303.48
Before You Know It. Bargh, John A — 154.2
Before You Say Anything. Wellman, Victoria — 808.5
The **Beggar's** *Opera.* Gay, John — 782.1
Begin Again. Glaude, Eddie S. — 305.800973
BEGIN, MENACHEM, 1913-1992
    Wright, Lawrence. *Thirteen Days in September* — 956.04
A **Beginner's** *Guide to America.* Hakkakiyan, Ruya — 646.7
The **Beginner's** *Guide to Growing Heirloom Vegetables.* Iannotti, Marie — 635
A **Beginner's** *Guide to Japan.* Iyer, Pico — 952.05
Beginner's Guide to Kirigami. Descamps, Ghylenn — 745.54
★*The* **Beginner's** *Photography Guide.* Gatcum, Chris — 770
★**Beginners**. Vanderbilt, Tom — 646.7
Begley, Adam
    The Great Nadar — B
Bego, Mark
    Aretha Franklin — B
Behan, Ren
    ★*The Sweet Polish Kitchen* — 641.594
Behar, Richard
    Madoff — 364.16
Behave. Sapolsky, Robert M. — 612.8
BEHAVIOR
    Fogg, B. J. *Tiny Habits* — 158
    Freud, Sigmund. *Civilization and Its Discontents* — 150.19
    Turbow, Jason. *The Baseball Codes* — 796.357
BEHAVIOR AND CULTURE
    Gilliam, Fatimah. *Race Rules* — 305.8
BEHAVIOR EVOLUTION
    Miller, Kenneth R. *The Human Instinct* — 155.7
    Wilson, Edward O. *Genesis* — 591.5
BEHAVIOR GENETICS
    Wilson, Edward O. *Genesis* — 591.5
BEHAVIOR MODIFICATION
    Clear, James. ★*Atomic Habits* — 155.24
    Fallon, Allison. *The Power of Writing It Down* — 158.1
    Gilliam, Fatimah. *Race Rules* — 305.8
    Miller, Caroline Adams. *Creating Your Best Life* — 158.1
    Norton, Michael. ★*The Ritual Effect* — 650.1
    Pryor, Karen. ★*Don't Shoot the Dog* — 153.8
BEHAVIOR THERAPY
    Boone, Matthew S. *Stop Avoiding Stuff* — 152.4
    McKay, Matthew. *Self-Esteem* — 155.2
    Pryor, Karen. ★*Don't Shoot the Dog* — 153.8
    Van der Kolk, Bessel A. *The Body Keeps the Score* — 616.85
BEHAVIORAL ECONOMICS
    Ariely, Dan. *The Honest Truth About Dishonesty* — 177
    Fox, Justin. *The Myth of the Rational Market* — 332.64

BEHAVIORISM (PSYCHOLOGY)
    Bjork, Daniel W. *B.F. Skinner* — B
    ★*Behemoth.* Freeman, Joshua Benjamin — 338.6
    ★*Behind The Beautiful Forevers.* Boo, Katherine — 305.5
Behind The Burly Q. Zemeckis, Leslie Harter — 792.7
Behind The Mask. Dennison, Matthew — B
★*Behind The Seams.* Parton, Dolly — B
Behold The Monster. Lauren, Jillian — 364.152
Behold, America. Churchwell, Sarah Bartlett — 973.9
★*Being A Dog.* Horowitz, Alexandra — 636.7
Being A Human. Foster, Charles — 155.7
★*Being and Nothingness.* Sartre, Jean-Paul — 111
★*Being and Time.* Heidegger, Martin — 111
Being Elvis. Connolly, Ray — B
★*Being Henry.* Winkler, Henry — B
Being Heumann. Heumann, Judith E. — B
Being Hindu. Sengupta, Hindol — 294.5
Being Jewish. Goldman, Ari L. — 296.4
Being John Lennon. Connolly, Ray — B
★*Being Mortal.* Gawande, Atul — 362.17
Being Muslim Today. Qureshi, Saqib Iqbal — 305.6
Being Nixon. Thomas, Evan — B
Being Seen. Sjunneson, Elsa — 362.4
Being Wrong. Schulz, Kathryn — 121
BEIRUT, LEBANON
    Friedman, Matti. *Spies of No Country* — 327.12
Belafonte, Harry
    ★*My Song* — 782.42164
BELAFONTE, HARRY, 1927-2023
    Belafonte, Harry. ★*My Song* — 782.42164
BELARUS
    Plokhy, Serhii. *Lost Kingdom* — 947
BELARUSIAN PEOPLE
    Fishman, Boris. *Savage Feast* — B
Belasco, Andrew
    The Enlightened College Applicant — 378.1
Belcher, Chris
    Pretty Baby — B
Belcourt, Billy-Ray
    ★*A History of My Brief Body* — B
BELCOURT, BILLY-RAY
    Belcourt, Billy-Ray. ★*A History of My Brief Body* — B
BELFAST, NORTHERN IRELAND
    Keefe, Patrick Radden. ★*Say Nothing* — 364.152
Belfort, Jordan
    ★*The Wolf of Investing* — 332.63
BELFORT, JORDAN
    Belfort, Jordan. ★*The Wolf of Investing* — 332.63
BELGIUM
    Cornwell, Bernard. *Waterloo* — 940.2
    Hochschild, Adam. *King Leopold's Ghost* — 967.51
    Hogan, William R. *Task Force Hogan* — 940.54
    Winder, Simon. *Lotharingia* — 944
    Wright, Alex. *Cataloging the World* — 020.9
Belichick. O'Connor, Ian — B
BELICHICK, BILL
    Benedict, Jeff. *The Dynasty* — 796.332
    O'Connor, Ian. *Belichick* — B
BELIEF AND DOUBT
    Andersen, Kurt. ★*Fantasyland* — 973
    Bignon, Guillaume. *Confessions of a French Atheist* — 239
    Brotherton, Rob. *Suspicious Minds* — 153.4
    Dickey, Colin. *The Unidentified* — 130
    Dweck, Carol S. ★*Mindset* — 153.8
    Egan, Timothy. *A Pilgrimage to Eternity* — 263
    Evans, Rachel Held. *Wholehearted Faith* — 248.4
    Grant, Adam M. ★*Think Again* — 153.4
    Hazleton, Lesley. *Agnostic* — 211
    Hecht, Jennifer Michael. *Doubt* — 121
    Hitchens, Christopher. *The Four Horsemen* — 211
    Jun, Tasha. ★*Tell Me the Dream Again* — 248
    Kugel, James L. *The Great Shift* — 296.3
    Le Guin, Ursula K. *No Time to Spare* — 814
    McLaren, Brian D. *Faith After Doubt* — 234
    Nye, Bill. *Everything All at Once* — 153.4
    Prejean, Helen. *River of Fire* — B
    Scoles, Sarah. *They Are Already Here* — 001.942
    Shermer, Michael. *The Believing Brain* — 153.4

PUBLIC LIBRARY CORE COLLECTION: NONFICTION
Twentieth Edition

Sullivan, Randall. *The Devil's Best Trick* — 235
Tyson, Neil deGrasse. *Starry Messenger* — 901
Wiesel, Elie. ★*Night* — B
Wiman, Christian. *Zero at the Bone* — 818
Believe It. Foles, Nick — B
Believe It. Lima, Jamie Kern — B
Believe Me. Izzard, Eddie — B
★*Believing.* Hill, Anita — 305.42
The Believing Brain. Shermer, Michael — 153.4
Believing Is Seeing. Morris, Errol — 770.9
BELIZE
   Marcum, Diana. *The Fallen Stones* — B
Belkin, Lisa
   Genealogy of a Murder — 362.88
BELL, ALEXANDER GRAHAM, 1847-1922
   Gray, Charlotte. ★*Reluctant Genius* — 920
Bell, Alice R.
   Our Biggest Experiment — 363.738
BELL, BERT, 1894-1959
   Eisenberg, John. *The League* — 796.332
BELL, BOBBY
   Kalb, Bess. ★*Nobody Will Tell You This but Me* — 306.874
Bell, Darrin
   ★*The Talk* — 741.5
BELL, DARRIN
   Bell, Darrin. ★*The Talk* — 741.5
BELL, GERTRUDE LOWTHIAN, 1868-1926
   Howell, Georgina. *Gertrude Bell* — B
   Wallach, Janet. *Desert Queen* — B
Bell, Jim
   The Interstellar Age — 919
Bell, Julian
   Van Gogh — B
Bell, Laura
   Claiming Ground — B
BELL, LAURA, 1954-
   Bell, Laura. *Claiming Ground* — B
BELL, MABEL HUBBARD, 1857-1923
   Gray, Charlotte. ★*Reluctant Genius* — 920
Bell, Madison Smartt
   Child of Light — B
   Toussaint Louverture — B
Bell, W. Kamau
   ★*Do the Work!* — 305.8
Bell-Scott, Patricia
   The Firebrand and the First Lady — 920
Bella Figura. Mohammadi, Kamin — 641.01
Bella Tuscany. Mayes, Frances — 945
Bella, Timothy
   Barkley — B
Bellamy, Andrea
   Small-Space Vegetable Gardens — 635
BELLAMY, RICHARD
   Stein, Judith E. *Eye of the Sixties* — B
BELLE EPOQUE (1871-1914)
   Barnes, Julian. *The Man in the Red Coat* — B
   Begley, Adam. *The Great Nadar* — B
   King, Greg. *Twilight of Empire* — 943.6
   Walsh, Stephen. ★*Debussy* — B
   Zygar, Mikhail. *The Empire Must Die* — 947.08
Bellevue. Oshinsky, David M. — 362.1109747
Belliveau, Denis
   In the Footsteps of Marco Polo — 915
BELLIVEAU, DENIS, 1964-
   Belliveau, Denis. *In the Footsteps of Marco Polo* — 915
Bellos, David
   The Novel of the Century — 843
   Who Owns This Sentence? — 346.73
BELLOW, SAUL
   Leader, Zachary. *The Life of Saul Bellow* — B
Bellows, Amanda Brickell
   The Explorers — 910.92
BELLS
   Sherman, Anna. *The Bells of Old Tokyo* — 952
The Bells of Old Tokyo. Sherman, Anna — 952
★*Belonging.* Krug, Nora — 741.5
Belonging. Miller, Michelle — B

BELONGING
   Abdelmahmoud, Elamin. *Son of Elsewhere* — B
   Ahuvia, Aaron. ★*The Things We Love* — 790.1
   Bailey, Desiree C. *What Noise Against the Cane* — 811
   Bamford, Maria. *Sure, I'll Join Your Cult* — B
   Bee, Vanessa A. *Home Bound* — B
   Belser, Julia Watts. ★*Loving Our Own Bones* — 296
   Brina, Elizabeth Miki. *Speak, Okinawa* — 305.48
   Brown, Brene. *Braving the Wilderness* — 305.8
   Campoverdi, Alejandra. *First Gen* — B
   Chang, David. ★*Eat a Peach* — 641.5
   Chittister, Joan. *Following the Path* — 248.4
   Coffin, Jaed. *Roughhouse Friday* — B
   Feldman, Noah. ★*To Be a Jew Today* — 296.3
   Geter, Hafizah. *Un-American* — 811
   Gottlieb, Lori. ★*Maybe You Should Talk to Someone* — B
   Gulman, Gary. *Misfit* — B
   Gupta, Prachi. ★*They Called Us Exceptional* — B
   H, Lamya. ★*Hijab Butch Blues* — B
   Hagberg, Eva. *How to Be Loved* — 616.7
   Hudes, Quiara Alegria. ★*My Broken Language* — B
   Jamison, Leslie. ★*Make It Scream, Make It Burn* — 814
   Jun, Tasha. ★*Tell Me the Dream Again* — 248
   Lawton, Georgina. *Raceless* — B
   Marshall, Greg. *Leg* — B
   Maupin, Armistead. *Logical Family* — B
   Miller, Kei. *Things I Have Withheld* — 814
   Miller, Michelle. *Belonging* — B
   Nagassar, Rohadi. *When We Belong* — 254
   Ng, Fae Myenne. *Orphan Bachelors* — B
   Nguyen, Bich Minh. *Owner of a Lonely Heart* — B
   O'Toole, Jennifer Cook. *Autism in Heels* — B
   Olivarez, Jose. *Promises of Gold = Promesas De Oro* — 811
   Rodgers, Jodi. ★*How to Find a Four-Leaf Clover* — 616.85
   Shanahan, Charif. *Trace Evidence* — 811
   Shields, Aomawa L. *Life on Other Planets* — B
   Suarez, Ray. ★*We Are Home* — 325.73
   Thomas, Joseph Earl. *Sink* — B
   Tran, Phuc. ★*Sigh, Gone* — B
   Wagamese, Richard. *For Joshua* — B
   Wang, Connie. *Oh My Mother!* — B
   Watts, Reggie. *Great Falls, MT* — B
   Williams, Bari A. *Seen yet Unseen* — 338.4
   Wong, Carmen Rita. *Why Didn't You Tell Me?* — B
Below The Edge of Darkness. Widder, Edith — 551.46092
Belser, Julia Watts
   ★*Loving Our Own Bones* — 296
BELSER, JULIA WATTS, 1978-
   Belser, Julia Watts. ★*Loving Our Own Bones* — 296
Belsinger, Susan
   Grow Your Own Herbs — 635
BELUSHI, JOHN, 1949-1982
   De Semlyen, Nick. *Wild and Crazy Guys* — 920
   De Vise, Daniel. ★*The Blues Brothers* — 791.43
Belva Lockwood. Norgren, Jill — B
Belyea, Patricia
   East-Meets-West Quilts — 746.46
Ben & Me. Weiner, Eric — B
Ben Jelloun, Tahar
   Islam Explained — 297
Ben-Ishay, Melissa
   Come Hungry — 641.5
Bender, Michael C.
   "Frankly, We Did Win This Election" — 973.933
Bending Adversity. Pilling, David — 952.0512
Bending Toward Justice. Jones, Doug — 323.1196
Beneath A Ruthless Sun. King, Gilbert — B
Benedict, Jeff
   The Dynasty — 796.332
   Lebron — B
   The System — 796.332
   ★*Tiger Woods* — B
BENEDICT, SAINT, 480?-547?
   Butcher, Carmen Acevedo. *Man of Blessing* — B
BENEDICT, SAINT, ABBOT OF MONTE CASSINO
   Chittister, Joan. *The Monastic Heart* — 248.8
BENEFACTORS
   Gup, Ted. *A Secret Gift* — 977.1

AUTHOR, TITLE, SERIES AND SUBJECT INDEX

Hartman, Darrell. *Battle of Ink and Ice* — 998
BENEFICIAL INSECTS
  Walliser, Jessica. ★*Attracting Beneficial Bugs to Your Garden* — 635
BENEVOLENCE
  Gup, Ted. *A Secret Gift* — 977.1
Benforado, Adam
  A Minor Revolution — 362.7
★*Benjamin Franklin*. Isaacson, Walter — B
Benjamin, A. K.
  Let Me Not Be Mad — 612.8
BENJAMIN, A. K.
  Benjamin, A. K. *Let Me Not Be Mad* — 612.8
Benjamin, Arthur
  The Magic of Math — 510
Benjamin, Ruha
  ★*Imagination* — 302
BENJAMIN, WALTER, 1892-1940
  Eilenberger, Wolfram. *Time of the Magicians* — 920
Benner, Erica
  Be Like the Fox — B
Bennett, Alexander
  Kendo — 796.86
Bennett, Jackie
  The Writer's Garden — 920
BENNETT, JAMES GORDON, 1841-1918
  Sides, Hampton. ★*In the Kingdom of Ice* — 910.4
Bennett, Michael
  *F*ck Feelings* — 158
  Things That Make White People Uncomfortable — 305.896
BENNETT, MICHAEL, 1985-
  Bennett, Michael. *Things That Make White People Uncomfortable* — 305.896
Bennett, Roger
  Men in Blazers Present Encyclopedia Blazertannica — 796.334
Bennetts, Leslie
  Last Girl Before Freeway — B
Bennis, Phyllis
  Understanding the Palestinian-Israeli Conflict — 956.9405
Bensinger, Ken
  ★*Red Card* — 796.334
Benson, Herbert
  The Relaxation Response — 155.9
Benson, Michael
  Space Odyssey — 791.43
Benzakein, Erin
  Floret Farm's Cut Flower Garden — 635.9
  Floret Farm's Discovering Dahlias — 635.9
Beranbaum, Rose Levy
  ★*The Baking Bible* — 641.81
  ★*The Cake Bible* — 641.8
  ★*The Cookie Bible* — 641.86
  ★*Rose's Baking Basics* — 641.81
  Rose's Ice Cream Bliss — 641.86
Bercovici, Jeff
  Play On — 613.7
Berenbaum, Michael
  The World Must Know — 940.53
Berendt, John
  The City of Falling Angels — 945
  Midnight in the Garden of Good and Evil — 975.8
★*Berenice Abbott*. Van Haaften, Julia — B
Berens, Abra
  Grist — 641.6
  Pulp — 641.6
  Ruffage — 641.5
Berens, Kimberly Nix
  Blind Spots — 370.15
Berenson, Alex
  ★*Tell Your Children* — 362.29
Beres, Derek
  Conspirituality — 001.9
Berfield, Susan
  The Hour of Fate — 973.91
BERG FAMILY
  Berg, Elizabeth. *I'll Be Seeing You* — 306.874
Berg, A. Scott
  Kate Remembered — B
  ★*Wilson* — B

BERG, A. SCOTT (ANDREW SCOTT)
  Berg, A. Scott. *Kate Remembered* — B
Berg, Anastasia
  ★*What Are Children For?* — 306.87
Berg, Elizabeth
  I'll Be Seeing You — 306.874
BERG, ELIZABETH
  Berg, Elizabeth. *I'll Be Seeing You* — 306.874
BERG, GERTRUDE, 1899-1966
  Armstrong, Jennifer Keishin. *When Women Invented Television* — 791.45
Berg, Mary
  The Diary of Mary Berg — B
BERG, MARY, 1924-2013
  Berg, Mary. *The Diary of Mary Berg* — B
Berg, Meliz
  Dinner Tonight — 641.595
Berg, Raffi
  Red Sea Spies — 327.125694
Berg, Ryan
  No House to Call My Home — B
BERG, RYAN, 1974-
  Berg, Ryan. *No House to Call My Home* — B
Berg, Scott W.
  ★*38 Nooses* — 973.7
  The Burning of the World — 977.311
Bergen, Mark
  Like, Comment, Subscribe — 338.7
Bergen, Peter L.
  The Longest War — 909.83
  Manhunt — 363.325
  The Rise and Fall of Osama Bin Laden — 958.104
Berger, Eric
  Liftoff — B
Berger, Karen
  America's Great Hiking Trails — 796.510973
Berger, Lynn
  Second Thoughts — 306.85
BERGER, LYNN, 1984-
  Berger, Lynn. *Second Thoughts* — 306.85
Berger, Sidney E
  The Dictionary of the Book — 002.03
Berger, William
  Puccini Without Excuses — 782.1
  Verdi with a Vengeance — B
BERGH, HENRY, 1811-1888
  Freeberg, Ernest. *A Traitor to His Species* — B
BERGMAN, INGRID, 1915-1982
  Thomson, David. *Ingrid Bergman* — B
Bergner, Daniel
  ★*Sing for Your Life* — B
Bergreen, Laurence
  In Search of a Kingdom — B
  Marco Polo — B
  Over the Edge of the World — B
Bergstein, Rachelle
  The Genius of Judy — 813
Bergstrom, Lauren
  Cute & Cuddly Crochet — 746.43
  Mini Crochet Creatures — 746.43
Bering, Jesse
  Suicidal — 362.2
BERKELEY, CALIFORNIA
  Waters, Alice. *Coming to My Senses* — B
BERKMAN, ALEXANDER, 1870-1936
  Avrich, Paul. *Sasha and Emma* — 920
  Johnson, Steven. *The Infernal Machine* — 335
Berkow, Ira
  How Life Imitates Sports — 070.4
BERKOW, IRA
  Berkow, Ira. *How Life Imitates Sports* — 070.4
Berkshire, Jennifer
  The Education Wars — 371.01
Berlin. MacLean, Rory — 943.155
Berlin. McKay, Sinclair — 943
Berlin At War. Moorhouse, Roger — 943
The Berlin Wall. Taylor, Fred — 943
BERLIN WALL
  Hoyer, Katja. ★*Beyond the Wall* — 943.087

PUBLIC LIBRARY CORE COLLECTION: NONFICTION
Twentieth Edition

Kershaw, Ian. *The Global Age*	940.55
Merriman, Helena. ★*Tunnel 29*	943
Sarotte, M. E. *The Collapse*	943.087
Taylor, Fred. *The Berlin Wall*	943
BERLIN, BATTLE OF, 1945	
Beevor, Antony. *The Fall of Berlin, 1945*	940.54
Moorhouse, Roger. *Berlin at War*	943
Read, Anthony. *The Fall of Berlin*	940.54
Berlin, Edward A.	
King of Ragtime	B
BERLIN, GERMANY	
Beevor, Antony. *The Fall of Berlin, 1945*	940.54
Dugard, Martin. *Taking Berlin*	940.54
Frenkel, Francoise. *A Bookshop in Berlin*	B
MacLean, Rory. *Berlin*	943.155
McKay, Sinclair. *Berlin*	943
Merriman, Helena. ★*Tunnel 29*	943
Milton, Giles. *Checkmate in Berlin*	943
Moorhouse, Roger. *Berlin at War*	943
Neumann, Ariana. *When Time Stopped*	B
Read, Anthony. *The Fall of Berlin*	940.54
Roth, Joseph. *What I Saw*	943
Sarotte, M. E. *The Collapse*	943.087
Simon, Marie. *Underground in Berlin*	B
Taylor, Fred. *The Berlin Wall*	943
Vogel, Steve. *Betrayal in Berlin*	327.1273043
Willner, Nina. *Forty Autumns*	B
Berlin, Ira	
The Making of African America	973
Berlin, Lucia	
★*Welcome Home*	B
BERLIN, LUCIA	
Berlin, Lucia. ★*Welcome Home*	B
Berlo, Janet Catherine	
★*Native North American Art*	704.03
Berman, Ari	
Give Us the Ballot	324.6
★*Minority Rule*	305.809
Berman, Bob	
Earth-Shattering	523.1
Berman, Geoffrey	
Holding the Line	345.73
BERMAN, GEOFFREY, 1959-	
Berman, Geoffrey. *Holding the Line*	345.73
Berman, Lea	
Treating People Well	395
Berman, Sarah	
Don't Call It a Cult	361.4
BERMUDA ISLANDS	
Hamill, Kirkland. *Filthy Beasts*	B
Bernanke, Ben	
★*21st Century Monetary Policy*	332.1
BERNANKE, BEN	
Wessel, David. *In Fed We Trust*	332.1
Bernard, Emily	
Black Is the Body	305.48
BERNARD, EMILY, 1967-	
Bernard, Emily. *Black Is the Body*	305.48
Bernard, Wendy	
Up, Down, All-Around Stitch Dictionary	746.43
Berners-Lee, Mike	
The Carbon Footprint of Everything	363.738
Bernstein, Andrea	
American Oligarchs	920
Bernstein, Burton	
★*Leonard Bernstein*	B
Bernstein, Carl	
★*All the President's Men*	364.1
★*Chasing History*	B
BERNSTEIN, CARL, 1944-	
Bernstein, Carl. ★*All the President's Men*	364.1
Bernstein, Carl. ★*Chasing History*	B
Bernstein, Ellen	
Toward a Holy Ecology	223
Bernstein, Gabrielle	
Judgment Detox	158
BERNSTEIN, LEONARD, 1918-1990	
Bernstein, Burton. ★*Leonard Bernstein*	B
Berr, Helene	
The Journal of Helene Berr	B
BERR, HELENE, 1921-1945	
Berr, Helene. *The Journal of Helene Berr*	B
BERRA, YOGI, 1925-2015	
Barra, Allen. ★*Yogi Berra*	B
Pessah, Jon. *Yogi*	B
BERRIES	
Whitman, John. *Fresh from the Garden*	635.9
Berry, Daina Ramey	
★*A Black Women's History of the United States*	305.48
Berry, Erica	
Wolfish	152.4
BERRY, ERICA (WRITER)	
Berry, Erica. *Wolfish*	152.4
Berry, Jason	
City of a Million Dreams	976.3
Berry, Joanne	
The Complete Pompeii	937
Berry, Mary	
Cooking with Mary Berry	641.5
Berry, Mary Frances	
My Face Is Black Is True	B
Berry, Wendell	
The Art of Loading Brush	338.10973
Imagination in Place	814
New Collected Poems	811
A Timbered Choir	811
★*The World-Ending Fire*	818
BERRY, WENDELL, 1934-	
Berry, Wendell. ★*The World-Ending Fire*	818
Berryman, John	
Collected Poems, 1937-1971	811
Berssenbrugge, Mei-Mei	
A Treatise on Stars	811
Bertch, Jane	
The French Ingredient	B
BERTCH, JANE	
Bertch, Jane. *The French Ingredient*	B
Bertinelli, Valerie	
Enough Already	B
BERTINELLI, VALERIE, 1960-	
Bertinelli, Valerie. *Enough Already*	B
Beschloss, Michael R.	
The Conquerors	940.53
★*Presidents of War*	355.00973
Bess of Hardwick. Lovell, Mary S.	B
The Best and the Brightest. Halberstam, David	973.92
BEST BOOKS	
Kakutani, Michiko. *Ex Libris*	028
★*The Best Cook in the World*. Bragg, Rick	641.5975
BEST FRIENDS	
Caldwell, Gail. *Let's Take the Long Way Home*	B
Pick-Goslar, Hannah Elizabeth. ★*My Friend Anne Frank*	B
Pittard, Hannah. *We Are Too Many*	B
The Best Homemade Kids' Snacks on the Planet. Fuentes, Laura	641.5
The Best Land Under Heaven. Wallis, Michael	978
★*The Best Minds*. Rosen, Jonathan	616.89
Best Minds of My Generation. Ginsberg, Allen	810.9
The Best of It. Ryan, Kay	811
★*The Best of Me*. Sedaris, David	818
Best of Vegan. Hansen, Kim-Julie	641.5
★*The Best Strangers in the World*. Shapiro, Ari	B
The Best Team Money Can Buy. Knight, Molly	796.357
★*The Best We Could Do*. Bui, Thi	741.5
Bestor, Leslie Ann	
Cast On, Bind Off	746.432
Betaball. Malinowski, Erik	796.323
Bethencourt, Kahran	
Glory	779.2
★*Bethlehem*. Kattan, Fadi	641.59
BETHLEHEM	
Kattan, Fadi. ★*Bethlehem*	641.59
Betrayal. Karl, Jonathan	973.933
BETRAYAL	
Ackroyd, Peter. *The Death of King Arthur*	823
Betz-Hamilton, Axton. *The Less People Know About Us*	364.16
Blum, Howard. *The Spy Who Knew Too Much*	327.12

AUTHOR, TITLE, SERIES AND SUBJECT INDEX

Branigan, Tania. *Red Memory*	951.05
Drabkin, Ronald. *Beverly Hills Spy*	940.54
Friedman, Matti. *Spies of No Country*	327.12
Gleeson, John. *The Gotti Wars*	364.1
Lownie, Andrew. *Traitor King*	920
Macintyre, Ben. *A Spy Among Friends*	B
McMurtry, Larry. *Crazy Horse*	B
Millard, Candice. ★*River of the Gods*	916.204
Peyser, Marc N. *Hissing Cousins*	B
Pittard, Hannah. *We Are Too Many*	B
Popkin, Jim. *Code Name Blue Wren*	327.12
Ribowsky, Mark. *The Supremes*	B
Sebag-Montefiore, Simon. ★*The World*	929.7
Smith, Maggie. ★*You Could Make This Place Beautiful*	B
Sullivan, Rosemary. *The Betrayal of Anne Frank*	940.53
Van Wijk-Voskuijl, Joop. *The Last Secret of the Secret Annex*	940.53
Viren, Sarah. *To Name the Bigger Lie*	B
Vogel, Steve. *Betrayal in Berlin*	327.1273043
Xue, XInran. *The Book of Secrets*	951.05
Betrayal in Berlin. Vogel, Steve	327.1273043
The Betrayal of Anne Frank. Sullivan, Rosemary	940.53
BETS	
Walters, Billy. *Gambler*	796.092
Betsy Ross and the Making of America. Miller, Marla	B
Bette Davis. Thomson, David	B
The Bettencourt Affair. Sancton, Thomas	B
BETTENCOURT, LILIANE	
Sancton, Thomas. *The Bettencourt Affair*	B
Better Balance for Life. Clements, Carol	617
Better Boys, Better Men. Reiner, Andrew	155.43
Better Days Will Come Again. Atria, Travis	B
Better Faster Farther. Mertens, Maggie	796.42
Better Git It in Your Soul. Gabbard, Krin	B
Better Living Through Birding. Cooper, Christian	B
Better Living Through Origami. Baard, Nellianna van den	736.982
A Better Man. Black, Michael Ian	305.31
Better, Not Bitter. Salaam, Yusef	B
Betts, Reginald Dwayne	
Felon	811
★*Redaction*	704.9
★*Betty Crocker Cookbook*. Crocker, Betty	641.5
Betty Ford. McCubbin, Lisa	B
Between A Rock and a Hard Place. Ralston, Aron	796.522
Between Harlem and Heaven. Johnson, J. J.	641.59
Between Hope and Fear. Kinch, Michael S.	614.4
Between Light and Storm. Woolfson, Esther	599.93
Between The Mountain and the Sky. Doyne, Maggie	B
BETWEEN THE WARS (1918-1939)	
Allen, Frederick Lewis. *Only Yesterday*	973.9
Bailey, Catherine. *A Castle in Wartime*	943.086
Bascomb, Neal. *Faster*	796.7209
Bryson, Bill. *One Summer*	973.91
Caesar, Ed. *The Moth and the Mountain*	B
Eilenberger, Wolfram. *Time of the Magicians*	920
Evans, Richard J. *The Coming of the Third Reich*	943.08
Evans, Walker. *American Photographs*	779
Fritzsche, Peter. *Life and Death in the Third Reich*	943.086
Haffner, Sebastian. *Defying Hitler*	943.085
Hett, Benjamin Carter. *The Death of Democracy*	943.085
Kemper, Steve. *Our Man in Tokyo*	952.03
Kershaw, Ian. *Hitler*	B
Kershaw, Ian. *Hitler*	B
King, David. *The Trial of Adolf Hitler*	345.43
MacMillan, Margaret. *Paris 1919*	940.3
Mazzeo, Tilar J. *Sisters in Resistance*	945.091
McNamara, Kevin J. *Dreams of a Great Small Nation*	355.009437
Moorhouse, Roger. *Berlin at War*	943
O'Brien, Keith. *Fly Girls*	920
Ohler, Norman. *The Bohemians*	940.53
Roth, Joseph. *What I Saw*	943
Sigmund, Karl. *Exact Thinking in Demented Times*	920
Snyder, Timothy. *The Red Prince*	B
Weber, Thomas. *Becoming Hitler*	B
★*Between The World and Me*. Coates, Ta-Nehisi	305.800973
Between Them. Ford, Richard	B
Between Two Fires. Yaffa, Joshua	920
★*Between Two Kingdoms*. Jaouad, Suleika	B
Between You and Me. Norris, Mary	428.2
Betz-Hamilton, Axton	
The Less People Know About Us	364.16
BETZ-HAMILTON, AXTON	
Betz-Hamilton, Axton. *The Less People Know About Us*	364.16
BEVEL, JAMES L. (JAMES LUTHER), 1936-2008	
Kix, Paul. ★*You Have to Be Prepared to Die Before You Can Begin to Live*	976.1
BEVERAGE INDUSTRY AND TRADE	
Rogers, Adam. *Proof*	663
BEVERAGES	
Kurlansky, Mark. *Milk!*	637
Ramirez, Elva. *Zero Proof*	641.87
Standage, Tom. *A History of the World in 6 Glasses*	394.1
Watson, Ted Kennedy. *Ted Kennedy Watson's Guide to Stylish Entertaining*	793.2
Beverly Hills Spy. Drabkin, Ronald	940.54
Beyer, Jinny	
A Quilter's Album of Patchwork Patterns	746.46
Beyer, Kurt	
Grace Hopper and the Invention of the Information Age	B
Beyonce in Formation. Tinsley, Omise'eke Natasha	782.42164
BEYONCE, 1981-	
Tinsley, Omise'eke Natasha. *Beyonce in Formation*	782.42164
Beyond. Walker, Stephen	629.45
Beyond Band of Brothers. Winters, Richard D.	B
Beyond Belief. Pagels, Elaine H.	229
Beyond Earth. Wohlforth, Charles P.	629.45
★*Beyond Innocence*. Goodall, Jane	B
Beyond Innocence. Zerwick, Phoebe	347
Beyond Measure. Vincent, James	530.8
Beyond The Baby Blues. Fox Starr, Rebecca	618.7
Beyond The Call. Trimble, Lee	940.54
Beyond The Sand and Sea. McCormick, Ty	920
Beyond The Square Crochet Motifs. Eckman, Edie	746.43
★*Beyond The Wall*. Hoyer, Katja	943.087
★*Beyond The Wand*. Felton, Tom	B
Beyond Valor. Erwin, Jon	B
Beyond Welcome. Gonzalez, Karen	261.8
Beyond Words. Safina, Carl	591.56
The Bezos Blueprint. Gallo, Carmine	658.4
BEZOS, JEFFREY	
Baron, Martin. ★*Collision of Power*	070.4
Davenport, Christian. *The Space Barons*	920
Gallo, Carmine. *The Bezos Blueprint*	658.4
MacGillis, Alec. *Fulfillment*	381
The Bhagavad Gita. Davis, Richard H.	294.5
Bharara, Preet	
Doing Justice	347.73
Bhattacharya, Ananyo	
The Man from the Future	B
Bhattacharya, Shaoni	
The Baby Book	649.1
Bhogal, Ravinder	
Comfort and Joy	641.5
Bhutto, Benazir	
Reconciliation	297.2
BHUTTO, BENAZIR, 1953-2007	
Bhutto, Benazir. *Reconciliation*	297.2
Bi. Shaw, Julia	306.76
Bialosky, Jill	
Poetry Will Save Your Life	B
BIALOSKY, JILL	
Bialosky, Jill. *Poetry Will Save Your Life*	B
Bianco. Bianco, Chris	641.5
Bianco, Chris	
Bianco	641.5
★*Biased*. Eberhardt, Jennifer L.	303.3
Bibbins, Mark	
13th Balloon	813
Bibi. Pfeffer, Anshel	B
The Bible. Armstrong, Karen	220.09
BIBLE AND FEMINISM	
Murphy, Cullen. *The Word According to Eve*	220.8
BIBLE AS LITERATURE	
Armstrong, Karen. *The Bible*	220.09
The Bible with and Without Jesus. Levine, Amy-Jill	220.6
BIBLICAL TEACHING	
Armstrong, Karen. *A History of God*	202

PUBLIC LIBRARY CORE COLLECTION: NONFICTION
Twentieth Edition

Bernstein, Ellen. *Toward a Holy Ecology* — 223
Bolz-Weber, Nadia. *Shameless* — 261.8
Pagels, Elaine H. *The Origin of Satan* — 235
Whittle, Lisa. *God Knows* — 231
Wray, T. J. *The Birth of Satan* — 235
Bibliocraft. Pigza, Jessica — 745.5
BICYCLE RACING
Balf, Todd. *Major* — B
De Vise, Daniel. *The Comeback* — B
Hamilton, Tyler. *The Secret Race* — 796.62
Kranish, Michael. *The World's Fastest Man* — B
Leonard, Max. *Lanterne Rouge* — 796.6
BICYCLE TOURING
Fabes, Stephen. *Signs of Life* — B
Harris, Kate. *Lands of Lost Borders* — 915.804
Jenkins, Jedidiah. *To Shake the Sleeping Self* — B
Moore, Tim. *The Cyclist Who Went Out in the Cold* — 796.6
Robb, Graham. *France* — 944
BICYCLES
Petersen, Grant. *Just Ride* — 796.6
Rosen, Jody. *Two Wheels Good* — 629.227
Standage, Tom. *A Brief History of Motion* — 388
Weiss, Eben. ★ *The Ultimate Bicycle Owner's Manual* — 796.6
BICYCLING
De Vise, Daniel. *The Comeback* — B
Dietrich, Sean. *You Are My Sunshine* — B
Harris, Kate. *Lands of Lost Borders* — 915.804
Herlihy, David V. *The Lost Cyclist* — B
Jenkins, Jedidiah. *To Shake the Sleeping Self* — B
Leonard, Max. *Lanterne Rouge* — 796.6
Oyeneyin, Tunde. *Speak* — 158.1
Rosen, Jody. *Two Wheels Good* — 629.227
BICYCLISTS
Balf, Todd. *Major* — B
De Vise, Daniel. *The Comeback* — B
Dietrich, Sean. *You Are My Sunshine* — B
Fabes, Stephen. *Signs of Life* — B
Herlihy, David V. *The Lost Cyclist* — B
Kranish, Michael. *The World's Fastest Man* — B
Leonard, Max. *Lanterne Rouge* — 796.6
Rosen, Jody. *Two Wheels Good* — 629.227
Bidart, Frank
  ★ *Half-Light* — 811
BIDEN OWENS, VALERIE, 1945-
Biden Owens, Valerie. *Growing up Biden* — B
BIDEN, BEAU, 1969-2015
Biden, Joseph R. *Promise Me, Dad* — B
Biden, Jill
  Where the Light Enters — B
BIDEN, JILL
Biden, Jill. *Where the Light Enters* — B
Biden, Joseph R.
  Promise Me, Dad — B
BIDEN, JOSEPH R., 1942-
Allen, Jonathan. *Lucky* — 324.973
Biden Owens, Valerie. *Growing up Biden* — B
Biden, Jill. *Where the Light Enters* — B
Biden, Joseph R. *Promise Me, Dad* — B
Bowden, Mark. *The Steal* — 973.933
Foer, Franklin. ★ *The Last Politician* — 973.934
Martin, Jonathan. *This Will Not Pass* — 973.933
Osnos, Evan. *Joe Biden* — B
Walker, Hunter. *The Truce* — 324.2736
Whipple, Chris. *The Fight of His Life* — 973.934
Woodward, Bob. *Peril* — 973.933
Biden, Robert Hunter
  Beautiful Things — B
BIDEN, ROBERT HUNTER, 1970-
Biden, Robert Hunter. *Beautiful Things* — B
Buhle, Kathleen. *If We Break* — B
Bidwell, Duane R.
  When One Religion Isn't Enough — 261.2
The Big Awesome Book of Hand & Chalk Lettering. Rodriguez, Dina — 745.6
BIG BANG THEORY (ASTRONOMY)
Berman, Bob. *Earth-Shattering* — 523.1
Cliff, Harry. *How to Make an Apple Pie from Scratch* — 523.01
Cox, Brian. *Universal* — 523.1
Greene, B. *Until the End of Time* — 523.1

Hawking, Stephen. *A Brief History of Time* — 523.1
Hawking, Stephen. ★ *A Briefer History of Time* — 523.1
Kaku, Michio. *The God Equation* — 523.1
Kaku, Michio. *Parallel Worlds* — 523.1
Big Bets. Shah, Rajiv Janardan — 303.4
The Big Book of a Miniature House. Frisoni, Christine-Lea — 745.592
★ *The Big Burn*. Egan, Timothy — 973.911
BIG BUSINESS
Cohan, William D. *Power Failure* — 338.7
Coll, Steve. *Private Empire* — 338.7
Dayen, David. *Monopolized* — 338.8
Hiltzik, Michael A. *Iron Empires* — 385.0973
Hoffman, Liz. *Crash Landing* — 330
Hvistendahl, Mara. ★ *The Scientist and the Spy* — 364.16
Lemann, Nicholas. *Transaction Man* — 330.973
Leonard, Christopher. *Kochland* — 338.7
Linden, Eugene. *Fire and Flood* — 304.2
MacGillis, Alec. *Fulfillment* — 381
Oller, John. *White Shoe* — 346.73
Teachout, Zephyr. *Break 'Em Up* — 338.8
BIG BUSINESS AND POLITICS
Dayen, David. *Monopolized* — 338.8
Teachout, Zephyr. *Break 'Em Up* — 338.8
The Big Cheat. Johnston, David Cay — 973.933
★ *The Big Con*. Mazzucato, Mariana — 650.1
BIG DATA
Hill, Kashmir. ★ *Your Face Belongs to Us* — 006.2
Law, Keith. *Smart Baseball* — 796.357
O'Neil, Cathy. *Weapons of Math Destruction* — 005.7
Tau, Byron. ★ *Means of Control* — 363.25
Wiggins, Christopher L. *How Data Happened* — 310
Big Data Baseball. Sawchik, Travis — 796.357
Big Day Coming. Jarnow, Jesse — B
Big Dirty Money. Taub, Jennifer — 364.16
The Big Fail. Nocera, Joseph — 362.1962
The Big Fella. Leavy, Jane — B
Big Fit Girl. Green, Louise — 613.7
Big Friendship. Sow, Aminatou — 177
BIG GAME ANIMALS
Rinella, Steven. *The Complete Guide to Hunting, Butchering, and Cooking Wild Game* — 799.2
The Big Goodbye. Wasson, Sam — 791.43
Big Knits Big Needles. Impelen, Helgrid van — 746.43
★ *Big Magic*. Gilbert, Elizabeth — 153.3
The Big Payback. Charnas, Dan — 306.4
The Big Picture. Carroll, Sean M. — 577
★ *The Big Reveal*. Velour, Sasha — 792.7
The Big Rich. Burrough, Bryan — 338.2
The Big Screen. Thomson, David — 791.430973
The Big Short. Lewis, Michael — 330.973
Big Sister, Little Sister, Red Sister. Chang, Jung — B
Big Vape. Ducharme, Jamie — 338.7
Big Week. Holland, James — 940.54
BIGAMY
Sisman, Adam. *The Professor and the Parson* — 364.16
Biggers, Jeff
  Reckoning at Eagle Creek — 333.73
The Biggest Bluff. Konnikova, Maria — 795.412
Biggest Brother. Alexander, Larry — B
The Biggest Ideas in the Universe. Carroll, Sean M. — 530.11
The Biggest Prison on Earth. Pappe, Ilan — 956.9405
Bignoli, Callan
  ★ *Responding to Rapid Change in Libraries* — 020
Bignon, Guillaume
  Confessions of a French Atheist — 239
BIGNON, GUILLAUME
Bignon, Guillaume. *Confessions of a French Atheist* — 239
Bigsby, Christopher William Edgar
  Arthur Miller — B
Bilal, Wafaa
  Shoot an Iraqi — B
BILAL, WAFAA
Bilal, Wafaa. *Shoot an Iraqi* — B
Bilefsky, Dan
  The Last Job — 364.16
Bilger, Burkhard
  Fatherland — B

AUTHOR, TITLE, SERIES AND SUBJECT INDEX

BILGER, BURKHARD
   Bilger, Burkhard. *Fatherland* — B
BILINGUAL MATERIALS — ENGLISH/GERMAN
   Celan, Paul. *Breathturn into Timestead* — 831
BILINGUAL MATERIALS — ENGLISH/ITALIAN
   Lahiri, Jhumpa. *In Other Words* — B
BILINGUAL MATERIALS — ENGLISH/SPANISH
   Baca, Jimmy Santiago. *Selected Poems* — 811
   Olivarez, Jose. *Promises of Gold = Promesas De Oro* — 811
   Paz, Octavio. ★*The Collected Poems of Octavio Paz, 1957-1987* — 861
BILINGUALISM
   Oliva, Alejandra. *Rivermouth* — 305.9
BILL COLLECTING
   Halpern, Jake. *Bad Paper* — 332.7
★*The **Bill** Gates Problem*. Schwab, Tim — 361.7
***Bill** Mauldin*. DePastino, Todd — B
*The **Bill** of the Century*. Risen, Clay — 342.7308
BILLIARD PLAYERS
   McCumber, David. *Playing off the Rail* — B
Billings, J. Todd
   Rejoicing in Lament — 248.8
BILLINGS, J. TODD
   Billings, J. Todd. *Rejoicing in Lament* — 248.8
***Billion** Dollar Loser*. Wiedeman, Reeves — 333.33
★*A **Billion** Years*. Rinder, Mike — B
***Billion**-Dollar Ball*. Gaul, Gilbert M. — 796.332
BILLIONAIRES
   Elwood, Phil. *All the Worst Humans* — 659.2
   Isaacson, Walter. ★*Elon Musk* — B
   Lewis, Michael. ★*Going Infinite* — 305.5
   Rempel, William C. *The Gambler* — B
   Schwab, Tim. ★*The Bill Gates Problem* — 361.7
***Billions** and Billions*. Sagan, Carl — 500
***Billy** Martin*. Pennington, Bill — B
***Billy** The Kid*. Wallis, Michael — B
BILLY, THE KID
   Wallis, Michael. *Billy the Kid* — B
Bilott, Robert
   Exposure — 344.04
BILOTT, ROBERT, 1965-
   Bilott, Robert. *Exposure* — 344.04
Bilton, Chrysta
   Normal Family — B
BILTON, CHRYSTA
   Bilton, Chrysta. *Normal Family* — B
Bilton, Nick
   Hatching Twitter — 006.7
BIN LADEN FAMILY
   Coll, Steve. *The Bin Ladens* — 920
BIN LADEN, OSAMA, 1957-2011
   Bergen, Peter L. *Manhunt* — 363.325
   Bergen, Peter L. *The Rise and Fall of Osama Bin Laden* — 958.104
   Coll, Steve. *The Bin Ladens* — 920
   Coll, Steve. ★*Ghost Wars* — 958.104
   O'Neill, Robert. *The Operator* — B
   Owen, Mark. *No Easy Day* — B
   Wallace, Chris. *Countdown Bin Laden* — 958.104
*The **Bin** Ladens*. Coll, Steve — 920
***Bing** Crosby*. Giddins, Gary — B
***Bing** Crosby*. Giddins, Gary — B
***Bing** Crosby (Gary Giddins)* [Series]. Giddins, Gary — B
***Binge** Times*. Hayes, Dade — 384.55
Bingen, Steven
   Easy Rider — 791.4372
Bingham, Clara
   Witness to the Revolution — 303.48
Bingham, Hiram
   ★*Lost City of the Incas* — 985
BINGHAM, HIRAM, 1875-1956
   Adams, Mark. *Turn Right at Machu Picchu* — 985
   Bingham, Hiram. ★*Lost City of the Incas* — 985
   Heaney, Christopher. *Cradle of Gold* — B
BINION, TED, DIED 1998
   McManus, James. ★*Positively Fifth Street* — 795.41
Binyon, T. J.
   Pushkin — B
BIOCHEMISTRY
   Cech, Thomas. *The Catalyst* — 572.8

   Harrington, Anne. *Mind Fixers* — 616.89
   Twilley, Nicola. ★*Frostbite* — 621
BIOCHEMISTS
   Kariko, Katalin. *Breaking Through* — B
BIODEGRADATION
   Doughty, Caitlin. *Will My Cat Eat My Eyeballs?* — 306.9
   Roman, Joe. *Eat, Poop, Die* — 577
BIODIVERSITY
   Attenborough, David. *A Life on Our Planet* — 508
   Jabr, Ferris. ★*Becoming Earth* — 570.1
   Rhodes, Richard. *Scientist* — B
   Saladino, Dan. *Eating to Extinction* — 641.3
   Struzik, Edward. *Swamplands* — 577.68
   Turvey, Samuel. ★*The Tomb of the Mili Mongga* — 398.24
   Wilson, Edward O. *The Diversity of Life* — 333.95
   Wilson, Edward O. *A Window on Eternity* — 333.95
   Wohlleben, Peter. *The Secret Wisdom of Nature* — 508
   Zimmer, Carl. *Life's Edge* — 570
BIODIVERSITY CONSERVATION
   Hiss, Tony. ★*Rescuing the Planet* — 333.75
   Wilson, Edward O. *Half-Earth* — 333.95
BIOETHICS
   Rieder, Travis. *In Pain* — 362.29
   Skloot, Rebecca. ★*The Immortal Life of Henrietta Lacks* — B
BIOGEOCHEMICAL CYCLES
   Townsend, Alan R. ★*This Ordinary Stardust* — B
BIOGEOGRAPHY
   Rawlence, Ben. *The Treeline* — 577.3
   Rhodes, Richard. *Scientist* — B
BIOGRAPHERS
   Caro, Robert A. ★*Working* — B
   Rowland, Ingrid D. *The Collector of Lives* — B
BIOGRAPHICAL COMICS
   Delisle, Guy. *Hostage* — 741.5
   Guibert, Emmanuel. *Alan's War* — 741.5
   Hesse, Maria. ★*Frida Kahlo* — 741.5
   Krimstein, Ken. *When I Grow Up* — 741.5
   Kupperman, Michael. *All the Answers* — 741.5
   Ottaviani, Jim. *Hawking* — 741.5
   Santiago, Wilfred. *"21"* — 741.5
   Spiegelman, Art. *Co-Mix* — 741.5
   Spiegelman, Art. *In the Shadow of No Towers* — 741.5
   Voloj, Julian. *Ghetto Brother* — 741.5
BIOGRAPHIES
   Abbott, Karen. *American Rose* — B
   Ackerman, Diane. ★*The Zookeeper's Wife* — 940.53
   Ackmann, Martha. ★*These Fevered Days* — B
   Ackroyd, Peter. *Charlie Chaplin* — B
   Adams, John. *Hallelujah Junction* — B
   Ahamed, Liaquat. *Lords of Finance* — 920
   Albers, Patricia. *Joan Mitchell* — B
   Albracht, William. *Abandoned in Hell* — 959.704
   Alden, Ginger. *Elvis and Ginger* — B
   Alderton, Dolly. *Everything I Know About Love* — B
   Aldrin, Buzz. *No Dream Is Too High* — B
   Alexander, Larry. *Biggest Brother* — B
   Alexander, Paul. *Bitter Crop* — B
   Alford, Henry. *And Then We Danced* — 792.8
   Alford, Terry. *Fortune's Fool* — B
   Ali, Wajahat. *Go Back to Where You Came From* — B
   Alinder, Mary Street. *Ansel Adams* — B
   Allgor, Catherine. *A Perfect Union* — B
   Alter, Jonathan. *His Very Best* — B
   Ambrose, Stephen E. *The Victors* — 940.54
   Anand, Anita. *The Patient Assassin* — B
   Andersen, Christopher P. *The Good Son* — B
   Andersen, Jens. *Astrid Lindgren* — B
   Anderson, Jon Lee. *Che Guevara* — B
   Andrews-Dyer, Helena. *Reclaiming Her Time* — B
   Angelou, Maya. *A Song Flung up to Heaven* — B
   Anolik, Lili. *Hollywood's Eve* — B
   Anthony, Carl Sferrazza. *Camera Girl* — B
   Anthony, Carl Sferrazza. *Nellie Taft* — B
   Aptowicz, Cristin O'Keefe. *Dr. Mutter's Marvels* — B
   Arana, Marie. *American Chica* — B
   Arana, Marie. *Bolivar* — B
   Arkin, Alan. *An Improvised Life* — B
   Armstrong, Karen. *Buddha* — B

PUBLIC LIBRARY CORE COLLECTION: NONFICTION
Twentieth Edition

Armstrong, Karen. *Muhammad*	B
Armstrong, Louis. *Louis Armstrong, in His Own Words*	B
Arrington, Leonard J. *Brigham Young*	B
Arsenault, Raymond. *John Lewis*	B
Asbridge, Thomas S. *The Greatest Knight*	942.03
Asbrink, Elisabeth. *And in the Vienna Woods the Trees Remain*	B
Asher, Zain E. *Where the Children Take Us*	942.1
Askwith, Richard. *Unbreakable*	B
Atria, Travis. *Better Days Will Come Again*	B
Attwell, David. *J. M. Coetzee and the Life of Writing*	823
Atwood, Margaret. *In Other Worlds*	813
Au-Yeung, Angel. *Wonder Boy*	B
Augustine. *Confessions*	B
Auletta, Ken. *Media Man*	B
Auster, Paul. *Burning Boy*	B
Avlon, John P. *Washington's Farewell*	973.4
Babb, Valerie Melissa. *The Book of James*	B
Bacall, Lauren. *By Myself and Then Some*	B
Baier, Bret. *Three Days in January*	B
Baier, Bret. *To Rescue the Constitution*	973.4
Baime, A. J. *The Accidental President*	B
Bair, Deirdre. *Al Capone*	B
Bair, Deirdre. *Saul Steinberg*	B
Baird, Julia. ★*Victoria the Queen*	B
Baker, Deborah. *The Convert*	B
Baker, Peter. *The Man Who Ran Washington*	B
Bakewell, Sarah. ★*At the Existentialist Cafe*	920
Bakewell, Sarah. *How to Live—Or—A Life of Montaigne*	B
Balf, Todd. *Major*	B
Ball, Lucille. *Love, Lucy*	B
Ball, Molly. ★*Pelosi*	B
Bamberger, Michael. *The Second Life of Tiger Woods*	B
Barbree, Jay. *Neil Armstrong*	B
Barnes, Julian. *The Man in the Red Coat*	B
Barra, Allen. *Inventing Wyatt Earp*	B
Barra, Allen. ★*The Last Coach*	B
Barra, Allen. ★*Yogi Berra*	B
Barry, John M. *Roger Williams and the Creation of the American Soul*	974.5
Barthel, Joan. *American Saint*	B
Bartlett, Rosamund. ★*Tolstoy*	B
Basbanes, Nicholas A. ★*Cross of Snow*	B
Basie, Count. *Good Morning Blues*	B
Basinger, Jeanine. *The Star Machine*	384
Bass, Rick. *Why I Came West*	333.78
Bate, Jonathan. *Radical Wordsworth*	B
Beeman, Richard R. *Our Lives, Our Fortunes and Our Sacred Honor*	973.3
Begley, Adam. *The Great Nadar*	B
Bego, Mark. *Aretha Franklin*	B
Behar, Richard. *Madoff*	364.16
Belafonte, Harry. ★*My Song*	782.42164
Bell, Julian. *Van Gogh*	B
Bell, Madison Smartt. *Child of Light*	B
Bell, Madison Smartt. *Toussaint Louverture*	B
Bella, Timothy. *Barkley*	B
Benedict, Jeff. *Lebron*	B
Benedict, Jeff. ★*Tiger Woods*	B
Benner, Erica. *Be Like the Fox*	B
Bennetts, Leslie. *Last Girl Before Freeway*	B
Berg, A. Scott. *Kate Remembered*	B
Berg, A. Scott. ★*Wilson*	B
Bergen, Peter L. *The Rise and Fall of Osama Bin Laden*	958.104
Berger, William. *Puccini Without Excuses*	782.1
Berger, William. *Verdi with a Vengeance*	B
Bergner, Daniel. ★*Sing for Your Life*	B
Bergreen, Laurence. *In Search of a Kingdom*	B
Bergreen, Laurence. *Marco Polo*	B
Bergstein, Rachelle. *The Genius of Judy*	813
Berlin, Edward A. *King of Ragtime*	B
Berlin, Lucia. *Welcome Home*	B
Bernard, Emily. *Black Is the Body*	305.48
Bernstein, Burton. ★*Leonard Bernstein*	B
Berry, Mary Frances. *My Face Is Black Is True*	B
Beyer, Kurt. *Grace Hopper and the Invention of the Information Age*	B
Bhattacharya, Ananyo. *The Man from the Future*	B
Bhutto, Benazir. *Reconciliation*	297.2
Biden, Joseph R. *Promise Me, Dad*	B
Bigsby, Christopher William Edgar. *Arthur Miller*	B
Binyon, T. J. *Pushkin*	B
Bird, Kai. *American Prometheus*	B
Bird, Kai. *The Outlier*	973.926
Birdsall, John. *The Man Who Ate Too Much*	B
Biskind, Peter. *Star*	B
Bix, Herbert P. *Hirohito and the Making of Modern Japan*	B
Bjork, Daniel W. *B.F. Skinner*	B
Black Elk. *Black Elk Speaks*	B
Black, Alexandra. *Scientists Who Changed History*	509.22
Black, Dustin Lance. *Mama's Boy*	B
Blais, Madeleine. *Queen of the Court*	B
Blaisdell, Robert. *Creating Anna Karenina*	891.7
Blanning, T. C. W. *Frederick the Great*	B
Blight, David W. ★*Frederick Douglass*	B
Blight, David W. *A Slave No More*	B
Blom, Onno. *Young Rembrandt*	B
Blount, Roy. *Robert E. Lee*	B
Blume, Lesley M. M. *Fallout*	940.54
Blumenthal, Sidney. ★*All the Powers of Earth*	B
Blumenthal, Sidney. *A Self-Made Man*	B
Blumenthal, Sidney. *Wrestling with His Angel*	B
Blunk, Jonathan. *James Wright*	B
Bobrow-Strain, Aaron. *The Death and Life of Aida Hernandez*	972
Boeheim, Jim. *Bleeding Orange*	B
Boessenecker, John. *Gentleman Bandit*	B
Boessenecker, John. *Texas Ranger*	B
Bogle, Donald. *Bright Boulevards, Bold Dreams*	791.43
Bogle, Donald. *Heat Wave*	782.42164
Bogus, Carl T. *Buckley*	B
Boles, John B. *Jefferson*	B
Bonanos, Christopher. *Flash*	B
Boot, Max. ★*The Road Not Taken*	B
Bordo, Susan. *The Creation of Anne Boleyn*	942.05
Borman, Tracy. *Crown & Sceptre*	941
Borman, Tracy. *Elizabeth's Women*	B
Borman, Tracy. *Henry VIII and the Men Who Made Him*	942.05
Borman, Tracy. *Thomas Cromwell*	B
Borneman, Walter R. *The Admirals*	B
Borneman, Walter R. *Macarthur at War*	B
Borneman, Walter R. *Polk*	B
Bostridge, Mark. *Florence Nightingale*	B
Boswell, James. ★*The Life of Samuel Johnson*	B
Boucheron, Patrick. *Machiavelli*	320.1092
Bowker, Gordon. ★*James Joyce*	B
Boylan, Jennifer Finney. *Good Boy*	B
Bradford, Sarah. *Lucrezia Borgia*	B
Bradlee, Ben. *The Kid*	B
Bradley, James. *Flags of Our Fathers*	940.54
Bradley, James. *Flyboys*	940.54
Brady, Frank. *Endgame*	B
Brady, James. *The Coldest War*	B
Brady, Patricia. *Martha Washington*	B
Branch, John. *Boy on Ice*	B
Branch, Taylor. ★*At Canaan's Edge*	323.1196
Branch, Taylor. *The Clinton Tapes*	973.929
Branch, Taylor. *Parting the Waters*	973
Branch, Taylor. ★*Pillar of Fire*	323.1
Brand, Christo. *Mandela*	B
Brands, H. W. ★*Andrew Jackson, His Life and Times*	B
Brands, H. W. *The First American*	B
Brands, H. W. ★*Heirs of the Founders*	973.5
Brands, H. W. ★*The Man Who Saved the Union*	B
Brands, H. W. *Reagan*	B
Brands, H. W. *Traitor to His Class*	B
Brands, H. W. *Woodrow Wilson*	B
Bremer, Francis J. *John Winthrop*	B
Brier, Bob. *The Murder of Tutankhamen*	B
Briggs, Julia. *Virginia Woolf*	823
Brighton, Terry. *Patton, Montgomery, Rommel*	B
Brinkley, Alan. *John F. Kennedy*	B
Brinkley, Alan. ★*The Publisher*	B
Brinkley, Douglas. ★*Cronkite*	B
Brinkley, Douglas. *Wheels for the World*	B
Brinkley, Douglas. *The Wilderness Warrior*	B
Broadwater, Jeff. ★*George Mason*	B
Broadwater, Jeff. *James Madison*	B
Broers, Michael. *Napoleon*	B
Broers, Michael. *Napoleon*	944.05
Broers, Michael. *Napoleon*	B

AUTHOR, TITLE, SERIES AND SUBJECT INDEX

Brokaw, Tom. *The Fall of Richard Nixon*	B
Brooks, Maegan Parker. *Fannie Lou Hamer*	B
Brooks, Michael. *The Quantum Astrologer's Handbook*	B
Brosh, Allie. ★*Hyperbole and a Half*	741.5
Brothers, Thomas David. ★*Louis Armstrong, Master of Modernism*	B
Brotherton, Marcus. *A Bright and Blinding Sun*	940.54
Brower, Kate Andersen. *Elizabeth Taylor*	B
Brown, Carolyn. *Chance and Circumstance*	B
Brown, Craig. *150 Glimpses of the Beatles*	920
Brown, Craig. *Ninety-Nine Glimpses of Princess Margaret*	B
Brown, Daniel James. ★*The Boys in the Boat*	797.12
Brown, David S. *Paradise Lost*	813
Brown, Jasmine. *Twice as Hard*	610.92
Brown, Mick. ★*Tearing Down the Wall of Sound*	B
Brown, Terence. *The Life of W.B. Yeats*	B
Brown, Theresa. *Healing*	616.99
Brown, Tina. *The Diana Chronicles*	B
Brown-Nagin, Tomiko. *Civil Rights Queen*	B
Browne, David. *So Many Roads*	B
Browne, E. J. *Charles Darwin*	B
Browne, E. J. *Charles Darwin*	B
Bruck, Connie. *When Hollywood Had a King*	B
Bruning, John R. *Indestructible*	B
Bruning, John R. *The Race of Aces*	940.54
Bryant, Howard. *The Last Hero*	B
Bryant, Howard. *Rickey*	B
Bryson, Bill. *Shakespeare*	B
Budiansky, Stephen. *Journey to the Edge of Reason*	B
Budiansky, Stephen. *Oliver Wendell Holmes*	B
Buford, Kate. *Native American Son*	B
Bundles, A'Lelia. *On Her Own Ground*	B
Bunker, Nick. *Young Benjamin Franklin*	B
Bunting, Josiah. ★*The Making of a Leader*	B
Bunting, Josiah. *Ulysses S. Grant*	B
Burger, Ariel. *Witness*	848
Burke, Carolyn. *Lee Miller*	B
Burke, Monte. *Saban*	796.332
Burkett, Elinor. *Golda*	B
Burlingame, Michael. *Abraham Lincoln*	B
Burns, Eric. *Someone to Watch Over Me*	973.917092
Burns, William J. *The Back Channel*	B
Burstein, Andrew. *Madison and Jefferson*	973.4
Bush, George W. *41*	B
Bush, George W. *Decision Points*	B
Butcher, Carmen Acevedo. *Man of Blessing*	B
Byrne, Eugene. *Darwin*	741.5
Byrne, Paula. *Kick*	B
Cadbury, Deborah. *Queen Victoria's Matchmaking*	941.081
Cadbury, Deborah. *The School That Escaped from the Nazis*	940.53
Caesar, Ed. *The Moth and the Mountain*	B
Caine, Michael. *Blowing the Bloody Doors Off*	B
Calcaterra, Regina. *Girl Unbroken*	B
Caldwell, Gail. *Let's Take the Long Way Home*	B
Callahan, Tom. *Arnie*	B
Callow, Simon. ★*Orson Welles*	B
Calloway, Colin G. *The Indian World of George Washington*	323.1197
Canellos, Peter S. *The Great Dissenter*	B
Cannadine, David. ★*Mellon*	B
Cannell, Michael T. *A Brotherhood Betrayed*	B
Capote, Truman. ★*Portraits and Observations*	814
Caputo, Philip. *A Rumor of War*	959.704
Carlin, Kelly. *A Carlin Home Companion*	B
Carlin, Peter Ames. *Bruce*	B
Carlisle, Clare. *Philosopher of the Heart*	B
Carlson, Brady. *Dead Presidents*	B
Carlson, W. Bernard. *Tesla*	B
Carmon, Irin. *Notorious RBG*	B
Caro, Robert A. ★*The Passage of Power*	B
Caro, Robert A. *The Power Broker*	B
Carr, C. *Candy Darling*	B
Carr, Erin Lee. *All That You Leave Behind*	B
Carretta, Vincent. *Equiano, the African*	B
Carroll, James. *Constantine's Sword*	261
Carter, Alice A. *The Red Rose Girls*	B
Carter, Ash. *Life Isn't Everything*	B
Carter, Jimmy. *Everything to Gain*	B
Carter, Jimmy. *A Full Life*	B
Carter, Jimmy. *An Hour Before Daylight*	B
Carter, Jimmy. *Keeping Faith*	B
Carter, Jimmy. *Sharing Good Times*	973.926
Carwardine, Richard. *Lincoln*	B
Cash, Rosanne. ★*Composed*	B
Casillo, Charles. *Marilyn Monroe*	B
Castor, Helen. *Joan of Arc*	B
Century, Douglas. *Barney Ross*	B
Cep, Casey N. ★*Furious Hours*	364.152
Cervini, Eric. *The Deviant's War*	B
Chabon, Michael. *Manhood for Amateurs*	B
Chafkin, Max. *The Contrarian*	B
Chang, Jung. *Big Sister, Little Sister, Red Sister*	B
Chang, Jung. *Empress Dowager Cixi*	B
Chang, Jung. *Mao*	B
Charter, David. *Royal Audience*	941.085
Chase, James. *Acheson*	B
Chen, Da. *Colors of the Mountain*	951.05
Cheney, Lynne V. *James Madison*	B
Cheney, Lynne V. *The Virginia Dynasty*	B
Chernaik, Judith. *Schumann*	B
Chernow, Ron. ★*Alexander Hamilton*	B
Chernow, Ron. ★*Grant*	B
Chernow, Ron. *The Warburgs*	B
Chernow, Ron. *Washington*	B
Chozick, Amy. *Chasing Hillary*	B
Chrisinger, David. *The Soldier's Truth*	940.54
Cisneros, Sandra. *A House of My Own*	B
Clapton, Eric. *Clapton*	B
Clarey, Christopher. ★*The Master*	B
Clark, Heather. ★*Red Comet*	B
Clarke, Thurston. *JFK's Last Hundred Days*	B
Clavin, Thomas. *The DiMaggios*	920
Clavin, Thomas. *Dodge City*	978.1
Clavin, Thomas. *Lightning Down*	940.54
Clavin, Thomas. *Wild Bill*	B
Cleaver, Eldridge. *Soul on Ice*	B
Cleveland, Pat. *Walking with the Muses*	B
Clinton, Bill. *My Life*	B
Clinton, Catherine. *Harriet Tubman*	B
Clinton, Hillary Rodham. *The Book of Gutsy Women*	920
Clinton, Hillary Rodham. *Living History*	B
Clinton, Hillary Rodham. *What Happened*	328.73
Coe, Alexis. ★*You Never Forget Your First*	B
Cohen, Andrew. *Two Days in June*	973.922
Cohen-Solal, Annie. *Mark Rothko*	759.13
Cohodas, Nadine. *Princess Noire*	782.42164
Cole, Jason. *Elway*	B
Cole, Natalie. *Angel on My Shoulder*	B
Coleman, Rick. ★*Blue Monday*	B
Collins, Gail. *William Henry Harrison*	B
Collins, Max Allan. *Eliot Ness and the Mad Butcher*	364.152
Collins, Max Allan. *Spillane*	B
Coltman, Leycester. *The Real Fidel Castro*	B
Colton, Larry. *Counting Coup*	796.323
Common. *One Day It'll All Make Sense*	B
Conant, Jennet. *Man of the Hour*	B
Connell, Evan S. *Son of the Morning Star*	973.8
Connolly, Ray. *Being Elvis*	B
Connolly, Ray. *Being John Lennon*	B
Conradi, Peter J. *Iris*	B
Conroy, Pat. *My Losing Season*	B
Cook, Blanche Wiesen. *Eleanor Roosevelt; Volume 2*	B
Cook, Blanche Wiesen. ★*Eleanor Roosevelt; Volume 3*	B
Cook, Jane Hampton. *American Phoenix*	973.5
Cook, Kevin. *The Burning Blue*	629.45
Cooper, Anderson. *The Rainbow Comes and Goes*	B
Cooper, Andrew Scott. *The Fall of Heaven*	B
Cooper, Helene. *Madame President*	966.62
Cooper, John Milton. *Woodrow Wilson*	B
Copeland, B. Jack. *Turing*	B
Cordery, Stacy A. *Alice*	B
Costa, James T. *Radical by Nature*	B
Costello, Elvis. *Unfaithful Music & Disappearing Ink*	B
Cott, Jonathan. *There's a Mystery There*	813
Courogen, Carrie. ★*Miss May Does Not Exist*	B
Cozzens, Peter. *Tecumseh and the Prophet*	920
Cramer, Richard Ben. *Joe DiMaggio*	B
Crawford, Bill. ★*All American*	B

PUBLIC LIBRARY CORE COLLECTION: NONFICTION
Twentieth Edition

Creamer, Robert W. *Babe*	B
Creamer, Robert W. *Stengel*	796.357
Crespino, Joseph. *Atticus Finch*	B
Croke, Vicki. *The Lady and the Panda*	599.789
Cronkite, Walter. *A Reporter's Life*	B
Cross, Charles R. *Room Full of Mirrors*	B
Cross, William R. *Winslow Homer*	759.13
Crouch, Gregory. *The Bonanza King*	B
Crouch, Stanley. *Kansas City Lightning*	B
Crowe, Lauren Goldstein. *The Towering World of Jimmy Choo*	391.4
Crowell, Rodney. *Chinaberry Sidewalks*	B
Cullen, Kevin. *Whitey Bulger*	B
Cumming, Laura. ★*The Vanishing Velazquez*	759.6
Curran, Andrew S. *Diderot and the Art of Thinking Freely*	194
Curtis, Edward S. *Edward S. Curtis*	770.92
Curtis, James. *Spencer Tracy*	B
Cusk, Rachel. *Aftermath*	B
D'Alessandro, Emilio. *Stanley Kubrick and Me*	791.4302
Dallek, Robert. ★*Franklin D. Roosevelt*	B
Dallek, Robert. *Harry S. Truman*	B
Dallek, Robert. *Let Every Nation Know*	B
Dallek, Robert. *An Unfinished Life*	B
Dance, Stanley. ★*The World of Earl Hines*	B
Danticat, Edwidge. ★*Brother, I'm Dying*	B
Darling, Ron. *The Complete Game*	B
Daugherty, Tracy. *Larry McMurtry*	B
Daugherty, Tracy. *The Last Love Song*	B
Davenport, Christian. *The Space Barons*	920
Davidson, Mark A. ★*Bob Dylan*	B
Davis, Jack E. *An Everglades Providence*	B
Davis, Seth. *Wooden*	B
Davis, Stephen. *Gold Dust Woman*	B
Davis, Viola. ★*Finding Me*	B
Davis, William C. *Crucible of Command*	920
Dawidziak, Mark. *A Mystery of Mysteries*	B
Dawkins, Richard. *An Appetite for Wonder*	B
Dawkins, Richard. *Brief Candle in the Dark*	B
Dawson, Kate Winkler. ★*American Sherlock*	B
De Courcy, Anne. *Chanel's Riviera*	944.9
De Hart, Jane Sherron. ★*Ruth Bader Ginsburg*	B
De Leon, Jason. ★*Soldiers and Kings*	364.1
De Stefano, Cristina. *The Child Is the Teacher*	B
De Vise, Daniel. *The Comeback*	B
Dean, John W. *The Nixon Defense*	973.924092
Dearborn, Mary V. *Carson McCullers*	B
Dearborn, Mary V. *Ernest Hemingway*	B
DeCurtis, Anthony. *Lou Reed*	B
Delany, Sarah Louise. *Having Our Say*	B
Dench, Judi. *Shakespeare*	792
Denevi, Timothy. *Freak Kingdom*	B
Dennison, Matthew. *Behind the Mask*	B
Dennison, Matthew. *The Man in the Willows*	B
DePastino, Todd. *Bill Mauldin*	B
Dery, Mark. *Born to Be Posthumous*	B
Didion, Joan. ★*The Year of Magical Thinking*	B
DiFranco, Ani. *No Walls and the Recurring Dream*	782.42164
Dilbeck, D. H. *Frederick Douglass*	B
Dillard, Annie. *An American Childhood*	B
Dillard, Annie. *The Writing Life*	B
Dittrich, Luke. ★*Patient H.M.*	616.85
Doggett, Peter. *You Never Give Me Your Money*	B
Donald, Aida DiPace. *Citizen Soldier*	B
Donald, David Herbert. *Lincoln*	B
Donner, Rebecca. *All the Frequent Troubles of Our Days*	943
Douglass, Frederick. *My Bondage and My Freedom*	B
Douglass, Frederick. *The Portable Frederick Douglass*	973.8
Downey, Kirstin. *Isabella*	B
Drabkin, Ronald. *Beverly Hills Spy*	940.54
Drape, Joe. *Black Maestro*	B
Dray, Philip. *Capitol Men*	973.8
Dregni, Michael. *Django*	B
Drury, Bob. *Blood and Treasure*	B
Drury, Bob. *The Heart of Everything That Is*	B
Drury, Bob. *Lucky 666*	B
Duberman, Martin B. *Howard Zinn*	B
Dubus, Andre. *Townie*	B
Duiker, William J. *Ho Chi Minh*	B
Dunaway, David King. ★*How Can I Keep from Singing?*	B
Dunbar, Erica Armstrong. ★*She Came to Slay*	B
Duncan, Michael. ★*Hero of Two Worlds*	B
Dunnavant, Keith. *Montana*	B
Dylan, Bob. *Chronicles; Volume 1*	B
Dyson, Michael Eric. *Holler If You Hear Me*	B
Eade, Philip. *Evelyn Waugh*	B
Ebert, Roger. *Scorsese by Ebert*	B
Eckert, Allan W. *A Sorrow in Our Heart*	B
Edmonds, Chris. *No Surrender*	B
Edmundson, Mark. *Why Football Matters*	B
Edwards, Anne. *Matriarch*	B
Edwards, Bob. *Edward R. Murrow and the Birth of Broadcast Journalism*	B
Egan, Timothy. ★*The Big Burn*	973.911
Egan, Timothy. ★*The Immortal Irishman*	B
Egan, Timothy. ★*Short Nights of the Shadow Catcher*	770.92
Eger, Edith Eva. *The Choice*	B
Eggers, Dave. *The Monk of Mokha*	B
Eig, Jonathan. *Get Capone*	364.1
Eig, Jonathan. ★*King*	B
Eisler, Benita. ★*Chopin's Funeral*	B
Eisler, Benita. *The Red Man's Bones*	B
Eizenstat, Stuart. ★*President Carter*	B
Eliot, Marc. *The Hag*	B
Elledge, Scott. *E.B. White*	B
Elliott, Andrea. ★*Invisible Child*	362.7
Ellis, Joseph J. *American Sphinx*	973.4
Ellis, Joseph J. *First Family*	973.4
Ellis, Joseph J. *Founding Brothers*	973.4
Ellis, Joseph J. ★*His Excellency*	B
Ellmann, Richard. *Oscar Wilde*	B
Emberton, Carole. *To Walk About in Freedom*	306.3
Enss, Chris. *Mochi's War*	B
Epstein, Franci. *Franci's War*	B
Erdrich, Louise. *Books and Islands in Ojibwe Country*	977
Erickson, Carolly. *Great Catherine*	B
Erwin, Jon. *Beyond Valor*	B
Essinger, James. *Ada's Algorithm*	B
Evans, R. Tripp. *Grant Wood*	B
Evanzz, Karl. *The Messenger*	B
Everitt, Anthony. *Alexander the Great*	B
Everitt, Anthony. *Cicero*	B
Everitt, Anthony. *Hadrian and the Triumph of Rome*	B
Eyman, Scott. *Cary Grant*	B
Eyman, Scott. *Charlie Chaplin vs. America*	B
Eyman, Scott. *Empire of Dreams*	B
Eyman, Scott. *John Wayne*	B
Fagone, Jason. *The Woman Who Smashed Codes*	B
Fairweather, Jack. *The Volunteer*	B
Farley, Audrey Clare. *The Unfit Heiress*	B
Farrell, John A. *Clarence Darrow*	B
Farrell, John A. ★*Richard Nixon*	B
Farrell, John A. *Ted Kennedy*	B
Fauber, L. S. *Heaven on Earth*	B
Feaver, William. ★*The Lives of Lucian Freud*	B
Feinstein, Adam. *Pablo Neruda*	B
Feinstein, Michael. *The Gershwins and Me*	782.42164
Felder, Deborah G. *The American Women's Almanac*	305.40973
Feldman, Deborah. *Unorthodox*	B
Feldman, Noah. *The Three Lives of James Madison*	B
Feldstein, Mark Avrom. *Poisoning the Press*	973.924092
Fellman, Michael. *The Making of Robert E. Lee*	B
Ferguson, Niall. *Kissinger*	973.924
Fernandez-Armesto, Felipe. ★*Amerigo*	B
Fernando, S. H., Jr. *From the Streets of Shaolin*	782.421
Fiennes, Ranulph. *Shackleton*	B
Fingeroth, Danny. *A Marvelous Life*	741.5
Finkel, David. *The Good Soldiers*	956.7044
Finkel, Michael. *The Art Thief*	364.1628
Finkel, Michael. *The Stranger in the Woods*	B
Finkelman, Paul. *Millard Fillmore*	B
Fischer, David Hackett. *Champlain's Dream*	B
Fischer, Paul. *A Kim Jong-Il Production*	791.43
Fischer, Paul. *The Man Who Invented Motion Pictures*	791.43
Fitzgerald, Matt. *Iron War*	796.42
Fitzharris, Lindsey. *The Butchering Art*	B
Fleming, Melissa. *A Hope More Powerful Than the Sea*	956.9104
Flexner, James Thomas. *George Washington and the New Nation, 1783-1793*	973.4

AUTHOR, TITLE, SERIES AND SUBJECT INDEX

Flexner, James Thomas. *George Washington*	B
Fogerty, John. *Fortunate Son*	B
Forbes, Nancy. *Faraday, Maxwell, and the Electromagnetic Field*	B
Ford, Ashley C. ★*Somebody's Daughter*	B
Ford, Tanisha C. *Our Secret Society*	B
Foreman, Amanda. *Georgiana, Duchess of Devonshire*	B
Forgosh, Linda B. *Louis Bamberger*	B
Fox, Margalit. *The Talented Mrs. Mandelbaum*	364.1
Frank, Barney. *Frank*	B
Frank, Jeffrey. *The Trials of Harry S. Truman*	973.918
Frank, Joseph. ★*Dostoevsky*	B
Frank, Lone. *The Pleasure Shock*	616.8
Franklin, Benjamin. ★*The Autobiography of Benjamin Franklin*	B
Franklin, Benjamin. ★*Autobiography, Poor Richard, and Later Writings*	973.2
Franklin, Benjamin. *The Compleated Autobiography*	B
Franklin, John Hope. *In Search of the Promised Land*	929
Franklin, Jonathan. *438 Days*	910.91
Franklin, Jonathan. *A Wild Idea*	B
Franklin, Ruth. *Shirley Jackson*	B
Franklin, Sara B. ★*The Editor*	B
Fraser, Antonia. *Love and Louis XIV*	B
Fraser, Antonia. *Marie Antoinette*	B
Fraser, Antonia. *Mary, Queen of Scots*	B
Fraser, Antonia. ★*The Wives of Henry VIII*	942.05
Fraser, Caroline. ★*Prairie Fires*	B
Fraser, Rebecca. *The Mayflower*	974.4
Fredriksen, Paula. *Jesus of Nazareth, King of the Jews*	B
Freeman, Douglas Southall. *Lee*	B
Freeman, Hadley. *House of Glass*	B
Freeman, Sally Mott. *The Jersey Brothers*	920
French, Patrick. *The World Is What It Is*	B
Frenkel, Francoise. *A Bookshop in Berlin*	B
Frey, Julia Bloch. *Toulouse-Lautrec*	B
Fried, Stephen. *Rush*	B
Friedman, Maurice S. *Encounter on the Narrow Ridge*	B
Friedwald, Will. ★*Sinatra! the Song Is You*	782.42164
Friedwald, Will. *Straighten up and Fly Right*	782.42164
Fuhrmann, Joseph T. *Rasputin*	B
Fuller, Alexandra. *Don't Let's Go to the Dogs Tonight*	B
Futterman, Matthew. *Running to the Edge*	796.42071
Gabbard, Krin. *Better Git It in Your Soul*	B
Gabler, Neal. ★*Against the Wind*	B
Gabler, Neal. *Catching the Wind*	B
Gabler, Neal. *Walt Disney*	B
Gabriel, Mary. *Madonna*	B
Gage, Beverly. *G-Man*	B
Gallego, Ruben. *They Called Us*	956.7044
Gandhi. *An Autobiography*	B
Garcia, Mayte. *The Most Beautiful*	920
Gardiner, John Eliot. *Bach*	B
Garelick, Rhonda K. *Mademoiselle*	B
Garrow, David J. *Rising Star*	B
Gary, Amy. *In the Great Green Room*	813
Gaskell, Elizabeth Cleghorn. *The Life of Charlotte Bronte*	B
Gates, Henry Louis. *Colored People*	B
Gavin, James. ★*Stormy Weather*	782.42164
Gay, Peter. *Freud*	B
Gaye, Jan. *After the Dance*	B
Geck, Martin. ★*Johann Sebastian Bach*	780.92
Gefter, Philip. *What Becomes a Legend Most*	B
Gehring, Wes D. *James Dean*	B
Gelles, David. *The Man Who Broke Capitalism*	330.12
George-Warren, Holly. ★*Janis*	B
Gerwarth, Robert. *Hitler's Hangman*	B
Gewen, Barry. ★*The Inevitability of Tragedy*	B
Ghez, Didier. *The Hidden Art of Disney's Golden Age*	741.5
Gibson, Larry S. *Young Thurgood*	B
Giddings, Paula. *Ida*	B
Giddins, Gary. *Bing Crosby*	B
Giddins, Gary. *Bing Crosby*	B
Gienapp, William E. *Abraham Lincoln and Civil War America*	B
Gilbert, Elizabeth. *Eat, Pray, Love*	B
Gildea, William. *The Longest Fight*	B
Gilder, Ginny. *Course Correction*	797.12
Gill, Anton. *Art Lover*	B
Gillette, Michael L. *Lady Bird Johnson*	B
Gilliam, Dorothy Butler. *Trailblazer*	B
Gillon, Steven M. *America's Reluctant Prince*	B
Ginzberg, Lori D. *Elizabeth Cady Stanton*	B
Glaude, Eddie S. *Begin Again*	305.800973
Glendinning, Victoria. *Leonard Woolf*	B
Goessel, Tracey. *The First King of Hollywood*	B
Goldberger, Paul. *Building Art*	B
Goldfarb, Bruce. ★*18 Tiny Deaths*	B
Goldsmith, Martin. *The Inextinguishable Symphony*	B
Goldstein, Nancy. *Jackie Ormes*	B
Goldstone, Nancy Bazelon. *The Rival Queens*	944
Goldsworthy, Adrian Keith. *Antony and Cleopatra*	937
Goldsworthy, Adrian Keith. *Augustus*	B
Goldsworthy, Adrian Keith. ★*Caesar*	B
Gooch, Brad. ★*Flannery*	B
Gooch, Brad. *Radiant*	B
Goodall, Jane. ★*Beyond Innocence*	B
Goodwin, Doris Kearns. *No Ordinary Time*	920
Goodyear, C. W. *President Garfield*	B
Gopnik, Blake. ★*Warhol*	B
Gordon, Charlotte. *Romantic Outlaws*	920
Gordon, Edmund. *The Invention of Angela Carter*	B
Gordon, Linda. *Dorothea Lange*	B
Gordon, Lyndall. ★*T.S. Eliot*	B
Gordon, Meryl. *Bunny Mellon*	B
Gordon-Reed, Annette. *Andrew Johnson*	B
Gordon-Reed, Annette. ★*The Hemingses of Monticello*	920
Gordon-Reed, Annette. ★*Most Blessed of the Patriarchs*	973.4
Gorra, Michael Edward. *The Saddest Words*	813
Gortemaker, Heike B. *Eva Braun*	B
Gotch, Jen. *The Upside of Being Down*	B
Gottlieb, Robert. *George Balanchine*	B
Goudsouzian, Aram. *Sidney Poitier*	B
Graff, Henry F. *Grover Cleveland*	B
Graham-Dixon, Andrew. *Caravaggio*	B
Grande, Reyna. ★*The Distance Between Us*	973
Grandin, Greg. *Kissinger's Shadow*	B
Grandmaster Flash. *The Adventures of Grandmaster Flash*	B
Grant, Colin. *The Natural Mystics*	B
Grant, Gail Milissa. *At the Elbows of My Elders*	B
Grant, James. ★*John Adams*	B
Grant, Ulysses S. ★*The Annotated Memoirs of Ulysses S. Grant*	B
Grant, Ulysses S. *Memoirs and Selected Letters*	B
Gray, Charlotte. ★*Reluctant Genius*	920
Gray, Michael. *Hand Me My Travelin' Shoes*	B
Greenberg, Amy S. *Lady First*	B
Greenblatt, Stephen. ★*Will in the World*	B
Greenburg, Zack O'Malley. *3 Kings*	782.421649
Greene, Joshua. *Unstoppable*	B
Greenfield, Martin. ★*Measure of a Man*	B
Greenfield, Robert. *True West*	B
Greenhouse, Linda. *Becoming Justice Blackmun*	B
Greenidge, Kerri. *Black Radical*	B
Greenman, Ben. *Dig If You Will the Picture*	B
Grey, Joel. *Master of Ceremonies*	B
Gristwood, Sarah. *The Tudors in Love*	941.05
Groom, Winston. *The Allies*	940.5309
Groom, Winston. *The Aviators*	920
Groom, Winston. *The Generals*	920
Guarnere, William. *Brothers in Battle, Best of Friends*	B
Guelzo, Allen C. *Robert E. Lee*	B
Guerrero, Jean. *Hatemonger*	B
Guha, Ramachandra. *Gandhi Before India*	B
Guha, Ramachandra. *Gandhi*	B
Guibert, Emmanuel. *Alan's War*	741.5
Guillermoprieto, Alma. *Dancing with Cuba*	972.9106
Guinn, Jeff. *Go Down Together*	B
Guinn, Jeff. ★*Manson*	B
Guinn, Jeff. *The Road to Jonestown*	289.9
Guralnick, Peter. ★*Sam Phillips*	B
Gutman, Robert W. *Mozart*	B
Guy, John. *Hunting the Falcon*	B
Gwynne, S. C. *Empire of the Summer Moon*	B
Gwynne, S. C. *Rebel Yell*	B
Hadlow, Janice. *A Royal Experiment*	B
Haffner, Sebastian. *Defying Hitler*	943.085
Hagan, Joe. *Sticky Fingers*	B
Hagstrom, Robert G. *The Warren Buffett Way*	332.6
Halberstam, David. *The Amateurs*	B

PUBLIC LIBRARY CORE COLLECTION: NONFICTION
Twentieth Edition

Halberstam, David. ★*The Children*	323.1
Halberstam, David. *The Teammates*	B
Hale, Sheila. *Titian*	B
Hales, Dianne R. *Mona Lisa*	B
Hamilton, Duncan. *For the Glory*	B
Hamilton, Lisa M. *The Hungry Season*	B
Hammer, Langdon. *James Merrill*	B
Harden, Blaine. *The Great Leader and the Fighter Pilot*	B
Harden, Marcia Gay. *The Seasons of My Mother*	B
Hardman, Robert. *Queen of Our Times*	B
Hardman, Robert. *Queen of the World*	B
Hargrove, Brantley. *The Man Who Caught the Storm*	B
Harig, Bob. *Drive*	796.352
Harlan, Elizabeth. *George Sand*	B
Harlan, Louis R. *Booker T. Washington*	B
Harlan, Louis R. *Booker T. Washington*	B
Harman, Claire. *Charlotte Bronte*	B
Harrington, Joel F. *Dangerous Mystic*	B
Harrington, Joel F. *The Faithful Executioner*	B
Harris, David. *The Genius*	B
Harris, Ellen T. *George Frideric Handel*	B
Harris, J. William. *The Hanging of Thomas Jeremiah*	B
Harris, Mark. *Mike Nichols*	B
Harris, Neil Patrick. *Neil Patrick Harris*	B
Harryhausen, Ray. *The Art of Ray Harryhausen*	778
Harss, Marina. *The Boy from Kyiv*	B
Hartigan, Patti. *August Wilson*	B
Haskell, Molly. *Steven Spielberg*	B
Hastings, Selina. *The Secret Lives of Somerset Maugham*	B
Havrilesky, Heather. *What If This Were Enough?*	152.4
Hawking, Stephen. ★*Black Holes and Baby Universes and Other Essays*	530.1
Hawksley, Lucinda. *Queen Victoria's Mysterious Daughter*	B
Hayes, Elaine M. ★*Queen of Bebop*	B
Haygood, Wil. *Showdown*	B
Haygood, Wil. ★*Sweet Thunder*	B
Hazelgrove, William Elliott. *Wright Brothers, Wrong Story*	920
Hazleton, Lesley. *The First Muslim*	B
Hazleton, Lesley. *Mary*	B
Heacox, Kim. ★*John Muir and the Ice That Started a Fire*	333.7209798
Heaney, Christopher. *Cradle of Gold*	B
Hecimovich, Gregg A. ★*The Life and Times of Hannah Crafts*	B
Hegar, Mary Jennings. *Shoot Like a Girl*	B
Helm, Sarah. *A Life in Secrets*	B
Hemon, Aleksandar. *My Parents*	814
Hemphill, Paul. *Lovesick Blues*	B
Hendershot, Heather. *Open to Debate*	B
Hendrix, Scott H. *Martin Luther*	B
Henig, Robin Marantz. *The Monk in the Garden*	B
Hennessy, Kate. *Dorothy Day*	B
Hensley, William L. Iggiagruk. *Fifty Miles from Tomorrow*	B
Hepworth, David. *Uncommon People*	B
Herbert, Brian. *Dreamer of Dune*	B
Herdrich, Stephanie L. ★*Sargent*	759.13
Herman, Arthur. ★*Douglas Macarthur*	B
Hermes, Will. *Lou Reed*	B
Hernandez, Daisy. *A Cup of Water Under My Bed*	B
Herrera, Hayden. *Frida*	B
Herrera, Hayden. *Listening to Stone*	B
Herriot, James. ★*All Creatures Great and Small*	B
Herriot, James. *All Things Wise and Wonderful*	B
Herriot, James. *Every Living Thing*	B
Herrmann, Dorothy. *Helen Keller*	B
Hesse, Maria. ★*Frida Kahlo*	B
Heumann, Judith E. *Being Heumann*	B
Hewitt, Catherine. *Renoir's Dancer*	B
Heyman, Stephen. *The Planter of Modern Life*	B
Hiaasen, Carl. *The Downhill Lie*	B
Hibbert, Christopher. *Edward VII*	B
Hilburn, Robert. ★*Johnny Cash*	B
Hilburn, Robert. ★*Paul Simon*	782.42164
Hilfiger, Tommy. *American Dreamer*	B
Hillenbrand, Laura. ★*Unbroken*	B
Hilsum, Lindsey. *In Extremis*	B
Hilton, Paris. *Paris*	B
Hirsch, James S. *Willie Mays*	B
Hirshey, Gerri. *Not Pretty Enough*	B
Hirshman, Linda R. *Sisters in Law*	347.73

Hirst, Michael. *Michelangelo*	B
Hitchcock, William I. *The Age of Eisenhower*	973.921092
Hitchens, Christopher. *Hitch-22*	920
Hitchens, Christopher. *Mortality*	304.6
Hitchens, Christopher. *Thomas Jefferson*	B
Hoban, Phoebe. *Alice Neel*	B
Hobbs, Jeff. ★*The Short and Tragic Life of Robert Peace*	B
Hochschild, Adam. *Rebel Cinderella*	B
Hoffman, Adina. ★*My Happiness Bears No Relation to Happiness*	B
Hoffman, David E. *Give Me Liberty*	B
Hogan, Linda. *The Woman Who Watches Over the World*	B
Hogan, William R. *Task Force Hogan*	940.54
Hollis, Matthew. *The Waste Land*	821
Holmes, Elizabeth. *HRH*	941.085
Holton, Woody. *Abigail Adams*	B
Holzer, Harold. *Brought Forth on This Continent*	973.7
Holzer, Harold. *A Just and Generous Nation*	973.7092
Holzer, Harold. *Monument Man*	B
Honey, Michael K. *To the Promised Land*	323
Hope, Bradley. *Blood and Oil*	B
Hopkins, Jerry. *No One Here Gets Out Alive*	B
Horn, Jonathan. *Washington's End*	B
Horwitz, Tony. ★*Midnight Rising*	973.7
Howard, Hugh. *Architects of an American Landscape*	712.092
Howard, Johnette. *The Rivals*	B
Howell, Georgina. *Gertrude Bell*	B
Huang, Yunte. *Daughter of the Dragon*	B
Hubbard, Ben (Journalist). *Mbs*	B
Huffman, Alan. *Here I Am*	B
Hughes, Bettany. ★*The Hemlock Cup*	B
Hughes, Langston. ★*I Wonder as I Wander*	B
Hughes, Robert. *Goya*	B
Humez, Jean McMahon. *Harriet Tubman*	B
Hunt, Patrick. *Hannibal*	B
Hunt, Tristram. *Marx's General*	335.4092
Hurston, Zora Neale. *Dust Tracks on a Road*	B
Huxley, Elspeth Joscelin Grant. *The Flame Trees of Thika*	B
Huxtable, Ada Louise. ★*Frank Lloyd Wright*	B
Hyland, William G. *George Gershwin*	B
Iandoli, Kathy. *Baby Girl*	B
Ignotofsky, Rachel. *Women in Science*	920
Iguodala, Andre. *The Sixth Man*	B
Inskeep, Steve. *Imperfect Union*	B
Isaacson, Walter. ★*Benjamin Franklin*	B
Isaacson, Walter. ★*The Code Breaker*	576.5
Isaacson, Walter. ★*Elon Musk*	B
Isaacson, Walter. ★*Leonardo Da Vinci*	B
Isaacson, Walter. ★*Steve Jobs*	B
Isacoff, Stuart. *Musical Revolutions*	780.9
Isenberg, Nancy. *The Problem of Democracy*	973.4
Itzkoff, Dave. ★*Robin*	B
Jackson, Angela. *A Surprised Queenhood in the New Black Sun*	B
Jackson, Curtis. *Hustle Harder, Hustle Smarter*	B
Jackson, Joe. *Black Elk*	978.004
Jackson, Julian. *De Gaulle*	B
Jackson, Lawrence Patrick. *Chester B. Himes*	B
Jackson, Ted. ★*You Ought to Do a Story About Me*	B
Jackson, Troy. *Becoming King*	B
Jacobs, Alexandra. *Still Here*	B
Jacobs, Harriet. ★*Incidents in the Life of a Slave Girl*	B
Jacobs, Sally H. *Althea*	B
Jacobson, Sidney. *Anne Frank*	741.5
Jacoby, Karl. *The Strange Career of William Ellis*	B
Jarrett, Valerie. *Finding My Voice*	B
Jeal, Tim. *Explorers of the Nile*	920
Jebara, Mohamad. *Muhammad, the World-Changer*	B
Jenkins, Peter. *A Walk Across America*	917.304
Jeter, Derek. *Jeter Unfiltered*	B
Jewel. *Never Broken*	782.42164
Jobb, Dean. *The Case of the Murderous Dr. Cream*	364.152
Jobrani, Maziyar. *I'm Not a Terrorist, but I've Played One on TV*	B
John, Elton. ★*Me*	B
Johnson, George. *Miss Leavitt's Stars*	522
Johnson, Graham. *Poulenc*	B
Johnson, Joyce. *The Voice Is All*	B
Johnson, Paul. *Churchill*	B
Johnson, Paul. *Eisenhower*	B
Johnson, Paul. *George Washington*	B

AUTHOR, TITLE, SERIES AND SUBJECT INDEX

Johnson, Paul. *Napoleon*	B
Johnson, Paul. *Socrates*	183
Johnson, Victoria. ★*American Eden*	580.973
Jollett, Mikel. ★*Hollywood Park*	B
Jones, Booker T. *Time Is Tight*	B
Jones, Brenda. *Alexandria Ocasio-Cortez*	B
Jones, Brenda. *Maxine Waters*	B
Jones, Brian Jay. ★*Becoming Dr. Seuss*	B
Jones, Brian Jay. *George Lucas*	B
Jones, Brian Jay. *Jim Henson*	B
Jones, Dylan. *David Bowie*	B
Jones, Gerard. *Men of Tomorrow*	741.5
Jones, Michael K. *The Black Prince*	B
Jones, Sharon L. *Critical Companion to Zora Neale Hurston*	813
Jordan, Jonathan W. *Brothers, Rivals, Victors*	940.54
Jordan, Mary. *The Art of Her Deal*	B
Kagan, Donald. *Thucydides*	938
Kakutani, Michiko. *Ex Libris*	028
Kaling, Mindy. *Why Not Me?*	B
Kamensky, Jane. *A Revolution in Color*	759.13
Kanfer, Stefan. *Tough Without a Gun*	B
Kanigel, Robert. *Eyes on the Street*	B
Kanigel, Robert. *The Man Who Knew Infinity*	B
Kaplan, Alice Yaeger. *Looking for the Stranger*	B
Kaplan, Fred. *John Quincy Adams*	B
Kaplan, James. *Sinatra*	782.42164
Kashner, Sam. *The Fabulous Bouvier Sisters*	920
Kashner, Sam. *Furious Love*	B
Kaufman, Kenn. *The Birds That Audubon Missed*	598
Kavanagh, Julie. *Nureyev*	B
Keaton, Diane. ★*Brother & Sister*	B
Keene, Donald. *Emperor of Japan*	952.03
Keiler, Allan. *Marian Anderson*	B
Keith, Philip A. *All Blood Runs Red*	B
Keller, Helen. ★*The Story of My Life*	B
Kemper, Steve. *Our Man in Tokyo*	952.03
Keneally, Thomas. *A Commonwealth of Thieves*	994
Kennedy, John F. *Profiles in Courage*	920
Kennedy, Kostya. *True*	B
Kennedy, Michael. *Richard Strauss*	B
Kenner, Rob. *The Marathon Don't Stop*	B
Kennicott, Philip. *Counterpoint*	B
Kershaw, Alex. *Against All Odds*	940.54
Kershaw, Alex. *Avenue of Spies*	940.53
Kershaw, Ian. *Hitler*	B
Kershaw, Ian. *Hitler*	B
Khan, Mahvish Rukhsana. *My Guantanamo Diary*	973.931
Khilnani, Sunil. *Incarnations*	920
Khlevniuk, Oleg V. *Stalin*	B
Kidder, Tracy. *A Truck Full of Money*	B
Kildea, Paul Francis. *Chopin's Piano*	B
Kimball, George. *Four Kings*	B
Kimberley, Hannah. *A Woman's Place Is at the Top*	B
King, B. B. ★*Blues All Around Me*	B
King, Billie Jean. ★*All In*	B
King, Coretta Scott. ★*My Life, My Love, My Legacy*	B
King, Martin Luther. *The Autobiography of Martin Luther King, Jr.*	B
King, Maxwell. *The Good Neighbor*	B
King, Ross. ★*Mad Enchantment*	759.4
King, Stephen. *On Writing*	B
Kingston, Maxine Hong. *The Woman Warrior*	B
Kinzer, Stephen. *Poisoner in Chief*	B
Kirtzman, Andrew. *Giuliani*	B
Kiser, Joy M. *America's Other Audubon*	B
Kix, Paul. *The Saboteur*	940.53
Kluger, Richard. *Indelible Ink*	B
Knight, Philip H. *Shoe Dog*	B
Kolker, Robert Phillip. *Kubrick*	B
Koppel, Lily. *The Astronaut Wives Club*	920
Korda, Michael. *Clouds of Glory*	B
Kornhauser, Jacob. *The Cup of Coffee Club*	796.357
Kot, Greg. *I'll Take You There*	B
Kotkin, Stephen. *Stalin*	B
Kotkin, Stephen. *Stalin*	B
Kozinn, Allan. *The McCartney Legacy*	B
Krakauer, Jon. *Into the Wild*	917.9804
Kram, Mark. *Smokin' Joe*	B
Kranish, Michael. *Trump Revealed*	B
Kranish, Michael. *The World's Fastest Man*	B
Krass, Peter. *Carnegie*	B
Kraus, Dita. *A Delayed Life*	B
Kriegel, Mark. *Pistol*	B
Kriss, Alexander. *Borderline*	616.85
Kroeber, Theodora. *Ishi in Two Worlds*	B
Kunetka, James W. *The General and the Genius*	355.8
Kupperman, Michael. *All the Answers*	741.5
Kurlansky, Mark. *Birdseye*	B
Kyle, Taya. *American Spirit*	B
Lal, Ruby. *Empress*	B
Lane, Charles. *Freedom's Detective*	B
Lane, Christina. *Phantom Lady*	B
Lanegan, Mark. *Sing Backwards and Weep*	B
Larman, Alexander. *The Windsors at War*	940.53
Larson, Edward J. *An Empire of Ice*	919.8
Larson, Edward J. *The Return of George Washington*	B
Larson, Erik. *In the Garden of Beasts*	B
Larson, Kate Clifford. *Bound for the Promised Land*	B
Larson, Kate Clifford. *Rosemary*	B
Larson, Kate Clifford. *Walk with Me*	B
Larson, Kay. *Where the Heart Beats*	700.1
Laskin, David. *The Children's Blizzard*	977
Lauterbach, Preston. *Bluff City*	B
Leader, Zachary. *The Life of Saul Bellow*	B
Leaming, Laurence. *The Kennedy Men*	920
Leaming, Barbara. *Jacqueline Bouvier Kennedy Onassis*	B
Leaming, Barbara. *Kick Kennedy*	B
Leaming, Barbara. *Mrs. Kennedy*	B
Lear, Linda J. *Beatrix Potter*	B
Leavy, Jane. *The Big Fella*	B
Leavy, Jane. *The Last Boy*	B
Leavy, Jane. *Sandy Koufax*	B
Lebo, Harlan. ★*Citizen Kane*	791.43
LeDuff, Charlie. *Detroit*	977.4
Lee, Sung-Yoon. *The Sister*	951.93
Leerhsen, Charles. ★*Butch Cassidy*	B
Lees, Gene. *You Can't Steal a Gift*	B
Lemmon, Gayle Tzemach. *Ashley's War*	B
Lemmon, Gayle Tzemach. *The Dressmaker of Khair Khana*	B
Lepore, Jill. *Book of Ages*	B
Lessing, Doris May. *Under My Skin*	823
Letts, Elizabeth. ★*The Ride of Her Life*	B
Lever, Evelyne. *Marie Antoinette*	B
Levin, Gail. *Edward Hopper*	759.13
Levin, Josh. *The Queen*	364.16
Levine, Bruce C. *Thaddeus Stevens*	B
Levingston, Steven. *Kennedy and King*	920
Levinsohn, Florence Hamlish. *Looking for Farrakhan*	B
Levy, Aidan. *Saxophone Colossus*	B
Levy, Reynold. *They Told Me Not to Take That Job*	792.09
Levy, Shawn. ★*In on the Joke*	792.7
Lewis, Damien. *Agent Josephine*	B
Lewis, David L. *W.E.B. Du Bois*	B
Lewis, John. ★*March; Book One*	741.5
Lewis, John. ★*March; Book Three*	741.5
Lewis, John. ★*March; Book Two*	741.5
Lewis, John. ★*Run; Book One*	741.5
Lewis, John. *Walking with the Wind*	B
Lewis, Michael. *The Blind Side*	B
Li, Zhuqing. *Daughters of the Flower Fragrant Garden*	951.04
Lichtblau, Eric. *Return to the Reich*	B
Liedman, Sven-Eric. *A World to Win*	B
Lindwer, Willy. *The Last Seven Months of Anne Frank*	B
Lineberry, Cate. *Be Free or Die*	B
Lively, Penelope. *Life in the Garden*	B
Lockley, Thomas. *African Samurai*	B
Lockwood, Lewis. *Beethoven*	B
Loftis, Larry. *Code Name*	B
Loftis, Larry. ★*The Watchmaker's Daughter*	940.53
Logevall, Fredrik. ★*JFK*	B
Longerich, Peter. *Goebbels*	B
Longerich, Peter. *Hitler*	B
Louvish, Simon. *Monkey Business*	B
Lovell, Mary S. *Bess of Hardwick*	B
Lovell, Mary S. *The Sisters*	920.72
Lowry, Beverly. *Deer Creek Drive*	364.152
Lozano, Luis-Martin. *Frida Kahlo*	759.972

PUBLIC LIBRARY CORE COLLECTION: NONFICTION
Twentieth Edition

Lubow, Arthur. *Diane Arbus*	B
Lucey, Donna M. *Sargent's Women*	920
Lusane, Clarence. *The Black History of the White House*	975.3
Luttrell, Marcus. *Service*	956.7044
Lynn, Loretta. *Still Woman Enough*	B
Maathai, Wangari. *Unbowed*	B
MacCulloch, Diarmaid. *Thomas Cromwell*	B
Macintyre, Ben. ★*Agent Sonya*	B
Macintyre, Ben. *Agent Zigzag*	B
Macintyre, Ben. *Double Cross*	940.54
Macintyre, Ben. *A Spy Among Friends*	B
Macintyre, Ben. ★*The Spy and the Traitor*	B
Mackeen, Dawn Anahid. *The Hundred-Year Walk*	956.6
MacPherson, Myra. *All Governments Lie*	B
Maddox, Brenda. *Rosalind Franklin*	B
Magida, Arthur J. *Code Name Madeleine*	940.54
Maguire, James. *Impresario*	B
Mahoney, Richard D. *Sons & Brothers*	920
Makos, Adam. *Spearhead*	B
Malarkey, Tucker. *Stronghold*	639.2
Malcolm X. ★*The Autobiography of Malcolm X*	B
Mallaby, Sebastian. *The Man Who Knew*	B
Manchester, William. *Goodbye, Darkness*	B
Manchester, William. *The Last Lion, Winston Spencer Churchill.*	B
Manchester, William. *The Last Lion, Winston Spencer Churchill.*	B
Manchester, William. *The Last Lion, Winston Spencer Churchill.*	B
Mankoff, Robert. *How About Never—Is Never Good for You?*	741.5
Mann, Jim. *The Rebellion of Ronald Reagan*	973.927092
Mann, William J. *The Contender*	B
Mann, William J. *Hello, Gorgeous*	B
Mann, William J. *Kate*	B
Manseau, Peter. *The Apparitionists*	B
Mansel, Philip. *King of the World*	B
Manzione, Gianmarc. *Pin Action*	B
Marable, Manning. ★*Malcolm X*	B
Maraniss, Andrew. *Strong Inside*	B
Maraniss, David. ★*Barack Obama*	B
Maraniss, David. *Clemente*	B
Maraniss, David. ★*Path Lit by Lightning*	B
Markel, Howard. *Origin Story*	576.8
Markel, Howard. *The Secret of Life*	572.86
Marks, Ann. *Vivian Maier Developed*	778.9
Marnham, Patrick. *Dreaming with His Eyes Open*	B
Marozzi, Justin. *Tamerlane*	950.2
Marsh, Charles. *Strange Glory*	B
Martin, Gerald. ★*Gabriel Garcia Marquez*	B
Martin, Steve. *Number One Is Walking*	B
Martin, Valerie. *Salvation*	B
Marton, Kati. ★*The Chancellor*	B
Marton, Kati. *The Great Escape*	920
Marton, Kati. *Hidden Power*	B
Marvel, William. *Lincoln's Autocrat*	B
Marwell, David G. *Mengele*	B
Mason, Nick. *Inside Out*	B
Massie, Robert K. *Catherine the Great*	B
Massing, Michael. *Fatal Discord*	920
Matthews, Christopher. *Bobby Kennedy*	B
Matzen, Robert. *Dutch Girl*	B
Maurer, Kevin. *Damn Lucky*	940.54
Max, D. T. *Finale*	782.1
May, Gary. *John Tyler*	B
May, Gregory. *A Madman's Will*	973.5
Mayes, Frances. *Bella Tuscany*	945
Mays, Willie. *24*	B
Mazzeo, Tilar J. ★*Eliza Hamilton*	B
Mazzeo, Tilar J. *Irena's Children*	B
McBride, James. *The Color of Water*	B
McBride, James. *Kill 'Em and Leave*	B
McBrien, William. *Cole Porter*	B
McCabe, John. *Cagney*	B
McCallum, Jack. *Dream Team*	796.323
McCarten, Anthony. *Darkest Hour*	941.084
McClelland, Mac. *Irritable Hearts*	B
McCormick, Mack. *Biography of a Phantom*	782.421643
McCourt, Frank. ★*Angela's Ashes*	929
McCourt, Frank. *'Tis*	B
McCourt, Malachy. *A Monk Swimming*	B
McCourt, Malachy. *Singing My Him Song*	B
McCubbin, Lisa. *Betty Ford*	B
McCullough, David G. ★*John Adams*	B
McCullough, David G. *Mornings on Horseback*	B
McCullough, David G. *Truman*	B
McCullough, David G. ★*The Wright Brothers*	B
McDonough, James L. *William Tecumseh Sherman*	B
McDonough, Jimmy. *Tammy Wynette*	B
McDowell, Marta. *The World of Laura Ingalls Wilder*	813
McGilligan, Patrick. *Funny Man*	B
McGilligan, Patrick. *Oscar Micheaux*	B
McGilligan, Patrick. *Young Orson*	B
McGinty, Brian. *Lincoln's Greatest Case*	346.7303
McGrath, Ben. *Riverman*	797.122
McGrath, Tim. *James Monroe*	B
McKean, David. *Suspected of Independence*	B
McLynn, Frank. *Genghis Khan*	950.2
McMurtry, Larry. *Crazy Horse*	B
McMurtry, Larry. *Custer*	B
McNamara, Eileen. ★*Eunice*	B
McPhee, Peter. *Robespierre*	B
McPherson, James M. ★*Abraham Lincoln*	B
McPherson, James M. ★*Tried by War*	973.7
Meacham, Jon. ★*American Lion*	B
Meacham, Jon. ★*And There Was Light*	B
Meacham, Jon. ★*Destiny and Power*	B
Meacham, Jon. *His Truth Is Marching On*	B
Meacham, Jon. ★*Thomas Jefferson*	B
Mealer, Bryan. *The Kings of Big Spring*	B
Megdal, Howard. *The Baseball Talmud*	796.357
Meltzer, Marisa. *This Is Big*	613.25
Merry, Robert W. *A Country of Vast Designs*	B
Merry, Robert W. *President McKinley*	B
Metatawabin, Edmund. *Up Ghost River*	B
Metaxas, Eric. *Martin Luther*	B
Meyer, Dakota. *Into the Fire*	958.104
Michaelis, David. ★*Eleanor*	973.917
Michaelis, David. *Schulz and Peanuts*	B
Miles, Tiya. ★*Night Flyer*	B
Milford, Nancy. *Savage Beauty*	B
Millard, Candice. *Destiny of the Republic*	973.8
Millard, Candice. ★*Hero of the Empire*	968.04
Millard, Candice. *River of Doubt*	918.1
Miller, Char. *Gifford Pinchot and the Making of Modern Environmentalism*	B
Miller, Jim. *Examined Lives*	B
Miller, Lucasta. ★*Keats*	821
Miller, Lulu. *Why Fish Don't Exist*	B
Miller, Marla. *Betsy Ross and the Making of America*	B
Miller, Scott. *The President and the Assassin*	973.8
Minutaglio, Bill. *The Most Dangerous Man in America*	B
Miraldi, Robert. *Seymour Hersh*	B
Mitchell, Jerry. ★*Race Against Time*	364.152
Mlodinow, Leonard. *Stephen Hawking*	B
Montillo, Roseanne. *Fire on the Track*	B
Montillo, Roseanne. *The Lady and Her Monsters*	823
Montville, Leigh. *Sting Like a Bee*	B
Moody, Anthony David. *Ezra Pound*	B
Mooney, Paul. *Black Is the New White*	792.7
Moore, Charles. *Margaret Thatcher*	941.085
Moore, Kate. ★*The Woman They Could Not Silence*	B
Moore, Marcus J. *The Butterfly Effect*	B
Moore, Wes. *The Work*	B
Mordden, Ethan. *Ziegfeld*	B
Morgan, Robert. *Boone*	B
Morgan, Robert. *Lions of the West*	978
Morgan-Owens, Jessie. *Girl in Black and White*	B
Morison, Samuel Eliot. *John Paul Jones*	B
Morley, Paul. *The Age of Bowie*	B
Morris, Edmund. *Beethoven*	B
Morris, Edmund. ★*Colonel Roosevelt*	B
Morris, Edmund. ★*Edison*	B
Morris, Edmund. ★*The Rise of Theodore Roosevelt*	B
Morris, Edmund. ★*Theodore Rex*	973.911
Morris, James McGrath. *Eye on the Struggle*	B
Morris, James McGrath. *Pulitzer*	B
Morris, Marc. *A Great and Terrible King*	B
Morris, Marc. *King John*	942.033
Morton, Andrew. *Diana*	B
Morton, Andrew. *Wallis in Love*	B

AUTHOR, TITLE, SERIES AND SUBJECT INDEX

Moser, Benjamin. ★*Sontag*	B
Moser, Benjamin. *Why This World*	B
Mowat, Farley. *Born Naked*	B
Moyle, Franny. *Turner*	B
Mueller, Melissa. *Alice's Piano*	B
Muir, John. *The Story of My Boyhood and Youth*	B
Mullen, Bill. ★*James Baldwin*	B
Muller, Melissa. *Anne Frank*	B
Mulley, Clare. *The Spy Who Loved*	B
Mulley, Clare. *The Women Who Flew for Hitler*	920
Munson, Richard. *Tesla*	B
Murdoch, Sierra Crane. ★*Yellow Bird*	364.152
Murphy, Andrew R. *William Penn*	B
Murphy, Brian. *81 Days Below Zero*	940.54
Murphy, Bruce Allen. *Scalia*	B
Murray, Charles Shaar. *Crosstown Traffic*	B
Myers, Steven Lee. *The New Tsar*	B
Nagorski, Andrew. *Saving Freud*	940.53
Naifeh, Steven W. *Van Gogh*	B
Namath, Joe Willie. ★*All the Way*	B
Nasaw, David. *Andrew Carnegie*	B
Nasaw, David. *The Chief*	B
Nasaw, David. ★*The Patriarch*	B
Nathan, Debbie. *Sybil Exposed*	B
Nelson, Willie. *It's a Long Story*	B
Neu, Charles E. *Colonel House*	B
Neumann, Ariana. *When Time Stopped*	B
Nevala-Lee, Alec. *Astounding*	809.3
Newman, Richard S. *Freedom's Prophet*	B
Niven, Jennifer. *Ada Blackjack*	B
Niven, Penelope. *Thornton Wilder*	B
Noah, Trevor. *Born a Crime*	B
Nolte, Nick. *Rebel*	B
Norgren, Jill. *Belva Lockwood*	B
Norman, Jesse. *Adam Smith*	B
Norman, Philip. *George Harrison*	B
Norman, Philip. *John Lennon*	B
Norman, Philip. ★*Wild Thing*	B
Norrell, Robert J. *Up from History*	B
Norris, Robert S. *Racing for the Bomb*	B
Northup, Solomon. *Twelve Years a Slave*	B
Nuland, Sherwin B. *Leonardo Da Vinci*	B
O'Brien, Keith. *Charlie Hustle*	796.357
O'Brien, Keith. *Fly Girls*	920
O'Brien, Phillips Payson. *The Second Most Powerful Man in the World*	B
O'Connell, Robert L. *Revolutionary*	B
O'Connor, Garry. *Ian McKellen*	B
O'Connor, Garry. *Universal Father*	B
O'Connor, Ian. *Belichick*	B
O'Connor, Ian. *Coach K*	B
O'Sullivan, Emer. *The Fall of the House of Wilde*	B
O'Toole, Patricia. *The Moralist*	B
Obama, Barack. ★*Dreams from My Father*	B
Oberman, Heiko Augustinus. *Luther*	B
Odell, Amy. *Anna*	B
Odenkirk, Bob. *Comedy Comedy Comedy Drama*	B
Oliphant, Thomas. ★*The Road to Camelot*	973.922092
Oller, John. *American Queen*	B
Olson, Lynne. ★*Madame Fourcade's Secret War*	B
Onassis, Jacqueline Kennedy. *Historic Conversations on Life with John F. Kennedy*	B
Oppedisano, Tony. *Sinatra and Me*	B
Orbanes, Philip. *The Game Makers*	338.7
Osborne, Richard. *Herbert Von Karajan*	B
Osbourne, Ozzy. *I Am Ozzy*	B
Osnos, Evan. *Joe Biden*	B
Ottaviani, Jim. *Hawking*	741.5
Owens, Delia. *The Eye of the Elephant*	639.9
Oz, Amos. *A Tale of Love and Darkness*	B
Packer, George. *Our Man*	B
Page, Susan. ★*The Matriarch*	B
Page, Susan. ★*The Rulebreaker*	B
Painter, Nell Irvin. ★*Sojourner Truth*	B
Pak, Jung H. *Becoming Kim Jong Un*	B
Pakula, Hannah. *The Last Empress*	B
Palahniuk, Chuck. *Consider This*	B
Palmer, Amanda. ★*The Art of Asking*	782.42164
Palmieri, Jennifer. *Dear Madam President*	158
Pantsov, Alexander. *Mao*	B
Paradis, Michel. *The Light of Battle*	940.54
Parini, Jay. *Robert Frost*	B
Patrick, James. *Robert Johnson*	B
Patton, George S. *War as I Knew It*	B
Paul, Joel R. ★*Without Precedent*	B
Pauling, Linus. *Linus Pauling*	081
Pawel, Miriam. *The Browns of California*	920
Pawel, Miriam. *The Crusades of Cesar Chavez*	B
Payne, Les. ★*The Dead Are Arising*	B
Pearlman, Jeff. *Gunslinger*	B
Pearlman, Jeff. *The Last Folk Hero*	B
Pearlman, Jeff. *Sweetness*	B
Pearson, Roger. *Voltaire Almighty*	B
Peer, Basharat. *Curfewed Night*	B
Penn, Thomas. *The Brothers York*	942.04
Pennington, Bill. *Billy Martin*	B
Pepin, Jacques. *The Apprentice*	B
Perl, Jed. *Calder*	B
Perl, Jed. ★*Calder*	B
Perlstein, Rick. *The Invisible Bridge*	973.924
Perlstein, Rick. ★*Nixonland*	973.924
Perry, Bruce. *Malcolm*	B
Perry, Imani. *Looking for Lorraine*	B
Perry, Mark. *The Most Dangerous Man in America*	B
Persico, Joseph E. *Franklin and Lucy*	973.917092
Person, Charles. *Buses Are a Comin'*	B
Pessah, Jon. *Yogi*	B
Peters, Charles. *Lyndon B. Johnson*	B
Petropoulos, Jonathan. *The Faustian Bargain*	709
Peyser, Marc N. *Hissing Cousins*	B
Pfeffer, Anshel. *Bibi*	B
Pham, Andrew X. ★*The Eaves of Heaven*	B
Philbrick, Nathaniel. ★*The Last Stand*	973.8
Philbrick, Nathaniel. ★*Valiant Ambition*	B
Philipps, Busy. *This Will Only Hurt a Little*	B
Philipps, David. *Alpha*	956.7044
Philipps, Roland. *A Spy Named Orphan*	B
Phillips, Julie. *James Tiptree, Jr.*	B
Philpott, Mary Laura. *Bomb Shelter*	B
Pitts, Mike. *Digging for Richard III*	942.046
Pitzer, Andrea. *The Secret History of Vladimir Nabokov*	813
Pivnik, Sam. *Survivor*	940.5318
Poehler, Amy. *Yes Please*	B
Politi, Marco. *Pope Francis Among the Wolves*	282.092
Pollack, Howard. ★*George Gershwin*	B
Polly, Matthew. ★*Bruce Lee*	B
Poole, W. Scott. *Vampira*	B
Popkin, Jim. *Code Name Blue Wren*	327.12
Popoff, Alexandra. *Vasily Grossman and the Soviet Century*	B
Porter, Carolyn. *Marcel's Letters*	940.54
Porter, Cecelia Hopkins. *Five Lives in Music*	B
Porter, Linda. *Katherine the Queen*	B
Posnanski, Joe. ★*The Life and Afterlife of Harry Houdini*	793.8
Posnanski, Joe. *The Soul of Baseball*	796.357
Povey, Glenn. *Echoes*	782.42166
Powers, Ann. ★*Traveling*	B
Prideaux, Sue. *Edvard Munch*	B
Prideaux, Sue. *I Am Dynamite!*	B
Prose, Francine. *Caravaggio*	759.5
Prothero, Stephen R. *God the Bestseller*	070.5
Proulx, Annie. *Bird Cloud*	B
Pryor, Elizabeth Brown. *Six Encounters with Lincoln*	973.7092
Purdum, Todd S. *Something Wonderful*	B
Purnell, Sonia. *Clementine*	B
Purnell, Sonia. ★*A Woman of No Importance*	B
Questlove. *Mo' Meta Blues*	782.42164
Quinn, Bridget. *Broad Strokes*	920
Radzinskii, Edvard. *Stalin*	947.084
Rampersad, Arnold. *The Life of Langston Hughes*	B
Rampersad, Arnold. ★*The Life of Langston Hughes*	B
Rampersad, Arnold. ★*Ralph Ellison*	B
Randall, Willard Sterne. *George Washington*	B
Ransby, Barbara. *Eslanda*	B
Rapoport, Ron. *Let's Play Two*	B
Rappleye, Charles. *Herbert Hoover in the White House*	B
Rasenberger, Jim. *Revolver*	B
Rathbone, John Paul. *The Sugar King of Havana*	B

PUBLIC LIBRARY CORE COLLECTION: NONFICTION
Twentieth Edition

Ratliff, Evan. *The Mastermind*	B
Rees, Laurence. *Auschwitz*	940.53
Reid, Joy-Ann Lomena. ★*Medgar and Myrlie*	920
Reiss, Tom. *The Black Count*	B
Remnick, David. *The Bridge*	B
Rempel, William C. *The Gambler*	B
Renehan, Edward. *Commodore*	B
Resendez, Andres. *Conquering the Pacific*	959.9
Reynolds, David S. ★*Abe*	B
Reynolds, David S. *John Brown, Abolitionist*	B
Reynolds, Simon. *Shock and Awe*	781.6609
Rhodes, Richard. *Scientist*	B
Ribowsky, Mark. *Dreams to Remember*	B
Ribowsky, Mark. *Howard Cosell*	070.449796
Ribowsky, Mark. *The Last Cowboy*	796.332
Ribowsky, Mark. *Shula*	B
Ribowsky, Mark. *Signed, Sealed, and Delivered*	B
Ribowsky, Mark. *The Supremes*	B
Ricanati, Elizabeth. *Braided*	B
Rice, Condoleezza. *Extraordinary, Ordinary People*	B
Rice, Condoleezza. *No Higher Honor*	B
Richardson, Edmund. *The King's Shadow*	958.1
Richardson, Lance. *House of Nutter*	B
Richardson, Robert D. *Emerson*	814
Richardson, Robert D. *William James*	B
Ricks, Thomas E. *Churchill and Orwell*	920
Ridley, Jane. *George V*	B
Ridley, Jane. *The Heir Apparent*	B
Riesman, Abraham. *True Believer*	741.5
Riess, Jana. *Flunking Sainthood*	248.4
Riley, Kathleen. *The Astaires*	B
Rinehart, Lorissa. *First to the Front*	B
Risen, James. ★*The Last Honest Man*	973.92
Roberts, Andrew. ★*Churchill*	B
Roberts, Andrew. *The Last King of America*	B
Roberts, Andrew. ★*Napoleon*	B
Roberts, Cokie. *Founding Mothers*	920
Roberts, David. *Alone on the Ice*	919.8904
Roberts, David. *Once They Moved Like the Wind*	B
Roberts, Jason. *A Sense of the World*	B
Roberts, Randy. *Blood Brothers*	920
Roberts, Randy. *Joe Louis*	B
Roberts, Steven V. *Cokie*	B
Robertson, James I. *Stonewall Jackson*	B
Robeson, Paul. *Here I Stand*	B
Robeson, Paul. *The Undiscovered Paul Robeson*	B
Robin, Corey. *The Enigma of Clarence Thomas*	347.73
Robinson, Jackie. *I Never Had It Made*	B
Robinson, Ray. *Iron Horse*	B
Robinson, Roxana. *Georgia O'Keeffe*	B
Robinson, Staci. ★*Tupac Shakur*	B
Roffman, Karin. *The Songs We Know Best*	B
Rogers, Robbie. *Coming Out to Play*	B
Roll, David L. *Ascent to Power*	973.918
Roll, David L. *George Marshall*	B
Ronald, Susan. *A Dangerous Woman*	B
Rose, Alexander. *Empires of the Sky*	920
Rose, Sarah. *D-Day Girls*	940.53
Rosen, Charles. *Sugar*	B
Rosen, Jeffrey. *Conversations with RBG*	B
Rosen, Richard A. *Julius Chambers*	B
Rosenberg, Rosalind. ★*Jane Crow*	B
Rosenblitt, J. Alison. *The Beauty of Living*	B
Rosenbloom, Joseph. *Redemption*	B
Rosnay, Tatiana de. *Manderley Forever*	B
Ross, John F. *The Promise of the Grand Canyon*	917.91
Roudinesco, Elisabeth. ★*Freud*	B
Rousseau, Jean-Jacques. *Confessions*	B
Rowe, Mickey. *Fearlessly Different*	B
Rowland, Ingrid D. *The Collector of Lives*	B
Rundell, Katherine. ★*Super-Infinite*	B
Rush, Chris. *The Light Years*	B
Russell, Gareth. *Young and Damned and Fair*	B
Rynecki, Elizabeth. *Chasing Portraits*	B
Sacks, Oliver. ★*Everything in Its Place*	B
Safranski, Rudiger. *Goethe*	B
Salisbury, Katie Gee. ★*Not Your China Doll*	B
Sallah, Michael. *The Yankee Comandante*	972.91
Sampson, Fiona. *In Search of Mary Shelley*	B
Sancton, Thomas. *The Bettencourt Affair*	B
Sandburg, Carl. *Abraham Lincoln*	B
Sands, Philippe. *The Ratline*	B
Santana, Carlos. *The Universal Tone*	B
Santiago, Wilfred. *"21"*	741.5
Saul, Scott. ★*Becoming Richard Pryor*	B
Saxton, Martha. *The Widow Washington*	B
Schaap, Jeremy. *Cinderella Man*	B
Schechter, Harold. *Hell's Princess*	B
Schiavi, Michael R. *Celluloid Activist*	B
Schiff, Stacy. ★*Cleopatra*	B
Schlender, Brent. *Becoming Steve Jobs*	B
Schmidt, Thomas. *The Saga of Lewis & Clark*	917.804
Schroeder, Alice. *The Snowball*	B
Schultz, Kevin Michael. *Buckley and Mailer*	920
Schumacher, Michael. *Will Eisner*	741.5
Schwartz, David N. *The Last Man Who Knew Everything*	B
Sears, Stephen W. *Lincoln's Lieutenants*	920
Sebag-Montefiore, Simon. *The Romanovs*	947
Sebag-Montefiore, Simon. *Stalin*	B
Sebag-Montefiore, Simon. *Young Stalin*	B
Sebba, Anne. *Ethel Rosenberg*	B
Sebestyen, Victor. *Lenin*	B
Secrest, Meryle. *Elsa Schiaparelli*	746.9
Secrest, Meryle. *Frank Lloyd Wright*	B
Secrest, Meryle. *Modigliani*	B
Seierstad, Asne. *The Bookseller of Kabul*	958.1
Seiple, Samantha. *Louisa on the Front Lines*	B
Senik, Troy. *A Man of Iron*	B
Servadio, Gaia. *Rossini*	B
Service, Robert. *Lenin—A Biography*	B
Shahidi, Afshin. *Prince*	B
Shakespeare, Nicholas. *Ian Fleming*	B
Shannon, Elaine. *Hunting Leroux*	364.1
Shapiro, James. *The Year of Lear*	822.33
Shapland, Jenn. *My Autobiography of Carson McCullers*	B
Shatz, Adam. *The Rebel's Clinic*	965
Shaw, Jennifer Laurie. *Exist Otherwise*	709.2
Shawcross, William. *The Queen Mother*	B
Shearer, Stephen Michael. *Beautiful*	B
Sheehan, Jason. *Cooking Dirty*	B
Sheehan, Neil. *A Bright Shining Lie*	959.704
Sheehan, Neil. *A Fiery Peace in a Cold War*	B
Sheff, David. *The Buddhist on Death Row*	B
Shelden, Michael. *Mark Twain*	B
Sherman, Casey. *Hunting Whitey*	B
Sherr, Lynn. *Sally Ride*	B
Shields, Charles J. *Lorraine Hansberry*	B
Shipnuck, Alan. *Phil*	B
Shirley, Craig. *Mary Ball Washington*	B
Shlaes, Amity. *Coolidge*	B
Shone, Tom. *The Nolan Variations*	791.4302
Short, Philip. *Putin*	B
Showalter, Elaine. ★*A Jury of Her Peers*	810.9
Shuster, Simon. ★*The Showman*	B
Sielski, Mike. *The Rise*	B
Simmons, Sylvie. *I'm Your Man*	B
Sims, Michael. *Arthur and Sherlock*	B
Sinise, Gary. *Grateful American*	B
Sisman, Adam. *The Professor and the Parson*	364.16
Sjunneson, Elsa. *Being Seen*	362.4
Skal, David J. *Something in the Blood*	823
Skloot, Rebecca. ★*The Immortal Life of Henrietta Lacks*	B
Slawenski, Kenneth. ★*Salinger*	B
Slevin, Peter. *Michelle Obama*	B
Smee, Sebastian. *The Art of Rivalry*	700.92
Smith, Chris. *The Daily Show (the Book)*	791.45
Smith, David James. *Young Mandela*	B
Smith, Douglas. *Rasputin*	B
Smith, Jean Edward. *Bush*	973.931
Smith, Jean Edward. *FDR*	B
Smith, Jean Edward. *John Marshall*	B
Smith, Jeremy N. *Breaking and Entering*	B
Smith, Mychal Denzel. *Invisible Man, Got the Whole World Watching*	305.242
Smith, Patti. ★*M Train*	B
Smith, R. J. *American Witness*	B

AUTHOR, TITLE, SERIES AND SUBJECT INDEX

Smith, Richard Norton. *On His Own Terms*	973.925092
Smith, Sally Bedell. *Elizabeth the Queen*	B
Smith, Sally Bedell. *Prince Charles*	B
Smith, Starr. *Jimmy Stewart*	B
Snyder, Brad. *A Well-Paid Slave*	B
Snyder, Laura J. *Eye of the Beholder*	920
Snyder, Timothy. *The Red Prince*	B
Sobel, Dava. *A More Perfect Heaven*	520.9
Sohn, Amy. *The Man Who Hated Women*	363.28
Sokol, Jason. *The Heavens Might Crack*	323.092
Solnit, Rebecca. *Orwell's Roses*	B
Solomon, Deborah. *American Mirror*	B
Solomon, Deborah. *Jackson Pollock*	B
Soni, Jimmy. *A Mind at Play*	B
Sorensen, Theodore C. *Counselor*	B
Sotomayor, Sonia. ★*My Beloved World*	B
Souder, William. *Mad at the World*	813
Souder, William. *On a Farther Shore*	B
Southon, Emma. *Agrippina*	B
Sperber, Jonathan. *Karl Marx*	B
Spiegel, Maura. *Sidney Lumet*	B
Spiegelman, Art. *Co-Mix*	741.5
Spiegelman, Art. ★*Maus*	741.5
Spiegelman, Art. *Metamaus*	B
Spitz, Bob. ★*The Beatles*	B
Spitz, Bob. ★*Dearie*	B
Spitz, Bob. ★*Reagan*	B
Spoto, Donald. *The Dark Side of Genius*	B
Spoto, Donald. *High Society*	B
Spoto, Donald. *Joan*	B
Springsteen, Bruce. ★*Born to Run*	B
Spurling, Hilary. *Anthony Powell*	B
Spurling, Hilary. *Matisse the Master*	B
Stahr, Celia. *Frida in America*	B
Stahr, Walter. *Seward*	B
Stahr, Walter. ★*Stanton*	B
Staiti, Paul J. *Of Arms and Artists*	B
Standiford, Les. *Bringing Adam Home*	364.15
Stangneth, Bettina. *Eichmann Before Jerusalem*	B
Stanley, Amy. *Stranger in the Shogun's City*	B
Stanley, Bob. ★*The Story of the Bee Gees*	782.42164
Stanton, Mike. ★*Unbeaten*	B
Stark, Peter. *Young Washington*	B
Starkey, David. *Six Wives*	942.05
Starks, Glenn L. *Thurgood Marshall*	B
Stauffer, John. *Picturing Fredrick Douglass*	B
Stavridis, James. *To Risk It All*	359
Stein, Judith E. *Eye of the Sixties*	B
Steinberg, Jonathan. *Bismarck*	B
Steinberg, Jonny. *A Man of Good Hope*	B
Steinem, Gloria. *My Life on the Road*	B
Steinem, Gloria. *Outrageous Acts and Everyday Rebellions*	305.42
Stern, Jessica. *My War Criminal*	341.6
Stevens, Dana. *Camera Man*	791.4302
Stevens, Norma. *Avedon*	B
Stewart, David O. *George Washington*	973.4
Stewart, David O. *Madison's Gift*	B
Stewart, Jeffrey C. ★*The New Negro*	191
Stiles, T. J. *Custer's Trials*	B
Stiles, T. J. ★*The First Tycoon*	B
Stiles, T. J. *Jesse James*	B
Stone, Daniel. *The Food Explorer*	B
Stourton, James. *Kenneth Clark*	B
Stratton, W. K. *Floyd Patterson*	B
Strauss, Barry S. *The Death of Caesar*	937
Stuart, Amanda Mackenzie. *Empress of Fashion*	B
Stump, Al. *Cobb*	B
Sturgis, Matthew. *Oscar Wilde*	B
Suchet, John. *Beethoven*	B
Suchet, John. *Mozart*	B
Suchet, John. *Verdi*	782.1092
Sullivan, Rosemary. *Stalin's Daughter*	B
Suny, Ronald Grigor. *Stalin*	B
Swafford, Jan. ★*Beethoven*	B
Swafford, Jan. *Charles Ives*	B
Swafford, Jan. *Johannes Brahms*	B
Swafford, Jan. *Mozart*	B
Swarns, Rachel L. ★*American Tapestry*	B
Sweig, Julia. *Lady Bird Johnson*	B
Swofford, Anthony. *Jarhead*	956.7044
Sykes, Christopher Simon. *David Hockney*	B
Sykes, Christopher Simon. *David Hockney*	B
Symonds, Craig L. *Lincoln and His Admirals*	B
Szerlip, Barbara. *The Man Who Designed the Future*	B
Szwed, John F. *Cosmic Scholar*	B
Tallent, Elizabeth. *Scratched*	B
Talley, Andre Leon. *The Chiffon Trenches*	B
Tallis, Frank. ★*Mortal Secrets*	B
Tallis, Nicola. *Crown of Blood*	B
Tallis, Nicola. *Uncrowned Queen*	B
Talty, Stephan. *Agent Garbo*	940.5
Tamblyn, Amber. ★*Era of Ignition*	B
Taraborrelli, J. Randy. *After Camelot*	B
Taraborrelli, J. Randy. ★*Jackie*	B
Taraborrelli, J. Randy. ★*The Secret Life of Marilyn Monroe*	B
Taubman, William. *Gorbachev*	B
Taubman, William. *Khrushchev*	B
Taylor, D. J. *Orwell*	B
Taylor, Jay. *The Generalissimo*	B
Taylor, Stephen. *Commander*	B
Teachout, Terry. ★*All in the Dances*	B
Teachout, Terry. *Duke*	B
Teachout, Terry. *Pops*	B
Tefertiller, Casey. *Wyatt Earp*	B
Telushkin, Joseph. *Rebbe*	296.833
Theoharis, Jeanne. *The Rebellious Life of Mrs. Rosa Parks*	B
Thomas, Evan. *Being Nixon*	B
Thomas, Evan. ★*First*	B
Thomas, Evan. ★*John Paul Jones*	B
Thomas, Evan. ★*Robert Kennedy*	B
Thomas, Louisa. *Louisa*	B
Thomas, R. Eric. *Here for It*	B
Thompson, Juan F. *Stories I Tell Myself*	B
Thompson, Nicholas. *The Hawk and the Dove*	973.92
Thompson, Wright. *The Cost of These Dreams*	B
Thomson, David. *Bette Davis*	B
Thomson, David. *Ingrid Bergman*	B
Thomson, Graeme. *George Harrison*	B
Thoreau, Henry David. ★*Walden, Or, Life in the Woods*	813
Thwaite, Ann. *Goodbye Christopher Robin*	B
Tisserand, Michael. *Krazy*	741.5
Tobin, James. *Ernie Pyle's War*	B
Todd, Olivier. *Albert Camus*	B
Tolan, Sandy. *Children of the Stone*	780
Tolan, Sandy. ★*The Lemon Tree*	B
Tolinski, Brad. *Light and Shade*	B
Tomalin, Claire. *Samuel Pepys*	B
Tomalin, Claire. *Thomas Hardy*	B
Tomlinson, Janis A. ★*Goya*	B
Toobin, Jeffrey. ★*Homegrown*	363.325
Traub, James. *John Quincy Adams*	B
Travisano, Thomas J. *Love Unknown*	B
Trebek, Alex. *The Answer Is ...*	791.4502
Tresch, John. *The Reason for the Darkness of the Night*	B
Trimble, Lee. *Beyond the Call*	940.54
Trimborn, Jurgen. *Leni Riefenstahl*	B
Trump, Mary L. *Too Much and Never Enough*	B
Tubbs, Michael. *The Deeper the Roots*	B
Tucci, Stanley. ★*Taste*	B
Tumulty, Karen. *The Triumph of Nancy Reagan*	B
Turan, Kenneth. ★*Free for All*	B
Turner, John G. *Brigham Young, Pioneer Prophet*	B
Turner, Tina. ★*Happiness Becomes You*	158.1
Twain, Mark. *Autobiography of Mark Twain*	B
Twain, Mark. ★*Autobiography of Mark Twain*	B
Twain, Mark. ★*Autobiography of Mark Twain*	B
Tye, Larry. ★*Bobby Kennedy*	B
Tye, Larry. ★*Demagogue*	B
Tye, Larry. *Satchel*	B
Tyson, Mike. *Iron Ambition*	B
Ulander, Perry A. *Walking Point*	B
Ullrich, Volker. *Hitler*	B
Ullrich, Volker. *Hitler*	B
Ung, Loung. *Lucky Child*	B
Unger, Debi. *George Marshall*	B
Unger, Harlow G. *First Founding Father*	B

PUBLIC LIBRARY CORE COLLECTION: NONFICTION
Twentieth Edition

Unger, Harlow G. *The Last Founding Father*	B
Unger, Miles. ★*Michelangelo*	B
Unger, Miles. *Picasso and the Painting That Shocked the World*	759.4
Updegrove, Mark K. *The Last Republicans*	973.928
Urofsky, Melvin I. *Louis D. Brandeis*	B
Ustvedt, Oystein. *Edvard Munch*	759.81
Utley, Robert M. ★*Geronimo*	B
Utley, Robert M. *Sitting Bull*	B
Vallely, Paul. *Pope Francis*	B
Van Haaften, Julia. ★*Berenice Abbott*	B
Vargas, Jose Antonio. *Dear America*	B
Varon, Elizabeth R. *Longstreet*	B
Vaughn, Ellen Santilli. ★*Becoming Elisabeth Elliot*	B
Vella, Christina. *George Washington Carver*	B
Vitale, Tom. *In the Weeds*	B
Vogel, Ezra F. *Deng Xiaoping and the Transformation of China*	B
Vogel, Joseph. *Man in the Music*	B
Von Drehle, Dave. ★*Triangle*	974.7
Von Furstenberg, Diane. *The Woman I Wanted to Be*	B
Vonnegut, Kurt. *Kurt Vonnegut*	813
Vonnegut, Kurt. ★*A Man Without a Country*	818
Vowell, Sarah. *Assassination Vacation*	B
Wacker, Grant. *America's Pastor*	B
Wagamese, Richard. *One Native Life*	B
Wald, Elijah. ★*Escaping the Delta*	B
Waldstreicher, David. *The Odyssey of Phillis Wheatley*	B
Walker, Stephen. *Beyond*	629.45
Walker-Hill, Helen. *From Spirituals to Symphonies*	780
Wallace, Christopher. *Twentieth-Century Man*	B
Wallach, Janet. *Desert Queen*	B
Waller, Douglas C. *Wild Bill Donovan*	B
Wallis, Michael. *Billy the Kid*	B
Walls, Jeannette. ★*The Glass Castle*	B
Walls, Laura Dassow. ★*Henry David Thoreau*	B
Walsh, Stephen. ★*Debussy*	B
Ward, Andrew. ★*The Slaves' War*	973.7
Ward, Geoffrey C. *A Disposition to Be Rich*	B
Ward, Geoffrey C. *Jazz*	781.6509
Ward, Geoffrey C. ★*The Roosevelts*	B
Ward, Geoffrey C. *Unforgivable Blackness*	B
Ward, Jesmyn. ★*Men We Reaped*	B
Warren, Louis S. *Buffalo Bill's America*	B
Warren, Rosanna. *Max Jacob*	B
Washington, Booker T. ★*Up from Slavery*	B
Waters, John. *Mr. Know-It-All*	814
Waters, John. *Role Models*	B
Watson, Richard A. *Cogito Ergo Sum*	B
Watts, Jill. *Hattie McDaniel*	B
Watts, Steven. *The People's Tycoon*	B
Watts, Steven. *Self-Help Messiah*	B
Weatherford, J. McIver. ★*Genghis Khan and the Making of the Modern World*	B
Weber, Thomas. *Becoming Hitler*	B
Weiner, Tim. *One Man Against the World*	B
Weingarten, Gene. ★*One Day*	973
Weinman, Sarah. *Scoundrel*	364.152
Weintraub, Robert. *No Better Friend*	940.54
Weir, Alison. *The Children of Henry VIII*	B
Weir, Alison. *Eleanor of Aquitaine*	B
Weir, Alison. *Henry VIII*	B
Weir, Alison. *The Lady in the Tower*	B
Weir, Alison. *The Life of Elizabeth I*	B
Weir, Alison. *The Lost Tudor Princess*	B
Weir, Alison. *The Six Wives of Henry VIII*	942.05
Weller, Sam. *The Bradbury Chronicles*	B
Weller, Sheila. *Carrie Fisher*	B
Welteroth, Elaine. *More Than Enough*	B
Welty, Eudora. *One Writer's Beginnings*	B
Wert, Jeffry D. *Cavalryman of the Lost Cause*	B
Wert, Jeffry D. *Custer*	B
Weschler, Lawrence. *And How Are You, Dr. Sacks?*	B
West, Lindy. *Shrill*	818
Wexler, Stuart. *Killing King*	323.092
Wheelan, Joseph. ★*Terrible Swift Sword*	B
Wheen, Francis. *Karl Marx*	B
White, Charles. *The Life and Times of Little Richard*	B
White, Elizabeth B. ★*The Counterfeit Countess*	940.53
White, Ronald C. *A. Lincoln*	B
White, Ronald C. ★*American Ulysses*	B
White, Ronald C. *Lincoln in Private*	B
White, Ronald C. *On Great Fields*	B
White, Ryan. *Jimmy Buffett*	782.42164
White, Shane. *Prince of Darkness*	B
Whitlock, Craig. ★*Fat Leonard*	364.16
Whyte, Kenneth. *Hoover*	B
Whyte, Kenneth. *The Uncrowned King*	B
Widmer, Edward L. *Lincoln on the Verge*	B
Widmer, Edward L. *Martin Van Buren*	B
Wiedeman, Reeves. *Billion Dollar Loser*	333.33
Wiehl, Lis W. *A Spy in Plain Sight*	327.1247
Wiesel, Elie. *All Rivers Run to the Sea*	B
Wiesel, Elie. *And the Sea Is Never Full*	B
Wilderson, Frank B. *Afropessimism*	B
Wilkinson, Alec. *The Protest Singer*	B
Willetts, Paul. *King Con*	B
Williams, Jay. *Life Is Not an Accident*	B
Williams, Juan. *Thurgood Marshall*	B
Williams, Kate. *Ambition and Desire*	B
Williamson, Edwin. *Borges*	B
Wills, Garry. *James Madison*	B
Wills, Garry. *Saint Augustine*	B
Wilson, A. N. *C.S. Lewis*	823
Wilson, A. N. *The Mystery of Charles Dickens*	823
Wilson, A. N. *Victoria*	B
Wilson, Chris. *The Master Plan*	B
Wilson, Derek. *Out of the Storm*	B
Wilson, Robert. *Barnum*	B
Wilson, Robert. *Mathew Brady*	B
Wilson, Victoria. *A Life of Barbara Stanwyck*	B
Wilson-Lee, Edward. ★*The Catalogue of Shipwrecked Books*	B
Winchester, Simon. *The Map That Changed the World*	B
Winchester, Simon. *The Professor and the Madman*	423
Winder, Elizabeth. *Pain, Parties, Work*	B
Winters, Kathleen C. *Amelia Earhart*	B
Winters, Richard D. *Beyond Band of Brothers*	B
Wojczuk, Tana. *Lady Romeo*	B
Wolfe, Charles K. ★*The Life and Legend of Leadbelly*	B
Wolff, Christoph. *Johann Sebastian Bach*	B
Wong, Ali. ★*Dear Girls*	B
Wong, Chun Han. *Party of One*	951.06
Woods, Randall Bennett. *Prisoners of Hope*	973.923
Woodward, Bob. *Peril*	973.933
Woolever, Laurie. *Bourdain*	B
Woolf, Virginia. *Moments of Being*	B
Worsley, Lucy. ★*Agatha Christie*	B
Worsley, Lucy. *Queen Victoria*	B
Worster, Donald. *A Passion for Nature the Life of John Muir*	B
Wright, Alex. *Cataloging the World*	020.9
Wright, Lawrence. *Going Clear*	299
Wright, Richard. ★*Black Boy*	B
Wulf, Andrea. *The Brother Gardeners*	920
Wulf, Andrea. *The Invention of Nature*	B
Wullschlager, Jackie. ★*Chagall*	B
Yaffe, David. *Reckless Daughter*	782.42164
Yeebo, Yepoka. *Anansi's Gold*	364.16
Young, Neil. *Waging Heavy Peace*	B
Yousse, Bower. *Freddie Steinmark*	796.332
Zack, Ian. *Odetta*	B
Zambone, Albert Louis. *Daniel Morgan*	B
Zamoyski, Adam. *Napoleon*	B
Zanes, Warren. *Petty*	B
Zapruder, Alexandra. *Twenty-Six Seconds*	973.922092
Zeitz, Joshua. *Building the Great Society*	973.923
Zemeckis, Leslie Harter. *Behind the Burly Q*	792.7
Zenith, Richard. *Pessoa*	B
Zimmerman, Paul. *Dr. Z*	B
Zoglin, Richard. *Hope*	B
Zwonitzer, Mark. *Will You Miss Me When I'm Gone?*	920
Biography of a Phantom. McCormick, Mack	782.421643
Biography of Resistance. Zaman, Muhammad H.	616.9
BIOGRAPHY WRITING	
Calhoun, Ada. *Also a Poet*	B
Rocca, Mo. *Mobituaries*	920
★*Biohack* Your Brain. Willeumier, Kristen	612.8
BIOHISTORY	
Kennedy, Jonathan. *Pathogenesis*	614.4

AUTHOR, TITLE, SERIES AND SUBJECT INDEX

BIOLOGICAL DISCOVERIES
    Darwin, Charles. *Charles Darwin*   576.8
    Schlanger, Zoe. ★*The Light Eaters*   571.2
BIOLOGICAL GROWTH
    Curtis, Glade B. *Your Pregnancy Week by Week*   618.2
    Eagleman, David. *Livewired*   612.8
    Eliot, Lise. *Pink Brain, Blue Brain*   612.6
    Horowitz, Alexandra. ★*The Year of the Puppy*   636.7
    Martinez Arias, Alfonso. *The Master Builder*   571.6
    Siegel, Daniel J. *Brainstorm*   155.5
    Zernicka-Goetz, Magdalena. *The Dance of Life*   591.56
BIOLOGICAL INVASIONS
    Anthony, Leslie. *The Aliens Among Us*   578.6
BIOLOGICAL RESEARCH
    Cech, Thomas. *The Catalyst*   572.8
    Martinez Arias, Alfonso. *The Master Builder*   571.6
BIOLOGICAL SYSTEMS
    Miller, Lulu. *Why Fish Don't Exist*   B
    Smil, Vaclav. *Size*   153.7
BIOLOGICAL TERRORISM
    Guillemin, Jeanne. *Biological Weapons*   358
BIOLOGICAL WARFARE
    Guillemin, Jeanne. *Biological Weapons*   358
    Tucker, Jonathan B. *War of Nerves*   358
Biological Weapons. Guillemin, Jeanne   358
BIOLOGICAL WEAPONS
    Baker, Nicholson. *Baseless*   358
    Tucker, Jonathan B. *War of Nerves*   358
BIOLOGISTS
    Costa, James T. *Radical by Nature*   B
    Dawkins, Richard. *An Appetite for Wonder*   B
    Dawkins, Richard. *Brief Candle in the Dark*   B
    Hanson, Thor. *Hurricane Lizards and Plastic Squid*   577.2
    Jahren, Hope. ★*Lab Girl*   B
    Lowman, Margaret. *Life in the Treetops*   B
    Markel, Howard. *Origin Story*   576.8
    Mustill, Tom. *How to Speak Whale*   591.59
    Rhodes, Richard. *Scientist*   B
    Wilson, Edward O. ★*Letters to a Young Scientist*   570.92
BIOLOGY
    Carson, Rachel. *The Edge of the Sea*   578.769
    Catania, Kenneth. *Great Adaptations*   576.8
    Dawkins, Richard. *The Greatest Show on Earth*   576.8
    Denworth, Lydia. *Friendship*   158.2
    Emlen, Douglas John. *Animal Weapons*   591.47
    Fossey, Dian. ★*Gorillas in the Mist*   599.884
    Harari, Yuval N. *Homo Deus*   909.83
    Harari, Yuval N. ★*Sapiens*   909
    Harrington, Anne. *Mind Fixers*   616.89
    Heinrich, Bernd. *A Naturalist at Large*   508
    Henig, Robin Marantz. *The Monk in the Garden*   B
    Jabr, Ferris. ★*Becoming Earth*   570.1
    Johnson, Sarah Stewart. *The Sirens of Mars*   576.8
    Levitt, Dan. *What's Gotten into You*   539.7
    McCalman, Iain. *Darwin's Armada*   576.8
    Miller, Lulu. *Why Fish Don't Exist*   B
    Roberts, Jason. ★*Every Living Thing*   578
    Schutt, Bill. *Pump*   612.1
    Stanger, Ben. *From One Cell*   571.6
    Toomey, David. *Kingdom of Play*   591.56
    Ward, Ashley. *Where We Meet the World*   612.8
BIOLUMINESCENCE
    Widder, Edith. *Below the Edge of Darkness*   551.46092
BIOMECHANICS
    Durrani, Matin. *Furry Logic*   591.5
BIOPHYSICS
    Durrani, Matin. *Furry Logic*   591.5
BIOSPHERE RESERVES
    Wilson, Edward O. *Half-Earth*   333.95
BIOTECHNOLOGY
    Aryee, Patrick. *30 Animals That Made Us Smarter*   590
    Carreyrou, John. ★*Bad Blood*   338.7
    Elmore, Bartow J. *Seed Money*   338.7
    Kaku, Michio. *Quantum Supremacy*   006.3
    Piore, Adam. *The Body Builders*   660.6
BIOTECHNOLOGY IN AGRICULTURE
    Elmore, Bartow J. *Seed Money*   338.7

BIOTECHNOLOGY INDUSTRY AND TRADE
    Loftus, Peter. *The Messenger*   338.4
BIOTIC COMMUNITIES
    Anthony, Leslie. *The Aliens Among Us*   578.6
    Black, Riley. *The Last Days of the Dinosaurs*   576.8
    Czerski, Helen. *The Blue Machine*   551.46
    Flyn, Cal. ★*Islands of Abandonment*   333.73
    Goldfarb, Ben. *Crossings*   333.77
    Goldfarb, Ben. *Eager*   333.95
    Hanson, Thor. *Hurricane Lizards and Plastic Squid*   577.2
    Kumar, Priyanka. *Conversations with Birds*   598
    Nicholls, Steve. *Alien Worlds*   595.7
    Roman, Joe. *Eat, Poop, Die*   577
    Schilthuizen, Menno. *Darwin Comes to Town*   577.5
    Sheldrake, Merlin. *Entangled Life*   579.5
    Struzik, Edward. *Swamplands*   577.68
    Webb, Kinari. *Guardians of the Trees*   B
    Wohlleben, Peter. *Forest Walking*   582.16
    Wohlleben, Peter. *The Secret Wisdom of Nature*   508
BIPOLAR DISORDER
    Gotch, Jen. *The Upside of Being Down*   B
    Ikpi, Bassey. *I'm Telling the Truth, but I'm Lying*   814
    Kissinger, Meg. *While You Were Out*   362.2
    Lewis, Jenifer. *Walking in My Joy*   B
    Lin, Jami Nakamura. *The Night Parade*   B
    Mailhot, Terese Marie. *Heart Berries*   B
    Waldman, Ayelet. *A Really Good Day*   B
    Weller, Sheila. *Carrie Fisher*   B
Birbiglia, Mike
    The New One   B
BIRBIGLIA, MIKE
    Birbiglia, Mike. *The New One*   B
Birch, Helen
    Freehand   741.2
BIRD ATTRACTING
    Barker, Margaret A. *Audubon Birdhouse Book*   728
    Burton, Robert. *Audubon North American Birdfeeder Guide*   598
    Erickson, Laura. ★*100 Plants to Feed the Birds*   635
BIRD BEHAVIOR
    Ackerman, Jennifer. *The Bird Way*   598.15
    Ackerman, Jennifer. ★*What an Owl Knows*   598.9
    Attenborough, David. *The Life of Birds*   598.15
    Burton, Robert. *Audubon North American Birdfeeder Guide*   598
    Dunn, Jon L. *The Glitter in the Green*   598.7
    Erickson, Laura. *The Love Lives of Birds*   598.15
    Heinrich, Bernd. *A Naturalist at Large*   508
    Heinrich, Bernd. *White Feathers*   598.8
    Lederer, Roger J. *Beaks, Bones, and Bird Songs*   598
    Nicolson, Adam. *The Seabird's Cry*   598.177
    Sibley, David. *The Sibley Guide to Birds*   598.097
    Strycker, Noah K. *The Thing with Feathers*   598.072
    Tan, Amy. ★*The Backyard Bird Chronicles*   598
Bird by Bird. Lamott, Anne   808
Bird Cloud. Proulx, Annie   B
BIRD ECOLOGY
    Attenborough, David. *The Life of Birds*   598.15
BIRD MIGRATION
    Dunn, Jon L. *The Glitter in the Green*   598.7
    Nicolson, Adam. *The Seabird's Cry*   598.177
    Tougias, Robert. *Birder on Berry Lane*   598.072
    Van Hemert, Caroline. *The Sun Is a Compass*   979.8
    Weidensaul, Scott. *A World on the Wing*   598.156
BIRD PROTECTION
    Birkhead, Tim. *Birds and Us*   598
    Gyllenhaal, Anders. *A Wing and a Prayer*   639.97
    Hirschfeld, Erik. *The World's Rarest Birds*   333.95822
Bird Sense. Birkhead, T. R.   598
BIRD SOUNDS AND CALLS
    Ackerman, Jennifer. ★*What an Owl Knows*   598.9
    Tougias, Robert. *Birder on Berry Lane*   598.072
Bird Uncaged. Peterson, Marlon   B
BIRD WATCHERS
    Cooper, Christian. *Better Living Through Birding*   B
    Craig, Mya-Rose. *Birdgirl*   B
    Kumar, Priyanka. *Conversations with Birds*   598
    Tougias, Robert. *Birder on Berry Lane*   598.072
BIRD WATCHING
    Alderfer, Jonathan K. *National Geographic Birding Essentials*   598.072

PUBLIC LIBRARY CORE COLLECTION: NONFICTION
Twentieth Edition

Attenborough, David. *The Life of Birds*	598.15
Cooper, Christian. *Better Living Through Birding*	B
Craig, Mya-Rose. *Birdgirl*	B
Dunn, Jon L. *The Glitter in the Green*	598.7
Erickson, Laura. *The Love Lives of Birds*	598.15
Floyd, Ted. *How to Know the Birds*	598.072
Gentile, Olivia. *Life List*	598.072
Kumar, Priyanka. *Conversations with Birds*	598
Sibley, David. ★*Sibley's Birding Basics*	598
Stokes, Donald W. *The New Stokes Field Guide to Birds.*	598
Strycker, Noah K. *The Thing with Feathers*	598.072
Tan, Amy. ★*The Backyard Bird Chronicles*	598
Tougias, Robert. *Birder on Berry Lane*	598.072
The Bird Way. Ackerman, Jennifer	598.15

Bird, Kai
American Prometheus	B
The Outlier	973.926

Birder *on Berry Lane.* Tougias, Robert — 598.072
Birdgirl. Craig, Mya-Rose — B

BIRDS
Ackerman, Jennifer. *The Bird Way*	598.15
Alderfer, Jonathan K. *National Geographic Birding Essentials*	598.072
Barnes, Simon. *The Meaning of Birds*	598
Birkhead, T. R. *Bird Sense*	598
Birkhead, Tim. *Birds and Us*	598
Bull, John L. ★*The National Audubon Society Field Guide to North American Birds.*	598.097
Davies, N. B. *Cuckoo*	598.7
Davis, Jack E. *The Bald Eagle*	598.9
Erickson, Laura. ★*100 Plants to Feed the Birds*	635
Erickson, Laura. *The Love Lives of Birds*	598.15
Floyd, Ted. *How to Know the Birds*	598.072
Floyd, Ted. *Smithsonian Field Guide to the Birds of North America*	598.097
Gyllenhaal, Anders. *A Wing and a Prayer*	639.97
Hammer, Joshua. *The Falcon Thief*	364.16
Johnson, Kirk W. *The Feather Thief*	364.16
Jones, Darryl N. *The Birds at My Table*	598.072
Kaufman, Kenn. *The Birds That Audubon Missed*	598
Kiser, Joy M. *America's Other Audubon*	B
Kumar, Priyanka. *Conversations with Birds*	598
Lederer, Roger J. *Beaks, Bones, and Bird Songs*	598
Meiburg, Jonathan. *A Most Remarkable Creature*	598.9
Montgomery, Sy. *The Hummingbirds' Gift*	598.7
Peterson, Roger Tory. *Peterson Field Guide to Birds of Eastern and Central North America*	598.097
Peterson, Roger Tory. *Peterson Field Guide to Birds of Western North America*	598.097
Robbins, Jim. *The Wonder of Birds*	598
Safina, Carl. ★*Alfie and Me*	598.9
Sibley, David. *Sibley Birds East*	598.097
Sibley, David. ★*Sibley Birds West*	598.097
Sibley, David. *The Sibley Guide to Birds*	598.097
Sibley, David. ★*Sibley's Birding Basics*	598
Stokes, Donald W. *The New Stokes Field Guide to Birds.*	598
Tan, Amy. ★*The Backyard Bird Chronicles*	598
Weidensaul, Scott. *A World on the Wing*	598.156

Birds *and Us.* Birkhead, Tim — 598

BIRDS AS PETS
Haupt, Lyanda Lynn. *Mozart's Starling*	B

The Birds At My Table. Jones, Darryl N. — 598.072

BIRDS IN ART
Kiser, Joy M. *America's Other Audubon*	B
Lapierre, Corinne. *Folk Embroidered Felt Birds*	746.0463
Zickefoose, Julie. *Baby Birds*	751.42

BIRDS OF PREY
Ackerman, Jennifer. ★*What an Owl Knows*	598.9
Meiburg, Jonathan. *A Most Remarkable Creature*	598.9
Montgomery, Sy. *The Hawk's Way*	598.9
Slaght, Jonathan C. *Owls of the Eastern Ice*	598.9

The Birds That Audubon Missed. Kaufman, Kenn — 598

Birdsall, John
The Man Who Ate Too Much	B

Birdseye. Kurlansky, Mark — B

BIRDSEYE, CLARENCE, 1886-1956
Kurlansky, Mark. *Birdseye*	B

BIRDSONGS
Tougias, Robert. *Birder on Berry Lane*	598.072

Birkhead, T. R.
Bird Sense	598

Birkhead, Tim
Birds and Us	598

BIRMINGHAM, ALABAMA
Erwin, Jon. *Beyond Valor*	B
Jones, Doug. *Bending Toward Justice*	323.1196
Kix, Paul. ★*You Have to Be Prepared to Die Before You Can Begin to Live*	976.1
McWhorter, Diane. *Carry Me Home*	976.1
Morrison, Melanie. *Murder on Shades Mountain*	345.761
Rice, Condoleezza. *Extraordinary, Ordinary People*	B

BIRTH CONTROL
Blair, Gabrielle Stanley. ★*Ejaculate Responsibly*	362.1988
Eig, Jonathan. *The Birth of the Pill*	618.1
Foster, Diana Greene. *The Turnaway Study*	362.1988
Prager, Joshua. *The Family Roe*	342.7308
Stone, Geoffrey R. ★*Sex and the Constitution*	345.7302
Wills, Garry. *The Future of the Catholic Church with Pope Francis*	282.09
Wright, Jennifer Ashley. ★*Madame Restell*	B

BIRTH DEFECTS
Joyce, Russell W. *His Face Like Mine*	248
Masters, Oksana. *The Hard Parts*	B
Stanley, Paul. *Face the Music*	B
Vanderbes, Jennifer. ★*Wonder Drug*	615

★*The Birth of a Nation.* Lehr, Dick — 305.800973
The Birth of an Opera. Rose, Michael — 782.1
The Birth of Loud. Port, Ian S — 787.87
The Birth of Satan. Wray, T. J. — 235
The Birth of the Pill. Eig, Jonathan — 618.1
Birth *Without Fear.* Harshe, January — 618.2

BIRTHDAYS
Crawford, Saffi. *The Power of Birthdays, Stars & Numbers*	133.5
Goldschneider, Gary. ★*The Secret Language of Birthdays*	133.5

BIRTHFATHERS
Calcaterra, Regina. *Etched in Sand*	B
Shapiro, Dani. ★*Inheritance*	B

Birthing *Liberation.* Wade, Sabia — 363.96

BIRTHMOTHERS
Carroll, Rebecca. *Surviving the White Gaze*	B
Fessler, Ann. *The Girls Who Went Away*	362.82
Sentilles, Sarah. *Stranger Care*	B

BIRTHPARENTS
Asgarian, Roxanna. *We Were Once a Family*	364.152
Brierley, Saroo. *A Long Way Home*	B
Chung, Nicole. *All You Can Ever Know*	B
Daley, Mark. *Safe*	B
Glaser, Gabrielle. *American Baby*	B
Oelhafen, Ingrid von. *Hitler's Stolen Children*	B
Sisson, Gretchen E. ★*Relinquished*	362.734

BISEXUAL MEN
Cumming, Alan. *Baggage*	B
Gehring, Wes D. *James Dean*	B

BISEXUAL PEOPLE
Funk, Mason. *The Book of Pride*	920
Gelwicks, Andrew. *The Queer Advantage*	920
Shaw, Julia. *Bi*	306.76

BISEXUAL WOMEN
Berg, A. Scott. *Kate Remembered*	B
Dearborn, Mary V. *Carson McCullers*	B
Hernandez, Daisy. *A Cup of Water Under My Bed*	B
Hill, Katie. *She Will Rise*	305.42
Shapland, Jenn. *My Autobiography of Carson McCullers*	B

BISEXUALITY
Shaw, Julia. *Bi*	306.76

Bishara, Rawia
Olives, Lemons & Za'atar	641.59

Bishop, Elizabeth
★*Poems*	811

BISHOP, ELIZABETH, 1911-1979
Hardwick, Elizabeth. *The Dolphin Letters, 1970-1979*	811
Travisano, Thomas J. *Love Unknown*	B

BISHOPS
Augustine. *Confessions*	B
Newman, Richard S. *Freedom's Prophet*	B
Wills, Garry. *Saint Augustine*	B

Biskind, Peter
Pandora's Box	791.45

AUTHOR, TITLE, SERIES AND SUBJECT INDEX

Star	B
Biskupic, Joan	
★*Nine Black Robes*	347.73
Bismarck. Steinberg, Jonathan	B
BISMARCK, OTTO, FURST VON, 1815-1898	
Steinberg, Jonathan. *Bismarck*	B
Biss, Eula	
Having and Being Had	306.3
Bissell, Tom	
Extra Lives	794.8
Bissinger, H. G.	
★*Friday Night Lights*	796.332
★*The Mosquito Bowl*	796.332
Bissonnette, Zac	
The Great Beanie Baby Bubble	338.7
Bitch. Cooke, Lucy	591.56
BITCOIN	
Greenberg, Andy. *Tracers in the Dark*	364.16
Bite by Bite. Nezhukumatathil, Aimee	641.3
A Bite-Sized History of France. Henaut, Stephane	394.1
Biting The Hand. Lee, Julia Sun-Joo	B
Bits and Pieces. Goldberg, Whoopi	B
Bitsoie, Freddie	
New Native Kitchen	641.59
Bitsui, Sherwin	
Dissolve	811
Bitter Brew. Knoedelseder, William	338.7
Bitter Crop. Alexander, Paul	B
The Bitter Taste of Victory. Feigel, Lara	320.943
Bitterly Divided. Williams, David	973.7
★*Bittersweet*. Cain, Susan	155.2
Bittle, Jake	
★*The Great Displacement*	362.87
★*Bittman Bread*. Bittman, Mark	641.81
Bittman, Mark	
Animal, Vegetable, Junk	394.1
★*Bittman Bread*	641.81
A Bone to Pick	338.10973
★*Dinner for Everyone*	641.5
★*How to Bake Everything*	641.81
How to Cook Everything Fast	641.5
★*How to Cook Everything Vegetarian*	641.5
★*How to Cook Everything*	641.5
How to Cook Everything	641.5
★*How to Grill Everything*	641.7
Mark Bittman's Kitchen Matrix	641.5
The VB6 Cookbook	641.5
VB6	641.5
Bix, Herbert P.	
Hirohito and the Making of Modern Japan	B
Bjarnason, Egill	
How Iceland Changed the World	949.12
Bjork, Daniel W.	
B.F. Skinner	B
Bjork, Katrin	
From the North	641.594
Bjornerud, Marcia	
Geopedia	551
BLACK AESTHETIC MOVEMENT	
Jackson, Angela. *A Surprised Queenhood in the New Black Sun*	B
★*Black AF History*. Harriot, Michael	973
Black and Female. Dangarembga, Tsitsi	305.48
The Black and the Blue. Horace, Matthew	B
Black and White. Williams, Richard	B
★*The Black Angels*. Smilios, Maria	610.73
Black Aperture. Rasmussen, Matt	811
Black Ball. Runstedtler, Theresa	796.323
The Black Banners Declassified. Soufan, Ali H.	363.325
BLACK BART, 1835-1917	
Boessenecker, John. *Gentleman Bandit*	B
The Black Book. Harris, M. A.	920
The Black Box. Gates, Henry Louis	908
★*Black Boy*. Wright, Richard	B
Black Boy Smile. Watkins, D.	B
BLACK BRITISH PEOPLE	
Asher, Zain E. *Where the Children Take Us*	942.1
BLACK BRITISH WOMEN	
Coel, Michaela. ★*Misfits*	158.2

Black Broadway. Lane, Stewart F.	792.089
BLACK CANADIANS	
Abdelmahmoud, Elamin. *Son of Elsewhere*	B
Black Chameleon. Mouton, Deborah D. E. E. P.	B
★*The Black Church*. Gates, Henry Louis	277
★*The Black Civil War Soldier*. Willis, Deborah	973.7
The Black Count. Reiss, Tom	B
BLACK DEATH	
Cantor, Norman F. *In the Wake of the Plague*	614.5
Kelly, John. *The Great Mortality*	614.5
Randall, David K. *Black Death at the Golden Gate*	616.9
Black Death at the Golden Gate. Randall, David K.	616.9
Black Detroit. Boyd, Herb	977.4
★*Black Diamond Queens*. Mahon, Maureen	782.421
Black Earth. Snyder, Timothy	940.53
★*Black Earth Wisdom*. Penniman, Leah	333.72
Black Edge. Kolhatkar, Sheelah	364.16
Black Elk	
Black Elk Speaks	B
Black Elk. Jackson, Joe	978.004
Black Elk Speaks. Black Elk	B
BLACK ELK, 1863-1950	
Black Elk. *Black Elk Speaks*	B
Jackson, Joe. *Black Elk*	978.004
Black Fatigue. Winters, Mary-Frances	305.896
Black Flags. Warrick, Joby	956.9104
Black Flags, Blue Waters. Dolin, Eric Jay	973.2
Black Folk. Kelley, Blair Murphy	331.6
Black Folk Could Fly. Kenan, Randall	813
Black Food. Terry, Bryant	394.1
Black Fortunes. Wills, Shomari	920
★*Black Friend*. Fumudoh, Ziwe	814
Black Girl Baking. Guy, Jerrelle	641.59
★*Black Girl Magic*. Browne, Mahogany L.	811.6
Black Girl, Call Home. Mans, Jasmine	811
Black Hawk. Trask, Kerry A.	973.5
Black Hawk Down. Bowden, Mark	967.7305
BLACK HAWK WAR, 1832	
Trask, Kerry A. *Black Hawk*	973.5
BLACK HAWK, SAUK CHIEF, 1767-1838	
Trask, Kerry A. *Black Hawk*	973.5
Black Hearts. Frederick, Jim	956.7044
BLACK HILLS	
Mort, T. A. *Thieves' Road*	978.3
The Black History of the White House. Lusane, Clarence	975.3
Black Hole Blues. Levin, Janna	539.7
BLACK HOLES (ASTRONOMY)	
Fletcher, Seth. *Einstein's Shadow*	523.8
Greene, B. *Until the End of Time*	523.1
Hawking, Stephen. ★*Black Holes and Baby Universes and Other Essays*	530.1
Hawking, Stephen. *A Brief History of Time*	523.1
Hawking, Stephen. ★*A Briefer History of Time*	523.1
Hawking, Stephen. *My Brief History*	B
Impey, Chris. *Einstein's Monsters*	523.8
Levin, Janna. *Black Hole Blues*	539.7
Tucker, Wallace H. *Chandra's Cosmos*	523.1
Tyson, Neil deGrasse. *Welcome to the Universe*	523.1
★*Black Holes and Baby Universes and Other Essays*. Hawking, Stephen	530.1
Black Is the Body. Bernard, Emily	305.48
Black Is the New White. Mooney, Paul	792.7
BLACK LIVES MATTER MOVEMENT	
Alexander, Kwame. *Light for the World to See*	811.6
Anderson, Carol. ★*White Rage*	305.800973
Carruthers, Charlene A. *Unapologetic*	305.48
Coates, Ta-Nehisi. *Between the World and Me*	305.800973
Dennis, David J., Jr. *The Movement Made Us*	B
Dyson, Michael Eric. *Long Time Coming*	305.800973
Garza, Alicia. *The Purpose of Power*	303.48
Glaude, Eddie S. *Begin Again*	305.800973
Lebron, Christopher J. *The Making of Black Lives Matter*	305.896
Oluo, Ijeoma. ★*So You Want to Talk About Race*	305.800973
Samuels, Robert. ★*His Name Is George Floyd*	B
Smith, Mychal Denzel. *Invisible Man, Got the Whole World Watching*	305.242
Taibbi, Matt. *I Can't Breathe*	363.2
Black Maestro. Drape, Joe	B
Black Magic. Sanders, Chad	305.896

PUBLIC LIBRARY CORE COLLECTION: NONFICTION
Twentieth Edition

The *Black* Man's President. Burlingame, Michael — 973.7
The *Black* Maria. Girmay, Aracelis — 811
BLACK MARKET
    Greenberg, Andy. *Tracers in the Dark* — 364.16
    Jacobs, Ryan McMahon. *The Truffle Underground* — 381
BLACK MUSLIMS
    Baldwin, James. ★*The Fire Next Time* — 305.896
    Eig, Jonathan. ★*Ali* — B
    Evanzz, Karl. *The Messenger* — B
    Levinsohn, Florence Hamlish. *Looking for Farrakhan* — B
    Malcolm X. ★*The Autobiography of Malcolm X* — B
    Marable, Manning. ★*Malcolm X* — B
    Montville, Leigh. *Sting Like a Bee* — B
    Payne, Les. ★*The Dead Are Arising* — B
    Perry, Bruce. *Malcolm* — B
    Roberts, Randy. *Blood Brothers* — 920
BLACK NATIONALISM
    Marable, Manning. ★*Malcolm X* — B
    Payne, Les. ★*The Dead Are Arising* — B
Black Nerd Problems. Evans, William — 814.6
BLACK PEOPLE
    Enninful, Edward. *A Visible Man* — B
    Gates, Henry Louis. *The Black Box* — 908
    Jackson, Jenn M. ★*Black Women Taught Us* — 305.48
    Royster, Francesca T. *Choosing Family* — B
    Shanahan, Charif. *Trace Evidence* — 811
    Wilson, A'ja. ★*Dear Black Girls* — 158.1
BLACK POWER
    Carruthers, Charlene A. *Unapologetic* — 305.48
    Joseph, Peniel E. *Waiting 'Til the Midnight Hour* — 323.1196
    Whitaker, Mark. ★*Saying It Loud* — 973.923
The *Black* Practice of Disbelief. Pinn, Anthony B. — 211
The *Black* Presidency. Dyson, Michael Eric — 305.800973
The *Black* Prince. Jones, Michael K. — B
Black Prophetic Fire. West, Cornel — 920
Black Radical. Greenidge, Kerri — B
Black Skinhead. Collins-Dexter, Brandi — 324.2734
Black Snow. Scott, James — 940.54
BLACK SOX SCANDAL, 1919
    Zminda, Don. *Double Plays and Double Crosses* — 796.357
Black Thought
    The Upcycled Self — B
BLACK THOUGHT, 1973-
    Black Thought. *The Upcycled Self* — B
Black Trials. Weiner, Mark Stuart — 342.7308
Black Tudors. Kaufmann, Miranda — 941
Black Wave. Ghattas, Kim — 955.05
★*Black Women Taught Us*. Jackson, Jenn M. — 305.48
★*A Black Women's History of the United States*. Berry, Daina Ramey — 305.48
Black, Alexandra
    Design — 745.4
    Scientists Who Changed History — 509.22
BLACK, ATLANTIS, 1976-2008
    Bonner, Betsy. *The Book of Atlantis Black* — 364.152
Black, Dustin Lance
    Mama's Boy — B
BLACK, DUSTIN LANCE
    Black, Dustin Lance. *Mama's Boy* — B
Black, George
    Empire of Shadows — 978.7
    ★*The Long Reckoning* — 959.704
Black, Michael Ian
    A Better Man — 305.31
BLACK, MICHAEL IAN, 1971-
    Black, Michael Ian. *A Better Man* — 305.31
Black, Riley
    The Last Days of the Dinosaurs — 576.8
Black, Sarah
    One Dough, Ten Breads — 641.81
Black, Scott Hoffman
    Gardening for Butterflies — 638
Blackacre. Youn, Monica — 811.6
Blackburn, Simon
    The Oxford Dictionary of Philosophy — 103
    Think — 100
Blackett's War. Budiansky, Stephen — 940.54

BLACKETT, P. M. S. (PATRICK MAYNARD STUART), BARON BLACKETT, 1897-1974
    Budiansky, Stephen. *Blackett's War* — 940.54
Blackhawk, Ned
    ★*The Rediscovery of America* — 973.04
BLACKLISTING OF AUTHORS
    Frankel, Glenn. *High Noon* — 791.43
Blackmon, Douglas A.
    Slavery by Another Name — 305.896
BLACKMUN, HARRY A., 1908-1999
    Greenhouse, Linda. *Becoming Justice Blackmun* — B
Blackstock, Uche
    Legacy — 610.92
BLACKSTOCK, UCHE
    Blackstock, Uche. *Legacy* — 610.92
Blackstone, Amy
    Childfree by Choice — 306.874
Blackstone-Ford, Jann
    Co-Parenting Through Separation and Divorce — 306.89
BLACKWELL, ELIZABETH, 1821-1910
    Campbell, Olivia. *Women in White Coats* — 610.92
    Nimura, Janice P. ★*The Doctors Blackwell* — 610.92
BLACKWELL, EMILY, 1826-1910
    Nimura, Janice P. ★*The Doctors Blackwell* — 610.92
BLACKWOOD, CAROLINE
    Hardwick, Elizabeth. *The Dolphin Letters, 1970-1979* — 811
Blain, Keisha N.
    Until I Am Free — B
Blair, Barb
    Furniture Makeovers — 684.1
BLAIR, EILEEN, 1905-1945
    Funder, Anna. *Wifedom* — B
Blair, Gabrielle Stanley
    ★*Ejaculate Responsibly* — 362.1988
Blair, Selma
    Mean Baby — B
BLAIR, SELMA, 1972-
    Blair, Selma. *Mean Baby* — B
Blair, Tony
    A Journey — B
BLAIR, TONY, 1953-
    Blair, Tony. *A Journey* — B
Blais, Madeleine
    In These Girls, Hope Is a Muscle — 796.323
    Queen of the Court — B
Blaisdell, Robert
    Creating Anna Karenina — 891.7
BLAKE, GEORGE, 1922-2020
    Vogel, Steve. *Betrayal in Berlin* — 327.1273043
Blake, Melissa
    Beautiful People — 362.4
BLAKE, MELISSA (BLOGGER)
    Blake, Melissa. *Beautiful People* — 362.4
Blake, William
    ★*The Complete Poetry and Prose of William Blake* — 821
Blakeney, Justina
    Jungalow — 747
    The New Bohemians Handbook — 747
Blakeslee, Nate
    American Wolf — 599.773
Blakinger, Keri
    Corrections in Ink — B
BLAKINGER, KERI
    Blakinger, Keri. *Corrections in Ink* — B
BLAME
    Johnson, Kirk W. *The Fishermen and the Dragon* — 976.4
    Nussbaum, Martha Craven. *The Monarchy of Fear* — 306.20973
    O'Neil, Cathy. *The Shame Machine* — 152.4
Blanco, Richard
    How to Love a Country — 811
    The Prince of Los Cocuyos — B
BLANCO, RICHARD, 1968-
    Blanco, Richard. *The Prince of Los Cocuyos* — B
Blanford, Nicholas
    Warriors of God — 956.9204
The *Blank* Slate. Pinker, Steven — 155.2
BLANKENSHIP, DONALD LEON
    Leamer, Laurence. *The Price of Justice* — 346.7302

AUTHOR, TITLE, SERIES AND SUBJECT INDEX

Maher, Kris. *Desperate* — 344
BLANKETS
   Hubert, Margaret. *10 Granny Squares, 30 Blankets* — 746.43
Blanning, T. C. W.
   Frederick the Great — B
Blanton, DeAnne
   They Fought Like Demons — 973.7
Blaser, Martin J.
   Missing Microbes — 615.7
BLASPHEMY
   Minois, Georges. *The Atheist's Bible* — 200
Blattman, Christopher
   Why We Fight — 303.6
Blau, Magda Hellinger
   The Nazis Knew My Name — 940.53
BLAU, MAGDA HELLINGER, 1916-2006
   Blau, Magda Hellinger. *The Nazis Knew My Name* — 940.53
Blay, Zeba
   Carefree Black Girls — 305.48
BLAY, ZEBA
   Blay, Zeba. *Carefree Black Girls* — 305.48
BLAY-MIEZAH, JOHN ACKAH
   Yeebo, Yepoka. *Anansi's Gold* — 364.16
BLAZER, CHUCK, 1945-2017
   Papenfuss, Mary. *American Huckster* — B
The Blazing World. Healey, Jonathan — 941.06
Bleeding Orange. Boeheim, Jim — B
BLENDED FAMILIES
   Doyle, Glennon. *Untamed* — B
   Santopietro, Tom. *The Sound of Music Story* — 791.43
   Union, Gabrielle. *You Got Anything Stronger?* — B
The Blessing and the Curse. Kirsch, Adam — 809
BLIGH, WILLIAM, 1754-1817
   Alexander, Caroline. *The Bounty* — 996.1
   Preston, Diana. *Paradise in Chains* — 996.18
★*Blight*. Monosson, Emily — 616.9
Blight, David W.
   ★*Frederick Douglass* — B
   A Slave No More — B
Blind Descent. Tabor, James M. — 796.52
The Blind Side. Lewis, Michael — B
Blind Spot. Cole, Teju — 770
Blind Spots. Berens, Kimberly Nix — 370.15
BLINDNESS
   Bruni, Frank. *The Beauty of Dusk* — B
   Leland, Andrew. ★*The Country of the Blind* — B
   Roberts, Jason. *A Sense of the World* — B
Blink. Gladwell, Malcolm — 153.4
Bliss, Debbie
   ★*The Knitter's Book of Knowledge* — 746.43
Blitzer, Jonathan
   Everyone Who Is Gone Is Here — 305.9
BLIZZARDS
   Bukreev, Anatolii Nikolaevich. *The Climb* — 796.52
   Krist, Gary. *The White Cascade* — 979.7
   Laskin, David. *The Children's Blizzard* — 977
BLOCHER, PAUL (MISSING PERSON)
   Levin, Daniel. *Proof of Life* — 956.9104
Block, Jennifer
   Everything Below the Waist — 613
BLOCKCHAINS (DATABASES)
   Small, Zachary. ★*Token Supremacy* — 332.4
Blockley, David
   Bridges — 725
BLOGGERS
   Doughty, Caitlin. *Smoke Gets in Your Eyes* — B
   Irby, Samantha. *We Are Never Meeting in Real Life* — 814
   Lebovitz, David. *My Paris Kitchen* — 641.594
   Mann, Jen. ★*Midlife Bites* — 305.244
   Manson, Mark. *The Subtle Art of Not Giving a F*ck* — 158.1
   Mitchell, Wendy. *Somebody I Used to Know* — B
   Momus. *Niche* — B
   Powell, Julie. *Julie and Julia* — 641.5
   Ramsey, Franchesca. *Well, That Escalated Quickly* — B
BLOGS
   Brosh, Allie. ★*Hyperbole and a Half* — 741.5
   Brosh, Allie. ★*Solutions and Other Problems* — 741.5

Blom, Onno
   Young Rembrandt — B
BLONDE WOMEN
   Leamer, Laurence. *Hitchcock's Blondes* — 791.43
★*Blood*. Gunter, Jen — 612.6
BLOOD
   George, Rose. *Nine Pints* — 612.1
Blood and Iron. Hoyer, Katja — 943.08
Blood and Oil. Hope, Bradley — B
Blood and Sand. Von Tunzelmann, Alex — 909.82
Blood and Thunder. Sides, Hampton — 978
Blood and Treasure. Drury, Bob — B
Blood At the Root. Phillips, Patrick — 305.8
BLOOD BANKS
   McLaughlin, Kathleen. *Blood Money* — 362.17
Blood Brothers. Roberts, Randy — 920
Blood Dazzler. Smith, Patricia — 811
BLOOD DISEASES
   Harpham, Heather Elise. *Happiness* — B
Blood Done Sign My Name. Tyson, Timothy B. — 975.6
BLOOD DONORS
   George, Rose. *Nine Pints* — 612.1
Blood in the Cage. Wertheim, L. Jon — 796.815
Blood in the Machine. Merchant, Brian — 303.48
Blood in the Water. Cameron, Silver Donald — 364.152
Blood in the Water. Thompson, Heather Ann — 365
Blood Memory. Duncan, Dayton — 599.64
Blood Money. McLaughlin, Kathleen — 362.17
Blood Moon. Sedgwick, John — 975.004
The Blood of Emmett Till. Tyson, Timothy B. — 364.1
The Blood of Heroes. Donovan, Jim — 976.4
Blood on the River. Kars, Marjoleine — 306.3
Blood on Their Hands. Matney, Mandy — 364.152
Blood Orange Night. Bond, Melissa — 616.8
Blood Papa. Hatzfeld, Jean — 967.5710431
Blood Royal. Jager, Eric — 944.026
Blood Runs Coal. Bradley, Mark A. — B
Blood Sisters. Gristwood, Sarah — 942.04092
BLOOD TRANSFUSION
   Harpham, Heather Elise. *Happiness* — B
Blood, Bones, and Butter. Hamilton, Gabrielle — B
Blood, Fire & Gold. Paranque, Estelle — 920
Bloodbath Nation. Auster, Paul — 363.33
★*The Bloodied Nightgown*. Acocella, Joan Ross — 814
★*Bloodlands*. Snyder, Timothy — 940.54
Bloom, Amy
   In Love — B
BLOOM, AMY, 1953-
   Bloom, Amy. *In Love* — B
Bloom, Harold
   Genius — 153.9
   Lear — 822.33
   Shakespeare — 822.33
   The Western Canon — 809
Bloom, Ken
   Broadway Musicals — 792.6
Bloom, Paul
   Psych — 150
Blount, Roy
   Robert E. Lee — B
Blount, Tommye
   Fantasia for the Man in Blue — 811
Blow Your House Down. Frangello, Gina — 813
Blowing The Bloody Doors Off. Caine, Michael — B
Blowout. Maddow, Rachel — 338.2
Blue Blood II. Chansky, Art — 796.323
BLUE COLLAR FAMILIES
   Arsenault, Kerri. *Mill Town* — B
BLUE COLLAR WOMEN
   Chang, Leslie T. *Factory Girls* — 331.4
   Smarsh, Sarah. *She Come by It Natural* — 782.42164
BLUE COLLAR WORKERS
   Arsenault, Kerri. *Mill Town* — B
   Case, Anne. *Deaths of Despair and the Future of Capitalism* — 362.28
   Chang, Leslie T. *Factory Girls* — 331.4
   Cullen, Art. *Storm Lake* — 071.7
   Ehrenreich, Barbara. ★*Nickel and Dimed* — B
   Goldstein, Amy. *Janesville* — 330.9775

PUBLIC LIBRARY CORE COLLECTION: NONFICTION
Twentieth Edition

Kelley, Blair Murphy. *Black Folk*	331.6
Kristof, Nicholas D. ★*Tightrope*	306.0973
MacGillis, Alec. *Fulfillment*	381
Marie, Jane. ★*Selling the Dream*	658.8
Miller, Scott. *The President and the Assassin*	973.8
Blue Dreams. Slater, Lauren	615.7
Blue Highways. Heat Moon, William Least	917.304
Blue Hour. Forche, Carolyn	811
The Blue Machine. Czerski, Helen	551.46
★*Blue Monday*. Coleman, Rick	B
Blue Ocean Shift. Kim, W. Chan	658.8
BLUE RIDGE MOUNTAINS	
Dillard, Annie. *Pilgrim at Tinker Creek*	508
Blue Sky Kingdom. Kirkby, Bruce	954.96
BLUEGRASS MUSIC	
Russell, Tony. *Country Music Originals*	B
BLUES (MUSIC)	
De Vise, Daniel. ★*The Blues Brothers*	791.43
Ferris, William R. *Give My Poor Heart Ease*	781.643
George-Warren, Holly. ★*Janis*	B
Gray, Michael. *Hand Me My Travelin' Shoes*	B
Lomax, Alan. ★*The Land Where the Blues Began*	781.643
McCormick, Mack. *Biography of a Phantom*	782.421643
Wald, Elijah. *American Epic*	781.64
Wald, Elijah. ★*Escaping the Delta*	B
★*Blues All Around Me*. King, B. B.	B
★*The Blues Brothers*. De Vise, Daniel	791.43
BLUES MUSIC	
Patrick, James. *Robert Johnson*	B
BLUES MUSICIANS	
Alexander, Paul. *Bitter Crop*	B
Ferris, William R. *Give My Poor Heart Ease*	781.643
Gray, Michael. *Hand Me My Travelin' Shoes*	B
King, B. B. ★*Blues All Around Me*	B
McCormick, Mack. *Biography of a Phantom*	782.421643
Patrick, James. *Robert Johnson*	B
Wald, Elijah. ★*Escaping the Delta*	B
Wolfe, Charles K. ★*The Life and Legend of Leadbelly*	B
Bluest Nude. Codjoe, Ama	811
Bluestein, Jane	
The Perfection Deception	155.2
Bluff City. Lauterbach, Preston	B
Bluhm, Lisa	
Creative Soldered Jewelry & Accessories	745.594
Blum, Deborah	
Ghost Hunters	133.9
The Poisoner's Handbook	614
Blum, Edward J.	
The Color of Christ	232
Blum, Howard	
The Spy Who Knew Too Much	327.12
BLUME, JUDY	
Bergstein, Rachelle. *The Genius of Judy*	813
Blume, Lesley M. M.	
Fallout	940.54
Blumenthal, Brett	
52 Small Changes for the Mind	616.89
Blumenthal, Eileen	
Puppetry	791.5
Blumenthal, Heston	
Is This a Cookbook?	641.5
Blumenthal, Sidney	
★*All the Powers of Earth*	B
A Self-Made Man	B
Wrestling with His Angel	B
Blunk, Jonathan	
James Wright	B
Blunt, Katherine	
California Burning	333.793
Blurred Lines. Grigoriadis, Vanessa	371.7
Bly, Robert	
Collected Poems	811
★*Iron John*	305.310973
More Than True	398.2
Blyth, Catherine	
The Art of Conversation	395.5
Boa, Kenneth D.	
Recalibrate Your Life	248.8
BOARD GAMES	
Goodridge, Michelle. *Librarian's Guide to Games and Gamers*	025.2
Orbanes, Philip. *The Game Makers*	338.7
Parkin, Simon. *A Game of Birds and Wolves*	940.54
Roeder, Oliver. *Seven Games*	794
Boardman, John	
★*Greek Art*	709
BOAS, FRANZ, 1858-1942	
King, Charles. ★*Gods of the Upper Air*	920
BOAT PEOPLE (SOUTHEAST ASIAN REFUGEES)	
Chung, Vinh. *Where the Wind Leads*	B
Yip-Williams, Julie. ★*The Unwinding of the Miracle*	973
BOATING	
Sciolino, Elaine. *The Seine*	944
BOATING ACCIDENTS	
Fairbanks, Amanda M. *The Lost Boys of Montauk*	910.91
★*Bob Dylan*. Davidson, Mark A.	B
Bobby At Home. Flay, Bobby	641.5
★*Bobby Fischer Teaches Chess*. Fischer, Bobby	794.1
Bobby Kennedy. Matthews, Christopher	B
★*Bobby Kennedy*. Tye, Larry	B
Bobrick, Benson	
Angel in the Whirlwind	973.3
Bobrow-Strain, Aaron	
The Death and Life of Aida Hernandez	972
BOCA RATON, FLORIDA	
Madden, T Kira. *Long Live the Tribe of Fatherless Girls*	814
Boccaletti, Giulio	
Water	909
Bodanis, David	
Electric Universe	537
Boden, Anne	
Female Founders' Playbook	658.4
BODIES OF WATER	
Boccaletti, Giulio. *Water*	909
Bodies on the Line. Rankin, Lauren	362.1988
BODINE, POLLY	
Hortis, C. Alexander. *The Witch of New York*	364.152
The Body. Bryson, Bill	612
BODY AWARENESS	
Briggs, Lyvonne. ★*Sensual Faith*	204
Gordon, Aubrey. *"You Just Need to Lose Weight"*	616.3
Teng, Tara. ★*Your Body Is a Revolution*	306.4
The Body Builders. Piore, Adam	660.6
BODY COVERING (ANATOMY)	
Hanson, Thor. *Feathers*	598.147
Lyman, Monty. *The Remarkable Life of the Skin*	612.7
BODY DYSMORPHIC DISORDER	
Kang, Mia. *Knockout*	B
Kazdin, Cole. ★*What's Eating Us*	616.85
Sole-Smith, Virginia. ★*Fat Talk*	649.1
BODY FLUIDS	
Everts, Sarah. *The Joy of Sweat*	612.7
BODY IMAGE	
Beck, Amanda Martinez. *More of You*	613
Bowen, Sesali. *Bad Fat Black Girl*	305.42
Briggs, Lyvonne. ★*Sensual Faith*	204
Brodeur, Michael Andor. ★*Swole*	155.3
Byas, Taylor. *I Done Clicked My Heels Three Times*	811
Chaudry, Rabia. *Fatty Fatty Boom Boom*	B
Clein, Emmeline. ★*Dead Weight*	616.85
Copaken, Deborah. *Ladyparts*	B
Feast, Fancy. *Naked*	792.7
Freeman, Hadley. *Good Girls*	616.85
Graham, Ashley. *A New Model*	B
Hari, Johann. ★*Magic Pill*	613.2
Jamieson, Alexandra. *Women, Food, and Desire*	155.3
Jones, Chloe Cooper. ★*Easy Beauty*	B
Kang, Mia. *Knockout*	B
Kazdin, Cole. ★*What's Eating Us*	616.85
King, Chrissy. *The Body Liberation Project*	306.4
Klein, Jessi. *I'll Show Myself Out*	B
Kneeland, Jessi. *Body Neutral*	306.4
Laing, Olivia. *Everybody*	323
Lieu, Susan. ★*The Manicurist's Daughter*	B
Lima, Jamie Kern. *Believe It*	B
Meltzer, Marisa. *This Is Big*	613.25
Michaud-Skog, Summer. *Fat Girls Hiking*	796.51

AUTHOR, TITLE, SERIES AND SUBJECT INDEX

Moran, Caitlin. *More Than a Woman*	B
Robb, Alice. ★*Don't Think, Dear*	792.8
Semenya, Caster. *The Race to Be Myself*	B
Sole-Smith, Virginia. ★*Fat Talk*	649.1
Specter, Emma. *More, Please*	616.85
Stone, Lillian. ★*Everybody's Favorite*	814.6
Teng, Tara. ★*Your Body Is a Revolution*	306.4
Van Ness, Jonathan. *Love That Story*	791.4502
Whitefield-Madrano, Autumn. *Face Value*	111
Wilson, Jessica. *It's Always Been Ours*	613
Yong, Sable. *Die Hot with a Vengeance*	646.7
The *Body Keeps the Score*. Van der Kolk, Bessel A.	616.85
BODY LANGUAGE	
Dimitrius, Jo-Ellan. *Reading People*	155.2
Lieberman, David J. *Mindreader*	401
Nowicki, Stephen. *Raising a Socially Successful Child*	649
Pease, Allan. *The Definitive Book of Body Language*	153.6
Scott, Andy. *One Kiss or Two?*	395.4
The *Body Liberation Project*. King, Chrissy	306.4
A *Body Made of Glass*. Crampton, Caroline	616.85
BODY MOVEMENT	
Brown, Molly McCully. *Places I've Taken My Body*	B
Michaud-Skog, Summer. *Fat Girls Hiking*	796.51
Body Neutral. Kneeland, Jessi	306.4
BODY ODOR	
Everts, Sarah. *The Joy of Sweat*	612.7
A *Body of Work*. Hallberg, David	B
BODY SIZE	
Gordon, Aubrey. *"You Just Need to Lose Weight"*	616.3
MacPhee, R. D. E. *End of the Megafauna*	591.4
BODY SNATCHING	
Craughwell, Thomas J. *Stealing Lincoln's Body*	973.7092
★*Body Work*. Febos, Melissa	808.06
BODYBUILDING	
Brodeur, Michael Andor. ★*Swole*	155.3
BODYGUARDS	
Hill, Clint. *My Travels with Mrs. Kennedy*	B
Meltzer, Brad. ★*The First Conspiracy*	973.4
Boeheim, Jim	
Bleeding Orange	B
BOEHEIM, JIM	
Boeheim, Jim. *Bleeding Orange*	B
BOER WAR, 1899-1902	
Millard, Candice. ★*Hero of the Empire*	968.04
Boessenecker, John	
Gentleman Bandit	B
Texas Ranger	B
BOG BODIES	
Proulx, Annie. ★*Fen, Bog and Swamp*	551.41
Struzik, Edward. *Swamplands*	577.68
BOGART, HUMPHREY, 1899-1957	
Kanfer, Stefan. *Tough Without a Gun*	B
Mann, William J. *Bogie & Bacall*	920
Bogdanich, Walt	
When McKinsey Comes to Town	001
Boggs, Jacey	
Spin Art	746.1
Boghosian, Heidi	
"i Have Nothing to Hide"	363.1
Bogie & Bacall. Mann, William J.	920
Bogira, Steve	
Courtroom 302	345.773
Bogle, Donald	
Bright Boulevards, Bold Dreams	791.43
Heat Wave	782.42164
Bogosian, Eric	
Operation Nemesis	956.62
BOGS	
Struzik, Edward. *Swamplands*	577.68
Bogus, Carl T.	
Buckley	B
Bohannon, Cat	
★*Eve*	613
BOHEMIANISM	
Blakeney, Justina. *The New Bohemians Handbook*	747
Martin, Justin. *Rebel Souls*	920
Milford, Nancy. *Savage Beauty*	B
Ohler, Norman. *The Bohemians*	940.53
Reid, David. *The Brazen Age*	974.7
The *Bohemians*. Ohler, Norman	940.53
Bohl, Loree	
Fearless Gardening	712
Bohme, Madelaine	
Ancient Bones	599.93
Bohmig, Franz	
★*The Month-By-Month Gardening Guide*	635
Boilen, Bob	
Your Song Changed My Life	780.92
Bok, Derek Curtis	
The Struggle to Reform Our Colleges	378.73
Boland, Becca	
Making the Most of Teen Library Volunteers	023
Boland, Eavan	
The Historians	821
New Collected Poems	821
A Woman Without a Country	821
★*The Bold Dry Garden*. Silver, Johanna	635.9
Boldly Go. Shatner, William	B
Boles, John B.	
Jefferson	B
Bolivar. Arana, Marie	B
BOLIVAR, SIMON, 1783-1830	
Arana, Marie. *Bolivar*	B
Bollywood. Ausaja, S. M. M.	791.43
Bolshoi Confidential. Morrison, Simon Alexander	792.8
Bolsta, Hyla Shifra	
The Illuminated Kaddish	296.4
Bolt, Robert	
A Man for All Seasons	822
Bolz-Weber, Nadia	
Accidental Saints	284.1
Shameless	261.8
BOLZ-WEBER, NADIA	
Bolz-Weber, Nadia. *Accidental Saints*	284.1
Bolz-Weber, Nadia. *Shameless*	261.8
The *Bomb*. Kaplan, Fred M.	355.8
Bomb. Sheinkin, Steve	623.4
Bomb Shelter. Philpott, Mary Laura	B
BOMB SQUADS	
Castner, Brian. *The Long Walk*	B
BOMBARDMENT	
Frank, Richard B. *Downfall*	940.54
Gladwell, Malcolm. ★*The Bomber Mafia*	940.54
Grayling, A. C. *Among the Dead Cities*	940.54
Hastings, Max. *Operation Pedestal*	940.54
Larson, Erik. ★*The Splendid and the Vile*	940.54
Maurer, Kevin. *Damn Lucky*	940.54
Moorhouse, Roger. *Berlin at War*	943
Reid, Anna. *Leningrad*	940.54
BOMBAY, SIDI MUBARAK	
Millard, Candice. ★*River of the Gods*	916.204
★The *Bomber Mafia*. Gladwell, Malcolm	940.54
BOMBER PILOTS	
Ambrose, Stephen E. *The Wild Blue*	940.54
Drury, Bob. *Lucky 666*	B
Makos, Adam. ★*A Higher Call*	940.54
Maurer, Kevin. *Damn Lucky*	940.54
Miller, Donald L. ★*Masters of the Air*	940.54
Simms, Brendan. *The Silver Waterfall*	940.54
Smith, Starr. *Jimmy Stewart*	B
Trimble, Lee. *Beyond the Call*	940.54
BOMBERS (AIRPLANES)	
Ambrose, Stephen E. *The Wild Blue*	940.54
Hastings, Max. *Operation Chastise*	940.54
Lewis, Damien. *The Dog Who Could Fly*	940.54
Toobin, Jeffrey. ★*Homegrown*	363.325
BOMBERS (PEOPLE)	
Wiehl, Lis W. *Hunting the Unabomber*	364.152
BOMBING INVESTIGATION	
Gage, Beverly. *The Day Wall Street Exploded*	974.7
Wiehl, Lis W. *Hunting the Unabomber*	364.152
BOMBING VICTIMS	
Wallace, Chris. *Countdown 1945*	940.54
BOMBINGS	
Burrough, Bryan. *Days of Rage*	303.48
Gage, Beverly. *The Day Wall Street Exploded*	974.7

1693

PUBLIC LIBRARY CORE COLLECTION: NONFICTION
Twentieth Edition

Gregory, Rebekah. *Taking My Life Back*	B
Johnson, Steven. *The Infernal Machine*	335
Jones, Doug. *Bending Toward Justice*	323.1196
Martin, Rachel Louise. *A Most Tolerant Little Town*	379.2
Melville, Wilma. ★*Hero Dogs*	636.7

BOMBS
Hersey, John. ★*Hiroshima*	940.54

Bomey, Nathan
Detroit Resurrected	977.4
The Bon Appetit Cookbook. Fairchild, Barbara	641.5

Bonanos, Christopher
Flash	B
The Bonanza King. Crouch, Gregory	B

Bond, Julian
★*Julian Bond's Time to Teach*	323.0975

Bond, Melissa
Blood Orange Night	616.8

BOND, MELISSA
Bond, Melissa. *Blood Orange Night*	616.8

BONDING (HUMAN-ANIMAL)
Bailey, Elisabeth. *The Sound of a Wild Snail Eating*	594
Bragg, Rick. *The Speckled Beauty*	636.7
Carr, Caleb. *My Beloved Monster*	B
Golbeck, Jennifer. *The Purest Bond*	636.7
Melville, Wilma. ★*Hero Dogs*	636.7
Myron, Vicki. ★*Dewey*	636.80092
Wynne, Clive D. L. ★*Dog Is Love*	636.7

BONDING (INTERPERSONAL RELATIONS)
Brand, Christo. *Mandela*	B
Gurdon, Meghan Cox. *The Enchanted Hour*	372.4
Way, Niobe. *Rebels with a Cause*	649

BONDS
Belfort, Jordan. ★*The Wolf of Investing*	332.63

Bondy, Dianne
Yoga Where You Are	613.7
The Bone and Sinew of the Land. Cox, Anna-Lisa	977

BONE CANCER
Ali, Fatima. ★*Savor*	B
Jaouad, Suleika. ★*Between Two Kingdoms*	B
Patchett, Ann. *Truth & Beauty*	B
A Bone to Pick. Bittman, Mark	338.10973
Bones. Meals, Roy A.	599.9

BONES
Hagerty, Alexa. ★*Still Life with Bones*	599.9
Meals, Roy A. *Bones*	599.9
Switek, Brian. *Skeleton Keys*	611

Bongiovanni, Archie
A Quick & Easy Guide to They/Them Pronouns	741.5

BONHOEFFER, DIETRICH, 1906-1945
Marsh, Charles. *Strange Glory*	B
Thomas, Gordon. *Defying Hitler*	920
Bonk. Roach, Mary	612.6

Bonner, Betsy
The Book of Atlantis Black	364.152

BONNER, BETSY
Bonner, Betsy. *The Book of Atlantis Black*	364.152

Bono
★*Surrender*	B

BONO, 1960-
Bono. ★*Surrender*	B
Bonobo. Waal, F. B. M. de	599.88

BONOBOS
Waal, F. B. M. de. *Bonobo*	599.88
Waal, F. B. M. de. *Our Inner Ape*	156

Boo, Katherine
★*Behind the Beautiful Forevers*	305.5

BOOGAARD, DEREK, 1982-2011
Branch, John. *Boy on Ice*	B
The Book. Houston, Keith	002.09

BOOK BURNING
Baez, Fernando. *Universal History of the Destruction of Books*	098

BOOK CLUB BEST BETS
Alexander, Michelle. *The New Jim Crow*	364.973
Baer, Kate. *What Kind of Woman*	811
Bailey, Desiree C. *What Noise Against the Cane*	811
Bauer, Shane. *American Prison*	365
Beck, Martha Nibley. *The Way of Integrity*	158.1
Blay, Zeba. *Carefree Black Girls*	305.48
Boo, Katherine. ★*Behind the Beautiful Forevers*	305.5
Broom, Sarah M. *The Yellow House*	B
Brown, Austin Channing. ★*I'm Still Here*	B
Brown, Daniel James. ★*The Boys in the Boat*	797.12
Browne, Mahogany L. ★*Black Girl Magic*	811.6
Bruder, Jessica. ★*Nomadland*	331.3
Brunson, Quinta. *She Memes Well*	B
Cain, Susan. ★*Bittersweet*	155.2
Carreyrou, John. ★*Bad Blood*	338.7
Carriere, Alice. *Everything/Nothing/Someone*	B
Carruthers, Charlene A. *Unapologetic*	305.48
Castillo, Elaine. ★*How to Read Now*	418
Cep, Casey N. ★*Furious Hours*	364.152
Chang, Emily. *Brotopia*	331.4
Chow, Kat. *Seeing Ghosts*	B
Chung, Nicole. ★*A Living Remedy*	B
Clay, Catrine. *King, Kaiser, Tsar*	B
Cottom, Tressie McMillan. *Thick*	301
Davis, Viola. ★*Finding Me*	B
De Waal, Edmund. *The Hare with Amber Eyes*	B
Desmond, Matthew. ★*Poverty, by America*	362.5
Doyle, Glennon. *Untamed*	B
Dunne, Griffin. ★*The Friday Afternoon Club*	B
Egan, Timothy. *The Worst Hard Time*	978
Eisen, Norman L. *The Last Palace*	920
Fagan, Kate. *All the Colors Came Out*	B
Finkel, David. *Thank You for Your Service*	920
Finnegan, William. *Barbarian Days*	B
Ford, Ashley C. ★*Somebody's Daughter*	B
Franklin, John Hope. *In Search of the Promised Land*	929
Garcia, Rodrigo. *A Farewell to Gabo and Mercedes*	B
Grann, David. ★*Killers of the Flower Moon*	976.6004
H, Lamya. ★*Hijab Butch Blues*	B
Halberstam, David. *The Coldest Winter*	951.904
Hardin, Lara Love. ★*The Many Lives of Mama Love*	B
Harry. ★*Spare*	B
Hauser, CJ. *The Crane Wife*	B
Havrilesky, Heather. *Foreverland*	306.81
Hendrickson, John. *Life on Delay*	B
Hong, Cathy Park. *Minor Feelings*	305.48
Horwitz, Tony. ★*Midnight Rising*	973.7
Hudes, Quiara Alegria. ★*My Broken Language*	B
Hurston, Zora Neale. ★*Barracoon*	B
Jauhar, Sandeep. *Heart*	612.1
Jefferson, Margo. *Negroland*	305.896
Kelly, Donika. *The Renunciations*	811
King, Ross. ★*Leonardo and the Last Supper*	759.5
Kolker, Robert. ★*Hidden Valley Road*	920
Krakauer, Jon. *Into the Wild*	917.9804
Larson, Erik. ★*The Devil in the White City*	364.15
Laymon, Kiese. ★*Heavy*	B
Lifford, Tina. *The Little Book of Big Lies*	155.2
Locke, Tembi. ★*From Scratch*	B
Mailhot, Terese Marie. *Heart Berries*	B
Mans, Jasmine. *Black Girl, Call Home*	811
McBride, James. *The Color of Water*	B
McColl, Sarah. *Joy Enough*	B
McGhee, Heather C. ★*The Sum of Us*	305.8
Moore, Wayetu. *The Dragons, the Giant, the Women*	B
Nafisi, Azar. *Things I've Been Silent About*	B
Nezhukumatathil, Aimee. *Bite by Bite*	641.3
Noah, Trevor. *Born a Crime*	B
Obama, Michelle. ★*Becoming*	B
Obama, Michelle. ★*The Light We Carry*	B
Oliva, Alejandra. *Rivermouth*	305.9
Orlean, Susan. ★*The Library Book*	027.4
Parrado, Nando. ★*Miracle in the Andes*	982
Patchett, Ann. ★*These Precious Days*	814
Pellegrino, Danny. *How Do I Un-Remember This?*	B
Perkins, Nichole. *Sometimes I Trip on How Happy We Could Be*	B
Perry, Imani. ★*South to America*	917
Raboteau, Emily. *Lessons for Survival*	814
Rankine, Claudia. ★*Citizen*	814
Renkl, Margaret. *The Comfort of Crows*	814.6
Robinson, Phoebe. *You Can't Touch My Hair and Other Things I Still Have to Explain*	792.7
Saad, Layla F. ★*Me and White Supremacy*	305.809
Schulz, Kathryn. ★*Lost & Found*	B

AUTHOR, TITLE, SERIES AND SUBJECT INDEX

Shapiro, Dani. ★*Inheritance*	B
Sinclair, Safiya. ★*How to Say Babylon*	B
Skloot, Rebecca. ★*The Immortal Life of Henrietta Lacks*	B
Sobel, Dava. *A More Perfect Heaven*	520.9
Taddeo, Lisa. *Three Women*	306.7082
Tate, Christie. ★*Group*	B
Thomas, R. Eric. *Here for It*	B
Tolentino, Jia. ★*Trick Mirror*	973.93
Vasquez-Lavado, Silvia. *In the Shadow of the Mountain*	B
Vedantam, Shankar. *Useful Delusions*	153.4
Wang, Qian Julie. ★*Beautiful Country*	B
Ward, Jesmyn. ★*The Fire This Time*	305.896
Westover, Tara. ★*Educated*	B
Wilkerson, Isabel. ★*Caste*	305.5
Winkler, Adam. *We the Corporations*	346.73
Yip-Williams, Julie. ★*The Unwinding of the Miracle*	973
Zamora, Javier. ★*Solito*	B

BOOK CLUBS
Brown, Noah. *Reading Together*	028.5
Nafisi, Azar. ★*Reading Lolita in Tehran*	B

BOOK COLLECTING
Berger, Sidney E. *The Dictionary of the Book*	002.03
Collins, Paul. *The Book of William*	016.8223
Lansky, Aaron. *Outwitting History*	002
Pettegree, Andrew. *The Library*	027.4

BOOK COLLECTORS
Davis, Margaret Leslie. *The Lost Gutenberg*	093
Kaag, John J. *American Philosophy*	191
Reed, Shannon. *Why We Read*	028

BOOK DESIGN
Lee, Marshall. *Bookmaking*	686
Rivers, Charlotte. *Little Book of Book Making*	686
The Book in the Renaissance. Pettegree, Andrew	070.5

BOOK INDUSTRY AND TRADE
De Hamel, Christopher. *The Manuscripts Club*	091
Larimer, Kevin. *The Poets & Writers Complete Guide to Being a Writer*	808
Palahniuk, Chuck. *Consider This*	B
Pettegree, Andrew. *The Book in the Renaissance*	070.5
Smyth, Adam. *The Book-Makers*	686.2
The Book of (more) Delights. Gay, Ross	814
Book of Ages. Lepore, Jill	B
The Book of Atlantis Black. Bonner, Betsy	364.152
The Book of Basketball. Simmons, Bill	796.323
Book of Blues. Kerouac, Jack	811
★*The Book of Charlie.* Von Drehle, David	B
★*A Book of Days.* Smith, Patti	779
The Book of Eels. Svensson, Patrik	597
The Book of Endings. Harrison, Leslie	811
The Book of Forgiving. Tutu, Desmond	179
The Book of Gutsy Women. Clinton, Hillary Rodham	920
★*The Book of Hope.* Goodall, Jane	128
Book of Hours. Young, Kevin	811
The Book of Hygge. Brits, Louisa Thomsen	747
The Book of James. Babb, Valerie Melissa	B
★*The Book of Jewish Food.* Roden, Claudia	641.5
The Book of Joy. Dalai Lama	294.3
The Book of Klezmer. Strom, Yale	781.62
The Book of Matt. Jimenez, Stephen	364.152
The Book of Miracles. Woodward, Kenneth L.	231.7
The Book of Mormon. Gutjahr, Paul C.	289.3
The Book of Numbers. Conway, John Horton	512
The Book of Phobias and Manias. Summerscale, Kate	616.85
The Book of Pride. Funk, Mason	920
The Book of Rosy. Pablo Cruz, Rosayra	B
The Book of Secrets. Xue, XInran	951.05
Book of Sketches, 1952-57. Kerouac, Jack	818
The Book of William. Collins, Paul	016.8223
★*The Book on Pie.* McDowell, Erin Jeanne	641.86
Book Repair. Lavender, Kenneth	025.8

BOOK REVIEWING
Mantel, Hilary. *Mantel Pieces*	824.914

BOOK REVIEWS
Mantel, Hilary. *Mantel Pieces*	824.914
The Book Smugglers. Fishman, David E.	940.53

BOOK THEFTS
Rydell, Anders. *The Book Thieves*	027
The Book Thieves. Rydell, Anders	027
★*The Book You Wish Your Parents Had Read.* Perry, Philippa	649

The Book-Makers. Smyth, Adam	686.2

BOOKBINDERS
Smyth, Adam. *The Book-Makers*	686.2

BOOKBINDING
Lavender, Kenneth. *Book Repair*	025.8
Rivers, Charlotte. *Little Book of Book Making*	686
Smyth, Adam. *The Book-Makers*	686.2
Bookends. Chabon, Michael	818
Booker T. Washington. Harlan, Louis R.	B
Booker T. Washington. Harlan, Louis R.	B
Bookmaking. Lee, Marshall	686

BOOKMAKING (BETTING)
Lang, Arne K. *Sports Betting and Bookmaking*	798.4010973

Bookman, Marc
A Descending Spiral	345.73

BOOKS
Bellos, David. *The Novel of the Century*	843
Bloom, Harold. *The Western Canon*	809
Bradford, Robin. ★*The Readers' Advisory Guide to Romance*	025.2
Breitenbach, Kathleen. ★*LGBTQIA+ Books for Children and Teens*	028.7
Cahill, Thomas. *How the Irish Saved Civilization*	941.501
Castleman, Michael. *The Untold Story of Books*	381
Collins, Paul. *The Book of William*	016.8223
Cox, Marge. *Kids' Books and Maker Activities*	372.41
Darkshire, Oliver. *Once Upon a Tome*	B
Dorr, Christina H. ★*Profiles in Resilience*	028.5
Duncan, Dennis. *Index, a History of The*	025.3
Fehrman, Craig. *Author in Chief*	920
Houston, Keith. *The Book*	002.09
Lansky, Aaron. *Outwitting History*	002
Lavender, Kenneth. *Book Repair*	025.8
Lee, Marshall. *Bookmaking*	686
Minois, Georges. *The Atheist's Bible*	200
Patterson, James. *The Secret Lives of Booksellers and Librarians*	381
Percy, Benjamin. *Thrill Me*	808.3
Pettegree, Andrew. *The Book in the Renaissance*	070.5
Pettegree, Andrew. *The Library*	027.4
Poe, Edgar Allan. *Essays and Reviews*	809
Reed, Shannon. *Why We Read*	028
Reynolds, David S. *Mightier Than the Sword*	813
Smith, Emma. *Portable Magic*	002
Smyth, Adam. *The Book-Makers*	686.2
Spence, Annie. *Dear Fahrenheit 451*	028.9
Spratford, Becky Siegel. *The Readers' Advisory Guide to Horror*	025.5
Wilde, Oscar. *The Artist as Critic*	809
Books and Islands in Ojibwe Country. Erdrich, Louise	977

BOOKS AND READING
Acocella, Joan Ross. ★*The Bloodied Nightgown*	814
Appleman, Deborah. *Literature and the New Culture Wars*	807
Basbanes, Nicholas A. *Every Book Its Reader*	028
Batuman, Elif. *The Possessed*	891.7
Bergstein, Rachelle. *The Genius of Judy*	813
Bloom, Harold. *The Western Canon*	809
Blumenthal, Sidney. *A Self-Made Man*	B
Bratt, Jessica Anne. *Let's Talk About Race in Storytimes*	027.62
Breitenbach, Kathleen. ★*LGBTQIA+ Books for Children and Teens*	028.7
Brown, Noah. *Reading Together*	028.5
Burt, Stephanie. *Don't Read Poetry*	811
Cart, Michael. *Young Adult Literature*	813.009
Castillo, Elaine. ★*How to Read Now*	418
Castleman, Michael. *The Untold Story of Books*	381
Chabon, Michael. *Bookends*	818
Chabon, Michael. *Maps and Legends*	801
Chance, Rosemary. *Young Adult Literature in Action*	011.62
Chee, Alexander. ★*How to Write an Autobiographical Novel*	B
Coetzee, J. M. *Late Essays, 2006-2017*	824
Corbett, Emily. *In Transition*	809
Damrosch, David. *Around the World in 80 Books*	809
Dehaene, Stanislas. *Reading in the Brain*	418
Dochartaigh, Kerri ni. *Cacophony of Bone*	B
Fehrman, Craig. *Author in Chief*	920
Gabbert, Elisa. *Any Person Is the Only Self*	814
Garner, Dwight. *The Upstairs Delicatessen*	B
Ghoting, Saroj Nadkarni. *Step into Storytime*	027.62
Gurdon, Meghan Cox. *The Enchanted Hour*	372.4
Harman, Claire. *Murder by the Book*	364.152
Hecht, Jennifer Michael. ★*The Wonder Paradox*	808.1
Highsmith, Patricia. ★*Patricia Highsmith's Diaries and Notebooks*	818

PUBLIC LIBRARY CORE COLLECTION: NONFICTION
Twentieth Edition

Houston, Keith. *The Book*	002.09
Hustvedt, Siri. *Mothers, Fathers, and Others*	814
Kaag, John J. *American Philosophy*	191
Kakutani, Michiko. *Ex Libris*	028
Kelly, Helena. *Jane Austen, the Secret Radical*	823
King, Ross. *Bookseller of Florence*	381
Kroger, Lisa. *Monster, She Wrote*	920
Kuo, Michelle. *Reading with Patrick*	B
Kurlansky, Mark. *Paper*	676
LaRue, James. ★*On Censorship*	025.2
Li, Yiyun. *Dear Friend, from My Life I Write to You in Your Life*	B
Manglik, Gauri. ★*Muslims in Story*	809
Mantel, Hilary. *Mantel Pieces*	824.914
McCann, Colum. *Letters to a Young Writer*	808.02
McDermott, Alice. *What About the Baby?*	814
Mead, Rebecca. *My Life in Middlemarch*	823
Moss, Gabrielle. *Paperback Crush*	813.009
Mustich, James. ★*1,000 Books to Read*	028
Nafisi, Azar. *Read Dangerously*	809
Nafisi, Azar. ★*Reading Lolita in Tehran*	B
Nafisi, Azar. *The Republic of Imagination*	B
Orner, Peter. *Am I Alone Here?*	814
Patchett, Ann. ★*These Precious Days*	814
Patterson, James. *The Secret Lives of Booksellers and Librarians*	381
Paul, Pamela. ★*How to Raise a Reader*	649
Percy, Benjamin. *Thrill Me*	808.3
Pettegree, Andrew. *The Library*	027.4
Prose, Francine. *What to Read and Why*	028
Puchner, Martin. *The Written World*	809
Reed, Shannon. *Why We Read*	028
Rehak, Melanie. *Girl Sleuth*	813
Rioux, Anne Boyd. *Meg, Jo, Beth, Amy*	813
Rosen, Jeffrey. *The Pursuit of Happiness*	973.3
Russo, Richard. *The Destiny Thief*	814
Ryback, Timothy W. *Hitler's Private Library*	027
Salter, James. *Don't Save Anything*	818
Scalzi, John. *Don't Live for Your Obituary*	808.02
Schwalbe, Will. ★*The End of Your Life Book Club*	B
Smiley, Jane. *Thirteen Ways of Looking at the Novel*	B
Smith, Emma. *Portable Magic*	002
Solnit, Rebecca. *The Faraway Nearby*	814
Spence, Annie. *Dear Fahrenheit 451*	028.9
Taylor, Goldie. *The Love You Save*	B
Thomson, Mike. *Syria's Secret Library*	956.9104
Tran, Phuc. ★*Sigh, Gone*	B
Wassef, Nadia. *Shelf Life*	B
Wilson-Lee, Edward. ★*The Catalogue of Shipwrecked Books*	B
Wolf, Maryanne. *Reader, Come Home*	418
Wood, James. *How Fiction Works*	808.3
Young, Damon. *The Art of Reading*	028.9
BOOKS FOR BROWSING	
Gottlieb, Iris. *Seeing Gender*	305.3
Magee, Bryan. *The Story of Philosophy*	190
Parker, Kate T. *Strong Is the New Pretty*	155.43
BOOKS FOR RELUCTANT READERS	
Burcaw, Shane. ★*Laughing at My Nightmare*	B
Felisbret, Eric. *Graffiti New York*	751.7
Ganz, Nicholas. ★*Graffiti World*	751.7
Munroe, Randall. ★*What If?*	500
Bookseller of Florence. King, Ross	381
The Bookseller of Kabul. Seierstad, Asne	958.1
BOOKSELLERS	
Castleman, Michael. *The Untold Story of Books*	381
Cumming, Laura. ★*The Vanishing Velazquez*	759.6
Darkshire, Oliver. *Once Upon a Tome*	B
Daugherty, Tracy. *Larry McMurtry*	B
King, Ross. *Bookseller of Florence*	381
Patterson, James. *The Secret Lives of Booksellers and Librarians*	381
Seierstad, Asne. *The Bookseller of Kabul*	958.1
BOOKSELLING	
Castleman, Michael. *The Untold Story of Books*	381
A Bookshop in Berlin. Frenkel, Francoise	B
BOOKSTORES	
Castleman, Michael. *The Untold Story of Books*	381
Darkshire, Oliver. *Once Upon a Tome*	B
Frenkel, Francoise. *A Bookshop in Berlin*	B
Wassef, Nadia. *Shelf Life*	B
Boom. Shnayerson, Michael	701
Boom Town. Anderson, Sam	976.6
Boone. Morgan, Robert	B
BOONE, DANIEL, 1734-1820	
Drury, Bob. *Blood and Treasure*	B
Morgan, Robert. *Boone*	B
Boone, Matthew S.	
Stop Avoiding Stuff	152.4
Boorstin, Daniel J.	
The Americans	973
The Americans	973
Boot, Max	
Invisible Armies	355.02
★*The Road Not Taken*	B
★*War Made New*	355.0209
BOOTH, EDWIN, 1833-1893	
Martin, Justin. *Rebel Souls*	920
BOOTH, JOHN WILKES, 1838-1865	
Alford, Terry. *Fortune's Fool*	B
Booth, Michael	
The Almost Nearly Perfect People	948.071
Booth, Wayne C.	
The Craft of Research	001.4
BOOTLEGGERS	
Hill, David. *The Vapors*	976.7
Okrent, Daniel. *Last Call*	363.4
Bootstrapped. Quart, Alissa	305.5
Bop Apocalypse. Torgoff, Martin	781.65
BORDEN, LIZZIE, 1860-1927	
Robertson, Cara. *The Trial of Lizzie Borden*	345.744
Border. Kassabova, Kapka	949.9
BORDER DISPUTES	
Taylor, Alan. *The Civil War of 1812*	973.5
Ullrich, Volker. *Germany 1923*	943.085
BORDER PATROL AGENTS	
Cantu, Francisco. *The Line Becomes a River*	B
Soboroff, Jacob. ★*Separated*	325.73
BORDER PATROLS	
Hernandez Castillo, Marcelo. *Children of the Land*	B
BORDER SECURITY	
Cantu, Francisco. *The Line Becomes a River*	B
Kassabova, Kapka. *Border*	949.9
Lekas Miller, Anna. *Love Across Borders*	323.6
Molnar, Petra. *The Walls Have Eyes*	363.28
Zamora, Javier. ★*Solito*	B
Borderland Apocrypha. Cody, Anthony	811
BORDERLANDS	
Bobrow-Strain, Aaron. *The Death and Life of Aida Hernandez*	972
Corral, Eduardo C. *Guillotine*	811.6
Grandin, Greg. *The End of the Myth*	973
Guinn, Jeff. ★*War on the Border*	972.08
Kassabova, Kapka. *Border*	949.9
Longo, Matthew. *The Picnic*	947.084
Phillips, Timothy. *Retracing the Iron Curtain*	909.82
Robb, Graham. *The Debatable Land*	941.3
Ronstadt, Linda. *Feels Like Home*	B
Stewart, Rory. *The Marches*	941.3
Borderline. Kriss, Alexander	616.85
BORDERLINE SYNDROME (PSYCHIATRY)	
Kriss, Alexander. *Borderline*	616.85
Scheier, Liz. *Never Simple*	B
Bordewich, Fergus M.	
America's Great Debate	973.6
Bound for Canaan	973.7
Congress at War	324.2734
Klan War	973.8
Washington	975.3
Bordo, Susan	
The Creation of Anne Boleyn	942.05
Bored and Brilliant. Zomorodi, Manoush	153.3
BOREDOM	
Zomorodi, Manoush. *Bored and Brilliant*	153.3
Borges. Williamson, Edwin	B
Borges and Me. Parini, Jay	813
Borges, Jorge Luis	
Selected Non-Fictions	864
★*Selected Poems*	861
BORGES, JORGE LUIS, 1899-1986	
Borges, Jorge Luis. *Selected Non-Fictions*	864

AUTHOR, TITLE, SERIES AND SUBJECT INDEX

Borges, Jorge Luis. ★*Selected Poems* ... 861
Parini, Jay. *Borges and Me* ... 813
Williamson, Edwin. *Borges* ... B
BORGIA FAMILY
  Hibbert, Christopher. *The Borgias and Their Enemies* ... 920
  Meyer, G. J. *The Borgias* ... 920
  Strathern, Paul. *The Borgias* ... 945.06
BORGIA, CESARE, 1476?-1507
  Strathern, Paul. *The Borgias* ... 945.06
BORGIA, LUCREZIA, 1480-1519
  Bradford, Sarah. *Lucrezia Borgia* ... B
  Strathern, Paul. *The Borgias* ... 945.06
The **Borgias**. Meyer, G. J. ... 920
The **Borgias**. Strathern, Paul ... 945.06
The **Borgias** *and Their Enemies*. Hibbert, Christopher ... 920
Borman, Tracy
  Anne Boleyn and Elizabeth I ... 920
  Crown & Sceptre ... 941
  Elizabeth's Women ... B
  Henry VIII and the Men Who Made Him ... 942.05
  The Private Lives of the Tudors ... 920
  Thomas Cromwell ... B
Born A Crime. Noah, Trevor ... B
Born in Blackness. French, Howard W. ... 960
Born in Blood and Fire. Chasteen, John Charles ... 980
Born Naked. Mowat, Farley ... B
★*Born of Lakes and Plains*. Hyde, Anne Farrar ... 978
Born on a Blue Day. Tammet, Daniel ... B
★*Born Survivors*. Holden, Wendy ... 940.53
Born to Be Good. Keltner, Dacher ... 155.2
Born to Be Hanged. Thomson, Keith ... 910.4
Born to Be Posthumous. Dery, Mark ... B
★*Born to Run*. McDougall, Christopher ... 796.42
★*Born to Run*. Springsteen, Bruce ... B
Born with Teeth. Mulgrew, Kate ... 791.45028
Borneman, Walter R.
  The Admirals ... B
  Alaska ... 979.8
  Macarthur at War ... B
  Polk ... B
BORREL, ANDREE, 1919-1944
  Rose, Sarah. *D-Day Girls* ... 940.53
Borrell, Brendan
  The First Shots ... 615.3
Borsato, Diane
  Mushrooming ... 579.6
Boruch, Marianne
  Eventually One Dreams the Real Thing ... 811
BORUP, GEORGE, 1885-1912
  Welky, David. *A Wretched and Precarious Situation* ... 910.911
Borzutzky, Daniel
  Lake Michigan ... 811
  The Performance of Becoming Human ... 811
Boschert, Sherry
  37 Words ... 344.73
Boser, Ulrich
  Learn Better ... 153.1
Bosh! Firth, Henry ... 641.5
Bosker, Bianca
  Cork Dork ... 641.2
  Get the Picture ... 701
BOSKER, BIANCA
  Bosker, Bianca. *Cork Dork* ... 641.2
  Bosker, Bianca. *Get the Picture* ... 701
BOSNIA AND HERCEGOVINA
  Hemon, Aleksandar. *My Parents* ... 814
  Maass, Peter. *Love Thy Neighbor* ... 949.702
  Stern, Jessica. *My War Criminal* ... 341.6
  Trebincevic, Kenan. *The Bosnia List* ... B
The **Bosnia** *List*. Trebincevic, Kenan ... B
BOSNIAN AMERICANS
  Hemon, Aleksandar. *My Parents* ... 814
  Trebincevic, Kenan. *The Bosnia List* ... B
Boss Cupid. Gunn, Thom ... 821
Boss Life. Downs, Paul ... 338.7
Bossiere, Zoe
  Cactus Country ... 306

BOSSIERE, ZOE, 1992-
  Bossiere, Zoe. *Cactus Country* ... 306
BOSTON MARATHON
  Gregory, Rebekah. *Taking My Life Back* ... B
BOSTON MARATHON BOMBING, BOSTON, MASS., 2013
  Gregory, Rebekah. *Taking My Life Back* ... B
BOSTON TEA PARTY, 1773
  Norton, Mary Beth. *1774* ... 973.3
  Unger, Harlow G. *American Tempest* ... 973.3
BOSTON, MASSACHUSETTS
  Kidder, Tracy. ★*Rough Sleepers* ... 362.5
  Lepore, Jill. *Book of Ages* ... B
  Shane, Scott. ★*Flee North* ... 973.7
  Sherman, Casey. *Hunting Whitey* ... B
  Stout, Glenn. *Fenway 1912* ... 796.357
  Unger, Harlow G. *American Tempest* ... 973.3
Bostridge, Ian
  Schubert's Winter Journey ... 782.4
BOSTRIDGE, IAN
  Bostridge, Ian. *Schubert's Winter Journey* ... 782.4
Bostridge, Mark
  Florence Nightingale ... B
Boswell, James
  ★*The Life of Samuel Johnson* ... B
BOSWELL, JAMES, 1740-1795
  Damrosch, Leopold. *The Club* ... 920
BOTANICAL GARDENS
  Holway, Tatiana M. *The Flower of Empire* ... 727
  Johnson, Victoria. ★*American Eden* ... 580.973
BOTANISTS
  Davis, Wade. *One River* ... 581.6
  Holway, Tatiana M. *The Flower of Empire* ... 727
  Johnson, Victoria. ★*American Eden* ... 580.973
  Lowman, Margaret. *The Arbornaut* ... 581.7
  Magdalena, Carlos. *The Plant Messiah* ... 333.95
  McNeur, Catherine. *Mischievous Creatures* ... 920
  Stone, Daniel. *The Food Explorer* ... B
BOTANY
  Drori, Jonathan. *Around the World in 80 Plants* ... 581.63
  Holway, Tatiana M. *The Flower of Empire* ... 727
  Johnson, Victoria. ★*American Eden* ... 580.973
  Kassinger, Ruth. ★*A Garden of Marvels* ... 580.92
  Kimmerer, Robin Wall. ★*Braiding Sweetgrass* ... 304.2
  Mabey, Richard. *The Cabaret of Plants* ... 580
  Schlanger, Zoe. ★*The Light Eaters* ... 571.2
  Sevigny, Melissa L. ★*Brave the Wild River* ... 580.9
  Sheldrake, Merlin. *Entangled Life* ... 579.5
  Stewart, Amy. *Wicked Plants* ... 581.6
Botelho, Elena L.
  The CEO Next Door ... 658.4
BOTSWANA
  Wood, Levison. *The Last Giants* ... 599.67
The **Bottom** *Line for Baby*. Bryson, Tina Payne ... 618.92
Bottom of the 33rd. Barry, Dan ... 796.357
Bottoms Up and the Devil Laughs. Howley, Kerry ... 352.37
Boucheron, Patrick
  Machiavelli ... 320.1092
Bouchon Bakery. Keller, Thomas ... 641.594
BOUDREAU, PHILLIP
  Cameron, Silver Donald. *Blood in the Water* ... 364.152
BOULLOCHE, ANDRE
  Kaiser, Charles. *The Cost of Courage* ... B
Bound by War. Capozzola, Christopher ... 355
Bound for Canaan. Bordewich, Fergus M. ... 973.7
Bound for the Promised Land. Larson, Kate Clifford ... B
Bound to the Fire. Deetz, Kelley Fanto ... 641.59
Bound, Mensun
  The Ship Beneath the Ice ... 919.8904
BOUND, MENSUN
  Bound, Mensun. *The Ship Beneath the Ice* ... 919.8904
BOUNDARIES
  Bregman, Rutger. *Utopia for Realists* ... 335
  Ehrenreich, Ben. *The Way to the Spring* ... 956.95
  Grandin, Greg. *The End of the Myth* ... 973
  Hoyer, Katja. ★*Beyond the Wall* ... 943.087
  Kassabova, Kapka. *Border* ... 949.9
  Khan, Yasmin. *Ripe Figs* ... 641.595
  Longo, Matthew. *The Picnic* ... 947.084

PUBLIC LIBRARY CORE COLLECTION: NONFICTION
Twentieth Edition

Malhotra, Aanchal. *Remnants of Partition*	954.04
Marshall, Tim. *The Power of Geography*	320.1
Robb, Graham. *The Debatable Land*	941.3
Scenters-Zapico, Natalie. *Lima*	811
Shehadeh, Raja. *Where the Line Is Drawn*	956.9405
Stewart, Rory. *The Marches*	941.3
Theroux, Paul. *On the Plain of Snakes*	917
Tolan, Sandy. *Children of the Stone*	780

BOUNDARIES (INTERPERSONAL RELATIONS)

Hustvedt, Siri. *Mothers, Fathers, and Others*	814
Stryker, Kitty. *Ask*	302
The Bounty. Alexander, Caroline	996.1

BOUNTY HUNTERS

Dubus, Andre. *Ghost Dogs*	814

BOUNTY MUTINY, 1789

Alexander, Caroline. *The Bounty*	996.1
Preston, Diana. *Paradise in Chains*	996.18
Bourdain. Woolever, Laurie	B

Bourdain, Anthony

★*Appetites*	641.5
★*Kitchen Confidential*	B
Medium Raw	B
The Nasty Bits	641.5092
★*World Travel*	641.59

BOURDAIN, ANTHONY, 1956-2018

Bourdain, Anthony. ★*World Travel*	641.59
Bourdain, Anthony. ★*Kitchen Confidential*	B
Bourdain, Anthony. *Medium Raw*	B
Vitale, Tom. *In the Weeds*	B
Woolever, Laurie. *Bourdain*	B

Bouverie, Tim

Appeasement	327.41043
Bovids of the World. Castello, Jose R.	599.64

Bowden, Mark

Black Hawk Down	967.7305
The Case of the Vanishing Blonde	364.10973
Guests of the Ayatollah	955.05
★*Hue 1968*	959.704
The Last Stone	363.25
Life Sentence	364.106
The Steal	973.933

Bowdler, Michelle

★*Is Rape a Crime?*	B

BOWDLER, MICHELLE

Bowdler, Michelle. ★*Is Rape a Crime?*	B

Bowe, Whitney

The Beauty of Dirty Skin	646.7

Bowen, Dana

Dynamite Kids Cooking School	641.5

Bowen, Sesali

Bad Fat Black Girl	305.42

BOWEN, SESALI

Bowen, Sesali. *Bad Fat Black Girl*	305.42

BOWERS, SAMUEL HOLLOWAY, 1924-2006

Wilkie, Curtis. *When Evil Lived in Laurel*	305.8

Bowers, Sharon

Home Ec for Everyone	640

BOWIE, DAVID, 1947-2016

Jones, Dylan. *David Bowie*	B
Morley, Paul. *The Age of Bowie*	B
Reynolds, Simon. *Shock and Awe*	781.6609

Bowien, Danny

Mission Vegan	641.5

Bowker, Gordon

★*James Joyce*	B
Bowl. Volger, Lukas	641.81

Bowler, Kate

No Cure for Being Human	B

BOWLER, KATE

Bowler, Kate. *No Cure for Being Human*	B

Bowles, Hamish

Vogue & the Metropolitan Museum of Art Costume Institute	746.9

Bowlin, Ben

Stuff They Don't Want You to Know	001.9

BOWLING

Manzione, Gianmarc. *Pin Action*	B
Mullen, Michelle. *Bowling Fundamentals*	794.6
Bowling Fundamentals. Mullen, Michelle	794.6

Bown, Stephen R.

Merchant Kings	338.8

BOWSER, MARY ELIZABETH, APPROXIMATELY 1840-

Abbott, Karen. *Liar, Temptress, Soldier, Spy*	920

BOXERS (SPORTS)

Assael, Shaun. *The Murder of Sonny Liston*	B
Century, Douglas. *Barney Ross*	B
Coffin, Jaed. *Roughhouse Friday*	B
Dubus, Andre. *Townie*	B
Eig, Jonathan. ★*Ali*	B
Gildea, William. *The Longest Fight*	B
Haygood, Wil. ★*Sweet Thunder*	B
Keith, Philip A. *All Blood Runs Red*	B
Kimball, George. *Four Kings*	B
Kram, Mark. *Smokin' Joe*	B
Liebling, A. J. ★*The Sweet Science*	796.83
Montville, Leigh. *Sting Like a Bee*	B
Roberts, Randy. *Blood Brothers*	920
Roberts, Randy. *Joe Louis*	B
Schaap, Jeremy. *Cinderella Man*	B
Stanton, Mike. ★*Unbeaten*	B
Stratton, W. K. *Floyd Patterson*	B
Tyson, Mike. *Iron Ambition*	B
Ward, Geoffrey C. *Unforgivable Blackness*	B

BOXING

Assael, Shaun. *The Murder of Sonny Liston*	B
Butler, Brin-Jonathan. *The Domino Diaries*	796.83
Century, Douglas. *Barney Ross*	B
Coffin, Jaed. *Roughhouse Friday*	B
Gildea, William. *The Longest Fight*	B
Haygood, Wil. ★*Sweet Thunder*	B
Kimball, George. *Four Kings*	B
Liebling, A. J. ★*The Sweet Science*	796.83
Roberts, Randy. *Joe Louis*	B
Schaap, Jeremy. *Cinderella Man*	B
Stanton, Mike. ★*Unbeaten*	B
Stratton, W. K. *Floyd Patterson*	B
Ward, Geoffrey C. *Unforgivable Blackness*	B

BOXING MATCHES

Gildea, William. *The Longest Fight*	B
Kimball, George. *Four Kings*	B
Kram, Mark. *Smokin' Joe*	B

BOXING TRAINERS

Tyson, Mike. *Iron Ambition*	B
The Boy from Kyiv. Harss, Marina	B
Boy on Ice. Branch, John	B
★*The Boy Who Harnessed the Wind*. Kamkwamba, William	B

Boyce, W. Thomas

The Orchid and the Dandelion	649

BOYD, BELLE, 1844-1900

Abbott, Karen. *Liar, Temptress, Soldier, Spy*	920

Boyd, Herb

Black Detroit	977.4
We Shall Overcome	323.1196

Boyd, Nikki

★*Beautifully Organized*	648

Boyer, Anne

The Undying	B

BOYER, ANNE, 1973-

Boyer, Anne. *The Undying*	B

Boyes, Alice

The Anxiety Toolkit	616.85

Boykin, Keith

Race Against Time	305.8
★*Why Does Everything Have to Be About Race?*	305.8

BOYKIN, KEITH

Boykin, Keith. ★*Why Does Everything Have to Be About Race?*	305.8

Boylan, Jennifer Finney

Good Boy	B

BOYLAN, JENNIFER FINNEY, 1958-

Boylan, Jennifer Finney. *Good Boy*	B

Boyle, Greg

Tattoos on the Heart	277

BOYLE, GREG

Boyle, Greg. *Tattoos on the Heart*	277

Boyle, Kevin

Arc of Justice	345.73
The Shattering	973.923

AUTHOR, TITLE, SERIES AND SUBJECT INDEX

Boyle, Rebecca
   Our Moon — 523.3
BOYLE, WILLIAM ANTHONY, 1904-1985
   Bradley, Mark A. *Blood Runs Coal* — B
★*Boymom*. Whippman, Ruth — 305.23
★*The Boys*. Howard, Ron — B
BOYS
   Austin, Nefertiti. *Motherhood so White* — B
   Brown, Emma. *To Raise a Boy* — 649
   Davis, Joshua. *Spare Parts* — 629.8
   Harris, Taylor. *This Boy We Made* — B
   Hobbs, Jeff. *Show Them You're Good* — 373
   Iggulden, Conn. *The Double Dangerous Book for Boys* — 031.02
   Kirkby, Bruce. *Blue Sky Kingdom* — 954.96
   Lockley, Thomas. *African Samurai* — B
   Macy, Beth. ★*Truevine* — B
   Manuel, Ian. *My Time Will Come* — B
   Moore, Wes. *The Other Wes Moore* — B
   Natterson, Cara Familian. ★*Decoding Boys* — 649
   Nelson, David B. *Boys Enter the House* — 364.152
   Porter, Billy. ★*Unprotected* — B
   Reiner, Andrew. *Better Boys, Better Men* — 155.43
   Rowe, Mickey. *Fearlessly Different* — B
   Sattouf, Riad. *The Arab of the Future 2* — 741.5
   Sattouf, Riad. *The Arab of the Future* — 741.5
   Watkins, D. *Black Boy Smile* — B
   Way, Niobe. *Rebels with a Cause* — 649
   Wegner, Bobbi. *Raising Feminist Boys* — 305.23
   Whippman, Ruth. ★*Boymom* — 305.23
★*Boys & Sex*. Orenstein, Peggy — 305.235
Boys Among Men. Abrams, Jonathan P. D. — 796.323
Boys Enter the House. Nelson, David B. — 364.152
★*The Boys in the Boat*. Brown, Daniel James — 797.12
The Boys in the Cave. Gutman, Matt — 796.52
★*Boys in the Trees*. Simon, Carly — 782.42164
★*The Boys of Winter*. Coffey, Wayne R. — 796.962
Boys Will Be Boys. Pearlman, Jeff — 796.332
BOYS' SCHOOLS
   Kimmerle, Erin H. *We Carry Their Bones* — 365
BRACELETS
   Gedeon, Jade. *Beautiful Bracelets by Hand* — 745.594
Bracken, Peg
   The I Hate to Cook Book — 641.5
★*Bracketology*. Lunardi, Joe — 796.323
Brackett, Marc A.
   Permission to Feel — 152.4
Bradburd, Rus
   All the Dreams We've Dreamed — 796.323
The Bradbury Chronicles. Weller, Sam — B
Bradbury, Dominic
   The Iconic Interior — 747
   Mountain Modern — 728
Bradbury, Neil
   A Taste for Poison — 615.9
Bradbury, Ray
   ★*Remembrance* — 813
BRADBURY, RAY, 1920-2012
   Bradbury, Ray. ★*Remembrance* — 813
   Weller, Sam. *The Bradbury Chronicles* — B
BRADDOCK, JAMES J., 1906-1974
   Schaap, Jeremy. *Cinderella Man* — B
Bradford, Joy Harden
   Sisterhood Heals — 158.2
Bradford, Robin
   ★*The Readers' Advisory Guide to Romance* — 025.2
Bradford, Sarah
   Lucrezia Borgia — B
BRADFORD, WILLIAM, 1590-1657
   Philbrick, Nathaniel. ★*Mayflower* — 973.2
   Whittock, Martyn. *Mayflower Lives* — 974.4
Bradlee, Ben
   The Kid — B
Bradley, Barbara
   Drawing People — 743.4
Bradley, James
   Deep Water — 578.77
   Flags of Our Fathers — 940.54
   Flyboys — 940.54

Bradley, Mark A.
   Blood Runs Coal — B
BRADLEY, OMAR NELSON, 1893-1981
   Jordan, Jonathan W. *Brothers, Rivals, Victors* — 940.54
Bradley, Steve
   Pruning Simplified — 631.5
Bradshaw, John
   ★*Cat Sense* — 636.8
   ★*Dog Sense* — 636.7
Brady vs. *Manning*. Myers, Gary — B
Brady, Amy
   Ice — 553.7
Brady, Frank
   Endgame — B
Brady, James
   The Coldest War — B
BRADY, JAMES, 1928-2009
   Brady, James. *The Coldest War* — B
BRADY, MATHEW B., CA. 1823-1896
   Wilson, Robert. *Mathew Brady* — B
Brady, Patricia
   Martha Washington — B
BRADY, TOM, 1977-
   Benedict, Jeff. *The Dynasty* — 796.332
   Myers, Gary. *Brady vs. Manning* — B
Brag Better. Fineman, Meredith — 650.1
Bragg, Melvyn
   ★*The Adventure of English* — 420
Bragg, Rick
   ★*The Best Cook in the World* — 641.5975
   The Speckled Beauty — 636.7
   Where I Come From — 975
BRAGG, RICK
   Bragg, Rick. ★*The Best Cook in the World* — 641.5975
   Bragg, Rick. *The Speckled Beauty* — 636.7
   Bragg, Rick. *Where I Come From* — 975
Bragg, Sarah
   Is Everyone Happier Than Me? — 248.4
BRAHE, TYCHO, 1546-1601
   Fauber, L. S. *Heaven on Earth* — B
BRAHMINS
   French, Patrick. *The World Is What It Is* — B
BRAHMS, JOHANNES, 1833-1897
   Swafford, Jan. *Johannes Brahms* — B
Braided. Ricanati, Elizabeth — B
★*Braiding Sweetgrass*. Kimmerer, Robin Wall — 304.2
The Brain. Eagleman, David — 612.8
BRAIN
   Barrett, Lisa Feldman. ★*How Emotions Are Made* — 152.4
   Bloom, Paul. *Psych* — 150
   Bullmore, Edward T. *The Inflamed Mind* — 616.85
   Burnett, Dean. *Idiot Brain* — 612.8
   Clark, Andy. *The Experience Machine* — 153
   Davis, Kevin. *The Brain Defense* — 345.747
   Dehaene, Stanislas. *Reading in the Brain* — 418
   Deisseroth, Karl. *Projections* — 616.89
   Dittrich, Luke. ★*Patient H.M.* — 616.85
   Eagleman, David. *The Brain* — 612.8
   Eagleman, David. *Incognito* — 153
   Eagleman, David. *Livewired* — 612.8
   Eliot, Lise. *Pink Brain, Blue Brain* — 612.6
   Fine, Cordelia. *Testosterone Rex* — 155.3
   Fleming, Renee. ★*Music and Mind* — 615.8
   Frank, Lone. *The Pleasure Shock* — 616.8
   Gupta, Sanjay. ★*Keep Sharp* — 153.4
   Hallinan, Joseph T. *Why We Make Mistakes* — 153
   Kean, Sam. *The Tale of the Dueling Neurosurgeons* — 617.4
   Kinzer, Stephen. *Poisoner in Chief* — B
   Konnikova, Maria. *Mastermind* — 153.4
   Kurzweil, Ray. ★*The Singularity Is Near* — 153.9
   Magsamen, Susan. *Your Brain on Art* — 111
   Marsh, Henry. *Admissions* — B
   Marsh, Henry. ★*Do No Harm* — B
   Medina, John. *Brain Rules* — 153
   Nakazawa, Donna Jackson. *The Angel and the Assassin* — 612.8
   Nerenberg, Jenara. *Divergent Mind* — 616.89
   Paul, Annie Murphy. *The Extended Mind* — 128
   Perlmutter, David. *The Grain Brain Cookbook* — 651.56

Rogers, Susan E. ★ *This Is What It Sounds Like*	781.1
Sagan, Carl. *Broca's Brain*	128
Sagan, Carl. *The Dragons of Eden*	153
Sapolsky, Robert M. *Behave*	612.8
Sarma, Sanjay E. *Grasp*	370.15
Siegel, Daniel J. *Brainstorm*	155.5
Taylor, Jill Bolte. *My Stroke of Insight*	362.19681
Willeumier, Kristen. ★ *Biohack Your Brain*	612.8
Wolf, Maryanne. *Reader, Come Home*	418

BRAIN CANCER
Quinn, Tallu Schuyler. *What We Wish Were True*	B
Townsend, Alan R. ★ *This Ordinary Stardust*	B

BRAIN CHEMISTRY
Guyenet, Stephan J. *The Hungry Brain*	616.85

BRAIN CONCUSSIONS
Fainaru-Wada, Mark. *League of Denial*	617.1
Laskas, Jeanne Marie. *Concussion*	617.5
The Brain Defense. Davis, Kevin	345.747

BRAIN DISEASES
Kandel, Eric R. ★ *The Disordered Mind*	616.89
Karlawish, Jason. ★ *The Problem of Alzheimer's*	616.8
Kean, Sam. *The Tale of the Dueling Neurosurgeons*	617.4
Kolata, Gina Bari. *Mercies in Disguise*	616
Nakazawa, Donna Jackson. *The Angel and the Assassin*	612.8
Thomson, Helen. *Unthinkable*	612.8
Willeumier, Kristen. ★ *Biohack Your Brain*	612.8

BRAIN INJURY
Chesney, Will. *No Ordinary Dog*	958.104
Brain on Fire. Cahalan, Susannah	616.8
Brain Rules. Medina, John	153

BRAIN TUMORS
Delaney, Rob. ★ *A Heart That Works*	B
Nordland, Rod. *Waiting for the Monsoon*	B
Brainstorm. Siegel, Daniel J.	155.5

BRAINSTORMING
Malone, Thomas W. *Superminds*	005.7

BRAINWASHING
Branigan, Tania. *Red Memory*	951.05
Huxley, Aldous. ★ *Brave New World Revisited*	823
Jones, Faith. *Sex Cult Nun*	B
Kinzer, Stephen. *Poisoner in Chief*	B
Lake, Dianne. *Member of the Family*	364.152
Simon, Matt. *Plight of the Living Dead*	591.6

Braitman, Laurel
Animal Madness	591.5
What Looks Like Bravery	B

BRAITMAN, LAUREL
Braitman, Laurel. *What Looks Like Bravery*	B

Bram, Christopher
Eminent Outlaws	920

BRAMANTE, ANDY
Tesoriero, Heather Won. *The Class*	507.1

Branch, John
Boy on Ice	B
The Last Cowboys	920

Branch, Taylor
★ *At Canaan's Edge*	323.1196
The Clinton Tapes	973.929
Parting the Waters	973
★ *Pillar of Fire*	323.1

BRANCUSI, CONSTANTIN, 1876-1957
Roe, Sue. *In Montmartre*	920

BRAND CHOICE
Vanderbilt, Tom. *You May Also Like*	153.8
Brand NFL. Oriard, Michael	796.332

Brand, Adele
The Hidden World of the Fox	599.775

Brand, Christo
Mandela	B

BRANDEIS, LOUIS DEMBITZ, 1856-1941
Cohen, Adam. ★ *Imbeciles*	344.7304
Urofsky, Melvin I. *Louis D. Brandeis*	B

BRANDO, MARLON, 1924-2004
Mann, William J. *The Contender*	B

Brandow, Todd
Edward Steichen	770.92

Brandreth, Gyles Daubeney
Have You Eaten Grandma?	428

Brands, H. W.
The Age of Gold	979.4
★ *Andrew Jackson, His Life and Times*	B
Dreams of El Dorado	978
The First American	B
★ *Founding Partisans*	973.3
The General vs. the President	973.918092
★ *Heirs of the Founders*	973.5
The Last Campaign	973.8
★ *The Man Who Saved the Union*	B
★ *Our First Civil War*	973.3
Reagan	B
Traitor to His Class	B
Woodrow Wilson	B
★ *The Zealot and the Emancipator*	920

Brandt, Anthony
The Man Who Ate His Boots	910.91

Brandt, Anthony K.
The Runaway Species	153.3

Brandvig, Jera
Quilt As-You-Go Made Vintage	746.46

Branhagen, Alan
Native Plants of the Midwest	635.9

Branigan, Tania
Red Memory	951.05

Brannen, Peter
The Ends of the World	576.8

Branson, Gary D.
Home, Water & Moisture Problems	643

BRANT, JOSEPH, MOHAWK CHIEF, 1742-1807
Taylor, Alan. *The Divided Ground*	974.7

Branum, Guy
My Life as a Goddess	B

BRANUM, GUY, 1975-
Branum, Guy. *My Life as a Goddess*	B

BRAQUE, GEORGES, 1882-1963
Roe, Sue. *In Montmartre*	920

Brasfield, Hope
Satisfying Stitches	746.44

Braswell, Porter
★ *Let Them See You*	650.1

Bratt, Jessica Anne
Let's Talk About Race in Storytimes	027.62

Braudy, Leo
Haunted	398.45

BRAUN, EVA
Gortemaker, Heike B. *Eva Braun*	B
Brave. McGowan, Rose	B
Brave Hearted. Hickman, Katie	978
★ *Brave New World Revisited*. Huxley, Aldous	823
★ *Brave The Wild River*. Sevigny, Melissa L.	580.9
★ *Bravetart*. Parks, Stella	641.86
Braving The Wilderness. Brown, Brene	305.8
Bravo Company. Kesling, Ben	958.104

Bravo, Reah
★ *Complicit*	331.4
The Brazen Age. Reid, David	974.7
Brazil. Skidmore, Thomas E.	981

BRAZIL
Moser, Benjamin. *Why This World*	B
Reel, Monte. *The Last of the Tribe*	981
Skidmore, Thomas E. *Brazil*	981
Talty, Stephan. *The Good Assassin*	364.15

Brazile, Donna
For Colored Girls Who Have Considered Politics	328.73

BRAZILIAN PEOPLE
Gracie, Rickson. *Breathe*	B
Breach of Faith. Horne, Jed	976.3

BREAD
Beranbaum, Rose Levy. ★ *Rose's Baking Basics*	641.81
Bittman, Mark. ★ *Bittman Bread*	641.81
Black, Sarah. *One Dough, Ten Breads*	641.81
Forkish, Ken. *Evolutions in Bread*	664
Forkish, Ken. *Flour Water Salt Yeast*	641.81
Forkish, Ken. ★ *Let's Make Bread!*	741.5
Francois, Zoe. *Holiday and Celebration Bread in Five Minutes a Day*	641.81
Hoffman, Brian Hart. ★ *Bake from Scratch; Volume Two*	641.81
Hollywood, Paul. ★ *Bake*	641.81

AUTHOR, TITLE, SERIES AND SUBJECT INDEX

Hussain, Nadiya. ★*Nadiya Bakes*	641.81
Kieffer, Sarah. *100 Morning Treats*	641.5
Kulaga, Agatha. *Ovenly*	641.81
Larsen, Jeffrey. ★*Gluten-Free Baking at Home*	641.5
Manning, Ivy. *Easy Soups from Scratch with Quick Breads to Match*	641.81
Rodriguez, Jessamyn Waldman. *The Hot Bread Kitchen Cookbook*	641.59
Wade, Greg. ★*Bread Head*	664
Weller, Melissa. *A Good Bake*	641.86
★*Bread Head*. Wade, Greg	664
Break 'Em Up. Teachout, Zephyr	338.8
Break The Cycle. Buque, Mariel	616.85
★*Break, Blow, Burn*. Paglia, Camille	821.009
BREAKFASTS	
Kieffer, Sarah. *100 Morning Treats*	641.5
Breaking and Entering. Smith, Jeremy N.	B
Breaking Night. Murray, Liz	B
Breaking Rockefeller. Doran, Peter B.	338.7
Breaking The Spell. Dennett, D. C.	200
Breaking Through. Kariko, Katalin	B
Breaking Through Bias. Kramer, Andrea S.	650.1
Breaking Twitter. Mezrich, Ben	338.7
BREAKING UP (INTERPERSONAL RELATIONS)	
Carson, Anne. *The Beauty of the Husband*	811
Felix, Camonghne. *Dyscalculia*	B
Olds, Sharon. *Stag's Leap*	811
Pico, Tommy. *Junk*	811
The Breaks. Singh, Julietta	B
The Breakthrough. Graeber, Charles	616.99
★*The Breakthrough Years*. Galinsky, Ellen	649
BREAST	
Love, Susan M. ★*Dr. Susan Love's Breast Book*	618.1
BREAST CANCER	
Boyer, Anne. *The Undying*	B
Brem, Rachel. *No Longer Radical*	616.99
Brown, Theresa. *Healing*	616.99
Campoverdi, Alejandra. *First Gen*	B
Funk, Kristi. *Breasts*	616.99
Hutton, Andrea. *Bald Is Better with Earrings*	362.19699
Love, Susan M. ★*Dr. Susan Love's Breast Book*	618.1
Mandel, Sarah. *Little Earthquakes*	B
Savage, Jodi M. *The Death of a Jaybird*	B
BREAST FEEDING	
Huggins, Kathleen. ★*The Nursing Mother's Companion*	649
Neifert, Marianne R. *The Essential Guide to Breastfeeding*	649
Breasts. Funk, Kristi	616.99
Breath Better Spent. Hill, DaMaris B.	811
Breathe. Gracie, Rickson	B
★*Breathless*. Quammen, David	614.5
Breathturn into Timestead. Celan, Paul	831
Breggin, Peter Roger	
Guilt, Shame, and Anxiety	152.4
Bregman, Rutger	
Utopia for Realists	335
Brehm, Matthew T.	
Drawing Perspective	742
Breihan, Tom	
★*The Number Ones*	782.42164
Breitenbach, Kathleen	
★*LGBTQIA+ Books for Children and Teens*	028.7
BREITWIESER, STÉPHANE, 1971-	
Finkel, Michael. *The Art Thief*	364.1628
Brem, Rachel	
No Longer Radical	616.99
Bremer, Francis J.	
John Winthrop	B
Brennan, Chad	
Faithful Antiracism	277.308
Brennan, Jason	
Libertarianism	320.51
Brennan, Kathy	
Keepers	641.5973
Brennan, Thomas J.	
Shooting Ghosts	B
BRENNAN, THOMAS J. (THOMAS JAMES)	
Brennan, Thomas J. *Shooting Ghosts*	B
Brenner, Andrea	
How to College	378.1
Brenner, Joel Glenn	
The Emperors of Chocolate	338.7
Brenner, Marie	
★*The Desperate Hours*	362.1962
Brenwall, Cynthia S	
The Central Park	974.7
Bress 'N' Nyam. Raiford, Matthew	641.59
Brettschneider, Corey Lang	
The Oath and the Office	342.73
The Presidents and the People	342.73
★*Brewer's Dictionary of Phrase & Fable*. Brewer, Ebenezer Cobham	423
Brewer, Ebenezer Cobham	
★*Brewer's Dictionary of Phrase & Fable*	423
Brewer, John	
The American Leonardo	759.5
BREWER, KENNEDY	
Balko, Radley. ★*The Cadaver King and the Country Dentist*	614
BREWERIES	
Hoalst-Pullen, Nancy. *National Geographic Atlas of Beer*	663
BREWING INDUSTRY AND TRADE	
Knoedelseder, William. *Bitter Brew*	338.7
O'Meara, Mallory. *Girly Drinks*	641.2
Brewster, Todd	
Lincoln's Gamble	973.7
Breyer, Stephen G.	
★*The Authority of the Court and the Peril of Politics*	347.73
Making Our Democracy Work	347.73
BRIBERY	
Bensinger, Ken. ★*Red Card*	796.334
Borman, Tracy. *Thomas Cromwell*	B
Conn, David. *The Fall of the House of FIFA*	796.334
Drabkin, Ronald. *Beverly Hills Spy*	940.54
Hughes, Evan. *The Hard Sell*	338.4
Maddow, Rachel. *Bag Man*	B
Whitlock, Craig. ★*Fat Leonard*	364.16
Brick by Brick. Robertson, David C.	338.7
Brickell, Francesca Cartier	
The Cartiers	B
BRICKLAYERS	
Waldman, Jonathan. *Sam*	629.8
Brickman, Sophie	
Baby, Unplugged	306.874
BRICKMAN, SOPHIE	
Brickman, Sophie. *Baby, Unplugged*	306.874
The Bride of E. Bang, Mary Jo	811
BRIDES	
Brown, Daniel James. *The Indifferent Stars Above*	B
The Bridge. Remnick, David	B
The Bridge At Andau. Michener, James A.	943.9
Bridge of Words. Schor, Esther H.	499
Bridge to the Sun. Henderson, Bruce B.	940.53
Bridges. Blockley, David	725
BRIDGES	
Blockley, David. *Bridges*	725
Bridges, Sheila	
Furnishing Forward	747
BRIDGETOWER, GEORGE AUGUSTUS POLGREEN	
Dove, Rita. *Sonata Mulattica*	811
Bried, Erin	
How to Sew a Button	640
★*Brief Answers to the Big Questions*. Hawking, Stephen	500
Brief Candle in the Dark. Dawkins, Richard	B
A Brief Guide to Islam. Grieve, Paul	297
Brief history (Facts on File) [Series]. Foster, Lynn V.	972
A Brief History of Angels and Demons. Bartlett, Sarah	202
A Brief History of Equality. Piketty, Thomas	305.09
A Brief History of Mexico. Foster, Lynn V.	972
A Brief History of Motion. Standage, Tom	388
A Brief History of the Female Body. Emera, Deena	612.6
A Brief History of Time. Hawking, Stephen	523.1
★*A Briefer History of Time*. Hawking, Stephen	523.1
★*Briefly Perfectly Human*. Arthur, Alua	306.9
Brier, Bob	
The Murder of Tutankhamen	B
Brierley, Saroo	
A Long Way Home	B
BRIERLEY, SAROO	
Brierley, Saroo. *A Long Way Home*	B

1701

PUBLIC LIBRARY CORE COLLECTION: NONFICTION
Twentieth Edition

BRIGGS, ARTHUR, 1901-1991
   Atria, Travis. *Better Days Will Come Again* — B
Briggs, Julia
   Virginia Woolf — 823
Briggs, Kate
   This Little Art — 418
BRIGGS, KATE
   Briggs, Kate. *This Little Art* — 418
Briggs, Lyvonne
   ★*Sensual Faith* — 204
Brigham *Young*. Arrington, Leonard J. — B
Brigham *Young, Pioneer Prophet*. Turner, John G. — B
A **Bright** *and Blinding Sun*. Brotherton, Marcus — 940.54
Bright *Boulevards, Bold Dreams*. Bogle, Donald — 791.43
Bright *Dead Things*. Limon, Ada — 811
The **Bright** *Hour*. Riggs, Nina — B
A **Bright** *Shining Lie*. Sheehan, Neil — 959.704
Bright-*Sided*. Ehrenreich, Barbara — 155.2
Brighten, Jolene
   Is This Normal? — 618.1
Brighton, Terry
   Patton, Montgomery, Rommel — B
Brill, Steven
   Class Warfare — 371.010973
   Tailspin — 306.0973
BRILLESLIJPER, JANNY
   Iperen, Roxane van. ★*The Sisters of Auschwitz* — 940.53
BRILLESLIJPER, LIEN
   Iperen, Roxane van. ★*The Sisters of Auschwitz* — 940.53
The **Brilliant** *Abyss*. Scales, Helen — 551.46
The **Brilliant** *Disaster*. Rasenberger, Jim — 972.9106
Brina, Elizabeth Miki
   Speak, Okinawa — 305.48
BRINA, ELIZABETH MIKI, 1981-
   Brina, Elizabeth Miki. *Speak, Okinawa* — 305.48
Bring *It!* Rosen, Ali — 641.5973
Bring *Your Baggage and Don't Pack Light*. Ellis, Helen — 814
Bringing *Adam Home*. Standiford, Les — 364.15
Bringing *Columbia Home*. Leinbach, Michael D. — 363.12
Bringing *up Race*. Asika, Uju — 155.4
The **Brink**. Ambinder, Marc — 355.5
Brinkley, Alan
   John F. Kennedy — B
   ★*The Publisher* — B
Brinkley, Douglas
   ★*American Moonshot* — 629.40973
   ★*Cronkite* — B
   The Great Deluge — 976.3
   Rightful Heritage — B
   Wheels for the World — B
   The Wilderness Warrior — B
Briody, Blaire
   The New Wild West — 338.2
The **Brisket** *Chronicles*. Raichlen, Steven — 641.6
Britain *At Bay*. Allport, Alan — 940.53
BRITAIN, BATTLE OF, 1940
   Churchill, Winston. *Their Finest Hour* — 940.53
   Holland, James. *Battle of Britain* — 940.54
   Korda, Michael. *With Wings Like Eagles* — 940.54
   McCarten, Anthony. *Darkest Hour* — 941.084
BRITISH AMERICANS
   Barrett, Duncan. *GI Brides* — 920
★*The* **British** *Are Coming*. Atkinson, Rick — 973.3
BRITISH COLUMBIA
   McDiarmid, Jessica. *Highway of Tears* — 364.152
BRITISH HISTORY
   Ackroyd, Peter. *The Death of King Arthur* — 823
   Ackroyd, Peter. *Foundation* — 942
   Ackroyd, Peter. *Innovation* — 942.082
   Ackroyd, Peter. *Rebellion* — 941.06
   Ackroyd, Peter. *Tudors* — 942.05
   Asbridge, Thomas S. *The Greatest Knight* — 942.03
   Baird, Julia. ★*Victoria the Queen* — B
   Barker, Juliet R. V. *Agincourt* — 944
   Bergreen, Laurence. *In Search of a Kingdom* — B
   Bolt, Robert. *A Man for All Seasons* — 822
   Bordo, Susan. *The Creation of Anne Boleyn* — 942.05
   Borman, Tracy. *Anne Boleyn and Elizabeth I* — 920

Borman, Tracy. *Crown & Sceptre* — 941
Borman, Tracy. *Elizabeth's Women* — B
Borman, Tracy. *Henry VIII and the Men Who Made Him* — 942.05
Borman, Tracy. *The Private Lives of the Tudors* — 920
Borman, Tracy. *Thomas Cromwell* — B
Bostridge, Mark. *Florence Nightingale* — B
Bremer, Francis J. *John Winthrop* — B
Brown, Tina. ★*The Palace Papers* — 920
Cadbury, Deborah. *Princes at War* — 920
Carter, Miranda. *George, Nicholas and Wilhelm* — 940.3
Charles-Edwards, T. M. *Wales and the Britons, 350-1064* — 942.901
Clay, Catrine. *King, Kaiser, Tsar* — B
Copeland, B. Jack. *Turing* — B
Damrosch, Leopold. *The Club* — 920
Edwards, Anne. *Matriarch* — B
Elkins, Caroline. *Legacy of Violence* — 909
Essinger, James. *Ada's Algorithm* — B
Foreman, Amanda. *Georgiana, Duchess of Devonshire* — B
Fowler, Corinne. ★*The Countryside* — 941
Fraser, Antonia. *Faith and Treason* — 942.06
Fraser, Antonia. *Mary, Queen of Scots* — B
Fraser, Antonia. ★*The Wives of Henry VIII* — 942.05
Gies, Joseph. *Life in a Medieval Castle* — 940.1
Gill, Gillian. *We Two* — 941.081
Glendinning, Victoria. *Leonard Woolf* — B
Goodman, Ruth. *How to Be a Tudor* — 942.05
Goodman, Ruth. *How to Be a Victorian* — 941.08
Green, Matthew. *Shadowlands* — 941.03
Gristwood, Sarah. *Blood Sisters* — 942.04092
Gristwood, Sarah. *The Tudors in Love* — 941.05
Guy, John. *Hunting the Falcon* — B
Hardman, Robert. *Queen of Our Times* — B
Hardman, Robert. *Queen of the World* — B
Hawksley, Lucinda. *Queen Victoria's Mysterious Daughter* — B
Healey, Jonathan. *The Blazing World* — 941.06
Hibbert, Christopher. *Edward VII* — B
Higgins, Charlotte. *Under Another Sky* — 936
Hochschild, Adam. *Bury the Chains* — 326
Holway, Tatiana M. *The Flower of Empire* — 727
Johnson, Steven. *Enemy of All Mankind* — 910.4
Jones, Dan. ★*The Plantagenets* — 942.03092
Jones, Dan. ★*The Wars of the Roses* — 942.04
Jones, Michael K. *The Black Prince* — B
Keefe, Patrick Radden. ★*Say Nothing* — 364.152
Knight, Sam. *The Premonitions Bureau* — 133.8
Koch, Bea. *Mad and Bad* — 920
Korda, Michael. *With Wings Like Eagles* — 940.54
Lacey, Robert. *Great Tales from English History 1* — 941
Lacey, Robert. *Great Tales from English History 2* — 941
Lacey, Robert. *Great Tales from English History 3* — 941
Larman, Alexander. ★*Power and Glory* — 941.085
Larson, Erik. ★*The Splendid and the Vile* — 940.54
Leavitt, David. *The Man Who Knew Too Much* — B
Lewis, Damien. *The Dog Who Could Fly* — 940.54
Lovell, Mary S. *Bess of Hardwick* — B
Lownie, Andrew. *Traitor King* — B
Lynskey, Dorian. *33 Revolutions per Minute* — 782.42
MacCulloch, Diarmaid. *Thomas Cromwell* — B
Macintyre, Ben. *Agent Zigzag* — B
Macintyre, Ben. *A Spy Among Friends* — B
McCalman, Iain. *Darwin's Armada* — 576.8
Meyer, G. J. *The Tudors* — 920
Moore, Peter. *Life, Liberty, and the Pursuit of Happiness* — 199
Moore, Wendy. *No Man's Land* — 940.4
Morris, Marc. ★*The Anglo-Saxons* — 942.01
Morris, Marc. *A Great and Terrible King* — B
Morris, Marc. *King John* — 942.033
Morris, Marc. *The Norman Conquest* — 942.02
Morrison, Robert. *The Regency Years* — 941.07
Mortimer, Ian. *The Time Traveler's Guide to Elizabethan England* — 942.05
Mortimer, Ian. *The Time Traveler's Guide to Restoration Britain* — 941.06
Morton, Andrew. *Diana* — B
Morton, Andrew. *Wallis in Love* — B
Nicolson, Juliet. *The Great Silence* — 941.083
Norwich, John Julius. *Shakespeare's Kings* — 822.33
O'Sullivan, Emer. *The Fall of the House of Wilde* — B
O'Toole, Fintan. ★*We Don't Know Ourselves* — 941.7
Parkin, Simon. *The Island of Extraordinary Captives* — 940.53

AUTHOR, TITLE, SERIES AND SUBJECT INDEX

Penn, Thomas. *The Brothers York*	942.04
Pepys, Samuel. *The Diary of Samuel Pepys*	B
Porter, Linda. *Katherine the Queen*	B
Purnell, Sonia. *Clementine*	B
Ridley, Jane. *The Heir Apparent*	B
Robb, Graham. *The Debatable Land*	941.3
Robb, John. *Punk Rock*	781.6609
Ronald, Susan. *The Pirate Queen*	B
Rounding, Virginia. *The Burning Time*	272
Russell, Gareth. *Young and Damned and Fair*	B
Sanghera, Sathnam. *Empireworld*	909
Satia, Priya. *Empire of Guns*	330.941
Schama, Simon. *A History of Britain; 2*	941
Shawcross, William. *The Queen Mother*	B
Smith, Sally Bedell. *Elizabeth the Queen*	B
Smith, Sally Bedell. *George VI and Elizabeth*	920
Smith, Sally Bedell. *Prince Charles*	B
Sobel, Dava. *Longitude*	526
Starkey, David. *Six Wives*	942.05
Stewart, Rory. *The Marches*	941.3
Tallis, Nicola. *Crown of Blood*	B
Tallis, Nicola. *Uncrowned Queen*	B
Tomalin, Claire. *Samuel Pepys*	B
Tombs, Robert. *The English and Their History*	942
Wallach, Janet. *Desert Queen*	B
Weir, Alison. *The Children of Henry VIII*	B
Weir, Alison. *Eleanor of Aquitaine*	B
Weir, Alison. *Henry VIII*	B
Weir, Alison. *The Lady in the Tower*	B
Weir, Alison. *The Life of Elizabeth I*	B
Weir, Alison. *The Lost Tudor Princess*	B
Weir, Alison. *Queens of the Age of Chivalry*	920
Weir, Alison. *The Six Wives of Henry VIII*	942.05
Weir, Alison. *The Wars of the Roses*	942.04
Wiederhorn, Jon. *Louder Than Hell*	781.6609
Wilson, A. N. *Victoria*	B
Winchester, Simon. *The Map That Changed the World*	B
Woolley, Benjamin. *The King's Assassin*	B
Worsley, Lucy. *Queen Victoria*	B
Wulf, Andrea. *The Brother Gardeners*	920
BRITISH PEOPLE	
Borman, Tracy. *Anne Boleyn and Elizabeth I*	920
Charter, David. *Royal Audience*	941.085
Coldstream, Catherine. ★*Cloistered*	B
Costa, James T. *Radical by Nature*	B
Craig, Mya-Rose. *Birdgirl*	B
Drabkin, Ronald. *Beverly Hills Spy*	940.54
Eyman, Scott. *Charlie Chaplin vs. America*	B
Finkelstein, Daniel. *Two Roads Home*	920
Hardman, Robert. *Queen of Our Times*	B
Harry. ★*Spare*	B
Heughan, Sam. *Waypoints*	B
Johnson, Brian. *The Lives of Brian*	B
Kozinn, Allan. *The McCartney Legacy*	B
Lessing, Doris May. *Under My Skin*	823
Loyn, David. *In Afghanistan*	958.1
Markel, Howard. *Origin Story*	576.8
Moore, Peter. *Life, Liberty, and the Pursuit of Happiness*	199
Raban, Jonathan. *Father and Son*	B
Sanghera, Sathnam. ★*Empireland*	941
Smith, Sally Bedell. *George VI and Elizabeth*	920
Stewart, Patrick. ★*Making It So*	B
Weir, Alison. *Queens of the Age of Chivalry*	920
BRITISH PEOPLE IN AFRICA	
Dinesen, Isak. *Out of Africa*	967.62
Fuller, Alexandra. *Don't Let's Go to the Dogs Tonight*	B
Fuller, Alexandra. *Travel Light, Move Fast*	B
Markham, Beryl. *West with the Night*	B
Millard, Candice. ★*River of the Gods*	916.204
BRITISH PEOPLE IN FOREIGN COUNTRIES	
Ansary, Mir Tamim. *Games Without Rules*	958.1
Dalrymple, William. *The Return of a King*	958.1
Lessing, Doris May. *Under My Skin*	823
Loyn, David. *In Afghanistan*	958.1
BRITISH PEOPLE IN FRANCE	
Mayle, Peter. *Encore Provence*	944
Mayle, Peter. *My Twenty-Five Years in Provence*	944.9
Mayle, Peter. ★*A Year in Provence*	944
BRITISH PEOPLE IN INDIA	
Dalrymple, William. *White Mughals*	954
BRITISH PEOPLE IN IRELAND	
Kelly, John. *The Graves Are Walking*	941.5081
BRITISH PEOPLE IN SOUTH AFRICA	
Millard, Candice. ★*Hero of the Empire*	968.04
BRITISH PEOPLE IN SOUTHWEST ASIA AND NORTH AFRICA (MIDDLE EAST)	
Lawrence, T. E. *Seven Pillars of Wisdom*	940.4
Mills, Dan. *Sniper One*	956.7044
Stewart, Rory. *The Prince of the Marshes*	956.7044
BRITISH PEOPLE IN THE UNITED STATES	
Brown, Tina. *The Vanity Fair Diaries*	B
Gunn, Thom. ★*The Letters of Thom Gunn*	821
Hitchens, Christopher. *Hitch-22*	920
BRITISH POETRY	
Auden, W. H. *Collected Poems*	811
Auden, W. H. *Selected Poems*	821
Browning, Robert. ★*Robert Browning's Poetry*	821
Browning, Robert. *Robert Browning*	821.8
Bunting, Basil. *Complete Poems*	821
Byron, George Gordon Byron. *Selected Poetry of Lord Byron*	821
Coleridge, Samuel Taylor. *The Complete Poems*	821
Day-Lewis, Cecil. *The Complete Poems of C. Day Lewis*	821
Dunmore, Helen. *Inside the Wave*	821
Fenton, James. *Selected Poems*	821
Hill, Geoffrey. *Selected Poems*	821
Keats, John. ★*The Complete Poems of John Keats*	821
Keats, John. *Poems*	821
Kipling, Rudyard. *Complete Verse*	821
Larkin, Philip. ★*Collected Poems*	821
Larkin, Philip. *The Complete Poems*	821
Oswald, Alice. *Falling Awake*	821
Rossetti, Christina Georgina. *Christina Rossetti*	821.8
Shelley, Percy Bysshe. *Shelley's Poetry and Prose*	821
Shelley, Percy Bysshe. *Shelley*	821
Tennyson, Alfred. *Poems*	821
BRITISH RAJ (1858-1947)	
Dalrymple, William. *White Mughals*	954
Guha, Ramachandra. *Rebels Against the Raj*	954.03
Brits, Louisa Thomsen	
The Book of Hygge	747
BRITT, MAURICE LEE	
Kershaw, Alex. *Against All Odds*	940.54
Britt, Ryan	
Phasers on Stun!	791.45
★*The Spice Must Flow*	813
BRITTON, JANE SANDERS, 1945-1969	
Cooper, Becky. *We Keep the Dead Close*	364.152
Britton, Sarah	
Naturally Nourished	641.5
Broad Band. Evans, Claire Lisa	920
Broad Strokes. Quinn, Bridget	920
★*Broadcast Hysteria*. Schwartz, A. Brad	791.44
BROADCAST JOURNALISM	
Austerlitz, Saul. *Kind of a Big Deal*	791.43
Couric, Katie. *Going There*	B
Fager, Jeffrey. *Fifty Years of 60 Minutes*	070.1
Gladstone, Brooke. *The Influencing Machine*	741.5
Napoli, Lisa. *Up All Night*	384.55
Tur, Katy. *Rough Draft*	B
Wenger, Debora Halpern. *Advancing the Story*	070.1
BROADCASTING	
Brinkley, Douglas. ★*Cronkite*	B
Edwards, Bob. *Edward R. Murrow and the Birth of Broadcast Journalism*	B
Broadwater, Jeff	
★*George Mason*	B
James Madison	B
★*Broadway*. Maslon, Laurence	782.1
Broadway Musicals. Bloom, Ken	792.6
BROADWAY, NEW YORK CITY	
Bernstein, Burton. ★*Leonard Bernstein*	B
Bloom, Ken. *Broadway Musicals*	792.6
Butler, Isaac. *The World Only Spins Forward*	812
Maslon, Laurence. ★*Broadway*	782.1
Miranda, Lin-Manuel. *Hamilton*	782.1
Mordden, Ethan. *Anything Goes*	782.1
Purdum, Todd S. *Something Wonderful*	B

PUBLIC LIBRARY CORE COLLECTION: NONFICTION
Twentieth Edition

Rannells, Andrew. *Too Much Is Not Enough* — 792.02
Riedel, Michael. *Razzle Dazzle* — 792.09
Riedel, Michael. *Singular Sensation* — 792
Viertel, Jack. *The Secret Life of the American Musical* — 792.609
Wallace, Mike. *Greater Gotham* — 974.7
Broca's Brain. Sagan, Carl — 128
BROCA, PAUL, 1824-1880
   Sagan, Carl. *Broca's Brain* — 128
Brock, James P.
   Kaufman Field Guide to Butterflies of North America — 595.7
Brock, Sean
   South — 641.5975
Brock-Broido, Lucie
   Stay, Illusion — 811
Brockett, Oscar G.
   History of the Theatre — 792
Brockman, Christian Frank
   Trees of North America — 582.16097
Brockman, John
   This Idea Is Brilliant — 500
Brodeur, Michael Andor
   ★*Swole* — 155.3
Brodsky, Alexandra
   Sexual Justice — 364.15
Brody, Jane E.
   Jane Brody's Guide to the Great Beyond — 616
Brody, Mark
   Mosaic Garden Projects — 712
Broers, Michael
   Napoleon — B
   Napoleon — 944.05
   Napoleon — B
Brokaw, Tom
   The Fall of Richard Nixon — B
BROKAW, TOM
   Brokaw, Tom. *The Fall of Richard Nixon* — B
★*Broke*. Kirshner, Jodie Adams — 336.3
★*Broke Millennial Talks Money*. Lowry, Erin — 332.024
Broke, Usa. Rivlin, Gary — 339.4
★*Broken*. Lawson, Jenny — B
★*Broken*. Pryce, Jessica — 362.7
★*Broken Code*. Horwitz, Jeff — 302.3
The Broken Constitution. Feldman, Noah — 973.7
Broken Horses. Carlile, Brandi — B
Broken Places & Outer Spaces. Okorafor, Nnedi — 153.6
BROKERS
   Fabre, Cin. *Wolf Hustle* — 332.6
   Schroeder, Alice. *The Snowball* — B
   Vaughan, Liam. *Flash Crash* — B
Brokhausen, Nick
   Whispers in the Tall Grass — 959.704
BROMFIELD, LOUIS, 1896-1956
   Heyman, Stephen. *The Planter of Modern Life* — B
Bronfman, Edgar M.
   Why Be Jewish? — 296
Bronski, Michael
   A Queer History of the United States — 306.76
BRONTE, CHARLOTTE, 1816-1855
   Gaskell, Elizabeth Cleghorn. *The Life of Charlotte Bronte* — B
   Harman, Claire. *Charlotte Bronte* — B
BRONX, NEW YORK CITY
   Abrams, Jonathan P. D. ★*The Come Up* — 782.421649
   Feige, David. *Indefensible* — B
   Onwuachi, Kwame. ★*Notes from a Young Black Chef* — 641.59
   Skelton, Marc. *Pounding the Rock* — 796.323
   Voloj, Julian. *Ghetto Brother* — 741.5
BRONZE AGE
   Cline, Eric H. *After 1177 B.C.* — 937
BRONZE AND IRON AGES (3500-27 B.C.E.)
   Alexander, Caroline. *The War That Killed Achilles* — 883
   Ceram, C. W. *Gods, Graves & Scholars* — 930.1
   Cline, Eric H. *After 1177 B.C.* — 937
   Firdawsi. *Shahnameh* — 891
   Fox, Margalit. *The Riddle of the Labyrinth* — 920
   Kriwaczek, Paul. *Babylon* — 935
   O'Connell, Robert L. *The Ghosts of Cannae* — 937
   Virgil. ★*The Aeneid* — 873

Brookhiser, Richard
   Give Me Liberty — 320.540973
BROOKLYN, NEW YORK CITY
   Anthony, Carmelo. *Where Tomorrows Aren't Promised* — B
   Feldman, Deborah. *Unorthodox* — B
   Howe, Ben Ryder. *My Korean Deli* — B
   Peterson, Marlon. *Bird Uncaged* — B
   Samaha, Albert. *Never Ran, Never Will* — 920
   Savage, Jodi M. *The Death of a Jaybird* — B
   Smith, Patti. ★*Just Kids* — B
   Streisand, Barbra. ★*My Name Is Barbra* — B
   Telushkin, Joseph. *Rebbe* — 296.833
   Tran, Ly. *House of Sticks* — B
   Wang, Qian Julie. ★*Beautiful Country* — B
Brooks, Amanda
   Run to the Finish — 613.7
Brooks, Arthur C.
   Build the Life You Want — 158.1
Brooks, David
   ★*How to Know a Person* — 158.2
   ★*The Second Mountain* — 302
   The Social Animal — 305.5
Brooks, Geraldine
   Nine Parts of Desire — 305.48
Brooks, Gwendolyn
   ★*The Essential Gwendolyn Brooks* — 811
   In Montgomery, and Other Poems — 811
BROOKS, GWENDOLYN, 1917-2000
   Jackson, Angela. *A Surprised Queenhood in the New Black Sun* — B
Brooks, James
   Mesa of Sorrows — 979.1004
BROOKS, LEVON, 1959-
   Balko, Radley. ★*The Cadaver King and the Country Dentist* — 614
Brooks, Maegan Parker
   Fannie Lou Hamer — B
Brooks, Mel
   ★*All About Me!* — B
BROOKS, MEL, 1926-
   Brooks, Mel. ★*All About Me!* — B
   McGilligan, Patrick. *Funny Man* — B
Brooks, Michael
   The Art of More — 510.9
   The Quantum Astrologer's Handbook — B
Brooks, Rosa
   How Everything Became War and the Military Became Everything — 355
Brookshire, Bethany
   Pests — 590
Brookwood, Marilyn
   The Orphans of Davenport — 305.231
Broom, Sarah M.
   The Yellow House — B
BROOM, SARAH M.
   Broom, Sarah M. *The Yellow House* — B
Broome, Brian
   ★*Punch Me up to the Gods* — B
BROOME, BRIAN
   Broome, Brian. ★*Punch Me up to the Gods* — B
Brosh, Allie
   ★*Hyperbole and a Half* — 741.5
   ★*Solutions and Other Problems* — 741.5
BROSH, ALLIE
   Brosh, Allie. ★*Hyperbole and a Half* — 741.5
   Brosh, Allie. ★*Solutions and Other Problems* — 741.5
★*Brother & Sister*. Keaton, Diane — B
The Brother Gardeners. Wulf, Andrea — 920
★*Brother, I'm Dying*. Danticat, Edwidge — B
A Brotherhood Betrayed. Cannell, Michael T. — B
BROTHERHOODS
   Fairbanks, Amanda M. *The Lost Boys of Montauk* — 910.91
BROTHERS
   B., David. *Epileptic* — 741.5
   Bechdel, Alison. ★*Fun Home* — 741.5
   Buck, Rinker. *Life on the Mississippi* — 917
   Clavin, Thomas. *The DiMaggios* — 920
   Dutta, Sunil. *Stealing Green Mangoes* — 973
   Freeman, Sally Mott. *The Jersey Brothers* — 920
   Goldberg, Whoopi. *Bits and Pieces* — B
   Hamill, Kirkland. *Filthy Beasts* — B

AUTHOR, TITLE, SERIES AND SUBJECT INDEX

Howard, Ron. ★*The Boys*	B
Kouchner, Camille. *The Familia Grande*	B
Lambert, Raymond. *Every Man a Hero*	B
Louvish, Simon. *Monkey Business*	B
Mahoney, Richard D. *Sons & Brothers*	920
Mansbach, Adam. *I Had a Brother Once*	811
Richardson, Lance. *House of Nutter*	B
Wise, Beau. *Three Wise Men*	958.104
Yancey, Philip. ★*Where the Light Fell*	B
Brothers At Arms. Ferreiro, Larrie D.	327.73
Brothers in Arms. Holland, James	940.54
Brothers in Battle, Best of Friends. Guarnere, William	B
Brothers on Three. Streep, Abe	306.85
The ***Brothers*** York. Penn, Thomas	942.04
Brothers, Rivals, Victors. Jordan, Jonathan W.	940.54
Brothers, Thomas David	
★*Louis Armstrong, Master of Modernism*	B
Brotherton, Marcus	
A Bright and Blinding Sun	940.54
Brotherton, Rob	
Suspicious Minds	153.4
Brotopia. Chang, Emily	331.4
Brought Forth on This Continent. Holzer, Harold	973.7
Brous, Sharon	
★*The Amen Effect*	296.3
Broven, John	
Record Makers and Breakers	B
Brower, Kate Andersen	
Elizabeth Taylor	B
First in Line	920
First Women	920
The Residence	975.3
Brown. Young, Kevin	811
Brown Album. Khakpour, Porochista	304.8
BROWN FAMILY	
Pawel, Miriam. *The Browns of California*	920
Brown, Amanda	
★*Spruce*	747
Brown, Archie	
★*The Rise and Fall of Communism*	320.53
Brown, Austin Channing	
★*I'm Still Here*	B
BROWN, AUSTIN CHANNING	
Brown, Austin Channing. ★*I'm Still Here*	B
Brown, Brene	
Braving the Wilderness	305.8
★*Dare to Lead*	658.4
The Gifts of Imperfection	158
Brown, Carolyn	
Chance and Circumstance	B
BROWN, CAROLYN, 1927-2025	
Brown, Carolyn. *Chance and Circumstance*	B
BROWN, CHARLIE, 1912-2008	
Makos, Adam. ★*A Higher Call*	940.54
Brown, Christopher C.	
Librarian's Guide to Online Searching	025.04
Brown, Claude	
Manchild in the Promised Land	B
BROWN, CLAUDE, 1937-2002	
Brown, Claude. *Manchild in the Promised Land*	B
Brown, Craig	
150 Glimpses of the Beatles	920
Ninety-Nine Glimpses of Princess Margaret	B
Brown, Daniel James	
★*The Boys in the Boat*	797.12
★*Facing the Mountain*	940.54
The Indifferent Stars Above	B
Brown, David S.	
Paradise Lost	813
Brown, Dee	
The American West	978
★*Bury My Heart at Wounded Knee*	978
BROWN, EDMUND G. (EDMUND GERALD), 1905-1996	
Pawel, Miriam. *The Browns of California*	920
Brown, Eliot	
The Cult of We	333.33
Brown, Emma	
To Raise a Boy	649

Brown, George E.	
Essential Pruning Techniques	635.9
BROWN, HELEN GURLEY	
Hirshey, Gerri. *Not Pretty Enough*	B
BROWN, HENRY BILLINGS, 1836-1913	
Luxenberg, Steve. ★*Separate*	342.7308
BROWN, JAMES, 1933-2006	
McBride, James. *Kill 'Em and Leave*	B
Wood, Damon. *Working for the Man, Playing in the Band*	782.42164
Brown, Jasmine	
Twice as Hard	610.92
Brown, Jericho	
★*The Tradition*	811
BROWN, JERRY, 1938-	
Pawel, Miriam. *The Browns of California*	920
BROWN, JESSE LEROY	
Makos, Adam. *Devotion*	920
BROWN, JOHN, 1800-1859	
Brands, H. W. ★*The Zealot and the Emancipator*	920
Horwitz, Tony. ★*Midnight Rising*	973.7
Meyer, Eugene L. *Five for Freedom*	973.7
Reynolds, David S. *John Brown, Abolitionist*	B
Brown, Kardea	
The Way Home	641.5975
Brown, Kendall H.	
Quiet Beauty	712.09
Brown, Leanne	
★*Good and Cheap*	641.5
Brown, Maressa	
Raising Baby by the Stars	133.5
BROWN, MARGARET WISE, 1910-1952	
Gary, Amy. *In the Great Green Room*	813
Brown, Mick	
★*Tearing Down the Wall of Sound*	B
Brown, Molly McCully	
Places I've Taken My Body	B
The Virginia State Colony for Epileptics and Feebleminded	811
BROWN, MOLLY MCCULLY, 1991-	
Brown, Molly McCully. *Places I've Taken My Body*	B
Brown, Nancy Marie	
The Abacus and the Cross	B
Ivory Vikings	736
The Real Valkyrie	948
Brown, Noah	
Reading Together	028.5
Brown, Peter	
Through the Eye of a Needle	270.2
Brown, Robert J.	
You Can't Go Wrong Doing Right	B
BROWN, ROBERT J. (ROBERT JOE), 1935-2020	
Brown, Robert J. *You Can't Go Wrong Doing Right*	B
Brown, Samuel Morris	
In Heaven as It Is on Earth	289.3
Brown, Sarah L.	
The Hidden Language of Cats	636.8
Brown, Stephen	
Glitterville's Handmade Christmas	B
Brown, Tabitha	
I Did a New Thing	158.1
Brown, Terence	
The Life of W.B. Yeats	B
Brown, Theresa	
Healing	616.99
BROWN, THERESA	
Brown, Theresa. *Healing*	616.99
Brown, Tim	
★*The Tao of the Backup Catcher*	796.357
Brown, Tina	
The Diana Chronicles	B
★*The Palace Papers*	920
The Vanity Fair Diaries	B
BROWN, TINA	
Brown, Tina. *The Vanity Fair Diaries*	B
Brown, Vanessa	
The Forest City Killer	364.152
Brown, White, Black. Mehra, Nishta	305.800973
Brown-Nagin, Tomiko	
Civil Rights Queen	B

Brownback, Lydia
   Finding God in My Loneliness — 248.8
Browne, David
   Crosby, Stills, Nash and Young — 920
   So Many Roads — B
Browne, E. J.
   Charles Darwin — B
   Charles Darwin — B
Browne, Mahogany L.
   ★*Black Girl Magic* — 811.6
Browning, Robert
   ★*Robert Browning's Poetry* — 821
   Robert Browning — 821.8
BROWNING, ROBERT, 1812-1889
   Browning, Robert. ★*Robert Browning's Poetry* — 821
The **Browns** *of California.* Pawel, Miriam — 920
Brownstein, Gabriel
   ★*The Secret Mind of Bertha Pappenheim* — 616.85
Brownworth, Lars
   Lost to the West — 949.5
Broyles, Michael
   ★*Revolutions in American Music* — 780.9
Bruce. Carlin, Peter Ames — B
★**Bruce** *Lee.* Polly, Matthew — B
Bruchac, Joseph
   Our Stories Remember — 973.04
Bruck, Connie
   When Hollywood Had a King — B
Bruder, Jessica
   ★*Nomadland* — 331.3
Brunelleschi's *Dome.* King, Ross — 726.6
BRUNELLESCHI, FILIPPO, 1377-1446
   King, Ross. *Brunelleschi's Dome* — 726.6
Bruner, Robert F.
   ★*The Panic of 1907, 2nd Ed.* — 330.973
Brunetti, Ivan
   Cartooning — 741.5
BRUNHILD
   Puhak, Shelley. *The Dark Queens* — 944
Bruni, Frank
   The Beauty of Dusk — B
   Where You Go Is Not Who You'll Be — 378.1
BRUNI, FRANK
   Bruni, Frank. *The Beauty of Dusk* — B
Bruning, John R.
   Indestructible — B
   The Race of Aces — 940.54
Brunson, Quinta
   She Memes Well — B
BRUNSON, QUINTA
   Brunson, Quinta. *She Memes Well* — B
Brunsting, Karen
   ★*Open Access Literature in Libraries* — 070.5
Brusatte, Stephen
   ★*The Rise and Fall of the Dinosaurs* — 567.9
   The Rise and Reign of the Mammals — 569
A **Brutal** *Reckoning.* Cozzens, Peter — 973.5
Brute. Skaja, Emily — 811.6
BRYANT, CARTER
   Lobel, Orly. *You Don't Own Me* — 346.7304
Bryant, Howard
   Full Dissidence — 306.20973
   The Last Hero — B
   Rickey — B
Bryant, Kobe
   The Mamba Mentality — B
BRYANT, KOBE, 1978-2020
   Bryant, Kobe. *The Mamba Mentality* — B
   Pearlman, Jeff. ★*Three-Ring Circus* — 796.323
   Sielski, Mike. *The Rise* — B
BRYANT, PAUL W.
   Barra, Allen. ★*The Last Coach* — B
Bryson, Bill
   ★*At Home* — 643
   The Body — 612
   In a Sunburned Country — 919
   The Life and Times of the Thunderbolt Kid — B
   Notes from a Small Island — 914

   One Summer — 973.91
   The Road to Little Dribbling — 914
   Shakespeare — B
   ★*A Short History of Nearly Everything* — 500
   ★*A Walk in the Woods* — 917
BRYSON, BILL
   Bryson, Bill. *In a Sunburned Country* — 919
   Bryson, Bill. *The Life and Times of the Thunderbolt Kid* — B
   Bryson, Bill. *Notes from a Small Island* — 914
   Bryson, Bill. *The Road to Little Dribbling* — 914
   Bryson, Bill. ★*A Walk in the Woods* — 917
Bryson, Lew
   Tasting Whiskey — 663
Bryson, Tina Payne
   The Bottom Line for Baby — 618.92
BUBER, MARTIN, 1878-1965
   Friedman, Maurice S. *Encounter on the Narrow Ridge* — B
BUCCANEERS
   Kritzler, Ed. *Jewish Pirates of the Caribbean* — 972.9
Buchanan, Rita
   Taylor's Master Guide to Landscaping — 712
BUCK, CARRIE, 1906-1983
   Cohen, Adam. ★*Imbeciles* — 344.7304
Buck, Joe
   Lucky Bastard — B
BUCK, JOE
   Buck, Joe. *Lucky Bastard* — B
Buck, Rinker
   Life on the Mississippi — 917
BUCK, RINKER, 1950-
   Buck, Rinker. *Life on the Mississippi* — 917
Buckland, Gail
   Who Shot Rock & Roll — 779
   Who Shot Sports — 779
Buckley. Bogus, Carl T. — B
Buckley *and Mailer.* Schultz, Kevin Michael — 920
BUCKLEY, WILLIAM F. (WILLIAM FRANK), 1925-2008
   Bogus, Carl T. *Buckley* — B
   Hendershot, Heather. *Open to Debate* — B
   Schultz, Kevin Michael. *Buckley and Mailer* — 920
Budapest. Sebestyen, Victor — 943.912
BUDAPEST, HUNGARY
   Katin, Miriam. *We Are on Our Own* — 741.5
   Marton, Kati. *The Great Escape* — 920
   Sebestyen, Victor. *Budapest* — 943.912
Budd, Ann
   The Knitter's Handy Book of Top-Down Sweaters — 746.43
   New Directions in Sock Knitting — 746.43
   Sock Knitting Master Class — 746.43
Buddha. Armstrong, Karen — B
The **Buddha** *Walks into a Bar.* Rinzler, Lodro — 294.3
★**Buddhish.** Salguero, C. Pierce — 294.3
Buddhism. Oliver, Joan Duncan — 294.3
BUDDHISM
   Armstrong, Karen. *Buddha* — B
   Armstrong, Karen. ★*The Great Transformation* — 200.9
   Chodron, Pema. *How We Live Is How We Die* — 294.3
   Chodron, Pema. *Practicing Peace* — 294.3
   Dalai Lama. *An Appeal to the World* — 170
   Dalai Lama. *Approaching the Buddhist Path* — 294.3
   Dalai Lama. *How to Be Compassionate* — 294.3
   Dalai Lama. *The Second Dalai Lama* — 294.3
   Emet, Joseph. *Finding the Blue Sky* — 294.3
   Epstein, Mark. *Advice Not Given* — 294.3
   Epstein, Mark. *The Zen of Therapy* — 294.3
   Gunaratana, Henepola. *Start Here, Start Now* — 294.3
   Han, Chenxing. *Be the Refuge* — 294.3
   Harris, Dan. ★*10% Happier* — 158.1
   Hase, Craig. *How Not to Be a Hot Mess* — 158.1
   Iyer, Pico. *The Lady and the Monk* — 952
   Iyer, Pico. *The Open Road* — B
   Keown, Damien. ★*A Dictionary of Buddhism* — 294.3
   Kerouac, Jack. ★*Some of the Dharma* — 294.3
   Kornfield, Jack. *The Wise Heart* — 294.3
   Lahn, Bussho. *Singing and Dancing Are the Voice of the Law* — 294.3
   Nhat Hanh. *The Art of Living* — 294.3
   Nhat Hanh. *Zen and the Art of Saving the Planet* — 294.3
   Oliver, Joan Duncan. *Buddhism* — 294.3

AUTHOR, TITLE, SERIES AND SUBJECT INDEX

Olson, Carl. *Historical Dictionary of Buddhism*	294.3
Rinzler, Lodro. *The Buddha Walks into a Bar*	294.3
Rinzler, Lodro. *Love Hurts*	294.3
Salguero, C. Pierce. ★*Buddhish*	294.3
Siff, Jason. *Thoughts Are Not the Enemy*	294.3
Simmons, Sylvie. *I'm Your Man*	B
Sogyal. *The Tibetan Book of Living and Dying*	294.3
Sutin, Lawrence. ★*All Is Change*	294.309
Turner, Tina. ★*Happiness Becomes You*	158.1
Tworkov, Helen. *Lotus Girl*	B
Van Buren, Mark. *A Fool's Guide to Actual Happiness*	294.3
Wright, Robert. *Why Buddhism Is True*	294.3

BUDDHIST DOCTRINES
Dalai Lama. *An Appeal to the World*	170
Epstein, Mark. *Advice Not Given*	294.3
Kongtrul, Dzigar. *Peaceful Heart*	294.3
Oliver, Joan Duncan. *Buddhism*	294.3
Sogyal. *The Tibetan Book of Living and Dying*	294.3

BUDDHIST MEDITATION
Gunaratana, Henepola. *Start Here, Start Now*	294.3
Harris, Dan. ★*10% Happier*	158.1
Nhat Hanh. *The Art of Living*	294.3
Oliver, Joan Duncan. *Buddhism*	294.3
Sawaki, Kodo. *Discovering the True Self*	294.3
Sheff, David. *The Buddhist on Death Row*	B
Siff, Jason. *Thoughts Are Not the Enemy*	294.3

BUDDHIST MONASTERIES
Kirkby, Bruce. *Blue Sky Kingdom*	954.96

BUDDHIST MONKS
Tenzin Priyadarshi. *Running Toward Mystery*	B
The Buddhist on Death Row. Sheff, David	B

BUDDHIST WOMEN
Turner, Tina. ★*Happiness Becomes You*	158.1
Tworkov, Helen. *Lotus Girl*	B

BUDDHISTS
Dalai Lama. *Freedom in Exile*	B
Epstein, Mark. *The Zen of Therapy*	294.3
Han, Chenxing. *Be the Refuge*	294.3
Iyer, Pico. *The Open Road*	B
Rinzler, Lodro. *The Buddha Walks into a Bar*	294.3
Sheff, David. *The Buddhist on Death Row*	B
Turner, Tina. ★*Happiness Becomes You*	158.1

BUDGET
Ariely, Dan. *Dollars and Sense*	332.024
Ramsey, Dave. *The Total Money Makeover*	332.024
Reid, T. R. *A Fine Mess*	336.200973

BUDGET DEFICITS
Phillips-Fein, Kim. *Fear City*	330.9747

Budiansky, Stephen
Blackett's War	940.54
Code Warriors	327.73047
Journey to the Edge of Reason	B
Oliver Wendell Holmes	B

Buell, Hal
Moments	070.4
Buffalo Bill's America. Warren, Louis S.	B

BUFFALO BILL, 1846-1917
Warren, Louis S. *Buffalo Bill's America*	B

BUFFALO, NEW YORK
Creighton, Margaret S. *The Electrifying Fall of Rainbow City*	607

BUFFALOES
Rinella, Steven. *American Buffalo*	599.64
Buffering. Hart, Hannah	B

BUFFETT, JIMMY 1946-2023
White, Ryan. *Jimmy Buffett*	782.42164

Buffett, Mary
Warren Buffett and the Art of Stock Arbitrage	332.645

BUFFETT, WARREN
Buffett, Mary. *Warren Buffett and the Art of Stock Arbitrage*	332.645
Hagstrom, Robert G. *The Warren Buffett Way*	332.6
Schroeder, Alice. *The Snowball*	B

BUFFON, GEORGES LOUIS LECLERC, COMTE DE, 1707-1788
Roberts, Jason. ★*Every Living Thing*	578

Buford, Bill
★*Dirt*	B

BUFORD, BILL
Buford, Bill. ★*Dirt*	B

Buford, Kate
Native American Son	B
Bugged. MacNeal, David	595.7

Bugliosi, Vincent
★*Helter Skelter*	364.1

Buhle, Kathleen
If We Break	B

BUHLE, KATHLEEN
Buhle, Kathleen. *If We Break*	B

Bui, Thi
★*The Best We Could Do*	741.5

BUI, THI
Bui, Thi. ★*The Best We Could Do*	741.5
Build Stuff with Wood. Christiana, Asa	684
Build The Life You Want. Brooks, Arthur C.	158.1
Build Your Running Body. Magill, Pete	796.42
Build Yourself a Boat. Felix, Camonghne	811

BUILDING
Denton, Sally. *The Profiteers*	B
Parker, Matthew. *Panama Fever*	972.87
Thorstensen, Ole. *Making Things Right*	690
Building Art. Goldberger, Paul	B

BUILDING BLOCKS (TOYS)
Still, Ben. *Particle Physics Brick by Brick*	539.7

BUILDING CONSERVATION AND RESTORATION
Bauermeister, Erica. *House Lessons*	B
Burroughs, Augusten. ★*Toil & Trouble*	B
Mayes, Frances. *Bella Tuscany*	945
Shadid, Anthony. *House of Stone*	306.0956

BUILDING FAILURES
Smith, Dennis. *Report from Ground Zero*	974.7
Building The Getty. Meier, Richard	727
Building The Great Society. Zeitz, Joshua	973.923

BUILDINGS
Cornille, Didier. *Who Built That?*	720
Dwyer, Jim. *102 Minutes*	974.7
Flaherty, Mary Grace. ★*The Disaster Planning Handbook for Libraries*	025.8
Goldberger, Paul. *Building Art*	B
Hammack, William Scott. ★*Things We Make*	620
Hollis, Edward. *The Secret Lives of Buildings*	720.9
Holzer, Harold. *Monument Man*	B
Howard, Hugh. *Architects of an American Landscape*	712.092
Khan, Yasmin Sabina. *Enlightening the World*	974.7
Kiernan, Denise. *The Last Castle*	975.6
King, Ross. *Brunelleschi's Dome*	726.6
Morris, Marc. *Castles*	728.81
Thenell, Jan. *The Library's Crisis Communications Planner*	021.7
Wing, Charles. *How Your House Works*	643
Built from the Fire. Luckerson, Victor	976.6

Bukreev, Anatolii Nikolaevich
The Climb	796.52

BUKREEV, ANATOLII NIKOLAEVICH, 1958-1997
Bukreev, Anatolii Nikolaevich. *The Climb*	796.52

BULGARIA
Kassabova, Kapka. *Border*	949.9
Szablowski, Witold. *Dancing Bears*	947.086

BULGER, WHITEY, 1929-2018
Cullen, Kevin. *Whitey Bulger*	B
Sherman, Casey. *Hunting Whitey*	B

BULIMIA
Clein, Emmeline. ★*Dead Weight*	616.85
Hornbacher, Marya. *Wasted*	B
Tate, Christie. ★*Group*	B

Bull, John L.
★*The National Audubon Society Field Guide to North American Birds.*	598.097

BULLARD, EUGENE JACQUES, 1895-1961
Keith, Philip A. *All Blood Runs Red*	B
★*The Bullet Journal Method.* Carroll, Ryder	640
Bullets and Opium. Liao, Yiwu	951.05

BULLIES AND BULLYING
Bazelon, Emily. *Sticks and Stones*	302.34
Blake, Melissa. *Beautiful People*	362.4
Cameron, Silver Donald. *Blood in the Water*	364.152
Quinn, Zoe. *Crash Override*	794.8
Velasquez, Lizzie. *Dare to Be Kind*	177

PUBLIC LIBRARY CORE COLLECTION: NONFICTION
Twentieth Edition

BULLITT, WILLIAM C. (WILLIAM CHRISTIAN), 1891-1967
   McKean, David. *Watching Darkness Fall* — 940.53
Bullmore, Edward T.
   The Inflamed Mind — 616.85
Bullock, Darryl W.
   David Bowie Made Me Gay — 780
Bullough, Oliver
   Moneyland — 364.1
   ★*The Bully Pulpit*. Goodwin, Doris Kearns — 973.91
BULLYING IN THE WORKPLACE
   Sutton, Robert I. *The Asshole Survival Guide* — 650.1
BUMBLEBEES
   Wilson, Joseph S. *The Bees in Your Backyard* — 595.79
Bundles, A'Lelia
   On Her Own Ground — B
BUNDY, TED, 1946-1989
   Rubin, Kathy Kleiner. *A Light in the Dark* — 364.152
   Rule, Ann. *The Stranger Beside Me* — B
BUNGLERS AND BUNGLING
   Bilefsky, Dan. *The Last Job* — 364.16
Bunk. Young, Kevin — 177
★*Bunker Hill*. Philbrick, Nathaniel — 973.3
BUNKER HILL, BATTLE OF, 1775
   Philbrick, Nathaniel. ★*Bunker Hill* — 973.3
Bunker, Nick
   ★*Making Haste from Babylon* — 974.4
   Young Benjamin Franklin — B
Bunnell, David
   Good Friday on the Rez — B
BUNNELL, DAVID
   Bunnell, David. *Good Friday on the Rez* — B
Bunny Mellon. Gordon, Meryl — B
Bunting, Basil
   Complete Poems — 821
Bunting, Josiah
   ★*The Making of a Leader* — B
   Ulysses S. Grant — B
Buque, Mariel
   Break the Cycle — 616.85
Burak, Asi
   Power Play — 794.8
Burcaw, Shane
   ★*Laughing at My Nightmare* — B
BURCAW, SHANE
   Burcaw, Shane. ★*Laughing at My Nightmare* — B
The Burden of Sports. Parry, John Weston — 796.01
Burdick, Alan
   Why Time Flies — 529
BUREAUCRACY
   Asgarian, Roxanna. *We Were Once a Family* — 364.152
   Daley, Mark. *Safe* — B
   Farmer, John J. *The Ground Truth* — 973.931
   Sarotte, M. E. *The Collapse* — 943.087
   Thrall, Nathan. ★*A Day in the Life of Abed Salama* — 956.05
   White, Ralph. *Getting Out of Saigon* — 959.704
The Burger Court and the Rise of the Judicial Right. Graetz, Michael J. — 347.73
Burger, Ariel
   Witness — 848
BURGER, WARREN EARL, 1907-1995
   Graetz, Michael J. *The Burger Court and the Rise of the Judicial Right* — 347.73
Burgess, Ann Wolbert
   A Killer by Design — 364.3
BURGESS, ANN WOLBERT
   Burgess, Ann Wolbert. *A Killer by Design* — 364.3
Burgin, R. V.
   Islands of the Damned — B
BURGIN, R. V.
   Burgin, R. V. *Islands of the Damned* — B
Burgis, Tom
   The Looting Machine — 338.2
BURGLARY
   Bilefsky, Dan. *The Last Job* — 364.16
Burgman, John
   High Drama — 796.522
BURIAL
   Doughty, Caitlin. *From Here to Eternity* — 393
   Doughty, Caitlin. *Smoke Gets in Your Eyes* — B

   Faust, Drew Gilpin. *This Republic of Suffering* — 973.7
   Herring, Lucinda. *Reimagining Death* — 393
   Hunt, Will. *Underground* — 624.1
   Poole, Robert M. *Section 60* — 975.5
   Raffa, Guy P. *Dante's Bones* — 851
The Buried. Hessler, Peter — 962.05
★*Buried in the Sky*. Zuckerman, Peter — 796.522
The Buried Mirror. Fuentes, Carlos — 946
Burke Harris, Nadine
   The Deepest Well — 618.92
Burke, Carolyn
   Lee Miller — B
Burke, Edmund
   Reflections on the Revolution in France — 944.04
BURKE, EDMUND, 1729-1797
   Paine, Thomas. ★*Rights of Man* — 320.5
Burke, Kelsy
   The Pornography Wars — 306.77
BURKE, MICHAEL, 1918-1987
   Anderson, Scott. ★*The Quiet Americans* — 327.12
Burke, Monte
   Lords of the Fly — 799.124
   Saban — 796.332
Burke, Tarana
   ★*Unbound* — B
BURKE, TARANA
   Burke, Tarana. ★*Unbound* — B
Burkett, Elinor
   Golda — B
Burkus, David
   Friend of a Friend... — 650.1
BURLESQUE
   Abbott, Karen. *American Rose* — B
   Johnson, Stephanie. *Tanqueray* — B
   Zemeckis, Leslie Harter. *Behind the Burly Q* — 792.7
Burlingame, Michael
   Abraham Lincoln — B
   The Black Man's President — 973.7
BURMA
   Alexander, Caroline. *Skies of Thunder* — 940.54
   Holland, James. ★*Burma '44* — 940.54
   Thant Myint-U. *The Hidden History of Burma* — 959.105
★*Burma '44*. Holland, James — 940.54
Burman, Leonard
   Taxes in America — 336.200973
Burn Book. Swisher, Kara — 303.48
Burn It Down. Ryan, Maureen — 791.43
BURN OUT (PSYCHOLOGY)
   Dooner, Caroline. *Tired as F*ck* — 152.1
   May, Katherine. *Enchantment* — 158.1
   Petersen, Anne Helen. *Can't Even* — 305.242
   Tur, Katy. *Rough Draft* — B
   Washington, Kate. ★*Already Toast* — 649.8
BURN VICTIMS
   Thi, Kim Phuc Phan. *Fire Road* — B
Burnett, Carol
   In Such Good Company — 791.45
BURNETT, CAROL
   Burnett, Carol. *In Such Good Company* — 791.45
Burnett, Dean
   Idiot Brain — 612.8
Burnett, Jason Bige
   Graphic Clay — 738.1
BURNETT, PATRICIA HILL
   Turk, Katherine. *The Women of Now* — 305.42
Burnett, William
   Designing Your Life — 650.1
BURNHAM, DANIEL HUDSON, 1846-1912
   Larson, Erik. ★*The Devil in the White City* — 364.15
Burnham, Margaret A.
   ★*By Hands Now Known* — 342.73
The Burning. Madigan, Tim — 976.6
The Burning Blue. Cook, Kevin — 629.45
Burning Boy. Auster, Paul — B
Burning Down the House. Zelizer, Julian E. — 328.73
The Burning of the World. Berg, Scott W. — 977.311
Burning Questions. Atwood, Margaret — 814
The Burning Tigris. Balakian, Peter — 956.6

AUTHOR, TITLE, SERIES AND SUBJECT INDEX

The *Burning Time*. Rounding, Virginia ... 272
Burns. Burns, Robert ... 821
BURNS AND SCALDS
   Erwin, Jon. *Beyond Valor* ... B
Burns, Cherie
   The Great Hurricane—1938 ... 974.7
Burns, Eric
   Infamous Scribblers ... 071
   Someone to Watch Over Me ... 973.917092
Burns, Ken
   ★*Our America* ... 973
Burns, Mike
   The Only One Living to Tell ... 305.897
BURNS, MIKE, 1865?-1934
   Burns, Mike. *The Only One Living to Tell* ... 305.897
Burns, Robert
   Burns ... 821
Burns, William J.
   The Back Channel ... B
BURNS, WILLIAM J. (WILLIAM JOSEPH), 1956-
   Burns, William J. *The Back Channel* ... B
BURR, AARON, 1756-1836
   Sedgwick, John. *War of Two* ... 973.4
BURR-HAMILTON DUEL, WEEHAWKEN, N.J., 1804
   Sedgwick, John. *War of Two* ... 973.4
Burrough, Bryan
   The Big Rich ... 338.2
   Days of Rage ... 303.48
   Forget the Alamo ... 976.043
Burroughs, Augusten
   ★*Toil & Trouble* ... B
BURROUGHS, AUGUSTEN
   Burroughs, Augusten. ★*Toil & Trouble* ... B
Burrows, James
   ★*Directed by James Burrows* ... 791.4502
BURROWS, JAMES, 1940-
   Burrows, James. ★*Directed by James Burrows* ... 791.4502
Burstein, Andrew
   Madison and Jefferson ... 973.4
Burt, Stephanie
   Don't Read Poetry ... 811
BURTON, RICHARD F., 1821-1890
   Jeal, Tim. *Explorers of the Nile* ... 920
BURTON, RICHARD FRANCIS, SIR, 1821-1890
   Millard, Candice. ★*River of the Gods* ... 916.204
BURTON, RICHARD, 1925-1984
   Kashner, Sam. *Furious Love* ... B
Burton, Robert
   Audubon North American Birdfeeder Guide ... 598
Burton, Susan
   Becoming Ms. Burton ... B
   Empty ... B
BURTON, SUSAN, 1973-
   Burton, Susan. *Empty* ... B
Burton-Hill, Clemency
   ★*Year of Wonder* ... 780.9
Buruma, Ian
   Inventing Japan, 1853-1964 ... 952.03
★*Bury My Heart at Wounded Knee*. Brown, Dee ... 978
Bury The Chains. Hochschild, Adam ... 326
BUS TRAVEL
   Stahl, Jerry. *Nein, Nein, Nein!* ... B
Busbee, Jay
   Earnhardt Nation ... B
Busby, Jill Louise
   Unfollow Me ... 305.08
BUSBY, JILL LOUISE
   Busby, Jill Louise. *Unfollow Me* ... 305.08
BUSCH FAMILY
   Knoedelseder, William. *Bitter Brew* ... 338.7
Busch, Robert
   The Wolf Almanac ... 599.773
Buses Are a Comin'. Person, Charles ... B
Bush. Smith, Jean Edward ... 973.931
BUSH FAMILY
   Hager, Jenna Bush. *Sisters First* ... B
   Page, Susan. ★*The Matriarch* ... B
   Updegrove, Mark K. *The Last Republicans* ... 973.928

BUSH, BARBARA PIERCE
   Hager, Jenna Bush. *Sisters First* ... B
BUSH, BARBARA, 1925-2018
   Page, Susan. ★*The Matriarch* ... B
Bush, George
   All the Best, George Bush ... 973.928
Bush, George W.
   41 ... B
   Decision Points ... B
BUSH, GEORGE W. (GEORGE WALKER), 1946-
   Bush, George W. *Decision Points* ... B
   Draper, Robert. *To Start a War* ... 956.7044
   Dyson, Michael Eric. *Come Hell or High Water* ... 976.3
   Smith, Jean Edward. *Bush* ... 973.931
   Updegrove, Mark K. *The Last Republicans* ... 973.928
BUSH, GEORGE, 1924-2018
   Bush, George. *All the Best, George Bush* ... 973.928
   Bush, George W. *41* ... B
   Meacham, Jon. ★*Destiny and Power* ... B
   Updegrove, Mark K. *The Last Republicans* ... 973.928
   Woodward, Bob. *Shadow* ... 973.92
Bushcraft 101. Canterbury, Dave ... 613.6
Bushman, Richard L.
   Mormonism ... 289.3
BUSINESS
   Bogdanich, Walt. *When McKinsey Comes to Town* ... 001
   Burgis, Tom. *The Looting Machine* ... 338.2
   Burrough, Bryan. *The Big Rich* ... 338.2
   Clark, Taylor. *Starbucked* ... 338
   De Botton, Alain. *The Pleasures and Sorrows of Work* ... 306.3
   Fineman, Meredith. *Brag Better* ... 650.1
   Gelles, David. *The Man Who Broke Capitalism* ... 330.12
   Keefe, Bob. *Clean Economy Now* ... 333.79
   Knight, Philip H. *Shoe Dog* ... B
   Lashinsky, Adam. *Wild Ride* ... 388.4
   Mazzucato, Mariana. ★*The Big Con* ... 650.1
   Mezrich, Ben. *Breaking Twitter* ... 338.7
   Micklethwait, John. *The Company* ... 338.7
   Nooyi, Indra. ★*My Life in Full* ... B
   Stone, Brad. *The Upstarts* ... 338.04
   Teachout, Zephyr. *Break 'Em Up* ... 338.8
   Vlasic, Bill. *Once Upon a Car* ... 338.4
   Wayland-Smith, Ellen. *Oneida* ... 307.77
   Winkler, Adam. *We the Corporations* ... 346.73
BUSINESS AND ECONOMICS — BUSINESS ADVICE
   Abrams, Stacey. *Level Up* ... 658.4
   Ariely, Dan. *Predictably Irrational* ... 153.8
   Berman, Lea. *Treating People Well* ... 395
   Burkus, David. *Friend of a Friend...* ... 650.1
   Carnegie, Dale. ★*How to Win Friends and Influence People* ... 158
   Cast, Carter. *The Right—And Wrong—Stuff* ... 650.1
   Covey, Stephen R. ★*The 7 Habits of Highly Effective People* ... 158
   Covey, Stephen R. *The 8th Habit* ... 158
   Dennis, Felix. *How to Get Rich* ... B
   Duke, Annie. *Thinking in Bets* ... 658.4
   Economy, Peter. *Wait, I'm Working with Who?!?* ... 650.1
   Fineman, Meredith. *Brag Better* ... 650.1
   Gallo, Carmine. *The Bezos Blueprint* ... 658.4
   Gentile, Mary C. *Giving Voice to Values* ... 174
   Goldman, Seth. *Mission in a Bottle* ... 741.5
   Grant, Adam M. *Give and Take* ... 158.2
   Grant, Adam M. *Originals* ... 153.3
   Green, Alison. *Ask a Manager* ... 650.1
   Greenberg, Sarah Stein. *Creative Acts for Curious People* ... 153.3
   Hamilton, Denise. ★*Indivisible* ... 658.3
   Henry, Alan. *Seen, Heard, and Paid* ... 650.1
   Lima, Jamie Kern. *Believe It* ... B
   Livingston, Robert W. *The Conversation* ... 305.8
   McAfee, Andrew. *The Geek Way* ... 658.3
   Pink, Daniel H. *Drive* ... 153.1
   Porath, Christine Lynne. *Mastering Civility* ... 650.1
   Rice, Condoleezza. *Political Risk* ... 658.15
   Rollag, Keith. *What to Do When You're New* ... 158.2
   Sally, David. *One Step Ahead* ... 658.4
   Sandberg, Sheryl. *Lean In* ... 658.4
   Sandberg, Sheryl. *Lean In* ... 658.4
   Schein, Edgar H. *Humble Inquiry* ... 302.2
   Schweitzer, Sharon. *Access to Asia* ... 395.5

PUBLIC LIBRARY CORE COLLECTION: NONFICTION
Twentieth Edition

Snow, Shane. *Dream Teams*	658.4
Solovic, Susan Wilson. *The One-Percent Edge*	658.4
Spetzler, Carl S. *Decision Quality*	658.4
Stanley, Mary J. *Managing Library Employees*	023
Steingold, Fred S. *The Employer's Legal Handbook, 16th Ed.*	344.7301
Sutton, Robert I. *The Asshole Survival Guide*	650.1
Walker, Sam. *The Captain Class*	796.07
Warzel, Charlie. *Out of Office*	658.3

BUSINESS AND ECONOMICS — BUSINESS ADVICE — LEADERSHIP AND MANAGEMENT

Bahcall, Safi. *Loonshots*	658.4
Barsh, Joanna. *Grow Wherever You Work*	658.4
Boden, Anne. *Female Founders' Playbook*	658.4
Botelho, Elena L. *The CEO Next Door*	658.4
Brown, Brene. ★*Dare to Lead*	658.4
Cerulo, Erica. *Work Wife*	658.4
Cox, Gena. *Leading Inclusion*	658.3
Economy, Peter. *Wait, I'm the Boss?!?*	658
Gaddis, John Lewis. *On Grand Strategy*	355.4
Gentile, Mary C. *Giving Voice to Values*	174
Gilkey, Charlie. *Start Finishing*	658.4
Gillard, Julia. ★*Women and Leadership*	158
Godin, Seth. *The Practice*	153.3
Goleman, Daniel. *Primal Leadership*	658.4
Goodall, Amanda. *Credible*	658.4
Gryta, Thomas. *Lights Out*	338.7
Hansen, Morten T. *Great at Work*	650.1
Hastings, Reed. *No Rules Rules*	384.55
Horstman, Mark. *The Effective Manager*	658.4
Ketheledge, Raymond Michael. *Lead Yourself First*	658.4
Kim, W. Chan. *Blue Ocean Shift*	658.8
Malone, Thomas W. *Superminds*	005.7
Peter, Laurence J. *The Peter Principle*	658
Phillips, Collette A. M. *The Incluters*	658.4
Richards, Shola. *Making Work Work*	658.3
Riel, Jennifer. *Creating Great Choices*	658.4
Rowan, Barry L. *The Spiritual Art of Business*	261.8
Scott, Kim Malone. *Radical Candor*	658.4
Shah, Rajiv Janardan. *Big Bets*	303.4
Smith, Clint. *How to Hire*	658.3
Suh, Krista. *DIY Rules for a WTF World*	158.1
Tracy, Brian. *Full Engagement!*	658.3
Varol, Ozan O. *Think Like a Rocket Scientist*	650.1
Washington, Ella F. *The Necessary Journey*	658.3
Webb, Maynard. *Dear Founder*	658
Wooldridge, Adrian. *Masters of Management*	658

BUSINESS AND ECONOMICS — BUSINESS LEADERS AND ENTREPRENEURS

Au-Yeung, Angel. *Wonder Boy*	B
Auletta, Ken. *Media Man*	B
Boden, Anne. *Female Founders' Playbook*	658.4
Brinkley, Alan. ★*The Publisher*	B
Brinkley, Douglas. *Wheels for the World*	B
Bundles, A'Lelia. *On Her Own Ground*	B
Burrough, Bryan. *The Big Rich*	338.2
Cannadine, David. ★*Mellon*	B
Chernow, Ron. *The Warburgs*	B
Crowe, Lauren Goldstein. *The Towering World of Jimmy Choo*	391.4
DeBord, Matthew. *Return to Glory*	338.4
Downs, Paul. *Boss Life*	338.7
Fuller, Pamela. ★*The Leader's Guide to Unconscious Bias*	658.3
Gelles, David. *The Man Who Broke Capitalism*	330.12
Greenburg, Zack O'Malley. *3 Kings*	782.421649
Greenfield, Martin. ★*Measure of a Man*	B
Higgins, Tim. *Power Play*	338.7
Hoffman, Liz. *Crash Landing*	330
Isaacson, Walter. ★*Elon Musk*	B
Isaacson, Walter. ★*Steve Jobs*	B
Jackson, Curtis. *Hustle Harder, Hustle Smarter*	B
Kawasaki, Guy. *The Art of the Start 2.0*	658.1
Knight, Philip H. *Shoe Dog*	B
Kolhatkar, Sheelah. *Black Edge*	364.16
Krass, Peter. *Carnegie*	B
Kurlansky, Mark. *Birdseye*	B
Levy, Reynold. *They Told Me Not to Take That Job*	792.09
Marshall, Cynthia. *You've Been Chosen*	B
Mulcahy, Diane. *The Gig Economy*	650.1
Nasaw, David. *Andrew Carnegie*	B
Nasaw, David. *The Chief*	B
Nooyi, Indra. ★*My Life in Full*	B
Rathbone, John Paul. *The Sugar King of Havana*	B
Renehan, Edward. *Commodore*	B
Satow, Julie. *When Women Ran Fifth Avenue*	381.141
Schroeder, Alice. *The Snowball*	B
Scott, Kim Malone. *Radical Candor*	658.4
Snow, Richard. *Disney's Land*	791.06
Stiles, T. J. ★*The First Tycoon*	B
Vaynerchuk, Gary. *Crushing It!*	650.1
Waterhouse, Benjamin C. *One Day I'll Work for Myself*	338
Watts, Steven. *The People's Tycoon*	B
Whyte, Kenneth. *The Uncrowned King*	B
Wiedeman, Reeves. *Billion Dollar Loser*	333.33
Wills, Garry. *Certain Trumpets*	303.3

BUSINESS AND ECONOMICS — CAREERS

Burnett, William. *Designing Your Life*	650.1
Ferrazzi, Keith. *Never Eat Alone*	658.4
Green, Alison. *Ask a Manager*	650.1
Moore, Rachel. *The Artist's Compass*	791
Mulcahy, Diane. *The Gig Economy*	650.1
Webb, Caroline. *How to Have a Good Day*	650.1

BUSINESS AND ECONOMICS — CORRUPTION AND SCANDAL

Arsenault, Kerri. *Mill Town*	B
Bauer, Shane. *American Prison*	365
Bensinger, Ken. ★*Red Card*	796.334
Bernstein, Andrea. *American Oligarchs*	920
Bilott, Robert. *Exposure*	344.04
Blunt, Katherine. *California Burning*	333.793
Bogdanich, Walt. *When McKinsey Comes to Town*	001
Brown, Eliot. *The Cult of We*	333.33
Bullough, Oliver. *Moneyland*	364.1
Carreyrou, John. ★*Bad Blood*	338.7
Cohan, William D. *Power Failure*	338.7
Conn, David. *The Fall of the House of FIFA*	796.334
Dayen, David. *Chain of Title*	330.973
Dayen, David. *Monopolized*	338.8
Ditmore, Melissa Hope. ★*Unbroken Chains*	306.74
Ducharme, Jamie. *Big Vape*	338.7
Etter, Lauren. ★*The Devil's Playbook*	338.7
Ewing, Jack. *Faster, Higher, Farther*	338.7
Fagin, Dan. *Toms River*	363.7209749
Flannery, Kate. *Strip Tees*	338.4
Goldacre, Ben. *Bad Science*	500
Hamby, Chris. *Soul Full of Coal Dust*	363.11
Hardy, Alyssa. *Worn Out*	338.4
Hart, Matt. *Win at All Costs*	338.7
Higham, Scott. *American Cartel*	338.4
Horwitz, Jeff. ★*Broken Code*	302.3
Hudson, Michael W. *The Monster*	332.63
Kolhatkar, Sheelah. *Black Edge*	364.16
Leamer, Laurence. *The Price of Justice*	346.7302
Lenzer, Jeanne. *The Danger Within Us*	338.4
Lewis, Michael. ★*Going Infinite*	305.5
Maddow, Rachel. *Blowout*	338.2
Maroney, Tyler. *The Modern Detective*	658.4
Mattioli, Dana. ★*The Everything War*	381.142
McGreal, Chris. *American Overdose*	362.29
McSwane, J. David. ★*Pandemic, Inc.*	362.1962
Mezrich, Ben. *Breaking Twitter*	338.7
Michel, Casey. *American Kleptocracy*	364.16
Moore, Kate. *The Radium Girls*	363.17
Morgenson, Gretchen. ★*These Are the Plunderers*	332.6
Mueller, Tom. *Crisis of Conscience*	364.16
Posner, Gerald L. ★*Pharma*	338.4
Robison, Peter. ★*Flying Blind*	338.7
Rosenthal, Elisabeth. *An American Sickness*	362.10973
Schwab, Tim. ★*The Bill Gates Problem*	361.7
Stewart, James B. *Unscripted*	658.1
Taub, Jennifer. *Big Dirty Money*	364.16
Ward, Geoffrey C. *A Disposition to Be Rich*	B
Wicker, Alden. ★*To Dye For*	746

BUSINESS AND ECONOMICS — ECONOMICS

Case, Anne. *Deaths of Despair and the Future of Capitalism*	362.28
Chang, Ha-Joon. *Economics*	330
Cox, Josie. *Women Money Power*	330.082
Gelles, David. *The Man Who Broke Capitalism*	330.12

AUTHOR, TITLE, SERIES AND SUBJECT INDEX

Keynes, John Maynard. ★*The General Theory of Employment, Interest, and Money* — 330.15
Krugman, Paul R. *Arguing with Zombies* — 330.973
Lanchester, John. *How to Speak Money* — 330.1
Levitt, Steven D. ★*Freakonomics* — 330
Levitt, Steven D. *Superfreakonomics* — 330
Romeo, Nick. *The Alternative* — 174
Roth, Alvin E. *Who Gets What—And Why* — 330.01
Schumacher, E. F. *Small Is Beautiful* — 330
Sen, Amartya. *Home in the World* — B
Smith, Adam. ★*The Wealth of Nations* — 330.15
Sowell, Thomas. *Basic Economics* — 330
Wheelan, Charles J. *Naked Economics* — 330

BUSINESS AND ECONOMICS — ECONOMICS — CONSUMERISM

Ariely, Dan. *Dollars and Sense* — 332.024
Auletta, Ken. *Frenemies* — 659.1
Berners-Lee, Mike. *The Carbon Footprint of Everything* — 363.738
Bissonnette, Zac. *The Great Beanie Baby Bubble* — 338.7
Cline, Elizabeth L. *The Conscious Closet* — 646
Cohen, Lizabeth. *A Consumers' Republic* — 339.4
Gerth, Karl. *As China Goes, so Goes the World* — 339.4
Haag, Pamela. ★*The Gunning of America* — 338.4
Hammond, Claudia. *Mind Over Money* — 332.401
Marie, Jane. ★*Selling the Dream* — 658.8
Minter, Adam. *Secondhand* — 381
Morduch, Jonathan. *The Financial Diaries* — 332.024
Schwartz, Nelson. *The Velvet Rope Economy* — 339.2
Tonti, Lucianne. *Sundressed* — 746.9
Vanderbilt, Tom. *You May Also Like* — 153.8
Wu, Tim. *The Attention Merchants* — 659.1

BUSINESS AND ECONOMICS — ECONOMICS — CONTEMPORARY U.S. ECONOMY

Bernanke, Ben. ★*21st Century Monetary Policy* — 332.1
Bomey, Nathan. *Detroit Resurrected* — 977.4
Ditmore, Melissa Hope. ★*Unbroken Chains* — 306.74
Fine, Doug. *Too High to Fail* — 338.4
Fox, Justin. *The Myth of the Rational Market* — 332.64
Goldstein, Amy. *Janesville* — 330.9775
Hoffman, Liz. *Crash Landing* — 330
Klobuchar, Amy. ★*Antitrust* — 343.73
Krugman, Paul R. *Arguing with Zombies* — 330.973
Kwak, James. *Economism* — 330
Lemann, Nicholas. *Transaction Man* — 330.973
Lewis, Michael. *The Big Short* — 330.973
Mallaby, Sebastian. *The Man Who Knew* — B
McGhee, Heather C. ★*The Sum of Us* — 305.8
McLean, Bethany. *All the Devils Are Here* — 330.973
Morduch, Jonathan. *The Financial Diaries* — 332.024
Morgenson, Gretchen. ★*These Are the Plunderers* — 332.6
Noah, Timothy. *The Great Divergence* — 339.2
Paulson, Henry M. *On the Brink* — 330.973
Peta, Joe. *Trading Bases* — 796.357
Quart, Alissa. *Squeezed* — 305.5
Small, Zachary. ★*Token Supremacy* — 332.4
Smialek, Jeanna. ★*Limitless* — 332.1
Stiglitz, Joseph E. *The Price of Inequality* — 305.50973
Teachout, Zephyr. *Break 'Em Up* — 338.8
Warren, Elizabeth. *This Fight Is Our Fight* — 305.5
Wessel, David. *In Fed We Trust* — 332.1
Winkler, Adam. *We the Corporations* — 346.73

BUSINESS AND ECONOMICS — ECONOMICS — HISTORY

Acemoglu, Daron. *Power and Progress* — 303.48
Ahamed, Liaquat. *Lords of Finance* — 920
Bogdanich, Walt. *When McKinsey Comes to Town* — 001
Bown, Stephen R. *Merchant Kings* — 338.8
Conway, Edmund. *The Summit* — 337.09
De Long, J. Bradford. *Slouching Towards Utopia* — 330.9
Doran, Peter B. *Breaking Rockefeller* — 338.7
Dougherty, Conor. *Golden Gates* — 363.509794
Fraser, Steve. *The Age of Acquiescence* — 973.91
Freeman, Joshua Benjamin. ★*Behemoth* — 338.6
Friedman, Benjamin M. *Religion and the Rise of Capitalism* — 330.12
Goldstein, Jacob. *Money* — 332.4
Gordon, Robert J. ★*The Rise and Fall of American Growth* — 339.4
Gramm, Jeff. *Dear Chairman* — 659.2
Greenspan, Alan. *Capitalism in America* — 330.973
Gryta, Thomas. *Lights Out* — 338.7
Hansen, Valerie. *The Year 1000* — 909

Harford, Tim. *50 Inventions That Shaped the Modern Economy* — 609
Heilbroner, Robert L. ★*The Worldly Philosophers* — B
Herman, Arthur. *Freedom's Forge* — 940.53
Hickel, Jason. *The Divide* — 330.9
Kennedy, Paul M. *The Rise and Fall of the Great Powers* — 909.82
Ledbetter, James. *One Nation Under Gold* — 332.4
Lemann, Nicholas. *Transaction Man* — 330.973
Levy, Jonathan. *Ages of American Capitalism* — 330.12
Lowenstein, Roger. *America's Bank* — 332.1
Lowenstein, Roger. *Ways and Means* — 973.7
Mazzucato, Mariana. ★*The Big Con* — 650.1
McCraw, Thomas K. ★*The Founders and Finance* — 330.973
McMillan, John. *Reinventing the Bazaar* — 330.12
Micklethwait, John. *The Company* — 338.7
Montero, David. ★*The Stolen Wealth of Slavery* — 381
Nations, Scott. *A History of the United States in Five Crashes* — 338.5
Norman, Jesse. *Adam Smith* — B
Oller, John. *White Shoe* — 346.73
Perino, Michael A. *The Hellhound of Wall Street* — 330.973
Phillips-Fein, Kim. *Fear City* — 330.9747
Piketty, Thomas. *A Brief History of Equality* — 305.09
Piketty, Thomas. ★*Capital in the Twenty-First Century* — 332
Piketty, Thomas. *The Economics of Inequality* — 339.2
Russell, Rupert. *Price Wars* — 332.64
Shlaes, Amity. *The Forgotten Man* — 973.91
Steil, Benn. *The Battle of Bretton Woods* — 339.5
Waterhouse, Benjamin C. *One Day I'll Work for Myself* — 338
Weatherall, James Owen. *The Physics of Wall Street* — 332.63

BUSINESS AND ECONOMICS — ECONOMICS — SOCIOECONOMICS

Biss, Eula. *Having and Being Had* — 306.3
Davies, Richard. *Extreme Economies* — 306.3
De Botton, Alain. *The Pleasures and Sorrows of Work* — 306.3
De Graaf, John. *What's the Economy For, Anyway?* — 330.973
Derks, Scott. *The Value of a Dollar* — 338.5
Derks, Scott. *The Value of a Dollar* — 338.5
Dougherty, Conor. *Golden Gates* — 363.509794
Flitter, Emily. *The White Wall* — 332.0973
Honey, Michael K. *To the Promised Land* — 323
Jacoby, Melissa B. ★*Unjust Debts* — 346.73
Jena, Anupam B. *Random Acts of Medicine* — 616.0072
Kardas-Nelson, Mara. *We Are Not Able to Live in the Sky* — 332.3
Leonhardt, David. ★*Ours Was the Shining Future* — 330.973
Lieber, Ron. *The Opposite of Spoiled* — 332.0240083
MacKinnon, J. B. ★*The Day the World Stops Shopping* — 339.4
Markovits, Daniel. *The Meritocracy Trap* — 305.5
McGhee, Heather C. ★*The Sum of Us* — 305.8
Mechanic, Michael. *Jackpot* — 305.5
Mishra, Pankaj. *Age of Anger* — 909.8
Monforton, Celeste. *On the Job* — 331.1
Morduch, Jonathan. *The Financial Diaries* — 332.024
Phillips-Fein, Kim. *Fear City* — 330.9747
Piketty, Thomas. *A Brief History of Equality* — 305.09
Piketty, Thomas. ★*Capital and Ideology* — 305
Piketty, Thomas. ★*Capital in the Twenty-First Century* — 332
Piketty, Thomas. *The Economics of Inequality* — 339.2
Romeo, Nick. *The Alternative* — 174
Sachs, Jeffrey. *The Age of Sustainable Development* — 338.9
Sandel, Michael J. *What Money Can't Buy* — 174
Shlaes, Amity. *The Forgotten Man* — 973.91
Smarsh, Sarah. ★*Heartland* — B
Stiglitz, Joseph E. *Globalization and Its Discontents* — 337
Taub, Jennifer. *Big Dirty Money* — 364.16
Thaler, Richard H. *Misbehaving* — 330.01
Turchin, Peter. *End Times* — 320.01
Wartzman, Rick. *Still Broke* — 381
Waterhouse, Benjamin C. *One Day I'll Work for Myself* — 338
Wingfield, Adia Harvey. *Gray Areas* — 331.6

BUSINESS AND ECONOMICS — ECONOMICS — WORLD ECONOMY

Burgis, Tom. *The Looting Machine* — 338.2
Daunton, M. J. ★*The Economic Government of the World* — 337
Davidson, Adam. *The Passion Economy* — 330.9
Davies, Richard. *Extreme Economies* — 306.3
De Long, J. Bradford. *Slouching Towards Utopia* — 330.9
Foroohar, Rana. *Homecoming* — 338.6
Gerth, Karl. *As China Goes, so Goes the World* — 339.4
Goodman, Peter S. ★*How the World Ran Out of Everything* — 658.7
Kershaw, Ian. *The Global Age* — 940.55
McMillan, John. *Reinventing the Bazaar* — 330.12

PUBLIC LIBRARY CORE COLLECTION: NONFICTION
Twentieth Edition

Miller, Chris. *Chip War*	338.4
Patterson, Scott. ★*Chaos Kings*	338.5
Piketty, Thomas. ★*Capital and Ideology*	305
Piketty, Thomas. ★*Capital in the Twenty-First Century*	332
Reid, T. R. *A Fine Mess*	336.200973
Russell, Rupert. *Price Wars*	332.64
Schweitzer, Sharon. *Access to Asia*	395.5
Sharma, Ruchir. *The Rise and Fall of Nations*	330.9
Sorkin, Andrew Ross. *Too Big to Fail*	330.973
Stiglitz, Joseph E. *Globalization and Its Discontents*	337
Wolf, Martin. ★*The Crisis of Democratic Capitalism*	330.12
Yunus, Muhammad. *A World of Three Zeros*	330

BUSINESS AND ECONOMICS — GENERAL

Auerbach, Annie. *Flex*	331.25
Becker, Joshua. *The More of Less*	241
Bellos, David. *Who Owns This Sentence?*	346.73
Burman, Leonard. *Taxes in America*	336.200973
Carroll, Ryder. ★*The Bullet Journal Method*	640
Chapin, Kari. ★*The Handmade Marketplace*	745.5
Davidds, Yasmin. *Your Own Terms*	658.4
Derks, Scott. *The Value of a Dollar*	338.5
Duke, Annie. *Thinking in Bets*	658.4
Elias, Stephen. *The Foreclosure Survival Guide, 9th Ed.*	346.7304
Fabritius, Friederike. *The Leading Brain*	158
Feiler, Bruce. ★*The Search*	306.3
Ferriss, Timothy. *Tools of Titans*	081
Fisher, Roger. ★*Getting to Yes*	158
Gilkey, Charlie. *Start Finishing*	658.4
Goleman, Daniel. *Ecological Intelligence*	333.7
Hansen, Morten T. *Great at Work*	650.1
Hill, Napoleon. *Think and Grow Rich*	650.1
Kawasaki, Guy. *The Art of the Start 2.0*	658.1
Kerpen, Dave. *Likeable Social Media*	658.8
Kowalsky, Michelle. *Creating Inclusive Library Environments*	027.6
Laughlin, Sara. *The Quality Library*	025.1
Leonard, Christopher. *Kochland*	338.7
Lindner, Dan. ★*A Guide to Federal Contracting, 2nd Ed.*	346.7302
Lobel, Orly. *You Don't Own Me*	346.7304
MacKellar, Pamela H. ★*Winning Grants*	025.1
McKeever, Mike P. *How to Write a Business Plan*	658.15
McKeown, Greg. *Essentialism*	153.8
Meltzer, Allan H. *A History of the Federal Reserve*	332.1
Morin, Amy. *13 Things Mentally Strong Women Don't Do*	158.1
Mulcahy, Diane. *The Gig Economy*	650.1
Nocera, Joseph. *The Big Fail*	362.1962
Richards, Shola. *Making Work Work*	658.3
Rubin, Robert Edward. *The Yellow Pad*	658.4
Sack, Steven Mitchell. *The Employee Rights Handbook*	344.7301
Schein, Edgar H. *Humble Inquiry*	302.2
Schneier, Bruce. *A Hacker's Mind*	364.16
Siegel, Joel G. *Accounting Handbook.*	657
Steib, Mike. *The Career Manifesto*	650.1
Steingold, Fred S. *The Employer's Legal Handbook, 16th Ed.*	344.7301
Stulberg, Brad. *Peak Performance*	158.1
Watkins, Alexandra. *Hello, My Name Is Awesome*	658.8
Webb, Caroline. *How to Have a Good Day*	650.1
Willink, Jocko. *Discipline Equals Freedom*	158.1

BUSINESS AND ECONOMICS — INDUSTRIES

Au-Yeung, Angel. *Wonder Boy*	B
Bissonnette, Zac. *The Great Beanie Baby Bubble*	338.7
Bogdanich, Walt. *When McKinsey Comes to Town*	001
Denton, Sally. *The Profiteers*	B
Fine, Doug. *Too High to Fail*	338.4
Franklin-Wallis, Oliver. ★*Wasteland*	363.72
Harrison, Christy. *The Wellness Trap*	613
Harrison, Scott. *Thirst*	B
Humes, Edward. ★*Total Garbage*	628.4
Mazzucato, Mariana. ★*The Big Con*	650.1
Mitford, Jessica. ★*The American Way of Death Revisited*	338.4
Morris, Jim. ★*The Cancer Factory*	658.3
Schoenfeld, Bruce. ★*Game of Edges*	796.04
Schultz, Howard. *From the Ground Up*	B
Teachout, Zephyr. *Break 'Em Up*	338.8
Yong, Sable. *Die Hot with a Vengeance*	646.7

BUSINESS AND ECONOMICS — INDUSTRIES — AGRICULTURE AND FOOD

Addison, Corban. *Wastelands*	346.73
Bittman, Mark. *Animal, Vegetable, Junk*	394.1
Brenner, Joel Glenn. *The Emperors of Chocolate*	338.7
Capparell, Stephanie. *The Real Pepsi Challenge*	338.7
Chatelain, Marcia. ★*Franchise*	339
Clark, Taylor. *Starbucked*	338
Ducharme, Jamie. *Big Vape*	338.7
Eggers, Dave. *The Monk of Mokha*	B
Elmore, Bartow J. *Citizen Coke*	338.7
Elmore, Bartow J. *Seed Money*	338.7
Freeman, Andrea. ★*Ruin Their Crops on the Ground*	338.1
Genoways, Ted. *The Chain*	338.7
Hvistendahl, Mara. ★*The Scientist and the Spy*	364.16
Knoedelseder, William. *Bitter Brew*	338.7
Kurlansky, Mark. *Birdseye*	B
Logsdon, Gene. *Letter to a Young Farmer*	338.10973
Lorr, Benjamin. *The Secret Life of Groceries*	381.4
Montgomery, David R. *What Your Food Ate*	631.4
Nordhaus, Hannah. *The Beekeeper's Lament*	638
Sedgewick, Augustine. *Coffeeland*	338.4
Sorvino, Chloe. *Raw Deal*	338.1
Stone, Daniel. *The Food Explorer*	B
Zimberoff, Larissa. *Technically Food*	613.2
Zuckerman, Jocelyn C. *Planet Palm*	633.8

BUSINESS AND ECONOMICS — INDUSTRIES — ENERGY

Bakke, Gretchen Anna. *The Grid*	333.793
Biggers, Jeff. *Reckoning at Eagle Creek*	333.73
Blunt, Katherine. *California Burning*	333.793
Briody, Blaire. *The New Wild West*	338.2
Burrough, Bryan. *The Big Rich*	338.2
Coll, Steve. *Private Empire*	338.7
Doran, Peter B. *Breaking Rockefeller*	338.7
Higgins, Tim. *Power Play*	338.7
Keefe, Bob. *Clean Economy Now*	333.79
Maass, Peter. *Crude World*	338.2
Maddow, Rachel. *Blowout*	338.2
Magner, Mike. *Poisoned Legacy*	338.7
Margonelli, Lisa. *Oil on the Brain*	338.2
Rao, Maya. *Great American Outpost*	338.2
Scheyder, Ernest. *The War Below*	333.7
Yergin, Daniel. *The New Map*	333.79

BUSINESS AND ECONOMICS — INDUSTRIES — ENTERTAINMENT AND MEDIA

Auletta, Ken. *Media Man*	B
Bergen, Mark. *Like, Comment, Subscribe*	338.7
Biskind, Peter. *Pandora's Box*	791.45
Burak, Asi. *Power Play*	794.8
Charnas, Dan. *The Big Payback*	306.4
Harris, Blake J. *Console Wars*	338.7
Hayes, Dade. *Binge Times*	384.55
Howe, Sean. *Marvel Comics*	741.5
Knight, Molly. *The Best Team Money Can Buy*	796.357
Napoli, Lisa. *Up All Night*	384.55
Schwartzel, Erich. *Red Carpet*	791.43
Smith, Ben. *Traffic*	070.4
Smith, Sam. *Hard Labor*	796.323
Snow, Richard. *Disney's Land*	791.06
Taplin, Jonathan. *Move Fast and Break Things*	330.9
Windhorst, Brian. *Lebron, Inc.*	B
Wu, Tim. *The Attention Merchants*	659.1

BUSINESS AND ECONOMICS — INDUSTRIES — FINANCE

Belfort, Jordan. ★*The Wolf of Investing*	332.63
Boden, Anne. *Female Founders' Playbook*	658.4
Dayen, David. *Chain of Title*	330.973
Enrich, David. *Dark Towers*	332.1
Fabre, Cin. *Wolf Hustle*	332.6
Graham, Benjamin. *The Intelligent Investor*	332.67
Grind, Kirsten. *The Lost Bank*	332.3
Hagstrom, Robert G. *The Warren Buffett Way*	332.6
Halpern, Jake. *Bad Paper*	332.7
Howard, Timothy. *The Mortgage Wars*	332.7
Hudson, Michael W. *The Monster*	332.63
Karabell, Zachary. *Inside Money*	332.1
Lewis, Michael. *The Big Short*	330.973
Lewis, Michael. ★*Going Infinite*	305.5
Michel, Casey. *American Kleptocracy*	364.16
Mitchell, Josh. *The Debt Trap*	378.3
O'Rourke, P. J. *None of My Business*	332
Schulman, Daniel. *The Money Kings*	332.0973
Sorkin, Andrew Ross. *Too Big to Fail*	330.973

AUTHOR, TITLE, SERIES AND SUBJECT INDEX

Sun, Carrie. *Private Equity*	B
Thorp, Edward O. *A Man for All Markets*	B
Weatherall, James Owen. *The Physics of Wall Street*	332.63

BUSINESS AND ECONOMICS — INDUSTRIES — MANUFACTURING

Cohan, William D. *Power Failure*	338.7
Gelles, David. *The Man Who Broke Capitalism*	330.12
Green, Hardy. *The Company Town*	307.76
Kurutz, Steven. *American Flannel*	338.4
Macy, Beth. ★*Factory Man*	338.7
Pang, Amelia. ★*Made in China*	331.11
Slade, Rachel. *American Hoodie*	338.4
Tonti, Lucianne. *Sundressed*	746.9

BUSINESS AND ECONOMICS — INDUSTRIES — MEDICAL

Abramson, John. *Sickening*	338.4
Allen, Marshall. ★*Never Pay the First Bill*	610.28
Brown, Theresa. *Healing*	616.99
Carreyrou, John. ★*Bad Blood*	338.7
Eyre, Eric. *Death in Mud Lick*	362.29
Hari, Johann. ★*Magic Pill*	613.2
Higham, Scott. *American Cartel*	338.4
Jena, Anupam B. *Random Acts of Medicine*	616.0072
Keefe, Patrick Radden. ★*Empire of Pain*	338.7
Lenzer, Jeanne. *The Danger Within Us*	338.4
Loftus, Peter. *The Messenger*	338.4
Macy, Beth. ★*Dopesick*	362.29
Macy, Beth. ★*Raising Lazarus*	362.29
McGreal, Chris. *American Overdose*	362.29
Otto, Mary. *Teeth*	617
Posner, Gerald L. ★*Pharma*	338.4
Quigley, Fran. *Prescription for the People*	338.4
Rosenthal, Elisabeth. *An American Sickness*	362.10973
Vanderbes, Jennifer. ★*Wonder Drug*	615
Villarosa, Linda. ★*Under the Skin*	362.1089
Zaitchik, Alexander. *Owning the Sun*	362.1
Zuckerman, Gregory. *A Shot to Save the World*	614.5

BUSINESS AND ECONOMICS — INDUSTRIES — RETAIL PRODUCTS AND SERVICES

Del Rey, Jason. *Winner Sells All*	381
Etter, Lauren. ★*The Devil's Playbook*	338.7
Gerber, Robin. *Barbie and Ruth*	B
Goodman, Peter S. ★*How the World Ran Out of Everything*	658.7
Guendelsberger, Emily. *On the Clock*	331.0973
Hardy, Alyssa. *Worn Out*	338.4
Hu, Elise. *Flawless*	646.7
Knight, Philip H. *Shoe Dog*	B
MacGillis, Alec. *Fulfillment*	381
Marie, Jane. ★*Selling the Dream*	658.8
Mattioli, Dana. ★*The Everything War*	381.142
Orbanes, Philip. *The Game Makers*	338.7
Pang, Amelia. ★*Made in China*	331.11
Raphael, Rina. *The Gospel of Wellness*	613
Robertson, David C. *Brick by Brick*	338.7
Satow, Julie. *When Women Ran Fifth Avenue*	381.141
Smith, Michael. *Cabin Fever*	614.5
Taplin, Jonathan. *Move Fast and Break Things*	330.9
Tonti, Lucianne. *Sundressed*	746.9
Wartzman, Rick. *Still Broke*	381
Wassef, Nadia. *Shelf Life*	B

BUSINESS AND ECONOMICS — INDUSTRIES — TECHNOLOGY

Auletta, Ken. *Frenemies*	659.1
Auletta, Ken. *Googled*	338.7
Bergen, Mark. *Like, Comment, Subscribe*	338.7
Bilton, Nick. *Hatching Twitter*	006.7
Burak, Asi. *Power Play*	794.8
Campbell-Kelly, Martin. *From Airline Reservations to Sonic the Hedgehog*	338.4
Chafkin, Max. *The Contrarian*	B
Chang, Emily. *Brotopia*	331.4
Citron, Danielle Keats. *The Fight for Privacy*	342.7308
Etter, Lauren. ★*The Devil's Playbook*	338.7
Galloway, Scott. *The Four*	338.7
Hill, Kashmir. ★*Your Face Belongs to Us*	006.2
Horwitz, Jeff. ★*Broken Code*	302.3
Isaacson, Walter. ★*Steve Jobs*	B
Lashinsky, Adam. *Wild Ride*	388.4
Mattioli, Dana. ★*The Everything War*	381.142
McAfee, Andrew. *The Geek Way*	658.3
McCourt, Frank H. ★*Our Biggest Fight*	303.48

Menuez, Doug. *Fearless Genius*	979.4
Mezrich, Ben. *Breaking Twitter*	338.7
Miller, Chris. *Chip War*	338.4
Nadella, Satya. *Hit Refresh*	B
Pein, Corey. *Live Work Work Work Die*	338.4
Schlender, Brent. *Becoming Steve Jobs*	B
Scott, Kevin. *Reprogramming the American Dream*	338
Stone, Brad. *The Upstarts*	338.04
Swisher, Kara. *Burn Book*	303.48
Taplin, Jonathan. *Move Fast and Break Things*	330.9
Tau, Byron. ★*Means of Control*	363.25
Vance, Ashlee. *When the Heavens Went on Sale*	621.43
Williams, Bari A. *Seen yet Unseen*	338.4

BUSINESS AND ECONOMICS — INDUSTRIES — TRANSPORTATION

Albert, Daniel M. *Are We There Yet?*	303.48
Brinkley, Douglas. *Wheels for the World*	B
Cooke, Julia. *Come Fly the World*	387.7
DeBord, Matthew. *Return to Glory*	338.4
Ewing, Jack. *Faster, Higher, Farther*	338.7
Goldstein, Amy. *Janesville*	330.9775
Goldstone, Lawrence. *Drive!*	338.4
Goodman, Peter S. ★*How the World Ran Out of Everything*	658.7
Higgins, Tim. *Power Play*	338.7
Hiltzik, Michael A. *Iron Empires*	385.0973
Humes, Edward. *Door to Door*	388.09
Lashinsky, Adam. *Wild Ride*	388.4
McPhee, John. *Uncommon Carriers*	388
McShane Wulfhart, Nell. *The Great Stewardess Rebellion*	331.4
Robison, Peter. ★*Flying Blind*	338.7
Ujifusa, Steven. *Barons of the Sea*	387.5
Vlasic, Bill. *Once Upon a Car*	338.4
Watts, Steven. *The People's Tycoon*	B

BUSINESS AND ECONOMICS — PERSONAL FINANCE

Belfort, Jordan. ★*The Wolf of Investing*	332.63
Buffett, Mary. *Warren Buffett and the Art of Stock Arbitrage*	332.645
Davenport, Anthony. *Your Score*	332.7
Fagan, Chelsea. *The Financial Diet*	332.024
Graham, Benjamin. *The Intelligent Investor*	332.67
Kobliner, Beth. *Make Your Kid a Money Genius (even If You're Not)*	332.024
Mecham, Jesse. *You Need a Budget*	332.024
O'Neill, Cara. *Chapter 13 Bankruptcy, 17th Ed.*	346.7307
Orman, Suze. *Women & Money*	332.0240082
Quinn, Jane Bryant. ★*How to Make Your Money Last*	332.024
Ramsey, Dave. *The Total Money Makeover*	332.024
Rick, Scott. *Tightwads and Spendthrifts*	332.024
Sabatier, Grant. *Financial Freedom*	332.024
Simmons, Lauren. *Make Money Move*	332.024
Stanley, Thomas J. *The Next Millionaire Next Door*	332.024
Tu, Vivian. *Rich Af*	332.024

BUSINESS AND ECONOMICS — POPULAR PSYCHOLOGY

Ariely, Dan. *Dollars and Sense*	332.024
Bahcall, Safi. *Loonshots*	658.4
Brown, Brene. ★*Dare to Lead*	658.4
Burkus, David. *Friend of a Friend...*	650.1
Callahan, David. *The Cheating Culture*	174
Cast, Carter. *The Right—And Wrong—Stuff*	650.1
Clear, James. ★*Atomic Habits*	155.24
Coggan, Philip. *Surviving the Daily Grind*	658.3
Crawford, Matthew B. *The World Beyond Your Head*	155.2
Duhigg, Charles. ★*The Power of Habit*	158.1
Duhigg, Charles. *Smarter Faster Better*	158
Duhigg, Charles. ★*Supercommunicators*	153.6
Dutton, Kevin. *Split-Second Persuasion*	153.8
Edmondson, Amy C. *The Right Kind of Wrong*	158.1
Epstein, David J. ★*Range*	153.9
Friedman, Ron. *Decoding Greatness*	650.1
Gallo, Amy. *Getting Along*	658.4
Gladwell, Malcolm. *Blink*	153.4
Gladwell, Malcolm. *David and Goliath*	155.2
Gladwell, Malcolm. *Outliers*	302
Godin, Seth. *The Practice*	153.3
Grant, Adam M. *Hidden Potential*	153.8
Grant, Adam M. ★*Think Again*	153.4
Green, Alison. *Ask a Manager*	650.1
Harford, Tim. *Messy*	153.3
Kahneman, Daniel. ★*Thinking, Fast and Slow*	153.4
Kethledge, Raymond Michael. *Lead Yourself First*	658.4
Konnikova, Maria. *The Biggest Bluff*	795.412

PUBLIC LIBRARY CORE COLLECTION: NONFICTION
Twentieth Edition

Livingston, Robert W. *The Conversation*	305.8
Mueller, Jennifer. *Creative Change*	658.4
Newkirk, Pamela. *Diversity, Inc.*	658.3
Pink, Daniel H. *When*	153.7
Price, Devon. ★*Laziness Does Not Exist*	158.1
Ridley, Matt. *The Rational Optimist*	339.2
Rosling, Hans. *Factfulness*	155.9
Shlain, Tiffany. *24/6*	158.1
Vanderbilt, Tom. *You May Also Like*	153.8
Webb, Maynard. *Dear Founder*	658
Williams, Joan. *What Works for Women at Work*	650.1
Wills, Garry. *Certain Trumpets*	303.3
Yoshino, Kenji. *Say the Right Thing*	305.3
Young, Scott H. *Get Better at Anything*	650.1

BUSINESS AND ECONOMICS — WOMEN AND THE WORKPLACE

Cerulo, Erica. *Work Wife*	658.4
Davidds, Yasmin. *Your Own Terms*	658.4
Dufu, Tiffany. *Drop the Ball*	650.1
Harts, Minda. *Right Within*	658.3
Kramer, Andrea S. *Breaking Through Bias*	650.1
Lipman, Joanne. *That's What She Said*	305.30973
Marcal, Katrine. *Mother of Invention*	604.82
McShane Wulfhart, Nell. *The Great Stewardess Rebellion*	331.4
Palmieri, Jennifer. *Dear Madam President*	158
Rueckert, Veronica. *Outspoken*	808.5
Sandberg, Sheryl. *Lean In*	658.4
Sandberg, Sheryl. *Lean In*	658.4
Vanek Smith, Stacey. *Machiavelli for Women*	650.1
Wasserman, Claire. *Ladies Get Paid*	650.1
Williams, Joan. *What Works for Women at Work*	650.1

BUSINESS AND MASS MEDIA

Teachout, Zephyr. *Break 'Em Up*	338.8

BUSINESS AND POLITICS

Bryant, Howard. *Full Dissidence*	306.20973
Hoffman, Liz. *Crash Landing*	330
Leonard, Christopher. *Kochland*	338.7
MacGillis, Alec. *Fulfillment*	381
Maddow, Rachel. *Blowout*	338.2
Michel, Casey. *American Kleptocracy*	364.16
Rice, Condoleezza. *Political Risk*	658.15
Winkler, Adam. *We the Corporations*	346.73

BUSINESS COMMUNICATION

Burkus, David. *Friend of a Friend...*	650.1
Fineman, Meredith. *Brag Better*	650.1
Gallo, Carmine. *The Bezos Blueprint*	658.4
Malone, Thomas W. *Superminds*	005.7

BUSINESS COMPETITION

Biskind, Peter. *Pandora's Box*	791.45
Brenner, Joel Glenn. *The Emperors of Chocolate*	338.7
DeBord, Matthew. *Return to Glory*	338.4
Hartman, Darrell. *Battle of Ink and Ice*	998
Higgins, Tim. *Power Play*	338.7
Kaufman, Jonathan. *The Last Kings of Shanghai*	951
Lobel, Orly. *You Don't Own Me*	346.7304
Pein, Corey. *Live Work Work Work Die*	338.4
Port, Ian S. *The Birth of Loud*	787.87
Ujifusa, Steven. *Barons of the Sea*	387.5

BUSINESS CONSULTANTS

Bogdanich, Walt. *When McKinsey Comes to Town*	001
Brown, Robert J. *You Can't Go Wrong Doing Right*	B
Mazzucato, Mariana. ★*The Big Con*	650.1

BUSINESS CORRUPTION

Arsenault, Kerri. *Mill Town*	B
Bullough, Oliver. *Moneyland*	364.1
Carreyrou, John. ★*Bad Blood*	338.7
Elmore, Bartow J. *Seed Money*	338.7
Ewing, Jack. *Faster, Higher, Farther*	338.7
Fagin, Dan. *Toms River*	363.7209749
Fainaru-Wada, Mark. *League of Denial*	617.1
Gee, Alastair. *Fire in Paradise*	363.37
Greenberg, Andy. *Tracers in the Dark*	364.16
Hamby, Chris. *Soul Full of Coal Dust*	363.11
Hewlett, Sylvia Ann. *#metoo in the Corporate World*	658.3
Hvistendahl, Mara. ★*The Scientist and the Spy*	364.16
Johnson, Lizzie. ★*Paradise*	363.37
Johnston, David Cay. *The Big Cheat*	973.933
Kolhatkar, Sheelah. *Black Edge*	364.16
Leamer, Laurence. *The Price of Justice*	346.7302

Maddow, Rachel. *Blowout*	338.2
Maher, Kris. *Desperate*	344
Mattioli, Dana. ★*The Everything War*	381.142
McSwane, J. David. ★*Pandemic, Inc.*	362.1962
Morgenson, Gretchen. ★*These Are the Plunderers*	332.6
Mueller, Tom. *Crisis of Conscience*	364.16
Murdoch, Sierra Crane. ★*Yellow Bird*	364.152
Perino, Michael A. *The Hellhound of Wall Street*	330.973
Posner, Gerald L. ★*Pharma*	338.4
Rosenthal, Elisabeth. *An American Sickness*	362.10973
Whitlock, Craig. ★*Fat Leonard*	364.16
Zuckerman, Jocelyn C. *Planet Palm*	633.8

BUSINESS ETHICS

Callahan, David. *The Cheating Culture*	174
Carter, Iain. *Golf Wars*	796.352
Dayen, David. *Monopolized*	338.8
Gentile, Mary C. *Giving Voice to Values*	174
Hardy, Alyssa. *Worn Out*	338.4
Hill, Kashmir. ★*Your Face Belongs to Us*	006.2
Kim, Anne. ★*Poverty for Profit*	302.5
Magner, Mike. *Poisoned Legacy*	338.7
Michel, Casey. *American Kleptocracy*	364.16
Romeo, Nick. *The Alternative*	174
Teachout, Zephyr. *Break 'Em Up*	338.8
Wartzman, Rick. *Still Broke*	381

BUSINESS ETIQUETTE

Berman, Lea. *Treating People Well*	395
Post, Lizzie. *Emily Post's Etiquette*	395
Post, Lizzie. *Emily Post's Etiquette*	395
Schweitzer, Sharon. *Access to Asia*	395.5

BUSINESS FAILURES

Brown, Eliot. *The Cult of We*	333.33
Carreyrou, John. ★*Bad Blood*	338.7
Sorkin, Andrew Ross. *Too Big to Fail*	330.973
Waterhouse, Benjamin C. *One Day I'll Work for Myself*	338
Wiedeman, Reeves. *Billion Dollar Loser*	333.33

BUSINESS INNOVATIONS

Greenspan, Alan. *Capitalism in America*	330.973
Hastings, Reed. *No Rules Rules*	384.55
Lashinsky, Adam. *Wild Ride*	388.4
McAfee, Andrew. *The Geek Way*	658.3
Mueller, Jennifer. *Creative Change*	658.4
Newkirk, Pamela. *Diversity, Inc.*	658.3
Stone, Brad. *The Upstarts*	338.04
Yunus, Muhammad. *A World of Three Zeros*	330

BUSINESS INTELLIGENCE

Hvistendahl, Mara. ★*The Scientist and the Spy*	364.16
Maroney, Tyler. *The Modern Detective*	658.4

BUSINESS LOSSES

Sorkin, Andrew Ross. *Too Big to Fail*	330.973

BUSINESS NETWORKS

Burkus, David. *Friend of a Friend...*	650.1
Ferrazzi, Keith. *Never Eat Alone*	658.4

BUSINESS PARTNERS

Smith, Clive Stafford. *The Injustice System*	345.759

BUSINESS PARTNERSHIP

Cerulo, Erica. *Work Wife*	658.4
Etter, Lauren. ★*The Devil's Playbook*	338.7

BUSINESS PRESENTATIONS

Gallo, Carmine. *Talk Like Ted*	658.4

BUSINESS PSYCHOLOGY

Malone, Thomas W. *Superminds*	005.7

BUSINESS REGULATION

Klobuchar, Amy. ★*Antitrust*	343.73

BUSINESS SECURITY

Maroney, Tyler. *The Modern Detective*	658.4

BUSINESSPEOPLE

Au-Yeung, Angel. *Wonder Boy*	B
Auletta, Ken. *Media Man*	B
Brands, H. W. *Dreams of El Dorado*	978
Brinkley, Alan. ★*The Publisher*	B
Bruck, Connie. *When Hollywood Had a King*	B
Chang, Leslie T. ★*Egyptian Made*	331.4
Davidds, Yasmin. *Your Own Terms*	658.4
Davidson, Adam. *The Passion Economy*	330.9
Doran, Peter B. *Breaking Rockefeller*	338.7
Dufu, Tiffany. *Drop the Ball*	650.1
Dykstra, Lenny. *House of Nails*	B

AUTHOR, TITLE, SERIES AND SUBJECT INDEX

Eggers, Dave. *The Monk of Mokha* — B
Follett, Ken. *On Wings of Eagles* — 955
Forgosh, Linda B. *Louis Bamberger* — B
Franklin, Jonathan. *A Wild Idea* — B
Gerber, Robin. *Barbie and Ruth* — B
Gotch, Jen. *The Upside of Being Down* — B
Greenberg, Amy S. *Lady First* — B
Greene, Joshua. *Unstoppable* — B
Greenfield, Martin. ★*Measure of a Man* — B
Hahn, Emanuel. *Koreatown Dreaming* — 979.4
Hilfiger, Tommy. *American Dreamer* — B
Howe, Ben Ryder. *My Korean Deli* — B
Isaacson, Walter. ★*Steve Jobs* — B
Jacoby, Karl. *The Strange Career of William Ellis* — B
Jarrett, Valerie. *Finding My Voice* — B
Kaufman, Jonathan. *The Last Kings of Shanghai* — 951
Kidder, Tracy. *A Truck Full of Money* — B
Knight, Philip H. *Shoe Dog* — B
Kranish, Michael. *Trump Revealed* — B
Kurlansky, Mark. *Birdseye* — B
Levy, Reynold. *They Told Me Not to Take That Job* — 792.09
Lipman, Joanne. *That's What She Said* — 305.30973
Malone, Jo. *Jo Malone* — B
Morris, James McGrath. *Pulitzer* — B
Nasaw, David. *The Chief* — B
Nasaw, David. ★*The Patriarch* — B
Oller, John. *White Shoe* — 346.73
Rathbone, John Paul. *The Sugar King of Havana* — B
Renehan, Edward. *Commodore* — B
Rothman, Joshua D. *The Ledger and the Chain* — 306.362
Saint John, Bozoma. *The Urgent Life* — B
Schlender, Brent. *Becoming Steve Jobs* — B
Schulman, Daniel. *The Money Kings* — 332.0973
Slade, Rachel. *American Hoodie* — 338.4
Smith, Clive Stafford. *The Injustice System* — 345.759
Smith, Richard Norton. *On His Own Terms* — 973.925092
Spitz, Bob. ★*Dearie* — B
Standiford, Les. ★*Battle for the Big Top* — 791.3
Stiles, T. J. ★*The First Tycoon* — B
Trump, Mary L. *Too Much and Never Enough* — B
Von Furstenberg, Diane. *The Woman I Wanted to Be* — B
Watts, Steven. *The People's Tycoon* — B
Whyte, Kenneth. *Hoover* — B
Wiedeman, Reeves. *Billion Dollar Loser* — 333.33
Wilson, Chris. *The Master Plan* — B
Wilson, Robert. *Barnum* — B
Windhorst, Brian. *Lebron, Inc.* — B
Zuckerman, Gregory. *The Frackers* — B
Busted in New York and Other Essays. Pinckney, Darryl — 305.800973
Buster Keaton. Curtis, James — B
But What If We're Wrong. Klosterman, Chuck — 909.83
★*But What Will People Say?.* Kohli, Sahaj Kaur — 616.89
★*Butch Cassidy.* Leerhsen, Charles — B
Butcher, Amy
   Mothertrucker — B
BUTCHER, AMY
   Butcher, Amy. *Mothertrucker* — B
Butcher, Barbara
   What the Dead Know — 614
BUTCHER, BARBARA
   Butcher, Barbara. *What the Dead Know* — 614
Butcher, Carmen Acevedo
   Man of Blessing — B
The Butchering Art. Fitzharris, Lindsey — B
Butchering Poultry, Rabbit, Lamb, Goat, and Pork. Danforth, Adam — 664
Butler, Brin-Jonathan
   The Domino Diaries — 796.83
BUTLER, BRIN-JONATHAN
   Butler, Brin-Jonathan. *The Domino Diaries* — 796.83
Butler, Daniel Allen
   "*Unsinkable*" — 910
Butler, Isaac
   The Method — 792.02
   The World Only Spins Forward — 812
Butler, Judith
   ★*Who's Afraid of Gender?* — 305.3
Butler, Katy
   The Art of Dying Well — 616.02

Butler, Marcia
   The Skin Above My Knee — B
BUTLER, MARCIA
   Butler, Marcia. *The Skin Above My Knee* — B
Butler, Paul
   Chokehold — 363.2
Butler, Rebecca P.
   ★*Copyright for Teachers & Librarians in the 21st Century* — 346.7304
Butter, Flour, Sugar, Joy. Kartes, Danielle — 641.86
BUTTERFLIES
   Black, Scott Hoffman. *Gardening for Butterflies* — 638
   Brock, James P. *Kaufman Field Guide to Butterflies of North America* — 595.7
   Marcum, Diana. *The Fallen Stones* — B
   Mooallem, Jon. *Wild Ones* — 333.95
   Williams, Wendy. *The Language of Butterflies* — 595.78
Butterfly. Mardini, Yusra — B
The Butterfly Effect. Moore, Marcus J. — B
BUTTERFLY GARDENING
   Black, Scott Hoffman. *Gardening for Butterflies* — 638
Buttermilk Graffiti. Lee, Edward — 641.59
Butterworth, Alex
   The World That Never Was — 335
Buttigieg, Pete
   Shortest Way Home — B
BUTTIGIEG, PETE, 1982-
   Buttigieg, Pete. *Shortest Way Home* — B
BUTTOCKS
   Radke, Heather. *Butts* — 611
Butts. Radke, Heather — 611
Buzz, Sting, Bite. Sverdrup-Thygeson, Anne — 595.7
Buzzed. Kuhn, Cynthia — 362.29
By All Means Available. Vickers, Michael G. — 355
By Chance Alone. Eisen, Max — 940.5318
★*By Hands Now Known.* Burnham, Margaret A. — 342.73
By Myself and Then Some. Bacall, Lauren — B
Byas, Taylor
   I Done Clicked My Heels Three Times — 811
Byers, Charles T.
   Ultimate Guide Home Repair and Improvement — 643
Byrn, Anne
   ★*American Cake* — 641.86
   ★*American Cookie* — 641.86
   A New Take on Cake — 641.86
   Skillet Love — 641.7
Byrne, Eugene
   Darwin — 741.5
Byrne, Paula
   Kick — B
Byron, George Gordon Byron
   Selected Poetry of Lord Byron — 821
BYZANTINE CIVILIZATION
   Brownworth, Lars. *Lost to the West* — 949.5
   Norwich, John Julius. *A Short History of Byzantium* — 949.5
BYZANTINE EMPIRE
   Brownworth, Lars. *Lost to the West* — 949.5
   Crowley, Roger. *1453* — 949.61
   Frankopan, Peter. *The First Crusade* — 956
   Gibbon, Edward. ★*The Decline and Fall of the Roman Empire* — 937
   Herrin, Judith. *Byzantium* — 949.5
   Madden, Thomas F. *Istanbul* — 949.61
   Norwich, John Julius. *Byzantium* — 949.5
   Norwich, John Julius. *Byzantium* — 949.5
   Norwich, John Julius. *Byzantium* — 949.5
   Norwich, John Julius. *A Short History of Byzantium* — 949.5
Byzantium. Herrin, Judith — 949.5
Byzantium. Norwich, John Julius — 949.5
Byzantium. Norwich, John Julius — 949.5
Byzantium. Norwich, John Julius — 949.5

C

C&B Crafts [Series]. Crowfoot, Jane — 746.43
C.S. Lewis. Wilson, A. N. — 823
The Cabaret of Plants. Mabey, Richard — 580
CABARETS
   Cohodas, Nadine. *Princess Noire* — 782.42164
Cabin Fever. Smith, Michael — 614.5

PUBLIC LIBRARY CORE COLLECTION: NONFICTION
Twentieth Edition

CABINET OFFICERS
    Baker, Peter. *The Man Who Ran Washington* — B
    Cannadine, David. ★*Mellon* — B
    Chase, James. *Acheson* — B
    Draper, Robert. *To Start a War* — 956.7044
    Eizenstat, Stuart. ★*President Carter* — B
    Gewen, Barry. ★*The Inevitability of Tragedy* — B
    Graff, Garrett M. *Watergate* — 973.924
    Kerry, John. *Every Day Is Extra* — B
    Marvel, William. *Lincoln's Autocrat* — B
    Matthews, Christopher. *Bobby Kennedy* — B
    Pepys, Samuel. *The Diary of Samuel Pepys* — B
    Schmidt, Michael S. ★*Donald Trump v. The United States* — 973.933
    Stahr, Walter. *Seward* — B
    Stahr, Walter. ★*Stanton* — B
    Tomalin, Claire. *Samuel Pepys* — B
    Zeitz, Joshua. *Building the Great Society* — 973.923

CABINETMAKERS
    Downs, Paul. *Boss Life* — 338.7

CABINS
    Auvinen, Karen. *Rough Beauty* — B
Cable Left, Cable Right. Durant, Judith — 746.43

CABLE TELEVISION
    Biskind, Peter. *Pandora's Box* — 791.45
    Martin, Brett. *Difficult Men* — 791.4509

CACAO BEANS
    Frank, Lois Ellen. *Seed to Plate, Soil to Sky* — 641.5

Cacciatore, Joanne
    Bearing the Unbearable — 155.9

CACIOPPO, JOHN T.
    Cacioppo, Stephanie. *Wired for Love* — 616.8

Cacioppo, Stephanie
    Wired for Love — 616.8

CACIOPPO, STEPHANIE, 1974-
    Cacioppo, Stephanie. *Wired for Love* — 616.8
Cacophony of Bone. Dochartaigh, Kerri ni — B
Cactus Country. Bossiere, Zoe — 306

Cadava, Geraldo L.
    The Hispanic Republican — 324.2734089
★*The Cadaver King and the Country Dentist*. Balko, Radley — 614

Cadbury, Deborah
    Princes at War — 920
    Queen Victoria's Matchmaking — 941.081
    The School That Escaped from the Nazis — 940.53

Caddick-Adams, Peter
    Sand and Steel — 940.54
Caddyshack. Nashawaty, Chris — 791.43
★*Caesar*. Goldsworthy, Adrian Keith — B
Caesar's Last Breath. Kean, Sam — 551.51

Caesar, Ed
    The Moth and the Mountain — B

CAESAR, JULIUS, 100-44 B.C.E
    Goldsworthy, Adrian Keith. ★*Caesar* — B
    Strauss, Barry S. *The Death of Caesar* — 937

CAFFEINE
    Pollan, Michael. ★*This Is Your Mind on Plants* — 581.6

CAGE, JOHN, 1912-1992
    Brown, Carolyn. *Chance and Circumstance* — B
    Larson, Kay. *Where the Heart Beats* — 700.1
Cagney. McCabe, John — B

CAGNEY, JAMES, 1899-1986
    McCabe, John. *Cagney* — B

Cahalan, Susannah
    Brain on Fire — 616.8
    ★*The Great Pretender* — 616.89

CAHALAN, SUSANNAH
    Cahalan, Susannah. *Brain on Fire* — 616.8

Cahan, Richard
    Un-American — 940.53

Cahill, Thomas
    How the Irish Saved Civilization — 941.501
    Sailing the Wine-Dark Sea — 909

Cahn, Naomi R.
    ★*Fair Shake* — 331.4

CAHUN, CLAUDE, 1894-1954
    Shaw, Jennifer Laurie. *Exist Otherwise* — 709.2

Cailan, Alvin
    Amboy — 641.595

CAILAN, ALVIN
    Cailan, Alvin. *Amboy* — 641.595

Cain, Susan
    ★*Bittersweet* — 155.2
    Quiet — 155.2

Caine, Michael
    Blowing the Bloody Doors Off — B

CAINE, MICHAEL
    Caine, Michael. *Blowing the Bloody Doors Off* — B

Cairns, Scott
    The End of Suffering — 231

CAIRO (DOG)
    Chesney, Will. *No Ordinary Dog* — 958.104

Cairo, Alberto
    How Charts Lie — 302.2

CAIRO, EGYPT
    Hessler, Peter. *The Buried* — 962.05
    Matar, Hisham. *The Return* — B
    Wassef, Nadia. *Shelf Life* — B

CAKE
    Adams, Jocelyn Delk. *Grandbaby Cakes* — 641.86
    Arefi, Yossy. *Snacking Cakes* — 641.86
    Beranbaum, Rose Levy. ★*The Cake Bible* — 641.8
    Byrn, Anne. ★*American Cake* — 641.86
    Byrn, Anne. *A New Take on Cake* — 641.86
    Day, Cheryl. *Back in the Day Bakery, Made with Love* — 641.81
    Dodge, Abigail Johnson. *Sheet Cake* — 641.86
    Francois, Zoe. *Zoe Bakes Cakes* — 641.86
    Nelson, Candace. *The Sprinkles Baking Book* — 641.81
    Nelson, Kim. *Daisy Cakes Bakes* — 641.86
    Saltz, Joanna. ★*Delish Insane Sweets* — 641.81
    Stewart, Martha. *Martha Stewart's Cake Perfection* — 641.86
    Tosi, Christina. *All About Cake* — 641.86
    Weller, Melissa. *A Good Bake* — 641.86
    Williams, Odette. *Simple Cake* — 641.86
    Wright, Caroline. *Cake Magic!* — 641.86
★*The Cake Bible*. Beranbaum, Rose Levy — 641.8

CAKE DECORATING
    Stewart, Martha. *Martha Stewart's Cake Perfection* — 641.86
Cake Magic! Wright, Caroline — 641.86

Calamar, Gary
    Record Store Days — 780.26

CALAMITY JANE, 1852-1903
    Clavin, Thomas. *Wild Bill* — B

Calasso, Roberto
    Ardor — 294.5

Calcaterra, Regina
    Etched in Sand — B
    Girl Unbroken — B

CALCATERRA, REGINA
    Calcaterra, Regina. *Etched in Sand* — B
    Calcaterra, Regina. *Girl Unbroken* — B

CALCULUS
    Alexander, Amir R. *Infinitesimal* — 511

CALCUTTA, INDIA
    Lapierre, Dominique. *The City of Joy* — 954
Calder. Perl, Jed — B
★*Calder*. Perl, Jed — B

CALDER, ALEXANDER, 1898-1976
    Perl, Jed. *Calder* — B
    Perl, Jed. ★*Calder* — B

Caldwell, Christopher
    The Age of Entitlement — 305.240973

Caldwell, Gail
    Let's Take the Long Way Home — B

CALDWELL, GAIL, 1951-
    Caldwell, Gail. *Let's Take the Long Way Home* — B

CALENDARS
    Boyle, Rebecca. *Our Moon* — 523.3

Calhoun, Ada
    Also a Poet — B
    Why We Can't Sleep — 305.244

CALHOUN, ADA
    Calhoun, Ada. *Also a Poet* — B

CALHOUN, JOHN C., 1782-1850
    Brands, H. W. ★*Heirs of the Founders* — 973.5

CALIFORNIA
    Akins, Damon B. ★*We Are the Land* — 978

AUTHOR, TITLE, SERIES AND SUBJECT INDEX

Alinder, Mary Street. *Group F.64*	770.92
Allende, Isabel. ★*Paula*	B
Aron, Nina Renata. *Good Morning, Destroyer of Men's Souls*	B
Atleework, Kendra. *Miracle Country*	979.4
Austerlitz, Saul. *Just a Shot Away*	781.66078
Black, Dustin Lance. *Mama's Boy*	B
Blunt, Katherine. *California Burning*	333.793
Boessenecker, John. *Gentleman Bandit*	B
Brands, H. W. *The Age of Gold*	979.4
Brown, Daniel James. *The Indifferent Stars Above*	B
Bugliosi, Vincent. ★*Helter Skelter*	364.1
Cross, Kim. *In Light of All Darkness*	363.25
Crouch, Gregory. *The Bonanza King*	B
Dana, Richard Henry. *Two Years Before the Mast*	910.4
Danler, Stephanie. *Stray*	B
Didion, Joan. *Where I Was from*	979.4
Dougherty, Conor. *Golden Gates*	363.509794
Dresner, Amy. *My Fair Junkie*	B
Dykstra, Lenny. *House of Nails*	B
Edwards, Adrienne L. *Firescaping Your Home*	635.9
Fadiman, Anne. *The Spirit Catches You and You Fall Down*	306.4
Fox, Jeremy. *On Vegetables*	641.6
Garrison, Jessica. *The Devil's Harvest*	B
Gee, Alastair. *Fire in Paradise*	363.37
Glatt, John. *The Family Next Door*	362.76092
Guinn, Jeff. ★*Manson*	B
Gutman, Matt. ★*No Time to Panic*	616.85
Hahn, Emanuel. *Koreatown Dreaming*	979.4
Hamilton, Lisa M. *The Hungry Season*	B
Hillenbrand, Laura. *Unbroken*	B
Holland, Tanya. ★*Tanya Holland's California Soul*	641.59
Johnson, Lizzie. ★*Paradise*	363.37
Kinch, David. *At Home in the Kitchen*	641.5973
Kingston, Maxine Hong. *The Woman Warrior*	B
Lankford, Andrea. *Trail of the Lost*	363.2
Lauren, Jillian. *Behold the Monster*	364.152
Lee, Helie. *In the Absence of Sun*	B
Lieu, Susan. ★*The Manicurist's Daughter*	B
Markham, Lauren. ★*The Far Away Brothers*	920
Martin, Manjula. *The Last Fire Season*	B
McKeen, William. *Everybody Had an Ocean*	781.6609
McMillan, Tracie. *The American Way of Eating*	338.4
Miranda, Deborah A. *Bad Indians*	305.8009794
Moore, Susanna. *Miss Aluminum*	813
Nusbaum, Eric. *Stealing Home*	796.357
Pawel, Miriam. *The Browns of California*	920
Pawel, Miriam. *The Crusades of Cesar Chavez*	B
Rae-Venter, Barbara. *I Know Who You Are*	364.152
Rosenfeld, Seth. *Subversives*	378.1
Rosenzweig, Laura B. *Hollywood's Spies*	791.43
Silver, Johanna. ★*The Bold Dry Garden*	635.9
Snow, Richard. *Disney's Land*	791.06
Standefer, Katherine E. *Lightning Flowers*	B
Stein, Jean. *West of Eden*	979.4
Taffa, Deborah Jackson. ★*Whiskey Tender*	B
Thompson-Hernandez, Walter. *The Compton Cowboys*	920
Trejo, Danny. *Trejo*	B
Tumulty, Karen. *The Triumph of Nancy Reagan*	B
Wariner, Ruth. *The Sound of Gravel*	B
Waters, Alice. *Coming to My Senses*	B
Watkins, Carleton E. *Carleton Watkins*	778.9
Wiehl, Lis W. *Hunting Charles Manson*	364.152
Winchester, Simon. *A Crack in the Edge of the World*	979.4
California Burning. Blunt, Katherine	333.793
CALIFORNIA IN LITERATURE	
Didion, Joan. *Where I Was from*	979.4
Caligula & Three Other Plays. Camus, Albert	842
CALIGULA, EMPEROR OF ROME, 12-41	
Camus, Albert. *Caligula & Three Other Plays*	842
CALIPHATE	
Hazleton, Lesley. *After the Prophet*	297.8
Call Me American. Iftin, Abdi Nor	305.893
Call Me Indian. Sasakamoose, Fred	B
The Call of the Tribe. Vargas Llosa, Mario	868
The Call of Trains. Shaughnessy, Jim	779
Call Them by Their True Names. Solnit, Rebecca	303.3
A Call to Mercy. Teresa	234
★*Call Us What We Carry.* Gorman, Amanda	811
Callahan, David	
The Cheating Culture	174
Callahan, Gail	
Hand Dyeing Yarn and Fleece	746.6
Callahan, Maureen	
American Predator	364.152
Callahan, Tom	
Arnie	B
Called Again. Davis, Jennifer Pharr	B
CALLEN, MICHAEL, 1955-1993	
Duberman, Martin B. *Hold Tight Gently*	920
CALLIGRAPHY	
Beard, Mary. ★*How Do We Look*	704.9
Owen, Imogen. *Modern Calligraphy Workshop*	745.6
Shepherd, Margaret. *Learn Calligraphy*	745.6
Thorpe, Molly Suber. *Modern Calligraphy*	745.6
Tsu, Jing. *Kingdom of Characters*	495.111
Calling A Wolf a Wolf. Akbar, Kaveh	811
Callings. Isay, David	920
Callow, Simon	
★*Orson Welles*	B
Calloway, Colin G.	
The Indian World of George Washington	323.1197
One Vast Winter Count	978
CALVES	
Connell, John. *The Farmer's Son*	630.9
Calvino, Italo	
Collection of Sand	854
CALVINO, ITALO	
Calvino, Italo. *Collection of Sand*	854
Calypso. Sedaris, David	814
Camara, Gabriela	
My Mexico City Kitchen	641.5972
CAMBODIA	
Taing, Mae Bunseng. *Under the Naga Tail*	B
Ung, Loung. *First They Killed My Father*	959.604
Ung, Loung. *Lucky Child*	B
CAMBODIAN AMERICANS	
Reang, Putsata. *Ma and Me*	B
Ung, Loung. *Lucky Child*	B
CAMBODIAN GENOCIDE, 1975-1979	
Taing, Mae Bunseng. *Under the Naga Tail*	B
CAMBODIAN PEOPLE	
So, Anthony Veasna. ★*Songs on Endless Repeat*	814
Taing, Mae Bunseng. *Under the Naga Tail*	B
The Cambridge Guide to the Solar System. Lang, Kenneth R.	523.2
The Cambridge Star Atlas. Tirion, Wil	523.8
CAMBRIDGE, MASSACHUSETTS	
Cooper, Becky. *We Keep the Dead Close*	364.152
Doherty, Maggie. *The Equivalents*	920
Garrett, Kent. *The Last Negroes at Harvard*	920
Nathans, Sydney. *To Free a Family*	B
Camera Girl. Anthony, Carl Sferrazza	
Camera Man. Stevens, Dana	791.4302
Cameron, Julia	
It's Never Too Late to Begin Again	155.67
★*The Listening Path*	153.6
Living the Artist's Way	153.3
Cameron, Silver Donald	
Blood in the Water	364.152
CAMINO DE SANTIAGO DE COMPOSTELA	
Mullins, Edwin. *The Four Roads to Heaven*	263
CAMOUFLAGE (BIOLOGY)	
Forbes, Peter. *Dazzled and Deceived*	578.4
CAMP DAVID, MARYLAND	
Giorgione, Michael. *Inside Camp David*	975.2
Camp Grandma. Day, Marianne Waggoner	306.8745
CAMPAIGN FUNDS	
Coyle, Marcia. *The Roberts Court*	347.73
CAMPAIGN MANAGEMENT	
Martini, Adrienne. *Somebody's Gotta Do It*	B
CAMPAIGNING	
Allen, Jonathan. *Shattered*	324.973
Barlow, John Perry. *Mother American Night*	782.42164
Chozick, Amy. *Chasing Hillary*	B
Dallek, Robert. *An Unfinished Life*	B
Gillette, Michael L. *Lady Bird Johnson*	B

PUBLIC LIBRARY CORE COLLECTION: NONFICTION
Twentieth Edition

Campany, David
   The Open Road — 770
Campbell, Deborah
   A Disappearance in Damascus — 365
CAMPBELL, DEBORAH, 1970-
   Campbell, Deborah. *A Disappearance in Damascus* — 365
Campbell, Hayley
   All the Living and the Dead — 363.7
   The Art of Neil Gaiman — B
Campbell, James
   The Ghost Mountain Boys — 940.54
Campbell, Jeremy
   The Liar's Tale — 177
CAMPBELL, JOHN WOOD, 1910-1971
   Nevala-Lee, Alec. *Astounding* — 809.3
Campbell, Joseph
   The Masks of God — 201.3
   The Power of Myth — 201.3
CAMPBELL, JOSEPH, 1904-1987
   Campbell, Joseph. *The Power of Myth* — 201.3
Campbell, Olivia
   Women in White Coats — 610.92
Campbell, T. Colin
   The China Study — 613.2
CAMPBELL, WILLIAM, 1745-1781
   Harris, J. William. *The Hanging of Thomas Jeremiah* — B
Campbell-Kelly, Martin
   From Airline Reservations to Sonic the Hedgehog — 338.4
CAMPING
   Canterbury, Dave. *Bushcraft 101* — 613.6
   Robinson, Kim Stanley. *The High Sierra* — 917.94
   White, Dan. *Under the Stars* — 796.54
Campoverdi, Alejandra
   First Gen — B
CAMPOVERDI, ALEJANDRA
   Campoverdi, Alejandra. *First Gen* — B
CAMPUS LIFE
   Hechinger, John. ★*True Gentlemen* — 371.85
   Mock, Janet. *Surpassing Certainty* — B
   Selingo, Jeffrey J. *College (un)bound* — 378
Camus, Albert
   Caligula & Three Other Plays — 842
   The Myth of Sisyphus and Other Essays — 844
   The Rebel — 303.6
   Resistance, Rebellion, and Death — 844
CAMUS, ALBERT, 1913-1960
   Kaplan, Alice Yaeger. *Looking for the Stranger* — B
   Todd, Olivier. *Albert Camus* — B
Can We Talk About Israel?. Sokatch, Daniel — 956.9405
Can't Even. Petersen, Anne Helen — 305.242
Can't Help Myself. Goldstein, Meredith — B
Can't Knock the Hustle. Sullivan, Matt — 796.323
Can't Nothing Bring Me Down. Keeling, Ida — B
Can't Stop, Won't Stop. Chang, Jeff — 306.4
★*Can't We Talk About Something More Pleasant?*. Chast, Roz — 741.5
CANADA
   Alvarez, Noe. *Spirit Run* — 796.42
   Beaton, Kate. ★*Ducks* — 741.5
   Branch, John. *Boy on Ice* — B
   Brockman, Christian Frank. *Trees of North America* — 582.16097
   Brown, Vanessa. *The Forest City Killer* — 364.152
   Cohen, Eliot A. *Conquered into Liberty* — 355.009747
   Fischer, David Hackett. *Champlain's Dream* — B
   Isen, Tajja. *Some of My Best Friends* — 305.8
   Kurlansky, Mark. *Cod* — 333.95
   Lim, Audrea. *Free the Land* — 333.73
   Lincoff, Gary. *The Audubon Society Field Guide to North American Mushrooms* — 579.6
   Little, Elbert L. *The Audubon Society Field Guide to North American Trees* — 582.16097
   Mendez, Antonio J. *Argo* — 955.05
   Messenger, Alex. *The Twenty-Ninth Day* — B
   Mowat, Farley. *Born Naked* — B
   Nesteroff, Kliph. *We Had a Little Real Estate Problem* — 970.004
   Norman, Michael. *Haunted America* — 133.1
   Plummer, Christopher. *In Spite of Myself* — B
   Robertson, Robbie. ★*Testimony* — B
   Wagamese, Richard. *One Native Life* — B

   Whitman, John. *Fresh from the Garden* — 635.9
   Wohlleben, Peter. *Forest Walking* — 582.16
CANADIAN FICTION
   Carson, Anne. *Autobiography of Red* — 811
CANADIAN HISTORY
   Bacon, John U. *The Great Halifax Explosion* — 971.6
   Castner, Brian. *Stampede* — 971.9
   Fischer, David Hackett. *Champlain's Dream* — B
   Lim, Audrea. *Free the Land* — 333.73
   Taylor, Alan. *American Civil Wars* — 973.7
   Taylor, Alan. *The Civil War of 1812* — 973.5
   Taylor, Alan. *The Divided Ground* — 974.7
   Tobin, Jacqueline. *From Midnight to Dawn* — 973.7
CANADIAN LITERATURE
   Abdelmahmoud, Elamin. *Son of Elsewhere* — B
   Abuelaish, Izzeldin. *I Shall Not Hate* — B
   Armstrong, Karen. *Fields of Blood* — 201
   Atwood, Margaret. *In Other Worlds* — 813
   Belcourt, Billy-Ray. ★*A History of My Brief Body* — B
   Bowler, Kate. *No Cure for Being Human* — B
   Bown, Stephen R. *Merchant Kings* — 338.8
   Brown, Vanessa. *The Forest City Killer* — 364.152
   Cameron, Silver Donald. *Blood in the Water* — 364.152
   Campbell, Deborah. *A Disappearance in Damascus* — 365
   Chapin, Sasha. *All the Wrong Moves* — 794.1092
   Cohen, Andrew. *Two Days in June* — 973.922
   Cusk, Rachel. *Aftermath* — B
   Cusk, Rachel. *A Life's Work* — 306.874
   Davis, Wade. *Into the Silence* — B
   Davis, Wade. *Magdalena* — 986.1
   Delisle, Guy. *Pyongyang* — 741.5
   Di Cintio, Marcello. *Pay No Heed to the Rockets* — 956.9405
   Eisen, Max. *By Chance Alone* — 940.5318
   Favro, Terri. *Generation Robot* — 006.3
   Fox, Michael J. *No Time Like the Future* — B
   Frum, David. *Trumpocracy* — 973.933
   Gladwell, Malcolm. *Blink* — 153.4
   Gladwell, Malcolm. *Outliers* — 302
   Gladwell, Malcolm. *The Tipping Point* — 302
   Gray, Charlotte. ★*Reluctant Genius* — 920
   Green, Stefanie. *This Is Assisted Dying* — 616.02
   Habib, Rodney. ★*The Forever Dog* — 636.7
   Harris, Kate. *Lands of Lost Borders* — 915.804
   Hayhoe, Katharine. *Saving Us* — 304.2
   Henry, John. *Great White Fleet* — 387.243
   Heti, Sheila. *Alphabetical Diaries* — 818
   Ignatieff, Michael. *On Consolation* — 152.4
   Isen, Tajja. *Some of My Best Friends* — 305.8
   Jang, Lucia. *Stars Between the Sun and Moon* — 365.45092
   Johnston, Ann Dowsett. *Drink* — 362.292
   Kaur, Rupi. *Milk and Honey* — 811
   King, Ross. ★*Leonardo and the Last Supper* — 759.5
   Kirkby, Bruce. *Blue Sky Kingdom* — 954.96
   Klein, Naomi. ★*Doppelganger* — 302.2
   Lin, Amy. *Here After* — B
   Mattson, Ingrid. ★*The Story of the Qur'an* — 297.122
   McCrum, Robert. ★*The Story of English* — 420
   McDiarmid, Jessica. *Highway of Tears* — 364.152
   Metatawabin, Edmund. *Up Ghost River* — B
   Mowat, Farley. *Born Naked* — B
   Nadeau, Jean-Benoit. ★*The Story of French* — 440
   Nadeau, Jean-Benoit. *The Story of Spanish* — 460
   Nawaz, Zarqa. *Laughing All the Way to the Mosque* — 791.45028
   Oelhafen, Ingrid von. *Hitler's Stolen Children* — B
   Orenstein, Ronald I. *Ivory, Horn and Blood* — 333.95
   Page, Elliot. *Pageboy* — B
   Paperny, Anna Mehler. *Hello I Want to Die Please Fix Me* — 362.2
   Plummer, Christopher. *In Spite of Myself* — B
   Robertson, Robbie. ★*Testimony* — B
   Sasakamoose, Fred. *Call Me Indian* — B
   Schatzker, Mark. *The Dorito Effect* — 641.3
   Shatner, William. *Boldly Go* — B
   Shatner, William. *Live Long And—* — B
   Shaw, Julia. *Bi* — 306.76
   Short, Martin. *I Must Say* — B
   Shraya, Vivek. *I'm Afraid of Men* — 813
   Smith, Bren. *Eat Like a Fish* — 338.3
   Stevenson, William. *A Man Called Intrepid* — 940.54

AUTHOR, TITLE, SERIES AND SUBJECT INDEX

Struzik, Edward. *Swamplands*	577.68
Sullivan, Rosemary. *The Betrayal of Anne Frank*	940.53
Thompson, Clive. *Coders*	005.1092
Trebek, Alex. *The Answer Is ...*	791.4502
Vaillant, John. *The Tiger*	599.756
Wagamese, Richard. *For Joshua*	B
Wagamese, Richard. *One Native Life*	B
Whyte, Kenneth. *Hoover*	B
Whyte, Kenneth. *The Uncrowned King*	B
Young, Neil. *Waging Heavy Peace*	B

CANADIAN PEOPLE

Heti, Sheila. *Alphabetical Diaries*	818
Kirkby, Bruce. *Blue Sky Kingdom*	954.96
Page, Elliot. *Pageboy*	B
Shane, Scott. ★*Flee North*	973.7
Wagamese, Richard. *For Joshua*	B

CANADIAN PEOPLE IN FOREIGN COUNTRIES

Delisle, Guy. *Pyongyang*	741.5

CANADIAN PEOPLE IN THE UNITED STATES

Velshi, Ali. *Small Acts of Courage*	B

CANADIAN POETRY

Atwood, Margaret. *Dearly*	811
Bitsui, Sherwin. *Dissolve*	811
Carson, Anne. *Decreation*	818
Carson, Anne. *Red Doc*	811
Cohen, Leonard. *The Flame*	810

CANALS

Madden, Thomas F. *Venice*	945
McCullough, David G. *The Path Between the Seas*	972.87
Parker, Matthew. *Panama Fever*	972.87
Shorto, Russell. *Amsterdam*	949.2

CANCER

Billings, J. Todd. *Rejoicing in Lament*	248.8
Boyer, Anne. *The Undying*	B
Brown, Theresa. *Healing*	616.99
Campoverdi, Alejandra. *First Gen*	B
Chow, Kat. *Seeing Ghosts*	B
Ephron, Delia. *Left on Tenth*	B
Fagin, Dan. *Toms River*	363.7209749
Frangello, Gina. *Blow Your House Down*	813
Fung, Jason. ★*The Cancer Code*	616.99
Gentile, Olivia. *Life List*	598.072
Graeber, Charles. *The Breakthrough*	616.99
Hutton, Andrea. *Bald Is Better with Earrings*	362.19699
Ingrassia, Lawrence. *A Fatal Inheritance*	616.99
Jaouad, Suleika. ★*Between Two Kingdoms*	B
Kingston, Genevieve. *Did I Ever Tell You?*	B
Lipska, Barbara K. *The Neuroscientist Who Lost Her Mind*	B
Love, Susan M. ★*Dr. Susan Love's Breast Book*	618.1
McCourt, Malachy. *Singing My Him Song*	B
Mukherjee, Siddhartha. ★*The Emperor of All Maladies*	616.99
Raza, Azra. *The First Cell*	616.99
Servan-Schreiber, David. *Anticancer*	616.99
Townsend, Alan R. ★*This Ordinary Stardust*	B
Yousse, Bower. *Freddie Steinmark*	796.332
★*The Cancer Code*. Fung, Jason	616.99
★*The Cancer Factory*. Morris, Jim	658.3

CANCER RESEARCH

Graeber, Charles. *The Breakthrough*	616.99
Ingrassia, Lawrence. *A Fatal Inheritance*	616.99
Skloot, Rebecca. ★*The Immortal Life of Henrietta Lacks*	B

CANCER SURVIVORS

Baskette, Molly Phinney. *How to Begin When Your World Is Ending*	248.8
Bragg, Rick. *The Speckled Beauty*	636.7
Dickinson, Bruce. *What Does This Button Do?*	B
Dutta, Sunil. *Stealing Green Mangoes*	973
Malone, Jo. *Jo Malone*	B
Mandel, Sarah. *Little Earthquakes*	B
Marshall, Cynthia. *You've Been Chosen*	B
McCubbin, Lisa. *Betty Ford*	B
Rubin, Kathy Kleiner. *A Light in the Dark*	364.152
Candace Pert. Ryckman, Pamela	B
The Candlemaker's Companion. Oppenheimer, Betty	745.593

CANDLEMAKING

Oppenheimer, Betty. *The Candlemaker's Companion*	745.593

CANDY

Almond, Steve. ★*Candyfreak*	338.4
Curl, Jami. *Candy Is Magic*	641.85
Candy Darling. Carr, C.	B

CANDY INDUSTRY AND TRADE

Almond, Steve. ★*Candyfreak*	338.4
Brenner, Joel Glenn. *The Emperors of Chocolate*	338.7
Candy Is Magic. Curl, Jami	641.85

CANDY, JOHN, 1950-1994

De Semlyen, Nick. *Wild and Crazy Guys*	920
★*Candyfreak*. Almond, Steve	338.4
Canellos, Peter S. *The Great Dissenter*	B
Canfield, Jack	
The 30 Day Sobriety Solution	616.89
The Success Principles	158
Cannadine, David	
★*Mellon*	B
Cannato, Vincent	
American Passage	325.73
Cannell, Michael T.	
A Brotherhood Betrayed	B
Cannibal. Sinclair, Safiya	811
Cannibalism. Schutt, Bill	394

CANNIBALISM

Hoffman, Carl. ★*Savage Harvest*	995.1
Parrado, Nando. ★*Miracle in the Andes*	982
Read, Piers Paul. ★*Alive*	982
Roach, Mary. ★*Stiff*	611
Schutt, Bill. *Cannibalism*	394

CANNING AND PRESERVING

Danforth, Adam. *Butchering Poultry, Rabbit, Lamb, Goat, and Pork*	664
Pleasant, Barbara. *Homegrown Pantry*	635
Rodriguez, Ashley. *Rooted Kitchen*	641.5
West, Kevin. *Saving the Season*	641.4

CANOE BUILDING

Preszler, Trent. *Little and Often*	B

CANOEING

McGrath, Ben. *Riverman*	797.122
Messenger, Alex. *The Twenty-Ninth Day*	B

CANOES

McGrath, Ben. *Riverman*	797.122
Preszler, Trent. *Little and Often*	B
Canon, Dan	
★*Pleading Out*	345.73

CANONIZATION

Woodward, Kenneth L. *Making Saints*	235.24
Canterbury, Dave	
Bushcraft 101	613.6
Cantor, Norman F.	
In the Wake of the Plague	614.5
Cantu, Francisco	
The Line Becomes a River	B

CANTU, FRANCISCO (ESSAYIST)

Cantu, Francisco. *The Line Becomes a River*	B
★*Canyon Dreams*. Powell, Michael	796.323

CAPE HORN

Dana, Richard Henry. *Two Years Before the Mast*	910.4
★*The Caped Crusade*. Weldon, Glen	741.5
Capelle, Philip B.	
★*Play Your Best Straight Pool*	790

CAPERTON, HUGH

Leamer, Laurence. *The Price of Justice*	346.7302
★*Capital*. Marx, Karl	335.4

CAPITAL

Marx, Karl. ★*Capital*	335.4
Piketty, Thomas. ★*Capital in the Twenty-First Century*	332
★*Capital and Ideology*. Piketty, Thomas	305
Capital Dames. Roberts, Cokie	920
★*Capital in the Twenty-First Century*. Piketty, Thomas	332

CAPITAL PUNISHMENT

Bardenwerper, William. *The Prisoner in His Palace*	956.7044
Bookman, Marc. *A Descending Spiral*	345.73
Chammah, Maurice. ★*Let the Lord Sort Them*	364.66
Harrington, Joel F. *The Faithful Executioner*	B
Hinton, Anthony Ray. *The Sun Does Shine*	B
Mandery, Evan J. *A Wild Justice*	345.73
Marzano-Lesnevich, Alexandria. *The Fact of a Body*	364.152
Prejean, Helen. *The Death of Innocents*	364.66
Stevenson, Bryan. *Just Mercy*	B
Turow, Scott. ★*Ultimate Punishment*	345.73

PUBLIC LIBRARY CORE COLLECTION: NONFICTION
Twentieth Edition

CAPITALISM
- Beckert, Sven. *Empire of Cotton* — 338.4
- Bellos, David. *Who Owns This Sentence?* — 346.73
- Berfield, Susan. *The Hour of Fate* — 973.91
- Burrough, Bryan. *The Big Rich* — 338.2
- Chang, Ha-Joon. *Economics* — 330
- Chayka, Kyle. *Filterworld* — 306
- Chomsky, Noam. *Global Discontents* — 410.92
- De Long, J. Bradford. *Slouching Towards Utopia* — 330.9
- Fox, Justin. *The Myth of the Rational Market* — 332.64
- Friedman, Benjamin M. *Religion and the Rise of Capitalism* — 330.12
- Green, Hardy. *The Company Town* — 307.76
- Greenspan, Alan. *Capitalism in America* — 330.973
- Karabell, Zachary. *Inside Money* — 332.1
- Leonhardt, David. ★*Ours Was the Shining Future* — 330.973
- Levy, Jonathan. *Ages of American Capitalism* — 330.12
- Linklater, Andro. *Owning the Earth* — 333.3
- Linn, Susan. *Who's Raising the Kids?* — 649
- Madden, Thomas F. *Venice* — 945
- McMillan, John. *Reinventing the Bazaar* — 330.12
- Montero, David. ★*The Stolen Wealth of Slavery* — 381
- Nocera, Joseph. *The Big Fail* — 362.1962
- Norman, Jesse. *Adam Smith* — B
- Pan, Philip P. *Out of Mao's Shadow* — 306.20951
- Petersen, Anne Helen. *Can't Even* — 305.242
- Piketty, Thomas. ★*Capital and Ideology* — 305
- Sandel, Michael J. *What Money Can't Buy* — 174
- Shapland, Jenn. ★*Thin Skin* — 814
- Taylor, Fred. *The Berlin Wall* — 943
- Tolentino, Jia. ★*Trick Mirror* — 973.93
- Vance, Ashlee. *When the Heavens Went on Sale* — 621.43
- Wartzman, Rick. *Still Broke* — 381
- Westad, Odd Arne. *The Cold War* — 909.825
- Wheelan, Charles J. *Naked Economics* — 330
- Wolf, Martin. ★*The Crisis of Democratic Capitalism* — 330.12
- Yunus, Muhammad. *A World of Three Zeros* — 330

CAPITALISM AND DEMOCRACY
- Norman, Jesse. *Adam Smith* — B

CAPITALISM AND INEQUALITY
- Case, Anne. *Deaths of Despair and the Future of Capitalism* — 362.28
- Piketty, Thomas. ★*Capital in the Twenty-First Century* — 332
- Piketty, Thomas. *The Economics of Inequality* — 339.2
- *Capitalism in America*. Greenspan, Alan — 330.973

CAPITALISTS AND FINANCIERS
- Ahamed, Liaquat. *Lords of Finance* — 920
- Berfield, Susan. *The Hour of Fate* — 973.91
- Chafkin, Max. *The Contrarian* — B
- Cooper, Anderson. *Vanderbilt* — 920
- Dalrymple, William. ★*The Anarchy* — 954.03
- Hagstrom, Robert G. *The Warren Buffett Way* — 332.6
- Hiltzik, Michael A. *Iron Empires* — 385.0973
- Lewis, Michael. ★*Going Infinite* — 305.5
- Rempel, William C. *The Gambler* — B
- Schroeder, Alice. *The Snowball* — B
- Stark, Peter. *Astoria* — 979.5
- Sun, Carrie. *Private Equity* — B
- Ward, Geoffrey C. *A Disposition to Be Rich* — B

CAPITALS (CITIES)
- Addis, Ferdinand. *The Eternal City* — 945.6
- Hughes, Bettany. *Istanbul* — 949.61
- *Capitol Men*. Dray, Philip — 973.8

CAPITOL RIOT, WASHINGTON, D.C., 2021
- Bade, Rachael. ★*Unchecked* — 342.73
- Cheney, Liz. *Oath and Honor* — 328.73
- Dunn, Harry. *Standing My Ground* — B
- Gonell, Aquilino. *American Shield* — B
- Hutchinson, Cassidy. *Enough* — B
- Mogelson, Luke. *The Storm Is Here* — 973.933
- Reilly, Ryan J. ★*Sedition Hunters* — 364.1

CAPONE, AL, 1899-1947
- Bair, Deirdre. *Al Capone* — B
- Eig, Jonathan. *Get Capone* — 364.1

Capote, Truman
- ★*In Cold Blood* — 364.1
- ★*Portraits and Observations* — 814
- *Too Brief a Treat* — B

CAPOTE, TRUMAN, 1924-1984
- Capote, Truman. ★*Portraits and Observations* — 814
- Capote, Truman. *Too Brief a Treat* — B
- Montillo, Roseanne. *Deliberate Cruelty* — 364.152

Capozzola, Christopher
- *Bound by War* — 355

Capparell, Stephanie
- *The Real Pepsi Challenge* — 338.7

CAPRA, FRANK, 1897-1991
- Harris, Mark. ★*Five Came Back* — 791.4302

The Captain Asks for a Show of Hands. Flynn, Nick — 811
The Captain Class. Walker, Sam — 796.07
The Captive Imagination. Dakwar, Elias — 616.85
Captive Paradise. Haley, James L. — 996.9

CAPTIVE WILD ANIMALS
- Attenborough, David. *Adventures of a Young Naturalist* — B
- Charman, Isobel. *The Zoo* — 590.73
- Neiwert, David A. *Of Orcas and Men* — 599.53

CAPTIVES
- Fischer, Paul. *A Kim Jong-Il Production* — 791.43
- Glatt, John. *The Family Next Door* — 362.76092

CAPTIVITY
- Demos, John. *The Unredeemed Captive* — 973.2
- Khalaf, Farida. *The Girl Who Escaped Isis* — B

Caputo, Philip
- *A Rumor of War* — 959.704

CAPUTO, PHILIP, 1941-
- Caputo, Philip. *A Rumor of War* — 959.704

Caravaggio. Graham-Dixon, Andrew — B
Caravaggio. Prose, Francine — 759.5

CARAVAGGIO, MICHELANGELO MERISI DA, 1573-1610
- Graham-Dixon, Andrew. *Caravaggio* — B
- Prose, Francine. *Caravaggio* — 759.5

Carballo, David M.
- *America* — 912

CARBOHYDRATES
- Perlmutter, David. *The Grain Brain Cookbook* — 651.56

CARBON
- Kean, Sam. *The Disappearing Spoon* — 546
- *The Carbon Footprint of Everything*. Berners-Lee, Mike — 363.738
- *Carbon ideologies* [Series]. Vollmann, William T. — 333.79

Carcaterra, Lorenzo
- *Three Dreamers* — B

CARCATERRA, LORENZO
- Carcaterra, Lorenzo. *Three Dreamers* — B

CARD GAMES
- Ho, Oliver. *The Ultimate Book of Family Card Games* — 795.4
- McManus, James. ★*Positively Fifth Street* — 795.41
- Roeder, Oliver. *Seven Games* — 794

CARD TRICKS
- Diaconis, Persi. *Magical Mathematics* — 793.8
- Owen, Oscar. *Mind-Blowing Magic Tricks for Everyone* — 793.8

CARDANO, GIROLAMO, 1501-1576
- Brooks, Michael. *The Quantum Astrologer's Handbook* — B

Cardenal, Ernesto
- *Pluriverse* — 861

CARDENAL, ERNESTO, 1925-2020
- Cardenal, Ernesto. *Pluriverse* — 861

CARDIOLOGY
- Jauhar, Sandeep. *Heart* — 612.1
- Swartz, Mimi. *Ticker* — 617.4

Cardwell, Diane
- *Rockaway* — B

CARDWELL, DIANE, 1964-
- Cardwell, Diane. *Rockaway* — B

CAREER BOOKS — GENERAL
- Morgan, Genevieve. *Undecided* — 331.702

CAREER CHANGES
- Elwood, Phil. *All the Worst Humans* — 659.2
- Finkle, Jane. *The Introvert's Complete Career Guide* — 650.14
- Germer, Fawn. *Coming Back* — 650.14
- Keller, Julia. *Quitting* — 650.14
- Louis, Matthew J. *Mission Transition* — 650.14
- Painter, Nell Irvin. *Old in Art School* — B
- Pollak, Lindsey. *Recalculating* — 650.1
- Thomson, Graeme. *George Harrison* — B

CAREER DEVELOPMENT
- Botelho, Elena L. *The CEO Next Door* — 658.4
- Braswell, Porter. ★*Let Them See You* — 650.1
- Burkus, David. *Friend of a Friend...* — 650.1

AUTHOR, TITLE, SERIES AND SUBJECT INDEX

Cast, Carter. *The Right—And Wrong—Stuff*	650.1
Coggan, Philip. *Surviving the Daily Grind*	658.3
Eikenberry, Kevin. *The Long-Distance Teammate*	650.1
Finkle, Jane. *The Introvert's Complete Career Guide*	650.14
Germer, Fawn. *Coming Back*	650.14
Mattel, Trixie. *Working Girls*	650.1
Morgan, Genevieve. *Undecided*	331.702
Mulcahy, Diane. *The Gig Economy*	650.1
Nevins, Sheila. *You Don't Look Your Age*	B
Pollak, Lindsey. *Recalculating*	650.1
Rueckert, Veronica. *Outspoken*	808.5
Steib, Mike. *The Career Manifesto*	650.1
Wasserman, Claire. *Ladies Get Paid*	650.1
Young, Scott H. *Get Better at Anything*	650.1
The Career Manifesto. Steib, Mike	650.1
Carefree Black Girls. Blay, Zeba	305.48

CAREGIVERS

Applebaum, Allison. *Stand by Me*	649.8
Case, Molly. *How to Treat People*	616.1
Coste, Joanne Koenig. *Learning to Speak Alzheimer's*	362.1
Davis, Patti. *Floating in the Deep End*	616.8
Garbes, Angela. *Essential Labor*	306.874
Karlawish, Jason. ★*The Problem of Alzheimer's*	616.8
Kiper, Dasha. ★*Travelers to Unimaginable Lands*	616.8
Morgan, Abi. *This Is Not a Pity Memoir*	B
Pataki, Allison. *Beauty in the Broken Places*	B
Washington, Kate. ★*Already Toast*	649.8

CARETAKERS

Zambreno, Kate. *The Light Room*	B

Carey, Benedict
How We Learn	153.1

Carey, Jenny Rose
The Ultimate Flower Gardener's Guide	635.9

Carey, John
A Little History of Poetry	809.1

Carey, Tanith
What's My Child Thinking?	155.4

Cargle, Rachel Elizabeth
A Renaissance of Our Own	B

CARGLE, RACHEL ELIZABETH
Cargle, Rachel Elizabeth. *A Renaissance of Our Own*	B

CARGO HANDLING
McPhee, John. *Uncommon Carriers*	388

CARIBBEAN AMERICANS
Bailey, Desiree C. *What Noise Against the Cane*	811

CARIBBEAN AREA
Irving, Apricot Anderson. *The Gospel of Trees*	B
Ruck, Rob. *Raceball*	796.357
Thomas, Hugh. *Rivers of Gold*	980

CARIBBEAN HISTORY
Bell, Madison Smartt. *Toussaint Louverture*	B
Castro, Fidel. *Fidel Castro*	B
Coltman, Leycester. *The Real Fidel Castro*	B
DePalma, Anthony. *The Cubans*	920
Ferrer, Ada. ★*Cuba*	972.91
Guevara, Che. *Diary of a Combatant*	972.91063
Guillermoprieto, Alma. *Dancing with Cuba*	972.9106
Kritzler, Ed. *Jewish Pirates of the Caribbean*	972.9
Kurlansky, Mark. *Havana*	972.91
Rathbone, John Paul. *The Sugar King of Havana*	B
Sallah, Michael. *The Yankee Comandante*	972.91

CARIBBEAN SEA
Slade, Rachel. *Into the Raging Sea*	910.91

CARING
Brous, Sharon. ★*The Amen Effect*	296.3
Hagglund, Martin. *This Life*	110
Jamison, Leslie. *The Empathy Exams*	813
Palmer, Amanda. ★*The Art of Asking*	782.42164
Caring for the Dying. Fersko-Weiss, Henry	616.02
Caring for Your Baby and Young Child. Trubo, Richard	618.92
Carla Hall's Soul Food. Hall, Carla	641.5975
Carla's Comfort Foods. Hall, Carla	641.59

Carle-Sanders, Theresa
Outlander Kitchen	641.5
Carleton Watkins. Watkins, Carleton E.	778.9

Carlile, Brandi
Broken Horses	B

CARLILE, BRANDI
Carlile, Brandi. *Broken Horses*	B
A Carlin Home Companion. Carlin, Kelly	B

CARLIN, GEORGE
Carlin, Kelly. *A Carlin Home Companion*	B

Carlin, John
Playing the Enemy	968.06

Carlin, Kelly
A Carlin Home Companion	B

CARLIN, KELLY, 1963-
Carlin, Kelly. *A Carlin Home Companion*	B

Carlin, Peter Ames
Bruce	B
Carlisle vs. Army. Anderson, Lars	796.332

Carlisle, Clare
Philosopher of the Heart	B

Carlo, Philip
Gaspipe	B

Carlsen, Spike
A Walk Around the Block	031

Carlsen, William
Jungle of Stone	B

CARLSEN, WILLIAM 1945-
Carlsen, William. *Jungle of Stone*	B

Carlson, Brady
Dead Presidents	B

Carlson, Erin
I'll Have What She's Having	791.43

Carlson, Julie
Remodelista	648

Carlson, Peter
K Blows Top	947.085

Carlson, W. Bernard
Tesla	B

Carmon, Irin
Notorious RBG	B
Carnegie. Krass, Peter	B

CARNEGIE, ANDREW, 1835-1919
Hill, Napoleon. *Think and Grow Rich*	650.1
Krass, Peter. *Carnegie*	B
Nasaw, David. *Andrew Carnegie*	B

Carnegie, Dale
★*How to Win Friends and Influence People*	158

CARNEGIE, DALE, 1888-1955
Watts, Steven. *Self-Help Messiah*	B

Carney, Scott
The Vortex	954.92
★*A Carnival of Snackery.* Sedaris, David	818

Caro, Robert A.
★*The Passage of Power*	B
The Power Broker	B
★*Working*	B

CARO, ROBERT A.
Caro, Robert A. ★*Working*	B

Carpenter, Amanda B.
Gaslighting America	973.933

Carpenter, Dale
Flagrant Conduct	342.7308

Carpenter, Kyle
You Are Worth It	B

CARPENTER, KYLE
Carpenter, Kyle. *You Are Worth It*	B

CARPENTERS
Thorstensen, Ole. *Making Things Right*	690

CARPETS
Badkhen, Anna. *The World Is a Carpet*	305.409581

Carr, C.
Candy Darling	B

Carr, Caleb
My Beloved Monster	B

CARR, CALEB, 1955-2024
Carr, Caleb. *My Beloved Monster*	B

Carr, David
The Night of the Gun	B

CARR, DAVID, 1956-2015
Carr, David. *The Night of the Gun*	B
Carr, Erin Lee. *All That You Leave Behind*	B

PUBLIC LIBRARY CORE COLLECTION: NONFICTION
Twentieth Edition

Carr, Erin Lee
  All That You Leave Behind — B
CARR, ERIN LEE
  Carr, Erin Lee. *All That You Leave Behind* — B
Carranca, Adriana
  Soul by Soul — 230
Carretta, Vincent
  Equiano, the African — B
Carreyrou, John
  ★*Bad Blood* — 338.7
Carrie Carolyn Coco. Gerard, Sarah — 364.152
Carrie Fisher. Weller, Sheila — B
Carriere, Alice
  Everything/Nothing/Someone — B
CARRIERE, ALICE
  Carriere, Alice. *Everything/Nothing/Someone* — B
Carroll, Andrew
  My Fellow Soldiers — 940.4
Carroll, Georgie
  The Mythology Book — 201
Carroll, James
  Constantine's Sword — 261
Carroll, Rebecca
  Surviving the White Gaze — B
CARROLL, REBECCA
  Carroll, Rebecca. *Surviving the White Gaze* — B
Carroll, Rory
  There Will Be Fire — 363.325
Carroll, Ryder
  ★*The Bullet Journal Method* — 640
Carroll, Sean M.
  The Big Picture — 577
  The Biggest Ideas in the Universe — 530.11
  From Eternity to Here — 530.11
  Something Deeply Hidden — 530.12
Carruthers, Charlene A.
  Unapologetic — 305.48
Carry Me Home. McWhorter, Diane — 976.1
Carry On. Fenn, Lisa — B
Carry On. Lewis, John — 328.73
★*The Carrying*. Limon, Ada — 811
Carson McCullers. Dearborn, Mary V. — B
Carson, Anne
  Autobiography of Red — 811
  The Beauty of the Husband — 811
  Decreation — 818
  Red Doc — 811
CARSON, KIT, 1809-1868
  Sides, Hampton. *Blood and Thunder* — 978
Carson, Rachel
  The Edge of the Sea — 578.769
  ★*Silent Spring* — 363.738
  Under the Sea Wind — 578.77
CARSON, RACHEL, 1907-1964
  Souder, William. *On a Farther Shore* — B
Cart, Michael
  Young Adult Literature — 813.009
CARTELS
  Ratliff, Evan. *The Mastermind* — B
  Shannon, Elaine. *Hunting Leroux* — 364.1
  Vorobyov, Niko. *Dopeworld* — 364.1
  Westhoff, Ben. *Fentanyl, Inc.* — 362.29
CARTER FAMILY
  Carter, Jimmy. *An Hour Before Daylight* — B
Carter, Alice A.
  The Red Rose Girls — B
CARTER, ANGELA, 1940-1992
  Gordon, Edmund. *The Invention of Angela Carter* — B
Carter, Ash
  Life Isn't Everything — B
Carter, Darryl
  The Collected Home — 747
  The New Traditional — 747
Carter, David
  Stonewall — 306.76
CARTER, EUNICE HUNTON, 1899-1970
  Carter, Stephen L. *Invisible* — B

Carter, Hilton
  Wild Interiors — 747.98
Carter, Iain
  Golf Wars — 796.352
Carter, Jimmy
  Everything to Gain — B
  Faith — OK T A
  A Full Life — B
  An Hour Before Daylight — B
  Keeping Faith — B
  Palestine — 956.04
  Sharing Good Times — 973.926
  Sources of Strength — 248.4
  White House Diary — 973.926
CARTER, JIMMY, 1924-
  Alter, Jonathan. *His Very Best* — B
  Bird, Kai. *The Outlier* — 973.926
  Carter, Jimmy. *Everything to Gain* — B
  Carter, Jimmy. *A Full Life* — B
  Carter, Jimmy. *An Hour Before Daylight* — B
  Carter, Jimmy. *Keeping Faith* — B
  Carter, Jimmy. *Palestine* — 956.04
  Carter, Jimmy. *Sharing Good Times* — 973.926
  Carter, Jimmy. *White House Diary* — 973.926
  Eizenstat, Stuart. ★*President Carter* — B
  Perlstein, Rick. ★*Reaganland* — 973.926
  Woodward, Bob. *Shadow* — 973.92
  Wright, Lawrence. *Thirteen Days in September* — 956.04
Carter, Miranda
  George, Nicholas and Wilhelm — 940.3
CARTER, ROSALYNN
  Carter, Jimmy. *Everything to Gain* — B
Carter, Ruth E.
  ★*The Art of Ruth E. Carter* — 746.9
CARTER, RUTH E.
  Carter, Ruthe. ★*The Art of Ruth E. Carter* — 746.9
Carter, Stephen L.
  Invisible — B
CARTER, STEPHEN L., 1954-
  Carter, Stephen L. *Invisible* — B
CARTHAGE (EXTINCT CITY)
  Hunt, Patrick. *Hannibal* — B
  O'Connell, Robert L. *The Ghosts of Cannae* — 937
  Virgil. ★*The Aeneid* — 873
CARTIER FAMILY
  Brickell, Francesca Cartier. *The Cartiers* — B
The Cartiers. Brickell, Francesca Cartier — B
CARTOGRAPHERS
  Winchester, Simon. *The Map That Changed the World* — B
CARTOGRAPHY
  Garfield, Simon. *On the Map* — 526.09
  Kaltenegger, Lisa. ★*Alien Earths* — 523.2
  Sides, Hampton. ★*The Wide Wide Sea* — 910.92
  Winchester, Simon. *The Map That Changed the World* — B
CARTOON CHARACTERS
  Ghez, Didier. *The Hidden Art of Disney's Golden Age* — 741.5
  Gitlin, Marty. *A Celebration of Animation* — 741.5
Cartooning. Brunetti, Ivan — 741.5
CARTOONING
  Brunetti, Ivan. *Cartooning* — 741.5
  McCloud, Scott. *Making Comics* — 741.5
Cartooning for the Beginner. Hart, Christopher — 741.5
CARTOONING TECHNIQUE
  Abel, Jessica. *Drawing Words, Writing Pictures* — 741.5
  Abel, Jessica. *Mastering Comics* — 741.5
  Brunetti, Ivan. *Cartooning* — 741.5
  Eisner, Will. ★*Comics and Sequential Art* — 741.5
  Hart, Christopher. *Cartooning for the Beginner* — 741.5
  Leong, Sonia. *101 Top Tips from Professional Manga Artists* — 741.5
  McCloud, Scott. ★*Understanding Comics* — 741.5
CARTOONISTS
  Bair, Deirdre. *Saul Steinberg* — B
  Bechdel, Alison. ★*Fun Home* — 741.5
  Bechdel, Alison. ★*The Secret to Superhuman Strength* — 741.5
  Bell, Darrin. ★*The Talk* — 741.5
  Chast, Roz. ★*Can't We Talk About Something More Pleasant?* — 741.5
  Delisle, Guy. *Pyongyang* — 741.5
  DePastino, Todd. *Bill Mauldin*

AUTHOR, TITLE, SERIES AND SUBJECT INDEX

Finch, Christopher. *The Art of Walt Disney*	791.43092
Goldstein, Nancy. *Jackie Ormes*	B
Jones, Gerard. *Men of Tomorrow*	741.5
Kitchen, Denis. *The Art of Harvey Kurtzman*	741.5
Mankoff, Robert. *How About Never—Is Never Good for You?*	741.5
Michaelis, David. *Schulz and Peanuts*	B
Riesman, Abraham. *True Believer*	741.5
Sattouf, Riad. *The Arab of the Future*	741.5
Sattouf, Riad. *The Arab of the Future 2*	741.5
Schumacher, Michael. *Will Eisner*	741.5
Sipress, David. *What's so Funny?*	B
Spiegelman, Art. *Metamaus*	B
Tomine, Adrian. *The Loneliness of the Long-Distance Cartoonist*	741.5
CARTOONS	
Mankoff, Robert. *How About Never—Is Never Good for You?*	741.5
McCloud, Scott. *Reinventing Comics*	741.5
Reiss, Mike. *Springfield Confidential*	791.45
Schumacher, Michael. *Will Eisner*	741.5
Sipress, David. *What's so Funny?*	B
Wood, Lawrence. *Your Caption Has Been Selected*	741.5
CARTOONS (ANIMATED FILMS)	
Delisle, Guy. *Pyongyang*	741.5
Gitlin, Marty. *A Celebration of Animation*	741.5
Caruana Galizia, Paul	
★*A Death in Malta*	364.15
CARUANA GALIZIA, PAUL, 1988-	
Caruana Galizia, Paul. ★*A Death in Malta*	364.15
CARVER, GEORGE WASHINGTON, 1864?-1943	
Vella, Christina. *George Washington Carver*	B
Carver, Raymond	
All of Us	811
A New Path to the Waterfall	811
Carville's Cure. Fessler, Pam	362.19699
Carwardine, Richard	
Lincoln	B
Cary Grant. Eyman, Scott	B
Casares, Sylvia	
The Enchilada Queen Cookbook	641.5926872073
Casares, Whitney	
The Working Mom Blueprint	306.8743
Casazza, Allie	
Declutter Like a Mother	648
The Case Against Reality. Hoffman, Donald D.	121
Case Closed. Posner, Gerald L.	364.1
★*The Case for Cancel Culture*. Owens, Ernest	303.3
The Case for God. Armstrong, Karen	211
The Case for Grace. Strobel, Lee	234
The Case of the Murderous Dr. Cream. Jobb, Dean	364.152
The Case of the Vanishing Blonde. Bowden, Mark	364.10973
Case, Anne	
Deaths of Despair and the Future of Capitalism	362.28
Case, Molly	
How to Treat People	616.1
CASE, MOLLY	
Case, Molly. *How to Treat People*	616.1
Casey, Susan	
The Underworld	551.46
CASH, JOHNNY, 1932-2003	
Hilburn, Robert. ★*Johnny Cash*	B
Cash, Rosanne	
★*Composed*	B
CASH, ROSANNE	
Cash, Rosanne. ★*Composed*	B
Casillo, Charles	
Marilyn Monroe	B
CASINO EMPLOYEES	
Hill, David. *The Vapors*	976.7
CASINOS	
Hill, David. *The Vapors*	976.7
Rempel, William C. *The Gambler*	B
Thorp, Edward O. *A Man for All Markets*	B
Cassell, Kay Ann	
★*Reference and Information Services*	025.5
CASSIDY, BUTCH, 1866-1908	
Leerhsen, Charles. ★*Butch Cassidy*	B
Cassidy, Cody	
And Then You're Dead	612
How to Survive History	904

CASSIRER, ERNST, 1874-1945	
Eilenberger, Wolfram. *Time of the Magicians*	920
CASSO, GASPIPE, 1942-2020	
Carlo, Philip. *Gaspipe*	B
Cast On, Bind Off. Bestor, Leslie Ann	746.432
Cast, Carter	
The Right—And Wrong—Stuff	650.1
Castaneda, Carlos	
The Teachings of Don Juan;	299
Castaway Mountain. Roy, Saumya	363.72
CASTAWAYS	
Severin, Timothy. *In Search of Robinson Crusoe*	996.1
★*Caste*. Wilkerson, Isabel	305.5
CASTE	
Faleiro, Sonia. *The Good Girls*	364.152
Gidla, Sujatha. *Ants Among Elephants*	305.5
Guha, Ramachandra. *Gandhi*	B
Jadhav, Narendra. *Untouchables*	305.5
Sharma, Nina. *The Way You Make Me Feel*	B
Wilkerson, Isabel. ★*Caste*	305.5
Castello, Jose R.	
Bovids of the World	599.64
Castillo, Elaine	
★*How to Read Now*	418
Casting into the Light. Messineo, Janet	799.1
A Castle in Wartime. Bailey, Catherine	943.086
★*The Castle on Sunset*. Levy, Shawn	647.95
Castleman, Michael	
The Untold Story of Books	381
Castles. Morris, Marc	728.81
CASTLES	
Bailey, Catherine. *A Castle in Wartime*	943.086
Gies, Joseph. *Life in a Medieval Castle*	940.1
Macintyre, Ben. ★*Prisoners of the Castle*	940.54
Morris, Marc. *Castles*	728.81
Castles of Steel. Massie, Robert K.	940.4
Castner, Brian	
The Long Walk	B
Stampede	971.9
CASTNER, BRIAN	
Castner, Brian. *The Long Walk*	B
Castor, Helen	
Joan of Arc	B
She-Wolves	942
Castro, Fidel	
Fidel Castro	B
CASTRO, FIDEL, 1926-2016	
Castro, Fidel. *Fidel Castro*	B
Coltman, Leycester. *The Real Fidel Castro*	B
Maier, Thomas. *Mafia Spies*	364.1060973
Rasenberger, Jim. *The Brilliant Disaster*	972.9106
Castro, M. Regina	
★*The Essential Diabetes Book*	616.4
CAT OWNERS	
Bradshaw, John. ★*Cat Sense*	636.8
★*Cat Sense*. Bradshaw, John	636.8
Cat Tale. Pittman, Craig	599.75
The Cat's Meow. Losos, Jonathan B.	636.8
★*Catalog of Unabashed Gratitude*. Gay, Ross	811
CATALOGING	
Kaag, John J. *American Philosophy*	191
Cataloging The World. Wright, Alex	020.9
★*The Catalogue of Shipwrecked Books*. Wilson-Lee, Edward	B
The Catalyst. Cech, Thomas	572.8
Catania, Kenneth	
Great Adaptations	576.8
Catastrophe 1914. Hastings, Max	940.3
CATASTROPHISM	
Berman, Bob. *Earth-Shattering*	523.1
The Catch. Myers, Gary	796.332
★*Catch and Kill*. Farrow, Ronan	331.4
Catch The Sparrow. Rear, Rachel	364.152
Catch-67. Goodman, Micah	956.04
CATCHERS (BASEBALL)	
Brown, Tim. ★*The Tao of the Backup Catcher*	796.357
Catching Fire. Wrangham, Richard W.	394.1
Catching The Light. Harjo, Joy	818
Catching The Sky. Moore, Colten	B

PUBLIC LIBRARY CORE COLLECTION: NONFICTION
Twentieth Edition

Catching The Wind. Gabler, Neal — B
CATHARINE PARR, QUEEN, CONSORT OF HENRY VIII, KING OF ENGLAND, 1512-1548
    Fraser, Antonia. ★*The Wives of Henry VIII* — 942.05
    Porter, Linda. *Katherine the Queen* — B
CATHARINE, OF ARAGON, QUEEN, CONSORT OF HENRY VIII, KING OF ENGLAND, 1485-1536
    Fraser, Antonia. ★*The Wives of Henry VIII* — 942.05
    Starkey, David. *Six Wives* — 942.05
CATHEDRALS
    King, Ross. *Brunelleschi's Dome* — 726.6
Cather, Willa
    The Selected Letters of Willa Cather — B
CATHER, WILLA, 1873-1947
    Cather, Willa. *The Selected Letters of Willa Cather* — B
    Woodress, James Leslie. *Willa Cather* — B
CATHERINE DE MEDICIS, QUEEN, CONSORT OF HENRY II, KING OF FRANCE, 1519-1589
    Goldstone, Nancy Bazelon. *The Rival Queens* — 944
    Paranque, Estelle. *Blood, Fire & Gold* — 920
CATHERINE HOWARD, QUEEN, CONSORT OF HENRY VIII, KING OF ENGLAND, D. 1542
    Fraser, Antonia. ★*The Wives of Henry VIII* — 942.05
    Russell, Gareth. *Young and Damned and Fair* — B
CATHERINE II, EMPRESS OF RUSSIA, 1729-1796
    Erickson, Carolly. *Great Catherine* — B
    Massie, Robert K. *Catherine the Great* — B
Catherine The Great. Massie, Robert K. — B
CATHERINE, PRINCESS OF WALES, 1982-
    Holmes, Elizabeth. *HRH* — 941.085
CATHERWOOD, FREDERICK
    Carlsen, William. *Jungle of Stone* — B
CATHOLIC CHURCH AND NAZISM
    Eisner, Peter. *The Pope's Last Crusade* — 282.092
CATHOLIC CHURCH RENEWAL
    Francis. *The Church of Mercy* — 252
    McGreevy, John T. ★*Catholicism* — 282.09
CATHOLIC FAMILIES
    Egan, Timothy. *A Pilgrimage to Eternity* — 263
CATHOLIC THEOLOGY
    Alexander, Amir R. *Infinitesimal* — 511
    Chaput, Charles J. *Things Worth Dying For* — 248.4
    Davies, Brian. *The Thought of Thomas Aquinas* — 230
    McGreevy, John T. ★*Catholicism* — 282.09
    Wintz, Jack. *Will I See My Dog in Heaven?* — 231.7
    Woodward, Kenneth L. *Making Saints* — 235.24
CATHOLIC WOMEN
    Barthel, Joan. *American Saint* — B
    Coldstream, Catherine. ★*Cloistered* — B
    Fraser, Antonia. *Mary, Queen of Scots* — B
    Gaffigan, Jeannie. *When Life Gives You Pears* — B
    Hennessy, Kate. *Dorothy Day* — B
CATHOLIC WORKER MOVEMENT
    Hennessy, Kate. *Dorothy Day* — B
★*Catholicism.* McGreevy, John T. — 282.09
CATHOLICS
    Byrne, Paula. *Kick* — B
    Francis. *Walking with Jesus* — 282.09
    Hennessy, Kate. *Dorothy Day* — B
    Hoffman, David E. *Give Me Liberty* — B
    Leaming, Barbara. *Kick Kennedy* — B
    Lockwood, Patricia. *Priestdaddy* — B
    Norris, Kathleen. *The Cloister Walk* — 255
    Phelan, Tom. *We Were Rich and We Didn't Know It* — B
    Shanley, John Patrick. *Doubt* — 812
CATLIN, GEORGE, 1796-1872
    Eisler, Benita. *The Red Man's Bones* — B
CATS
    Bradshaw, John. ★*Cat Sense* — 636.8
    Brown, Sarah L. *The Hidden Language of Cats* — 636.8
    Carr, Caleb. *My Beloved Monster* — B
    Galaxy, Jackson. ★*Total Cat Mojo* — 636.8
    Herriot, James. *James Herriot's Cat Stories* — 636.8
    Le Guin, Ursula K. *No Time to Spare* — 814
    Losos, Jonathan B. *The Cat's Meow* — 636.8
    Myron, Vicki. ★*Dewey* — 636.80092
    Schotz, Susanne. *The Secret Language of Cats* — 636.8
    Tucker, Abigail. *The Lion in the Living Room* — 636.8

CATS AS PETS
    Bradshaw, John. ★*Cat Sense* — 636.8
    Brown, Sarah L. *The Hidden Language of Cats* — 636.8
    Carr, Caleb. *My Beloved Monster* — B
    Herriot, James. *James Herriot's Cat Stories* — 636.8
    Losos, Jonathan B. *The Cat's Meow* — 636.8
    Tucker, Abigail. *The Lion in the Living Room* — 636.8
CATTLE
    Connell, John. *The Farmer's Son* — 630.9
CATTLE RANCHERS
    Barlow, John Perry. *Mother American Night* — 782.42164
    Branch, John. *The Last Cowboys* — 920
CATTLE RANCHES
    Branch, John. *The Last Cowboys* — 920
Catullus, Gaius Valerius
    The Poems of Catullus — 874
CATULLUS, GAIUS VALERIUS
    Catullus, Gaius Valerius. *The Poems of Catullus* — 874
Caught in the Revolution. Rappaport, Helen — 355.00947
CAUSATION
    Gladwell, Malcolm. *The Tipping Point* — 302
    Hirsch, Jennifer S. *Sexual Citizens* — 371.7
    Levitt, Steven D. ★*Freakonomics* — 330
    Levitt, Steven D. *Superfreakonomics* — 330
    MacPhee, R. D. E. *End of the Megafauna* — 591.4
    Pinker, Steven. *Rationality* — 153.4
The Cause. Ellis, Joseph J. — 973.3
CAUSES OF WAR
    Aly, Gotz. *Europe Against the Jews* — 305.892
    Ansary, Mir Tamim. *Games Without Rules* — 958.1
    Bordewich, Fergus M. *America's Great Debate* — 973.6
    Bouverie, Tim. *Appeasement* — 327.41043
    Brands, H. W. ★*Our First Civil War* — 973.3
    Brands, H. W. *Woodrow Wilson* — B
    Brands, H. W. ★*The Zealot and the Emancipator* — 920
    Carter, Miranda. *George, Nicholas and Wilhelm* — 940.3
    Childers, Thomas. *The Third Reich* — 943.086
    Delbanco, Andrew. *The War Before the War* — 973.7
    Draper, Robert. *To Start a War* — 956.7044
    Dwork, Deborah. ★*Holocaust* — 940
    Evans, Richard J. *The Pursuit of Power* — 940.2
    Finkelman, Paul. *Millard Fillmore* — B
    Fritzsche, Peter. *Life and Death in the Third Reich* — 943.086
    Goldhagen, Daniel Jonah. *Hitler's Willing Executioners* — 940.53
    Goodheart, Adam. *1861* — 973.7
    Hastings, Max. *Catastrophe 1914* — 940.3
    Hayes, Peter. *Why?* — 940.53
    Hogeland, William. *Declaration* — 973.3
    Holzer, Harold. *A Just and Generous Nation* — 973.7092
    Keegan, John. *The First World War* — 940.3
    King, Greg. *The Assassination of the Archduke* — B
    Maier, Pauline. *American Scripture* — 973.3
    McCullough, David G. ★*1776* — 973.3
    McMeekin, Sean. *July 1914* — 940.3
    McPherson, James M. *Battle Cry of Freedom* — 973.7
    Nixon, John. *Debriefing the President* — 956.7044
    Phillips, Adrian. *Fighting Churchill, Appeasing Hitler* — 327.41043
    Sebag-Montefiore, Simon. *Jerusalem* — 956.94
    Snyder, Timothy. *Black Earth* — 940.53
    Taylor, Fred. *1939* — 940.53
    Unger, Harlow G. *American Tempest* — 973.3
    Wineapple, Brenda. *Ecstatic Nation* — 973.6
    Yergin, Daniel. ★*The Prize* — 338.2
Cavafy, Constantine
    The Collected Poems — 889
CAVAFY, CONSTANTINE, 1863-1933
    Cavafy, Constantine. *The Collected Poems* — 889
Cavalier, Stephen
    The World History of Animation — 791.43
Cavallari, Kristin
    True Roots — 641.5
CAVALRY
    Wert, Jeffry D. *Cavalryman of the Lost Cause* — B
    Wheelan, Joseph. ★*Terrible Swift Sword* — B
Cavalryman of the Lost Cause. Wert, Jeffry D. — B
CAVE DIVING
    Gutman, Matt. *The Boys in the Cave* — 796.52

AUTHOR, TITLE, SERIES AND SUBJECT INDEX

CAVENDISH, GEORGIANA SPENCER, DUCHESS OF DEVONSHIRE, 1757-1806
    Foreman, Amanda. *Georgiana, Duchess of Devonshire* — B
CAVES
    Gutman, Matt. *The Boys in the Cave* — 796.52
    Hunt, Will. *Underground* — 624.1
    Tabor, James M. *Blind Descent* — 796.52
CAVING
    Gutman, Matt. *The Boys in the Cave* — 796.52
    Tabor, James M. *Blind Descent* — 796.52
Cayne, Alison
    The Haven's Kitchen Cooking School — 641.5
Cayton-Holland, Adam
    Tragedy Plus Time — B
CAYTON-HOLLAND, ADAM
    Cayton-Holland, Adam. *Tragedy Plus Time* — B
Cecchi-Azzolina, Michael
    Your Table Is Ready — 647.95
CECCHI-AZZOLINA, MICHAEL
    Cecchi-Azzolina, Michael. *Your Table Is Ready* — 647.95
Cech, Thomas
    The Catalyst — 572.8
Celan, Paul
    Breathturn into Timestead — 831
    ★*Memory Rose into Threshold Speech* — 831
A Celebration of Animation. Gitlin, Marty — 741.5
CELEBRATIONS
    Ondaatje, Michael. *A Year of Last Things* — 811
    Sagan, Sasha. *For Small Creatures Such as We* — 390.09
CELEBRITIES
    Anthony, Carl Sferrazza. *Camera Girl* — B
    Attas, Amy. *Pets and the City* — B
    Bacall, Lauren. *By Myself and Then Some* — B
    Bamberger, Michael. *The Second Life of Tiger Woods* — B
    Beaty, Katelyn. *Celebrities for Jesus* — 261
    Begley, Adam. *The Great Nadar* — B
    Benedict, Jeff. ★*Tiger Woods* — B
    Biskind, Peter. *Star* — B
    Cecchi-Azzolina, Michael. *Your Table Is Ready* — 647.95
    Chan, Jackie. *Never Grow Up* — B
    Connolly, Ray. *Being John Lennon* — B
    Cooper, Anderson. *The Rainbow Comes and Goes* — B
    Curtis, James. *Spencer Tracy* — B
    Dederer, Claire. ★*Monsters* — 700.1
    Ditum, Sarah. *Toxic* — 920.72
    Dunne, Griffin. ★*The Friday Afternoon Club* — B
    Ebert, Roger. *Life Itself* — B
    Eyman, Scott. *Charlie Chaplin vs. America* — B
    Field, Sally. *In Pieces* — B
    Fisher, Todd. *My Girls* — B
    Gillon, Steven M. *America's Reluctant Prince* — B
    Gruen, Bob. *Right Place, Right Time* — B
    Hagan, Joe. *Sticky Fingers* — B
    Harris, Mark. *Mike Nichols* — B
    Hilton, Paris. *Paris* — B
    Jones, Dylan. *David Bowie* — B
    Jones, Marie D. *Celebrity Ghosts and Notorious Hauntings* — 133.1
    Kalb, Claudia. *Andy Warhol Was a Hoarder* — 920
    Kaling, Mindy. *Why Not Me?* — B
    Kashner, Sam. *The Fabulous Bouvier Sisters* — 920
    Kavanagh, Julie. *Nureyev* — B
    Kemper, Ellie. *My Squirrel Days* — B
    Leaming, Barbara. *Jacqueline Bouvier Kennedy Onassis* — B
    Leavy, Jane. *The Big Fella* — B
    Levy, Shawn. ★*The Castle on Sunset* — 647.95
    Mann, William J. *Bogie & Bacall* — 920
    Martin, Steve. *Number One Is Walking* — B
    Moore, Marcus J. *The Butterfly Effect* — B
    Moore, Susanna. *Miss Aluminum* — 813
    Morley, Paul. *The Age of Bowie* — B
    Morton, Andrew. *Diana* — B
    Norman, Philip. *John Lennon* — B
    O'Brien, Keith. *Charlie Hustle* — 796.357
    Oppedisano, Tony. *Sinatra and Me* — B
    Patterson, James. *What Really Happens in Vegas* — 920
    Philipps, Busy. *This Will Only Hurt a Little* — B
    Poniewozik, James. *Audience of One* — 324.7
    Reynolds, Debbie. *Make 'Em Laugh* — B
    Rocca, Mo. *Mobituaries* — 920
    Schulman, Michael. ★*Oscar Wars* — 791.43
    Schumer, Amy. *The Girl with the Lower Back Tattoo* — B
    Segura, Tom. ★*I'd Like to Play Alone, Please* — B
    Seinfeld, Jerry. *Is This Anything?* — 818
    Selleck, Tom. *You Never Know* — B
    Springsteen, Bruce. ★*Born to Run* — B
    Stamos, John. *If You Would Have Told Me* — B
    Stone, Sharon. *The Beauty of Living Twice* — B
    Tammet, Daniel. *Born on a Blue Day* — B
    Taborrelli, J. Randy. *Jackie, Janet & Lee* — 920
    Taborrelli, J. Randy. ★*Jackie* — B
    Taborrelli, J. Randy. ★*The Secret Life of Marilyn Monroe* — B
    Vitale, Tom. *In the Weeds* — B
    Washington, Kerry. *Thicker Than Water* — B
    Waters, John. *Mr. Know-It-All* — 814
    Woolever, Laurie. *Bourdain* — B
Celebrities for Jesus. Beaty, Katelyn — 261
CELEBRITY CHEFS
    Bourdain, Anthony. ★*World Travel* — 641.59
    Fall, Jeremy. *Falling Upwards* — 158.1
    Sanchez, Aaron. *Where I Come From* — 641.5092
Celebrity Ghosts and Notorious Hauntings. Jones, Marie D. — 133.1
CELEBRITY PROMOTION
    Begley, Adam. *The Great Nadar* — B
★*Celestial Bodies*. Jacobs, Laura — 792.8
CELL CULTURE
    Skloot, Rebecca. ★*The Immortal Life of Henrietta Lacks* — B
CELL DIVISION
    Cech, Thomas. *The Catalyst* — 572.8
CELL PHONES
    Cox, Joseph. *Dark Wire* — 363.2
CELL PHYSIOLOGY
    Cech, Thomas. *The Catalyst* — 572.8
CELLS
    Martinez Arias, Alfonso. *The Master Builder* — 571.6
    Mukherjee, Siddhartha. ★*The Song of the Cell* — 571.6
    Nakazawa, Donna Jackson. *The Angel and the Assassin* — 612.8
    Stanger, Ben. *From One Cell* — 571.6
Celluloid Activist. Schiavi, Michael R. — B
CEMETERIES
    Cotton, Tom. *Sacred Duty* — 355.6
    Kimmerle, Erin H. *We Carry Their Bones* — 365
    McElya, Micki. *The Politics of Mourning* — 975.5
    Neighbors, Joy. *The Family Tree Cemetery Field Guide* — 929
    Poole, Robert M. *Section 60* — 975.5
CENSORSHIP
    Ai, Weiwei. *Zodiac* — 741.5
    Appleman, Deborah. *Literature and the New Culture Wars* — 807
    Baez, Fernando. *Universal History of the Destruction of Books* — 098
    Bergstein, Rachelle. *The Genius of Judy* — 813
    Ellis, Bret Easton. *White* — 814
    English, Charlie. *The Gallery of Miracles and Madness* — 709.04
    Gold, Judy. *Yes I Can Say That* — 792.7
    Lane, Christina. *Phantom Lady* — B
    LaRue, James. *On Censorship* — 025.2
    Lehr, Dick. ★*The Birth of a Nation* — 305.800973
    McCraw, David Edward. *Truth in Our Times* — 342.7308
    McHangama, Jacob. ★*Free Speech* — 323.44
    Mitchell, Elizabeth. *Lincoln's Lie* — 973.7092
    Rushdie, Salman. *Joseph Anton* — B
    Rushdie, Salman. *Languages of Truth* — 824
    Strittmatter, Kai. *We Have Been Harmonized* — 323.44
    Strossen, Nadine. *Hate* — 342.7308
CENSUS
    Whitby, Andrew. *The Sum of the People* — 001.4
CENTENARIANS
    Day, John D. *The Longevity Plan* — 612.6
    Jaku, Eddie. ★*The Happiest Man on Earth* — B
    Von Drehle, David. ★*The Book of Charlie* — B
Centeno, Josef
    Ama — 641.5979
CENTRAL AFRICA
    Cooper, Helene. *Madame President* — 966.62
    Jeal, Tim. *Explorers of the Nile* — 920
CENTRAL AMERICA
    Alvarez, Noe. *Spirit Run* — 796.42
    Beard, Mary. ★*How Do We Look* — 704.9

PUBLIC LIBRARY CORE COLLECTION: NONFICTION
Twentieth Edition

Blitzer, Jonathan. *Everyone Who Is Gone Is Here* — 305.9
Carlsen, William. *Jungle of Stone* — B
Coe, Michael D. *The Maya* — 972
Jenkins, Jedidiah. *To Shake the Sleeping Self* — B
Marcum, Diana. *The Fallen Stones* — B

CENTRAL AMERICAN HISTORY
Dodds Pennock, Caroline. ★*On Savage Shores* — 970.004
Foster, Lynn V. *A Brief History of Mexico* — 972
McCullough, David G. *The Path Between the Seas* — 972.87
Morris, Edmund. ★*Theodore Rex* — 973.911
Parker, Matthew. *Panama Fever* — 972.87
Sedgewick, Augustine. *Coffeeland* — 338.4

CENTRAL AMERICAN PEOPLE
Blitzer, Jonathan. *Everyone Who Is Gone Is Here* — 305.9
Mojica Rodriguez, Prisca Dorcas. *For Brown Girls with Sharp Edges and Tender Hearts* — 305.48

CENTRAL ASIA
Badkhen, Anna. *The World Is a Carpet* — 305.409581
Dalai Lama. *Freedom in Exile* — B
Frankopan, Peter. *The Silk Roads* — 909
Kaplan, Robert D. *The Loom of Time* — 327

CENTRAL BANKING
Lowenstein, Roger. *America's Bank* — 332.1
Wessel, David. *In Fed We Trust* — 332.1

CENTRAL EUROPE
Judson, Pieter M. *The Habsburg Empire* — 943.6
Rady, Martyn C. *The Middle Kingdoms* — 943
Sebestyen, Victor. *Budapest* — 943.912
The Central Park. Brenwall, Cynthia S — 974.7

CENTRAL PARK, NEW YORK CITY
Brenwall, Cynthia S. *The Central Park* — 974.7
★*A Century of Recorded Music.* Day, Timothy — 780

Century, Douglas
Barney Ross — B

Cenziper, Debbie
★*Love Wins* — 346.7301
The Ceo Next Door. Botelho, Elena L. — 658.4

Cep, Casey N.
★*Furious Hours* — 364.152

Ceram, C. W.
Gods, Graves & Scholars — 930.1
Ceramics. Nelson, Glenn C. — 738

CERAMICS
Nelson, Glenn C. *Ceramics* — 738

Cercas, Javier
Lord of All the Dead — 868

CERCAS, JAVIER, 1962-
Cercas, Javier. *Lord of All the Dead* — 868

CEREBRAL DOMINANCE
Edwards, Betty. *Drawing on the Right Side of the Brain* — 741.2

CEREBRAL PALSY
Brown, Molly McCully. *Places I've Taken My Body* — B

Cermele, Joe
★*The Total Fishing Manual* — 799.1
Certain Magical Acts. Notley, Alice — 811
Certain Trumpets. Wills, Garry — 303.3

Cerulo, Erica
Work Wife — 658.4

Cervantes, Fernando
Conquistadores — 970.01

Cervini, Eric
The Deviant's War — B

CESAREAN SECTION
Somerstein, Rachel. ★*Invisible Labor* — 618.8

CETACEA
Hoyt, Erich. *Encyclopedia of Whales, Dolphins and Porpoises* — 599.5

Cetti, Livia
The Exquisite Book of Paper Flowers — 745.594

CH'OE, UN-HUI, 1930-2018
Fischer, Paul. *A Kim Jong-Il Production* — 791.43

Chabon, Michael
Bookends — 818
Manhood for Amateurs — B
Maps and Legends — 801
Pops — 306.874

CHABON, MICHAEL
Chabon, Michael. *Manhood for Amateurs* — B
Chabon, Michael. *Pops* — 306.874

Chace, Teri Dunn
Seeing Seeds — 581.4

Chachra, Deb
How Infrastructure Works — 363

Chachula, Robyn
Unexpected Afghans — 746.43

CHACO CULTURE NATIONAL HISTORICAL PARK, NEW MEXICO
Childs, Craig. *House of Rain* — 978.9

Chafkin, Max
The Contrarian — B
★*Chagall.* Wullschlager, Jackie — B

CHAGALL, MARC, 1887-1985
Wullschlager, Jackie. ★*Chagall* — B
The Chain. Genoways, Ted — 338.7
Chain of Title. Dayen, David — 330.973

CHAIN RESTAURANTS
Chatelain, Marcia. ★*Franchise* — 339

CHAIN STORES
Wartzman, Rick. *Still Broke* — 381

CHAIN-GANGS
Bauer, Shane. *American Prison* — 365

CHAINS (JEWELRY)
Karon, Karen. *Advanced Chain Maille Jewelry Workshop* — 745.594

Chait, Jonathan
Audacity — 973.932

CHAKRAS
Dale, Cyndi. *Llewellyn's Complete Book of Chakras* — 131
Gupta, Suneel. *Everyday Dharma* — 158.1
Shumsky, Susan G. *Earth Energy Meditations* — 133.8

CHALK DRAWING
Gooch, Brad. *Radiant* — B

CHALLAH
Ricanati, Elizabeth. *Braided* — B
The Challenge of Library Management. VanDuinkerken, Wyoma — 025.1

CHALLENGED BOOKS
Appleman, Deborah. *Literature and the New Culture Wars* — 807
★*Challenger.* Higginbotham, Adam — 629.45

CHALLENGER (SPACE SHUTTLE)
Cook, Kevin. *The Burning Blue* — 629.45
Higginbotham, Adam. ★*Challenger* — 629.45

CHALLENGER (SPACE SHUTTLE) ACCIDENT, JANUARY 28, 1986
Cook, Kevin. *The Burning Blue* — 629.45
Higginbotham, Adam. ★*Challenger* — 629.45

Challoner, Jack
The Elements — 546

Chalmers, David Mark
Hooded Americanism — 322.4

Cham, Jorge
Frequently Asked Questions About the Universe — 523.1
Chamber Divers. Lance, Rachel — 940.54
Chamber Music. Ashon, Will — 782.421649

CHAMBER MUSIC
Servadio, Gaia. *Rossini* — B

CHAMBERLAIN, JOSHUA LAWRENCE, 1828-1914
White, Ronald C. *On Great Fields* — B

CHAMBERLAIN, NEVILLE, 1869-1940
Bouverie, Tim. *Appeasement* — 327.41043
Olson, Lynne. *Troublesome Young Men* — 941.084
Phillips, Adrian. *Fighting Churchill, Appeasing Hitler* — 327.41043

CHAMBERLAIN, WILT, 1936-1999
Montville, Leigh. *Tall Men, Short Shorts* — 796.323

Chamberlin, Paul Thomas
The Cold War's Killing Fields — 355.009

Chamberlin, Silas
On the Trail — 796.510973

CHAMBERS, JULIUS L. (JULIUS LEVONNE), 1936-2013
Rosen, Richard A. *Julius Chambers* — B
The Chameleon Couch. Komunyakaa, Yusef — 811

Chammah, Maurice
★*Let the Lord Sort Them* — 364.66
The Champion's Mind. Afremow, James A. — 796.01
Champions Way. McIntire, Mike — 796.043
Champlain's Dream. Fischer, David Hackett — B

CHAMPLAIN, SAMUEL DE, 1567-1635
Fischer, David Hackett. *Champlain's Dream* — B

CHAMPOLLION, JEAN-FRANCOIS, 1790-1832
Dolnick, Edward. *The Writing of the Gods* — 493

AUTHOR, TITLE, SERIES AND SUBJECT INDEX

Chan, Jackie
  Never Grow Up   B
CHAN, JACKIE, 1954-
  Chan, Jackie. *Never Grow Up*   B
CHANCE
  Mazur, Joseph. *Fluke*   519.2
Chance and Circumstance. Brown, Carolyn   B
CHANCE, FRANK L. (FRANK LEROY), 1877-1924
  Rapp, David. *Tinker to Evers to Chance*   796.357
Chance, Rosemary
  Young Adult Literature in Action   011.62
★*The Chancellor*. Marton, Kati   B
★*Chancellorsville*. Sears, Stephen W.   973.7
CHANCELLORSVILLE, BATTLE OF, 1863
  Sears, Stephen W. ★*Chancellorsville*   973.7
Chandler, Adam
  Drive-Thru Dreams   647.95
Chandra's Cosmos. Tucker, Wallace H.   523.1
Chandrasekaran, Rajiv
  Imperial Life in the Emerald City   956.7044
Chanel's Riviera. De Courcy, Anne   944.9
CHANEL, COCO, 1883-1971
  De Courcy, Anne. *Chanel's Riviera*   944.9
  Garelick, Rhonda K. *Mademoiselle*   B
  Mazzeo, Tilar J. *The Secret of Chanel No. 5*   338.7
Chang, David
  ★*Eat a Peach*   641.5
CHANG, DAVID, 1977-
  Chang, David. ★*Eat a Peach*   641.5
Chang, Emily
  Brotopia   331.4
Chang, Gordon H.
  Ghosts of Gold Mountain   331.6
Chang, Ha-Joon
  Economics   330
Chang, Iris
  ★*The Rape of Nanking*   951.04
Chang, Jeff
  Can't Stop, Won't Stop   306.4
Chang, Joanne
  Pastry Love   641.86
Chang, Jung
  Big Sister, Little Sister, Red Sister   B
  Empress Dowager Cixi   B
  Mao   B
  ★*Wild Swans*   B
CHANG, JUNG, 1952-
  Chang, Jung. ★*Wild Swans*   B
Chang, Leslie T.
  ★*Egyptian Made*   331.4
  Factory Girls   331.4
Chang, Tina
  Hybrida   811
Chang, Victoria
  Obit   811
CHANGE
  Berg, Elizabeth. *I'll Be Seeing You*   306.874
  Boa, Kenneth D. *Recalibrate Your Life*   248.8
  Douthat, Ross Gregory. *To Change the Church*   230
  Levine, Bruce C. *The Fall of the House of Dixie*   973.7
  Mueller, Jennifer. *Creative Change*   658.4
  Phillips, Adam. *On Giving up*   158.2
  Pipher, Mary Bray. *A Life in Light*   B
  Sante, Lucy. *I Heard Her Call My Name*   B
  Sherman, Anna. *The Bells of Old Tokyo*   952
  Waldman, Jonathan. *Sam*   629.8
  Wills, Garry. *The Future of the Catholic Church with Pope Francis*   282.09
CHANGE (PSYCHOLOGY)
  Bergner, Daniel. ★*Sing for Your Life*   B
  Brooks, Arthur C. *Build the Life You Want*   158.1
  Brown, Brene. *The Gifts of Imperfection*   158
  Brown, Tabitha. *I Did a New Thing*   158.1
  Chodron, Pema. *How We Live Is How We Die*   294.3
  Clarke, Thurston. *JFK's Last Hundred Days*   B
  Conley, Chip. ★*Learning to Love Midlife*   646.7
  Duhigg, Charles. ★*The Power of Habit*   158.1
  Dutton, Kevin. *Split-Second Persuasion*   153.8
  Feiler, Bruce. *Life Is in the Transitions*   392

  Ferriss, Timothy. *Tools of Titans*   081
  Fogg, B. J. *Tiny Habits*   158
  Goldsmith, Marshall. *Triggers*   155.2
  Healy, Thomas. *The Great Dissent*   342.7308
  Keltner, Dacher. ★*Awe*   152.4
  Lerner, Harriet Goldhor. *The Dance of Intimacy*   155.6
  McGraw, Phillip C. *Life Strategies*   158
  Miller, Caroline Adams. *Creating Your Best Life*   158.1
  Norton, Michael. ★*The Ritual Effect*   650.1
  Rakoff, Joanna Smith. *My Salinger Year*   B
  Rusbridger, Alan. ★*Play It Again*   B
  Rush, Chris. *The Light Years*   B
  Vollmer, Becky. *You Are Not Stuck*   158.1
  Westheimer, Ruth. *The Doctor Is In*   B
  Wood, Wendy. *Good Habits, Bad Habits*   152.3
Changing Lives. Tunstall, Tricia   780.71
Chanin, Natalie
  ★*The Geometry of Hand-Sewing*   746.44
CHANNEL TUNNEL
  Denton, Sally. *The Profiteers*   B
Chansky, Art
  Blue Blood II   796.323
CHAO, BUWEI YANG, 1889-1981
  Sen, Mayukh. *Taste Makers*   641.5092
★*Chaos*. O'Neill, Tom   364.152
CHAOS
  Harford, Tim. *Messy*   153.3
  Patterson, Scott. ★*Chaos Kings*   338.5
★*Chaos Kings*. Patterson, Scott   338.5
The Chaos Cure*. Cilley, Marla   648
CHAPELLE, DICKEY, 1919-1965
  Rinehart, Lorissa. *First to the Front*   B
Chapin, Kari
  ★*The Handmade Marketplace*   745.5
Chapin, Sasha
  All the Wrong Moves   794.1092
CHAPIN, SASHA
  Chapin, Sasha. *All the Wrong Moves*   794.1092
Chaplin, Amy
  Whole Food Cooking Every Day   641.3
CHAPLIN, CHARLIE, 1889-1977
  Ackroyd, Peter. *Charlie Chaplin*   B
  Eyman, Scott. *Charlie Chaplin vs. America*   B
Chapman, Baylor
  ★*Decorating with Plants*   635.9
CHAPMAN, EDDIE
  Macintyre, Ben. *Agent Zigzag*   B
CHAPMAN, ELIZABETH WINTHROP CHANLER, 1866-1937
  Lucey, Donna M. *Sargent's Women*   920
Chapman, Gary D.
  Love as a Way of Life   241
Chapman, Rex
  ★*It's Hard for Me to Live with Me*   B
Chappell, Jon
  ★*Guitar All-In-One for Dummies*   787.87
Chapter 13 Bankruptcy, 17th Ed. O'Neill, Cara   346.7307
Chaput, Charles J.
  Things Worth Dying For   248.4
CHARACTER
  Bordo, Susan. *The Creation of Anne Boleyn*   942.05
  Brands, H. W. ★*Andrew Jackson, His Life and Times*   B
  Brooks, David. ★*The Second Mountain*   302
  Brooks, David. *The Social Animal*   305.5
  Covey, Stephen R. ★*The 7 Habits of Highly Effective People*   158
  Dederer, Claire. ★*Monsters*   700.1
  Edmundson, Mark. *Why Football Matters*   B
  Goodwin, Doris Kearns. ★*Leadership in Turbulent Times*   973.09
  Grant, Adam M. *Hidden Potential*   153.8
  Pryor, Elizabeth Brown. *Six Encounters with Lincoln*   973.7092
  Rusbridger, Alan. ★*Play It Again*   B
CHARACTER EDUCATION
  Wegner, Bobbi. *Raising Feminist Boys*   305.23
  Whippman, Ruth. ★*Boymom*   305.23
CHARACTERS AND CHARACTERISTICS
  Tough, Paul. ★*How Children Succeed*   372.210973
CHARACTERS AND CHARACTERISTICS IN FAIRY TALES
  Chang, Tina. *Hybrida*   811

PUBLIC LIBRARY CORE COLLECTION: NONFICTION
Twentieth Edition

CHARACTERS AND CHARACTERISTICS IN FILMS
    Austerlitz, Saul. *Kind of a Big Deal* — 791.43
    Wasson, Sam. *The Big Goodbye* — 791.43
CHARACTERS AND CHARACTERISTICS IN LITERATURE
    Blaisdell, Robert. *Creating Anna Karenina* — 891.7
    Bloom, Harold. *Shakespeare* — 822.33
    Corbett, Emily. *In Transition* — 809
    James, P. D. *Talking About Detective Fiction* — 823
    Konnikova, Maria. *Mastermind* — 153.4
    McIlwaine, Catherine. *Tolkien* — 002.09
    Philbrick, Nathaniel. *Why Read Moby-Dick?* — 813
    Reiss, Tom. *The Black Count* — B
    Tatar, Maria. *The Heroine with 1001 Faces* — 809
    Wilson, A. N. *The Mystery of Charles Dickens* — 823
CHARACTERS AND CHARACTERISTICS IN MYTHOLOGY
    Hughes, Bettany. *Venus and Aphrodite* — 292
    Larrington, Carolyne. *The Norse Myths* — 293
    Reed, Justin Phillip. *The Malevolent Volume* — 811
    Tatar, Maria. *The Heroine with 1001 Faces* — 809
    Zimmerman, Jess. *Women and Other Monsters* — 155.3
CHARACTERS AND CHARACTERISTICS IN TELEVISION
    Key, Keegan-Michael. ★*The History of Sketch Comedy* — 792.2
★*Charged*. Bazelon, Emily — 345.73
Chariot. Cotterell, Arthur — 357
CHARISMA
    Hill, Clint. *Mrs. Kennedy and Me* — 973.922092
CHARISMATIC POLITICAL LEADERSHIP
    Zygar, Mikhail. *All the Kremlin's Men* — 947.086
CHARITABLE CONTRIBUTIONS
    Schwab, Tim. ★*The Bill Gates Problem* — 361.7
CHARITIES
    Doyne, Maggie. *Between the Mountain and the Sky* — B
    Harrison, Scott. *Thirst* — B
    Schwab, Tim. ★*The Bill Gates Problem* — 361.7
CHARITY
    Chittister, Joan. *Following the Path* — 248.4
    Francis. *The Church of Mercy* — 252
Charles Darwin. Browne, E. J. — B
Charles Darwin. Browne, E. J. — B
Charles Darwin. Darwin, Charles — 576.8
CHARLES I, KING OF ENGLAND, 1600-1649
    Ackroyd, Peter. *Rebellion* — 941.06
CHARLES II, KING OF ENGLAND, 1630-1685
    Mortimer, Ian. *The Time Traveler's Guide to Restoration Britain* — 941.06
Charles Ives. Swafford, Jan — B
CHARLES, III, KING OF GREAT BRITAIN, 1948-
    Smith, Sally Bedell. *Prince Charles* — B
Charles, Jos
    Feeld — 811
Charles-Edwards, T. M.
    Wales and the Britons, 350-1064 — 942.901
Charleson, Susannah
    Where the Lost Dogs Go — 636.7
CHARLESON, SUSANNAH
    Charleson, Susannah. *Where the Lost Dogs Go* — 636.7
CHARLESTON, SOUTH CAROLINA
    Ball, Edward. *Slaves in the Family* — 975.7
    Conroy, Pat. *My Losing Season* — B
    Harris, J. William. *The Hanging of Thomas Jeremiah* — B
    Kytle, Ethan J. *Denmark Vesey's Garden* — 975.7
    Lance, Rachel. *In the Waves* — 973.7
Charlie Chaplin. Ackroyd, Peter — B
Charlie Chaplin vs. America. Eyman, Scott — B
Charlie Hustle. O'Brien, Keith — 796.357
Charlotte Bronte. Harman, Claire — B
CHARLOTTESVILLE, VIRGINIA
    Neus, Nora. *24 Hours in Charlottesville* — 973.933
    Signer, Michael. *Cry Havoc* — 305.800973
★*Charm* School. Goertzen, Vanessa — 746.46
Charman, Isobel
    The Zoo — 590.73
CHARMS
    Abrev, Ileana. *The Little Big Book of White Spells* — 133.4
Charnas, Dan
    The Big Payback — 306.4
CHARNEY, DOV, 1969-
    Flannery, Kate. *Strip Tees* — 338.4

CHARTER SCHOOLS
    Fitzpatrick, Cara. *The Death of Public School* — 379.73
Charter, David
    Royal Audience — 941.085
CHARTS
    Cairo, Alberto. *How Charts Lie* — 302.2
CHASE, CHEVY, 1943-
    De Semlyen, Nick. *Wild and Crazy Guys* — 920
CHASE, DAVID, 1945 AUGUST 22-
    Seitz, Matt Zoller. *The Sopranos Sessions* — 791.45
Chase, James
    Acheson — B
CHASE, SALMON PORTLAND, 1808-1873
    Goodwin, Doris Kearns. ★*Team of Rivals* — B
    Oller, John. *American Queen* — B
Chasing Gideon. Houppert, Karen — 345.73
Chasing Hillary. Chozick, Amy — B
★*Chasing* History. Bernstein, Carl — B
★*Chasing* Hope. Kristof, Nicholas D. — B
Chasing Me to My Grave. Rembert, Winfred — B
Chasing New Horizons. Stern, Alan — 629.43
Chasing Perfection. Glockner, Andy — 796.323
Chasing Portraits. Rynecki, Elizabeth — B
Chasing Shadows. Skomal, Gregory — 597.3
Chasing Space. Melvin, Leland — B
Chasing The Demon. Hampton, Dan — 629.132
Chasing The Moon. Stone, Robert — 629.45
Chasing The Thrill. Barbarisi, Daniel — 796.1
Chast, Roz
    ★*Can't We Talk About Something More Pleasant?* — 741.5
CHAST, ROZ
    Chast, Roz. ★*Can't We Talk About Something More Pleasant?* — 741.5
Chasteen, John Charles
    Americanos — 980
    Born in Blood and Fire — 980
Chatelain, Marcia
    ★*Franchise* — 339
★*Chatter*. Kross, Ethan — 158.1
Chaucer, Geoffrey
    ★*The Complete Poetry and Prose of Geoffrey Chaucer* — 821
CHAUCER, GEOFFREY, D. 1400
    Chaucer, Geoffrey. ★*The Complete Poetry and Prose of Geoffrey Chaucer* — 821
Chaudry, Rabia
    Fatty Fatty Boom Boom — B
CHAUDRY, RABIA
    Chaudry, Rabia. *Fatty Fatty Boom Boom* — B
Chavez Perez, Inti
    Respect — 176
CHAVEZ, CESAR, 1927-1993
    Pawel, Miriam. *The Crusades of Cesar Chavez* — B
Chayka, Kyle
    Filterworld — 306
    The Longing for Less — 179.9
Che Guevara. Anderson, Jon Lee — B
Che, Hannah
    ★*The Vegan Chinese Kitchen* — 641.5
Cheap Old Houses. Finkelstein, Elizabeth — 643
CHEATING (INTERPERSONAL RELATIONS)
    Pittard, Hannah. *We Are Too Many* — B
The Cheating Culture. Callahan, David — 174
CHECHNYA, RUSSIA
    Igort. *The Ukrainian and Russian Notebooks* — 741.5
    Seierstad, Asne. *Angel of Grozny* — 947.086
Checking In. Williams, Michelle — B
Checkmate in Berlin. Milton, Giles — 943
Checkoway, Julie
    The Three-Year Swim Club — 797.2
Chee, Alexander
    ★*How to Write an Autobiographical Novel* — B
Cheers to the Publican, Repast and Present. Kahan, Paul — 641.594
CHEESE
    Aron, Jules. *Vegan Cheese* — 641.5
    Mullen, Marissa. *That Cheese Plate Wants to Party* — 641.6
Cheever, Susan
    American Bloomsbury — 920
    Drinking in America — 394.1
The Chef and the Slow Cooker. Acheson, Hugh — 641.5

AUTHOR, TITLE, SERIES AND SUBJECT INDEX

Chekhov. Chekhov, Anton Pavlovich ... 891.72
Chekhov, Anton Pavlovich
   Chekhov ... 891.72
   The Complete Plays ... 891.72
CHEKHOV, ANTON PAVLOVICH, 1860-1904
   Chekhov, Anton Pavlovich. *Chekhov* ... 891.72
   Chekhov, Anton Pavlovich. *The Complete Plays* ... 891.72
   Malcolm, Janet. *Reading Chekhov* ... 891.72
   Saunders, George. ★*A Swim in a Pond in the Rain* ... 891.7
Chelsea, David
   Perspective in Action ... 741.5
Chemaly, Soraya L.
   Rage Becomes Her ... 155.3
Chemerinsky, Erwin
   Closing the Courthouse Door ... 347.73
   Presumed Guilty ... 344.7305
CHEMICAL ELEMENTS
   Challoner, Jack. *The Elements* ... 546
   Gray, Theodore W. ★*The Elements* ... 546
   Gray, Theodore W. *Reactions* ... 530
   Kean, Sam. *Caesar's Last Breath* ... 551.51
   Kean, Sam. *The Disappearing Spoon* ... 546
   Levi, Primo. *The Periodic Table* ... 858
   Levitt, Dan. *What's Gotten into You* ... 539.7
CHEMICAL INDUSTRY AND TRADE
   Bilott, Robert. *Exposure* ... 344.04
   Fagin, Dan. *Toms River* ... 363.7209749
   Fields, Micah. ★*We Hold Our Breath* ... 976.4
   Westhoff, Ben. *Fentanyl, Inc.* ... 362.29
CHEMICAL PLANTS
   O'Brien, Keith. *Paradise Falls* ... 363.738
CHEMICAL WARFARE
   Emery, Theo. *Hellfire Boys* ... 358
   Tucker, Jonathan B. *War of Nerves* ... 358
   Warrick, Joby. *Red Line* ... 956.9104
CHEMICAL WEAPONS
   Emery, Theo. *Hellfire Boys* ... 358
   Preston, Diana. *A Higher Form of Killing* ... 940.4
   Tucker, Jonathan B. *War of Nerves* ... 358
   Warrick, Joby. *Red Line* ... 956.9104
CHEMICALS
   Kean, Sam. *The Disappearing Spoon* ... 546
CHEMISTRY
   Cliff, Harry. *How to Make an Apple Pie from Scratch* ... 523.01
   Gray, Theodore W. ★*The Elements* ... 546
   Gray, Theodore W. *Reactions* ... 530
   Kean, Sam. *Caesar's Last Breath* ... 551.51
   Kean, Sam. *The Disappearing Spoon* ... 546
   Miodownik, Mark. *Liquid Rules* ... 530.4
   Miodownik, Mark. *Stuff Matters* ... 620.1
CHEMISTS
   Dawson, Kate Winkler. ★*American Sherlock* ... B
   Levi, Primo. *The Periodic Table* ... 858
CHEMOTHERAPY
   Boyer, Anne. *The Undying* ... B
   Mukherjee, Siddhartha. ★*The Emperor of All Maladies* ... 616.99
CHEN FAMILY
   Li, Zhuqing. *Daughters of the Flower Fragrant Garden* ... 951.04
Chen, Da
   Colors of the Mountain ... 951.05
CHEN, DA, 1962-2019
   Chen, Da. *Colors of the Mountain* ... 951.05
CHEN, HONG (PSEUDONYM)
   Li, Zhuqing. *Daughters of the Flower Fragrant Garden* ... 951.04
CHEN, WENJUN, 1923-2014
   Li, Zhuqing. *Daughters of the Flower Fragrant Garden* ... 951.04
Cheney, Liz
   Oath and Honor ... 328.73
CHENEY, LIZ, 1966-
   Cheney, Liz. *Oath and Honor* ... 328.73
Cheney, Lynne V.
   James Madison ... B
   The Virginia Dynasty ... B
Cheng, Eugenia
   How to Bake Pi ... 510
Cheng, Nien
   Life and Death in Shanghai ... B

CHENG, NIEN, 1915-2009
   Cheng, Nien. *Life and Death in Shanghai* ... B
Chernaik, Judith
   Schumann ... B
CHERNOBYL NUCLEAR ACCIDENT, 1986
   Higginbotham, Adam. ★*Midnight in Chernobyl* ... 363.17
Chernow, Ron
   ★*Alexander Hamilton* ... B
   ★*Grant* ... B
   The Warburgs ... B
   Washington ... B
CHEROKEE (NORTH AMERICAN PEOPLE)
   Inskeep, Steve. *Jacksonland* ... 973.56
   McLoughlin, William Gerald. *After the Trail of Tears* ... 973
   Sedgwick, John. *Blood Moon* ... 975.004
Chertoff, Michael
   Exploding Data ... 343.7309
Cheryl Day's Treasury of Southern Baking. Day, Cheryl ... 641.81
CHESAPEAKE BAY
   Swift, Earl. *Chesapeake Requiem* ... 639
Chesapeake Requiem. Swift, Earl ... 639
Cheshire, James
   Where the Animals Go ... 591.47
Chesney, Will
   No Ordinary Dog ... 958.104
CHESNEY, WILL, 1984-
   Chesney, Will. *No Ordinary Dog* ... 958.104
CHESS
   Ashley, Maurice. *Move by Move* ... 158
   Brady, Frank. *Endgame* ... B
   Brown, Nancy Marie. *Ivory Vikings* ... 736
   Chapin, Sasha. *All the Wrong Moves* ... 794.1092
   Fischer, Bobby. ★*Bobby Fischer Teaches Chess* ... 794.1
   Kasparov, G. K. *Deep Thinking* ... 006.3
CHESS PLAYERS
   Ashley, Maurice. *Move by Move* ... 158
   Brady, Frank. *Endgame* ... B
   Chapin, Sasha. *All the Wrong Moves* ... 794.1092
   Kasparov, G. K. *Deep Thinking* ... 006.3
CHESS SETS
   Brown, Nancy Marie. *Ivory Vikings* ... 736
Chesshire, Charles
   Japanese Gardening ... 712
Chester B. Himes. Jackson, Lawrence Patrick ... B
Cheung, Karen
   The Impossible City ... 951.25
CHEUNG, KAREN, 1993-
   Cheung, Karen. *The Impossible City* ... 951.25
Chevallier, Andrew
   Encyclopedia of Herbal Medicine ... 615.3
Chevannes, Barry
   Rastafari ... 299
CHEYENNE (NORTH AMERICAN PEOPLE)
   Connell, Evan S. *Son of the Morning Star* ... 973.8
   Enss, Chris. *Mochi's War* ... B
   Grathwohl, Marya. *This Wheel of Rocks* ... 271
   Philbrick, Nathaniel. ★*The Last Stand* ... 973.8
Chezar, Ariella
   ★*Seasonal Flower Arranging* ... 635.9
CHIANG, KAI-SHEK, 1887-1975
   Mitter, Rana. *Forgotten Ally* ... 951.04
   Pakula, Hannah. *The Last Empress* ... B
   Taylor, Jay. *The Generalissimo* ... B
CHIANG, MAY-LING SOONG, 1897-2003
   Chang, Jung. *Big Sister, Little Sister, Red Sister* ... B
   Pakula, Hannah. *The Last Empress* ... B
CHIAPAS, MEXICO (STATE)
   Franklin, Jonathan. *438 Days* ... 910.91
The Chicago Cubs. Cohen, Rich ... 796.357
The Chicago Guide to Grammar, Usage, and Punctuation. Garner, Bryan A ... 428.2
CHICAGO, ILLINOIS
   Bair, Deirdre. *Al Capone* ... B
   Berg, Scott W. *The Burning of the World* ... 977.311
   Bruck, Connie. *When Hollywood Had a King* ... B
   Byas, Taylor. *I Done Clicked My Heels Three Times* ... 811
   Cohen, Rich. *The Chicago Cubs* ... 796.357
   Common. *One Day It'll All Make Sense* ... B
   Dyja, Tom. *The Third Coast* ... 977.311

PUBLIC LIBRARY CORE COLLECTION: NONFICTION
Twentieth Edition

Eig, Jonathan. *Get Capone*	364.1
Ewing, Eve L. *1919*	811
Ewing, Eve L. *Ghosts in the Schoolyard*	370.89
Fisher, Thomas. ★*The Emergency*	362.1089
Garrow, David J. *Rising Star*	B
Hansberry, Lorraine. ★*A Raisin in the Sun*	812
Jefferson, Margo. *Negroland*	305.896
King, Greg. *Nothing but the Night*	364.152
Larson, Erik. ★*The Devil in the White City*	364.15
Levin, Josh. *The Queen*	364.16
Marovich, Robert M. *A City Called Heaven*	782.25
Miller, Donald L. *City of the Century*	977.311
Nelson, David B. *Boys Enter the House*	364.152
Obama, Barack. ★*Dreams from My Father*	B
Rapoport, Ron. *Let's Play Two*	B
Royster, Francesca T. *Choosing Family*	B
Simon, Scott. *My Cubs*	796.357
Tate, Christie. ★*Group*	B
Trice, Dawn Turner. ★*Three Girls from Bronzeville*	977.311
Zminda, Don. *Double Plays and Double Crosses*	796.357

CHICKASAW (NORTH AMERICAN PEOPLE)
Hogan, Linda. *The Woman Who Watches Over the World*	B
Chicken with Plums. Satrapi, Marjane	741.5

CHICKENS
Pepin, Jacques. *Art of the Chicken*	641.665
Rude, Emelyn. *Tastes Like Chicken*	338.1
Stark, Lizzie. ★*Egg*	641.3
Webb, Leah M. *The Seven-Step Homestead*	635
The Chief. Nasaw, David	B

CHIEF EXECUTIVE OFFICERS
Botelho, Elena L. *The CEO Next Door*	658.4
Brown, Eliot. *The Cult of We*	333.33
Bruck, Connie. *When Hollywood Had a King*	B
Cohan, William D. *Power Failure*	338.7
DeBord, Matthew. *Return to Glory*	338.4
Flannery, Kate. *Strip Tees*	338.4
Gelles, David. *The Man Who Broke Capitalism*	330.12
Hastings, Reed. *No Rules Rules*	384.55
Isaacson, Walter. ★*Steve Jobs*	B
Schultz, Howard. *From the Ground Up*	B
Tenzin Priyadarshi. *Running Toward Mystery*	B

CHIEFS (POLITICAL ANTHROPOLOGY)
Gardner, Mark L. *The Earth Is All That Lasts*	978.004
Gwynne, S. C. *Empire of the Summer Moon*	B
★Philbrick, Nathaniel. ★*The Last Stand*	973.8
Utley, Robert M. *Sitting Bull*	B
The Chiffon Trenches. Talley, Andre Leon	B

Chiger, Krystyna
The Girl in the Green Sweater	B

CHIGER, KRYSTYNA, 1935-
Chiger, Krystyna. *The Girl in the Green Sweater*	B
Chihuly. Ward, Gerald W. R.	709

CHIHULY, DALE, 1941-
Ward, Gerald W. R. *Chihuly*	709

CHILD ABUSE
Asgarian, Roxanna. *We Were Once a Family*	364.152
Benforado, Adam. *A Minor Revolution*	362.7
Bergner, Daniel. ★*Sing for Your Life*	B
Calcaterra, Regina. *Etched in Sand*	B
Calcaterra, Regina. *Girl Unbroken*	B
Glatt, John. *The Family Next Door*	362.76092
Hilton, Paris. *Paris*	B
Kelly, Donika. *The Renunciations*	811
Kenneally, Christine. *Ghosts of the Orphanage*	362.73
Shorter, Frank. *My Marathon*	796.42
Soboroff, Jacob. ★*Separated*	325.73
V. *The Apology*	818
Watkins, D. *Black Boy Smile*	B

CHILD ABUSE VICTIMS
Calcaterra, Regina. *Etched in Sand*	B
Calcaterra, Regina. *Girl Unbroken*	B
Farley, Audrey Clare. ★*Girls and Their Monsters*	306.875
Glatt, John. *The Family Next Door*	362.76092
Grande, Reyna. ★*The Distance Between Us*	973
Jewel. *Never Broken*	782.42164
Lake, Dianne. *Member of the Family*	364.152
Metatawabin, Edmund. *Up Ghost River*	B
Qu, Anna. *Made in China*	B

Scheeres, Julia. *Jesus Land*	B
Tran, Phuc. ★*Sigh, Gone*	B
West, Cait. ★*Rift*	B
Williams, Mary. *The Lost Daughter*	B

CHILD ABUSERS
Glatt, John. *The Family Next Door*	362.76092

CHILD ACTORS AND ACTRESSES
Harris, Neil Patrick. *Neil Patrick Harris*	B
Mills, Hayley. *Forever Young*	B

CHILD ADVOCACY
Haidt, Jonathan. ★*The Anxious Generation*	305.23

CHILD ARTISTS
B., David. *Epileptic*	741.5
Mankoff, Robert. *How About Never—Is Never Good for You?*	741.5
Van't Hul, Jean. *The Artful Parent*	745.5083

CHILD BALLET DANCERS
Robb, Alice. ★*Don't Think, Dear*	792.8

CHILD CARE
Albom, Mitch. *Finding Chika*	B
Bhattacharya, Shaoni. *The Baby Book*	649.1
Senior, Jennifer. *All Joy and No Fun*	306.874
Trubo, Richard. *Caring for Your Baby and Young Child*	618.92

CHILD CELEBRITIES
Jackson family. *The Jacksons*	782.421644
Jefferson, Margo. *On Michael Jackson*	B
Kupperman, Michael. *All the Answers*	741.5

CHILD CUSTODY
Asgarian, Roxanna. *We Were Once a Family*	364.152

CHILD DEVELOPMENT
Boyce, W. Thomas. *The Orchid and the Dandelion*	649
Brookwood, Marilyn. *The Orphans of Davenport*	305.231
Clinton, Hillary Rodham. *It Takes a Village*	305.23
Davis, Lisa Selin. *Tomboy*	305.409
Day, Marianne Waggoner. *Camp Grandma*	306.8745
Eliot, Lise. *Pink Brain, Blue Brain*	612.6
Fleming, Renee. ★*Music and Mind*	615.8
Galinsky, Ellen. ★*The Breakthrough Years*	649
Haelle, Tara. *The Informed Parent*	649
Haidt, Jonathan. ★*The Anxious Generation*	305.23
Koenig, Joan. *The Musical Child*	780.71
Ramesh, Jaya. *Parenting at the Intersections*	649
Reiner, Andrew. *Better Boys, Better Men*	155.43
Ruthsatz, Joanne. *The Prodigy's Cousin*	155.45
Santomero, Angela C. *Preschool Clues*	305.233
Seldin, Tim. *How to Raise an Amazing Child the Montessori Way*	649
Siegel, Daniel J. *Brainstorm*	155.5
Sole-Smith, Virginia. ★*Fat Talk*	649.1
Ticktin, Allie. *Play to Progress*	370.15
Trubo, Richard. *Caring for Your Baby and Young Child*	618.92
Wegner, Bobbi. *Raising Feminist Boys*	305.23
Whippman, Ruth. ★*Boymom*	305.23
Wojcicki, Esther. *How to Raise Successful People*	649
Wolf, Maryanne. *Reader, Come Home*	418
Yang, Charles D. *The Infinite Gift*	401

CHILD GYMNASTS
Barr, John. *Start by Believing*	364.15

CHILD HEALTH
Klass, Perri. *A Good Time to Be Born*	362.19892

CHILD HOLOCAUST SURVIVORS
Van Es, Bart. *The Cut Out Girl*	B

CHILD IMMIGRANTS
Bobrow-Strain, Aaron. *The Death and Life of Aida Hernandez*	972
Bui, Thi. ★*The Best We Could Do*	741.5
Hernandez Castillo, Marcelo. *Children of the Land*	B
Luiselli, Valeria. *Tell Me How It Ends*	305.23086
Qu, Anna. *Made in China*	B
Talusan, Meredith. *Fairest*	305.30973
Wides-Munoz, Laura. *The Making of a Dream*	920

CHILD INTERNET USERS
Haidt, Jonathan. ★*The Anxious Generation*	305.23
A Child Is Born. Nilsson, Lennart	612.6
The Child Is the Teacher. De Stefano, Cristina	B

CHILD KIDNAPPING VICTIMS
Douglas, John E. *When a Killer Calls*	364.152
Tjipombo, Tupa. *I Am Not Your Slave*	B

CHILD MENTAL HEALTH
Haidt, Jonathan. ★*The Anxious Generation*	305.23
Linn, Susan. *Who's Raising the Kids?*	649

CHILD MURDER VICTIMS
Asgarian, Roxanna. *We Were Once a Family* — 364.152
Douglas, John E. *When a Killer Calls* — 364.152
Faleiro, Sonia. *The Good Girls* — 364.152
Glatt, John. ★*The Perfect Father* — 364.152
Nelson, David B. *Boys Enter the House* — 364.152

CHILD MURDERS
Glatt, John. *The Doomsday Mother* — 364.152
Kaminsky, Ilya. ★*Deaf Republic* — 811
McGinniss, Joe. *Fatal Vision* — B

CHILD NEGLECT
Asgarian, Roxanna. *We Were Once a Family* — 364.152
Calcaterra, Regina. *Etched in Sand* — B
Calcaterra, Regina. *Girl Unbroken* — B
Crais, Clifton C. *History Lessons* — B
Hamill, Kirkland. *Filthy Beasts* — B
Henderson, Rob Kim. *Troubled* — B

CHILD NEGLECT VICTIMS
Crais, Clifton C. *History Lessons* — B
Walls, Jeannette. ★*The Glass Castle* — B
Child of Light. Bell, Madison Smartt — B

CHILD PORNOGRAPHY
DeRogatis, Jim. *Soulless* — B

CHILD PRISONERS
Kimmerle, Erin H. *We Carry Their Bones* — 365
Soboroff, Jacob. ★*Separated* — 325.73

CHILD PRODIGIES
Butler, Marcia. *The Skin Above My Knee* — B
Kupperman, Michael. *All the Answers* — 741.5
Ruthsatz, Joanne. *The Prodigy's Cousin* — 155.45

CHILD PROTECTIVE SERVICES
Asgarian, Roxanna. *We Were Once a Family* — 364.152
Pryce, Jessica. ★*Broken* — 362.7
Qu, Anna. *Made in China* — B

CHILD PSYCHOLOGY
Brookwood, Marilyn. *The Orphans of Davenport* — 305.231
Carey, Tanith. *What's My Child Thinking?* — 155.4
Christakis, Erika. *The Importance of Being Little* — 372.21
De Stefano, Cristina. *The Child Is the Teacher* — B
Gopnik, Alison. *The Gardener and the Carpenter* — 155.4
Linn, Susan. *Who's Raising the Kids?* — 649
Ruthsatz, Joanne. *The Prodigy's Cousin* — 155.45
Spofford, Tim. *What the Children Told Us* — 150.92
Wojcicki, Esther. *How to Raise Successful People* — 649

CHILD REARING
Adichie, Chimamanda Ngozi. *Dear Ijeawele* — 649
Asika, Uju. *Bringing up Race* — 155.4
Barkley, Russell A. *Taking Charge of ADHD* — 618.92
Baxley, Traci. *Social Justice Parenting* — 649
Brickman, Sophie. *Baby, Unplugged* — 306.874
Brown, Emma. *To Raise a Boy* — 649
Dubin, Minna. ★*Mom Rage* — 306.874
Emswiler, Mary Ann. *Guiding Your Child Through Grief* — 155.9
Ezzo, Gary. *On Becoming Baby Wise* — 649
Farris, Grace. *Mom Milestones* — 306.87
Gopnik, Alison. *The Gardener and the Carpenter* — 155.4
Haelle, Tara. *The Informed Parent* — 649
Hawthorne, Britt. ★*Raising Antiracist Children* — 649
Hillsberg, Christina. *License to Parent* — 649.1
Klein, Tovah P. *How Toddlers Thrive* — 305.232
Kurcinka, Mary Sheedy. *Raising Your Spirited Baby* — 306.874
Lahey, Jessica. *The Addiction Inoculation* — 649
Lahey, Jessica. *The Gift of Failure* — 649
Levine, Madeline. ★*Ready or Not* — 649
Morin, Amy. *13 Things Mentally Strong Parents Don't Do* — 649
Murkoff, Heidi Eisenberg. *What to Expect the First Year* — 305.232
Murkoff, Heidi Eisenberg. ★*What to Expect the Second Year* — 649
Natterson, Cara Familian. ★*Decoding Boys* — 649
Nowicki, Stephen. *Raising a Socially Successful Child* — 649
Phelan, Thomas W. *1-2-3 Magic* — 649
Pressman, Aliza. *The 5 Principles of Parenting* — 649.1
Pritchett, Georgia. *My Mess Is a Bit of a Life* — B
Ramesh, Jaya. *Parenting at the Intersections* — 649
Rippon, Kelly. *Parent Up* — 649
Santomero, Angela C. *Preschool Clues* — 305.233
Seldin, Tim. *How to Raise an Amazing Child the Montessori Way* — 649
Siegel, Daniel J. ★*The Yes Brain* — 155.4
Stixrud, William R. *The Self-Driven Child* — 155.4

Traig, Jennifer. *Act Natural* — 306.874
Wegner, Bobbi. *Raising Feminist Boys* — 305.23
Whippman, Ruth. ★*Boymom* — 305.23

CHILD REFUGEES
Eire, Carlos M. N. *Learning to Die in Miami* — B
Mufleh, Luma. ★*Learning America* — 371.826
Nayeri, Dina. ★*The Ungrateful Refugee* — 362.87
Passarlay, Gulwali. *The Lightless Sky* — B
Paxson, Margaret. *The Plateau* — 362.87
St. John, Warren. *Outcasts United* — B

CHILD SAFETY
Shaughnessy, Brenda. *The Octopus Museum* — 811

CHILD SEXUAL ABUSE
Barr, John. *Start by Believing* — 364.15
Bass, Ellen. ★*The Courage to Heal* — 616.85
Casillo, Charles. *Marilyn Monroe* — B
Jones, Faith. *Sex Cult Nun* — B
Kouchner, Camille. *The Familia Grande* — B
Mills, Stephen Tukel. *Chosen* — B
Porter, Billy. ★*Unprotected* — B
Shanley, John Patrick. *Doubt* — 812

CHILD SEXUAL ABUSE INVESTIGATION
Rabinowitz, Dorothy. *No Crueler Tyrannies* — 345.73

CHILD SEXUAL ABUSERS
Barr, John. *Start by Believing* — 364.15
Bowden, Mark. *The Last Stone* — 363.25

CHILD SOLDIERS
Aleksievich, Svetlana. *Last Witnesses* — 940.53
Beah, Ishmael. ★*A Long Way Gone* — B
Lockley, Thomas. *African Samurai* — B
Mohan, Rohini. *The Seasons of Trouble* — 954.9303

CHILD WAR VICTIMS
Aleksievich, Svetlana. *Last Witnesses* — 940.53

CHILD WELFARE
Asgarian, Roxanna. *We Were Once a Family* — 364.152
Benforado, Adam. *A Minor Revolution* — 362.7
Clinton, Hillary Rodham. *It Takes a Village* — 305.23
Daley, Mark. *Safe* — B
Jaffe, Sarah W. *Wanting What's Best* — 649
Kamenetz, Anya. *The Stolen Year* — 306.43
Kozol, Jonathan. *Fire in the Ashes* — 362.77
Linn, Susan. *Who's Raising the Kids?* — 649
Madrick, Jeffrey G. *Invisible Americans* — 362.7086
Moody, Anne. *The Children Money Can Buy* — 362.73
Pryce, Jessica. ★*Broken* — 362.7
Roberts, Dorothy E. *Torn Apart* — 362.7

CHILD WITNESSES
Aleksievich, Svetlana. *Last Witnesses* — 940.53
Rabinowitz, Dorothy. *No Crueler Tyrannies* — 345.73
A Child's Christmas in Wales. Thomas, Dylan — B

Child, Julia
Julia and Jacques Cooking at Home — 641.594
★*Mastering the Art of French Cooking* — 641.594
★*My Life in France* — B
★*The Way to Cook* — 641.5

CHILD, JULIA
Child, Julia. *Julia and Jacques Cooking at Home* — 641.594
Child, Julia. ★*My Life in France* — B
Conant, Jennet. *The Lotus Eaters* — 940.54
Powell, Julie. *Julie and Julia* — 641.5
Prud'homme, Alex. *The French Chef in America* — B
Sen, Mayukh. *Taste Makers* — 641.5092
Spitz, Bob. ★*Dearie* — B

CHILD, PAUL, 1902-1994
Conant, Jennet. *The Lotus Eaters* — 940.54

CHILD-FREE LIFESTYLE
Blackstone, Amy. *Childfree by Choice* — 306.874

CHILD-SEPARATED FATHERS
Taraborrelli, J. Randy. ★*The Secret Life of Marilyn Monroe* — B

CHILD-SEPARATED MOTHERS
Glaser, Gabrielle. *American Baby* — B

CHILDBIRTH
Addario, Lynsey. *Of Love & War* — 779
Bhattacharya, Shaoni. *The Baby Book* — 649.1
Brown, Tina. ★*The Palace Papers* — 920
Farris, Grace. *Mom Milestones* — 306.87
Fisher, Susan J. *Taking Charge of Your Pregnancy* — 618.2
Harshe, January. *Birth Without Fear* — 618.2

PUBLIC LIBRARY CORE COLLECTION: NONFICTION
Twentieth Edition

Jones, Lucy. ★*Matrescence*	306.874
Millwood, Molly. *To Have and to Hold*	306.874
Murkoff, Heidi Eisenberg. ★*What to Expect When You're Expecting*	618.2
Nilsson, Lennart. *A Child Is Born*	612.6
Somerstein, Rachel. ★*Invisible Labor*	618.8
Wade, Sabia. *Birthing Liberation*	363.96

Childers, Thomas
The Third Reich	943.086

***Childfree* by Choice.** Blackstone, Amy 306.874

CHILDHOOD
Albright, Madeleine Korbel. *Prague Winter*	943.71
Archibald, John. *Shaking the Gates of Hell*	B
B., David. *Epileptic*	741.5
Barra, Allen. ★*The Last Coach*	B
Bilton, Chrysta. *Normal Family*	B
Blom, Onno. *Young Rembrandt*	B
Blumenthal, Sidney. *A Self-Made Man*	B
Bossiere, Zoe. *Cactus Country*	306
Broome, Brian. ★*Punch Me up to the Gods*	B
Calcaterra, Regina. *Etched in Sand*	B
Calcaterra, Regina. *Girl Unbroken*	B
Carlile, Brandi. *Broken Horses*	B
Carriere, Alice. *Everything/Nothing/Someone*	B
Chabon, Michael. *Pops*	306.874
Chaudry, Rabia. *Fatty Fatty Boom Boom*	B
Chude-Sokei, Louis Onuorah. *Floating in a Most Peculiar Way*	979.4
Common. *One Day It'll All Make Sense*	B
Davis, Geena. *Dying of Politeness*	B
Devantez, Chelsea. ★*I Shouldn't Be Telling You This*	B
Dillard, Annie. *An American Childhood*	B
Doty, Cate. *Mergers and Acquisitions*	395.2
Dunne, Griffin. ★*The Friday Afternoon Club*	B
Felix, Camonghne. *Dyscalculia*	B
Findakly, Brigitte. *Poppies of Iraq*	741.5
Foxx, Jamie. *Act Like You Got Some Sense*	B
Fuller, Alexandra. *Don't Let's Go to the Dogs Tonight*	B
Garcia, Angela. ★*The Way That Leads Among the Lost*	362.29
Geller, Danielle. *Dog Flowers*	B
Giovanni, Nikki. *Make Me Rain*	811
Goetsch, Diana. *This Body I Wore*	B
Goldberg, Whoopi. *Bits and Pieces*	B
Gulman, Gary. *Misfit*	B
Hartigan, Patti. *August Wilson*	B
Heaney, Seamus. *District and Circle*	821
Hensley, William L. Iggiagruk. *Fifty Miles from Tomorrow*	B
Hickam, Homer H. ★*Rocket Boys*	B
Hill, DaMaris B. *Breath Better Spent*	811
Hill, Jemele. *Uphill*	B
Hough, Lauren. *Leaving Isn't the Hardest Thing*	B
Hudes, Quiara Alegria. ★*My Broken Language*	B
Jackson, Bruce. *Never Far from Home*	B
Johnson, Katherine G. *My Remarkable Journey*	B
Kelly, Donika. *The Renunciations*	811
Lewis, Jenifer. *Walking in My Joy*	B
Macdonald, Helen. ★*Vesper Flights*	508
Mans, Jasmine. *Black Girl, Call Home*	811
McCourt, Frank. ★*Angela's Ashes*	929
Messud, Claire. *Kant's Little Prussian Head and Other Reasons Why I Write*	B
Mills, Hayley. *Forever Young*	B
Mouton, Deborah D. E. E. P. *Black Chameleon*	B
Mowat, Farley. *Born Naked*	B
O'Connor, Sinead. ★*Rememberings*	B
Oluseyi, Hakeem M. *A Quantum Life*	B
Owusu, Nadia. *Aftershocks*	B
Patchett, Ann. *This Is the Story of a Happy Marriage*	B
Rainbow, Randy. *Playing with Myself*	B
RuPaul. ★*The House of Hidden Meanings*	B
Sattouf, Riad. *The Arab of the Future*	741.5
Scheer, Paul. *Joyful Recollections of Trauma*	B
Sedaris, David. ★*The Best of Me*	818
Shankar, Shalini. *Beeline*	155.4
Shatner, William. *Live Long And—*	B
Sinclair, Safiya. ★*How to Say Babylon*	B
Smith, Clint. ★*Above Ground*	811
Szczeszak-Brewer, Agata. *The Hunger Book*	B
Taylor, Goldie. *The Love You Save*	B
Tran, Ly. *House of Sticks*	B

Tumulty, Karen. *The Triumph of Nancy Reagan*	B
Tur, Katy. *Rough Draft*	B
Wariner, Ruth. *The Sound of Gravel*	B
Williams, Lucinda. *Don't Tell Anybody the Secrets I Told You*	B
Williams, Zach. *Rescue Story*	B
Winfrey, Oprah. *What Happened to You?*	616.85
Wong, Jane. ★*Meet Me Tonight in Atlantic City*	B
Wu, Constance. *Making a Scene*	B

CHILDHOOD FRIENDS
Baker, Billy. *We Need to Hang Out*	177
Potts, Monica. *The Forgotten Girls*	B

CHILDHOOD INNOCENCE (CONCEPT)
Sattouf, Riad. *The Arab of the Future 2*	741.5

***Childhood* Leukemia.** Keene, Nancy 618.92

CHILDLESSNESS
Blackstone, Amy. *Childfree by Choice*	306.874
O'Donnell Heffington, Peggy. *Without Children*	306.85

CHILDREN
Aleksievich, Svetlana. *Last Witnesses*	940.53
Amer, Lindz. *Rainbow Parenting*	649
Arment, Ainsley. *The Wild + Free Family*	649
Brown, Noah. *Reading Together*	028.5
Cadbury, Deborah. *The School That Escaped from the Nazis*	940.53
Chiger, Krystyna. *The Girl in the Green Sweater*	B
Christakis, Erika. *The Importance of Being Little*	372.21
Cox, Marge. *Kids' Books and Maker Activities*	372.41
Dorr, Christina H. ★*Profiles in Resilience*	028.5
Doyne, Maggie. *Between the Mountain and the Sky*	B
Edelman, Marian Wright. *Lanterns*	362.7
Fletcher, Susan A. *Exploring the History of Childhood and Play Through 50 Historic Treasures*	790
Goyal, Nikhil. ★*Live to See the Day*	305.5
Hendrickson, Debra. ★*The Air They Breathe*	363.7
Hillsberg, Christina. *License to Parent*	649.1
Hirsch, Edward. *Gabriel*	811
Ho, Oliver. *The Ultimate Book of Family Card Games*	795.4
Kamenetz, Anya. *The Stolen Year*	306.43
Kamp, David. *Sunny Days*	791.4502
Klass, Perri. *A Good Time to Be Born*	362.19892
Kobliner, Beth. *Make Your Kid a Money Genius (even If You're Not)*	332.024
Kozol, Jonathan. *Fire in the Ashes*	362.77
Kraus, Dita. *A Delayed Life*	B
Lahey, Jessica. *The Addiction Inoculation*	649
Lee, Jennifer Tyler. *Half the Sugar, All the Love*	641.5
Lieber, Ron. *The Opposite of Spoiled*	332.0240083
Manglik, Gauri. *Muslims in Story*	809
Mazzeo, Tilar J. *Irena's Children*	B
McCarthy, Catherine. *Raising a Kid Who Can*	649
Mead, Margaret. *Coming of Age in Samoa*	306
Nowicki, Stephen. *Raising a Socially Successful Child*	649
Oelhafen, Ingrid von. *Hitler's Stolen Children*	B
Paul, Pamela. ★*How to Raise a Reader*	649
Porto, Anthony. *The Pediatrician's Guide to Feeding Babies & Toddlers*	618.92
Pulde, Alona. *Forks Over Knives Family*	641.5
Smart, Maya Payne. *Reading for Our Lives*	372.4
St. John, Warren. *Outcasts United*	B
Van Es, Bart. *The Cut Out Girl*	B
Zambreno, Kate. *The Light Room*	B

★*The* **Children.** Halberstam, David 323.1

CHILDREN AND ADULTS
Kline, Emily. ★*The School of Hard Talks*	155.5

CHILDREN AND DEATH
Emswiler, Mary Ann. *Guiding Your Child Through Grief*	155.9

CHILDREN AND MUSIC
Koenig, Joan. *The Musical Child*	780.71
Tunstall, Tricia. *Changing Lives*	780.71

CHILDREN AND SPORTS
Samaha, Albert. *Never Ran, Never Will*	920

CHILDREN AND WAR
Aleksievich, Svetlana. *Last Witnesses*	940.53
Katin, Miriam. *We Are on Our Own*	741.5
Satrapi, Marjane. ★*The Complete Persepolis*	741.5
Thi, Kim Phuc Phan. *Fire Road*	B

CHILDREN IN COMAS
Didion, Joan. ★*The Year of Magical Thinking*	B

The **Children** *Money Can Buy.* Moody, Anne 362.73

AUTHOR, TITLE, SERIES AND SUBJECT INDEX

CHILDREN OF ABUSED WOMEN
    Trethewey, Natasha D. ★*Memorial Drive* — B
CHILDREN OF AGING PARENTS
    Berg, Elizabeth. *I'll Be Seeing You* — 306.874
    Chast, Roz. ★*Can't We Talk About Something More Pleasant?* — 741.5
CHILDREN OF ALCOHOLIC MOTHERS
    Kang, Mia. *Knockout* — B
    Williams, Patricia. *Rabbit* — B
CHILDREN OF ALCOHOLICS
    Alexie, Sherman. *You Don't Have to Say You Love Me* — 818
    Danler, Stephanie. *Stray* — B
    Madden, T Kira. *Long Live the Tribe of Fatherless Girls* — 814
    McCourt, Frank. ★*Angela's Ashes* — 929
    Walls, Jeannette. ★*The Glass Castle* — B
★*Children of Ash and Elm*. Price, Neil S. — 948
CHILDREN OF CELEBRITIES
    Pentland, Jenny. *This Will Be Funny Later* — B
    Sagan, Sasha. *For Small Creatures Such as We* — 390.09
CHILDREN OF CLERGY
    Archibald, John. *Shaking the Gates of Hell* — B
    Ward, Geoffrey C. *A Disposition to Be Rich* — B
    Ward, Jon. *Testimony* — 277.308
CHILDREN OF CRIMINALS
    Wetherall, Tyler. *No Way Home* — B
CHILDREN OF DIVORCED PARENTS
    Bechdel, Alison. ★*Fun Home* — 741.5
    Blackstone-Ford, Jann. *Co-Parenting Through Separation and Divorce* — 306.89
    Danler, Stephanie. *Stray* — B
    Driver, Minnie. *Managing Expectations* — B
    May, Meredith. *The Honey Bus* — B
CHILDREN OF DRUG ABUSERS
    Danler, Stephanie. *Stray* — B
    Murray, Liz. *Breaking Night* — B
    Thomas, Joseph Earl. *Sink* — B
Children of Dust. Eteraz, Ali — B
CHILDREN OF ENSLAVED PEOPLE
    Hall, Rebecca. ★*Wake* — 741.5
CHILDREN OF FARMERS
    Phelan, Tom. *We Were Rich and We Didn't Know It* — B
CHILDREN OF HEADS OF STATE
    Sullivan, Rosemary. *Stalin's Daughter* — B
The Children of Henry VIII. Weir, Alison — B
CHILDREN OF HOLOCAUST SURVIVORS
    Finkelstein, Daniel. *Two Roads Home* — 920
    Foer, Esther Safran. *I Want You to Know We're Still Here* — B
    Fremont, Helen. *The Escape Artist* — B
    Spiegelman, Art. ★*Maus* — 741.5
CHILDREN OF IMMIGRANTS
    Ali, Wajahat. *Go Back to Where You Came From* — B
    Alvarez, Noe. *Spirit Run* — 796.42
    Cailan, Alvin. *Amboy* — 641.595
    Campoverdi, Alejandra. *First Gen* — B
    Gupta, Prachi. ★*They Called Us Exceptional* — B
    Henderson, Bruce B. *Bridge to the Sun* — 940.53
    Hong, Cathy Park. *Minor Feelings* — 305.48
    Hsu, Hua. ★*Stay True* — B
    Kalb, Bess. ★*Nobody Will Tell You This but Me* — 306.874
    Koh, EJ. *The Magical Language of Others* — 813
    Lang, Maya. *What We Carry* — B
    Lee, Julia Sun-Joo. *Biting the Hand* — B
    Lieu, Susan. ★*The Manicurist's Daughter* — B
    Peterson, Marlon. *Bird Uncaged* — B
    Ribowsky, Mark. *Shula* — B
    Sanchez, Erika L. *Crying in the Bathroom* — B
    Sarsour, Linda. *We Are Not Here to Be Bystanders* — B
    Shih, David. *Chinese Prodigal* — B
    Soboroff, Jacob. ★*Separated* — 325.73
    Sun, Carrie. *Private Equity* — B
    Wang, Connie. *Oh My Mother!* — B
    Wong, Carmen Rita. *Why Didn't You Tell Me?* — B
CHILDREN OF LGBTQIA+ PARENTS
    Bilton, Chrysta. *Normal Family* — B
CHILDREN OF MISSIONARIES
    Irving, Apricot Anderson. *The Gospel of Trees* — B
CHILDREN OF MURDER VICTIMS
    Caruana Galizia, Paul. ★*A Death in Malta* — 364.15
    Ervin, Kristine S. *Rabbit Heart* — 364.152

    Shehadeh, Raja. ★*We Could Have Been Friends, My Father and I* — B
    Steinberg, Jonny. *A Man of Good Hope* — B
CHILDREN OF MUSICIANS
    Villarreal, Vanessa Anglica. *Magical/Realism* — 814
The Children of Nazis. Crasnianski, Tania — 943.086
CHILDREN OF NAZIS
    Crasnianski, Tania. *The Children of Nazis* — 943.086
CHILDREN OF PEOPLE WITH MENTAL ILLNESSES
    Cho, Grace M. *Tastes Like War* — 305.48
    May, Meredith. *The Honey Bus* — B
CHILDREN OF POLITICIANS
    Buhle, Kathleen. *If We Break* — B
    Katz, Catherine Grace. *The Daughters of Yalta* — 920
    Taraborrelli, J. Randy. *The Kennedy Heirs* — 920
CHILDREN OF PRESIDENTS
    Andersen, Christopher P. *The Good Son* — B
    Brower, Kate Andersen. *The Residence* — 975.3
    Cordery, Stacy A. *Alice* — B
    Gillon, Steven M. *America's Reluctant Prince* — 649
    Good, Cassandra A. *First Family* — 920
    Peyser, Marc N. *Hissing Cousins* — B
CHILDREN OF PRISONERS
    Ford, Ashley C. ★*Somebody's Daughter* — B
The Children of Sanchez. Lewis, Oscar — 306.85
CHILDREN OF SINGLE PARENTS
    Laymon, Kiese. ★*Heavy* — B
    Tubbs, Michael. *The Deeper the Roots* — B
    Ward, Jesmyn. ★*Men We Reaped* — B
CHILDREN OF SPERM DONORS
    Bilton, Chrysta. *Normal Family* — B
    Shapiro, Dani. ★*Inheritance* — B
Children of the Land. Hernandez Castillo, Marcelo — B
Children of the State. Hobbs, Jeff — 364.36
Children of the Stone. Tolan, Sandy — 780
CHILDREN OF UNDOCUMENTED IMMIGRANTS
    Cornejo Villavicencio, Karla. ★*The Undocumented Americans* — 920
Children Under Fire. Cox, John Woodrow — 371.7
CHILDREN WHO ARE DEAF
    Marschark, Marc. ★*How Deaf Children Learn* — 371.91
CHILDREN WHO ARE HYPERACTIVE
    Scheeres, Julia. *Jesus Land* — B
CHILDREN WITH ADHD
    Nigg, Joel T. *Getting Ahead of ADHD* — 618.92
    Ramesh, Jaya. *Parenting at the Intersections* — 649
    Saline, Sharon. *What Your ADHD Child Wishes You Knew* — 618.92
CHILDREN WITH CANCER
    Townsend, Alan R. ★*This Ordinary Stardust* — B
CHILDREN WITH DEVELOPMENTAL DISABILITIES
    Fradin, Kelly. *Advanced Parenting* — 649
    Ramesh, Jaya. *Parenting at the Intersections* — 649
CHILDREN WITH DISABILITIES
    Anderson, Amelia. *Library Programming for Autistic Children and Teens* — 027.6
    Bond, Melissa. *Blood Orange Night* — 616.8
    Fradin, Kelly. *Advanced Parenting* — 649
    Marcus, Amy Dockser. *We the Scientists* — 618.92
    Solomon, Andrew. *Far from the Tree* — 362.4083
CHILDREN WITH DYSLEXIA
    Winkler, Henry. ★*Being Henry* — B
CHILDREN WITH EMOTIONAL ILLNESSES
    Fradin, Kelly. *Advanced Parenting* — 649
CHILDREN WITH EPILEPSY
    B., David. *Epileptic* — 741.5
    Fadiman, Anne. *The Spirit Catches You and You Fall Down* — 306.4
CHILDREN WITH LEARNING DISABILITIES
    Flink, David. *Thinking Differently* — 371.9
    Fradin, Kelly. *Advanced Parenting* — 649
    Mooney, Jonathan. *Normal Sucks* — B
CHILDREN WITH MENTAL ILLNESSES
    Haidt, Jonathan. ★*The Anxious Generation* — 305.23
CHILDREN WITH TERMINAL ILLNESSES
    Albom, Mitch. *Finding Chika* — B
The Children's Blizzard. Laskin, David — 977
CHILDREN'S BOOK ILLUSTRATORS
    Cott, Jonathan. *There's a Mystery There* — 813
    Jones, Brian Jay. ★*Becoming Dr. Seuss* — B
    Marcus, Leonard S. ★*Pictured Worlds* — 741.6

PUBLIC LIBRARY CORE COLLECTION: NONFICTION
Twentieth Edition

CHILDREN'S CLOTHING
    Yaker, Rebecca. *Little One-Yard Wonders* — 646.2

CHILDREN'S LIBRARIES
    Bratt, Jessica Anne. *Let's Talk About Race in Storytimes* — 027.62
    Del Negro, Janice. *Folktales Aloud* — 027.62
    Ghoting, Saroj Nadkarni. *Step into Storytime* — 027.62
    Knoll, Debra J. *Engaging Babies in the Library* — 027.62
    Maxwell, Lucas. *Podcasting with Youth* — 006.7
    Reid, Rob. ★*200+ Original and Adapted Story Program Activities* — 027.62

CHILDREN'S LIBRARY SERVICES
    Bratt, Jessica Anne. *Let's Talk About Race in Storytimes* — 027.62
    Breitenbach, Kathleen. ★*LGBTQIA+ Books for Children and Teens* — 028.7

CHILDREN'S LITERATURE AUTHORS
    Andersen, Jens. *Astrid Lindgren* — B
    Cott, Jonathan. *There's a Mystery There* — 813
    Dennison, Matthew. *The Man in the Willows* — B
    Gary, Amy. *In the Great Green Room* — 813
    Handler, Daniel. ★*And Then? and Then? What Else?* — 813
    Jones, Brian Jay. ★*Becoming Dr. Seuss* — B
    Lear, Linda J. *Beatrix Potter* — B

CHILDREN'S LITERATURE WRITING
    Cott, Jonathan. *There's a Mystery There* — 813
    Elledge, Scott. *E.B. White* — B
    Gary, Amy. *In the Great Green Room* — 813
    Jones, Brian Jay. ★*Becoming Dr. Seuss* — B
    Klein, Cheryl B. *The Magic Words* — 808.06
    Lear, Linda J. *Beatrix Potter* — B
    Manglik, Gauri. ★*Muslims in Story* — 809
    Wilder, Laura Ingalls. *Pioneer Girl* — B

CHILDREN'S RIGHTS
    Benforado, Adam. *A Minor Revolution* — 362.7
    Kozol, Jonathan. ★*An End to Inequality* — 379.2
    Yousafzai, Malala. *I Am Malala* — B

CHILDREN'S TELEVISION PERSONALITIES
    King, Maxwell. *The Good Neighbor* — B

Childs, Craig
    Atlas of a Lost World — 551.7
    House of Rain — 978.9

CHILE
    Allende, Isabel. *My Invented Country* — B
    Allende, Isabel. ★*Paula* — B
    Feinstein, Adam. *Pablo Neruda* — B

CHILE PEPPERS
    Frank, Lois Ellen. *Seed to Plate, Soil to Sky* — 641.5
    Kang, Mingoo. *Jang* — 641.595

CHILEAN PEOPLE
    Allende, Isabel. *My Invented Country* — B
    Allende, Isabel. ★*Paula* — B
    Allende, Isabel. *The Sum of Our Days* — B
    Feinstein, Adam. *Pablo Neruda* — B

CHILEAN POETRY
    Neruda, Pablo. *All the Odes* — 861
    Neruda, Pablo. *Then Come Back* — 861
    Neruda, Pablo. ★*Twenty Love Poems and a Song of Despair* — 861
    Neruda, Pablo. *World's End* — 861

CHIMPANZEES
    Fouts, Roger. *Next of Kin* — 156
    Goodall, Jane. ★*Beyond Innocence* — B
    Goodall, Jane. ★*In the Shadow of Man* — 599.8
    Safina, Carl. ★*Becoming Wild* — 591.7
    Waal, F. B. M. de. *Our Inner Ape* — 156

Chin, Ava
    ★*Mott Street* — 974.7

Chin, Curtis
    Everything I Learned, I Learned in a Chinese Restaurant — B

CHIN, CURTIS
    Chin, Curtis. *Everything I Learned, I Learned in a Chinese Restaurant* — B

CHINA
    Ai, Weiwei. *Zodiac* — 741.5
    Alexander, Caroline. *Skies of Thunder* — 940.54
    Armstrong, Karen. ★*The Great Transformation* — 200.9
    Brands, H. W. *The General vs. the President* — 973.918092
    Chang, Jung. *Big Sister, Little Sister, Red Sister* — B
    Chang, Jung. *Empress Dowager Cixi* — B
    Chang, Jung. *Mao* — B
    Chang, Jung. ★*Wild Swans* — B
    Chang, Leslie T. *Factory Girls* — 331.4
    Chen, Da. *Colors of the Mountain* — 951.05
    Cheng, Nien. *Life and Death in Shanghai* — B
    Chin, Ava. ★*Mott Street* — 974.7
    Chu, Lenora. *Little Soldiers* — 370
    Croke, Vicki. *The Lady and the Panda* — 599.789
    Day, John D. *The Longevity Plan* — 612.6
    Demick, Barbara. *Eat the Buddha* — 951
    Dikotter, Frank. *China After Mao* — 951.05
    Dikotter, Frank. *The Cultural Revolution* — 951.056
    Dikotter, Frank. *Mao's Great Famine* — 951.05
    Gerth, Karl. *As China Goes, so Goes the World* — 339.4
    Guo, XIaolu. *Nine Continents* — B
    Haitiwaji, Gulbahar. *How I Survived a Chinese "Reeducation" Camp* — 305.8
    Hessler, Peter. *Oracle Bones* — 951
    Hessler, Peter. *Other Rivers* — 378.1
    Hoja, Gulchehra. *A Stone Is Most Precious Where It Belongs* — B
    Hulls, Tessa. ★*Feeding Ghosts* — 741.5
    Hvistendahl, Mara. ★*The Scientist and the Spy* — 364.16
    Izgil, Tahir Hamut. *Waiting to Be Arrested at Night* — B
    Johnson, Ian. *The Souls of China* — 200.951
    Juan, Li. *Winter Pasture* — 951.06
    Kan, Karoline. *Under Red Skies* — B
    Krakauer, Jon. ★*Into Thin Air* — 796.52
    Kurtz-Phelan, Daniel. *The China Mission* — 951.04
    Li, Zhuqing. *Daughters of the Flower Fragrant Garden* — 951.04
    Liao, Yiwu. *Bullets and Opium* — 951.05
    Lim, Louisa. *The People's Republic of Amnesia* — 951.05
    Lovell, Julia. *Maoism* — 335.43
    Macy, Beth. ★*Factory Man* — 338.7
    Mahtani, Shibani. *Among the Braves* — 951.25
    Min, Anchee. *Red Azalea* — B
    Mitter, Rana. *Forgotten Ally* — 951.04
    Osnos, Evan. *Age of Ambition* — 951.06
    Pan, Philip P. *Out of Mao's Shadow* — 306.20951
    Pang, Amelia. ★*Made in China* — 331.11
    Pantsov, Alexander. *Mao* — B
    Platt, Stephen R. *Autumn in the Heavenly Kingdom* — 951
    Scharre, Paul. *Four Battlegrounds* — 006.3
    Schell, Orville. *Wealth and Power* — 920
    Schmitz, Rob. *Street of Eternal Happiness* — 951
    Schwartzel, Erich. *Red Carpet* — 791.43
    Spence, Jonathan D. *God's Chinese Son* — 951
    Strittmatter, Kai. *We Have Been Harmonized* — 323.44
    Theroux, Paul. *Riding the Iron Rooster* — 915
    Tsu, Jing. *Kingdom of Characters* — 495.111
    Tuchman, Barbara W. *Stilwell and the American Experience in China, 1911-45* — B
    Vogel, Ezra F. *Deng XIaoping and the Transformation of China* — B
    Walton, Calder. *Spies* — 327.1247
    Wang, Qian Julie. ★*Beautiful Country* — B
    Wong, Chun Han. *Party of One* — 951.06
    Wood, Michael. *The Story of China* — 951
    Xue, XInran. *The Book of Secrets* — 951.05
    Yang, Jisheng. *The World Turned Upside Down* — 951.05

China After Mao. Dikotter, Frank — 951.05
The China Mission. Kurtz-Phelan, Daniel — 951.04
The China Study. Campbell, T. Colin — 613.2
Chinaberry Sidewalks. Crowell, Rodney — B

CHINATOWN, NEW YORK CITY
    Chin, Ava. ★*Mott Street* — 974.7

CHINATOWN, SAN FRANCISCO, CALIFORNIA
    Ng, Fae Myenne. *Orphan Bachelors* — B

Chinen, Nate
    Playing Changes — 781.6509

CHINESE AMERICAN FAMILIES
    Chin, Ava. ★*Mott Street* — 974.7
    Chin, Curtis. *Everything I Learned, I Learned in a Chinese Restaurant* — B
    Chow, Kat. *Seeing Ghosts* — B
    Hulls, Tessa. ★*Feeding Ghosts* — 741.5
    Ng, Fae Myenne. *Orphan Bachelors* — B

CHINESE AMERICAN WOMEN
    Chow, Kat. *Seeing Ghosts* — B
    Li, Fei-Fei. *The Worlds I See* — B
    Qu, Anna. *Made in China* — B
    Sun, Carrie. *Private Equity* — B
    Wang, Qian Julie. ★*Beautiful Country* — B
    Wong, Jane. ★*Meet Me Tonight in Atlantic City* — B

CHINESE AMERICANS
    Chang, Gordon H. *Ghosts of Gold Mountain* — 331.6

AUTHOR, TITLE, SERIES AND SUBJECT INDEX

Chin, Ava. ★*Mott Street*	974.7
Chin, Curtis. *Everything I Learned, I Learned in a Chinese Restaurant*	B
Huang, Yunte. *Daughter of the Dragon*	B
Kingston, Maxine Hong. *The Woman Warrior*	B
Rekdal, Paisley. *West*	811
Salisbury, Katie Gee. ★*Not Your China Doll*	B
Shih, David. *Chinese Prodigal*	B
Wang, Qian Julie. ★*Beautiful Country*	B
Wong, Jane. ★*Meet Me Tonight in Atlantic City*	B
Chinese Art. Tregear, Mary	709.51
CHINESE AUSTRALIANS	
Zhu, Mimi. *Be Not Afraid of Love*	152.4
Chinese Brush Painting. Jung, Kwan	751.4
Chinese Brush Painting. Self, Caroline	751.4
CHINESE CHARACTERS	
Tsu, Jing. *Kingdom of Characters*	495.111
CHINESE CIVIL WAR, 1945-1949	
Kurtz-Phelan, Daniel. *The China Mission*	951.04
Li, Zhuqing. *Daughters of the Flower Fragrant Garden*	951.04
Zia, Helen. *Last Boat Out of Shanghai*	951.04
CHINESE CULTURAL REVOLUTION (1966-1976)	
Branigan, Tania. *Red Memory*	951.05
Chen, Da. *Colors of the Mountain*	951.05
Cheng, Nien. *Life and Death in Shanghai*	B
Dikotter, Frank. *The Cultural Revolution*	951.056
Min, Anchee. *Red Azalea*	B
Yang, Jisheng. *The World Turned Upside Down*	951.05
CHINESE HISTORY	
Ai, Weiwei. *1000 Years of Joys and Sorrows*	709.2
Armstrong, Karen. *The Great Transformation*	200.9
Branigan, Tania. *Red Memory*	951.05
Chang, Gordon H. *Ghosts of Gold Mountain*	331.6
Chang, Iris. ★*The Rape of Nanking*	951.04
Chang, Jung. *Big Sister, Little Sister, Red Sister*	B
Chang, Jung. *Empress Dowager Cixi*	B
Chang, Jung. *Mao*	B
Chen, Da. *Colors of the Mountain*	951.05
Cheng, Nien. *Life and Death in Shanghai*	B
Demick, Barbara. *Eat the Buddha*	951
Dikotter, Frank. *China After Mao*	951.05
Dikotter, Frank. *The Cultural Revolution*	951.056
Hulls, Tessa. ★*Feeding Ghosts*	741.5
Kaufman, Jonathan. *The Last Kings of Shanghai*	951
Liao, Yiwu. *Bullets and Opium*	951.05
Liao, Yiwu. *God Is Red*	275
Lim, Louisa. *The People's Republic of Amnesia*	951.05
Logevall, Fredrik. *Embers of War*	959.704
Lovell, Julia. *Maoism*	335.43
Min, Anchee. *Red Azalea*	B
Mitter, Rana. *Forgotten Ally*	951.04
Pakula, Hannah. *The Last Empress*	B
Pan, Philip P. *Out of Mao's Shadow*	306.20951
Platt, Stephen R. *Autumn in the Heavenly Kingdom*	951
Platt, Stephen R. *Imperial Twilight*	951
Schell, Orville. *Wealth and Power*	920
Spence, Jonathan D. *God's Chinese Son*	951
Spence, Jonathan D. *The Search for Modern China*	951
Taylor, Jay. *The Generalissimo*	B
Tsu, Jing. *Kingdom of Characters*	495.111
Tuchman, Barbara W. *Stilwell and the American Experience in China, 1911-45*	B
Wood, Michael. *The Story of China*	951
Yang, Jisheng. *The World Turned Upside Down*	951.05
Zia, Helen. *Last Boat Out of Shanghai*	951.04
CHINESE LANGUAGE	
Tsu, Jing. *Kingdom of Characters*	495.111
CHINESE PEOPLE	
Ai, Weiwei. *Zodiac*	741.5
Chang, Gordon H. *Ghosts of Gold Mountain*	331.6
Chin, Ava. ★*Mott Street*	974.7
Chin, Curtis. *Everything I Learned, I Learned in a Chinese Restaurant*	B
Chung, Vinh. *Where the Wind Leads*	B
Hoja, Gulchehra. *A Stone Is Most Precious Where It Belongs*	B
Hulls, Tessa. ★*Feeding Ghosts*	741.5
Hvistendahl, Mara. ★*The Scientist and the Spy*	364.16
Li, Fei-Fei. *The Worlds I See*	B
Ng, Fae Myenne. *Orphan Bachelors*	B
Qu, Anna. *Made in China*	B

Siler, Julia Flynn. *The White Devil's Daughters*	306.3
Sun, Carrie. *Private Equity*	B
CHINESE PEOPLE IN FOREIGN COUNTRIES	
Chung, Vinh. *Where the Wind Leads*	B
CHINESE PEOPLE IN THE UNITED STATES	
Chang, Gordon H. *Ghosts of Gold Mountain*	331.6
Chung, Vinh. *Where the Wind Leads*	B
Hvistendahl, Mara. ★*The Scientist and the Spy*	364.16
Qu, Anna. *Made in China*	B
Siler, Julia Flynn. *The White Devil's Daughters*	306.3
Chinese Prodigal. Shih, David	B
CHINESE RESTAURANTS	
Chin, Curtis. *Everything I Learned, I Learned in a Chinese Restaurant*	B
Chinese Soul Food. Chou, Hsiao-Ching	641.595
CHINESE WOMEN	
Chang, Jung. *Big Sister, Little Sister, Red Sister*	B
Chang, Jung. ★*Wild Swans*	B
Kan, Karoline. *Under Red Skies*	B
CHINESE ZODIAC	
Ai, Weiwei. *Zodiac*	741.5
Smith, Patti. ★*Year of the Monkey*	B
Ching, Francis D. K.	
★*A Global History of Architecture*	720.9
CHINN, MAY EDWARD, 1896-1980	
Brown, Jasmine. *Twice as Hard*	610.92
Chip War. Miller, Chris	338.4
Chisholm, Edward	
A Waiter in Paris	B
CHISHOLM, EDWARD	
Chisholm, Edward. *A Waiter in Paris*	B
Chittister, Joan	
Following the Path	248.4
The Gift of Years	200
The Monastic Heart	248.8
Chivers, C. J.	
The Fighters	920
Chloe Flavor. Coscarelli, Chloe	641.5
Cho, Grace M.	
Tastes Like War	305.48
CHO, GRACE M.	
Cho, Grace M. *Tastes Like War*	305.48
Cho, Kristina	
Mooncakes + Milk Bread	641.595
CHOCOLATE	
Almond, Steve. ★*Candyfreak*	338.4
CHOCOLATE CANDY	
Brenner, Joel Glenn. *The Emperors of Chocolate*	338.7
CHOCOLATE INDUSTRY AND TRADE	
Brenner, Joel Glenn. *The Emperors of Chocolate*	338.7
Chodron, Pema	
How We Live Is How We Die	294.3
Practicing Peace	294.3
Choi, Don Mee	
DMZ Colony	818
Hardly War	811
Choi, Franny	
The World Keeps Ending, and the World Goes On	811
The Choice. Eger, Edith Eva	B
CHOICE OF TRANSPORTATION	
Rosen, Jody. *Two Wheels Good*	629.227
The Choice Point. Grover, Joanna	158.1
Choice Theory. Glasser, William	150
Chokehold. Butler, Paul	363.2
CHOLERA	
Johnson, Steven. *The Ghost Map*	614.5
Chomsky, Noam	
Global Discontents	410.92
Who Rules the World?	327.73
CHOO, JIMMY, 1961-	
Crowe, Lauren Goldstein. *The Towering World of Jimmy Choo*	391.4
Choosing Family. Royster, Francesca T.	B
Choosing Hope. Roig-Debellis, Kaitlin	371.7
★*Chopin's Funeral*. Eisler, Benita	B
Chopin's Piano. Kildea, Paul Francis	B
CHOPIN, FREDERIC, 1810-1849	
Eisler, Benita. ★*Chopin's Funeral*	B
Kildea, Paul Francis. *Chopin's Piano*	B
Rusbridger, Alan. ★*Play It Again*	B

Chopra, Deepak
  Metahuman — 204

CHOREOGRAPHERS
  Brown, Carolyn. *Chance and Circumstance* — B
  Duncan, Isadora. *My Life* — B
  Gottlieb, Robert. *George Balanchine* — B
  Harss, Marina. *The Boy from Kyiv* — B
  Morris, Mark. *Out Loud* — B
  Teachout, Terry. ★*All in the Dances* — B

CHOREOGRAPHY
  Duncan, Isadora. *My Life* — B
  Jacobs, Laura. ★*Celestial Bodies* — 792.8
  Mordden, Ethan. *Anything Goes* — 782.1
  Morris, Mark. *Out Loud* — B

Chosen. Mills, Stephen Tukel — B
The Chosen Wars. Weisman, Steven R. — 296.0973

Chou, Hsiao-Ching
  Chinese Soul Food — 641.595

Chow, Kat
  Seeing Ghosts — B

CHOW, KAT
  Chow, Kat. *Seeing Ghosts* — B

Chown, Marcus
  Infinity in the Palm of Your Hand — 523.1

Choy, Catherine Ceniza
  ★*Asian American Histories of the United States* — 973

Chozick, Amy
  Chasing Hillary — B

Chrisinger, David
  The Soldier's Truth — 940.54

CHRISINGER, DAVID, 1986-
  Chrisinger, David. *The Soldier's Truth* — 940.54

Christakis, Erika
  The Importance of Being Little — 372.21

Christakis, Nicholas A.
  Apollo's Arrow — 362.1962

Christensen, Ashley
  It's Always Freezer Season — 641.5

Christensen, Jo Ippolito
  ★*The Needlepoint Book* — 746.44

CHRISTIAN AFRICAN AMERICANS
  Baraka, Sho. *He Saw That It Was Good* — 261.5

CHRISTIAN APOLOGETICS
  Armstrong, Karen. *The Case for God* — 211
  Augustine. *Concerning the City of God Against the Pagans* — 239
  Chaput, Charles J. *Things Worth Dying For* — 248.4
  Collins, Francis S. *The Language of God* — 215
  Keller, Timothy J. *The Reason for God* — 239
  Lewis, C. S. *Mere Christianity* — 230
  McLaren, Brian D. *Do I Stay Christian?* — 270.8

CHRISTIAN CHURCH AND RACE RELATIONS
  Archibald, John. *Shaking the Gates of Hell* — B
  Brennan, Chad. *Faithful Antiracism* — 277.308
  Jones, Robert P. *White Too Long* — 277

CHRISTIAN CHURCH RENEWAL
  Smietana, Bob. *Reorganized Religion* — 262.001

CHRISTIAN CHURCH WORK WITH POOR PEOPLE
  Vallely, Paul. *Pope Francis* — B

CHRISTIAN CHURCH WORK WITH PRISONERS
  McCloskey, Jim. *When Truth Is All You Have* — B

CHRISTIAN CONSERVATISM
  Griffith, R. Marie. *Moral Combat* — 261.8
  Ward, Jon. *Testimony* — 277.308

CHRISTIAN COUPLES
  Duggar, Jill. *Counting the Cost* — B

CHRISTIAN DOCTRINES
  Armstrong, Karen. *A History of God* — 202
  Bolz-Weber, Nadia. *Accidental Saints* — 284.1
  Douthat, Ross Gregory. *To Change the Church* — 230
  Eire, Carlos M. N. *A Very Brief History of Eternity* — 236
  Francis. *Walking with Jesus* — 282.09
  Griffin, Chante. *Loving Your Black Neighbor as Yourself* — 261
  Roberts, Matthias. *Holy Runaways* — 262
  Wills, Garry. *The Future of the Catholic Church with Pope Francis* — 282.09
  Wintz, Jack. *Will I See My Dog in Heaven?* — 231.7

CHRISTIAN EDUCATION
  Scheeres, Julia. *Jesus Land* — B

CHRISTIAN ETHICS
  Armstrong, Karen. *Twelve Steps to a Compassionate Life* — 177
  Lamott, Anne. ★*Hallelujah Anyway* — 241
  Lewis, C. S. *Mere Christianity* — 230
  Meyaard-Schaap, Kyle. *Following Jesus in a Warming World* — 241
  Price, Reynolds. *A Serious Way of Wondering* — 241

CHRISTIAN FAMILIES
  Findakly, Brigitte. *Poppies of Iraq* — 741.5
  Yancey, Philip. ★*Where the Light Fell* — B

CHRISTIAN FICTION
  Lewis, C. S. ★*The Screwtape Letters* — 248.4

CHRISTIAN GAY MEN AND LESBIANS
  Chu, Jeff. *Does Jesus Really Love Me?* — 261.8
  Thomas, R. Eric. *Here for It* — B

CHRISTIAN HERETICS
  Rounding, Virginia. *The Burning Time* — 272

CHRISTIAN HISTORY
  Barry, John M. *Roger Williams and the Creation of the American Soul* — 974.5
  Holifield, E. Brooks. *Theology in America* — 230
  Holland, Tom. *Dominion* — 261
  MacCulloch, Diarmaid. *Christianity* — 270
  MacCulloch, Diarmaid. *The Reformation* — 270.6

CHRISTIAN HUMANISM
  Massing, Michael. *Fatal Discord* — 920

CHRISTIAN LIFE
  Armstrong, Karen. *The Case for God* — 211
  Bailey, Jennifer. *To My Beloveds* — 261.8
  Baraka, Sho. *He Saw That It Was Good* — 261.5
  Batterson, Mark. *Please, Sorry, Thanks* — 179
  Beaty, Katelyn. *Celebrities for Jesus* — 261
  Beck, Amanda Martinez. *More of You* — 613
  Billings, J. Todd. *Rejoicing in Lament* — 248.8
  Bolz-Weber, Nadia. *Accidental Saints* — 284.1
  Boyle, Greg. *Tattoos on the Heart* — 277
  Bragg, Sarah. *Is Everyone Happier Than Me?* — 248.4
  Brennan, Chad. *Faithful Antiracism* — 277.308
  Cairns, Scott. *The End of Suffering* — 231
  Carter, Jimmy. *Sources of Strength* — 248.4
  Chaput, Charles J. *Things Worth Dying For* — 248.4
  Chittister, Joan. *Following the Path* — 248.4
  Darling, Daniel. *Agents of Grace* — 158.2
  DiFelice, Bekah. *Almost There* — 248.8
  Dilbeck, D. H. *Frederick Douglass* — B
  Evans, Jimmy. *Strengths Based Marriage* — 248.8
  Evans, Rachel Held. *Wholehearted Faith* — 248.4
  Francis. *Happiness in This Life* — 248.4
  Francis. *Let Us Dream* — 282.092
  Franklin, Missy. *Relentless Spirit* — B
  Gilliard, Dominique Dubois. *Rethinking Incarceration* — 261.8
  Girzone, Joseph F. *Never Alone* — 248.4
  Girzone, Joseph F. *A Portrait of Jesus* — 232.9
  Hatmaker, Jen. *Of Mess and Moxie* — 248.8
  Jakes, T. D. *Destiny* — 248.4
  Joyce, Russell W. *His Face Like Mine* — 248
  Karon, Jan. *Bathed in Prayer* — 242
  Lamott, Anne. ★*Dusk, Night, Dawn* — B
  Lamott, Anne. ★*Hallelujah Anyway* — 241
  Lamott, Anne. *Small Victories* — 248
  Lewis, C. S. *Letters to Malcolm* — 248.3
  Lucado, Max. *Before Amen* — 248.3
  Lucado, Max. *Unshakable Hope* — 248.4
  Lucado, Max. *You Are Never Alone* — 248.4
  Martin, James. *Learning to Pray* — 248.3
  McLaren, Brian D. *Faith After Doubt* — 234
  Meyer, Joyce. *Seize the Day* — 248.4
  Namath, Joe Willie. ★*All the Way* — B
  Orji, Yvonne. *Bamboozled by Jesus* — B
  Risner, Vaneetha Rendall. *Walking Through Fire* — B
  Rivera, Mariano. *The Closer* — B
  Rohr, Richard. *The Universal Christ* — 232
  Rowan, Barry L. *The Spiritual Art of Business* — 261.8
  Smietana, Bob. *Reorganized Religion* — 262.001
  Strobel, Lee. *The Case for Grace* — 234
  Villodas, Rich. *The Deeply Formed Life* — 248.4
  Villodas, Rich. *Good and Beautiful and Kind* — 232.9
  Williams, Zach. *Rescue Story* — B
  Winkler, Kyle. *Permission to Be Imperfect* — 170
  Yancey, Philip. ★*Where the Light Fell* — B

AUTHOR, TITLE, SERIES AND SUBJECT INDEX

CHRISTIAN MARRIAGE
   Evans, Jimmy. *Strengths Based Marriage* — 248.8
CHRISTIAN MARTYRS
   Marsh, Charles. *Strange Glory* — B
   Rounding, Virginia. *The Burning Time* — 272
CHRISTIAN MEN
   Boyle, Greg. *Tattoos on the Heart* — 277
   Hartke, Austen. *Transforming* — 277
   Lecrae. ★*I Am Restored* — B
   Moby. *Porcelain* — B
   Ribowsky, Mark. *The Last Cowboy* — 796.332
   Rivera, Mariano. *The Closer* — B
   Ward, Jon. *Testimony* — 277.308
CHRISTIAN MISSIONARIES
   Carranca, Adriana. *Soul by Soul* — 230
   Hamilton, Duncan. *For the Glory* — B
CHRISTIAN MISSIONS
   Hamilton, Duncan. *For the Glory* — B
CHRISTIAN PHILOSOPHY
   Massing, Michael. *Fatal Discord* — 920
   Teilhard de Chardin, Pierre. ★*The Divine Milieu* — 233
CHRISTIAN SAINTS
   Augustine. *Confessions* — B
   Barthel, Joan. *American Saint* — B
   Butcher, Carmen Acevedo. *Man of Blessing* — B
   Farmer, David Hugh. *The Oxford Dictionary of Saints* — 270
   Martin, Valerie. *Salvation* — B
   Wills, Garry. *Saint Augustine* — B
   Woodward, Kenneth L. *Making Saints* — 235.24
CHRISTIAN SCIENCE
   Nesmith, Michael. *Infinite Tuesday* — B
CHRISTIAN SCIENTISTS
   Eddy, Mary Baker. ★*Mary Baker Eddy* — 289.5
   Nesmith, Michael. *Infinite Tuesday* — B
CHRISTIAN SECTS
   Jones, Faith. *Sex Cult Nun* — B
   McGuckin, John Anthony. ★*The Eastern Orthodox Church* — 281.909
   Olson, Roger E. ★*Handbook of Denominations in the United States* — 200.973
CHRISTIAN THEOLOGIANS
   Barry, John M. *Roger Williams and the Creation of the American Soul* — 974.5
CHRISTIAN VALUES
   Bolz-Weber, Nadia. *Accidental Saints* — 284.1
   Smith, James K. A. *How to Inhabit Time* — 223
CHRISTIAN WOMEN
   Armas, Kat. *Abuelita Faith* — 248.8
   Brownback, Lydia. *Finding God in My Loneliness* — 248.8
   Castor, Helen. *Joan of Arc* — B
   Davis, Jennifer Pharr. *Called Again* — B
   Dokun, Chanel. *Life Starts Now* — 248.8
   Downey, Kirstin. *Isabella* — B
   Doyle, Glennon. *Untamed* — B
   Evans, Rachel Held. *Wholehearted Faith* — 248.4
   Goudeau, Jessica. ★*After the Last Border* — 362.83
   Guthrie, Savannah. *Mostly What God Does* — 248.4
   Henny, Ally. *I Won't Shut Up* — 305.896
   Jun, Tasha. ★*Tell Me the Dream Again* — 248
   King, Coretta Scott. ★*My Life, My Love, My Legacy* — B
   Loftis, Larry. ★*The Watchmaker's Daughter* — 940.53
   Mojica Rodriguez, Prisca Dorcas. *For Brown Girls with Sharp Edges and Tender Hearts* — 305.48
   Moore, Beth. *All My Knotted-Up Life* — B
   Nockels, Christy. *The Life You Long For* — 248.8
   Orji, Yvonne. *Bamboozled by Jesus* — B
   Rush, Charaia. *Courageously Soft* — 234
   Vaughn, Ellen Santilli. ★*Becoming Elisabeth Elliot* — B
   West, Cait. ★*Rift* — B
CHRISTIAN WRITING
   Merton, Thomas. ★*The Seven Storey Mountain* — B
Christian, Brian
   Algorithms to Live By — 153.4
Christian, Carol
   A Question and Answer Guide to Astronomy — 520
Christian, David
   Origin Story — 909
CHRISTIAN, FLETCHER, 1764-1793
   Alexander, Caroline. *The Bounty* — 996.1
Christiana, Asa
   Build Stuff with Wood — 684

Christianity. MacCulloch, Diarmaid — 270
CHRISTIANITY
   Akyol, Mustafa. *The Islamic Jesus* — 297.2
   Alberta, Tim. *The Kingdom, the Power, and the Glory* — 270.8
   Armstrong, Karen. *The Battle for God* — 200
   Armstrong, Karen. *A History of God* — 202
   Armstrong, Karen. *Jerusalem* — 956.94
   Armstrong, Karen. *Twelve Steps to a Compassionate Life* — 177
   Asbridge, Thomas S. ★*The Crusades* — 909.07
   Augustine. *Confessions* — B
   Baraka, Sho. *He Saw That It Was Good* — 261.5
   Barton, John. *A History of the Bible* — 220.09
   Becker, Joshua. *The Minimalist Home* — 241
   Becker, Joshua. *The More of Less* — 241
   Belser, Julia Watts. ★*Loving Our Own Bones* — 296
   Billings, J. Todd. *Rejoicing in Lament* — 248.8
   Blum, Edward J. *The Color of Christ* — 232
   Brennan, Chad. *Faithful Antiracism* — 277.308
   Briggs, Lyvonne. ★*Sensual Faith* — 204
   Brownback, Lydia. *Finding God in My Loneliness* — 248.8
   Cairns, Scott. *The End of Suffering* — 231
   Carlisle, Clare. *Philosopher of the Heart* — B
   Carter, Jimmy. *Faith* — OK T A
   Chapman, Gary D. *Love as a Way of Life* — 241
   Chaput, Charles J. *Things Worth Dying For* — 248.4
   Chittister, Joan. *The Gift of Years* — 200
   Chu, Jeff. *Does Jesus Really Love Me?* — 261.8
   Cliff, Nigel. *Holy War* — 909
   Curry, Michael B. *Love Is the Way* — 241
   Dante Alighieri. *The Paradiso* — 851
   Dokun, Chanel. *Life Starts Now* — 248.8
   Edman, Elizabeth M. *Queer Virtue* — 230
   Ehrman, Bart D. ★*Armageddon* — 236
   Ehrman, Bart D. *The Triumph of Christianity* — 270.1
   Eire, Carlos M. N. *A Very Brief History of Eternity* — 236
   Evans, Jimmy. *Strengths Based Marriage* — 248.8
   Evans, Rachel Held. *Wholehearted Faith* — 248.4
   Francis. *Happiness in This Life* — 248.4
   Francis. *Life* — B
   Francois, Willie Dwayne. *Silencing White Noise* — 277
   Frankopan, Peter. *The First Crusade* — 956
   Fredriksen, Paula. *Jesus of Nazareth, King of the Jews* — B
   Friedman, Benjamin M. *Religion and the Rise of Capitalism* — 330.12
   Fusco, Daniel. *Crazy Happy* — 248.4
   Garcia, Damon. *The God Who Riots* — 269
   Gates, Henry Louis. ★*The Black Church* — 277
   Girzone, Joseph F. *Never Alone* — 248.4
   Gonzalez, Karen. *Beyond Welcome* — 261.8
   Grieve, Paul. *A Brief Guide to Islam* — 297
   Griffin, Chante. *Loving Your Black Neighbor as Yourself* — 261
   Griswold, Eliza. *The Tenth Parallel* — 297.2
   Hardwick, Lamar. *How Ableism Fuels Racism* — 261.8
   Hartke, Austen. *Transforming* — 277
   Hirst, J. B. *The Shortest History of Europe* — 940
   Jones, Dan. *Crusaders* — 909.07
   Jones, Robert P. *The Hidden Roots of White Supremacy* — 305.8
   Jones, Robert P. *White Too Long* — 277
   Keller, Timothy J. *The Reason for God* — 239
   Kierkegaard, Soren. *Fear and Trembling* — 248
   Lambert, Malcolm. *God's Armies* — 956
   Lamott, Anne. *Small Victories* — 248
   Levine, Amy-Jill. *The Bible with and Without Jesus* — 220.6
   Levine, Amy-Jill. *Short Stories by Jesus* — 226.8
   Lewis, C. S. ★*A Grief Observed* — 242
   Lewis, C. S. *Mere Christianity* — 230
   Lewis, C. S. *Miracles* — 231.7
   Lewis, C. S. ★*The Screwtape Letters* — 248.4
   Liao, Yiwu. *God Is Red* — 275
   Lucado, Max. *Before Amen* — 248.3
   Marty, Martin E. *Pilgrims in Their Own Land* — 200
   McLaren, Brian D. *Faith After Doubt* — 234
   Meyaard-Schaap, Kyle. *Following Jesus in a Warming World* — 241
   Miles, Jack. *Religion as We Know It* — 200.9
   Nockels, Christy. *The Life You Long For* — 248.8
   Norris, Kathleen. *Acedia & Me* — 248.8
   Norris, Kathleen. *The Cloister Walk* — 255
   Pagels, Elaine H. *Beyond Belief* — 229
   Pagels, Elaine H. ★*The Gnostic Gospels* — 273

PUBLIC LIBRARY CORE COLLECTION: NONFICTION
Twentieth Edition

Park, Benjamin E. *American Zion*	289.3
Peters, Rebecca Todd. *Trust Women*	362.1988
Rashid, Jonny. *Jesus Takes a Side*	261.7
Riess, Jana. *Flunking Sainthood*	248.4
Riley, Gregory J. *The River of God*	270.1
Robinson, Marilynne. ★*Reading Genesis*	222
Rohr, Richard. *The Universal Christ*	232
Rowan, Barry L. *The Spiritual Art of Business*	261.8
Ryrie, Alec. *Protestants*	280
Samatar, Sofia. *The White Mosque*	B
Sauls, Scott. *Beautiful People Don't Just Happen*	248.8
Seiffert, Amy. *Starved*	248
Shulevitz, Judith. *The Sabbath World*	296.4
Smietana, Bob. *Reorganized Religion*	262.001
Smith, James K. A. *How to Inhabit Time*	223
Spong, John Shelby. *Eternal Life*	236
Stanley, Brian. *Christianity in the Twentieth Century*	270.8
Stavrakopoulou, Francesca. *God*	231
Teilhard de Chardin, Pierre. ★*The Divine Milieu*	233
Tickle, Phyllis. *The Great Emergence*	270.8
Tutu, Desmond. *The Book of Forgiving*	179
Villodas, Rich. *The Deeply Formed Life*	248.4
Wallis, Jim. *The False White Gospel*	261.7
West, Cait. ★*Rift*	B
Wintz, Jack. *Will I See My Dog in Heaven?*	231.7
Zahl, David. *Low Anthropology*	233

CHRISTIANITY AND ART
Beard, Mary. ★*How Do We Look*	704.9

CHRISTIANITY AND CAPITALISM
Friedman, Benjamin M. *Religion and the Rise of Capitalism*	330.12

CHRISTIANITY AND CULTURE
Beaty, Katelyn. *Celebrities for Jesus*	261
Carter, Jimmy. *Faith*	OK T A
Du Mez, Kristin Kobes. *Jesus and John Wayne*	277.308
Garcia, Damon. *The God Who Riots*	269
Holland, Tom. *Dominion*	261
Stanley, Brian. *Christianity in the Twentieth Century*	270.8
Wacker, Grant. *America's Pastor*	B

CHRISTIANITY AND DEMOCRACY
Griffith, R. Marie. *Moral Combat*	261.8

CHRISTIANITY AND HOMOSEXUALITY
Chu, Jeff. *Does Jesus Really Love Me?*	261.8
Hays, Katie. *Family of Origin, Family of Choice*	248.8086

CHRISTIANITY AND JUSTICE
Francis. *Let Us Dream*	282.092

CHRISTIANITY AND POLITICS
Barber, William J. *We Are Called to Be a Movement*	261.8
Du Mez, Kristin Kobes. *Jesus and John Wayne*	277.308
FitzGerald, Frances. *The Evangelicals*	277
Garcia, Damon. *The God Who Riots*	269
Griffith, R. Marie. *Moral Combat*	261.8
Liao, Yiwu. *God Is Red*	275
Rashid, Jonny. *Jesus Takes a Side*	261.7
Spencer, Kyle. *Raising Them Right*	320.5
Volf, Miroslav. *Public Faith in Action*	261.7

CHRISTIANITY AND SEXUALITY
Bolz-Weber, Nadia. *Shameless*	261.8
Edman, Elizabeth M. *Queer Virtue*	230
Hays, Katie. *Family of Origin, Family of Choice*	248.8086
Stone, Geoffrey R. ★*Sex and the Constitution*	345.7302

CHRISTIANITY AND THE ARTS
Baraka, Sho. *He Saw That It Was Good*	261.5

CHRISTIANITY AND WOMEN
Armas, Kat. *Abuelita Faith*	248.8
Christianity in the Twentieth Century. Stanley, Brian	270.8

CHRISTIANS
Alberta, Tim. *The Kingdom, the Power, and the Glory*	270.8
Chu, Jeff. *Does Jesus Really Love Me?*	261.8
Griffith, R. Marie. *Moral Combat*	261.8
Hays, Katie. *Family of Origin, Family of Choice*	248.8086
Jones, Robert P. *White Too Long*	277
MacCulloch, Diarmaid. *Christianity*	270
Roberts, Matthias. *Holy Runaways*	262
Volf, Miroslav. *Public Faith in Action*	261.7
Yancey, Philip. *Where the Light Fell*	B

CHRISTIE, AGATHA, 1890-1976
Worsley, Lucy. ★*Agatha Christie*	B

Christie, Chris
Let Me Finish	B
Christina Rossetti. Rossetti, Christina Georgina	821.8
Christmas. Flanders, Judith	394.2663
Christmas. Forbes, Bruce David	394.2663

CHRISTMAS
Flanders, Judith. *Christmas*	394.2663
Forbes, Bruce David. *Christmas*	394.2663
Stibbe, Nina. *An Almost Perfect Christmas*	394.2663
Thomas, Dylan. *A Child's Christmas in Wales*	B

CHRISTMAS COOKING
Kieffer, Sarah. ★*Baking for the Holidays*	641.5
Stibbe, Nina. *An Almost Perfect Christmas*	394.2663

CHRISTMAS DECORATIONS
Brown, Stephen. *Glitterville's Handmade Christmas*	B
Pester, Sophie. *Homemade Holiday*	745.594

CHRISTMAS PRESENTS
Stibbe, Nina. *An Almost Perfect Christmas*	394.2663
Christopher Kimball's Milk Street. Kimball, Christopher	641.5
Christopher Kimball's Milk Street. Kimball, Christopher	641.5

CHRONIC DISEASES
Abril, Andy. *Mayo Clinic Guide to Fibromyalgia*	616.7
Castro, M. Regina. ★*The Essential Diabetes Book*	616.4
Crais, Clifton C. *History Lessons*	B
Dearborn, Mary V. *Carson McCullers*	B
Gupta, Shalene. *The Cycle*	618.1
Lustig, Robert H. *Metabolical*	616
O'Rourke, Meghan. ★*The Invisible Kingdom*	616
Ramey, Sarah. *The Lady's Handbook for Her Mysterious Illness*	B
Ruhl, Sarah. *Smile*	B

CHRONIC PAIN
Lalkhen, Abdul-Ghaaliq. *An Anatomy of Pain*	616
McGreal, Chris. *American Overdose*	362.29
Norman, Abby. *Ask Me About My Uterus*	618.1
Parker, Lara. *Vagina Problems*	618.1
Ramey, Sarah. *The Lady's Handbook for Her Mysterious Illness*	B
Warraich, Haider. *The Song of Our Scars*	616

CHRONIC PAIN SYNDROME
Ramey, Sarah. *The Lady's Handbook for Her Mysterious Illness*	B
The Chronicle of Jazz. Cooke, Mervyn	781.6509
Chronicles; Volume 1. Dylan, Bob	B

CHRONOLOGY, HISTORICAL
Grun, Bernard. ★*The Timetables of History*	902

Chu, Jeff
Does Jesus Really Love Me?	261.8

CHU, JEFF
Chu, Jeff. *Does Jesus Really Love Me?*	261.8

Chu, Lenora
Little Soldiers	370

CHU, LENORA
Chu, Lenora. *Little Soldiers*	370
Chuck D Presents This Day in Rap and Hip-Hop History. Chuck D.	782.421649

Chuck D.
Chuck D Presents This Day in Rap and Hip-Hop History	782.421649

Chude-Sokei, Louis Onuorah
Floating in a Most Peculiar Way	979.4

CHUDE-SOKEI, LOUIS ONUORAH, 1967-
Chude-Sokei, Louis Onuorah. *Floating in a Most Peculiar Way*	979.4

Chung, Nicole
All You Can Ever Know	B
★*A Living Remedy*	B

CHUNG, NICOLE
Chung, Nicole. *All You Can Ever Know*	B

Chung, Vinh
Where the Wind Leads	B

CHUNG, VINH, 1975-
Chung, Vinh. *Where the Wind Leads*	B

CHURCH AND EDUCATION
Hixenbaugh, Michael. ★*They Came for the Schools*	371.9

CHURCH AND SOCIAL PROBLEMS
Barber, William J. *We Are Called to Be a Movement*	261.8
Gonzalez, Karen. *Beyond Welcome*	261.8
Nagassar, Rohadi. *When We Belong*	254
Vallely, Paul. *Pope Francis*	B
Volf, Miroslav. *Public Faith in Action*	261.7

CHURCH AND STATE
Kamen, Henry. *The Spanish Inquisition*	272
Rounding, Virginia. *The Burning Time*	272

Waldman, Steven. *Sacred Liberty*		341.4
Wexler, Jay. *Holy Hullabaloos*		342.7308
Wills, Garry. *The Future of the Catholic Church with Pope Francis*		282.09

CHURCH AND THE WORLD
Vallely, Paul. *Pope Francis*		B
Ward, Jon. *Testimony*		277.308

CHURCH ATTENDANCE
McCammon, Sarah. ★*The Exvangelicals*		277.308
Smietana, Bob. *Reorganized Religion*		262.001

CHURCH HISTORY
Asbridge, Thomas S. ★*The Crusades*		909.07
Aslan, Reza. *God*		211
Blum, Edward J. *The Color of Christ*		232
Bremer, Francis J. *John Winthrop*		B
Brown, Peter. *Through the Eye of a Needle*		270.2
Campbell, Joseph. *The Masks of God*		201.3
Douthat, Ross Gregory. *To Change the Church*		230
Ehrman, Bart D. *The Triumph of Christianity*		270.1
FitzGerald, Frances. *The Evangelicals*		277
Jones, Robert P. *The Hidden Roots of White Supremacy*		305.8
Jones, Robert P. *White Too Long*		277
Kamen, Henry. *The Spanish Inquisition*		272
Kertzer, David I. *The Pope at War*		940.53
Kertzer, David I. *The Pope Who Would Be King*		282.092
MacCulloch, Diarmaid. *Christianity*		270
Manseau, Peter. *Objects of Devotion*		277
Marty, Martin E. *Pilgrims in Their Own Land*		200
Metaxas, Eric. *Martin Luther*		B
Oberman, Heiko Augustinus. *Luther*		B
Riley, Gregory J. *The River of God*		270.1
Rounding, Virginia. *The Burning Time*		272
Smietana, Bob. *Reorganized Religion*		262.001
Stanley, Brian. *Christianity in the Twentieth Century*		270.8
Tickle, Phyllis. *The Great Emergence*		270.8
Wills, Garry. *The Future of the Catholic Church with Pope Francis*		282.09
Wilson, Derek. *Out of the Storm*		B

CHURCH MEMBERSHIP
McCammon, Sarah. ★*The Exvangelicals*		277.308
Nagassar, Rohadi. *When We Belong*		254
The Church of Baseball. Shelton, Ron		791.43
The Church of Mercy. Francis		252
Church of the Small Things. Shankle, Melanie		248.8

CHURCH WORK
Boyle, Greg. *Tattoos on the Heart*		277
Vaughn, Ellen Santilli. ★*Becoming Elisabeth Elliot*		B

CHURCH, BENJAMIN, 1639-1718
Philbrick, Nathaniel. ★*Mayflower*		973.2

CHURCH, FRANK
Risen, James. ★*The Last Honest Man*		973.92

CHURCH, ROBERT REED, 1839-1912
Lauterbach, Preston. *Beale Street Dynasty*		976.8

CHURCHES
Baskette, Molly Phinney. *How to Begin When Your World Is Ending*		248.8
Smietana, Bob. *Reorganized Religion*		262.001
Van Hensbergen, Gijs. *The Sagrada Familia*		726.5
★*Churchill.* Roberts, Andrew		B
Churchill. Johnson, Paul		B
Churchill and Orwell. Ricks, Thomas E.		920
Churchill's Hellraisers. Lewis, Damien		940.54
Churchill's Ministry of Ungentlemanly Warfare. Milton, Giles		940.54

CHURCHILL, CLEMENTINE, 1885-1977
Purnell, Sonia. *Clementine*		B

CHURCHILL, SARAH, 1914-1982
Katz, Catherine Grace. *The Daughters of Yalta*		920

Churchill, Winston
The Grand Alliance		940.53
Their Finest Hour		940.53
Triumph and Tragedy		940.53

CHURCHILL, WINSTON, 1874-1965
Beschloss, Michael R. *The Conquerors*		940.53
Bouverie, Tim. *Appeasement*		327.41043
Churchill, Winston. *The Grand Alliance*		940.53
Churchill, Winston. *Their Finest Hour*		940.53
Churchill, Winston. *Triumph and Tragedy*		940.53
Groom, Winston. *The Allies*		940.5309
Johnson, Paul. *Churchill*		B
Larson, Erik. ★*The Splendid and the Vile*		940.54
Lukacs, John. *Five Days in London, May 1940*		940.53
Manchester, William. *The Last Lion, Winston Spencer Churchill.*		B
Manchester, William. *The Last Lion, Winston Spencer Churchill.*		B
Manchester, William. *The Last Lion, Winston Spencer Churchill.*		B
McCarten, Anthony. *Darkest Hour*		941.084
Meacham, Jon. *Franklin and Winston*		940.53
Meltzer, Brad. ★*The Nazi Conspiracy*		940.53
Millard, Candice. ★*Hero of the Empire*		968.04
Milton, Giles. *Churchill's Ministry of Ungentlemanly Warfare*		940.54
Olson, Lynne. *Citizens of London*		940.54012
Olson, Lynne. *Troublesome Young Men*		941.084
Phillips, Adrian. *Fighting Churchill, Appeasing Hitler*		327.41043
Preston, Diana. *Eight Days at Yalta*		940.53
Purnell, Sonia. *Clementine*		B
Ricks, Thomas E. *Churchill and Orwell*		920
Roberts, Andrew. ★*Churchill*		B
Roberts, Andrew. *Masters and Commanders*		940.5322

Churchwell, Sarah Bartlett
Behold, America		973.9
The CIA. Wilford, Hugh		327.1273

CIA AGENTS
Blum, Howard. *The Spy Who Knew Too Much*		327.12
Hillsberg, Christina. *License to Parent*		649.1
Morley, Jefferson. *Scorpions' Dance*		973.924

Cialdini, Robert B.
Influence		153.8

CIANO, EDDA MUSSOLINI, CONTESSA
Mazzeo, Tilar J. *Sisters in Resistance*		945.091

CIANO, GALEAZZO, CONTE, 1903-1944
Mazzeo, Tilar J. *Sisters in Resistance*		945.091
Cicero. Everitt, Anthony		B

Cicero, Marcus Tullius
★*The Republic*		320.1
Selected Works		875

CICERO, MARCUS TULLIUS
Cicero, Marcus Tullius. *Selected Works*		875
Everitt, Anthony. *Cicero*		B

CIDER
White, April. *Apples to Cider*		663

Cilley, Marla
The Chaos* Cure		648

CINCINNATI, OHIO
O'Brien, Keith. *Charlie Hustle*		796.357
Cinderella Ate My Daughter. Orenstein, Peggy		305.23082
Cinderella Man. Schaap, Jeremy		B
Cinema Speculation. Tarantino, Quentin		791.43

CINEMATOGRAPHY
Fischer, Paul. *The Man Who Invented Motion Pictures*		791.43
Lumet, Sidney. *Making Movies*		791.43
Pincus, Edward. *The Filmmaker's Handbook*		777
Thomson, David. ★*How to Watch a Movie*		791.43

Cioletti, Jeff
Sakepedia		663
The Circuit. Phillips, Rowan Ricardo		796.342
Circular Knitting Workshop. Radcliffe, Margaret		746.43

CIRCUS
Macy, Beth. ★*Truevine*		B
Standiford, Les. ★*Battle for the Big Top*		791.3
Wall, Duncan. *The Ordinary Acrobat*		B
Wilson, Robert. *Barnum*		B

CIRCUS ANIMALS
Standiford, Les. ★*Battle for the Big Top*		791.3

CIRCUS OWNERS
Standiford, Les. ★*Battle for the Big Top*		791.3
Wilson, Robert. *Barnum*		B

CIRCUS PERFORMERS
Standiford, Les. ★*Battle for the Big Top*		791.3
Wall, Duncan. *The Ordinary Acrobat*		B

Cisneros, Sandra
A House of My Own		B

CISNEROS, SANDRA
Cisneros, Sandra. *A House of My Own*		B

CITIES AND TOWNS
Anderson, Sam. *Boom Town*		976.6
Berg, Scott W. *The Burning of the World*		977.311
Bomey, Nathan. *Detroit Resurrected*		977.4
Boyd, Herb. *Black Detroit*		977.4
Brenner, Marie. ★*The Desperate Hours*		362.1962
Briody, Blaire. *The New Wild West*		338.2

PUBLIC LIBRARY CORE COLLECTION: NONFICTION
Twentieth Edition

Collins, Max Allan. *Eliot Ness and the Mad Butcher*	364.152
Currid-Halkett, Elizabeth. *The Overlooked Americans*	307.76
Desmond, Matthew. ★*Evicted*	339.4
Dyja, Tom. *The Third Coast*	977.311
Edin, Kathryn. ★*The Injustice of Place*	339.4
Emanuel, Rahm. *The Nation City*	352.23
Fields, Micah. ★*We Hold Our Breath*	976.4
Grant, Richard. *The Deepest South of All*	976.2
Hanna-Attisha, Mona. *What the Eyes Don't See*	615.9
Hughes, Bettany. *Istanbul*	949.61
Johnson, Lizzie. ★*Paradise*	363.37
Kattan, Fadi. ★*Bethlehem*	641.59
Kiernan, Denise. *The Girls of Atomic City*	976.8
Kimble, Megan. ★*City Limits*	388.1
King, Charles. *Odessa*	947.7
Kirshner, Jodie Adams. ★*Broke*	336.3
Lauterbach, Preston. *Beale Street Dynasty*	976.8
LeDuff, Charlie. *Detroit*	977.4
Lunenfeld, Peter. *City at the Edge of Forever*	979.4
Madden, Thomas F. *Istanbul*	949.61
Madden, Thomas F. *Venice*	945
Marozzi, Justin. *Islamic Empires*	909
Mars, Roman. ★*The 99% Invisible City*	720
McKay, Sinclair. *Berlin*	943
Miles, Jonathan. *St. Petersburg*	947
Moss, Jeremiah. *Feral City*	B
Mumford, Lewis. *The City in History*	307.76
Norwich, John Julius. *A History of Venice*	945
Podemski, Max. *A Paradise of Small Houses*	363.5
Rajchel, Diana. *Urban Magick*	133.4
Riedel, Michael. *Razzle Dazzle*	792.09
Robb, Graham. *The Discovery of France*	944
Robb, Graham. *Parisians*	944
Rudacille, Deborah. *Roots of Steel*	338.4
Rybczynski, Witold. *Mysteries of the Mall*	720
Schilthuizen, Menno. *Darwin Comes to Town*	577.5
Sciolino, Elaine. *The Only Street in Paris*	944
Sciolino, Elaine. *The Seine*	944
Sebag-Montefiore, Simon. *Jerusalem*	956.94
Shackle, Samira. *Karachi Vice*	954.91
Stashower, Daniel. *American Demon*	364.152
Vanhoenacker, Mark. *Imagine a City*	629.13
★*Citizen*. Rankine, Claudia	814
Citizen Coke. Elmore, Bartow J.	338.7
★*Citizen Kane*. Lebo, Harlan	791.43
CITIZEN PARTICIPATION IN GOVERNMENT	
Barkan, Ady. *Eyes to the Wind*	B
Litt, David. *Democracy in One Book or Less*	321.8
Mahtani, Shibani. *Among the Braves*	951.25
Plouffe, David. *A Citizen's Guide to Beating Donald Trump*	324.0973
Rousseau, Jean-Jacques. ★*The Social Contract*	320.1
Smith, Erin Geiger. ★*Thank You for Voting*	324.973
Citizen Soldier. Donald, Aida DiPace	B
Citizen Soldiers. Ambrose, Stephen E.	940.54
A Citizen's Guide to Beating Donald Trump. Plouffe, David	324.0973
Citizens. Schama, Simon	944.04
Citizens of London. Olson, Lynne	940.54012
CITIZENSHIP	
Beard, Mary. ★*S.P.Q.R.*	937
Gomez, Laura E. ★*Inventing Latinos*	305.868
Immerwahr, Daniel. *How to Hide an Empire*	973
Kershner, Isabel. *The Land of Hope and Fear*	956.9405
Klay, Phil. *Uncertain Ground*	359.9
Lalami, Laila. *Conditional Citizens*	323.60973
Luiselli, Valeria. *Tell Me How It Ends*	305.23086
McCullough, David G. ★*The American Spirit*	973
Ramos, Jorge. *Stranger*	325.73
Rather, Dan. *What Unites Us*	323.6
Skach, C. L. *How to Be a Citizen*	323.6
Suarez, Ray. ★*We Are Home*	325.73
Willis, Deborah. ★*The Black Civil War Soldier*	973.7
Citro, Asia	
150+ Screen-Free Activities for Kids	796.5
Citron, Danielle Keats	
The Fight for Privacy	342.7308
City At the Edge of Forever. Lunenfeld, Peter	979.4
A City Called Heaven. Marovich, Robert M.	782.25
CITY DWELLERS	
Baum, Dan. *Nine Lives*	B
Laing, Olivia. ★*The Lonely City*	700.1
Rajchel, Diana. *Urban Magick*	133.4
Robb, Graham. *Parisians*	944
Shackle, Samira. *Karachi Vice*	954.91
The City Game. Goodman, Matthew	796.323
The City in History. Mumford, Lewis	307.76
CITY LIFE	
Anbinder, Tyler. ★*City of Dreams*	974.7
Arceneaux, Michael. *I Finally Bought Some Jordans*	306.76
Beard, Mary. *The Fires of Vesuvius*	937
Bergner, Daniel. ★*Sing for Your Life*	B
Day, Daniel R. *Dapper Dan*	B
Dusoulier, Clotilde. *Tasting Paris*	641.594
Dyja, Tom. *The Third Coast*	977.311
Figes, Orlando. ★*The Whisperers*	306.850947
Hessler, Peter. *The Buried*	962.05
Kanigel, Robert. *Eyes on the Street*	B
Kimble, Megan. ★*City Limits*	388.1
King, Charles. *Midnight at the Pera Palace*	949.61
Kurlansky, Mark. *Havana*	972.91
Laing, Olivia. ★*The Lonely City*	700.1
Malek, Alia. *The Home That Was Our Country*	B
Martin, Wednesday. *Primates of Park Avenue*	974.7
Mehta, Suketu. *Maximum City*	954
Miller, Donald L. *Supreme City*	974.7
Moss, Jeremiah. *Feral City*	B
Mumford, Lewis. *The City in History*	307.76
Rajchel, Diana. *Urban Magick*	133.4
Rivlin, Gary. *Katrina*	976.3
Schmitz, Rob. *Street of Eternal Happiness*	951
Shackle, Samira. *Karachi Vice*	954.91
Shorto, Russell. *Amsterdam*	949.2
Stewart, Nikita. *Troop 6000*	369
Wallace, Mike. *Greater Gotham*	974.7
Wilder, Thornton. *Our Town*	812
Woolf, Virginia. *The London Scene*	942.1
★*City Limits*. Kimble, Megan	388.1
City of a Million Dreams. Berry, Jason	976.3
★*City of Dreams*. Anbinder, Tyler	974.7
The City of Falling Angels. Berendt, John	945
City of Fortune. Crowley, Roger	945
The City of Joy. Lapierre, Dominique	954
City of Lies. Navai, Ramita	955
City of Oranges. LeBor, Adam	956.94
City of the Century. Miller, Donald L.	977.311
City of Thorns. Rawlence, Ben	967.7305
★*A City on Mars*. Weinersmith, Kelly	629.4
CITY-STATES	
Aristotle. ★*Politics, 2nd Ed*	320
Roberts, Jennifer Tolbert. *The Plague of War*	938
CIVICS	
Packer, George. *Last Best Hope*	973.93
Sage, Sami. *Democracy in Retrograde*	324
Skach, C. L. *How to Be a Citizen*	323.6
Smith, Erin Geiger. ★*Thank You for Voting*	324.973
Will, George F. *The Conservative Sensibility*	320.520973
CIVIL RIGHTS	
Adayfi, Mansoor. *Don't Forget Us Here*	B
Becker, Jo. ★*Forcing the Spring*	346.79401
Bowdler, Michelle. ★*Is Rape a Crime?*	B
Brodsky, Alexandra. *Sexual Justice*	364.15
Carpenter, Dale. *Flagrant Conduct*	342.7308
Cenziper, Debbie. ★*Love Wins*	346.7301
Engelhart, Katie. *The Inevitable*	179.7
Funk, Mason. *The Book of Pride*	920
Goldberg, Carrie. *Nobody's Victim*	345.73
Grigoriadis, Vanessa. *Blurred Lines*	371.7
Kaplan, Roberta A. *Then Comes Marriage*	346.7301
Khan, Mahvish Rukhsana. *My Guantanamo Diary*	973.931
Krakauer, Jon. *Missoula*	362.883
Lemay, Mimi. *What We Will Become*	306.874
Nutt, Amy Ellis. *Becoming Nicole*	920
Thompson, Heather Ann. *Blood in the Water*	365
Yoshino, Kenji. *Speak Now*	346.79401
CIVIL DEFENSE	
Graff, Garrett M. *Raven Rock*	363.350973

AUTHOR, TITLE, SERIES AND SUBJECT INDEX

CIVIL DISOBEDIENCE
Hinton, Elizabeth Kai. ★*America on Fire* — 305.800973
CIVIL ENGINEERING
Chachra, Deb. *How Infrastructure Works* — 363
McCullough, David G. *The Path Between the Seas* — 972.87
CIVIL RIGHTS
Adayfi, Mansoor. *Don't Forget Us Here* — B
Anderson, Carol. ★*One Person, No Vote* — 324.6
Anderson, Carol. ★*White Rage* — 305.800973
Avlon, John P. *Lincoln and the Fight for Peace* — 973.7
Baime, A. J. *White Lies* — B
Baker, Calvin. *A More Perfect Reunion* — 305.800973
Baldwin, James. ★*Collected Essays* — 814
Baldwin, James. ★*The Fire Next Time* — 305.896
Baldwin, James. ★*Notes of a Native Son* — 305.8
Becker, Jo. ★*Forcing the Spring* — 346.79401
Berman, Ari. *Give Us the Ballot* — 324.6
Blackmon, Douglas A. *Slavery by Another Name* — 305.896
Blain, Keisha N. *Until I Am Free* — B
Blais, Madeleine. *Queen of the Court* — B
Blight, David W. ★*Frederick Douglass* — B
Boghosian, Heidi. *"i Have Nothing to Hide"* — 363.1
Bond, Julian. ★*Julian Bond's Time to Teach* — 323.0975
Boyd, Herb. *We Shall Overcome* — 323.1196
Boyle, Kevin. *Arc of Justice* — 345.73
Branch, Taylor. ★*At Canaan's Edge* — 323.1196
Brazile, Donna. *For Colored Girls Who Have Considered Politics* — 328.73
Brettschneider, Corey Lang. *The Presidents and the People* — 342.73
Brodsky, Alexandra. *Sexual Justice* — 364.15
Bryant, Howard. *Full Dissidence* — 306.20973
Butler, Paul. *Chokehold* — 363.2
Canellos, Peter S. *The Great Dissenter* — B
Carmon, Irin. *Notorious RBG* — B
Cenziper, Debbie. ★*Love Wins* — 346.7301
Chemerinsky, Erwin. *Closing the Courthouse Door* — 347.73
Chemerinsky, Erwin. *Presumed Guilty* — 344.7305
Citron, Danielle Keats. *The Fight for Privacy* — 342.7308
Cleaver, Eldridge. *Soul on Ice* — B
Cohodas, Nadine. *Princess Noire* — 782.42164
Colaiaco, James A. *Frederick Douglass and the Fourth of July* — 973.7
Collins, Gail. *When Everything Changed* — 305.40973
Crump, Benjamin. *Open Season* — 364
Davis, Angela Y. *Abolition* — 364.6
De Hart, Jane Sherron. ★*Ruth Bader Ginsburg* — B
Dennis, David J., Jr. *The Movement Made Us* — B
Douglass, Frederick. ★*Frederick Douglass* — 973.8
Driver, Justin. *The Schoolhouse Gate* — 344.73
Euchner, Charles C. *Nobody Turn Me Around* — 975.3
Faust, Drew Gilpin. *Necessary Trouble* — B
Foner, Eric. ★*Reconstruction* — 973.8
Ford, Richard T. *Rights Gone Wrong* — 342.7308
Francis. *Happiness in This Life* — 248.4
Friedman, Barry. ★*Unwarranted* — 344.7305
Garza, Alicia. *The Purpose of Power* — 303.48
Gergel, Richard. *Unexampled Courage* — 323.1196
Gibson, Larry S. *Young Thurgood* — B
Giddings, Paula. *Ida* — B
Ginsburg, Ruth Bader. ★*My Own Words* — 347.73
Grant, Gail Milissa. *At the Elbows of My Elders* — B
Greene, Jamal. *How Rights Went Wrong* — 342.7308
Gregory, Dick. *Defining Moments in Black History* — 973
Griffith, Elisabeth. *Formidable* — 305.42
Halberstam, David. ★*The Children* — 323.1
Hayes, Christopher. *A Colony in a Nation* — 364.3
Haygood, Wil. *Showdown* — B
Hensley, William L. Iggiagruk. *Fifty Miles from Tomorrow* — B
Hirshman, Linda R. *Sisters in Law* — 347.73
Houppert, Karen. *Chasing Gideon* — 345.73
Immerwahr, Daniel. *How to Hide an Empire* — 973
Jackson, Jenn M. ★*Black Women Taught Us* — 305.48
Jackson, Troy. *Becoming King* — B
Jacoby, Melissa B. ★*Unjust Debts* — 346.73
Jones, Doug. *Bending Toward Justice* — 323.1196
Jones, Nathaniel R. *Answering the Call* — B
Keith, Philip A. *All Blood Runs Red* — B
Kelly, Kate. *Ordinary Equality* — 920
Kennedy, Kostya. *True* — B
Kennedy, Robert Francis. *RFK* — 973.92

King, Coretta Scott. ★*My Life, My Love, My Legacy* — B
King, Martin Luther. *The Autobiography of Martin Luther King, Jr.* — B
Kotz, Nick. *Judgment Days* — 323
Larson, Kate Clifford. *Walk with Me* — B
Lemann, Nicholas. *Redemption* — 975
Levine, Bruce C. *Thaddeus Stevens* — B
Lewis, David L. *W.E.B. Du Bois* — B
Lewis, John. ★*March; Book One* — 741.5
Lewis, John. ★*March; Book Three* — 741.5
Lewis, John. ★*March; Book Two* — 741.5
Luxenberg, Steve. ★*Separate* — 342.7308
Mahtani, Shibani. *Among the Braves* — 951.25
Maier, Pauline. *Ratification* — 342.7302
Maraniss, Andrew. *Strong Inside* — B
Masur, Kate. *Until Justice Be Done* — 323.1196
Mattlin, Ben. *Disability Pride* — 323.3
McWhorter, Diane. *Carry Me Home* — 976.1
Metzl, Jonathan M. ★*What We've Become* — 364.152
Moore, Wes. ★*Five Days* — 363.32
Morrison, Melanie. *Murder on Shades Mountain* — 345.761
Mullen, Bill. ★*James Baldwin* — B
Pappe, Ilan. *The Biggest Prison on Earth* — 956.9405
Perry, Imani. *May We Forever Stand* — 782.25
Person, Charles. *Buses Are a Comin'* — B
Plant, Deborah G. *Of Greed and Glory* — 326
Purdum, Todd S. *An Idea Whose Time Has Come* — 342.7308
Reese, Anney. ★*Stuff Mom Never Told You* — 305.42
Risen, Clay. *The Bill of the Century* — 342.7308
Roll, David L. *Ascent to Power* — 973.918
Rosenbloom, Joseph. *Redemption* — B
Roundtree, Dovey Johnson. ★*Mighty Justice* — B
Roy, Arundhati. *Walking with the Comrades* — 954
Sefarad, Mikhael. *The Wall and the Gate* — 341.48
Sharfstein, Daniel J. ★*Thunder in the Mountains* — 979.5
Simon, James F. *Eisenhower vs. Warren* — 347.73
Smith, Mychal Denzel. *Stakes Is High* — 973.933
Sokol, Jason. *The Heavens Might Crack* — 323.092
Soyinka, Wole. *Of Africa* — 960
Spofford, Tim. *What the Children Told Us* — 150.92
Stone, Geoffrey R. *Perilous Times* — 323.44
Strittmatter, Kai. *We Have Been Harmonized* — 323.44
Sullivan, Patricia. *Lift Every Voice* — 973
Theoharis, Jeanne. *A More Beautiful and Terrible History* — 323.1196
Thompson, Heather Ann. *Blood in the Water* — 365
Tubbs, Anna Malaika. *The Three Mothers* — 306.874
Urofsky, Melvin I. *The Affirmative Action Puzzle* — 331.13
Van Meter, Matthew. *Deep Delta Justice* — 345.763
Waldman, Michael. *The Supermajority* — 347.73
Ward, Jesmyn. ★*The Fire This Time* — 305.896
Watson, Bruce. *Freedom Summer* — 323.1196
Wexler, Stuart. *Killing King* — 323.092
Wilkins, Robert L. *Long Road to Hard Truth* — 069
Will, George F. *The Conservative Sensibility* — 320.520973
Williams, Juan. *Eyes on the Prize* — 323.4
Williams, Kidada E. *I Saw Death Coming* — 973.8
Willis, Raquel. *The Risk It Takes to Bloom* — B
Wise, Tim J. *Dispatches from the Race War* — 305.8
Worth, Robert Forsyth. ★*A Rage for Order* — 909
Yoshino, Kenji. *Speak Now* — 346.79401
Zeitz, Joshua. *Building the Great Society* — 973.923
CIVIL RIGHTS DEMONSTRATIONS
Bond, Julian. ★*Julian Bond's Time to Teach* — 323.0975
Euchner, Charles C. *Nobody Turn Me Around* — 975.3
Meacham, Jon. *His Truth Is Marching On* — B
Wright, C. D. *One with Others* — 811
CIVIL RIGHTS LAWYERS
Aguon, Julian. *No Country for Eight-Spot Butterflies* — 305.89
Crump, Benjamin. *Open Season* — 364
Rosen, Richard A. *Julius Chambers* — B
Van Meter, Matthew. *Deep Delta Justice* — 345.763
CIVIL RIGHTS MOVEMENT
Angelou, Maya. *A Song Flung up to Heaven* — B
Archibald, John. *Shaking the Gates of Hell* — B
Arsenault, Raymond. *John Lewis* — B
Avlon, John P. *Lincoln and the Fight for Peace* — 973.7
Baldwin, James. ★*Collected Essays* — 814
Blain, Keisha N. *Until I Am Free* — B
Bond, Julian. ★*Julian Bond's Time to Teach* — 323.0975

PUBLIC LIBRARY CORE COLLECTION: NONFICTION
Twentieth Edition

Boyd, Herb. *We Shall Overcome*	323.1196		Brand, Christo. *Mandela*	B
Boyle, Kevin. *The Shattering*	973.923		Brooks, Maegan Parker. *Fannie Lou Hamer*	B
Branch, Taylor. ★*At Canaan's Edge*	323.1196		Eig, Jonathan. ★*King*	B
Branch, Taylor. *Parting the Waters*	973		Garza, Alicia. *The Purpose of Power*	303.48
Branch, Taylor. ★*Pillar of Fire*	323.1		Halberstam, David. ★*The Children*	323.1
Brooks, Maegan Parker. *Fannie Lou Hamer*	B		Honey, Michael K. *To the Promised Land*	323
Brown-Nagin, Tomiko. *Civil Rights Queen*	B		King, Coretta Scott. ★*My Life, My Love, My Legacy*	B
Dennis, David J., Jr. *The Movement Made Us*	B		King, Martin Luther. *The Autobiography of Martin Luther King, Jr.*	B
Eig, Jonathan. ★*King*	B		Levingston, Steven. *Kennedy and King*	920
Else, Jon. *True South*	305.800973		Lewis, John. *Walking with the Wind*	B
Euchner, Charles C. *Nobody Turn Me Around*	975.3		Luxenberg, Steve. ★*Separate*	342.7308
Faust, Drew Gilpin. *Necessary Trouble*	B		Mallory, Tamika D. *State of Emergency*	305.896
Ford, Tanisha C. *Our Secret Society*	B		Mitchell, Jerry. ★*Race Against Time*	364.152
Garrett, Kent. *The Last Negroes at Harvard*	920		Morris, James McGrath. *Eye on the Struggle*	B
Gates, Henry Louis. *And Still I Rise*	305.896		Reid, Joy-Ann Lomena. ★*Medgar and Myrlie*	920
Gergel, Richard. *Unexampled Courage*	323.1196		Sarsour, Linda. *We Are Not Here to Be Bystanders*	B
Glaude, Eddie S. *Begin Again*	305.800973		Shields, Charles J. *Lorraine Hansberry*	B
Grant, Gail Milissa. *At the Elbows of My Elders*	B		Smith, David James. *Young Mandela*	B
Green, Kristen. *Something Must Be Done About Prince Edward County*	379.2		Theoharis, Jeanne. *The Rebellious Life of Mrs. Rosa Parks*	B
Halberstam, David. ★*The Children*	323.1		Watson, Bruce. *Freedom Summer*	323.1196
Honey, Michael K. *To the Promised Land*	323		Williams, Juan. *Thurgood Marshall*	B
Hunter-Gault, Charlayne. ★*My People*	305.48		**CIVIL SERVICE WORKERS**	
Jackson, Troy. *Becoming King*	973		Caro, Robert A. *The Power Broker*	B
Jacobs, Sally H. *Althea*	B		Cervini, Eric. *The Deviant's War*	B
Jefferson, Margo. *Negroland*	305.896		*The Civil War.* Foote, Shelby	973.7
Joseph, Peniel E. *The Sword and the Shield*	B		*The Civil War.* Masur, Louis P.	973.7
Joseph, Peniel E. *Waiting 'Til the Midnight Hour*	323.1196		*The Civil War.* Ward, Geoffrey C.	973.7
King, Coretta Scott. ★*My Life, My Love, My Legacy*	B		**CIVIL WAR**	
King, Martin Luther. *Why We Can't Wait*	305.8		Abouzeid, Rania. *No Turning Back*	956.9104
Kix, Paul. ★*You Have to Be Prepared to Die Before You Can Begin to Live*	976.1		Achebe, Chinua. *There Was a Country*	B
Kot, Greg. *I'll Take You There*	B		Ackroyd, Peter. *Rebellion*	941.06
Lauterbach, Preston. *Bluff City*	B		Ahmad, Aeham. *The Pianist from Syria*	B
Levingston, Steven. *Kennedy and King*	920		AL Samawi, Mohammed. *The Fox Hunt*	953
Lewis, David L. ★*W.E.B. Du Bois*	B		Armitage, David. *Civil Wars*	355.02
Lewis, John. ★*March; Book One*	741.5		Ash, Stephen V. *Firebrand of Liberty*	973.7
Lewis, John. ★*March; Book Three*	741.5		Beah, Ishmael. ★*A Long Way Gone*	B
Lewis, John. ★*March; Book Two*	741.5		Beevor, Antony. *Russia*	947.084
Lewis, John. *Walking with the Wind*	B		Blanton, DeAnne. *They Fought Like Demons*	973.7
McWhorter, Diane. *Carry Me Home*	976.1		Blight, David W. *A Slave No More*	973.7
Meacham, Jon. *His Truth Is Marching On*	B		Blount, Roy. *Robert E. Lee*	B
Mitchell, Jerry. ★*Race Against Time*	364.152		Burlingame, Michael. *Abraham Lincoln*	B
Montville, Leigh. *Sting Like a Bee*	B		Carwardine, Richard. *Lincoln*	B
Parker, Morgan. *Magical Negro*	811		Cooper, Helene. *Madame President*	966.62
Payne, Les. ★*The Dead Are Arising*	B		Cwiklik, Robert. *Sheridan's Secret Mission*	973.8
Purdum, Todd S. *An Idea Whose Time Has Come*	342.7308		Dagher, Sam. *Assad or We Burn the Country*	956.9104
Reid, Joy-Ann Lomena. ★*Medgar and Myrlie*	920		Davis, William C. *Crucible of Command*	920
Reid, Joy-Ann Lomena. ★*Medgar and Myrlie*	920		Delbanco, Andrew. *The War Before the War*	973.7
Rembert, Winfred. *Chasing Me to My Grave*	B		Deng, Alephonsion. *They Poured Fire on Us from the Sky*	B
Roberts, Randy. *Blood Brothers*	920		Di Giovanni, Janine. *The Morning They Came for Us*	956.9104
Rosen, Richard A. *Julius Chambers*	B		Donald, David Herbert. *Lincoln*	B
Rosenberg, Rosalind. ★*Jane Crow*	B		Egerton, Douglas R. *Thunder at the Gates*	973.7
Rosenbloom, Joseph. *Redemption*	B		Everitt, Anthony. *The Rise of Rome*	937
Roundtree, Dovey Johnson. ★*Mighty Justice*	B		Faust, Drew Gilpin. *This Republic of Suffering*	973.7
Sides, Hampton. *Hellhound on His Trail*	364.152		Fields-Black, Edda L. *Combee*	973.7
Simon, James F. *Eisenhower vs. Warren*	347.73		Finkelman, Paul. *Millard Fillmore*	B
Sokol, Jason. *The Heavens Might Crack*	323.092		Foner, Eric. *Forever Free*	973.8
Sorin, Gretchen Sullivan. *Driving While Black*	323.1196		Foote, Shelby. *The Civil War*	973.7
Sullivan, Patricia. *Lift Every Voice*	973		Forche, Carolyn. *What You Have Heard Is True*	B
Theoharis, Jeanne. *A More Beautiful and Terrible History*	323.1196		Goodheart, Adam. *1861*	973.7
Theoharis, Jeanne. *The Rebellious Life of Mrs. Rosa Parks*	B		Gristwood, Sarah. *Blood Sisters*	942.04092
Tye, Larry. ★*The Jazzmen*	781.6509		Groom, Winston. *Shiloh, 1862*	973.7
Tyson, Timothy B. *The Blood of Emmett Till*	364.1		Guelzo, Allen C. *Gettysburg*	973.7
Van Meter, Matthew. *Deep Delta Justice*	345.763		Gwynne, S. C. *Hymns of the Republic*	973.7
Walker, Vanessa Siddle. *The Lost Education of Horace Tate*	370.92		Gwynne, S. C. *Rebel Yell*	B
Watson, Bruce. *Freedom Summer*	323.1196		Hochschild, Adam. *Spain in Our Hearts*	946.081
Wexler, Stuart. *Killing King*	323.092		Horwitz, Tony. *Confederates in the Attic*	973.7
Whitaker, Mark. ★*Saying It Loud*	973.923		Huffman, Alan. *Here I Am*	B
Williams, Juan. *Eyes on the Prize*	323.4		Jones, Jacqueline. *Saving Savannah*	975.8
Wright, C. D. *One with Others*	811		Keegan, John. *The American Civil War*	973.7
Zack, Ian. *Odetta*	B		Korda, Michael. *Clouds of Glory*	B
CIVIL RIGHTS ORGANIZATIONS			Kurtz-Phelan, Daniel. *The China Mission*	951.04
Kix, Paul. ★*You Have to Be Prepared to Die Before You Can Begin to Live*	976.1		Levine, Bruce C. *The Fall of the House of Dixie*	973.7
Civil Rights Queen. Brown-Nagin, Tomiko	B		Levine, Bruce C. *Thaddeus Stevens*	B
CIVIL RIGHTS WORKERS			Li, Zhuqing. *Daughters of the Flower Fragrant Garden*	951.04
Blain, Keisha N. *Until I Am Free*	B		Lockley, Thomas. *African Samurai*	B
Bond, Julian. ★*Julian Bond's Time to Teach*	323.0975		Malala, Justice. *The Plot to Save South Africa*	968.07
			Man, John. *Ninja*	355.5
			Matloff, Judith. *No Friends but the Mountains*	355.009

AUTHOR, TITLE, SERIES AND SUBJECT INDEX

McPherson, James M. *Battle Cry of Freedom*	973.7
McPherson, James M. *Drawn with the Sword*	973.7
McPherson, James M. *For Cause and Comrades*	973.7
McPherson, James M. *Hallowed Ground*	973.7
McPherson, James M. ★*Tried by War*	973.7
Miller, Donald L. *Vicksburg*	973.7
Mohan, Rohini. *The Seasons of Trouble*	954.9303
Moore, Wayetu. *The Dragons, the Giant, the Women*	B
Oakes, James. *Freedom National*	973.7
Packer, George. *The Assassins' Gate*	956.7044
Platt, Stephen R. *Autumn in the Heavenly Kingdom*	951
Rawlence, Ben. *City of Thorns*	967.7305
Reid, Stuart A. *The Lumumba Plot*	967.51
Reynolds, David S. *Mightier Than the Sword*	813
Sandburg, Carl. *Abraham Lincoln*	B
Sears, Stephen W. ★*Chancellorsville*	973.7
Sears, Stephen W. *Gettysburg*	973.7
Sears, Stephen W. ★*Landscape Turned Red*	973.7
Sears, Stephen W. *Lincoln's Lieutenants*	920
Seierstad, Asne. *Angel of Grozny*	947.086
Seierstad, Asne. *Two Sisters*	956.9104
Stiles, T. J. *Jesse James*	B
Strauss, Barry S. ★*The War That Made the Roman Empire*	937
Subramanian, Sammanth. *This Divided Island*	954.9303
Symonds, Craig L. *Lincoln and His Admirals*	B
Taylor, Alan. *American Civil Wars*	973.7
Taylor, Jay. *The Generalissimo*	B
Thomson, Mike. *Syria's Secret Library*	956.9104
Varon, Elizabeth R. *Longstreet*	B
Ward, Andrew. ★*The Slaves' War*	973.7
Ward, Geoffrey C. *The Civil War*	973.7
Watling, Sarah. *Tomorrow Perhaps the Future*	946.081
Wert, Jeffry D. *Cavalryman of the Lost Cause*	B
Wheelan, Joseph. ★*Terrible Swift Sword*	B
Wickenden, Dorothy. *The Agitators*	920
Williams, David. *Bitterly Divided*	973.7
Willis, Deborah. ★*The Black Civil War Soldier*	973.7
Wills, Garry. *Lincoln at Gettysburg*	973.7
Winik, Jay. *April 1865*	973.7
Ypi, Lea. ★*Free*	B
Zamora, Javier. ★*Solito*	B
Zia, Helen. *Last Boat Out of Shanghai*	951.04
The Civil War and American Art. Harvey, Eleanor Jones	740.9
The Civil War of 1812. Taylor, Alan	973.5
CIVIL WAR VETERANS	
White, Ronald C. *On Great Fields*	B
Winchester, Simon. *The Professor and the Madman*	423
Civil Wars. Armitage, David	355.02
CIVILIANS IN WAR	
Ayers, Edward L. ★*The Thin Light of Freedom*	975.5
Chrisinger, David. *The Soldier's Truth*	940.54
Harding, Luke. *Invasion*	947.7
McKay, Sinclair. *The Fire and the Darkness*	940.54
Miller, Christopher. *The War Came to Us*	947.7
Scott, James. *Black Snow*	940.54
Thomson, Mike. *Syria's Secret Library*	956.9104
White, Ralph. *Getting Out of Saigon*	959.704
The Civility Solution. Forni, Pier Massimo	395
CIVILIZATION	
Addis, Ferdinand. *The Eternal City*	945.6
Alt, Matt. *Pure Invention*	306.0952
Appy, Christian G. *American Reckoning*	959.704
Barnes, Julian. *The Man in the Red Coat*	B
Baron, David. *American Eclipse*	523.7
Barzun, Jacques. *From Dawn to Decadence*	940.2
Beard, Mary. ★*Emperor of Rome*	937
Bittman, Mark. *Animal, Vegetable, Junk*	394.1
Boccaletti, Giulio. *Water*	909
Boorstin, Daniel J. *The Americans*	973
Boorstin, Daniel J. *The Americans*	973
Boyle, Rebecca. *Our Moon*	523.3
Brooks, Michael. *The Art of More*	510.9
Brownworth, Lars. *Lost to the West*	949.5
Bryson, Bill. *Notes from a Small Island*	914
Bryson, Bill. *The Road to Little Dribbling*	914
Cahill, Thomas. *How the Irish Saved Civilization*	941.501
Cassidy, Cody. *How to Survive History*	904
Cline, Eric H. *After 1177 B.C.*	937
Cohen, Roger. *An Affirming Flame*	071
Collingham, E. M. *Curry*	394.1
Cooney, Kara. *When Women Ruled the World*	920
Darnell, John Coleman. *Egypt's Golden Couple*	932
Desilva, Jeremy. *First Steps*	599.93
Diamond, Jared M. *Guns, Germs, and Steel*	303.4
DuVal, Kathleen. ★*Native Nations*	970.004
Fagan, Brian M. *Fishing*	338.3
Ferrara, Silvia. *The Greatest Invention*	411
Fischer, David Hackett. ★*African Founders*	973
Frank, Adam. *Light of the Stars*	523.1
Freud, Sigmund. *Civilization and Its Discontents*	150.19
Fuentes, Carlos. *The Buried Mirror*	946
Gates, Henry Louis. ★*Life Upon These Shores*	973
Gleick, James. *The Information*	020.9
Gleick, Peter H. *The Three Ages of Water*	333.91
Goldsworthy, Adrian Keith. *Pax Romana*	937
Goodheart, Adam. *The Last Island*	954
Graeber, David. *The Dawn of Everything*	901
Hansen, Valerie. *The Year 1000*	909
Harper, Kyle. *The Fate of Rome*	937
Herman, Arthur. *How the Scots Invented the Modern World*	941.1
Hessler, Peter. *Oracle Bones*	951
Hirst, J. B. *The Shortest History of Europe*	940
Hughes, Robert. *Rome*	945.6
Johansen, Signe. ★*How to Hygge*	646.7
Joyce, Patrick. *Remembering Peasants*	305.5
Kenny, Charles. *The Plague Cycle*	614.4
Khilnani, Sunil. *Incarnations*	920
Kriwaczek, Paul. *Babylon*	935
Kurlansky, Mark. *Paper*	676
Lacey, Robert. *Inside the Kingdom*	953.805
Le Guin, Ursula K. *No Time to Spare*	814
Le Guin, Ursula K. *Ursula K. Le Guin*	B
Lunenfeld, Peter. *City at the Edge of Forever*	979.4
Mac Sweeney, Naoise. *The West*	909
MacGregor, Neil. *Germany*	943
MacGregor, Neil. *A History of the World in 100 Objects*	930.1
Marchant, Jo. *The Human Cosmos*	523.1
Marozzi, Justin. *Islamic Empires*	909
McCullough, David G. ★*The American Spirit*	973
Meals, Roy A. *Bones*	599.9
Menand, Louis. *The Free World*	306.0973
Mikanowski, Jacob. ★*Goodbye, Eastern Europe*	947
Morrison, Robert. *The Regency Years*	941.07
Osnos, Evan. *Wildland*	973.93
Packer, George. *Last Best Hope*	973.93
Rady, Martyn C. *The Middle Kingdoms*	943
Reed, Julia. *Dispatches from the Gilded Age*	B
Ricks, Thomas E. ★*First Principles*	973.09
Sanghera, Sathnam. *Empireworld*	909
Schama, Simon. *A History of Britain; 2*	941
Schulman, Bruce J. *The Seventies*	973.92
Sebag-Montefiore, Simon. ★*The World*	929.7
Sen, Amartya. *The Argumentative Indian*	954
Shaw, Ian. *The Princeton Dictionary of Ancient Egypt*	932
Spitzer, Michael. *The Musical Human*	780.9
Stone, I. F. *The Trial of Socrates*	183
Strathern, Paul. *The Florentines*	945
Strauss, Barry S. *Ten Caesars*	937
Sundeen, Mark. *The Unsettlers*	640
Tallis, Frank. ★*Mortal Secrets*	B
Tanais. *In Sensorium*	B
Tolentino, Jia. ★*Trick Mirror*	973.93
Townsend, Richard F. *The Aztecs*	972
Trentmann, Frank. *Out of the Darkness*	943.08
Tsu, Jing. *Kingdom of Characters*	495.111
Tyson, Neil deGrasse. *Starry Messenger*	901
Vince, Gaia. *Transcendence*	599.93
Ward, Peter Douglas. *Life as We Do Not Know It*	576.839
Watson, Peter. *The German Genius*	943
Weatherford, J. McIver. *Genghis Khan and the Quest for God*	323.44
Wilkerson, Isabel. ★*The Warmth of Other Suns*	304.80973
Winchester, Simon. *Atlantic*	551.46
Winchester, Simon. *Knowing What We Know*	306.4
Wood, Gordon S. *Empire of Liberty*	973.4
Wood, Michael. *The Story of China*	951
Civilization and Its Discontents. Freud, Sigmund	150.19

PUBLIC LIBRARY CORE COLLECTION: NONFICTION
Twentieth Edition

CIVILIZATION, ANCIENT
- Beard, Mary. ★*Emperor of Rome* — 937
- Beard, Mary. *How Do We Look* — 704.9
- Brownworth, Lars. *Lost to the West* — 949.5
- Cline, Eric H. *After 1177 B.C.* — 937
- Cooney, Kara. *When Women Ruled the World* — 920
- Everitt, Anthony. *The Rise of Rome* — 937
- Fagan, Brian M. *Climate Chaos* — 304.2
- Garfinkel, Yosef. *In the Footsteps of King David* — 933
- Gibbon, Edward. ★*The Decline and Fall of the Roman Empire* — 937
- Goldsworthy, Adrian Keith. *Antony and Cleopatra* — 937
- Goldsworthy, Adrian Keith. *Pax Romana* — 937
- Herodotus. *The Histories* — 938
- Homer. ★*The Odyssey* — 883
- Kagan, Donald. *Thucydides* — 938
- Kriwaczek, Paul. *Babylon* — 935
- Nicolson, Adam. *How to Be* — 180
- Preston, Douglas J. *The Lost Tomb* — 930.1
- Richardson, Edmund. *The King's Shadow* — 958.1
- Romer, John. *A History of Ancient Egypt* — 932
- Schiff, Stacy. ★*Cleopatra* — B
- Shaw, Ian. *The Princeton Dictionary of Ancient Egypt* — 932
- Stone, I. F. *The Trial of Socrates* — 183
- Strauss, Barry S. *The Death of Caesar* — 937
- Townsend, Richard F. *The Aztecs* — 972
- Wilkinson, Toby A. H. *The Nile* — 962
- Wilkinson, Toby A. H. ★*The Rise and Fall of Ancient Egypt* — 932
- Wilkinson, Toby A. H. *A World Beneath the Sands* — 932
- Woolf, Greg. *Rome* — 937

CIVILIZATION, ANGLO-SAXON
- Morris, Marc. ★*The Anglo-Saxons* — 942.01

CIVILIZATION, ARABIC
- Mackintosh-Smith, Tim. *Arabs* — 909.04

CIVILIZATION, CHRISTIAN
- Holland, Tom. *Dominion* — 261

CIVILIZATION, CLASSICAL
- Beard, Mary. ★*S.P.Q.R.* — 937
- Everitt, Anthony. *The Rise of Rome* — 937
- MacGregor, Neil. *A History of the World in 100 Objects* — 930.1
- Woolf, Greg. *Rome* — 937

CIVILIZATION, GRECO-ROMAN
- Beard, Mary. ★*S.P.Q.R.* — 937

CIVILIZATION, INDIGENOUS
- DuVal, Kathleen. ★*Native Nations* — 970.004

CIVILIZATION, ISLAMIC
- Akyol, Mustafa. ★*Reopening Muslim Minds* — 297.09
- Crowley, Roger. *1453* — 949.61
- Finkel, Caroline. *Osman's Dream* — 956.1
- Lal, Ruby. *Empress* — B
- Madden, Thomas F. *Istanbul* — 949.61
- Marozzi, Justin. *Islamic Empires* — 909
- Nasr, Seyyed Hossein. *Islam* — 297
- Pamuk, Orhan. *Istanbul* — 949.61
- Sebag-Montefiore, Simon. *Jerusalem* — 956.94
- Sluglett, Peter. *Atlas of Islamic History* — 912.19

CIVILIZATION, MEDIEVAL
- Ackroyd, Peter. *Foundation* — 942
- Asbridge, Thomas S. ★*The Crusades* — 909.07
- Barker, Juliet R. V. *Agincourt* — 944
- Brown, Nancy Marie. *The Abacus and the Cross* — B
- Brown, Nancy Marie. *Ivory Vikings* — 736
- Brown, Nancy Marie. *The Real Valkyrie* — 948
- Brownworth, Lars. *Lost to the West* — 949.5
- Bryson, Bill. *Notes from a Small Island* — 914
- Bryson, Bill. *The Road to Little Dribbling* — 914
- Cahill, Thomas. *How the Irish Saved Civilization* — 941.501
- Cantor, Norman F. *In the Wake of the Plague* — 614.5
- Charles-Edwards, T. M. *Wales and the Britons, 350-1064* — 942.901
- Crowley, Roger. *1453* — 949.61
- Crowley, Roger. *City of Fortune* — 945
- De Hamel, Christopher. ★*Meetings with Remarkable Manuscripts* — 091
- Gertsman, Elina. *The Middle Ages in 50 Objects* — 909.07
- Gies, Joseph. *Life in a Medieval Castle* — 940.1
- Haag, Michael. *The Tragedy of the Templars* — 271.7913
- Herrin, Judith. *Byzantium* — 949.5
- Jones, Dan. *Crusaders* — 909.07
- Jones, Dan. ★*The Plantagenets* — 942.03092
- Lacey, Robert. *Great Tales from English History 1* — 941

- Lambert, Malcolm. *God's Armies* — 956
- MacGregor, Neil. *A History of the World in 100 Objects* — 930.1
- Manchester, William. *A World Lit Only by Fire* — 940.2
- Morris, Marc. ★*The Anglo-Saxons* — 942.01
- Morris, Marc. *King John* — 942.033
- Morrison, Robert. *The Regency Years* — 941.07
- Norwich, John Julius. *A Short History of Byzantium* — 949.5
- Ramirez, Janina. *Femina* — 940.1
- Tuchman, Barbara W. ★*A Distant Mirror* — 944
- Weir, Alison. *Queens of the Conquest* — 920
- Wickham, Chris. *The Inheritance of Rome* — 940.1
- Winder, Simon. *Lotharingia* — 944

CIVILIZATION, PRE-COLUMBIAN
- Mann, Charles C. ★*1491* — 970.01

CIVILIZATION, STONE AGE
- Armstrong, Karen. ★*A Short History of Myth* — 201

CIVILIZATION, VIKING
- Brown, Nancy Marie. *The Real Valkyrie* — 948
- Herman, Arthur. *The Viking Heart* — 948
- Price, Neil S. ★*Children of Ash and Elm* — 948
- Winroth, Anders. *The Age of the Vikings* — 948

CIVILIZATION, WESTERN
- Armstrong, Karen. ★*A Short History of Myth* — 201
- Barzun, Jacques. *From Dawn to Decadence* — 940.2
- Cahill, Thomas. *Sailing the Wine-Dark Sea* — 909
- Crowley, Roger. *1453* — 949.61
- Eire, Carlos M. N. *A Very Brief History of Eternity* — 236
- Gaddis, John Lewis. *On Grand Strategy* — 355.4
- Greenblatt, Stephen. ★*The Swerve* — 940.2
- Harari, Yuval N. ★*21 Lessons for the 21st Century* — 909.82
- Herman, Arthur. *How the Scots Invented the Modern World* — 941.1
- Holland, Tom. *Dominion* — 261
- Mac Sweeney, Naoise. *The West* — 909
- Madden, Thomas F. *Venice* — 945
- McKibben, Bill. *Falter* — 909.83
- McLaren, Brian D. *Life After Doom* — 200.1
- Miles, Jack. *Religion as We Know It* — 200.9
- Mortimer, Ian. *The Time Traveler's Guide to Elizabethan England* — 942.05
- Mortimer, Ian. *The Time Traveler's Guide to Restoration Britain* — 941.06
- Strathern, Paul. *The Florentines* — 945
- Wilson-Lee, Edward. ★*The Catalogue of Shipwrecked Books* — B

CIXI, EMPRESS DOWAGER OF CHINA, 1835-1908
- Chang, Jung. *Empress Dowager Cixi* — B

Clague, Mark
- *O Say Can You Hear?* — 782.42

Claiborne, Jenne
- ★*Sweet Potato Soul* — 641.5

Claim Your Confidence. Fenet, Lydia — 158.1
Claiming Ground. Bell, Laura — B
Clapton. Clapton, Eric — B

Clapton, Eric
- *Clapton* — B

CLAPTON, ERIC
- Clapton, Eric. *Clapton* — B
- Womack, Kenneth. *All Things Must Pass Away* — 781.66

Clara's War. Kramer, Clara — B
Clarence Darrow. Farrell, John A. — B

CLARENCE, GEORGE, DUKE OF, 1449-1478
- Penn, Thomas. *The Brothers York* — 942.04

Clarey, Christopher
- ★*The Master* — B

Clark, Andy
- *The Experience Machine* — 153

Clark, Anna
- *The Poisoned City* — 363.6

Clark, Doug Bock
- *The Last Whalers* — 639.2

Clark, Heather
- ★*Red Comet* — B

Clark, John Lee
- *Touch the Future* — B

CLARK, JOHN LEE, 1978-
- Clark, John Lee. *Touch the Future* — B

CLARK, KENNETH BANCROFT, 1914-2005
- Spofford, Tim. *What the Children Told Us* — 150.92

CLARK, KENNETH, 1903-1983
- Stourton, James. *Kenneth Clark* — B

1744

AUTHOR, TITLE, SERIES AND SUBJECT INDEX

Clark, Liz
  Swell — B
CLARK, LIZ
  Clark, Liz. *Swell* — B
Clark, Lloyd
  The Commanders — 940.53
CLARK, MAMIE PHIPPS
  Spofford, Tim. *What the Children Told Us* — 150.92
Clark, Melissa
  Comfort in an Instant — 641.5
  ★*Dinner in an Instant* — 641.5
  Dinner in French — 641.594
  ★*Dinner in One* — 641.82
  Dinner — 641.5
  Kid in the Kitchen — 641.5
Clark, Taylor
  Starbucked — 338
Clark, Tiana
  I Can't Talk About the Trees Without the Blood — 811
CLARK, WILLIAM, 1770-1838
  Ambrose, Stephen E. ★*Undaunted Courage* — 917.804
CLARKE, ARTHUR C. (ARTHUR CHARLES), 1917-2008
  Benson, Michael. *Space Odyssey* — 791.43
Clarke, Gemma
  Soccerwomen — 796.334
CLARKE, KRISTOPHER
  Murdoch, Sierra Crane. ★*Yellow Bird* — 364.152
Clarke, Rachel
  Dear Life — B
CLARKE, RACHEL (PHYSICIAN)
  Clarke, Rachel. *Dear Life* — B
Clarke, Thurston
  Honorable Exit — 959.704
  JFK's Last Hundred Days — B
  The Last Campaign — B
CLARKSON, THOMAS 1760-1846
  Hochschild, Adam. *Bury the Chains* — 326
*The **Class***. Tesoriero, Heather Won — 507.1
CLASS ACTIONS (CIVIL PROCEDURE)
  Johnson, Kirk W. *The Fishermen and the Dragon* — 976.4
CLASS CONFLICT
  Land, Stephanie. *Maid* — B
  Price, David A. ★*Love and Hate in Jamestown* — 975.5
  Schwartz, Nelson. *The Velvet Rope Economy* — 339.2
  Smarsh, Sarah. ★*Heartland* — B
CLASS STRUGGLE
  Branigan, Tania. *Red Memory* — 951.05
  Brown, Archie. ★*The Rise and Fall of Communism* — 320.53
  McMeekin, Sean. *The Russian Revolution* — 947.084
  Zygar, Mikhail. *The Empire Must Die* — 947.08
Class Warfare. Brill, Steven — 371.010973
Classic German Baking. Weiss, Luisa — 641.594
Classic Human Anatomy. Winslow, Valerie L. — 743.4
Classic Krakauer. Krakauer, Jon — 814
Classical Literature. Jenkyns, Richard — 880.09
CLASSICAL MUSIC
  Berger, William. *Puccini Without Excuses* — 782.1
  Berger, William. *Verdi with a Vengeance* — B
  Chernaik, Judith. *Schumann* — B
  Gardiner, John Eliot. *Bach* — B
  Hamilton-Paterson, James. ★*Beethoven's Eroica* — 784.18
  Harris, Ellen T. *George Frideric Handel* — B
  Horowitz, Joseph. ★*Classical Music in America* — 781.6
  Hough, Stephen. *Rough Ideas* — 786.2092
  Johnson, Graham. *Poulenc* — B
  Kennicott, Philip. *Counterpoint* — B
  Kildea, Paul Francis. *Chopin's Piano* — B
  Mauceri, John. *For the Love of Music* — 781.1
  Morris, Edmund. *Beethoven* — B
  Murakami, Haruki. ★*Absolutely on Music* — 784.2
  Servadio, Gaia. *Rossini* — B
  Suchet, John. *Mozart* — B
  Suchet, John. *Verdi* — 782.1092
  Swafford, Jan. *Mozart* — B
  Walsh, Stephen. ★*Debussy* — B
  Warsaw-Fan Rauch, Arianna. ★*Declassified* — 781.1
★*Classical* Music in America. Horowitz, Joseph — 781.6

*The **Classical** Music Lover's Companion to Orchestral Music*. Philip, Robert — 784.2
CLASSICAL MUSICIANS
  Gardiner, John Eliot. *Bach* — B
  Hough, Stephen. *Rough Ideas* — 786.2092
  Morris, Edmund. *Beethoven* — B
  Warsaw-Fan Rauch, Arianna. ★*Declassified* — 781.1
  White, Richard Antoine. *I'm Possible* — B
*The **Classical** Style*. Rosen, Charles — 780.9
CLASSICS
  Dinesen, Isak. *Out of Africa* — 967.62
  Gibran, Kahlil. *And the Prophet Said* — 811
  Goethe, Johann Wolfgang von. *Goethe's Faust* — 832
  Hansberry, Lorraine. ★*A Raisin in the Sun* — 812
  Homer. *The Iliad* — 883
  Homer. *The Iliad* — 883
  Homer. *Iliad* — 883
  Homer. *The Odyssey* — 883
  Homer. *The Odyssey* — 883
  Homer. *Odyssey* — 883
  Homer. ★*The Odyssey* — 883
  Ovid. *Tales from Ovid* — 873
  Virgil. ★*The Aeneid* — 873
  Virgil. *The Aeneid* — 873
CLASSIFICATION
  Roberts, Jason. ★*Every Living Thing* — 578
CLASSISM
  Berg, Scott W. *The Burning of the World* — 977.311
  Dyson, Michael Eric. *Come Hell or High Water* — 976.3
  Eddo-Lodge, Reni. *Why I'm No Longer Talking to White People About Race* — 305.8
  Glenconner, Anne. ★*Lady in Waiting* — B
  Hay, Carol. *Think Like a Feminist* — 305.42
  Ishikawa, Masaji. ★*A River in Darkness* — B
  Moore, Wes. ★*Five Days* — 363.32
  Nusbaum, Eric. *Stealing Home* — 796.357
  Rutherford, Adam. *Control* — 363.9
  Schwartz, Nelson. *The Velvet Rope Economy* — 339.2
  Smarsh, Sarah. ★*Heartland* — B
  Stevens, Stuart. *It Was All a Lie* — 324.2734
CLASSROOM MANAGEMENT
  Baker, Nicholson. *Substitute* — 371.14
CLAUDIUS I, EMPEROR OF ROME, 10 B.C.E.-54 C.E
  Southon, Emma. *Agrippina* — B
Clavin, Thomas
  The DiMaggios — 920
  Dodge City — 978.1
  Lightning Down — 940.54
  Wild Bill — B
Clavin, Tom
  The Last Hill — 940.54
Clay, Catrine
  King, Kaiser, Tsar — B
CLAY, HENRY, 1777-1852
  Bordewich, Fergus M. *America's Great Debate* — 973.6
  Brands, H. W. ★*Heirs of the Founders* — 973.5
Cleage, Pearl
  Things I Should Have Told My Daughter — B
CLEAGE, PEARL
  Cleage, Pearl. *Things I Should Have Told My Daughter* — B
Clean. Hamblin, James — 613
Clean Economy Now. Keefe, Bob — 333.79
CLEAN ENERGY
  Bakke, Gretchen Anna. *The Grid* — 333.793
CLEAN ENERGY INDUSTRY AND TRADE
  Keefe, Bob. *Clean Economy Now* — 333.79
  Scheyder, Ernest. *The War Below* — 333.7
CLEANING
  White, Dana. *How to Manage Your Home Without Losing Your Mind* — 648
Clear, James
  ★*Atomic Habits* — 155.24
Cleaver, Eldridge
  Soul on Ice — B
CLEAVER, ELDRIDGE, 1935-1998
  Cleaver, Eldridge. *Soul on Ice* — B
Cleaver, Samantha
  Raising an Active Reader — 372.4

PUBLIC LIBRARY CORE COLLECTION: NONFICTION
Twentieth Edition

Clegg, Brian
  Are Numbers Real?   510
  Extra Sensory   133.8
Cleghorn, Elinor
  Unwell Women   613
CLEGHORN, ELINOR
  Cleghorn, Elinor. *Unwell Women*   613
Clein, Emmeline
  ★*Dead Weight*   616.85
CLEIN, EMMELINE
  Clein, Emmeline. ★*Dead Weight*   616.85
CLEMENCEAU, GEORGES, 1841-1929
  MacMillan, Margaret. *Paris 1919*   940.3
CLEMENCY
  Barnett, Brittany K. ★*A Knock at Midnight*   B
  Minow, Martha. *When Should Law Forgive?*   345
Clemente. Maraniss, David   B
CLEMENTE, ROBERTO, 1934-1972
  Maraniss, David. *Clemente*   B
  Santiago, Wilfred. *"21"*   741.5
Clementine. Purnell, Sonia   B
Clements, Carol
  Better Balance for Life   617
Clements, Jonathan
  The Anime Encyclopedia   791.43
Clemmons, Francois S.
  Officer Clemmons   B
CLEMMONS, FRANCOIS S.
  Clemmons, Francois S. *Officer Clemmons*   B
★*Cleopatra*. Schiff, Stacy   B
CLEOPATRA, QUEEN OF EGYPT, 69-30 B.C.E
  Goldsworthy, Adrian Keith. *Antony and Cleopatra*   937
  Schiff, Stacy. ★*Cleopatra*   B
  Strauss, Barry S. ★*The War That Made the Roman Empire*   937
CLERGY
  Billings, J. Todd. *Rejoicing in Lament*   248.8
  Eig, Jonathan. ★*King*   B
  Francis. *Life*   B
  Harrington, Joel F. *Dangerous Mystic*   B
  Jackson, Troy. *Becoming King*   B
  King, Martin Luther. *The Autobiography of Martin Luther King, Jr.*   B
  King, Maxwell. *The Good Neighbor*   B
  McCloskey, Jim. *When Truth Is All You Have*   B
  Metaxas, Eric. *Martin Luther*   B
  Shanley, John Patrick. *Doubt*   812
  Sharpton, Al. *Rise Up*   973.933
  Wacker, Grant. *America's Pastor*   B
  Warren, James A. *God, War, and Providence*   974.5
CLERGYWOMEN
  Baskette, Molly Phinney. *How to Begin When Your World Is Ending*   248.8
  Cobbs-Leonard, Tasha. *Do It Anyway*   241
  Moore, Beth. *All My Knotted-Up Life*   B
  Quinn, Tallu Schuyler. *What We Wish Were True*   B
  Rosenberg, Rosalind. ★*Jane Crow*   B
  Taylor, Barbara Brown. *Holy Envy*   B
CLEVELAND, GROVER, 1837-1908
  Graff, Henry F. *Grover Cleveland*   B
  Senik, Troy. *A Man of Iron*   B
CLEVELAND, OHIO
  Collins, Max Allan. *Eliot Ness and the Mad Butcher*   364.152
  Fenn, Lisa. *Carry On*   B
  Stashower, Daniel. *American Demon*   364.152
Cleveland, Pat
  Walking with the Muses   B
CLEVELAND, PAT
  Cleveland, Pat. *Walking with the Muses*   B
Cliff, Harry
  How to Make an Apple Pie from Scratch   523.01
Cliff, Nigel
  Holy War   909
CLIFF-DWELLINGS
  Roberts, David. *The Bears Ears*   979.2
Clifton, Lucille
  How to Carry Water   811
  Mercy   811
CLIMATE AND CIVILIZATION
  Frankopan, Peter. *The Earth Transformed*   304.2
★*The Climate Book*. Thunberg, Greta   363.738

CLIMATE CHANGE
  Aguon, Julian. *No Country for Eight-Spot Butterflies*   305.89
  Atleework, Kendra. *Miracle Country*   979.4
  Atwood, Margaret. *Burning Questions*   814
  Barnett, Cynthia. *Rain*   551.57
  Barnett, Cynthia. ★*The Sound of the Sea*   591.47
  Bell, Alice R. *Our Biggest Experiment*   363.738
  Berners-Lee, Mike. *The Carbon Footprint of Everything*   363.738
  Bittle, Jake. ★*The Great Displacement*   362.87
  Brannen, Peter. *The Ends of the World*   576.8
  Casey, Susan. *The Underworld*   551.46
  Chachra, Deb. *How Infrastructure Works*   363
  Chomsky, Noam. *Global Discontents*   410.92
  Dickie, Gloria. *Eight Bears*   599.78
  Dolin, Eric Jay. *A Furious Sky*   363.34
  Ehrlich, Gretel. *Unsoloaced*   B
  Fagan, Brian M. *Climate Chaos*   304.2
  Fagan, Brian M. *The Long Summer*   551.6
  Farmer, Jared. *Elderflora*   582.16
  Flowers, Catherine Coleman. *Waste*   363.72
  Foer, Jonathan Safran. ★*We Are the Weather*   636
  Fox, Porter. *The Last Winter*   363.738
  Frankopan, Peter. *The Earth Transformed*   304.2
  Franzen, Jonathan. *The End of the End of the Earth*   814
  Friedman, Thomas L. ★*Thank You for Being Late*   303.48
  Gee, Alastair. *Fire in Paradise*   363.37
  Ghosh, Amitav. *The Great Derangement*   809
  Gleick, Peter H. *The Three Ages of Water*   333.91
  Goodell, Jeff. *The Heat Will Kill You First*   363.738
  Goodell, Jeff. *The Water Will Come*   551.45
  Graham, Jorie. *To 2040*   811
  Gyllenhaal, Anders. *A Wing and a Prayer*   639.97
  Hanson, Thor. *Hurricane Lizards and Plastic Squid*   577.2
  Harper, Kyle. *The Fate of Rome*   937
  Hayhoe, Katharine. *Saving Us*   304.2
  Heacox, Kim. ★*John Muir and the Ice That Started a Fire*   333.7209798
  Heacox, Kim. *Rhythm of the Wild*   979.8
  Hendrickson, Debra. ★*The Air They Breathe*   363.7
  Hiss, Tony. ★*Rescuing the Planet*   333.75
  Holthaus, Eric. *The Future Earth*   363.738
  Jabr, Ferris. ★*Becoming Earth*   570.1
  Kenny, Charles. *The Plague Cycle*   614.4
  Klare, Michael T. *All Hell Breaking Loose*   355.20973
  Kolbert, Elizabeth. *Field Notes from a Catastrophe*   363.738
  Kostigen, Thomas. *Hacking Planet Earth*   628
  Lacovara, Kenneth. *Why Dinosaurs Matter*   567.9
  Lewis, Daniel. *Twelve Trees*   582.16
  Lim, Audrea. *Free the Land*   333.73
  Linden, Eugene. *Fire and Flood*   304.2
  Lipsky, David. ★*The Parrot and the Igloo*   304.2
  Lowman, Margaret. *The Arbornaut*   581.7
  Lustgarten, Abrahm. *On the Move*   363.7
  Lynas, Mark. *Six Degrees*   551.6
  Macdonald, Helen. ★*Vesper Flights*   508
  Martin, Manjula. *The Last Fire Season*   B
  Mathews, Daniel. *Trees in Trouble*   634.9
  McKibben, Bill. *Falter*   909.83
  McLaren, Brian D. *Life After Doom*   200.1
  Millet, Lydia. *We Loved It All*   813
  Monbiot, George. ★*Regenesis*   338.1
  Moore, Kathleen Dean. *Earth's Wild Music*   576.8
  Nhat Hanh. *Zen and the Art of Saving the Planet*   294.3
  Owens, Jay. *Dust*   551.51
  Patterson, Scott. ★*Chaos Kings*   338.5
  Pearce, Fred. *A Trillion Trees*   577.3
  Pollack, H. N. *A World Without Ice*   551.31
  Preston, Christopher J. *Tenacious Beasts*   591.68
  Proulx, Annie. ★*Fen, Bog and Swamp*   551.41
  Raboteau, Emily. *Lessons for Survival*   814
  Rawlence, Ben. *The Treeline*   577.3
  Rich, Nathaniel. *Second Nature*   304.2
  Ritchie, Hannah. *Not the End of the World*   338.9
  Rush, Elizabeth A. *Rising*   551.45
  Smith, Clint. ★*Above Ground*   811
  Swift, Earl. *Chesapeake Requiem*   639
  Thunberg, Greta. ★*The Climate Book*   363.738
  Vaillant, John. ★*Fire Weather*   363.37
  Vigliotti, Jonathan. *Before It's Gone*   577

AUTHOR, TITLE, SERIES AND SUBJECT INDEX

Vince, Gaia. *Nomad Century*	362.87
Vollmann, William T. *No Immediate Danger*	333.79
Waldman, Michael. *The Supermajority*	347.73
Wallace-Wells, David. *The Uninhabitable Earth*	304.2
Welz, Adam. *The End of Eden*	577.2
Williams, Kale. *The Loneliest Polar Bear*	599.786
Wood, Gillen D'Arcy. *Land of Wondrous Cold*	919.89
Woolfson, Esther. *Between Light and Storm*	599.93
Wray, Britt. *Generation Dread*	155.9
Yergin, Daniel. *The New Map*	333.79
CLIMATE CHANGE MITIGATION	
Jabr, Ferris. ★*Becoming Earth*	570.1
Ritchie, Hannah. *Not the End of the World*	338.9
Roman, Joe. *Eat, Poop, Die*	577
Thunberg, Greta. ★*The Climate Book*	363.738
Climate Chaos. Fagan, Brian M.	304.2
CLIMATIC EXTREMES	
Frankopan, Peter. *The Earth Transformed*	304.2
Goodell, Jeff. *The Heat Will Kill You First*	363.738
Kostigen, Thomas. *Hacking Planet Earth*	628
CLIMATOLOGISTS	
Hayhoe, Katharine. *Saving Us*	304.2
CLIMATOLOGY	
Bell, Alice R. *Our Biggest Experiment*	363.738
Fagan, Brian M. *The Long Summer*	551.6
Goodell, Jeff. *The Water Will Come*	551.45
Holthaus, Eric. *The Future Earth*	363.738
Redniss, Lauren. *Thunder & Lightning*	741.5
Williams, Jack. ★*The Ams Weather Book*	551.5
The Climb. Bukreev, Anatolii Nikolaevich	796.52
Cline, Elizabeth L.	
The Conscious Closet	646
Cline, Eric H.	
After 1177 B.C.	937
CLINE, PATSY, 1932-1963	
Lynn, Loretta. ★*Me & Patsy Kickin' up Dust*	B
CLINICAL PSYCHOLOGISTS	
Thompson, J. M. *Running Is a Kind of Dreaming*	B
CLINICAL TRIALS	
Goldacre, Ben. *Bad Science*	500
Offit, Paul A. *You Bet Your Life*	615.5
CLINICS	
Webb, Kinari. *Guardians of the Trees*	B
CLINTON FAMILY	
Clinton, Bill. *My Life*	B
The Clinton Tapes. Branch, Taylor	973.929
Clinton, Bill	
My Life	B
CLINTON, BILL, 1946-	
Branch, Taylor. *The Clinton Tapes*	973.929
Clinton, Bill. *My Life*	B
Clinton, Hillary Rodham. *Living History*	B
Kornacki, Steve. *The Red and the Blue*	306.20973
Woodward, Bob. *Shadow*	973.92
Clinton, Catherine	
Harriet Tubman	B
CLINTON, HENRY, SIR, 1738?-1795	
Ferling, John E. *Winning Independence*	973.3
Clinton, Hillary Rodham	
The Book of Gutsy Women	920
It Takes a Village	305.23
Living History	B
What Happened	328.73
CLINTON, HILLARY RODHAM	
Allen, Jonathan. *Shattered*	324.973
Chozick, Amy. *Chasing Hillary*	B
Clinton, Hillary Rodham. *It Takes a Village*	305.23
Clinton, Hillary Rodham. *Living History*	B
Clinton, Hillary Rodham. *What Happened*	328.73
D'Antonio, Michael. *The Hunting of Hillary*	B
CLIPPER-SHIPS	
Ujifusa, Steven. *Barons of the Sea*	387.5
CLOCK AND WATCH MAKERS	
Loftis, Larry. ★*The Watchmaker's Daughter*	940.53
Sobel, Dava. *Longitude*	526
The Cloister Walk. Norris, Kathleen	255
★*Cloistered*. Coldstream, Catherine	B
Close Encounters of the Third Kind. Klastorin, Michael	791.43
Close Encounters with Humankind. Yi, Sang-Hui	599.93
The Closer. Rivera, Mariano	B
CLOSETED GAY MEN	
Bechdel, Alison. ★*Fun Home*	741.5
Closing The Courthouse Door. Chemerinsky, Erwin	347.73
Clothes, Clothes, Clothes. Music, Music, Music. Albertine, Viv	B
CLOTHING	
Baca, Salena. *Oversize Fashion Crochet*	746.43
Bari, Shahidha K. *Dressed*	391
Carter, Ruth E. ★*The Art of Ruth E. Carter*	746.9
Cline, Elizabeth L. *The Conscious Closet*	646
Cox, Caroline. *The World Atlas of Street Fashion*	391.009
Dirix, Emmanuelle. *Dressing the Decades*	746.92
Edwards, Zoe. *Mend It, Wear It, Love It!*	646
Faerm, Steven. *Fashion Design Course*	746.9
Ford, Tanisha C. *Dressed in Dreams*	391
Holmes, Elizabeth. *HRH*	941.085
Ishida, Sanae. *Sewing Love*	646
Karen, Dawnn. *Dress Your Best Life*	646
Leventon, Melissa. *What People Wore When*	391.009
Misumi, Noriko. *Mending with Love*	646.6
Montenegro, Sonya. *Mending Life*	646
Murphy, Marilyn. *Woven to Wear*	746.1
Parton, Dolly. ★*Behind the Seams*	B
Thanhauser, Sofi. *Worn*	391
Tonti, Lucianne. *Sundressed*	746.9
Wicker, Alden. ★*To Dye For*	746
Yang, April. *DIY Thrift Flip*	646.2
CLOTHING INDUSTRY AND TRADE	
Au-Yeung, Angel. *Wonder Boy*	B
Cline, Elizabeth L. *The Conscious Closet*	646
Enninful, Edward. *A Visible Man*	B
Flannery, Kate. *Strip Tees*	338.4
Gucci, Patricia. *In the Name of Gucci*	B
Hardy, Alyssa. *Worn Out*	338.4
Kurutz, Steven. *American Flannel*	338.4
Mizrahi, Isaac. *I.M.*	B
Secrest, Meryle. *Elsa Schiaparelli*	746.9
Slade, Rachel. *American Hoodie*	338.4
Talley, Andre Leon. *The Chiffon Trenches*	B
Thomas, Dana. *Gods and Kings*	920
Tonti, Lucianne. *Sundressed*	746.9
Wicker, Alden. ★*To Dye For*	746
Yong, Sable. *Die Hot with a Vengeance*	646.7
CLOTHING WORKERS	
Hardy, Alyssa. *Worn Out*	338.4
CLOUDS	
Redniss, Lauren. *Thunder & Lightning*	741.5
Clouds of Glory. Korda, Michael	B
CLOVER, ELZADA	
Sevigny, Melissa L. ★*Brave the Wild River*	580.9
The Club. Damrosch, Leopold	920
CLUBS	
Damrosch, Leopold. *The Club*	920
CLUES	
Bonner, Betsy. *The Book of Atlantis Black*	364.152
Clutter. Howard, Jennifer	306.3
CLUTTER	
Howard, Jennifer. *Clutter*	306.3
Kondo, Marie. ★*The Life-Changing Magic of Tidying Up*	648
McCubbin, Tracy. *Make Space for Happiness*	179
White, Dana. *How to Manage Your Home Without Losing Your Mind*	648
CLUTTER FAMILY	
Capote, Truman. ★*In Cold Blood*	364.1
Co-Mix. Spiegelman, Art	741.5
Co-Parenting Through Separation and Divorce. Blackstone-Ford, Jann	306.89
COACH AND ATHLETE	
Thompson, Wright. *The Cost of These Dreams*	B
Tyson, Mike. *Iron Ambition*	B
Coach K. O'Connor, Ian	B
Coach Wooden and Me. Abdul-Jabbar, Kareem	B
COACHING (ATHLETICS)	
Checkoway, Julie. *The Three-Year Swim Club*	797.2
Davis, Seth. *Getting to Us*	796.07
Davis, Seth. *Wooden*	B
O'Connor, Ian. *Belichick*	B
COAL INDUSTRY AND TRADE	
Leamer, Laurence. *The Price of Justice*	346.7302

PUBLIC LIBRARY CORE COLLECTION: NONFICTION
Twentieth Edition

COAL MINERS
    Berfield, Susan. *The Hour of Fate*   973.91
    Bradley, Mark A. *Blood Runs Coal*   B
    Hamby, Chris. *Soul Full of Coal Dust*   363.11
COAL MINES AND MINING
    Biggers, Jeff. *Reckoning at Eagle Creek*   333.73
    Leamer, Laurence. *The Price of Justice*   346.7302
    Maher, Kris. *Desperate*   344
COAL MINING TOWNS
    Hickam, Homer H. ★*Rocket Boys*   B
COAST CHANGES
    Dean, Cornelia. *Against the Tide*   333.91
    Goodell, Jeff. *The Water Will Come*   551.45
    Rush, Elizabeth A. *Rising*   551.45
COAST SALISH (NORTH AMERICAN PEOPLE)
    LaPointe, Sasha taqwseblu. *Red Paint*   B
    LaPointe, Sasha taqwseblu. *Thunder Song*   814
COASTAL ECOLOGY
    Carson, Rachel. *The Edge of the Sea*   578.769
    Davis, Jack E. ★*The Gulf*   909
    Rush, Elizabeth A. *Rising*   551.45
    Steelquist, Robert. *The Northwest Coastal Explorer*   508
COASTAL TOWNS
    Cameron, Silver Donald. *Blood in the Water*   364.152
    Dean, Cornelia. *Against the Tide*   333.91
    Hohn, Donovan. *The Inner Coast*   304.20973
    Swift, Earl. *Chesapeake Requiem*   639
COASTS
    Ash, Lamorna. *Dark, Salt, Clear*   942.3
    Davis, Jack E. ★*The Gulf*   909
    Rush, Elizabeth A. *Rising*   551.45
    Shorto, Russell. *Amsterdam*   949.2
COATES, DASANI, 2001-
    Elliott, Andrea. ★*Invisible Child*   362.7
Coates, Laura Gayle
    Just Pursuit   345.73
COATES, LAURA GAYLE
    Coates, Laura Gayle. *Just Pursuit*   345.73
Coates, Ta-Nehisi
    The Beautiful Struggle   B
    ★*Between the World and Me*   305.800973
    ★*We Were Eight Years in Power*   305.896
COATES, TA-NEHISI
    Coates, Ta-Nehisi. *The Beautiful Struggle*   B
COBAIN, KURT, 1967-1994
    Cross, Charles R. *Here We Are Now*   782.42166
Cobalt Red. Kara, Siddharth   338.2
Cobb. Stump, Al   B
COBB, JERRIE
    Teitel, Amy Shira. *Fighting for Space*   920
COBB, TY, 1886-1961
    Stump, Al. *Cobb*   B
Cobbs-Leonard, Tasha
    Do It Anyway   241
COBBS-LEONARD, TASHA, 1981-
    Cobbs-Leonard, Tasha. *Do It Anyway*   241
Coburn, Broughton
    Everest   796.5
COCA INDUSTRY AND TRADE
    Muse, Toby. *Kilo*   363.4509861
COCAINE
    Ramsey, Donovan X. ★*When Crack Was King*   362.29
COCAINE ABUSE
    Carr, David. *The Night of the Gun*   B
COCAINE SMUGGLING
    Muse, Toby. *Kilo*   363.4509861
COCAINE TRAFFIC
    Muse, Toby. *Kilo*   363.4509861
    Westhoff, Ben. *Original Gangstas*   782.421649
COCHISE, APACHE CHIEF, DIED 1874
    Roberts, David. *Once They Moved Like the Wind*   B
COCHLEAR IMPLANTS
    Owen, David. *Volume Control*   617.8
COCHRAN, JACQUELINE
    Teitel, Amy Shira. *Fighting for Space*   920
COCKTAILS
    Hoffman, Maggie. *Batch Cocktails*   641.87
    Mullen, Marissa. *That Cheese Plate Wants to Party*   641.6

    Rollich, Christiaan. *Bar Chef*   641.87
    Tipton-Martin, Toni. *Juke Joints, Jazz Clubs & Juice*   641.87
Cod. Kurlansky, Mark   333.95
COD
    Greenberg, Paul. *Four Fish*   333.95
    Kurlansky, Mark. *Cod*   333.95
COD FISHING
    Kurlansky, Mark. *Cod*   333.95
★*The **Code** Breaker.* Isaacson, Walter   576.5
***Code** Dependent.* Murgia, Madhumita   303.48
***Code** Girls.* Mundy, Liza   940.54
***Code** Name.* Loftis, Larry   B
***Code** Name Blue Wren.* Popkin, Jim   327.12
***Code** Name Madeleine.* Magida, Arthur J.   940.54
***Code** of Silence.* Olsen, Lise   347.73
***Code** Talker.* Nez, Chester   B
***Code** Warriors.* Budiansky, Stephen   327.73047
CODEPENDENCY
    Aron, Nina Renata. *Good Morning, Destroyer of Men's Souls*   B
    Beattie, Melody. *Codependent No More*   616.86
    Buhle, Kathleen. *If We Break*   B
***Codependent** No More.* Beattie, Melody   616.86
Coders. Thompson, Clive   005.1092
CODES (COMMUNICATION)
    Barbarisi, Daniel. *Chasing the Thrill*   796.1
    Budiansky, Stephen. *Code Warriors*   327.73047
    Copeland, B. Jack. *Turing*   B
    Fagone, Jason. *The Woman Who Smashed Codes*   B
    Lee, Heath Hardage. ★*The League of Wives*   959.704
    Nez, Chester. *Code Talker*   B
    Tobin, Jacqueline. *Hidden in Plain View*   973.7
Codina, Carles
    The Complete Book of Jewelry Making   739.27
Codjoe, Ama
    Bluest Nude   811
Cody, Anthony
    Borderland Apocrypha   811
Coe, Alexis
    ★*You Never Forget Your First*   B
Coe, Michael D.
    The Maya   972
Coel, Michaela
    ★*Misfits*   158.2
COEL, MICHAELA
    Coel, Michaela. ★*Misfits*   158.2
COERCION
    Auletta, Ken. ★*Hollywood Ending*   791.43
    Berman, Sarah. *Don't Call It a Cult*   361.4
    Farrow, Ronan. ★*Catch and Kill*   331.4
    Rinder, Mike. ★*A Billion Years*   B
Coetzee, J. M.
    Late Essays, 2006-2017   824
COETZEE, J. M., 1940-
    Attwell, David. *J. M. Coetzee and the Life of Writing*   823
COFFEE
    Clark, Taylor. *Starbucked*   338
    Easto, Jessica. *How to Taste Coffee*   663
    Sedgewick, Augustine. *Coffeeland*   338.4
    Standage, Tom. *A History of the World in 6 Glasses*   394.1
COFFEE INDUSTRY AND TRADE
    Clark, Taylor. *Starbucked*   338
    Eggers, Dave. *The Monk of Mokha*   B
    Sedgewick, Augustine. *Coffeeland*   338.4
COFFEE PLANTATIONS
    Kars, Marjoleine. *Blood on the River*   306.3
    Sedgewick, Augustine. *Coffeeland*   338.4
COFFEE SHOPS
    Clark, Taylor. *Starbucked*   338
***Coffee** with Hitler.* Spicer, Charles   941.084
Coffeeland. Sedgewick, Augustine   338.4
Coffey, Wayne R.
    ★*The Boys of Winter*   796.962
Coffin, Jaed
    Roughhouse Friday   B
COFFIN, JAED
    Coffin, Jaed. *Roughhouse Friday*   B
Coffin, Judith G.
    Sex, Love, and Letters   848

AUTHOR, TITLE, SERIES AND SUBJECT INDEX

Cogeval, Guy
   Edouard Vuillard   759.4
Coggan, Philip
   Surviving the Daily Grind   658.3
Cogito Ergo Sum. Watson, Richard A.   B
COGNITION
   Bargh, John A. *Before You Know It*   154.2
   Dobelli, Rolf. *The Art of Thinking Clearly*   153.4
   Dunbar, R. I. M. *Human Evolution*   155.7
   Gupta, Sanjay. ★*Keep Sharp*   153.4
   Harari, Yuval N. ★*Sapiens*   909
   Iyengar, Sheena. *The Art of Choosing*   153.8
   Jacobs, A. J. *The Puzzler*   793.73
   Johnson, Steven. *Farsighted*   153.8
   Pink, Daniel H. *Drive*   153.1
   Pinker, Steven. *The Blank Slate*   155.2
   Pinker, Steven. *Rationality*   153.4
   Ranganath, Charan. ★*Why We Remember*   153.1
   Rosling, Hans. *Factfulness*   155.9
   Sarma, Sanjay E. *Grasp*   370.15
   Seldin, Tim. *How to Raise an Amazing Child the Montessori Way*   649
   Spitzer, Michael. *The Musical Human*   780.9
   Willeumier, Kristen. ★*Biohack Your Brain*   612.8
   Wolf, Maryanne. *Reader, Come Home*   418
COGNITION AND CULTURE
   Harari, Yuval N. ★*Sapiens*   909
   Wertheim, L. Jon. *This Is Your Brain on Sports*   796.01
COGNITION IN ANIMALS
   Golbeck, Jennifer. *The Purest Bond*   636.7
   Horowitz, Alexandra. ★*Being a Dog*   636.7
COGNITIVE NEUROSCIENCE
   Ahuvia, Aaron. ★*The Things We Love*   790.1
   Fainaru-Wada, Mark. *League of Denial*   617.1
   Fleming, Renee. ★*Music and Mind*   615.8
   Gurdon, Meghan Cox. *The Enchanted Hour*   372.4
   Laskas, Jeanne Marie. *Concussion*   617.5
   Lewis, Michael. ★*The Undoing Project*   920
   Pinker, Steven. *How the Mind Works*   153
   Sarma, Sanjay E. *Grasp*   370.15
   Shermer, Michael. *The Believing Brain*   153.4
   Wood, Wendy. *Good Habits, Bad Habits*   152.3
   Wright, Robert. *Why Buddhism Is True*   294.3
COGNITIVE SCIENCE
   Bloom, Paul. *Psych*   150
   Clark, Andy. *The Experience Machine*   153
   Fine, Cordelia. *Testosterone Rex*   155.3
   Hoffman, Donald D. *The Case Against Reality*   121
   Hofstadter, Douglas R. *Surfaces and Essences*   169
COGNITIVE STYLES
   Seldin, Tim. *How to Raise an Amazing Child the Montessori Way*   649
COGNITIVE THERAPY
   Grover, Joanna. *The Choice Point*   158.1
   Mandel, Sarah. *Little Earthquakes*   B
   Navab, Pedram. *Sleep Reimagined*   616.8
The Cognoscenti's Guide to Florence. Fili, Louise   381
Cohan, William D.
   Power Failure   338.7
Cohen, Adam
   ★*Imbeciles*   344.7304
   ★*Supreme Inequality*   347.73
Cohen, Andrew
   Two Days in June   973.922
Cohen, Deborah
   Last Call at the Hotel Imperial   070.92
Cohen, Eliot A.
   Conquered into Liberty   355.009747
Cohen, Jake
   Jew-Ish   641.5
Cohen, Jared
   Accidental Presidents   973.09
   Life After Power   973.09
Cohen, Leonard
   The Flame   810
COHEN, LEONARD, 1934-2016
   Simmons, Sylvie. *I'm Your Man*   B
Cohen, Lizabeth
   A Consumers' Republic   339.4

Cohen, Rhaina
   ★*The Other Significant Others*   177
Cohen, Rich
   The Chicago Cubs   796.357
   The Sun and the Moon and the Rolling Stones   782.42166
Cohen, Robert
   Acting Power   792.02
Cohen, Roger
   An Affirming Flame   071
COHEN, STEVEN A., 1956-
   Kolhatkar, Sheelah. *Black Edge*   364.16
Cohen-Solal, Annie
   Mark Rothko   759.13
COHN, BILLY
   Swartz, Mimi. *Ticker*   617.4
Cohn, Jonathan
   The Ten Year War   368.38
COHN, ROY M.
   Kushner, Tony. *Angels in America*   812
Cohodas, Nadine
   Princess Noire   782.42164
Coile, D. Caroline
   Encyclopedia of Dog Breeds   636.7
COIN TRICKS
   Owen, Oscar. *Mind-Blowing Magic Tricks for Everyone*   793.8
COINCIDENCE
   Mazur, Joseph. *Fluke*   519.2
Coker, Margaret
   The Spymaster of Baghdad   956.7044
Cokie. Roberts, Steven V.   B
Colaiaco, James A.
   Frederick Douglass and the Fourth of July   973.7
COLD
   Hogge, Fred. *Of Ice and Men*   338.4
   Twilley, Nicola. ★*Frostbite*   621
COLD CASES (CRIMINAL INVESTIGATION)
   Bowden, Mark. *The Case of the Vanishing Blonde*   364.10973
   Bowden, Mark. *The Last Stone*   363.25
   Brown, Vanessa. *The Forest City Killer*   364.152
   Cooper, Becky. *We Keep the Dead Close*   364.152
   Corcoran, Katherine. *In the Mouth of the Wolf*   364.152
   Eisenberg, Emma Copley. ★*The Third Rainbow Girl*   364.152
   Holes, Paul. *Unmasked*   363.25
   Humes, Edward. *The Forever Witness*   363.25
   Lankford, Andrea. *Trail of the Lost*   363.2
   McGough, Matthew. *The Lazarus Files*   364.152
   McNamara, Michelle. *I'll Be Gone in the Dark*   364.152
   Mitchell, Jerry. ★*Race Against Time*   364.152
   Norton, Laurah. *Lay Them to Rest*   363.25
   Rae-Venter, Barbara. *I Know Who You Are*   364.152
   Sullivan, Rosemary. *The Betrayal of Anne Frank*   940.53
   White, Richard. *Who Killed Jane Stanford?*   364.152
Cold Crematorium. Debreczeni, Jozsef   940.53
The Cold War. Westad, Odd Arne   909.825
COLD WAR
   Ambinder, Marc. *The Brink*   355.5
   Anderson, Scott. ★*The Quiet Americans*   327.12
   Baime, A. J. *The Accidental President*   B
   Baker, Nicholson. *Baseless*   358
   Brands, H. W. *The General vs. the President*   973.918092
   Brinkley, Douglas. ★*American Moonshot*   629.40973
   Budiansky, Stephen. *Code Warriors*   327.73047
   Carlson, Peter. *K Blows Top*   947.085
   Carney, Scott. *The Vortex*   954.92
   Chamberlin, Paul Thomas. *The Cold War's Killing Fields*   355.009
   Cunningham, Benjamin. *The Liar*   327.1273
   Donovan, Jim. ★*Shoot for the Moon*   629.45
   Finn, Peter. *The Zhivago Affair*   891.73
   Gordin, Michael D. *Red Cloud at Dawn*   355.02
   Graff, Garrett M. *Raven Rock*   363.350973
   Hampton, Dan. *Chasing the Demon*   629.132
   Hitchcock, William I. *The Age of Eisenhower*   973.921092
   Hornfischer, James D. *Who Can Hold the Sea*   359.00973
   Hoyer, Katja. ★*Beyond the Wall*   943.087
   Humphreys, Richard. *Under Pressure*   B
   Jacobsen, Annie. ★*Operation Paperclip*   940.54
   Judt, Tony. *Postwar*   940.55
   Kershaw, Ian. *The Global Age*   940.55

PUBLIC LIBRARY CORE COLLECTION: NONFICTION
Twentieth Edition

Kluger, Jeffrey. ★*Apollo 8* — 629.45
Logevall, Fredrik. *Embers of War* — 959.704
Longo, Matthew. *The Picnic* — 947.084
Lynskey, Dorian. *The Ministry of Truth* — 823
Macintyre, Ben. ★*Agent Sonya* — B
Macintyre, Ben. ★*The Spy and the Traitor* — B
Mann, Jim. *The Rebellion of Ronald Reagan* — 973.927092
McKay, Sinclair. *Berlin* — 943
Menand, Louis. *The Free World* — 306.0973
Merriman, Helena. ★*Tunnel 29* — 943
Milton, Giles. *Checkmate in Berlin* — 943
Navarro, Joe. *Three Minutes to Doomsday* — B
Petraeus, David Howell. *Conflict* — 355
Phillips, Timothy. *Retracing the Iron Curtain* — 909.82
Plokhy, Serhii. ★*Nuclear Folly* — 972.9106
Reagan, Ronald. *The Reagan Diaries* — B
Reynolds, Nicholas E. *Need to Know* — 940.54
Sarotte, M. E. *The Collapse* — 943.087
Schlosser, Eric. *Command and Control* — 363.17
Sebestyen, Victor. *Revolution 1989* — 947.085
Service, Robert. *The End of the Cold War 1985-1991* — 909.82
Sheehan, Neil. *A Fiery Peace in a Cold War* — B
Sherman, Casey. *Above and Beyond* — 973.922092
Taubman, William. *Gorbachev* — B
Taubman, William. *Khrushchev* — B
Taylor, Fred. *The Berlin Wall* — 943
Thomas, Evan. *Ike's Bluff* — 973.921092
Thompson, Nicholas. *The Hawk and the Dove* — 973.92
Trahair, R. C. S. *Encyclopedia of Cold War Espionage, Spies, and Secret Operations 3rd Ed.* — 327.12
Vogel, Steve. *Betrayal in Berlin* — 327.1273043
Von Tunzelmann, Alex. *Blood and Sand* — 909.82
Walker, Stephen. *Beyond* — 629.45
Walton, Calder. *Spies* — 327.1247
Warren, James A. *Year of the Hawk* — 959.704
Weiner, Tim. *The Folly and the Glory* — 327.73047
Westad, Odd Arne. *The Cold War* — 909.825
Wilford, Hugh. *The CIA* — 327.1273
Willner, Nina. *Forty Autumns* — B
The Cold War's Killing Fields. Chamberlin, Paul Thomas — 355.009
The Coldest War. Brady, James — B
The Coldest Winter. Halberstam, David — 951.904
Coldstream, Catherine
　★*Cloistered* — B
COLDSTREAM, CATHERINE
　Coldstream, Catherine. ★*Cloistered* — B
Cole Porter. McBrien, William — B
Cole, Jason
　Elway — B
COLE, NAT
　Lees, Gene. *You Can't Steal a Gift* — B
COLE, NAT KING, 1919-1965
　Friedwald, Will. *Straighten up and Fly Right* — 782.42164
Cole, Natalie
　Angel on My Shoulder — B
　★*Transforming Summer Programs at Your Library* — 028
COLE, NATALIE, 1950-2014
　Cole, Natalie. *Angel on My Shoulder* — B
Cole, Samantha
　How the Internet Changed Sex and Sex Changed the Internet — 306.7
Cole, Teju
　Blind Spot — 770
COLE, TEJU
　Cole, Teju. *Blind Spot* — 770
Coleman, David G.
　The Fourteenth Day — 973.922092
Coleman, Eliot
　★*The New Organic Grower* — 635
Coleman, Rick
　★*Blue Monday* — B
Coleridge, Samuel Taylor
　The Complete Poems — 821
COLERIDGE, SAMUEL TAYLOR, 1772-1834
　Nicolson, Adam. *The Making of Poetry* — 821.709
Coles, Robert
　Lives of Moral Leadership — 170
Coll, Steve
　★*The Achilles Trap* — 956.7044

The Bin Ladens — 920
Directorate S — 958.104
★*Ghost Wars* — 958.104
Private Empire — 338.7
The Collaboration. Urwand, Ben — 791.430973
COLLABORATION
　Benjamin, Ruha. ★*Imagination* — 302
　Cerulo, Erica. *Work Wife* — 658.4
　Lessig, Lawrence. *Remix* — 346.7304
　Levine, Madeline. ★*Ready or Not* — 649
　Malone, Thomas W. *Superminds* — 005.7
　McAfee, Andrew. *The Geek Way* — 658.3
　Mlodinow, Leonard. *Stephen Hawking* — B
　Teachout, Terry. *Duke* — B
COLLAGE
　Matisse, Henri. *Henri Matisse* — 709.2
Collapse. Diamond, Jared M. — 304.2
The Collapse. Sarotte, M. E — 943.087
COLLAZO, JULIE SCHWIETERT
　Pablo Cruz, Rosayra. *The Book of Rosy* — B
★*The Collected Dialogues of Plato, Including the Letters*. Plato — 184
Collected Early Poems, 1950-1970. Rich, Adrienne — 811
★*Collected Essays*. Baldwin, James — 814
★*Collected Essays and Poems*. Thoreau, Henry David — 818
★*The Collected Essays of Ralph Ellison*. Ellison, Ralph — 814
The Collected Home. Carter, Darryl — 747
The Collected Letters of Thomas Hardy. Hardy, Thomas — 823
Collected Lyrics. Smith, Patti — 782
Collected Poems. Rich, Adrienne — 811
★*Collected Poems*. Larkin, Philip — 821
Collected Poems. Swenson, May — 811
Collected Poems. Garcia Lorca, Federico — 861
The Collected Poems. Cavafy, Constantine — 889
Collected Poems. Kinnell, Galway — 811
Collected Poems. Hayden, Robert — 811
Collected Poems. Auden, W. H. — 811
Collected Poems. Millay, Edna St. Vincent — 811
Collected Poems. Lowell, Robert — 811
Collected Poems. Gilbert, Jack — 811
Collected Poems. Padgett, Ron — 811
Collected Poems. Schuyler, James — 811
★*The Collected Poems*. Kunitz, Stanley — 811
★*Collected Poems*. Williams, C. K. — 811
Collected Poems. Bly, Robert — 811
★*The Collected Poems*. Plath, Sylvia — 811
Collected Poems. Strand, Mark — 811
★*Collected Poems and Translations*. Emerson, Ralph Waldo — 811
Collected Poems in English and French. Beckett, Samuel — 841
★*The Collected Poems of Octavio Paz, 1957-1987*. Paz, Octavio — 861
The Collected Poems of Theodore Roethke. Roethke, Theodore — 811
The Collected Poems of W.B. Yeats. Yeats, W. B. — 821
Collected Poems, 1909-1962. Eliot, T. S. — 821.912
Collected Poems, 1912-1944. H. D. — 811
Collected Poems, 1937-1971. Berryman, John — 811
★*Collected Poems, 1943-2004*. Wilbur, Richard — 811
The Collected Poems, 1956-1998. Herbert, Zbigniew — 891.8
Collected Poetry and Prose. Stevens, Wallace — 811
★*The Collected Poetry of Nikki Giovanni, 1968-1998*. Giovanni, Nikki — 811
The Collected Works. Gibran, Kahlil — 811
COLLECTIBLES
　Garfield, Simon. *In Miniature* — 745.5928
　Jamieson, David. *Mint Condition* — 796.357
　Wong, Stephen. *Smithsonian Baseball* — 796.357
COLLECTION MANAGEMENT (LIBRARIES)
　Brunsting, Karen. ★*Open Access Literature in Libraries* — 070.5
　Evans, G. Edward. *Collection Management Basics* — 025.2
　Goodridge, Michelle. *Librarian's Guide to Games and Gamers* — 025.2
　Johnson, Peggy. ★*Fundamentals of Collection Development and Management* — 025

Collection Management Basics. Evans, G. Edward — 025.2
★*Collection Management for Youth*. Hughes-Hassell, Sandra — 025.2
Collection of Sand. Calvino, Italo — 854
COLLECTIVE AUTOBIOGRAPHIES AND MEMOIRS
　Blight, David W. *A Slave No More* — B
　Chang, Jung. ★*Wild Swans* — B
　Di Giovanni, Janine. *The Morning They Came for Us* — 956.9104
　Duggar, Jill. *Counting the Cost* — B
　Fischer, Jenna. *The Office BFFs* — 791.45

AUTHOR, TITLE, SERIES AND SUBJECT INDEX

Howard, Ron. ★*The Boys*	B
Ice-T. *Split Decision*	920
Isay, David. *Callings*	920
Jackson family. *The Jacksons*	782.421644
Pablo Cruz, Rosayra. *The Book of Rosy*	B
Pearlman, Wendy. *We Crossed a Bridge and It Trembled*	956.9104
Quinn, Susan. *Eleanor and Hick*	B
Somerstein, Rachel. ★*Invisible Labor*	618.8
Spera, Keith. *Groove Interrupted*	B
Stanton, Brandon. *Humans*	779
Strobel, Lee. *The Case for Grace*	234
A *Collective* Bargain. McAlevey, Jane	331.890973
COLLECTIVE BARGAINING	
McAlevey, Jane. *A Collective Bargain*	331.890973
COLLECTIVE BEHAVIOR	
Lowery, Brian S. *Selfless*	155.2
COLLECTIVE BIOGRAPHIES	
Abbott, Karen. *Liar, Temptress, Soldier, Spy*	920
Ackmann, Martha. *The Mercury 13*	920
Ahamed, Liaquat. *Lords of Finance*	920
Ambrose, Stephen E. ★*Band of Brothers*	920
Armstrong, Jennifer Keishin. *When Women Invented Television*	791.45
Avrich, Paul. *Sasha and Emma*	920
Bakewell, Sarah. ★*At the Existentialist Cafe*	920
Barr, Luke. *Ritz & Escoffier*	920
Barrett, Duncan. *GI Brides*	920
Becker, Adam. *What Is Real?*	920
Bell-Scott, Patricia. *The Firebrand and the First Lady*	920
Bellows, Amanda Brickell. *The Explorers*	910.92
Bennett, Jackie. *The Writer's Garden*	920
Bernstein, Andrea. *American Oligarchs*	920
Borman, Tracy. *Anne Boleyn and Elizabeth I*	920
Borman, Tracy. *Crown & Sceptre*	941
Borman, Tracy. *The Private Lives of the Tudors*	920
Bram, Christopher. *Eminent Outlaws*	920
Branch, John. *The Last Cowboys*	920
Brands, H. W. ★*The Zealot and the Emancipator*	920
Brower, Kate Andersen. *First in Line*	920
Brower, Kate Andersen. *First Women*	920
Brown, Craig. *150 Glimpses of the Beatles*	920
Brown, Tina. ★*The Palace Papers*	920
Browne, David. *Crosby, Stills, Nash and Young*	920
Cadbury, Deborah. *Princes at War*	920
Campbell, Olivia. *Women in White Coats*	610.92
Caruana Galizia, Paul. ★*A Death in Malta*	364.15
Cheever, Susan. *American Bloomsbury*	920
Chivers, C. J. *The Fighters*	920
Clark, Lloyd. *The Commanders*	940.53
Clavin, Thomas. *The DiMaggios*	920
Clinton, Hillary Rodham. *The Book of Gutsy Women*	920
Cohen, Deborah. *Last Call at the Hotel Imperial*	070.92
Cohen, Jared. *Life After Power*	973.09
Coll, Steve. *The Bin Ladens*	920
Cooke, Julia. *Come Fly the World*	387.7
Cooney, Kara. *When Women Ruled the World*	920
Cooper, Anderson. *Vanderbilt*	920
Cornejo Villavicencio, Karla. ★*The Undocumented Americans*	920
Cozzens, Peter. *Tecumseh and the Prophet*	920
Crasnianski, Tania. *The Children of Nazis*	943.086
Crowther, Gail. *Three-Martini Afternoons at the Ritz*	920
Damrosch, Leopold. *The Club*	920
Darnton, Robert. *The Revolutionary Temper*	944
Davenport, Christian. *The Space Barons*	920
Davis, William C. *Crucible of Command*	920
De Courcy, Anne. *The Husband Hunters*	920
De Hamel, Christopher. *The Manuscripts Club*	091
De Semlyen, Nick. *Wild and Crazy Guys*	920
Demick, Barbara. ★*Nothing to Envy*	920
DePalma, Anthony. *The Cubans*	920
Doherty, Maggie. *The Equivalents*	920
Duberman, Martin B. *Hold Tight Gently*	920
Eder, Mari K. *The Girls Who Stepped Out of Line*	920
Eig, Jonathan. *The Birth of the Pill*	618.1
Eilenberger, Wolfram. *Time of the Magicians*	920
Eisen, Norman L. *The Last Palace*	920
Epplin, Luke. *Our Team*	796.357
Evans, Claire Lisa. *Broad Band*	920
Eyman, Scott. *Hank and Jim*	920
Fehrman, Craig. *Author in Chief*	920
Figes, Orlando. *The Europeans*	920
Finkel, David. *Thank You for Your Service*	920
Finkelstein, Daniel. *Two Roads Home*	920
Fox, Margalit. *The Riddle of the Labyrinth*	920
Frankel, Rebecca. *Into the Forest*	940.53
Fraser, Antonia. ★*The Wives of Henry VIII*	942.05
Freeman, Sally Mott. *The Jersey Brothers*	920
Funk, Mason. *The Book of Pride*	920
Gabriel, Mary. *Love and Capital*	920
Gabriel, Mary. *Ninth Street Women*	920
Garcia, Mayte. *The Most Beautiful*	920
Gardner, Mark L. *The Earth Is All That Lasts*	978.004
Garrett, Kent. *The Last Negroes at Harvard*	920
Gelwicks, Andrew. *The Queer Advantage*	920
Goldstone, Nancy Bazelon. *Daughters of the Winter Queen*	920
Goldstone, Nancy Bazelon. *In the Shadow of the Empress*	920
Good, Cassandra A. *First Family*	920
Goodwin, Doris Kearns. *No Ordinary Time*	920
Gopal, Anand. *No Good Men Among the Living*	920
Gordon, Charlotte. *Romantic Outlaws*	920
Gordon-Reed, Annette. ★*The Hemingses of Monticello*	920
Gray, Charlotte. ★*Reluctant Genius*	920
Greenidge, Kerri. ★*The Grimkes*	973.5
Groom, Winston. *The Allies*	940.5309
Groom, Winston. *The Aviators*	920
Groom, Winston. *The Generals*	920
Groom, Winston. *The Patriots*	920
Grush, Loren. ★*The Six*	629.4
Guha, Ramachandra. *Rebels Against the Raj*	954.03
Gutzman, Kevin R. C. *The Jeffersonians*	973.5
Gwynne, S. C. *The Perfect Pass*	920
Hallman, J. C. *Say Anarcha*	618.1
Hayasaki, Erika. *Somewhere Sisters*	362.7
Hazelgrove, William Elliott. *Wright Brothers, Wrong Story*	920
Hibbert, Christopher. *The Borgias and Their Enemies*	920
Hibbert, Christopher. *The House of Medici*	920
Hickman, Katie. *Brave Hearted*	978
Holley, Santi Elijah. *An Amerikan Family*	920
Holt, Nathalia. *The Queens of Animation*	920
Howard, Hugh. *Architects of an American Landscape*	712.092
Hurowitz, Richard. *In the Garden of the Righteous*	940.53
Ignotofsky, Rachel. *Women in Science*	920
Iperen, Roxane van. ★*The Sisters of Auschwitz*	940.53
Jeal, Tim. *Explorers of the Nile*	920
Kalb, Claudia. *Andy Warhol Was a Hoarder*	920
Kaplan, James. *3 Shades of Blue*	920
Kaplan, Janice. *The Genius of Women*	920
Karbo, Karen. *In Praise of Difficult Women*	920
Kashner, Sam. *The Fabulous Bouvier Sisters*	920
Katz, Catherine Grace. *The Daughters of Yalta*	920
Kaufman, Jonathan. *The Last Kings of Shanghai*	951
Kearse, Bettye. *The Other Madisons*	920
Keefe, Patrick Radden. ★*Empire of Pain*	338.7
Keene, Adrienne. *Notable Native People*	920
Kempowski, Walter. *Swansong 1945*	940.54
Kennedy, John F. *Profiles in Courage*	920
Kerrison, Catherine. *Jefferson's Daughters*	920
Kershaw, Alex. *Against All Odds*	940.54
Khilnani, Sunil. *Incarnations*	920
King, Charles. ★*Gods of the Upper Air*	920
King, Greg. *Twilight of Empire*	943.6
Kissinger, Henry. *Leadership*	303.3
Kleiman, Kathy. *Proving Ground*	4.092
Klinenberg, Eric. ★*2020*	306
Koch, Bea. *Mad and Bad*	920
Kolker, Robert. ★*Hidden Valley Road*	920
Koppel, Lily. *The Astronaut Wives Club*	920
Korda, Michael. *Muse of Fire*	940.4
Krimstein, Ken. *When I Grow Up*	741.5
Krist, Gary. *The Mirage Factory*	920
Kroger, Lisa. *Monster, She Wrote*	920
Kunetka, James W. *The General and the Genius*	355.8
Landdeck, Katherine Sharp. *The Women with Silver Wings*	920
Larman, Alexander. ★*Power and Glory*	941.085
Leamer, Laurence. *Hitchcock's Blondes*	791.43
Leamer, Laurence. *The Kennedy Men*	920
Levingston, Steven. *Kennedy and King*	920

PUBLIC LIBRARY CORE COLLECTION: NONFICTION
Twentieth Edition

Lewis, Michael. ★*The Undoing Project*	920
Li, Zhuqing. *Daughters of the Flower Fragrant Garden*	951.04
Lovell, Mary S. *The Sisters*	920.72
Lownie, Andrew. *Traitor King*	920
Lucey, Donna M. *Sargent's Women*	920
MacKrell, Judith. *The Correspondents*	070.4
Mahoney, Richard D. *Sons & Brothers*	920
Makos, Adam. *Devotion*	920
Mann, William J. *Bogie & Bacall*	920
Markel, Howard. *The Secret of Life*	572.86
Markham, Lauren. ★*The Far Away Brothers*	920
Martin, Justin. *Rebel Souls*	920
Marton, Kati. *The Great Escape*	920
Massing, Michael. *Fatal Discord*	920
Matteson, John. *Eden's Outcasts*	920
McCalman, George. *Illustrated Black History*	920
McCormick, Ty. *Beyond the Sand and Sea*	920
McCullough, David G. *The Pioneers*	920
McDonald, Greg (Producer). *Elvis and the Colonel*	920
McKean, David. *Watching Darkness Fall*	940.53
McNeur, Catherine. *Mischievous Creatures*	920
Mehr, Bob. *Trouble Boys*	920
Meyer, G. J. *The Borgias*	920
Meyer, G. J. *The Tudors*	920
Mikhaiil, Dunya. *The Beekeeper*	956.7044
Moore, Peter. *Life, Liberty, and the Pursuit of Happiness*	199
Mulley, Clare. *The Women Who Flew for Hitler*	920
Myers, Paul. *The Kids in the Hall*	920
Nadeau, Barbie Latza. *The Godmother*	364.106
Napoli, Lisa. *Susan, Linda, Nina & Cokie*	920
Nicolson, Adam. *The Making of Poetry*	821.709
Nimura, Janice P. *Daughters of the Samurai*	920
Nimura, Janice P. ★*The Doctors Blackwell*	610.92
Nutt, Amy Ellis. *Becoming Nicole*	920
O'Brien, Keith. *Fly Girls*	920
O'Brien, Keith. *Paradise Falls*	363.738
Pappu, Sridhar. *The Year of the Pitcher*	920
Paranque, Estelle. *Blood, Fire & Gold*	920
Patterson, James. *The Secret Lives of Booksellers and Librarians*	381
Patterson, James. *Walk in My Combat Boots*	920
Paul, Richard. *We Could Not Fail*	920
Pawel, Miriam. *The Browns of California*	920
Peiffer, Prudence. *The Slip*	709.73
Poirier, Agnes. *Left Bank*	944
Popova, Maria. *Figuring*	920
Posnanski, Joe. *The Baseball 100*	796.357
Puhak, Shelley. *The Dark Queens*	944
Quinn, Bridget. *Broad Strokes*	920
Rappaport, Helen. *The Romanov Sisters*	920
Rees, Laurence. *Hitler and Stalin*	940.53
Reid, Joy-Ann Lomena. ★*Medgar and Myrlie*	920
Remnick, David. *Holding the Note*	781.64
Reser, Anna. *Forces of Nature*	509.2
Ricks, Thomas E. *Churchill and Orwell*	920
Roberts, Andrew. *Leadership in War*	920
Roberts, Cokie. *Capital Dames*	920
Roberts, Cokie. *Founding Mothers*	920
Roberts, Cokie. *Ladies of Liberty*	920
Roberts, Jason. ★*Every Living Thing*	578
Roberts, Randy. *Blood Brothers*	920
Rocca, Mo. *Mobituaries*	920
Roe, Sue. *In Montmartre*	920
Roe, Sue. *The Private Lives of the Impressionists*	920
Rogers, Katie. ★*American Woman*	973.09
Rose, Alexander. *Empires of the Sky*	920
Rose, Sarah. *D-Day Girls*	940.53
Rothman, Joshua D. *The Ledger and the Chain*	306.362
Rubenhold, Hallie. ★*The Five*	362.88
Sakamoto, Pamela Rotner. *Midnight in Broad Daylight*	940.53
Samaha, Albert. *Never Ran, Never Will*	920
Sando, Mike. *The Football 100*	796.332
Sankovitch, Nina. *American Rebels*	920
Schatz, Kate. *Rad Women Worldwide*	920
Schell, Orville. *Wealth and Power*	920
Schulman, Daniel. *The Money Kings*	332.0973
Schultz, Kevin Michael. *Buckley and Mailer*	920
Sears, Stephen W. *Lincoln's Lieutenants*	920
Sen, Mayukh. *Taste Makers*	641.5092
Sevigny, Melissa L. ★*Brave the Wild River*	580.9
Shane, Scott. ★*Flee North*	973.7
Sigmund, Karl. *Exact Thinking in Demented Times*	920
Simmons, Nadirah. ★*First Things First*	782.42164
Singer, Matt. *Opposable Thumbs*	791.43
Smilios, Maria. ★*The Black Angels*	610.73
Smith, Sally Bedell. *George VI and Elizabeth*	920
Snyder, Laura J. *Eye of the Beholder*	920
Spitz, Bob. *Led Zeppelin*	782.42166
Spofford, Tim. *What the Children Told Us*	150.92
Steinberg, Jonny. *Winnie and Nelson*	920
Strauss, Barry S. *Ten Caesars*	937
Strauss, Gwen. *The Nine*	940.53
Taraborrelli, J. Randy. *Jackie, Janet & Lee*	920
Taraborrelli, J. Randy. *The Kennedy Heirs*	920
Teitel, Amy Shira. *Fighting for Space*	920
Terkel, Studs. *Working*	920
Thomas, Dana. *Gods and Kings*	920
Thomas, Gordon. *Defying Hitler*	920
Thompson-Hernandez, Walter. *The Compton Cowboys*	920
Todd, Kim. *Sensational*	920
Toibin, Colm. *Mad, Bad, Dangerous to Know*	920
Tubbs, Anna Malaika. *The Three Mothers*	306.874
Tye, Larry. ★*The Jazzmen*	781.6509
Valby, Karen. *The Swans of Harlem*	792.8
Weir, Alison. *Queens of the Age of Chivalry*	920
Weir, Alison. *Queens of the Conquest*	920
West, Cornel. *Black Prophetic Fire*	920
Whipple, Chris. *The Spymasters*	920
Wickenden, Dorothy. *The Agitators*	920
Wides-Munoz, Laura. *The Making of a Dream*	920
Wills, Shomari. *Black Fortunes*	920
Winder, Elizabeth. *Parachute Women*	782.42164
Wolff, Daniel J. *Grown-Up Anger*	920
Womack, Kenneth. *All Things Must Pass Away*	781.66
Woo, Ilyon. ★*Master Slave Husband Wife*	920
Wood, Gordon S. *Friends Divided*	920
Wulf, Andrea. *The Brother Gardeners*	920
Yaffa, Joshua. *Between Two Fires*	920
Zwonitzer, Mark. *Will You Miss Me When I'm Gone?*	920

COLLECTIVE MEMORY
Benjamin, Ruha. ★*Imagination*	302
Cercas, Javier. *Lord of All the Dead*	868
Fritzsche, Peter. *Life and Death in the Third Reich*	943.086
Jones, Saeed. *Alive at the End of the World*	811
Klein, Naomi. ★*Doppelganger*	302.2
Kytle, Ethan J. *Denmark Vesey's Garden*	975.7
Lowe, Keith. *Prisoners of History*	940.54
Oppenheimer, Mark. *Squirrel Hill*	364.152
Rosner, Elizabeth. *Survivor Cafe*	940.53
Samet, Elizabeth D. *Looking for the Good War*	940.53
Sexton, Jared Yates. *American Rule*	973
Smith, Clint. ★*How the Word Is Passed*	973
Thompson, Erin L. *Smashing Statues*	725
Zapruder, Alexandra. *Twenty-Six Seconds*	973.922092

COLLECTIVE SETTLEMENTS
Stille, Alexander. *The Sullivanians*	307.77

The Collector of Lives. Rowland, Ingrid D. — B

COLLECTORS AND COLLECTING
Barron, James. *The One-Cent Magenta*	769.569
Collins, Paul. *The Book of William*	016.8223
Darwin, Charles. *Charles Darwin*	576.8
Davis, Margaret Leslie. *The Lost Gutenberg*	093
De Hamel, Christopher. *The Manuscripts Club*	091
De Waal, Edmund. *The Hare with Amber Eyes*	B
Garfield, Simon. *In Miniature*	745.5928
Hook, Philip. *Rogues' Gallery*	709.2
Jamieson, David. *Mint Condition*	796.357
Pettegree, Andrew. *The Library*	027.4
Raab, Nathan. *The Hunt for History*	790.1
Wong, Stephen. *Smithsonian Baseball*	796.357

College (un)bound. Selingo, Jeffrey J. — 378

COLLEGE APPLICANTS
Hobbs, Jeff. *Show Them You're Good*	373
Selingo, Jeffrey J. *Who Gets in and Why*	378.1

COLLEGE APPLICATION ESSAYS
Belasco, Andrew. *The Enlightened College Applicant*	378.1

AUTHOR, TITLE, SERIES AND SUBJECT INDEX

COLLEGE APPLICATIONS
   Belasco, Andrew. *The Enlightened College Applicant* — 378.1
COLLEGE ATHLETES
   Feinstein, John. ★*Last Dance* — 796.323
   McIntire, Mike. *Champions Way* — 796.043
   Nocera, Joseph. *Indentured* — 796.04
   Okorafor, Nnedi. *Broken Places & Outer Spaces* — 153.3
COLLEGE BASKETBALL
   Boeheim, Jim. *Bleeding Orange* — B
   Chansky, Art. *Blue Blood II* — 796.323
   Davis, Seth. *Wooden* — B
   Feinstein, John. ★*The Back Roads to March* — 796.323
   Feinstein, John. ★*Last Dance* — 796.323
   Feinstein, John. *A March to Madness* — 796.323
   Lunardi, Joe. ★*Bracketology* — 796.323
   Maraniss, Andrew. *Strong Inside* — B
   O'Connor, Ian. *Coach K* — B
   Summitt, Pat Head. *Sum It Up* — B
COLLEGE BASKETBALL COACHES
   Feinstein, John. ★*The Back Roads to March* — 796.323
   Feinstein, John. ★*Last Dance* — 796.323
   Feinstein, John. *A March to Madness* — 796.323
COLLEGE BASKETBALL COACHING
   Boeheim, Jim. *Bleeding Orange* — B
COLLEGE BASKETBALL PLAYERS
   Abrams, Jonathan P. D. *Boys Among Men* — 796.323
   Feinstein, John. ★*The Back Roads to March* — 796.323
   Feinstein, John. ★*Last Dance* — 796.323
COLLEGE CHOICE
   Belasco, Andrew. *The Enlightened College Applicant* — 378.1
   Bruni, Frank. *Where You Go Is Not Who You'll Be* — 378.1
   Fiske, Edward B. *Fiske Guide to Getting into the Right College* — 378.1
COLLEGE COSTS
   Goldrick-Rab, Sara. *Paying the Price* — 378.3
   Mitchell, Josh. *The Debt Trap* — 378.3
   Selingo, Jeffrey J. *College (un)bound* — 378
COLLEGE DROPOUTS
   Fleming, Brandon P. *Miseducated* — B
COLLEGE FOOTBALL
   Barra, Allen. ★*The Last Coach* — B
   Benedict, Jeff. *The System* — 796.332
   Burke, Monte. *Saban* — 796.332
   Colt, George Howe. *The Game* — 796.332
   Easterbrook, Gregg. ★*The King of Sports* — 796.332
   Eatman, Nicholas. *Friday, Saturday, Sunday in Texas* — 796.332
   Gaul, Gilbert M. *Billion-Dollar Ball* — 796.332
   Krakauer, Jon. *Missoula* — 362.883
   Lewis, Michael. *The Blind Side* — B
   McIntire, Mike. *Champions Way* — 796.043
   Savage, Phil. *4th and Goal Every Day* — 796.332
   Weinreb, Michael. *Season of Saturdays* — 796.332
COLLEGE FOOTBALL COACHES
   Barra, Allen. ★*The Last Coach* — B
COLLEGE FOOTBALL PLAYERS
   Bissinger, H. G. ★*The Mosquito Bowl* — 796.332
   Eatman, Nicholas. *Friday, Saturday, Sunday in Texas* — 796.332
   Yousse, Bower. *Freddie Steinmark* — 796.332
COLLEGE FRESHMEN
   Brenner, Andrea. *How to College* — 378.1
COLLEGE FRIENDS
   Baker, Billy. *We Need to Hang Out* — 177
COLLEGE GRADUATES
   Gerald, Casey. *There Will Be No Miracles Here* — B
   Rakoff, Joanna Smith. *My Salinger Year* — B
COLLEGE PRESIDENTS
   Miller, Lulu. *Why Fish Don't Exist* — B
   Simmons, Ruth. ★*Up Home* — B
   White, Ronald C. *On Great Fields* — B
COLLEGE SPORTS
   Benedict, Jeff. *The System* — 796.332
   Chansky, Art. *Blue Blood II* — 796.323
   Colt, George Howe. *The Game* — 796.332
   Conroy, Pat. *My Losing Season* — B
   Davis, Seth. *Wooden* — B
   Feinstein, John. ★*The Back Roads to March* — 796.323
   Feinstein, John. ★*The Legends Club* — B
   Feinstein, John. *A March to Madness* — 796.323
   Gaul, Gilbert M. *Billion-Dollar Ball* — 796.332

   Goodman, Matthew. *The City Game* — 796.323
   Lewis, Michael. *The Blind Side* — B
   McIntire, Mike. *Champions Way* — 796.043
   Nocera, Joseph. *Indentured* — 796.04
   O'Connor, Ian. *Coach K* — B
   Savage, Phil. *4th and Goal Every Day* — 796.332
   Weinreb, Michael. *Season of Saturdays* — 796.332
COLLEGE STUDENT ORIENTATION
   Brenner, Andrea. *How to College* — 378.1
   Tough, Paul. *The Years That Matter Most* — 378.1
COLLEGE STUDENT RAPE VICTIMS
   Grigoriadis, Vanessa. *Blurred Lines* — 371.7
   Krakauer, Jon. *Missoula* — 362.883
   Miller, Chanel. *Know My Name* — B
COLLEGE STUDENTS
   Appelman, J. Reuben. *While Idaho Slept* — 364.152
   Bain, Ken. *What the Best College Students Do* — 378.1
   Brenner, Andrea. *How to College* — 378.1
   Colt, George Howe. *The Game* — 796.332
   Derf. *Kent State* — 741.5
   Fleming, Jory. *How to Be Human* — 616.85
   Hechinger, John. ★*True Gentlemen* — 371.85
   Hibbs, B. Janet. *The Stressed Years of Their Lives* — 616.8900835
   Hirsch, Jennifer S. *Sexual Citizens* — 371.7
   Hobbs, Jeff. ★*The Short and Tragic Life of Robert Peace* — B
   Hsu, Hua. ★*Stay True* — B
   Marshall, McMillan. *Among the Bros* — 362.29
   Rosenfeld, Seth. *Subversives* — 378.1
   Selingo, Jeffrey J. *College (un)bound* — 378
   Tough, Paul. *The Years That Matter Most* — 378.1
COLLEGE TEACHERS
   Albee, Edward. ★*Who's Afraid of Virginia Woolf?* — 812
   Albom, Mitch. *Tuesdays with Morrie* — B
   Edmonds, David. *Wittgenstein's Poker* — 192
   Fleming, Brandon P. *Miseducated* — B
   Freitas, Donna. *Consent* — 364.158092
   Grue, Jan. *I Live a Life Like Yours* — B
   Klemperer, Victor. *I Will Bear Witness* — B
   Miller, Lulu. *Why Fish Don't Exist* — B
   Parini, Jay. *The Art of Teaching* — 378.1
   Rhodes, Richard. *Scientist* — B
   Rosenberg, Justus. *The Art of Resistance* — B
   Tenzin Priyadarshi. *Running Toward Mystery* — B
   Viren, Sarah. *To Name the Bigger Lie* — B
   Wilderson, Frank B. *Afropessimism* — B
COLLEGE TEACHING
   Parini, Jay. *The Art of Teaching* — 378.1
Collen, Alanna
   10% Human — 612.3
Collingham, E. M.
   Curry — 394.1
Collins, Billy
   Aimless Love — 811
   Sailing Alone Around the Room — 811
   The Trouble with Poetry and Other Poems — 811
   Whale Day — 811
Collins, Francis S.
   The Language of God — 215
Collins, Gail
   When Everything Changed — 305.40973
   William Henry Harrison — B
Collins, Larry
   O Jerusalem! — 956
Collins, Lauren
   When in French — B
COLLINS, LAUREN (JOURNALIST)
   Collins, Lauren. *When in French* — B
Collins, Martha
   Admit One — 811
COLLINS, MARY JEAN
   Turk, Katherine. *The Women of Now* — 305.42
Collins, Max Allan
   Eliot Ness and the Mad Butcher — 364.152
   Spillane — B
Collins, Paul
   The Book of William — 016.8223
Collins-Dexter, Brandi
   Black Skinhead — 324.2734

PUBLIC LIBRARY CORE COLLECTION: NONFICTION
Twentieth Edition

Collision Low Crossers. Dawidoff, Nicholas — 796.332
★*Collision of Power*. Baron, Martin — 070.4
COLLISIONS (ASTROPHYSICS)
  Black, Riley. *The Last Days of the Dinosaurs* — 576.8
Collusion. Harding, Luke — 324.70973
COLOMBIA
  Davis, Wade. *Magdalena* — 986.1
  Garcia Marquez, Gabriel. *Living to Tell the Tale* — B
  Muse, Toby. *Kilo* — 363.4509861
  Rojas Contreras, Ingrid. ★*The Man Who Could Move Clouds* — B
COLOMBIAN AMERICANS
  Hernandez, Daisy. *A Cup of Water Under My Bed* — B
  Rojas Contreras, Ingrid. ★*The Man Who Could Move Clouds* — B
Colombiana. Velasquez, Mariana — 641.59861
COLON CANCER
  Bowler, Kate. *No Cure for Being Human* — B
  Yip-Williams, Julie. ★*The Unwinding of the Miracle* — 973
COLON, FERNANDO, 1488-1539
  Wilson-Lee, Edward. ★*The Catalogue of Shipwrecked Books* — B
Colonel House. Neu, Charles E. — B
★*Colonel Roosevelt*. Morris, Edmund — B
COLONIAL ADMINISTRATORS
  Dolin, Eric Jay. *Black Flags, Blue Waters* — 973.2
  Howell, Georgina. *Gertrude Bell* — B
  Wallach, Janet. *Desert Queen* — B
COLONIAL AMERICA (1600-1775)
  Barry, John M. *Roger Williams and the Creation of the American Soul* — 974.5
  Brands, H. W. *The First American* — B
  Bremer, Francis J. *John Winthrop* — B
  Broadwater, Jeff. ★*George Mason* — B
  Bunker, Nick. ★*Making Haste from Babylon* — 974.4
  Bunker, Nick. *Young Benjamin Franklin* — B
  Dolin, Eric Jay. *Black Flags, Blue Waters* — 973.2
  Ellis, Joseph J. ★*His Excellency* — B
  Eustace, Nicole. ★*Covered with Night* — 364.152
  Franklin, Benjamin. *The Compleated Autobiography* — B
  Fraser, Rebecca. *The Mayflower* — 974.4
  Hogeland, William. *Declaration* — 973.3
  Horn, James P. P. *Land as God Made It* — 975.5
  Kelly, Joseph. *Marooned* — 975.5
  Kluger, Richard. *Indelible Ink* — B
  Lawler, Andrew. *The Secret Token* — 975.6
  Lepore, Jill. *The Name of War* — 973.2
  Lepore, Jill. *New York Burning* — 974.7
  McDonnell, Michael. *Masters of Empire* — 977.4
  Moore, Peter. *Life, Liberty, and the Pursuit of Happiness* — 199
  Murphy, Andrew R. *William Penn* — B
  Norton, Mary Beth. *1774* — 973.3
  Pestana, Carla Gardina. *The World of Plymouth Plantation* — 974.4
  Philbrick, Nathaniel. ★*Mayflower* — 973.2
  Price, David A. ★*Love and Hate in Jamestown* — 975.5
  Roberts, Cokie. *Founding Mothers* — 920
  Saxton, Martha. *The Widow Washington* — B
  Schiff, Stacy. *The Witches* — 345
  Schultz, Eric B. *King Philip's War* — 973.2
  Shirley, Craig. *Mary Ball Washington* — B
  Silverman, David J. ★*This Land Is Their Land* — 974.4
  Taylor, Alan. *American Revolutions* — 973.3
  Warren, James A. *God, War, and Providence* — 974.5
  Whittock, Martyn. *Mayflower Lives* — 974.4
COLONIAL AUSTRALIA (1788-1901)
  Preston, Diana. *Paradise in Chains* — 996.18
COLONIALISM
  Alexander, Will. *Refractive Africa* — 811
  Anand, Anita. *The Patient Assassin* — B
  Barr, James. *Lords of the Desert* — 956
  Belcourt, Billy-Ray. ★*A History of My Brief Body* — B
  Blackhawk, Ned. ★*The Rediscovery of America* — 973.04
  Capozzola, Christopher. *Bound by War* — 355
  Cervantes, Fernando. *Conquistadores* — 970.01
  Dalrymple, William. ★*The Anarchy* — 954.03
  Dalrymple, William. *The Return of a King* — 958.1
  Diaz, Natalie. ★*Postcolonial Love Poem* — 811
  Dinesen, Isak. *Out of Africa* — 967.62
  Duiker, William J. *Ho Chi Minh* — B
  Dunbar-Ortiz, Roxanne. ★*An Indigenous Peoples' History of the United States* — 970.004
  Evans, Martin. *Algeria* — 965

  Faloyin, Dipo. ★*Africa Is Not a Country* — 960.33
  Ferrer, Ada. ★*Cuba* — 972.91
  Fischer, David Hackett. *Champlain's Dream* — B
  Flores, Dan L. *Wild New World* — 591.9709
  Fowler, Corinne. ★*The Countryside* — 941
  Frank, Richard B. *Tower of Skulls* — 940.54
  French, Howard W. *Born in Blackness* — 960
  Gayle, Caleb. *We Refuse to Forget* — 975.004
  Gibson, Marion. *Witchcraft* — 133.4
  Guha, Ramachandra. *Gandhi* — B
  Guha, Ramachandra. *Rebels Against the Raj* — 954.03
  Hajari, Nisid. *Midnight's Furies* — 954.04
  Harriot, Michael. ★*Black AF History* — 973
  Hoffman, Carl. ★*Savage Harvest* — 995.1
  Horn, James P. P. *A Kingdom Strange* — 975.6
  Immerwahr, Daniel. *How to Hide an Empire* — 973
  Johnson, Steven. *Enemy of All Mankind* — 910.4
  Jones, Robert P. *The Hidden Roots of White Supremacy* — 305.8
  Jordan, June. ★*The Essential June Jordan* — 811
  Kars, Marjoleine. *Blood on the River* — 306.3
  Kuper, Adam. *The Museum of Other People* — 305.8
  Laing, Olivia. *The Garden Against Time* — 635
  LaPointe, Sasha taqwseblu. *Thunder Song* — 814
  Lawler, Andrew. *The Secret Token* — 975.6
  Mansel, Philip. *King of the World* — B
  Mays, Kyle. ★*An Afro-Indigenous History of the United States* — 973
  Millard, Candice. ★*Hero of the Empire* — 968.04
  Millard, Candice. ★*River of the Gods* — 916.204
  Mishra, Pankaj. *Age of Anger* — 909.8
  Murphy, Andrew R. *William Penn* — B
  Nguyen, Viet Thanh. ★*A Man of Two Faces* — B
  Norton, Mary Beth. *1774* — 973.3
  Olivarez, Jose. *Promises of Gold = Promesas De Oro* — 811
  Platt, Stephen R. *Imperial Twilight* — 951
  Prendergast, John. *Congo Stories* — 967.5103
  Proenza-Coles, Christina. *American Founders* — 973
  Richardson, Edmund. *The King's Shadow* — 958.1
  Rojas Contreras, Ingrid. ★*The Man Who Could Move Clouds* — B
  Samaha, Albert. *Concepcion* — 929
  Sanghera, Sathnam. ★*Empireland* — 941
  Sanghera, Sathnam. *Empireworld* — 909
  Santos Perez, Craig. *From Unincorporated Territory [amot]* — 811
  Sedgewick, Augustine. *Coffeeland* — 338.4
  Thomas, Hugh. *Rivers of Gold* — 980
  Thomson, Keith. *Born to Be Hanged* — 910.4
  Villarreal, Vanessa Anglica. *Magical/Realism* — 814
  Wainaina, Binyavanga. ★*How to Write About Africa* — 814
  Warren, James A. *Year of the Hawk* — 959.704
  Zakaria, Rafia. *Against White Feminism* — 305.42
COLONIES
  Atkinson, Rick. ★*The British Are Coming* — 973.3
  Bunker, Nick. ★*Making Haste from Babylon* — 974.4
  Elkins, Caroline. *Legacy of Violence* — 909
  Ellis, Joseph J. *The Cause* — 973.3
  Ellis, Joseph J. ★*Revolutionary Summer* — 973.3
  Evans, Martin. *Algeria* — 965
  Fowler, Corinne. ★*The Countryside* — 941
  Fraser, Rebecca. *The Mayflower* — 974.4
  Fuentes, Carlos. *The Buried Mirror* — 946
  Hochschild, Adam. *King Leopold's Ghost* — 967.51
  Horn, James P. P. *A Kingdom Strange* — 975.6
  Immerwahr, Daniel. *How to Hide an Empire* — 973
  Kelly, Joseph. *Marooned* — 975.5
  Kluger, Richard. *Indelible Ink* — B
  Lawler, Andrew. *The Secret Token* — 975.6
  Lepore, Jill. *The Name of War* — 973.2
  Logevall, Fredrik. *Embers of War* — 959.704
  Murphy, Andrew R. *William Penn* — B
  Roberts, Andrew. *The Last King of America* — B
  Sanghera, Sathnam. *Empireworld* — 909
  Thomas, Hugh. *Rivers of Gold* — 980
COLONISTS
  Bobrick, Benson. *Angel in the Whirlwind* — 973.3
  Brands, H. W. ★*Our First Civil War* — 973.3
  Bremer, Francis J. *John Winthrop* — B
  Bunker, Nick. ★*Making Haste from Babylon* — 974.4
  Crawford, Alan Pell. *This Fierce People* — 975
  Dolin, Eric Jay. *Black Flags, Blue Waters* — 973.2

AUTHOR, TITLE, SERIES AND SUBJECT INDEX

Ellis, Joseph J. *The Cause*	973.3
Fraser, Rebecca. *The Mayflower*	974.4
Horn, James P. P. *A Kingdom Strange*	975.6
Kars, Marjoleine. *Blood on the River*	306.3
Kelly, Joseph. *Marooned*	975.5
Lawler, Andrew. *The Secret Token*	975.6
Philbrick, Nathaniel. ★*Mayflower*	973.2
Warren, James A. *God, War, and Providence*	974.5
Whittock, Martyn. *Mayflower Lives*	974.4

COLONIZATION
Dunbar-Ortiz, Roxanne. ★*An Indigenous Peoples' History of the United States*	970.004
Fisk, Robert. *The Great War for Civilisation*	956.04
Sanghera, Sathnam. *Empireworld*	909

COLONIZED PEOPLES
Dunbar-Ortiz, Roxanne. ★*An Indigenous Peoples' History of the United States*	970.004

The Colony. Denton, Sally	364.152
A Colony in a Nation. Hayes, Christopher	364.3
Color. Edwards, Betty	752

COLOR
Rogers, Adam. *Full Spectrum*	152.14
Color Concrete Garden Projects. Smith, Nathan	721

COLOR IN ART
Edwards, Betty. *Color*	752
Griffel, Lois. *Painting the Impressionist Landscape*	751.45
Rogers, Adam. *Full Spectrum*	152.14

COLOR IN DESIGN
Brody, Mark. *Mosaic Garden Projects*	712
Color Me Floral. Underwood, Kiana	745.92

COLOR OF AFRICAN AMERICANS
Morgan-Owens, Jessie. *Girl in Black and White*	B
The Color of Christ. Blum, Edward J.	232
★*The Color of Law*. Rothstein, Richard	305.800973
The Color of Water. McBride, James	B
Color Recipes for Painted Furniture and More. Sloan, Annie	745.7

COLORADO
Cullen, David. *Columbine*	373
Dungy, Camille T. *Soil*	635.0978
Enss, Chris. *Mochi's War*	B
Houston, Pam. *Deep Creek*	814
Iversen, Kristen. *Full Body Burden*	363.17
Kenda, Joe. *Killer Triggers*	364.152

COLORADO RIVER
Fedarko, Kevin. *A Walk in the Park*	917.91
Owen, David. *Where the Water Goes*	917.91
Ross, John F. *The Promise of the Grand Canyon*	917.91
Sevigny, Melissa L. ★*Brave the Wild River*	580.9
Colored People. Gates, Henry Louis	B

COLORISM
Sharma, Nina. *The Way You Make Me Feel*	B
★*Colorization*. Haygood, Wil	791.43
Colors of the Mountain. Chen, Da	951.05

COLT REVOLVER
Rasenberger, Jim. *Revolver*	B

Colt, George Howe
The Game	796.332

COLT, SAMUEL, 1814-1862
Rasenberger, Jim. *Revolver*	B

Coltman, Leycester
The Real Fidel Castro	B

Colton, Larry
Counting Coup	796.323

COLTRANE, JOHN, 1926-1967
Kahn, Ashley. *The House That Trane Built*	781.6509
Kaplan, James. *3 Shades of Blue*	920

COLUMBIA RIVER
Sullivan, Randall. *Graveyard of the Pacific*	979.7

COLUMBIA RIVER REGION
Sullivan, Randall. *Graveyard of the Pacific*	979.7
Columbine. Cullen, David	373

COLUMBINE HIGH SCHOOL SHOOTING, LITTLETON, COLO., 1999
Cullen, David. *Columbine*	373

COLUMBUS, CHRISTOPHER, 1451-1506
Wilson-Lee, Edward. ★*The Catalogue of Shipwrecked Books*	B

COLUMNISTS
Reed, Julia. *Dispatches from the Gilded Age*	B

COLVIN, MARIE
Hilsum, Lindsey. *In Extremis*	B

Colwell, Rita R.
A Lab of One's Own	B

COLWELL, RITA R., 1934-
Colwell, Rita R. *A Lab of One's Own*	B

COMA
Morgan, Abi. *This Is Not a Pity Memoir*	B

COMANCHE (NORTH AMERICAN PEOPLE)
Gwynne, S. C. *Empire of the Summer Moon*	B

COMBAT
Ackerman, Elliot. *Places and Names*	B
Chrisinger, David. *The Soldier's Truth*	940.54
Gallego, Ruben. *They Called Us*	956.7044
Hastings, Max. *Warriors*	355
Henderson, Bruce B. *Bridge to the Sun*	940.53
Hogan, William R. *Task Force Hogan*	940.54
Kershaw, Alex. *The First Wave*	940.54
Kindsvatter, Peter S. *American Soldiers*	355
McManus, John C. *Island Infernos*	940.54
McManus, John C. *To the End of the Earth*	940.54
McPherson, James M. *For Cause and Comrades*	973.7
Meyer, Dakota. *Into the Fire*	958.104
Miller, Christopher. *The War Came to Us*	947.7
Milton, Giles. *Soldier, Sailor, Frogman, Spy, Airman, Gangster, Kill or Die*	940.54
Morris, David J. *The Evil Hours*	616.85
Owen, Mark. *No Hero*	B
Patterson, James. *Walk in My Combat Boots*	920
Raban, Jonathan. *Father and Son*	B
Wheelan, Joseph. *Midnight in the Pacific*	940.54

COMBAT SURVIVAL
Maurer, Kevin. *Damn Lucky*	940.54

COMBATANTS AND NONCOMBATANTS (INTERNATIONAL LAW)
Khan, Mahvish Rukhsana. *My Guantanamo Diary*	973.931
Combee. Fields-Black, Edda L.	973.7

Combs, Rebecca Ann
Kumihimo	745.594
Come Back in September. Pinckney, Darryl	B
Come Closer and Listen. Simic, Charles	811
Come Fly the World. Cooke, Julia	387.7
Come Hell or High Water. Dyson, Michael Eric	976.3
Come Hungry. Ben-Ishay, Melissa	641.5
Come on All You Ghosts. Zapruder, Matthew	811
Come on Over. Mauro, Jeff	641.5
Come to This Court and Cry. Kinstler, Linda	940.53
★*The Come Up*. Abrams, Jonathan P. D.	782.421649
The Comeback. De Vise, Daniel	B
★*Comeback Season*. Perron, Cam	796.357
The Comedians. Nesteroff, Kliph	792.7

COMEDIANS
Ackroyd, Peter. *Charlie Chaplin*	B
Bamford, Maria. *Sure, I'll Join Your Cult*	B
Bennetts, Leslie. *Last Girl Before Freeway*	B
Birbiglia, Mike. *The New One*	B
Branum, Guy. *My Life as a Goddess*	B
Brooks, Mel. ★*All About Me!*	B
Brosh, Allie. ★*Hyperbole and a Half*	741.5
Brosh, Allie. ★*Solutions and Other Problems*	741.5
Brunson, Quinta. *She Memes Well*	B
Carlin, Kelly. *A Carlin Home Companion*	B
Cayton-Holland, Adam. *Tragedy Plus Time*	B
Courogen, Carrie. ★*Miss May Does Not Exist*	B
Curtis, James. *Buster Keaton*	B
De Semlyen, Nick. *Wild and Crazy Guys*	920
De Vise, Daniel. ★*The Blues Brothers*	791.43
Eyman, Scott. *Charlie Chaplin vs. America*	B
Fox, Jesse David. *Comedy Book*	792.7
Foxx, Jamie. *Act Like You Got Some Sense*	B
Gold, Judy. *Yes I Can Say That*	792.7
Gregory, Dick. ★*The Essential Dick Gregory*	818
Hart, Kevin. *I Can't Make This Up*	B
Itzkoff, Dave. ★*Robin*	B
Izzard, Eddie. *Believe Me*	B
Jennings, Ken. *Planet Funny*	809.7
Jobrani, Maziyar. *I'm Not a Terrorist, but I've Played One on TV*	B
Key, Keegan-Michael. ★*The History of Sketch Comedy*	792.2
Lawson, Jenny. ★*Broken*	B

PUBLIC LIBRARY CORE COLLECTION: NONFICTION
Twentieth Edition

Levy, Shawn. ★*In on the Joke*	792.7
Louvish, Simon. *Monkey Business*	B
Martin, Steve. *Number One Is Walking*	B
McGilligan, Patrick. *Funny Man*	B
Myers, Paul. *The Kids in the Hall*	920
Nesteroff, Kliph. *The Comedians*	792.7
Nesteroff, Kliph. *We Had a Little Real Estate Problem*	970.004
Noah, Trevor. *Born a Crime*	B
Odenkirk, Bob. *Comedy Comedy Comedy Drama*	B
Pellegrino, Danny. *How Do I Un-Remember This?*	B
Poehler, Amy. *Yes Please*	B
Rainbow, Randy. *Playing with Myself*	B
Ramsey, Franchesca. *Well, That Escalated Quickly*	B
Retta. *So Close to Being the Sh*t, Y'all Don't Even Know*	B
Saul, Scott. ★*Becoming Richard Pryor*	B
Scheer, Paul. *Joyful Recollections of Trauma*	B
Schumer, Amy. *The Girl with the Lower Back Tattoo*	B
Segura, Tom. ★*I'd Like to Play Alone, Please*	B
Shales, Tom. *Live from New York*	791.45
Shannon, Molly. ★*Hello, Molly!*	B
Short, Martin. *I Must Say*	B
Smith, Chris. *The Daily Show (the Book)*	791.45
Stevens, Dana. *Camera Man*	791.4302
Thompson, Kenan. *When I Was Your Age*	B
Wasson, Sam. ★*Improv Nation*	792.02
Watts, Reggie. *Great Falls, MT*	B
Williams, Patricia. *Rabbit*	B
Wong, Ali. ★*Dear Girls*	B
Zoglin, Richard. *Hope*	B
Zweibel, Alan. *Laugh Lines*	B
Comedy Book. Fox, Jesse David	792.7
Comedy Comedy Comedy Drama. Odenkirk, Bob	B
COMEDY FILMS	
Austerlitz, Saul. *Kind of a Big Deal*	791.43
Carlson, Erin. *I'll Have What She's Having*	791.43
De Semlyen, Nick. *Wild and Crazy Guys*	920
De Vise, Daniel. ★*The Blues Brothers*	791.43
Meslow, Scott. *From Hollywood with Love*	791.43
Nashawaty, Chris. *Caddyshack*	791.43
Zucker, David. *Surely You Can't Be Serious*	791.43
COMEDY WRITING	
Armstrong, Jennifer Keishin. *Seinfeldia*	791.45
Armstrong, Jennifer Keishin. *Sex and the City and Us*	791.45
Dauber, Jeremy Asher. *Jewish Comedy*	809.7
Fox, Jesse David. *Comedy Book*	792.7
Greene, Andy. *The Office*	791.45
Key, Keegan-Michael. ★*The History of Sketch Comedy*	792.2
Seinfeld, Jerry. *Is This Anything?*	818
Zucker, David. *Surely You Can't Be Serious*	791.43
Comen, Elizabeth	
★*All in Her Head*	613
Comerford, Hope	
Fix-It and Forget-It Healthy 5-Ingredient Cookbook	641.5
Comfort and Joy. Bhogal, Ravinder	641.5
COMFORT FOOD	
Adams, Jocelyn Delk. *Everyday Grand*	641.5975
Adarme, Adrianna. *The Year of Cozy*	641.3
Ali, Laila. *Food for Life*	641.5
Bhogal, Ravinder. *Comfort and Joy*	641.5
Byrn, Anne. *Skillet Love*	641.7
Clark, Melissa. *Comfort in an Instant*	641.5
Garten, Ina. ★*Modern Comfort Food*	641.5
Gerard, Tieghan. ★*Half Baked Harvest Every Day*	641.5
Guarnaschelli, Alex. ★*Cook It Up*	641.5
Hall, Carla. *Carla's Comfort Foods*	641.59
Holland, Tanya. ★*Tanya Holland's California Soul*	641.59
Lawson, Nigella. ★*Cook, Eat, Repeat*	641.5
Lawson, Nigella. ★*Simply Nigella*	641.5
Noyes, Brian. *The Red Truck Bakery Farmhouse Cookbook*	641.5973
Nunn, Emily. *The Comfort Food Diaries*	641.5973
Rodale, Maria. *Scratch*	641.3
Sarna, Shannon. *Modern Jewish Comfort Food*	641.5
Snoop Dogg. *Goon with the Spoon*	641.59
Tandoh, Ruby. ★*Cook as You Are*	641.59
Turshen, Julia. *Simply Julia*	641.3
Wilson, Melba. ★*Melba's American Comfort*	641.5973
Yearwood, Trisha. *Trisha's Kitchen*	641.5
The Comfort Food Diaries. Nunn, Emily	641.5973
Comfort in an Instant. Clark, Melissa	641.5
Comfort Me with Apples. Reichl, Ruth	B
The Comfort of Crows. Renkl, Margaret	814.6
Comforts of the Abyss. Schultz, Philip	801
COMIC BOOK CHARACTERS	
Howe, Sean. *Marvel Comics*	741.5
Lepore, Jill. ★*The Secret History of Wonder Woman*	741.5
Phillips, Maya. *Nerd*	302.23
Weldon, Glen. ★*The Caped Crusade*	741.5
COMIC BOOK ILLUSTRATION	
Abel, Jessica. *Drawing Words, Writing Pictures*	741.5
Abel, Jessica. *Mastering Comics*	741.5
McCloud, Scott. *Reinventing Comics*	741.5
O'Neil, Dennis. *The DC Comics Guide to Writing Comics*	808
Spiegelman, Art. *Co-Mix*	741.5
COMIC BOOK ILLUSTRATORS	
Fingeroth, Danny. *A Marvelous Life*	741.5
Howe, Sean. *Marvel Comics*	741.5
Riesman, Abraham. *True Believer*	741.5
Spiegelman, Art. *Co-Mix*	741.5
Spiegelman, Art. ★*Maus*	741.5
COMIC BOOKS, STRIPS, ETC.	
Abel, Jessica. *Drawing Words, Writing Pictures*	741.5
Abel, Jessica. *Mastering Comics*	741.5
Fingeroth, Danny. *A Marvelous Life*	741.5
Howe, Sean. *Marvel Comics*	741.5
Jones, Gerard. *Men of Tomorrow*	741.5
Kakalios, James. *The Amazing Story of Quantum Mechanics*	530.12
Kneece, Mark. *The Art of Comic Book Writing*	741.5
Lepore, Jill. ★*The Secret History of Wonder Woman*	741.5
McCloud, Scott. ★*Understanding Comics*	741.5
Pawuk, Michael. *Graphic Novels*	016.74
Riesman, Abraham. *True Believer*	741.5
Spiegelman, Art. *Co-Mix*	741.5
Tisserand, Michael. *Krazy*	741.5
Weldon, Glen. ★*The Caped Crusade*	741.5
Wolk, Douglas. ★*All of the Marvels*	741.5
COMIC ROUTINES	
Levy, Shawn. ★*In on the Joke*	792.7
COMIC STRIP CHARACTERS	
Leong, Sonia. *101 Top Tips from Professional Manga Artists*	741.5
COMIC STRIP ILLUSTRATORS	
Tisserand, Michael. *Krazy*	741.5
COMICS AND GRAPHIC NOVEL WRITERS	
Cooper, Christian. *Better Living Through Birding*	B
Fingeroth, Danny. *A Marvelous Life*	741.5
Howe, Sean. *Marvel Comics*	741.5
Lepore, Jill. ★*The Secret History of Wonder Woman*	741.5
Riesman, Abraham. *True Believer*	741.5
Spiegelman, Art. *Co-Mix*	741.5
Spiegelman, Art. ★*Maus*	741.5
Tisserand, Michael. *Krazy*	741.5
COMICS AND GRAPHIC NOVEL WRITING	
Abel, Jessica. *Drawing Words, Writing Pictures*	741.5
Abel, Jessica. *Mastering Comics*	741.5
Chelsea, David. *Perspective in Action*	741.5
Goldsmith, Francisca. *The Readers' Advisory Guide to Graphic Novels*	025.2
McCloud, Scott. *Making Comics*	741.5
McCloud, Scott. *Reinventing Comics*	741.5
O'Neil, Dennis. *The DC Comics Guide to Writing Comics*	808
Spiegelman, Art. *Co-Mix*	741.5
Spiegelman, Art. *Metamaus*	B
Tisserand, Michael. *Krazy*	741.5
COMICS AND GRAPHIC NOVELS	
Abel, Jessica. *Drawing Words, Writing Pictures*	741.5
Abel, Jessica. *Mastering Comics*	741.5
Ai, Weiwei. *Zodiac*	741.5
Amano, Hugh. *Let's Make Dumplings!*	741.5
B., David. *Epileptic*	741.5
Beaton, Kate. ★*Ducks*	741.5
Bechdel, Alison. ★*Fun Home*	741.5
Bechdel, Alison. ★*The Secret to Superhuman Strength*	741.5
Bell, Darrin. ★*The Talk*	741.5
Bongiovanni, Archie. *A Quick & Easy Guide to They/Them Pronouns*	741.5
Brosh, Allie. ★*Hyperbole and a Half*	741.5
Brosh, Allie. ★*Solutions and Other Problems*	741.5
Bui, Thi. ★*The Best We Could Do*	741.5
Byrne, Eugene. *Darwin*	741.5

AUTHOR, TITLE, SERIES AND SUBJECT INDEX

Chast, Roz. ★*Can't We Talk About Something More Pleasant?* ... 741.5
Chelsea, David. *Perspective in Action* ... 741.5
Delisle, Guy. *Hostage* ... 741.5
Delisle, Guy. *Pyongyang* ... 741.5
Derf. *Kent State* ... 741.5
Findakly, Brigitte. *Poppies of Iraq* ... 741.5
Forkish, Ken. ★*Let's Make Bread!* ... 741.5
Gladstone, Brooke. *The Influencing Machine* ... 741.5
Goldman, Seth. *Mission in a Bottle* ... 741.5
Guibert, Emmanuel. *Alan's War* ... 741.5
Guibert, Emmanuel. *The Photographer* ... 741.5
Hall, Rebecca. ★*Wake* ... 741.5
Hedges, Chris. *Days of Destruction, Days of Revolt* ... 741.5
Hennessey, Jonathan. *The United States Constitution* ... 741.5
Hulls, Tessa. ★*Feeding Ghosts* ... 741.5
Igort. *The Ukrainian and Russian Notebooks* ... 741.5
Inman, Matthew. *The Terrible and Wonderful Reasons Why I Run Long Distances* ... 741.5
Jacob, Mira. *Good Talk* ... 741.5
Jacobson, Sidney. *The 9-11 Report* ... 741.5
Jacobson, Sidney. *Anne Frank* ... 741.5
Katin, Miriam. *We Are on Our Own* ... 741.5
Kawa, Abraham. *Democracy* ... 741.5
Kobabe, Maia. *Gender Queer* ... 741.5
Krimstein, Ken. *When I Grow Up* ... 741.5
Krug, Nora. ★*Belonging* ... 741.5
Kupperman, Michael. *All the Answers* ... 741.5
Lewis, John. ★*March; Book One* ... 741.5
Lewis, John. ★*March; Book Three* ... 741.5
Lewis, John. ★*March; Book Two* ... 741.5
Lewis, John. ★*Run; Book One* ... 741.5
Mankoff, Robert. *How About Never—Is Never Good for You?* ... 741.5
Martin, Steve. *Number One Is Walking* ... B
Mauldin, Bill. *Willie & Joe* ... 741.5
McCloud, Scott. *Making Comics* ... 741.5
McCloud, Scott. *Reinventing Comics* ... 741.5
McCloud, Scott. ★*Understanding Comics* ... 741.5
Mizuki, Shigeru. *Showa 1926-1939* ... 741.5
Neufeld, Josh. *A.D.* ... 741.5
Ottaviani, Jim. *Hawking* ... 741.5
Parker, Meghan. *Teaching Artfully* ... 741.5
Powell, Nate. ★*Lies My Teacher Told Me* ... 741.5
Radtke, Kristen. *Seek You* ... 741.5
Redniss, Lauren. *Thunder & Lightning* ... 741.5
Sacco, Joe. *Footnotes in Gaza* ... 741.5
Sacco, Joe. *Paying the Land* ... 741.5
Santiago, Wilfred. *"21"* ... 741.5
Satrapi, Marjane. *Chicken with Plums* ... 741.5
Satrapi, Marjane. ★*The Complete Persepolis* ... 741.5
Satrapi, Marjane. *Embroideries* ... 741.5
Sattouf, Riad. *The Arab of the Future 2* ... 741.5
Sattouf, Riad. *The Arab of the Future* ... 741.5
Spiegelman, Art. *Co-Mix* ... 741.5
Spiegelman, Art. *In the Shadow of No Towers* ... 741.5
Spiegelman, Art. ★*Maus* ... 741.5
Tomine, Adrian. *The Loneliness of the Long-Distance Cartoonist* ... 741.5
Voloj, Julian. *Ghetto Brother* ... 741.5
Witte, Christina De. ★*Noodles, Rice, and Everything Spice* ... 641.595
★*Comics* and Sequential Art. Eisner, Will ... 741.5
Coming Apart. Murray, Charles A. ... 305.8
Coming Back. Germer, Fawn ... 650.14
Coming of Age in Samoa. Mead, Margaret ... 306
The ***Coming*** of the Third Reich. Evans, Richard J. ... 943.08
COMING OUT (SEXUAL OR GENDER IDENTITY)
Bechdel, Alison. ★*Fun Home* ... 741.5
Black, Dustin Lance. *Mama's Boy* ... B
Frank, Barney. *Frank* ... B
Greene, Benjamin. ★*My Child Is Trans, Now What?* ... 649
Gutowitz, Jill. *Girls Can Kiss Now* ... 814
Hamill, Kirkland. *Filthy Beasts* ... B
Marshall, Greg. *Leg* ... B
Page, Elliot. *Pageboy* ... B
Pellegrino, Danny. *How Do I Un-Remember This?* ... B
Rogers, Robbie. *Coming Out to Play* ... B
Soloway, Jill. *She Wants It* ... B
Tobia, Jacob. *Sissy* ... 305.30973
Weigel, Alicia Roth. *Inverse Cowgirl* ... B
Wizenberg, Molly. *Fixed Stars* ... B

Coming Out to Play. Rogers, Robbie ... B
Coming to My Senses. Waters, Alice ... B
Coming up for Air. Daley, Tom ... B
The ***Coming*** Wave. Suleyman, Mustafa ... 303.48
Command and Control. Schlosser, Eric ... 363.17
COMMAND OF TROOPS
Albracht, William. *Abandoned in Hell* ... 959.704
Ambrose, Stephen E. *The Victors* ... 940.54
Arana, Marie. *Bolivar* ... B
Baier, Bret. *To Rescue the Constitution* ... 973.4
Beevor, Antony. *The Battle of Arnhem* ... 940.54
Blount, Roy. *Robert E. Lee* ... B
Borneman, Walter R. *The Admirals* ... B
Borneman, Walter R. *Macarthur at War* ... B
Broers, Michael. *Napoleon* ... B
Broers, Michael. *Napoleon* ... 944.05
Broers, Michael. *Napoleon* ... B
Bunting, Josiah. ★*The Making of a Leader* ... B
Chernow, Ron. ★*Grant* ... B
Clark, Lloyd. *The Commanders* ... 940.53
Coe, Alexis. ★*You Never Forget Your First* ... B
Crawford, Alan Pell. *This Fierce People* ... 975
Davis, William C. *Crucible of Command* ... 920
Drury, Bob. *Valley Forge* ... 973.3
Ellis, Joseph J. ★*His Excellency* ... B
Everitt, Anthony. *Alexander the Great* ... B
Fischer, David Hackett. *Washington's Crossing* ... 973.3
Freeman, Douglas Southall. *Lee* ... B
Gardner, Mark L. *Rough Riders* ... 973.911
Groom, Winston. *The Generals* ... 920
Guelzo, Allen C. *Robert E. Lee* ... B
Hamilton, Nigel. *The Mantle of Command* ... 940.54
Hanson, Victor Davis. *The Soul of Battle* ... 355
Holland, James. *The Savage Storm* ... 940.53
Horn, Jonathan. *Washington's End* ... B
Hunt, Patrick. *Hannibal* ... B
Johnson, Paul. *George Washington* ... B
Johnson, Paul. *Napoleon* ... B
Jones, Michael K. *The Black Prince* ... B
Korda, Michael. *Clouds of Glory* ... B
Loyn, David. *The Long War* ... 958.104
McDonough, James L. *William Tecumseh Sherman* ... B
McLynn, Frank. *Genghis Khan* ... 950.2
McManus, John C. *Island Infernos* ... 940.54
McManus, John C. *To the End of the Earth* ... 940.54
McMurtry, Larry. *Custer* ... B
Meacham, Jon. *Franklin and Winston* ... 940.53
Morison, Samuel Eliot. *John Paul Jones* ... B
Morris, Marc. *King John* ... 942.033
O'Connell, Robert L. *Revolutionary* ... B
Paradis, Michel. *The Light of Battle* ... 940.54
Patton, George S. *War as I Knew It* ... B
Perry, Mark. *The Most Dangerous Man in America* ... B
Petraeus, David Howell. *Conflict* ... 355
Philbrick, Nathaniel. ★*In the Hurricane's Eye* ... 973.3
Philbrick, Nathaniel. ★*Valiant Ambition* ... B
Randall, Willard Sterne. *George Washington* ... B
Ricks, Thomas E. ★*The Generals* ... B
Roberts, Andrew. *Leadership in War* ... 920
Roberts, Andrew. *Masters and Commanders* ... 940.5322
Roberts, Andrew. ★*Napoleon* ... B
Robertson, James I. *Stonewall Jackson* ... B
Sears, Stephen W. *Lincoln's Lieutenants* ... 920
Simms, Brendan. *The Silver Waterfall* ... 940.54
Stark, Peter. *Young Washington* ... B
Stiles, T. J. *Custer's Trials* ... B
Symonds, Craig L. *Lincoln and His Admirals* ... B
Thomas, Evan. ★*John Paul Jones* ... B
Thomas, Evan. *Sea of Thunder* ... 940.54
Unger, Debi. *George Marshall* ... B
Wallace, Chris. *Countdown 1945* ... 940.54
Weintraub, Stanley. *Iron Tears* ... 973.3
Wert, Jeffry D. *Cavalryman of the Lost Cause* ... B
Wert, Jeffry D. *Custer* ... B
White, Ronald C. ★*American Ulysses* ... B
Winik, Jay. *1944* ... 940.53
Zambone, Albert Louis. *Daniel Morgan* ... B
Zamoyski, Adam. *Napoleon* ... B

PUBLIC LIBRARY CORE COLLECTION: NONFICTION
Twentieth Edition

Commander. Taylor, Stephen — B
The Commanders. Clark, Lloyd — 940.53
COMMANDO OPERATIONS
    Bascomb, Neal. *The Winter Fortress* — 940.54
    Hastings, Max. *The Secret War* — 940.54
    O'Donnell, Patrick K. *The Unvanquished* — 973.7
    O'Neill, Robert. *The Operator* — B
    Owen, Mark. *No Easy Day* — B
COMMANDO TROOPS
    Couch, Dick. *The Warrior Elite* — 359.9
    Garrett, Leah. *X Troop* — 940.54
    Kershaw, Alex. *The First Wave* — 940.54
    Macintyre, Ben. ★*Rogue Heroes* — 940.54
    McRaven, William H. *Sea Stories* — B
COMMERCE
    Crowley, Roger. *City of Fortune* — 945
    Dodds Pennock, Caroline. ★*On Savage Shores* — 970.004
    Frankopan, Peter. *The Silk Roads* — 909
    Hughes, Bettany. *Istanbul* — 949.61
    Micklethwait, John. *The Company* — 338.7
    Sowell, Thomas. *Basic Economics* — 330
COMMERCIAL AVIATION
    Cooke, Julia. *Come Fly the World* — 387.7
    Robison, Peter. ★*Flying Blind* — 338.7
    Rose, Alexander. *Empires of the Sky* — 920
    Vanhoenacker, Mark. *Imagine a City* — 629.13
COMMERCIAL POLICY
    Stiglitz, Joseph E. *Globalization and Its Discontents* — 337
COMMERCIAL PRODUCTS
    Lorr, Benjamin. *The Secret Life of Groceries* — 381.4
COMMERCIALIZATION
    Crawford, Matthew B. *The World Beyond Your Head* — 155.2
    Del Rey, Jason. *Winner Sells All* — 381
COMMITMENT (PSYCHOLOGY)
    Brooks, David. ★*The Second Mountain* — 302
    Davis, Jennifer Pharr. *Called Again* — 158.1
    Davis, Pete. *Dedicated* — 158.1
    Hagglund, Martin. *This Life* — 110
Committed. Stern, Adam — 616.89
COMMODITY EXCHANGES
    Kurlansky, Mark. *Salt* — 553.6
    Russell, Rupert. *Price Wars* — 332.64
Commodore. Renehan, Edward — B
Common
    ★*And Then We Rise* — 613
    One Day It'll All Make Sense — B
COMMON (MUSICIAN)
    Common. *One Day It'll All Make Sense* — B
COMMON GOOD
    Beeman, Richard R. ★*Plain, Honest Men* — 342.7302
    Crawford, Matthew B. *The World Beyond Your Head* — 155.2
    Frank, Thomas. *The People, No* — 320.56
    Sandel, Michael J. *Justice* — 172
    Tutu, Desmond. *Made for Goodness* — 170
COMMON SENSE
    Tyson, Neil deGrasse. *Starry Messenger* — 901
A Commonwealth of Thieves. Keneally, Thomas — 994
Commotion of the Birds. Ashbery, John — 811
COMMUNES
    Rush, Chris. *The Light Years* — B
COMMUNICABLE DISEASES
    Barry, John M. ★*The Great Influenza* — 614.5
    Brenner, Marie. ★*The Desperate Hours* — 362.1962
    Deer, Brian. *The Doctor Who Fooled the World* — 610.92
    Farmer, Paul. *Fevers, Feuds, and Diamonds* — 614.5
    Gates, Bill. ★*How to Prevent the Next Pandemic* — 614.5
    Goldberg, Emma. *Life on the Line* — 362.1962
    Hernandez, Daisy. *The Kissing Bug* — 616.9
    Honigsbaum, Mark. *The Pandemic Century* — 614.4
    Hotez, Peter J. *Preventing the Next Pandemic* — 362.1969
    Ireland, Tom. *The Good Virus* — 579.2
    Johnson, Steven. *The Ghost Map* — 614.5
    Kennedy, Jonathan. *Pathogenesis* — 614.4
    Kenny, Charles. *The Plague Cycle* — 614.4
    Kinch, Michael S. *Between Hope and Fear* — 614.4
    Monosson, Emily. ★*Blight* — 616.9
    Price, Polly J. *Plagues in the Nation* — 614.4
    Quammen, David. ★*Breathless* — 614.5

    Quammen, David. ★*Spillover* — 614.4
    Senthilingam, Meera. *Outbreaks and Epidemics* — 614.4
    Wadman, Meredith. *The Vaccine Race* — 614.5
COMMUNICATION
    Alda, Alan. *If I Understood You, Would I Have This Look on My Face?* — 153.6
    Armantrout, Rae. *Wobble* — 811
    Clark, John Lee. *Touch the Future* — B
    Duhigg, Charles. ★*Supercommunicators* — 153.6
    Ellis, Bret Easton. *White* — 814
    Farmer, Lesley S. J. ★*Impactful Community-Based Literacy Projects* — 372.6
    Ferrara, Silvia. *The Greatest Invention* — 411
    Fineman, Meredith. *Brag Better* — 650.1
    Henry, Jo. *Cultivating Civility* — 023
    Hunger, Christina. *How Stella Learned to Talk* — 636.7
    Ingall, Marjorie. *Sorry, Sorry, Sorry* — 158.2
    Jackson, Danielle Bayard. *Fighting for Our Friendships* — 302.34
    Kross, Ethan. ★*Chatter* — 158.1
    Lowry, Erin. ★*Broke Millennial Talks Money* — 332.024
    Lyons, Daniel. *STFU* — 302.2
    McHangama, Jacob. ★*Free Speech* — 323.44
    Mukantabana, Yseult P. ★*Real Friends Talk About Race* — 305.8
    Murthy, Vivek Hallegere. *Together* — 158.2
    Oyler, Lauren. *No Judgment* — 814
    Pease, Allan. *The Definitive Book of Body Language* — 153.6
    Rueckert, Veronica. *Outspoken* — 808.5
    Sale, Anna. ★*Let's Talk About Hard Things* — 153.6
    Schlanger, Zoe. ★*The Light Eaters* — 571.2
    Scott, Andy. *One Kiss or Two?* — 395.4
    Soep, Elisabeth. *Other People's Words* — 155.9
    Stone, Douglas. *Difficult Conversations* — 158.2
    Tatum, Beverly Daniel. ★*"Why Are All the Black Kids Sitting Together in the Cafeteria?"* — 305.800973
    Vince, Gaia. *Transcendence* — 599.93
    Woods, Geraldine. *25 Great Sentences and How They Got That Way* — 808
COMMUNICATION AND TECHNOLOGY
    Ramsey, Franchesca. *Well, That Escalated Quickly* — B
    Smith, Patti. ★*A Book of Days* — 779
COMMUNICATION IN ART
    Micklewright, Keith. *Drawing* — 741.2
    Updike, John. *Always Looking* — 700
COMMUNICATION IN MANAGEMENT
    Gallo, Carmine. *The Bezos Blueprint* — 658.4
    Kramer, Andrea S. *Breaking Through Bias* — 650.1
COMMUNICATION IN MARRIAGE
    Dunn, Jancee. ★*How Not to Hate Your Husband After Kids* — 646.7
COMMUNICATION IN MEDICINE
    Goldberg, Sana. *How to Be a Patient* — 610.69
COMMUNICATION IN ORGANIZATIONS
    Hastings, Reed. *No Rules Rules* — 384.55
    Kramer, Andrea S. *Breaking Through Bias* — 650.1
COMMUNICATION IN POLITICS
    Carpenter, Amanda B. *Gaslighting America* — 973.933
    Elwood, Phil. *All the Worst Humans* — 659.2
    Zelizer, Julian E. *Burning Down the House* — 328.73
COMMUNICATION TECHNOLOGY
    Boghosian, Heidi. *"i Have Nothing to Hide"* — 363.1
Communism. Pipes, Richard — 335.43
COMMUNISM
    Aleksievich, Svetlana. ★*Secondhand Time* — 947.086
    Applebaum, Anne. *Iron Curtain* — 947
    Branigan, Tania. *Red Memory* — 951.05
    Brown, Archie. ★*The Rise and Fall of Communism* — 320.53
    Chang, Jung. *Big Sister, Little Sister, Red Sister* — B
    Chang, Jung. *Mao* — B
    Chang, Jung. ★*Wild Swans* — B
    Cheng, Nien. *Life and Death in Shanghai* — B
    Delisle, Guy. *Pyongyang* — 741.5
    Dikotter, Frank. *China After Mao* — 951.05
    Dikotter, Frank. *The Cultural Revolution* — 951.056
    Duiker, William J. *Ho Chi Minh* — B
    Eisen, Norman L. *The Last Palace* — 920
    Ferrer, Ada. ★*Cuba* — 972.91
    Figes, Orlando. ★*The Whisperers* — 306.850947
    Frankel, Glenn. *High Noon* — 791.43
    Gessen, Masha. *Never Remember* — 365
    Harden, Blaine. *The Great Leader and the Fighter Pilot* — B
    Hoffman, David E. *Give Me Liberty* — B
    Hoyer, Katja. ★*Beyond the Wall* — 943.087

AUTHOR, TITLE, SERIES AND SUBJECT INDEX

Hunt, Tristram. *Marx's General*	335.4092
Igort. *The Ukrainian and Russian Notebooks*	741.5
Kotkin, Stephen. *Stalin*	B
Kotkin, Stephen. *Stalin*	B
Kurtz-Phelan, Daniel. *The China Mission*	951.04
Lankov, A. N. *The Real North Korea*	951.9304
Liao, Yiwu. *God Is Red*	275
Liedman, Sven-Eric. *A World to Win*	B
Lovell, Julia. *Maoism*	335.43
Marx, Karl. ★*The Communist Manifesto*	355.4
McMeekin, Sean. *The Russian Revolution*	947.084
McMeekin, Sean. *Stalin's War*	940.53
Merriman, Helena. ★*Tunnel 29*	943
Mieville, China. *October*	947.084
Min, Anchee. *Red Azalea*	B
Pantsov, Alexander. *Mao*	B
Petrushevskaia, Liudmila. *The Girl from the Metropol Hotel*	B
Phillips, Timothy. *Retracing the Iron Curtain*	909.82
Pipes, Richard. *Communism*	335.43
Rasenberger, Jim. *The Brilliant Disaster*	972.9106
Sallah, Michael. *The Yankee Comandante*	972.91
Satter, David. *The Less You Know, the Better You Sleep*	947.086
Sebag-Montefiore, Simon. *Stalin*	B
Sebestyen, Victor. *Lenin*	B
Sebestyen, Victor. *Revolution 1989*	947.085
Service, Robert. *Lenin—A Biography*	B
Slezkine, Yuri. *The House of Government*	947.084
Sperber, Jonathan. *Karl Marx*	B
Sullivan, Rosemary. *Stalin's Daughter*	B
Szczszak-Brewer, Agata. *The Hunger Book*	B
Taubman, William. *Gorbachev*	B
Taylor, Fred. *The Berlin Wall*	943
Vogel, Ezra F. *Deng Xiaoping and the Transformation of China*	B
Warren, James A. *Year of the Hawk*	959.704
Westad, Odd Arne. *The Cold War*	909.825
Wheen, Francis. *Karl Marx*	B
Willner, Nina. *Forty Autumns*	B
Xue, XInran. *The Book of Secrets*	951.05
Ypi, Lea. ★*Free*	B
COMMUNISM AND CHRISTIANITY	
Johnson, Ian. *The Souls of China*	200.951
Liao, Yiwu. *God Is Red*	275
COMMUNISM AND CULTURE	
Yang, Jisheng. *The World Turned Upside Down*	951.05
COMMUNISM AND RELIGION	
Johnson, Ian. *The Souls of China*	200.951
Liao, Yiwu. *God Is Red*	275
O'Connor, Garry. *Universal Father*	B
COMMUNIST COUNTRIES	
Applebaum, Anne. *Iron Curtain*	947
Fifield, Anna. *The Great Successor*	B
★*The Communist Manifesto*. Marx, Karl	355.4
COMMUNISTS	
Gabriel, Mary. *Love and Capital*	920
Hunt, Tristram. *Marx's General*	335.4092
Liedman, Sven-Eric. *A World to Win*	B
Pantsov, Alexander. *Mao*	B
Sebba, Anne. *Ethel Rosenberg*	B
Sebestyen, Victor. *Lenin*	B
Service, Robert. *Lenin—A Biography*	B
Slezkine, Yuri. *The House of Government*	947.084
Sperber, Jonathan. *Karl Marx*	B
Suny, Ronald Grigor. *Stalin*	B
Vogel, Ezra F. *Deng Xiaoping and the Transformation of China*	B
Wheen, Francis. *Karl Marx*	B
Zia, Helen. *Last Boat Out of Shanghai*	951.04
COMMUNITIES	
Bamford, Maria. *Sure, I'll Join Your Cult*	B
Black Thought. *The Upcycled Self*	
Bradford, Joy Harden. *Sisterhood Heals*	158.2
Brous, Sharon. ★*The Amen Effect*	296.3
Brown, Brene. *Braving the Wilderness*	305.8
Bruder, Jessica. ★*Nomadland*	331.3
Connell, John. *The Farmer's Son*	630.9
Eisenberg, Emma Copley. ★*The Third Rainbow Girl*	364.152
Field, Andy. *Encounterism*	302
Gates, Henry Louis. *The Black Box*	908
Gerson, Merissa Nathan. *Forget Prayers, Bring Cake*	155.9
Glass, Sara. *Kissing Girls on Shabbat*	B
Gorrindo, Simone. ★*The Wives*	B
Harding, Thomas. *The House by the Lake*	943
Hobbs, Jeff. ★*The Short and Tragic Life of Robert Peace*	B
Hoja, Gulchehra. *A Stone Is Most Precious Where It Belongs*	B
Hudes, Quiara Alegria. ★*My Broken Language*	B
Kristof, Nicholas D. ★*Tightrope*	306.0973
Kyle, Taya. *American Spirit*	B
Lin, Jami Nakamura. *The Night Parade*	B
Maddigan, Beth. *Community Library Programs That Work*	021.2
Mans, Jasmine. *Black Girl, Call Home*	811
McCaulley, Esau. *How Far to the Promised Land*	B
Murthy, Vivek Hallegere. *Together*	158.2
O'Brien, Keith. *Paradise Falls*	363.738
Palmer, Amanda. ★*The Art of Asking*	782.42164
Parkin, Simon. *The Island of Extraordinary Captives*	940.53
Pinn, Anthony B. *The Black Practice of Disbelief*	211
Quinn, Tallu Schuyler. *What We Wish Were True*	B
Quinones, John. ★*One Year in Uvalde*	371.7
Rodgers, Jodi. ★*How to Find a Four-Leaf Clover*	616.85
Safina, Carl. ★*Becoming Wild*	591.7
Samatar, Sofia. *The White Mosque*	B
Sanchez, Sonia. *Homegirls & Handgrenades*	811
Sankovitch, Nina. *American Rebels*	920
Saunt, Claudio. *Unworthy Republic*	323.1197
Shange, Ntozake. ★*Sing a Black Girl's Song*	818
Slezkine, Yuri. *The House of Government*	947.084
Smith, Danez. ★*Homie*	811
Thomson, Mike. *Syria's Secret Library*	956.9104
Twenge, Jean M. *Generations*	305.2
Vance, J. D. *Hillbilly Elegy*	B
Vasquez, Karla Tatiana. ★*The Salvisoul Cookbook*	641.598
Velour, Sasha. ★*The Big Reveal*	792.7
Wariner, Ruth. *The Sound of Gravel*	B
Wolf, Brandon J. *A Place for Us*	B
COMMUNITY ACTIVISM	
Allen, Brigette. *Living Without Plastic*	640
Beavan, Colin. *No Impact Man*	B
Chatelain, Marcia. ★*Franchise*	339
Jackson, Jenn M. ★*Black Women Taught Us*	305.48
Mattlin, Ben. *Disability Pride*	323.3
O'Brien, Keith. *Paradise Falls*	363.738
Sokolik, Vicki. ★*If You See Them*	362.5
Wilbur, Matika. *Project 562*	970.004
COMMUNITY ACTIVISTS	
Kanigel, Robert. *Eyes on the Street*	B
Moore, Wes. *The Work*	B
COMMUNITY DEVELOPMENT	
Garbes, Angela. *Essential Labor*	306.874
Lunenfeld, Peter. *City at the Edge of Forever*	979.4
Rubinstein, Julian. ★*The Holly*	364.106
Community Library Programs That Work. Maddigan, Beth	021.2
COMMUNITY LIFE	
Auvinen, Karen. *Rough Beauty*	B
Baskette, Molly Phinney. *How to Begin When Your World Is Ending*	248.8
Gill, Jonathan. *Harlem*	974.7
Narayan, Shoba. *The Milk Lady of Bangalore*	390
Swift, Earl. *Chesapeake Requiem*	639
COMMUNITY ORGANIZATION	
Maher, Kris. *Desperate*	344
Samaha, Albert. *Never Ran, Never Will*	920
COMMUNITY ORGANIZERS	
Obama, Barack. ★*Dreams from My Father*	B
Obama, Barack. ★*A Promised Land*	B
Remnick, David. *The Bridge*	B
Wong, Alice. ★*Year of the Tiger*	B
COMMUNITY SERVICE (PUNISHMENT)	
Dresner, Amy. *My Fair Junkie*	B
COMODAS, ROSALIE	
DeParle, Jason. ★*A Good Provider Is One Who Leaves*	305.899
COMPANIONSHIP	
Bailey, Elisabeth. *The Sound of a Wild Snail Eating*	594
Denworth, Lydia. *Friendship*	158.2
Golbeck, Jennifer. *The Purest Bond*	636.7
The Company. Micklethwait, John	338.7
The Company Town. Green, Hardy	307.76
COMPANY TOWNS	
Green, Hardy. *The Company Town*	307.76

PUBLIC LIBRARY CORE COLLECTION: NONFICTION
Twentieth Edition

Macy, Beth. ★*Factory Man*	338.7

COMPARATIVE CIVILIZATION
Diamond, Jared M. *Upheaval*	303.48

COMPARATIVE GOVERNMENT
Aristotle. ★*Politics, 2nd Ed*	320
Fukuyama, Francis. *Political Order and Political Decay*	320.1

COMPARATIVE PSYCHOLOGY
Safina, Carl. *Beyond Words*	591.56
Suddendorf, Thomas. *The Gap*	156
Waal, F. B. M. de. *Our Inner Ape*	156

COMPARISON
Chu, Lenora. *Little Soldiers*	370
Miles, Jack. *God in the Qur'an*	297.2

COMPASSION
Aptowicz, Cristin O'Keefe. *Dr. Mutter's Marvels*	B
Armstrong, Karen. *Twelve Steps to a Compassionate Life*	177
Bardenwerper, William. *The Prisoner in His Palace*	956.7044
Bragg, Rick. *The Speckled Beauty*	636.7
Brous, Sharon. ★*The Amen Effect*	296.3
Brown, Theresa. *Healing*	616.99
Clarke, Rachel. *Dear Life*	B
Dalai Lama. *How to Be Compassionate*	294.3
Goldblatt, Duchess. *Becoming Duchess Goldblatt*	B
Grose, Peter. *A Good Place to Hide*	940.53
Hardin, Lara Love. ★*The Many Lives of Mama Love*	B
Lamott, Anne. ★*Hallelujah Anyway*	241
Lamott, Anne. ★*Somehow*	814
Lewis, C. S. *Mere Christianity*	230
Naumburg, Carla. ★*You Are Not a Sh*tty Parent*	649
Obama, Michelle. ★*The Light We Carry*	B
Olivares, Efren C. *My Boy Will Die of Sorrow*	305.9
Rakel, David. *The Compassionate Connection*	610.1
Raza, Azra. *The First Cell*	616.99
Shlain, Tiffany. *24/6*	158.1
Teresa. *A Call to Mercy*	234
Van Ness, Jonathan. *Love That Story*	791.4502
Waal, F. B. M. de. ★*Mama's Last Hug*	599.885
The Compassionate Connection. Rakel, David	610.1

COMPENSATION FOR JUDICIAL ERROR
Hinton, Anthony Ray. *The Sun Does Shine*	B

COMPETITION
Askwith, Richard. *Unbreakable*	B
Barbarisi, Daniel. *Chasing the Thrill*	796.1
Bruni, Frank. *Where You Go Is Not Who You'll Be*	378.1
Burgman, John. *High Drama*	796.522
Burke, Monte. *Lords of the Fly*	799.124
Cadbury, Deborah. *Princes at War*	920
Chapin, Sasha. *All the Wrong Moves*	794.1092
Cole, Jason. *Elway*	B
Crowther, Gail. *Three-Martini Afternoons at the Ritz*	920
Ellis, Bret Easton. *White*	814
Feinstein, John. *The Back Roads to March*	796.323
Fischer, Paul. *The Man Who Invented Motion Pictures*	791.43
Gessner, David. *Ultimate Glory*	796.2
Goldstone, Nancy Bazelon. *The Rival Queens*	944
Hartman, Darrell. *Battle of Ink and Ice*	998
Howard, Johnette. *The Rivals*	B
Jaher, David. *The Witch of Lime Street*	B
Johnson, Kirk W. *The Fishermen and the Dragon*	976.4
Kohan, Rafi. ★*Trash Talk*	179
Masters, Oksana. *The Hard Parts*	B
McIntyre, Rick. *The Reign of Wolf 21*	599.773
McPhee, John. *Levels of the Game*	796.34
Millard, Candice. ★*River of the Gods*	916.204
O'Brady, Colin. ★*The Impossible First*	919.8904
Ollestad, Norman. *Crazy for the Storm*	B
Phillips, Rowan Ricardo. *The Circuit*	796.342
Port, Ian S. *The Birth of Loud*	787.87
Prior-Palmer, Lara. *Rough Magic*	798.4
Rippon, Adam. *Beautiful on the Outside*	B
Rose, Alexander. *Empires of the Sky*	920
Smith, Ben. *Traffic*	070.4
Stelter, Brian. *Top of the Morning*	791.456
Taraborrelli, J. Randy. *Jackie, Janet & Lee*	920
Tomlinson, Tommy. *Dogland*	636.7
Wertheim, L. Jon. *This Is Your Brain on Sports*	796.01
Womack, Kenneth. *All Things Must Pass Away*	781.66

COMPETITION (BIOLOGY)
Anthony, Leslie. *The Aliens Among Us*	578.6
Wohlleben, Peter. *The Secret Wisdom of Nature*	508
The Compleated Autobiography. Franklin, Benjamin	B
The Complete Book of Jewelry Making. Codina, Carles	739.27
The Complete Book of Polymer Clay. Pavelka, Lisa	738.1
The Complete Compost Gardening Guide. Pleasant, Barbara	631.8
Complete Copyright for K-12 Librarians and Educators. Russell, Carrie	346.73
★*Complete Crochet Course.* Mullett-Bowlsby, Shannon	746.43
The Complete Game. Darling, Ron	B
★*The Complete Gods and Goddesses of Ancient Egypt.* Wilkinson, Richard H.	299
The Complete Guide to Absolutely Everything. Rutherford, Adam	500
The Complete Guide to Acquisitions Management. Wilkinson, Frances C.	025.2
The Complete Guide to Drawing for Beginners. Ogura, Yoshiko	740
The Complete Guide to Hunting, Butchering, and Cooking Wild Game. Rinella, Steven	799.2
The Complete Guide to Saving Seeds. Gough, Robert E.	631.5
The Complete Houseplant Survival Manual. Pleasant, Barbara	635.9
The Complete Jewelry Making Course. McGrath, Jinks	739.27028
The Complete Lesbian & Gay Parenting Guide. Lev, Arlene Istar	649
★*The Complete Persepolis.* Satrapi, Marjane	741.5
Complete Photo Guide [Series]. Watanabe, Judi	745.594
The Complete Photo Guide to Cardmaking. Watanabe, Judi	745.594
The Complete Photo Guide to Crochet. Hubert, Margaret	746.43
The Complete Photo Guide to Framing and Displaying Artwork. Kistler, Vivian Carli	749
The Complete Plays. Chekhov, Anton Pavlovich	891.72
The Complete Plays. Marlowe, Christopher	822
Complete Poems. Melville, Herman	811
★*The Complete Poems.* Jarrell, Randall	811
Complete Poems. Poe, Edgar Allan	810
Complete Poems. Bunting, Basil	821
The Complete Poems. Larkin, Philip	821
The Complete Poems. Coleridge, Samuel Taylor	821
Complete Poems. Johnson, James Weldon	811
★*Complete Poems and Plays.* Eliot, T. S.	810
★*The Complete Poems of Anna Akhmatova.* Akhmatova, Anna Andreevna	891.71
The Complete Poems of C. Day Lewis. Day-Lewis, Cecil	821
★*The Complete Poems of Carl Sandburg.* Sandburg, Carl	811
★*The Complete Poems of John Keats.* Keats, John	821
★*Complete Poems, 1904-1962.* Cummings, E. E.	811
★*The Complete Poems.* Dickinson, Emily	811.4
The Complete Poetry. Angelou, Maya	811
★*The Complete Poetry and Prose of Geoffrey Chaucer.* Chaucer, Geoffrey	821
★*The Complete Poetry and Prose of William Blake.* Blake, William	821
The Complete Pompeii. Berry, Joanne	937
The Complete Sailing Manual. Sleight, Steve	797.1
Complete Verse. Kipling, Rudyard	821
The Complete Verse and Other Nonsense. Lear, Edward	821
★*The Complete Works.* Shakespeare, William	822.33
Complications. Gawande, Atul	B
★*Complicit.* Bravo, Reah	331.4
★*Composed.* Cash, Rosanne	B

COMPOSERS
Adams, John. *Hallelujah Junction*	B
Berger, William. *Puccini Without Excuses*	782.1
Berger, William. *Verdi with a Vengeance*	B
Berlin, Edward A. *King of Ragtime*	B
Bernstein, Burton. ★*Leonard Bernstein*	B
Bostridge, Ian. *Schubert's Winter Journey*	782.4
Brown, Carolyn. *Chance and Circumstance*	B
Chernaik, Judith. *Schumann*	B
Dolby, Thomas. *The Speed of Sound*	B
Eisler, Benita. ★*Chopin's Funeral*	B
Gabbard, Krin. *Better Git It in Your Soul*	B
Gardiner, John Eliot. *Bach*	B
Geck, Martin. ★*Johann Sebastian Bach*	780.92
Glass, Philip. *Words Without Music*	B
Gutman, Robert W. *Mozart*	B
Harris, Ellen T. *George Frideric Handel*	B
Haupt, Lyanda Lynn. *Mozart's Starling*	B
Hough, Stephen. *Rough Ideas*	786.2092
Hyland, William G. *George Gershwin*	B
Johnson, Graham. *Poulenc*	B
Kennedy, Michael. *Richard Strauss*	B
Kennicott, Philip. *Counterpoint*	B

AUTHOR, TITLE, SERIES AND SUBJECT INDEX

Kildea, Paul Francis. *Chopin's Piano* — B
Larson, Kay. *Where the Heart Beats* — 700.1
Lloyd Webber, Andrew. *Unmasked* — B
Lockwood, Lewis. *Beethoven* — B
Max, D. T. *Finale* — 782.1
McBrien, William. *Cole Porter* — B
Morris, Edmund. *Beethoven* — B
Norman, Philip. *George Harrison* — B
Pollack, Howard. ★*George Gershwin* — B
Porter, Cecelia Hopkins. *Five Lives in Music* — B
Purdum, Todd S. *Something Wonderful* — B
Rodgers, Mary. *Shy* — B
Rose, Michael. *The Birth of an Opera* — 782.1
Ross, Alex. *Wagnerism* — B
Sachs, Harvey. *The Ninth* — 784.2
Schonberg, Harold C. ★*The Lives of the Great Composers* — 780
Servadio, Gaia. *Rossini* — B
Suchet, John. *Beethoven* — B
Suchet, John. *Mozart* — B
Suchet, John. *Verdi* — 782.1092
Swafford, Jan. ★*Beethoven* — B
Swafford, Jan. *Charles Ives* — B
Swafford, Jan. *Johannes Brahms* — B
Swafford, Jan. *Mozart* — B
Teachout, Terry. *Duke* — B
Threadgill, Henry. *Easily Slip into Another World* — B
Walker-Hill, Helen. *From Spirituals to Symphonies* — 780
Walsh, Stephen. ★*Debussy* — B
Wolff, Christoph. *Johann Sebastian Bach* — B

COMPOSITION (MUSIC)
Bostridge, Ian. *Schubert's Winter Journey* — 782.4
Feinstein, Michael. *The Gershwins and Me* — 782.42164
Glass, Philip. *Words Without Music* — B
Guesdon, Jean-Michel. *All the Songs* — 782.42166
Johnson, Graham. *Poulenc* — B
Kennicott, Philip. *Counterpoint* — B
Max, D. T. *Finale* — 782.1
Mordden, Ethan. *Anything Goes* — 782.1
Pollack, Howard. ★*George Gershwin* — B
Purdum, Todd S. *Something Wonderful* — B
Rose, Michael. *The Birth of an Opera* — 782.1
Sloan, Nate. *Switched on Pop* — 781.64
Sondheim, Stephen. *Look, I Made a Hat* — 782.1
Spitzer, Michael. *The Musical Human* — 780.9

COMPOST
Pleasant, Barbara. *The Complete Compost Gardening Guide* — 631.8

COMPREHENSION
Dehaene, Stanislas. *Reading in the Brain* — 418

COMPROMISE
Beeman, Richard R. ★*Plain, Honest Men* — 342.7302
Blattman, Christopher. *Why We Fight* — 303.6
Wolf, Martin. ★*The Crisis of Democratic Capitalism* — 330.12

The Compton Cowboys. Thompson-Hernandez, Walter — 920

COMPULSIVE BEHAVIOR
Adam, David. *The Man Who Couldn't Stop* — 616.85
Fisher, Carl Erik. ★*The Urge* — 362.29
Kalb, Claudia. *Andy Warhol Was a Hoarder* — 920
Lembke, Anna. *Dopamine Nation* — 152.4
Stone, Lillian. ★*Everybody's Favorite* — 814.6
Summerscale, Kate. *The Book of Phobias and Manias* — 616.85
Tammet, Daniel. *Born on a Blue Day* — B
Tate, Christie. ★*Group* — B

COMPULSIVE EATING
Burton, Susan. *Empty* — B
Freeman, Hadley. *Good Girls* — 616.85
Moss, Michael. ★*Hooked* — 613.2
Moss, Michael. *Salt, Sugar, Fat* — 613.2
Specter, Emma. *More, Please* — 616.85

COMPULSIVE GAMBLERS
O'Brien, Keith. *Charlie Hustle* — 796.357

COMPULSIVE HOARDING
Howard, Jennifer. *Clutter* — 306.3
Stewart, Alison. *Junk* — 616.85

COMPUTATIONAL COMPLEXITY
Fortnow, Lance. *The Golden Ticket* — 511.3

COMPUTER ALGORITHMS
Christian, Brian. *Algorithms to Live By* — 153.4
Fortnow, Lance. *The Golden Ticket* — 511.3

Wiggins, Christopher L. *How Data Happened* — 310

COMPUTER ART
Bilal, Wafaa. *Shoot an Iraqi* — B

COMPUTER CRIMES
Dudley, Renee. *The Ransomware Hunting Team* — 363.25
Goldberg, Carrie. *Nobody's Victim* — 345.73
Greenberg, Andy. *Sandworm* — 364.16
Greenberg, Andy. *Tracers in the Dark* — 364.16
Mitnick, Kevin D. *The Art of Invisibility* — 005.8
Mitnick, Kevin D. *Ghost in the Wires* — B
Ratliff, Evan. *The Mastermind* — B
Shannon, Elaine. *Hunting Leroux* — 364.1
Shapiro, Scott J. ★*Fancy Bear Goes Phishing* — 364.16
Smith, Jeremy N. *Breaking and Entering* — B
Vaughan, Liam. *Flash Crash* — B

COMPUTER CRIMINALS
Smith, Jeremy N. *Breaking and Entering* — B

COMPUTER ENGINEERS
Beyer, Kurt. *Grace Hopper and the Invention of the Information Age* — B
Schlender, Brent. *Becoming Steve Jobs* — B

COMPUTER ERRORS
Russell, Stuart J. *Human Compatible* — 006.301

COMPUTER FILE SHARING
Taplin, Jonathan. *Move Fast and Break Things* — 330.9

COMPUTER GAMES
Miller, Megan. ★*The Ultimate Unofficial Encyclopedia for Minecrafters* — 794.8

COMPUTER INDUSTRY AND TRADE
Isaacson, Walter. ★*Steve Jobs* — B
Lashinsky, Adam. *Wild Ride* — 388.4
Nadella, Satya. *Hit Refresh* — B
Schlender, Brent. *Becoming Steve Jobs* — B
Stone, Brad. *The Upstarts* — 338.04
Swisher, Kara. *Burn Book* — 303.48
Wiener, Anna. ★*Uncanny Valley* — B

COMPUTER NETWORKS
Cox, Joseph. *Dark Wire* — 363.2
Dudley, Renee. *The Ransomware Hunting Team* — 363.25

COMPUTER PROGRAMMERS
Evans, Claire Lisa. *Broad Band* — 920
Kidder, Tracy. *A Truck Full of Money* — B
Pein, Corey. *Live Work Work Work Die* — 338.4
Ratliff, Evan. *The Mastermind* — B
Thompson, Clive. *Coders* — 005.1092
Ullman, Ellen. *Life in Code* — B

COMPUTER PROGRAMMING
Kleiman, Kathy. *Proving Ground* — 4.092
Lloyd, Seth. *Programming the Universe* — 530.12
Thompson, Clive. *Coders* — 005.1092
Ullman, Ellen. *Life in Code* — B

COMPUTER SCIENCE
Beyer, Kurt. *Grace Hopper and the Invention of the Information Age* — B
Fortnow, Lance. *The Golden Ticket* — 511.3
Isaacson, Walter. ★*The Innovators* — B
Roeder, Oliver. *Seven Games* — 794
Soni, Jimmy. *A Mind at Play* — B

COMPUTER SCIENTISTS
Evans, Claire Lisa. *Broad Band* — 920
Price, David A. *Geniuses at War* — 940.54

COMPUTER SECURITY
Chertoff, Michael. *Exploding Data* — 343.7309
Cox, Joseph. *Dark Wire* — 363.2
Dudley, Renee. *The Ransomware Hunting Team* — 363.25
Greenberg, Andy. *Sandworm* — 364.16
Hasen, Richard L. *Election Meltdown* — 324.973
Mitnick, Kevin D. *The Art of Invisibility* — 005.8
Mitnick, Kevin D. *Ghost in the Wires* — B
Shapiro, Scott J. ★*Fancy Bear Goes Phishing* — 364.16
Smith, Jeremy N. *Breaking and Entering* — B
Wiehl, Lis W. *A Spy in Plain Sight* — 327.1247

COMPUTER SIMULATION
Christian, Brian. *Algorithms to Live By* — 153.4
Pontzen, Andrew. *The Universe in a Box* — 523.1

COMPUTER SOFTWARE
Hill, Kashmir. ★*Your Face Belongs to Us* — 006.2

COMPUTER SOFTWARE INDUSTRY AND TRADE
Campbell-Kelly, Martin. *From Airline Reservations to Sonic the Hedgehog* — 338.4

PUBLIC LIBRARY CORE COLLECTION: NONFICTION
Twentieth Edition

COMPUTER TECHNICIANS
   Dudley, Renee. *The Ransomware Hunting Team*   363.25
COMPUTER TECHNOLOGY
   Dyson, George. *Turing's Cathedral*   004
   Wiggins, Christopher L. *How Data Happened*   310
COMPUTERS
   Auletta, Ken. *Googled*   338.7
   Campbell-Kelly, Martin. *From Airline Reservations to Sonic the Hedgehog*   338.4
   Copeland, B. Jack. *Turing*   B
   Dyson, George. *Turing's Cathedral*   004
   Essinger, James. *Ada's Algorithm*   B
   Galloway, Scott. *The Four*   338.7
   Isaacson, Walter. ★*The Innovators*   B
   Kasparov, G. K. *Deep Thinking*   006.3
   Leavitt, David. *The Man Who Knew Too Much*   B
   Li, Fei-Fei. *The Worlds I See*   B
   Price, David A. *Geniuses at War*   940.54
   Russell, Stuart J. *Human Compatible*   006.301
COMPUTERS AND CHILDREN
   Linn, Susan. *Who's Raising the Kids?*   649
COMPUTERS AND CIVILIZATION
   Galloway, Scott. *The Four*   338.7
   Kaku, Michio. *Quantum Supremacy*   006.3
   Malone, Thomas W. *Superminds*   005.7
   Merchant, Brian. *Blood in the Machine*   303.48
   Miller, Chris. *Chip War*   338.4
   Mishra, Pankaj. *Age of Anger*   909.8
   Russell, Stuart J. *Human Compatible*   006.301
   Thompson, Clive. *Coders*   005.1092
   Ullman, Ellen. *Life in Code*   B
COMSTOCK, ANTHONY, 1844-1915
   Sohn, Amy. *The Man Who Hated Women*   363.28
Con/Artist. Tetro, Tony   B
Conaboy, Chelsea
   Mother Brain   306.874
Conaboy, Kelly
   The Particulars of Peter   636.7
CONABOY, KELLY
   Conaboy, Kelly. *The Particulars of Peter*   636.7
Conahan, Gillian
   The Hero's Closet   646.2
CONANT, JAMES, 1893-1978
   Conant, Jennet. *Man of the Hour*   B
Conant, Jennet
   The Lotus Eaters   940.54
   Man of the Hour   B
CONANT, RICHARD PERRY
   McGrath, Ben. *Riverman*   797.122
Conason, Joe
   The Longest Con   320.52
Conaway, James
   America's Library   027.5
CONCENTRATION CAMP COMMANDANTS
   Teege, Jennifer. *My Grandfather Would Have Shot Me*   929.2
CONCENTRATION CAMP RESISTANCE AND REVOLTS
   Fairweather, Jack. *The Volunteer*   B
CONCENTRATION CAMP SURVIVORS
   Frank, Michael. ★*One Hundred Saturdays*   B
   Frankl, Viktor E. ★*Man's Search for Meaning*   B
   Greenfield, Martin. ★*Measure of a Man*   B
   Mueller, Melissa. *Alice's Piano*   B
   Nasaw, David. *The Last Million*   940.53
   Rees, Laurence. *Auschwitz*   940.53
   Wiesel, Elie. ★*Night*   B
CONCENTRATION CAMPS
   Applebaum, Anne. ★*Gulag*   365
   Cahan, Richard. *Un-American*   940.53
   Clavin, Thomas. *Lightning Down*   940.54
   Debreczeni, Jozsef. *Cold Crematorium*   940.53
   Fairweather, Jack. *The Volunteer*   B
   Freedland, Jonathan. ★*The Escape Artist*   940.53
   Gessen, Masha. *Never Remember*   365
   Haitiwaji, Gulbahar. *How I Survived a Chinese "Reeducation" Camp*   305.8
   Helm, Sarah. *Ravensbruck*   940.53
   Henderson, Bruce B. *Bridge to the Sun*   940.53
   Holden, Wendy. ★*Born Survivors*   940.53
   Jaku, Eddie. ★*The Happiest Man on Earth*   B

   Kaiser, Charles. *The Cost of Courage*   B
   Karski, Jan. *Story of a Secret State*   940.53
   Kraus, Dita. *A Delayed Life*   B
   Lindwer, Willy. *The Last Seven Months of Anne Frank*   B
   Loftis, Larry. ★*The Watchmaker's Daughter*   940.53
   Macadam, Heather Dune. *999*   940.53
   Magida, Arthur J. *Code Name Madeleine*   940.54
   Moorehead, Caroline. *A Train in Winter*   940.53
   Parkin, Simon. *The Island of Extraordinary Captives*   940.53
   Pivnik, Sam. *Survivor*   940.5318
   Rajchman, Chil. *The Last Jew of Treblinka*   940.53
   Rees, Laurence. *Auschwitz*   940.53
   Reeves, Richard. *Infamy*   940.53
   Ross, Steve. *From Broken Glass*   B
   Sides, Hampton. ★*Ghost Soldiers*   940.54
   Solzhenitsyn, Aleksandr Isaevich. ★*The Gulag Archipelago 1918-1956*   365
   Solzhenitsyn, Aleksandr Isaevich. ★*The Gulag Archipelago, 1918-1956*   365
   Stahl, Jerry. *Nein, Nein, Nein!*   B
   Van De Perre, Selma. *My Name Is Selma*   940.53
   Wachsmann, Nikolaus. *Kl*   940.53
   Weintraub, Robert. *No Better Friend*   940.54
   Weiss, Helga. *Helga's Diary*   B
   Wiesenthal, Simon. ★*The Sunflower*   179.7
   Winters, Richard D. *Beyond Band of Brothers*   B
Concepcion. Samaha, Albert   929
CONCEPCION FAMILY
   Samaha, Albert. *Concepcion*   929
CONCEPTION
   Dolnick, Edward. *Seeds of Life*   612.6
   Schrock, Leslie. *Fertility Rules*   613.9
CONCEPTUAL ART
   Bilal, Wafaa. *Shoot an Iraqi*   B
Concerning The City of God Against the Pagans. Augustine   239
CONCERT AGENTS
   McDonald, Greg (Producer). *Elvis and the Colonel*   920
CONCERT TOURS
   McCartney, Paul. ★*1964*   782.42166
Concerto Al-Quds. Adunis   892.7
Concise Encyclopedia of Amish, Brethren, Hutterites, and Mennonites. Kraybill, Donald B.   289.7
The Concise Guide to Hip-Hop Music. Edwards, Paul   782.421649
A Concise History of the Russian Revolution. Pipes, Richard   947.084
CONCORD, BATTLE OF, 1775
   Fischer, David Hackett. *Paul Revere's Ride*   973.3
   Norton, Mary Beth. *1774*   973.3
   Phillips, Kevin. *1775*   973.3
CONCORD, MASSACHUSETTS
   Cheever, Susan. *American Bloomsbury*   920
CONCRETE CONSTRUCTION
   Smith, Nathan. *Color Concrete Garden Projects*   721
Concussion. Laskas, Jeanne Marie   617.5
The Condemnation of Blackness. Muhammad, Khalil Gibran   364.2
CONDIMENTS
   Murad, Noor. ★*Ottolenghi Test Kitchen*   641.3
Conditional Citizens. Lalami, Laila   323.60973
CONDOLENCE
   Corrigan, Kelly. *Glitter and Glue*   B
CONDUCTING
   Mauceri, John. *Maestros and Their Music*   781.45
Conducting The Reference Interview. Ross, Catherine Sheldrick   025.5
CONDUCTORS (MUSIC)
   Bernstein, Burton. ★*Leonard Bernstein*   B
   Mauceri, John. *Maestros and Their Music*   781.45
   Osborne, Richard. *Herbert Von Karajan*   B
Conefrey, Mick
   The Ghosts of K2   796.522
CONFECTIONERY
   Curl, Jami. *Candy Is Magic*   641.85
   Nederlanden, Elisabet der. ★*Holiday Cookies*   641.86
   Ottolenghi, Yotam. *Sweet*   641.86
CONFEDERATE SOLDIERS
   Blount, Roy. *Robert E. Lee*   B
   Gwynne, S. C. *Rebel Yell*   B
   Korda, Michael. *Clouds of Glory*   B
   McPherson, James M. *For Cause and Comrades*   973.7
   Robertson, James I. *Stonewall Jackson*   B
   Varon, Elizabeth R. *Longstreet*   B
   Wert, Jeffry D. *Cavalryman of the Lost Cause*   B

AUTHOR, TITLE, SERIES AND SUBJECT INDEX

CONFEDERATE STATES OF AMERICA
    Horwitz, Tony. *Confederates in the Attic* — 973.7
    Levine, Bruce C. *The Fall of the House of Dixie* — 973.7
    Williams, David. *Bitterly Divided* — 973.7
Confederates in the Attic. Horwitz, Tony — 973.7
CONFESSION
    Heti, Sheila. *Alphabetical Diaries* — 818
    Ng, Fae Myenne. *Orphan Bachelors* — B
CONFESSION (LAW)
    Glatt, John. ★*The Perfect Father* — 364.152
    Harman, Claire. *Murder by the Book* — 364.152
    Lauren, Jillian. *Behold the Monster* — 364.152
    Mayer, Jane. *The Dark Side* — 973.931
    Trainum, James L. *How the Police Generate False Confessions* — 345.73
Confessions. Augustine — B
Confessions. Rousseau, Jean-Jacques — B
Confessions of a French Atheist. Bignon, Guillaume — 239
The Confidence Men. Fox, Margalit — 940.4
The Confidence Trap. Runciman, David — 321.8
Conflict. Petraeus, David Howell — 355
CONFLICT (PSYCHOLOGY)
    Nordland, Rod. *Waiting for the Monsoon* — B
CONFLICT IN FAMILIES
    Black, Dustin Lance. *Mama's Boy* — B
    Cooper, Anderson. *Vanderbilt* — 920
    Fremont, Helen. *The Escape Artist* — B
    Irving, Apricot Anderson. *The Gospel of Trees* — B
    Laux, Dorianne. *Only as the Day Is Long* — 811
    Maupin, Armistead. *Logical Family* — B
    Preszler, Trent. *Little and Often* — B
    Schindler, Meriel. *The Lost Cafe Schindler* — 943.64
    Stewart, James B. *Unscripted* — 658.1
CONFLICT OF INTERESTS
    Hartman, Darrell. *Battle of Ink and Ice* — 998
CONFLICT RESOLUTION
    Beeman, Richard R. ★*Plain, Honest Men* — 342.7302
    Economy, Peter. *Wait, I'm Working with Who?!?* — 650.1
    Gallo, Amy. *Getting Along* — 658.4
    Gottman, Julie Schwartz. *Fight Right* — 616.89
    Green, Alison. *Ask a Manager* — 650.1
    Henry, Jo. *Cultivating Civility* — 023
    Jackson, Danielle Bayard. *Fighting for Our Friendships* — 302.34
    Seo, Bo. *Good Arguments* — 808.53
    Tenzin Priyadarshi. *Running Toward Mystery* — B
    Waxman, Jamye. *How to Break up with Anyone* — 158.2
CONFRONTATION (INTERPERSONAL RELATIONS)
    Stone, Douglas. *Difficult Conversations* — 158.2
CONFUCIANISM
    Armstrong, Karen. ★*The Great Transformation* — 200.9
Congdon, Lisa
    Art Inc. — 702
CONGO (DEMOCRATIC REPUBLIC)
    Addario, Lynsey. *Of Love & War* — 779
    Hochschild, Adam. *King Leopold's Ghost* — 967.51
    Jeal, Tim. *Explorers of the Nile* — 920
    Kara, Siddharth. *Cobalt Red* — 338.2
    Prendergast, John. *Congo Stories* — 967.5103
    Reid, Stuart A. *The Lumumba Plot* — 967.51
    Standefer, Katherine E. *Lightning Flowers* — B
Congo Stories. Prendergast, John — 967.5103
★*Congratulations, The Best Is Over!* Thomas, R. Eric — B
Congress At War. Bordewich, Fergus M. — 324.2734
CONIFERS
    Brown, George E. *Essential Pruning Techniques* — 635.9
Conley, Chip
    ★*Learning to Love Midlife* — 646.7
Conn, David
    The Fall of the House of FIFA — 796.334
Connect The Shapes Crochet Motifs. Eckman, Edie — 746.43
CONNECTICUT
    Belkin, Lisa. *Genealogy of a Murder* — 362.88
    Lysiak, Matthew. *Newtown* — 371.7
    Williamson, Elizabeth. ★*Sandy Hook* — 364.152
★*The Connection Cure*. Hotz, Julia — 610
Connell, Evan S.
    Son of the Morning Star — 973.8
Connell, John
    The Farmer's Son — 630.9

CONNELL, JOHN, 1986-
    Connell, John. *The Farmer's Son* — 630.9
Connelly, Ben
    Inside Vasubandhu's Yogacara — 294.3
Connelly, Matthew James
    The Declassification Engine — 352.3
Conner, Polly
    ★*From Freezer to Cooker* — 641.6
Conners, Rachel
    Bakerita — 641.81
Conniff, Richard
    House of Lost Worlds — 069
Connolly, Ray
    Being Elvis — B
    Being John Lennon — B
CONNOR, EUGENE, 1897-1973
    McWhorter, Diane. *Carry Me Home* — 976.1
Conquered into Liberty. Cohen, Eliot A. — 355.009747
Conquering The Pacific. Resendez, Andres — 959.9
The Conquering Tide. Toll, Ian W. — 940.54
The Conquerors. Beschloss, Michael R. — 940.53
CONQUERORS
    Cervantes, Fernando. *Conquistadores* — 970.01
    Kennedy, Hugh. ★*The Great Arab Conquests* — 297.09
    Marozzi, Justin. *Tamerlane* — 950.2
    McLynn, Frank. *Genghis Khan* — 950.2
    Morris, Marc. *A Great and Terrible King* — B
    Weatherford, J. McIver. *Genghis Khan and the Quest for God* — 323.44
    Woolf, Greg. *Rome* — 937
CONQUEST OF MEXICO (1519-1540)
    Diaz del Castillo, Bernal. *The Discovery and Conquest of Mexico, 1517-1521* — 972
    Restall, Matthew. *When Montezuma Met Cortes* — 972
Conquistadores. Cervantes, Fernando — 970.01
CONQUISTADORS
    Cervantes, Fernando. *Conquistadores* — 970.01
Conradi, Peter J.
    Iris — B
    Who Lost Russia? — 947.086
Conroy, Pat
    My Losing Season — B
CONROY, PAT
    Conroy, Pat. *My Losing Season* — B
CONSCIENCE
    Bilger, Burkhard. *Fatherland* — B
    Elwood, Phil. *All the Worst Humans* — 659.2
CONSCIENTIOUS OBJECTORS
    Azad. *Long Shot* — B
    Edstrom, Erik. *Un-American* — B
    Montville, Leigh. *Sting Like a Bee* — B
    Tucker, Todd. *The Great Starvation Experiment* — 174.2
The Conscious Closet. Cline, Elizabeth L. — 646
Conscious Luck. Hendricks, Gay — 158.1
CONSCIOUSNESS
    Armantrout, Rae. *Wobble* — 811
    Bloom, Paul. *Psych* — 150
    Burnett, Dean. *Idiot Brain* — 612.8
    Clark, Andy. *The Experience Machine* — 153
    Damasio, Antonio R. *The Feeling of What Happens* — 153
    Eagleman, David. *Incognito* — 153
    Foster, Charles. *Being a Human* — 155.7
    Gladwell, Malcolm. *Blink* — 153.4
    Greene, B. *Until the End of Time* — 523.1
    Hofstadter, Douglas R. *I Am a Strange Loop* — 153
    Kandel, Eric R. ★*The Disordered Mind* — 616.89
    Miller, Kenneth R. *The Human Instinct* — 155.7
    Sapolsky, Robert M. *Determined* — 123
    Thomson, Helen. *Unthinkable* — 612.8
    Whitehouse, David. *The Alien Perspective* — 523.1
CONSCIOUSNESS IN ANIMALS
    Grandin, Temple. ★*Animals Make Us Human* — 636.08
CONSENSUS (SOCIAL SCIENCES)
    Beeman, Richard R. ★*Plain, Honest Men* — 342.7302
    Hayhoe, Katharine. *Saving Us* — 304.2
Consent. Freitas, Donna — 364.158092
Consequence. Fair, Eric — B
CONSEQUENCES
    Bergreen, Laurence. *Over the Edge of the World* — B

PUBLIC LIBRARY CORE COLLECTION: NONFICTION
Twentieth Edition

Brands, H. W. *The Age of Gold*	979.4
Hallinan, Joseph T. *Why We Make Mistakes*	153
Ice-T. *Split Decision*	920
Lacovara, Kenneth. *Why Dinosaurs Matter*	567.9
Vance, J. D. *Hillbilly Elegy*	B

CONSERVATION OF NATURAL RESOURCES

D'Agata, John. *About a Mountain*	979.3
Freeman, Scott. *Saving Tarboo Creek*	333.72
Gleick, Peter H. *The Three Ages of Water*	333.91
Hiss, Tony. ★*Rescuing the Planet*	333.75
Kumar, Priyanka. *Conversations with Birds*	598
Miller, Char. *Gifford Pinchot and the Making of Modern Environmentalism*	B
Momaday, N. Scott. *Earth Keeper*	814
Morris, Edmund. ★*Theodore Rex*	973.911
Park, Chris C. *A Dictionary of Environment and Conservation*	333.703
Reid, John W. *Ever Green*	634.9
Roberts, David. *The Bears Ears*	979.2
Wilson, Edward O. *The Diversity of Life*	333.95
Wohlforth, Charles P. *The Fate of Nature*	304.209798
Wulf, Andrea. *The Invention of Nature*	B

CONSERVATISM

Alberta, Tim. *American Carnage*	324.2734
Alberta, Tim. *The Kingdom, the Power, and the Glory*	270.8
Allitt, Patrick. *The Conservatives*	320.520973
Berman, Ari. ★*Minority Rule*	305.809
Blair, Tony. *A Journey*	B
Bogus, Carl T. *Buckley*	B
Cadava, Geraldo L. *The Hispanic Republican*	324.2734089
Conason, Joe. *The Longest Con*	320.52
Coyle, Marcia. *The Roberts Court*	347.73
FitzGerald, Frances. *The Evangelicals*	277
Fitzpatrick, Cara. *The Death of Public School*	379.73
Gabler, Neal. ★*Against the Wind*	B
Ganz, John. *When the Clock Broke*	320.52
Hendershot, Heather. *Open to Debate*	B
Masciotra, David. *Exurbia Now*	320.973
Mayer, Jane. ★*Dark Money*	973.932
Perlstein, Rick. *The Invisible Bridge*	973.924
Perlstein, Rick. ★*Reaganland*	973.926
Richardson, Heather Cox. *Democracy Awakening*	320.473
Richardson, Heather Cox. ★*How the South Won the Civil War*	306.20973
Robin, Corey. *The Enigma of Clarence Thomas*	347.73
Spencer, Kyle. *Raising Them Right*	320.5
Spitz, Bob. ★*Reagan*	B
Stelter, Brian. *Hoax*	070.4
Stevens, Stuart. *It Was All a Lie*	324.2734
Toobin, Jeffrey. *The Nine*	347.73
Vladeck, Stephen I. *The Shadow Docket*	347.73
Waldman, Michael. *The Supermajority*	347.73
Will, George F. *The Conservative Sensibility*	320.520973
The Conservative Sensibility. Will, George F.	320.520973

CONSERVATIVE WRITING

Caldwell, Christopher. *The Age of Entitlement*	305.240973
Christie, Chris. *Let Me Finish*	B
Douthat, Ross Gregory. *To Change the Church*	230
Johnson, Paul. *Eisenhower*	B
Murray, Charles A. *Coming Apart*	305.8
O'Rourke, P. J. *None of My Business*	332
Shlaes, Amity. *The Forgotten Man*	973.91
Sowell, Thomas. *Wealth, Poverty and Politics*	330.1
Will, George F. *The Conservative Sensibility*	320.520973
The Conservatives. Allitt, Patrick	320.520973

CONSERVATIVES

Allitt, Patrick. *The Conservatives*	320.520973
Blair, Tony. *A Journey*	B
Chafkin, Max. *The Contrarian*	B
Christie, Chris. *Let Me Finish*	B
Conason, Joe. *The Longest Con*	320.52
Hendershot, Heather. *Open to Debate*	B
Spencer, Kyle. *Raising Them Right*	320.5
Spruill, Marjorie Julian. *Divided We Stand*	305.42

CONSERVATORIES OF MUSIC

Tolan, Sandy. *Children of the Stone*	780
Consider The Lobster. Wallace, David Foster	814
Consider This. Palahniuk, Chuck	B
Consilience. Wilson, Edward O.	121

CONSOLATION

Corrigan, Kelly. *Glitter and Glue*	B
Ignatieff, Michael. *On Consolation*	152.4
Lewis, C. S. ★*A Grief Observed*	242
Rinzler, Lodro. *Love Hurts*	294.3
Roig-Debellis, Kaitlin. *Choosing Hope*	371.7
Console Wars. Harris, Blake J.	338.7

CONSPIRACIES

Barron, Justine. *They Killed Freddie Gray*	363.32
Beres, Derek. *Conspirituality*	001.9
Bowlin, Ben. *Stuff They Don't Want You to Know*	001.9
Brotherton, Rob. *Suspicious Minds*	153.4
Crawford, Lacy. *Notes on a Silencing*	B
Deer, Brian. *The Doctor Who Fooled the World*	610.92
Draper, Robert. *To Start a War*	956.7044
Graff, Garrett M. *Watergate*	973.924
Hoffman, Carl. ★*Savage Harvest*	995.1
Jager, Eric. *Blood Royal*	944.026
Kavanagh, Julie. *The Irish Assassins*	941.5
Lane, Charles. *Freedom's Detective*	B
Leamer, Laurence. *The Price of Justice*	346.7302
Lehr, Dick. *White Hot Hate*	363.325
Maddow, Rachel. *Bag Man*	B
Meltzer, Brad. ★*The First Conspiracy*	973.4
Meltzer, Brad. *The Lincoln Conspiracy*	973.7092
Meltzer, Brad. ★*The Nazi Conspiracy*	940.53
O'Connell, Mark. *A Thread of Violence*	364.152
O'Neill, Tom. ★*Chaos*	364.152
Posner, Gerald L. *Case Closed*	364.1
Satter, David. *The Less You Know, the Better You Sleep*	947.086
Strang, Dean A. *Worse Than the Devil*	345.775
Toobin, Jeffrey. *True Crimes and Misdemeanors*	973.933
Viren, Sarah. *To Name the Bigger Lie*	B
Wexler, Stuart. *Killing King*	323.092
White, Richard. *Who Killed Jane Stanford?*	364.152

CONSPIRACY THEORIES

Abrams, Dan. *Kennedy's Avenger*	973.922
Andersen, Kurt. ★*Fantasyland*	973
Bowlin, Ben. *Stuff They Don't Want You to Know*	001.9
Brotherton, Rob. *Suspicious Minds*	153.4
Dickey, Colin. *The Unidentified*	130
DiResta, Renee. *Invisible Rulers*	320
Fraser, Antonia. *Faith and Treason*	942.06
Graff, Garrett M. *UFO*	001.942
Jacobsen, Annie. *Phenomena*	133.8
Kroll, Andy. *A Death on W Street*	364.152
Novella, Steven. *The Skeptics' Guide to the Universe*	500
Prothero, Donald R. *UFOs, Chemtrails, and Aliens*	001.94
Rothschild, Mike. *The Storm Is Upon Us*	973.933
Sharlet, Jeff. ★*The Undertow*	322
Sommer, Will. ★*Trust the Plan*	973.933
Weill, Kelly. *Off the Edge*	001.9
Williamson, Elizabeth. ★*Sandy Hook*	364.152
Zapruder, Alexandra. *Twenty-Six Seconds*	973.922092
The Conspiracy to End America. Stevens, Stuart	324.2734
Conspirituality. Beres, Derek	001.9

CONSTANTINE I, EMPEROR OF ROME, DIED 337

Ehrman, Bart D. *The Triumph of Christianity*	270.1
Constantine's Sword. Carroll, James	261

CONSTELLATIONS

Shore, Linda. *The Total Skywatcher's Manual*	523
The Constitution. Paulsen, Michael Stokes	342.7302
The Constitution Today. Amar, Akhil Reed	342.73

CONSTITUTIONAL AMENDMENTS

Anderson, Carol. ★*The Second*	344.7305
Jacobs, A. J. ★*The Year of Living Constitutionally*	342.73
Kelly, Kate. *Ordinary Equality*	920
Vile, John R. *Encyclopedia of Constitutional Amendments, Proposed Amendments, and Amending Issues, 1789-2010*	342.7303
★*The Constitutional Convention*. Madison, James	342.7302

CONSTITUTIONAL HISTORY

Amar, Akhil Reed. ★*America's Constitution*	342.7302
Amar, Akhil Reed. *The Constitution Today*	342.73
Amar, Akhil Reed. *The Words That Made Us*	342.7302
Baier, Bret. *To Rescue the Constitution*	973.4
Barron, David J. *Waging War*	342.73
Beeman, Richard R. ★*Plain, Honest Men*	342.7302
Brands, H. W. ★*Heirs of the Founders*	973.5
Brettschneider, Corey Lang. *The Oath and the Office*	342.73
Brettschneider, Corey Lang. *The Presidents and the People*	342.73

AUTHOR, TITLE, SERIES AND SUBJECT INDEX

Breyer, Stephen G. *Making Our Democracy Work*	347.73
Broadwater, Jeff. ★*George Mason*	B
Colaiaco, James A. *Frederick Douglass and the Fourth of July*	973.7
Delbanco, Andrew. *The War Before the War*	973.7
Foner, Eric. *The Second Founding*	342.73
Greenhouse, Linda. *Becoming Justice Blackmun*	B
Hennessey, Jonathan. *The United States Constitution*	741.5
Jacobs, A. J. ★*The Year of Living Constitutionally*	342.73
Kelly, Kate. *Ordinary Equality*	920
Klarman, Michael J. *The Framers' Coup*	342.7302
Maddex, Robert L. *The U.S. Constitution A to Z*	342.730203
Madison, James. ★*The Constitutional Convention*	342.7302
Maier, Pauline. *Ratification*	342.7302
Meyerson, Michael. *Liberty's Blueprint*	342.7302
Paulsen, Michael Stokes. *The Constitution*	342.7302
Randall, Willard Sterne. *The Founders' Fortunes*	973.3
Raphael, Ray. *Constitutional Myths*	342.7302
Simon, James F. *What Kind of Nation*	342.73
Vile, John R. *Encyclopedia of Constitutional Amendments, Proposed Amendments, and Amending Issues, 1789-2010*	342.7303
Will, George F. *The Conservative Sensibility*	320.520973

CONSTITUTIONAL LAW

Amar, Akhil Reed. ★*America's Constitution*	342.7302
Amar, Akhil Reed. *The Constitution Today*	342.73
Amar, Akhil Reed. *The Words That Made Us*	342.7302
Biskupic, Joan. ★*Nine Black Robes*	347.73
Brettschneider, Corey Lang. *The Oath and the Office*	342.73
Brettschneider, Corey Lang. *The Presidents and the People*	342.73
Chemerinsky, Erwin. *Closing the Courthouse Door*	347.73
Dennie, Madiba K. *The Originalism Trap*	342.73
Driver, Justin. *The Schoolhouse Gate*	344.73
Erdozain, Dominic. *One Nation Under Guns*	363.33
Finkelman, Paul. ★*Landmark Decisions of the United States Supreme Court*	347.73
Foner, Eric. *The Second Founding*	342.73
Friedman, Barry. ★*Unwarranted*	344.7305
Graetz, Michael J. *The Burger Court and the Rise of the Judicial Right*	347.73
Jacobs, A. J. ★*The Year of Living Constitutionally*	342.73
Kaplan, David A. *The Most Dangerous Branch*	347.73
Maddex, Robert L. *The U.S. Constitution A to Z*	342.730203
Meyerson, Michael. *Liberty's Blueprint*	342.7302
Murphy, Bruce Allen. *Scalia*	B
Paulsen, Michael Stokes. *The Constitution*	342.7302
Randall, Willard Sterne. *The Founders' Fortunes*	973.3
Raphael, Ray. *Mr. President*	352.230973
Rapping, Jonathan. *Gideon's Promise*	345.73
Rosenberg, Ian. *The Fight for Free Speech*	342.73
Schultz, David A. *Encyclopedia of the United States Constitution*	342.730203
Stone, Geoffrey R. ★*Sex and the Constitution*	345.7302
Strossen, Nadine. *Hate*	342.7308
Sunstein, Cass R. *Impeachment*	342.73
Tribe, Laurence H. *Uncertain Justice*	342.73
Urofsky, Melvin I. *Dissent and the Supreme Court*	342.7302
Constitutional Myths. Raphael, Ray	342.7302

CONSTITUTIONS

Aristotle. ★*Politics, 2nd Ed*	320
Cicero, Marcus Tullius. ★*The Republic*	320.1
Klarman, Michael J. *The Framers' Coup*	342.7302

CONSTRUCTION INDUSTRY AND TRADE

Fabey, Michael. *Heavy Metal*	338.4
Waldman, Jonathan. *Sam*	629.8

CONSULS

Everitt, Anthony. *Cicero*	B

CONSULTANTS

Mazzucato, Mariana. ★*The Big Con*	650.1

CONSULTING FIRMS

Bogdanich, Walt. *When McKinsey Comes to Town*	001
Mazzucato, Mariana. ★*The Big Con*	650.1

CONSUMER BEHAVIOR

Ahuvia, Aaron. ★*The Things We Love*	790.1
Ariely, Dan. *Predictably Irrational*	153.8
Auletta, Ken. *Frenemies*	659.1
Cohen, Lizabeth. *A Consumers' Republic*	339.4
Gerth, Karl. *As China Goes, so Goes the World*	339.4
Goleman, Daniel. *Ecological Intelligence*	333.7
Minter, Adam. *Secondhand*	381
Wu, Tim. *The Attention Merchants*	659.1

CONSUMER CREDIT

Davenport, Anthony. *Your Score*	332.7
Halpern, Jake. *Bad Paper*	332.7

CONSUMER ECONOMICS

Berners-Lee, Mike. *The Carbon Footprint of Everything*	363.738
Cline, Elizabeth L. *The Conscious Closet*	646
Cohen, Lizabeth. *A Consumers' Republic*	339.4
Gerth, Karl. *As China Goes, so Goes the World*	339.4
Hardy, Alyssa. *Worn Out*	338.4
MacKinnon, J. B. ★*The Day the World Stops Shopping*	339.4
Tonti, Lucianne. *Sundressed*	746.9

CONSUMER EDUCATION

Olmsted, Larry. *Real Food/Fake Food*	641.3

CONSUMER SOCIETY

Chayka, Kyle. *Filterworld*	306
Howard, Jennifer. *Clutter*	306.3
MacKinnon, J. B. ★*The Day the World Stops Shopping*	339.4
Stewart, Alison. *Junk*	616.85
A Consumer's Dictionary of Food Additives. Winter, Ruth	664

CONSUMERISM

Biss, Eula. *Having and Being Had*	306.3
Crawford, Matthew B. *The World Beyond Your Head*	155.2
Del Rey, Jason. *Winner Sells All*	381
Gerth, Karl. *As China Goes, so Goes the World*	339.4
Howard, Jennifer. *Clutter*	306.3
Hu, Elise. *Flawless*	646.7
Langlands, Alex. *Craeft*	306.4
MacKinnon, J. B. ★*The Day the World Stops Shopping*	339.4
Marie, Jane. ★*Selling the Dream*	658.8
Minter, Adam. *Secondhand*	381
Raphael, Rina. *The Gospel of Wellness*	613
Roy, Saumya. *Castaway Mountain*	363.72
Satow, Julie. *When Women Ran Fifth Avenue*	381.141
Schwartz, Nelson. *The Velvet Rope Economy*	339.2
Sedgewick, Augustine. *Coffeeland*	338.4
Watts, Steven. *The People's Tycoon*	B
Wu, Tim. *The Attention Merchants*	659.1

CONSUMERS

Cecchi-Azzolina, Michael. *Your Table Is Ready*	647.95

CONSUMERS' PREFERENCES

Vanderbilt, Tom. *You May Also Like*	153.8
A Consumers' Republic. Cohen, Lizabeth	339.4

CONTAGION (SOCIAL PSYCHOLOGY)

Gladwell, Malcolm. *The Tipping Point*	302
★*Container Gardener's Handbook.* Tophill, Frances	635.9

CONTAINER GARDENING

Ondra, Nancy J. *Container Theme Gardens*	635.9
Smith, Edward C. *The Vegetable Gardener's Container Bible*	635
Stuckey, Maggie. *The Container Victory Garden*	635.9
Tophill, Frances. ★*Container Gardener's Handbook*	635.9
Container Theme Gardens. Ondra, Nancy J	635.9
The Container Victory Garden. Stuckey, Maggie	635.9

CONTEMPORARY FANTASY

Harkness, Deborah E. *The World of All Souls*	813
The Contender. Mann, William J.	B

CONTENTMENT

Covey, Stephen R. ★*The 7 Habits of Highly Effective People*	158
Covey, Stephen R. *The 8th Habit*	158
Gopnik, Adam. *All That Happiness Is*	158.1
Holmes, Cassie. *Happier Hour*	158.1
Langshur, Eric. *Start Here*	158
Vollmer, Becky. *You Are Not Stuck*	158.1
Waldinger, Robert J. ★*The Good Life*	158.1
Walker, Alice. *We Are the Ones We Have Been Waiting For*	811
Weir, Laura. *Cosy*	646.7009
Wiking, Meik. *The Little Book of Lykke*	646.7
Contested Will. Shapiro, James	822.33

CONTESTS

Wood, Lawrence. *Your Caption Has Been Selected*	741.5

CONTEXT EFFECTS (PSYCHOLOGY)

Gladwell, Malcolm. *The Tipping Point*	302
Continental Divide. Isserman, Maurice	796.52

CONTINENTS

Faloyin, Dipo. ★*Africa Is Not a Country*	960.33

CONTRACEPTION

Eig, Jonathan. *The Birth of the Pill*	618.1

CONTRACTORS

Denton, Sally. *The Profiteers*	B

PUBLIC LIBRARY CORE COLLECTION: NONFICTION
Twentieth Edition

Follett, Ken. *On Wings of Eagles* — 955
CONTRACTS
  Goethe, Johann Wolfgang von. *Goethe's Faust* — 832
  Lindner, Dan. ★*A Guide to Federal Contracting, 2nd Ed.* — 346.7302
  Mendelson, Cheryl. ★*Vows* — 203
  Norton, Hughes. ★*Rainmaker* — 796.352
  Pessah, Jon. *The Game* — 796.357
The Contrarian. Chafkin, Max — B
Control. Rutherford, Adam — 363.9
CONTROL
  Berman, Sarah. *Don't Call It a Cult* — 361.4
  Garfield, Simon. *In Miniature* — 745.5928
  Raphael, Rina. *The Gospel of Wellness* — 613
  Russell, Stuart J. *Human Compatible* — 006.301
  Schwab, Tim. ★*The Bill Gates Problem* — 361.7
  Selvaratnam, Tanya. *Assume Nothing* — B
  Solnit, Rebecca. *Men Explain Things to Me* — 305.42
  Stout, Martha. *Outsmarting the Sociopath Next Door* — 155.2
Controlling Women. Kolbert, Kathryn — 362.1988
CONVALESCENCE
  Bragg, Rick. *The Speckled Beauty* — 636.7
  Braitman, Laurel. *Animal Madness* — 591.5
  Gregory, Rebekah. *Taking My Life Back* — B
  Morgan, Abi. *This Is Not a Pity Memoir* — B
  Pataki, Allison. *Beauty in the Broken Places* — B
CONVENIENCE FOODS
  Waters, Alice. ★*We Are What We Eat* — 641.01
CONVENIENCE STORES
  Howe, Ben Ryder. *My Korean Deli* — B
CONVENTIONAL WARFARE
  Barrett, David Dean. *140 Days to Hiroshima* — 940.54
CONVENTS
  Coldstream, Catherine. ★*Cloistered* — B
The Conversation. Livingston, Robert W. — 305.8
The Conversation. Volandes, Angelo E. — 616.02
CONVERSATION
  Blyth, Catherine. *The Art of Conversation* — 395.5
  Corrigan, Kelly. *Tell Me More* — 153.6
  Damrosch, Leopold. *The Club* — 920
  Duhigg, Charles. ★*Supercommunicators* — 153.6
  Evans, Rachel Held. *Wholehearted Faith* — 248.4
  Headlee, Celeste Anne. *We Need to Talk* — 153.6
  Imperioli, Michael. *Woke up This Morning* — 791.45
  Kross, Ethan. ★*Chatter* — 158.1
  Lyons, Daniel. *STFU* — 302.2
  Mann, Jen. ★*Midlife Bites* — 305.244
  Pryor, Elizabeth Brown. *Six Encounters with Lincoln* — 973.7092
  Soep, Elisabeth. *Other People's Words* — 155.9
  Yoshino, Kenji. *Say the Right Thing* — 305.3
Conversation At Princeton. Vargas Llosa, Mario — 868
Conversations At the American Film Institute with the Great Moviemakers.
  Stevens, George, Jr — 791.4302
Conversations with Birds. Kumar, Priyanka — 598
Conversations with Myself. Mandela, Nelson — B
Conversations with RBG. Rosen, Jeffrey — B
CONVERSION THERAPY
  Cooper, Alex. *Saving Alex* — B
CONVERSION TO CHRISTIANITY
  Risner, Vaneetha Rendall. *Walking Through Fire* — B
  Woolf, Greg. *Rome* — 937
CONVERSION TO ISLAM
  Kennedy, Hugh. ★*The Great Arab Conquests* — 297.09
CONVERSION TO JUDAISM
  Reuben, Steven Carr. ★*Becoming Jewish* — 296.7
The Convert. Baker, Deborah — B
CONVERTS TO BUDDHISM
  Tworkov, Helen. *Lotus Girl* — B
CONVERTS TO CATHOLICISM
  Barthel, Joan. *American Saint* — B
CONVERTS TO CHRISTIANITY
  Thi, Kim Phuc Phan. *Fire Road* — B
CONVERTS TO CHRISTIANITY FROM ISLAM
  Carranca, Adriana. *Soul by Soul* — 230
CONVERTS TO ISLAM
  Baker, Deborah. *The Convert* — B
  Power, Carla. *If the Oceans Were Ink* — B
CONVERTS TO JUDAISM
  Reuben, Steven Carr. ★*Becoming Jewish* — 296.7

CONVICT LABOR
  Applebaum, Anne. ★*Gulag* — 365
  Blackmon, Douglas A. *Slavery by Another Name* — 305.896
  White, Neil. *In the Sanctuary of Outcasts* — B
CONVICT SHIPS
  Keneally, Thomas. *A Commonwealth of Thieves* — 994
The Conviction of Richard Nixon. Reston, James — 973.924092
Conway, Edmund
  Material World — 333.7
  The Summit — 337.09
Conway, John Horton
  The Book of Numbers — 512
Conyers, Jonathan
  I Wasn't Supposed to Be Here — B
CONYERS, JONATHAN, 1994-
  Conyers, Jonathan. *I Wasn't Supposed to Be Here* — B
★*Cook as You Are*. Tandoh, Ruby — 641.59
★*Cook It Up*. Guarnaschelli, Alex — 641.5
Cook Like a Local. Shepherd, Chris — 641.59
★*Cook Like a Pro*. Garten, Ina — 641.5
Cook Real Hawai?i. Simeon, Sheldon — 641.59969
Cook This Book. Baz, Molly — 641.5
The Cook's Book. McKoy, Bri — 641.3
Cook, Blanche Wiesen
  Eleanor Roosevelt; Volume 2 — B
  ★*Eleanor Roosevelt; Volume 3* — B
★*Cook, Eat, Repeat*. Lawson, Nigella — 641.5
COOK, FREDERICK ALBERT, 1865-1940
  Hartman, Darrell. *Battle of Ink and Ice* — 998
  Sancton, Julian. *Madhouse at the End of the Earth* — 919.8904
COOK, JAMES, 1728-1779
  Sides, Hampton. ★*The Wide Wide Sea* — 910.92
Cook, Jane Hampton
  American Phoenix — 973.5
Cook, Kevin
  The Burning Blue — 629.45
  Ten Innings at Wrigley — 796.357
  Waco Rising — 299
Cook, M. A.
  The Koran — 297.122
COOKBOOK WRITING
  Tipton-Martin, Toni. *The Jemima Code* — 641.59
COOKBOOKS
  Acheson, Hugh. *The Chef and the Slow Cooker* — 641.5
  Adams, Jocelyn Delk. *Everyday Grand* — 641.5975
  Adams, Jocelyn Delk. *Grandbaby Cakes* — 641.86
  Adarme, Adrianna. *The Year of Cozy* — 641.3
  Admony, Einat. *Shuk* — 641.595
  Ali, Laila. *Food for Life* — 641.5
  Alikhani, Nasim. *Sofreh* — 641.595
  Allibhoy, Omar. *Spanish Made Simple* — 641.594
  Anderson, Pam. *How to Cook Without a Book* — 641.5
  Andres, Jose. *Vegetables Unleashed* — 641.5
  Anthony, Michael. *V Is for Vegetables* — 641.6
  Apfelbaum, Chanie. ★*Totally Kosher* — 641.5
  Arefi, Yossy. *Snacking Cakes* — 641.86
  Aron, Jules. *Vegan Cheese* — 641.5
  Assil, Reem. *Arabiyya* — 641.595
  Barrett, Pearl. *Trim Healthy Mama Trim Healthy Table* — 613.2
  Barrow, Cathy. ★*Pie Squared* — 641.86
  Bastianich, Lidia. *Felidia* — 641.594
  Bastianich, Lidia. *Lidia Cooks from the Heart of Italy* — 641.594
  Bastianich, Lidia. ★*Lidia's a Pot, a Pan, and a Bowl* — 641.82
  Bastianich, Lidia. *Lidia's Commonsense Italian Cooking* — 641.594
  Bastianich, Lidia. *Lidia's Family Table* — 641.594
  Bastianich, Lidia. *Lidia's Favorite Recipes* — 641.594
  Bastianich, Lidia. ★*Lidia's from Our Family Table to Yours* — 641.594
  Bastianich, Lidia. *Lidia's Mastering the Art of Italian Cuisine* — 641.594
  Bastianich, Lidia. *Lidia's* — 641.594
  Batali, Mario. *Mario Batali Big American Cookbook* — 641.5973
  Bayless, Rick. *Authentic Mexican* — 641.5972
  Bayless, Rick. ★*Fiesta at Rick's* — 641.5972
  Bayless, Rick. *Mexican Everyday* — 641.5972
  Bayless, Rick. ★*More Mexican Everyday* — 641.5972
  Bayless, Rick. *Rick Bayless Mexico One Plate at a Time* — 641.5972
  Baz, Molly. *Cook This Book* — 641.5
  Behan, Ren. ★*The Sweet Polish Kitchen* — 641.594
  Ben-Ishay, Melissa. *Come Hungry* — 641.5

AUTHOR, TITLE, SERIES AND SUBJECT INDEX

Beranbaum, Rose Levy. ★*The Baking Bible*	641.81
Beranbaum, Rose Levy. ★*The Cookie Bible*	641.86
Beranbaum, Rose Levy. ★*Rose's Baking Basics*	641.81
Beranbaum, Rose Levy. *Rose's Ice Cream Bliss*	641.86
Berens, Abra. *Grist*	641.6
Berens, Abra. *Pulp*	641.6
Berry, Mary. *Cooking with Mary Berry.*	641.5
Bianco, Chris. *Bianco*	641.5
Bishara, Rawia. *Olives, Lemons & Za'atar*	641.59
Bittman, Mark. ★*Bittman Bread*	641.81
Bittman, Mark. ★*Dinner for Everyone*	641.5
Bittman, Mark. ★*How to Bake Everything*	641.81
Bittman, Mark. *How to Cook Everything Fast*	641.5
Bittman, Mark. ★*How to Cook Everything Vegetarian*	641.5
Bittman, Mark. ★*How to Cook Everything*	641.5
Bittman, Mark. *How to Cook Everything*	641.5
Bittman, Mark. ★*How to Grill Everything*	641.7
Bittman, Mark. *Mark Bittman's Kitchen Matrix*	641.5
Bittman, Mark. *The VB6 Cookbook*	641.5
Bittman, Mark. *VB6*	641.5
Bjork, Katrin. *From the North*	641.594
Black, Sarah. *One Dough, Ten Breads*	641.81
Blumenthal, Heston. *Is This a Cookbook?*	641.5
Bowen, Dana. *Dynamite Kids Cooking School*	641.5
Bowien, Danny. *Mission Vegan*	641.5
Brennan, Kathy. *Keepers*	641.5973
Britton, Sarah. *Naturally Nourished*	641.5
Brock, Sean. *South*	641.5975
Brown, Kardea. *The Way Home*	641.5975
Brown, Leanne. ★*Good and Cheap*	641.5
Byrn, Anne. ★*American Cake*	641.86
Byrn, Anne. ★*American Cookie*	641.86
Byrn, Anne. *A New Take on Cake*	641.86
Byrn, Anne. *Skillet Love*	641.7
Camara, Gabriela. *My Mexico City Kitchen*	641.5972
Carle-Sanders, Theresa. *Outlander Kitchen*	641.5
Casares, Sylvia. *The Enchilada Queen Cookbook*	641.5926872073
Cavallari, Kristin. *True Roots*	641.5
Cayne, Alison. *The Haven's Kitchen Cooking School*	641.5
Centeno, Josef. *Ama*	641.5979
Chang, Joanne. *Pastry Love*	641.86
Chaplin, Amy. *Whole Food Cooking Every Day*	641.3
Che, Hannah. ★*The Vegan Chinese Kitchen*	641.5
Child, Julia. *Julia and Jacques Cooking at Home*	641.594
Child, Julia. ★*Mastering the Art of French Cooking*	641.594
Chou, Hsiao-Ching. *Chinese Soul Food*	641.595
Claiborne, Jenne. ★*Sweet Potato Soul*	641.5
Clark, Melissa. *Comfort in an Instant*	641.5
Clark, Melissa. ★*Dinner in an Instant*	641.5
Clark, Melissa. *Dinner in French*	641.594
Clark, Melissa. ★*Dinner in One*	641.82
Clark, Melissa. *Dinner*	641.5
Comerford, Hope. *Fix-It and Forget-It Healthy 5-Ingredient Cookbook*	641.5
Conner, Polly. ★*From Freezer to Cooker*	641.6
Conners, Rachel. *Bakerita*	641.81
Coscarelli, Chloe. *Chloe Flavor*	641.5
Crocker, Betty. ★*Betty Crocker Cookbook*	641.5
Curl, Jami. *Candy Is Magic*	641.85
Curry, Kevin. *Fit Men Cook*	641.5
Dada, Samah. *Dada Eats Love to Cook It*	641.5
Damuck, Jess. *Salad Freak*	641.83
Danford, Natalie. *How to Eataly*	641.594
David, Laurie. *The Family Cooks*	641.3
Day, Cheryl. *Back in the Day Bakery, Made with Love*	641.81
Day, Cheryl. *Cheryl Day's Treasury of Southern Baking*	641.81
De Laurentiis, Giada. ★*Giada's Italy*	641.594
De Laurentiis, Giada. *Giada's Kitchen*	641.594
De Laurentiis, Giada. *Happy Cooking*	641.5
Diaz, Von. ★*Islas*	641.59
DiGregorio, Sarah. *Adventures in Slow Cooking*	641.5
Dinki, Nikki. *Meat on the Side*	641.3
Disbrowe, Paula. *Thank You for Smoking*	641.5
DiSpirito, Rocco. *Now Eat This!*	641.5
DiSpirito, Rocco. *Rocco's Healthy+Delicious*	641.3
Dissen, William Stark. *Thoughtful Cooking*	641.5975
Dodge, Abigail Johnson. *Sheet Cake*	641.86
Donofrio, Jeanine. ★*Love & Lemons*	641.5
Dragonwagon, Crescent. *Bean by Bean*	641.6
Drummond, Ree. ★*The Pioneer Woman Cooks*	641.5
Dunlop, Fuchsia. *The Food of Sichuan*	641.595
Eckhardt, Robyn. *Istanbul & Beyond*	641.595
Emberling, Amy. *Zingerman's Bakehouse*	641.81
Esposito, Jennifer. *Jennifer's Way Kitchen*	641.5
Falk, Daina. *The Hungry Fan's Game Day Cookbook*	641.5973
Fearnley-Whittingstall, Hugh. *River Cottage Veg*	641.5
Feinberg, Andrew. *Franny's*	641.594
Firth, Henry. *Bosh!*	641.5
Flanagan, Shalane. *Run Fast, Cook Fast, Eat Slow*	641.5
Flay, Bobby. *Bobby at Home*	641.5
Flay, Bobby. *Sundays with Sophie*	641.5
Forkish, Ken. *Evolutions in Bread*	664
Forkish, Ken. *Flour Water Salt Yeast*	641.81
Forte, Sara. *The Sprouted Kitchen*	641.3
Fox, Jeremy. *On Vegetables*	641.6
Francois, Zoe. *Holiday and Celebration Bread in Five Minutes a Day*	641.81
Frank, Lois Ellen. *Seed to Plate, Soil to Sky*	641.5
Franklin, Aaron. *Franklin Barbecue*	641.7
Franklin, Aaron. *Franklin Steak*	641.6
Fuentes, Laura. *The Best Homemade Kids' Snacks on the Planet*	641.5
Fuhrman, Joel. *Eat to Live Quick & Easy Cookbook*	641.5
Gaines, Joanna. ★*Magnolia Table*	641.5975
Ganeshram, Ramin. *Future Chefs*	641.3
Garten, Ina. *Barefoot Contessa at Home*	641.5
Garten, Ina. ★*Barefoot Contessa, How Easy Is That?*	641.5
Garten, Ina. *Barefoot in Paris*	641.594
Garten, Ina. ★*Cook Like a Pro*	641.5
Garten, Ina. *Cooking for Jeffrey*	641.5
Garten, Ina. ★*Go-To Dinners*	641.5
Garten, Ina. ★*Make It Ahead*	641.5
Gaw, Frankie. *First Generation*	641.595
Gerard, Tieghan. *A Half Baked Harvest Every Day*	641.5
Gerson, Fany. *Mexican Ice Cream*	641.86
Gerson, Fany. *My Sweet Mexico*	641.5972
Gill, Sasha. *East Meets Vegan*	641.5
Goldman, Duff. *Duff Bakes*	641.81
Goldstein, Joyce Esersky, author. *Jam Session*	641.85
Goldwyn, Meathead. ★*Meathead*	641.7
Good, Phyllis Pellman. *Fix-It and Forget-It New Cookbook*	641.5
Gourdet, Gregory. *Everyone's Table*	641.5
Gray, Jon. *Ghetto Gastro Black Power Kitchen*	641.5
Greenspan, Dorie. *Baking Chez Moi*	641.86
Greenspan, Dorie. ★*Baking with Dorie*	641.81
Greenspan, Dorie. *Baking with Julia*	641.8
Greenspan, Dorie. *Baking*	641.8
Greenspan, Dorie. ★*Dorie's Cookies*	641.86
Greenspan, Dorie. ★*Everyday Dorie*	641.5
Greenspan, Eric. *The Great Grilled Cheese Book*	641.6
Griffin, Brooke. *Skinny Suppers*	641.5
Guarnaschelli, Alex. ★*Cook It Up*	641.5
Guarnaschelli, Alex. *The Home Cook*	641.5973
Guetta, Benedetta Jasmine. *Cooking Alla Giudia*	641.5
Gutierrez, Sandra A. *Latinisimo*	641.598
Guy, Jerrelle. *Black Girl Baking*	641.59
Hage, Salma. ★*The Levantine Vegetarian*	641.595
Hall, Carla. *Carla Hall's Soul Food*	641.5975
Hall, Carla. *Carla's Comfort Foods*	641.59
Hamilton, Gabrielle. *Prune*	641.3
Hamshaw, Gena. *Food 52 Vegan*	641.5
Hansen, Kim-Julie. *Best of Vegan*	641.5
Hartnett, Angela. *The Weekend Cook*	641.5
Hartwig, Melissa. *The Whole30 Fast & Easy*	641.5
Hartwig, Melissa. *The Whole30 Slow Cooker*	641.5
Hassan, Hawa. *In Bibi's Kitchen*	641.596
Hazan, Jack. *Mind Over Batter*	641.81
Hazan, Marcella. ★*Essentials of Classic Italian Cooking*	641.594
Headley, Brooks. *Superiority Burger Cookbook*	641.5
Heatter, Maida. ★*Happiness Is Baking*	641.86
Helou, Anissa. *Feast*	641.595
Henry, Diana. *From the Oven to the Table*	641.82
Hernandez, Eddie. *Turnip Greens & Tortillas*	641.5972
Hesser, Amanda. ★*The Essential New York Times Cook Book*	641.5
Heuck, Lidey. ★*Cooking in Real Life*	641.5
Hill, McKel. *Nutrition Stripped*	641.3
Hoffman, Brian Hart. ★*Bake from Scratch; Volume Two*	641.81
Holland, Tanya. ★*Tanya Holland's California Soul*	641.59
Hollis, B. Dylan. ★*Baking Yesteryear*	641.81

1767

PUBLIC LIBRARY CORE COLLECTION: NONFICTION
Twentieth Edition

Author	Title	Dewey
Hollywood, Paul.	★Bake	641.81
Holmberg, Martha.	★Simply Tomato	641.6
Homolka, Gina.	Skinnytaste Fast and Slow	641.5
Homolka, Gina.	Skinnytaste One & Done	641.5
Hong, Deuki.	Koreatown	641.595
Hudson, Kate.	Pretty Fun	642
Hunt, Lindsay Maitland.	Healthyish	641.5
Hunt, Lindsay Maitland.	Help Yourself	641.5
Hussain, Nadiya.	★Nadiya Bakes	641.81
Iyer, Raghavan.	Indian Cooking Unfolded	641.595
Jade, Holly.	The Essential Book of Vegan Bakes	641.5
Jaffrey, Madhur.	★Madhur Jaffrey's Instantly Indian Cookbook	641.595
Jaffrey, Madhur.	Madhur Jaffrey's World Vegetarian.	641.5
Jaffrey, Madhur.	Vegetarian India	641.595
Jenkins, Nancy Harmon.	The New Mediterranean Diet Cookbook	641.59
Jinich, Pati.	Mexican Today	641.5972
Jinich, Pati.	★Treasures of the Mexican Table	641.5972
Johnson, J. J.	Between Harlem and Heaven	641.59
Jones, Anna.	One	641.5
Joo, Judy.	Korean Food Made Simple	641.595
Kahan, Paul.	Cheers to the Publican, Repast and Present	641.594
Kane, Cyndi.	Save-It-Forward Suppers	641.5
Kanell, John.	Preppy Kitchen	641.5
Kang, Mingoo.	Jang	641.595
Karadsheh, Suzy.	★The Mediterranean Dish	641.59
Kartes, Danielle.	Butter, Flour, Sugar, Joy	641.86
Katzen, Mollie.	The Heart of the Plate	641.5
Katzen, Mollie.	★The Moosewood Cookbook	641.5
Keller, Thomas.	Bouchon Bakery	641.594
Keller, Thomas.	The French Laundry Cookbook	641.5
Khan, Asma.	Ammu	641.595
Khan, Yasmin.	Ripe Figs	641.595
Khan, Yasmin.	★Zaitoun	641.595
Kieffer, Sarah.	100 Morning Treats	641.5
Kim, Bill.	Korean BBQ	641.595
Kim, Eric.	★Korean American	641.595
Kim, Hooni.	My Korea	641.595
Kimball, Christopher.	Christopher Kimball's Milk Street	641.5
Kimball, Christopher.	Christopher Kimball's Milk Street	641.5
Kimball, Christopher.	★Milk Street 365	641.5
Kimball, Christopher.	Milk Street	641.5
Kimball, Christopher.	Milk Street	641.5
Kimball, Christopher.	Milk Street	641.7
Kimball, Christopher.	Tuesday Nights Mediterranean	641.59
Klein, Dini.	Prep + Rally	641.5
Klopotenko, Yevhen.	★The Authentic Ukrainian Kitchen	641.594
Kochilas, Diane.	The Ikaria Way	641.5
Koenig, Leah.	Portico	641.5
Korkosz, Michał.	Fresh from Poland	641.594
Krieger, Ellie.	You Have It Made!	641.5
Krishna, Priya.	★Indian-ish	641.595
Kulaga, Agatha.	Ovenly	641.81
Kysar, Alana.	Aloha Kitchen	641.59969
Ladner, Mark.	The Del Posto Cookbook	641.594
Lagasse, Emeril.	Essential Emeril	641.5
Lahey, Jim.	The Sullivan Street Bakery Cookbook	641.81
Lambert, Miranda.	Y'all Eat Yet?	641.5976
Lancaster, Bridget.	Cooking at Home with Bridget & Julia	641.5
Lane, Christina.	Dessert for Two	641.86
Langholtz, Gabrielle.	America	641.5973
Lanza, Fabrizia.	The Food of Sicily	641.594
Laperruque, Emma.	Food52 Big Little Recipes	641.5
Larsen, Jeffrey.	★Gluten-Free Baking at Home	641.5
Lawson, Nigella.	At My Table	641.59
Lawson, Nigella.	★Simply Nigella	641.5
Le, Mike.	That Noodle Life	641.82
Leake, Lisa.	100 Days of Real Food on a Budget	641.5
Leake, Lisa.	★100 Days of Real Food	641.5
Lee Molinaro, Joanne.	★The Korean Vegan Cookbook	641.595
Lee, Jennifer Tyler.	Half the Sugar, All the Love	641.5
Lee, Lara.	A Splash of Soy	641.595
Leung, Bill.	★The Woks of Life	641.7
Lewis, John.	Badass Vegan	641.5
Lightner, Jill.	Cooking from Scratch	641.5
Lillien, Lisa.	Hungry Girl 1-2-3	641.5
Lillien, Lisa.	Hungry Girl Simply 6	641.5
Lomas, Vallery.	★Life Is What You Bake It	641.81
Lopez-Alt, J. Kenji.	★The Wok	641.595
Ludwinski, Lisa.	Sister Pie	641.86
Lukas, Albert.	★Sweet Home Cafe Cookbook	641.59
Maangchi.	Maangchi's Real Korean Cooking	641.595
Madison, Deborah.	In My Kitchen	641.5
Madison, Deborah.	Vegetable Literacy	641.6
Maisonet, Illyanna.	★Diasporican	641.597295
Mangini, Cara.	The Vegetable Butcher	641.6
Mangini, Cara.	★The Vegetable Eater	641.6
Manning, Ivy.	Easy Soups from Scratch with Quick Breads to Match	641.81
Martin, Pat.	Life of Fire	641.5
Martinez, Rick.	★Mi Cocina	641.5972
Massih, Edy.	★Keep It Zesty	641.595
Massov, Olga.	★Hot Sheet	641.82
Mauro, Jeff.	Come on Over	641.5
McAlpine, Skye.	A Table Full of Love	641.5
McBride, Martina.	Martina's Kitchen Mix	641.5973
McDermott, Kate.	★Art of the Pie	641.86
McDowell, Erin Jeanne.	The Fearless Baker	641.81
McFadden, Joshua.	★Grains for Every Season	641.3
McFadden, Joshua.	Six Seasons	641.5
McKenney, Sally.	★Sally's Cookie Addiction	641.86
McKoy, Bri.	The Cook's Book	641.3
Meehan, Peter.	Lucky Peach Presents 101 Easy Asian Recipes	641.595
Merchant, Jessica.	Everyday Dinners	641.82
Miglore, Kristen.	Food52 Genius Desserts	641.86
Miglore, Kristen.	★Food52 Genius Recipes	641.5
Miglore, Kristen.	★Food52 Simply Genius	641.5
Miller, Klancy.	★For the Culture	641.59
Mitchell, Andie.	Eating in the Middle	641.3
Moore, Matt.	Serial Griller	641.7
Morales, Bonnie Frumkin.	Kachka	641.594
Morimoto, Masaharu.	Mastering the Art of Japanese Home Cooking	641.595
Moskowitz, Isa Chandra.	The Superfun Times Vegan Holiday Cookbook	651.56
Moskowitz, Isa Chandra.	Veganomicon	641
Moulton, Sara.	Sara Moulton's Home Cooking 101	641.5973
Mubarak, Heather.	Stuffed	641.86
Mullen, Marissa.	That Cheese Plate Wants to Party	641.6
Mullins, Brittany.	Mostly Veggies	641.5
Munno, Nadia Caterina.	The Pasta Queen	641.82
Murad, Noor.	★Ottolenghi Test Kitchen	641.3
Murad, Noor.	Ottolenghi Test Kitchen	641.5
Music, Carla Lalli.	That Sounds so Good	641.5
Music, Carla Lalli.	Where Cooking Begins	641.5
Myers, Amy.	The Autoimmune Solution Cookbook	641.5
Nederlanden, Elisabet der.	★Holiday Cookies	641.86
Nelson, Candace.	The Sprinkles Baking Book	641.81
Nelson, Kim.	Daisy Cakes Bakes	641.86
Nguyen, Andrea Quynhgiao.	Ever-Green Vietnamese	641.595
Nguyen, Andrea Quynhgiao.	The Pho Cookbook	641.595
Nguyen, Andrea Quynhgiao.	★Vietnamese Food Any Day	641.595
Nolen, Jeremy.	New German Cooking	641.594
Noyes, Brian.	The Red Truck Bakery Farmhouse Cookbook	641.5973
Oliver, Jamie.	Together	641.5
Orkin, Ivan.	The Gaijin Cookbook	641.595
Ottolenghi, Yotam.	★Jerusalem	641.5
Ottolenghi, Yotam.	Ottolenghi Simple	641.59
Ottolenghi, Yotam.	Ottolenghi	641.59
Ottolenghi, Yotam.	★Plenty More	641.6
Ottolenghi, Yotam.	Plenty	641.6
Ottolenghi, Yotam.	Sweet	641.86
Oz, Daphne.	The Happy Cook	641.5
Paltrow, Gwyneth.	It's All Easy	641.5
Pang, Kevin.	A Very Chinese Cookbook	641.595
Pansino, Rosanna.	Baking All Year Round	641.86
Parks, Stella.	★Bravetart	641.86
Parla, Katie.	Tasting Rome	641.59
Pashman, Dan.	Anything's Pastable	641.82
Patel, Palak.	Food Is Love	641.5
Pauline, Kathryn.	A Dish for All Seasons	641.5
Pauline, Kathryn.	★Piecemeal	641.5
Pelaez, Ana Sofia.	The Cuban Table	641.597291
Pepin, Jacques.	Essential Pepin	641.5
Pepin, Jacques.	★Jacques Pepin	641.5
Pepin, Jacques.	★Jacques Pepin	641.594
Pepin, Jacques.	★Jacques Pépin Cooking My Way	641.5
Peppler, Rebekah.	Le Sud	641.594
Perelman, Deb.	★The Smitten Kitchen Cookbook	641.5

AUTHOR, TITLE, SERIES AND SUBJECT INDEX

Perelman, Deb. ★*Smitten Kitchen Every Day*	641.5
Perelman, Deb. ★*Smitten Kitchen Keepers*	641.5
Perlmutter, David. *The Grain Brain Cookbook*	651.56
Perry Lang, Adam. *Serious Barbecue*	641.5
Perry, Dawn. *Ready, Set, Cook*	641.5
Peters, Meike. *Noon*	641.5
Peterson, James. *Sauces*	641.81
Pfeiffer, Jacquy. *The Art of French Pastry*	641.86
Pierson, Joy. *Vegan Holiday Cooking from Candle Cafe*	641.5
Pittman, Ann Taylor. *The Global Pantry Cookbook*	641.59
Poliafito, Renato. ★*Dolci!*	641.81
Pollan, Corky. *The Pollan Family Table*	641.5
Ponseca, Nicole. *I Am a Filipino and This Is How We Cook*	641.595
Porowski, Antoni. *Antoni*	641.5
Prescott, Matthew. *Food Is the Solution*	613.2
Presilla, Maricel E. *Gran Cocina Latina*	641.5972
Pulde, Alona. *Forks Over Knives Family*	641.5
Pulde, Alona. ★*The Forks Over Knives Plan*	641.5
Purviance, Jamie. *Weber's Greatest Hits*	641.5
Purviance, Jamie. *Weber's Ultimate Grilling*	641.5
Raichlen, Steven. *The Brisket Chronicles*	641.6
Raichlen, Steven. *How to Grill Vegetables*	641.6
Raines, Abigail Sotto. *Rice. Noodles. Yum.*	641.595
Ramirez, Elva. *Zero Proof*	641.87
Rapoport, Adam. *The Grilling Book*	641.7
Ray, Rachael. *Everyone Is Italian on Sunday*	641.594
Ray, Rachael. ★*This Must Be the Place*	641.5
Reinhart, Peter. *Perfect Pan Pizza*	641.82
Rettke, Amanda. *Homestead Recipes*	641.5977
Richards, Todd. *Soul*	641.59296073
Ripert, Eric. *Seafood Simple*	641.6
Rodale, Maria. *Scratch*	641.3
Roddy, Rachel. ★*An A-Z of Pasta*	641.82
Rodriguez, Ashley. *Rooted Kitchen*	641.5
Rodriguez, Jessamyn Waldman. *The Hot Bread Kitchen Cookbook*	641.59
Roll, Rich. *The Plantpower Way*	641.5
Roman, Alison. *Dining In*	641.5
Roman, Alison. ★*Nothing Fancy*	642
Roman, Alison. *Sweet Enough*	641.86
Rombauer, Irma S. ★*Joy of Cooking*	641.5973
Rombauer, Irma S. ★*Joy of Cooking*	641.5973
Rondinelli-Hamilton, Lara. *The Diabetes Cookbook*	641.5
Rosen, Ali. *Bring It!*	641.5973
Rosen, Ilene. *Saladish*	641.83
Rosenstrach, Jenny. *How to Celebrate Everything*	641.5
Rosenstrach, Jenny. ★*The Weekday Vegetarians*	641.5
Rosenthal, Phil. ★*Somebody Feed Phil the Book*	641.59
Rosso, Julee. *The New Basics Cookbook*	641.5
Rosso, Julee. *The Silver Palate Cookbook*	641.5
Ruhlman, Michael. *Ratio*	641.5
Saffitz, Claire. ★*What's for Dessert*	641.86
Sakai, Sonoko. *Japanese Home Cooking*	641.595
Saltz, Joanna. ★*Delish Insane Sweets*	641.81
Saltz, Joanna. *Delish*	641.5
Samuelsson, Marcus. *Marcus off Duty*	641.5
Samuelsson, Marcus. *The Red Rooster Cookbook*	641.5977
Sarna, Shannon. *Modern Jewish Comfort Food*	641.5
Sarno, Chad. *The Wicked Healthy Cookbook*	651.56
Scarpaleggia, Giulia. ★*Cucina Povera*	641.594
Schinner, Miyoko Nishimoto. *The Vegan Meat Cookbook*	641.5
Schrijver, Darlene. *The Salad Lab*	641.83
Scott, Chris. *Homage*	641.5
Scott, Ryan. *The No-Fuss Family Cookbook*	641.5
Segnit, Niki. ★*The Flavor Thesaurus*	641.5
Selengut, Becky. ★*Misunderstood Vegetables*	641.6
Seneviratne, Samantha. *Bake Smart*	641.81
Serpico, Peter. *Learning Korean*	641.595
Setareh, Saghar. *Pomegranates & Artichokes*	641.5
Sever, Shauna. ★*Midwest Made*	641.5977
Sharma, Nik. *Veg-Table*	641.6
Sheehan, Jessie. ★*Snackable Bakes*	641.7
Shepherd, Chris. *Cook Like a Local*	641.59
Sherman, Sean. *The Sioux Chef's Indigenous Kitchen*	641.59
Shumski, Daniel. *How to Instant Pot*	641.5
Sifton, Sam. ★*See You on Sunday*	641.5
Sifton, Sam. *Thanksgiving*	641.5
Silverton, Nancy. ★*The Cookie That Changed My Life*	641.81
Siva, Micah. *Nosh*	641.5
Smalls, Alexander. *Meals, Music, and Muses*	641.59
Smith, Michelle. *The Whole Smiths Good Food Cookbook*	641.5
Smith, R. Garth. *Asd, the Complete Autism Spectrum Disorder Health & Diet Guide*	616.85
Snodgrass, Alex. ★*The Defined Dish*	641.5
Snoop Dogg. *Goon with the Spoon*	641.59
Snyder, Sabrina. *Dinner Then Dessert*	641.5
Sodha, Meera. *East*	641.595
Sodha, Meera. *Made in India*	641.595
Steele, Lisa. ★*The Fresh Eggs Daily Cookbook*	641.6
Stewart, Martha. ★*Martha Stewart's Baking Handbook*	641.8
Stewart, Martha. *Martha Stewart's Cake Perfection*	641.86
Stewart, Martha. *Martha Stewart's Cooking School*	641.5
Stone, Robyn. *Add a Pinch Cookbook*	641.5975
Sussman, Adeena. *Sababa*	641.5
Sussman, Adeena. ★*Shabbat*	641.5
Symon, Michael. ★*Fix It with Food*	641.5
Symon, Michael. *Michael Symon's Playing with Fire*	641.7
Tam, Michelle. *Ready or Not!*	641.5
Tamimi, Sami. *Falastin*	641.595
Tandoh, Ruby. ★*Cook as You Are*	641.59
Taylor, Kathryne. *Love Real Food*	641.5
Taylor, Nicole A. ★*Watermelon & Red Birds*	641.5
Teigen, Pepper (Vilailuck). *The Pepper Thai Cookbook*	641.595
Terry, Bryant. *Afro-Vegan*	641.59
Terry, Bryant. *Vegan Soul Kitchen*	641.5
Terry, Bryant. ★*Vegetable Kingdom*	641.5
Thiessen, Tiffani. *Pull up a Chair*	641.5
Thomas, Anna. *Vegan Vegetarian Omnivore*	641.5
Thomas, Haile. *Living Lively*	641.5
Thompson, Jennifer Trainer. *Fresh Fish*	641.3
Thorisson, Mimi. *A Kitchen in France*	641.594
Tila, Jet. *101 Asian Dishes You Need to Cook Before You Die*	641.595
Timothy, Duval. *Food from Across Africa*	641.596
Tosi, Christina. *All About Cake*	641.86
Tosi, Christina. *All About Cookies*	641.86
Trejo, Danny. *Trejo's Tacos*	641.5979
Turshen, Julia. *Feed the Resistance*	641.5
Turshen, Julia. *Now & Again*	641.5
Turshen, Julia. *Small Victories*	641.5
Umah-Shaylor, Lerato. *Africana*	641.596
Urban, Melissa. *The Whole30 Friends & Family*	641.5
Van't Hul, Jean. *The Artful Year*	745.594
Velasquez, Mariana. *Colombiana*	641.59861
Vetri, Marc. *Mastering Pizza*	641.82
Vicenzino, Cettina. *The Sicily Cookbook*	641.59458
Villanova, Thibaud. *Disney Enchanted Recipes*	641.5
Villasuso, Susana. *Sobremesa*	641.5972
Volger, Lukas. *Bowl*	641.81
Wade, Greg. ★*Bread Head*	664
Walch, Aubry. *The Herbivorous Butcher Cookbook*	641.5
Walker, Danielle. *Danielle Walker's Against All Grain*	641.5
Walker, Danielle. *Danielle Walker's Healthy in a Hurry*	641.5
Wang, Jason. *Xl'an Famous Foods*	641.595
Wangler, Justin. *Season*	641.5979
Weil, Andrew. *Fast Food, Good Food*	641.3
Weinstein, Bruce. *The Great Big Pressure Cooker Book*	641.5
Weinstein, Bruce. *The Kitchen Shortcut Bible*	641.555
Weiss, Luisa. *Classic German Baking*	641.594
Wells, Patricia. *My Master Recipes*	641.5
West, Kevin. *Saving the Season*	641.4
Westerhausen, Shelly. *Every Season Is Soup Season*	641.81
White, Marco Pierre. *White Heat*	641.594
Wilkinson, Crystal. *Praisesong for the Kitchen Ghosts*	641.5975
Williams, Odette. *Simple Cake*	641.86
Williams, Odette. ★*Simple Pasta*	641.822
Wilson, Melba. ★*Melba's American Comfort*	641.5973
Winfrey, Oprah. *Food, Health, and Happiness*	641.5
Witte, Christina De. ★*Noodles, Rice, and Everything Spice*	641.595
Woo, Ronnie. *Did You Eat Yet?*	641.595
Workman, Katie. *Dinner Solved!*	641.5
Workman, Katie. *The Mom 100 Cookbook*	641.5
Wright, Caroline. *Cake Magic!*	641.86
Yeh, Molly. *Home Is Where the Eggs Are*	641.5
Zizka, Maria. *The Hostess Handbook*	642

Cooke, Alistair

The American Home Front, 1941-1942	940.53

PUBLIC LIBRARY CORE COLLECTION: NONFICTION
Twentieth Edition

COOKE, ALISTAIR, 1908-2004
   Cooke, Alistair. *The American Home Front, 1941-1942* — 940.53
Cooke, Julia
   Come Fly the World — 387.7
Cooke, Lucy
   Bitch — 591.56
   The Truth About Animals — 590.2
Cooke, Mervyn
   The Chronicle of Jazz — 781.6509
Cooked. Pollan, Michael — 641.5
★ *The **Cookie** Bible*. Beranbaum, Rose Levy — 641.86
★ *The **Cookie** That Changed My Life*. Silverton, Nancy — 641.81
COOKIES
   Beranbaum, Rose Levy. ★ *The Cookie Bible* — 641.86
   Beranbaum, Rose Levy. ★ *Rose's Baking Basics* — 641.81
   Byrn, Anne. ★ *American Cookie* — 641.86
   Cho, Kristina. *Mooncakes + Milk Bread* — 641.595
   Greenspan, Dorie. ★ *Dorie's Cookies* — 641.86
   Hussain, Nadiya. ★ *Nadiya Bakes* — 641.81
   Larsen, Jeffrey. ★ *Gluten-Free Baking at Home* — 641.5
   McKenney, Sally. ★ *Sally's Cookie Addiction* — 641.86
   Mubarak, Heather. *Stuffed* — 641.86
   Nederlanden, Elisabet der. ★ *Holiday Cookies* — 641.86
   Saltz, Joanna. ★ *Delish Insane Sweets* — 641.81
   Silverton, Nancy. ★ *The Cookie That Changed My Life* — 641.81
   Tosi, Christina. *All About Cookies* — 641.86
   Weller, Melissa. *A Good Bake* — 641.86
COOKING
   Adler, Tamar. *An Everlasting Meal* — 641.5
   Ali, Laila. *Food for Life* — 641.5
   Angelou, Maya. *Hallelujah! the Welcome Table* — 641.5973
   Ayubi, Durkhanai. *Parwana* — 641.595
   Bastianich, Lidia. *Lidia Cooks from the Heart of Italy* — 641.594
   Baz, Molly. *Cook This Book* — 641.5
   Behan, Ren. ★ *The Sweet Polish Kitchen* — 641.594
   Ben-Ishay, Melissa. *Come Hungry* — 641.5
   Berry, Mary. *Cooking with Mary Berry* — 641.5
   Bianco, Chris. *Bianco* — 641.5
   Bittman, Mark. ★ *Dinner for Everyone* — 641.5
   Bittman, Mark. ★ *How to Cook Everything* — 641.5
   Bittman, Mark. *How to Cook Everything* — 641.5
   Bittman, Mark. *Mark Bittman's Kitchen Matrix* — 641.5
   Blumenthal, Heston. *Is This a Cookbook?* — 641.5
   Bourdain, Anthony. ★ *Appetites* — 641.5
   Bourdain, Anthony. ★ *Kitchen Confidential* — B
   Bourdain, Anthony. *Medium Raw* — 664
   Bourdain, Anthony. *The Nasty Bits* — 641.5092
   Bowen, Dana. *Dynamite Kids Cooking School* — 641.5
   Bracken, Peg. *The I Hate to Cook Book* — 641.5
   Brennan, Kathy. *Keepers* — 641.5973
   Buford, Bill. ★ *Dirt* — B
   Carle-Sanders, Theresa. *Outlander Kitchen* — 641.5
   Cayne, Alison. *The Haven's Kitchen Cooking School* — 641.5
   Chang, David. ★ *Eat a Peach* — 641.5
   Cheng, Eugenia. *How to Bake Pi* — 510
   Child, Julia. ★ *My Life in France* — B
   Child, Julia. ★ *The Way to Cook* — 641.5
   Clark, Melissa. *Dinner* — 641.5
   Clark, Melissa. *Kid in the Kitchen* — 641.5
   Crocker, Betty. ★ *Betty Crocker Cookbook* — 641.5
   Curry, Kevin. *Fit Men Cook* — 641.5
   De Laurentiis, Giada. *Happy Cooking* — 641.5
   Diaz, Von. ★ *Islas* — 641.59
   DiGregorio, Sarah. *Adventures in Slow Cooking* — 641.5
   Disbrowe, Paula. *Thank You for Smoking* — 641.5
   Dissen, William Stark. *Thoughtful Cooking* — 641.5975
   Dragonwagon, Crescent. *Bean by Bean* — 641.6
   El-Waylly, Sohla. ★ *Start Here* — 641.3
   Fairchild, Barbara. *The Bon Appetit Cookbook* — 641.5
   Feinberg, Andrew. *Franny's* — 641.594
   Flay, Bobby. *Bobby at Home* — 641.5
   Flay, Bobby. *Sundays with Sophie* — 641.5
   Forte, Sara. *The Sprouted Kitchen* — 641.3
   Franklin, Aaron. *Franklin Barbecue* — 641.7
   Ganeshram, Ramin. *Future Chefs* — 641.3
   Gardner, Lindsay. *Why We Cook* — 641.5
   Garten, Ina. *Barefoot Contessa at Home* — 641.5
   Garten, Ina. *Barefoot Contessa Family Style* — 641.5

Garten, Ina. ★ *Barefoot Contessa, How Easy Is That?* — 641.5
Garten, Ina. ★ *Cook Like a Pro* — 641.5
Garten, Ina. *Cooking for Jeffrey* — 641.5
Garten, Ina. ★ *Go-To Dinners* — 641.5
Good, Phyllis Pellman. *Fix-It and Forget-It New Cookbook* — 641.5
Goulding, Matt. *Grape, Olive, Pig* — 394.1
Gourdet, Gregory. *Everyone's Table* — 641.5
Greenspan, Dorie. ★ *Everyday Dorie* — 641.5
Guarnaschelli, Alex. ★ *Cook It Up* — 641.5
Hamilton, Gabrielle. *Blood, Bones, and Butter* — B
Hartnett, Angela. *The Weekend Cook* — 641.5
Hartwig, Melissa. *The Whole30 Slow Cooker* — 641.5
Hassan, Hawa. *In Bibi's Kitchen* — 641.596
Helou, Anissa. *Feast* — 641.595
Henaut, Stephane. *A Bite-Sized History of France* — 394.1
Henry, Diana. *From the Oven to the Table* — 641.82
Hesser, Amanda. ★ *The Essential New York Times Cook Book* — 641.5
Holmberg, Martha. ★ *Simply Tomato* — 641.6
Hood, Ann. *Kitchen Yarns* — 641.5
Howard, Vivian. *Deep Run Roots* — 641.5975
Huang, Eddie. *Fresh off the Boat* — B
Hudson, Kate. *Pretty Fun* — 642
Hunt, Lindsay Maitland. *Healthyish* — 641.5
Hunt, Lindsay Maitland. *Help Yourself* — 641.5
Hussain, Nadiya. ★ *Nadiya's Everyday Baking* — 641.5
Jacobs, Ryan McMahon. *The Truffle Underground* — 381
Kimball, Christopher. ★ *Milk Street 365* — 641.5
Kimball, Christopher. *Milk Street* — 641.5
Kimball, Christopher. *Milk Street* — 641.5
King, Maren Ellingboe. *Fresh Midwest* — 641.5977
King, Niloufer Ichaporia. *My Bombay Kitchen* — 641.595
Kingsley, Lisa. *Smithsonian American Table* — 641.5
Klein, Dini. *Prep + Rally* — 641.5
Klopotenko, Yevhen. ★ *The Authentic Ukrainian Kitchen* — 641.594
Korkosz, Michal. *Fresh from Poland* — 641.594
Kysar, Alana. *Aloha Kitchen* — 641.59969
Lagasse, Emeril. *Essential Emeril* — 641.5
Lakshmi, Padma. *Love, Loss, and What We Ate* — 791.4502
Lancaster, Bridget. *Cooking at Home with Bridget & Julia* — 641.5
Lawson, Nigella. *At My Table* — 641.59
Lawson, Nigella. ★ *Cook, Eat, Repeat* — 641.5
Lawson, Nigella. ★ *Simply Nigella* — 641.5
Lebovitz, David. *My Paris Kitchen* — 641.594
Lee, Edward. *Buttermilk Graffiti* — 641.59
Lee, Jennifer Tyler. *Half the Sugar, All the Love* — 641.5
Lopez-Alt, J. Kenji. *The Food Lab* — 664
Lopez-Alt, J. Kenji. ★ *The Wok* — 641.595
Madison, Deborah. *In My Kitchen* — 641.5
Maisonet, Illyanna. ★ *Diasporican* — 641.597295
Martin, Pat. *Life of Fire* — 641.5
Massov, Olga. ★ *Hot Sheet* — 641.82
Mauro, Jeff. *Come on Over* — 641.5
McAlpine, Skye. *A Table Full of Love* — 641.5
McGee, Harold. ★ *On Food and Cooking* — 641.5
McKinnon, Hetty. ★ *Tenderheart* — 641.5
McKoy, Bri. *The Cook's Book* — 641.3
Miglore, Kristen. ★ *Food52 Genius Recipes* — 641.5
Miglore, Kristen. ★ *Food52 Simply Genius* — 641.5
Miller, Max. ★ *Tasting History* — 641.509
Murad, Noor. ★ *Ottolenghi Test Kitchen* — 641.3
Murad, Noor. *Ottolenghi Test Kitchen* — 641.5
Music, Carla Lalli. *That Sounds so Good* — 641.5
Music, Carla Lalli. *Where Cooking Begins* — 641.5
Nathan, Joan. ★ *My Life in Recipes* — 641.5
Nosrat, Samin. ★ *Salt, Fat, Acid, Heat* — 641.5
Onwuachi, Kwame. ★ *Notes from a Young Black Chef* — 641.59
Oz, Daphne. *The Happy Cook* — 641.5
Page, Karen. *The Flavor Bible* — 641.5
Pepin, Jacques. *The Apprentice* — B
Pepin, Jacques. *Essential Pepin* — 641.5
Pepin, Jacques. ★ *Jacques Pepin* — 641.5
Pepin, Jacques. ★ *Jacques Pepin* — 641.594
Pepin, Jacques. ★ *Jacques Pépin Cooking My Way* —
Peppler, Rebekah. *Le Sud* — 641.594
Perelman, Deb. ★ *The Smitten Kitchen Cookbook* — 641.5
Pollan, Corky. *The Pollan Family Table* — 641.5
Pollan, Michael. *Cooked* — 641.5
Ray, Rachael. ★ *This Must Be the Place* — 641.5

AUTHOR, TITLE, SERIES AND SUBJECT INDEX

Reichl, Ruth. *Comfort Me with Apples*	B
Reichl, Ruth. *Garlic and Sapphires*	B
Reichl, Ruth. *My Kitchen Year*	641.5
Reichl, Ruth. ★*Save Me the Plums*	B
Ripert, Eric. *32 Yolks*	B
Rodale, Maria. *Scratch*	641.3
Roman, Alison. *Dining In*	641.5
Roman, Alison. ★*Nothing Fancy*	642
Rosso, Julee. *The Silver Palate Cookbook*	641.5
Ruhlman, Michael. *Ratio*	641.5
Saltz, Joanna. *Delish*	641.5
Samuelsson, Marcus. *Marcus off Duty*	641.5
Samuelsson, Marcus. *The Red Rooster Cookbook*	641.5974
Samuelsson, Marcus. *Yes, Chef*	B
Sanchez, Aaron. *Where I Come From*	641.5092
Sen, Mayukh. *Taste Makers*	641.5092
Sheehan, Jason. *Cooking Dirty*	B
Shepherd, Chris. *Cook Like a Local*	641.59
Siegel, Matt. *The Secret History of Food*	641.3
Sifton, Sam. ★*See You on Sunday*	641.5
Simeon, Sheldon. *Cook Real Hawai?i*	641.59969
Spitz, Bob. ★*Dearie*	B
Stewart, Martha. *Martha Stewart's Cake Perfection*	641.86
Stewart, Martha. *Martha Stewart's Cooking School*	641.5
Symon, Michael. ★*Fix It with Food*	641.5
Tandoh, Ruby. ★*Eat Up*	641.3
Teigen, Chrissy. *Cravings*	641.5
Terry, Bryant. *Black Food*	394.1
Terry, Bryant. *Vegan Soul Kitchen*	641.5
Thiessen, Tiffani. *Pull up a Chair*	641.5
Thomas, Anna. *Vegan Vegetarian Omnivore*	641.5
Thorisson, Mimi. *A Kitchen in France*	641.594
Turshen, Julia. *Feed the Resistance*	641.5
Turshen, Julia. *Now & Again*	641.5
Turshen, Julia. *Simply Julia*	641.3
Turshen, Julia. *Small Victories*	641.5
Vasquez, Karla Tatiana. ★*The Salvisoul Cookbook*	641.598
Velasquez, Mariana. *Colombiana*	641.59861
Villanova, Thibaud. *Disney Enchanted Recipes*	641.5
Walker, Danielle. *Danielle Walker's Healthy in a Hurry*	641.5
Waters, Alice. *The Art of Simple Food*	641.5
Watson, Ted Kennedy. *Ted Kennedy Watson's Guide to Stylish Entertaining*	793.2
Wells, Patricia. *My Master Recipes*	641.5
Wilson, Katherine. *Only in Naples*	B
Winfrey, Oprah. *Food, Health, and Happiness*	641.5
Workman, Katie. *Dinner Solved!*	641.5
Workman, Katie. *The Mom 100 Cookbook*	641.5
Wrangham, Richard W. *Catching Fire*	394.1
Yearwood, Trisha. *Trisha's Kitchen*	641.5
Yeh, Molly. *Home Is Where the Eggs Are*	641.5
Zizka, Maria. *The Hostess Handbook*	642

COOKING (BEEF)
Franklin, Aaron. *Franklin Steak*	641.6
Raichlen, Steven. *The Brisket Chronicles*	641.6

COOKING (BREAD)
Bittman, Mark. ★*Bittman Bread*	641.81
Forkish, Ken. ★*Let's Make Bread!*	741.5

COOKING (CEREALS)
Berens, Abra. *Grist*	641.6
Forte, Sara. *The Sprouted Kitchen*	641.3
McFadden, Joshua. ★*Grains for Every Season*	641.3

COOKING (CHEESE)
Greenspan, Eric. *The Great Grilled Cheese Book*	641.6
Mullen, Marissa. *That Cheese Plate Wants to Party*	641.6

COOKING (CHICKEN)
Pepin, Jacques. *Art of the Chicken*	641.665
Wilson, Melba. ★*Melba's American Comfort*	641.5973

COOKING (CURRY)
Collingham, E. M. *Curry*	394.1

COOKING (EGGS)
Stark, Lizzie. ★*Egg*	641.3
Steele, Lisa. ★*The Fresh Eggs Daily Cookbook*	641.6

COOKING (FISH)
Ripert, Eric. *Seafood Simple*	641.6
Thompson, Jennifer Trainer. *Fresh Fish*	641.3

COOKING (FRUIT)
Berens, Abra. *Pulp*	641.6

COOKING (GAME)
Rinella, Steven. *The Complete Guide to Hunting, Butchering, and Cooking Wild Game*	799.2
Rinella, Steven. *The Complete Guide to Hunting, Butchering, and Cooking Wild Game; Volume 2*	799.2

COOKING (HERBS)
Belsinger, Susan. *Grow Your Own Herbs*	635
Lakshmi, Padma. *The Encyclopedia of Spices and Herbs*	641.3

COOKING (MEAT)
Danforth, Adam. *Butchering Poultry, Rabbit, Lamb, Goat, and Pork*	664
Symon, Michael. *Michael Symon's Playing with Fire*	641.7

COOKING (NATURAL FOODS)
Barber, Dan. *The Third Plate*	641.3
Britton, Sarah. *Naturally Nourished*	641.5
Cavallari, Kristin. *True Roots*	641.5
Chaplin, Amy. *Whole Food Cooking Every Day*	641.3
Cristofano, Jana. *Eat Well, Be Well*	641.5
David, Laurie. *The Family Cooks*	641.5
DiSpirito, Rocco. *Rocco's Healthy+Delicious*	641.5
Esposito, Jennifer. *Jennifer's Way Kitchen*	641.5
Flanagan, Shalane. *Run Fast, Cook Fast, Eat Slow*	641.5
Forte, Sara. *The Sprouted Kitchen*	641.3
Fuentes, Laura. *The Best Homemade Kids' Snacks on the Planet*	641.5
Guy, Jerrelle. *Black Girl Baking*	641.59
Hill, McKel. *Nutrition Stripped*	641.3
Katzen, Mollie. *The Heart of the Plate*	641.5
Katzen, Mollie. ★*The Moosewood Cookbook*	641.5
Kauffman, Jonathan. *Hippie Food*	394.1
Leake, Lisa. *100 Days of Real Food on a Budget*	641.5
Leake, Lisa. ★*100 Days of Real Food*	641.5
Lightner, Jill. *Cooking from Scratch*	641.5
McFadden, Joshua. ★*Grains for Every Season*	641.3
Murad, Noor. ★*Ottolenghi Test Kitchen*	641.3
Murad, Noor. *Ottolenghi Test Kitchen*	641.5
Pollan, Corky. *The Pollan Family Table*	641.5
Pulde, Alona. ★*The Forks Over Knives Plan*	641.5
Roll, Rich. *The Plantpower Way*	641.5
Sanfilippo, Diane. *Practical Paleo*	613.2
Sarno, Chad. *The Wicked Healthy Cookbook*	651.56
Smith, Michelle. *The Whole Smiths Good Food Cookbook*	641.5
Snodgrass, Alex. ★*The Defined Dish*	641.5
Tam, Michelle. *Ready or Not!*	641.5
Terry, Bryant. ★*Vegetable Kingdom*	641.5
Thomas, Haile. *Living Lively*	641.5
Urban, Melissa. *The Whole30 Friends & Family*	641.5
Walker, Danielle. *Danielle Walker's Against All Grain*	641.5
Weil, Andrew. *Fast Food, Good Food*	641.3
Winfrey, Oprah. *Food, Health, and Happiness*	641.5

COOKING (NOODLES)
Le, Mike. *That Noodle Life*	641.82
Wang, Jason. *Xi'an Famous Foods*	641.595

COOKING (PASTA)
Le, Mike. *That Noodle Life*	641.82
Munno, Nadia Caterina. *The Pasta Queen*	641.82
Pashman, Dan. *Anything's Pastable*	641.82
Roddy, Rachel. ★*An A-Z of Pasta*	641.82
Williams, Odette. ★*Simple Pasta*	641.822
Zanini De Vita, Oretta. *Encyclopedia of Pasta*	641.822

COOKING (SEAFOOD)
Ripert, Eric. *Seafood Simple*	641.6

COOKING (SPICES)
Lakshmi, Padma. *The Encyclopedia of Spices and Herbs*	641.3
Sodha, Meera. *Made in India*	641.595

COOKING (VEGETABLES)
Andres, Jose. *Vegetables Unleashed*	641.5
Anthony, Michael. *V Is for Vegetables*	641.6
Berens, Abra. *Grist*	641.6
Berens, Abra. *Pulp*	641.6
Berens, Abra. *Ruffage*	641.5
Bittman, Mark. ★*How to Cook Everything Vegetarian*	641.5
Dinki, Nikki. *Meat on the Side*	641.3
Firth, Henry. *Bosh!*	641.5
Fox, Jeremy. *On Vegetables*	641.6
Hamshaw, Gena. *Food 52 Vegan*	641.5
Jones, Anna. *One*	641.5
Lewis, John. *Badass Vegan*	641.5
Madison, Deborah. *Vegetable Literacy*	641.6
Mangini, Cara. *The Vegetable Butcher*	641.6

PUBLIC LIBRARY CORE COLLECTION: NONFICTION
Twentieth Edition

Mangini, Cara. ★*The Vegetable Eater*	641.6
McFadden, Joshua. *Six Seasons*	641.5
Mullins, Brittany. *Mostly Veggies*	641.5
Nguyen, Andrea Quynhgiao. *Ever-Green Vietnamese*	641.595
Ottolenghi, Yotam. ★*Plenty More*	641.6
Ottolenghi, Yotam. *Plenty*	641.6
Prescott, Matthew. *Food Is the Solution*	613.2
Raichlen, Steven. *How to Grill Vegetables*	641.6
Rodriguez, Ashley. *Rooted Kitchen*	641.5
Sarno, Chad. *The Wicked Healthy Cookbook*	651.56
Segnit, Niki. ★*The Flavor Thesaurus*	641.5
Selengut, Becky. ★*Misunderstood Vegetables*	641.6
Sharma, Nik. *Veg-Table*	641.6
Westerhausen, Shelly. *Every Season Is Soup Season*	641.81

COOKING (WILD FOODS)
Rodriguez, Ashley. *Rooted Kitchen*	641.5
Cooking Alla Giudia. Guetta, Benedetta Jasmine	641.5

COOKING AND CHILDREN
Scott, Ryan. *The No-Fuss Family Cookbook*	641.5

COOKING AND TEENAGERS
Guarnaschelli, Alex. ★*Cook It Up*	641.5
Cooking At Home with Bridget & Julia. Lancaster, Bridget	641.5
Cooking Dirty. Sheehan, Jason	B

COOKING FOR FAMILIES
Bourdain, Anthony. ★*Appetites*	641.5
Howard, Vivian. *This Will Make It Taste Good*	641.5
Merchant, Jessica. *Everyday Dinners*	641.82
Pelosi, Dan. *Let's Eat*	641.5
Pulde, Alona. *Forks Over Knives Family*	641.5
Teigen, Pepper (Vilailuck). *The Pepper Thai Cookbook*	641.595
Yearwood, Trisha. *Trisha's Kitchen*	641.5
Cooking for Jeffrey. Garten, Ina	641.5
Cooking from Scratch. Lightner, Jill	641.5
★*The Cooking Gene*. Twitty, Michael	641.59
★*Cooking in Real Life*. Heuck, Lidey	641.5

COOKING SCHOOLS
Bertch, Jane. *The French Ingredient*	B
Cooking with Mary Berry. Berry, Mary	641.5

COOKING, AFRICAN
Hassan, Hawa. *In Bibi's Kitchen*	641.596
Samuelsson, Marcus. ★*The Rise*	641.59
Terry, Bryant. *Afro-Vegan*	641.59
Timothy, Duval. *Food from Across Africa*	641.596
Umah-Shaylor, Lerato. *Africana*	641.596

COOKING, AFRICAN AMERICAN
Brown, Kardea. *The Way Home*	641.5975
Claiborne, Jenne. ★*Sweet Potato Soul*	641.5
Deetz, Kelley Fanto. *Bound to the Fire*	641.59
Gray, Jon. *Ghetto Gastro Black Power Kitchen*	641.5
Guy, Jerrelle. *Black Girl Baking*	641.59
Hall, Carla. *Carla Hall's Soul Food*	641.5975
Harris, Jessica B. *High on the Hog*	641.59
Holland, Tanya. ★*Tanya Holland's California Soul*	641.59
Johnson, J. J. *Between Harlem and Heaven*	641.59
Lukas, Albert. ★*Sweet Home Cafe Cookbook*	641.59
Miller, Klancy. ★*For the Culture*	641.59
Onwuachi, Kwame. ★*Notes from a Young Black Chef*	641.59
Raiford, Matthew. *Bress 'N' Nyam*	641.59
Richards, Todd. *Soul*	641.59296073
Samuelsson, Marcus. ★*The Rise*	641.59
Scott, Chris. *Homage*	641.5
Smalls, Alexander. *Meals, Music, and Muses*	641.59
Taylor, Nicole A. ★*Watermelon & Red Birds*	641.5
Terry, Bryant. *Afro-Vegan*	641.59
Terry, Bryant. *Black Food*	394.1
Terry, Bryant. *Vegan Soul Kitchen*	641.5
Tipton-Martin, Toni. *The Jemima Code*	641.59
Tipton-Martin, Toni. *Jubilee*	641.59
Twitty, Michael. ★*The Cooking Gene*	641.59
Twitty, Michael. ★*Koshersoul*	641.5
Wilkinson, Crystal. *Praisesong for the Kitchen Ghosts*	641.5975
Wilson, Melba. ★*Melba's American Comfort*	641.5973

COOKING, AMERICAN
Adams, Jocelyn Delk. *Everyday Grand*	641.5975
Angelou, Maya. *Great Food, All Day Long*	641.5973
Angelou, Maya. *Hallelujah! the Welcome Table*	641.5973
Barber, Dan. *The Third Plate*	641.3
Batali, Mario. *Mario Batali Big American Cookbook*	641.5973
Birdsall, John. *The Man Who Ate Too Much*	B
Bitsoie, Freddie. *New Native Kitchen*	641.59
Bragg, Rick. ★*The Best Cook in the World*	641.5975
Brennan, Kathy. *Keepers*	641.5973
Brock, Sean. *South*	641.5975
Brown, Kardea. *The Way Home*	641.5975
Centeno, Josef. *Ama*	641.5979
Claiborne, Jenne. ★*Sweet Potato Soul*	641.5
Day, Cheryl. *Cheryl Day's Treasury of Southern Baking*	641.81
Deetz, Kelley Fanto. *Bound to the Fire*	641.59
DiSpirito, Rocco. *Now Eat This!*	641.5
Dissen, William Stark. *Thoughtful Cooking*	641.5975
Falk, Daina. *The Hungry Fan's Game Day Cookbook*	641.5973
Ferguson, Jesse Tyler. ★*Food Between Friends*	641.5973
Fox, Jeremy. *On Vegetables*	641.6
Frank, Lois Ellen. *Seed to Plate, Soil to Sky*	641.5
Gaines, Joanna. ★*Magnolia Table*	641.5975
Guarnaschelli, Alex. *The Home Cook*	641.5973
Hall, Carla. *Carla Hall's Soul Food*	641.5975
Hamilton, Gabrielle. *Prune*	641.3
Hereford, Mason. *Turkey and the Wolf*	641.5976
Holland, Tanya. ★*Tanya Holland's California Soul*	641.59
Howard, Vivian. *Deep Run Roots*	641.5975
Kauffman, Jonathan. *Hippie Food*	394.1
Kim, Hooni. *My Korea*	641.595
Kinch, David. *At Home in the Kitchen*	641.5973
King, Maren Ellingboe. *Fresh Midwest*	641.5977
Krishna, Priya. ★*Indian-ish*	641.595
Lambert, Miranda. *Y'all Eat Yet?*	641.5976
Langholtz, Gabrielle. *America*	641.5973
Lewis, Edna. *In Pursuit of Flavor*	641.5975
Lopez-Alt, J. Kenji. *The Food Lab*	664
Lukas, Albert. ★*Sweet Home Cafe Cookbook*	641.59
McBride, Martina. *Martina's Kitchen Mix*	641.5973
Miller, Klancy. ★*For the Culture*	641.59
Mitchell, Andie. *Eating in the Middle*	641.3
Moore, Matt. *Serial Griller*	641.7
Moulton, Sara. *Sara Moulton's Home Cooking 101*	641.5973
Noyes, Brian. *The Red Truck Bakery Farmhouse Cookbook*	641.5973
Nunn, Emily. *The Comfort Food Diaries*	641.5973
Onwuachi, Kwame. ★*Notes from a Young Black Chef*	641.59
Parks, Stella. ★*Bravetart*	641.86
Pelosi, Dan. *Let's Eat*	641.5
Pepin, Jacques. *Art of the Chicken*	641.665
Perelman, Deb. ★*Smitten Kitchen Every Day*	641.5
Perelman, Deb. ★*Smitten Kitchen Keepers*	641.5
Poliafito, Renato. ★*Dolci*	641.81
Raiford, Matthew. *Bress 'N' Nyam*	641.59
Rettke, Amanda. *Homestead Recipes*	641.5977
Richards, Todd. *Soul*	641.59296073
Rombauer, Irma S. ★*Joy of Cooking*	641.5973
Rombauer, Irma S. ★*Joy of Cooking*	641.5973
Rosen, Ali. *Bring It!*	641.5973
Rosso, Julee. *The New Basics Cookbook*	641.5
Samuelsson, Marcus. ★*The Rise*	641.59
Scott, Chris. *Homage*	641.5
Scott, Rodney. ★*Rodney Scott's World of BBQ*	641.7
Sever, Shauna. ★*Midwest Made*	641.5977
Sifton, Sam. *Thanksgiving*	641.5
Smalls, Alexander. *Meals, Music, and Muses*	641.59
Snoop Dogg. *Goon with the Spoon*	641.59
Stone, Robyn. *Add a Pinch Cookbook*	641.5975
Terry, Bryant. *Afro-Vegan*	641.59
Terry, Bryant. *Vegan Soul Kitchen*	641.5
Twitty, Michael. ★*The Cooking Gene*	641.59
Wangler, Justin. *Season*	641.5979
Wilkinson, Crystal. *Praisesong for the Kitchen Ghosts*	641.5975
Wilson, Melba. ★*Melba's American Comfort*	641.5973
Woo, Ronnie. *Did You Eat Yet?*	641.595
Workman, Katie. *Dinner Solved!*	641.5

COOKING, ARABIC
Roden, Claudia. *Arabesque*	641.59

COOKING, ASIAN
Amano, Hugh. *Let's Make Dumplings!*	741.5
Bowien, Danny. *Mission Vegan*	641.5
Gill, Sasha. *East Meets Vegan*	641.5
Lee, Lara. *A Splash of Soy*	641.595
Meehan, Peter. *Lucky Peach Presents 101 Easy Asian Recipes*	641.595

AUTHOR, TITLE, SERIES AND SUBJECT INDEX

Raines, Abigail Sotto. *Rice. Noodles. Yum.*	641.595
Sodha, Meera. *East*	641.595
Tila, Jet. *101 Asian Dishes You Need to Cook Before You Die*	641.595
Volger, Lukas. *Bowl*	641.81
Woo, Ronnie. *Did You Eat Yet?*	641.595
COOKING, BRITISH	
Hollywood, Paul. ★*Bake*	641.81
Hussain, Nadiya. ★*Nadiya's Everyday Baking*	641.5
COOKING, CARIBBEAN	
Maisonet, Illyanna. ★*Diasporican*	641.597295
Presilla, Maricel E. *Gran Cocina Latina*	641.5972
Terry, Bryant. *Afro-Vegan*	641.59
COOKING, CHINESE	
Che, Hannah. ★*The Vegan Chinese Kitchen*	641.5
Cho, Kristina. *Mooncakes + Milk Bread*	641.595
Chou, Hsiao-Ching. *Chinese Soul Food*	641.595
Dunlop, Fuchsia. *The Food of Sichuan*	641.595
Gaw, Frankie. *First Generation*	641.595
Leung, Bill. ★*The Woks of Life*	641.7
Lopez-Alt, J. Kenji. ★*The Wok*	641.595
Pang, Kevin. *A Very Chinese Cookbook*	641.595
Wang, Jason. *XI'an Famous Foods*	641.595
Yeh, Molly. *Home Is Where the Eggs Are*	641.5
COOKING, CUBAN	
Pelaez, Ana Sofia. *The Cuban Table*	641.597291
COOKING, ENGLISH	
Lawson, Nigella. *At My Table*	641.59
Roberts, Julius. *The Farm Table*	641.594
White, Marco Pierre. *White Heat*	641.594
COOKING, EUROPEAN	
Kahan, Paul. *Cheers to the Publican, Repast and Present*	641.594
COOKING, FRENCH	
Bard, Elizabeth. *Lunch in Paris*	B
Bard, Elizabeth. *Picnic in Provence*	B
Bertch, Jane. *The French Ingredient*	B
Buford, Bill. ★*Dirt*	B
Child, Julia. *Julia and Jacques Cooking at Home*	641.594
Child, Julia. ★*Mastering the Art of French Cooking*	641.594
Child, Julia. ★*My Life in France*	B
Clark, Melissa. *Dinner in French*	641.594
DeJean, Joan E. *The Essence of Style*	391
Downie, David. *A Taste of Paris*	394.1
Dusoulier, Clotilde. *Tasting Paris*	641.594
Garten, Ina. *Barefoot in Paris*	641.594
Greenspan, Dorie. *Around My French Table*	641.594
Greenspan, Dorie. *Baking Chez Moi*	641.86
Hamilton, Gabrielle. *Prune*	641.3
Henaut, Stephane. *A Bite-Sized History of France*	394.1
Keller, Thomas. *The French Laundry Cookbook*	641.5
Lebovitz, David. *My Paris Kitchen*	641.594
Pepin, Jacques. *Art of the Chicken*	641.665
Pepin, Jacques. *Essential Pepin*	641.594
Peppler, Rebekah. *Le Sud*	641.594
Pfeiffer, Jacquy. *The Art of French Pastry*	641.86
Powell, Julie. *Julie and Julia*	641.5
Prud'homme, Alex. *The French Chef in America*	B
Ripert, Eric. *32 Yolks*	B
Spitz, Bob. ★*Dearie*	B
Thorisson, Mimi. *A Kitchen in France*	641.594
Waters, Alice. *Coming to My Senses*	B
COOKING, GERMAN	
Nolen, Jeremy. *New German Cooking*	641.594
Weiss, Luisa. *Classic German Baking*	641.594
COOKING, GREEK	
Hayden, Georgina. *Greekish*	641.594
Kochilas, Diane. *The Ikaria Way*	641.5
COOKING, INDIC	
Collingham, E. M. *Curry*	394.1
Diaz, Von. ★*Islas*	641.59
Helou, Anissa. *Feast*	641.595
Iyer, Raghavan. *Indian Cooking Unfolded*	641.595
Jaffrey, Madhur. ★*Madhur Jaffrey's Instantly Indian Cookbook*	641.595
Jaffrey, Madhur. *Vegetarian India*	641.595
Kahate, Ruta. *6 Spices 60 Dishes*	641.595
Khan, Asma. *Ammu*	641.595
King, Niloufer Ichaporia. *My Bombay Kitchen*	641.595
Krishna, Priya. ★*Indian-ish*	641.595
Patel, Palak. *Food Is Love*	641.595
Sodha, Meera. *Made in India*	641.595
COOKING, INDIGENOUS	
Bitsoie, Freddie. *New Native Kitchen*	641.59
Frank, Lois Ellen. *Seed to Plate, Soil to Sky*	641.5
COOKING, IRANIAN	
Alikhani, Nasim. *Sofreh*	641.595
Setareh, Saghar. *Pomegranates & Artichokes*	641.5
COOKING, IRISH	
Andrews, Colman. *The Country Cooking of Ireland*	641.594
COOKING, ISRAELI	
Admony, Einat. *Shuk*	641.595
Solomonov, Michael. *Israeli Soul*	641.595
Solomonov, Michael. *Zahav*	641.595
COOKING, ITALIAN	
Bastianich, Lidia. *Felidia*	641.594
Bastianich, Lidia. *Lidia Cooks from the Heart of Italy*	641.594
Bastianich, Lidia. ★*Lidia's a Pot, a Pan, and a Bowl*	641.82
Bastianich, Lidia. *Lidia's Commonsense Italian Cooking*	641.594
Bastianich, Lidia. *Lidia's Family Table*	641.594
Bastianich, Lidia. *Lidia's Favorite Recipes*	641.594
Bastianich, Lidia. ★*Lidia's from Our Family Table to Yours*	641.594
Bastianich, Lidia. *Lidia's Mastering the Art of Italian Cuisine*	641.594
Bastianich, Lidia. *Lidia's*	641.594
Bastianich, Lidia. *My American Dream*	B
Bianco, Chris. *Bianco*	641.5
Danford, Natalie. *How to Eataly*	641.594
De Laurentiis, Giada. ★*Giada's Italy*	641.594
De Laurentiis, Giada. *Giada's Kitchen*	641.594
Feinberg, Andrew. *Franny's*	641.594
Gilbert, Elizabeth. *Eat, Pray, Love*	B
Guetta, Benedetta Jasmine. *Cooking Alla Giudia*	641.5
Hazan, Marcella. ★*Essentials of Classic Italian Cooking*	641.594
Hood, Ann. *Kitchen Yarns*	641.5
Koenig, Leah. *Portico*	641.5
Ladner, Mark. *The Del Posto Cookbook*	641.594
Lanza, Fabrizia. *The Food of Sicily*	641.594
Locke, Tembi. ★*From Scratch*	B
Mayes, Frances. *Under the Tuscan Sun*	945
Mohammadi, Kamin. *Bella Figura*	641.01
Munno, Nadia Caterina. *The Pasta Queen*	641.82
Parla, Katie. *Tasting Rome*	641.59
Pashman, Dan. *Anything's Pastable*	641.82
Pelosi, Dan. *Let's Eat*	641.5
Poliafito, Renato. ★*Dolci!*	641.81
Ray, Rachael. *Everyone Is Italian on Sunday*	641.594
Reinhart, Peter. *Perfect Pan Pizza*	641.82
Roddy, Rachel. ★*An A-Z of Pasta*	641.82
Scarpaleggia, Giulia. ★*Cucina Povera*	641.594
Setareh, Saghar. *Pomegranates & Artichokes*	641.5
Tucci, Stanley. ★*Taste*	B
Vetri, Marc. *Mastering Pizza*	641.82
Vicenzino, Cettina. *The Sicily Cookbook*	641.59458
Williams, Odette. ★*Simple Pasta*	641.822
COOKING, ITALIAN-AMERICAN	
De Laurentiis, Giada. *Giada's Kitchen*	641.594
COOKING, JAPANESE	
Goulding, Matt. *Rice, Noodle, Fish*	394.1
Morimoto, Masaharu. *Mastering the Art of Japanese Home Cooking*	641.595
Orkin, Ivan. *The Gaijin Cookbook*	641.595
Sakai, Sonoko. *Japanese Home Cooking*	641.595
COOKING, JEWISH	
Apfelbaum, Chanie. ★*Totally Kosher*	641.5
Cohen, Jake. *Jew-Ish*	641.5
Guetta, Benedetta Jasmine. *Cooking Alla Giudia*	641.5
Koenig, Leah. *Portico*	641.5
Nathan, Joan. *King Solomon's Table*	641.5
Nathan, Joan. ★*My Life in Recipes*	641.5
Ricanati, Elizabeth. *Braided*	B
Roden, Claudia. ★*The Book of Jewish Food*	641.5
Sarna, Shannon. *Modern Jewish Comfort Food*	641.5
Setareh, Saghar. *Pomegranates & Artichokes*	641.5
Siva, Micah. *Nosh*	641.5
Sussman, Adeena. ★*Shabbat*	641.5
Twitty, Michael. ★*Koshersoul*	641.5
Yeh, Molly. *Home Is Where the Eggs Are*	641.5
COOKING, KOREAN	
Cho, Grace M. *Tastes Like War*	305.48
Hong, Deuki. *Koreatown*	641.595

PUBLIC LIBRARY CORE COLLECTION: NONFICTION
Twentieth Edition

Joo, Judy. *Korean Food Made Simple*	641.595
Kang, Mingoo. *Jang*	641.595
Kim, Bill. *Korean BBQ*	641.595
Kim, Eric. ★*Korean American*	641.595
Kim, Hooni. *My Korea*	641.595
Lee Molinaro, Joanne. ★*The Korean Vegan Cookbook*	641.595
Maangchi. *Maangchi's Real Korean Cooking*	641.595
Serpico, Peter. *Learning Korean*	641.595
COOKING, KOSHER	
Apfelbaum, Chanie. ★*Totally Kosher*	641.5
COOKING, LATIN AMERICAN	
Gutierrez, Sandra A. *Latinísimo*	641.598
Presilla, Maricel E. *Gran Cocina Latina*	641.5972
Sanchez, Aaron. *Where I Come From*	641.5092
COOKING, LEBANESE	
Massih, Edy. ★*Keep It Zesty*	641.595
Roden, Claudia. *Arabesque*	641.59
COOKING, MEDITERRANEAN	
Berg, Meliz. *Dinner Tonight*	641.595
Hayden, Georgina. *Greekish*	641.594
Hayden, Georgina. *Nistisima*	641.5
Jenkins, Nancy Harmon. *The New Mediterranean Diet Cookbook*	641.59
Karadsheh, Suzy. ★*The Mediterranean Dish*	641.59
Kimball, Christopher. *Tuesday Nights Mediterranean*	641.59
Kochilas, Diane. *The Ikaria Way*	641.5
Lawson, Nigella. *At My Table*	641.59
Ottolenghi, Yotam. *Ottolenghi*	641.59
Vicenzino, Cettina. *The Sicily Cookbook*	641.59458
COOKING, MEXICAN	
Bayless, Rick. *Authentic Mexican*	641.5972
Bayless, Rick. ★*Fiesta at Rick's*	641.5972
Bayless, Rick. *Mexican Everyday*	641.5972
Bayless, Rick. ★*More Mexican Everyday*	641.5972
Bayless, Rick. *Rick Bayless Mexico One Plate at a Time*	641.5972
Camara, Gabriela. *My Mexico City Kitchen*	641.5972
Gerson, Fany. *Mexican Ice Cream*	641.86
Gerson, Fany. *My Sweet Mexico*	641.5972
Hernandez, Eddie. *Turnip Greens & Tortillas*	641.5972
Jinich, Pati. *Mexican Today*	641.5972
Jinich, Pati. ★*Treasures of the Mexican Table*	641.5972
Martinez, Rick. ★*Mi Cocina*	641.5972
Presilla, Maricel E. *Gran Cocina Latina*	641.5972
Ronstadt, Linda. *Feels Like Home*	B
Villasuso, Susana. *Sobremesa*	641.5972
COOKING, MEXICAN AMERICAN	
Casares, Sylvia. *The Enchilada Queen Cookbook*	641.5926872073
Centeno, Josef. *Ama*	641.5979
Trejo, Danny. *Trejo's Tacos*	641.5979
COOKING, MOROCCAN	
Roden, Claudia. *Arabesque*	641.59
COOKING, NORTH AFRICAN	
Helou, Anissa. *Feast*	641.595
COOKING, PHILIPPINE	
Cailan, Alvin. *Amboy*	641.595
Ponseca, Nicole. *I Am a Filipino and This Is How We Cook*	641.595
COOKING, RUSSIAN	
Morales, Bonnie Frumkin. *Kachka*	641.594
COOKING, SCANDINAVIAN	
Bjork, Katrin. *From the North*	641.594
King, Maren Ellingboe. *Fresh Midwest*	641.5977
COOKING, SOUTHEAST ASIAN	
Raines, Abigail Sotto. *Rice. Noodles. Yum.*	641.595
COOKING, SOUTHWEST ASIAN AND NORTH AFRICAN	
Bishara, Rawia. *Olives, Lemons & Za'atar*	641.59
Hage, Salma. ★*The Levantine Vegetarian*	641.595
Hayden, Georgina. *Nistisima*	641.5
Helou, Anissa. *Feast*	641.595
Kattan, Fadi. ★*Bethlehem*	641.59
Khan, Yasmin. *Ripe Figs*	641.595
Khan, Yasmin. ★*Zaitoun*	641.595
Murad, Noor. *Ottolenghi Test Kitchen*	641.5
Ottolenghi, Yotam. ★*Jerusalem*	641.5
Ottolenghi, Yotam. *Ottolenghi Simple*	641.59
Ottolenghi, Yotam. *Ottolenghi*	641.59
Sahadi Whelan, Christine. *Flavors of the Sun*	641.595
Solomonov, Michael. *Israeli Soul*	641.595
Solomonov, Michael. *Zahav*	641.595
COOKING, SPANISH	
Allibhoy, Omar. *Spanish Made Simple*	641.594
COOKING, THAI	
Teigen, Pepper (Vilailuck). *The Pepper Thai Cookbook*	641.595
Witte, Christina De. ★*Noodles, Rice, and Everything Spice*	641.595
COOKING, TURKISH	
Eckhardt, Robyn. *Istanbul & Beyond*	641.595
Roden, Claudia. *Arabesque*	641.59
COOKING, VIETNAMESE	
Nguyen, Andrea Quynhgiao. *Ever-Green Vietnamese*	641.595
Nguyen, Andrea Quynhgiao. *The Pho Cookbook*	641.595
Nguyen, Andrea Quynhgiao. ★*Vietnamese Food Any Day*	641.595
COOKS	
Ali, Fatima. ★*Savor*	B
Bastianich, Lidia. *My American Dream*	B
Bertch, Jane. *The French Ingredient*	B
Birdsall, John. *The Man Who Ate Too Much*	B
Bourdain, Anthony. ★*Appetites*	641.5
Bourdain, Anthony. ★*Kitchen Confidential*	B
Bourdain, Anthony. *Medium Raw*	B
Buford, Bill. ★*Dirt*	B
Cailan, Alvin. *Amboy*	641.595
Child, Julia. ★*My Life in France*	B
Hamilton, Gabrielle. *Blood, Bones, and Butter*	B
Jacobs, Ryan McMahon. *The Truffle Underground*	381
Lakshmi, Padma. *Love, Loss, and What We Ate*	791.4502
Lee, Edward. *Buttermilk Graffiti*	641.59
Lopez-Alt, J. Kenji. *The Food Lab*	664
Martinez, Rick. ★*Mi Cocina*	641.5972
Narayan, Shoba. *The Milk Lady of Bangalore*	390
Nosrat, Samin. ★*Salt, Fat, Acid, Heat*	641.5
Onwuachi, Kwame. ★*Notes from a Young Black Chef*	641.59
Pepin, Jacques. *The Apprentice*	B
Pepin, Jacques. *Art of the Chicken*	641.665
Pollan, Michael. *Cooked*	641.5
Regan, Iliana. *Fieldwork*	B
Ripert, Eric. *32 Yolks*	B
Samuelsson, Marcus. *Yes, Chef*	B
Sanchez, Aaron. *Where I Come From*	641.5092
Sheehan, Jason. *Cooking Dirty*	B
Solomonov, Michael. *Zahav*	641.595
Spitz, Bob. ★*Dearie*	B
Teigen, Chrissy. *Cravings*	641.5
Tipton-Martin, Toni. *The Jemima Code*	641.59
White, Marco Pierre. *White Heat*	641.594
Woolever, Laurie. *Bourdain*	B
COOKWARE	
McKoy, Bri. *The Cook's Book*	641.3
The Cool Factor. Linett, Andrea	746.9
Coolidge. Shlaes, Amity	B
COOLIDGE, CALVIN, 1872-1933	
Cohen, Jared. *Accidental Presidents*	973.09
Shlaes, Amity. *Coolidge*	B
COOLING	
Hogge, Fred. *Of Ice and Men*	338.4
Coombes, Joshua	
Do Something for Nothing	362.5
COOMBES, JOSHUA	
Coombes, Joshua. *Do Something for Nothing*	362.5
Cooney, Kara	
When Women Ruled the World	920
Cooper, Alex	
Saving Alex	B
COOPER, ALEX, 1994-	
Cooper, Alex. *Saving Alex*	B
Cooper, Anderson	
The Rainbow Comes and Goes	B
Vanderbilt	920
COOPER, ANDERSON	
Cooper, Anderson. *The Rainbow Comes and Goes*	B
Cooper, Anderson. *Vanderbilt*	920
Cooper, Andrew Scott	
The Fall of Heaven	B
Cooper, Becky	
We Keep the Dead Close	364.152
Cooper, Brittney C.	
Eloquent Rage	B

AUTHOR, TITLE, SERIES AND SUBJECT INDEX

COOPER, BRITTNEY C., 1980-
   Cooper, Brittney C. *Eloquent Rage* — B
Cooper, Christian
   Better Living Through Birding — B
COOPER, CHRISTIAN
   Cooper, Christian. *Better Living Through Birding* — B
Cooper, Helene
   The House at Sugar Beach — 921
   Madame President — 966.62
COOPER, HELENE
   Cooper, Helene. *The House at Sugar Beach* — 921
Cooper, John Milton
   Woodrow Wilson — B
COOPER, PAULA
   Mar, Alex. *Seventy Times Seven* — 362.88
Cooper, Sean Patrick
   The Shooter at Midnight — 363.25
COOPERATION
   Aktipis, Athena. ★*A Field Guide to the Apocalypse* — 155.2
   Baer, Daniel Brooks. *The Four Tests* — 320.973
   Benjamin, Ruha. ★*Imagination* — 302
   Berman, Lea. *Treating People Well* — 395
   Hamilton, Denise. *Indivisible* — 658.3
   Kasparov, G. K. *Deep Thinking* — 006.3
   Keltner, Dacher. *Born to Be Good* — 155.2
   McAfee, Andrew. *The Geek Way* — 658.3
   McDougall, Christopher. *Running with Sherman* — 636.1
   McIntyre, Rick. *The Reign of Wolf 21* — 599.773
   Skach, C. L. *How to Be a Citizen* — 323.6
   Snow, Shane. *Dream Teams* — 658.4
   Stanley, Matthew. *Einstein's War* — 530
Copaken, Deborah
   Ladyparts — B
COPAKEN, DEBORAH
   Copaken, Deborah. *Ladyparts* — B
COPARENTING
   Dais, Dawn. *The Sh!t No One Tells You About Divorce* — 306.89
COPE, ALAN INGRAM, 1925-1999
   Guibert, Emmanuel. *Alan's War* — 741.5
Copeland, B. Jack
   Turing — B
COPELAND, JOHN A. (JOHN ANTHONY), 1834-1859
   Meyer, Eugene L. *Five for Freedom* — 973.7
Copeland, Misty
   ★*Ballerina Body* — 792.8
   ★*Life in Motion* — B
   The Wind at My Back — B
COPELAND, MISTY
   Copeland, Misty. ★*Life in Motion* — B
   Copeland, Misty. *The Wind at My Back* — B
COPERNICUS, NICOLAUS, 1473-1543
   Fauber, L. S. *Heaven on Earth* — B
   Sobel, Dava. *A More Perfect Heaven* — 520.9
Copi, Irving M.
   ★*Introduction to Logic* — 160
COPING
   Adam, David. *The Man Who Couldn't Stop* — 616.85
   Allende, Isabel. ★*Paula* — B
   Allende, Isabel. *The Sum of Our Days* — B
   Armstrong, Karen. *The Spiral Staircase* — B
   Atleework, Kendra. *Miracle Country* — 979.4
   Barnes, Cinelle. *Monsoon Mansion* — B
   Biden, Joseph R. *Promise Me, Dad* — B
   Bui, Thi. ★*The Best We Could Do* — 741.5
   Danler, Stephanie. *Stray* — B
   Danticat, Edwidge. *The Art of Death* — 809
   Delaney, Brigid. *Reasons Not to Worry* — 158.1
   Diamond, Jared M. *Upheaval* — 303.48
   DiFelice, Bekah. *Almost There* — 248.8
   Dutta, Sunil. *Stealing Green Mangoes* — 973
   Eger, Edith Eva. *The Choice* — B
   Fuller, Alexandra. *Travel Light, Move Fast* — B
   Gawande, Atul. *Complications* — B
   Greitens, Eric. *Resilience* — 155.2
   Haig, Matt. *Notes on a Nervous Planet* — 616.89
   Harden, Marcia Gay. *The Seasons of My Mother* — B
   Holloway, Richard. *Waiting for the Last Bus* — 202
   Irby, Samantha. ★*Quietly Hostile* — 814
   Junger, Sebastian. *War* — 958.104
   Kaur, Rupi. *Milk and Honey* — 811
   Kaur, Rupi. *The Sun and Her Flowers* — 811.6
   Kubler-Ross, Elisabeth. ★*On Death and Dying* — 155.9
   Lamott, Anne. ★*Dusk, Night, Dawn* — B
   Madden, T Kira. *Long Live the Tribe of Fatherless Girls* — 814
   Mankell, Henning. *Quicksand* — B
   McColl, Sarah. *Joy Enough* — B
   O'Toole, Jennifer Cook. *Autism in Heels* — B
   Pagels, Elaine H. ★*Why Religion?* — B
   Reichl, Ruth. *My Kitchen Year* — 641.5
   Sandberg, Sheryl. *Option B* — 155.9
   Saunders, John. *Playing Hurt* — B
   Teege, Jennifer. *My Grandfather Would Have Shot Me* — 929.2
   Terkel, Studs. *Hope Dies Last* — 920
   Wagamese, Richard. *One Native Life* — B
   Wilson, Sarah. *First, We Make the Beast Beautiful* — 616.85
   Winch, Guy. *How to Fix a Broken Heart* — 155.9
   Zerwick, Phoebe. *Beyond Innocence* — 347
COPING IN CHILDREN
   B., David. *Epileptic* — 741.5
COPLEY, JOHN SINGLETON, 1738-1815
   Kamensky, Jane. *A Revolution in Color* — 759.13
   Staiti, Paul J. *Of Arms and Artists* — B
COPPER
   Conway, Edmund. *Material World* — 333.7
   Redniss, Lauren. ★*Oak Flat* — 970.5
COPPER MINERS
   Wolff, Daniel J. *Grown-Up Anger* — 920
Coppola, Francis Ford
   Live Cinema and Its Techniques — 791.4302
COPPOLA, FRANCIS FORD, 1939-
   Seal, Mark. ★*Leave the Gun, Take the Cannoli* — 791.43
COPYRIGHT
   Bellos, David. *Who Owns This Sentence?* — 346.73
   Butler, Rebecca P. ★*Copyright for Teachers & Librarians in the 21st Century* — 346.7304
   Castleman, Michael. *The Untold Story of Books* — 381
   Crews, Kenneth D. ★*Copyright Law for Librarians and Educators* — 346.7304
   Decherney, Peter. *Hollywood's Copyright Wars* — 346.7304
   Fishman, Stephen. ★*The Copyright Handbook, 15th Ed.* — 346.7304
   Gasaway, Laura N. *Copyright Questions and Answers for Information Professionals* — 346.7304
   Harris, Lesley Ellen. *Licensing Digital Content* — 346.7304
   Howe, Sean. *Marvel Comics* — 741.5
   Lessig, Lawrence. *Remix* — 346.7304
   Norwick, Kenneth P. *The Legal Guide for Writers, Artists and Other Creative People* — 346.04
   Russell, Carrie. *Complete Copyright for K-12 Librarians and Educators* — 346.73
COPYRIGHT AND ELECTRONIC DATA PROCESSING
   Lessig, Lawrence. *The Future of Ideas* — 346.04
   Lessig, Lawrence. *Remix* — 346.7304
★*Copyright for Teachers & Librarians in the 21st Century.* Butler, Rebecca P. — 346.7304
★*The Copyright Handbook, 15th Ed.* Fishman, Stephen — 346.7304
★*Copyright Law for Librarians and Educators.* Crews, Kenneth D. — 346.7304
Copyright Questions and Answers for Information Professionals. Gasaway, Laura N. — 346.7304
Corbeil, Jean-Claude
   ★*Merriam-Webster's Visual Dictionary* — 423
Corbett, Emily
   In Transition — 809
Corcoran, Katherine
   In the Mouth of the Wolf — 364.152
Cordery, Stacy A.
   Alice — B
Cordes, Kelly
   The Tower — 796.522
Cordingly, David
   Under the Black Flag — 910.4
COREEN, ACTIVE 18TH CENTURY
   Kearse, Bettye. *The Other Madisons* — 920
Corinna, Heather
   What Fresh Hell Is This? — 618.1
Cork Dork. Bosker, Bianca — 641.2
Corkhill, Betsan
   Crochet Therapy — 746.43

PUBLIC LIBRARY CORE COLLECTION: NONFICTION
Twentieth Edition

★*Corky* Lee's Asian America. Lee, Corky — 770
CORN
  Frank, Lois Ellen. *Seed to Plate, Soil to Sky* — 641.5
  Pollan, Michael. *The Omnivore's Dilemma* — 394.1
Cornejo Villavicencio, Karla
  ★*The Undocumented Americans* — 920
CORNEJO VILLAVICENCIO, KARLA
  Cornejo Villavicencio, Karla. ★*The Undocumented Americans* — 920
Cornelius, Maria M.
  The Final Season — B
Cornille, Didier
  Who Built That? — 720
CORNWALL, ENGLAND
  Ash, Lamorna. *Dark, Salt, Clear* — 942.3
  Winn, Raynor. *The Wild Silence* — B
Cornwell, Bernard
  Waterloo — 940.2
Cornwell, John
  Hitler's Pope — B
Cornwell, Patricia Daniels
  Ripper — 364.152
CORONAVIRUS INFECTIONS
  Leonnig, Carol. *I Alone Can Fix It* — 973.933
  Senthilingam, Meera. *Outbreaks and Epidemics* — 614.4
  Werb, Dan. *The Invisible Siege* — 614.5
CORONAVIRUSES
  Quammen, David. ★*Breathless* — 614.5
  Werb, Dan. *The Invisible Siege* — 614.5
CORONERS
  Goldfarb, Bruce. ★*18 Tiny Deaths* — B
CORPORAL PUNISHMENT
  Harrington, Joel F. *The Faithful Executioner* — B
CORPORATE ACCOUNTABILITY
  Auletta, Ken. *Frenemies* — 659.1
  Elmore, Bartow J. *Citizen Coke* — 338.7
  Hardy, Alyssa. *Worn Out* — 338.4
  Higham, Scott. *American Cartel* — 338.4
  Leamer, Laurence. *The Price of Justice* — 346.7302
  Montero, David. ★*The Stolen Wealth of Slavery* — 381
  Schultz, Howard. *From the Ground Up* — B
  Wartzman, Rick. *Still Broke* — 381
  Wooldridge, Adrian. *Masters of Management* — 658
CORPORATE ACQUISITIONS
  Gelles, David. *The Man Who Broke Capitalism* — 330.12
  Mezrich, Ben. *Breaking Twitter* — 338.7
CORPORATE COVER-UPS
  Bilott, Robert. *Exposure* — 344.04
  Fagin, Dan. *Toms River* — 363.7209749
  Fainaru-Wada, Mark. *League of Denial* — 617.1
  Hamby, Chris. *Soul Full of Coal Dust* — 363.11
  Laskas, Jeanne Marie. *Concussion* — 617.5
CORPORATE CRIME
  Kolhatkar, Sheelah. *Black Edge* — 364.16
CORPORATE CULTURE
  Busby, Jill Louise. *Unfollow Me* — 305.08
  Clark, Taylor. *Starbucked* — 338
  Cox, Gena. *Leading Inclusion* — 658.3
  Flannery, Kate. *Strip Tees* — 338.4
  Hamilton, Denise. ★*Indivisible* — 658.3
  Hastings, Reed. *No Rules Rules* — 384.55
  McAfee, Andrew. *The Geek Way* — 658.3
  Price, Devon. *Laziness Does Not Exist* — 158.1
  Robison, Peter. ★*Flying Blind* — 338.7
  Schultz, Howard. *From the Ground Up* — B
  Schweitzer, Sharon. *Access to Asia* — 395.5
  Solovic, Susan Wilson. *The One-Percent Edge* — 658.4
  Sun, Carrie. *Private Equity* — B
  Warzel, Charlie. *Out of Office* — 658.3
  Webb, Maynard. *Dear Founder* — 658
  Wiener, Anna. ★*Uncanny Valley* — B
  Wingfield, Adia Harvey. *Gray Areas* — 331.6
  Yoshino, Kenji. *Say the Right Thing* — 305.3
CORPORATE DOWNSIZING
  Gelles, David. *The Man Who Broke Capitalism* — 330.12
CORPORATE GOVERNANCE
  Gramm, Jeff. *Dear Chairman* — 659.2
CORPORATE GREED
  Leamer, Laurence. *The Price of Justice* — 346.7302

  Mattioli, Dana. ★*The Everything War* — 381.142
  Posner, Gerald L. ★*Pharma* — 338.4
  Sorvino, Chloe. *Raw Deal* — 338.1
  Taplin, Jonathan. *Move Fast and Break Things* — 330.9
CORPORATE LAWYERS
  Jackson, Bruce. *Never Far from Home* — B
  Oller, John. *White Shoe* — 346.73
CORPORATE MERGERS
  Knoedelseder, William. *Bitter Brew* — 338.7
  Sorvino, Chloe. *Raw Deal* — 338.1
CORPORATE NEGLIGENCE
  Blunt, Katherine. *California Burning* — 333.793
CORPORATE POWER
  Bellos, David. *Who Owns This Sentence?* — 346.73
  Carter, Iain. *Golf Wars* — 796.352
  Coll, Steve. *Private Empire* — 338.7
  Dalrymple, William. ★*The Anarchy* — 954.03
  Dayen, David. *Monopolized* — 338.8
  Desmond, Matthew. ★*Poverty, by America* — 362.5
  Jacoby, Melissa B. ★*Unjust Debts* — 346.73
  Leonard, Christopher. *Kochland* — 338.7
  Maddow, Rachel. *Blowout* — 338.2
  Posner, Gerald L. ★*Pharma* — 338.4
  Sun, Carrie. *Private Equity* — B
  Teachout, Zephyr. *Break 'Em Up* — 338.8
  Zuckerman, Jocelyn C. *Planet Palm* — 633.8
CORPORATE PROFITS
  MacGillis, Alec. *Fulfillment* — 381
CORPORATE SPONSORSHIP
  Norton, Hughes. ★*Rainmaker* — 796.352
  Oriard, Michael. *Brand NFL* — 796.332
The **Corporation**. English, T. J. — 364.106089
CORPORATIONS
  Addison, Corban. *Wastelands* — 346.73
  Berger, Eric. *Liftoff* — B
  Bilott, Robert. *Exposure* — 344.04
  Blunt, Katherine. *California Burning* — 333.793
  Citron, Danielle Keats. *The Fight for Privacy* — 342.7308
  Cohan, William D. *Power Failure* — 338.7
  Dalrymple, William. ★*The Anarchy* — 954.03
  Dayen, David. *Monopolized* — 338.8
  Ducharme, Jamie. *Big Vape* — 338.7
  Etter, Lauren. ★*The Devil's Playbook* — 338.7
  Flannery, Kate. *Strip Tees* — 338.4
  Gelles, David. *The Man Who Broke Capitalism* — 330.12
  Gramm, Jeff. *Dear Chairman* — 659.2
  Hill, Kashmir. ★*Your Face Belongs to Us* — 006.2
  Hoffman, Liz. *Crash Landing* — 330
  Hu, Elise. *Flawless* — 646.7
  Johnson, Steven. *Enemy of All Mankind* — 910.4
  Johnston, David Cay. *The Big Cheat* — 973.933
  Kim, Anne. ★*Poverty for Profit* — 302.5
  Lemann, Nicholas. *Transaction Man* — 330.973
  Leonard, Christopher. *Kochland* — 338.7
  Magner, Mike. *Poisoned Legacy* — 338.7
  Marie, Jane. ★*Selling the Dream* — 658.8
  Mattioli, Dana. ★*The Everything War* — 381.142
  Micklethwait, John. *The Company* — 338.7
  Molnar, Petra. *The Walls Have Eyes* — 363.28
  Montero, David. ★*The Stolen Wealth of Slavery* — 381
  Oller, John. *White Shoe* — 346.73
  Posner, Gerald L. ★*Pharma* — 338.4
  Stewart, James B. *Unscripted* — 658.1
  Teachout, Zephyr. *Break 'Em Up* — 338.8
  Vance, Ashlee. *When the Heavens Went on Sale* — 621.43
CORPORATIONS, AMERICAN
  Green, Hardy. *The Company Town* — 307.76
  Kim, Anne. ★*Poverty for Profit* — 302.5
Corral, Eduardo C.
  Guillotine — 811.6
Correction. Austen, Ben — 364.6
CORRECTIONAL INSTITUTIONS
  Fedderly, Eva. *These Walls* — 365
  Rayman, Graham. ★*Rikers* — 365
CORRECTIONAL PERSONNEL
  Bauer, Shane. *American Prison* — 365
  Hobbs, Jeff. *Children of the State* — 364.36

AUTHOR, TITLE, SERIES AND SUBJECT INDEX

CORRECTIONS
   Austen, Ben. *Correction* — 364.6
   Bauer, Shane. *American Prison* — 365
   ***Corrections** in Ink*. Blakinger, Keri — B
   *The **Correspondents***. MacKrell, Judith — 070.4
Corrigan, Kelly
   Glitter and Glue — B
   Tell Me More — 153.6
CORRIGAN, KELLY, 1967-
   Corrigan, Kelly. *Glitter and Glue* — B
   Corrigan, Kelly. *Tell Me More* — 153.6
CORRUPTION
   Abramson, John. *Sickening* — 338.4
   Bauer, Shane. *American Prison* — 365
   Berman, Sarah. *Don't Call It a Cult* — 361.4
   Bernstein, Andrea. *American Oligarchs* — 920
   Bogdanich, Walt. *When McKinsey Comes to Town* — 001
   Bradley, Mark A. *Blood Runs Coal* — B
   Coldstream, Catherine. ★*Cloistered*
   Conason, Joe. *The Longest Con* — 320.52
   Conn, David. *The Fall of the House of FIFA* — 796.334
   Corcoran, Katherine. *In the Mouth of the Wolf* — 364.152
   Crawford, Lacy. *Notes on a Silencing* — B
   Dayen, David. *Chain of Title* — 330.973
   Deer, Brian. *The Doctor Who Fooled the World* — 610.92
   Dybdahl, Thomas L. *When Innocence Is Not Enough* — 345.73
   Enrich, David. *Dark Towers* — 332.1
   Enrich, David. *Servants of the Damned* — 340.023
   Eyre, Eric. *Death in Mud Lick* — 362.29
   Fox, Margalit. *The Talented Mrs. Mandelbaum* — 364.1
   Glaser, Gabrielle. *American Baby* — B
   Glatt, John. *Tangled Vines* — 364.152
   Goodman, Matthew. *The City Game* — 796.323
   Hart, Matt. *Win at All Costs* — 338.7
   Hope, Bradley. *Blood and Oil* — B
   Horwitz, Jeff. ★*Broken Code* — 302.3
   Karl, Jonathan. *Front Row at the Trump Show* — 973.933
   Kean, Sam. *The Icepick Surgeon* — 509
   Keefe, Patrick Radden. ★*Rogues* — 364.16
   Lenzer, Jeanne. *The Danger Within Us* — 338.4
   Matney, Mandy. *Blood on Their Hands* — 364.152
   McGarrahan, Ellen. *Two Truths and a Lie* — 364.152
   McGreal, Chris. *American Overdose* — 362.29
   McIntire, Mike. *Champions Way* — 796.043
   McLaughlin, Kathleen. *Blood Money* — 362.17
   Michel, Casey. *American Kleptocracy* — 364.16
   O'Brien, Keith. *Charlie Hustle* — 796.357
   O'Toole, Fintan. ★*We Don't Know Ourselves* — 941.7
   Papenfuss, Mary. *American Huckster* — B
   Posner, Gerald L. *God's Bankers* — 364.16
   Posner, Gerald L. ★*Pharma* — 338.4
   Randall, David K. *Black Death at the Golden Gate* — 616.9
   Rao, Maya. *Great American Outpost* — 338.2
   Rudolf, David S. *American Injustice* — 345.73
   Schwartz, Joanna C. ★*Shielded* — 344.7305
   Sexton, Jared Yates. *American Rule* — 973
   Shackle, Samira. *Karachi Vice* — 954.91
   Stanton, Mike. ★*Unbeaten* — B
   Taub, Jennifer. *Big Dirty Money* — 364.16
   Tetro, Tony. *Con/Artist* — B
   Vanderbes, Jennifer. ★*Wonder Drug* — 615
   White, Richard. *Who Killed Jane Stanford?* — 364.152
CORRUPTION INVESTIGATION
   Bensinger, Ken. ★*Red Card* — 796.334
   Carreyrou, John. ★*Bad Blood* — 338.7
   Maroney, Tyler. *The Modern Detective* — 658.4
   Weissmann, Andrew. ★*Where Law Ends* — 324.7
CORTES, HERNAN, 1485-1547
   Diaz del Castillo, Bernal. *The Discovery and Conquest of Mexico, 1517-1521* — 972
   Restall, Matthew. *When Montezuma Met Cortes* — 972
Corwin, Lena
   Lena Corwin's Made by Hand — 746.6
   Printing by Hand — 745.5
Cory, Steve
   Ultimate Guide — 690
Coscarelli, Chloe
   Chloe Flavor — 641.5

COSELL, HOWARD, 1918-1995
   Ribowsky, Mark. *Howard Cosell* — 070.449796
COSMETICS
   Godas, Maru. *Organic Beauty* — 646.7
   Hankir, Zahra. *Eyeliner* — 391.6
   Herman, Eleanor. *The Royal Art of Poison* — 364.152
   Sancton, Thomas. *The Bettencourt Affair* — B
COSMETICS INDUSTRY AND TRADE
   Bundles, A'Lelia. *On Her Own Ground* — B
   Hankir, Zahra. *Eyeliner* — 391.6
   Hu, Elise. *Flawless* — 646.7
   Lima, Jamie Kern. *Believe It* — B
   Zuckerman, Jocelyn C. *Planet Palm* — 633.8
   *Cosmic **Queries***. Tyson, Neil deGrasse — 523.1
   *Cosmic **Scholar***. Szwed, John F. — B
COSMOBIOLOGY
   Kershenbaum, Arik. *The Zoologist's Guide to the Galaxy* — 576.8
   Shields, Aomawa L. *Life on Other Planets* — B
COSMOGONY
   Hawking, Stephen. ★*Brief Answers to the Big Questions* — 500
   Jabr, Ferris. ★*Becoming Earth* — 570.1
   Krauss, Lawrence Maxwell. *The Greatest Story Ever Told—So Far* — 530.01
   Tonelli, Guido. *Genesis* — 523.1
   Tyson, Neil deGrasse. ★*Astrophysics for People in a Hurry* — 523.01
   Tyson, Neil deGrasse. *Letters from an Astrophysicist* — 520.92
COSMOLOGY
   Alexander, Stephon. *Fear of a Black Universe* — 523.1
   Berman, Bob. *Earth-Shattering* — 523.1
   Carroll, Sean M. *The Biggest Ideas in the Universe* — 530.11
   Carroll, Sean M. *The Big Picture* — 577
   Cham, Jorge. *Frequently Asked Questions About the Universe* — 523.1
   Christian, David. *Origin Story* — 909
   Cliff, Harry. *How to Make an Apple Pie from Scratch* — 523.01
   Cox, Brian. *Universal* — 523.1
   Frank, Adam. *Light of the Stars* — 523.1
   Green, Jaime. *The Possibility of Life* — 576.8
   Greene, B. ★*The Elegant Universe* — 539.7
   Greene, B. *The Fabric of the Cosmos* — 523.1
   Greene, B. ★*The Hidden Reality* — 530.12
   Greene, B. *Until the End of Time* — 523.1
   Hawking, Stephen. ★*Black Holes and Baby Universes and Other Essays* — 530.1
   Hawking, Stephen. *A Brief History of Time* — 523.1
   Hawking, Stephen. ★*A Briefer History of Time* — 523.1
   Hawking, Stephen. ★*The Grand Design* — 530.14
   Hawking, Stephen. *My Brief History* — B
   Hawking, Stephen. *The Nature of Space and Time* — 530.1
   Hawking, Stephen. ★*The Universe in a Nutshell* — 530.12
   Holt, Jim. *Why Does the World Exist?* — 113
   Kaku, Michio. *The God Equation* — 523.1
   Kaku, Michio. *Parallel Worlds* — 523.1
   Kaltenegger, Lisa. ★*Alien Earths* — 523.2
   Krauss, Lawrence Maxwell. *The Greatest Story Ever Told—So Far* — 530.01
   Lightman, Alan P. *Searching for Stars on an Island in Maine* — 523.1
   Lintott, Chris. *Accidental Astronomy* — 520
   Mack, Katie. *The End of Everything* — 523.1
   Marchant, Jo. *The Human Cosmos* — 523.1
   McTier, Moiya. *The Milky Way* — 523.1
   Plait, Philip C. *Under Alien Skies* — 520
   Pontzen, Andrew. *The Universe in a Box* — 523.1
   Prescod-Weinstein, Chanda. *The Disordered Cosmos* — 523.01
   Rovelli, Carlo. *The Order of Time* — 530.11
   Rutherford, Adam. *The Complete Guide to Absolutely Everything* — 500
   Sagan, Carl. *Broca's Brain* — 128
   Sanders, Ella Frances. *Eating the Sun* — 520
   Still, Ben. *Particle Physics Brick by Brick* — 539.7
   Tegmark, Max. *Our Mathematical Universe* — 523.1
   Tonelli, Guido. *Genesis* — 523.1
   Tyson, Neil deGrasse. ★*Astrophysics for People in a Hurry* — 523.01
   Tyson, Neil deGrasse. *Cosmic Queries* — 523.1
   Tyson, Neil deGrasse. *Letters from an Astrophysicist* — 520.92
   Tyson, Neil deGrasse. *Starry Messenger* — 901
   Tyson, Neil deGrasse. *Startalk* — 523.1
   Tyson, Neil deGrasse. *To Infinity and Beyond* — 520
   Tyson, Neil deGrasse. *Welcome to the Universe* — 523.1
   Whitehouse, David. *The Alien Perspective* — 523.1
   Wilczek, Frank. *Fundamentals* — 530.01

PUBLIC LIBRARY CORE COLLECTION: NONFICTION
Twentieth Edition

COSMOPOLITANISM
   Figes, Orlando. *The Europeans* — 920
   King, Charles. *Midnight at the Pera Palace* — 949.61
   King, Charles. *Odessa* — 947.7
Cosmos. Sagan, Carl — 520
COSPLAY
   Conahan, Gillian. *The Hero's Closet* — 646.2
   Quindt, Svetlana. *The Costume Making Guide* — 646.4
COST AND STANDARD OF LIVING
   Derks, Scott. *The Value of a Dollar* — 338.5
   Derks, Scott. *The Value of a Dollar* — 338.5
   Gordon, Robert J. ★*The Rise and Fall of American Growth* — 339.4
   Morduch, Jonathan. *The Financial Diaries* — 332.024
   Quart, Alissa. *Squeezed* — 305.5
Cost Control for Nonprofits in Crisis. Smith, G. Stevenson — 025.1
The Cost of Courage. Kaiser, Charles — B
The Cost of Living. Levy, Deborah — B
The Cost of These Dreams. Thompson, Wright — B
COST OF WAR
   Lowenstein, Roger. *Ways and Means* — 973.7
   MacMillan, Margaret. *War* — 355.0209
COSTA RICA
   Dial, Roman. *The Adventurer's Son* — 917.286
Costa, James T.
   Darwin's Backyard — 576.8
   Radical by Nature — B
Coste, Joanne Koenig
   Learning to Speak Alzheimer's — 362.1
Costello, Elvis
   Unfaithful Music & Disappearing Ink — B
COSTELLO, ELVIS
   Costello, Elvis. *Unfaithful Music & Disappearing Ink* — B
COSTUME
   Bari, Shahidha K. *Dressed* — 391
   Bowles, Hamish. *Vogue & the Metropolitan Museum of Art Costume Institute* — 746.9
   Carter, Ruth E. ★*The Art of Ruth E. Carter* — 746.9
   Conahan, Gillian. *The Hero's Closet* — 646.2
COSTUME DESIGN
   Carter, Ruth E. ★*The Art of Ruth E. Carter* — 746.9
   Quindt, Svetlana. *The Costume Making Guide* — 646.4
COSTUME JEWELRY
   Crowther, Janet. *Make a Statement* — 745.594
The Costume Making Guide. Quindt, Svetlana — 646.4
Cosy. Weir, Laura — 646.7009
COTE D'IVOIRE
   Erdman, Sarah. *Nine Hills to Nambonkaha* — 966.68
Cott, Jonathan
   There's a Mystery There — 813
COTTAGES
   Dochartaigh, Kerri ni. *Cacophony of Bone* — B
Cotterell, Arthur
   Chariot — 357
Cottom, Tressie McMillan
   Lower Ed — 378.73
   Thick — 301
COTTOM, TRESSIE MCMILLAN
   Cottom, Tressie McMillan. *Thick* — 301
COTTON INDUSTRY AND TRADE
   Beckert, Sven. *Empire of Cotton* — 338.4
COTTON MANUFACTURE
   Beckert, Sven. *Empire of Cotton* — 338.4
★*Cotton Tenants*. Agee, James — 976.1
Cotton, Tom
   Sacred Duty — 355.6
COTTON, TOM
   Cotton, Tom. *Sacred Duty* — 355.6
Couch, Dick
   The Warrior Elite — 359.9
Couchsurfing in Iran. Orth, Stephan — 955.06
COUCY, ENGUERRAND DE, 1340-1397
   Tuchman, Barbara W. ★*A Distant Mirror* — 944
COUNEY, MARTIN A.
   Raffel, Dawn. *The Strange Case of Dr. Couney* — B
COUNSELING
   Kim, Anne. ★*Abandoned* — 305.2350973
   Park, J. S. *As Long as You Need* — 248.8
Counselor. Sorensen, Theodore C. — B

COUNSELORS
   Berg, Ryan. *No House to Call My Home* — B
Countdown 1945. Wallace, Chris — 940.54
Countdown Bin Laden. Wallace, Chris — 958.104
Countdown to Pearl Harbor. Twomey, Steve — 940.54
COUNTERCULTURE
   Austerlitz, Saul. *Just a Shot Away* — 781.66078
   Burrough, Bryan. *Days of Rage* — 303.48
   Harry, Debbie. *Face It* — B
   Johnson, Joyce. *The Voice Is All* — B
   Kauffman, Jonathan. *Hippie Food* — 394.1
   Lang, Michael. *The Road to Woodstock* — 781.66
   Lattin, Don. *The Harvard Psychedelic Club* — 973.922092
   Minutaglio, Bill. *The Most Dangerous Man in America* — B
   Moser, Benjamin. ★*Sontag* — B
   Rush, Chris. *The Light Years* — B
   Savage, Jon. ★*1966* — 781.6609
   Tolokonnikova, Nadezhda. *Rules for Rulebreakers* — 782.42166
   Waters, Alice. *Coming to My Senses* — B
   Wiederhorn, Jon. *Louder Than Hell* — 781.6609
★*The Counterfeit Countess*. White, Elizabeth B. — 940.53
COUNTERFEITS AND COUNTERFEITING
   Craughwell, Thomas J. *Stealing Lincoln's Body* — 973.7092
   Jacobs, Ryan McMahon. *The Truffle Underground* — 381
COUNTERINTELLIGENCE
   Andrew, Christopher M. *The Secret World* — 327.1209
   Harmon, Mark. *Ghosts of Honolulu* — 940.54
Counterpoint. Kennicott, Philip — B
Counting. Stone, Deborah A. — 001.4
COUNTING
   Stone, Deborah A. *Counting* — 001.4
Counting Coup. Colton, Larry — 796.323
Counting The Cost. Duggar, Jill — B
COUNTRIES
   Dikotter, Frank. *China After Mao* — 951.05
   Ellis, Joseph J. *The Cause* — 973.3
   Hoyer, Katja. ★*Beyond the Wall* — 943.087
   Kershner, Isabel. *The Land of Hope and Fear* — 956.9405
   Marshall, Tim. *The Power of Geography* — 320.1
   Mikanowski, Jacob. ★*Goodbye, Eastern Europe* — 947
   Trentmann, Frank. *Out of the Darkness* — 943.08
The Country Cooking of Ireland. Andrews, Colman — 641.594
★*Country Music*. Duncan, Dayton — 781.642
COUNTRY MUSIC
   Cash, Rosanne. ★*Composed* — B
   Duncan, Dayton. ★*Country Music* — 781.642
   Eliot, Marc. *The Hag* — B
   Hilburn, Robert. ★*Johnny Cash* — B
   Louvin, Charlie. *Satan Is Real* — 920
   Lynn, Loretta. ★*Me & Patsy Kickin' up Dust* — B
   McDonough, Jimmy. *Tammy Wynette* — B
   Moss, Marissa R. *Her Country* — 781.642
   Parton, Dolly. ★*Dolly Parton, Songteller* — B
   Russell, Tony. *Country Music Originals* — B
   Travis, Randy. *Forever and Ever, Amen* — B
COUNTRY MUSIC INDUSTRY AND TRADE
   Louvin, Charlie. *Satan Is Real* — 920
   Lynn, Loretta. ★*Me & Patsy Kickin' up Dust* — B
   Nelson, Willie. *It's a Long Story* — B
Country Music Originals. Russell, Tony — B
COUNTRY MUSICIANS
   Cash, Rosanne. ★*Composed* — B
   Crowell, Rodney. *Chinaberry Sidewalks* — B
   Duncan, Dayton. ★*Country Music* — 781.642
   Eliot, Marc. *The Hag* — B
   Hemphill, Paul. *Lovesick Blues* — B
   Hilburn, Robert. ★*Johnny Cash* — B
   Lambert, Miranda. *Y'all Eat Yet?* — 641.5976
   Lynn, Loretta. *Still Woman Enough* — B
   McDonough, Jimmy. *Tammy Wynette* — B
   Nelson, Willie. *It's a Long Story* — B
   Parton, Dolly. ★*Behind the Seams* — B
   Parton, Dolly. ★*Dolly Parton, Songteller* — B
   Russell, Tony. *Country Music Originals* — B
   Travis, Randy. *Forever and Ever, Amen* — B
   Zwonitzer, Mark. *Will You Miss Me When I'm Gone?* — 920
★*The Country of the Blind*. Leland, Andrew — B
A Country of Vast Designs. Merry, Robert W. — B

AUTHOR, TITLE, SERIES AND SUBJECT INDEX

★*The Countryside*. Fowler, Corinne — 941
COUNTS AND COUNTESSES
  Askwith, Richard. *Unbreakable* — B
  Barnes, Julian. *The Man in the Red Coat* — B
  Lovell, Mary S. *Bess of Hardwick* — B
The Coup. Abrahamian, Ervand — 955.05
COUPLES
  Adams, John. *My Dearest Friend* — 973.4
  Buhle, Kathleen. *If We Break* — B
  Dochartaigh, Kerri ni. *Cacophony of Bone* — B
  Finkel, Michael. *The Art Thief* — 364.1628
  Garcia, Mayte. *The Most Beautiful* — 920
  Gottman, Julie Schwartz. *Fight Right* — 616.89
  Hewitt, Sean. *All Down Darkness Wide* — B
  Lekas Miller, Anna. *Love Across Borders* — 323.6
  Mann, William J. *Bogie & Bacall* — 920
  Morgan, Abi. *This Is Not a Pity Memoir* — B
  Offerman, Nick. *The Greatest Love Story Ever Told* — B
  Rallo, Eli. *I Didn't Know I Needed This* — 306.73
  Real, Terrence. *Us* — 646.7
  Reid, Joy-Ann Lomena. ★*Medgar and Myrlie* — 920
  Soep, Elisabeth. *Other People's Words* — 155.9
  Viren, Sarah. *To Name the Bigger Lie* — B
  Woo, Ilyon. ★*Master Slave Husband Wife* — 920
COUPS D'ETAT
  Abrahamian, Ervand. *The Coup* — 955.05
  Carney, Scott. *The Vortex* — 954.92
  King, David. *The Trial of Adolf Hitler* — 345.43
  Mieville, China. *October* — 947.084
  Preston, Paul. *The Spanish Holocaust* — 946.081
  Zucchino, David. *Wilmington's Lie* — 305.8009756
COURAGE
  Ackerman, Elliot. *Places and Names* — B
  Addario, Lynsey. *Of Love & War* — 779
  Albracht, William. *Abandoned in Hell* — 959.704
  Ambrose, Stephen E. ★*Band of Brothers* — 920
  Bascomb, Neal. *The Escape Artists* — 940.4
  Batalion, Judith. *The Light of Days* — 940.53
  Berry, Erica. *Wolfish* — 152.4
  Brenner, Marie. ★*The Desperate Hours* — 362.1962
  Brown, Brene. ★*Dare to Lead* — 658.4
  Carcaterra, Lorenzo. *Three Dreamers* — B
  Carpenter, Kyle. *You Are Worth It* — B
  Castor, Helen. *Joan of Arc* — B
  Clinton, Hillary Rodham. *The Book of Gutsy Women* — 920
  Donovan, Jim. *The Blood of Heroes* — 976.4
  Dunbar, Erica Armstrong. ★*She Came to Slay* — B
  Edmundson, Mark. *Why Football Matters* — B
  Gies, Miep. ★*Anne Frank Remembered* — B
  Gilbert, Elizabeth. ★*Big Magic* — 153.3
  Girma, Haben. *Haben* — B
  Hillenbrand, Laura. ★*Unbroken* — B
  Kennedy, John F. *Profiles in Courage* — 920
  Kershaw, Alex. *Against All Odds* — 940.54
  Kershaw, Alex. *Avenue of Spies* — 940.53
  Kyle, Taya. *American Spirit* — B
  Lambert, Raymond. *Every Man a Hero* — B
  Lewis, John. *Carry On* — 328.73
  Lichtblau, Eric. *Return to the Reich* — B
  Lineberry, Cate. *Be Free or Die* — B
  Lineberry, Cate. *The Secret Rescue* — 940.54
  Macadam, Heather Dune. *999* — 940.53
  Magida, Arthur J. *Code Name Madeleine* — 940.54
  Masters, Oksana. *The Hard Parts* — B
  Miller, Chanel. *Know My Name* — B
  Mock, Janet. *Surpassing Certainty* — B
  Mulley, Clare. *The Spy Who Loved* — B
  Mulley, Clare. *The Women Who Flew for Hitler* — 920
  Sides, Hampton. *On Desperate Ground* — 951.904
  Tillich, Paul. ★*The Courage to Be* — 179
  Toler, Pamela D. *Women Warriors* — 355.0092
  Vasquez-Lavado, Silvia. *In the Shadow of the Mountain* — B
  Velshi, Ali. *Small Acts of Courage* — B
  Willner, Nina. *Forty Autumns* — B
  Winters, Richard D. *Beyond Band of Brothers* — B
  Wolfe, Tom. ★*The Right Stuff* — 629.4
  Yousafzai, Malala. *I Am Malala* — B
  Zia, Helen. *Last Boat Out of Shanghai* — 951.04

COURAGE IN CHILDREN
  Glatt, John. *The Family Next Door* — 362.76092
★*The Courage to Be*. Tillich, Paul — 179
The Courage to Be Disliked. Kishimi, Ichiro — 158
★*The Courage to Heal*. Bass, Ellen — 616.85
Courageously Soft. Rush, Charaia — 234
Couric, Katie
  Going There — B
COURIC, KATIE, 1957-
  Couric, Katie. *Going There* — B
  Stelter, Brian. *Top of the Morning* — 791.456
Courogen, Carrie
  ★*Miss May Does Not Exist* — B
A Course Called Scotland. Coyne, Tom — 796.352
Course Correction. Gilder, Ginny — 797.12
COURTESY
  Alkon, Amy. *Good Manners for Nice People* — 395
  Berman, Lea. *Treating People Well* — 395
  Forni, Pier Massimo. *The Civility Solution* — 395
  Post, Lizzie. *Emily Post's Etiquette* — 395
  Post, Lizzie. *Emily Post's Etiquette* — 395
COURTLY LOVE
  Gristwood, Sarah. *The Tudors in Love* — 941.05
Courtroom 302. Bogira, Steve — 345.773
COURTS
  Biskupic, Joan. ★*Nine Black Robes* — 347.73
  Graetz, Michael J. *The Burger Court and the Rise of the Judicial Right* — 347.73
  O'Connor, Sandra Day. ★*Out of Order* — 347.73
COURTS AND COURTIERS
  Borman, Tracy. *Elizabeth's Women* — B
  Borman, Tracy. *Henry VIII and the Men Who Made Him* — 942.05
  Borman, Tracy. *Thomas Cromwell* — B
  Fuhrmann, Joseph T. *Rasputin* — B
  Gies, Joseph. *Life in a Medieval Castle* — 940.1
  Glenconner, Anne. ★*Lady in Waiting* — B
  Goldstone, Nancy Bazelon. *In the Shadow of the Empress* — 920
  Goldstone, Nancy Bazelon. *The Rival Queens* — 944
  Herman, Eleanor. *The Royal Art of Poison* — 364.152
  MacCulloch, Diarmaid. *Thomas Cromwell* — B
  Mansel, Philip. *King of the World* — B
  Roberts, Andrew. ★*Napoleon* — B
  Smith, Douglas. *Rasputin* — B
  Weir, Alison. *Henry VIII* — B
COURTS-MARTIAL AND COURTS OF INQUIRY
  Alexander, Caroline. *The Bounty* — 996.1
  Grann, David. ★*The Wager* — 910.91
  Philipps, David. *Alpha* — 956.7044
  Vincent, Lynn. *Indianapolis* — 940.54
COURTSHIP
  Cacioppo, Stephanie. *Wired for Love* — 616.8
  De Courcy, Anne. *The Husband Hunters* — 920
  Guy, John. *Hunting the Falcon* — B
  Narayan, R. K. ★*The Ramayana* — 294.5
COURTSHIP OF ANIMALS
  Erickson, Laura. *The Love Lives of Birds* — 598.15
  McIntyre, Rick. *The Reign of Wolf 21* — 599.773
COURVOISIER, FRANCOIS BENJAMIN, D. 1840
  Harman, Claire. *Murder by the Book* — 364.152
COUSINS
  Faleiro, Sonia. *The Good Girls* — 364.152
  Meyer, Robert. *Every Minute Is a Day* — 362.1962
  Peyser, Marc N. *Hissing Cousins* — B
Cousteau, Jacques Yves
  The Human, the Orchid, and the Octopus — B
COUSTEAU, JACQUES YVES
  Cousteau, Jacques Yves. *The Human, the Orchid, and the Octopus* — B
COUTURE CLOTHING
  Thomas, Dana. *Gods and Kings* — 920
  Trubert-Tollu, Chantal. ★*The House of Worth 1858-1954* — 746.92
Coventry. Cusk, Rachel — 814
★*Covered with Night*. Eustace, Nicole — 364.152
Covey, Stephen R.
  ★*The 7 Habits of Highly Effective People* — 158
  The 8th Habit — 158
COVID 19 DISEASE
  Fisher, Thomas. ★*The Emergency* — 362.1089
Covid-19. Mackenzie, Debora — 616.2

PUBLIC LIBRARY CORE COLLECTION: NONFICTION
Twentieth Edition

COVID-19 (DISEASE)
    Ashton, Jennifer. *The New Normal* — 613
    Borrell, Brendan. *The First Shots* — 615.3
    Brenner, Marie. ★*The Desperate Hours* — 362.1962
    Christakis, Nicholas A. *Apollo's Arrow* — 362.1962
    Ferguson, Niall. *Doom* — 362.1962
    Francis. *Let Us Dream* — 282.092
    Gates, Bill. ★*How to Prevent the Next Pandemic* — 614.5
    Goldberg, Emma. *Life on the Line* — 362.1962
    Kariko, Katalin. *Breaking Through* — B
    Leonnig, Carol. *I Alone Can Fix It* — 973.933
    Lewis, Michael. ★*The Premonition* — 614.5
    Loftus, Peter. *The Messenger* — 338.4
    MacGillis, Alec. *Fulfillment* — 381
    Mackenzie, Debora. *Covid-19* — 616.2
    Manaugh, Geoff. *Until Proven Safe* — 614.4
    McNeil, Donald G. ★*The Wisdom of Plagues* — 614.4
    Meyer, Robert. *Every Minute Is a Day* — 362.1962
    Price, Polly J. *Plagues in the Nation* — 614.4
    Quammen, David. ★*Breathless* — 614.5
    Sedaris, David. ★*Happy-Go-Lucky* — 814
    Smith, Michael. *Cabin Fever* — 614.5
    Sullivan, Matt. *Can't Knock the Hustle* — 796.323
    Werb, Dan. *The Invisible Siege* — 614.5
    Wright, Lawrence. ★*The Plague Year* — 614.5
    Xuecun, Murong. *Deadly Quiet City* — 614.5
    Zaitchik, Alexander. *Owning the Sun* — 362.1
    Zuckerman, Gregory. *A Shot to Save the World* — 614.5

COVID-19 PANDEMIC, 2020-
    Arceneaux, Michael. *I Finally Bought Some Jordans* — 306.76
    Atwood, Margaret. *Burning Questions* — 814
    Borrell, Brendan. *The First Shots* — 615.3
    Brenner, Marie. ★*The Desperate Hours* — 362.1962
    Dochartaigh, Kerri ni. *Cacophony of Bone* — B
    Gates, Bill. ★*How to Prevent the Next Pandemic* — 614.5
    Goodman, Peter S. ★*How the World Ran Out of Everything* — 658.7
    Hoffman, Liz. *Crash Landing* — 330
    Irby, Samantha. ★*Quietly Hostile* — 814
    Kamenetz, Anya. *The Stolen Year* — 306.43
    Kelley, Margot Anne. *A Gardener at the End of the World* — 615.8
    Klinenberg, Eric. ★*2020* — 306
    McNeil, Donald G. ★*The Wisdom of Plagues* — 614.4
    McSwane, J. David. ★*Pandemic, Inc.* — 362.1962
    Meyer, Robert. *Every Minute Is a Day* — 362.1962
    Mogelson, Luke. *The Storm Is Here* — 973.933
    Moss, Jeremiah. *Feral City* — B
    Nocera, Joseph. *The Big Fail* — 362.1962
    Orenstein, Peggy. *Unraveling* — B
    Quammen, David. ★*Breathless* — 614.5
    Smith, Freda Love. *I Quit Everything* — B
    Smith, Michael. *Cabin Fever* — 614.5
    Sullivan, Matt. *Can't Knock the Hustle* — 796.323
    Thrasher, Steven W. ★*The Viral Underclass* — 362.1962
    Werb, Dan. *The Invisible Siege* — 614.5
    Wright, Lawrence. ★*The Plague Year* — 614.5
    Xuecun, Murong. *Deadly Quiet City* — 614.5
    Zambreno, Kate. *The Light Room* — B
    Zuckerman, Gregory. *A Shot to Save the World* — 614.5

Coward, Noel
    Three Plays — 822

COWBOYS
    Branch, John. *The Last Cowboys* — 920
    Grant, Will. *The Last Ride of the Pony Express* — 917.804
    Parke, Henry C. *The Greatest Westerns Ever Made and the People Who Made Them* — 791.43
    Thompson-Hernandez, Walter. *The Compton Cowboys* — 920

Cowden, Meg McAndrews
    ★*Plant Grow Harvest Repeat* — 635.9

Cowen, Tyler
    An Economist Gets Lunch — 394.1

COWS
    Narayan, Shoba. *The Milk Lady of Bangalore* — 390

Cox, Anna-Lisa
    The Bone and Sinew of the Land — 977

Cox, Brian
    The Quantum Universe — 530.12
    Universal — 523.1

Cox, Caroline
    The World Atlas of Street Fashion — 391.009

Cox, Gena
    Leading Inclusion — 658.3

Cox, John Woodrow
    Children Under Fire — 371.7

Cox, Joseph
    Dark Wire — 363.2

Cox, Josie
    Women Money Power — 330.082

Cox, Lynne
    Swimming to Antarctica — B

COX, LYNNE, 1957-
    Cox, Lynne. *Swimming to Antarctica* — B

Cox, Marge
    Kids' Books and Maker Activities — 372.41

Cox, Michael
    Zonal Marking — 796

Cox, Shelley
    Bead Embroidery — 746.5

Coyle, Marcia
    The Roberts Court — 347.73

Coyne, Tom
    A Course Called Scotland — 796.352

COYNE, TOM
    Coyne, Tom. *A Course Called Scotland* — 796.352

Cozzens, Peter
    A Brutal Reckoning — 973.5
    The Earth Is Weeping — 978
    Tecumseh and the Prophet — 920

Crabapple, Molly
    Drawing Blood — B

CRABAPPLE, MOLLY
    Crabapple, Molly. *Drawing Blood* — B

CRABBING
    Swift, Earl. *Chesapeake Requiem* — 639

CRABS
    Swift, Earl. *Chesapeake Requiem* — 639

CRACK (DRUG)
    Ramsey, Donovan X. ★*When Crack Was King* — 362.29

A Crack in the Edge of the World. Winchester, Simon — 979.4
Cradle of Gold. Heaney, Christopher — B
Craeft. Langlands, Alex — 306.4
★*Craft in the Real World.* Salesses, Matthew — 808.3
The Craft of Research. Booth, Wayne C. — 001.4

CRAFT, ELLEN
    Woo, Ilyon. ★*Master Slave Husband Wife* — 920

CRAFT, WILLIAM
    Woo, Ilyon. ★*Master Slave Husband Wife* — 920

Crafting A Patterned Home. Nicholas, Kristin — 745.5

CRAFTS, HANNAH
    Hecimovich, Gregg A. ★*The Life and Times of Hannah Crafts* — B

A Craftsman's Legacy. Gorges, Eric — 745.5
Craig & Fred. Grossi, Craig — B

Craig, Mya-Rose
    Birdgirl — B

CRAIG, MYA-ROSE
    Craig, Mya-Rose. *Birdgirl* — B

Craig, William
    Yankee Come Home — 972.9107

Craine, Debra
    The Oxford Dictionary of Dance — 792.8

Crais, Clifton C.
    History Lessons — B

CRAIS, CLIFTON C.
    Crais, Clifton C. *History Lessons* — B

Cramer, Richard Ben
    Joe DiMaggio — B

Crampton, Caroline
    A Body Made of Glass — 616.85

CRAMPTON, CAROLINE
    Crampton, Caroline. *A Body Made of Glass* — 616.85

The Crane Wife. Hauser, CJ — B

CRANE, LEON, 1919-2002
    Murphy, Brian. *81 Days Below Zero* — 940.54

CRANE, STEPHEN, 1871-1900
    Auster, Paul. *Burning Boy* — B

AUTHOR, TITLE, SERIES AND SUBJECT INDEX

Cranshaw, Whitney
  Garden Insects of North America — 635
Crary, Calvert
  The Encyclopedia of Cut Flowers — 745.92
Crase, Douglas
  On Autumn Lake — 809
Crash Course in Collection Development. Disher, Wayne — 025.2
Crash Course in Contemporary Reference. Goldsmith, Francisca — 025.5
Crash Course in Library Supervision. Tucker, Dennis C. — 023
★*Crash Course in Readers' Advisory*. Orr, Cynthia — 025.5
Crash Landing. Hoffman, Liz — 330
Crash Override. Quinn, Zoe — 794.8
Crasnianski, Tania
  The Children of Nazis — 943.086
Craughwell, Thomas J.
  Stealing Lincoln's Body — 973.7092
Crave Radiance. Alexander, Elizabeth — 811
Cravings. Teigen, Chrissy — 641.5
Crawford, Alan Pell
  This Fierce People — 975
Crawford, Bill
  ★*All American* — B
Crawford, Lacy
  Notes on a Silencing — B
CRAWFORD, LACY
  Crawford, Lacy. *Notes on a Silencing* — B
Crawford, Matthew B.
  The World Beyond Your Head — 155.2
Crawford, Richard
  America's Musical Life — 780
Crawford, Robert
  Eliot After the Waste Land — B
Crawford, Saffi
  The Power of Birthdays, Stars & Numbers — 133.5
Crazy Brave. Harjo, Joy — B
Crazy for the Storm. Ollestad, Norman — B
Crazy Happy. Fusco, Daniel — 248.4
Crazy Horse. McMurtry, Larry — B
CRAZY HORSE, APPROXIMATELY 1842-1877
  Gardner, Mark L. *The Earth Is All That Lasts* — 978.004
  McMurtry, Larry. *Crazy Horse* — B
  Powers, Thomas. *The Killing of Crazy Horse* — B
CREAM, THOMAS NEILL, 1850-1892
  Jobb, Dean. *The Case of the Murderous Dr. Cream* — 364.152
Creamer, Robert W.
  Babe — B
  Stengel — 796.357
Crease, Robert P.
  The Quantum Moment — 530.12
Creating A New Old House. Versaci, Russell — 728
Creating Anna Karenina. Blaisdell, Robert — 891.7
Creating Great Choices. Riel, Jennifer — 658.4
Creating Inclusive Library Environments. Kowalsky, Michelle — 027.6
Creating The Not so Big House. Susanka, Sarah — 728
Creating Their Own Image. Farrington, Lisa E. — 704
Creating Your Best Life. Miller, Caroline Adams — 158.1
CREATION
  Grabbe, Lester L. *Faith and Fossils* — 231.7
  Greenblatt, Stephen. *The Rise and Fall of Adam and Eve* — 233
  Hawking, Stephen. ★*The Grand Design* — 530.14
CREATION (CHRISTIANITY)
  Meyaard-Schaap, Kyle. *Following Jesus in a Warming World* — 241
CREATION (LITERARY, ARTISTIC, ETC.)
  Ai, Weiwei. *Zodiac* — 741.5
  Anders, Charlie Jane. ★*Never Say You Can't Survive* — 808.02
  Baker, Nicholson. *Finding a Likeness* — B
  Baraka, Sho. *He Saw That It Was Good* — 261.5
  Basbanes, Nicholas A. ★*Cross of Snow* — B
  Bellos, David. *Who Owns This Sentence?* — 346.73
  Birch, Helen. *Freehand* — 741.2
  Blaisdell, Robert. *Creating Anna Karenina* — 891.7
  Bosker, Bianca. *Get the Picture* — 701
  Bradbury, Ray. ★*Remembrance* — 813
  Cameron, Julia. *Living the Artist's Way* — 153.3
  Codjoe, Ama. *Bluest Nude* — 811
  Cusk, Rachel. *Coventry* — 814
  Damon-Moore, Laura C. *The Artist's Library* — 021.2
  Doherty, Maggie. *The Equivalents* — 920

Falick, Melanie. *Making a Life* — 745.5
Fox, Dan. *Pretentiousness* — 700
Gabbert, Elisa. *Any Person Is the Only Self* — 814
Gluck, Louise. *American Originality* — 814
Godin, Seth. *The Practice* — 153.3
Gopnik, Adam. *The Real Work* — 153.9
Gorges, Eric. *A Craftsman's Legacy* — 745.5
Gunn, Thom. ★*The Letters of Thom Gunn* — 821
Harjo, Joy. *Catching the Light* — 818
Harss, Marina. *The Boy from Kyiv* — B
Knausgaard, Karl Ove. *So Much Longing in so Little Space* — 759.81
LaPointe, Sasha taqwseblu. *Thunder Song* — 814
Larimer, Kevin. *The Poets & Writers Complete Guide to Being a Writer* — 808
Lynch, David. *Room to Dream* — B
McIlwaine, Catherine. *Tolkien* — 002.09
Mead, Rebecca. *My Life in Middlemarch* — 823
Miller, Lucasta. ★*Keats* — 821
Moss, Adam. ★*The Work of Art* — 701
Murakami, Haruki. ★*Novelist as a Vocation* — 895.64
Nelson, Maggie. ★*Like Love* — 814
Nichtern, David. *Creativity, Spirituality & Making a Buck* — 294.3
Nicolson, Adam. *The Making of Poetry* — 821.709
Patchett, Ann. ★*These Precious Days* — 814
Rose, Michael. *The Birth of an Opera* — 782.1
Rubin, Rick. ★*The Creative Act* — 153.3
Sabatini Sloan, Aisha. *Dreaming of Ramadi in Detroit* — 814
Salesses, Matthew. ★*Craft in the Real World* — 808.3
Schultz, Philip. *Comforts of the Abyss* — 801
Shone, Tom. *The Nolan Variations* — 791.4302
Smee, Sebastian. *The Art of Rivalry* — 700.92
Smith, Zadie. *Intimations* — 824
Spitzer, Michael. *The Musical Human* — 780.9
Unger, Miles. *Picasso and the Painting That Shocked the World* — 759.4
Wilson, A. N. *The Mystery of Charles Dickens* — 823
Zwick, Edward. ★*Hits, Flops, and Other Illusions* — B
The Creation of Anne Boleyn. Bordo, Susan — 942.05
CREATIONISM
  Nye, Bill. *Undeniable* — 576.8
  ★*The Creative Act*. Rubin, Rick — 153.3
CREATIVE ACTIVITIES AND SEAT WORK
  Citro, Asia. *150+ Screen-Free Activities for Kids* — 796.5
  Doorley, Rachelle. *Tinkerlab* — 600
  Van't Hul, Jean. *The Artful Parent* — 745.5083
CREATIVE ACTIVITIES FOR CHILDREN AND STUDENTS
  Cox, Marge. *Kids' Books and Maker Activities* — 372.41
Creative Acts for Curious People. Greenberg, Sarah Stein — 153.3
Creative Change. Mueller, Jennifer — 658.4
Creative Homeowner Ultimate Guide to.. [Series]. Cory, Steve — 690
Creative Lettering. Doh, Jenny — 745.6
Creative Schools. Robinson, Ken — 370.973
The Creative Shrub Garden. McIndoe, Andrew — 635.9
Creative Soldered Jewelry & Accessories. Bluhm, Lisa — 745.594
Creative Stained Glass. Stevenson, Christine Kellman — 748.50282
★*The Creative Tarot*. Crispin, Jessa — 133.3
CREATIVE THINKING
  Grant, Adam M. *Originals* — 153.3
  Greenberg, Sarah Stein. *Creative Acts for Curious People* — 153.3
  Rubin, Rick. ★*The Creative Act* — 153.3
★*Creative Visualization*. Gawain, Shakti — 153.3
CREATIVE WRITING
  Dufresne, John. *Storyville!* — 808.3
  Griffin, Susan. *Out of Silence, Sound. Out of Nothing, Something* — 808.02
  Kidder, Tracy. *Good Prose* — 808.02
  Larimer, Kevin. *The Poets & Writers Complete Guide to Being a Writer* — 808
  Le Guin, Ursula K. *Words Are My Matter* — 818
  McCann, Colum. *Letters to a Young Writer* — 808.02
  Mosley, Walter. *Elements of Fiction* — 808.3
  Palahniuk, Chuck. *Consider This* — B
  Salesses, Matthew. ★*Craft in the Real World* — 808.3
  Saunders, George. ★*A Swim in a Pond in the Rain* — 891.7
  Vogler, Christopher. ★*The Writer's Journey* — 808.2
CREATIVE WRITING TEACHERS
  McCourt, Frank. *'Tis* — B
  McPhee, John. *Tabula Rasa; V.1* — 818
  Sabatini Sloan, Aisha. *Dreaming of Ramadi in Detroit* — 814
CREATIVITY
  Ackmann, Martha. ★*These Fevered Days* — B
  Adams, John. *Hallelujah Junction* — B

PUBLIC LIBRARY CORE COLLECTION: NONFICTION
Twentieth Edition

Ai, Weiwei. *1000 Years of Joys and Sorrows*	709.2
Anders, Charlie Jane. ★*Never Say You Can't Survive*	808.02
Arceneaux, Michael. *I Finally Bought Some Jordans*	306.76
Baker, Nicholson. *Finding a Likeness*	B
Baraka, Sho. *He Saw That It Was Good*	261.5
Benjamin, Ruha. ★*Imagination*	302
Black Thought. *The Upcycled Self*	B
Brandt, Anthony K. *The Runaway Species*	153.3
Cameron, Julia. *It's Never Too Late to Begin Again*	155.67
Cameron, Julia. ★*The Listening Path*	153.6
Cameron, Julia. *Living the Artist's Way*	153.3
Cep, Casey N. ★*Furious Hours*	364.152
Chayka, Kyle. *Filterworld*	306
Cott, Jonathan. *There's a Mystery There*	813
Crease, Robert P. *The Quantum Moment*	530.12
Epstein, David J. ★*Range*	153.9
Evaristo, Bernardine. *Manifesto*	B
Fall, Jeremy. *Falling Upwards*	158.1
Fox, Dan. *Pretentiousness*	700
Friedman, Rachel. ★*And Then We Grew Up*	305.24
Friedman, Ron. *Decoding Greatness*	650.1
Gabriel, Mary. *Madonna*	B
Gabriel, Mary. *Ninth Street Women*	920
Garcia, Mayte. *The Most Beautiful*	920
Gilbert, Elizabeth. ★*Big Magic*	153.3
Goldman, William. *Adventures in the Screen Trade*	384
Gopnik, Blake. ★*Warhol*	B
Gotch, Jen. *The Upside of Being Down*	B
Grant, Adam M. *Originals*	153.3
Greenberg, Sarah Stein. *Creative Acts for Curious People*	153.3
Griffin, Susan. *Out of Silence, Sound. Out of Nothing, Something*	808.02
Harford, Tim. *Messy*	153.3
Harvey, Samantha. *The Shapeless Unease*	B
Herzog, Werner. ★*Every Man for Himself and God Against All*	B
Hesse, Maria. ★*Frida Kahlo*	B
Hester, Diarmuid. *Nothing Ever Just Disappears*	306.76
Jones, Dylan. *David Bowie*	B
Kaplan, Janice. *The Genius of Women*	920
Lessig, Lawrence. *Remix*	346.7304
Livio, Mario. *Why?*	153.3
Lynch, David. *Room to Dream*	B
Max, D. T. *Finale*	782.1
McIlwaine, Catherine. *Tolkien*	002.09
Moore, Thurston. *Sonic Life*	B
Moss, Adam. ★*The Work of Art*	701
Mueller, Jennifer. *Creative Change*	658.4
Murakami, Haruki. ★*Novelist as a Vocation*	895.64
Nichtern, David. *Creativity, Spirituality & Making a Buck*	294.3
Niven, Penelope. *Thornton Wilder*	B
Okorafor, Nnedi. *Broken Places & Outer Spaces*	153.3
Oliver, Mary. ★*Upstream*	814
Parker, Kate T. *Strong Is the New Pretty*	155.43
Paul, Annie Murphy. *The Extended Mind*	128
Powers, Ann. ★*Traveling*	B
Remnick, David. *Holding the Note*	781.64
Rodsky, Eve. *Find Your Unicorn Space*	158.1
Rubin, Rick. ★*The Creative Act*	153.3
Rushdie, Salman. *Languages of Truth*	824
Schama, Simon. *The Power of Art*	709
Seal, Mark. ★*Leave the Gun, Take the Cannoli*	791.43
Seidelman, Susan. *Desperately Seeking Something*	B
Shlain, Tiffany. *24/6*	158.1
Slate, Jenny. *Little Weirds*	B
Slawenski, Kenneth. ★*Salinger*	B
Smith, Patti. ★*M Train*	B
Sonenshein, Scott. *Stretch*	153.3
Spiegel, Maura. *Sidney Lumet*	B
Suh, Krista. *DIY Rules for a WTF World*	158.1
Tan, Amy. ★*Where the Past Begins*	B
Tweedy, Jeff. *How to Write One Song*	782.42
Varol, Ozan O. *Think Like a Rocket Scientist*	650.1
Welty, Eudora. *One Writer's Beginnings*	B
Williams, Florence. *The Nature Fix*	155.9
Wilson, Brian. *I Am Brian Wilson*	B
Wood, Lawrence. *Your Caption Has Been Selected*	741.5
Zomorodi, Manoush. *Bored and Brilliant*	153.3

CREATIVITY IN ART

Baker, Nicholson. *Finding a Likeness*	B
Smith, Patti. ★*M Train*	B

CREATIVITY IN BUSINESS

Bahcall, Safi. *Loonshots*	658.4
Boden, Anne. *Female Founders' Playbook*	658.4
Godin, Seth. *The Practice*	153.3
Grant, Adam M. *Originals*	153.3
Isaacson, Walter. ★*Elon Musk*	B
Varol, Ozan O. *Think Like a Rocket Scientist*	650.1

CREATIVITY IN MUSIC

Thomas, Richard F. ★*Why Bob Dylan Matters*	782.42164

CREATIVITY IN SCIENCE

Shermer, Michael. *Why People Believe Weird Things*	133

Creativity, Spirituality & Making a Buck. Nichtern, David   294.3
Credible. Goodall, Amanda   658.4
Credible. Tuerkheimer, Deborah   363.25

CREDIT CARDS

Ariely, Dan. *Dollars and Sense*	332.024

CREE (EEYOU) (NORTH AMERICAN PEOPLE)

Belcourt, Billy-Ray. ★*A History of My Brief Body*	B
Metatawabin, Edmund. *Up Ghost River*	B
Sasakamoose, Fred. *Call Me Indian*	B

CREEK (MUSKOGEE) (NORTH AMERICAN PEOPLE)

Cozzens, Peter. *A Brutal Reckoning*	973.5
Gayle, Caleb. *We Refuse to Forget*	975.004
Harjo, Joy. *An American Sunrise*	811
Inskeep, Steve. *Jacksonland*	973.56

CREEK WAR, 1813-1814

Cozzens, Peter. *A Brutal Reckoning*	973.5
Inskeep, Steve. *Jacksonland*	973.56

Cregan, Mary
  The Scar   616.85

CREGAN, MARY

Cregan, Mary. *The Scar*	616.85

Creighton, Margaret S.
  The Electrifying Fall of Rainbow City   607

CREOLES (LOUISIANA)

Ball, Edward. *Life of a Klansman*	305.8009763

Crespino, Joseph
  Atticus Finch   B

CRETE

Fox, Margalit. *The Riddle of the Labyrinth*	920

Crews, Kenneth D.
  ★*Copyright Law for Librarians and Educators*   346.7304
★***Cribsheet***. Oster, Emily   618.2

CRICK, FRANCIS, 1916-2004

Markel, Howard. *The Secret of Life*	572.86

Crilley, Mark
  The Realism Challenge   751.4

CRIME

Bharara, Preet. *Doing Justice*	347.73
Bowden, Mark. *The Case of the Vanishing Blonde*	364.10973
Brettschneider, Corey Lang. *The Presidents and the People*	342.73
Fenton, Justin. *We Own This City*	364.1
Glatt, John. *Tangled Vines*	364.152
Harrington, Joel F. *The Faithful Executioner*	B
Hedges, Chris. *Days of Destruction, Days of Revolt*	741.5
Holes, Paul. *Unmasked*	363.25
Honig, Elie. *Untouchable*	364.1
Ice-T. *Split Decision*	920
Jager, Eric. *Blood Royal*	944.026
Keefe, Patrick Radden. ★*Rogues*	364.16
Kenda, Joe. *Killer Triggers*	364.152
Krist, Gary. *Empire of Sin*	976.3
Leerhsen, Charles. ★*Butch Cassidy*	B
Lowe, Keith. *Savage Continent*	940.55
Matney, Mandy. *Blood on Their Hands*	364.152
Oluseyi, Hakeem M. *A Quantum Life*	B
Pardlo, Gregory. *Spectral Evidence*	811
Rear, Rachel. *Catch the Sparrow*	364.152
Roth, Joseph. *What I Saw*	943
Schechter, Harold. ★*Ripped from the Headlines!*	791.43
Sebba, Anne. *Ethel Rosenberg*	B
Sered, Danielle. *Until We Reckon*	364.6
Shannon, Elaine. *Hunting Leroux*	364.1
Shaw, Bernard. *Major Barbara*	822
Stout, David. *The Kidnap Years*	364.15
Trejo, Danny. *Trejo*	B
Weinman, Sarah. *Scoundrel*	364.152

AUTHOR, TITLE, SERIES AND SUBJECT INDEX

CRIME AND RACE
    Crump, Benjamin. *Open Season* — 364
    Leovy, Jill. *Ghettoside* — 364.152

CRIME AND THE PRESS
    Craughwell, Thomas J. *Stealing Lincoln's Body* — 973.7092
    McGarrahan, Ellen. *Two Truths and a Lie* — 364.152

CRIME BOSSES
    Bair, Deirdre. *Al Capone* — B
    Carlo, Philip. *Gaspipe* — B
    Eig, Jonathan. *Get Capone* — 364.1
    English, T. J. *The Corporation* — 364.106089
    Gleeson, John. *The Gotti Wars* — 364.1
    Ratliff, Evan. *The Mastermind* — B
    Shannon, Elaine. *Hunting Leroux* — 364.1
    Sherman, Casey. *Hunting Whitey* — B

CRIME FORECASTING
    Burgess, Ann Wolbert. *A Killer by Design* — 364.3

CRIME IN THE NEWS MEDIA
    Guinn, Jeff. *Go Down Together* — B
    O'Connell, Mark. *A Thread of Violence* — 364.152

CRIME LABORATORIES
    Bass, William M. *Death's Acre* — 614
    Dawson, Kate Winkler. ★*American Sherlock* — B
    Fabricant, M. Chris. *Junk Science and the American Criminal Justice System* — 363.25

CRIME PREVENTION
    Bullough, Oliver. *Moneyland* — 364.1
    Dudley, Renee. *The Ransomware Hunting Team* — 363.25

CRIME SCENES
    Bonanos, Christopher. *Flash* — B
    Capote, Truman. ★*In Cold Blood* — 364.1
    Goldfarb, Bruce. ★*18 Tiny Deaths* — B
The Crimean War. Figes, Orlando — 947

CRIMEAN WAR, 1853-1856
    Bostridge, Mark. *Florence Nightingale* — B
    Figes, Orlando. *The Crimean War* — 947

CRIMES AGAINST AFRICAN AMERICANS
    Alexander, Elizabeth. ★*The Trayvon Generation* — 305.896
    Bailey, Issac J. *Why Didn't We Riot?* — 305.800973
    Blackmon, Douglas A. *Slavery by Another Name* — 305.896
    Currie, Elliott. *A Peculiar Indifference* — 305.800973
    Dray, Philip. *At the Hands of Persons Unknown* — 364.1
    Hawes, Jennifer. *Grace Will Lead Us Home* — 364.152
    Lane, Charles. *The Day Freedom Died* — 976.3
    Morrison, Melanie. *Murder on Shades Mountain* — 345.761
    Tyson, Timothy B. *Blood Done Sign My Name* — 975.6
    Tyson, Timothy B. *The Blood of Emmett Till* — 364.1
    Wilkie, Curtis. *When Evil Lived in Laurel* — 305.8

CRIMES AGAINST CHILDREN
    Lysiak, Matthew. *Newtown* — 371.7
    Roig-Debellis, Kaitlin. *Choosing Hope* — 371.7
    Standiford, Les. *Bringing Adam Home* — 364.15
    Williamson, Elizabeth. ★*Sandy Hook* — 364.152

CRIMES AGAINST GAY MEN AND LESBIANS
    Green, Elon. *Last Call* — 363.15

CRIMES AGAINST HUMANITY
    Childers, Thomas. *The Third Reich* — 943.086
    Igort. *The Ukrainian and Russian Notebooks* — 741.5
    Mackeen, Dawn Anahid. *The Hundred-Year Walk* — 956.6
    Newton, Michael A. *Enemy of the State* — 345.567
    Sands, Philippe. *East West Street* — 345
    Thant Myint-U. *The Hidden History of Burma* — 959.105

CRIMES AGAINST IMMIGRANTS
    Garrison, Jessica. *The Devil's Harvest* — B
    Walker, Ronald W. ★*Massacre at Mountain Meadows* — 979.2

CRIMES AGAINST PEOPLE
    Stryker, Kitty. *Ask* — 302

CRIMES AGAINST UNDOCUMENTED WORKERS
    Urrea, Luis Alberto. *The Devil's Highway* — 304.8

CRIMES AGAINST WOMEN
    Brodsky, Alexandra. *Sexual Justice* — 364.15
    Kristof, Nicholas D. *Half the Sky* — 362.83
    McNamara, Michelle. *I'll Be Gone in the Dark* — 364.152
    Miller, Chanel. *Know My Name* — B

CRIMINAL BEHAVIOR
    Dutta, Sunil. *Stealing Green Mangoes* — 973
    Franscell, Ron. *Shadowman* — 362.88
    Kean, Sam. *The Icepick Surgeon* — 509

    Monroe, Jana. *Hearts of Darkness* — 363.25

CRIMINAL COURTS
    Bogira, Steve. *Courtroom 302* — 345.773

CRIMINAL EVIDENCE
    Barron, Justine. *They Killed Freddie Gray* — 363.32
    Dawson, Kate Winkler. ★*American Sherlock* — B

CRIMINAL INVESTIGATION
    Bernstein, Carl. ★*All the President's Men* — 364.1
    Bowden, Mark. *The Case of the Vanishing Blonde* — 364.10973
    Cox, Joseph. *Dark Wire* — 363.2
    Dawson, Kate Winkler. ★*American Sherlock* — B
    Di Maio, Vincent J. M. *Morgue* — B
    Fabricant, M. Chris. *Junk Science and the American Criminal Justice System* — 363.25
    Faleiro, Sonia. *The Good Girls* — 364.152
    Finkel, Michael. *The Art Thief* — 364.1628
    Franscell, Ron. *Shadowman* — 362.88
    Goldfarb, Bruce. ★*18 Tiny Deaths* — B
    Holes, Paul. *Unmasked* — 363.25
    Hughes, Evan. *The Hard Sell* — 338.4
    Humes, Edward. *The Forever Witness* — 363.25
    Kenda, Joe. *Killer Triggers* — 364.152
    Kinstler, Linda. *Come to This Court and Cry* — 940.53
    McNamara, Michelle. *I'll Be Gone in the Dark* — 364.152
    Murdoch, Sierra Crane. ★*Yellow Bird* — 364.152
    Norton, Laurah. *Lay Them to Rest* — 363.25
    Rae-Venter, Barbara. *I Know Who You Are* — 364.152
    Sherman, Casey. *Hunting Whitey* — B
    Weinman, Sarah. ★*Unspeakable Acts* — 364.1

CRIMINAL JUDGMENTS
    Egan, Timothy. ★*A Fever in the Heartland* — 322.4

CRIMINAL JUSTICE PERSONNEL
    Bogira, Steve. *Courtroom 302* — 345.773

CRIMINAL JUSTICE POLICY
    Austen, Ben. *Correction* — 364.6
    Barnett, Brittany K. ★*A Knock at Midnight* — B
    Forman, James. *Locking up Our Own* — 364.973

CRIMINAL JUSTICE REFORM
    Barnett, Brittany K. ★*A Knock at Midnight* — B
    Fedderly, Eva. *These Walls* — 365
    Gross, Neil. *Walk the Walk* — 363.2
    Kaba, Mariame. *No More Police* — 363.2
    Messenger, Tony. *Profit and Punishment* — 362.5
    Miller, Reuben Jonathan. *Halfway Home* — 364.8
    Peterson, Marlon. *Bird Uncaged* — B
    Pratt, Victoria. *The Power of Dignity* — 364.973
    Raymond, Edwin. *An Inconvenient Cop* — 363.2
    Schwartz, Joanna C. ★*Shielded* — 344.7305

CRIMINAL JUSTICE SYSTEM
    Alexander, Michelle. *The New Jim Crow* — 364.973
    Austen, Ben. *Correction* — 364.6
    Balko, Radley. ★*The Cadaver King and the Country Dentist* — 614
    Barnett, Brittany K. ★*A Knock at Midnight* — B
    Bauer, Shane. *American Prison* — 365
    Bazelon, Emily. ★*Charged* — 345.73
    Belkin, Lisa. *Genealogy of a Murder* — 362.88
    Betts, Reginald Dwayne. ★*Redaction* — 704.9
    Bharara, Preet. *Doing Justice* — 347.73
    Bogira, Steve. *Courtroom 302* — 345.773
    Bookman, Marc. *A Descending Spiral* — 345.73
    Bowden, Mark. *Life Sentence* — 364.106
    Brodsky, Alexandra. *Sexual Justice* — 364.15
    Butler, Paul. *Chokehold* — 363.2
    Canon, Dan. ★*Pleading Out* — 345.73
    Chammah, Maurice. ★*Let the Lord Sort Them* — 364.66
    Coates, Laura Gayle. *Just Pursuit* — 345.73
    Davis, Angela Y. *Abolition* — 364.6
    Dudley, Steven S. *MS-13* — 364.106
    Dybdahl, Thomas L. *When Innocence Is Not Enough* — 345.73
    Eberhardt, Jennifer L. ★*Biased* — 303.3
    Eustace, Nicole. ★*Covered with Night* — 364.152
    Fedderly, Eva. *These Walls* — 365
    Feige, David. *Indefensible* — B
    Forman, James. *Locking up Our Own* — 364.973
    Gilliard, Dominique Dubois. *Rethinking Incarceration* — 261.8
    Gross, Neil. *Walk the Walk* — 363.2
    Hardin, Lara Love. ★*The Many Lives of Mama Love* — B
    Harrington, Joel F. *The Faithful Executioner* — B

PUBLIC LIBRARY CORE COLLECTION: NONFICTION
Twentieth Edition

Hayes, Christopher. *A Colony in a Nation*	364.3
Honig, Elie. *Untouchable*	364.1
Horton, Michelle. *Dear Sister*	B
Jackson, Bruce. *Never Far from Home*	B
Kaba, Mariame. *No More Police*	363.2
Kadri, Sadakat. *The Trial*	345
Manuel, Ian. *My Time Will Come*	B
Mar, Alex. *Seventy Times Seven*	362.88
McDiarmid, Jessica. *Highway of Tears*	364.152
Messenger, Tony. *Profit and Punishment*	362.5
Miller, Reuben Jonathan. *Halfway Home*	364.8
Minow, Martha. *When Should Law Forgive?*	345
Morton, Michael. *Getting Life*	B
Norton, Jack. *The Jail Is Everywhere*	365
Oshinsky, David M. *Worse Than Slavery*	365
Pratt, Victoria. *The Power of Dignity*	364.973
Ramsey, Donovan X. ★ *When Crack Was King*	362.29
Rapping, Jonathan. *Gideon's Promise*	345.73
Rear, Rachel. *Catch the Sparrow*	364.152
Rudolf, David S. *American Injustice*	345.73
Salaam, Yusef. *Better, Not Bitter*	B
Schwartz, Joanna C. ★ *Shielded*	344.7305
Sered, Danielle. *Until We Reckon*	364.6
Shahani, Aarti Namdev. *Here We Are*	B
Smith, Clive Stafford. *The Injustice System*	345.759
Smith, Mychal Denzel. *Stakes Is High*	973.933
Stevens, John Paul. *The Making of a Justice*	B
Stevenson, Bryan. *Just Mercy*	B
Taibbi, Matt. *I Can't Breathe*	363.2
Thompson, Heather Ann. *Blood in the Water*	365
Turow, Scott. ★ *Ultimate Punishment*	345.73
Woodfox, Albert. *Solitary*	B
Zerwick, Phoebe. *Beyond Innocence*	347

CRIMINAL LAW
Canon, Dan. ★ *Pleading Out*	345.73
Goldberg, Carrie. *Nobody's Victim*	345.73
Stone, Geoffrey R. ★ *Sex and the Constitution*	345.7302

CRIMINAL PROCEDURE
Harrington, Joel F. *The Faithful Executioner*	B

CRIMINAL PROFILERS
Douglas, John E. *When a Killer Calls*	364.152
Monroe, Jana. *Hearts of Darkness*	363.25

CRIMINAL PROFILING
Burgess, Ann Wolbert. *A Killer by Design*	364.3
Douglas, John E. *The Killer Across the Table*	B
Franscell, Ron. *Shadowman*	362.88

CRIMINAL PSYCHOLOGY
Douglas, John E. *The Killer Across the Table*	B
Franscell, Ron. *Shadowman*	362.88

CRIMINALS
Bair, Deirdre. *Al Capone*	B
Betts, Reginald Dwayne. *Felon*	811
Bogira, Steve. *Courtroom 302*	345.773
Cameron, Silver Donald. *Blood in the Water*	364.152
Capote, Truman. ★ *In Cold Blood*	364.1
Carlo, Philip. *Gaspipe*	B
Diamond, Cheryl. *Nowhere Girl*	B
Dolin, Eric Jay. *Black Flags, Blue Waters*	973.2
Eig, Jonathan. *Get Capone*	364.1
English, T. J. *The Corporation*	364.106089
Ford, Elizabeth. *Sometimes Amazing Things Happen*	B
Fox, Margalit. *The Talented Mrs. Mandelbaum*	364.1
Gaffney, Ginger. *Half Broke*	B
Guinn, Jeff. *Go Down Together*	B
Guinn, Jeff. ★ *Manson*	B
Hardy, Jason Matthew. ★ *The Second Chance Club*	364.6
Harman, Claire. *Murder by the Book*	364.152
Ice-T. *Split Decision*	920
Keefe, Patrick Radden. ★ *Rogues*	364.16
Kizzia, Tom. *Pilgrim's Wilderness*	B
Leerhsen, Charles. ★ *Butch Cassidy*	B
Levin, Daniel Barban. *Slonim Woods 9*	B
Ratliff, Evan. *The Mastermind*	B
Rule, Ann. *The Stranger Beside Me*	B
Sered, Danielle. *Until We Reckon*	364.6
Shannon, Elaine. *Hunting Leroux*	364.1
Wetherall, Tyler. *No Way Home*	B
Wilson, Chris. *The Master Plan*	B

Cringeworthy. Dahl, Melissa	158.2
Crisis in the Red Zone. Preston, Richard	614.5

CRISIS INTERVENTION
Ripley, Amanda. *The Unthinkable*	155.9
Tweedy, Damon. *Facing the Unseen*	362.2

CRISIS MANAGEMENT
Diamond, Jared M. *Upheaval*	303.48
Eggers, Dave. *Zeitoun*	305.892
Goodwin, Doris Kearns. ★ *Leadership in Turbulent Times*	973.09
Graff, Garrett M. *Raven Rock*	363.350973
Hoffman, Liz. *Crash Landing*	330
Rubin, Robert Edward. *The Yellow Pad*	658.4
Stephanopoulos, George. ★ *The Situation Room*	973.09
Thenell, Jan. *The Library's Crisis Communications Planner*	021.7

CRISIS MANAGEMENT IN GOVERNMENT
Stephanopoulos, George. ★ *The Situation Room*	973.09
Crisis of Conscience. Mueller, Tom	364.16
★ *The Crisis of Democratic Capitalism*. Wolf, Martin	330.12

Crispin, Jessa
★ *The Creative Tarot*	133.3

CRISPR (GENETICS)
Isaacson, Walter. ★ *The Code Breaker*	576.5

Cristofano, Jana
Eat Well, Be Well	641.5

CRITICAL CARE
Ely, Wes. *Every Deep-Drawn Breath*	616.02
Lamas, Daniela J. *You Can Stop Humming Now*	616.02
Critical Companion to Maya Angelou. Thursby, Jacqueline S.	818
Critical Companion to Ralph Waldo Emerson. Wayne, Tiffany K.	814
Critical Companion to Toni Morrison. Gillespie, Carmen	813
Critical Companion to Zora Neale Hurston. Jones, Sharon L.	813
A *Critical* issue [Series]. Daniels, Roger	940.53

CRITICAL RACE THEORY
Ray, Victor. *On Critical Race Theory*	305.8

CRITICAL THINKING
Grant, Adam M. ★ *Think Again*	153.4
Kasparov, G. K. *Deep Thinking*	006.3
Kethledge, Raymond Michael. *Lead Yourself First*	658.4
LaGarde, Jennifer. *Fact vs. Fiction*	370.15
Levine, Madeline. ★ *Ready or Not*	649
Levitin, Daniel J. ★ *A Field Guide to Lies*	153.4
Lyons, Daniel. *STFU*	302.2
Morrison, Toni. ★ *The Source of Self-Regard*	814
Nye, Bill. *Everything All at Once*	153.4
Pinker, Steven. *Rationality*	153.4
Wolf, Maryanne. *Reader, Come Home*	418

CRITICISM
Baldick, Chris. ★ *The Oxford Dictionary of Literary Terms*	803
Moore, Lorrie. *See What Can Be Done*	801
Ozick, Cynthia. *Critics, Monsters, Fanatics, and Other Literary Essays*	801
Wilde, Oscar. *The Artist as Critic*	809

CRITICS
Caldwell, Gail. *Let's Take the Long Way Home*	B
Ebert, Roger. *Life Itself*	B
Gates, Henry Louis. *Colored People*	B
Gordon, Lyndall. ★ *T.S. Eliot*	B
hooks, bell. *Remembered Rapture*	808
Kakutani, Michiko. *Ex Libris*	028
Nussbaum, Emily. *I Like to Watch*	791.45
Critics, Monsters, Fanatics, and Other Literary Essays. Ozick, Cynthia	801
Crochet Animal Rugs. Rott, Ira	746.7
The Crochet Answer Book. Eckman, Edie	746.43
Crochet Therapy. Corkhill, Betsan	746.43
Crochet, Learn It. Love It. Todhunter, Tracey	746.43
The Crocheter's Skill-Building Workshop. Ohrenstein, Dora	746.43

CROCHETING
Abbondio, Sarah. *Mini Amigurumi Animals*	746.43
Baca, Salena. *Oversize Fashion Crochet*	746.43
Bergstrom, Lauren. *Cute & Cuddly Crochet*	746.43
Bergstrom, Lauren. *Mini Crochet Creatures*	746.43
Chachula, Robyn. *Unexpected Afghans*	746.43
Corkhill, Betsan. *Crochet Therapy*	746.43
Crowfoot, Jane. *Ultimate Crochet Bible*	746.43
Eaton, Jan. *350+ Crochet Tips, Techniques, and Trade Secrets*	746.432
Eckman, Edie. *Around the Corner Crochet Borders*	746.43
Eckman, Edie. *Beyond the Square Crochet Motifs*	746.43
Eckman, Edie. *Connect the Shapes Crochet Motifs*	746.43
Eckman, Edie. *The Crochet Answer Book*	746.43

AUTHOR, TITLE, SERIES AND SUBJECT INDEX

Green-Hite, Vincent. *Knot Bad Amigurumi* — 746.43
Gullberg, Maria. *Tapestry Crochet and More* — 746.43
Hatchard, Gurinder Kaur. *Hooked on Shakespeare* — 746.43
Hubert, Margaret. *10 Granny Squares, 30 Blankets* — 746.43
Hubert, Margaret. *The Complete Photo Guide to Crochet* — 746.43
Hubert, Margaret. *The Granny Square Book* — 746.43
Knight, Erika. *500 Crochet Stitches* — 746.43
Mullett-Bowlsby, Shannon. ★*Complete Crochet Course* — 746.43
Ohrenstein, Dora. *The Crocheter's Skill-Building Workshop* — 746.43
Righetti, Maggie. *Crocheting in Plain English* — 746.43
Rott, Ira. *Crochet Animal Rugs* — 746.7
Stanfield, Lesley. *100 Flowers to Knit & Crochet* — 746.43
Todhunter, Tracey. *Crochet, Learn It. Love It.* — 746.43
Werker, Kim P. *Teach Yourself Visually Crochet* — 746.43
Crocheting in Plain English. Righetti, Maggie
Crocker, Betty
  ★*Betty Crocker Cookbook* — 641.5
CROCKETT, DARTANYON
  Fenn, Lisa. *Carry On* — B
Croke, Ken
  Riding with Evil — 364.106
CROKE, KEN
  Croke, Ken. *Riding with Evil* — 364.106
Croke, Vicki
  The Lady and the Panda — 599.789
CROMWELL, OLIVER, 1599-1658
  Ackroyd, Peter. *Rebellion* — 941.06
CROMWELL, THOMAS, EARL OF ESSEX, 1485?-1540
  Borman, Tracy. *Thomas Cromwell* — B
  MacCulloch, Diarmaid. *Thomas Cromwell* — B
★*Cronkite*. Brinkley, Douglas — B
Cronkite's War. Cronkite, Walter — 070.4
CRONKITE, BETSY, -2005
  Cronkite, Walter. *Cronkite's War* — 070.4
Cronkite, Walter
  Cronkite's War — 070.4
  A Reporter's Life — B
CRONKITE, WALTER
  Brinkley, Douglas. ★*Cronkite* — B
  Cronkite, Walter. *Cronkite's War* — 070.4
  Cronkite, Walter. *A Reporter's Life* — B
CROONING
  Giddins, Gary. *Bing Crosby* — B
  Giddins, Gary. *Bing Crosby* — B
CROPS AND CLIMATE
  Frankopan, Peter. *The Earth Transformed* — 304.2
CROSBY, BING, 1904-1977
  Giddins, Gary. *Bing Crosby* — B
  Giddins, Gary. *Bing Crosby* — B
Crosby, Molly Caldwell
  The American Plague — 614.5
Crosby, Stills, Nash and Young. Browne, David — 920
Crosley, Sloane
  Grief Is for People — B
  I Was Told There'd Be Cake — 814
  ★*Look Alive Out There* — 814
CROSLEY, SLOANE
  Crosley, Sloane. *Grief Is for People* — B
  Crosley, Sloane. *I Was Told There'd Be Cake* — 814
  Crosley, Sloane. ★*Look Alive Out There* — 814
★*Cross of Snow*. Basbanes, Nicholas A. — B
CROSS, BARTON, 1918-1945
  Freeman, Sally Mott. *The Jersey Brothers* — 920
Cross, Charles R.
  Here We Are Now — 782.42166
  Room Full of Mirrors — B
Cross, Kim
  In Light of All Darkness — 363.25
Cross, Tiffany D.
  ★*Say It Louder!* — 324.6
Cross, William R.
  Winslow Homer — 759.13
CROSS-COUNTRY AUTOMOBILE TRIPS
  Hall, Alvin D. *Driving the Green Book* — 917.304
  Heat Moon, William Least. *Blue Highways* — 917.304
  Jaouad, Suleika. ★*Between Two Kingdoms* — B
CROSS-COUNTRY RUNNERS
  Wade, Becky. *Run the World* — 796.42

CROSS-COUNTRY RUNNING
  Finn, Adharanand. *The Rise of the Ultra Runners* — B
  Wade, Becky. *Run the World* — 796.42
CROSS-CULTURAL STUDIES
  Damrosch, David. *Around the World in 80 Books* — 809
  Iyer, Pico. ★*The Half Known Life* — 203
Crossing The River. Smith, Carol — B
Crossings. Goldfarb, Ben — 333.77
Crosson, Monica
  The Magikal Family — 299
Crosstown Traffic. Murray, Charles Shaar — B
Crouch, Gregory
  The Bonanza King — B
Crouch, Stanley
  Kansas City Lightning — B
Crouse, Karen
  Norwich — 796
CROW (APSÁALOOKE) (NORTH AMERICAN PEOPLE)
  Colton, Larry. *Counting Coup* — 796.323
  Grathwohl, Marya. *This Wheel of Rocks* — 271
Crowe, Lauren Goldstein
  The Towering World of Jimmy Choo — 391.4
Crowell, Rodney
  Chinaberry Sidewalks — B
CROWELL, RODNEY
  Crowell, Rodney. *Chinaberry Sidewalks* — B
Crowfoot, Jane
  Ultimate Crochet Bible — 746.43
Crowley, Bill
  Defending Professionalism — 020.92
Crowley, Chris
  Younger Next Year — 613
Crowley, Roger
  1453 — 949.61
  City of Fortune — 945
Crown & Sceptre. Borman, Tracy — 941
Crown of Blood. Tallis, Nicola — B
Crowther, Gail
  Three-Martini Afternoons at the Ritz — 920
Crowther, Janet
  Make a Statement — 745.594
Crucible of Command. Davis, William C. — 920
Crude World. Maass, Peter — 338.2
CRUELTY
  Hoock, Holger. *Scars of Independence* — 973.3
  King, Charles. *Odessa* — 947.7
Cruikshank, Tiffany
  Meditate Your Weight — 613.2
CRUISE SHIPS
  Larson, Erik. ★*Dead Wake* — 940.4
  Smith, Michael. *Cabin Fever* — 614.5
Crumb, R.
  R. Crumb — 741.6
CRUMB, R.
  Crumb, R. *R. Crumb* — 741.6
Crump, Benjamin
  Open Season — 364
CRUMP, BENJAMIN, 1969-
  Crump, Benjamin. *Open Season* — 364
CRUMPLER, REBECCA LEE, 1835-1895
  Brown, Jasmine. *Twice as Hard* — 610.92
Crusaders. Jones, Dan — 909.07
CRUSADERS (MIDDLE AGES)
  Haag, Michael. *The Tragedy of the Templars* — 271.7913
  Jones, Dan. *The Templars* — 271
★*The Crusades*. Asbridge, Thomas S. — 909.07
CRUSADES
  Asbridge, Thomas S. ★*The Crusades* — 909.07
  Frankopan, Peter. *The First Crusade* — 956
  Haag, Michael. *The Tragedy of the Templars* — 271.7913
  Jones, Dan. *Crusaders* — 909.07
  Jones, Dan. *The Templars* — 271
  Lambert, Malcolm. *God's Armies* — 956
The Crusades of Cesar Chavez. Pawel, Miriam — B
CRUSHES
  Carson, Anne. *Autobiography of Red* — 811
Crushing It! Vaynerchuk, Gary — 650.1

PUBLIC LIBRARY CORE COLLECTION: NONFICTION
Twentieth Edition

CRUSTACEA
   Nicolson, Adam. *Life Between the Tides* — 577.69
Crutchfield, James A.
   Revolt at Taos — 972
Cry Havoc. Signer, Michael — 305.800973
★*Crying in H Mart.* Zauner, Michelle — B
Crying in the Bathroom. Sanchez, Erika L. — B
CRYPTOCURRENCIES
   Greenberg, Andy. *Tracers in the Dark* — 364.16
   Lewis, Michael. ★*Going Infinite* — 305.5
   Small, Zachary. ★*Token Supremacy* — 332.4
CRYPTOGRAPHERS
   Fagone, Jason. *The Woman Who Smashed Codes* — B
   Mundy, Liza. *Code Girls* — 940.54
CRYPTOGRAPHY
   Budiansky, Stephen. *Code Warriors* — 327.73047
   Copeland, B. Jack. *Turing* — B
   Fagone, Jason. *The Woman Who Smashed Codes* — B
   McKay, Sinclair. *The Secret Lives of Codebreakers* — 940.54
   Mundy, Liza. *Code Girls* — 940.54
   Nez, Chester. *Code Talker* — B
   Price, David A. *Geniuses at War* — 940.54
CRYPTOZOOLOGY
   Dickey, Colin. *The Unidentified* — 130
   Loxton, Daniel. *Abominable Science!* — 001.944
   O'Connor, John. *The Secret History of Bigfoot* — 001.944
Crystal, David
   ★*English as a Global Language* — 427
   ★*How Language Works* — 410
   Spell It Out — 421
   ★*The Stories of English* — 427
   The Story of English in 100 Words — 422
★*Cuba.* Ferrer, Ada — 972.91
CUBA
   Butler, Brin-Jonathan. *The Domino Diaries* — 796.83
   Castro, Fidel. *Fidel Castro* — B
   Coleman, David G. *The Fourteenth Day* — 973.922092
   Coltman, Leycester. *The Real Fidel Castro* — B
   Craig, William. *Yankee Come Home* — 972.9107
   DePalma, Anthony. *The Cubans* — 920
   Ferrer, Ada. ★*Cuba* — 972.91
   Guevara, Che. *Diary of a Combatant* — 972.91063
   Guillermoprieto, Alma. *Dancing with Cuba* — 972.9106
   Hoffman, David E. *Give Me Liberty* — B
   Kennedy, Robert F. *Thirteen Days* — 327.73
   Maier, Thomas. *Mafia Spies* — 364.1060973
   Plokhy, Serhii. ★*Nuclear Folly* — 972.9106
   Rasenberger, Jim. *The Brilliant Disaster* — 972.9106
   Rathbone, John Paul. *The Sugar King of Havana* — B
   Sallah, Michael. *The Yankee Comandante* — 972.91
   Sherman, Casey. *Above and Beyond* — 973.922092
   Szablowski, Witold. *Dancing Bears* — 947.086
CUBAN AMERICANS
   Armas, Kat. *Abuelita Faith* — 248.8
   Eire, Carlos M. N. *Learning to Die in Miami* — B
   English, T. J. *The Corporation* — 364.106089
   Hernandez, Daisy. *A Cup of Water Under My Bed* — B
CUBAN MISSILE CRISIS, 1962
   Coleman, David G. *The Fourteenth Day* — 973.922092
   Hastings, Max. *The Abyss* — 972.9106
   Plokhy, Serhii. ★*Nuclear Folly* — 972.9106
   Sherman, Casey. *Above and Beyond* — 973.922092
   Sherwin, Martin J. *Gambling with Armageddon* — 972.9106
   Sorensen, Theodore C. *Counselor* — B
CUBAN PEOPLE IN THE UNITED STATES
   English, T. J. *The Corporation* — 364.106089
The Cuban Table. Pelaez, Ana Sofia — 641.597291
The Cubans. DePalma, Anthony — 920
CUBISM
   Unger, Miles. *Picasso and the Painting That Shocked the World* — 759.4
   Warren, Rosanna. *Max Jacob* — B
★*Cucina Povera.* Scarpaleggia, Giulia — 641.594
Cuckoo. Davies, N. B. — 598.7
CUCKOOS
   Davies, N. B. *Cuckoo* — 598.7
Cuddy, Amy
   Presence — 158.1
Cue the Sun! Nussbaum, Emily — 791.45

CUKURS, HERBERT, 1900-1965
   Talty, Stephan. *The Good Assassin* — 364.15
Cullen, Art
   Storm Lake — 071.7
CULLEN, ART
   Cullen, Art. *Storm Lake* — 071.7
Cullen, David
   Columbine — 373
   Parkland — 371.7
Cullen, Kevin
   Whitey Bulger — B
CULT FILMS
   Hendrix, Grady. *These Fists Break Bricks* — 791
   Schechter, Harold. ★*Ripped from the Headlines!* — 791.43
CULT LEADERS
   Cook, Kevin. *Waco Rising* — 299
   Cutler, Max. *Cults* — 364.15
   Jones, Faith. *Sex Cult Nun* — B
CULT MEMBERS
   Berman, Sarah. *Don't Call It a Cult* — 361.4
   Cutler, Max. *Cults* — 364.15
   Hough, Lauren. *Leaving Isn't the Hardest Thing* — B
   Jones, Faith. *Sex Cult Nun* — B
   Young, Daniella Mestyanek. *Uncultured* — B
The Cult of We. Brown, Eliot — 333.33
Cultivating Civility. Henry, Jo — 023
Cultivating Garden Style. Greayer, Rochelle — 712
Cults. Cutler, Max — 364.15
CULTS
   Berman, Sarah. *Don't Call It a Cult* — 361.4
   Cook, Kevin. *Waco Rising* — 299
   Cutler, Max. *Cults* — 364.15
   Guinn, Jeff. *The Road to Jonestown* — 289.9
   Hough, Lauren. *Leaving Isn't the Hardest Thing* — B
   Jollett, Mikel. ★*Hollywood Park* — B
   Jones, Faith. *Sex Cult Nun* — B
   Kizzia, Tom. *Pilgrim's Wilderness* — B
   Lake, Dianne. *Member of the Family* — 364.152
   Levin, Daniel Barban. *Slonim Woods 9* — B
   Lewis, James R. *Legitimating New Religions* — 200
   Stille, Alexander. *The Sullivanians* — 307.77
   Wariner, Ruth. *The Sound of Gravel* — B
   Wiehl, Lis W. *Hunting Charles Manson* — 364.152
   Young, Daniella Mestyanek. *Uncultured* — B
CULTURAL APPROPRIATION
   Ford, Tanisha C. *Dressed in Dreams* — 391
   Gaddy, K. R. ★*Well of Souls* — 787
   Gilliam, Fatimah. *Race Rules* — 305.8
   Oluo, Ijeoma. *So You Want to Talk About Race* — 305.800973
CULTURAL DIFFERENCES
   Bryson, Bill. *The Road to Little Dribbling* — 914
   Collins, Lauren. *When in French* — B
   Dodds Pennock, Caroline. ★*On Savage Shores* — 970.004
   Fadiman, Anne. *The Spirit Catches You and You Fall Down* — 306.4
   Ferrer, Ada. ★*Cuba* — 972.91
   Fishman, Elly. *Refugee High* — 370.8
   Geter, Hafizah. *Un-American* — 811
   Horwitz, Tony. *Spying on the South* — 917
   Kois, Dan. *How to Be a Family* — 910.4
   Mahjoub, Jamal. *A Line in the River* — 962.404
   Nimura, Janice P. *Daughters of the Samurai* — 920
   Norris, Michele. ★*Our Hidden Conversations* — 305
   Sedaris, David. ★*A Carnival of Snackery* — 818
   Wagner, Alex. *Futureface* — B
   Wilson, Katherine. *Only in Naples* — B
CULTURAL DIFFUSION
   Diamond, Jared M. *Guns, Germs, and Steel* — 303.4
CULTURAL FUSION
   Dusoulier, Clotilde. *Tasting Paris* — 641.594
CULTURAL INDUSTRY AND TRADE
   Lessig, Lawrence. *Remix* — 346.7304
CULTURAL PROPERTY
   Adams, Mark. *Turn Right at Machu Picchu* — 985
   Edsel, Robert M. *The Monuments Men* — 940.53
   Fishman, David E. *The Book Smugglers* — 940.53
   Hammer, Joshua. *The Bad-Ass Librarians of Timbuktu* — 025.8
   Heaney, Christopher. *Cradle of Gold* — B
   Mooallem, Jon. *Wild Ones* — 333.95

AUTHOR, TITLE, SERIES AND SUBJECT INDEX

CULTURAL RELATIONS
Hansen, Valerie. *The Year 1000*	909
Husain, Ed. ★*The House of Islam*	297
The **Cultural** *Revolution*. Dikotter, Frank	951.056

CULTURE
Acocella, Joan Ross. ★*The Bloodied Nightgown*	814
Atwood, Margaret. *Burning Questions*	814
Ayers, Edward L. *American Visions*	973.5
Barnes, Julian. *The Man in the Red Coat*	B
Boyle, Rebecca. *Our Moon*	523.3
Campbell, Hayley. *All the Living and the Dead*	363.7
Chayka, Kyle. *Filterworld*	306
Chisholm, Edward. *A Waiter in Paris*	B
Crampton, Caroline. *A Body Made of Glass*	616.85
De Bres, Helena. *How to Be Multiple*	155.44
Dikotter, Frank. *China After Mao*	951.05
Ditum, Sarah. *Toxic*	920.72
Ellison, Ralph. ★*The Collected Essays of Ralph Ellison*	814
Feast, Fancy. *Naked*	792.7
Feldman, Noah. ★*To Be a Jew Today*	296.3
Findakly, Brigitte. *Poppies of Iraq*	741.5
Foster, Charles. *Being a Human*	155.7
Foster, Lynn V. *A Brief History of Mexico*	972
Fuentes, Carlos. *The Buried Mirror*	946
Gay, Roxane. *Bad Feminist*	814
Goldsworthy, Adrian Keith. *Pax Romana*	937
Gross, Neil. *Walk the Walk*	363.2
Harris, Mark. *Pictures at a Revolution*	791.43
Hirst, J. B. *The Shortest History of Europe*	940
Hough, Stephen. *Rough Ideas*	786.2092
Hoyer, Katja. ★*Beyond the Wall*	943.087
Hurston, Zora Neale. ★*You Don't Know Us Negroes and Other Essays*	814
Huxley, Aldous. ★*Brave New World Revisited*	823
Iyer, Pico. *A Beginner's Guide to Japan*	952.05
Jebara, Mohamad. ★*The Life of the Qur'an*	297.122
Joyce, Patrick. *Remembering Peasants*	305.5
Jun, Tasha. ★*Tell Me the Dream Again*	248
Kassabova, Kapka. *Border*	949.9
Kattan, Fadi. ★*Bethlehem*	641.59
Kenan, Randall. *Black Folk Could Fly*	813
Khan, Yasmin. ★*Zaitoun*	641.595
Kingsley, Lisa. *Smithsonian American Table*	641.5
Klein, Naomi. ★*Doppelganger*	302.2
Kohli, Sahaj Kaur. ★*But What Will People Say?*	616.89
Leland, Andrew. ★*The Country of the Blind*	B
Liu, Simu. ★*We Were Dreamers*	B
Lorenz, Taylor. ★*Extremely Online*	302.23
MacGregor, Neil. *Germany*	943
Marchant, Jo. *The Human Cosmos*	523.1
Marx, W. David. ★*Status and Culture*	305
Mayes, Frances. *See You in the Piazza*	914.5
McGrath, Tom. *Triumph of the Yuppies*	305.242
McKay, Sinclair. *Berlin*	943
Meals, Roy A. *Bones*	599.9
Mikanowski, Jacob. ★*Goodbye, Eastern Europe*	947
Montell, Amanda. ★*The Age of Magical Overthinking*	153.4
Myers, Leah. *Thinning Blood*	B
Nelson, Maggie. ★*Like Love*	814
Nezhukumatathil, Aimee. *Bite by Bite*	641.3
Oakes, John G. H. ★*The Fast*	613.2
Olivarez, Jose. *Promises of Gold = Promesas De Oro*	811
Orth, Stephan. *Couchsurfing in Iran*	955.06
Parker, Morgan. ★*You Get What You Pay For*	305.896
Perlin, Ross. ★*Language City*	306.44
Perry, Imani. ★*South to America*	917
Pipher, Mary Bray. *A Life in Light*	B
Rady, Martyn C. *The Middle Kingdoms*	943
Rothfeld, Becca. ★*All Things Are Too Small*	814
Rubenstein, David M. *The American Experiment*	973
Safina, Carl. *Becoming Wild*	591.7
Saldana, Stephanie. *What We Remember Will Be Saved*	362.7
Santos Perez, Craig. *From Unincorporated Territory [amot]*	811
Savage, Jon. ★*1966*	781.6609
Schneier, Bruce. *A Hacker's Mind*	364.16
Schulman, Michael. ★*Oscar Wars*	791.43
Sciolino, Elaine. *The Only Street in Paris*	944
Sciolino, Elaine. *The Seine*	944
Sebestyen, Victor. *Budapest*	943.912
Sharif, Solmaz. *Customs*	811
Sinclair, Safiya. ★*How to Say Babylon*	B
Smyth, Adam. *The Book-Makers*	686.2
Soyinka, Wole. *Of Africa*	960
Specter, Emma. *More, Please*	616.85
Stanley, Amy. *Stranger in the Shogun's City*	B
Tallis, Frank. ★*Mortal Secrets*	B
Taplin, Jonathan. *Move Fast and Break Things*	330.9
Tobar, Hector. ★*Our Migrant Souls*	305.868
Tolentino, Jia. ★*Trick Mirror*	973.93
Trentmann, Frank. *Out of the Darkness*	943.08
Turvey, Samuel. ★*The Tomb of the Mili Mongga*	398.24
Vince, Gaia. *Transcendence*	599.93
Von Bremzen, Anya. *National Dish*	641.3
Walvin, James. *Sugar*	338.17361
Way, Niobe. *Rebels with a Cause*	649
Wickham, Chris. *The Inheritance of Rome*	940.1
Wilbur, Matika. *Project 562*	970.004
Wilson, Jessica. *It's Always Been Ours*	613
Wragg Sykes, Rebecca. *Kindred*	569.9
Wright, Lawrence. *God Save Texas*	917.64
Yong, Sable. *Die Hot with a Vengeance*	646.7

CULTURE AND CUSTOMS — ASIA AND THE SOUTH PACIFIC — CHINA
Self, Caroline. *Chinese Brush Painting*	751.4

CULTURE AND GLOBALIZATION
Figes, Orlando. *The Europeans*	920

CULTURE CONFLICT
Berkshire, Jennifer. *The Education Wars*	371.01
Blanco, Richard. *The Prince of Los Cocuyos*	B
Brands, H. W. *Dreams of El Dorado*	978
Dalrymple, William. *The Return of a King*	958.1
Demick, Barbara. *Eat the Buddha*	951
Friedman, George. *Flashpoints*	940.56
Goodheart, Adam. *The Last Island*	954
Hanes, Stephanie. *White Man's Game*	333.95
Howe, Ben Ryder. *My Korean Deli*	B
Johnson, Akemi. *Night in the American Village*	305.40952
Kassabova, Kapka. *Border*	949.9
Moore, Susanna. *Paradise of the Pacific*	996.9
Mort, T. A. *Thieves' Road*	978.3
Myers, Leah. *Thinning Blood*	B
Nawaz, Zarqa. *Laughing All the Way to the Mosque*	791.45028
Nimura, Janice P. *Daughters of the Samurai*	920
Price, David A. ★*Love and Hate in Jamestown*	975.5
Rehman, Sabeeha. *Threading My Prayer Rug*	305.8
Sebag-Montefiore, Simon. *Jerusalem*	956.94
Shapiro, James. ★*The Playbook*	792
Taffa, Deborah Jackson. ★*Whiskey Tender*	B
Thomas, Louisa. *Louisa*	B

CULTURE SHOCK
Abdelmahmoud, Elamin. *Son of Elsewhere*	B
Cultures of War. Dower, John W.	355.00973

Cumings, Bruce
The Korean War	951.904

Cumming, Alan
Baggage	B

CUMMING, ALAN, 1965-
Cumming, Alan. *Baggage*	B

Cumming, Laura
★*The Vanishing Velazquez*	759.6

Cumming, Robert
Art	700

CUMMINGS, BRENT
Finkel, David. *An American Dreamer*	975.8

Cummings, E. E.
★*Complete Poems, 1904-1962*	811

CUMMINGS, E. E. (EDWARD ESTLIN), 1894-1962
Rosenblitt, J. Alison. *The Beauty of Living*	B

Cummings, Elijah
★*We're Better Than This*	B

CUMMINGS, ELIJAH
Cummings, Elijah. ★*We're Better Than This*	B

Cunningham, Benjamin
The Liar	327.1273

CUNNINGHAM, MERCE, 1919-2009
Brown, Carolyn. *Chance and Circumstance*	B

PUBLIC LIBRARY CORE COLLECTION: NONFICTION
Twentieth Edition

Cunningham, William J.
   ★*Fashion Climbing*   B
CUNNINGHAM, WILLIAM J.
   Cunningham, William J. ★*Fashion Climbing*   B
The Cup of Coffee Club. Kornhauser, Jacob   796.357
A Cup of Water Under My Bed. Hernandez, Daisy   B
CUPCAKES
   Nelson, Candace. *The Sprinkles Baking Book*   641.81
   Saltz, Joanna. ★*Delish Insane Sweets*   641.81
Cupp, Lundy
   Realistic Pumpkin Carving   745.5941646
CURANDERISMO
   Rojas Contreras, Ingrid. ★*The Man Who Could Move Clouds*   B
Cure. Marchant, Jo   616.89
★*A Cure for Darkness*. Riley, Alex   616.85
Cured. Holt, Nathalia   614.5
Curfewed Night. Peer, Basharat   B
CURIOSITIES AND WONDERS
   Carlsen, Spike. *A Walk Around the Block*   031
   Dasal, Jennifer. *Artcurious*   709
   Dickey, Colin. *Ghostland*   133.1
   Dickey, Colin. *The Unidentified*   130
   Foer, Joshua. *Atlas Obscura*   910.41
   Foer, Joshua. ★*Atlas Obscura 2nd Ed.*   910.41
   Graff, Garrett M. *UFO*   001.942
   Preston, Douglas J. *The Lost Tomb*   930.1
   Prothero, Donald R. *UFOs, Chemtrails, and Aliens*   001.94
   Scoles, Sarah. *They Are Already Here*   001.942
   Smith, Richard MacLean. *Unexplained*   130
   Tyson, Neil deGrasse. *Cosmic Queries*   523.1
   Wong, Cecily. ★*Gastro Obscura*   641.3
CURIOSITIES, MARVELS, AND WONDERS — MYTHICAL PLACES AND BEINGS
   Guiley, Rosemary. *The Encyclopedia of Demons and Demonology*   133.4
CURIOSITY
   Benjamin, Ruha. ★*Imagination*   302
   Leland, Andrew. ★*The Country of the Blind*   B
   Levine, Madeline. ★*Ready or Not*   649
   Li, Fei-Fei. *The Worlds I See*   B
   Livio, Mario. *Why?*   153.3
   McAfee, Andrew. *The Geek Way*   658.3
   McPhee, John. *Tabula Rasa; V.1*   818
   Schneider, Amy. *In the Form of a Question*   B
Curious Behavior. Provine, Robert R.   152.3
Curl, Jami
   Candy Is Magic   641.85
Curran, Andrew S.
   Diderot and the Art of Thinking Freely   194
CURRENT EVENTS
   Kristof, Nicholas D. ★*Chasing Hope*   B
   Napoli, Lisa. *Up All Night*   384.55
   Petri, Alexandra. *Nothing Is Wrong and Here Is Why*   973.933
   Smith, Ben. *Traffic*   070.4
   Smith, Zadie. *Intimations*   824
Current, Austin
   Science of Strength Training   613.7
CURRICULUM PLANNING
   Baker, Nicholson. *Substitute*   371.14
   Hughes-Hassell, Sandra. ★*Collection Management for Youth*   025.2
Currid-Halkett, Elizabeth
   The Overlooked Americans   307.76
Currie, Elliott
   A Peculiar Indifference   305.800973
Curry. Collingham, E. M.   394.1
Curry, Kevin
   Fit Men Cook   641.5
Curry, Michael B.
   Love Is the Way   241
CURRY, MICHAEL B.
   Curry, Michael B. *Love Is the Way*   241
CURRY, STEPHEN, 1988-
   McCallum, Jack. *Golden Days*   796.323
★*The Curtain*. Kundera, Milan   801
Curtis, Edward E.
   Muslims in America   305.6
Curtis, Edward S.
   Edward S. Curtis   770.92

CURTIS, EDWARD S., 1868-1952
   Curtis, Edward S. *Edward S. Curtis*   770.92
   Egan, Timothy. ★*Short Nights of the Shadow Catcher*   770.92
   Gulbrandsen, Don. *Edward Sheriff Curtis*   970.004
Curtis, Glade B.
   Your Pregnancy Week by Week   618.2
Curtis, James
   Buster Keaton   B
   Spencer Tracy   B
Curtis, William J. R.
   Modern Architecture Since 1900   724
Curzan, Anne
   ★*Says Who?*   428
Curzon, Susan Carol
   What Every Library Director Should Know   025.1
The Cushion in the Road. Walker, Alice   814
CUSHMAN, CHARLOTTE, 1816-1876
   Wojczuk, Tana. *Lady Romeo*   B
Cushman, Kathleen
   Fires in Our Lives   373.1102
Cusk, Rachel
   Aftermath   B
   Coventry   814
   A Life's Work   306.874
CUSK, RACHEL, 1967-
   Cusk, Rachel. *Aftermath*   B
   Cusk, Rachel. *Coventry*   814
Custer. Wert, Jeffry D.   B
Custer. McMurtry, Larry   B
Custer's Trials. Stiles, T. J.   B
CUSTER, GEORGE A. (GEORGE ARMSTRONG), 1839-1876
   Connell, Evan S. *Son of the Morning Star*   973.8
   Donovan, Jim. *A Terrible Glory*   973.8
   McMurtry, Larry. *Custer*   B
   Philbrick, Nathaniel. ★*The Last Stand*   973.8
   Stiles, T. J. *Custer's Trials*   B
   Wert, Jeffry D. *Custer*   B
CUSTIS FAMILY
   Good, Cassandra A. *First Family*   920
Customs. Sharif, Solmaz   811
The Cut Out Girl. Van Es, Bart   B
Cut The Clutter. Ewer, Cynthia Townley   648
Cute & Cuddly Crochet. Bergstrom, Lauren   746.43
Cutler, Max
   Cults   364.15
Cwiklik, Robert
   Sheridan's Secret Mission   973.8
CY YOUNG AWARD WINNERS
   Turbow, Jason. *They Bled Blue*   796.357
CYBERBULLYING
   Quinn, Zoe. *Crash Override*   794.8
CYBERCULTURE
   Acemoglu, Daron. *Power and Progress*   303.48
CYBERTERRORISM
   Dudley, Renee. *The Ransomware Hunting Team*   363.25
   Greenberg, Andy. *Sandworm*   364.16
   Hasen, Richard L. *Election Meltdown*   324.973
   Walton, Calder. *Spies*   327.1247
   Wiehl, Lis W. *A Spy in Plain Sight*   327.1247
The Cycle. Gupta, Shalene   618.1
The Cyclist Who Went Out in the Cold. Moore, Tim   796.6
CYCLONES
   Carney, Scott. *The Vortex*   954.92
Cylinder, Carly
   The Flower Chef   745.92
CYNICISM
   Montell, Amanda. ★*The Age of Magical Overthinking*   153.4
CYTOLOGY
   Cech, Thomas. *The Catalyst*   572.8
   Sinclair, David A. *Lifespan*   570
CZECH AMERICANS
   Slouka, Mark. *Nobody's Son*   B
CZECH PEOPLE
   Eisen, Max. *By Chance Alone*   940.5318
   Greenfield, Martin. ★*Measure of a Man*   B
   Kraus, Dita. *A Delayed Life*   B
   Neumann, Ariana. *When Time Stopped*   B

AUTHOR, TITLE, SERIES AND SUBJECT INDEX

CZECH REPUBLIC
   McNamara, Kevin J. *Dreams of a Great Small Nation* — 355.009437
CZECHOSLOVAKIA
   Albright, Madeleine Korbel. *Prague Winter* — 943.71
   Askwith, Richard. *Unbreakable* — B
   Eisen, Norman L. *The Last Palace* — 920
   Epstein, Franci. *Franci's War* — B
   Gerwarth, Robert. *Hitler's Hangman* — B
   Kraus, Dita. *A Delayed Life* — B
   McNamara, Kevin J. *Dreams of a Great Small Nation* — 355.009437
   Neumann, Ariana. *When Time Stopped* — B
Czerski, Helen
   The Blue Machine — 551.46
   Storm in a Teacup — 530
CZOLGOSZ, LEON F., 1873?-1901
   Miller, Scott. *The President and the Assassin* — 973.8

D

D'Agata, John
   About a Mountain — 979.3
D'Alessandro, Emilio
   Stanley Kubrick and Me — 791.4302
D'ALESSANDRO, EMILIO
   D'Alessandro, Emilio. *Stanley Kubrick and Me* — 791.4302
D'AMATO, CUS
   Tyson, Mike. *Iron Ambition* — B
D'Antonio, Michael
   The Hunting of Hillary — B
D-Day. Beevor, Antony — 940.54
D-Day Girls. Rose, Sarah — 940.53
D-Day, June 6, 1944. Ambrose, Stephen E. — 940.54
Da Vinci's Ghost. Lester, Toby — 741.092
Dabiri, Emma
   Twisted — 391.5
Dad Is Fat. Gaffigan, Jim — 814
Dada. Dickerman, Leah — 709
Dada Eats Love to Cook It. Dada, Samah — 641.5
Dada, Samah
   Dada Eats Love to Cook It — 641.5
DADAISM
   Dickerman, Leah. *Dada* — 709
Dagher, Sam
   Assad or We Burn the Country — 956.9104
Dahl, Melissa
   Cringeworthy — 158.2
DAHMER, VERNON FERDINAND, 1908-1966
   Wilkie, Curtis. *When Evil Lived in Laurel* — 305.8
Daily Painting. Marine, Carol — 751.4
The Daily Show (the Book). Smith, Chris — 791.45
DAIRY PRODUCTS
   Kurlansky, Mark. *Milk!* — 637
DAIRYING
   Kurlansky, Mark. *Milk!* — 637
Dais, Dawn
   The Sh!t No One Tells You About Divorce — 306.89
Daisy Cakes Bakes. Nelson, Kim — 641.86
DAKOTA (NORTH AMERICAN PEOPLE)
   Berg, Scott W. ★*38 Nooses* — 973.7
   Connell, Evan S. *Son of the Morning Star* — 973.8
   Mort, T. A. *Thieves' Road* — 978.3
   Philbrick, Nathaniel. ★*The Last Stand* — 973.8
   Utley, Robert M. *Sitting Bull* — B
DAKOTA TERRITORY
   Raban, Jonathan. *Bad Land* — 978
Dakwar, Elias
   The Captive Imagination — 616.85
Dalai Lama
   An Appeal to the World — 170
   Approaching the Buddhist Path — 294.3
   The Book of Joy — 294.3
   Freedom in Exile — B
   How to Be Compassionate — 294.3
   The Second Dalai Lama — 294.3
DALAI LAMA II, 1476-1542
   Dalai Lama. *The Second Dalai Lama* — 294.3

DALAI LAMA XIV, 1935-
   Dalai Lama. *Freedom in Exile* — B
   Iyer, Pico. *The Open Road* — B
DALAI LAMAS
   Dalai Lama. *Freedom in Exile* — B
   Dalai Lama. *The Second Dalai Lama* — 294.3
Dale, Cyndi
   Llewellyn's Complete Book of Chakras — 131
Daley, Mark
   Safe — B
DALEY, MARK (FOSTER CHILD ADVOCATE)
   Daley, Mark. *Safe* — B
Daley, Tom
   Coming up for Air — B
DALEY, TOM, 1994-
   Daley, Tom. *Coming up for Air* — B
Daley-Ward, Yrsa
   The How — 158.1
DALITS (INDIAN SCHEDULED CASTES)
   Gidla, Sujatha. *Ants Among Elephants* — 305.5
   Jadhav, Narendra. *Untouchables* — 305.5
Dallas 1963. Minutaglio, Bill — 973.922092
DALLAS, TEXAS
   Minutaglio, Bill. *Dallas 1963* — 973.922092
   Pearlman, Jeff. *Boys Will Be Boys* — 796.332
   Shih, David. *Chinese Prodigal* — B
   Swanson, James L. *End of Days* — 973.922092
   Thompson, Jamie. *Standoff* — 364.152
Dallek, Robert
   ★*Franklin D. Roosevelt* — B
   Harry S. Truman — B
   Let Every Nation Know — B
   Nixon and Kissinger — B
   An Unfinished Life — B
Dalrymple, William
   ★*The Anarchy* — 954.03
   Nine Lives — 294
   The Return of a King — 958.1
   White Mughals — 954
Daly, Fiona
   Weaving on a Little Loom — 746.1
DALY, MICHAEL J., 1924-2008
   Kershaw, Alex. *Against All Odds* — 940.54
DAMASCUS, SYRIA
   Ahmad, Aeham. *The Pianist from Syria* — B
   Malek, Alia. *The Home That Was Our Country* — B
   Thomson, Mike. *Syria's Secret Library* — 956.9104
Damasio, Antonio R.
   The Feeling of What Happens — 153
   Looking for Spinoza — 152.4
Damn Lucky. Maurer, Kevin — 940.54
Damon-Moore, Laura C.
   The Artist's Library — 021.2
Damour, Lisa
   The Emotional Lives of Teenagers — 155.5
   ★*Under Pressure* — 155.5
   Untangled — 305.235
Damrosch, David
   Around the World in 80 Books — 809
Damrosch, Leopold
   The Club — 920
DAMS
   Hastings, Max. *Operation Chastise* — 940.54
   Roker, Al. *Ruthless Tide* — 974.8
DAMSELFLIES
   Paulson, Dennis. *Dragonflies & Damselflies* — 595.7
Damuck, Jess
   Salad Freak — 641.83
Dana, Richard Henry
   Two Years Before the Mast — 910.4
DANA, RICHARD HENRY 1815-1882
   Dana, Richard Henry. *Two Years Before the Mast* — 910.4
DANCE COMPANIES
   Brown, Carolyn. *Chance and Circumstance* — B
   Hallberg, David. *A Body of Work* — B
   Morris, Mark. *Out Loud* — B
   Morrison, Simon Alexander. *Bolshoi Confidential* — 792.8

PUBLIC LIBRARY CORE COLLECTION: NONFICTION
Twentieth Edition

DANCE MUSIC
   Matos, Michaelangelo. *The Underground Is Massive* — 781.648
   Moby. *Porcelain* — B
   Prince. *The Beautiful Ones* — B
★*The Dance of Anger*. Lerner, Harriet Goldhor — 152.4
The Dance of Intimacy. Lerner, Harriet Goldhor — 155.6
The Dance of Life. Zernicka-Goetz, Magdalena — 591.56
DANCE TEACHERS
   Guillermoprieto, Alma. *Dancing with Cuba* — 972.9106
   Valby, Karen. *The Swans of Harlem* — 792.8
Dance, Stanley
   ★*The World of Earl Hines* — B
DANCERS
   Alford, Henry. *And Then We Danced* — 792.8
   Brown, Carolyn. *Chance and Circumstance* — B
   Copeland, Misty. *The Wind at My Back* — B
   Duncan, Isadora. *My Life* — B
   Garcia, Mayte. *The Most Beautiful* — 920
   Hallberg, David. *A Body of Work* — B
   Homans, Jennifer. ★*Apollo's Angels* — 792.8
   Morris, Mark. *Out Loud* — B
   Riley, Kathleen. *The Astaires* — B
   Robb, Alice. ★*Don't Think, Dear* — 792.8
   Teachout, Terry. ★*All in the Dances* — B
   Williams, Michael Kenneth. *Scenes from My Life* — B
   Zemeckis, Leslie Harter. *Behind the Burly Q* — 792.7
DANCING
   Alford, Henry. *And Then We Danced* — 792.8
   Angyal, Chloe. *Turning Pointe* — 792.8
   Craine, Debra. *The Oxford Dictionary of Dance* — 792.8
   Duncan, Isadora. *My Life* — B
   Flaherty, Meghan. *Tango Lessons* — 793.3
   Hallberg, David. *A Body of Work* — B
   Homans, Jennifer. ★*Apollo's Angels* — 792.8
   Jacobs, Laura. ★*Celestial Bodies* — 792.8
   Mordden, Ethan. *Anything Goes* — 782.1
   Morris, Mark. *Out Loud* — B
   Powers, Ann. *Good Booty* — 781.64
   Riley, Kathleen. *The Astaires* — B
   Robb, Alice. ★*Don't Think, Dear* — 792.8
Dancing Bears. Szablowski, Witold — 947.086
Dancing in the Mosque. Qadiri, Humayra — B
Dancing on My Own. Wu, Simon — 700.1
Dancing with Cuba. Guillermoprieto, Alma — 972.9106
Danford, Natalie
   How to Eataly — 641.594
Danforth, Adam
   Butchering Poultry, Rabbit, Lamb, Goat, and Pork — 664
Dangarembga, Tsitsi
   Black and Female — 305.48
The Danger Within Us. Lenzer, Jeanne — 338.4
DANGEROUS ANIMALS
   Sprinkle, Timothy. *Lost and Stranded* — 613.6
Dangerous Mystic. Harrington, Joel F. — B
DANGEROUS PLANTS
   Stewart, Amy. *Wicked Plants* — 581.6
A Dangerous Woman. Ronald, Susan — B
Daniel Morgan. Zambone, Albert Louis — B
Danielle Walker's Against All Grain. Walker, Danielle — 641.5
Danielle Walker's Healthy in a Hurry. Walker, Danielle — 641.5
DANIELS, JESSE DELBERT, 1938-2018
   King, Gilbert. *Beneath a Ruthless Sun* — B
Daniels, Roger
   Prisoners Without Trial — 940.53
Daniels, Stormy
   Full Disclosure — B
DANIELS, STORMY, 1979-
   Daniels, Stormy. *Full Disclosure* — B
Danler, Stephanie
   Stray — B
DANLER, STEPHANIE
   Danler, Stephanie. *Stray* — B
Dante Alighieri
   ★*The Divine Comedy* — 851
   Inferno — 851
   The Paradiso — 851
   Paradiso — 851
   Purgatorio — 851

DANTE ALIGHIERI, 1265-1321
   Raffa, Guy P. *Dante's Bones* — 851
   Strathern, Paul. *The Florentines* — 945
Dante's Bones. Raffa, Guy P. — 851
Danticat, Edwidge
   The Art of Death — 809
   ★*Brother, I'm Dying* — B
DANTICAT, EDWIDGE, 1969-
   Danticat, Edwidge. *The Art of Death* — 809
   Danticat, Edwidge. ★*Brother, I'm Dying* — B
Dapper Dan. Day, Daniel R. — B
Darby, Seyward
   ★*Sisters in Hate* — 305.800973
Darcey, Cheralyn
   Flowerpaedia — 580
The Darcy Myth. Feder, Rachel — 823
DARCY, FITZWILLIAM (FICTITIOUS CHARACTER)
   Feder, Rachel. *The Darcy Myth* — 823
Dare Not Linger. Mandela, Nelson — B
Dare to Be Kind. Velasquez, Lizzie — 177
★*Dare to Lead*. Brown, Brene — 658.4
Dare to Sketch. Scheinberger, Felix — 741.2
DARE, VIRGINIA, 1587-
   Lawler, Andrew. *The Secret Token* — 975.6
Dark biology [Series]. Preston, Richard — 614.5
DARK MATTER (ASTRONOMY)
   Mack, Katie. *The End of Everything* — 523.1
   Prescod-Weinstein, Chanda. *The Disordered Cosmos* — 523.01
   Randall, Lisa. *Dark Matter and the Dinosaurs* — 523.1
   Tucker, Wallace H. *Chandra's Cosmos* — 523.1
Dark Matter and the Dinosaurs. Randall, Lisa — 523.1
★*Dark Mirror*. Gellman, Barton — B
★*Dark Money*. Mayer, Jane — 973.932
The Dark Queens. Puhak, Shelley — 944
The Dark Side. Mayer, Jane — 973.931
The Dark Side of Genius. Spoto, Donald — B
Dark Towers. Enrich, David — 332.1
Dark Wire. Cox, Joseph — 363.2
Dark, Salt, Clear. Ash, Lamorna — 942.3
Darke, Rick
   The Living Landscape — 712
Darkest Hour. McCarten, Anthony — 941.084
The Darkness Manifesto. Eklof, Johan — 363.7
Darkshire, Oliver
   Once Upon a Tome — B
DARKSHIRE, OLIVER
   Darkshire, Oliver. *Once Upon a Tome* — B
DARLING, CANDY, 1944-1974
   Carr, C. *Candy Darling* — B
Darling, Daniel
   Agents of Grace — 158.2
Darling, Ron
   The Complete Game — B
DARLING, RON
   Darling, Ron. *The Complete Game* — B
Darlington, Miriam
   Otter Country — 599.769
DARLINGTON, MIRIAM
   Darlington, Miriam. *Otter Country* — 599.769
Darnell, John Coleman
   Egypt's Golden Couple — 932
DARNLEY, HENRY STUART, LORD, 1545-1567
   Weir, Alison. *Mary, Queen of Scots, and the Murder of Lord Darnley* — 941.105
Darnton, Robert
   The Revolutionary Temper — 944
DARROW, CLARENCE, 1857-1938
   Boyle, Kevin. *Arc of Justice* — 345.73
   Farrell, John A. *Clarence Darrow* — B
   Strang, Dean A. *Worse Than the Devil* — 345.775
Darwin. Byrne, Eugene — 741.5
Darwin Comes to Town. Schilthuizen, Menno — 577.5
Darwin's Armada. McCalman, Iain — 576.8
Darwin's Backyard. Costa, James T. — 576.8
Darwin's Dangerous Idea. Dennett, D. C. — 146
Darwin's Fossils. Lister, Adrian — 576.8
★*Darwin's Ghosts*. Stott, Rebecca — 576.8
Darwin, Charles
   Charles Darwin — 576.8

AUTHOR, TITLE, SERIES AND SUBJECT INDEX

★*The Origin of Species by Means of Natural Selection, Or, the Preservation of Favored Races in the Struggle for Life* 575
★*The Voyage of the Beagle* 508
DARWIN, CHARLES, 1809-1882
  Browne, E. J. *Charles Darwin* B
  Browne, E. J. *Charles Darwin* B
  Byrne, Eugene. *Darwin* 741.5
  Costa, James T. *Darwin's Backyard* 576.8
  Darwin, Charles. *Charles Darwin* 576.8
  Dennett, D. C. *Darwin's Dangerous Idea* 146
  Lister, Adrian. *Darwin's Fossils* 576.8
  Markel, Howard. *Origin Story* 576.8
  McCalman, Iain. *Darwin's Armada* 576.8
  Preston, Diana. *The Evolution of Charles Darwin* 508
  Stott, Rebecca. ★*Darwin's Ghosts* 576.8
Darwish, Mamoud
  If I Were Another 892.7
  ★*Unfortunately, It Was Paradise* 892
Das Reboot. Honigstein, Raphael 796.334
Das, Gaur Gopal
  The Way of the Monk 294.5
Dasal, Jennifer
  Artcurious 709
Dassau, Jennifer
  Knitting Short Rows 746.43
DATA ENCRYPTION (COMPUTER SCIENCE)
  Cox, Joseph. *Dark Wire* 363.2
DATA MINING
  Cole, Samantha. *How the Internet Changed Sex and Sex Changed the Internet* 306.7
  Page, Scott E. *The Model Thinker* 001.4
  Waldinger, Robert J. ★*The Good Life* 158.1
DATA PROCESSING
  Murgia, Madhumita. *Code Dependent* 303.48
  Schoenfeld, Bruce. ★*Game of Edges* 796.04
DATA PROTECTION
  Boghosian, Heidi. *"i Have Nothing to Hide"* 363.1
  Chertoff, Michael. *Exploding Data* 343.7309
  Mitnick, Kevin D. *The Art of Invisibility* 005.8
DATE RAPE
  Grigoriadis, Vanessa. *Blurred Lines* 371.7
  Krakauer, Jon. *Missoula* 362.883
Dateable. Slice, Jessica 646.7
DATING
  Alderton, Dolly. *Everything I Know About Love* B
  Arceneaux, Michael. *I Finally Bought Some Jordans* 306.76
  Cole, Samantha. *How the Internet Changed Sex and Sex Changed the Internet* 306.7
  Hoffman, Damona. *F the Fairy Tale* 306.73
  Isenberg, Sheila. *Women Who Love Men Who Kill* 362.83
  Monger, George. *Marriage Customs of the World* 392.5
  Offerman, Nick. *The Greatest Love Story Ever Told* B
  Rallo, Eli. *I Didn't Know I Needed This* 306.73
  Raskin, Allison. *Overthinking About You* 646.7
  Robinson, Phoebe. *Please Don't Sit on My Bed in Your Outside Clothes* 818
  Slice, Jessica. *Dateable* 646.7
  Smiler, Andrew P. *Dating and Sex* 613.9071
  Tate, Christie. ★*Group* B
Dating and Sex. Smiler, Andrew P. 613.9071
Dauber, Jeremy Asher
  Jewish Comedy 809.7
Daughan, George C.
  Revolution on the Hudson 974.7
Daugherty, Tracy
  Larry McMurtry B
  The Last Love Song B
★*The Daughter of Auschwitz*. Friedman, Tova B
Daughter of the Dragon. Huang, Yunte B
DAUGHTERS
  Diamond, Cheryl. *Nowhere Girl* B
  Foxx, Jamie. *Act Like You Got Some Sense* B
  Mans, Jasmine. *Black Girl, Call Home* 811
  Williams, Richard. *Black and White* B
The Daughters of Kobani. Lemmon, Gayle Tzemach 956.9104
Daughters of the Flower Fragrant Garden. Li, Zhuqing 951.04
Daughters of the Samurai. Nimura, Janice P. 920
Daughters of the Winter Queen. Goldstone, Nancy Bazelon 920
The Daughters of Yalta. Katz, Catherine Grace 920

DAUGHTERS-IN-LAW
  Wilson, Katherine. *Only in Naples* B
Daunton, M. J.
  ★*The Economic Government of the World* 337
Davenport, Anthony
  Your Score 332.7
Davenport, Christian
  The Space Barons 920
Davenport, Matthew J.
  First Over There 940.4
  The Longest Minute 979.4
David and Goliath. Gladwell, Malcolm 155.2
David Bowie. Jones, Dylan B
David Bowie Made Me Gay. Bullock, Darryl W. 780
David Hockney. Sykes, Christopher Simon B
David Hockney. Sykes, Christopher Simon B
DAVID, KING OF ISRAEL
  Garfinkel, Yosef. *In the Footsteps of King David* 933
David, Laurie
  The Family Cooks 641.3
Davidds, Yasmin
  Your Own Terms 658.4
DAVIDMAN, JOY, 1915-1960
  Lewis, C. S. ★*A Grief Observed* 242
Davidson, Adam
  The Passion Economy 330.9
Davidson, Ian
  The French Revolution 944.04
Davidson, Mark A.
  ★*Bob Dylan* B
Davidson, Tish
  The Vaccine Debate 615.3
Davies, Brian
  The Thought of Thomas Aquinas 230
DAVIES, MARION, 1897-1961
  Nasaw, David. *The Chief* B
Davies, N. B.
  Cuckoo 598.7
Davies, Richard
  Extreme Economies 306.3
Davies, Simone
  The Montessori Toddler 371.39
Davis, Angela Y.
  Abolition 364.6
DAVIS, BETTE, 1908-1989
  Thomson, David. *Bette Davis* B
Davis, Burke
  Sherman's March 973.7
Davis, Geena
  Dying of Politeness B
DAVIS, GEENA
  Davis, Geena. *Dying of Politeness* B
Davis, Jack E.
  The Bald Eagle 598.9
  An Everglades Providence B
  ★*The Gulf* 909
Davis, Jennifer Pharr
  Called Again B
  The Pursuit of Endurance 796.51
DAVIS, JENNIFER PHARR
  Davis, Jennifer Pharr. *Called Again* B
  Davis, Jennifer Pharr. *The Pursuit of Endurance* 796.51
Davis, Joshua
  Spare Parts 629.8
Davis, KC
  ★*How to Keep House While Drowning* 648
Davis, Kevin
  The Brain Defense 345.747
Davis, Lennard J.
  Enabling Acts 342.7308
Davis, Lisa
  ★*Housewife* 331.4
Davis, Lisa Selin
  Tomboy 305.409
Davis, Margaret Leslie
  The Lost Gutenberg 093
Davis, Michael
  Street Gang 791.43

PUBLIC LIBRARY CORE COLLECTION: NONFICTION
Twentieth Edition

DAVIS, MILES
    Kaplan, James. *3 Shades of Blue* — 920
Davis, Patti
    Floating in the Deep End — 616.8
DAVIS, PATTI, 1952-
    Davis, Patti. *Floating in the Deep End* — 616.8
Davis, Pete
    Dedicated — 158.1
Davis, Richard H.
    The Bhagavad Gita — 294.5
Davis, Seth
    Getting to Us — 796.07
    Wooden — B
Davis, Stephen
    Gold Dust Woman — B
Davis, Thomas J.
    History of African Americans — 973
Davis, Viola
    ★*Finding Me* — B
DAVIS, VIOLA, 1965-
    Davis, Viola. ★*Finding Me* — B
Davis, Wade
    Into the Silence — B
    Magdalena — 986.1
    One River — 581.6
Davis, William C.
    Crucible of Command — 920
DAVY, HUMPHRY, SIR, 1778-1829
    Holmes, Richard. *The Age of Wonder* — 509
Dawidoff, Nicholas
    Collision Low Crossers — 796.332
Dawidziak, Mark
    A Mystery of Mysteries — B
Dawkins, Richard
    ★*The Ancestor's Tale* — 576.8
    An Appetite for Wonder — B
    Brief Candle in the Dark — B
    The Greatest Show on Earth — 576.8
    Science in the Soul — 500
DAWKINS, RICHARD, 1941-
    Dawkins, Richard. *An Appetite for Wonder* — B
    Dawkins, Richard. *Brief Candle in the Dark* — B
*The **Dawn** of Detroit*. Miles, Tiya — 977.4
*The **Dawn** of Everything*. Graeber, David — 901
Dawson, Kate Winkler
    ★*American Sherlock* — B
*The **Day** Freedom Died*. Lane, Charles — 976.3
*The **Day** I Die*. Hannig, Anita — 364.152
★*A **Day** in the Life of Abed Salama*. Thrall, Nathan — 956.05
*The **Day** of Battle*. Atkinson, Rick — 940.54
★*The **Day** The World Stops Shopping*. MacKinnon, J. B. — 339.4
*The **Day** Wall Street Exploded*. Gage, Beverly — 974.7
Day, Cheryl
    Back in the Day Bakery, Made with Love — 641.81
    Cheryl Day's Treasury of Southern Baking — 641.81
Day, Daniel R.
    Dapper Dan — B
DAY, DANIEL R.
    Day, Daniel R. *Dapper Dan* — B
DAY, DOROTHY, 1897-1980
    Hennessy, Kate. *Dorothy Day* — B
Day, John D.
    The Longevity Plan — 612.6
DAY, JOHN D., DR
    Day, John D. *The Longevity Plan* — 612.6
Day, Marianne Waggoner
    Camp Grandma — 306.8745
Day, Timothy
    ★*A Century of Recorded Music* — 780
Day-Lewis, Cecil
    The Complete Poems of C. Day Lewis — 821
DAYBELL, CHAD, 1968-
    Glatt, John. *The Doomsday Mother* — 364.152
Dayen, David
    Chain of Title — 330.973
    Monopolized — 338.8
DAYS
    Weingarten, Gene. ★*One Day* — 973

Days of Destruction, Days of Revolt. Hedges, Chris — 741.5
Days of Rage. Burrough, Bryan — 303.48
Dazzled and Deceived. Forbes, Peter — 578.4
The DC Comics Guide to Writing Comics. O'Neil, Dennis — 808
De Botton, Alain
    The Pleasures and Sorrows of Work — 306.3
    Religion for Atheists — 200
De Bres, Helena
    How to Be Multiple — 155.44
De Courcy, Anne
    Chanel's Riviera — 944.9
    The Husband Hunters — 920
De Gaulle. Jackson, Julian — B
De Graaf, John
    What's the Economy For, Anyway? — 330.973
De Hamel, Christopher
    The Manuscripts Club — 091
    ★*Meetings with Remarkable Manuscripts* — 091
De Hart, Jane Sherron
    ★*Ruth Bader Ginsburg* — B
DE JONG, HESSELINE
    Van Es, Bart. *The Cut Out Girl* — B
DE KLERK, F. W., 1936-2021
    Malala, Justice. *The Plot to Save South Africa* — 968.07
DE KOONING, WILLEM, 1904-1997
    Smee, Sebastian. *The Art of Rivalry* — 700.92
De Laurentiis, Giada
    ★*Giada's Italy* — 641.594
    Giada's Kitchen — 641.594
    Happy Cooking — 641.5
De Leon, Jason
    ★*Soldiers and Kings* — 364.1
De Leon, Paco
    Finance for the People — 332.024
DE LONG, GEORGE W. (GEORGE WASHINGTON), 1844-1881
    Sides, Hampton. ★*In the Kingdom of Ice* — 910.4
De Long, J. Bradford
    Slouching Towards Utopia — 330.9
De Reyna, Rudy
    How to Draw What You See — 741.2
De Semlyen, Nick
    Wild and Crazy Guys — 920
De Stefano, Cristina
    The Child Is the Teacher — B
De Vise, Daniel
    ★*The Blues Brothers* — 791.43
    The Comeback — B
De Waal, Edmund
    The Hare with Amber Eyes — B
DEAD
    Bass, William M. *Death's Acre* — 614
    Butcher, Barbara. *What the Dead Know* — 614
    Campbell, Hayley. *All the Living and the Dead* — 363.7
    Craughwell, Thomas J. *Stealing Lincoln's Body* — 973.7092
    Dante Alighieri. *Purgatorio* — 851
    Doughty, Caitlin. *Will My Cat Eat My Eyeballs?* — 306.9
    Hagerty, Alexa. ★*Still Life with Bones* — 599.9
    Jensen, Robert A. *Personal Effects* — 363.34
    Norton, Laurah. *Lay Them to Rest* — 363.25
    Prickett, Pamela J. ★*The Unclaimed* — 363.7
    Roach, Mary. ★*Stiff* — 611
★*The **Dead** Are Arising*. Payne, Les — B
Dead Men Do Tell Tales. Maples, William R. — 614
Dead Mountain. Eichar, Donnie — 914
Dead Presidents. Carlson, Brady — B
DEAD SEA SCROLLS
    Schiffman, Lawrence H. *Reclaiming the Dead Sea Scrolls* — 296.1
★*Dead Wake*. Larson, Erik — 940.4
★*Dead Weight*. Clein, Emmeline — 616.85
★*The **Deadline***. Lepore, Jill — 814
Deadly Quiet City. Xuecun, Murong — 614.5
DEAF CULTURE
    DiMarco, Nyle. ★*Deaf Utopia* — B
★*Deaf Republic*. Kaminsky, Ilya — 811
★*Deaf Utopia*. DiMarco, Nyle — B
DEAFNESS
    Hay, Matt. *Soundtrack of Silence* — B
    Kaminsky, Ilya. ★*Deaf Republic* — 811

AUTHOR, TITLE, SERIES AND SUBJECT INDEX

Melvin, Leland. *Chasing Space* — B
Owen, David. *Volume Control* — 617.8
Dean, Cornelia
  Against the Tide — 333.91
DEAN, JAMES, 1931-1955
  Gehring, Wes D. *James Dean* — B
Dean, John W.
  The Nixon Defense — 973.924092
Dean, Josh
  The Taking of K-129 — 910.91
Dear America. Vargas, Jose Antonio — B
★*Dear Black Girls*. Wilson, A'ja — 158.1
Dear Chairman. Gramm, Jeff — 659.2
Dear Fahrenheit 451. Spence, Annie — 028.9
Dear Founder. Webb, Maynard — 658
Dear Friend, from My Life I Write to You in Your Life. Li, Yiyun — B
Dear Ghosts. Gallagher, Tess — 811
★*Dear Girls*. Wong, Ali — B
Dear Ijeawele. Adichie, Chimamanda Ngozi — 649
Dear Leader. Jang, Jin-Sung — B
Dear Life. Clarke, Rachel — B
Dear Madam President. Palmieri, Jennifer — 158
Dear Papa. Hemingway, Ernest — 813
Dear Prudence. Lavery, Daniel M. — 170
★*Dear Senthuran*. Emezi, Akwaeke — B
Dear Sister. Horton, Michelle — B
Dearborn, Mary V.
  Carson McCullers — B
  Ernest Hemingway — B
Deardorff, David C
  What's Wrong with My Houseplant? — 635.9
Dearen, Jason
  Kill Shot — 616.8
★*Dearie*. Spitz, Bob — B
Dearly. Atwood, Margaret — 811
DEATH
  Adichie, Chimamanda Ngozi. *Notes on Grief* — 155.9
  Albom, Mitch. *Tuesdays with Morrie* — B
  Allende, Isabel. ★*Paula* — B
  Arthur, Alua. ★*Briefly Perfectly Human* — 306.9
  Auster, Paul. *Bloodbath Nation* — 363.33
  Barron, Justine. *They Killed Freddie Gray* — 363.32
  Bechdel, Alison. ★*Fun Home* — 741.5
  Becker, Ernest. ★*The Denial of Death* — 128
  Bloom, Amy. *In Love* — B
  Bowler, Kate. *No Cure for Being Human* — B
  Brenner, Marie. ★*The Desperate Hours* — 362.1962
  Brown, Samuel Morris. *In Heaven as It Is on Earth* — 289.3
  Brown, Tina. ★*The Palace Papers* — 920
  Butcher, Barbara. *What the Dead Know* — 614
  Butler, Katy. *The Art of Dying Well* — 616.02
  Campbell, Hayley. *All the Living and the Dead* — 363.7
  Clarke, Rachel. *Dear Life* — B
  Danticat, Edwidge. *The Art of Death* — 809
  Delaney, Rob. ★*A Heart That Works* — B
  Doughty, Caitlin. *From Here to Eternity* — 393
  Doughty, Caitlin. *Will My Cat Eat My Eyeballs?* — 306.9
  Dugdale, Lydia S. *The Lost Art of Dying* — 155.9
  Egan, Kerry. *On Living* — 170
  Eisler, Benita. ★*Chopin's Funeral* — B
  Faust, Drew Gilpin. *This Republic of Suffering* — 973.7
  Fink, Sheri. *Five Days at Memorial* — 362.1109763
  Forche, Carolyn. *In the Lateness of the World* — 811
  Garcia, Rodrigo. *A Farewell to Gabo and Mercedes* — B
  Gawande, Atul. *Complications* — B
  Gilbert, Sandra M. *Death's Door* — 155.9
  Godwin, Gail. *Getting to Know Death* — B
  Goldberg, Emma. *Life on the Line* — 362.1962
  Green, Stefanie. *This Is Assisted Dying* — 616.02
  Hitchens, Christopher. *Mortality* — 304.6
  Holloway, Richard. *Waiting for the Last Bus* — 202
  Homer. ★*The Iliad* — 883
  Horn, Dara. ★*People Love Dead Jews* — 909
  Jensen, Robert A. *Personal Effects* — 363.34
  Junger, Sebastian. ★*In My Time of Dying* — 304.6
  Kalanithi, Paul. ★*When Breath Becomes Air* — B
  Kenneally, Christine. *Ghosts of the Orphanage* — 362.73
  Kerr, Christopher. *Death Is but a Dream* — 155.9

Kessler, David. *Finding Meaning* — 155.9
King, Charles. *Odessa* — 947.7
King, Charles Monroe. *A Journal for Jordan* — 956.7044
Krakauer, Jon. *Into the Wild* — 917.9804
Kubler-Ross, Elisabeth. *Life Lessons* — 170
Kubler-Ross, Elisabeth. ★*On Death and Dying* — 155.9
Leder, Steven Z. *The Beauty of What Remains* — 306.9
Lyons, Anna. *We All Know How This Ends* — 362.17
Mankell, Henning. *Quicksand* — B
Mannix, Kathryn. *With the End in Mind* — 304.6
Marwell, David G. *Mengele* — B
McCormick, Mack. *Biography of a Phantom* — 782.421643
McInerny, Nora. *The Hot Young Widows Club* — 155.9
McKay, Sinclair. *The Fire and the Darkness* — 940.54
Minami, Jikisai. *It's Okay Not to Look for the Meaning of Life* — 158.1
Mitford, Jessica. ★*The American Way of Death Revisited* — 338.4
Norman, Philip. ★*Wild Thing* — B
Park, J. S. ★*As Long as You Need* — 248.8
Powers, Thomas. *The Killing of Crazy Horse* — B
Prickett, Pamela J. ★*The Unclaimed* — 363.7
Rees, Laurence. *Auschwitz* — 940.53
Riggs, Nina. *The Bright Hour* — B
Ritvo, Max. *The Final Voicemails* — 811
Roiphe, Katie. *The Violet Hour* — 809
Rosenblatt, Roger. *Kayak Morning* — 155.9
Sacks, Oliver. *Gratitude* — 306.9
Sale, Anna. ★*Let's Talk About Hard Things* — 153.6
Samuel, Julia. *Grief Works* — 155.9
Satrapi, Marjane. *Chicken with Plums* — 741.5
Schulz, Kathryn. ★*Lost & Found* — B
Soep, Elisabeth. *Other People's Words* — 155.9
Sogyal. *The Tibetan Book of Living and Dying* — 294.3
Solnit, Rebecca. *The Faraway Nearby* — 814
Speerstra, Karen. *The Divine Art of Dying* — 202
Spong, John Shelby. *Eternal Life* — 236
Stephenson, Michael. *The Last Full Measure* — 305.9
Taylor, Cory. *Dying* — B
Terkel, Studs. *Will the Circle Be Unbroken?* — 128
Thomas, Elizabeth Marshall. *Growing Old* — 305.26
Volandes, Angelo E. *The Conversation* — 616.02
Ward, Jesmyn. ★*Men We Reaped* — B
Wilder, Thornton. *Our Town* — 812
Williams, C. K. *Falling Ill* — 811
Wiman, Christian. *He Held Radical Light* — 814
Yalom, Irvin D. *Staring at the Sun* — 155.9
The Death and Life of Aida Hernandez. Bobrow-Strain, Aaron — 972
The Death and Life of the Great American School System. Ravitch, Diane — 379.1
★*The Death and Life of the Great Lakes*. Egan, Dan — 577.6
DEATH CONTROL
  Forman, James. *Locking up Our Own* — 364.973
DEATH EDUCATION
  Doughty, Caitlin. *From Here to Eternity* — 393
  Doughty, Caitlin. *Smoke Gets in Your Eyes* — B
  Ehrenreich, Barbara. *Natural Causes* — 613.2
  Warraich, Haider. *Modern Death* — 179.7
★*A Death in Malta*. Caruana Galizia, Paul — 364.15
Death in Mud Lick. Eyre, Eric — 362.29
Death in the City of Light. King, David — 364.152
Death Is but a Dream. Kerr, Christopher — 155.9
DEATH METAL MUSIC
  Wiederhorn, Jon. *Louder Than Hell* — 781.6609
The Death of a Jaybird. Savage, Jodi M. — B
DEATH OF ARTISTS
  Roiphe, Katie. *The Violet Hour* — 809
DEATH OF AUNTS
  Hernandez, Daisy. *The Kissing Bug* — 616.9
DEATH OF AUTHORS
  Roiphe, Katie. *The Violet Hour* — 809
DEATH OF BABIES
  Cregan, Mary. *The Scar* — 616.85
DEATH OF BROTHERS
  Gupta, Prachi. ★*They Called Us Exceptional* — B
  Moore, Colten. *Catching the Sky* — B
  Ng, Fae Myenne. *Orphan Bachelors* — B
The Death of Caesar. Strauss, Barry S. — 937
DEATH OF CHILDREN
  Delaney, Rob. ★*A Heart That Works* — B
  Deraniyagala, Sonali. *Wave* — B

PUBLIC LIBRARY CORE COLLECTION: NONFICTION
Twentieth Edition

Greene, Jayson. *Once More We Saw Stars*	155.9
Laskin, David. *The Children's Blizzard*	977
Markel, Howard. *Origin Story*	576.8
Pagels, Elaine H. ★*Why Religion?*	B
DEATH OF DAUGHTERS	
Allende, Isabel. ★*Paula*	B
O'Hara, Maryanne. *Little Matches*	B
The Death of Democracy. Hett, Benjamin Carter	943.085
DEATH OF FAMILY MEMBERS	
Hernandez, Daisy. *The Kissing Bug*	616.9
DEATH OF FATHERS	
Adichie, Chimamanda Ngozi. *Notes on Grief*	155.9
Auburn, David. *Proof*	812
Braitman, Laurel. *What Looks Like Bravery*	B
Carr, Erin Lee. *All That You Leave Behind*	B
Clarke, Rachel. *Dear Life*	B
Coldstream, Catherine. ★*Cloistered*	B
Fagan, Kate. *All the Colors Came Out*	B
Fuller, Alexandra. *Travel Light, Move Fast*	B
Gerson, Merissa Nathan. *Forget Prayers, Bring Cake*	155.9
Hirshey, Gerri. *Not Pretty Enough*	B
Leder, Steven Z. *The Beauty of What Remains*	306.9
Madden, T Kira. *Long Live the Tribe of Fatherless Girls*	814
Ollestad, Norman. *Crazy for the Storm*	B
Passarlay, Gulwali. *The Lightless Sky*	B
Preszler, Trent. *Little and Often*	B
Russert, Luke. *Look for Me There*	B
Sedaris, David. ★*Happy-Go-Lucky*	814
Shehadeh, Raja. ★*We Could Have Been Friends, My Father and I*	B
Smyth, Katharine. *All the Lives We Ever Lived*	B
Stoppard, Tom. ★*Rosencrantz & Guildenstern Are Dead*	822
Wieseltier, Leon. *Kaddish*	296.4
DEATH OF FRIENDS	
Crosley, Sloane. *Grief Is for People*	B
Gerard, Sarah. *Carrie Carolyn Coco*	364.152
Lynn, Loretta. *Me & Patsy Kickin' up Dust*	B
DEATH OF GIRLFRIENDS	
Gardner, Chris. ★*Permission to Dream*	158.1
The Death of Innocents. Prejean, Helen	364.66
The Death of King Arthur. Ackroyd, Peter	823
DEATH OF MARRIED MEN	
Cacioppo, Stephanie. *Wired for Love*	616.8
Goodwin, Doris Kearns. ★*An Unfinished Love Story*	B
Lin, Amy. *Here After*	B
Pagels, Elaine H. ★*Why Religion?*	B
Saint John, Bozoma. *The Urgent Life*	B
Seager, Sara. *The Smallest Lights in the Universe*	B
DEATH OF MARRIED WOMEN	
Guy, John. *Hunting the Falcon*	B
Rosenthal, Jason. *My Wife Said You May Want to Marry Me*	B
Weir, Alison. *The Lady in the Tower*	B
DEATH OF MOTHERS	
Alexander, Kwame. *Why Fathers Cry at Night*	B
Alexie, Sherman. *You Don't Have to Say You Love Me*	818
Atleework, Kendra. *Miracle Country*	979.4
Biden, Robert Hunter. *Beautiful Things*	B
Chow, Kat. *Seeing Ghosts*	B
Corrigan, Kelly. *Glitter and Glue*	B
Danticat, Edwidge. *The Art of Death*	809
Ervin, Kristine S. *Rabbit Heart*	364.152
Gander, Forrest. ★*Be With*	811
Geller, Danielle. *Dog Flowers*	B
Granata, Vince. *Everything Is Fine*	B
Harry. ★*Spare*	B
Kingston, Genevieve. *Did I Ever Tell You?*	B
Lieu, Susan. ★*The Manicurist's Daughter*	B
McColl, Sarah. *Joy Enough*	B
McCurdy, Jennette. ★*I'm Glad My Mom Died*	B
Moore, Susanna. *Miss Aluminum*	813
O'Reilly, Seamas. ★*Did Ye Hear Mammy Died?*	B
Strayed, Cheryl. ★*Wild*	B
Trethewey, Natasha D. ★*Memorial Drive*	B
Vuong, Ocean. ★*Time Is a Mother*	811
Williams, Marlena. *Night Mother*	791.43
Zauner, Michelle. ★*Crying in H Mart*	B
DEATH OF PARENTS	
Chung, Nicole. ★*A Living Remedy*	B
Deraniyagala, Sonali. *Wave*	B
Garcia, Rodrigo. *A Farewell to Gabo and Mercedes*	B
Ng, Fae Myenne. *Orphan Bachelors*	B
DEATH OF PETS	
Masson, J. Moussaieff. *Lost Companions*	636.088
Sife, Wallace. *The Loss of a Pet*	155.9
The Death of Public School. Fitzpatrick, Cara	379.73
DEATH OF RULERS	
Woolley, Benjamin. *The King's Assassin*	B
★*The Death of Sitting Bear.* Momaday, N. Scott	811
DEATH OF SONS	
Delaney, Rob. ★*A Heart That Works*	B
Etheridge, Melissa. *Talking to My Angels*	B
Gracie, Rickson. *Breathe*	B
McCann, Colum. *American Mother*	956.9104
Pagels, Elaine H. ★*Why Religion?*	B
Smith, Carol. *Crossing the River*	B
DEATH OF WOMEN	
Leach, Samantha. ★*The Elissas*	362.73
A Death on W Street. Kroll, Andy	364.152
DEATH ROW	
Hinton, Anthony Ray. *The Sun Does Shine*	B
Mar, Alex. *Seventy Times Seven*	362.88
DEATH ROW PRISONERS	
Chammah, Maurice. ★*Let the Lord Sort Them*	364.66
Fabricant, M. Chris. *Junk Science and the American Criminal Justice System*	363.25
Hinton, Anthony Ray. *The Sun Does Shine*	B
Isenberg, Sheila. *Women Who Love Men Who Kill*	362.83
Mar, Alex. *Seventy Times Seven*	362.88
Prejean, Helen. *The Death of Innocents*	364.66
Sheff, David. *The Buddhist on Death Row*	B
DEATH SQUADS	
Forche, Carolyn. *What You Have Heard Is True*	B
DEATH THREATS	
Rushdie, Salman. *Joseph Anton*	B
Trebincevic, Kenan. *The Bosnia List*	B
Death's Acre. Bass, William M.	614
Death's Door. Gilbert, Sandra M.	155.9
Deaths of Despair and the Future of Capitalism. Case, Anne	362.28
The Debatable Land. Robb, Graham	941.3
DEBATES AND DEBATING	
Blumenthal, Sidney. ★*All the Powers of Earth*	B
Blumenthal, Sidney. *Wrestling with His Angel*	B
Bordewich, Fergus M. *America's Great Debate*	973.6
Boykin, Keith. ★*Why Does Everything Have to Be About Race?*	305.8
Conyers, Jonathan. *I Wasn't Supposed to Be Here*	B
Edmonds, David. *Wittgenstein's Poker*	192
Engelhart, Katie. *The Inevitable*	179.7
Fish, Stanley Eugene. *Winning Arguments*	808
Freeman, Joanne B. *The Field of Blood*	973.7
Guelzo, Allen C. *Lincoln and Douglas*	973.6
Markel, Howard. *Origin Story*	576.8
McHangama, Jacob. ★*Free Speech*	323.44
Raphael, Ray. *Mr. President*	352.230973
Seo, Bo. *Good Arguments*	808.53
Singer, Matt. *Opposable Thumbs*	791.43
DeBord, Matthew	
Return to Glory	338.4
Debreczeni, Jozsef	
Cold Crematorium	940.53
DEBRECZENI, JOZSEF, 1905-1978	
Debreczeni, Jozsef. *Cold Crematorium*	940.53
Debriefing The President. Nixon, John	956.7044
DEBT	
Ariely, Dan. *Dollars and Sense*	332.024
Betz-Hamilton, Axton. *The Less People Know About Us*	364.16
Biss, Eula. *Having and Being Had*	306.3
De Leon, Paco. *Finance for the People*	332.024
Halpern, Jake. *Bad Paper*	332.7
Horn, Jonathan. *Washington's End*	B
Marie, Jane. ★*Selling the Dream*	658.8
Mitchell, Josh. *The Debt Trap*	378.3
Morgenson, Gretchen. ★*These Are the Plunderers*	332.6
O'Connell, Mark. *A Thread of Violence*	364.152
Petersen, Anne Helen. *Can't Even*	305.242
Ramsey, Dave. *The Total Money Makeover*	332.024
Swift, Earl. *Hell Put to Shame*	364.15
The Debt Trap. Mitchell, Josh	378.3

AUTHOR, TITLE, SERIES AND SUBJECT INDEX

★*Debussy*. Walsh, Stephen	B
DEBUSSY, CLAUDE, 1862-1918	
Walsh, Stephen. ★*Debussy*	B
DEBUT TITLE	
Abdul-Ahad, Ghaith. *A Stranger in Your Own City*	956.7044
Ackmann, Martha. *The Mercury 13*	920
Arnsdorf, Isaac. ★*Finish What We Started*	320.52
Asgarian, Roxanna. *We Were Once a Family*	364.152
Baron, Martin. ★*Collision of Power*	070.4
Barron, Justine. *They Killed Freddie Gray*	363.32
Bell, Darrin. ★*The Talk*	741.5
Berry, Erica. *Wolfish*	152.4
Bertch, Jane. *The French Ingredient*	B
Bittle, Jake. ★*The Great Displacement*	362.87
Black Thought. *The Upcycled Self*	B
Blackstock, Uche. *Legacy*	610.92
Blount, Tommye. *Fantasia for the Man in Blue*	811
Blunt, Katherine. *California Burning*	333.793
Bohannon, Cat. ★*Eve*	613
Bound, Mensun. *The Ship Beneath the Ice*	919.8904
Boyle, Rebecca. *Our Moon*	523.3
Bradbury, Neil. *A Taste for Poison*	615.9
Bradford, Joy Harden. *Sisterhood Heals*	158.2
Briggs, Lyvonne. ★*Sensual Faith*	204
Broome, Brian. ★*Punch Me up to the Gods*	B
Brown, Jasmine. *Twice as Hard*	610.92
Carriere, Alice. *Everything/Nothing/Someone*	B
Cech, Thomas. *The Catalyst*	572.8
Chachra, Deb. *How Infrastructure Works*	363
Chin, Curtis. *Everything I Learned, I Learned in a Chinese Restaurant*	B
Clein, Emmeline. ★*Dead Weight*	616.85
Cobbs-Leonard, Tasha. *Do It Anyway*	241
Codjoe, Ama. *Bluest Nude*	811
Cohen, Rhaina. ★*The Other Significant Others*	177
Coldstream, Catherine. ★*Cloistered*	B
Cooper, Becky. *We Keep the Dead Close*	364.152
Corbett, Emily. *In Transition*	809
Craig, Mya-Rose. *Birdgirl*	B
Daley, Mark. *Safe*	B
Emera, Deena. *A Brief History of the Female Body*	612.6
Evangelista, Patricia. ★*Some People Need Killing*	364.4
Fall, Jeremy. *Falling Upwards*	158.1
Fitzpatrick, Cara. *The Death of Public School*	379.73
Flannery, Kate. *Strip Tees*	338.4
Ganz, John. *When the Clock Broke*	320.52
Goodan, Chelsey. *Underestimated*	305.235
Goodman, Elyssa. *Glitter and Concrete*	792.7
Grann, David. *The Lost City of Z*	918.1
Grant, Will. *The Last Ride of the Pony Express*	917.804
greathouse, torrin a. *Wound from the Mouth of a Wound*	811
Green, Matthew. *Shadowlands*	941.03
Greenfieldboyce, Nell. ★*Transient and Strange*	501
Grush, Loren. ★*The Six*	629.4
H, Lamya. ★*Hijab Butch Blues*	B
Hagerty, Alexa. ★*Still Life with Bones*	599.9
Hamad, Ruby. *White Tears/Brown Scars*	305.8
Hardy, Alyssa. *Worn Out*	338.4
Harriot, Michael. ★*Black AF History*	973
Harss, Marina. *The Boy from Kyiv*	B
Hartman, Darrell. *Battle of Ink and Ice*	998
Harvilla, Rob. *60 Songs That Explain the '90s*	782.42164
Hazrat, Florence. *An Admirable Point*	411
Henderson, Rob Kim. *Troubled*	B
Henny, Ally. *I Won't Shut Up*	305.896
Herold, Benjamin. *Disillusioned*	307.76
Hickey, Walt. *You Are What You Watch*	791.4
Hill, Kashmir. ★*Your Face Belongs to Us*	006.2
Horton, Michelle. *Dear Sister*	B
Hu, Elise. *Flawless*	646.7
Hulls, Tessa. ★*Feeding Ghosts*	741.5
Hylton, Antonia. *Madness*	362.2
Izgil, Tahir Hamut. *Waiting to Be Arrested at Night*	B
Jabr, Ferris. ★*Becoming Earth*	570.1
Jackson, Curtis. *Hustle Harder, Hustle Smarter*	B
Johnson, Lizzie. ★*Paradise*	363.37
Jones, Faith. *Sex Cult Nun*	B
Kennedy, Jonathan. *Pathogenesis*	614.4
Kingston, Genevieve. *Did I Ever Tell You?*	B
Kissinger, Meg. *While You Were Out*	362.2
Kleiman, Kathy. *Proving Ground*	4.092
Kroll, Andy. *A Death on W Street*	364.152
Lahey, Jessica. *The Gift of Failure*	649
Leach, Samantha. ★*The Elissas*	362.73
Leland, Andrew. ★*The Country of the Blind*	B
Lisle, John. *The Dirty Tricks Department*	940.54
Luckerson, Victor. *Built from the Fire*	976.6
Marshall, McMillan. *Among the Bros*	362.29
Means, Brittany. *Hell If We Don't Change Our Ways*	B
Meyaard-Schaap, Kyle. *Following Jesus in a Warming World*	241
Mikanowski, Jacob. ★*Goodbye, Eastern Europe*	947
Miller, Christopher. *The War Came to Us*	947.7
Molnar, Petra. *The Walls Have Eyes*	363.28
Monroe, Jana. *Hearts of Darkness*	363.25
Morris, Jim. ★*The Cancer Factory*	658.3
Myers, Leah. *Thinning Blood*	B
Nuila, Ricardo. *The People's Hospital*	362.1
Olds, Sally. ★*People Who Lunch*	824
Oliva, Alejandra. *Rivermouth*	305.9
Owens, Jay. *Dust*	551.51
Page, Elliot. *Pageboy*	B
Pelosi, Dan. *Let's Eat*	641.5
Penaluna, Regan. ★*How to Think Like a Woman*	190.82
Podemski, Max. *A Paradise of Small Houses*	363.5
Possanza, Amelia. *Lesbian Love Story*	B
Prescod, Danielle. *Token Black Girl*	B
Preszler, Trent. *Little and Often*	B
Price, Margo. *Maybe We'll Make It*	B
Psaki, Jen. *Say More*	B
Ramsey, Donovan X. ★*When Crack Was King*	362.29
Renner, Rebecca. ★*Gator Country*	364.16
Rinehart, Lorissa. *First to the Front*	B
Rubin, Kathy Kleiner. *A Light in the Dark*	364.152
Rush, Charaia. *Courageously Soft*	234
Schneider, Amy. *In the Form of a Question*	B
Schwab, Tim. ★*The Bill Gates Problem*	361.7
Shelton, Ron. *The Church of Baseball*	791.43
Sinise, Gary. *Grateful American*	B
Stamos, John. *If You Would Have Told Me*	B
Stone, Lillian. ★*Everybody's Favorite*	814.6
Sumner, Seirian. *Endless Forms*	595.79
Sun, Carrie. *Private Equity*	B
Tang, Karen. ★*It's Not Hysteria*	618.2
Toll, Ian W. ★*Six Frigates*	359.00973
Tucker, Abigail. *The Lion in the Living Room*	636.8
Vasquez, Karla Tatiana. ★*The Salvisoul Cookbook*	641.598
Vigliotti, Jonathan. *Before It's Gone*	577
Vladeck, Stephen I. *The Shadow Docket*	347.73
Wade, Sabia. *Birthing Liberation*	363.96
Watts, Reggie. *Great Falls, MT*	B
Weber, Charlotte Fox. *Tell Me What You Want*	153.8
Weigel, Alicia Roth. *Inverse Cowgirl*	B
Williams, Kidada E. *I Saw Death Coming*	973.8
Young, Daniella Mestyanek. *Uncultured*	B
Zwick, Edward. ★*Hits, Flops, and Other Illusions*	B
DECENTRALIZATION IN GOVERNMENT	
Acemoglu, Daron. *The Narrow Corridor*	320.01
DECEPTION	
Abbott, Karen. *Liar, Temptress, Soldier, Spy*	920
Betz-Hamilton, Axton. *The Less People Know About Us*	364.16
Bowden, Mark. *The Last Stone*	363.25
Carpenter, Amanda B. *Gaslighting America*	973.933
Conason, Joe. *The Longest Con*	320.52
Davies, N. B. *Cuckoo*	598.7
Deer, Brian. *The Doctor Who Fooled the World*	610.92
DiResta, Renee. *Invisible Rulers*	320
Karl, Jonathan. *Front Row at the Trump Show*	973.933
Katin, Miriam. *We Are on Our Own*	741.5
Kroll, Andy. *A Death on W Street*	364.152
Larson, Erik. ★*The Devil in the White City*	364.15
Leamer, Laurence. *The Price of Justice*	346.7302
Lieberman, David J. *Mindreader*	401
Macintyre, Ben. ★*Operation Mincemeat*	940.54
Maddox, Brenda. *Rosalind Franklin*	B
Nafisi, Azar. ★*Reading Lolita in Tehran*	B
Ng, Fae Myenne. *Orphan Bachelors*	B
Nussbaum, Emily. *Cue the Sun!*	791.45

PUBLIC LIBRARY CORE COLLECTION: NONFICTION
Twentieth Edition

O'Brien, Keith. *Charlie Hustle*	796.357
Raphael, Rina. *The Gospel of Wellness*	613
Rule, Ann. *The Stranger Beside Me*	B
Saunt, Claudio. *Unworthy Republic*	323.1197
Scheier, Liz. *Never Simple*	B
Schwartz, A. Brad. ★*Broadcast Hysteria*	791.44
Shultz, Richard H. *The Secret War Against Hanoi*	959.704
Simon, Marie. *Underground in Berlin*	B
Vedantam, Shankar. *Useful Delusions*	153.4
White, Richard. *Who Killed Jane Stanford?*	364.152
Willetts, Paul. *King Con*	B
Young, Kevin. *Bunk*	177
Decherney, Peter	
Hollywood's Copyright Wars	346.7304
DECISION MAKING	
Burnett, William. *Designing Your Life*	650.1
Davis, Pete. *Dedicated*	158.1
Dobelli, Rolf. *The Art of Thinking Clearly*	153.4
Duhigg, Charles. *Smarter Faster Better*	158
Duke, Annie. *Thinking in Bets*	658.4
Gladwell, Malcolm. *Blink*	153.4
Iyengar, Sheena. *The Art of Choosing*	153.8
Kahneman, Daniel. ★*Thinking, Fast and Slow*	153.4
Kethledge, Raymond Michael. *Lead Yourself First*	658.4
McGinnis, Patrick J. *Fear of Missing Out*	153.8
McKeown, Greg. *Essentialism*	153.8
Mueller, Jennifer. *Creative Change*	658.4
Mullainathan, Sendhil. *Scarcity*	338.5
Murgia, Madhumita. *Code Dependent*	303.48
Riel, Jennifer. *Creating Great Choices*	658.4
Rosling, Hans. *Factfulness*	155.9
Spetzler, Carl S. *Decision Quality*	658.4
Wan, Bonnie. *The Life Brief*	158.1
Decision Points. Bush, George W.	B
Decision Quality. Spetzler, Carl S.	658.4
DECISION-MAKING	
Ariely, Dan. *Dollars and Sense*	332.024
Ariely, Dan. *The Honest Truth About Dishonesty*	177
Ariely, Dan. *Predictably Irrational*	153.8
Barron, David J. *Waging War*	342.73
Berg, Anastasia. ★*What Are Children For?*	306.87
Bush, George W. *Decision Points*	B
Butler, Katy. *The Art of Dying Well*	616.02
Chayka, Kyle. *Filterworld*	306
Chittister, Joan. *Following the Path*	248.4
Draper, Robert. *To Start a War*	956.7044
Dutton, Kevin. *Split-Second Persuasion*	153.8
Eagleman, David. *Incognito*	153
Gardner, Dan. *The Science of Fear*	152.4
Gawande, Atul. *Complications*	B
Gilbert, Daniel Todd. ★*Stumbling on Happiness*	158
Gladwell, Malcolm. ★*The Bomber Mafia*	940.54
Hoffman, Liz. *Crash Landing*	330
Jacobs, Alan. *How to Think*	153.4
Johnson, Steven. *Farsighted*	153.8
Jordan, Mary. *The Art of Her Deal*	B
Kandel, Eric R. ★*The Disordered Mind*	616.89
Kasparov, G. K. *Deep Thinking*	006.3
Law, Keith. *The Inside Game*	796.35764
Law, Keith. *Smart Baseball*	796.357
Lewis, Michael. ★*The Undoing Project*	920
Mlodinow, Leonard. *Emotional*	152.4
Oster, Emily. ★*Cribsheet*	618.2
Pinker, Steven. *Rationality*	153.4
Ricks, Thomas E. *Fiasco*	956.7044
Rubin, Robert Edward. *The Yellow Pad*	658.4
Sapolsky, Robert M. *Determined*	123
Sasakamoose, Fred. *Call Me Indian*	B
Satrapi, Marjane. *Chicken with Plums*	741.5
Scott, Kim Malone. *Radical Candor*	658.4
Shah, Rajiv Janardan. *Big Bets*	303.4
Smith, Jean Edward. *Bush*	973.931
Stavridis, James. *To Risk It All*	359
Stephanopoulos, George. ★*The Situation Room*	973.09
Thaler, Richard H. *Misbehaving*	330.01
Von Tunzelmann, Alex. *Blood and Sand*	909.82
Zia, Helen. *Last Boat Out of Shanghai*	951.04
Declaration. Hogeland, William	973.3
The Declassification Engine. Connelly, Matthew James	352.3
★*Declassified*. Warsaw-Fan Rauch, Arianna	781.1
★*The Decline and Fall of the Roman Empire*. Gibbon, Edward	937
Declutter Like a Mother. Casazza, Allie	648
★*Decoding Boys*. Natterson, Cara Familian	649
Decoding Greatness. Friedman, Ron	650.1
DECOLONIZATION	
Tesfamariam, Rahiel. ★*Imagine Freedom*	305.896
Decorate. Becker, Holly	747
★*Decorating with Plants*. Chapman, Baylor	635.9
DECORATIVE ARTS	
Logan, M. David. *Mat, Mount, and Frame It Yourself*	749
Rodriguez, Dina. *The Big Awesome Book of Hand & Chalk Lettering*	745.6
DeCoster, Marcia	
★*Marcia Decoster's Beaded Opulence*	739.27
Decreation. Carson, Anne	818
DECRIMINALIZATION OF DRUGS	
Vorobyov, Niko. *Dopeworld*	364.1
DECRIMINALIZATION OF MARIJUANA	
Berenson, Alex. ★*Tell Your Children*	362.29
Dufton, Emily. *Grass Roots*	362.29
DeCurtis, Anthony	
Lou Reed	B
Dederer, Claire	
★*Monsters*	700.1
Dedicated. Davis, Pete	158.1
Deep. Nestor, James	797.2
Deep Creek. Houston, Pam	814
Deep Delta Justice. Van Meter, Matthew	345.763
DEEP DIVING	
Kurson, Robert. *Pirate Hunters*	910.91
Lance, Rachel. *Chamber Divers*	940.54
Deep Lane. Doty, Mark	811
Deep Run Roots. Howard, Vivian	641.5975
Deep South. Theroux, Paul	975
Deep Thinking. Kasparov, G. K.	006.3
Deep Water. Bradley, James	578.77
DEEP-SEA SOUNDING	
Casey, Susan. *The Underworld*	551.46
The Deeper The Roots. Tubbs, Michael	B
The Deepest South of All. Grant, Richard	976.2
The Deepest Well. Burke Harris, Nadine	618.92
The Deeply Formed Life. Villodas, Rich	248.4
Deeply Rooted. Hamilton, Lisa M.	338.10973
DEER	
Delorme, Geoffroy. *Deer Man*	599.65
Howsare, Erika. *The Age of Deer*	599.65
Deer Creek Drive. Lowry, Beverly	364.152
Deer Man. Delorme, Geoffroy	599.65
Deer, Brian	
The Doctor Who Fooled the World	610.92
Deetz, Kelley Fanto	
Bound to the Fire	641.59
DEFECTION	
Golinkin, Lev. *A Backpack, a Bear, and Eight Crates of Vodka*	B
DEFECTORS	
Golinkin, Lev. *A Backpack, a Bear, and Eight Crates of Vodka*	B
Harden, Blaine. *The Great Leader and the Fighter Pilot*	B
Ishikawa, Masaji. ★*A River in Darkness*	B
Jang, Jin-Sung. *Dear Leader*	B
Kavanagh, Julie. *Nureyev*	B
Longo, Matthew. *The Picnic*	947.084
Sullivan, Rosemary. *Stalin's Daughter*	B
Defending Professionalism. Crowley, Bill	020.92
DEFENSE ATTORNEYS	
Adams, Jarrett. *Redeeming Justice*	340.092
Fabricant, M. Chris. *Junk Science and the American Criminal Justice System*	363.25
Farrell, John A. *Clarence Darrow*	B
DEFENSE CONTRACTS	
Whitlock, Craig. ★*Fat Leonard*	364.16
DEFENSE INDUSTRY AND TRADE	
Miller, Chris. *Chip War*	338.4
Tyson, Neil deGrasse. *Accessory to War*	355.001
DEFENSE PLANNING	
Gans, John. *White House Warriors*	355
Kaplan, Fred M. *The Bomb*	355.8

AUTHOR, TITLE, SERIES AND SUBJECT INDEX

DEFENSIVE (MILITARY SCIENCE)
    Emlen, Douglas John. *Animal Weapons* — 591.47
★*The Defined Dish*. Snodgrass, Alex — 641.5
Defining Moments in Black History. Gregory, Dick — 973
The Definitive Book of Body Language. Pease, Allan — 153.6
DEFOE, DANIEL, 1661?-1731
    Severin, Timothy. *In Search of Robinson Crusoe* — 996.1
DEFORESTATION
    Irving, Apricot Anderson. *The Gospel of Trees* — B
    Webb, Kinari. *Guardians of the Trees* — B
Defying Hitler. Haffner, Sebastian — 943.085
Defying Hitler. Thomas, Gordon — 920
DEGAS, EDGAR, 1834-1917
    Smee, Sebastian. *The Art of Rivalry* — 700.92
DEGENERATION (PATHOLOGY)
    Leland, Andrew. ★*The Country of the Blind* — B
Degrees of Inequality. Mettler, Suzanne — 378.73
Dehaene, Stanislas
    Reading in the Brain — 418
DEINDUSTRIALIZATION
    Price, S. L. *Playing Through the Whistle* — 796.332
Deisseroth, Karl
    Projections — 616.89
DeJean, Joan E.
    The Essence of Style — 391
    How Paris Became Paris — 944
DEL GIOCONDO, LISA, 1479-
    Hales, Dianne R. *Mona Lisa* — B
Del Negro, Janice
    Folktales Aloud — 027.62
The Del Posto Cookbook. Ladner, Mark — 641.594
Del Rey, Jason
    Winner Sells All — 381
Delaney, Brigid
    Reasons Not to Worry — 158.1
Delaney, Rob
    ★*A Heart That Works* — B
DELANEY, ROB, 1977-
    Delaney, Rob. ★*A Heart That Works* — B
DELANY FAMILY
    Delany, Sarah Louise. *Having Our Say* — B
DELANY, ANNIE ELIZABETH, 1891-1995
    Delany, Sarah Louise. *Having Our Say* — B
Delany, Sarah Louise
    Having Our Say — B
DELANY, SARAH LOUISE, 1889-1999
    Delany, Sarah Louise. *Having Our Say* — B
A Delayed Life. Kraus, Dita — B
Delbanco, Andrew
    The War Before the War — 973.7
Deliberate Cruelty. Montillo, Roseanne — 364.152
DELICATESSENS
    Howe, Ben Ryder. *My Korean Deli* — B
Delights & Shadows. Kooser, Ted — 811
Delish. Saltz, Joanna — 641.5
★*Delish Insane Sweets*. Saltz, Joanna — 641.81
Delisle, Guy
    Hostage — 741.5
    Pyongyang — 741.5
DELISLE, GUY
    Delisle, Guy. *Pyongyang* — 741.5
Deliver Me from Nowhere. Zanes, Warren — 782.42164
Deliver Us from Evil. Ford, Lacy K. — 973.7
Dell, Christopher
    The Occult, Witchcraft & Magic — 130
DELMER, SEFTON, 1904-1979
    Pomerantsev, Peter. ★*How to Win an Information War* — 940.53
Delmont, Matthew F.
    Half American — 940.54
Delorme, Geoffroy
    Deer Man — 599.65
DELORME, GEOFFROY
    Delorme, Geoffroy. *Deer Man* — 599.65
DELTA REGION, MISSISSIPPI
    Lomax, Alan. ★*The Land Where the Blues Began* — 781.643
    Wald, Elijah. ★*Escaping the Delta* — B
DELUSIONS
    Glatt, John. *The Doomsday Mother* — 364.152
    Lieberman, Jeffrey A. *Malady of the Mind* — 616.89
    Vedantam, Shankar. *Useful Delusions* — 153.4
★*Demagogue*. Tye, Larry — B
DEMAGOGUISM AND DEMAGOGUES
    Mishra, Pankaj. *Age of Anger* — 909.8
    Tye, Larry. ★*Demagogue* — B
DEMBELE, MONIQUE
    Holloway, Kris. *Monique and the Mango Rains* — B
DEMENTIA
    Karlawish, Jason. ★*The Problem of Alzheimer's* — 616.8
    Kiper, Dasha. ★*Travelers to Unimaginable Lands* — 616.8
    Mace, Nancy L. ★*The 36-Hour Day* — 616.8
    Mitchell, Wendy. *Somebody I Used to Know* — B
    Powell, Tia. *Dementia Reimagined* — 616.8
Dementia Reimagined. Powell, Tia — 616.8
Demick, Barbara
    Eat the Buddha — 951
    ★*Nothing to Envy* — 920
DEMILLE, CECIL B., 1881-1959
    Eyman, Scott. *Empire of Dreams* — B
DEMOCRACY
    Abrams, Stacey. *Our Time Is Now* — 324.60973
    Acemoglu, Daron. *The Narrow Corridor* — 320.01
    Applebaum, Anne. *Twilight of Democracy* — 321.9
    Aristotle. ★*Politics, 2nd Ed* — 320
    Baer, Daniel Brooks. *The Four Tests* — 320.973
    Baker, Calvin. *A More Perfect Reunion* — 305.800973
    Barber, William J. *We Are Called to Be a Movement* — 261.8
    Berman, Ari. ★*Minority Rule* — 305.809
    Bhutto, Benazir. *Reconciliation* — 297.2
    Boorstin, Daniel J. *The Americans* — 973
    Brands, H. W. ★*Andrew Jackson, His Life and Times* — B
    Brettschneider, Corey Lang. *The Presidents and the People* — 342.73
    Brill, Steven. *Tailspin* — 306.0973
    Cheney, Liz. *Oath and Honor* — 328.73
    Cheung, Karen. *The Impossible City* — 951.25
    Chomsky, Noam. *Global Discontents* — 410.92
    Chomsky, Noam. *Who Rules the World?* — 327.73
    Cohen, Roger. *An Affirming Flame* — 071
    Cross, Tiffany D. *Say It Louder!* — 324.6
    Cummings, Elijah. ★*We're Better Than This* — B
    Du Mez, Kristin Kobes. *Jesus and John Wayne* — 277.308
    Dunn, Harry. *Standing My Ground* — B
    Faloyin, Dipo. ★*Africa Is Not a Country* — 960.33
    Finan, Christopher M. *How Free Speech Saved Democracy* — 342.73
    Foner, Eric. ★*Reconstruction* — 973.8
    Frank, Thomas. *The People, No* — 320.56
    Freeman, Joanne B. *The Field of Blood* — 973.7
    Fukuyama, Francis. *Liberalism and Its Discontents* — 320.51
    Fukuyama, Francis. *Political Order and Political Decay* — 320.1
    Gessen, Masha. *Surviving Autocracy* — 973.933
    Giridharadas, Anand. ★*The Persuaders* — 320.973
    Griffin, Farah Jasmine. *Read Until You Understand* — 810.9
    Hasen, Richard L. *Election Meltdown* — 324.973
    Hill, Fiona. *There Is Nothing for You Here* — 327.2
    Hochschild, Adam. *American Midnight* — 973.91
    Hochschild, Adam. *Spain in Our Hearts* — 946.081
    Hoffman, David E. *Give Me Liberty* — B
    Hutchinson, Cassidy. *Enough* — B
    Isenberg, Nancy. *The Problem of Democracy* — 973.4
    Kawa, Abraham. *Democracy* — 741.5
    Kelly, Joseph. *Marooned* — 975.5
    Kissinger, Henry. *Leadership* — 303.3
    LaRue, James. ★*On Censorship* — 025.2
    Lasch, Christopher. ★*The Revolt of the Elites* — 306
    Lim, Louisa. *The People's Republic of Amnesia* — 951.05
    Litt, David. *Democracy in One Book or Less* — 321.8
    Maddow, Rachel. *Blowout* — 338.2
    Mahtani, Shibani. *Among the Braves* — 951.25
    Martin, Jonathan. *This Will Not Pass* — 973.933
    McAlevey, Jane. *A Collective Bargain* — 331.890973
    Meacham, Jon. ★*The Soul of America* — 973
    Nafisi, Azar. *The Republic of Imagination* — B
    Nance, Malcolm W. *The Plot to Betray America* — 973.933
    Neiwert, David A. ★*The Age of Insurrection* — 303.48
    O'Neil, Cathy. *Weapons of Math Destruction* — 005.7
    Owens, Ernest. ★*The Case for Cancel Culture* — 303.3
    Packer, George. *Last Best Hope* — 973.93

PUBLIC LIBRARY CORE COLLECTION: NONFICTION
Twentieth Edition

Pan, Philip P. *Out of Mao's Shadow*	306.20951
Preston, Paul. *The Spanish Holocaust*	946.081
Raphael, Ray. *Constitutional Myths*	342.7302
Richardson, Heather Cox. *Democracy Awakening*	320.473
Ricks, Thomas E. *Churchill and Orwell*	920
Rosenberg, Ian. *The Fight for Free Speech*	342.73
Rothkopf, David J. *American Resistance*	973.933
Roy, Arundhati. *Walking with the Comrades*	954
Rubenstein, David M. *The American Experiment*	973
Runciman, David. *The Confidence Trap*	321.8
Sage, Sami. *Democracy in Retrograde*	324
Sebestyen, Victor. *Revolution 1989*	947.085
Sexton, Jared Yates. *American Rule*	973
Shapiro, James. ★*The Playbook*	792
Sinha, Manisha. ★*The Rise and Fall of the Second American Republic*	973.8
Smith, Erin Geiger. ★*Thank You for Voting*	324.973
Smith, J. Douglas. *On Democracy's Doorstep*	342.73
Stevens, Stuart. *The Conspiracy to End America*	324.2734
Tocqueville, Alexis de. ★*Democracy in America*	320.973
Trentmann, Frank. *Out of the Darkness*	943.08
Ullrich, Volker. *Germany 1923*	943.085
Velshi, Ali. *Small Acts of Courage*	B
Waldman, Michael. *The Supermajority*	347.73
Wallis, Jim. *The False White Gospel*	261.7
Westad, Odd Arne. *The Cold War*	909.825
Widmer, Edward L. *Lincoln on the Verge*	B
Wolf, Martin. ★*The Crisis of Democratic Capitalism*	330.12
Young, Ralph F. *Dissent*	303.48
Democracy. Kawa, Abraham	741.5
***Democracy** Awakening*. Richardson, Heather Cox	320.473
★***Democracy** in America*. Tocqueville, Alexis de	320.973
***Democracy** in One Book or Less*. Litt, David	321.8
***Democracy** in Retrograde*. Sage, Sami	324
DEMOCRATIC SOCIALISM	
Hagglund, Martin. *This Life*	110
DEMOCRATIZATION	
Worth, Robert Forsyth. ★*A Rage for Order*	909
DEMOCRATS	
Berg, A. Scott. ★*Wilson*	B
Brinkley, Alan. *John F. Kennedy*	B
Caro, Robert A. ★*The Passage of Power*	B
Collins-Dexter, Brandi. *Black Skinhead*	324.2734
Cooper, John Milton. *Woodrow Wilson*	B
Farrell, John A. *Ted Kennedy*	B
Frank, Barney. *Frank*	B
Gabler, Neal. ★*Against the Wind*	B
Kazin, Michael. *What It Took to Win*	324.2736
Plouffe, David. *A Citizen's Guide to Beating Donald Trump*	324.0973
Remnick, David. *The Bridge*	B
Wilson, Rick. *Running Against the Devil*	973.933
DEMOGRAPHIC TRANSITION	
Sciubba, Jennifer Dabbs. *8 Billion and Counting*	304.6
DEMOGRAPHY	
Cross, Tiffany D. ★*Say It Louder!*	324.6
Currid-Halkett, Elizabeth. *The Overlooked Americans*	307.76
Diamond, Jared M. *Guns, Germs, and Steel*	303.4
Holzer, Harold. *Brought Forth on This Continent*	973.7
Sciubba, Jennifer Dabbs. *8 Billion and Counting*	304.6
Stone, Deborah A. *Counting*	001.4
Whitby, Andrew. *The Sum of the People*	001.4
★*The **Demon** of Unrest*. Larson, Erik	973.7
***Demonic** Foes*. Gallagher, Richard E.	133.42
DEMONIC POSSESSION	
Gallagher, Richard E. *Demonic Foes*	133.42
Guiley, Rosemary. *The Encyclopedia of Demons and Demonology*	133.4
DEMONS	
Bartlett, Sarah. *A Brief History of Angels and Demons*	202
Guiley, Rosemary. *The Encyclopedia of Demons and Demonology*	133.4
***Demons**, The Devil, and Fallen Angels*. Jones, Marie D.	133.4
Demos, John	
The Unredeemed Captive	973.2
***Demystifying** Disability*. Ladau, Emily	305.9
***Demystifying** Islam*. Zafar, Harris	297
★***Demystifying** Online Instruction in Libraries*. Turnbow, Dominique	028.7
***Demystifying** Shariah*. Ali-Karamali, Sumbul	340.5
DENALI NATIONAL PARK AND PRESERVE (ALASKA)	
Hall, Andy. *Denali's Howl*	796.522
***Denali's** Howl*. Hall, Andy	796.522
Dench, Judi	
Shakespeare	792
DENCH, JUDI, 1934-	
Dench, Judi. *Shakespeare*	792
DENESULINE (NORTH AMERICAN PEOPLE)	
Sacco, Joe. ★*Paying the Land*	741.5
Denevi, Timothy	
Freak Kingdom	B
***Deng** XIaoping and the Transformation of China*. Vogel, Ezra F.	B
Deng, Alephonsion	
They Poured Fire on Us from the Sky	B
DENG, ALEPHONSION	
Deng, Alephonsion. *They Poured Fire on Us from the Sky*	B
DENG, BENSON	
Deng, Alephonsion. *They Poured Fire on Us from the Sky*	B
DENG, XIAOPING, 1904-1997	
Vogel, Ezra F. *Deng XIaoping and the Transformation of China*	B
DENIAL (PSYCHOLOGY)	
Barnett, Erica C. *Quitter*	B
Becker, Ernest. ★*The Denial of Death*	128
Braitman, Laurel. *What Looks Like Bravery*	B
Ferguson, Niall. *Doom*	362.1962
Ghosh, Amitav. *The Great Derangement*	809
Khar, Erin. *Strung Out*	B
Lipsky, David. ★*The Parrot and the Igloo*	304.2
Schwarz, Geraldine. *Those Who Forget*	940.53
Smith, Clint. ★*How the Word Is Passed*	973
★*The **Denial** of Death*. Becker, Ernest	128
DENMARK	
Booth, Michael. *The Almost Nearly Perfect People*	948.071
Stoppard, Tom. ★*Rosencrantz & Guildenstern Are Dead*	822
***Denmark** Vesey's Garden*. Kytle, Ethan J.	975.7
Dennett, D. C.	
Breaking the Spell	200
Darwin's Dangerous Idea	146
Intuition Pumps and Other Tools for Thinking	121
Dennie, Madiba K.	
The Originalism Trap	342.73
Dennis, David J., Jr	
The Movement Made Us	B
DENNIS, DAVID J., JR	
Dennis, David J., Jr. *The Movement Made Us*	B
DENNIS, DAVID J., SR	
Dennis, David J., Jr. *The Movement Made Us*	B
Dennis, Felix	
How to Get Rich	B
DENNIS, FELIX, 1947-2014	
Dennis, Felix. *How to Get Rich*	B
Dennis, Jerry	
The Living Great Lakes	977
DENNIS, JERRY, 1954-	
Dennis, Jerry. *The Living Great Lakes*	977
Dennison, Matthew	
Behind the Mask	B
The Man in the Willows	B
DENTAL CARE	
Otto, Mary. *Teeth*	617
DENTISTRY	
Otto, Mary. *Teeth*	617
DENTON, NICHOLAS	
Smith, Ben. *Traffic*	070.4
Denton, Sally	
The Colony	364.152
The Profiteers	B
DENVER, COLORADO	
Cayton-Holland, Adam. *Tragedy Plus Time*	B
Glatt, John. ★*The Perfect Father*	364.152
Rubinstein, Julian. ★*The Holly*	364.106
Denver, Rorke	
Worth Dying For	359.9
DENVER, RORKE	
Denver, Rorke. *Worth Dying For*	359.9
Denworth, Lydia	
Friendship	158.2
DePalma, Anthony	
The Cubans	920
DeParle, Jason	
★*A Good Provider Is One Who Leaves*	305.899

AUTHOR, TITLE, SERIES AND SUBJECT INDEX

DEPARTMENT STORES
   Forgosh, Linda B. *Louis Bamberger* — B
   Satow, Julie. *When Women Ran Fifth Avenue* — 381.141
DePastino, Todd
   Bill Mauldin — B
DEPENDENCY
   LeFavour, Cree. *Lights On, Rats Out* — 616.85
   Wilder-Taylor, Stefanie. ★*Drunk-Ish* — B
DEPORTATION
   Bobrow-Strain, Aaron. *The Death and Life of Aida Hernandez* — 972
   Frank, Michael. ★*One Hundred Saturdays* — B
   Hernandez Castillo, Marcelo. *Children of the Land* — B
   Luiselli, Valeria. *Tell Me How It Ends* — 305.23086
   Mackeen, Dawn Anahid. *The Hundred-Year Walk* — 956.6
   Ramos, Jorge. *Stranger* — 325.73
   Saunt, Claudio. *Unworthy Republic* — 323.1197
   Wides-Munoz, Laura. *The Making of a Dream* — 920
DEPRESSION
   Bering, Jesse. *Suicidal* — 362.2
   Bullmore, Edward T. *The Inflamed Mind* — 616.85
   Case, Anne. *Deaths of Despair and the Future of Capitalism* — 362.28
   Cayton-Holland, Adam. *Tragedy Plus Time* — B
   Cheung, Karen. *The Impossible City* — 951.25
   Cregan, Mary. *The Scar* — 616.85
   Cross, Charles R. *Here We Are Now* — 782.42166
   Davis, KC. ★*How to Keep House While Drowning* — 648
   Elwood, Phil. *All the Worst Humans* — 659.2
   Finkel, David. *Thank You for Your Service* — 920
   Gupta, Shalene. *The Cycle* — 618.1
   Haidt, Jonathan. ★*The Anxious Generation* — 305.23
   Haig, Matt. *Notes on a Nervous Planet* — 616.89
   Hewitt, Sean. *All Down Darkness Wide* — B
   Kissinger, Meg. *While You Were Out* — 362.2
   Kramer, Peter D. ★*Ordinarily Well* — 615.7
   Lawson, Jenny. ★*Broken* — B
   Lawson, Jenny. *Furiously Happy* — B
   Lecrae. ★*I Am Restored* — B
   Mandel, Sarah. *Little Earthquakes* — B
   Mizrahi, Isaac. *I.M.* — B
   Norris, Kathleen. *Acedia & Me* — 248.8
   Paperny, Anna Mehler. *Hello I Want to Die Please Fix Me* — 362.2
   Raskin, Allison. *Overthinking About You* — 646.7
   Rauch, Jonathan. *The Happiness Curve* — 155.6
   Riley, Alex. ★*A Cure for Darkness* — 616.85
   Rothenberg, Ben. *Naomi Osaka* — B
   Saunders, John. *Playing Hurt* — B
   Sehee, Baek. *I Want to Die but I Want to Eat Tteokbokki* — B
   Solomon, Deborah. *American Mirror* — B
   Taylor, Madisyn. *Unmedicated* — 615.8
   Thompson, J. M. *Running Is a Kind of Dreaming* — B
   Way, Niobe. *Rebels with a Cause* — 649
DEPRESSION ERA (1929-1941)
   Allen, Frederick Lewis. *Only Yesterday* — 973.9
   Brookwood, Marilyn. *The Orphans of Davenport* — 305.231
   Bryson, Bill. *One Summer* — 973.91
   Collins, Max Allan. *Eliot Ness and the Mad Butcher* — 364.152
   Cooke, Alistair. *The American Home Front, 1941-1942* — 940.53
   Egan, Timothy. *The Worst Hard Time* — 978
   Golay, Michael. *America 1933* — B
   Gordon, Robert J. ★*The Rise and Fall of American Growth* — 339.4
   Hughes, Langston. ★*I Wonder as I Wander* — B
   Rappleye, Charles. *Herbert Hoover in the White House* — B
   Shlaes, Amity. *The Forgotten Man* — 973.91
   Stout, David. *The Kidnap Years* — 364.15
DEPRESSIONS
   Ahamed, Liaquat. *Lords of Finance* — 920
   Bruner, Robert F. ★*The Panic of 1907, 2nd Ed.* — 330.973
   De Long, J. Bradford. *Slouching Towards Utopia* — 330.9
   Nations, Scott. *A History of the United States in Five Crashes* — 338.5
   Welty, Eudora. *One Time, One Place* — 976.2
DEPRESSIONS, 1929-1941
   Agee, James. ★*Cotton Tenants* — 976.1
   Agee, James. *Let Us Now Praise Famous Men* — 976.1
   Brands, H. W. *Traitor to His Class* — B
   Brookwood, Marilyn. *The Orphans of Davenport* — 305.231
   Collins, Max Allan. *Eliot Ness and the Mad Butcher* — 364.152
   Egan, Timothy. *The Worst Hard Time* — 978
   Galbraith, John Kenneth. ★*The Great Crash, 1929* — 338.5
   Golay, Michael. *America 1933* — B
   Gup, Ted. *A Secret Gift* — 977.1
   Katznelson, Ira. *Fear Itself* — 973.917
   Kennedy, David M. ★*Freedom from Fear* — 973.91
   Rappleye, Charles. *Herbert Hoover in the White House* — B
   Schaap, Jeremy. *Cinderella Man* — B
   Shlaes, Amity. *The Forgotten Man* — 973.91
   Simon, James F. *FDR and Chief Justice Hughes* — 973.917092
   Stout, David. *The Kidnap Years* — 364.15
   Terkel, Studs. ★*Hard Times* — 973.91
   Whyte, Kenneth. *Hoover* — B
DEPRIVATION (PSYCHOLOGY)
   Edelman, Hope. *Motherless Daughters* — 155.9
DERAIN, ANDRE, 1880-1954
   Roe, Sue. *In Montmartre* — 920
Deraniyagala, Sonali
   Wave — B
DERANIYAGALA, SONALI
   Deraniyagala, Sonali. *Wave* — B
DEREGULATION
   Blunt, Katherine. *California Burning* — 333.793
   Goodman, Peter S. ★*How the World Ran Out of Everything* — 658.7
Derf
   Kent State — 741.5
Derks, Scott
   The Value of a Dollar — 338.5
   The Value of a Dollar — 338.5
DeRogatis, Jim
   Soulless — B
Derricotte, Toi
   I — 811
DERRICOTTE, TOI, 1941-
   Derricotte, Toi. *I* — 811
Dery, Mark
   Born to Be Posthumous — B
DES MOINES, IOWA
   Bryson, Bill. *The Life and Times of the Thunderbolt Kid* — B
Descamps, Ghylenn
   Beginner's Guide to Kirigami — 745.54
★*Descartes*. Descartes, Rene — 194
Descartes, Rene
   ★*Descartes* — 194
DESCARTES, RENE, 1596-1650
   Bloom, Paul. *Psych* — 150
   Descartes, Rene. ★*Descartes* — 194
   Watson, Richard A. *Cogito Ergo Sum* — B
A Descending Spiral. Bookman, Marc — 345.73
The Desert and the Sea. Moore, Michael Scott — 364.15
Desert Queen. Wallach, Janet — B
DESERT SURVIVAL
   Ralston, Aron. *Between a Rock and a Hard Place* — 796.522
   Urrea, Luis Alberto. *The Devil's Highway* — 304.8
DESERTERS
   Azad. *Long Shot* — B
   Richardson, Edmund. *The King's Shadow* — 958.1
DESERTS
   Atleework, Kendra. *Miracle Country* — 979.4
   Owens, Jay. *Dust* — 551.51
   Rawlence, Ben. *City of Thorns* — 967.7305
   Ronstadt, Linda. *Feels Like Home* — B
   Williams, Terry Tempest. *Erosion* — 814
Design. Black, Alexandra — 745.4
DESIGN
   Aronson, Joseph. *The Encyclopedia of Furniture* — 749
   Black, Alexandra. *Design* — 745.4
   Burnett, William. *Designing Your Life* — 650.1
   Howard, Hugh. *Architects of an American Landscape* — 712.092
   Khan, Yasmin Sabina. *Enlightening the World* — 974.7
   Lee, Vinny. *Kitchenalia* — 747.7
   Mars, Roman. ★*The 99% Invisible City* — 720
   Miller, Judith. *Furniture* — 749
   Szerlip, Barbara. *The Man Who Designed the Future* — B
DESIGN AND CONSTRUCTION
   Alexander, Rosemary. ★*The Essential Garden Design Workbook* — 712
   Baime, A. J. ★*Go Like Hell* — 796.7209
   Bauermeister, Erica. *House Lessons* — B
   Brenwall, Cynthia S. *The Central Park* — 974.7
   Brody, Mark. *Mosaic Garden Projects* — 712

PUBLIC LIBRARY CORE COLLECTION: NONFICTION
Twentieth Edition

Byers, Charles T. *Ultimate Guide Home Repair and Improvement*	643
Caro, Robert A. *The Power Broker*	B
Chesshire, Charles. *Japanese Gardening*	712
Feldmann, Erica. *Hausmagick*	133.4
Greayer, Rochelle. *Cultivating Garden Style*	712
Hafner, Katie. *A Romance on Three Legs*	786.2092
Hirsch, William J. *Designing Your Perfect House*	728
Holmes, Roger. *Midwest Home Landscaping*	712
Howcroft, Heidi. *Garden Design*	712
Jordan, Wendy Adler. *Universal Design for the Home*	728
King, Ross. *Brunelleschi's Dome*	726.6
Koones, Sheri. *Prefabulous Small Houses*	728
Langewiesche, William. *American Ground*	974.7
Mayes, Frances. *Under the Tuscan Sun*	945
McCullough, David G. *The Path Between the Seas*	972.87
Pember, Mat. *DIY Garden Projects*	712
Petersik, Sherry. *Lovable Livable Home*	645
Pierce, D. *The Accessible Home*	728
Ploszajski, Anna. *Handmade*	620.1
Schwartz, Bobbie. *Garden Renovation*	635
Scott, Jonathan. ★*Dream Home*	643
Slatalla, Michelle. *Gardenista*	635
Smith, Nathan. *Color Concrete Garden Projects*	721
Snow, Richard. *Disney's Land*	791.06
Thorstensen, Ole. *Making Things Right*	690
Ujifusa, Steven. *Barons of the Sea*	387.5
Whitney, Craig R. *All the Stops*	786.5
Williams, Bunny. *On Garden Style*	712
Design by Nature. Tanov, Erica	747
The Designer Within. McClain, John	645
DESIGNERS	
Szerlip, Barbara. *The Man Who Designed the Future*	B
Designing History. Smith, Michael S.	975.3
Designing with Light. Gillette, J. Michael	792
Designing Your Life. Burnett, William	650.1
Designing Your Perfect House. Hirsch, William J.	728
Desilva, Jeremy	
First Steps	599.93
DESIRE	
Belcher, Chris. *Pretty Baby*	B
Cain, Susan. ★*Bittersweet*	155.2
Carson, Anne. *The Beauty of the Husband*	811
Diaz, Natalie. ★*Postcolonial Love Poem*	811
Faliveno, Melissa. *Tomboyland*	B
Feast, Fancy. *Naked*	792.7
Febos, Melissa. *Girlhood*	818
Finkel, Michael. *The Art Thief*	364.1628
Frangello, Gina. *Blow Your House Down*	813
Godin, Seth. *The Practice*	153.3
Krimstein, Ken. *When I Grow Up*	741.5
Leamer, Laurence. *Hitchcock's Blondes*	791.43
Olds, Sharon. *Odes*	811
Perkins, Nichole. *Sometimes I Trip on How Happy We Could Be*	B
Pham, Larissa. *Pop Song*	709.2
Rothfeld, Becca. ★*All Things Are Too Small*	814
Sale, Anna. ★*Let's Talk About Hard Things*	153.6
Shanahan, Charif. *Trace Evidence*	811
Shapland, Jenn. ★*Thin Skin*	814
So, Anthony Veasna. ★*Songs on Endless Repeat*	814
Specter, Emma. *More, Please*	616.85
Taddeo, Lisa. *Three Women*	306.7082
Tallis, Frank. *The Incurable Romantic*	152.4
Volf, Miroslav. *Life Worth Living*	113
Ward, Maitland. *Rated X*	B
Weber, Charlotte Fox. *Tell Me What You Want*	153.8
Wenner, Jann. *Like a Rolling Stone*	B
Winter, Molly Roden. *More*	B
Desmond, Matthew	
★*Evicted*	339.4
★*Poverty, by America*	362.5
DESPAIR	
Hobbs, Jeff. *Children of the State*	364.36
Kyle, Taya. *American Spirit*	B
Manson, Mark. *Everything Is F*cked*	152.4
Morgan, Abi. *This Is Not a Pity Memoir*	B
Ralph, Laurence. *Sito*	364.152
Wiman, Christian. *Zero at the Bone*	818
Zamora, Javier. ★*Solito*	B
Desperate. Maher, Kris	344
★*The Desperate Hours.* Brenner, Marie	362.1962
Desperately Seeking Something. Seidelman, Susan	B
DESPOTISM	
Figes, Orlando. ★*The Story of Russia*	947
Gessen, Masha. *The Future Is History*	947.086
Gessen, Masha. *Never Remember*	365
Hochschild, Adam. *Lessons from a Dark Time*	909.82
Rothkopf, David J. *American Resistance*	973.933
DESROCHES-NOBLECOURT, CHRISTIANE, 1913-2011	
Olson, Lynne. ★*Empress of the Nile*	B
Dessert for Two. Lane, Christina	641.86
DESSERTS	
Arefi, Yossy. *Snacking Cakes*	641.86
Barrow, Cathy. ★*Pie Squared*	641.86
Behan, Ren. ★*The Sweet Polish Kitchen*	641.594
Beranbaum, Rose Levy. ★*The Cookie Bible*	641.86
Berens, Abra. *Pulp*	641.6
Chang, Joanne. *Pastry Love*	641.86
Cho, Kristina. *Mooncakes + Milk Bread*	641.595
Conners, Rachel. *Bakerita*	641.81
Gerson, Fany. *Mexican Ice Cream*	641.86
Gerson, Fany. *My Sweet Mexico*	641.5972
Goldman, Duff. *Duff Bakes*	641.81
Greenspan, Dorie. *Baking Chez Moi*	641.86
Heatter, Maida. *Happiness Is Baking*	641.86
Hoffman, Brian Hart. ★*Bake from Scratch; Volume Two*	641.81
Hollywood, Paul. ★*Bake*	641.81
Kartes, Danielle. *Butter, Flour, Sugar, Joy*	641.86
Lane, Christina. *Dessert for Two*	641.86
Lloyd, Bobbie. *The Magnolia Bakery Handbook*	641.86
Lomas, Vallery. ★*Life Is What You Bake It*	641.81
McDermott, Kate. ★*Art of the Pie*	641.86
McDowell, Erin Jeanne. ★*The Book on Pie*	641.86
Miglore, Kristen. *Food52 Genius Desserts*	641.86
Mubarak, Heather. *Stuffed*	641.86
Nelson, Candace. *The Sprinkles Baking Book*	641.81
Nelson, Kim. *Daisy Cakes Bakes*	641.86
Ottolenghi, Yotam. *Sweet*	641.86
Pansino, Rosanna. *Baking All Year Round*	641.86
Parks, Stella. ★*Bravetart*	641.86
Poliafito, Renato. ★*Dolci!*	641.81
Roman, Alison. *Sweet Enough*	641.86
Saffitz, Claire. ★*What's for Dessert*	641.86
Saltz, Joanna. ★*Delish Insane Sweets*	641.81
Seneviratne, Samantha. *Bake Smart*	641.81
Sheehan, Jessie. ★*Snackable Bakes*	641.7
Silverton, Nancy. ★*The Cookie That Changed My Life*	641.81
Snyder, Sabrina. *Dinner Then Dessert*	641.5
Tosi, Christina. *All About Cake*	641.86
Wright, Caroline. *Cake Magic!*	641.86
DeSteno, David	
How God Works	200.1
Destination Casablanca. Hindley, Meredith	940.54
Destiny. Jakes, T. D	248.4
★*Destiny and Power.* Meacham, Jon	B
Destiny of the Republic. Millard, Candice	973.8
The Destiny Thief. Russo, Richard	814
DESTROYERS (WARSHIPS)	
Sullivan, James. *Unsinkable*	940.54
DETECTIVES	
Boessenecker, John. *Gentleman Bandit*	B
Bowden, Mark. *The Case of the Vanishing Blonde*	364.10973
Bowden, Mark. *The Last Stone*	363.25
Callahan, Maureen. *American Predator*	364.152
Collins, Max Allan. *Eliot Ness and the Mad Butcher*	364.152
Hammer, Joshua. *The Falcon Thief*	364.16
Holes, Paul. *Unmasked*	363.25
Johnson, Steven. *The Infernal Machine*	335
Kenda, Joe. *Killer Triggers*	364.152
Leovy, Jill. *Ghettoside*	364.152
Stashower, Daniel. *American Demon*	364.152
DETECTIVES IN LITERATURE	
James, P. D. *Talking About Detective Fiction*	823
Sims, Michael. *Arthur and Sherlock*	B
DETENTION OF PEOPLE	
Adayfi, Mansoor. *Don't Forget Us Here*	B
Khan, Mahvish Rukhsana. *My Guantanamo Diary*	973.931

AUTHOR, TITLE, SERIES AND SUBJECT INDEX

Slahi, Mohamedou Ould. *The Mauritanian*   958.104
DETERDING, HENRI, 1866-1939
  Doran, Peter B. *Breaking Rockefeller*   338.7
DETERMINATION
  Anthony, Carmelo. *Where Tomorrows Aren't Promised*   B
  Bertch, Jane. *The French Ingredient*   B
  Brown, Daniel James. ★*The Boys in the Boat*   797.12
  Brown, Jasmine. *Twice as Hard*   610.92
  Cahalan, Susannah. *Brain on Fire*   616.8
  Carpenter, Kyle. *You Are Worth It*   B
  Clinton, Hillary Rodham. *The Book of Gutsy Women*   920
  Couric, Katie. *Going There*   B
  Downey, Kirstin. *Isabella*   B
  Drury, Bob. *Valley Forge*   973.3
  Eggers, Dave. *The Monk of Mokha*   B
  Everitt, Anthony. *Alexander the Great*   B
  Fitzmaurice, Simon. *It's Not yet Dark*   616.8
  Foles, Nick. *Believe It*   B
  Gaffigan, Jeannie. *When Life Gives You Pears*   B
  Gillette, Michael L. *Lady Bird Johnson*   B
  Girma, Haben. *Haben*   B
  Hart, Kevin. *I Can't Make This Up*   B
  Heminsley, Alexandra. *Running Like a Girl*   B
  Heumann, Judith E. *Being Heumann*   B
  Johnson, Katherine G. *My Remarkable Journey*   B
  Kalb, Bess. ★*Nobody Will Tell You This but Me*   306.874
  Keflezighi, Meb. *26 Marathons*   B
  Lee, Heath Hardage. ★*The League of Wives*   959.704
  Masters, Oksana. *The Hard Parts*   B
  Moore, Wes. *The Work*   B
  Morris, Edmund. ★*Edison*   B
  Mulgrew, Kate. *Born with Teeth*   791.45028
  Murray, Liz. *Breaking Night*   B
  Nyamayaro, Elizabeth. *I Am a Girl from Africa*   B
  O'Brien, Vanessa. *To the Greatest Heights*   B
  Obama, Barack. ★*A Promised Land*   B
  Odenkirk, Bob. *Comedy Comedy Comedy Drama*   B
  Onwuachi, Kwame. ★*Notes from a Young Black Chef*   641.59
  Petersen, Andrea. *On Edge*   616.85
  Porter, Billy. ★*Unprotected*   B
  Rahmani, Niloofar. *Open Skies*   B
  Rusbridger, Alan. ★*Play It Again*   B
  Sasakamoose, Fred. *Call Me Indian*   B
  Sweig, Julia. *Lady Bird Johnson*   B
  Thi, Kim Phuc Phan. *Fire Road*   B
  Thomas, Evan. ★*First*   B
  Thomas, Louisa. *Louisa*   B
  Welteroth, Elaine. *More Than Enough*   B
  Williams, Jay. *Life Is Not an Accident*   B
  Wilson, Chris. *The Master Plan*   B
  Yousafzai, Malala. *I Am Malala*   B
Determined. Sapolsky, Robert M.   123
DETOXIFICATION (HEALTH)
  Lee, Jennifer Tyler. *Half the Sugar, All the Love*   641.5
  Oakes, John G. H. ★*The Fast*   613.2
Detroit. LeDuff, Charlie   977.4
Detroit Resurrected. Bomey, Nathan   977.4
DETROIT, MICHIGAN
  Bomey, Nathan. *Detroit Resurrected*   977.4
  Boyd, Herb. *Black Detroit*   977.4
  Boyle, Kevin. *Arc of Justice*   345.73
  Chin, Curtis. *Everything I Learned, I Learned in a Chinese Restaurant*   B
  Kirshner, Jodie Adams. ★*Broke*   336.3
  LeDuff, Charlie. *Detroit*   977.4
  McMillan, Tracie. *The American Way of Eating*   338.4
  Miles, Tiya. *The Dawn of Detroit*   977.4
  Stahr, Celia. *Frida in America*   B
Dettmer, Philipp
  Immune   616.07
Deutsch, Babette
  Poetry Handbook   808.1
Deutscher, Guy
  ★*Through the Language Glass*   410
Devantez, Chelsea
  ★*I Shouldn't Be Telling You This*   B
DEVANTEZ, CHELSEA
  Devantez, Chelsea. ★*I Shouldn't Be Telling You This*   B

DeVeaux, Scott Knowles
  Jazz   781.65
Developing an Outstanding Core Collection. Alabaster, Carol   025.2
DEVELOPING COUNTRIES
  Kristof, Nicholas D. *Half the Sky*   362.83
  Sharma, Ruchir. *The Rise and Fall of Nations*   330.9
Developing Library Collections for Today's Young Adults. Pattee, Amy   027.62
DEVELOPMENTAL BIOLOGY
  Brookwood, Marilyn. *The Orphans of Davenport*   305.231
  Martinez Arias, Alfonso. *The Master Builder*   571.6
DEVELOPMENTAL NEUROBIOLOGY
  Eliot, Lise. *Pink Brain, Blue Brain*   612.6
  Sapolsky, Robert M. *Behave*   612.8
DEVELOPMENTAL PSYCHOLOGY
  Boyce, W. Thomas. *The Orchid and the Dandelion*   649
  Brookwood, Marilyn. *The Orphans of Davenport*   305.231
  Gopnik, Alison. *The Gardener and the Carpenter*   155.4
  Way, Niobe. *Rebels with a Cause*   649
DEVIANT BEHAVIOR
  Kalb, Claudia. *Andy Warhol Was a Hoarder*   920
The Deviant's War. Cervini, Eric   B
DEVIL
  Goethe, Johann Wolfgang von. *Goethe's Faust*   832
  Lewis, C. S. ★*The Screwtape Letters*   248.4
  Pagels, Elaine H. *The Origin of Satan*   235
  Sullivan, Randall. *The Devil's Best Trick*   235
  Wray, T. J. *The Birth of Satan*   235
★*Devil in the Grove*. King, Gilbert   305.896
★*The Devil in the Shape of a Woman*. Karlsen, Carol F.   133.4
★*The Devil in the White City*. Larson, Erik   364.15
The Devil Within. Levack, Brian P.   133.4
The Devil's Best Trick. Sullivan, Randall   235
The Devil's Harvest. Garrison, Jessica   B
The Devil's Highway. Urrea, Luis Alberto   304.8
★*The Devil's Playbook*. Etter, Lauren   338.7
The Devils' Alliance. Moorhouse, Roger   940.53
DEVONSHIRE, WILLIAM CAVENDISH, DUKE OF, 1748-1811
  Foreman, Amanda. *Georgiana, Duchess of Devonshire*   B
DEVOTEDNESS
  Cohen, Rhaina. ★*The Other Significant Others*   177
  Jebara, Mohamad. *Muhammad, the World-Changer*   B
Devotion. Makos, Adam   920
★*Devotions*. Oliver, Mary   811
★*Dewey*. Myron, Vicki   636.80092
DEWEY (MARMALADE CAT)
  Myron, Vicki. ★*Dewey*   636.80092
DEWEY, THOMAS E., (THOMAS EDMUND), 1902-1971
  Carter, Stephen L. *Invisible*   B
DGE-LUGS-PA DOCTRINES
  Dalai Lama. *The Second Dalai Lama*   294.3
DHARMA (BUDDHISM)
  Chodron, Pema. *Practicing Peace*   294.3
  Dalai Lama. *Approaching the Buddhist Path*   294.3
  Gupta, Suneel. *Everyday Dharma*   158.1
Di Cintio, Marcello
  Pay No Heed to the Rockets   956.9405
DI CINTIO, MARCELLO, 1973-
  Di Cintio, Marcello. *Pay No Heed to the Rockets*   956.9405
Di Giovanni, Janine
  The Morning They Came for Us   956.9104
Di Maio, Vincent J. M.
  Morgue   B
DI MAIO, VINCENT J. M., 1941-2022
  Di Maio, Vincent J. M. *Morgue*   B
DIABETES
  Castro, M. Regina. ★*The Essential Diabetes Book*   616.4
  Rondinelli-Hamilton, Lara. *The Diabetes Cookbook*   641.5
  Taubes, Gary. ★*Rethinking Diabetes*   616.462
The Diabetes Cookbook. Rondinelli-Hamilton, Lara   641.5
Diaconis, Persi
  Magical Mathematics   793.8
DIAGNOSIS
  Cahalan, Susannah. ★*The Great Pretender*   616.89
  Foulkes, Lucy. ★*Losing Our Minds*   616.89
  Gentile, Olivia. *Life List*   598.072
  Gooch, Brad. ★*Flannery*   B
  Jaouad, Suleika. ★*Between Two Kingdoms*   B
  Kelly, Christopher R. *Am I Dying?!*   362.1

PUBLIC LIBRARY CORE COLLECTION: NONFICTION
Twentieth Edition

Lieberman, Jeffrey A. *Malady of the Mind* — 616.89
Love, Susan M. ★*Dr. Susan Love's Breast Book* — 618.1
McCourt, Malachy. *Singing My Him Song* — B
Nerenberg, Jenara. *Divergent Mind* — 616.89
O'Rourke, Meghan. ★*The Invisible Kingdom* — 616
Saul, Richard. *ADHD Does Not Exist* — 618.92
DIAGNOSTIC ERRORS
　Cahalan, Susannah. *Brain on Fire* — 616.8
　Cleghorn, Elinor. *Unwell Women* — 613
　Ramey, Sarah. *The Lady's Handbook for Her Mysterious Illness* — B
　Schwarz, Alan. *ADHD Nation* — 618.92
Dial, Roman
　The Adventurer's Son — 917.286
DIAL, ROMAN
　Dial, Roman. *The Adventurer's Son* — 917.286
Dialogue. McKee, Robert — 809
DIAMANDIS, PETER H.
　Guthrie, Julian. *How to Make a Spaceship* — 629.47
Diamant, Anita
　The Jewish Wedding Now — 296.4
　★*Period. End of Sentence* — 612.6
　Pitching My Tent — 296.7
DIAMANT, ANITA
　Diamant, Anita. *Pitching My Tent* — 296.7
DIAMOND INDUSTRY AND TRADE
　Junger, Sebastian. *Fire* — 909.82
Diamond, Cheryl
　Nowhere Girl — B
DIAMOND, CHERYL
　Diamond, Cheryl. *Nowhere Girl* — B
Diamond, Jared M.
　Collapse — 304.2
　Guns, Germs, and Steel — 303.4
　Swing Kings — 796.357
　Upheaval — 303.48
Diana. Morton, Andrew — B
The Diana Chronicles. Brown, Tina — B
DIANA, PRINCESS OF WALES, 1961-1997
　Brown, Tina. *The Diana Chronicles* — B
　Holmes, Elizabeth. *HRH* — 941.085
　Morton, Andrew. *Diana* — B
Diane Arbus. Lubow, Arthur — B
DIANETICS
　Reitman, Janet. *Inside Scientology* — 299
　Rinder, Mike. ★*A Billion Years* — B
　Wright, Lawrence. *Going Clear* — 299
DiAngelo, Robin J.
　White Fragility — 305.8
DIARIES
　Berr, Helene. *The Journal of Helene Berr* — B
　Berry, Wendell. ★*The World-Ending Fire* — 818
　Brown, Tina. *The Vanity Fair Diaries* — B
　Englund, Peter. *November 1942* — 940.53
　Frank, Anne. *The Diary of Anne Frank* — B
　Harrington, Joel F. *The Faithful Executioner* — B
　Highsmith, Patricia. ★*Patricia Highsmith's Diaries and Notebooks* — 818
　Kahlo, Frida. *The Diary of Frida Kahlo* — B
　Kempowski, Walter. *Swansong 1945* — 940.54
　Orwell, George. *Diaries* — 828
　Pepys, Samuel. *The Diary of Samuel Pepys* — B
　Reagan, Ronald. *The Reagan Diaries* — B
　Rusbridger, Alan. ★*Play It Again* — B
　Samer. *The Raqqa Diaries* — 956.9104
　Sedaris, David. ★*A Carnival of Snackery* — 818
　Sedaris, David. *Theft by Finding* — B
　Siegal, Nina. *The Diary Keepers* — 940.54
　Tomalin, Claire. *Samuel Pepys* — B
　Walker, Alice. *Gathering Blossoms Under Fire* — B
　Weiss, Helga. *Helga's Diary* — B
Diaries. Orwell, George — 828
The Diaries of Victor Klemperer [Series]. Klemperer, Victor — B
The Diary Keepers. Siegal, Nina — 940.54
Diary of a Combatant. Guevara, Che — 972.91063
Diary of a Misfit. Parks, Casey — B
★*The Diary of a Young Girl*. Frank, Anne — 940.53
Diary of a Young Naturalist. McAnulty, Dara — 508.092
The Diary of Anne Frank. Frank, Anne — B
The Diary of Anne Frank. Goodrich, Frances — 812
The Diary of Frida Kahlo. Kahlo, Frida — B
The Diary of Mary Berg. Berg, Mary — B
The Diary of Samuel Pepys. Pepys, Samuel — B
DIARY WRITING
　Burton, Susan. *Empty* — B
　Englund, Peter. *November 1942* — 940.53
　Gabbert, Elisa. *Any Person Is the Only Self* — 814
　Heti, Sheila. *Alphabetical Diaries* — 818
　Highsmith, Patricia. ★*Patricia Highsmith's Diaries and Notebooks* — 818
　Mazzeo, Tilar J. *Sisters in Resistance* — 945.091
　V. ★*Reckoning* — 814
★*Diasporican*. Maisonet, Illyanna — 641.597295
Diaz del Castillo, Bernal
　The Discovery and Conquest of Mexico, 1517-1521 — 972
Diaz, Jaquira
　Ordinary Girls — 818
DIAZ, JAQUIRA
　Diaz, Jaquira. *Ordinary Girls* — 818
Diaz, Natalie
　★*Postcolonial Love Poem* — 811
Diaz, Tom
　The Last Gun — 338.4
Diaz, Von
　★*Islas* — 641.59
DICKENS, CHARLES, 1812-1870
　Wilson, A. N. *The Mystery of Charles Dickens* — 823
Dickerman, Leah
　Dada — 709
Dickey, Bronwen
　Pit Bull — 636.755
Dickey, Colin
　Ghostland — 133.1
　The Unidentified — 130
Dickie, Gloria
　Eight Bears — 599.78
Dickinson. Dickinson, Emily — 811
Dickinson, Amy
　Strangers Tend to Tell Me Things — B
DICKINSON, AMY
　Dickinson, Amy. *Strangers Tend to Tell Me Things* — B
Dickinson, Bruce
　What Does This Button Do? — B
DICKINSON, BRUCE, 1958-
　Dickinson, Bruce. *What Does This Button Do?* — B
Dickinson, Emily
　★*The Complete Poems* — 811.4
　Dickinson — 811
DICKINSON, EMILY, 1830-1886
　Ackmann, Martha. ★*These Fevered Days* — B
　Dickinson, Emily. *Dickinson* — 811
Dickinson, Richard
　Weeds of North America — 632
Dickson, Paul
　The Rise of the G.I. Army 1940-1941 — 940.54
DICTATORS
　Bardenwerper, William. *The Prisoner in His Palace* — 956.7044
　Cercas, Javier. *Lord of All the Dead* — 868
　Elwood, Phil. *All the Worst Humans* — 659.2
　Fifield, Anna. *The Great Successor* — B
　Findakly, Brigitte. *Poppies of Iraq* — 741.5
　Harden, Blaine. *The Great Leader and the Fighter Pilot* — B
　Hubbard, Ben (Journalist). *Mbs* — B
　Kalder, Daniel. *The Infernal Library* — 321.9
　Kershaw, Ian. *Hitler* — B
　Khlevniuk, Oleg V. *Stalin* — B
　Lankov, A. N. *The Real North Korea* — 951.9304
　Nixon, John. *Debriefing the President* — 956.7044
　Pak, Jung H. *Becoming Kim Jong Un* — B
　Rees, Laurence. *Hitler and Stalin* — 940.53
　Sebag-Montefiore, Simon. *Young Stalin* — B
　Sebestyen, Victor. *Lenin* — B
　Snyder, Timothy. ★*Bloodlands* — 940.54
　Suny, Ronald Grigor. *Stalin* — B
　Ullrich, Volker. *Hitler* — B
　Ullrich, Volker. *Hitler* — B
DICTATORSHIP
　Dagher, Sam. *Assad or We Burn the Country* — 956.9104
　Demick, Barbara. ★*Nothing to Envy* — 920

AUTHOR, TITLE, SERIES AND SUBJECT INDEX

Faloyin, Dipo. ★*Africa Is Not a Country*	960.33
Fifield, Anna. *The Great Successor*	B
Hessler, Peter. *Other Rivers*	378.1
Hochschild, Adam. *Spain in Our Hearts*	946.081
Hubbard, Ben (Journalist). *Mbs*	B
Jang, Lucia. *Stars Between the Sun and Moon*	365.45092
Jeppesen, Travis. *See You Again in Pyongyang*	951.93
Kalder, Daniel. *The Infernal Library*	321.9
McDonough, Frank. *The Hitler Years*	943.086
Pak, Jung H. *Becoming Kim Jong Un*	B
Preston, Paul. *The Spanish Holocaust*	946.081
Rees, Laurence. *Hitler and Stalin*	940.53
Sattouf, Riad. *The Arab of the Future 2*	741.5
Sattouf, Riad. *The Arab of the Future*	741.5
Snyder, Timothy. ★*Bloodlands*	940.54
Trentmann, Frank. *Out of the Darkness*	943.08
Tudor, Daniel. *North Korea Confidential*	951.93

DICTIONARIES

Atherley, Kate. *The Knitter's Dictionary*	746.43
Baldick, Chris. ★*The Oxford Dictionary of Literary Terms*	803
Brewer, Ebenezer Cobham. ★*Brewer's Dictionary of Phrase & Fable*	423
Darcey, Cheralyn. *Flowerpaedia*	580
Espy, Willard R. *Words to Rhyme With*	423
Garner, Bryan A. *Garner's Modern English Usage*	423
Park, Chris C. *A Dictionary of Environment and Conservation*	333.703
Pukui, Mary Kawena. *Hawaiian Dictionary*	499
Shaw, Ian. *The Princeton Dictionary of Ancient Egypt*	932
Simpson, J. A. *The Word Detective*	B
Stamper, Kory. *Word by Word*	413.028
Tennant, Richard A. *The American Sign Language Handshape Dictionary*	419
★*A Dictionary of Buddhism*. Keown, Damien	294.3
A Dictionary of Environment and Conservation. Park, Chris C.	333.703
Dictionary of Gods and Goddesses. Jordan, Michael	202
The Dictionary of Imaginary Places. Manguel, Alberto	809
The Dictionary of the Book. Berger, Sidney E	002.03
The Dictionary People. Ogilvie, Sarah	423
Did I Ever Tell You?. Kingston, Genevieve	B
★*Did Ye Hear Mammy Died?*. O'Reilly, Seamas	B
Did You Eat Yet?. Woo, Ronnie	641.595

DIDDY, 1969-

Greenburg, Zack O'Malley. *3 Kings*	782.421649
Diderot and the Art of Thinking Freely. Curran, Andrew S.	194

DIDEROT, DENIS, 1713-1784

Curran, Andrew S. *Diderot and the Art of Thinking Freely*	194

Didion, Joan

★*Let Me Tell You What I Mean*	814
Where I Was from	979.4
★*The Year of Magical Thinking*	B

DIDION, JOAN, 1934-2021

Daugherty, Tracy. *The Last Love Song*	B
Didion, Joan. ★*Let Me Tell You What I Mean*	814
Didion, Joan. *Where I Was from*	979.4
Didion, Joan. ★*The Year of Magical Thinking*	B
Die Hot with a Vengeance. Yong, Sable	646.7

DIET

Bittman, Mark. *A Bone to Pick*	338.10973
Dooner, Caroline. *Tired as F*ck*	152.1
Guyenet, Stephan J. *The Hungry Brain*	616.85
Harrison, Christy. *The Wellness Trap*	613
Kauffman, Jonathan. *Hippie Food*	394.1
Kingsolver, Barbara. ★*Animal, Vegetable, Miracle*	641
Meltzer, Marisa. *This Is Big*	613.25
Mitchell, Andie. *Eating in the Middle*	641.3
Moss, Michael. ★*Hooked*	613.2
Pollan, Michael. *The Omnivore's Dilemma*	394.1
Taubes, Gary. ★*Rethinking Diabetes*	616.462
Tomlinson, Tommy. *The Elephant in the Room*	B
Wilson, Bee. *The Way We Eat Now*	641.01

DIET AND DISEASE

Freeman, Andrea. ★*Ruin Their Crops on the Ground*	338.1
Urban, Melissa. *The Whole30 Friends & Family*	641.5

DIET INDUSTRY AND TRADE

Kazdin, Cole. ★*What's Eating Us*	616.85
King, Chrissy. *The Body Liberation Project*	306.4
Meltzer, Marisa. *This Is Big*	613.25

DIETING

Barrett, Pearl. *Trim Healthy Mama Trim Healthy Table*	613.2
Bittman, Mark. *The VB6 Cookbook*	641.5
Bittman, Mark. *VB6*	641.5
Clein, Emmeline. ★*Dead Weight*	616.85
Curry, Kevin. *Fit Men Cook*	641.5
Fuhrman, Joel. *Eat to Live Quick & Easy Cookbook*	641.5
Greger, Michael. ★*The How Not to Diet Cookbook*	641.5
Hartwig, Melissa. *The Whole30 Fast & Easy*	641.5
Homolka, Gina. *Skinnytaste Fast and Slow*	641.5
Homolka, Gina. *Skinnytaste One & Done*	641.5
Kazdin, Cole. ★*What's Eating Us*	616.85
Ludwig, David. *Always Hungry?*	613.2
Meltzer, Marisa. *This Is Big*	613.25
Schatzker, Mark. *The Dorito Effect*	641.3
Sole-Smith, Virginia. ★*Fat Talk*	649.1
Tandoh, Ruby. ★*Eat Up*	641.3
Urban, Melissa. *The Whole30 Friends & Family*	641.5
Wolf, Robb. *Wired to Eat*	641.5

Dietrich, Sean

You Are My Sunshine	B

DIETRICH, SEAN, 1982-

Dietrich, Sean. *You Are My Sunshine*	B

DiFelice, Bekah

Almost There	248.8

DIFELICE, BEKAH

DiFelice, Bekah. *Almost There*	248.8

DIFFERENCE

Morrison, Toni. ★*The Origin of Others*	809
Rodgers, Jodi. ★*How to Find a Four-Leaf Clover*	616.85

DIFFERENCE (PHILOSOPHY)

Karim-Cooper, Farah. ★*The Great White Bard*	822.33
A Different Kind of Daughter. Toorpakai, Maria	B
Difficult Conversations. Stone, Douglas	158.2
Difficult Men. Martin, Brett	791.4509

DIFFUSION OF INNOVATIONS

Bahcall, Safi. *Loonshots*	658.4

DiFranco, Ani

No Walls and the Recurring Dream	782.42164

DIFRANCO, ANI

DiFranco, Ani. *No Walls and the Recurring Dream*	782.42164
Dig If You Will the Picture. Greenman, Ben	B

DIGESTION

Roach, Mary. *Gulp*	612.3
Roman, Joe. *Eat, Poop, Die*	577

DIGESTIVE ORGANS

Roach, Mary. *Gulp*	612.3
Scarlata, Kate. *Mind Your Gut*	616.3
Digging for Richard III. Pitts, Mike	942.046

DIGITAL ART

Small, Zachary. ★*Token Supremacy*	332.4

DIGITAL CAMERAS

Ang, Tom. *Digital Photographer's Handbook*	771
Freeman, Michael. *The Photographer's Mind*	770

DIGITAL CINEMATOGRAPHY

Pincus, Edward. *The Filmmaker's Handbook*	777

DIGITAL COMMUNICATIONS

Duncan, Dennis. *Index, a History of The*	025.3

DIGITAL CURRENCY

Lewis, Michael. ★*Going Infinite*	305.5

DIGITAL MAPPING

Cheshire, James. *Where the Animals Go*	591.47

DIGITAL MEDIA

DiResta, Renee. *Invisible Rulers*	320
Galloway, Scott. *The Four*	338.7
Haidt, Jonathan. ★*The Anxious Generation*	305.23
Hill, Marc Lamont. *Seen and Unseen*	303.3
Smith, Ben. *Traffic*	070.4
Taplin, Jonathan. *Move Fast and Break Things*	330.9
Wolf, Maryanne. *Reader, Come Home*	418

DIGITAL MUSIC

Calamar, Gary. *Record Store Days*	780.26
Dolby, Thomas. *The Speed of Sound*	B
Digital Photographer's Handbook. Ang, Tom	771
Digital Photography. Horenstein, Henry	770

DIGITAL PHOTOGRAPHY

Ang, Tom. *Digital Photographer's Handbook*	771
Ang, Tom. *Digital Photography Masterclass*	770
Fagans, Michael. *iPhone Photography for Everybody*	770

PUBLIC LIBRARY CORE COLLECTION: NONFICTION
Twentieth Edition

Fordham, Demetrius. ★*If You're Bored with Your Camera Read This Book*   770.23
  Freeman, Michael. *The Photographer's Mind*   770
  Gatcum, Chris. ★*The Beginner's Photography Guide*   770
  Horenstein, Henry. *Digital Photography*   770
  Taylor, David. *Digital Photography Complete Course*   770
Digital Photography Complete Course. Taylor, David   770
Digital Photography Masterclass. Ang, Tom   770
DIGITAL VIDEO
  Pincus, Edward. *The Filmmaker's Handbook*   777
DiGiulian, Sasha
  Take the Lead   B
DIGIULIAN, SASHA
  DiGiulian, Sasha. *Take the Lead*   B
DIGNITY
  Jackson, Major. *Razzle Dazzle*   811
  Mannix, Kathryn. *With the End in Mind*   304.6
  Pratt, Victoria. *The Power of Dignity*   364.973
DiGregorio, Sarah
  Adventures in Slow Cooking   641.5
  Early   618.92
  ★*Taking Care*   610.73
DIGREGORIO, SARAH
  DiGregorio, Sarah. *Early*   618.92
Dikotter, Frank
  China After Mao   951.05
  The Cultural Revolution   951.056
  Mao's Great Famine   951.05
Dilbeck, D. H.
  Frederick Douglass   B
DILIGENCE
  Duckworth, Angela. *Grit*   158.1
Dillard, Annie
  The Abundance   814
  An American Childhood   B
  Pilgrim at Tinker Creek   508
  Teaching a Stone to Talk   508
  The Writing Life   B
DILLARD, ANNIE
  Dillard, Annie. *An American Childhood*   B
  Dillard, Annie. *The Writing Life*   B
DILLARD, DERICK
  Duggar, Jill. *Counting the Cost*   B
DIMAGGIO, DOM
  Clavin, Thomas. *The DiMaggios*   920
  Halberstam, David. *The Teammates*   B
DIMAGGIO, JOE, 1914-1999
  Clavin, Thomas. *The DiMaggios*   920
  Cramer, Richard Ben. *Joe DiMaggio*   B
DIMAGGIO, VINCE
  Clavin, Thomas. *The DiMaggios*   920
The DiMaggios. Clavin, Thomas   920
DiMarco, Nyle
  ★*Deaf Utopia*   B
DIMARCO, NYLE, 1989-
  DiMarco, Nyle. ★*Deaf Utopia*   B
Dimbleby, Jonathan
  The Battle of the Atlantic   940.54
DIMENSIONS
  Weill, Kelly. *Off the Edge*   001.9
Dimestore. Smith, Lee   975.5
Dimitrius, Jo-Ellan
  Reading People   155.2
Dine. Iverson, Peter   979.1004
Dinesen, Isak
  Out of Africa   967.62
DINESEN, ISAK, 1885-1962
  Dinesen, Isak. *Out of Africa*   967.62
Dining In. Roman, Alison   641.5
Dinki, Nikki
  Meat on the Side   641.3
Dinner. Clark, Melissa   641.5
★*Dinner for Everyone*. Bittman, Mark   641.5
★*Dinner in an Instant*. Clark, Melissa   641.5
Dinner in French. Clark, Melissa   641.594
★*Dinner in One*. Clark, Melissa   641.82
Dinner Solved! Workman, Katie   641.5
Dinner Then Dessert. Snyder, Sabrina   641.5

Dinner Tonight. Berg, Meliz   641.595
Dinner Tonight. Snodgrass, Alex   641.5
★*Dinner with the President*. Prud'homme, Alex   973
DINNERS AND DINING
  Bass, Rick. *The Traveling Feast*   B
  Bourdain, Anthony. ★*Appetites*   641.5
  Bowen, Dana. *Dynamite Kids Cooking School*   641.5
  Cecchi-Azzolina, Michael. *Your Table Is Ready*   647.95
  Harrison, Jim. *The Search for the Genuine*   814
  Henaut, Stephane. *A Bite-Sized History of France*   394.1
  Heuck, Lidey. ★*Cooking in Real Life*   641.5
  Hussain, Nadiya. ★*Nadiya's Everyday Baking*   641.5
  Merchant, Jessica. *Everyday Dinners*   641.82
  Porowski, Antoni. *Antoni*   641.5
  Rosenstrach, Jenny. *How to Celebrate Everything*   641.5
  Snodgrass, Alex. *Dinner Tonight*   641.5
  Villasuso, Susana. *Sobremesa*   641.5972
  Wong, Cecily. ★*Gastro Obscura*   641.3
  Zizka, Maria. *The Hostess Handbook*   642
★*Dinners with Ruth*. Totenberg, Nina   B
DINOSAURS
  Black, Riley. *The Last Days of the Dinosaurs*   576.8
  Brusatte, Stephen. ★*The Rise and Fall of the Dinosaurs*   567.9
  Lacovara, Kenneth. *Why Dinosaurs Matter*   567.9
  Paul, Gregory S. *The Princeton Field Guide to Dinosaurs*   567.9
  Pim, Keiron. *Dinosaurs the Grand Tour*   567.9
Dinosaurs The Grand Tour. Pim, Keiron   567.9
DIORAMAS
  Goldfarb, Bruce. ★*18 Tiny Deaths*   B
DIPLOMACY
  Albright, Madeleine Korbel. *Hell and Other Destinations*   B
  Beschloss, Michael R. *The Conquerors*   940.53
  Bouverie, Tim. *Appeasement*   327.41043
  Brands, H. W. *The First American*   B
  Burns, William J. *The Back Channel*   B
  Charter, David. *Royal Audience*   941.085
  Churchill, Winston. *The Grand Alliance*   940.53
  Churchill, Winston. *Their Finest Hour*   940.53
  Churchill, Winston. *Triumph and Tragedy*   940.53
  Conradi, Peter J. *Who Lost Russia?*   947.086
  Dodds Pennock, Caroline. ★*On Savage Shores*   970.004
  Farrow, Ronan. *War on Peace*   327.73
  Fischer, David Hackett. *Champlain's Dream*   B
  Fullilove, Michael. *Rendezvous with Destiny*   973.917092
  Gates, Robert Michael. ★*Exercise of Power*   973.929
  Gewen, Barry. ★*The Inevitability of Tragedy*   B
  Hindley, Meredith. *Destination Casablanca*   940.54
  Horn, Jonathan. *Washington's End*   B
  Indyk, Martin. *Master of the Game*   327.73
  Katz, Catherine Grace. *The Daughters of Yalta*   920
  Kemper, Steve. *Our Man in Tokyo*   952.03
  Kertzer, David I. *The Pope at War*   940.53
  Loyn, David. *The Long War*   958.104
  Lukacs, John. *Five Days in London, May 1940*   940.53
  Mann, Jim. *The Rebellion of Ronald Reagan*   973.927092
  McCarten, Anthony. *Darkest Hour*   941.084
  McKean, David. *Watching Darkness Fall*   940.53
  McMeekin, Sean. *July 1914*   940.3
  McMeekin, Sean. *Stalin's War*   940.53
  Meacham, Jon. *Franklin and Winston*   940.53
  Moorhouse, Roger. *The Devils' Alliance*   940.53
  Olson, Lynne. *Citizens of London*   940.54012
  Olson, Lynne. *Last Hope Island*   940.53
  Olson, Lynne. *Those Angry Days*   940.53
  Paradis, Michel. *The Light of Battle*   940.54
  Plokhy, Serhii. *Yalta*   940.53
  Preston, Diana. *Eight Days at Yalta*   940.53
  Roberts, Andrew. *Masters and Commanders*   940.5322
DIPLOMATIC AND CONSULAR SERVICE
  Albright, Madeleine Korbel. *Hell and Other Destinations*   B
  Bailey, Catherine. *A Castle in Wartime*   943.086
  Eisen, Norman L. *The Last Palace*   920
  Moorhouse, Roger. *The Forgers*   940.53
  Shimer, David. *Rigged*   324.60973
DIPLOMATIC NEGOTIATIONS IN INTERNATIONAL DISPUTES
  Barrett, David Dean. *140 Days to Hiroshima*   940.54
  Conradi, Peter J. *Who Lost Russia?*   947.086
  Halevi, Yossi Klein. ★*Letters to My Palestinian Neighbor*   956.94054

AUTHOR, TITLE, SERIES AND SUBJECT INDEX

Rezaian, Jason. *Prisoner* — B
Von Tunzelmann, Alex. *Blood and Sand* — 909.82
DIPLOMATS
  Boucheron, Patrick. *Machiavelli* — 320.1092
  Burns, William J. *The Back Channel* — B
  Cannadine, David. ★*Mellon* — B
  Clarke, Thurston. *Honorable Exit* — 959.704
  Cook, Jane Hampton. *American Phoenix* — 973.5
  Eisen, Norman L. *The Last Palace* — 920
  Fasulo, Linda M. *An Insider's Guide to the Un, 4th Ed.* — 341.23
  Grandin, Greg. *Kissinger's Shadow* — B
  Larson, Erik. *In the Garden of Beasts* — B
  McGrath, Tim. *James Monroe* — B
  Meacham, Jon. ★*Thomas Jefferson* — B
  Mendez, Antonio J. *Argo* — 955.05
  Packer, George. *Our Man* — B
  Rakove, Jack N. *Revolutionaries* — 973.3
  Unger, Harlow G. *The Last Founding Father* — B
  Yovanovitch, Marie. *Lessons from the Edge* — 973.933
  Zuckoff, Mitchell. *The Secret Gate* — 958.104
★*Directed* by James Burrows. Burrows, James — 791.4502
DIRECTIONS (GEOGRAPHY)
  Sobel, Dava. *Longitude* — 526
Directorate S. Coll, Steve — 958.104
DIRECTORS OF CENTRAL INTELLIGENCE
  Whipple, Chris. *The Spymasters* — 920
DiResta, Renee
  Invisible Rulers — 320
Dirix, Emmanuelle
  Dressing the Decades — 746.92
★*Dirt*. Buford, Bill — B
Dirtbag, Massachusetts. Fitzgerald, Isaac — B
DIRTINESS
  Herman, Eleanor. *The Royal Art of Poison* — 364.152
Dirty South. Westhoff, Ben — 782.421649
The Dirty Tricks Department. Lisle, John — 940.54
Dirty Wars. Scahill, Jeremy — 355.00973
★*Dirty Work*. Press, Eyal — 331.7
DISABILITIES
  Belser, Julia Watts. ★*Loving Our Own Bones* — 296
  Burcaw, Shane. ★*Laughing at My Nightmare* — B
  Fleming, Jory. *How to Be Human* — 616.85
  greathouse, torrin a. *Wound from the Mouth of a Wound* — 811
  Grue, Jan. *I Live a Life Like Yours* — B
  Hardwick, Lamar. *How Ableism Fuels Racism* — 261.8
  Ladau, Emily. *Demystifying Disability* — 305.9
  Nielsen, Kim E. *A Disability History of the United States* — 362.40973
  Taussig, Rebekah. *Sitting Pretty* — B
  Wong, Alice. ★*Year of the Tiger* — B
A Disability History of the United States. Nielsen, Kim E. — 362.40973
Disability Pride. Mattlin, Ben — 323.3
DISABILITY RIGHTS ADVOCATES
  Girma, Haben. *Haben* — B
  Ndopu, Eddie. *Sipping Dom Pérignon Through a Straw* — B
  Taussig, Rebekah. *Sitting Pretty* — B
DISABILITY RIGHTS MOVEMENT
  Blake, Melissa. *Beautiful People* — 362.4
  Heumann, Judith E. *Being Heumann* — B
DISAGREEMENT
  Arnsdorf, Isaac. ★*Finish What We Started* — 320.52
  Freeman, Joanne B. *The Field of Blood* — 973.7
  Hayhoe, Katharine. *Saving Us* — 304.2
A Disappearance in Damascus. Campbell, Deborah — 365
DISAPPEARED PEOPLE
  Ahmed, Azam. *Fear Is Just a Word* — 364.152
  Hochschild, Adam. *The Unquiet Ghost* — 947.084
  Hoja, Gulchehra. *A Stone Is Most Precious Where It Belongs* — B
  Mohan, Rohini. *The Seasons of Trouble* — 954.9303
  Ypi, Lea. ★*Free* — B
The Disappearing Spoon. Kean, Sam — 546
DISAPPOINTMENT
  Kushner, Harold S. *Overcoming Life's Disappointments* — 296.7
The Disaster Artist. Sestero, Greg — 791.43
DISASTER FORECASTING
  Brannen, Peter. *The Ends of the World* — 576.8
★*Disaster Planning*. Halsted, Deborah D. — 025.8
★*The Disaster Planning Handbook for Libraries*. Flaherty, Mary Grace — 025.8

DISASTER RELIEF
  Bittle, Jake. ★*The Great Displacement* — 362.87
  Brinkley, Douglas. *The Great Deluge* — 976.3
  Ferguson, Niall. *Doom* — 362.1962
  Fink, Sheri. *Five Days at Memorial* — 362.1109763
  Horne, Jed. *Breach of Faith* — 976.3
  Jensen, Robert A. *Personal Effects* — 363.34
  Langewiesche, William. *American Ground* — 974.7
  Ripley, Amanda. *The Unthinkable* — 155.9
DISASTER VICTIMS
  Berg, Scott W. *The Burning of the World* — 977.311
  Brinkley, Douglas. *The Great Deluge* — 976.3
  Deraniyagala, Sonali. *Wave* — B
  Eggers, Dave. *Zeitoun* — 305.892
  Horne, Jed. *Breach of Faith* — 976.3
  Jensen, Robert A. *Personal Effects* — 363.34
  Johnson, Lizzie. ★*Paradise* — 363.37
  Neufeld, Josh. *A.D.* — 741.5
  Ripley, Amanda. *The Unthinkable* — 155.9
  Spera, Keith. *Groove Interrupted* — B
DISASTERS
  Aktipis, Athena. ★*A Field Guide to the Apocalypse* — 155.2
  Berg, Scott W. *The Burning of the World* — 977.311
  Cassidy, Cody. *How to Survive History* — 904
  Ferguson, Niall. *Doom* — 362.1962
  Gee, Alastair. *Fire in Paradise* — 363.37
  Hargrove, Brantley. *The Man Who Caught the Storm* — B
  Horne, Jed. *Breach of Faith* — 976.3
  Jensen, Robert A. *Personal Effects* — 363.34
  Johnson, Earl. *Finding Comfort During Hard Times* — 155.9
  Johnson, Lizzie. ★*Paradise* — 363.37
  Junger, Sebastian. *Fire* — 909.82
  Knight, Sam. *The Premonitions Bureau* — 133.8
  Ripley, Amanda. *The Unthinkable* — 155.9
  Schlosser, Eric. *Command and Control* — 363.17
  Singer, Jessie. *There Are No Accidents* — 363.1
  Slade, Rachel. *Into the Raging Sea* — 910.91
  Smith, Zadie. *Intimations* — 824
  Solnit, Rebecca. *A Paradise Built in Hell* — 303.48
  Winchester, Simon. *A Crack in the Edge of the World* — 979.4
Disbrowe, Paula
  Thank You for Smoking — 641.5
DISC JOCKEYS
  Moby. *Porcelain* — B
  Moby. *Then It Fell Apart* — B
DISCIPLINE
  Willink, Jocko. *Discipline Equals Freedom* — 158.1
Discipline Equals Freedom. Willink, Jocko — 158.1
DISCO MUSIC
  Stanley, Bob. ★*The Story of the Bee Gees* — 782.42164
DISCONTENT
  Chomsky, Noam. *Global Discontents* — 410.92
DISCOVERIES (IN GEOGRAPHY)
  Bellows, Amanda Brickell. *The Explorers* — 910.92
  Bound, Mensun. *The Ship Beneath the Ice* — 919.8904
  Cliff, Nigel. *Holy War* — 909
  Larson, Edward J. *An Empire of Ice* — 919.8
  Millard, Candice. ★*River of the Gods* — 916.204
  Turney, Chris. *1912* — 998
The Discoveries. Lightman, Alan P. — 509
Discovering The True Self. Sawaki, Kodo — 294.3
The Discovery and Conquest of Mexico, 1517-1521. Diaz del Castillo, Bernal — 972
The Discovery of Being. May, Rollo — 150.19
The Discovery of France. Robb, Graham — 944
DISCRIMINATION
  Agarwal, Pragya. *Sway* — 177
  Alexander, Stephon. *Fear of a Black Universe* — 523.1
  Asher, Zain E. *Where the Children Take Us* — 942.1
  Baker, Calvin. *A More Perfect Reunion* — 305.800973
  Butler, Paul. *Chokehold* — 363.2
  Cohen, Adam. ★*Imbeciles* — 344.7304
  Cohen, Adam. ★*Supreme Inequality* — 347.73
  Cornejo Villavicencio, Karla. ★*The Undocumented Americans* — 920
  Cross, Tiffany D. ★*Say It Louder!* — 324.6
  Dabiri, Emma. *Twisted* — 391.5
  Davis, Lennard J. *Enabling Acts* — 342.7308
  DiGregorio, Sarah. ★*Taking Care* — 610.73
  Eberhardt, Jennifer L. ★*Biased* — 303.3

PUBLIC LIBRARY CORE COLLECTION: NONFICTION
Twentieth Edition

Eichenwald, Kurt. *A Mind Unraveled*	B
Fuller, Pamela. ★*The Leader's Guide to Unconscious Bias*	658.3
Fumudoh, Ziwe. ★*Black Friend*	814
Gordon, Aubrey. *"You Just Need to Lose Weight"*	616.3
Grann, David. ★*Killers of the Flower Moon*	976.6004
Greene, Jamal. *How Rights Went Wrong*	342.7308
Gregory, Dick. ★*The Essential Dick Gregory*	818
Hardwick, Lamar. *How Ableism Fuels Racism*	261.8
Hayes, Christopher. *A Colony in a Nation*	364.3
Hernandez, Daisy. *The Kissing Bug*	616.9
Jackson, Regina. *White Women*	305.8
Kaba, Mariame. *No More Police*	363.2
Kendi, Ibram X. ★*How to Be an Antiracist*	305.8
Kendi, Ibram X. ★*Stamped from the Beginning*	305.8
Lalami, Laila. *Conditional Citizens*	323.60973
Laymon, Kiese. ★*Heavy*	B
Lichtman, Allan J. *The Embattled Vote in America*	324.6
Lim, Audrea. *Free the Land*	333.73
Liverpool, Layal. *Systemic*	362.1
Livingston, Robert W. *The Conversation*	305.8
Mattlin, Ben. *Disability Pride*	323.3
McGregor, Alyson J. *Sex Matters*	613
Miller, Kei. *Things I Have Withheld*	814
Miller, Reuben Jonathan. *Halfway Home*	364.8
Neiman, Garrett. *Rich White Men*	305.5
Norris, Michele. ★*Our Hidden Conversations*	305
Nussbaum, Martha Craven. *The New Religious Intolerance*	201.723
O'Neil, Cathy. *The Shame Machine*	152.4
Okrent, Daniel. *The Guarded Gate*	344.73
Petrosino, Kiki. *White Blood*	811
Postel, Charles. *Equality*	305.50973
Ricketts, Rachel. ★*Do Better*	305.800973
Rothstein, Richard. ★*The Color of Law*	305.800973
Rowe, Mickey. *Fearlessly Different*	B
Shaw, Julia. *Bi*	306.76
Urofsky, Melvin I. *The Affirmative Action Puzzle*	331.13
Watson, Bruce. *Freedom Summer*	323.1196
Wides-Munoz, Laura. *The Making of a Dream*	920
Williams, Billy Dee. ★*What Have We Here*	B
Williams, Sophie. *Anti-Racist Ally*	305.8
Zernike, Kate. *The Exceptions*	331.4

DISCRIMINATION IN EDUCATION

Boschert, Sherry. *37 Words*	344.73
Duncan, Arne. *How Schools Work*	379
Givens, Jarvis R. ★*School Clothes*	371.829
Love, Bettina L. *Punished for Dreaming*	371.829
McMillan, Tracie. ★*The White Bonus*	305.8
Picower, Bree. *Reading, Writing, and Racism*	371.829
Urofsky, Melvin I. *The Affirmative Action Puzzle*	331.13
Yacovone, Donald. ★*Teaching White Supremacy*	370.89

DISCRIMINATION IN EMPLOYMENT

Cervini, Eric. *The Deviant's War*	B
Chang, Emily. *Brotopia*	331.4
Cox, Josie. *Women Money Power*	330.082
DeParle, Jason. ★*A Good Provider Is One Who Leaves*	305.899
Eberhardt, Jennifer L. ★*Biased*	303.3
Henry, Alan. *Seen, Heard, and Paid*	650.1
Honey, Michael K. *To the Promised Land*	323
McMillan, Tracie. ★*The White Bonus*	305.8
Paul, Richard. *We Could Not Fail*	920

DISCRIMINATION IN HOUSING

Dougherty, Conor. *Golden Gates*	363.509794
McMillan, Tracie. ★*The White Bonus*	305.8
Meckler, Laura. ★*Dream Town*	305.8

DISCRIMINATION IN LAW ENFORCEMENT

Anderson, Carol. ★*The Second*	344.7305
Bailey, Issac J. *Why Didn't We Riot?*	305.800973
Butler, Paul. *Chokehold*	363.2
Kaba, Mariame. *No More Police*	363.2
Taibbi, Matt. *I Can't Breathe*	363.2

DISCRIMINATION IN SPORTS

Bascomb, Neal. *Faster*	796.7209
Runstedtler, Theresa. *Black Ball*	796.323

DISCRIMINATION IN UNIVERSITIES AND COLLEGES

Garrett, Kent. *The Last Negroes at Harvard*	920
Harris, Adam. ★*The State Must Provide*	379.2
Selingo, Jeffrey J. *Who Gets in and Why*	378.1

DISCUSSION

DiAngelo, Robin J. *White Fragility*	305.8
Hayhoe, Katharine. *Saving Us*	304.2

DISEASES

Ashton, Jennifer. *The New Normal*	613
Black, George. ★*The Long Reckoning*	959.704
Blaser, Martin J. *Missing Microbes*	615.7
Christakis, Nicholas A. *Apollo's Arrow*	362.1962
Fauci, Anthony S. *Expect the Unexpected*	610.92
Hagberg, Eva. *How to Be Loved*	616.7
Harper, Kyle. *The Fate of Rome*	937
Herman, Eleanor. *The Royal Art of Poison*	364.152
Honigsbaum, Mark. *The Pandemic Century*	614.4
Johnson, Steven. *The Ghost Map*	614.5
Kang, Lydia. *Patient Zero*	614.4
Kennedy, Jonathan. *Pathogenesis*	614.4
Kenny, Charles. *The Plague Cycle*	614.4
Kolata, Gina Bari. *Mercies in Disguise*	616
Leland, Andrew. ★*The Country of the Blind*	B
Love, Susan M. ★*Dr. Susan Love's Breast Book*	618.1
Mackenzie, Debora. *Covid-19*	616.2
May, Katherine. *Wintering*	155.9
Meyer, Robert. *Every Minute Is a Day*	362.1962
Mukherjee, Siddhartha. ★*The Emperor of All Maladies*	616.99
Mukherjee, Siddhartha. ★*The Song of the Cell*	571.6
O'Sullivan, Suzanne. *The Sleeping Beauties*	616.85
Porter, Roy. *The Greatest Benefit to Mankind*	610
Preston, Douglas J. ★*The Lost City of the Monkey God*	972.85
Preston, Richard. *Crisis in the Red Zone*	614.5
Preston, Richard. *The Hot Zone*	614.5
Quave, Cassandra Leah. *The Plant Hunter*	581.6
Randall, David K. *Black Death at the Golden Gate*	616.9
Roy, Saumya. *Castaway Mountain*	363.72
Ruhl, Sarah. *Smile*	B
Sancton, Julian. *Madhouse at the End of the Earth*	919.8904
Scarlata, Kate. *Mind Your Gut*	616.3
Schama, Simon. *Foreign Bodies*	614.4
Schwarz, Alan. *ADHD Nation*	618.92
Senthilingam, Meera. *Outbreaks and Epidemics*	614.4
Standefer, Katherine E. *Lightning Flowers*	B
Wasik, Bill. *Rabid*	614.5

DISGUISES

Abbott, Karen. *Liar, Temptress, Soldier, Spy*	920
Katin, Miriam. *We Are on Our Own*	741.5
Moore, Susanna. *Miss Aluminum*	813
Nordberg, Jenny. *The Underground Girls of Kabul*	305.3
Todd, Kim. *Sensational*	920
Woo, Ilyon. ★*Master Slave Husband Wife*	920

The Dish. Friedman, Andrew 647.95
A Dish for All Seasons. Pauline, Kathryn 641.5
Disher, Wayne
Crash Course in Collection Development 025.2

DISHONESTY

Andersen, Kurt. ★*Fantasyland*	973
Ariely, Dan. *The Honest Truth About Dishonesty*	177
Fremont, Helen. *The Escape Artist*	B
Hardin, Lara Love. ★*The Many Lives of Mama Love*	B
Lifford, Tina. *The Little Book of Big Lies*	155.2
Scheier, Liz. *Never Simple*	B
Viren, Sarah. *To Name the Bigger Lie*	B

Disillusioned. Herold, Benjamin 307.76

DISILLUSIONMENT

Coldstream, Catherine. ★*Cloistered*	B
Finkel, David. *An American Dreamer*	975.8
Kaag, John J. *American Philosophy*	191
McCammon, Sarah. ★*The Exvangelicals*	277.308
Ward, Jon. *Testimony*	277.308

DISMEMBERMENT

Stashower, Daniel. *American Demon*	364.152

DISNEY CHARACTERS

Ghez, Didier. *The Hidden Art of Disney's Golden Age*	741.5
Villanova, Thibaud. *Disney Enchanted Recipes*	641.5

Disney Enchanted Recipes. Villanova, Thibaud 641.5
Disney's Land. Snow, Richard 791.06

DISNEY, WALT, 1901-1966

Finch, Christopher. *The Art of Walt Disney*	791.43092
Gabler, Neal. *Walt Disney*	B
Snow, Richard. *Disney's Land*	791.06

AUTHOR, TITLE, SERIES AND SUBJECT INDEX

The *Disordered* Cosmos. Prescod-Weinstein, Chanda	523.01
★The *Disordered* Mind. Kandel, Eric R.	616.89
DISORIENTATION	
Codjoe, Ama. *Bluest Nude*	811
Dispatches from the Gilded Age. Reed, Julia	B
Dispatches from the Race War. Wise, Tim J.	305.8
DiSpirito, Rocco	
Now Eat This!	641.5
Rocco's Healthy+Delicious	641.3
DISPLACEMENT (PSYCHOLOGY)	
Bittle, Jake. ★*The Great Displacement*	362.87
A *Disposition* to Be Rich. Ward, Geoffrey C.	B
Dissen, William Stark	
Thoughtful Cooking	641.5975
Dissent. Young, Ralph F.	303.48
Dissent and the Supreme Court. Urofsky, Melvin I.	342.7302
DISSENTERS	
Ai, Weiwei. *Zodiac*	741.5
Ayers, Edward L. *American Visions*	973.5
Canellos, Peter S. *The Great Dissenter*	
Chomsky, Noam. *Global Discontents*	410.92
Finn, Peter. *The Zhivago Affair*	891.73
Guha, Ramachandra. *Rebels Against the Raj*	954.03
Levi, Primo. *The Periodic Table*	858
Lim, Louisa. *Indelible City*	951.25
Mahtani, Shibani. *Among the Braves*	951.25
Matar, Hisham. *The Return*	B
Popoff, Alexandra. *Vasily Grossman and the Soviet Century*	B
Yaffa, Joshua. *Between Two Fires*	920
Young, Ralph F. *Dissent*	303.48
DISSENTERS, ARTISTIC	
Ai, Weiwei. *1000 Years of Joys and Sorrows*	709.2
McPhee, John. *The Ransom of Russian Art*	709
DISSENTING OPINIONS	
King, Charles. ★*Gods of the Upper Air*	920
Stone, Geoffrey R. *Perilous Times*	323.44
Urofsky, Melvin I. *Dissent and the Supreme Court*	342.7302
DISSOCIATIVE DISORDERS	
Carriere, Alice. *Everything/Nothing/Someone*	B
Mandel, Sarah. *Little Earthquakes*	B
Nathan, Debbie. *Sybil Exposed*	B
DISSOCIATIVE IDENTITY DISORDER	
Nathan, Debbie. *Sybil Exposed*	B
Schreiber, Flora Rheta. *Sybil*	616.85
Dissolve. Bitsui, Sherwin	811
★The *Distance* Between Us. Grande, Reyna	973
DISTANCE EDUCATION	
Turnbow, Dominique. ★*Demystifying Online Instruction in Libraries*	028.7
DISTANCE RUNNING	
Alvarez, Noe. *Spirit Run*	796.42
Davis, Jennifer Pharr. *The Pursuit of Endurance*	796.51
Murakami, Haruki. *What I Talk About When I Talk About Running*	B
★A *Distant* Mirror. Tuchman, Barbara W.	944
DISTILLATION	
Rogers, Adam. *Proof*	663
DISTILLING INDUSTRY AND TRADE	
O'Meara, Mallory. *Girly Drinks*	641.2
DISTRACTION (PSYCHOLOGY)	
Allen, Cory. *Now Is the Way*	158.1
Shlain, Tiffany. *24/6*	158.1
Zorn, Justin. *Golden*	128
DISTRACTIONS	
Goleman, Daniel. *Focus*	153.7
Kethledge, Raymond Michael. *Lead Yourself First*	658.4
DISTRESS (PSYCHOLOGY)	
Winfrey, Oprah. *What Happened to You?*	616.85
District and Circle. Heaney, Seamus	821
DISTRICT ATTORNEYS	
Berman, Geoffrey. *Holding the Line*	345.73
Ditmore, Melissa Hope	
★*Unbroken Chains*	306.74
Dittrich, Luke	
★*Patient H.M.*	616.85
Ditum, Sarah	
Toxic	920.72
Divergent Mind. Nerenberg, Jenara	616.89
The *Diversity* of Life. Wilson, Edward O.	333.95
Diversity, Inc. Newkirk, Pamela	658.3
The *Divide.* Hickel, Jason	330.9
DIVIDED GOVERNMENT	
Nussbaum, Martha Craven. *The Monarchy of Fear*	306.20973
The *Divided* Ground. Taylor, Alan	974.7
Divided We Stand. Spruill, Marjorie Julian	305.42
The *Divider.* Baker, Peter	973.933
The *Divine* Art of Dying. Speerstra, Karen	202
★The *Divine* Comedy. Dante Alighieri	851
★The *Divine* Milieu. Teilhard de Chardin, Pierre	233
DIVISION OF LABOR	
Dubin, Minna. ★*Mom Rage*	306.874
Hartley, Gemma. *Fed Up*	155.3
Wrangham, Richard W. *Catching Fire*	394.1
DIVORCE	
Alexander, Kwame. *Why Fathers Cry at Night*	B
Bechdel, Alison. ★*Fun Home*	741.5
Blackstone-Ford, Jann. *Co-Parenting Through Separation and Divorce*	306.89
Buhle, Kathleen. *If We Break*	B
Copaken, Deborah. *Ladyparts*	B
Cusk, Rachel. *Aftermath*	B
Dais, Dawn. *The Sh!t No One Tells You About Divorce*	306.89
Foster, Sutton. *Hooked*	B
Frangello, Gina. *Blow Your House Down*	813
Fuller, Alexandra. *Leaving Before the Rains Come*	B
Green, Janice. ★*Divorce After 50*	306.89
Levy, Deborah. *The Cost of Living*	B
Levy, Deborah. ★*Real Estate*	B
McCourt, Malachy. *A Monk Swimming*	B
Patchett, Ann. *This Is the Story of a Happy Marriage*	B
Pittard, Hannah. *We Are Too Many*	B
Reichl, Ruth. *Comfort Me with Apples*	B
Reynolds, Debbie. *Make 'Em Laugh*	B
Rush, Charaia. *Courageously Soft*	234
Smith, Maggie. ★*You Could Make This Place Beautiful*	B
Starkey, David. *Six Wives*	942.05
Steinberg, Jonny. *Winnie and Nelson*	920
Williams, Florence. *Heartbreak*	306.7
Wizenberg, Molly. *Fixed Stars*	B
★*Divorce* After 50. Green, Janice	306.89
DIVORCED MEN	
Bass, Rick. *The Traveling Feast*	B
Travis, Randy. *Forever and Ever, Amen*	B
DIVORCED MOTHERS	
Margulies, Julianna. *Sunshine Girl*	B
Tallent, Elizabeth. *Scratched*	B
DIVORCED WOMEN	
Cardwell, Diane. *Rockaway*	B
Cole, Natalie. *Angel on My Shoulder*	B
Cusk, Rachel. *Aftermath*	B
Danler, Stephanie. *Stray*	B
Doyle, Glennon. *Untamed*	B
Gilbert, Elizabeth. *Eat, Pray, Love*	B
Harper, Michele. *The Beauty in Breaking*	B
Mayes, Frances. *Bella Tuscany*	945
Mayes, Frances. *Under the Tuscan Sun*	945
Pace, Kristin Knight. *This Much Country*	B
Qadiri, Humayra. *Dancing in the Mosque*	B
Dixon, Anne	
The Handweaver's Pattern Directory	746.1
The Weaver's Inkle Pattern Directory	746.1
Dixon, Matt	
The Well-Built Triathlete	796.42
Dixon, Wheeler W.	
A Short History of Film	791.43
DIY Garden Projects. Pember, Mat	712
DIY Rules for a WTF World. Suh, Krista	158.1
DIY Thrift Flip. Yang, April	646.2
Django. Dregni, Michael	B
DMZ Colony. Choi, Don Mee	818
DNA	
Hagerty, Alexa. ★*Still Life with Bones*	599.9
Heine, Steven J. *DNA Is Not Destiny*	572.8
Humes, Edward. *The Forever Witness*	363.25
Markel, Howard. *The Secret of Life*	572.86
Rae-Venter, Barbara. *I Know Who You Are*	364.152
Raff, Jennifer. *Origin*	576.5
Stanger, Ben. *From One Cell*	571.6

PUBLIC LIBRARY CORE COLLECTION: NONFICTION
Twentieth Edition

DNA FINGERPRINTING
    Kimmerle, Erin H. *We Carry Their Bones* — 365
Dna Is Not Destiny. Heine, Steven J. — 572.8
DNA RESEARCH
    Finkel, Elizabeth. *The Genome Generation* — 599.93
    Maddox, Brenda. *Rosalind Franklin* — B
    Rae-Venter, Barbara. *I Know Who You Are* — 364.152
    ★*Do Better*. Ricketts, Rachel — 305.800973
Do I Stay Christian?. McLaren, Brian D. — 270.8
Do It Anyway. Cobbs-Leonard, Tasha — 241
★*Do No Harm*. Marsh, Henry — B
Do Right by Me. Harrison, Valerie J. — 649
Do Something for Nothing. Coombes, Joshua — 362.5
★*Do The Work!* Bell, W. Kamau — 305.8
Do Unto Animals. Stewart, Tracey — 590
DO-IT-YOURSELF WORK
    Adarme, Adrianna. *The Year of Cozy* — 641.3
    Bowers, Sharon. *Home Ec for Everyone* — 640
    Brown, Amanda. ★*Spruce* — 747
    Horwood, Roger. *Woodworker's Handbook* — 684
Dobbs, Michael
    King Richard — 973.924
Dobelli, Rolf
    The Art of Thinking Clearly — 153.4
DOBY, LARRY
    Epplin, Luke. *Our Team* — 796.357
Dochartaigh, Kerri ni
    Cacophony of Bone — B
DOCHARTAIGH, KERRI NI, 1983-
    Dochartaigh, Kerri ni. *Cacophony of Bone* — B
The Doctor Is In. Westheimer, Ruth — B
The Doctor Who Fooled the World. Deer, Brian — 610.92
Doctors and Distillers. English, Camper — 615.7
★*The Doctors Blackwell*. Nimura, Janice P. — 610.92
DOCUMENTARY EVIDENCE
    Holton, Woody. *Liberty Is Sweet* — 973.3
DOCUMENTARY FILMMAKERS
    Chin, Curtis. *Everything I Learned, I Learned in a Chinese Restaurant* — B
    Mustill, Tom. *How to Speak Whale* — 591.59
DOCUMENTARY FILMS
    Morris, Errol. *Believing Is Seeing* — 770.9
    Wilkman, Jon. *Screening Reality* — 070.1
DOCUMENTARY PHOTOGRAPHY
    Friend, David. *Watching the World Change* — 974.7
    Gordon, Linda. *Dorothea Lange* — B
    Menuez, Doug. *Fearless Genius* — 979.4
    Morris, Errol. *Believing Is Seeing* — 770.9
    Welty, Eudora. *One Time, One Place* — 976.2
    Willis, Deborah. *Envisioning Emancipation* — 973.7
DOCUMENTARY TELEVISION PROGRAMS
    Else, Jon. *True South* — 305.800973
    Nussbaum, Emily. *Cue the Sun!* — 791.45
DODD, WILLIAM, 1869-1940
    Larson, Erik. *In the Garden of Beasts* — B
    McKean, David. *Watching Darkness Fall* — 940.53
Dodds Pennock, Caroline
    ★*On Savage Shores* — 970.004
Dodge City. Clavin, Thomas — 978.1
DODGE CITY, KANSAS
    Clavin, Thomas. *Dodge City* — 978.1
Dodge, Abigail Johnson
    Sheet Cake — 641.86
DODGE, NORTON TOWNSHEND, 1927-2011
    McPhee, John. *The Ransom of Russian Art* — 709
Dodging Energy Vampires. Northrup, Christiane — 155.2
DOERR, BOBBY, 1918-2017
    Halberstam, David. *The Teammates* — B
Does Jesus Really Love Me?. Chu, Jeff — 261.8
DOG ADOPTION
    Achterberg, Cara Sue. *Another Good Dog* — 636.7
    Conaboy, Kelly. *The Particulars of Peter* — 636.7
DOG BREEDING
    Kavin, Kim. *The Dog Merchants* — 636.7
    Tomlinson, Tommy. *Dogland* — 636.7
DOG BREEDS
    Coile, D. Caroline. *Encyclopedia of Dog Breeds* — 636.7
Dog Flowers. Geller, Danielle — B

DOG HEROES
    Lewis, Damien. *The Dog Who Could Fly* — 940.54
★*Dog Is Love*. Wynne, Clive D. L. — 636.7
The Dog Merchants. Kavin, Kim — 636.7
A Dog Named Beautiful. Kugler, Rob — B
DOG OWNERS
    Boylan, Jennifer Finney. *Good Boy* — B
    Dickey, Bronwen. *Pit Bull* — 636.755
    Golbeck, Jennifer. *The Purest Bond* — 636.7
    Herriot, James. *James Herriot's Dog Stories* — 636.7
    Herriot, James. *James Herriot's Favorite Dog Stories* — 636.7
    Horowitz, Alexandra. ★*Inside of a Dog* — 636.7
    Horowitz, Alexandra. *Our Dogs, Ourselves* — 636.7
    Horowitz, Alexandra. ★*The Year of the Puppy* — 636.7
    Kugler, Rob. *A Dog Named Beautiful* — B
    McConnell, Patricia B. ★*The Other End of the Leash* — 636.7
DOG RESCUE
    Melville, Wilma. ★*Hero Dogs* — 636.7
★*Dog Sense*. Bradshaw, John — 636.7
DOG SHOWS
    Tomlinson, Tommy. *Dogland* — 636.7
DOG TRAINERS
    Melville, Wilma. ★*Hero Dogs* — 636.7
DOG TRAINING
    Horowitz, Alexandra. ★*The Year of the Puppy* — 636.7
    Hunger, Christina. *How Stella Learned to Talk* — 636.7
    McConnell, Patricia B. ★*The Other End of the Leash* — 636.7
    Melville, Wilma. ★*Hero Dogs* — 636.7
    Miller, Pat. ★*The Power of Positive Dog Training* — 636.7
    Monks of New Skete. *The Art of Raising a Puppy* — 636.7
    Nichols, Kerry. *Puppy Brain* — 636.7
A Dog Walks into a Nursing Home. Halpern, Sue — B
The Dog Who Could Fly. Lewis, Damien — 940.54
Doggett, Peter
    Electric Shock — 781.64
    You Never Give Me Your Money — B
The Dogist. Friedman, Elias Weiss — 779
Dogland. Tomlinson, Tommy — 636.7
Dogon, Mondiant
    Those We Throw Away Are Diamonds — B
DOGON, MONDIANT
    Dogon, Mondiant. *Those We Throw Away Are Diamonds* — B
DOGS
    Boylan, Jennifer Finney. *Good Boy* — B
    Bradshaw, John. ★*Dog Sense* — 636.7
    Chesney, Will. *No Ordinary Dog* — 958.104
    Conaboy, Kelly. *The Particulars of Peter* — 636.7
    Golbeck, Jennifer. *The Purest Bond* — 636.7
    Grogan, John. ★*Marley & Me* — 636.752
    Grossi, Craig. *Craig & Fred* — B
    Habib, Rodney. ★*The Forever Dog* — 636.7
    Halpern, Sue. *A Dog Walks into a Nursing Home* — B
    Herriot, James. *James Herriot's Dog Stories* — 636.7
    Herriot, James. *James Herriot's Favorite Dog Stories* — 636.7
    Horowitz, Alexandra. ★*Being a Dog* — 636.7
    Horowitz, Alexandra. ★*Inside of a Dog* — 636.7
    Horowitz, Alexandra. *Our Dogs, Ourselves* — 636.7
    Horowitz, Alexandra. ★*The Year of the Puppy* — 636.7
    Kavin, Kim. *The Dog Merchants* — 636.7
    Kugler, Rob. *A Dog Named Beautiful* — B
    Letts, Elizabeth. ★*The Ride of Her Life* — B
    Lewis, Damien. *The Dog Who Could Fly* — 940.54
    McConnell, Patricia B. ★*The Other End of the Leash* — 636.7
    Miller, Pat. ★*The Power of Positive Dog Training* — 636.7
    Nichols, Kerry. *Puppy Brain* — 636.7
    Steinbeck, John. *Travels with Charley* — B
    Wynne, Clive D. L. ★*Dog Is Love* — 636.7
DOGS AS PETS
    Bragg, Rick. *The Speckled Beauty* — 636.7
    Conaboy, Kelly. *The Particulars of Peter* — 636.7
    Dickey, Bronwen. *Pit Bull* — 636.755
    Golbeck, Jennifer. *The Purest Bond* — 636.7
    Grogan, John. ★*Marley & Me* — 636.752
    Herriot, James. *James Herriot's Dog Stories* — 636.7
    Herriot, James. *James Herriot's Favorite Dog Stories* — 636.7
    Horowitz, Alexandra. *Our Dogs, Ourselves* — 636.7
    Hunger, Christina. *How Stella Learned to Talk* — 636.7
    Kavin, Kim. *The Dog Merchants* — 636.7

AUTHOR, TITLE, SERIES AND SUBJECT INDEX

Tomlinson, Tommy. *Dogland*	636.7
DOGS IN FILMS	
Orlean, Susan. *Rin Tin Tin*	636.737
DOGSLEDDING	
Pace, Kristin Knight. *This Much Country*	B
Doh, Jenny	
Creative Lettering	745.6
DOHENY, ESTELLE, 1875-1958	
Davis, Margaret Leslie. *The Lost Gutenberg*	093
Doherty, Maggie	
The Equivalents	920
Dohrmann, George	
★*Play Their Hearts Out*	796.323
Switching Fields	796.334
Doing Justice. Bharara, Preet	347.73
DOING THINGS	
Epstein, David J. ★*Range*	153.9
Gopnik, Adam. *All That Happiness Is*	158.1
Dokun, Chanel	
Life Starts Now	248.8
Dolby, Thomas	
The Speed of Sound	B
DOLBY, THOMAS	
Dolby, Thomas. *The Speed of Sound*	B
★*Dolci!* Poliafito, Renato	641.81
Dolin, Eric Jay	
Black Flags, Blue Waters	973.2
A Furious Sky	363.34
★*Rebels at Sea*	973.3
A Doll for Throwing. Bang, Mary Jo	811
DOLL INDUSTRY AND TRADE	
Gerber, Robin. *Barbie and Ruth*	B
Dollars and Sense. Ariely, Dan	332.024
DOLLHOUSES	
Frisoni, Christine-Lea. *The Big Book of a Miniature House*	745.592
Garfield, Simon. *In Miniature*	745.5928
Smith, Sally J. *Fairy Houses*	745.592
DOLLMAKERS	
Gerber, Robin. *Barbie and Ruth*	B
★*Dolly Parton, Songteller*. Parton, Dolly	B
Dolnick, Edward	
The Rescue Artist	364.16
Seeds of Life	612.6
The Writing of the Gods	493
The Dolphin Letters, 1970-1979. Hardwick, Elizabeth	811
DOLPHINS	
Hoyt, Erich. *Encyclopedia of Whales, Dolphins and Porpoises*	599.5
DOMES	
King, Ross. *Brunelleschi's Dome*	726.6
DOMESTIC ANIMALS	
Grandin, Temple. *Temple Grandin's Guide to Working with Farm Animals*	636
Herriot, James. *James Herriot's Animal Stories*	B
Rude, Emelyn. *Tastes Like Chicken*	338.1
DOMESTIC TERRORISM	
Bordewich, Fergus M. *Klan War*	973.8
Burrough, Bryan. *Days of Rage*	303.48
Keefe, Patrick Radden. ★*Say Nothing*	364.152
Kushner, Jacob. *Look Away*	305.9
Lehr, Dick. *White Hot Hate*	363.325
Mishra, Pankaj. *Age of Anger*	909.8
Neiwert, David A. ★*The Age of Insurrection*	303.48
Phillips, Patrick. *Blood at the Root*	305.8
Reilly, Ryan J. ★*Sedition Hunters*	364.1
Stephanopoulos, George. ★*The Situation Room*	973.09
Toobin, Jeffrey. ★*Homegrown*	363.325
Wiehl, Lis W. *Hunting the Unabomber*	364.152
Williams, Kidada E. *I Saw Death Coming*	973.8
DOMESTICATION	
Brown, Sarah L. *The Hidden Language of Cats*	636.8
Losos, Jonathan B. *The Cat's Meow*	636.8
DOMINANCE (PSYCHOLOGY)	
Berman, Sarah. *Don't Call It a Cult*	361.4
DOMINICAN AMERICAN WOMEN	
Alvarez, Julia. *The Woman I Kept to Myself*	811
DOMINICAN AMERICANS	
Gonell, Aquilino. *American Shield*	B

DOMINICAN REPUBLIC	
Kurlansky, Mark. *The Eastern Stars*	796.357
Scheeres, Julia. *Jesus Land*	B
Dominion. Holland, Tom	261
The Dominion of War. Anderson, Fred	973
The Domino Diaries. Butler, Brin-Jonathan	796.83
DOMINO, FATS, 1928-2017	
Coleman, Rick. ★*Blue Monday*	B
Don't Call It a Cult. Berman, Sarah	361.4
Don't Call Me Princess. Orenstein, Peggy	305.42
★*Don't Call Us Dead*. Smith, Danez	811.6
Don't Forget Us Here. Adayfi, Mansoor	B
Don't Let's Go to the Dogs Tonight. Fuller, Alexandra	B
Don't Live for Your Obituary. Scalzi, John	808.02
Don't Read Poetry. Burt, Stephanie	811
Don't Save Anything. Salter, James	818
★*Don't Shoot the Dog*. Pryor, Karen	153.8
Don't Tell Anybody the Secrets I Told You. Williams, Lucinda	B
★*Don't Think, Dear*. Robb, Alice	792.8
★*Donald Trump v. The United States*. Schmidt, Michael S.	973.933
Donald, Aida DiPace	
Citizen Soldier	B
Donald, David Herbert	
Lincoln	B
Donaldson-Pressman, Stephanie	
The Learning Habit	371.30281
DONATION OF ORGANS, TISSUES, ETC.	
Mezrich, Joshua D. *When Death Becomes Life*	617.9
Doniger, Wendy	
On Hinduism	294.5
DONKEYS	
McDougall, Christopher. *Running with Sherman*	636.1
DONNE, JOHN, 1572-1631	
Rundell, Katherine. ★*Super-Infinite*	B
DONNER PARTY	
Brown, Daniel James. *The Indifferent Stars Above*	B
Wallis, Michael. *The Best Land Under Heaven*	978
Donner, Rebecca	
All the Frequent Troubles of Our Days	943
Donofrio, Jeanine	
★*Love & Lemons*	641.5
Donovan, Jim	
The Blood of Heroes	976.4
★*Shoot for the Moon*	629.45
A Terrible Glory	973.8
DONOVAN, WILLIAM J. (WILLIAM JOSEPH), 1883-1959	
Fullilove, Michael. *Rendezvous with Destiny*	973.917092
Waller, Douglas C. *Wild Bill Donovan*	B
Donvan, John	
In a Different Key	616.85
DOOLITTLE, JAMES HAROLD, 1896-1993	
Groom, Winston. *The Aviators*	920
Scott, James. *Target Tokyo*	940.54
Doom. Ferguson, Niall	362.1962
The Doomsday Mother. Glatt, John	364.152
Dooner, Caroline	
*Tired as F*ck*	152.1
Door in the Mountain. Valentine, Jean	811
Door to Door. Humes, Edward	388.09
Doorley, Rachelle	
Tinkerlab	600
Dopamine Nation. Lembke, Anna	152.4
★*Dopesick*. Macy, Beth	362.29
Dopeworld. Vorobyov, Niko	364.1
DOPING IN SPORTS	
Hamilton, Tyler. *The Secret Race*	796.62
Hart, Matt. *Win at All Costs*	338.7
Shorter, Frank. *My Marathon*	796.42
★*Doppelganger*. Klein, Naomi	302.2
DOPPELGANGERS	
Klein, Naomi. ★*Doppelganger*	302.2
Doran, Peter B.	
Breaking Rockefeller	338.7
Dorey-Stein, Beck	
From the Corner of the Oval	B
DOREY-STEIN, BECK	
Dorey-Stein, Beck. *From the Corner of the Oval*	B
★*Dorie's Cookies*. Greenspan, Dorie	641.86

PUBLIC LIBRARY CORE COLLECTION: NONFICTION
Twentieth Edition

*The **Dorito** Effect.* Schatzker, Mark — 641.3
***Dorothea** Lange.* Gordon, Linda — B
***Dorothy** Day.* Hennessy, Kate — B
Dorr, Christina H.
    ★*Profiles in Resilience* — 028.5
DORSEY, JACK, 1976-
    Bilton, Nick. *Hatching Twitter* — 006.7
★***Dostoevsky.*** Frank, Joseph — B
DOSTOYEVSKY, FYODOR, 1821-1881
    Frank, Joseph. ★*Dostoevsky* — B
Doty, Cate
    Mergers and Acquisitions — 395.2
DOTY, CATE
    Doty, Cate. *Mergers and Acquisitions* — 395.2
Doty, Mark
    Deep Lane — 811
    Fire to Fire — 811
    What Is the Grass — 811
DOTY, MARK
    Doty, Mark. *What Is the Grass* — 811
DOUBLE AGENTS
    Cunningham, Benjamin. *The Liar* — 327.1273
    Drabkin, Ronald. *Beverly Hills Spy* — 940.54
    Macintyre, Ben. *A Spy Among Friends* — B
    Macintyre, Ben. ★*The Spy and the Traitor* — B
    Sallah, Michael. *The Yankee Comandante* — 972.91
***Double** Cross.* Macintyre, Ben — 940.54
*The **Double** Dangerous Book for Boys.* Iggulden, Conn — 031.02
***Double** Plays and Double Crosses.* Zminda, Don — 796.357
***Double** Victory.* Takaki, Ronald T. — 940.53
Doubt. Hecht, Jennifer Michael — 121
Doubt. Shanley, John Patrick — 812
DOUDNA, JENNIFER A.
    Isaacson, Walter. ★*The Code Breaker* — 576.5
Dougherty, Conor
    Golden Gates — 363.509794
Doughty, Caitlin
    From Here to Eternity — 393
    Smoke Gets in Your Eyes — B
    Will My Cat Eat My Eyeballs? — 306.9
DOUGHTY, CAITLIN
    Doughty, Caitlin. *From Here to Eternity* — 393
    Doughty, Caitlin. *Smoke Gets in Your Eyes* — B
Doughty, Kathy
    Adding Layers — 746.46
★***Douglas** Macarthur.* Herman, Arthur — B
Douglas, John E.
    The Killer Across the Table — B
    When a Killer Calls — 364.152
DOUGLAS, JOHN E.
    Douglas, John E. *The Killer Across the Table* — B
    Douglas, John E. *When a Killer Calls* — 364.152
Douglas, Marjory Stoneman
    The Everglades — 975.9
DOUGLAS, MARJORY STONEMAN, 1890-1998
    Davis, Jack E. *An Everglades Providence* — B
DOUGLAS, STEPHEN A. (STEPHEN ARNOLD), 1813-1861
    Bordewich, Fergus M. *America's Great Debate* — 973.6
    Guelzo, Allen C. *Lincoln and Douglas* — 973.6
Douglass, Frederick
    ★*Frederick Douglass* — 973.8
    My Bondage and My Freedom — B
    Narrative of the Life of Frederick Douglass, an American Slave — B
    The Portable Frederick Douglass — 973.8
DOUGLASS, FREDERICK, 1818-1895
    Blight, David W. ★*Frederick Douglass* — B
    Colaiaco, James A. *Frederick Douglass and the Fourth of July* — 973.7
    Dilbeck, D. H. *Frederick Douglass* — B
    Douglass, Frederick. *My Bondage and My Freedom* — B
    Douglass, Frederick. *Narrative of the Life of Frederick Douglass, an American Slave* — B
    Douglass, Frederick. *The Portable Frederick Douglass* — 973.8
    Levine, Robert S. ★*The Failed Promise* — 973.8
    Stauffer, John. *Picturing Fredrick Douglass* — B
    West, Cornel. *Black Prophetic Fire* — 920
Doust, Kelly
    The Power Age — 305.244

Douthat, Ross Gregory
    To Change the Church — 230
Dove, Rita
    Playlist for the Apocalypse — 811
    ★*Selected Poems* — 811
    Sonata Mulattica — 811
Dower, John W.
    Cultures of War — 355.00973
    Embracing Defeat — 952.04
***Down** The Drain.* Fox, Julia — B
Downeast. Georges, Gigi — 974.1
Downey, Kirstin
    Isabella — B
Downfall. Frank, Richard B. — 940.54
*The **Downhill** Lie.* Hiaasen, Carl — B
Downie, David
    A Taste of Paris — 394.1
Downs, Paul
    Boss Life — 338.7
DOWNS, PAUL
    Downs, Paul. *Boss Life* — 338.7
DOYLE, ARTHUR CONAN, SIR, 1859-1930
    Jaher, David. *The Witch of Lime Street* — B
    Sims, Michael. *Arthur and Sherlock* — B
Doyle, Glennon
    Untamed — B
DOYLE, GLENNON, 1976-
    Doyle, Glennon. *Untamed* — B
Doyle, Martin
    The Source — 333.91
Doyne, Maggie
    Between the Mountain and the Sky — B
DOYNE, MAGGIE
    Doyne, Maggie. *Between the Mountain and the Sky* — B
DR. DRE, 1965-
    Greenburg, Zack O'Malley. *3 Kings* — 782.421649
    Westhoff, Ben. *Original Gangstas* — 782.421649
Dr. Mutter's Marvels. Aptowicz, Cristin O'Keefe — B
Dr. Patrick Walsh's Guide to Surviving Prostate Cancer. Walsh, Patrick C. — 616.99
★***Dr. Susan Love's Breast Book.*** Love, Susan M. — 618.1
Dr. Z. Zimmerman, Paul — B
Drabkin, Ronald
    Beverly Hills Spy — 940.54
DRACULA, COUNT (FICTITIOUS CHARACTER)
    Braudy, Leo. *Haunted* — 398.45
    Skal, David J. *Something in the Blood* — 823
DRAG KINGS
    Goodman, Elyssa. *Glitter and Concrete* — 792.7
    Hall, Jake. *The Art of Drag* — 792.8
DRAG QUEENS
    Goodman, Elyssa. *Glitter and Concrete* — 792.7
    Hall, Jake. *The Art of Drag* — 792.8
    Mattel, Trixie. *Working Girls* — 650.1
    Olsen, Craig. *P.S. Burn This Letter Please* — 306.76
    RuPaul. ★*The House of Hidden Meanings* — B
    Seligman, Craig. *Who Does That Bitch Think She Is?* — 792.02
    Velour, Sasha. ★*The Big Reveal* — 792.7
DRAG SHOWS
    Goodman, Elyssa. *Glitter and Concrete* — 792.7
    Hall, Jake. *The Art of Drag* — 792.8
    Seligman, Craig. *Who Does That Bitch Think She Is?* — 792.02
    Velour, Sasha. ★*The Big Reveal* — 792.7
DRAGONFLIES
    Paulson, Dennis. *Dragonflies & Damselflies* — 595.7
***Dragonflies** & Damselflies.* Paulson, Dennis — 595.7
*The **Dragons** of Eden.* Sagan, Carl — 153
*The **Dragons**, The Giant, the Women.* Moore, Wayetu — B
Dragonwagon, Crescent
    Bean by Bean — 641.6
DRAGSTERS
    Hawley, Sam. *Speed Duel* — 796.72
DRAKE, FRANCIS, SIR, 1540?-1596
    Bergreen, Laurence. *In Search of a Kingdom* — B
DRAMA
    Aeschylus. *The Oresteia* — 882
    Albee, Edward. ★*Who's Afraid of Virginia Woolf?* — 812
    Auburn, David. *Proof* — 812
    Bloom, Harold. *Shakespeare* — 822.33

AUTHOR, TITLE, SERIES AND SUBJECT INDEX

Bolt, Robert. *A Man for All Seasons* — 822
Brockett, Oscar G. *History of the Theatre* — 792
Butler, Isaac. *The World Only Spins Forward* — 812
Dromgoole, Dominic. *Hamlet Globe to Globe* — 792.9
Fugard, Athol. ★ *"master Harold"—And the Boys* — 822
Gay, John. *The Beggar's Opera* — 782.1
Gibson, William. ★ *The Miracle Worker* — 812
Goodrich, Frances. *The Diary of Anne Frank* — 812
Harris, Neil Patrick. *Neil Patrick Harris* — B
Karim-Cooper, Farah. ★ *The Great White Bard* — 822.33
Kushner, Tony. *Angels in America* — 812
Lane, Stewart F. *Black Broadway* — 792.089
Miranda, Lin-Manuel. *Hamilton* — 782.1
Norwich, John Julius. *Shakespeare's Kings* — 822.33
Ottemiller, John H. *Ottemiller's Index to Plays in Collections* — 016
Rankine, Claudia. *The White Card* — 812
Riedel, Michael. *Singular Sensation* — 792
Shaffer, Peter. ★ *Equus* — 822
Shapiro, James. ★ *The Playbook* — 792
Shapiro, James. *The Year of Lear* — 822.33
Shaw, Bernard. *Major Barbara* — 822
Shaw, Bernard. *Saint Joan* — 822
Smith, Emma. *This Is Shakespeare* — 822.33
Stoppard, Tom. *Arcadia* — 822
Thomas, Dylan. *Under Milk Wood* — 822.91
Wilder, Thornton. *Our Town* — 812
Williams, Tennessee. ★ *A Streetcar Named Desire* — 812
Wilson, August. *King Hedley II* — 812
Wilson, August. *Two Trains Running* — 812

Drape, Joe
  American Pharoah — 798.40092
  Black Maestro — B

Draper, Robert
  To Start a War — 956.7044

***Draw* Fashion Now**. Meder, Danielle — 741.6
***Draw* Horses in 15 Minutes**. Hand, Diana — 743.6
Drawing. Micklewright, Keith — 741.2

DRAWING
  De Reyna, Rudy. *How to Draw What You See* — 741.2
  Kline, Fred R. *Leonardo's Holy Child* — 741.09
  Lester, Toby. *Da Vinci's Ghost* — 741.092
  McCloud, Scott. *Making Comics* — 741.5
  Ogura, Yoshiko. *The Complete Guide to Drawing for Beginners* — 740

***Drawing* Blood**. Crabapple, Molly — B
***Drawing* Down the Moon**. Adler, Margot — 299
***Drawing* for the Absolute Beginner**. Willenbrink, Mark — 741.2
***Drawing* on the Right Side of the Brain**. Edwards, Betty — 741.2
***Drawing* People**. Bradley, Barbara — 743.4
***Drawing* Perspective**. Brehm, Matthew T. — 742

DRAWING TECHNIQUE
  Birch, Helen. *Freehand* — 741.2
  Bradley, Barbara. *Drawing People* — 743.4
  Brehm, Matthew T. *Drawing Perspective* — 742
  Crilley, Mark. *The Realism Challenge* — 751.4
  Edwards, Betty. *Drawing on the Right Side of the Brain* — 741.2
  Eisner, Will. ★ *Comics and Sequential Art* — 741.5
  Hand, Diana. *Draw Horses in 15 Minutes* — 743.6
  Hart, Christopher. *Human Anatomy Made Amazingly Easy* — 743.4
  Huston, Steve. *Figure Drawing for Artists* — 743.4
  Lee, Stan. *Stan Lee's How to Draw Comics* — 741.5
  Loomis, Andrew. *Figure Drawing for All It's Worth* — 743.4
  Micklewright, Keith. *Drawing* — 741.2
  Parks, Carrie. *Secrets to Drawing Realistic Faces* — 743.4
  Ryder, Anthony. *The Artist's Complete Guide to Figure Drawing* — 743.4
  Scheinberger, Felix. *Dare to Sketch* — 741.2
  Willenbrink, Mark. *Drawing for the Absolute Beginner* — 741.2
  Williams, Richard. *The Animator's Survival Kit* — 778
  Winslow, Valerie L. *Classic Human Anatomy* — 743.4

***Drawing* Words, Writing Pictures**. Abel, Jessica — 741.5
***Drawn* with the Sword**. McPherson, James M. — 973.7

Dray, Philip
  At the Hands of Persons Unknown — 364.1
  Capitol Men — 973.8

***Dream* Hoarders**. Reeves, Richard V. — 305.5
★ ***Dream* Home**. Scott, Jonathan — 643

DREAM INTERPRETATION
  Freud, Sigmund. ★ *The Interpretation of Dreams* — 154.6
  Kerr, Christopher. *Death Is but a Dream* — 155.9

★ *The **Dream** of Enlightenment*. Gottlieb, Anthony — 190
*The **Dream** of Reason*. Gottlieb, Anthony — 180
*The **Dream** of the Unified Field*. Graham, Jorie — 811
***Dream* Team**. McCallum, Jack — 796.323
***Dream* Teams**. Snow, Shane — 658.4
★ ***Dream* Town**. Meckler, Laura — 305.8
***Dream* Work**. Oliver, Mary — 811
***Dreamer* of Dune**. Herbert, Brian — B
***Dreaming* of Ramadi in Detroit**. Sabatini Sloan, Aisha — 814
***Dreaming* with His Eyes Open**. Marnham, Patrick — B
Dreamland. Quinones, Sam — 362.29

DREAMS
  Knight, Sam. *The Premonitions Bureau* — 133.8
  Okorafor, Nnedi. *Broken Places & Outer Spaces* — 153.3
  Smith, Patti. ★ *M Train* — B
  Wang, Jackie. *The Sunflower Cast a Spell to Save Us from the Void* — 811
  Zadra, Antonio. *When Brains Dream* — 613.7

★ ***Dreams* from My Father**. Obama, Barack — B
***Dreams* of a Great Small Nation**. McNamara, Kevin J. — 355.009437
***Dreams* of El Dorado**. Brands, H. W. — 978
***Dreams* to Remember**. Ribowsky, Mark — B

DRED SCOTT CASE
  Delbanco, Andrew. *The War Before the War* — 973.7

Dregni, Michael
  Django — B

***Dresden* Quilt Blocks Reimagined**. Grisham, Candyce Copp — 746.46

DRESDEN, GERMANY
  Klemperer, Victor. *I Will Bear Witness* — B
  McKay, Sinclair. *The Fire and the Darkness* — 940.54

Dresner, Amy
  My Fair Junkie — B

DRESNER, AMY
  Dresner, Amy. *My Fair Junkie* — B

DRESS ACCESSORIES
  Hewett, Jen. *Print, Pattern, Sew* — 646.4

***Dress* Your Best Life**. Karen, Dawnn — 646
Dressed. Bari, Shahidha K. — 391
***Dressed* in Dreams**. Ford, Tanisha C. — 391

Dresser, Norine
  Multicultural Manners — 395

***Dressing* The Decades**. Dirix, Emmanuelle — 746.92
*The **Dressmaker** of Khair Khana*. Lemmon, Gayle Tzemach — B

DRESSMAKERS
  Lemmon, Gayle Tzemach. *The Dressmaker of Khair Khana* — B

DRESSMAKING
  Hewett, Jen. *Print, Pattern, Sew* — 646.4

Drew, Liam
  I, Mammal — 599

DREW, NANCY (FICTITIOUS CHARACTER)
  Rehak, Melanie. *Girl Sleuth* — 813

***Dreyer's* English**. Dreyer, Benjamin — 808.02

Dreyer, Benjamin
  Dreyer's English — 808.02

DREYFUS, RENE
  Bascomb, Neal. *Faster* — 796.7209

Drink. Johnston, Ann Dowsett — 362.292

DRINKING
  English, Camper. *Doctors and Distillers* — 615.7
  Harrison, Jim. *The Search for the Genuine* — 814
  Johnston, Ann Dowsett. *Drink* — 362.292
  O'Meara, Mallory. *Girly Drinks* — 641.2
  Okrent, Daniel. *Last Call* — 363.4
  Standage, Tom. *A History of the World in 6 Glasses* — 394.1

DRINKING CUSTOMS
  Cheever, Susan. *Drinking in America* — 394.1
  Tipton-Martin, Toni. *Juke Joints, Jazz Clubs & Juice* — 641.87

***Drinking* in America**. Cheever, Susan — 394.1
Drive. Harig, Bob — 796.352
Drive. Pink, Daniel H. — 153.1
Drive! Goldstone, Lawrence — 338.4
***Drive-Thru* Dreams**. Chandler, Adam — 647.95

Driver, Justin
  The Schoolhouse Gate — 344.73

Driver, Minnie
  Managing Expectations — B

DRIVER, MINNIE
  Driver, Minnie. *Managing Expectations* — B

***Driving* Over Lemons**. Stewart, Chris — 946

PUBLIC LIBRARY CORE COLLECTION: NONFICTION
Twentieth Edition

Driving over lemons [Series]. Stewart, Chris — 946
Driving The Green Book. Hall, Alvin D. — 917.304
Driving While Black. Sorin, Gretchen Sullivan — 323.1196
Dromgoole, Dominic
    Hamlet Globe to Globe — 792.9
The ***Drone*** Eats with Me. Abu Sayf, Atif — B
Drop The Ball. Dufu, Tiffany — 650.1
Drori, Jonathan
    Around the World in 80 Plants — 581.63
    Around the World in 80 Trees — 582.16
DROUGHT-TOLERANT PLANTS
    Baldwin, Debra Lee. *Succulents Simplified* — 635.9
    Penick, Pam. *The Water-Saving Garden* — 635.9
DROUGHTS
    Barnett, Cynthia. *Rain* — 551.57
    Bittle, Jake. ★*The Great Displacement* — 362.87
    Egan, Timothy. *The Worst Hard Time* — 978
    Fagan, Brian M. *Climate Chaos* — 304.2
    Harper, Kyle. *The Fate of Rome* — 937
    Klare, Michael T. *All Hell Breaking Loose* — 355.20973
    Solomon, Steven. *Water* — 553.7
★The ***Drowned*** and the Saved. Levi, Primo — 940.53
DRUG ABUSE
    Aron, Nina Renata. *Good Morning, Destroyer of Men's Souls* — B
    Au-Yeung, Angel. *Wonder Boy* — B
    Barnett, Erica C. *Quitter* — B
    Biden, Robert Hunter. *Beautiful Things* — B
    Bonner, Betsy. *The Book of Atlantis Black* — 364.152
    Bossiere, Zoe. *Cactus Country* — 306
    Carlin, Kelly. *A Carlin Home Companion* — B
    Carr, David. *The Night of the Gun* — B
    Etter, Lauren. ★*The Devil's Playbook* — 338.7
    Fisher, Carl Erik. ★*The Urge* — 362.29
    Garcia, Angela. ★*The Way That Leads Among the Lost* — 362.29
    Hardin, Lara Love. ★*The Many Lives of Mama Love* — B
    Kuhn, Cynthia. *Buzzed* — 362.29
    Lahey, Jessica. *The Addiction Inoculation* — 649
    Legler, Casey. ★*Godspeed* — B
    Lembke, Anna. *Dopamine Nation* — 152.4
    Marshall, McMillan. *Among the Bros* — 362.29
    McGreal, Chris. *American Overdose* — 362.29
    Moby. *Then It Fell Apart* — B
    Perry, Matthew. *Friends, Lovers, and the Big Terrible Thing* — B
    Quinones, Sam. ★*The Least of Us* — 362.29
    Rosen, Charles. *Sugar* — B
    Smith, Freda Love. *I Quit Everything* — B
    Thompson, Juan F. *Stories I Tell Myself* — B
    Vorobyov, Niko. *Dopeworld* — 364.1
    Williams, Zach. *Rescue Story* — B
    Zara, Christopher. *Uneducated* — B
DRUG ABUSE TREATMENT CENTERS AND CLINICS
    Garcia, Angela. ★*The Way That Leads Among the Lost* — 362.29
DRUG ADDICTION
    Aron, Nina Renata. *Good Morning, Destroyer of Men's Souls* — B
    Bell, Madison Smartt. *Child of Light* — B
    Biden, Robert Hunter. *Beautiful Things* — B
    Century, Douglas. *Barney Ross* — B
    Dykstra, Lenny. *House of Nails* — B
    Garcia, Angela. ★*The Way That Leads Among the Lost* — 362.29
    George-Warren, Holly. ★*Janis* — B
    Grandmaster Flash. *The Adventures of Grandmaster Flash* — B
    Jackson, Mitchell S. *Survival Math* — B
    Jackson, Ted. ★*You Ought to Do a Story About Me* — B
    Kang, Mia. *Knockout* — B
    Macy, Beth. ★*Dopesick* — 362.29
    Macy, Beth. ★*Raising Lazarus* — 362.29
    McDonald, Michael. ★*What a Fool Believes* — B
    McGreal, Chris. *American Overdose* — 362.29
    Mealer, Bryan. *The Kings of Big Spring* — B
    Milch, David. *Life's Work* — B
    Quinones, Sam. *Dreamland* — 362.29
    Quinones, Sam. ★*The Least of Us* — 362.29
    Rieder, Travis. *In Pain* — 362.29
    Sacks, Oliver. *On the Move* — B
    Schemel, Patty. *Hit so Hard* — B
    Stone, Sly. *Thank You (Falettinme Be Mice Elf Agin)* — B
    Weller, Sheila. *Carrie Fisher* — B

DRUG ADDICTS
    Aron, Nina Renata. *Good Morning, Destroyer of Men's Souls* — B
    Blakinger, Keri. *Corrections in Ink* — B
    Carr, David. *The Night of the Gun* — B
    Dresner, Amy. *My Fair Junkie* — B
    Evangelista, Patricia. ★*Some People Need Killing* — 364.4
    Garcia, Angela. ★*The Way That Leads Among the Lost* — 362.29
    Khar, Erin. *Strung Out* — B
    Lanegan, Mark. *Sing Backwards and Weep* — B
    Macy, Beth. ★*Dopesick* — 362.29
    Macy, Beth. ★*Raising Lazarus* — 362.29
    Quinones, Sam. ★*The Least of Us* — 362.29
    Rao, Cheeni. *In Hanuman's Hands* — B
    Thomas, Joseph Earl. *Sink* — B
    Westhoff, Ben. *Fentanyl, Inc.* — 362.29
DRUG CARTELS
    Muse, Toby. *Kilo* — 363.4509861
    Shahani, Aarti Namdev. *Here We Are* — B
DRUG CONTROL
    Dufton, Emily. *Grass Roots* — 362.29
    Evangelista, Patricia. ★*Some People Need Killing* — 364.4
    Ramsey, Donovan X. ★*When Crack Was King* — 362.29
    Vorobyov, Niko. *Dopeworld* — 364.1
    Westhoff, Ben. *Fentanyl, Inc.* — 362.29
DRUG CULTURE
    Dufton, Emily. *Grass Roots* — 362.29
    Vorobyov, Niko. *Dopeworld* — 364.1
DRUG DEALERS
    Ahmed, Azam. *Fear Is Just a Word* — 364.152
    Evangelista, Patricia. ★*Some People Need Killing* — 364.4
    Garrison, Jessica. *The Devil's Harvest* — B
    Vorobyov, Niko. *Dopeworld* — 364.1
    Watkins, D. *Black Boy Smile* — B
    Westhoff, Ben. *Fentanyl, Inc.* — 362.29
DRUG ENFORCEMENT AGENTS
    Higham, Scott. *American Cartel* — 338.4
    Shannon, Elaine. *Hunting Leroux* — 364.1
DRUG INDUSTRY AND TRADE
    Abramson, John. *Sickening* — 338.4
    Dearen, Jason. *Kill Shot* — 616.8
    Eyre, Eric. *Death in Mud Lick* — 362.29
    Fine, Doug. *Too High to Fail* — 338.4
    Hari, Johann. ★*Magic Pill* — 613.2
    Jackson, Bruce. *Never Far from Home* — B
    Jimenez, Stephen. *The Book of Matt* — 364.152
    Keefe, Patrick Radden. ★*Empire of Pain* — 338.7
    Loftus, Peter. *The Messenger* — 338.4
    Macy, Beth. ★*Dopesick* — 362.29
    Macy, Beth. ★*Raising Lazarus* — 362.29
    McGreal, Chris. *American Overdose* — 362.29
    Posner, Gerald L. ★*Pharma* — 338.4
    Quigley, Fran. *Prescription for the People* — 338.4
    Quinones, Sam. ★*The Least of Us* — 362.29
    Schwarz, Alan. *ADHD Nation* — 618.92
    Slater, Lauren. *Blue Dreams* — 615.7
    Vanderbes, Jennifer. ★*Wonder Drug* — 615
    Westhoff, Ben. *Fentanyl, Inc.* — 362.29
    Zaitchik, Alexander. *Owning the Sun* — 362.1
DRUG INDUSTRY CORRUPTION
    Goldacre, Ben. *Bad Science* — 500
    Higham, Scott. *American Cartel* — 338.4
    Hughes, Evan. *The Hard Sell* — 338.4
    Keefe, Patrick Radden. ★*Empire of Pain* — 338.7
    Vanderbes, Jennifer. ★*Wonder Drug* — 615
DRUG OVERDOSES
    Case, Anne. *Deaths of Despair and the Future of Capitalism* — 362.28
    Higham, Scott. *American Cartel* — 338.4
    Westhoff, Ben. *Fentanyl, Inc.* — 362.29
DRUG PRICES
    Quigley, Fran. *Prescription for the People* — 338.4
DRUG RESISTANCE IN MICROORGANISMS
    Blaser, Martin J. *Missing Microbes* — 615.7
    Zaman, Muhammad H. *Biography of Resistance* — 616.9
DRUG SMUGGLING
    Croke, Ken. *Riding with Evil* — 364.106
    Marshall, McMillan. *Among the Bros* — 362.29
DRUG TESTING
    Kempner, Joanna. *Psychedelic Outlaws* — 615.7

AUTHOR, TITLE, SERIES AND SUBJECT INDEX

DRUG TRAFFIC
    Ahmed, Azam. *Fear Is Just a Word* — 364.152
    Bowden, Mark. *Life Sentence* — 364.106
    Brown, Claude. *Manchild in the Promised Land* — B
    Dudley, Steven S. *MS-13* — 364.106
    Fenton, Justin. *We Own This City* — 364.1
    Jackson, Mitchell S. *Survival Math* — B
    Quinones, Sam. *Dreamland* — 362.29
    Ratliff, Evan. *The Mastermind* — B
    Shannon, Elaine. *Hunting Leroux* — 364.1
    Vorobyov, Niko. *Dopeworld* — 364.1

DRUG USE
    Cole, Natalie. *Angel on My Shoulder* — B
    Duran, Elvis. *Where Do I Begin?* — B
    Gaye, Jan. *After the Dance* — B
    Hamilton, Tyler. *The Secret Race* — 796.62
    Harry, Debbie. *Face It* — B
    Hechinger, John. ★*True Gentlemen* — 371.85
    Inglis, Lucy. *Milk of Paradise* — 362.29
    Jimenez, Stephen. *The Book of Matt* — 364.152
    Lahey, Jessica. *The Addiction Inoculation* — 649
    Legler, Casey. ★*Godspeed* — B
    Osbourne, Ozzy. *I Am Ozzy* — B
    Pollan, Michael. *How to Change Your Mind* — 615.7
    Pollan, Michael. ★*This Is Your Mind on Plants* — 581.6
    Rush, Chris. *The Light Years* — B
    Ulander, Perry A. *Walking Point* — B

DRUG WITHDRAWAL SYMPTOMS
    Rieder, Travis. *In Pain* — 362.29

DRUGS
    Abramson, John. *Sickening* — 338.4
    Dearen, Jason. *Kill Shot* — 616.8
    Fleming, Brandon P. *Miseducated* — B
    Garcia, Angela. ★*The Way That Leads Among the Lost* — 362.29
    Keefe, Patrick Radden. ★*Empire of Pain* — 338.7
    Kuhn, Cynthia. *Buzzed* — 362.29
    Lisle, John. *The Dirty Tricks Department* — 940.54
    Pollan, Michael. ★*This Is Your Mind on Plants* — 581.6
    Ramsey, Donovan X. ★*When Crack Was King* — 362.29
    Suvari, Mena. *The Great Peace* — B
    Torgoff, Martin. *Bop Apocalypse* — 781.65
    Vanderbes, Jennifer. ★*Wonder Drug* — 615
    Vorobyov, Niko. *Dopeworld* — 364.1
    Westhoff, Ben. *Original Gangstas* — 782.421649

DRUMMERS
    Questlove. *Mo' Meta Blues* — 782.42164
    Schemel, Patty. *Hit so Hard* — B

Drummond, Ree
    ★*The Pioneer Woman Cooks* — 641.5
★*Drunk-Ish*. Wilder-Taylor, Stefanie — B

Drury, Bob
    Blood and Treasure — B
    The Heart of Everything That Is — B
    Lucky 666 — B
    Valley Forge — 973.3

Druse, Kenneth
    The New Shade Garden — 635.9

Du Bois, W. E. B.
    The Oxford W.E.B. Du Bois Reader — 305.896
    ★*The Souls of Black Folk* — 973
    ★*Writings* — 973

DU BOIS, W. E. B. (WILLIAM EDWARD BURGHARDT), 1868-1963
    Lewis, David L. ★*W.E.B. Du Bois* — B
    West, Cornel. *Black Prophetic Fire* — 920

DU MAURIER, DAPHNE, 1907-1989
    Rosnay, Tatiana de. *Manderley Forever* — B

Du Mez, Kristin Kobes
    Jesus and John Wayne — 277.308

Du Sautoy, Marcus
    ★*Around the World in Eighty Games* — 790.1
    The Great Unknown — 500

DUALISM
    Scenters-Zapico, Natalie. *Lima* — 811

DUBAI
    Tjipombo, Tupa. *I Am Not Your Slave* — B

Duberman, Martin B.
    Andrea Dworkin — B
    Hold Tight Gently — 920

    Howard Zinn — B

Dubin, Minna
    ★*Mom Rage* — 306.874

DUBLIN, IRELAND
    Banville, John. *Time Pieces* — 914.1
    O'Connell, Mark. *A Thread of Violence* — 364.152

Dubofsky, Melvyn
    Labor in America — 331.880973

DuBois, Ellen Carol
    Suffrage — 324.6

Dubus, Andre
    Ghost Dogs — 814
    Townie — B

DUBUS, ANDRE, III, 1959-
    Dubus, Andre. *Townie* — B

Ducharme, Jamie
    Big Vape — 338.7
★*Ducks*. Beaton, Kate — 741.5

Duckworth, Angela
    Grit — 158.1

Duckworth, Tammy
    Every Day Is a Gift — B

DUCKWORTH, TAMMY, 1968-
    Duckworth, Tammy. *Every Day Is a Gift* — B

DUCT TAPE
    Akiyama, Lance. *Duct Tape Engineer* — 745.5
Duct Tape Engineer. Akiyama, Lance — 745.5

DUDAMEL, GUSTAVO
    Tunstall, Tricia. *Changing Lives* — 780.71

Dudley, Renee
    The Ransomware Hunting Team — 363.25

Dudley, Steven S.
    MS-13 — 364.106

DUE PROCESS OF LAW
    Brodsky, Alexandra. *Sexual Justice* — 364.15
    Khan, Mahvish Rukhsana. *My Guantanamo Diary* — 973.931
    Minian, Ana Raquel. ★*In the Shadow of Liberty* — 365

DUELING
    Freeman, Joanne B. *The Field of Blood* — 973.7
    Sedgwick, John. *War of Two* — 973.4
Dueling with Kings. Barbarisi, Daniel — 793.93
Duende. Smith, Tracy K. — 811

Duerr, Sasha
    Natural Color — 746.6
Duff Bakes. Goldman, Duff — 641.81

Duffy, Eamon
    Saints & Sinners — 262

Dufresne, John
    Storyville! — 808.3

Dufton, Emily
    Grass Roots — 362.29

Dufu, Tiffany
    Drop the Ball — 650.1

DUFU, TIFFANY
    Dufu, Tiffany. *Drop the Ball* — 650.1

Dugard, Martin
    Taking Berlin — 940.54
    Taking Paris — 940.54

Dugdale, Lydia S.
    The Lost Art of Dying — 155.9

Duggan, Christopher
    The Force of Destiny — 945

Duggar, Jill
    Counting the Cost — B

DUGGAR, JILL
    Duggar, Jill. *Counting the Cost* — B

DUHAMEL, OLIVIER, 1950-
    Kouchner, Camille. *The Familia Grande* — B

Duhigg, Charles
    ★*The Power of Habit* — 158.1
    Smarter Faster Better — 158
    ★*Supercommunicators* — 153.6

Duiker, William J.
    Ho Chi Minh — B
★*Duino Elegies*. Rilke, Rainer Maria — 831
Duke. Teachout, Terry — B

Duke, Annie
    Thinking in Bets — 658.4

PUBLIC LIBRARY CORE COLLECTION: NONFICTION
Twentieth Edition

DUKES AND DUCHESSES
   Lownie, Andrew. *Traitor King* — 920
DUMAS, ALEXANDRE, 1802-1870
   Reiss, Tom. *The Black Count* — B
DUMAS, THOMAS ALEXANDRE, 1762-1806
   Reiss, Tom. *The Black Count* — B
Dumb Luck and the Kindness of Strangers. Gierach, John — 799.124
Dumbach, Annette E.
   Sophie Scholl and the White Rose — 943.086
DUMPLINGS
   Amano, Hugh. *Let's Make Dumplings!* — 741.5
Dunaway, David King
   ★*How Can I Keep from Singing?* — B
DUNAWAY, FAYE, 1941-
   Wasson, Sam. *The Big Goodbye* — 791.43
Dunbar, Erica Armstrong
   ★*Never Caught* — B
   ★*She Came to Slay* — B
Dunbar, R. I. M.
   Human Evolution — 155.7
Dunbar-Ortiz, Roxanne
   ★*An Indigenous Peoples' History of the United States* — 970.004
Duncan, Arne
   How Schools Work — 379
Duncan, Dayton
   Blood Memory — 599.64
   ★*Country Music* — 781.642
   The National Parks — 333.78
Duncan, Dennis
   Index, a History of The — 025.3
DUNCAN, GARY
   Van Meter, Matthew. *Deep Delta Justice* — 345.763
Duncan, Isadora
   My Life — B
DUNCAN, ISADORA, 1877-1927
   Duncan, Isadora. *My Life* — B
Duncan, James R.
   Owls of the World — 598.9
Duncan, Michael
   ★*Hero of Two Worlds* — B
Duncan, Robert
   Selected Poems — 811
Dunce. Ruefle, Mary — 811
DUNE (IMAGINARY PLACE)
   Britt, Ryan. ★*The Spice Must Flow* — 813
   Herbert, Brian. *Dreamer of Dune* — B
Dungy, Camille T.
   Soil — 635.0978
DUNGY, CAMILLE T., 1972-
   Dungy, Camille T. *Soil* — 635.0978
Dunham, William
   The Mathematical Universe — 510
DUNKIRK, FRANCE, BATTLE OF, 1940
   Korda, Michael. *Alone* — 940.54
Dunlop, Fuchsia
   The Food of Sichuan — 641.595
Dunmore, Helen
   Inside the Wave — 821
Dunn, Harry
   Standing My Ground — B
DUNN, HARRY (POLICE OFFICER)
   Dunn, Harry. *Standing My Ground* — B
Dunn, Jancee
   Hot and Bothered — 618.1
   ★*How Not to Hate Your Husband After Kids* — 646.7
DUNN, JANCEE
   Dunn, Jancee. ★*How Not to Hate Your Husband After Kids* — 646.7
Dunn, Jon L.
   The Glitter in the Green — 598.7
Dunn, Stephen
   Local Visitations — 811
   New & Selected Poems — 811
Dunnavant, Keith
   Montana — B
Dunne, Griffin
   ★*The Friday Afternoon Club* — B
DUNNE, GRIFFIN
   Dunne, Griffin. ★*The Friday Afternoon Club* — B

DUNNE, JOHN GREGORY, 1932-2003
   Didion, Joan. ★*The Year of Magical Thinking* — B
Dunne, Linnea
   Lagom — 158.1
Dunning, John
   On the Air — 791.44
Duran, Elvis
   Where Do I Begin? — B
DURAN, ELVIS
   Duran, Elvis. *Where Do I Begin?* — B
DURAN, ROBERTO, 1951-
   Kimball, George. *Four Kings* — B
Durant, Judith
   Cable Left, Cable Right — 746.43
   Increase, Decrease — 746.43
DURANT, KEVIN, 1988-
   Sullivan, Matt. *Can't Knock the Hustle* — 796.323
Durant, Will
   ★*The Story of Philosophy* — 190
Durber, Sarah
   Make Your Own Indoor Garden — 635
Durkheim, Emile
   ★*Suicide* — 394.8
Durkin, Hannah
   ★*The Survivors of the Clotilda* — 306.362
Durrani, Matin
   Furry Logic — 591.5
Durvasula, Ramani
   ★*It's Not You* — 155.2
★*Dusk, Night, Dawn*. Lamott, Anne — B
Dusoulier, Clotilde
   Tasting Paris — 641.594
Dust. Owens, Jay — 551.51
DUST
   Owens, Jay. *Dust* — 551.51
DUST BOWL (SOUTH CENTRAL UNITED STATES)
   Egan, Timothy. *The Worst Hard Time* — 978
DUST BOWL ERA, 1931-1939
   Egan, Timothy. *The Worst Hard Time* — 978
DUST STORMS
   Egan, Timothy. *The Worst Hard Time* — 978
Dust Tracks on a Road. Hurston, Zora Neale — B
Dutch Girl. Matzen, Robert — B
DUTCH PEOPLE
   Blom, Onno. *Young Rembrandt* — B
   Iperen, Roxane van. ★*The Sisters of Auschwitz* — 940.53
   Loftis, Larry. ★*The Watchmaker's Daughter* — 940.53
   McDonald, Greg (Producer). *Elvis and the Colonel* — 920
   Pick-Goslar, Hannah Elizabeth. ★*My Friend Anne Frank* — B
   Siegal, Nina. *The Diary Keepers* — 940.54
   Sullivan, Rosemary. *The Betrayal of Anne Frank* — 940.53
   Van Es, Bart. *The Cut Out Girl* — B
DUTERTE, RODRIGO ROA, 1945-
   Evangelista, Patricia. ★*Some People Need Killing* — 364.4
Dutta, Sunil
   Stealing Green Mangoes — 973
DUTTA, SUNIL
   Dutta, Sunil. *Stealing Green Mangoes* — 973
Dutton, Kevin
   Split-Second Persuasion — 153.8
DUTY
   Brenner, Marie. ★*The Desperate Hours* — 362.1962
   Bunting, Josiah. ★*The Making of a Leader* — B
   Roll, David L. *Ascent to Power* — 973.918
   Weir, Alison. *Queens of the Age of Chivalry* — 920
DuVal, Kathleen
   ★*Native Nations* — 970.004
Dweck, Carol S.
   ★*Mindset* — 153.8
Dwork, Deborah
   ★*Holocaust* — 940
DWORKIN, ANDREA
   Duberman, Martin B. *Andrea Dworkin* — B
Dwyer, Jim
   102 Minutes — 974.7
Dybdahl, Thomas L.
   When Innocence Is Not Enough — 345.73

AUTHOR, TITLE, SERIES AND SUBJECT INDEX

DYE INDUSTRY AND TRADE
    Fagin, Dan. *Toms River* — 363.7209749
    Wicker, Alden. ★*To Dye For* — 746
Dyer, Wayne W.
    ★*The Power of Intention* — 158.1
DYES AND DYEING
    Callahan, Gail. *Hand Dyeing Yarn and Fleece* — 746.6
    Corwin, Lena. *Lena Corwin's Made by Hand* — 746.6
    Duerr, Sasha. *Natural Color* — 746.6
    Joyce, Anna. *Hand Dyed* — 746.6
    Wicker, Alden. ★*To Dye For* — 746
Dying. Taylor, Cory — B
Dying of Politeness. Davis, Geena — B
Dyja, Tom
    The Third Coast — 977.311
Dykstra, Lenny
    House of Nails — B
DYKSTRA, LENNY, 1963-
    Dykstra, Lenny. *House of Nails* — B
Dylan Goes Electric! Wald, Elijah — 782.42164
Dylan, Bob
    Chronicles; Volume 1 — B
    ★*The Philosophy of Modern Song* — 782.42
DYLAN, BOB, 1941-
    Davidson, Mark A. ★*Bob Dylan* — B
    Dylan, Bob. *Chronicles; Volume 1* — B
    Thomas, Richard F. ★*Why Bob Dylan Matters* — 782.42164
    Wald, Elijah. *Dylan Goes Electric!* — 782.42164
    Wolff, Daniel J. *Grown-Up Anger* — 920
DYNAMITE
    Johnson, Steven. *The Infernal Machine* — 335
Dynamite Kids Cooking School. Bowen, Dana — 641.5
The Dynasty. Benedict, Jeff — 796.332
Dyscalculia. Felix, Camoghne — B
DYSCALCULIA
    Felix, Camoghne. *Dyscalculia* — B
DYSFUNCTIONAL FAMILIES
    Alexie, Sherman. *You Don't Have to Say You Love Me* — 818
    Auvinen, Karen. *Rough Beauty* — B
    Barnes, Cinelle. *Monsoon Mansion* — B
    Bilton, Chrysta. *Normal Family* — B
    Conyers, Jonathan. *I Wasn't Supposed to Be Here* — B
    Dais, Dawn. *The Sh!t No One Tells You About Divorce* — 306.89
    Danler, Stephanie. *Stray* — B
    Duggar, Jill. *Counting the Cost* — B
    Fitzgerald, Isaac. *Dirtbag, Massachusetts* — B
    Fremont, Helen. *The Escape Artist* — B
    Grande, Reyna. ★*The Distance Between Us* — 973
    Gupta, Prachi. ★*They Called Us Exceptional* — B
    Hamill, Kirkland. *Filthy Beasts* — B
    Hilfiger, Tommy. *American Dreamer* — B
    Jollett, Mikel. ★*Hollywood Park* — B
    Kizzia, Tom. *Pilgrim's Wilderness* — B
    Laux, Dorianne. *Only as the Day Is Long* — 811
    Machado, Carmen Maria. ★*In the Dream House* — B
    Madden, T Kira. *Long Live the Tribe of Fatherless Girls* — 814
    Mann, William J. *The Wars of the Roosevelts* — B
    Margulies, Julianna. *Sunshine Girl* — B
    Means, Brittany. *Hell If We Don't Change Our Ways* — B
    Nietfeld, Emi. *Acceptance* — B
    O'Connor, Sinead. ★*Rememberings* — B
    Pentland, Jenny. *This Will Be Funny Later* — B
    Rowe, Mickey. *Fearlessly Different* — B
    Scheier, Liz. *Never Simple* — B
    Selvaratnam, Tanya. *Assume Nothing* — B
    Shorter, Frank. *My Marathon* — 796.42
    Sipress, David. *What's so Funny?* — B
    Tometich, Annabelle. *The Mango Tree* — B
    Trump, Mary L. *Too Much and Never Enough* — B
    V. *The Apology* — 818
    Walls, Jeannette. ★*The Glass Castle* — B
    Williams, Mary. *The Lost Daughter* — B
DYSLEXIA
    Ballard, Robert D. *Into the Deep* — 551.46092
Dyson, Freeman J.
    Maker of Patterns — B
DYSON, FREEMAN J.
    Dyson, Freeman J. *Maker of Patterns* — B

Dyson, George
    Turing's Cathedral — 004
Dyson, Michael Eric
    The Black Presidency — 305.800973
    Come Hell or High Water — 976.3
    Holler If You Hear Me — B
    Long Time Coming — 305.800973
    Tears We Cannot Stop — 305.800973
    What Truth Sounds Like — 305.800973
DYSTOPIAS
    Choi, Franny. *The World Keeps Ending, and the World Goes On* — 811

E

E.B. White. Elledge, Scott — B
Eade, Philip
    Evelyn Waugh — B
EADS, JAMES BUCHANAN, 1820-1887
    Barry, John M. *Rising Tide* — 977
Eager. Goldfarb, Ben — 333.95
Eagle, Ellen
    Pastel Painting Atelier — 741.2
Eagleman, David
    The Brain — 612.8
    Incognito — 153
    Livewired — 612.8
EAKINS, THOMAS, 1844-1916
    Sewell, Darrel. *Thomas Eakins* — 759.13
EARHART, AMELIA, 1897-1937
    O'Brien, Keith. *Fly Girls* — 920
    Winters, Kathleen C. *Amelia Earhart* — B
    Zanglein, Jayne E. *The Girl Explorers* — B
Early. DiGregorio, Sarah — 618.92
EARLY AMERICA (1784-1819)
    Adams, Abigail. *Abigail Adams* — 973.4
    Adams, John. *My Dearest Friend* — 973.4
    Avlon, John P. *Washington's Farewell* — 973.4
    Baier, Bret. *To Rescue the Constitution* — 973.4
    Boles, John B. *Jefferson* — B
    Brands, H. W. ★*Founding Partisans* — 973.3
    Cheney, Lynne V. *The Virginia Dynasty* — B
    Chernow, Ron. ★*Alexander Hamilton* — B
    Dunbar, Erica Armstrong. ★*Never Caught* — B
    Ellis, Joseph J. *American Creation* — 973.3
    Ellis, Joseph J. *First Family* — 973.4
    Ellis, Joseph J. *Founding Brothers* — 973.4
    Ellis, Joseph J. *The Quartet* — 342.7302
    Flexner, James Thomas. *George Washington and the New Nation, 1783-1793* — 973.4
    Flexner, James Thomas. *George Washington* — B
    Good, Cassandra A. *First Family* — 920
    Gordon-Reed, Annette. *Most Blessed of the Patriarchs* — 973.4
    Groom, Winston. *The Patriots* — 920
    Horn, Jonathan. *Washington's End* — B
    Isaacson, Walter. ★*Benjamin Franklin* — B
    Jefferson, Thomas. *Writings* — 973.3
    Johnson, Victoria. ★*American Eden* — 580.973
    Kerrison, Catherine. *Jefferson's Daughters* — 920
    Kilmeade, Brian. ★*Thomas Jefferson and the Tripoli Pirates* — 973.4
    Larson, Edward J. *The Return of George Washington* — B
    McCullough, David G. ★*John Adams* — B
    McCullough, David G. *The Pioneers* — 920
    Meacham, Jon. ★*Thomas Jefferson* — B
    Paul, Joel R. ★*Without Precedent* — B
    Randall, Willard Sterne. *The Founders' Fortunes* — 973.3
    Raphael, Ray. *Constitutional Myths* — 342.7302
    Raphael, Ray. *Mr. President* — 352.230973
    Roberts, Cokie. *Founding Mothers* — 920
    Rosen, Jeffrey. *The Pursuit of Happiness* — 973.3
    Simon, James F. *What Kind of Nation* — 342.73
    Snow, Peter. *When Britain Burned the White House* — 975.3
    Stewart, David O. *George Washington* — 973.4
    Taylor, Alan. *American Republics* — 973.3
    Taylor, Alan. *American Revolutions* — 973.3
    Taylor, Alan. *The Civil War of 1812* — 973.5
    Taylor, Alan. ★*The Internal Enemy* — 975.5
    Thomas, Louisa. *Louisa* — B

PUBLIC LIBRARY CORE COLLECTION: NONFICTION
Twentieth Edition

Wills, Garry. *James Madison*	B
Wood, Gordon S. *Empire of Liberty*	973.4

EARLY CHILDHOOD EDUCATION

Alvarez, Celine. *The Natural Laws of Children*	372.21
Christakis, Erika. *The Importance of Being Little*	372.21
Chu, Lenora. *Little Soldiers*	370
Ghoting, Saroj Nadkarni. *Step into Storytime*	027.62
Koenig, Joan. *The Musical Child*	780.71
Lahey, Jessica. *The Gift of Failure*	649
Seldin, Tim. *How to Raise an Amazing Child the Montessori Way*	649
Tough, Paul. ★*How Children Succeed*	372.210973

EARNHARDT FAMILY

Busbee, Jay. *Earnhardt Nation*	B
Earnhardt Nation. Busbee, Jay	B

EARNHARDT, DALE, 1951-2001

Busbee, Jay. *Earnhardt Nation*	B

EARP, WYATT, 1848-1929

Barra, Allen. *Inventing Wyatt Earp*	B
Clavin, Thomas. *Dodge City*	978.1
Tefertiller, Casey. *Wyatt Earp*	B

EARTH

Foster, Craig. ★*Amphibious Soul*	155.9
Frank, Adam. *Light of the Stars*	523.1
Jabr, Ferris. ★*Becoming Earth*	570.1
Sanders, Ella Frances. *Eating the Sun*	520
Weill, Kelly. *Off the Edge*	001.9
Earth Almanac. Keffer, Ken	508
Earth Energy Meditations. Shumsky, Susan G.	133.8

EARTH HISTORY

Gee, Henry. *A (Very) Short History of Life on Earth*	576.8
Randall, Lisa. *Dark Matter and the Dinosaurs*	523.1
The Earth Is All That Lasts. Gardner, Mark L.	978.004
The Earth Is Weeping. Cozzens, Peter	978
Earth Keeper. Momaday, N. Scott	814

EARTH SCIENCES

Barnett, Cynthia. *Rain*	551.57
Bell, Alice R. *Our Biggest Experiment*	363.738
Conway, Edmund. *Material World*	333.7
Tyson, Neil deGrasse. *Startalk*	523.1
The Earth Transformed. Frankopan, Peter	304.2
Earth's Wild Music. Moore, Kathleen Dean	576.8
Earth-Shattering. Berman, Bob	523.1

EARTHQUAKES

Davenport, Matthew J. *The Longest Minute*	979.4
Gates, Alexander E. *Encyclopedia of Earthquakes and Volcanoes*	551.2
McClelland, Mac. *Irritable Hearts*	B
Winchester, Simon. *A Crack in the Edge of the World*	979.4
Easily Slip into Another World. Threadgill, Henry	B
East. Sodha, Meera	641.595

EAST AFRICA

Deng, Alephonsion. *They Poured Fire on Us from the Sky*	B
Hassan, Hawa. *In Bibi's Kitchen*	641.596
Markham, Beryl. *West with the Night*	B
Wallace, Christopher. *Twentieth-Century Man*	B

EAST AFRICAN PEOPLE

Berg, Raffi. *Red Sea Spies*	327.125694
Wainaina, Binyavanga. ★*How to Write About Africa*	814

EAST AND WEST

Cliff, Nigel. *Holy War*	909
Crowley, Roger. *1453*	949.61
Guha, Ramachandra. *Rebels Against the Raj*	954.03
Hessler, Peter. *Oracle Bones*	951
Hughes, Bettany. *Istanbul*	949.61
Platt, Stephen R. *Imperial Twilight*	951

EAST ASIA

Spence, Jonathan D. *God's Chinese Son*	951

EAST ASIAN AMERICANS

Brina, Elizabeth Miki. *Speak, Okinawa*	305.48
Brown, Daniel James. ★*Facing the Mountain*	940.54
Cahan, Richard. *Un-American*	940.53
Chang, David. ★*Eat a Peach*	641.5
Chang, Gordon H. *Ghosts of Gold Mountain*	331.6
Checkoway, Julie. *The Three-Year Swim Club*	797.2
Daniels, Roger. *Prisoners Without Trial*	940.53
Henderson, Bruce B. *Bridge to the Sun*	940.53
Herrera, Hayden. *Listening to Stone*	B
Howe, Ben Ryder. *My Korean Deli*	B
Hsu, Hua. ★*Stay True*	B
Huang, Eddie. *Fresh off the Boat*	B
Huang, Yunte. *Daughter of the Dragon*	B
Kingston, Maxine Hong. *The Woman Warrior*	B
Lee, Helie. *In the Absence of Sun*	B
Reeves, Richard. *Infamy*	940.53
Russell, Jan Jarboe. *The Train to Crystal City*	940.53
Salisbury, Katie Gee. ★*Not Your China Doll*	B
Sone, Monica Itoi. *Nisei Daughter*	979.7
Wang, Qian Julie. ★*Beautiful Country*	B
Zauner, Michelle. ★*Crying in H Mart*	B

EAST ASIAN PEOPLE

Ai, Weiwei. *Zodiac*	741.5
Chin, Curtis. *Everything I Learned, I Learned in a Chinese Restaurant*	B
Gaines, Joanna. *The Stories We Tell*	B
Hoja, Gulchehra. *A Stone Is Most Precious Where It Belongs*	B
Hulls, Tessa. ★*Feeding Ghosts*	741.5
Jun, Tasha. ★*Tell Me the Dream Again*	248
Kemper, Steve. *Our Man in Tokyo*	952.03
Li, Fei-Fei. *The Worlds I See*	B
Ng, Fae Myenne. *Orphan Bachelors*	B
Sehee, Baek. *I Want to Die but I Want to Eat Tteokbokki*	B
Sun, Carrie. *Private Equity*	B

EAST BERLIN, GERMANY

Vogel, Steve. *Betrayal in Berlin*	327.1273043

EAST GERMANY

Hoyer, Katja. ★*Beyond the Wall*	943.087
Longo, Matthew. *The Picnic*	947.084
Taylor, Fred. *The Berlin Wall*	943
Willner, Nina. *Forty Autumns*	B
East Meets Vegan. Gill, Sasha	641.5
East West Street. Sands, Philippe	345
East-Meets-West Quilts. Belyea, Patricia	746.46

EAST-WEST RELATIONS

Service, Robert. *The End of the Cold War 1985-1991*	909.82

EASTER ISLAND

Treister, Kenneth. *Easter Island's Silent Sentinels*	996.18
Easter Island's Silent Sentinels. Treister, Kenneth	996.18

Easterbrook, Gregg

★*The King of Sports*	796.332

EASTERN EUROPE

Applebaum, Anne. *Iron Curtain*	947
Applebaum, Anne. ★*Red Famine*	947.708
Eisen, Norman L. *The Last Palace*	920
Golinkin, Lev. *A Backpack, a Bear, and Eight Crates of Vodka*	B
Krimstein, Ken. *When I Grow Up*	741.5
Mikanowski, Jacob. *Goodbye, Eastern Europe*	947
Moore, Tim. *The Cyclist Who Went Out in the Cold*	796.6
Plokhy, Serhii. ★*The Gates of Europe*	947.7
Rady, Martyn C. *The Middle Kingdoms*	943
Rees, Laurence. *Hitler and Stalin*	940.53
Snyder, Timothy. ★*Bloodlands*	940.54
Snyder, Timothy. *The Red Prince*	B
Szablowski, Witold. *Dancing Bears*	947.086

EASTERN EUROPEAN PEOPLE

Chiger, Krystyna. *The Girl in the Green Sweater*	B
Eisen, Max. *By Chance Alone*	940.5318
Faludi, Susan. *In the Darkroom*	B
Finkelstein, Daniel. *Two Roads Home*	920
Fishman, Boris. *Savage Feast*	B
Greenfield, Martin. ★*Measure of a Man*	B
Harss, Marina. *The Boy from Kyiv*	B
Katin, Miriam. *We Are on Our Own*	741.5
Klopotenko, Yevhen. ★*The Authentic Ukrainian Kitchen*	641.594
Kraus, Dita. *A Delayed Life*	B
Masters, Oksana. *The Hard Parts*	B
Neumann, Ariana. *When Time Stopped*	B
Szczeszak-Brewer, Agata. *The Hunger Book*	B
Thubron, Colin. *In Siberia*	957

EASTERN FRONT (WORLD WAR II)

Churchill, Winston. *The Grand Alliance*	940.53
Merridale, Catherine. *Ivan's War*	940.54
★*The Eastern Orthodox Church.* McGuckin, John Anthony	281.909
The Eastern Stars. Kurlansky, Mark	796.357

Easto, Jessica

How to Taste Coffee	663
★*Easy Beauty.* Jones, Chloe Cooper	B
Easy Fair Isle Knitting. Storey, Martin	746.43
Easy Homemade Pottery. Stone, Francesca	738.1

AUTHOR, TITLE, SERIES AND SUBJECT INDEX

Easy Rider. Bingen, Steven	791.4372
Easy Soups from Scratch with Quick Breads to Match. Manning, Ivy	641.81
★*Eat & Flourish.* Albright, Mary Beth	612.3
★*Eat A Peach.* Chang, David	641.5
Eat Like a Fish. Smith, Bren	338.3
Eat The Buddha. Demick, Barbara	951
Eat to Live Quick & Easy Cookbook. Fuhrman, Joel	641.5
★*Eat Up.* Tandoh, Ruby	641.3
Eat Well, Be Well. Cristofano, Jana	641.5
Eat, Poop, Die. Roman, Joe	577
Eat, Pray, Love. Gilbert, Elizabeth	B
Eating Animals. Foer, Jonathan Safran	641.3
EATING DISORDERS	
Burton, Susan. *Empty*	B
Freeman, Hadley. *Good Girls*	616.85
Hornbacher, Marya. *Wasted*	B
Kang, Mia. *Knockout*	B
Kazdin, Cole. ★*What's Eating Us*	616.85
McCurdy, Jennette. ★*I'm Glad My Mom Died*	B
Sole-Smith, Virginia. ★*Fat Talk*	649.1
Specter, Emma. *More, Please*	616.85
Tate, Christie. ★*Group*	B
Wilson, Jessica. *It's Always Been Ours*	613
Eating in the Middle. Mitchell, Andie	641.3
Eating on the Wild Side. Robinson, Jo	641.3
EATING OUT	
Dusoulier, Clotilde. *Tasting Paris*	641.594
Eating The Sun. Sanders, Ella Frances	520
Eating to Extinction. Saladino, Dan	641.3
Eatman, Nicholas	
Friday, Saturday, Sunday in Texas	796.332
Eaton, Jan	
350+ Crochet Tips, Techniques, and Trade Secrets	746.432
Mary Thomas's Dictionary of Embroidery Stitches.	746.44
Eats, Shoots & Leaves. Truss, Lynne	428.2
★*The Eaves of Heaven.* Pham, Andrew X.	B
Eberhardt, Jennifer L.	
★*Biased*	303.3
Ebersol, Dick	
From Saturday Night to Sunday Night	B
Ebert, Roger	
Life Itself	B
Scorsese by Ebert	B
EBERT, ROGER	
Ebert, Roger. *Life Itself*	B
Singer, Matt. *Opposable Thumbs*	791.43
EBOLA VIRUS DISEASE	
Farmer, Paul. *Fevers, Feuds, and Diamonds*	614.5
Honigsbaum, Mark. *The Pandemic Century*	614.4
Preston, Richard. *Crisis in the Red Zone*	614.5
Preston, Richard. *The Hot Zone*	614.5
Quammen, David. ★*Spillover*	614.4
Ebony and Ivy. Wilder, Craig Steven	379.2
ECCENTRIC MEN	
Herbert, Brian. *Dreamer of Dune*	B
Sisman, Adam. *The Professor and the Parson*	364.16
ECCENTRICS AND ECCENTRICITIES	
Alterman, Sara Faith. *Let's Never Talk About This Again*	616.8
Berendt, John. *Midnight in the Garden of Good and Evil*	975.8
Burroughs, Augusten. ★*Toil & Trouble*	B
Dennison, Matthew. *Behind the Mask*	B
Dery, Mark. *Born to Be Posthumous*	B
Finkel, Michael. *The Stranger in the Woods*	B
Fuller, Alexandra. *Travel Light, Move Fast*	B
Grant, Richard. *The Deepest South of All*	976.2
Kalb, Claudia. *Andy Warhol Was a Hoarder*	920
Krakauer, Jon. *Classic Krakauer*	814
McGrath, Ben. *Riverman*	797.122
Morton, Brian. *Tasha*	B
O'Sullivan, Emer. *The Fall of the House of Wilde*	B
Prideaux, Sue. *I Am Dynamite!*	B
Rao, Maya. *Great American Outpost*	338.2
Walls, Jeannette. ★*The Glass Castle*	B
Zenith, Richard. *Pessoa*	B
Echoes. Povey, Glenn	782.42166
ECKENER, HUGO, 1868-1954	
Rose, Alexander. *Empires of the Sky*	920

Eckert, Allan W.	
A Sorrow in Our Heart	B
ECKFORD, ELIZABETH, 1941-	
Margolick, David. *Elizabeth and Hazel*	379.2
Eckhardt, Robyn	
Istanbul & Beyond	641.595
ECKHART, MEISTER, -1327	
Harrington, Joel F. *Dangerous Mystic*	B
Eckman, Edie	
Around the Corner Crochet Borders	746.43
Beyond the Square Crochet Motifs	746.43
Connect the Shapes Crochet Motifs	746.43
The Crochet Answer Book	746.43
ECLIPSES	
Baron, David. *American Eclipse*	523.7
Nordgren, Tyler E. *Sun, Moon, Earth*	523.7
The Eclogues of Virgil. Virgil	871
Eco, Umberto	
History of Beauty	111
On Ugliness	111
ECOLOGICAL HOUSES	
Koones, Sheri. *Prefabulous Small Houses*	728
Ecological Intelligence. Goleman, Daniel	333.7
ECOLOGISTS	
Lowman, Margaret. *Life in the Treetops*	B
Safina, Carl. ★*Alfie and Me*	598.9
Simard, S. ★*Finding the Mother Tree*	582.16
ECOLOGY	
Darlington, Miriam. *Otter Country*	599.769
Francis. *Life*	B
Goldfarb, Ben. *Crossings*	333.77
Goldfarb, Ben. *Eager*	333.95
Kumar, Priyanka. *Conversations with Birds*	598
Leopold, Aldo. ★*A Sand County Almanac & Other Writings on Ecology and Conservation*	814
Roman, Joe. *Eat, Poop, Die*	577
Wohlleben, Peter. *The Secret Wisdom of Nature*	508
Wynn-Grant, Rae. *Wild Life*	B
ECONOMIC ASSISTANCE	
Milanovic, Branko. *The Have and the Have-Nots*	339.2
Steil, Benn. ★*The Marshall Plan*	338.91
ECONOMIC ASSISTANCE, AMERICAN	
Puleo, Stephen. *Voyage of Mercy*	363.8
Steil, Benn. ★*The Marshall Plan*	338.91
ECONOMIC DEVELOPMENT	
Ackroyd, Peter. *Revolution*	941.07
Burgis, Tom. *The Looting Machine*	338.2
Conway, Edmund. *The Summit*	337.09
Daunton, M. J. ★*The Economic Government of the World*	337
De Graaf, John. *What's the Economy For, Anyway?*	330.973
De Long, J. Bradford. *Slouching Towards Utopia*	330.9
Dikotter, Frank. *China After Mao*	951.05
Fields, Micah. ★*We Hold Our Breath*	976.4
Fowler, Corinne. ★*The Countryside*	941
Hessler, Peter. *Oracle Bones*	951
Hessler, Peter. *Other Rivers*	378.1
Holzer, Harold. *A Just and Generous Nation*	973.7092
Kershaw, Ian. *The Global Age*	940.55
Morris, Ian. *Geography Is Destiny*	941
Osnos, Evan. *Age of Ambition*	951.06
Roy, Arundhati. *Walking with the Comrades*	954
Schell, Orville. *Wealth and Power*	920
Scott, Kevin. *Reprogramming the American Dream*	338
Winchester, Simon. *The Men Who United the States*	973
Yunus, Muhammad. *A World of Three Zeros*	330
ECONOMIC FORECASTING	
Davidson, Adam. *The Passion Economy*	330.9
Davies, Richard. *Extreme Economies*	306.3
Lankov, A. N. *The Real North Korea*	951.9304
Sharma, Ruchir. *The Rise and Fall of Nations*	330.9
★*The Economic Government of the World.* Daunton, M. J.	337
ECONOMIC HISTORY	
Ahamed, Liaquat. *Lords of Finance*	920
Berfield, Susan. *The Hour of Fate*	973.91
Conway, Edmund. *The Summit*	337.09
Daunton, M. J. ★*The Economic Government of the World*	337
De Long, J. Bradford. *Slouching Towards Utopia*	330.9
Freeman, Joshua Benjamin. ★*Behemoth*	338.6

PUBLIC LIBRARY CORE COLLECTION: NONFICTION
Twentieth Edition

Gerth, Karl. *As China Goes, so Goes the World*	339.4
Gordon, Robert J. ★*The Rise and Fall of American Growth*	339.4
Harford, Tim. *50 Inventions That Shaped the Modern Economy*	609
Kennedy, Paul M. *The Rise and Fall of the Great Powers*	909.82
Krugman, Paul R. *Arguing with Zombies*	330.973
McMillan, John. *Reinventing the Bazaar*	330.12
Micklethwait, John. *The Company*	338.7
Nations, Scott. *A History of the United States in Five Crashes*	338.5
Sharma, Ruchir. *The Rise and Fall of Nations*	330.9

ECONOMIC INDICATORS

Jena, Anupam B. *Random Acts of Medicine*	616.0072
Nations, Scott. *A History of the United States in Five Crashes*	338.5

ECONOMIC POLICY

Bernanke, Ben. ★*21st Century Monetary Policy*	332.1
Booth, Michael. *The Almost Nearly Perfect People*	948.071
Chang, Ha-Joon. *Economics*	330
Daunton, M. J. ★*The Economic Government of the World*	337
Dayen, David. *Chain of Title*	330.973
De Graaf, John. *What's the Economy For, Anyway?*	330.973
Goldstein, Amy. *Janesville*	330.9775
Goldstein, Jacob. *Money*	332.4
Hayek, Friedrich A. von. *The Road to Serfdom*	330.1
Herman, Arthur. *Freedom's Forge*	940.53
Kelly, John. *The Graves Are Walking*	941.5081
Kemper, Steve. *Our Man in Tokyo*	952.03
Krugman, Paul R. *Arguing with Zombies*	330.973
Kwak, James. *Economism*	330
Lemann, Nicholas. *Transaction Man*	330.973
Leonard, Christopher. *Kochland*	338.7
Madrick, Jeffrey G. *Invisible Americans*	362.7086
McCraw, Thomas K. ★*The Founders and Finance*	330.973
McLean, Bethany. *All the Devils Are Here*	330.973
Noah, Timothy. *The Great Divergence*	339.2
Packer, George. ★*The Unwinding*	973.924
Paulson, Henry M. *On the Brink*	330.973
Phillips-Fein, Kim. *Fear City*	330.9747
Pilling, David. *Bending Adversity*	952.0512
Quart, Alissa. *Squeezed*	305.5
Reid, T. R. *A Fine Mess*	336.200973
Remnick, David. *Lenin's Tomb*	947.085
Romeo, Nick. *The Alternative*	174
Scott, Kevin. *Reprogramming the American Dream*	338
Shlaes, Amity. *Coolidge*	B
Smialek, Jeanna. ★*Limitless*	332.1
Warren, Elizabeth. *This Fight Is Our Fight*	305.5
Waterhouse, Benjamin C. *One Day I'll Work for Myself*	338
Wessel, David. *In Fed We Trust*	332.1
Wheelan, Charles J. *Naked Economics*	330

ECONOMIC SECURITY

Bruder, Jessica. ★*Nomadland*	331.3
Cox, Josie. *Women Money Power*	330.082
Economics. Chang, Ha-Joon	330

ECONOMICS

Agee, James. ★*Cotton Tenants*	976.1
Ahamed, Liaquat. *Lords of Finance*	920
Ahuvia, Aaron. ★*The Things We Love*	790.1
Allen, Frederick Lewis. *Only Yesterday*	973.9
Berfield, Susan. *The Hour of Fate*	973.91
Bernanke, Ben. ★*21st Century Monetary Policy*	332.1
Boorstin, Daniel J. *The Americans*	973
Bruder, Jessica. ★*Nomadland*	331.3
Burgis, Tom. *The Looting Machine*	338.2
Burrough, Bryan. *The Big Rich*	338.2
Case, Anne. *Deaths of Despair and the Future of Capitalism*	362.28
Chang, Ha-Joon. *Economics*	330
Chang, Leslie T. *Factory Girls*	331.4
Cohen, Lizabeth. *A Consumers' Republic*	339.4
Conway, Edmund. *Material World*	333.7
Cowen, Tyler. *An Economist Gets Lunch*	394.1
Davidson, Adam. *The Passion Economy*	330.9
Davies, Richard. *Extreme Economies*	306.3
De Graaf, John. *What's the Economy For, Anyway?*	330.973
Desmond, Matthew. ★*Poverty, by America*	362.5
Dikotter, Frank. *China After Mao*	951.05
Ditmore, Melissa Hope. *Unbroken Chains*	306.74
Edin, Kathryn. ★*The Injustice of Place*	339.4
Egan, Timothy. *The Worst Hard Time*	978
Ehrenreich, Barbara. ★*Nickel and Dimed*	B
Freeman, Amanda. *Getting Me Cheap*	362.83
Friedman, Benjamin M. *Religion and the Rise of Capitalism*	330.12
Gerth, Karl. *As China Goes, so Goes the World*	339.4
Golay, Michael. *America 1933*	B
Goldstein, Amy. *Janesville*	330.9775
Gordon, Robert J. ★*The Rise and Fall of American Growth*	339.4
Greenspan, Alan. *Capitalism in America*	330.973
Halberstam, David. *The Fifties*	973.92
Hayek, Friedrich A. von. *The Road to Serfdom*	330.1
Heilbroner, Robert L. ★*The Worldly Philosophers*	B
Herman, Arthur. *Freedom's Forge*	940.53
Hiltzik, Michael A. *Iron Empires*	385.0973
Hoffman, Liz. *Crash Landing*	330
Howe, Daniel Walker. *What Hath God Wrought*	973.5
Jena, Anupam B. *Random Acts of Medicine*	616.0072
Judt, Tony. *Postwar*	940.55
Karabell, Zachary. *Inside Money*	332.1
Keefe, Bob. *Clean Economy Now*	333.79
Keynes, John Maynard. ★*The General Theory of Employment, Interest, and Money*	330.15
Kirshner, Jodie Adams. ★*Broke*	336.3
Krugman, Paul R. *Arguing with Zombies*	330.973
Kuper, Simon. *Soccernomics*	796.334
Kwak, James. *Economism*	330
Lanchester, John. *How to Speak Money*	330.1
Ledbetter, James. *One Nation Under Gold*	332.4
Lemann, Nicholas. *Transaction Man*	330.973
Leonhardt, David. ★*Ours Was the Shining Future*	330.973
Levitt, Steven D. ★*Freakonomics*	330
Levitt, Steven D. *Superfreakonomics*	330
Levy, Jonathan. *Ages of American Capitalism*	330.12
Lewis, Michael. *The Big Short*	330.973
Linklater, Andro. *Owning the Earth*	333.3
Lovell, Julia. *Maoism*	335.43
Lowenstein, Roger. *Ways and Means*	973.7
MacGillis, Alec. *Fulfillment*	381
Marx, Karl. ★*Capital*	335.4
McCraw, Thomas K. ★*The Founders and Finance*	330.973
McLean, Bethany. *All the Devils Are Here*	330.973
Mitchell, Josh. *The Debt Trap*	378.3
Mitford, Jessica. ★*The American Way of Death Revisited*	338.4
Nations, Scott. *A History of the United States in Five Crashes*	338.5
Neiman, Garrett. *Rich White Men*	305.5
Nelson, Craig. ★*V Is for Victory*	973.917
Noah, Timothy. *The Great Divergence*	339.2
Norman, Jesse. *Adam Smith*	B
O'Rourke, P. J. *None of My Business*	332
Osnos, Evan. *Wildland*	973.93
Paulson, Henry M. *On the Brink*	330.973
Phillips-Fein, Kim. *Fear City*	330.9747
Piketty, Thomas. ★*Capital and Ideology*	305
Press, Eyal. ★*Dirty Work*	331.7
Putnam, Robert D. *Our Kids*	305.5
Quart, Alissa. *Squeezed*	305.5
Randall, Willard Sterne. *The Founders' Fortunes*	973.3
Reid, T. R. *A Fine Mess*	336.200973
Rivlin, Gary. *Broke, Usa*	339.4
Romeo, Nick. *The Alternative*	174
Roth, Alvin E. *Who Gets What—And Why*	330.01
Sachs, Jeffrey. *The Age of Sustainable Development*	338.9
Sandel, Michael J. *What Money Can't Buy*	174
Schumacher, E. F. *Small Is Beautiful*	330
Schwartz, Nelson. *The Velvet Rope Economy*	339.2
Servon, Lisa J. *The Unbanking of America*	332.10973
Sharma, Ruchir. *The Rise and Fall of Nations*	330.9
Shlaes, Amity. *Coolidge*	B
Shlaes, Amity. *The Forgotten Man*	973.91
Short, Philip. *Putin*	B
Smialek, Jeanna. ★*Limitless*	332.1
Smith, Adam. ★*The Wealth of Nations*	330.15
Sorkin, Andrew Ross. *Too Big to Fail*	330.973
Sowell, Thomas. *Basic Economics*	330
Sowell, Thomas. *Wealth, Poverty and Politics*	330.1
Steil, Benn. *The Battle of Bretton Woods*	339.5
Steil, Benn. ★*The Marshall Plan*	338.91
Stiglitz, Joseph E. *The Price of Inequality*	305.50973
Taub, Jennifer. *Big Dirty Money*	364.16
Thaler, Richard H. *Misbehaving*	330.01

AUTHOR, TITLE, SERIES AND SUBJECT INDEX

Weatherall, James Owen. *The Physics of Wall Street*	332.63
Wessel, David. *In Fed We Trust*	332.1
Wheelan, Charles J. *Naked Economics*	330
Wood, Michael. *The Story of China*	951
The Economics of Inequality. Piketty, Thomas	339.2
Economism. Kwak, James	330
An Economist Gets Lunch. Cowen, Tyler	394.1

ECONOMISTS

Heilbroner, Robert L. ★*The Worldly Philosophers*	B
Jadhav, Narendra. *Untouchables*	305.5
Lemann, Nicholas. *Transaction Man*	330.973
Mallaby, Sebastian. *The Man Who Knew*	B
Norman, Jesse. *Adam Smith*	B
Sen, Amartya. *Home in the World*	B

Economy, Peter

Wait, I'm the Boss?!?	658
Wait, I'm Working with Who?!?	650.1

ECOSYSTEM MANAGEMENT

Goldfarb, Ben. *Eager*	333.95

ECOTOURISM

McClanahan, Paige. *The New Tourist*	338.4

ECSTASY (DRUG)

Matos, Michaelangelo. *The Underground Is Massive*	781.648
Ecstatic Nation. Wineapple, Brenda	973.6

EDDINGTON, ARTHUR STANLEY, SIR, 1882-1944

Stanley, Matthew. *Einstein's War*	530

Eddo-Lodge, Reni

Why I'm No Longer Talking to White People About Race	305.8

Eddy, Mary Baker

★*Mary Baker Eddy*	289.5

EDDY, MARY BAKER, 1821-1910

Eddy, Mary Baker. ★*Mary Baker Eddy*	289.5

Edelman, Hope

The Aftergrief	155.9
Motherless Daughters	155.9

Edelman, Marian Wright

Lanterns	362.7

EDELMAN, MARIAN WRIGHT, 1939-

Edelman, Marian Wright. *Lanterns*	362.7

EDEN

Kushner, Harold S. *How Good Do We Have to Be?*	296.7
Eden's Outcasts. Matteson, John	920

Eder, Mari K.

The Girls Who Stepped Out of Line	920
The Edge of Every Day. Sardy, Marin	B
The Edge of the Sea. Carson, Rachel	578.769
An Edible History of Humanity. Standage, Tom	394.1

EDIBLE MUSHROOMS

Borsato, Diane. *Mushrooming*	579.6

Edin, Kathryn

$2.00 a Day	339.4
★*The Injustice of Place*	339.4
★*Edison*. Morris, Edmund	B

EDISON, THOMAS A. (THOMAS ALVA), 1847-1931

Baron, David. *American Eclipse*	523.7
Morris, Edmund. ★*Edison*	B

EDITING

Dreyer, Benjamin. *Dreyer's English*	808.02
Lee, Marshall. *Bookmaking*	686
★*The Editor*. Franklin, Sara B.	B

EDITORIALS

Gay, Roxane. ★*Opinions*	814

EDITORS

Brinkley, Alan. ★*The Publisher*	B
Franklin, Sara B. ★*The Editor*	B
Hagan, Joe. *Sticky Fingers*	B
Hirshey, Gerri. *Not Pretty Enough*	B
Howe, Ben Ryder. *My Korean Deli*	B
Norris, Mary. *Between You and Me*	428.2
Prothero, Stephen R. *God the Bestseller*	070.5
Reed, Julia. *Dispatches from the Gilded Age*	B
Shafrir, Doree. *Thanks for Waiting*	B
Talley, Andre Leon. *The Chiffon Trenches*	B
Wenner, Jann. *Like a Rolling Stone*	B

Edman, Elizabeth M.

Queer Virtue	230

Edmonds, Chris

No Surrender	B

Edmonds, David

Wittgenstein's Poker	192

EDMONDS, RODDIE (RODERICK WARING), 1919-1985

Edmonds, Chris. *No Surrender*	B

Edmondson, Amy C.

The Right Kind of Wrong	158.1

Edmundson, Mark

Why Football Matters	B

EDMUNDSON, MARK, 1952-

Edmundson, Mark. *Why Football Matters*	B
Edouard Vuillard. Cogeval, Guy	759.4

Edsel, Robert M.

The Monuments Men	940.53

Edson, Margaret

Wit	812

Edstrom, Erik

Un-American	B

EDSTROM, ERIK

Edstrom, Erik. *Un-American*	B
★*Educated*. Westover, Tara	B

EDUCATION

Addario, Lynsey. *Of Love & War*	779
Alvarez, Celine. *The Natural Laws of Children*	372.21
Bauer, Susan Wise. *Rethinking School*	371.19
Berens, Kimberly Nix. *Blind Spots*	370.15
Berkshire, Jennifer. *The Education Wars*	371.01
Brill, Steven. *Class Warfare*	371.010973
Burak, Asi. *Power Play*	794.8
Chu, Lenora. *Little Soldiers*	370
Cottom, Tressie McMillan. *Lower Ed*	378.73
Cushman, Kathleen. *Fires in Our Lives*	373.1102
Duncan, Arne. *How Schools Work*	379
Eberhardt, Jennifer L. ★*Biased*	303.3
Elliott, Andrea. ★*Invisible Child*	362.7
Emdin, Christopher. *Ratchetdemic*	370.1
Ewing, Eve L. *Ghosts in the Schoolyard*	370.89
Fishman, Elly. *Refugee High*	370.8
Franklin, Benjamin. ★*The Autobiography of Benjamin Franklin*	B
Garrett, Kent. *The Last Negroes at Harvard*	920
Givens, Jarvis R. ★*School Clothes*	371.829
Goldstein, Dana. *The Teacher Wars*	371.1020973
Grandin, Temple. *Visual Thinking*	152.14
Hechinger, John. ★*True Gentlemen*	371.85
Hixenbaugh, Michael. ★*They Came for the Schools*	371.9
Kamenetz, Anya. *The Stolen Year*	306.43
Kamp, David. *Sunny Days*	791.4502
Keizer, Garret. *Getting Schooled*	373.1102
Kozol, Jonathan. ★*An End to Inequality*	379.2
Kozol, Jonathan. *Fire in the Ashes*	362.77
Kozol, Jonathan. *Letters to a Young Teacher*	371.1
Kuo, Michelle. *Reading with Patrick*	B
Lickona, Thomas. *How to Raise Kind Kids*	649
Love, Bettina L. *Punished for Dreaming*	371.829
McCourt, Frank. *Teacher Man*	B
Mitchell, Josh. *The Debt Trap*	378.3
Mooney, Jonathan. *Normal Sucks*	B
Mufleh, Luma. ★*Learning America*	371.826
Norrell, Robert J. *Up from History*	B
Rademacher, Tom. *It Won't Be Easy*	B
Ravitch, Diane. *Slaying Goliath*	371.010973
Robinson, Ken. *Creative Schools*	370.973
Rose, Mike. *Back to School*	374
Sarma, Sanjay E. *Grasp*	370.15
Scheeres, Julia. *Jesus Land*	B
Selingo, Jeffrey J. *College (un)bound*	378
Selingo, Jeffrey J. *Who Gets in and Why*	378.1
Simmons, Ruth. ★*Up Home*	B
Smart, Maya Payne. *Reading for Our Lives*	372.4
Sweeney, Jennifer. *Literacy*	027.62
Ventrone, Jillian. *From the Marine Corps to College*	378.1
Williams, Juan. *I'll Find a Way or Make One*	378.73
Wojcicki, Esther. *How to Raise Successful People*	649
Yousafzai, Malala. *I Am Malala*	B
Yousafzai, Ziauddin. *Let Her Fly*	B
Zara, Christopher. *Uneducated*	B

EDUCATION AND CULTURE

Kozol, Jonathan. ★*An End to Inequality*	379.2
The Education of a British-Protected Child. Achebe, Chinua	B

PUBLIC LIBRARY CORE COLLECTION: NONFICTION
Twentieth Edition

The Education of Kendrick Perkins. Perkins, Kendrick   B
The Education Wars. Berkshire, Jennifer   371.01
EDUCATIONAL GUIDANCE
   Morgan, Genevieve. *Undecided*   331.702
EDUCATIONAL INNOVATIONS
   De Stefano, Cristina. *The Child Is the Teacher*   B
   Hughes-Hassell, Sandra. ★*Collection Management for Youth*   025.2
   Mettler, Suzanne. *Degrees of Inequality*   378.73
   Robinson, Ken. *Creative Schools*   370.973
EDUCATIONAL LAW AND LEGISLATION
   Driver, Justin. *The Schoolhouse Gate*   344.73
EDUCATIONAL POLICY
   Berkshire, Jennifer. *The Education Wars*   371.01
   Boschert, Sherry. *37 Words*   344.73
   Brill, Steven. *Class Warfare*   371.010973
   Christakis, Erika. *The Importance of Being Little*   372.21
   Duncan, Arne. *How Schools Work*   379
   Fitzpatrick, Cara. *The Death of Public School*   379.73
   Friedman, Thomas L. ★*Thank You for Being Late*   303.48
   Hixenbaugh, Michael. ★*They Came for the Schools*   371.9
   Kozol, Jonathan. ★*An End to Inequality*   379.2
   Love, Bettina L. *Punished for Dreaming*   371.829
   Ravitch, Diane. *The Death and Life of the Great American School System*   379.1
   Ravitch, Diane. *Slaying Goliath*   371.010973
   Robinson, Ken. *Creative Schools*   370.973
   Selingo, Jeffrey J. *College (un)bound*   378
   Yacovone, Donald. ★*Teaching White Supremacy*   370.89
EDUCATIONAL REFORM
   Berens, Kimberly Nix. *Blind Spots*   370.15
   Bok, Derek Curtis. *The Struggle to Reform Our Colleges*   378.73
   Boschert, Sherry. *37 Words*   344.73
   Brill, Steven. *Class Warfare*   371.010973
   Christakis, Erika. *The Importance of Being Little*   372.21
   Goldstein, Dana. *The Teacher Wars*   371.1020973
   Love, Bettina L. *Punished for Dreaming*   371.829
   Ravitch, Diane. *The Death and Life of the Great American School System*   379.1
   Robinson, Ken. *Creative Schools*   370.973
   Selingo, Jeffrey J. *College (un)bound*   378
   Selingo, Jeffrey J. *Who Gets in and Why*   378.1
EDUCATIONAL SOCIOLOGY
   Kamenetz, Anya. *The Stolen Year*   306.43
EDUCATIONAL TECHNOLOGY
   Turnbow, Dominique. ★*Demystifying Online Instruction in Libraries*   028.7
EDUCATIONAL TESTS AND MEASUREMENTS
   Christakis, Erika. *The Importance of Being Little*   372.21
   Chu, Lenora. *Little Soldiers*   370
   Murdoch, Stephen. *IQ*   153.9
   Ravitch, Diane. *The Death and Life of the Great American School System*   379.1
   Reese, William J. *Testing Wars in the Public Schools*   371.260973
   Robinson, Ken. *Creative Schools*   370.973
EDUCATOR RESOURCES — ARTS & HUMANITIES
   Parker, Meghan. *Teaching Artfully*   741.5
EDUCATOR RESOURCES — ENGLISH LANGUAGE ARTS
   Cleaver, Samantha. *Raising an Active Reader*   372.4
   Trelease, Jim. ★*Jim Trelease's Read-Aloud Handbook*   372.4
EDUCATOR RESOURCES — GENERAL
   Alvarez, Celine. *The Natural Laws of Children*   372.21
   Bauer, Susan Wise. *Rethinking School*   371.19
   Boser, Ulrich. *Learn Better*   153.1
   Butler, Rebecca P. ★*Copyright for Teachers & Librarians in the 21st Century*   346.7304
   Cushman, Kathleen. *Fires in Our Lives*   373.1102
   Fagell, Phyllis L. ★*Middle School Matters*   373.236
   Flink, David. *Thinking Differently*   371.9
   Grandin, Temple. *Navigating Autism*   618.92
   Hibbs, B. Janet. *The Stressed Years of Their Lives*   616.8900835
   LaGarde, Jennifer. *Fact vs. Fiction*   370.15
   Marschark, Marc. ★*How Deaf Children Learn*   371.91
   Montessori, Maria. ★*The Montessori Method*   372
   Parini, Jay. *The Art of Teaching*   378.1
   Reid, Rob. ★*200+ Original and Adapted Story Program Activities*   027.62
   Simmons, Rachel. *Odd Girl Out*   302.5
   Stixrud, William R. *The Self-Driven Child*   155.4
   Sweeney, Jennifer. *Literacy*   027.62

Tennant, Richard A. *The American Sign Language Handshape Dictionary*   419
   Thenell, Jan. *The Library's Crisis Communications Planner*   021.7
   Vernacchio, Al. *For Goodness Sex*   613.9071
   Wiseman, Rosalind. *Masterminds & Wingmen*   305.235
EDUCATOR RESOURCES — PRIMARY EDUCATION
   Marschark, Marc. ★*How Deaf Children Learn*   371.91
   Reid, Rob. ★*200+ Original and Adapted Story Program Activities*   027.62
   Santomero, Angela C. *Preschool Clues*   305.233
   Trelease, Jim. ★*Jim Trelease's Read-Aloud Handbook*   372.4
EDUCATOR RESOURCES — SECONDARY EDUCATION
   Belasco, Andrew. *The Enlightened College Applicant*   378.1
   Cushman, Kathleen. *Fires in Our Lives*   373.1102
   Ventrone, Jillian. *From the Marine Corps to College*   378.1
EDUCATORS
   Brown, Emma. *To Raise a Boy*   649
   Conant, Jennet. *Man of the Hour*   B
   Harlan, Louis R. *Booker T. Washington*   B
   Washington, Booker T. ★*Up from Slavery*   B
   Yousafzai, Ziauddin. *Let Her Fly*   B
Edvard Munch. Prideaux, Sue   B
Edvard Munch. Ustvedt, Oystein   759.81
Edvard Hopper. Levin, Gail   759.13
EDWARD I, KING OF ENGLAND, 1239-1307
   Morris, Marc. *A Great and Terrible King*   B
EDWARD IV, KING OF ENGLAND, 1442-1483
   Penn, Thomas. *The Brothers York*   942.04
Edward R. Murrow and the Birth of Broadcast Journalism. Edwards, Bob   B
Edward S. Curtis. Curtis, Edward S.   770.92
Edward Sheriff Curtis. Gulbrandsen, Don   970.004
Edward Steichen. Brandow, Todd   770.92
Edward Steichen. Smith, Joel   779
EDWARD VI, KING OF ENGLAND, 1537-1553
   Rounding, Virginia. *The Burning Time*   272
   Weir, Alison. *The Children of Henry VIII*   B
Edward VII. Hibbert, Christopher   B
EDWARD VII, KING OF GREAT BRITAIN, 1841-1910
   Carter, Miranda. *George, Nicholas and Wilhelm*   940.3
   Hibbert, Christopher. *Edward VII*   B
   Ridley, Jane. *The Heir Apparent*   B
EDWARD, PRINCE OF WALES, 1330-1376
   Jones, Michael K. *The Black Prince*   B
EDWARDIAN ERA (1901-1914)
   Carter, Miranda. *George, Nicholas and Wilhelm*   940.3
   Hibbert, Christopher. *Edward VII*   B
   Ridley, Jane. *The Heir Apparent*   B
   Russell, Gareth. *The Ship of Dreams*   910.91
Edwards, Adrienne L.
   Firescaping Your Home   635.9
Edwards, Anne
   Matriarch   B
Edwards, Betty
   Color   752
   Drawing on the Right Side of the Brain   741.2
Edwards, Bob
   Edward R. Murrow and the Birth of Broadcast Journalism   B
Edwards, Lydia
   How to Read a Dress   391
Edwards, Paul
   The Concise Guide to Hip-Hop Music   782.421649
Edwards, Zoe
   Mend It, Wear It, Love It!   646
EELS
   Svensson, Patrik. *The Book of Eels*   597
EFFECT OF ENVIRONMENT ON HUMANS
   Ackerman, Diane. *The Human Age*   304.2
   Atleework, Kendra. *Miracle Country*   979.4
   Baszile, Natalie. *We Are Each Other's Harvest*   630.89
   Bernstein, Ellen. *Toward a Holy Ecology*   223
   Boccaletti, Giulio. *Water*   909
   Davis, Jack E. ★*The Gulf*   909
   Delorme, Geoffroy. *Deer Man*   599.65
   Diamond, Jared M. *Guns, Germs, and Steel*   303.4
   Dolin, Eric Jay. *A Furious Sky*   363.34
   Doyle, Martin. *The Source*   333.91
   Ehrlich, Gretel. *Unsolaced*   B
   Fagan, Brian M. *The Long Summer*   551.6
   Foster, Craig. ★*Amphibious Soul*   155.9

AUTHOR, TITLE, SERIES AND SUBJECT INDEX

Ghosh, Amitav. *The Great Derangement*	809
Grathwohl, Marya. *This Wheel of Rocks*	271
Harper, Kyle. *The Fate of Rome*	937
Houston, Pam. *Deep Creek*	814
Lynas, Mark. *Six Degrees*	551.6
Macdonald, Helen. ★*Vesper Flights*	508
MacPhail, Theresa. *Allergic*	616.97
Marchant, Jo. *The Human Cosmos*	523.1
Martin, Manjula. *The Last Fire Season*	B
Matloff, Judith. *No Friends but the Mountains*	355.009
Momaday, N. Scott. *Earth Keeper*	814
Nezhukumatathil, Aimee. *World of Wonders*	590
Renkl, Margaret. *The Comfort of Crows*	814.6
Rich, Nathaniel. *Second Nature*	304.2
Rubin, Gretchen Craft. ★*Life in Five Senses*	152.1
Scales, Helen. *The Brilliant Abyss*	551.46
Vigliotti, Jonathan. *Before It's Gone*	577
Vince, Gaia. *Nomad Century*	362.87
Vince, Gaia. *Transcendence*	599.93
Webb, Kinari. *Guardians of the Trees*	B
Williams, Florence. *The Nature Fix*	155.9
Wohlleben, Peter. *The Heartbeat of Trees*	582.16
EFFECT OF HUMANS ON NATURE	
Alexander, Jane. *Wild Things, Wild Places*	333.95
Anthony, Leslie. *The Aliens Among Us*	578.6
Attenborough, David. *A Life on Our Planet*	508
Barnett, Cynthia. ★*The Sound of the Sea*	591.47
Bernstein, Ellen. *Toward a Holy Ecology*	223
Blakeslee, Nate. *American Wolf*	599.773
Brand, Adele. *The Hidden World of the Fox*	599.775
Briody, Blaire. *The New Wild West*	338.2
Cousteau, Jacques Yves. *The Human, the Orchid, and the Octopus*	B
Duncan, Dayton. *Blood Memory*	599.64
Eklof, Johan. *The Darkness Manifesto*	363.7
Fagan, Brian M. *Climate Chaos*	304.2
Fagan, Brian M. *The Long Summer*	551.6
Flores, Dan L. *Wild New World*	591.9709
Flyn, Cal. ★*Islands of Abandonment*	333.73
Fox, Porter. *The Last Winter*	363.738
Freeman, Scott. *Saving Tarboo Creek*	333.72
Goodall, Jane. ★*The Ten Trusts*	333.95
Hohn, Donovan. *The Inner Coast*	304.20973
Houston, Pam. *Deep Creek*	814
Howsare, Erika. *The Age of Deer*	599.65
Jabr, Ferris. ★*Becoming Earth*	570.1
Kimmerer, Robin Wall. ★*Braiding Sweetgrass*	304.2
Kolbert, Elizabeth. ★*Under a White Sky*	304.2
Kostigen, Thomas. *Hacking Planet Earth*	628
Lacovara, Kenneth. *Why Dinosaurs Matter*	567.9
Laing, Olivia. *The Garden Against Time*	635
Martin, Manjula. *The Last Fire Season*	B
McKibben, Bill. *Falter*	909.83
Neiwert, David A. *Of Orcas and Men*	599.53
Owens, Jay. *Dust*	551.51
Rich, Nathaniel. *Second Nature*	304.2
Scales, Helen. *What the Wild Sea Can Be*	577.7
Standefer, Katherine E. *Lightning Flowers*	B
Svensson, Patrik. *The Book of Eels*	597
Thanhauser, Sofi. *Worn*	391
Vigliotti, Jonathan. *Before It's Gone*	577
Wilson, Edward O. *The Diversity of Life*	333.95
Wilson, Edward O. *Half-Earth*	333.95
Wood, Levison. *The Last Giants*	599.67
Woolfson, Esther. *Between Light and Storm*	599.93
Wynn-Grant, Rae. *Wild Life*	B
Yergin, Daniel. *The New Map*	333.79
The Effective Manager. Horstman, Mark	658.4
Egan, Dan	
★*The Death and Life of the Great Lakes*	577.6
Egan, Kerry	
On Living	170
Egan, Timothy	
★*The Big Burn*	973.911
★*A Fever in the Heartland*	322.4
★*The Immortal Irishman*	B
A Pilgrimage to Eternity	263
★*Short Nights of the Shadow Catcher*	770.92
The Worst Hard Time	978
Eger, Edith Eva	
The Choice	B
Egerton, Douglas R.	
Thunder at the Gates	973.7
★*Egg.* Stark, Lizzie	641.3
EGG DECORATION	
Stark, Lizzie. ★*Egg*	641.3
Eggers, Dave	
The Monk of Mokha	B
Zeitoun	305.892
EGGS	
Hammer, Joshua. *The Falcon Thief*	364.16
Stark, Lizzie. ★*Egg*	641.3
Ego Is the Enemy. Holiday, Ryan	158.1
EGOTISM	
Epstein, Mark. *Advice Not Given*	294.3
Holiday, Ryan. *Ego Is the Enemy*	158.1
Rand, Ayn. ★*The Virtue of Selfishness*	149
EGYPT	
Brier, Bob. *The Murder of Tutankhamen*	B
Chang, Leslie T. ★*Egyptian Made*	331.4
Cooney, Kara. *When Women Ruled the World*	920
Darnell, John Coleman. *Egypt's Golden Couple*	932
Goldsworthy, Adrian Keith. *Antony and Cleopatra*	937
Hessler, Peter. *The Buried*	962.05
Mertz, Barbara. *Temples, Tombs, & Hieroglyphs*	932
Millard, Candice. ★*River of the Gods*	916.204
Olson, Lynne. ★*Empress of the Nile*	B
Sacco, Joe. *Footnotes in Gaza*	741.5
Shaw, Ian. *The Princeton Dictionary of Ancient Egypt*	932
Von Tunzelmann, Alex. *Blood and Sand*	909.82
Wilkinson, Richard H. ★*The Complete Gods and Goddesses of Ancient Egypt*	299
Wilkinson, Toby A. H. *The Nile*	962
Wilkinson, Toby A. H. *A World Beneath the Sands*	932
Egypt's Golden Couple. Darnell, John Coleman	932
EGYPTIAN HIEROGLYPHICS	
Dolnick, Edward. *The Writing of the Gods*	493
Mertz, Barbara. *Temples, Tombs, & Hieroglyphs*	932
★*Egyptian Made.* Chang, Leslie T.	331.4
EGYPTOLOGISTS	
Olson, Lynne. ★*Empress of the Nile*	B
Wilkinson, Toby A. H. *A World Beneath the Sands*	932
EGYPTOLOGY	
Darnell, John Coleman. *Egypt's Golden Couple*	932
Dolnick, Edward. *The Writing of the Gods*	493
Wilkinson, Toby A. H. *A World Beneath the Sands*	932
Ehrenreich, Barbara	
Bright-Sided	155.2
Had I Known	814
Natural Causes	613.2
★*Nickel and Dimed*	B
Ehrenreich, Ben	
The Way to the Spring	956.95
Ehrlich, Gretel	
This Cold Heaven	998.2
Unsolaced	B
EHRLICH, GRETEL	
Ehrlich, Gretel. *This Cold Heaven*	998.2
Ehrlich, Gretel. *Unsolaced*	B
Ehrman, Bart D.	
★*Armageddon*	236
The Triumph of Christianity	270.1
Eichar, Donnie	
Dead Mountain	914
EICHAR, DONNIE	
Eichar, Donnie. *Dead Mountain*	914
Eichenwald, Kurt	
A Mind Unraveled	B
EICHENWALD, KURT, 1961-	
Eichenwald, Kurt. *A Mind Unraveled*	B
Eichmann Before Jerusalem. Stangneth, Bettina	B
The Eichmann Trial. Lipstadt, Deborah E.	345.5694
EICHMANN, ADOLF, 1906-1962	
Bascomb, Neal. *Hunting Eichmann*	943.086
Lipstadt, Deborah E. *The Eichmann Trial*	345.5694
Rees, Laurence. *Auschwitz*	940.53
Stangneth, Bettina. *Eichmann Before Jerusalem*	B

PUBLIC LIBRARY CORE COLLECTION: NONFICTION
Twentieth Edition

Eig, Jonathan
   ★*Ali* — B
   The Birth of the Pill — 618.1
   Get Capone — 364.1
   ★*King* — B
Eight Bears. Dickie, Gloria — 599.78
Eight Days at Yalta. Preston, Diana — 940.53
★**Eight** Days in May. Ullrich, Volker — 943.086
Eight World Cups. Vecsey, George — 796.334
Eighteen Days of October. Kaufmann, Uri R. — 956.04
Eightysomethings. Esty, Katharaine C. — 612.6
Eikenberry, Kevin
   The Long-Distance Teammate — 650.1
Eilenberger, Wolfram
   Time of the Magicians — 920
Einstein's Monsters. Impey, Chris — 523.8
Einstein's Shadow. Fletcher, Seth — 523.8
Einstein's War. Stanley, Matthew — 530
Einstein, Albert
   ★*The Evolution of Physics* — 530
   Ideas and Opinions — 081
   The Meaning of Relativity — 530.11
   ★*A Stubbornly Persistent Illusion* — 530.092
   The Ultimate Quotable Einstein — 530.092
EINSTEIN, ALBERT, 1879-1955
   Einstein, Albert. ★*A Stubbornly Persistent Illusion* — 530.092
   Einstein, Albert. *The Ultimate Quotable Einstein* — 530.092
   Stanley, Matthew. *Einstein's War* — 530
Eire, Carlos M. N.
   Learning to Die in Miami — B
   A Very Brief History of Eternity — 236
EIRE, CARLOS M. N.
   Eire, Carlos M. N. *Learning to Die in Miami* — B
Eisen, Max
   By Chance Alone — 940.5318
EISEN, MAX
   Eisen, Max. *By Chance Alone* — 940.5318
Eisen, Norman L.
   The Last Palace — 920
EISEN, NORMAN L., 1961-
   Eisen, Norman L. *The Last Palace* — 920
Eisenberg, Emma Copley
   ★*The Third Rainbow Girl* — 364.152
Eisenberg, John
   The League — 796.332
   The Streak — 796.357
Eisenhower. Johnson, Paul — B
Eisenhower vs. Warren. Simon, James F. — 347.73
EISENHOWER, DWIGHT D. (DWIGHT DAVID), 1890-1969
   Ambrose, Stephen E. *The Victors* — 940.54
   Baier, Bret. *Three Days in January* — B
   Hitchcock, William I. *The Age of Eisenhower* — 973.921092
   Johnson, Paul. *Eisenhower* — B
   Jordan, Jonathan W. *Brothers, Rivals, Victors* — 940.54
   Paradis, Michel. *The Light of Battle* — 940.54
   Simon, James F. *Eisenhower vs. Warren* — 347.73
   Thomas, Evan. *Ike's Bluff* — 973.921092
   Von Tunzelmann, Alex. *Blood and Sand* — 909.82
Eisler, Benita
   ★*Chopin's Funeral* — B
   The Red Man's Bones — B
Eisner, Peter
   The Pope's Last Crusade — 282.092
Eisner, Will
   ★*Comics and Sequential Art* — 741.5
EISNER, WILL
   Schumacher, Michael. *Will Eisner* — 741.5
Eizenstat, Stuart
   ★*President Carter* — B
★***Ejaculate*** Responsibly. Blair, Gabrielle Stanley — 362.1988
EJIOFOR, OBIAJULU
   Asher, Zain E. *Where the Children Take Us* — 942.1
Ekirch, A. Roger
   ★*At Day's Close* — 306.4
Eklof, Johan
   The Darkness Manifesto — 363.7
EL DORADO (LEGENDARY LAND)
   Grann, David. *The Lost City of Z* — 918.1

EL PASO, TEXAS
   Sanchez, Aaron. *Where I Come From* — 641.5092
EL SALVADOR
   Dudley, Steven S. *MS-13* — 364.106
   Forche, Carolyn. *What You Have Heard Is True* — B
   Lovato, Roberto. *Unforgetting* — B
   Markham, Lauren. *The Far Away Brothers* — 920
   Sedgewick, Augustine. *Coffeeland* — 338.4
   Vasquez, Karla Tatiana. ★*The Salvisoul Cookbook* — 641.598
   Zamora, Javier. ★*Solito* — B
El-Waylly, Sohla
   ★*Start Here* — 641.3
ELASTICITY
   Davies, Richard. *Extreme Economies* — 306.3
ELATION
   Keltner, Dacher. ★*Awe* — 152.4
ELDER, RUTH, 1902-1977
   O'Brien, Keith. *Fly Girls* — 920
Elderflora. Farmer, Jared — 582.16
Elderhood. Aronson, Louise — 362.60973
ELDERS (INDIGENOUS LEADERS)
   Gayle, Caleb. *We Refuse to Forget* — 975.004
ELDERS, JOYCELYN, 1933-
   Brown, Jasmine. *Twice as Hard* — 610.92
Eldredge, Niles
   Why We Do It — 155.3
★***Eleanor***. Michaelis, David — 973.917
Eleanor and Hick. Quinn, Susan — B
Eleanor of Aquitaine. Weir, Alison — B
Eleanor Roosevelt; Volume 2. Cook, Blanche Wiesen — B
★***Eleanor*** Roosevelt; Volume 3. Cook, Blanche Wiesen — B
ELEANOR, OF AQUITAINE, QUEEN, CONSORT OF HENRY II, KING OF ENGLAND, 1122?-1204
   Weir, Alison. *Eleanor of Aquitaine* — B
ELECTION CORRUPTION
   Abrams, Stacey. *Our Time Is Now* — 324.60973
   Bowden, Mark. *The Steal* — 973.933
   Hasen, Richard L. *Election Meltdown* — 324.973
   Isikoff, Michael. *Russian Roulette* — 973.933
   Shimer, David. *Rigged* — 324.60973
   Weiner, Tim. *The Folly and the Glory* — 327.73047
   Weissmann, Andrew. ★*Where Law Ends* — 324.7
ELECTION LAW
   Berman, Ari. *Give Us the Ballot* — 324.6
   Cohen, Adam. ★*Supreme Inequality* — 347.73
   Wehle, Kim. *What You Need to Know About Voting and Why* — 324.60973
Election Meltdown. Hasen, Richard L. — 324.973
ELECTIONS
   Allen, Jonathan. *Lucky* — 324.973
   Allen, Jonathan. *Shattered* — 324.973
   Anderson, Carol. ★*One Person, No Vote* — 324.6
   Arnsdorf, Isaac. ★*Finish What We Started* — 320.52
   Balz, Daniel J. *The Battle for America, 2008* — 973.932
   Bhutto, Benazir. *Reconciliation* — 297.2
   Bowden, Mark. *The Steal* — 973.933
   Brazile, Donna. *For Colored Girls Who Have Considered Politics* — 328.73
   Brettschneider, Corey Lang. *The Oath and the Office* — 342.73
   Brettschneider, Corey Lang. *The Presidents and the People* — 342.73
   Chozick, Amy. *Chasing Hillary* — B
   Clinton, Hillary Rodham. *What Happened* — 328.73
   Cook, Blanche Wiesen. *Eleanor Roosevelt; Volume 2* — B
   Cook, Blanche Wiesen. ★*Eleanor Roosevelt; Volume 3* — B
   Cross, Tiffany D. ★*Say It Louder!* — 324.6
   Hasen, Richard L. *Election Meltdown* — 324.973
   Karl, Jonathan. *Tired of Winning* — 973.933
   Lichtman, Allan J. *The Embattled Vote in America* — 324.6
   Oliphant, Thomas. ★*The Road to Camelot* — 973.922092
   Perlstein, Rick. ★*Nixonland* — 973.924
   Perlstein, Rick. ★*Reaganland* — 973.926
   Plouffe, David. *A Citizen's Guide to Beating Donald Trump* — 324.0973
   Schieffer, Bob. *Overload* — 070.4
   Stevens, Stuart. *It Was All a Lie* — 324.2734
   Wehle, Kim. *What You Need to Know About Voting and Why* — 324.60973
   Woodward, Bob. *Peril* — 973.933
ELECTORAL COLLEGE
   Berman, Ari. ★*Minority Rule* — 305.809
ELECTRA (GREEK MYTHOLOGY)
   Aeschylus. *The Oresteia* — 882

AUTHOR, TITLE, SERIES AND SUBJECT INDEX

ELECTRIC COOKING
   Acheson, Hugh. *The Chef and the Slow Cooker*   641.5
   DiGregorio, Sarah. *Adventures in Slow Cooking*   641.5
   Homolka, Gina. *Skinnytaste Fast and Slow*   641.5
Electric Eden. Young, Rob   781.62
ELECTRIC EEL
   Catania, Kenneth. *Great Adaptations*   576.8
ELECTRIC EQUIPMENT
   McAlister, Michael. *Taunton's Wiring Complete*   621.3
ELECTRIC GUITAR
   Norman, Philip. ★*Wild Thing*   B
   Port, Ian S. *The Birth of Loud*   787.87
ELECTRIC POWER
   Carlson, W. Bernard. *Tesla*   B
ELECTRIC POWER DISTRIBUTION
   Bakke, Gretchen Anna. *The Grid*   333.793
   Blunt, Katherine. *California Burning*   333.793
ELECTRIC POWER PRODUCTION
   Kamkwamba, William. ★*The Boy Who Harnessed the Wind*   B
Electric Shock. Doggett, Peter   781.64
Electric Universe. Bodanis, David   537
ELECTRIC UTILITIES
   Blunt, Katherine. *California Burning*   333.793
ELECTRIC VEHICLES
   Higgins, Tim. *Power Play*   338.7
   Humes, Edward. ★*Total Garbage*   628.4
   Isaacson, Walter. ★*Elon Musk*   B
ELECTRIC WIRING
   McAlister, Michael. *Taunton's Wiring Complete*   621.3
ELECTRICAL ENGINEERING
   Carlson, W. Bernard. *Tesla*   B
   Cohan, William D. *Power Failure*   338.7
   Munson, Richard. *Tesla*   B
ELECTRICAL ENGINEERS
   Carlson, W. Bernard. *Tesla*   B
   Morris, Edmund. ★*Edison*   B
   Munson, Richard. *Tesla*   B
   Soni, Jimmy. *A Mind at Play*   B
ELECTRICITY
   Bodanis, David. *Electric Universe*   537
   Forbes, Nancy. *Faraday, Maxwell, and the Electromagnetic Field*   B
The Electrifying Fall of Rainbow City. Creighton, Margaret S.   607
ELECTROMAGNETISM
   Forbes, Nancy. *Faraday, Maxwell, and the Electromagnetic Field*   B
ELECTRONIC BOOKS
   Wolf, Maryanne. *Reader, Come Home*   418
ELECTRONIC COMMERCE
   Au-Yeung, Angel. *Wonder Boy*   B
   Del Rey, Jason. *Winner Sells All*   381
   MacGillis, Alec. *Fulfillment*   381
   Mattioli, Dana. ★*The Everything War*   381.142
   Taplin, Jonathan. *Move Fast and Break Things*   330.9
ELECTRONIC GAMES
   Bissell, Tom. *Extra Lives*   794.8
ELECTRONIC INFORMATION RESOURCES
   Evans, G. Edward. *Collection Management Basics*   025.2
   Howley, Kerry. *Bottoms Up and the Devil Laughs*   352.37
   Pettegree, Andrew. *The Library*   027.4
   Ross, Catherine Sheldrick. *Conducting the Reference Interview*   025.5
   Verminski, Alana. ★*Fundamentals of Electronic Resources Management*   025.2
ELECTRONIC INTELLIGENCE
   Greenberg, Andy. *Sandworm*   364.16
   Mundy, Liza. *Code Girls*   940.54
   Walton, Calder. *Spies*   327.1247
ELECTRONIC MUSIC
   Matos, Michaelangelo. *The Underground Is Massive*   781.648
   Warner, Daniel. *Live Wires*   786.7
ELECTRONIC NEWSPAPERS
   Schieffer, Bob. *Overload*   070.4
ELECTRONIC SURVEILLANCE
   Boghosian, Heidi. *"i Have Nothing to Hide"*   363.1
   Cox, Joseph. *Dark Wire*   363.2
   Friedman, Barry. ★*Unwarranted*   344.7305
   Gellman, Barton. ★*Dark Mirror*   B
   Gleeson, John. *The Gotti Wars*   364.1
   Howley, Kerry. *Bottoms Up and the Devil Laughs*   352.37
   Molnar, Petra. *The Walls Have Eyes*   363.28

   Strittmatter, Kai. *We Have Been Harmonized*   323.44
ELECTRONS
   Bodanis, David. *Electric Universe*   537
   ★*An Elegant Defense*. Richtel, Matt   616.07
   ★*The Elegant Universe*. Greene, B.   539.7
ELEGIAC POETRY
   Bang, Mary Jo. *Elegy*   811
   Forsythe, Kelly. *Perennial*   811
   Hall, Donald. *The Selected Poems of Donald Hall*.   811
   Harrison, Leslie. *The Book of Endings*   811
   Hirsch, Edward. *Stranger by Night*   811
   Ritvo, Max. *Four Reincarnations*   811
   Simic, Charles. *Come Closer and Listen*   811
   Williams, C. K. *Falling Ill*   811
Elegy. Bang, Mary Jo   811
Elemental Knits. Spainhower, Courtney   746.43
ELEMENTARY SCHOOL LIBRARIES
   Del Negro, Janice. *Folktales Aloud*   027.62
ELEMENTARY SCHOOLS
   Lysiak, Matthew. *Newtown*   371.7
   Quinones, John. ★*One Year in Uvalde*   371.7
   Williamson, Elizabeth. ★*Sandy Hook*   364.152
The Elements. Challoner, Jack   546
★*The Elements*. Gray, Theodore W.   546
★*Elements of Family Style*. Gates, Erin T   747
Elements of Fiction. Mosley, Walter   808.3
★*The Elements of Style*. Strunk, William   808
The Elephant in the Room. Tomlinson, Tommy   B
ELEPHANTS
   Orenstein, Ronald I. *Ivory, Horn and Blood*   333.95
   Owens, Delia. *The Eye of the Elephant*   639.9
   Safina, Carl. *Beyond Words*   591.56
   Wood, Levison. *The Last Giants*   599.67
ELEVEN-YEAR-OLD GIRLS
   Weinman, Sarah. *The Real Lolita*   362.88092
Elias, Stephen
   The Foreclosure Survival Guide, 9th Ed.   346.7304
ELIJAH MUHAMMAD, 1897-1975
   Evanzz, Karl. *The Messenger*   B
Eliot After the Waste Land. Crawford, Robert   B
Eliot Ness and the Mad Butcher. Collins, Max Allan   364.152
ELIOT, GEORGE, 1819-1880
   Mead, Rebecca. *My Life in Middlemarch*   823
Eliot, Lise
   Pink Brain, Blue Brain   612.6
Eliot, Marc
   The Hag   B
Eliot, T. S.
   Collected Poems, 1909-1962.   821.912
   ★*Complete Poems and Plays.*   810
ELIOT, T. S. (THOMAS STEARNS), 1888-1965
   Crawford, Robert. *Eliot After the Waste Land*   B
   Gordon, Lyndall. ★*T.S. Eliot*   B
   Hollis, Matthew. *The Waste Land*   821
ELISABETH, COUNTESS PALATINE, 1618-1680
   Goldstone, Nancy Bazelon. *Daughters of the Winter Queen*   920
★*The Elissas*. Leach, Samantha   362.73
ELITE (SOCIAL SCIENCES)
   Berg, Scott W. *The Burning of the World*   977.311
   Bosker, Bianca. *Get the Picture*   701
   Brooks, David. *The Social Animal*   305.5
   Frank, Thomas. *The People, No*   320.56
   Fraser, Steve. *The Age of Acquiescence*   973.91
   Honig, Elie. *Untouchable*   364.1
   Isenberg, Nancy. *The Problem of Democracy*   973.4
   Jefferson, Margo. *Negroland*   305.896
   Jones, Jacqueline. *Saving Savannah*   975.8
   Kouchner, Camille. *The Familia Grande*   B
   Lasch, Christopher. ★*The Revolt of the Elites*   306
   Levine, Bruce C. *The Fall of the House of Dixie*   973.7
   Mann, William J. *The Wars of the Roosevelts*   B
   Markovits, Daniel. *The Meritocracy Trap*   305.5
   Marshall, McMillan. *Among the Bros*   362.29
   Richardson, Heather Cox. *Democracy Awakening*   320.473
   Richardson, Heather Cox. ★*How the South Won the Civil War*   306.20973
   Ronald, Susan. *Hitler's Aristocrats*   940.53
   Turchin, Peter. *End Times*   320.01
   Zygar, Mikhail. *The Empire Must Die*   947.08

PUBLIC LIBRARY CORE COLLECTION: NONFICTION
Twentieth Edition

ELITE OPERATIVES
    Jacobsen, Annie. *Surprise, Kill, Vanish* — 327.1273
    Wallace, Chris. *Countdown Bin Laden* — 958.104
ELITISM
    Gerald, Casey. *There Will Be No Miracles Here* — B
    Jaffe, Sarah W. *Wanting What's Best* — 649
    Warsaw-Fan Rauch, Arianna. ★*Declassified* — 781.1
★*Eliza Hamilton*. Mazzeo, Tilar J. — B
Elizabeth and Hazel. Margolick, David — 379.2
Elizabeth Cady Stanton. Ginzberg, Lori D. — B
ELIZABETH I, QUEEN OF ENGLAND, 1533-1603
    Bergreen, Laurence. *In Search of a Kingdom* — B
    Borman, Tracy. *Anne Boleyn and Elizabeth I* — 920
    Borman, Tracy. *Elizabeth's Women* — B
    Paranque, Estelle. *Blood, Fire & Gold* — 920
    Ronald, Susan. *The Pirate Queen* — B
    Weir, Alison. *The Children of Henry VIII* — B
    Weir, Alison. *The Life of Elizabeth I* — B
ELIZABETH II, QUEEN OF GREAT BRITAIN, 1926-2022
    Charter, David. *Royal Audience* — 941.085
    Glenconner, Anne. ★*Lady in Waiting* — B
    Hardman, Robert. *Queen of Our Times* — B
    Hardman, Robert. *Queen of the World* — B
    Holmes, Elizabeth. *HRH* — 941.085
    Larman, Alexander. ★*Power and Glory* — 941.085
    Smith, Sally Bedell. *Elizabeth the Queen* — B
Elizabeth Taylor. Brower, Kate Andersen — B
Elizabeth The Queen. Smith, Sally Bedell — B
Elizabeth's Women. Borman, Tracy — B
ELIZABETH, QUEEN, CONSORT OF EDWARD IV, KING OF ENGLAND, 1437?-1492
    Gristwood, Sarah. *Blood Sisters* — 942.04092
    Jones, Dan. ★*The Wars of the Roses* — 942.04
ELIZABETH, QUEEN, CONSORT OF FREDERICK I, KING OF BOHEMIA, 1596-1662
    Goldstone, Nancy Bazelon. *Daughters of the Winter Queen* — 920
ELIZABETH, QUEEN, CONSORT OF GEORGE VI, KING OF GREAT BRITAIN, 1900-2002
    Shawcross, William. *The Queen Mother* — B
    Smith, Sally Bedell. *George VI and Elizabeth* — 920
ELIZABETH, QUEEN, CONSORT OF HENRY VII, KING OF ENGLAND, 1465-1503
    Gristwood, Sarah. *Blood Sisters* — 942.04092
ELIZABETHAN ERA (1558-1603)
    Bergreen, Laurence. *In Search of a Kingdom* — B
    Borman, Tracy. *Anne Boleyn and Elizabeth I* — 920
    Borman, Tracy. *Elizabeth's Women* — B
    Fraser, Antonia. *Mary, Queen of Scots* — B
    Goodman, Ruth. *How to Behave Badly in Elizabethan England* — 942.05
    Lovell, Mary S. *Bess of Hardwick* — B
    Mortimer, Ian. *The Time Traveler's Guide to Elizabethan England* — 942.05
    Paranque, Estelle. *Blood, Fire & Gold* — 920
    Ronald, Susan. *The Pirate Queen* — B
    Tallis, Nicola. *Uncrowned Queen* — B
    Weir, Alison. *The Life of Elizabeth I* — B
Elkind, David
    The Power of Play — 155.4
Elkins, Caroline
    Legacy of Violence — 909
Ellard, Colin
    You Are Here — 153.7
Elledge, Scott
    E.B. White — B
Ellenberg, Jordan
    ★*How Not to Be Wrong* — 510
Ellenhorn, Ross D.
    ★*Purple Crayons* — 153.3
ELLINGTON, DUKE, 1899-1974
    Teachout, Terry. *Duke* — B
    Tye, Larry. ★*The Jazzmen* — 781.6509
ELLIOT, ELISABETH
    Vaughn, Ellen Santilli. ★*Becoming Elisabeth Elliot* — B
Elliott, Andrea
    ★*Invisible Child* — 362.7
Elliott, Carl
    ★*The Occasional Human Sacrifice* — 174.2
ELLIOTT, CARL, 1961-
    Elliott, Carl. ★*The Occasional Human Sacrifice* — 174.2

ELLIOTT, ELIZABETH SHIPPEN GREEN
    Carter, Alice A. *The Red Rose Girls* — B
ELLIOTT, NICHOLAS, 1916-1994
    Macintyre, Ben. *A Spy Among Friends* — B
ELLIS ISLAND, NEW YORK
    Cannato, Vincent. *American Passage* — 325.73
Ellis, Bret Easton
    White — 814
ELLIS, BRET EASTON
    Ellis, Bret Easton. *White* — 814
Ellis, Helen
    Bring Your Baggage and Don't Pack Light — 814
    Southern Lady Code — 814
ELLIS, HELEN
    Ellis, Helen. *Bring Your Baggage and Don't Pack Light* — 814
    Ellis, Helen. *Southern Lady Code* — 814
Ellis, Joseph J.
    American Creation — 973.3
    ★*American Dialogue* — 973.3
    American Sphinx — 973.3
    The Cause — 973.3
    First Family — 973.4
    Founding Brothers — 973.4
    ★*His Excellency* — B
    The Quartet — 342.7302
    ★*Revolutionary Summer* — 973.3
Ellis, Richard
    ★*The Empty Ocean* — 577.7
    Tuna — 333.95
Ellis, Thomas Sayers
    Skin, Inc. — 811
ELLIS, WILLIAM HENRY, 1864-1923
    Jacoby, Karl. *The Strange Career of William Ellis* — B
Ellison, Ralph
    ★*The Collected Essays of Ralph Ellison* — 814
    The Selected Letters of Ralph Ellison — 813
ELLISON, RALPH
    Ellison, Ralph. *The Selected Letters of Ralph Ellison* — 813
    Rampersad, Arnold. ★*Ralph Ellison* — B
Ellmann, Richard
    Oscar Wilde — B
Ellsworth, Scott
    The Ground Breaking — 976.6
    The World Beneath Their Feet — 796.522
Elmore, Bartow J.
    Citizen Coke — 338.7
    Seed Money — 338.7
Elnoury, Tamer
    American Radical — B
★*Elon Musk*. Isaacson, Walter — B
Eloquent Rage. Cooper, Brittney C. — B
Elsa Schiaparelli. Secrest, Meryle — 746.9
Else, Jon
    True South — 305.800973
ELSE, JON
    Else, Jon. *True South* — 305.800973
Elster, Charles Harrington
    How to Tell Fate from Destiny — 428.1
Eltahawy, Mona
    The Seven Necessary Sins for Women and Girls — 305.42
Elvis and Ginger. Alden, Ginger — B
Elvis and the Colonel. McDonald, Greg (Producer) — 920
Elway. Cole, Jason — B
ELWAY, JOHN, 1960-
    Cole, Jason. *Elway* — B
Elwes, Cary
    As You Wish — 791.43
ELWES, CARY, 1962-
    Elwes, Cary. *As You Wish* — 791.43
Elwood, Phil
    All the Worst Humans — 659.2
ELWOOD, PHIL (PHILIP)
    Elwood, Phil. *All the Worst Humans* — 659.2
Ely, Wes
    Every Deep-Drawn Breath — 616.02
ELY, WES
    Ely, Wes. *Every Deep-Drawn Breath* — 616.02

AUTHOR, TITLE, SERIES AND SUBJECT INDEX

Emanuel, Rahm
   The Nation City   352.23
EMANUEL, RAHM, 1959-
   Emanuel, Rahm. *The Nation City*   352.23
EMBARRASSMENT
   Dahl, Melissa. *Cringeworthy*   158.2
   Knight, Keltie. *Lady Secrets*   305.4
The Embarrassment of Riches. Schama, Simon   949.2
The Embattled Vote in America. Lichtman, Allan J.   324.6
Emberling, Amy
   Zingerman's Bakehouse   641.81
Embers of War. Logevall, Fredrik   959.704
Emberton, Carole
   To Walk About in Freedom   306.3
EMBEZZLEMENT
   Bensinger, Ken. ★*Red Card*   796.334
   Conn, David. *The Fall of the House of FIFA*   796.334
Embracing Defeat. Dower, John W.   952.04
Embroider Your Life. Mornu, Nathalie   746.44
Embroidered Animals. Higuchi, Yumiko   746.44
Embroideries. Satrapi, Marjane   741.5
EMBROIDERY
   Brasfield, Hope. *Satisfying Stitches*   746.44
   Christensen, Jo Ippolito. ★*The Needlepoint Book*   746.44
   Eaton, Jan. *Mary Thomas's Dictionary of Embroidery Stitches.*   746.44
   Frazer, Amy L. *Empowered Embroidery*   746.44
   Galbraith, Melissa. *How to Embroider Texture and Pattern*   746.44
   Ganderton, Lucinda. ★*Embroidery*   746.44
   Higuchi, Yumiko. *Embroidered Animals*   746.44
   Lapierre, Corinne. *Folk Embroidered Felt Birds*   746.0463
   Lowry, Melissa. *Vibrant Punch Needle Decor*   746.44
   Mornu, Nathalie. *Embroider Your Life*   746.44
   Ringquist, Rebecca. ★*Rebecca Ringquist's Embroidery Workshops*   746.44
   Shimoda, Naoko. *Artfully Embroidered*   746.44
   Watson, Sarah. *Pen to Thread*   746.44
★*Embroidery.* Ganderton, Lucinda   746.44
EMBRYOLOGY
   Zernicka-Goetz, Magdalena. *The Dance of Life*   591.56
EMBRYONIC STEM CELLS
   Zernicka-Goetz, Magdalena. *The Dance of Life*   591.56
Emdin, Christopher
   Ratchetdemic   370.1
Emera, Deena
   A Brief History of the Female Body   612.6
EMERGENCIES
   Jensen, Robert A. *Personal Effects*   363.34
   Sprinkle, Timothy. *Lost and Stranded*   613.6
★*The Emergency.* Fisher, Thomas   362.1089
EMERGENCY MEDICAL SERVICES
   Fisher, Thomas. ★*The Emergency*   362.1089
   Meyer, Robert. *Every Minute Is a Day*   362.1962
   Patterson, James. *ER Nurses*   610.73
EMERGENCY PHYSICIANS
   Harper, Michele. *The Beauty in Breaking*   B
   Meyer, Robert. *Every Minute Is a Day*   362.1962
EMERGENCY PLANNING
   Brinkley, Douglas. *The Great Deluge*   976.3
   Dyson, Michael Eric. *Come Hell or High Water*   976.3
   Fagan, Brian M. *Climate Chaos*   304.2
   Ferguson, Niall. *Doom*   362.1962
   Flaherty, Mary Grace. ★*The Disaster Planning Handbook for Libraries*   025.8
   Gates, Bill. ★*How to Prevent the Next Pandemic*   614.5
   Graff, Garrett M. *Raven Rock*   363.350973
   Halsted, Deborah D. ★*Disaster Planning*   025.8
   Horne, Jed. *Breach of Faith*   976.3
   Price, Polly J. *Plagues in the Nation*   614.4
   Ripley, Amanda. *The Unthinkable*   155.9
EMERGING INFECTIOUS DISEASES
   Kang, Lydia. *Patient Zero*   614.4
Emerson. Richardson, Robert D.   814
Emerson, Ralph Waldo
   ★*Collected Poems and Translations*   811
EMERSON, RALPH WALDO, 1803-1882
   Richardson, Robert D. *Emerson*   814
   Wayne, Tiffany K. *Critical Companion to Ralph Waldo Emerson*   814
Emery, Theo
   Hellfire Boys   358

Emet, Joseph
   Finding the Blue Sky   294.3
Emezi, Akwaeke
   ★*Dear Senthuran*   B
EMEZI, AKWAEKE
   Emezi, Akwaeke. ★*Dear Senthuran*   B
Emily Post's Etiquette. Post, Lizzie   395
Emily Post's Etiquette. Post, Lizzie   395
Eminent lives [Series]. Gottlieb, Robert   B
Eminent Outlaws. Bram, Christopher   920
Emlen, Douglas John
   Animal Weapons   591.47
Emotional. Mlodinow, Leonard   152.4
EMOTIONAL ABUSE
   Coldstream, Catherine. ★*Cloistered*   B
   Durvasula, Ramani. ★*It's Not You*   155.2
   McCurdy, Jennette. ★*I'm Glad My Mom Died*   B
   Sutton, Robert I. *The Asshole Survival Guide*   650.1
   West, Cait. ★*Rift*   B
Emotional Healing. Barry, Harry   158.1
EMOTIONAL INTELLIGENCE
   Brackett, Marc A. *Permission to Feel*   152.4
   Goleman, Daniel. *Emotional Intelligence*   152.4
   Goleman, Daniel. *Primal Leadership*   658.4
   Mlodinow, Leonard. *Emotional*   152.4
Emotional Intelligence. Goleman, Daniel   152.4
★*Emotional Labor.* Hackman, Rose   155.3
The Emotional Lives of Teenagers. Damour, Lisa   155.5
EMOTIONS
   Barrett, Lisa Feldman. ★*How Emotions Are Made*   152.4
   Barry, Harry. *Emotional Healing*   158.1
   Bloom, Paul. *Psych*   150
   Breggin, Peter Roger. *Guilt, Shame, and Anxiety*   152.4
   Brooks, Arthur C. *Build the Life You Want*   158.1
   Cain, Susan. ★*Bittersweet*   155.2
   Damasio, Antonio R. *The Feeling of What Happens*   153
   Damasio, Antonio R. *Looking for Spinoza*   152.4
   Deisseroth, Karl. *Projections*   616.89
   Duhigg, Charles. ★*Supercommunicators*   153.6
   Goleman, Daniel. ★*Social Intelligence*   158.2
   Goodan, Chelsey. *Underestimated*   305.235
   Hackman, Rose. ★*Emotional Labor*   155.3
   Hartley, Gemma. *Fed Up*   155.3
   Howes, Molly. *A Good Apology*   158.2
   Keltner, Dacher. ★*Awe*   152.4
   Keltner, Dacher. *Born to Be Good*   155.2
   Lifford, Tina. *The Little Book of Big Lies*   155.2
   Mlodinow, Leonard. *Emotional*   152.4
   Obama, Barack. ★*The Audacity of Hope*   B
   Waal, F. B. M. de. ★*Mama's Last Hug*   599.885
   Weber, Charlotte Fox. *Tell Me What You Want*   153.8
   Winch, Guy. *How to Fix a Broken Heart*   155.9
EMOTIONS AND COGNITION
   Barrett, Lisa Feldman. ★*How Emotions Are Made*   152.4
EMOTIONS IN ANIMALS
   Grandin, Temple. ★*Animals Make Us Human*   636.08
   Waal, F. B. M. de. ★*Mama's Last Hug*   599.885
   Wynne, Clive D. L. ★*Dog Is Love*   636.7
EMOTIONS IN CHILDREN
   McCarthy, Catherine. *Raising a Kid Who Can*   649
EMOTIONS IN TEENAGERS
   Damour, Lisa. *The Emotional Lives of Teenagers*   155.5
EMPATHY
   Adler, Kevin F. *When We Walk By*   362.5
   Alda, Alan. *If I Understood You, Would I Have This Look on My Face?*   153.6
   Asika, Uju. *Bringing up Race*   155.4
   Burke, Tarana. ★*Unbound*   B
   DeSteno, David. *How God Works*   200.1
   Gaines, Joanna. *The Stories We Tell*   B
   Jamison, Kay Redfield. *Fires in the Dark*   616.89
   Jamison, Leslie. *The Empathy Exams*   813
   Jordan, June. ★*The Essential June Jordan*   811
   Montgomery, Sy. *How to Be a Good Creature*   590
   Northrup, Christiane. *Dodging Energy Vampires*   155.2
   Oliva, Alejandra. *Rivermouth*   305.9
   Rippon, Kelly. *Parent Up*   649
   Ruttenberg, Danya. *On Repentance and Repair*   202
   Solnit, Rebecca. *The Faraway Nearby*   814

PUBLIC LIBRARY CORE COLLECTION: NONFICTION
Twentieth Edition

Souder, William. *Mad at the World*	813
Van Ness, Jonathan. *Love That Story*	791.4502
Waal, F. B. M. de. ★*Mama's Last Hug*	599.885
The Empathy Exams. Jamison, Leslie	813
★*The Emperor of All Maladies*. Mukherjee, Siddhartha	616.99
Emperor of Japan. Keene, Donald	952.03
★*Emperor of Rome*. Beard, Mary	937
The Emperors of Chocolate. Brenner, Joel Glenn	338.7
The Empire Must Die. Zygar, Mikhail	947.08
Empire of Cotton. Beckert, Sven	338.4
Empire of Dreams. Eyman, Scott	B
Empire of Guns. Satia, Priya	330.941
An Empire of Ice. Larson, Edward J.	919.8
Empire of Liberty. Wood, Gordon S.	973.4
★*Empire of Pain*. Keefe, Patrick Radden	338.7
Empire of Shadows. Black, George	978.7
Empire of Sin. Krist, Gary	976.3
Empire of the Scalpel. Rutkow, Ira M.	617
Empire of the Summer Moon. Gwynne, S. C.	B
★*Empireland*. Sanghera, Sathnam	941
Empires of the Sky. Rose, Alexander	920
Empires, Nations, and Families. Hyde, Anne Farrar	978
Empireworld. Sanghera, Sathnam	909
EMPIRICISM	
Andersen, Kurt. ★*Fantasyland*	973
Cox, Brian. *Universal*	523.1
Robertson, Ritchie. *The Enlightenment*	190
EMPLOYEE MORALE	
Coggan, Philip. *Surviving the Daily Grind*	658.3
Porath, Christine Lynne. *Mastering Civility*	650.1
EMPLOYEE MOTIVATION	
Coggan, Philip. *Surviving the Daily Grind*	658.3
Scott, Kim Malone. *Radical Candor*	658.4
Tracy, Brian. *Full Engagement!*	658.3
EMPLOYEE OWNERSHIP	
Monforton, Celeste. *On the Job*	331.1
EMPLOYEE RIGHTS	
McShane Wulfhart, Nell. *The Great Stewardess Rebellion*	331.4
Monforton, Celeste. *On the Job*	331.1
Moore, Kate. *The Radium Girls*	363.17
Sack, Steven Mitchell. *The Employee Rights Handbook*	344.7301
The Employee Rights Handbook. Sack, Steven Mitchell	344.7301
EMPLOYEE SELECTION	
Newkirk, Pamela. *Diversity, Inc.*	658.3
Smith, Clint. *How to Hire*	658.3
EMPLOYEE TERMINATION	
Gelles, David. *The Man Who Broke Capitalism*	330.12
Norton, Hughes. ★*Rainmaker*	796.352
EMPLOYEES	
Coggan, Philip. *Surviving the Daily Grind*	658.3
Guendelsberger, Emily. *On the Clock*	331.0973
Rowan, Barry L. *The Spiritual Art of Business*	261.8
Terkel, Studs. *Working*	920
The Employer's Legal Handbook, 16th Ed. Steingold, Fred S.	344.7301
EMPLOYMENT INTERVIEWING	
Finkle, Jane. *The Introvert's Complete Career Guide*	650.14
Pollak, Lindsey. *Recalculating*	650.1
Smith, Clint. *How to Hire*	658.3
Empowered Embroidery. Frazer, Amy L.	746.44
EMPOWERMENT	
Adichie, Chimamanda Ngozi. *Dear Ijeawele*	649
Adichie, Chimamanda Ngozi. *We Should All Be Feminists*	305.42
Blake, Melissa. *Beautiful People*	362.4
Flock, Elizabeth. ★*The Furies*	305.48
Garcia, Amanda Yates. *Initiated*	B
Goodan, Chelsey. *Underestimated*	305.235
Hill, Katie. *She Will Rise*	305.42
Kantor, Jodi. *She Said*	364.15
Lehrer, Riva. *Golem Girl*	B
Marshall, Cynthia. *You've Been Chosen*	B
Miller, Chanel. *Know My Name*	B
Mojica Rodriguez, Prisca Dorcas. *For Brown Girls with Sharp Edges and Tender Hearts*	305.48
Parker, Lara. *Vagina Problems*	618.1
Suvari, Mena. *The Great Peace*	B
Vanek Smith, Stacey. *Machiavelli for Women*	650.1
Empress. Lal, Ruby	B
Empress Dowager Cixi. Chang, Jung	B
Empress of Fashion. Stuart, Amanda Mackenzie	B
★*Empress of the Nile*. Olson, Lynne	B
Empty. Burton, Susan	B
EMPTY NESTERS	
Achterberg, Cara Sue. *Another Good Dog*	636.7
★*The Empty Ocean*. Ellis, Richard	577.7
Emswiler, Mary Ann	
Guiding Your Child Through Grief	155.9
EMWAZI, MOHAMMED, -2015	
Mekhennet, Souad. *I Was Told to Come Alone*	363.3250956
ENABLING (PSYCHOLOGY)	
Aron, Nina Renata. *Good Morning, Destroyer of Men's Souls*	B
Enabling Acts. Davis, Lennard J.	342.7308
The Enchanted Hour. Gurdon, Meghan Cox	372.4
Enchantment. May, Katherine	158.1
The Enchilada Queen Cookbook. Casares, Sylvia	641.5926872073
Encore Provence. Mayle, Peter	944
Encounter. Kundera, Milan	809
Encounter on the Narrow Ridge. Friedman, Maurice S.	B
Encounterism. Field, Andy	302
ENCOURAGEMENT	
Brownback, Lydia. *Finding God in My Loneliness*	248.8
Roberts, Matthias. *Holy Runaways*	262
The Encyclopedia of Animated Cartoons. Lenburg, Jeff	791.43
Encyclopedia of Cold War Espionage, Spies, and Secret Operations 3rd Ed. Trahair, R. C. S.	327.12
Encyclopedia of Constitutional Amendments, Proposed Amendments, and Amending Issues, 1789-2010 (apr. Vile, John R.	342.7303
The Encyclopedia of Cut Flowers. Crary, Calvert	745.92
The Encyclopedia of Demons and Demonology. Guiley, Rosemary	133.4
Encyclopedia of Dog Breeds. Coile, D. Caroline	636.7
Encyclopedia of Earthquakes and Volcanoes. Gates, Alexander E.	551.2
The Encyclopedia of Furniture. Aronson, Joseph	749
★*The Encyclopedia of Ghosts and Spirits*. Guiley, Rosemary	133.1
Encyclopedia of Herbal Medicine. Chevallier, Andrew	615.3
Encyclopedia of Native Tribes of North America. Johnson, Michael	970.00497
Encyclopedia of Pasta. Zanini De Vita, Oretta	641.822
The Encyclopedia of Spices and Herbs. Lakshmi, Padma	641.3
The Encyclopedia of Superheroes on Film and Television. Muir, John Kenneth	791.43
Encyclopedia of the Enlightenment. Wilson, Ellen Judy	940.2
Encyclopedia of the United States Constitution. Schultz, David A.	342.730203
Encyclopedia of Whales, Dolphins and Porpoises. Hoyt, Erich	599.5
The Encyclopedia of Witches, Witchcraft and Wicca. Guiley, Rosemary	133.4
ENCYCLOPEDIAS	
Aronson, Joseph. *The Encyclopedia of Furniture*	749
Garfield, Simon. ★*All the Knowledge in the World*	030.9
Gates, Alexander E. *Encyclopedia of Earthquakes and Volcanoes*	551.2
Guiley, Rosemary. *The Encyclopedia of Demons and Demonology*	133.4
Hoyt, Erich. *Encyclopedia of Whales, Dolphins and Porpoises*	599.5
Lenburg, Jeff. *The Encyclopedia of Animated Cartoons*	791.43
Maddex, Robert L. *The U.S. Constitution A to Z*	342.730203
Monger, George. *Marriage Customs of the World*	392.5
Vile, John R. *Encyclopedia of Constitutional Amendments, Proposed Amendments, and Amending Issues, 1789-2010*	342.7303
Wilson, Ellen Judy. *Encyclopedia of the Enlightenment*	940.2
The End of Country. McGraw, Seamus	333.7909748
End of Days. Swanson, James L.	973.922092
The End of Eden. Welz, Adam	577.2
The End of Everything. Mack, Katie	523.1
The End of Love. Strings, Sabrina	155.3
The End of Suffering. Cairns, Scott	231
The End of the Cold War 1985-1991. Service, Robert	909.82
The End of the End of the Earth. Franzen, Jonathan	814
End of the Megafauna. MacPhee, R. D. E.	591.4
The End of the Myth. Grandin, Greg	973
END OF THE UNIVERSE	
Mack, Katie. *The End of Everything*	523.1
END OF THE WORLD	
Choi, Franny. *The World Keeps Ending, and the World Goes On*	811
Jones, Saeed. *Alive at the End of the World*	811
Newitz, Annalee. *Scatter, Adapt, and Remember*	576.8
END OF THE WORLD (CHRISTIAN THEOLOGY)	
Ehrman, Bart D. ★*Armageddon*	236
★*The End of Your Life Book Club*. Schwalbe, Will	B
End Times. Turchin, Peter	320.01
★*An End to Inequality*. Kozol, Jonathan	379.2
★*Endangered Eating*. Lohman, Sarah	641.5973

AUTHOR, TITLE, SERIES AND SUBJECT INDEX

ENDANGERED ECOSYSTEMS
    Struzik, Edward. *Swamplands*   577.68
Endgame. Brady, Frank   B
Endgame. Rohde, David   949.703
Ending The Vietnam War. Kissinger, Henry   959.704
Endless Forms. Sumner, Seirian   595.79
ENDOMETRIOSIS
    Norman, Abby. *Ask Me About My Uterus*   618.1
    Parker, Lara. *Vagina Problems*   618.1
The Ends of the World. Brannen, Peter   576.8
The Endurance. Alexander, Caroline   919.8
★*Endurance*. Kelly, Scott   B
ENDURANCE
    Velshi, Ali. *Small Acts of Courage*   B
ENDURANCE SPORTS
    Alvarez, Noe. *Spirit Run*   796.42
    Cox, Lynne. *Swimming to Antarctica*   B
    Davis, Jennifer Pharr. *The Pursuit of Endurance*   796.51
    Finn, Adharanand. *The Rise of the Ultra Runners*   B
    Fitzgerald, Matt. *Iron War*   796.42
    Foreman, Tom. *My Year of Running Dangerously*   B
    Karnazes, Dean. *The Legend of Marathon*   796.42
    Keeling, Ida. *Can't Nothing Bring Me Down*   B
    McDougall, Christopher. *Born to Run*   796.42
    McDougall, Christopher. *Natural Born Heroes*   940.53
    Mortimer, Gavin. *The Great Swim*   B
    Murakami, Haruki. *What I Talk About When I Talk About Running*   B
    Nyad, Diana. *Find a Way*   B
    Pace, Kristin Knight. *This Much Country*   B
    Paulsen, Gary. *Winterdance*   B
    Shorter, Frank. *My Marathon*   796.42
    Wade, Becky. *Run the World*   796.42
★*Enduring* Vietnam. Wright, James Edward   959.704
ENEMIES
    Hampton, Dan. *Operation Vengeance*   940.54
    Morley, Jefferson. *Scorpions' Dance*   973.924
    Sedgwick, John. *War of Two*   973.4
Enemy of All Mankind. Johnson, Steven   910.4
Enemy of the State. Newton, Michael A.   345.567
★*Energy*. Rhodes, Richard   333.7909
ENERGY
    Bodanis, David. *Electric Universe*   537
    Rhodes, Richard. ★*Energy*   333.7909
    Wilczek, Frank. *Fundamentals*   530.01
ENERGY CONSUMPTION
    Humes, Edward. ★*Total Garbage*   628.4
    Margonelli, Lisa. *Oil on the Brain*   338.2
    Sachs, Jeffrey. *The Age of Sustainable Development*   338.9
ENERGY DEVELOPMENT
    Rhodes, Richard. ★*Energy*   333.7909
ENERGY INDUSTRY AND TRADE
    Blunt, Katherine. *California Burning*   333.793
    Keefe, Bob. *Clean Economy Now*   333.79
    Leonard, Christopher. *Kochland*   338.7
    Scheyder, Ernest. *The War Below*   333.7
    Zuckerman, Gregory. *The Frackers*   B
ENERGY POLICY
    Bakke, Gretchen Anna. *The Grid*   333.793
    Ewing, Jack. *Faster, Higher, Farther*   338.7
    Keefe, Bob. *Clean Economy Now*   333.79
    Kershaw, Ian. *The Global Age*   940.55
    Maddow, Rachel. *Blowout*   338.2
    Yergin, Daniel. *The New Map*   333.79
ENERGY PRODUCTION
    Kaku, Michio. *Quantum Supremacy*   006.3
    Maass, Peter. *Crude World*   338.2
    Rhodes, Richard. ★*Energy*   333.7909
ENERGY RESOURCES
    Rhodes, Richard. ★*Energy*   333.7909
    Yergin, Daniel. *The Quest*   333.79
ENERGY TECHNOLOGY
    Humes, Edward. ★*Total Garbage*   628.4
ENGAGED PEOPLE
    Alden, Ginger. *Elvis and Ginger*   B
★*The Engagement*. Issenberg, Sasha   346.7301
Engaging Babies in the Library. Knoll, Debra J.   027.62
Engel, Richard
    And Then All Hell Broke Loose   956.05

ENGEL, RICHARD, 1973-
    Engel, Richard. *And Then All Hell Broke Loose*   956.05
ENGELBERG, MORRIS
    Cramer, Richard Ben. *Joe DiMaggio*   B
Engelhart, Katie
    The Inevitable   179.7
ENGELS, FRIEDRICH, 1820-1895
    Hunt, Tristram. *Marx's General*   335.4092
Engine Empire. Hong, Cathy Park   811
ENGINEERING
    Agrawal, Roma. *Nuts and Bolts*   609
    Denton, Sally. *The Profiteers*   B
    Hammack, William Scott. ★*Things We Make*   620
    Parker, Matthew. *Panama Fever*   972.87
    Ploszajski, Anna. *Handmade*   620.1
    Smil, Vaclav. *Size*   153.7
    Standage, Tom. *A Brief History of Motion*   388
ENGINEERING DESIGN
    Aryee, Patrick. *30 Animals That Made Us Smarter*   590
    DeBord, Matthew. *Return to Glory*   338.4
    Lauretta, D. S. *The Asteroid Hunter*   523.44
    Ploszajski, Anna. *Handmade*   620.1
ENGINEERS
    Berger, Eric. *Liftoff*   B
    Fishman, Charles. ★*One Giant Leap*   629.45
    McWhirter, Cameron. *American Gun*   683.4
    Price, David A. *Geniuses at War*   940.54
    Swift, Earl. *Across the Airless Wilds*   629.45
    Waldman, Jonathan. *Sam*   629.8
Engineers of Victory. Kennedy, Paul   940.54
ENGLAND
    Ackroyd, Peter. *Rebellion*   941.06
    Ackroyd, Peter. *Tudors*   942.05
    Alderton, Dolly. *Everything I Know About Love*   B
    Armstrong, Karen. *The Spiral Staircase*   B
    Ash, Lamorna. *Dark, Salt, Clear*   942.3
    Borman, Tracy. *Thomas Cromwell*   B
    Bremer, Francis J. *John Winthrop*   B
    Briggs, Julia. *Virginia Woolf*   823
    Bryson, Bill. *Notes from a Small Island*   914
    Bryson, Bill. *The Road to Little Dribbling*   914
    Bryson, Bill. *Shakespeare*   B
    Castor, Helen. *She-Wolves*   942
    Clapton, Eric. *Clapton*   B
    Connolly, Ray. *Being John Lennon*   B
    Costello, Elvis. *Unfaithful Music & Disappearing Ink*   B
    Dennison, Matthew. *The Man in the Willows*   B
    Doggett, Peter. *You Never Give Me Your Money*   B
    Flanders, Judith. *The Victorian City*   942.1
    Funder, Anna. *Wifedom*   B
    Gaskell, Elizabeth Cleghorn. *The Life of Charlotte Bronte*   B
    Gies, Frances. *Life in a Medieval Village*   306
    Greenblatt, Stephen. ★*Will in the World*   B
    Harris, Ellen T. *George Frideric Handel*   B
    Hastings, Selina. *The Secret Lives of Somerset Maugham*   B
    Herriot, James. *All Things Wise and Wonderful*   B
    John, Elton. ★*Me*   B
    Jones, Dylan. *David Bowie*   B
    Koch, Bea. *Mad and Bad*   920
    Lane, Christina. *Phantom Lady*   B
    Lessing, Doris May. *Under My Skin*   823
    MacColl, Gail. *To Marry an English Lord*   974.7
    Margotin, Philippe. *The Rolling Stones*   782.42166
    McKay, Sinclair. *The Secret Lives of Codebreakers*   940.54
    Montillo, Roseanne. *The Lady and Her Monsters*   823
    Morley, Paul. *The Age of Bowie*   B
    Morris, Marc. ★*The Anglo-Saxons*   942.01
    Morris, Marc. *Castles*   728.81
    Morrison, Robert. *The Regency Years*   941.07
    Mortimer, Ian. *The Time Traveler's Guide to Elizabethan England*   942.05
    Nicolson, Adam. *The Making of Poetry*   821.709
    Norman, Philip. *John Lennon*   B
    Nuttall, A. D. *Shakespeare the Thinker*   822.33
    Offerman, Nick. *Where the Deer and the Antelope Play*   973.93
    Osbourne, Ozzy. *I Am Ozzy*   B
    Parker Pearson, Michael. *Stonehenge*   936.2
    Pitts, Mike. *Digging for Richard III*   942.046
    Povey, Glenn. *Echoes*   782.42166

PUBLIC LIBRARY CORE COLLECTION: NONFICTION
Twentieth Edition

Pryor, Francis. ★*Stonehenge* — 936.2
Reynolds, Simon. *Shock and Awe* — 781.6609
Roberts, Julius. *The Farm Table* — 641.594
Rounding, Virginia. *The Burning Time* — 272
Smith, Emma. *This Is Shakespeare* — 822.33
Smith, Sally Bedell. *Elizabeth the Queen* — B
Spitz, Bob. ★*The Beatles* — B
Starkey, David. *Six Wives* — 942.05
Stewart, Rory. *The Marches* — 941.3
Tammet, Daniel. *Born on a Blue Day* — B
Thomson, Graeme. *George Harrison* — B
Winn, Raynor. ★*The Salt Path* — B

ENGLAND IN LITERATURE
Norwich, John Julius. *Shakespeare's Kings* — 822.33
England's medieval queens [Series]. Weir, Alison — 920

Engle, Charlie
   Running Man — B

ENGLE, CHARLIE
Engle, Charlie. *Running Man* — B

*The **English** and Their History.* Tombs, Robert — 942
★***English** as a Global Language.* Crystal, David — 427

ENGLISH CIVIL WAR, 1642-1649
Ackroyd, Peter. *Rebellion* — 941.06

ENGLISH HISTORY
Ackroyd, Peter. *Revolution* — 941.07
Albertine, Viv. *Clothes, Clothes, Clothes. Music, Music, Music* — B
Asbridge, Thomas S. *The Greatest Knight* — 942.03
Borman, Tracy. *Thomas Cromwell* — B
Browne, E. J. *Charles Darwin* — B
Browne, E. J. *Charles Darwin* — B
Byrne, Eugene. *Darwin* — 741.5
Greenblatt, Stephen. ★*Will in the World* — B
Gwynne, S. C. *His Majesty's Airship* — 363.12
Larson, Erik. ★*The Splendid and the Vile* — 940.54
Macintyre, Ben. ★*Operation Mincemeat* — 940.54
Manchester, William. *The Last Lion, Winston Spencer Churchill.* — B
Manchester, William. *The Last Lion, Winston Spencer Churchill.* — B
Manchester, William. *The Last Lion, Winston Spencer Churchill.* — B
Parker Pearson, Michael. *Stonehenge* — 936.2
Povey, Glenn. *Echoes* — 782.42166
Price, David A. *Geniuses at War* — 940.54
Shapiro, James. *The Year of Lear* — 822.33
Spitz, Bob. ★*The Beatles* — B
Tallis, Nicola. *Crown of Blood* — B
Tolinski, Brad. *Light and Shade* — B
Weir, Alison. *The Lady in the Tower* — B
Weir, Alison. *Queens of the Conquest* — 920
Wise, Steven M. *Though the Heavens May Fall* — 342.42
Wulf, Andrea. *The Brother Gardeners* — 920

ENGLISH LANGUAGE
Ammer, Christine. *The American Heritage Dictionary of Idioms* — 423
Bailey, Richard W. *Speaking American* — 427
Baldick, Chris. ★*The Oxford Dictionary of Literary Terms* — 803
Baron, Dennis E. *What's Your Pronoun?* — 425.55
Bragg, Melvyn. ★*The Adventure of English* — 420
Brandreth, Gyles Daubeney. *Have You Eaten Grandma?* — 428
Brewer, Ebenezer Cobham. ★*Brewer's Dictionary of Phrase & Fable* — 423
Crystal, David. ★*English as a Global Language* — 427
Crystal, David. *Spell It Out* — 421
Crystal, David. ★*The Stories of English* — 427
Crystal, David. *The Story of English in 100 Words* — 422
Curzan, Anne. ★*Says Who?* — 428
Dreyer, Benjamin. *Dreyer's English* — 808.02
Elster, Charles Harrington. *How to Tell Fate from Destiny* — 428.1
Espy, Willard R. *Words to Rhyme With* — 423
Fridland, Valerie. ★*Like, Literally, Dude* — 420.141
Garner, Bryan A. *The Chicago Guide to Grammar, Usage, and Punctuation* — 428.2
Garner, Bryan A. *Garner's Modern English Usage* — 423
Greenblatt, Stephen. ★*Will in the World* — B
Hitchings, Henry. *The Language Wars* — 420.9
Holder, R. W. *How Not to Say What You Mean* — 427
Hult, Christine A. *The Handy English Grammar Answer Book* — 428.2
McCrum, Robert. ★*The Story of English* — 420
McWhorter, John H. *Talking Back, Talking Black* — 427
Ogilvie, Sarah. *The Dictionary People* — 423
Oliver, Mary. *A Poetry Handbook* — 808.1
Pukui, Mary Kawena. *Hawaiian Dictionary* — 499

Rosten, Leo. *The New Joys of Yiddish* — 422
Sharif, Solmaz. *Customs* — 811
Stamper, Kory. *Word by Word* — 413.028
Strunk, William. ★*The Elements of Style* — 808
Thorpe, Helen. *The Newcomers* — 373.18
Truss, Lynne. *Eats, Shoots & Leaves* — 428.2
Wood, James. *How Fiction Works* — 808.3
Woods, Geraldine. *25 Great Sentences and How They Got That Way* — 808
Zinsser, William Knowlton. *Writing to Learn* — 808

ENGLISH LANGUAGE TEACHERS
Hessler, Peter. *Other Rivers* — 378.1
Nafisi, Azar. ★*Reading Lolita in Tehran* — B

ENGLISH LITERATURE
Morrison, Robert. *The Regency Years* — 941.07

ENGLISH PEOPLE
Borman, Tracy. *Anne Boleyn and Elizabeth I* — 920
Charter, David. *Royal Audience* — 941.085
Coldstream, Catherine. ★*Cloistered* — B
Costa, James T. *Radical by Nature* — B
Eyman, Scott. *Charlie Chaplin vs. America* — B
Finkelstein, Daniel. *Two Roads Home* — 920
Hardman, Robert. *Queen of Our Times* — B
Harry. ★*Spare* — B
Johnson, Brian. *The Lives of Brian* — B
Kozinn, Allan. *The McCartney Legacy* — B
Markel, Howard. *Origin Story* — 576.8
Norman, Philip. *George Harrison* — B
Raban, Jonathan. *Father and Son* — B
Smith, Sally Bedell. *George VI and Elizabeth* — 920
Stewart, Patrick. ★*Making It So* — B
Weir, Alison. *Queens of the Age of Chivalry* — 920

English, Camper
   Doctors and Distillers — 615.7

English, Charlie
   The Gallery of Miracles and Madness — 709.04

ENGLISH, PAUL M., 1963-
Kidder, Tracy. *A Truck Full of Money* — B

English, T. J.
   The Corporation — 364.106089

Englund, Peter
   The Beauty and the Sorrow — 940.309
   November 1942 — 940.53

ENIAC (COMPUTER)
Kleiman, Kathy. *Proving Ground* — 4.092

*The **Enigma** of Clarence Thomas.* Robin, Corey — 347.73

ENJOYMENT
McColl, Sarah. *Joy Enough* — B
Rinaldi, Karen. *It's Great to Suck at Something* — 158.1

*The **Enlightened** College Applicant.* Belasco, Andrew — 378.1
***Enlightened** Journey.* Thondup — 294.3
***Enlightening** The World.* Khan, Yasmin Sabina — 974.7
*The **Enlightenment**.* Gay, Peter — 190
*The **Enlightenment**.* Gay, Peter — 190

ENLIGHTENMENT (BUDDHISM)
Armstrong, Karen. *Buddha* — B
Dalai Lama. *Approaching the Buddhist Path* — 294.3

ENLIGHTENMENT (EUROPEAN INTELLECTUAL MOVEMENT)
Blanning, T. C. W. *Frederick the Great* — B
Curran, Andrew S. *Diderot and the Art of Thinking Freely* — 194
Gottlieb, Anthony. ★*The Dream of Enlightenment* — 190
Herman, Arthur. *How the Scots Invented the Modern World* — 941.1
Moore, Peter. *Life, Liberty, and the Pursuit of Happiness* — 199
Purnell, Carolyn. *The Sensational Past* — 152.109
Robertson, Ritchie. *The Enlightenment* — 190
Swafford, Jan. ★*Beethoven* — B
Wilson, Derek K. *A Magical World* — 261.55

*The **Enlightenment**.* Robertson, Ritchie — 190
★***Enlightenment** Now.* Pinker, Steven — 303.44

Enninful, Edward
   A Visible Man — B

Enough. Hutchinson, Cassidy — B
Enough Already. Bertinelli, Valerie — B
★*Enough as She Is.* Simmons, Rachel — 155.5

Enrich, David
   Dark Towers — 332.1
   Servants of the Damned — 340.023

Enright, Lynn
   Vagina — 612.6

AUTHOR, TITLE, SERIES AND SUBJECT INDEX

ENSLAVED CHILDREN
   Morgan-Owens, Jessie. *Girl in Black and White* — B

ENSLAVED PEOPLE
   Ball, Edward. *Slaves in the Family* — 975.7
   Beard, Mary. ★*S.P.Q.R.* — 937
   Beckert, Sven. *Empire of Cotton* — 338.4
   Blight, David W. ★*Frederick Douglass* — B
   Blight, David W. *A Slave No More* — B
   Carretta, Vincent. *Equiano, the African* — B
   Clinton, Catherine. *Harriet Tubman* — B
   Deetz, Kelley Fanto. *Bound to the Fire* — 641.59
   Delbanco, Andrew. *The War Before the War* — 973.7
   Dilbeck, D. H. *Frederick Douglass* — B
   Douglass, Frederick. ★*Frederick Douglass* — 973.8
   Douglass, Frederick. *My Bondage and My Freedom* — B
   Douglass, Frederick. *The Portable Frederick Douglass* — 973.8
   Dunbar, Erica Armstrong. ★*She Came to Slay* — B
   Durkin, Hannah. ★*The Survivors of the Clotilda* — 306.362
   Fields-Black, Edda L. *Combee* — 973.7
   Fischer, David Hackett. *African Founders* — 973
   Franklin, John Hope. ★*From Slavery to Freedom* — 973
   Franklin, John Hope. *In Search of the Promised Land* — 929
   Gaddy, K. R. ★*Well of Souls* — 787
   Genovese, Eugene D. *Roll, Jordan, Roll* — 975
   Gordon-Reed, Annette. ★*The Hemingses of Monticello* — 920
   Humez, Jean McMahon. *Harriet Tubman* — B
   Hurston, Zora Neale. ★*Barracoon* — B
   Jacobs, Harriet. ★*Incidents in the Life of a Slave Girl* — B
   Jacoby, Karl. *The Strange Career of William Ellis* — B
   Johnson, Walter. *Soul by Soul* — 976.3
   Kars, Marjoleine. *Blood on the River* — 306.3
   Kearse, Bettye. *The Other Madisons* — 920
   Kelley, Blair Murphy. *Black Folk* — 331.6
   Kerrison, Catherine. *Jefferson's Daughters* — 920
   Larson, Kate Clifford. *Bound for the Promised Land* — B
   Lockley, Thomas. *African Samurai* — B
   Manegold, Catherine S. *Ten Hills Farm* — 974.4
   May, Gregory. *A Madman's Will* — 973.5
   McGill, Joseph. *Sleeping with the Ancestors* — 306.362
   Miles, Tiya. ★*Night Flyer* — B
   Nathans, Sydney. *To Free a Family* — B
   Northup, Solomon. *Twelve Years a Slave* — B
   Plant, Deborah G. *Of Greed and Glory* — 326
   Price, David A. ★*Love and Hate in Jamestown* — 975.5
   Rae, Noel. ★*The Great Stain* — 306.3
   Raines, Ben. *The Last Slave Ship* — 306.362
   Rediker, Marcus. *The Amistad Rebellion* — 326.0973
   Sinha, Manisha. *The Slave's Cause* — 326
   Smith, Clint. ★*How the Word Is Passed* — 973
   Stuart, Andrea. *Sugar in the Blood* — 338.1
   Swarns, Rachel L. *The 272* — 975.2
   Tabor, Nick. *Africatown* — 976.1
   Taylor, Alan. *The Internal Enemy* — 975.5
   Tipton-Martin, Toni. ★*Jubilee* — 641.59
   Waldstreicher, David. *The Odyssey of Phillis Wheatley* — B
   Ward, Andrew. ★*The Slaves' War* — 973.7
   White, Gayle Jessup. *Reclamation* — B
   Wiencek, Henry. *Master of the Mountain* — 973.4
   Willis, Deborah. *Envisioning Emancipation* — 973.7
   Wise, Steven M. *Though the Heavens May Fall* — 342.42
   Young, Kevin. *Ardency* — 811

ENSLAVED PEOPLE'S RESISTANCE AND REVOLTS
   Hall, Rebecca. ★*Wake* — 741.5
   Kars, Marjoleine. *Blood on the River* — 306.3
   Lepore, Jill. *New York Burning* — 974.7
   Rasmussen, Daniel. *American Uprising* — 976.3
   Rediker, Marcus. *The Amistad Rebellion* — 326.0973
   Sinha, Manisha. *The Slave's Cause* — 326
   Young, Kevin. *Ardency* — 811

ENSLAVED WOMEN
   Dunbar, Erica Armstrong. ★*Never Caught* — B
   Hall, Rebecca. ★*Wake* — 741.5
   Hallman, J. C. *Say Anarcha* — 618.1
   Hecimovich, Gregg A. ★*The Life and Times of Hannah Crafts* — B
   Jeffers, Honorée Fanonne. *The Age of Phillis* — 811
   Nathans, Sydney. *To Free a Family* — B

Enss, Chris
   Mochi's War — B

Entangled Life. Sheldrake, Merlin — 579.5

ENTERTAINERS
   Bennetts, Leslie. *Last Girl Before Freeway* — B
   Gehring, Wes D. *James Dean* — B
   Izzard, Eddie. *Believe Me* — B
   Kashner, Sam. *Furious Love* — B
   Martin, Steve. *Number One Is Walking* — B
   McBride, James. *Kill 'Em and Leave* — B
   Patterson, Pat. *Accepted* — B
   Poole, W. Scott. *Vampira* — B
   Posnanski, Joe. ★*The Life and Afterlife of Harry Houdini* — 793.8
   RuPaul. ★*The House of Hidden Meanings* — B
   Wall, Duncan. *The Ordinary Acrobat* — B
   Warren, Louis S. *Buffalo Bill's America* — B

ENTERTAINING
   Bayless, Rick. ★*Fiesta at Rick's* — 641.5972
   Bjork, Katrin. *From the North* — 641.594
   Hartnett, Angela. *The Weekend Cook* — 641.5
   Heuck, Lidey. ★*Cooking in Real Life* — 641.5
   Hudson, Kate. *Pretty Fun* — 642
   McAlpine, Skye. *A Table Full of Love* — 641.5
   Mullen, Marissa. *That Cheese Plate Wants to Party* — 641.6
   Oliver, Jamie. *Together* — 641.5
   Post, Lizzie. *Emily Post's Etiquette* — 395
   Post, Lizzie. *Emily Post's Etiquette* — 395
   Roman, Alison. ★*Nothing Fancy* — 642
   Rosenstrach, Jenny. *How to Celebrate Everything* — 641.5
   Saltz, Joanna. *Delish* — 641.5
   Sifton, Sam. ★*See You on Sunday* — 641.5
   Stewart, Martha. ★*The Martha Manual* — 640
   Watson, Ted Kennedy. *Ted Kennedy Watson's Guide to Stylish Entertaining* — 793.2
   Zizka, Maria. *The Hostess Handbook* — 642

ENTERTAINMENT INDUSTRY AND TRADE
   Andrews, Julie. *Home Work* — B
   Bacall, Lauren. *By Myself and Then Some* — B
   Basinger, Jeanine. *Hollywood* — 791.43
   Berg, A. Scott. *Kate Remembered* — B
   De Semlyen, Nick. *Wild and Crazy Guys* — 920
   Fisher, Todd. *My Girls* — B
   Fumudoh, Ziwe. ★*Black Friend* — 814
   Haddish, Tiffany. *The Last Black Unicorn* — B
   Hayes, Dade. *Binge Times* — 384.55
   Isen, Tajja. *Some of My Best Friends* — 305.8
   Johnson, Steven. *Wonderland* — 790.1
   Levy, Shawn. ★*The Castle on Sunset* — 647.95
   Lunenfeld, Peter. *City at the Edge of Forever* — 979.4
   Patterson, James. *What Really Happens in Vegas* — 920
   Patterson, Pat. *Accepted* — B
   Penn, Kal. *You Can't Be Serious* — B
   Ratajkowski, Emily. ★*My Body* — B
   Ripa, Kelly. *Live Wire* — B
   Ryan, Maureen. *Burn It Down* — 791.43
   Schulman, Michael. ★*Oscar Wars* — 791.43
   Scovell, Nell. *Just the Funny Parts* — B
   Zweibel, Alan. *Laugh Lines* — B
   Zwick, Edward. ★*Hits, Flops, and Other Illusions* — B

ENTERTAINMENTS
   Owen, Oscar. *Mind-Blowing Magic Tricks for Everyone* — 793.8

ENTHUSIASM
   Miranda, Lin-Manuel. *Gmorning, Gnight!* — 811

ENTITLEMENT ATTITUDES
   Caldwell, Christopher. *The Age of Entitlement* — 305.240973
   Hamad, Ruby. *White Tears/Brown Scars* — 305.8

ENTOMOLOGISTS
   MacNeal, David. *Bugged* — 595.7
   McNeur, Catherine. *Mischievous Creatures* — 920
   Wilson, Edward O. *Tales from the Ant World* — 595.79

ENTOMOLOGY
   MacNeal, David. *Bugged* — 595.7
   Nicholls, Steve. *Alien Worlds* — 595.7
   Sverdrup-Thygeson, Anne. *Buzz, Sting, Bite* — 595.7
   Waldbauer, Gilbert. *What Good Are Bugs?* — 595.717

ENTREPRENEURS
   Cailan, Alvin. *Amboy* — 641.595
   Davenport, Christian. *The Space Barons* — 920
   Dickinson, Bruce. *What Does This Button Do?* — B
   Downs, Paul. *Boss Life* — 338.7

PUBLIC LIBRARY CORE COLLECTION: NONFICTION
Twentieth Edition

Ducharme, Jamie. *Big Vape*	338.7
Fall, Jeremy. *Falling Upwards*	158.1
Franklin, Jonathan. *A Wild Idea*	B
Harrison, Scott. *Thirst*	B
Hewitt, Ben. ★*The Town That Food Saved*	338.1
Howe, Ben Ryder. *My Korean Deli*	B
Isaacson, Walter. ★*Elon Musk*	B
Kaufman, Jonathan. *The Last Kings of Shanghai*	951
Kenner, Rob. *The Marathon Don't Stop*	B
Kidder, Tracy. *A Truck Full of Money*	B
Knight, Philip H. *Shoe Dog*	B
Kurutz, Steven. *American Flannel*	338.4
Snow, Richard. *Disney's Land*	791.06
Umar, Ousman. *North to Paradise*	B
Waterhouse, Benjamin C. *One Day I'll Work for Myself*	338
Webb, Maynard. *Dear Founder*	658
Wilson, Robert. *Barnum*	B
Zuckerman, Gregory. *The Frackers*	B

ENTREPRENEURSHIP

Abrams, Stacey. *Level Up*	658.4
Bahcall, Safi. *Loonshots*	658.4
Dennis, Felix. *How to Get Rich*	B
Galloway, Scott. *The Four*	338.7
Godin, Seth. *The Practice*	153.3
Grant, Adam M. *Originals*	153.3
Greenspan, Alan. *Capitalism in America*	330.973
Harrison, Scott. *Thirst*	B
Hewitt, Ben. ★*The Town That Food Saved*	338.1
Kawasaki, Guy. *The Art of the Start 2.0*	658.1
Knight, Philip H. *Shoe Dog*	B
Lashinsky, Adam. *Wild Ride*	388.4
Micklethwait, John. *The Company*	338.7
Nadella, Satya. *Hit Refresh*	B
Pein, Corey. *Live Work Work Work Die*	338.4
Stone, Brad. *The Upstarts*	338.04
Vaynerchuk, Gary. *Crushing It!*	650.1
Waterhouse, Benjamin C. *One Day I'll Work for Myself*	338
Webb, Maynard. *Dear Founder*	658
Wiener, Anna. ★*Uncanny Valley*	B
Yunus, Muhammad. *A World of Three Zeros*	330

ENTROPY

Greene, B. *Until the End of Time*	523.1

ENVIRONMENTAL DEGRADATION

Ackerman, Diane. *The Human Age*	304.2
Aguon, Julian. *No Country for Eight-Spot Butterflies*	305.89
Attenborough, David. *A Life on Our Planet*	508
Berners-Lee, Mike. *The Carbon Footprint of Everything*	363.738
Bittle, Jake. ★*The Great Displacement*	362.87
Black, George. ★*The Long Reckoning*	959.704
Burke, Monte. *Lords of the Fly*	799.124
Carson, Rachel. ★*Silent Spring*	363.738
Craig, Mya-Rose. *Birdgirl*	B
Cullen, Art. *Storm Lake*	071.7
Davis, Jack E. *An Everglades Providence*	B
Diamond, Jared M. *Collapse*	304.2
Ehrlich, Gretel. *Unsolaced*	B
Erdrich, Heid E. ★*Little Big Bully*	811
Fields, Micah. ★*We Hold Our Breath*	976.4
Flowers, Catherine Coleman. *Waste*	363.72
Franklin-Wallis, Oliver. ★*Wasteland*	363.72
Ghosh, Amitav. *The Great Derangement*	809
Goldfarb, Ben. *Crossings*	333.77
Hardy, Alyssa. *Worn Out*	338.4
Jabr, Ferris. ★*Becoming Earth*	570.1
Jones, Saeed. *Alive at the End of the World*	811
Kara, Siddharth. *Cobalt Red*	338.2
Kumar, Priyanka. *Conversations with Birds*	598
Lopez, Barry Holstun. *Horizon*	B
Millet, Lydia. *We Loved It All*	813
Monbiot, George. ★*Regenesis*	338.1
Owens, Jay. *Dust*	551.51
Pasternak, Judy. *Yellow Dirt*	979.1004
Pearce, Fred. *A Trillion Trees*	577.3
Proulx, Annie. ★*Fen, Bog and Swamp*	551.41
Sorvino, Chloe. *Raw Deal*	338.1
Vaillant, John. ★*Fire Weather*	363.37
Welz, Adam. *The End of Eden*	577.2
Wilson, Edward O. *The Future of Life*	333.95
Wohlforth, Charles P. *The Fate of Nature*	304.209798
Wynn-Grant, Rae. *Wild Life*	B
Zuckerman, Jocelyn C. *Planet Palm*	633.8

ENVIRONMENTAL DESIGN

Tonti, Lucianne. *Sundressed*	746.9

ENVIRONMENTAL DISASTERS

Attenborough, David. *A Life on Our Planet*	508
Bittle, Jake. ★*The Great Displacement*	362.87
Brannen, Peter. *The Ends of the World*	576.8
Flyn, Cal. ★*Islands of Abandonment*	333.73
Johnson, Kirk W. *The Fishermen and the Dragon*	976.4
Lustgarten, Abrahm. ★*On the Move*	363.7
Shaughnessy, Brenda. *The Octopus Museum*	811
Vaillant, John. ★*Fire Weather*	363.37

ENVIRONMENTAL ENGINEERING

Ackerman, Diane. *The Human Age*	304.2
Humes, Edward. ★*Total Garbage*	628.4
Kostigen, Thomas. *Hacking Planet Earth*	628
Rosen, Jody. *Two Wheels Good*	629.227

ENVIRONMENTAL ETHICS

Ackerman, Diane. *The Human Age*	304.2
Cline, Elizabeth L. *The Conscious Closet*	646
Souder, William. *On a Farther Shore*	B
Tonti, Lucianne. *Sundressed*	746.9

ENVIRONMENTAL FORECASTING

Bittle, Jake. ★*The Great Displacement*	362.87
Brannen, Peter. *The Ends of the World*	576.8

ENVIRONMENTAL HEALTH

Hotz, Julia. ★*The Connection Cure*	610
Webb, Kinari. *Guardians of the Trees*	B

ENVIRONMENTAL JUSTICE

Aguon, Julian. *No Country for Eight-Spot Butterflies*	305.89
Dungy, Camille T. *Soil*	635.0978
Flowers, Catherine Coleman. *Waste*	363.72

ENVIRONMENTAL MOVEMENT

Beavan, Colin. *No Impact Man*	B

ENVIRONMENTAL POLICY

Bittle, Jake. ★*The Great Displacement*	362.87
Davis, Jack E. *An Everglades Providence*	B
Diamond, Jared M. *Collapse*	304.2
Flowers, Catherine Coleman. *Waste*	363.72
Ghosh, Amitav. *The Great Derangement*	809
Hilborn, Ray. *Overfishing*	338.3
Hiss, Tony. ★*Rescuing the Planet*	333.75
Humes, Edward. ★*Total Garbage*	628.4
Klare, Michael T. *All Hell Breaking Loose*	355.20973
Linden, Eugene. *Fire and Flood*	304.2
Morris, Jim. ★*The Cancer Factory*	658.3

ENVIRONMENTAL PROTECTION

Aguon, Julian. *No Country for Eight-Spot Butterflies*	305.89
Allen, Brigette. *Living Without Plastic*	640
Beavan, Colin. *No Impact Man*	B
Estes, Nick. *Our History Is the Future*	978.004
Franklin, Jonathan. *A Wild Idea*	B
Ghosh, Amitav. *The Great Derangement*	809
Gleick, Peter H. *The Three Ages of Water*	333.91
Horn, Miriam. *Rancher, Farmer, Fisherman*	B
Kolbert, Elizabeth. ★*Under a White Sky*	304.2
Lewis, Daniel. *Twelve Trees*	582.16
Meyaard-Schaap, Kyle. *Following Jesus in a Warming World*	241
Moore, Kathleen Dean. *Earth's Wild Music*	576.8
Nhat Hanh. *Zen and the Art of Saving the Planet*	294.3
Renner, Rebecca. ★*Gator Country*	364.16
Thunberg, Greta. ★*The Climate Book*	363.738
Wohlforth, Charles P. *The Fate of Nature*	304.209798

ENVIRONMENTAL PSYCHOLOGY

Williams, Florence. *The Nature Fix*	155.9

ENVIRONMENTAL REFUGEES

Lustgarten, Abrahm. ★*On the Move*	363.7

ENVIRONMENTAL RESPONSIBILITY

Aguon, Julian. *No Country for Eight-Spot Butterflies*	305.89
Berners-Lee, Mike. *The Carbon Footprint of Everything*	363.738
Cline, Elizabeth L. *The Conscious Closet*	646
Goleman, Daniel. *Ecological Intelligence*	333.7
Herring, Lucinda. *Reimagining Death*	393
Smil, Vaclav. *How the World Really Works*	500
Tonti, Lucianne. *Sundressed*	746.9

AUTHOR, TITLE, SERIES AND SUBJECT INDEX

ENVIRONMENTAL SCIENCES
   Bell, Alice R. *Our Biggest Experiment*   363.738
   Oreskes, Naomi. *Merchants of Doubt*   174
   Park, Chris C. *A Dictionary of Environment and Conservation*   333.703
ENVIRONMENTAL STEWARDSHIP
   Wilbur, Matika. *Project 562*   970.004
ENVIRONMENTALISM
   Allen, Brigette. *Living Without Plastic*   640
   Amos, Tori. *Resistance*   B
   Arsenault, Kerri. *Mill Town*   B
   Attenborough, David. *A Life on Our Planet*   508
   Beavan, Colin. *No Impact Man*   B
   Becker, Elizabeth. *Overbooked*   338.4
   Bernstein, Ellen. *Toward a Holy Ecology*   223
   Berry, Wendell. *The Art of Loading Brush*   338.10973
   Bittman, Mark. *Animal, Vegetable, Junk*   394.1
   Bradley, James. *Deep Water*   578.77
   Carson, Rachel. ★*Silent Spring*   363.738
   Cline, Elizabeth L. *The Conscious Closet*   646
   Cullen, Art. *Storm Lake*   071.7
   Davis, Jack E. ★*The Gulf*   909
   Ewing, Jack. *Faster, Higher, Farther*   338.7
   Fagan, Brian M. *The Long Summer*   551.6
   Fox, Porter. *The Last Winter*   363.738
   Franklin, Jonathan. *A Wild Idea*   B
   Goldfarb, Ben. *Eager*   333.95
   Goleman, Daniel. *Ecological Intelligence*   333.7
   Goodall, Jane. ★*Beyond Innocence*   B
   Goodall, Jane. ★*The Book of Hope*   128
   Hardy, Alyssa. *Worn Out*   338.4
   Hayhoe, Katharine. *Saving Us*   304.2
   Heacox, Kim. ★*John Muir and the Ice That Started a Fire*   333.7209798
   Hirshfield, Jane. *Ledger*   811
   Keefe, Bob. *Clean Economy Now*   333.79
   King, Greg. *The Ghost Forest*   333.75
   Lacovara, Kenneth. *Why Dinosaurs Matter*   567.9
   Linden, Eugene. *Fire and Flood*   304.2
   Lynas, Mark. *Six Degrees*   551.6
   MacKinnon, J. B. ★*The Day the World Stops Shopping*   339.4
   Marcum, Diana. *The Fallen Stones*   B
   Meyaard-Schaap, Kyle. *Following Jesus in a Warming World*   241
   Miller, Char. *Gifford Pinchot and the Making of Modern Environmentalism*   B
   Millet, Lydia. *We Loved It All*   813
   Momaday, N. Scott. *Earth Keeper*   814
   Monosson, Emily. ★*Blight*   616.9
   Nooyi, Indra. ★*My Life in Full*   B
   Penniman, Leah. ★*Black Earth Wisdom*   333.72
   Raboteau, Emily. *Lessons for Survival*   814
   Rawlence, Ben. *The Treeline*   577.3
   Rich, Nathaniel. *Losing Earth*   363.738
   Rich, Nathaniel. *Second Nature*   304.2
   Rinella, Steven. ★*Outdoor Kids in an Inside World*   649
   Sachs, Jeffrey. *The Age of Sustainable Development*   338.9
   Santos Perez, Craig. *From Unincorporated Territory [amot]*   811
   Scales, Helen. *What the Wild Sea Can Be*   577.7
   Scheyder, Ernest. *The War Below*   333.7
   Smith, Bren. *Eat Like a Fish*   338.3
   Solnit, Rebecca. *Call Them by Their True Names*   303.3
   Souder, William. *On a Farther Shore*   B
   Standage, Tom. *A Brief History of Motion*   388
   Taylor, Joseph E. *Pilgrims of the Vertical*   796.52
   Thunberg, Greta. ★*The Climate Book*   363.738
   Tonti, Lucianne. *Sundressed*   746.9
   Williams, Terry Tempest. *Erosion*   814
   Wilson, Edward O. *The Diversity of Life*   333.95
   Worster, Donald. *A Passion for Nature the Life of John Muir*   B
ENVIRONMENTALISTS
   Addison, Corban. *Wastelands*   346.73
   Alexander, Jane. *Wild Things, Wild Places*   333.95
   Alinder, Mary Street. *Ansel Adams*   B
   Bell, Alice R. *Our Biggest Experiment*   363.738
   Brinkley, Douglas. *The Wilderness Warrior*   B
   Egan, Timothy. ★*The Big Burn*   973.911
   Flowers, Catherine Coleman. *Waste*   363.72
   Franklin, Jonathan. *A Wild Idea*   B
   Freeman, Scott. *Saving Tarboo Creek*   333.72
   Hanes, Stephanie. *White Man's Game*   333.95
   Horn, Miriam. *Rancher, Farmer, Fisherman*

   King, Dean. *Guardians of the Valley*   333.72
   Lowman, Margaret. *The Arbornaut*   581.7
   Malarkey, Tucker. *Stronghold*   639.2
   McAnulty, Dara. *Diary of a Young Naturalist*   508.092
   Miller, Char. *Gifford Pinchot and the Making of Modern Environmentalism*   B
   Mooallem, Jon. *Wild Ones*   333.95
   Morris, Edmund. ★*The Rise of Theodore Roosevelt*   B
   Muir, John. *Nature Writings*   B
   Muir, John. *The Story of My Boyhood and Youth*   B
   Penniman, Leah. ★*Black Earth Wisdom*   333.72
   Simard, S. ★*Finding the Mother Tree*   582.16
   Souder, William. *On a Farther Shore*   B
   Taylor, Joseph E. *Pilgrims of the Vertical*   796.52
   Thunberg, Greta. ★*The Climate Book*   363.738
   Webb, Kinari. *Guardians of the Trees*   B
   Wheelan, Joseph. ★*Terrible Swift Sword*   B
   Worster, Donald. *A Passion for Nature the Life of John Muir*   B
ENVIRONMENTALLY INDUCED DISEASES
   O'Brien, Keith. *Paradise Falls*   363.738
Envisioning Emancipation. Willis, Deborah   973.7
EPAMINONDAS, B. CA. 420 B.C.E
   Hanson, Victor Davis. *The Soul of Battle*   355
Ephron, Dan
   Killing a King   956.9405
Ephron, Delia
   Left on Tenth   B
EPHRON, DELIA
   Ephron, Delia. *Left on Tenth*   B
Ephron, Nora
   The Most of Nora Ephron   814
EPHRON, NORA
   Carlson, Erin. *I'll Have What She's Having*   791.43
   Ephron, Nora. *The Most of Nora Ephron*   814
EPIC POETRY
   Carson, Anne. *Red Doc*   811
   Dante Alighieri. ★*The Divine Comedy*   851
   Dante Alighieri. *The Paradiso*   851
   Dante Alighieri. *Paradiso*   851
   Dante Alighieri. *Purgatorio*   851
   Homer. *The Iliad*   883
   Homer. *The Iliad*   883
   Homer. *Iliad*   883
   Homer. ★*The Iliad*   883
   Homer. *The Odyssey*   883
   Homer. *The Odyssey*   883
   Homer. *Odyssey*   883
   Homer. ★*The Odyssey*   883
   Homer. *The Odyssey*   883
   Ovid. *Tales from Ovid*   873
   Satyamurti, Carole. *Mahabharata*   821
   Virgil. ★*The Aeneid*   873
   Virgil. *The Aeneid*   873
Epic Surf Breaks of the World. Mackinnon, Al   797.32
Epic Tomatoes. LeHoullier, Craig   635
EPICS AND HERO TALES — ASIA
   Narayan, R. K. ★*The Ramayana*   294.5
EPICS AND HERO TALES — GREECE
   Homer. *The Iliad*   883
   Homer. *Iliad*   883
   Homer. *Odyssey*   883
EPIDEMIC ENCEPHALITIS
   Cahalan, Susannah. *Brain on Fire*   616.8
EPIDEMICS
   Ashton, Jennifer. *The New Normal*   613
   Barry, John M. ★*The Great Influenza*   614.5
   Brenner, Marie. *The Desperate Hours*   362.1962
   Christakis, Nicholas A. *Apollo's Arrow*   362.1962
   Crosby, Molly Caldwell. *The American Plague*   614.5
   Dearen, Jason. *Kill Shot*   616.8
   Farmer, Paul. *Fevers, Feuds, and Diamonds*   614.5
   Ferguson, Niall. *Doom*   362.1962
   Gates, Bill. ★*How to Prevent the Next Pandemic*   614.5
   Goldberg, Emma. *Life on the Line*   362.1962
   Hernandez, Daisy. *The Kissing Bug*   616.9
   Hoffman, Liz. *Crash Landing*   330
   Honigsbaum, Mark. *The Pandemic Century*   614.4
   Hotez, Peter J. *Preventing the Next Pandemic*   362.1969
   Johnson, Steven. *The Ghost Map*   614.5

PUBLIC LIBRARY CORE COLLECTION: NONFICTION
Twentieth Edition

Kang, Lydia. *Patient Zero*	614.4
Kelley, Margot Anne. *A Gardener at the End of the World*	615.8
Kelly, John. *The Great Mortality*	614.5
Kennedy, Jonathan. *Pathogenesis*	614.4
Kenny, Charles. *The Plague Cycle*	614.4
Kinch, Michael S. *Between Hope and Fear*	614.4
Klare, Michael T. *All Hell Breaking Loose*	355.20973
Leonnig, Carol. *I Alone Can Fix It*	973.933
Lewis, Michael. ★*The Premonition*	614.5
Mackenzie, Debora. *Covid-19*	616.2
Manaugh, Geoff. *Until Proven Safe*	614.4
Marcum, Diana. *The Fallen Stones*	B
McNeil, Donald G. ★*The Wisdom of Plagues*	614.4
Nocera, Joseph. *The Big Fail*	362.1962
Preston, Richard. *Crisis in the Red Zone*	614.5
Preston, Richard. *The Hot Zone*	614.5
Price, Polly J. *Plagues in the Nation*	614.4
Quammen, David. ★*Breathless*	614.5
Quammen, David. ★*Spillover*	614.4
Ramsey, Donovan X. ★*When Crack Was King*	362.29
Schama, Simon. *Foreign Bodies*	614.4
Senthilingam, Meera. *Outbreaks and Epidemics*	614.4
Smith, Zadie. *Intimations*	824
Spinney, Laura. ★*Pale Rider*	614.5
Werb, Dan. *The Invisible Siege*	614.5
Wright, Lawrence. ★*The Plague Year*	614.5
Zambreno, Kate. *The Light Room*	B

EPIDEMIOLOGY

Christakis, Nicholas A. *Apollo's Arrow*	362.1962
Gates, Bill. ★*How to Prevent the Next Pandemic*	614.5
Honigsbaum, Mark. *The Pandemic Century*	614.4
Mackenzie, Debora. *Covid-19*	616.2
McNeil, Donald G. ★*The Wisdom of Plagues*	614.4
Spinney, Laura. ★*Pale Rider*	614.5

EPIGENETICS

Heine, Steven J. *DNA Is Not Destiny*	572.8

EPILEPSY

B., David. *Epileptic*	741.5
Dittrich, Luke. ★*Patient H.M.*	616.85
Eichenwald, Kurt. *A Mind Unraveled*	B
Epileptic. B., David	741.5

EPISTOLARY NOVELS

Lewis, C. S. ★*The Screwtape Letters*	248.4

EPITHETS

Kohan, Rafi. ★*Trash Talk*	179

EPPES, MARIA, 1778-1804

Kerrison, Catherine. *Jefferson's Daughters*	920

Epplin, Luke

Our Team	796.357

EPSTEIN, BARBARA, 1928-2006

Pinckney, Darryl. *Come Back in September*	B

Epstein, David J.

★*Range*	153.9

Epstein, Franci

Franci's War	B

EPSTEIN, FRANCI

Epstein, Franci. *Franci's War*	B

Epstein, Lawrence J.

The Basic Beliefs of Judaism	296.3

Epstein, Mark

Advice Not Given	294.3
The Zen of Therapy	294.3

EPSTEIN, MARK, 1953-

Epstein, Mark. *The Zen of Therapy*	294.3

Epstein, Nicky

Nicky Epstein, the Essential Edgings Collection	746.43

EQUAL EDUCATION POLICY

Kozol, Jonathan. ★*An End to Inequality*	379.2
Martin, Rachel Louise. *A Most Tolerant Little Town*	379.2
Meckler, Laura. ★*Dream Town*	305.8
Mettler, Suzanne. *Degrees of Inequality*	378.73
Tough, Paul. *The Years That Matter Most*	378.1
★*Equal Partners*. Mangino, Kate	305.3

EQUAL PAY FOR EQUAL WORK

Wasserman, Claire. *Ladies Get Paid*	650.1

EQUAL RIGHTS AMENDMENTS

Kelly, Kate. *Ordinary Equality*	920
Equality. Postel, Charles	305.50973

EQUALITY

Arana, Marie. *Bolivar*	B
Baker, Calvin. *A More Perfect Reunion*	305.800973
Barber, William J. *We Are Called to Be a Movement*	261.8
Blumenthal, Sidney. *Wrestling with His Angel*	B
Brill, Steven. *Tailspin*	306.0973
Brown-Nagin, Tomiko. *Civil Rights Queen*	B
Canellos, Peter S. *The Great Dissenter*	B
Chung, Nicole. ★*A Living Remedy*	B
Cohen, Adam. ★*Supreme Inequality*	347.73
Cohen, Lizabeth. *A Consumers' Republic*	339.4
Cox, Josie. *Women Money Power*	330.082
Cummings, Elijah. ★*We're Better Than This*	B
Dohrmann, George. *Switching Fields*	796.334
Dubin, Minna. ★*Mom Rage*	306.874
Fisher, Thomas. ★*The Emergency*	362.1089
Garza, Alicia. *The Purpose of Power*	303.48
Gates, Melinda. ★*The Moment of Lift*	305.42
Griffith, Elisabeth. *Formidable*	305.42
Hickel, Jason. *The Divide*	330.9
Hill, Katie. *She Will Rise*	305.42
Holzer, Harold. *A Just and Generous Nation*	973.7092
Honey, Michael K. *To the Promised Land*	323
Jackson, Troy. *Becoming King*	B
Johnson, Theodore R. *When the Stars Begin to Fall*	305.800973
Kaplan, Fred. *Lincoln and the Abolitionists*	973.7092
Kelly, Kate. *Ordinary Equality*	920
Klinenberg, Eric. ★*2020*	306
Lebron, Christopher J. *The Making of Black Lives Matter*	305.896
Levine, Bruce C. *Thaddeus Stevens*	B
MacGillis, Alec. *Fulfillment*	381
Mandela, Nelson. *Dare Not Linger*	B
McGrath, Tom. *Triumph of the Yuppies*	305.242
Meacham, Jon. *His Truth Is Marching On*	B
Nolan, Hamilton. *The Hammer*	331.8
Nuttall, Jennifer Anne. ★*Mother Tongue*	422
Packer, George. *Last Best Hope*	973.93
Piketty, Thomas. *A Brief History of Equality*	305.09
Piketty, Thomas. ★*Capital and Ideology*	305
Piketty, Thomas. *The Economics of Inequality*	339.2
Postel, Charles. *Equality*	305.50973
Press, Eyal. ★*Dirty Work*	331.7
Proenza-Coles, Christina. *American Founders*	973
Quinn, Bridget. *She Votes*	324.6
Reeves, Richard V. *Dream Hoarders*	305.5
Richardson, Heather Cox. *Democracy Awakening*	320.473
Rubenstein, David M. *The American Experiment*	973
Saad, Layla F. ★*Me and White Supremacy*	305.809
Smith, Mychal Denzel. *Stakes Is High*	973.933
Thrasher, Steven W. ★*The Viral Underclass*	362.1962
Urofsky, Melvin I. *The Affirmative Action Puzzle*	331.13
Washington, Ella F. *The Necessary Journey*	658.3

EQUALITY BEFORE THE LAW

Cohen, Adam. ★*Supreme Inequality*	347.73
Watson, Bruce. *Freedom Summer*	323.1196

EQUATIONS

Brooks, Michael. *The Art of More*	510.9
Fortnow, Lance. *The Golden Ticket*	511.3

EQUESTRIAN THERAPY

Gaffney, Ginger. *Half Broke*	B
Thompson-Hernandez, Walter. *The Compton Cowboys*	920

EQUESTRIANISM

Grant, Will. *The Last Ride of the Pony Express*	917.804
Letts, Elizabeth. ★*The Ride of Her Life*	B
Nir, Sarah Maslin. *Horse Crazy*	B

EQUESTRIANS

Nir, Sarah Maslin. *Horse Crazy*	B

EQUIANO, OLAUDAH, 1745-1797

Carretta, Vincent. *Equiano, the African*	B
Equiano, The African. Carretta, Vincent	B
The Equivalents. Doherty, Maggie	920
★*Equus*. Shaffer, Peter	822
ER Nurses. Patterson, James	610.73
★*Era of Ignition*. Tamblyn, Amber	B

ERASMUS, DESIDERIUS, DIED 1536

Massing, Michael. *Fatal Discord*	920

Erdman, Sarah

Nine Hills to Nambonkaha	966.68

AUTHOR, TITLE, SERIES AND SUBJECT INDEX

ERDMAN, SARAH
   Erdman, Sarah. *Nine Hills to Nambonkaha* — 966.68
Erdozain, Dominic
   One Nation Under Guns — 363.33
Erdrich, Heid E.
   ★*Little Big Bully* — 811
Erdrich, Louise
   Books and Islands in Ojibwe Country — 977
ERDRICH, LOUISE
   Erdrich, Louise. *Books and Islands in Ojibwe Country* — 977
Erickson, Carolly
   Great Catherine — B
Erickson, Laura
   ★*100 Plants to Feed the Birds* — 635
   The Love Lives of Birds — 598.15
Ericsson, K. Anders
   Peak — 153.9
ERITREAN PEOPLE
   Girma, Haben. *Haben* — B
Ernaux, Annie
   ★*The Years* — B
ERNAUX, ANNIE, 1940-
   Ernaux, Annie. ★*The Years* — B
Ernest Hemingway. Dearborn, Mary V. — B
Ernie Pyle's War. Tobin, James — B
Ernst, Carl W.
   The Shambhala Guide to Sufism — 297.4
Erosion. Williams, Terry Tempest — 814
EROSION
   Dean, Cornelia. *Against the Tide* — 333.91
   Goldfarb, Ben. *Eager* — 333.95
   Williams, Terry Tempest. *Erosion* — 814
EROTIC FICTION WRITING
   Alterman, Sara Faith. *Let's Never Talk About This Again* — 616.8
ERRORS
   Brandreth, Gyles Daubeney. *Have You Eaten Grandma?* — 428
   Cairo, Alberto. *How Charts Lie* — 302.2
   Dobelli, Rolf. *The Art of Thinking Clearly* — 153.4
   Hallinan, Joseph T. *Why We Make Mistakes* — 153
   Mooallem, Jon. *Serious Face* — 814
   Parker, Matt. *Humble Pi* — 510
   Pinker, Steven. *Rationality* — 153.4
   Robison, Peter. ★*Flying Blind* — 338.7
   Schulz, Kathryn. *Being Wrong* — 121
   Sentilles, Sarah. *Stranger Care* — B
   Suvari, Mena. *The Great Peace* — B
   Yates, Kit. *The Math of Life and Death* — 510
Eruzione, Mike
   The Making of a Miracle — B
ERUZIONE, MIKE
   Eruzione, Mike. *The Making of a Miracle* — B
Ervin, Kristine S.
   Rabbit Heart — 364.152
ERVIN, KRISTINE S.
   Ervin, Kristine S. *Rabbit Heart* — 364.152
ERWIN, HENRY EUGENE, 1921-2002
   Erwin, Jon. *Beyond Valor* — B
Erwin, Jon
   Beyond Valor — B
★*The Escape Artist*. Freedland, Jonathan — 940.53
The Escape Artist. Fremont, Helen — B
The Escape Artists. Bascomb, Neal — 940.4
ESCAPE ARTISTS
   Posnanski, Joe. ★*The Life and Afterlife of Harry Houdini* — 793.8
Escape from Model Land. Thompson, Erica — 511
ESCAPED PRISONERS OF WAR
   Bascomb, Neal. *The Escape Artists* — 940.4
   Fox, Margalit. *The Confidence Men* — 940.4
   Millard, Candice. ★*Hero of the Empire* — 968.04
ESCAPES
   AL Samawi, Mohammed. *The Fox Hunt* — 953
   Albracht, William. *Abandoned in Hell* — 959.704
   Bascomb, Neal. *The Escape Artists* — 940.4
   Follett, Ken. *On Wings of Eagles* — 955
   Freedland, Jonathan. ★*The Escape Artist* — 940.53
   Frenkel, Francoise. *A Bookshop in Berlin* — B
   Izgil, Tahir Hamut. *Waiting to Be Arrested at Night* — B
   Jacobs, Harriet. ★*Incidents in the Life of a Slave Girl* — B
   Jaku, Eddie. ★*The Happiest Man on Earth* — B
   Jobb, Dean. *A Gentleman and a Thief* — 364.16
   Means, Brittany. *Hell If We Don't Change Our Ways* — B
   Merriman, Helena. ★*Tunnel 29* — 943
   Mikhaiil, Dunya. *The Beekeeper* — 956.7044
   Millard, Candice. ★*Hero of the Empire* — 968.04
   Minutaglio, Bill. *The Most Dangerous Man in America* — B
   Passarlay, Gulwali. *The Lightless Sky* — B
   Preston, Diana. *Paradise in Chains* — 996.18
   Rinder, Mike. ★*A Billion Years* — B
   Taing, Mae Bunseng. *Under the Naga Tail* — B
   Tjipombo, Tupa. *I Am Not Your Slave* — B
   Toorpakai, Maria. *A Different Kind of Daughter* — B
   White, Ralph. *Getting Out of Saigon* — 959.704
   Wise, Steven M. *Though the Heavens May Fall* — 342.42
   Young, Daniella Mestyanek. *Uncultured* — B
★*Escaping* The Delta. Wald, Elijah — B
ESCAPISM
   B., David. *Epileptic* — 741.5
ESCOFFIER, A. (AUGUSTE), 1846-1935
   Barr, Luke. *Ritz & Escoffier* — 920
Eslanda. Ransby, Barbara — B
Esmonde-White, Miranda
   Aging Backwards — 613.7
Espada, Martin
   ★*Floaters* — 811
ESPIONAGE
   Anderson, Scott. ★*The Quiet Americans* — 327.12
   Andrew, Christopher M. *The Secret World* — 327.1209
   Batalion, Judith. *The Light of Days* — 940.53
   Berg, Raffi. *Red Sea Spies* — 327.125694
   Brokhausen, Nick. *Whispers in the Tall Grass* — 959.704
   Coker, Margaret. *The Spymaster of Baghdad* — 956.7044
   Cunningham, Benjamin. *The Liar* — 327.1273
   Drabkin, Ronald. *Beverly Hills Spy* — 940.54
   Dugard, Martin. *Taking Paris* — 940.54
   Elnoury, Tamer. *American Radical* — B
   Fairweather, Jack. *The Volunteer* — B
   Friedman, Barry. ★*Unwarranted* — 344.7305
   Friedman, Matti. *Spies of No Country* — 327.12
   Harmon, Mark. *Ghosts of Honolulu* — 940.54
   Hemming, Henry. *Agents of Influence* — 940.54
   Hindley, Meredith. *Destination Casablanca* — 940.54
   Kean, Sam. *The Bastard Brigade* — 355.8
   Kix, Paul. *The Saboteur* — 940.53
   Lichtblau, Eric. *Return to the Reich* — B
   Lisle, John. *The Dirty Tricks Department* — 940.54
   Loftis, Larry. *Code Name* — B
   Macintyre, Ben. *Double Cross* — 940.54
   Magida, Arthur J. *Code Name Madeleine* — 940.54
   Maier, Thomas. *Mafia Spies* — 364.1060973
   Mazzeo, Tilar J. *Sisters in Resistance* — 945.091
   Merridale, Catherine. *Lenin on the Train* — B
   Mundy, Liza. ★*The Sisterhood* — 327.12
   Navarro, Joe. *Three Minutes to Doomsday* — B
   Ohler, Norman. *The Bohemians* — 940.53
   Olson, Lynne. ★*Madame Fourcade's Secret War* — B
   Popkin, Jim. *Code Name Blue Wren* — 327.12
   Purnell, Sonia. ★*A Woman of No Importance* — B
   Reynolds, Nicholas E. *Need to Know* — 940.54
   Richardson, Edmund. *The King's Shadow* — 958.1
   Rose, Sarah. *D-Day Girls* — 940.53
   Shapiro, Scott J. ★*Fancy Bear Goes Phishing* — 364.16
   Shultz, Richard H. *The Secret War Against Hanoi* — 959.704
   Talty, Stephan. *Agent Garbo* — 940.5
   Trahair, R. C. S. *Encyclopedia of Cold War Espionage, Spies, and Secret Operations 3rd Ed.* — 327.12
   Trimble, Lee. *Beyond the Call* — 940.54
   Vogel, Steve. *Betrayal in Berlin* — 327.1273043
   Waller, Douglas C. *Lincoln's Spies* — 973.7
   Walton, Calder. *Spies* — 327.1247
   Weiner, Tim. *The Folly and the Glory* — 327.73047
   Weiner, Tim. *Legacy of Ashes* — 327.1273009
   Wiehl, Lis W. *A Spy in Plain Sight* — 327.1247
Esposito, Jennifer
   Jennifer's Way Kitchen — 641.5
Espy, Willard R.
   Words to Rhyme With — 423

PUBLIC LIBRARY CORE COLLECTION: NONFICTION
Twentieth Edition

An Essay Concerning Human Understanding. Locke, John	121
ESSAY WRITING	
Addario, Lynsey. *Of Love & War*	779
McPhee, John. *Tabula Rasa; V.1*	818
Mehra, Nishta. *Brown, White, Black*	305.800973
Morrison, Toni. ★*The Source of Self-Regard*	814
Purnell, Carolyn. *The Sensational Past*	152.109
ESSAYISTS	
Bee, Vanessa A. *Home Bound*	B
Nelson, Maggie. ★*Like Love*	814
Shane, Scott. ★*Flee North*	973.7
ESSAYS	
Abdelmahmoud, Elamin. *Son of Elsewhere*	B
Achebe, Chinua. *The Education of a British-Protected Child*	B
Ackerman, Elliot. *Places and Names*	B
Acocella, Joan Ross. ★*The Bloodied Nightgown*	814
Adichie, Chimamanda Ngozi. *We Should All Be Feminists*	305.42
Adler, Tamar. *An Everlasting Meal*	641.5
Aguon, Julian. *No Country for Eight-Spot Butterflies*	305.89
Ahdoot, Dan. *Undercooked*	647.95
Alford, Henry. *And Then We Danced*	792.8
Alvis-Walker, Marcie. *Everybody Come Alive*	B
Amar, Akhil Reed. *The Constitution Today*	342.73
Amis, Martin. *The Rub of Time*	824
Anders, Charlie Jane. ★*Never Say You Can't Survive*	808.02
Angelou, Maya. *Letter to My Daughter*	814
Angelou, Maya. *Wouldn't Take Nothing for My Journey Now*	814
Arceneaux, Michael. *I Finally Bought Some Jordans*	306.76
Asim, Jabari. *We Can't Breathe*	305.896
Attenberg, Jami. *1000 Words*	808.02
Atwood, Margaret. *Burning Questions*	814
Atwood, Margaret. *In Other Worlds*	813
Auvinen, Karen. *Rough Beauty*	B
Backman, Fredrik. *Things My Son Needs to Know About the World*	B
Bailey, Issac J. *Why Didn't We Riot?*	305.800973
Bailey, Jennifer. *To My Beloveds*	261.8
Baldwin, James. ★*Collected Essays*	814
Baldwin, James. *I Am Not Your Negro*	323.1196
Baldwin, James. ★*Notes of a Native Son*	305.8
Barker, Elspeth. ★*Notes from the Henhouse*	828
Barnes, Julian. *Keeping an Eye Open*	709.04
Baszile, Natalie. *We Are Each Other's Harvest*	630.89
Batuman, Elif. *The Possessed*	891.7
Bauermeister, Erica. *House Lessons*	B
Belcourt, Billy-Ray. ★*A History of My Brief Body*	B
Berg, Anastasia. ★*What Are Children For?*	306.87
Berkow, Ira. *How Life Imitates Sports*	070.4
Bernard, Emily. *Black Is the Body*	305.48
Bernstein, Burton. ★*Leonard Bernstein*	B
Berry, Erica. *Wolfish*	152.4
Berry, Wendell. *The Art of Loading Brush*	338.10973
Berry, Wendell. *Imagination in Place*	814
Berry, Wendell. ★*The World-Ending Fire*	818
Biss, Eula. *Having and Being Had*	306.3
Bittman, Mark. *A Bone to Pick*	338.10973
Blay, Zeba. *Carefree Black Girls*	305.48
Bly, Robert. *More Than True*	398.2
Borges, Jorge Luis. *Selected Non-Fictions*	864
Bowden, Mark. *The Case of the Vanishing Blonde*	364.10973
Bragg, Rick. *Where I Come From*	975
Briggs, Julia. *Virginia Woolf*	823
Briggs, Kate. *This Little Art*	418
Brockman, John. *This Idea Is Brilliant*	500
Brown, Molly McCully. *Places I've Taken My Body*	B
Brunson, Quinta. *She Memes Well*	B
Bryant, Howard. *Full Dissidence*	306.20973
Busby, Jill Louise. *Unfollow Me*	305.08
Calvino, Italo. *Collection of Sand*	854
Camus, Albert. *The Myth of Sisyphus and Other Essays*	844
Camus, Albert. *The Rebel*	303.6
Capote, Truman. ★*Portraits and Observations*	814
Caro, Robert A. ★*Working*	B
Castillo, Elaine. ★*How to Read Now*	418
Chabon, Michael. *Bookends*	818
Chabon, Michael. *Maps and Legends*	801
Chabon, Michael. *Pops*	306.874
Chee, Alexander. ★*How to Write an Autobiographical Novel*	B
Chomsky, Noam. *Who Rules the World?*	327.73
Cisneros, Sandra. *A House of My Own*	B
Clark, John Lee. *Touch the Future*	B
Cleaver, Eldridge. *Soul on Ice*	B
Clinton, Hillary Rodham. *The Book of Gutsy Women*	920
Clinton, Hillary Rodham. *What Happened*	328.73
Coates, Ta-Nehisi. ★*We Were Eight Years in Power*	305.896
Coetzee, J. M. *Late Essays, 2006-2017*	824
Cohen, Roger. *An Affirming Flame*	071
Collins-Dexter, Brandi. *Black Skinhead*	324.2734
Cottom, Tressie McMillan. *Thick*	301
Crase, Douglas. *On Autumn Lake*	809
Crosley, Sloane. *I Was Told There'd Be Cake*	814
Crosley, Sloane. ★*Look Alive Out There*	814
Cusk, Rachel. *Coventry*	814
Dangarembga, Tsitsi. *Black and Female*	305.48
Darwin, Charles. ★*The Origin of Species by Means of Natural Selection, Or, the Preservation of Favored Races in the Struggle for Life*	575
Davis, Angela Y. *Abolition*	364.6
Dawkins, Richard. *Science in the Soul*	500
De Bres, Helena. *How to Be Multiple*	155.44
Devantez, Chelsea. ★*I Shouldn't Be Telling You This*	B
Diamant, Anita. ★*Period. End of Sentence*	612.6
Didion, Joan. ★*Let Me Tell You What I Mean*	814
Dillard, Annie. *The Abundance*	814
Dillard, Annie. *Pilgrim at Tinker Creek*	508
Dochartaigh, Kerri ni. *Cacophony of Bone*	B
Doniger, Wendy. *On Hinduism*	294.5
Downie, David. *A Taste of Paris*	394.1
Driver, Minnie. *Managing Expectations*	B
Du Bois, W. E. B. ★*The Souls of Black Folk*	973
Dubus, Andre. *Ghost Dogs*	814
Dylan, Bob. ★*The Philosophy of Modern Song*	782.42
Ehrenreich, Barbara. *Had I Known*	814
Einstein, Albert. *Ideas and Opinions*	081
Einstein, Albert. ★*A Stubbornly Persistent Illusion*	530.092
Ellis, Bret Easton. *White*	814
Ellis, Helen. *Bring Your Baggage and Don't Pack Light*	814
Ellis, Helen. *Southern Lady Code*	814
Ellison, Ralph. ★*The Collected Essays of Ralph Ellison*	814
Else, Jon. *True South*	305.800973
Ephron, Nora. *The Most of Nora Ephron*	814
Evans, Rachel Held. *Wholehearted Faith*	248.4
Evans, William. *Black Nerd Problems*	814.6
Faliveno, Melissa. *Tomboyland*	B
Feast, Fancy. *Naked*	792.7
Febos, Melissa. ★*Body Work*	808.06
Febos, Melissa. *Girlhood*	818
Felder, Deborah G. *The American Women's Almanac*	305.40973
Finkel, David. *Thank You for Your Service*	920
Fitzgerald, Isaac. *Dirtbag, Massachusetts*	B
Fleming, Renee. ★*Music and Mind*	615.8
Forman, James. *Locking Up Our Own*	364.973
Francis. *The Church of Mercy*	252
Franzen, Jonathan. *The End of the End of the Earth*	814
Franzen, Jonathan. *Farther Away*	814
Frazier, Ian. *Hogs Wild*	814
Frey, Kate. *Ground Rules*	635
Fumudoh, Ziwe. ★*Black Friend*	814
Gabbard, Krin. *Better Git It in Your Soul*	B
Gabbert, Elisa. *Any Person Is the Only Self*	814
Gaiman, Neil. *The View from the Cheap Seats*	824
Gawande, Atul. *Complications*	B
Gay, Ross. *The Book of (more) Delights*	814
Gay, Ross. *Inciting Joy*	814
Gay, Roxane. *Bad Feminist*	814
Gay, Roxane. ★*Opinions*	814
Gerard, Sarah. *Sunshine State*	814
Gerson, Fany. *Mexican Ice Cream*	641.86
Gierach, John. *All Fishermen Are Liars*	799.12
Gierach, John. *Dumb Luck and the Kindness of Strangers*	799.124
Gierach, John. *A Fly Rod of Your Own*	799.12
Ginsburg, Ruth Bader. ★*My Own Words*	347.73
Gluck, Louise. *American Originality*	814
Gopnik, Adam. *The Real Work*	153.9
Grass, Gunter. *Of All That Ends*	838
Gray, Jon. *Ghetto Gastro Black Power Kitchen*	641.5
Green, Jaime. *The Possibility of Life*	576.8
Greenfieldboyce, Nell. ★*Transient and Strange*	501

AUTHOR, TITLE, SERIES AND SUBJECT INDEX

Gregory, Dick. *Defining Moments in Black History*	973
Gregory, Dick. ★*The Essential Dick Gregory*	818
Griffin, Farah Jasmine. ★*In Search of a Beautiful Freedom*	814
Gunst, Kathy. *Rage Baking*	641.86
Gutowitz, Jill. *Girls Can Kiss Now*	814
Gutting, Gary. *What Philosophy Can Do*	100
Hanson, Victor Davis. *The Father of Us All*	355.0209
Harford, Tim. *50 Inventions That Shaped the Modern Economy*	609
Harriot, Michael. ★*Black AF History*	973
Harrison, Jim. *The Search for the Genuine*	814
Hart, Hannah. *Buffering*	B
Hauser, CJ. *The Crane Wife*	B
Havrilesky, Heather. *What If This Were Enough?*	152.4
Hawking, Stephen. ★*Black Holes and Baby Universes and Other Essays*	530.1
Heinrich, Bernd. *A Naturalist at Large*	508
Hitchens, Christopher. *The Four Horsemen*	211
Hochschild, Adam. *Lessons from a Dark Time*	909.82
Hodgman, John. *Medallion Status*	B
Hodgman, John. *Vacationland*	B
Hohn, Donovan. *The Inner Coast*	304.20973
Hollis, Edward. *The Secret Lives of Buildings*	720.9
Holt, Jim. ★*When Einstein Walked with Godel*	814
Hong, Cathy Park. *Minor Feelings*	305.48
Hood, Ann. *Kitchen Yarns*	641.5
hooks, bell. *Remembered Rapture*	808
Hopper, Jessica. *The First Collection of Criticism by a Living Female Rock Critic*	781.66
Hough, Lauren. *Leaving Isn't the Hardest Thing*	B
Hough, Stephen. *Rough Ideas*	786.2092
Houston, Pam. *Deep Creek*	814
Hunter-Gault, Charlayne. ★*My People*	305.48
Hurston, Zora Neale. ★*You Don't Know Us Negroes and Other Essays*	814
Hustvedt, Siri. *Mothers, Fathers, and Others*	814
Huxtable, Ada Louise. *On Architecture*	724
Hyden, Steven. *Twilight of the Gods*	781.6609
Ikpi, Bassey. *I'm Telling the Truth, but I'm Lying*	814
Imbler, Sabrina. *How Far the Light Reaches*	591.77
Irby, Samantha. ★*Quietly Hostile*	814
Irby, Samantha. *We Are Never Meeting in Real Life*	814
Isen, Tajja. *Some of My Best Friends*	305.8
Iyer, Pico. *A Beginner's Guide to Japan*	952.05
Jackson, Jenn M. ★*Black Women Taught Us*	305.48
Jackson, Shirley. *Let Me Tell You*	818
Jamison, Leslie. *The Empathy Exams*	813
Jamison, Leslie. *Make It Scream, Make It Burn*	814
Jefferson, Thomas. *Writings*	973.3
Jeppesen, Travis. *See You Again in Pyongyang*	951.93
Jun, Tasha. ★*Tell Me the Dream Again*	248
Junger, Sebastian. *Fire*	909.82
Kakutani, Michiko. *Ex Libris*	028
Keefe, Patrick Radden. ★*Rogues*	364.16
Kenan, Randall. *Black Folk Could Fly*	813
Kendall, Mikki. *Hood Feminism*	305.420973
Khakpour, Porochista. *Brown Album*	304.8
Khan, Yasmin. *Ripe Figs*	641.595
Kimmerer, Robin Wall. ★*Braiding Sweetgrass*	304.2
Klay, Phil. *Uncertain Ground*	359.9
Klosterman, Chuck. *But What If We're Wrong*	909.83
Klosterman, Chuck. ★*The Nineties*	306.0973
Krakauer, Jon. *Classic Krakauer*	814
Kumar, Priyanka. *Conversations with Birds*	598
Kundera, Milan. *Encounter*	809
Lahiri, Jhumpa. *Translating Myself and Others*	418
Lamott, Anne. ★*Dusk, Night, Dawn*	B
Lamott, Anne. *Small Victories*	248
Lamott, Anne. ★*Somehow*	814
LaPointe, Sasha taqwseblu. *Thunder Song*	814
LaRue, James. ★*On Censorship*	025.2
Lavery, Daniel M. *Dear Prudence*	170
Lavery, Daniel M. *Something That May Shock and Discredit You*	814
Laymon, Kiese. *How to Slowly Kill Yourself and Others in America*	814.6
Le Guin, Ursula K. *No Time to Spare*	814
Le Guin, Ursula K. *Words Are My Matter*	818
Leon, Donna. *My Venice and Other Essays*	945
Leopold, Aldo. ★*A Sand County Almanac & Other Writings on Ecology and Conservation*	814
Lepore, Jill. ★*The Deadline*	814
Lewis, Jenifer. *Walking in My Joy*	B
Li, Yiyun. *Dear Friend, from My Life I Write to You in Your Life*	B
Liebling, A. J. ★*The Sweet Science*	796.83
Lightman, Alan P. *The Discoveries*	509
Lippman, Laura. *My Life as a Villainess*	B
Lopez, Barry Holstun. ★*Of Wolves and Men*	599.773
Lorde, Audre. ★*The Selected Works of Audre Lorde*	814
Lorde, Audre. *Sister Outsider*	814
Luiselli, Valeria. *Tell Me How It Ends*	305.23086
Macdonald, Helen. ★*Vesper Flights*	508
Mamet, David. *True and False*	792
Mandela, Nelson. *In His Own Words*	B
Mankell, Henning. *Quicksand*	B
Mantel, Hilary. *Mantel Pieces*	824.914
McCann, Colum. *Letters to a Young Writer*	808.02
McCullough, David G. ★*The American Spirit*	973
McDermott, Alice. *What About the Baby?*	814
McPherson, James M. *Drawn with the Sword*	973.7
McWhorter, John H. *Talking Back, Talking Black*	427
Messud, Claire. *Kant's Little Prussian Head and Other Reasons Why I Write*	B
Miller, Kei. *Things I Have Withheld*	814
Minami, Jikisai. *It's Okay Not to Look for the Meaning of Life*	158.1
Montell, Amanda. ★*The Age of Magical Overthinking*	153.4
Mooallem, Jon. *Serious Face*	814
Moore, Kathleen Dean. *Earth's Wild Music*	576.8
Moore, Lorrie. *See What Can Be Done*	801
Moran, Caitlin. *More Than a Woman*	B
Morrison, Toni. ★*The Origin of Others*	809
Morrison, Toni. *Playing in the Dark*	810.9
Moss, Jeremiah. *Feral City*	B
Muir, John. *Nature Writings*	508
Munroe, Randall. *How To*	500
Murakami, Haruki. ★*Novelist as a Vocation*	895.64
Myers, David G. *How Do We Know Ourselves?*	155.2
Napier, Erin. *Heirloom Rooms*	747
Nelson, Maggie. ★*Like Love*	814
Nevins, Sheila. *You Don't Look Your Age*	B
Nezhukumatathil, Aimee. *Bite by Bite*	641.3
Nezhukumatathil, Aimee. *World of Wonders*	590
Noah, Trevor. *Born a Crime*	B
Norton, Jack. *The Jail Is Everywhere*	365
Nye, Bill. *Everything All at Once*	153.4
O'Farrell, Maggie. *I Am, I Am, I Am*	B
Obama, Michelle. *American Grown*	635.09
Olds, Sally. ★*People Who Lunch*	824
Oliver, Mary. ★*Upstream*	814
Orenstein, Peggy. *Don't Call Me Princess*	305.42
Orlean, Susan. *On Animals*	590
Oyler, Lauren. *No Judgment*	814
Ozick, Cynthia. *Critics, Monsters, Fanatics, and Other Literary Essays*	801
Painter, Nell Irvin. ★*I Just Keep Talking*	814
Parke, Henry C. *The Greatest Westerns Ever Made and the People Who Made Them*	791.43
Parker, James. ★*Get Me Through the Next Five Minutes*	158.1
Parker, Morgan. *You Get What You Pay For*	305.896
Patchett, Ann. ★*These Precious Days*	814
Patchett, Ann. *This Is the Story of a Happy Marriage*	B
Pellegrino, Charles R. *To Hell and Back*	940.54
Percy, Benjamin. *Thrill Me*	808.3
Perkins, Nichole. *Sometimes I Trip on How Happy We Could Be*	B
Pesca, Mike. *Upon Further Review*	796
Petri, Alexandra. *Alexandra Petri's US History*	817
Petri, Alexandra. *Nothing Is Wrong and Here Is Why*	973.933
Phillips, Maya. *Nerd*	302.23
Philpott, Mary Laura. *Bomb Shelter*	B
Pinckney, Darryl. *Busted in New York and Other Essays*	305.800973
Pipher, Mary Bray. *A Life in Light*	B
Porizkova, Paulina. *No Filter*	B
Pratchett, Terry. *A Slip of the Keyboard*	824
Prose, Francine. *What to Read and Why*	028
Pyle, Robert Michael. *Nature Matrix*	508
Qashu, Sayed. *Native*	892.4
Questlove. *Music Is History*	782.42164
Quinn, Tallu Schuyler. *What We Wish Were True*	B
Rabinowitz, Dorothy. *No Crueler Tyrannies*	345.73
Rademacher, Tom. *It Won't Be Easy*	B
Rankine, Claudia. ★*Citizen*	814

PUBLIC LIBRARY CORE COLLECTION: NONFICTION
Twentieth Edition

Rankine, Claudia. ★*Just Us*	305.896
Rannells, Andrew. *Uncle of the Year*	B
Ratajkowski, Emily. ★*My Body*	B
Rather, Dan. *What Unites Us*	323.6
Ray, Victor. *On Critical Race Theory*	305.8
Reed, Julia. *Dispatches from the Gilded Age*	B
Reed, Shannon. *Why We Read*	028
Reichl, Ruth. *My Kitchen Year*	641.5
Remnick, David. *Holding the Note*	781.64
Renkl, Margaret. *The Comfort of Crows*	814.6
Retta. *So Close to Being the Sh*t, Y'all Don't Even Know*	B
Rich, Adrienne. *Essential Essays*	814
Robinson, Phoebe. *Please Don't Sit on My Bed in Your Outside Clothes*	818
Rogen, Seth. ★*Yearbook*	B
Rose, Jacqueline. *On Violence and on Violence Against Women*	362.88
Ross, Dax-Devlon. *Letters to My White Male Friends*	305.8
Rothfeld, Becca. ★*All Things Are Too Small*	814
Rovelli, Carlo. *There Are Places in the World Where Rules Are Less Important Than Kindness*	500
Rushdie, Salman. *Languages of Truth*	824
Russo, Richard. *The Destiny Thief*	814
Rybczynski, Witold. *Mysteries of the Mall*	720
Sabatini Sloan, Aisha. *Dreaming of Ramadi in Detroit*	814
Sachs, Harvey. *Ten Masterpieces of Music*	780.9
Sacks, Oliver. ★*Everything in Its Place*	B
Sacks, Oliver. *Gratitude*	306.9
Sagan, Carl. *Billions and Billions*	500
Salle, David. *How to See*	709.04
Salter, James. *Don't Save Anything*	818
Sanchez, Erika L. *Crying in the Bathroom*	B
Sanders, Chad. *Black Magic*	305.896
Sando, Mike. *The Football 100*	796.332
Sartre, Jean-Paul. *We Have Only This Life to Live*	848
Sato, Hiroaki. *On Haiku*	809.1
Savage, Jodi M. *The Death of a Jaybird*	B
Scalzi, John. *Don't Live for Your Obituary*	808.02
Schechter, Harold. ★*Ripped from the Headlines!*	791.43
Schneider, Amy. *In the Form of a Question*	B
Schumer, Amy. *The Girl with the Lower Back Tattoo*	B
Sedaris, David. ★*The Best of Me*	818
Sedaris, David. *Calypso*	814
Sedaris, David. ★*Happy-Go-Lucky*	814
Seitz, Matt Zoller. *The Sopranos Sessions*	791.45
Sepinwall, Alan. ★*TV (the Book)*	791.45
Shange, Ntozake. ★*Sing a Black Girl's Song*	818
Shankle, Melanie. *Church of the Small Things*	248.8
Shapiro, Ari. ★*The Best Strangers in the World*	B
Shapland, Jenn. ★*Thin Skin*	814
Sharlet, Jeff. ★*The Undertow*	322
Sharma, Nina. *The Way You Make Me Feel*	B
Shepard, Jim. *The Tunnel at the End of the Light*	791.43
Silver, Johanna. *The Bold Dry Garden*	635.9
Simon, Matt. *The Wasp That Brainwashed the Caterpillar*	578.4
Slate, Jenny. *Little Weirds*	B
Smith, Emma. *This Is Shakespeare*	822.33
Smith, Mychal Denzel. *Stakes Is High*	973.933
Smith, Zadie. ★*Feel Free*	824
Smith, Zadie. *Intimations*	824
So, Anthony Veasna. ★*Songs on Endless Repeat*	814
Sol, Adam. *How a Poem Moves*	808.1
Solnit, Rebecca. *Call Them by Their True Names*	303.3
Solnit, Rebecca. *Men Explain Things to Me*	305.42
Solnit, Rebecca. *The Mother of All Questions*	305.42
Somerstein, Rachel. ★*Invisible Labor*	618.8
Sontag, Susan. *At the Same Time*	814
Soyinka, Wole. *Of Africa*	960
Spence, Annie. *Dear Fahrenheit 451*	028.9
Srinivasan, Amia. *The Right to Sex*	305.42
Stein, Gertrude. *Writings, 1932-1946*	818
Steinem, Gloria. *Outrageous Acts and Everyday Rebellions*	305.42
Steinem, Gloria. *The Truth Will Set You Free, but First It Will Piss You Off*	305.42
Stewart, Ian. *Professor Stewart's Casebook of Mathematical Mysteries*	793.74
Stone, Lillian. ★*Everybody's Favorite*	814.6
Strobel, Lee. *The Case for Grace*	234
Styron, William. *My Generation*	814
Tamblyn, Amber. ★*Era of Ignition*	B
Taussig, Rebekah. *Sitting Pretty*	B
Tea, Michelle. *Against Memoir*	B
Teicher, Craig Morgan. *We Begin in Gladness*	808.1
Thomas, Etan. *We Matter*	796.08
Thomas, R. Eric. ★*Congratulations, the Best Is Over!*	B
Thomas, R. Eric. *Here for It*	B
Thompson, Wright. *The Cost of These Dreams*	B
Thoreau, Henry David. ★*Collected Essays and Poems*	818
Thurman, Judith. ★*A Left-Handed Woman*	814
Tobar, Hector. ★*Our Migrant Souls*	305.868
Tolentino, Jia. ★*Trick Mirror*	973.93
Tomlinson, Tommy. *The Elephant in the Room*	B
Trillin, Calvin. *The Lede*	071
Union, Gabrielle. *We're Going to Need More Wine*	B
Union, Gabrielle. *You Got Anything Stronger?*	B
Updike, John. *Always Looking*	700
V. ★*Reckoning*	814
Van Ness, Jonathan. *Love That Story*	791.4502
Vargas Llosa, Mario. *Sabers and Utopias*	980.03
Villarreal, Vanessa Anglica. *Magical/Realism*	814
Villoro, Juan. *God Is Round*	796.334
Virts, Terry. *How to Astronaut*	629.45
Vonnegut, Kurt. ★*A Man Without a Country*	818
Wainaina, Binyavanga. ★*How to Write About Africa*	814
Walker, Alice. *The Cushion in the Road*	814
Wallace, David Foster. *Consider the Lobster*	814
Waters, John. *Mr. Know-It-All*	814
Waters, John. *Role Models*	B
Weinman, Sarah. ★*Unspeakable Acts*	364.1
West, Lindy. *The Witches Are Coming*	305.420973
White, E. B. *Essays of E.B. White*	814
Williams, Marlena. *Night Mother*	791.43
Williams, Terry Tempest. *Erosion*	814
Wills, Garry. *Certain Trumpets*	303.3
Wiman, Christian. *Zero at the Bone*	818
Wise, Tim J. *Dispatches from the Race War*	305.8
Wong, Alice. ★*Year of the Tiger*	B
Woolf, Virginia. *The London Scene*	942.1
Wu, Simon. *Dancing on My Own*	700.1
Yong, Sable. *Die Hot with a Vengeance*	646.7
Young, Damon. ★*What Doesn't Kill You Makes You Blacker*	B
Zhu, Mimi. *Be Not Afraid of Love*	152.4
Essays and Reviews. Poe, Edgar Allan	809
Essays of E.B. White. White, E. B.	814
The **Essence** of Style. DeJean, Joan E.	391
The **Essential** Book of Vegan Bakes. Jade, Holly	641.5
★**Essential** Cinema. Rosenbaum, Jonathan	791.43
★The **Essential** Diabetes Book. Castro, M. Regina	616.4
★The **Essential** Dick Gregory. Gregory, Dick	818
Essential Emeril. Lagasse, Emeril	641.5
Essential Essays. Rich, Adrienne	814
★The **Essential** Garden Design Workbook. Alexander, Rosemary	712
The **Essential** Guide to Breastfeeding. Neifert, Marianne R.	649
★The **Essential** Gwendolyn Brooks. Brooks, Gwendolyn	811
★The **Essential** June Jordan. Jordan, June	811
Essential Knit Sweaters. Ludwig, Frauke	746.43
Essential Labor. Garbes, Angela	306.874
★The **Essential** New York Times Cook Book. Hesser, Amanda	641.5
Essential Pepin. Pepin, Jacques	641.594
The **Essential** Poems of Jim Harrison. Harrison, Jim	811
Essential Pruning Techniques. Brown, George E.	635.9
The **Essential** Rumi. Jalal al-Din Rumi, Maulana	891
Essentialism. McKeown, Greg	153.8
★**Essentials** of Classic Italian Cooking. Hazan, Marcella	641.594
Essin, Christin	
Stage Designers in Early Twentieth-Century America	792.02
ESSINGER, ANNA	
Cadbury, Deborah. *The School That Escaped from the Nazis*	940.53
Essinger, James	
Ada's Algorithm	B
Estes, Nick	
Our History Is the Future	978.004
Esty, Katharaine C.	
Eightysomethings	612.6
Etched in Sand. Calcaterra, Regina	B
Eteraz, Ali	
Children of Dust	B
The **Eternal** City. Addis, Ferdinand	945.6
Eternal Enemies. Zagajewski, Adam	891.8

AUTHOR, TITLE, SERIES AND SUBJECT INDEX

Eternal Life. Spong, John Shelby — 236
ETERNITY
  Borges, Jorge Luis. *Selected Non-Fictions* — 864
  Eire, Carlos M. N. *A Very Brief History of Eternity* — 236
  Jennings, Ken. ★*100 Places to See After You Die* — 202
  Le Guin, Ursula K. *So Far so Good* — 811
  Spong, John Shelby. *Eternal Life* — 236
  Wiman, Christian. *He Held Radical Light* — 814
Ethel Rosenberg. Sebba, Anne — B
Etheridge, Melissa
  Talking to My Angels — B
ETHERIDGE, MELISSA
  Etheridge, Melissa. *Talking to My Angels* — B
ETHICAL PROBLEMS
  Zapruder, Alexandra. *Twenty-Six Seconds* — 973.922092
ETHICS
  Aristotle. ★*Nicomachean Ethics* — 171
  Armstrong, Karen. *Fields of Blood* — 201
  Armstrong, Karen. *Twelve Steps to a Compassionate Life* — 177
  Austen, Ben. *Correction* — 364.6
  Barber, William J. *We Are Called to Be a Movement* — 261.8
  Bignon, Guillaume. *Confessions of a French Atheist* — 239
  Brooks, David. ★*How to Know a Person* — 158.2
  Brooks, David. ★*The Second Mountain* — 302
  Carter, Iain. *Golf Wars* — 796.352
  Coles, Robert. *Lives of Moral Leadership* — 170
  Dederer, Claire. ★*Monsters* — 700.1
  Eilenberger, Wolfram. *Time of the Magicians* — 920
  Elwood, Phil. *All the Worst Humans* — 659.2
  Engelhart, Katie. *The Inevitable* — 179.7
  Griffith, R. Marie. *Moral Combat* — 261.8
  Harari, Yuval N. *Homo Deus* — 909.83
  Held, Shai. *Judaism Is About Love* — 296.3
  Hendrickson, Debra. ★*The Air They Breathe* — 363.7
  Hitchens, Christopher. *The Four Horsemen* — 211
  Holland, Tom. *Dominion* — 261
  Husain, Ed. ★*The House of Islam* — 297
  Kalanithi, Paul. ★*When Breath Becomes Air* — B
  Kara, Siddharth. *Cobalt Red* — 338.2
  Kim, Anne. ★*Poverty for Profit* — 302.5
  Le Guin, Ursula K. *No Time to Spare* — 814
  Lewis, C. S. *Mere Christianity* — 230
  Lisle, John. *The Dirty Tricks Department* — 940.54
  Marcus Aurelius. ★*Meditations* — 188
  Maroney, Tyler. *The Modern Detective* — 658.4
  Martin, Clancy W. *How Not to Kill Yourself* — 362.28
  McLaren, Brian D. *Do I Stay Christian?* — 270.8
  Meacham, Jon. ★*And There Was Light* — B
  Mueller, Tom. *Crisis of Conscience* — 364.16
  Paxson, Margaret. *The Plateau* — 362.87
  Peterson, Dale. *The Moral Lives of Animals* — 156
  Phillips, Adam. *On Giving up* — 158.2
  Phillips, Carl. ★*Then the War* — 811
  Phillips, Collette A. M. *The Includers* — 658.4
  Price, Reynolds. *A Serious Way of Wondering* — 241
  Prideaux, Sue. *I Am Dynamite!* — B
  Ruttenberg, Danya. *On Repentance and Repair* — 202
  Sandel, Michael J. *Justice* — 172
  Sapolsky, Robert M. *Determined* — 123
  Shahvisi, Arianne. *Arguing for a Better World* — 170
  Skach, C. L. *How to Be a Citizen* — 323.6
  Stanley, Brian. *Christianity in the Twentieth Century* — 270.8
  Suleyman, Mustafa. *The Coming Wave* — 303.48
  Sullivan, Meghan. *The Good Life Method* — 170
  Tenzin Priyadarshi. *Running Toward Mystery* — B
  Vanderbes, Jennifer. *Wonder Drug* — 615
  Wasik, Bill. ★*Our Kindred Creatures* — 179
  Weiner, Eric. *Ben & Me* — B
  Wiman, Christian. *Zero at the Bone* — 818
  Woolfson, Esther. *Between Light and Storm* — 599.93
  Zakaria, Rafia. *Against White Feminism* — 305.42
  Zimberoff, Larissa. *Technically Food* — 613.2
  Zuckerman, Phil. *Living the Secular Life* — 211
ETHICS, JEWISH
  Leibovitz, Liel. ★*How the Talmud Can Change Your Life* — 296.1
ETHIOPIA
  Johanson, Donald C. *Lucy* — 569

ETHIOPIAN PEOPLE
  Berg, Raffi. *Red Sea Spies* — 327.125694
ETHNIC GROUPS
  Kurlansky, Mark. *The Basque History of the World* — 946
  Mackintosh-Smith, Tim. *Arabs* — 909.04
ETHNIC IDENTITY
  Abdelmahmoud, Elamin. *Son of Elsewhere* — B
  Baylor, Elgin. *Hang Time* — B
  Bayoumi, Moustafa. *How Does It Feel to Be a Problem?* — 305.892
  Bernard, Emily. *Black Is the Body* — 305.48
  Chang, Tina. *Hybrida* — 811
  Choy, Catherine Ceniza. ★*Asian American Histories of the United States* — 973
  Chude-Sokei, Louis Onuorah. *Floating in a Most Peculiar Way* — 979.4
  Collins-Dexter, Brandi. *Black Skinhead* — 324.2734
  Davis, Thomas J. *History of African Americans* — 973
  Gates, Henry Louis. *The Black Box* — 908
  Gayle, Caleb. *We Refuse to Forget* — 975.004
  Gomez, Laura E. ★*Inventing Latinos* — 305.868
  Guida-Richards, Melissa. *What White Parents Should Know About Transracial Adoption* — 362.734
  Huang, Eddie. *Fresh off the Boat* — B
  Isen, Tajja. *Some of My Best Friends* — 305.8
  Jun, Tasha. ★*Tell Me the Dream Again* — 248
  Kendi, Ibram X. ★*How to Be an Antiracist* — 305.8
  LaPointe, Sasha taqwseblu. *Thunder Song* — 814
  McBride, James. *The Color of Water* — B
  Mojica Rodriguez, Prisca Dorcas. *For Brown Girls with Sharp Edges and Tender Hearts* — 305.48
  Nawaz, Zarqa. *Laughing All the Way to the Mosque* — 791.45028
  Nguyen, Viet Thanh. ★*A Man of Two Faces* — B
  Norris, Michele. ★*Our Hidden Conversations* — 305
  Nye, Naomi Shihab. *The Tiny Journalist* — 811
  Prescod, Danielle. *Token Black Girl* — B
  Rose, Jacqueline. *On Violence and on Violence Against Women* — 362.88
  Royster, Francesca T. *Choosing Family* — B
  Samaha, Albert. *Concepcion* — 929
  Shehadeh, Raja. ★*We Could Have Been Friends, My Father and I* — B
  So, Anthony Veasna. ★*Songs on Endless Repeat* — 814
  Taffa, Deborah Jackson. ★*Whiskey Tender* — B
  Thompson, Tracy. *The New Mind of the South* — 305.800975
  Tobar, Hector. ★*Our Migrant Souls* — 305.868
  Wagner, Alex. *Futureface* — B
  Wilbur, Matika. *Project 562* — 970.004
  Yoshino, Kenji. *Say the Right Thing* — 305.3
ETHNIC NEIGHBORHOODS
  Hahn, Emanuel. *Koreatown Dreaming* — 979.4
ETHNIC POLICY
  Kuper, Adam. *The Museum of Other People* — 305.8
ETHNICITY
  Wilkerson, Isabel. ★*Caste* — 305.5
ETHNOBOTANISTS
  Davis, Wade. *One River* — 581.6
  Quave, Cassandra Leah. *The Plant Hunter* — 581.6
ETHNOBOTANY
  Davis, Wade. *One River* — 581.6
  Quave, Cassandra Leah. *The Plant Hunter* — 581.6
ETHNOLOGY
  Diamond, Jared M. *Guns, Germs, and Steel* — 303.4
  Hoffman, Carl. ★*Savage Harvest* — 995.1
ETHNOPSYCHOLOGY
  Levi-Strauss, Claude. ★*The Savage Mind* — 155.8
ETIQUETTE
  Alkon, Amy. *Good Manners for Nice People* — 395
  Baron, Dennis E. *What's Your Pronoun?* — 425.55
  Berman, Lea. *Treating People Well* — 395
  Davis, Geena. *Dying of Politeness* — B
  Dresser, Norine. *Multicultural Manners* — 395
  Forni, Pier Massimo. *The Civility Solution* — 395
  Gilliam, Fatimah. *Race Rules* — 305.8
  Goodman, Ruth. *How to Behave Badly in Elizabethan England* — 942.05
  Post, Lizzie. *Emily Post's Etiquette* — 395
  Post, Lizzie. *Emily Post's Etiquette* — 395
Etter, Lauren
  ★*The Devil's Playbook* — 338.7
ETYMOLOGY
  Bragg, Melvyn. ★*The Adventure of English* — 420
  Crystal, David. *The Story of English in 100 Words* — 422
  Winchester, Simon. *The Professor and the Madman* — 423

PUBLIC LIBRARY CORE COLLECTION: NONFICTION
Twentieth Edition

Euchner, Charles C.
   Nobody Turn Me Around — 975.3
Eugene Onegin. Pushkin, Aleksandr Sergeevich — 891.71
EUGENICS
   Brookwood, Marilyn. *The Orphans of Davenport* — 305.231
   Cohen, Adam. ★*Imbeciles* — 344.7304
   Collins, Martha. *Admit One* — 811
   Nourse, Victoria F. *In Reckless Hands* — 344.7304
   Oelhafen, Ingrid von. *Hitler's Stolen Children* — B
   Okrent, Daniel. *The Guarded Gate* — 344.73
   Rutherford, Adam. *Control* — 363.9
★*Eunice*. McNamara, Eileen — B
Europe. Flannery, Tim F. — 508.4
EUROPE
   Aly, Gotz. *Europe Against the Jews* — 305.892
   Asbridge, Thomas S. ★*The Crusades* — 909.07
   Barzun, Jacques. *From Dawn to Decadence* — 940.2
   Bowker, Gordon. ★*James Joyce* — B
   Bown, Stephen R. *Merchant Kings* — 338.8
   Brighton, Terry. *Patton, Montgomery, Rommel* — B
   Cahill, Thomas. *How the Irish Saved Civilization* — 941.501
   Camus, Albert. *Resistance, Rebellion, and Death* — 844
   Carter, Miranda. *George, Nicholas and Wilhelm* — 940.3
   Clay, Catrine. *King, Kaiser, Tsar* — B
   Cornwell, John. *Hitler's Pope* — B
   Cox, Michael. *Zonal Marking* — 796
   Crowley, Roger. *1453* — 949.61
   Curran, Andrew S. *Diderot and the Art of Thinking Freely* — 194
   De Hamel, Christopher. ★*Meetings with Remarkable Manuscripts* — 091
   Drape, Joe. *Black Maestro* — B
   Dugard, Martin. *Taking Berlin* — 940.54
   Edsel, Robert M. *The Monuments Men* — 940.54
   Egan, Timothy. *A Pilgrimage to Eternity* — 263
   Evans, Richard J. *The Pursuit of Power* — 940.2
   Figes, Orlando. *The Europeans* — 920
   Finkel, Michael. *The Art Thief* — 364.1628
   Flannery, Tim F. *Europe* — 508.4
   Friedman, George. *Flashpoints* — 940.56
   Gies, Joseph. *Life in a Medieval Castle* — 940.1
   Gill, Anton. *Art Lover* — B
   Grayling, A. C. *The Age of Genius* — 940.2
   Guibert, Emmanuel. *Alan's War* — 741.5
   Hastings, Max. *Operation Chastise* — 940.54
   Hirst, J. B. *The Shortest History of Europe* — 940
   Jackson, Julian. *De Gaulle* — B
   Jaku, Eddie. ★*The Happiest Man on Earth* — B
   Jones, Dan. *Crusaders* — 909.07
   Jordan, Jonathan W. *Brothers, Rivals, Victors* — 940.54
   Joyce, Patrick. *Remembering Peasants* — 305.5
   Judt, Tony. *Postwar* — 940.55
   Kelly, John. *The Great Mortality* — 614.5
   Kershaw, Alex. *Against All Odds* — 940.54
   Kertzer, David I. *The Pope Who Would Be King* — 282.092
   Krause, Johannes. *A Short History of Humanity* — 599.9
   Larson, Erik. ★*Dead Wake* — 940.4
   Lowe, Keith. *Savage Continent* — 940.55
   Lower, Wendy. *Hitler's Furies* — 940.53
   Mac Sweeney, Naoise. *The West* — 909
   Marton, Kati. ★*The Chancellor* — B
   Maurer, Kevin. *Damn Lucky* — 940.54
   Mazower, Mark. *The Greek Revolution* — 949.5
   McKean, David. *Watching Darkness Fall* — 940.53
   Morris, Ian. *Geography Is Destiny* — 941
   Nasaw, David. *The Last Million* — 940.53
   Nicolson, Adam. *Why Homer Matters* — 883
   Olson, Lynne. *Last Hope Island* — 940.53
   Paxton, Robert O. *The Anatomy of Fascism* — 320.53
   Pettegree, Andrew. *The Book in the Renaissance* — 070.5
   Phillips, Timothy. *Retracing the Iron Curtain* — 909.82
   Preston, Diana. *Eight Days at Yalta* — 940.53
   Ramirez, Janina. *Femina* — 940.1
   Saldana, Stephanie. *What We Remember Will Be Saved* — 362.7
   Schwarz, Geraldine. *Those Who Forget* — 940.53
   Smyth, Adam. *The Book-Makers* — 686.2
   Steil, Benn. ★*The Marshall Plan* — 338.91
   Svensson, Patrik. *The Book of Eels* — 597
   Taylor, Fred. *1939* — 940.53
   Tuchman, Barbara W. *The Proud Tower* — 909.82

Umar, Ousman. *North to Paradise* — B
Warren, Rosanna. *Max Jacob* — B
Winters, Richard D. *Beyond Band of Brothers* — B
Europe Against the Jews. Aly, Gotz — 305.892
EUROPEAN AMERICAN MEN
   Archibald, John. *Shaking the Gates of Hell* — B
   Neiman, Garrett. *Rich White Men* — 305.5
   Oluo, Ijeoma. *Mediocre* — 305.310973
   Ross, Dax-Devlon. *Letters to My White Male Friends* — 305.8
   Shane, Scott. ★*Flee North* — 973.7
EUROPEAN AMERICAN WOMEN
   Darby, Seyward. ★*Sisters in Hate* — 305.800973
EUROPEAN AMERICANS
   DiAngelo, Robin J. *White Fragility* — 305.8
   Enss, Chris. *Mochi's War* — B
   Fischer, David Hackett. *African Founders* — 973
   Ford, Lacy K. *Deliver Us from Evil* — 973.7
   Griffin, Chante. *Loving Your Black Neighbor as Yourself* — 261
   Hamalainen, Pekka. *Indigenous Continent* — 970.004
   Horn, James P. P. *Land as God Made It* — 975.5
   Hyde, Anne Farrar. ★*Born of Lakes and Plains* — 978
   Isenberg, Nancy. *White Trash* — 305.5
   McDonnell, Michael. *Masters of Empire* — 977.4
   Morrison, Toni. *Playing in the Dark* — 810.9
   Mort, T. A. *Thieves' Road* — 978.3
   Murray, Charles A. *Coming Apart* — 305.8
   Row, Jess. *White Flights* — 813
   Saad, Layla F. ★*Me and White Supremacy* — 305.809
   Seidule, Ty. *Robert E. Lee and Me* — 973.7
   Sharfstein, Daniel J. ★*Thunder in the Mountains* — 979.5
   Tyson, Timothy B. *Blood Done Sign My Name* — 975.6
EUROPEAN HISTORY
   Ackerman, Diane. ★*The Zookeeper's Wife* — 940.53
   Albright, Madeleine Korbel. *Prague Winter* — 943.71
   Aleksievich, Svetlana. *Last Witnesses* — 940.53
   Aleksievich, Svetlana. ★*The Unwomanly Face of War* — 940.53
   Alexander, Amir R. *Infinitesimal* — 511
   Aly, Gotz. *Europe Against the Jews* — 305.892
   Ambrose, Stephen E. *Citizen Soldiers* — 940.54
   Applebaum, Anne. ★*Red Famine* — 947.708
   Asbrink, Elisabeth. *And in the Vienna Woods the Trees Remain* — B
   Askwith, Richard. *Unbreakable* — B
   Atkinson, Rick. *The Day of Battle* — 940.54
   Barzun, Jacques. *From Dawn to Decadence* — 940.2
   Batalion, Judith. *The Light of Days* — 940.53
   Berg, Mary. *The Diary of Mary Berg* — B
   Bergreen, Laurence. *Marco Polo* — B
   Bjarnason, Egill. *How Iceland Changed the World* — 949.12
   Bown, Stephen R. *Merchant Kings* — 338.8
   Broers, Michael. *Napoleon* — 944.05
   Brown, Nancy Marie. *The Real Valkyrie* — 948
   Castor, Helen. *Joan of Arc* — B
   Chiger, Krystyna. *The Girl in the Green Sweater* — B
   Churchill, Winston. *The Grand Alliance* — 940.53
   Churchill, Winston. *Their Finest Hour* — 940.53
   Churchill, Winston. *Triumph and Tragedy* — 940.53
   Cornwell, John. *Hitler's Pope* — B
   Crasnianski, Tania. *The Children of Nazis* — 943.086
   Darnton, Robert. *The Revolutionary Temper* — 944
   De Hamel, Christopher. *The Manuscripts Club* — 091
   De Hamel, Christopher. ★*Meetings with Remarkable Manuscripts* — 091
   Dodds Pennock, Caroline. ★*On Savage Shores* — 970.004
   Eisen, Norman L. *The Last Palace* — 920
   Epstein, Franci. *Franci's War* — B
   Fauber, L. S. *Heaven on Earth* — B
   Fishman, David E. *The Book Smugglers* — 940.53
   Flannery, Tim F. *Europe* — 508.4
   Frankopan, Peter. *The First Crusade* — 956
   French, Howard W. *Born in Blackness* — B
   Friedman, George. *Flashpoints* — 940.56
   Gatrell, Peter. *The Unsettling of Europe* — 304.8
   Gilbert, Martin. *The Second World War* — 940.53
   Goldstone, Nancy Bazelon. *In the Shadow of the Empress* — 920
   Goodrich, Frances. *The Diary of Anne Frank* — 812
   Greenblatt, Stephen. ★*The Swerve* — 940.2
   Guarnere, William. *Brothers in Battle, Best of Friends* — B
   Harding, Luke. *Invasion* — 947.7
   Hastings, Max. *Catastrophe 1914* — 940.3

AUTHOR, TITLE, SERIES AND SUBJECT INDEX

Hemon, Aleksandar. *My Parents*	814
Henderson, Bruce B. *Sons and Soldiers*	940.53
Herman, Arthur. *The Viking Heart*	948
Herrin, Judith. *Byzantium*	949.5
Higginbotham, Adam. ★*Midnight in Chernobyl*	363.17
Hirst, J. B. *The Shortest History of Europe*	940
Holland, James. *Big Week*	940.54
Holland, James. *Brothers in Arms*	940.54
Igort. *The Ukrainian and Russian Notebooks*	741.5
Iperen, Roxane van. ★*The Sisters of Auschwitz*	940.53
Jones, Dan. *Crusaders*	909.07
Judt, Tony. *Postwar*	940.55
Kaiser, Menachem. *Plunder*	940.53
Kandel, Eric R. *The Age of Insight*	154.2
Karski, Jan. *Story of a Secret State*	940.53
Keegan, John. *The First World War*	940.3
Keith, Philip A. *All Blood Runs Red*	B
Kelly, John. *The Great Mortality*	614.5
King, Greg. *The Assassination of the Archduke*	B
Kix, Paul. *The Saboteur*	940.53
Kotkin, Stephen. *Stalin*	B
Kotkin, Stephen. *Stalin*	B
Kramer, Clara. *Clara's War*	B
Kraus, Dita. *A Delayed Life*	B
Kurtz, Glenn. *Three Minutes in Poland*	947.7
Lovell, Mary S. *The Sisters*	920.72
Lowe, Keith. *Savage Continent*	940.55
Maass, Peter. *Love Thy Neighbor*	949.702
MacMillan, Margaret. *Paris 1919*	940.3
Manchester, William. *A World Lit Only by Fire*	940.2
Marton, Kati. *The Great Escape*	920
Matzen, Robert. *Dutch Girl*	B
Mazower, Mark. *The Balkans*	949.6
Mazower, Mark. *The Greek Revolution*	949.5
Mazower, Mark. *Hitler's Empire*	940.53
Mazower, Mark. *Salonica, City of Ghosts*	949.5
Mazzeo, Tilar J. *Irena's Children*	B
McCarten, Anthony. *Darkest Hour*	941.084
McMeekin, Sean. *July 1914*	940.3
McNamara, Kevin J. *Dreams of a Great Small Nation*	355.009437
Michener, James A. *The Bridge at Andau*	943.9
Mikanowski, Jacob. ★*Goodbye, Eastern Europe*	947
Miller, Christopher. *The War Came to Us*	947.7
Norwich, John Julius. *Byzantium*	949.5
Norwich, John Julius. *Byzantium*	949.5
Norwich, John Julius. *Byzantium*	949.5
Norwich, John Julius. *A History of France*	944
Norwich, John Julius. *A Short History of Byzantium*	949.5
O'Keeffe, Paul. *Waterloo*	940.2
Patton, George S. *War as I Knew It*	B
Plokhy, Serhii. ★*The Gates of Europe*	947.7
Plokhy, Serhii. *Lost Kingdom*	947
Plokhy, Serhii. ★*The Russo-Ukrainian War*	947.7
Rady, Martyn C. *The Middle Kingdoms*	943
Rees, Laurence. *Auschwitz*	940.53
Reston, James. *The Last Apocalypse*	940.1
Sachs, Harvey. *The Ninth*	784.2
Schama, Simon. *The Embarrassment of Riches*	949.2
Schindler, Meriel. *The Lost Cafe Schindler*	943.64
Siegal, Nina. *The Diary Keepers*	940.54
Smith, Sally Bedell. *Prince Charles*	B
Snyder, Laura J. *Eye of the Beholder*	920
Snyder, Timothy. ★*Bloodlands*	940.54
Snyder, Timothy. *The Red Prince*	B
Spiegel, Renia. *Renia's Diary*	B
Stern, Jessica. *My War Criminal*	341.6
Tallis, Frank. ★*Mortal Secrets*	B
Taylor, Fred. *1939*	940.53
Trentmann, Frank. *Out of the Darkness*	943.08
Trofimov, Yaroslav. ★*Our Enemies Will Vanish*	947.7
Tuchman, Barbara W. ★*The Guns of August*	940.4
Tuchman, Barbara W. *The Proud Tower*	909.82
Van Es, Bart. *The Cut Out Girl*	B
Wickham, Chris. *The Inheritance of Rome*	940.1
Wilson, Derek K. *A Magical World*	261.55
Wilson, Peter H. *Heart of Europe*	943
Winder, Simon. *Lotharingia*	944
Winroth, Anders. *The Age of the Vikings*	948
Zelensky, Volodymyr. *A Message from Ukraine*	947.7
EUROPEAN PEOPLE	
Aly, Gotz. *Europe Against the Jews*	305.892
Fishman, Boris. *Savage Feast*	B
Kertzer, David I. *The Pope at War*	940.53
Platt, Stephen R. *Autumn in the Heavenly Kingdom*	951
Rees, Laurence. *Auschwitz*	940.53
EUROPEAN PEOPLE IN FOREIGN COUNTRIES	
Guha, Ramachandra. *Rebels Against the Raj*	954.03
Lamb, Christina. *House of Stone*	968.91
Orth, Stephan. *Couchsurfing in Iran*	955.06
EUROPEAN RENAISSANCE	
Al-Khalili, Jim. *The House of Wisdom*	509
Brooks, Michael. *The Quantum Astrologer's Handbook*	B
Frampton, Saul. *When I Am Playing with My Cat, How Do I Know She Is Not Playing with Me?*	844
Greenblatt, Stephen. ★*The Swerve*	940.2
Hibbert, Christopher. *The Borgias and Their Enemies*	920
King, Ross. *Brunelleschi's Dome*	726.6
Manchester, William. *A World Lit Only by Fire*	940.2
Meyer, G. J. *The Borgias*	920
Mortimer, Ian. *The Time Traveler's Guide to Elizabethan England*	942.05
Norwich, John Julius. *A History of Venice*	945
Pettegree, Andrew. *The Book in the Renaissance*	070.5
Rowland, Ingrid D. *The Collector of Lives*	B
Strathern, Paul. *The Borgias*	945.06
Strathern, Paul. *The Florentines*	945
Strathern, Paul. *The Medici*	945.5
Unger, Miles. ★*Michelangelo*	B
The Europeans. Figes, Orlando	920
EUROPEANS	
Olson, Lynne. *Last Hope Island*	940.53
Eustace, Nicole	
★*Covered with Night*	364.152
EUTHANASIA	
Engelhart, Katie. *The Inevitable*	179.7
Fink, Sheri. *Five Days at Memorial*	362.1109763
Hannig, Anita. *The Day I Die*	364.152
Wanzer, Sidney H. ★*To Die Well*	179.7
Eva Braun. Gortemaker, Heike B.	B
EVACUATION OF CIVILIANS	
Ackerman, Elliot. *The Fifth Act*	958.104
Clarke, Thurston. *Honorable Exit*	959.704
White, Ralph. *Getting Out of Saigon*	959.704
Zuckoff, Mitchell. *The Secret Gate*	958.104
Evaluating Teen Services and Programs. Flowers, Sarah	027.62
EVANGELICAL THEOLOGY	
FitzGerald, Frances. *The Evangelicals*	277
EVANGELICALISM	
Alberta, Tim. *The Kingdom, the Power, and the Glory*	270.8
Beaty, Katelyn. *Celebrities for Jesus*	261
Bunker, Nick. ★*Making Haste from Babylon*	974.4
Carranca, Adriana. *Soul by Soul*	230
Du Mez, Kristin Kobes. *Jesus and John Wayne*	277.308
FitzGerald, Frances. *The Evangelicals*	277
MacCulloch, Diarmaid. *Christianity*	270
Massing, Michael. *Fatal Discord*	920
McCammon, Sarah. ★*The Exvangelicals*	277.308
Stone, Lillian. ★*Everybody's Favorite*	814.6
Wacker, Grant. *America's Pastor*	B
Ward, Jon. *Testimony*	277.308
The Evangelicals. FitzGerald, Frances	277
Evangelista, Patricia	
★*Some People Need Killing*	364.4
EVANGELISTA, PATRICIA	
Evangelista, Patricia. ★*Some People Need Killing*	364.4
EVANGELISTIC WORK (CHRISTIANITY)	
Wacker, Grant. *America's Pastor*	B
EVANGELISTS	
Wacker, Grant. *America's Pastor*	B
EVANS, ARTHUR, SIR, 1851-1941	
Fox, Margalit. *The Riddle of the Labyrinth*	920
Evans, Bec	
Written	808
EVANS, BILL, 1929-1980	
Kaplan, James. *3 Shades of Blue*	920
Evans, Claire Lisa	
Broad Band	920

PUBLIC LIBRARY CORE COLLECTION: NONFICTION
Twentieth Edition

EVANS, ERNEST EDWIN, 1908-1944
   Thomas, Evan. *Sea of Thunder* — 940.54
Evans, G. Edward
   Collection Management Basics — 025.2
Evans, Jimmy
   Strengths Based Marriage — 248.8
Evans, Martin
   Algeria — 965
Evans, R. Tripp
   Grant Wood — B
Evans, Rachel Held
   Wholehearted Faith — 248.4
EVANS, RACHEL HELD, 1981-2019
   Evans, Rachel Held. *Wholehearted Faith* — 248.4
Evans, Richard J.
   The Coming of the Third Reich — 943.08
   The Pursuit of Power — 940.2
   The Third Reich at War — 940.53
   The Third Reich in Power, 1933-1939 — 943.086
EVANS, ROBERT, 1930-2019
   Wasson, Sam. *The Big Goodbye* — 791.43
Evans, Walker
   American Photographs — 779
EVANS, WALKER, 1903-1975
   Evans, Walker. *American Photographs* — 779
Evans, William
   Black Nerd Problems — 814.6
   We Inherit What the Fires Left — 811
Evanzz, Karl
   The Messenger — B
Evaristo, Bernardine
   Manifesto — B
EVARISTO, BERNARDINE, 1959-
   Evaristo, Bernardine. *Manifesto* — B
★*Eve*. Bohannon, Cat — 613
EVE (BIBLICAL FIGURE)
   Feiler, Bruce. *The First Love Story* — 222
   Greenblatt, Stephen. *The Rise and Fall of Adam and Eve* — 233
Evelyn Waugh. Eade, Philip — B
Even This I Get to Experience. Lear, Norman — B
Eventually One Dreams the Real Thing. Boruch, Marianne — 811
Ever Green. Reid, John W. — 634.9
Ever-Green Vietnamese. Nguyen, Andrea Quynhgiao — 641.595
Everest. Coburn, Broughton — 796.5
Everett, Daniel Leonard
   How Language Began — 401
The Everglades. Douglas, Marjory Stoneman — 975.9
An Everglades Providence. Davis, Jack E. — B
EVERGLADES, FLORIDA
   Davis, Jack E. *An Everglades Providence* — B
   Douglas, Marjory Stoneman. *The Everglades* — 975.9
   Renner, Rebecca. ★*Gator Country* — 364.16
Everitt, Anthony
   Alexander the Great — B
   Cicero — B
   Hadrian and the Triumph of Rome — B
   The Rise of Athens — 938
   The Rise of Rome — 937
An Everlasting Meal. Adler, Tamar — 641.5
EVERS, JOHNNY
   Rapp, David. *Tinker to Evers to Chance* — 796.357
EVERS, MEDGAR WILEY, 1925-1963
   Reid, Joy-Ann Lomena. ★*Medgar and Myrlie* — 920
EVERS, MYRLIE
   Reid, Joy-Ann Lomena. ★*Medgar and Myrlie* — 920
EVERT, CHRIS, 1955-
   Howard, Johnette. *The Rivals* — B
Everts, Sarah
   The Joy of Sweat — 612.7
Every Body Yoga. Stanley, Jessamyn — 613.7
Every Book Its Reader. Basbanes, Nicholas A. — 028
Every Day Is a Gift. Duckworth, Tammy — B
Every Day Is Extra. Kerry, John — B
Every Day We Get More Illegal. Herrera, Juan Felipe — 811
Every Deep-Drawn Breath. Ely, Wes — 616.02
★*Every Living Thing*. Roberts, Jason — 578
Every Living Thing. Herriot, James — B
Every Man a Hero. Lambert, Raymond — B

★*Every Man for Himself and God Against All*. Herzog, Werner — B
Every Minute Is a Day. Meyer, Robert — 362.1962
Every Season Is Soup Season. Westerhausen, Shelly — 641.81
Everybody. Laing, Olivia — 323
Everybody Come Alive. Alvis-Walker, Marcie — B
Everybody Had an Ocean. McKeen, William — 781.6609
★*Everybody's Favorite*. Stone, Lillian — 814.6
Everyday Dharma. Gupta, Suneel — 158.1
Everyday Dinners. Merchant, Jessica — 641.82
★*Everyday Dorie*. Greenspan, Dorie — 641.5
Everyday Grand. Adams, Jocelyn Delk — 641.5975
EVERYDAY LIFE
   Atwood, Margaret. *Dearly* — 811
   Carlsen, Spike. *A Walk Around the Block* — 031
   Cornejo Villavicencio, Karla. ★*The Undocumented Americans* — 920
   Crosley, Sloane. ★*Look Alive Out There* — 814
   DePalma, Anthony. *The Cubans* — 920
   Ellenberg, Jordan. ★*How Not to Be Wrong* — 510
   Ephron, Nora. *The Most of Nora Ephron* — 814
   Fennelly, Beth Ann. *Heating & Cooling* — B
   Franklin, Missy. *Relentless Spirit* — B
   Gay, Ross. *The Book of (more) Delights* — 814
   Georges, Gigi. *Downeast* — 974.1
   Ghodsee, Kristen Rogheh. *Everyday Utopia* — 335
   Greenfieldboyce, Nell. ★*Transient and Strange* — 501
   Hatmaker, Jen. *Of Mess and Moxie* — 248.8
   Havrilesky, Heather. *What If This Were Enough?* — 152.4
   Irby, Samantha. ★*Quietly Hostile* — 814
   Irby, Samantha. *We Are Never Meeting in Real Life* — 814
   Jackson, Shirley. ★*The Letters of Shirley Jackson* — 813
   Jones, Saeed. *Alive at the End of the World* — 811
   Kershner, Isabel. *The Land of Hope and Fear* — 956.9405
   Knausgaard, Karl Ove. *Spring* — B
   Leon, Donna. *My Venice and Other Essays* — 945
   Millet, Lydia. *We Loved It All* — 813
   Mooallem, Jon. *Serious Face* — 814
   Myers, David G. *How Do We Know Ourselves?* — 155.2
   Nhat Hanh. *The Art of Living* — 294.3
   Osnos, Evan. *Wildland* — 973.93
   Parker, James. ★*Get Me Through the Next Five Minutes* — 158.1
   Ruffin, Amber. ★*The World Record Book of Racist Stories* — 305.896
   Ruffin, Amber. *You'll Never Believe What Happened to Lacey* — 305.896
   Sanders, Ella Frances. *Eating the Sun* — 520
   Schulz, Kathryn. ★*Lost & Found* — B
   Sedaris, David. ★*A Carnival of Snackery* — 818
   Sedaris, David. ★*Happy-Go-Lucky* — 814
   Shankle, Melanie. *Church of the Small Things* — 248.8
   Sharot, Tali. *Look Again* — 158.1
   Stanton, Brandon. *Humans* — 779
   Weir, Laura. *Cosy* — 646.7009
★*Everyday Mojo Songs of Earth*. Komunyakaa, Yusef — 811
Everyday Utopia. Ghodsee, Kristen Rogheh — 335
Everyone Is Italian on Sunday. Ray, Rachael — 641.594
Everyone Who Is Gone Is Here. Blitzer, Jonathan — 305.9
Everyone's Table. Gourdet, Gregory — 641.5
Everything All at Once. Nye, Bill — 153.4
Everything Below the Waist. Block, Jennifer — 613
Everything I Know About Love. Alderton, Dolly — B
Everything I Learned, I Learned in a Chinese Restaurant. Chin, Curtis — B
★*Everything in Its Place*. Sacks, Oliver — B
*Everything Is F*cked*. Manson, Mark — 152.4
Everything Is Fine. Granata, Vince — B
Everything to Gain. Carter, Jimmy — B
★*The Everything War*. Mattioli, Dana — 381.142
Everything You Wanted to Know About Indians but Were Afraid to Ask. Treuer, Anton — 970.1
Everything/Nothing/Someone. Carriere, Alice — B
★*Evicted*. Desmond, Matthew — 339.4
EVICTION
   Desmond, Matthew. ★*Evicted* — 339.4
The Evil Hours. Morris, David J. — 616.85
Evolution. Larson, Edward J. — 576.8
EVOLUTION
   Black, Riley. *The Last Days of the Dinosaurs* — 576.8
   Bohme, Madelaine. *Ancient Bones* — 599.93
   Browne, E. J. *Charles Darwin* — B
   Browne, E. J. *Charles Darwin* — B
   Brusatte, Stephen. ★*The Rise and Fall of the Dinosaurs* — 567.9

AUTHOR, TITLE, SERIES AND SUBJECT INDEX

Brusatte, Stephen. *The Rise and Reign of the Mammals*	569
Byrne, Eugene. *Darwin*	741.5
Carroll, Sean M. *The Big Picture*	577
Catania, Kenneth. *Great Adaptations*	576.8
Cooke, Lucy. *Bitch*	591.56
Costa, James T. *Darwin's Backyard*	576.8
Costa, James T. *Radical by Nature*	B
Darwin, Charles. ★*The Origin of Species by Means of Natural Selection, Or, the Preservation of Favored Races in the Struggle for Life*	575
Dawkins, Richard. ★*The Ancestor's Tale*	576.8
Dawkins, Richard. *An Appetite for Wonder*	B
Dawkins, Richard. *The Greatest Show on Earth*	576.8
Dawkins, Richard. *Science in the Soul*	500
Dennett, D. C. *Darwin's Dangerous Idea*	146
Denworth, Lydia. *Friendship*	158.2
Dunbar, R. I. M. *Human Evolution*	155.7
Foster, Charles. *Being a Human*	155.7
Gee, Henry. *A (Very) Short History of Life on Earth*	576.8
Gould, Stephen Jay. *The Richness of Life*	508
Gould, Stephen Jay. *The Structure of Evolutionary Theory*	576.8
Greenblatt, Stephen. *The Rise and Fall of Adam and Eve*	233
Hanson, Thor. *Hurricane Lizards and Plastic Squid*	577.2
Harari, Yuval N. *Homo Deus*	909.83
Harari, Yuval N. ★*Sapiens*	909
Harman, Oren Solomon. *Evolutions*	201
Hawking, Stephen. ★*The Grand Design*	530.14
Higgins, Jackie. *Sentient*	573.8
Hoffman, Donald D. *The Case Against Reality*	121
Jabr, Ferris. ★*Becoming Earth*	570.1
Johanson, Donald C. *Lucy*	569
Kershenbaum, Arik. *The Zoologist's Guide to the Galaxy*	576.8
Kurzweil, Ray. ★*The Singularity Is Near*	153.9
Larson, Edward J. *Evolution*	576.8
Leakey, Richard E. *The Origin of Humankind*	599.93
Lederer, Roger J. *Beaks, Bones, and Bird Songs*	598
Lister, Adrian. *Darwin's Fossils*	576.8
Losos, Jonathan B. *Improbable Destinies*	576.8
MacPhee, R. D. E. *End of the Megafauna*	591.4
Margulis, Lynn. *Symbiotic Planet*	576.8
Markel, Howard. *Origin Story*	576.8
McCalman, Iain. *Darwin's Armada*	576.8
Nicholls, Steve. *Alien Worlds*	595.7
Nye, Bill. *Undeniable*	576.8
O'Connor, Maura R. *Resurrection Science*	591.68
Pinker, Steven. *The Blank Slate*	155.2
Preston, Diana. *The Evolution of Charles Darwin*	508
Pyenson, Nick. *Spying on Whales*	599.5
Randall, Lisa. *Dark Matter and the Dinosaurs*	523.1
Rutherford, Adam. *Humanimal*	599.93
Sanders, Ella Frances. *Eating the Sun*	520
Schilthuizen, Menno. *Darwin Comes to Town*	577.5
Simon, Matt. *Plight of the Living Dead*	591.6
Stott, Rebecca. ★*Darwin's Ghosts*	576.8
Sumner, Seirian. *Endless Forms*	595.79
Switek, Brian. *Skeleton Keys*	611
Tattersall, Ian. *Masters of the Planet*	599.93
Tonelli, Guido. *Genesis*	523.1
Toomey, David. *Kingdom of Play*	591.56
Turvey, Samuel. ★*The Tomb of the Mili Mongga*	398.24
Ward, Ashley. *Where We Meet the World*	612.8
Wilson, David Sloan. *Evolution for Everyone*	576.801
Wilson, Edward O. *Genesis*	591.5
Wilson, Edward O. *Half-Earth*	333.95
Wilson, Edward O. ★*The Social Conquest of Earth*	599.93
Wragg Sykes, Rebecca. *Kindred*	569.9
Evolution for Everyone. Wilson, David Sloan	576.801
The Evolution of Charles Darwin. Preston, Diana	508
★*The Evolution of Physics*. Einstein, Albert	530
Evolutions. Harman, Oren Solomon	201
Evolutions in Bread. Forkish, Ken	664
Ewer, Cynthia Townley	
Cut the Clutter	648
Ewing, Eve L.	
1919	811
Ghosts in the Schoolyard	370.89
Ewing, Jack	
Faster, Higher, Farther	338.7
Ex Libris. Kakutani, Michiko	028

Exact Thinking in Demented Times. Sigmund, Karl	920
Examined Lives. Miller, Jim	B
Examining Tuskegee. Reverby, Susan M.	174.2
EXCAVATION	
Hunt, Will. *Underground*	624.1
EXCAVATIONS (ARCHAEOLOGY)	
Brooks, James. *Mesa of Sorrows*	979.1004
Brown, Nancy Marie. *The Real Valkyrie*	948
Fox, Margalit. *The Riddle of the Labyrinth*	920
Garfinkel, Yosef. *In the Footsteps of King David*	933
Griswold, Mac K. *The Manor*	974.7
Hessler, Peter. *The Buried*	962.05
Lance, Rachel. *In the Waves*	973.7
Lawler, Andrew. *Under Jerusalem*	956.94
Pattison, Kermit. *Fossil Men*	569.9
Pitts, Mike. *Digging for Richard III*	942.046
Preston, Douglas J. ★*The Lost City of the Monkey God*	972.85
Wilkinson, Toby A. H. *A World Beneath the Sands*	932
EXCAVATIONS (PALEONTOLOGY)	
Black, Riley. *The Last Days of the Dinosaurs*	576.8
EXCELLENCE	
Robinson, Phoebe. *Please Don't Sit on My Bed in Your Outside Clothes*	818
★*Excellent Advice for Living*. Kelly, Kevin	158.1
Excellent Daughters. Zoepf, Katherine	305.42
The Exceptions. Zernike, Kate	331.4
EXCESS (PHILOSOPHY)	
Reynolds, Simon. *Shock and Awe*	781.6609
Rothfeld, Becca. ★*All Things Are Too Small*	814
Excuse Me While I Disappear. Notaro, Laurie	B
EXECUTIONS AND EXECUTIONERS	
Berg, Scott W. ★*38 Nooses*	973.7
Borman, Tracy. *Thomas Cromwell*	B
Chammah, Maurice. ★*Let the Lord Sort Them*	364.66
Donner, Rebecca. *All the Frequent Troubles of Our Days*	943
Guy, John. *Hunting the Falcon*	B
Harrington, Joel F. *The Faithful Executioner*	B
Rhodes, Richard. *Masters of Death*	940.53
Sebba, Anne. *Ethel Rosenberg*	B
Toobin, Jeffrey. ★*Homegrown*	363.325
Weir, Alison. *The Lady in the Tower*	B
EXECUTIVE ABILITY	
Botelho, Elena L. *The CEO Next Door*	658.4
Cast, Carter. *The Right—And Wrong—Stuff*	650.1
Goleman, Daniel. *Primal Leadership*	658.4
Horstman, Mark. *The Effective Manager*	658.4
Peter, Laurence J. *The Peter Principle*	658
EXECUTIVE POWER	
Acemoglu, Daron. *The Narrow Corridor*	320.01
Barron, David J. *Waging War*	342.73
Beeman, Richard R. ★*Plain, Honest Men*	342.7302
Beschloss, Michael R. ★*Presidents of War*	355.00973
Brettschneider, Corey Lang. *The Oath and the Office*	342.73
Brettschneider, Corey Lang. *The Presidents and the People*	342.73
Carter, Jimmy. *White House Diary*	973.926
Hennessey, Susan. *Unmaking the Presidency*	973.933
McPherson, James M. ★*Tried by War*	973.7
Raphael, Ray. *Mr. President*	352.230973
Schmidt, Michael S. ★*Donald Trump v. The United States*	973.933
Simon, James F. *FDR and Chief Justice Hughes*	973.917092
Simon, James F. *What Kind of Nation*	342.73
Stephanopoulos, George. ★*The Situation Room*	973.09
Wolff, Michael. *Landslide*	973.933
EXECUTIVES	
Cole, Jason. *Elway*	B
Etter, Lauren. ★*The Devil's Playbook*	338.7
Gelles, David. *The Man Who Broke Capitalism*	330.12
Hoffman, Liz. *Crash Landing*	330
Hughes, Evan. *The Hard Sell*	338.4
Jensen, Robert A. *Personal Effects*	363.34
Leonard, Christopher. *Kochland*	338.7
McDonald, Greg (Producer). *Elvis and the Colonel*	920
Posner, Gerald L. ★*Pharma*	338.4
Scott, Kim Malone. *Radical Candor*	658.4
EXERCISE	
Attia, Peter. ★*Outlive*	612.6
Current, Austin. *Science of Strength Training*	613.7
Hayes, Bill. *Sweat*	613.7
Lacerda, Daniel. *2,100 Asanas*	613.7

PUBLIC LIBRARY CORE COLLECTION: NONFICTION
Twentieth Edition

Lieberman, Daniel. *Exercised*	612.044
Meals, Roy A. *Muscle*	612.7
Nigg, Joel T. *Getting Ahead of ADHD*	618.92
Stanley, Jessamyn. *Every Body Yoga*	613.7
Stanley, Jessamyn. ★*Yoke*	613.7
Streets, Annabel. *52 Ways to Walk*	796.51
★*Exercise of Power*. Gates, Robert Michael	973.929

EXERCISE THERAPY

Fishman, Loren. *Yoga for Arthritis*	616.7
Wayne, Peter. *The Harvard Medical School Guide to Tai Chi*	613.7
Exercised. Lieberman, Daniel	612.044

EXHIBITION CATALOGS

Shackelford, George T. M. *Monet*	759.4

EXHIBITIONS

Creighton, Margaret S. *The Electrifying Fall of Rainbow City*	607
Raffel, Dawn. *The Strange Case of Dr. Couney*	B

EXHUMATION

Kimmerle, Erin H. *We Carry Their Bones*	365

EXILE (PUNISHMENT)

Bellos, David. *The Novel of the Century*	843
Broers, Michael. *Napoleon*	944.05
Cooper, Helene. *Madame President*	966.62
Eyman, Scott. *Charlie Chaplin vs. America*	B
Malek, Alia. *The Home That Was Our Country*	B
Warren, James A. *God, War, and Providence*	974.5

EXILES

Ai, Weiwei. *Zodiac*	741.5
Allende, Isabel. *My Invented Country*	B
Callow, Simon. ★*Orson Welles*	B
Diamond, Cheryl. *Nowhere Girl*	B
Egan, Timothy. ★*The Immortal Irishman*	B
Hughes, Robert. *The Fatal Shore*	994
Kertzer, David I. *The Pope Who Would Be King*	282.092
King, Charles. *Midnight at the Pera Palace*	949.61
Mao, Sally Wen. *Oculus*	811
Marton, Kati. *The Great Escape*	920
Matar, Hisham. *The Return*	B
Merridale, Catherine. *Lenin on the Train*	B
Olson, Lynne. *Last Hope Island*	940.53
Rappaport, Helen. *After the Romanovs*	944
Rathbone, John Paul. *The Sugar King of Havana*	B
Zia, Helen. *Last Boat Out of Shanghai*	951.04
Exist Otherwise. Shaw, Jennifer Laurie	709.2

EXISTENTIALISM

Bakewell, Sarah. ★*At the Existentialist Cafe*	920
Barrett, William. *Irrational Man*	142
Carlisle, Clare. *Philosopher of the Heart*	B
Heidegger, Martin. ★*Being and Time*	111
Hitchens, Christopher. *The Four Horsemen*	211
Nicolson, Adam. *How to Be*	180
Sartre, Jean-Paul. ★*Being and Nothingness*	111
Sartre, Jean-Paul. *Existentialism and Human Emotions*	111
Tillich, Paul. ★*The Courage to Be*	179
Yalom, Irvin D. *Staring at the Sun*	155.9
Existentialism and Human Emotions. Sartre, Jean-Paul	111

EXMAN, EUGENE

Prothero, Stephen R. *God the Bestseller*	070.5

EXMOUTH, EDWARD PELLEW, VISCOUNT, 1757-1833

Taylor, Stephen. *Commander*	B

EXOBIOLOGY

Frank, Adam. *Light of the Stars*	523.1
Exodus. Feldman, Deborah	B
Exoplanets. Summers, Michael E.	523.2

EXORCISM

Gallagher, Richard E. *Demonic Foes*	133.42
Levack, Brian P. *The Devil Within*	133.4
Sullivan, Randall. *The Devil's Best Trick*	235

EXPATRIATE ARTISTS

Ai, Weiwei. *1000 Years of Joys and Sorrows*	709.2
Bilal, Wafaa. *Shoot an Iraqi*	B
Stahr, Celia. *Frida in America*	B

EXPATRIATE WOMEN

Irving, Apricot Anderson. *The Gospel of Trees*	B
Watling, Sarah. *Tomorrow Perhaps the Future*	946.081

EXPATRIATES

Bertch, Jane. *The French Ingredient*	B
Bowker, Gordon. ★*James Joyce*	B
Callow, Simon. ★*Orson Welles*	B
Drabkin, Ronald. *Beverly Hills Spy*	940.54
Eyman, Scott. *Charlie Chaplin vs. America*	B
Hoja, Gulchehra. *A Stone Is Most Precious Where It Belongs*	B
Irving, Apricot Anderson. *The Gospel of Trees*	B
James, Jamie. *The Glamour of Strangeness*	700.1
Mayle, Peter. *My Twenty-Five Years in Provence*	944.9
Parkin, Simon. *The Island of Extraordinary Captives*	940.53
Stewart, Chris. *Driving Over Lemons*	946
Expect The Unexpected. Fauci, Anthony S.	610.92

EXPECTATION

Browne, Mahogany L. ★*Black Girl Magic*	811.6
Clark, Andy. *The Experience Machine*	153
Codjoe, Ama. *Bluest Nude*	811
Cohen, Rhaina. ★*The Other Significant Others*	177
Duckworth, Angela. *Grit*	158.1
Grose, Jessica. *Screaming on the Inside*	306.874
Gupta, Prachi. ★*They Called Us Exceptional*	B
Klein, Jessi. *I'll Show Myself Out*	B
Loh, Sandra Tsing. *The Madwoman and the Roomba*	B
Lythcott-Haims, Julie. *Your Turn*	305.24
Montgomery, Patrick. *Baseball's Great Expectations*	796.357
Shockley, Evie. *Suddenly We*	811
Zimmerman, Jess. *Women and Other Monsters*	155.3

EXPEDITIONS

Bergreen, Laurence. *Over the Edge of the World*	B
Carlsen, William. *Jungle of Stone*	B
Conefrey, Mick. *The Ghosts of K2*	796.522
Darwin, Charles. *Charles Darwin*	576.8
Ellsworth, Scott. *The World Beneath Their Feet*	796.522
Grann, David. *The Lost City of Z*	918.1
Krakauer, Jon. ★*Into Thin Air*	796.52
Larson, Edward J. *An Empire of Ice*	919.8
Lowe, George. *Letters from Everest*	796.522
Millard, Candice. ★*River of the Gods*	916.204
Niven, Jennifer. *Ada Blackjack*	B
O'Brady, Colin. ★*The Impossible First*	919.8904
O'Connor, John. *The Secret History of Bigfoot*	001.944
Resendez, Andres. *Conquering the Pacific*	959.9
Sancton, Julian. *Madhouse at the End of the Earth*	919.8904
Stark, Peter. *Astoria*	979.5
Turney, Chris. *1912*	998
Wallace, Scott. *The Unconquered*	981
Wood, Gillen D'Arcy. *Land of Wondrous Cold*	919.89

EXPERIENCE

Clark, Andy. *The Experience Machine*	153
Handler, Daniel. ★*And Then? and Then? What Else?*	813

EXPERIENCE (RELIGION)

James, William. ★*The Varieties of Religious Experience*	204
The Experience Machine. Clark, Andy	153

EXPERIMENTAL FILMS

Lynch, David. *Room to Dream*	B

EXPERIMENTAL MEDICINE

Dittrich, Luke. ★*Patient H.M.*	616.85
Elliott, Carl. ★*The Occasional Human Sacrifice*	174.2
Goldacre, Ben. *Bad Science*	500

EXPERIMENTS

Ananthaswamy, Anil. *Through Two Doors at Once*	530.12
Costa, James T. *Darwin's Backyard*	576.8
Dolnick, Edward. *Seeds of Life*	612.6
Einstein, Albert. ★*A Stubbornly Persistent Illusion*	530.092
Goldacre, Ben. *Bad Science*	500
Gray, Charlotte. ★*Reluctant Genius*	920
Heti, Sheila. *Alphabetical Diaries*	818
Kean, Sam. *The Icepick Surgeon*	509
McAfee, Andrew. *The Geek Way*	658.3
Schwartz, David N. *The Last Man Who Knew Everything*	B
Toomey, David. *Kingdom of Play*	591.56

EXPERT EVIDENCE

Fabricant, M. Chris. *Junk Science and the American Criminal Justice System*	363.25

EXPERTISE

Epstein, David J. ★*Range*	153.9
Ericsson, K. Anders. *Peak*	153.9
Gopnik, Adam. *The Real Work*	153.9

EXPERTS

Gopnik, Adam. *The Real Work*	153.9
Exploding Data. Chertoff, Michael	343.7309

AUTHOR, TITLE, SERIES AND SUBJECT INDEX

EXPLOITATION
    Beaton, Kate. ★*Ducks*   741.5
    Citron, Danielle Keats. *The Fight for Privacy*   342.7308
    Dalrymple, William. ★*The Anarchy*   954.03
    Farmer, Paul. *Fevers, Feuds, and Diamonds*   614.5
    Guendelsberger, Emily. *On the Clock*   331.0973
    Hurston, Zora Neale. ★*Barracoon*   B
    Jacobs, Sally H. *Althea*   B
    Leamer, Laurence. *The Price of Justice*   346.7302
    Macy, Beth. ★*Truevine*   B
    Marie, Jane. ★*Selling the Dream*   658.8
    Prendergast, John. *Congo Stories*   967.5103
    Puglionesi, Alicia. *In Whose Ruins*   973
    Rae, Noel. ★*The Great Stain*   306.3
    Raphael, Rina. *The Gospel of Wellness*   613
    Sanghera, Sathnam. *Empireworld*   909
    Schneier, Bruce. *A Hacker's Mind*   364.16
    Siler, Julia Flynn. *The White Devil's Daughters*   306.3
    Umar, Ousman. *North to Paradise*   B
    Wilkinson, Toby A. H. *A World Beneath the Sands*   932

EXPLORATION
    Adams, Mark. *Turn Right at Machu Picchu*   985
    Aldrin, Buzz. *Mission to Mars*   523.43
    Alexander, Caroline. *The Endurance*   919.8
    Ambrose, Stephen E. ★*Undaunted Courage*   917.804
    Bell, Jim. *The Interstellar Age*   919
    Bergreen, Laurence. *Over the Edge of the World*   B
    Bound, Mensun. *The Ship Beneath the Ice*   919.8904
    Brinkley, Douglas. ★*American Moonshot*   629.40973
    Cliff, Nigel. *Holy War*   909
    Darwin, Charles. ★*The Voyage of the Beagle*   508
    Dodds Pennock, Caroline. ★*On Savage Shores*   970.004
    Donovan, Jim. ★*Shoot for the Moon*   629.45
    Fernandez-Armesto, Felipe. ★*Amerigo*   B
    Fiennes, Ranulph. *Shackleton*   B
    Fischer, David Hackett. *Champlain's Dream*   B
    Fishman, Charles. ★*One Giant Leap*   629.45
    Grann, David. *The Lost City of Z*   918.1
    Grann, David. *The White Darkness*   B
    Hartman, Darrell. *Battle of Ink and Ice*   998
    Holway, Tatiana M. *The Flower of Empire*   727
    Horwitz, Tony. ★*A Voyage Long and Strange*   970.01
    Hunt, Will. *Underground*   624.1
    Hyde, Anne Farrar. *Empires, Nations, and Families*   978
    Jeal, Tim. *Explorers of the Nile*   920
    Kitmacher, Gary. *Space Stations*   629.44
    Larson, Edward J. *An Empire of Ice*   919.8
    Levy, Buddy. *Labyrinth of Ice*   910.91
    Lowe, George. *Letters from Everest*   796.522
    Niven, Jennifer. *Ada Blackjack*   B
    O'Brady, Colin. ★*The Impossible First*   919.8904
    Resendez, Andres. *Conquering the Pacific*   959.9
    Roberts, David. *Alone on the Ice*   919.8904
    Sancton, Julian. *Madhouse at the End of the Earth*   919.8904
    Schmidt, Thomas. *The Saga of Lewis & Clark*   917.804
    Sevigny, Melissa L. ★*Brave the Wild River*   580.9
    Shatner, William. *Boldly Go*   B
    Sides, Hampton. ★*The Wide Wide Sea*   910.92
    Thomas, Hugh. *Rivers of Gold*   980
    Turney, Chris. *1912*   998
    Turvey, Samuel. ★*The Tomb of the Mili Mongga*   398.24
    Watson, Paul. *Ice Ghosts*   917
    Wilkinson, Toby A. H. *A World Beneath the Sands*   932
    Wilson-Lee, Edward. ★*The Catalogue of Shipwrecked Books*   B
    Wood, Gillen D'Arcy. *Land of Wondrous Cold*   919.89
    Wulf, Andrea. *The Invention of Nature*   508
The **Explorers**. Bellows, Amanda Brickell   910.92

EXPLORERS
    Alexander, Caroline. *The Endurance*   919.8
    Ambrose, Stephen E. ★*Undaunted Courage*   917.804
    Belliveau, Denis. *In the Footsteps of Marco Polo*   915
    Bellows, Amanda Brickell. *The Explorers*   910.92
    Bergreen, Laurence. *In Search of a Kingdom*   B
    Bergreen, Laurence. *Marco Polo*   B
    Bergreen, Laurence. *Over the Edge of the World*   B
    Bound, Mensun. *The Ship Beneath the Ice*   919.8904
    Brandt, Anthony. *The Man Who Ate His Boots*   910.91
    Carlsen, William. *Jungle of Stone*   B
    Cliff, Nigel. *Holy War*   909
    Davis, Wade. *Into the Silence*   B
    Drury, Bob. *Blood and Treasure*   B
    Ehrlich, Gretel. *This Cold Heaven*   998.2
    Fernandez-Armesto, Felipe. ★*Amerigo*   B
    Fiennes, Ranulph. *Shackleton*   B
    Fischer, David Hackett. *Champlain's Dream*   B
    Grann, David. *The Lost City of Z*   918.1
    Grann, David. *The White Darkness*   B
    Hansen, Valerie. *The Year 1000*   909
    Hartman, Darrell. *Battle of Ink and Ice*   998
    Horwitz, Tony. ★*A Voyage Long and Strange*   970.01
    Inskeep, Steve. *Imperfect Union*   B
    Jeal, Tim. *Explorers of the Nile*   920
    Kurson, Robert. *Pirate Hunters*   910.91
    Larson, Edward J. *An Empire of Ice*   919.8
    Lawler, Andrew. *Under Jerusalem*   956.94
    Levy, Buddy. *Labyrinth of Ice*   910.91
    Millard, Candice. ★*River of the Gods*   916.204
    Morgan, Robert. *Boone*   B
    Morgan, Robert. *Lions of the West*   978
    Niven, Jennifer. *Ada Blackjack*   B
    Resendez, Andres. *Conquering the Pacific*   959.9
    Roberts, David. *Alone on the Ice*   919.8904
    Ross, John F. *The Promise of the Grand Canyon*   917.91
    Sancton, Julian. *Madhouse at the End of the Earth*   919.8904
    Sides, Hampton. ★*The Wide Wide Sea*   910.92
    Synnott, Mark. *The Third Pole*   796.522
    Turney, Chris. *1912*   998
    Watson, Paul. *Ice Ghosts*   917
    Welky, David. ★*A Wretched and Precarious Situation*   910.911
    Wilson-Lee, Edward. ★*The Catalogue of Shipwrecked Books*   B
    Winchester, Simon. *The Men Who United the States*   973
    Wood, Gillen D'Arcy. *Land of Wondrous Cold*   919.89
***Explorers** of the Nile.* Jeal, Tim   920
***Exploring** The History of Childhood and Play Through 50 Historic Treasures.*
    Fletcher, Susan A.   790
***Exploring** Women's Suffrage Through 50 Historic Treasures.* Jenkins, Jessica D.
    324.6

EXPLOSIONS
    Bacon, John U. *The Great Halifax Explosion*   971.6
    Berman, Bob. *Earth-Shattering*   523.1
    Leinbach, Michael D. *Bringing Columbia Home*   363.12

EXPLOSIVES
    Castner, Brian. *The Long Walk*   B
    Lehr, Dick. *White Hot Hate*   363.325
***Exposure**.* Bilott, Robert   344.04

EXPRESSIONISM (ART)
    Albers, Patricia. *Joan Mitchell*   B
    Knausgaard, Karl Ove. *So Much Longing in so Little Space*   759.81
*The **Exquisite** Book of Paper Flowers.* Cetti, Livia   745.594

EXTENDED FAMILIES
    Chin, Curtis. *Everything I Learned, I Learned in a Chinese Restaurant*   B
    Chow, Kat. *Seeing Ghosts*   B
    DeParle, Jason. ★*A Good Provider Is One Who Leaves*   305.899
    Duggar, Jill. *Counting the Cost*   B
    Jacobs, A. J. *It's All Relative*   929.1
    Means, Brittany. *Hell If We Don't Change Our Ways*   B
    Salama, Jordan. ★*Stranger in the Desert*   982
*The **Extended** Mind.* Paul, Annie Murphy   128

EXTINCT ANIMALS
    Halliday, Thomas. ★*Otherlands*   560
    MacPhee, R. D. E. *End of the Megafauna*   591.4

EXTINCT BIRDS
    Attenborough, David. *The Life of Birds*   598.15
    Hirschfeld, Erik. *The World's Rarest Birds*   333.95822

EXTINCT CITIES
    Garfinkel, Yosef. *In the Footsteps of King David*   933
    Green, Matthew. *Shadowlands*   941.03
    Preston, Douglas J. ★*The Lost City of the Monkey God*   972.85
    Richardson, Edmund. *The King's Shadow*   958.1
    Robb, Graham. *The Debatable Land*   941.3

EXTINCT LANGUAGES
    Dolnick, Edward. *The Writing of the Gods*   493
    Ferrara, Silvia. *The Greatest Invention*   411

EXTINCT MAMMALS
    Brusatte, Stephen. *The Rise and Reign of the Mammals*   569
    MacPhee, R. D. E. *End of the Megafauna*   591.4

PUBLIC LIBRARY CORE COLLECTION: NONFICTION
Twentieth Edition

EXTINCTION
- Attenborough, David. *A Life on Our Planet* — 508
- Barrow, Mark V. *Nature's Ghosts* — 333.95
- Black, Riley. *The Last Days of the Dinosaurs* — 576.8
- Brannen, Peter. *The Ends of the World* — 576.8
- Duncan, Dayton. *Blood Memory* — 599.64
- Flores, Dan L. *Wild New World* — 591.9709
- Gyllenhaal, Anders. *A Wing and a Prayer* — 639.97
- Lacovara, Kenneth. *Why Dinosaurs Matter* — 567.9
- MacPhee, R. D. E. *End of the Megafauna* — 591.4
- Millet, Lydia. *We Loved It All* — 813
- Monosson, Emily. ★*Blight* — 616.9
- Moore, Kathleen Dean. *Earth's Wild Music* — 576.8
- Newitz, Annalee. *Scatter, Adapt, and Remember* — 576.8
- Nicolson, Adam. *The Seabird's Cry* — 598.177
- Pittman, Craig. *Cat Tale* — 599.75
- Welz, Adam. *The End of Eden* — 577.2
- Wilson, Edward O. *The Future of Life* — 333.95

EXTORTION
- Berman, Sarah. *Don't Call It a Cult* — 361.4
- Goldberg, Carrie. *Nobody's Victim* — 345.73
- Levin, Daniel Barban. *Slonim Woods 9* — B
- Maddow, Rachel. *Bag Man* — B
- Whitlock, Craig. ★*Fat Leonard* — 364.16

Extra Life. Johnson, Steven — 362.1
Extra Lives. Bissell, Tom — 794.8
Extra Sensory. Clegg, Brian — 133.8

EXTRAJUDICIAL EXECUTIONS
- Evangelista, Patricia. ★*Some People Need Killing* — 364.4

EXTRAMARITAL AFFAIRS
- Aron, Nina Renata. *Good Morning, Destroyer of Men's Souls* — B
- Crawford, Robert. *Eliot After the Waste Land* — B
- Daniels, Stormy. *Full Disclosure* — B
- Eyman, Scott. *Charlie Chaplin vs. America* — B
- Frangello, Gina. *Blow Your House Down* — 813
- Glatt, John. ★*The Perfect Father* — 364.152
- Koppel, Lily. *The Astronaut Wives Club* — 920
- Mansel, Philip. *King of the World* — B
- Mazzeo, Tilar J. ★*Eliza Hamilton* — B
- Oller, John. *American Queen* — B
- Peyser, Marc N. *Hissing Cousins* — B
- Pittard, Hannah. *We Are Too Many* — B
- Teachout, Terry. *Duke* — B
- Wilson, A. N. *The Mystery of Charles Dickens* — 823

The Extraordinary Life of an Ordinary Man. Newman, Paul — B
Extraordinary, Ordinary People. Rice, Condoleezza — B

EXTRASENSORY PERCEPTION
- Clegg, Brian. *Extra Sensory* — 133.8
- Jacobsen, Annie. *Phenomena* — 133.8

EXTRASOLAR PLANETS
- Kaltenegger, Lisa. ★*Alien Earths* — 523.2
- Seager, Sara. *The Smallest Lights in the Universe* — B
- Summers, Michael E. *Exoplanets* — 523.2
- Tucker, Wallace H. *Chandra's Cosmos* — 523.1

Extraterrestrial. Loeb, Abraham — 576.8

EXTRATERRESTRIAL ANTHROPOLOGY
- Kaltenegger, Lisa. ★*Alien Earths* — 523.2
- Kershenbaum, Arik. *The Zoologist's Guide to the Galaxy* — 576.8

Extreme Economies. Davies, Richard — 306.3

EXTREME ENVIRONMENTS
- Cordes, Kelly. *The Tower* — 796.522
- Johnson, Sarah Stewart. *The Sirens of Mars* — 576.8

Extreme Sports. McCormick, Brad — 791.457

EXTREME SPORTS
- Bukreev, Anatolii Nikolaevich. *The Climb* — 796.52
- Burgman, John. *High Drama* — 796.522
- Coburn, Broughton. *Everest* — 796.5
- Cordes, Kelly. *The Tower* — 796.522
- Cox, Lynne. *Swimming to Antarctica* — B
- Krakauer, Jon. *Classic Krakauer* — 814
- Krakauer, Jon. ★*Into Thin Air* — 796.52
- McCormick, Brad. *Extreme Sports* — 791.457
- Moore, Colten. *Catching the Sky* — B
- Mortimer, Gavin. *The Great Swim* — B
- Ralston, Aron. *Between a Rock and a Hard Place* — 796.522
- Roberts, David. *Limits of the Known* — B

The Extremely Busy Woman's Guide to Self-Care. Falter, Suzanne — 613
★*Extremely Online*. Lorenz, Taylor — 302.23

EXTREMISM
- Alberta, Tim. *The Kingdom, the Power, and the Glory* — 270.8
- Finkel, David. *An American Dreamer* — 975.8
- Ganz, John. *When the Clock Broke* — 320.52
- Harris, Sam. *Islam and the Future of Tolerance* — 297.2
- Lehr, Dick. *White Hot Hate* — 363.325
- Mekhennet, Souad. *I Was Told to Come Alone* — 363.3250956
- Neiwert, David A. ★*The Age of Insurrection* — 303.48
- Rothschild, Mike. *The Storm Is Upon Us* — 973.933
- Toobin, Jeffrey. ★*Homegrown* — 363.325
- Verini, James. *They Will Have to Die Now* — 956.7044
- Walsh, Declan. *The Nine Lives of Pakistan* — 954.91
- Yancey, Philip. ★*Where the Light Fell* — B

EXTREMISTS
- Bates, Laura. *Men Who Hate Women* — 305.3
- Bergen, Peter L. *The Rise and Fall of Osama Bin Laden* — 958.104
- Harris, Sam. *Islam and the Future of Tolerance* — 297.2
- Minutaglio, Bill. *Dallas 1963* — 973.922092

Exurbia Now. Masciotra, David — 320.973
★*The Exvangelicals*. McCammon, Sarah — 277.308
Eye Level. Xle, Jenny — 811
Eye of the Beholder. Snyder, Laura J. — 920
The Eye of the Elephant. Owens, Delia — 639.9
Eye of the Sixties. Stein, Judith E. — B
Eye on the Struggle. Morris, James McGrath — B
Eyeliner. Hankir, Zahra — 391.6
Eyes on the Prize. Williams, Juan — 323.4
Eyes on the Street. Kanigel, Robert — B
Eyes to the Wind. Barkan, Ady — B

Eyman, Scott
- *Cary Grant* — B
- *Charlie Chaplin vs. America* — B
- *Empire of Dreams* — B
- *Hank and Jim* — 920
- *John Wayne* — B

Eyre, Eric
- *Death in Mud Lick* — 362.29

Ezra Pound. Moody, Anthony David — B

Ezzo, Gary
- *On Becoming Baby Wise* — 649

F

F The Fairy Tale. Hoffman, Damona — 306.73
*F*ck Feelings*. Bennett, Michael — 158

Faber, Adele
- ★*How to Talk so Kids Will Listen & Listen so Kids Will Talk* — 649

FABERGE EGGS
- Stark, Lizzie. ★*Egg* — 641.3

Fabes, Stephen
- *Signs of Life* — B

FABES, STEPHEN
- Fabes, Stephen. *Signs of Life* — B

Fabey, Michael
- *Heavy Metal* — 338.4

Fabre, Cin
- *Wolf Hustle* — 332.6

FABRE, CIN
- Fabre, Cin. *Wolf Hustle* — 332.6

The Fabric of the Cosmos. Greene, B. — 523.1

Fabricant, M. Chris
- *Junk Science and the American Criminal Justice System* — 363.25

FABRICANT, M. CHRIS
- Fabricant, M. Chris. *Junk Science and the American Criminal Justice System* — 363.25

Fabritius, Friederike
- *The Leading Brain* — 158

The Fabulous Bouvier Sisters. Kashner, Sam — 920

FACE
- Joyce, Russell W. *His Face Like Mine* — 248
- Ruhl, Sarah. *Smile* — B

FACE IN ART
- Parks, Carrie. *Secrets to Drawing Realistic Faces* — 743.4

Face It. Harry, Debbie — B
The Face of Water. Ruden, Sarah — 220.5
Face The Music. Stanley, Paul — B
Face Value. Whitefield-Madrano, Autumn — 111

AUTHOR, TITLE, SERIES AND SUBJECT INDEX

FACIAL EXPRESSION
   Ruhl, Sarah. *Smile*   B
FACIAL PARALYSIS
   Ruhl, Sarah. *Smile*   B
★ *Facing The Mountain*. Brown, Daniel James   940.54
Facing The Unseen. Tweedy, Damon   362.2
The Fact of a Body. Marzano-Lesnevich, Alexandria   364.152
Fact vs. Fiction. LaGarde, Jennifer   370.15
Factfulness. Rosling, Hans   155.9
FACTORIES
   Ditmore, Melissa Hope. ★ *Unbroken Chains*   306.74
   Freeman, Joshua Benjamin. ★ *Behemoth*   338.6
   Goldstein, Amy. *Janesville*   330.9775
   Merchant, Brian. *Blood in the Machine*   303.48
   Von Drehle, Dave. ★ *Triangle*   974.7
FACTORY FARMING
   Faruqi, Sonia. *Project Animal Farm*   338.1
   Genoways, Ted. *The Chain*   338.7
Factory Girls. Chang, Leslie T.   331.4
★ *Factory Man*. Macy, Beth   338.7
Fadiman, Anne
   The Spirit Catches You and You Fall Down   306.4
FADS AND CRAZES
   Bechdel, Alison. ★ *The Secret to Superhuman Strength*   741.5
   Holway, Tatiana M. *The Flower of Empire*   727
Faerm, Steven
   Fashion Design Course   746.9
Fagan, Brian M.
   Climate Chaos   304.2
   Fishing   338.3
   The Long Summer   551.6
Fagan, Chelsea
   The Financial Diet   332.024
Fagan, Kate
   All the Colors Came Out   B
FAGAN, KATE (SPORTS WRITER)
   Fagan, Kate. *All the Colors Came Out*   B
Fagans, Michael
   iPhone Photography for Everybody   770
Fagell, Phyllis L.
   ★ *Middle School Matters*   373.236
Fager, Jeffrey
   Fifty Years of 60 Minutes   070.1
Fagin, Dan
   Toms River   363.7209749
Fagone, Jason
   The Woman Who Smashed Codes   B
★ *The Failed Promise*. Levine, Robert S.   973.8
Failing Law Schools. Tamanaha, Brian Z.   340.071
FAILURE
   Bade, Rachael. ★ *Unchecked*   342.73
   Barnett, Erica C. *Quitter*   B
   Conroy, Pat. *My Losing Season*   B
   Edmondson, Amy C. *The Right Kind of Wrong*   158.1
   Ferguson, Niall. *Doom*   362.1962
   Hallinan, Joseph T. *Why We Make Mistakes*   153
   Hammack, William Scott. ★ *Things We Make*   620
   Manson, Mark. *The Subtle Art of Not Giving a F*ck*   158.1
   Montgomery, Patrick. *Baseball's Great Expectations*   796.357
   Phillips, Adam. *On Giving up*   158.2
   Riess, Jana. *Flunking Sainthood*   248.4
   Rinaldi, Karen. *It's Great to Suck at Something*   158.1
Failure to Launch. McConville, Mark   155.6
Fainaru-Wada, Mark
   League of Denial   617.1
★ *Fair Play*. Barnes, Katie   796.082
★ *Fair Shake*. Cahn, Naomi R.   331.4
FAIR TRIAL
   Leamer, Laurence. *The Price of Justice*   346.7302
FAIR USE (COPYRIGHT)
   Bellos, David. *Who Owns This Sentence?*   346.73
   Butler, Rebecca P. ★ *Copyright for Teachers & Librarians in the 21st Century*   346.7304
   Crews, Kenneth D. ★ *Copyright Law for Librarians and Educators*   346.7304
   Gasaway, Laura N. *Copyright Questions and Answers for Information Professionals*   346.7304
   Russell, Carrie. *Complete Copyright for K-12 Librarians and Educators*   346.73

   Zapruder, Alexandra. *Twenty-Six Seconds*   973.922092
Fair, Eric
   Consequence   B
FAIR, ERIC
   Fair, Eric. *Consequence*   B
Fairbanks, Amanda M.
   The Lost Boys of Montauk   910.91
FAIRBANKS, DOUGLAS, 1883-1939
   Goessel, Tracey. *The First King of Hollywood*   B
Fairchild, Barbara
   The Bon Appetit Cookbook   641.5
FAIRCHILD, DAVID, 1869-1954
   Stone, Daniel. *The Food Explorer*   B
Fairest. Talusan, Meredith   305.30973
FAIRIES
   Smith, Sally J. *Fairy Houses*   745.592
FAIRIES IN ART
   Smith, Sally J. *Fairy Houses*   745.592
FAIRNESS
   Baer, Daniel Brooks. *The Four Tests*   320.973
   Baron, Dennis E. *What's Your Pronoun?*   425.55
   Bharara, Preet. *Doing Justice*   347.73
   Breyer, Stephen G. ★ *The Authority of the Court and the Peril of Politics*   347.73
   Minow, Martha. *When Should Law Forgive?*   345
   Pratt, Victoria. *The Power of Dignity*   364.973
   Romeo, Nick. *The Alternative*   174
   Waal, F. B. M. de. ★ *Mama's Last Hug*   599.885
Fairweather, Jack
   The Volunteer   B
Fairy Houses. Smith, Sally J.   745.592
FAIRY TALE WRITING
   Bly, Robert. *More Than True*   398.2
★ *Fairy Tales from the Brothers Grimm*. Pullman, Philip   398.2
Faith. Carter, Jimmy   OK T A
FAITH
   Akbar, Kaveh. *Pilgrim Bell*   811
   Akyol, Mustafa. *The Islamic Jesus*   297.2
   Armstrong, Karen. *The Spiral Staircase*   B
   Bailey, Jennifer. *To My Beloveds*   261.8
   Bidwell, Duane R. *When One Religion Isn't Enough*   261.2
   Bignon, Guillaume. *Confessions of a French Atheist*   239
   Briggs, Lyvonne. ★ *Sensual Faith*   204
   Brown, Molly McCully. *Places I've Taken My Body*   B
   Carter, Jimmy. *Faith*   OK T A
   Cole, Natalie. *Angel on My Shoulder*   B
   Curtis, James. *Spencer Tracy*   B
   Dennett, D. C. *Breaking the Spell*   200
   DeSteno, David. *How God Works*   200.1
   Erwin, Jon. *Beyond Valor*   B
   Griswold, Eliza. *The Tenth Parallel*   297.2
   H, Lamya. ★ *Hijab Butch Blues*   B
   Hagglund, Martin. *This Life*   110
   Hitchens, Christopher. *The Four Horsemen*   211
   Husain, Ed. ★ *The House of Islam*   297
   Keflezighi, Meb. *26 Marathons*   B
   Keller, Timothy J. *The Reason for God*   239
   Kushner, Harold S. *Overcoming Life's Disappointments*   296.7
   Kyle, Taya. *American Spirit*   B
   Lemay, Mimi. *What We Will Become*   306.874
   Lewis, C. S. ★ *A Grief Observed*   242
   Lewis, C. S. *Miracles*   231.7
   Lewis, John. *Carry On*   328.73
   Loftis, Larry. ★ *The Watchmaker's Daughter*   940.53
   Mar, Alex. *Seventy Times Seven*   362.88
   Marsh, Charles. *Strange Glory*   B
   McCaulley, Esau. *How Far to the Promised Land*   B
   Merton, Thomas. ★ *The Seven Storey Mountain*   B
   Norris, Kathleen. *The Cloister Walk*   255
   Oliva, Alejandra. *Rivermouth*   305.9
   Poitier, Sidney. *The Measure of a Man*   B
   Samatar, Sofia. *The White Mosque*   B
   Savage, Jodi M. *The Death of a Jaybird*   B
   Smietana, Bob. *Reorganized Religion*   262.001
   Stanley, Brian. *Christianity in the Twentieth Century*   270.8
   Taylor, Barbara Brown. *Holy Envy*   B
   Taylor, Goldie. *The Love You Save*   B
   Taylor, Justin. *Riding with the Ghost*   B

PUBLIC LIBRARY CORE COLLECTION: NONFICTION
Twentieth Edition

Teresa. *A Call to Mercy*	234
Terkel, Studs. *Hope Dies Last*	920
Terkel, Studs. *Will the Circle Be Unbroken?*	128
Tippett, Krista. ★*Becoming Wise*	158.1
Turner, John G. *Brigham Young, Pioneer Prophet*	B
Vasquez-Lavado, Silvia. *In the Shadow of the Mountain*	B
Vaughn, Ellen Santilli. ★*Becoming Elisabeth Elliot*	B
Walsh, Declan. *The Nine Lives of Pakistan*	954.91
Warren, Rosanna. *Max Jacob*	B
Wiman, Christian. *He Held Radical Light*	814
Wiman, Christian. *Zero at the Bone*	818
Wray, T. J. *The Birth of Satan*	235

FAITH (CHRISTIANITY)

Armas, Kat. *Abuelita Faith*	248.8
Augustine. *Confessions*	B
Baskette, Molly Phinney. *How to Begin When Your World Is Ending*	248.8
Bass, Diana Butler. *Grateful*	241
Beaty, Katelyn. *Celebrities for Jesus*	261
Bee, Vanessa A. *Home Bound*	B
Billings, J. Todd. *Rejoicing in Lament*	248.8
Boa, Kenneth D. *Recalibrate Your Life*	248.8
Bolz-Weber, Nadia. *Accidental Saints*	284.1
Bono. ★*Surrender*	B
Bowler, Kate. *No Cure for Being Human*	B
Carlile, Brandi. *Broken Horses*	B
Carter, Jimmy. *Faith*	OK T A
Chaput, Charles J. *Things Worth Dying For*	248.4
Cobbs-Leonard, Tasha. *Do It Anyway*	241
Coldstream, Catherine. ★*Cloistered*	
Connell, John. *The Farmer's Son*	630.9
Crawford, Robert. *Eliot After the Waste Land*	B
Darling, Daniel. *Agents of Grace*	158.2
DiFelice, Bekah. *Almost There*	248.8
Dilbeck, D. H. *Frederick Douglass*	B
Duggar, Jill. *Counting the Cost*	B
Egan, Timothy. *A Pilgrimage to Eternity*	263
Evans, Rachel Held. *Wholehearted Faith*	248.4
Foles, Nick. *Believe It*	B
Francis. *Happiness in This Life*	248.4
Franklin, Missy. *Relentless Spirit*	B
Gaffigan, Jeannie. *When Life Gives You Pears*	B
Gregory, Rebekah. *Taking My Life Back*	B
Guthrie, Savannah. *Mostly What God Does*	248.4
Harris, Taylor. *This Boy We Made*	B
Hatmaker, Jen. *Of Mess and Moxie*	248.8
Hill, Jemele. *Uphill*	B
Irving, Apricot Anderson. *The Gospel of Trees*	B
Jenkins, Jedidiah. *To Shake the Sleeping Self*	B
Joyce, Russell W. *His Face Like Mine*	248
Jun, Tasha. ★*Tell Me the Dream Again*	248
Karon, Jan. *Bathed in Prayer*	242
Keeling, Ida. *Can't Nothing Bring Me Down*	B
Kriegel, Mark. *Pistol*	B
Lamott, Anne. ★*Dusk, Night, Dawn*	B
Lamott, Anne. ★*Hallelujah Anyway*	241
Lecrae. ★*I Am Restored*	B
Lima, Jamie Kern. *Believe It*	B
Loftis, Larry. ★*The Watchmaker's Daughter*	940.53
Lucado, Max. *Before Amen*	248.3
Manseau, Peter. *The Apparitionists*	B
Marshall, Cynthia. *You've Been Chosen*	B
McCammon, Sarah. ★*The Exvangelicals*	277.308
McCloskey, Jim. *When Truth Is All You Have*	B
McGuckin, John Anthony. ★*The Eastern Orthodox Church*	281.909
McLaren, Brian D. *Do I Stay Christian?*	270.8
McLaren, Brian D. *Faith After Doubt*	234
Means, Brittany. *Hell If We Don't Change Our Ways*	B
Merritt, Tyler. *I Take My Coffee Black*	791.4302
Merton, Thomas. ★*The Seven Storey Mountain*	B
Moore, Beth. *All My Knotted-Up Life*	B
Morton, Michael. *Getting Life*	B
Neville, Aaron. *Tell It Like It Is*	B
Orji, Yvonne. *Bamboozled by Jesus*	B
Pablo Cruz, Rosayra. *The Book of Rosy*	B
Pagels, Elaine H. ★*Why Religion?*	B
Park, J. S. ★*As Long as You Need*	248.8
Perry, Imani. *May We Forever Stand*	782.25
Peters, Rebecca Todd. *Trust Women*	362.1988
Plantinga, Cornelius. *Gratitude*	179
Prejean, Helen. *River of Fire*	B
Risner, Vaneetha Rendall. *Walking Through Fire*	B
Roberts, Matthias. *Holy Runaways*	262
Rohr, Richard. *The Universal Christ*	232
Rush, Charaia. *Courageously Soft*	234
Saxton, Martha. *The Widow Washington*	B
Shankle, Melanie. *Church of the Small Things*	248.8
Shirley, Craig. *Mary Ball Washington*	B
Smith, Jean Edward. *Bush*	973.931
Thi, Kim Phuc Phan. *Fire Road*	B
Thomas, R. Eric. *Here for It*	B
Travis, Randy. *Forever and Ever, Amen*	B
Vaughn, Ellen Santilli. ★*Becoming Elisabeth Elliot*	B
Wallis, Jim. *The False White Gospel*	261.7
Warren, W. Lee. *No Place to Hide*	B
Williams, Michelle. *Checking In*	B
Williams, Zach. *Rescue Story*	B

FAITH (ISLAM)

Ghobash, Omar Saif. *Letters to a Young Muslim*	297.09
Jalal al-Din Rumi, Maulana. *Rumi*	891
Moghul, Haroon. *How to Be a Muslim*	B
Ramadan, Tariq. ★*Introduction to Islam*	297

FAITH (JUDAISM)

Freedman, H. ★*The Talmud*	296.1
Kushner, Harold S. *Who Needs God*	296.7
Pogrebin, Abigail. *My Jewish Year*	296.4
Faith After Doubt. McLaren, Brian D.	234
Faith and Fossils. Grabbe, Lester L	231.7

FAITH AND REASON

Hagglund, Martin. *This Life*	110
Faith and Treason. Fraser, Antonia	942.06

FAITH HEALING

Brownback, Lydia. *Finding God in My Loneliness*	248.8
Eddy, Mary Baker. ★*Mary Baker Eddy*	289.5
Faithful Antiracism. Brennan, Chad	277.308
The Faithful Executioner. Harrington, Joel F.	B

FAITHFULL, MARIANNE

Winder, Elizabeth. *Parachute Women*	782.42164
Faizullah, Tarfia	
Registers of Illuminated Villages	811

FAKE NEWS

Hasen, Richard L. *Election Meltdown*	324.973
LaGarde, Jennifer. *Fact vs. Fiction*	370.15
Levitin, Daniel J. ★*A Field Guide to Lies*	153.4
McCraw, David Edward. *Truth in Our Times*	342.7308
Newitz, Annalee. *Stories Are Weapons*	355.3
Stengel, Richard. *Information Wars*	355.3
van der Linden, Sander. ★*Foolproof*	302.3
Falastin. Tamimi, Sami	641.595
The Falcon Thief. Hammer, Joshua	364.16

FALCONS

Hammer, Joshua. *The Falcon Thief*	364.16
Faleiro, Sonia	
The Good Girls	364.152
Falick, Melanie	
Making a Life	745.5
Faliveno, Melissa	
Tomboyland	B

FALIVENO, MELISSA, 1983-

Faliveno, Melissa. *Tomboyland*	B
Falk, Daina	
The Hungry Fan's Game Day Cookbook	641.5973
★*Fall and Rise.* Zuckoff, Mitchell	973.931
The Fall Line. Vinton, Nathaniel	796.93
The Fall of Berlin. Read, Anthony	940.54
The Fall of Berlin, 1945. Beevor, Antony	940.54
The Fall of Heaven. Cooper, Andrew Scott	B
The Fall of Richard Nixon. Brokaw, Tom	B
The Fall of the House of Dixie. Levine, Bruce C.	973.7
The Fall of the House of FIFA. Conn, David	796.334
The Fall of the House of Wilde. O'Sullivan, Emer	B
The Fall of the Ottomans. Rogan, Eugene L.	940.3
Fall, Jeremy	
Falling Upwards	158.1

FALL, JEREMY, 1990-

Fall, Jeremy. *Falling Upwards*	158.1

AUTHOR, TITLE, SERIES AND SUBJECT INDEX

FALLACIES (LOGIC)
    Levitin, Daniel J. ★*A Field Guide to Lies*   153.4
*The **Fallen** Stones*. Marcum, Diana   B
***Falling** Awake*. Oswald, Alice   821
***Falling** Back in Love with Being Human*. Thom, Kai Cheng   811
***Falling** Ill*. Williams, C. K.   811
***Falling** Upwards*. Fall, Jeremy   158.1
***Falling** Upwards*. Holmes, Richard   387.7
Fallon, Allison
    The Power of Writing It Down   158.1
Fallout. Blume, Lesley M. M.   940.54
FALLOWS, DEBORAH
    Fallows, James M. *Our Towns*   306.0973
Fallows, James M.
    Our Towns   306.0973
FALLOWS, JAMES M., 1949-
    Fallows, James M. *Our Towns*   306.0973
Faloyin, Dipo
    ★*Africa Is Not a Country*   960.33
FALSE IMPRISONMENT
    Adams, Jarrett. *Redeeming Justice*   340.092
    Cheng, Nien. *Life and Death in Shanghai*   B
    King, Gilbert. *Beneath a Ruthless Sun*   B
    Salaam, Yusef. *Better, Not Bitter*   B
    Smith, Clive Stafford. *The Injustice System*   345.759
    Woodfox, Albert. *Solitary*   B
FALSE PERSONATION
    White, Elizabeth B. ★*The Counterfeit Countess*   940.53
    Willetts, Paul. *King Con*   B
*A **False** Report*. Miller, T. Christian   364.15
FALSE TESTIMONY
    Rabinowitz, Dorothy. *No Crueler Tyrannies*   345.73
*The **False** White Gospel*. Wallis, Jim   261.7
Falter. McKibben, Bill   909.83
Falter, Suzanne
    The Extremely Busy Woman's Guide to Self-Care   613
Faludi, Susan
    In the Darkroom   B
FALUDI, SUSAN
    Faludi, Susan. *In the Darkroom*   B
FAME
    Andrews, Julie. *Home Work*   B
    Babb, Valerie Melissa. *The Book of James*   B
    Beaty, Katelyn. *Celebrities for Jesus*   261
    Bergstein, Rachelle. *The Genius of Judy*   813
    Bono. ★*Surrender*   B
    Brickell, Francesca Cartier. *The Cartiers*   B
    Brown, Craig. *Ninety-Nine Glimpses of Princess Margaret*   B
    Browne, David. *Crosby, Stills, Nash and Young*   920
    Busby, Jill Louise. *Unfollow Me*   305.08
    Carlin, Kelly. *A Carlin Home Companion*   B
    Casillo, Charles. *Marilyn Monroe*   B
    Costello, Elvis. *Unfaithful Music & Disappearing Ink*   B
    Dearborn, Mary V. *Carson McCullers*   B
    Ditum, Sarah. *Toxic*   920.72
    Driver, Minnie. *Managing Expectations*   B
    Duggar, Jill. *Counting the Cost*   B
    Farley, Audrey Clare. ★*Girls and Their Monsters*   306.875
    Felton, Tom. ★*Beyond the Wand*   B
    Field, Sally. *In Pieces*   B
    Fischer, Jenna. *The Office BFFs*   791.45
    Fox, Julia. *Down the Drain*   B
    Gless, Sharon. *Apparently There Were Complaints*   B
    Grey, Jennifer. *Out of the Corner*   B
    Guinn, Jeff. *Go Down Together*   B
    Harris, Mark. *Mike Nichols*   B
    Harry, Debbie. *Face It*   B
    Hodgman, John. *Medallion Status*   B
    Howard, Ron. ★*The Boys*   B
    Hussey, Olivia. *The Girl on the Balcony*   B
    Ice-T. *Split Decision*   920
    Jackson family. *The Jacksons*   782.421644
    Jefferson, Margo. *On Michael Jackson*   B
    John, Elton. ★*Me*   B
    Johnson, Brian. *The Lives of Brian*   B
    Kalb, Claudia. *Andy Warhol Was a Hoarder*   920
    Kemper, Ellie. *My Squirrel Days*   B
    King, David. *The Trial of Adolf Hitler*   345.43

    Kupperman, Michael. *All the Answers*   741.5
    Leavy, Jane. *The Big Fella*   B
    Letts, Elizabeth. ★*The Ride of Her Life*   B
    Lewis, Jenifer. *Walking in My Joy*   B
    Lorenz, Taylor. ★*Extremely Online*   302.23
    Lynn, Loretta. *Me & Patsy Kickin' up Dust*   B
    Mann, William J. *Hello, Gorgeous*   B
    Mans, Jasmine. *Black Girl, Call Home*   811
    Martin, Steve. *Number One Is Walking*   B
    Mills, Hayley. *Forever Young*   B
    Moby. *Then It Fell Apart*   B
    Moore, Marcus J. *The Butterfly Effect*   B
    Morton, Andrew. *Diana*   B
    Moser, Benjamin. ★*Sontag*   B
    Newman, Paul. *The Extraordinary Life of an Ordinary Man*   B
    Norman, Philip. ★*Wild Thing*   B
    Odenkirk, Bob. *Comedy Comedy Comedy Drama*   B
    Page, Elliot. *Pageboy*   B
    Perry, Joe. *Rocks*   B
    Philipps, Busy. *This Will Only Hurt a Little*   B
    Poniewozik, James. *Audience of One*   324.7
    Posey, Parker. *You're on an Airplane*   B
    Prince. *The Beautiful Ones*   B
    Prud'homme, Alex. *The French Chef in America*   B
    Rannells, Andrew. *Uncle of the Year*   B
    Reynolds, Simon. *Shock and Awe*   781.6609
    Ripa, Kelly. *Live Wire*   B
    Rosen, Charles. *Sugar*   B
    Sabathia, CC. *Till the End*   796.357
    Schemel, Patty. *Hit so Hard*   B
    Selleck, Tom. *You Never Know*   B
    Sestero, Greg. *The Disaster Artist*   791.43
    Smith, Jada Pinkett. *Worthy*   B
    Smith, Will. ★*Will*   B
    Spears, Britney. *The Woman in Me*   B
    Stamos, John. *If You Would Have Told Me*   B
    Stewart, Patrick. ★*Making It So*   B
    Stone, Sly. *Thank You (Falettinme Be Mice Elf Agin)*   B
    Sullivan, Matt. *Can't Knock the Hustle*   796.323
    Suvari, Mena. *The Great Peace*   B
    Taraborrelli, J. Randy. ★*Jackie*   B
    Taraborrelli, J. Randy. *The Kennedy Heirs*   920
    Tomine, Adrian. *The Loneliness of the Long-Distance Cartoonist*   741.5
    Travis, Randy. *Forever and Ever, Amen*   B
    Trebek, Alex. *The Answer Is ...*   791.4502
    Trejo, Danny. *Trejo*   B
    Union, Gabrielle. *We're Going to Need More Wine*   B
    Valby, Karen. *The Swans of Harlem*   792.8
    Waters, John. *Mr. Know-It-All*   814
    Weinman, Sarah. *Scoundrel*   364.152
    Wilson, A. N. *The Mystery of Charles Dickens*   823
    Winkler, Henry. ★*Being Henry*   B
    Woolever, Laurie. *Bourdain*   B
*The **Familia** Grande*. Kouchner, Camille   B
FAMILIAL LOVE
    Alexie, Sherman. *You Don't Have to Say You Love Me*   818
    Black, Dustin Lance. *Mama's Boy*   B
    Ford, Ashley C. ★*Somebody's Daughter*   B
    Hamill, Kirkland. *Filthy Beasts*   B
    Horton, Michelle. *Dear Sister*   B
    Hulls, Tessa. ★*Feeding Ghosts*   741.5
    Locke, Tembi. ★*From Scratch*   B
    Marshall, Greg. *Leg*   B
    Rippon, Kelly. *Parent Up*   649
    Simmons, Ruth. ★*Up Home*   B
FAMILIES
    Abdelmahmoud, Elamin. *Son of Elsewhere*   B
    Agee, James. ★*Cotton Tenants*   976.1
    Ai, Weiwei. *1000 Years of Joys and Sorrows*   709.2
    Akbar, Kaveh. *Pilgrim Bell*   811
    Albom, Mitch. *Finding Chika*   B
    Ali, Fatima. ★*Savor*   B
    Alyan, Hala. *The Moon That Turns You Back*   811
    Arment, Ainsley. *The Wild + Free Family*   649
    B., David. *Epileptic*   741.5
    Badkhen, Anna. *The World Is a Carpet*   305.409581
    Bailey, Catherine. *A Castle in Wartime*   943.086
    Bauermeister, Erica. *House Lessons*   B

PUBLIC LIBRARY CORE COLLECTION: NONFICTION
Twentieth Edition

Beaton, Kate. ★*Ducks*	741.5
Bell, Madison Smartt. *Child of Light*	B
Berger, Lynn. *Second Thoughts*	306.85
Betz-Hamilton, Axton. *The Less People Know About Us*	364.16
Bilger, Burkhard. *Fatherland*	B
Bilton, Chrysta. *Normal Family*	B
Birbiglia, Mike. *The New One*	B
Blair, Selma. *Mean Baby*	B
Bragg, Rick. ★*The Best Cook in the World*	641.5975
Bragg, Rick. *The Speckled Beauty*	636.7
Brower, Kate Andersen. *The Residence*	975.3
Buford, Bill. ★*Dirt*	B
Buque, Mariel. *Break the Cycle*	616.85
Byrne, Paula. *Kick*	B
Carriere, Alice. *Everything/Nothing/Someone*	B
Carter, Jimmy. *Sharing Good Times*	973.926
Caruana Galizia, Paul. ★*A Death in Malta*	364.15
Chaudry, Rabia. *Fatty Fatty Boom Boom*	B
Choi, Don Mee. *Hardly War*	811
Chow, Kat. *Seeing Ghosts*	B
Chung, Nicole. *All You Can Ever Know*	B
Clark, John Lee. *Touch the Future*	B
Clinton, Hillary Rodham. *It Takes a Village*	305.23
Crosson, Monica. *The Magikal Family*	299
Crowell, Rodney. *Chinaberry Sidewalks*	B
David, Laurie. *The Family Cooks*	641.3
De Bres, Helena. *How to Be Multiple*	155.44
Diamond, Cheryl. *Nowhere Girl*	B
Diaz, Jaquira. *Ordinary Girls*	818
Dogon, Mondiant. *Those We Throw Away Are Diamonds*	B
Donaldson-Pressman, Stephanie. *The Learning Habit*	371.30281
Dunne, Griffin. ★*The Friday Afternoon Club*	B
Ervin, Kristine S. *Rabbit Heart*	364.152
Fairbanks, Amanda M. *The Lost Boys of Montauk*	910.91
Faliveno, Melissa. *Tomboyland*	B
Faust, Drew Gilpin. *Necessary Trouble*	B
Finkel, David. *An American Dreamer*	975.8
Fleming, Melissa. *A Hope More Powerful Than the Sea*	956.9104
Foo, Stephanie. ★*What My Bones Know*	B
Frangello, Gina. *Blow Your House Down*	813
Franklin, Missy. *Relentless Spirit*	B
Gaffigan, Jim. *Dad Is Fat*	814
Garcia, Angela. ★*The Way That Leads Among the Lost*	362.29
Gates, Henry Louis. *In Search of Our Roots*	973
Gidla, Sujatha. *Ants Among Elephants*	305.5
Glass, Sara. *Kissing Girls on Shabbat*	B
Glatt, John. *The Family Next Door*	362.76092
Glatt, John. *Tangled Vines*	364.152
Gless, Sharon. *Apparently There Were Complaints*	B
Goldberg, Whoopi. *Bits and Pieces*	B
Good, Cassandra A. *First Family*	920
Gracie, Rickson. *Breathe*	B
Greene, Jayson. *Once More We Saw Stars*	155.9
Gupta, Prachi. ★*They Called Us Exceptional*	B
Hadlow, Janice. *A Royal Experiment*	B
Haelle, Tara. *The Informed Parent*	649
Hager, Jenna Bush. *Sisters First*	B
Hale, Grace Elizabeth. *In the Pines*	364.13
Harding, Thomas. *The House by the Lake*	943
Harjo, Joy. ★*Poet Warrior*	B
Hayasaki, Erika. *Somewhere Sisters*	362.7
Hays, Katie. *Family of Origin, Family of Choice*	248.8086
Hempel, Jessi. *The Family Outing*	B
Hernandez, Daisy. *The Kissing Bug*	616.9
Herold, Benjamin. *Disillusioned*	307.76
Hessler, Peter. *Other Rivers*	378.1
Heughan, Sam. *Waypoints*	B
Hudes, Quiara Alegria. ★*My Broken Language*	B
Hyde, Anne Farrar. *Empires, Nations, and Families*	978
Imbler, Sabrina. *How Far the Light Reaches*	591.77
Ingrassia, Lawrence. *A Fatal Inheritance*	616.99
Izgil, Tahir Hamut. *Waiting to Be Arrested at Night*	B
Jackson, Shirley. *Let Me Tell You*	818
Jackson, Shirley. ★*The Letters of Shirley Jackson*	813
Jacob, Mira. *Good Talk*	741.5
Jacobs, A. J. *It's All Relative*	929.1
James, Victoria. *Wine Girl*	B
Kaiser, Charles. *The Cost of Courage*	B
Kander, Jason. *Invisible Storm*	B
Kattan, Fadi. ★*Bethlehem*	641.59
Kearse, Bettye. *The Other Madisons*	920
Keaton, Diane. ★*Brother & Sister*	B
Keefe, Patrick Radden. ★*Empire of Pain*	338.7
Kelly, Donika. *The Renunciations*	811
Kershaw, Alex. *Avenue of Spies*	940.53
Kirkby, Bruce. *Blue Sky Kingdom*	954.96
Kissinger, Meg. *While You Were Out*	362.2
Kohli, Sahaj Kaur. *But What Will People Say?*	616.89
Kois, Dan. *How to Be a Family*	910.4
Kolata, Gina Bari. *Mercies in Disguise*	616
LaPointe, Sasha taqwseblu. *Red Paint*	B
Larman, Alexander. *The Windsors at War*	940.53
Lawton, Georgina. *Raceless*	B
Leaming, Barbara. *Kick Kennedy*	B
Lee, Helie. *In the Absence of Sun*	B
Lee, Sung-Yoon. *The Sister*	951.93
Lemay, Mimi. *What We Will Become*	306.874
Lev, Arlene Istar. *The Complete Lesbian & Gay Parenting Guide*	649
Levine, Philip. *The Simple Truth*	811
Lewis, Oscar. *The Children of Sanchez*	306.85
Li, Zhuqing. *Daughters of the Flower Fragrant Garden*	951.04
Lippman, Laura. *My Life as a Villainess*	B
Lovato, Roberto. *Unforgetting*	B
Mann, Sally. ★*Hold Still*	B
Mann, William J. *The Wars of the Roosevelts*	B
Mans, Jasmine. *Black Girl, Call Home*	811
Mansbach, Adam. *I Had a Brother Once*	811
Margulies, Julianna. *Sunshine Girl*	B
Matney, Mandy. *Blood on Their Hands*	364.152
Maupin, Armistead. *Logical Family*	B
McCormick, Ty. *Beyond the Sand and Sea*	920
Meacham, Jon. ★*American Lion*	B
Messud, Claire. *Kant's Little Prussian Head and Other Reasons Why I Write*	B
Miller, Kei. *Things I Have Withheld*	814
Mills, Hayley. *Forever Young*	B
Moore, Wayetu. *The Dragons, the Giant, the Women*	B
Morgan, Abi. *This Is Not a Pity Memoir*	B
Mowat, Farley. *Born Naked*	B
Nelson, Maggie. ★*The Argonauts*	B
Neumann, Ariana. *When Time Stopped*	B
Newman, Magdalena. *Normal*	611
Nguyen, Hieu Minh. *Not Here*	811
Nutt, Amy Ellis. *Becoming Nicole*	920
O'Reilly, Seamas. ★*Did Ye Hear Mammy Died?*	B
Olds, Sharon. *Arias*	811
Orenstein, Peggy. *Unraveling*	B
Page, Susan. ★*The Matriarch*	B
Paul, Pamela. ★*How to Raise a Reader*	649
Pawel, Miriam. *The Browns of California*	920
Porter, Carolyn. *Marcel's Letters*	940.54
Possanza, Amelia. *Lesbian Love Story*	B
Qadiri, Humayra. *Dancing in the Mosque*	B
Quinn, Tallu Schuyler. *What We Wish Were True*	B
Raboteau, Emily. *Lessons for Survival*	814
Rannells, Andrew. *Uncle of the Year*	B
Rear, Rachel. *Catch the Sparrow*	364.152
Rice, Condoleezza. *Extraordinary, Ordinary People*	B
Rosenstrach, Jenny. *How to Celebrate Everything*	641.5
Roy, Jessica. *American Girls*	305.48
RuPaul. ★*The House of Hidden Meanings*	B
Sabathia, CC. *Till the End*	796.357
Sale, Anna. ★*Let's Talk About Hard Things*	153.6
Sankovitch, Nina. *American Rebels*	920
Sattouf, Riad. *The Arab of the Future 2*	741.5
Sattouf, Riad. *The Arab of the Future*	741.5
Saxton, Martha. *The Widow Washington*	B
Scottoline, Lisa. *I See Life Through Rose-Colored Glasses*	813
Sebag-Montefiore, Simon. ★*The World*	929.7
Sedaris, David. ★*The Best of Me*	818
Sedaris, David. *Calypso*	814
Self, Robert O. *All in the Family*	320.50973
Sentilles, Sarah. *Stranger Care*	B
Shirley, Craig. *Mary Ball Washington*	B
Sinclair, Safiya. ★*How to Say Babylon*	B
Singh, Julietta. *The Breaks*	B

AUTHOR, TITLE, SERIES AND SUBJECT INDEX

Snyder, Rachel Louise. *Women We Buried, Women We Burned*	B
Som, Brandon. *Tripas*	811
Stewart, Chris. *Driving Over Lemons*	946
Szczeszak-Brewer, Agata. *The Hunger Book*	B
Taing, Mae Bunseng. *Under the Naga Tail*	B
Tallent, Elizabeth. *Scratched*	B
Taylor, Goldie. *The Love You Save*	B
Tometich, Annabelle. *The Mango Tree*	B
Townsend, Alan R. ★*This Ordinary Stardust*	B
Tran, Ly. *House of Sticks*	B
Tumulty, Karen. *The Triumph of Nancy Reagan*	B
Tur, Katy. *Rough Draft*	B
Vance, J. D. *Hillbilly Elegy*	B
Vuong, Ocean. ★*Time Is a Mother*	811
Weller, Sheila. *Carrie Fisher*	B
White, Ralph. *Getting Out of Saigon*	959.704
Wilkinson, Crystal. *Praisesong for the Kitchen Ghosts*	641.5975
Williams, Richard. *Black and White*	B
Willner, Nina. *Forty Autumns*	B
Wills, Clair. ★*Missing Persons*	929.2
Wilson, Katherine. *Only in Naples*	B
Wong, Jane. ★*Meet Me Tonight in Atlantic City*	B
Wu, Constance. *Making a Scene*	B
Wu, Simon. *Dancing on My Own*	700.1
Xue, XInran. *The Book of Secrets*	951.05
Young, Kevin. *Stones*	811
Zauner, Michelle. ★*Crying in H Mart*	B

FAMILIES OF MILITARY PERSONNEL

Finkel, David. *Thank You for Your Service*	920
Lee, Heath Hardage. *The League of Wives*	959.704
Poole, Robert M. *Section 60*	975.5
Wise, Beau. *Three Wise Men*	958.104
Wright, James Edward. *Enduring Vietnam*	959.704

FAMILIES OF MURDER VICTIMS

Ervin, Kristine S. *Rabbit Heart*	364.152
Gerard, Sarah. *Carrie Carolyn Coco*	364.152
Hagerty, Alexa. ★*Still Life with Bones*	599.9
Leaming, Barbara. *Jacqueline Bouvier Kennedy Onassis*	B
Nelson, David B. *Boys Enter the House*	364.152
Stoppard, Tom. ★*Rosencrantz & Guildenstern Are Dead*	822
Trethewey, Natasha D. ★*Memorial Drive*	B

FAMILIES OF MURDERERS

Gerard, Sarah. *Carrie Carolyn Coco*	364.152

FAMILY AND ADDICTION

Bond, Melissa. *Blood Orange Night*	616.8
Hamill, Kirkland. *Filthy Beasts*	B

FAMILY AND DEATH

Cayton-Holland, Adam. *Tragedy Plus Time*	B
Danticat, Edwidge. *The Art of Death*	809
Riggs, Nina. *The Bright Hour*	B
Rosenthal, Jason. *My Wife Said You May Want to Marry Me*	B

FAMILY AND MENTAL ILLNESS

Sardy, Marin. *The Edge of Every Day*	B

FAMILY AND RELATIONSHIPS — ABUSE

Bass, Ellen. ★*The Courage to Heal*	616.85
Calcaterra, Regina. *Etched in Sand*	B
Calcaterra, Regina. *Girl Unbroken*	B
Durvasula, Ramani. ★*It's Not You*	155.2
Freitas, Donna. *Consent*	364.158092
Gupta, Prachi. ★*They Called Us Exceptional*	B
Hamill, Kirkland. *Filthy Beasts*	B
Horton, Michelle. *Dear Sister*	B
Kenneally, Christine. *Ghosts of the Orphanage*	362.73
Kouchner, Camille. *The Familia Grande*	B
McCurdy, Jennette. ★*I'm Glad My Mom Died*	B
Robison, John Elder. *Look Me in the Eye*	B
Roy, Jessica. *American Girls*	305.48
Schreiber, Flora Rheta. *Sybil*	616.85
Selvaratnam, Tanya. *Assume Nothing*	B
Shorter, Frank. *My Marathon*	796.42
Snyder, Rachel Louise. *No Visible Bruises*	362.82
Taylor, Goldie. *The Love You Save*	B
V. *The Apology*	818
West, Cait. ★*Rift*	B
Wolff, Tobias. *This Boy's Life*	B
Zhu, Mimi. *Be Not Afraid of Love*	152.4

FAMILY AND RELATIONSHIPS — AGING AND DEATH

Adichie, Chimamanda Ngozi. *Notes on Grief*	155.9
Albom, Mitch. *Tuesdays with Morrie*	B
Alterman, Sara Faith. *Let's Never Talk About This Again*	616.8
Angelou, Maya. *Wouldn't Take Nothing for My Journey Now*	814
Applewhite, Ashton. *This Chair Rocks*	155.67
Aronson, Louise. *Elderhood*	362.60973
Berg, Elizabeth. *I'll Be Seeing You*	306.874
Bloom, Amy. *In Love*	B
Boa, Kenneth D. *Recalibrate Your Life*	248.8
Brody, Jane E. *Jane Brody's Guide to the Great Beyond*	616
Butler, Katy. *The Art of Dying Well*	616.02
Cacciatore, Joanne. *Bearing the Unbearable*	155.9
Chast, Roz. ★*Can't We Talk About Something More Pleasant?*	741.5
Chittister, Joan. *The Gift of Years*	200
Chow, Kat. *Seeing Ghosts*	B
Clarke, Rachel. *Dear Life*	B
Crosley, Sloane. *Grief Is for People*	B
Danticat, Edwidge. *The Art of Death*	809
Day, John D. *The Longevity Plan*	612.6
Delaney, Rob. ★*A Heart That Works*	B
Didion, Joan. ★*The Year of Magical Thinking*	B
Dugdale, Lydia S. *The Lost Art of Dying*	155.9
Edelman, Hope. *Motherless Daughters*	155.9
Ellis, Helen. *Bring Your Baggage and Don't Pack Light*	B
Emswiler, Mary Ann. *Guiding Your Child Through Grief*	155.9
Esty, Katharaine C. *Eightysomethings*	612.6
Fagan, Kate. *All the Colors Came Out*	B
Fersko-Weiss, Henry. *Caring for the Dying*	616.02
Frampton, Saul. *When I Am Playing with My Cat, How Do I Know She Is Not Playing with Me?*	844
Garcia, Rodrigo. *A Farewell to Gabo and Mercedes*	B
Gawande, Atul. ★*Being Mortal*	362.17
Gilbert, Sandra M. *Death's Door*	155.9
Godwin, Gail. *Getting to Know Death*	B
Green, Stefanie. *This Is Assisted Dying*	616.02
Hagerty, Barbara Bradley. *Life Reimagined*	155.6
Hannig, Anita. *The Day I Die*	364.152
Henderson, Artis. *Unremarried Widow*	B
Herring, Lucinda. *Reimagining Death*	393
James, John W. ★*The Grief Recovery Handbook*	155.9
Kerr, Christopher. *Death Is but a Dream*	155.9
Kessler, David. *Finding Meaning*	155.9
Kingston, Genevieve. *Did I Ever Tell You?*	B
Kubler-Ross, Elisabeth. *Life Lessons*	170
Kubler-Ross, Elisabeth. ★*On Death and Dying*	155.9
Lang, Maya. *What We Carry*	B
Leder, Steven Z. *The Beauty of What Remains*	306.9
Lewis, C. S. ★*A Grief Observed*	242
Lin, Amy. *Here After*	B
Locke, Tembi. ★*From Scratch*	B
Loh, Sandra Tsing. *The Madwoman and the Roomba*	B
Lyons, Anna. *We All Know How This Ends*	362.17
Mann, Jen. ★*Midlife Bites*	305.244
McColl, Sarah. *Joy Enough*	B
Mitford, Jessica. ★*The American Way of Death Revisited*	338.4
Moore, Thomas. *Ageless Soul*	155.67
Morton, Brian. *Tasha*	B
Norris, Kathleen. *Acedia & Me*	248.8
Notaro, Laurie. *Excuse Me While I Disappear*	B
O'Hara, Maryanne. *Little Matches*	B
Pagels, Elaine H. ★*Why Religion?*	B
Park, J. S. ★*As Long as You Need*	248.8
Pipher, Mary Bray. *Women Rowing North*	305.26
Preszler, Trent. *Little and Often*	B
Prickett, Pamela J. ★*The Unclaimed*	363.7
Rasmussen, Christina. *Where Did You Go?*	133.9
Rehm, Diane. *On My Own*	B
Rehm, Diane. ★*When My Time Comes*	179.7
Riggs, Nina. *The Bright Hour*	B
Roiphe, Katie. *The Violet Hour*	809
Rosenblatt, Roger. *Kayak Morning*	155.9
Rosenthal, Jason. *My Wife Said You May Want to Marry Me*	B
Saint John, Bozoma. *The Urgent Life*	B
Samuel, Julia. *Grief Works*	155.9
Seager, Sara. *The Smallest Lights in the Universe*	B
Smith, Carol. *Crossing the River*	B
Speerstra, Karen. *The Divine Art of Dying*	202
Taylor, Justin. *Riding with the Ghost*	B
Terkel, Studs. *Will the Circle Be Unbroken?*	128

PUBLIC LIBRARY CORE COLLECTION: NONFICTION
Twentieth Edition

Thomas, Elizabeth Marshall. *Growing Old*	305.26
Wanzer, Sidney H. ★*To Die Well*	179.7
Warraich, Haider. *Modern Death*	179.7
Yalom, Irvin D. *Staring at the Sun*	155.9

FAMILY AND RELATIONSHIPS — DATING AND MARRIAGE

Adams, John. *My Dearest Friend*	973.4
Bard, Elizabeth. *Lunch in Paris*	B
Bard, Elizabeth. *Picnic in Provence*	B
Cacioppo, Stephanie. *Wired for Love*	616.8
Collins, Lauren. *When in French*	B
Cronkite, Walter. *Cronkite's War*	070.4
Doty, Cate. *Mergers and Acquisitions*	395.2
Dunn, Jancee. *How Not to Hate Your Husband After Kids*	646.7
Ellis, Helen. *Bring Your Baggage and Don't Pack Light*	814
Feiler, Bruce. *The First Love Story*	222
Fraser, Antonia. *Love and Louis XIV*	B
Gabriel, Mary. *Love and Capital*	920
Garcia, Mayte. *The Most Beautiful*	920
Goldsmith, Martin. *The Inextinguishable Symphony*	B
Goodwin, Doris Kearns. *No Ordinary Time*	920
Gottlieb, Lori. ★*Maybe You Should Talk to Someone*	B
Gottman, Julie Schwartz. *Fight Right*	616.89
Gristwood, Sarah. *The Tudors in Love*	941.05
Havrilesky, Heather. *Foreverland*	306.81
Hoffman, Damona. *F the Fairy Tale*	306.73
Isenberg, Sheila. *Women Who Love Men Who Kill*	362.83
Jacob, Mira. *Good Talk*	741.5
Kerner, Ian. *She Comes First*	613.9
Lerner, Harriet Goldhor. *The Dance of Intimacy*	155.6
MacColl, Gail. *To Marry an English Lord*	974.7
Machado, Carmen Maria. ★*In the Dream House*	B
Marton, Kati. *Hidden Power*	B
McClelland, Mac. *Irritable Hearts*	B
Mendelson, Cheryl. ★*Vows*	203
Millwood, Molly. *To Have and to Hold*	306.874
Offerman, Nick. *The Greatest Love Story Ever Told*	B
Patchett, Ann. *This Is the Story of a Happy Marriage*	B
Persico, Joseph E. *Franklin and Lucy*	973.917092
Rallo, Eli. *I Didn't Know I Needed This*	306.73
Real, Terrence. *Us*	646.7
Rinzler, Lodro. *Love Hurts*	294.3
Schwartz, David Joseph. ★*The Magic of Thinking Big*	158
Slice, Jessica. *Dateable*	646.7
Strings, Sabrina. *The End of Love*	155.3
Verant, Samantha. *Seven Letters from Paris*	B
Winter, Molly Roden. *More*	B

FAMILY AND RELATIONSHIPS — DISABLED FAMILY MEMBERS

Clark, John Lee. *Touch the Future*	B
DiMarco, Nyle. ★*Deaf Utopia*	B
Grandin, Temple. *Navigating Autism*	618.92
Grue, Jan. *I Live a Life Like Yours*	B
Mace, Nancy L. ★*The 36-Hour Day*	616.8
Moorer, Allison. *I Dream He Talks to Me*	782.42164
Solomon, Andrew. *Far from the Tree*	362.4083

FAMILY AND RELATIONSHIPS — DIVORCE

Blackstone-Ford, Jann. *Co-Parenting Through Separation and Divorce*	306.89
Cusk, Rachel. *Aftermath*	B
Frangello, Gina. *Blow Your House Down*	813
Green, Janice. ★*Divorce After 50*	306.89
Smith, Maggie. ★*You Could Make This Place Beautiful*	B

FAMILY AND RELATIONSHIPS — FAMILIES

Alexander, Kwame. *Why Fathers Cry at Night*	B
Alterman, Sara Faith. *Let's Never Talk About This Again*	616.8
Ball, Edward. *Slaves in the Family*	975.7
Bechdel, Alison. ★*Fun Home*	B
Betz-Hamilton, Axton. *The Less People Know About Us*	364.16
Bilton, Chrysta. *Normal Family*	B
Birbiglia, Mike. *The New One*	B
Black, Michael Ian. *A Better Man*	305.31
Brina, Elizabeth Miki. *Speak, Okinawa*	305.48
Bui, Thi. *The Best We Could Do*	741.5
Buque, Mariel. *Break the Cycle*	616.85
Chernow, Ron. *The Warburgs*	B
Cho, Grace M. *Tastes Like War*	305.48
Chow, Kat. *Seeing Ghosts*	B
Coll, Steve. *The Bin Ladens*	920
Connell, John. *The Farmer's Son*	630.9
Cooper, Anderson. *The Rainbow Comes and Goes*	B
Cooper, Helene. *The House at Sugar Beach*	921
Danticat, Edwidge. ★*Brother, I'm Dying*	B
Day, Marianne Waggoner. *Camp Grandma*	306.8745
Diamond, Cheryl. *Nowhere Girl*	B
Dunne, Griffin. ★*The Friday Afternoon Club*	B
Foer, Esther Safran. *I Want You to Know We're Still Here*	B
Ford, Ashley C. ★*Somebody's Daughter*	B
Ford, Richard. *Between Them*	B
Franklin, John Hope. *In Search of the Promised Land*	929
Franklin, Missy. *Relentless Spirit*	B
Fremont, Helen. *The Escape Artist*	B
Geller, Danielle. *Dog Flowers*	B
Genoways, Ted. *This Blessed Earth*	630.9
Goldberg, Whoopi. *Bits and Pieces*	B
Gordon-Reed, Annette. ★*The Hemingses of Monticello*	920
Grant, Gail Milissa. *At the Elbows of My Elders*	B
Greene, Jayson. *Once More We Saw Stars*	155.9
Hadlow, Janice. *A Royal Experiment*	B
Hemon, Aleksandar. *My Parents*	814
Hempel, Jessi. *The Family Outing*	B
Hood, Ann. *Kitchen Yarns*	641.5
Howe, Ben Ryder. *My Korean Deli*	B
Irving, Apricot Anderson. *The Gospel of Trees*	B
Kamkwamba, William. ★*The Boy Who Harnessed the Wind*	B
Koh, EJ. *The Magical Language of Others*	813
Kois, Dan. *How to Be a Family*	910.4
Kozol, Jonathan. *The Theft of Memory*	B
Lamb, Christina. *House of Stone*	968.91
Leamer, Laurence. *The Kennedy Men*	920
Lee, Helie. *In the Absence of Sun*	B
Lewis, Oscar. *The Children of Sanchez*	306.85
Lockwood, Patricia. *Priestdaddy*	B
Mahoney, Richard D. *Sons & Brothers*	920
McBride, James. *The Color of Water*	B
McBride, Karyl. *Will I Ever Be Good Enough?*	616.85
McCauley, Esau. *How Far to the Promised Land*	B
McConville, Mark. *Failure to Launch*	155.6
McCourt, Malachy. *A Monk Swimming*	B
McCourt, Malachy. *Singing My Him Song*	B
Means, Brittany. *Hell If We Don't Change Our Ways*	B
Mehra, Nishta. *Brown, White, Black*	305.800973
Meyer, G. J. *The Borgias*	920
Miller, Michelle. *Belonging*	B
Miranda, Deborah A. *Bad Indians*	305.8009794
Morton, Brian. *Tasha*	B
Mouton, Deborah D. E. E. P. *Black Chameleon*	B
Nguyen, Bich Minh. *Owner of a Lonely Heart*	B
O'Reilly, Seamas. ★*Did Ye Hear Mammy Died?*	B
Owusu, Nadia. *Aftershocks*	B
Pryce, Jessica. ★*Broken*	362.7
Reang, Putsata. *Ma and Me*	B
Sabar, Ariel. *My Father's Paradise*	B
Salama, Jordan. ★*Stranger in the Desert*	982
Satrapi, Marjane. *Chicken with Plums*	741.5
Savage, Jodi M. *The Death of a Jaybird*	B
Sedaris, David. ★*The Best of Me*	818
Sentilles, Sarah. *Stranger Care*	B
Shankle, Melanie. *Church of the Small Things*	248.8
Shapiro, Dani. ★*Inheritance*	B
Shih, David. *Chinese Prodigal*	B
Shlain, Tiffany. *24/6*	158.1
Sipress, David. *What's so Funny?*	B
Szczeszak-Brewer, Agata. *The Hunger Book*	B
Tan, Amy. ★*Where the Past Begins*	B
Thomas, Joseph Earl. *Sink*	B
Tometich, Annabelle. *The Mango Tree*	B
Wang, Connie. *Oh My Mother!*	B
Williams, Richard. *Black and White*	B
Willner, Nina. *Forty Autumns*	B
Wills, Clair. ★*Missing Persons*	929.2
Wong, Carmen Rita. *Why Didn't You Tell Me?*	B
Yousafzai, Ziauddin. *Let Her Fly*	B

FAMILY AND RELATIONSHIPS — FRIENDSHIP

Albom, Mitch. *Tuesdays with Morrie*	B
Baker, Billy. *We Need to Hang Out*	177
Bradford, Joy Harden. *Sisterhood Heals*	158.2
Cohen, Rhaina. ★*The Other Significant Others*	177

AUTHOR, TITLE, SERIES AND SUBJECT INDEX

Crosley, Sloane. *Grief Is for People*	B
Guarnere, William. *Brothers in Battle, Best of Friends*	B
Hagberg, Eva. *How to Be Loved*	616.7
Halberstam, David. *The Teammates*	B
Holloway, Kris. *Monique and the Mango Rains*	B
Jackson, Danielle Bayard. *Fighting for Our Friendships*	302.34
Meacham, Jon. *Franklin and Winston*	940.53
Nagorski, Andrew. *Saving Freud*	940.53
Patchett, Ann. *Truth & Beauty*	B
Rosen, Jonathan. ★*The Best Minds*	616.89
Schwalbe, Will. *We Should Not Be Friends*	B
Shankle, Melanie. *Church of the Small Things*	248.8
Smee, Sebastian. *The Art of Rivalry*	700.92
Sow, Aminatou. *Big Friendship*	177
Tate, Christie. *B.F.F.*	B
Totenberg, Nina. ★*Dinners with Ruth*	B
Trice, Dawn Turner. ★*Three Girls from Bronzeville*	977.311
Wenzke, Ali. ★*The Art of Happy Moving*	648

FAMILY AND RELATIONSHIPS — GENERAL

Bauermeister, Erica. *House Lessons*	B
Belasco, Andrew. *The Enlightened College Applicant*	378.1
Blackstone, Amy. *Childfree by Choice*	306.874
Blair, Selma. *Mean Baby*	B
Blyth, Catherine. *The Art of Conversation*	395.5
Brooks, David. ★*How to Know a Person*	158.2
Brooks, David. *The Social Animal*	305.5
Cain, Susan. *Quiet*	155.2
Carcaterra, Lorenzo. *Three Dreamers*	B
Citro, Asia. *150+ Screen-Free Activities for Kids*	796.5
Craig, William. *Yankee Come Home*	972.9107
Dahl, Melissa. *Cringeworthy*	158.2
Dickinson, Amy. *Strangers Tend to Tell Me Things*	B
Doorley, Rachelle. *Tinkerlab*	600
Doyne, Maggie. *Between the Mountain and the Sky*	B
Felix, Camonghne. *Dyscalculia*	B
Flink, David. *Thinking Differently*	371.9
Foo, Stephanie. *What My Bones Know*	B
Foster, Sutton. *Hooked*	B
Franzen, Jonathan. *The End of the End of the Earth*	814
Goodin, Tanya. *Stop Staring at Screens*	004.67
Hackman, Rose. ★*Emotional Labor*	155.3
Hatmaker, Jen. *Of Mess and Moxie*	248.8
Headlee, Celeste Anne. *We Need to Talk*	153.6
Jamison, Leslie. *The Empathy Exams*	813
Kohli, Sahaj Kaur. ★*But What Will People Say?*	616.89
Lekas Miller, Anna. *Love Across Borders*	323.6
Lev, Arlene Istar. *The Complete Lesbian & Gay Parenting Guide*	649
Lieberman, David J. *Never Get Angry Again*	152.4
Maisel, Ivan. *I Keep Trying to Catch His Eye*	B
McInerny, Nora. *The Hot Young Widows Club*	155.9
Murray, Liz. *Breaking Night*	B
Oster, Emily. ★*The Unexpected*	618.2
Pease, Allan. *The Definitive Book of Body Language*	153.6
Philpott, Mary Laura. *Bomb Shelter*	B
Pipher, Mary Bray. *A Life in Light*	B
Post, Lizzie. *Emily Post's Etiquette*	395
Post, Lizzie. *Emily Post's Etiquette*	395
Rakel, David. *The Compassionate Connection*	610.1
Saline, Sharon. *What Your ADHD Child Wishes You Knew*	618.92
Sancton, Thomas. *The Bettencourt Affair*	B
Schulz, Kathryn. ★*Lost & Found*	B
Sederer, Lloyd I. *The Family Guide to Mental Health Care*	616.89
Smith, R. Garth. *Asd, the Complete Autism Spectrum Disorder Health & Diet Guide*	616.85
Snyder, Rachel Louise. *Women We Buried, Women We Burned*	B
Solnit, Rebecca. *The Faraway Nearby*	814
Stone, Douglas. *Difficult Conversations*	158.2
Stryker, Kitty. *Ask*	302
Tolan, Sandy. ★*The Lemon Tree*	B
Van Es, Bart. *The Cut Out Girl*	B
Van't Hul, Jean. *The Artful Parent*	745.5083
Van't Hul, Jean. *The Artful Year*	745.594
Velasquez, Lizzie. *Dare to Be Kind*	177
Waxman, Jamye. *How to Break up with Anyone*	158.2
Williams, Florence. *Heartbreak*	306.7
Zauner, Michelle. ★*Crying in H Mart*	B

FAMILY AND RELATIONSHIPS — GROWING UP

Abdurraqib, Hanif. ★*There's Always This Year*	796.323

Alderton, Dolly. *Everything I Know About Love*	B
Allmen, Tara. *Menopause Confidential*	618.1
Alvarez, Celine. *The Natural Laws of Children*	372.21
Arana, Marie. *American Chica*	B
Brina, Elizabeth Miki. *Speak, Okinawa*	305.48
Broom, Sarah M. *The Yellow House*	B
Broome, Brian. ★*Punch Me up to the Gods*	B
Brown, Emma. *To Raise a Boy*	649
Burke Harris, Nadine. *The Deepest Well*	618.92
Burton, Susan. *Empty*	B
Calcaterra, Regina. *Etched in Sand*	B
Calcaterra, Regina. *Girl Unbroken*	B
Cameron, Julia. *It's Never Too Late to Begin Again*	155.67
Carey, Tanith. *What's My Child Thinking?*	155.4
Carter, Jimmy. *An Hour Before Daylight*	B
Chavez Perez, Inti. *Respect*	176
Coates, Ta-Nehisi. *The Beautiful Struggle*	B
Crais, Clifton C. *History Lessons*	B
Damour, Lisa. ★*Under Pressure*	155.5
Damour, Lisa. *Untangled*	305.235
Davies, Simone. *The Montessori Toddler*	371.39
Devantez, Chelsea. ★*I Shouldn't Be Telling You This*	B
Diamant, Anita. *Pitching My Tent*	296.7
Dillard, Annie. *An American Childhood*	B
Dunne, Griffin. ★*The Friday Afternoon Club*	B
Eire, Carlos M. N. *Learning to Die in Miami*	B
Fagell, Phyllis L. ★*Middle School Matters*	373.236
Faliveno, Melissa. *Tomboyland*	B
Findakly, Brigitte. *Poppies of Iraq*	741.5
Ford, Ashley C. ★*Somebody's Daughter*	B
Goodan, Chelsey. *Underestimated*	305.235
H, Lamya. ★*Hijab Butch Blues*	B
Haelle, Tara. *The Informed Parent*	649
Haidt, Jonathan. ★*The Anxious Generation*	305.23
Helwig, Jenna. *Baby-Led Feeding*	641.3
Henning, Kristin. *The Rage of Innocence*	364.36
Huggins, Kathleen. ★*The Nursing Mother's Companion*	649
Jawando, Will. ★*My Seven Black Fathers*	B
Klein, Tovah P. *How Toddlers Thrive*	305.232
Lythcott-Haims, Julie. *Your Turn*	305.24
McConville, Mark. *Failure to Launch*	155.6
McCourt, Frank. ★*Angela's Ashes*	929
Miller, Michelle. *Belonging*	B
Mogel, Wendy. *Voice Lessons for Parents*	649
Moore, Wes. *The Other Wes Moore*	B
Mouton, Deborah D. E. E. P. *Black Chameleon*	B
Mowat, Farley. *Born Naked*	B
Murkoff, Heidi Eisenberg. *What to Expect the First Year*	305.232
Murkoff, Heidi Eisenberg. ★*What to Expect When You're Expecting*	618.2
Nafisi, Azar. *Things I've Been Silent About*	B
Natterson, Cara Familian. ★*Decoding Boys*	649
Noah, Trevor. *Born a Crime*	B
Ockwell-Smith, Sarah. *Ready, Set, Go!*	649
Patchett, Ann. *This Is the Story of a Happy Marriage*	B
Pattee, Amy. *Developing Library Collections for Today's Young Adults*	027.62
Phelan, Tom. *We Were Rich and We Didn't Know It*	B
Satrapi, Marjane. ★*The Complete Persepolis*	741.5
Scheier, Liz. *Never Simple*	B
Shteyngart, Gary. ★*Little Failure*	B
Simmons, Rachel. ★*Enough as She Is*	155.5
Sinclair, Safiya. ★*How to Say Babylon*	B
Sipress, David. *What's so Funny?*	B
Sone, Monica Itoi. *Nisei Daughter*	979.7
Stern, Amanda. *Little Panic*	616.8522
Taylor, Goldie. *The Love You Save*	B
Thomas, Joseph Earl. *Sink*	B
Tometich, Annabelle. *The Mango Tree*	B
Tran, Ly. *House of Sticks*	B
Walls, Jeannette. ★*The Glass Castle*	B
Watts, Reggie. *Great Falls, MT*	B
Whitney, Emerson. *Heaven*	B
Williams, Mary. *The Lost Daughter*	B
Wolff, Tobias. *This Boy's Life*	B

FAMILY AND RELATIONSHIPS — ILLNESS AND THE FAMILY

Albom, Mitch. *Finding Chika*	B
Allende, Isabel. ★*Paula*	B
Applebaum, Allison. *Stand by Me*	649.8

PUBLIC LIBRARY CORE COLLECTION: NONFICTION
Twentieth Edition

B., David. *Epileptic*	741.5
Bond, Melissa. *Blood Orange Night*	616.8
Bowler, Kate. *No Cure for Being Human*	B
Davis, Patti. *Floating in the Deep End*	616.8
Didion, Joan. ★*The Year of Magical Thinking*	B
DiGregorio, Sarah. *Early*	618.92
Granata, Vince. *Everything Is Fine*	B
Harpham, Heather Elise. *Happiness*	B
Harris, Taylor. *This Boy We Made*	B
Hernandez, Daisy. *The Kissing Bug*	616.9
Ingrassia, Lawrence. *A Fatal Inheritance*	616.99
Kander, Jason. *Invisible Storm*	B
Kiper, Dasha. ★*Travelers to Unimaginable Lands*	616.8
Kissinger, Meg. *While You Were Out*	362.2
Kolata, Gina Bari. *Mercies in Disguise*	616
Kolker, Robert. ★*Hidden Valley Road*	920
Lang, Maya. *What We Carry*	B
Lin, Jami Nakamura. *The Night Parade*	B
May, Katherine. *Wintering*	155.9
Morgan, Abi. *This Is Not a Pity Memoir*	B
O'Hara, Maryanne. *Little Matches*	B
Quinn, Tallu Schuyler. *What We Wish Were True*	B
Riggs, Nina. *The Bright Hour*	B
Schwalbe, Will. ★*The End of Your Life Book Club*	B
Townsend, Alan R. ★*This Ordinary Stardust*	B
Washington, Kate. ★*Already Toast*	649.8
Winn, Raynor. *The Wild Silence*	B

FAMILY AND RELATIONSHIPS — LGBTQIA+

Amer, Lindz. *Rainbow Parenting*	649
Greene, Benjamin. ★*My Child Is Trans, Now What?*	649
Hays, Katie. *Family of Origin, Family of Choice*	248.8086
Hewitt, Sean. *All Down Darkness Wide*	B
Mock, Janet. *Surpassing Certainty*	B
Wizenberg, Molly. *Fixed Stars*	B

FAMILY AND RELATIONSHIPS — PARENTING

Adichie, Chimamanda Ngozi. *Dear Ijeawele*	649
Airton, Lee. ★*Gender*	305.3
Allende, Isabel. ★*Paula*	B
Altmann, Tanya Remer. *What to Feed Your Baby*	649
Amer, Lindz. *Rainbow Parenting*	649
Apter, T. E. *The Teen Interpreter*	306.874
Arment, Ainsley. *The Wild + Free Family*	649
Asika, Uju. *Bringing up Race*	155.4
Backman, Fredrik. *Things My Son Needs to Know About the World*	B
Barkley, Russell A. *Taking Charge of ADHD*	618.92
Baxley, Traci. *Social Justice Parenting*	306.87
Berg, Anastasia. ★*What Are Children For?*	306.87
Berger, Lynn. *Second Thoughts*	306.85
Bhattacharya, Shaoni. *The Baby Book*	649.1
Blackstone-Ford, Jann. *Co-Parenting Through Separation and Divorce*	306.89
Boyce, W. Thomas. *The Orchid and the Dandelion*	649
Brackett, Marc A. *Permission to Feel*	152.4
Brickman, Sophie. *Baby, Unplugged*	306.874
Brown, Emma. *To Raise a Boy*	649
Brown, Maressa. *Raising Baby by the Stars*	133.5
Brown, Noah. *Reading Together*	028.5
Bryson, Tina Payne. *The Bottom Line for Baby*	618.92
Carey, Tanith. *What's My Child Thinking?*	155.4
Casares, Whitney. *The Working Mom Blueprint*	306.8743
Chabon, Michael. *Pops*	306.874
Christakis, Erika. *The Importance of Being Little*	372.21
Citro, Asia. *150+ Screen-Free Activities for Kids*	796.5
Conaboy, Chelsea. *Mother Brain*	306.874
Corrigan, Kelly. *Glitter and Glue*	B
Curtis, Glade B. *Your Pregnancy Week by Week*	618.2
Cusk, Rachel. *A Life's Work*	306.874
Damour, Lisa. *The Emotional Lives of Teenagers*	155.5
Damour, Lisa. ★*Under Pressure*	155.5
Damour, Lisa. *Untangled*	305.235
Davies, Simone. *The Montessori Toddler*	371.39
Day, Marianne Waggoner. *Camp Grandma*	306.8745
Delaney, Rob. ★*A Heart That Works*	B
Dial, Roman. *The Adventurer's Son*	917.286
DiGregorio, Sarah. *Early*	618.92
Donaldson-Pressman, Stephanie. *The Learning Habit*	371.30281
Dubin, Minna. ★*Mom Rage*	306.874
Elkind, David. *The Power of Play*	155.4
Emswiler, Mary Ann. *Guiding Your Child Through Grief*	155.9
Ezzo, Gary. *On Becoming Baby Wise*	649
Faber, Adele. ★*How to Talk so Kids Will Listen & Listen so Kids Will Talk*	649
Fagell, Phyllis L. ★*Middle School Matters*	373.236
Farris, Grace. *Mom Milestones*	306.87
Finlay, B. Brett. *Let Them Eat Dirt*	616.9
Flink, David. *Thinking Differently*	371.9
Foxx, Jamie. *Act Like You Got Some Sense*	B
Fradin, Kelly. *Advanced Parenting*	649
Gaffigan, Jim. *Dad Is Fat*	814
Galanti, Regine. ★*Parenting Anxious Kids*	155.4
Galinsky, Ellen. ★*The Breakthrough Years*	649
Garbes, Angela. *Essential Labor*	306.874
Goh, Suzanne. *Magnificent Minds*	618.92
Goodan, Chelsey. *Underestimated*	305.235
Goodin, Tanya. *Stop Staring at Screens*	004.67
Gopnik, Alison. *The Gardener and the Carpenter*	155.4
Greene, Benjamin. ★*My Child Is Trans, Now What?*	649
Grose, Jessica. *Screaming on the Inside*	306.874
Haelle, Tara. *The Informed Parent*	649
Haidt, Jonathan. ★*The Anxious Generation*	305.23
Hawthorne, Britt. ★*Raising Antiracist Children*	649
Hibbs, B. Janet. *The Stressed Years of Their Lives*	616.8900835
Hibbs, B. Janet. *You're Not Done Yet*	649
Hillsberg, Christina. *License to Parent*	649.1
Jaffe, Sarah W. *Wanting What's Best*	649
Jones, Lucy. ★*Matrescence*	306.874
Kendi, Ibram X. ★*How to Raise an Antiracist*	649
Kennedy-Moore, Eileen. ★*Kid Confidence*	155.4
King, Charles Monroe. *A Journal for Jordan*	956.7044
Kingston, Genevieve. *Did I Ever Tell You?*	B
Klein, Jessi. *I'll Show Myself Out*	B
Klein, Tovah P. *How Toddlers Thrive*	305.232
Kline, Emily. ★*The School of Hard Talks*	155.5
Kobliner, Beth. *Make Your Kid a Money Genius (even If You're Not)*	332.024
Koenig, Joan. *The Musical Child*	780.71
Kowal-Connelly, Suanne. *Parenting Through Puberty*	649
Kurcinka, Mary Sheedy. *Raising Your Spirited Baby*	306.874
Lahey, Jessica. *The Addiction Inoculation*	649
Lahey, Jessica. *The Gift of Failure*	649
Lang, Maya. *What We Carry*	B
Lemay, Mimi. *What We Will Become*	306.874
Lev, Arlene Istar. *The Complete Lesbian & Gay Parenting Guide*	649
Levine, Madeline. ★*Ready or Not*	649
Lickona, Thomas. *How to Raise Kind Kids*	649
Lieber, Ron. *The Opposite of Spoiled*	332.0240083
Linn, Susan. *Who's Raising the Kids?*	649
McCarthy, Catherine. *Raising a Kid Who Can*	649
Medini, Shari. *Parenting While Working from Home*	650.1
Millwood, Molly. *To Have and to Hold*	306.874
Mogel, Wendy. *Voice Lessons for Parents*	649
Moorer, Allison. *I Dream He Talks to Me*	782.42164
Morgenstern, Julie. *Time to Parent*	649
Morin, Amy. *13 Things Mentally Strong Parents Don't Do*	649
Murkoff, Heidi Eisenberg. *What to Expect the First Year*	305.232
Murkoff, Heidi Eisenberg. ★*What to Expect the Second Year*	649
Murkoff, Heidi Eisenberg. ★*What to Expect When You're Expecting*	618.2
Natterson, Cara Familian. ★*Decoding Boys*	649
Naumburg, Carla. ★*You Are Not a Sh*tty Parent*	649
Nguyen, Bich Minh. *Owner of a Lonely Heart*	B
Nowicki, Stephen. *Raising a Socially Successful Child*	649
Ockwell-Smith, Sarah. *Ready, Set, Go!*	649
Orenstein, Peggy. *Cinderella Ate My Daughter*	305.23082
Oster, Emily. ★*Cribsheet*	618.2
Paul, Pamela. ★*How to Raise a Reader*	649
Perry, Philippa. ★*The Book You Wish Your Parents Had Read*	649
Phelan, Thomas W. *1-2-3 Magic*	649
Pressman, Aliza. *The 5 Principles of Parenting*	649.1
Prizant, Barry M. ★*Uniquely Human*	618.92
Quindlen, Anna. ★*Nanaville*	B
Ramesh, Jaya. *Parenting at the Intersections*	649
Rinella, Steven. ★*Outdoor Kids in an Inside World*	649
Rippon, Kelly. *Parent Up*	649
Rowe, Peggy. *About My Mother*	B
Russert, Luke. *Look for Me There*	B
Santomero, Angela C. *Preschool Clues*	305.233
Seldin, Tim. *How to Raise an Amazing Child the Montessori Way*	649

AUTHOR, TITLE, SERIES AND SUBJECT INDEX

Senator, Susan. *Autism Adulthood*	616.85
Senior, Jennifer. *All Joy and No Fun*	306.874
Serrallach, Oscar. *The Postnatal Depletion Cure*	618.6
Siegel, Daniel J. *Parenting from the Inside Out*	649
Siegel, Daniel J. *The Power of Showing Up*	649
Siegel, Daniel J. ★*The Yes Brain*	155.4
Simmons, Rachel. ★*Enough as She Is*	155.5
Singh, Julietta. *The Breaks*	B
Smart, Maya Payne. *Reading for Our Lives*	372.4
Sole-Smith, Virginia. ★*Fat Talk*	649.1
Stixrud, William R. *The Self-Driven Child*	155.4
Stixrud, William R. ★*What Do You Say?*	155.4
Taylor, Justin. *Riding with the Ghost*	B
Ticktin, Allie. *Play to Progress*	370.15
Traig, Jennifer. *Act Natural*	306.874
Trubo, Richard. *Caring for Your Baby and Young Child*	618.92
Vlock, Deborah. *Parenting Children with Mental Health Challenges*	618.92
Wagamese, Richard. *For Joshua*	B
Warner, Judith. *Perfect Madness*	306.874
Wegner, Bobbi. *Raising Feminist Boys*	305.23
Whippman, Ruth. ★*Boymom*	305.23
Wiseman, Rosalind. *Masterminds & Wingmen*	305.235
Wojcicki, Esther. *How to Raise Successful People*	649
Wong, Ali. ★*Dear Girls*	B
Workman, Katie. *Dinner Solved!*	641.5
Ziegler, Sheryl. ★*Mommy Burnout*	646.7

FAMILY AND RELATIONSHIPS — PARENTING — ADOPTION

Albom, Mitch. *Finding Chika*	B
Asgarian, Roxanna. *We Were Once a Family*	364.152
Austin, Nefertiti. *Motherhood so White*	B
Bee, Vanessa A. *Home Bound*	B
Brierley, Saroo. *A Long Way Home*	B
Carroll, Rebecca. *Surviving the White Gaze*	B
Daley, Mark. *Safe*	B
Fessler, Ann. *The Girls Who Went Away*	362.82
Glaser, Gabrielle. *American Baby*	B
Guida-Richards, Melissa. *What White Parents Should Know About Transracial Adoption*	362.734
Harrison, Valerie I. *Do Right by Me*	649
Hayasaki, Erika. *Somewhere Sisters*	362.7
Moody, Anne. *The Children Money Can Buy*	362.73
Mulgrew, Kate. *Born with Teeth*	791.45028
Scheeres, Julia. *Jesus Land*	B
Sentilles, Sarah. *Stranger Care*	B
Sisson, Gretchen E. ★*Relinquished*	362.734
Williams, Mary. *The Lost Daughter*	B

FAMILY AND RELATIONSHIPS — PETS AND OWNERS

Achterberg, Cara Sue. *Another Good Dog*	636.7
Attas, Amy. *Pets and the City*	B
Bailey, Elisabeth. *The Sound of a Wild Snail Eating*	594
Boylan, Jennifer Finney. *Good Boy*	B
Bradshaw, John. ★*Cat Sense*	636.8
Bradshaw, John. ★*Dog Sense*	636.7
Bragg, Rick. *The Speckled Beauty*	636.7
Brown, Sarah L. *The Hidden Language of Cats*	636.8
Carr, Caleb. *My Beloved Monster*	B
Charleson, Susannah. *Where the Lost Dogs Go*	636.7
Chesney, Will. *No Ordinary Dog*	958.104
Conaboy, Kelly. *The Particulars of Peter*	636.7
Dickey, Bronwen. *Pit Bull*	636.755
Golbeck, Jennifer. *The Purest Bond*	636.7
Grogan, John. ★*Marley & Me*	636.752
Grossi, Craig. *Craig & Fred*	B
Habib, Rodney. ★*The Forever Dog*	636.7
Halpern, Sue. *A Dog Walks into a Nursing Home*	B
Haupt, Lyanda Lynn. *Mozart's Starling*	B
Herriot, James. ★*All Creatures Great and Small*	B
Herriot, James. *Every Living Thing*	B
Herriot, James. *James Herriot's Animal Stories*	B
Herriot, James. *James Herriot's Cat Stories*	636.8
Herriot, James. *James Herriot's Dog Stories*	636.7
Herriot, James. *James Herriot's Favorite Dog Stories*	636.7
Hillenbrand, Laura. ★*Seabiscuit*	798.4
Horowitz, Alexandra. *Our Dogs, Ourselves*	636.7
Horowitz, Alexandra. ★*The Year of the Puppy*	636.7
Hunger, Christina. *How Stella Learned to Talk*	636.7
Kavin, Kim. *The Dog Merchants*	636.7
Kugler, Rob. *A Dog Named Beautiful*	B
Masson, J. Moussaieff. *Lost Companions*	636.088
McConnell, Patricia B. ★*The Other End of the Leash*	636.7
Montgomery, Sy. *The Good Good Pig*	636.4
Myron, Vicki. ★*Dewey*	636.80092
Nir, Sarah Maslin. *Horse Crazy*	B
Novello, Carol. *Mutual Rescue*	636.088
Orlean, Susan. *On Animals*	590
Schott, Philipp. *The Accidental Veterinarian*	B
Tomlinson, Tommy. *Dogland*	636.7
Tucker, Abigail. *The Lion in the Living Room*	636.8
Wynne, Clive D. L. ★*Dog Is Love*	636.7

FAMILY AND RELATIONSHIPS — SIBLINGS

Berger, Lynn. *Second Thoughts*	306.85
Bilton, Chrysta. *Normal Family*	B
Cayton-Holland, Adam. *Tragedy Plus Time*	B
Clavin, Thomas. *The DiMaggios*	920
De Bres, Helena. *How to Be Multiple*	155.44
Howard, Ron. ★*The Boys*	B
Kashner, Sam. *The Fabulous Bouvier Sisters*	920
Keaton, Diane. ★*Brother & Sister*	B
Louvish, Simon. *Monkey Business*	B
O'Reilly, Seamas. ★*Did Ye Hear Mammy Died?*	B
Scheeres, Julia. *Jesus Land*	B
Ung, Loung. *Lucky Child*	B
Wise, Beau. *Three Wise Men*	958.104

FAMILY AND SCHIZOPHRENIA

Granata, Vince. *Everything Is Fine*	B

FAMILY AND SUICIDE

Maisel, Ivan. *I Keep Trying to Catch His Eye*	B
Moe, John. *The Hilarious World of Depression*	616.85

FAMILY AND WAR

Alyan, Hala. *The Moon That Turns You Back*	811
Russell, Jan Jarboe. *The Train to Crystal City*	940.53

FAMILY AND WORK

Medini, Shari. *Parenting While Working from Home*	650.1
Nooyi, Indra. ★*My Life in Full*	B
Searcey, Dionne. *In Pursuit of Disobedient Women*	B

FAMILY BUSINESSES

Bernstein, Andrea. *American Oligarchs*	920
Howe, Ben Ryder. *My Korean Deli*	B
Macy, Beth. ★*Factory Man*	338.7
Schindler, Meriel. *The Lost Cafe Schindler*	943.64
The Family Cooks. David, Laurie	641.3

FAMILY FARMS

Connell, John. *The Farmer's Son*	630.9
Genoways, Ted. *This Blessed Earth*	630.9
McDowell, Marta. *The World of Laura Ingalls Wilder*	813

FAMILY FORTUNES

Cooper, Anderson. *Vanderbilt*	920
Hamill, Kirkland. *Filthy Beasts*	B
Mealer, Bryan. *The Kings of Big Spring*	B
Strathern, Paul. *The Borgias*	945.06
The Family Guide to Mental Health Care. Sederer, Lloyd I.	616.89

FAMILY HISTORY

Cercas, Javier. *Lord of All the Dead*	868
Chin, Ava. ★*Mott Street*	974.7
Cooper, Anderson. *Vanderbilt*	920
Craig, William. *Yankee Come Home*	972.9107
Foer, Esther Safran. *I Want You to Know We're Still Here*	B
Gucci, Patricia. *In the Name of Gucci*	B
Jerkins, Morgan. *Wandering in Strange Lands*	305.896
Kearse, Bettye. *The Other Madisons*	920
Koh, EJ. *The Magical Language of Others*	813
Krug, Nora. ★*Belonging*	741.5
Luckerson, Victor. *Built from the Fire*	976.6
Malhotra, Aanchal. *Remnants of Partition*	954.04
McMillan, Tracie. ★*The White Bonus*	305.8
Myers, Leah. *Thinning Blood*	B
Nathan, Joan. ★*My Life in Recipes*	641.5
Ng, Fae Myenne. *Orphan Bachelors*	B
Petrosino, Kiki. *White Blood*	811
Raines, Ben. *The Last Slave Ship*	306.362
Rojas Contreras, Ingrid. ★*The Man Who Could Move Clouds*	B
Salama, Jordan. ★*Stranger in the Desert*	982
Samaha, Albert. *Concepcion*	929
Schindler, Meriel. *The Lost Cafe Schindler*	943.64
Schwarz, Geraldine. *Those Who Forget*	940.53
Simard, S. ★*Finding the Mother Tree*	582.16

PUBLIC LIBRARY CORE COLLECTION: NONFICTION
Twentieth Edition

Smarsh, Sarah. ★*Heartland*	B
Smith, Clint. ★*Above Ground*	811
Stuart, Andrea. *Sugar in the Blood*	338.1
Swarns, Rachel L. ★*American Tapestry*	B
Trethewey, Natasha D. ★*Memorial Drive*	B
Trethewey, Natasha D. ★*Monument*	811
Van Es, Bart. *The Cut Out Girl*	B
Velshi, Ali. *Small Acts of Courage*	B

FAMILY LEAVE

Grose, Jessica. *Screaming on the Inside*	306.874

FAMILY LORE

Wagner, Alex. *Futureface*	B
The *Family* Next Door. Glatt, John	362.76092
Family of Origin, Family of Choice. Hays, Katie	248.8086
The *Family* Outing. Hempel, Jessi	B

FAMILY PLANNING

Shah, Meera. *You're the Only One I've Told*	362.1988

FAMILY POLICY

Self, Robert O. *All in the Family*	320.50973

FAMILY PROBLEMS

B., David. *Epileptic*	741.5
Diaz, Jaquira. *Ordinary Girls*	818
Kolker, Robert. ★*Hidden Valley Road*	920

FAMILY RECIPES

Locke, Tembi. ★*From Scratch*	B
Stibbe, Nina. *An Almost Perfect Christmas*	394.2663

FAMILY RECREATION

Van't Hul, Jean. *The Artful Year*	745.594

FAMILY RELATIONSHIPS

Abdurraqib, Hanif. ★*There's Always This Year*	796.323
Adichie, Chimamanda Ngozi. *Notes on Grief*	155.9
Ahdoot, Dan. *Undercooked*	647.95
Alderton, Dolly. *Everything I Know About Love*	B
Allende, Isabel. ★*Paula*	B
Alterman, Sara Faith. *Let's Never Talk About This Again*	616.8
Andrews, Julie. *Home Work*	B
Applebaum, Allison. *Stand by Me*	649.8
Arceneaux, Michael. *I Finally Bought Some Jordans*	306.76
Archibald, John. *Shaking the Gates of Hell*	B
Asher, Zain E. *Where the Children Take Us*	942.1
B., David. *Epileptic*	741.5
Backman, Fredrik. *Things My Son Needs to Know About the World*	B
Bair, Deirdre. *Al Capone*	B
Bard, Elizabeth. *Picnic in Provence*	B
Berg, A. Scott. *Kate Remembered*	B
Berg, Elizabeth. *I'll Be Seeing You*	306.874
Berger, Lynn. *Second Thoughts*	306.85
Biden Owens, Valerie. *Growing up Biden*	B
Biden, Jill. *Where the Light Enters*	B
Biden, Joseph R. *Promise Me, Dad*	B
Biden, Robert Hunter. *Beautiful Things*	B
Blackstone, Amy. *Childfree by Choice*	306.874
Blaisdell, Robert. *Creating Anna Karenina*	891.7
Bonner, Betsy. *The Book of Atlantis Black*	364.152
Bono. ★*Surrender*	B
Bowler, Kate. *No Cure for Being Human*	B
Brina, Elizabeth Miki. *Speak, Okinawa*	305.48
Brooks, Mel. ★*All About Me!*	B
Browne, E. J. *Charles Darwin*	B
Browne, E. J. *Charles Darwin*	B
Bui, Thi. ★*The Best We Could Do*	741.5
Burton, Susan. *Empty*	B
Byas, Taylor. *I Done Clicked My Heels Three Times*	811
Byrne, Paula. *Kick*	B
Calhoun, Ada. *Also a Poet*	B
Carcaterra, Lorenzo. *Three Dreamers*	B
Carlin, Kelly. *A Carlin Home Companion*	B
Carter, Jimmy. *Sharing Good Times*	973.926
Chan, Jackie. *Never Grow up*	B
Chee, Alexander. ★*How to Write an Autobiographical Novel*	B
Cheung, Karen. *The Impossible City*	951.25
Chung, Nicole. *A Living Remedy*	B
Coates, Ta-Nehisi. *The Beautiful Struggle*	B
Coffin, Jaed. *Roughhouse Friday*	B
Common. *One Day It'll All Make Sense*	B
Connell, John. *The Farmer's Son*	630.9
Crasnianski, Tania. *The Children of Nazis*	943.086
Curtis, James. *Spencer Tracy*	B
Cusk, Rachel. *Coventry*	814
Dais, Dawn. *The Sh!t No One Tells You About Divorce*	306.89
Daley, Mark. *Safe*	B
Daley, Tom. *Coming up for Air*	B
Danticat, Edwidge. ★*Brother, I'm Dying*	B
Davis, Patti. *Floating in the Deep End*	616.8
Diamond, Cheryl. *Nowhere Girl*	B
Dickinson, Amy. *Strangers Tend to Tell Me Things*	B
Didion, Joan. ★*The Year of Magical Thinking*	B
DiFelice, Bekah. *Almost There*	248.8
Dunne, Griffin. ★*The Friday Afternoon Club*	B
Eade, Philip. *Evelyn Waugh*	B
Eyman, Scott. *Hank and Jim*	920
Fagan, Kate. *All the Colors Came Out*	B
Field, Sally. *In Pieces*	B
Finkel, David. *Thank You for Your Service*	920
Fisher, Todd. *My Girls*	B
Fishman, Boris. *Savage Feast*	B
Foster, Sutton. *Hooked*	B
Fox, Michael J. *No Time Like the Future*	B
Franzen, Jonathan. *The End of the End of the Earth*	814
Fuller, Alexandra. *Don't Let's Go to the Dogs Tonight*	B
Fuller, Alexandra. *Travel Light, Move Fast*	B
Gabriel, Mary. *Madonna*	B
Gaines, Joanna. *The Stories We Tell*	B
Garcia, Angela. *The Way That Leads Among the Lost*	362.29
Garcia, Rodrigo. *A Farewell to Gabo and Mercedes*	B
Gay, Ross. *Inciting Joy*	814
Geller, Danielle. *Dog Flowers*	B
Gracie, Rickson. *Breathe*	B
Granata, Vince. *Everything Is Fine*	B
Greene, Benjamin. ★*My Child Is Trans, Now What?*	649
Hamill, Kirkland. *Filthy Beasts*	B
Hamilton, Lisa M. *The Hungry Season*	B
Hansberry, Lorraine. ★*A Raisin in the Sun*	812
Hardman, Robert. *Queen of Our Times*	B
Harry. ★*Spare*	B
Havrilesky, Heather. *Foreverland*	306.81
Hayasaki, Erika. *Somewhere Sisters*	362.7
Hays, Katie. *Family of Origin, Family of Choice*	248.8086
Hemingway, Ernest. *Dear Papa*	813
Hempel, Jessi. *The Family Outing*	B
Henderson, Danielle. ★*The Ugly Cry*	B
Hernandez, Daisy. *A Cup of Water Under My Bed*	B
Hill, Jemele. *Uphill*	B
Hobbs, Jeff. *Show Them You're Good*	373
Hogan, Linda. *The Woman Who Watches Over the World*	B
Hustvedt, Siri. *Mothers, Fathers, and Others*	814
Irby, Samantha. ★*Quietly Hostile*	814
Jackson, Shirley. *Let Me Tell You*	818
Jackson, Shirley. ★*The Letters of Shirley Jackson*	813
Jawando, Will. ★*My Seven Black Fathers*	B
Jones, Faith. *Sex Cult Nun*	B
Jones, Saeed. *How We Fight for Our Lives*	B
Kalb, Bess. ★*Nobody Will Tell You This but Me*	306.874
Kan, Karoline. *Under Red Skies*	B
Keaton, Diane. ★*Brother & Sister*	B
Kelly, Minka. ★*Tell Me Everything*	B
Kingston, Genevieve. *Did I Ever Tell You?*	B
Koh, EJ. *The Magical Language of Others*	813
Kolker, Robert. ★*Hidden Valley Road*	920
Kouchner, Camille. *La Familia Grande*	B
Kram, Mark. *Smokin' Joe*	B
Lang, Maya. *What We Carry*	B
Lawson, Jenny. *Furiously Happy*	B
Lawton, Georgina. *Raceless*	B
Lewis, Oscar. *The Children of Sanchez*	306.85
Lieu, Susan. ★*The Manicurist's Daughter*	B
Limon, Ada. ★*The Hurting Kind*	811
Lin, Jami Nakamura. *The Night Parade*	B
Liu, Simu. ★*We Were Dreamers*	B
Locke, Tembi. ★*From Scratch*	B
Lockwood, Patricia. *Priestdaddy*	B
Loh, Sandra Tsing. *The Madwoman and the Roomba*	B
Louvin, Charlie. *Satan Is Real*	920
Louvish, Simon. *Monkey Business*	B
Mann, William J. *Hello, Gorgeous*	B
Mann, William J. *The Wars of the Roosevelts*	B

AUTHOR, TITLE, SERIES AND SUBJECT INDEX

Mansbach, Adam. *I Had a Brother Once*	811	
Margulies, Julianna. *Sunshine Girl*	B	
Marshall, Greg. *Leg*	B	
Matteson, John. *Eden's Outcasts*	920	
May, Katherine. *Wintering*	155.9	
May, Meredith. *The Honey Bus*	B	
McAnulty, Dara. *Diary of a Young Naturalist*	508.092	
McConville, Mark. *Failure to Launch*	155.6	
McCourt, Frank. *'Tis*	B	
Messud, Claire. *Kant's Little Prussian Head and Other Reasons Why I Write*	B	
Millet, Lydia. *We Loved It All*	813	
Moorer, Allison. *I Dream He Talks to Me*	782.42164	
Morton, Brian. *Tasha*	B	
Nafisi, Azar. *Things I've Been Silent About*	B	
Newman, Magdalena. *Normal*	611	
Newman, Paul. *The Extraordinary Life of an Ordinary Man*	B	
Nezhukumatathil, Aimee. *Bite by Bite*	641.3	
Nguyen, Bich Minh. *Owner of a Lonely Heart*	B	
Nguyen, Viet Thanh. ★*A Man of Two Faces*	B	
Niven, Penelope. *Thornton Wilder*	B	
O'Donnell, Svenja. *Inge's War*	943.086	
O'Reilly, Seamas. ★*Did Ye Hear Mammy Died?*	B	
O'Sullivan, Emer. *The Fall of the House of Wilde*	B	
Olivares, Efren C. *My Boy Will Die of Sorrow*	305.9	
Osnos, Evan. *Joe Biden*	B	
Owusu, Nadia. *Aftershocks*	B	
Oz, Amos. *A Tale of Love and Darkness*	B	
Patchett, Ann. ★*These Precious Days*	814	
Pepin, Jacques. *The Apprentice*	B	
Petersen, Sara. *Momfluenced*	306.87	
Poitier, Sidney. *The Measure of a Man*	B	
Prideaux, Sue. *I Am Dynamite!*	B	
Qu, Anna. *Made in China*	B	
Raban, Jonathan. *Father and Son*	B	
Ralph, Laurence. *Sito*	364.152	
Reang, Putsata. *Ma and Me*	B	
Regan, Iliana. *Fieldwork*	B	
Rehm, Diane. *On My Own*	B	
Ripa, Kelly. *Live Wire*	B	
Robison, John Elder. *Look Me in the Eye*	B	
Rogen, Seth. ★*Yearbook*	B	
RuPaul. ★*The House of Hidden Meanings*	B	
Sabar, Ariel. *My Father's Paradise*	B	
Sagan, Sasha. *For Small Creatures Such as We*	390.09	
Salama, Jordan. ★*Stranger in the Desert*	982	
Sardy, Marin. *The Edge of Every Day*	B	
Sasakamoose, Fred. *Call Me Indian*	B	
Satrapi, Marjane. *Embroideries*	741.5	
Scheier, Liz. *Never Simple*	B	
Schulz, Kathryn. ★*Lost & Found*	B	
Schwalbe, Will. ★*The End of Your Life Book Club*	B	
Scottoline, Lisa. *I See Life Through Rose-Colored Glasses*	813	
Sedaris, David. ★*The Best of Me*	818	
Sedaris, David. ★*A Carnival of Snackery*	818	
Sedaris, David. ★*Happy-Go-Lucky*	814	
Sedaris, David. *Theft by Finding*	B	
Senator, Susan. *Autism Adulthood*	616.85	
Shadid, Anthony. *House of Stone*	306.0956	
Shakur, Prince. *When They Tell You to Be Good*	B	
Shankle, Melanie. *Church of the Small Things*	248.8	
Shannon, Molly. ★*Hello, Molly!*	B	
Shehadeh, Raja. *We Could Have Been Friends, My Father and I*	B	
Shlain, Tiffany. *24/6*	158.1	
Singh, Julietta. *The Breaks*	B	
Sipress, David. *What's so Funny?*	B	
Smith, Jada Pinkett. *Worthy*	B	
Smith, Sally Bedell. *George VI and Elizabeth*	920	
So, Anthony Veasna. ★*Songs on Endless Repeat*	814	
Sole-Smith, Virginia. ★*Fat Talk*	649.1	
Solnit, Rebecca. *The Faraway Nearby*	814	
Spitz, Bob. ★*Dearie*	B	
Stone, Sharon. *The Beauty of Living Twice*	B	
Streep, Abe. *Brothers on Three*	306.85	
Stump, Al. *Cobb*	B	
Taffa, Deborah Jackson. ★*Whiskey Tender*	B	
Taraborrelli, J. Randy. *After Camelot*	B	
Taraborrelli, J. Randy. *The Kennedy Heirs*	920	
Taylor, Goldie. *The Love You Save*	B	
Taylor, Justin. *Riding with the Ghost*	B	
Thomas, Evan. ★*Robert Kennedy*	B	
Thomas, Joseph Earl. *Sink*	B	
Threadgill, Henry. *Easily Slip into Another World*	B	
Tibble, Tayi. *Poukahangatus*	821	
Toibin, Colm. *Mad, Bad, Dangerous to Know*	920	
Tometich, Annabelle. *The Mango Tree*	B	
Tomlinson, Janis A. ★*Goya*	B	
Tran, Ly. *House of Sticks*	B	
Tran, Phuc. ★*Sigh, Gone*	B	
Trebek, Alex. *The Answer Is ...*	791.4502	
Trump, Mary L. *Too Much and Never Enough*	B	
Tubbs, Michael. *The Deeper the Roots*	B	
Tur, Katy. *Rough Draft*	B	
Tye, Larry. ★*Bobby Kennedy*	B	
Union, Gabrielle. *You Got Anything Stronger?*	B	
Vasquez-Lavado, Silvia. *In the Shadow of the Mountain*	B	
Wainaina, Binyavanga. *One Day I Will Write About This Place*	B	
Walls, Jeannette. ★*The Glass Castle*	B	
Wang, Connie. *Oh My Mother!*	B	
Ward, Jon. *Testimony*	277.308	
Washington, Kate. ★*Already Toast*	649.8	
Weller, Sheila. *Carrie Fisher*	B	
Whitney, Emerson. *Heaven*	B	
Williams, Marlena. *Night Mother*	791.43	
Wilson, A. N. *The Mystery of Charles Dickens*	823	
Wiman, Christian. *Zero at the Bone*	818	
Wong, Carmen Rita. *Why Didn't You Tell Me?*	B	
Worsley, Lucy. *Queen Victoria*	B	

FAMILY REUNIONS
Nathans, Sydney. *To Free a Family*	B	
Willner, Nina. *Forty Autumns*	B	
The **Family** *Roe*. Prager, Joshua	342.7308	

FAMILY SECRETS
Alterman, Sara Faith. *Let's Never Talk About This Again*	616.8	
Betz-Hamilton, Axton. *The Less People Know About Us*	364.16	
Bilton, Chrysta. *Normal Family*	B	
Denton, Sally. *The Colony*	364.152	
Diamond, Cheryl. *Nowhere Girl*	B	
Duggar, Jill. *Counting the Cost*	B	
Foer, Esther Safran. *I Want You to Know We're Still Here*	B	
Foo, Stephanie. ★*What My Bones Know*	B	
Ford, Ashley C. ★*Somebody's Daughter*	B	
Freeman, Hadley. *House of Glass*	B	
Fremont, Helen. *The Escape Artist*	B	
Green, Kristen. *Something Must Be Done About Prince Edward County*	379.2	
Gucci, Patricia. *In the Name of Gucci*	B	
Hale, Grace Elizabeth. *In the Pines*	364.13	
Hamill, Kirkland. *Filthy Beasts*	B	
Hempel, Jessi. *The Family Outing*	B	
Kan, Karoline. *Under Red Skies*	B	
Kearse, Bettye. *The Other Madisons*	920	
King, Greg. *Twilight of Empire*	943.6	
Kissinger, Meg. *While You Were Out*	362.2	
Kolker, Robert. ★*Hidden Valley Road*	920	
Kouchner, Camille. *The Familia Grande*	B	
Krug, Nora. ★*Belonging*	741.5	
Lang, Maya. *What We Carry*	B	
Lawton, Georgina. *Raceless*	B	
Mann, Sally. ★*Hold Still*	B	
Mann, William J. *The Wars of the Roosevelts*	B	
Marshall, Greg. *Leg*	B	
Marzano-Lesnevich, Alexandria. *The Fact of a Body*	364.152	
Oelhafen, Ingrid von. *Hitler's Stolen Children*	B	
Owusu, Nadia. *Aftershocks*	B	
Sands, Philippe. *East West Street*	345	
Scheier, Liz. *Never Simple*	B	
Shakur, Prince. *When They Tell You to Be Good*	B	
Shapiro, Dani. ★*Inheritance*	B	
Slouka, Mark. *Nobody's Son*	B	
Teege, Jennifer. *My Grandfather Would Have Shot Me*	929.2	
Van Es, Bart. *The Cut Out Girl*	B	
Van Wijk-Voskuijl, Joop. *The Last Secret of the Secret Annex*	940.53	
Wills, Clair. ★*Missing Persons*	929.2	
Wong, Carmen Rita. *Why Didn't You Tell Me?*	B	
Yancey, Philip. ★*Where the Light Fell*	B	
Ypi, Lea. ★*Free*	B	

PUBLIC LIBRARY CORE COLLECTION: NONFICTION
Twentieth Edition

FAMILY TRADITIONS
    Locke, Tembi. ★*From Scratch* — B
    Stibbe, Nina. *An Almost Perfect Christmas* — 394.2663

FAMILY TRAVEL
    Kirkby, Bruce. *Blue Sky Kingdom* — 954.96
    Kois, Dan. *How to Be a Family* — 910.4
    The Family Tree Cemetery Field Guide. Neighbors, Joy — 929

FAMILY VIOLENCE
    Butler, Marcia. *The Skin Above My Knee* — B
    Dutta, Sunil. *Stealing Green Mangoes* — 973
    Foo, Stephanie. ★*What My Bones Know* — B
    Glatt, John. *The Family Next Door* — 362.76092
    Glatt, John. ★*The Perfect Father* — 364.152
    Harjo, Joy. ★*Poet Warrior* — B
    Harper, Michele. *The Beauty in Breaking* — B
    Horton, Michelle. *Dear Sister* — B
    Kolker, Robert. ★*Hidden Valley Road* — 920
    Liu, Simu. ★*We Were Dreamers* — B
    Machado, Carmen Maria. *In the Dream House* — B
    Matney, Mandy. *Blood on Their Hands* — 364.152
    Roy, Jessica. *American Girls* — 305.48
    Scheer, Paul. *Joyful Recollections of Trauma* — B
    Selvaratnam, Tanya. *Assume Nothing* — B
    Sinclair, Safiya. ★*How to Say Babylon* — B
    Snyder, Rachel Louise. *No Visible Bruises* — 362.82
    Snyder, Rachel Louise. *Women We Buried, Women We Burned* — B
    Sundberg, Kelly. *Goodbye, Sweet Girl* — B
    Taylor, Goldie. *The Love You Save* — B
    Thomas, Joseph Earl. *Sink* — B
    Tran, Phuc. ★*Sigh, Gone* — B
    Travis, Randy. *Forever and Ever, Amen* — B
    Trethewey, Natasha D. ★*Memorial Drive* — B
    Westover, Tara. ★*Educated* — B
    Wolff, Tobias. *This Boy's Life* — B

FAMILY VIOLENCE VICTIMS
    Cooper, Helene. *Madame President* — 966.62
    Herman, Judith Lewis. *Truth and Repair* — 362.883
    Snyder, Rachel Louise. *No Visible Bruises* — 362.82
    Westover, Tara. ★*Educated* — B

FAMILY-KILLING
    Bradley, Mark A. *Blood Runs Coal* — B

FAMINES
    Applebaum, Anne. ★*Red Famine* — 947.708
    Dikotter, Frank. *Mao's Great Famine* — 951.05
    Igort. *The Ukrainian and Russian Notebooks* — 741.5
    Jang, Lucia. *Stars Between the Sun and Moon* — 365.45092
    Kamkwamba, William. ★*The Boy Who Harnessed the Wind* — B
    Kelly, John. *The Graves Are Walking* — 941.5081
    Kotkin, Stephen. *Stalin* — B
    Puleo, Stephen. *Voyage of Mercy* — 363.8
    Smith, Douglas. *The Russian Job* — 947.084

FAN MAIL
    Rakoff, Joanna Smith. *My Salinger Year* — B

FANATICISM
    Jones, Dan. *Crusaders* — 909.07
    ★*Fancy Bear Goes Phishing*. Shapiro, Scott J. — 364.16
    Fannie Lou Hamer. Brooks, Maegan Parker — B

FANON, FRANTZ, 1925-1961
    Shatz, Adam. *The Rebel's Clinic* — 965

FANS (PEOPLE)
    Almond, Steve. *Rock and Roll Will Save Your Life* — 781.6
    Jameson, A. D. *I Find Your Lack of Faith Disturbing* — 791.43
    Katz, Evan Ross. *Into Every Generation a Slayer Is Born* — 791.45
    Pesca, Mike. *Upon Further Review* — 796
    Phillips, Maya. *Nerd* — 302.23
    Posnanski, Joe. ★*The Life and Afterlife of Harry Houdini* — 793.8
    Tarantino, Quentin. *Cinema Speculation* — 791.43
    Weldon, Glen. ★*The Caped Crusade* — 741.5
    Fantasia for the Man in Blue. Blount, Tommye — 811
    ★*The Fantastic Laboratory of Dr. Weigl*. Allen, Arthur — 614.5

FANTASY
    Villarreal, Vanessa Anglica. *Magical/Realism* — 814

FANTASY FICTION AUTHORS
    Kroger, Lisa. *Monster, She Wrote* — 920

FANTASY FICTION WRITING
    McIlwaine, Catherine. *Tolkien* — 002.09
    Pratchett, Terry. *A Slip of the Keyboard* — 824

FANTASY FOOTBALL (GAME)
    Barbarisi, Daniel. *Dueling with Kings* — 793.93

FANTASY SPORTS
    Barbarisi, Daniel. *Dueling with Kings* — 793.93
    ★*Fantasyland*. Andersen, Kurt — 973
    ★*The Far Away Brothers*. Markham, Lauren — 920
    Far from the Tree. Solomon, Andrew — 362.4083
    Faraday, Maxwell, and the Electromagnetic Field. Forbes, Nancy — B

FARADAY, MICHAEL, 1791-1867
    Forbes, Nancy. *Faraday, Maxwell, and the Electromagnetic Field* — B

FARAH, EMPRESS, CONSORT OF MOHAMMAD REZA PAHLAVI, SHAH OF IRAN, 1938-
    Cooper, Andrew Scott. *The Fall of Heaven* — B
    The Faraway Nearby. Solnit, Rebecca — 814
    A Farewell to Gabo and Mercedes. Garcia, Rodrigo — B

Farley, Audrey Clare
    ★*Girls and Their Monsters* — 306.875
    The Unfit Heiress — B

FARM ANIMAL WELFARE
    Williams, Wyatt. *Springer Mountain* — 394.1

FARM ANIMALS
    Orlean, Susan. *On Animals* — 590

FARM LIFE
    Agee, James. *Let Us Now Praise Famous Men* — 976.1
    Barker, Elspeth. ★*Notes from the Henhouse* — 828
    Berry, Wendell. ★*The World-Ending Fire* — 818
    Calcaterra, Regina. *Girl Unbroken* — B
    Carter, Jimmy. *An Hour Before Daylight* — B
    Connell, John. *The Farmer's Son* — 630.9
    Genoways, Ted. *This Blessed Earth* — 630.9
    Heyman, Stephen. *The Planter of Modern Life* — B
    Kingsolver, Barbara. ★*Animal, Vegetable, Miracle* — 641
    Logsdon, Gene. *Letter to a Young Farmer* — 338.10973
    Phelan, Tom. *We Were Rich and We Didn't Know It* — B
    Regan, Iliana. *Fieldwork* — B
    Roberts, Julius. *The Farm Table* — 641.594
    Stewart, Chris. *Driving Over Lemons* — 946
    Wariner, Ruth. *The Sound of Gravel* — B
    Yeh, Molly. *Home Is Where the Eggs Are* — 641.5

FARM MANAGEMENT
    Berry, Wendell. *The Art of Loading Brush* — 338.10973
    Farm Sanctuary. Baur, Gene — 179
    The Farm Table. Roberts, Julius — 641.594
    The Farmer's Son. Connell, John — 630.9

Farmer, David Hugh
    The Oxford Dictionary of Saints — 270

Farmer, Jared
    Elderflora — 582.16

Farmer, John J.
    The Ground Truth — 973.931

Farmer, Lesley S. J.
    ★*Impactful Community-Based Literacy Projects* — 372.6

Farmer, Paul
    Fevers, Feuds, and Diamonds — 614.5

FARMERS
    Baszile, Natalie. *We Are Each Other's Harvest* — 630.89
    Carter, Jimmy. *An Hour Before Daylight* — B
    Ehrenreich, Ben. *The Way to the Spring* — 956.95
    Genoways, Ted. *This Blessed Earth* — 630.9
    Hamilton, Lisa M. *Deeply Rooted* — 338.10973
    Heyman, Stephen. *The Planter of Modern Life* — B
    Horn, Miriam. *Rancher, Farmer, Fisherman* — B
    Jacobs, Ryan McMahon. *The Truffle Underground* — 381
    Logsdon, Gene. *Letter to a Young Farmer* — 338.10973
    Muse, Toby. *Kilo* — 363.4509861
    Raban, Jonathan. *Bad Land* — 978
    Tester, Jon. *Grounded* — B

FARMS
    Cullen, Art. *Storm Lake* — 071.7
    Egan, Timothy. *The Worst Hard Time* — 978
    Faruqi, Sonia. *Project Animal Farm* — 338.1
    Marcum, Diana. *The Fallen Stones* — B
    Monbiot, George. ★*Regenesis* — 338.1

FARRAKHAN, LOUIS
    Levinsohn, Florence Hamlish. *Looking for Farrakhan* — B

Farrell, John A.
    Clarence Darrow — B
    ★*Richard Nixon* — B

AUTHOR, TITLE, SERIES AND SUBJECT INDEX

Ted Kennedy	B
FARREN, ROY	
Lewis, Damien. *Churchill's Hellraisers*	940.54
Farrington, Lisa E.	
Creating Their Own Image	704
Farris, Grace	
Mom Milestones	306.87
Farris, Scott	
Almost President	324.973
Farrow, Ronan	
★*Catch and Kill*	331.4
War on Peace	327.73
FARROW, RONAN, 1987-	
Farrow, Ronan. ★*Catch and Kill*	331.4
Farsighted. Johnson, Steven	153.8
Farther Away. Franzen, Jonathan	814
Faruqi, Sonia	
Project Animal Farm	338.1
FASCISM	
Cercas, Javier. *Lord of All the Dead*	868
Fifield, Anna. *The Great Successor*	B
Jeppesen, Travis. *See You Again in Pyongyang*	951.93
Kertzer, David I. *The Pope and Mussolini*	322
Kushner, Jacob. *Look Away*	305.9
Maddow, Rachel. ★*Prequel*	320.53
Mazzeo, Tilar J. *Sisters in Resistance*	945.091
McKean, David. *Watching Darkness Fall*	940.53
Neiwert, David A. ★*The Age of Insurrection*	303.48
Paxton, Robert O. *The Anatomy of Fascism*	320.53
Preston, Paul. *A People Betrayed*	946
Stanley, Jason. *How Fascism Works*	321.9
FASCISTS	
Ronald, Susan. *Hitler's Aristocrats*	940.53
FASHION	
Bari, Shahidha K. *Dressed*	391
Cleveland, Pat. *Walking with the Muses*	B
Cline, Elizabeth L. *The Conscious Closet*	646
Cross, Charles R. *Here We Are Now*	782.42166
Crowe, Lauren Goldstein. *The Towering World of Jimmy Choo*	391.4
Crowther, Janet. *Make a Statement*	745.594
Cunningham, William J. ★*Fashion Climbing*	B
Day, Daniel R. *Dapper Dan*	B
DeJean, Joan E. *The Essence of Style*	391
Dirix, Emmanuelle. *Dressing the Decades*	746.92
Edwards, Lydia. *How to Read a Dress*	391
Enninful, Edward. *A Visible Man*	B
Flannery, Kate. *Strip Tees*	338.4
Ford, Tanisha C. *Dressed in Dreams*	391
Gabriel, Mary. *Madonna*	B
Grumbach, Didier. *History of International Fashion*	746.9
Hardy, Alyssa. *Worn Out*	338.4
Hilfiger, Tommy. *American Dreamer*	B
Holmes, Elizabeth. *HRH*	941.085
Karen, Dawnn. *Dress Your Best Life*	646
Linett, Andrea. *The Cool Factor*	746.9
Prescod, Danielle. *Token Black Girl*	B
Richardson, Lance. *House of Nutter*	B
Satow, Julie. *When Women Ran Fifth Avenue*	381.141
Talley, Andre Leon. *The Chiffon Trenches*	B
Thanhauser, Sofi. *Worn*	391
Thurman, Judith. ★*A Left-Handed Woman*	814
Tonti, Lucianne. *Sundressed*	746.9
Wu, Simon. *Dancing on My Own*	700.1
Yang, April. *DIY Thrift Flip*	646.2
Yong, Sable. *Die Hot with a Vengeance*	646.7
★*Fashion Climbing*. Cunningham, William J.	B
FASHION DESIGN	
Carter, Ruth E. ★*The Art of Ruth E. Carter*	746.9
Cleveland, Pat. *Walking with the Muses*	B
Crowe, Lauren Goldstein. *The Towering World of Jimmy Choo*	391.4
Day, Daniel R. *Dapper Dan*	B
Dirix, Emmanuelle. *Dressing the Decades*	746.92
Faerm, Steven. *Fashion Design Course*	746.9
Garelick, Rhonda K. *Mademoiselle*	B
Givhan, Robin. *The Battle of Versailles*	746.9
Greenfield, Martin. ★*Measure of a Man*	B
Grumbach, Didier. *History of International Fashion*	746.9
Hilfiger, Tommy. *American Dreamer*	B
Lowit, Roxanne. *Yves Saint Laurent*	746.9
Parton, Dolly. ★*Behind the Seams*	B
Secrest, Meryle. *Elsa Schiaparelli*	746.9
Trubert-Tollu, Chantal. ★*The House of Worth 1858-1954*	746.92
Fashion Design Course. Faerm, Steven	746.9
FASHION DESIGNERS	
Carter, Ruth E. ★*The Art of Ruth E. Carter*	746.9
Cleveland, Pat. *Walking with the Muses*	B
Cunningham, William J. ★*Fashion Climbing*	B
Day, Daniel R. *Dapper Dan*	B
De Courcy, Anne. *Chanel's Riviera*	944.9
Epstein, Franci. *Franci's War*	B
Garelick, Rhonda K. *Mademoiselle*	B
Givhan, Robin. *The Battle of Versailles*	746.9
Greenfield, Martin. ★*Measure of a Man*	B
Gucci, Patricia. *In the Name of Gucci*	B
Hilfiger, Tommy. *American Dreamer*	B
Lowit, Roxanne. *Yves Saint Laurent*	746.9
Mazzeo, Tilar J. *The Secret of Chanel No. 5*	338.7
Mizrahi, Isaac. *I.M.*	B
Richardson, Lance. *House of Nutter*	B
Secrest, Meryle. *Elsa Schiaparelli*	746.9
Thomas, Dana. *Gods and Kings*	920
Trubert-Tollu, Chantal. ★*The House of Worth 1858-1954*	746.92
Von Furstenberg, Diane. *The Woman I Wanted to Be*	B
FASHION DRAWING	
Meder, Danielle. *Draw Fashion Now*	741.6
FASHION HISTORY	
Barker, Nigel. *Models of Influence*	746.92092
Cox, Caroline. *The World Atlas of Street Fashion*	391.009
Stuart, Amanda Mackenzie. *Empress of Fashion*	B
Fashion Jewelry. Legenhausen, Courtney	745.594
FASHION MERCHANDISING	
Givhan, Robin. *The Battle of Versailles*	746.9
FASHION MODELING	
Graham, Ashley. *A New Model*	B
FASHION MODELS	
Barker, Nigel. *Models of Influence*	746.92092
Beauvais, Garcelle. *Love Me as I Am*	B
Burke, Carolyn. *Lee Miller*	B
Fox, Julia. *Down the Drain*	B
Graham, Ashley. *A New Model*	B
Kang, Mia. *Knockout*	B
Moore, Susanna. *Miss Aluminum*	813
Porizkova, Paulina. *No Filter*	B
Ratajkowski, Emily. ★*My Body*	B
Winder, Elizabeth. *Parachute Women*	782.42164
FASHION PERIODICAL EDITORS	
Stuart, Amanda Mackenzie. *Empress of Fashion*	B
Talley, Andre Leon. *The Chiffon Trenches*	B
FASHION PERIODICALS	
Brown, Tina. *The Vanity Fair Diaries*	B
Enninful, Edward. *A Visible Man*	B
Odell, Amy. *Anna*	B
Stuart, Amanda Mackenzie. *Empress of Fashion*	B
FASHION PHOTOGRAPHERS	
Gefter, Philip. *What Becomes a Legend Most*	B
FASHION PHOTOGRAPHY	
Bowles, Hamish. *Vogue & the Metropolitan Museum of Art Costume Institute*	746.9
Cox, Caroline. *The World Atlas of Street Fashion*	391.009
Parton, Dolly. ★*Behind the Seams*	B
FASHION SHOWS	
Cleveland, Pat. *Walking with the Muses*	B
Givhan, Robin. *The Battle of Versailles*	746.9
★*The Fast*. Oakes, John G. H.	613.2
Fast. Graham, Jorie	811
FAST FOOD RESTAURANTS, CHAINS, ETC.	
Chandler, Adam. *Drive-Thru Dreams*	647.95
Chatelain, Marcia. ★*Franchise*	339
FAST FOOD RESTAURATEURS	
Chandler, Adam. *Drive-Thru Dreams*	647.95
FAST FOOD WORKERS	
Chandler, Adam. *Drive-Thru Dreams*	647.95
Fast Food, Good Food. Weil, Andrew	641.3
FAST FOODS	
Chandler, Adam. *Drive-Thru Dreams*	647.95
Tulleken, Chris van. *Ultra-Processed People*	664

PUBLIC LIBRARY CORE COLLECTION: NONFICTION
Twentieth Edition

Faster. Bascomb, Neal — 796.7209
Faster, Higher, Farther. Ewing, Jack — 338.7
FASTING
   Oakes, John G. H. ★*The Fast* — 613.2
FASTS AND FEASTS
   Axelrod, Matt. *Your Guide to the Jewish Holidays* — 296.4
Fasulo, Linda M.
   An Insider's Guide to the Un, 4th Ed. — 341.23
FAT CHILDREN
   Kang, Mia. *Knockout* — B
   Sole-Smith, Virginia. ★*Fat Talk* — 649.1
Fat Girls Hiking. Michaud-Skog, Summer — 796.51
★*Fat Leonard*. Whitlock, Craig — 364.16
FAT MEN
   Branum, Guy. *My Life as a Goddess* — B
   Tomlinson, Tommy. *The Elephant in the Room* — B
FAT PEOPLE
   Chaudry, Rabia. *Fatty Fatty Boom Boom* — B
   Gordon, Aubrey. *"You Just Need to Lose Weight"* — 616.3
   Specter, Emma. *More, Please* — 616.85
★*Fat Talk*. Sole-Smith, Virginia — 649.1
FAT WOMEN
   Beck, Amanda Martinez. *More of You* — 613
   Gadsby, Hannah. ★*Ten Steps to Nanette* — B
   Graham, Ashley. *A New Model* — B
   Green, Louise. *Big Fit Girl* — 613.7
   Michaud-Skog, Summer. *Fat Girls Hiking* — 796.51
The Fatal Alliance. Thomson, David — 791.43
Fatal Discord. Massing, Michael — 920
A Fatal Inheritance. Ingrassia, Lawrence — 616.99
Fatal Purity. Scurr, Ruth — B
The Fatal Shore. Hughes, Robert — 994
FATAL TRAFFIC ACCIDENTS
   Gehring, Wes D. *James Dean* — B
Fatal Vision. McGinniss, Joe — B
FATE AND FATALISM
   Homer. ★*The Iliad* — 883
   Jakes, T. D. *Destiny* — 248.4
   Trice, Dawn Turner. ★*Three Girls from Bronzeville* — 977.311
The Fate of Nature. Wohlforth, Charles P. — 304.209798
The Fate of Rome. Harper, Kyle — 937
FATHER AND ADULT DAUGHTER
   Case, Molly. *How to Treat People* — 616.1
   Lockwood, Patricia. *Priestdaddy* — B
   Schindler, Meriel. *The Lost Cafe Schindler* — 943.64
FATHER AND ADULT SON
   Preszler, Trent. *Little and Often* — B
   Sabar, Ariel. *My Father's Paradise* — B
   Wilson-Lee, Edward. ★*The Catalogue of Shipwrecked Books* — B
FATHER AND CHILD
   Chabon, Michael. *Pops* — 306.874
   Gaffigan, Jim. *Dad Is Fat* — 814
   Satrapi, Marjane. *Chicken with Plums* — 741.5
Father and Son. Raban, Jonathan — B
FATHER FIGURES
   Jawando, Will. ★*My Seven Black Fathers* — B
The Father of Us All. Hanson, Victor Davis — 355.0209
FATHER-DESERTED CHILDREN
   Koh, EJ. *The Magical Language of Others* — 813
FATHER-DESERTED FAMILIES
   Barnes, Cinelle. *Monsoon Mansion* — B
FATHER-SEPARATED CHILDREN
   Hernandez Castillo, Marcelo. *Children of the Land* — B
   Moore, Wes. *The Other Wes Moore* — B
FATHER-SEPARATED FAMILIES
   Porter, Carolyn. *Marcel's Letters* — 940.54
FATHERHOOD
   Alexander, Kwame. *Why Fathers Cry at Night* — B
   Backman, Fredrik. *Things My Son Needs to Know About the World* — B
   Bell, Darrin. ★*The Talk* — 741.5
   Birbiglia, Mike. *The New One* — B
   Chabon, Michael. *Manhood for Amateurs* — B
   Chabon, Michael. *Pops* — 306.874
   Daley, Tom. *Coming up for Air* — B
   Dubus, Andre. *Ghost Dogs* — 814
   Foxx, Jamie. *Act Like You Got Some Sense* — B
   Gaffigan, Jim. *Dad Is Fat* — 814
   Hadlow, Janice. *A Royal Experiment* — B

Harry. ★*Spare* — B
Hayes, Terrance. *So to Speak* — 811
Kendi, Ibram X. ★*How to Raise an Antiracist* — 649
King, Charles Monroe. *A Journal for Jordan* — 956.7044
Knausgaard, Karl Ove. *Spring* — B
Pardlo, Gregory. *Air Traffic* — B
Perkins, Kendrick. *The Education of Kendrick Perkins* — B
Scheer, Paul. *Joyful Recollections of Trauma* — B
Smith, Clint. ★*Above Ground* — 811
Taylor, Justin. *Riding with the Ghost* — B
Fatherland. Bilger, Burkhard
FATHERS
   Archibald, John. *Shaking the Gates of Hell* — B
   Chabon, Michael. *Manhood for Amateurs* — B
   Chabon, Michael. *Pops* — 306.874
   Fagan, Kate. *All the Colors Came Out* — B
   Gaffigan, Jim. *Dad Is Fat* — 814
   Greene, Jayson. *Once More We Saw Stars* — 155.9
   Kalanithi, Paul. ★*When Breath Becomes Air* — B
   Leland, Andrew. ★*The Country of the Blind* — B
FATHERS AND DAUGHTERS
   Alexander, Kwame. *Why Fathers Cry at Night* — B
   Alterman, Sara Faith. *Let's Never Talk About This Again* — 616.8
   Bechdel, Alison. ★*Fun Home* — 741.5
   Birbiglia, Mike. *The New One* — B
   Blum, Howard. *The Spy Who Knew Too Much* — 327.12
   Burns, Eric. *Someone to Watch Over Me* — 973.917092
   Calhoun, Ada. *Also a Poet* — B
   Carlin, Kelly. *A Carlin Home Companion* — B
   Carr, Erin Lee. *All That You Leave Behind* — B
   Clarke, Rachel. *Dear Life* — B
   Cole, Natalie. *Angel on My Shoulder* — B
   Davis, Patti. *Floating in the Deep End* — 616.8
   Fagan, Kate. *All the Colors Came Out* — B
   Faludi, Susan. *In the Darkroom* — B
   Foreman, Tom. *My Year of Running Dangerously* — B
   Foxx, Jamie. *Act Like You Got Some Sense* — B
   Irving, Apricot Anderson. *The Gospel of Trees* — B
   Katz, Catherine Grace. *The Daughters of Yalta* — 920
   Kerrison, Catherine. *Jefferson's Daughters* — 920
   Knausgaard, Karl Ove. *Spring* — B
   Leader, Zachary. *The Life of Saul Bellow* — B
   Madden, T Kira. *Long Live the Tribe of Fatherless Girls* — 814
   Matteson, John. *Eden's Outcasts* — 920
   Nafisi, Azar. *Read Dangerously* — 809
   Neumann, Ariana. *When Time Stopped* — B
   Ng, Fae Myenne. *Orphan Bachelors* — B
   Roy, Saumya. *Castaway Mountain* — 363.72
   Schulz, Kathryn. *Lost & Found* — B
   Seierstad, Asne. *Two Sisters* — 956.9104
   Shahani, Aarti Namdev. *Here We Are* — B
   Shapiro, Dani. ★*Inheritance* — B
   Shaw, Bernard. *Major Barbara* — 822
   Sinclair, Safiya. ★*How to Say Babylon* — B
   Smyth, Katharine. *All the Lives We Ever Lived* — B
   Stewart, James B. *Unscripted* — 658.1
   V. *The Apology* — 818
   Vanderbilt, Tom. ★*Beginners* — 646.7
   Wetherall, Tyler. *No Way Home* — B
   Yousafzai, Ziauddin. *Let Her Fly* — B
FATHERS AND SONS
   Backman, Fredrik. *Things My Son Needs to Know About the World* — B
   Biden, Joseph R. *Promise Me, Dad* — B
   Black, Michael Ian. *A Better Man* — 305.31
   Bush, George W. *41* — B
   Coates, Ta-Nehisi. *The Beautiful Struggle* — B
   Coffin, Jaed. *Roughhouse Friday* — B
   Dennis, David J., Jr. *The Movement Made Us* — B
   Dial, Roman. *The Adventurer's Son* — 917.286
   Dubus, Andre. *Townie* — B
   Edmundson, Mark. *Why Football Matters* — B
   Enrich, David. *Dark Towers* — 332.1
   Firdawsi. *Shahnameh* — 891
   Ghobash, Omar Saif. *Letters to a Young Muslim* — 297.09
   Hemingway, Ernest. *Dear Papa* — 813
   Herbert, Brian. *Dreamer of Dune* — B
   Hilfiger, Tommy. *American Dreamer* — B
   Hodgman, John. *Medallion Status* — B

AUTHOR, TITLE, SERIES AND SUBJECT INDEX

Jawando, Will. ★*My Seven Black Fathers*	B
King, Charles Monroe. *A Journal for Jordan*	956.7044
Kozol, Jonathan. *The Theft of Memory*	B
Kupperman, Michael. *All the Answers*	741.5
Leader, Zachary. *The Life of Saul Bellow*	B
Lovato, Roberto. *Unforgetting*	B
Matar, Hisham. *The Return*	B
Ollestad, Norman. *Crazy for the Storm*	B
Pardlo, Gregory. *Air Traffic*	B
Phelan, Tom. *We Were Rich and We Didn't Know It*	B
Raban, Jonathan. *Father and Son*	B
Reiss, Tom. *The Black Count*	B
Russert, Luke. *Look for Me There*	B
Sattouf, Riad. *The Arab of the Future 2*	741.5
Sattouf, Riad. *The Arab of the Future*	741.5
Shehadeh, Raja. ★*We Could Have Been Friends, My Father and I*	B
Shih, David. *Chinese Prodigal*	B
Spiegelman, Art. ★*Maus*	741.5
Taylor, Justin. *Riding with the Ghost*	B
Thompson, Juan F. *Stories I Tell Myself*	B
Thompson, Wright. *The Cost of These Dreams*	B
Thrall, Nathan. ★*A Day in the Life of Abed Salama*	956.05
Thwaite, Ann. *Goodbye Christopher Robin*	B
Toibin, Colm. *Mad, Bad, Dangerous to Know*	920
Tran, Phuc. ★*Sigh, Gone*	B
Trump, Mary L. *Too Much and Never Enough*	B
Updegrove, Mark K. *The Last Republicans*	973.928
Wagamese, Richard. *For Joshua*	B
Watkins, D. *Black Boy Smile*	B
FATIGUE	
Davis, KC. ★*How to Keep House While Drowning*	648
Hubbard, Shanita. ★*Ride-Or-Die*	305.48
Keyes, Corey L. M. ★*Languishing*	152.1
Winters, Mary-Frances. *Black Fatigue*	305.896
Fatty Fatty Boom Boom. Chaudry, Rabia	B
Fauber, L. S.	
Heaven on Earth	B
Fauci, Anthony S.	
Expect the Unexpected	610.92
FAUCI, ANTHONY S., 1940-	
Fauci, Anthony S. *Expect the Unexpected*	610.92
FAULKNER, WILLIAM, 1897-1962	
Gorra, Michael Edward. *The Saddest Words*	813
Fault Lines. Kruse, Kevin Michael	973.92
Faust, Drew Gilpin	
Mothers of Invention	973.7
Necessary Trouble	
This Republic of Suffering	973.7
FAUST, DREW GILPIN	
Faust, Drew Gilpin. *Necessary Trouble*	B
The Faustian Bargain. Petropoulos, Jonathan	709
FAUSTIAN BARGAINS	
Goethe, Johann Wolfgang von. *Goethe's Faust*	832
FAVORITES, ROYAL	
Fraser, Antonia. *Love and Louis XIV*	B
Woolley, Benjamin. *The King's Assassin*	B
FAVRE, BRETT	
Pearlman, Jeff. *Gunslinger*	B
Favro, Terri	
Generation Robot	006.3
FAVRO, TERRI	
Favro, Terri. *Generation Robot*	006.3
FAWCETT, PERCY HARRISON, 1867-1925?	
Grann, David. *The Lost City of Z*	918.1
FAWKES, GUY, 1570-1606	
Fraser, Antonia. *Faith and Treason*	942.06
FBI AGENTS	
Douglas, John E. *The Killer Across the Table*	B
Douglas, John E. *When a Killer Calls*	364.152
Elnoury, Tamer. *American Radical*	B
Lehr, Dick. *White Hot Hate*	363.325
Wiehl, Lis W. *Hunting the Unabomber*	364.152
FBI INFORMANTS	
Lauterbach, Preston. *Bluff City*	B
FDR. Smith, Jean Edward	B
FDR and Chief Justice Hughes. Simon, James F.	973.917092
Fear. Woodward, Bob	973.933

FEAR	
Aktipis, Athena. ★*A Field Guide to the Apocalypse*	155.2
Berry, Erica. *Wolfish*	152.4
Boone, Matthew S. *Stop Avoiding Stuff*	152.4
Braudy, Leo. *Haunted*	398.45
Butcher, Amy. *Mothertrucker*	B
Butler, Judith. ★*Who's Afraid of Gender?*	305.3
Fenet, Lydia. *Claim Your Confidence*	158.1
Gardner, Dan. *The Science of Fear*	152.4
Gay, Ross. *Inciting Joy*	814
Goldberg, Emma. *Life on the Line*	362.1962
Heti, Sheila. *Alphabetical Diaries*	818
Jeffers, Susan J. *Feel the Fear— and Do It Anyway*	152.4
Kubler-Ross, Elisabeth. *Life Lessons*	170
Nussbaum, Martha Craven. *The Monarchy of Fear*	306.20973
Nussbaum, Martha Craven. *The New Religious Intolerance*	201.723
Sauls, Scott. *Beautiful People Don't Just Happen*	248.8
Shaughnessy, Brenda. *The Octopus Museum*	811
Spurling, Hilary. *Matisse the Master*	B
Stern, Amanda. *Little Panic*	616.8522
Stern, Jessica. *My War Criminal*	341.6
Summerscale, Kate. *The Book of Phobias and Manias*	616.85
Zambreno, Kate. *The Light Room*	B
Zamora, Javier. ★*Solito*	B
Zhu, Mimi. *Be Not Afraid of Love*	152.4
Fear and Loathing at Rolling Stone. Thompson, Hunter S.	070.1
★*Fear and Loathing in America.* Thompson, Hunter S.	B
Fear and Trembling. Kierkegaard, Soren	248
Fear City. Phillips-Fein, Kim	330.9747
Fear Is Just a Word. Ahmed, Azam	364.152
Fear Itself. Katznelson, Ira	973.917
Fear of a Black Universe. Alexander, Stephon	523.1
FEAR OF DEATH	
Spong, John Shelby. *Eternal Life*	236
Yalom, Irvin D. *Staring at the Sun*	155.9
Fear of Missing Out. McGinnis, Patrick J.	153.8
FEAR OF NUCLEAR WAR	
Sherman, Casey. *Above and Beyond*	973.922092
The Fearless Baker. McDowell, Erin Jeanne	641.81
Fearless Gardening. Bohl, Loree	712
Fearless Genius. Menuez, Doug	979.4
Fearless with Fabric. Maxwell, Sarah	746.46
Fearlessly Different. Rowe, Mickey	B
Fearnley-Whittingstall, Hugh	
River Cottage Veg	641.5
Feast. Helou, Anissa	641.595
Feast, Fancy	
Naked	792.7
FEAST, FANCY, 1988-	
Feast, Fancy. *Naked*	792.7
The Feather Thief. Johnson, Kirk W.	364.16
Feathers. Hanson, Thor	598.147
FEATHERS	
Hanson, Thor. *Feathers*	598.147
Johnson, Kirk W. *The Feather Thief*	364.16
Feaver, William	
★*The Lives of Lucian Freud*	B
Febos, Melissa	
★*Body Work*	808.06
Girlhood	818
FEBOS, MELISSA	
Febos, Melissa. ★*Body Work*	808.06
Febos, Melissa. *Girlhood*	818
FECES	
Nelson, Bryn. *Flush*	612.3
Fed Up. Hartley, Gemma	155.3
Fedarko, Kevin	
A Walk in the Park	917.91
FEDARKO, KEVIN	
Fedarko, Kevin. *A Walk in the Park*	917.91
Fedderly, Eva	
These Walls	365
Feder, Rachel	
The Darcy Myth	823
FEDERAL COURTS	
Olsen, Lise. *Code of Silence*	347.73
Stevens, John Paul. *The Making of a Justice*	B

PUBLIC LIBRARY CORE COLLECTION: NONFICTION
Twentieth Edition

FEDERAL GOVERNMENT
    Ellis, Joseph J. *American Creation* — 973.3
    Ellis, Joseph J. *Founding Brothers* — 973.4
    Feldman, Noah. *The Broken Constitution* — 973.7
    Nelson, Megan Kate. *The Three-Cornered War* — 978
    Raphael, Ray. *Mr. President* — 352.230973
    Simon, James F. *What Kind of Nation* — 342.73

FEDERAL JUDGES
    Olsen, Lise. *Code of Silence* — 347.73
    Stevens, John Paul. *The Making of a Justice* — B
    Urofsky, Melvin I. *Louis D. Brandeis* — B

FEDERAL RESERVE BANKS
    Bernanke, Ben. ★*21st Century Monetary Policy* — 332.1
    Lowenstein, Roger. *America's Bank* — 332.1
    Meltzer, Allan H. *A History of the Federal Reserve* — 332.1
    Smialek, Jeanna. ★*Limitless* — 332.1
    Wheelan, Charles J. *Naked Economics* — 330

FEDERER, ROGER, 1981-
    Clarey, Christopher. ★*The Master* — B

Feed. Pico, Tommy — 811
Feed The Resistance. Turshen, Julia — 641.5
★*Feeding Ghosts*. Hulls, Tessa — 741.5
★*Feel Free*. Smith, Zadie — 824
Feel The Fear— and Do It Anyway. Jeffers, Susan J. — 152.4
Feeld. Charles, Jos — 811
The Feeling of What Happens. Damasio, Antonio R. — 153
Feels Like Home. Ronstadt, Linda — B

Fehrman, Craig
    Author in Chief — 920

Feifer, Gregory
    The Great Gamble — 958.104

Feige, David
    Indefensible — B

FEIGE, DAVID
    Feige, David. *Indefensible* — B

Feigel, Lara
    The Bitter Taste of Victory — 320.943

Feiler, Bruce
    The First Love Story — 222
    Life Is in the Transitions — 392
    ★*The Search* — 306.3
    Walking the Bible — 915

FEILER, BRUCE, 1964-
    Feiler, Bruce. *Walking the Bible* — 915

Feinberg, Andrew
    Franny's — 641.594

Feinstein, Adam
    Pablo Neruda — B

Feinstein, John
    ★*The Back Roads to March* — 796.323
    The First Major — 796.352
    ★*Last Dance* — 796.323
    ★*The Legends Club* — B
    A March to Madness — 796.323
    Quarterback — B
    Where Nobody Knows Your Name — 796.357

Feinstein, Michael
    The Gershwins and Me — 782.42164

FEINSTEIN, MICHAEL
    Feinstein, Michael. *The Gershwins and Me* — 782.42164

Felder, Deborah G
    The American Women's Almanac — 305.40973

Feldman, Deborah
    Exodus — B
    Unorthodox — B

FELDMAN, DEBORAH, 1986-
    Feldman, Deborah. *Exodus* — B
    Feldman, Deborah. *Unorthodox* — B

Feldman, Noah
    The Broken Constitution — 973.7
    The Three Lives of James Madison — B
    ★*To Be a Jew Today* — 296.3

Feldmann, Erica
    Hausmagick — 133.4

Feldstein, Mark Avrom
    Poisoning the Press — 973.924092

Felidia. Bastianich, Lidia — 641.594

Felisbret, Eric
    Graffiti New York — 751.7

Felix, Camonghne
    Build Yourself a Boat — 811
    Dyscalculia — B

FELLER, BOB, 1918-2010
    Epplin, Luke. *Our Team* — 796.357

Fellman, Michael
    The Making of Robert E. Lee — B

Felon. Betts, Reginald Dwayne — 811

FELT WORK
    Adams, Liza. *Needle Felting* — 746
    Lapierre, Corinne. *Folk Embroidered Felt Birds* — 746.0463
    Susa, Sachiko. *Sweet & Simple Needle Felted Animals* — 746

Felton, Tom
    ★*Beyond the Wand* — B

FELTON, TOM, 1987-
    Felton, Tom. ★*Beyond the Wand* — B

FEMALE DOMINATION (SEXUALITY)
    Belcher, Chris. *Pretty Baby* — B

Female Founders' Playbook. Boden, Anne — 658.4

FEMALE FRIENDSHIP
    Adichie, Chimamanda Ngozi. *Dear Ijeawele* — 649
    Batalion, Judith. *The Light of Days* — 940.53
    Bell-Scott, Patricia. *The Firebrand and the First Lady* — 920
    Bradford, Joy Harden. *Sisterhood Heals* — 158.2
    Brown, Tina. *The Diana Chronicles* — B
    Butcher, Amy. *Mothertrucker* — B
    Caldwell, Gail. *Let's Take the Long Way Home* — B
    Cerulo, Erica. *Work Wife* — 658.4
    Crowther, Gail. *Three-Martini Afternoons at the Ritz* — 920
    Doherty, Maggie. *The Equivalents* — 920
    Gerard, Sarah. *Carrie Carolyn Coco* — 364.152
    Gorrindo, Simone. ★*The Wives* — B
    Jackson, Danielle Bayard. *Fighting for Our Friendships* — 302.34
    Koppel, Lily. *The Astronaut Wives Club* — 920
    Leach, Samantha. ★*The Elissas* — 362.73
    Lynn, Loretta. ★*Me & Patsy Kickin' up Dust* — B
    Margolick, David. *Elizabeth and Hazel* — 379.2
    McKeon, Kathy. *Jackie's Girl* — B
    Nafisi, Azar. ★*Reading Lolita in Tehran* — B
    Narayan, Shoba. *The Milk Lady of Bangalore* — 390
    Patchett, Ann. *Truth & Beauty* — B
    Poehler, Amy. *Yes Please* — B
    Quinn, Susan. *Eleanor and Hick* — B
    Satrapi, Marjane. *Embroideries* — 741.5
    Slate, Jenny. *Little Weirds* — B
    Sow, Aminatou. *Big Friendship* — 177
    Tate, Christie. *B.F.F.* — B
    Totenberg, Nina. ★*Dinners with Ruth* — B
    Trice, Dawn Turner. ★*Three Girls from Bronzeville* — 977.311
    Verdelle, A. J. *Miss Chloe* — B

FEMALE IMPERSONATORS
    Mattel, Trixie. *Working Girls* — 650.1
    Velour, Sasha. ★*The Big Reveal* — 792.7

FEMALE INFERTILITY
    Union, Gabrielle. *You Got Anything Stronger?* — B

FEMALE REPRODUCTIVE SYSTEM
    Gross, Rachel E. *Vagina Obscura* — 618.1
    Gunter, Jen. ★*Blood* — 612.6
    Gunter, Jen. *The Vagina Bible* — 612.6
    Hazard, Leah. *Womb* — 612.6
    Mendelson, Zoe. *Pussypedia* — 612.6

Femina. Ramirez, Janina — 940.1

FEMININE BEAUTY (AESTHETICS)
    Clein, Emmeline. ★*Dead Weight* — 616.85
    Hankir, Zahra. *Eyeliner* — 391.6
    Hu, Elise. *Flawless* — 646.7
    Jones, Chloe Cooper. ★*Easy Beauty* — B
    Lieu, Susan. ★*The Manicurist's Daughter* — B
    Mifflin, Margot. *Looking for Miss America* — 791.6
    Moran, Caitlin. *How to Be a Woman* — B
    Ratajkowski, Emily. ★*My Body* — B
    Whitefield-Madrano, Autumn. *Face Value* — 111

★*The Feminine Mystique*. Friedan, Betty — 305.42

FEMININITY
    Baer, Kate. *What Kind of Woman* — 811
    Belcher, Chris. *Pretty Baby* — B

AUTHOR, TITLE, SERIES AND SUBJECT INDEX

Berry, Erica. *Wolfish*	152.4
Byas, Taylor. *I Done Clicked My Heels Three Times*	811
Clifton, Lucille. *How to Carry Water*	811
Codjoe, Ama. *Bluest Nude*	811
Davis, Lisa Selin. *Tomboy*	305.409
Ellis, Helen. *Bring Your Baggage and Don't Pack Light*	814
Febos, Melissa. *Girlhood*	818
Goodan, Chelsey. *Underestimated*	305.235
Hay, Carol. *Think Like a Feminist*	305.42
Levy, Deborah. *The Cost of Living*	B
Levy, Deborah. ★*Real Estate*	B
Levy, Deborah. ★*Things I Don't Want to Know*	B
Loh, Sandra Tsing. *The Madwoman and the Roomba*	B
Lorde, Audre. ★*The Selected Works of Audre Lorde*	814
Mann, Jen. ★*Midlife Bites*	305.244
Mifflin, Margot. *Looking for Miss America*	791.6
Moran, Caitlin. *How to Be a Woman*	B
Moran, Caitlin. *More Than a Woman*	B
Mouton, Deborah D. E. E. P. *Black Chameleon*	B
O'Donnell Heffington, Peggy. *Without Children*	306.85
Orenstein, Peggy. *Cinderella Ate My Daughter*	305.23082
Porizkova, Paulina. *No Filter*	B
Ramirez, Janina. *Femina*	940.1
Ratajkowski, Emily. ★*My Body*	B
Robb, Alice. ★*Don't Think, Dear*	792.8
Savage, Jodi M. *The Death of a Jaybird*	B
Scenters-Zapico, Natalie. *Lima*	811
Skaja, Emily. *Brute*	811.6
Tatar, Maria. *The Heroine with 1001 Faces*	809
Zimmerman, Jess. *Women and Other Monsters*	155.3

FEMINISM

Adichie, Chimamanda Ngozi. *Dear Ijeawele*	649
Adichie, Chimamanda Ngozi. *We Should All Be Feminists*	305.42
Ahmed, Sara. *The Feminist Killjoy Handbook*	305.42
Amos, Tori. *Resistance*	B
Austerlitz, Saul. *Kind of a Big Deal*	791.43
Beauvoir, Simone de. ★*The Second Sex*	305.4
Block, Jennifer. *Everything Below the Waist*	613
Bowen, Sesali. *Bad Fat Black Girl*	305.42
Campbell, Olivia. *Women in White Coats*	610.92
Cargle, Rachel Elizabeth. *A Renaissance of Our Own*	B
Carruthers, Charlene A. *Unapologetic*	305.48
Chang, Leslie T. ★*Egyptian Made*	331.4
Chemaly, Soraya L. *Rage Becomes Her*	155.3
Cook, Blanche Wiesen. *Eleanor Roosevelt; Volume 2*	B
Cook, Blanche Wiesen. ★*Eleanor Roosevelt; Volume 3*	B
Cooper, Brittney C. *Eloquent Rage*	B
Cottom, Tressie McMillan. *Thick*	301
Dabiri, Emma. *Twisted*	391.5
Davis, Angela Y. *Abolition*	364.6
Doherty, Maggie. *The Equivalents*	920
Duberman, Martin B. *Andrea Dworkin*	B
Dubin, Minna. ★*Mom Rage*	306.874
Eig, Jonathan. *The Birth of the Pill*	618.1
Eltahawy, Mona. *The Seven Necessary Sins for Women and Girls*	305.42
Evaristo, Bernardine. *Manifesto*	B
Febos, Melissa. *Girlhood*	818
Filipovic, Jill. *The H-Spot*	155.3
Flock, Elizabeth. ★*The Furies*	305.48
Frangello, Gina. *Blow Your House Down*	813
Friedan, Betty. ★*The Feminine Mystique*	305.42
Gabriel, Mary. *Madonna*	B
Garcia, Amanda Yates. *Initiated*	B
Gates, Melinda. ★*The Moment of Lift*	305.42
Gay, Roxane. *Bad Feminist*	814
Gay, Roxane. ★*Opinions*	814
Ghodsee, Kristen Rogheh. *Everyday Utopia*	335
Gilbert, Sandra M. ★*Still Mad*	810.9
Ginzberg, Lori D. *Elizabeth Cady Stanton*	B
Griffin, Farah Jasmine. ★*In Search of a Beautiful Freedom*	814
Griffith, Elisabeth. *Formidable*	305.42
Grossman, Pam. *Waking the Witch*	133.4
Hackman, Rose. ★*Emotional Labor*	155.3
Hanna, Kathleen. *Rebel Girl*	B
Hartley, Gemma. *Fed Up*	155.3
Hay, Carol. *Think Like a Feminist*	305.42
Hester, Diarmuid. *Nothing Ever Just Disappears*	306.76
Hill, Katie. *She Will Rise*	305.42
Hirshey, Gerri. *Not Pretty Enough*	B
Hirshman, Linda R. *Reckoning*	305.420973
hooks, bell. *Remembered Rapture*	808
hooks, bell. *Wounds of Passion*	B
Hubbard, Shanita. ★*Ride-Or-Die*	305.48
Jackson, Jenn M. ★*Black Women Taught Us*	305.48
Jackson, Regina. *White Women*	305.8
Kantor, Jodi. *She Said*	364.15
Karbo, Karen. *In Praise of Difficult Women*	920
Kelly, Helena. *Jane Austen, the Secret Radical*	823
Kendall, Mikki. *Hood Feminism*	305.420973
Lahti, Christine. *True Stories from an Unreliable Eyewitness*	B
Lepore, Jill. ★*The Secret History of Wonder Woman*	741.5
Lorde, Audre. ★*The Selected Works of Audre Lorde*	814
Lorde, Audre. *Sister Outsider*	814
Mans, Jasmine. *Black Girl, Call Home*	811
McGowan, Rose. *Brave*	B
Michaelis, David. ★*Eleanor*	973.917
Mifflin, Margot. *Looking for Miss America*	791.6
Moran, Caitlin. *How to Be a Woman*	B
Moran, Caitlin. *More Than a Woman*	B
Morris, Bonnie J. ★*The Feminist Revolution*	305.4209
Nuttall, Jennifer Anne. ★*Mother Tongue*	422
O'Meara, Mallory. *Girly Drinks*	641.2
Orenstein, Peggy. *Don't Call Me Princess*	305.42
Palmieri, Jennifer. *She Proclaims*	305.42
Perkins, Anne Gardiner. *Yale Needs Women*	378
Pham, Larissa. *Pop Song*	709.2
Popova, Maria. *Figuring*	920
Quinn, Bridget. *She Votes*	324.6
Reese, Anney. ★*Stuff Mom Never Told You*	305.42
Rose, Jacqueline. *On Violence and on Violence Against Women*	362.88
Saini, Angela. *Inferior*	305.4
Schuller, Kyla. *The Trouble with White Women*	305.42
Sisson, Gretchen E. ★*Relinquished*	362.734
Smarsh, Sarah. *She Come by It Natural*	782.42164
Solnit, Rebecca. *Call Them by Their True Names*	303.3
Solnit, Rebecca. *Men Explain Things to Me*	305.42
Solnit, Rebecca. *The Mother of All Questions*	305.42
Solnit, Rebecca. ★*Recollections of My Nonexistence*	B
Spruill, Marjorie Julian. *Divided We Stand*	305.42
Srinivasan, Amia. *The Right to Sex*	305.42
Steinem, Gloria. *My Life on the Road*	B
Steinem, Gloria. *Outrageous Acts and Everyday Rebellions*	305.42
Steinem, Gloria. *The Truth Will Set You Free, but First It Will Piss You Off*	305.42
Stryker, Kitty. *Ask*	302
Suh, Krista. *DIY Rules for a WTF World*	158.1
Tatar, Maria. *The Heroine with 1001 Faces*	809
Tinsley, Omise'eke Natasha. *Beyonce in Formation*	782.42164
Tolokonnikova, Nadezhda. *Rules for Rulebreakers*	782.42166
Traister, Rebecca. *Good and Mad*	305.420973
Turk, Katherine. *The Women of Now*	305.42
Union, Gabrielle. *We're Going to Need More Wine*	B
Wegner, Bobbi. *Raising Feminist Boys*	305.23
West, Lindy. *The Witches Are Coming*	305.420973
Whitefield-Madrano, Autumn. *Face Value*	111
Williams, Marlena. *Night Mother*	791.43
Worley, Jennifer. *Neon Girls*	792.7
Zakaria, Rafia. *Against White Feminism*	305.42
Zimmerman, Jess. *Women and Other Monsters*	155.3

FEMINISM AND RACISM

Hay, Carol. *Think Like a Feminist*	305.42

FEMINIST CRITICISM

Gilbert, Sandra M. ★*Still Mad*	810.9
The Feminist Killjoy Handbook. Ahmed, Sara	305.42
★*The Feminist Revolution*. Morris, Bonnie J.	305.4209

FEMINIST SPIRITUALITY

Garcia, Amanda Yates. *Initiated*	B

FEMINIST THEORY

Adichie, Chimamanda Ngozi. *Dear Ijeawele*	649
Filipovic, Jill. *The H-Spot*	155.3
Hay, Carol. *Think Like a Feminist*	305.42
Stryker, Kitty. *Ask*	302

FEMINISTS

Adichie, Chimamanda Ngozi. *Dear Ijeawele*	649
Bates, Laura. *Men Who Hate Women*	305.3
Beauvoir, Simone de. ★*The Second Sex*	305.4

PUBLIC LIBRARY CORE COLLECTION: NONFICTION
Twentieth Edition

Bell-Scott, Patricia. *The Firebrand and the First Lady*	920
Brownstein, Gabriel. ★*The Secret Mind of Bertha Pappenheim*	616.85
Carmon, Irin. *Notorious RBG*	B
Davis, Jack E. *An Everglades Providence*	B
De Stefano, Cristina. *The Child Is the Teacher*	B
Duberman, Martin B. *Andrea Dworkin*	B
Ginsburg, Ruth Bader. ★*My Own Words*	347.73
Ginzberg, Lori D. *Elizabeth Cady Stanton*	B
Gordon, Charlotte. *Romantic Outlaws*	920
Gray, Emma. *A Girl's Guide to Joining the Resistance*	303.48
Greenidge, Kerri. ★*The Grimkes*	973.5
Hochschild, Adam. *Rebel Cinderella*	B
hooks, bell. *Wounds of Passion*	B
Jones, Brenda. *Alexandria Ocasio-Cortez*	B
Jones, Brenda. *Maxine Waters*	B
Kelly, Kate. *Ordinary Equality*	920
Kimberley, Hannah. *A Woman's Place Is at the Top*	B
King, Billie Jean. ★*All In*	B
Lahti, Christine. *True Stories from an Unreliable Eyewitness*	B
Moser, Benjamin. ★*Sontag*	B
Painter, Nell Irvin. ★*Sojourner Truth*	B
Rosenberg, Rosalind. ★*Jane Crow*	B
Royster, Francesca T. *Choosing Family*	B
Ryckman, Pamela. *Candace Pert*	B
Sarsour, Linda. *We Are Not Here to Be Bystanders*	B
Schuller, Kyla. *The Trouble with White Women*	305.42
Steinem, Gloria. *My Life on the Road*	B
Steinem, Gloria. *Outrageous Acts and Everyday Rebellions*	305.42
Tamblyn, Amber. ★*Era of Ignition*	B
Tinsley, Omise'eke Natasha. *Beyonce in Formation*	782.42164
V. ★*Reckoning*	814
West, Lindy. *Shrill*	818
★*Fen, Bog and Swamp*. Proulx, Annie	551.41
FENCERS	
Muhammad, Ibtihaj. *Proud*	B
Fences. Wilson, August	812
FENDER GUITAR	
Port, Ian S. *The Birth of Loud*	787.87
FENDER, LEO, 1909-1991	
Port, Ian S. *The Birth of Loud*	787.87
Fenet, Lydia	
Claim Your Confidence	158.1
FENN, FORREST	
Barbarisi, Daniel. *Chasing the Thrill*	796.1
Fenn, Lisa	
Carry On	B
FENN, LISA	
Fenn, Lisa. *Carry On*	B
Fennelly, Beth Ann	
Heating & Cooling	B
FENNELLY, BETH ANN, 1971-	
Fennelly, Beth Ann. *Heating & Cooling*	B
FENTANYL	
Hughes, Evan. *The Hard Sell*	338.4
Macy, Beth. ★*Raising Lazarus*	362.29
Quinones, Sam. ★*The Least of Us*	362.29
Fentanyl, Inc. Westhoff, Ben	362.29
Fenton, James	
Selected Poems	821
Fenton, Justin	
We Own This City	364.1
Fenway 1912. Stout, Glenn	796.357
Feral. Pennington, Emily	B
FERAL CATS	
Carr, Caleb. *My Beloved Monster*	B
Feral City. Moss, Jeremiah	B
Ferguson, Charles D.	
Nuclear Energy	333.792
Ferguson, Jane	
No Ordinary Assignment	B
FERGUSON, JANE	
Ferguson, Jane. *No Ordinary Assignment*	B
Ferguson, Jesse Tyler	
★*Food Between Friends*	641.5973
Ferguson, Niall	
Doom	362.1962
Kissinger	973.924
Ferling, John E.	
Winning Independence	973.3
Ferlinghetti, Lawrence	
These Are My Rivers	811
Fermat's Enigma. Singh, Simon	512
FERMENTATION	
Redzepi, Rene. *The Noma Guide to Fermentation*	664
FERMENTED FOODS	
Kang, Mingoo. *Jang*	641.595
Redzepi, Rene. *The Noma Guide to Fermentation*	664
FERMI, ENRICO, 1901-1954	
Schwartz, David N. *The Last Man Who Knew Everything*	B
Fernandez-Armesto, Felipe	
★*Amerigo*	B
Our America	973
Fernando, S. H., Jr	
From the Streets of Shaolin	782.421
Ferrante, Elena	
In the Margins	809
FERRANTE, ELENA	
Ferrante, Elena. *In the Margins*	809
Ferrara, Silvia	
The Greatest Invention	411
FERRARI AUTOMOBILE	
Baime, A. J. ★*Go Like Hell*	796.7209
Ferrazzi, Keith	
Never Eat Alone	658.4
Ferreiro, Larrie D.	
Brothers at Arms	327.73
Ferrer, Ada	
★*Cuba*	972.91
Ferris, William R.	
Give My Poor Heart Ease	781.643
Ferriss, Timothy	
Tools of Titans	081
Fersko, Diana	
★*We Need to Talk About Antisemitism*	305.892
Fersko-Weiss, Henry	
Caring for the Dying	616.02
FERTILITY	
Foster, Sutton. *Hooked*	B
Hughes, Bettany. *Venus and Aphrodite*	292
Wilson, Rebel. *Rebel Rising*	B
Fertility Rules. Schrock, Leslie	613.9
Fessler, Ann	
The Girls Who Went Away	362.82
Fessler, Pam	
Carville's Cure	362.19699
FETUS	
Curtis, Glade B. *Your Pregnancy Week by Week*	618.2
Zernicka-Goetz, Magdalena. *The Dance of Life*	591.56
FEUDALISM	
Lockley, Thomas. *African Samurai*	B
Man, John. *Ninja*	355.5
FEUDS	
Freeman, Joanne B. *The Field of Blood*	973.7
Satyamurti, Carole. *Mahabharata*	821
★*A Fever in the Heartland*. Egan, Timothy	322.4
Fevers, Feuds, and Diamonds. Farmer, Paul	614.5
The Few. Kershaw, Alex	940.54
Feynman, Richard P.	
★*The Meaning of It All*	500
★*Six Easy Pieces*	530
FEYNMAN, RICHARD P., (RICHARD PHILLIPS), 1918-1988	
Feynman, Richard P. ★*The Meaning of It All*	500
Fiasco. Ricks, Thomas E.	956.7044
FIBROMYALGIA	
Abril, Andy. *Mayo Clinic Guide to Fibromyalgia*	616.7
FICTION AND CULTURE	
Houston, Keith. *The Book*	002.09
Nafisi, Azar. *The Republic of Imagination*	B
FICTION IN LIBRARIES	
Bradford, Robin. ★*The Readers' Advisory Guide to Romance*	025.2
Spratford, Becky Siegel. *The Readers' Advisory Guide to Horror*	025.5
FICTION WRITING	
Anders, Charlie Jane. ★*Never Say You Can't Survive*	808.02
Attwell, David. *J. M. Coetzee and the Life of Writing*	823
Blaisdell, Robert. *Creating Anna Karenina*	891.7

AUTHOR, TITLE, SERIES AND SUBJECT INDEX

Collins, Max Allan. *Spillane*	B
Damrosch, David. *Around the World in 80 Books*	809
Dufresne, John. *Storyville!*	808.3
Griffin, Susan. *Out of Silence, Sound. Out of Nothing, Something*	808.02
Hecimovich, Gregg A. ★*The Life and Times of Hannah Crafts*	B
Highsmith, Patricia. ★*Patricia Highsmith's Diaries and Notebooks*	818
Koch, Stephen. *The Modern Library Writer's Workshop*	808.3
Larimer, Kevin. *The Poets & Writers Complete Guide to Being a Writer*	808
McDermott, Alice. *What About the Baby?*	814
McKee, Robert. *Dialogue*	809
Mosley, Walter. *Elements of Fiction*	808.3
Nafisi, Azar. *The Republic of Imagination*	B
Palahniuk, Chuck. *Consider This*	B
Percy, Benjamin. *Thrill Me*	808.3
Piercy, Marge. *So You Want to Write*	808.3
Prose, Francine. *What to Read and Why*	028
Salesses, Matthew. ★*Craft in the Real World*	808.3
Saunders, George. ★*A Swim in a Pond in the Rain*	891.7
Sepetys, Ruta. ★*You*	808.02
Shange, Ntozake. ★*Sing a Black Girl's Song*	818
Smiley, Jane. *Thirteen Ways of Looking at the Novel*	B
Fidel Castro. Castro, Fidel	
A Field Guide to American Houses. McAlester, Virginia	728
★*A Field Guide to Animal Tracks.* Murie, Olaus J.	599
The Field Guide to Fleece. Robson, Deborah	677
The Field Guide to Geology. Lambert, David	550
★*A Field Guide to Lies.* Levitin, Daniel J.	153.4
A Field Guide to Mushrooms, North America. McKnight, Kent H.	579.6
★*A Field Guide to Rocks and Minerals.* Pough, Frederick H.	549
★*A Field Guide to the Apocalypse.* Aktipis, Athena	155.2
The Field Guide to Trains. Solomon, Brian	625.2
A Field Guide to Western Trees. Petrides, George A.	582.16
Field Notes from a Catastrophe. Kolbert, Elizabeth	363.738
The Field of Blood. Freeman, Joanne B.	973.7
Field, Andy	
Encounterism	302
Field, Sally	
In Pieces	B
FIELD, SALLY	
Field, Sally. *In Pieces*	B
Fields of Blood. Armstrong, Karen	201
Fields, Micah	
★*We Hold Our Breath*	976.4
FIELDS, MICAH	
Fields, Micah. ★*We Hold Our Breath*	976.4
Fields-Black, Edda L.	
Combee	973.7
Fieldwork. Regan, Iliana	B
Fiennes, Ranulph	
Shackleton	B
A Fiery Peace in a Cold War. Sheehan, Neil	B
The Fiery Trial. Foner, Eric	973.7092
Fieseler, Robert W.	
Tinderbox	364.152
★*Fiesta At Rick's.* Bayless, Rick	641.5972
Fifield, Anna	
The Great Successor	B
The Fifth Act. Ackerman, Elliot	958.104
Fifth Avenue, 5 A.M. Wasson, Sam	791.43
The Fifties. Halberstam, David	973.92
Fifty Miles from Tomorrow. Hensley, William L. Iggiagruk	B
Fifty Ships That Changed the Course of History. Graham, Ian	387.2
The Fifty Year Mission. Gross, Edward	791.45
Fifty Years of 60 Minutes. Fager, Jeffrey	070.1
Figes, Orlando	
The Crimean War	947
The Europeans	920
A People's Tragedy	947.08
★*The Story of Russia*	947
★*The Whisperers*	306.850947
The Fight for Free Speech. Rosenberg, Ian	342.73
The Fight for Privacy. Citron, Danielle Keats	342.7308
The Fight of His Life. Whipple, Chris	973.934
Fight Right. Gottman, Julie Schwartz	616.89
FIGHTER PILOTS	
Bruning, John R. *The Race of Aces*	940.54
Clavin, Thomas. *Lightning Down*	940.54
Hampton, Dan. *Operation Vengeance*	940.54
Harden, Blaine. *The Great Leader and the Fighter Pilot*	B
Hynes, Samuel. *The Unsubstantial Air*	940.4
Makos, Adam. ★*A Higher Call*	940.54
FIGHTER PLANES	
Bruning, John R. *The Race of Aces*	940.54
Hamilton-Paterson, James. *Marked for Death*	358.400941
Harden, Blaine. *The Great Leader and the Fighter Pilot*	B
The Fighters. Chivers, C. J.	920
Fighting Churchill, Appeasing Hitler. Phillips, Adrian	327.41043
Fighting for Our Friendships. Jackson, Danielle Bayard	302.34
Fighting for Space. Teitel, Amy Shira	920
FIGURE DRAWING	
Hale, Robert Beverly. *Anatomy Lessons from the Great Masters*	743.4
Huston, Steve. *Figure Drawing for Artists*	743.4
Loomis, Andrew. *Figure Drawing for All It's Worth*	743.4
Ryder, Anthony. *The Artist's Complete Guide to Figure Drawing*	743.4
Vanderpoel, John Henry. *The Human Figure*	743
Winslow, Valerie L. *Classic Human Anatomy*	743.4
Figure Drawing for All It's Worth. Loomis, Andrew	743.4
Figure Drawing for Artists. Huston, Steve	743.4
FIGURE SKATERS	
Blakinger, Keri. *Corrections in Ink*	B
Rippon, Adam. *Beautiful on the Outside*	B
FIGURE SKATING	
Rippon, Adam. *Beautiful on the Outside*	B
The Figured Wheel. Pinsky, Robert	811
Figuring. Popova, Maria	920
Fili, Louise	
The Cognoscenti's Guide to Florence	381
FILICIDE	
Glatt, John. *The Doomsday Mother*	364.152
FILIPINO AMERICAN WOMEN	
Garbes, Angela. *Essential Labor*	306.874
FILIPINO AMERICANS	
Cailan, Alvin. *Amboy*	641.595
Nezhukumatathil, Aimee. *Bite by Bite*	641.3
Ressa, Maria. ★*How to Stand up to a Dictator*	070.92
Samaha, Albert. *Concepcion*	929
Talusan, Meredith. *Fairest*	305.30973
Tometich, Annabelle. *The Mango Tree*	B
Vargas, Jose Antonio. *Dear America*	B
FILIPINO PEOPLE	
DeParle, Jason. ★*A Good Provider Is One Who Leaves*	305.899
Nezhukumatathil, Aimee. *Bite by Bite*	641.3
Ressa, Maria. ★*How to Stand up to a Dictator*	070.92
Filipovic, Jill	
The H-Spot	155.3
Filkins, Dexter	
The Forever War	956.7044
FILLMORE, MILLARD, 1800-1874	
Cohen, Jared. *Accidental Presidents*	973.09
Finkelman, Paul. *Millard Fillmore*	B
FILM	
Carter, Ruth E. ★*The Art of Ruth E. Carter*	746.9
Leamer, Laurence. *Hitchcock's Blondes*	791.43
Peiffer, Prudence. *The Slip*	709.73
Schwartzel, Erich. *Red Carpet*	791.43
Seidelman, Susan. *Desperately Seeking Something*	B
Yomota, Inuhiko. *What Is Japanese Cinema?*	791.43
FILM ACTING	
Bacall, Lauren. *By Myself and Then Some*	B
FILM AUDIENCES	
Goetz, Kevin. *Audienceology*	791.43
FILM CRITICS	
Gleiberman, Owen. *Movie Freak*	B
Singer, Matt. *Opposable Thumbs*	791.43
FILM EDITING	
Hirsch, Paul. *A Long Time Ago in a Cutting Room Far, Far Away*	B
FILM EDITORS	
Hirsch, Paul. *A Long Time Ago in a Cutting Room Far, Far Away*	B
FILM EVALUATION	
Kael, Pauline. ★*The Age of Movies*	791.43
Schickel, Richard. *Keepers*	791.430973
Thomson, David. ★*How to Watch a Movie*	791.43
FILM HISTORY AND CRITICISM	
Ausaja, S. M. M. *Bollywood*	791.43
Britt, Ryan. ★*The Spice Must Flow*	813
Brockett, Oscar G. *History of the Theatre*	792

PUBLIC LIBRARY CORE COLLECTION: NONFICTION
Twentieth Edition

Carlson, Erin. *I'll Have What She's Having*	791.43
Cavalier, Stephen. *The World History of Animation*	791.43
Davis, Michael. *Street Gang*	791.43
De Vise, Daniel. ★*The Blues Brothers*	791.43
Ebert, Roger. *Life Itself*	B
Ebert, Roger. *Scorsese by Ebert*	B
Fournier-Lanzoni, Remi. *French Cinema, 2nd Ed.*	791.43
Gitlin, Marty. *A Celebration of Animation*	741.5
Goetz, Kevin. *Audienceology*	791.43
Harris, Mark. *Pictures at a Revolution*	791.43
Hendrix, Grady. *These Fists Break Bricks*	791
Hirsch, Foster. ★*Hollywood and the Movies of the Fifties*	791.43
Hirsch, Paul. *A Long Time Ago in a Cutting Room Far, Far Away*	B
Holt, Nathalia. *The Queens of Animation*	920
Johnson, Mindy. *Ink & Paint*	B
Kael, Pauline. ★*The Age of Movies*	791.43
Kenny, Glenn. *Made Men*	791.43
Kenny, Glenn. *The World Is Yours*	791.43
Kroger, Lisa. *Monster, She Wrote*	920
Lenburg, Jeff. *The Encyclopedia of Animated Cartoons*	791.43
McGilligan, Patrick. *Oscar Micheaux*	B
Meslow, Scott. *From Hollywood with Love*	791.43
Norwich, John Julius. *Shakespeare's Kings*	822.33
O'Meara, Mallory. *The Lady from the Black Lagoon*	921
Riedel, Michael. *Singular Sensation*	792
Rosenbaum, Jonathan. ★*Essential Cinema*	791.43
Row, Jess. *White Flights*	813
Schechter, Harold. ★*Ripped from the Headlines!*	791.43
Shelton, Ron. *The Church of Baseball*	791.43
Silver, Alain. ★*From the Moment They Met It Was Murder*	791.43
Smith, Emma. *This Is Shakespeare*	822.33
Spoto, Donald. *The Dark Side of Genius*	B
Stratton, W. K. *The Wild Bunch*	791.43
Tarantino, Quentin. *Cinema Speculation*	791.43
Thomson, David. *The Fatal Alliance*	791.43
Wasson, Sam. *The Big Goodbye*	791.43
Weismann, Brad. *Lost in the Dark*	791.43
Wilkman, Jon. *Screening Reality*	070.1
Williams, Marlena. *Night Mother*	791.43
Yang, Jeff. *The Golden Screen*	791.43
Yomota, Inuhiko. *What Is Japanese Cinema?*	791.43

FILM INDUSTRY AND TRADE

Arkin, Alan. *An Improvised Life*	B
Ausaja, S. M. M. *Bollywood*	791.43
Basinger, Jeanine. *Hollywood*	791.43
Basinger, Jeanine. *The Star Machine*	384
Berg, A. Scott. *Kate Remembered*	B
Brooks, Mel. ★*All About Me!*	B
Caine, Michael. *Blowing the Bloody Doors Off*	B
Callow, Simon. ★*Orson Welles*	B
Coppola, Francis Ford. *Live Cinema and Its Techniques*	791.4302
D'Alessandro, Emilio. *Stanley Kubrick and Me*	791.4302
De Semlyen, Nick. *Wild and Crazy Guys*	920
De Vise, Daniel. ★*The Blues Brothers*	791.43
Dixon, Wheeler W. *A Short History of Film*	791.43
Ebert, Roger. *Scorsese by Ebert*	B
Eyman, Scott. *Empire of Dreams*	B
Finch, Christopher. *The Art of Walt Disney*	791.43092
Fournier-Lanzoni, Remi. *French Cinema, 2nd Ed.*	791.43
Frankel, Glenn. *High Noon*	791.43
Goetz, Kevin. *Audienceology*	791.43
Goldman, William. *Adventures in the Screen Trade*	384
Harris, Mark. ★*Five Came Back*	791.4302
Hayes, Dade. *Binge Times*	384.55
Hirsch, Foster. ★*Hollywood and the Movies of the Fifties*	791.43
Hirsch, Paul. *A Long Time Ago in a Cutting Room Far, Far Away*	B
Hussey, Olivia. *The Girl on the Balcony*	B
Jones, Brian Jay. *George Lucas*	B
Kanfer, Stefan. *Tough Without a Gun*	B
Levy, Shawn. ★*The Castle on Sunset*	647.95
Liu, Simu. ★*We Were Dreamers*	B
Longworth, Karina. *Seduction*	B
Nolte, Nick. *Rebel*	B
O'Meara, Mallory. *The Lady from the Black Lagoon*	921
Parke, Henry C. *The Greatest Westerns Ever Made and the People Who Made Them*	791.43
Rempel, William C. *The Gambler*	B
Rosenzweig, Laura B. *Hollywood's Spies*	791.43
Schickel, Richard. *Keepers*	791.430973
Schulman, Michael. ★*Oscar Wars*	791.43
Schwartzel, Erich. *Red Carpet*	791.43
Seal, Mark. ★*Leave the Gun, Take the Cannoli*	791.43
Stevens, Dana. *Camera Man*	791.4302
Stratton, W. K. *The Wild Bunch*	791.43
Tarantino, Quentin. *Cinema Speculation*	791.43
Thomson, David. *Bette Davis*	B
Thomson, David. *The Fatal Alliance*	791.43
Thomson, David. *How to Watch a Movie*	791.43
Thomson, David. *Ingrid Bergman*	B
Tietjen, Jill S. *Hollywood, Her Story*	791.43
Turan, Kenneth. *Not to Be Missed*	791.43
Union, Gabrielle. *You Got Anything Stronger?*	B
Urwand, Ben. *The Collaboration*	791.430973
Van Zandt, Steve. *Unrequited Infatuations*	B
Vick, Tom. *Asian Cinema*	791.43
Wasson, Sam. *The Big Goodbye*	791.43
Waxman, Sharon. *Rebels on the Backlot*	791.4302
Weismann, Brad. *Lost in the Dark*	791.43
Williams, Billy Dee. ★*What Have We Here*	B
Yang, Jeff. *The Golden Screen*	791.43

FILM NOIR

Kenny, Glenn. *Made Men*	791.43
Lane, Christina. *Phantom Lady*	B
Silver, Alain. ★*From the Moment They Met It Was Murder*	791.43
Spoto, Donald. *The Dark Side of Genius*	B

FILM PRODUCERS AND DIRECTORS

Auletta, Ken. ★*Hollywood Ending*	791.43
Benson, Michael. *Space Odyssey*	791.43
Brooks, Mel. ★*All About Me!*	B
Callow, Simon. ★*Orson Welles*	B
Carter, Ash. *Life Isn't Everything*	B
Chan, Jackie. *Never Grow Up*	B
Courogen, Carrie. ★*Miss May Does Not Exist*	B
D'Alessandro, Emilio. *Stanley Kubrick and Me*	791.4302
DiMarco, Nyle. ★*Deaf Utopia*	B
Ebert, Roger. *Scorsese by Ebert*	B
Eyman, Scott. *Charlie Chaplin vs. America*	B
Eyman, Scott. *Empire of Dreams*	B
Farrow, Ronan. ★*Catch and Kill*	331.4
Fischer, Paul. *A Kim Jong-Il Production*	791.43
Fisher, Todd. *My Girls*	B
Harris, Mark. *Mike Nichols*	B
Harryhausen, Ray. *The Art of Ray Harryhausen*	778
Haskell, Molly. *Steven Spielberg*	B
Herzog, Werner. ★*Every Man for Himself and God Against All*	B
Jones, Brian Jay. *George Lucas*	B
Karp, Josh. *Orson Welles's Last Movie*	791.43
Kenny, Glenn. *Made Men*	791.43
Kenny, Glenn. *The World Is Yours*	791.43
Kolker, Robert Phillip. *Kubrick*	B
Kurosawa, Akira. *Something Like an Autobiography*	B
Lanzmann, Claude. *The Patagonian Hare*	B
Lebo, Harlan. ★*Citizen Kane*	791.43
Longworth, Karina. *Seduction*	B
Lumet, Sidney. *Making Movies*	791.43
Lynch, David. *Room to Dream*	B
McGilligan, Patrick. *Funny Man*	B
McGilligan, Patrick. *Young Orson*	B
Meslow, Scott. *From Hollywood with Love*	791.43
Parke, Henry C. *The Greatest Westerns Ever Made and the People Who Made Them*	791.43
Rogen, Seth. ★*Yearbook*	B
Schechter, Harold. ★*Ripped from the Headlines!*	791.43
Seal, Mark. ★*Leave the Gun, Take the Cannoli*	791.43
Seidelman, Susan. *Desperately Seeking Something*	B
Shelton, Ron. *The Church of Baseball*	791.43
Shone, Tom. *The Nolan Variations*	791.4302
Silver, Alain. ★*From the Moment They Met It Was Murder*	791.43
Spiegel, Maura. *Sidney Lumet*	B
Spoto, Donald. *The Dark Side of Genius*	B
Stevens, Dana. *Camera Man*	791.4302
Stevens, George, Jr. *Conversations at the American Film Institute with the Great Moviemakers*	791.4302
Stratton, W. K. *The Wild Bunch*	791.43
Szwed, John F. *Cosmic Scholar*	B
Thomson, David. *The Big Screen*	791.430973

AUTHOR, TITLE, SERIES AND SUBJECT INDEX

Trimborn, Jurgen. *Leni Riefenstahl*	B
Wasson, Sam. *The Big Goodbye*	791.43
Waters, John. *Mr. Know-It-All*	814
Waters, John. *Role Models*	B
Waxman, Sharon. *Rebels on the Backlot*	791.4302
Zucker, David. *Surely You Can't Be Serious*	791.43
Zwick, Edward. ★*Hits, Flops, and Other Illusions*	B

FILM REVIEWS

Kael, Pauline. ★*The Age of Movies*	791.43
Turan, Kenneth. *Not to Be Missed*	791.43
The Filmmaker's Handbook. Pincus, Edward	777

FILMMAKERS

Al-Maria, Sophia. *The Girl Who Fell to Earth*	B
Callow, Simon. ★*Orson Welles*	B
Carter, Ash. *Life Isn't Everything*	B
Coppola, Francis Ford. *Live Cinema and Its Techniques*	791.4302
Curtis, James. *Buster Keaton*	B
D'Alessandro, Emilio. *Stanley Kubrick and Me*	791.4302
Eyman, Scott. *Empire of Dreams*	B
Harris, Mark. *Mike Nichols*	B
Howard, Ron. ★*The Boys*	B
Kolker, Robert Phillip. *Kubrick*	B
Lumet, Sidney. *Making Movies*	791.43
Parke, Henry C. *The Greatest Westerns Ever Made and the People Who Made Them*	791.43
Scheer, Paul. *Joyful Recollections of Trauma*	B
Sestero, Greg. *The Disaster Artist*	791.43
Shone, Tom. *The Nolan Variations*	791.4302
Thomson, Graeme. *George Harrison*	B
Yang, Jeff. *The Golden Screen*	791.43

FILMMAKING

Al-Maria, Sophia. *The Girl Who Fell to Earth*	B
Arkin, Alan. *An Improvised Life*	B
Benson, Michael. *Space Odyssey*	791.43
Brooks, Mel. ★*All About Me!*	B
Coppola, Francis Ford. *Live Cinema and Its Techniques*	791.4302
Curtis, James. *Buster Keaton*	B
D'Alessandro, Emilio. *Stanley Kubrick and Me*	791.4302
Elwes, Cary. *As You Wish*	791.43
Frankel, Glenn. *Shooting Midnight Cowboy*	791.43
Harris, Mark. *Pictures at a Revolution*	791.43
Haskell, Molly. *Steven Spielberg*	B
Hirsch, Paul. *A Long Time Ago in a Cutting Room Far, Far Away*	B
Jones, Brian Jay. *George Lucas*	B
Karp, Josh. *Orson Welles's Last Movie*	791.43
Kenny, Glenn. *Made Men*	791.43
Kenny, Glenn. *The World Is Yours*	791.43
Lumet, Sidney. *Making Movies*	791.43
Lynch, David. *Room to Dream*	B
McGilligan, Patrick. *Funny Man*	B
Meslow, Scott. *From Hollywood with Love*	791.43
O'Meara, Mallory. *The Lady from the Black Lagoon*	921
Pincus, Edward. *The Filmmaker's Handbook*	777
Rinzler, J. W. *The Making of Aliens*	791.4372
Robinson, Joanna. ★*McU*	791.43
Seal, Mark. ★*Leave the Gun, Take the Cannoli*	791.43
Seidelman, Susan. *Desperately Seeking Something*	B
Sestero, Greg. *The Disaster Artist*	791.43
Shelton, Ron. *The Church of Baseball*	791.43
Shone, Tom. *The Nolan Variations*	791.4302
Spiegel, Maura. *Sidney Lumet*	B
Stevens, George, Jr. *Conversations at the American Film Institute with the Great Moviemakers*	791.4302
Stratton, W. K. *The Wild Bunch*	791.43
Thomson, David. *The Big Screen*	791.430973
Tietjen, Jill S. *Hollywood, Her Story*	791.43
Wilkman, Jon. *Screening Reality*	070.1
Zwick, Edward. ★*Hits, Flops, and Other Illusions*	B

FILMS

Ackroyd, Peter. *Charlie Chaplin*	B
Andrews, Julie. *Home Work*	B
Andrews, Julie. *Home*	B
Arkin, Alan. *An Improvised Life*	B
Arnold, Jeremy. *Turner Classic Movies*	791.43
Ausaja, S. M. M. *Bollywood*	791.43
Austerlitz, Saul. *Kind of a Big Deal*	791.43
Bacall, Lauren. *By Myself and Then Some*	B
Basinger, Jeanine. *The Star Machine*	384
Benson, Michael. *Space Odyssey*	791.43
Berg, A. Scott. *Kate Remembered*	B
Biskind, Peter. *Star*	B
Bogle, Donald. *Bright Boulevards, Bold Dreams*	791.43
Brower, Kate Andersen. *Elizabeth Taylor*	B
Caine, Michael. *Blowing the Bloody Doors Off*	B
Carlson, Erin. *I'll Have What She's Having*	791.43
Casillo, Charles. *Marilyn Monroe*	B
Chan, Jackie. *Never Grow Up*	B
Coppola, Francis Ford. *Live Cinema and Its Techniques*	791.4302
Curtis, James. *Buster Keaton*	B
Dixon, Wheeler W. *A Short History of Film*	791.43
Eyman, Scott. *Cary Grant*	B
Eyman, Scott. *Hank and Jim*	920
Eyman, Scott. *John Wayne*	B
Felton, Tom. ★*Beyond the Wand*	B
Fischer, Paul. *A Kim Jong-Il Production*	791.43
Fisher, Todd. *My Girls*	B
Fournier-Lanzoni, Remi. *French Cinema, 2nd Ed.*	791.43
Frankel, Glenn. *Shooting Midnight Cowboy*	791.43
Gehring, Wes D. *James Dean*	B
Gleiberman, Owen. *Movie Freak*	B
Goessel, Tracey. *The First King of Hollywood*	B
Goetz, Kevin. *Audienceology*	791.43
Grey, Jennifer. *Out of the Corner*	B
Harris, Mark. ★*Five Came Back*	791.4302
Haskell, Molly. *Steven Spielberg*	B
Hayes, Dade. *Binge Times*	384.55
Haygood, Wil. ★*Colorization*	791.43
Hendrix, Grady. *These Fists Break Bricks*	791
Hirsch, Foster. ★*Hollywood and the Movies of the Fifties*	791.43
Huang, Yunte. *Daughter of the Dragon*	B
Huston, Anjelica. *Watch Me*	B
Iandoli, Kathy. *Baby Girl*	B
Kanfer, Stefan. *Tough Without a Gun*	B
Kashner, Sam. *Furious Love*	B
Keaton, Diane. ★*Brother & Sister*	B
Kolker, Robert Phillip. *Kubrick*	B
Lane, Christina. *Phantom Lady*	B
Levy, Shawn. ★*The Castle on Sunset*	647.95
Longworth, Karina. *Seduction*	B
Louvish, Simon. *Monkey Business*	B
Lumet, Sidney. *Making Movies*	791.43
Mamet, David. *True and False*	792
Mann, William J. *Hello, Gorgeous*	B
Mann, William J. *Kate*	B
Martin, Steve. *Number One Is Walking*	B
McCabe, John. *Cagney*	B
McConaughey, Matthew. *Greenlights*	B
McGilligan, Patrick. *Funny Man*	B
Meslow, Scott. *From Hollywood with Love*	791.43
Nashawaty, Chris. *Caddyshack*	791.43
Newman, Paul. *The Extraordinary Life of an Ordinary Man*	B
Nolte, Nick. *Rebel*	B
O'Connor, Garry. *Ian McKellen*	B
Osborne, Robert. *85 Years of the Oscar*	791.43079
Parke, Henry C. *The Greatest Westerns Ever Made and the People Who Made Them*	791.43
Phillips, Maya. *Nerd*	302.23
Polly, Matthew. ★*Bruce Lee*	B
Rhodes, Richard. *Hedy's Folly*	B
Rinzler, J. W. *The Making of Aliens*	791.4372
Rogen, Seth. ★*Yearbook*	B
Rosenbaum, Jonathan. ★*Essential Cinema*	791.43
Salisbury, Katie Gee. ★*Not Your China Doll*	B
Saul, Scott. ★*Becoming Richard Pryor*	B
Schechter, Harold. ★*Ripped from the Headlines!*	791.43
Schickel, Richard. *Keepers*	791.430973
Schulman, Michael. ★*Oscar Wars*	791.43
Sestero, Greg. *The Disaster Artist*	791.43
Shearer, Stephen Michael. *Beautiful*	B
Shepard, Jim. *The Tunnel at the End of the Light*	791.43
Silver, Alain. ★*From the Moment They Met It Was Murder*	791.43
Singer, Matt. *Opposable Thumbs*	791.43
Smith, Starr. *Jimmy Stewart*	B
Spiegel, Maura. *Sidney Lumet*	B
Spitz, Bob. ★*Reagan*	B
Spoto, Donald. *High Society*	B

PUBLIC LIBRARY CORE COLLECTION: NONFICTION
Twentieth Edition

Stevens, Dana. *Camera Man*	791.4302
Stewart, Patrick. ★*Making It So*	B
Taraborrelli, J. Randy. ★*The Secret Life of Marilyn Monroe*	B
Tarantino, Quentin. *Cinema Speculation*	791.43
Thomson, David. *Bette Davis*	B
Thomson, David. *The Big Screen*	791.430973
Thomson, David. ★*How to Watch a Movie*	791.43
Thomson, David. *Ingrid Bergman*	B
Thomson, David. *The New Biographical Dictionary of Film*	791.4302
Tietjen, Jill S. *Hollywood, Her Story*	791.43
Trimborn, Jurgen. *Leni Riefenstahl*	B
Turan, Kenneth. *Not to Be Missed*	791.43
Urwand, Ben. *The Collaboration*	791.430973
Wasson, Sam. *The Big Goodbye*	791.43
Watts, Jill. *Hattie McDaniel*	B
Weismann, Brad. *Lost in the Dark*	791.43
Wilson, Victoria. *A Life of Barbara Stanwyck*	B
Yang, Jeff. *The Golden Screen*	791.43

FILMS AND HISTORY

De Vise, Daniel. ★*The Blues Brothers*	791.43
Zapruder, Alexandra. *Twenty-Six Seconds*	973.922092

FILMS, AMERICAN

Ebert, Roger. *Scorsese by Ebert*	B
Harris, Mark. ★*Five Came Back*	791.4302
Harris, Mark. *Pictures at a Revolution*	791.43
Hirsch, Paul. *A Long Time Ago in a Cutting Room Far, Far Away*	B
Kolker, Robert Phillip. *Kubrick*	B
Ross, Steven Joseph. ★*Hitler in Los Angeles*	979.4
Urwand, Ben. *The Collaboration*	791.430973
Filterworld. Chayka, Kyle	306
Filthy Beasts. Hamill, Kirkland	B
The Final Days. Woodward, Bob	B
The Final Season. Cornelius, Maria M.	B
The Final Voicemails. Ritvo, Max	811
Finale. Max, D. T.	782.1
Finan, Christopher M.	
How Free Speech Saved Democracy	342.73

FINANCE

Boden, Anne. *Female Founders' Playbook*	658.4
Flitter, Emily. *The White Wall*	332.0973
Fox, Justin. *The Myth of the Rational Market*	332.64
Goldstein, Jacob. *Money*	332.4
Lewis, Michael. ★*Going Infinite*	305.5
McCraw, Thomas K. ★*The Founders and Finance*	330.973
McKeever, Mike P. *How to Write a Business Plan*	658.15
Mitchell, Josh. *The Debt Trap*	378.3
O'Rourke, P. J. *None of My Business*	332
Peta, Joe. *Trading Bases*	796.357
Schulman, Daniel. *The Money Kings*	332.0973
Schwartzel, Erich. *Red Carpet*	791.43
Small, Zachary. ★*Token Supremacy*	332.4
Smith, G. Stevenson. *Cost Control for Nonprofits in Crisis*	025.1
Sowell, Thomas. *Basic Economics*	330
Thorp, Edward O. *A Man for All Markets*	B
Finance for the People. De Leon, Paco	332.024

FINANCIAL CRISES

Atwood, Margaret. *Burning Questions*	814
Bomey, Nathan. *Detroit Resurrected*	977.4
Bruner, Robert F. ★*The Panic of 1907, 2nd Ed.*	330.973
Conway, Edmund. *The Summit*	337.09
Dayen, David. *Chain of Title*	330.973
Hudson, Michael W. *The Monster*	332.63
Kershaw, Ian. *The Global Age*	940.55
Lewis, Michael. *The Big Short*	330.973
McLean, Bethany. *All the Devils Are Here*	330.973
Nations, Scott. *A History of the United States in Five Crashes*	338.5
O'Toole, Fintan. ★*We Don't Know Ourselves*	941.7
Patterson, Scott. ★*Chaos Kings*	338.5
Paulson, Henry M. *On the Brink*	330.973
Perino, Michael A. *The Hellhound of Wall Street*	330.973
Phillips-Fein, Kim. *Fear City*	330.9747
Sorkin, Andrew Ross. *Too Big to Fail*	330.973
Vaughan, Liam. *Flash Crash*	B
Vlasic, Bill. *Once Upon a Car*	338.4
Ward, Geoffrey C. *A Disposition to Be Rich*	B
Wessel, David. *In Fed We Trust*	332.1
Zygar, Mikhail. *The Empire Must Die*	947.08
The Financial Diaries. Morduch, Jonathan	332.024
The Financial Diet. Fagan, Chelsea	332.024

FINANCIAL FORECASTING

Patterson, Scott. ★*Chaos Kings*	338.5
Weatherall, James Owen. *The Physics of Wall Street*	332.63
Financial Freedom. Sabatier, Grant	332.024

FINANCIAL INSTITUTIONS

Daunton, M. J. ★*The Economic Government of the World*	337
McLean, Bethany. *All the Devils Are Here*	330.973
Michel, Casey. *American Kleptocracy*	364.16
Morgenson, Gretchen. ★*These Are the Plunderers*	332.6
Paulson, Henry M. *On the Brink*	330.973
Wheelan, Charles J. *Naked Economics*	330

FINANCIAL LITERACY

Cox, Josie. *Women Money Power*	330.082
Lowry, Erin. ★*Broke Millennial Talks Money*	332.024

FINANCIAL SERVICES INDUSTRY AND TRADE

Kaiser, Robert G. *Act of Congress*	346.73
Finch, Christopher	
The Art of Walt Disney	791.43092
Fincham-Gray, Suzanne	
My Patients and Other Animals	B

FINCHAM-GRAY, SUZANNE

Fincham-Gray, Suzanne. *My Patients and Other Animals*	B
Find A Way. Nyad, Diana	B
Find Your Unicorn Space. Rodsky, Eve	158.1
Findakly, Brigitte	
Poppies of Iraq	741.5
Finding A Likeness. Baker, Nicholson	B
Finding Chika. Albom, Mitch	B
Finding Comfort During Hard Times. Johnson, Earl	155.9
Finding God in My Loneliness. Brownback, Lydia	248.8
★*Finding Me*. Davis, Viola	B
Finding Meaning. Kessler, David	155.9
Finding My Voice. Jarrett, Valerie	B
Finding The Answers to Legal Questions. Tucker, Virginia	340.072
Finding The Blue Sky. Emet, Joseph	294.3
★*Finding The Mother Tree*. Simard, S.	582.16
The Fine Art of Paper Flowers. Turner, Tiffanie	745.92
A Fine Mess. Reid, T. R.	336.200973
A Fine Romance. Lehman, David	781.64
Fine, Cordelia	
Testosterone Rex	155.3
Fine, Doug	
Too High to Fail	338.4
Fineman, Meredith	
Brag Better	650.1
Fingeroth, Danny	
A Marvelous Life	741.5
★*Finish What We Started*. Arnsdorf, Isaac	320.52
Finishing School. Newton, Deborah	746.43

FINISHING THINGS

McPhee, John. *Tabula Rasa; V.1*	818
Fink, Sheri	
Five Days at Memorial	362.1109763
Finkel, Caroline	
Osman's Dream	956.1
Finkel, David	
An American Dreamer	975.8
The Good Soldiers	956.7044
Thank You for Your Service	920
Finkel, Elizabeth	
The Genome Generation	599.93
Finkel, Michael	
The Art Thief	364.1628
The Stranger in the Woods	B
Finkelman, Paul	
★*Landmark Decisions of the United States Supreme Court*	347.73
Millard Fillmore	B

FINKELSTEIN FAMILY

Finkelstein, Daniel. *Two Roads Home*	920
Finkelstein, Daniel	
Two Roads Home	920
Finkelstein, Elizabeth	
Cheap Old Houses	643

FINKELSTEIN, LUDWIK, 1929-2011

Finkelstein, Daniel. *Two Roads Home*	920

FINKELSTEIN, MIRJAM, 1933-2017

Finkelstein, Daniel. *Two Roads Home*	920

AUTHOR, TITLE, SERIES AND SUBJECT INDEX

Finkle, Jane
   The Introvert's Complete Career Guide   650.14
FINLAND
   Booth, Michael. *The Almost Nearly Perfect People*   948.071
Finlay, B. Brett
   Let Them Eat Dirt   616.9
Finn, Adharanand
   The Rise of the Ultra Runners   B
   The Way of the Runner   796.42
FINN, ADHARANAND
   Finn, Adharanand. *The Rise of the Ultra Runners*   B
Finn, Peter
   The Zhivago Affair   891.73
Finna. Marshall, Nate   811
Finnegan, William
   Barbarian Days   B
Finney, Nikky
   Love Child's Hotbed of Occasional Poetry   811
Firdawsi
   Shahnameh   891
FIRE
   Wrangham, Richard W. *Catching Fire*   394.1
Fire. Junger, Sebastian   909.82
Fire and Flood. Linden, Eugene   304.2
Fire and Fortitude. McManus, John C.   940.54
Fire and Fury. Wolff, Michael   973.933
The Fire and the Darkness. McKay, Sinclair   940.54
FIRE DEPARTMENTS
   Smith, Dennis. *Report from Ground Zero*   974.7
FIRE ECOLOGY
   Martin, Manjula. *The Last Fire Season*   B
FIRE FIGHTERS
   Johnson, Lizzie. ★*Paradise*   363.37
   Pfeifer, Joseph. *Ordinary Heroes*   973.931
FIRE FIGHTING
   Martin, Manjula. *The Last Fire Season*   B
Fire in Paradise. Gee, Alastair   363.37
Fire in the Ashes. Kozol, Jonathan   362.77
Fire in the Lake. FitzGerald, Frances   959.704
FIRE INVESTIGATION
   Berendt, John. *The City of Falling Angels*   945
★*The Fire Next Time*. Baldwin, James   305.896
Fire on the Track. Montillo, Roseanne   B
FIRE PREVENTION
   Martin, Manjula. *The Last Fire Season*   B
   Orlean, Susan. ★*The Library Book*   027.4
Fire Road. Thi, Kim Phuc Phan
★*The Fire This Time*. Ward, Jesmyn   305.896
Fire to Fire. Doty, Mark   811
★*Fire Weather*. Vaillant, John   363.37
FIREBOMBING
   Scott, James. *Black Snow*   940.54
The Firebrand and the First Lady. Bell-Scott, Patricia   920
Firebrand of Liberty. Ash, Stephen V.   973.7
FIREFLIES
   Lewis, Sara. *Silent Sparks*   595.76
FIRES
   Auvinen, Karen. *Rough Beauty*   B
   Berendt, John. *The City of Falling Angels*   945
   Berg, Scott W. *The Burning of the World*   977.311
   Davenport, Matthew J. *The Longest Minute*   979.4
   James, Scott. *Trial by Fire*   363.3709745
   Johnson, Lizzie. ★*Paradise*   363.37
   Lepore, Jill. *New York Burning*   974.7
   McKay, Sinclair. *The Fire and the Darkness*   940.54
   Orlean, Susan. ★*The Library Book*   027.4
   Von Drehle, Dave. ★*Triangle*   974.7
   Winchester, Simon. *A Crack in the Edge of the World*   979.4
Fires in Our Lives. Cushman, Kathleen   373.1102
Fires in the Dark. Jamison, Kay Redfield   616.89
The Fires of Vesuvius. Beard, Mary   937
Firescaping Your Home. Edwards, Adrienne L.   635.9
FIREWORKS
   James, Scott. *Trial by Fire*   363.3709745
★*First*. Thomas, Evan   B
The First American. Brands, H. W.   B
FIRST BASE PLAYERS (BASEBALL)
   Eisenberg, John. *The Streak*   796.357

Posnanski, Joe. *The Soul of Baseball*   796.357
Robinson, Ray. *Iron Horse*   B
The First Cell. Raza, Azra   616.99
The First Collection of Criticism by a Living Female Rock Critic. Hopper, Jessica   781.66
★*The First Conspiracy*. Meltzer, Brad   973.4
FIRST CONTACT (ANTHROPOLOGY)
   Price, David A. ★*Love and Hate in Jamestown*   975.5
   Sides, Hampton. ★*The Wide Wide Sea*   910.92
   Silverman, David J. ★*This Land Is Their Land*   974.4
FIRST CONTACT OF INDIGENOUS PEOPLES WITH EUROPEANS
   Cervantes, Fernando. *Conquistadores*   970.01
   DuVal, Kathleen. ★*Native Nations*   970.004
   Price, David A. ★*Love and Hate in Jamestown*   975.5
   Sides, Hampton. ★*The Wide Wide Sea*   910.92
   Silverman, David J. ★*This Land Is Their Land*   974.4
The First Crusade. Frankopan, Peter   956
FIRST CRUSADE, 1096-1099
   Frankopan, Peter. *The First Crusade*   956
First Family. Ellis, Joseph J.   973.4
First Family. Good, Cassandra A.   920
First Founding Father. Unger, Harlow G.   B
First Gen. Campoverdi, Alejandra   B
First Generation. Gaw, Frankie   641.595
The First Idea. Greenspan, Stanley I.   153.7
FIRST IMPRESSIONS
   Dahl, Melissa. *Cringeworthy*   158.2
First in Line. Brower, Kate Andersen   920
The First King of Hollywood. Goessel, Tracey   B
The First Love Story. Feiler, Bruce   222
FIRST LOVES
   Mock, Janet. *Surpassing Certainty*   B
The First Major. Feinstein, John   796.352
The First Muslim. Hazleton, Lesley   B
FIRST NATIONS (CANADA)
   Alvarez, Noe. *Spirit Run*   796.42
   Belcourt, Billy-Ray. ★*A History of My Brief Body*   B
   Mailhot, Terese Marie. *Heart Berries*   B
   McDiarmid, Jessica. *Highway of Tears*   364.152
   Metatawabin, Edmund. *Up Ghost River*   B
   Sacco, Joe. ★*Paying the Land*   741.5
   Sasakamoose, Fred. *Call Me Indian*   B
   Taylor, Alan. *The Divided Ground*   974.7
   Wagamese, Richard. *For Joshua*   B
   Wagamese, Richard. *One Native Life*   B
First Over There. Davenport, Matthew J.   940.4
★*First Principles*. Ricks, Thomas E.   973.09
FIRST RESPONDERS
   Dunn, Harry. *Standing My Ground*   B
   Graff, Garrett M. ★*The Only Plane in the Sky*   973.931
   Hazzard, Kevin M. *American Sirens*   362.18
The First Shots. Borrell, Brendan   615.3
First Steps. Desilva, Jeremy   599.93
First They Killed My Father. Ung, Loung   959.604
★*First Things First*. Simmons, Nadirah   782.42164
First to the Front. Rinehart, Lorissa   B
★*The First Tycoon*. Stiles, T. J.   B
The First Wave. Kershaw, Alex   940.54
First Women. Brower, Kate Andersen   920
The First World War. Keegan, John   940.3
FIRST WORLD WAR ERA (1914-1918)
   Bascomb, Neal. *The Escape Artists*   940.4
   Carroll, Andrew. *My Fellow Soldiers*   940.4
   Emery, Theo. *Hellfire Boys*   358
   Hochschild, Adam. *American Midnight*   973.91
   Johnson, Steven. *The Infernal Machine*   335
   Korda, Michael. *Muse of Fire*   940.4
   Lloyd, Nick. *The Western Front*   940.4
   Moore, Wendy. *No Man's Land*   940.4
   Zygar, Mikhail. *The Empire Must Die*   947.08
FIRST YEAR TEACHERS
   Kozol, Jonathan. *Letters to a Young Teacher*   371.1
   Rademacher, Tom. *It Won't Be Easy*   B
First, We Make the Beast Beautiful. Wilson, Sarah   616.85
The Firsts. Steinhauer, Jennifer   320.082
Firth, Henry
   Bosh!   641.5

PUBLIC LIBRARY CORE COLLECTION: NONFICTION
Twentieth Edition

FISCAL POLICY
   Phillips-Fein, Kim. *Fear City* — 330.9747
   Warren, Elizabeth. *This Fight Is Our Fight* — 305.5
Fischer, Bobby
   ★*Bobby Fischer Teaches Chess* — 794.1
FISCHER, BOBBY, 1943-2008
   Brady, Frank. *Endgame* — B
Fischer, David Hackett
   ★*African Founders* — 973
   Champlain's Dream — B
   Paul Revere's Ride — 973.3
   Washington's Crossing — 973.3
Fischer, Jenna
   The Actor's Life — 792.02
   The Office BFFs — 791.45
FISCHER, JENNA, 1974-
   Fischer, Jenna. *The Office BFFs* — 791.45
Fischer, Paul
   A Kim Jong-Il Production — 791.43
   The Man Who Invented Motion Pictures — 791.43
FISH AS FOOD
   Lanza, Fabrizia. *The Food of Sicily* — 641.594
   Ripert, Eric. *Seafood Simple* — 641.6
FISH FARMING
   Ellis, Richard. *Tuna* — 333.95
   Greenberg, Paul. *Four Fish* — 333.95
FISH, DORIS, 1952-1991
   Seligman, Craig. *Who Does That Bitch Think She Is?* — 792.02
Fish, Stanley Eugene
   Winning Arguments — 808
FISHER, ANNA LEE
   Grush, Loren. ★*The Six* — 629.4
Fisher, Carl Erik
   ★*The Urge* — 362.29
FISHER, CARL ERIK
   Fisher, Carl Erik. ★*The Urge* — 362.29
FISHER, CARRIE
   Fisher, Todd. *My Girls* — B
   Weller, Sheila. *Carrie Fisher* — B
Fisher, Marshall Jon
   A Terrible Splendor — 796.342
Fisher, Roger
   ★*Getting to Yes* — 158
Fisher, Susan J.
   Taking Charge of Your Pregnancy — 618.2
Fisher, Thomas
   ★*The Emergency* — 362.1089
FISHER, THOMAS, (BOARD-CERTIFIED EMERGENCY MEDICINE PHYSICIAN)
   Fisher, Thomas. ★*The Emergency* — 362.1089
Fisher, Todd
   My Girls — B
FISHER, TODD, 1958-
   Fisher, Todd. *My Girls* — B
FISHERIES
   Ash, Lamorna. *Dark, Salt, Clear* — 942.3
   Ellis, Richard. *Tuna* — 333.95
   Fagan, Brian M. *Fishing* — 338.3
   Franklin, Jonathan. *438 Days* — 910.91
   Hilborn, Ray. *Overfishing* — 338.3
   Johnson, Kirk W. *The Fishermen and the Dragon* — 976.4
   Kurlansky, Mark. *Cod* — 333.95
*The **Fishermen** and the Dragon*. Johnson, Kirk W.
FISHERS
   Ash, Lamorna. *Dark, Salt, Clear* — 942.3
   Burke, Monte. *Lords of the Fly* — 799.124
   Cameron, Silver Donald. *Blood in the Water* — 364.152
   Fairbanks, Amanda M. *The Lost Boys of Montauk* — 910.91
   Franklin, Jonathan. *438 Days* — 910.91
   Gierach, John. *All Fishermen Are Liars* — 799.12
   Horn, Miriam. *Rancher, Farmer, Fisherman* — B
   Johnson, Kirk W. *The Fishermen and the Dragon* — 976.4
   Junger, Sebastian. *The Perfect Storm* — 974.4
   Smith, Bren. *Eat Like a Fish* — 338.3
   Swift, Earl. *Chesapeake Requiem* — 639
FISHERY CONSERVATION
   Malarkey, Tucker. *Stronghold* — 639.2

FISHERY MANAGEMENT
   Greenberg, Paul. *Four Fish* — 333.95
FISHES
   Balcombe, Jonathan P. *What a Fish Knows* — 597.15
   Gilbert, Carter Rowell. ★*National Audubon Society Field Guide to Fishes.* — 597
   Schultz, Ken. *Ken Schultz's Essentials of Fishing* — 799.1
Fishing. Fagan, Brian M. — 338.3
FISHING
   Burke, Monte. *Lords of the Fly* — 799.124
   Cermele, Joe. ★*The Total Fishing Manual* — 799.1
   Ellis, Richard. *Tuna* — 333.95
   Fagan, Brian M. *Fishing* — 338.3
   Fairbanks, Amanda M. *The Lost Boys of Montauk* — 910.91
   Gierach, John. *All Fishermen Are Liars* — 799.12
   Gierach, John. *Dumb Luck and the Kindness of Strangers* — 799.124
   Gierach, John. *A Fly Rod of Your Own* — 799.12
   Greenberg, Paul. *Four Fish* — 333.95
   Harrison, Jim. *The Search for the Genuine* — 814
   Kurlansky, Mark. *Cod* — 333.95
   Messineo, Janet. *Casting into the Light* — 799.1
   Schultz, Ken. *Ken Schultz's Essentials of Fishing* — 799.1
   Strøksnes, Morten Andreas. *Shark Drunk* — 338.3
FISHING BOAT CAPTAINS
   Fairbanks, Amanda M. *The Lost Boys of Montauk* — 910.91
FISHING BOATS
   Franklin, Jonathan. *438 Days* — 910.91
FISHING EQUIPMENT
   Fagan, Brian M. *Fishing* — 338.3
FISHING INDUSTRY AND TRADE
   Ash, Lamorna. *Dark, Salt, Clear* — 942.3
   Greenberg, Paul. *Four Fish* — 333.95
FISHING RODS
   Schultz, Ken. *Ken Schultz's Essentials of Fishing* — 799.1
FISHING TACKLE
   Schultz, Ken. *Ken Schultz's Essentials of Fishing* — 799.1
FISHING VILLAGES
   Ash, Lamorna. *Dark, Salt, Clear* — 942.3
Fishman, Boris
   Savage Feast — B
FISHMAN, BORIS, 1979-
   Fishman, Boris. *Savage Feast* — B
Fishman, Charles
   ★*One Giant Leap* — 629.45
Fishman, David E.
   The Book Smugglers — 940.53
Fishman, Elly
   Refugee High — 370.8
Fishman, Loren
   Yoga for Arthritis — 616.7
Fishman, Stephen
   ★*The Copyright Handbook, 15th Ed.* — 346.7304
Fisk, Robert
   The Great War for Civilisation — 956.04
Fiske Guide to Getting into the Right College. Fiske, Edward B. — 378.1
Fiske, Edward B.
   Fiske Guide to Getting into the Right College — 378.1
Fit Men Cook. Curry, Kevin — 641.5
FITZGERALD, F. SCOTT (FRANCIS SCOTT), 1896-1940
   Brown, David S. *Paradise Lost* — 813
FitzGerald, Frances
   The Evangelicals — 277
   Fire in the Lake — 959.704
Fitzgerald, Isaac
   Dirtbag, Massachusetts — B
Fitzgerald, Matt
   Iron War — 796.42
FitzGerald, Michael C.
   ★*Picasso and American Art* — 709.73
FITZGERALD, ZELDA, 1900-1948
   Brown, David S. *Paradise Lost* — 813
Fitzharris, Lindsey
   The Butchering Art — B
Fitzmaurice, Simon
   It's Not yet Dark — 616.8
FITZMAURICE, SIMON
   Fitzmaurice, Simon. *It's Not yet Dark* — 616.8

AUTHOR, TITLE, SERIES AND SUBJECT INDEX

Fitzpatrick, Cara
   The Death of Public School   379.73
★*The Five*. Rubenhold, Hallie   362.88
★*Five Came Back*. Harris, Mark   791.4302
★*Five Days*. Moore, Wes   363.32
Five Days at Memorial. Fink, Sheri   362.1109763
Five Days in London, May 1940. Lukacs, John   940.53
Five Days in November. Hill, Clint   973.922092
Five for Freedom. Meyer, Eugene L.   973.7
★*Five Lessons*. Hogan, Ben   796.352
Five Lives in Music. Porter, Cecelia Hopkins   B
Five Presidents. Hill, Clint   B
★*Fix It with Food*. Symon, Michael   641.5
Fix-It and Forget-It [Series]. Good, Phyllis Pellman   641.5
Fix-It and Forget-It Healthy 5-Ingredient Cookbook. Comerford, Hope   641.5
Fix-It and Forget-It New Cookbook. Good, Phyllis Pellman   641.5
Fixed Stars. Wizenberg, Molly   B
Flagrant Conduct. Carpenter, Dale   342.7308
FLAGS
   Miller, Marla. *Betsy Ross and the Making of America*   B
   Znamierowski, Alfred. *The World Encyclopedia of Flags*   903
Flags of Our Fathers. Bradley, James   940.54
Flaherty, Mary Grace
   ★*The Disaster Planning Handbook for Libraries*   025.8
Flaherty, Meghan
   Tango Lessons   793.3
FLAHERTY, MEGHAN
   Flaherty, Meghan. *Tango Lessons*   793.3
FLAMBOYANCE (PERSONAL QUALITY)
   Duncan, Isadora. *My Life*   B
The Flame. Cohen, Leonard   810
The Flame Trees of Thika. Huxley, Elspeth Joscelin Grant   B
Flanagan, Shalane
   Run Fast, Cook Fast, Eat Slow   641.5
Flanders, Judith
   Christmas   394.2663
   The Victorian City   942.1
The Flaneur. White, Edmund   944
★*Flannery*. Gooch, Brad   B
Flannery, Kate
   Strip Tees   338.4
FLANNERY, KATE
   Flannery, Kate. *Strip Tees*   338.4
Flannery, Tim F.
   Europe   508.4
Flash. Bonanos, Christopher   B
Flash Crash. Vaughan, Liam   B
Flashpoints. Friedman, George   940.56
Flavor. Holmes, Bob   612.8
FLAVOR
   Easto, Jessica. *How to Taste Coffee*   663
   Holmes, Bob. *Flavor*   612.8
   Howard, Vivian. *This Will Make It Taste Good*   641.5
   Nezhukumatathil, Aimee. *Bite by Bite*   641.3
   Page, Karen. *The Flavor Bible*   641.5
   Redzepi, Rene. *The Noma Guide to Fermentation*   664
   Segnit, Niki. ★*The Flavor Thesaurus*   641.5
The Flavor Bible. Page, Karen   641.5
★*The Flavor Thesaurus*. Segnit, Niki   641.5
Flavors of the Sun. Sahadi Whelan, Christine   641.595
Flawless. Hu, Elise   646.7
Flay, Bobby
   Bobby at Home   641.5
   Sundays with Sophie   641.5
Flea Market Fabulous. Spencer, Lara   747
FLEA MARKETS
   Spencer, Lara. *Flea Market Fabulous*   747
FLECK, LUDWIK, 1896-1961
   Allen, Arthur. ★*The Fantastic Laboratory of Dr. Weigl*   614.5
★*Flee North*. Shane, Scott   973.7
Fleming, Brandon P.
   Miseducated   B
FLEMING, BRANDON P.
   Fleming, Brandon P. *Miseducated*   B
Fleming, Crystal Marie
   How to Be Less Stupid About Race   305.800973
FLEMING, IAN, 1908-1964
   Shakespeare, Nicholas. *Ian Fleming*   B

Fleming, Jory
   How to Be Human   616.85
FLEMING, JORY
   Fleming, Jory. *How to Be Human*   616.85
Fleming, Melissa
   A Hope More Powerful Than the Sea   956.9104
Fleming, Renee
   ★*Music and Mind*   615.8
Fleshman, Lauren
   ★*Good for a Girl*   B
FLESHMAN, LAUREN
   Fleshman, Lauren. ★*Good for a Girl*   B
Fletcher, Emily
   Stress Less, Accomplish More   155.9
Fletcher, Seth
   Einstein's Shadow   523.8
Fletcher, Susan A.
   Exploring the History of Childhood and Play Through 50 Historic Treasures   790
Flex. Auerbach, Annie   331.25
FLEX TIME
   Auerbach, Annie. *Flex*   331.25
   Mulcahy, Diane. *The Gig Economy*   650.1
   Warzel, Charlie. *Out of Office*   658.3
Flexner, James Thomas
   George Washington and the New Nation, 1783-1793   973.4
   George Washington   B
FLIES
   Balcombe, Jonathan P. *Super Fly*   595.77
FLIES, ARTIFICIAL
   Whitelaw, Ian. *The History of Fly-Fishing in Fifty Flies*   688.7
FLIGHT
   Hazelgrove, William Elliott. *Wright Brothers, Wrong Story*   920
   McCullough, David G. ★*The Wright Brothers*   B
   Teitel, Amy Shira. *Fighting for Space*   920
   Winters, Kathleen C. *Amelia Earhart*   B
FLIGHT ATTENDANTS
   Cooke, Julia. *Come Fly the World*   387.7
   McShane Wulfhart, Nell. *The Great Stewardess Rebellion*   331.4
   Nolan, Hamilton. *The Hammer*   331.8
FLIGHT CREWS
   Ambrose, Stephen E. *The Wild Blue*   940.54
FLIGHTLESS BIRDS
   Attenborough, David. *The Life of Birds*   598.15
Flink, David
   Thinking Differently   371.9
FLINT, MICHIGAN
   Clark, Anna. *The Poisoned City*   363.6
   Hanna-Attisha, Mona. *What the Eyes Don't See*   615.9
FLIRTATION
   Rallo, Eli. *I Didn't Know I Needed This*   306.73
Flitter, Emily
   The White Wall   332.0973
★*Floaters*. Espada, Martin   811
Floating Collections. Bartlett, Wendy K.   025.2
Floating in a Most Peculiar Way. Chude-Sokei, Louis Onuorah   979.4
Floating in the Deep End. Davis, Patti   616.8
Flock, Elizabeth
   ★*The Furies*   305.48
FLOOD CONTROL
   Barry, John M. *Rising Tide*   977
FLOOD, CURT, 1938-1997
   Snyder, Brad. *A Well-Paid Slave*   B
FLOODS
   Barry, John M. *Rising Tide*   977
   Bittle, Jake. ★*The Great Displacement*   362.87
   Brinkley, Douglas. *The Great Deluge*   976.3
   Dyson, Michael Eric. *Come Hell or High Water*   976.3
   Fagan, Brian M. *Climate Chaos*   304.2
   Fields, Micah. ★*We Hold Our Breath*   976.4
   Goodell, Jeff. *The Water Will Come*   551.45
   Hastings, Max. *Operation Chastise*   940.54
   Horne, Jed. *Breach of Faith*   976.3
   Kelly, John. *The Great Mortality*   614.5
   Roker, Al. *Ruthless Tide*   974.8
Flor, Martina
   The Golden Secrets of Lettering   745.6
Florence. King, Ross   759.5

Florence Nightingale. Bostridge, Mark — B
FLORENCE, ITALY
   Benner, Erica. *Be Like the Fox* — B
   Fernandez-Armesto, Felipe. ★*Amerigo* — B
   Fili, Louise. *The Cognoscenti's Guide to Florence* — 381
   Hales, Dianne R. *Mona Lisa* — B
   Hibbert, Christopher. *The House of Medici* — 920
   King, Ross. *Bookseller of Florence* — 381
   King, Ross. *Brunelleschi's Dome* — 726.6
   King, Ross. *Florence* — 759.5
   Strathern, Paul. *The Florentines* — 945
The Florentines. Strathern, Paul — 945
FLORES MAGON, RICARDO, 1873-1922
   Hernandez, Kelly Lytle. ★*Bad Mexicans* — 972
Flores, Dan L.
   Wild New World — 591.9709
FLORES, ERNESTO, 1997-
   Markham, Lauren. ★*The Far Away Brothers* — 920
FLORES, RAUL, 1997-
   Markham, Lauren. ★*The Far Away Brothers* — 920
Floret Farm's Cut Flower Garden. Benzakein, Erin — 635.9
Floret Farm's Discovering Dahlias. Benzakein, Erin — 635.9
FLORIDA
   Ash, Stephen V. *Firebrand of Liberty* — 973.7
   Burke, Monte. *Lords of the Fly* — 799.124
   Cullen, David. *Parkland* — 371.7
   Davis, Jack E. *An Everglades Providence* — B
   Douglas, Marjory Stoneman. *The Everglades* — 975.9
   Gerard, Sarah. *Sunshine State* — 814
   Gomez, Edgar. *High-Risk Homosexual* — B
   Grogan, John. ★*Marley & Me* — 636.752
   King, Gilbert. *Beneath a Ruthless Sun* — B
   King, Gilbert. ★*Devil in the Grove* — 305.896
   McGarrahan, Ellen. *Two Truths and a Lie* — 364.152
   McIntire, Mike. *Champions Way* — 796.043
   Pittman, Craig. *Cat Tale* — 599.75
   Renner, Rebecca. ★*Gator Country* — 364.16
   Ross, Andrew. *Sunbelt Blues* — 363.5
   Sokolik, Vicki. ★*If You See Them* — 362.5
   Standiford, Les. *Bringing Adam Home* — 364.15
   Tometich, Annabelle. *The Mango Tree* — B
FLORIDA PANTHER
   Pittman, Craig. *Cat Tale* — 599.75
Flottum, Kim
   The Backyard Beekeeper — 638
Flour Water Salt Yeast. Forkish, Ken — 641.81
FLOWER ARRANGEMENT
   Benzakein, Erin. *Floret Farm's Cut Flower Garden* — 635.9
   Benzakein, Erin. *Floret Farm's Discovering Dahlias* — 635.9
   Chezar, Ariella. ★*Seasonal Flower Arranging* — 635.9
   Crary, Calvert. *The Encyclopedia of Cut Flowers* — 745.92
   Cylinder, Carly. *The Flower Chef* — 745.92
   Harampolis, Alethea. *The Flower Recipe Book* — 745.92
   McLeary, Susan. *Flowers for All* — 745.92
   Stewart, Martha. ★*Martha's Flowers* — 635.9
   Turner, Tiffanie. *The Fine Art of Paper Flowers* — 745.92
   Underwood, Kiana. *Color Me Floral* — 745.92
The Flower Chef. Cylinder, Carly — 745.92
FLOWER GARDENING
   Benzakein, Erin. *Floret Farm's Discovering Dahlias* — 635.9
   Carey, Jenny Rose. *The Ultimate Flower Gardener's Guide* — 635.9
   Chezar, Ariella. ★*Seasonal Flower Arranging* — 635.9
   Stewart, Martha. ★*Martha's Flowers* — 635.9
The Flower of Empire. Holway, Tatiana M. — 727
The Flower Recipe Book. Harampolis, Alethea — 745.92
Flowerpaedia. Darcey, Cheralyn — 580
FLOWERS
   Bohmig, Franz. ★*The Month-By-Month Gardening Guide* — 635
   Carey, Jenny Rose. *The Ultimate Flower Gardener's Guide* — 635.9
   Crary, Calvert. *The Encyclopedia of Cut Flowers* — 745.92
   Darcey, Cheralyn. *Flowerpaedia* — 580
   Holway, Tatiana M. *The Flower of Empire* — 727
   McLeary, Susan. *Flowers for All* — 745.92
   Stewart, Martha. ★*Martha's Flowers* — 635.9
   Ziegler, Lisa Mason. *Vegetables Love Flowers* — 635
Flowers for All. McLeary, Susan — 745.92
Flowers, Catherine Coleman
   Waste — 363.72
FLOWERS, CATHERINE COLEMAN
   Flowers, Catherine Coleman. *Waste* — 363.72
Flowers, Sarah
   Evaluating Teen Services and Programs — 027.62
FLOWERS, T. H. (THOMAS HAROLD), 1905-1998
   Price, David A. *Geniuses at War* — 940.54
Floyd Patterson. Stratton, W. K. — B
FLOYD, GEORGE, 1974-2020
   Alexander, Kwame. *Light for the World to See* — 811.6
   Samuels, Robert. ★*His Name Is George Floyd* — B
Floyd, Ted
   How to Know the Birds — 598.072
   Smithsonian Field Guide to the Birds of North America — 598.097
Fluke. Mazur, Joseph — 519.2
★*Flunk, Start*. Hall, Sands — B
FLUNKING
   Zara, Christopher. *Uneducated* — B
Flunking Sainthood. Riess, Jana — 248.4
Flush. Nelson, Bryn — 612.3
FLY FISHING
   Burke, Monte. *Lords of the Fly* — 799.124
   Gierach, John. *All Fishermen Are Liars* — 799.12
   Gierach, John. *Dumb Luck and the Kindness of Strangers* — 799.124
   Gierach, John. *A Fly Rod of Your Own* — 799.12
   Malarkey, Tucker. *Stronghold* — 639.2
   Meyers, Charlie. *The Little Red Book of Fly Fishing* — 799.12
   Rosenbauer, Tom. *The Orvis Fly-Fishing Guide* — 799.12
   Whitelaw, Ian. *The History of Fly-Fishing in Fifty Flies* — 688.7
Fly Girls. O'Brien, Keith — 920
A Fly Rod of Your Own. Gierach, John — 799.12
FLY TYING
   Johnson, Kirk W. *The Feather Thief* — 364.16
Flyboys. Bradley, James — 940.54
★*Flying Blind*. Robison, Peter — 338.7
Flyn, Cal
   ★*Islands of Abandonment* — 333.73
Flynn, Nick
   The Captain Asks for a Show of Hands — 811
Focus. Goleman, Daniel — 153.7
Foer, Esther Safran
   I Want You to Know We're Still Here — B
FOER, ESTHER SAFRAN
   Foer, Esther Safran. *I Want You to Know We're Still Here* — B
Foer, Franklin
   ★*The Last Politician* — 973.934
Foer, Jonathan Safran
   Eating Animals — 641.3
   ★*We Are the Weather* — 636
Foer, Joshua
   Atlas Obscura — 910.41
   ★*Atlas Obscura 2nd Ed.* — 910.41
   Moonwalking with Einstein — 153.1
FOG
   Redniss, Lauren. *Thunder & Lightning* — 741.5
Fogerty, John
   Fortunate Son — B
FOGERTY, JOHN, 1945-
   Fogerty, John. *Fortunate Son* — B
Fogg, B. J.
   Tiny Habits — 158
FOGG, B. J.
   Fogg, B. J. *Tiny Habits* — 158
Fogler, Janet
   Improving Your Memory — 153.1
Foles, Nick
   Believe It — B
FOLES, NICK
   Foles, Nick. *Believe It* — B
Foley, Caroline
   Topiary, Knots and Parterres — 715
FOLEY, DAVE, 1963-
   Myers, Paul. *The Kids in the Hall* — 920
FOLEY, DIANE MARIE, 1956-
   McCann, Colum. *American Mother* — 956.9104
FOLK ART
   Hoffman, Carl. ★*Savage Harvest* — 995.1
Folk Embroidered Felt Birds. Lapierre, Corinne — 746.0463

AUTHOR, TITLE, SERIES AND SUBJECT INDEX

FOLK MUSIC
    Dylan, Bob. *Chronicles; Volume 1* — B
    Garfunkel, Art. *What Is It All but Luminous* — 782.42164
    McCormick, Mack. *Biography of a Phantom* — 782.421643
    Polenberg, Richard. *Hear My Sad Story* — 782.42162
    Powers, Ann. ★*Traveling* — B
    Sandburg, Carl. *The American Songbag* — 782.42162
    Santopietro, Tom. *The Sound of Music Story* — 791.43
    Strom, Yale. *The Book of Klezmer* — 781.62
    Wald, Elijah. *American Epic* — 781.64
    Wolff, Daniel J. *Grown-Up Anger* — 920
    Yaffe, David. *Reckless Daughter* — 782.42164
    Young, Rob. *Electric Eden* — 781.62

FOLK MUSIC, AMERICAN
    Dunaway, David King. ★*How Can I Keep from Singing?* — B
    Thomas, Richard F. ★*Why Bob Dylan Matters* — 782.42164
    Wald, Elijah. *Dylan Goes Electric!* — 782.42164
    Wilkinson, Alec. *The Protest Singer* — B

FOLK MUSICIANS
    Dylan, Bob. *Chronicles; Volume 1* — B
    Garfunkel, Art. *What Is It All but Luminous* — 782.42164
    Powers, Ann. ★*Traveling* — B
    Wilkinson, Alec. *The Protest Singer* — B
    Yaffe, David. *Reckless Daughter* — 782.42164

FOLK SINGERS
    Dunaway, David King. ★*How Can I Keep from Singing?* — B
    Wilkinson, Alec. *The Protest Singer* — B
    Zack, Ian. *Odetta* — B

FOLK-ROCK MUSIC
    Wald, Elijah. *Dylan Goes Electric!* — 782.42164

FOLKLORE, INDIGENOUS
    Turvey, Samuel. ★*The Tomb of the Mili Mongga* — 398.24

FOLKLORE, INDIGENOUS — HISTORY AND CRITICISM
    Bruchac, Joseph. *Our Stories Remember* — 973.04

FOLKLORISTS
    Hurston, Zora Neale. *Dust Tracks on a Road* — B

FOLKLORISTS, AMERICAN
    Hurston, Zora Neale. *Zora Neale Hurston* — B

Folktales Aloud. Del Negro, Janice — 027.62

Follett, Ken
    On Wings of Eagles — 955
Following Jesus in a Warming World. Meyaard-Schaap, Kyle — 241
Following The Path. Chittister, Joan — 248.4
The Folly and the Glory. Weiner, Tim — 327.73047

FONDA, HENRY, 1905-1982
    Eyman, Scott. *Hank and Jim* — 920

FONDA, JANE, 1937-
    Williams, Mary. *The Lost Daughter* — B

Foner, Eric
    The Fiery Trial — 973.7092
    Forever Free — 973.8
    ★*Gateway to Freedom* — 973.7
    ★*Reconstruction* — 973.8
    The Second Founding — 342.73

Foo, Stephanie
    ★*What My Bones Know* — B

FOO, STEPHANIE
    Foo, Stephanie. ★*What My Bones Know* — B

FOOD
    Ahdoot, Dan. *Undercooked* — 647.95
    Albright, Mary Beth. ★*Eat & Flourish* — 612.3
    Ali, Fatima. ★*Savor* — B
    Bass, Rick. *The Traveling Feast* — B
    Bourdain, Anthony. ★*Kitchen Confidential* — B
    Bourdain, Anthony. *Medium Raw* — B
    Bourdain, Anthony. *The Nasty Bits* — 641.5092
    Bourdain, Anthony. ★*World Travel* — 641.59
    Burton, Susan. *Empty* — B
    Cheng, Eugenia. *How to Bake Pi* — 510
    Downie, David. *A Taste of Paris* — 394.1
    Fagan, Brian M. *Fishing* — 338.3
    Fishman, Boris. *Savage Feast* — B
    Foer, Jonathan Safran. *Eating Animals* — 641.3
    Gardner, Lindsay. *Why We Cook* — 641.5
    Goulding, Matt. *Grape, Olive, Pig* — 394.1
    Henaut, Stephane. *A Bite-Sized History of France* — 394.1
    Kattan, Fadi. ★*Bethlehem* — 641.59
    Kingsley, Lisa. *Smithsonian American Table* — 641.5
    Lawson, Nigella. ★*Cook, Eat, Repeat* — 641.5
    Lohman, Sarah. ★*Endangered Eating* — 641.5973
    Lorr, Benjamin. *The Secret Life of Groceries* — 381.4
    McGee, Harold. ★*On Food and Cooking* — 641.5
    Mitchell, Andie. *Eating in the Middle* — 641.3
    Moss, Michael. *Salt, Sugar, Fat* — 613.2
    Nathan, Joan. *King Solomon's Table* — 641.5
    Nezhukumatathil, Aimee. *Bite by Bite* — 641.3
    Olmsted, Larry. *Real Food/Fake Food* — 641.3
    Pittman, Ann Taylor. *The Global Pantry Cookbook* — 641.59
    Pleasant, Barbara. *Homegrown Pantry* — 635
    Pollan, Michael. *The Omnivore's Dilemma* — 394.1
    Price, Catherine. *Vitamania* — 612.3
    Prud'homme, Alex. ★*Dinner with the President* — 973
    Reichl, Ruth. *Garlic and Sapphires* — B
    Reichl, Ruth. ★*Save Me the Plums* — B
    Rude, Emelyn. *Tastes Like Chicken* — 338.1
    Saladino, Dan. *Eating to Extinction* — 641.3
    Samuelsson, Marcus. *The Red Rooster Cookbook* — 641.5974
    Segnit, Niki. ★*The Flavor Thesaurus* — 641.5
    Sen, Mayukh. *Taste Makers* — 641.5092
    Siegel, Matt. *The Secret History of Food* — 641.3
    Standage, Tom. *An Edible History of Humanity* — 394.1
    Tamimi, Sami. *Falastin* — 641.595
    Tandoh, Ruby. ★*Eat Up* — 641.3
    Tipton-Martin, Toni. ★*Jubilee* — 641.59
    Tulleken, Chris van. *Ultra-Processed People* — 664
    Von Bremzen, Anya. *National Dish* — 641.3
    Walvin, James. *Sugar* — 338.17361
    Waters, Alice. *Coming to My Senses* — B
    Wilson, Bee. *The Way We Eat Now* — 641.01
    Wilson, Jessica. *It's Always Been Ours* — 613
    Wong, Cecily. ★*Gastro Obscura* — 641.3

Food 52 Vegan. Hamshaw, Gena — 641.5

FOOD ADDITIVES
    Moss, Michael. ★*Hooked* — 613.2
    Olmsted, Larry. *Real Food/Fake Food* — 641.3
    Winter, Ruth. *A Consumer's Dictionary of Food Additives* — 664

FOOD ALLERGY
    MacPhail, Theresa. *Allergic* — 616.97

FOOD AND WINE PAIRING
    Wangler, Justin. *Season* — 641.5979
    ★*Food Between Friends*. Ferguson, Jesse Tyler — 641.5973

FOOD BOOKS — COOKBOOKS
    Bowen, Dana. *Dynamite Kids Cooking School* — 641.5

FOOD BOOKS — HISTORY AND CULTURE
    Witte, Christina De. ★*Noodles, Rice, and Everything Spice* — 641.595

FOOD CHAINS (ECOLOGY)
    Roman, Joe. *Eat, Poop, Die* — 577

FOOD CONSUMPTION
    Foer, Jonathan Safran. *Eating Animals* — 641.3
    Garner, Dwight. *The Upstairs Delicatessen* — B
    Oakes, John G. H. ★*The Fast* — 613.2
    Pollan, Michael. *The Omnivore's Dilemma* — 394.1
    Saladino, Dan. *Eating to Extinction* — 641.3
    Wilson, Bee. *The Way We Eat Now* — 641.01

FOOD CROPS
    Elmore, Bartow J. *Seed Money* — 338.7
    Jabbour, Niki. ★*Groundbreaking Food Gardens* — 635
    Madison, Deborah. *Vegetable Literacy* — 641.6
    Pleasant, Barbara. *Homegrown Pantry* — 635

The Food Explorer. Stone, Daniel — B
Food for Life. Ali, Laila — 641.5
Food from Across Africa. Timothy, Duval — 641.596

FOOD HABITS
    Ahdoot, Dan. *Undercooked* — 647.95
    Albright, Mary Beth. ★*Eat & Flourish* — 612.3
    Altmann, Tanya Remer. *What to Feed Your Baby* — 649
    Angelou, Maya. *Great Food, All Day Long* — 641.5973
    Anthony, Jason C. *Hoosh* — 394.1
    Bard, Elizabeth. *Lunch in Paris* — B
    Bard, Elizabeth. *Picnic in Provence* — B
    Bittman, Mark. *Animal, Vegetable, Junk* — 394.1
    Bourdain, Anthony. ★*Appetites* — 641.5
    Bourdain, Anthony. ★*World Travel* — 641.59
    Buford, Bill. ★*Dirt* — B
    Burton, Susan. *Empty* — B
    Camara, Gabriela. *My Mexico City Kitchen* — 641.5972

PUBLIC LIBRARY CORE COLLECTION: NONFICTION
Twentieth Edition

Chandler, Adam. *Drive-Thru Dreams*	647.95
Chaudry, Rabia. *Fatty Fatty Boom Boom*	B
Cho, Grace M. *Tastes Like War*	305.48
Collingham, E. M. *Curry*	394.1
Cowen, Tyler. *An Economist Gets Lunch*	394.1
Downie, David. *A Taste of Paris*	394.1
Dusoulier, Clotilde. *Tasting Paris*	641.594
Foer, Jonathan Safran. *Eating Animals*	641.3
Freeman, Andrea. ★*Ruin Their Crops on the Ground*	338.1
Freeman, Hadley. *Good Girls*	616.85
Gardner, Lindsay. *Why We Cook*	641.5
Garner, Dwight. *The Upstairs Delicatessen*	B
Goulding, Matt. *Grape, Olive, Pig*	394.1
Goulding, Matt. *Rice, Noodle, Fish*	394.1
Greenberg, Paul. *American Catch*	333.95
Greger, Michael. *The How Not to Diet Cookbook*	641.5
Hamilton, Gabrielle. *Blood, Bones, and Butter*	B
Harris, Jessica B. *High on the Hog*	641.59
Hartwig, Melissa. *The Whole30 Fast & Easy*	641.5
Hartwig, Melissa. *The Whole30 Slow Cooker*	641.5
Henaut, Stephane. *A Bite-Sized History of France*	394.1
Hussain, Nadiya. ★*Nadiya's Everyday Baking*	641.5
Kattan, Fadi. ★*Bethlehem*	641.5
Kauffman, Jonathan. *Hippie Food*	394.1
Khan, Yasmin. ★*Zaitoun*	641.595
Kingsley, Lisa. *Smithsonian American Table*	641.5
Kingsolver, Barbara. ★*Animal, Vegetable, Miracle*	641
Kurlansky, Mark. *Milk!*	637
Lebovitz, David. *My Paris Kitchen*	641.594
Lewis, Edna. *In Pursuit of Flavor*	641.5975
Locke, Tembi. ★*From Scratch*	B
Lohman, Sarah. ★*Endangered Eating*	641.5973
McGee, Harold. ★*On Food and Cooking*	641.5
McMillan, Tracie. *The American Way of Eating*	338.4
Miller, Max. ★*Tasting History*	641.509
Moss, Michael. ★*Hooked*	613.2
Moss, Michael. *Salt, Sugar, Fat*	613.2
Nathan, Joan. *King Solomon's Table*	641.5
Nosrat, Samin. ★*Salt, Fat, Acid, Heat*	641.5
Oakes, John G. H. ★*The Fast*	613.2
Pepin, Jacques. *The Apprentice*	B
Pollan, Michael. *Cooked*	641.5
Pollan, Michael. *The Omnivore's Dilemma*	394.1
Porto, Anthony. *The Pediatrician's Guide to Feeding Babies & Toddlers*	618.92
Powell, Julie. *Julie and Julia*	641.5
Prud'homme, Alex. ★*Dinner with the President*	973
Reichl, Ruth. *Comfort Me with Apples*	B
Roach, Mary. *Gulp*	612.3
Siegel, Matt. *The Secret History of Food*	641.3
Specter, Emma. *More, Please*	616.85
Standage, Tom. *An Edible History of Humanity*	394.1
Stone, Daniel. *The Food Explorer*	B
Tandoh, Ruby. ★*Eat Up*	641.3
Terry, Bryant. *Black Food*	394.1
Tipton-Martin, Toni. *The Jemima Code*	641.59
Tipton-Martin, Toni. ★*Jubilee*	641.59
Tomlinson, Tommy. *The Elephant in the Room*	B
Tulleken, Chris van. *Ultra-Processed People*	664
Twilley, Nicola. ★*Frostbite*	621
Twitty, Michael. ★*The Cooking Gene*	641.59
Vitale, Tom. *In the Weeds*	B
Von Bremzen, Anya. *National Dish*	641.3
Walvin, James. *Sugar*	338.17361
Waters, Alice. ★*We Are What We Eat*	641.01
Wilkinson, Crystal. *Praisesong for the Kitchen Ghosts*	641.5975
Wilson, Bee. *The Way We Eat Now*	641.01
Wilson, Jessica. *It's Always Been Ours*	613
Woolever, Laurie. *Bourdain*	B
Wrangham, Richard W. *Catching Fire*	394.1
Zimberoff, Larissa. *Technically Food*	613.2

FOOD IN LITERATURE

McGee, Harold. ★*On Food and Cooking*	641.5

FOOD INDUSTRY AND TRADE

Bittman, Mark. *A Bone to Pick*	338.10973
Bourdain, Anthony. ★*Kitchen Confidential*	B
Bourdain, Anthony. *Medium Raw*	B
Bourdain, Anthony. *The Nasty Bits*	641.5092
Bourdain, Anthony. ★*World Travel*	641.59
Chisholm, Edward. *A Waiter in Paris*	B
Cowen, Tyler. *An Economist Gets Lunch*	394.1
Freeman, Andrea. ★*Ruin Their Crops on the Ground*	338.1
Friedman, Andrew. *The Dish*	647.95
Genoways, Ted. *The Chain*	338.7
Hewitt, Ben. ★*The Town That Food Saved*	338.1
Jacobs, Ryan McMahon. *The Truffle Underground*	381
Lorr, Benjamin. *The Secret Life of Groceries*	381.4
Monbiot, George. ★*Regenesis*	338.1
Moss, Michael. ★*Hooked*	613.2
Moss, Michael. *Salt, Sugar, Fat*	613.2
Saladino, Dan. *Eating to Extinction*	641.3
Standage, Tom. *An Edible History of Humanity*	394.1
Tulleken, Chris van. *Ultra-Processed People*	664
Twilley, Nicola. ★*Frostbite*	621
Waters, Alice. ★*We Are What We Eat*	641.01
Zimberoff, Larissa. *Technically Food*	613.2
Zuckerman, Jocelyn C. *Planet Palm*	633.8
Food Is Love. Patel, Palak	641.595
Food Is the Solution. Prescott, Matthew	613.2
The Food Lab. Lopez-Alt, J. Kenji	664
The Food of Sichuan. Dunlop, Fuchsia	641.595
The Food of Sicily. Lanza, Fabrizia	641.594

FOOD POLICY

Freeman, Andrea. ★*Ruin Their Crops on the Ground*	338.1

FOOD PORTIONS

Schatzker, Mark. *The Dorito Effect*	641.3

FOOD PREPARATION

Adler, Tamar. *An Everlasting Meal*	641.5
Bitsoie, Freddie. *New Native Kitchen*	641.59
Cailan, Alvin. *Amboy*	641.595
El-Waylly, Sohla. ★*Start Here*	641.3
Kingsley, Lisa. *Smithsonian American Table*	641.5
Lawson, Nigella. ★*Cook, Eat, Repeat*	641.5
Lewis, Edna. *In Pursuit of Flavor*	641.5975
Nathan, Joan. ★*My Life in Recipes*	641.5
Samuelsson, Marcus. ★*The Rise*	641.59
Vasquez, Karla Tatiana. ★*The Salvisoul Cookbook*	641.598

FOOD RELIEF

Puleo, Stephen. *Voyage of Mercy*	363.8
Smith, Douglas. *The Russian Job*	947.084

FOOD SCIENCE

Lopez-Alt, J. Kenji. *The Food Lab*	664
McGee, Harold. ★*On Food and Cooking*	641.5
Moss, Michael. ★*Hooked*	613.2
Nosrat, Samin. ★*Salt, Fat, Acid, Heat*	641.5
Twilley, Nicola. ★*Frostbite*	621

FOOD SECURITY

Ackerman-Leist, Philip. *Rebuilding the Foodshed*	338.1
Freeman, Andrea. ★*Ruin Their Crops on the Ground*	338.1
Saladino, Dan. *Eating to Extinction*	641.3
Szczeszak-Brewer, Agata. *The Hunger Book*	B

FOOD SERVICE

Cecchi-Azzolina, Michael. *Your Table Is Ready*	647.95

FOOD SUBSTITUTES

Olmsted, Larry. *Real Food/Fake Food*	641.3
Zimberoff, Larissa. *Technically Food*	613.2

FOOD SUPPLEMENTS

Price, Catherine. *Vitamania*	612.3

FOOD SUPPLY

Ackerman-Leist, Philip. *Rebuilding the Foodshed*	338.1
Dikotter, Frank. *Mao's Great Famine*	951.05
Freeman, Andrea. ★*Ruin Their Crops on the Ground*	338.1
Hewitt, Ben. ★*The Town That Food Saved*	338.1
Kauffman, Jonathan. *Hippie Food*	394.1
Klare, Michael T. *All Hell Breaking Loose*	355.20973
Monbiot, George. ★*Regenesis*	338.1
Montgomery, David R. *What Your Food Ate*	631.4
Saladino, Dan. *Eating to Extinction*	641.3
Smith, Bren. *Eat Like a Fish*	338.3
Twilley, Nicola. ★*Frostbite*	621
Wilson, Bee. *The Way We Eat Now*	641.01

FOOD TOURISM

Goulding, Matt. *Rice, Noodle, Fish*	394.1

FOOD VALUES

Wrangham, Richard W. *Catching Fire*	394.1

AUTHOR, TITLE, SERIES AND SUBJECT INDEX

FOOD WASTE
- Humes, Edward. ★ *Total Garbage* — 628.4

FOOD WRITERS
- Garner, Dwight. *The Upstairs Delicatessen* — B
- Nunn, Emily. *The Comfort Food Diaries* — 641.5973
- Reichl, Ruth. *Garlic and Sapphires* — B
- Reichl, Ruth. ★ *Save Me the Plums* — B
- Sheehan, Jason. *Cooking Dirty* — B
- Tucci, Stanley. ★ *Taste* — B

FOOD WRITING
- Garner, Dwight. *The Upstairs Delicatessen* — B

FOOD WRITING — BEER, WINE, AND LIQUOR
- Bryson, Lew. *Tasting Whiskey* — 663
- Cioletti, Jeff. *Sakepedia* — 663
- Hoalst-Pullen, Nancy. *National Geographic Atlas of Beer* — 663
- Hoffman, Maggie. *Batch Cocktails* — 641.87
- Hudson, Kate. *Pretty Fun* — 642
- Neiman, Ophelie. *Wine Isn't Rocket Science* — 641.2
- O'Meara, Mallory. *Girly Drinks* — 641.2
- Risen, Clay. *American Whiskey, Bourbon, & Rye* — 641.2
- Rollich, Christiaan. *Bar Chef* — 641.87
- Standage, Tom. *A History of the World in 6 Glasses* — 394.1
- Tipton-Martin, Toni. *Juke Joints, Jazz Clubs & Juice* — 641.87
- White, April. *Apples to Cider* — 663
- Zraly, Kevin. *Windows on the World Complete Wine Course* — 641.2

FOOD WRITING — COOKING AND COOKBOOKS
- Baz, Molly. *Cook This Book* — 641.5
- Beranbaum, Rose Levy. ★ *The Baking Bible* — 641.81
- Clark, Melissa. *Kid in the Kitchen* — 641.5
- Crocker, Betty. ★ *Betty Crocker Cookbook* — 641.5
- Gerard, Tieghan. ★ *Half Baked Harvest Every Day* — 641.5
- Khan, Yasmin. ★ *Zaitoun* — 641.595
- Lomas, Vallery. ★ *Life Is What You Bake It* — 641.81
- McDowell, Erin Jeanne. ★ *The Book on Pie* — 641.86
- Miglore, Kristen. ★ *Food52 Genius Recipes* — 641.5
- Miller, Klancy. ★ *For the Culture* — 641.59
- Miller, Max. ★ *Tasting History* — 641.509
- Pauline, Kathryn. *A Dish for All Seasons* — 641.5
- Perelman, Deb. ★ *Smitten Kitchen Keepers* — 641.5
- Rombauer, Irma S. ★ *Joy of Cooking* — 641.5973
- Stewart, Martha. *Martha Stewart's Cake Perfection* — 641.86
- Turshen, Julia. *Now & Again* — 641.5
- Villanova, Thibaud. *Disney Enchanted Recipes* — 641.5
- Weller, Melissa. *A Good Bake* — 641.86
- Yearwood, Trisha. *Trisha's Kitchen* — 641.5

FOOD WRITING — COOKING AND COOKBOOKS — CHEFS AND RESTAURANTS
- Acheson, Hugh. *The Chef and the Slow Cooker* — 641.5
- Admony, Einat. *Shuk* — 641.595
- Alikhani, Nasim. *Sofreh* — 641.595
- Andres, Jose. *Vegetables Unleashed* — 641.5
- Assil, Reem. *Arabiyya* — 641.595
- Bastianich, Lidia. *Felidia* — 641.594
- Bastianich, Lidia. *Lidia's Commonsense Italian Cooking* — 641.594
- Bastianich, Lidia. *Lidia's Favorite Recipes* — 641.594
- Bastianich, Lidia. ★ *Lidia's from Our Family Table to Yours* — 641.594
- Bastianich, Lidia. *Lidia's Mastering the Art of Italian Cuisine* — 641.594
- Bastianich, Lidia. *Lidia's* — 641.594
- Batali, Mario. *Mario Batali Big American Cookbook* — 641.5973
- Berry, Mary. *Cooking with Mary Berry* — 641.5
- Blumenthal, Heston. *Is This a Cookbook?* — 641.5
- Bourdain, Anthony. ★ *Appetites* — 641.5
- Brock, Sean. *South* — 641.5975
- Brown, Kardea. *The Way Home* — 641.5975
- Buford, Bill. ★ *Dirt* — B
- Camara, Gabriela. *My Mexico City Kitchen* — 641.5972
- Cayne, Alison. *The Haven's Kitchen Cooking School* — 641.5
- Centeno, Josef. *Ama* — 641.5979
- Chaplin, Amy. *Whole Food Cooking Every Day* — 641.3
- Christensen, Ashley. *It's Always Freezer Season* — 641.5
- Danford, Natalie. *How to Eataly* — 641.594
- Day, Cheryl. *Cheryl Day's Treasury of Southern Baking* — 641.81
- De Laurentiis, Giada. *Giada's Kitchen* — 641.594
- De Laurentiis, Giada. *Happy Cooking* — 641.5
- DiSpirito, Rocco. *Rocco's Healthy+Delicious* — 641.3
- Dissen, William Stark. *Thoughtful Cooking* — 641.5975
- Drummond, Ree. ★ *The Pioneer Woman Cooks* — 641.5
- Emberling, Amy. *Zingerman's Bakehouse* — 641.81

- Esposito, Jennifer. *Jennifer's Way Kitchen* — 641.5
- Flay, Bobby. *Bobby at Home* — 641.5
- Flay, Bobby. *Sundays with Sophie* — 641.5
- Fox, Jeremy. *On Vegetables* — 641.6
- Garten, Ina. *Barefoot Contessa at Home* — 641.5
- Garten, Ina. ★ *Cook Like a Pro* — 641.5
- Garten, Ina. *Cooking for Jeffrey* — 641.5
- Garten, Ina. ★ *Go-To Dinners* — 641.5
- Garten, Ina. ★ *Modern Comfort Food* — 641.5
- Goldman, Duff. *Duff Bakes* — 641.81
- Gourdet, Gregory. *Everyone's Table* — 641.5
- Gray, Jon. *Ghetto Gastro Black Power Kitchen* — 641.5
- Greenspan, Dorie. ★ *Everyday Dorie* — 641.5
- Hall, Carla. *Carla Hall's Soul Food* — 641.5975
- Hamilton, Gabrielle. *Prune* — 641.3
- Headley, Brooks. *Superiority Burger Cookbook* — 641.5
- Heatter, Maida. ★ *Happiness Is Baking* — 641.86
- Henry, Diana. *From the Oven to the Table* — 641.82
- Hereford, Mason. *Turkey and the Wolf* — 641.5976
- Howard, Vivian. *Deep Run Roots* — 641.5975
- Howard, Vivian. *This Will Make It Taste Good* — 641.5
- Hussain, Nadiya. ★ *Nadiya Bakes* — 641.81
- Jinich, Pati. ★ *Treasures of the Mexican Table* — 641.5972
- Johnson, J. J. *Between Harlem and Heaven* — 641.59
- Kahan, Paul. *Cheers to the Publican, Repast and Present* — 641.594
- Kang, Mingoo. *Jang* — 641.595
- Keller, Thomas. *Bouchon Bakery* — 641.594
- Keller, Thomas. *The French Laundry Cookbook* — 641.5
- Kim, Hooni. *My Korea* — 641.595
- Kimball, Christopher. *Christopher Kimball's Milk Street* — 641.5
- Kimball, Christopher. *Christopher Kimball's Milk Street* — 641.5
- Kimball, Christopher. *Milk Street* — 641.5
- Kimball, Christopher. *Milk Street* — 641.5
- Kinch, David. *At Home in the Kitchen* — 641.5973
- Klopotenko, Yevhen. ★ *The Authentic Ukrainian Kitchen* — 641.594
- Ladner, Mark. *The Del Posto Cookbook* — 641.594
- Lagasse, Emeril. *Essential Emeril* — 641.5
- Lahey, Jim. *The Sullivan Street Bakery Cookbook* — 641.81
- Lancaster, Bridget. *Cooking at Home with Bridget & Julia* — 641.5
- Lawson, Nigella. *At My Table* — 641.59
- Lawson, Nigella. ★ *Simply Nigella* — 641.5
- Lee, Edward. *Buttermilk Graffiti* — 641.59
- Lewis, Edna. *In Pursuit of Flavor* — 641.5975
- Lloyd, Bobbie. *The Magnolia Bakery Handbook* — 641.86
- Lukas, Albert. ★ *Sweet Home Cafe Cookbook* — 641.59
- Massih, Edy. ★ *Keep It Zesty* — 641.595
- Mauro, Jeff. *Come on Over* — 641.5
- McFadden, Joshua. ★ *Grains for Every Season* — 641.3
- McFadden, Joshua. *Six Seasons* — 641.5
- Miglore, Kristen. ★ *Food52 Genius Recipes* — 641.5
- Morales, Bonnie Frumkin. *Kachka* — 641.594
- Moulton, Sara. *Sara Moulton's Home Cooking 101* — 641.5973
- Murad, Noor. ★ *Ottolenghi Test Kitchen* — 641.3
- Murad, Noor. *Ottolenghi Test Kitchen* — 641.5
- Nelson, Candace. *The Sprinkles Baking Book* — 641.81
- Noyes, Brian. *The Red Truck Bakery Farmhouse Cookbook* — 641.5973
- Oliver, Jamie. *Together* — 641.5
- Orkin, Ivan. *The Gaijin Cookbook* — 641.595
- Ottolenghi, Yotam. *Ottolenghi Simple* — 641.59
- Ottolenghi, Yotam. ★ *Plenty More* — 641.6
- Ottolenghi, Yotam. *Plenty* — 641.6
- Ottolenghi, Yotam. *Sweet* — 641.86
- Pepin, Jacques. ★ *Jacques Pepin* — 641.5
- Pepin, Jacques. ★ *Jacques Pepin* — 641.594
- Pepin, Jacques. ★ *Jacques Pépin Cooking My Way* — 641.5
- Perelman, Deb. ★ *The Smitten Kitchen Cookbook* — 641.5
- Perelman, Deb. ★ *Smitten Kitchen Every Day* — 641.5
- Pierson, Joy. *Vegan Holiday Cooking from Candle Cafe* — 641.5
- Ponseca, Nicole. *I Am a Filipino and This Is How We Cook* — 641.595
- Porowski, Antoni. *Antoni* — 641.5
- Ramsay, Gordon. ★ *Quick and Delicious* — 641.5
- Ray, Rachael. *Everyone Is Italian on Sunday* — 641.594
- Ray, Rachael. ★ *This Must Be the Place* — 641.5
- Redzepi, Rene. *The Noma Guide to Fermentation* — 664
- Ripert, Eric. *Seafood Simple* — 641.6
- Rosen, Ilene. *Saladish* — 641.83
- Samuelsson, Marcus. *Marcus off Duty* — 641.5
- Scott, Rodney. ★ *Rodney Scott's World of BBQ* — 641.7

Shepherd, Chris. *Cook Like a Local*	641.59
Sherman, Sean. ★*The Sioux Chef's Indigenous Kitchen*	641.59
Silverton, Nancy. ★*The Cookie That Changed My Life*	641.81
Simeon, Sheldon. *Cook Real Hawai?i*	641.59969
Smalls, Alexander. *Meals, Music, and Muses*	641.59
Snoop Dogg. *Goon with the Spoon*	641.59
Solomonov, Michael. *Israeli Soul*	641.595
Tamimi, Sami. *Falastin*	641.595
Tandoh, Ruby. ★*Cook as You Are*	641.59
Tila, Jet. *101 Asian Dishes You Need to Cook Before You Die*	641.595
Tosi, Christina. *All About Cake*	641.86
Trejo, Danny. *Trejo's Tacos*	641.5979
Vetri, Marc. *Mastering Pizza*	641.82
Walch, Aubry. *The Herbivorous Butcher Cookbook*	641.5
Wang, Jason. *XI'an Famous Foods*	641.595
Waters, Alice. *Coming to My Senses*	B
Wells, Patricia. *My Master Recipes*	641.5
White, Marco Pierre. *White Heat*	641.594
Wilson, Melba. ★*Melba's American Comfort*	641.5973
Woo, Ronnie. *Did You Eat Yet?*	641.595

FOOD WRITING — COOKING AND COOKBOOKS — COOKING FOR HEALTH

Ali, Laila. *Food for Life*	641.5
Barrett, Pearl. *Trim Healthy Mama Trim Healthy Table*	613.2
Bittman, Mark. *The VB6 Cookbook*	641.5
Bittman, Mark. *VB6*	641.5
Britton, Sarah. *Naturally Nourished*	641.5
Cavallari, Kristin. *True Roots*	641.5
Chaplin, Amy. *Whole Food Cooking Every Day*	641.3
Conners, Rachel. *Bakerita*	641.81
Cristofano, Jana. *Eat Well, Be Well*	641.5
Curry, Kevin. *Fit Men Cook*	641.5
Dada, Samah. *Dada Eats Love to Cook It*	641.5
David, Laurie. *The Family Cooks*	641.3
DiSpirito, Rocco. *Now Eat This!*	641.5
DiSpirito, Rocco. *Rocco's Healthy+Delicious*	641.3
Esposito, Jennifer. *Jennifer's Way Kitchen*	641.5
Flanagan, Shalane. *Run Fast, Cook Fast, Eat Slow*	641.5
Forte, Sara. *The Sprouted Kitchen*	641.3
Fuhrman, Joel. *Eat to Live Quick & Easy Cookbook*	641.5
Gourdet, Gregory. *Everyone's Table*	641.5
Greger, Michael. ★*The How Not to Diet Cookbook*	641.5
Griffin, Brooke. *Skinny Suppers*	641.5
Hartwig, Melissa. *The Whole30 Fast & Easy*	641.5
Hartwig, Melissa. *The Whole30 Slow Cooker*	641.5
Hill, McKel. *Nutrition Stripped*	641.3
Homolka, Gina. *Skinnytaste One & Done*	641.5
Hunt, Lindsay Maitland. *Help Yourself*	641.5
Jenkins, Nancy Harmon. *The New Mediterranean Diet Cookbook*	641.59
Krieger, Ellie. *You Have It Made!*	641.5
Larsen, Jeffrey. ★*Gluten-Free Baking at Home*	641.5
Lee, Jennifer Tyler. *Half the Sugar, All the Love*	641.5
Lewis, John. *Badass Vegan*	641.5
Lillien, Lisa. *Hungry Girl 1-2-3*	641.5
Lillien, Lisa. *Hungry Girl Simply 6*	641.5
Mitchell, Andie. *Eating in the Middle*	641.3
Mullen, Seamus. *Real Food Heals*	641.5
Myers, Amy. *The Autoimmune Solution Cookbook*	641.5
Perlmutter, David. *The Grain Brain Cookbook*	651.56
Pollan, Corky. *The Pollan Family Table*	641.5
Pulde, Alona. *Forks Over Knives Family*	641.5
Rodale, Maria. *Scratch*	641.3
Rondinelli-Hamilton, Lara. *The Diabetes Cookbook*	641.5
Sanfilippo, Diane. *Practical Paleo*	613.2
Smith, Michelle. *The Whole Smiths Good Food Cookbook*	641.5
Smith, R. Garth. *Asd, the Complete Autism Spectrum Disorder Health & Diet Guide*	616.85
Snodgrass, Alex. ★*The Defined Dish*	641.5
Snodgrass, Alex. *Dinner Tonight*	641.5
Symon, Michael. ★*Fix It with Food*	641.5
Terry, Bryant. *Vegan Soul Kitchen*	641.5
Thomas, Haile. *Living Lively*	641.5
Turshen, Julia. *Simply Julia*	641.3
Urban, Melissa. *The Whole30 Friends & Family*	641.5
Walker, Danielle. *Danielle Walker's Against All Grain*	641.5
Walker, Danielle. *Danielle Walker's Healthy in a Hurry*	641.5
Weil, Andrew. *Fast Food, Good Food*	641.3
Winfrey, Oprah. *Food, Health, and Happiness*	641.5
Wolf, Robb. *Wired to Eat*	641.5

FOOD WRITING — COOKING AND COOKBOOKS — COOKING FOR THE FAMILY

Bastianich, Lidia. *Lidia's Family Table*	641.594
David, Laurie. *The Family Cooks*	641.3
Flay, Bobby. *Sundays with Sophie*	641.5
Guarnaschelli, Alex. ★*Cook It Up*	641.5
Helwig, Jenna. *Baby-Led Feeding*	641.3
Hussain, Nadiya. *Time to Eat*	641.5
Klein, Dini. *Prep + Rally*	641.5
Lancaster, Bridget. *Cooking at Home with Bridget & Julia*	641.5
Lee, Jennifer Tyler. *Half the Sugar, All the Love*	641.5
Merchant, Jessica. *Everyday Dinners*	641.82
Pulde, Alona. *Forks Over Knives Family*	641.5
Scott, Ryan. *The No-Fuss Family Cookbook*	641.5
Thiessen, Tiffani. *Pull up a Chair*	641.5
Workman, Katie. *The Mom 100 Cookbook*	641.5

FOOD WRITING — COOKING AND COOKBOOKS — COURSES

Adams, Jocelyn Delk. *Grandbaby Cakes*	641.86
Arefi, Yossy. *Snacking Cakes*	641.86
Barrow, Cathy. *Bagels, Schmears, and a Nice Piece of Fish*	641.81
Barrow, Cathy. ★*Pie Squared*	641.86
Behan, Ren. ★*The Sweet Polish Kitchen*	641.594
Ben-Ishay, Melissa. *Come Hungry*	641.5
Beranbaum, Rose Levy. ★*The Cake Bible*	641.8
Beranbaum, Rose Levy. ★*The Cookie Bible*	641.86
Beranbaum, Rose Levy. *Rose's Ice Cream Bliss*	641.86
Bianco, Chris. *Bianco*	641.5
Bittman, Mark. ★*Bittman Bread*	641.81
Black, Sarah. *One Dough, Ten Breads*	641.81
Brown, Leanne. ★*Good and Cheap*	641.5
Byrn, Anne. ★*American Cake*	641.86
Byrn, Anne. ★*American Cookie*	641.86
Byrn, Anne. *A New Take on Cake*	641.86
Chang, Joanne. *Pastry Love*	641.86
Clark, Melissa. *Dinner*	641.5
Comerford, Hope. *Fix-It and Forget-It Healthy 5-Ingredient Cookbook*	641.5
Damuck, Jess. *Salad Freak*	641.83
Dodge, Abigail Johnson. *Sheet Cake*	641.86
Fairchild, Barbara. *The Bon Appetit Cookbook*	641.5
Forkish, Ken. *Evolutions in Bread*	664
Forkish, Ken. *Flour Water Salt Yeast*	641.81
Francois, Zoe. *Holiday and Celebration Bread in Five Minutes a Day*	641.81
Francois, Zoe. *Zoe Bakes Cakes*	641.86
Ganeshram, Ramin. *Future Chefs*	641.3
Garten, Ina. *Cooking for Jeffrey*	641.5
Gerson, Fany. *Mexican Ice Cream*	641.86
Gerson, Fany. *My Sweet Mexico*	641.5972
Greenspan, Dorie. ★*Baking with Dorie*	641.81
Guarnaschelli, Alex. *The Home Cook*	641.5973
Heatter, Maida. ★*Happiness Is Baking*	641.86
Hoffman, Brian Hart. ★*Bake from Scratch; Volume Two*	641.81
Hollis, B. Dylan. ★*Baking Yesteryear*	641.81
Hollywood, Paul. ★*Bake*	641.81
Hunt, Lindsay Maitland. *Healthyish*	641.5
Hussain, Nadiya. ★*Nadiya Bakes*	641.81
Iyer, Raghavan. *Indian Cooking Unfolded*	641.595
Kartes, Danielle. *Butter, Flour, Sugar, Joy*	641.86
Kieffer, Sarah. *100 Morning Treats*	641.5
Kieffer, Sarah. ★*Baking for the Holidays*	641.5
Kimball, Christopher. ★*Milk Street 365*	641.5
Lahey, Jim. *The Sullivan Street Bakery Cookbook*	641.81
Lane, Christina. *Dessert for Two*	641.86
Ludwinski, Lisa. *Sister Pie*	641.86
Manning, Ivy. *Easy Soups from Scratch with Quick Breads to Match*	641.81
McDermott, Kate. ★*Art of the Pie*	641.86
McKenney, Sally. ★*Sally's Cookie Addiction*	641.86
Moskowitz, Isa Chandra. *Veganomicon*	641
Mubarak, Heather. *Stuffed*	641.86
Music, Carla Lalli. *That Sounds so Good*	641.5
Nederlanden, Elisabet der. ★*Holiday Cookies*	641.86
Nguyen, Andrea Quynhgiao. *The Pho Cookbook*	641.595
Parks, Stella. ★*Bravetart*	641.86
Peters, Meike. *Noon*	641.5
Peterson, James. *Sauces*	641.81
Pfeiffer, Jacquy. *The Art of French Pastry*	641.86
Reinhart, Peter. *Perfect Pan Pizza*	641.82
Rodriguez, Jessamyn Waldman. *The Hot Bread Kitchen Cookbook*	641.59

AUTHOR, TITLE, SERIES AND SUBJECT INDEX

Roman, Alison. *Dining In*	641.5
Roman, Alison. ★*Nothing Fancy*	642
Roman, Alison. *Sweet Enough*	641.86
Rosso, Julee. *The Silver Palate Cookbook*	641.5
Saffitz, Claire. ★*What's for Dessert*	641.86
Saltz, Joanna. ★*Delish Insane Sweets*	641.81
Sarno, Chad. *The Wicked Healthy Cookbook*	651.56
Schrijver, Darlene. *The Salad Lab*	641.83
Seneviratne, Samantha. *Bake Smart*	641.81
Sheehan, Jessie. ★*Snackable Bakes*	641.7
Silverton, Nancy. ★*The Cookie That Changed My Life*	641.81
Snodgrass, Alex. ★*The Defined Dish*	641.5
Snyder, Sabrina. *Dinner Then Dessert*	641.5
Tosi, Christina. *All About Cake*	641.86
Tosi, Christina. *All About Cookies*	641.86
Weiss, Luisa. *Classic German Baking*	641.594
Westerhausen, Shelly. *Every Season Is Soup Season*	641.81
Williams, Odette. *Simple Cake*	641.86
Zizka, Maria. *The Hostess Handbook*	642

FOOD WRITING — COOKING AND COOKBOOKS — ENTERTAINING

Bastianich, Lidia. *Lidia's*	641.594
Bracken, Peg. *The I Hate to Cook Book*	641.5
Flay, Bobby. *Bobby at Home*	641.5
Gaines, Joanna. ★*Magnolia Table*	641.5975
Garten, Ina. *Barefoot Contessa at Home*	641.5
Garten, Ina. *Barefoot Contessa Family Style*	641.5
Hartnett, Angela. *The Weekend Cook*	641.5
Heuck, Lidey. ★*Cooking in Real Life*	641.5
Hudson, Kate. *Pretty Fun*	642
Mauro, Jeff. *Come on Over*	641.5
McAlpine, Skye. *A Table Full of Love*	641.5
Moskowitz, Isa Chandra. *The Superfun Times Vegan Holiday Cookbook*	651.56
Mullen, Marissa. *That Cheese Plate Wants to Party*	641.6
Neiman, Ophelie. *Wine Isn't Rocket Science*	641.2
Pepin, Jacques. ★*Jacques Pepin*	641.594
Purviance, Jamie. *Weber's Ultimate Grilling*	641.5
Roman, Alison. ★*Nothing Fancy*	642
Rosen, Ali. *Bring It!*	641.5973
Rosenstrach, Jenny. *How to Celebrate Everything*	641.5
Saltz, Joanna. *Delish*	641.5
Sifton, Sam. ★*See You on Sunday*	641.5
Snoop Dogg. *Goon with the Spoon*	641.59
Taylor, Nicole A. ★*Watermelon & Red Birds*	641.5
Thiessen, Tiffani. *Pull up a Chair*	641.5
Tower, Jeremiah. ★*Table Manners*	395.5
Urban, Melissa. *The Whole30 Friends & Family*	641.5
Watson, Ted Kennedy. *Ted Kennedy Watson's Guide to Stylish Entertaining*	793.2
Zizka, Maria. *The Hostess Handbook*	642

FOOD WRITING — COOKING AND COOKBOOKS — INGREDIENTS

Andres, Jose. *Vegetables Unleashed*	641.5
Anthony, Michael. *V Is for Vegetables*	641.6
Belsinger, Susan. *Grow Your Own Herbs*	635
Berens, Abra. *Grist*	641.6
Berens, Abra. *Pulp*	641.6
Bittman, Mark. ★*How to Cook Everything Vegetarian*	641.5
Cavallari, Kristin. *True Roots*	641.5
Chaplin, Amy. *Whole Food Cooking Every Day*	641.3
Conner, Polly. ★*From Freezer to Cooker*	641.6
Curl, Jami. *Candy Is Magic*	641.85
Damuck, Jess. *Salad Freak*	641.83
Danforth, Adam. *Butchering Poultry, Rabbit, Lamb, Goat, and Pork*	664
De Laurentiis, Giada. ★*Giada's Italy*	641.594
Dinki, Nikki. *Meat on the Side*	641.3
DiSpirito, Rocco. *Rocco's Healthy+Delicious*	641.3
Dragonwagon, Crescent. *Bean by Bean*	641.6
Fearnley-Whittingstall, Hugh. *River Cottage Veg*	641.5
Firth, Henry. *Bosh!*	641.5
Fox, Jeremy. *On Vegetables*	641.6
Franklin, Aaron. *Franklin Steak*	641.6
Fuentes, Laura. *The Best Homemade Kids' Snacks on the Planet*	641.5
Goldstein, Joyce Esersky, author. *Jam Session*	641.85
Greenspan, Eric. *The Great Grilled Cheese Book*	641.6
Hall, Carla. *Carla's Comfort Foods*	641.59
Hamshaw, Gena. *Food 52 Vegan*	641.5
Hill, McKel. *Nutrition Stripped*	641.3
Holmberg, Martha. ★*Simply Tomato*	641.6
Howard, Vivian. *This Will Make It Taste Good*	641.5
Kahate, Ruta. *6 Spices 60 Dishes*	641.595
Kim, Bill. *Korean BBQ*	641.595
Korkosz, Michal. *Fresh from Poland*	641.594
Lakshmi, Padma. *The Encyclopedia of Spices and Herbs*	641.3
Le, Mike. *That Noodle Life*	641.82
Leake, Lisa. ★*100 Days of Real Food*	641.5
Madison, Deborah. *Vegetable Literacy*	641.6
Mangini, Cara. *The Vegetable Butcher*	641.6
Mangini, Cara. ★*The Vegetable Eater*	641.6
McFadden, Joshua. ★*Grains for Every Season*	641.3
McFadden, Joshua. *Six Seasons*	641.5
Mullen, Marissa. *That Cheese Plate Wants to Party*	641.6
Munno, Nadia Caterina. *The Pasta Queen*	641.82
Pashman, Dan. *Anything's Pastable*	641.82
Perelman, Deb. ★*Smitten Kitchen Every Day*	641.5
Pittman, Ann Taylor. *The Global Pantry Cookbook*	641.59
Prescott, Matthew. *Food Is the Solution*	613.2
Purviance, Jamie. *Weber's Greatest Hits*	641.5
Raichlen, Steven. *The Brisket Chronicles*	641.6
Raichlen, Steven. *How to Grill Vegetables*	641.6
Rinella, Steven. *The Complete Guide to Hunting, Butchering, and Cooking Wild Game*	799.2
Rinella, Steven. *The Complete Guide to Hunting, Butchering, and Cooking Wild Game; Volume 2*	799.2
Ripert, Eric. *Seafood Simple*	641.6
Rodale, Maria. *Scratch*	641.3
Roddy, Rachel. ★*An A-Z of Pasta*	641.82
Rodriguez, Ashley. *Rooted Kitchen*	641.5
Roll, Rich. *The Plantpower Way*	641.5
Sahadi Whelan, Christine. *Flavors of the Sun*	641.595
Sarno, Chad. *The Wicked Healthy Cookbook*	651.56
Schinner, Miyoko Nishimoto. *The Vegan Meat Cookbook*	641.5
Selengut, Becky. ★*Misunderstood Vegetables*	641.6
Sharma, Nik. *Veg-Table*	641.6
Steele, Lisa. ★*The Fresh Eggs Daily Cookbook*	641.6
Tam, Michelle. *Ready or Not!*	641.5
Thomas, Anna. *Vegan Vegetarian Omnivore*	641.5
Thompson, Jennifer Trainer. *Fresh Fish*	641.3
Walker, Danielle. *Danielle Walker's Against All Grain*	641.5
Waters, Alice. *The Art of Simple Food*	641.5
Williams, Odette. ★*Simple Pasta*	641.822
Zanini De Vita, Oretta. *Encyclopedia of Pasta*	641.822

FOOD WRITING — COOKING AND COOKBOOKS — METHODS

Acheson, Hugh. *The Chef and the Slow Cooker*	641.5
Adams, Jocelyn Delk. *Grandbaby Cakes*	641.86
Anderson, Pam. *How to Cook Without a Book*	641.5
Arefi, Yossy. *Snacking Cakes*	641.86
Barrow, Cathy. *Bagels, Schmears, and a Nice Piece of Fish*	641.81
Barrow, Cathy. ★*Pie Squared*	641.86
Bastianich, Lidia. ★*Lidia's a Pot, a Pan, and a Bowl*	641.82
Bayless, Rick. ★*More Mexican Everyday*	641.5972
Behan, Ren. ★*The Sweet Polish Kitchen*	641.594
Beranbaum, Rose Levy. ★*The Cookie Bible*	641.86
Beranbaum, Rose Levy. ★*Rose's Baking Basics*	641.81
Beranbaum, Rose Levy. *Rose's Ice Cream Bliss*	641.86
Berg, Meliz. *Dinner Tonight*	641.595
Bittman, Mark. ★*Bittman Bread*	641.81
Bittman, Mark. ★*Dinner for Everyone*	641.5
Bittman, Mark. ★*How to Bake Everything*	641.81
Bittman, Mark. *How to Cook Everything Fast*	641.5
Bittman, Mark. ★*How to Cook Everything*	641.5
Bittman, Mark. *How to Cook Everything*	641.5
Bittman, Mark. ★*How to Grill Everything*	641.7
Bittman, Mark. *Mark Bittman's Kitchen Matrix*	641.5
Black, Sarah. *One Dough, Ten Breads*	641.81
Brennan, Kathy. *Keepers*	641.5973
Britton, Sarah. *Naturally Nourished*	641.5
Brown, Leanne. ★*Good and Cheap*	641.5
Byrn, Anne. ★*American Cookie*	641.86
Byrn, Anne. *A New Take on Cake*	641.86
Byrn, Anne. *Skillet Love*	641.7
Cayne, Alison. *The Haven's Kitchen Cooking School*	641.5
Chang, Joanne. *Pastry Love*	641.86
Cho, Kristina. *Mooncakes + Milk Bread*	641.595
Christensen, Ashley. *It's Always Freezer Season*	641.5
Clark, Melissa. *Comfort in an Instant*	641.5
Clark, Melissa. ★*Dinner in an Instant*	641.5

PUBLIC LIBRARY CORE COLLECTION: NONFICTION
Twentieth Edition

Clark, Melissa. *Dinner in French*	641.594	
Clark, Melissa. ★*Dinner in One*	641.82	
Clark, Melissa. *Dinner*	641.5	
Clark, Melissa. *Kid in the Kitchen*	641.5	
Comerford, Hope. *Fix-It and Forget-It Healthy 5-Ingredient Cookbook*	641.5	
Conner, Polly. ★*From Freezer to Cooker*	641.6	
Conners, Rachel. *Bakerita*	641.81	
Coscarelli, Chloe. *Chloe Flavor*	641.5	
Day, Cheryl. *Back in the Day Bakery, Made with Love*	641.81	
Day, Cheryl. *Cheryl Day's Treasury of Southern Baking*	641.81	
DiGregorio, Sarah. *Adventures in Slow Cooking*	641.5	
Disbrowe, Paula. *Thank You for Smoking*	641.5	
Dodge, Abigail Johnson. *Sheet Cake*	641.86	
Drummond, Ree. ★*The Pioneer Woman Cooks*	641.5	
El-Waylly, Sohla. ★*Start Here*	641.3	
Emberling, Amy. *Zingerman's Bakehouse*	641.81	
Falk, Daina. *The Hungry Fan's Game Day Cookbook*	641.5973	
Forkish, Ken. *Evolutions in Bread*	664	
Forkish, Ken. *Flour Water Salt Yeast*	641.81	
Francois, Zoe. *Holiday and Celebration Bread in Five Minutes a Day*	641.81	
Francois, Zoe. *Zoe Bakes Cakes*	641.86	
Franklin, Aaron. *Franklin Barbecue*	641.7	
Franklin, Aaron. *Franklin Steak*	641.6	
Fuentes, Laura. *The Best Homemade Kids' Snacks on the Planet*	641.5	
Garten, Ina. ★*Barefoot Contessa, How Easy Is That?*	641.5	
Garten, Ina. ★*Cook Like a Pro*	641.5	
Garten, Ina. ★*Go-To Dinners*	641.5	
Garten, Ina. ★*Make It Ahead*	641.5	
Goldman, Duff. *Duff Bakes*	641.81	
Goldstein, Joyce Esersky, author. *Jam Session*	641.85	
Goldwyn, Meathead. ★*Meathead*	641.7	
Good, Phyllis Pellman. *Fix-It and Forget-It New Cookbook*	641.5	
Greenspan, Dorie. *Baking Chez Moi*	641.86	
Greenspan, Dorie. ★*Baking with Dorie*	641.81	
Greenspan, Dorie. *Baking with Julia*	641.8	
Greenspan, Dorie. *Baking*	641.8	
Greenspan, Dorie. ★*Dorie's Cookies*	641.86	
Greenspan, Eric. *The Great Grilled Cheese Book*	641.6	
Guy, Jerrelle. *Black Girl Baking*	641.59	
Hamilton, Gabrielle. *Prune*	641.3	
Hartnett, Angela. *The Weekend Cook*	641.5	
Hartwig, Melissa. *The Whole30 Fast & Easy*	641.5	
Hartwig, Melissa. *The Whole30 Slow Cooker*	641.5	
Hayden, Georgina. *Greekish*	641.594	
Hazan, Jack. *Mind Over Batter*	641.81	
Henry, Diana. *From the Oven to the Table*	641.82	
Heuck, Lidey. ★*Cooking in Real Life*	641.5	
Hoffman, Brian Hart. ★*Bake from Scratch; Volume Two*	641.81	
Hollis, B. Dylan. ★*Baking Yesteryear*	641.81	
Hollywood, Paul. ★*Bake*	641.81	
Homolka, Gina. *Skinnytaste Fast and Slow*	641.5	
Homolka, Gina. *Skinnytaste One & Done*	641.5	
Hunt, Lindsay Maitland. *Healthyish*	641.5	
Hussain, Nadiya. ★*Nadiya Bakes*	641.81	
Iyer, Raghavan. *Indian Cooking Unfolded*	641.595	
Jade, Holly. *The Essential Book of Vegan Bakes*	641.5	
Jaffrey, Madhur. ★*Madhur Jaffrey's Instantly Indian Cookbook*	641.595	
Kane, Cyndi. *Save-It-Forward Suppers*	641.5	
Kanell, John. *Preppy Kitchen*	641.5	
Kartes, Danielle. *Butter, Flour, Sugar, Joy*	641.86	
Keller, Thomas. *Bouchon Bakery*	641.594	
Kieffer, Sarah. *100 Morning Treats*	641.81	
Kieffer, Sarah. ★*Baking for the Holidays*	641.81	
Kim, Bill. *Korean BBQ*	641.595	
Kimball, Christopher. *Christopher Kimball's Milk Street*	641.5	
Kimball, Christopher. *Milk Street*	641.5	
Kimball, Christopher. *Milk Street*	641.7	
Klein, Dini. *Prep + Rally*	641.5	
Krieger, Ellie. *You Have It Made!*	641.5	
Kulaga, Agatha. *Ovenly*	641.81	
Lane, Christina. *Dessert for Two*	641.86	
Laperruque, Emma. *Food52 Big Little Recipes*	641.5	
Larsen, Jeffrey. ★*Gluten-Free Baking at Home*	641.5	
Lawson, Nigella. *At My Table*	641.59	
Leake, Lisa. *100 Days of Real Food on a Budget*	641.5	
Lee, Lara. *A Splash of Soy*	641.595	
Lloyd, Bobbie. *The Magnolia Bakery Handbook*	641.86	
Lopez-Alt, J. Kenji. ★*The Wok*	641.595	
Ludwinski, Lisa. *Sister Pie*	641.86
Martin, Pat. *Life of Fire*	641.5
Massov, Olga. ★*Hot Sheet*	641.82
McDermott, Kate. ★*Art of the Pie*	641.86
McDowell, Erin Jeanne. *The Fearless Baker*	641.81
McKoy, Bri. *The Cook's Book*	641.3
Meehan, Peter. *Lucky Peach Presents 101 Easy Asian Recipes*	641.595
Miglore, Kristen. *Food52 Genius Desserts*	641.86
Miglore, Kristen. ★*Food52 Simply Genius*	641.5
Moore, Matt. *Serial Griller*	641.7
Morimoto, Masaharu. *Mastering the Art of Japanese Home Cooking*	641.595
Moulton, Sara. *Sara Moulton's Home Cooking 101*	641.5973
Mullins, Brittany. *Mostly Veggies*	641.5
Music, Carla Lalli. *That Sounds so Good*	641.5
Music, Carla Lalli. *Where Cooking Begins*	641.5
Nederlanden, Elisabet der. ★*Holiday Cookies*	641.86
Nelson, Candace. *The Sprinkles Baking Book*	641.81
Nelson, Kim. *Daisy Cakes Bakes*	641.86
Nguyen, Andrea Quynhgiao. ★*Vietnamese Food Any Day*	641.595
Ottolenghi, Yotam. *Ottolenghi Simple*	641.59
Ottolenghi, Yotam. *Sweet*	641.86
Oz, Daphne. *The Happy Cook*	641.5
Paltrow, Gwyneth. *It's All Easy*	641.5
Pansino, Rosanna. *Baking All Year Round*	641.86
Pauline, Kathryn. ★*Piecemeal*	641.5
Pepin, Jacques. *Essential Pepin*	641.594
Pepin, Jacques. ★*Jacques Pepin*	641.5
Pepin, Jacques. ★*Jacques Pépin Cooking My Way*	641.5
Perry Lang, Adam. *Serious Barbecue*	641.7
Perry, Dawn. *Ready, Set, Cook*	641.5
Peters, Meike. *Noon*	641.5
Pleasant, Barbara. *Homegrown Pantry*	635
Poliafito, Renato. ★*Dolci!*	641.81
Purviance, Jamie. *Weber's Greatest Hits*	641.5
Purviance, Jamie. *Weber's Ultimate Grilling*	641.5
Raichlen, Steven. *The Brisket Chronicles*	641.6
Ramsay, Gordon. ★*Quick and Delicious*	641.5
Rapoport, Adam. *The Grilling Book*	641.7
Redzepi, Rene. *The Noma Guide to Fermentation*	664
Roberts, Julius. *The Farm Table*	641.594
Rodriguez, Ashley. *Rooted Kitchen*	641.5
Rodriguez, Jessamyn Waldman. *The Hot Bread Kitchen Cookbook*	641.59
Roman, Alison. ★*Nothing Fancy*	642
Roman, Alison. *Sweet Enough*	641.86
Rosso, Julee. *The New Basics Cookbook*	641.5
Rosso, Julee. *The Silver Palate Cookbook*	641.5
Ruhlman, Michael. *Ratio*	641.5
Saffitz, Claire. ★*What's for Dessert*	641.86
Saltz, Joanna. *Delish*	641.5
Scott, Rodney. ★*Rodney Scott's World of BBQ*	641.7
Seneviratne, Samantha. *Bake Smart*	641.81
Sever, Shauna. ★*Midwest Made*	641.5977
Sheehan, Jessie. ★*Snackable Bakes*	641.7
Shumski, Daniel. *How to Instant Pot*	641.5
Sifton, Sam. ★*The New York Times Cooking No-Recipe Recipes*	641.5
Silverton, Nancy. *The Cookie That Changed My Life*	641.81
Snodgrass, Alex. ★*The Defined Dish*	641.5
Snodgrass, Alex. *Dinner Tonight*	641.5
Snyder, Sabrina. *Dinner Then Dessert*	641.5
Stewart, Martha. ★*Martha Stewart's Baking Handbook*	641.8
Stewart, Martha. *Martha Stewart's Cooking School*	641.5
Symon, Michael. *Michael Symon's Playing with Fire*	641.7
Tam, Michelle. *Ready or Not!*	641.5
Tandoh, Ruby. ★*Cook as You Are*	641.59
Teigen, Chrissy. *Cravings*	641.5
Tosi, Christina. *All About Cake*	641.86
Tosi, Christina. *All About Cookies*	641.86
Turshen, Julia. *Small Victories*	641.5
Villasuso, Susana. *Sobremesa*	641.5972
Wade, Greg. ★*Bread Head*	664
Weil, Andrew. *Fast Food, Good Food*	641.3
Weinstein, Bruce. *The Great Big Pressure Cooker Book*	641.5
Weinstein, Bruce. *The Kitchen Shortcut Bible*	641.555
Weiss, Luisa. *Classic German Baking*	641.594
Wells, Patricia. *My Master Recipes*	641.5
West, Kevin. *Saving the Season*	641.4
Williams, Odette. *Simple Cake*	641.86
Workman, Katie. *The Mom 100 Cookbook*	641.5

AUTHOR, TITLE, SERIES AND SUBJECT INDEX

Wright, Caroline. *Cake Magic!*	641.86

FOOD WRITING — COOKING AND COOKBOOKS — NARRATIVE COOKBOOKS

Adarme, Adrianna. *The Year of Cozy*	641.3
Amano, Hugh. *Let's Make Dumplings!*	741.5
Angelou, Maya. *Great Food, All Day Long*	641.5973
Angelou, Maya. *Hallelujah! the Welcome Table*	641.5973
Ayubi, Durkhanai. *Parwana*	641.595
Bitsoie, Freddie. *New Native Kitchen*	641.59
Bourdain, Anthony. ★*Appetites*	641.5
Cailan, Alvin. *Amboy*	641.595
Diaz, Von. ★*Islas*	641.59
Dusoulier, Clotilde. *Tasting Paris*	641.594
Forkish, Ken. ★*Let's Make Bread!*	741.5
Gardner, Lindsay. *Why We Cook*	641.5
Gerson, Fany. *Mexican Ice Cream*	641.86
Gray, Jon. *Ghetto Gastro Black Power Kitchen*	641.5
Gunst, Kathy. *Rage Baking*	641.86
Hassan, Hawa. *In Bibi's Kitchen*	641.596
Howard, Vivian. *Deep Run Roots*	641.5975
Hussain, Nadiya. ★*Nadiya's Everyday Baking*	641.5
Kattan, Fadi. ★*Bethlehem*	641.59
Khan, Yasmin. *Ripe Figs*	641.595
King, Niloufer Ichaporia. *My Bombay Kitchen*	641.595
Lawson, Nigella. ★*Cook, Eat, Repeat*	641.5
Lebovitz, David. *My Paris Kitchen*	641.594
Lewis, Edna. *In Pursuit of Flavor*	641.5975
Lopez-Alt, J. Kenji. *The Food Lab*	664
Nathan, Joan. *King Solomon's Table*	641.5
Nathan, Joan. *My Life in Recipes*	641.5
Nosrat, Samin. ★*Salt, Fat, Acid, Heat*	641.5
Nunn, Emily. *The Comfort Food Diaries*	641.5973
Pepin, Jacques. *Art of the Chicken*	641.665
Pepin, Jacques. ★*Jacques Pepin*	641.594
Raiford, Matthew. *Bress 'N' Nyam*	641.59
Ray, Rachael. ★*This Must Be the Place*	641.5
Reichl, Ruth. *My Kitchen Year*	641.5
Ricanati, Elizabeth. *Braided*	B
Risbridger, Ella. *The Year of Miracles*	641.5
Roden, Claudia. *Arabesque*	641.59
Samuelsson, Marcus. ★*The Rise*	641.59
Solomonov, Michael. *Israeli Soul*	641.595
Solomonov, Michael. *Zahav*	641.595
Teigen, Chrissy. *Cravings*	641.5
Teigen, Pepper (Vilailuck). *The Pepper Thai Cookbook*	641.595
Tipton-Martin, Toni. *The Jemima Code*	641.59
Tipton-Martin, Toni. ★*Jubilee*	641.59
Turshen, Julia. *Feed the Resistance*	641.5
Twitty, Michael. ★*Koshersoul*	641.5
Vasquez, Karla Tatiana. ★*The Salvisoul Cookbook*	641.598
Wang, Jason. *XI'an Famous Foods*	641.595
Wilkinson, Crystal. *Praisesong for the Kitchen Ghosts*	641.5975

FOOD WRITING — COOKING AND COOKBOOKS — REFERENCE

Bastianich, Lidia. *Lidia's Mastering the Art of Italian Cuisine*	641.594
Bracken, Peg. *The I Hate to Cook Book*	641.5
Child, Julia. ★*The Way to Cook*	641.5
Diaz, Von. ★*Islas*	641.59
Goldstein, Joyce Esersky, author. *Jam Session*	641.85
Guarnaschelli, Alex. *The Home Cook*	641.5973
Hesser, Amanda. ★*The Essential New York Times Cook Book*	641.5
Kimball, Christopher. ★*Milk Street 365*	641.5
Lakshmi, Padma. *The Encyclopedia of Spices and Herbs*	641.3
Lloyd, Bobbie. *The Magnolia Bakery Handbook*	641.86
McKoy, Bri. *The Cook's Book*	641.3
Page, Karen. *The Flavor Bible*	641.5
Pepin, Jacques. ★*Jacques Pepin*	641.5
Perry, Dawn. *Ready, Set, Cook*	641.5
Rosso, Julee. *The New Basics Cookbook*	641.5
Segnit, Niki. ★*The Flavor Thesaurus*	641.5

FOOD WRITING — COOKING AND COOKBOOKS — REGIONAL

Adams, Jocelyn Delk. *Everyday Grand*	641.5975
Adams, Jocelyn Delk. *Grandbaby Cakes*	641.86
Admony, Einat. *Shuk*	641.595
Alikhani, Nasim. *Sofreh*	641.595
Allibhoy, Omar. *Spanish Made Simple*	641.594
Andrews, Colman. *The Country Cooking of Ireland*	641.594
Apfelbaum, Chanie. ★*Totally Kosher*	641.5
Assil, Reem. *Arabiyya*	641.595

Ayubi, Durkhanai. *Parwana*	641.595
Bastianich, Lidia. *Felidia*	641.594
Bastianich, Lidia. *Lidia Cooks from the Heart of Italy*	641.594
Bastianich, Lidia. ★*Lidia's a Pot, a Pan, and a Bowl*	641.82
Bastianich, Lidia. *Lidia's Commonsense Italian Cooking*	641.594
Bastianich, Lidia. *Lidia's Family Table*	641.594
Bastianich, Lidia. *Lidia's Favorite Recipes*	641.594
Bastianich, Lidia. ★*Lidia's from Our Family Table to Yours*	641.594
Bastianich, Lidia. *Lidia's Mastering the Art of Italian Cuisine*	641.594
Bastianich, Lidia. *Lidia's*	641.594
Batali, Mario. *Mario Batali Big American Cookbook*	641.5973
Bayless, Rick. *Authentic Mexican*	641.5972
Bayless, Rick. ★*Fiesta at Rick's*	641.5972
Bayless, Rick. *Mexican Everyday*	641.5972
Bayless, Rick. ★*More Mexican Everyday*	641.5972
Bayless, Rick. *Rick Bayless Mexico One Plate at a Time*	641.5972
Behan, Ren. ★*The Sweet Polish Kitchen*	641.594
Berg, Meliz. *Dinner Tonight*	641.595
Berry, Mary. *Cooking with Mary Berry*	641.5
Bianco, Chris. *Bianco*	641.5
Bishara, Rawia. *Olives, Lemons & Za'atar*	641.59
Bjork, Katrin. *From the North*	641.594
Bowien, Danny. *Mission Vegan*	641.5
Brock, Sean. *South*	641.5975
Brown, Kardea. *The Way Home*	641.5975
Byrn, Anne. ★*American Cake*	641.86
Camara, Gabriela. *My Mexico City Kitchen*	641.5972
Carle-Sanders, Theresa. *Outlander Kitchen*	641.5
Casares, Sylvia. *The Enchilada Queen Cookbook*	641.5926872073
Centeno, Josef. *Ama*	641.5979
Che, Hannah. ★*The Vegan Chinese Kitchen*	641.5
Child, Julia. *Julia and Jacques Cooking at Home*	641.594
Child, Julia. ★*Mastering the Art of French Cooking*	641.594
Cho, Kristina. *Mooncakes + Milk Bread*	641.595
Chou, Hsiao-Ching. *Chinese Soul Food*	641.595
Clark, Melissa. *Dinner in French*	641.594
Clark, Melissa. *Dinner*	641.5
Cohen, Jake. *Jew-Ish*	641.5
Danford, Natalie. *How to Eataly*	641.594
Day, Cheryl. *Back in the Day Bakery, Made with Love*	641.81
De Laurentiis, Giada. ★*Giada's Italy*	641.594
De Laurentiis, Giada. *Giada's Kitchen*	641.594
Diaz, Von. ★*Islas*	641.59
Disbrowe, Paula. *Thank You for Smoking*	641.5
Dissen, William Stark. *Thoughtful Cooking*	641.5975
Dunlop, Fuchsia. *The Food of Sichuan*	641.595
Eckhardt, Robyn. *Istanbul & Beyond*	641.595
Feinberg, Andrew. *Franny's*	641.594
Ferguson, Jesse Tyler. ★*Food Between Friends*	641.5973
Fox, Jeremy. *On Vegetables*	641.6
Frank, Lois Ellen. *Seed to Plate, Soil to Sky*	641.5
Franklin, Aaron. *Franklin Barbecue*	641.7
Franklin, Aaron. *Franklin Steak*	641.6
Gaines, Joanna. ★*Magnolia Table*	641.5975
Garten, Ina. *Barefoot in Paris*	641.594
Garten, Ina. *Cooking for Jeffrey*	641.5
Gaw, Frankie. *First Generation*	641.595
Gerson, Fany. *Mexican Ice Cream*	641.86
Gerson, Fany. *My Sweet Mexico*	641.5972
Gill, Sasha. *East Meets Vegan*	641.5
Greenspan, Dorie. *Around My French Table*	641.594
Greenspan, Dorie. *Baking Chez Moi*	641.86
Guetta, Benedetta Jasmine. *Cooking Alla Giudia*	641.5
Gutierrez, Sandra A. *Latinísimo*	641.598
Hage, Salma. ★*The Levantine Vegetarian*	641.595
Hall, Carla. *Carla Hall's Soul Food*	641.5975
Hall, Carla. *Carla's Comfort Foods*	641.59
Hamilton, Gabrielle. *Prune*	641.3
Hassan, Hawa. *In Bibi's Kitchen*	641.596
Hayden, Georgina. *Greekish*	641.594
Hayden, Georgina. *Nistisima*	641.5
Hazan, Marcella. ★*Essentials of Classic Italian Cooking*	641.594
Helou, Anissa. *Feast*	641.595
Hereford, Mason. *Turkey and the Wolf*	641.5976
Hernandez, Eddie. *Turnip Greens & Tortillas*	641.5972
Hong, Deuki. *Koreatown*	641.595
Iyer, Raghavan. *Indian Cooking Unfolded*	641.595
Jaffrey, Madhur. ★*Madhur Jaffrey's Instantly Indian Cookbook*	641.595

PUBLIC LIBRARY CORE COLLECTION: NONFICTION
Twentieth Edition

Jaffrey, Madhur. *Vegetarian India* — 641.595
Jinich, Pati. *Mexican Today* — 641.5972
Jinich, Pati. ★*Treasures of the Mexican Table* — 641.5972
Johnson, J. J. *Between Harlem and Heaven* — 641.59
Joo, Judy. *Korean Food Made Simple* — 641.595
Kahate, Ruta. *6 Spices 60 Dishes* — 641.595
Kang, Mingoo. *Jang* — 641.595
Karadsheh, Suzy. ★*The Mediterranean Dish* — 641.59
Keller, Thomas. *The French Laundry Cookbook* — 641.5
Khan, Asma. *Ammu* — 641.595
Kim, Bill. *Korean BBQ* — 641.595
Kim, Eric. ★*Korean American* — 641.595
Kim, Hooni. *My Korea* — 641.595
Kimball, Christopher. *Milk Street* — 641.5
Kimball, Christopher. *Tuesday Nights Mediterranean* — 641.59
Kinch, David. *At Home in the Kitchen* — 641.5973
King, Maren Ellingboe. *Fresh Midwest* — 641.5977
Klopotenko, Yevhen. ★*The Authentic Ukrainian Kitchen* — 641.594
Kochilas, Diane. *The Ikaria Way* — 641.5
Koenig, Leah. *Portico* — 641.5
Korkosz, Michal. *Fresh from Poland* — 641.594
Krishna, Priya. ★*Indian-ish* — 641.595
Kysar, Alana. *Aloha Kitchen* — 641.59969
Ladner, Mark. *The Del Posto Cookbook* — 641.594
Lambert, Miranda. *Y'all Eat Yet?* — 641.5976
Langholtz, Gabrielle. *America* — 641.5973
Le, Mike. *That Noodle Life* — 641.82
Lee Molinaro, Joanne. ★*The Korean Vegan Cookbook* — 641.595
Lee, Lara. *A Splash of Soy* — 641.595
Leung, Bill. ★*The Woks of Life* — 641.7
Lightner, Jill. *Cooking from Scratch* — 641.5
Lukas, Albert. ★*Sweet Home Cafe Cookbook* — 641.59
Maangchi. *Maangchi's Real Korean Cooking* — 641.595
Maisonet, Illyanna. ★*Diasporican* — 641.597295
Martinez, Rick. ★*Mi Cocina* — 641.5972
Massih, Edy. ★*Keep It Zesty* — 641.595
McBride, Martina. *Martina's Kitchen Mix* — 641.5973
Meehan, Peter. *Lucky Peach Presents 101 Easy Asian Recipes* — 641.595
Mitchell, Andie. *Eating in the Middle* — 641.3
Morimoto, Masaharu. *Mastering the Art of Japanese Home Cooking* — 641.595
Munno, Nadia Caterina. *The Pasta Queen* — 641.82
Murad, Noor. ★*Ottolenghi Test Kitchen* — 641.3
Murad, Noor. *Ottolenghi Test Kitchen* — 641.5
Nguyen, Andrea Quynhgiao. *Ever-Green Vietnamese* — 641.595
Nguyen, Andrea Quynhgiao. *The Pho Cookbook* — 641.595
Nguyen, Andrea Quynhgiao. ★*Vietnamese Food Any Day* — 641.595
Nolen, Jeremy. *New German Cooking* — 641.594
Noyes, Brian. *The Red Truck Bakery Farmhouse Cookbook* — 641.5973
Orkin, Ivan. *The Gaijin Cookbook* — 641.595
Ottolenghi, Yotam. ★*Jerusalem* — 641.5
Ottolenghi, Yotam. *Ottolenghi Simple* — 641.59
Ottolenghi, Yotam. *Ottolenghi* — 641.59
Parks, Stella. ★*Bravetart* — 641.86
Parla, Katie. *Tasting Rome* — 641.59
Pashman, Dan. *Anything's Pastable* — 641.82
Patel, Palak. *Food Is Love* — 641.595
Pelaez, Ana Sofia. *The Cuban Table* — 641.597291
Pelosi, Dan. *Let's Eat* — 641.5
Pepin, Jacques. *Essential Pepin* — 641.594
Peppler, Rebekah. *Le Sud* — 641.594
Perelman, Deb. ★*Smitten Kitchen Every Day* — 641.5
Pfeiffer, Jacquy. *The Art of French Pastry* — 641.86
Pittman, Ann Taylor. *The Global Pantry Cookbook* — 641.59
Poliafito, Renato. ★*Dolci!* — 641.81
Ponseca, Nicole. *I Am a Filipino and This Is How We Cook* — 641.595
Presilla, Maricel E. *Gran Cocina Latina* — 641.5972
Raines, Abigail Sotto. *Rice. Noodles. Yum.* — 641.595
Ray, Rachael. *Everyone Is Italian on Sunday* — 641.594
Reinhart, Peter. *Perfect Pan Pizza* — 641.82
Rettke, Amanda. *Homestead Recipes* — 641.5977
Richards, Todd. *Soul* — 641.59296073
Roberts, Julius. *The Farm Table* — 641.594
Roddy, Rachel. ★*An A-Z of Pasta* — 641.82
Roden, Claudia. ★*The Book of Jewish Food* — 641.5
Rodriguez, Jessamyn Waldman. *The Hot Bread Kitchen Cookbook* — 641.59
Rombauer, Irma S. ★*Joy of Cooking* — 641.5973
Rosenthal, Phil. ★*Somebody Feed Phil the Book* — 641.59
Sahadi Whelan, Christine. *Flavors of the Sun* — 641.595
Sakai, Sonoko. *Japanese Home Cooking* — 641.595
Samuelsson, Marcus. *Marcus off Duty* — 641.5
Samuelsson, Marcus. *The Red Rooster Cookbook* — 641.5974
Sarna, Shannon. *Modern Jewish Comfort Food* — 641.5
Scarpaleggia, Giulia. ★*Cucina Povera* — 641.594
Scott, Chris. *Homage* — 641.5
Scott, Rodney. ★*Rodney Scott's World of BBQ* — 641.7
Serpico, Peter. *Learning Korean* — 641.595
Setareh, Saghar. *Pomegranates & Artichokes* — 641.5
Sever, Shauna. ★*Midwest Made* — 641.5977
Shepherd, Chris. *Cook Like a Local* — 641.59
Sherman, Sean. ★*The Sioux Chef's Indigenous Kitchen* — 641.59
Sifton, Sam. *Thanksgiving* — 641.5
Simeon, Sheldon. *Cook Real Hawai?i* — 641.59969
Siva, Micah. *Nosh* — 641.5
Smalls, Alexander. *Meals, Music, and Muses* — 641.59
Sodha, Meera. *East* — 641.595
Sodha, Meera. *Made in India* — 641.595
Stone, Robyn. *Add a Pinch Cookbook* — 641.5975
Sussman, Adeena. *Sababa* — 641.5
Sussman, Adeena. ★*Shabbat* — 641.5
Tamimi, Sami. *Falastin* — 641.595
Taylor, Nicole A. ★*Watermelon & Red Birds* — 641.5
Teigen, Pepper (Vilailuck). *The Pepper Thai Cookbook* — 641.595
Terry, Bryant. *Afro-Vegan* — 641.59
Thompson, Jennifer Trainer. *Fresh Fish* — 641.3
Thorisson, Mimi. *A Kitchen in France* — 641.594
Tila, Jet. *101 Asian Dishes You Need to Cook Before You Die* — 641.595
Trejo, Danny. *Trejo's Tacos* — 641.5979
Turshen, Julia. *Feed the Resistance* — 641.5
Umah-Shaylor, Lerato. *Africana* — 641.596
Velasquez, Mariana. *Colombiana* — 641.59861
Vetri, Marc. *Mastering Pizza* — 641.82
Vicenzino, Cettina. *The Sicily Cookbook* — 641.59458
Villasuso, Susana. *Sobremesa* — 641.5972
Wang, Jason. *XI'an Famous Foods* — 641.595
Wangler, Justin. *Season* — 641.5979
Weiss, Luisa. *Classic German Baking* — 641.594
White, Marco Pierre. *White Heat* — 641.594
Williams, Odette. ★*Simple Pasta* — 641.822
Wilson, Melba. ★*Melba's American Comfort* — 641.5973
Witte, Christina De. ★*Noodles, Rice, and Everything Spice* — 641.595
Woo, Ronnie. *Did You Eat Yet?* — 641.595
Workman, Katie. *Dinner Solved!* — 641.5
Yeh, Molly. *Home Is Where the Eggs Are* — 641.5

FOOD WRITING — COOKING AND COOKBOOKS — VEGETARIAN AND VEGAN

Andres, Jose. *Vegetables Unleashed* — 641.5
Anthony, Michael. *V Is for Vegetables* — 641.6
Aron, Jules. *Vegan Cheese* — 641.5
Ben-Ishay, Melissa. *Come Hungry* — 641.5
Berens, Abra. *Grist* — 641.6
Berens, Abra. *Ruffage* — 641.5
Bhogal, Ravinder. *Comfort and Joy* — 641.5
Bittman, Mark. ★*How to Cook Everything Vegetarian* — 641.5
Bittman, Mark. *The VB6 Cookbook* — 641.5
Bittman, Mark. *VB6* — 641.5
Bowien, Danny. *Mission Vegan* — 641.5
Britton, Sarah. *Naturally Nourished* — 641.5
Che, Hannah. ★*The Vegan Chinese Kitchen* — 641.5
Claiborne, Jenne. ★*Sweet Potato Soul* — 641.5
Coscarelli, Chloe. *Chloe Flavor* — 641.5
Cristofano, Jana. *Eat Well, Be Well* — 641.5
Dada, Samah. *Dada Eats Love to Cook It* — 641.5
Fearnley-Whittingstall, Hugh. *River Cottage Veg* — 641.5
Firth, Henry. *Bosh!* — 641.5
Frank, Lois Ellen. *Seed to Plate, Soil to Sky* — 641.5
Gill, Sasha. *East Meets Vegan* — 641.5
Hage, Salma. ★*The Levantine Vegetarian* — 641.595
Hamshaw, Gena. *Food 52 Vegan* — 641.5
Hansen, Kim-Julie. *Best of Vegan* — 641.5
Hayden, Georgina. *Nistisima* — 641.5
Headley, Brooks. *Superiority Burger Cookbook* — 641.5
Jade, Holly. *The Essential Book of Vegan Bakes* — 641.5
Jaffrey, Madhur. *Madhur Jaffrey's World Vegetarian.* — 641.5
Jaffrey, Madhur. *Vegetarian India* — 641.595
Jones, Anna. *One* — 641.5
Katzen, Mollie. *The Heart of the Plate* — 641.5

AUTHOR, TITLE, SERIES AND SUBJECT INDEX

Katzen, Mollie. ★*The Moosewood Cookbook*	641.5
Kochilas, Diane. *The Ikaria Way*	641.5
Korkosz, Michal. *Fresh from Poland*	641.594
Lee Molinaro, Joanne. ★*The Korean Vegan Cookbook*	641.595
Lewis, John. *Badass Vegan*	641.5
Madison, Deborah. *In My Kitchen*	641.5
Madison, Deborah. *Vegetable Literacy*	641.6
Madison, Deborah. *Vegetarian Cooking for Everyone*	641.5
Mangini, Cara. *The Vegetable Butcher*	641.6
Mangini, Cara. ★*The Vegetable Eater*	641.6
McKinnon, Hetty. ★*Tenderheart*	641.5
Moskowitz, Isa Chandra. *The Superfun Times Vegan Holiday Cookbook*	651.56
Moskowitz, Isa Chandra. *Veganomicon*	641
Mullins, Brittany. *Mostly Veggies*	641.5
Nguyen, Andrea Quynhgiao. *Ever-Green Vietnamese*	641.595
Ottolenghi, Yotam. ★*Plenty More*	641.6
Ottolenghi, Yotam. *Plenty*	641.6
Patel, Palak. *Food Is Love*	641.595
Pierson, Joy. *Vegan Holiday Cooking from Candle Cafe*	641.5
Pulde, Alona. ★*The Forks Over Knives Plan*	641.5
Roll, Rich. *The Plantpower Way*	641.5
Rosen, Ilene. *Saladish*	641.83
Rosenstrach, Jenny. ★*The Weekday Vegetarians*	641.5
Sarno, Chad. *The Wicked Healthy Cookbook*	651.56
Schinner, Miyoko Nishimoto. *The Vegan Meat Cookbook*	641.5
Segnit, Niki. ★*The Flavor Thesaurus*	641.5
Selengut, Becky. ★*Misunderstood Vegetables*	641.6
Siva, Micah. *Nosh*	641.5
Sodha, Meera. *East*	641.595
Taylor, Kathryne. *Love Real Food*	641.5
Terry, Bryant. *Afro-Vegan*	641.59
Terry, Bryant. *Vegan Soul Kitchen*	641.5
Terry, Bryant. ★*Vegetable Kingdom*	641.5
Thomas, Anna. *Vegan Vegetarian Omnivore*	641.5
Thomas, Haile. *Living Lively*	641.5
Volger, Lukas. *Bowl*	641.81
Walch, Aubry. *The Herbivorous Butcher Cookbook*	641.5
Workman, Katie. *Dinner Solved!*	641.5

FOOD WRITING — FOOD AND CULTURE

Amano, Hugh. *Let's Make Dumplings!*	741.5
Anthony, Jason C. *Hoosh*	394.1
Bitsoie, Freddie. *New Native Kitchen*	641.59
Bourdain, Anthony. ★*World Travel*	641.59
Buford, Bill. ★*Dirt*	B
Cailan, Alvin. *Amboy*	641.595
Chandler, Adam. *Drive-Thru Dreams*	647.95
Cheever, Susan. *Drinking in America*	394.1
Collingham, E. M. *Curry*	394.1
Downie, David. *A Taste of Paris*	394.1
Dusoulier, Clotilde. *Tasting Paris*	641.594
Forkish, Ken. ★*Let's Make Bread!*	741.5
Gardner, Lindsay. *Why We Cook*	641.5
Gilbert, Elizabeth. *Eat, Pray, Love*	B
Goulding, Matt. *Grape, Olive, Pig*	394.1
Goulding, Matt. *Rice, Noodle, Fish*	394.1
Hassan, Hawa. *In Bibi's Kitchen*	641.596
Henaut, Stephane. *A Bite-Sized History of France*	394.1
Howard, Vivian. *Deep Run Roots*	641.5975
Hussain, Nadiya. ★*Nadiya's Everyday Baking*	641.5
Jacobs, Ryan McMahon. *The Truffle Underground*	381
Kattan, Fadi. ★*Bethlehem*	641.59
Khan, Yasmin. *Ripe Figs*	641.595
Khan, Yasmin. ★*Zaitoun*	641.595
Kingsley, Lisa. *Smithsonian American Table*	641.5
Lebovitz, David. *My Paris Kitchen*	641.594
Lee, Edward. *Buttermilk Graffiti*	641.59
Lohman, Sarah. ★*Endangered Eating*	641.5973
Martinez, Rick. ★*Mi Cocina*	641.5972
Miller, Klancy. ★*For the Culture*	641.59
Narayan, Shoba. *The Milk Lady of Bangalore*	390
Nezhukumatathil, Aimee. *Bite by Bite*	641.3
Raiford, Matthew. *Bress 'N' Nyam*	641.59
Samuelsson, Marcus. ★*The Rise*	641.59
Sen, Mayukh. *Taste Makers*	641.5092
Solomonov, Michael. *Israeli Soul*	641.595
Standage, Tom. *An Edible History of Humanity*	394.1
Stark, Lizzie. ★*Egg*	641.3
Stibbe, Nina. *An Almost Perfect Christmas*	394.2663
Tandoh, Ruby. ★*Eat Up*	641.3
Terry, Bryant. *Black Food*	394.1
Tipton-Martin, Toni. ★*Jubilee*	641.59
Tucci, Stanley. ★*Taste*	B
Twilley, Nicola. ★*Frostbite*	621
Twitty, Michael. ★*The Cooking Gene*	641.59
Twitty, Michael. ★*Koshersoul*	641.5
Vasquez, Karla Tatiana. ★*The Salvisoul Cookbook*	641.598
Vitale, Tom. *In the Weeds*	B
Von Bremzen, Anya. *National Dish*	641.3
Williams, Wyatt. *Springer Mountain*	394.1
Wilson, Bee. *The Way We Eat Now*	641.01
Wong, Cecily. ★*Gastro Obscura*	641.3

FOOD WRITING — GENERAL

Adler, Tamar. *An Everlasting Meal*	641.5
Albright, Mary Beth. ★*Eat & Flourish*	612.3
Bourdain, Anthony. *The Nasty Bits*	641.5092
Cheng, Eugenia. *How to Bake Pi*	510
Cowen, Tyler. *An Economist Gets Lunch*	394.1
Friedman, Andrew. *The Dish*	647.95
Garner, Dwight. *The Upstairs Delicatessen*	B
Harris, Jessica B. *High on the Hog*	641.59
Hewitt, Ben. ★*The Town That Food Saved*	338.1
McGee, Harold. ★*Nose Dive*	612.8
McGee, Harold. ★*On Food and Cooking*	641.5
Prud'homme, Alex. ★*Dinner with the President*	973
Rogers, Adam. *Proof*	663
Siegel, Matt. *The Secret History of Food*	641.3
Tower, Jeremiah. ★*Table Manners*	395.5

FOOD WRITING — HISTORY AND MICROHISTORY

Brenner, Joel Glenn. *The Emperors of Chocolate*	338.7
Byrn, Anne. ★*American Cake*	641.86
Byrn, Anne. ★*American Cookie*	641.86
Chandler, Adam. *Drive-Thru Dreams*	647.95
Collingham, E. M. *Curry*	394.1
Deetz, Kelley Fanto. *Bound to the Fire*	641.59
Ellis, Richard. *Tuna*	333.95
English, Camper. *Doctors and Distillers*	615.7
Fagan, Brian M. *Fishing*	338.3
Frank, Lois Ellen. *Seed to Plate, Soil to Sky*	641.5
Freeman, Andrea. ★*Ruin Their Crops on the Ground*	338.1
Henaut, Stephane. *A Bite-Sized History of France*	394.1
Kauffman, Jonathan. *Hippie Food*	394.1
Kingsley, Lisa. *Smithsonian American Table*	641.5
Kurlansky, Mark. *Cod*	333.95
Kurlansky, Mark. *Milk!*	637
Kurlansky, Mark. *Salt*	553.6
Miller, Max. ★*Tasting History*	641.509
O'Meara, Mallory. *Girly Drinks*	641.2
Rude, Emelyn. *Tastes Like Chicken*	338.1
Standage, Tom. *A History of the World in 6 Glasses*	394.1
Stark, Lizzie. ★*Egg*	641.3
Tipton-Martin, Toni. *The Jemima Code*	641.59
Tipton-Martin, Toni. ★*Jubilee*	641.59
Tipton-Martin, Toni. *Juke Joints, Jazz Clubs & Juice*	641.87
Twilley, Nicola. ★*Frostbite*	621
Twitty, Michael. ★*The Cooking Gene*	641.59
Walvin, James. *Sugar*	338.17361
Wilson, Bee. *The Way We Eat Now*	641.01
Wrangham, Richard W. *Catching Fire*	394.1

FOOD WRITING — INVESTIGATIONS

Ackerman-Leist, Philip. *Rebuilding the Foodshed*	338.1
Almond, Steve. ★*Candyfreak*	338.4
Barber, Dan. *The Third Plate*	641.3
Bittman, Mark. *A Bone to Pick*	338.10973
Elmore, Bartow J. *Seed Money*	338.7
Faruqi, Sonia. *Project Animal Farm*	338.1
Foer, Jonathan Safran. *Eating Animals*	641.3
Genoways, Ted. *The Chain*	338.7
Greenberg, Paul. *American Catch*	333.95
Greenberg, Paul. *Four Fish*	333.95
Hamilton, Lisa M. *Deeply Rooted*	338.10973
Jacobs, Ryan McMahon. *The Truffle Underground*	381
Kazdin, Cole. ★*What's Eating Us*	616.85
Knoedelseder, William. *Bitter Brew*	338.7
Lorr, Benjamin. *The Secret Life of Groceries*	381.4
McMillan, Tracie. *The American Way of Eating*	338.4

PUBLIC LIBRARY CORE COLLECTION: NONFICTION
Twentieth Edition

Moss, Michael. ★*Hooked*	613.2
Moss, Michael. *Salt, Sugar, Fat*	613.2
Olmsted, Larry. *Real Food/Fake Food*	641.3
Pollan, Michael. *Cooked*	641.5
Pollan, Michael. *The Omnivore's Dilemma*	394.1
Roach, Mary. *Gulp*	612.3
Saladino, Dan. *Eating to Extinction*	641.3
Schatzker, Mark. *The Dorito Effect*	641.3
Sorvino, Chloe. *Raw Deal*	338.1
Tulleken, Chris van. *Ultra-Processed People*	664
Waters, Alice. ★*We Are What We Eat*	641.01
Zuckerman, Jocelyn C. *Planet Palm*	633.8

FOOD WRITING — MEMOIRS AND BIOGRAPHIES

Ahdoot, Dan. *Undercooked*	647.95
Ali, Fatima. ★*Savor*	B
Bard, Elizabeth. *Lunch in Paris*	B
Bard, Elizabeth. *Picnic in Provence*	B
Bass, Rick. *The Traveling Feast*	B
Bastianich, Lidia. *My American Dream*	B
Bertch, Jane. *The French Ingredient*	B
Birdsall, John. *The Man Who Ate Too Much*	B
Bosker, Bianca. *Cork Dork*	641.2
Bourdain, Anthony. ★*Kitchen Confidential*	B
Bourdain, Anthony. *Medium Raw*	B
Bragg, Rick. ★*The Best Cook in the World*	641.5975
Buford, Bill. ★*Dirt*	B
Cecchi-Azzolina, Michael. *Your Table Is Ready*	647.95
Chang, David. ★*Eat a Peach*	641.5
Child, Julia. *My Life in France*	B
Chin, Curtis. *Everything I Learned, I Learned in a Chinese Restaurant*	B
Chisholm, Edward. *A Waiter in Paris*	B
Cho, Grace M. *Tastes Like War*	305.48
Fall, Jeremy. *Falling Upwards*	158.1
Fishman, Boris. *Savage Feast*	B
Gardner, Lindsay. *Why We Cook*	641.5
Hamilton, Gabrielle. *Blood, Bones, and Butter*	B
Hood, Ann. *Kitchen Yarns*	641.5
Huang, Eddie. *Fresh off the Boat*	B
James, Victoria. *Wine Girl*	B
Kingsolver, Barbara. ★*Animal, Vegetable, Miracle*	641
Locke, Tembi. ★*From Scratch*	B
Mayes, Frances. *See You in the Piazza*	914.5
Mayes, Frances. *Under the Tuscan Sun*	945
Miller, Klancy. ★*For the Culture*	641.59
Nathan, Joan. ★*My Life in Recipes*	641.5
Nezhukumatathil, Aimee. *Bite by Bite*	641.3
Onwuachi, Kwame. ★*Notes from a Young Black Chef*	641.59
Pepin, Jacques. *The Apprentice*	B
Pepin, Jacques. *Art of the Chicken*	641.665
Powell, Julie. *Julie and Julia*	641.5
Prud'homme, Alex. *The French Chef in America*	B
Reichl, Ruth. *Comfort Me with Apples*	B
Reichl, Ruth. *Garlic and Sapphires*	B
Reichl, Ruth. ★*Save Me the Plums*	B
Ripert, Eric. *32 Yolks*	B
Samuelsson, Marcus. *Yes, Chef*	B
Sanchez, Aaron. *Where I Come From*	641.5092
Sen, Mayukh. *Taste Makers*	641.5092
Sheehan, Jason. *Cooking Dirty*	B
Smith, Bren. *Eat Like a Fish*	338.3
Solomonov, Michael. *Zahav*	641.595
Teigen, Chrissy. *Cravings*	641.5
Tucci, Stanley. ★*Taste*	B
Waters, Alice. *Coming to My Senses*	B
Woolever, Laurie. *Bourdain*	B

FOOD WRITING — NON-ALCOHOLIC BEVERAGES

Clark, Taylor. *Starbucked*	338
Easto, Jessica. *How to Taste Coffee*	663
Ramirez, Elva. *Zero Proof*	641.87
Sedgewick, Augustine. *Coffeeland*	338.4
Standage, Tom. *A History of the World in 6 Glasses*	394.1
White, April. *Apples to Cider*	663
Food, Health, and Happiness. Winfrey, Oprah	641.5
Food52 Big Little Recipes. Laperruque, Emma	641.5
Food52 Genius Desserts. Miglore, Kristen	641.86
★*Food52 Genius Recipes*. Miglore, Kristen	641.5
★*Food52 Simply Genius*. Miglore, Kristen	641.5
Food52 Works [Series]. Miglore, Kristen	641.86

A *Fool's* Guide to Actual Happiness. Van Buren, Mark	294.3
Fooling Houdini. Stone, Alex	B
★*Foolproof*. van der Linden, Sander	302.3

FOOTBALL

Benedict, Jeff. *The Dynasty*	796.332
Benedict, Jeff. *The System*	796.332
Bissinger, H. G. ★*Friday Night Lights*	796.332
Bissinger, H. G. ★*The Mosquito Bowl*	796.332
Dawidoff, Nicholas. *Collision Low Crossers*	796.332
Dunnavant, Keith. *Montana*	B
Easterbrook, Gregg. ★*The King of Sports*	796.332
Eatman, Nicholas. *Friday, Saturday, Sunday in Texas*	796.332
Edmundson, Mark. *Why Football Matters*	B
Eisenberg, John. *The League*	796.332
Fainaru-Wada, Mark. *League of Denial*	617.1
Gaul, Gilbert M. *Billion-Dollar Ball*	796.332
Gwynne, S. C. *The Perfect Pass*	920
Horrigan, Joe. *NFL Century*	796.332
Jaworksi, Ron. *The Games That Changed the Game*	796.332
Laskas, Jeanne Marie. *Concussion*	617.5
Lewis, Michael. *The Blind Side*	B
Maraniss, David. ★*Path Lit by Lightning*	B
Myers, Gary. *Brady vs. Manning*	B
Myers, Gary. *The Catch*	796.332
O'Connor, Ian. *Belichick*	B
Oriard, Michael. *Brand NFL*	796.332
Parcells, Bill. *Parcells*	B
Pearlman, Jeff. *Boys Will Be Boys*	796.332
Pearlman, Jeff. *Football for a Buck*	796.332
Rice, Jerry. *America's Game*	796.332
Samaha, Albert. *Never Ran, Never Will*	920
Sando, Mike. *The Football 100*	796.332
Schwartzman, Nancy. *Roll Red Roll*	364.15
Spurrier, Steve. *Head Ball Coach*	B
Weinreb, Michael. *Season of Saturdays*	796.332
Young, Steve. *QB*	B
Yousse, Bower. *Freddie Steinmark*	796.332
Zimmerman, Paul. *Dr. Z*	B
The Football 100. Sando, Mike	796.332

FOOTBALL COACHES

Barra, Allen. ★*The Last Coach*	B
Benedict, Jeff. *The Dynasty*	796.332
Burke, Monte. *Saban*	796.332
Gwynne, S. C. *The Perfect Pass*	920
Harris, David. *The Genius*	B
O'Connor, Ian. *Belichick*	B
Ribowsky, Mark. *Shula*	B
Rice, Jerry. *America's Game*	796.332
Samaha, Albert. *Never Ran, Never Will*	920
Spurrier, Steve. *Head Ball Coach*	B

FOOTBALL COACHING

Barra, Allen. ★*The Last Coach*	B
Football for a Buck. Pearlman, Jeff	796.332

FOOTBALL HISTORY

Anderson, Lars. *Carlisle vs. Army*	796.332
Sando, Mike. *The Football 100*	796.332

FOOTBALL INJURIES

Fainaru-Wada, Mark. *League of Denial*	617.1
Laskas, Jeanne Marie. *Concussion*	617.5
The Football Man. Hopcraft, Arthur	796.334

FOOTBALL PLAYERS

Bennett, Michael. *Things That Make White People Uncomfortable*	305.896
Bissinger, H. G. ★*The Mosquito Bowl*	796.332
Cole, Jason. *Elway*	B
Crawford, Bill. ★*All American*	B
Dunnavant, Keith. *Montana*	B
Easterbrook, Gregg. ★*The King of Sports*	796.332
Eatman, Nicholas. *Friday, Saturday, Sunday in Texas*	796.332
Edmundson, Mark. *Why Football Matters*	B
Foles, Nick. *Believe It*	B
Jaworksi, Ron. *The Games That Changed the Game*	796.332
Lewis, Michael. *The Blind Side*	B
Maraniss, David. ★*Path Lit by Lightning*	B
Melvin, Leland. *Chasing Space*	B
Myers, Gary. *Brady vs. Manning*	B
Myers, Gary. *The Catch*	796.332
Namath, Joe Willie. ★*All the Way*	B
Pearlman, Jeff. *Gunslinger*	B

AUTHOR, TITLE, SERIES AND SUBJECT INDEX

Pearlman, Jeff. *The Last Folk Hero*	B
Pearlman, Jeff. *Sweetness*	B
Rice, Jerry. *America's Game*	796.332
Sando, Mike. *The Football 100*	796.332
Savage, Phil. *4th and Goal Every Day*	796.332
Young, Steve. *QB*	B

FOOTBALL TEAM OWNERS
Pearlman, Jeff. *Football for a Buck*	796.332

FOOTBALL TEAMS
Benedict, Jeff. *The Dynasty*	796.332
Bissinger, H. G. ★*Friday Night Lights*	796.332
Eatman, Nicholas. *Friday, Saturday, Sunday in Texas*	796.332
Harris, David. *The Genius*	B
O'Connor, Ian. *Belichick*	B
Pearlman, Jeff. *Boys Will Be Boys*	796.332
Rice, Jerry. *America's Game*	796.332
Samaha, Albert. *Never Ran, Never Will*	920
Wickersham, Seth. ★*It's Better to Be Feared*	796.332

Foote, Shelby
The Civil War	973.7
Stars in Their Courses	973.7

Footnotes in Gaza. Sacco, Joe	741.5
For Brown Girls with Sharp Edges and Tender Hearts. Mojica Rodriguez, Prisca Dorcas	305.48
For Cause and Comrades. McPherson, James M.	973.7
For Colored Girls Who Have Considered Politics. Brazile, Donna	328.73
For Goodness Sex. Vernacchio, Al	613.9071
For Joshua. Wagamese, Richard	B
For Liberty and Glory. Gaines, James R.	B
For Small Creatures Such as We. Sagan, Sasha	390.09
★*For The Culture.* Miller, Klancy	641.59
For The Glory. Hamilton, Duncan	B
For The Love of Music. Mauceri, John	781.1
★*For The Prevention of Cruelty.* Beers, Diane L.	179

FOR-PROFIT UNIVERSITIES AND COLLEGES
Cottom, Tressie McMillan. *Lower Ed*	378.73
Mettler, Suzanne. *Degrees of Inequality*	378.73

Forbes, Bruce David
Christmas	394.2663

Forbes, Nancy
Faraday, Maxwell, and the Electromagnetic Field	B

Forbes, Peter
Dazzled and Deceived	578.4

FORBES, R. B. (ROBERT BENNET), 1804-1889
Puleo, Stephen. *Voyage of Mercy*	363.8

FORCE
Bodanis, David. *Electric Universe*	537
The Force of Destiny. Duggan, Christopher	945

FORCED LABOR
Applebaum, Anne. ★*Gulag*	365
Berman, Sarah. *Don't Call It a Cult*	361.4
Blackmon, Douglas A. *Slavery by Another Name*	305.896
Dikotter, Frank. *Mao's Great Famine*	951.05
Ditmore, Melissa Hope. ★*Unbroken Chains*	306.74
Hochschild, Adam. *King Leopold's Ghost*	967.51
Humbert, Agnes. *Resistance*	B
Jaku, Eddie. ★*The Happiest Man on Earth*	B
Jang, Lucia. *Stars Between the Sun and Moon*	365.45092
Kars, Marjoleine. *Blood on the River*	306.3
Kimmerle, Erin H. *We Carry Their Bones*	365
Pang, Amelia. ★*Made in China*	331.11
Qu, Anna. *Made in China*	B
Siler, Julia Flynn. *The White Devil's Daughters*	306.3
Swarns, Rachel L. *The 272*	975.2
Zuckerman, Jocelyn C. *Planet Palm*	633.8

FORCED RELOCATIONS
Finkelstein, Daniel. *Two Roads Home*	920
Lowe, Keith. *Savage Continent*	940.55
Lustgarten, Abrahm. ★*On the Move*	363.7
McMurtry, Larry. *Crazy Horse*	B
Molnar, Petra. *The Walls Have Eyes*	363.28
Parkin, Simon. *The Island of Extraordinary Captives*	940.53
Russell, Jan Jarboe. *The Train to Crystal City*	940.53
Saldana, Stephanie. *What We Remember Will Be Saved*	362.7
Sanghera, Sathnam. *Empireworld*	909
Saunt, Claudio. *Unworthy Republic*	323.1197
Sedgwick, John. *Blood Moon*	975.004
Trebincevic, Kenan. *The Bosnia List*	B

Forces of Nature. Reser, Anna	509.2

Forche, Carolyn
Blue Hour	811
In the Lateness of the World	811
What You Have Heard Is True	B

★*Forcing The Spring.* Becker, Jo	346.79401

Ford, Ashley C.
★*Somebody's Daughter*	B

FORD, ASHLEY C.
Ford, Ashley C. ★*Somebody's Daughter*	B

FORD, BETTY, 1918-2011
McCubbin, Lisa. *Betty Ford*	B

Ford, Christine Blasey
One Way Back	B

Ford, Elizabeth
Sometimes Amazing Things Happen	B

FORD, ELIZABETH (ELIZABETH B.)
Ford, Elizabeth. *Sometimes Amazing Things Happen*	B

FORD, GERALD R., 1913-2006
Rumsfeld, Donald. *When the Center Held*	973.925092
Smith, Richard Norton. *An Ordinary Man*	B
Woodward, Bob. *Shadow*	973.92

FORD, HENRY, 1863-1947
Baime, A. J. ★*Go Like Hell*	796.7209
Brinkley, Douglas. *Wheels for the World*	B
Goldstone, Lawrence. *Drive!*	338.4
Watts, Steven. *The People's Tycoon*	B

FORD, JOHN, 1894-1973
Harris, Mark. ★*Five Came Back*	791.4302

Ford, Lacy K.
Deliver Us from Evil	973.7

Ford, Richard
Between Them	B

Ford, Richard T.
Rights Gone Wrong	342.7308

FORD, RICHARD, 1944-
Ford, Richard. *Between Them*	B

Ford, Tanisha C.
Dressed in Dreams	391
Our Secret Society	B

FORD, TANISHA C.
Fordham, Tanisha C. *Dressed in Dreams*	391

Fordham, Demetrius
★*If You're Bored with Your Camera Read This Book*	770.23

FORECASTING
Clark, Andy. *The Experience Machine*	153
Friedman, George. *Flashpoints*	940.56
Graham, Jorie. *To 2040*	811
Harari, Yuval N. ★*21 Lessons for the 21st Century*	909.82
Harari, Yuval N. *Homo Deus*	909.83
Law, Keith. *Smart Baseball*	796.357
Scales, Helen. *What the Wild Sea Can Be*	577.7
Schwartz, Samuel I. *No One at the Wheel*	629.2
Tegmark, Max. *Life 3.0*	006.301
Wallace-Wells, David. *The Uninhabitable Earth*	304.2
Weinersmith, Kelly. ★*A City on Mars*	629.4

FORECLOSURE
Dayen, David. *Chain of Title*	330.973
Elias, Stephen. *The Foreclosure Survival Guide, 9th Ed.*	346.7304
The Foreclosure Survival Guide, 9th Ed. Elias, Stephen	346.7304
Foreign Bodies. Schama, Simon	614.4

FOREIGN CORRESPONDENTS
Cohen, Deborah. *Last Call at the Hotel Imperial*	070.92
Engel, Richard. *And Then All Hell Broke Loose*	956.05
Hilsum, Lindsey. *In Extremis*	B
Mekhennet, Souad. *I Was Told to Come Alone*	363.3250956

FOREIGN INTERFERENCE IN ELECTIONS
Hennessey, Susan. *Unmaking the Presidency*	973.933
Petri, Alexandra. *Nothing Is Wrong and Here Is Why*	973.933
Rohde, David. *In Deep*	973.933
Toobin, Jeffrey. *True Crimes and Misdemeanors*	973.933

Foreman, Amanda
Georgiana, Duchess of Devonshire	B

FOREMAN, CARL
Frankel, Glenn. *High Noon*	791.43

Foreman, Tom
My Year of Running Dangerously	B

PUBLIC LIBRARY CORE COLLECTION: NONFICTION
Twentieth Edition

FOREMAN, TOM
   Foreman, Tom. *My Year of Running Dangerously* — B

FORENSIC ANTHROPOLOGISTS
   Kimmerle, Erin H. *We Carry Their Bones* — 365

FORENSIC ANTHROPOLOGY
   Bass, William M. *Death's Acre* — 614
   Hagerty, Alexa. ★*Still Life with Bones* — 599.9
   Herman, Eleanor. *The Royal Art of Poison* — 364.152
   Maples, William R. *Dead Men Do Tell Tales* — 614
   Norton, Laurah. *Lay Them to Rest* — 363.25
   Pattison, Kermit. *Fossil Men* — 569.9
   Pringle, Heather Anne. *The Mummy Congress* — 393
   Raffa, Guy P. *Dante's Bones* — 851
   Switek, Brian. *Skeleton Keys* — 611
   Yi, Sang-Hui. *Close Encounters with Humankind* — 599.93

FORENSIC MEDICINE
   Blum, Deborah. *The Poisoner's Handbook* — 614
   Burgess, Ann Wolbert. *A Killer by Design* — 364.3
   Dawson, Kate Winkler. ★*American Sherlock* — B
   Roach, Mary. ★*Stiff* — 611

FORENSIC PATHOLOGY
   Fabricant, M. Chris. *Junk Science and the American Criminal Justice System* — 363.25

FORENSIC PSYCHIATRY
   Ford, Elizabeth. *Sometimes Amazing Things Happen* — B

FORENSIC PSYCHOLOGY
   Monroe, Jana. *Hearts of Darkness* — 363.25

FORENSIC SCIENCES
   Blum, Deborah. *The Poisoner's Handbook* — 614
   Dawson, Kate Winkler. ★*American Sherlock* — B
   Di Maio, Vincent J. M. *Morgue* — B
   Goldfarb, Bruce. ★*18 Tiny Deaths* — B
   Jobb, Dean. *The Case of the Murderous Dr. Cream* — 364.152
   Roach, Mary. ★*Stiff* — 611

FORENSIC SCIENTISTS
   Goldfarb, Bruce. ★*18 Tiny Deaths* — B
   Norton, Laurah. *Lay Them to Rest* — 363.25
   Rae-Venter, Barbara. *I Know Who You Are* — 364.152
   Roach, Mary. ★*Stiff* — 611

FORENSIC TOXICOLOGY
   Blum, Deborah. *The Poisoner's Handbook* — 614

FOREST ANIMALS
   Wohlleben, Peter. *Forest Walking* — 582.16
   Wohlleben, Peter. *The Hidden Life of Trees* — 582.16

FOREST BIRDS
   Attenborough, David. *The Life of Birds* — 598.15

FOREST CANOPY ECOLOGY
   Lowman, Margaret. *The Arbornaut* — 581.7
   Lowman, Margaret. *Life in the Treetops* — B
The Forest City Killer. Brown, Vanessa — 364.152

FOREST CONSERVATION
   Egan, Timothy. ★*The Big Burn* — 973.911
   Irving, Apricot Anderson. *The Gospel of Trees* — B
   Pearce, Fred. *A Trillion Trees* — 577.3
   Preston, Richard. *The Wild Trees* — 585
   Simard, S. ★*Finding the Mother Tree* — 582.16

FOREST ECOLOGY
   Mathews, Daniel. *Trees in Trouble* — 634.9
   Wohlleben, Peter. *Forest Walking* — 582.16

FOREST FIRES
   Egan, Timothy. ★*The Big Burn* — 973.911
   Junger, Sebastian. *Fire* — 909.82
   Martin, Manjula. *The Last Fire Season* — B
   Mathews, Daniel. *Trees in Trouble* — 634.9
   Vaillant, John. ★*Fire Weather* — 363.37

FOREST MANAGEMENT
   Martin, Manjula. *The Last Fire Season* — B
   Mathews, Daniel. *Trees in Trouble* — 634.9

FOREST PLANTS
   Regan, Iliana. *Fieldwork* — B
Forest Walking. Wohlleben, Peter — 582.16

FORESTRY
   Farmer, Jared. *Elderflora* — 582.16
   Logan, William Bryant. *Sprout Lands* — 582.16
   Mathews, Daniel. *Trees in Trouble* — 634.9
   Miller, Char. *Gifford Pinchot and the Making of Modern Environmentalism* — B
   Reid, John W. *Ever Green* — 634.9
   Webb, Kinari. *Guardians of the Trees* — B

FORESTS
   Farmer, Jared. *Elderflora* — 582.16
   King, Greg. *The Ghost Forest* — 333.75
   Lewis, Daniel. *Twelve Trees* — 582.16
   Mathews, Daniel. *Trees in Trouble* — 634.9
   Pearce, Fred. *A Trillion Trees* — 577.3
   Preston, Richard. *The Wild Trees* — 585
   Rawlence, Ben. *The Treeline* — 577.3
   Regan, Iliana. *Fieldwork* — B
   Reid, John W. *Ever Green* — 634.9
   Wohlleben, Peter. *Forest Walking* — 582.16
   Wohlleben, Peter. *The Hidden Life of Trees* — 582.16
Forever and Ever, Amen. Travis, Randy — B
★*The Forever Dog*. Habib, Rodney — 636.7
Forever Free. Foner, Eric — 973.8
The Forever Prisoner. Scott-Clark, Cathy — 364.6
The Forever War. Filkins, Dexter — 956.7044
The Forever Witness. Humes, Edward — 363.25
Forever Young. Mills, Hayley — B
Foreverland. Havrilesky, Heather — 306.81
The Forgers. Moorhouse, Roger — 940.53

FORGERS
   Tigay, Chanan. *The Lost Book of Moses* — 098

FORGERY
   Moorhouse, Roger. *The Forgers* — 940.53
   Tigay, Chanan. *The Lost Book of Moses* — 098
Forget Prayers, Bring Cake. Gerson, Merissa Nathan — 155.9
Forget The Alamo. Burrough, Bryan — 976.043

FORGIVENESS
   Batterson, Mark. *Please, Sorry, Thanks* — 179
   Cercas, Javier. *Lord of All the Dead* — 868
   Fitzgerald, Isaac. *Dirtbag, Massachusetts* — B
   Frangello, Gina. *Blow Your House Down* — 813
   Girzone, Joseph F. *Never Alone* — 248.4
   Granata, Vince. *Everything Is Fine* — B
   Green, Kristen. *Something Must Be Done About Prince Edward County* — 379.2
   Hawes, Jennifer. *Grace Will Lead Us Home* — 364.152
   Hempel, Jessi. *The Family Outing* — B
   Koh, EJ. *The Magical Language of Others* — 813
   Kubler-Ross, Elisabeth. *Life Lessons* — 170
   Kushner, Harold S. *How Good Do We Have to Be?* — 296.7
   Kushner, Harold S. *Overcoming Life's Disappointments* — 296.7
   Lewis, John. *Carry On* — 328.73
   Mansbach, Adam. *I Had a Brother Once* — 811
   Mar, Alex. *Seventy Times Seven* — 362.88
   Minow, Martha. *When Should Law Forgive?* — 345
   Rush, Charaia. *Courageously Soft* — 234
   Shapiro, Susan. *The Forgiveness Tour* — 158.2
   Thom, Kai Cheng. *Falling Back in Love with Being Human* — 811
   Tutu, Desmond. *The Book of Forgiving* — 179
   Tutu, Desmond. *Made for Goodness* — 170
   Wiesenthal, Simon. ★*The Sunflower* — 179.7

FORGIVENESS (CHRISTIANITY)
   Morton, Michael. *Getting Life* — B
The Forgiveness Tour. Shapiro, Susan — 158.2
Forgosh, Linda B.
   Louis Bamberger — B
Forgotten. Hervieux, Linda — 940.54
Forgotten Ally. Mitter, Rana — 951.04
The Forgotten Girls. Potts, Monica — B
The Forgotten Man. Shlaes, Amity — 973.91
Forkish, Ken
   Evolutions in Bread — 664
   Flour Water Salt Yeast — 641.81
   ★*Let's Make Bread!* — 741.5
Forks Over Knives Family. Pulde, Alona — 641.5
★*The Forks Over Knives Plan*. Pulde, Alona — 641.5
Forman, James
   Locking up Our Own — 364.973

FORMER BASEBALL PLAYERS
   Shelton, Ron. *The Church of Baseball* — 791.43

FORMER BASKETBALL PLAYERS
   Smith, Kenny. *Talk of Champions* — B
   Thomas, Etan. *We Matter* — 796.08

FORMER CAPTIVES
   Khalaf, Farida. *The Girl Who Escaped Isis* — B

FORMER CHILD ACTORS AND ACTRESSES
   Howard, Ron. ★*The Boys* — B

AUTHOR, TITLE, SERIES AND SUBJECT INDEX

FORMER CHURCH MEMBERS
   Roberts, Matthias. *Holy Runaways*   262
FORMER CIA AGENTS
   Blum, Howard. *The Spy Who Knew Too Much*   327.12
   Mendez, Antonio J. *Argo*   955.05
FORMER COLLEGE TEACHERS
   Wiehl, Lis W. *Hunting the Unabomber*   364.152
FORMER COMMUNISTS
   Szablowski, Witold. *Dancing Bears*   947.086
FORMER CONVICTS
   Betts, Reginald Dwayne. *Felon*   811
   Blakinger, Keri. *Corrections in Ink*   B
   Dykstra, Lenny. *House of Nails*   B
   Hardy, Jason Matthew. ★*The Second Chance Club*   364.6
   Hopwood, Shon. *Law Man*   B
   Jackson, Lawrence Patrick. *Chester B. Himes*   B
   Manuel, Ian. *My Time Will Come*   B
   Wilson, August. *King Hedley II*   812
   Wilson, Chris. *The Master Plan*   B
FORMER CULT MEMBERS
   Rinder, Mike. ★*A Billion Years*   B
FORMER DRUG ADDICTS
   Burton, Susan. *Becoming Ms. Burton*   B
FORMER FRIENDS
   Pittard, Hannah. *We Are Too Many*   B
   Roberts, Randy. *Blood Brothers*   920
FORMER GANG MEMBERS
   Onwuachi, Kwame. ★*Notes from a Young Black Chef*   641.59
   Rubinstein, Julian. ★*The Holly*   364.106
FORMER GIRLFRIENDS
   McGough, Matthew. *The Lazarus Files*   364.152
FORMER GOVERNORS
   Christie, Chris. *Let Me Finish*   B
FORMER LAWYERS
   Shlaes, Amity. *Coolidge*   B
FORMER MARINES
   Carpenter, Kyle. *You Are Worth It*   B
FORMER NAVY SEALS
   Owen, Mark. *No Hero*   B
FORMER NAZIS
   Bilger, Burkhard. *Fatherland*   B
FORMER NUNS
   Armstrong, Karen. *The Spiral Staircase*   B
FORMER PHYSICIANS
   Deer, Brian. *The Doctor Who Fooled the World*   610.92
   Von Drehle, David. ★*The Book of Charlie*   B
FORMER PRESIDENTS
   Abrams, Dan. *Theodore Roosevelt for the Defense*   345.73
   Bardenwerper, William. *The Prisoner in His Palace*   956.7044
   Carter, Jimmy. *A Full Life*   B
   Cohen, Jared. *Life After Power*   973.09
   Karl, Jonathan. *Tired of Winning*   973.933
   Reston, James. *The Conviction of Richard Nixon*   973.924092
FORMER PRIESTS
   Carroll, James. *Constantine's Sword*   261
   Girzone, Joseph F. *Never Alone*   248.4
FORMER PROFESSIONAL FOOTBALL PLAYERS
   Jackson, Ted. ★*You Ought to Do a Story About Me*   B
   Spurrier, Steve. *Head Ball Coach*   B
FORMER SOVIET REPUBLICS
   Plokhy, Serhii. ★*The Gates of Europe*   947.7
Formidable. Griffith, Elisabeth   305.42
Formosa, Dan
   Baseball Field Guide   796.357
Forni, Pier Massimo
   The Civility Solution   395
Foroohar, Rana
   Homecoming   338.6
Forsythe, Kelly
   Perennial   811
Forte, Sara
   The Sprouted Kitchen   641.3
FORTITUDE
   Morin, Amy. *13 Things Mentally Strong Women Don't Do*   158.1
Fortnow, Lance
   The Golden Ticket   511.3
Fortunate Son. Fogerty, John   B
A Fortune for Your Disaster. Abdurraqib, Hanif   811

Fortune's Fool. Alford, Terry   B
The Fortunes of Africa. Meredith, Martin   960
Forty Autumns. Willner, Nina   B
Forward. Wambach, Abby   B
FOSDICK, SARAH GRAVES, 1825-1871
   Brown, Daniel James. *The Indifferent Stars Above*   B
Fossey, Dian
   ★*Gorillas in the Mist*   599.884
FOSSEY, DIAN, 1932-1985
   Fossey, Dian. ★*Gorillas in the Mist*   599.884
FOSSIL FUELS
   Bell, Alice R. *Our Biggest Experiment*   363.738
   Jabr, Ferris. ★*Becoming Earth*   570.1
   Maddow, Rachel. *Blowout*   338.2
   Yergin, Daniel. *The New Map*   333.79
FOSSIL MAMMALS
   Childs, Craig. *Atlas of a Lost World*   551.7
Fossil Men. Pattison, Kermit   569.9
FOSSILS
   Darwin, Charles. *Charles Darwin*   576.8
   Halliday, Thomas. ★*Otherlands*   560
   Lacovara, Kenneth. *Why Dinosaurs Matter*   567.9
   Lister, Adrian. *Darwin's Fossils*   576.8
   Pattison, Kermit. *Fossil Men*   569.9
   Thompson, Ida. ★*The Audubon Society Field Guide to North American Fossils*   560
FOSTER CARE
   Asgarian, Roxanna. *We Were Once a Family*   364.152
   Calcaterra, Regina. *Etched in Sand*   B
   Calcaterra, Regina. *Girl Unbroken*   B
   Haddish, Tiffany. *The Last Black Unicorn*   B
   Sentilles, Sarah. *Stranger Care*   B
FOSTER CHILDREN
   Ambroz, David. *A Place Called Home*   B
   Asgarian, Roxanna. *We Were Once a Family*   364.152
   Casillo, Charles. *Marilyn Monroe*   B
   Daley, Mark. *Safe*   B
   Eire, Carlos M. N. *Learning to Die in Miami*   B
   Henderson, Rob Kim. *Troubled*   B
   Moody, Anne. *The Children Money Can Buy*   362.73
   Nietfeld, Emi. *Acceptance*   B
   Sentilles, Sarah. *Stranger Care*   B
   Van Es, Bart. *The Cut Out Girl*   B
FOSTER HOME CARE
   Daley, Mark. *Safe*   B
   Henderson, Rob Kim. *Troubled*   B
   Moody, Anne. *The Children Money Can Buy*   362.73
   Wagamese, Richard. *For Joshua*   B
FOSTER PARENTS
   Calcaterra, Regina. *Etched in Sand*   B
   Calcaterra, Regina. *Girl Unbroken*   B
   Daley, Mark. *Safe*   B
   Sentilles, Sarah. *Stranger Care*   B
Foster, Charles
   Being a Human   155.7
FOSTER, CHARLES, 1962-
   Foster, Charles. *Being a Human*   155.7
Foster, Craig
   ★*Amphibious Soul*   155.9
FOSTER, CRAIG (FILMMAKER)
   Foster, Craig. ★*Amphibious Soul*   155.9
Foster, Diana Greene
   The Turnaway Study   362.1988
Foster, Lynn V.
   A Brief History of Mexico   972
Foster, Sutton
   Hooked   B
FOSTER, SUTTON
   Foster, Sutton. *Hooked*   B
Foster, Thomas C
   How to Read Poetry Like a Professor   808.1
★*Fostering Wellness in the Workplace*. Newman, Bobbi L.   023
Foulkes, Lucy
   ★*Losing Our Minds*   616.89
Foundation. Ackroyd, Peter   942
FOUNDATIONS
   Doyne, Maggie. *Between the Mountain and the Sky*   B
★*The Founders and Finance*. McCraw, Thomas K.   330.973

PUBLIC LIBRARY CORE COLLECTION: NONFICTION
Twentieth Edition

The Founders' Fortunes. Randall, Willard Sterne	973.3
Founding Brothers. Ellis, Joseph J.	973.4
FOUNDING FATHERS OF THE UNITED STATES	
Baier, Bret. *To Rescue the Constitution*	973.4
Boles, John B. *Jefferson*	B
Brands, H. W. *The First American*	B
Brands, H. W. ★*Founding Partisans*	973.3
Bunker, Nick. *Young Benjamin Franklin*	B
Burstein, Andrew. *Madison and Jefferson*	973.4
Cheney, Lynne V. *James Madison*	B
Cheney, Lynne V. *The Virginia Dynasty*	B
Coe, Alexis. ★*You Never Forget Your First*	B
Ellis, Joseph J. ★*American Dialogue*	973.3
Ellis, Joseph J. *First Family*	973.4
Ellis, Joseph J. *The Quartet*	342.7302
Feldman, Noah. *The Three Lives of James Madison*	B
Fried, Stephen. *Rush*	B
Grant, James. ★*John Adams*	B
Groom, Winston. *The Patriots*	920
Johnson, Paul. *George Washington*	B
Kearse, Bettye. *The Other Madisons*	920
Klarman, Michael J. *The Framers' Coup*	342.7302
Larson, Edward J. *The Return of George Washington*	B
Lepore, Jill. ★*These Truths*	973
Maier, Pauline. *Ratification*	342.7302
McCullough, David G. ★*John Adams*	B
McGrath, Tim. *James Monroe*	B
McKean, David. *Suspected of Independence*	B
Meyerson, Michael. *Liberty's Blueprint*	342.7302
Miranda, Lin-Manuel. *Hamilton*	782.1
Randall, Willard Sterne. *The Founders' Fortunes*	973.3
Randall, Willard Sterne. *George Washington*	B
Ricks, Thomas E. ★*First Principles*	973.09
Rosen, Jeffrey. *The Pursuit of Happiness*	973.3
Rubenstein, David M. *The American Story*	973.07202
Sankovitch, Nina. *American Rebels*	920
Stewart, David O. *George Washington*	973.4
Stewart, David O. *Madison's Gift*	B
Taylor, Alan. *American Revolutions*	973.3
Toll, Ian W. ★*Six Frigates*	359.00973
Unger, Harlow G. *First Founding Father*	B
Unger, Harlow G. *The Last Founding Father*	B
Will, George F. *The Conservative Sensibility*	320.520973
Founding Mothers. Roberts, Cokie	920
★*Founding Partisans*. Brands, H. W.	973.3
The Four. Galloway, Scott	338.7
Four Battlegrounds. Scharre, Paul	006.3
FOUR ELEMENTS	
Pollan, Michael. *Cooked*	641.5
Four Fish. Greenberg, Paul	333.95
The Four Horsemen. Hitchens, Christopher	211
Four Kings. Kimball, George	B
The Four Noble Truths. Thubten Zopa	294.3
FOUR NOBLE TRUTHS	
Thubten Zopa. *The Four Noble Truths*	294.3
Four Reincarnations. Ritvo, Max	811
The Four Roads to Heaven. Mullins, Edwin	263
Four seasons encyclopedia [Series]. Knausgaard, Karl Ove	B
The Four Tests. Baer, Daniel Brooks	320.973
FOURCADE, MARIE-MADELEINE, 1909-1989	
Olson, Lynne. ★*Madame Fourcade's Secret War*	B
Fournier-Lanzoni, Remi	
French Cinema, 2nd Ed.	791.43
The Fourteenth Day. Coleman, David G.	973.922092
FOURTH DIMENSION	
Kaku, Michio. *Parallel Worlds*	523.1
FOURTH OF JULY	
Colaiaco, James A. *Frederick Douglass and the Fourth of July*	973.7
Fouts, Roger	
Next of Kin	156
FOUTS, ROGER	
Fouts, Roger. *Next of Kin*	156
Fowlds, Grant	
Saving the Last Rhinos	599.66
FOWLDS, GRANT	
Fowlds, Grant. *Saving the Last Rhinos*	599.66
Fowler, Corinne	
★*The Countryside*	941

FOWLING	
Rinella, Steven. *The Complete Guide to Hunting, Butchering, and Cooking Wild Game; Volume 2*	799.2
FOX (MESKWAKI) (NORTH AMERICAN PEOPLE)	
Trask, Kerry A. *Black Hawk*	973.5
The Fox Hunt. AL Samawi, Mohammed	953
Fox Starr, Rebecca	
Beyond the Baby Blues	618.7
Fox, Amaryllis	
Life Undercover	B
FOX, AMARYLLIS	
Fox, Amaryllis. *Life Undercover*	B
Fox, Dan	
Pretentiousness	700
FOX, GUSTAVUS VASA, 1821-1883	
Symonds, Craig L. *Lincoln and His Admirals*	B
Fox, Jeremy	
On Vegetables	641.6
Fox, Jesse David	
Comedy Book	792.7
Fox, Julia	
Down the Drain	B
FOX, JULIA, 1990-	
Fox, Julia. *Down the Drain*	B
Fox, Justin	
The Myth of the Rational Market	332.64
Fox, Margalit	
The Confidence Men	940.4
The Riddle of the Labyrinth	920
The Talented Mrs. Mandelbaum	364.1
Fox, Michael J.	
No Time Like the Future	B
FOX, MICHAEL J., 1961-	
Fox, Michael J. *No Time Like the Future*	B
Fox, Porter	
The Last Winter	363.738
FOXES	
Brand, Adele. *The Hidden World of the Fox*	599.775
Foxx, Jamie	
Act Like You Got Some Sense	B
FOXX, JAMIE	
Foxx, Jamie. *Act Like You Got Some Sense*	B
The Frackers. Zuckerman, Gregory	B
Fradin, Kelly	
Advanced Parenting	649
Fragmented. Yurkiewicz, Ilana	362.1
The Framers' Coup. Klarman, Michael J.	342.7302
FRAMEUPS	
King, Gilbert. *Beneath a Ruthless Sun*	B
Kushner, Jacob. *Look Away*	305.9
Frampton, Saul	
When I Am Playing with My Cat, How Do I Know She Is Not Playing with Me?	844
France. Robb, Graham	944
FRANCE	
Ambrose, Stephen E. *D-Day, June 6, 1944*	940.54
Arnold, James R. *Jungle of Snakes*	355.02
B., David. *Epileptic*	741.5
Bard, Elizabeth. *Lunch in Paris*	B
Bard, Elizabeth. *Picnic in Provence*	B
Barker, Juliet R. V. *Agincourt*	944
Barnes, Julian. *The Man in the Red Coat*	B
Barr, James. *A Line in the Sand*	956
Berr, Helene. *The Journal of Helene Berr*	B
Broers, Michael. *Napoleon*	B
Broers, Michael. *Napoleon*	B
Buford, Bill. ★*Dirt*	B
Burke, Edmund. *Reflections on the Revolution in France*	944.04
Caddick-Adams, Peter. *Sand and Steel*	940.54
Collins, Lauren. *When in French*	B
Cornwell, Bernard. *Waterloo*	940.2
Curran, Andrew S. *Diderot and the Art of Thinking Freely*	194
Darnton, Robert. *The Revolutionary Temper*	944
Davenport, Matthew J. *First Over There*	940.4
De Courcy, Anne. *Chanel's Riviera*	944.9
DeJean, Joan E. *The Essence of Style*	391
Downie, David. *A Taste of Paris*	394.1
Evans, Martin. *Algeria*	965

AUTHOR, TITLE, SERIES AND SUBJECT INDEX

Ferreiro, Larrie D. *Brothers at Arms*	327.73
Fournier-Lanzoni, Remi. *French Cinema, 2nd Ed.*	791.43
Fraser, Antonia. *Love and Louis XIV*	B
Fraser, Antonia. *Marie Antoinette*	B
Freeman, Hadley. *House of Glass*	B
Frenkel, Francoise. *A Bookshop in Berlin*	B
Frey, Julia Bloch. *Toulouse-Lautrec*	B
Garelick, Rhonda K. *Mademoiselle*	B
Grose, Peter. *A Good Place to Hide*	940.53
Guibert, Emmanuel. *Alan's War*	741.5
Haitiwaji, Gulbahar. *How I Survived a Chinese "Reeducation" Camp*	305.8
Harlan, Elizabeth. *George Sand*	B
Henaut, Stephane. *A Bite-Sized History of France*	394.1
Hindley, Meredith. *Destination Casablanca*	940.54
Hogan, William R. *Task Force Hogan*	940.54
Holland, James. *Brothers in Arms*	940.54
Holland, James. *Normandy '44*	940.54
Jackson, Julian. *De Gaulle*	B
Jacobs, Ryan McMahon. *The Truffle Underground*	381
Johnson, Paul. *Napoleon*	B
Kelder, Diane. *The Great Book of French Impressionism*	759.4
Khan, Yasmin Sabina. *Enlightening the World*	974.7
King, David. *Death in the City of Light*	364.152
King, Ross. *The Judgment of Paris*	759.4
Korda, Michael. *Alone*	940.54
Kouchner, Camille. *The Familia Grande*	B
Lebovitz, David. *My Paris Kitchen*	641.594
Logevall, Fredrik. *Embers of War*	959.704
Mansel, Philip. *King of the World*	B
Mayle, Peter. *Encore Provence*	944
Mayle, Peter. *My Twenty-Five Years in Provence*	944.9
Mayle, Peter. *Provence A-Z*	944
Mayle, Peter. ★*A Year in Provence*	944
Mazzeo, Tilar J. *The Secret of Chanel No. 5*	338.7
McCullough, David G. *The Greater Journey*	920
McPhee, Peter. *Robespierre*	B
Olson, Lynne. ★*Madame Fourcade's Secret War*	B
Paine, Thomas. ★*Rights of Man*	320.5
Paradis, Michel. *The Light of Battle*	940.54
Paxson, Margaret. *The Plateau*	362.87
Pearson, Roger. *Voltaire Almighty*	B
Pepin, Jacques. *The Apprentice*	B
Philbrick, Nathaniel. ★*In the Hurricane's Eye*	973.3
Reiss, Tom. *The Black Count*	B
Robb, Graham. *The Discovery of France*	944
Robb, Graham. *France*	944
Roberts, Andrew. ★*Napoleon*	B
Roe, Sue. *The Private Lives of the Impressionists*	920
Rosbottom, Ronald C. *When Paris Went Dark*	944.0816
Rosenberg, Justus. *The Art of Resistance*	B
Schama, Simon. *Citizens*	944.04
Sciolino, Elaine. *The Only Street in Paris*	944
Sciolino, Elaine. *The Seine*	944
Scurr, Ruth. *Fatal Purity*	B
Shaw, Jennifer Laurie. *Exist Otherwise*	709.2
Strauss, Gwen. *The Nine*	940.53
Todd, Olivier. *Albert Camus*	B
Tuchman, Barbara W. ★*A Distant Mirror*	944
Von Bremzen, Anya. *National Dish*	641.3
Zamoyski, Adam. *Napoleon*	B

France, David
How to Survive a Plague	362.196

France, John
Perilous Glory	355
★*Franchise*. Chatelain, Marcia	339
Franci's War. Epstein, Franci	B

Francis
The Church of Mercy	252
Happiness in This Life	248.4
Let Us Dream	282.092
Life	B
Walking with Jesus	282.09

FRANCIS, OF ASSISI, SAINT, 1182-1226
Martin, Valerie. *Salvation*	B

FRANCIS, POPE, 1936-
Douthat, Ross Gregory. *To Change the Church*	230
Francis. *Let Us Dream*	282.092
Francis. *Life*	B
Politi, Marco. *Pope Francis Among the Wolves*	282.092
Vallely, Paul. *Pope Francis*	B
Wills, Garry. *The Future of the Catholic Church with Pope Francis*	282.09

FRANCO, FRANCISCO, 1892-1975
Preston, Paul. *A People Betrayed*	946
Preston, Paul. *The Spanish Holocaust*	946.081

Franco, Marisa G.
Platonic	302.34

Francois, Willie Dwayne
Silencing White Noise	277

Francois, Zoe
Holiday and Celebration Bread in Five Minutes a Day	641.81
Zoe Bakes Cakes	641.86

Frangello, Gina
Blow Your House Down	813

FRANGELLO, GINA
Frangello, Gina. *Blow Your House Down*	813

Frank. Frank, Barney	B
★*Frank*. Seuss, Diane	811

FRANK FAMILY
Van Wijk-Voskuijl, Joop. *The Last Secret of the Secret Annex*	940.53
Frank Lloyd Wright. Secrest, Meryle	B
★*Frank Lloyd Wright*. Huxtable, Ada Louise	B
The Frank Lloyd Wright Companion. Storrer, William Allin	720.92
Frank Sinatra (James Kaplan) [Series]. Kaplan, James	782.42164

Frank, Adam
Light of the Stars	523.1

Frank, Anne
★*The Diary of a Young Girl*	940.53
The Diary of Anne Frank	B

FRANK, ANNE, 1929-1945
Frank, Anne. ★*The Diary of a Young Girl*	940.53
Frank, Anne. *The Diary of Anne Frank*	B
Gies, Miep. ★*Anne Frank Remembered*	B
Goodrich, Frances. *The Diary of Anne Frank*	812
Jacobson, Sidney. *Anne Frank*	741.5
Lindwer, Willy. *The Last Seven Months of Anne Frank*	B
Muller, Melissa. *Anne Frank*	B
Pick-Goslar, Hannah Elizabeth. ★*My Friend Anne Frank*	B
Sullivan, Rosemary. *The Betrayal of Anne Frank*	940.53
Van Wijk-Voskuijl, Joop. *The Last Secret of the Secret Annex*	940.53

Frank, Barney
Frank	B

FRANK, BARNEY, 1940-
Frank, Barney. *Frank*	B

Frank, Jeffrey
The Trials of Harry S. Truman	973.918

Frank, Joseph
★*Dostoevsky*	B

Frank, Lois Ellen
Seed to Plate, Soil to Sky	641.5

Frank, Lone
The Pleasure Shock	616.8

Frank, Michael
★*One Hundred Saturdays*	B

Frank, Richard B.
Downfall	940.54
Tower of Skulls	940.54

FRANK, ROBERT, 1924-2019
Smith, R. J. *American Witness*	B

Frank, Thomas
The People, No	320.56

Frankel, Glenn
High Noon	791.43
Shooting Midnight Cowboy	791.43

Frankel, Rebecca
Into the Forest	940.53

FRANKENSTEIN'S MONSTER (FICTITIOUS CHARACTER)
Braudy, Leo. *Haunted*	398.45
Montillo, Roseanne. *The Lady and Her Monsters*	823

Frankl, Viktor E.
★*Man's Search for Meaning*	B
Yes to Life	150.19

FRANKL, VIKTOR E. (VIKTOR EMIL), 1905-1997
Frankl, Viktor E. ★*Man's Search for Meaning*	B
Franklin and Lucy. Persico, Joseph E.	973.917092
Franklin and Winston. Meacham, Jon	940.53
Franklin Barbecue. Franklin, Aaron	641.7

★*Franklin D. Roosevelt*. Dallek, Robert — B
Franklin Steak. Franklin, Aaron — 641.6
Franklin, Aaron
    Franklin Barbecue — 641.7
    Franklin Steak — 641.6
FRANKLIN, ARETHA, 1942-2018
    Bego, Mark. *Aretha Franklin* — B
Franklin, Benjamin
    ★*The Autobiography of Benjamin Franklin* — B
    ★*Autobiography, Poor Richard, and Later Writings* — 973.2
    The Compleated Autobiography — B
FRANKLIN, BENJAMIN, 1706-1790
    Brands, H. W. *The First American* — B
    Bunker, Nick. *Young Benjamin Franklin* — B
    Franklin, Benjamin. ★*The Autobiography of Benjamin Franklin* — B
    Franklin, Benjamin. ★*Autobiography, Poor Richard, and Later Writings* — 973.2
    Franklin, Benjamin. *The Compleated Autobiography* — B
    Isaacson, Walter. ★*Benjamin Franklin* — B
    Lepore, Jill. *Book of Ages* — B
    Moore, Peter. *Life, Liberty, and the Pursuit of Happiness* — 199
    Weiner, Eric. *Ben & Me* — B
FRANKLIN, ISAAC, 1789-1846
    Rothman, Joshua D. *The Ledger and the Chain* — 306.362
Franklin, John Hope
    ★*From Slavery to Freedom* — 973
    In Search of the Promised Land — 929
Franklin, Jonathan
    438 Days — 910.91
    A Wild Idea — B
Franklin, Missy
    Relentless Spirit — B
FRANKLIN, MISSY, 1995-
    Franklin, Missy. *Relentless Spirit* — B
FRANKLIN, ROSALIND, 1920-1958
    Maddox, Brenda. *Rosalind Franklin* — B
    Markel, Howard. *The Secret of Life* — 572.86
Franklin, Ruth
    Shirley Jackson — B
Franklin, Sara B.
    ★*The Editor* — B
Franklin-Wallis, Oliver
    ★*Wasteland* — 363.72
Frankly, We Did Win This Election". Bender, Michael C. — 973.933
Frankopan, Peter
    The Earth Transformed — 304.2
    The First Crusade — 956
    The Silk Roads — 909
Franny's. Feinberg, Andrew — 641.594
Franscell, Ron
    Shadowman — 362.88
FRANZ FERDINAND, ARCHDUKE OF AUSTRIA, 1863-1914
    King, Greg. *The Assassination of the Archduke* — B
Franzen, Jonathan
    The End of the End of the Earth — 814
    Farther Away — 814
Fraser, Antonia
    Faith and Treason — 942.06
    Love and Louis XIV — B
    Marie Antoinette — B
    Mary, Queen of Scots — B
    ★*The Wives of Henry VIII* — 942.05
Fraser, Caroline
    ★*Prairie Fires* — B
Fraser, Rebecca
    The Mayflower — 974.4
Fraser, Steve
    The Age of Acquiescence — 973.91
FRATERNITIES
    Hechinger, John. ★*True Gentlemen* — 371.85
    Marshall, McMillan. *Among the Bros* — 362.29
FRAUD
    Behar, Richard. *Madoff* — 364.16
    Bensinger, Ken. ★*Red Card* — 796.334
    Carreyrou, John. ★*Bad Blood* — 338.7
    Conason, Joe. *The Longest Con* — 320.52
    Johnston, David Cay. *The Big Cheat* — 973.933
    Levin, Josh. *The Queen* — 364.16
    Mueller, Tom. *Crisis of Conscience* — 364.16
    Olmsted, Larry. *Real Food/Fake Food* — 641.3
    Ritchie, Stuart. *Science Fictions* — 500
    Sisman, Adam. *The Professor and the Parson* — 364.16
    White, Neil. *In the Sanctuary of Outcasts* — B
    Whitlock, Craig. ★*Fat Leonard* — 364.16
    Willetts, Paul. *King Con* — B
    Yeebo, Yepoka. *Anansi's Gold* — 364.16
    Young, Kevin. *Bunk* — 177
Frazer, Amy L.
    Empowered Embroidery — 746.44
Frazier, Ian
    Hogs Wild — 814
    Travels in Siberia — 957
FRAZIER, IAN
    Frazier, Ian. *Travels in Siberia* — 957
FRAZIER, JOE, 1944-2011
    Kram, Mark. *Smokin' Joe* — B
FRAZIER, O. HOWARD
    Swartz, Mimi. *Ticker* — 617.4
Freak Kingdom. Denevi, Timothy — B
★*Freakonomics*. Levitt, Steven D. — 330
The **Fred** W. Morrison series in Southern studies [Series]. Faust, Drew Gilpin — 973.7
Freddie Steinmark. Yousse, Bower — 796.332
FREDEGUND, — QUEEN, CONSORT OF CHILPERIC I, KING OF NEUSTRIA, -- -597
    Puhak, Shelley. *The Dark Queens* — 944
★*Frederick Douglass*. Blight, David W. — B
Frederick Douglass. Dilbeck, D. H. — B
★*Frederick Douglass*. Douglass, Frederick — 973.8
Frederick Douglass and the Fourth of July. Colaiaco, James A. — 973.7
FREDERICK II, THE GREAT, KING OF PRUSSIA, 1712-1786
    Blanning, T. C. W. *Frederick the Great* — B
★*Frederick Seidel Selected Poems*. Seidel, Frederick — 811
Frederick The Great. Blanning, T. C. W. — B
Frederick, Jim
    Black Hearts — 956.7044
Fredrickson, Barbara
    Positivity — 158.1
Fredriksen, Paula
    Jesus of Nazareth, King of the Jews — B
★*Free*. Ypi, Lea — B
FREE AFRICAN AMERICANS
    Franklin, John Hope. ★*From Slavery to Freedom* — 973
    Harris, J. William. *The Hanging of Thomas Jeremiah* — B
    Masur, Kate. *Until Justice Be Done* — 323.1196
    Willis, Deborah. *Envisioning Emancipation* — 973.7
FREE AGENTS (SPORTS)
    Snyder, Brad. *A Well-Paid Slave* — B
FREE CLIMBING
    Burgman, John. *High Drama* — 796.522
FREE ENTERPRISE
    McMillan, John. *Reinventing the Bazaar* — 330.12
    Oller, John. *White Shoe* — 346.73
    Yunus, Muhammad. *A World of Three Zeros* — 330
★*Free for All*. Turan, Kenneth — B
★*Free Speech*. McHangama, Jacob — 323.44
Free Speech in Its Forgotten Years. Rabban, David M. — 342.73
Free The Land. Lim, Audrea — 333.73
Free Thinker. Hamlin, Kimberly A — B
FREE THOUGHT
    Zuckerman, Phil. *Living the Secular Life* — 211
★*Free to Be*. Turban, Jack L. — 616.85
FREE TRADE
    Slade, Rachel. *American Hoodie* — 338.4
    Yunus, Muhammad. *A World of Three Zeros* — 330
FREE WILL AND DETERMINISM
    Chayka, Kyle. *Filterworld* — 306
    Hagglund, Martin. *This Life* — 110
    Jacobs, Alan. *Original Sin* — 233
    Miller, Kenneth R. *The Human Instinct* — 155.7
    Sapolsky, Robert M. *Determined* — 123
    Wulf, Andrea. *Magnificent Rebels* — 830.9
The Free World. Menand, Louis — 306.0973
Free-Motion Meandering. Walters, Angela — 746.46
Freeberg, Ernest
    A Traitor to His Species — B

AUTHOR, TITLE, SERIES AND SUBJECT INDEX

FREED PEOPLE
    Bellows, Amanda Brickell. *The Explorers* — 910.92
    Brewster, Todd. *Lincoln's Gamble* — 973.7
    Burlingame, Michael. *The Black Man's President* — 973.7
    Carretta, Vincent. *Equiano, the African* — B
    Emberton, Carole. *To Walk About in Freedom* — 306.3
    Feldman, Noah. *The Broken Constitution* — 973.7
    Fields-Black, Edda L. *Combee* — 973.7
    Fischer, David Hackett. ★*African Founders* — 973
    Foner, Eric. *Forever Free* — 973.8
    Gayle, Caleb. *We Refuse to Forget* — 975.004
    Greenidge, Kerri. ★*The Grimkes* — 973.5
    Hahn, Steven. *A Nation Under Our Feet* — 975
    Hurston, Zora Neale. ★*Barracoon* — B
    Jones, Jacqueline. *Saving Savannah* — 975.8
    Kearse, Bettye. *The Other Madisons* — 920
    Levine, Robert S. ★*The Failed Promise* — 973.8
    Manning, Chandra. *Troubled Refuge* — 973.7
    Meacham, Jon. ★*And There Was Light* — B
    Morgan-Owens, Jessie. *Girl in Black and White* — B
    Plant, Deborah G. *Of Greed and Glory* — 326
    Rae, Noel. ★*The Great Stain* — 306.3
    Raiford, Matthew. *Bress 'N' Nyam* — 641.59
    Richards, Leonard L. *Who Freed the Slaves?* — 342.7308
    Shane, Scott. ★*Flee North* — 973.7
    Taylor, Alan. *American Civil Wars* — 973.7
    Taylor, Alan. ★*The Internal Enemy* — 975.5
    Ward, Andrew. ★*The Slaves' War* — 973.7
    Washington, Booker T. ★*Up from Slavery* — B
    Williams, Kidada E. *I Saw Death Coming* — 973.8
    Wills, Shomari. *Black Fortunes* — 920

Freedland, Jonathan
    ★*The Escape Artist* — 940.53

Freedman, H.
    ★*The Talmud* — 296.1

Freedman, Samuel G.
    Jew vs. Jew — 296

FREEDOM
    Acemoglu, Daron. *The Narrow Corridor* — 320.01
    Arana, Marie. *Bolivar* — B
    Bakewell, Sarah. ★*At the Existentialist Cafe* — 920
    Belcourt, Billy-Ray. ★*A History of My Brief Body* — B
    Boland, Eavan. *The Historians* — 821
    Brookhiser, Richard. *Give Me Liberty* — 320.540973
    Chemerinsky, Erwin. *Closing the Courthouse Door* — 347.73
    Cox, Josie. *Women Money Power* — 330.082
    Davis, Angela Y. *Abolition* — 364.6
    Dungy, Camille T. *Soil* — 635.0978
    Erdozain, Dominic. *One Nation Under Guns* — 363.33
    Finan, Christopher M. *How Free Speech Saved Democracy* — 342.73
    Fukuyama, Francis. *Liberalism and Its Discontents* — 320.51
    Gorman, Amanda. ★*Call Us What We Carry* — 811
    Hagglund, Martin. *This Life* — 110
    Harris, J. William. *The Hanging of Thomas Jeremiah* — B
    Hester, Diarmuid. *Nothing Ever Just Disappears* — 306.76
    Hoffman, David E. *Give Me Liberty* — B
    Holton, Woody. *Liberty Is Sweet* — 973.3
    Jones, Faith. *Sex Cult Nun* — B
    Laing, Olivia. *Everybody* — 323
    Longo, Matthew. *The Picnic* — 947.084
    May, Gregory. *A Madman's Will* — 973.5
    Mazower, Mark. *The Greek Revolution* — 949.5
    Metzl, Jonathan M. ★*What We've Become* — 364.152
    Miles, Tiya. ★*Wild Girls* — 304.2
    Moore, Peter. *Life, Liberty, and the Pursuit of Happiness* — 199
    Moss, Jeremiah. *Feral City* — B
    Oakes, James. *Freedom National* — 973.7
    Plant, Deborah G. *Of Greed and Glory* — 326
    Proenza-Coles, Christina. *American Founders* — 973
    Rousseau, Jean-Jacques. ★*The Social Contract* — 320.1
    Ruttenberg, Danya. *On Repentance and Repair* — 202
    Sankovitch, Nina. *American Rebels* — 920
    Smith, Patricia. *Unshuttered* — 811
    Smith, Tracy K. ★*To Free the Captives* — 818
    Sullivan, Rosemary. *Stalin's Daughter* — B
    Tesfamariam, Rahiel. ★*Imagine Freedom* — 305.896
    Watling, Sarah. *Tomorrow Perhaps the Future* — 946.081
    Watson, Bruce. *Freedom Summer* — 323.1196
    Will, George F. *The Conservative Sensibility* — 320.520973
    Woo, Ilyon. ★*Master Slave Husband Wife* — 920
    Ypi, Lea. ★*Free* — B
    Zygar, Mikhail. *The Empire Must Die* — 947.08

FREEDOM AND ART
    Ai, Weiwei. *Zodiac* — 741.5
    ★*Freedom from Fear*. Kennedy, David M. — 973.91
    Freedom in Exile. Dalai Lama — B
    Freedom National. Oakes, James — 973.7

FREEDOM OF EXPRESSION
    Eltahawy, Mona. *The Seven Necessary Sins for Women and Girls* — 305.42
    Febos, Melissa. ★*Body Work* — 808.06
    Goodman, Elyssa. *Glitter and Concrete* — 792.7
    McHangama, Jacob. ★*Free Speech* — 323.44
    Rosenberg, Ian. *The Fight for Free Speech* — 342.73

FREEDOM OF INFORMATION
    Connelly, Matthew James. *The Declassification Engine* — 352.3

FREEDOM OF RELIGION
    Barry, John M. *Roger Williams and the Creation of the American Soul* — 974.5
    Nussbaum, Martha Craven. *The New Religious Intolerance* — 201.723
    Waldman, Steven. *Sacred Liberty* — 341.4
    Warren, James A. *God, War, and Providence* — 974.5
    Weatherford, J. McIver. *Genghis Khan and the Quest for God* — 323.44
    Wexler, Jay. *Holy Hullabaloos* — 342.7308

FREEDOM OF SPEECH
    Finan, Christopher M. *How Free Speech Saved Democracy* — 342.73
    Gold, Judy. *Yes I Can Say That* — 792.7
    Healy, Thomas. *The Great Dissent* — 342.7308
    Kluger, Richard. *Indelible Ink* — B
    McHangama, Jacob. ★*Free Speech* — 323.44
    Rabban, David M. *Free Speech in Its Forgotten Years* — 342.73
    Rosenberg, Ian. *The Fight for Free Speech* — 342.73
    Rushdie, Salman. *Joseph Anton* — B
    Signer, Michael. *Cry Havoc* — 305.800973
    Sohn, Amy. *The Man Who Hated Women* — 363.28
    Stone, Geoffrey R. *Perilous Times* — 323.44
    Strossen, Nadine. *Hate* — 342.7308

FREEDOM OF THE PRESS
    Baron, Martin. ★*Collision of Power* — 070.4
    Hersh, Seymour M. *Reporter* — B
    Kluger, Richard. *Indelible Ink* — B
    McCraw, David Edward. *Truth in Our Times* — 342.7308
    Rosenberg, Ian. *The Fight for Free Speech* — 342.73
    Rushdie, Salman. *Joseph Anton* — B

FREEDOM RIDERS (CIVIL RIGHTS MOVEMENT)
    Arsenault, Raymond. *John Lewis* — B
    Branch, Taylor. ★*Pillar of Fire* — 323.1
    Dennis, David J., Jr. *The Movement Made Us* — B
    McWhorter, Diane. *Carry Me Home* — 976.1
    Person, Charles. *Buses Are a Comin'* — B

FREEDOM RIDES (CIVIL RIGHTS MOVEMENT)
    Person, Charles. *Buses Are a Comin'* — B

FREEDOM SEEKERS
    Blight, David W. *A Slave No More* — B
    Bordewich, Fergus M. *Bound for Canaan* — 973.7
    Delbanco, Andrew. *The War Before the War* — 973.7
    Douglass, Frederick. *My Bondage and My Freedom* — B
    Dunbar, Erica Armstrong. ★*Never Caught* — B
    Dunbar, Erica Armstrong. ★*She Came to Slay* — B
    Foner, Eric. ★*Gateway to Freedom* — 973.7
    Hecimovich, Gregg A. ★*The Life and Times of Hannah Crafts* — B
    Jacobs, Harriet. ★*Incidents in the Life of a Slave Girl* — B
    Larson, Kate Clifford. *Bound for the Promised Land* — B
    Lineberry, Cate. *Be Free or Die* — B
    Miles, Tiya. ★*Night Flyer* — B
    Nathans, Sydney. *To Free a Family* — B
    Painter, Nell Irvin. ★*Sojourner Truth* — B
    Shane, Scott. ★*Flee North* — 973.7
    Snodgrass, Mary Ellen. *The Underground Railroad* — 973.7
    Stiles, T. J. *Custer's Trials* — B
    Tobin, Jacqueline. *From Midnight to Dawn* — 973.7
    Tobin, Jacqueline. *Hidden in Plain View* — 973.7
    Woo, Ilyon. ★*Master Slave Husband Wife* — 920

Freedom Summer. Watson, Bruce — 323.1196
Freedom's Battle. Bass, Gary Jonathan — 341.5
Freedom's Detective. Lane, Charles — B
Freedom's Forge. Herman, Arthur — 940.53
Freedom's Prophet. Newman, Richard S. — B

PUBLIC LIBRARY CORE COLLECTION: NONFICTION
Twentieth Edition

Freehand. Birch, Helen	741.2
Freeing The Natural Voice. Linklater, Kristin	808.5
FREEMAN FAMILY	
Freeman, Scott. *Saving Tarboo Creek*	333.72
Freeman, Amanda	
Getting Me Cheap	362.83
Freeman, Andrea	
★*Ruin Their Crops on the Ground*	338.1
Freeman, Douglas Southall	
Lee	B
Freeman, Hadley	
Good Girls	616.85
House of Glass	B
FREEMAN, HADLEY	
Freeman, Hadley. *Good Girls*	616.85
Freeman, Joanne B.	
The Field of Blood	973.7
Freeman, Joshua Benjamin	
★*Behemoth*	338.6
Freeman, Michael	
The Photographer's Mind	770
Freeman, Sally Mott	
The Jersey Brothers	920
Freeman, Scott	
Saving Tarboo Creek	333.72
FREEWAYS	
Goldfarb, Ben. *Crossings*	333.77
Heat Moon, William Least. *Blue Highways*	917.304
Kimble, Megan. ★*City Limits*	388.1
FREIGHT AND FREIGHTAGE	
Goodman, Peter S. ★*How the World Ran Out of Everything*	658.7
McPhee, John. *Uncommon Carriers*	388
FREIGHTERS	
Geroux, William. *The Ghost Ships of Archangel*	940.54
McPhee, John. *Uncommon Carriers*	388
Freitas, Donna	
Consent	364.158092
FREITAS, DONNA	
Freitas, Donna. *Consent*	364.158092
Fremont, Helen	
The Escape Artist	B
FREMONT, HELEN	
Fremont, Helen. *The Escape Artist*	B
FREMONT, JESSIE BENTON, 1824-1902	
Inskeep, Steve. *Imperfect Union*	B
FREMONT, JOHN CHARLES, 1813-1890	
Inskeep, Steve. *Imperfect Union*	B
FRENCH ALPS	
Peppler, Rebekah. *Le Sud*	641.594
FRENCH AND INDIAN WAR, 1754-1763	
Calloway, Colin G. *The Indian World of George Washington*	323.1197
Demos, John. *The Unredeemed Captive*	973.2
Ellis, Joseph J. ★*His Excellency*	B
Stark, Peter. *Young Washington*	B
The **French** *Beauty Solution*. Thomas, Mathilde	646.7
FRENCH CANADIAN LITERATURE	
Nadeau, Jean-Benoit. ★*The Story of French*	440
Nadeau, Jean-Benoit. *The Story of Spanish*	460
The **French** *Chef in America*. Prud'homme, Alex	B
French *Cinema, 2nd Ed.* Fournier-Lanzoni, Remi	791.43
FRENCH HISTORY	
Bakewell, Sarah. *How to Live—Or—A Life of Montaigne*	B
Beevor, Antony. *D-Day*	940.54
Bellos, David. *The Novel of the Century*	843
Bilger, Burkhard. *Fatherland*	B
Broers, Michael. *Napoleon*	B
Broers, Michael. *Napoleon*	944.05
Broers, Michael. *Napoleon*	B
Burke, Edmund. *Reflections on the Revolution in France*	944.04
Castor, Helen. *Joan of Arc*	B
Churchill, Winston. *Their Finest Hour*	940.53
Darnton, Robert. *The Revolutionary Temper*	944
Davidson, Ian. *The French Revolution*	944.04
Dugard, Martin. *Taking Paris*	940.54
Duncan, Michael. ★*Hero of Two Worlds*	B
Ernaux, Annie. ★*The Years*	B
Fournier-Lanzoni, Remi. *French Cinema, 2nd Ed.*	791.43
Fraser, Antonia. *Love and Louis XIV*	B
Fraser, Antonia. *Marie Antoinette*	B
Gaines, James R. *For Liberty and Glory*	B
Goldstone, Nancy Bazelon. *The Rival Queens*	944
Graff, Garrett M. ★*When the Sea Came Alive*	940.54
Grose, Peter. *A Good Place to Hide*	940.53
Helm, Sarah. *A Life in Secrets*	B
Humbert, Agnes. *Resistance*	B
Jager, Eric. *Blood Royal*	944.026
Johnson, Paul. *Napoleon*	B
Kaiser, Charles. *The Cost of Courage*	B
Kershaw, Alex. *Avenue of Spies*	940.53
King, David. *Death in the City of Light*	364.152
Kix, Paul. *The Saboteur*	940.53
Lambert, Raymond. *Every Man a Hero*	B
Lever, Evelyne. *Marie Antoinette*	B
Magida, Arthur J. *Code Name Madeleine*	940.54
Mansel, Philip. *King of the World*	B
McPhee, Peter. *Robespierre*	B
Moorehead, Caroline. *A Train in Winter*	940.53
Moorehead, Caroline. *Village of Secrets*	944
Norwich, John Julius. *A History of France*	944
Olson, Lynne. ★*Madame Fourcade's Secret War*	B
Paxson, Margaret. *The Plateau*	362.87
Popkin, Jeremy D. *A New World Begins*	944.04
Porter, Carolyn. *Marcel's Letters*	940.54
Purnell, Sonia. ★*A Woman of No Importance*	B
Reiss, Tom. *The Black Count*	B
Robb, Graham. *The Discovery of France*	944
Robb, Graham. *France*	944
Roberts, Andrew. ★*Napoleon*	B
Rosbottom, Ronald C. *When Paris Went Dark*	944.0816
Rosenberg, Justus. *The Art of Resistance*	B
Schama, Simon. *Citizens*	944.04
Schwarz, Geraldine. *Those Who Forget*	940.53
Scurr, Ruth. *Fatal Purity*	B
Shaw, Bernard. *Saint Joan*	822
Spoto, Donald. *Joan*	B
Tuchman, Barbara W. ★*A Distant Mirror*	944
Weir, Alison. *Eleanor of Aquitaine*	B
Zamoyski, Adam. *Napoleon*	B
The **French** *Ingredient*. Bertch, Jane	B
FRENCH LANGUAGE	
Collins, Lauren. *When in French*	B
Nadeau, Jean-Benoit. ★*The Story of French*	440
The **French** *Laundry Cookbook*. Keller, Thomas	641.5
FRENCH PARTICIPATION IN WARS	
Duncan, Michael. ★*Hero of Two Worlds*	B
Ferreiro, Larrie D. *Brothers at Arms*	327.73
FRENCH PEOPLE	
Berr, Helene. *The Journal of Helene Berr*	B
Bertch, Jane. *The French Ingredient*	B
Darnton, Robert. *The Revolutionary Temper*	944
Finkel, Michael. *The Art Thief*	364.1628
Grose, Peter. *A Good Place to Hide*	940.53
Olson, Lynne. ★*Empress of the Nile*	B
Pepin, Jacques. *Art of the Chicken*	641.665
Weir, Alison. *Queens of the Age of Chivalry*	920
FRENCH PEOPLE IN THE UNITED STATES	
Tocqueville, Alexis de. *Democracy in America*	320.973
FRENCH RESISTANCE (WORLD WAR II)	
Dugard, Martin. *Taking Paris*	940.54
Helm, Sarah. *A Life in Secrets*	B
Humbert, Agnes. *Resistance*	B
Jackson, Julian. *De Gaulle*	B
Kaiser, Charles. *The Cost of Courage*	B
Kershaw, Alex. *Avenue of Spies*	940.53
Kix, Paul. *The Saboteur*	940.53
Loftis, Larry. *Code Name*	B
Magida, Arthur J. *Code Name Madeleine*	940.54
Moorehead, Caroline. *A Train in Winter*	940.53
Moorehead, Caroline. *Village of Secrets*	944
Olson, Lynne. ★*Madame Fourcade's Secret War*	B
Purnell, Sonia. ★*A Woman of No Importance*	B
Rosbottom, Ronald C. *When Paris Went Dark*	944.0816
Rose, Sarah. *D-Day Girls*	940.53
Rosenberg, Justus. *The Art of Resistance*	B
The **French** *Revolution*. Davidson, Ian	944.04

AUTHOR, TITLE, SERIES AND SUBJECT INDEX

FRENCH REVOLUTION, 1789-1799
    Burke, Edmund. *Reflections on the Revolution in France*   944.04
    Cornwell, Bernard. *Waterloo*   940.2
    Darnton, Robert. *The Revolutionary Temper*   944
    Popkin, Jeremy D. *A New World Begins*   944.04
FRENCH RIVIERA
    De Courcy, Anne. *Chanel's Riviera*   944.9
    Peppler, Rebekah. *Le Sud*   641.594
FRENCH, DANIEL CHESTER, 1850-1931
    Holzer, Harold. *Monument Man*   B
French, Howard W.
    Born in Blackness   960
French, Patrick
    The World Is What It Is   B
Frenemies. Auletta, Ken   659.1
Frenkel, Francoise
    A Bookshop in Berlin   B
FRENKEL, FRANCOISE, 1889-1975
    Frenkel, Francoise. *A Bookshop in Berlin*   B
Frequently Asked Questions About the Universe. Cham, Jorge   523.1
FRESCOES
    King, Ross. *Michelangelo & the Pope's Ceiling*   759.5
★*The Fresh Eggs Daily Cookbook*. Steele, Lisa   641.6
Fresh Fish. Thompson, Jennifer Trainer   641.3
Fresh from Poland. Korkosz, Michal   641.594
Fresh from the Garden. Whitman, John   635.9
Fresh Midwest. King, Maren Ellingboe   641.5977
Fresh off the Boat. Huang, Eddie   B
FRESHWATER FISHES
    Malarkey, Tucker. *Stronghold*   639.2
    Page, Lawrence M. ★*Peterson Field Guide to Freshwater Fishes of North America North of Mexico*   597.176
Freud. Gay, Peter   B
★*Freud*. Roudinesco, Elisabeth   B
FREUD, LUCIAN
    Feaver, William. ★*The Lives of Lucian Freud*   B
    Smee, Sebastian. *The Art of Rivalry*   700.92
Freud, Sigmund
    ★*The Basic Writings of Sigmund Freud*   150.19
    Civilization and Its Discontents   150.19
    ★*The Interpretation of Dreams*   154.6
FREUD, SIGMUND, 1856-1939
    Bloom, Paul. *Psych*   150
    Brownstein, Gabriel. ★*The Secret Mind of Bertha Pappenheim*   616.85
    Gay, Peter. *Freud*   B
    Gay, Peter. *A Godless Jew*   150.19
    Nagorski, Andrew. *Saving Freud*   940.53
    Roudinesco, Elisabeth. ★*Freud*   B
    Tallis, Frank. ★*Mortal Secrets*   B
Frey, Julia Bloch
    Toulouse-Lautrec   B
Frey, Kate
    The Bee-Friendly Garden   595.79
    Ground Rules   635
Frida. Herrera, Hayden   B
Frida in America. Stahr, Celia   B
★*Frida Kahlo*. Hesse, Maria   B
Frida Kahlo. Lozano, Luis-Martin   759.972
★*The Friday Afternoon Club*. Dunne, Griffin   B
★*Friday Night Lights*. Bissinger, H. G.   796.332
Friday, Saturday, Sunday in Texas. Eatman, Nicholas   796.332
Fridland, Valerie
    ★*Like, Literally, Dude*   420.141
Fried, Stephen
    Rush   B
Friedan, Betty
    ★*The Feminine Mystique*   305.42
Friedlander, Saul
    Nazi Germany and the Jews   940.53
    Nazi Germany and the Jews   940.53
Friedman, Andrew
    The Dish   647.95
FRIEDMAN, ANN
    Sow, Aminatou. *Big Friendship*   177
Friedman, Barry
    ★*Unwarranted*   344.7305
    The Will of the People   347.73

Friedman, Benjamin M.
    Religion and the Rise of Capitalism   330.12
Friedman, Elias Weiss
    The Dogist   779
FRIEDMAN, ELIZABETH, 1892-1980
    Fagone, Jason. *The Woman Who Smashed Codes*   B
Friedman, George
    Flashpoints   940.56
Friedman, Matti
    Pumpkinflowers   B
    Spies of No Country   327.12
FRIEDMAN, MATTI
    Friedman, Matti. *Pumpkinflowers*   B
Friedman, Maurice S.
    Encounter on the Narrow Ridge   B
Friedman, Rachel
    ★*And Then We Grew Up*   305.24
FRIEDMAN, RACHEL, 1981-
    Friedman, Rachel. ★*And Then We Grew Up*   305.24
Friedman, Ron
    Decoding Greatness   650.1
Friedman, Thomas L.
    ★*From Beirut to Jerusalem*   956.04
    ★*Thank You for Being Late*   303.48
FRIEDMAN, THOMAS L.
    Friedman, Thomas L. ★*From Beirut to Jerusalem*   956.04
Friedman, Tova
    ★*The Daughter of Auschwitz*   B
Friedwald, Will
    The Great Jazz and Pop Vocal Albums   016.78
    ★*Sinatra! the Song Is You*   782.42164
    Straighten up and Fly Right   782.42164
Friel, Joe
    The Triathlete's Training Bible   796.42
Friend of a Friend.. Burkus, David   650.1
Friend, David
    Watching the World Change   974.7
Friendly Reminders. Tatum, Scott   158.1
Friends Divided. Wood, Gordon S.   920
Friends, Lovers, and the Big Terrible Thing. Perry, Matthew   B
Friendship. Denworth, Lydia   158.2
FRIENDSHIP
    Abdul-Jabbar, Kareem. *Coach Wooden and Me*   B
    Abdurraqib, Hanif. *A Fortune for Your Disaster*   811
    Ackerman, Elliot. *Places and Names*   B
    Albom, Mitch. *Tuesdays with Morrie*   B
    Alderton, Dolly. *Everything I Know About Love*   B
    Baker, Billy. *We Need to Hang Out*   177
    Bass, Rick. *The Traveling Feast*   B
    Bilton, Nick. *Hatching Twitter*   006.7
    Black Thought. *The Upcycled Self*   B
    Bradbury, Ray. ★*Remembrance*   813
    Bradford, Joy Harden. *Sisterhood Heals*   158.2
    Brand, Christo. *Mandela*   B
    Brennan, Thomas J. *Shooting Ghosts*   B
    Brown, Daniel James. ★*The Boys in the Boat*   797.12
    Caldwell, Gail. *Let's Take the Long Way Home*   B
    Capote, Truman. *Too Brief a Treat*   B
    Clemmons, Francois S. *Officer Clemmons*   B
    Cohen, Rhaina. ★*The Other Significant Others*   177
    Copeland, Misty. *The Wind at My Back*   B
    De Vise, Daniel. ★*The Blues Brothers*   791.43
    Denworth, Lydia. *Friendship*   158.2
    Ebert, Roger. *Life Itself*   B
    Ellis, Helen. *Bring Your Baggage and Don't Pack Light*   814
    Eyman, Scott. *Hank and Jim*   920
    Fenn, Lisa. *Carry On*   B
    Fischer, Jenna. *The Office BFFs*   791.45
    Fox, Margalit. *The Confidence Men*   940.4
    Fox, Michael J. *No Time Like the Future*   B
    Franco, Marisa G. *Platonic*   302.34
    Gerson, Merissa Nathan. *Forget Prayers, Bring Cake*   155.9
    Glass, Charles. *Soldiers Don't Go Mad*   616.85
    Greitens, Eric. *Resilience*   155.2
    Gunn, Thom. ★*The Letters of Thom Gunn*   821
    Hagberg, Eva. *How to Be Loved*   616.7
    Halberstam, David. *The Teammates*   B
    Hardwick, Elizabeth. *The Dolphin Letters, 1970-1979*   811

PUBLIC LIBRARY CORE COLLECTION: NONFICTION
Twentieth Edition

Heughan, Sam. *Waypoints*	B
Hill, Clint. *My Travels with Mrs. Kennedy*	B
Hobbs, Jeff. *Show Them You're Good*	373
Howard, Hugh. *Architects of an American Landscape*	712.092
Jackson, Danielle Bayard. *Fighting for Our Friendships*	302.34
Jahren, Hope. ★*Lab Girl*	B
James, Victoria. *Wine Girl*	B
Jaouad, Suleika. ★*Between Two Kingdoms*	B
Killam, Kasley. *The Art and Science of Connection*	302
King, Ross. ★*Mad Enchantment*	759.4
Lewis, Damien. *The Dog Who Could Fly*	940.54
McAnulty, Dara. *Diary of a Young Naturalist*	508.092
Millet, Lydia. *We Loved It All*	813
Mlodinow, Leonard. *Stephen Hawking*	B
Mortimer, Frank. *Bee People and the Bugs They Love*	B
Mukantabana, Yseult P. ★*Real Friends Talk About Race*	305.8
Nagorski, Andrew. *Saving Freud*	940.53
Obama, Michelle. ★*The Light We Carry*	B
Olivarez, Jose. *Promises of Gold = Promesas De Oro*	811
Oppedisano, Tony. *Sinatra and Me*	B
Patchett, Ann. ★*These Precious Days*	814
Patchett, Ann. *Truth & Beauty*	B
Perron, Cam. ★*Comeback Season*	796.357
Pinckney, Darryl. *Come Back in September*	B
Poehler, Amy. *Yes Please*	B
Power, Carla. *If the Oceans Were Ink*	B
Reynolds, Debbie. *Make 'Em Laugh*	B
Rosen, Jonathan. ★*The Best Minds*	616.89
Ruhl, Sarah. *Letters from Max*	811
Russo, Richard. *The Destiny Thief*	814
Safina, Carl. ★*Alfie and Me*	598.9
Sankovitch, Nina. *American Rebels*	920
Schafer, John R. *The Like Switch*	158.2
Schloss, Edith. *The Loft Generation*	700.9
Schwalbe, Will. *We Should Not Be Friends*	B
Shafrir, Doree. *Thanks for Waiting*	B
Singer, Matt. *Opposable Thumbs*	791.43
Smee, Sebastian. *The Art of Rivalry*	700.92
Smith, Danez. ★*Homie*	811
Smith, Patti. ★*Just Kids*	B
Soep, Elisabeth. *Other People's Words*	155.9
Sow, Aminatou. *Big Friendship*	177
Spicer, Charles. *Coffee with Hitler*	941.084
Tenzin Priyadarshi. *Running Toward Mystery*	B
Tolan, Sandy. ★*The Lemon Tree*	B
Verdelle, A. J. *Miss Chloe*	B
Von Drehle, David. ★*The Book of Charlie*	B
Watts, Reggie. *Great Falls, MT*	B
Waxman, Jamye. *How to Break up with Anyone*	158.2
FRIGATES	
Taylor, Stephen. *Commander*	B
Toll, Ian W. ★*Six Frigates*	359.00973
FRISBEE (GAME)	
Gessner, David. *Ultimate Glory*	796.2
Frisoni, Christine-Lea	
The Big Book of a Miniature House	745.592
Fritz, Ian	
What the Taliban Told Me	B
Fritzsche, Peter	
Life and Death in the Third Reich	943.086
From Airline Reservations to Sonic the Hedgehog. Campbell-Kelly, Martin	338.4
★*From Beirut to Jerusalem.* Friedman, Thomas L.	956.04
From Broken Glass. Ross, Steve	B
From Dawn to Decadence. Barzun, Jacques	940.2
From Eternity to Here. Carroll, Sean M.	530.11
★*From Freezer to Cooker.* Conner, Polly	641.6
From Here to Eternity. Doughty, Caitlin	393
From Hollywood with Love. Meslow, Scott	791.43
From Midnight to Dawn. Tobin, Jacqueline	973.7
From One Cell. Stanger, Ben	571.6
From Saturday Night to Sunday Night. Ebersol, Dick	B
★*From Scratch.* Locke, Tembi	B
★*From Slavery to Freedom.* Franklin, John Hope	973
From Spirituals to Symphonies. Walker-Hill, Helen	780
From The Corner of the Oval. Dorey-Stein, Beck	B
From The Folks Who Brought You the Weekend. Murolo, Priscilla	331
From The Ground Up. Schultz, Howard	B
From The Marine Corps to College. Ventrone, Jillian	378.1
★*From The Moment They Met It Was Murder.* Silver, Alain	791.43
From The New World. Graham, Jorie	811
From The North. Bjork, Katrin	641.594
From The Oven to the Table. Henry, Diana	641.82
From The Ruins of Empire. Mishra, Pankaj	950.4
From The Streets of Shaolin. Fernando, S. H., Jr	782.421
From Unincorporated Territory [amot]. Santos Perez, Craig	811
Front Row at the Trump Show. Karl, Jonathan	973.933
FRONTAL LOBOTOMY	
Larson, Kate Clifford. *Rosemary*	B
FRONTIER AND PIONEER LIFE	
Barra, Allen. *Inventing Wyatt Earp*	B
Boessenecker, John. *Gentleman Bandit*	B
Borneman, Walter R. *Alaska*	979.8
Brands, H. W. *The Age of Gold*	979.4
Brands, H. W. *Dreams of El Dorado*	978
Brands, H. W. *The Last Campaign*	973.8
Brown, Daniel James. *The Indifferent Stars Above*	B
Castner, Brian. *Stampede*	971.9
Clavin, Thomas. *Dodge City*	978.1
Clavin, Thomas. *Wild Bill*	B
Cox, Anna-Lisa. *The Bone and Sinew of the Land*	977
Crouch, Gregory. *The Bonanza King*	B
Drury, Bob. *Blood and Treasure*	B
Eisler, Benita. *The Red Man's Bones*	B
Fraser, Caroline. ★*Prairie Fires*	B
Gallagher, Winifred. *New Women in the Old West*	978.02
Grandin, Greg. *The End of the Myth*	973
Gwynne, S. C. *Empire of the Summer Moon*	B
Hyde, Anne Farrar. *Empires, Nations, and Families*	978
Kelly, Joseph. *Marooned*	975.5
Keneally, Thomas. *A Commonwealth of Thieves*	994
Laskin, David. *The Children's Blizzard*	977
McCullough, David G. *The Pioneers*	920
McDowell, Marta. *The World of Laura Ingalls Wilder*	813
Morgan, Robert. *Boone*	B
Nelson, Megan Kate. *The Three-Cornered War*	978
Raban, Jonathan. *Bad Land*	978
Roberts, David. *Once They Moved Like the Wind*	B
Sides, Hampton. *Blood and Thunder*	978
Stiles, T. J. *Custer's Trials*	B
Wallis, Michael. *The Best Land Under Heaven*	978
Wallis, Michael. *Billy the Kid*	B
Ward, Geoffrey C. *The West*	978
Warren, Louis S. *Buffalo Bill's America*	B
Wilder, Laura Ingalls. *Pioneer Girl*	B
FRONTIER THESIS	
Grandin, Greg. *The End of the Myth*	973
FROST, DAVID	
Reston, James. *The Conviction of Richard Nixon*	973.924092
Frost, Mark	
The Match	796.352
FROST, ROBERT, 1874-1963	
Parini, Jay. *Robert Frost*	B
★*Frostbite.* Twilley, Nicola	621
FROZEN DESSERTS	
Gerson, Fany. *Mexican Ice Cream*	641.86
Frozen Earth. Macdougall, J. D.	551.7
FROZEN FOODS	
Christensen, Ashley. *It's Always Freezer Season*	641.5
Frozen in Time. Zuckoff, Mitchell	998.2
FRUIT	
Berens, Abra. *Pulp*	641.6
Jabbour, Niki. ★*Groundbreaking Food Gardens*	635
Pleasant, Barbara. *Homegrown Pantry*	635
FRUIT GROWING	
Webb, Leah M. *The Seven-Step Homestead*	635
FRUIT TREES	
Ralph, Ann. *Grow a Little Fruit Tree*	634
Webb, Leah M. *The Seven-Step Homestead*	635
Frum, David	
Trumpocracy	973.933
FRUSTRATION	
Irby, Samantha. *We Are Never Meeting in Real Life*	814
FRY, VARIAN, 1908-1967	
Rosenberg, Justus. *The Art of Resistance*	B
Fuentes, Carlos	
The Buried Mirror	946

AUTHOR, TITLE, SERIES AND SUBJECT INDEX

Fuentes, Laura
   The Best Homemade Kids' Snacks on the Planet — 641.5
Fugard, Athol
   ★*"master Harold"—And the Boys* — 822
FUGATE, CARIL ANN
   MacLean, Harry N. *Starkweather* — 364.152
FUGITIVES
   Bascomb, Neal. *Hunting Eichmann* — 943.086
   Bergen, Peter L. *The Rise and Fall of Osama Bin Laden* — 958.104
   Cullen, Kevin. *Whitey Bulger* — B
   Diamond, Cheryl. *Nowhere Girl* — B
   Hutton, Paul Andrew. *The Apache Wars* — 979
   Jaku, Eddie. ★*The Happiest Man on Earth* — B
   Jobb, Dean. *A Gentleman and a Thief* — 364.16
   Minutaglio, Bill. *The Most Dangerous Man in America* — B
   Sands, Philippe. *The Ratline* — B
   Sherman, Casey. *Hunting Whitey* — B
   Talty, Stephan. *The Good Assassin* — 364.15
   Wallace, Chris. *Countdown Bin Laden* — 958.104
   Wetherall, Tyler. *No Way Home* — B
Fuhrer, Margaret
   ★*American Dance* — 792.809
Fuhrman, Joel
   Eat to Live Quick & Easy Cookbook — 641.5
Fuhrmann, Joseph T.
   Rasputin — B
FUKUHARA, FRANK, 1924-2015
   Sakamoto, Pamela Rotner. *Midnight in Broad Daylight* — 940.53
FUKUHARA, HARRY K., 1920-2015
   Sakamoto, Pamela Rotner. *Midnight in Broad Daylight* — 940.53
FUKUHARA, PIERCE, 1922-2008
   Sakamoto, Pamela Rotner. *Midnight in Broad Daylight* — 940.53
FUKUSHIMA NUCLEAR DISASTER, JAPAN, 2011
   Parry, Richard Lloyd. *Ghosts of the Tsunami* — 952.05
   Pilling, David. *Bending Adversity* — 952.0512
   Roripaugh, Lee Ann. *Tsunami vs. the Fukushima 50* — 811
   Vollmann, William T. *No Immediate Danger* — 333.79
Fukuyama, Francis
   Liberalism and Its Discontents — 320.51
   Political Order and Political Decay — 320.1
Fulfillment. MacGillis, Alec — 381
Full Body Burden. Iversen, Kristen — 363.17
Full Disclosure. Daniels, Stormy — B
Full Dissidence. Bryant, Howard — 306.20973
Full Engagement! Tracy, Brian — 658.3
A Full Life. Carter, Jimmy — B
Full Spectrum. Rogers, Adam — 152.14
Fuller, Alexandra
   Don't Let's Go to the Dogs Tonight — B
   Leaving Before the Rains Come — B
   Travel Light, Move Fast — B
FULLER, ALEXANDRA, 1969-
   Fuller, Alexandra. *Don't Let's Go to the Dogs Tonight* — B
   Fuller, Alexandra. *Leaving Before the Rains Come* — B
   Fuller, Alexandra. *Travel Light, Move Fast* — B
FULLER, LUCIA FAIRCHILD, 1872-1924
   Lucey, Donna M. *Sargent's Women* — 920
Fuller, Pamela
   ★*The Leader's Guide to Unconscious Bias* — 658.3
FULLER, TIM (TIMOTHY DONALD), 1940-2015
   Fuller, Alexandra. *Travel Light, Move Fast* — B
Fullilove, Michael
   Rendezvous with Destiny — 973.917092
Fully Alive. Shriver, Timothy P. — 796.087
Fumudoh, Ziwe
   ★*Black Friend* — 814
★*Fun Home*. Bechdel, Alison — 741.5
FUND RAISING
   Ford, Tanisha C. *Our Secret Society* — B
   Givhan, Robin. *The Battle of Versailles* — 746.9
   Nelson, Willie. *It's a Long Story* — B
FUNDAMENTALISM
   Abou El Fadl, Khaled. *The Great Theft* — 297.09
   Armstrong, Karen. *The Battle for God* — 200
   Armstrong, Karen. *The Lost Art of Scripture* — 208
   Baker, Deborah. *The Convert* — B
   Bowden, Mark. *Guests of the Ayatollah* — 955.05
   Denton, Sally. *The Colony* — 364.152
   Eteraz, Ali. *Children of Dust* — B
   FitzGerald, Frances. *The Evangelicals* — 277
   Ghobash, Omar Saif. *Letters to a Young Muslim* — 297.09
   Griffith, R. Marie. *Moral Combat* — 261.8
   Rashid, Ahmed. *Taliban* — 958.104
   Ryrie, Alec. *Protestants* — 280
   Warrick, Joby. *Black Flags* — 956.9104
   Wood, Graeme. *The Way of the Strangers* — 363.325
   Yancey, Philip. ★*Where the Light Fell* — B
FUNDAMENTALISTS
   Baker, Deborah. *The Convert* — B
   Blanford, Nicholas. *Warriors of God* — 956.9204
   Feldman, Deborah. *Unorthodox* — B
   Rashid, Ahmed. *Taliban* — 958.104
Fundamentals. Wilczek, Frank — 530.01
★*Fundamentals of Collection Development and Management*. Johnson, Peggy — 025
★*Fundamentals of Electronic Resources Management*. Verminski, Alana — 025.2
Fundamentals of Library Supervision. McNeil, Beth — 023
Fundamentals of Reference. Mulac, Carolyn — 025.5
Funder, Anna
   Wifedom — B
FUNERAL HOMES
   Bechdel, Alison. ★*Fun Home* — 741.5
FUNERALS
   Cotton, Tom. *Sacred Duty* — 355.6
   Doughty, Caitlin. *From Here to Eternity* — 393
   Doughty, Caitlin. *Will My Cat Eat My Eyeballs?* — 306.9
   Eisler, Benita. ★*Chopin's Funeral* — B
   Lyons, Anna. *We All Know How This Ends* — 362.17
   McElya, Micki. *The Politics of Mourning* — 975.5
   Mitford, Jessica. ★*The American Way of Death Revisited* — 338.4
Fung, Jason
   ★*The Cancer Code* — 616.99
FUNGI
   Lincoff, Gary. *The Audubon Society Field Guide to North American Mushrooms* — 579.6
   Monosson, Emily. ★*Blight* — 616.9
   Sheldrake, Merlin. *Entangled Life* — 579.5
FUNK MUSIC
   Prince. *The Beautiful Ones* — B
   Stone, Sly. *Thank You (Falettinme Be Mice Elf Agin)* — B
Funk, Kristi
   Breasts — 616.99
Funk, Mason
   The Book of Pride — 920
Funny Man. McGilligan, Patrick — B
FUR INDUSTRY AND TRADE
   Miles, Tiya. *The Dawn of Detroit* — 977.4
   Stark, Peter. *Astoria* — 979.5
FUR TRADERS
   Hyde, Anne Farrar. ★*Born of Lakes and Plains* — 978
★*The Furies*. Flock, Elizabeth — 305.48
★*Furious Hours*. Cep, Casey N. — 364.152
Furious Love. Kashner, Sam — B
A Furious Sky. Dolin, Eric Jay — 363.34
Furiously Happy. Lawson, Jenny — B
FURNISH, DAVID
   John, Elton. ★*Me* — B
Furnishing Forward. Bridges, Sheila — 747
FURNITURE
   Aronson, Joseph. *The Encyclopedia of Furniture* — 749
   Bryson, Bill. ★*At Home* — 643
   Hingley, Brian D. *Furniture Repair & Restoration* — 684.1
   Lee, Vinny. *Kitchenalia* — 747.7
   Miller, Judith. *Furniture* — 749
   Pourny, Christophe. ★*The Furniture Bible* — 684.1
Furniture. Miller, Judith — 749
★*The Furniture Bible*. Pourny, Christophe — 684.1
FURNITURE FINISHING
   Blair, Barb. *Furniture Makeovers* — 684.1
   Hingley, Brian D. *Furniture Repair & Restoration* — 684.1
   Pourny, Christophe. ★*The Furniture Bible* — 684.1
FURNITURE INDUSTRY AND TRADE
   Aronson, Joseph. *The Encyclopedia of Furniture* — 749
   Macy, Beth. ★*Factory Man* — 338.7
   Miller, Judith. *Furniture* — 749
   Pourny, Christophe. ★*The Furniture Bible* — 684.1

PUBLIC LIBRARY CORE COLLECTION: NONFICTION
Twentieth Edition

Furniture Makeovers. Blair, Barb — 684.1
FURNITURE MAKERS
    Aronson, Joseph. *The Encyclopedia of Furniture* — 749
    Miller, Judith. *Furniture* — 749
Furniture Repair & Restoration. Hingley, Brian D. — 684.1
Furry Logic. Durrani, Matin — 591.5
Fury, Shawn
    Rise and Fire — 796.323
Fusco, Daniel
    Crazy Happy — 248.4
Futterman, Matthew
    Running to the Edge — 796.42071
Future Chefs. Ganeshram, Ramin — 641.3
The *Future* Earth. Holthaus, Eric — 363.738
The *Future* Is History. Gessen, Masha — 947.086
★The *Future* of Humanity. Kaku, Michio — 629.45
The *Future* of Ideas. Lessig, Lawrence — 346.04
The *Future* of Life. Wilson, Edward O. — 333.95
The *Future* of the Catholic Church with Pope Francis. Wills, Garry — 282.09
The *Future* of the Race. Gates, Henry Louis — 305.896
Futureface. Wagner, Alex — B
★*Fuzz*. Roach, Mary — 591.5

G

G-Man. Gage, Beverly — B
GABALDON, DIANA
    Carle-Sanders, Theresa. *Outlander Kitchen* — 641.5
Gabbard, Krin
    Better Git It in Your Soul — B
Gabbert, Elisa
    Any Person Is the Only Self — 814
GABBERT, ELISA
    Gabbert, Elisa. *Any Person Is the Only Self* — 814
Gabler, Neal
    ★*Against the Wind* — B
    Catching the Wind — B
    Walt Disney — B
Gabriel. Hirsch, Edward — 811
★*Gabriel* Garcia Marquez. Martin, Gerald — B
Gabriel, Mary
    Love and Capital — 920
    Madonna — B
    Ninth Street Women — 920
GACY, JOHN WAYNE, 1942-1994
    Nelson, David B. *Boys Enter the House* — 364.152
Gaddis, John Lewis
    On Grand Strategy — 355.4
Gaddy, K. R.
    ★*Well of Souls* — 787
Gadsby, Hannah
    ★*Ten Steps to Nanette* — B
Gaffigan, Jeannie
    When Life Gives You Pears — B
GAFFIGAN, JEANNIE, 1970-
    Gaffigan, Jeannie. *When Life Gives You Pears* — B
Gaffigan, Jim
    Dad Is Fat — 814
GAFFIGAN, JIM
    Gaffigan, Jim. *Dad Is Fat* — 814
Gaffney, Ginger
    Half Broke — B
GAFFNEY, GINGER
    Gaffney, Ginger. *Half Broke* — B
GAGARIN, YURI ALEKSEYEVICH, 1934-1968
    Walker, Stephen. *Beyond* — 629.45
Gage, Beverly
    The Day Wall Street Exploded — 974.7
    G-Man — B
Gagne, Patric
    Sociopath — B
GAGNE, PATRIC
    Gagne, Patric. *Sociopath* — B
The *Gaijin* Cookbook. Orkin, Ivan — 641.595
Gaiman, Neil
    The View from the Cheap Seats — 824

GAIMAN, NEIL
    Campbell, Hayley. *The Art of Neil Gaiman* — B
Gaines, James R.
    For Liberty and Glory — B
Gaines, Joanna
    ★*Magnolia Table* — 641.5975
    The Stories We Tell — B
GAINES, JOANNA, 1978-
    Gaines, Joanna. *The Stories We Tell* — B
Galanti, Regine
    ★*Parenting Anxious Kids* — 155.4
Galassi, Peter
    Ansel Adams in Yosemite Valley — 770.92
GALAXIES
    McTier, Moiya. *The Milky Way* — 523.1
    Tyson, Neil deGrasse. *To Infinity and Beyond* — 520
    Tyson, Neil deGrasse. *Welcome to the Universe* — 523.1
Galaxy, Jackson
    ★*Total Cat Mojo* — 636.8
Galbraith, John Kenneth
    ★*The Great Crash, 1929* — 338.5
Galbraith, Melissa
    How to Embroider Texture and Pattern — 746.44
Galeano, Eduardo
    Soccer in Sun and Shadow — 796.334
Galeotti, Mark
    A Short History of Russia — 947.086
GALILEI, GALILEO, 1564-1642
    Fauber, L. S. *Heaven on Earth* — B
    Strathern, Paul. *The Florentines* — 945
Galinsky, Ellen
    ★*The Breakthrough Years* — 649
GALIZIA, DAPHNE CARUANA, 1964-2017
    Caruana Galizia, Paul. ★*A Death in Malta* — 364.15
GALLAGHER, EDDIE, 1979-
    Philipps, David. *Alpha* — 956.7044
Gallagher, Richard E.
    Demonic Foes — 133.42
Gallagher, Tess
    Dear Ghosts — 811
    Is, Is Not — 811
Gallagher, Winifred
    New Women in the Old West — 978.02
GALLATIN, ALBERT, 1761-1849
    McCraw, Thomas K. ★*The Founders and Finance* — 330.973
Gallego, Ruben
    They Called Us — 956.7044
GALLEGO, RUBEN, 1979-
    Gallego, Ruben. *They Called Us* — 956.7044
The *Galleons*. Barot, Rick — 811
The *Gallery* of Miracles and Madness. English, Charlie — 709.04
GALLIANO, JOHN
    Thomas, Dana. *Gods and Kings* — 920
Gallo, Amy
    Getting Along — 658.4
Gallo, Carmine
    The Bezos Blueprint — 658.4
    Talk Like Ted — 658.4
GALLOWAY, JOSEPH L.
    Moore, Harold G. *We Are Soldiers Still* — 959.704
Galloway, Scott
    The Four — 338.7
Gallwey, W. Timothy
    ★*The Inner Game of Tennis* — 796.342
GALVESTON, TEXAS
    Johnson, Kirk W. *The Fishermen and the Dragon* — 976.4
GALVIN FAMILY
    Kolker, Robert. ★*Hidden Valley Road* — 920
GAMA, VASCO DA, 1469-1524
    Cliff, Nigel. *Holy War* — 909
The *Gambler*. Rempel, William C. — B
Gambler. Walters, Billy — 796.092
GAMBLERS
    Brooks, Michael. *The Quantum Astrologer's Handbook* — B
    McManus, James. ★*Positively Fifth Street* — 795.41
    Ridley, Jane. *The Heir Apparent* — B
    Thorp, Edward O. *A Man for All Markets* — B
    Walters, Billy. *Gambler* — 796.092

AUTHOR, TITLE, SERIES AND SUBJECT INDEX

GAMBLING
    Barbarisi, Daniel. *Dueling with Kings* — 793.93
    Goodman, Matthew. *The City Game* — 796.323
    Hill, David. *The Vapors* — 976.7
    Konnikova, Maria. *The Biggest Bluff* — 795.412
    Lang, Arne K. *Sports Betting and Bookmaking* — 798.4010973
    Manzione, Gianmarc. *Pin Action* — B
    Peta, Joe. *Trading Bases* — 796.357
    Rempel, William C. *The Gambler* — B
    Thorp, Edward O. *A Man for All Markets* — B
    Walters, Billy. *Gambler* — 796.092

GAMBLING SYSTEMS
    Thorp, Edward O. *A Man for All Markets* — B

Gambling with Armageddon. Sherwin, Martin J. — 972.9106
The Game. Colt, George Howe — 796.332
The Game. Pessah, Jon — 796.357

GAME AND GAME BIRDS
    Rinella, Steven. *The Complete Guide to Hunting, Butchering, and Cooking Wild Game; Volume 2* — 799.2

Game Changers. Asprey, Dave — 158.1
The Game Makers. Orbanes, Philip — 338.7
A Game of Birds and Wolves. Parkin, Simon — 940.54
★*Game of Edges.* Schoenfeld, Bruce — 796.04

GAME THEORY
    Du Sautoy, Marcus. ★*Around the World in Eighty Games* — 790.1
    Roth, Alvin E. *Who Gets What—And Why* — 330.01

Game Worn. Wong, Stephen — 796.357
The Games. Goldblatt, David — 796.4809

GAMES
    Du Sautoy, Marcus. ★*Around the World in Eighty Games* — 790.1
    Fletcher, Susan A. *Exploring the History of Childhood and Play Through 50 Historic Treasures* — 790
    Goodridge, Michelle. *Librarian's Guide to Games and Gamers* — 025.2
    Ho, Oliver. *The Ultimate Book of Family Card Games* — 795.4
    Miller, Megan. ★*The Ultimate Unofficial Encyclopedia for Minecrafters* — 794.8
    Roeder, Oliver. *Seven Games* — 794

GAMES OF CHANCE
    Thorp, Edward O. *A Man for All Markets* — B

The Games That Changed the Game. Jaworksi, Ron — 796.332
Games Without Rules. Ansary, Mir Tamim — 958.1

Gander, Forrest
    ★*Be With* — 811

Ganderton, Lucinda
    ★*Embroidery* — 746.44

Gandhi
    An Autobiography — B
    ★*Gandhi on Non-Violence* — 179.7

Gandhi. Guha, Ramachandra — B
Gandhi Before India. Guha, Ramachandra — B
★*Gandhi on Non-Violence.* Gandhi — 179.7

GANDHI, MAHATMA, 1869-1948
    Gandhi. *An Autobiography* — B
    Guha, Ramachandra. *Gandhi Before India* — B
    Guha, Ramachandra. *Gandhi* — B

Ganeshram, Ramin
    Future Chefs — 641.3

GANG LEADERS
    Voloj, Julian. *Ghetto Brother* — 741.5

GANG MEMBERS
    Bowden, Mark. *Life Sentence* — 364.106
    Dudley, Steven S. *MS-13* — 364.106

GANG RAPE
    Faleiro, Sonia. *The Good Girls* — 364.152
    Schwartzman, Nancy. *Roll Red Roll* — 364.15

GANGS
    Bowden, Mark. *Life Sentence* — 364.106
    Dudley, Steven S. *MS-13* — 364.106
    Flock, Elizabeth. ★*The Furies* — 305.48
    Ralph, Laurence. *Sito* — 364.152
    Roy, Saumya. *Castaway Mountain* — 363.72
    Rubinstein, Julian. ★*The Holly* — 364.106
    Voloj, Julian. *Ghetto Brother* — 741.5

GANGSTA RAP
    Westhoff, Ben. *Original Gangstas* — 782.421649

GANGSTER FILMS
    Kenny, Glenn. *Made Men* — 791.43
    Kenny, Glenn. *The World Is Yours* — 791.43

GANGSTERS
    Bair, Deirdre. *Al Capone* — B
    Carlo, Philip. *Gaspipe* — B
    Cullen, Kevin. *Whitey Bulger* — B
    Eig, Jonathan. *Get Capone* — 364.1
    English, T. J. *The Corporation* — 364.106089
    Hill, David. *The Vapors* — 976.7
    Ice-T. *Split Decision* — 920
    Maier, Thomas. *Mafia Spies* — 364.1060973
    Muse, Toby. *Kilo* — 363.4509861
    Stout, David. *The Kidnap Years* — 364.15

GANS, JOE
    Gildea, William. *The Longest Fight* — B

Gans, John
    White House Warriors — 355

GANS, MANFRED
    Garrett, Leah. *X Troop* — 940.54

Ganz, John
    When the Clock Broke — 320.52

Ganz, Nicholas
    ★*Graffiti World* — 751.7

The Gap. Suddendorf, Thomas — 156

GARBAGE COLLECTION
    Franklin-Wallis, Oliver. ★*Wasteland* — 363.72

Garbes, Angela
    Essential Labor — 306.874

GARBES, ANGELA
    Garbes, Angela. *Essential Labor* — 306.874

Garcia Lorca, Federico
    Collected Poems — 861
    Poet in New York — 861

GARCIA LORCA, FEDERICO, 1898-1936
    Garcia Lorca, Federico. *Collected Poems* — 861
    Garcia Lorca, Federico. *Poet in New York* — 861

Garcia Marquez, Gabriel
    Living to Tell the Tale — B

GARCIA MARQUEZ, GABRIEL, 1928-2014
    Garcia Marquez, Gabriel. *Living to Tell the Tale* — B
    Garcia, Rodrigo. *A Farewell to Gabo and Mercedes* — B
    Martin, Gerald. ★*Gabriel Garcia Marquez* — B

Garcia, Amanda Yates
    Initiated — B

GARCIA, AMANDA YATES
    Garcia, Amanda Yates. *Initiated* — B

Garcia, Angela
    ★*The Way That Leads Among the Lost* — 362.29

GARCIA, ANGELA, 1971-
    Garcia, Angela. ★*The Way That Leads Among the Lost* — 362.29

Garcia, Damon
    The God Who Riots — 269

Garcia, Mayte
    The Most Beautiful — 920

GARCIA, MAYTE, 1973-
    Garcia, Mayte. *The Most Beautiful* — 920

Garcia, Rodrigo
    A Farewell to Gabo and Mercedes — B

GARCIA, RODRIGO, 1959-
    Garcia, Rodrigo. *A Farewell to Gabo and Mercedes* — B

The Garden Against Time. Laing, Olivia — 635
Garden Allies. Lavoipierre, Frederique — 635
Garden Design. Howcroft, Heidi — 712

GARDEN ECOLOGY
    Lawson, Nancy. *The Humane Gardener* — 577.5

Garden Insects of North America. Cranshaw, Whitney — 635
Garden Inspirations. Moss, Charlotte — 747

GARDEN OF EDEN (BIBLICAL PLACE)
    Greenblatt, Stephen. *The Rise and Fall of Adam and Eve* — 233

★*A Garden of Marvels.* Kassinger, Ruth — 580.92

GARDEN ORNAMENTS AND FURNITURE
    Brody, Mark. *Mosaic Garden Projects* — 712
    Smith, Nathan. *Color Concrete Garden Projects* — 721

GARDEN PESTS
    Cranshaw, Whitney. *Garden Insects of North America* — 635
    Walliser, Jessica. ★*Attracting Beneficial Bugs to Your Garden* — 635

The Garden Refresh. Holmes, Kier — 635
Garden Renovation. Schwartz, Bobbie — 635

GARDEN STRUCTURES
    Pember, Mat. *DIY Garden Projects* — 712

Williams, Bunny. *On Garden Style*	712
The Gardener and the Carpenter. Gopnik, Alison	155.4
A Gardener At the End of the World. Kelley, Margot Anne	615.8

GARDENER, HELEN H. (HELEN HAMILTON), 1853-1925
Hamlin, Kimberly A. *Free Thinker*	B

GARDENERS
Dennison, Matthew. *Behind the Mask*	B
Gordon, Meryl. *Bunny Mellon*	B
Kassinger, Ruth. ★*A Garden of Marvels*	580.92
Wulf, Andrea. *The Brother Gardeners*	920

GARDENING
Bainbridge, David A. *Gardening with Less Water*	635.9
Bennett, Jackie. *The Writer's Garden*	920
Bohl, Loree. *Fearless Gardening*	712
Bohmig, Franz. ★*The Month-By-Month Gardening Guide*	635
Cowden, Meg McAndrews. ★*Plant Grow Harvest Repeat*	635.9
Dennison, Matthew. *Behind the Mask*	B
Erickson, Laura. ★*100 Plants to Feed the Birds*	635
Frey, Kate. *Ground Rules*	635
Gidding, John. *At Home with Nature*	635.9
Greayer, Rochelle. *Cultivating Garden Style*	712
Holmes, Kier. *The Garden Refresh*	635
Kelley, Margot Anne. *A Gardener at the End of the World*	615.8
Laing, Olivia. *The Garden Against Time*	635
Lavelle, Christine. *How to Create a Wildlife Garden*	635
Lavoipierre, Frederique. *Garden Allies*	635
Lively, Penelope. *Life in the Garden*	B
Loades, Greg. *The Modern Cottage Garden*	635
McDowell, Marta. *The World of Laura Ingalls Wilder*	813
McLaughlin, Chris. *The Good Garden*	635
Murphy, Emily. *Grow Now*	635
Roach, Margaret. ★*A Way to Garden*	635
Schwartz, Bobbie. *Garden Renovation*	635
Solnit, Rebecca. *Orwell's Roses*	B
Stewart, Martha. ★*The Martha Manual*	640
Webb, Leah M. *The Seven-Step Homestead*	635
Williams, Bunny. *On Garden Style*	712
Wulf, Andrea. *The Brother Gardeners*	920
Gardening for Butterflies. Black, Scott Hoffman	638

GARDENING TO ATTRACT WILDLIFE
Frey, Kate. *The Bee-Friendly Garden*	595.79
Lavelle, Christine. *How to Create a Wildlife Garden*	635
Lawson, Nancy. *The Humane Gardener*	577.5
McLaughlin, Chris. *The Good Garden*	635
Gardening with Less Water. Bainbridge, David A	635.9
Gardenista. Slatalla, Michelle	635
Gardenlust. Woods, Christopher	635.022

GARDENS
Alexander, Rosemary. ★*The Essential Garden Design Workbook*	712
Bennett, Jackie. *The Writer's Garden*	920
Brenwall, Cynthia S. *The Central Park*	974.7
Brody, Mark. *Mosaic Garden Projects*	712
Carey, Jenny Rose. *The Ultimate Flower Gardener's Guide*	635.9
Chesshire, Charles. *Japanese Gardening*	712
Dungy, Camille T. *Soil*	635.0978
Greayer, Rochelle. *Cultivating Garden Style*	712
Holmes, Roger. *Midwest Home Landscaping*	712
Howcroft, Heidi. *Garden Design*	712
Kassinger, Ruth. ★*A Garden of Marvels*	580.92
Kelley, Margot Anne. *A Gardener at the End of the World*	615.8
Laing, Olivia. *The Garden Against Time*	635
Moss, Charlotte. *Garden Inspirations*	747
Obama, Michelle. *American Grown*	635.09
Pember, Mat. *DIY Garden Projects*	712
Roach, Margaret. ★*A Way to Garden*	635
Schwartz, Bobbie. *Garden Renovation*	635
Slatalla, Michelle. *Gardenista*	635
Williams, Bunny. *On Garden Style*	712
Woods, Christopher. *Gardenlust*	635.022
Wulf, Andrea. *The Brother Gardeners*	920
★*Gardentopia*. Johnsen, Jan	635.9

Gardiner, John Eliot
Bach	B

Gardner, Chris
★*Permission to Dream*	158.1

Gardner, Dan
The Science of Fear	152.4

GARDNER, ISABELLA STEWART, 1840-1924
Lucey, Donna M. *Sargent's Women*	920

Gardner, Lindsay
Why We Cook	641.5

Gardner, Mark L.
The Earth Is All That Lasts	978.004
Rough Riders	973.911

Garelick, Rhonda K.
Mademoiselle	B

GARFIELD, JAMES ABRAM, 1831-1881
Goodyear, C. W. *President Garfield*	B
Millard, Candice. *Destiny of the Republic*	973.8

Garfield, Simon
★*All the Knowledge in the World*	030.9
In Miniature	745.5928
On the Map	526.09

Garfinkel, Yosef
In the Footsteps of King David	933

Garfunkel, Art
What Is It All but Luminous	782.42164

GARFUNKEL, ART, 1941-
Garfunkel, Art. *What Is It All but Luminous*	782.42164

GARIBALDI, GIUSEPPE, 1807-1882
Parks, Tim. *The Hero's Way*	945

Garlic and Sapphires. Reichl, Ruth	B
Garner's Modern English Usage. Garner, Bryan A.	423

Garner, Bryan A
The Chicago Guide to Grammar, Usage, and Punctuation	428.2
Garner's Modern English Usage	423

Garner, Dwight
The Upstairs Delicatessen	B

GARNER, ERIC, 1970-2014
Taibbi, Matt. *I Can't Breathe*	363.2

Garnice, Michael
The Ultimate Guide to Great Reggae	781.646

Garrels, Anne
Putin Country	947

GARRELS, ANNE, 1951-2022
Garrels, Anne. *Putin Country*	947

Garrett, Kent
The Last Negroes at Harvard	920

GARRETT, KENT
Garrett, Kent. *The Last Negroes at Harvard*	920

Garrett, Leah
X Troop	940.54

Garrison, Jessica
The Devil's Harvest	B

Garrow, David J.
Rising Star	B

Garten, Ina
Barefoot Contessa at Home	641.5
Barefoot Contessa Family Style	641.5
★*Barefoot Contessa, How Easy Is That?*	641.5
Barefoot in Paris	641.594
★*Cook Like a Pro*	641.5
Cooking for Jeffrey	641.5
★*Go-To Dinners*	641.5
★*Make It Ahead*	641.5
★*Modern Comfort Food*	641.5

Gary, Amy
In the Great Green Room	813

Garza, Alicia
The Purpose of Power	303.48

GARZA, ALICIA, 1981-
Garza, Alicia. *The Purpose of Power*	303.48

GAS WELLS
Zuckerman, Gregory. *The Frackers*	B

Gasaway, Laura N.
Copyright Questions and Answers for Information Professionals	346.7304

Gaskell, Elizabeth Cleghorn
The Life of Charlotte Bronte	B

Gaslighting America. Carpenter, Amanda B.	973.933
Gaspipe. Carlo, Philip	B

Gasser, Nolan
Why You Like It	781.1

★*Gastro Obscura*. Wong, Cecily	641.3

GASTROINTESTINAL SYSTEM
Roach, Mary. *Gulp*	612.3

AUTHOR, TITLE, SERIES AND SUBJECT INDEX

GASTRONOMY
    Adler, Tamar. *An Everlasting Meal* — 641.5
    Ahdoot, Dan. *Undercooked* — 647.95
    Downie, David. *A Taste of Paris* — 394.1
    Garner, Dwight. *The Upstairs Delicatessen* — B
    Harrison, Jim. *The Search for the Genuine* — 814
    Henaut, Stephane. *A Bite-Sized History of France* — 394.1
    Mohammadi, Kamin. *Bella Figura* — 641.01
    Page, Karen. *The Flavor Bible* — 641.5
    Waters, Alice. ★*We Are What We Eat* — 641.01
Gatcum, Chris
    ★*The Beginner's Photography Guide* — 770
*The **Gatekeepers***. Whipple, Chris — 973.92092
★*The **Gates** of Europe*. Plokhy, Serhii — 947.7
Gates, Alexander E.
    Encyclopedia of Earthquakes and Volcanoes — 551.2
Gates, Bill
    ★*How to Prevent the Next Pandemic* — 614.5
GATES, BILL, 1955-
    Schwab, Tim. ★*The Bill Gates Problem* — 361.7
Gates, Erin T
    ★*Elements of Family Style* — 747
Gates, Henry Louis
    100 Amazing Facts About the Negro — 973
    And Still I Rise — 305.896
    The Black Box — 908
    ★*The Black Church* — 277
    Colored People — B
    The Future of the Race — 305.896
    In Search of Our Roots — 973
    ★*Life Upon These Shores* — 973
    ★*Stony the Road* — 973
GATES, HENRY LOUIS, 1950-
    Gates, Henry Louis. *Colored People* — B
Gates, Melinda
    ★*The Moment of Lift* — 305.42
Gates, Robert Michael
    ★*Exercise of Power* — 973.929
★***Gateway** to Freedom*. Foner, Eric — 973.7
GATHERING (OF WILD FOODS, SEEDS, MEDICINAL PLANTS, ETC.)
    Quave, Cassandra Leah. *The Plant Hunter* — 581.6
    Rodriguez, Ashley. *Rooted Kitchen* — 641.5
Gathering Blossoms Under Fire. Walker, Alice — B
★*Gator Country*. Renner, Rebecca — 364.16
Gatrell, Peter
    The Unsettling of Europe — 304.8
GAUDI, ANTONI, 1852-1926
    Van Hensbergen, Gijs. *The Sagrada Familia* — 726.5
Gaughan, Norah
    Norah Gaughan's Knitted Cable Sourcebook — 746.43
GAUL
    Norwich, John Julius. *A History of France* — 944
Gaul, Gilbert M.
    Billion-Dollar Ball — 796.332
GAULLE, CHARLES DE, 1890-1970
    Jackson, Julian. *De Gaulle* — B
    Kissinger, Henry. *Leadership* — 303.3
GAUTAMA BUDDHA
    Armstrong, Karen. *Buddha* —
    Dalai Lama. *Approaching the Buddhist Path* — 294.3
    Oliver, Joan Duncan. *Buddhism* — 294.3
Gavin, James
    ★*Stormy Weather* — 782.42164
Gaw, Frankie
    First Generation — 641.595
Gawain, Shakti
    ★*Creative Visualization* — 153.3
Gawande, Atul
    ★*Being Mortal* — 362.17
    Complications — B
GAWANDE, ATUL
    Gawande, Atul. *Complications* — B
GAY ACTIVISTS
    Duberman, Martin B. *Hold Tight Gently* — 920
    Funk, Mason. *The Book of Pride* — 920
    Kugle, Scott Alan. *Living Out Islam* — 297
    Okporo, Edafe. *Asylum* — B
    Schiavi, Michael R. *Celluloid Activist* — B

    Windsor, Edie. *A Wild and Precious Life* — B
GAY AND LESBIAN MOVEMENT
    Becker, Jo. ★*Forcing the Spring* — 346.79401
    Carter, David. *Stonewall* — 306.76
    Fieseler, Robert W. *Tinderbox* — 364.152
    France, David. *How to Survive a Plague* — 362.196
    Funk, Mason. *The Book of Pride* — 920
    Yoshino, Kenji. *Speak Now* — 346.79401
GAY ATHLETES
    Rogers, Robbie. *Coming Out to Play* — B
GAY AUTHORS
    Bram, Christopher. *Eminent Outlaws* — 920
    Jones, Saeed. *How We Fight for Our Lives* — B
    Schiavi, Michael R. *Celluloid Activist* — B
GAY BARS AND RESTAURANTS
    Fieseler, Robert W. *Tinderbox* — 364.152
GAY COLLEGE STUDENTS
    Talusan, Meredith. *Fairest* — 305.30973
GAY COMMUNITIES
    Olsen, Craig. *P.S. Burn This Letter Please* — 306.76
    Seligman, Craig. *Who Does That Bitch Think She Is?* — 792.02
GAY COUPLES
    Burroughs, Augusten. ★*Toil & Trouble* — B
    Cenziper, Debbie. ★*Love Wins* — 346.7301
    Kaplan, Roberta A. *Then Comes Marriage* — 346.7301
GAY CULTURE
    Bullock, Darryl W. *David Bowie Made Me Gay* — 780
    Dery, Mark. *Born to Be Posthumous* — B
    Gooch, Brad. *Radiant* — B
    Ruberg, Bonnie. ★*The Queer Games Avant-Garde* — 794.8
    Velour, Sasha. ★*The Big Reveal* — 792.7
GAY HUSBANDS
    Hastings, Selina. *The Secret Lives of Somerset Maugham* — B
GAY MARRIAGE
    Becker, Jo. ★*Forcing the Spring* — 346.79401
    Kaplan, Roberta A. *Then Comes Marriage* — 346.7301
    Windsor, Edie. *A Wild and Precious Life* — B
    Yoshino, Kenji. *Speak Now* — 346.79401
GAY MEN
    Ambroz, David. *A Place Called Home* — B
    Bechdel, Alison. ★*Fun Home* — 741.5
    Becker, Jo. ★*Forcing the Spring* — 346.79401
    Birdsall, John. *The Man Who Ate Too Much* — B
    Black, Dustin Lance. *Mama's Boy* — B
    Blanco, Richard. *The Prince of Los Cocuyos* — B
    Branum, Guy. *My Life as a Goddess* — B
    Bronski, Michael. *A Queer History of the United States* — 306.76
    Broome, Brian. ★*Punch Me up to the Gods* — B
    Carpenter, Dale. *Flagrant Conduct* — 342.7308
    Carter, David. *Stonewall* — 306.76
    Cenziper, Debbie. ★*Love Wins* — 346.7301
    Cervini, Eric. *The Deviant's War* — B
    Chee, Alexander. ★*How to Write an Autobiographical Novel* — B
    Chin, Curtis. *Everything I Learned, I Learned in a Chinese Restaurant* — B
    Chu, Jeff. *Does Jesus Really Love Me?* — 261.8
    Clemmons, Francois S. *Officer Clemmons* — B
    Cooper, Christian. *Better Living Through Birding* — B
    Daley, Mark. *Safe* — B
    Daley, Tom. *Coming up for Air* — B
    Doty, Mark. *What Is the Grass* — 811
    Duberman, Martin B. *Hold Tight Gently* — 920
    Duran, Elvis. *Where Do I Begin?* — B
    Enninful, Edward. *A Visible Man* — B
    France, David. *How to Survive a Plague* — 362.196
    Funk, Mason. *The Book of Pride* — 920
    Gefter, Philip. *What Becomes a Legend Most* — B
    Gehring, Wes D. *James Dean* — B
    Gelwicks, Andrew. *The Queer Advantage* — 920
    Glass, Charles. *Soldiers Don't Go Mad* — 616.85
    Gomez, Edgar. *High-Risk Homosexual* — B
    Gooch, Brad. *Radiant* — B
    Gunn, Thom. ★*The Letters of Thom Gunn* — 821
    Hamill, Kirkland. *Filthy Beasts* — B
    Hammer, Langdon. *James Merrill* — B
    Hastings, Selina. *The Secret Lives of Somerset Maugham* — B
    Hester, Diarmuid. *Nothing Ever Just Disappears* — 306.76
    Hewitt, Sean. *All Down Darkness Wide* — B
    Jenkins, Jedidiah. *To Shake the Sleeping Self* — B

PUBLIC LIBRARY CORE COLLECTION: NONFICTION
Twentieth Edition

John, Elton. ★*Me*	B
Johnson, Graham. *Poulenc*	B
Jones, Saeed. *How We Fight for Our Lives*	B
Kavanagh, Julie. *Nureyev*	B
Keene, John. ★*Punks*	811
Kenan, Randall. *Black Folk Could Fly*	813
Kugle, Scott Alan. *Living Out Islam*	297
Kushner, Tony. *Angels in America*	812
Leavitt, David. *The Man Who Knew Too Much*	B
Marshall, Greg. *Leg*	B
Maupin, Armistead. *Logical Family*	B
Max, D. T. *Finale*	782.1
McBrien, William. *Cole Porter*	B
Mizrahi, Isaac. *I.M.*	B
Morris, Mark. *Out Loud*	B
Mullen, Bill. ★*James Baldwin*	B
O'Connor, Garry. *Ian McKellen*	B
O'Sullivan, Emer. *The Fall of the House of Wilde*	B
Okporo, Edafe. *Asylum*	B
Pellegrino, Danny. *How Do I Un-Remember This?*	B
Pico, Tommy. *Junk*	811
Preszler, Trent. *Little and Often*	B
Rannells, Andrew. *Uncle of the Year*	B
Richardson, Lance. *House of Nutter*	B
Rigsby, Cody. ★*XOXO, Cody*	B
Rippon, Adam. *Beautiful on the Outside*	B
Roberts, Matthias. *Holy Runaways*	262
Rogers, Robbie. *Coming Out to Play*	B
RuPaul. ★*The House of Hidden Meanings*	B
Schiavi, Michael R. *Celluloid Activist*	B
Shanahan, Charif. *Trace Evidence*	811
Shapiro, Ari. ★*The Best Strangers in the World*	B
Smith, Danez. ★*Don't Call Us Dead*	811.6
Sturgis, Matthew. *Oscar Wilde*	B
Sykes, Christopher Simon. *David Hockney*	B
Sykes, Christopher Simon. *David Hockney*	B
Wainaina, Binyavanga. ★*How to Write About Africa*	814
Warren, Rosanna. *Max Jacob*	B
Weschler, Lawrence. *And How Are You, Dr. Sacks?*	B
Yoshino, Kenji. *Speak Now*	346.79401

GAY PARENTS
John, Elton. ★*Me*	B
Lev, Arlene Istar. *The Complete Lesbian & Gay Parenting Guide*	649

GAY POETS
Hammer, Langdon. *James Merrill*	B

GAY POLITICIANS
Buttigieg, Pete. *Shortest Way Home*	B
Frank, Barney. *Frank*	B

GAY TEENAGERS
Berg, Ryan. *No House to Call My Home*	B
Porter, Billy. ★*Unprotected*	B

Gay, John
The Beggar's Opera	782.1

Gay, Peter
The Enlightenment	190
The Enlightenment	190
Freud	B
A Godless Jew	150.19

Gay, Ross
The Book of (more) Delights	814
★*Catalog of Unabashed Gratitude*	811
Inciting Joy	814

GAY, ROSS, 1974-
Gay, Ross. *The Book of (more) Delights*	814
Gay, Ross. *Inciting Joy*	814

Gay, Roxane
Bad Feminist	814
★*Opinions*	814

GAY, ROXANE
Gay, Roxane. ★*Opinions*	814

Gaye, Jan
After the Dance	B

GAYE, JAN
Gaye, Jan. *After the Dance*	B

GAYE, MARVIN
Gaye, Jan. *After the Dance*	B

Gayle, Caleb
We Refuse to Forget	975.004

GAZA STRIP
Abu Sayf, Atif. *The Drone Eats with Me*	B
Abuelaish, Izzeldin. *I Shall Not Hate*	B
Di Cintio, Marcello. *Pay No Heed to the Rockets*	956.9405
Oren, Michael B. *Six Days of War*	956.04
Pappe, Ilan. *The Biggest Prison on Earth*	956.9405
Sacco, Joe. *Footnotes in Gaza*	741.5
Sefarad, Mikhael. *The Wall and the Gate*	341.48

Geary, Theresa Flores
The Illustrated Bead Bible	745.594

Geck, Martin
★*Johann Sebastian Bach*	780.92

GEDDES, NORMAN BEL, 1893-1958
Szerlip, Barbara. *The Man Who Designed the Future*	B

Gedeon, Jade
Beautiful Bracelets by Hand	745.594

Gee, Alastair
Fire in Paradise	363.37

Gee, Henry
A (Very) Short History of Life on Earth	576.8

The **Geek** *Way.* McAfee, Andrew — 658.3

GEEKS (COMPUTER ENTHUSIASTS)
Thomas, Joseph Earl. *Sink*	B

Gefter, Philip
What Becomes a Legend Most	B

Gehrig, Lou
The Lost Memoir	B

GEHRIG, LOU, 1903-1941
Eisenberg, John. *The Streak*	796.357
Gehrig, Lou. *The Lost Memoir*	B
Robinson, Ray. *Iron Horse*	B

Gehring, Wes D.
James Dean	B

GEHRY, FRANK O., 1929-
Goldberger, Paul. *Building Art*	B

Geist, William
Little League Confidential	796.357

Geller, Danielle
Dog Flowers	B

GELLER, DANIELLE
Geller, Danielle. *Dog Flowers*	B

Gelles, David
The Man Who Broke Capitalism	330.12

Gellman, Barton
★*Dark Mirror*	B

GELLMAN, BARTON, 1960-
Gellman, Barton. ★*Dark Mirror*	B

Gelwicks, Andrew
The Queer Advantage	920

GEM THEFT
Jobb, Dean. *A Gentleman and a Thief*	364.16

GEMS
Judah, Hettie. *Lapidarium*	553.8

★*Gender.* Airton, Lee — 305.3

GENDER DYSPHORIA
Turban, Jack L. ★*Free to Be*	616.85

GENDER EQUITY
Adichie, Chimamanda Ngozi. *We Should All Be Feminists*	305.42
Agarwal, Pragya. *Sway*	177
Baron, Dennis E. *What's Your Pronoun?*	425.55
Block, Jennifer. *Everything Below the Waist*	613
Boschert, Sherry. *37 Words*	344.73
Cahn, Naomi R. ★*Fair Shake*	331.4
Chemaly, Soraya L. *Rage Becomes Her*	155.3
Davis, Geena. *Dying of Politeness*	B
Felder, Deborah G. *The American Women's Almanac*	305.40973
Gates, Melinda. ★*The Moment of Lift*	305.42
Gilliam, Dorothy Butler. *Trailblazer*	B
Griffith, Elisabeth. *Formidable*	305.42
Kelly, Kate. *Ordinary Equality*	920
Kimberley, Hannah. *A Woman's Place Is at the Top*	B
King, Billie Jean. ★*All In*	B
Mangino, Kate. ★*Equal Partners*	305.3
Mendelson, Cheryl. ★*Vows*	203
Nyamayaro, Elizabeth. *I Am a Girl from Africa*	B
Quinn, Bridget. *She Votes*	324.6
Schuller, Kyla. *The Trouble with White Women*	305.42
Semenya, Caster. *The Race to Be Myself*	B

AUTHOR, TITLE, SERIES AND SUBJECT INDEX

Solnit, Rebecca. *Men Explain Things to Me*	305.42
Teitel, Amy Shira. *Fighting for Space*	920
Traister, Rebecca. *Good and Mad*	305.420973
Wayland-Smith, Ellen. *Oneida*	307.77
Weiss, Elaine F. *The Woman's Hour*	324.6

GENDER EXPRESSION

Bongiovanni, Archie. *A Quick & Easy Guide to They/Them Pronouns*	741.5
Gottlieb, Iris. *Seeing Gender*	305.3
Velour, Sasha. ★*The Big Reveal*	792.7

GENDER FLUID

Bossiere, Zoe. *Cactus Country*	306
Tea, Michelle. *Against Memoir*	B
Whitney, Emerson. *Heaven*	B

GENDER GAP

Cahn, Naomi R. ★*Fair Shake*	331.4
Eliot, Lise. *Pink Brain, Blue Brain*	612.6
Lipman, Joanne. *That's What She Said*	305.30973
Solnit, Rebecca. *The Mother of All Questions*	305.42

GENDER IDENTITY

Airton, Lee. ★*Gender*	305.3
Amer, Lindz. *Rainbow Parenting*	649
Barnes, Katie. ★*Fair Play*	796.082
Baron, Dennis E. *What's Your Pronoun?*	425.55
Bongiovanni, Archie. *A Quick & Easy Guide to They/Them Pronouns*	741.5
Brown, Emma. *To Raise a Boy*	649
Butler, Judith. ★*Who's Afraid of Gender?*	305.3
Charles, Jos. *Feeld*	811
Citron, Danielle Keats. *The Fight for Privacy*	342.7308
Corbett, Emily. *In Transition*	809
Davis, Lisa Selin. *Tomboy*	305.409
Faliveno, Melissa. *Tomboyland*	B
Fremont, Helen. *The Escape Artist*	B
Gay, Roxane. ★*Opinions*	814
Gelwicks, Andrew. *The Queer Advantage*	920
Goetsch, Diana. *This Body I Wore*	B
Goodman, Elyssa. *Glitter and Concrete*	792.7
Gottlieb, Iris. *Seeing Gender*	305.3
greathouse, torrin a. *Wound from the Mouth of a Wound*	811
Greene, Benjamin. ★*My Child Is Trans, Now What?*	649
Griffin, Farah Jasmine. ★*In Search of a Beautiful Freedom*	814
Hall, Jake. *The Art of Drag*	792.8
Hartke, Austen. *Transforming*	277
Hester, Diarmuid. *Nothing Ever Just Disappears*	306.76
Hurston, Zora Neale. ★*You Don't Know Us Negroes and Other Essays*	814
Imani, Blair. *Read This to Get Smarter*	303.3
Isen, Tajja. *Some of My Best Friends*	305.8
Kobabe, Maia. *Gender Queer*	741.5
Lemay, Mimi. *What We Will Become*	306.874
Manning, Chelsea. *Readme.Txt*	B
Moran, Caitlin. *What About Men?*	155.3
Nelson, Maggie. ★*The Argonauts*	B
Nordberg, Jenny. *The Underground Girls of Kabul*	305.3
Parks, Casey. *Diary of a Misfit*	B
Phillips, Maya. *Nerd*	302.23
Rose, Jacqueline. *On Violence and on Violence Against Women*	362.88
Royster, Francesca T. *Choosing Family*	B
Ruberg, Bonnie. ★*The Queer Games Avant-Garde*	794.8
Sante, Lucy. *I Heard Her Call My Name*	B
Scenters-Zapico, Natalie. *Lima*	811
Semenya, Caster. *The Race to Be Myself*	B
Shaw, Julia. *Bi*	306.76
Shraya, Vivek. *I'm Afraid of Men*	813
Skaja, Emily. *Brute*	811.6
Solnit, Rebecca. ★*Recollections of My Nonexistence*	B
Soloway, Jill. *She Wants It*	B
Talusan, Meredith. *Fairest*	305.30973
Tea, Michelle. *Against Memoir*	B
Tobia, Jacob. *Sissy*	305.30973
Town, Caren J. *LGBTQ Young Adult Fiction*	813.009
Turban, Jack L. ★*Free to Be*	616.85
Velour, Sasha. ★*The Big Reveal*	792.7
Whitney, Emerson. *Heaven*	B
Wilson, Rebel. *Rebel Rising*	B
Worley, Jennifer. *Neon Girls*	792.7
Yoshino, Kenji. *Say the Right Thing*	305.3

GENDER NONCONFORMITY

Bongiovanni, Archie. *A Quick & Easy Guide to They/Them Pronouns*	741.5
Davis, Lisa Selin. *Tomboy*	305.409

Gottlieb, Iris. *Seeing Gender*	305.3
Greene, Benjamin. ★*My Child Is Trans, Now What?*	649
Hartke, Austen. *Transforming*	277
Kobabe, Maia. *Gender Queer*	741.5
Semenya, Caster. *The Race to Be Myself*	B
Weigel, Alicia Roth. *Inverse Cowgirl*	B

Gender Queer. Kobabe, Maia   741.5

GENDER ROLE

Adichie, Chimamanda Ngozi. *We Should All Be Feminists*	305.42
Albertine, Viv. *Clothes, Clothes, Clothes. Music, Music, Music*	B
Baer, Kate. *What Kind of Woman*	811
Beard, Mary. ★*Women & Power*	305.409
Beauvoir, Simone de. ★*The Second Sex*	305.4
Black, Michael Ian. *A Better Man*	305.31
Bossiere, Zoe. *Cactus Country*	306
Boyle, Kevin. *The Shattering*	973.923
Brown, Nancy Marie. *The Real Valkyrie*	948
Codjoe, Ama. *Bluest Nude*	811
Collins, Gail. *When Everything Changed*	305.40973
Cooke, Lucy. *Bitch*	591.56
Cooney, Kara. *When Women Ruled the World*	920
Cooper, Helene. *Madame President*	966.62
Crowther, Gail. *Three-Martini Afternoons at the Ritz*	920
Cusk, Rachel. *Coventry*	814
Dangarembga, Tsitsi. *Black and Female*	305.48
Davis, Lisa. ★*Housewife*	331.4
Doherty, Maggie. *The Equivalents*	920
Dubin, Minna. ★*Mom Rage*	306.874
Faleiro, Sonia. *The Good Girls*	364.152
Faliveno, Melissa. *Tomboyland*	B
Faust, Drew Gilpin. *Necessary Trouble*	B
Febos, Melissa. *Girlhood*	818
Filipovic, Jill. *The H-Spot*	155.3
Fine, Cordelia. *Testosterone Rex*	155.3
Fitzgerald, Isaac. *Dirtbag, Massachusetts*	B
Frangello, Gina. *Blow Your House Down*	813
Friedan, Betty. ★*The Feminine Mystique*	305.42
Funder, Anna. *Wifedom*	B
Georges, Gigi. *Downeast*	974.1
Gomez, Edgar. *High-Risk Homosexual*	B
Griffith, R. Marie. *Moral Combat*	261.8
Haddish, Tiffany. *The Last Black Unicorn*	B
Hartley, Gemma. *Fed Up*	155.3
Hatmaker, Jen. *Of Mess and Moxie*	248.8
Hay, Carol. *Think Like a Feminist*	305.42
Hoban, Phoebe. *Alice Neel*	B
Holt, Nathalia. *The Queens of Animation*	920
Holt, Nathalia. ★*Rise of the Rocket Girls*	629.4
Hope, Clover. *The Motherlode*	920
Iandoli, Kathy. *God Save the Queens*	782.421649
Kaplan, Janice. *The Genius of Women*	920
Kerrison, Catherine. *Jefferson's Daughters*	920
Kimberley, Hannah. *A Woman's Place Is at the Top*	B
Kruse, Kevin Michael. *Fault Lines*	973.92
Lemay, Mimi. *What We Will Become*	306.874
Levy, Deborah. *The Cost of Living*	B
Levy, Deborah. ★*Real Estate*	B
Lucey, Donna M. *Sargent's Women*	920
Mangino, Kate. ★*Equal Partners*	305.3
Mans, Jasmine. *Black Girl, Call Home*	811
Mertens, Maggie. *Better Faster Farther*	796.42
Miles, Tiya. ★*Wild Girls*	304.2
Miller, Adrienne. *In the Land of Men*	070.5
Miller, Kei. *Things I Have Withheld*	814
Moorehead, Caroline. *A House in the Mountains*	940.53
Moran, Caitlin. *What About Men?*	155.3
Moran, Rachel. *Paid For*	306.74082
Morrison, Toni. ★*The Source of Self-Regard*	814
Moss, Marissa R. *Her Country*	781.642
Mulley, Clare. *The Women Who Flew for Hitler*	920
Neiman, Garrett. *Rich White Men*	305.5
Nordberg, Jenny. *The Underground Girls of Kabul*	305.3
O'Donnell Heffington, Peggy. *Without Children*	306.85
O'Meara, Mallory. *Girly Drinks*	641.2
Orenstein, Peggy. *Cinderella Ate My Daughter*	305.23082
Petersen, Sara. *Momfluenced*	306.87
Pratt, Misty. *All in Her Head*	616.89
Rahmani, Niloofar. *Open Skies*	B

PUBLIC LIBRARY CORE COLLECTION: NONFICTION
Twentieth Edition

Schumer, Amy. *The Girl with the Lower Back Tattoo*	B
Sen, Mayukh. *Taste Makers*	641.5092
Shapland, Jenn. ★*Thin Skin*	814
Shraya, Vivek. *I'm Afraid of Men*	813
Sinclair, Safiya. ★*How to Say Babylon*	B
Tea, Michelle. *Against Memoir*	B
Teitel, Amy Shira. *Fighting for Space*	920
Thomas, Louisa. *Louisa*	B
Thurman, Judith. ★*A Left-Handed Woman*	814
Turban, Jack L. ★*Free to Be*	616.85
Wojczuk, Tana. *Lady Romeo*	B
Worsley, Lucy. *Queen Victoria*	B
Yousafzai, Ziauddin. *Let Her Fly*	B
Zimmerman, Jess. *Women and Other Monsters*	155.3

GENDER ROLE AND CHILDREN

Turban, Jack L. ★*Free to Be*	616.85

GENDER ROLE IN THE WORK ENVIRONMENT

Cooke, Julia. *Come Fly the World*	387.7
McShane Wulfhart, Nell. *The Great Stewardess Rebellion*	331.4
Williams, Joan. *What Works for Women at Work*	650.1

GENDER WARS

Adichie, Chimamanda Ngozi. *Dear Ijeawele*	649
Feiler, Bruce. *The First Love Story*	222
Filipovic, Jill. *The H-Spot*	155.3
Solnit, Rebecca. *The Mother of All Questions*	305.42

GENDER-NONCONFORMING PEOPLE

Gottlieb, Iris. *Seeing Gender*	305.3
Hartke, Austen. *Transforming*	277
Smith, Danez. ★*Homie*	811
Soloway, Jill. *She Wants It*	B
Whitney, Emerson. *Heaven*	B

GENDERQUEER PEOPLE

Bossiere, Zoe. *Cactus Country*	306
Emezi, Akwaeke. ★*Dear Senthuran*	B
Faliveno, Melissa. *Tomboyland*	B
Kobabe, Maia. *Gender Queer*	741.5
Tobia, Jacob. *Sissy*	305.30973
Wolf, Brandon J. *A Place for Us*	B
★*The Gene*. Mukherjee, Siddhartha	616

GENE EDITING

Isaacson, Walter. ★*The Code Breaker*	576.5
McKibben, Bill. *Falter*	909.83
Mukherjee, Siddhartha. ★*The Song of the Cell*	571.6
Rutherford, Adam. *Control*	363.9
Zernicka-Goetz, Magdalena. *The Dance of Life*	591.56

GENE MAPPING

Finkel, Elizabeth. *The Genome Generation*	599.93

GENE THERAPY

Holt, Nathalia. *Cured*	614.5

GENEALOGY

Gates, Henry Louis. *In Search of Our Roots*	973
Jacobs, A. J. *It's All Relative*	929.1
Jerkins, Morgan. *Wandering in Strange Lands*	305.896
Kearse, Bettye. *The Other Madisons*	920
Lee, Helie. *In the Absence of Sun*	B
Myers, Leah. *Thinning Blood*	B
Neighbors, Joy. *The Family Tree Cemetery Field Guide*	929
Pennavaria, Katherine. *Genealogy for Beginners*	929.1
Petrosino, Kiki. *White Blood*	811
Porter, Carolyn. *Marcel's Letters*	940.54
Raines, Ben. *The Last Slave Ship*	306.362
Salama, Jordan. ★*Stranger in the Desert*	982
Schindler, Meriel. *The Lost Cafe Schindler*	943.64
Shapiro, Dani. ★*Inheritance*	B
Wagner, Alex. *Futureface*	B
White, Gayle Jessup. *Reclamation*	B
Genealogy for Beginners. Pennavaria, Katherine	929.1
Genealogy of a Murder. Belkin, Lisa	362.88
The General and the Genius. Kunetka, James W.	355.8

GENERAL RELATIVITY (PHYSICS)

Carroll, Sean M. *The Biggest Ideas in the Universe*	530.11
Cox, Brian. *Universal*	523.1
Impey, Chris. *Einstein's Monsters*	523.8
★*The General Theory of Employment, Interest, and Money*. Keynes, John Maynard	330.15
The General vs. the President. Brands, H. W.	973.918092
The Generalissimo. Taylor, Jay	B
The Generals. Groom, Winston	920
★*The Generals*. Ricks, Thomas E.	B

GENERALS

Ambrose, Stephen E. *The Victors*	940.54
Baier, Bret. *Three Days in January*	B
Baier, Bret. *To Rescue the Constitution*	973.4
Barrett, David Dean. *140 Days to Hiroshima*	940.54
Bell, Madison Smartt. *Toussaint Louverture*	B
Blount, Roy. *Robert E. Lee*	B
Boot, Max. ★*The Road Not Taken*	B
Borneman, Walter R. *Macarthur at War*	B
Brands, H. W. *The General vs. the President*	973.918092
Brands, H. W. *The Last Campaign*	973.8
Brands, H. W. ★*The Man Who Saved the Union*	B
Brighton, Terry. *Patton, Montgomery, Rommel*	B
Broers, Michael. *Napoleon*	B
Broers, Michael. *Napoleon*	B
Bunting, Josiah. ★*The Making of a Leader*	B
Chernow, Ron. ★*Grant*	B
Chernow, Ron. *Washington*	B
Clark, Lloyd. *The Commanders*	940.53
Coe, Alexis. ★*You Never Forget Your First*	B
Connell, Evan S. *Son of the Morning Star*	973.8
Crawford, Alan Pell. *This Fierce People*	975
Davis, William C. *Crucible of Command*	920
Drury, Bob. *Valley Forge*	973.3
Duncan, Michael. ★*Hero of Two Worlds*	B
Egan, Timothy. ★*The Immortal Irishman*	B
Eisen, Norman L. *The Last Palace*	920
Ellis, Joseph J. ★*His Excellency*	B
Fellman, Michael. *The Making of Robert E. Lee*	B
Ferling, John E. *Winning Independence*	973.3
Fischer, David Hackett. *Washington's Crossing*	973.3
Flexner, James Thomas. *George Washington*	B
Freeman, Douglas Southall. *Lee*	B
Gladwell, Malcolm. ★*The Bomber Mafia*	940.54
Goldsworthy, Adrian Keith. *Antony and Cleopatra*	937
Goldsworthy, Adrian Keith. ★*Caesar*	B
Grant, Ulysses S. ★*The Annotated Memoirs of Ulysses S. Grant*	B
Grant, Ulysses S. *Memoirs and Selected Letters*	B
Groom, Winston. *The Generals*	920
Guelzo, Allen C. *Robert E. Lee*	B
Guinn, Jeff. ★*War on the Border*	972.08
Gwynne, S. C. *Rebel Yell*	B
Herman, Arthur. ★*Douglas Macarthur*	B
Homer. ★*The Iliad*	883
Hunt, Patrick. *Hannibal*	B
Jackson, Julian. *De Gaulle*	B
Johnson, Paul. *Eisenhower*	B
Johnson, Paul. *George Washington*	B
Johnson, Paul. *Napoleon*	B
Jordan, Jonathan W. *Brothers, Rivals, Victors*	940.54
Kilmeade, Brian. ★*Andrew Jackson and the Miracle of New Orleans*	973.5
Korda, Michael. *Clouds of Glory*	B
Kunetka, James W. *The General and the Genius*	355.8
Loyn, David. *The Long War*	958.104
McDonough, James L. *William Tecumseh Sherman*	B
McManus, John C. *Fire and Fortitude*	940.54
McManus, John C. *Island Infernos*	940.54
McMurtry, Larry. *Custer*	B
Meacham, Jon. ★*American Lion*	B
Norris, Robert S. *Racing for the Bomb*	B
O'Connell, Robert L. *Revolutionary*	B
Paradis, Michel. *The Light of Battle*	940.54
Patton, George S. *War as I Knew It*	B
Perry, Mark. *The Most Dangerous Man in America*	B
Philbrick, Nathaniel. ★*The Last Stand*	973.8
Philbrick, Nathaniel. ★*Valiant Ambition*	B
Randall, Willard Sterne. *George Washington*	B
Ricks, Thomas E. ★*The Generals*	B
Roberts, Andrew. ★*Napoleon*	B
Robertson, James I. *Stonewall Jackson*	B
Roll, David L. *George Marshall*	B
Scott, James. *Black Snow*	940.54
Sears, Stephen W. *Lincoln's Lieutenants*	920
Sheehan, Neil. *A Fiery Peace in a Cold War*	B
Stark, Peter. *Young Washington*	B
Stewart, David O. *George Washington*	973.4
Stiles, T. J. *Custer's Trials*	B

AUTHOR, TITLE, SERIES AND SUBJECT INDEX

Strauss, Barry S. ★*The War That Made the Roman Empire*	937
Unger, Debi. *George Marshall*	B
Varon, Elizabeth R. *Longstreet*	B
Wallace, Chris. *Countdown 1945*	940.54
Wert, Jeffry D. *Cavalryman of the Lost Cause*	B
Wert, Jeffry D. *Custer*	B
White, Ronald C. ★*American Ulysses*	B
White, Ronald C. *On Great Fields*	B
Zambone, Albert Louis. *Daniel Morgan*	B
Zamoyski, Adam. *Napoleon*	B
Generation Dread. Wray, Britt	155.9

GENERATION GAP
Irving, Apricot Anderson. *The Gospel of Trees*	B
Koh, EJ. *The Magical Language of Others*	813
Shirley, Craig. *Mary Ball Washington*	B
Twenge, Jean M. *Generations*	305.2
Generation Kill. Wright, Evan	956.7044
Generation Robot. Favro, Terri	006.3

GENERATION X
Calhoun, Ada. *Why We Can't Sleep*	305.244
Germer, Fawn. *Coming Back*	650.14
Hyden, Steven. *Long Road*	782.42166

GENERATION Z.
Shankar, Shalini. *Beeline*	155.4
Generations. Twenge, Jean M.	305.2

GENERATIONS
Ernaux, Annie. ★*The Years*	B
Gates, Henry Louis. *In Search of Our Roots*	973
Hessler, Peter. *Other Rivers*	378.1
Shankar, Shalini. *Beeline*	155.4
Swarns, Rachel L. ★*American Tapestry*	B
Twenge, Jean M. *Generations*	305.2
Waldinger, Robert J. ★*The Good Life*	158.1

GENEROSITY
Ferrazzi, Keith. *Never Eat Alone*	658.4
Grant, Adam M. *Give and Take*	158.2
Lieber, Ron. *The Opposite of Spoiled*	332.0240083
Visser, Margaret. *The Gift of Thanks*	394

GENES
Heine, Steven J. *DNA Is Not Destiny*	572.8
Mukherjee, Siddhartha. ★*The Gene*	616
Nigg, Joel T. *Getting Ahead of ADHD*	618.92
Stanger, Ben. *From One Cell*	571.6
Genesis. Tonelli, Guido	523.1
Genesis. Wilson, Edward O.	591.5

GENETIC CODE
Finkel, Elizabeth. *The Genome Generation*	599.93
Markel, Howard. *The Secret of Life*	572.86
Norton, Laurah. *Lay Them to Rest*	363.25

GENETIC ENGINEERING
Finkel, Elizabeth. *The Genome Generation*	599.93
Piore, Adam. *The Body Builders*	660.6

GENETIC GENEALOGY
Humes, Edward. *The Forever Witness*	363.25
Jacobs, A. J. *It's All Relative*	929.1

GENETIC PSYCHOLOGY
Dunbar, R. I. M. *Human Evolution*	155.7
Foster, Charles. *Being a Human*	155.7
Miller, Kenneth R. *The Human Instinct*	155.7
Pinker, Steven. *The Blank Slate*	155.2
Provine, Robert R. *Curious Behavior*	152.3
Sagan, Carl. *The Dragons of Eden*	153
Tattersall, Ian. *Masters of the Planet*	599.93

GENETIC RESEARCH
Finkel, Elizabeth. *The Genome Generation*	599.93
Isaacson, Walter. ★*The Code Breaker*	576.5
Zimmer, Carl. *She Has Her Mother's Laugh*	576.5

GENETIC RESOURCES CONSERVATION
Wilson, Edward O. *The Diversity of Life*	333.95

GENETIC SCREENING
Kolata, Gina Bari. *Mercies in Disguise*	616
Semenya, Caster. *The Race to Be Myself*	B

GENETICALLY ENGINEERED FOOD
Elmore, Bartow J. *Seed Money*	338.7

GENETICALLY ENGINEERED ORGANISMS
Kurlansky, Mark. *Milk!*	637

GENETICALLY ENGINEERED PLANTS
Elmore, Bartow J. *Seed Money*	338.7

GENETICISTS
Henig, Robin Marantz. *The Monk in the Garden*	B

GENETICS
Dawkins, Richard. *The Greatest Show on Earth*	576.8
Desilva, Jeremy. *First Steps*	599.93
Farley, Audrey Clare. ★*Girls and Their Monsters*	306.875
Heine, Steven J. *DNA Is Not Destiny*	572.8
Henig, Robin Marantz. *The Monk in the Garden*	B
Ingrassia, Lawrence. *A Fatal Inheritance*	616.99
Isaacson, Walter. ★*The Code Breaker*	576.5
Kolata, Gina Bari. *Mercies in Disguise*	616
Kolker, Robert. ★*Hidden Valley Road*	920
Kurzweil, Ray. ★*The Singularity Is Near*	153.9
Larson, Edward J. *Evolution*	576.8
Markel, Howard. *The Secret of Life*	572.86
Mukherjee, Siddhartha. ★*The Gene*	616
Nesse, Randolph M. *Good Reasons for Bad Feelings*	616.89
Raff, Jennifer. *Origin*	576.5
Tabery, James. ★*Tyranny of the Gene*	572.8
Zimmer, Carl. *She Has Her Mother's Laugh*	576.5

GENEVA, SWITZERLAND
Collins, Lauren. *When in French*	B
Genghis Khan. McLynn, Frank	950.2
★*Genghis* Khan and the Making of the Modern World. Weatherford, J. McIver	B
Genghis Khan and the Quest for God. Weatherford, J. McIver	323.44

GENGHIS KHAN, 1162-1227
McLynn, Frank. *Genghis Khan*	950.2
Weatherford, J. McIver. ★*Genghis Khan and the Making of the Modern World*	B
Weatherford, J. McIver. *Genghis Khan and the Quest for God*	323.44

GENIES
Seale, Yasmine. *Aladdin*	398.2
Genius. Bloom, Harold	153.9
The Genius. Harris, David	B

GENIUS
Bloom, Harold. *Genius*	153.9
Dederer, Claire. ★*Monsters*	700.1
Goodwin, Doris Kearns. ★*Team of Rivals*	B
Kanigel, Robert. *The Man Who Knew Infinity*	B
Kaplan, Janice. *The Genius of Women*	920
King, Charles. *Odessa*	947.7
Suchet, John. *Mozart*	B
Swafford, Jan. *Mozart*	B
The Genius of Judy. Bergstein, Rachelle	813
The Genius of Women. Kaplan, Janice	920
Geniuses At War. Price, David A.	940.54

GENOCIDE
Akcam, Taner. *A Shameful Act*	956.6
Aly, Gotz. *Europe Against the Jews*	305.892
Applebaum, Anne. ★*Red Famine*	947.708
Balakian, Peter. *The Burning Tigris*	956.6
Carney, Scott. *The Vortex*	954.92
Chang, Iris. ★*The Rape of Nanking*	951.04
Crump, Benjamin. *Open Season*	364
Deng, Alephonsion. *They Poured Fire on Us from the Sky*	B
Erdrich, Heid E. ★*Little Big Bully*	811
French, Howard W. *Born in Blackness*	960
Gourevitch, Philip. *We Wish to Inform You That Tomorrow We Will Be Killed with Our Families*	364.15
Hagerty, Alexa. ★*Still Life with Bones*	599.9
Hari, Daoud. *The Translator*	B
Hatzfeld, Jean. *Blood Papa*	967.5710431
Hatzfeld, Jean. *Machete Season*	967.57104
Hayes, Peter. *Why?*	940.53
Igort. *The Ukrainian and Russian Notebooks*	741.5
Izgil, Tahir Hamut. *Waiting to Be Arrested at Night*	B
Jones, Robert P. *The Hidden Roots of White Supremacy*	305.8
Maass, Peter. *Love Thy Neighbor*	949.702
Mackeen, Dawn Anahid. *The Hundred-Year Walk*	956.6
Mikhaiil, Dunya. *The Beekeeper*	956.7044
Murad, Nadia. ★*The Last Girl*	B
Myers, Leah. *Thinning Blood*	B
Pappe, Ilan. *The Biggest Prison on Earth*	956.9405
Rajchman, Chil. *The Last Jew of Treblinka*	940.53
Rees, Laurence. *Auschwitz*	940.53
Rhodes, Richard. *Masters of Death*	940.53
Sands, Philippe. *East West Street*	345
Snyder, Timothy. *Black Earth*	940.53

PUBLIC LIBRARY CORE COLLECTION: NONFICTION
Twentieth Edition

Snyder, Timothy. ★*Bloodlands*	940.54
Stern, Jessica. *My War Criminal*	341.6
Thant Myint-U. *The Hidden History of Burma*	959.105
Trebincevic, Kenan. *The Bosnia List*	
Trentmann, Frank. *Out of the Darkness*	943.08
Ung, Loung. *First They Killed My Father*	959.604
Ung, Loung. *Lucky Child*	B
Wiesenthal, Simon. ★*The Sunflower*	179.7
The Genome Generation. Finkel, Elizabeth	599.93
GENOMES	
Heine, Steven J. *DNA Is Not Destiny*	572.8
Markel, Howard. *The Secret of Life*	572.86
Tabery, James. ★*Tyranny of the Gene*	572.8
Genovese, Eugene D.	
Roll, Jordan, Roll	975
Genoways, Ted	
The Chain	338.7
This Blessed Earth	630.9
Gentile, Mary C.	
Giving Voice to Values	174
Gentile, Olivia	
Life List	598.072
A Gentleman and a Thief. Jobb, Dean	364.16
Gentleman Bandit. Boessenecker, John	B
GENTRIFICATION OF CITIES	
Elliott, Andrea. ★*Invisible Child*	362.7
Lim, Audrea. *Free the Land*	333.73
Luckerson, Victor. *Built from the Fire*	976.6
Moss, Jeremiah. *Feral City*	B
Podemski, Max. *A Paradise of Small Houses*	363.5
Rubinstein, Julian. ★*The Holly*	364.106
Samaha, Albert. *Never Ran, Never Will*	920
GENTRY	
Fellman, Michael. *The Making of Robert E. Lee*	B
GEOBIOLOGY	
Jahren, Hope. ★*Lab Girl*	B
GEODYNAMICS	
Jabr, Ferris. ★*Becoming Earth*	570.1
GEOGRAPHICAL PERCEPTION	
Ellard, Colin. *You Are Here*	153.7
Nabokov, Peter. *Where the Lightning Strikes*	299.7
GEOGRAPHY	
Carballo, David M. *America*	912
Diamond, Jared M. *Guns, Germs, and Steel*	303.4
Hayes, Derek. *Historical Atlas of the United States*	911
Keegan, John. *The American Civil War*	973.7
Marshall, Tim. *The Power of Geography*	320.1
Morris, Ian. *Geography Is Destiny*	941
Sluglett, Peter. *Atlas of Islamic History*	912.19
Winchester, Simon. *Pacific*	909
Geography Is Destiny. Morris, Ian	941
GEOLOGICAL TIME	
Halliday, Thomas. ★*Otherlands*	560
GEOLOGISTS	
Ross, John F. *The Promise of the Grand Canyon*	917.91
Winchester, Simon. *The Map That Changed the World*	B
GEOLOGY	
Bjornerud, Marcia. *Geopedia*	551
Conway, Edmund. *Material World*	333.7
Darwin, Charles. ★*The Voyage of the Beagle*	508
Flannery, Tim F. *Europe*	508.4
Heacox, Kim. ★*John Muir and the Ice That Started a Fire*	333.7209798
Jabr, Ferris. ★*Becoming Earth*	570.1
Johnson, Sarah Stewart. *The Sirens of Mars*	576.8
Judah, Hettie. *Lapidarium*	553.8
Lambert, David. *The Field Guide to Geology*	550
GEOLOGY, STRATIGRAPHIC	
Winchester, Simon. *The Map That Changed the World*	B
GEOMETRY IN NATURE	
Ball, Philip. *Patterns in Nature*	500.201
★*The Geometry of Hand-Sewing*. Chanin, Natalie	746.44
GEOMYTHOLOGY	
Manguel, Alberto. *The Dictionary of Imaginary Places*	809
Geopedia. Bjornerud, Marcia	551
GEOPOLITICS	
Bergen, Peter L. *The Rise and Fall of Osama Bin Laden*	958.104
Beschloss, Michael R. *The Conquerors*	940.53
Capozzola, Christopher. *Bound by War*	355
Carney, Scott. *The Vortex*	954.92
Englund, Peter. *November 1942*	940.53
Friedman, George. *Flashpoints*	940.56
Gates, Robert Michael. ★*Exercise of Power*	973.929
Goldblatt, David. ★*The Age of Football*	796.334
Hansen, Valerie. *The Year 1000*	909
Harding, Luke. *Invasion*	947.7
Hubbard, Ben (Journalist). *Mbs*	B
Hughes, Bettany. *Istanbul*	949.61
Khodorkovsky, Mikhail. *The Russia Conundrum*	947.086
Kissinger, Henry. *Leadership*	303.3
Marshall, Tim. *The Power of Geography*	320.1
Mikanowski, Jacob. ★*Goodbye, Eastern Europe*	947
Miller, Chris. *Chip War*	338.4
Mirski, Sean A. *We May Dominate the World*	973.91
Roll, David L. *Ascent to Power*	973.918
Sanghera, Sathnam. *Empireworld*	909
Stavridis, James. *Sea Power*	359
Winchester, Simon. *Pacific*	909
Yergin, Daniel. *The New Map*	333.79
George Balanchine. Gottlieb, Robert	B
George Frideric Handel. Harris, Ellen T.	B
George Gershwin. Hyland, William G.	B
★*George Gershwin*. Pollack, Howard	B
George Harrison. Norman, Philip	B
George Harrison. Thomson, Graeme	B
GEORGE I, KING OF GREAT BRITAIN, 1660-1727	
Ackroyd, Peter. *Revolution*	941.07
GEORGE II KING OF GREAT BRITAIN 1683-1760	
Ackroyd, Peter. *Revolution*	941.07
GEORGE III, KING OF GREAT BRITAIN, 1738-1820	
Ackroyd, Peter. *Revolution*	941.07
Hadlow, Janice. *A Royal Experiment*	B
McCullough, David G. ★*1776*	973.3
Roberts, Andrew. *The Last King of America*	B
GEORGE IV, KING OF GREAT BRITAIN, 1762-1830	
Ackroyd, Peter. *Revolution*	941.07
George Lucas. Jones, Brian Jay	B
George Marshall. Roll, David L.	B
George Marshall. Unger, Debi	B
★*George Mason*. Broadwater, Jeff	B
George Sand. Harlan, Elizabeth	B
George V. Ridley, Jane	B
GEORGE V, KING OF GREAT BRITAIN, 1865-1936	
Clay, Catrine. *King, Kaiser, Tsar*	B
Ridley, Jane. *George V*	B
George VI and Elizabeth. Smith, Sally Bedell	920
GEORGE VI, KING OF GREAT BRITAIN, 1895-1952	
Cadbury, Deborah. *Princes at War*	920
Larman, Alexander. *The Windsors at War*	940.53
Smith, Sally Bedell. *George VI and Elizabeth*	920
George Washington. Flexner, James Thomas	B
George Washington. Johnson, Paul	B
George Washington. Randall, Willard Sterne	B
George Washington. Stewart, David O.	973.4
George Washington and the New Nation, 1783-1793. Flexner, James Thomas	973.4
George Washington Carver. Vella, Christina	B
★*George Washington's Secret Six*. Kilmeade, Brian	973.4
George, Nicholas and Wilhelm. Carter, Miranda	940.3
George, Rose	
Nine Pints	612.1
George-Warren, Holly	
★*Janis*	B
Georges, Gigi	
Downeast	974.1
GEORGIA	
Carter, Jimmy. *An Hour Before Daylight*	B
Finkel, David. *An American Dreamer*	975.8
Gooch, Brad. ★*Flannery*	B
Gray, Michael. *Hand Me My Travelin' Shoes*	B
Jones, Jacqueline. *Saving Savannah*	975.8
Lewis, John. ★*Run; Book One*	741.5
Phillips, Patrick. *Blood at the Root*	305.8
Pressly, Paul M. *On the Rim of the Caribbean*	975.8
Rembert, Winfred. *Chasing Me to My Grave*	B
St. John, Warren. *Outcasts United*	B
Swift, Earl. *Hell Put to Shame*	364.15

AUTHOR, TITLE, SERIES AND SUBJECT INDEX

Walker, Vanessa Siddle. *The Lost Education of Horace Tate*	370.92
Georgia O'Keeffe. Robinson, Roxana	B
Georgia O'Keeffe Museum Collections. Lynes, Barbara Buhler	759.13

GEORGIAN ERA (1714-1837)

Ackroyd, Peter. *Revolution*	941.07
Charman, Isobel. *The Zoo*	590.73
Foreman, Amanda. *Georgiana, Duchess of Devonshire*	B
Hogeland, William. *Declaration*	973.3
Koch, Bea. *Mad and Bad*	920
Morrison, Robert. *The Regency Years*	941.07
Paine, Thomas. ★*Rights of Man*	320.5
Roberts, Andrew. *The Last King of America*	B

Georgiana, Duchess of Devonshire. Foreman, Amanda B

Gerald, Casey
There Will Be No Miracles Here B

GERALD, CASEY
Gerald, Casey. *There Will Be No Miracles Here* B

Gerard, Sarah
Carrie Carolyn Coco	364.152
Sunshine State	814

GERARD, SARAH
Gerard, Sarah. *Carrie Carolyn Coco*	364.152
Gerard, Sarah. *Sunshine State*	814

Gerard, Tieghan
★*Half Baked Harvest Every Day* 641.5

Gerber, Robin
Barbie and Ruth B

Gerdts, William H.
American Impressionism 759.13

Gergel, Richard
Unexampled Courage 323.1196

GERIATRICS
Aronson, Louise. *Elderhood* 362.60973

Gering, Jacquie
Quilting Modern	746.46
Walk	746.46

GERLACHE DE GOMERY, A. DE (ADRIEN), COMMANDANT, 1866-1934
Sancton, Julian. *Madhouse at the End of the Earth* 919.8904

GERMAN AMERICAN FAMILIES
Krug, Nora. ★*Belonging* 741.5

GERMAN AMERICANS
Jacobsen, Annie. ★*Operation Paperclip*	940.54
Krug, Nora. ★*Belonging*	741.5
Russell, Jan Jarboe. *The Train to Crystal City*	940.53
Simms, Brendan. *The Silver Waterfall*	940.54

The German Genius. Watson, Peter 943

GERMAN HISTORY

Beevor, Antony. *The Fall of Berlin, 1945*	940.54
Carter, Miranda. *George, Nicholas and Wilhelm*	940.3
Clay, Catrine. *King, Kaiser, Tsar*	B
Edsel, Robert M. *The Monuments Men*	940.53
Einstein, Albert. ★*A Stubbornly Persistent Illusion*	530.092
English, Charlie. *The Gallery of Miracles and Madness*	709.04
Evans, Richard J. *The Coming of the Third Reich*	943.08
Evans, Richard J. *The Third Reich at War*	940.53
Feigel, Lara. *The Bitter Taste of Victory*	320.943
Fritzsche, Peter. *Life and Death in the Third Reich*	943.086
Geck, Martin. ★*Johann Sebastian Bach*	780.92
Goldsmith, Martin. *The Inextinguishable Symphony*	B
Goodman, Simon. *The Orpheus Clock*	940.53
Haffner, Sebastian. *Defying Hitler*	943.085
Harding, Thomas. *The House by the Lake*	943
Hastings, Max. *Operation Chastise*	940.54
Hoyer, Katja. *Blood and Iron*	943.08
Jahner, Harald. ★*Aftermath*	943.087
Kempowski, Walter. *Swansong 1945*	940.54
Kershaw, Ian. *Hitler*	B
Kershaw, Ian. *Hitler*	B
King, David. *The Trial of Adolf Hitler*	345.43
Krug, Nora. ★*Belonging*	741.5
MacGregor, Neil. *Germany*	943
Macintyre, Ben. *Agent Zigzag*	
Macintyre, Ben. ★*Prisoners of the Castle*	940.54
MacLean, Rory. *Berlin*	943.155
MacMillan, Margaret. *Paris 1919*	940.3
McKay, Sinclair. *Berlin*	943
Merriman, Helena. ★*Tunnel 29*	943
Milton, Giles. *Checkmate in Berlin*	943
Moorhouse, Roger. *Berlin at War*	943
Petropoulos, Jonathan. *The Faustian Bargain*	709
Read, Anthony. *The Fall of Berlin*	940.54
Safranski, Rudiger. *Goethe*	B
Sarotte, M. E. *The Collapse*	943.087
Schwarz, Geraldine. *Those Who Forget*	940.53
Smith, Helmut Walser. *Germany, a Nation in Its Time*	943
Taylor, Fred. *The Berlin Wall*	943
Trentmann, Frank. *Out of the Darkness*	943.08
Vogel, Steve. *Betrayal in Berlin*	327.1273043
Watson, Peter. *The German Genius*	943
Willner, Nina. *Forty Autumns*	B
Winder, Simon. *Lotharingia*	944

GERMAN OCCUPATION, WORLD WAR II

Berg, Mary. *The Diary of Mary Berg*	B
Bilger, Burkhard. *Fatherland*	B
Chiger, Krystyna. *The Girl in the Green Sweater*	B
Dugard, Martin. *Taking Paris*	940.54
Goodrich, Frances. *The Diary of Anne Frank*	812
Grose, Peter. *A Good Place to Hide*	940.53
Humbert, Agnes. *Resistance*	B
Iperen, Roxane van. ★*The Sisters of Auschwitz*	940.53
Kaiser, Charles. *The Cost of Courage*	B
Kaiser, Menachem. *Plunder*	940.53
Karski, Jan. *Story of a Secret State*	940.53
Kershaw, Alex. *Avenue of Spies*	940.53
King, David. *Death in the City of Light*	364.152
Kix, Paul. *The Saboteur*	940.53
Lewis, Damien. *Churchill's Hellraisers*	940.54
Magida, Arthur J. *Code Name Madeleine*	940.54
Matzen, Robert. *Dutch Girl*	B
Mazzeo, Tilar J. *Irena's Children*	B
Mazzeo, Tilar J. *Sisters in Resistance*	945.091
Moorehead, Caroline. *A House in the Mountains*	940.53
Moorehead, Caroline. *A Train in Winter*	940.53
Moorehead, Caroline. *Village of Secrets*	944
Olson, Lynne. ★*Madame Fourcade's Secret War*	B
Porter, Carolyn. *Marcel's Letters*	940.54
Purnell, Sonia. ★*A Woman of No Importance*	B
Rosbottom, Ronald C. *When Paris Went Dark*	944.0816
Rosenberg, Justus. *The Art of Resistance*	B
Schwarz, Geraldine. *Those Who Forget*	940.53
Siegal, Nina. *The Diary Keepers*	940.53
Spiegel, Renia. *Renia's Diary*	B
Van Es, Bart. *The Cut Out Girl*	B

GERMAN PEOPLE

Bilger, Burkhard. *Fatherland*	B
Chernow, Ron. *The Warburgs*	B
Finkelstein, Daniel. *Two Roads Home*	920
Friedlander, Saul. *Nazi Germany and the Jews*	940.53
Herzog, Werner. ★*Every Man for Himself and God Against All*	B
Klemperer, Victor. *I Will Bear Witness*	B
Krug, Nora. ★*Belonging*	741.5
Lichtblau, Eric. *Return to the Reich*	B
MacGregor, Iain. *The Lighthouse of Stalingrad*	940.54
Nathan, Joan. ★*My Life in Recipes*	641.5
Pick-Goslar, Hannah Elizabeth. ★*My Friend Anne Frank*	
Schulman, Daniel. *The Money Kings*	332.0973
Simon, Marie. *Underground in Berlin*	B
Stargardt, Nicholas. *The German War*	940.53

GERMAN PEOPLE IN FOREIGN COUNTRIES

Bailey, Catherine. *A Castle in Wartime*	943.086
Marsh, Charles. *Strange Glory*	B

GERMAN PEOPLE IN ITALY
Bailey, Catherine. *A Castle in Wartime* 943.086

GERMAN PEOPLE IN THE UNITED STATES
Marsh, Charles. *Strange Glory* B

GERMAN REUNIFICATION

Hoyer, Katja. ★*Beyond the Wall*	943.087
Sarotte, M. E. *The Collapse*	943.087
Taylor, Fred. *The Berlin Wall*	943

GERMAN SHEPHERD DOG

Lewis, Damien. *The Dog Who Could Fly*	940.54
Orlean, Susan. *Rin Tin Tin*	636.737

The German War. Stargardt, Nicholas 940.53
Germany. MacGregor, Neil 943

GERMANY
Ahmad, Aeham. *The Pianist from Syria* B

PUBLIC LIBRARY CORE COLLECTION: NONFICTION
Twentieth Edition

Ambrose, Stephen E. *The Wild Blue*	940.54
Bascomb, Neal. *The Winter Fortress*	940.54
Beevor, Antony. *The Fall of Berlin, 1945*	940.54
Beschloss, Michael R. *The Conquerors*	940.53
Bouverie, Tim. *Appeasement*	327.41043
Cadbury, Deborah. *The School That Escaped from the Nazis*	940.53
Childers, Thomas. *The Third Reich*	943.086
Cornwell, Bernard. *Waterloo*	940.2
Donner, Rebecca. *All the Frequent Troubles of Our Days*	943
Dumbach, Annette E. *Sophie Scholl and the White Rose*	943.086
Dwork, Deborah. ★*Holocaust*	940
Edmonds, Chris. *No Surrender*	B
Eisner, Peter. *The Pope's Last Crusade*	282.092
English, Charlie. *The Gallery of Miracles and Madness*	709.04
Enrich, David. *Dark Towers*	332.1
Evans, Richard J. *The Third Reich at War*	940.53
Evans, Richard J. *The Third Reich in Power, 1933-1939*	943.086
Feigel, Lara. *The Bitter Taste of Victory*	320.943
Finkelstein, Daniel. *Two Roads Home*	920
Friedlander, Saul. *Nazi Germany and the Jews*	940.53
Friedlander, Saul. *Nazi Germany and the Jews*	940.53
Fritzsche, Peter. *Life and Death in the Third Reich*	943.086
Gerwarth, Robert. *Hitler's Hangman*	B
Goldhagen, Daniel Jonah. *Hitler's Willing Executioners*	940.53
Grayling, A. C. *Among the Dead Cities*	940.54
Harding, Thomas. *The House by the Lake*	943
Hayes, Peter. *Why?*	940.53
Hendrix, Scott H. *Martin Luther*	B
Hitler, Adolf. *Mein Kampf*	B
Hogan, William R. *Task Force Hogan*	940.54
Holland, James. *Brothers in Arms*	940.54
Holland, James. *The Rise of Germany, 1939-1941; Vol. 1*	940.54
Honigstein, Raphael. *DAS Reboot*	796.334
Hoyer, Katja. *Blood and Iron*	943.08
Jahner, Harald. ★*Aftermath*	943.087
Kean, Sam. *The Bastard Brigade*	355.8
Kempowski, Walter. *Swansong 1945*	940.54
Kennedy, Michael. *Richard Strauss*	B
Kershaw, Ian. *Hitler*	B
Kershaw, Ian. *Hitler*	B
Klemperer, Victor. *I Will Bear Witness*	B
Krug, Nora. ★*Belonging*	741.5
Kushner, Jacob. *Look Away*	305.9
Larson, Erik. *In the Garden of Beasts*	B
Levi, Primo. *The Periodic Table*	858
Levi, Primo. ★*Survival in Auschwitz*	B
Lichtblau, Eric. *Return to the Reich*	B
Longerich, Peter. *Goebbels*	B
Longerich, Peter. *Hitler*	B
MacGregor, Iain. *The Lighthouse of Stalingrad*	940.54
MacGregor, Neil. *Germany*	943
Macintyre, Ben. *Double Cross*	940.54
MacLean, Rory. *Berlin*	943.155
MacMillan, Margaret. *Paris 1919*	940.3
Marsh, Charles. *Strange Glory*	B
Marton, Kati. ★*The Chancellor*	B
Mazower, Mark. *Hitler's Empire*	940.53
McDonough, Frank. *The Hitler Years*	943.086
McKay, Sinclair. *The Fire and the Darkness*	940.54
Meltzer, Brad. ★*The Nazi Conspiracy*	940.53
Merridale, Catherine. *Lenin on the Train*	B
Metaxas, Eric. *Martin Luther*	B
Miller, Donald L. ★*Masters of the Air*	940.54
Milton, Giles. *Checkmate in Berlin*	943
Moorhouse, Roger. *The Devils' Alliance*	940.53
Oberman, Heiko Augustinus. *Luther*	B
Oelhafen, Ingrid von. *Hitler's Stolen Children*	B
Ohler, Norman. *The Bohemians*	940.53
Phillips, Adrian. *Fighting Churchill, Appeasing Hitler*	327.41043
Pick-Goslar, Hannah Elizabeth. ★*My Friend Anne Frank*	B
Read, Anthony. *The Fall of Berlin*	940.54
Rees, Laurence. *Hitler and Stalin*	940.53
Ronald, Susan. *Hitler's Aristocrats*	940.53
Roth, Joseph. *What I Saw*	943
Ryback, Timothy W. *Takeover*	943.086
Sarotte, M. E. *The Collapse*	943.087
Shirer, William L. ★*The Rise and Fall of the Third Reich*	943.086
Smith, Helmut Walser. *Germany, a Nation in Its Time*	943
Speer, Albert. *Inside the Third Reich*	B
Spicer, Charles. *Coffee with Hitler*	941.084
Stahl, Jerry. *Nein, Nein, Nein!*	B
Stargardt, Nicholas. *The German War*	940.53
Steinberg, Jonathan. *Bismarck*	B
Strauss, Gwen. *The Nine*	940.53
Swafford, Jan. ★*Beethoven*	B
Talty, Stephan. *Agent Garbo*	940.5
Taylor, Fred. *The Berlin Wall*	943
Thomas, Gordon. *Defying Hitler*	920
Trentmann, Frank. *Out of the Darkness*	943.08
Trimborn, Jurgen. *Leni Riefenstahl*	B
Ullrich, Volker. ★*Eight Days in May*	943.086
Ullrich, Volker. *Germany 1923*	943.085
Ullrich, Volker. *Hitler*	B
Urwand, Ben. *The Collaboration*	791.430973
Wachsmann, Nikolaus. *Kl*	940.53
Watson, Peter. *The German Genius*	943
Weale, Adrian. *Army of Evil*	940.54
Weber, Thomas. *Becoming Hitler*	B
Wulf, Andrea. *Magnificent Rebels*	830.9
Germany 1923. Ullrich, Volker	943.085
Germany, A Nation in Its Time. Smith, Helmut Walser	943
Germer, Fawn	
Coming Back	650.14
★***Geronimo.*** Utley, Robert M.	B
GERONIMO, APACHE CHIEF, 1829-1909	
Brands, H. W. *The Last Campaign*	973.8
Hutton, Paul Andrew. *The Apache Wars*	979
Roberts, David. *Once They Moved Like the Wind*	B
Utley, Robert M. ★*Geronimo*	B
Geronimus, Arline T.	
★*Weathering*	362.1089
Geroux, William	
The Ghost Ships of Archangel	940.54
GERRYMANDERING	
Anderson, Carol. ★*One Person, No Vote*	324.6
Seabrook, Nicholas R. *One Person, One Vote*	328.3
Wehle, Kim. *What You Need to Know About Voting and Why*	324.60973
GERSHWIN, GEORGE, 1898-1937	
Feinstein, Michael. *The Gershwins and Me*	782.42164
Hyland, William G. *George Gershwin*	B
Pollack, Howard. ★*George Gershwin*	B
GERSHWIN, IRA, 1896-1983	
Feinstein, Michael. *The Gershwins and Me*	782.42164
The Gershwins and Me. Feinstein, Michael	782.42164
Gerson, Fany	
Mexican Ice Cream	641.86
My Sweet Mexico	641.5972
Gerson, Merissa Nathan	
Forget Prayers, Bring Cake	155.9
GERSON, MERISSA NATHAN	
Gerson, Merissa Nathan. *Forget Prayers, Bring Cake*	155.9
GERSTEIN, KURT, 1905-1945	
Thomas, Gordon. *Defying Hitler*	920
Gerth, Karl	
As China Goes, so Goes the World	339.4
Gertrude Bell. Howell, Georgina	B
Gertsman, Elina	
The Middle Ages in 50 Objects	909.07
Gerwarth, Robert	
Hitler's Hangman	B
Gessen, Masha	
The Future Is History	947.086
Never Remember	365
Surviving Autocracy	973.933
Gessner, David	
Ultimate Glory	796.2
GESSNER, DAVID, 1961-	
Gessner, David. *Ultimate Glory*	796.2
Get Better at Anything. Young, Scott H.	650.1
Get Capone. Eig, Jonathan	364.1
★***Get Me Through the Next Five Minutes.*** Parker, James	158.1
Get The Picture. Bosker, Bianca	701
Geter, Hafizah	
Un-American	811
Gethin, Rosanna Clare	
Sew Luxe Leather	745.53

AUTHOR, TITLE, SERIES AND SUBJECT INDEX

Getting Ahead of ADHD. Nigg, Joel T. — 618.92
Getting Along. Gallo, Amy — 658.4
Getting Life. Morton, Michael — B
Getting Me Cheap. Freeman, Amanda — 362.83
Getting Out of Saigon. White, Ralph — 959.704
Getting Schooled. Keizer, Garret — 373.1102
★*Getting* Things Done. Allen, David — 646.7
Getting to Know Death. Godwin, Gail — B
Getting to Us. Davis, Seth — 796.07
★*Getting* to Yes. Fisher, Roger — 158
Gettysburg. Guelzo, Allen C. — 973.7
Gettysburg. Sears, Stephen W. — 973.7
GETTYSBURG CAMPAIGN, 1863
    Foote, Shelby. *Stars in Their Courses* — 973.7
GETTYSBURG, BATTLE OF, 1863
    Guelzo, Allen C. *Gettysburg* — 973.7
    McPherson, James M. *Hallowed Ground* — 973.7
    Miller, Donald L. *Vicksburg* — 973.7
    Sears, Stephen W. *Gettysburg* — 973.7
    White, Ronald C. *On Great Fields* — B
Gevisser, Mark
    A Legacy of Liberation — B
Gewen, Barry
    ★*The Inevitability of Tragedy* — B
Ghafari, Zarifa
    Zarifa — B
GHANA
    Umar, Ousman. *North to Paradise* — B
    Yeebo, Yepoka. *Anansi's Gold* — 364.16
GHANAIAN PEOPLE
    Yeebo, Yepoka. *Anansi's Gold* — 364.16
Ghattas, Kim
    Black Wave — 955.05
Ghazvinian, John
    America and Iran — 327
Ghetto Brother. Voloj, Julian — 741.5
Ghetto Gastro Black Power Kitchen. Gray, Jon — 641.5
GHETTOES, AFRICAN AMERICAN
    Brown, Claude. *Manchild in the Promised Land* — B
    Jackson, Mitchell S. *Survival Math* — B
    Leovy, Jill. *Ghettoside* — 364.152
GHETTOES, JEWISH
    Mazzeo, Tilar J. *Irena's Children* — B
    Spiegel, Renia. *Renia's Diary* — B
Ghettoside. Leovy, Jill — 364.152
Ghez, Didier
    The Hidden Art of Disney's Golden Age — 741.5
GHIBERTI, LORENZO, 1378-1455
    King, Ross. *Brunelleschi's Dome* — 726.6
Ghobash, Omar Saif
    Letters to a Young Muslim — 297.09
GHOBASH, OMAR SAIF, 1971-
    Ghobash, Omar Saif. *Letters to a Young Muslim* — 297.09
Ghodsee, Kristen Rogheh
    Everyday Utopia — 335
Ghosh, Amitav
    The Great Derangement — 809
Ghost. Ramsland, Katherine M. — 133.1
Ghost Dogs. Dubus, Andre — 814
The Ghost Forest. King, Greg — 333.75
Ghost Hunters. Blum, Deborah — 133.9
Ghost in the Wires. Mitnick, Kevin D. — B
The Ghost Map. Johnson, Steven — 614.5
The Ghost Mountain Boys. Campbell, James — 940.54
Ghost of. Nguyen, Diana Khoi — 811
The Ghost Ships of Archangel. Geroux, William — 940.54
★*Ghost Soldiers*. Sides, Hampton — 940.54
★*Ghost Wars*. Coll, Steve — 958.104
Ghostface Killah
    Rise of a Killah — B
GHOSTFACE KILLAH (RAPPER)
    Ghostface Killah. *Rise of a Killah* — B
Ghostland. Dickey, Colin — 133.1
GHOSTS
    Aykroyd, Peter. *A History of Ghosts* — 133.1
    Blum, Deborah. *Ghost Hunters* — 133.9
    Guiley, Rosemary. ★*The Encyclopedia of Ghosts and Spirits* — 133.1
    Jones, Marie D. *Celebrity Ghosts and Notorious Hauntings* — 133.1
    Nguyen, Hoa. *A Thousand Times You Lose Your Treasure* — 811
    Norman, Michael. *Haunted America* — 133.1
    Ramsland, Katherine M. *Ghost* — 133.1
    Whitmer, Jamie Davis. *America's Most Haunted Hotels* — 133.1
Ghosts in the Schoolyard. Ewing, Eve L. — 370.89
The Ghosts of Cannae. O'Connell, Robert L. — 937
Ghosts of Gold Mountain. Chang, Gordon H. — 331.6
Ghosts of Honolulu. Harmon, Mark — 940.54
The Ghosts of K2. Conefrey, Mick — 796.522
Ghosts of Spain. Tremlett, Giles — 946.08
Ghosts of the Orphanage. Kenneally, Christine — 362.73
Ghosts of the Tsunami. Parry, Richard Lloyd — 952.05
GHOSTWRITERS
    Hardin, Lara Love. ★*The Many Lives of Mama Love* — B
Ghoting, Saroj Nadkarni
    Step into Storytime — 027.62
GI Brides. Barrett, Duncan — 920
★*Giada's Italy*. De Laurentiis, Giada — 641.594
Giada's Kitchen. De Laurentiis, Giada — 641.594
GIANCANA, SAM, 1908-1975
    Maier, Thomas. *Mafia Spies* — 364.1060973
Giangreco, D. M.
    Hell to Pay — 940.54
GIANT PANDA
    Croke, Vicki. *The Lady and the Panda* — 599.789
GIBB, BARRY, 1947-
    Stanley, Bob. ★*The Story of the Bee Gees* — 782.42164
GIBB, MAURICE, 1949-2003
    Stanley, Bob. ★*The Story of the Bee Gees* — 782.42164
GIBB, ROBIN, 1949-2012
    Stanley, Bob. ★*The Story of the Bee Gees* — 782.42164
Gibbins, David J. L.
    A History of the World in Twelve Shipwrecks — 909
Gibbon, Edward
    ★*The Decline and Fall of the Roman Empire* — 937
Gibney, John
    A Short History of Ireland, 1500-2000 — 941.7
Gibran, Kahlil
    And the Prophet Said — 811
    The Collected Works — 811
    ★*The Prophet* — 811
GIBSON, ALTHEA, 1927-2003
    Jacobs, Sally H. *Althea* — B
GIBSON, BOB, 1935-2020
    Pappu, Sridhar. *The Year of the Pitcher* — 920
GIBSON, CHARLES, 1943-
    Stelter, Brian. *Top of the Morning* — 791.456
Gibson, Larry S.
    Young Thurgood — B
Gibson, Marion
    Witchcraft — 133.4
Gibson, William
    ★*The Miracle Worker* — 812
Gidding, John
    At Home with Nature — 635.9
Giddings, Paula
    Ida — B
Giddins, Gary
    Bing Crosby — B
    Bing Crosby — B
    Weather Bird — 781.6509
Gideon's Promise. Rapping, Jonathan — 345.73
Gideon's Trumpet. Lewis, Anthony — 345.73
GIDEON, CLARENCE EARL
    Lewis, Anthony. *Gideon's Trumpet* — 345.73
Gidla, Sujatha
    Ants Among Elephants — 305.5
GIDLA, SUJATHA, 1963-
    Gidla, Sujatha. *Ants Among Elephants* — 305.5
Gienapp, William E.
    Abraham Lincoln and Civil War America — B
Gierach, John
    All Fishermen Are Liars — 799.12
    Dumb Luck and the Kindness of Strangers — 799.124
    A Fly Rod of Your Own — 799.12
Gies, Frances
    Life in a Medieval Village — 306

PUBLIC LIBRARY CORE COLLECTION: NONFICTION
Twentieth Edition

Gies, Joseph
   Life in a Medieval Castle — 940.1
Gies, Miep
   ★*Anne Frank Remembered* — B
GIES, MIEP, 1909-2010
   Gies, Miep. ★*Anne Frank Remembered* — B
Gifford Pinchot and the Making of Modern Environmentalism. Miller, Char — B
★*The Gift*. Hafiz — 891
The Gift of Failure. Lahey, Jessica — 649
The Gift of Thanks. Visser, Margaret — 394
The Gift of Years. Chittister, Joan — 200
GIFTED PEOPLE
   Bloom, Harold. *Genius* — 153.9
   Isaacson, Walter. ★*Leonardo Da Vinci* — B
GIFTED TEENAGERS
   Tesoriero, Heather Won. *The Class* — 507.1
GIFTED WOMEN
   Kaplan, Janice. *The Genius of Women* — 920
GIFTS
   Kingston, Genevieve. *Did I Ever Tell You?* — B
Gifts Differing. Myers, Isabel Briggs — 155.2
The Gifts of Imperfection. Brown, Brene — 158
The Gig Economy. Mulcahy, Diane — 650.1
Gilbert, Carter Rowell
   ★*National Audubon Society Field Guide to Fishes.* — 597
Gilbert, Daniel Todd
   ★*Stumbling on Happiness* — 158
Gilbert, Elizabeth
   ★*Big Magic* — 153.3
   Eat, Pray, Love — B
GILBERT, ELIZABETH, 1969-
   Gilbert, Elizabeth. *Eat, Pray, Love* — B
Gilbert, Jack
   Collected Poems — 811
Gilbert, Martin
   The Second World War — 940.53
Gilbert, Sandra M.
   Death's Door — 155.9
   ★*Still Mad* — 810.9
Gilchrist, Abby
   Modern Fabric — 746.092
Gildea, William
   The Longest Fight — B
GILDED AGE (1865-1898)
   Boorstin, Daniel J. *The Americans* — 973
   Freeberg, Ernest. *A Traitor to His Species* — B
   Hiltzik, Michael A. *Iron Empires* — 385.0973
   Jacoby, Karl. *The Strange Career of William Ellis* — B
   Manseau, Peter. *The Apparitionists* — B
   Mort, T. A. *Thieves' Road* — 978.3
   Painter, Nell Irvin. ★*Sojourner Truth* — B
   Postel, Charles. *Equality* — 305.50973
   Senik, Troy. *A Man of Iron* — B
   Sinha, Manisha. ★*The Rise and Fall of the Second American Republic* — 973.8
   Todd, Kim. *Sensational* — 920
   Ward, Geoffrey C. *A Disposition to Be Rich* — B
   Wright, Jennifer Ashley. ★*Madame Restell* — B
Gilder, Ginny
   Course Correction — 797.12
GILDER, GINNY
   Gilder, Ginny. *Course Correction* — 797.12
Gildiner, Catherine
   Good Morning, Monster — 616.89
GILDINER, CATHERINE, 1948-
   Gildiner, Catherine. *Good Morning, Monster* — 616.89
Gilkey, Charlie
   Start Finishing — 658.4
Gill, A. A.
   To America with Love — 973.93
GILL, A. A., 1954-2016
   Gill, A. A. *To America with Love* — 973.93
Gill, Anton
   Art Lover — B
Gill, Gillian
   We Two — 941.081
Gill, Jonathan
   Harlem — 974.7

Gill, Sasha
   East Meets Vegan — 641.5
Gill, Shira
   Organized Living — 747
Gillard, Julia
   ★*Women and Leadership* — 158
Gilleland, Diane
   All Points Patchwork — 746.46
Gillespie, Carmen
   Critical Companion to Toni Morrison — 813
GILLESPIE, DIZZY, 1917-1993
   Lees, Gene. *You Can't Steal a Gift* — B
Gillette, J. Michael
   Designing with Light — 792
   Theatrical Design and Production — 792.02
Gillette, Michael L.
   Lady Bird Johnson — B
Gilliam, Dorothy Butler
   Trailblazer — B
GILLIAM, DOROTHY BUTLER, 1936-
   Gilliam, Dorothy Butler. *Trailblazer* — B
Gilliam, Fatimah
   Race Rules — 305.8
Gilliard, Dominique Dubois
   Rethinking Incarceration — 261.8
Gillon, Steven M.
   America's Reluctant Prince — B
GILPIN FAMILY
   Faust, Drew Gilpin. *Necessary Trouble* — B
Gimenez Smith, Carmen
   Be Recorder — 811
GINGERBREAD
   Samuell, Kristine. *A Year of Gingerbread Houses* — 745.5
GINGERBREAD HOUSES
   Samuell, Kristine. *A Year of Gingerbread Houses* — 745.5
Gingrich, Dayne
   Pickleball Mindset — 796.34
GINGRICH, NEWT
   Zelizer, Julian E. *Burning Down the House* — 328.73
Ginsberg, Allen
   Best Minds of My Generation — 810.9
   ★*Howl* — 811.54
Ginsburg, Ruth Bader
   ★*My Own Words* — 347.73
GINSBURG, RUTH BADER, 1933-2020
   Carmon, Irin. *Notorious RBG* — B
   De Hart, Jane Sherron. ★*Ruth Bader Ginsburg* — B
   Ginsburg, Ruth Bader. ★*My Own Words* — 347.73
   Hirshman, Linda R. *Sisters in Law* — 347.73
   Rosen, Jeffrey. *Conversations with RBG* — B
   Totenberg, Nina. ★*Dinners with Ruth* — B
Ginzberg, Lori D.
   Elizabeth Cady Stanton — B
Gioia, Dana
   99 Poems — 811
Gioia, Ted
   The History of Jazz — 781.6509
   Music — 780.9
   Work Songs — 782.42
Giorgione, Michael
   Inside Camp David — 975.2
Giovanni, Nikki
   ★*The Collected Poetry of Nikki Giovanni, 1968-1998* — 811
   A Good Cry — 811
   Make Me Rain — 811
   Quilting the Black-Eyed Pea — 811
Giraffe Reflections. Peterson, Dale — 599.638
Giridharadas, Anand
   ★*The Persuaders* — 320.973
The Girl Explorers. Zanglein, Jayne E. — B
The Girl from the Metropol Hotel. Petrushevskaia, Liudmila — B
Girl in a Band. Gordon, Kim — B
Girl in Black and White. Morgan-Owens, Jessie — B
The Girl in the Green Sweater. Chiger, Krystyna — B
The Girl on the Balcony. Hussey, Olivia — B
Girl Sleuth. Rehak, Melanie — 813
Girl Unbroken. Calcaterra, Regina — B
The Girl Who Escaped Isis. Khalaf, Farida — B

AUTHOR, TITLE, SERIES AND SUBJECT INDEX

*The **Girl** Who Fell to Earth*. Al-Maria, Sophia — B
*The **Girl** with the Lower Back Tattoo*. Schumer, Amy — B
*A **Girl**'s Guide to Joining the Resistance*. Gray, Emma — 303.48
Girlhood. Febos, Melissa — 818

GIRLS
   Barr, John. *Start by Believing* — 364.15
   Blais, Madeleine. *In These Girls, Hope Is a Muscle* — 796.323
   Bowden, Mark. *The Last Stone* — 363.25
   Browne, Mahogany L. ★*Black Girl Magic* — 811.6
   Clein, Emmeline. ★*Dead Weight* — 616.85
   Davis, Lisa Selin. *Tomboy* — 305.409
   DeRogatis, Jim. *Soulless* — B
   Diamant, Anita. ★*Period. End of Sentence* — 612.6
   Douglas, John E. *When a Killer Calls* — 364.152
   Faleiro, Sonia. *The Good Girls* — 364.152
   Febos, Melissa. *Girlhood* — 818
   Finney, Nikky. *Love Child's Hotbed of Occasional Poetry* — 811
   Fuller, Alexandra. *Don't Let's Go to the Dogs Tonight* — B
   Henderson, Danielle. ★*The Ugly Cry* — B
   Hill, DaMaris B. *Breath Better Spent* — 811
   Jacobson, Sidney. *Anne Frank* — 741.5
   Jones, Faith. *Sex Cult Nun* — B
   Mans, Jasmine. *Black Girl, Call Home* — 811
   Mar, Alex. *Seventy Times Seven* — 362.88
   May, Meredith. *The Honey Bus* — B
   McDiarmid, Jessica. *Highway of Tears* — 364.152
   Mead, Margaret. *Coming of Age in Samoa* — 306
   Muller, Melissa. *Anne Frank* — B
   Murray, Liz. *Breaking Night* — B
   Nayeri, Dina. ★*The Ungrateful Refugee* — 362.87
   Nordberg, Jenny. *The Underground Girls of Kabul* — 305.3
   Orenstein, Peggy. *Cinderella Ate My Daughter* — 305.23082
   Orenstein, Peggy. *Don't Call Me Princess* — 305.42
   Parker, Kate T. *Strong Is the New Pretty* — 155.43
   Pick-Goslar, Hannah Elizabeth. ★*My Friend Anne Frank* — B
   Rehak, Melanie. *Girl Sleuth* — 813
   Robb, Alice. ★*Don't Think, Dear* — 792.8
   Simmons, Rachel. *Odd Girl Out* — 302.5
   Stewart, Nikita. *Troop 6000* — 369
   Tjipombo, Tupa. *I Am Not Your Slave* — 818
   V. *The Apology* — 818
   Wallace, Chris. *Countdown 1945* — 940.54
   Yousafzai, Malala. *I Am Malala* — B
   Yousafzai, Ziauddin. *Let Her Fly* — B

★*Girls and Their Monsters*. Farley, Audrey Clare — 306.875
Girls Can Kiss Now. Gutowitz, Jill — 814
*The **Girls** in the Wild Fig Tree*. Leng'ete, Nice — B
*The **Girls** of Atomic City*. Kiernan, Denise — 976.8
*The **Girls** Who Stepped Out of Line*. Eder, Mari K. — 920
*The **Girls** Who Went Away*. Fessler, Ann — 362.82

GIRLS' SCHOOLS
   Yousafzai, Malala. *I Am Malala* — B

Girly Drinks. O'Meara, Mallory — 641.2
Girma, Haben
   Haben — B
GIRMA, HABEN, 1988-
   Girma, Haben. *Haben* — B
Girmay, Aracelis
   The Black Maria — 811
Girzone, Joseph F.
   Never Alone — 248.4
   A Portrait of Jesus — 232.9
GIRZONE, JOSEPH F.
   Girzone, Joseph F. *Never Alone* — 248.4
Gitlin, Marty
   A Celebration of Animation — 741.5
Giuliani. Kirtzman, Andrew — B
GIULIANI, RUDOLPH W.
   Kirtzman, Andrew. *Giuliani* — B
Give and Take. Grant, Adam M. — 158.2
Give Me Liberty. Brookhiser, Richard — 320.540973
Give Me Liberty. Hoffman, David E. — B
Give My Poor Heart Ease. Ferris, William R. — 781.643
Give Us the Ballot. Berman, Ari — 324.6
Givens, Jarvis R.
   ★*School Clothes* — 371.829
Givhan, Robin
   The Battle of Versailles — 746.9

Giving Voice to Values. Gentile, Mary C. — 174
GLACIER NATIONAL PARK
   Offerman, Nick. *Where the Deer and the Antelope Play* — 973.93
GLACIERS
   Heacox, Kim. ★*John Muir and the Ice That Started a Fire* — 333.7209798
   Pollack, H. N. *A World Without Ice* — 551.31
Gladstone, Brooke
   The Influencing Machine — 741.5
Gladwell, Malcolm
   Blink — 153.4
   ★*The Bomber Mafia* — 940.54
   David and Goliath — 155.2
   Outliers — 302
   ★*Talking to Strangers* — 302
   The Tipping Point — 302
*The **Glamour** of Strangeness*. James, Jamie — 700.1
Glancey, Jonathan
   The Story of Architecture — 720
Glaser, Gabrielle
   American Baby — B
GLASNOST
   Remnick, David. *Lenin's Tomb* — 947.085
   Taubman, William. *Gorbachev* — B
★*The **Glass** Castle*. Walls, Jeannette — B
GLASS CEILING
   Williams, Joan. *What Works for Women at Work* — 650.1
   Wingfield, Adia Harvey. *Gray Areas* — 331.6
GLASS CRAFT
   Rich, Chris. *Stained Glass Basics* — 748.5
GLASS FAMILY
   Freeman, Hadley. *House of Glass* — B
GLASS PAINTING
   Rich, Chris. *Stained Glass Basics* — 748.5
GLASS SCULPTURE
   Ward, Gerald W. R. *Chihuly* — 709
Glass, Alison
   Alison Glass Applique — 746.44
Glass, Brent D
   50 Great American Places — 973
Glass, Charles
   Soldiers Don't Go Mad — 616.85
GLASS, NOAH
   Bilton, Nick. *Hatching Twitter* — 006.7
Glass, Philip
   Words Without Music — B
GLASS, PHILIP, 1937-
   Glass, Philip. *Words Without Music* — B
Glass, Sara
   Kissing Girls on Shabbat — B
GLASS, SARA
   Glass, Sara. *Kissing Girls on Shabbat* — B
Glasse, Cyril
   The New Encyclopedia of Islam — 297.03
Glasser, William
   Choice Theory — 150
Glatt, John
   The Doomsday Mother — 364.152
   The Family Next Door — 362.76092
   ★*The Perfect Father* — 364.152
   Tangled Vines — 364.152
Glatthaar, Joseph T.
   The American Military — 355.00973
Glaude, Eddie S.
   Begin Again — 305.800973
Glaze. Taylor, Brian J. — 738.1
Gleeson, John
   The Gotti Wars — 364.1
GLEESON, JOHN, 1953 JULY 14-
   Gleeson, John. *The Gotti Wars* — 364.1
Gleiberman, Owen
   Movie Freak — B
GLEIBERMAN, OWEN
   Gleiberman, Owen. *Movie Freak* — B
Gleick, James
   The Information — 020.9
   Time Travel — 530.11
Gleick, Peter H.
   The Three Ages of Water — 333.91

PUBLIC LIBRARY CORE COLLECTION: NONFICTION
Twentieth Edition

Glenconner, Anne
  ★*Lady in Waiting* — B
GLENCONNER, ANNE
  Glenconner, Anne. ★*Lady in Waiting* — B
Glendinning, Victoria
  Leonard Woolf — B
GLENN, JOHN, 1921-2016
  Shesol, Jeff. *Mercury Rising* — 629.45
Gless, Sharon
  Apparently There Were Complaints — B
GLESS, SHARON
  Gless, Sharon. *Apparently There Were Complaints* — B
Glinert, Lewis
  The Story of Hebrew — 492.4
Glitter and Concrete. Goodman, Elyssa — 792.7
Glitter and Glue. Corrigan, Kelly — B
The *Glitter* in the Green. Dunn, Jon L. — 598.7
Glitterville's Handmade Christmas. Brown, Stephen — B
The *Global* Age. Kershaw, Ian — 940.55
Global Discontents. Chomsky, Noam — 410.92
GLOBAL ENVIRONMENTAL CHANGE
  Fox, Porter. *The Last Winter* — 363.738
  Frankopan, Peter. *The Earth Transformed* — 304.2
  Hanson, Thor. *Hurricane Lizards and Plastic Squid* — 577.2
  Holthaus, Eric. *The Future Earth* — 363.738
  Klare, Michael T. *All Hell Breaking Loose* — 355.20973
  Kolbert, Elizabeth. *Field Notes from a Catastrophe* — 363.738
  Kolbert, Elizabeth. ★*Under a White Sky* — 304.2
  Linden, Eugene. *Fire and Flood* — 304.2
  Macdougall, J. D. *Frozen Earth* — 551.7
  Reid, John W. *Ever Green* — 634.9
  Rich, Nathaniel. *Losing Earth* — 363.738
  Ritchie, Hannah. *Not the End of the World* — 338.9
  Wallace-Wells, David. *The Uninhabitable Earth* — 304.2
GLOBAL FINANCIAL CRISIS, 2008-2009
  Dayen, David. *Chain of Title* — 330.973
  Howard, Timothy. *The Mortgage Wars* — 332.7
  Kaiser, Robert G. *Act of Congress* — 346.73
  Kershaw, Ian. *The Global Age* — 940.55
  McLean, Bethany. *All the Devils Are Here* — 330.973
  Paulson, Henry M. *On the Brink* — 330.973
  Sorkin, Andrew Ross. *Too Big to Fail* — 330.973
★A *Global* History of Architecture. Ching, Francis D. K. — 720.9
The *Global* Pantry Cookbook. Pittman, Ann Taylor — 641.59
GLOBAL TEMPERATURE CHANGES
  Kolbert, Elizabeth. *Field Notes from a Catastrophe* — 363.738
GLOBAL WARMING
  Bell, Alice R. *Our Biggest Experiment* — 363.738
  Berners-Lee, Mike. *The Carbon Footprint of Everything* — 363.738
  Dolin, Eric Jay. *A Furious Sky* — 363.34
  Fagan, Brian M. *The Long Summer* — 551.6
  Foer, Jonathan Safran. ★*We Are the Weather* — 636
  Ghosh, Amitav. *The Great Derangement* — 809
  Goodell, Jeff. *The Heat Will Kill You First* — 363.738
  Goodell, Jeff. *The Water Will Come* — 551.45
  Hiss, Tony. ★*Rescuing the Planet* — 333.75
  Hogge, Fred. *Of Ice and Men* — 338.4
  Kolbert, Elizabeth. *Field Notes from a Catastrophe* — 363.738
  Kostigen, Thomas. *Hacking Planet Earth* — 628
  Lustgarten, Abrahm. ★*On the Move* — 363.7
  Lynas, Mark. *Six Degrees* — 551.6
  Manson, Marla. *Everything Is F*cked* — 152.4
  Martin, Manjula. *The Last Fire Season* — B
  McKibben, Bill. *Falter* — 909.83
  Meyaard-Schaap, Kyle. *Following Jesus in a Warming World* — 241
  Pollack, H. N. *A World Without Ice* — 551.31
  Rawlence, Ben. *The Treeline* — 577.3
  Rich, Nathaniel. *Losing Earth* — 363.738
  Rich, Nathaniel. *Second Nature* — 304.2
  Swift, Earl. *Chesapeake Requiem* — 639
  Vigliotti, Jonathan. *Before It's Gone* — 577
  Vince, Gaia. *Nomad Century* — 362.87
  Vollmann, William T. *No Immediate Danger* — 333.79
  Wallace-Wells, David. *The Uninhabitable Earth* — 304.2
GLOBALIZATION
  Becker, Elizabeth. *Overbooked* — 338.4
  De Long, J. Bradford. *Slouching Towards Utopia* — 330.9
  Figes, Orlando. *The Europeans* — 920
  Friedman, Thomas L. ★*Thank You for Being Late* — 303.48
  Hickel, Jason. *The Divide* — 330.9
  Immerwahr, Daniel. *How to Hide an Empire* — 973
  Kenny, Charles. *The Plague Cycle* — 614.4
  Kershaw, Ian. *The Global Age* — 940.55
  Mishra, Pankaj. *Age of Anger* — 909.8
  Saladino, Dan. *Eating to Extinction* — 641.3
  Yergin, Daniel. *The Quest* — 333.79
GLOBALIZATION (ECONOMICS)
  Daunton, M. J. ★*The Economic Government of the World* — 337
  Hansen, Valerie. *The Year 1000* — 909
  Macy, Beth. ★*Factory Man* — 338.7
  Pang, Amelia. ★*Made in China* — 331.11
  Pilling, David. *Bending Adversity* — 952.0512
  Stiglitz, Joseph E. *Globalization and Its Discontents* — 337
  Wheelan, Charles J. *Naked Economics* — 330
Globalization and Its Discontents. Stiglitz, Joseph E. — 337
Glockner, Andy
  Chasing Perfection — 796.323
The *Glorious* Cause. Middlekauff, Robert — 973.3
A *Glorious* Enterprise. Peck, Robert McCracken — 508
Glory. Bethencourt, Kahran — 779.2
Glory Days. Wertheim, L. Jon — 796.09
Gluck, Louise
  American Originality — 814
  Averno — 811
  ★*Poems 1962-2012* — 811
  Winter Recipes from the Collective — 811
★*Gluten-Free* Baking at Home. Larsen, Jeffrey — 641.5
GLUTEN-FREE DIET
  Cavallari, Kristin. *True Roots* — 641.5
  Conners, Rachel. *Bakerita* — 641.81
  Cristofano, Jana. *Eat Well, Be Well* — 641.5
  Dada, Samah. *Dada Eats Love to Cook It* — 641.5
  Esposito, Jennifer. *Jennifer's Way Kitchen* — 641.5
  Gourdet, Gregory. *Everyone's Table* — 641.5
  Larsen, Jeffrey. ★*Gluten-Free Baking at Home* — 641.5
  Moskowitz, Isa Chandra. *Veganomicon* — 641
  Perlmutter, David. *The Grain Brain Cookbook* — 651.56
  Smith, R. Garth. *Asd, the Complete Autism Spectrum Disorder Health & Diet Guide* — 616.85
  Snodgrass, Alex. ★*The Defined Dish* — 641.5
  Walker, Danielle. *Danielle Walker's Against All Grain* — 641.5
Glynn, Kathy
  Hand Lettering Step by Step — 745.6
Gmorning, Gnight! Miranda, Lin-Manuel — 811
★The *Gnostic* Gospels. Pagels, Elaine H. — 273
GNOSTICISM
  Pagels, Elaine H. *Beyond Belief* — 229
  Pagels, Elaine H. ★*The Gnostic Gospels* — 273
Go Ahead in the Rain. Abdurraqib, Hanif — 782.421649
Go Back to Where You Came From. Ali, Wajahat — B
Go Down Together. Guinn, Jeff — B
★*Go* Like Hell. Baime, A. J. — 796.7209
★*Go-To* Dinners. Garten, Ina — 641.5
GOALS AND OBJECTIVES
  Davidson, Adam. *The Passion Economy* — 330.9
  Gardner, Chris. ★*Permission to Dream* — 158.1
  Gladwell, Malcolm. *David and Goliath* — 155.2
  Grant, Adam M. *Give and Take* — 158.2
  Grover, Joanna. *The Choice Point* — 158.1
  Kelly, Kevin. ★*Excellent Advice for Living* — 158.1
  O'Brady, Colin. ★*The Impossible First* — 919.8904
  Pink, Daniel H. *Drive* — 153.1
  Rodsky, Eve. *Find Your Unicorn Space* — 158.1
  Volf, Miroslav. *Life Worth Living* — 113
  Wilson, Chris. *The Master Plan* — B
GOBETTI, ADA, 1902-1968
  Moorehead, Caroline. *A House in the Mountains* — 940.53
God. Aslan, Reza — 211
God. Stavrakopoulou, Francesca — 231
GOD
  Armstrong, Karen. *The Battle for God* — 200
  Armstrong, Karen. *The Case for God* — 211
  Armstrong, Karen. *A History of God* — 202
  Aslan, Reza. *God* — 211
  Bignon, Guillaume. *Confessions of a French Atheist* — 239
  Heidegger, Martin. ★*Being and Time* — 111

AUTHOR, TITLE, SERIES AND SUBJECT INDEX

Kugel, James L. *The Great Shift*	296.3
Kushner, Harold S. *Who Needs God*	296.7
Stavrakopoulou, Francesca. *God*	231
Wiman, Christian. *Zero at the Bone*	818

GOD (CHRISTIANITY)
Armstrong, Karen. *The Case for God*	211
Armstrong, Karen. *A History of God*	202
Bolz-Weber, Nadia. *Accidental Saints*	284.1
Chittister, Joan. *Following the Path*	248.4
Guthrie, Savannah. *Mostly What God Does*	248.4
Strobel, Lee. *The Case for Grace*	234
Whittle, Lisa. *God Knows*	231
Winkler, Kyle. *Permission to Be Imperfect*	170

GOD (ISLAM)
Armstrong, Karen. *A History of God*	202
Miles, Jack. *God in the Qur'an*	297.2

GOD (JUDAISM)
Armstrong, Karen. *A History of God*	202
Feldman, Noah. ★*To Be a Jew Today*	296.3
Held, Shai. ★*Judaism Is About Love*	296.3
Kushner, Harold S. *Who Needs God*	296.7
Wiesel, Elie. ★*Night*	B

The God Equation. Kaku, Michio	523.1
God in the Qur'an. Miles, Jack	297.2
God Is in the Crowd. Keinan, Tal	305.892
God Is Not One. Prothero, Stephen R.	200
God Is Red. Liao, Yiwu	275
God Is Round. Villoro, Juan	796.334
God Knows. Whittle, Lisa	231
God Save Texas. Wright, Lawrence	917.64
God Save the Queens. Iandoli, Kathy	782.421649
God The Bestseller. Prothero, Stephen R.	070.5
The God Who Riots. Garcia, Damon	269
God's Armies. Lambert, Malcolm	956
God's Bankers. Posner, Gerald L.	364.16
God's Chinese Son. Spence, Jonathan D.	951
God's Shadow. Mikhail, Alan	B
God, Human, Animal, Machine. O'Gieblyn, Meghan	814
God, War, and Providence. Warren, James A.	974.5

Godas, Maru	
Organic Beauty	646.7

GODDESS WORSHIP
Garcia, Amanda Yates. *Initiated*	B

GODEL, KURT, 1906-1978
Budiansky, Stephen. *Journey to the Edge of Reason*	B

Godin, Seth	
The Practice	153.3
A Godless Jew. Gay, Peter	150.19
The Godmother. Nadeau, Barbie Latza	364.106

GODS AND GODDESSES
Campbell, Joseph. *The Masks of God*	201.3
Hamilton, Edith. ★*Mythology*	292.1
Homer. ★*The Iliad*	883
Hughes, Bettany. *Venus and Aphrodite*	292
Jennings, Ken. ★*100 Places to See After You Die*	202
Jordan, Michael. *Dictionary of Gods and Goddesses*	202

GODS AND GODDESSES, EGYPTIAN
Wilkinson, Richard H. ★*The Complete Gods and Goddesses of Ancient Egypt*	299

GODS AND GODDESSES, GREEK
Homer. *The Odyssey*	883
Homer. *The Odyssey*	883
Homer. *Odyssey*	883
Homer. ★*The Odyssey*	883

GODS AND GODDESSES, HINDU
Satyamurti, Carole. *Mahabharata*	821

GODS AND GODDESSES, NORSE
Larrington, Carolyne. *The Norse Myths*	293

GODS AND GODDESSES, ROMAN
Virgil. ★*The Aeneid*	873
Woolf, Greg. *Rome*	937

Gods and Kings. Thomas, Dana	920
★*Gods of the Upper Air.* King, Charles	920
Gods, Graves & Scholars. Ceram, C. W.	930.1
★*Godspeed.* Legler, Casey	B

Godwin, Gail	
Getting to Know Death	B

GODWIN, GAIL
Godwin, Gail. *Getting to Know Death*	B
Goebbels. Longerich, Peter	B

GOEBBELS, JOSEPH, 1897-1945
Longerich, Peter. *Goebbels*	B

Goertzen, Vanessa	
★*Charm School*	746.46
Goessel, Tracey	
The First King of Hollywood	B
Goethe. Safranski, Rudiger	B
Goethe's Faust. Goethe, Johann Wolfgang von	832
Goethe, Johann Wolfgang von	
Goethe's Faust	832
Selected Poetry	831

GOETHE, JOHANN WOLFGANG VON, 1749-1832
Safranski, Rudiger. *Goethe*	B

Goetsch, Diana	
This Body I Wore	B

GOETSCH, DIANA
Goetsch, Diana. *This Body I Wore*	B

Goetz, Kevin	
Audienceology	791.43

GOGH, VINCENT VAN, 1853-1890
Bell, Julian. *Van Gogh*	B
Naifeh, Steven W. *Van Gogh*	B

GOGOL, NIKOLAI VASILIEVICH, 1809-1852
Saunders, George. ★*A Swim in a Pond in the Rain*	891.7

Goh, Suzanne	
Magnificent Minds	618.92
Gohr, Siegfried	
★*Magritte*	759.9493
Going Clear. Wright, Lawrence	299
★*Going Infinite.* Lewis, Michael	305.5
Going There. Couric, Katie	B
Golay, Michael	
America 1933	B
Golbeck, Jennifer	
The Purest Bond	636.7

GOLD
Kean, Sam. *The Disappearing Spoon*	546
Ledbetter, James. *One Nation Under Gold*	332.4
Gold Dust Woman. Davis, Stephen	B

GOLD MINERS
Castner, Brian. *Stampede*	971.9

GOLD MINES AND MINING
Brands, H. W. *The Age of Gold*	979.4
Castner, Brian. *Stampede*	971.9
Crouch, Gregory. *The Bonanza King*	B
Mort, T. A. *Thieves' Road*	978.3

GOLD PROSPECTING
Mort, T. A. *Thieves' Road*	978.3

GOLD RUSH
Brands, H. W. *The Age of Gold*	979.4
Crouch, Gregory. *The Bonanza King*	B
Mort, T. A. *Thieves' Road*	978.3

GOLD STANDARD
Ahamed, Liaquat. *Lords of Finance*	920
Ledbetter, James. *One Nation Under Gold*	332.4

Gold, Jamie	
Taunton's New Bathroom Idea Book	747.7
Gold, Judy	
Yes I Can Say That	792.7
Golda. Burkett, Elinor	B
Goldacre, Ben	
Bad Science	500
Goldberg, Carrie	
Nobody's Victim	345.73

GOLDBERG, CARRIE
Goldberg, Carrie. *Nobody's Victim*	345.73

Goldberg, Emma	
Life on the Line	362.1962
Goldberg, Philip	
American Veda	294.509
Goldberg, Sana	
How to Be a Patient	610.69
Goldberg, Whoopi	
Bits and Pieces	B

PUBLIC LIBRARY CORE COLLECTION: NONFICTION
Twentieth Edition

GOLDBERG, WHOOPI, 1955-
    Goldberg, Whoopi. *Bits and Pieces* — B
Goldberger, Paul
    Ballpark — 796.357
    Building Art — B
Goldblatt, David
    ★*The Age of Football* — 796.334
    The Games — 796.4809
Goldblatt, Duchess
    Becoming Duchess Goldblatt — B
GOLDBLATT, DUCHESS
    Goldblatt, Duchess. *Becoming Duchess Goldblatt* — B
Golden. Zorn, Justin — 128
Golden Days. McCallum, Jack — 796.323
Golden Gates. Dougherty, Conor — 363.509794
A *golden* guide [Series]. Brockman, Christian Frank — 582.16
GOLDEN RULE
    Griffin, Chante. *Loving Your Black Neighbor as Yourself* — 261
The Golden Screen. Yang, Jeff — 791.43
The Golden Secrets of Lettering. Flor, Martina — 745.6
The Golden Ticket. Fortnow, Lance — 511.3
Goldfarb, Ben
    Crossings — 333.77
    Eager — 333.95
Goldfarb, Bruce
    ★*18 Tiny Deaths* — B
Goldhagen, Daniel Jonah
    Hitler's Willing Executioners — 940.53
Goldhagen, Sarah Williams
    Welcome to Your World — 720.1
Goldman, Ari L.
    Being Jewish — 296.4
Goldman, Duff
    Duff Bakes — 641.81
GOLDMAN, EMMA, 1869-1940
    Avrich, Paul. *Sasha and Emma* — 920
    Johnson, Steven. *The Infernal Machine* — 335
Goldman, Seth
    Mission in a Bottle — 741.5
Goldman, William
    Adventures in the Screen Trade — 384
GOLDMAN, WILLIAM, 1931-2018
    Goldman, William. *Adventures in the Screen Trade* — 384
Goldrick-Rab, Sara
    Paying the Price — 378.3
Goldschneider, Gary
    ★*The Secret Language of Birthdays* — 133.5
Goldsmith, Becky
    The Ultimate Thread Guide — 677
Goldsmith, Francisca
    Crash Course in Contemporary Reference — 025.5
    The Readers' Advisory Guide to Graphic Novels — 025.2
GOLDSMITH, GEORGE, 1913-2009
    Goldsmith, Martin. *The Inextinguishable Symphony* — B
Goldsmith, Marshall
    Triggers — 155.2
Goldsmith, Martin
    The Inextinguishable Symphony — B
GOLDSMITH, ROSEMARY, 1917-1984
    Goldsmith, Martin. *The Inextinguishable Symphony* — B
Goldstein, Amy
    Janesville — 330.9775
Goldstein, Dana
    The Teacher Wars — 371.1020973
Goldstein, Jacob
    Money — 332.4
Goldstein, Joyce Esersky, author
    Jam Session — 641.85
Goldstein, Meredith
    Can't Help Myself — B
GOLDSTEIN, MEREDITH
    Goldstein, Meredith. *Can't Help Myself* — B
Goldstein, Nancy
    Jackie Ormes — B
Goldstone, Lawrence
    Drive! — 338.4
    On Account of Race — 342.7308

Goldstone, Nancy Bazelon
    Daughters of the Winter Queen — 920
    In the Shadow of the Empress — 920
    The Rival Queens — 944
Goldsworthy, Adrian Keith
    Antony and Cleopatra — 937
    Augustus — B
    ★*Caesar* — B
    Pax Romana — 937
Goldsworthy, Lynne
    Quick & Easy Quilts — 746.46
GOLDWATER, BARRY M. 1909-1998
    Stevens, Stuart. *It Was All a Lie* — 324.2734
Goldwyn, Meathead
    ★*Meathead* — 641.7
Golem Girl. Lehrer, Riva — B
Goleman, Daniel
    Ecological Intelligence — 333.7
    Emotional Intelligence — 152.4
    Focus — 153.7
    Primal Leadership — 658.4
    ★*Social Intelligence* — 158.2
    Why We Meditate — 158.1
Golembesky, Michael
    Level Zero Heroes — 958.104
GOLEMBESKY, MICHAEL
    Golembesky, Michael. *Level Zero Heroes* — 958.104
GOLF
    Bamberger, Michael. *The Second Life of Tiger Woods* — B
    Callahan, Tom. *Arnie* — B
    Carter, Iain. *Golf Wars* — 796.352
    Coyne, Tom. *A Course Called Scotland* — 796.352
    Feinstein, John. *The First Major* — 796.352
    Frost, Mark. *The Match* — 796.352
    Hiaasen, Carl. *The Downhill Lie* — B
    Hogan, Ben. ★*Five Lessons* — 796.352
    Norton, Hughes. ★*Rainmaker* — 796.352
    Palmer, Arnold. *A Golfer's Life* — B
    Rotella, Robert J. *Golf Is Not a Game of Perfect* — 796.352
    Shipnuck, Alan. *Phil* — B
    Woods, Tiger. *The 1997 Masters* — B
GOLF COURSES
    Coyne, Tom. *A Course Called Scotland* — 796.352
Golf Is Not a Game of Perfect. Rotella, Robert J. — 796.352
Golf Wars. Carter, Iain — 796.352
A Golfer's Life. Palmer, Arnold — B
GOLFERS
    Bamberger, Michael. *The Second Life of Tiger Woods* — B
    Benedict, Jeff. ★*Tiger Woods* — B
    Callahan, Tom. *Arnie* — B
    Coyne, Tom. *A Course Called Scotland* — 796.352
    Frost, Mark. *The Match* — 796.352
    Harig, Bob. *Drive* — 796.352
    Hiaasen, Carl. *The Downhill Lie* — B
    Palmer, Arnold. *A Golfer's Life* — B
    Rotella, Robert J. *Golf Is Not a Game of Perfect* — 796.352
    Shipnuck, Alan. *Phil* — B
Golinkin, Lev
    A Backpack, a Bear, and Eight Crates of Vodka — B
GOLINKIN, LEV
    Golinkin, Lev. *A Backpack, a Bear, and Eight Crates of Vodka* — B
Gombrich, E. H.
    ★*The Story of Art* — 709
Gomez, Edgar
    High-Risk Homosexual — B
GOMEZ, EDGAR
    Gomez, Edgar. *High-Risk Homosexual* — B
Gomez, Laura E.
    ★*Inventing Latinos* — 305.868
Gompertz, Will
    What Are You Looking At? — 709
Gonell, Aquilino
    American Shield — B
Gonzalez, Karen
    Beyond Welcome — 261.8
GONZO JOURNALISM
    Thompson, Hunter S. *Fear and Loathing at Rolling Stone* — 070.1
    Thompson, Juan F. *Stories I Tell Myself* — B

AUTHOR, TITLE, SERIES AND SUBJECT INDEX

Gooch, Brad
  ★*Flannery* — B
  Radiant — B
Good and Beautiful and Kind. Villodas, Rich — 232.9
★*Good and Cheap.* Brown, Leanne — 641.5
GOOD AND EVIL
  Camus, Albert. *Resistance, Rebellion, and Death* — 844
  Jacobs, Alan. *Original Sin* — 233
  Keltner, Dacher. *Born to Be Good* — 155.2
  Kushner, Harold S. *How Good Do We Have to Be?* — 296.7
  Lewis, C. S. ★*The Screwtape Letters* — 248.4
  Sullivan, Randall. *The Devil's Best Trick* — 235
  Wray, T. J. *The Birth of Satan* — 235
  Zimbardo, Philip G. *The Lucifer Effect* — 155.9
Good and Mad. Traister, Rebecca — 305.420973
A Good Apology. Howes, Molly — 158.2
Good Arguments. Seo, Bo — 808.53
The Good Assassin. Talty, Stephan — 364.15
A Good Bake. Weller, Melissa — 641.86
Good Booty. Powers, Ann — 781.64
Good Boy. Boylan, Jennifer Finney — B
A Good Cry. Giovanni, Nikki — 811
★*Good for a Girl.* Fleshman, Lauren — B
Good Friday on the Rez. Bunnell, David — B
The Good Garden. McLaughlin, Chris — 635
The Good Girls. Faleiro, Sonia — 364.152
Good Girls. Freeman, Hadley — 616.85
The Good Good Pig. Montgomery, Sy — 636.4
Good Habits, Bad Habits. Wood, Wendy — 152.3
★*The Good Life.* Waldinger, Robert J. — 158.1
The Good Life Method. Sullivan, Meghan — 170
GOOD LUCK
  Lintott, Chris. *Accidental Astronomy* — 520
Good Manners for Nice People. Alkon, Amy — 395
Good Morning Blues. Basie, Count — B
Good Morning, Destroyer of Men's Souls. Aron, Nina Renata — B
Good Morning, Monster. Gildiner, Catherine — 616.89
The Good Neighbor. King, Maxwell — B
A Good Place to Hide. Grose, Peter — 940.53
Good Prose. Kidder, Tracy — 808.02
★*A Good Provider Is One Who Leaves.* DeParle, Jason — 305.899
Good Reasons for Bad Feelings. Nesse, Randolph M. — 616.89
The Good Soldiers. Finkel, David — 956.7044
The Good Son. Andersen, Christopher P. — B
Good Talk. Jacob, Mira — 741.5
A Good Time to Be Born. Klass, Perri — 362.19892
Good to Go. Aschwanden, Christie — 617.1
The Good Virus. Ireland, Tom — 579.2
The Good War. Terkel, Studs — 940.54
Good, Cassandra A.
  First Family — 920
Good, Phyllis Pellman
  Fix-It and Forget-It New Cookbook — 641.5
Goodall, Amanda
  Credible — 658.4
Goodall, Jane
  ★*Beyond Innocence* — B
  ★*The Book of Hope* — 128
  ★*In the Shadow of Man* — 599.8
  ★*The Ten Trusts* — 333.95
GOODALL, JANE, 1934-
  Goodall, Jane. ★*Beyond Innocence* — B
  Goodall, Jane. ★*The Book of Hope* — 128
Goodan, Chelsey
  Underestimated — 305.235
Goodbye Christopher Robin. Thwaite, Ann — B
Goodbye, Darkness. Manchester, William — B
★*Goodbye, Eastern Europe.* Mikanowski, Jacob — 947
Goodbye, Sweet Girl. Sundberg, Kelly — B
Goodell, Jeff
  The Heat Will Kill You First — 363.738
  The Water Will Come — 551.45
Goodheart, Adam
  1861 — 973.7
  The Last Island — 954
Goodin, Tanya
  Stop Staring at Screens — 004.67

Goodman, Elyssa
  Glitter and Concrete — 792.7
Goodman, Linda
  Linda Goodman's Star Signs — 133.5
  Linda Goodman's Sun Signs — 133.5
Goodman, Martin
  ★*A History of Judaism* — 296.09
Goodman, Matthew
  The City Game — 796.323
Goodman, Micah
  Catch-67 — 956.04
Goodman, Peter S.
  ★*How the World Ran Out of Everything* — 658.7
Goodman, Ruth
  How to Be a Tudor — 942.05
  How to Be a Victorian — 941.08
  How to Behave Badly in Elizabethan England — 942.05
Goodman, Simon
  The Orpheus Clock — 940.53
GOODMAN, SIMON
  Goodman, Simon. *The Orpheus Clock* — 940.53
Goodrich, Frances
  The Diary of Anne Frank — 812
Goodridge, Michelle
  Librarian's Guide to Games and Gamers — 025.2
GOODWIN FAMILY
  Luckerson, Victor. *Built from the Fire* — 976.6
Goodwin, Doris Kearns
  ★*The Bully Pulpit* — 973.91
  ★*Leadership in Turbulent Times* — 973.09
  No Ordinary Time — 920
  ★*Team of Rivals* — B
  ★*An Unfinished Love Story* — B
Goodyear, C. W.
  President Garfield — B
Googled. Auletta, Ken — 338.7
Goon with the Spoon. Snoop Dogg — 641.59
Gopal, Anand
  No Good Men Among the Living — 920
Gopnik, Adam
  All That Happiness Is — 158.1
  The Real Work — 153.9
GOPNIK, ADAM
  Gopnik, Adam. *All That Happiness Is* — 158.1
  Gopnik, Adam. *The Real Work* — 153.9
Gopnik, Alison
  The Gardener and the Carpenter — 155.4
Gopnik, Blake
  ★*Warhol* — B
Gorbachev. Taubman, William — B
Gorbachev, Mikhail
  On My Country and the World — 947.085
GORBACHEV, MIKHAIL, 1931-2022
  Gorbachev, Mikhail. *On My Country and the World* — 947.085
  Remnick, David. *Lenin's Tomb* — 947.085
  Taubman, William. *Gorbachev* — B
GORDIEVSKY, OLEG
  Macintyre, Ben. ★*The Spy and the Traitor* — B
Gordin, Michael D.
  Red Cloud at Dawn — 355.02
Gordis, Daniel
  Impossible Takes Longer — 956.94
  Israel — 956.9405
Gordon, Andrew
  A Modern History of Japan — 952
Gordon, Aubrey
  "You Just Need to Lose Weight" — 616.3
Gordon, Charlotte
  Romantic Outlaws — 920
Gordon, Edmund
  The Invention of Angela Carter — B
Gordon, Kim
  Girl in a Band — B
GORDON, KIM, 1953-
  Gordon, Kim. *Girl in a Band* — B
Gordon, Linda
  Dorothea Lange — B

PUBLIC LIBRARY CORE COLLECTION: NONFICTION
Twentieth Edition

Gordon, Lyndall
   ★*T.S. Eliot* — B
Gordon, Matthew
   Understanding Islam — 297
Gordon, Meryl
   Bunny Mellon — B
Gordon, Robert J.
   ★*The Rise and Fall of American Growth* — 339.4
Gordon-Reed, Annette
   Andrew Johnson — B
   ★*The Hemingses of Monticello* — 920
   ★*Most Blessed of the Patriarchs* — 973.4
GOREY, EDWARD, 1925-2000
   Dery, Mark. *Born to Be Posthumous* — B
Gorges, Eric
   A Craftsman's Legacy — 745.5
GORGES, ERIC
   Gorges, Eric. *A Craftsman's Legacy* — 745.5
GORILLAS
   Fossey, Dian. ★*Gorillas in the Mist* — 599.884
   ★*Gorillas in the Mist*. Fossey, Dian — 599.884
Gorman, Amanda
   ★*Call Us What We Carry* — 811
Gorra, Michael Edward
   The Saddest Words — 813
Gorrindo, Simone
   ★*The Wives* — B
Gortemaker, Heike B.
   Eva Braun — B
Gosden, Chris
   Magic — 133.4
GOSPEL MUSIC
   Marovich, Robert M. *A City Called Heaven* — 782.25
   Wald, Elijah. *American Epic* — 781.64
GOSPEL MUSICIANS
   Kot, Greg. *I'll Take You There* — B
The Gospel of Trees. Irving, Apricot Anderson — B
The Gospel of Wellness. Raphael, Rina — 613
GOSSIPS AND GOSSIPING
   Oyler, Lauren. *No Judgment* — 814
Gotch, Jen
   The Upside of Being Down — B
GOTCH, JEN, 1971-
   Gotch, Jen. *The Upside of Being Down* — B
GOTH, AMON, 1908-1946
   Teege, Jennifer. *My Grandfather Would Have Shot Me* — 929.2
The Gotti Wars. Gleeson, John — 364.1
GOTTI, JOHN
   Gleeson, John. *The Gotti Wars* — 364.1
Gottlieb, Anthony
   ★*The Dream of Enlightenment* — 190
   The Dream of Reason — 180
Gottlieb, Iris
   Seeing Gender — 305.3
Gottlieb, Lori
   ★*Maybe You Should Talk to Someone* — B
GOTTLIEB, LORI
   Gottlieb, Lori. ★*Maybe You Should Talk to Someone* — B
Gottlieb, Robert
   George Balanchine — B
GOTTLIEB, SIDNEY, 1918-1999
   Kinzer, Stephen. *Poisoner in Chief* — B
Gottman, Julie Schwartz
   Fight Right — 616.89
Goudeau, Jessica
   ★*After the Last Border* — 362.83
Goudsouzian, Aram
   Sidney Poitier — B
Gough, Robert E.
   The Complete Guide to Saving Seeds — 631.5
GOULD, FLORENCE, 1895-1983
   Ronald, Susan. *A Dangerous Woman* — B
GOULD, GLENN
   Hafner, Katie. *A Romance on Three Legs* — 786.2092
Gould, Stephen Jay
   The Mismeasure of Man — 153.9
   The Richness of Life — 508
   The Structure of Evolutionary Theory — 576.8

GOULD, STEPHEN JAY
   Gould, Stephen Jay. *The Richness of Life* — 508
Goulding, Matt
   Grape, Olive, Pig — 394.1
   Rice, Noodle, Fish — 394.1
GOULDING, MATT
   Goulding, Matt. *Rice, Noodle, Fish* — 394.1
Goulston, Mark
   Talking to Crazy — 158.2
Gourdet, Gregory
   Everyone's Table — 641.5
Gourevitch, Philip
   We Wish to Inform You That Tomorrow We Will Be Killed with Our Families — 364.15
GOURMET COOKING
   Buford, Bill. ★*Dirt* — B
   Rosso, Julee. *The Silver Palate Cookbook* — 641.5
   Wells, Patricia. *My Master Recipes* — 641.5
GOVERNMENT ACCOUNTABILITY
   Clark, Anna. *The Poisoned City* — 363.6
   Connelly, Matthew James. *The Declassification Engine* — 352.3
   Emanuel, Rahm. *The Nation City* — 352.23
   Fitzpatrick, Cara. *The Death of Public School* — 379.73
   Manning, Chelsea. *Readme.Txt* — B
   Vladeck, Stephen I. *The Shadow Docket* — 347.73
GOVERNMENT AND POLITICS — EUROPE — UKRAINE
   Trofimov, Yaroslav. ★*Our Enemies Will Vanish* — 947.7
GOVERNMENT AND POLITICS — SUPREME COURT AND THE JUDICIAL BRANCH — BIOGRAPHIES — UNITED STATES
   Starks, Glenn L. *Thurgood Marshall* — B
GOVERNMENT CONSPIRACIES
   Rohde, David. *In Deep* — 973.933
GOVERNMENT CONTRACTORS
   Fair, Eric. *Consequence* — B
   Tau, Byron. ★*Means of Control* — 363.25
GOVERNMENT CONTRACTS
   Lindner, Dan. ★*A Guide to Federal Contracting, 2nd Ed.* — 346.7302
GOVERNMENT COVER-UPS
   Dobbs, Michael. *King Richard* — 973.924
   Farrell, John A. ★*Richard Nixon* — B
   Graff, Garrett M. *Watergate* — 973.924
   Higginbotham, Adam. ★*Midnight in Chernobyl* — 363.17
   Morton, Andrew. *17 Carnations* — 941.084
   Randall, David K. *Black Death at the Golden Gate* — 616.9
   Vincent, Lynn. *Indianapolis* — 940.54
   Woodward, Bob. *The Final Days* — B
GOVERNMENT ECONOMISTS
   Mallaby, Sebastian. *The Man Who Knew* — B
GOVERNMENT EMPLOYEES
   Thompson, Nicholas. *The Hawk and the Dove* — 973.92
GOVERNMENT EXECUTIVES
   Gage, Beverly. *G-Man* — B
GOVERNMENT INFORMATION
   Baker, Nicholson. *Baseless* — 358
   Connelly, Matthew James. *The Declassification Engine* — 352.3
   Gellman, Barton. ★*Dark Mirror* — B
   Graff, Garrett M. *UFO* — 001.942
GOVERNMENT INVESTIGATORS
   Butcher, Barbara. *What the Dead Know* — 614
   Croke, Ken. *Riding with Evil* — 364.106
GOVERNMENT REGULATION
   Klobuchar, Amy. ★*Antitrust* — 343.73
   Perino, Michael A. *The Hellhound of Wall Street* — 330.973
   Posner, Gerald L. ★*Pharma* — 338.4
   Shlaes, Amity. *Coolidge* — B
GOVERNMENT RELATIONS WITH INDIGENOUS PEOPLES
   Calloway, Colin G. *The Indian World of George Washington* — 323.1197
   Calloway, Colin G. *One Vast Winter Count* — 978
   Cozzens, Peter. *A Brutal Reckoning* — 973.5
   Cozzens, Peter. *The Earth Is Weeping* — 978
   Cozzens, Peter. *Tecumseh and the Prophet* — 920
   Donovan, Jim. *A Terrible Glory* — 973.8
   Drury, Bob. *The Heart of Everything That Is* — B
   Hamalainen, Pekka. ★*Indigenous Continent* — 970.004
   Inskeep, Steve. *Jacksonland* — 973.56
   Long Soldier, Layli. ★*Whereas* — 811
   McLoughlin, William Gerald. *After the Trail of Tears* — 973
   Nelson, Megan Kate. *The Three-Cornered War* — 978

AUTHOR, TITLE, SERIES AND SUBJECT INDEX

Pasternak, Judy. *Yellow Dirt*	979.1004
Philbrick, Nathaniel. ★*The Last Stand*	973.8
Redniss, Lauren. ★*Oak Flat*	970.5
Sacco, Joe. ★*Paying the Land*	741.5
Saunt, Claudio. *Unworthy Republic*	323.1197
Schultz, Eric B. *King Philip's War*	973.2
Sedgwick, John. *Blood Moon*	975.004
Sharfstein, Daniel J. ★*Thunder in the Mountains*	979.5
Silverman, David J. ★*This Land Is Their Land*	974.4
Taylor, Alan. *The Divided Ground*	974.7
Warren, James A. *God, War, and Providence*	974.5
GOVERNMENT SERVICES	
Demick, Barbara. ★*Nothing to Envy*	920
GOVERNMENT SPENDING POLICY	
Phillips-Fein, Kim. *Fear City*	330.9747
Reid, T. R. *A Fine Mess*	336.200973
GOVERNMENTAL INVESTIGATIONS	
Cheney, Liz. *Oath and Honor*	328.73
Graff, Garrett M. *Watergate*	973.924
Hvistendahl, Mara. ★*The Scientist and the Spy*	364.16
Risen, James. ★*The Last Honest Man*	973.92
Stephanopoulos, George. ★*The Situation Room*	973.09
GOVERNMENTAL REFORM	
Desmond, Matthew. ★*Poverty, by America*	362.5
Remnick, David. *Lenin's Tomb*	947.085
GOVERNORS	
Bremer, Francis J. *John Winthrop*	B
Collins, Gail. *William Henry Harrison*	B
Egan, Timothy. ★*The Immortal Irishman*	B
Keneally, Thomas. *A Commonwealth of Thieves*	994
May, Gary. *John Tyler*	B
McKean, David. *Suspected of Independence*	B
Morris, Edmund. ★*The Rise of Theodore Roosevelt*	B
Pawel, Miriam. *The Browns of California*	920
Stahr, Walter. *Seward*	B
Stewart, Rory. *The Prince of the Marshes*	956.7044
Swift, Earl. *Hell Put to Shame*	364.15
White, Ronald C. *On Great Fields*	B
GOVERNORS' SPOUSES	
Greenberg, Amy S. *Lady First*	B
★*Goya*. Tomlinson, Janis A.	B
Goya. Hughes, Robert	B
GOYA, FRANCISCO, 1746-1828	
Hughes, Robert. *Goya*	B
Tomlinson, Janis A. ★*Goya*	B
Goyal, Nikhil	
★*Live to See the Day*	305.5
Grabar, Henry	
Paved Paradise	388.474
Grabbe, Lester L	
Faith and Fossils	231.7
Grace. Keenan, Cody	973.932
GRACE (CHRISTIAN THEOLOGY)	
Baraka, Sho. *He Saw That It Was Good*	261.5
Bolz-Weber, Nadia. *Accidental Saints*	284.1
Curry, Michael B. *Love Is the Way*	241
Lamott, Anne. *Small Victories*	248
Strobel, Lee. *The Case for Grace*	234
Grace Hopper and the Invention of the Information Age. Beyer, Kurt	B
Grace Will Lead Us Home. Hawes, Jennifer	364.152
Grace Without God. Ozment, Katherine	200.973
GRACE, PRINCESS OF MONACO, 1929-1982	
Spoto, Donald. *High Society*	B
Gracie, Rickson	
Breathe	B
GRACIE, RICKSON	
Gracie, Rickson. *Breathe*	B
Graeber, Charles	
The Breakthrough	616.99
Graeber, David	
The Dawn of Everything	901
GRAEBNER, CLARK, 1943-	
McPhee, John. *Levels of the Game*	796.34
Graetz, Michael J.	
The Burger Court and the Rise of the Judicial Right	347.73
Graff, Garrett M.	
★*The Only Plane in the Sky*	973.931
Raven Rock	363.350973
UFO	001.942
Watergate	973.924
★*When the Sea Came Alive*	940.54
Graff, Henry F.	
Grover Cleveland	B
GRAFFITI	
Felisbret, Eric. *Graffiti New York*	751.7
Ganz, Nicholas. ★*Graffiti World*	751.7
Graffiti New York. Felisbret, Eric	751.7
★*Graffiti World*. Ganz, Nicholas	751.7
Graham Greene. Greene, Graham	823
Graham, Ashley	
A New Model	B
GRAHAM, ASHLEY	
Graham, Ashley. *A New Model*	B
Graham, Benjamin	
The Intelligent Investor	332.67
GRAHAM, BILLY, 1918-2018	
Wacker, Grant. *America's Pastor*	B
Graham, Ian	
Fifty Ships That Changed the Course of History	387.2
Graham, Jasmin	
Sharks Don't Sink	597.3
GRAHAM, JASMIN	
Graham, Jasmin. *Sharks Don't Sink*	597.3
Graham, Jorie	
The Dream of the Unified Field	811
Fast	811
From the New World	811
Overlord	811
To 2040	811
Graham-Dixon, Andrew	
Caravaggio	B
GRAHAME, KENNETH, 1859-1932	
Dennison, Matthew. *The Man in the Willows*	B
GRAIL	
Ackroyd, Peter. *The Death of King Arthur*	823
GRAIN	
McFadden, Joshua. ★*Grains for Every Season*	641.3
The Grain Brain Cookbook. Perlmutter, David	651.56
★*Grains for Every Season*. McFadden, Joshua	641.3
Gramm, Jeff	
Dear Chairman	659.2
GRAMMAR	
Baron, Dennis E. *What's Your Pronoun?*	425.55
Brandreth, Gyles Daubeney. *Have You Eaten Grandma?*	428
Curzan, Anne. ★*Says Who?*	428
Deutscher, Guy. ★*Through the Language Glass*	410
Dreyer, Benjamin. *Dreyer's English*	808.02
Everett, Daniel Leonard. *How Language Began*	401
Garner, Bryan A. *The Chicago Guide to Grammar, Usage, and Punctuation*	428.2
Hult, Christine A. *The Handy English Grammar Answer Book*	428.2
McCrum, Robert. ★*The Story of English*	420
Norris, Mary. *Between You and Me*	428.2
Truss, Lynne. *Eats, Shoots & Leaves*	428.2
Watson, Cecelia. *Semicolon*	428.2
GRAMMAR, COMPARATIVE AND GENERAL	
Baron, Dennis E. *What's Your Pronoun?*	425.55
Hitchings, Henry. *The Language Wars*	420.9
Pinker, Steven. *Words and Rules*	415
GRAMMY AWARD WINNERS	
Streisand, Barbra. ★*My Name Is Barbra*	B
Gran Cocina Latina. Presilla, Maricel E.	641.5972
Granata, Vince	
Everything Is Fine	B
GRANATA, VINCE	
Granata, Vince. *Everything Is Fine*	B
The Grand Alliance. Churchill, Winston	940.53
GRAND CANYON	
Ross, John F. *The Promise of the Grand Canyon*	917.91
Sevigny, Melissa L. ★*Brave the Wild River*	580.9
GRAND CANYON NATIONAL PARK	
Fedarko, Kevin. *A Walk in the Park*	917.91
★*The Grand Design*. Hawking, Stephen	530.14
GRAND PRIX RACING	
Baime, A. J. ★*Go Like Hell*	796.7209
Bascomb, Neal. *Faster*	796.7209

PUBLIC LIBRARY CORE COLLECTION: NONFICTION
Twentieth Edition

GRAND UNIFIED THEORIES (NUCLEAR PHYSICS)
    Hawking, Stephen. ★*A Briefer History of Time*   523.1
Grandbaby Cakes. Adams, Jocelyn Delk   641.86
Grande, Reyna
    ★*The Distance Between Us*   973
GRANDE, REYNA
    Grande, Reyna. ★*The Distance Between Us*   973
GRANDFATHER AND GRANDDAUGHTER
    Gardner, Chris. ★*Permission to Dream*   158.1
    Jones, Faith. *Sex Cult Nun*   B
    May, Meredith. *The Honey Bus*   B
    Teege, Jennifer. *My Grandfather Would Have Shot Me*   929.2
GRANDFATHERS
    Bilger, Burkhard. *Fatherland*   B
    Rojas Contreras, Ingrid. ★*The Man Who Could Move Clouds*   B
Grandin, Greg
    The End of the Myth   973
    Kissinger's Shadow   B
Grandin, Temple
    ★*Animals in Translation*   591.5
    ★*Animals Make Us Human*   636.08
    Navigating Autism   618.92
    Temple Grandin's Guide to Working with Farm Animals   636
    ★*Visual Thinking*   152.14
Grandmaster Flash
    The Adventures of Grandmaster Flash   B
GRANDMASTER FLASH
    Grandmaster Flash. *The Adventures of Grandmaster Flash*   B
GRANDMOTHER AND GRANDCHILD
    Quindlen, Anna. ★*Nanaville*   B
    Whitney, Emerson. *Heaven*   B
GRANDMOTHER AND GRANDDAUGHTER
    Henderson, Danielle. ★*The Ugly Cry*   B
    Kalb, Bess. ★*Nobody Will Tell You This but Me*   306.874
GRANDMOTHERS
    Armas, Kat. *Abuelita Faith*   248.8
    Brown, Robert J. *You Can't Go Wrong Doing Right*   B
    Carcaterra, Lorenzo. *Three Dreamers*   B
    Foxx, Jamie. *Act Like You Got Some Sense*   B
    Kalb, Bess. ★*Nobody Will Tell You This but Me*   306.874
    Koh, EJ. *The Magical Language of Others*   813
    O'Donnell, Svenja. *Inge's War*   943.086
    Quindlen, Anna. ★*Nanaville*   B
GRANDPARENT AND CHILD
    Brown, Robert J. *You Can't Go Wrong Doing Right*   B
    Day, Marianne Waggoner. *Camp Grandma*   306.8745
    Quindlen, Anna. ★*Nanaville*   B
GRANDPARENTING
    Day, Marianne Waggoner. *Camp Grandma*   306.8745
GRANDPARENTS
    Means, Brittany. *Hell If We Don't Change Our Ways*   B
Grann, David
    ★*Killers of the Flower Moon*   976.6004
    The Lost City of Z   918.1
    ★*The Wager*   910.91
    The White Darkness   B
GRANN, DAVID
    Grann, David. *The Lost City of Z*   918.1
The Granny Square Book. Hubert, Margaret   746.43
★*Grant.* Chernow, Ron   B
Grant Wood. Evans, R. Tripp   B
Grant, Adam M.
    Give and Take   158.2
    Hidden Potential   153.8
    Originals   153.3
    ★*Think Again*   153.4
GRANT, CARY, 1904-1986
    Eyman, Scott. *Cary Grant*   B
Grant, Colin
    The Natural Mystics   B
Grant, Edward
    Science and Religion, 400 B.C. To A.D. 1550   201
Grant, Gail Milissa
    At the Elbows of My Elders   B
GRANT, GAIL MILISSA, 1949-
    Grant, Gail Milissa. *At the Elbows of My Elders*   B
Grant, James
    ★*John Adams*   B

Grant, R. G.
    World War I   940.3
Grant, Richard
    The Deepest South of All   976.2
Grant, Ulysses S.
    ★*The Annotated Memoirs of Ulysses S. Grant*   B
    Memoirs and Selected Letters   B
GRANT, ULYSSES S., 1822-1885
    Bordewich, Fergus M. *Klan War*   973.8
    Brands, H. W. ★*The Man Who Saved the Union*   B
    Bunting, Josiah. *Ulysses S. Grant*   B
    Chernow, Ron. ★*Grant*   B
    Davis, William C. *Crucible of Command*   920
    Grant, Ulysses S. ★*The Annotated Memoirs of Ulysses S. Grant*   B
    Grant, Ulysses S. *Memoirs and Selected Letters*   B
    Gwynne, S. C. *Hymns of the Republic*   973.7
    Miller, Donald L. *Vicksburg*   973.7
    Ward, Geoffrey C. *A Disposition to Be Rich*   B
    White, Ronald C. ★*American Ulysses*   B
Grant, Will
    The Last Ride of the Pony Express   917.804
GRANT, WILL, (JOURNALIST)
    Grant, Will. *The Last Ride of the Pony Express*   917.804
Grape, Olive, Pig. Goulding, Matt   394.1
GRAPHIC ARTS
    Rendgen, Sandra. *Understanding the World*   741.6
Graphic Clay. Burnett, Jason Bige   738.1
GRAPHIC DESIGN
    Porter, Carolyn. *Marcel's Letters*   940.54
GRAPHIC DESIGNERS
    Porter, Carolyn. *Marcel's Letters*   940.54
GRAPHIC METHODS
    Cairo, Alberto. *How Charts Lie*   302.2
    Rendgen, Sandra. *Understanding the World*   741.6
Graphic Novels. Pawuk, Michael   016.74
Grasp. Sarma, Sanjay E.   370.15
Grass Roots. Dufton, Emily   362.29
Grass, Gunter
    Of All That Ends   838
GRASS, GUNTER, 1927-2015
    Grass, Gunter. *Of All That Ends*   838
GRASSROOTS MOVEMENT
    Arnsdorf, Isaac. ★*Finish What We Started*   320.52
    Barkan, Ady. *Eyes to the Wind*   B
    Kimble, Megan. ★*City Limits*   388.1
    Ryan, Maureen. *Burn It Down*   791.43
Grateful. Bass, Diana Butler   241
Grateful American. Sinise, Gary   B
Grathwohl, Marya
    This Wheel of Rocks   271
GRATHWOHL, MARYA, SISTER
    Grathwohl, Marya. *This Wheel of Rocks*   271
Gratitude. Plantinga, Cornelius   179
GRATITUDE
    Bass, Diana Butler. *Grateful*   241
    Bass, Rick. *The Traveling Feast*   B
    Batterson, Mark. *Please, Sorry, Thanks*   179
    Gay, Ross. *The Book of (more) Delights*   814
    Jaku, Eddie. ★*The Happiest Man on Earth*   B
    Parker, James. ★*Get Me Through the Next Five Minutes*   158.1
    Plantinga, Cornelius. *Gratitude*   179
    Sacks, Oliver. *Gratitude*   306.9
    Sanchez, Erika L. *Crying in the Bathroom*   B
    Schulz, Kathryn. ★*Lost & Found*   B
    Stone, Sly. *Thank You (Falettinme Be Mice Elf Agin)*   B
    Visser, Margaret. *The Gift of Thanks*   394
Gratitude. Sacks, Oliver   306.9
GRAVE ROBBING
    Craughwell, Thomas J. *Stealing Lincoln's Body*   973.7092
Graver, Dennis
    Scuba Diving   797.2
The Graves Are Walking. Kelly, John   941.5081
GRAVESTONES, MAUSOLEUMS, ETC.
    Carlson, Brady. *Dead Presidents*   B
Graveyard of the Pacific. Sullivan, Randall   979.7
GRAVITATIONAL WAVES
    Levin, Janna. *Black Hole Blues*   539.7
    Panek, Richard. *The Trouble with Gravity*   531

AUTHOR, TITLE, SERIES AND SUBJECT INDEX

GRAVITY
- Boyle, Rebecca. *Our Moon* — 523.3
- Impey, Chris. *Einstein's Monsters* — 523.8
- Krauss, Lawrence Maxwell. *The Greatest Story Ever Told—So Far* — 530.01
- Panek, Richard. *The Trouble with Gravity* — 531
- Roach, Mary. *Packing for Mars* — 571.0919
- Rovelli, Carlo. *Reality Is Not What It Seems* — 530.14
- Rovelli, Carlo. ★*Seven Brief Lessons on Physics* — 530

Gray Areas. Wingfield, Adia Harvey — 331.6

GRAY WOLVES
- Berry, Erica. *Wolfish* — 152.4
- McIntyre, Rick. *The Reign of Wolf 21* — 599.773

Gray, Charlotte
- ★*Reluctant Genius* — 920

Gray, Emma
- *A Girl's Guide to Joining the Resistance* — 303.48

GRAY, FREDDIE 1989-2015
- Barron, Justine. *They Killed Freddie Gray* — 363.32
- Moore, Wes. ★*Five Days* — 363.32

Gray, Jon
- *Ghetto Gastro Black Power Kitchen* — 641.5

Gray, Michael
- *Hand Me My Travelin' Shoes* — B

Gray, Theodore W.
- ★*The Elements* — 546
- *Molecules* — 541
- *Reactions* — 530

Grayling, A. C.
- *The Age of Genius* — 940.2
- *Among the Dead Cities* — 940.54
- *The History of Philosophy* — 109

GREALY, LUCY
- Patchett, Ann. *Truth & Beauty* — B

Great Adaptations. Catania, Kenneth — 576.8
Great American Outpost. Rao, Maya — 338.2
A Great and Terrible King. Morris, Marc — B
★*The Great Arab Conquests*. Kennedy, Hugh — 297.09
Great At Work. Hansen, Morten T — 650.1
The Great Beanie Baby Bubble. Bissonnette, Zac — 338.7
The Great Big Pressure Cooker Book. Weinstein, Bruce — 641.5
The Great Book of French Impressionism. Kelder, Diane — 759.4

GREAT BRITAIN
- Abrahamian, Ervand. *The Coup* — 955.05
- Adam, David. *The Man Who Couldn't Stop* — 616.85
- Albertine, Viv. *Clothes, Clothes, Clothes. Music, Music, Music* — B
- Allport, Alan. *Britain at Bay* — 940.53
- Arnold, James R. *Jungle of Snakes* — 355.02
- Atkinson, Rick. ★*The British Are Coming* — 973.3
- Baird, Julia. ★*Victoria the Queen* — B
- Barker, Juliet R. V. *Agincourt* — 944
- Barr, James. *A Line in the Sand* — 956
- Barr, James. *Lords of the Desert* — 956
- Bate, Jonathan. *Radical Wordsworth* — B
- Bennett, Jackie. *The Writer's Garden* — 920
- Bergreen, Laurence. *In Search of a Kingdom* — B
- Blair, Tony. *A Journey* — B
- Borman, Tracy. *Crown & Sceptre* — 941
- Borman, Tracy. *Elizabeth's Women* — B
- Borman, Tracy. *Henry VIII and the Men Who Made Him* — 942.05
- Borman, Tracy. *The Private Lives of the Tudors* — 920
- Borman, Tracy. *Thomas Cromwell* — B
- Bouverie, Tim. *Appeasement* — 327.41043
- Brown, Craig. *Ninety-Nine Glimpses of Princess Margaret* — B
- Brown, Tina. *The Diana Chronicles* — B
- Brown, Tina. ★*The Palace Papers* — 920
- Byrne, Paula. *Kick* — B
- Cadbury, Deborah. *Princes at War* — 920
- Carretta, Vincent. *Equiano, the African* — B
- Carroll, Rory. *There Will Be Fire* — 363.325
- Castor, Helen. *She-Wolves* — 942
- Charter, David. *Royal Audience* — 941.085
- Coldstream, Catherine. ★*Cloistered* — B
- Connolly, Ray. *Being John Lennon* — B
- Conradi, Peter J. *Iris* — B
- Dalrymple, William. ★*The Anarchy* — 954.03
- Darlington, Miriam. *Otter Country* — 599.769
- De Courcy, Anne. *The Husband Hunters* — 920
- Dickinson, Bruce. *What Does This Button Do?* — B

Dolin, Eric Jay. *Black Flags, Blue Waters* — 973.2
Eddo-Lodge, Reni. *Why I'm No Longer Talking to White People About Race* — 305.8
Edwards, Anne. *Matriarch* — B
Elkins, Caroline. *Legacy of Violence* — 909
Ellis, Joseph J. *The Cause* — 973.3
Enninful, Edward. *A Visible Man* — B
Ferreiro, Larrie D. *Brothers at Arms* — 327.73
Foreman, Amanda. *Georgiana, Duchess of Devonshire* — B
Fowler, Corinne. ★*The Countryside* — 941
Fraser, Antonia. *Faith and Treason* — 942.06
Fraser, Antonia. *Mary, Queen of Scots* — B
Fraser, Antonia. ★*The Wives of Henry VIII* — 942.05
Garrett, Leah. *X Troop* — 940.54
Gies, Frances. *Life in a Medieval Village* — 306
Gies, Joseph. *Life in a Medieval Castle* — 940.1
Gill, Gillian. *We Two* — 941.081
Glenconner, Anne. ★*Lady in Waiting* — B
Goodman, Ruth. *How to Be a Tudor* — 942.05
Goodman, Ruth. *How to Be a Victorian* — 941.08
Goodman, Ruth. *How to Behave Badly in Elizabethan England* — 942.05
Green, Matthew. *Shadowlands* — 941.03
Gristwood, Sarah. *The Tudors in Love* — 941.05
Guesdon, Jean-Michel. *All the Songs* — 782.42166
Hamilton, Nigel. *The Mantle of Command* — 940.54
Hardman, Robert. *Queen of Our Times* — B
Hardman, Robert. *Queen of the World* — B
Hastings, Max. *Operation Pedestal* — 940.54
Hawksley, Lucinda. *Queen Victoria's Mysterious Daughter* — B
Healey, Jonathan. *The Blazing World* — 941.06
Helm, Sarah. *A Life in Secrets* — B
Hibbert, Christopher. *Edward VII* — B
Hochschild, Adam. *Bury the Chains* — 326
Hoffman, Bruce. *Anonymous Soldiers* — 956.94
Hogeland, William. *Declaration* — 973.3
Holland, James. *Brothers in Arms* — 940.54
Holmes, Elizabeth. *HRH* — 941.085
Holmes, Richard. *The Age of Wonder* — 509
Hutton, Ronald. *The Triumph of the Moon* — 133.4
Johnson, Paul. *Churchill* — B
Jones, Dan. ★*The Plantagenets* — 942.03092
Kanigel, Robert. *The Man Who Knew Infinity* — B
Kershaw, Alex. *The Few* — 940.54
Kluger, Richard. *Indelible Ink* — B
Korda, Michael. *Alone* — 940.54
Lacey, Robert. *Great Tales from English History 3* — 941
Laing, Olivia. *The Garden Against Time* — 635
Lance, Rachel. *Chamber Divers* — 940.54
Larman, Alexander. ★*Power and Glory* — 941.085
Larman, Alexander. *The Windsors at War* — 940.53
Larson, Erik. ★*The Splendid and the Vile* — 940.54
Leaming, Barbara. *Kick Kennedy* — B
Lepore, Jill. *The Name of War* — 973.2
Lovell, Mary S. *Bess of Hardwick* — B
Lovell, Mary S. *The Sisters* — 920.72
Lownie, Andrew. *Traitor King* — B
Lukacs, John. *Five Days in London, May 1940* — 940.53
MacColl, Gail. *To Marry an English Lord* — 974.7
Macintyre, Ben. ★*Operation Mincemeat* — 940.54
Macintyre, Ben. *A Spy Among Friends* — B
Magida, Arthur J. *Code Name Madeleine* — 940.54
Manchester, William. *The Last Lion, Winston Spencer Churchill.* — B
Manchester, William. *The Last Lion, Winston Spencer Churchill.* — B
Manchester, William. *The Last Lion, Winston Spencer Churchill.* — B
McCartney, Paul. ★*1964* — 782.42166
Meacham, Jon. *Franklin and Winston* — 940.53
Meyer, G. J. *The Tudors* — 920
Millard, Candice. ★*Hero of the Empire* — 968.04
Millard, Candice. ★*River of the Gods* — 916.204
Mills, Dan. *Sniper One* — 956.7044
Moore, Charles. *Margaret Thatcher* — 941.085
Morgan, Abi. *This Is Not a Pity Memoir* — B
Morris, Ian. *Geography Is Destiny* — 941
Morris, Marc. *Castles* — 728.81
Morrison, Robert. *The Regency Years* — 941.07
Morton, Andrew. *Diana* — B
Mulley, Clare. *The Spy Who Loved* — B
Murphy, Andrew R. *William Penn* — B

PUBLIC LIBRARY CORE COLLECTION: NONFICTION
Twentieth Edition

Nicolson, Adam. *Life Between the Tides*	577.69
Nicolson, Juliet. *The Great Silence*	941.083
Norman, Philip. *George Harrison*	B
Norwich, John Julius. *Shakespeare's Kings*	822.33
Nyamayaro, Elizabeth. *I Am a Girl from Africa*	B
Olson, Lynne. *Citizens of London*	940.54012
Olson, Lynne. *Last Hope Island*	940.53
Olson, Lynne. *Troublesome Young Men*	941.084
Paine, Thomas. ★*Rights of Man*	320.5
Penn, Thomas. *The Brothers York*	942.04
Pepys, Samuel. *The Diary of Samuel Pepys*	B
Philipps, Roland. *A Spy Named Orphan*	B
Phillips, Adrian. *Fighting Churchill, Appeasing Hitler*	327.41043
Pritchett, Georgia. *My Mess Is a Bit of a Life*	B
Purnell, Sonia. *Clementine*	B
Ridley, Jane. *George V*	B
Ridley, Jane. *The Heir Apparent*	B
Robb, Graham. *The Debatable Land*	941.3
Roberts, Andrew. ★*Churchill*	B
Roberts, Andrew. *The Last King of America*	B
Ronald, Susan. *The Pirate Queen*	B
Rose, Sarah. *D-Day Girls*	940.53
Russell, Gareth. *Young and Damned and Fair*	B
Sanghera, Sathnam. ★*Empireland*	941
Sanghera, Sathnam. *Empireworld*	909
Schama, Simon. *A History of Britain; 2*	941
Severin, Timothy. *In Search of Robinson Crusoe*	996.1
Shawcross, William. *The Queen Mother*	B
Smith, Sally Bedell. *Elizabeth the Queen*	B
Smith, Sally Bedell. *Prince Charles*	B
Spicer, Charles. *Coffee with Hitler*	941.084
Starkey, David. *Six Wives*	942.05
Sturgis, Matthew. *Oscar Wilde*	B
Tallis, Nicola. *Crown of Blood*	B
Tallis, Nicola. *Uncrowned Queen*	B
Talty, Stephan. *Agent Garbo*	940.5
Taylor, Stephen. *Commander*	B
Thomson, Graeme. *George Harrison*	B
Tomalin, Claire. *Samuel Pepys*	B
Vogel, Steve. *Betrayal in Berlin*	327.1273043
Walton, Calder. *Spies*	327.1247
Weintraub, Stanley. *Iron Tears*	973.3
Weir, Alison. *The Children of Henry VIII*	B
Weir, Alison. *Eleanor of Aquitaine*	B
Weir, Alison. *Henry VIII*	B
Weir, Alison. *The Life of Elizabeth I*	B
Weir, Alison. *The Six Wives of Henry VIII*	942.05
Weir, Laura. *Cosy*	646.7009
Wilson, A. N. *Victoria*	B
Winn, Raynor. ★*The Salt Path*	B
Worsley, Lucy. *Queen Victoria*	B
Wulf, Andrea. *The Brother Gardeners*	920
Great Catherine. Erickson, Carolly	B
Great Christian Thinkers. Kung, Hans	230
★*The Great* Crash, 1929. Galbraith, John Kenneth	338.5
Great Crossings. Snyder, Christina	976.9
The Great Deluge. Brinkley, Douglas	976.3
The Great Derangement. Ghosh, Amitav	809
Great discoveries [Series]. Johnson, George	522
★*The Great* Displacement. Bittle, Jake	362.87
The Great Dissent. Healy, Thomas	342.7308
The Great Dissenter. Canellos, Peter S.	B
The Great Divergence. Noah, Timothy	339.2
The Great Emergence. Tickle, Phyllis	270.8
The Great Enigma. Transtromer, Tomas	839.71
The Great Escape. Marton, Kati	920
Great Falls, MT. Watts, Reggie	B
GREAT FIRE, CHICAGO, ILL., 1871	
Berg, Scott W. *The Burning of the World*	977.311
Great Food, All Day Long. Angelou, Maya	641.5973
The Great Gamble. Feifer, Gregory	958.104
The Great Grilled Cheese Book. Greenspan, Eric	641.6
The Great Halifax Explosion. Bacon, John U.	971.6
The Great Hurricane—1938. Burns, Cherie	974.7
★*The Great* Influenza. Barry, John M.	614.5
The Great Jazz and Pop Vocal Albums. Friedwald, Will	016.78
GREAT LAKES	
Dennis, Jerry. *The Living Great Lakes*	977
Egan, Dan. ★*The Death and Life of the Great Lakes*	577.6
GREAT LAKES REGION	
Cozzens, Peter. *Tecumseh and the Prophet*	920
Dennis, Jerry. *The Living Great Lakes*	977
Egan, Dan. ★*The Death and Life of the Great Lakes*	577.6
McDonnell, Michael. *Masters of Empire*	977.4
The Great Leader and the Fighter Pilot. Harden, Blaine	B
The Great Mortality. Kelly, John	614.5
The Great Nadar. Begley, Adam	B
The Great Partnership. Sacks, Jonathan	201
The Great Peace. Suvari, Mena	B
GREAT PLAINS (UNITED STATES)	
Bunnell, David. *Good Friday on the Rez*	B
Duncan, Dayton. *Blood Memory*	599.64
Egan, Timothy. *The Worst Hard Time*	978
Gardner, Mark L. *The Earth Is All That Lasts*	978.004
GREAT POWERS	
Ansary, Mir Tamim. *Games Without Rules*	958.1
Chamberlin, Paul Thomas. *The Cold War's Killing Fields*	355.009
Dikotter, Frank. *China After Mao*	951.05
Gates, Robert Michael. ★*Exercise of Power*	973.929
McMeekin, Sean. *July 1914*	940.3
Mirski, Sean A. *We May Dominate the World*	973.91
Walton, Calder. *Spies*	327.1247
★*The Great* Pretender. Cahalan, Susannah	616.89
The Great Railway Bazaar. Theroux, Paul	915
The Great Shift. Kugel, James L.	296.3
The Great Silence. Nicolson, Juliet	941.083
★*The Great* Stain. Rae, Noel	306.3
The Great Starvation Experiment. Tucker, Todd	174.2
The Great Stewardess Rebellion. McShane Wulfhart, Nell	331.4
The Great Successor. Fifield, Anna	B
The Great Swim. Mortimer, Gavin	B
Great Tales from English History 1. Lacey, Robert	941
Great Tales from English History 2. Lacey, Robert	941
Great Tales from English History 3. Lacey, Robert	941
The Great Theft. Abou El Fadl, Khaled	297.09
★*The Great* Transformation. Armstrong, Karen	200.9
The Great Unknown. Du Sautoy, Marcus	500
The Great War for Civilisation. Fisk, Robert	956.04
★*The Great* White Bard. Karim-Cooper, Farah	822.33
Great White Fleet. Henry, John	387.243
GREAT WHITE SHARK	
Skomal, Gregory. *Chasing Shadows*	597.3
GREAT-GRANDFATHERS	
Salama, Jordan. ★*Stranger in the Desert*	982
Greater Gotham. Wallace, Mike	974.7
The Greater Journey. McCullough, David G.	920
The Greatest Benefit to Mankind. Porter, Roy	610
The Greatest Invention. Ferrara, Silvia	411
The Greatest Knight. Asbridge, Thomas S.	942.03
The Greatest Love Story Ever Told. Offerman, Nick	B
The Greatest Show on Earth. Dawkins, Richard	576.8
The Greatest Story Ever Told—So Far. Krauss, Lawrence Maxwell	530.01
The Greatest Westerns Ever Made and the People Who Made Them. Parke, Henry C.	791.43
greathouse, torrin a	
Wound from the Mouth of a Wound	811
Greayer, Rochelle	
Cultivating Garden Style	712
GREECE	
Armstrong, Karen. ★*The Great Transformation*	200.9
Karnazes, Dean. *The Legend of Marathon*	796.42
Kassabova, Kapka. *Border*	949.9
Kochilas, Diane. *The Ikaria Way*	641.5
Mazower, Mark. *The Greek Revolution*	949.5
Mazower, Mark. *Salonica, City of Ghosts*	949.5
Roberts, Jennifer Tolbert. *The Plague of War*	938
Weinberg, Steven. *To Explain the World*	509
GREED	
Beaty, Katelyn. *Celebrities for Jesus*	261
Bradley, Mark A. *Blood Runs Coal*	B
Brown, Eliot. *The Cult of We*	333.33
Etter, Lauren. ★*The Devil's Playbook*	338.7
Gaul, Gilbert M. *Billion-Dollar Ball*	796.332
Hansberry, Lorraine. ★*A Raisin in the Sun*	812
Hughes, Evan. *The Hard Sell*	338.4
Leamer, Laurence. *The Price of Justice*	346.7302

AUTHOR, TITLE, SERIES AND SUBJECT INDEX

Marshall, McMillan. *Among the Bros* — 362.29
McGraw, Seamus. *The End of Country* — 333.7909748
McGreal, Chris. *American Overdose* — 362.29
Mealer, Bryan. *The Kings of Big Spring* — B
Sancton, Thomas. *The Bettencourt Affair* — B
Sun, Carrie. *Private Equity* — B
Urwand, Ben. *The Collaboration* — 791.430973
★*Greek Art*. Boardman, John — 709

GREEK CIVILIZATION
Cahill, Thomas. *Sailing the Wine-Dark Sea* — 909
Everitt, Anthony. *The Rise of Athens* — 938
Ricks, Thomas E. ★*First Principles* — 973.09

GREEK LANGUAGE
Liddell, Henry George. *A Greek-English Lexicon* — 483
Strong, James. *The New Strong's Expanded Exhaustive Concordance of the Bible* — 220.5

The Greek Revolution. Mazower, Mark — 949.5
Greek, C. Ray
  Sacred Cows and Golden Geese — 179
A Greek-English Lexicon. Liddell, Henry George — 483
Greekish. Hayden, Georgina — 641.594

GREELY, A. W. (ADOLPHUS WASHINGTON), 1844-1935
Levy, Buddy. *Labyrinth of Ice* — 910.91

GREEN CONSUMERISM
Cline, Elizabeth L. *The Conscious Closet* — 646
MacKinnon, J. B. ★*The Day the World Stops Shopping* — 339.4
Tonti, Lucianne. *Sundressed* — 746.9

GREEN ECONOMICS
Scheyder, Ernest. *The War Below* — 333.7

GREEN PRODUCTS
Cline, Elizabeth L. *The Conscious Closet* — 646

Green, Alison
  Ask a Manager — 650.1
Green, Elon
  Last Call — 363.15
Green, Hardy
  The Company Town — 307.76
Green, Jaime
  The Possibility of Life — 576.8
Green, Janice
  ★*Divorce After 50* — 306.89
Green, Kristen
  Something Must Be Done About Prince Edward County — 379.2
GREEN, KRISTEN
  Green, Kristen. *Something Must Be Done About Prince Edward County* — 379.2
Green, Louise
  Big Fit Girl — 613.7
Green, Matthew
  Shadowlands — 941.03
Green, Robin
  The Only Girl — 070.92
GREEN, ROBIN
  Green, Robin. *The Only Girl* — 070.92
GREEN, RYAN SPEEDO
  Bergner, Daniel. ★*Sing for Your Life* — B
GREEN, SHIELDS, APPROXIMATELY 1836-1859
  Meyer, Eugene L. *Five for Freedom* — 973.7
Green, Stefanie
  This Is Assisted Dying — 616.02
GREEN, STEFANIE
  Green, Stefanie. *This Is Assisted Dying* — 616.02
Green-Hite, Vincent
  Knot Bad Amigurumi — 746.43
Greenberg, Amy S.
  Lady First — B
Greenberg, Andy
  Sandworm — 364.16
  Tracers in the Dark — 364.16
Greenberg, Paul
  American Catch — 333.95
  Four Fish — 333.95
Greenberg, Sarah Stein
  Creative Acts for Curious People — 153.3
Greenblatt, Stephen
  The Rise and Fall of Adam and Eve — 233
  ★*The Swerve* — 940.2
  ★*Will in the World* — B

Greenburg, Zack O'Malley
  3 Kings — 782.421649
Greene, Andy
  The Office — 791.45
Greene, B.
  ★*The Elegant Universe* — 539.7
  The Fabric of the Cosmos — 523.1
  ★*The Hidden Reality* — 530.12
  Until the End of Time — 523.1
Greene, Benjamin
  ★*My Child Is Trans, Now What?* — 649
Greene, David
  Midnight in Siberia — 914
GREENE, DAVID, 1976-
  Greene, David. *Midnight in Siberia* — 914
Greene, Graham
  Graham Greene — 823
GREENE, GRAHAM, 1904-1991
  Greene, Graham. *Graham Greene* — 823
Greene, Jamal
  How Rights Went Wrong — 342.7308
Greene, Jayson
  Once More We Saw Stars — 155.9
GREENE, JAYSON
  Greene, Jayson. *Once More We Saw Stars* — 155.9
Greene, Joshua
  Unstoppable — B
GREENE, NATHANAEL, 1742-1786
  Crawford, Alan Pell. *This Fierce People* — 975
Greenfield, Martin
  ★*Measure of a Man* — B
GREENFIELD, MARTIN, 1928-2024
  Greenfield, Martin. ★*Measure of a Man* — B
Greenfield, Robert
  True West — B
Greenfieldboyce, Nell
  ★*Transient and Strange* — 501
GREENFIELDBOYCE, NELL
  Greenfieldboyce, Nell. ★*Transient and Strange* — 501
GREENHOUSE EFFECT, ATMOSPHERIC
  Rich, Nathaniel. *Losing Earth* — 363.738
GREENHOUSE GAS MITIGATION
  Ewing, Jack. *Faster, Higher, Farther* — 338.7
GREENHOUSE GASES
  Hiss, Tony. ★*Rescuing the Planet* — 333.75
  Proulx, Annie. ★*Fen, Bog and Swamp* — 551.41
  Vaillant, John. ★*Fire Weather* — 363.37
Greenhouse, Linda
  Becoming Justice Blackmun — B
GREENHOW, ROSE O'NEAL, 1814-1864
  Abbott, Karen. *Liar, Temptress, Soldier, Spy* — 920
Greenidge, Kerri
  Black Radical — B
  ★*The Grimkes* — 973.5
GREENLAND
  Ehrlich, Gretel. *This Cold Heaven* — 998.2
  Ehrlich, Gretel. *Unsolaced* — B
Greenlights. McConaughey, Matthew — B
Greenman, Ben
  Dig If You Will the Picture — B
Greenspan, Alan
  Capitalism in America — 330.973
GREENSPAN, ALAN, 1926-
  Mallaby, Sebastian. *The Man Who Knew* — B
Greenspan, Dorie
  Around My French Table — 641.594
  Baking Chez Moi — 641.86
  ★*Baking with Dorie* — 641.81
  Baking with Julia — 641.8
  Baking — 641.8
  ★*Dorie's Cookies* — 641.86
  ★*Everyday Dorie* — 641.5
Greenspan, Eric
  The Great Grilled Cheese Book — 641.6
Greenspan, Stanley I.
  The First Idea — 153.7
Greenstein, Edward L.
  Job — 223

PUBLIC LIBRARY CORE COLLECTION: NONFICTION
Twentieth Edition

GREENWICH VILLAGE, NEW YORK CITY
    Carter, David. *Stonewall* — 306.76
    Milford, Nancy. *Savage Beauty* — B
    Reid, David. *The Brazen Age* — 974.7
GREENWICH, CONNECTICUT
    Tesoriero, Heather Won. *The Class* — 507.1
Greenwood biographies [Series]. Starks, Glenn L. — B
GREETING CARDS
    Watanabe, Judi. *The Complete Photo Guide to Cardmaking* — 745.594
Greger, Michael
    ★*The How Not to Diet Cookbook* — 641.5
Gregg, Linda
    All of It Singing — 811.54
Gregory, Dick
    Defining Moments in Black History — 973
    ★*The Essential Dick Gregory* — 818
Gregory, Rebekah
    Taking My Life Back — B
GREGORY, REBEKAH
    Gregory, Rebekah. *Taking My Life Back* — B
Greitens, Eric
    Resilience — 155.2
Gretzky, Wayne
    99 — B
GRETZKY, WAYNE, 1961-
    Gretzky, Wayne. *99* — B
GREY, JANE, LADY, 1537-1554
    Tallis, Nicola. *Crown of Blood* — B
    Weir, Alison. *The Children of Henry VIII* — B
Grey, Jennifer
    Out of the Corner — B
GREY, JENNIFER, 1960-
    Grey, Jennifer. *Out of the Corner* — B
Grey, Joel
    Master of Ceremonies — B
GREY, JOEL, 1932-
    Grey, Joel. *Master of Ceremonies* — B
The Grid. Bakke, Gretchen Anna — 333.793
GRIEF
    Adichie, Chimamanda Ngozi. *Notes on Grief* — 155.9
    Alexander, Kwame. *Why Fathers Cry at Night* — B
    Bailey, Jennifer. *To My Beloveds* — 261.8
    Barry, Harry. *Emotional Healing* — 158.1
    Baskette, Molly Phinney. *How to Begin When Your World Is Ending* — 248.8
    Bibbins, Mark. *13th Balloon* — 813
    Biden, Robert Hunter. *Beautiful Things* — B
    Braitman, Laurel. *What Looks Like Bravery* — B
    Cacciatore, Joanne. *Bearing the Unbearable* — 155.9
    Cacioppo, Stephanie. *Wired for Love* — 616.8
    Cain, Susan. ★*Bittersweet* — 155.2
    Caldwell, Gail. *Let's Take the Long Way Home* — B
    Campbell, Hayley. *All the Living and the Dead* — 363.7
    Cayton-Holland, Adam. *Tragedy Plus Time* — B
    Chow, Kat. *Seeing Ghosts* — B
    Chung, Nicole. ★*A Living Remedy* — B
    Clarke, Rachel. *Dear Life* — B
    Coldstream, Catherine. ★*Cloistered* — B
    Corral, Eduardo C. *Guillotine* — 811.6
    Corrigan, Kelly. *Glitter and Glue* — B
    Crosley, Sloane. *Grief Is for People* — B
    Danler, Stephanie. *Stray* — B
    Danticat, Edwidge. *The Art of Death* — 809
    Delaney, Rob. ★*A Heart That Works* — B
    Deraniyagala, Sonali. *Wave* — B
    Dial, Roman. *The Adventurer's Son* — 917.286
    Didion, Joan. ★*The Year of Magical Thinking* — B
    Edelman, Hope. *The Aftergrief* — 155.9
    Edelman, Hope. *Motherless Daughters* — 155.9
    Ephron, Delia. *Left on Tenth* — B
    Ervin, Kristine S. *Rabbit Heart* — 364.152
    Faust, Drew Gilpin. *This Republic of Suffering* — 973.7
    Frampton, Saul. *When I Am Playing with My Cat, How Do I Know She Is Not Playing with Me?* — 844
    Fuller, Alexandra. *Travel Light, Move Fast* — B
    Garcia, Rodrigo. *A Farewell to Gabo and Mercedes* — B
    Gay, Ross. *Inciting Joy* — 814
    Geller, Danielle. *Dog Flowers* — B
    Gerson, Merissa Nathan. *Forget Prayers, Bring Cake* — 155.9

    Geter, Hafizah. *Un-American* — 811
    Gilbert, Sandra M. *Death's Door* — 155.9
    Gorman, Amanda. ★*Call Us What We Carry* — 811
    Granata, Vince. *Everything Is Fine* — B
    Greene, Jayson. *Once More We Saw Stars* — 155.9
    Hawes, Jennifer. *Grace Will Lead Us Home* — 364.152
    Henderson, Artis. *Unremarried Widow* — B
    Hernandez, Daisy. *The Kissing Bug* — 616.9
    Hirsch, Edward. *Gabriel* — 811
    Holloway, Richard. *Waiting for the Last Bus* — 202
    Homer. ★*The Iliad* — 883
    Hood, Ann. *Kitchen Yarns* — 641.5
    Ignatieff, Michael. *On Consolation* — 152.4
    James, John W. ★*The Grief Recovery Handbook* — 155.9
    Jones, Saeed. *Alive at the End of the World* — 811
    Kalanithi, Paul. ★*When Breath Becomes Air* — B
    Kaur, Rupi. *The Sun and Her Flowers* — 811.6
    Kennicott, Philip. *Counterpoint* — B
    Kessler, David. *Finding Meaning* — 155.9
    Kubler-Ross, Elisabeth. ★*On Death and Dying* — 155.9
    Kugler, Rob. *A Dog Named Beautiful* — B
    Leder, Steven Z. *The Beauty of What Remains* — 306.9
    Lewis, C. S. ★*A Grief Observed* — 242
    Lieu, Susan. ★*The Manicurist's Daughter* — B
    Lin, Amy. *Here After* — B
    Lin, Jami Nakamura. *The Night Parade* — B
    Locke, Tembi. ★*From Scratch* — B
    Lyons, Anna. *We All Know How This Ends* — 362.17
    Maisel, Ivan. *I Keep Trying to Catch His Eye* — B
    Mannix, Kathryn. *With the End in Mind* — 304.6
    Mansbach, Adam. *I Had a Brother Once* — 811
    Markel, Howard. *Origin Story* — 576.8
    Masson, J. Moussaieff. *Lost Companions* — 636.088
    McColl, Sarah. *Joy Enough* — B
    McGarrahan, Ellen. *Two Truths and a Lie* — 364.152
    McInerny, Nora. *The Hot Young Widows Club* — 155.9
    Moe, John. *The Hilarious World of Depression* — 616.85
    Nunn, Emily. *The Comfort Food Diaries* — 641.5973
    O'Hara, Maryanne. *Little Matches* — B
    O'Reilly, Seamas. ★*Did Ye Hear Mammy Died?* — B
    Orenstein, Peggy. *Unraveling* — B
    Pagels, Elaine H. ★*Why Religion?* — B
    Park, J. S. ★*As Long as You Need* — 248.8
    Pfeifer, Joseph. *Ordinary Heroes* — 973.931
    Porizkova, Paulina. *No Filter* — B
    Preszler, Trent. *Little and Often* — B
    Qadiri, Humayra. *Dancing in the Mosque* — B
    Quinones, John. ★*One Year in Uvalde* — 371.7
    Rehm, Diane. *On My Own* — B
    Rekdal, Paisley. *Nightingale* — 811
    Risbridger, Ella. *The Year of Miracles* — 641.5
    Roig-Debellis, Kaitlin. *Choosing Hope* — 371.7
    Rosenblatt, Roger. *Kayak Morning* — 155.9
    Russert, Luke. *Look for Me There* — B
    Saint John, Bozoma. *The Urgent Life* — B
    Samuel, Julia. *Grief Works* — 155.9
    Sandberg, Sheryl. *Option B* — 155.9
    Savage, Jodi M. *The Death of a Jaybird* — B
    Schulz, Kathryn. ★*Lost & Found* — B
    Sentilles, Sarah. *Stranger Care* — B
    Sife, Wallace. *The Loss of a Pet* — 155.9
    Smith, Carol. *Crossing the River* — B
    Smith, Clint. ★*Above Ground* — 811
    Smith, Patricia. *Unshuttered* — 811
    Smith, Patti. ★*M Train* — B
    Smith, Tracy K. ★*Such Color* — 811
    Smyth, Katharine. *All the Lives We Ever Lived* — B
    Snyder, Rachel Louise. *Women We Buried, Women We Burned* — B
    Spiegelman, Art. *In the Shadow of No Towers* — 741.5
    Stamos, John. *If You Would Have Told Me* — B
    Standefer, Katherine E. *Lightning Flowers* — B
    Strayed, Cheryl. ★*Wild* — B
    Townsend, Alan R. ★*This Ordinary Stardust* — B
    Trethewey, Natasha D. ★*Memorial Drive* — B
    Van Ness, Jonathan. *Love That Story* — 791.4502
    Vitale, Tom. *In the Weeds* — B
    Vuong, Ocean. ★*Time Is a Mother* — 811
    White, Kate. *Your Guide to Miscarriage & Pregnancy Loss* — 618.3

AUTHOR, TITLE, SERIES AND SUBJECT INDEX

Wieseltier, Leon. *Kaddish*	296.4
Williams, Florence. *Heartbreak*	306.7
Williams, Marlena. *Night Mother*	791.43
Young, Kevin. ★*The Art of Losing*	811
Zauner, Michelle. ★*Crying in H Mart*	B
GRIEF IN CHILDREN	
Emswiler, Mary Ann. *Guiding Your Child Through Grief*	155.9
GRIEF IN FAMILIES	
Schwalbe, Will. ★*The End of Your Life Book Club*	B
GRIEF IN PARENTS	
Delaney, Rob. ★*A Heart That Works*	B
Maisel, Ivan. *I Keep Trying to Catch His Eye*	B
GRIEF IN TEENAGERS	
Emswiler, Mary Ann. *Guiding Your Child Through Grief*	155.9
Grief Is for People. Crosley, Sloane	B
★*A Grief Observed*. Lewis, C. S.	242
★*The Grief Recovery Handbook*. James, John W.	155.9
GRIEF THERAPY	
Greene, Jayson. *Once More We Saw Stars*	155.9
Leder, Steven Z. *The Beauty of What Remains*	306.9
Samuel, Julia. *Grief Works*	155.9
Grief Works. Samuel, Julia	155.9
Grieve, Paul	
A Brief Guide to Islam	297
Griffel, Lois	
Painting the Impressionist Landscape	751.45
Griffin, Brooke	
Skinny Suppers	641.5
Griffin, Chante	
Loving Your Black Neighbor as Yourself	261
Griffin, Farah Jasmine	
★*In Search of a Beautiful Freedom*	814
Read Until You Understand	810.9
GRIFFIN, FARAH JASMINE	
Griffin, Farah Jasmine. *Read Until You Understand*	810.9
Griffin, Susan	
Out of Silence, Sound. Out of Nothing, Something	808.02
GRIFFIN, SUSAN	
Griffin, Susan. *Out of Silence, Sound. Out of Nothing, Something*	808.02
GRIFFITH, D. W. (DAVID WARK), 1875-1948	
Krist, Gary. *The Mirage Factory*	920
Lehr, Dick. ★*The Birth of a Nation*	305.800973
Griffith, Elisabeth	
Formidable	305.42
Griffith, R. Marie	
Moral Combat	261.8
Grigoriadis, Vanessa	
Blurred Lines	371.7
The Grilling Book. Rapoport, Adam	641.7
Grimassi, Raven	
What We Knew in the Night	133.4
GRIMKE, ANGELINA EMILY, 1805-1879	
Greenidge, Kerri. ★*The Grimkes*	973.5
GRIMKE, SARAH MOORE, 1792-1873	
Greenidge, Kerri. ★*The Grimkes*	973.5
★*The Grimkes*. Greenidge, Kerri	973.5
The Grind. Svrluga, Barry	796.357
Grind, Kirsten	
The Lost Bank	332.3
Grinker, Roy Richard	
Nobody's Normal	616.89
GRINKER, ROY RICHARD, 1961-	
Grinker, Roy Richard. *Nobody's Normal*	616.89
Grinspan, Jon	
Wide Awake	973.7
Grisham, Candyce Copp	
Dresden Quilt Blocks Reimagined	746.46
Grist. Berens, Abra	641.6
Gristwood, Sarah	
Blood Sisters	942.04092
The Tudors in Love	941.05
Griswold, Eliza	
The Tenth Parallel	297.2
Griswold, Mac K.	
The Manor	974.7
Grit. Duckworth, Angela	158.1
GRIZZLY BEAR	
Messenger, Alex. *The Twenty-Ninth Day*	B
GROCERS	
Massih, Edy. ★*Keep It Zesty*	641.595
GROCERY INDUSTRY AND TRADE	
Lorr, Benjamin. *The Secret Life of Groceries*	381.4
GROCERY INDUSTRY AND TRADE EMPLOYEES	
Lorr, Benjamin. *The Secret Life of Groceries*	381.4
GROCERY SHOPPING	
Lorr, Benjamin. *The Secret Life of Groceries*	381.4
Grogan, John	
★*Marley & Me*	636.752
GROGAN, JOHN, 1957-	
Grogan, John. ★*Marley & Me*	636.752
Groom, Winston	
The Allies	940.5309
The Aviators	920
The Generals	920
The Patriots	920
Shiloh, 1862	973.7
Groove Interrupted. Spera, Keith	B
Grose, Jessica	
Screaming on the Inside	306.874
Grose, Peter	
A Good Place to Hide	940.53
Gross, Edward	
The Fifty Year Mission	791.45
Gross, Jan Tomasz	
Neighbors	940.53
Gross, Neil	
Walk the Walk	363.2
Gross, Rachel E.	
Vagina Obscura	618.1
Grossi, Craig	
Craig & Fred	B
GROSSI, CRAIG	
Grossi, Craig. *Craig & Fred*	B
Grossman, David	
The Yellow Wind	956.95
GROSSMAN, DAVID	
Grossman, David. *The Yellow Wind*	956.95
Grossman, Gail Boorstein	
Restorative Yoga for Life	613.7
Grossman, Pam	
Waking the Witch	133.4
GROSSMAN, PAM	
Grossman, Pam. *Waking the Witch*	133.4
GROSSMAN, VASILII SEMENOVICH	
Popoff, Alexandra. *Vasily Grossman and the Soviet Century*	B
The Ground Breaking. Ellsworth, Scott	976.6
Ground Rules. Frey, Kate	635
The Ground Truth. Farmer, John J.	973.931
★*Groundbreaking Food Gardens*. Jabbour, Niki	635
Grounded. Tester, Jon	B
★*Group*. Tate, Christie	B
Group F.64. Alinder, Mary Street	770.92
GROUP HOMES FOR TEENAGERS	
Berg, Ryan. *No House to Call My Home*	B
GROUP IDENTITY	
Alberta, Tim. *American Carnage*	324.2734
Baer, Daniel Brooks. *The Four Tests*	320.973
Benjamin, Ruha. ★*Imagination*	302
Blanco, Richard. *How to Love a Country*	811
Brookhiser, Richard. *Give Me Liberty*	320.540973
Brown, Brene. *Braving the Wilderness*	305.8
Darby, Seyward. ★*Sisters in Hate*	305.800973
Johnson, Akemi. *Night in the American Village*	305.40952
Paul, Joel R. *Indivisible*	973.5
Perry, Imani. ★*South to America*	917
Petersen, Anne Helen. *Can't Even*	305.242
Thompson, Tracy. *The New Mind of the South*	305.800975
Van Bavel, Jay J. *The Power of Us*	155.2
Young, Daniella Mestyanek. *Uncultured*	B
GROUP PSYCHOTHERAPY	
Tate, Christie. ★*Group*	B
Grove, Kirsten	
Simply Styling	747
Grover Cleveland. Graff, Henry F.	B
Grover, Joanna	
The Choice Point	158.1

PUBLIC LIBRARY CORE COLLECTION: NONFICTION
Twentieth Edition

GROVES, LESLIE R., 1896-1970
    Kunetka, James W. *The General and the Genius* — 355.8
    Norris, Robert S. *Racing for the Bomb* — B
Grow A Little Fruit Tree. Ralph, Ann — 634
Grow Now. Murphy, Emily — 635
Grow Wherever You Work. Barsh, Joanna — 658.4
Grow Your Own Herbs. Belsinger, Susan — 635
Growing Old. Thomas, Elizabeth Marshall — 305.26
Growing Under Cover. Jabbour, Niki — 635
GROWING UP
    Abdelmahmoud, Elamin. *Son of Elsewhere* — B
    Abdurraqib, Hanif. ★*There's Always This Year* — 796.323
    Ai, Weiwei. *Zodiac* — 741.5
    Al-Maria, Sophia. *The Girl Who Fell to Earth* — B
    Alderton, Dolly. *Everything I Know About Love* — B
    Alexander, Kwame. *Why Fathers Cry at Night* — B
    Alexie, Sherman. *You Don't Have to Say You Love Me* — 818
    Andrews, Julie. *Home* — B
    Angelou, Maya. *Letter to My Daughter* — 814
    Anthony, Carmelo. *Where Tomorrows Aren't Promised* — B
    Arana, Marie. *American Chica* — B
    Atleework, Kendra. *Miracle Country* — 979.4
    B., David. *Epileptic* — 741.5
    Barnes, Cinelle. *Monsoon Mansion* — B
    Bastianich, Lidia. *My American Dream* — B
    Bechdel, Alison. ★*The Secret to Superhuman Strength* — 741.5
    Belcourt, Billy-Ray. ★*A History of My Brief Body* — B
    Bell, Darrin. ★*The Talk* — 741.5
    Bella, Timothy. *Barkley* — B
    Bergner, Daniel. ★*Sing for Your Life* — B
    Bernard, Emily. *Black Is the Body* — 305.48
    Bialosky, Jill. *Poetry Will Save Your Life* — B
    Black Thought. *The Upcycled Self* — B
    Black, Dustin Lance. *Mama's Boy* — B
    Blair, Selma. *Mean Baby* — B
    Blanco, Richard. *The Prince of Los Cocuyos* — B
    Bono. ★*Surrender* — B
    Bossiere, Zoe. *Cactus Country* — 306
    Brina, Elizabeth Miki. *Speak, Okinawa* — 305.48
    Brooks, Mel. ★*All About Me!* — B
    Broome, Brian. ★*Punch Me up to the Gods* — B
    Brosh, Allie. *Hyperbole and a Half* — 741.5
    Brosh, Allie. ★*Solutions and Other Problems* — 741.5
    Brown, Claude. *Manchild in the Promised Land* — B
    Brown, Emma. *To Raise a Boy* — 649
    Bryson, Bill. *The Life and Times of the Thunderbolt Kid* — B
    Calcaterra, Regina. *Etched in Sand* — B
    Calcaterra, Regina. *Girl Unbroken* — B
    Carlile, Brandi. *Broken Horses* — B
    Carriere, Alice. *Everything/Nothing/Someone* — B
    Carter, Jimmy. *An Hour Before Daylight* — B
    Chabon, Michael. *Pops* — 306.874
    Chan, Jackie. *Never Grow Up* — B
    Chee, Alexander. ★*How to Write an Autobiographical Novel* — B
    Cheung, Karen. *The Impossible City* — 951.25
    Chin, Curtis. *Everything I Learned, I Learned in a Chinese Restaurant* — B
    Chude-Sokei, Louis Onuorah. *Floating in a Most Peculiar Way* — 979.4
    Coates, Ta-Nehisi. *The Beautiful Struggle* — B
    Coel, Michaela. ★*Misfits* — 158.2
    Conyers, Jonathan. *I Wasn't Supposed to Be Here* — B
    Crouse, Karen. *Norwich* — 796
    Crowell, Rodney. *Chinaberry Sidewalks* — B
    Davis, Viola. ★*Finding Me* — B
    Day, Daniel R. *Dapper Dan* — B
    Diamond, Cheryl. *Nowhere Girl* — B
    Dickinson, Bruce. *What Does This Button Do?* — B
    Dillard, Annie. *An American Childhood* — B
    Driver, Minnie. *Managing Expectations* — B
    Dubus, Andre. *Townie* — B
    Duckworth, Tammy. *Every Day Is a Gift* — B
    Dunne, Griffin. ★*The Friday Afternoon Club* — B
    Dutta, Sunil. *Stealing Green Mangoes* — 973
    Eire, Carlos M. N. *Learning to Die in Miami* — B
    Ellis, Helen. *Southern Lady Code* — 814
    Eruzione, Mike. *The Making of a Miracle* — B
    Etheridge, Melissa. *Talking to My Angels* — B
    Fall, Jeremy. *Falling Upwards* — 158.1
    Febos, Melissa. *Girlhood* — 818

Felton, Tom. ★*Beyond the Wand* — B
Findakly, Brigitte. *Poppies of Iraq* — 741.5
Fisher, Todd. *My Girls* — B
Fleming, Brandon P. *Miseducated* — B
Ford, Ashley C. ★*Somebody's Daughter* — B
Ford, Richard. *Between Them* — B
Ford, Tanisha C. *Dressed in Dreams* — 391
Fox, Julia. *Down the Drain* — B
Frank, Michael. ★*One Hundred Saturdays* — B
Fuller, Alexandra. *Don't Let's Go to the Dogs Tonight* — B
Garfunkel, Art. *What Is It All but Luminous* — 782.42164
Garza, Alicia. *The Purpose of Power* — 303.48
Gates, Henry Louis. *Colored People* — B
Gerald, Casey. *There Will Be No Miracles Here* — B
Goldberg, Whoopi. *Bits and Pieces* — B
Goodan, Chelsey. *Underestimated* — 305.235
Grande, Reyna. ★*The Distance Between Us* — 973
Grey, Jennifer. *Out of the Corner* — B
Gulman, Gary. *Misfit* — B
Guo, XIaolu. *Nine Continents* — B
H, Lamya. ★*Hijab Butch Blues* — B
Hager, Jenna Bush. *Sisters First* — B
Hamill, Kirkland. *Filthy Beasts* — B
Hanna, Kathleen. *Rebel Girl* — B
Harriot, Michael. ★*Black AF History* — 973
Harry. ★*Spare* — B
Henderson, Danielle. ★*The Ugly Cry* — B
Henderson, Rob Kim. *Troubled* — B
Hewitt, Sean. *All Down Darkness Wide* — B
Hill, Fiona. *There Is Nothing for You Here* — 327.2
Howard, Ron. ★*The Boys* — B
Hsu, Hua. ★*Stay True* — B
Ikpi, Bassey. *I'm Telling the Truth, but I'm Lying* — 814
Irving, Apricot Anderson. *The Gospel of Trees* — B
Iversen, Kristen. *Full Body Burden* — 363.17
Jackson family. *The Jacksons* — 782.421644
Jackson, Mitchell S. *Survival Math* — B
James, Victoria. *Wine Girl* — B
Jarrett, Valerie. *Finding My Voice* — B
Johnson, Brian. *The Lives of Brian* — B
Johnson, Katherine G. *My Remarkable Journey* — B
Jollett, Mikel. ★*Hollywood Park* — B
Jones, Faith. *Sex Cult Nun* — B
Jones, Saeed. *How We Fight for Our Lives* — B
Kemper, Ellie. *My Squirrel Days* — B
Kenan, Randall. *Black Folk Could Fly* — 813
Khar, Erin. *Strung Out* — B
Krimstein, Ken. *When I Grow Up* — 741.5
Kweli, Talib. *Vibrate Higher* — B
Lahti, Christine. *True Stories from an Unreliable Eyewitness* — B
Lake, Dianne. *Member of the Family* — 364.152
Lakshmi, Padma. *Love, Loss, and What We Ate* — 791.4502
Lawton, Georgina. *Raceless* — B
Laymon, Kiese. *How to Slowly Kill Yourself and Others in America* — 814.6
Legler, Casey. ★*Godspeed* — B
Lessing, Doris May. *Under My Skin* — 823
Li, Fei-Fei. *The Worlds I See* — B
Lockwood, Patricia. *Priestdaddy* — B
Lythcott-Haims, Julie. *Your Turn* — 305.24
Madden, T Kira. *Long Live the Tribe of Fatherless Girls* — 814
Malone, Jo. *Jo Malone* — B
Mankoff, Robert. *How About Never—Is Never Good for You?* — 741.5
Mans, Jasmine. *Black Girl, Call Home* — 811
Margulies, Julianna. *Sunshine Girl* — B
Marshall, Greg. *Leg* — B
May, Meredith. *The Honey Bus* — B
McConville, Mark. *Failure to Launch* — 155.6
McCourt, Frank. ★*Angela's Ashes* — 929
Means, Brittany. *Hell If We Don't Change Our Ways* — B
Merritt, Tyler. *I Take My Coffee Black* — 791.4302
Mills, Hayley. *Forever Young* — B
Min, Anchee. *Red Azalea* — B
Mojica Rodriguez, Prisca Dorcas. *For Brown Girls with Sharp Edges and Tender Hearts* — 305.48
Moore, Beth. *All My Knotted-Up Life* — B
Mouton, Deborah D. E. E. P. *Black Chameleon* — B
Mulgrew, Kate. *Born with Teeth* — 791.45028
Nafisi, Azar. *Things I've Been Silent About* — B

AUTHOR, TITLE, SERIES AND SUBJECT INDEX

Newman, Paul. *The Extraordinary Life of an Ordinary Man* — B
Ng, Fae Myenne. *Orphan Bachelors* — B
Noah, Trevor. *Born a Crime* — B
O'Reilly, Seamas. ★*Did Ye Hear Mammy Died?* — B
Oz, Amos. *A Tale of Love and Darkness* — B
Pardlo, Gregory. *Air Traffic* — B
Patchett, Ann. *This Is the Story of a Happy Marriage* — B
Patterson, James. *James Patterson by James Patterson* — B
Pellegrino, Danny. *How Do I Un-Remember This?* — B
Pentland, Jenny. *This Will Be Funny Later* — B
Peterson, Marlon. *Bird Uncaged* — B
Petrushevskaia, Liudmila. *The Girl from the Metropol Hotel* — B
Phelan, Tom. *We Were Rich and We Didn't Know It* — B
Pipher, Mary Bray. *A Life in Light* — B
Porter, Billy. ★*Unprotected* — B
Prince. *The Beautiful Ones* — B
Qu, Anna. *Made in China* — B
Rainbow, Randy. *Playing with Myself* — B
Retta. *So Close to Being the Sh*t, Y'all Don't Even Know* — B
Reynolds, David S. ★*Abe* — B
Rippon, Adam. *Beautiful on the Outside* — B
Rogen, Seth. ★*Yearbook* — B
Ronstadt, Linda. *Feels Like Home* — B
Rowe, Mickey. *Fearlessly Different* — B
Rowe, Peggy. *About My Mother* — B
RuPaul. ★*The House of Hidden Meanings* — B
Rush, Chris. *The Light Years* — B
Sanchez, Aaron. *Where I Come From* — 641.5092
Sanchez, Erika L. *Crying in the Bathroom* — B
Sattouf, Riad. *The Arab of the Future 2* — 741.5
Sattouf, Riad. *The Arab of the Future* — 741.5
Scheeres, Julia. *Jesus Land* — B
Schlesinger, Arthur M. *A Life in the Twentieth Century* — B
Seidelman, Susan. *Desperately Seeking Something* — B
Shafrir, Doree. *Thanks for Waiting* — B
Shankar, Shalini. *Beeline* — 155.4
Shannon, Molly. ★*Hello, Molly!* — B
Shriver, Timothy P. *Fully Alive* — 796.087
Shteyngart, Gary. ★*Little Failure* — B
Simmons, Ruth. ★*Up Home* — B
Sinclair, Safiya. ★*How to Say Babylon* — B
Sipress, David. *What's so Funny?* — B
Slate, Jenny. *Little Weirds* — B
Smith, Jada Pinkett. *Worthy* — B
Smith, Lee. *Dimestore* — 975.5
Smith, Will. ★*Will* — B
Snyder, Rachel Louise. *Women We Buried, Women We Burned* — B
Specter, Emma. *More, Please* — 616.85
Stern, Amanda. *Little Panic* — 616.8522
Stone, Lillian. ★*Everybody's Favorite* — 814.6
Talley, Andre Leon. *The Chiffon Trenches* — B
Taylor, Goldie. *The Love You Save* — B
Threadgill, Henry. *Easily Slip into Another World* — B
Tobia, Jacob. *Sissy* — 305.30973
Tometich, Annabelle. *The Mango Tree* — B
Tran, Ly. *House of Sticks* — B
Tran, Phuc. ★*Sigh, Gone* — B
Trebek, Alex. *The Answer Is ...* — 791.4502
Trice, Dawn Turner. ★*Three Girls from Bronzeville* — 977.311
Tubbs, Michael. *The Deeper the Roots* — B
Tur, Katy. *Rough Draft* — B
Wagamese, Richard. *For Joshua* — B
Walls, Jeannette. ★*The Glass Castle* — B
Wang, Qian Julie. ★*Beautiful Country* — B
Ward, Jon. *Testimony* — 277.308
Watkins, D. *Black Boy Smile* — B
Watts, Reggie. *Great Falls, MT* — B
Weigel, Alicia Roth. *Inverse Cowgirl* — B
Wetherall, Tyler. *No Way Home* — B
White, Richard Antoine. *I'm Possible* — B
Whitney, Emerson. *Heaven* — B
Wiesel, Elie. ★*Night* — B
Williams, Mary. *The Lost Daughter* — B
Williams, Patricia. *Rabbit* — B
Williams, Zach. *Rescue Story* — B
Winfrey, Oprah. *What Happened to You?* — 616.85
Winkler, Henry. ★*Being Henry* — B
Wolff, Tobias. *This Boy's Life* — B

Wu, Constance. *Making a Scene* — B
Yancey, Philip. ★*Where the Light Fell* — B
Young, Damon. ★*What Doesn't Kill You Makes You Blacker* — B
Young, Daniella Mestyanek. *Uncultured* — B
Ypi, Lea. ★*Free* — B
Zauner, Michelle. ★*Crying in H Mart* — B

GROWING UP — CHARACTER BUILDING
Parker, Kate T. *Strong Is the New Pretty* — 155.43

GROWING UP — LGBTQIA+
Bongiovanni, Archie. *A Quick & Easy Guide to They/Them Pronouns* — 741.5
Gottlieb, Iris. *Seeing Gender* — 305.3
Kobabe, Maia. *Gender Queer* — 741.5

GROWING UP — MY BODY — LET'S TALK ABOUT SEX
Smiler, Andrew P. *Dating and Sex* — 613.9071

GROWING UP — RELATIONSHIPS — DATING
Smiler, Andrew P. *Dating and Sex* — 613.9071

Growing up Biden. Biden Owens, Valerie — B
Grown Woman Talk. Malone, Sharon — 362.1
Grown-Up Anger. Wolff, Daniel J. — 920

GROWTH DISORDERS
Marcus, Amy Dockser. *We the Scientists* — 618.92

Grue, Jan
  I Live a Life Like Yours — B
GRUE, JAN, 1981-
  Grue, Jan. *I Live a Life Like Yours* — B
Gruen, Bob
  Right Place, Right Time — B
GRUEN, BOB
  Gruen, Bob. *Right Place, Right Time* — B
Grumbach, Didier
  History of International Fashion — 746.9
Grun, Bernard
  ★*The Timetables of History* — 902

GRUNGE GROUPS
Cross, Charles R. *Here We Are Now* — 782.42166
Lanegan, Mark. *Sing Backwards and Weep* — B

GRUNGE MUSIC
Cross, Charles R. *Here We Are Now* — 782.42166

★*Grunt*. Roach, Mary — 355
Grush, Loren
  ★*The Six* — 629.4
Grylls, Bear
  Never Give Up — B
GRYLLS, BEAR
  Grylls, Bear. *Never Give Up* — B
Gryta, Thomas
  Lights Out — 338.7

GUADALCANAL ISLAND
Hornfischer, James D. *Neptune's Inferno* — 940.54
Wheelan, Joseph. *Midnight in the Pacific* — 940.54

GUADALCANAL, BATTLE OF, 1942-1943
Hornfischer, James D. *Neptune's Inferno* — 940.54
Wheelan, Joseph. *Midnight in the Pacific* — 940.54

GUAM
Aguon, Julian. *No Country for Eight-Spot Butterflies* — 305.89
Immerwahr, Daniel. *How to Hide an Empire* — 973
Santos Perez, Craig. *From Unincorporated Territory [amot]* — 811

GUANTANAMO BAY NAVAL BASE, CUBA
Adayfi, Mansoor. *Don't Forget Us Here* — B
Khan, Mahvish Rukhsana. *My Guantanamo Diary* — 973.931
Slahi, Mohamedou Ould. *The Mauritanian* — 958.104

The Guarded Gate. Okrent, Daniel — 344.73
Guardians of the Trees. Webb, Kinari — B
Guardians of the Valley. King, Dean — 333.72
Guarnaschelli, Alex
  ★*Cook It Up* — 641.5
  The Home Cook — 641.5973
Guarnere, William
  Brothers in Battle, Best of Friends — B
GUARNERE, WILLIAM
  Guarnere, William. *Brothers in Battle, Best of Friends* — B

GUATEMALA
Alvarez, Noe. *Spirit Run* — 796.42
Hagerty, Alexa. ★*Still Life with Bones* — 599.9

GUATEMALAN PEOPLE IN THE UNITED STATES
Pablo Cruz, Rosayra. *The Book of Rosy* — B

GUCCI FAMILY
Gucci, Patricia. *In the Name of Gucci* — B

PUBLIC LIBRARY CORE COLLECTION: NONFICTION
Twentieth Edition

Gucci, Patricia
    In the Name of Gucci   B
GUCCI, PATRICIA
    Gucci, Patricia. *In the Name of Gucci*   B
Guelzo, Allen C.
    Gettysburg   973.7
    Lincoln and Douglas   973.6
    Robert E. Lee   B
Guendelsberger, Emily
    On the Clock   331.0973
Guerrero, Jean
    Hatemonger   B
GUERRILLA WARFARE
    Batalion, Judith. *The Light of Days*   940.53
    Boot, Max. *Invisible Armies*   355.02
    Crawford, Alan Pell. *This Fierce People*   975
    Kars, Marjoleine. *Blood on the River*   306.3
    Lovato, Roberto. *Unforgetting*   B
    Milton, Giles. *Churchill's Ministry of Ungentlemanly Warfare*   940.54
    Petraeus, David Howell. *Conflict*   355
    Stanton, Doug. *The Odyssey of Echo Company*   959.704
    Wright, Evan. *Generation Kill*   956.7044
GUERRILLAS
    Anderson, Jon Lee. *Che Guevara*   B
    Burrough, Bryan. *Days of Rage*   303.48
    Kaiser, Charles. *The Cost of Courage*   940.53
    O'Donnell, Patrick K. *The Unvanquished*   973.7
    Roy, Arundhati. *Walking with the Comrades*   954
    Stiles, T. J. *Jesse James*   B
    Strauss, Gwen. *The Nine*   940.53
Guesdon, Jean-Michel
    All the Songs   782.42166
Guests of the Ayatollah. Bowden, Mark   955.05
Guetta, Benedetta Jasmine
    Cooking Alla Giudia   641.5
Guevara, Che
    Diary of a Combatant   972.91063
GUEVARA, CHE, 1928-1967
    Anderson, Jon Lee. *Che Guevara*   B
    Guevara, Che. *Diary of a Combatant*   972.91063
GUGGENHEIM, PEGGY, 1898-1979
    Gill, Anton. *Art Lover*   B
Guha, Ramachandra
    Gandhi Before India   B
    Gandhi   B
    India After Gandhi   954.04
    Rebels Against the Raj   954.03
Guibert, Emmanuel
    Alan's War   741.5
    The Photographer   741.5
Guida-Richards, Melissa
    What White Parents Should Know About Transracial Adoption   362.734
★*A Guide to Federal Contracting, 2nd Ed*. Lindner, Dan   346.7302
The Guide to Period Styles for Interiors. Gura, Judith   747
GUIDES (PEOPLE)
    Millard, Candice. ★*River of the Gods*   916.204
GUIDETTI SERRA, BIANA
    Moorehead, Caroline. *A House in the Mountains*   940.53
Guiding Your Child Through Grief. Emswiler, Mary Ann   155.9
Guiley, Rosemary
    The Encyclopedia of Demons and Demonology   133.4
    ★*The Encyclopedia of Ghosts and Spirits*   133.1
    The Encyclopedia of Witches, Witchcraft and Wicca   133.4
Guillemin, Jeanne
    Biological Weapons   358
Guillermoprieto, Alma
    Dancing with Cuba   972.9106
GUILLERMOPRIETO, ALMA, 1949-
    Guillermoprieto, Alma. *Dancing with Cuba*   972.9106
Guillotine. Corral, Eduardo C.   811.6
GUILT
    Breggin, Peter Roger. *Guilt, Shame, and Anxiety*   152.4
    Fair, Eric. *Consequence*   B
    Greenidge, Kerri. ★*The Grimkes*   973.5
    Henderson, Artis. *Unremarried Widow*   B
    Kohli, Sahaj Kaur. ★*But What Will People Say?*   616.89
    Kouchner, Camille. *The Familia Grande*   B
    Krug, Nora. ★*Belonging*   741.5

    Kushner, Harold S. *How Good Do We Have to Be?*   296.7
    Ruttenberg, Danya. *On Repentance and Repair*   202
    Schwarz, Geraldine. *Those Who Forget*   940.53
    Warner, Judith. *Perfect Madness*   306.874
    Williams, Marlena. *Night Mother*   791.43
GUILT (LAW)
    Harman, Claire. *Murder by the Book*   364.152
GUILT IN CHILDREN
    Black Thought. *The Upcycled Self*   B
GUILT IN TEENAGERS
    Wiesel, Elie. ★*Night*   B
Guilt, Shame, and Anxiety. Breggin, Peter Roger   152.4
Guinn, Jeff
    Go Down Together   B
    ★*Manson*   B
    The Road to Jonestown   289.9
    ★*War on the Border*   972.08
GUITAR
    Chappell, Jon. ★*Guitar All-In-One for Dummies*   787.87
    Port, Ian S. *The Birth of Loud*   787.87
★*Guitar All-In-One for Dummies*. Chappell, Jon   787.87
GUITARISTS
    Clapton, Eric. *Clapton*   B
    Dregni, Michael. *Django*   B
    Gray, Michael. *Hand Me My Travelin' Shoes*   B
    Moore, Thurston. *Sonic Life*   B
    Norman, Philip. ★*Wild Thing*   B
    Patrick, James. *Robert Johnson*   B
    Perry, Joe. *Rocks*   B
    Santana, Carlos. *The Universal Tone*   B
    Thomson, Graeme. *George Harrison*   B
    Tweedy, Jeff. *Let's Go (so We Can Get Back)*   B
    Wald, Elijah. ★*Escaping the Delta*   B
    Wood, Damon. *Working for the Man, Playing in the Band*   782.42164
★*Gulag*. Applebaum, Anne   365
★*The Gulag Archipelago 1918-1956*. Solzhenitsyn, Aleksandr Isaevich   365
★*The Gulag Archipelago, 1918-1956*. Solzhenitsyn, Aleksandr Isaevich   365
Gulbrandsen, Don
    Edward Sheriff Curtis   970.004
★*The Gulf*. Davis, Jack E.   909
GULF OF MEXICO
    Davis, Jack E. ★*The Gulf*   909
    Dolin, Eric Jay. *A Furious Sky*   363.34
    Johnson, Kirk W. *The Fishermen and the Dragon*   976.4
GULLAHS
    Brown, Kardea. *The Way Home*   641.5975
Gullberg, Maria
    Tapestry Crochet and More   746.43
GULLIBILITY
    Andersen, Kurt. ★*Fantasyland*   973
Gulman, Gary
    Misfit   B
GULMAN, GARY
    Gulman, Gary. *Misfit*   B
Gulp. Roach, Mary   612.3
GUN ACCIDENTS
    Auster, Paul. *Bloodbath Nation*   363.33
    Diaz, Tom. *The Last Gun*   338.4
GUN CONTROL
    Anderson, Carol. ★*The Second*   344.7305
    Auster, Paul. *Bloodbath Nation*   363.33
    Cox, John Woodrow. *Children Under Fire*   371.7
    Coyle, Marcia. *The Roberts Court*   347.73
    Cullen, David. *Parkland*   371.7
    Diaz, Tom. *The Last Gun*   338.4
    Erdozain, Dominic. *One Nation Under Guns*   363.33
    McWhirter, Cameron. *American Gun*   683.4
    Metzl, Jonathan M. ★*What We've Become*   364.152
    Murphy, Chris. ★*The Violence Inside Us*   303.60973
    Satia, Priya. *Empire of Guns*   330.941
    Waldman, Michael. *The Supermajority*   347.73
GUN INDUSTRY AND TRADE
    Diaz, Tom. *The Last Gun*   338.4
    Haag, Pamela. ★*The Gunning of America*   338.4
    McWhirter, Cameron. *American Gun*   683.4
GUN OWNERSHIP
    Anderson, Carol. ★*The Second*   344.7305
    Auster, Paul. *Bloodbath Nation*   363.33

AUTHOR, TITLE, SERIES AND SUBJECT INDEX

Diaz, Tom. *The Last Gun* — 338.4
Dubus, Andre. *Ghost Dogs* — 814
Erdozain, Dominic. *One Nation Under Guns* — 363.33
Murphy, Chris. ★*The Violence Inside Us* — 303.60973
Satia, Priya. *Empire of Guns* — 330.941
Gunaratana, Henepola
   Start Here, Start Now — 294.3
GUNFIGHTERS
   Clavin, Thomas. *Wild Bill* — B
GUNFIGHTS
   Clavin, Thomas. *Wild Bill* — B
GUNN, PAUL IRVIN, 1899-1957
   Bruning, John R. *Indestructible* — B
Gunn, Thom
   Boss Cupid — 821
   ★*The Letters of Thom Gunn* — 821
GUNN, THOM
   Gunn, Thom. ★*The Letters of Thom Gunn* — 821
Gunnels, Claire B.
   Joint Libraries — 027.4
GUNNESS, BELLE, 1859-1908
   Schechter, Harold. *Hell's Princess* — B
★*The Gunning of America*. Haag, Pamela — 338.4
GUNPOWDER PLOT, 1605
   Fraser, Antonia. *Faith and Treason* — 942.06
   Shapiro, James. *The Year of Lear* — 822.33
GUNS
   Bradburd, Rus. *All the Dreams We've Dreamed* — 796.323
   Diaz, Tom. *The Last Gun* — 338.4
   Erdozain, Dominic. *One Nation Under Guns* — 363.33
   Haag, Pamela. ★*The Gunning of America* — 338.4
   Rasenberger, Jim. *Revolver* — B
The Guns At Last Light. Atkinson, Rick — 940.54
★*The Guns of August*. Tuchman, Barbara W. — 940.4
Guns, Germs, and Steel. Diamond, Jared M. — 303.4
GUNSHOT VICTIMS
   Auster, Paul. *Bloodbath Nation* — 363.33
   Quinones, John. ★*One Year in Uvalde* — 371.7
GUNSHOT WOUNDS
   Auster, Paul. *Bloodbath Nation* — 363.33
Gunslinger. Pearlman, Jeff — B
GUNSMITHS
   McWhirter, Cameron. *American Gun* — 683.4
   Rasenberger, Jim. *Revolver* — B
Gunst, Kathy
   Rage Baking — 641.86
Gunter, Jen
   ★*Blood* — 612.6
   The Menopause Manifesto — 618.175
   The Vagina Bible — 612.6
GUNTHER, FRANCES
   Cohen, Deborah. *Last Call at the Hotel Imperial* — 070.92
GUNTHER, JOHN, 1901-1970
   Cohen, Deborah. *Last Call at the Hotel Imperial* — 070.92
Guo, XIaolu
   Nine Continents — B
GUO, XIAOLU, 1973-
   Guo, XIaolu. *Nine Continents* — B
Gup, Ted
   A Secret Gift — 977.1
Gupta, Prachi
   ★*They Called Us Exceptional* — B
GUPTA, PRACHI (JOURNALIST)
   Gupta, Prachi. ★*They Called Us Exceptional* — B
Gupta, Sanjay
   ★*Keep Sharp* — 153.4
Gupta, Shalene
   The Cycle — 618.1
GUPTA, SHALENE
   Gupta, Shalene. *The Cycle* — 618.1
Gupta, Suneel
   Everyday Dharma — 158.1
Gura, Judith
   The Guide to Period Styles for Interiors — 747
Guralnick, Margot
   Remodelista — 747
Guralnick, Peter
   ★*Sam Phillips* — B

Gurdon, Meghan Cox
   The Enchanted Hour — 372.4
Guthrie, Julian
   How to Make a Spaceship — 629.47
Guthrie, Savannah
   Mostly What God Does — 248.4
GUTHRIE, SAVANNAH
   Guthrie, Savannah. *Mostly What God Does* — 248.4
GUTHRIE, WOODY, 1912-1967
   Wolff, Daniel J. *Grown-Up Anger* — 920
Gutierrez, Sandra A.
   Latinísimo — 641.598
Gutjahr, Paul C.
   The Book of Mormon — 289.3
Gutman, Matt
   The Boys in the Cave — 796.52
   ★*No Time to Panic* — 616.85
GUTMAN, MATT, 1977-
   Gutman, Matt. ★*No Time to Panic* — 616.85
Gutman, Robert W.
   Mozart — B
Gutowitz, Jill
   Girls Can Kiss Now — 814
GUTOWITZ, JILL
   Gutowitz, Jill. *Girls Can Kiss Now* — 814
Gutting, Gary
   What Philosophy Can Do — 100
Gutzman, Kevin R. C.
   The Jeffersonians — 973.5
Guy, Jerrelle
   Black Girl Baking — 641.59
GUY, JERRELLE, 1990-
   Guy, Jerrelle. *Black Girl Baking* — 641.59
Guy, John
   Hunting the Falcon — B
GUYANA
   Barron, James. *The One-Cent Magenta* — 769.569
   Kars, Marjoleine. *Blood on the River* — 306.3
Guyenet, Stephan J.
   The Hungry Brain — 616.85
Gwynne, S. C.
   Empire of the Summer Moon — B
   His Majesty's Airship — 363.12
   Hymns of the Republic — 973.7
   The Perfect Pass — 920
   Rebel Yell — B
Gyllenhaal, Anders
   A Wing and a Prayer — 639.97
GYNECOLOGISTS
   Abuelaish, Izzeldin. *I Shall Not Hate* — B
   Barnes, Julian. *The Man in the Red Coat* — B
   Hallman, J. C. *Say Anarcha* — 618.1
GYNECOLOGY
   Brighten, Jolene. *Is This Normal?* — 618.1
   Gunter, Jen. *The Vagina Bible* — 612.6
   Hallman, J. C. *Say Anarcha* — 618.1
   Tang, Karen. ★*It's Not Hysteria* — 618.2
GÖNNER, KARL, 1899-1979
   Bilger, Burkhard. *Fatherland* — B

H

H, Lamya
   ★*Hijab Butch Blues* — B
H, LAMYA
   H, Lamya. ★*Hijab Butch Blues* — B
The H-Spot. Filipovic, Jill — 155.3
H. D.
   Collected Poems, 1912-1944 — 811
H. M., 1926-2008
   Dittrich, Luke. ★*Patient H.M.* — 616.85
Haab, Sherri
   The Art of Metal Clay — 739.27
Haag, Michael
   The Tragedy of the Templars — 271.7913
Haag, Pamela
   ★*The Gunning of America* — 338.4

PUBLIC LIBRARY CORE COLLECTION: NONFICTION
Twentieth Edition

Haben. Girma, Haben — B
Habib, Rodney
   ★*The Forever Dog* — 636.7
HABIT
   Brown, Tabitha. *I Did a New Thing* — 158.1
   Duhigg, Charles. ★*The Power of Habit* — 158.1
   Evans, Bec. *Written* — 808
   Fogg, B. J. *Tiny Habits* — 158
   Norton, Michael. ★*The Ritual Effect* — 650.1
   Wood, Wendy. *Good Habits, Bad Habits* — 152.3
HABIT BREAKING
   Wood, Wendy. *Good Habits, Bad Habits* — 152.3
HABITABLE PLANETS
   Summers, Michael E. *Exoplanets* — 523.2
HABITAT CONSERVATION
   Anthony, Leslie. *The Aliens Among Us* — 578.6
   Gyllenhaal, Anders. *A Wing and a Prayer* — 639.97
   Struzik, Edward. *Swamplands* — 577.68
HABITATS
   Dunn, Jon L. *The Glitter in the Green* — 598.7
   Flyn, Cal. ★*Islands of Abandonment* — 333.73
   Goldfarb, Ben. *Crossings* — 333.77
   Goldfarb, Ben. *Eager* — 333.95
   Montgomery, Sy. *The Hummingbirds' Gift* — 598.7
   Roman, Joe. *Eat, Poop, Die* — 577
   Wilson, Edward O. *Tales from the Ant World* — 595.79
   Wohlleben, Peter. *The Secret Wisdom of Nature* — 508
The Habsburg Empire. Judson, Pieter M. — 943.6
HABSBURG, HOUSE OF
   Goldstone, Nancy Bazelon. *In the Shadow of the Empress* — 920
   Judson, Pieter M. *The Habsburg Empire* — 943.6
   King, Greg. *Twilight of Empire* — 943.6
   Snyder, Timothy. *The Red Prince* — B
HABSBURG-LOTHRINGEN, WILHELM, 1895-1949
   Snyder, Timothy. *The Red Prince* — B
A Hacker's Mind. Schneier, Bruce — 364.16
Hacker, Marilyn
   Selected Poems, 1965-1990 — 811
   A Stranger's Mirror — 811
HACKERS
   Greenberg, Andy. *Sandworm* — 364.16
   Mitnick, Kevin D. *Ghost in the Wires* — B
   Schneier, Bruce. *A Hacker's Mind* — 364.16
   Shapiro, Scott J. ★*Fancy Bear Goes Phishing* — 364.16
   Smith, Jeremy N. *Breaking and Entering* — B
HACKING
   Hasen, Richard L. *Election Meltdown* — 324.973
   Nance, Malcolm W. *The Plot to Betray America* — 973.933
   Schneier, Bruce. *A Hacker's Mind* — 364.16
   Shapiro, Scott J. ★*Fancy Bear Goes Phishing* — 364.16
   Smith, Jeremy N. *Breaking and Entering* — B
Hacking Planet Earth. Kostigen, Thomas — 628
Hackman, Rose
   ★*Emotional Labor* — 155.3
Had I Known. Ehrenreich, Barbara — 814
Haddish, Tiffany
   The Last Black Unicorn — B
HADDISH, TIFFANY, 1979-
   Haddish, Tiffany. *The Last Black Unicorn* — B
Hadlow, Janice
   A Royal Experiment — B
Hadrian and the Triumph of Rome. Everitt, Anthony — B
HADRIAN, EMPEROR OF ROME, 76-138
   Everitt, Anthony. *Hadrian and the Triumph of Rome* — B
Haelle, Tara
   The Informed Parent — 649
Haffner, Sebastian
   Defying Hitler — 943.085
HAFFNER, SEBASTIAN, 1907-1999
   Haffner, Sebastian. *Defying Hitler* — 943.085
Hafiz
   ★*The Gift* — 891
HAFIZ, 1320-1389
   Housden, Roger. *Saved by Beauty* — 955
Hafner, Katie
   A Romance on Three Legs — 786.2092
The Hag. Eliot, Marc — B

Hagan, Joe
   Sticky Fingers — B
Hagberg, Eva
   How to Be Loved — 616.7
HAGBERG, EVA
   Hagberg, Eva. *How to Be Loved* — 616.7
Hage, Salma
   ★*The Levantine Vegetarian* — 641.595
Hagen, Uta
   ★*Respect for Acting* — 792.02
Hager, Jenna Bush
   Sisters First — B
HAGER, JENNA BUSH, 1981-
   Hager, Jenna Bush. *Sisters First* — B
Hagerty, Alexa
   ★*Still Life with Bones* — 599.9
HAGERTY, ALEXA
   Hagerty, Alexa. ★*Still Life with Bones* — 599.9
Hagerty, Barbara Bradley
   Life Reimagined — 155.6
HAGGARD, MERLE
   Eliot, Marc. *The Hag* — B
Hagglund, Martin
   This Life — 110
HAGLER, MARVELOUS MARVIN, 1954-
   Kimball, George. *Four Kings* — B
Hagstrom, Robert G.
   The Warren Buffett Way — 332.6
Hahn, Emanuel
   Koreatown Dreaming — 979.4
HAHN, HARRY (HARRY J.), B. 1897
   Brewer, John. *The American Leonardo* — 759.5
Hahn, Steven
   A Nation Under Our Feet — 975
Haidt, Jonathan
   ★*The Anxious Generation* — 305.23
Haig, Matt
   Notes on a Nervous Planet — 616.89
The Haiku Handbook. Higginson, William J. — 808.1
HAIR
   Robinson, Phoebe. *Please Don't Sit on My Bed in Your Outside Clothes* — 818
HAIR CARE PRODUCTS
   Bundles, A'Lelia. *On Her Own Ground* — B
HAIRCUTTING
   Coombes, Joshua. *Do Something for Nothing* — 362.5
HAIRDRESSERS
   Coombes, Joshua. *Do Something for Nothing* — 362.5
HAIRSTYLES
   Dabiri, Emma. *Twisted* — 391.5
HAITI
   Albom, Mitch. *Finding Chika* — B
   Bell, Madison Smartt. *Toussaint Louverture* — B
   Danticat, Edwidge. ★*Brother, I'm Dying* — B
   Irving, Apricot Anderson. *The Gospel of Trees* — B
HAITI EARTHQUAKE, HAITI, 2010
   McClelland, Mac. *Irritable Hearts* — B
HAITIAN AMERICANS
   Beauvais, Garcelle. *Love Me as I Am* — B
   Rothenberg, Ben. *Naomi Osaka* — B
HAITIAN PEOPLE IN THE UNITED STATES
   Danticat, Edwidge. ★*Brother, I'm Dying* — B
   Raymond, Edwin. *An Inconvenient Cop* — 363.2
Haitiwaji, Gulbahar
   How I Survived a Chinese "Reeducation" Camp — 305.8
HAITIWAJI, GULBAHAR
   Haitiwaji, Gulbahar. *How I Survived a Chinese "Reeducation" Camp* — 305.8
Hajari, Nisid
   Midnight's Furies — 954.04
Hakkakiyan, Ruya
   A Beginner's Guide to America — 646.7
HAKKAKIYAN, RUYA
   Hakkakiyan, Ruya. *A Beginner's Guide to America* — 646.7
HAKUIN, 1686-1769
   Lahn, Bussho. *Singing and Dancing Are the Voice of the Law* — 294.3
HALAS, GEORGE STANLEY, 1895-1983
   Eisenberg, John. *The League* — 796.332
Halberstam, David
   The Amateurs — B

AUTHOR, TITLE, SERIES AND SUBJECT INDEX

    The Best and the Brightest   973.92
    ★The Children   323.1
    The Coldest Winter   951.904
    The Fifties   973.92
    Summer of '49   796.357
    The Teammates   B
HALDANE, J. B. S. (JOHN BURDON SANDERSON), 1892-1964
    Lance, Rachel. *Chamber Divers*   940.54
Hale, Grace Elizabeth
    In the Pines   364.13
HALE, GRACE ELIZABETH
    Hale, Grace Elizabeth. *In the Pines*   364.13
Hale, Kathleen
    ★*Slenderman*   364.152
HALE, ROBERT (ROBERT ALLEN), 1941-2008
    Kizzia, Tom. *Pilgrim's Wilderness*   B
Hale, Robert Beverly
    Anatomy Lessons from the Great Masters   743.4
Hale, Sheila
    Titian   B
Haleem, M. A. S. Abdel
    ★*The Qur'an*   297.122
Hales, Dianne R.
    Mona Lisa   B
Halevi, Yossi Klein
    ★*Letters to My Palestinian Neighbor*   956.94054
Haley, James L.
    Captive Paradise   996.9
Half American. Delmont, Matthew F.   940.54
★*Half Baked Harvest Every Day*. Gerard, Tieghan   641.5
Half Broke. Gaffney, Ginger   B
★*The Half Known Life*. Iyer, Pico   203
HALF SISTERS
    Kerrison, Catherine. *Jefferson's Daughters*   920
Half The Sky. Kristof, Nicholas D.   362.83
Half The Sugar, All the Love. Lee, Jennifer Tyler   641.5
HALF-BROTHERS
    Canellos, Peter S. *The Great Dissenter*   B
Half-Earth. Wilson, Edward O.   333.95
★*Half-Light*. Bidart, Frank   811
Halfway Home. Miller, Reuben Jonathan   364.8
HALIFAX EXPLOSION, DECEMBER 6, 1917
    Bacon, John U. *The Great Halifax Explosion*   971.6
HALIFAX, EDWARD FREDERICK LINDLEY WOOD, EARL OF, 1881-1959
    Lukacs, John. *Five Days in London, May 1940*   940.53
HALIFAX, NOVA SCOTIA
    Bacon, John U. *The Great Halifax Explosion*   971.6
Hall, Alvin D.
    Driving the Green Book   917.304
HALL, ALVIN D.
    Hall, Alvin D. *Driving the Green Book*   917.304
Hall, Andy
    Denali's Howl   796.522
Hall, Carla
    Carla Hall's Soul Food   641.5975
    Carla's Comfort Foods   641.59
Hall, Donald
    The Back Chamber   811
    The Selected Poems of Donald Hall.   811
    White Apples and the Taste of Stone   811
Hall, Jake
    The Art of Drag   792.8
Hall, James
    The Self-Portrait   704.9
Hall, Rebecca
    ★*Wake*   741.5
HALL, REBECCA, 1963-
    Hall, Rebecca. ★*Wake*   741.5
Hall, Sands
    ★*Flunk, Start*   B
HALL, SANDS
    Hall, Sands. ★*Flunk, Start*   B
HALL, VIRGINIA, 1906-1982
    Purnell, Sonia. ★*A Woman of No Importance*   B
Hallberg, David
    A Body of Work   B
HALLBERG, DAVID
    Hallberg, David. *A Body of Work*   B

Halleck, Leslie F.
    Plant Parenting   631.5
★*Hallelujah Anyway*. Lamott, Anne   241
Hallelujah Junction. Adams, John   B
Hallelujah! The Welcome Table. Angelou, Maya   641.5973
Halliday, Thomas
    ★*Otherlands*   560
Hallinan, Joseph T.
    Why We Make Mistakes   153
Hallman, J. C.
    Say Anarcha   618.1
Hallowed Ground. McPherson, James M.   973.7
HALLOWEEN
    Morton, Lisa. *Trick or Treat*   394.2646
HALLOWEEN DECORATIONS
    Cupp, Lundy. *Realistic Pumpkin Carving*   745.5941646
HALLUCINATIONS AND ILLUSIONS
    Farley, Audrey Clare. ★*Girls and Their Monsters*   306.875
HALLUCINOGENIC DRUG USE
    Lattin, Don. *The Harvard Psychedelic Club*   973.922092
HALLUCINOGENIC DRUGS
    Dakwar, Elias. *The Captive Imagination*   616.85
    Kinzer, Stephen. *Poisoner in Chief*   B
    Lattin, Don. *The Harvard Psychedelic Club*   973.922092
    Waldman, Ayelet. *A Really Good Day*   B
HALLUCINOGENIC DRUGS AND RELIGIOUS EXPERIENCE
    Castaneda, Carlos. *The Teachings of Don Juan;*   299
HALLUCINOGENIC MUSHROOMS
    Kempner, Joanna. *Psychedelic Outlaws*   615.7
HALLUCINOGENIC PLANTS
    Davis, Wade. *One River*   581.6
Halpern, Jake
    Bad Paper   332.7
Halpern, Sue
    A Dog Walks into a Nursing Home   B
HALSEY, WILLIAM FREDERICK, 1882-1959
    Borneman, Walter R. *The Admirals*   B
    Thomas, Evan. *Sea of Thunder*   940.54
Halsted, Deborah D.
    ★*Disaster Planning*   025.8
Ham, Paul
    Hiroshima Nagasaki   940.54
Hamad, Ruby
    White Tears/Brown Scars   305.8
Hamalainen, Pekka
    ★*Indigenous Continent*   970.004
HAMBLETON, GENE (ICEAL EUGENE), 1918-2004
    Talty, Stephan. *Saving Bravo*   959.704
Hamblin, James
    Clean   613
    If Our Bodies Could Talk   613
HAMBURGER
    Headley, Brooks. *Superiority Burger Cookbook*   641.5
Hamby, Chris
    Soul Full of Coal Dust   363.11
HAMER, FANNIE LOU, 1917-1977
    Blain, Keisha N. *Until I Am Free*   B
    Brooks, Maegan Parker. *Fannie Lou Hamer*   B
    Larson, Kate Clifford. *Walk with Me*   B
HAMER, FRANK, 1884-1955
    Boessenecker, John. *Texas Ranger*   B
Hamill, Kirkland
    Filthy Beasts   B
HAMILL, KIRKLAND
    Hamill, Kirkland. *Filthy Beasts*   B
Hamilton. Miranda, Lin-Manuel   782.1
HAMILTON, ALEXANDER, 1757-1804
    Brands, H. W. ★*Founding Partisans*   973.3
    Chernow, Ron. ★*Alexander Hamilton*   B
    Ellis, Joseph J. *The Quartet*   342.7302
    Groom, Winston. *The Patriots*   920
    Mazzeo, Tilar J. ★*Eliza Hamilton*   B
    McCraw, Thomas K. ★*The Founders and Finance*   330.973
    Meyerson, Michael. *Liberty's Blueprint*   342.7302
    Miranda, Lin-Manuel. *Hamilton*   782.1
    Sedgwick, John. *War of Two*   973.4
Hamilton, Denise
    ★*Indivisible*   658.3

PUBLIC LIBRARY CORE COLLECTION: NONFICTION
Twentieth Edition

Hamilton, Duncan
  For the Glory — B
Hamilton, Edith
  ★*Mythology* — 292.1
HAMILTON, ELIZABETH SCHUYLER, 1757-1854
  Mazzeo, Tilar J. ★*Eliza Hamilton* — B
Hamilton, Gabrielle
  Blood, Bones, and Butter — B
  Prune — 641.3
HAMILTON, GABRIELLE
  Hamilton, Gabrielle. *Blood, Bones, and Butter* — B
HAMILTON, JEREMIAH G., -1875
  White, Shane. *Prince of Darkness* — B
Hamilton, Lisa M.
  Deeply Rooted — 338.10973
  The Hungry Season — B
Hamilton, Nigel
  The Mantle of Command — 940.54
Hamilton, Tyler
  The Secret Race — 796.62
HAMILTON, TYLER, 1971-
  Hamilton, Tyler. *The Secret Race* — 796.62
Hamilton-Paterson, James
  ★*Beethoven's Eroica* — 784.18
  Marked for Death — 358.400941
HAMLET (LEGENDARY CHARACTER)
  Stoppard, Tom. ★*Rosencrantz & Guildenstern Are Dead* — 822
***Hamlet** Globe to Globe*. Dromgoole, Dominic — 792.9
Hamlin, Kimberly A
  Free Thinker — B
Hamm, Thomas D.
  ★*The Quakers in America* — 289.6
Hammack, William Scott
  ★*Things We Make* — 620
*The **Hammer***. Nolan, Hamilton — 331.8
Hammer, Joshua
  The Bad-Ass Librarians of Timbuktu — 025.8
  The Falcon Thief — 364.16
Hammer, Langdon
  James Merrill — B
HAMMERSTEIN, OSCAR, II, 1895-1960
  Purdum, Todd S. *Something Wonderful* — B
HAMMOND FAMILY
  Genoways, Ted. *This Blessed Earth* — 630.9
Hammond, Claudia
  Mind Over Money — 332.401
HAMMURABI, KING OF BABYLONIA
  Kriwaczek, Paul. *Babylon* — 935
Hample, Zack
  The Baseball — 796.357
Hampton, Dan
  Chasing the Demon — 629.132
  Operation Vengeance — 940.54
HAMPTON, HENRY, 1940-1998
  Else, Jon. *True South* — 305.800973
Hamshaw, Gena
  Food 52 Vegan — 641.5
Han, Chenxing
  Be the Refuge — 294.3
HAN, CHENXING, 1986-
  Han, Chenxing. *Be the Refuge* — 294.3
HANCOCK FAMILY
  Sankovitch, Nina. *American Rebels* — 920
HANCOCK, DOROTHY QUINCY, 1747-1830
  Sankovitch, Nina. *American Rebels* — 920
HANCOCK, JOHN, 1737-1793
  Sankovitch, Nina. *American Rebels* — 920
***Hand** Dyed*. Joyce, Anna — 746.6
***Hand** Dyeing Yarn and Fleece*. Callahan, Gail — 746.6
***Hand** Lettering Step by Step*. Glynn, Kathy — 745.6
***Hand** Me My Travelin' Shoes*. Gray, Michael — B
HAND WEAVING
  Bassetti, Amanda. *Arm Knitting* — 746.43
  Dixon, Anne. *The Handweaver's Pattern Directory* — 746.1
  Jarchow, Deborah. *The Weaving Explorer* — 746.1
  Mezoff, Rebecca. ★*The Art of Tapestry Weaving* — 746.7
  Mitchell, Syne. *Inventive Weaving on a Little Loom* — 746.1
  Murphy, Marilyn. *Woven to Wear* — 746.1

  Patrick, Jane. *The Weaver's Idea Book* — 746.1
Hand, Diana
  Draw Horses in 15 Minutes — 743.6
HAND-TO-HAND FIGHTING
  Freeman, Joanne B. *The Field of Blood* — 973.7
HANDBAGS
  Alicia, Anna. *Bags* — 646.4
★***Handbook** of Chinese Mythology*. Yang, Lihui — 299.5
★***Handbook** of Denominations in the United States*. Olson, Roger E. — 200.973
HANDEL, GEORG FRIEDRICH, 1685-1759
  Harris, Ellen T. *George Frideric Handel* — B
HANDICRAFT
  Adarme, Adrianna. *The Year of Cozy* — 641.3
  Akiyama, Lance. *Rubber Band Engineer* — 745.57
  Bried, Erin. *How to Sew a Button* — 640
  Brown, Stephen. *Glitterville's Handmade Christmas* — 745.5
  Chapin, Kari. ★*The Handmade Marketplace* — 745.5
  Corwin, Lena. *Lena Corwin's Made by Hand* — 746.6
  Corwin, Lena. *Printing by Hand* — 745.5
  Cox, Marge. *Kids' Books and Maker Activities* — 372.41
  Crawford, Matthew B. *The World Beyond Your Head* — 155.2
  Falick, Melanie. *Making a Life* — 745.5
  Foster, Sutton. *Hooked* — B
  Gethin, Rosanna Clare. *Sew Luxe Leather* — 745.53
  Glynn, Kathy. *Hand Lettering Step by Step* — 745.6
  Gorges, Eric. *A Craftsman's Legacy* — 745.5
  Horwood, Roger. *Woodworker's Handbook* — 684
  Joyce, Anna. *Stamp Stencil Paint* — 745.7
  Katz, Emily. *Modern Macrame* — 746.42
  Langlands, Alex. *Cræft* — 306.4
  Larson, Elsie. *A Beautiful Mess Happy Handmade Home* — 745
  Minter, Laura. *Mini Makers* — 745.5
  Nicholas, Kristin. *Crafting a Patterned Home* — 745.5
  Orenstein, Peggy. *Unraveling* — B
  Pester, Sophie. *Homemade Holiday* — 745.594
  Pester, Sophie. *Supercraft* — 745.5
  Ploszajski, Anna. *Handmade* — 620.1
  Rodabaugh, Katrina. *The Paper Playhouse* — 745.5
  Susa, Sachiko. *Sweet & Simple Needle Felted Animals* — 746
  Van't Hul, Jean. *The Artful Year* — 745.594
  Yamazaki, Hiromi. *Japanese Paper Flowers* — 745.594
  Zedenius, Fanny. *Macrame* — 746.42
HANDICRAFT FOR CHILDREN
  Cox, Marge. *Kids' Books and Maker Activities* — 372.41
  Minter, Laura. *Mini Makers* — 745.5
  Neuburger, Emily K. *Show Me a Story* — 745.5083
  Van't Hul, Jean. *The Artful Parent* — 745.5083
Handler, Daniel
  ★*And Then? and Then? What Else?* — 813
HANDLER, DANIEL
  Handler, Daniel. ★*And Then? and Then? What Else?* — 813
HANDLER, RUTH
  Gerber, Robin. *Barbie and Ruth* — B
Handmade. Ploszajski, Anna — 620.1
★*The **Handmade** Marketplace*. Chapin, Kari — 745.5
*The **Handweaver's** Pattern Directory*. Dixon, Anne — 746.1
HANDWRITING
  Porter, Carolyn. *Marcel's Letters* — 940.54
*The **Handy** English Grammar Answer Book*. Hult, Christine A — 428.2
*The **Handy** Islam Answer Book*. Renard, John — 297
Hanes, Stephanie
  White Man's Game — 333.95
***Hang** Time*. Baylor, Elgin — B
*The **Hanging** of Thomas Jeremiah*. Harris, J. William — B
***Hank** and Jim*. Eyman, Scott — 920
Hankir, Zahra
  Eyeliner — 391.6
Hanna, Kathleen
  Rebel Girl — B
HANNA, KATHLEEN, 1968-
  Hanna, Kathleen. *Rebel Girl* — B
Hanna-Attisha, Mona
  What the Eyes Don't See — 615.9
HANNA-ATTISHA, MONA
  Hanna-Attisha, Mona. *What the Eyes Don't See* — 615.9
Hannibal. Hunt, Patrick — B
HANNIBAL, 247-182 B.C.E
  Hunt, Patrick. *Hannibal* — B

AUTHOR, TITLE, SERIES AND SUBJECT INDEX

O'Connell, Robert L. *The Ghosts of Cannae*	937
Hannig, Anita	
The Day I Die	364.152
HANNITY, SEAN, 1961-	
Stelter, Brian. *Hoax*	070.4
HANOI, VIETNAM	
Lee, Heath Hardage. ★*The League of Wives*	959.704
HANOVER, HOUSE OF	
Ackroyd, Peter. *Revolution*	941.07
Hansberry, Lorraine	
★*A Raisin in the Sun*	812
HANSBERRY, LORRAINE, 1930-1965	
Nemiroff, Robert. *To Be Young, Gifted, and Black*	B
Perry, Imani. *Looking for Lorraine*	B
Shields, Charles J. *Lorraine Hansberry*	B
Hansen, Kim-Julie	
Best of Vegan	641.5
Hansen, Morten T	
Great at Work	650.1
Hansen, Valerie	
The Year 1000	909
Hanson, Thor	
Feathers	598.147
Hurricane Lizards and Plastic Squid	577.2
HANSON, THOR	
Hanson, Thor. *Hurricane Lizards and Plastic Squid*	577.2
Hanson, Victor Davis	
The Father of Us All	355.0209
The Second World Wars	940.54
The Soul of Battle	355
HANSSEN, ROBERT	
Wiehl, Lis W. *A Spy in Plain Sight*	327.1247
HANUKKAH	
Ashton, Dianne. *Hanukkah in America*	296.4
Hanukkah in America. Ashton, Dianne	296.4
HANUMAN (HINDU DEITY)	
Rao, Cheeni. *In Hanuman's Hands*	B
Happier Hour. Holmes, Cassie	158.1
★*The Happiest Man on Earth.* Jaku, Eddie	B
Happiness. Harpham, Heather Elise	B
HAPPINESS	
Asprey, Dave. *Game Changers*	158.1
Beck, Martha Nibley. *The Way of Integrity*	158.1
Bernstein, Gabrielle. *Judgment Detox*	158
Bragg, Sarah. *Is Everyone Happier Than Me?*	248.4
Brooks, Arthur C. *Build the Life You Want*	158.1
Brooks, David. ★*The Second Mountain*	302
Chittister, Joan. *Following the Path*	248.4
Cohen, Rhaina. ★*The Other Significant Others*	177
Dalai Lama. *The Book of Joy*	294.3
Dalai Lama. *How to Be Compassionate*	294.3
De Graaf, John. *What's the Economy For, Anyway?*	330.973
Ehrenreich, Barbara. *Bright-Sided*	155.2
Emet, Joseph. *Finding the Blue Sky*	294.3
Filipovic, Jill. *The H-Spot*	155.3
Francis. *Happiness in This Life*	248.4
Fusco, Daniel. *Crazy Happy*	248.4
Ghodsee, Kristen Rogheh. *Everyday Utopia*	335
Gilbert, Daniel Todd. ★*Stumbling on Happiness*	158
Gilbert, Elizabeth. *Eat, Pray, Love*	B
Golbeck, Jennifer. *The Purest Bond*	636.7
Gopnik, Adam. *All That Happiness Is*	158.1
Gorges, Eric. *A Craftsman's Legacy*	745.5
Halpern, Sue. *A Dog Walks into a Nursing Home*	B
Harris, Dan. *Meditation for Fidgety Skeptics*	158.1
Hatmaker, Jen. *Of Mess and Moxie*	248.4
Havrilesky, Heather. *What If This Were Enough?*	152.4
Heller, Rick. *Secular Meditation*	158.1
Jamie, Poppy. *Happy Not Perfect*	158.1
Johansen, Signe. ★*How to Hygge*	646.7
Keyes, Corey L. M. ★*Languishing*	152.1
King, Vanessa. *10 Keys to Happier Living*	158
Kois, Dan. *How to Be a Family*	910.4
Kondo, Marie. ★*Marie Kondo's Kurashi at Home*	648
Lamott, Anne. *Small Victories*	248
Lancaster, Jen. *Welcome to the United States of Anxiety*	155.4
Langshur, Eric. *Start Here*	158
Lyubomirsky, Sonja. *The How of Happiness*	158
May, Katherine. *Enchantment*	158.1
Miller, Caroline Adams. *Creating Your Best Life*	158.1
Nhat Hanh. *The Art of Living*	294.3
Popova, Maria. *Figuring*	920
Quindlen, Anna. ★*Nanaville*	B
Rauch, Jonathan. *The Happiness Curve*	155.6
Rinaldi, Karen. *It's Great to Suck at Something*	158.1
Rubin, Gretchen. *Outer Order, Inner Calm*	158
Rubin, Gretchen Craft. ★*Life in Five Senses*	152.1
Smith, Patricia. *Unshuttered*	811
Stanley, Paul. *Backstage Pass*	B
Streets, Annabel. *52 Ways to Walk*	796.51
Stutz, Phil. *Lessons for Living*	158.1
Tatum, Scott. *Friendly Reminders*	158.1
Tuama, Padraig O. ★*Poetry Unbound*	808.1
Van Buren, Mark. *A Fool's Guide to Actual Happiness*	294.3
Waldinger, Robert J. ★*The Good Life*	158.1
Walker, Alice. *We Are the Ones We Have Been Waiting For*	811
Wiking, Meik. *The Art of Making Memories*	153.1
Wiking, Meik. *The Little Book of Hygge*	158.1
Wiking, Meik. *The Little Book of Lykke*	646.7
Winkler, Kyle. *Permission to Be Imperfect*	170
Wu, Simon. *Dancing on My Own*	700.1
Zambreno, Kate. *The Light Room*	B
★*Happiness Becomes You.* Turner, Tina	158.1
The Happiness Curve. Rauch, Jonathan	155.6
Happiness in This Life. Francis	248.4
★*Happiness Is Baking.* Heatter, Maida	641.86
The Happy Cook. Oz, Daphne	641.5
Happy Cooking. De Laurentiis, Giada	641.5
Happy Not Perfect. Jamie, Poppy	158.1
★*Happy-Go-Lucky.* Sedaris, David	814
Harampolis, Alethea	
The Flower Recipe Book	745.92
Harari, Yuval N.	
★*21 Lessons for the 21st Century*	909.82
Homo Deus	909.83
★*Sapiens*	909
HARASSMENT	
Copaken, Deborah. *Ladyparts*	B
Farrow, Ronan. ★*Catch and Kill*	331.4
Hill, Katie. *She Will Rise*	305.42
Quinn, Zoe. *Crash Override*	794.8
Ryan, Maureen. *Burn It Down*	791.43
HARBORS	
Sciolino, Elaine. *The Seine*	944
Hard Labor. Smith, Sam	796.323
The Hard Parts. Masters, Oksana	B
The Hard Sell. Hughes, Evan	338.4
★*Hard Times.* Terkel, Studs	973.91
Hard Times Require Furious Dancing. Walker, Alice	811
Hardacre, Helen	
Shinto	299.5
Harden, Blaine	
The Great Leader and the Fighter Pilot	B
Harden, Marcia Gay	
The Seasons of My Mother	B
The Hardest Place. Morgan, Wesley	958.104
Hardin, Lara Love	
★*The Many Lives of Mama Love*	B
HARDIN, LARA LOVE	
Hardin, Lara Love. ★*The Many Lives of Mama Love*	B
Harding, Luke	
Collusion	324.70973
Invasion	947.7
HARDING, LUKE, 1968-	
Harding, Luke. *Invasion*	947.7
Harding, Thomas	
The House by the Lake	943
Hardly War. Choi, Don Mee	811
Hardman, Robert	
Queen of Our Times	B
Queen of the World	B
Hardwick, Elizabeth	
The Dolphin Letters, 1970-1979	811
HARDWICK, ELIZABETH	
Hardwick, Elizabeth. *The Dolphin Letters, 1970-1979*	811
Pinckney, Darryl. *Come Back in September*	B

PUBLIC LIBRARY CORE COLLECTION: NONFICTION
Twentieth Edition

Hardwick, Lamar
   How Ableism Fuels Racism — 261.8
Hardy, Alyssa
   Worn Out — 338.4
Hardy, Benjamin
   Willpower Doesn't Work — 158
HARDY, G. H. (GODFREY HAROLD), 1877-1947
   Kanigel, Robert. *The Man Who Knew Infinity* — B
Hardy, Grant
   Understanding the Book of Mormon — 289.3
Hardy, Jason Matthew
   ★*The Second Chance Club* — 364.6
HARDY, JASON MATTHEW
   Hardy, Jason Matthew. ★*The Second Chance Club* — 364.6
Hardy, Thomas
   The Collected Letters of Thomas Hardy — 823
   Thomas Hardy — 821
HARDY, THOMAS, 1840-1928
   Hardy, Thomas. *The Collected Letters of Thomas Hardy* — 823
   Tomalin, Claire. *Thomas Hardy* — B
The *Hare* with Amber Eyes. De Waal, Edmund — B
Hare, R. M.
   ★*Plato* — 184
Harford, Tim
   50 Inventions That Shaped the Modern Economy — 609
   Messy — 153.3
Hargrove, Brantley
   The Man Who Caught the Storm — B
Hari, Daoud
   The Translator — B
HARI, DAOUD
   Hari, Daoud. *The Translator* — B
Hari, Johann
   ★*Magic Pill* — 613.2
HARI, JOHANN
   Hari, Johann. ★*Magic Pill* — 613.2
Harig, Bob
   Drive — 796.352
HARING, KEITH, 1958-1990
   Gooch, Brad. *Radiant* — B
Harjo, Joy
   An American Sunrise — 811
   Catching the Light — 818
   Crazy Brave — B
   A Map to the Next World — 811
   ★*Poet Warrior* — B
HARJO, JOY, 1951-
   Harjo, Joy. *Catching the Light* — 818
   Harjo, Joy. *Crazy Brave* — B
   Harjo, Joy. ★*Poet Warrior* — B
Harkness, Deborah E.
   The World of All Souls — 813
HARKNESS, RUTH
   Croke, Vicki. *The Lady and the Panda* — 599.789
Harlan, Elizabeth
   George Sand — B
HARLAN, JOHN MARSHALL, 1833-1911
   Canellos, Peter S. *The Great Dissenter* — B
   Luxenberg, Steve. ★*Separate* — 342.7308
Harlan, Louis R.
   Booker T. Washington — B
   Booker T. Washington — B
HARLAN, ROBERT J.
   Canellos, Peter S. *The Great Dissenter* — B
Harlem. Gill, Jonathan — 974.7
HARLEM RENAISSANCE
   Hurston, Zora Neale. *Dust Tracks on a Road* — B
   Stewart, Jeffrey C. ★*The New Negro* — 191
HARLEM, NEW YORK CITY
   Brown, Claude. *Manchild in the Promised Land* — B
   Day, Daniel R. *Dapper Dan* — B
   Gill, Jonathan. *Harlem* — 974.7
   Stewart, Jeffrey C. ★*The New Negro* — 191
   Valby, Karen. *The Swans of Harlem* — 792.8
   Williams, Billy Dee. ★*What Have We Here* — B
   Wilson, Melba. ★*Melba's American Comfort* — 641.5973
Harman, Claire
   Charlotte Bronte — B
   Murder by the Book — 364.152
Harman, Oren Solomon
   Evolutions — 201
Harmon, Katharine A.
   The Map as Art — 760
Harmon, Mark
   Ghosts of Honolulu — 940.54
HARMONICA
   Gardner, Chris. ★*Permission to Dream* — 158.1
HARMONY
   Ghodsee, Kristen Rogheh. *Everyday Utopia* — 335
HARNACK-FISH, MILDRED, 1902-1943
   Donner, Rebecca. *All the Frequent Troubles of Our Days* — 943
   Thomas, Gordon. *Defying Hitler* — 920
Harper, Kyle
   The Fate of Rome — 937
Harper, Michele
   The Beauty in Breaking — B
HARPER, MICHELE
   Harper, Michele. *The Beauty in Breaking* — B
A **HarperResource** book [Series]. Hellmuth, Phil — 795.41
HARPERS FERRY, BATTLE OF, HARPERS FERRY, W. VA., 1862
   Brands, H. W. ★*The Zealot and the Emancipator* — 920
   Horwitz, Tony. ★*Midnight Rising* — 973.7
   Meyer, Eugene L. *Five for Freedom* — 973.7
   Reynolds, David S. *John Brown, Abolitionist* — B
Harpham, Heather Elise
   Happiness — B
HARPHAM, HEATHER ELISE, 1967-
   Harpham, Heather Elise. *Happiness* — B
Harriet Tubman. Clinton, Catherine — B
Harriet Tubman. Humez, Jean McMahon — B
HARRIMAN, W. AVERELL (WILLIAM AVERELL), 1891-1986
   Fullilove, Michael. *Rendezvous with Destiny* — 973.917092
   Olson, Lynne. *Citizens of London* — 940.54012
Harrington, Anne
   Mind Fixers — 616.89
Harrington, Joel F.
   Dangerous Mystic — B
   The Faithful Executioner — B
HARRINGTON, SHAWN
   Bradburd, Rus. *All the Dreams We've Dreamed* — 796.323
Harriot, Michael
   ★*Black AF History* — 973
HARRIOT, MICHAEL
   Harriot, Michael. ★*Black AF History* — 973
Harris, Adam
   ★*The State Must Provide* — 379.2
Harris, Blake J.
   Console Wars — 338.7
Harris, Dan
   ★*10% Happier* — 158.1
   Meditation for Fidgety Skeptics — 158.1
Harris, David
   The Genius — B
Harris, Ellen T.
   George Frideric Handel — B
Harris, J. William
   The Hanging of Thomas Jeremiah — B
Harris, Jessica B.
   High on the Hog — 641.59
Harris, Kate
   Lands of Lost Borders — 915.804
HARRIS, KATE, 1982-
   Harris, Kate. *Lands of Lost Borders* — 915.804
Harris, Lesley Ellen
   Licensing Digital Content — 346.7304
Harris, M. A.
   The Black Book — 920
Harris, Mark
   ★*Five Came Back* — 791.4302
   Mike Nichols — B
   Pictures at a Revolution — 791.43
Harris, Neil Patrick
   Neil Patrick Harris — B
HARRIS, NEIL PATRICK, 1973-
   Harris, Neil Patrick. *Neil Patrick Harris* — B

AUTHOR, TITLE, SERIES AND SUBJECT INDEX

Harris, Sam
   Islam and the Future of Tolerance   297.2
Harris, Taylor
   This Boy We Made   B
HARRIS, TAYLOR
   Harris, Taylor. *This Boy We Made*   B
Harrison, Christy
   The Wellness Trap   613
HARRISON, GEORGE, 1943-2001
   Brown, Craig. *150 Glimpses of the Beatles*   920
   Doggett, Peter. *You Never Give Me Your Money*   B
   Norman, Philip. *George Harrison*   B
   Thomson, Graeme. *George Harrison*   B
   Womack, Kenneth. *All Things Must Pass Away*   781.66
Harrison, Jim
   The Essential Poems of Jim Harrison   811
   The Search for the Genuine   814
   Songs of Unreason   811
HARRISON, JIM, 1937-2016
   Harrison, Jim. *The Search for the Genuine*   814
HARRISON, JOAN, 1907-1994
   Lane, Christina. *Phantom Lady*   B
HARRISON, JOHN, 1693-1776
   Sobel, Dava. *Longitude*   526
Harrison, Leslie
   The Book of Endings   811
Harrison, Scott
   Thirst   B
HARRISON, SCOTT
   Harrison, Scott. *Thirst*   B
Harrison, Valerie I.
   Do Right by Me   649
HARRISON, WILLIAM HENRY, 1773-1841
   Collins, Gail. *William Henry Harrison*   B
Harry
   ★*Spare*
HARRY POTTER FILMS
   Felton, Tom. ★*Beyond the Wand*   B
Harry S. Truman. Dallek, Robert
Harry, Debbie
   Face It   B
HARRY, DEBBIE
   Harry, Debbie. *Face It*   B
HARRY, PRINCE, DUKE OF SUSSEX, 1984-
   Harry. ★*Spare*   B
Harryhausen, Ray
   The Art of Ray Harryhausen   778
HARRYHAUSEN, RAY
   Harryhausen, Ray. *The Art of Ray Harryhausen*   778
Harshe, January
   Birth Without Fear   618.2
Harss, Marina
   The Boy from Kyiv   B
Hart, Christopher
   Cartooning for the Beginner   741.5
   Human Anatomy Made Amazingly Easy   743.4
Hart, Hannah
   Buffering   B
HART, HANNAH, 1986-
   Hart, Hannah. *Buffering*   B
Hart, James David
   The Oxford Companion to American Literature   810.9
Hart, Kevin
   I Can't Make This Up   B
HART, KEVIN, 1979-
   Hart, Kevin. *I Can't Make This Up*   B
Hart, Matt
   Win at All Costs   338.7
Hartigan, Patti
   August Wilson   B
Hartke, Austen
   Transforming   277
HARTKE, AUSTEN
   Hartke, Austen. *Transforming*   277
Hartley, Gemma
   Fed Up   155.3
Hartman, Darrell
   Battle of Ink and Ice   998

Hartman, Elizabeth
   Modern Patchwork   746.46
Hartnett, Angela
   The Weekend Cook   641.5
Harts, Minda
   Right Within   658.3
Hartwig, Melissa
   The Whole30 Fast & Easy   641.5
   The Whole30 Slow Cooker   641.5
The Harvard Medical School Guide to Tai Chi. Wayne, Peter   613.7
The Harvard Psychedelic Club. Lattin, Don   973.922092
Harvey, Eleanor Jones
   The Civil War and American Art   740.9
Harvey, Samantha
   The Shapeless Unease   B
HARVEY, SAMANTHA, 1975-
   Harvey, Samantha. *The Shapeless Unease*   B
Harvilla, Rob
   60 Songs That Explain the '90s   782.42164
Hase, Craig
   How Not to Be a Hot Mess   158.1
Hasen, Richard L.
   Election Meltdown   324.973
HASIDIM
   Feldman, Deborah. *Unorthodox*   B
HASIDISM
   Telushkin, Joseph. *Rebbe*   296.833
HASKELL, KATHARINE WRIGHT, 1874-1929
   Hazelgrove, William Elliott. *Wright Brothers, Wrong Story*   920
Haskell, Molly
   Steven Spielberg   B
Hass, Robert
   The Apple Trees at Olema   811
   Summer Snow   811.6
Hassan, Hawa
   In Bibi's Kitchen   641.596
HASSELL, ULRICH VON, 1881-1944
   Bailey, Catherine. *A Castle in Wartime*   943.086
HASTINGS, BATTLE OF, ENGLAND, 1066
   Morris, Marc. *The Norman Conquest*   942.02
Hastings, Max
   The Abyss   972.9106
   Armageddon   940.54
   Catastrophe 1914   940.3
   Inferno   940.54
   Operation Chastise   940.54
   Operation Pedestal   940.54
   Overlord   940.54
   Retribution   940.54
   The Secret War   940.54
   ★*Vietnam*   959.704
   Warriors   355
Hastings, Reed
   No Rules Rules   384.55
HASTINGS, REED, 1960-
   Hastings, Reed. *No Rules Rules*   384.55
Hastings, Selina
   The Secret Lives of Somerset Maugham   B
Hatchard, Gurinder Kaur
   Hooked on Shakespeare   746.43
Hatching Twitter. Bilton, Nick   006.7
Hate. Strossen, Nadine   342.7308
HATE
   Darby, Seyward. ★*Sisters in Hate*   305.800973
HATE CRIMES
   Gergel, Richard. *Unexampled Courage*   323.1196
   Hawes, Jennifer. *Grace Will Lead Us Home*   364.152
   Jimenez, Stephen. *The Book of Matt*   364.152
   Kushner, Jacob. *Look Away*   305.9
   Morrison, Melanie. *Murder on Shades Mountain*   345.761
   Oppenheimer, Mark. *Squirrel Hill*   364.152
   Phillips, Patrick. *Blood at the Root*   305.8
   Tyson, Timothy B. *The Blood of Emmett Till*   364.1
HATE GROUPS
   Bates, Laura. *Men Who Hate Women*   305.3
   Chalmers, David Mark. *Hooded Americanism*   322.4
   Darby, Seyward. ★*Sisters in Hate*   305.800973
   Egan, Timothy. ★*A Fever in the Heartland*   322.4

PUBLIC LIBRARY CORE COLLECTION: NONFICTION
Twentieth Edition

Minutaglio, Bill. *Dallas 1963*	973.922092
HATE SPEECH	
Strossen, Nadine. *Hate*	342.7308
Hatemonger. Guerrero, Jean	B
HATHA YOGA	
Bondy, Dianne. *Yoga Where You Are*	613.7
Grossman, Gail Boorstein. *Restorative Yoga for Life*	613.7
Lacerda, Daniel. *2,100 Asanas*	613.7
Lasater, Judith. *Yoga Myths*	613.7
Pohlman, Dean. *Yoga Fitness for Men*	613.7
Stanley, Jessamyn. *Every Body Yoga*	613.7
Stanley, Jessamyn. ★*Yoke*	613.7
Hatmaker, Jen	
Of Mess and Moxie	248.8
Hattie McDaniel. Watts, Jill	B
Hatzfeld, Jean	
Blood Papa	967.5710431
Machete Season	967.57104
Haunted. Braudy, Leo	398.45
Haunted America. Norman, Michael	133.1
HAUNTED HOTELS	
Whitmer, Jamie Davis. *America's Most Haunted Hotels*	133.1
HAUNTED HOUSES	
Norman, Michael. *Haunted America*	133.1
HAUNTED PLACES	
Dickey, Colin. *Ghostland*	133.1
Haupt, Lyanda Lynn	
Mozart's Starling	B
HAUPT, LYANDA LYNN	
Haupt, Lyanda Lynn. *Mozart's Starling*	B
Hauser, CJ	
The Crane Wife	B
HAUSER, CJ	
Hauser, CJ. *The Crane Wife*	B
Hausmagick. Feldmann, Erica	133.4
HAUTE CUISINE	
DeJean, Joan E. *The Essence of Style*	391
Keller, Thomas. *The French Laundry Cookbook*	641.5
Havana. Kurlansky, Mark	972.91
HAVANA, CUBA	
DePalma, Anthony. *The Cubans*	920
Kurlansky, Mark. *Havana*	972.91
The Have and the Have-Nots. Milanovic, Branko	339.2
Have You Eaten Grandma?. Brandreth, Gyles Daubeney	428
The Haven's Kitchen Cooking School. Cayne, Alison	641.5
Haver, Mary Claire	
★*The New Menopause*	618.1
Having and Being Had. Biss, Eula	306.3
Having Our Say. Delany, Sarah Louise	B
Havrilesky, Heather	
Foreverland	306.81
What If This Were Enough?	152.4
HAVRILESKY, HEATHER	
Havrilesky, Heather. *Foreverland*	306.81
Havrilesky, Heather. *What If This Were Enough?*	152.4
HAWAII	
Checkoway, Julie. *The Three-Year Swim Club*	797.2
Drabkin, Ronald. *Beverly Hills Spy*	940.54
Garrow, David J. *Rising Star*	B
Glatt, John. *The Doomsday Mother*	364.152
Haley, James L. *Captive Paradise*	996.9
Hirono, Mazie. *Heart of Fire*	B
Maraniss, David. ★*Barack Obama*	B
Moore, Susanna. *Paradise of the Pacific*	996.9
Prange, Gordon W. *At Dawn We Slept*	940.54
Twomey, Steve. *Countdown to Pearl Harbor*	940.54
White, Richard. *Who Killed Jane Stanford?*	364.152
Hawaiian Dictionary. Pukui, Mary Kawena	499
Hawes, Jennifer	
Grace Will Lead Us Home	364.152
The Hawk and the Dove. Thompson, Nicholas	973.92
The Hawk's Way. Montgomery, Sy	598.9
Hawking. Ottaviani, Jim	741.5
Hawking, Stephen	
★*Black Holes and Baby Universes and Other Essays*	530.1
★*Brief Answers to the Big Questions*	500
A Brief History of Time	523.1
★*A Briefer History of Time*	523.1
★*The Grand Design*	530.14
My Brief History	B
The Nature of Space and Time	530.1
★*The Universe in a Nutshell*	530.12
HAWKING, STEPHEN, 1942-2018	
Hawking, Stephen. ★*Black Holes and Baby Universes and Other Essays*	530.1
Hawking, Stephen. *My Brief History*	B
Mlodinow, Leonard. *Stephen Hawking*	B
Ottaviani, Jim. *Hawking*	741.5
HAWKS	
Montgomery, Sy. *The Hawk's Way*	598.9
Hawksley, Lucinda	
Queen Victoria's Mysterious Daughter	B
Hawley, Sam	
Speed Duel	796.72
Hawthorne, Britt	
★*Raising Antiracist Children*	649
HAWTHORNE, CHARLES WEBSTER, 1872-1930	
Griffel, Lois. *Painting the Impressionist Landscape*	751.45
Hay Hinsdale, Emily L.	
What Is My Plant Telling Me?	635.9
Hay, Carol	
Think Like a Feminist	305.42
Hay, Matt	
Soundtrack of Silence	B
HAY, MATT, 1973-	
Hay, Matt. *Soundtrack of Silence*	B
Hayakawa, Hiroshi	
Kirigami Menagerie	736.98
Hayasaki, Erika	
Somewhere Sisters	362.7
Hayden, Georgina	
Greekish	641.594
Nistisima	641.5
Hayden, Robert	
Collected Poems	811
HAYDN, FRANZ JOSEPH, 1732-1809	
Rosen, Charles. *The Classical Style*	780.9
Hayek, Friedrich A. von	
The Road to Serfdom	330.1
Hayes, Bill	
Sweat	613.7
Hayes, Christopher	
A Colony in a Nation	364.3
Hayes, Dade	
Binge Times	384.55
Hayes, Derek	
Historical Atlas of the American West	911
Historical Atlas of the United States	911
Hayes, Elaine M.	
★*Queen of Bebop*	B
Hayes, Peter	
Why?	940.53
Hayes, Terrance	
★*American Sonnets for My Past and Future Assassin*	811
How to Be Drawn	811
★*Lighthead*	811
So to Speak	811
Haygood, Wil	
★*Colorization*	791.43
Showdown	B
★*Sweet Thunder*	B
Hayhoe, Katharine	
Saving Us	304.2
HAYHOE, KATHARINE	
Hayhoe, Katharine. *Saving Us*	304.2
HAYNE, STEVEN (FORENSIC PATHOLOGIST)	
Balko, Radley. ★*The Cadaver King and the Country Dentist*	614
Hays, Jeanine	
Remix	747
Hays, Katie	
Family of Origin, Family of Choice	248.8086
Hayward, Gordon	
Stone in the Garden	717
Hazan, Jack	
Mind Over Batter	641.81

AUTHOR, TITLE, SERIES AND SUBJECT INDEX

Hazan, Marcella
   ★*Essentials of Classic Italian Cooking*   641.594
HAZAN, MARCELLA
   Sen, Mayukh. *Taste Makers*   641.5092
Hazard, Leah
   Womb   612.6
HAZARDOUS MATERIALS
   Morris, Jim. ★*The Cancer Factory*   658.3
HAZARDOUS OCCUPATIONS
   Morris, Jim. ★*The Cancer Factory*   658.3
HAZARDOUS WASTE
   Bilott, Robert. *Exposure*   344.04
HAZARDOUS WASTE SITES
   O'Brien, Keith. *Paradise Falls*   363.738
   Roy, Saumya. *Castaway Mountain*   363.72
Hazelgrove, William Elliott
   Wright Brothers, Wrong Story   920
HAZING
   Hechinger, John. ★*True Gentlemen*   371.85
Hazleton, Lesley
   After the Prophet   297.8
   Agnostic   211
   The First Muslim   B
   Mary   B
Hazrat, Florence
   An Admirable Point   411
Hazzard, Kevin
   A Thousand Naked Strangers   B
HAZZARD, KEVIN
   Hazzard, Kevin. *A Thousand Naked Strangers*   B
Hazzard, Kevin M.
   American Sirens   362.18
He Held Radical Light. Wiman, Christian   814
He Saw That It Was Good. Baraka, Sho   261.5
Heacox, Kim
   ★*John Muir and the Ice That Started a Fire*   333.7209798
   National Geographic the National Parks   363.6
   Rhythm of the Wild   979.8
HEACOX, KIM
   Heacox, Kim. *Rhythm of the Wild*   979.8
HEAD
   Fainaru-Wada, Mark. *League of Denial*   617.1
   Laskas, Jeanne Marie. *Concussion*   617.5
Head Ball Coach. Spurrier, Steve   B
HEADACHE
   Kempner, Joanna. *Psychedelic Outlaws*   615.7
Headlee, Celeste Anne
   Speaking of Race   305.8
   We Need to Talk   153.6
Headley, Brooks
   Superiority Burger Cookbook   641.5
HEADS OF STATE
   Arana, Marie. *Bolivar*   B
   Castro, Fidel. *Fidel Castro*   B
   Chang, Jung. *Mao*   B
   Clay, Fidel. *King, Kaiser, Tsar*   B
   Coltman, Leycester. *The Real Fidel Castro*   B
   Dugard, Martin. *Taking Berlin*   940.54
   Goldsworthy, Adrian Keith. ★*Caesar*   B
   Groom, Winston. *The Allies*   940.5309
   Katz, Catherine Grace. *The Daughters of Yalta*   920
   Kershaw, Ian. *Hitler*   B
   Kershaw, Ian. *Hitler*   B
   Khlevniuk, Oleg V. *Stalin*   B
   Kotkin, Stephen. *Stalin*   B
   Kotkin, Stephen. *Stalin*   B
   Longerich, Peter. *Hitler*   B
   Olson, Lynne. *Last Hope Island*   940.53
   Pantsov, Alexander. *Mao*   B
   Pfeffer, Anshel. *Bibi*   B
   Radzinskii, Edvard. *Stalin*   947.084
   Sebag-Montefiore, Simon. *Stalin*   B
   Sebag-Montefiore, Simon. *Young Stalin*   B
   Service, Robert. *Lenin—A Biography*   B
   Suny, Ronald Grigor. *Stalin*   B
   Taubman, William. *Gorbachev*   B
   Taubman, William. *Khrushchev*   B
   Ullrich, Volker. *Hitler*   B

   Ullrich, Volker. *Hitler*   B
   Vogel, Ezra F. *Deng XIaoping and the Transformation of China*   B
   Weber, Thomas. *Becoming Hitler*   B
HEALERS
   Black Elk. *Black Elk Speaks*   B
   Fuhrmann, Joseph T. *Rasputin*   B
   Jackson, Joe. *Black Elk*   978.004
   Rojas Contreras, Ingrid. ★*The Man Who Could Move Clouds*   B
Healey, Jonathan
   The Blazing World   941.06
Healing. Brown, Theresa   616.99
Healing. Insel, Thomas R.   362.2
HEALING
   Barry, Harry. *Emotional Healing*   158.1
   Baskette, Molly Phinney. *How to Begin When Your World Is Ending*   248.8
   Bond, Melissa. *Blood Orange Night*   616.8
   Bradford, Joy Harden. *Sisterhood Heals*   158.2
   Braitman, Laurel. *What Looks Like Bravery*   B
   Brownstein, Gabriel. ★*The Secret Mind of Bertha Pappenheim*   616.85
   Buhle, Kathleen. *If We Break*   B
   Burke, Tarana. ★*Unbound*   B
   Campoverdi, Alejandra. *First Gen*   B
   Carpenter, Kyle. *You Are Worth It*   B
   Crosley, Sloane. *Grief Is for People*   B
   Doyne, Maggie. *Between the Mountain and the Sky*   B
   Etheridge, Melissa. *Talking to My Angels*   B
   Febos, Melissa. ★*Body Work*   808.06
   Felix, Camonghne. *Dyscalculia*   B
   Foo, Stephanie. ★*What My Bones Know*   B
   Gaffney, Ginger. *Half Broke*   B
   Gaines, Joanna. *The Stories We Tell*   B
   Gildiner, Catherine. *Good Morning, Monster*   616.89
   Godwin, Gail. *Getting to Know Death*   B
   Golbeck, Jennifer. *The Purest Bond*   636.7
   Gulman, Gary. *Misfit*   B
   Hardin, Lara Love. ★*The Many Lives of Mama Love*   B
   Hilton, Paris. *Paris*   B
   Hubbard, Shanita. ★*Ride-Or-Die*   305.48
   Jamison, Kay Redfield. *Fires in the Dark*   616.89
   Jaouad, Suleika. ★*Between Two Kingdoms*   B
   Johnson, Earl. *Finding Comfort During Hard Times*   155.9
   Joyce, Russell W. *His Face Like Mine*   248
   Kander, Jason. *Invisible Storm*   B
   Kelly, Donika. *The Renunciations*   811
   Kessler, David. *Finding Meaning*   155.9
   Kidder, Tracy. ★*Rough Sleepers*   362.5
   Lecrae. ★*I Am Restored*   B
   LeFavour, Cree. *Lights On, Rats Out*   616.85
   Mandel, Sarah. *Little Earthquakes*   B
   Marchant, Jo. *Cure*   616.89
   May, Katherine. *Wintering*   155.9
   May, Meredith. *The Honey Bus*   B
   McCurdy, Jennette. ★*I'm Glad My Mom Died*   B
   McDougall, Christopher. *Running with Sherman*   636.1
   Means, Brittany. *Hell If We Don't Change Our Ways*   B
   Nakazawa, Donna Jackson. *The Angel and the Assassin*   612.8
   Novello, Carol. *Mutual Rescue*   636.088
   Oppenheimer, Mark. *Squirrel Hill*   364.152
   Pittard, Hannah. *We Are Too Many*   B
   Prescod, Danielle. *Token Black Girl*   B
   Preszler, Trent. *Little and Often*   B
   Rakel, David. *The Compassionate Connection*   610.1
   Rhodes, James. *Instrumental*   B
   Risbridger, Ella. *The Year of Miracles*   641.5
   Rosenblatt, Roger. *Kayak Morning*   155.9
   Rosenthal, Jason. *My Wife Said You May Want to Marry Me*   B
   Rush, Charaia. *Courageously Soft*   234
   Servan-Schreiber, David. *Anticancer*   616.99
   Smith, Carol. *Crossing the River*   B
   Snyder, Rachel Louise. *Women We Buried, Women We Burned*   B
   Stone, Sharon. *The Beauty of Living Twice*   B
   Tanais. *In Sensorium*   B
   Tesfamariam, Rahiel. ★*Imagine Freedom*   305.896
   Tran, Paul. *All the Flowers Kneeling*   811
   Trebincevic, Kenan. *The Bosnia List*   B
   V. *The Apology*   818
   Wallace, Carvell. *Another Word for Love*   B
   Winfrey, Oprah. *What Happened to You?*   616.85

PUBLIC LIBRARY CORE COLLECTION: NONFICTION
Twentieth Edition

HEALTH
- Aronson, Louise. *Elderhood* — 362.60973
- Aschwanden, Christie. *Good to Go* — 617.1
- Ashton, Jennifer. *The New Normal* — 613
- Bamberger, Michael. *The Second Life of Tiger Woods* — B
- Bechdel, Alison. ★*The Secret to Superhuman Strength* — 741.5
- Beres, Derek. *Conspirituality* — 001.9
- Block, Jennifer. *Everything Below the Waist* — 613
- Castro, M. Regina. ★*The Essential Diabetes Book* — 616.4
- Citron, Danielle Keats. *The Fight for Privacy* — 342.7308
- Collen, Alanna. *10% Human* — 612.3
- Copaken, Deborah. *Ladyparts* — B
- Cox, Lynne. *Swimming to Antarctica* — B
- Current, Austin. *Science of Strength Training* — 613.7
- Curry, Kevin. *Fit Men Cook* — 641.5
- Dooner, Caroline. *Tired as F*ck* — 152.1
- Dunn, Jancee. *Hot and Bothered* — 618.1
- Ehrenreich, Barbara. *Natural Causes* — 613.2
- Enright, Lynn. *Vagina* — 612.6
- Fisher, Thomas. ★*The Emergency* — 362.1089
- Galaxy, Jackson. ★*Total Cat Mojo* — 636.8
- Geronimus, Arline T. ★*Weathering* — 362.1089
- Gunter, Jen. *The Menopause Manifesto* — 618.175
- Habib, Rodney. ★*The Forever Dog* — 636.7
- Hamblin, James. *If Our Bodies Could Talk* — 613
- Hari, Johann. *Magic Pill* — 613.2
- Harvey, Samantha. *The Shapeless Unease* — B
- Haver, Mary Claire. ★*The New Menopause* — 618.1
- Hecht, M. E. *Two Old Broads* — 613
- Hendrickson, Debra. ★*The Air They Breathe* — 363.7
- Hernandez, Daisy. *The Kissing Bug* — 616.9
- Hotz, Julia. ★*The Connection Cure* — 610
- Hunt, Lindsay Maitland. *Help Yourself* — 641.5
- Kelly, Christopher R. *Am I Dying?!* — 362.1
- Kelly, John. *The Great Mortality* — 614.5
- Killam, Kasley. *The Art and Science of Connection* — 302
- Kolata, Gina Bari. *Mercies in Disguise* — 616
- Lawson, Jenny. ★*Broken* — B
- Lieberman, Daniel. *Exercised* — 612.044
- Luger, Chelsey. ★*The Seven Circles* — 610
- Magsamen, Susan. *Your Brain on Art* — 111
- Malone, Sharon. *Grown Woman Talk* — 362.1
- Mansberg, Ginni. *The M Word* — 612.6
- McGee, Harold. ★*On Food and Cooking* — 641.5
- McGregor, Alyson J. *Sex Matters* — 613
- Mendelson, Zoe. *Pussypedia* — 612.6
- Mitchell, Andie. *Eating in the Middle* — 641.3
- Montgomery, David R. *What Your Food Ate* — 631.4
- Mukherjee, Siddhartha. ★*The Song of the Cell* — 571.6
- Newman, Bobbi L. ★*Fostering Wellness in the Workplace* — 023
- Oakes, John G. H. ★*The Fast* — 613.2
- Oster, Emily. ★*The Unexpected* — 618.2
- Parker, Lara. *Vagina Problems* — 618.1
- Ramey, Sarah. *The Lady's Handbook for Her Mysterious Illness* — B
- Raphael, Rina. *The Gospel of Wellness* — 613
- Shatner, William. *Live Long And—* — B
- Sheldrake, Rupert. *Science and Spiritual Practices* — 201
- Smith, Freda Love. *I Quit Everything* — B
- Streets, Annabel. *52 Ways to Walk* — 796.51
- Symon, Michael. ★*Fix It with Food* — 641.5
- Tsui, Bonnie. *Why We Swim* — 797.2
- Tulleken, Chris van. *Ultra-Processed People* — 664
- Walker, Danielle. *Danielle Walker's Healthy in a Hurry* — 641.5
- Wayne, Peter. *The Harvard Medical School Guide to Tai Chi* — 613.7
- Weitzman, Gary. *National Geographic Complete Guide to Pet Health, Behavior, and Happiness* — 636.088
- Williams, Florence. *The Nature Fix* — 155.9
- Wilson, Bee. *The Way We Eat Now* — 641.01
- Wilson, F. Perry. *How Medicine Works and When It Doesn't* — 610.69
- Wilson, Jessica. *It's Always Been Ours* — 613
- Wilson, Rebel. *Rebel Rising* — B
- Winfrey, Oprah. *What Happened to You?* — 616.85
- Winters, Mary-Frances. *Black Fatigue* — 305.896

HEALTH FOOD INDUSTRY AND TRADE
- Kauffman, Jonathan. *Hippie Food* — 394.1

HEALTH FOODS
- Angelou, Maya. *Great Food, All Day Long* — 641.5973
- Lewis, John. *Badass Vegan* — 641.5
- Mullins, Brittany. *Mostly Veggies* — 641.5

HEALTH HAZARDS
- Clark, Anna. *The Poisoned City* — 363.6
- Ducharme, Jamie. *Big Vape* — 338.7
- Etter, Lauren. ★*The Devil's Playbook* — 338.7
- Fagin, Dan. *Toms River* — 363.7209749
- Hanna-Attisha, Mona. *What the Eyes Don't See* — 615.9
- Higginbotham, Adam. ★*Midnight in Chernobyl* — 363.17
- Iversen, Kristen. *Full Body Burden* — 363.17
- Moore, Kate. *The Radium Girls* — 363.17
- O'Brien, Keith. *Paradise Falls* — 363.738

HEALTH INSURANCE
- Allen, Marshall. ★*Never Pay the First Bill* — 610.28
- Cohn, Jonathan. *The Ten Year War* — 368.38
- Nuila, Ricardo. *The People's Hospital* — 362.1
- Rosenthal, Elisabeth. *An American Sickness* — 362.10973

HEALTH PLANNING
- Mackenzie, Debora. *Covid-19* — 616.2

HEALTH POLICY
- Alexander, Brian. ★*The Hospital* — 362.10973
- Clark, Anna. *The Poisoned City* — 363.6
- Deer, Brian. *The Doctor Who Fooled the World* — 610.92
- Hendrickson, Debra. ★*The Air They Breathe* — 363.7
- Jena, Anupam B. *Random Acts of Medicine* — 616.0072
- Kinch, Michael S. *Between Hope and Fear* — 614.4
- Krugman, Paul R. *Arguing with Zombies* — 330.973
- Mackenzie, Debora. *Covid-19* — 616.2
- Matthews, Hannah. *You or Someone You Love* — 362.1988
- McNeil, Donald E. ★*The Wisdom of Plagues* — 614.4
- Nocera, Joseph. *The Big Fail* — 362.1962
- Otto, Mary. *Teeth* — 617
- Preston, Richard. *Crisis in the Red Zone* — 614.5
- Quigley, Fran. *Prescription for the People* — 338.4
- Rosenthal, Elisabeth. *An American Sickness* — 362.10973
- Wadman, Meredith. *The Vaccine Race* — 614.5

HEALTH RISK ASSESSMENT
- Kelly, Christopher R. *Am I Dying?!* — 362.1

HEALTH SERVICES ACCESSIBILITY
- Liverpool, Layal. *Systemic* — 362.1
- Nocera, Joseph. *The Big Fail* — 362.1962

Healthyish. Hunt, Lindsay Maitland — 641.5

Healy, Thomas
- *The Great Dissent* — 342.7308

Heaney, Christopher
- *Cradle of Gold* — B

Heaney, Seamus
- *District and Circle* — 821
- *Human Chain* — 821
- *Opened Ground* — 821

Hear My Sad Story. Polenberg, Richard — 782.42162

HEARING
- Ackerman, Diane. *A Natural History of the Senses* — 152.1
- Gray, Charlotte. ★*Reluctant Genius* — 920
- Owen, David. *Volume Control* — 617.8

HEARING DISORDERS
- Hay, Matt. *Soundtrack of Silence* — B

HEARNS, THOMAS
- Kimball, George. *Four Kings* — B

HEARST, MILLICENT WILLSON
- Nasaw, David. *The Chief* — B

HEARST, WILLIAM RANDOLPH, 1863-1951
- Nasaw, David. *The Chief* — B
- Whyte, Kenneth. *The Uncrowned King* — B

Heart. Jauhar, Sandeep — 612.1

HEART
- Jauhar, Sandeep. *Heart* — 612.1
- Jones, Chip. *The Organ Thieves* — 617.4
- Schutt, Bill. *Pump* — 612.1
- Swartz, Mimi. *Ticker* — 617.4

Heart Berries. Mailhot, Terese Marie — B
Heart of Europe. Wilson, Peter H. — 943
The Heart of Everything That Is. Drury, Bob — B
Heart of Fire. Hirono, Mazie — B
The Heart of the Plate. Katzen, Mollie — 641.5

HEART SURGEONS
- Swartz, Mimi. *Ticker* — 617.4
- ★*A Heart That Works*. Delaney, Rob — B

The Heartbeat of Trees. Wohlleben, Peter — 582.16

AUTHOR, TITLE, SERIES AND SUBJECT INDEX

★The **Heartbeat** of Wounded Knee. Treuer, David — 970.004
Heartbreak. Williams, Florence — 306.7
Heartbreak House. Shaw, Bernard — 822
★**Heartland**. Smarsh, Sarah — B
Hearts of Darkness. Monroe, Jana — 363.25
Heaser, Sue
   The Polymer Clay Techniques Book — 731.4
HEAT
   Goodell, Jeff. *The Heat Will Kill You First* — 363.738
Heat Moon, William Least
   Blue Highways — 917.304
   Roads to Quoz — 917.3
HEAT MOON, WILLIAM LEAST
   Heat Moon, William Least. *Blue Highways* — 917.304
   Heat Moon, William Least. *Roads to Quoz* — 917.3
Heat Wave. Bogle, Donald — 782.42164
The **Heat** Will Kill You First. Goodell, Jeff — 363.738
Heath, Chip
   The Power of Moments — 128
HEATH, ROBERT G. (ROBERT GALBRAITH), 1915-1999
   Frank, Lone. *The Pleasure Shock* — 616.8
Heating & Cooling. Fennelly, Beth Ann — B
Heatter, Maida
   ★*Happiness Is Baking* — 641.86
HEAVEN
   Dante Alighieri. *The Paradiso* — 851
   Jennings, Ken. ★*100 Places to See After You Die* — 202
Heaven. Whitney, Emerson — B
Heaven Is Beautiful. Panagore, Peter Baldwin — B
Heaven on Earth. Fauber, L. S. — B
The **Heavens** Might Crack. Sokol, Jason — 323.092
★**Heavy**. Laymon, Kiese — B
Heavy Metal. Fabey, Michael — 338.4
HEAVY METAL GROUPS
   Spitz, Bob. *Led Zeppelin* — 782.42166
   Wiederhorn, Jon. *Louder Than Hell* — 781.6609
HEAVY METAL MUSIC
   Dickinson, Bruce. *What Does This Button Do?* — B
   Johnson, Brian. *The Lives of Brian* — B
   Osbourne, Ozzy. *I Am Ozzy* — B
   Waksman, Steve. *This Ain't the Summer of Love* — 781.66
   Wiederhorn, Jon. *Louder Than Hell* — 781.6609
HEAVY METAL MUSICIANS
   Osbourne, Ozzy. *I Am Ozzy* — B
HEBREW LANGUAGE
   Glinert, Lewis. *The Story of Hebrew* — 492.4
   Strong, James. *The New Strong's Expanded Exhaustive Concordance of the Bible* — 220.5
HEBRIDES
   Nicolson, Adam. *Sea Room* — 941.1
   Nicolson, Adam. *The Seabird's Cry* — 598.177
Hechinger, John
   ★*True Gentlemen* — 371.85
Hecht, Jennifer Michael
   Doubt — 121
   ★*The Wonder Paradox* — 808.1
Hecht, M. E.
   Two Old Broads — 613
Hecimovich, Gregg A.
   ★*The Life and Times of Hannah Crafts* — B
HECTOR (LEGENDARY CHARACTER)
   Homer. ★*The Iliad* — 883
HEDGE FUNDS
   Kolhatkar, Sheelah. *Black Edge* — 364.16
   Sun, Carrie. *Private Equity* — B
HEDGES
   Foley, Caroline. *Topiary, Knots and Parterres* — 715
Hedges, Chris
   Days of Destruction, Days of Revolt — 741.5
   War Is a Force That Gives Us Meaning — 355.02
HEDGES, CHRIS
   Hedges, Chris. *War Is a Force That Gives Us Meaning* — 355.02
Hedy's Folly. Rhodes, Richard — B
HEFFRON, EDWARD
   Guarnere, William. *Brothers in Battle, Best of Friends* — B
Hegar, Mary Jennings
   Shoot Like a Girl — B

HEGAR, MARY JENNINGS
   Hegar, Mary Jennings. *Shoot Like a Girl* — B
HEGEMONY
   Mirski, Sean A. *We May Dominate the World* — 973.91
Heidegger, Martin
   Basic Writings — 193
   ★*Being and Time* — 111
HEIDEGGER, MARTIN, 1889-1976
   Eilenberger, Wolfram. *Time of the Magicians* — 920
Heil Hitler. Allert, Tilman — 395.4
Heilbroner, Robert L.
   ★*The Worldly Philosophers* — B
Heine, Steven J.
   DNA Is Not Destiny — 572.8
HEINLEIN, ROBERT A. (ROBERT ANSON), 1907-1988
   Nevala-Lee, Alec. *Astounding* — 809.3
Heinrich, Bernd
   A Naturalist at Large — 508
   White Feathers — 598.8
HEINRICH, EDWARD OSCAR, 1881-1953
   Dawson, Kate Winkler. ★*American Sherlock* — B
The **Heir** Apparent. Ridley, Jane — B
Heirloom Rooms. Napier, Erin — 747
HEIRLOOMS
   Malhotra, Aanchal. *Remnants of Partition* — 954.04
HEIRS AND HEIRESSES
   De Courcy, Anne. *The Husband Hunters* — 920
   Farley, Audrey Clare. *The Unfit Heiress* — B
   Goldstone, Nancy Bazelon. *The Rival Queens* — 944
   Gucci, Patricia. *In the Name of Gucci* — B
   MacColl, Gail. *To Marry an English Lord* — 974.7
   O'Connell, Mark. *A Thread of Violence* — 364.152
   Parkin, Simon. *The Island of Extraordinary Captives* — 940.53
   Sancton, Thomas. *The Bettencourt Affair* — B
★**Heirs** of the Founders. Brands, H. W. — 973.5
HEISENBERG UNCERTAINTY PRINCIPLE
   Greene, B. *The Fabric of the Cosmos* — 523.1
Held, Shai
   ★*Judaism Is About Love* — 296.3
Helen Keller. Herrmann, Dorothy — B
HELEN OF TROY (GREEK MYTHOLOGY)
   Homer. ★*The Iliad* — 883
Helga's Diary. Weiss, Helga — B
Helgoe, Laurie A.
   Introvert Power — 155.2
Helgoland. Rovelli, Carlo — 530.12
HELICOPTER PILOTS
   Hegar, Mary Jennings. *Shoot Like a Girl* — B
   Henderson, Artis. *Unremarried Widow* — B
HELL
   Dante Alighieri. *Inferno* — 851
   Dante Alighieri. *Paradiso* — 851
   Jennings, Ken. ★*100 Places to See After You Die* — 202
   Turner, Alice K. *The History of Hell* — 236
Hell and Other Destinations. Albright, Madeleine Korbel — B
Hell If We Don't Change Our Ways. Means, Brittany — B
Hell Put to Shame. Swift, Earl — 364.15
Hell to Pay. Giangreco, D. M. — 940.54
Hell's Princess. Schechter, Harold — B
Heller, Jason
   Strange Stars — 781.6609
Heller, Rick
   Secular Meditation — 158.1
Hellfire Boys. Emery, Theo — 358
The **Hellhound** of Wall Street. Perino, Michael A. — 330.973
Hellhound on His Trail. Sides, Hampton — 364.152
Hellmuth, Phil
   Play Poker Like the Pros — 795.41
Hello I Want to Die Please Fix Me. Paperny, Anna Mehler — 362.2
Hello, Gorgeous. Mann, William J. — B
★**Hello**, Molly! Shannon, Molly — B
Hello, My Name Is Awesome. Watkins, Alexandra — 658.8
Helm, Ben
   The Water Gardener's Bible — 635.9
Helm, Sarah
   A Life in Secrets — B
   Ravensbruck — 940.53

PUBLIC LIBRARY CORE COLLECTION: NONFICTION
Twentieth Edition

HELMS, RICHARD
    Morley, Jefferson. *Scorpions' Dance* — 973.924
Helou, Anissa
    Feast — 641.595
Help Me! Power, Marianne — 158.1
Help Yourself. Hunt, Lindsay Maitland — 641.5
HELPFULNESS
    Brous, Sharon. ★ *The Amen Effect* — 296.3
    Keltner, Dacher. *Born to Be Good* — 155.2
    Pablo Cruz, Rosayra. *The Book of Rosy* — B
    Sinise, Gary. *Grateful American* — B
    Solnit, Rebecca. *A Paradise Built in Hell* — 303.48
★ ***Helter Skelter***. Bugliosi, Vincent — 364.1
Helwig, Jenna
    Baby-Led Feeding — 641.3
HEMINGS FAMILY
    Gordon-Reed, Annette. ★ *The Hemingses of Monticello* — 920
HEMINGS, HARRIET, 1801-
    Kerrison, Catherine. *Jefferson's Daughters* — 920
HEMINGS, SALLY, 1773-1835?
    Gordon-Reed, Annette. ★ *The Hemingses of Monticello* — 920
    White, Gayle Jessup. *Reclamation* — B
    Wiencek, Henry. *Master of the Mountain* — 973.4
★ *The **Hemingses** of Monticello*. Gordon-Reed, Annette — 920
Hemingway, Ernest
    Dear Papa — 813
HEMINGWAY, ERNEST, 1899-1961
    Dearborn, Mary V. *Ernest Hemingway* — B
    Hemingway, Ernest. *Dear Papa* — 813
HEMINGWAY, PATRICK
    Hemingway, Ernest. *Dear Papa* — 813
Heminsley, Alexandra
    Running Like a Girl — B
HEMINSLEY, ALEXANDRA, 1976-
    Heminsley, Alexandra. *Running Like a Girl* — B
★ *The **Hemlock** Cup*. Hughes, Bettany — B
Hemming, Henry
    Agents of Influence — 940.54
Hemon, Aleksandar
    My Parents — 814
HEMON, ALEKSANDAR, 1964-
    Hemon, Aleksandar. *My Parents* — 814
Hempel, Jessi
    The Family Outing — B
HEMPEL, JESSI
    Hempel, Jessi. *The Family Outing* — B
HEMPHILL, ESSEX
    Duberman, Martin B. *Hold Tight Gently* — 920
Hemphill, Paul
    Lovesick Blues — B
Henaut, Stephane
    A Bite-Sized History of France — 394.1
Hendershot, Heather
    Open to Debate — B
Henderson, Artis
    Unremarried Widow — B
HENDERSON, ARTIS
    Henderson, Artis. *Unremarried Widow* — B
Henderson, Bruce B.
    Bridge to the Sun — 940.53
    Sons and Soldiers — 940.53
Henderson, Danielle
    ★ *The Ugly Cry* — B
HENDERSON, DANIELLE
    Henderson, Danielle. ★ *The Ugly Cry* — B
HENDERSON, RICKEY, 1958-
    Bryant, Howard. *Rickey* — B
Henderson, Rob Kim
    Troubled — B
HENDERSON, ROB KIM
    Henderson, Rob Kim. *Troubled* — B
Hendricks, Gay
    Conscious Luck — 158.1
Hendricks, Steve
    The Unquiet Grave — 323.1197
Hendrickson, Debra
    ★ *The Air They Breathe* — 363.7

Hendrickson, John
    Life on Delay — B
HENDRICKSON, JOHN (ATLANTIC SENIOR EDITOR)
    Hendrickson, John. *Life on Delay* — B
Hendrickson, Paul
    The Living and the Dead — 959.704
Hendrix, Grady
    These Fists Break Bricks — 791
HENDRIX, JIMI, 1942-1970
    Cross, Charles R. *Room Full of Mirrors* — B
    Murray, Charles Shaar. *Crosstown Traffic* — B
    Norman, Philip. ★ *Wild Thing* — B
Hendrix, Scott H.
    Martin Luther — B
Henig, Robin Marantz
    The Monk in the Garden — B
Hennessey, Jonathan
    The United States Constitution — 741.5
Hennessey, Patrick
    The Junior Officers' Reading Club — B
HENNESSEY, PATRICK, 1982-
    Hennessey, Patrick. *The Junior Officers' Reading Club* — B
Hennessey, Susan
    Unmaking the Presidency — 973.933
Hennessy, Kate
    Dorothy Day — B
Henning, Kristin
    The Rage of Innocence — 364.36
Henny, Ally
    I Won't Shut Up — 305.896
HENNY, ALLY, 1985-
    Henny, Ally. *I Won't Shut Up* — 305.896
Henri Matisse. Matisse, Henri — 709.2
★ *Henry David Thoreau*. Walls, Laura Dassow — B
HENRY IV, KING OF FRANCE, 1553-1610
    DeJean, Joan E. *How Paris Became Paris* — 944
HENRY V, KING OF ENGLAND, 1387-1422
    Barker, Juliet R. V. *Agincourt* — 944
HENRY VI, KING OF ENGLAND, 1421-1471
    Weir, Alison. *The Wars of the Roses* — 942.04
HENRY VII, KING OF ENGLAND, 1457-1509
    Starkey, David. *Six Wives* — 942.05
HENRY VII, KING OF ENGLAND, 1491-1547
    Bordo, Susan. *The Creation of Anne Boleyn* — 942.05
    Borman, Tracy. *Henry VIII and the Men Who Made Him* — 942.05
    Borman, Tracy. *Thomas Cromwell* — B
    MacCulloch, Diarmaid. *Thomas Cromwell* — B
    Porter, Linda. *Katherine the Queen* — B
    Rounding, Virginia. *The Burning Time* — 272
    Weir, Alison. *Henry VIII* — B
Henry VIII. Weir, Alison — B
Henry VIII and the Men Who Made Him. Borman, Tracy — 942.05
HENRY VIII, KING OF ENGLAND, 1491-1547
    Bolt, Robert. *A Man for All Seasons* — 822
    Bordo, Susan. *The Creation of Anne Boleyn* — 942.05
    Borman, Tracy. *Anne Boleyn and Elizabeth I* — 920
    Borman, Tracy. *Henry VIII and the Men Who Made Him* — 942.05
    Borman, Tracy. *Thomas Cromwell* — B
    Fraser, Antonia. ★ *The Wives of Henry VIII* — 942.05
    Guy, John. *Hunting the Falcon* — B
    Porter, Linda. *Katherine the Queen* — B
    Rounding, Virginia. *The Burning Time* — 272
    Russell, Gareth. *Young and Damned and Fair* — B
    Starkey, David. *Six Wives* — 942.05
    Weir, Alison. *The Children of Henry VIII* — B
    Weir, Alison. *Henry VIII* — B
    Weir, Alison. *The Lady in the Tower* — B
    Weir, Alison. *The Lost Tudor Princess* — B
    Weir, Alison. *The Six Wives of Henry VIII* — 942.05
Henry, Alan
    Seen, Heard, and Paid — 650.1
Henry, Diana
    From the Oven to the Table — 641.82
Henry, Jo
    Cultivating Civility — 023
Henry, John
    Great White Fleet — 387.243

AUTHOR, TITLE, SERIES AND SUBJECT INDEX

Hensley, William L. Iggiagruk
   Fifty Miles from Tomorrow — B
HENSLEY, WILLIAM L. IGGIAGRUK
   Hensley, William L. Iggiagruk. *Fifty Miles from Tomorrow* — B
HENSON, JIM
   Jones, Brian Jay. *Jim Henson* — B
Henson, Taraji P.
   Around the Way Girl — B
HENSON, TARAJI P.
   Henson, Taraji P. *Around the Way Girl* — B
HEPBURN, AUDREY, 1929-1993
   Matzen, Robert. *Dutch Girl* — B
   Wasson, Sam. *Fifth Avenue, 5 A.M.* — 791.43
HEPBURN, KATHARINE, 1907-2003
   Berg, A. Scott. *Kate Remembered* — B
   Mann, William J. *Kate* — B
Hepworth, David
   Uncommon People — B
Her Country. Moss, Marissa R. — 781.642
HERB GARDENING
   Belsinger, Susan. *Grow Your Own Herbs* — 635
   Whitman, John. *Fresh from the Garden* — 635.9
HERBAL MEDICINE
   Quave, Cassandra Leah. *The Plant Hunter* — 581.6
Herbert Hoover in the White House. Rappleye, Charles — B
Herbert Von Karajan. Osborne, Richard — B
Herbert, Brian
   Dreamer of Dune — B
HERBERT, FRANK
   Britt, Ryan. ★*The Spice Must Flow* — 813
   Herbert, Brian. *Dreamer of Dune* — B
Herbert, Zbigniew
   The Collected Poems, 1956-1998 — 891.8
Herbertson, Angie
   Sewing Face Masks, Scrub Caps, Arm Slings, and More — 646.4
The Herbivorous Butcher Cookbook. Walch, Aubry — 641.5
HERBS
   Belsinger, Susan. *Grow Your Own Herbs* — 635
   Bohmig, Franz. ★*The Month-By-Month Gardening Guide* — 635
   Lakshmi, Padma. *The Encyclopedia of Spices and Herbs* — 641.3
   Pleasant, Barbara. *Homegrown Pantry* — 635
   Roth, Harold. *The Witching Herbs* — 133.4
HERCULES (ROMAN MYTHOLOGY)
   Carson, Anne. *Autobiography of Red* — 811
HERDERS
   Juan, Li. *Winter Pasture* — 951.06
Herdrich, Stephanie L
   ★*Sargent* — 759.13
Here. Szymborska, Wislawa — 891.8
Here After. Lin, Amy — B
Here for It. Thomas, R. Eric — B
Here I Am. Huffman, Alan — B
Here I Stand. Robeson, Paul — B
Here Is Real Magic. Staniforth, Nate — B
Here We Are. Shahani, Aarti Namdev — B
Here We Are Now. Cross, Charles R. — 782.42166
HEREDITY
   Kolata, Gina Bari. *Mercies in Disguise* — 616
   Mukherjee, Siddhartha. ★*The Gene* — 616
   Zimmer, Carl. *She Has Her Mother's Laugh* — 576.5
HEREDITY AND ENVIRONMENT (PSYCHOLOGY)
   Boyce, W. Thomas. *The Orchid and the Dandelion* — 649
   Brookwood, Marilyn. *The Orphans of Davenport* — 305.231
   Dunbar, R. I. M. *Human Evolution* — 155.7
   Freud, Sigmund. *Civilization and Its Discontents* — 150.19
   Pinker, Steven. *The Blank Slate* — 155.2
   Ruthsatz, Joanne. *The Prodigy's Cousin* — 155.45
Hereford, Mason
   Turkey and the Wolf — 641.5976
HERESY
   Harrington, Joel F. *Dangerous Mystic* — B
   Jones, Dan. *The Templars* — 271
   Minois, Georges. *The Atheist's Bible* — 200
HERETICS
   Brooks, Michael. *The Quantum Astrologer's Handbook* — B
HERITAGE TOURISM
   McClanahan, Paige. *The New Tourist* — 338.4

Herlihy, David V.
   The Lost Cyclist — B
Herman, Amy
   Visual Intelligence — 152.14
Herman, Arthur
   1917 — 940.3
   ★*Douglas Macarthur* — B
   Freedom's Forge — 940.53
   How the Scots Invented the Modern World — 941.1
   The Viking Heart — 948
Herman, Eleanor
   The Royal Art of Poison — 364.152
Herman, Judith Lewis
   Truth and Repair — 362.883
Hermes, Will
   Lou Reed — B
   Love Goes to Buildings on Fire — 781.64
HERMITS
   Finkel, Michael. *The Stranger in the Woods* — B
Hernandez Castillo, Marcelo
   Children of the Land — B
HERNANDEZ CASTILLO, MARCELO, 1988-
   Hernandez Castillo, Marcelo. *Children of the Land* — B
HERNANDEZ, AIDA
   Bobrow-Strain, Aaron. *The Death and Life of Aida Hernandez* — 972
HERNANDEZ, AILEEN
   Turk, Katherine. *The Women of Now* — 305.42
Hernandez, Daisy
   A Cup of Water Under My Bed — B
   The Kissing Bug — 616.9
HERNANDEZ, DAISY
   Hernandez, Daisy. *A Cup of Water Under My Bed* — B
   Hernandez, Daisy. *The Kissing Bug* — 616.9
Hernandez, Eddie
   Turnip Greens & Tortillas — 641.5972
Hernandez, Keith
   I'm Keith Hernandez — B
HERNANDEZ, KEITH
   Hernandez, Keith. *I'm Keith Hernandez* — B
Hernandez, Kelly Lytle
   ★*Bad Mexicans* — 972
Hernon, Peter
   Assessing Service Quality — 025.5
★*Hero Dogs.* Melville, Wilma — 636.7
★*Hero of the Empire.* Millard, Candice — 968.04
★*Hero of Two Worlds.* Duncan, Michael — B
The Hero's Closet. Conahan, Gillian — 646.2
The Hero's Way. Parks, Tim — 945
Herodotus
   The Histories — 938
HEROES AND HEROINES
   Becker, Ernest. ★*The Denial of Death* — 128
   Campbell, Joseph. *The Masks of God* — 201.3
   Campbell, Joseph. *The Power of Myth* — 201.3
   Eder, Mari K. *The Girls Who Stepped Out of Line* — 920
   Firdawsi. *Shahnameh* — 891
   Homer. ★*The Iliad* — 883
   Keith, Philip A. *All Blood Runs Red* — B
   Lambert, Raymond. *Every Man a Hero* — B
   Pfeifer, Joseph. *Ordinary Heroes* — 973.931
   Tatar, Maria. *The Heroine with 1001 Faces* — 809
HEROES AND HEROINES IN MYTHOLOGY
   Hamilton, Edith. ★*Mythology* — 292.1
HEROES AND HEROINES, AMERICAN
   Albracht, William. *Abandoned in Hell* — 959.704
   Egan, Timothy. ★*The Immortal Irishman* — B
   Groom, Winston. *The Aviators* — 920
   Longman, Jere. *Among the Heroes* — 974.8
HEROES AND HEROINES, GREEK
   Homer. *The Odyssey* — 883
   Homer. *The Odyssey* — 883
   Homer. *Odyssey* — 883
   Homer. ★*The Odyssey* — 883
HEROES AND HEROINES, ROMAN
   Virgil. ★*The Aeneid* — 873
HEROIN
   Assael, Shaun. *The Murder of Sonny Liston* — B
   Macy, Beth. ★*Dopesick* — 362.29

Macy, Beth. ★*Raising Lazarus* ... 362.29
HEROIN ADDICTION
    Crouch, Stanley. *Kansas City Lightning* ... B
    Khar, Erin. *Strung Out* ... B
    Neville, Aaron. *Tell It Like It Is* ... B
    Quinones, Sam. *Dreamland* ... 362.29
    Schemel, Patty. *Hit so Hard* ... B
HEROIN ADDICTS
    Blakinger, Keri. *Corrections in Ink* ... B
HEROIN SMUGGLING
    McGreal, Chris. *American Overdose* ... 362.29
HEROIN USERS
    Crouch, Stanley. *Kansas City Lightning* ... B
The *Heroine* with 1001 Faces. Tatar, Maria ... 809
Heroines of Mercy Street. Toler, Pamela D. ... 973.7
Herold, Benjamin
    Disillusioned ... 307.76
Herrera, Hayden
    Frida ... B
    Listening to Stone ... B
Herrera, Juan Felipe
    Every Day We Get More Illegal ... 811
HERRIMAN, GEORGE, 1880-1944
    Tisserand, Michael. *Krazy* ... 741.5
Herrin, Judith
    Byzantium ... 949.5
Herring, Lucinda
    Reimagining Death ... 393
Herriot, James
    ★*All Creatures Great and Small* ... B
    All Things Wise and Wonderful ... B
    Every Living Thing ... B
    James Herriot's Animal Stories ... B
    James Herriot's Cat Stories ... 636.8
    James Herriot's Dog Stories ... 636.7
    James Herriot's Favorite Dog Stories ... 636.7
HERRIOT, JAMES 1916-1995
    Herriot, James. ★*All Creatures Great and Small* ... B
    Herriot, James. *All Things Wise and Wonderful* ... B
    Herriot, James. *Every Living Thing* ... B
    Herriot, James. *James Herriot's Animal Stories* ... B
    Herriot, James. *James Herriot's Cat Stories* ... 636.8
    Herriot, James. *James Herriot's Dog Stories* ... 636.7
    Herriot, James. *James Herriot's Favorite Dog Stories* ... 636.7
Herrmann, Dorothy
    Helen Keller ... B
HERSCHEL, CAROLINE LUCRETIA, 1750-1848
    Holmes, Richard. *The Age of Wonder* ... 509
HERSCHEL, WILLIAM, 1738-1822
    Holmes, Richard. *The Age of Wonder* ... 509
Hersey, John
    ★*Hiroshima* ... 940.54
HERSEY, JOHN, 1914-1993
    Blume, Lesley M. M. *Fallout* ... 940.54
Hersh, Seymour M.
    Reporter ... B
HERSH, SEYMOUR M., 1937-
    Hersh, Seymour M. *Reporter* ... B
    Miraldi, Robert. *Seymour Hersh* ... B
HERSHEY, MILTON SNAVELY, 1857-1945
    Brenner, Joel Glenn. *The Emperors of Chocolate* ... 338.7
Hervieux, Linda
    Forgotten ... 940.54
HERZ-SOMMER, ALICE, 1903-2014
    Mueller, Melissa. *Alice's Piano* ... B
Herzog, Amy
    Knit Wear Love ... 746.43
    You Can Knit That ... 746.432
Herzog, Werner
    ★*Every Man for Himself and God Against All* ... B
HERZOG, WERNER, 1942-
    Herzog, Werner. ★*Every Man for Himself and God Against All* ... B
Hesiod
    Works and Days and Theogony ... 881
HESIOD
    Hesiod. *Works and Days and Theogony* ... 881
Hesse, Maria
    ★*Frida Kahlo* ... B

Hesser, Amanda
    ★*The Essential New York Times Cook Book* ... 641.5
Hessler, Peter
    The Buried ... 962.05
    Oracle Bones ... 951
    Other Rivers ... 378.1
HESSLER, PETER, 1969-
    Hessler, Peter. *The Buried* ... 962.05
    Hessler, Peter. *Other Rivers* ... 378.1
Hester, Diarmuid
    Nothing Ever Just Disappears ... 306.76
HETHERINGTON, TIM
    Huffman, Alan. *Here I Am* ... B
Heti, Sheila
    Alphabetical Diaries ... 818
HETI, SHEILA, 1976-
    Heti, Sheila. *Alphabetical Diaries* ... 818
Hett, Benjamin Carter
    The Death of Democracy ... 943.085
Heuck, Lidey
    ★*Cooking in Real Life* ... 641.5
Heughan, Sam
    Waypoints ... B
HEUGHAN, SAM, 1980-
    Heughan, Sam. *Waypoints* ... B
Heumann, Judith E.
    Being Heumann ... B
HEUMANN, JUDITH E.
    Heumann, Judith E. *Being Heumann* ... B
HEUZÉ, MARCEL, 1912-1992
    Porter, Carolyn. *Marcel's Letters* ... 940.54
Hewett, Jen
    Print, Pattern, Sew ... 646.4
HEWITT, ANN COOPER, 1914-1956
    Farley, Audrey Clare. *The Unfit Heiress* ... B
Hewitt, Ben
    ★*The Town That Food Saved* ... 338.1
Hewitt, Catherine
    Renoir's Dancer ... B
HEWITT, JOHN H., 1924-2000
    Stanislaus, Grace C. *Instill & Inspire* ... 704.03
Hewitt, Sean
    All Down Darkness Wide ... B
HEWITT, SEAN
    Hewitt, Sean. *All Down Darkness Wide* ... B
HEWITT, VIVIAN D.
    Stanislaus, Grace C. *Instill & Inspire* ... 704.03
Hewlett, Sylvia Ann
    #metoo in the Corporate World ... 658.3
Hexham, Irving
    Understanding World Religions ... 200
HEYDRICH, REINHARD, 1904-1942
    Gerwarth, Robert. *Hitler's Hangman* ... B
Heyman, Stephen
    The Planter of Modern Life ... B
Hiaasen, Carl
    The Downhill Lie ... B
HIAASEN, CARL
    Hiaasen, Carl. *The Downhill Lie* ... B
Hiatt, June
    The Principles of Knitting ... 746.43
HIBAKUSHA
    Blume, Lesley M. M. *Fallout* ... 940.54
    Ham, Paul. *Hiroshima Nagasaki* ... 940.54
    Pellegrino, Charles R. *To Hell and Back* ... 940.54
    Southard, Susan. *Nagasaki* ... 940.54
Hibbert, Christopher
    The Borgias and Their Enemies ... 920
    Edward VII ... B
    The House of Medici ... 920
Hibbs, B. Janet
    The Stressed Years of Their Lives ... 616.8900835
    You're Not Done Yet ... 649
Hickam, Homer H.
    ★*Rocket Boys* ... B
HICKAM, HOMER H., 1943-
    Hickam, Homer H. ★*Rocket Boys* ... B

AUTHOR, TITLE, SERIES AND SUBJECT INDEX

Hickel, Jason
   The Divide — 330.9
Hickey, Walt
   ★*You Are What You Watch* — 791.4
Hickman, Katie
   Brave Hearted — 978
HICKOK, LORENA ALICE, 1893-1968
   Golay, Michael. *America 1933* — B
   Quinn, Susan. *Eleanor and Hick* — B
HICKOK, RICHARD EUGENE, 1931-1965
   Capote, Truman. ★*In Cold Blood* — 364.1
HICKOK, WILD BILL, 1837-1876
   Clavin, Thomas. *Wild Bill* — B
*The **Hidden** Art of Disney's Golden Age*. Ghez, Didier — 741.5
HIDDEN CHILDREN (HOLOCAUST)
   Frank, Anne. ★*The Diary of a Young Girl* — 940.53
   Gies, Miep. ★*Anne Frank Remembered* — B
   Moorehead, Caroline. *Village of Secrets* — 944
   Spiegel, Renia. *Renia's Diary* — B
★***Hidden** Figures*. Shetterly, Margot Lee — 510.92
*The **Hidden** History of Burma*. Thant Myint-U — 959.105
*The **Hidden** History of the White House*. Mead, Corey — 975.3
***Hidden** in Plain View*. Tobin, Jacqueline — 973.7
*The **Hidden** Language of Cats*. Brown, Sarah L. — 636.8
*The **Hidden** Life of Trees*. Wohlleben, Peter — 582.16
***Hidden** Potential*. Grant, Adam M. — 153.8
***Hidden** Power*. Marton, Kati — B
★*The **Hidden** Reality*. Greene, B. — 530.12
*The **Hidden** Roots of White Supremacy*. Jones, Robert P. — 305.8
★***Hidden** Valley Road*. Kolker, Robert — 920
*The **Hidden** World of the Fox*. Brand, Adele — 599.775
HIDING
   Chiger, Krystyna. *The Girl in the Green Sweater* — B
   Freeman, Hadley. *House of Glass* — B
   Frenkel, Francoise. *A Bookshop in Berlin* — B
   Grose, Peter. *A Good Place to Hide* — 940.53
   Rushdie, Salman. *Joseph Anton* — B
   Simon, Marie. *Underground in Berlin* — B
   Wetherall, Tyler. *No Way Home* — B
HIERARCHY (SOCIAL SCIENCES)
   Wilkerson, Isabel. ★*Caste* — 305.5
Higdon, Hal
   ★*Marathon* — 796.42
Higginbotham, Adam
   ★*Challenger* — 629.45
   ★*Midnight in Chernobyl* — 363.17
Higgins, Charlotte
   Under Another Sky — 936
Higgins, Jackie
   Sentient — 573.8
Higgins, Tim
   Power Play — 338.7
Higginson, William J.
   The Haiku Handbook — 808.1
HIGGS BOSONS
   Cliff, Harry. *How to Make an Apple Pie from Scratch* — 523.01
HIGH ACHIEVEMENT
   Epstein, David J. ★*Range* — 153.9
   Gladwell, Malcolm. *Outliers* — 302
   Gupta, Prachi. ★*They Called Us Exceptional* — B
   Rippon, Kelly. *Parent Up* — 649
***High** Drama*. Burgman, John — 796.522
***High** Noon*. Frankel, Glenn — 791.43
***High** on the Hog*. Harris, Jessica B. — 641.59
★***High** School*. Quin, Tegan — B
HIGH SCHOOL BASKETBALL
   Blais, Madeleine. *In These Girls, Hope Is a Muscle* — 796.323
   Skelton, Marc. *Pounding the Rock* — 796.323
HIGH SCHOOL BASKETBALL COACHES
   Skelton, Marc. *Pounding the Rock* — 796.323
HIGH SCHOOL BASKETBALL PLAYERS
   Streep, Abe. *Brothers on Three* — 306.85
HIGH SCHOOL FOOTBALL
   Bissinger, H. G. ★*Friday Night Lights* — 796.332
   Eatman, Nicholas. *Friday, Saturday, Sunday in Texas* — 796.332
   Price, S. L. *Playing Through the Whistle* — 796.332
HIGH SCHOOL FOOTBALL PLAYERS
   Eatman, Nicholas. *Friday, Saturday, Sunday in Texas* — 796.332

   Schwartzman, Nancy. *Roll Red Roll* — 364.15
HIGH SCHOOL LIBRARIES
   Chance, Rosemary. *Young Adult Literature in Action* — 011.62
HIGH SCHOOL SENIORS
   Hobbs, Jeff. *Show Them You're Good* — 373
HIGH SCHOOL STUDENTS
   Colton, Larry. *Counting Coup* — 796.323
   Cullen, David. *Parkland* — 371.7
   Cushman, Kathleen. *Fires in Our Lives* — 373.1102
   Hickam, Homer H. ★*Rocket Boys* — B
   Hobbs, Jeff. *Show Them You're Good* — 373
   Margolick, David. *Elizabeth and Hazel* — 379.2
   Powell, Michael. *Canyon Dreams* — 796.323
   Skelton, Marc. *Pounding the Rock* — 796.323
   Tesoriero, Heather Won. *The Class* — 507.1
   Thorpe, Helen. *The Newcomers* — 373.18
HIGH SCHOOL TEACHERS
   Keizer, Garret. *Getting Schooled* — 373.1102
   McCourt, Frank. *Teacher Man* — B
   McCourt, Frank. *'Tis* — B
   Skelton, Marc. *Pounding the Rock* — 796.323
   Tran, Phuc. ★*Sigh, Gone* — B
HIGH SCHOOLS
   Ewing, Eve L. *Ghosts in the Schoolyard* — 370.89
   Fishman, Elly. *Refugee High* — 370.8
   Keizer, Garret. *Getting Schooled* — 373.1102
   Powell, Nate. ★*Lies My Teacher Told Me* — 741.5
*The **High** Sierra*. Robinson, Kim Stanley — 917.94
***High** Society*. Spoto, Donald — B
HIGH TECHNOLOGY
   Citron, Danielle Keats. *The Fight for Privacy* — 342.7308
   Greenberg, Andy. *Tracers in the Dark* — 364.16
   Hill, Kashmir. ★*Your Face Belongs to Us* — 006.2
   Kaku, Michio. ★*The Future of Humanity* — 629.45
   Lashinsky, Adam. *Wild Ride* — 388.4
   Menuez, Doug. *Fearless Genius* — 979.4
   Stone, Brad. *The Upstarts* — 338.04
   Williams, Bari A. *Seen yet Unseen* — 338.4
HIGH TECHNOLOGY INDUSTRY AND TRADE
   Brown, Eliot. *The Cult of We* — 333.33
   Chafkin, Max. *The Contrarian* — B
   Chayka, Kyle. *Filterworld* — 306
   Citron, Danielle Keats. *The Fight for Privacy* — 342.7308
   Etter, Lauren. ★*The Devil's Playbook* — 338.7
   Li, Fei-Fei. *The Worlds I See* — B
   Linn, Susan. *Who's Raising the Kids?* —
   McAfee, Andrew. *The Geek Way* — 658.3
   Molnar, Petra. *The Walls Have Eyes* — 363.28
   Swisher, Kara. *Burn Book* — 303.48
   Tau, Byron. ★*Means of Control* — 363.25
   Vance, Ashlee. *When the Heavens Went on Sale* — 621.43
   Wiener, Anna. ★*Uncanny Valley* — B
HIGH-PROTEIN DIET
   Mullen, Seamus. *Real Food Heals* — 641.5
   Sanfilippo, Diane. *Practical Paleo* — 613.2
   Tam, Michelle. *Ready or Not!* — 641.5
   Walker, Danielle. *Danielle Walker's Against All Grain* — 641.5
***High-Risk** Homosexual*. Gomez, Edgar — B
HIGH-SPEED AVIATION
   Hampton, Dan. *Chasing the Demon* — 629.132
HIGH-TECHNOLOGY INDUSTRY AND TRADE
   Pein, Corey. *Live Work Work Work Die* — 338.4
Higham, Scott
   American Cartel — 338.4
★*A **Higher** Call*. Makos, Adam — 940.54
HIGHER EDUCATION
   Bawer, Bruce. *The Victims' Revolution* — 320.973
   Bok, Derek Curtis. *The Struggle to Reform Our Colleges* — 378.73
   Brenner, Andrea. *How to College* — 378.1
   Bruni, Frank. *Where You Go Is Not Who You'll Be* — 378.1
   Cottom, Tressie McMillan. *Lower Ed* — 378.73
   Gaul, Gilbert M. *Billion-Dollar Ball* — 796.332
   Goldrick-Rab, Sara. *Paying the Price* — 378.3
   Harris, Adam. ★*The State Must Provide* — 379.2
   Hechinger, John. ★*True Gentlemen* — 371.85
   Henderson, Rob Kim. *Troubled* — B
   Hirsch, Jennifer S. *Sexual Citizens* — 371.7
   Hobbs, Jeff. *Show Them You're Good* — 373

PUBLIC LIBRARY CORE COLLECTION: NONFICTION
Twentieth Edition

Mettler, Suzanne. *Degrees of Inequality*	378.73
Mitchell, Josh. *The Debt Trap*	378.3
Rose, Mike. *Back to School*	374
Selingo, Jeffrey J. *College (un)bound*	378
Urofsky, Melvin I. *The Affirmative Action Puzzle*	331.13
Wilder, Craig Steven. *Ebony and Ivy*	379.2

HIGHER EDUCATION POLICY

Mettler, Suzanne. *Degrees of Inequality*	378.73
Mitchell, Josh. *The Debt Trap*	378.3
Selingo, Jeffrey J. *Who Gets in and Why*	378.1

A *Higher Form of Killing*. Preston, Diana — 940.4

Highsmith, Patricia

★*Patricia Highsmith's Diaries and Notebooks*	818

HIGHSMITH, PATRICIA, 1921-1995

Highsmith, Patricia. ★*Patricia Highsmith's Diaries and Notebooks*	818

Highway of Tears. McDiarmid, Jessica — 364.152

Higuchi, Yumiko

Embroidered Animals	746.44

HIJAB (ISLAMIC CLOTHING)

Alinizhad, Masih. *The Wind in My Hair*	B
Muhammad, Ibtihaj. *Proud*	B
★*Hijab Butch Blues*. H, Lamya	B

HIJACKING OF AIRCRAFT

Jacobson, Sidney. *The 9-11 Report*	741.5
Longman, Jere. *Among the Heroes*	974.8

HIJACKING OF SHIPS

Kilmeade, Brian. ★*Thomas Jefferson and the Tripoli Pirates*	973.4

HIKERS

Davis, Jennifer Pharr. *Called Again*	B
Lankford, Andrea. *Trail of the Lost*	363.2
Miles, Kathryn. *Trailed*	364.152
Winn, Raynor. ★*The Salt Path*	B
Winn, Raynor. *The Wild Silence*	B

HIKING

Berger, Karen. *America's Great Hiking Trails*	796.510973
Bryson, Bill. ★*A Walk in the Woods*	917
Chamberlin, Silas. *On the Trail*	796.510973
Davis, Jennifer Pharr. *Called Again*	B
Eichar, Donnie. *Dead Mountain*	914
Fedarko, Kevin. *A Walk in the Park*	917.91
Kaag, John J. *Hiking with Nietzsche*	193
Kirkby, Bruce. *Blue Sky Kingdom*	954.96
Michaud-Skog, Summer. *Fat Girls Hiking*	796.51
Offerman, Nick. *Where the Deer and the Antelope Play*	973.93
Robinson, Kim Stanley. *The High Sierra*	917.94
Solnit, Rebecca. *Wanderlust*	796.51
Spira, Timothy P. *Waterfalls and Wildflowers in the Southern Appalachians*	796.5109756
Strayed, Cheryl. ★*Wild*	B

Hiking with Nietzsche. Kaag, John J. — 193
The *Hilarious World of Depression*. Moe, John — 616.85

Hilborn, Ray

Overfishing	338.3

Hilburn, Robert

★*Johnny Cash*	B
★*Paul Simon*	782.42164

Hilfiger, Tommy

American Dreamer	B

HILFIGER, TOMMY

Hilfiger, Tommy. *American Dreamer*	B

Hill, Anita

★*Believing*	305.42

HILL, ANITA

Hill, Anita. ★*Believing*	305.42

HILL, C. W. (CEDRIC WATERS), 1891-1975

Fox, Margalit. *The Confidence Men*	940.4

Hill, Clint

Five Days in November	973.922092
Five Presidents	B
Mrs. Kennedy and Me	973.922092
My Travels with Mrs. Kennedy	B

HILL, CLINT

Hill, Clint. *Five Presidents*	B
Hill, Clint. *Mrs. Kennedy and Me*	973.922092
Hill, Clint. *My Travels with Mrs. Kennedy*	B

Hill, DaMaris B.

Breath Better Spent	811

Hill, David

The Vapors	976.7

HILL, DAVID

Hill, David. *The Vapors*	976.7

Hill, Fiona

There Is Nothing for You Here	327.2

HILL, FIONA, 1965-

Hill, Fiona. *There Is Nothing for You Here*	327.2

Hill, Geoffrey

Selected Poems	821

Hill, Jemele

Uphill	B

HILL, JEMELE

Hill, Jemele. *Uphill*	B

Hill, Kashmir

★*Your Face Belongs to Us*	006.2

Hill, Katie

She Will Rise	305.42

HILL, KATIE, (FORMER CONGRESSIONAL REPRESENTATIVE)

Hill, Katie. *She Will Rise*	305.42

Hill, Marc Lamont

Seen and Unseen	303.3

Hill, McKel

Nutrition Stripped	641.3

Hill, Napoleon

Think and Grow Rich	650.1

Hillbilly Elegy. Vance, J. D. — B

Hillenbrand, Laura

★*Seabiscuit*	798.4
★*Unbroken*	B

Hillsberg, Christina

License to Parent	649.1

HILLSBERG, CHRISTINA

Hillsberg, Christina. *License to Parent*	649.1

Hillstrom, Laurie Collier

The Thanksgiving Book	394.2649

Hilsum, Lindsey

In Extremis	B

Hilton, Paris

Paris	B

HILTON, PARIS, 1981-

Hilton, Paris. *Paris*	B

Hiltzik, Michael A.

Iron Empires	385.0973

HIMALAYA MOUNTAINS

Alexander, Caroline. *Skies of Thunder*	940.54
Ellsworth, Scott. *The World Beneath Their Feet*	796.522
Kirkby, Bruce. *Blue Sky Kingdom*	954.96
Krakauer, Jon. ★*Into Thin Air*	796.52

HIMES, CHESTER B., 1909-1984

Jackson, Lawrence Patrick. *Chester B. Himes*	B

Hindley, Meredith

Destination Casablanca	940.54

HINDUISM

Armstrong, Karen. ★*The Great Transformation*	200.9
Davis, Richard H. *The Bhagavad Gita*	294.5
Doniger, Wendy. *On Hinduism*	294.5
Goldberg, Philip. *American Veda*	294.509
Satyamurti, Carole. *Mahabharata*	821
Sengupta, Hindol. *Being Hindu*	294.5

HINDUS

Rao, Cheeni. *In Hanuman's Hands*	B
Sengupta, Hindol. *Being Hindu*	294.5

Hing, Bill Ong

★*Humanizing Immigration*	342.7308

Hinges of history [Series]. Cahill, Thomas — 941.501

Hingley, Brian D.

Furniture Repair & Restoration	684.1

Hinkson, Jim

Lacrosse for Dummies	796.34

Hinojosa, Maria

Once I Was You	B

HINOJOSA, MARIA, 1961-

Hinojosa, Maria. *Once I Was You*	B

Hinton, Anthony Ray

The Sun Does Shine	B

HINTON, ANTHONY RAY

Hinton, Anthony Ray. *The Sun Does Shine*	B

AUTHOR, TITLE, SERIES AND SUBJECT INDEX

Hinton, Elizabeth Kai
  ★*America on Fire*   305.800973
HINTON, MILT, 1910-2000
  Lees, Gene. *You Can't Steal a Gift*   B
HIP HOP CULTURE
  Abrams, Jonathan P. D. ★*The Come Up*   782.421649
  Simmons, Nadirah. ★*First Things First*   782.42164
HIP-HOP CULTURE
  Abdurraqib, Hanif. *Go Ahead in the Rain*   782.421649
  Ashon, Will. *Chamber Music*   782.421649
  Black Thought. *The Upcycled Self*   B
  Bowen, Sesali. *Bad Fat Black Girl*   305.42
  Chang, Jeff. *Can't Stop, Won't Stop*   306.4
  Charnas, Dan. *The Big Payback*   306.4
  Chuck D. *Chuck D Presents This Day in Rap and Hip-Hop History*   782.421649
  Day, Daniel R. *Dapper Dan*   B
  Fernando, S. H., Jr. *From the Streets of Shaolin*   782.421
  Ghostface Killah. *Rise of a Killah*   B
  Grandmaster Flash. *The Adventures of Grandmaster Flash*   B
  Greenburg, Zack O'Malley. *3 Kings*   782.421649
  Hope, Clover. *The Motherlode*   920
  Hubbard, Shanita. ★*Ride-Or-Die*   305.48
  Iandoli, Kathy. *God Save the Queens*   782.421649
  Kenner, Rob. *The Marathon Don't Stop*   B
  Kweli, Talib. *Vibrate Higher*   B
  Miranda, Lin-Manuel. *Hamilton*   782.1
  Questlove. ★*Hip-Hop Is History*   782.421649
  Questlove. *Mo' Meta Blues*   782.42164
  Robinson, Staci. ★*Tupac Shakur*   B
  Westhoff, Ben. *Dirty South*   782.421649
  Westhoff, Ben. *Original Gangstas*   782.421649
★*Hip-Hop Is History*. Questlove   782.421649
Hippie Food. Kauffman, Jonathan   394.1
Hirohito and the Making of Modern Japan. Bix, Herbert P.   B
HIROHITO, EMPEROR OF JAPAN, 1901-1989
  Bix, Herbert P. *Hirohito and the Making of Modern Japan*   B
  Dower, John W. *Embracing Defeat*   952.04
Hirono, Mazie
  Heart of Fire   B
★*Hiroshima*. Hersey, John   940.54
Hiroshima Nagasaki. Ham, Paul   940.54
HIROSHIMA, JAPAN
  Barrett, David Dean. *140 Days to Hiroshima*   940.54
  Blume, Lesley M. M. *Fallout*   940.54
  Ham, Paul. *Hiroshima Nagasaki*   940.54
  Hersey, John. ★*Hiroshima*   940.54
  Pellegrino, Charles R. *To Hell and Back*   940.54
  Preston, Diana. *Before the Fallout*   303.48
  Sakamoto, Pamela Rotner. *Midnight in Broad Daylight*   940.53
  Smith, Jim B. *The Last Mission*   940.54
  Southard, Susan. *Nagasaki*   940.54
  Wallace, Chris. *Countdown 1945*   940.54
Hirsch, Edward
  Gabriel   811
  How to Read a Poem   808.1
  The Living Fire   811
  Poet's Choice   808.81
  A Poet's Glossary   808.1
  Special Orders   811
  Stranger by Night   811
Hirsch, Foster
  ★*Hollywood and the Movies of the Fifties*   791.43
Hirsch, James S.
  Riot and Remembrance   976.6
  Willie Mays   B
Hirsch, Jennifer S.
  Sexual Citizens   371.7
Hirsch, Paul
  A Long Time Ago in a Cutting Room Far, Far Away   B
HIRSCH, PAUL, 1945-
  Hirsch, Paul. *A Long Time Ago in a Cutting Room Far, Far Away*   B
Hirsch, William J.
  Designing Your Perfect House   728
Hirschfeld, Erik
  The World's Rarest Birds   333.95822
Hirshey, Gerri
  Not Pretty Enough   B

Hirshfield, Jane
  After   811
  The Beauty   811
  Ledger   811
Hirshman, Linda R.
  Reckoning   305.420973
  Sisters in Law   347.73
Hirsi Ali, Ayaan
  ★*Infidel*   B
HIRSI ALI, AYAAN, 1969-
  Hirsi Ali, Ayaan. ★*Infidel*   B
Hirst, J. B
  The Shortest History of Europe   940
Hirst, Michael
  Michelangelo.   B
★*His Excellency*. Ellis, Joseph J.   B
His Face Like Mine. Joyce, Russell W.   248
His Majesty's Airship. Gwynne, S. C.   363.12
★*His Name Is George Floyd*. Samuels, Robert   B
His Truth Is Marching On. Meacham, Jon   B
His Very Best. Alter, Jonathan   B
Hischak, Thomas S.
  The Oxford Companion to the American Musical   782.1
HISPANIC AMERICAN BASEBALL PLAYERS
  Ruck, Rob. *Raceball*   796.357
HISPANIC AMERICAN CHILDREN
  Hobbs, Jeff. *Show Them You're Good*   373
HISPANIC AMERICAN GANGS
  Dudley, Steven S. *MS-13*   364.106
HISPANIC AMERICAN WOMEN
  Hernandez, Daisy. *A Cup of Water Under My Bed*   B
  Hudes, Quiara Alegria. ★*My Broken Language*   B
  Jones, Brenda. *Alexandria Ocasio-Cortez*   B
  Mojica Rodriguez, Prisca Dorcas. *For Brown Girls with Sharp Edges and Tender Hearts*   305.48
  Rojas Contreras, Ingrid. ★*The Man Who Could Move Clouds*   B
  Sotomayor, Sonia. ★*My Beloved World*   B
  Vasquez-Lavado, Silvia. *In the Shadow of the Mountain*   B
HISPANIC AMERICANS
  Arana, Marie. ★*Latinoland*   973
  Blanco, Richard. *The Prince of Los Cocuyos*   B
  Cadava, Geraldo L. *The Hispanic Republican*   324.2734089
  Cornejo Villavicencio, Karla. ★*The Undocumented Americans*   920
  Corral, Eduardo C. *Guillotine*   811.6
  Espada, Martin. ★*Floaters*   811
  Fernandez-Armesto, Felipe. *Our America*   973
  Gallego, Ruben. *They Called Us*   956.7044
  Gomez, Laura E. ★*Inventing Latinos*   305.868
  Mojica Rodriguez, Prisca Dorcas. *For Brown Girls with Sharp Edges and Tender Hearts*   305.48
  Ortiz, Paul. *An African American and Latinx History of the United States*   305.8
  Otfinoski, Steven. *Latinos in the Arts*   700.89
  Ramos, Jorge. *Stranger*   325.73
  Sanchez, Erika L. *Crying in the Bathroom*   B
  Sotomayor, Sonia. ★*My Beloved World*   B
  Tobar, Hector. ★*Our Migrant Souls*   305.868
The Hispanic Republican. Cadava, Geraldo L.   324.2734089
Hiss, Tony
  ★*Rescuing the Planet*   333.75
Hissing Cousins. Peyser, Marc N.   B
The Historians. Boland, Eavan   821
HISTORIANS
  Ceram, C. W. *Gods, Graves & Scholars*   930.1
  Duberman, Martin B. *Howard Zinn*   B
  Ferguson, Niall. *Kissinger*   973.924
  Haffner, Sebastian. *Defying Hitler*   943.085
  Kagan, Donald. *Thucydides*   938
  Larson, Erik. *In the Garden of Beasts*   B
  McGill, Joseph. *Sleeping with the Ancestors*   306.362
  Rubenstein, David M. *The American Story*   973.07202
  Schlesinger, Arthur M. *Journals, 1952-2000*   973.91092
  Schlesinger, Arthur M. *A Life in the Twentieth Century*   B
  Seidule, Ty. *Robert E. Lee and Me*   973.7
  Zinn, Howard. ★*A People's History of the United States*   973
HISTORIC BUILDINGS
  Finkelstein, Elizabeth. *Cheap Old Houses*   643
  Goldberger, Paul. *Ballpark*   796.357

PUBLIC LIBRARY CORE COLLECTION: NONFICTION
Twentieth Edition

McGill, Joseph. *Sleeping with the Ancestors*	306.362
Satow, Julie. *The Plaza*	917.47
Historic Conversations on Life with John F. Kennedy. Onassis, Jacqueline Kennedy	B

HISTORIC DOCUMENTS

Brookhiser, Richard. *Give Me Liberty*	320.540973
Klarman, Michael J. *The Framers' Coup*	342.7302
Raab, Nathan. *The Hunt for History*	790.1

HISTORIC PRESERVATION

Bechdel, Alison. ★*Fun Home*	741.5
Finkelstein, Elizabeth. *Cheap Old Houses*	643
Olson, Lynne. ★*Empress of the Nile*	B

HISTORIC SITES

Akins, Damon B. ★*We Are the Land*	978
Carlson, Brady. *Dead Presidents*	B
Fowler, Corinne. ★*The Countryside*	941
Frankopan, Peter. *The Silk Roads*	909
Glass, Brent D. *50 Great American Places*	973
McGill, Joseph. *Sleeping with the Ancestors*	306.362
Puglionesi, Alicia. *In Whose Ruins*	973
Robb, Graham. *France*	944
Smith, Clint. ★*How the Word Is Passed*	973
Vowell, Sarah. *Assassination Vacation*	B
Historical Atlas of the American West. Hayes, Derek	911
Historical Atlas of the United States. Hayes, Derek	911

HISTORICAL COMICS

Hall, Rebecca. ★*Wake*	741.5
Igort. *The Ukrainian and Russian Notebooks*	741.5
Mizuki, Shigeru. *Showa 1926-1939*	741.5
Sacco, Joe. ★*Paying the Land*	741.5
Historical Dictionary of Buddhism. Olson, Carl	294.3

HISTORICAL FICTION WRITING

Daugherty, Tracy. *Larry McMurtry*	B

HISTORICAL MUSEUMS

Wilkins, Robert L. *Long Road to Hard Truth*	069

HISTORICAL REENACTMENTS

Goodman, Ruth. *How to Be a Tudor*	942.05
Goodman, Ruth. *How to Be a Victorian*	941.08
Horwitz, Tony. *Confederates in the Attic*	973.7
Philbrick, Nathaniel. *Travels with George*	973.4

HISTORICAL RESEARCH

Caro, Robert A. ★*Working*	B
Hall, Rebecca. ★*Wake*	741.5
McCormick, Mack. *Biography of a Phantom*	782.421643
Porter, Carolyn. *Marcel's Letters*	940.54
White, Gayle Jessup. *Reclamation*	B
Wilkman, Jon. *Screening Reality*	070.1

HISTORICAL REVISIONISM

Burrough, Bryan. *Forget the Alamo*	976.043
Else, Jon. *True South*	305.800973
Fernandez-Armesto, Felipe. *Our America*	973
Powell, Nate. ★*Lies My Teacher Told Me*	741.5
Seidule, Ty. *Robert E. Lee and Me*	973.7
Smith, Clint. ★*How the Word Is Passed*	973
Theoharis, Jeanne. *A More Beautiful and Terrible History*	323.1196
The Histories. Herodotus	938
Histories of the Hanged. Anderson, David	967.62

HISTORIOGRAPHY

Else, Jon. *True South*	305.800973
French, Howard W. *Born in Blackness*	960
Friedman, Thomas L. ★*From Beirut to Jerusalem*	956.04
Grossman, David. *The Yellow Wind*	956.95
Jebara, Mohamad. ★*The Life of the Qur'an*	297.122
Kimmerling, Baruch. *The Palestinian People*	956.94
Lightman, Alan P. *The Discoveries*	509
Lipstadt, Deborah E. *History on Trial*	940.53
Mac Sweeney, Naoise. *The West*	909
Novick, Peter. *The Holocaust in American Life*	940.53
Powell, Nate. ★*Lies My Teacher Told Me*	741.5
Qashu, Sayed. *Native*	892.4
Sacco, Joe. *Footnotes in Gaza*	741.5
Smith, Clint. ★*How the Word Is Passed*	973
Theoharis, Jeanne. *A More Beautiful and Terrible History*	323.1196
Wald, Elijah. *How the Beatles Destroyed Rock 'N' Roll*	781.64
White, Gayle Jessup. *Reclamation*	B
Willis, Deborah. *Envisioning Emancipation*	973.7

HISTORY

Bellos, David. *Who Owns This Sentence?*	346.73
Boyle, Rebecca. *Our Moon*	523.3
Branigan, Tania. *Red Memory*	951.05
Brooks, Michael. *The Art of More*	510.9
Brownstein, Gabriel. ★*The Secret Mind of Bertha Pappenheim*	616.85
Carballo, David M. *America*	912
Carter, Jimmy. *Faith*	OK T A
Cassidy, Cody. *How to Survive History*	904
Chasteen, John Charles. *Born in Blood and Fire*	980
Dixon, Wheeler W. *A Short History of Film*	791.43
DuVal, Kathleen. ★*Native Nations*	970.004
Englund, Peter. *The Beauty and the Sorrow*	940.309
Foster, Lynn V. *A Brief History of Mexico*	972
Francis. *Life*	B
Garfield, Simon. *In Miniature*	745.5928
Gibbins, David J. L. *A History of the World in Twelve Shipwrecks*	909
Gleick, Peter H. *The Three Ages of Water*	333.91
Goodheart, Adam. *The Last Island*	954
Graeber, David. *The Dawn of Everything*	901
Hanson, Victor Davis. *The Father of Us All*	355.0209
Hester, Diarmuid. *Nothing Ever Just Disappears*	306.76
Hirst, J. B. *The Shortest History of Europe*	940
Hollis, B. Dylan. ★*Baking Yesteryear*	641.81
Jebara, Mohamad. ★*The Life of the Qur'an*	297.122
Johnson, Steven. *Wonderland*	790.1
Judah, Hettie. *Lapidarium*	553.8
Kelley, Blair Murphy. *Black Folk*	331.6
Kingsley, Lisa. *Smithsonian American Table*	641.5
Laing, Olivia. *The Garden Against Time*	635
Lepore, Jill. ★*The Deadline*	814
Lieven, Dominic. *In the Shadow of the Gods*	352.23
Mac Sweeney, Naoise. *The West*	909
Mendelson, Cheryl. ★*Vows*	203
Miller, Max. *Tasting History*	641.509
Mortimer, Ian. *The Time Traveler's Guide to Restoration Britain*	941.06
Perry, Imani. ★*South to America*	917
Prasad, Aarathi. *Silk*	677
Raab, Nathan. *The Hunt for History*	790.1
Rady, Martyn C. *The Middle Kingdoms*	943
Schama, Simon. ★*The Story of the Jews; Volume One*	909
Schama, Simon. ★*The Story of the Jews; Volume Two*	909
Sciolino, Elaine. *The Seine*	944
Sebag-Montefiore, Simon. ★*The World*	929.7
Smith, Tracy K. ★*Such Color*	811
Thurman, Judith. ★*A Left-Handed Woman*	814
Tombs, Robert. *The English and Their History*	942
Tuama, Padraig O. ★*Poetry Unbound*	808.1
Tuchman, Barbara W. *March of Folly*	909.08
Vincent, James. *Beyond Measure*	530.8
Walton, Calder. *Spies*	327.1247
Wickham, Chris. *The Inheritance of Rome*	940.1
Wood, Michael. *The Story of China*	951
Young, R. J. *Requiem for the Massacre*	305.8
Zakaria, Fareed. *Age of Revolutions*	303.6

HISTORY BOOKS — AFRICAN AMERICANS — SLAVERY

Rae, Noel. ★*The Great Stain*	306.3

HISTORY BOOKS — AFRICAN AMERICANS — SLAVERY — ABOLITIONIST MOVEMENTS AND THE UNDERGROUND RAILROAD

Miles, Tiya. ★*Night Flyer*	B

HISTORY BOOKS — CENTRAL AND SOUTH AMERICA — MEXICO

Foster, Lynn V. *A Brief History of Mexico*	972

HISTORY BOOKS — EUROPE — GERMANY

Speer, Albert. *Inside the Third Reich*	B

HISTORY BOOKS — UNITED STATES

Powell, Nate. ★*Lies My Teacher Told Me*	741.5
Schultz, David A. *Encyclopedia of the United States Constitution*	342.730203

HISTORY BOOKS — WARS — ATOMIC BOMB — WORLD WAR II

Sheinkin, Steve. *Bomb*	623.4

HISTORY BOOKS — WARS — HOLOCAUST — WORLD WAR II

Frank, Anne. ★*The Diary of a Young Girl*	940.53
Jacobson, Sidney. *Anne Frank*	741.5
Muller, Melissa. *Anne Frank*	B
Van De Perre, Selma. *My Name Is Selma*	940.53
History Lessons. Crais, Clifton C.	B
History of African Americans. Davis, Thomas J.	973
A *History* of Ancient Egypt. Romer, John	932

HISTORY OF ANTI-SLAVERY MOVEMENTS

Brands, H. W. ★*The Zealot and the Emancipator*	920

AUTHOR, TITLE, SERIES AND SUBJECT INDEX

Brewster, Todd. *Lincoln's Gamble*	973.7
Clinton, Catherine. *Harriet Tubman*	B
Douglass, Frederick. *My Bondage and My Freedom*	B
Dunbar, Erica Armstrong. ★*She Came to Slay*	B
Larson, Kate Clifford. *Bound for the Promised Land*	B
Meyer, Eugene L. *Five for Freedom*	973.7
Sinha, Manisha. *The Slave's Cause*	326
History of Beauty. Eco, Umberto	111
A History of Britain; 2. Schama, Simon	941

HISTORY OF CIVILIZATION

Diamond, Jared M. *Upheaval*	303.48
Fagan, Brian M. *The Long Summer*	551.6
Graeber, David. *The Dawn of Everything*	901
Piketty, Thomas. *A Brief History of Equality*	305.09
Puchner, Martin. *The Written World*	809
History of England [Series]. Ackroyd, Peter	941.07
The History of Fly-Fishing in Fifty Flies. Whitelaw, Ian	688.7
A History of France. Norwich, John Julius	944
A History of Ghosts. Aykroyd, Peter	133.1
A History of God. Armstrong, Karen	202
The History of Hell. Turner, Alice K.	236

HISTORY OF IMMIGRANTS

Cannato, Vincent. *American Passage*	325.73
Lee, Erika. *America for Americans*	305.800973
Minian, Ana Raquel. ★*In the Shadow of Liberty*	365
History of International Fashion. Grumbach, Didier	746.9
The History of Jazz. Gioia, Ted	781.6509
★*A History of Judaism*. Goodman, Martin	296.09
A History of Mathematics. Merzbach, Uta C.	510.9

HISTORY OF MEDICINE

Barnes, Julian. *The Man in the Red Coat*	B
Campbell, Olivia. *Women in White Coats*	610.92
Cleghorn, Elinor. *Unwell Women*	613
DiGregorio, Sarah. ★*Taking Care*	610.73
Honigsbaum, Mark. *The Pandemic Century*	614.4
Jauhar, Sandeep. *Heart*	612.1
Lieberman, Jeffrey A. *Malady of the Mind*	616.89
Markel, Howard. *The Secret of Life*	572.86
Meals, Roy A. *Muscle*	612.7
Millard, Candice. *Destiny of the Republic*	973.8
Oshinsky, David M. *Bellevue*	362.1109747
Preston, Richard. *The Hot Zone*	614.5
Randall, David K. *Black Death at the Golden Gate*	616.9
Richtel, Matt. ★*An Elegant Defense*	616.07
Riley, Alex. ★*A Cure for Darkness*	616.85
Taubes, Gary. ★*Rethinking Diabetes*	616.462
Zaitchik, Alexander. *Owning the Sun*	362.1
★*History of Modern Art*. Arnason, H. Harvard	709.04
★*A History of My Brief Body*. Belcourt, Billy-Ray	B
The History of Philosophy. Grayling, A. C.	109
A History of Russia. Riasanovsky, Nicholas V.	947
★*The History of Sketch Comedy*. Key, Keegan-Michael	792.2
A History of the Bible. Barton, John	220.09
A History of the Federal Reserve. Meltzer, Allan H.	332.1
History of the Theatre. Brockett, Oscar G.	792
A History of the United States in Five Crashes. Nations, Scott	338.5
A History of the World in 100 Objects. MacGregor, Neil	930.1
A History of the World in 6 Glasses. Standage, Tom	394.1
A History of the World in Twelve Shipwrecks. Gibbins, David J. L.	909
A History of Venice. Norwich, John Julius	945
A History of Western Architecture. Watkin, David	720
A History of Western Philosophy, and Its Connection with Political and Social Circumstances from The. Russell, Bertrand	109

HISTORY OF WOMEN'S RIGHTS

Gallagher, Winifred. *New Women in the Old West*	978.02
Lepore, Jill. ★*The Secret History of Wonder Woman*	741.5
Schatz, Kate. *Rad Women Worldwide*	920
Wickenden, Dorothy. *The Agitators*	920
History on Trial. Lipstadt, Deborah E.	940.53

HISTORY WRITING — 1960S — UNITED STATES

Abrams, Dan. *Kennedy's Avenger*	973.922
Appy, Christian G. *American Reckoning*	959.704
Archibald, John. *Shaking the Gates of Hell*	B
Austerlitz, Saul. *Just a Shot Away*	781.66078
Berman, Ari. *Give Us the Ballot*	324.6
Boyle, Kevin. *The Shattering*	973.923
Branch, Taylor. ★*At Canaan's Edge*	323.1196
Branch, Taylor. *Parting the Waters*	973
Branch, Taylor. ★*Pillar of Fire*	323.1
Brinkley, Douglas. ★*American Moonshot*	629.40973
Caro, Robert A. ★*The Passage of Power*	B
Carter, David. *Stonewall*	306.76
Cervini, Eric. *The Deviant's War*	B
Clarke, Thurston. *JFK's Last Hundred Days*	B
Clarke, Thurston. *The Last Campaign*	B
Cohen, Andrew. *Two Days in June*	973.922
Coleman, David G. *The Fourteenth Day*	973.922092
Colt, George Howe. *The Game*	796.332
Dallek, Robert. *Let Every Nation Know*	B
Dallek, Robert. *An Unfinished Life*	B
Denevi, Timothy. *Freak Kingdom*	B
Fishman, Charles. ★*One Giant Leap*	629.45
Grant, Gail Milissa. *At the Elbows of My Elders*	B
Hastings, Max. *The Abyss*	972.9106
Hill, Clint. *Mrs. Kennedy and Me*	973.922092
Johnson, Lyndon B. *Taking Charge*	973.923
Jones, Doug. *Bending Toward Justice*	323.1196
Joseph, Peniel E. *The Sword and the Shield*	B
Kennedy, Robert Francis. *RFK*	973.92
Kinzer, Stephen. *Poisoner in Chief*	B
Kix, Paul. ★*You Have to Be Prepared to Die Before You Can Begin to Live*	976.1
Kluger, Jeffrey. ★*Apollo 8*	629.45
Kurlansky, Mark. *1968*	909.82
Larson, Kate Clifford. *Walk with Me*	B
Lattin, Don. *The Harvard Psychedelic Club*	973.922092
Leaming, Barbara. *Jacqueline Bouvier Kennedy Onassis*	B
Leaming, Barbara. *Mrs. Kennedy*	B
Maier, Thomas. *Mafia Spies*	364.1060973
Maraniss, David. *They Marched into Sunlight*	959.704
Matthews, Christopher. *Kennedy & Nixon*	973.922
McKeen, William. *Everybody Had an Ocean*	781.6609
Minutaglio, Bill. *Dallas 1963*	973.922092
Minutaglio, Bill. *The Most Dangerous Man in America*	B
Oliphant, Thomas. ★*The Road to Camelot*	973.922092
Perlstein, Rick. ★*Nixonland*	973.924
Person, Charles. *Buses Are a Comin'*	B
Peters, Charles. *Lyndon B. Johnson*	B
Purdum, Todd S. *An Idea Whose Time Has Come*	342.7308
Rasenberger, Jim. *The Brilliant Disaster*	972.9106
Reid, Joy-Ann Lomena. ★*Medgar and Myrlie*	920
Rosenbloom, Joseph. *Redemption*	B
Rosenfeld, Seth. *Subversives*	378.1
Rudd, Mark. *Underground*	378.1
Schultz, Kevin Michael. *Buckley and Mailer*	920
Sokol, Jason. *The Heavens Might Crack*	323.092
Sorensen, Theodore C. *Counselor*	B
Swanson, James L. *End of Days*	973.922092
Theoharis, Jeanne. *The Rebellious Life of Mrs. Rosa Parks*	B
Thomas, Evan. ★*Robert Kennedy*	B
Tye, Larry. ★*Bobby Kennedy*	B
Warren, James A. *Year of the Hawk*	959.704
Wexler, Stuart. *Killing King*	323.092
Whitaker, Mark. ★*Saying It Loud*	973.923
Wolfe, Tom. ★*The Right Stuff*	629.4
Woods, Randall Bennett. *Prisoners of Hope*	973.923
Zeitz, Joshua. *Building the Great Society*	973.923

HISTORY WRITING — 1970S — UNITED STATES

Appy, Christian G. *American Reckoning*	959.704
Bernstein, Carl. ★*All the President's Men*	364.1
Bowden, Mark. *Guests of the Ayatollah*	955.05
Brokaw, Tom. *The Fall of Richard Nixon*	B
Burrough, Bryan. *Days of Rage*	303.48
Carter, Jimmy. *Keeping Faith*	B
Carter, Jimmy. *Sharing Good Times*	973.926
Carter, Jimmy. *White House Diary*	973.926
Dean, John W. *The Nixon Defense*	973.924092
Denevi, Timothy. *Freak Kingdom*	B
Derf. *Kent State*	741.5
Dobbs, Michael. *King Richard*	973.924
Feldstein, Mark Avrom. *Poisoning the Press*	973.924092
Fieseler, Robert W. *Tinderbox*	364.152
Follett, Ken. *On Wings of Eagles*	955
Graff, Garrett M. *Watergate*	973.924
Kinzer, Stephen. *Poisoner in Chief*	B
Levin, Josh. *The Queen*	364.16

PUBLIC LIBRARY CORE COLLECTION: NONFICTION
Twentieth Edition

McCubbin, Lisa. *Betty Ford*	B
Minutaglio, Bill. *The Most Dangerous Man in America*	B
Perlstein, Rick. *The Invisible Bridge*	973.924
Perlstein, Rick. ★*Reaganland*	973.926
Phillips-Fein, Kim. *Fear City*	330.9747
Reston, James. *The Conviction of Richard Nixon*	973.924092
Risen, James. ★*The Last Honest Man*	973.92
Rumsfeld, Donald. *When the Center Held*	973.925092
Schulman, Bruce J. *The Seventies*	973.92
Thompson, Heather Ann. *Blood in the Water*	365
Weiner, Tim. *One Man Against the World*	B
Woodward, Bob. *The Final Days*	B

HISTORY WRITING — 1980S — UNITED STATES

Brands, H. W. *Reagan*	B
Carter, Jimmy. *White House Diary*	973.926
Mann, Jim. *The Rebellion of Ronald Reagan*	973.927092
McGrath, Tom. *Triumph of the Yuppies*	305.242
Mealer, Bryan. *The Kings of Big Spring*	B
Reagan, Ronald. *The Reagan Diaries*	B
Spitz, Bob. ★*Reagan*	B

HISTORY WRITING — 1990S — UNITED STATES

Branch, Taylor. *The Clinton Tapes*	973.929
Bush, George. *All the Best, George Bush*	973.928
Clinton, Bill. *My Life*	B
Cook, Kevin. *Waco Rising*	299
Ganz, John. *When the Clock Broke*	320.52
Harvilla, Rob. *60 Songs That Explain the '90s*	782.42164
Klosterman, Chuck. ★*The Nineties*	306.0973
Kornacki, Steve. *The Red and the Blue*	306.20973
Meacham, Jon. ★*Destiny and Power*	B
Zelizer, Julian E. *Burning Down the House*	328.73

HISTORY WRITING — AFRICA

Evans, Martin. *Algeria*	965
Kamkwamba, William. ★*The Boy Who Harnessed the Wind*	B
Kara, Siddharth. *Cobalt Red*	338.2
Maathai, Wangari. *Unbowed*	B
Mahjoub, Jamal. *A Line in the River*	962.404
Meredith, Martin. *The Fortunes of Africa*	960
Raines, Ben. *The Last Slave Ship*	306.362
Soyinka, Wole. *Of Africa*	960
Tutu, Desmond. *The Book of Forgiving*	179

HISTORY WRITING — AFRICA — SOUTH AFRICA

Carlin, John. *Playing the Enemy*	968.06
Gevisser, Mark. *A Legacy of Liberation*	B
Mandela, Nelson. *Conversations with Myself*	B
Mandela, Nelson. *Dare Not Linger*	B
Mandela, Nelson. *In His Own Words*	B
Mandela, Nelson. ★*Long Walk to Freedom*	B
Mandela, Nelson. *Mandela*	B
Mandela, Nelson. *The Prison Letters of Nelson Mandela*	968.06092
Smith, David James. *Young Mandela*	B
Steinberg, Jonny. *Winnie and Nelson*	920

HISTORY WRITING — AFRICAN AMERICAN — CIVIL RIGHTS — UNITED STATES

Alexander, Michelle. *The New Jim Crow*	364.973
Arsenault, Raymond. *John Lewis*	B
Baker, Calvin. *A More Perfect Reunion*	305.800973
Baldwin, James. ★*Collected Essays*	814
Baldwin, James. ★*Notes of a Native Son*	305.8
Berman, Ari. *Give Us the Ballot*	324.6
Berry, Mary Frances. *My Face Is Black Is True*	B
Blain, Keisha N. *Until I Am Free*	B
Bond, Julian. ★*Julian Bond's Time to Teach*	323.0975
Boyd, Herb. *We Shall Overcome*	323.1196
Boyle, Kevin. *Arc of Justice*	345.73
Branch, Taylor. ★*At Canaan's Edge*	323.1196
Branch, Taylor. *Parting the Waters*	973
Branch, Taylor. ★*Pillar of Fire*	323.1
Brooks, Maegan Parker. *Fannie Lou Hamer*	B
Canellos, Peter S. *The Great Dissenter*	B
Crump, Benjamin. *Open Season*	364
Dennis, David J., Jr. *The Movement Made Us*	B
Dray, Philip. *At the Hands of Persons Unknown*	364.1
Dray, Philip. *Capitol Men*	973.8
Du Bois, W. E. B. ★*The Souls of Black Folk*	973
Eig, Jonathan. ★*King*	B
Else, Jon. *True South*	305.800973
Euchner, Charles C. *Nobody Turn Me Around*	975.3

Evanzz, Karl. *The Messenger*	B
Foner, Eric. *Forever Free*	973.8
Ford, Tanisha C. *Our Secret Society*	B
Garrett, Kent. *The Last Negroes at Harvard*	920
Gates, Henry Louis. *Colored People*	B
Gates, Henry Louis. *The Future of the Race*	305.896
Gates, Henry Louis. *In Search of Our Roots*	973
Gates, Henry Louis. ★*Life Upon These Shores*	973
Gates, Henry Louis. ★*Stony the Road*	973
Gergel, Richard. *Unexampled Courage*	323.1196
Gibson, Larry S. *Young Thurgood*	B
Giddings, Paula. *Ida*	B
Goldstone, Lawrence. *On Account of Race*	342.7308
Grant, Gail Milissa. *At the Elbows of My Elders*	B
Greenidge, Kerri. *Black Radical*	B
Hahn, Steven. *A Nation Under Our Feet*	975
Halberstam, David. ★*The Children*	323.1
Harlan, Louis R. *Booker T. Washington*	B
Haygood, Wil. *Showdown*	B
Hirsch, James S. *Riot and Remembrance*	976.6
Honey, Michael K. *To the Promised Land*	323
Jackson, Troy. *Becoming King*	B
Jones, Doug. *Bending Toward Justice*	323.1196
Jones, Nathaniel R. *Answering the Call*	B
Joseph, Peniel E. *The Sword and the Shield*	B
Joseph, Peniel E. *Waiting 'Til the Midnight Hour*	323.1196
Keith, Philip A. *All Blood Runs Red*	B
Kennedy, Kostya. *True*	B
King, Coretta Scott. ★*My Life, My Love, My Legacy*	B
King, Gilbert. ★*Devil in the Grove*	305.896
King, Martin Luther. *The Autobiography of Martin Luther King, Jr.*	B
King, Martin Luther. *Why We Can't Wait*	305.8
Kix, Paul. ★*You Have to Be Prepared to Die Before You Can Begin to Live*	976.1
Kotz, Nick. *Judgment Days*	323
Lane, Charles. *The Day Freedom Died*	976.3
Larson, Kate Clifford. *Walk with Me*	B
Lauterbach, Preston. *Bluff City*	B
Levine, Robert S. ★*The Failed Promise*	973.8
Levingston, Steven. *Kennedy and King*	920
Lewis, David L. *W.E.B. Du Bois*	B
Lewis, John. ★*March; Book One*	741.5
Lewis, John. ★*March; Book Three*	741.5
Lewis, John. ★*March; Book Two*	741.5
Lewis, John. *Walking with the Wind*	B
Luxenberg, Steve. ★*Separate*	342.7308
Macy, Beth. ★*Truevine*	B
Madigan, Tim. *The Burning*	976.6
Malcolm X. ★*The Autobiography of Malcolm X*	B
Margolick, David. *Elizabeth and Hazel*	379.2
Martin, Rachel Louise. *A Most Tolerant Little Town*	379.2
Masur, Kate. *Until Justice Be Done*	323.1196
McWhorter, Diane. *Carry Me Home*	976.1
Meacham, Jon. *His Truth Is Marching On*	B
Morrison, Melanie. *Murder on Shades Mountain*	345.761
Muhammad, Khalil Gibran. *The Condemnation of Blackness*	364.2
Norrell, Robert J. *Up from History*	B
Oshinsky, David M. *Worse Than Slavery*	365
Payne, Les. ★*The Dead Are Arising*	B
Perry, Bruce. *Malcolm*	B
Person, Charles. *Buses Are a Comin'*	B
Phillips, Patrick. *Blood at the Root*	305.8
Purdum, Todd S. *An Idea Whose Time Has Come*	342.7308
Reid, Joy-Ann Lomena. ★*Medgar and Myrlie*	920
Reverby, Susan M. *Examining Tuskegee*	174.2
Rhoden, William C. *$40 Million Slaves*	796
Risen, Clay. *The Bill of the Century*	342.7308
Robeson, Paul. *The Undiscovered Paul Robeson*	B
Rosen, Richard A. *Julius Chambers*	B
Rosenbloom, Joseph. *Redemption*	B
Rothstein, Richard. ★*The Color of Law*	305.800973
Roundtree, Dovey Johnson. ★*Mighty Justice*	B
Sides, Hampton. *Hellhound on His Trail*	364.152
Simon, James F. *Eisenhower vs. Warren*	347.73
Sokol, Jason. *The Heavens Might Crack*	323.092
Sullivan, Patricia. *Lift Every Voice*	973
Theoharis, Jeanne. *A More Beautiful and Terrible History*	323.1196
Theoharis, Jeanne. *The Rebellious Life of Mrs. Rosa Parks*	B

AUTHOR, TITLE, SERIES AND SUBJECT INDEX

Tyson, Timothy B. *Blood Done Sign My Name*	975.6
Tyson, Timothy B. *The Blood of Emmett Till*	364.1
Urofsky, Melvin I. *The Affirmative Action Puzzle*	331.13
Van Meter, Matthew. *Deep Delta Justice*	345.763
Walker, Vanessa Siddle. *The Lost Education of Horace Tate*	370.92
Washington, Booker T. ★*Up from Slavery*	B
Watson, Bruce. *Freedom Summer*	323.1196
Wexler, Stuart. *Killing King*	323.092
Whitaker, Mark. ★*Saying It Loud*	973.923
Wilkie, Curtis. *When Evil Lived in Laurel*	305.8
Williams, Juan. *Eyes on the Prize*	323.4
Williams, Juan. *Thurgood Marshall*	B
Willis, Deborah. *Envisioning Emancipation*	973.7
Woodward, C. Vann. *The Strange Career of Jim Crow*	305.896
Wright, Richard. ★*Black Boy*	B
Zack, Ian. *Odetta*	B

HISTORY WRITING — AFRICAN AMERICAN — ENSLAVEMENT — UNITED STATES

Ball, Edward. *Slaves in the Family*	975.7
Blackmon, Douglas A. *Slavery by Another Name*	305.896
Blight, David W. ★*Frederick Douglass*	B
Blight, David W. *A Slave No More*	B
Bordewich, Fergus M. *Bound for Canaan*	973.7
Brewster, Todd. *Lincoln's Gamble*	973.7
Burlingame, Michael. *The Black Man's President*	973.7
Carretta, Vincent. *Equiano, the African*	B
Clinton, Catherine. *Harriet Tubman*	B
Deetz, Kelley Fanto. *Bound to the Fire*	641.59
Delbanco, Andrew. *The War Before the War*	973.7
Dilbeck, D. H. *Frederick Douglass*	B
Douglass, Frederick. *My Bondage and My Freedom*	B
Dunbar, Erica Armstrong. ★*Never Caught*	B
Dunbar, Erica Armstrong. ★*She Came to Slay*	B
Durkin, Hannah. ★*The Survivors of the Clotilda*	306.362
Feldman, Noah. *The Broken Constitution*	973.7
Fischer, David Hackett. ★*African Founders*	973
Foner, Eric. ★*Gateway to Freedom*	973.7
Ford, Lacy K. *Deliver Us from Evil*	973.7
French, Howard W. *Born in Blackness*	960
Greenidge, Kerri. ★*The Grimkes*	973.5
Griswold, Mac K. *The Manor*	974.7
Hall, Rebecca. ★*Wake*	741.5
Hallman, J. C. *Say Anarcha*	618.1
Harris, J. William. *The Hanging of Thomas Jeremiah*	B
Horwitz, Tony. ★*Midnight Rising*	973.7
Humez, Jean McMahon. *Harriet Tubman*	B
Hurston, Zora Neale. ★*Barracoon*	B
Jacobs, Harriet. ★*Incidents in the Life of a Slave Girl*	B
Johnson, Walter. *Soul by Soul*	976.3
Kaplan, Fred. *Lincoln and the Abolitionists*	973.7092
Kytle, Ethan J. *Denmark Vesey's Garden*	975.7
Larson, Kate Clifford. *Bound for the Promised Land*	B
Lepore, Jill. *New York Burning*	974.7
Lineberry, Cate. *Be Free or Die*	B
Manegold, Catherine S. *Ten Hills Farm*	974.4
May, Gregory. *A Madman's Will*	973.5
McGill, Joseph. *Sleeping with the Ancestors*	306.362
Meacham, Jon. ★*And There Was Light*	973.7
Meyer, Eugene L. *Five for Freedom*	B
Miles, Tiya. *The Dawn of Detroit*	977.4
Montero, David. ★*The Stolen Wealth of Slavery*	381
Morgan-Owens, Jessie. *Girl in Black and White*	B
Nathans, Sydney. *To Free a Family*	B
Northup, Solomon. *Twelve Years a Slave*	B
Oakes, James. *Freedom National*	973.7
Painter, Nell Irvin. ★*Sojourner Truth*	B
Plant, Deborah G. *Of Greed and Glory*	326
Raines, Ben. *The Last Slave Ship*	306.362
Rasmussen, Daniel. *American Uprising*	976.3
Rediker, Marcus. *The Amistad Rebellion*	326.0973
Reynolds, David S. *John Brown, Abolitionist*	B
Richards, Leonard L. *Who Freed the Slaves?*	342.7308
Rothman, Joshua D. *The Ledger and the Chain*	306.362
Shane, Scott. ★*Flee North*	973.7
Sinha, Manisha. *The Slave's Cause*	326
Smith, Clint. ★*How the Word Is Passed*	973
Snodgrass, Mary Ellen. *The Underground Railroad*	973.7
Snyder, Christina. *Great Crossings*	976.9

Stauffer, John. *Picturing Fredrick Douglass*	B
Stuart, Andrea. *Sugar in the Blood*	338.1
Swarns, Rachel L. *The 272*	975.2
Tabor, Nick. *Africatown*	976.1
Taylor, Alan. ★*The Internal Enemy*	975.5
Tobin, Jacqueline. *From Midnight to Dawn*	973.7
Tobin, Jacqueline. *Hidden in Plain View*	973.7
Ward, Andrew. ★*The Slaves' War*	973.7
Weiner, Mark Stuart. *Black Trials*	342.7308
White, Gayle Jessup. *Reclamation*	B
Wiencek, Henry. *Master of the Mountain*	973.4
Wilder, Craig Steven. *Ebony and Ivy*	379.2
Wineapple, Brenda. *Ecstatic Nation*	973.6
Woo, Ilyon. ★*Master Slave Husband Wife*	920
Young, Kevin. *Ardency*	811

HISTORY WRITING — AFRICAN AMERICAN — UNITED STATES

Anderson, Carol. ★*White Rage*	305.800973
Ash, Stephen V. *Firebrand of Liberty*	973.7
Asim, Jabari. *We Can't Breathe*	305.896
Baime, A. J. *White Lies*	B
Baldwin, James. ★*The Fire Next Time*	305.896
Baldwin, James. *I Am Not Your Negro*	323.1196
Barnett, Brittany K. ★*A Knock at Midnight*	B
Berlin, Ira. *The Making of African America*	973
Berry, Daina Ramey. ★*A Black Women's History of the United States*	305.48
Boykin, Keith. *Race Against Time*	305.8
Brazile, Donna. *For Colored Girls Who Have Considered Politics*	328.73
Capparell, Stephanie. *The Real Pepsi Challenge*	338.7
Carruthers, Charlene A. *Unapologetic*	305.48
Chatelain, Marcia. ★*Franchise*	339
Cleaver, Eldridge. *Soul on Ice*	B
Colaiaco, James A. *Frederick Douglass and the Fourth of July*	973.7
Cox, Anna-Lisa. *The Bone and Sinew of the Land*	977
Currie, Elliott. *A Peculiar Indifference*	305.800973
Delany, Sarah Louise. *Having Our Say*	B
Delmont, Matthew F. *Half American*	940.54
Edelman, Marian Wright. *Lanterns*	362.7
Ellison, Ralph. *The Selected Letters of Ralph Ellison*	813
Ellsworth, Scott. *The Ground Breaking*	976.6
Emberton, Carole. *To Walk About in Freedom*	306.3
Farrington, Lisa E. *Creating Their Own Image*	704
Fields-Black, Edda L. *Combee*	973.7
Forman, James. *Locking up Our Own*	364.973
Franklin, John Hope. ★*From Slavery to Freedom*	973
Franklin, John Hope. *In Search of the Promised Land*	929
Gaddy, K. R. ★*Well of Souls*	787
Gates, Henry Louis. *100 Amazing Facts About the Negro*	973
Gates, Henry Louis. ★*The Black Church*	277
Gayle, Caleb. *We Refuse to Forget*	975.004
Genovese, Eugene D. *Roll, Jordan, Roll*	975
Gill, Jonathan. *Harlem*	974.7
Givens, Jarvis R. ★*School Clothes*	371.829
Glaude, Eddie S. *Begin Again*	305.800973
Gordon-Reed, Annette. ★*The Hemingses of Monticello*	920
Gregory, Dick. *Defining Moments in Black History*	973
Griffin, Farah Jasmine. *Read Until You Understand*	810.9
Hale, Grace Elizabeth. *In the Pines*	364.13
Hall, Alvin D. *Driving the Green Book*	917.304
Harlan, Louis R. *Booker T. Washington*	B
Harriot, Michael. ★*Black AF History*	973
Harris, Jessica B. *High on the Hog*	641.59
Haygood, Wil. ★*Colorization*	791.43
Hazzard, Kevin M. *American Sirens*	362.18
Hecimovich, Gregg A. ★*The Life and Times of Hannah Crafts*	B
Hervieux, Linda. *Forgotten*	940.54
Hinton, Elizabeth Kai. ★*America on Fire*	305.800973
Hunter-Gault, Charlayne. ★*My People*	305.48
Hurston, Zora Neale. ★*You Don't Know Us Negroes and Other Essays*	814
Hylton, Antonia. *Madness*	362.2
Jackson, Lawrence Patrick. *Chester B. Himes*	B
Jacobs, Sally H. *Althea*	B
Jerkins, Morgan. *Wandering in Strange Lands*	305.896
Johnson, Katherine G. *My Remarkable Journey*	B
Johnson, Theodore R. *When the Stars Begin to Fall*	305.800973
Jones, Chip. *The Organ Thieves*	617.4
Jones, Jacqueline. *Saving Savannah*	975.8
Kearse, Bettye. *The Other Madisons*	920
Kelley, Blair Murphy. *Black Folk*	331.6

PUBLIC LIBRARY CORE COLLECTION: NONFICTION
Twentieth Edition

Kendrick, Kathleen M. *Official Guide to the Smithsonian National Museum of African American History & Culture*	975.3
Lane, Stewart F. *Black Broadway*	792.089
Lemann, Nicholas. *Redemption*	975
Lemon, Don. *This Is the Fire*	305.896
Levinsohn, Florence Hamlish. *Looking for Farrakhan*	B
Levy, Aidan. *Saxophone Colossus*	B
Luckerson, Victor. *Built from the Fire*	976.6
Mahon, Maureen. ★*Black Diamond Queens*	782.421
Mays, Kyle. ★*An Afro-Indigenous History of the United States*	973
McNally, Dennis. *On Highway 61*	781.64
Morris, James McGrath. *Eye on the Struggle*	B
Morrison, Toni. *Playing in the Dark*	810.9
Ortiz, Paul. *An African American and Latinx History of the United States*	305.8
Perron, Cam. ★*Comeback Season*	796.357
Perry, Imani. *May We Forever Stand*	782.25
Pinn, Anthony B. *The Black Practice of Disbelief*	211
Proenza-Coles, Christina. *American Founders*	973
Raiford, Matthew. *Bress 'N' Nyam*	641.59
Ransby, Barbara. *Eslanda*	B
Rembert, Winfred. *Chasing Me to My Grave*	B
Ribowsky, Mark. *The Supremes*	B
Rosenberg, Rosalind. ★*Jane Crow*	B
Runstedtler, Theresa. *Black Ball*	796.323
Sharpe, Christina Elizabeth. *Ordinary Notes*	305.896
Shetterly, Margot Lee. ★*Hidden Figures*	510.92
Smilios, Maria. ★*The Black Angels*	610.73
Sorin, Gretchen Sullivan. *Driving While Black*	323.1196
Souza, Pete. *Shade*	973.932
Stewart, Jeffrey C. ★*The New Negro*	191
Swift, Earl. *Hell Put to Shame*	364.15
Terry, Bryant. *Black Food*	394.1
Tesfamariam, Rahiel. ★*Imagine Freedom*	305.896
Thomas, Franklin A. *An Unplanned Life*	B
Thompson-Hernandez, Walter. *The Compton Cowboys*	920
Tipton-Martin, Toni. *The Jemima Code*	641.59
Tipton-Martin, Toni. ★*Jubilee*	641.59
Tubbs, Anna Malaika. *The Three Mothers*	306.874
Tuccille, Jerome. *The Roughest Riders*	973.8
Twitty, Michael. ★*The Cooking Gene*	641.59
Valby, Karen. *The Swans of Harlem*	792.8
Vella, Christina. *George Washington Carver*	B
Waldstreicher, David. *The Odyssey of Phillis Wheatley*	B
West, Cornel. *Black Prophetic Fire*	920
Westhoff, Ben. *Original Gangstas*	782.421649
Whitaker, Mark. *Smoketown*	305.896
White, Shane. *Prince of Darkness*	B
Wickenden, Dorothy. *The Agitators*	920
Wilkerson, Isabel. ★*The Warmth of Other Suns*	304.80973
Wilkins, Robert L. *Long Road to Hard Truth*	069
Williams, Kidada E. *I Saw Death Coming*	973.8
Willis, Deborah. ★*The Black Civil War Soldier*	973.7
Wills, Shomari. *Black Fortunes*	920
Wilson, Jessica. *It's Always Been Ours*	613
Young, R. J. *Requiem for the Massacre*	305.8
Zucchino, David. *Wilmington's Lie*	305.8009756

HISTORY WRITING — ANCIENT

Beard, Mary. ★*How Do We Look*	704.9
Bohme, Madelaine. *Ancient Bones*	599.93
Ceram, C. W. *Gods, Graves & Scholars*	930.1
Childs, Craig. *Atlas of a Lost World*	551.7
Cline, Eric H. *After 1177 B.C.*	937
Fagan, Brian M. *Climate Chaos*	304.2
Fagan, Brian M. *Fishing*	338.3
Ferrara, Silvia. *The Greatest Invention*	411
Frankopan, Peter. *The Silk Roads*	909
Garfinkel, Yosef. *In the Footsteps of King David*	933
Herodotus. *The Histories*	938
Holland, Tom. *Dominion*	261
Hughes, Bettany. *Venus and Aphrodite*	292
Johanson, Donald C. *Lucy*	569
Kriwaczek, Paul. *Babylon*	935
Leakey, Richard E. *The Origin of Humankind*	599.93
Mackintosh-Smith, Tim. *Arabs*	909.04
O'Connell, Robert L. *The Ghosts of Cannae*	937
Pryor, Francis. ★*Stonehenge*	936.2
Wragg Sykes, Rebecca. *Kindred*	569.9

Wrangham, Richard W. *Catching Fire*	394.1

HISTORY WRITING — ANCIENT — EGYPT

Brier, Bob. *The Murder of Tutankhamen*	B
Cooney, Kara. *When Women Ruled the World*	920
Darnell, John Coleman. *Egypt's Golden Couple*	932
Dolnick, Edward. *The Writing of the Gods*	493
Goldsworthy, Adrian Keith. *Antony and Cleopatra*	937
Mertz, Barbara. *Temples, Tombs, & Hieroglyphs*	932
Robins, Gay. *The Art of Ancient Egypt*	709
Romer, John. *A History of Ancient Egypt*	932
Schiff, Stacy. ★*Cleopatra*	B
Shaw, Ian. *The Princeton Dictionary of Ancient Egypt*	932
Wilkinson, Richard H. ★*The Complete Gods and Goddesses of Ancient Egypt*	299
Wilkinson, Toby A. H. *The Nile*	962
Wilkinson, Toby A. H. ★*The Rise and Fall of Ancient Egypt*	932
Wilkinson, Toby A. H. *A World Beneath the Sands*	932

HISTORY WRITING — ANCIENT — GREECE

Adler, Mortimer Jerome. *Aristotle for Everybody*	185
Alexander, Caroline. *The War That Killed Achilles*	883
Cahill, Thomas. *Sailing the Wine-Dark Sea*	909
Everitt, Anthony. *Alexander the Great*	B
Everitt, Anthony. *The Rise of Athens*	938
Hughes, Bettany. ★*The Hemlock Cup*	B
Jenkyns, Richard. *Classical Literature*	880.09
Johnson, Paul. *Socrates*	183
Kagan, Donald. *The Peloponnesian War*	938
Kagan, Donald. *Thucydides*	938
Kawa, Abraham. *Democracy*	741.5
Nicolson, Adam. *How to Be*	180
Nicolson, Adam. *Why Homer Matters*	883
Roberts, Jennifer Tolbert. *The Plague of War*	938
Stone, I. F. *The Trial of Socrates*	183
Wroe, Ann. *Orpheus*	398.2093802

HISTORY WRITING — ANCIENT — ROME

Addis, Ferdinand. *The Eternal City*	945.6
Augustine. *Concerning the City of God Against the Pagans*	239
Beard, Mary. ★*Emperor of Rome*	937
Beard, Mary. *The Fires of Vesuvius*	937
Beard, Mary. ★*S.P.Q.R.*	937
Berry, Joanne. *The Complete Pompeii*	937
Brown, Peter. *Through the Eye of a Needle*	270.2
Brownworth, Lars. *Lost to the West*	949.5
Cicero, Marcus Tullius. ★*The Republic*	320.1
Cicero, Marcus Tullius. *Selected Works*	875
Everitt, Anthony. *Cicero*	B
Everitt, Anthony. *Hadrian and the Triumph of Rome*	B
Everitt, Anthony. *The Rise of Rome*	937
Gibbon, Edward. ★*The Decline and Fall of the Roman Empire*	937
Goldsworthy, Adrian Keith. *Augustus*	B
Goldsworthy, Adrian Keith. ★*Caesar*	B
Goldsworthy, Adrian Keith. *Pax Romana*	937
Harper, Kyle. *The Fate of Rome*	937
Higgins, Charlotte. *Under Another Sky*	936
Hunt, Patrick. *Hannibal*	B
Jenkyns, Richard. *Classical Literature*	880.09
Southon, Emma. *Agrippina*	B
Strauss, Barry S. *The Death of Caesar*	937
Strauss, Barry S. *Ten Caesars*	937
Strauss, Barry S. ★*The War That Made the Roman Empire*	937
Suetonius. ★*The Twelve Caesars*	B
Woolf, Greg. *Rome*	937

HISTORY WRITING — ANTEBELLUM AMERICA — UNITED STATES

Ayers, Edward L. *American Visions*	973.5
Borneman, Walter R. *Polk*	B
Brands, H. W. *Andrew Jackson, His Life and Times*	B
Brands, H. W. ★*The Zealot and the Emancipator*	920
Colaiaco, James A. *Frederick Douglass and the Fourth of July*	973.7
Collins, Gail. *William Henry Harrison*	B
Delbanco, Andrew. *The War Before the War*	973.7
Douglass, Frederick. ★*Frederick Douglass*	973.8
Douglass, Frederick. *Narrative of the Life of Frederick Douglass, an American Slave*	B
Faust, Drew Gilpin. *Mothers of Invention*	973.7
Feldman, Noah. *The Broken Constitution*	973.7
Finkelman, Paul. *Millard Fillmore*	B
Foote, Shelby. *Stars in Their Courses*	973.7
Ford, Lacy K. *Deliver Us from Evil*	973.7

AUTHOR, TITLE, SERIES AND SUBJECT INDEX

Freeman, Joanne B. *The Field of Blood*	973.7
Goodwin, Doris Kearns. ★ *Team of Rivals*	B
Greenidge, Kerri. ★ *The Grimkes*	973.5
Grinspan, Jon. *Wide Awake*	973.7
Guelzo, Allen C. *Lincoln and Douglas*	973.6
Harvey, Eleanor Jones. *The Civil War and American Art*	740.9
Horwitz, Tony. ★ *Midnight Rising*	973.7
Howe, Daniel Walker. *What Hath God Wrought*	973.5
Johnson, Victoria. ★ *American Eden*	580.973
Kytle, Ethan J. *Denmark Vesey's Garden*	975.7
Masur, Kate. *Until Justice Be Done*	323.1196
McGinty, Brian. *Lincoln's Greatest Case*	346.7303
Meacham, Jon. ★ *American Lion*	B
Meltzer, Brad. *The Lincoln Conspiracy*	973.7092
Merry, Robert W. *A Country of Vast Designs*	B
Meyer, Eugene L. *Five for Freedom*	973.7
Paul, Joel R. *Indivisible*	973.5
Puleo, Stephen. *Voyage of Mercy*	363.8
Randall, Willard Sterne. *The Founders' Fortunes*	973.3
Rasenberger, Jim. *Revolver*	B
Reynolds, David S. *John Brown, Abolitionist*	B
Reynolds, David S. *Mightier Than the Sword*	813
Sandburg, Carl. *Abraham Lincoln*	B
Taylor, Alan. *American Revolutions*	973.3
Thompson, Bob. *Revolutionary Roads*	973.3
Widmer, Edward L. *Martin Van Buren*	B
Woo, Ilyon. ★ *Master Slave Husband Wife*	920

HISTORY WRITING — ARAB-ISRAELI RELATIONS — SOUTHWEST ASIA AND NORTH AFRICA (MIDDLE EAST)

Abuelaish, Izzeldin. *I Shall Not Hate*	B
Armstrong, Karen. *Jerusalem*	956.94
Bascomb, Neal. *Hunting Eichmann*	943.086
Bennis, Phyllis. *Understanding the Palestinian-Israeli Conflict*	956.9405
Berg, Raffi. *Red Sea Spies*	327.125694
Blanford, Nicholas. *Warriors of God*	956.9204
Burkett, Elinor. *Golda*	B
Collins, Larry. *O Jerusalem!*	956
Ehrenreich, Ben. *The Way to the Spring*	956.95
Ephron, Dan. *Killing a King*	956.9405
Friedman, Thomas L. ★ *From Beirut to Jerusalem*	956.04
Gordis, Daniel. *Impossible Takes Longer*	956.94
Gordis, Daniel. *Israel*	956.9405
Grossman, David. *The Yellow Wind*	956.95
Hoffman, Bruce. *Anonymous Soldiers*	956.94
Indyk, Martin. *Master of the Game*	327.73
Kaufmann, Uri R. *Eighteen Days of October*	956.04
Khalidi, Rashid. ★ *The Hundred Years' War on Palestine*	956.9405
Kimmerling, Baruch. *The Palestinian People*	956.94
Klagsbrun, Francine. *Lioness*	B
LeBor, Adam. *City of Oranges*	956.94
Mead, Walter Russell. *The Arc of a Covenant*	327.73
Mitchell, George J. *A Path to Peace*	956.9405
Morris, Benny. *1948*	956.04
Morris, Benny. *Righteous Victims*	956
Nusseibeh, Sari. *Once Upon a Country*	B
Oren, Michael B. *Six Days of War*	956.04
Oz, Amos. *A Tale of Love and Darkness*	B
Pappe, Ilan. *The Biggest Prison on Earth*	956.9405
Sacco, Joe. *Footnotes in Gaza*	741.5
Sebag-Montefiore, Simon. *Jerusalem*	956.94
Sefarad, Mikhael. *The Wall and the Gate*	341.48
Shavit, Ari. *My Promised Land*	956.05
Shehadeh, Raja. ★ *We Could Have Been Friends, My Father and I*	B
Shehadeh, Raja. *Where the Line Is Drawn*	956.9405
Shlaim, Avi. *The Iron Wall*	956.04
Sokatch, Daniel. *Can We Talk About Israel?*	956.9405
Thrall, Nathan. ★ *A Day in the Life of Abed Salama*	956.05
Tolan, Sandy. ★ *The Lemon Tree*	B
Wright, Lawrence. *Thirteen Days in September*	956.04

HISTORY WRITING — ARCHAEOLOGY

Beard, Mary. ★ *Emperor of Rome*	937
Bound, Mensun. *The Ship Beneath the Ice*	919.8904
Brown, Nancy Marie. *The Real Valkyrie*	948
Ceram, C. W. *Gods, Graves & Scholars*	930.1
Childs, Craig. *Atlas of a Lost World*	551.7
Childs, Craig. *House of Rain*	978.9
Cline, Eric H. *After 1177 B.C.*	937
Coe, Michael D. *The Maya*	972
Darnell, John Coleman. *Egypt's Golden Couple*	932
Dolnick, Edward. *The Writing of the Gods*	493
Fox, Margalit. *The Riddle of the Labyrinth*	920
Garfinkel, Yosef. *In the Footsteps of King David*	933
Gibbins, David J. L. *A History of the World in Twelve Shipwrecks*	909
Graeber, David. *The Dawn of Everything*	901
Hughes, Bettany. *Istanbul*	949.61
Krause, Johannes. *A Short History of Humanity*	599.9
Mann, Charles C. ★ *1491*	970.01
Meals, Roy A. *Bones*	599.9
Olson, Lynne. ★ *Empress of the Nile*	B
Parker Pearson, Michael. *Stonehenge*	936.2
Pitts, Mike. *Digging for Richard III*	942.046
Preston, Douglas J. *The Lost Tomb*	930.1
Pringle, Heather Anne. *The Mummy Congress*	393
Richardson, Edmund. *The King's Shadow*	958.1
Tigay, Chanan. *The Lost Book of Moses*	098
Treister, Kenneth. *Easter Island's Silent Sentinels*	996.18
Wilkinson, Toby A. H. *A World Beneath the Sands*	932
Wragg Sykes, Rebecca. *Kindred*	569.9

HISTORY WRITING — ARTS AND CULTURE

Abrams, Jonathan P. D. ★ *The Come Up*	782.421649
Aitken-Smith, Trent. *The Tattoo Dictionary*	391.6
Bari, Shahidha K. *Dressed*	391
Barr, Luke. *Ritz & Escoffier*	920
Barron, James. *The One-Cent Magenta*	769.569
Basinger, Jeanine. *Hollywood*	791.43
Begley, Adam. *The Great Nadar*	B
Bellos, David. *The Novel of the Century*	843
Bellos, David. *Who Owns This Sentence?*	346.73
Berlo, Janet Catherine. ★ *Native North American Art*	704.03
Berry, Jason. *City of a Million Dreams*	976.3
Birkhead, Tim. *Birds and Us*	598
Boardman, John. ★ *Greek Art*	709
Brickell, Francesca Cartier. *The Cartiers*	B
Brown, Nancy Marie. *Ivory Vikings*	736
Broyles, Michael. ★ *Revolutions in American Music*	780.9
Bullock, Darryl W. *David Bowie Made Me Gay*	780
Butler, Isaac. *The Method*	792.02
Casillo, Charles. *Marilyn Monroe*	B
Charman, Isobel. *The Zoo*	590.73
Chuck D. *Chuck D Presents This Day in Rap and Hip-Hop History*	782.421649
Coffin, Judith G. *Sex, Love, and Letters*	848
Collingham, E. M. *Curry*	394.1
Cumming, Robert. *Art*	700
Cunningham, William J. ★ *Fashion Climbing*	B
Damrosch, Leopold. *The Club*	920
Dasal, Jennifer. *Artcurious*	709
Dauber, Jeremy Asher. *Jewish Comedy*	809.7
Davis, Margaret Leslie. *The Lost Gutenberg*	093
Dickerman, Leah. *Dada*	709
Doggett, Peter. *Electric Shock*	781.64
Doherty, Maggie. *The Equivalents*	920
Duncan, Dennis. *Index, a History of The*	025.3
Easterbrook, Gregg. ★ *The King of Sports*	796.332
Eilenberger, Wolfram. *Time of the Magicians*	920
English, Charlie. *The Gallery of Miracles and Madness*	709.04
Ernaux, Annie. ★ *The Years*	844
Flanders, Judith. *Christmas*	394.2663
Fletcher, Susan A. *Exploring the History of Childhood and Play Through 50 Historic Treasures*	790
Fox, Jesse David. *Comedy Book*	792.7
Garfield, Simon. *In Miniature*	745.5928
Ghez, Didier. *The Hidden Art of Disney's Golden Age*	741.5
Gioia, Ted. *Music*	780.9
Goldblatt, David. *The Games*	796.4809
Gombrich, E. H. ★ *The Story of Art*	709
Gompertz, Will. *What Are You Looking At?*	709
Goodman, Ruth. *How to Behave Badly in Elizabethan England*	942.05
Greenblatt, Stephen. *The Rise and Fall of Adam and Eve*	233
Hall, Jake. *The Art of Drag*	792.8
Hammer, Joshua. *The Bad-Ass Librarians of Timbuktu*	025.8
Harvey, Eleanor Jones. *The Civil War and American Art*	740.9
Hepworth, David. *Uncommon People*	B
Hewitt, Catherine. *Renoir's Dancer*	B
Hirsch, Foster. ★ *Hollywood and the Movies of the Fifties*	791.43
Hook, Philip. *Rogues' Gallery*	709.2

Hope, Clover. *The Motherlode*	920
Hoving, Thomas. *Art for Dummies*	709
Howard, Hugh. *Architects of an American Landscape*	712.092
Hughes, Bettany. *Venus and Aphrodite*	292
Isenberg, Nancy. *White Trash*	305.5
Isserman, Maurice. *Continental Divide*	796.52
Jacobs, Laura. ★*Celestial Bodies*	792.8
Janson, H. W. ★*Janson's History of Art*	709
Jennings, Ken. *Planet Funny*	809.7
Kapilow, Robert. ★*Listening for America*	782.42164
Kaye, Lenny. ★*Lightning Striking*	781.66
Khalili, Nasser D. *Islamic Art and Culture*	709.1
King, Charles. ★*Gods of the Upper Air*	920
Kohan, Rafi. *The Arena*	796.06
Krause, Johannes. *A Short History of Humanity*	599.9
Levy, Shawn. ★*The Castle on Sunset*	647.95
Lunenfeld, Peter. *City at the Edge of Forever*	979.4
Lynskey, Dorian. *The Ministry of Truth*	823
MacGregor, Neil. *A History of the World in 100 Objects*	930.1
Mahon, Maureen. ★*Black Diamond Queens*	782.421
Manseau, Peter. *The Apparitionists*	B
Marchant, Jo. *The Human Cosmos*	523.1
Martin, Justin. *Rebel Souls*	920
McKeen, William. *Everybody Had an Ocean*	781.6609
Meacham, Jon. *Songs of America*	782.42
Menand, Louis. *The Free World*	306.0973
Mordden, Ethan. *Anything Goes*	782.1
Nadeau, Jean-Benoit. ★*The Story of French*	440
Nevala-Lee, Alec. *Astounding*	809.3
Norwich, John Julius. *Shakespeare's Kings*	822.33
Nuttall, Jennifer Anne. ★*Mother Tongue*	422
Ogilvie, Sarah. *The Dictionary People*	423
Orlean, Susan. ★*The Library Book*	027.4
Patterson, James. *The Secret Lives of Booksellers and Librarians*	381
Patton, Sharon F. *African-American Art*	704.03
Peiffer, Prudence. *The Slip*	709.73
Perlin, Ross. ★*Language City*	306.44
Petropoulos, Jonathan. *The Faustian Bargain*	709
Pettegree, Andrew. *The Library*	027.4
Poole, W. Scott. *Vampira*	B
Powers, Ann. *Good Booty*	781.64
Questlove. ★*Hip-Hop Is History*	782.421649
Questlove. *Music Is History*	782.42164
Riedel, Michael. *Singular Sensation*	792
Rioux, Anne Boyd. *Meg, Jo, Beth, Amy*	813
Robins, Gay. *The Art of Ancient Egypt*	709
Rogers, Adam. *Full Spectrum*	152.14
Romano, Carlin. *America the Philosophical*	191
Ross, Alex. *Wagnerism*	B
Rothko, Mark. *Rothko*	759.13
Sampson, Fiona. *In Search of Mary Shelley*	B
Sato, Hiroaki. *On Haiku*	809.1
Schloss, Edith. *The Loft Generation*	700.9
Schwartzel, Erich. *Red Carpet*	791.43
Shackelford, George T. M. *Monet*	759.4
Shapiro, James. ★*The Playbook*	792
Siegel, Matt. *The Secret History of Food*	641.3
Smith, Emma. *Portable Magic*	002
Spitzer, Michael. *The Musical Human*	780.9
Stamper, Kory. *Word by Word*	413.028
Standiford, Les. ★*Battle for the Big Top*	791.3
Szerlip, Barbara. *The Man Who Designed the Future*	B
Thanhauser, Sofi. *Worn*	391
Thomson, David. *The Fatal Alliance*	791.43
Torgoff, Martin. *Bop Apocalypse*	781.65
Tregear, Mary. *Chinese Art*	709.51
Wald, Elijah. *American Epic*	781.64
Ward, Ossian. *Look Again*	750.1
Wayland-Smith, Ellen. *Oneida*	307.77
Whistler, Catherine. *Venice and Drawing, 1500-1800*	741.09
White, Dan. *Under the Stars*	796.54
Wilkman, Jon. *Screening Reality*	070.1
Wolk, Douglas. ★*All of the Marvels*	741.5
Wroe, Ann. *Orpheus*	398.2093802
Wu, Simon. *Dancing on My Own*	700.1
Wulf, Andrea. *Magnificent Rebels*	830.9
Young, Ralph F. *Dissent*	303.48

HISTORY WRITING — ASIA

Dalai Lama. *Freedom in Exile*	B
Frankopan, Peter. *The Silk Roads*	909
Hughes, Bettany. *Istanbul*	949.61
Kaplan, Robert D. *The Loom of Time*	327
Mahtani, Shibani. *Among the Braves*	951.25
Marozzi, Justin. *Tamerlane*	950.2
McLynn, Frank. *Genghis Khan*	950.2
Mishra, Pankaj. *From the Ruins of Empire*	950.4
Ollivier, Bernard. *Out of Istanbul*	B
Samatar, Sofia. *The White Mosque*	B
Weatherford, J. McIver. ★*Genghis Khan and the Making of the Modern World*	B
Weatherford, J. McIver. *Genghis Khan and the Quest for God*	323.44

HISTORY WRITING — ASIA — CHINA

Ai, Weiwei. *1000 Years of Joys and Sorrows*	709.2
Chang, Jung. *Big Sister, Little Sister, Red Sister*	B
Chang, Jung. ★*Wild Swans*	B
Demick, Barbara. *Eat the Buddha*	951
Haitiwaji, Gulbahar. *How I Survived a Chinese "Reeducation" Camp*	305.8
Izgil, Tahir Hamut. *Waiting to Be Arrested at Night*	B
Johnson, Ian. *The Souls of China*	200.951
Kaufman, Jonathan. *The Last Kings of Shanghai*	951
Li, Zhuqing. *Daughters of the Flower Fragrant Garden*	951.04
Lim, Louisa. *Indelible City*	951.25
Pan, Philip P. *Out of Mao's Shadow*	306.20951
Platt, Stephen R. *Autumn in the Heavenly Kingdom*	951
Schell, Orville. *Wealth and Power*	920
Spence, Jonathan D. *The Search for Modern China*	951
Tsu, Jing. *Kingdom of Characters*	495.111
Wood, Michael. *The Story of China*	951
Xuecun, Murong. *Deadly Quiet City*	614.5

HISTORY WRITING — ASIA — JAPAN

Alt, Matt. *Pure Invention*	306.0952
Barrett, David Dean. *140 Days to Hiroshima*	940.54
Bass, Gary Jonathan. ★*Judgment at Tokyo*	952.04
Bennett, Alexander. *Kendo*	796.86
Bix, Herbert P. *Hirohito and the Making of Modern Japan*	B
Blume, Lesley M. M. *Fallout*	940.54
Buruma, Ian. *Inventing Japan, 1853-1964*	952.03
Dower, John W. *Embracing Defeat*	952.04
Gordon, Andrew. *A Modern History of Japan*	952
Hardacre, Helen. *Shinto*	299.5
Hotta, Eri. *Japan 1941*	940.54
Iyer, Pico. *A Beginner's Guide to Japan*	952.05
Jansen, Marius. *The Making of Modern Japan*	952
Keene, Donald. *Emperor of Japan*	952.03
Lockley, Thomas. *African Samurai*	B
Man, John. *Ninja*	355.5
McClain, James. *Japan*	952.03
McManus, John C. *To the End of the Earth*	940.54
Mizuki, Shigeru. *Showa 1926-1939*	741.5
Murakami, Haruki. *Underground*	364.15
Scott, James. *Black Snow*	940.54
Sherman, Anna. *The Bells of Old Tokyo*	952
Stanley, Amy. *Stranger in the Shogun's City*	B
Wallace, Chris. *Countdown 1945*	940.54

HISTORY WRITING — ASIA — NORTH AND SOUTH KOREA

Demick, Barbara. ★*Nothing to Envy*	920
Fifield, Anna. *The Great Successor*	B
Fischer, Paul. *A Kim Jong-Il Production*	791.43
Harden, Blaine. *The Great Leader and the Fighter Pilot*	B
Ishikawa, Masaji. ★*A River in Darkness*	B
Jang, Lucia. *Stars Between the Sun and Moon*	365.45092
Jeppesen, Travis. *See You Again in Pyongyang*	951.93
Lankov, A. N. *The Real North Korea*	951.9304
Lee, Sung-Yoon. *The Sister*	951.93
Oberdorfer, Don. *The Two Koreas 3rd Ed.*	951.904
Pak, Jung H. *Becoming Kim Jong Un*	B

HISTORY WRITING — ASIA — SOUTH ASIA

Gandhi. ★*Gandhi on Non-Violence*	179.7
Mohan, Rohini. *The Seasons of Trouble*	954.9303
Richardson, Edmund. *The King's Shadow*	958.1
Subramanian, Sammanth. *This Divided Island*	954.9303

HISTORY WRITING — ASIA — SOUTH ASIA — AFGHANISTAN

Ansary, Mir Tamim. *Games Without Rules*	958.1
Badkhen, Anna. *The World Is a Carpet*	305.409581
Coll, Steve. *Directorate S*	958.104

AUTHOR, TITLE, SERIES AND SUBJECT INDEX

Coll, Steve. ★*Ghost Wars*	958.104
Dalrymple, William. *The Return of a King*	958.1
Feifer, Gregory. *The Great Gamble*	958.104
Guibert, Emmanuel. *The Photographer*	741.5
Loyn, David. *In Afghanistan*	958.1
Whitlock, Craig. *The Afghanistan Papers*	958.104

HISTORY WRITING — ASIA — SOUTH ASIA — INDIA

Anand, Anita. *The Patient Assassin*	B
Collingham, E. M. *Curry*	394.1
Dalrymple, William. ★*The Anarchy*	954.03
Dalrymple, William. *White Mughals*	954
Gandhi. *An Autobiography*	B
Gidla, Sujatha. *Ants Among Elephants*	305.5
Guha, Ramachandra. *Gandhi*	B
Guha, Ramachandra. *India After Gandhi*	954.04
Guha, Ramachandra. *Rebels Against the Raj*	954.03
Jadhav, Narendra. *Untouchables*	305.5
Keay, John. *India*	954
Khilnani, Sunil. *Incarnations*	920
Lal, Ruby. *Empress*	B
Malhotra, Aanchal. *Remnants of Partition*	954.04
Mehta, Suketu. *Maximum City*	954
Peer, Basharat. *Curfewed Night*	B
Sen, Amartya. *The Argumentative Indian*	954

HISTORY WRITING — ASIA — SOUTH ASIA — PAKISTAN

Carney, Scott. *The Vortex*	954.92
Coll, Steve. *Directorate S*	958.104
Hajari, Nisid. *Midnight's Furies*	954.04
Malhotra, Aanchal. *Remnants of Partition*	954.04

HISTORY WRITING — ASIA — SOUTHEAST ASIA

Alexander, Caroline. *Skies of Thunder*	940.54
Capozzola, Christopher. *Bound by War*	355
Duiker, William J. *Ho Chi Minh*	B
Evangelista, Patricia. ★*Some People Need Killing*	364.4
Logevall, Fredrik. *Embers of War*	959.704
Taing, Mae Bunseng. *Under the Naga Tail*	B
Thant Myint-U. *The Hidden History of Burma*	959.105
Turvey, Samuel. ★*The Tomb of the Mili Mongga*	398.24
Ung, Loung. *First They Killed My Father*	959.604
Warren, James A. *Year of the Hawk*	959.704
White, Ralph. *Getting Out of Saigon*	959.704

HISTORY WRITING — CANADA

Castner, Brian. *Stampede*	971.9
Childs, Craig. *Atlas of a Lost World*	551.7
Flores, Dan L. *Wild New World*	591.9709
Henry, John. *Great White Fleet*	387.243

HISTORY WRITING — CIVIL WARS AND GENOCIDE — AFRICA

Achebe, Chinua. *There Was a Country*	B
Beah, Ishmael. ★*A Long Way Gone*	B
Cooper, Helene. *The House at Sugar Beach*	921
Cooper, Helene. *Madame President*	966.62
Deng, Alephonsion. *They Poured Fire on Us from the Sky*	B
Dogon, Mondiant. *Those We Throw Away Are Diamonds*	B
Gourevitch, Philip. *We Wish to Inform You That Tomorrow We Will Be Killed with Our Families*	364.15
Hatzfeld, Jean. *Machete Season*	967.57104
Lamb, Christina. *House of Stone*	968.91
Rawlence, Ben. *City of Thorns*	967.7305
Reid, Stuart A. *The Lumumba Plot*	967.51
Steinberg, Jonny. *A Man of Good Hope*	B

HISTORY WRITING — COLD WAR

Ambinder, Marc. *The Brink*	355.5
Baker, Nicholson. *Baseless*	358
Brinkley, Douglas. ★*American Moonshot*	629.40973
Budiansky, Stephen. *Code Warriors*	327.73047
Carlson, Peter. *K Blows Top*	947.085
Carney, Scott. *The Vortex*	954.92
Chamberlin, Paul Thomas. *The Cold War's Killing Fields*	355.009
Coleman, David G. *The Fourteenth Day*	973.922092
Dallek, Robert. *Nixon and Kissinger*	B
Dean, Josh. *The Taking of K-129*	910.91
Donovan, Jim. ★*Shoot for the Moon*	629.45
Finn, Peter. *The Zhivago Affair*	891.73
Gordin, Michael D. *Red Cloud at Dawn*	355.02
Graff, Garrett M. *Raven Rock*	363.350973
Hastings, Max. *The Abyss*	972.9106
Hornfischer, James D. *Who Can Hold the Sea*	359.00973
Hoyer, Katja. ★*Beyond the Wall*	943.087
Kluger, Jeffrey. ★*Apollo 8*	629.45
Longo, Matthew. *The Picnic*	947.084
Macintyre, Ben. ★*Agent Sonya*	B
Macintyre, Ben. ★*The Spy and the Traitor*	B
Mann, Jim. *The Rebellion of Ronald Reagan*	973.927092
Menand, Louis. *The Free World*	306.0973
Milton, Giles. *Checkmate in Berlin*	943
Navarro, Joe. *Three Minutes to Doomsday*	B
Philipps, Roland. *A Spy Named Orphan*	B
Plokhy, Serhii. ★*Nuclear Folly*	972.9106
Rasenberger, Jim. *The Brilliant Disaster*	972.9106
Sarotte, M. E. *The Collapse*	943.087
Sebestyen, Victor. *Revolution 1989*	947.085
Service, Robert. *The End of the Cold War 1985-1991*	909.82
Sheehan, Neil. *A Fiery Peace in a Cold War*	B
Sherman, Casey. *Above and Beyond*	973.922092
Sherwin, Martin J. *Gambling with Armageddon*	972.9106
Taubman, William. *Gorbachev*	B
Taubman, William. *Khrushchev*	B
Taylor, Fred. *The Berlin Wall*	943
Thomas, Evan. *Ike's Bluff*	973.921092
Thompson, Nicholas. *The Hawk and the Dove*	973.92
Vogel, Steve. *Betrayal in Berlin*	327.1273043
Von Tunzelmann, Alex. *Blood and Sand*	909.82
Weiner, Tim. *The Folly and the Glory*	327.73047
Westad, Odd Arne. *The Cold War*	909.825
Ypi, Lea. ★*Free*	B

HISTORY WRITING — COLONIAL AMERICA — UNITED STATES

Barry, John M. *Roger Williams and the Creation of the American Soul*	974.5
Brands, H. W. *The First American*	B
Brands, H. W. ★*Our First Civil War*	973.3
Bremer, Francis J. *John Winthrop*	B
Broadwater, Jeff. ★*George Mason*	B
Bunker, Nick. ★*Making Haste from Babylon*	974.4
Bunker, Nick. *Young Benjamin Franklin*	B
Chernow, Ron. *Washington*	B
Demos, John. *The Unredeemed Captive*	973.2
Dolin, Eric Jay. *Black Flags, Blue Waters*	973.2
Ellis, Joseph J. *American Sphinx*	973.4
Ellis, Joseph J. ★*His Excellency*	B
Ellis, Joseph J. ★*Revolutionary Summer*	973.3
Eustace, Nicole. ★*Covered with Night*	364.152
Franklin, Benjamin. ★*The Autobiography of Benjamin Franklin*	B
Franklin, Benjamin. *The Compleated Autobiography*	B
Fraser, Rebecca. *The Mayflower*	974.4
Hitchens, Christopher. *Thomas Jefferson*	B
Hogeland, William. *Declaration*	973.3
Holton, Woody. *Liberty Is Sweet*	973.3
Horn, James P. P. *A Kingdom Strange*	975.6
Horn, James P. P. *Land as God Made It*	975.5
Isaacson, Walter. ★*Benjamin Franklin*	B
Jefferson, Thomas. *Writings*	973.3
Karlsen, Carol F. ★*The Devil in the Shape of a Woman*	133.4
Kelly, Joseph. *Marooned*	975.5
Kluger, Richard. *Indelible Ink*	B
Lawler, Andrew. *The Secret Token*	975.6
Lepore, Jill. *The Name of War*	973.2
Maier, Pauline. *American Scripture*	973.3
Meacham, Jon. ★*Thomas Jefferson*	B
Moore, Peter. *Life, Liberty, and the Pursuit of Happiness*	199
Murphy, Andrew R. *William Penn*	B
Norton, Mary Beth. *1774*	973.3
Pestana, Carla Gardina. *The World of Plymouth Plantation*	974.4
Philbrick, Nathaniel. ★*Bunker Hill*	973.3
Philbrick, Nathaniel. ★*Mayflower*	973.2
Pressly, Paul M. *On the Rim of the Caribbean*	975.8
Price, David A. ★*Love and Hate in Jamestown*	975.5
Rosen, Jeffrey. *The Pursuit of Happiness*	973.3
Sankovitch, Nina. *American Rebels*	920
Schiff, Stacy. *The Witches*	345
Schultz, Eric B. *King Philip's War*	973.2
Silverman, David J. ★*This Land Is Their Land*	974.4
Stewart, David O. *George Washington*	973.4
Taylor, Alan. *American Revolutions*	973.3
Unger, Harlow G. *American Tempest*	973.3
Waldstreicher, David. *The Odyssey of Phillis Wheatley*	B
Warren, James A. *God, War, and Providence*	974.5
Whittock, Martyn. *Mayflower Lives*	974.4

PUBLIC LIBRARY CORE COLLECTION: NONFICTION
Twentieth Edition

HISTORY WRITING — COLONIALISM — EUROPE
Cervantes, Fernando. *Conquistadores*	970.01
Dalrymple, William. *The Return of a King*	958.1
Elkins, Caroline. *Legacy of Violence*	909
Fowler, Corinne. ★*The Countryside*	941
French, Howard W. *Born in Blackness*	960
Kars, Marjoleine. *Blood on the River*	306.3
Kelly, Joseph. *Marooned*	975.5
Mishra, Pankaj. *Age of Anger*	909.8
Sanghera, Sathnam. *Empireworld*	909
Thomas, Hugh. *Rivers of Gold*	980
Wise, Steven M. *Though the Heavens May Fall*	342.42

HISTORY WRITING — COLONIZATION — AFRICA
Anderson, David. *Histories of the Hanged*	967.62
French, Howard W. *Born in Blackness*	960
Fuller, Alexandra. *Don't Let's Go to the Dogs Tonight*	B
Hochschild, Adam. *King Leopold's Ghost*	967.51
Huxley, Elspeth Joscelin Grant. *The Flame Trees of Thika*	B
Markham, Beryl. *West with the Night*	B
Millard, Candice. ★*River of the Gods*	916.204
Ngugi wa Thiong'o. *In the House of the Interpreter*	B
Wilkinson, Toby A. H. *A World Beneath the Sands*	932
Wise, Steven M. *Though the Heavens May Fall*	342.42

HISTORY WRITING — COMMUNISM — EUROPE — RUSSIA
Aleksievich, Svetlana. ★*Secondhand Time*	947.086
Applebaum, Anne. ★*Gulag*	365
Applebaum, Anne. *Iron Curtain*	947
Applebaum, Anne. ★*Red Famine*	947.708
Figes, Orlando. ★*The Whisperers*	306.850947
Hochschild, Adam. *The Unquiet Ghost*	947.084
Igort. *The Ukrainian and Russian Notebooks*	741.5
Kotkin, Stephen. *Stalin*	B
Kotkin, Stephen. *Stalin*	B
McMeekin, Sean. *The Russian Revolution*	947.084
Medvedev, Roy Aleksandrovich. *Let History Judge*	947.084
Petrushevskaia, Liudmila. *The Girl from the Metropol Hotel*	B
Phillips, Timothy. *Retracing the Iron Curtain*	909.82
Rees, Laurence. *Hitler and Stalin*	940.53
Remnick, David. *Lenin's Tomb*	947.085
Sebag-Montefiore, Simon. *Stalin*	B
Sebag-Montefiore, Simon. *Young Stalin*	B
Sebestyen, Victor. *Lenin*	B
Sebestyen, Victor. *Revolution 1989*	947.085
Service, Robert. *Lenin—A Biography*	B
Slezkine, Yuri. *The House of Government*	947.084
Solzhenitsyn, Aleksandr Isaevich. ★*The Gulag Archipelago 1918-1956*	365
Solzhenitsyn, Aleksandr Isaevich. ★*The Gulag Archipelago, 1918-1956*	365
Sullivan, Rosemary. *Stalin's Daughter*	B
Suny, Ronald Grigor. *Stalin*	B
Taubman, William. *Gorbachev*	B
Taubman, William. *Khrushchev*	B

HISTORY WRITING — COMMUNIST CHINA — ASIA — CHINA
Branigan, Tania. *Red Memory*	951.05
Chang, Jung. *Mao*	B
Chen, Da. *Colors of the Mountain*	951.05
Cheng, Nien. *Life and Death in Shanghai*	B
Dikotter, Frank. *China After Mao*	951.05
Dikotter, Frank. *The Cultural Revolution*	951.056
Dikotter, Frank. *Mao's Great Famine*	951.05
Hulls, Tessa. ★*Feeding Ghosts*	741.5
Kan, Karoline. *Under Red Skies*	B
Kurtz-Phelan, Daniel. *The China Mission*	951.04
Liao, Yiwu. *Bullets and Opium*	951.05
Lim, Louisa. *The People's Republic of Amnesia*	951.05
Lovell, Julia. *Maoism*	335.43
Min, Anchee. *Red Azalea*	B
Mitter, Rana. *Forgotten Ally*	951.04
Pakula, Hannah. *The Last Empress*	B
Pantsov, Alexander. *Mao*	B
Taylor, Jay. *The Generalissimo*	B
Tuchman, Barbara W. *Stilwell and the American Experience in China, 1911-45*	B
Vogel, Ezra F. *Deng Xlaoping and the Transformation of China*	B
Wong, Chun Han. *Party of One*	951.06
Xue, XInran. *The Book of Secrets*	951.05
Yang, Jisheng. *The World Turned Upside Down*	951.05
Zia, Helen. *Last Boat Out of Shanghai*	951.04

HISTORY WRITING — CONFEDERACY — UNITED STATES
Guelzo, Allen C. *Robert E. Lee*	B
Gwynne, S. C. *Rebel Yell*	B
Jones, Jacqueline. *Saving Savannah*	975.8
Wheelan, Joseph. ★*Terrible Swift Sword*	B
Williams, David. *Bitterly Divided*	973.7

HISTORY WRITING — CONSPIRACY THEORIES
Abrams, Dan. *Kennedy's Avenger*	973.922
Baker, Nicholson. *Baseless*	358
Beres, Derek. *Conspirituality*	001.9
Jacobsen, Annie. *Phenomena*	133.8
Kroll, Andy. *A Death on W Street*	364.152
Posner, Gerald L. *Case Closed*	364.1

HISTORY WRITING — EARLY 20TH CENTURY — UNITED STATES
Abrams, Dan. *Theodore Roosevelt for the Defense*	345.73
Berfield, Susan. *The Hour of Fate*	973.91
Berg, A. Scott. ★*Wilson*	B
Brands, H. W. *Woodrow Wilson*	B
Bruner, Robert F. ★*The Panic of 1907, 2nd Ed.*	330.973
Budiansky, Stephen. *Oliver Wendell Holmes*	B
Cooper, John Milton. *Woodrow Wilson*	B
Cordery, Stacy A. *Alice*	B
Creighton, Margaret S. *The Electrifying Fall of Rainbow City*	607
Gage, Beverly. *The Day Wall Street Exploded*	974.7
Goldstone, Lawrence. *Drive!*	338.4
Goodwin, Doris Kearns. ★*The Bully Pulpit*	973.91
Greenidge, Kerri. *Black Radical*	B
Guinn, Jeff. ★*War on the Border*	972.08
Haley, James L. *Captive Paradise*	996.9
Healy, Thomas. *The Great Dissent*	342.7308
Hernandez, Kelly Lytle. ★*Bad Mexicans*	972
Johnson, Steven. *The Infernal Machine*	335
Kinzer, Stephen. ★*The True Flag*	327.73
Krist, Gary. *Empire of Sin*	976.3
Lehr, Dick. ★*The Birth of a Nation*	305.800973
Mann, William J. *The Wars of the Roosevelts*	B
McCormick, Mack. *Biography of a Phantom*	782.421643
Morris, Edmund. ★*Colonel Roosevelt*	B
Morris, Edmund. ★*The Rise of Theodore Roosevelt*	B
Morris, Edmund. ★*Theodore Rex*	973.911
Neu, Charles E. *Colonel House*	B
Okrent, Daniel. *Last Call*	363.4
Oller, John. *White Shoe*	346.73
Peyser, Marc N. *Hissing Cousins*	B
Raffel, Dawn. *The Strange Case of Dr. Couney*	B
Randall, David K. *Black Death at the Golden Gate*	616.9
Renehan, Edward. *Commodore*	B
Schlesinger, Arthur M. *A Life in the Twentieth Century*	B
Sebba, Anne. *Ethel Rosenberg*	B
Tye, Larry. ★*Demagogue*	B
Von Drehle, Dave. ★*Triangle*	974.7
Watts, Steven. *The People's Tycoon*	B
White, Richard. *Who Killed Jane Stanford?*	364.152
Whyte, Kenneth. *Hoover*	B
Winchester, Simon. *A Crack in the Edge of the World*	979.4

HISTORY WRITING — EARLY 21ST CENTURY — UNITED STATES
Albright, Madeleine Korbel. *Hell and Other Destinations*	B
Baer, Daniel Brooks. *The Four Tests*	320.973
Baker, Peter. *The Divider*	973.933
Bender, Michael C. *"Frankly, We Did Win This Election"*	973.933
Boykin, Keith. *Race Against Time*	305.8
Brenner, Marie. ★*The Desperate Hours*	362.1962
Brinkley, Douglas. *The Great Deluge*	976.3
Bush, George W. *Decision Points*	B
Finkel, David. *An American Dreamer*	975.8
Hawes, Jennifer. *Grace Will Lead Us Home*	364.152
Hoffman, Liz. *Crash Landing*	330
Issenberg, Sasha. ★*The Engagement*	346.7301
Lee, Corky. ★*Corky Lee's Asian America*	770
Lehr, Dick. *White Hot Hate*	363.325
Leonnig, Carol. *I Alone Can Fix It*	973.933
Linden, Eugene. *Fire and Flood*	304.2
Lithwick, Dahlia. *Lady Justice*	345.73
Lowery, Wesley. ★*American Whitelash*	305.8
Loyn, David. *The Long War*	958.104
Mogelson, Luke. *The Storm Is Here*	973.933
Oppenheimer, Mark. *Squirrel Hill*	364.152
Reilly, Ryan J. ★*Sedition Hunters*	364.1

AUTHOR, TITLE, SERIES AND SUBJECT INDEX

Soboroff, Jacob. ★*Separated*	325.73
Steinhauer, Jennifer. *The Firsts*	320.082
Thompson, Jamie. *Standoff*	364.152
Van Agtmael, Peter. *Look at the USA*	070
Wallace, Chris. *Countdown Bin Laden*	958.104
Wise, Tim J. *Dispatches from the Race War*	305.8
Woodward, Bob. *Peril*	973.933

HISTORY WRITING — EARLY AMERICA — UNITED STATES

Adams, Abigail. *Abigail Adams*	973.4
Adams, John. *My Dearest Friend*	973.4
Allgor, Catherine. *A Perfect Union*	B
Amar, Akhil Reed. *The Words That Made Us*	342.7302
Ambrose, Stephen E. ★*Undaunted Courage*	917.804
Ayers, Edward L. *American Visions*	973.5
Baier, Bret. *To Rescue the Constitution*	973.4
Beeman, Richard R. ★*Plain, Honest Men*	342.7302
Brady, Patricia. *Martha Washington*	B
Brands, H. W. *The First American*	B
Brands, H. W. ★*Founding Partisans*	973.3
Brands, H. W. ★*Heirs of the Founders*	973.5
Broadwater, Jeff. ★*George Mason*	B
Broadwater, Jeff. *James Madison*	B
Cheney, Lynne V. *James Madison*	B
Cheney, Lynne V. *The Virginia Dynasty*	B
Chernow, Ron. ★*Alexander Hamilton*	B
Dunbar, Erica Armstrong. ★*Never Caught*	B
Ellis, Joseph J. *American Creation*	973.3
Ellis, Joseph J. ★*American Dialogue*	973.3
Ellis, Joseph J. *American Sphinx*	973.4
Ellis, Joseph J. *The Cause*	973.3
Ellis, Joseph J. *First Family*	973.4
Ellis, Joseph J. *Founding Brothers*	973.4
Ellis, Joseph J. ★*His Excellency*	B
Ellis, Joseph J. *The Quartet*	342.7302
Feldman, Noah. *The Three Lives of James Madison*	B
Flexner, James Thomas. *George Washington and the New Nation, 1783-1793*	973.4
Flexner, James Thomas. *George Washington*	B
Franklin, Benjamin. ★*The Autobiography of Benjamin Franklin*	B
Franklin, Benjamin. *The Compleated Autobiography*	B
Fried, Stephen. *Rush*	B
Good, Cassandra A. *First Family*	920
Gordon-Reed, Annette. ★*Most Blessed of the Patriarchs*	973.4
Grant, James. ★*John Adams*	B
Groom, Winston. *The Patriots*	920
Gutzman, Kevin R. C. *The Jeffersonians*	973.5
Hitchens, Christopher. *Thomas Jefferson*	B
Holton, Woody. *Abigail Adams*	B
Horn, Jonathan. *Washington's End*	973.3
Jefferson, Thomas. *Writings*	B
Kamensky, Jane. *A Revolution in Color*	759.13
Kaplan, Fred. *John Quincy Adams*	B
Kerrison, Catherine. *Jefferson's Daughters*	920
Klarman, Michael J. *The Framers' Coup*	342.7302
Larson, Edward J. *The Return of George Washington*	B
Madison, James. ★*The Constitutional Convention*	342.7302
Maier, Pauline. *Ratification*	342.7302
Masur, Kate. *Until Justice Be Done*	323.1196
Mazzeo, Tilar J. ★*Eliza Hamilton*	B
McCraw, Thomas K. ★*The Founders and Finance*	330.973
McCullough, David G. ★*John Adams*	B
McCullough, David G. *The Pioneers*	920
Meacham, Jon. ★*Thomas Jefferson*	B
Meltzer, Brad. ★*The First Conspiracy*	973.4
Meyerson, Michael. *Liberty's Blueprint*	342.7302
Paul, Joel R. ★*Without Precedent*	B
Philbrick, Nathaniel. *Travels with George*	973.4
Randall, Willard Sterne. *The Founders' Fortunes*	973.3
Randall, Willard Sterne. *George Washington*	B
Rasmussen, Daniel. *American Uprising*	976.3
Roberts, Cokie. *Founding Mothers*	920
Rosen, Jeffrey. *The Pursuit of Happiness*	973.3
Schmidt, Thomas. *The Saga of Lewis & Clark*	917.804
Sedgwick, John. *War of Two*	973.4
Simon, James F. *What Kind of Nation*	342.73
Snow, Peter. *When Britain Burned the White House*	975.3
Stark, Peter. *Astoria*	979.5
Stewart, David O. *Madison's Gift*	B
Taylor, Alan. *The Civil War of 1812*	973.5
Taylor, Alan. ★*The Internal Enemy*	975.5
Unger, Harlow G. *First Founding Father*	B
Wiencek, Henry. *Master of the Mountain*	973.4
Wills, Garry. *James Madison*	B
Wood, Gordon S. *Empire of Liberty*	973.4
Wood, Gordon S. *Friends Divided*	920

HISTORY WRITING — EARLY AUSTRALIA — AUSTRALIA

Hughes, Robert. *The Fatal Shore*	994
Keneally, Thomas. *A Commonwealth of Thieves*	994
Preston, Diana. *Paradise in Chains*	996.18

HISTORY WRITING — EARLY CANADA TO CONFEDERATION (1867) — CANADA

Fischer, David Hackett. *Champlain's Dream*	B
Tobin, Jacqueline. *From Midnight to Dawn*	973.7

HISTORY WRITING — ENLIGHTENMENT — EUROPE

Curran, Andrew S. *Diderot and the Art of Thinking Freely*	194
Gay, Peter. *The Enlightenment*	190
Gottlieb, Anthony. ★*The Dream of Enlightenment*	190
Purnell, Carolyn. *The Sensational Past*	152.109
Robertson, Ritchie. *The Enlightenment*	190
Sachs, Harvey. *The Ninth*	784.2
Sobel, Dava. *Longitude*	526
Wilson, Derek K. *A Magical World*	261.55

HISTORY WRITING — EUROPE

Alexander, Amir R. *Infinitesimal*	511
Aly, Gotz. *Europe Against the Jews*	305.892
Barzun, Jacques. *From Dawn to Decadence*	940.2
Bascomb, Neal. *Faster*	796.7209
Bjarnason, Egill. *How Iceland Changed the World*	949.12
Bown, Stephen R. *Merchant Kings*	338.8
Butterworth, Alex. *The World That Never Was*	335
Cadbury, Deborah. *Queen Victoria's Matchmaking*	941.081
Carter, Miranda. *George, Nicholas and Wilhelm*	940.3
Caruana Galizia, Paul. ★*A Death in Malta*	364.15
De Waal, Edmund. *The Hare with Amber Eyes*	B
Dugard, Martin. *Taking Berlin*	940.54
Evans, Richard J. *The Pursuit of Power*	940.2
Figes, Orlando. *The Europeans*	920
Flannery, Tim F. *Europe*	508.4
Frank, Michael. ★*One Hundred Saturdays*	B
Gabriel, Mary. *Love and Capital*	920
Gatrell, Peter. *The Unsettling of Europe*	304.8
Gertsman, Elina. *The Middle Ages in 50 Objects*	909.07
Goldstone, Nancy Bazelon. *Daughters of the Winter Queen*	920
Goldstone, Nancy Bazelon. *In the Shadow of the Empress*	920
Grayling, A. C. *The Age of Genius*	940.2
Herman, Eleanor. *The Royal Art of Poison*	364.152
Hirst, J. B. *The Shortest History of Europe*	940
Joyce, Patrick. *Remembering Peasants*	305.5
Judson, Pieter M. *The Habsburg Empire*	943.6
Judt, Tony. *Postwar*	940.55
Kershaw, Ian. *The Global Age*	940.55
Kertzer, David I. *The Pope at War*	940.53
Kertzer, David I. *The Pope Who Would Be King*	282.092
King, Greg. *The Assassination of the Archduke*	B
Lowe, Keith. *Savage Continent*	940.55
Mazower, Mark. *The Greek Revolution*	949.5
McMeekin, Sean. *July 1914*	940.3
Mullins, Edwin. *The Four Roads to Heaven*	263
Nasaw, David. *The Last Million*	940.53
Olson, Lynne. *Last Hope Island*	940.53
Price, Neil S. ★*Children of Ash and Elm*	948
Rady, Martyn C. *The Middle Kingdoms*	943
Reston, James. *The Last Apocalypse*	940.1
Schama, Simon. *The Embarrassment of Riches*	949.2
Schwarz, Geraldine. *Those Who Forget*	940.53
Sebestyen, Victor. *Budapest*	943.912
Shorto, Russell. *Amsterdam*	949.2
Shuster, Simon. ★*The Showman*	B
Siegal, Nina. *The Diary Keepers*	940.54
Smyth, Adam. *The Book-Makers*	686.2
Snyder, Laura J. *Eye of the Beholder*	920
Snyder, Timothy. *The Red Prince*	B
Spoto, Donald. *High Society*	B
Szczeszak-Brewer, Agata. *The Hunger Book*	B
Tallis, Frank. ★*Mortal Secrets*	B
Wilson, Peter H. *Heart of Europe*	943

PUBLIC LIBRARY CORE COLLECTION: NONFICTION
Twentieth Edition

Winder, Simon. *Lotharingia*	944

HISTORY WRITING — EUROPE — EASTERN EUROPE

Aleksievich, Svetlana. ★*Secondhand Time*	947.086
Applebaum, Anne. *Iron Curtain*	947
Askwith, Richard. *Unbreakable*	B
Beevor, Antony. *Russia*	947.084
Bogosian, Eric. *Operation Nemesis*	956.62
Eisen, Norman L. *The Last Palace*	920
Golinkin, Lev. *A Backpack, a Bear, and Eight Crates of Vodka*	B
Gorbachev, Mikhail. *On My Country and the World*	947.085
Harding, Luke. *Invasion*	947.7
Igort. *The Ukrainian and Russian Notebooks*	741.5
Karski, Jan. *Story of a Secret State*	940.53
Kassabova, Kapka. *Border*	949.9
King, Charles. *Odessa*	947.7
King, Greg. *Twilight of Empire*	943.6
Kraus, Dita. *A Delayed Life*	B
Krimstein, Ken. *When I Grow Up*	741.5
Mazower, Mark. *The Balkans*	949.6
Mazower, Mark. *Salonica, City of Ghosts*	949.5
McNamara, Kevin J. *Dreams of a Great Small Nation*	355.009437
Michener, James A. *The Bridge at Andau*	943.9
Mikanowski, Jacob. ★*Goodbye, Eastern Europe*	947
Miller, Christopher. *The War Came to Us*	947.7
Norwich, John Julius. *Byzantium*	949.5
Norwich, John Julius. *Byzantium*	949.5
Plokhy, Serhii. ★*The Gates of Europe*	947.7
Seierstad, Asne. *Angel of Grozny*	947.086
Stern, Jessica. *My War Criminal*	341.6
Trebincevic, Kenan. *The Bosnia List*	B
Trofimov, Yaroslav. ★*Our Enemies Will Vanish*	947.7
Ypi, Lea. ★*Free*	B

HISTORY WRITING — EUROPE — FRANCE

Barnes, Julian. *The Man in the Red Coat*	B
Begley, Adam. *The Great Nadar*	B
Broers, Michael. *Napoleon*	944.05
Castor, Helen. *Joan of Arc*	B
Darnton, Robert. *The Revolutionary Temper*	944
De Courcy, Anne. *Chanel's Riviera*	944.9
De Waal, Edmund. *The Hare with Amber Eyes*	B
DeJean, Joan E. *The Essence of Style*	391
DeJean, Joan E. *How Paris Became Paris*	944
Dugard, Martin. *Taking Paris*	940.54
Duncan, Michael. ★*Hero of Two Worlds*	B
Ernaux, Annie. ★*The Years*	B
Evans, Martin. *Algeria*	965
Fraser, Antonia. *Love and Louis XIV*	B
Fraser, Antonia. *Marie Antoinette*	B
Goldstone, Nancy Bazelon. *The Rival Queens*	944
Henaut, Stephane. *A Bite-Sized History of France*	394.1
Horne, Alistair. *Seven Ages of Paris*	944
Jackson, Julian. *De Gaulle*	B
Lever, Evelyne. *Marie Antoinette*	B
Mansel, Philip. *King of the World*	B
McCullough, David G. *The Greater Journey*	920
McPhee, Peter. *Robespierre*	B
Moorehead, Caroline. *A Train in Winter*	940.53
Moorehead, Caroline. *Village of Secrets*	944
Norwich, John Julius. *A History of France*	944
Paxson, Margaret. *The Plateau*	362.87
Poirier, Agnes. *Left Bank*	944
Popkin, Jeremy D. *A New World Begins*	944.04
Rappaport, Helen. *After the Romanovs*	944
Reiss, Tom. *The Black Count*	B
Robb, Graham. *The Discovery of France*	944
Robb, Graham. *France*	944
Robb, Graham. *Parisians*	944
Sciolino, Elaine. *The Seine*	944
Weir, Alison. *Eleanor of Aquitaine*	B
Williams, Kate. *Ambition and Desire*	B
Zamoyski, Adam. *Napoleon*	B

HISTORY WRITING — EUROPE — GERMANY

Allert, Tilman. *Heil Hitler*	395.4
Blanning, T. C. W. *Frederick the Great*	B
Crasnianski, Tania. *The Children of Nazis*	943.086
Dumbach, Annette E. *Sophie Scholl and the White Rose*	943.086
Eisner, Peter. *The Pope's Last Crusade*	282.092
English, Charlie. *The Gallery of Miracles and Madness*	709.04
Evans, Richard J. *The Coming of the Third Reich*	943.08
Evans, Richard J. *The Third Reich at War*	940.53
Evans, Richard J. *The Third Reich in Power, 1933-1939*	943.086
Feigel, Lara. *The Bitter Taste of Victory*	320.943
Friedlander, Saul. *Nazi Germany and the Jews*	940.53
Fritzsche, Peter. *Life and Death in the Third Reich*	943.086
Gerwarth, Robert. *Hitler's Hangman*	B
Gortemaker, Heike B. *Eva Braun*	B
Harding, Thomas. *The House by the Lake*	943
Harrington, Joel F. *The Faithful Executioner*	B
Hett, Benjamin Carter. *The Death of Democracy*	943.085
Hitler, Adolf. *Mein Kampf*	B
Hoyer, Katja. ★*Beyond the Wall*	943.087
Hoyer, Katja. *Blood and Iron*	943.08
Jahner, Harald. ★*Aftermath*	943.087
Kershaw, Ian. *Hitler*	B
Kershaw, Ian. *Hitler*	B
King, David. *The Trial of Adolf Hitler*	345.43
Kushner, Jacob. *Look Away*	305.9
Larson, Erik. *In the Garden of Beasts*	B
Longerich, Peter. *Hitler*	B
MacGregor, Neil. *Germany*	943
MacLean, Rory. *Berlin*	943.155
Mazower, Mark. *Hitler's Empire*	940.53
McDonough, Frank. *The Hitler Years*	943.086
McKay, Sinclair. *Berlin*	943
Merriman, Helena. ★*Tunnel 29*	943
Milton, Giles. *Checkmate in Berlin*	943
Moorhouse, Roger. *Berlin at War*	943
Mulley, Clare. *The Women Who Flew for Hitler*	920
Oelhafen, Ingrid von. *Hitler's Stolen Children*	B
Ohler, Norman. *The Bohemians*	940.53
Rees, Laurence. *Hitler and Stalin*	940.53
Ronald, Susan. *Hitler's Aristocrats*	940.53
Roth, Joseph. *What I Saw*	943
Ryback, Timothy W. *Hitler's Private Library*	027
Ryback, Timothy W. *Takeover*	943.086
Safranski, Rudiger. *Goethe*	B
Sarotte, M. E. *The Collapse*	943.087
Shirer, William L. ★*The Rise and Fall of the Third Reich*	943.086
Smith, Helmut Walser. *Germany, a Nation in Its Time*	943
Sperber, Jonathan. *Karl Marx*	B
Spicer, Charles. *Coffee with Hitler*	941.084
Steinberg, Jonathan. *Bismarck*	B
Taylor, Fred. *The Berlin Wall*	943
Trentmann, Frank. *Out of the Darkness*	943.08
Ullrich, Volker. ★*Eight Days in May*	943.086
Ullrich, Volker. *Germany 1923*	943.085
Ullrich, Volker. *Hitler*	B
Ullrich, Volker. *Hitler*	B
Watson, Peter. *The German Genius*	943
Weale, Adrian. *Army of Evil*	940.54
Weber, Thomas. *Becoming Hitler*	B
Wheen, Francis. *Karl Marx*	B
Willner, Nina. *Forty Autumns*	B
Wilson, Derek. *Out of the Storm*	B

HISTORY WRITING — EUROPE — IRELAND

Banville, John. *Time Pieces*	914.1
Gibney, John. *A Short History of Ireland, 1500-2000*	941.7
Kavanagh, Julie. *The Irish Assassins*	941.5
Kelly, John. *The Graves Are Walking*	941.5081
O'Toole, Fintan. ★*We Don't Know Ourselves*	941.7
Puleo, Stephen. *Voyage of Mercy*	363.8
Wills, Clair. ★*Missing Persons*	929.2

HISTORY WRITING — EUROPE — ITALY

Addis, Ferdinand. *The Eternal City*	945.6
Bailey, Catherine. *A Castle in Wartime*	943.086
Berendt, John. *The City of Falling Angels*	945
Bradford, Sarah. *Lucrezia Borgia*	B
Crowley, Roger. *City of Fortune*	945
Duggan, Christopher. *The Force of Destiny*	945
Hales, Dianne R. *Mona Lisa*	B
Hibbert, Christopher. *The Borgias and Their Enemies*	920
Hibbert, Christopher. *The House of Medici*	920
Hooper, John. *The Italians*	945.093
Hughes, Robert. *Rome*	945.6
Kertzer, David I. *The Pope and Mussolini*	322
King, Ross. *Bookseller of Florence*	381

AUTHOR, TITLE, SERIES AND SUBJECT INDEX

King, Ross. *Brunelleschi's Dome*	726.6
Madden, Thomas F. *Venice*	945
McGregor, James H. *Rome from the Ground up*	711
Meyer, G. J. *The Borgias*	920
Moorehead, Caroline. *A House in the Mountains*	940.53
Norwich, John Julius. *A History of Venice*	945
Norwich, John Julius. *Sicily*	945.8
Raffa, Guy P. *Dante's Bones*	851
Strathern, Paul. *The Borgias*	945.06
Strathern, Paul. *The Florentines*	945
Strathern, Paul. *The Medici*	945.5
Unger, Miles. ★*Michelangelo*	B
Wickham, Chris. *The Inheritance of Rome*	940.1

HISTORY WRITING — EUROPE — RUSSIA

Alekhina, Marija. *Riot Days*	B
Amis, Martin. *Koba the Dread*	947.084
Beevor, Antony. *Russia*	947.084
Erickson, Carolly. *Great Catherine*	B
Figes, Orlando. ★*The Story of Russia*	947
Finn, Peter. *The Zhivago Affair*	891.73
Fuhrmann, Joseph T. *Rasputin*	B
Galeotti, Mark. *A Short History of Russia*	947.086
Garrels, Anne. *Putin Country*	947
Gessen, Masha. *The Future Is History*	947.086
Gessen, Masha. *Never Remember*	365
Hill, Fiona. *There Is Nothing for You Here*	327.2
Kasparov, Gary. *Winter Is Coming*	947.086
Khlevniuk, Oleg V. *Stalin*	B
Khodorkovsky, Mikhail. *The Russia Conundrum*	947.086
MacGregor, Iain. *The Lighthouse of Stalingrad*	940.54
Massie, Robert K. *Catherine the Great*	B
Massie, Robert K. *Nicholas and Alexandra*	B
Massie, Robert K. *The Romanovs*	947
McMeekin, Sean. *Stalin's War*	940.53
Miles, Jonathan. *St. Petersburg*	947
Myers, Steven Lee. *The New Tsar*	B
Pipes, Richard. *The Russian Revolution*	947.084
Plokhy, Serhii. *Lost Kingdom*	947
Politkovskaya, Anna. *A Russian Diary*	947.086
Popoff, Alexandra. *Vasily Grossman and the Soviet Century*	B
Radzinskii, Edvard. *Stalin*	947.084
Rappaport, Helen. *After the Romanovs*	944
Rappaport, Helen. *Caught in the Revolution*	355.00947
Rappaport, Helen. *The Race to Save the Romanovs*	947.08
Rappaport, Helen. *The Romanov Sisters*	920
Riasanovsky, Nicholas V. *A History of Russia*	947
Satter, David. *The Less You Know, the Better You Sleep*	947.086
Sebag-Montefiore, Simon. *The Romanovs*	947
Short, Philip. *Putin*	B
Smith, Douglas. *Rasputin*	B
Smith, Douglas. *The Russian Job*	947.084
Walker, Stephen. *Beyond*	629.45
Yaffa, Joshua. *Between Two Fires*	920
Zygar, Mikhail. *All the Kremlin's Men*	947.086
Zygar, Mikhail. *The Empire Must Die*	947.08

HISTORY WRITING — EUROPE — SPAIN

Cercas, Javier. *Lord of All the Dead*	868
Downey, Kirstin. *Isabella*	B
Hochschild, Adam. *Spain in Our Hearts*	946.081
Hughes, Robert. *Barcelona*	946
Kurlansky, Mark. *The Basque History of the World*	946
Perez, Joseph. ★*The Spanish Inquisition*	272
Preston, Paul. *A People Betrayed*	946
Preston, Paul. *The Spanish Holocaust*	946.081
Resendez, Andres. *Conquering the Pacific*	959.9
Thomas, Hugh. *Rivers of Gold*	980
Tremlett, Giles. *Ghosts of Spain*	946.08
Van Hensbergen, Gijs. *The Sagrada Familia*	726.5

HISTORY WRITING — EUROPE — UNITED KINGDOM

Ackroyd, Peter. *Foundation*	942
Ackroyd, Peter. *Innovation*	942.082
Ackroyd, Peter. *London*	942.1
Ackroyd, Peter. *Rebellion*	941.06
Ackroyd, Peter. *Revolution*	941.07
Ackroyd, Peter. *Tudors*	942.05
Allport, Alan. *Britain at Bay*	940.53
Asbridge, Thomas S. *The Greatest Knight*	942.03
Baird, Julia. ★*Victoria the Queen*	B
Blair, Tony. *A Journey*	B
Bordo, Susan. *The Creation of Anne Boleyn*	942.05
Borman, Tracy. *Anne Boleyn and Elizabeth I*	920
Borman, Tracy. *Crown & Sceptre*	941
Borman, Tracy. *Elizabeth's Women*	B
Borman, Tracy. *Henry VIII and the Men Who Made Him*	942.05
Borman, Tracy. *The Private Lives of the Tudors*	920
Borman, Tracy. *Thomas Cromwell*	B
Bostridge, Mark. *Florence Nightingale*	B
Bouverie, Tim. *Appeasement*	327.41043
Brown, Tina. ★*The Palace Papers*	920
Bryson, Bill. *Shakespeare*	B
Cadbury, Deborah. *Princes at War*	920
Cadbury, Deborah. *Queen Victoria's Matchmaking*	941.081
Cadbury, Deborah. *The School That Escaped from the Nazis*	940.53
Castor, Helen. *She-Wolves*	942
Charles-Edwards, T. M. *Wales and the Britons, 350-1064*	942.901
Charman, Isobel. *The Zoo*	590.73
Charter, David. *Royal Audience*	941.085
Churchill, Winston. *Their Finest Hour*	940.53
Dalrymple, William. ★*The Anarchy*	954.03
Dalrymple, William. *The Return of a King*	958.1
Damrosch, Leopold. *The Club*	920
De Courcy, Anne. *The Husband Hunters*	920
Edwards, Anne. *Matriarch*	B
Flanders, Judith. *The Victorian City*	942.1
Foreman, Amanda. *Georgiana, Duchess of Devonshire*	B
Fowler, Corinne. ★*The Countryside*	941
Fraser, Antonia. *Faith and Treason*	942.06
Fraser, Antonia. *Mary, Queen of Scots*	B
Fraser, Antonia. ★*The Wives of Henry VIII*	942.05
Gill, Gillian. *We Two*	941.081
Glenconner, Anne. ★*Lady in Waiting*	B
Glendinning, Victoria. *Leonard Woolf*	B
Goodman, Ruth. *How to Be a Tudor*	942.05
Goodman, Ruth. *How to Be a Victorian*	941.08
Goodman, Ruth. *How to Behave Badly in Elizabethan England*	942.05
Greenblatt, Stephen. ★*Will in the World*	B
Gristwood, Sarah. *Blood Sisters*	942.04092
Gristwood, Sarah. *The Tudors in Love*	941.05
Guy, John. *Hunting the Falcon*	B
Gwynne, S. C. *His Majesty's Airship*	363.12
Hadlow, Janice. *A Royal Experiment*	B
Hardman, Robert. *Queen of Our Times*	B
Harris, Ellen T. *George Frideric Handel*	B
Hawksley, Lucinda. *Queen Victoria's Mysterious Daughter*	B
Healey, Jonathan. *The Blazing World*	941.06
Herman, Arthur. *How the Scots Invented the Modern World*	941.1
Hibbert, Christopher. *Edward VII*	B
Higgins, Charlotte. *Under Another Sky*	936
Hochschild, Adam. *Bury the Chains*	326
Holland, James. *Brothers in Arms*	940.54
Holway, Tatiana M. *The Flower of Empire*	727
Hunt, Tristram. *Marx's General*	335.4092
Johnson, Paul. *Churchill*	B
Johnson, Steven. *The Ghost Map*	614.5
Jones, Dan. ★*The Wars of the Roses*	942.04
Jones, Michael K. *The Black Prince*	B
Kaufmann, Miranda. *Black Tudors*	941
Kelly, John. *The Graves Are Walking*	941.5081
Knight, Sam. *The Premonitions Bureau*	133.8
Koch, Bea. *Mad and Bad*	920
Lacey, Robert. *Great Tales from English History 1*	941
Lacey, Robert. *Great Tales from English History 2*	941
Lacey, Robert. *Great Tales from English History 3*	941
Larman, Alexander. *The Windsors at War*	940.53
Lovell, Mary S. *Bess of Hardwick*	B
Lovell, Mary S. *The Sisters*	920.72
Lownie, Andrew. *Traitor King*	B
MacColl, Gail. *To Marry an English Lord*	974.7
MacCulloch, Diarmaid. *Thomas Cromwell*	B
Maiklem, Lara. *Mudlark*	B
Manchester, William. *The Last Lion, Winston Spencer Churchill.*	B
Manchester, William. *The Last Lion, Winston Spencer Churchill.*	B
Manchester, William. *The Last Lion, Winston Spencer Churchill.*	B
McCarten, Anthony. *Darkest Hour*	941.084
Meacham, Jon. *Franklin and Winston*	940.53
Meyer, G. J. *The Tudors*	920

PUBLIC LIBRARY CORE COLLECTION: NONFICTION
Twentieth Edition

Moore, Charles. *Margaret Thatcher*	941.085
Moore, Peter. *Life, Liberty, and the Pursuit of Happiness*	199
Moore, Wendy. *No Man's Land*	940.4
Morris, Ian. *Geography Is Destiny*	941
Morris, Marc. ★*The Anglo-Saxons*	942.01
Morris, Marc. *A Great and Terrible King*	B
Morris, Marc. *The Norman Conquest*	942.02
Morrison, Robert. *The Regency Years*	941.07
Mortimer, Ian. *The Time Traveler's Guide to Elizabethan England*	942.05
Mortimer, Ian. *The Time Traveler's Guide to Restoration Britain*	941.06
Morton, Andrew. *17 Carnations*	941.084
Morton, Andrew. *Wallis in Love*	B
Murphy, Russell R. *William Penn*	B
Nicolson, Juliet. *The Great Silence*	941.083
O'Sullivan, Emer. *The Fall of the House of Wilde*	B
Ogilvie, Sarah. *The Dictionary People*	423
Olson, Lynne. *Troublesome Young Men*	941.084
Parker Pearson, Michael. *Stonehenge*	936.2
Parkin, Simon. *The Island of Extraordinary Captives*	940.53
Penn, Thomas. *The Brothers York*	942.04
Phillips, Adrian. *Fighting Churchill, Appeasing Hitler*	327.41043
Porter, Linda. *Katherine the Queen*	B
Pryor, Francis. ★*Stonehenge*	936.2
Ridley, Jane. *George V*	B
Ridley, Jane. *The Heir Apparent*	B
Robb, Graham. *The Debatable Land*	941.3
Robb, John. *Punk Rock*	781.6609
Roberts, Andrew. *The Last King of America*	B
Ronald, Susan. *The Pirate Queen*	B
Rounding, Virginia. *The Burning Time*	272
Rubenhold, Hallie. ★*The Five*	362.88
Russell, Gareth. ★*The Palace*	942.1
Russell, Gareth. *Young and Damned and Fair*	B
Sanghera, Sathnam. ★*Empireland*	941
Sanghera, Sathnam. *Empireworld*	909
Satia, Priya. *Empire of Guns*	330.941
Schama, Simon. *A History of Britain; 2*	941
Shapiro, James. *The Year of Lear*	822.33
Shawcross, William. *The Queen Mother*	B
Sisman, Adam. *The Professor and the Parson*	364.16
Smith, Emma. *This Is Shakespeare*	822.33
Smith, Sally Bedell. *George VI and Elizabeth*	920
Smith, Sally Bedell. *Prince Charles*	B
Sobel, Dava. *Longitude*	526
Spicer, Charles. *Coffee with Hitler*	941.084
Starkey, David. *Six Wives*	942.05
Tallis, Nicola. *Uncrowned Queen*	B
Tombs, Robert. *The English and Their History*	942
Weintraub, Stanley. *Iron Tears*	973.3
Weir, Alison. *The Children of Henry VIII*	B
Weir, Alison. *The Lady in the Tower*	B
Weir, Alison. *The Life of Elizabeth I*	B
Weir, Alison. *The Lost Tudor Princess*	B
Weir, Alison. *Mary, Queen of Scots, and the Murder of Lord Darnley*	941.105
Weir, Alison. *Queens of the Age of Chivalry*	920
Weir, Alison. *Queens of the Conquest*	920
Weir, Alison. *The Six Wives of Henry VIII*	942.05
Wilson, A. N. *Victoria*	B
Winkler, Elizabeth. *Shakespeare Was a Woman & Other Heresies*	822.33
Woolley, Benjamin. *The King's Assassin*	B
Worsley, Lucy. *Queen Victoria*	B

HISTORY WRITING — EUROPE — UNITED KINGDOM — NORTHERN IRELAND

Carroll, Rory. *There Will Be Fire*	363.325
Keefe, Patrick Radden. ★*Say Nothing*	364.152

HISTORY WRITING — EXPLORATION

Adams, Simon. *Journey*	910.9
Alexander, Caroline. *The Endurance*	919.8
Bellows, Amanda Brickell. *The Explorers*	910.92
Bergreen, Laurence. *In Search of a Kingdom*	B
Bergreen, Laurence. *Marco Polo*	B
Bergreen, Laurence. *Over the Edge of the World*	B
Bound, Mensun. *The Ship Beneath the Ice*	919.8904
Brandt, Anthony. *The Man Who Ate His Boots*	910.91
Castner, Brian. *Stampede*	971.9
Cervantes, Fernando. *Conquistadores*	970.01
Cliff, Nigel. *Holy War*	909
Dana, Richard Henry. *Two Years Before the Mast*	910.4
Dodds Pennock, Caroline. ★*On Savage Shores*	970.004
Ellsworth, Scott. *The World Beneath Their Feet*	796.522
Fernandez-Armesto, Felipe. ★*Amerigo*	B
Fischer, David Hackett. *Champlain's Dream*	B
Graham, Ian. *Fifty Ships That Changed the Course of History*	387.2
Hansen, Valerie. *The Year 1000*	909
Heaney, Christopher. *Cradle of Gold*	B
Horwitz, Tony. ★*A Voyage Long and Strange*	970.01
Jeal, Tim. *Explorers of the Nile*	920
Larson, Edward J. *An Empire of Ice*	919.8
Levy, Buddy. *Labyrinth of Ice*	910.91
Lister, Adrian. *Darwin's Fossils*	576.8
Lowe, George. *Letters from Everest*	796.522
Millard, Candice. ★*River of the Gods*	916.204
Niven, Jennifer. *Ada Blackjack*	B
Preston, Diana. *The Evolution of Charles Darwin*	508
Preston, Diana. *Paradise in Chains*	996.18
Preston, Douglas J. *The Lost Tomb*	930.1
Resendez, Andres. *Conquering the Pacific*	959.9
Roberts, David. *Alone on the Ice*	919.8904
Sancton, Julian. *Madhouse at the End of the Earth*	919.8904
Severin, Timothy. *In Search of Robinson Crusoe*	996.1
Sides, Hampton. ★*The Wide Wide Sea*	910.92
Stark, Peter. *Astoria*	979.5
Turney, Chris. *1912*	998
Turvey, Samuel. ★*The Tomb of the Mili Mongga*	398.24
Watson, Paul. *Ice Ghosts*	917
Wilkinson, Toby A. H. *A World Beneath the Sands*	932
Wilson-Lee, Edward. ★*The Catalogue of Shipwrecked Books*	B
Winchester, Simon. *The Men Who United the States*	973
Wood, Gillen D'Arcy. *Land of Wondrous Cold*	919.89
Zanglein, Jayne E. *The Girl Explorers*	B

HISTORY WRITING — GENERAL

Arendt, Hannah. *The Origins of Totalitarianism*	320.53
Armstrong, Karen. ★*The Great Transformation*	200.9
Armstrong, Karen. *The Lost Art of Scripture*	208
Armstrong, Karen. ★*A Short History of Myth*	201
Aslan, Reza. *God*	211
Atwood, Margaret. *Burning Questions*	814
Aykroyd, Peter. *A History of Ghosts*	133.1
Baez, Fernando. *Universal History of the Destruction of Books*	098
Bittman, Mark. *Animal, Vegetable, Junk*	394.1
Brookshire, Bethany. *Pests*	590
Buell, Hal. *Moments*	070.4
Cassidy, Cody. *How to Survive History*	904
Coles, Robert. *Lives of Moral Leadership*	170
Crystal, David. ★*The Stories of English*	427
Desilva, Jeremy. *First Steps*	599.93
Deutscher, Guy. ★*Through the Language Glass*	410
Diamond, Jared M. *Collapse*	304.2
Diamond, Jared M. *Guns, Germs, and Steel*	303.4
Diamond, Jared M. *Upheaval*	303.48
Dickinson, Richard. *Weeds of North America*	632
Durant, Will. ★*The Story of Philosophy*	190
Edwards, Lydia. *How to Read a Dress*	391
Everett, Daniel Leonard. *How Language Began*	401
Fasulo, Linda M. *An Insider's Guide to the Un, 4th Ed.*	341.23
Francis. *Life*	B
Frankopan, Peter. *The Earth Transformed*	304.2
Gaddis, John Lewis. *On Grand Strategy*	355.4
Gibson, Marion. *Witchcraft*	133.4
Gosden, Chris. *Magic*	133.4
Graeber, David. *The Dawn of Everything*	901
Grant, R. G. *World War I*	940.3
Grayling, A. C. *The History of Philosophy*	109
Harari, Yuval N. ★*Sapiens*	909
Harris, M. A. *The Black Book*	920
Hayes, Bill. *Sweat*	613.7
Herman, Arthur. *1917*	940.3
Herman, Arthur. *The Viking Heart*	948
Holmes, Richard. *The Age of Wonder*	509
Howard, Jennifer. *Clutter*	306.3
Jobb, Dean. *The Case of the Murderous Dr. Cream*	364.152
Johnson, Steven. *Wonderland*	790.1
Kennedy, Paul M. *The Rise and Fall of the Great Powers*	909.82
Kennedy, Robert F. *Thirteen Days*	327.73
Kitagawa, Kate. *The Secret Lives of Numbers*	510.9
Laing, Olivia. *Everybody*	323

AUTHOR, TITLE, SERIES AND SUBJECT INDEX

Langlands, Alex. *Craeft*	306.4
Lieven, Dominic. *In the Shadow of the Gods*	352.23
Linklater, Andro. *Owning the Earth*	333.3
Mac Sweeney, Naoise. *The West*	909
MacGregor, Neil. *A History of the World in 100 Objects*	930.1
Minois, Georges. *The Atheist's Bible*	200
Moran, Joe. *Shrinking Violets*	155.2
Morton, Lisa. *Trick or Treat*	394.2646
Mumford, Lewis. *The City in History*	307.76
Norwich, John Julius. *Byzantium*	949.5
Ostertag, Bob. *People's Movements, People's Press*	071
Ostler, Nicholas. *Ad Infinitum*	470
Philbrick, Nathaniel. *Why Read Moby-Dick?*	813
Pipes, Richard. *Communism*	335.43
Raab, Nathan. *The Hunt for History*	790.1
Radke, Heather. *Butts*	611
Ridley, Matt. *The Rational Optimist*	339.2
Roeder, Oliver. *Seven Games*	794
Rohde, David. *Endgame*	949.703
Rose, Michael. *The Birth of an Opera*	782.1
Rosner, Elizabeth. *Survivor Cafe*	940.53
Runciman, David. *The Confidence Trap*	321.8
Savage, Jon. ★*1966*	781.6609
Schor, Esther H. *Bridge of Words*	499
Schulman, Michael. ★*Oscar Wars*	791.43
Sebag-Montefiore, Simon. ★*The World*	929.7
Solomon, Steven. *Water*	553.7
Standage, Tom. *An Edible History of Humanity*	394.1
Stiglitz, Joseph E. *Globalization and Its Discontents*	337
Stott, Rebecca. ★*Darwin's Ghosts*	576.8
Summerscale, Kate. *The Book of Phobias and Manias*	616.85
Swarns, Rachel L. ★*American Tapestry*	B
Tuchman, Barbara W. *March of Folly*	909.08
Tuchman, Barbara W. *The Proud Tower*	909.82
Weill, Kelly. *Off the Edge*	001.9
Weinberg, Steven. *To Explain the World*	509
Whitby, Andrew. *The Sum of the People*	001.4
Winchester, Simon. *Knowing What We Know*	306.4
Winchester, Simon. *Pacific*	909
Winchester, Simon. *The Professor and the Madman*	423

HISTORY WRITING — GILDED AGE — UNITED STATES

Boorstin, Daniel J. *The Americans*	973
Brinkley, Douglas. *The Wilderness Warrior*	B
Bunting, Josiah. *Ulysses S. Grant*	B
Freeberg, Ernest. *A Traitor to His Species*	B
Hiltzik, Michael A. *Iron Empires*	385.0973
Howard, Hugh. *Architects of an American Landscape*	712.092
Jacoby, Karl. *The Strange Career of William Ellis*	B
Khan, Yasmin Sabina. *Enlightening the World*	974.7
Kiernan, Denise. *The Last Castle*	975.6
Larson, Erik. ★*The Devil in the White City*	364.15
Manseau, Peter. *The Apparitionists*	B
Merry, Robert W. *President McKinley*	B
Miller, Donald L. *City of the Century*	977.311
Miller, Scott. *The President and the Assassin*	973.8
Morris, James McGrath. *Pulitzer*	B
Nasaw, David. *The Chief*	B
Norgren, Jill. *Belva Lockwood*	B
Oller, John. *American Queen*	B
Sohn, Amy. *The Man Who Hated Women*	363.28
Todd, Kim. *Sensational*	920
Ward, Geoffrey C. *A Disposition to Be Rich*	B

HISTORY WRITING — GREAT DEPRESSION — UNITED STATES

Agee, James. ★*Cotton Tenants*	976.1
Ahamed, Liaquat. *Lords of Finance*	920
Burns, Cherie. *The Great Hurricane—1938*	974.7
Collins, Max Allan. *Eliot Ness and the Mad Butcher*	364.152
Egan, Timothy. *The Worst Hard Time*	978
Galbraith, John Kenneth. ★*The Great Crash, 1929*	338.5
Golay, Michael. *America 1933*	B
Gup, Ted. *A Secret Gift*	977.1
Katznelson, Ira. *Fear Itself*	973.917
Kennedy, David M. ★*Freedom from Fear*	973.91
Perino, Michael A. *The Hellhound of Wall Street*	330.973
Quinn, Susan. *Eleanor and Hick*	B
Rappleye, Charles. *Herbert Hoover in the White House*	B
Schwartz, A. Brad. ★*Broadcast Hysteria*	791.44
Shlaes, Amity. *The Forgotten Man*	973.91
Simon, James F. *FDR and Chief Justice Hughes*	973.917092
Stout, David. *The Kidnap Years*	364.15
Taylor, Nick. *American Made*	331.13
Terkel, Studs. ★*Hard Times*	973.91

HISTORY WRITING — HISTORICAL MYSTERIES

Brier, Bob. *The Murder of Tutankhamen*	B
Dolnick, Edward. *The Writing of the Gods*	493
Grann, David. *The Lost City of Z*	918.1
Grann, David. ★*The Wager*	910.91
Horn, James P. P. *A Kingdom Strange*	975.6
Lawler, Andrew. *The Secret Token*	975.6
Maples, William R. *Dead Men Do Tell Tales*	614
Massie, Robert K. *The Romanovs*	947
Nicholl, Charles. *The Reckoning*	B
Rappaport, Helen. *The Romanov Sisters*	920
Smith, Richard MacLean. *Unexplained*	130
Watson, Paul. *Ice Ghosts*	917
Weir, Alison. *Mary, Queen of Scots, and the Murder of Lord Darnley*	941.105

HISTORY WRITING — IMMIGRATION — UNITED STATES

Anbinder, Tyler. ★*City of Dreams*	974.7
Cannato, Vincent. *American Passage*	325.73
Chang, Gordon H. *Ghosts of Gold Mountain*	331.6
Eire, Carlos M. N. *Learning to Die in Miami*	B
Henderson, Bruce B. *Bridge to the Sun*	940.53
Holzer, Harold. *Brought Forth on This Continent*	973.7
Jacobsen, Annie. ★*Operation Paperclip*	940.54
Kingston, Maxine Hong. *The Woman Warrior*	B
Lee, Erika. *America for Americans*	305.800973
Lee, Erika. *The Making of Asian America*	973
Lovato, Roberto. *Unforgetting*	B
McCourt, Malachy. *Singing My Him Song*	B
Minian, Ana Raquel. ★*In the Shadow of Liberty*	365
Nayeri, Dina. ★*The Ungrateful Refugee*	362.87
Ng, Fae Myenne. *Orphan Bachelors*	B
Okrent, Daniel. *The Guarded Gate*	344.73
Pawel, Miriam. *The Crusades of Cesar Chavez*	B
Pham, Andrew X. ★*The Eaves of Heaven*	B
Pipher, Mary Bray. *The Middle of Everywhere*	305.9
St. John, Warren. *Outcasts United*	B
Suarez, Ray. ★*We Are Home*	325.73
Ung, Loung. *Lucky Child*	B
Urrea, Luis Alberto. *The Devil's Highway*	304.8
Yang, Jia Lynn. ★*One Mighty and Irresistible Tide*	325.73

HISTORY WRITING — IMPERIAL CHINA — ASIA — CHINA

Chang, Jung. *Empress Dowager Cixi*	B
Platt, Stephen R. *Imperial Twilight*	951
Spence, Jonathan D. *God's Chinese Son*	951

HISTORY WRITING — INDIGENOUS PEOPLES — CANADA

Dodds Pennock, Caroline. ★*On Savage Shores*	970.004
Erdrich, Louise. *Books and Islands in Ojibwe Country*	977
McDiarmid, Jessica. *Highway of Tears*	364.152
Sacco, Joe. ★*Paying the Land*	741.5
Sasakamoose, Fred. *Call Me Indian*	B
Wagamese, Richard. *One Native Life*	B

HISTORY WRITING — INDIGENOUS PEOPLES — LATIN AMERICA

Bingham, Hiram. ★*Lost City of the Incas*	985
Cervantes, Fernando. *Conquistadores*	970.01
Dodds Pennock, Caroline. ★*On Savage Shores*	970.004
Heaney, Christopher. *Cradle of Gold*	B
Mann, Charles C. ★*1491*	970.01
Preston, Douglas J. ★*The Lost City of the Monkey God*	972.85
Reel, Monte. *The Last of the Tribe*	981
Restall, Matthew. *When Montezuma Met Cortes*	972
Townsend, Richard F. *The Aztecs*	972

HISTORY WRITING — INDIGENOUS PEOPLES — UNITED STATES

Akins, Damon B. ★*We Are the Land*	978
Berg, Scott W. ★*38 Nooses*	973.7
Black Elk. *Black Elk Speaks*	B
Blackhawk, Ned. ★*The Rediscovery of America*	973.04
Brands, H. W. *The Last Campaign*	973.8
Brooks, James. *Mesa of Sorrows*	979.1004
Brown, Dee. ★*Bury My Heart at Wounded Knee*	978
Bruchac, Joseph. *Our Stories Remember*	973.04
Bunnell, David. *Good Friday on the Rez*	B
Burns, Mike. *The Only One Living to Tell*	305.897
Calloway, Colin G. *One Vast Winter Count*	978
Childs, Craig. *House of Rain*	978.9
Cozzens, Peter. *A Brutal Reckoning*	973.5

PUBLIC LIBRARY CORE COLLECTION: NONFICTION
Twentieth Edition

Cozzens, Peter. *The Earth Is Weeping*	978
Cozzens, Peter. *Tecumseh and the Prophet*	920
Crutchfield, James A. *Revolt at Taos*	972
Dodds Pennock, Caroline. ★*On Savage Shores*	970.004
Drury, Bob. *The Heart of Everything That Is*	B
Dunbar-Ortiz, Roxanne. ★*An Indigenous Peoples' History of the United States*	970.004
DuVal, Kathleen. ★*Native Nations*	970.004
Eckert, Allan W. *A Sorrow in Our Heart*	B
Egan, Timothy. ★*Short Nights of the Shadow Catcher*	770.92
Enss, Chris. *Mochi's War*	B
Erdrich, Louise. *Books and Islands in Ojibwe Country*	977
Estes, Nick. *Our History Is the Future*	978.004
Eustace, Nicole. ★*Covered with Night*	364.152
Gardner, Mark L. *The Earth Is All That Lasts*	978.004
Gayle, Caleb. *We Refuse to Forget*	975.004
Grann, David. ★*Killers of the Flower Moon*	976.6004
Hamalainen, Pekka. ★*Indigenous Continent*	970.004
Hendricks, Steve. *The Unquiet Grave*	323.1197
Hensley, William L. Iggiagruk. *Fifty Miles from Tomorrow*	B
Hutton, Paul Andrew. *The Apache Wars*	979
Hyde, Anne Farrar. ★*Born of Lakes and Plains*	978
Inskeep, Steve. *Jacksonland*	973.56
Iverson, Peter. *Dine*	979.1004
Jackson, Joe. *Black Elk*	978.004
LaPointe, Sasha taqwseblu. *Red Paint*	B
LaPointe, Sasha taqwseblu. *Thunder Song*	814
Lepore, Jill. *The Name of War*	973.2
Mays, Kyle. ★*An Afro-Indigenous History of the United States*	973
McDonnell, Michael. *Masters of Empire*	977.4
McLoughlin, William Gerald. *After the Trail of Tears*	973
McMurtry, Larry. *Crazy Horse*	B
Miranda, Deborah A. *Bad Indians*	305.8009794
Mort, T. A. *Thieves' Road*	978.3
Myers, Leah. *Thinning Blood*	B
Nelson, Megan Kate. *The Three-Cornered War*	978
Nesteroff, Kliph. *We Had a Little Real Estate Problem*	970.004
Pasternak, Judy. *Yellow Dirt*	979.1004
Philbrick, Nathaniel. ★*The Last Stand*	973.8
Powers, Thomas. *The Killing of Crazy Horse*	B
Price, David A. ★*Love and Hate in Jamestown*	975.5
Saunt, Claudio. *Unworthy Republic*	323.1197
Schultz, Eric B. *King Philip's War*	973.2
Sedgwick, John. *Blood Moon*	975.004
Sharfstein, Daniel J. ★*Thunder in the Mountains*	979.5
Sides, Hampton. *Blood and Thunder*	978
Silverman, David J. ★*This Land Is Their Land*	974.4
Snyder, Christina. *Great Crossings*	976.9
Taylor, Alan. *The Divided Ground*	974.7
Trask, Kerry A. *Black Hawk*	973.5
Treuer, Anton. *Everything You Wanted to Know About Indians but Were Afraid to Ask*	970.1
Treuer, David. ★*The Heartbeat of Wounded Knee*	970.004
Utley, Robert M. ★*Geronimo*	B
Utley, Robert M. *Sitting Bull*	B
Warren, James A. *God, War, and Providence*	974.5

HISTORY WRITING — JEWISH HISTORY

Aly, Gotz. *Europe Against the Jews*	305.892
Ashton, Dianne. *Hanukkah in America*	296.4
Batalion, Judith. *The Light of Days*	940.53
Berg, Raffi. *Red Sea Spies*	327.125694
Chernow, Ron. *The Warburgs*	B
Dauber, Jeremy Asher. *Jewish Comedy*	809.7
Debreczeni, Jozsef. *Cold Crematorium*	940.53
Frank, Michael. ★*One Hundred Saturdays*	B
Frankel, Rebecca. *Into the Forest*	940.53
Freedland, Jonathan. ★*The Escape Artist*	940.53
Frenkel, Francoise. *A Bookshop in Berlin*	B
Garrett, Leah. *X Troop*	940.54
Glinert, Lewis. *The Story of Hebrew*	492.4
Henderson, Bruce B. *Sons and Soldiers*	940.53
Hoffman, Adina. *Sacred Trash*	296.09
Horn, Dara. ★*People Love Dead Jews*	909
Iperen, Roxane van. ★*The Sisters of Auschwitz*	940.53
Kirsch, Adam. *The Blessing and the Curse*	809
Kirsch, Adam. ★*The People and the Books*	809
Krimstein, Ken. *When I Grow Up*	741.5
Kritzler, Ed. *Jewish Pirates of the Caribbean*	972.9
Lehman, David. *A Fine Romance*	781.64
Lichtblau, Eric. *Return to the Reich*	B
Macadam, Heather Dune. *999*	940.53
Marton, Kati. *The Great Escape*	920
Megdal, Howard. *The Baseball Talmud*	796.357
Neumann, Ariana. *When Time Stopped*	B
Oppenheimer, Mark. *Squirrel Hill*	364.152
Rosenzweig, Laura B. *Hollywood's Spies*	791.43
Rynecki, Elizabeth. *Chasing Portraits*	B
Sabar, Ariel. *My Father's Paradise*	B
Sarna, Jonathan D. ★*American Judaism*	296
Schama, Simon. ★*The Story of the Jews; Volume One*	909
Schama, Simon. ★*The Story of the Jews; Volume Two*	909
Stone, Dan. ★*The Holocaust*	940.53
Sullivan, Rosemary. *The Betrayal of Anne Frank*	940.53
Van De Perre, Selma. *My Name Is Selma*	940.53
White, Elizabeth B. ★*The Counterfeit Countess*	940.53
Wiesel, Elie. *And the Sea Is Never Full*	B

HISTORY WRITING — JUDICIAL BRANCH — UNITED STATES

Anderson, Carol. ★*One Person, No Vote*	324.6
Biskupic, Joan. ★*Nine Black Robes*	347.73
Breyer, Stephen G. *Making Our Democracy Work*	347.73
Budiansky, Stephen. *Oliver Wendell Holmes*	B
Canellos, Peter S. *The Great Dissenter*	B
Chemerinsky, Erwin. *Presumed Guilty*	344.7305
Cohen, Adam. ★*Imbeciles*	344.7304
Cohen, Adam. ★*Supreme Inequality*	347.73
De Hart, Jane Sherron. ★*Ruth Bader Ginsburg*	B
Driver, Justin. *The Schoolhouse Gate*	344.73
Farrell, John A. *Clarence Darrow*	B
Friedman, Barry. *The Will of the People*	347.73
Gibson, Larry S. *Young Thurgood*	B
Goldstone, Lawrence. *On Account of Race*	342.7308
Graetz, Michael J. *The Burger Court and the Rise of the Judicial Right*	347.73
Greenhouse, Linda. *Becoming Justice Blackmun*	B
Haygood, Wil. *Showdown*	B
Healy, Thomas. *The Great Dissent*	342.7308
Hirshman, Linda R. *Sisters in Law*	347.73
Kaplan, David A. *The Most Dangerous Branch*	347.73
Lane, Charles. *The Day Freedom Died*	976.3
Lewis, Anthony. *Gideon's Trumpet*	345.73
Luxenberg, Steve. ★*Separate*	342.7308
Nourse, Victoria F. *In Reckless Hands*	344.7304
Robin, Corey. *The Enigma of Clarence Thomas*	347.73
Rosenberg, Ian. *The Fight for Free Speech*	342.73
Shesol, Jeff. *Supreme Power*	347.73
Simon, James F. *FDR and Chief Justice Hughes*	973.917092
Smith, Jean Edward. *John Marshall*	B
Stevens, John Paul. *The Making of a Justice*	B
Thomas, Evan. ★*First*	B
Urofsky, Melvin I. *Dissent and the Supreme Court*	342.7302
Urofsky, Melvin I. *Louis D. Brandeis*	B
Waldman, Michael. *The Supermajority*	347.73

HISTORY WRITING — LATIN AMERICA

Arana, Marie. *Bolivar*	B
Bell, Madison Smartt. *Toussaint Louverture*	B
Carlsen, William. *Jungle of Stone*	B
Chasteen, John Charles. *Americanos*	980
Chasteen, John Charles. *Born in Blood and Fire*	980
Fuentes, Carlos. *The Buried Mirror*	946
Grann, David. *The Lost City of Z*	918.1
Guevara, Che. *Diary of a Combatant*	972.91063
Kars, Marjoleine. *Blood on the River*	306.3
Martinez Wood, Jamie. *Latino Writers and Journalists*	B
McConahay, Mary Jo. *The Tango War*	940.53
McCullough, David G. *The Path Between the Seas*	972.87
Ortiz, Paul. *An African American and Latinx History of the United States*	305.8
Otfinoski, Steven. *Latinos in the Arts*	700.89
Parker, Matthew. *Panama Fever*	972.87
Pressly, Paul M. *On the Rim of the Caribbean*	975.8
Sedgewick, Augustine. *Coffeeland*	338.4
Skidmore, Thomas E. *Brazil*	981
Stuart, Andrea. *Sugar in the Blood*	338.1
Thomas, Hugh. *Rivers of Gold*	980
Thomson, Keith. *Born to Be Hanged*	910.4
Vargas Llosa, Mario. *Sabers and Utopias*	980.03

AUTHOR, TITLE, SERIES AND SUBJECT INDEX

HISTORY WRITING — LATIN AMERICA — CUBA
- Castro, Fidel. *Fidel Castro* — B
- Coleman, David G. *The Fourteenth Day* — 973.922092
- Coltman, Leycester. *The Real Fidel Castro* — B
- Craig, William. *Yankee Come Home* — 972.9107
- DePalma, Anthony. *The Cubans* — 920
- Ferrer, Ada. ★*Cuba* — 972.91
- Guillermoprieto, Alma. *Dancing with Cuba* — 972.9106
- Hastings, Max. *The Abyss* — 972.9106
- Hoffman, David E. *Give Me Liberty* — B
- Kurlansky, Mark. *Havana* — 972.91
- Rathbone, John Paul. *The Sugar King of Havana* — B
- Sallah, Michael. *The Yankee Comandante* — 972.91

HISTORY WRITING — LATIN AMERICA — MEXICO
- Ahmed, Azam. *Fear Is Just a Word* — 364.152
- Coe, Michael D. *The Maya* — 972
- Corcoran, Katherine. *In the Mouth of the Wolf* — 364.152
- Denton, Sally. *The Colony* — 364.152
- Diaz del Castillo, Bernal. *The Discovery and Conquest of Mexico, 1517-1521* — 972
- Flores, Dan L. *Wild New World* — 591.9709
- Garcia, Angela. ★*The Way That Leads Among the Lost* — 362.29
- Guinn, Jeff. ★*War on the Border* — 972.08
- Hernandez, Kelly Lytle. ★*Bad Mexicans* — 972
- Restall, Matthew. *When Montezuma Met Cortes* — 972
- Womack, John. *Zapata and the Mexican Revolution* — B

HISTORY WRITING — LATIN AMERICA — SOUTH AMERICA
- Bingham, Hiram. ★*Lost City of the Incas* — 985
- Millard, Candice. *River of Doubt* — 918.1
- Rojas Contreras, Ingrid. ★*The Man Who Could Move Clouds* — B

HISTORY WRITING — LGBTQIA+
- Bronski, Michael. *A Queer History of the United States* — 306.76
- Bullock, Darryl W. *David Bowie Made Me Gay* — 780
- Carter, David. *Stonewall* — 306.76
- Cenziper, Debbie. ★*Love Wins* — 346.7301
- Cervini, Eric. *The Deviant's War* — B
- Fieseler, Robert W. *Tinderbox* — 364.152
- France, David. *How to Survive a Plague* — 362.196
- Funk, Mason. *The Book of Pride* — 920
- Goodman, Elyssa. *Glitter and Concrete* — 792.7
- Hall, Jake. *The Art of Drag* — 792.8
- Hester, Diarmuid. *Nothing Ever Just Disappears* — 306.76
- Issenberg, Sasha. ★*The Engagement* — 346.7301
- Olsen, Craig. *P.S. Burn This Letter Please* — 306.76
- Possanza, Amelia. *Lesbian Love Story* — B
- Seligman, Craig. *Who Does That Bitch Think She Is?* — 792.02
- Shaw, Julia. *Bi* — 306.76
- Windsor, Edie. *A Wild and Precious Life* — B

HISTORY WRITING — MAORI — NEW ZEALAND
- Thompson, Christina. *Sea People* — 305.8994

HISTORY WRITING — MEDIEVAL — EUROPE
- Barker, Juliet R. V. *Agincourt* — 944
- Borman, Tracy. *Thomas Cromwell* — B
- Brown, Nancy Marie. *The Abacus and the Cross* — B
- Brown, Nancy Marie. *Ivory Vikings* — 736
- Brown, Nancy Marie. *The Real Valkyrie* — 948
- Brownworth, Lars. *Lost to the West* — 949.5
- Cahill, Thomas. *How the Irish Saved Civilization* — 941.501
- Cantor, Norman F. *In the Wake of the Plague* — 614.5
- Castor, Helen. *Joan of Arc* — B
- Charles-Edwards, T. M. *Wales and the Britons, 350-1064* — 942.901
- De Hamel, Christopher. ★*Meetings with Remarkable Manuscripts* — 091
- Dell, Christopher. *The Occult, Witchcraft & Magic* — 130
- Gies, Frances. *Life in a Medieval Village* — 306
- Gies, Joseph. *Life in a Medieval Castle* — 940.1
- Gristwood, Sarah. *Blood Sisters* — 942.04092
- Herrin, Judith. *Byzantium* — 949.5
- Jager, Eric. *Blood Royal* — 944.026
- Jones, Dan. *Crusaders* — 909.07
- Jones, Dan. ★*The Plantagenets* — 942.03092
- Jones, Dan. *The Templars* — 271
- Jones, Michael K. *The Black Prince* — B
- Kelly, John. *The Great Mortality* — 614.5
- Larrington, Carolyne. *The Norse Myths* — 293
- Manchester, William. *A World Lit Only by Fire* — 940.2
- Morris, Marc. ★*The Anglo-Saxons* — 942.01
- Morris, Marc. *Castles* — 728.81
- Morris, Marc. *King John* — 942.033
- Morris, Marc. *The Norman Conquest* — 942.02
- Norwich, John Julius. *Shakespeare's Kings* — 822.33
- Norwich, John Julius. *A Short History of Byzantium* — 949.5
- Puhak, Shelley. *The Dark Queens* — 944
- Ramirez, Janina. *Femina* — 940.1
- Tuchman, Barbara W. ★*A Distant Mirror* — 944
- Weir, Alison. *Eleanor of Aquitaine* — B
- Weir, Alison. *Queens of the Age of Chivalry* — 920
- Weir, Alison. *Queens of the Conquest* — 920
- Weir, Alison. *The Wars of the Roses* — 942.04
- Winroth, Anders. *The Age of the Vikings* — 948

HISTORY WRITING — MICROHISTORY
- Albert, Daniel M. *Are We There Yet?* — 303.48
- Almond, Steve. ★*Candyfreak* — 338.4
- Armstrong, Karen. *Fields of Blood* — 201
- Baker, James W. *Thanksgiving* — 394.2649
- Basbanes, Nicholas A. *On Paper* — 676
- Becker, Ernest. ★*The Denial of Death* — 128
- Beckert, Sven. *Empire of Cotton* — 338.4
- Boccaletti, Giulio. *Water* — 909
- Boot, Max. *Invisible Armies* — 355.02
- Boyle, Rebecca. *Our Moon* — 523.3
- Brady, Amy. *Ice* — 553.7
- Brenner, Joel Glenn. *The Emperors of Chocolate* — 338.7
- Bryson, Bill. ★*At Home* — 643
- Castleman, Michael. *The Untold Story of Books* — 381
- Chamberlin, Silas. *On the Trail* — 796.510973
- Conway, Edmund. *Material World* — 333.7
- Doyle, Martin. *The Source* — 333.91
- Ekirch, A. Roger. ★*At Day's Close* — 306.4
- Ellis, Richard. *Tuna* — 333.95
- Fagan, Brian M. *Fishing* — 338.3
- Farmer, Jared. *Elderflora* — 582.16
- Ferrara, Silvia. *The Greatest Invention* — 411
- Flanders, Judith. *Christmas* — 394.2663
- Forbes, Bruce David. *Christmas* — 394.2663
- Freeman, Joshua Benjamin. ★*Behemoth* — 338.6
- Garfield, Simon. ★*All the Knowledge in the World* — 030.9
- Garfield, Simon. *In Miniature* — 745.5928
- Garfield, Simon. *On the Map* — 526.09
- Gerber, Robin. *Barbie and Ruth* — B
- Gleick, Peter H. *The Three Ages of Water* — 333.91
- Goldstein, Jacob. *Money* — 332.4
- Hample, Zack. *The Baseball* — 796.357
- Hanson, Thor. *Feathers* — 598.147
- Hazard, Leah. *Womb* — 612.6
- Hazrat, Florence. *An Admirable Point* — 411
- Hecht, Jennifer Michael. *Doubt* — 121
- Hitchings, Henry. *The Language Wars* — 420.9
- Houston, Keith. *The Book* — 002.09
- Houston, Keith. *Shady Characters* — 411
- Inglis, Lucy. *Milk of Paradise* — 362.29
- Judah, Hettie. *Lapidarium* — 553.8
- Kurlansky, Mark. *The Basque History of the World* — 946
- Kurlansky, Mark. *Cod* — 333.95
- Kurlansky, Mark. *Paper* — 676
- Kurlansky, Mark. *Salt* — 553.6
- Laar, Arnold van de. *Under the Knife* — 617
- Laing, Olivia. *The Garden Against Time* — 635
- Lieberman, Jeffrey A. *Shrinks* — 616.89
- Mazzeo, Tilar J. *The Secret of Chanel No. 5* — 338.7
- McHangama, Jacob. ★*Free Speech* — 323.44
- Means, Howard B. ★*Splash!* — 797.2
- Mendelson, Cheryl. ★*Vows* — 203
- Murdoch, Stephen. *IQ* — 153.9
- Nadeau, Jean-Benoit. *The Story of Spanish* — 460
- Pettegree, Andrew. *The Library* — 027.4
- Pollan, Michael. ★*This Is Your Mind on Plants* — 581.6
- Prasad, Aarathi. *Silk* — 677
- Puchner, Martin. *The Written World* — 809
- Rogers, Adam. *Full Spectrum* — 152.14
- Rosen, Jody. *Two Wheels Good* — 629.227
- Rosen, Michael. *Alphabetical* — 421
- Rutkow, Ira M. *Empire of the Scalpel* — 617
- Schutt, Bill. *Cannibalism* — 394
- Solnit, Rebecca. *Wanderlust* — 796.51
- Spitzer, Michael. *The Musical Human* — 780.9
- Stamper, Kory. *Word by Word* — 413.028

PUBLIC LIBRARY CORE COLLECTION: NONFICTION
Twentieth Edition

Standage, Tom. *A History of the World in 6 Glasses*	394.1
Stark, Lizzie. ★*Egg*	641.3
Thomson, David. *The Big Screen*	791.430973
Tucker, Abigail. *The Lion in the Living Room*	636.8
Vorobyov, Niko. *Dopeworld*	364.1
Walvin, James. *Sugar*	338.17361
White, Dan. *Under the Stars*	796.54
Winchester, Simon. *Atlantic*	551.46
Winchester, Simon. *The Map That Changed the World*	B
Yergin, Daniel. ★*The Prize*	338.2
Yergin, Daniel. *The Quest*	333.79
Young, Kevin. *Bunk*	177
Zoellner, Tom. *Train*	385.09

HISTORY WRITING — MILITARY

Alexander, Caroline. *Skies of Thunder*	940.54
Ash, Stephen V. *Firebrand of Liberty*	973.7
Atkinson, Rick. ★*The British Are Coming*	973.3
Bacevich, Andrew J. *America's War for the Greater Middle East*	956.05
Barrett, David Dean. *140 Days to Hiroshima*	940.54
Bass, Gary Jonathan. ★*Judgment at Tokyo*	952.04
Caddick-Adams, Peter. *Sand and Steel*	940.54
Capozzola, Christopher. *Bound by War*	355
Clarke, Thurston. *Honorable Exit*	959.704
Dickson, Paul. *The Rise of the G.I. Army 1940-1941*	940.54
France, John. *Perilous Glory*	355
Frank, Richard B. *Tower of Skulls*	940.54
Glatthaar, Joseph T. *The American Military*	355.00973
Graff, Garrett M. *Raven Rock*	363.350973
Hampton, Dan. *Operation Vengeance*	940.54
Hastings, Max. *Warriors*	355
Henderson, Bruce B. *Bridge to the Sun*	940.53
Hogeland, William. *Autumn of the Black Snake*	970.004
Holland, James. ★*Burma '44*	940.54
Holland, James. *The Savage Storm*	940.53
Horwitz, Josh. *War of the Whales*	333.95
Kershaw, Alex. *The First Wave*	940.54
Kindsvatter, Peter S. *American Soldiers*	355
McElya, Micki. *The Politics of Mourning*	975.5
McKay, Sinclair. *The Fire and the Darkness*	940.54
McManus, John C. *Island Infernos*	940.54
McManus, John C. *To the End of the Earth*	940.54
Milton, Giles. *Soldier, Sailor, Frogman, Spy, Airman, Gangster, Kill or Die*	940.54
Nolan, Cathal J. *The Allure of Battle*	355.409
Petraeus, David Howell. *Conflict*	355
Raines, Howell. *Silent Cavalry*	973.7
Ricks, Thomas E. ★*The Generals*	B
Scharre, Paul. *Four Battlegrounds*	006.3
Simms, Brendan. *The Silver Waterfall*	940.54
Strauss, Barry S. ★*The War That Made the Roman Empire*	937
Wheelan, Joseph. *Midnight in the Pacific*	940.54
Wukovits, John F. *Lost at Sea*	940.54

HISTORY WRITING — MILITARY — AVIATION HISTORY

Ambrose, Stephen E. *The Wild Blue*	940.54
Bruning, John R. *Indestructible*	B
Bruning, John R. *The Race of Aces*	940.54
Gladwell, Malcolm. ★*The Bomber Mafia*	940.54
Groom, Winston. *The Aviators*	920
Gwynne, S. C. *His Majesty's Airship*	363.12
Hamilton-Paterson, James. *Marked for Death*	358.400941
Hampton, Dan. *Chasing the Demon*	629.132
Hastings, Max. *Operation Chastise*	940.54
Holland, James. *Big Week*	940.54
Maurer, Kevin. *Damn Lucky*	940.54
O'Brien, Keith. *Fly Girls*	920
Scott, James. *Black Snow*	940.54
Snyder, Steve. *Shot Down*	940.54
Teitel, Amy Shira. *Fighting for Space*	920

HISTORY WRITING — MILITARY — MILITARY LEADERSHIP

Blount, Roy. *Robert E. Lee*	B
Broers, Michael. *Napoleon*	B
Broers, Michael. *Napoleon*	B
Bunting, Josiah. ★*The Making of a Leader*	B
Clark, Lloyd. *The Commanders*	940.53
Drury, Bob. *Valley Forge*	973.3
Ellis, Joseph J. ★*His Excellency*	B
Ferling, John E. *Winning Independence*	973.3
Freeman, Douglas Southall. *Lee*	B
Groom, Winston. *The Generals*	920
Guelzo, Allen C. *Robert E. Lee*	B
Hanson, Victor Davis. *The Soul of Battle*	355
Hunt, Patrick. *Hannibal*	B
Johnson, Paul. *George Washington*	B
Johnson, Paul. *Napoleon*	B
Korda, Michael. *Clouds of Glory*	B
McLynn, Frank. *Genghis Khan*	950.2
McRaven, William H. *Sea Stories*	B
Morison, Samuel Eliot. *John Paul Jones*	B
Patton, George S. *War as I Knew It*	B
Perry, Mark. *The Most Dangerous Man in America*	B
Randall, Willard Sterne. *George Washington*	B
Roberts, Andrew. *Leadership in War*	920
Roberts, Andrew. ★*Napoleon*	B
Robertson, James I. *Stonewall Jackson*	B
Stiles, T. J. *Custer's Trials*	B
Thomas, Evan. ★*John Paul Jones*	B
Unger, Debi. *George Marshall*	B
Wert, Jeffry D. *Cavalryman of the Lost Cause*	B
Wert, Jeffry D. *Custer*	B
Zambone, Albert Louis. *Daniel Morgan*	B

HISTORY WRITING — MILITARY — MILITARY TODAY

Ackerman, Elliot. *Places and Names*	B
Finkel, David. *The Good Soldiers*	956.7044
Finkel, David. *Thank You for Your Service*	920
Hennessey, Patrick. *The Junior Officers' Reading Club*	B
Johnson, Akemi. *Night in the American Village*	305.40952
Klay, Phil. *Uncertain Ground*	359.9
Patterson, James. *Walk in My Combat Boots*	920
Poole, Robert M. *Section 60*	975.5
Roach, Mary. ★*Grunt*	355

HISTORY WRITING — MILITARY — MILITARY UNITS

Ambrose, Stephen E. *The Wild Blue*	940.54
Brown, Daniel James. ★*Facing the Mountain*	940.54
Clavin, Tom. *The Last Hill*	940.54
Cotton, Tom. *Sacred Duty*	355.6
Emery, Theo. *Hellfire Boys*	358
Gallego, Ruben. *They Called Us*	956.7044
Hogan, William R. *Task Force Hogan*	940.54
Holland, James. *Brothers in Arms*	940.54
Kershaw, Alex. *Against All Odds*	940.54
Kesling, Ben. *Bravo Company*	958.104
O'Donnell, Patrick K. *The Indispensables*	973.3
Sears, Stephen W. *Lincoln's Lieutenants*	920
Stanton, Doug. *The Odyssey of Echo Company*	959.704
Tuccille, Jerome. *The Roughest Riders*	973.8

HISTORY WRITING — MILITARY — NAVAL HISTORY

Alexander, Caroline. *The Bounty*	996.1
Budiansky, Stephen. *Blackett's War*	940.54
Crowley, Roger. *City of Fortune*	945
Fabey, Michael. *Heavy Metal*	338.4
Geroux, William. *The Ghost Ships of Archangel*	940.54
Hastings, Max. *Operation Pedestal*	940.54
Hornfischer, James D. *Who Can Hold the Sea*	359.00973
Humphreys, Richard. *Under Pressure*	B
Kilmeade, Brian. ★*Thomas Jefferson and the Tripoli Pirates*	973.4
Lance, Rachel. *In the Waves*	973.7
Morison, Samuel Eliot. *John Paul Jones*	B
Parkin, Simon. *A Game of Birds and Wolves*	940.54
Parrish, Thomas D. *The Submarine*	359.9
Stavridis, James. *To Risk It All*	359
Sullivan, James. *Unsinkable*	940.54
Symonds, Craig L. *World War II at Sea*	940.54
Taylor, Stephen. *Commander*	B
Thomas, Evan. ★*John Paul Jones*	B
Toll, Ian W. *The Conquering Tide*	940.54
Toll, Ian W. *Pacific Crucible*	940.54
Toll, Ian W. ★*Six Frigates*	359.00973
Toll, Ian W. *Twilight of the Gods*	940.54
Vincent, Lynn. *Indianapolis*	940.54
Whitlock, Craig. ★*Fat Leonard*	364.16

HISTORY WRITING — MILITARY — SPECIAL FORCES

Berg, Raffi. *Red Sea Spies*	327.125694
Bowden, Mark. *Black Hawk Down*	967.7305
Couch, Dick. *The Warrior Elite*	359.9
Denver, Rorke. *Worth Dying For*	359.9
Frederick, Jim. *Black Hearts*	956.7044

AUTHOR, TITLE, SERIES AND SUBJECT INDEX

Golembesky, Michael. *Level Zero Heroes*	958.104
Henderson, Bruce B. *Sons and Soldiers*	940.53
Lance, Rachel. *Chamber Divers*	940.54
Lemmon, Gayle Tzemach. *Ashley's War*	B
Lemmon, Gayle Tzemach. *The Daughters of Kobani*	956.9104
Luttrell, Marcus. *Lone Survivor*	958.104
Macintyre, Ben. ★*Rogue Heroes*	940.54
Mills, Dan. *Sniper One*	956.7044
O'Donnell, Patrick K. *The Unvanquished*	973.7
O'Neill, Robert. *The Operator*	B
Owen, Mark. *No Hero*	B
Philipps, David. *Alpha*	956.7044
Stanton, Doug. *12 Strong*	958.104
Talty, Stephan. *Saving Bravo*	959.704
Wallace, Chris. *Countdown Bin Laden*	958.104

HISTORY WRITING — MILITARY — WEAPONS

Boot, Max. ★*War Made New*	355.0209
Cotterell, Arthur. *Chariot*	357
Emery, Theo. *Hellfire Boys*	358
Gordin, Michael D. *Red Cloud at Dawn*	355.02
Guillemin, Jeanne. *Biological Weapons*	358
Kaplan, Fred M. *The Bomb*	355.8
Kean, Sam. *The Bastard Brigade*	355.8
Langewiesche, William. *The Atomic Bazaar*	355.02
Lloyd, Nick. *The Western Front*	940.4
McWhirter, Cameron. *American Gun*	683.4
Plokhy, Serhii. ★*Nuclear Folly*	972.9106
Schlosser, Eric. *Command and Control*	363.17
Sheehan, Neil. *A Fiery Peace in a Cold War*	B
Sherwin, Martin J. *Gambling with Armageddon*	972.9106
Tucker, Jonathan B. *War of Nerves*	358
Tyson, Neil deGrasse. *Accessory to War*	355.001

HISTORY WRITING — NATIONALISM — SOUTHWEST ASIA AND NORTH AFRICA (MIDDLE EAST)

Abrahamian, Ervand. *The Coup*	955.05
Anderson, Scott. *Lawrence in Arabia*	B
Azad. *Long Shot*	B
Bacevich, Andrew J. *America's War for the Greater Middle East*	956.05
Barr, James. *A Line in the Sand*	956
Bowden, Mark. *Guests of the Ayatollah*	955.05
Coll, Steve. *The Bin Ladens*	920
Cooper, Andrew Scott. *The Fall of Heaven*	B
Dagher, Sam. *Assad or We Burn the Country*	956.9104
Di Giovanni, Janine. *The Morning They Came for Us*	956.9104
Fisk, Robert. *The Great War for Civilisation*	956.04
Ghattas, Kim. *Black Wave*	955.05
Hubbard, Ben (Journalist). *Mbs*	B
King, Charles. *Midnight at the Pera Palace*	949.61
Kinzer, Stephen. ★*All the Shah's Men*	955.05
Lacey, Robert. *Inside the Kingdom*	953.805
Nafisi, Azar. ★*Reading Lolita in Tehran*	B
Nasr, Seyyed Vali Reza. *The Shia Revival*	297.8
Navai, Ramita. *City of Lies*	955
Nemat, Marina. *Prisoner of Tehran*	B
Noor. *Leap of Faith*	B
Pearlman, Wendy. *We Crossed a Bridge and It Trembled*	956.9104
Sabar, Ariel. *My Father's Paradise*	B
Satrapi, Marjane. ★*The Complete Persepolis*	741.5
Shadid, Anthony. *House of Stone*	306.0956
Shehadeh, Raja. *Where the Line Is Drawn*	956.9405
Trofimov, Yaroslav. *The Siege of Mecca*	953.805
Von Tunzelmann, Alex. *Blood and Sand*	909.82

HISTORY WRITING — NATURAL DISASTERS AND TRAGEDIES

Bacon, John U. *The Great Halifax Explosion*	971.6
Barry, John M. *Rising Tide*	977
Berendt, John. *The City of Falling Angels*	945
Berg, Scott W. *The Burning of the World*	977.311
Blunt, Katherine. *California Burning*	333.793
Brinkley, Douglas. *The Great Deluge*	976.3
Burns, Cherie. *The Great Hurricane—1938*	974.7
Butler, Daniel Allen. *"Unsinkable"*	910
Carney, Scott. *The Vortex*	954.92
Davenport, Matthew J. *The Longest Minute*	979.4
Deraniyagala, Sonali. *Wave*	B
Dolin, Eric Jay. *A Furious Sky*	363.34
Eichar, Donnie. *Dead Mountain*	914
Fairbanks, Amanda M. *The Lost Boys of Montauk*	910.91
Ferguson, Niall. *Doom*	362.1962
Fink, Sheri. *Five Days at Memorial*	362.1109763
Gibbins, David J. L. *A History of the World in Twelve Shipwrecks*	909
Graff, Garrett M. ★*The Only Plane in the Sky*	973.931
Harper, Kyle. *The Fate of Rome*	937
Higginbotham, Adam. ★*Midnight in Chernobyl*	363.17
Horne, Jed. *Breach of Faith*	976.3
James, Scott. *Trial by Fire*	363.3709745
Johnson, Lizzie. ★*Paradise*	363.37
Knight, Sam. *The Premonitions Bureau*	133.8
Krist, Gary. *The White Cascade*	979.7
Larson, Erik. ★*Dead Wake*	940.4
Laskin, David. *The Children's Blizzard*	977
Leinbach, Michael D. *Bringing Columbia Home*	363.12
Lord, Walter. ★*A Night to Remember*	910
McKay, Sinclair. *The Fire and the Darkness*	940.54
Melville, Wilma. ★*Hero Dogs*	636.7
Neufeld, Josh. *A.D.*	741.5
Parry, Richard Lloyd. *Ghosts of the Tsunami*	952.05
Rivlin, Gary. *Katrina*	976.3
Russell, Gareth. *The Ship of Dreams*	910.91
Schlosser, Eric. *Command and Control*	363.17
Spera, Keith. *Groove Interrupted*	B
Stone, Daniel. *Sinkable*	910.91
Vaillant, John. ★*Fire Weather*	363.37
Von Drehle, Dave. ★*Triangle*	974.7
Young, R. J. *Requiem for the Massacre*	305.8

HISTORY WRITING — PIRATES

Cordingly, David. *Under the Black Flag*	910.4
Dolin, Eric Jay. *Black Flags, Blue Waters*	973.2
Johnson, Steven. *Enemy of All Mankind*	910.4
Kilmeade, Brian. ★*Thomas Jefferson and the Tripoli Pirates*	973.4
Kritzler, Ed. *Jewish Pirates of the Caribbean*	972.9
Thomson, Keith. *Born to Be Hanged*	910.4

HISTORY WRITING — PLAGUE AND FAMINE

Barry, John M. ★*The Great Influenza*	614.5
Cantor, Norman F. *In the Wake of the Plague*	614.5
Crosby, Molly Caldwell. *The American Plague*	614.5
Ferguson, Niall. *Doom*	362.1962
Holt, Nathalia. *Cured*	614.5
Honigsbaum, Mark. *The Pandemic Century*	614.4
Johnson, Steven. *The Ghost Map*	614.5
Kelly, John. *The Graves Are Walking*	941.5081
Kelly, John. *The Great Mortality*	614.5
Kennedy, Jonathan. *Pathogenesis*	614.4
Manaugh, Geoff. *Until Proven Safe*	614.4
Oshinsky, David M. ★*Polio*	614.5
Randall, David K. *Black Death at the Golden Gate*	616.9
Reverby, Susan M. *Examining Tuskegee*	174.2
Schama, Simon. *Foreign Bodies*	614.4
Senthilingam, Meera. *Outbreaks and Epidemics*	614.4
Spinney, Laura. ★*Pale Rider*	614.5
Wright, Lawrence. ★*The Plague Year*	614.5

HISTORY WRITING — POLITICIANS — UNITED STATES

Allitt, Patrick. *The Conservatives*	320.520973
Arsenault, Raymond. *John Lewis*	B
Bordewich, Fergus M. *Congress at War*	324.2734
Brands, H. W. ★*Founding Partisans*	973.3
Brands, H. W. ★*The Man Who Saved the Union*	B
Chernow, Ron. ★*Alexander Hamilton*	B
Clarke, Thurston. *The Last Campaign*	B
Farris, Scott. *Almost President*	324.973
Fehrman, Craig. *Author in Chief*	920
Ferguson, Niall. *Kissinger*	973.924
Freeman, Joanne B. *The Field of Blood*	973.7
Gabler, Neal. ★*Against the Wind*	B
Gabler, Neal. *Catching the Wind*	B
Goodwin, Doris Kearns. ★*An Unfinished Love Story*	B
Grandin, Greg. *Kissinger's Shadow*	B
Hayek, Friedrich A. von. *The Road to Serfdom*	330.1
Hendrickson, Paul. *The Living and the Dead*	959.704
Kennedy, John F. *Profiles in Courage*	920
Kennedy, Robert Francis. *RFK*	973.92
Larson, Erik. *In the Garden of Beasts*	B
Leamer, Laurence. *The Kennedy Men*	920
Lewis, John. ★*Run; Book One*	741.5
Maddow, Rachel. *Bag Man*	B
Mahoney, Richard D. *Sons & Brothers*	920
McKean, David. *Suspected of Independence*	B

PUBLIC LIBRARY CORE COLLECTION: NONFICTION
Twentieth Edition

Nasaw, David. ★*The Patriarch*	B
Rice, Condoleezza. *Extraordinary, Ordinary People*	B
Rice, Condoleezza. *No Higher Honor*	B
Richards, Leonard L. *Who Freed the Slaves?*	342.7308
Schlesinger, Arthur M. *Journals, 1952-2000*	973.91092
Self, Robert O. *All in the Family*	320.50973
Shlaes, Amity. *The Forgotten Man*	973.91
Stahr, Walter. *Seward*	B
Steinhauer, Jennifer. *The Firsts*	320.082
Thomas, Evan. ★*Robert Kennedy*	B
Thompson, Nicholas. *The Hawk and the Dove*	973.92
Tye, Larry. ★*Bobby Kennedy*	B
Will, George F. *The Conservative Sensibility*	320.520973
Yovanovitch, Marie. *Lessons from the Edge*	973.933
Zelizer, Julian E. *Burning Down the House*	328.73

HISTORY WRITING — POST WORLD WAR II - 1959 — UNITED STATES

Baier, Bret. *Three Days in January*	B
Baime, A. J. *The Accidental President*	B
Brands, H. W. *The General vs. the President*	973.918092
Dallek, Robert. *Harry S. Truman*	B
Donald, Aida DiPace. *Citizen Soldier*	B
Gillette, Michael L. *Lady Bird Johnson*	B
Goodman, Matthew. *The City Game*	796.323
Halberstam, David. *The Fifties*	973.92
Hitchcock, William I. *The Age of Eisenhower*	973.921092
Kinzer, Stephen. ★*All the Shah's Men*	955.05
Kurtz-Phelan, Daniel. *The China Mission*	951.04
Letts, Elizabeth. ★*The Ride of Her Life*	B
Martin, Rachel Louise. *A Most Tolerant Little Town*	379.2
McCullough, David G. *Truman*	B
Roll, David L. *Ascent to Power*	973.918
Samet, Elizabeth D. *Looking for the Good War*	940.53
Steil, Benn. ★*The Marshall Plan*	338.91
Thomas, Evan. *Ike's Bluff*	973.921092

HISTORY WRITING — PRESIDENCY — 18TH CENTURY — UNITED STATES

Adams, John. *My Dearest Friend*	973.4
Avlon, John P. *Washington's Farewell*	973.4
Baier, Bret. *To Rescue the Constitution*	973.4
Boles, John B. *Jefferson*	B
Brady, Patricia. *Martha Washington*	B
Broadwater, Jeff. *James Madison*	B
Burstein, Andrew. *Madison and Jefferson*	973.4
Calloway, Colin G. *The Indian World of George Washington*	323.1197
Chernow, Ron. *Washington*	B
Coe, Alexis. ★*You Never Forget Your First*	B
Dunbar, Erica Armstrong. ★*Never Caught*	B
Ellis, Joseph J. *First Family*	973.4
Ellis, Joseph J. ★*His Excellency*	B
Feldman, Noah. *The Three Lives of James Madison*	B
Flexner, James Thomas. *George Washington and the New Nation, 1783-1793*	973.4
Flexner, James Thomas. *George Washington*	B
Gordon-Reed, Annette. ★*Most Blessed of the Patriarchs*	973.4
Grant, James. ★*John Adams*	B
Horn, Jonathan. *Washington's End*	B
Isenberg, Nancy. *The Problem of Democracy*	973.4
Johnson, Paul. *George Washington*	B
Larson, Edward J. *The Return of George Washington*	B
McCullough, David G. ★*John Adams*	B
Meltzer, Brad. ★*The First Conspiracy*	973.4
Philbrick, Nathaniel. *Travels with George*	973.4
Randall, Willard Sterne. *George Washington*	B
Simon, James F. *What Kind of Nation*	342.73
Stark, Peter. *Young Washington*	B
Stewart, David O. *George Washington*	973.4
Stewart, David O. *Madison's Gift*	B
Unger, Harlow G. *The Last Founding Father*	B
Wiencek, Henry. *Master of the Mountain*	973.4
Wills, Garry. *James Madison*	B

HISTORY WRITING — PRESIDENCY — 19TH CENTURY — UNITED STATES

Achorn, Edward. *The Lincoln Miracle*	973.6
Allgor, Catherine. *A Perfect Union*	B
Blumenthal, Sidney. ★*All the Powers of Earth*	B
Blumenthal, Sidney. *A Self-Made Man*	B
Blumenthal, Sidney. *Wrestling with His Angel*	B
Borneman, Walter R. *Polk*	B
Brands, H. W. ★*Andrew Jackson, His Life and Times*	B
Brands, H. W. ★*The Man Who Saved the Union*	B
Brands, H. W. ★*The Zealot and the Emancipator*	920
Bunting, Josiah. *Ulysses S. Grant*	B
Burlingame, Michael. *Abraham Lincoln*	B
Burlingame, Michael. *The Black Man's President*	973.7
Carwardine, Richard. *Lincoln*	B
Chernow, Ron. ★*Grant*	B
Collins, Gail. *William Henry Harrison*	B
Cook, Jane Hampton. *American Phoenix*	973.5
Cozzens, Peter. *A Brutal Reckoning*	973.5
Craughwell, Thomas J. *Stealing Lincoln's Body*	973.7092
Donald, David Herbert. *Lincoln*	B
Ellis, Joseph J. *American Sphinx*	973.4
Feldman, Noah. *The Broken Constitution*	973.7
Finkelman, Paul. *Millard Fillmore*	B
Foner, Eric. *The Fiery Trial*	973.7092
Gienapp, William E. *Abraham Lincoln and Civil War America*	B
Goodyear, C. W. *President Garfield*	B
Gordon-Reed, Annette. *Andrew Johnson*	B
Grant, Ulysses S. ★*The Annotated Memoirs of Ulysses S. Grant*	B
Greenberg, Amy S. *Lady First*	B
Guelzo, Allen C. *Lincoln and Douglas*	973.6
Gutzman, Kevin R. C. *The Jeffersonians*	973.5
Hitchens, Christopher. *Thomas Jefferson*	B
Holzer, Harold. *Brought Forth on This Continent*	973.7
Holzer, Harold. *A Just and Generous Nation*	973.7092
Inskeep, Steve. *Jacksonland*	973.56
Isenberg, Nancy. *The Problem of Democracy*	973.4
Kaplan, Fred. *John Quincy Adams*	B
Kaplan, Fred. *Lincoln and the Abolitionists*	973.7092
Kearse, Bettye. *The Other Madisons*	920
Levine, Robert S. ★*The Failed Promise*	973.8
Lincoln, Abraham. *Speeches and Writings, 1859-1865*	973.6
Lowenstein, Roger. *Ways and Means*	973.7
McGrath, Tim. *James Monroe*	B
McPherson, James M. ★*Abraham Lincoln*	B
McPherson, James M. ★*Tried by War*	973.7
Meacham, Jon. ★*American Lion*	B
Meacham, Jon. ★*And There Was Light*	B
Meacham, Jon. ★*Thomas Jefferson*	B
Meltzer, Brad. *The Lincoln Conspiracy*	973.7092
Merry, Robert W. *A Country of Vast Designs*	B
Merry, Robert W. *President McKinley*	B
Millard, Candice. *Destiny of the Republic*	973.8
Miller, Scott. *The President and the Assassin*	973.8
Pryor, Elizabeth Brown. *Six Encounters with Lincoln*	973.7092
Reynolds, David S. ★*Abe*	B
Sandburg, Carl. *Abraham Lincoln*	B
Senik, Troy. *A Man of Iron*	B
Simon, James F. *What Kind of Nation*	342.73
Symonds, Craig L. *Lincoln and His Admirals*	B
Thomas, Louisa. *Louisa*	B
Traub, James. *John Quincy Adams*	B
White, Gayle Jessup. *Reclamation*	B
White, Ronald C. *A. Lincoln*	B
White, Ronald C. ★*American Ulysses*	B
White, Ronald C. *Lincoln in Private*	B
Widmer, Edward L. *Lincoln on the Verge*	B
Widmer, Edward L. *Martin Van Buren*	B
Wills, Garry. *Lincoln at Gettysburg*	973.7
Wineapple, Brenda. *The Impeachers*	973.8

HISTORY WRITING — PRESIDENCY — 20TH CENTURY — UNITED STATES

Abrams, Dan. *Theodore Roosevelt for the Defense*	345.73
Alter, Jonathan. *His Very Best*	B
Anthony, Carl Sferrazza. *Nellie Taft*	B
Baier, Bret. *Three Days in January*	B
Baime, A. J. *The Accidental President*	B
Baker, Peter. *The Man Who Ran Washington*	B
Berfield, Susan. *The Hour of Fate*	973.91
Berg, A. Scott. ★*Wilson*	B
Bernstein, Carl. ★*All the President's Men*	364.1
Bird, Kai. *The Outlier*	973.926
Branch, Taylor. *The Clinton Tapes*	973.929
Brands, H. W. *Reagan*	B
Brands, H. W. *Traitor to His Class*	B
Brands, H. W. *Woodrow Wilson*	B

1956

AUTHOR, TITLE, SERIES AND SUBJECT INDEX

Brinkley, Alan. *John F. Kennedy*	B
Brokaw, Tom. *The Fall of Richard Nixon*	B
Bush, George. *All the Best, George Bush*	973.928
Bush, George W. *41*	B
Caro, Robert A. ★*The Passage of Power*	B
Carter, Jimmy. *A Full Life*	B
Carter, Jimmy. *An Hour Before Daylight*	B
Carter, Jimmy. *Sharing Good Times*	973.926
Carter, Jimmy. *White House Diary*	973.926
Clarke, Thurston. *JFK's Last Hundred Days*	B
Clinton, Bill. *My Life*	B
Cohen, Andrew. *Two Days in June*	973.922
Cook, Blanche Wiesen. *Eleanor Roosevelt; Volume 2*	B
Cook, Blanche Wiesen. ★*Eleanor Roosevelt; Volume 3*	B
Cooper, John Milton. *Woodrow Wilson*	B
Dallek, Robert. ★*Franklin D. Roosevelt*	B
Dallek, Robert. *Harry S. Truman*	B
Dallek, Robert. *Let Every Nation Know*	B
Dallek, Robert. *Nixon and Kissinger*	B
Dallek, Robert. *An Unfinished Life*	B
Dean, John W. *The Nixon Defense*	973.924092
Denevi, Timothy. *Freak Kingdom*	B
Dobbs, Michael. *King Richard*	973.924
Donald, Aida DiPace. *Citizen Soldier*	B
Egan, Timothy. ★*The Big Burn*	973.911
Eizenstat, Stuart. ★*President Carter*	B
Farrell, John A. ★*Richard Nixon*	B
Feldstein, Mark Avrom. *Poisoning the Press*	973.924092
Frank, Jeffrey. *The Trials of Harry S. Truman*	973.918
Fullilove, Michael. *Rendezvous with Destiny*	973.917092
Gillette, Michael L. *Lady Bird Johnson*	B
Goodwin, Doris Kearns. ★*The Bully Pulpit*	973.91
Goodwin, Doris Kearns. *No Ordinary Time*	920
Graff, Garrett M. *Watergate*	973.924
Hager, Jenna Bush. *Sisters First*	B
Hill, Clint. *Five Days in November*	973.922092
Hill, Clint. *Five Presidents*	B
Hill, Clint. *Mrs. Kennedy and Me*	973.922092
Hitchcock, William I. *The Age of Eisenhower*	973.921092
Hochschild, Adam. *Rebel Cinderella*	B
Johnson, Lyndon B. *Taking Charge*	973.923
Johnson, Paul. *Eisenhower*	B
Leaming, Barbara. *Jacqueline Bouvier Kennedy Onassis*	B
Leaming, Barbara. *Mrs. Kennedy*	B
Mann, Jim. *The Rebellion of Ronald Reagan*	973.927092
Marton, Kati. *Hidden Power*	B
Matthews, Christopher. *Kennedy & Nixon*	973.922
McCullough, David G. *Truman*	B
McKean, David. *Watching Darkness Fall*	940.53
Meacham, Jon. ★*Destiny and Power*	B
Meacham, Jon. *Franklin and Winston*	940.53
Michaelis, David. ★*Eleanor*	973.917
Minutaglio, Bill. *Dallas 1963*	973.922092
Morley, Jefferson. *Scorpions' Dance*	973.924
Morris, Edmund. ★*Colonel Roosevelt*	B
Morris, Edmund. ★*The Rise of Theodore Roosevelt*	B
Morris, Edmund. ★*Theodore Rex*	973.911
Nelson, Craig. ★*V Is for Victory*	973.917
O'Brien, Phillips Payson. *The Second Most Powerful Man in the World*	B
O'Toole, Patricia. *The Moralist*	B
Onassis, Jacqueline Kennedy. *Historic Conversations on Life with John F. Kennedy*	B
Paradis, Michel. *The Light of Battle*	940.54
Perlstein, Rick. *The Invisible Bridge*	973.924
Perlstein, Rick. ★*Nixonland*	973.924
Perlstein, Rick. ★*Reaganland*	973.926
Persico, Joseph E. *Franklin and Lucy*	973.917092
Peters, Charles. *Lyndon B. Johnson*	B
Posner, Gerald L. *Case Closed*	364.1
Rappleye, Charles. *Herbert Hoover in the White House*	B
Reagan, Ronald. *The Reagan Diaries*	B
Reston, James. *The Conviction of Richard Nixon*	973.924092
Roll, David L. *Ascent to Power*	973.918
Roll, David L. *George Marshall*	B
Rumsfeld, Donald. *When the Center Held*	973.925092
Sherman, Casey. *Above and Beyond*	973.922092
Shesol, Jeff. *Supreme Power*	347.73
Shlaes, Amity. *Coolidge*	B
Smith, Jean Edward. *FDR*	B
Smith, Richard Norton. *An Ordinary Man*	B
Sorensen, Theodore C. *Counselor*	B
Spitz, Bob. ★*Reagan*	B
Swanson, James L. *End of Days*	973.922092
Sweig, Julia. *Lady Bird Johnson*	B
Thomas, Evan. *Being Nixon*	B
Thomas, Evan. *Ike's Bluff*	973.921092
Updegrove, Mark K. *The Last Republicans*	973.928
Von Tunzelmann, Alex. *Blood and Sand*	909.82
Wallace, Chris. *Countdown 1945*	940.54
Ward, Geoffrey C. ★*The Roosevelts*	B
Weiner, Tim. *One Man Against the World*	B
Whipple, Chris. *The Gatekeepers*	973.92092
Whyte, Kenneth. *Hoover*	B
Woods, Randall Bennett. *Prisoners of Hope*	973.923
Woodward, Bob. *The Final Days*	B
Woodward, Bob. *Shadow*	973.92
Zapruder, Alexandra. *Twenty-Six Seconds*	973.922092
Zeitz, Joshua. *Building the Great Society*	973.923

HISTORY WRITING — PRESIDENCY — 21ST CENTURY — UNITED STATES

Alberta, Tim. *American Carnage*	324.2734
Allen, Jonathan. *Lucky*	324.973
Bade, Rachael. ★*Unchecked*	342.73
Bush, George W. *41*	B
Bush, George W. *Decision Points*	B
Carpenter, Amanda B. *Gaslighting America*	973.933
Chait, Jonathan. *Audacity*	973.932
D'Antonio, Michael. *The Hunting of Hillary*	B
Daniels, Stormy. *Full Disclosure*	B
Dorey-Stein, Beck. *From the Corner of the Oval*	B
Draper, Robert. *To Start a War*	956.7044
Foer, Franklin. ★*The Last Politician*	973.934
Gessen, Masha. *Surviving Autocracy*	973.933
Hennessey, Susan. *Unmaking the Presidency*	973.933
Hoffman, Carl. *Liar's Circus*	973.933
Jarrett, Valerie. *Finding My Voice*	B
Johnston, David Cay. *The Big Cheat*	973.933
Jordan, Mary. *The Art of Her Deal*	B
Karl, Jonathan. *Betrayal*	973.933
Litt, David. *Thanks, Obama*	B
Martin, Jonathan. *This Will Not Pass*	973.933
Obama, Barack. ★*A Promised Land*	B
Obama, Michelle. ★*Becoming*	B
Poniewozik, James. *Audience of One*	324.7
Rhodes, Benjamin J. *The World as It Is*	973.932
Rothkopf, David J. *American Resistance*	973.933
Schmidt, Michael S. ★*Donald Trump v. The United States*	973.933
Slevin, Peter. *Michelle Obama*	B
Smith, Jean Edward. *Bush*	973.931
Souza, Pete. *The West Wing and Beyond*	917.53
Sullivan, Kevin. *Trump on Trial*	342.73
Toobin, Jeffrey. *True Crimes and Misdemeanors*	973.933
Trump, Mary L. *Too Much and Never Enough*	B
Weissmann, Andrew. ★*Where Law Ends*	324.7
Whipple, Chris. *The Fight of His Life*	973.934
Wilson, Rick. *Running Against the Devil*	973.933
Wolff, Michael. *Fire and Fury*	973.933
Wolff, Michael. *Landslide*	973.933
Woodward, Bob. *Fear*	973.933
Woodward, Bob. *Peril*	973.933

HISTORY WRITING — PRESIDENCY — UNITED STATES

Beschloss, Michael R. ★*Presidents of War*	355.00973
Borneman, Walter R. *Polk*	B
Brettschneider, Corey Lang. *The Presidents and the People*	342.73
Brower, Kate Andersen. *First in Line*	920
Brower, Kate Andersen. *First Women*	920
Brower, Kate Andersen. *The Residence*	975.3
Bunting, Josiah. *Ulysses S. Grant*	B
Carlson, Brady. *Dead Presidents*	B
Charter, David. *Royal Audience*	941.085
Cohen, Jared. *Accidental Presidents*	973.09
Cohen, Jared. *Life After Power*	973.09
Dallek, Robert. *Harry S. Truman*	B
Dallek, Robert. *Let Every Nation Know*	B
Donald, Aida DiPace. *Citizen Soldier*	B
Fehrman, Craig. *Author in Chief*	920

PUBLIC LIBRARY CORE COLLECTION: NONFICTION
Twentieth Edition

Feldstein, Mark Avrom. *Poisoning the Press*	973.924092
Flexner, James Thomas. *George Washington*	B
Garrow, David J. *Rising Star*	B
Gienapp, William E. *Abraham Lincoln and Civil War America*	B
Giorgione, Michael. *Inside Camp David*	975.2
Goodwin, Doris Kearns. ★*Leadership in Turbulent Times*	973.09
Karl, Jonathan. *Front Row at the Trump Show*	973.933
Lozada, Carlos. *The Washington Book*	320
Lusane, Clarence. *The Black History of the White House*	975.3
Meacham, Jon. ★*The Soul of America*	973
Oliphant, Thomas. ★*The Road to Camelot*	973.922092
Page, Susan. ★*The Matriarch*	B
Perlstein, Rick. *The Invisible Bridge*	973.924
Persico, Joseph E. *Franklin and Lucy*	973.917092
Peters, Charles. *Lyndon B. Johnson*	B
Prud'homme, Alex. ★*Dinner with the President*	973
Raphael, Ray. *Mr. President*	352.230973
Ricks, Thomas E. ★*First Principles*	973.09
Rogers, Katie. ★*American Woman*	973.09
Sandburg, Carl. *Abraham Lincoln*	B
Saxton, Martha. *The Widow Washington*	B
Shirley, Craig. *Mary Ball Washington*	B
Smith, Jean Edward. *FDR*	B
Thomas, Evan. *Ike's Bluff*	973.921092
Vowell, Sarah. *Assassination Vacation*	B
Widmer, Edward L. *Martin Van Buren*	B
Woodward, Bob. *The Final Days*	B

HISTORY WRITING — RECONSTRUCTION — UNITED STATES

Ayers, Edward L. ★*The Thin Light of Freedom*	975.5
Ball, Edward. *Life of a Klansman*	305.8009763
Blight, David W. ★*Frederick Douglass*	B
Bordewich, Fergus M. *Klan War*	973.8
Brewster, Todd. *Lincoln's Gamble*	973.7
Bunting, Josiah. *Ulysses S. Grant*	B
Dray, Philip. *Capitol Men*	973.8
Foner, Eric. *Forever Free*	973.8
Foner, Eric. ★*Reconstruction*	973.8
Foner, Eric. *The Second Founding*	342.73
Gordon-Reed, Annette. *Andrew Johnson*	B
Lane, Charles. *Freedom's Detective*	B
Langguth, A. J. *After Lincoln*	973.8
Levine, Bruce C. *The Fall of the House of Dixie*	973.7
Levine, Bruce C. *Thaddeus Stevens*	B
Levine, Robert S. ★*The Failed Promise*	973.8
Nimura, Janice P. *Daughters of the Samurai*	920
Sinha, Manisha. *The Rise and Fall of the Second American Republic*	973.8
Varon, Elizabeth R. *Longstreet*	B
Williams, Kidada E. *I Saw Death Coming*	973.8
Wineapple, Brenda. *Ecstatic Nation*	973.6
Wineapple, Brenda. *The Impeachers*	973.8
Woodward, C. Vann. *The Strange Career of Jim Crow*	305.896
Zucchino, David. *Wilmington's Lie*	305.8009756

HISTORY WRITING — REGIMES AND POLITICAL VIOLENCE — LATIN AMERICA

Allende, Isabel. *My Invented Country*	B
Forche, Carolyn. *What You Have Heard Is True*	B
Hagerty, Alexa. ★*Still Life with Bones*	599.9

HISTORY WRITING — REGIONAL HISTORY — CANADA

Bacon, John U. *The Great Halifax Explosion*	971.6

HISTORY WRITING — REGIONAL HISTORY — UNITED STATES

Abdurraqib, Hanif. ★*There's Always This Year*	796.323
Appelman, J. Reuben. *While Idaho Slept*	364.152
Berry, Jason. *City of a Million Dreams*	976.3
Biggers, Jeff. *Reckoning at Eagle Creek*	333.73
Blitzer, Jonathan. *Everyone Who Is Gone Is Here*	305.9
Bordewich, Fergus M. *Washington*	975.3
Borneman, Walter R. *Alaska*	979.8
Boyd, Herb. *Black Detroit*	977.4
Brookwood, Marilyn. *The Orphans of Davenport*	305.231
Buck, Rinker. *Life on the Mississippi*	917
Burrough, Bryan. *The Big Rich*	338.2
Burrough, Bryan. *Forget the Alamo*	976.043
Crawford, Alan Pell. *This Fierce People*	975
Crouse, Karen. *Norwich*	796
Cwiklik, Robert. *Sheridan's Secret Mission*	973.8
Davenport, Matthew J. *The Longest Minute*	979.4
Doyle, Martin. *The Source*	333.91
Dyja, Tom. *The Third Coast*	977.311
Ellsworth, Scott. *The Ground Breaking*	976.6
Fairbanks, Amanda M. *The Lost Boys of Montauk*	910.91
Fessler, Pam. *Carville's Cure*	362.19699
Fields-Black, Edda L. *Combee*	973.7
Fieseler, Robert W. *Tinderbox*	364.152
Fischer, David Hackett. ★*African Founders*	973
Gallagher, Winifred. *New Women in the Old West*	978.02
Grant, Richard. *The Deepest South of All*	976.2
Grant, Will. *The Last Ride of the Pony Express*	917.804
Hale, Grace Elizabeth. *In the Pines*	364.13
Hayes, Derek. *Historical Atlas of the American West*	911
Heacox, Kim. ★*John Muir and the Ice That Started a Fire*	333.7209798
Hill, David. *The Vapors*	976.7
Hortis, C. Alexander. *The Witch of New York*	364.152
Horwitz, Tony. *Spying on the South*	917
Johnson, Kirk W. *The Fishermen and the Dragon*	976.4
Johnson, Lizzie. ★*Paradise*	363.37
Kimmerle, Erin H. *We Carry Their Bones*	365
King, Greg. *The Ghost Forest*	333.75
Krist, Gary. *The Mirage Factory*	920
Lauterbach, Preston. *Beale Street Dynasty*	976.8
LeDuff, Charlie. *Detroit*	977.4
Levy, Shawn. ★*The Castle on Sunset*	647.95
Luckerson, Victor. *Built from the Fire*	976.6
Lunenfeld, Peter. *City at the Edge of Forever*	979.4
Martin, Rachel Louise. *A Most Tolerant Little Town*	379.2
Meckler, Laura. ★*Dream Town*	305.8
Miles, Kathryn. *Trailed*	364.152
Miles, Tiya. *The Dawn of Detroit*	977.4
Moore, Susanna. *Paradise of the Pacific*	996.9
Moss, Jeremiah. *Feral City*	B
Neus, Nora. *24 Hours in Charlottesville*	973.933
Nusbaum, Eric. *Stealing Home*	796.357
Orlean, Susan. ★*The Library Book*	027.4
Patterson, James. *What Really Happens in Vegas*	920
Pawel, Miriam. *The Browns of California*	920
Perry, Imani. ★*South to America*	917
Price, S. L. *Playing Through the Whistle*	796.332
Randall, David K. *The King and Queen of Malibu*	B
Reid, David. *The Brazen Age*	974.7
Rivlin, Gary. *Katrina*	976.3
Roker, Al. *Ruthless Tide*	974.8
Rubinstein, Julian. ★*The Holly*	364.106
Rudacille, Deborah. *Roots of Steel*	338.4
Satow, Julie. *The Plaza*	917.47
Sevigny, Melissa L. ★*Brave the Wild River*	580.9
Stempel, Larry. ★*Showtime*	792.609
Sullivan, Randall. *Graveyard of the Pacific*	979.7
Swift, Earl. *Chesapeake Requiem*	639
Vigliotti, Jonathan. *Before It's Gone*	577
Wallace, Mike. *Greater Gotham*	974.7
Wallis, Michael. *Route 66*	917.804
Wilkie, Curtis. *When Evil Lived in Laurel*	305.8
Wright, Lawrence. *God Save Texas*	917.64

HISTORY WRITING — RENAISSANCE — EUROPE

Bakewell, Sarah. *How to Live—Or—A Life of Montaigne*	B
Benner, Erica. *Be Like the Fox*	B
Bergreen, Laurence. *Marco Polo*	B
Bergreen, Laurence. *Over the Edge of the World*	B
Borman, Tracy. *The Private Lives of the Tudors*	920
Boucheron, Patrick. *Machiavelli*	320.1092
Bradford, Sarah. *Lucrezia Borgia*	B
Brooks, Michael. *The Quantum Astrologer's Handbook*	B
Dodds Pennock, Caroline. ★*On Savage Shores*	970.004
Downey, Kirstin. *Isabella*	B
Fauber, L. S. *Heaven on Earth*	B
Frampton, Saul. *When I Am Playing with My Cat, How Do I Know She Is Not Playing with Me?*	844
Fraser, Antonia. *Faith and Treason*	942.06
Fraser, Antonia. *Mary, Queen of Scots*	B
Fraser, Antonia. ★*The Wives of Henry VIII*	942.05
Goldstone, Nancy Bazelon. *The Rival Queens*	944
Goodman, Ruth. *How to Be a Tudor*	942.05
Goodman, Ruth. *How to Behave Badly in Elizabethan England*	942.05
Greenblatt, Stephen. ★*The Swerve*	940.2
Greenblatt, Stephen. ★*Will in the World*	B
Guy, John. *Hunting the Falcon*	B
Hibbert, Christopher. *The Borgias and Their Enemies*	920

AUTHOR, TITLE, SERIES AND SUBJECT INDEX

Hibbert, Christopher. *The House of Medici*	920
Isaacson, Walter. ★*Leonardo Da Vinci*	B
Kamen, Henry. *The Spanish Inquisition*	272
Kaufmann, Miranda. *Black Tudors*	941
King, Ross. *Bookseller of Florence*	381
King, Ross. *Brunelleschi's Dome*	726.6
King, Ross. *Michelangelo & the Pope's Ceiling*	759.5
Lester, Toby. *Da Vinci's Ghost*	741.092
Lovell, Mary S. *Bess of Hardwick*	B
MacCulloch, Diarmaid. *The Reformation*	270.6
Manchester, William. *A World Lit Only by Fire*	940.2
Massing, Michael. *Fatal Discord*	920
Metaxas, Eric. *Martin Luther*	B
Meyer, G. J. *The Borgias*	920
Mortimer, Ian. *The Time Traveler's Guide to Elizabethan England*	942.05
Norwich, John Julius. *A History of Venice*	945
Norwich, John Julius. *Shakespeare's Kings*	822.33
Nuland, Sherwin B. *Leonardo Da Vinci*	B
Paranque, Estelle. *Blood, Fire & Gold*	920
Pettegree, Andrew. *The Book in the Renaissance*	070.5
Porter, Linda. *Katherine the Queen*	B
Ronald, Susan. *The Pirate Queen*	B
Rounding, Virginia. *The Burning Time*	272
Russell, Gareth. *Young and Damned and Fair*	B
Spoto, Donald. *Joan*	B
Starkey, David. *Six Wives*	942.05
Strathern, Paul. *The Borgias*	945.06
Strathern, Paul. *The Florentines*	945
Strathern, Paul. *The Medici*	945.5
Tallis, Nicola. *Crown of Blood*	B
Weir, Alison. *The Children of Henry VIII*	B
Weir, Alison. *Henry VIII*	B
Weir, Alison. *The Lady in the Tower*	B
Weir, Alison. *The Life of Elizabeth I*	B
Weir, Alison. *The Lost Tudor Princess*	B
Weir, Alison. *Mary, Queen of Scots, and the Murder of Lord Darnley*	941.105
Weir, Alison. *The Six Wives of Henry VIII*	942.05
Weir, Alison. *The Wars of the Roses*	942.04
Wilson, Derek. *Out of the Storm*	B
Wilson, Derek K. *A Magical World*	261.55
Wilson, Ellen Judy. *Encyclopedia of the Enlightenment*	940.2

HISTORY WRITING — ROARING 20S — UNITED STATES

Abbott, Karen. *American Rose*	B
Allen, Frederick Lewis. *Only Yesterday*	973.9
Barry, John M. *Rising Tide*	977
Blum, Deborah. *The Poisoner's Handbook*	614
Boyle, Kevin. *Arc of Justice*	345.73
Bryson, Bill. *One Summer*	973.91
Egan, Timothy. ★*A Fever in the Heartland*	322.4
Eig, Jonathan. *Get Capone*	364.1
Jaher, David. *The Witch of Lime Street*	B
Madigan, Tim. *The Burning*	976.6
Miller, Donald L. *Supreme City*	974.7

HISTORY WRITING — SCANDALS

Bade, Rachael. ★*Unchecked*	342.73
Bernstein, Carl. ★*All the President's Men*	364.1
Brokaw, Tom. *The Fall of Richard Nixon*	B
Brown, Tina. ★*The Palace Papers*	920
Conason, Joe. *The Longest Con*	320.52
Craughwell, Thomas J. *Stealing Lincoln's Body*	973.7092
Dobbs, Michael. *King Richard*	973.924
Egan, Timothy. ★*A Fever in the Heartland*	322.4
Elliott, Carl. ★*The Occasional Human Sacrifice*	174.2
Goodman, Matthew. *The City Game*	796.323
Graff, Garrett M. *Watergate*	973.924
Jager, Eric. *Blood Royal*	944.026
Kertzer, David I. *The Pope and Mussolini*	322
King, Greg. *Twilight of Empire*	943.6
Maddow, Rachel. *Bag Man*	B
Maddow, Rachel. ★*Prequel*	320.53
Morley, Jefferson. *Scorpions' Dance*	973.924
Mueller, Tom. *Crisis of Conscience*	364.16
Reston, James. *The Conviction of Richard Nixon*	973.924092
Risen, James. ★*The Last Honest Man*	973.92
Rohde, David. *In Deep*	973.933
Strang, Dean A. *Worse Than the Devil*	345.775
Sullivan, Kevin. *Trump on Trial*	342.73
Toobin, Jeffrey. *True Crimes and Misdemeanors*	973.933
Ward, Geoffrey C. *A Disposition to Be Rich*	B
Zminda, Don. *Double Plays and Double Crosses*	796.357

HISTORY WRITING — SCIENCE, TECHNOLOGY AND MEDICINE

HISTORY WRITING — SCIENCE, TECHNOLOGY, AND MEDICINE

Al-Khalili, Jim. *The House of Wisdom*	509
Aryee, Patrick. *30 Animals That Made Us Smarter*	590
Baron, David. *American Eclipse*	523.7
Becker, Adam. *What Is Real?*	920
Bell, Alice R. *Our Biggest Experiment*	363.738
Black, Alexandra. *Scientists Who Changed History*	509.22
Bradbury, Neil. *A Taste for Poison*	615.9
Brinkley, Douglas. ★*American Moonshot*	629.40973
Brooks, Michael. *The Art of More*	510.9
Brooks, Michael. *The Quantum Astrologer's Handbook*	B
Brownstein, Gabriel. ★*The Secret Mind of Bertha Pappenheim*	616.85
Bryson, Bill. ★*A Short History of Nearly Everything*	500
Cahalan, Susannah. ★*The Great Pretender*	616.89
Campbell, Olivia. *Women in White Coats*	610.92
Cleghorn, Elinor. *Unwell Women*	613
Comen, Elizabeth. ★*All in Her Head*	613
Conniff, Richard. *House of Lost Worlds*	069
Crosby, Molly Caldwell. *The American Plague*	614.5
DiGregorio, Sarah. ★*Taking Care*	610.73
Dolnick, Edward. *Seeds of Life*	612.6
Donovan, Jim. ★*Shoot for the Moon*	629.45
Du Sautoy, Marcus. *The Great Unknown*	500
Dyson, Freeman J. *Maker of Patterns*	B
Elliott, Carl. ★*The Occasional Human Sacrifice*	174.2
Farley, Audrey Clare. ★*Girls and Their Monsters*	306.875
Fauber, L. S. *Heaven on Earth*	B
Favro, Terri. *Generation Robot*	006.3
Fishman, Charles. ★*One Giant Leap*	629.45
Fitzharris, Lindsey. *The Butchering Art*	B
Frank, Lone. *The Pleasure Shock*	616.8
Gross, Rachel E. *Vagina Obscura*	618.1
Hallman, J. C. *Say Anarcha*	618.1
Harford, Tim. *50 Inventions That Shaped the Modern Economy*	609
Harrington, Anne. *Mind Fixers*	616.89
Hazelgrove, William Elliott. *Wright Brothers, Wrong Story*	920
Hogge, Fred. *Of Ice and Men*	338.4
Honigsbaum, Mark. *The Pandemic Century*	614.4
Hotez, Peter J. *Preventing the Next Pandemic*	362.1969
Inglis, Lucy. *Milk of Paradise*	362.29
Jamison, Kay Redfield. *Fires in the Dark*	616.89
Jauhar, Sandeep. *Heart*	612.1
Johnson, Steven. *The Ghost Map*	614.5
Jones, Chip. *The Organ Thieves*	617.4
Kang, Lydia. *Patient Zero*	614.4
Kean, Sam. *The Icepick Surgeon*	509
Kean, Sam. *The Tale of the Dueling Neurosurgeons*	617.4
Kenny, Charles. *The Plague Cycle*	614.4
Kinch, Michael S. *Between Hope and Fear*	614.4
Kinzer, Stephen. *Poisoner in Chief*	B
Kitmacher, Gary. *Space Stations*	629.44
Klass, Perri. *A Good Time to Be Born*	362.19892
Laar, Arnold van de. *Under the Knife*	617
Launius, Roger D. *Apollo's Legacy*	629.45
Lieberman, Jeffrey A. *Malady of the Mind*	616.89
Lisle, John. *The Dirty Tricks Department*	940.54
Mahaffey, James A. *Atomic Adventures*	333.792
Markel, Howard. *Origin Story*	576.8
Markel, Howard. *The Secret of Life*	572.86
McNeur, Catherine. *Mischievous Creatures*	920
Mezrich, Joshua D. *When Death Becomes Life*	617.9
Munson, Richard. *Tesla*	B
Nimura, Janice P. ★*The Doctors Blackwell*	610.92
Nordgren, Tyler E. *Sun, Moon, Earth*	523.7
O'Sullivan, Suzanne. *The Sleeping Beauties*	616.85
Offit, Paul A. *You Bet Your Life*	615.5
Oshinsky, David M. *Bellevue*	362.1109747
Panek, Richard. *The Trouble with Gravity*	531
Peck, Robert McCracken. *A Glorious Enterprise*	508
Popova, Maria. *Figuring*	920
Price, David A. *Geniuses at War*	940.54
Randall, David K. *Black Death at the Golden Gate*	616.9
Reser, Anna. *Forces of Nature*	509.2

PUBLIC LIBRARY CORE COLLECTION: NONFICTION
Twentieth Edition

Rhodes, Richard. ★*Energy*	333.7909
Richtel, Matt. ★*An Elegant Defense*	616.07
Rutherford, Adam. *Control*	363.9
Rutkow, Ira M. *Empire of the Scalpel*	617
Schutt, Bill. *Pump*	612.1
Senthilingam, Meera. *Outbreaks and Epidemics*	614.4
Shapiro, Scott J. ★*Fancy Bear Goes Phishing*	364.16
Sheehy, Suzie. *The Matter of Everything*	539.7
Shesol, Jeff. *Mercury Rising*	629.45
Slater, Lauren. *Blue Dreams*	615.7
Soni, Jimmy. *A Mind at Play*	B
Spinney, Laura. ★*Pale Rider*	614.5
Standage, Tom. *A Brief History of Motion*	388
Stanley, Matthew. *Einstein's War*	530
Stone, Daniel. *The Food Explorer*	B
Strevens, Michael. *The Knowledge Machine*	500
Swift, Earl. *Across the Airless Wilds*	629.45
Taubes, Gary. ★*Rethinking Diabetes*	616.462
Ullman, Ellen. *Life in Code*	B
Vanderbes, Jennifer. ★*Wonder Drug*	615
Vincent, James. *Beyond Measure*	530.8
Wadman, Meredith. *The Vaccine Race*	614.5
Weinberg, Steven. *To Explain the World*	509
Werb, Dan. *The Invisible Siege*	614.5
Winchester, Simon. ★*The Perfectionists*	620.009
Zernike, Kate. *The Exceptions*	331.4

HISTORY WRITING — SEPTEMBER 11, 2001 — UNITED STATES

Dwyer, Jim. *102 Minutes*	974.7
Farmer, John J. *The Ground Truth*	973.931
Friend, David. *Watching the World Change*	974.7
Graff, Garrett M. ★*The Only Plane in the Sky*	973.931
Jacobson, Sidney. *The 9-11 Report*	741.5
Langewiesche, William. *American Ground*	974.7
Longman, Jere. *Among the Heroes*	974.8
Pfeifer, Joseph. *Ordinary Heroes*	973.931
Smith, Dennis. *Report from Ground Zero*	974.7
Soufan, Ali H. *The Black Banners Declassified*	363.325
Spiegelman, Art. *In the Shadow of No Towers*	741.5
Wright, Lawrence. ★*The Looming Tower*	973.931
Zuckoff, Mitchell. ★*Fall and Rise*	973.931

HISTORY WRITING — SOUTHWEST ASIA AND NORTH AFRICA (MIDDLE EAST)

Abdul-Ahad, Ghaith. *A Stranger in Your Own City*	956.7044
Akcam, Taner. *A Shameful Act*	956.6
Al-Khalili, Jim. *The House of Wisdom*	509
Amanat, Abbas. *Iran*	955
Armstrong, Karen. ★*Islam*	297
Balakian, Peter. *The Burning Tigris*	956.6
Barr, James. *Lords of the Desert*	956
Brownworth, Lars. *Lost to the West*	949.5
Crowley, Roger. *1453*	949.61
Di Cintio, Marcello. *Pay No Heed to the Rockets*	956.9405
Finkel, Caroline. *Osman's Dream*	956.1
Friedman, Matti. *Spies of No Country*	327.12
Garfinkel, Yosef. *In the Footsteps of King David*	933
Ghazvinian, John. *America and Iran*	327
Haag, Michael. *The Tragedy of the Templars*	271.7913
Herrin, Judith. *Byzantium*	949.5
Howell, Georgina. *Gertrude Bell*	B
Hughes, Bettany. *Istanbul*	949.61
Kaplan, Robert D. *The Loom of Time*	327
Kassabova, Kapka. *Border*	949.9
Kennedy, Hugh. ★*The Great Arab Conquests*	297.09
Lawler, Andrew. *Under Jerusalem*	956.94
Lawrence, T. E. *Seven Pillars of Wisdom*	940.4
Lemmon, Gayle Tzemach. *The Daughters of Kobani*	956.9104
Levin, Daniel. *Proof of Life*	956.9104
Lewis, Bernard. *The Middle East*	956
Mackeen, Dawn Anahid. *The Hundred-Year Walk*	956.6
Mackintosh-Smith, Tim. *Arabs*	909.04
Madden, Thomas F. *Istanbul*	949.61
Malek, Alia. *The Home That Was Our Country*	B
Marozzi, Justin. *Islamic Empires*	909
Mikhaiil, Dunya. *The Beekeeper*	956.7044
Mikhail, Alan. *God's Shadow*	B
Pamuk, Orhan. *Istanbul*	949.61
Peres, Shimon. *No Room for Small Dreams*	B
Rogan, Eugene L. *The Fall of the Ottomans*	940.3
Satrapi, Marjane. *Embroideries*	741.5
Thomson, Mike. *Syria's Secret Library*	956.9104
Verini, James. *They Will Have to Die Now*	956.7044
Wallach, Janet. *Desert Queen*	B
Warrick, Joby. *Red Line*	956.9104
Wilkinson, Toby A. H. *The Nile*	962
Zuckoff, Mitchell. *The Secret Gate*	958.104

HISTORY WRITING — SPIES AND SPYING

Abbott, Karen. *Liar, Temptress, Soldier, Spy*	920
Anderson, Scott. ★*The Quiet Americans*	327.12
Andrew, Christopher M. *The Secret World*	327.1209
Bascomb, Neal. *Hunting Eichmann*	943.086
Coker, Margaret. *The Spymaster of Baghdad*	956.7044
Conant, Jennet. *The Lotus Eaters*	940.54
Cunningham, Benjamin. *The Liar*	327.1273
Drabkin, Ronald. *Beverly Hills Spy*	940.54
Fagone, Jason. *The Woman Who Smashed Codes*	B
Hastings, Max. *The Secret War*	940.54
Helm, Sarah. *A Life in Secrets*	B
Hemming, Henry. *Agents of Influence*	940.54
Jacobsen, Annie. *Surprise, Kill, Vanish*	327.1273
Kershaw, Alex. *Avenue of Spies*	940.53
Kilmeade, Brian. ★*George Washington's Secret Six*	973.4
Levin, Daniel. *Proof of Life*	956.9104
Lewis, Damien. *Agent Josephine*	B
Lichtblau, Eric. *Return to the Reich*	B
Lisle, John. *The Dirty Tricks Department*	940.54
Loftis, Larry. *Code Name*	B
Macintyre, Ben. ★*Agent Sonya*	B
Macintyre, Ben. *Agent Zigzag*	B
Macintyre, Ben. *Double Cross*	940.54
Macintyre, Ben. *A Spy Among Friends*	B
Macintyre, Ben. ★*The Spy and the Traitor*	B
Magida, Arthur J. *Code Name Madeleine*	940.54
Maier, Thomas. *Mafia Spies*	364.1060973
McCoy, Alfred W. *A Question of Torture*	323.4
Meltzer, Brad. ★*The Nazi Conspiracy*	940.53
Mendez, Antonio J. *Argo*	955.05
Morley, Jefferson. *Scorpions' Dance*	973.924
Mulley, Clare. *The Spy Who Loved*	B
Mundy, Liza. *Code Girls*	940.54
Mundy, Liza. ★*The Sisterhood*	327.12
Nicholl, Charles. *The Reckoning*	B
Olson, Lynne. ★*Madame Fourcade's Secret War*	B
Philipps, Roland. *A Spy Named Orphan*	B
Popkin, Jim. *Code Name Blue Wren*	327.12
Price, David A. *Geniuses at War*	940.54
Purnell, Sonia. ★*A Woman of No Importance*	B
Ronald, Susan. *Hitler's Aristocrats*	940.53
Rose, Sarah. *D-Day Girls*	940.53
Ross, Steven Joseph. ★*Hitler in Los Angeles*	979.4
Scott-Clark, Cathy. *The Forever Prisoner*	364.6
Sebba, Anne. *Ethel Rosenberg*	B
Sherman, Casey. *Above and Beyond*	973.922092
Shimer, David. *Rigged*	324.60973
Shultz, Richard H. *The Secret War Against Hanoi*	959.704
Stevenson, William. *A Man Called Intrepid*	940.54
Talty, Stephan. *Agent Garbo*	940.5
Talty, Stephan. *The Good Assassin*	364.15
Vickers, Michael G. *By All Means Available*	355
Vogel, Steve. *Betrayal in Berlin*	327.1273043
Waller, Douglas C. *Lincoln's Spies*	973.7
Walton, Calder. *Spies*	327.1247
Weiner, Tim. *Legacy of Ashes*	327.1273009
Whipple, Chris. *The Spymasters*	920
Wiehl, Lis W. *A Spy in Plain Sight*	327.1247
Wilford, Hugh. *The CIA*	327.1273
Xue, XInran. *The Book of Secrets*	951.05

HISTORY WRITING — TECHNOLOGICAL INNOVATIONS

Agrawal, Roma. *Nuts and Bolts*	609
Albert, Daniel M. *Are We There Yet?*	303.48
Ambrose, Stephen E. *Nothing Like It in the World*	385
Boot, Max. ★*War Made New*	355.0209
Brinkley, Douglas. *Wheels for the World*	B
Brooks, Michael. *The Art of More*	510.9
Carlsen, Spike. *A Walk Around the Block*	031
Conway, Edmund. *Material World*	333.7
Copeland, B. Jack. *Turing*	B

1960

AUTHOR, TITLE, SERIES AND SUBJECT INDEX

Ferrara, Silvia. *The Greatest Invention*	411
Fischer, Paul. *The Man Who Invented Motion Pictures*	791.43
Fishman, Charles. ★*One Giant Leap*	629.45
Hammack, William Scott. ★*Things We Make*	620
Hampton, Dan. *Chasing the Demon*	629.132
Kasparov, G. K. *Deep Thinking*	006.3
King, Ross. *Brunelleschi's Dome*	726.6
Kleiman, Kathy. *Proving Ground*	4.092
Launius, Roger D. *Apollo's Legacy*	629.45
Marcal, Katrine. *Mother of Invention*	604.82
McCullough, David G. *The Path Between the Seas*	972.87
McCullough, David G. ★*The Wright Brothers*	B
McWhirter, Cameron. *American Gun*	683.4
Merchant, Brian. *Blood in the Machine*	303.48
Munson, Richard. *Tesla*	B
Parissien, Steven. *The Life of the Automobile*	629.222
Parker, Matthew. *Panama Fever*	972.87
Rose, Alexander. *Empires of the Sky*	920
Smil, Vaclav. *How the World Really Works*	500
Sobel, Dava. *Longitude*	526
Standage, Tom. *A Brief History of Motion*	388
Wolfe, Tom. ★*The Right Stuff*	629.4

HISTORY WRITING — UNITED STATES

Agee, James. *Let Us Now Praise Famous Men*	976.1
Andersen, Kurt. ★*Fantasyland*	973
Andrews, Lena S. ★*Valiant Women*	940.53
Armstrong, Jennifer Keishin. *When Women Invented Television*	791.45
Atkinson, Rick. ★*The British Are Coming*	973.3
Bader, Philip. *African-American Writers*	810.9
Barron, David J. *Waging War*	342.73
Beam, Alex. *American Crucifixion*	B
Berg, Scott W. *The Burning of the World*	977.311
Bingen, Steven. *Easy Rider*	791.4372
Blum, Edward J. *The Color of Christ*	232
Bonanos, Christopher. *Flash*	B
Boorstin, Daniel J. *The Americans*	973
Bordewich, Fergus M. *America's Great Debate*	973.6
Brady, Amy. *Ice*	553.7
Brettschneider, Corey Lang. *The Oath and the Office*	342.73
Brinkley, Douglas. *Rightful Heritage*	B
Brinkley, Douglas. *Wheels for the World*	B
Bronski, Michael. *A Queer History of the United States*	306.76
Brookhiser, Richard. *Give Me Liberty*	320.540973
Broyles, Michael. ★*Revolutions in American Music*	780.9
Burnham, Margaret A. ★*By Hands Now Known*	342.73
Burns, Ken. ★*Our America*	973
Cadava, Geraldo L. *The Hispanic Republican*	324.2734089
Cahan, Richard. *Un-American*	940.53
Caldwell, Christopher. *The Age of Entitlement*	305.240973
Capozzola, Christopher. *Bound by War*	355
Carballo, David M. *America*	912
Carter, Jimmy. *Everything to Gain*	B
Chalmers, David Mark. *Hooded Americanism*	322.4
Cheever, Susan. *Drinking in America*	394.1
Childs, Craig. *Atlas of a Lost World*	551.7
Choy, Catherine Ceniza. *Asian American Histories of the United States*	973
Churchwell, Sarah Bartlett. *Behold, America*	973.9
Clague, Mark. *O Say Can You Hear?*	782.42
Clavin, Tom. *The Last Hill*	940.54
Collins, Gail. *When Everything Changed*	305.40973
Conant, Jennet. *Man of the Hour*	B
Conaway, James. *America's Library*	027.5
Connelly, Matthew James. *The Declassification Engine*	352.3
Cook, Kevin. *The Burning Blue*	629.45
Cooper, Anderson. *Vanderbilt*	920
Crosby, Molly Caldwell. *The American Plague*	614.5
Curtis, Edward E. *Muslims in America*	305.6
Daniels, Roger. *Prisoners Without Trial*	940.53
Davis, Jack E. *The Bald Eagle*	598.9
Dawidziak, Mark. *A Mystery of Mysteries*	B
Dennie, Madiba K. *The Originalism Trap*	342.73
Dickson, Paul. *The Rise of the G.I. Army 1940-1941*	940.54
Dirix, Emmanuelle. *Dressing the Decades*	746.92
Drury, Bob. *Blood and Treasure*	B
Drury, Bob. *Valley Forge*	973.3
Dubofsky, Melvyn. *Labor in America*	331.880973
Duncan, Dayton. ★*Country Music*	781.642
Easterbrook, Gregg. ★*The King of Sports*	796.332
Edin, Kathryn. ★*The Injustice of Place*	339.4
English, T. J. *The Corporation*	364.106089
Epplin, Luke. *Our Team*	796.357
Erdozain, Dominic. *One Nation Under Guns*	363.33
Essin, Christin. *Stage Designers in Early Twentieth-Century America*	792.02
Farley, Audrey Clare. *The Unfit Heiress*	B
Faust, Drew Gilpin. *Necessary Trouble*	B
Fedderly, Eva. *These Walls*	365
Fernandez-Armesto, Felipe. *Our America*	973
Ferrer, Ada. ★*Cuba*	972.91
Finan, Christopher M. *How Free Speech Saved Democracy*	342.73
Finkel, David. *An American Dreamer*	975.8
FitzGerald, Frances. *The Evangelicals*	277
Fitzpatrick, Cara. *The Death of Public School*	379.73
Flores, Dan L. *Wild New World*	591.9709
Frank, Thomas. *The People, No*	320.56
Franscell, Ron. *Shadowman*	362.88
Fraser, Steve. *The Age of Acquiescence*	973.91
Freeman, Andrea. ★*Ruin Their Crops on the Ground*	338.1
Fuhrer, Margaret. ★*American Dance*	792.809
Gage, Beverly. *G-Man*	B
Ghazvinian, John. *America and Iran*	327
Ginzberg, Lori D. *Elizabeth Cady Stanton*	B
Glatthaar, Joseph T. *The American Military*	355.00973
Goldstein, Dana. *The Teacher Wars*	371.1020973
Gomez, Laura E. ★*Inventing Latinos*	305.868
Goyal, Nikhil. ★*Live to See the Day*	305.5
Green, Hardy. *The Company Town*	307.76
Haag, Pamela. ★*The Gunning of America*	338.4
Harris, Adam. ★*The State Must Provide*	379.2
Harris, M. A. *The Black Book*	920
Hayes, Derek. *Historical Atlas of the United States*	911
Heacox, Kim. *National Geographic the National Parks*	363.6
Hickman, Katie. *Brave Hearted*	978
Higginbotham, Adam. ★*Challenger*	629.45
Hirono, Mazie. *Heart of Fire*	B
Hirsch, Foster. ★*Hollywood and the Movies of the Fifties*	791.43
Hochschild, Adam. *American Midnight*	973.91
Holzer, Harold. *Monument Man*	B
Hongoltz-Hetling, Matthew. *If It Sounds Like a Quack*	615.8
Huang, Yunte. *Daughter of the Dragon*	B
Immerwahr, Daniel. *How to Hide an Empire*	973
Isenberg, Nancy. *White Trash*	305.5
Jacobsen, Annie. *Phenomena*	133.8
Jenkins, Jessica D. *Exploring Women's Suffrage Through 50 Historic Treasures*	324.6
Johnson, Michael. *Encyclopedia of Native Tribes of North America*	970.00497
Jones, Robert P. *The Hidden Roots of White Supremacy*	305.8
Karabell, Zachary. *Inside Money*	332.1
Kazin, Michael. *What It Took to Win*	324.2736
Kemper, Steve. *Our Man in Tokyo*	952.03
Kendi, Ibram X. ★*Stamped from the Beginning*	305.8
Kenneally, Christine. *Ghosts of the Orphanage*	362.73
Kennedy, Robert F. *Thirteen Days*	327.73
King, Coretta Scott. ★*My Life, My Love, My Legacy*	B
King, Dean. *Guardians of the Valley*	333.72
King, Martin Luther. ★*A Testament of Hope*	323.1
Kirsch, Adam. *The Blessing and the Curse*	809
Klinenberg, Eric. ★*2020*	306
Kolbert, Kathryn. *Controlling Women*	362.1988
Kozol, Jonathan. ★*An End to Inequality*	379.2
Kruse, Kevin Michael. *Fault Lines*	973.92
Launius, Roger D. *Apollo's Legacy*	629.45
Ledbetter, James. *One Nation Under Gold*	332.4
Lee, Corky. ★*Corky Lee's Asian America*	770
Leinbach, Michael D. *Bringing Columbia Home*	363.12
Lepore, Jill. ★*These Truths*	973
Levy, Jonathan. *Ages of American Capitalism*	330.12
Lichtman, Allan J. *The Embattled Vote in America*	324.6
Lincoln, Abraham. *Speeches and Writings, 1832-1858*	973.5
Lisle, John. *The Dirty Tricks Department*	940.54
Lowenstein, Roger. *America's Bank*	332.1
Maddow, Rachel. ★*Prequel*	320.53
Mandery, Evan J. *A Wild Justice*	345.73
Manseau, Peter. *Objects of Devotion*	277
Mar, Alex. *Seventy Times Seven*	362.88
Martin, Justin. *Rebel Souls*	920

1961

PUBLIC LIBRARY CORE COLLECTION: NONFICTION
Twentieth Edition

Marty, Martin E. *Pilgrims in Their Own Land*	200
Meacham, Jon. *Songs of America*	782.42
Meacham, Jon. ★*The Soul of America*	973
Mead, Corey. *The Hidden History of the White House*	975.3
Metzl, Jonathan M. ★*What We've Become*	364.152
Mirski, Sean A. *We May Dominate the World*	973.91
Mordden, Ethan. *Anything Goes*	782.1
Mundy, Liza. ★*The Sisterhood*	327.12
Murolo, Priscilla. *From the Folks Who Brought You the Weekend*	331
Norrell, Robert J. *Up from History*	B
O'Donnell, Patrick K. *The Indispensables*	973.3
Olsen, Craig. *P.S. Burn This Letter Please*	306.76
Oshinsky, David M. *Bellevue*	362.1109747
Oshinsky, David M. ★*Polio*	614.5
Painter, Nell Irvin. ★*I Just Keep Talking*	814
Park, Benjamin E. *American Zion*	289.3
Paulsen, Michael Stokes. *The Constitution*	342.7302
Petri, Alexandra. *Alexandra Petri's US History*	817
Poole, W. Scott. *Vampira*	B
Porter, Eduardo. *American Poison*	305.800973
Prager, Joshua. *The Family Roe*	342.7308
Price, Polly J. *Plagues in the Nation*	614.4
Prothero, Stephen R. *The American Bible*	973
Prothero, Stephen R. *God the Bestseller*	070.5
Puglionesi, Alicia. *In Whose Ruins*	973
Questlove. *Music Is History*	782.42164
Quinn, Bridget. *She Votes*	324.6
Quinones, John. ★*One Year in Uvalde*	371.7
Rabban, David M. *Free Speech in Its Forgotten Years*	342.73
Raines, Howell. *Silent Cavalry*	973.7
Ramsey, Donovan X. ★*When Crack Was King*	362.29
Raphael, Ray. *Constitutional Myths*	342.7302
Rashke, Richard. *Useful Enemies*	341.69
Rayman, Graham. ★*Rikers*	365
Reese, William J. *Testing Wars in the Public Schools*	371.260973
Reeves, Richard. *Infamy*	940.53
Reynolds, Nicholas E. *Need to Know*	940.54
Richardson, Heather Cox. *Democracy Awakening*	320.473
Roberts, Cokie. *Ladies of Liberty*	920
Rohde, David. *In Deep*	973.933
Romano, Carlin. *America the Philosophical*	191
Rubenstein, David M. *The American Experiment*	973
Rubenstein, David M. *The American Story*	973.07202
Rubin, Kathy Kleiner. *A Light in the Dark*	364.152
Sarna, Jonathan D. ★*American Judaism*	296
Schulman, Daniel. *The Money Kings*	332.0973
Seabrook, Nicholas R. *One Person, One Vote*	328.3
Sexton, Jared Yates. *American Rule*	973
Shapiro, James. ★*The Playbook*	792
Shapiro, James. *Shakespeare in a Divided America*	822.33
Shesol, Jeff. *Mercury Rising*	629.45
Siler, Julia Flynn. *The White Devil's Daughters*	306.3
Singer, Jessie. *There Are No Accidents*	363.1
Smith, Tracy K. ★*To Free the Captives*	818
Standiford, Les. ★*Battle for the Big Top*	791.3
Stephanopoulos, George. ★*The Situation Room*	973.09
Stevens, Stuart. *It Was All a Lie*	324.2734
Stille, Alexander. *The Sullivanians*	307.77
Stone, Geoffrey R. ★*Sex and the Constitution*	345.7302
Strang, Dean A. *Worse Than the Devil*	345.775
Swift, Earl. *Across the Airless Wilds*	629.45
Taraborrelli, J. Randy. *After Camelot*	B
Taylor, Alan. *American Republics*	973.3
Terkel, Studs. *Hope Dies Last*	920
Thompson, Erin L. *Smashing Statues*	725
Tobar, Hector. ★*Our Migrant Souls*	305.868
Torgoff, Martin. *Bop Apocalypse*	781.65
Trahair, R. C. S. *Encyclopedia of Cold War Espionage, Spies, and Secret Operations 3rd Ed.*	327.12
Trillin, Calvin. *The Lede*	071
Tumulty, Karen. *The Triumph of Nancy Reagan*	B
Twenge, Jean M. *Generations*	305.2
Van Doren, Adam. *The House Tells the Story*	728
Vile, John R. *Encyclopedia of Constitutional Amendments, Proposed Amendments, and Amending Issues, 1789-2010*	342.7303
Wald, Elijah. *American Epic*	781.64
Waldman, Steven. *Sacred Liberty*	341.4
Wasik, Bill. ★*Our Kindred Creatures*	179
Wayland-Smith, Ellen. *Oneida*	307.77
Weingarten, Gene. ★*One Day*	973
Weisman, Steven R. *The Chosen Wars*	296.0973
Wexler, Jay. *Holy Hullabaloos*	342.7308
Whipple, Chris. *The Spymasters*	920
Wickenden, Dorothy. *The Agitators*	920
Wilkman, Jon. *Screening Reality*	070.1
Williamson, Elizabeth. ★*Sandy Hook*	364.152
Winik, Jay. *1944*	940.53
Wolff, Daniel J. *Grown-Up Anger*	920
Yacovone, Donald. ★*Teaching White Supremacy*	370.89
Yang, Jeff. ★*Rise*	973
Young, Ralph F. *Dissent*	303.48
Zieger, Robert H. *American Workers, American Unions, 4th Ed.*	331.88
Zinn, Howard. ★*A People's History of the United States*	973

HISTORY WRITING — WARS AND CONFLICTS

Addario, Lynsey. *Of Love & War*	779
Anderson, Fred. *The Dominion of War*	973
Arnold, James R. *Jungle of Snakes*	355.02
Barron, David J. *Waging War*	342.73
Bass, Gary Jonathan. *Freedom's Battle*	341.5
Beschloss, Michael R. ★*Presidents of War*	355.00973
Blanning, T. C. W. *Frederick the Great*	B
Boot, Max. *Invisible Armies*	355.02
Capozzola, Christopher. *Bound by War*	355
Cohen, Eliot A. *Conquered into Liberty*	355.009747
Coker, Margaret. *The Spymaster of Baghdad*	956.7044
Dalrymple, William. *The Return of a King*	958.1
Dower, John W. *Cultures of War*	355.00973
Feifer, Gregory. *The Great Gamble*	958.104
Filkins, Dexter. *The Forever War*	956.7044
Guinn, Jeff. ★*War on the Border*	972.08
Hajari, Nisid. *Midnight's Furies*	954.04
Hanson, Victor Davis. *The Father of Us All*	355.0209
Harding, Luke. *Invasion*	947.7
Hedges, Chris. *War Is a Force That Gives Us Meaning*	355.02
Hornfischer, James D. *Who Can Hold the Sea*	359.00973
Jones, Dan. ★*The Wars of the Roses*	942.04
Kalder, Daniel. *The Infernal Library*	321.9
Khan, Mahvish Rukhsana. *My Guantanamo Diary*	973.931
Klay, Phil. *Uncertain Ground*	359.9
Kneale, Matthew. *Rome*	945.6
MacMillan, Margaret. *War*	355.0209
Matloff, Judith. *No Friends but the Mountains*	355.009
McCann, Colum. *American Mother*	956.9104
Millard, Candice. ★*Hero of the Empire*	968.04
Miller, Christopher. *The War Came to Us*	947.7
Mirski, Sean A. *We May Dominate the World*	973.91
Petraeus, David Howell. *Conflict*	355
Phillips, Timothy. *Retracing the Iron Curtain*	909.82
Platt, Stephen R. *Imperial Twilight*	951
Plokhy, Serhii. ★*The Russo-Ukrainian War*	947.7
Rinehart, Lorissa. *First to the Front*	B
Roberts, Andrew. *Leadership in War*	920
Samet, Elizabeth D. *Looking for the Good War*	940.53
Slahi, Mohamedou Ould. *The Mauritanian*	958.104
Stavridis, James. *Sea Power*	359
Stephenson, Michael. *The Last Full Measure*	305.9
Stone, Geoffrey R. *Perilous Times*	323.44
Taing, Mae Bunseng. *Under the Naga Tail*	B
Thompson, Bob. *Revolutionary Roads*	973.3
Thomson, David. *The Fatal Alliance*	791.43
Toler, Pamela D. *Women Warriors*	355.0092
Trofimov, Yaroslav. ★*Our Enemies Will Vanish*	947.7
Ventrone, Jillian. *From the Marine Corps to College*	378.1
Verini, James. *They Will Have to Die Now*	956.7044
Ward, Clarissa. *On All Fronts*	B
Wilford, Hugh. *The CIA*	327.1273
Wood, David Bowne. ★*What Have We Done*	616.85
Zelensky, Volodymyr. *A Message from Ukraine*	947.7

HISTORY WRITING — WARS AND CONFLICTS — AMERICAN CIVIL WAR

Abbott, Karen. *Liar, Temptress, Soldier, Spy*	920
Achorn, Edward. *The Lincoln Miracle*	973.6
Ash, Stephen V. *Firebrand of Liberty*	973.7
Avlon, John P. *Lincoln and the Fight for Peace*	973.7
Ayers, Edward L. ★*The Thin Light of Freedom*	975.5
Blanton, DeAnne. *They Fought Like Demons*	973.7

AUTHOR, TITLE, SERIES AND SUBJECT INDEX

Blount, Roy. *Robert E. Lee*	B
Bordewich, Fergus M. *Congress at War*	324.2734
Burlingame, Michael. *Abraham Lincoln*	B
Burlingame, Michael. *The Black Man's President*	973.7
Carwardine, Richard. *Lincoln*	B
Cwiklik, Robert. *Sheridan's Secret Mission*	973.8
Davis, Burke. *Sherman's March*	973.7
Davis, William C. *Crucible of Command*	920
Delbanco, Andrew. *The War Before the War*	973.7
Donald, David Herbert. *Lincoln*	B
Egan, Timothy. ★ *The Immortal Irishman*	B
Egerton, Douglas R. *Thunder at the Gates*	973.7
Faust, Drew Gilpin. *This Republic of Suffering*	973.7
Fellman, Michael. *The Making of Robert E. Lee*	B
Fields-Black, Edda L. *Combee*	973.7
Foner, Eric. *The Fiery Trial*	973.7092
Foote, Shelby. *The Civil War*	973.7
Freeman, Douglas Southall. *Lee*	B
Gienapp, William E. *Abraham Lincoln and Civil War America*	B
Goodheart, Adam. *1861*	973.7
Goodwin, Doris Kearns. ★ *Team of Rivals*	B
Gorra, Michael Edward. *The Saddest Words*	813
Grinspan, Jon. *Wide Awake*	973.7
Groom, Winston. *Shiloh, 1862*	973.7
Guelzo, Allen C. *Gettysburg*	973.7
Gwynne, S. C. *Hymns of the Republic*	973.7
Horwitz, Tony. *Confederates in the Attic*	973.7
Keegan, John. *The American Civil War*	973.7
Korda, Michael. *Clouds of Glory*	B
Lance, Rachel. *In the Waves*	973.7
Larson, Erik. ★ *The Demon of Unrest*	973.7
Lemann, Nicholas. *Redemption*	975
Lineberry, Cate. *Be Free or Die*	973.7
Lowenstein, Roger. *Ways and Means*	973.7
Manning, Chandra. *Troubled Refuge*	973.7
Marvel, William. *Lincoln's Autocrat*	B
Masur, Kate. *Until Justice Be Done*	323.1196
Masur, Louis P. *The Civil War*	973.7
McDonough, James L. *William Tecumseh Sherman*	B
McMurtry, Larry. *Custer*	B
McPherson, James M. ★ *Abraham Lincoln*	B
McPherson, James M. *Battle Cry of Freedom*	973.7
McPherson, James M. *Drawn with the Sword*	973.7
McPherson, James M. *For Cause and Comrades*	973.7
McPherson, James M. *Hallowed Ground*	973.7
McPherson, James M. ★ *Tried by War*	973.7
Miller, Donald L. *Vicksburg*	973.7
Mitchell, Elizabeth. *Lincoln's Lie*	973.7092
Nelson, Megan Kate. *The Three-Cornered War*	978
Oakes, James. *Freedom National*	973.7
Pryor, Elizabeth Brown. *Six Encounters with Lincoln*	973.7092
Raines, Howell. *Silent Cavalry*	973.7
Reynolds, David S. *Mightier Than the Sword*	813
Roberts, Cokie. *Capital Dames*	920
Robertson, James I. *Stonewall Jackson*	B
Sandburg, Carl. *Abraham Lincoln*	B
Sears, Stephen W. ★ *Chancellorsville*	973.7
Sears, Stephen W. *Gettysburg*	973.7
Sears, Stephen W. ★ *Landscape Turned Red*	973.7
Sears, Stephen W. *Lincoln's Lieutenants*	920
Seidule, Ty. *Robert E. Lee and Me*	973.7
Seiple, Samantha. *Louisa on the Front Lines*	B
Stahr, Walter. ★ *Stanton*	B
Stiles, T. J. *Jesse James*	B
Symonds, Craig L. *Lincoln and His Admirals*	B
Taylor, Alan. *American Civil Wars*	973.7
Toler, Pamela D. *Heroines of Mercy Street*	973.7
Waller, Douglas C. *Lincoln's Spies*	973.7
Ward, Andrew. *The Slaves' War*	973.7
Ward, Geoffrey C. *The Civil War*	973.7
Wert, Jeffry D. *Cavalryman of the Lost Cause*	B
Wheelan, Joseph. ★ *Terrible Swift Sword*	B
White, Ronald C. *A. Lincoln*	B
White, Ronald C. *On Great Fields*	B
Williams, David. *Bitterly Divided*	973.7
Willis, Deborah. ★ *The Black Civil War Soldier*	973.7
Willis, Deborah. *Envisioning Emancipation*	973.7
Wills, Garry. *Lincoln at Gettysburg*	973.7
Wilson, Robert. *Mathew Brady*	B
Wineapple, Brenda. *Ecstatic Nation*	973.6
Winik, Jay. *April 1865*	973.7
Witt, John Fabian. *Lincoln's Code*	343.73

HISTORY WRITING — WARS AND CONFLICTS — AMERICAN INDIGENOUS WARS

Berg, Scott W. ★ *38 Nooses*	973.7
Brands, H. W. *The Last Campaign*	973.8
Brown, Dee. ★ *Bury My Heart at Wounded Knee*	978
Burns, Mike. *The Only One Living to Tell*	305.897
Connell, Evan S. *Son of the Morning Star*	973.8
Cozzens, Peter. *A Brutal Reckoning*	973.5
Crutchfield, James A. *Revolt at Taos*	972
Donovan, Jim. *A Terrible Glory*	973.8
Drury, Bob. *The Heart of Everything That Is*	B
Gardner, Mark L. *The Earth Is All That Lasts*	978.004
Gwynne, S. C. *Empire of the Summer Moon*	B
Inskeep, Steve. *Jacksonland*	973.56
Lepore, Jill. *The Name of War*	973.2
Nelson, Megan Kate. *The Three-Cornered War*	978
Philbrick, Nathaniel. ★ *The Last Stand*	973.8
Roberts, David. *Once They Moved Like the Wind*	B
Schultz, Eric B. *King Philip's War*	973.2
Sharfstein, Daniel J. ★ *Thunder in the Mountains*	979.5
Trask, Kerry A. *Black Hawk*	973.5

HISTORY WRITING — WARS AND CONFLICTS — ARAB-ISRAELI CONFLICT

Carter, Jimmy. *Palestine*	956.04
Collins, Larry. *O Jerusalem!*	956
Friedman, Matti. *Spies of No-Country*	327.12
Indyk, Martin. *Master of the Game*	327.73
Kaufmann, Uri R. *Eighteen Days of October*	956.04
Morris, Benny. *1948*	956.04
Morris, Benny. *Righteous Victims*	956
Oren, Michael B. *Six Days of War*	956.04
Shehadeh, Raja. ★ *We Could Have Been Friends, My Father and I*	B
Sokatch, Daniel. *Can We Talk About Israel?*	956.9405
Wright, Lawrence. *Thirteen Days in September*	956.04

HISTORY WRITING — WARS AND CONFLICTS — ATOMIC BOMB — WORLD WAR II

Barrett, David Dean. *140 Days to Hiroshima*	940.54
Bird, Kai. *American Prometheus*	B
Blume, Lesley M. M. *Fallout*	940.54
Conant, Jennet. *Man of the Hour*	B
Ham, Paul. *Hiroshima Nagasaki*	940.54
Hersey, John. ★ *Hiroshima*	940.54
Kaplan, Fred M. *The Bomb*	355.8
Kiernan, Denise. *The Girls of Atomic City*	976.8
Kunetka, James W. *The General and the Genius*	355.8
Norris, Robert S. *Racing for the Bomb*	B
Pellegrino, Charles R. *To Hell and Back*	940.54
Preston, Diana. *Before the Fallout*	303.48
Southard, Susan. *Nagasaki*	940.54
Wallace, Chris. *Countdown 1945*	940.54

HISTORY WRITING — WARS AND CONFLICTS — BATTLES

Ambrose, Stephen E. *D-Day, June 6, 1944*	940.54
Barker, Juliet R. V. *Agincourt*	944
Beeman, Richard R. *Our Lives, Our Fortunes and Our Sacred Honor*	973.3
Beevor, Antony. *D-Day*	940.54
Beevor, Antony. *The Fall of Berlin, 1945*	940.54
Bowden, Mark. ★ *Hue 1968*	959.704
Burrough, Bryan. *Forget the Alamo*	976.043
Cornwell, Bernard. *Waterloo*	940.2
Donovan, Jim. *The Blood of Heroes*	976.4
Donovan, Jim. *A Terrible Glory*	973.8
Graff, Garrett M. *When the Sea Came Alive*	940.54
Groom, Winston. *Shiloh, 1862*	973.7
Hastings, Max. *Operation Pedestal*	940.54
Hastings, Max. *Overlord*	940.54
Holland, James. ★ *Burma '44*	940.54
Holland, James. *Sicily '43*	940.54
Lambert, Raymond. *Every Man a Hero*	B
Lucas, Jack. *Indestructible*	B
MacGregor, Iain. *The Lighthouse of Stalingrad*	940.54
McPherson, James M. *Hallowed Ground*	973.7
Miller, Donald L. *Vicksburg*	973.7
Moore, Harold G. *We Were Soldiers Once—And Young*	959.704
O'Connell, Robert L. *The Ghosts of Cannae*	937

PUBLIC LIBRARY CORE COLLECTION: NONFICTION
Twentieth Edition

Philbrick, Nathaniel. ★*The Last Stand*	973.8
Phillips, Kevin. *1775*	973.3
Read, Anthony. *The Fall of Berlin*	940.54
Sears, Stephen W. ★*Chancellorsville*	973.7
Sears, Stephen W. *Gettysburg*	973.7
Sears, Stephen W. *Landscape Turned Red*	973.7
Sides, Hampton. *On Desperate Ground*	951.904
Simms, Brendan. *The Silver Waterfall*	940.54
Smith, Jim B. *The Last Mission*	940.54
Strauss, Barry S. ★*The War That Made the Roman Empire*	937
Symonds, Craig L. *The Battle of Midway*	940.54
Thomas, Evan. *Sea of Thunder*	940.54
Winik, Jay. *April 1865*	973.7

HISTORY WRITING — WARS AND CONFLICTS — CIVIL WARS

Ackroyd, Peter. *Rebellion*	941.06
Armitage, David. *Civil Wars*	355.02
Beah, Ishmael. ★*A Long Way Gone*	B
Beevor, Antony. *Russia*	947.084
Cercas, Javier. *Lord of All the Dead*	868
Cooper, Helene. *The House at Sugar Beach*	921
Deng, Alephonsion. *They Poured Fire on Us from the Sky*	B
Gourevitch, Philip. *We Wish to Inform You That Tomorrow We Will Be Killed with Our Families*	364.15
Hari, Daoud. *The Translator*	B
Hatzfeld, Jean. *Machete Season*	967.57104
Hochschild, Adam. *Spain in Our Hearts*	946.081
Maass, Peter. *Love Thy Neighbor*	949.702
Mohan, Rohini. *The Seasons of Trouble*	954.9303
O'Donnell, Patrick K. *The Unvanquished*	973.7
Platt, Stephen R. *Autumn in the Heavenly Kingdom*	951
Preston, Paul. *The Spanish Holocaust*	946.081
Seierstad, Asne. *Angel of Grozny*	947.086
Stern, Jessica. *My War Criminal*	341.6
Subramanian, Sammanth. *This Divided Island*	954.9303
Taylor, Alan. *American Civil Wars*	973.7
Trebincevic, Kenan. *The Bosnia List*	B
Ung, Loung. *First They Killed My Father*	959.604
Warrick, Joby. *Red Line*	956.9104
Willis, Deborah. ★*The Black Civil War Soldier*	973.7

HISTORY WRITING — WARS AND CONFLICTS — CRIMEAN WAR

Figes, Orlando. *The Crimean War*	947

HISTORY WRITING — WARS AND CONFLICTS — CRUSADES

Asbridge, Thomas S. ★*The Crusades*	909.07
Frankopan, Peter. *The First Crusade*	956
Jones, Dan. *Crusaders*	909.07
Lambert, Malcolm. *God's Armies*	956

HISTORY WRITING — WARS AND CONFLICTS — FRENCH AND INDIAN WAR

Calloway, Colin G. *The Indian World of George Washington*	323.1197

HISTORY WRITING — WARS AND CONFLICTS — FRENCH REVOLUTION

Burke, Edmund. *Reflections on the Revolution in France*	944.04
Darnton, Robert. *The Revolutionary Temper*	944
Davidson, Ian. *The French Revolution*	944.04
Gaines, James R. *For Liberty and Glory*	B
Lever, Evelyne. *Marie Antoinette*	B
McPhee, Peter. *Robespierre*	B
Popkin, Jeremy D. *A New World Begins*	944.04
Schama, Simon. *Citizens*	944.04
Scurr, Ruth. *Fatal Purity*	B

HISTORY WRITING — WARS AND CONFLICTS — HOLOCAUST — WORLD WAR II

Ackerman, Diane. ★*The Zookeeper's Wife*	940.53
Albright, Madeleine Korbel. *Prague Winter*	943.71
Asbrink, Elisabeth. *And in the Vienna Woods the Trees Remain*	B
Atria, Travis. *Better Days Will Come Again*	B
Batalion, Judith. *The Light of Days*	940.53
Berenbaum, Michael. *The World Must Know*	940.53
Berr, Helene. *The Journal of Helene Berr*	B
Blau, Magda Hellinger. *The Nazis Knew My Name*	940.53
Cadbury, Deborah. *The School That Escaped from the Nazis*	940.53
Chiger, Krystyna. *The Girl in the Green Sweater*	B
Crasnianski, Tania. *The Children of Nazis*	943.086
Debreczeni, Jozsef. *Cold Crematorium*	940.53
Dwork, Deborah. ★*Holocaust*	940
Edmonds, Chris. *No Surrender*	B
Eisen, Max. *By Chance Alone*	940.5318
Fairweather, Jack. *The Volunteer*	B
Finkelstein, Daniel. *Two Roads Home*	920
Fishman, David E. *The Book Smugglers*	940.53
Frank, Anne. *The Diary of Anne Frank*	B
Frankel, Rebecca. *Into the Forest*	940.53
Frankl, Viktor E. ★*Man's Search for Meaning*	B
Frankl, Viktor E. *Yes to Life*	150.19
Freedland, Jonathan. ★*The Escape Artist*	940.53
Frenkel, Francoise. *A Bookshop in Berlin*	B
Friedlander, Saul. *Nazi Germany and the Jews*	940.53
Friedlander, Saul. *Nazi Germany and the Jews*	940.53
Goldhagen, Daniel Jonah. *Hitler's Willing Executioners*	940.53
Goldsmith, Martin. *The Inextinguishable Symphony*	B
Grose, Peter. *A Good Place to Hide*	940.53
Gross, Jan Tomasz. *Neighbors*	940.53
Hayes, Peter. *Why?*	940.53
Holden, Wendy. ★*Born Survivors*	940.53
Hurowitz, Richard. *In the Garden of the Righteous*	940.53
Iperen, Roxane van. ★*The Sisters of Auschwitz*	940.53
Jaku, Eddie. ★*The Happiest Man on Earth*	B
Kaiser, Menachem. *Plunder*	940.53
Katin, Miriam. *We Are on Our Own*	741.5
Kertzer, David I. *The Pope at War*	940.53
Kinstler, Linda. *Come to This Court and Cry*	940.53
Klemperer, Victor. *I Will Bear Witness*	B
Kramer, Clara. *Clara's War*	B
Kraus, Dita. *A Delayed Life*	B
Kurtz, Glenn. *Three Minutes in Poland*	947.7
Levi, Primo. ★*The Drowned and the Saved*	940.53
Levi, Primo. *The Periodic Table*	858
Levi, Primo. *The Reawakening*	B
Levi, Primo. ★*Survival in Auschwitz*	B
Lindwer, Willy. *The Last Seven Months of Anne Frank*	B
Lipstadt, Deborah E. *The Eichmann Trial*	345.5694
Lipstadt, Deborah E. *History on Trial*	B
Loftis, Larry. ★*The Watchmaker's Daughter*	940.53
Longerich, Peter. *Goebbels*	B
Lower, Wendy. *Hitler's Furies*	940.53
Macadam, Heather Dune. *999*	940.53
Marwell, David G. *Mengele*	B
Mazzeo, Tilar J. *Irena's Children*	
Moorehead, Caroline. *Village of Secrets*	944
Mueller, Melissa. *Alice's Piano*	B
Neumann, Ariana. *When Time Stopped*	B
Novick, Peter. *The Holocaust in American Life*	940.53
Pick-Goslar, Hannah Elizabeth. ★*My Friend Anne Frank*	B
Pivnik, Sam. *Survivor*	940.5318
Pressman, Steven. *50 Children*	B
Rajchman, Chil. *The Last Jew of Treblinka*	940.53
Rees, Laurence. *Auschwitz*	940.53
Rees, Laurence. *The Holocaust*	940.53
Rhodes, Richard. *Masters of Death*	940.53
Rydell, Anders. *The Book Thieves*	027
Rynecki, Elizabeth. *Chasing Portraits*	B
Sands, Philippe. *East West Street*	345
Sands, Philippe. *The Ratline*	B
Schindler, Meriel. *The Lost Cafe Schindler*	943.64
Simon, Marie. *Underground in Berlin*	B
Snyder, Timothy. *Black Earth*	940.53
Snyder, Timothy. ★*Bloodlands*	940.54
Spiegel, Renia. *Renia's Diary*	B
Spiegelman, Art. ★*Maus*	741.5
Stangneth, Bettina. *Eichmann Before Jerusalem*	B
Stone, Dan. ★*The Holocaust*	940.53
Sullivan, Rosemary. *The Betrayal of Anne Frank*	940.53
Talty, Stephan. *The Good Assassin*	364.15
Van Es, Bart. *The Cut Out Girl*	B
Van Wijk-Voskuijl, Joop. *The Last Secret of the Secret Annex*	940.53
Wachsmann, Nikolaus. *Kl*	940.53
Weiss, Helga. *Helga's Diary*	B
White, Elizabeth B. ★*The Counterfeit Countess*	940.53
Wiesel, Elie. *All Rivers Run to the Sea*	B
Wiesel, Elie. ★*Night*	B
Wiesenthal, Simon. ★*The Sunflower*	179.7

HISTORY WRITING — WARS AND CONFLICTS — HOMEFRONT — AMERICAN CIVIL WAR

Jones, Jacqueline. *Saving Savannah*	975.8

AUTHOR, TITLE, SERIES AND SUBJECT INDEX

HISTORY WRITING — WARS AND CONFLICTS — HOMEFRONT — WORLD WAR II
- Ackerman, Diane. ★*The Zookeeper's Wife* — 940.53
- Berg, Mary. *The Diary of Mary Berg* — B
- Cooke, Alistair. *The American Home Front, 1941-1942* — 940.53
- Crasnianski, Tania. *The Children of Nazis* — 943.086
- Dumbach, Annette E. *Sophie Scholl and the White Rose* — 943.086
- Englund, Peter. *November 1942* — 940.53
- Gies, Miep. ★*Anne Frank Remembered* — B
- Goodwin, Doris Kearns. *No Ordinary Time* — 920
- Grose, Peter. *A Good Place to Hide* — 940.53
- Haffner, Sebastian. *Defying Hitler* — 943.085
- Hemming, Henry. *Agents of Influence* — 940.54
- Humbert, Agnes. *Resistance* — B
- Jahner, Harald. ★*Aftermath* — 943.087
- Kennedy, David M. ★*Freedom from Fear* — 973.91
- Kiernan, Denise. *The Girls of Atomic City* — 976.8
- Kupperman, Michael. *All the Answers* — 741.5
- Moorhouse, Roger. *Berlin at War* — 943
- O'Donnell, Svenja. *Inge's War* — 943.086
- Oelhafen, Ingrid von. *Hitler's Stolen Children* — B
- Porter, Carolyn. *Marcel's Letters* — 940.54
- Reeves, Richard. *Infamy* — 940.53
- Ricks, Thomas E. *Churchill and Orwell* — 920
- Ronald, Susan. *Hitler's Aristocrats* — 940.53
- Rosenzweig, Laura B. *Hollywood's Spies* — 791.43
- Ross, Steven Joseph. ★*Hitler in Los Angeles* — 979.4
- Russell, Jan Jarboe. *The Train to Crystal City* — 940.53
- Schwarz, Geraldine. *Those Who Forget* — 940.53
- Sone, Monica Itoi. *Nisei Daughter* — 979.7
- Takaki, Ronald T. *Double Victory* — 940.53
- Yellin, Emily. *Our Mothers' War* — 940.53

HISTORY WRITING — WARS AND CONFLICTS — HUNDRED YEARS WAR
- Barker, Juliet R. V. *Agincourt* — 944

HISTORY WRITING — WARS AND CONFLICTS — IRAQ WAR
- Abdul-Ahad, Ghaith. *A Stranger in Your Own City* — 956.7044
- Bardenwerper, William. *The Prisoner in His Palace* — 956.7044
- Campbell, Deborah. *A Disappearance in Damascus* — 365
- Castner, Brian. *The Long Walk* — B
- Chandrasekaran, Rajiv. *Imperial Life in the Emerald City* — 956.7044
- Chivers, C. J. *The Fighters* — 920
- Coll, Steve. ★*The Achilles Trap* — 956.7044
- Draper, Robert. *To Start a War* — 956.7044
- Finkel, David. *The Good Soldiers* — 956.7044
- Finkel, David. *Thank You for Your Service* — 920
- Frederick, Jim. *Black Hearts* — 956.7044
- Gallego, Ruben. *They Called Us* — 956.7044
- Newton, Michael A. *Enemy of the State* — 345.567
- Packer, George. *The Assassins' Gate* — 956.7044
- Philipps, David. *Alpha* — 956.7044
- Raddatz, Martha. *The Long Road Home* — B
- Ricks, Thomas E. *Fiasco* — 956.7044
- Seierstad, Asne. *A Hundred and One Days* — 956.70443
- Stewart, Rory. *The Prince of the Marshes* — 956.7044
- Wright, Evan. *Generation Kill* — 956.7044

HISTORY WRITING — WARS AND CONFLICTS — KOREAN WAR
- Brady, James. *The Coldest War* — B
- Cumings, Bruce. *The Korean War* — 951.904
- Halberstam, David. *The Coldest Winter* — 951.904
- Hutton, Robin L. *Sgt. Reckless* — 951.904
- Makos, Adam. *Devotion* — 920
- Sides, Hampton. *On Desperate Ground* — 951.904

HISTORY WRITING — WARS AND CONFLICTS — MEXICAN-AMERICAN WAR
- Donovan, Jim. *The Blood of Heroes* — 976.4

HISTORY WRITING — WARS AND CONFLICTS — NAPOLEONIC WARS
- Broers, Michael. *Napoleon* — B
- Broers, Michael. *Napoleon* — 944.05
- Broers, Michael. *Napoleon* — B
- Cornwell, Bernard. *Waterloo* — 940.2
- Johnson, Paul. *Napoleon* — B
- O'Keeffe, Paul. *Waterloo* — 940.2
- Roberts, Andrew. ★*Napoleon* — B
- Zamoyski, Adam. *Napoleon* — B

HISTORY WRITING — WARS AND CONFLICTS — PELOPONNESIAN WAR
- Kagan, Donald. *The Peloponnesian War* — 938

- Roberts, Jennifer Tolbert. *The Plague of War* — 938

HISTORY WRITING — WARS AND CONFLICTS — PERSIAN GULF WAR
- Swofford, Anthony. *Jarhead* — 956.7044

HISTORY WRITING — WARS AND CONFLICTS — PROTESTS — VIETNAM WAR
- Bingham, Clara. *Witness to the Revolution* — 303.48
- Maraniss, David. *They Marched into Sunlight* — 959.704

HISTORY WRITING — WARS AND CONFLICTS — RESISTANCE — WORLD WAR II
- Allen, Arthur. ★*The Fantastic Laboratory of Dr. Weigl* — 614.5
- Bailey, Catherine. *A Castle in Wartime* — 943.086
- Bascomb, Neal. *The Winter Fortress* — 940.54
- Batalion, Judith. *The Light of Days* — 940.53
- Donner, Rebecca. *All the Frequent Troubles of Our Days* — 943
- Dumbach, Annette E. *Sophie Scholl and the White Rose* — 943.086
- Helm, Sarah. *A Life in Secrets* — B
- Humbert, Agnes. *Resistance* — B
- Hurowitz, Richard. *In the Garden of the Righteous* — 940.53
- Kaiser, Charles. *The Cost of Courage* — B
- Kershaw, Alex. *Avenue of Spies* — 940.53
- Kix, Paul. *The Saboteur* — 940.53
- Magida, Arthur J. *Code Name Madeleine* — 940.54
- Marsh, Charles. *Strange Glory* — B
- Mazzeo, Tilar J. *Sisters in Resistance* — 945.091
- Moorehead, Caroline. *A House in the Mountains* — 940.53
- Moorehead, Caroline. *A Train in Winter* — 940.53
- Moorehead, Caroline. *Village of Secrets* — 944
- Ohler, Norman. *The Bohemians* — 940.53
- Olson, Lynne. *Last Hope Island* — 940.53
- Pomerantsev, Peter. ★*How to Win an Information War* — 940.53
- Purnell, Sonia. ★*A Woman of No Importance* — B
- Rosbottom, Ronald C. *When Paris Went Dark* — 944.0816
- Rosenberg, Justus. *The Art of Resistance* — B

HISTORY WRITING — WARS AND CONFLICTS — REVOLUTIONARY WAR (AMERICA)
- Atkinson, Rick. ★*The British Are Coming* — 973.3
- Baier, Bret. *To Rescue the Constitution* — 973.4
- Beeman, Richard R. *Our Lives, Our Fortunes and Our Sacred Honor* — 973.3
- Bobrick, Benson. *Angel in the Whirlwind* — 973.3
- Brands, H. W. ★*Our First Civil War* — 973.3
- Broadwater, Jeff. ★*George Mason* — B
- Crawford, Alan Pell. *This Fierce People* — 975
- Daughan, George C. *Revolution on the Hudson* — 974.7
- Dolin, Eric Jay. ★*Rebels at Sea* — 973.3
- Drury, Bob. *Valley Forge* — 973.3
- Duncan, Michael. ★*Hero of Two Worlds* — B
- Ellis, Joseph J. *American Creation* — 973.3
- Ellis, Joseph J. *The Cause* — 973.3
- Ferling, John E. *Winning Independence* — 973.3
- Ferreiro, Larrie D. *Brothers at Arms* — 327.73
- Fischer, David Hackett. *Paul Revere's Ride* — 973.3
- Fischer, David Hackett. *Washington's Crossing* — 973.3
- Fried, Stephen. *Rush* — B
- Gaines, James R. *For Liberty and Glory* — B
- Hogeland, William. *Declaration* — 973.3
- Holton, Woody. *Liberty Is Sweet* — 973.3
- Hoock, Holger. *Scars of Independence* — 973.3
- Ketchum, Richard M. *Saratoga* — 973.3
- Kilmeade, Brian. ★*George Washington's Secret Six* — 973.4
- McCullough, David G. ★*1776* — 973.3
- Meltzer, Brad. ★*The First Conspiracy* — 973.4
- Middlekauff, Robert. *The Glorious Cause* — 973.3
- Miller, Marla. *Betsy Ross and the Making of America* — B
- Morison, Samuel Eliot. *John Paul Jones* — B
- Norton, Mary Beth. *1774* — 973.3
- O'Connell, Robert L. *Revolutionary* — B
- O'Donnell, Patrick K. *The Indispensables* — 973.3
- Philbrick, Nathaniel. ★*Bunker Hill* — 973.3
- Philbrick, Nathaniel. ★*In the Hurricane's Eye* — 973.3
- Philbrick, Nathaniel. ★*Valiant Ambition* — B
- Phillips, Kevin. *1775* — 973.3
- Rakove, Jack N. *Revolutionaries* — 973.3
- Raphael, Ray. *A People's History of the American Revolution* — 973.3
- Sankovitch, Nina. *American Rebels* — 920
- Staiti, Paul J. *Of Arms and Artists* — B
- Taylor, Alan. *American Revolutions* — 973.3
- Taylor, Alan. *The Divided Ground* — 974.7
- Weintraub, Stanley. *Iron Tears* — 973.3

PUBLIC LIBRARY CORE COLLECTION: NONFICTION
Twentieth Edition

Zambone, Albert Louis. *Daniel Morgan* — B

HISTORY WRITING — WARS AND CONFLICTS — REVOLUTIONS
Arana, Marie. *Bolivar* — B
Guevara, Che. *Diary of a Combatant* — 972.91063
Hernandez, Kelly Lytle. ★*Bad Mexicans* — 972
Kars, Marjoleine. *Blood on the River* — 306.3
Mazower, Mark. *The Greek Revolution* — 949.5
Michener, James A. *The Bridge at Andau* — 943.9
Spence, Jonathan D. *God's Chinese Son* — 951
Watling, Sarah. *Tomorrow Perhaps the Future* — 946.081
Zakaria, Fareed. *Age of Revolutions* — 303.6

HISTORY WRITING — WARS AND CONFLICTS — RUSSIAN REVOLUTION
Figes, Orlando. *A People's Tragedy* — 947.08
McMeekin, Sean. *The Russian Revolution* — 947.084
Merridale, Catherine. *Lenin on the Train* — B
Mieville, China. *October* — 947.084
Pipes, Richard. *A Concise History of the Russian Revolution* — 947.084
Rappaport, Helen. *Caught in the Revolution* — 355.00947
Reed, John. *Ten Days That Shook the World* — 947.084
Teffi, N. A. *Memories* — B

HISTORY WRITING — WARS AND CONFLICTS — SPANISH-AMERICAN WAR
Gardner, Mark L. *Rough Riders* — 973.911
Miller, Scott. *The President and the Assassin* — 973.8
Tuccille, Jerome. *The Roughest Riders* — 973.8

HISTORY WRITING — WARS AND CONFLICTS — TRIPOLITAN WAR
Kilmeade, Brian. ★*Thomas Jefferson and the Tripoli Pirates* — 973.4

HISTORY WRITING — WARS AND CONFLICTS — VIETNAM WAR
Albracht, William. *Abandoned in Hell* — 959.704
Appy, Christian G. *American Reckoning* — 959.704
Black, George. ★*The Long Reckoning* — 959.704
Boot, Max. ★*The Road Not Taken* — B
Bowden, Mark. ★*Hue 1968* — 959.704
Brokhausen, Nick. *Whispers in the Tall Grass* — 959.704
Caputo, Philip. *A Rumor of War* — 959.704
Clarke, Thurston. *Honorable Exit* — 959.704
Duiker, William J. *Ho Chi Minh* — B
FitzGerald, Frances. *Fire in the Lake* — 959.704
Gewen, Barry. ★*The Inevitability of Tragedy* — B
Halberstam, David. *The Best and the Brightest* — 973.92
Hastings, Max. ★*Vietnam* — 959.704
Hendrickson, Paul. *The Living and the Dead* — 959.704
Karnow, Stanley. *Vietnam, a History* — 959.704
Kissinger, Henry. *Ending the Vietnam War* — 959.704
Kurlansky, Mark. *1968* — 909.82
Lee, Heath Hardage. ★*The League of Wives* — 959.704
Logevall, Fredrik. *Embers of War* — 959.704
McNamara, Robert S. *In Retrospect* — 959.704
Moore, Harold G. *We Are Soldiers Still* — 959.704
Moore, Harold G. *We Were Soldiers Once—And Young* — 959.704
Nguyen, Viet Thanh. *Nothing Ever Dies* — 959.704
Pham, Andrew X. ★*The Eaves of Heaven* — B
Sheehan, Neil. *A Bright Shining Lie* — 959.704
Shultz, Richard H. *The Secret War Against Hanoi* — 959.704
Stanton, Doug. *The Odyssey of Echo Company* — 959.704
Talty, Stephan. *Saving Bravo* — 959.704
Ulander, Perry A. *Walking Point* — B
Ward, Geoffrey C. ★*The Vietnam War* — 959.704
Warren, James A. *Year of the Hawk* — 959.704
White, Ralph. *Getting Out of Saigon* — 959.704
Wright, James Edward. ★*Enduring Vietnam* — 959.704

HISTORY WRITING — WARS AND CONFLICTS — WAR IN AFGHANISTAN
Ackerman, Elliot. *The Fifth Act* — 958.104
Bergen, Peter L. *Manhunt* — 363.325
Brennan, Thomas J. *Shooting Ghosts* — B
Chivers, C. J. *The Fighters* — 920
Edstrom, Erik. *Un-American* — B
Fritz, Ian. *What the Taliban Told Me* — B
Golembesky, Michael. *Level Zero Heroes* — 958.104
Gopal, Anand. *No Good Men Among the Living* — 920
Junger, Sebastian. *War* — 958.104
Kesling, Ben. *Bravo Company* — 958.104
Lemmon, Gayle Tzemach. *Ashley's War* — B
Lemmon, Gayle Tzemach. *The Dressmaker of Khair Khana* — B
Loyn, David. *The Long War* — 958.104
Luttrell, Marcus. *Lone Survivor* — 958.104
Meyer, Dakota. *Into the Fire* — 958.104
Morgan, Wesley. *The Hardest Place* — 958.104
O'Neill, Robert. *The Operator* — B
Owen, Mark. *No Easy Day* — B
Passarlay, Gulwali. *The Lightless Sky* — B
Romesha, Clinton. *Red Platoon* — 958.104
Stanton, Doug. *12 Strong* — 958.104
Whitlock, Craig. *The Afghanistan Papers* — 958.104

HISTORY WRITING — WARS AND CONFLICTS — WAR OF 1812
Kilmeade, Brian. ★*Andrew Jackson and the Miracle of New Orleans* — 973.5
Snow, Peter. *When Britain Burned the White House* — 975.3
Taylor, Alan. *The Civil War of 1812* — 973.5
Taylor, Alan. ★*The Internal Enemy* — 975.5
Wills, Garry. *James Madison* — B

HISTORY WRITING — WARS AND CONFLICTS — WORLD WAR I
Anderson, Scott. *Lawrence in Arabia* — B
Bascomb, Neal. *The Escape Artists* — 940.4
Bogosian, Eric. *Operation Nemesis* — 956.62
Brotherton, Marcus. *A Bright and Blinding Sun* — 940.54
Carroll, Andrew. *My Fellow Soldiers* — 940.4
Carter, Miranda. *George, Nicholas and Wilhelm* — 940.3
Clay, Catrine. *King, Kaiser, Tsar* — B
Davenport, Matthew J. *First Over There* — 940.4
Emery, Theo. *Hellfire Boys* — 358
Englund, Peter. *The Beauty and the Sorrow* — 940.309
Fox, Margalit. *The Confidence Men* — 940.4
Glass, Charles. *Soldiers Don't Go Mad* — 616.85
Grant, R. G. *World War I* — 940.3
Hamilton-Paterson, James. *Marked for Death* — 358.400941
Hastings, Max. *Catastrophe 1914* — 940.3
Hynes, Samuel. *The Unsubstantial Air* — 940.4
Keegan, John. *The First World War* — 940.3
Korda, Michael. *Muse of Fire* — 940.4
Larson, Erik. ★*Dead Wake* — 940.4
Lawrence, T. E. *Seven Pillars of Wisdom* — 940.4
Lloyd, Nick. *The Western Front* — 940.4
MacMillan, Margaret. *Paris 1919* — 940.3
Massie, Robert K. *Castles of Steel* — 940.4
McMeekin, Sean. *July 1914* — 940.3
Moore, Wendy. *No Man's Land* — 940.4
Preston, Diana. *A Higher Form of Killing* — 940.4
Rogan, Eugene L. *The Fall of the Ottomans* — 940.3
Stanley, Matthew. *Einstein's War* — 530
Tuchman, Barbara W. ★*The Guns of August* — 940.4

HISTORY WRITING — WARS AND CONFLICTS — WORLD WAR II
Alexander, Caroline. *Skies of Thunder* — 940.54
Alexander, Larry. *Biggest Brother* — B
Allen, Arthur. ★*The Fantastic Laboratory of Dr. Weigl* — 614.5
Andrews, Lena S. ★*Valiant Women* — 940.53
Atkinson, Rick. *An Army at Dawn* — 940.54
Atkinson, Rick. *The Guns at Last Light* — 940.54
Barrett, Duncan. *GI Brides* — 920
Bass, Gary Jonathan. ★*Judgment at Tokyo* — 952.04
Beevor, Antony. *Ardennes 1944* — 940.54
Beevor, Antony. *D-Day* — 940.54
Beevor, Antony. *The Second World War* — 940.54
Beschloss, Michael R. *The Conquerors* — 940.53
Bilger, Burkhard. *Fatherland* — B
Bissinger, H. G. ★*The Mosquito Bowl* — 796.332
Borneman, Walter R. *The Admirals* — B
Borneman, Walter R. *Macarthur at War* — B
Bouverie, Tim. *Appeasement* — 327.41043
Brighton, Terry. *Patton, Montgomery, Rommel* — B
Brown, Daniel James. ★*Facing the Mountain* — 940.54
Budiansky, Stephen. *Blackett's War* — 940.54
Chrisinger, David. *The Soldier's Truth* — 940.54
Churchill, Winston. *The Grand Alliance* — 940.53
Clark, Lloyd. *The Commanders* — 940.53
Clavin, Thomas. *Lightning Down* — 940.54
Clavin, Tom. *The Last Hill* — 940.54
Cohen, Deborah. *Last Call at the Hotel Imperial* — 070.92
Copeland, B. Jack. *Turing* — B
Cornwell, John. *Hitler's Pope* — B
Daniels, Roger. *Prisoners Without Trial* — 940.53
Delmont, Matthew F. *Half American* — 940.54
Dickson, Paul. *The Rise of the G.I. Army 1940-1941* — 940.54
Dimbleby, Jonathan. *The Battle of the Atlantic* — 940.54
Drabkin, Ronald. *Beverly Hills Spy* — 940.54

AUTHOR, TITLE, SERIES AND SUBJECT INDEX

Eder, Mari K. *The Girls Who Stepped Out of Line*	920
Edsel, Robert M. *The Monuments Men*	940.53
Eisner, Peter. *The Pope's Last Crusade*	282.092
Evans, Richard J. *The Third Reich in Power, 1933-1939*	943.086
Fullilove, Michael. *Rendezvous with Destiny*	973.917092
Geroux, William. *The Ghost Ships of Archangel*	940.54
Giangreco, D. M. *Hell to Pay*	940.54
Gilbert, Martin. *The Second World War*	940.53
Goodman, Simon. *The Orpheus Clock*	940.53
Gortemaker, Heike B. *Eva Braun*	B
Graff, Garrett M. ★*When the Sea Came Alive*	940.54
Grayling, A. C. *Among the Dead Cities*	940.54
Groom, Winston. *The Allies*	940.5309
Groom, Winston. *The Generals*	920
Guibert, Emmanuel. *Alan's War*	741.5
Hamilton, Nigel. *The Mantle of Command*	940.54
Hanson, Victor Davis. *The Second World Wars*	940.54
Harris, Mark. ★*Five Came Back*	791.4302
Hastings, Max. *Inferno*	940.54
Hastings, Max. *The Secret War*	940.54
Helm, Sarah. *Ravensbruck*	940.53
Herman, Arthur. ★*Douglas Macarthur*	B
Herman, Arthur. *Freedom's Forge*	940.53
Hervieux, Linda. *Forgotten*	940.54
Hindley, Meredith. *Destination Casablanca*	940.54
Holden, Wendy. ★*Born Survivors*	940.53
Holland, James. *Battle of Britain*	940.54
Holland, James. *The Rise of Germany, 1939-1941; Vol. 1*	940.54
Hotta, Eri. *Japan 1941*	940.54
Jacobsen, Annie. ★*Operation Paperclip*	940.54
Johnson, Paul. *Churchill*	B
Jordan, Jonathan W. *Brothers, Rivals, Victors*	940.54
Kaiser, Charles. *The Cost of Courage*	940.54
Katz, Catherine Grace. *The Daughters of Yalta*	920
Kean, Sam. *The Bastard Brigade*	355.8
Keegan, John. *The Second World War*	940.53
Kempowski, Walter. *Swansong 1945*	940.54
Kennedy, Paul. *Engineers of Victory*	940.54
King, David. *Death in the City of Light*	364.152
Kramer, Clara. *Clara's War*	B
Landdeck, Katherine Sharp. *The Women with Silver Wings*	920
Larman, Alexander. *The Windsors at War*	940.53
Larson, Erik. ★*The Splendid and the Vile*	940.54
Lewis, Damien. *Agent Josephine*	B
Lineberry, Cate. *The Secret Rescue*	940.54
Lisle, John. *The Dirty Tricks Department*	940.54
Loftis, Larry. *Code Name*	B
Loftis, Larry. ★*The Watchmaker's Daughter*	940.53
Longerich, Peter. *Goebbels*	B
Longerich, Peter. *Hitler*	B
Lowe, Keith. *Prisoners of History*	940.54
Lowe, Keith. *Savage Continent*	940.55
Lower, Wendy. *Hitler's Furies*	940.53
MacGregor, Iain. *The Lighthouse of Stalingrad*	940.54
Macintyre, Ben. *Agent Zigzag*	B
Macintyre, Ben. ★*Operation Mincemeat*	940.54
Macintyre, Ben. ★*Rogue Heroes*	940.54
MacKrell, Judith. *The Correspondents*	070.4
Maddow, Rachel. ★*Prequel*	320.53
Makos, Adam. ★*A Higher Call*	940.54
Makos, Adam. *Spearhead*	B
Marsh, Charles. *Strange Glory*	B
Matzen, Robert. *Dutch Girl*	B
Mazower, Mark. *Hitler's Empire*	940.53
McConahay, Mary Jo. *The Tango War*	940.53
McKay, Sinclair. *Berlin*	943
McMeekin, Sean. *Stalin's War*	940.53
Meacham, Jon. *Franklin and Winston*	940.53
Meltzer, Brad. ★*The Nazi Conspiracy*	940.53
Moorehead, Caroline. *A House in the Mountains*	940.53
Moorehead, Caroline. *A Train in Winter*	940.53
Moorehead, Caroline. *Village of Secrets*	944
Moorhouse, Roger. *The Devils' Alliance*	940.53
Morton, Andrew. *17 Carnations*	941.084
Moynahan, Brian. *Leningrad*	780.92
Mulley, Clare. *The Spy Who Loved*	B
Mulley, Clare. *The Women Who Flew for Hitler*	920
Mundy, Liza. *Code Girls*	940.54
Nasaw, David. *The Last Million*	940.53
Nelson, Craig. *Pearl Harbor*	940.54
Nelson, Craig. ★*V Is for Victory*	973.917
Nez, Chester. *Code Talker*	B
O'Brien, Phillips Payson. *The Second Most Powerful Man in the World*	B
O'Reilly, Bill. *Killing the SS*	940.53
Olson, Lynne. *Citizens of London*	940.54012
Olson, Lynne. ★*Madame Fourcade's Secret War*	B
Olson, Lynne. *Those Angry Days*	940.53
Overy, R. J. *Why the Allies Won*	940.53
Paradis, Michel. *The Light of Battle*	940.54
Parkin, Simon. *A Game of Birds and Wolves*	940.54
Parkin, Simon. *The Island of Extraordinary Captives*	940.53
Patton, George S. *War as I Knew It*	B
Phillips, Adrian. *Fighting Churchill, Appeasing Hitler*	327.41043
Pivnik, Sam. *Survivor*	940.5318
Plokhy, Serhii. *Yalta*	940.53
Prange, Gordon W. *At Dawn We Slept*	940.54
Preston, Diana. *Eight Days at Yalta*	940.53
Price, David A. *Geniuses at War*	940.54
Purnell, Sonia. *Clementine*	B
Rajchman, Chil. *The Last Jew of Treblinka*	940.53
Reid, Anna. *Leningrad*	940.54
Roberts, Andrew. ★*Churchill*	B
Roberts, Andrew. *Masters and Commanders*	940.5322
Rogoyska, Jane. *Surviving Katyn*	940.54
Roll, David L. *George Marshall*	B
Ronald, Susan. *A Dangerous Woman*	B
Rose, Sarah. *D-Day Girls*	940.53
Ryback, Timothy W. *Takeover*	943.086
Sakamoto, Pamela Rotner. *Midnight in Broad Daylight*	940.53
Scott, James. *Target Tokyo*	940.54
Shirer, William L. ★*The Rise and Fall of the Third Reich*	943.086
Siegal, Nina. *The Diary Keepers*	940.54
Smith, Starr. *Jimmy Stewart*	B
Snyder, Steve. *Shot Down*	940.54
Snyder, Timothy. *Black Earth*	940.53
Snyder, Timothy. ★*Bloodlands*	940.54
Spicer, Charles. *Coffee with Hitler*	941.084
Stargardt, Nicholas. *The German War*	940.53
Stevenson, William. *A Man Called Intrepid*	940.54
Strauss, Gwen. *The Nine*	940.53
Taylor, Fred. *1939*	940.53
Terkel, Studs. *The Good War*	940.54
Thomas, Gordon. *Defying Hitler*	920
Tobin, James. *Ernie Pyle's War*	B
Toll, Ian W. *The Conquering Tide*	940.54
Toll, Ian W. *Twilight of the Gods*	940.54
Trimborn, Jurgen. *Leni Riefenstahl*	B
Tucker, Todd. *The Great Starvation Experiment*	174.2
Urwand, Ben. *The Collaboration*	791.430973
Waller, Douglas C. *Wild Bill Donovan*	B
Weale, Adrian. *Army of Evil*	940.54
Winik, Jay. *1944*	940.53
Zuckoff, Mitchell. *Frozen in Time*	998.2
Zuckoff, Mitchell. *Lost in Shangri-La*	940.54

HISTORY WRITING — WARS AND CONFLICTS — WORLD WAR II — EUROPEAN THEATER

Aleksievich, Svetlana. *Last Witnesses*	940.53
Aleksievich, Svetlana. ★*The Unwomanly Face of War*	940.53
Allport, Alan. *Britain at Bay*	940.53
Ambrose, Stephen E. ★*Band of Brothers*	920
Ambrose, Stephen E. *Citizen Soldiers*	940.54
Ambrose, Stephen E. *D-Day, June 6, 1944*	940.54
Ambrose, Stephen E. *The Victors*	940.54
Ambrose, Stephen E. *The Wild Blue*	940.54
Atkinson, Rick. *The Day of Battle*	940.54
Beevor, Antony. *The Battle of Arnhem*	940.54
Beevor, Antony. *The Fall of Berlin, 1945*	940.54
Beevor, Antony. *Stalingrad*	940.54
Caddick-Adams, Peter. *Sand and Steel*	940.54
Childers, Thomas. *The Third Reich*	943.086
Churchill, Winston. *Their Finest Hour*	940.53
Churchill, Winston. *Triumph and Tragedy*	940.53
Cronkite, Walter. *Cronkite's War*	070.4
Donner, Rebecca. *All the Frequent Troubles of Our Days*	943
Dugard, Martin. *Taking Berlin*	940.54
Dugard, Martin. *Taking Paris*	940.54

PUBLIC LIBRARY CORE COLLECTION: NONFICTION
Twentieth Edition

Englund, Peter. *November 1942*	940.53
Evans, Richard J. *The Third Reich at War*	940.53
Garrett, Leah. *X Troop*	940.53
Gerwarth, Robert. *Hitler's Hangman*	B
Guarnere, William. *Brothers in Battle, Best of Friends*	B
Hastings, Max. *Armageddon*	940.54
Hastings, Max. *Operation Chastise*	940.54
Hastings, Max. *Operation Pedestal*	940.54
Hastings, Max. *Overlord*	940.54
Helm, Sarah. *A Life in Secrets*	B
Henderson, Bruce B. *Sons and Soldiers*	940.53
Hogan, William R. *Task Force Hogan*	940.54
Holland, James. *Big Week*	940.54
Holland, James. *Brothers in Arms*	940.54
Holland, James. *Normandy '44*	940.54
Holland, James. *The Savage Storm*	940.54
Holland, James. *Sicily '43*	940.54
Iperen, Roxane van. ★*The Sisters of Auschwitz*	940.53
Isserman, Maurice. *The Winter Army*	940.54
Jackson, Julian. *De Gaulle*	B
Karski, Jan. *Story of a Secret State*	940.53
Keith, Philip A. *All Blood Runs Red*	B
Kershaw, Alex. *Against All Odds*	940.54
Kershaw, Alex. *Avenue of Spies*	940.53
Kershaw, Alex. *The Few*	940.54
Kershaw, Alex. *The First Wave*	940.54
Kershaw, Ian. *Hitler*	B
Kix, Paul. *The Saboteur*	940.53
Korda, Michael. *Alone*	940.54
Korda, Michael. *With Wings Like Eagles*	940.54
Lambert, Raymond. *Every Man a Hero*	B
Lance, Rachel. *Chamber Divers*	940.54
Letts, Elizabeth. *The Perfect Horse*	940.54
Lewis, Damien. *Churchill's Hellraisers*	940.54
Lichtblau, Eric. *Return to the Reich*	B
Lukacs, John. *Five Days in London, May 1940*	940.53
Macintyre, Ben. *Double Cross*	940.54
Macintyre, Ben. ★*Prisoners of the Castle*	940.54
Maurer, Kevin. *Damn Lucky*	940.54
McCarten, Anthony. *Darkest Hour*	941.084
McDonough, Frank. *The Hitler Years*	943.086
McKay, Sinclair. *The Fire and the Darkness*	940.54
McKay, Sinclair. *The Secret Lives of Codebreakers*	940.54
McKean, David. *Watching Darkness Fall*	940.53
Merridale, Catherine. *Ivan's War*	940.54
Miller, Donald L. ★*Masters of the Air*	940.54
Milton, Giles. *Churchill's Ministry of Ungentlemanly Warfare*	940.54
Milton, Giles. *Soldier, Sailor, Frogman, Spy, Airman, Gangster, Kill or Die*	940.54
Ohler, Norman. *The Bohemians*	940.53
Pavlychenko, Liudmyla Mykhailivna. *Lady Death*	B
Price, David A. *Geniuses at War*	940.54
Raban, Jonathan. *Father and Son*	B
Read, Anthony. *The Fall of Berlin*	940.54
Rees, Laurence. *Hitler and Stalin*	940.53
Rhodes, Richard. *Masters of Death*	940.53
Roberts, Andrew. *The Storm of War*	940.54
Rosbottom, Ronald C. *When Paris Went Dark*	944.0816
Sullivan, James. *Unsinkable*	940.54
Talty, Stephan. *Agent Garbo*	940.5
Toll, Ian W. *Pacific Crucible*	940.54
Trimble, Lee. *Beyond the Call*	940.54
Ullrich, Volker. ★*Eight Days in May*	943.086
Ullrich, Volker. *Hitler*	B
Ullrich, Volker. *Hitler*	B
Wiesenthal, Simon. ★*The Sunflower*	179.7
Winters, Richard D. *Beyond Band of Brothers*	B

HISTORY WRITING — WARS AND CONFLICTS — WORLD WAR II — PACIFIC THEATER

Bradley, James. *Flags of Our Fathers*	940.54
Bradley, James. *Flyboys*	940.54
Bruning, John R. *Indestructible*	B
Bruning, John R. *The Race of Aces*	940.54
Burgin, R. V. *Islands of the Damned*	B
Campbell, James. *The Ghost Mountain Boys*	940.54
Chang, Iris. ★*The Rape of Nanking*	951.04
Drury, Bob. *Lucky 666*	B
Englund, Peter. *November 1942*	940.53
Erwin, Jon. *Beyond Valor*	B
Frank, Richard B. *Downfall*	940.54
Frank, Richard B. *Tower of Skulls*	940.54
Freeman, Sally Mott. *The Jersey Brothers*	920
Gladwell, Malcolm. ★*The Bomber Mafia*	940.54
Ham, Paul. *Hiroshima Nagasaki*	940.54
Hampton, Dan. *Operation Vengeance*	940.54
Harmon, Mark. *Ghosts of Honolulu*	940.54
Hastings, Max. *Retribution*	940.54
Henderson, Bruce B. *Bridge to the Sun*	940.53
Hillenbrand, Laura. ★*Unbroken*	B
Holland, James. ★*Burma '44*	940.54
Hornfischer, James D. *Neptune's Inferno*	940.54
Iredale, Will. *The Kamikaze Hunters*	940.54
Lucas, Jack. *Indestructible*	B
Manchester, William. *Goodbye, Darkness*	B
McManus, John C. *Fire and Fortitude*	940.54
McManus, John C. *Island Infernos*	940.54
McManus, John C. *To the End of the Earth*	940.54
Mitter, Rana. *Forgotten Ally*	951.04
Norman, Elizabeth M. *We Band of Angels*	940.54
Norman, Michael. *Tears in the Darkness*	940.54
Scott, James. *Black Snow*	940.54
Scott, James. *Rampage*	940.54
Sides, Hampton. ★*Ghost Soldiers*	940.54
Simms, Brendan. *The Silver Waterfall*	940.54
Smith, Jim B. *The Last Mission*	940.54
Stanton, Doug. *In Harm's Way*	940.54
Symonds, Craig L. *The Battle of Midway*	940.54
Thomas, Evan. *Sea of Thunder*	940.54
Twomey, Steve. *Countdown to Pearl Harbor*	940.54
Wallace, Chris. *Countdown 1945*	940.54
Wheelan, Joseph. *Midnight in the Pacific*	940.54
Wukovits, John F. *Lost at Sea*	940.54

HISTORY WRITING — WESTWARD EXPANSION — UNITED STATES

Ambrose, Stephen E. *Nothing Like It in the World*	385
Ambrose, Stephen E. ★*Undaunted Courage*	917.804
Barra, Allen. *Inventing Wyatt Earp*	B
Boessenecker, John. *Gentleman Bandit*	B
Brands, H. W. *The Age of Gold*	979.4
Brands, H. W. *Dreams of El Dorado*	978
Brands, H. W. *The Last Campaign*	973.8
Brown, Daniel James. *The Indifferent Stars Above*	B
Brown, Dee. *The American West*	978
Clavin, Thomas. *Dodge City*	978.1
Clavin, Thomas. *Wild Bill*	B
Cozzens, Peter. *The Earth Is Weeping*	978
Crouch, Gregory. *The Bonanza King*	B
Donovan, Jim. *The Blood of Heroes*	976.4
Duncan, Dayton. *Blood Memory*	599.64
Eisler, Benita. *The Red Man's Bones*	B
Gallagher, Winifred. *New Women in the Old West*	978.02
Grandin, Greg. *The End of the Myth*	973
Gwynne, S. C. *Empire of the Summer Moon*	B
Hickman, Katie. *Brave Hearted*	978
Hyde, Anne Farrar. *Empires, Nations, and Families*	978
Inskeep, Steve. *Imperfect Union*	B
Laskin, David. *The Children's Blizzard*	977
Leerhsen, Charles. ★*Butch Cassidy*	B
Morgan, Robert. *Boone*	B
Morgan, Robert. *Lions of the West*	978
Mort, T. A. *Thieves' Road*	978.3
Nelson, Megan Kate. *The Three-Cornered War*	978
Raban, Jonathan. *Bad Land*	978
Richardson, Heather Cox. ★*How the South Won the Civil War*	306.20973
Sides, Hampton. *Blood and Thunder*	978
Snyder, Christina. *Great Crossings*	976.9
Stiles, T. J. *Custer's Trials*	B
Stiles, T. J. *Jesse James*	B
Tefertiller, Casey. *Wyatt Earp*	B
Walker, Ronald W. ★*Massacre at Mountain Meadows*	979.2
Wallis, Michael. *The Best Land Under Heaven*	978
Wallis, Michael. *Billy the Kid*	B
Ward, Geoffrey C. *The West*	978
Warren, Louis S. *Buffalo Bill's America*	B
Wilder, Laura Ingalls. *Pioneer Girl*	B

HISTORY WRITING — WOMEN'S HISTORY

Abbott, Karen. *Liar, Temptress, Soldier, Spy*	920

AUTHOR, TITLE, SERIES AND SUBJECT INDEX

Author	Call #
Ackmann, Martha. *The Mercury 13*	920
Aleksievich, Svetlana. ★*The Unwomanly Face of War*	940.53
Allgor, Catherine. *A Perfect Union*	B
Andrews, Lena S. ★*Valiant Women*	940.53
Anthony, Carl Sferrazza. *Nellie Taft*	B
Armstrong, Jennifer Keishin. *When Women Invented Television*	791.45
Askwith, Richard. *Unbreakable*	B
Ball, Molly. ★*Pelosi*	B
Batalion, Judith. *The Light of Days*	940.53
Bell-Scott, Patricia. *The Firebrand and the First Lady*	920
Berry, Daina Ramey. ★*A Black Women's History of the United States*	305.48
Berry, Mary Frances. *My Face Is Black Is True*	B
Blais, Madeleine. *Queen of the Court*	B
Blanton, DeAnne. *They Fought Like Demons*	973.7
Borman, Tracy. *Anne Boleyn and Elizabeth I*	920
Bostridge, Mark. *Florence Nightingale*	B
Bradford, Sarah. *Lucrezia Borgia*	B
Brown, Nancy Marie. *The Real Valkyrie*	948
Campbell, Olivia. *Women in White Coats*	610.92
Carmon, Irin. *Notorious RBG*	B
Castor, Helen. *She-Wolves*	942
Chang, Jung. *Big Sister, Little Sister, Red Sister*	B
Chang, Jung. ★*Wild Swans*	B
Cleghorn, Elinor. *Unwell Women*	613
Clinton, Catherine. *Harriet Tubman*	B
Clinton, Hillary Rodham. *The Book of Gutsy Women*	920
Collins, Gail. *When Everything Changed*	305.40973
Cook, Blanche Wiesen. *Eleanor Roosevelt; Volume 2*	B
Cook, Blanche Wiesen. ★*Eleanor Roosevelt; Volume 3*	B
Cooney, Kara. *When Women Ruled the World*	920
Cooper, Helene. *Madame President*	966.62
Cordery, Stacy A. *Alice*	B
Crowther, Gail. *Three-Martini Afternoons at the Ritz*	920
De Hart, Jane Sherron. ★*Ruth Bader Ginsburg*	B
Doherty, Maggie. *The Equivalents*	920
Downey, Kirstin. *Isabella*	B
DuBois, Ellen Carol. *Suffrage*	324.6
Dunbar, Erica Armstrong. ★*She Came to Slay*	B
Eder, Mari K. *The Girls Who Stepped Out of Line*	920
Enright, Lynn. *Vagina*	612.6
Evans, Claire Lisa. *Broad Band*	920
Farley, Audrey Clare. *The Unfit Heiress*	B
Felder, Deborah G. *The American Women's Almanac*	305.40973
Foreman, Amanda. *Georgiana, Duchess of Devonshire*	B
Fox, Margalit. *The Riddle of the Labyrinth*	920
Fraser, Antonia. *Marie Antoinette*	B
Friedan, Betty. ★*The Feminine Mystique*	305.42
Funder, Anna. *Wifedom*	B
Gallagher, Winifred. *New Women in the Old West*	978.02
Giddings, Paula. *Ida*	B
Gilbert, Sandra M. ★*Still Mad*	810.9
Ginzberg, Lori D. *Elizabeth Cady Stanton*	B
Goldstone, Nancy Bazelon. *The Rival Queens*	944
Gortemaker, Heike B. *Eva Braun*	B
Greenberg, Amy S. *Lady First*	B
Griffith, Elisabeth. *Formidable*	305.42
Gristwood, Sarah. *Blood Sisters*	942.04092
Gross, Rachel E. *Vagina Obscura*	618.1
Grush, Loren. ★*The Six*	629.4
Guy, John. *Hunting the Falcon*	B
Hall, Rebecca. ★*Wake*	741.5
Hallman, J. C. *Say Anarcha*	618.1
Hamlin, Kimberly A. *Free Thinker*	B
Hay, Carol. *Think Like a Feminist*	305.42
Hickman, Katie. *Brave Hearted*	978
Hirono, Mazie. *Heart of Fire*	B
Hirshman, Linda R. *Reckoning*	305.420973
Hirshman, Linda R. *Sisters in Law*	347.73
Hochschild, Adam. *Rebel Cinderella*	B
Holt, Nathalia. *The Queens of Animation*	920
Holt, Nathalia. ★*Rise of the Rocket Girls*	629.4
Holton, Woody. *Abigail Adams*	B
Hope, Clover. *The Motherlode*	920
Howell, Georgina. *Gertrude Bell*	B
Huang, Yunte. *Daughter of the Dragon*	B
Hughes, Bettany. *Venus and Aphrodite*	292
Humez, Jean McMahon. *Harriet Tubman*	B
Iandoli, Kathy. *God Save the Queens*	782.421649
Jacobs, Sally H. *Althea*	B
Kaplan, Janice. *The Genius of Women*	920
Karbo, Karen. *In Praise of Difficult Women*	920
Katz, Catherine Grace. *The Daughters of Yalta*	920
Kelly, Kate. *Ordinary Equality*	920
Kendall, Mikki. *Hood Feminism*	305.420973
Kerrison, Catherine. *Jefferson's Daughters*	920
Kessler-Harris, Alice. ★*Out to Work*	331.4
Kiernan, Denise. *The Girls of Atomic City*	976.8
Kimberley, Hannah. *A Woman's Place Is at the Top*	B
King, Coretta Scott. ★*My Life, My Love, My Legacy*	B
Kleiman, Kathy. *Proving Ground*	4.092
Koch, Bea. *Mad and Bad*	920
Kolbert, Kathryn. *Controlling Women*	362.1988
Koppel, Lily. *The Astronaut Wives Club*	920
Kroeger, Brooke. *Undaunted*	070.4
Kroger, Lisa. *Monster, She Wrote*	920
LaFollette, Marcel C. *Writing for Their Lives*	071.3
Landdeck, Katherine Sharp. *The Women with Silver Wings*	920
Larson, Kate Clifford. *Bound for the Promised Land*	B
Larson, Kate Clifford. *Walk with Me*	B
Lemmon, Gayle Tzemach. *The Daughters of Kobani*	956.9104
Lepore, Jill. *Book of Ages*	B
Levy, Shawn. ★*In on the Joke*	792.7
Lewis, Damien. *Agent Josephine*	B
Lovell, Mary S. *Bess of Hardwick*	B
Lucey, Donna M. *Sargent's Women*	920
Macintyre, Ben. ★*Agent Sonya*	B
MacKrell, Judith. *The Correspondents*	070.4
Magida, Arthur J. *Code Name Madeleine*	940.54
Mahon, Maureen. ★*Black Diamond Queens*	782.421
Marcal, Katrine. *Mother of Invention*	604.82
Markel, Howard. *The Secret of Life*	572.86
Markham, Beryl. *West with the Night*	B
Marton, Kati. *Hidden Power*	B
Massie, Robert K. *Catherine the Great*	B
McNeur, Catherine. *Mischievous Creatures*	920
McShane Wulfhart, Nell. *The Great Stewardess Rebellion*	331.4
Mertens, Maggie. *Better Faster Farther*	796.42
Miles, Tiya. ★*Wild Girls*	304.2
Miller, Marla. *Betsy Ross and the Making of America*	B
Min, Anchee. *Red Azalea*	B
Moore, Kate. *The Radium Girls*	363.17
Moore, Kate. ★*The Woman They Could Not Silence*	B
Moore, Wendy. *No Man's Land*	940.4
Moorehead, Caroline. *A House in the Mountains*	940.53
Morris, Bonnie J. ★*The Feminist Revolution*	305.4209
Mulley, Clare. *The Women Who Flew for Hitler*	920
Mundy, Liza. ★*The Sisterhood*	327.12
Napoli, Lisa. *Susan, Linda, Nina & Cokie*	920
Nemat, Marina. *Prisoner of Tehran*	B
Nimura, Janice P. ★*The Doctors Blackwell*	610.92
Noor. *Leap of Faith*	B
Norgren, Jill. *Belva Lockwood*	B
Norman, Elizabeth M. *We Band of Angels*	940.54
Nuttall, Jennifer Anne. ★*Mother Tongue*	422
O'Brien, Keith. *Fly Girls*	920
O'Donnell Heffington, Peggy. *Without Children*	306.85
O'Meara, Mallory. *Girly Drinks*	641.2
O'Meara, Mallory. *The Lady from the Black Lagoon*	921
Oller, John. *American Queen*	B
Painter, Nell Irvin. ★*Sojourner Truth*	B
Paranque, Estelle. *Blood, Fire & Gold*	920
Parkin, Simon. *A Game of Birds and Wolves*	940.54
Perkins, Anne Gardiner. *Yale Needs Women*	378
Popkin, Jim. *Code Name Blue Wren*	327.12
Pratt, Misty. *All in Her Head*	616.89
Puhak, Shelley. *The Dark Queens*	944
Quinn, Bridget. *She Votes*	324.6
Rahmani, Niloofar. *Open Skies*	B
Ramirez, Janina. *Femina*	940.1
Ransby, Barbara. *Eslanda*	B
Reese, Anney. ★*Stuff Mom Never Told You*	305.42
Rehak, Melanie. *Girl Sleuth*	813
Reser, Anna. *Forces of Nature*	509.2
Richards, Cecile. *Make Trouble*	B
Rinehart, Lorissa. *First to the Front*	B
Roberts, Cokie. *Capital Dames*	920

Roberts, Cokie. *Founding Mothers*	920
Roberts, Cokie. *Ladies of Liberty*	920
Rogers, Katie. ★*American Woman*	973.09
Rosenberg, Rosalind. ★*Jane Crow*	B
Rubenhold, Hallie. ★*The Five*	362.88
Rueckert, Veronica. *Outspoken*	808.5
Ryckman, Pamela. *Candace Pert*	B
Salisbury, Katie Gee. ★*Not Your China Doll*	B
Satow, Julie. *When Women Ran Fifth Avenue*	381.141
Satrapi, Marjane. *Embroideries*	741.5
Schiff, Stacy. ★*Cleopatra*	B
Schiff, Stacy. *The Witches*	345
Schuller, Kyla. *The Trouble with White Women*	305.42
Sevigny, Melissa L. ★*Brave the Wild River*	580.9
Sherr, Lynn. *Sally Ride*	B
Simmons, Nadirah. ★*First Things First*	782.42164
Smith, Danyel. *Shine Bright*	782.42164
Sohn, Amy. *The Man Who Hated Women*	363.28
Sollee, Kristen J. *Witch Hunt*	133
Spruill, Marjorie Julian. *Divided We Stand*	305.42
Stanley, Amy. *Stranger in the Shogun's City*	B
Strauss, Gwen. *The Nine*	940.53
Tallis, Nicola. *Uncrowned Queen*	B
Taraborrelli, J. Randy. *Jackie, Janet & Lee*	920
Taraborrelli, J. Randy. ★*Jackie*	B
Teitel, Amy Shira. *Fighting for Space*	920
Thomas, Gillian. *Because of Sex*	344.7301
Tietjen, Jill S. *Hollywood, Her Story*	791.43
Toler, Pamela D. *Women Warriors*	355.0092
Traister, Rebecca. *Good and Mad*	305.420973
Tubbs, Anna Malaika. *The Three Mothers*	306.874
Tumulty, Karen. *The Triumph of Nancy Reagan*	B
Turk, Katherine. *The Women of Now*	305.42
Waldstreicher, David. *The Odyssey of Phillis Wheatley*	B
Wallach, Janet. *Desert Queen*	B
Wasson, Sam. *Fifth Avenue, 5 A.M.*	791.43
Weir, Alison. *Eleanor of Aquitaine*	B
Weir, Alison. *The Lady in the Tower*	B
Weir, Alison. *The Life of Elizabeth I*	B
Weir, Alison. *Queens of the Age of Chivalry*	920
Weiss, Elaine F. *The Woman's Hour*	324.6
Wickenden, Dorothy. *The Agitators*	920
Wilder, Laura Ingalls. *Pioneer Girl*	B
Williams, Kate. *Ambition and Desire*	B
Winder, Elizabeth. *Parachute Women*	782.42164
Wright, Jennifer Ashley. ★*Madame Restell*	
Yellin, Emily. *Our Mothers' War*	940.53
Zanglein, Jayne E. *The Girl Explorers*	B
Zernike, Kate. *The Exceptions*	331.4
Hit Refresh. Nadella, Satya	B
Hit so Hard. Schemel, Patty	B
Hitch-22. Hitchens, Christopher	920
Hitchcock's Blondes. Leamer, Laurence	791.43
HITCHCOCK, ALFRED, 1899-1980	
Lane, Christina. *Phantom Lady*	B
Leamer, Laurence. *Hitchcock's Blondes*	791.43
Spoto, Donald. *The Dark Side of Genius*	B
Hitchcock, William I.	
The Age of Eisenhower	973.921092
Hitchens, Christopher	
The Four Horsemen	211
Hitch-22	920
Mortality	304.6
Thomas Jefferson	B
HITCHENS, CHRISTOPHER, 1949-2011	
Hitchens, Christopher. *Hitch-22*	920
Hitchens, Christopher. *Mortality*	304.6
HITCHHIKING	
Krakauer, Jon. *Into the Wild*	917.9804
Hitchings, Henry	
The Language Wars	420.9
Hitler. Kershaw, Ian	B
Hitler. Kershaw, Ian	B
Hitler. Longerich, Peter	B
Hitler. Ullrich, Volker	B
Hitler. Ullrich, Volker	B
Hitler and Stalin. Rees, Laurence	940.53
★*Hitler in Los Angeles*. Ross, Steven Joseph	979.4
The Hitler Years. McDonough, Frank	943.086
Hitler's Aristocrats. Ronald, Susan	940.53
Hitler's Empire. Mazower, Mark	940.53
Hitler's Furies. Lower, Wendy	940.53
Hitler's Hangman. Gerwarth, Robert	B
Hitler's Pope. Cornwell, John	B
Hitler's Private Library. Ryback, Timothy W.	027
Hitler's Stolen Children. Oelhafen, Ingrid von	B
Hitler's Willing Executioners. Goldhagen, Daniel Jonah	940.53
Hitler, Adolf	
Mein Kampf	B
HITLER, ADOLF, 1889-1945	
Bouverie, Tim. *Appeasement*	327.41043
Eisner, Peter. *The Pope's Last Crusade*	282.092
Evans, Richard J. *The Coming of the Third Reich*	943.08
Evans, Richard J. *The Third Reich in Power, 1933-1939*	943.086
Gortemaker, Heike B. *Eva Braun*	B
Hett, Benjamin Carter. *The Death of Democracy*	943.085
Hitler, Adolf. *Mein Kampf*	B
Kershaw, Ian. *Hitler*	B
Kershaw, Ian. *Hitler*	B
King, David. *The Trial of Adolf Hitler*	345.43
Longerich, Peter. *Hitler*	B
McDonough, Frank. *The Hitler Years*	943.086
Phillips, Adrian. *Fighting Churchill, Appeasing Hitler*	327.41043
Rees, Laurence. *Hitler and Stalin*	940.53
Roberts, Andrew. *The Storm of War*	940.54
Ronald, Susan. *Hitler's Aristocrats*	940.53
Ryback, Timothy W. *Hitler's Private Library*	027
Ryback, Timothy W. *Takeover*	943.086
Shirer, William L. ★*The Rise and Fall of the Third Reich*	943.086
Snyder, Timothy. ★*Bloodlands*	940.54
Speer, Albert. *Inside the Third Reich*	B
Spicer, Charles. *Coffee with Hitler*	941.084
Stargardt, Nicholas. *The German War*	940.53
Ullrich, Volker. ★*Eight Days in May*	943.086
Ullrich, Volker. *Hitler*	B
Ullrich, Volker. *Hitler*	B
Weber, Thomas. *Becoming Hitler*	B
★*Hits, Flops, and Other Illusions*. Zwick, Edward	B
HIV (VIRUSES)	
Holt, Nathalia. *Cured*	614.5
Smith, Danez. ★*Homie*	811
Hixenbaugh, Michael	
★*They Came for the Schools*	371.9
HMONG (SOUTHEAST ASIAN PEOPLE)	
Hamilton, Lisa M. *The Hungry Season*	B
HMONG AMERICANS	
Fadiman, Anne. *The Spirit Catches You and You Fall Down*	306.4
Ho Chi Minh. Duiker, William J.	B
HO CHI MINH CITY, VIETNAM	
White, Ralph. *Getting Out of Saigon*	959.704
HO, CHI MINH, 1890-1969	
Duiker, William J. *Ho Chi Minh*	B
Ho, Oliver	
The Ultimate Book of Family Card Games	795.4
Hoagland, Tony	
Priest Turned Therapist Treats Fear of God	811
Unincorporated Persons in the Late Honda Dynasty	811
Hoalst-Pullen, Nancy	
National Geographic Atlas of Beer	663
Hoare, Philip	
The Whale	599.5
Hoax. Stelter, Brian	070.4
HOAXES	
Fox, Margalit. *The Confidence Men*	940.4
Schwartz, A. Brad. ★*Broadcast Hysteria*	791.44
Young, Kevin. *Bunk*	177
Hoban, Phoebe	
Alice Neel	B
HOBART, TASMANIA	
Brierley, Saroo. *A Long Way Home*	B
Hobbes, Thomas	
★*Leviathan*	320.01
HOBBIES	
Friedman, Rachel. ★*And Then We Grew Up*	305.24
Gopnik, Adam. *All That Happiness Is*	158.1

AUTHOR, TITLE, SERIES AND SUBJECT INDEX

Hobbs, Jeff
  Children of the State — 364.36
  ★*The Short and Tragic Life of Robert Peace* — B
  Show Them You're Good — 373
HOBBS, JEFF, 1980-
  Hobbs, Jeff. ★*The Short and Tragic Life of Robert Peace* — B
Hochschild, Adam
  American Midnight — 973.91
  Bury the Chains — 326
  King Leopold's Ghost — 967.51
  Lessons from a Dark Time — 909.82
  Rebel Cinderella — B
  Spain in Our Hearts — 946.081
  The Unquiet Ghost — 947.084
HOCKEY
  Branch, John. *Boy on Ice* — B
  Coffey, Wayne R. ★*The Boys of Winter* — 796.962
  Eruzione, Mike. *The Making of a Miracle* — B
  Gretzky, Wayne. *99* — B
HOCKEY PLAYERS
  Branch, John. *Boy on Ice* — B
  Coffey, Wayne R. ★*The Boys of Winter* — 796.962
  Eruzione, Mike. *The Making of a Miracle* — B
  Gretzky, Wayne. *99* — B
  Sasakamoose, Fred. *Call Me Indian* — B
HOCKEY TEAMS
  Coffey, Wayne R. ★*The Boys of Winter* — 796.962
  Eruzione, Mike. *The Making of a Miracle* — B
  Gretzky, Wayne. *99* — B
HOCKNEY, DAVID, 1937-
  Sykes, Christopher Simon. *David Hockney* — B
  Sykes, Christopher Simon. *David Hockney* — B
Hodgman, John
  Medallion Status — B
  Vacationland — B
HODGMAN, JOHN
  Hodgman, John. *Medallion Status* — B
  Hodgman, John. *Vacationland* — B
Hoffman, Adina
  ★*My Happiness Bears No Relation to Happiness* — B
  Sacred Trash — 296.09
Hoffman, Brian Hart
  ★*Bake from Scratch; Volume Two* — 641.81
Hoffman, Bruce
  Anonymous Soldiers — 956.94
Hoffman, Carl
  Liar's Circus — 973.933
  ★*Savage Harvest* — 995.1
Hoffman, Damona
  F the Fairy Tale — 306.73
Hoffman, David E.
  Give Me Liberty — B
Hoffman, Donald D.
  The Case Against Reality — 121
  Visual Intelligence — 152.14
Hoffman, Liz
  Crash Landing — 330
Hoffman, Maggie
  Batch Cocktails — 641.87
Hoffman, Miles
  The NPR Classical Music Companion — 780.3
Hofstadter, Douglas R.
  I Am a Strange Loop — 153
  Surfaces and Essences — 169
Hogan, Ben
  ★*Five Lessons* — 796.352
Hogan, Linda
  The Woman Who Watches Over the World — B
HOGAN, LINDA
  Hogan, Linda. *The Woman Who Watches Over the World* — B
HOGAN, SAMUEL MASON, 1915-2005
  Hogan, William R. *Task Force Hogan* — 940.54
Hogan, William R.
  Task Force Hogan — 940.54
Hogeland, William
  Autumn of the Black Snake — 970.004
  Declaration — 973.3

Hogge, Fred
  Of Ice and Men — 338.4
Hogs Wild. Frazier, Ian — 814
Hohn, Donovan
  The Inner Coast — 304.20973
Hoja, Gulchehra
  A Stone Is Most Precious Where It Belongs — B
HOJA, GULCHEHRA
  Hoja, Gulchehra. *A Stone Is Most Precious Where It Belongs* — B
Hokusai. Katsushika, Hokusai — 769.92
HOLBROOKE, RICHARD C., 1941-2010
  Packer, George. *Our Man* — B
★*Hold Still*. Mann, Sally — B
Hold Tight Gently. Duberman, Martin B. — 920
Holden, Wendy
  ★*Born Survivors* — 940.53
Holder, R. W.
  How Not to Say What You Mean — 427
Holding The Line. Berman, Geoffrey — 345.73
Holding The Note. Remnick, David — 781.64
Holes, Paul
  Unmasked — 363.25
Holiday and Celebration Bread in Five Minutes a Day. Francois, Zoe — 641.81
★*Holiday Cookies*. Nederlanden, Elisabet der — 641.86
HOLIDAY COOKING
  Francois, Zoe. *Holiday and Celebration Bread in Five Minutes a Day* — 641.81
  Kieffer, Sarah. ★*Baking for the Holidays* — 641.5
  Lawson, Nigella. ★*Cook, Eat, Repeat* — 641.5
  Moskowitz, Isa Chandra. *The Superfun Times Vegan Holiday Cookbook* — 651.56
  Nederlanden, Elisabet der. ★*Holiday Cookies* — 641.86
  Pansino, Rosanna. *Baking All Year Round* — 641.86
  Pierson, Joy. *Vegan Holiday Cooking from Candle Cafe* — 641.5
  Rosenstrach, Jenny. *How to Celebrate Everything* — 641.5
  Sifton, Sam. *Thanksgiving* — 641.5
HOLIDAY DECORATIONS
  Van't Hul, Jean. *The Artful Year* — 745.594
HOLIDAY, BILLIE, 1915-1959
  Alexander, Paul. *Bitter Crop* — B
Holiday, Ryan
  Ego Is the Enemy — 158.1
  Lives of the Stoics — 188
HOLIDAYS
  Baker, James W. *Thanksgiving* — 394.2649
  Flanders, Judith. *Christmas* — 394.2663
  Forbes, Bruce David. *Christmas* — 394.2663
  Morton, Lisa. *Trick or Treat* — 394.2646
  Stibbe, Nina. *An Almost Perfect Christmas* — 394.2663
Holifield, E. Brooks
  Theology in America — 230
HOLISTIC MEDICINE
  Buque, Mariel. *Break the Cycle* — 616.85
  Hotz, Julia. ★*The Connection Cure* — 610
Holladay, Wilhelmina Cole
  A Museum of Their Own — 704
HOLLADAY, WILHELMINA COLE, 1922-2021
  Holladay, Wilhelmina Cole. *A Museum of Their Own* — 704
Holland, James
  Battle of Britain — 940.54
  Big Week — 940.54
  Brothers in Arms — 940.54
  ★*Burma '44* — 940.54
  Normandy '44 — 940.54
  The Rise of Germany, 1939-1941; Vol. 1 — 940.54
  The Savage Storm — 940.53
  Sicily '43 — 940.54
Holland, Tanya
  ★*Tanya Holland's California Soul* — 641.59
Holland, Tom
  Dominion — 261
Holldobler, Bert
  The Superorganism — 595.7
Holler If You Hear Me. Dyson, Michael Eric — B
Holley, Santi Elijah
  An Amerikan Family — 920
HOLLINGSWORTH, DENNIS, 1967-
  Yoshino, Kenji. *Speak Now* — 346.79401

PUBLIC LIBRARY CORE COLLECTION: NONFICTION
Twentieth Edition

Hollis, B. Dylan
  ★*Baking Yesteryear* — 641.81
Hollis, Edward
  The Secret Lives of Buildings — 720.9
Hollis, Matthew
  The Waste Land — 821
Holloway, Kris
  Monique and the Mango Rains — B
Holloway, Richard
  Waiting for the Last Bus — 202
★*The Holly*. Rubinstein, Julian — 364.106
Hollywood. Basinger, Jeanine — 791.43
★*Hollywood and the Movies of the Fifties*. Hirsch, Foster — 791.43
HOLLYWOOD BLACKLIST
  Frankel, Glenn. *High Noon* — 791.43
  Lane, Christina. *Phantom Lady* — B
★*Hollywood Ending*. Auletta, Ken — 791.43
★*Hollywood Park*. Jollett, Mikel — B
Hollywood's Copyright Wars. Decherney, Peter — 346.7304
Hollywood's Eve. Anolik, Lili — B
Hollywood's Spies. Rosenzweig, Laura B. — 791.43
HOLLYWOOD, CALIFORNIA
  Anolik, Lili. *Hollywood's Eve* — B
  Auletta, Ken. ★*Hollywood Ending* — 791.43
  Basinger, Jeanine. *Hollywood* — 791.43
  Bruck, Connie. *When Hollywood Had a King* — B
  Callow, Simon. ★*Orson Welles* — B
  Davis, Geena. *Dying of Politeness* — B
  Drabkin, Ronald. *Beverly Hills Spy* — 940.54
  Eyman, Scott. *Empire of Dreams* — B
  Eyman, Scott. *Hank and Jim* — 920
  Farrow, Ronan. ★*Catch and Kill* — 331.4
  Fisher, Todd. *My Girls* — B
  Frankel, Glenn. *Shooting Midnight Cowboy* — 791.43
  Giddins, Gary. *Bing Crosby* — B
  Giddins, Gary. *Bing Crosby* — B
  Hirsch, Foster. ★*Hollywood and the Movies of the Fifties* — 791.43
  Lahti, Christine. *True Stories from an Unreliable Eyewitness* — B
  Lane, Christina. *Phantom Lady* — B
  Levy, Shawn. ★*The Castle on Sunset* — 647.95
  Longworth, Karina. *Seduction* — B
  Meslow, Scott. *From Hollywood with Love* — 791.43
  Moore, Susanna. *Miss Aluminum* — 813
  Ryan, Maureen. *Burn It Down* — 791.43
  Schulman, Michael. ★*Oscar Wars* — 791.43
  Scovell, Nell. *Just the Funny Parts* — B
  Stein, Jean. *West of Eden* — 979.4
  Taraborrelli, J. Randy. ★*The Secret Life of Marilyn Monroe* — B
  Thomson, David. *Bette Davis* — B
  Thomson, David. *Ingrid Bergman* — B
  Ward, Maitland. *Rated X* — B
  Waxman, Sharon. *Rebels on the Backlot* — 791.4302
Hollywood, Her Story. Tietjen, Jill S — 791.43
Hollywood, Paul
  ★*Bake* — 641.81
HOLMAN, JAMES, 1786-1857
  Roberts, Jason. *A Sense of the World* — B
Holmberg, Martha
  ★*Simply Tomato* — 641.6
Holmes, Bob
  Flavor — 612.8
Holmes, Cassie
  Happier Hour — 158.1
Holmes, Elizabeth
  HRH — 941.085
Holmes, Kier
  The Garden Refresh — 635
HOLMES, OLIVER WENDELL, 1841-1935
  Budiansky, Stephen. *Oliver Wendell Holmes* — B
  Cohen, Adam. ★*Imbeciles* — 344.7304
  Healy, Thomas. *The Great Dissent* — 342.7308
Holmes, Richard
  The Age of Wonder — 509
  Falling Upwards — 387.7
Holmes, Roger
  Midwest Home Landscaping — 712
HOLMES, SHERLOCK (FICTITIOUS CHARACTER)
  Konnikova, Maria. *Mastermind* — 153.4

Sims, Michael. *Arthur and Sherlock* — B
★*Holocaust*. Dwork, Deborah — 940
The Holocaust. Rees, Laurence — 940.53
★*The Holocaust*. Stone, Dan — 940.53
HOLOCAUST (1933-1945)
  Ackerman, Diane. ★*The Zookeeper's Wife* — 940.53
  Aly, Gotz. *Europe Against the Jews* — 305.892
  Asbrink, Elisabeth. *And in the Vienna Woods the Trees Remain* — B
  Batalion, Judith. *The Light of Days* — 940.53
  Berenbaum, Michael. *The World Must Know* — 940.53
  Berg, Mary. *The Diary of Mary Berg* — B
  Berr, Helene. *The Journal of Helene Berr* — B
  Blau, Magda Hellinger. *The Nazis Knew My Name* — 940.53
  Burger, Ariel. *Witness* — 848
  Chiger, Krystyna. *The Girl in the Green Sweater* — B
  Childers, Thomas. *The Third Reich* — 943.086
  Crasnianski, Tania. *The Children of Nazis* — 943.086
  Debreczeni, Jozsef. *Cold Crematorium* — 940.53
  Dwork, Deborah. ★*Holocaust* — 940
  Eisen, Max. *By Chance Alone* — 940.5318
  Epstein, Franci. *Franci's War* — B
  Fairweather, Jack. *The Volunteer* — B
  Finkelstein, Daniel. *Two Roads Home* — 920
  Fishman, David E. *The Book Smugglers* — 940.53
  Frank, Anne. ★*The Diary of a Young Girl* — 940.53
  Frank, Anne. *The Diary of Anne Frank* — B
  Frank, Michael. ★*One Hundred Saturdays* — B
  Frankl, Viktor E. ★*Man's Search for Meaning* — B
  Freedland, Jonathan. ★*The Escape Artist* — 940.53
  Freeman, Hadley. *House of Glass* — B
  Frenkel, Francoise. *A Bookshop in Berlin* — B
  Friedlander, Saul. *Nazi Germany and the Jews* — 940.53
  Friedlander, Saul. *Nazi Germany and the Jews* — 940.53
  Fritzsche, Peter. *Life and Death in the Third Reich* — 943.086
  Gerwarth, Robert. *Hitler's Hangman* — B
  Gies, Miep. ★*Anne Frank Remembered* — B
  Goldhagen, Daniel Jonah. *Hitler's Willing Executioners* — 940.53
  Goldsmith, Martin. *The Inextinguishable Symphony* — B
  Goodrich, Frances. *The Diary of Anne Frank* — 812
  Greenfield, Martin. ★*Measure of a Man* — B
  Grose, Peter. *A Good Place to Hide* — 940.53
  Gross, Jan Tomasz. *Neighbors* — 940.53
  Hayes, Peter. *Why?* — 940.53
  Holden, Wendy. ★*Born Survivors* — 940.53
  Hurowitz, Richard. *In the Garden of the Righteous* — 940.53
  Iperen, Roxane van. ★*The Sisters of Auschwitz* — 940.53
  Jacobson, Sidney. *Anne Frank* — 741.5
  Kertzer, David I. *The Pope at War* — 940.53
  Kinstler, Linda. *Come to This Court and Cry* — 940.53
  Klemperer, Victor. *I Will Bear Witness* — B
  Kramer, Clara. *Clara's War* — B
  Kraus, Dita. *A Delayed Life* — B
  Krimstein, Ken. *When I Grow Up* — 741.5
  Krug, Nora. ★*Belonging* — 741.5
  Kurtz, Glenn. *Three Minutes in Poland* — 947.7
  Levi, Primo. ★*The Drowned and the Saved* — 940.53
  Levi, Primo. *The Periodic Table* — 858
  Levi, Primo. *The Reawakening* — B
  Levi, Primo. ★*Survival in Auschwitz* — B
  Lindwer, Willy. *The Last Seven Months of Anne Frank* — B
  Lipstadt, Deborah E. *The Eichmann Trial* — 345.5694
  Lipstadt, Deborah E. *History on Trial* — 940.53
  Loftis, Larry. ★*The Watchmaker's Daughter* — 940.53
  Longerich, Peter. *Goebbels* — B
  Longerich, Peter. *Hitler* — B
  Lower, Wendy. *Hitler's Furies* — 940.53
  Macadam, Heather Dune. *999* — 940.53
  Mazzeo, Tilar J. *Irena's Children* — B
  Moorehead, Caroline. *Village of Secrets* — 944
  Moorhouse, Roger. *The Forgers* — 940.53
  Mueller, Melissa. *Alice's Piano* — B
  Muller, Melissa. *Anne Frank* — B
  Neumann, Ariana. *When Time Stopped* — B
  Novick, Peter. *The Holocaust in American Life* — 940.53
  Pick-Goslar, Hannah Elizabeth. ★*My Friend Anne Frank* — B
  Pivnik, Sam. *Survivor* — 940.5318
  Rajchman, Chil. *The Last Jew of Treblinka* — 940.53
  Rees, Laurence. *Auschwitz* — 940.53

AUTHOR, TITLE, SERIES AND SUBJECT INDEX

Rees, Laurence. *The Holocaust*	940.53
Rhodes, Richard. *Masters of Death*	940.53
Rosenberg, Justus. *The Art of Resistance*	B
Ross, Steve. *From Broken Glass*	B
Sands, Philippe. *The Ratline*	B
Schindler, Meriel. *The Lost Cafe Schindler*	943.64
Schwarz, Geraldine. *Those Who Forget*	940.53
Simon, Marie. *Underground in Berlin*	B
Snyder, Timothy. *Black Earth*	940.53
Snyder, Timothy. ★*Bloodlands*	940.54
Spiegel, Renia. *Renia's Diary*	B
Spiegelman, Art. ★*Maus*	741.5
Stahl, Jerry. *Nein, Nein, Nein!*	B
Stangneth, Bettina. *Eichmann Before Jerusalem*	B
Stone, Dan. ★*The Holocaust*	940.53
Sullivan, Rosemary. *The Betrayal of Anne Frank*	940.53
Talty, Stephan. *The Good Assassin*	364.15
Van Es, Bart. *The Cut Out Girl*	B
Van Wijk-Voskuijl, Joop. *The Last Secret of the Secret Annex*	940.53
Wachsmann, Nikolaus. *Kl*	940.53
Weiss, Helga. *Helga's Diary*	B
White, Elizabeth B. ★*The Counterfeit Countess*	940.53
Wiesel, Elie. *All Rivers Run to the Sea*	B
Wiesel, Elie. *And the Sea Is Never Full*	B
Wiesel, Elie. ★*Night*	B
Winik, Jay. *1944*	940.53
HOLOCAUST DENIAL	
Lipstadt, Deborah E. *History on Trial*	940.53
The **Holocaust** *in American Life*. Novick, Peter	940.53
HOLOCAUST SURVIVORS	
Batalion, Judith. *The Light of Days*	940.53
Blau, Magda Hellinger. *The Nazis Knew My Name*	940.53
Burger, Ariel. *Witness*	848
Eger, Edith Eva. *The Choice*	B
Eisen, Max. *By Chance Alone*	940.5318
Epstein, Franci. *Franci's War*	B
Finkelstein, Daniel. *Two Roads Home*	920
Foer, Esther Safran. *I Want You to Know We're Still Here*	B
Frank, Michael. ★*One Hundred Saturdays*	B
Frankel, Rebecca. *Into the Forest*	940.53
Freeman, Hadley. *House of Glass*	B
Friedman, Tova. ★*The Daughter of Auschwitz*	B
Greene, Joshua. *Unstoppable*	B
Greenfield, Martin. ★*Measure of a Man*	B
Holden, Wendy. ★*Born Survivors*	940.53
Jaku, Eddie. ★*The Happiest Man on Earth*	B
Kaiser, Menachem. *Plunder*	B
Kinstler, Linda. *Come to This Court and Cry*	940.53
Kramer, Clara. *Clara's War*	B
Kraus, Dita. *A Delayed Life*	B
Kurtz, Glenn. *Three Minutes in Poland*	947.7
Levi, Primo. *The Reawakening*	B
Lindwer, Willy. *The Last Seven Months of Anne Frank*	B
Mueller, Melissa. *Alice's Piano*	B
Neumann, Ariana. *When Time Stopped*	B
Pivnik, Sam. *Survivor*	940.5318
Rees, Laurence. *Auschwitz*	940.53
Ross, Steve. *From Broken Glass*	B
Spiegelman, Art. ★*Maus*	741.5
Wiesel, Elie. *All Rivers Run to the Sea*	B
Wiesel, Elie. *And the Sea Is Never Full*	B
Wiesel, Elie. ★*Night*	B
HOLOCAUST VICTIMS	
Fairweather, Jack. *The Volunteer*	B
Sands, Philippe. *East West Street*	345
Spiegel, Renia. *Renia's Diary*	B
Van Wijk-Voskuijl, Joop. *The Last Secret of the Secret Annex*	940.53
Holt, Jim	
★*When Einstein Walked with Godel*	814
Why Does the World Exist?	113
Holt, Nathalia	
Cured	614.5
The Queens of Animation	920
★*Rise of the Rocket Girls*	629.4
Holthaus, Eric	
The Future Earth	363.738
Holton, Woody	
Abigail Adams	B
Liberty Is Sweet	973.3
Holway, Tatiana M.	
The Flower of Empire	727
Holy Envy. Taylor, Barbara Brown	B
Holy Hullabaloos. Wexler, Jay	342.7308
HOLY ROMAN EMPIRE	
Wilson, Peter H. *Heart of Europe*	943
Holy Runaways. Roberts, Matthias	262
Holy War. Cliff, Nigel	909
Holzer, Harold	
Brought Forth on This Continent	973.7
A Just and Generous Nation	973.7092
Monument Man	B
HOLZMAN, JAC	
Houghton, Mick. *Becoming Elektra*	781.64
Homage. Scott, Chris	641.5
Homans, Jennifer	
★*Apollo's Angels*	792.8
Home. Andrews, Julie	B
HOME (CONCEPT)	
Abdurraqib, Hanif. ★*There's Always This Year*	796.323
Alyan, Hala. *The Moon That Turns You Back*	811
Arceneaux, Michael. *I Finally Bought Some Jordans*	306.76
Bauermeister, Erica. *House Lessons*	B
Bee, Vanessa A. *Home Bound*	B
Broom, Sarah M. *The Yellow House*	B
Bryson, Bill. ★*At Home*	643
Dochartaigh, Kerri ni. *Cacophony of Bone*	B
Ehrlich, Gretel. *Unsoloced*	B
Georges, Gigi. *Downeast*	974.1
Hudes, Quiara Alegria. ★*My Broken Language*	B
Levy, Deborah. ★*Real Estate*	B
Malek, Alia. *The Home That Was Our Country*	B
Mans, Jasmine. *Black Girl, Call Home*	811
McCormick, Ty. *Beyond the Sand and Sea*	920
Morris, Jan. *A Writer's House in Wales*	942.9
Napier, Erin. *Heirloom Rooms*	747
Saldana, Stephanie. *What We Remember Will Be Saved*	362.7
Shadid, Anthony. *House of Stone*	306.0956
Suarez, Ray. ★*We Are Home*	325.73
Thomas, R. Eric. ★*Congratulations, the Best Is Over!*	B
Tworkov, Helen. *Lotus Girl*	B
Von Bremzen, Anya. *National Dish*	641.3
Watts, Reggie. *Great Falls, MT*	B
Weir, Laura. *Cosy*	646.7009
Young, Kevin. *Stones*	811
HOME (SOCIAL SCIENCES)	
Bryson, Bill. ★*At Home*	643
Hadlow, Janice. *A Royal Experiment*	B
HOME AND SCHOOL	
Fagell, Phyllis L. ★*Middle School Matters*	373.236
Home Bound. Bee, Vanessa A.	B
★*Home Comforts*. Mendelson, Cheryl	640
The Home Cook. Guarnaschelli, Alex	641.5973
Home Ec for Everyone. Bowers, Sharon	640
★*The Home Edit Life*. Shearer, Clea	648
HOME FURNISHINGS	
Larson, Elsie. *A Beautiful Mess Happy Handmade Home*	745
Linsley, Leslie. *Salvage Style*	747
Napier, Erin. *Heirloom Rooms*	747
Nicholas, Kristin. *Crafting a Patterned Home*	745.5
Parrella-Van Den Berg, Janet. *White & Faded*	645
Rott, Ira. *Crochet Animal Rugs*	746.7
Woodford, Chris. *Atoms Under the Floorboards*	500
Zedenius, Fanny. *Macrame*	746.42
HOME HEALTH CARE	
Davis, Patti. *Floating in the Deep End*	616.8
Karlawish, Jason. ★*The Problem of Alzheimer's*	616.8
Washington, Kate. ★*Already Toast*	649.8
Home in the World. Sen, Amartya	B
HOME INVASIONS	
McNamara, Michelle. *I'll Be Gone in the Dark*	364.152
Home Is Where the Eggs Are. Yeh, Molly	641.5
HOME LIBRARIES	
Ryback, Timothy W. *Hitler's Private Library*	027
HOME OWNERSHIP	
Dougherty, Conor. *Golden Gates*	363.509794

PUBLIC LIBRARY CORE COLLECTION: NONFICTION
Twentieth Edition

HOME RUNS (BASEBALL)
    Diamond, Jared M. *Swing Kings* — 796.357
HOME SCHOOLING
    Westover, Tara. ★*Educated* — B
The Home That Was Our Country. Malek, Alia — B
Home with Rue. Lamb, Kelli — 747
Home Work. Andrews, Julie — B
Home, Water & Moisture Problems. Branson, Gary D. — 643
Homecoming. Foroohar, Rana — 338.6
HOMECOMINGS
    Fields, Micah. ★*We Hold Our Breath* — 976.4
    Finkel, David. *Thank You for Your Service* — 920
    Kesling, Ben. *Bravo Company* — 958.104
    Lockwood, Patricia. *Priestdaddy* — B
    Mahjoub, Jamal. *A Line in the River* — 962.404
    Perry, Imani. ★*South to America* — 917
Homegirls & Handgrenades. Sanchez, Sonia — 811
★*Homegrown*. Toobin, Jeffrey — 363.325
Homegrown Pantry. Pleasant, Barbara — 635
HOMELESS CHILDREN
    Ambroz, David. *A Place Called Home* — B
    Elliott, Andrea. ★*Invisible Child* — 362.7
    Lockhart, Chris. ★*Walking the Bowl* — 362.7
    Sokolik, Vicki. ★*If You See Them* — 362.5
    Stewart, Nikita. *Troop 6000* — 369
HOMELESS MEN
    Jackson, Ted. ★*You Ought to Do a Story About Me* — B
HOMELESS PEOPLE
    Adler, Kevin F. *When We Walk By* — 362.5
    Berg, Scott W. *The Burning of the World* — 977.311
    Bruder, Jessica. ★*Nomadland* — 331.3
    Coombes, Joshua. *Do Something for Nothing* — 362.5
    Kidder, Tracy. ★*Rough Sleepers* — 362.5
    Kozol, Jonathan. *Rachel and Her Children* — 362.5
    Murray, Liz. *Breaking Night* — B
    Rao, Cheeni. *In Hanuman's Hands* — B
    Sokolik, Vicki. ★*If You See Them* — 362.5
    Walls, Jeannette. ★*The Glass Castle* — B
    Winn, Raynor. ★*The Salt Path* — B
HOMELESS TEENAGERS
    Sokolik, Vicki. ★*If You See Them* — 362.5
HOMELESS WOMEN
    Sandler, Lauren. *This Is All I Got* — B
HOMELESSNESS
    Adler, Kevin F. *When We Walk By* — 362.5
    Ambroz, David. *A Place Called Home* — B
    Conyers, Jonathan. *I Wasn't Supposed to Be Here* — B
    Coombes, Joshua. *Do Something for Nothing* — 362.5
    Elliott, Andrea. ★*Invisible Child* — 362.7
    Gerard, Sarah. *Sunshine State* — 814
    Jackson, Ted. ★*You Ought to Do a Story About Me* — B
    Kidder, Tracy. ★*Rough Sleepers* — 362.5
    Kim, Anne. ★*Abandoned* — 305.2350973
    Nietfeld, Emi. *Acceptance* — B
    Prickett, Pamela J. ★*The Unclaimed* — 363.7
    Ross, Andrew. *Sunbelt Blues* — 363.5
    Sandler, Lauren. *This Is All I Got* — B
    Schemel, Patty. *Hit so Hard* — B
    Sokolik, Vicki. ★*If You See Them* — 362.5
    Stewart, Nikita. *Troop 6000* — 369
    Vargas, Jose Antonio. *Dear America* — B
    Wallace, Carvell. *Another Word for Love* — B
    White, Richard Antoine. *I'm Possible* — B
Homemade Holiday. Pester, Sophie — 745.594
HOMEMAKERS
    Davis, Lisa. ★*Housewife* — 331.4
    Gopal, Anand. *No Good Men Among the Living* — 920
    Mangino, Kate. ★*Equal Partners* — 305.3
    Worsley, Lucy. ★*Agatha Christie* — B
HOMEMAKING
    Bowers, Sharon. *Home Ec for Everyone* — 640
    Bried, Erin. *How to Sew a Button* — 640
    Kondo, Marie. ★*The Life-Changing Magic of Tidying Up* — 648
    Kondo, Marie. ★*Marie Kondo's Kurashi at Home* — 648
    Kondo, Marie. ★*Spark Joy* — 648
    Mendelson, Cheryl. ★*Home Comforts* — 640
    Stewart, Martha. ★*The Martha Manual* — 640
    Watkins, Julia. *Simply Living Well* — 640

HOMEOWNERS
    Elias, Stephen. *The Foreclosure Survival Guide, 9th Ed.* — 346.7304
    Finkelstein, Elizabeth. *Cheap Old Houses* — 643
Homer
    The Iliad — 883
    The Iliad — 883
    Iliad — 883
    ★*The Iliad* — 883
    The Odyssey — 883
    The Odyssey — 883
    Odyssey — 883
    ★*The Odyssey* — 883
    The Odyssey — 883
HOMER
    Alexander, Caroline. *The War That Killed Achilles* — 883
    Manguel, Alberto. *Homer's Iliad and the Odyssey* — 883
    Nicolson, Adam. *Why Homer Matters* — 883
Homer's The Iliad and the Odyssey. Manguel, Alberto — 883
HOMER, WINSLOW, 1836-1910
    Cross, William R. *Winslow Homer* — 759.13
Homestead Recipes. Rettke, Amanda — 641.5977
HOMESTEADERS
    McGraw, Seamus. *The End of Country* — 333.7909748
    Raban, Jonathan. *Bad Land* — 978
HOMESTEADING
    Logsdon, Gene. *Letter to a Young Farmer* — 338.10973
    Raban, Jonathan. *Bad Land* — 978
    Sundeen, Mark. *The Unsettlers* — 640
HOMEWORK
    Donaldson-Pressman, Stephanie. *The Learning Habit* — 371.30281
Homey Don't Play That! Peisner, David — 791.45
★*Homie*. Smith, Danez — 811
Homo Deus. Harari, Yuval N. — 909.83
HOMO ERECTUS
    Tattersall, Ian. *Masters of the Planet* — 599.93
Homolka, Gina
    Skinnytaste Fast and Slow — 641.5
    Skinnytaste One & Done — 641.5
HOMOPHOBIA
    Broome, Brian. ★*Punch Me up to the Gods* — B
    Cervini, Eric. *The Deviant's War* — B
    Fieseler, Robert W. *Tinderbox* — 364.152
    Green, Elon. *Last Call* — 363.15
    Gutowitz, Jill. *Girls Can Kiss Now* — 814
    Hewitt, Sean. *All Down Darkness Wide* — B
    Lorde, Audre. *Sister Outsider* — 814
    Rogers, Robbie. *Coming Out to Play* — B
    Shakur, Prince. *When They Tell You to Be Good* — B
HOMOSEXUALITY
    Belcourt, Billy-Ray. ★*A History of My Brief Body* — B
    Bronski, Michael. *A Queer History of the United States* — 306.76
    Butler, Isaac. *The World Only Spins Forward* — 812
    Carpenter, Dale. *Flagrant Conduct* — 342.7308
    Cervini, Eric. *The Deviant's War* — B
    Chu, Jeff. *Does Jesus Really Love Me?* — 261.8
    Cooper, Alex. *Saving Alex* — B
    Davis, Lisa Selin. *Tomboy* — 305.409
    Dennison, Matthew. *Behind the Mask* — B
    Doty, Mark. *What Is the Grass* — 811
    Eade, Philip. *Evelyn Waugh* — B
    Evans, R. Tripp. *Grant Wood* — B
    Fieseler, Robert W. *Tinderbox* — 364.152
    Geter, Hafizah. *Un-American* — 811
    Gopnik, Blake. ★*Warhol* — B
    Gutowitz, Jill. *Girls Can Kiss Now* — 814
    O'Sullivan, Emer. *The Fall of the House of Wilde* — B
    Price, Reynolds. *A Serious Way of Wondering* — 241
    Schemel, Patty. *Hit so Hard* — B
    Stone, Geoffrey R. *Sex and the Constitution* — 345.7302
HOMOSEXUALITY AND LITERATURE
    Hastings, Selina. *The Secret Lives of Somerset Maugham* — B
    Town, Caren J. *LGBTQ Young Adult Fiction* — 813.009
HOMOSEXUALITY IN FILMS
    Schiavi, Michael R. *Celluloid Activist* — B
HOMOSEXUALITY IN LITERATURE
    Town, Caren J. *LGBTQ Young Adult Fiction* — 813.009
HONDURAS
    Preston, Douglas J. ★*The Lost City of the Monkey God* — 972.85

AUTHOR, TITLE, SERIES AND SUBJECT INDEX

The **Honest** *Truth About Dishonesty.* Ariely, Dan   177
HONESTY
    Ariely, Dan. *The Honest Truth About Dishonesty*   177
    Coel, Michaela. ★*Misfits*   158.2
    Duggar, Jill. *Counting the Cost*   B
    Goodan, Chelsey. *Underestimated*   305.235
    Griffin, Chante. *Loving Your Black Neighbor as Yourself*   261
    Knight, Keltie. *Lady Secrets*   305.4
    McAfee, Andrew. *The Geek Way*   658.3
    Scott, Kim Malone. *Radical Candor*   658.4
    Viren, Sarah. *To Name the Bigger Lie*   B
The **Honey** *Bus.* May, Meredith   B
Honey, Michael K
    To the Promised Land   323
HONEYBEE
    Flottum, Kim. *The Backyard Beekeeper*   638
    Wilson, Joseph S. *The Bees in Your Backyard*   595.79
HONG KONG
    Chan, Jackie. *Never Grow Up*   B
    Cheung, Karen. *The Impossible City*   951.25
    Hulls, Tessa. ★*Feeding Ghosts*   741.5
    Kaufman, Jonathan. *The Last Kings of Shanghai*   951
    Lim, Louisa. *Indelible City*   951.25
    Mahtani, Shibani. *Among the Braves*   951.25
Hong, Cathy Park
    Engine Empire   811
    Minor Feelings   305.48
HONG, CATHY PARK
    Hong, Cathy Park. *Minor Feelings*   305.48
Hong, Deuki
    Koreatown   641.595
Hongoltz-Hetling, Matthew
    If It Sounds Like a Quack   615.8
Honig, Elie
    Untouchable   364.1
Honigsbaum, Mark
    The Pandemic Century   614.4
Honigstein, Raphael
    DAS Reboot   796.334
Honnold, Alex
    Alone on the Wall   B
HONNOLD, ALEX
    Honnold, Alex. *Alone on the Wall*   B
HONOR
    Ronson, Jon. *So You've Been Publicly Shamed*   152.4
HONOR KILLINGS
    Faleiro, Sonia. *The Good Girls*   364.152
Honorable Exit. Clarke, Thurston   959.704
Hoock, Holger
    Scars of Independence   973.3
Hood Feminism. Kendall, Mikki   305.420973
Hood, Ann
    Kitchen Yarns   641.5
HOOD, ANN, 1956-
    Hood, Ann. *Kitchen Yarns*   641.5
Hooded Americanism. Chalmers, David Mark   322.4
Hook, Philip
    Rogues' Gallery   709.2
Hooked. Foster, Sutton   B
★*Hooked.* Moss, Michael   613.2
Hooked on Shakespeare. Hatchard, Gurinder Kaur   746.43
HOOKER, JOSEPH DALTON, SIR, 1817-1911
    McCalman, Iain. *Darwin's Armada*   576.8
hooks, bell
    Remembered Rapture   808
    Wounds of Passion   B
HOOKS, BELL, 1952-2021
    hooks, bell. *Remembered Rapture*   808
    hooks, bell. *Wounds of Passion*   B
Hooper, John
    The Italians   945.093
The **Hoops** *Whisperer.* Ravin, Idan   796.323
Hoosh. Anthony, Jason C.   394.1
Hoover. Whyte, Kenneth   B
HOOVER DAM
    Denton, Sally. *The Profiteers*   B
HOOVER, HERBERT, 1874-1964
    Rappleye, Charles. *Herbert Hoover in the White House*   B

Whyte, Kenneth. *Hoover*   B
HOOVER, J. EDGAR, 1895-1972
    Gage, Beverly. *G-Man*   B
    Rosenfeld, Seth. *Subversives*   378.1
Hopcraft, Arthur
    The Football Man   796.334
Hope. Zoglin, Richard   B
HOPE
    Alexander, Kwame. *Why Fathers Cry at Night*   B
    Bailey, Jennifer. *To My Beloveds*   261.8
    Biden, Joseph R. *Promise Me, Dad*   B
    Blanco, Richard. *How to Love a Country*   811
    Burke, Tarana. ★*Unbound*   B
    Dalai Lama. *The Book of Joy*   294.3
    Diaz, Natalie. ★*Postcolonial Love Poem*   811
    Doyne, Maggie. *Between the Mountain and the Sky*   B
    Fox, Michael J. *No Time Like the Future*   B
    Francis. *The Church of Mercy*   252
    Gay, Ross. *The Book of (more) Delights*   814
    Goodall, Jane. ★*The Book of Hope*   128
    Gorman, Amanda. ★*Call Us What We Carry*   811
    Heti, Sheila. *Alphabetical Diaries*   818
    Hobbs, Jeff. *Children of the State*   364.36
    Lamott, Anne. *Almost Everything*   170
    Lamott, Anne. ★*Dusk, Night, Dawn*   B
    Lamott, Anne. *Small Victories*   248
    Lewis, John. *Carry On*   328.73
    Manson, Mark. *Everything Is F*cked*   152.4
    Marshall, Nate. *Finna*   811
    Millet, Lydia. *We Loved It All*   813
    Morgan, Abi. *This Is Not a Pity Memoir*   B
    O'Hara, Maryanne. *Little Matches*   B
    Obama, Barack. ★*A Promised Land*   B
    Obama, Michelle. ★*The Light We Carry*   B
    Oluseyi, Hakeem M. *A Quantum Life*   B
    Plantinga, Cornelius. *Gratitude*   179
    Quinones, John. ★*One Year in Uvalde*   371.7
    Reang, Putsata. *Ma and Me*   B
    Rush, Charaia. *Courageously Soft*   234
    Setiya, Kieran. *Life Is Hard*   128
    Smith, Carol. *Crossing the River*   B
    Solnit, Rebecca. *Call Them by Their True Names*   303.3
    Terkel, Studs. *Hope Dies Last*   920
    Thom, Kai Cheng. *Falling Back in Love with Being Human*   811
    Tutu, Desmond. *Made for Goodness*   170
HOPE (CHRISTIANITY)
    Curry, Michael B. *Love Is the Way*   241
Hope Dies Last. Terkel, Studs   920
A **Hope** *More Powerful Than the Sea.* Fleming, Melissa   956.9104
HOPE, BOB, 1903-2003
    Zoglin, Richard. *Hope*   B
Hope, Bradley
    Blood and Oil   B
Hope, Clover
    The Motherlode   920
HOPI (NORTH AMERICAN PEOPLE)
    Brooks, James. *Mesa of Sorrows*   979.1004
HOPKINS, HARRY L. (HARRY LLOYD), 1890-1946
    Fullilove, Michael. *Rendezvous with Destiny*   973.917092
Hopkins, Jerry
    No One Here Gets Out Alive   B
HOPKINS, STEPHEN, 1581-1644
    Kelly, Joseph. *Marooned*   975.5
    Whittock, Martyn. *Mayflower Lives*   974.4
HOPP, STEVEN L., 1954-
    Kingsolver, Barbara. ★*Animal, Vegetable, Miracle*   641
HOPPER, EDWARD, 1882-1967
    Levin, Gail. *Edward Hopper*   759.13
HOPPER, GRACE MURRAY, 1906-1992
    Beyer, Kurt. *Grace Hopper and the Invention of the Information Age*   B
Hopper, Jessica
    The First Collection of Criticism by a Living Female Rock Critic   781.66
Hopwood, Shon
    Law Man   B
Horace
    Odes and Epodes   874
HORACE
    Horace. *Odes and Epodes*   874

PUBLIC LIBRARY CORE COLLECTION: NONFICTION
Twentieth Edition

Horace, Matthew
   The Black and the Blue — B
Horenstein, Henry
   Digital Photography — 770
Horizon. Lopez, Barry Holstun — B
HORMONES, SEX
   Semenya, Caster. *The Race to Be Myself* — B
Horn, Dara
   ★*People Love Dead Jews* — 909
HORN, DARA, 1977-
   Horn, Dara. ★*People Love Dead Jews* — 909
Horn, James P. P.
   A Kingdom Strange — 975.6
   Land as God Made It — 975.5
Horn, Jonathan
   Washington's End — B
Horn, Miriam
   Rancher, Farmer, Fisherman — B
Hornbacher, Marya
   Wasted — B
HORNBACHER, MARYA, 1974-
   Hornbacher, Marya. *Wasted* — B
Horne, Alistair
   Seven Ages of Paris — 944
Horne, Jed
   Breach of Faith — 976.3
HORNE, LENA
   Gavin, James. ★*Stormy Weather* — 782.42164
HORNER, SALLY
   Weinman, Sarah. *The Real Lolita* — 362.88092
Hornfischer, James D.
   Neptune's Inferno — 940.54
   Who Can Hold the Sea — 359.00973
HOROVITZ, ADAM
   Mike D. *Beastie Boys Book* — 782.42164
Horowitz, Alexandra
   ★*Being a Dog* — 636.7
   ★*Inside of a Dog* — 636.7
   Our Dogs, Ourselves — 636.7
   ★*The Year of the Puppy* — 636.7
HOROWITZ, ALEXANDRA
   Horowitz, Alexandra. ★*The Year of the Puppy* — 636.7
Horowitz, Joseph
   ★*Classical Music in America* — 781.6
Horrigan, Joe
   NFL Century — 796.332
HORROR AUTHORS
   Spratford, Becky Siegel. *The Readers' Advisory Guide to Horror* — 025.5
HORROR FILMS
   O'Meara, Mallory. *The Lady from the Black Lagoon* — 921
   Poole, W. Scott. *Vampira* — B
   Schechter, Harold. ★*Ripped from the Headlines!* — 791.43
   Weismann, Brad. *Lost in the Dark* — 791.43
   Williams, Marlena. *Night Mother* — 791.43
HORROR IN LITERATURE
   Spratford, Becky Siegel. *The Readers' Advisory Guide to Horror* — 025.5
Horror Stories. Phair, Liz — B
HORROR WRITING
   King, Stephen. *On Writing* — B
   Skal, David J. *Something in the Blood* — 823
HORSE BREEDERS
   Markham, Beryl. *West with the Night* — B
HORSE BREEDING
   Letts, Elizabeth. *The Perfect Horse* — 940.54
   Markham, Beryl. *West with the Night* — B
Horse Crazy. Nir, Sarah Maslin
HORSE OWNERS
   Nir, Sarah Maslin. *Horse Crazy* — B
HORSE RACE BETTING
   Lang, Arne K. *Sports Betting and Bookmaking* — 798.4010973
HORSE RACING
   Askwith, Richard. *Unbreakable* — B
   Drape, Joe. *American Pharoah* — 798.40092
   Drape, Joe. *Black Maestro* — B
   Hillenbrand, Laura. ★*Seabiscuit* — 798.4
   Lang, Arne K. *Sports Betting and Bookmaking* — 798.4010973
   Ours, Dorothy. *Man O' War* — 798.400929
   Prior-Palmer, Lara. *Rough Magic* — 798.4

HORSE TRAINERS
   Gaffney, Ginger. *Half Broke* — B
   Hillenbrand, Laura. ★*Seabiscuit* — 798.4
HORSE TRAINING
   Gaffney, Ginger. *Half Broke* — B
HORSES
   Askwith, Richard. *Unbreakable* — B
   Hutton, Robin L. *Sgt. Reckless* — 951.904
   Letts, Elizabeth. ★*The Ride of Her Life* — B
   Nir, Sarah Maslin. *Horse Crazy* — B
   Shaffer, Peter. ★*Equus* — 822
   Thompson-Hernandez, Walter. *The Compton Cowboys* — 920
HORSES IN ART
   Hand, Diana. *Draw Horses in 15 Minutes* — 743.6
Horstman, Mark
   The Effective Manager — 658.4
HORTICULTURE
   Bainbridge, David A. *Gardening with Less Water* — 635.9
   Johnson, Victoria. ★*American Eden* — 580.973
   Kassinger, Ruth. ★*A Garden of Marvels* — 580.92
   Lavoipierre, Frederique. *Garden Allies* — 635
   Solnit, Rebecca. *Orwell's Roses* — B
HORTICULTURISTS
   Magdalena, Carlos. *The Plant Messiah* — 333.95
   Wulf, Andrea. *The Brother Gardeners* — 920
Hortis, C. Alexander
   The Witch of New York — 364.152
Horton, Michelle
   Dear Sister — B
HORTON, MICHELLE
   Horton, Michelle. *Dear Sister* — B
HORVATH, FERDINAND, 1891-1973
   Ghez, Didier. *The Hidden Art of Disney's Golden Age* — 741.5
Horwitz, Jeff
   ★*Broken Code* — 302.3
Horwitz, Josh
   War of the Whales — 333.95
Horwitz, Tony
   Confederates in the Attic — 973.7
   ★*Midnight Rising* — 973.7
   Spying on the South — 917
   ★*A Voyage Long and Strange* — 970.01
HORWITZ, TONY, 1958-
   Horwitz, Tony. *Confederates in the Attic* — 973.7
   Horwitz, Tony. *Spying on the South* — 917
Horwood, Roger
   Woodworker's Handbook — 684
HOSACK, DAVID, 1769-1835
   Johnson, Victoria. ★*American Eden* — 580.973
HOSPICE CARE
   Clarke, Rachel. *Dear Life* — B
   Kerr, Christopher. *Death Is but a Dream* — 155.9
   Speerstra, Karen. *The Divine Art of Dying* — 202
★*The Hospital*. Alexander, Brian — 362.10973
HOSPITAL ADMINISTRATORS
   Alexander, Brian. ★*The Hospital* — 362.10973
HOSPITAL CARE
   Manheimer, Eric. *Twelve Patients* — 362.1109747
   Oshinsky, David M. *Bellevue* — 362.1109747
HOSPITAL CHAPLAINS
   Park, J. S. ★*As Long as You Need* — 248.8
HOSPITAL PATIENTS
   Brenner, Marie. ★*The Desperate Hours* — 362.1962
   Case, Molly. *How to Treat People* — 616.1
   Ely, Wes. *Every Deep-Drawn Breath* — 616.02
   Gawande, Atul. *Complications* — B
   Jena, Anupam B. *Random Acts of Medicine* — 616.0072
   Manheimer, Eric. *Twelve Patients* — 362.1109747
   Meyer, Robert. *Every Minute Is a Day* — 362.1962
   Oshinsky, David M. *Bellevue* — 362.1109747
HOSPITAL WORKERS
   Brenner, Marie. ★*The Desperate Hours* — 362.1962
HOSPITALITY
   Orth, Stephan. *Couchsurfing in Iran* — 955.06
HOSPITALITY INDUSTRY AND TRADE
   Barr, Luke. *Ritz & Escoffier* — 920
   James, Victoria. *Wine Girl* — B

AUTHOR, TITLE, SERIES AND SUBJECT INDEX

HOSPITALS
- Alexander, Brian. ★*The Hospital* — 362.10973
- Brenner, Marie. ★*The Desperate Hours* — 362.1962
- Fink, Sheri. *Five Days at Memorial* — 362.1109763
- Fisher, Thomas. ★*The Emergency* — 362.1089
- Goldberg, Emma. *Life on the Line* — 362.1962
- Jena, Anupam B. *Random Acts of Medicine* — 616.0072
- Manheimer, Eric. *Twelve Patients* — 362.1109747
- Meyer, Robert. *Every Minute Is a Day* — 362.1962
- Oshinsky, David M. *Bellevue* — 362.1109747
- Patterson, James. *ER Nurses* — 610.73
- Smilios, Maria. ★*The Black Angels* — 610.73

Hostage. Delisle, Guy — 741.5

HOSTAGE NEGOTIATIONS
- Follett, Ken. *On Wings of Eagles* — 955
- King, David. *Six Days in August* — 364.15
- Thompson, Jamie. *Standoff* — 364.152

HOSTAGE RESCUE UNITS
- Follett, Ken. *On Wings of Eagles* — 955

HOSTAGE TAKING
- Follett, Ken. *On Wings of Eagles* — 955
- Moore, Michael Scott. *The Desert and the Sea* — 364.15

HOSTAGES
- Bowden, Mark. *Guests of the Ayatollah* — 955.05
- Bruning, John R. *Indestructible* — B
- Delisle, Guy. *Hostage* — 741.5
- Follett, Ken. *On Wings of Eagles* — 955
- King, David. *Six Days in August* — 364.15
- McCann, Colum. *American Mother* — 956.9104
- Moore, Michael Scott. *The Desert and the Sea* — 364.15
- Rezaian, Jason. *Prisoner* — B

The Hostess Handbook. Zizka, Maria — 642

HOSTILITY (PSYCHOLOGY)
- Goodheart, Adam. *The Last Island* — 954

Hot and Bothered. Dunn, Jancee — 618.1
The Hot Bread Kitchen Cookbook. Rodriguez, Jessamyn Waldman — 641.59
★*Hot Sheet*. Massov, Olga — 641.82

HOT SPRINGS, ARKANSAS
- Hill, David. *The Vapors* — 976.7

The Hot Young Widows Club. McInerny, Nora — 155.9
The Hot Zone. Preston, Richard — 614.5

HOTEL OWNERS
- Levy, Shawn. ★*The Castle on Sunset* — 647.95

HOTELS
- Barr, Luke. *Ritz & Escoffier* — 920
- Delisle, Guy. *Pyongyang* — 741.5
- Levy, Shawn. ★*The Castle on Sunset* — 647.95
- Satow, Julie. *The Plaza* — 917.47

Hotez, Peter J.
- *Preventing the Next Pandemic* — 362.1969

Hotta, Eri
- *Japan 1941* — 940.54

Hotz, Julia
- ★*The Connection Cure* — 610

HOUDINI, HARRY, 1874-1926
- Jaher, David. *The Witch of Lime Street* — B
- Posnanski, Joe. ★*The Life and Afterlife of Harry Houdini* — 793.8

Hough, Lauren
- *Leaving Isn't the Hardest Thing* — B

HOUGH, LAUREN, 1977-
- Hough, Lauren. *Leaving Isn't the Hardest Thing* — B

HOUGH, NIGEL
- Lamb, Christina. *House of Stone* — 968.91

Hough, Stephen
- *Rough Ideas* — 786.2092

HOUGH, STEPHEN, 1961-
- Hough, Stephen. *Rough Ideas* — 786.2092

Houghton, Mick
- *Becoming Elektra* — 781.64

Houppert, Karen
- *Chasing Gideon* — 345.73

An Hour Before Daylight. Carter, Jimmy — B
The Hour of Fate. Berfield, Susan — 973.91

Housden, Roger
- *Saved by Beauty* — 955

HOUSDEN, ROGER
- Housden, Roger. *Saved by Beauty* — 955

HOUSE AND HOME — CLEANING, CARETAKING, AND ORGANIZING
- Becker, Joshua. *The Minimalist Home* — 241
- Boyd, Nikki. ★*Beautifully Organized* — 648
- Carlson, Julie. *Remodelista* — 648
- Casazza, Allie. *Declutter Like a Mother* — 648
- Chayka, Kyle. *The Longing for Less* — 179.9
- Cilley, Marla. *The Chaos* Cure* — 648
- Davis, KC. ★*How to Keep House While Drowning* — 648
- Ewer, Cynthia Townley. *Cut the Clutter* — 648
- Gill, Shira. *Organized Living* — 747
- Kondo, Marie. ★*The Life-Changing Magic of Tidying Up* — 648
- Kondo, Marie. ★*Marie Kondo's Kurashi at Home* — 648
- Kondo, Marie. ★*Spark Joy* — 648
- McCubbin, Tracy. *Make Space for Happiness* — 179
- McCubbin, Tracy. *Making Space, Clutter Free* — 648
- Mendelson, Cheryl. ★*Home Comforts* — 640
- Morgenstern, Julie. *Time to Parent* — 649
- Richardson, Patric. *Laundry Love* — 648
- Rubin, Gretchen. *Outer Order, Inner Calm* — 158
- Shearer, Clea. ★*The Home Edit Life* — 648
- Stewart, Martha. ★*The Martha Manual* — 640
- White, Dana. *How to Manage Your Home Without Losing Your Mind* — 648

HOUSE AND HOME — DIY, MAINTENANCE, AND REPAIR
- Akiyama, Lance. *Duct Tape Engineer* — 745.5
- Blakeney, Justina. *The New Bohemians Handbook* — 747
- Branson, Gary D. *Home, Water & Moisture Problems* — 643
- Byers, Charles T. *Ultimate Guide Home Repair and Improvement* — 643
- Grove, Kirsten. *Simply Styling* — 747
- Holmes, Roger. *Midwest Home Landscaping* — 712
- McAlister, Michael. *Taunton's Wiring Complete* — 621.3
- Milchtein, Chaya M. ★*Mechanic Shop Femme's Guide to Car Ownership* — 629.222
- Mitchell, Ryan. *Tiny House Living* — 728.37
- Pierce, D. *The Accessible Home* — 728
- Pourny, Christophe. ★*The Furniture Bible* — 684.1
- Scott, Jonathan. ★*Dream Home* — 643
- Stewart, Martha. ★*The Martha Manual* — 640
- Susanka, Sarah. *Creating the Not so Big House* — 728
- Toht, David. ★*Stanley Decks* — 690
- Wing, Charles. *How Your House Works* — 643

HOUSE AND HOME — GENERAL
- Bowers, Sharon. *Home Ec for Everyone* — 640
- Cilley, Marla. *The Chaos* Cure* — 648
- Gates, Erin T. ★*Elements of Family Style* — 747
- Hirsch, William J. *Designing Your Perfect House* — 728
- Koones, Sheri. *Prefabulous Small Houses* — 728
- Kotite, Erika. *She Sheds* — 728
- Napier, Erin. *Heirloom Rooms* — 747
- Pierce, D. *The Accessible Home* — 728
- Scott, Jonathan. ★*Dream Home* — 643
- Spencer, Lara. *Flea Market Fabulous* — 747
- Susanka, Sarah. *Creating the Not so Big House* — 728
- Susanka, Sarah. *Not so Big Solutions for Your Home* — 728
- Toht, David. ★*Stanley Decks* — 690
- Wenzke, Ali. ★*The Art of Happy Moving* — 648

HOUSE AND HOME — INTERIOR DECORATING AND FURNISHINGS
- Adams, Michael Henry. *Style and Grace* — 747
- Becker, Holly. *Decorate* — 747
- Blair, Barb. *Furniture Makeovers* — 684.1
- Blakeney, Justina. *Jungalow* — 747
- Blakeney, Justina. *The New Bohemians Handbook* — 747
- Bridges, Sheila. *Furnishing Forward* — 747
- Brits, Louisa Thomsen. *The Book of Hygge* — 747
- Brown, Amanda. ★*Spruce* — 747
- Carter, Darryl. *The Collected Home* — 747
- Carter, Darryl. *The New Traditional* — 747
- Carter, Hilton. *Wild Interiors* — 747.98
- Chapman, Baylor. ★*Decorating with Plants* — 635.9
- Chayka, Kyle. *The Longing for Less* — 179.9
- Feldmann, Erica. *Hausmagick* — 133.4
- Finkelstein, Elizabeth. *Cheap Old Houses* — 643
- Frisoni, Christine-Lea. *The Big Book of a Miniature House* — 745.592
- Gates, Erin T. ★*Elements of Family Style* — 747
- Gold, Jamie. *Taunton's New Bathroom Idea Book* — 747.7
- Greayer, Rochelle. *Cultivating Garden Style* — 712
- Hays, Jeanine. *Remix* — 747
- Hudson, Kate. *Pretty Fun* — 642
- Khemsurov, Monica. *How to Live with Objects* — 747

PUBLIC LIBRARY CORE COLLECTION: NONFICTION
Twentieth Edition

Kotite, Erika. *She Sheds*	728
Lamb, Kelli. *Home with Rue*	747
Larson, Elsie. *A Beautiful Mess Happy Handmade Home*	745
Linsley, Leslie. *Salvage Style*	747
Martin, Tovah. ★*The Indestructible Houseplant*	635.9
Martin, Tovah. *The Unexpected Houseplant*	635.9
McClain, John. *The Designer Within*	645
Merhi, Farah. ★*Inspire Your Home*	747
Needleman, Deborah. *The Perfectly Imperfect Home*	747
Nicholas, Kristin. *Crafting a Patterned Home*	745.5
Parrella-Van Den Berg, Janet. *White & Faded*	645
Petersik, Sherry. *Lovable Livable Home*	645
Smith, Michael S. *Designing History*	975.3
Spencer, Lara. *Flea Market Fabulous*	747
Tanov, Erica. *Design by Nature*	747
Taylor, Claude. *How to Zoom Your Room*	747
Watson, Ted Kennedy. *Ted Kennedy Watson's Guide to Stylish Entertaining*	793.2
Wilhide, Elizabeth. *Scandinavian Home*	728

HOUSE AND HOME — OUTDOOR AREAS
Cory, Steve. *Ultimate Guide*	690
Edwards, Adrienne L. *Firescaping Your Home*	635.9
Gidding, John. *At Home with Nature*	635.9
Greayer, Rochelle. *Cultivating Garden Style*	712
Holmes, Kier. *The Garden Refresh*	635
Kotite, Erika. *She Sheds*	728
Schwartz, Bobbie. *Garden Renovation*	635
Slatalla, Michelle. *Gardenista*	635
Striniste, Nancy. *Nature Play at Home*	796.083
Toht, David. ★*Stanley Decks*	690

HOUSE AND HOME — REMODELING AND RENOVATION
Branson, Gary D. *Home, Water & Moisture Problems*	643
Edwards, Adrienne L. *Firescaping Your Home*	635.9
Finkelstein, Elizabeth. *Cheap Old Houses*	643
Gold, Jamie. *Taunton's New Bathroom Idea Book*	747.7
Petersik, Sherry. *Lovable Livable Home*	645
Pierce, D. *The Accessible Home*	728
Scott, Jonathan. ★*Dream Home*	643

HOUSE AND HOME — SUSTAINABLE LIVING
Branhagen, Alan. *Native Plants of the Midwest*	635.9
Crosson, Monica. *The Magikal Family*	299
Edwards, Zoe. *Mend It, Wear It, Love It!*	646
Flottum, Kim. *The Backyard Beekeeper*	638
Guralnick, Margot, *Remodelista*	747
Mitchell, Ryan. *Tiny House Living*	728.37
Watkins, Julia. *Simply Living Well*	640
The House At Sugar Beach. Cooper, Helene	921

HOUSE BUYING
Scott, Jonathan. ★*Dream Home*	643
The House by the Lake. Harding, Thomas	943

HOUSE CLEANING
Becker, Joshua. *The Minimalist Home*	241
Casazza, Allie. *Declutter Like a Mother*	648
Cilley, Marla. *The Chaos* Cure*	648
Davis, KC. ★*How to Keep House While Drowning*	648
Ewer, Cynthia Townley. *Cut the Clutter*	648
McCubbin, Tracy. *Making Space, Clutter Free*	648
Watkins, Julia. *Simply Living Well*	640
White, Dana. *How to Manage Your Home Without Losing Your Mind*	648

HOUSE CONSTRUCTION
Proulx, Annie. *Bird Cloud*	B
Susanka, Sarah. *Not so Big Solutions for Your Home*	728
A House in the Mountains. Moorehead, Caroline	940.53
House Lessons. Bauermeister, Erica	B
House of Glass. Freeman, Hadley	B
The House of Government. Slezkine, Yuri	947.084
★*The House of Hidden Meanings*. RuPaul	B
★*The House of Islam*. Husain, Ed	297
House of Lords and Commons. Hutchinson, Ishion	811
House of Lost Worlds. Conniff, Richard	069
The House of Medici. Hibbert, Christopher	920
A House of My Own. Cisneros, Sandra	B
House of Nails. Dykstra, Lenny	B
House of Nutter. Richardson, Lance	B
House of Rain. Childs, Craig	978.9
House of Sticks. Tran, Ly	B
House of Stone. Lamb, Christina	968.91
House of Stone. Shadid, Anthony	306.0956

The House of Wisdom. Al-Khalili, Jim	509
★*The House of Worth 1858-1954*. Trubert-Tollu, Chantal	746.92

HOUSE PLANTS
Bohmig, Franz. ★*The Month-By-Month Gardening Guide*	635
Carter, Hilton. *Wild Interiors*	747.98
Chapman, Baylor. ★*Decorating with Plants*	635.9
Deardorff, David C. *What's Wrong with My Houseplant?*	635.9
Durber, Sarah. *Make Your Own Indoor Garden*	635
Hay Hinsdale, Emily L. *What Is My Plant Telling Me?*	635.9
Isabel, Agatha. *Houseplant Hookups*	635.9
Martin, Tovah. ★*The Indestructible Houseplant*	635.9
Martin, Tovah. *The Unexpected Houseplant*	635.9
Offolter, Enid. *Welcome to the Jungle*	635.9
Pleasant, Barbara. *The Complete Houseplant Survival Manual*	635.9
Stearns, Jen. *The Inspired Houseplant*	635.9

HOUSE SELLING
Elias, Stephen. *The Foreclosure Survival Guide, 9th Ed.*	346.7304
The House Tells the Story. Van Doren, Adam	728
The House That Trane Built. Kahn, Ashley	781.6509

HOUSE, CALLIE, 1861-1928
Berry, Mary Frances. *My Face Is Black Is True*	B

HOUSE, EDWARD MANDELL, 1858-1938
Neu, Charles E. *Colonel House*	B

HOUSEHOLD ACTIVITIES
Bryson, Bill. ★*At Home*	643
Gurdon, Meghan Cox. *The Enchanted Hour*	372.4
Smith, Zadie. *Intimations*	824

HOUSEHOLD EMPLOYEES
Brower, Kate Andersen. *The Residence*	975.3
Katin, Miriam. *We Are on Our Own*	741.5
Land, Stephanie. *Maid*	B
Stiles, T. J. *Custer's Trials*	B

HOUSEHOLD FINANCES
Ariely, Dan. *Dollars and Sense*	332.024
Morduch, Jonathan. *The Financial Diaries*	332.024
Quart, Alissa. *Squeezed*	305.5

HOUSEHOLDS
Bryson, Bill. ★*At Home*	643

HOUSEHUSBANDS
Mangino, Kate. ★*Equal Partners*	305.3

HOUSEKEEPERS
Katin, Miriam. *We Are on Our Own*	741.5

HOUSEKEEPING
Cilley, Marla. *The Chaos* Cure*	648
Davis, KC. ★*How to Keep House While Drowning*	648
Howard, Jennifer. *Clutter*	306.3
Kondo, Marie. ★*The Life-Changing Magic of Tidying Up*	648
Kondo, Marie. ★*Spark Joy*	648
Loh, Sandra Tsing. *The Madwoman and the Roomba*	B
Moran, Caitlin. *More Than a Woman*	B
Stewart, Alison. *Junk*	616.85
White, Dana. *How to Manage Your Home Without Losing Your Mind*	648
Houseplant Hookups. Isabel, Agatha	635.9

HOUSES
Bauermeister, Erica. *House Lessons*	B
Bowers, Sharon. *Home Ec for Everyone*	640
Branson, Gary D. *Home, Water & Moisture Problems*	643
Broom, Sarah M. *The Yellow House*	B
Bryson, Bill. ★*At Home*	643
Burroughs, Augusten. ★*Toil & Trouble*	B
Byers, Charles T. *Ultimate Guide Home Repair and Improvement*	643
Edwards, Adrienne L. *Firescaping Your Home*	635.9
Feldmann, Erica. *Hausmagick*	133.4
Finkelstein, Elizabeth. *Cheap Old Houses*	643
Harding, Thomas. *The House by the Lake*	943
Hirsch, William J. *Designing Your Perfect House*	728
Howard, Hugh. *Architects of an American Landscape*	712.092
Jordan, Wendy Adler. *Universal Design for the Home*	728
Koones, Sheri. *Prefabulous Small Houses*	728
Levy, Deborah. ★*Real Estate*	B
Mayes, Frances. *Bella Tuscany*	945
Mayes, Frances. *Under the Tuscan Sun*	945
McAlister, Michael. *Taunton's Wiring Complete*	621.3
McGill, Joseph. *Sleeping with the Ancestors*	306.362
Napier, Erin. *Heirloom Rooms*	747
Petersik, Sherry. *Lovable Livable Home*	645
Pierce, D. *The Accessible Home*	728
Podemski, Max. *A Paradise of Small Houses*	363.5

AUTHOR, TITLE, SERIES AND SUBJECT INDEX

Scott, Jonathan. ★*Dream Home*	643
Shadid, Anthony. *House of Stone*	306.0956
Stewart, Martha. *The Martha Manual*	640
Thorstensen, Ole. *Making Things Right*	690
Wing, Charles. *How Your House Works*	643
★*Housewife*. Davis, Lisa	331.4
HOUSING	
Bruder, Jessica. ★*Nomadland*	331.3
Dougherty, Conor. *Golden Gates*	363.509794
Howard, Timothy. *The Mortgage Wars*	332.7
Ross, Andrew. *Sunbelt Blues*	363.5
HOUSING POLICY	
Adler, Kevin F. *When We Walk By*	362.5
Podemski, Max. *A Paradise of Small Houses*	363.5
Ross, Andrew. *Sunbelt Blues*	363.5
HOUSMAN, A. E. (ALFRED EDWARD), 1859-1936	
Stoppard, Tom. *The Invention of Love*	822
Houston, Keith	
The Book	002.09
Shady Characters	411
Houston, Pam	
Deep Creek	814
HOUSTON, TEXAS	
Crowell, Rodney. *Chinaberry Sidewalks*	B
Fields, Micah. ★*We Hold Our Breath*	976.4
Koppel, Lily. *The Astronaut Wives Club*	920
Swartz, Mimi. *Ticker*	617.4
Hoving, Thomas	
Art for Dummies	709
The How. Daley-Ward, Yrsa	158.1
How A Poem Moves. Sol, Adam	808.1
How Ableism Fuels Racism. Hardwick, Lamar	261.8
How About Never—Is Never Good for You?. Mankoff, Robert	741.5
★*How Can I Keep from Singing?*. Dunaway, David King	B
How Champions Think. Rotella, Robert J.	796.01
How Charts Lie. Cairo, Alberto	302.2
★*How Children Succeed*. Tough, Paul	372.210973
How Data Happened. Wiggins, Christopher L.	310
★*How Deaf Children Learn*. Marschark, Marc	371.91
How Do I Un-Remember This?. Pellegrino, Danny	B
How Do We Know Ourselves?. Myers, David G.	155.2
★*How Do We Look*. Beard, Mary	704.9
How Does It Feel to Be a Problem?. Bayoumi, Moustafa	305.892
★*How Emotions Are Made*. Barrett, Lisa Feldman	152.4
How Everything Became War and the Military Became Everything. Brooks, Rosa	355
How Far the Light Reaches. Imbler, Sabrina	591.77
How Far to the Promised Land. McCaulley, Esau	B
How Fascism Works. Stanley, Jason	321.9
How Fiction Works. Wood, James	808.3
How Free Speech Saved Democracy. Finan, Christopher M.	342.73
How God Works. DeSteno, David	200.1
How Good Do We Have to Be?. Kushner, Harold S.	296.7
How I Survived a Chinese "Reeducation" Camp. Haitiwaji, Gulbahar	305.8
How Iceland Changed the World. Bjarnason, Egill	949.12
How Infrastructure Works. Chachra, Deb	363
How Language Began. Everett, Daniel Leonard	401
★*How Language Works*. Crystal, David	410
How Life Imitates Sports. Berkow, Ira	070.4
How Medicine Works and When It Doesn't. Wilson, F. Perry	610.69
How Not to Be a Hot Mess. Hase, Craig	158.1
★*How Not to Be Wrong*. Ellenberg, Jordan	510
★*The How Not to Diet Cookbook*. Greger, Michael	641.5
★*How Not to Hate Your Husband After Kids*. Dunn, Jancee	646.7
How Not to Kill Yourself. Martin, Clancy W.	362.28
How Not to Say What You Mean. Holder, R. W.	427
The How of Happiness. Lyubomirsky, Sonja	158
How Paris Became Paris. DeJean, Joan E.	944
How Rights Went Wrong. Greene, Jamal	342.7308
How Schools Work. Duncan, Arne	379
How Stella Learned to Talk. Hunger, Christina	636.7
How The Beatles Destroyed Rock 'N' Roll. Wald, Elijah	781.64
How The Internet Changed Sex and Sex Changed the Internet. Cole, Samantha	306.7
How The Irish Saved Civilization. Cahill, Thomas	941.501
How The Mind Works. Pinker, Steven	153
How The Police Generate False Confessions. Trainum, James L.	345.73
How The Scots Invented the Modern World. Herman, Arthur	941.1
★*How The South Won the Civil War*. Richardson, Heather Cox	306.20973
★*How The Talmud Can Change Your Life*. Leibovitz, Liel	296.1
★*How The Word Is Passed*. Smith, Clint	973
★*How The World Ran Out of Everything*. Goodman, Peter S.	658.7
How The World Really Works. Smil, Vaclav	500
How To. Munroe, Randall	500
How to Astronaut. Virts, Terry	629.45
★*How to Bake Everything*. Bittman, Mark	641.81
How to Bake Pi. Cheng, Eugenia	510
How to Be. Nicolson, Adam	180
How to Be a Citizen. Skach, C. L.	323.6
How to Be a Family. Kois, Dan	910.4
How to Be a Good Creature. Montgomery, Sy	590
How to Be a Muslim. Moghul, Haroon	B
How to Be a Patient. Goldberg, Sana	610.69
How to Be a Tudor. Goodman, Ruth	942.05
How to Be a Victorian. Goodman, Ruth	941.08
How to Be a Woman. Moran, Caitlin	B
★*How to Be an Antiracist*. Kendi, Ibram X.	305.8
How to Be an Illustrator. Rees, Darrel	741.6
How to Be Compassionate. Dalai Lama	294.3
How to Be Drawn. Hayes, Terrance	811
How to Be Human. Fleming, Jory	616.85
How to Be Less Stupid About Race. Fleming, Crystal Marie	305.800973
How to Be Loved. Hagberg, Eva	616.7
How to Be Multiple. De Bres, Helena	155.44
How to Begin When Your World Is Ending. Baskette, Molly Phinney	248.8
How to Behave Badly in Elizabethan England. Goodman, Ruth	942.05
How to Break up with Anyone. Waxman, Jamye	158.2
How to Carry Water. Clifton, Lucille	811
How to Celebrate Everything. Rosenstrach, Jenny	641.5
How to Change Your Mind. Pollan, Michael	615.7
How to College. Brenner, Andrea	378.1
★*How to Cook Everything*. Bittman, Mark	641.5
How to Cook Everything. Bittman, Mark	641.5
How to Cook Everything Fast. Bittman, Mark	641.5
★*How to Cook Everything Vegetarian*. Bittman, Mark	641.5
How to Cook Without a Book. Anderson, Pam	641.5
How to Create a Wildlife Garden. Lavelle, Christine	635
How to Draw What You See. De Reyna, Rudy	741.2
How to Eataly. Danford, Natalie	641.594
How to Embroider Texture and Pattern. Galbraith, Melissa	746.44
★*How to Find a Four-Leaf Clover*. Rodgers, Jodi	616.85
How to Fix a Broken Heart. Winch, Guy	155.9
How to Get Rich. Dennis, Felix	B
★*How to Grill Everything*. Bittman, Mark	641.7
How to Grill Vegetables. Raichlen, Steven	641.6
How to Have a Good Day. Webb, Caroline	650.1
How to Hide an Empire. Immerwahr, Daniel	973
How to Hire. Smith, Clint	658.3
★*How to Hygge*. Johansen, Signe	646.7
How to Inhabit Time. Smith, James K. A.	223
How to Instant Pot. Shumski, Daniel	641.5
★*How to Keep House While Drowning*. Davis, KC	648
★*How to Know a Person*. Brooks, David	158.2
How to Know the Birds. Floyd, Ted	598.072
How to Live in Space. Stuart, Colin	629.45
How to Live with Objects. Khemsurov, Monica	747
How to Live—Or—A Life of Montaigne. Bakewell, Sarah	B
How to Love a Country. Blanco, Richard	811
How to Make a Spaceship. Guthrie, Julian	629.47
How to Make an Apple Pie from Scratch. Cliff, Harry	523.01
★*How to Make Your Money Last*. Quinn, Jane Bryant	332.024
How to Manage Your Home Without Losing Your Mind. White, Dana	648
How to Play the 5-String Banjo. Seeger, Pete	787
★*How to Prevent the Next Pandemic*. Gates, Bill	614.5
★*How to Raise a Reader*. Paul, Pamela	649
How to Raise an Amazing Child the Montessori Way. Seldin, Tim	649
★*How to Raise an Antiracist*. Kendi, Ibram X.	649
How to Raise Kind Kids. Lickona, Thomas	649
How to Raise Successful People. Wojcicki, Esther	649
How to Read a Dress. Edwards, Lydia	391
How to Read a Poem. Hirsch, Edward	808.1
★*How to Read Now*. Castillo, Elaine	418
How to Read Poetry Like a Professor. Foster, Thomas C	808.1
★*How to Say Babylon*. Sinclair, Safiya	B
How to See. Salle, David	709.04
How to Self Publish Your Book. Yager, Jan	070.5

PUBLIC LIBRARY CORE COLLECTION: NONFICTION
Twentieth Edition

How to Sew a Button. Bried, Erin	640
★*How to Sleep*. Pelayo, Rafael	616.8
How to Slowly Kill Yourself and Others in America. Laymon, Kiese	814.6
How to Speak Money. Lanchester, John	330.1
How to Speak Whale. Mustill, Tom	591.59
★*How to Stand up to a Dictator*. Ressa, Maria	070.92
How to Survive a Plague. France, David	362.196
How to Survive History. Cassidy, Cody	904
★*How to Talk so Kids Will Listen & Listen so Kids Will Talk*. Faber, Adele	649
How to Taste Coffee. Easto, Jessica	663
How to Tell Fate from Destiny. Elster, Charles Harrington	428.1
How to Think. Jacobs, Alan	153.4
★*How to Think Like a Woman*. Penaluna, Regan	190.82
How to Treat People. Case, Molly	616.1
★*How to Watch a Movie*. Thomson, David	791.43
★*How to Win an Information War*. Pomerantsev, Peter	940.53
How to Win Friends and Influence Fungi. Balakrishnan, Chris	502
★*How to Win Friends and Influence People*. Carnegie, Dale	158
How to Write a Business Plan. McKeever, Mike P	658.15
★*How to Write About Africa*. Wainaina, Binyavanga	814
★*How to Write an Autobiographical Novel*. Chee, Alexander	B
How to Write One Song. Tweedy, Jeff	782.42
How to Zoom Your Room. Taylor, Claude	747
How Toddlers Thrive. Klein, Tovah P.	305.232
How We Fight for Our Lives. Jones, Saeed	B
How We Learn. Carey, Benedict	153.1
How We Live Is How We Die. Chodron, Pema	294.3
How You Say It. Kinzler, Katherine D.	302.2
How Your House Works. Wing, Charles	643
HOW-TO BOOKS	
Abel, Jessica. *Drawing Words, Writing Pictures*	741.5
Abel, Jessica. *Mastering Comics*	741.5
Lee, Stan. *Stan Lee's How to Draw Comics*	741.5
Leong, Sonia. *101 Top Tips from Professional Manga Artists*	741.5
O'Neil, Dennis. *The DC Comics Guide to Writing Comics*	808
Self, Caroline. *Chinese Brush Painting*	751.4
Witte, Christina De. ★*Noodles, Rice, and Everything Spice*	641.595
Howard Cosell. Ribowsky, Mark	070.449796
Howard Zinn. Duberman, Martin B.	B
HOWARD, CLINT, 1959-	
Howard, Ron. ★*The Boys*	B
Howard, Hugh	
Architects of an American Landscape	712.092
Howard, Jennifer	
Clutter	306.3
HOWARD, JENNIFER (JOURNALIST)	
Howard, Jennifer. *Clutter*	306.3
Howard, Johnette	
The Rivals	B
HOWARD, O. O. (OLIVER OTIS), 1830-1909	
Sharfstein, Daniel J. ★*Thunder in the Mountains*	979.5
Howard, Ron	
★*The Boys*	B
HOWARD, RON, 1954-	
Howard, Ron. ★*The Boys*	B
Howard, Timothy	
The Mortgage Wars	332.7
Howard, Vivian	
Deep Run Roots	641.5975
This Will Make It Taste Good	641.5
HOWARD, VIVIAN (VIVIAN S.), 1978-	
Howard, Vivian. *Deep Run Roots*	641.5975
Howcroft, Heidi	
Garden Design	712
Howe, Ben Ryder	
My Korean Deli	B
HOWE, BEN RYDER	
Howe, Ben Ryder. *My Korean Deli*	B
Howe, Daniel Walker	
What Hath God Wrought	973.5
Howe, Fanny	
Second Childhood	811
Howe, Sean	
Marvel Comics	741.5
Howell, Georgina	
Gertrude Bell	B
Howes, Molly	
A Good Apology	158.2

★*Howl*. Ginsberg, Allen	811.54
HOWLAND, JOHN, 1592?-1672	
Whittock, Martyn. *Mayflower Lives*	974.4
Howley, Kerry	
Bottoms Up and the Devil Laughs	352.37
Howsare, Erika	
The Age of Deer	599.65
Hoyer, Katja	
★*Beyond the Wall*	943.087
Blood and Iron	943.08
Hoyt, Erich	
Encyclopedia of Whales, Dolphins and Porpoises	599.5
HRH. Holmes, Elizabeth	941.085
HSIEH, TONY	
Au-Yeung, Angel. *Wonder Boy*	B
Hsu, Hua	
★*Stay True*	B
HSU, HUA, 1977-	
Hsu, Hua. ★*Stay True*	B
Hu, Elise	
Flawless	646.7
HU, ELISE	
Hu, Elise. *Flawless*	646.7
Huang, Eddie	
Fresh off the Boat	B
HUANG, EDDIE, 1982-	
Huang, Eddie. *Fresh off the Boat*	B
Huang, Yunte	
Daughter of the Dragon	B
Hubbard, Ben (Journalist)	
Mbs	B
HUBBARD, L. RON (LA FAYETTE RON), 1911-1986	
Nevala-Lee, Alec. *Astounding*	809.3
Wright, Lawrence. *Going Clear*	299
Hubbard, Shanita	
★*Ride-Or-Die*	305.48
Hubert, Margaret	
10 Granny Squares, 30 Blankets	746.43
The Complete Photo Guide to Crochet	746.43
The Granny Square Book	746.43
Hudes, Quiara Alegria	
★*My Broken Language*	B
HUDES, QUIARA ALEGRIA	
Hudes, Quiara Alegria. ★*My Broken Language*	B
HUDNER, TOM	
Makos, Adam. *Devotion*	920
HUDSON VALLEY	
Daughan, George C. *Revolution on the Hudson*	974.7
Hudson, Kate	
Pretty Fun	642
Hudson, Michael W.	
The Monster	332.63
★*Hue 1968*. Bowden, Mark	959.704
Huff, Mary Scott	
The Mitten Handbook	746.43
Huffman, Alan	
Here I Am	B
Huggins, Kathleen	
★*The Nursing Mother's Companion*	649
Hughes, Bettany	
★*The Hemlock Cup*	B
Istanbul	949.61
Venus and Aphrodite	292
HUGHES, CHARLES EVANS, 1862-1948	
Simon, James F. *FDR and Chief Justice Hughes*	973.917092
Hughes, Evan	
The Hard Sell	338.4
HUGHES, HOWARD, 1905-1976	
Dean, Josh. *The Taking of K-129*	910.91
Longworth, Karina. *Seduction*	B
Hughes, Langston	
★*I Wonder as I Wander*	B
★*Selected Poems of Langston Hughes*	811
HUGHES, LANGSTON, 1902-1967	
Hughes, Langston. ★*I Wonder as I Wander*	B
Rampersad, Arnold. *The Life of Langston Hughes*	B
Rampersad, Arnold. ★*The Life of Langston Hughes*	B

AUTHOR, TITLE, SERIES AND SUBJECT INDEX

Hughes, Robert
  American Visions — 709
  Barcelona — 946
  The Fatal Shore — 994
  Goya — B
  Rome — 945.6
Hughes-Hassell, Sandra
  ★*Collection Management for Youth* — 025.2
Hugo, Nancy R.
  Seeing Trees — 582.16
HUGO, VICTOR, 1802-1885
  Bellos, David. *The Novel of the Century* — 843
Hulls, Tessa
  ★*Feeding Ghosts* — 741.5
HULLS, TESSA, 1984-
  Hulls, Tessa. ★*Feeding Ghosts* — 741.5
Hult, Christine A
  The Handy English Grammar Answer Book — 428.2
The **Human** *Age*. Ackerman, Diane — 304.2
HUMAN ANATOMY
  Bryson, Bill. *The Body* — 612
  Cassidy, Cody. *And Then You're Dead* — 612
  Dolnick, Edward. *Seeds of Life* — 612.6
  Drew, Liam. *I, Mammal* — 599
  Enright, Lynn. *Vagina* — 612.6
  Kandel, Eric R. ★*The Disordered Mind* — 616.89
  Meals, Roy A. *Bones* — 599.9
  Meals, Roy A. *Muscle* — 612.7
  Switek, Brian. *Skeleton Keys* — 611
Human *Anatomy Made Amazingly Easy*. Hart, Christopher — 743.4
HUMAN BEHAVIOR
  Ackerman, Diane. *A Natural History of the Senses* — 152.1
  Ariely, Dan. *The Honest Truth About Dishonesty* — 177
  Ariely, Dan. *Predictably Irrational* — 153.8
  Bargh, John A. *Before You Know It* — 154.2
  Bishop, Elizabeth. ★*Poems* — 811
  Bohannon, Cat. ★*Eve* — 613
  Brotherton, Rob. *Suspicious Minds* — 153.4
  Campbell, Joseph. *The Masks of God* — 201.3
  Campbell, Joseph. *The Power of Myth* — 201.3
  Christian, Brian. *Algorithms to Live By* — 153.4
  Clear, James. ★*Atomic Habits* — 155.24
  Cuddy, Amy. *Presence* — 158.1
  Dahl, Melissa. *Cringeworthy* — 158.2
  De Botton, Alain. *The Pleasures and Sorrows of Work* — 306.3
  Denworth, Lydia. *Friendship* — 158.2
  Epstein, David J. ★*Range* — 153.9
  Foster, Charles. *Being a Human* — 155.7
  Franco, Marisa G. *Platonic* — 302.34
  Freud, Sigmund. *Civilization and Its Discontents* — 150.19
  Gardner, Dan. *The Science of Fear* — 152.4
  Gladwell, Malcolm. *Outliers* — 302
  Gladwell, Malcolm. ★*Talking to Strangers* — 302
  Gladwell, Malcolm. *The Tipping Point* — 302
  Grant, Adam M. *Give and Take* — 158.2
  Grant, Adam M. *Hidden Potential* — 153.8
  Grant, Adam M. ★*Think Again* — 153.4
  Hagglund, Martin. *This Life* — 110
  Hallinan, Joseph T. *Why We Make Mistakes* — 153
  Iyengar, Sheena. *The Art of Choosing* — 153.8
  Jacobs, Alan. *How to Think* — 153.4
  Jennings, Ken. *Planet Funny* — 809.7
  Jordan, June. ★*The Essential June Jordan* — 811
  Konnikova, Maria. *The Biggest Bluff* — 795.412
  Lembke, Anna. *Dopamine Nation* — 152.4
  Miller, Kenneth R. *The Human Instinct* — 155.7
  Mlodinow, Leonard. *Emotional* — 152.4
  Myers, David G. *How Do We Know Ourselves?* — 155.2
  Norton, Michael. ★*The Ritual Effect* — 650.1
  Pinker, Steven. *The Stuff of Thought* — 401
  Provine, Robert R. *Curious Behavior* — 152.3
  Pryor, Karen. ★*Don't Shoot the Dog* — 153.8
  Radtke, Kristen. *Seek You* — 741.5
  Ronson, Jon. *So You've Been Publicly Shamed* — 152.4
  Rosling, Hans. *Factfulness* — 155.9
  Ryan, Alan. *On Politics* — 320.01
  Sacks, Oliver. ★*Everything in Its Place* — B
  Sapolsky, Robert M. *Behave* — 612.8

  Sapolsky, Robert M. *Determined* — 123
  Schulz, Kathryn. *Being Wrong* — 121
  Schutt, Bill. *Cannibalism* — 394
  Scott, Andy. *One Kiss or Two?* — 395.4
  Skach, C. L. *How to Be a Citizen* — 323.6
  Stanton, Brandon. *Humans* — 779
  Suddendorf, Thomas. *The Gap* — 156
  Sullivan, Randall. *The Devil's Best Trick* — 235
  Thaler, Richard H. *Misbehaving* — 330.01
  Van Bavel, Jay J. *The Power of Us* — 155.2
  Vedantam, Shankar. *Useful Delusions* — 153.4
  Waal, F. B. M. de. ★*Mama's Last Hug* — 599.885
  Waal, F. B. M. de. *Our Inner Ape* — 156
  Wertheim, L. Jon. *This Is Your Brain on Sports* — 796.01
  Wiking, Meik. *The Art of Making Memories* — 153.1
  Williams, Joan. *What Works for Women at Work* — 650.1
  Wragg Sykes, Rebecca. *Kindred* — 569.9
HUMAN BIOLOGY
  Doughty, Caitlin. *Will My Cat Eat My Eyeballs?* — 306.9
  Provine, Robert R. *Curious Behavior* — 152.3
HUMAN BODY
  Bass, William M. *Death's Acre* — 614
  Beck, Amanda Martinez. *More of You* — 613
  Brown, Molly McCully. *Places I've Taken My Body* — B
  Bryson, Bill. *The Body* — 612
  Collen, Alanna. *10% Human* — 612.3
  Everts, Sarah. *The Joy of Sweat* — 612.7
  Grue, Jan. *I Live a Life Like Yours* — B
  Hamblin, James. *If Our Bodies Could Talk* — 613
  Hazard, Leah. *Womb* — 612.6
  Laing, Olivia. *Everybody* — 323
  Levitt, Dan. *What's Gotten into You* — 539.7
  Lyman, Monty. *The Remarkable Life of the Skin* — 612.7
  Norman, Abby. *Ask Me About My Uterus* — 618.1
  Pringle, Heather Anne. *The Mummy Congress* — 393
  Radke, Heather. *Butts* — 611
  Shapland, Jenn. ★*Thin Skin* — 814
  Sinclair, Safiya. *Cannibal* — 811
  Stanger, Ben. *From One Cell* — 571.6
  Thomas, Mathilde. *The French Beauty Solution* — 646.7
  Walters, Jacqueline. *The Queen V* — 612.6
Human *Chain*. Heaney, Seamus — 821
HUMAN COMFORT
  Brits, Louisa Thomsen. *The Book of Hygge* — 747
  Butler, Katy. *The Art of Dying Well* — 616.02
  Weir, Laura. *Cosy* — 646.7009
Human *Compatible*. Russell, Stuart J. — 006.301
The **Human** *Cosmos*. Marchant, Jo — 523.1
HUMAN DISSECTION
  Roach, Mary. ★*Stiff* — 611
HUMAN ECOLOGY
  Bernstein, Ellen. *Toward a Holy Ecology* — 223
  Farmer, Jared. *Elderflora* — 582.16
  Flores, Dan L. *Wild New World* — 591.9709
  Frank, Adam. *Light of the Stars* — 523.1
  Hohn, Donovan. *The Inner Coast* — 304.20973
  Houston, Pam. *Deep Creek* — 814
  Kelley, Margot Anne. *A Gardener at the End of the World* — 615.8
  Kimmerer, Robin Wall. ★*Braiding Sweetgrass* — 304.2
  Kolbert, Elizabeth. ★*Under a White Sky* — 304.2
  McKibben, Bill. *Falter* — 909.83
  Tallamy, Douglas W. ★*Nature's Best Hope* — 635.9
  Webb, Kinari. *Guardians of the Trees* — B
  Wilson, Edward O. *Half-Earth* — 333.95
  Wilson, Edward O. *In Search of Nature* — 113
  Wilson, Edward O. *The Meaning of Human Existence* — 128
  Wohlforth, Charles P. *The Fate of Nature* — 304.209798
HUMAN ENGINEERING
  Piore, Adam. *The Body Builders* — 660.6
Human *Evolution*. Dunbar, R. I. M. — 155.7
HUMAN EVOLUTION
  Alvarez, Walter. *A Most Improbable Journey* — 550
  Bohannon, Cat. ★*Eve* — 613
  Bohme, Madelaine. *Ancient Bones* — 599.93
  Deisseroth, Karl. *Projections* — 616.89
  Dennett, D. C. *Darwin's Dangerous Idea* — 146
  Desilva, Jeremy. *First Steps* — 599.93
  Drew, Liam. *I, Mammal* — 599

PUBLIC LIBRARY CORE COLLECTION: NONFICTION
Twentieth Edition

Eldredge, Niles. *Why We Do It*	155.3
Emera, Deena. *A Brief History of the Female Body*	612.6
Fleming, Renee. ★*Music and Mind*	615.8
Foster, Charles. *Being a Human*	155.7
Gee, Henry. *A (Very) Short History of Life on Earth*	576.8
Gould, Stephen Jay. *The Structure of Evolutionary Theory*	576.8
Kurzweil, Ray. ★*The Singularity Is Near*	153.9
Leakey, Richard E. *The Origin of Humankind*	599.93
Lieberman, Daniel. *Exercised*	612.044
Miller, Kenneth R. *The Human Instinct*	155.7
Nesse, Randolph M. *Good Reasons for Bad Feelings*	616.89
Pattison, Kermit. *Fossil Men*	569.9
Pinker, Steven. *How the Mind Works*	153
Rutherford, Adam. *Humanimal*	599.93
Spitzer, Michael. *The Musical Human*	780.9
Tattersall, Ian. *Masters of the Planet*	599.93
Vince, Gaia. *Transcendence*	599.93
Whitehouse, David. *The Alien Perspective*	523.1
Wilson, Edward O. *Half-Earth*	333.95
Wilson, Edward O. *The Meaning of Human Existence*	128
Wilson, Edward O. ★*The Social Conquest of Earth*	599.93
Wolfe, Tom. *The Kingdom of Speech*	401
Wrangham, Richard W. *Catching Fire*	394.1
Yi, Sang-Hui. *Close Encounters with Humankind*	599.93
Zimmer, Carl. *She Has Her Mother's Laugh*	576.5
HUMAN EXPERIMENTATION IN MEDICINE	
Elliott, Carl. ★*The Occasional Human Sacrifice*	174.2
Hallman, J. C. *Say Anarcha*	618.1
Jones, Chip. *The Organ Thieves*	617.4
Kinzer, Stephen. *Poisoner in Chief*	B
Lisle, John. *The Dirty Tricks Department*	940.54
Offit, Paul A. *You Bet Your Life*	615.5
Reverby, Susan M. *Examining Tuskegee*	174.2
Roach, Mary. ★*Stiff*	611
Skloot, Rebecca. ★*The Immortal Life of Henrietta Lacks*	B
Swartz, Mimi. *Ticker*	617.4
Tucker, Todd. *The Great Starvation Experiment*	174.2
Wadman, Meredith. *The Vaccine Race*	614.5
HUMAN EXPERIMENTATION IN PSYCHOLOGY	
Cahalan, Susannah. ★*The Great Pretender*	616.89
Farley, Audrey Clare. ★*Girls and Their Monsters*	306.875
Zimbardo, Philip G. *The Lucifer Effect*	155.9
HUMAN FERTILITY	
Schrock, Leslie. *Fertility Rules*	613.9
Zernicka-Goetz, Magdalena. *The Dance of Life*	591.56
*The **Human** Figure.* Vanderpoel, John Henry	743
HUMAN FIGURE IN ART	
Bradley, Barbara. *Drawing People*	743.4
Hart, Christopher. *Human Anatomy Made Amazingly Easy*	743.4
Huston, Steve. *Figure Drawing for Artists*	743.4
HUMAN GENETICS	
Finkel, Elizabeth. *The Genome Generation*	599.93
Isaacson, Walter. ★*The Code Breaker*	576.5
Krause, Johannes. *A Short History of Humanity*	599.9
HUMAN GENOME	
Isaacson, Walter. ★*The Code Breaker*	576.5
Tabery, James. ★*Tyranny of the Gene*	572.8
HUMAN GEOGRAPHY	
Anderson, Sam. *Boom Town*	976.6
Khilnani, Sunil. *Incarnations*	920
Vince, Gaia. *Nomad Century*	362.87
HUMAN INFORMATION PROCESSING	
Gupta, Sanjay. ★*Keep Sharp*	153.4
Hoffman, Donald D. *Visual Intelligence*	152.14
Medina, John. *Brain Rules*	153
*The **Human** Instinct.* Miller, Kenneth R.	155.7
HUMAN LIFE CYCLE	
Feiler, Bruce. *Life Is in the Transitions*	392
HUMAN NATURE	
Bloom, Harold. *Shakespeare*	822.33
Dunbar, R. I. M. *Human Evolution*	155.7
Goodall, Jane. ★*The Book of Hope*	128
Mao, Sally Wen. *Oculus*	811
Pinker, Steven. *The Blank Slate*	155.2
Pinker, Steven. *The Stuff of Thought*	401
Sapolsky, Robert M. *Behave*	612.8
Suddendorf, Thomas. *The Gap*	156
Waal, F. B. M. de. ★*Mama's Last Hug*	599.885
Wilson, Edward O. *The Meaning of Human Existence*	128
HUMAN PHYSIOLOGY	
Bryson, Bill. *The Body*	612
Cassidy, Cody. *And Then You're Dead*	612
Desilva, Jeremy. *First Steps*	599.93
Dettmer, Philipp. *Immune*	616.07
Drew, Liam. *I, Mammal*	599
Emera, Deena. *A Brief History of the Female Body*	612.6
Enright, Lynn. *Vagina*	612.6
Everts, Sarah. *The Joy of Sweat*	612.7
Gunter, Jen. ★*Blood*	612.6
Meals, Roy A. *Muscle*	612.7
Mukherjee, Siddhartha. ★*The Song of the Cell*	571.6
HUMAN POPULATION GENETICS	
Krause, Johannes. *A Short History of Humanity*	599.9
HUMAN REMAINS (ARCHAEOLOGY)	
Krause, Johannes. *A Short History of Humanity*	599.9
Meals, Roy A. *Bones*	599.9
Pitts, Mike. *Digging for Richard III*	942.046
Pringle, Heather Anne. *The Mummy Congress*	393
Switek, Brian. *Skeleton Keys*	611
HUMAN REPRODUCTION	
Blair, Gabrielle Stanley. ★*Ejaculate Responsibly*	362.1988
Dolnick, Edward. *Seeds of Life*	612.6
Gunter, Jen. ★*Blood*	612.6
HUMAN RIGHTS	
Adayfi, Mansoor. *Don't Forget Us Here*	B
Addario, Lynsey. *Of Love & War*	779
Andrews, Becca. ★*No Choice*	362.1988
Avlon, John P. *Lincoln and the Fight for Peace*	973.7
Balakian, Peter. *The Burning Tigris*	956.6
Becker, Jo. ★*Forcing the Spring*	346.79401
Blight, David W. ★*Frederick Douglass*	B
Bowdler, Michelle. ★*Is Rape a Crime?*	B
Brazile, Donna. *For Colored Girls Who Have Considered Politics*	328.73
Brodsky, Alexandra. *Sexual Justice*	364.15
Carpenter, Dale. *Flagrant Conduct*	342.7308
Cenziper, Debbie. ★*Love Wins*	346.7301
Engelhart, Katie. *The Inevitable*	179.7
Funk, Mason. *The Book of Pride*	920
Goldberg, Carrie. *Nobody's Victim*	345.73
Grayling, A. C. *The Age of Genius*	940.2
Grigoriadis, Vanessa. *Blurred Lines*	371.7
Hing, Bill Ong. ★*Humanizing Immigration*	342.7308
Hochschild, Adam. *Bury the Chains*	326
Hochschild, Adam. *King Leopold's Ghost*	967.51
Kaplan, Roberta A. *Then Comes Marriage*	346.7301
Kara, Siddharth. *Cobalt Red*	338.2
Kershner, Isabel. *The Land of Hope and Fear*	956.9405
Khan, Mahvish Rukhsana. *My Guantanamo Diary*	973.931
Krakauer, Jon. *Missoula*	362.883
Kristof, Nicholas D. *Half the Sky*	362.83
Laing, Olivia. *Everybody*	323
Lemay, Mimi. *What We Will Become*	306.874
Lithwick, Dahlia. *Lady Justice*	345.73
Mandela, Nelson. *The Prison Letters of Nelson Mandela*	968.06092
Morrison, Toni. ★*The Source of Self-Regard*	814
Ndopu, Eddie. *Sipping Dom Pérignon Through a Straw*	B
Nutt, Amy Ellis. *Becoming Nicole*	920
Pearlman, Wendy. *We Crossed a Bridge and It Trembled*	956.9104
Rapinoe, Megan. *One Life*	B
Rawlence, Ben. *City of Thorns*	967.7305
Sefarad, Mikhael. *The Wall and the Gate*	341.48
Semenya, Caster. *The Race to Be Myself*	B
Shatz, Adam. *The Rebel's Clinic*	965
Shehadeh, Raja. ★*We Could Have Been Friends, My Father and I*	B
Stanley, Brian. *Christianity in the Twentieth Century*	270.8
Thompson, Heather Ann. *Blood in the Water*	365
Watson, Bruce. *Freedom Summer*	323.1196
Wides-Munoz, Laura. *The Making of a Dream*	920
Worth, Robert Forsyth. ★*A Rage for Order*	909
Yoshino, Kenji. *Speak Now*	346.79401
Zimbardo, Philip G. *The Lucifer Effect*	155.9
HUMAN RIGHTS (INTERNATIONAL LAW)	
Sands, Philippe. *East West Street*	345
HUMAN RIGHTS ACTIVISTS	
Blake, Melissa. *Beautiful People*	362.4
Dogon, Mondiant. *Those We Throw Away Are Diamonds*	B

AUTHOR, TITLE, SERIES AND SUBJECT INDEX

Euchner, Charles C. *Nobody Turn Me Around*	975.3
Garza, Alicia. *The Purpose of Power*	303.48
Ghafari, Zarifa. *Zarifa*	B
Heumann, Judith E. *Being Heumann*	B
Igort. *The Ukrainian and Russian Notebooks*	741.5
Leng'ete, Nice. *The Girls in the Wild Fig Tree*	B
Okporo, Edafe. *Asylum*	B
Pawel, Miriam. *The Crusades of Cesar Chavez*	B
Vargas, Jose Antonio. *Dear America*	B

HUMAN RIGHTS ADVOCACY

Murad, Nadia. ★*The Last Girl*	B

HUMAN RIGHTS POLICY

Bass, Gary Jonathan. *Freedom's Battle*	341.5
Minian, Ana Raquel. ★*In the Shadow of Liberty*	365

HUMAN SKIN COLOR

Lyman, Monty. *The Remarkable Life of the Skin*	612.7
Morrison, Toni. *Playing in the Dark*	810.9

HUMAN SMUGGLING

De Leon, Jason. ★*Soldiers and Kings*	364.1
Umar, Ousman. *North to Paradise*	B
Urrea, Luis Alberto. *The Devil's Highway*	304.8

HUMAN TRAFFICKING

Ditmore, Melissa Hope. ★*Unbroken Chains*	306.74
Durkin, Hannah. ★*The Survivors of the Clotilda*	306.362
Jang, Lucia. *Stars Between the Sun and Moon*	365.45092
Mikhaiil, Dunya. *The Beekeeper*	956.7044
Murad, Nadia. ★*The Last Girl*	B
Siler, Julia Flynn. *The White Devil's Daughters*	306.3
Tjipombo, Tupa. *I Am Not Your Slave*	B

HUMAN TRAFFICKING VICTIMS

Ditmore, Melissa Hope. ★*Unbroken Chains*	306.74
Jang, Lucia. *Stars Between the Sun and Moon*	365.45092
Kruzan, Sara. *I Cried to Dream Again*	B
Siler, Julia Flynn. *The White Devil's Daughters*	306.3
Tjipombo, Tupa. *I Am Not Your Slave*	B
*The **Human**, The Orchid, and the Octopus.* Cousteau, Jacques Yves	B

HUMAN-ALIEN ENCOUNTERS

Loeb, Abraham. *Extraterrestrial*	576.8
Mezrich, Ben. *The 37th Parallel*	001.942
Prothero, Donald R. *UFOs, Chemtrails, and Aliens*	001.94
Scoles, Sarah. *They Are Already Here*	001.942

HUMAN-ANIMAL COMMUNICATION

Brown, Sarah L. *The Hidden Language of Cats*	636.8
Fouts, Roger. *Next of Kin*	156
Gaffney, Ginger. *Half Broke*	B
Golbeck, Jennifer. *The Purest Bond*	636.7
Hunger, Christina. *How Stella Learned to Talk*	636.7
Louv, Richard. *Our Wild Calling*	615.8
Mustill, Tom. *How to Speak Whale*	591.59
Schotz, Susanne. *The Secret Language of Cats*	636.8

HUMAN-ANIMAL RELATIONSHIPS

Achterberg, Cara Sue. *Another Good Dog*	636.7
Bailey, Elisabeth. *The Sound of a Wild Snail Eating*	594
Barnes, Simon. *The Meaning of Birds*	598
Berry, Erica. *Wolfish*	152.4
Birkhead, Tim. *Birds and Us*	598
Boylan, Jennifer Finney. *Good Boy*	B
Bradshaw, John. ★*Cat Sense*	636.8
Bradshaw, John. ★*Dog Sense*	636.7
Brand, Adele. *The Hidden World of the Fox*	599.775
Carr, Caleb. *My Beloved Monster*	B
Charleson, Susannah. *Where the Lost Dogs Go*	636.7
Chesney, Will. *No Ordinary Dog*	958.104
Conaboy, Kelly. *The Particulars of Peter*	636.7
Dinesen, Isak. *Out of Africa*	967.62
Duncan, Dayton. *Blood Memory*	599.64
Fincham-Gray, Suzanne. *My Patients and Other Animals*	B
Flores, Dan L. *Wild New World*	591.9709
Fouts, Roger. *Next of Kin*	156
Freeberg, Ernest. *A Traitor to His Species*	B
Gaffney, Ginger. *Half Broke*	B
Golbeck, Jennifer. *The Purest Bond*	636.7
Goodall, Jane. ★*The Ten Trusts*	333.95
Grandin, Temple. ★*Animals Make Us Human*	636.08
Grogan, John. ★*Marley & Me*	636.752
Grossi, Craig. *Craig & Fred*	B
Halpern, Sue. *A Dog Walks into a Nursing Home*	B
Herriot, James. ★*All Creatures Great and Small*	B

Herriot, James. *All Things Wise and Wonderful*	B
Herriot, James. *Every Living Thing*	B
Herriot, James. *James Herriot's Animal Stories*	B
Herriot, James. *James Herriot's Cat Stories*	636.8
Herriot, James. *James Herriot's Dog Stories*	636.7
Herriot, James. *James Herriot's Favorite Dog Stories*	636.7
Horowitz, Alexandra. ★*Being a Dog*	636.7
Horowitz, Alexandra. *Our Dogs, Ourselves*	636.7
Howsare, Erika. *The Age of Deer*	599.65
Hutton, Robin L. *Sgt. Reckless*	951.904
Jones, Darryl N. *The Birds at My Table*	598.072
Keim, Brandon. *Meet the Neighbors*	591.5
Kugler, Rob. *A Dog Named Beautiful*	577.69
Kumar, Priyanka. *Conversations with Birds*	598
Lewis, Damien. *The Dog Who Could Fly*	940.54
Louv, Richard. *Our Wild Calling*	615.8
McConnell, Patricia B. ★*The Other End of the Leash*	636.7
McDougall, Christopher. *Running with Sherman*	636.1
Melville, Wilma. ★*Hero Dogs*	636.7
Millet, Lydia. *We Loved It All*	813
Montgomery, Sy. *The Good Good Pig*	636.4
Montgomery, Sy. *How to Be a Good Creature*	590
Montgomery, Sy. ★*Of Time and Turtles*	597.92
Mooallem, Jon. *Wild Ones*	333.95
Mortimer, Frank. *Bee People and the Bugs They Love*	B
Mustill, Tom. *How to Speak Whale*	591.59
Myron, Vicki. ★*Dewey*	636.80092
Neiwert, David A. *Of Orcas and Men*	599.53
Nicolson, Adam. *Life Between the Tides*	577.69
Nir, Sarah Maslin. *Horse Crazy*	B
Novello, Carol. *Mutual Rescue*	636.088
Orlean, Susan. *On Animals*	590
Preston, Christopher J. *Tenacious Beasts*	591.68
Roach, Mary. ★*Fuzz*	591.5
Robbins, Jim. *The Wonder of Birds*	598
Safina, Carl. ★*Alfie and Me*	598.9
Schott, Philipp. *The Accidental Veterinarian*	B
Shapland, Jenn. ★*Thin Skin*	814
Skaife, Christopher. *The Ravenmaster*	B
Stewart, Tracey. *Do Unto Animals*	590
Strycker, Noah K. *The Thing with Feathers*	598.072
Suddendorf, Thomas. *The Gap*	156
Tomlinson, Tommy. *Dogland*	636.7
Tucker, Abigail. *The Lion in the Living Room*	636.8
Waal, F. B. M. de. ★*Mama's Last Hug*	599.885
Weintraub, Robert. *No Better Friend*	940.54
Williams, Kale. *The Loneliest Polar Bear*	599.786
Woolfson, Esther. *Between Light and Storm*	599.93
Wynn-Grant, Rae. *Wild Life*	B
Wynne, Clive D. L. ★*Dog Is Love*	636.7

HUMAN-COMPUTER INTERACTION

Citron, Danielle Keats. *The Fight for Privacy*	342.7308
Friedman, Thomas L. ★*Thank You for Being Late*	303.48
Kasparov, G K. *Deep Thinking*	006.3
Malone, Thomas W. *Superminds*	005.7
Murgia, Madhumita. *Code Dependent*	303.48
O'Gieblyn, Meghan. *God, Human, Animal, Machine*	814
Russell, Stuart J. *Human Compatible*	006.301
*The **Humane** Gardener.* Lawson, Nancy	577.5
***Humanimal**.* Rutherford, Adam	599.93

HUMANISM

Burger, Ariel. *Witness*	848
Kundera, Milan. *Encounter*	809
Massing, Michael. *Fatal Discord*	920
Pinn, Anthony B. *The Black Practice of Disbelief*	211
Robertson, Ritchie. *The Enlightenment*	190
Soyinka, Wole. *Of Africa*	960
Zuckerman, Phil. *Living the Secular Life*	211

HUMANISM (14TH-16TH CENTURIES)

Greenblatt, Stephen. ★*The Swerve*	940.2

HUMANISTS

Aptowicz, Cristin O'Keefe. *Dr. Mutter's Marvels*	B

HUMANITARIAN ASSISTANCE

Bass, Gary Jonathan. *Freedom's Battle*	341.5
Ditmore, Melissa Hope. ★*Unbroken Chains*	306.74
Farmer, Paul. *Fevers, Feuds, and Diamonds*	614.5
Guibert, Emmanuel. *The Photographer*	741.5
Nyamayaro, Elizabeth. *I Am a Girl from Africa*	B

PUBLIC LIBRARY CORE COLLECTION: NONFICTION
Twentieth Edition

Preston, Richard. *Crisis in the Red Zone* — 614.5
Smith, Douglas. *The Russian Job* — 947.084
Whyte, Kenneth. *Hoover* — B
HUMANITARIANISM
    Benjamin, Ruha. ★*Imagination* — 302
    Carter, Jimmy. *A Full Life* — B
    Irving, Apricot Anderson. *The Gospel of Trees* — B
    Nasaw, David. *The Last Million* — 940.53
    Prendergast, John. *Congo Stories* — 967.5103
    Puleo, Stephen. *Voyage of Mercy* — 363.8
    Stone, Sharon. *The Beauty of Living Twice* — B
    Walker, Alice. *The Cushion in the Road* — 814
    ★*Humanizing Immigration.* Hing, Bill Ong — 342.7308
HUMANKIND (CHRISTIAN THEOLOGY)
    Zahl, David. *Low Anthropology* — 233
HUMANS
    Bohme, Madelaine. *Ancient Bones* — 599.93
    Dawkins, Richard. ★*The Ancestor's Tale* — 576.8
    Dawkins, Richard. *The Greatest Show on Earth* — 576.8
    Desilva, Jeremy. *First Steps* — 599.93
    Drew, Liam. *I, Mammal* — 599
    Eagleman, David. *The Brain* — 612.8
    Greenblatt, Stephen. *The Rise and Fall of Adam and Eve* — 233
    Harari, Yuval N. *Homo Deus* — 909.83
    Harari, Yuval N. ★*Sapiens* — 909
    Hitchens, Christopher. *The Four Horsemen* — 211
    Levitt, Dan. *What's Gotten into You* — 539.7
    Marchant, Jo. *The Human Cosmos* — 523.1
    Mooallem, Jon. *Serious Face* — 814
    Newitz, Annalee. *Scatter, Adapt, and Remember* — 576.8
    Rutherford, Adam. *Humanimal* — 599.93
    Sapolsky, Robert M. *Behave* — 612.8
    Stanton, Brandon. *Humans* — 779
    Svensson, Patrik. *The Book of Eels* — 597
    Tattersall, Ian. *Masters of the Planet* — 599.93
    Thurman, Judith. ★*A Left-Handed Woman* — 814
    Tyson, Neil deGrasse. *Startalk* — 523.1
    Whitehouse, David. *The Alien Perspective* — 523.1
    Wilson, Edward O. *The Meaning of Human Existence* — 128
    Humans. Stanton, Brandon — 779
HUMANS AND BIRDS
    Barnes, Simon. *The Meaning of Birds* — 598
    Birkhead, Tim. *Birds and Us* — 598
    Robbins, Jim. *The Wonder of Birds* — 598
HUMANS AND CATS
    Brown, Sarah L. *The Hidden Language of Cats* — 636.8
    Herriot, James. *James Herriot's Cat Stories* — 636.8
    Losos, Jonathan B. *The Cat's Meow* — 636.8
    Myron, Vicki. ★*Dewey* — 636.80092
    Tucker, Abigail. *The Lion in the Living Room* — 636.8
HUMANS AND DOGS
    Charleson, Susannah. *Where the Lost Dogs Go* — 636.7
    Grossi, Craig. *Craig & Fred* — B
    Habib, Rodney. ★*The Forever Dog* — 636.7
    Halpern, Sue. *A Dog Walks into a Nursing Home* — B
    Horowitz, Alexandra. *Our Dogs, Ourselves* — 636.7
    Hunger, Christina. *How Stella Learned to Talk* — 636.7
    Miller, Pat. ★*The Power of Positive Dog Training* — 636.7
    Tomlinson, Tommy. *Dogland* — 636.7
    Wynne, Clive D. L. ★*Dog Is Love* — 636.7
HUMANS AND FISH
    Fagan, Brian M. *Fishing* — 338.3
    Gierach, John. *All Fishermen Are Liars* — 799.12
HUMANS AND GORILLAS
    Fossey, Dian. ★*Gorillas in the Mist* — 599.884
HUMANS AND HORSES
    Hutton, Robin L. *Sgt. Reckless* — 951.904
    Nir, Sarah Maslin. *Horse Crazy* — B
HUMANS AND INSECTS
    MacNeal, David. *Bugged* — 595.7
    Sverdrup-Thygeson, Anne. *Buzz, Sting, Bite* — 595.7
    Wilson, Edward O. *Tales from the Ant World* — 595.79
HUMANS AND NATURE
    Foster, Craig. ★*Amphibious Soul* — 155.9
    Tan, Amy. *The Backyard Bird Chronicles* — 598
HUMANS AND PETS
    Novello, Carol. *Mutual Rescue* — 636.088
    Orlean, Susan. *On Animals* — 590

Schott, Philipp. *The Accidental Veterinarian* — B
HUMANS AND PLANTS
    Drori, Jonathan. *Around the World in 80 Plants* — 581.63
    Kimmerer, Robin Wall. ★*Braiding Sweetgrass* — 304.2
    Logan, William Bryant. *Sprout Lands* — 582.16
HUMANS AND TREES
    Logan, William Bryant. *Sprout Lands* — 582.16
    Wohlleben, Peter. *The Heartbeat of Trees* — 582.16
HUMANS AND WHALES
    Mustill, Tom. *How to Speak Whale* — 591.59
    Neiwert, David A. *Of Orcas and Men* — 599.53
HUMANS AND WILD ANIMALS
    Neiwert, David A. *Of Orcas and Men* — 599.53
    Roach, Mary. ★*Fuzz* — 591.5
HUMANS AND WOLVES
    Lopez, Barry Holstun. ★*Of Wolves and Men* — 599.773
Humbert, Agnes
    Resistance — B
HUMBERT, AGNES
    Humbert, Agnes. *Resistance* — B
Humble Inquiry. Schein, Edgar H. — 302.2
Humble Pi. Parker, Matt — 510
HUMBOLDT, ALEXANDER VON, 1769-1859
    Wulf, Andrea. *The Invention of Nature* — B
Humes, Edward
    Door to Door — 388.09
    The Forever Witness — 363.25
    ★*Total Garbage* — 628.4
Humez, Jean McMahon
    Harriet Tubman — B
HUMILIATION
    Knight, Sam. *The Premonitions Bureau* — 133.8
    Macy, Beth. ★*Truevine* — B
    Stashower, Daniel. *American Demon* — 364.152
HUMILITY
    Evans, Rachel Held. *Wholehearted Faith* — 248.4
    Griffin, Chante. *Loving Your Black Neighbor as Yourself* — 261
    Schein, Edgar H. *Humble Inquiry* — 302.2
HUMMINGBIRDS
    Dunn, Jon L. *The Glitter in the Green* — 598.7
    Montgomery, Sy. *The Hummingbirds' Gift* — 598.7
The Hummingbirds' Gift. Montgomery, Sy — 598.7
HUMOR WRITING — CLASSIC HUMORISTS
    Bryson, Bill. ★*At Home* — 643
    Bryson, Bill. *The Body* — 612
    Bryson, Bill. *In a Sunburned Country* — 919
    Bryson, Bill. *The Life and Times of the Thunderbolt Kid* — B
    Bryson, Bill. *Notes from a Small Island* — 914
    Bryson, Bill. *One Summer* — 973.91
    Bryson, Bill. *The Road to Little Dribbling* — 914
    Bryson, Bill. *Shakespeare* — B
    Bryson, Bill. ★*A Short History of Nearly Everything* — 500
    Bryson, Bill. ★*A Walk in the Woods* — 917
    White, E. B. *Essays of E.B. White* — 814
HUMOR WRITING — FAMILY AND RELATIONSHIP HUMOR
    Birbiglia, Mike. *The New One* — B
    Dunn, Jancee. ★*How Not to Hate Your Husband After Kids* — 646.7
    Ellis, Helen. *Bring Your Baggage and Don't Pack Light* — 814
    Ellis, Helen. *Southern Lady Code* — 814
    Farris, Grace. *Mom Milestones* — 306.87
    Foxx, Jamie. *Act Like You Got Some Sense* — B
    Gaffigan, Jim. *Dad Is Fat* — 814
    Hatmaker, Jen. *Of Mess and Moxie* — 248.8
    Jacobs, A. J. *It's All Relative* — 929.1
    Kaling, Mindy. *Why Not Me?* — B
    Loh, Sandra Tsing. *The Madwoman and the Roomba* — B
    Noah, Trevor. *Born a Crime* — B
    Scottoline, Lisa. *I See Life Through Rose-Colored Glasses* — 813
    Sedaris, David. ★*The Best of Me* — 818
    Traig, Jennifer. *Act Natural* — 306.874
    Wong, Ali. ★*Dear Girls* — B
HUMOR WRITING — GENERAL
    Arceneaux, Michael. *I Finally Bought Some Jordans* — 306.76
    Brosh, Allie. ★*Hyperbole and a Half* — 741.5
    Brosh, Allie. ★*Solutions and Other Problems* — 741.5
    Burroughs, Augusten. ★*Toil & Trouble* — B
    Cassidy, Cody. *How to Survive History* — 904
    Conaboy, Kelly. *The Particulars of Peter* — 636.7

AUTHOR, TITLE, SERIES AND SUBJECT INDEX

Hiaasen, Carl. *The Downhill Lie*	B
Holder, R. W. *How Not to Say What You Mean*	427
Jennings, Ken. ★*100 Places to See After You Die*	202
Jennings, Ken. *Planet Funny*	809.7
Key, Keegan-Michael. ★*The History of Sketch Comedy*	792.2
Knight, Sarah. *The Life-Changing Magic of Not Giving a F*ck*	818
Manson, Mark. *Everything Is F*cked*	152.4
Manson, Mark. *The Subtle Art of Not Giving a F*ck*	158.1
Martin, Steve. *Number One Is Walking*	B
Miranda, Lin-Manuel. *Gmorning, Gnight!*	811
Munroe, Randall. *How To*	500
Munroe, Randall. *What If? 2*	500
Munroe, Randall. ★*What If?*	500
O'Rourke, P. J. *None of My Business*	332
Peter, Laurence J. *The Peter Principle*	658
Pratchett, Terry. *A Slip of the Keyboard*	824
Rannells, Andrew. *Uncle of the Year*	B
Rocca, Mo. *Mobituaries*	920
Sedaris, David. *Calypso*	814
Sedaris, David. ★*A Carnival of Snackery*	818
Sedaris, David. *Theft by Finding*	B
Serrano, Shea. *Basketball (and Other Things)*	796.323
Spence, Annie. *Dear Fahrenheit 451*	028.9
Truss, Lynne. *Eats, Shoots & Leaves*	428.2
HUMOR WRITING — POLITICAL SATIRE	
Jacobs, A. J. ★*The Year of Living Constitutionally*	342.73
HUMOR WRITING — SOCIAL HUMOR	
Ahdoot, Dan. *Undercooked*	647.95
Alford, Henry. *And Then We Danced*	792.8
Brunson, Quinta. *She Memes Well*	B
Crosley, Sloane. *I Was Told There'd Be Cake*	814
Crosley, Sloane. ★*Look Alive Out There*	814
Fumudoh, Ziwe. ★*Black Friend*	814
Geist, William. *Little League Confidential*	796.357
Gold, Judy. *Yes I Can Say That*	792.7
Inman, Matthew. *The Terrible and Wonderful Reasons Why I Run Long Distances*	741.5
Irby, Samantha. ★*Quietly Hostile*	814
Irby, Samantha. *We Are Never Meeting in Real Life*	814
Jobrani, Maziyar. *I'm Not a Terrorist, but I've Played One on TV*	B
Knight, Keltie. *Lady Secrets*	305.4
Lancaster, Jen. *Welcome to the United States of Anxiety*	155.4
Lavery, Daniel M. *Something That May Shock and Discredit You*	814
Mann, Jen. ★*Midlife Bites*	305.244
Mattel, Trixie. *Working Girls*	650.1
Moran, Caitlin. *How to Be a Woman*	B
Movsesian, Sona. *The World's Worst Assistant*	791.4302
Nawaz, Zarqa. *Laughing All the Way to the Mosque*	791.45028
Notaro, Laurie. *Excuse Me While I Disappear*	B
Parker, James. *Get Me Through the Next Five Minutes*	158.1
Petri, Alexandra. *Alexandra Petri's US History*	817
Posey, Parker. *You're on an Airplane*	B
Robinson, Phoebe. *Please Don't Sit on My Bed in Your Outside Clothes*	818
Ruffin, Amber. ★*The World Record Book of Racist Stories*	305.896
Ruffin, Amber. *You'll Never Believe What Happened to Lacey*	305.896
Schumer, Amy. *The Girl with the Lower Back Tattoo*	B
Sedaris, David. ★*Happy-Go-Lucky*	814
Segura, Tom. ★*I'd Like to Play Alone, Please*	B
Seinfeld, Jerry. *Is This Anything?*	818
Stibbe, Nina. *An Almost Perfect Christmas*	394.2663
Stone, Lillian. ★*Everybody's Favorite*	814.6
Thomas, R. Eric. ★*Congratulations, the Best Is Over!*	B
West, Lindy. *Shrill*	818
Zara, Christopher. *Uneducated*	B
HUMORISTS	
Henderson, Danielle. ★*The Ugly Cry*	B
Litt, David. *Thanks, Obama*	B
Sedaris, David. ★*A Carnival of Snackery*	818
Sedaris, David. ★*Happy-Go-Lucky*	814
Shelden, Michael. *Mark Twain*	B
Twain, Mark. *Autobiography of Mark Twain*	B
Twain, Mark. ★*Autobiography of Mark Twain*	B
Twain, Mark. ★*Autobiography of Mark Twain*	B
HUMOROUS WRITING	
Brunson, Quinta. *She Memes Well*	B
Farris, Grace. *Mom Milestones*	306.87
Goldblatt, Duchess. *Becoming Duchess Goldblatt*	B
Irby, Samantha. ★*Quietly Hostile*	814
Jennings, Ken. ★*100 Places to See After You Die*	202
Key, Keegan-Michael. ★*The History of Sketch Comedy*	792.2
Mattel, Trixie. *Working Girls*	650.1
Munroe, Randall. *What If? 2*	500
Rocca, Mo. *Mobituaries*	920
Ruffin, Amber. *You'll Never Believe What Happened to Lacey*	305.896
Sedaris, David. ★*Happy-Go-Lucky*	814
Seinfeld, Jerry. *Is This Anything?*	818
Wood, Lawrence. *Your Caption Has Been Selected*	741.5
Zweibel, Alan. *Laugh Lines*	B
HUMPHREYS, ANDREW ATKINSON, 1810-1883	
Barry, John M. *Rising Tide*	977
Humphreys, Richard	
Under Pressure	B
HUMPHREYS, RICHARD, 1967-	
Humphreys, Richard. *Under Pressure*	B
A **Hundred** *and One Days*. Seierstad, Asne	956.70443
★*The* **Hundred** *Years' War on Palestine*. Khalidi, Rashid	956.9405
HUNDRED YEARS' WAR, 1339-1453	
Barker, Juliet R. V. *Agincourt*	944
Castor, Helen. *Joan of Arc*	B
Spoto, Donald. *Joan*	B
The **Hundred-Year** *Walk*. Mackeen, Dawn Anahid	956.6
HUNG, HSIU-CHUAN, 1814-1864	
Spence, Jonathan D. *God's Chinese Son*	951
HUNGARIAN AMERICANS	
Kariko, Katalin. *Breaking Through*	B
HUNGARIAN PEOPLE	
Debreczeni, Jozsef. *Cold Crematorium*	940.53
Faludi, Susan. *In the Darkroom*	B
Kariko, Katalin. *Breaking Through*	B
Katin, Miriam. *We Are on Our Own*	741.5
HUNGARY	
Longo, Matthew. *The Picnic*	947.084
Michener, James A. *The Bridge at Andau*	943.9
Sebestyen, Victor. *Budapest*	943.912
Von Tunzelmann, Alex. *Blood and Sand*	909.82
HUNGER	
Kelly, John. *The Graves Are Walking*	941.5081
Lowe, Keith. *Savage Continent*	940.55
McCourt, Frank. ★*Angela's Ashes*	929
Tucker, Todd. *The Great Starvation Experiment*	174.2
The **Hunger** *Book*. Szczeszak-Brewer, Agata	B
Hunger, Christina	
How Stella Learned to Talk	636.7
HUNGER, CHRISTINA	
Hunger, Christina. *How Stella Learned to Talk*	636.7
The **Hungry** *Brain*. Guyenet, Stephan J.	616.85
The **Hungry** *Fan's Game Day Cookbook*. Falk, Daina	641.5973
Hungry *Girl 1-2-3*. Lillien, Lisa	641.5
Hungry *Girl Simply 6*. Lillien, Lisa	641.5
The **Hungry** *Season*. Hamilton, Lisa M.	B
The **Hunt** *for History*. Raab, Nathan	790.1
Hunt, Lindsay Maitland	
Healthyish	641.5
Help Yourself	641.5
HUNT, MARSHA	
Winder, Elizabeth. *Parachute Women*	782.42164
Hunt, Patrick	
Hannibal	B
Hunt, Tristram	
Marx's General	335.4092
Hunt, Will	
Underground	624.1
Hunter, Bonnie K.	
String Frenzy	746.46
Hunter-Gault, Charlayne	
★*My People*	305.48
HUNTERS	
Rinella, Steven. *Meat Eater*	B
HUNTING	
Duncan, Dayton. *Blood Memory*	599.64
Harrison, Jim. *The Search for the Genuine*	814
Howsare, Erika. *The Age of Deer*	599.65
Markham, Beryl. *West with the Night*	B
Rinella, Steven. *American Buffalo*	599.64
Rinella, Steven. *The Complete Guide to Hunting, Butchering, and Cooking Wild Game*	799.2

PUBLIC LIBRARY CORE COLLECTION: NONFICTION
Twentieth Edition

Rinella, Steven. *The Complete Guide to Hunting, Butchering, and Cooking Wild Game; Volume 2* — 799.2
Rinella, Steven. *Meat Eater* — B
Vaillant, John. *The Tiger* — 599.756
Williams, Wyatt. *Springer Mountain* — 394.1

HUNTING AND GATHERING SOCIETIES
Clark, Doug Bock. *The Last Whalers* — 639.2
Hunting Charles Manson. Wiehl, Lis W. — 364.152
Hunting Eichmann. Bascomb, Neal — 943.086

HUNTING EQUIPMENT
Rinella, Steven. *The Complete Guide to Hunting, Butchering, and Cooking Wild Game* — 799.2
Rinella, Steven. *The Complete Guide to Hunting, Butchering, and Cooking Wild Game; Volume 2* — 799.2
Hunting Leroux. Shannon, Elaine — 364.1
The **Hunting** *of Hillary.* D'Antonio, Michael — B
Hunting *The Falcon.* Guy, John — B
Hunting *The Unabomber.* Wiehl, Lis W. — 364.152
Hunting *Whitey.* Sherman, Casey — B

HUNTSVILLE, ALABAMA
McCaulley, Esau. *How Far to the Promised Land* — B

Hurowitz, Richard
In the Garden of the Righteous — 940.53

HURRICANE KATRINA, 2005
Brinkley, Douglas. *The Great Deluge* — 976.3
Broom, Sarah M. *The Yellow House* — B
Dyson, Michael Eric. *Come Hell or High Water* — 976.3
Eggers, Dave. *Zeitoun* — 305.892
Fink, Sheri. *Five Days at Memorial* — 362.1109763
Horne, Jed. *Breach of Faith* — 976.3
Neufeld, Josh. *A.D.* — 741.5
Rivlin, Gary. *Katrina* — 976.3
Smith, Patricia. *Blood Dazzler* — 811
Spera, Keith. *Groove Interrupted* — B
Hurricane Lizards and Plastic Squid. Hanson, Thor — 577.2

HURRICANE SANDY, 2012
Cardwell, Diane. *Rockaway* — B

HURRICANES
Baum, Dan. *Nine Lives* — B
Brinkley, Douglas. *The Great Deluge* — 976.3
Burns, Cherie. *The Great Hurricane—1938* — 974.7
Dolin, Eric Jay. *A Furious Sky* — 363.34
Fields, Micah. ★ *We Hold Our Breath* — 976.4
Fink, Sheri. *Five Days at Memorial* — 362.1109763
Horne, Jed. *Breach of Faith* — 976.3
Neufeld, Josh. *A.D.* — 741.5
Rush, Elizabeth A. *Rising* — 551.45
Slade, Rachel. *Into the Raging Sea* — 910.91

Hurston, Zora Neale
★*Barracoon* — B
Dust Tracks on a Road — B
★*You Don't Know Us Negroes and Other Essays* — 814
Zora Neale Hurston — B

HURSTON, ZORA NEALE
Hurston, Zora Neale. *Dust Tracks on a Road* — B
Hurston, Zora Neale. *Zora Neale Hurston* — B
Jones, Sharon L. *Critical Companion to Zora Neale Hurston* — 813

HURTER, ALBERT
Ghez, Didier. *The Hidden Art of Disney's Golden Age* — 741.5

★*The* **Hurting** *Kind.* Limon, Ada — 811

Husain, Ed
★*The House of Islam* — 297

HUSBAND AND WIFE
Bailey, Catherine. *A Castle in Wartime* — 943.086
Baird, Julia. ★*Victoria the Queen* — B
Bard, Elizabeth. *Lunch in Paris* — B
Bard, Elizabeth. *Picnic in Provence* — B
Berg, Elizabeth. *I'll Be Seeing You* — 306.874
Birbiglia, Mike. *The New One* — B
Bloom, Amy. *In Love* — B
Collins, Lauren. *When in French* — B
Cook, Blanche Wiesen. *Eleanor Roosevelt; Volume 2* — B
Cook, Blanche Wiesen. ★*Eleanor Roosevelt; Volume 3* — B
Cook, Jane Hampton. *American Phoenix* — 973.5
Darnell, John Coleman. *Egypt's Golden Couple* — 932
Dietrich, Sean. *You Are My Sunshine* — B
Duggar, Jill. *Counting the Cost* — B
Ellis, Joseph J. *First Family* — 973.4

Erwin, Jon. *Beyond Valor* — B
Gabriel, Mary. *Love and Capital* — 920
Gill, Gillian. *We Two* — 941.081
Glatt, John. *The Doomsday Mother* — 364.152
Glatt, John. ★*The Perfect Father* — 364.152
Goodwin, Doris Kearns. *No Ordinary Time* — 920
Gray, Charlotte. ★*Reluctant Genius* — 920
Henderson, Artis. *Unremarried Widow* — B
Herriot, James. *All Things Wise and Wonderful* — B
Hillsberg, Christina. *License to Parent* — 649.1
Holton, Woody. *Abigail Adams* — B
Homer. ★*The Odyssey* — 883
Inskeep, Steve. *Imperfect Union* — B
Mann, William J. *Bogie & Bacall* — 920
Marton, Kati. *Hidden Power* — B
McBrien, William. *Cole Porter* — B
Noor. *Leap of Faith* — B
Palmer, Arnold. *A Golfer's Life* — B
Pataki, Allison. *Beauty in the Broken Places* — B
Porter, Linda. *Katherine the Queen* — B
Pressman, Steven. *50 Children* — 940.53
Raban, Jonathan. *Father and Son* — B
Rehm, Diane. *On My Own* — B
Ricanati, Elizabeth. *Braided* — B
Ridley, Jane. *George V* — B
Sampson, Fiona. *In Search of Mary Shelley* — B
Satrapi, Marjane. *Chicken with Plums* — 741.5
Stahr, Celia. *Frida in America* — B
Steinberg, Jonny. *Winnie and Nelson* — 920
Van Hemert, Caroline. *The Sun Is a Compass* — 979.8
Winn, Raynor. ★*The Salt Path* — B
Winn, Raynor. *The Wild Silence* — B
Worsley, Lucy. *Queen Victoria* — B
The **Husband** Hunters. De Courcy, Anne — 920

Hussain, Nadiya
★*Nadiya Bakes* — 641.81
★*Nadiya's Everyday Baking* — 641.5
Time to Eat — 641.5

HUSSEIN, ASAD, 1995-
McCormick, Ty. *Beyond the Sand and Sea* — 920

HUSSEIN, KING OF JORDAN, 1935-1999
Noor. *Leap of Faith* — B

HUSSEIN, SADDAM, 1937-2006
Bardenwerper, William. *The Prisoner in His Palace* — 956.7044
Coll, Steve. ★*The Achilles Trap* — 956.7044
Newton, Michael A. *Enemy of the State* — 345.567
Nixon, John. *Debriefing the President* — 956.7044

Hussey, Olivia
The Girl on the Balcony — B

HUSSEY, OLIVIA
Hussey, Olivia. *The Girl on the Balcony* — B

HUSSLE, NIPSEY
Kenner, Rob. *The Marathon Don't Stop* — B
Hustle Harder, Hustle Smarter. Jackson, Curtis — B

Huston, Anjelica
Watch Me — B

HUSTON, ANJELICA
Huston, Anjelica. *Watch Me* — B

HUSTON, JOHN, 1906-1987
Harris, Mark. ★*Five Came Back* — 791.4302

Huston, Steve
Figure Drawing for Artists — 743.4

Hustvedt, Siri
Mothers, Fathers, and Others — 814

Hutchinson, Cassidy
Enough — B

HUTCHINSON, CASSIDY
Hutchinson, Cassidy. *Enough* — B

Hutchinson, Ishion
House of Lords and Commons — 811

Hutton, Andrea
Bald Is Better with Earrings — 362.19699

Hutton, Paul Andrew
The Apache Wars — 979

Hutton, Robin L.
Sgt. Reckless — 951.904

Hutton, Ronald
The Triumph of the Moon — 133.4

AUTHOR, TITLE, SERIES AND SUBJECT INDEX

HUTU (AFRICAN PEOPLE)
   Gourevitch, Philip. *We Wish to Inform You That Tomorrow We Will Be Killed*
      with Our Families   364.15
   Hatzfeld, Jean. *Machete Season*   967.57104
Huxley, Aldous
   ★*Brave New World Revisited*   823
Huxley, Elspeth Joscelin Grant
   The Flame Trees of Thika   B
HUXLEY, ELSPETH, 1907-1997
   Huxley, Elspeth Joscelin Grant. *The Flame Trees of Thika*   B
HUXLEY, THOMAS HENRY, 1825-1895
   McCalman, Iain. *Darwin's Armada*   576.8
Huxtable, Ada Louise
   ★*Frank Lloyd Wright*   B
   On Architecture   724
Hvistendahl, Mara
   ★*The Scientist and the Spy*   364.16
Hybrida. Chang, Tina   811
Hyde, Anne Farrar
   ★*Born of Lakes and Plains*   978
   Empires, Nations, and Families   978
Hyden, Steven
   Long Road   782.42166
   Twilight of the Gods   781.6609
HYDRAULIC FRACTURING
   Briody, Blaire. *The New Wild West*   338.2
   Zuckerman, Gregory. *The Frackers*   B
HYDROGEN BOMB
   Schlosser, Eric. *Command and Control*   363.17
HYDROLOGY
   Gleick, Peter H. *The Three Ages of Water*   333.91
HYGIENE
   Hamblin, James. *Clean*   613
   Harshe, January. *Birth Without Fear*   618.2
   Oster, Emily. ★*Cribsheet*   618.2
   Randall, David K. *Black Death at the Golden Gate*   616.9
   Rope, Kate. *Strong as a Mother*   618.2
Hyland, William G.
   George Gershwin   B
Hylton, Antonia
   Madness   362.2
Hymns of the Republic. Gwynne, S. C.   973.7
Hynes, Samuel
   The Unsubstantial Air   940.4
★*Hyperbole and a Half*. Brosh, Allie   741.5
★*Hyperspace*. Kaku, Michio   530.1
HYPERSPACE
   Kaku, Michio. ★*Hyperspace*   530.1
   Kaku, Michio. *Parallel Worlds*   523.1
HYPOCHONDRIA
   Crampton, Caroline. *A Body Made of Glass*   616.85
HYPOCRISY
   Busby, Jill Louise. *Unfollow Me*   305.08
   Gaul, Gilbert M. *Billion-Dollar Ball*   796.332
   Greenidge, Kerri. ★*The Grimkes*   973.5
   Smith, Mychal Denzel. *Stakes Is High*   973.933
   Solnit, Rebecca. *Call Them by Their True Names*   303.3
HYPOTHERMIA
   Laskin, David. *The Children's Blizzard*   977
   Panagore, Peter Baldwin. *Heaven Is Beautiful*   B
HYPOTHESIS
   Lintott, Chris. *Accidental Astronomy*   520
   Markel, Howard. *Origin Story*   576.8
   Munroe, Randall. *What If? 2*   500
HYSTERIA
   Brownstein, Gabriel. ★*The Secret Mind of Bertha Pappenheim*   616.85
HYSTERIA (SOCIAL PSYCHOLOGY)
   Branigan, Tania. *Red Memory*   951.05
   Gibson, Marion. *Witchcraft*   133.4
   O'Sullivan, Suzanne. *The Sleeping Beauties*   616.85
   Schiff, Stacy. *The Witches*   345
Hytner, Nicholas
   Balancing Acts   B
HYTNER, NICHOLAS
   Hytner, Nicholas. *Balancing Acts*   B

I

I. Derricotte, Toi   811
I Alone Can Fix It. Leonnig, Carol   973.933
I Am a Filipino and This Is How We Cook. Ponseca, Nicole   641.595
I Am a Girl from Africa. Nyamayaro, Elizabeth   B
I Am a Strange Loop. Hofstadter, Douglas R.   153
I Am Brian Wilson. Wilson, Brian   B
I Am Dynamite! Prideaux, Sue   B
I Am Malala. Yousafzai, Malala   B
I Am Not Your Negro. Baldwin, James   323.1196
I Am Not Your Slave. Tjipombo, Tupa   B
I Am Ozzy. Osbourne, Ozzy   B
★*I Am Restored*. Lecrae   B
I Am, I Am, I Am. O'Farrell, Maggie   B
I Can't Breathe. Taibbi, Matt   363.2
I Can't Make This Up. Hart, Kevin   B
I Can't Talk About the Trees Without the Blood. Clark, Tiana   811
I Cried to Dream Again. Kruzan, Sara   B
I Did a New Thing. Brown, Tabitha   158.1
I Didn't Know I Needed This. Rallo, Eli   306.73
I Done Clicked My Heels Three Times. Byas, Taylor   811
I Dream He Talks to Me. Moorer, Allison   782.42164
I Finally Bought Some Jordans. Arceneaux, Michael   306.76
I Find Your Lack of Faith Disturbing. Jameson, A. D.   791.43
I Had a Brother Once. Mansbach, Adam   811
The I Hate to Cook Book. Bracken, Peg   641.5
I Have Nothing to Hide". Boghosian, Heidi   363.1
I Heard Her Call My Name. Sante, Lucy   B
★*I Just Keep Talking*. Painter, Nell Irvin   814
I Keep Trying to Catch His Eye. Maisel, Ivan   B
I Know Who You Are. Rae-Venter, Barbara   364.152
★*I Know Why the Caged Bird Sings*. Angelou, Maya   B
I Like to Watch. Nussbaum, Emily   791.45
I Live a Life Like Yours. Grue, Jan   B
I Must Be Living Twice. Myles, Eileen   811.54
I Must Say. Short, Martin   B
I Never Had It Made. Robinson, Jackie   B
I Quit Everything. Smith, Freda Love   B
I Saw Death Coming. Williams, Kidada E.   973.8
I See Life Through Rose-Colored Glasses. Scottoline, Lisa   813
I Shall Not Hate. Abuelaish, Izzeldin   B
★*I Shouldn't Be Telling You This*. Devantez, Chelsea   B
I Take My Coffee Black. Merritt, Tyler   791.4302
I Want to Die but I Want to Eat Tteokbokki. Sehee, Baek   B
I Want You to Know We're Still Here. Foer, Esther Safran   B
I Was Told There'd Be Cake. Crosley, Sloane   814
I Was Told to Come Alone. Mekhennet, Souad   363.3250956
I Wasn't Supposed to Be Here. Conyers, Jonathan   B
I Will Bear Witness. Klemperer, Victor   B
I Won't Shut Up. Henny, Ally   305.896
★*I Wonder as I Wander*. Hughes, Langston   B
★*I'd Like to Play Alone, Please*. Segura, Tom   B
I'll Be Gone in the Dark. McNamara, Michelle   364.152
I'll Be Seeing You. Berg, Elizabeth   306.874
I'll Find a Way or Make One. Williams, Juan   378.73
I'll Have What She's Having. Carlson, Erin   791.43
I'll Show Myself Out. Klein, Jessi   B
I'll Take You There. Kot, Greg   B
I'm Afraid of Men. Shraya, Vivek   813
I'm Fascinated by Sacrifice Flies. Kurkjian, Tim   796.357
★*I'm Glad My Mom Died*. McCurdy, Jennette   B
I'm Keith Hernandez. Hernandez, Keith   B
I'm Not a Terrorist, but I've Played One on TV. Jobrani, Maziyar   B
I'm Possible. White, Richard Antoine   B
★*I'm Still Here*. Brown, Austin Channing   B
★*I'm Supposed to Protect You from All This*. Spiegelman, Nadja   741.5
I'm Telling the Truth, but I'm Lying. Ikpi, Bassey   814
I'm Your Man. Simmons, Sylvie   B
I've Been Thinking .. Shriver, Maria   170
I, Mammal. Drew, Liam   599
I.M. Mizrahi, Isaac   B
IACOCCA, LEE A., 1924-2019
   Baime, A. J. ★*Go Like Hell*   796.7209
Ian Fleming. Shakespeare, Nicholas   B
Ian McKellen. O'Connor, Garry   B
Iandoli, Kathy
   Baby Girl   B

PUBLIC LIBRARY CORE COLLECTION: NONFICTION
Twentieth Edition

God Save the Queens	782.421649
Iannotti, Marie	
The Beginner's Guide to Growing Heirloom Vegetables	635
Ice. Brady, Amy	553.7
ICE	
Brady, Amy. *Ice*	553.7
Fox, Porter. *The Last Winter*	363.738
Hogge, Fred. *Of Ice and Men*	338.4
Pollack, H. N. *A World Without Ice*	551.31
ICE AGE (GEOLOGY)	
Childs, Craig. *Atlas of a Lost World*	551.7
Macdougall, J. D. *Frozen Earth*	551.7
ICE CAPS	
Wood, Gillen D'Arcy. *Land of Wondrous Cold*	919.89
ICE CREAM, ICES, ETC.	
Beranbaum, Rose Levy. *Rose's Ice Cream Bliss*	641.86
Gerson, Fany. *Mexican Ice Cream*	641.86
ICE CUBE	
Westhoff, Ben. *Original Gangstas*	782.421649
Ice Ghosts. Watson, Paul	917
Ice-T	
Split Decision	920
ICE-T (MUSICIAN)	
Ice-T. *Split Decision*	920
ICELAND	
Bjarnason, Egill. *How Iceland Changed the World*	949.12
Winn, Raynor. *The Wild Silence*	B
The Icepick Surgeon. Kean, Sam	509
ICHTHYOLOGISTS	
Miller, Lulu. *Why Fish Don't Exist*	B
ICINGS, CAKE	
Stewart, Martha. *Martha Stewart's Cake Perfection*	641.86
The Iconic Interior. Bradbury, Dominic	747
The Iconic Photographs. McCurry, Steve	779.092
Ida. Giddings, Paula	B
IDAHO	
Appelman, J. Reuben. *While Idaho Slept*	364.152
Calcaterra, Regina. *Girl Unbroken*	B
Egan, Timothy. ★*The Big Burn*	973.911
Glatt, John. *The Doomsday Mother*	364.152
Westover, Tara. ★*Educated*	B
An Idea Whose Time Has Come. Purdum, Todd S.	342.7308
IDEALISM	
Brands, H. W. *Woodrow Wilson*	B
Ellis, Joseph J. *American Sphinx*	973.4
Irving, Apricot Anderson. *The Gospel of Trees*	B
Krakauer, Jon. *Into the Wild*	917.9804
Smith, James K. A. *How to Inhabit Time*	223
Taylor, Alan. *American Civil Wars*	973.7
IDEAS (PHILOSOPHY)	
Bahcall, Safi. *Loonshots*	658.4
Friedman, Ron. *Decoding Greatness*	650.1
McHangama, Jacob. ★*Free Speech*	323.44
Rubenstein, David M. *The American Experiment*	973
Russell, Bertrand. *The Problems of Philosophy*	110
Wilson, Derek K. *A Magical World*	261.5
Ideas and Opinions. Einstein, Albert	081
IDENTICAL TWINS	
De Bres, Helena. *How to Be Multiple*	155.44
Hayasaki, Erika. *Somewhere Sisters*	362.7
Nutt, Amy Ellis. *Becoming Nicole*	920
IDENTIFICATION	
Bass, William M. *Death's Acre*	614
Brierley, Saroo. *A Long Way Home*	B
Brockman, Christian Frank. *Trees of North America*	582.16097
Bull, John L. ★*The National Audubon Society Field Guide to North American Birds*.	598.097
Calcaterra, Regina. *Etched in Sand*	B
Chung, Nicole. *All You Can Ever Know*	B
Gilbert, Carter Rowell. ★*National Audubon Society Field Guide to Fishes*.	597
Glaser, Gabrielle. *American Baby*	B
Hagerty, Alexa. ★*Still Life with Bones*	599.9
Hill, Kashmir. ★*Your Face Belongs to Us*	006.2
Hugo, Nancy R. *Seeing Trees*	582.16
Jensen, Robert A. *Personal Effects*	363.34
Little, Elbert L. *The Audubon Society Field Guide to North American Trees*	582.16097
McKnight, Kent H. *A Field Guide to Mushrooms, North America*	579.6
Milne, Lorus Johnson. ★*The Audubon Society Field Guide to North American Insects and Spiders*	595.7097
Norton, Laurah. *Lay Them to Rest*	363.25
Petrides, George A. *A Field Guide to Western Trees*	582.16
Rehder, Harald Alfred. *The Audubon Society Field Guide to North American Seashells*	594
Sibley, David. *The Sibley Guide to Birds*	598.097
Stokes, Donald W. *The New Stokes Field Guide to Birds*.	598
Whitaker, John O. ★*National Audubon Society Field Guide to North American Mammals*	599.097
IDENTIFICATION CARDS	
Moorhouse, Roger. *The Forgers*	940.53
IDENTITY	
Abdelmahmoud, Elamin. *Son of Elsewhere*	B
Abdurraqib, Hanif. ★*There's Always This Year*	796.323
Abrams, Stacey. *Our Time Is Now*	324.60973
Ahuvia, Aaron. ★*The Things We Love*	790.1
Akbar, Kaveh. *Pilgrim Bell*	811
Alexander, Kwame. *Why Fathers Cry at Night*	B
Ali, Fatima. ★*Savor*	B
Ali, Wajahat. *Go Back to Where You Came From*	B
Alvis-Walker, Marcie. *Everybody Come Alive*	B
Arana, Marie. ★*Latinoland*	973
Arce, Julissa. *You Sound Like a White Girl*	303.48
Arceneaux, Michael. *I Finally Bought Some Jordans*	306.76
Aviv, Rachel. ★*Strangers to Ourselves*	616.89
Baer, Kate. *What Kind of Woman*	811
Baird, Julia. ★*Victoria the Queen*	B
Baraka, Sho. *He Saw That It Was Good*	261.5
Bari, Shahidha K. *Dressed*	391
Baron, Dennis E. *What's Your Pronoun?*	425.55
Barot, Rick. *The Galleons*	811
Bauermeister, Erica. *House Lessons*	B
Beauvoir, Simone de. ★*The Second Sex*	305.4
Bee, Vanessa A. *Home Bound*	B
Belcher, Chris. *Pretty Baby*	B
Bell, Darrin. ★*The Talk*	741.5
Berry, Erica. *Wolfish*	152.4
Betts, Reginald Dwayne. *Felon*	811
Betz-Hamilton, Axton. *The Less People Know About Us*	364.16
Bidwell, Duane R. *When One Religion Isn't Enough*	261.2
Bitsui, Sherwin. *Dissolve*	811
Black, Michael Ian. *A Better Man*	305.31
Blount, Tommye. *Fantasia for the Man in Blue*	811
Bossiere, Zoe. *Cactus Country*	306
Bowen, Sesali. *Bad Fat Black Girl*	305.42
Bragg, Rick. *Where I Come From*	975
Brina, Elizabeth Miki. *Speak, Okinawa*	305.48
Bronfman, Edgar M. *Why Be Jewish?*	296
Broom, Sarah M. *The Yellow House*	B
Broome, Brian. ★*Punch Me up to the Gods*	B
Brown, Brene. *Braving the Wilderness*	305.8
Brown, Brene. *The Gifts of Imperfection*	158
Brown, Jericho. ★*The Tradition*	811
Bui, Thi. ★*The Best We Could Do*	741.5
Busby, Jill Louise. *Unfollow Me*	305.08
Cahalan, Susannah. *Brain on Fire*	616.8
Cargle, Rachel Elizabeth. *A Renaissance of Our Own*	B
Carlile, Brandi. *Broken Horses*	B
Carroll, Rebecca. *Surviving the White Gaze*	B
Carson, Anne. *Autobiography of Red*	811
Chee, Alexander. ★*How to Write an Autobiographical Novel*	B
Chin, Curtis. *Everything I Learned, I Learned in a Chinese Restaurant*	B
Chude-Sokei, Louis Onuorah. *Floating in a Most Peculiar Way*	979.4
Chung, Nicole. *All You Can Ever Know*	B
Clark, Tiana. *I Can't Talk About the Trees Without the Blood*	811
Clemmons, Francois S. *Officer Clemmons*	B
Coates, Ta-Nehisi. ★*Between the World and Me*	305.800973
Coel, Michaela. ★*Misfits*	158.2
Coffin, Jaed. *Roughhouse Friday*	B
Collins-Dexter, Brandi. *Black Skinhead*	324.2734
Crais, Clifton C. *History Lessons*	B
Dabiri, Emma. *Twisted*	391.5
Dahl, Melissa. *Cringeworthy*	158.2
Dangarembga, Tsitsi. *Black and Female*	305.48
Davis, Viola. ★*Finding Me*	B
De Bres, Helena. *How to Be Multiple*	155.44

AUTHOR, TITLE, SERIES AND SUBJECT INDEX

Dearborn, Mary V. *Ernest Hemingway*	B
Doty, Mark. *What Is the Grass*	811
Dubin, Minna. ★*Mom Rage*	306.874
Dyson, Michael Eric. *The Black Presidency*	305.800973
Emdin, Christopher. *Ratchetdemic*	370.1
Enright, Lynn. *Vagina*	612.6
Ervin, Kristine S. *Rabbit Heart*	364.152
Faliveno, Melissa. *Tomboyland*	B
Faludi, Susan. *In the Darkroom*	B
Febos, Melissa. *Girlhood*	818
Feldman, Deborah. *Exodus*	B
Feldman, Noah. ★*To Be a Jew Today*	296.3
Fersko, Diana. ★*We Need to Talk About Antisemitism*	305.892
Fitzgerald, Isaac. *Dirtbag, Massachusetts*	B
Ford, Tanisha C. *Dressed in Dreams*	391
Freedman, Samuel G. *Jew vs. Jew*	296
Fumudoh, Ziwe. ★*Black Friend*	814
Galeotti, Mark. *A Short History of Russia*	947.086
Garrett, Kent. *The Last Negroes at Harvard*	920
Gates, Henry Louis. *In Search of Our Roots*	973
Gay, Ross. *Inciting Joy*	814
Gay, Roxane. ★*Opinions*	814
Geller, Danielle. *Dog Flowers*	B
Gelwicks, Andrew. *The Queer Advantage*	920
Georges, Gigi. *Downeast*	974.1
Gerald, Casey. *There Will Be No Miracles Here*	B
Gimenez Smith, Carmen. *Be Recorder*	811
Glaser, Gabrielle. *American Baby*	B
Glass, Sara. *Kissing Girls on Shabbat*	B
Glaude, Eddie S. *Begin Again*	305.800973
Goetsch, Diana. *This Body I Wore*	B
Golinkin, Lev. *A Backpack, a Bear, and Eight Crates of Vodka*	B
Gomez, Edgar. *High-Risk Homosexual*	B
Gomez, Laura E. ★*Inventing Latinos*	305.868
Gorman, Amanda. ★*Call Us What We Carry*	811
Gottlieb, Iris. *Seeing Gender*	305.3
Grue, Jan. *I Live a Life Like Yours*	B
H, Lamya. ★*Hijab Butch Blues*	B
Han, Chenxing. *Be the Refuge*	294.3
Hardy, Benjamin. *Willpower Doesn't Work*	158
Harjo, Joy. *Catching the Light*	818
Harjo, Joy. *Crazy Brave*	B
Harris, Jessica B. *High on the Hog*	641.59
Harry, Debbie. *Face It*	B
Hayasaki, Erika. *Somewhere Sisters*	362.7
Hemon, Aleksandar. *My Parents*	814
Hempel, Jessi. *The Family Outing*	B
Henny, Ally. *I Won't Shut Up*	305.896
Hernandez, Daisy. *A Cup of Water Under My Bed*	B
Herrera, Juan Felipe. *Every Day We Get More Illegal*	811
Hewitt, Sean. *All Down Darkness Wide*	B
Hill, Kashmir. ★*Your Face Belongs to Us*	006.2
Hixenbaugh, Michael. ★*They Came for the Schools*	371.9
Hoffman, Carl. *Liar's Circus*	973.933
Hong, Cathy Park. *Minor Feelings*	305.48
Horowitz, Alexandra. ★*The Year of the Puppy*	636.7
Hough, Lauren. *Leaving Isn't the Hardest Thing*	B
Hoyer, Katja. ★*Beyond the Wall*	943.087
Hubbard, Shanita. ★*Ride-Or-Die*	305.48
Hudes, Quiara Alegría. ★*My Broken Language*	B
Iverson, Peter. *Dine*	979.1004
Jackson, Jenn M. ★*Black Women Taught Us*	305.48
Jacob, Mira. *Good Talk*	741.5
Jamison, Leslie. ★*Make It Scream, Make It Burn*	814
Jefferson, Margo. *Negroland*	305.896
Jenkins, Jedidiah. *To Shake the Sleeping Self*	B
Jerkins, Morgan. *Wandering in Strange Lands*	305.896
Jones, Chloe Cooper. ★*Easy Beauty*	B
Jones, Saeed. *How We Fight for Our Lives*	B
Joseph, Peniel E. *The Sword and the Shield*	B
Kandel, Eric R. ★*The Disordered Mind*	616.89
Keinan, Tal. *God Is in the Crowd*	305.892
Kenan, Randall. *Black Folk Could Fly*	813
Kendi, Ibram X. ★*How to Be an Antiracist*	305.8
Khakpour, Porochista. *Brown Album*	304.8
Khan, Yasmin. *Ripe Figs*	641.595
Kingsley, Lisa. *Smithsonian American Table*	641.5
Klein, Ezra. ★*Why We're Polarized*	306.0973
Klein, Jessi. *I'll Show Myself Out*	B
Kneeland, Jessi. *Body Neutral*	306.4
Kohli, Sahaj Kaur. ★*But What Will People Say?*	616.89
Krug, Nora. ★*Belonging*	741.5
LaPointe, Sasha taqwseblu. *Red Paint*	B
Lavery, Daniel M. *Something That May Shock and Discredit You*	814
Lawson, Jenny. *Furiously Happy*	B
Lawton, Georgina. *Raceless*	B
Le Guin, Ursula K. *So Far so Good*	811
Lee, Julia Sun-Joo. *Biting the Hand*	B
Leland, Andrew. ★*The Country of the Blind*	B
Lemay, Mimi. *What We Will Become*	306.874
Levy, Deborah. ★*Real Estate*	B
Li, Zhuqing. *Daughters of the Flower Fragrant Garden*	951.04
Limon, Ada. *Bright Dead Things*	811
Liu, Simu. ★*We Were Dreamers*	B
Lockwood, Patricia. *Priestdaddy*	B
Lowery, Brian S. *Selfless*	155.2
Lozada, Carlos. *The Washington Book*	320
Mahjoub, Jamal. *A Line in the River*	962.404
Manly, Carla Marie. *Aging Joyfully*	305.26
Mans, Jasmine. *Black Girl, Call Home*	811
Mariani, Mike. *What Doesn't Kill Us Makes Us*	155.9
Marshall, Greg. *Leg*	B
Marshall, Nate. *Finna*	811
Marx, W. David. ★*Status and Culture*	305
Maupin, Armistead. *Logical Family*	B
Mays, Kyle. ★*An Afro-Indigenous History of the United States*	973
McLaren, Brian D. *Do I Stay Christian?*	270.8
Mehra, Nishta. *Brown, White, Black*	305.800973
Merritt, Tyler. *I Take My Coffee Black*	791.4302
Miller, Adrienne. *In the Land of Men*	070.5
Miller, Kei. *Things I Have Withheld*	814
Miller, Michelle. *Belonging*	B
Moghul, Haroon. *How to Be a Muslim*	B
Morrison, Toni. ★*The Origin of Others*	809
Morrison, Toni. ★*The Source of Self-Regard*	814
Mouton, Deborah D. E. E. P. *Black Chameleon*	B
Myers, Leah. *Thinning Blood*	B
Nawaz, Zarqa. *Laughing All the Way to the Mosque*	791.45028
Nayeri, Dina. ★*The Ungrateful Refugee*	362.87
Ng, Fae Myenne. *Orphan Bachelors*	B
Nguyen, Viet Thanh. *Nothing Ever Dies*	959.704
Norris, Michele. ★*Our Hidden Conversations*	305
Nutt, Amy Ellis. *Becoming Nicole*	920
O'Donnell, Svenja. *Inge's War*	943.086
O'Gieblyn, Meghan. *God, Human, Animal, Machine*	814
Oelhafen, Ingrid von. *Hitler's Stolen Children*	B
Olivares, Efren C. *My Boy Will Die of Sorrow*	305.9
Olivarez, Jose. *Promises of Gold = Promesas De Oro*	811
Oluo, Ijeoma. *Mediocre*	305.310973
Osnos, Evan. *Wildland*	973.93
Owusu, Nadia. *Aftershocks*	B
Packer, George. *Last Best Hope*	973.93
Pardlo, Gregory. *Spectral Evidence*	811
Parks, Casey. *Diary of a Misfit*	B
Payne, Les. ★*The Dead Are Arising*	B
Perkins, Kendrick. *The Education of Kendrick Perkins*	B
Petrosino, Kiki. *White Blood*	811
Pham, Larissa. *Pop Song*	709.2
Pinn, Anthony B. *The Black Practice of Disbelief*	211
Pipher, Mary Bray. *Women Rowing North*	305.26
Prose, Francine. *1974*	B
Questlove. *Music Is History*	782.42164
Quinn, Tallu Schuyler. *What We Wish Were True*	B
Ramos, Jorge. *Stranger*	325.73
Rankine, Claudia. ★*Just Us*	305.896
Ratajkowski, Emily. ★*My Body*	B
Reang, Putsata. *Ma and Me*	B
Ritvo, Max. *The Final Voicemails*	811
Rogers, Susan E. ★*This Is What It Sounds Like*	781.1
Row, Jess. *White Flights*	813
Russert, Luke. *Look for Me There*	B
Sabatini Sloan, Aisha. *Dreaming of Ramadi in Detroit*	814
Salama, Jordan. ★*Stranger in the Desert*	982
Sale, Anna. ★*Let's Talk About Hard Things*	153.6
Samaha, Albert. *Never Ran, Never Will*	920
Samatar, Sofia. *The White Mosque*	B

PUBLIC LIBRARY CORE COLLECTION: NONFICTION
Twentieth Edition

Sanders, Chad. *Black Magic*	305.896
Santos Perez, Craig. *From Unincorporated Territory [amot]*	811
Savage, Jodi M. *The Death of a Jaybird*	B
Schama, Simon. *The Embarrassment of Riches*	949.2
Scheier, Liz. *Never Simple*	B
Schneider, Amy. *In the Form of a Question*	B
Seidule, Ty. *Robert E. Lee and Me*	973.7
Shadid, Anthony. *House of Stone*	306.0956
Shanahan, Charif. *Trace Evidence*	811
Shapiro, Ari. ★ *The Best Strangers in the World*	B
Shapiro, Dani. ★ *Inheritance*	B
Shapland, Jenn. ★ *Thin Skin*	814
Sharif, Solmaz. *Customs*	811
Sharlet, Jeff. ★ *The Undertow*	322
Sharpe, Christina Elizabeth. *Ordinary Notes*	305.896
Shaw, Julia. *Bi*	306.76
Shields, Aomawa L. *Life on Other Planets*	B
Shih, David. *Chinese Prodigal*	B
Shockley, Evie. *Suddenly We*	811
Simmons, Ruth. ★ *Up Home*	B
Sinclair, Safiya. ★ *How to Say Babylon*	B
Smith, Clint. ★ *Above Ground*	811
Smith, Danez. ★ *Don't Call Us Dead*	811.6
Smith, Mychal Denzel. *Invisible Man, Got the Whole World Watching*	305.242
Smith, Mychal Denzel. *Stakes Is High*	973.933
Smith, Patricia. *Unshuttered*	811
So, Anthony Veasna. ★ *Songs on Endless Repeat*	814
Solomon, Andrew. *Far from the Tree*	362.4083
Specter, Emma. *More, Please*	616.85
Spencer, Kyle. *Raising Them Right*	320.5
Standefer, Katherine E. *Lightning Flowers*	B
Storr, Will. *Selfie*	155.2
Strings, Sabrina. *The End of Love*	155.3
Suarez, Ray. ★ *We Are Home*	325.73
Sullivan, Randall. *Graveyard of the Pacific*	979.7
Talusan, Meredith. *Fairest*	305.30973
Tanais. *In Sensorium*	B
Tatum, Beverly Daniel. ★ *"Why Are All the Black Kids Sitting Together in the Cafeteria?"*	305.800973
Taussig, Rebekah. *Sitting Pretty*	B
Tesfamariam, Rahiel. *Imagine Freedom*	305.896
Thomas, R. Eric. ★ *Congratulations, the Best Is Over!*	B
Thomas, R. Eric. *Here for It*	B
Thompson, Tracy. *The New Mind of the South*	305.800975
Thompson-Hernandez, Walter. *The Compton Cowboys*	920
Tibble, Tayi. *Poukahangatus*	821
Tobia, Jacob. *Sissy*	305.30973
Tolentino, Jia. ★ *Trick Mirror*	973.93
Tometich, Annabelle. *The Mango Tree*	B
Tran, Ly. *House of Sticks*	B
Treuer, David. ★ *The Heartbeat of Wounded Knee*	970.004
Tuama, Padraig O. ★ *Poetry Unbound*	808.1
Van Bavel, Jay J. *The Power of Us*	155.2
Van Ness, Jonathan. *Love That Story*	791.4502
Von Bremzen, Anya. *National Dish*	641.3
Von Furstenberg, Diane. *The Woman I Wanted to Be*	B
Wagner, Alex. *Futureface*	B
Wainaina, Binyavanga. ★ *How to Write About Africa*	814
Walsh, Declan. *The Nine Lives of Pakistan*	954.91
Washington, Kerry. *Thicker Than Water*	B
Watts, Reggie. *Great Falls, MT*	B
Weiner, Eric. *Ben & Me*	B
Wilderson, Frank B. *Afropessimism*	B
Williams, Bari A. *Seen yet Unseen*	338.4
Williams, Terry Tempest. *Erosion*	814
Willis, Raquel. *The Risk It Takes to Bloom*	B
Wizenberg, Molly. *Fixed Stars*	B
Wolf, Brandon J. *A Place for Us*	B
Wong, Carmen Rita. *Why Didn't You Tell Me?*	B
Wong, Jane. ★ *Meet Me Tonight in Atlantic City*	B
Wu, Constance. *Making a Scene*	B
Wu, Simon. *Dancing on My Own*	700.1
XIe, Jenny. *Eye Level*	811
Yong, Sable. *Die Hot with a Vengeance*	646.7
Yoshino, Kenji. *Say the Right Thing*	305.3
Young, Damon. ★ *What Doesn't Kill You Makes You Blacker*	B
Young, R. J. *Requiem for the Massacre*	305.8
Ypi, Lea. ★ *Free*	B
Zara, Christopher. *Uneducated*	B
Zauner, Michelle. ★ *Crying in H Mart*	B

IDENTITY THEFT
Betz-Hamilton, Axton. *The Less People Know About Us*	364.16

IDEOLOGY
Benner, Erica. *Be Like the Fox*	B
Biskupic, Joan. ★ *Nine Black Robes*	347.73
Bogus, Carl T. *Buckley*	B
Branigan, Tania. *Red Memory*	951.05
Broadwater, Jeff. *James Madison*	B
Brown, Archie. ★ *The Rise and Fall of Communism*	320.53
Conradi, Peter J. *Who Lost Russia?*	947.086
Du Mez, Kristin Kobes. *Jesus and John Wayne*	277.308
Eisner, Peter. *The Pope's Last Crusade*	282.092
Figes, Orlando. ★ *The Story of Russia*	947
Fritzsche, Peter. *Life and Death in the Third Reich*	943.086
Hunt, Tristram. *Marx's General*	335.4092
Klein, Naomi. ★ *Doppelganger*	302.2
Lovell, Julia. *Maoism*	335.43
Menand, Louis. *The Free World*	306.0973
Neiwert, David A. ★ *The Age of Insurrection*	303.48
Perlstein, Rick. *The Invisible Bridge*	973.924
Picower, Bree. *Reading, Writing, and Racism*	371.829
Piketty, Thomas. ★ *Capital and Ideology*	305
Pryor, Elizabeth Brown. *Six Encounters with Lincoln*	973.7092
Reynolds, David S. ★ *Abe*	B
Ricks, Thomas E. *Churchill and Orwell*	920
Ryan, Alan. *On Politics*	320.01
Shahvisi, Arianne. *Arguing for a Better World*	170
Smith, Mychal Denzel. *Stakes Is High*	973.933

IDIOMS
Ammer, Christine. *The American Heritage Dictionary of Idioms*	423

Idiot Brain. Burnett, Dean   612.8

IDITAROD TRAIL SLED DOG RACE, ALASKA
Pace, Kristin Knight. *This Much Country*	B
Paulsen, Gary. *Winterdance*	B

If I Understood You, Would I Have This Look on My Face?. Alda, Alan   153.6
If I Were Another. Darwish, Mamoud   892.7
If It Sounds Like a Quack. Hongoltz-Hetling, Matthew   615.8
If Not, Winter. Sappho   884
If Our Bodies Could Talk. Hamblin, James   613
If The Oceans Were Ink. Power, Carla   B
If They Come for Us. Asghar, Fatimah   811
If We Break. Buhle, Kathleen   B
★*If You See Them.* Sokolik, Vicki   362.5
If You Would Have Told Me. Stamos, John   B
★*If You're Bored with Your Camera Read This Book.* Fordham, Demetrius   770.23
If Your Adolescent Has ADHD. Power, Thomas J.   616.85

Iftin, Abdi Nor
Call Me American	305.893

IFTIN, ABDI NOR
Iftin, Abdi Nor. *Call Me American*	305.893

IGBO (AFRICAN PEOPLE)
Adichie, Chimamanda Ngozi. *Notes on Grief*	155.9

Iggulden, Conn
The Double Dangerous Book for Boys	031.02

Ignatieff, Michael
On Consolation	152.4

IGNATIUS, OF LOYOLA, SAINT, 1491-1556
Martin, James. *The Jesuit Guide to (Almost) Everything*	248.4

IGNORANCE
Fleming, Crystal Marie. *How to Be Less Stupid About Race*	305.800973

Ignotofsky, Rachel
Women in Science	920

Igort
The Ukrainian and Russian Notebooks	741.5

Iguodala, Andre
The Sixth Man	B

IGUODALA, ANDRE, 1984–
Iguodala, Andre. *The Sixth Man*	B

The Ikaria Way. Kochilas, Diane   641.5
Ike's Bluff. Thomas, Evan   973.921092

Ikpi, Bassey
I'm Telling the Truth, but I'm Lying	814

IKPI, BASSEY
Ikpi, Bassey. *I'm Telling the Truth, but I'm Lying*	814

AUTHOR, TITLE, SERIES AND SUBJECT INDEX

The *Iliad*. Homer	883
The *Iliad*. Homer	883
Iliad. Homer	883
★The *Iliad*. Homer	883

ILLEGAL HAZARDOUS WASTE DISPOSAL
Bilott, Robert. *Exposure*	344.04
Fagin, Dan. *Toms River*	363.7209749

ILLEGITIMACY
Gucci, Patricia. *In the Name of Gucci*	B
Hewitt, Catherine. *Renoir's Dancer*	B

ILLEGITIMATE CHILDREN OF ROYALTY
Hawksley, Lucinda. *Queen Victoria's Mysterious Daughter*	B

ILLINOIS
Beam, Alex. *American Crucifixion*	B
Biggers, Jeff. *Reckoning at Eagle Creek*	333.73
Craughwell, Thomas J. *Stealing Lincoln's Body*	973.7092
Dyja, Tom. *The Third Coast*	977.311
Guelzo, Allen C. *Lincoln and Douglas*	973.6
Lincoln, Abraham. *Speeches and Writings, 1832-1858*	973.5
Moore, Kate. ★*The Woman They Could Not Silence*	B
Nelson, David B. *Boys Enter the House*	364.152
Obama, Barack. ★*Dreams from My Father*	B
Sandburg, Carl. *Abraham Lincoln*	B
Trice, Dawn Turner. ★*Three Girls from Bronzeville*	977.311

ILLITERATE WOMEN
Painter, Nell Irvin. ★*Sojourner Truth*	B
The *Illuminated* Kaddish. Bolsta, Hyla Shifra	296.4

ILLUMINATION OF BOOKS AND MANUSCRIPTS
King, Ross. *Bookseller of Florence*	381

ILLUMINATION OF BOOKS AND MANUSCRIPTS, MEDIEVAL
De Hamel, Christopher. *The Manuscripts Club*	091
The *Illuminations*. Rimbaud, Arthur	841
The *Illustrated* Bead Bible. Geary, Theresa Flores	745.594
Illustrated Black History. McCalman, George	920

ILLUSTRATED BOOKS
Baker, Nicholson. *Finding a Likeness*	B
Gosden, Chris. *Magic*	133.4
Hall, Jake. *The Art of Drag*	792.8
Holmes, Elizabeth. *HRH*	941.085
Ignotofsky, Rachel. *Women in Science*	920
Launius, Roger D. *The Smithsonian History of Space Exploration*	629.4
Macfarlane, Robert. *The Lost Spells*	811
McIlwaine, Catherine. *Tolkien*	002.09
Mead, Corey. *The Hidden History of the White House*	975.3
Parton, Dolly. ★*Dolly Parton, Songteller*	B
Quinn, Bridget. *She Votes*	324.6
Redniss, Lauren. ★*Oak Flat*	970.5
Reser, Anna. *Forces of Nature*	509.2
Schmidt, Thomas. *The Saga of Lewis & Clark*	917.804
Shahidi, Afshin. *Prince*	B
Tan, Amy. ★*The Backyard Bird Chronicles*	598
Willis, Deborah. ★*The Black Civil War Soldier*	973.7

ILLUSTRATED CHILDREN'S BOOKS
Bang, Molly. ★*Picture This*	741.6
Marcus, Leonard S. ★*Pictured Worlds*	741.6
An *Illustrated* History of 151 Video Games. Parkin, Simon	794.8

ILLUSTRATION OF BOOKS
Bang, Molly. ★*Picture This*	741.6
Marcus, Leonard S. ★*Pictured Worlds*	741.6

ILLUSTRATORS
Cross, William R. *Winslow Homer*	759.13
De Hamel, Christopher. *The Manuscripts Club*	091
Jones, Brian Jay. ★*Becoming Dr. Seuss*	B
Lear, Linda J. *Beatrix Potter*	B
Rees, Darrel. *How to Be an Illustrator*	741.6
Schumacher, Michael. *Will Eisner*	741.5
Solomon, Deborah. *American Mirror*	B

IMAGE
Bordo, Susan. *The Creation of Anne Boleyn*	942.05
Hu, Elise. *Flawless*	646.7

IMAGE PROCESSING
Ang, Tom. *Digital Photography Masterclass*	770
Freeman, Michael. *The Photographer's Mind*	770

IMAGERY (PSYCHOLOGY)
Bly, Robert. *Collected Poems*	811

IMAGINARY CREATURES
Dickey, Colin. *The Unidentified*	130

IMAGINARY PLACES
Manguel, Alberto. *The Dictionary of Imaginary Places*	809
★*Imagination*. Benjamin, Ruha	302

IMAGINATION
Benjamin, Ruha. ★*Imagination*	302
Cott, Jonathan. *There's a Mystery There*	813
Damrosch, David. *Around the World in 80 Books*	809
Gopnik, Adam. *All That Happiness Is*	158.1
Griffin, Susan. *Out of Silence, Sound. Out of Nothing, Something*	808.02
Harjo, Joy. *Crazy Brave*	B
Laing, Olivia. *The Garden Against Time*	635
Suddendorf, Thomas. *The Gap*	156
Imagination in Place. Berry, Wendell	814
Imagine A City. Vanhoenacker, Mark	629.13
★*Imagine* Freedom. Tesfamariam, Rahiel	305.896

Imani, Blair
Read This to Get Smarter	303.3
★*Imbeciles*. Cohen, Adam	344.7304

Imbler, Sabrina
How Far the Light Reaches	591.77

IMBLER, SABRINA
Imbler, Sabrina. *How Far the Light Reaches*	591.77
★An *Immense* World. Yong, Ed	591.5

Immerwahr, Daniel
How to Hide an Empire	973

IMMIGRANT FAMILIES
Asher, Zain E. *Where the Children Take Us*	942.1
Bui, Thi. ★*The Best We Could Do*	741.5
Chaudry, Rabia. *Fatty Fatty Boom Boom*	B
Cho, Grace M. *Tastes Like War*	305.48
Cornejo Villavicencio, Karla. ★*The Undocumented Americans*	920
Fishman, Boris. *Savage Feast*	B
Hernandez Castillo, Marcelo. *Children of the Land*	B
Lakshmi, Padma. *Love, Loss, and What We Ate*	791.4502
Li, Fei-Fei. *The Worlds I See*	B
Nathan, Joan. ★*My Life in Recipes*	641.5
Nayeri, Dina. ★*The Ungrateful Refugee*	362.87
Ronstadt, Linda. *Feels Like Home*	B
Samaha, Albert. *Concepcion*	929
Tran, Ly. *House of Sticks*	B
Zamora, Javier. ★*Solito*	B

IMMIGRANT WORKERS
Chang, Gordon H. *Ghosts of Gold Mountain*	331.6
DeParle, Jason. ★*A Good Provider Is One Who Leaves*	305.899
Genoways, Ted. *The Chain*	338.7

IMMIGRANTS
Abdelmahmoud, Elamin. *Son of Elsewhere*	B
Ali, Wajahat. *Go Back to Where You Came From*	B
Allende, Isabel. *My Invented Country*	B
Anbinder, Tyler. ★*City of Dreams*	974.7
Armas, Kat. *Abuelita Faith*	248.8
Bair, Deirdre. *Saul Steinberg*	B
Barot, Rick. *The Galleons*	811
Bass, Amy. *One Goal*	796.334
Berlin, Ira. *The Making of African America*	973
Blanco, Richard. *The Prince of Los Cocuyos*	B
Blitzer, Jonathan. *Everyone Who Is Gone Is Here*	305.9
Bobrow-Strain, Aaron. *The Death and Life of Aida Hernandez*	972
Chin, Ava. ★*Mott Street*	974.7
Chude-Sokei, Louis Onuorah. *Floating in a Most Peculiar Way*	979.4
Cohen-Solal, Annie. *Mark Rothko*	759.13
Cornejo Villavicencio, Karla. ★*The Undocumented Americans*	920
Corral, Eduardo C. *Guillotine*	811.6
Cullen, Art. *Storm Lake*	071.7
DeParle, Jason. ★*A Good Provider Is One Who Leaves*	305.899
Dudley, Steven S. *MS-13*	364.106
Eire, Carlos M. N. *Learning to Die in Miami*	B
Enninful, Edward. *A Visible Man*	B
Espada, Martin. ★*Floaters*	811
Eteraz, Ali. *Children of Dust*	B
Ferguson, Niall. *Kissinger*	973.924
Gatrell, Peter. *The Unsettling of Europe*	304.8
Geter, Hafizah. *Un-American*	811
Gibran, Kahlil. *And the Prophet Said*	811
Gibran, Kahlil. ★*The Prophet*	811
Gonzalez, Karen. *Beyond Welcome*	261.8
Grande, Reyna. ★*The Distance Between Us*	973
H, Lamya. ★*Hijab Butch Blues*	B

PUBLIC LIBRARY CORE COLLECTION: NONFICTION
Twentieth Edition

Hahn, Emanuel. *Koreatown Dreaming*	979.4
Hakkakiyan, Ruya. *A Beginner's Guide to America*	646.7
Harris, Mark. *Mike Nichols*	B
Hemon, Aleksandar. *My Parents*	814
Herrera, Juan Felipe. *Every Day We Get More Illegal*	811
Hinojosa, Maria. *Once I Was You*	B
Hitchens, Christopher. *Hitch-22*	920
Holzer, Harold. *Brought Forth on This Continent*	973.7
Iftin, Abdi Nor. *Call Me American*	305.893
Ikpi, Bassey. *I'm Telling the Truth, but I'm Lying*	814
Jaku, Eddie. ★*The Happiest Man on Earth*	B
James, Jamie. *The Glamour of Strangeness*	700.1
Johnson, Steven. *The Infernal Machine*	335
Jordan, Mary. *The Art of Her Deal*	B
Kariko, Katalin. *Breaking Through*	B
Kavanagh, Julie. *Nureyev*	B
Khakpour, Porochista. *Brown Album*	304.8
Krug, Nora. ★*Belonging*	741.5
Lakshmi, Padma. *Love, Loss, and What We Ate*	791.4502
Laskin, David. *The Children's Blizzard*	977
Lawler, Andrew. *The Secret Token*	975.6
Lee, Erika. *The Making of Asian America*	973
Lehr, Dick. *White Hot Hate*	363.325
Levy, Deborah. ★*Things I Don't Want to Know*	B
Lichtblau, Eric. *Return to the Reich*	B
Markham, Lauren. ★*The Far Away Brothers*	920
Minian, Ana Raquel. ★*In the Shadow of Liberty*	365
Morrison, Toni. ★*The Source of Self-Regard*	814
Nafisi, Azar. *Things I've Been Silent About*	B
Nayeri, Dina. ★*The Ungrateful Refugee*	362.87
Nguyen, Viet Thanh. ★*A Man of Two Faces*	B
Oliva, Alejandra. *Rivermouth*	305.9
Olivares, Efren C. *My Boy Will Die of Sorrow*	305.9
Perlin, Ross. ★*Language City*	306.44
Pipher, Mary Bray. *The Middle of Everywhere*	305.9
Ramos, Jorge. *Stranger*	325.73
Randall, David K. *Black Death at the Golden Gate*	616.9
Rehman, Sabeeha. *Threading My Prayer Rug*	305.8
Salama, Jordan. ★*Stranger in the Desert*	982
Sanchez, Erika L. *Lessons on Expulsion*	811
Santopietro, Tom. *The Sound of Music Story*	791.43
Scenters-Zapico, Natalie. *Lima*	811
Schulman, Daniel. *The Money Kings*	332.0973
Schwartz, David N. *The Last Man Who Knew Everything*	B
Seierstad, Asne. *Two Sisters*	956.9104
Shadid, Anthony. *House of Stone*	306.0956
Shahani, Aarti Namdev. *Here We Are*	B
Shankar, Shalini. *Beeline*	155.4
Soboroff, Jacob. ★*Separated*	325.73
Stanton, Mike. ★*Unbeaten*	B
Suarez, Ray. ★*We Are Home*	325.73
Tobar, Hector. ★*Our Migrant Souls*	305.868
Vargas, Jose Antonio. *Dear America*	B
Vasquez, Karla Tatiana. ★*The Salvisoul Cookbook*	641.598
Velshi, Ali. *Small Acts of Courage*	B
Wang, Qian Julie. ★*Beautiful Country*	B
Wides-Munoz, Laura. *The Making of a Dream*	920
Wiedeman, Reeves. *Billion Dollar Loser*	333.33
Wright, Jennifer Ashley. ★*Madame Restell*	B
Yang, Jia Lynn. ★*One Mighty and Irresistible Tide*	325.73

IMMIGRANTS' RIGHTS
Canellos, Peter S. *The Great Dissenter*	B

IMMIGRANTS, ARAB
Lalami, Laila. *Conditional Citizens*	323.60973

IMMIGRANTS, CHINESE
Chang, Gordon H. *Ghosts of Gold Mountain*	331.6
Liu, Simu. ★*We Were Dreamers*	B

IMMIGRANTS, GERMAN
Russell, Jan Jarboe. *The Train to Crystal City*	940.53

IMMIGRANTS, INDIAN
Shahani, Aarti Namdev. *Here We Are*	B

IMMIGRANTS, IRISH
Kelly, John. *The Graves Are Walking*	941.5081
McCourt, Frank. *'Tis*	B
McCourt, Malachy. *A Monk Swimming*	B
McCourt, Malachy. *Singing My Him Song*	B
McKeon, Kathy. *Jackie's Girl*	B

IMMIGRANTS, ITALIAN
Krist, Gary. *Empire of Sin*	976.3
Russell, Jan Jarboe. *The Train to Crystal City*	940.53

IMMIGRANTS, JAPANESE
Russell, Jan Jarboe. *The Train to Crystal City*	940.53

IMMIGRANTS, JEWISH
Fishman, Boris. *Savage Feast*	B
Foer, Esther Safran. *I Want You to Know We're Still Here*	B
Weisman, Steven R. *The Chosen Wars*	296.0973

IMMIGRANTS, KOREAN
Hahn, Emanuel. *Koreatown Dreaming*	979.4

IMMIGRANTS, MEXICAN
Alvarez, Noe. *Spirit Run*	796.42
Arce, Julissa. *You Sound Like a White Girl*	303.48
Bobrow-Strain, Aaron. *The Death and Life of Aida Hernandez*	972

IMMIGRANTS, PUERTO-RICAN
Voloj, Julian. *Ghetto Brother*	741.5

IMMIGRANTS, RUSSIAN
Shteyngart, Gary. ★*Little Failure*	B
Sullivan, Rosemary. *Stalin's Daughter*	B

IMMIGRANTS, VIETNAMESE
Bui, Thi. ★*The Best We Could Do*	741.5
Tran, Ly. *House of Sticks*	B
Tran, Phuc. ★*Sigh, Gone*	B

IMMIGRATION AND EMIGRATION
Anbinder, Tyler. ★*City of Dreams*	974.7
Baer, Daniel Brooks. *The Four Tests*	320.973
Berlin, Ira. *The Making of African America*	973
Blitzer, Jonathan. *Everyone Who Is Gone Is Here*	305.9
Bobrow-Strain, Aaron. *The Death and Life of Aida Hernandez*	972
Bui, Thi. ★*The Best We Could Do*	741.5
Cannato, Vincent. *American Passage*	325.73
Cantu, Francisco. *The Line Becomes a River*	B
Chang, Gordon H. *Ghosts of Gold Mountain*	331.6
Chin, Ava. ★*Mott Street*	974.7
Chow, Kat. *Seeing Ghosts*	B
Choy, Catherine Ceniza. ★*Asian American Histories of the United States*	973
Cornejo Villavicencio, Karla. ★*The Undocumented Americans*	920
Coyle, Marcia. *The Roberts Court*	347.73
Danticat, Edwidge. ★*Brother, I'm Dying*	B
De Leon, Jason. ★*Soldiers and Kings*	364.1
DeParle, Jason. ★*A Good Provider Is One Who Leaves*	305.899
Ditmore, Melissa Hope. *Unbroken Chains*	306.74
Eteraz, Ali. *Children of Dust*	B
Fagan, Brian M. *Climate Chaos*	304.2
Fishman, Elly. *Refugee High*	370.8
Fleming, Melissa. *A Hope More Powerful Than the Sea*	956.9104
Gatrell, Peter. *The Unsettling of Europe*	304.8
Gomez, Laura E. ★*Inventing Latinos*	305.868
Gonzalez, Karen. *Beyond Welcome*	261.8
Grande, Reyna. ★*The Distance Between Us*	973
Guerrero, Jean. *Hatemonger*	B
Hakkakiyan, Ruya. *A Beginner's Guide to America*	646.7
Hamilton, Lisa M. *The Hungry Season*	B
Hernandez Castillo, Marcelo. *Children of the Land*	B
Hing, Bill Ong. ★*Humanizing Immigration*	342.7308
Hinojosa, Maria. *Once I Was You*	B
Holzer, Harold. *Brought Forth on This Continent*	973.7
Hulls, Tessa. ★*Feeding Ghosts*	741.5
Iftin, Abdi Nor. *Call Me American*	305.893
Ishikawa, Masaji. ★*A River in Darkness*	B
Jerkins, Morgan. *Wandering in Strange Lands*	305.896
Kassabova, Kapka. *Border*	949.9
Kelly, John. *The Graves Are Walking*	941.5081
Khan, Yasmin. *Ripe Figs*	641.595
Krause, Johannes. *A Short History of Humanity*	599.9
Kushner, Jacob. *Look Away*	305.9
Lalami, Laila. *Conditional Citizens*	323.60973
Lee, Erika. *America for Americans*	305.800973
Lee, Erika. *The Making of Asian America*	973
Lekas Miller, Anna. *Love Across Borders*	323.6
Lovato, Roberto. *Unforgetting*	B
Luiselli, Valeria. *Tell Me How It Ends*	305.23086
Malhotra, Aanchal. *Remnants of Partition*	954.04
Martinez, Rick. ★*Mi Cocina*	641.5972
McCormick, Ty. *Beyond the Sand and Sea*	920
McCourt, Frank. *'Tis*	B
Mehra, Nishta. *Brown, White, Black*	305.800973

AUTHOR, TITLE, SERIES AND SUBJECT INDEX

Minian, Ana Raquel. ★*In the Shadow of Liberty*	365
Molnar, Petra. *The Walls Have Eyes*	363.28
Morris, Ian. *Geography Is Destiny*	941
Nasaw, David. *The Last Million*	940.53
Nayeri, Dina. ★*The Ungrateful Refugee*	362.87
Ng, Fae Myenne. *Orphan Bachelors*	B
Okporo, Edafe. *Asylum*	B
Oliva, Alejandra. *Rivermouth*	305.9
Olivares, Efren C. *My Boy Will Die of Sorrow*	305.9
Pablo Cruz, Rosayra. *The Book of Rosy*	B
Passarlay, Gulwali. *The Lightless Sky*	B
Pham, Andrew X. ★*The Eaves of Heaven*	B
Pipher, Mary Bray. *The Middle of Everywhere*	305.9
Ramos, Jorge. *Stranger*	325.73
Rashke, Richard. *Useful Enemies*	341.69
Rekdal, Paisley. *West*	811
Saldana, Stephanie. *What We Remember Will Be Saved*	362.7
Samaha, Albert. *Concepcion*	929
Sciubba, Jennifer Dabbs. *8 Billion and Counting*	304.6
Sen, Mayukh. *Taste Makers*	641.5092
Setareh, Saghar. *Pomegranates & Artichokes*	641.5
Siler, Julia Flynn. *The White Devil's Daughters*	306.3
Soboroff, Jacob. ★*Separated*	325.73
Suarez, Ray. ★*We Are Home*	325.73
Trentmann, Frank. *Out of the Darkness*	943.08
Umar, Ousman. *North to Paradise*	B
Urrea, Luis Alberto. *The Devil's Highway*	304.8
Vargas, Jose Antonio. *Dear America*	B
Vince, Gaia. *Nomad Century*	362.87
White, Ralph. *Getting Out of Saigon*	959.704
Wides-Munoz, Laura. *The Making of a Dream*	920
Wilkerson, Isabel. ★*The Warmth of Other Suns*	304.80973
Yang, Jia Lynn. ★*One Mighty and Irresistible Tide*	325.73
Ypi, Lea. ★*Free*	B
Zamora, Javier. ★*Solito*	B
Zia, Helen. *Last Boat Out of Shanghai*	951.04
IMMIGRATION AND EMIGRATION LAW	
Blitzer, Jonathan. *Everyone Who Is Gone Is Here*	305.9
Goudeau, Jessica. ★*After the Last Border*	362.83
Guerrero, Jean. *Hatemonger*	B
Hing, Bill Ong. ★*Humanizing Immigration*	342.7308
Markham, Lauren. ★*The Far Away Brothers*	920
McCormick, Ty. *Beyond the Sand and Sea*	920
Okporo, Edafe. *Asylum*	B
Okrent, Daniel. *The Guarded Gate*	344.73
Rekdal, Paisley. *West*	811
Yang, Jia Lynn. ★*One Mighty and Irresistible Tide*	325.73
IMMIGRATION AND EMIGRATION LAW REFORM	
Yang, Jia Lynn. ★*One Mighty and Irresistible Tide*	325.73
IMMIGRATION ENFORCEMENT	
Yang, Jia Lynn. ★*One Mighty and Irresistible Tide*	325.73
IMMIGRATION POLICY	
Blitzer, Jonathan. *Everyone Who Is Gone Is Here*	305.9
Bobrow-Strain, Aaron. *The Death and Life of Aida Hernandez*	972
Gatrell, Peter. *The Unsettling of Europe*	304.8
Goudeau, Jessica. ★*After the Last Border*	362.83
Guerrero, Jean. *Hatemonger*	B
Hernandez Castillo, Marcelo. *Children of the Land*	B
Hinojosa, Maria. *Once I Was You*	B
Iftin, Abdi Nor. *Call Me American*	305.893
Lee, Erika. *America for Americans*	305.800973
Markham, Lauren. ★*The Far Away Brothers*	920
Minian, Ana Raquel. ★*In the Shadow of Liberty*	365
Okporo, Edafe. *Asylum*	B
Okrent, Daniel. *The Guarded Gate*	344.73
Olivares, Efren C. *My Boy Will Die of Sorrow*	305.9
Ramos, Jorge. *Stranger*	325.73
Soboroff, Jacob. ★*Separated*	325.73
IMMIGRATION PRISONS	
Hinojosa, Maria. *Once I Was You*	B
Minian, Ana Raquel. ★*In the Shadow of Liberty*	365
★*The Immortal Irishman*. Egan, Timothy	B
★*The Immortal Life of Henrietta Lacks*. Skloot, Rebecca	B
Immune. Dettmer, Philipp	616.07
IMMUNE SYSTEM	
Dettmer, Philipp. *Immune*	616.07
MacPhail, Theresa. *Allergic*	616.97
Richtel, Matt. ★*An Elegant Defense*	616.07
IMMUNITY	
Christakis, Nicholas A. *Apollo's Arrow*	362.1962
Kinch, Michael S. *Between Hope and Fear*	614.4
IMMUNOLOGIC DISEASES	
Hagberg, Eva. *How to Be Loved*	616.7
Richtel, Matt. ★*An Elegant Defense*	616.07
IMMUNOLOGY	
Dettmer, Philipp. *Immune*	616.07
Kinch, Michael S. *Between Hope and Fear*	614.4
Richtel, Matt. ★*An Elegant Defense*	616.07
IMMUNOTHERAPY	
Bowler, Kate. *No Cure for Being Human*	B
Graeber, Charles. *The Breakthrough*	616.99
★*Impactful Community-Based Literacy Projects*. Farmer, Lesley S. J.	372.6
IMPARTIAL WRITING	
Allen, Jonathan. *Lucky*	324.973
Bade, Rachael. ★*Unchecked*	342.73
Baier, Bret. *To Rescue the Constitution*	973.4
Bamberger, Michael. *The Second Life of Tiger Woods*	B
Bardenwerper, William. *The Prisoner in His Palace*	956.7044
Barton, John. *A History of the Bible*	220.09
Batalion, Judith. *The Light of Days*	940.53
Bidwell, Duane R. *When One Religion Isn't Enough*	261.2
Bix, Herbert P. *Hirohito and the Making of Modern Japan*	B
Borman, Tracy. *Crown & Sceptre*	941
Brands, H. W. *The General vs. the President*	973.918092
Braudy, Leo. *Haunted*	398.45
Brower, Kate Andersen. *First in Line*	920
Brower, Kate Andersen. *First Women*	920
Burke, Kelsy. *The Pornography Wars*	306.77
Burns, William J. *The Back Channel*	B
Burrough, Bryan. *Forget the Alamo*	976.043
Cadava, Geraldo L. *The Hispanic Republican*	324.2734089
Chammah, Maurice. ★*Let the Lord Sort Them*	364.66
Chu, Lenora. *Little Soldiers*	370
Coe, Alexis. ★*You Never Forget Your First*	B
Conradi, Peter J. *Who Lost Russia?*	947.086
Cozzens, Peter. *The Earth Is Weeping*	978
Cross, Kim. *In Light of All Darkness*	363.25
Dallek, Robert. ★*Franklin D. Roosevelt*	B
Daugherty, Tracy. *Larry McMurtry*	B
De Stefano, Cristina. *The Child Is the Teacher*	B
Draper, Robert. *To Start a War*	956.7044
Ellis, Joseph J. *American Sphinx*	973.4
Engelhart, Katie. *The Inevitable*	179.7
Ferrer, Ada. ★*Cuba*	972.91
FitzGerald, Frances. *The Evangelicals*	277
Foster, Diana Greene. *The Turnaway Study*	362.1988
Frankopan, Peter. *The Earth Transformed*	304.2
Frederick, Jim. *Black Hearts*	956.7044
Fukuyama, Francis. *Liberalism and Its Discontents*	320.51
Gans, John. *White House Warriors*	355
Ghazvinian, John. *America and Iran*	327
Glockner, Andy. *Chasing Perfection*	796.323
Goldblatt, David. *The Games*	796.4809
Good, Cassandra A. *First Family*	920
Graff, Garrett M. ★*The Only Plane in the Sky*	973.931
Guelzo, Allen C. *Robert E. Lee*	B
Gwynne, S. C. *Empire of the Summer Moon*	B
Hajari, Nisid. *Midnight's Furies*	954.04
Hardacre, Helen. *Shinto*	299.5
Harrington, Anne. *Mind Fixers*	616.89
Harris, Mark. *Mike Nichols*	B
Hasen, Richard L. *Election Meltdown*	324.973
Hendershot, Heather. *Open to Debate*	B
Hendricks, Steve. *The Unquiet Grave*	323.1197
Herman, Arthur. ★*Douglas Macarthur*	B
Hermes, Will. *Lou Reed*	B
Hessler, Peter. *Other Rivers*	378.1
Horn, Jonathan. *Washington's End*	B
Inskeep, Steve. *Jacksonland*	973.56
Isaacson, Walter. ★*Elon Musk*	B
Kauffman, Jonathan. *Hippie Food*	394.1
Klagsbrun, Francine. *Lioness*	B
Korda, Michael. *With Wings Like Eagles*	940.54
Kranish, Michael. *Trump Revealed*	B
Launius, Roger D. *Apollo's Legacy*	629.45
Leonard, Christopher. *Kochland*	338.7

PUBLIC LIBRARY CORE COLLECTION: NONFICTION
Twentieth Edition

Loyn, David. *The Long War*	958.104
MacMillan, Margaret. *Paris 1919*	940.3
Marchant, Jo. *Cure*	616.89
Martin, Wednesday. *Primates of Park Avenue*	974.7
Marton, Kati. ★*The Chancellor*	B
McHangama, Jacob. ★*Free Speech*	323.44
McKay, Sinclair. *The Fire and the Darkness*	940.54
McWhirter, Cameron. *American Gun*	683.4
Meacham, Jon. ★*Destiny and Power*	B
Mechanic, Michael. *Jackpot*	305.5
Mekhennet, Souad. *I Was Told to Come Alone*	363.3250956
Minow, Martha. *When Should Law Forgive?*	345
Mitchell, George J. *A Path to Peace*	956.9405
Myers, Steven Lee. *The New Tsar*	
O'Brien, Keith. *Charlie Hustle*	796.357
O'Toole, Patricia. *The Moralist*	
Osnos, Evan. *Joe Biden*	B
Osnos, Evan. *Wildland*	973.93
Packer, George. *The Assassins' Gate*	956.7044
Page, Susan. ★*The Rulebreaker*	B
Postel, Charles. *Equality*	305.50973
Reitman, Janet. *Inside Scientology*	299
Rogan, Eugene L. *The Fall of the Ottomans*	940.3
Rohde, David. *In Deep*	973.933
Scheyder, Ernest. *The War Below*	333.7
Schwartz, Nelson. *The Velvet Rope Economy*	339.2
Scoles, Sarah. *They Are Already Here*	001.942
Sharma, Ruchir. *The Rise and Fall of Nations*	330.9
Simon, James F. *Eisenhower vs. Warren*	347.73
Smith, Erin Geiger. ★*Thank You for Voting*	324.973
Sokatch, Daniel. *Can We Talk About Israel?*	956.9405
Souder, William. *Mad at the World*	813
Spitz, Bob. ★*Reagan*	B
Stargardt, Nicholas. *The German War*	940.53
Sunstein, Cass R. *Impeachment*	342.73
Thompson, Jamie. *Standoff*	364.152
Tobin, James. *Ernie Pyle's War*	B
Turchin, Peter. *End Times*	320.01
Tye, Larry. ★*Demagogue*	B
Urofsky, Melvin I. *The Affirmative Action Puzzle*	331.13
Urrea, Luis Alberto. *The Devil's Highway*	304.8
Wallace, Chris. *Countdown 1945*	940.54
The Impeachers. Wineapple, Brenda	973.8
Impeachment. Sunstein, Cass R.	342.73
IMPEACHMENTS	
Bade, Rachael. ★*Unchecked*	342.73
Brokaw, Tom. *The Fall of Richard Nixon*	B
Graff, Garrett M. *Watergate*	973.924
Olsen, Lise. *Code of Silence*	347.73
Sullivan, Kevin. *Trump on Trial*	342.73
Sunstein, Cass R. *Impeachment*	342.73
Toobin, Jeffrey. *True Crimes and Misdemeanors*	973.933
Wineapple, Brenda. *The Impeachers*	973.8
Woodward, Bob. *Shadow*	973.92
Impelen, Helgrid van	
Big Knits Big Needles	746.43
Imperfect Union. Inskeep, Steve	B
IMPERFECTION	
Guthrie, Savannah. *Mostly What God Does*	248.4
Hass, Robert. *Summer Snow*	811.6
Rinaldi, Karen. *It's Great to Suck at Something*	158.1
Imperial Life in the Emerald City. Chandrasekaran, Rajiv	956.7044
Imperial Twilight. Platt, Stephen R.	951
IMPERIALISM	
Akins, Damon B. ★*We Are the Land*	978
Anderson, Fred. *The Dominion of War*	973
Ansary, Mir Tamim. *Games Without Rules*	958.1
Arendt, Hannah. *The Origins of Totalitarianism*	320.53
Barr, James. *A Line in the Sand*	956
Broers, Michael. *Napoleon*	944.05
Castillo, Elaine. ★*How to Read Now*	418
Elkins, Caroline. *Legacy of Violence*	909
Everitt, Anthony. *The Rise of Rome*	937
Fowler, Corinne. ★*The Countryside*	941
Hernandez, Kelly Lytle. ★*Bad Mexicans*	972
Immerwahr, Daniel. *How to Hide an Empire*	973
Judson, Pieter M. *The Habsburg Empire*	943.6
Kaplan, Robert D. *The Loom of Time*	327
Kinzer, Stephen. ★*The True Flag*	327.73
Kuper, Adam. *The Museum of Other People*	305.8
Lieven, Dominic. *In the Shadow of the Gods*	352.23
Mikanowski, Jacob. ★*Goodbye, Eastern Europe*	947
Morris, Ian. *Geography Is Destiny*	941
Plokhy, Serhii. *Lost Kingdom*	947
Sanghera, Sathnam. ★*Empireland*	941
Sanghera, Sathnam. *Empireworld*	909
Sides, Hampton. ★*The Wide Wide Sea*	910.92
Solnit, Rebecca. *Orwell's Roses*	B
Woolf, Greg. *Rome*	937
IMPERIALISM, AMERICAN	
Blackhawk, Ned. ★*The Rediscovery of America*	973.04
Craig, William. *Yankee Come Home*	972.9107
Kinzer, Stephen. ★*The True Flag*	327.73
McCullough, David G. *The Path Between the Seas*	972.87
Morris, Edmund. *Theodore Rex*	973.911
Tran, Paul. *All the Flowers Kneeling*	811
Zinn, Howard. ★*A People's History of the United States*	973
IMPERIALISM, BRITISH	
Dalrymple, William. *The Return of a King*	958.1
Lawrence, T. E. *Seven Pillars of Wisdom*	940.4
Millard, Candice. ★*Hero of the Empire*	968.04
Ngugi wa Thiong'o. *In the House of the Interpreter*	B
IMPERIALISM, FRENCH	
Logevall, Fredrik. *Embers of War*	959.704
Robb, Graham. *The Discovery of France*	944
IMPERIALISM, JAPANESE	
Bix, Herbert P. *Hirohito and the Making of Modern Japan*	B
Imperioli, Michael	
Woke up This Morning	791.45
IMPERSONATION	
Diamond, Cheryl. *Nowhere Girl*	B
Impey, Chris	
Einstein's Monsters	523.8
IMPLANTS, ARTIFICIAL	
Swartz, Mimi. *Ticker*	617.4
IMPORT EXPORT BUSINESS	
Knight, Philip H. *Shoe Dog*	B
Ujifusa, Steven. *Barons of the Sea*	387.5
★*The Importance of Being Earnest and Other Plays*. Wilde, Oscar	822
The Importance of Being Little. Christakis, Erika	372.21
IMPORTS	
Greenberg, Paul. *American Catch*	333.95
The Impossible City. Cheung, Karen	951.25
★*The Impossible First*. O'Brady, Colin	919.8904
Impossible Takes Longer. Gordis, Daniel	956.94
IMPOSTORS	
Diamond, Cheryl. *Nowhere Girl*	B
Simon, Marie. *Underground in Berlin*	B
Sisman, Adam. *The Professor and the Parson*	364.16
Willetts, Paul. *King Con*	B
Impresario. Maguire, James	
IMPRESARIOS	
McDonald, Greg (Producer). *Elvis and the Colonel*	920
Mordden, Ethan. *Ziegfeld*	B
IMPRESSIONISM (ART)	
Gerdts, William H. *American Impressionism*	759.13
Griffel, Lois. *Painting the Impressionist Landscape*	751.45
Kelder, Diane. *The Great Book of French Impressionism*	759.4
King, Ross. *The Judgment of Paris*	759.4
King, Ross. ★*Mad Enchantment*	759.4
Moyle, Franny. *Turner*	B
Naifeh, Steven W. *Van Gogh*	B
Roe, Sue. *The Private Lives of the Impressionists*	920
IMPRESSMENT	
Taylor, Alan. *The Civil War of 1812*	973.5
IMPRISONMENT	
Adayfi, Mansoor. *Don't Forget Us Here*	B
Alekhina, Mariija. *Riot Days*	B
Bardenwerper, William. *The Prisoner in His Palace*	956.7044
Bauer, Shane. *American Prison*	365
Bazelon, Emily. ★*Charged*	345.73
Bergner, Daniel. ★*Sing for Your Life*	B
Betts, Reginald Dwayne. *Felon*	811
Betts, Reginald Dwayne. ★*Redaction*	704.9
Fessler, Pam. *Carville's Cure*	362.19699
Gerard, Sarah. *Sunshine State*	814

AUTHOR, TITLE, SERIES AND SUBJECT INDEX

Gilliard, Dominique Dubois. *Rethinking Incarceration*	261.8
Hardin, Lara Love. ★*The Many Lives of Mama Love*	B
Ice-T. *Split Decision*	920
Jackson, Mitchell S. *Survival Math*	B
Lee, Heath Hardage. ★*The League of Wives*	959.704
Manuel, Ian. *My Time Will Come*	B
Minian, Ana Raquel. ★*In the Shadow of Liberty*	365
Norton, Jack. *The Jail Is Everywhere*	365
Peterson, Marlon. *Bird Uncaged*	B
Ralph, Laurence. *Sito*	364.152
Rapping, Jonathan. *Gideon's Promise*	345.73
Rezaian, Jason. *Prisoner*	B
Sebba, Anne. *Ethel Rosenberg*	B
Sered, Danielle. *Until We Reckon*	364.6
Shahani, Aarti Namdev. *Here We Are*	B
Tamimi, Ahed. ★*They Called Me a Lioness*	B
Trejo, Danny. *Trejo*	B
Weir, Alison. *The Lady in the Tower*	B
Improbable Destinies. Losos, Jonathan B.	576.8
The Improv Handbook for Modern Quilters. Wood, Sherri	746.46
★*Improv Nation*. Wasson, Sam	792.02
Improving Your Memory. Fogler, Janet	153.1
IMPROVISATION (ACTING)	
De Vise, Daniel. ★*The Blues Brothers*	791.43
An Improvised Life. Arkin, Alan	B
In A Day's Work. Yeung, Bernice	362.88086
In A Different Key. Donvan, John	616.85
In A Sunburned Country. Bryson, Bill	919
In Afghanistan. Loyn, David	958.1
In Bibi's Kitchen. Hassan, Hawa	641.596
★*In Cold Blood*. Capote, Truman	364.1
In Deep. Rohde, David	973.933
In Extremis. Hilsum, Lindsey	B
In Fed We Trust. Wessel, David	332.1
In Hanuman's Hands. Rao, Cheeni	B
In Harm's Way. Stanton, Doug	940.54
In Heaven as It Is on Earth. Brown, Samuel Morris	289.3
In His Own Words. Mandela, Nelson	B
In Light of All Darkness. Cross, Kim	363.25
In Love. Bloom, Amy	B
In Miniature. Garfield, Simon	745.5928
In Montgomery, and Other Poems. Brooks, Gwendolyn	811
In Montmartre. Roe, Sue	920
In My Kitchen. Madison, Deborah	641.5
★*In My Time of Dying*. Junger, Sebastian	304.6
★*In on the Joke*. Levy, Shawn	792.7
In Other Words. Lahiri, Jhumpa	B
In Other Worlds. Atwood, Margaret	813
In Pain. Rieder, Travis	362.29
In Pieces. Field, Sally	B
In Praise of Difficult Women. Karbo, Karen	920
In Pursuit of Disobedient Women. Searcey, Dionne	B
In Pursuit of Flavor. Lewis, Edna	641.5975
In Reckless Hands. Nourse, Victoria F.	344.7304
In Retrospect. McNamara, Robert S.	959.704
★*In Search of a Beautiful Freedom*. Griffin, Farah Jasmine	814
In Search of a Kingdom. Bergreen, Laurence	B
In Search of Mary Shelley. Sampson, Fiona	B
In Search of Memory. Kandel, Eric R.	B
In Search of Nature. Wilson, Edward O.	113
In Search of Our Roots. Gates, Henry Louis	973
In Search of Robinson Crusoe. Severin, Timothy	996.1
In Search of the Promised Land. Franklin, John Hope	929
In Sensorium. Tanais	B
In Siberia. Thubron, Colin	957
In Spite of Myself. Plummer, Christopher	B
In Such Good Company. Burnett, Carol	791.45
In The Absence of Sun. Lee, Helie	B
In The Darkroom. Faludi, Susan	B
★*In The Dream House*. Machado, Carmen Maria	B
In The Footsteps of King David. Garfinkel, Yosef	933
In The Footsteps of Marco Polo. Belliveau, Denis	915
In The Form of a Question. Schneider, Amy	B
In The Garden of Beasts. Larson, Erik	B
In The Garden of the Righteous. Hurowitz, Richard	940.53
In The Great Green Room. Gary, Amy	813
In The House of the Interpreter. Ngugi wa Thiong'o	B
★*In The Hurricane's Eye*. Philbrick, Nathaniel	973.3
★*In The Kingdom of Ice*. Sides, Hampton	910.4
In The Land of Men. Miller, Adrienne	070.5
In The Language of My Captor. McCrae, Shane	811
In The Lateness of the World. Forche, Carolyn	811
In The Margins. Ferrante, Elena	809
In The Mouth of the Wolf. Corcoran, Katherine	364.152
In The Name of Gucci. Gucci, Patricia	B
In The Pines. Hale, Grace Elizabeth	364.13
In The Sanctuary of Outcasts. White, Neil	B
★*In The Shadow of Liberty*. Minian, Ana Raquel	365
★*In The Shadow of Man*. Goodall, Jane	599.8
In The Shadow of No Towers. Spiegelman, Art	741.5
In The Shadow of the Empress. Goldstone, Nancy Bazelon	920
In The Shadow of the Gods. Lieven, Dominic	352.23
In The Shadow of the Mountain. Vasquez-Lavado, Silvia	B
In The Wake of the Plague. Cantor, Norman F.	614.5
In The Waves. Lance, Rachel	973.7
In The Weeds. Vitale, Tom	B
In These Girls, Hope Is a Muscle. Blais, Madeleine	796.323
In Transition. Corbett, Emily	809
In Whose Ruins. Puglionesi, Alicia	973
INCA (SOUTH AMERICAN PEOPLE)	
Bingham, Hiram. ★*Lost City of the Incas*	985
Cervantes, Fernando. *Conquistadores*	970.01
Heaney, Christopher. *Cradle of Gold*	B
INCANTATIONS	
Abrev, Ileana. *The Little Big Book of White Spells*	133.4
Incarnations. Khilnani, Sunil	920
★*Incendiary Art*. Smith, Patricia	811.54
INCEST	
Kizzia, Tom. *Pilgrim's Wilderness*	B
Kouchner, Camille. *The Familia Grande*	B
INCEST VICTIMS	
V. *The Apology*	818
★*Incidents in the Life of a Slave Girl*. Jacobs, Harriet	B
Inciting Joy. Gay, Ross	814
The Includers. Phillips, Collette A. M.	658.4
INCLUSIVE EDUCATION	
Zakaria, Rafia. *Against White Feminism*	305.42
Incognito. Eagleman, David	153
INCOME	
Bregman, Rutger. *Utopia for Realists*	335
Rivlin, Gary. *Broke, Usa*	339.4
Sowell, Thomas. *Wealth, Poverty and Politics*	330.1
INCOME INEQUALITY	
Chung, Nicole. ★*A Living Remedy*	B
Cox, Josie. *Women Money Power*	330.082
Daunton, M. J. ★*The Economic Government of the World*	337
De Long, J. Bradford. *Slouching Towards Utopia*	330.9
Desmond, Matthew. ★*Poverty, by America*	362.5
Edin, Kathryn. *$2.00 a Day*	339.4
Fraser, Steve. *The Age of Acquiescence*	973.91
Gelles, David. *The Man Who Broke Capitalism*	330.12
Geronimus, Arline T. ★*Weathering*	362.1089
Hill, Fiona. *There Is Nothing for You Here*	327.2
Honey, Michael K. *To the Promised Land*	323
Jacoby, Melissa B. ★*Unjust Debts*	346.73
Kruse, Kevin Michael. *Fault Lines*	973.92
Linklater, Andro. *Owning the Earth*	333.3
McGhee, Heather C. ★*The Sum of Us*	305.8
McGrath, Tom. *Triumph of the Yuppies*	305.242
McMillan, Tracie. ★*The White Bonus*	305.8
Mechanic, Michael. *Jackpot*	305.5
Mettler, Suzanne. *Degrees of Inequality*	378.73
Milanovic, Branko. *The Have and the Have-Nots*	339.2
Moss, Jeremiah. *Feral City*	
Neiman, Garrett. *Rich White Men*	305.5
Noah, Timothy. *The Great Divergence*	339.2
Nolan, Hamilton. *The Hammer*	331.8
Norris, Michele. ★*Our Hidden Conversations*	305
Packer, George. *Last Best Hope*	973.93
Piketty, Thomas. *A Brief History of Equality*	305.09
Piketty, Thomas. ★*Capital in the Twenty-First Century*	332
Piketty, Thomas. *The Economics of Inequality*	339.2
Reeves, Richard V. *Dream Hoarders*	305.5
Romeo, Nick. *The Alternative*	174
Sandler, Lauren. *This Is All I Got*	B
Schwartz, Nelson. *The Velvet Rope Economy*	339.2

PUBLIC LIBRARY CORE COLLECTION: NONFICTION
Twentieth Edition

Smarsh, Sarah. ★*Heartland*	B
Sowell, Thomas. *Wealth, Poverty and Politics*	330.1
Stiglitz, Joseph E. *The Price of Inequality*	305.50973
Taub, Jennifer. *Big Dirty Money*	364.16
Turchin, Peter. *End Times*	320.01
Waterhouse, Benjamin C. *One Day I'll Work for Myself*	338

INCOME TAX

Bair, Deirdre. *Al Capone*	B
Lowenstein, Roger. *Ways and Means*	973.7
Reid, T. R. *A Fine Mess*	336.200973

INCOMPETENCE

Eichenwald, Kurt. *A Mind Unraveled*	B
Rudolf, David S. *American Injustice*	345.73
*An **Inconvenient** Cop*. Raymond, Edwin	363.2

INCORPORATION

Micklethwait, John. *The Company*	338.7
Increase, Decrease. Durant, Judith	746.43
*The **Incurable** Romantic*. Tallis, Frank	152.4
Indecency. Reed, Justin Phillip	811
Indefensible. Feige, David	B
Indelible City. Lim, Louisa	951.25
Indelible Ink. Kluger, Richard	B
Indentured. Nocera, Joseph	796.04

INDENTURED SERVANTS

Swift, Earl. *Hell Put to Shame*	364.15

INDEPENDENCE

Burns, Eric. *Someone to Watch Over Me*	973.917092
Cargle, Rachel Elizabeth. *A Renaissance of Our Own*	B
Clifton, Lucille. *How to Carry Water*	811
Cook, Blanche Wiesen. *Eleanor Roosevelt; Volume 2*	B
Cook, Blanche Wiesen. ★*Eleanor Roosevelt; Volume 3*	B
Cox, Josie. *Women Money Power*	330.082
De Stefano, Cristina. *The Child Is the Teacher*	B
Delany, Sarah Louise. *Having Our Say*	B
Didion, Joan. *Where I Was from*	979.4
Doyle, Glennon. *Untamed*	B
Feldman, Deborah. *Exodus*	B
Grandin, Greg. *The End of the Myth*	973
Gupta, Prachi. ★*They Called Us Exceptional*	B
Harry. ★*Spare*	B
Heumann, Judith E. *Being Heumann*	B
Hirshey, Gerri. *Not Pretty Enough*	B
Holton, Woody. *Abigail Adams*	B
Jordan, Mary. *The Art of Her Deal*	B
Kalb, Bess. ★*Nobody Will Tell You This but Me*	306.874
Lucey, Donna M. *Sargent's Women*	920
McConville, Mark. *Failure to Launch*	155.6
Michaelis, David. ★*Eleanor*	973.917
Nooyi, Indra. ★*My Life in Full*	B
Parker, Kate T. *Strong Is the New Pretty*	155.43
Pentland, Jenny. *This Will Be Funny Later*	B
Ransby, Barbara. *Eslanda*	B
Roberts, Cokie. *Capital Dames*	920
Rosnay, Tatiana de. *Manderley Forever*	B
Satrapi, Marjane. ★*The Complete Persepolis*	741.5
Senik, Troy. *A Man of Iron*	B
Tammet, Daniel. *Born on a Blue Day*	B
Trofimov, Yaroslav. ★*Our Enemies Will Vanish*	947.7
Tuama, Padraig O. ★*Poetry Unbound*	808.1

INDEPENDENCE IN CHILDREN

Hillsberg, Christina. *License to Parent*	649.1

INDEPENDENT BOOKSTORES

Wassef, Nadia. *Shelf Life*	B

INDEPENDENT FILMS

McGilligan, Patrick. *Oscar Micheaux*	B
Seidelman, Susan. *Desperately Seeking Something*	B
Indestructible. Bruning, John R.	B
Indestructible. Lucas, Jack	B
★*The **Indestructible** Houseplant*. Martin, Tovah	635.9
Index, A History of The. Duncan, Dennis	025.3
India. Keay, John	954

INDIA

Alexander, Caroline. *Skies of Thunder*	940.54
Anand, Anita. *The Patient Assassin*	B
Armstrong, Karen. ★*The Great Transformation*	200.9
Ausaja, S. M. M. *Bollywood*	791.43
Cliff, Nigel. *Holy War*	909
Collingham, E. M. *Curry*	394.1
Dalrymple, William. *Nine Lives*	294
Dalrymple, William. *White Mughals*	954
Faleiro, Sonia. *The Good Girls*	364.152
Gandhi. *An Autobiography*	B
Gidla, Sujatha. *Ants Among Elephants*	305.5
Gilbert, Elizabeth. *Eat, Pray, Love*	B
Guha, Ramachandra. *Gandhi Before India*	B
Guha, Ramachandra. *Gandhi*	B
Guha, Ramachandra. *India After Gandhi*	954.04
Guha, Ramachandra. *Rebels Against the Raj*	954.03
Jadhav, Narendra. *Untouchables*	305.5
Kanigel, Robert. *The Man Who Knew Infinity*	B
Keay, John. *India*	954
Khilnani, Sunil. *Incarnations*	920
Mehta, Suketu. *Maximum City*	954
Narayan, Shoba. *The Milk Lady of Bangalore*	390
Peer, Basharat. *Curfewed Night*	B
Roy, Arundhati. *Walking with the Comrades*	954
Sen, Amartya. *The Argumentative Indian*	954
Tenzin Priyadarshi. *Running Toward Mystery*	B
India After Gandhi. Guha, Ramachandra	954.04

INDIA-PAKISTAN CONFLICT, 1971

Carney, Scott. *The Vortex*	954.92

INDIAN AMERICANS

Dutta, Sunil. *Stealing Green Mangoes*	973
Gupta, Prachi. ★*They Called Us Exceptional*	B
Jacob, Mira. *Good Talk*	741.5
Jayapal, Pramila. *Use the Power You Have*	B
Lakshmi, Padma. *Love, Loss, and What We Ate*	791.4502
Lang, Maya. *What We Carry*	B
Mehra, Nishta. *Brown, White, Black*	305.800973
Nezhukumatathil, Aimee. *Bite by Bite*	641.3
Nooyi, Indra. ★*My Life in Full*	B
Penn, Kal. *You Can't Be Serious*	B
Rao, Cheeni. *In Hanuman's Hands*	B
Shahani, Aarti Namdev. *Here We Are*	B
Sharma, Nina. *The Way You Make Me Feel*	B
Indian Cooking Unfolded. Iyer, Raghavan	641.595

INDIAN ELEPHANT

Orenstein, Ronald I. *Ivory, Horn and Blood*	333.95

INDIAN HISTORY

Armstrong, Karen. ★*The Great Transformation*	200.9
Dalrymple, William. ★*The Anarchy*	954.03
Dalrymple, William. *White Mughals*	954
Dutta, Sunil. *Stealing Green Mangoes*	973
Guha, Ramachandra. *Gandhi*	B
Guha, Ramachandra. *India After Gandhi*	954.04
Guha, Ramachandra. *Rebels Against the Raj*	954.03
Hajari, Nisid. *Midnight's Furies*	954.04
Keay, John. *India*	954
Khilnani, Sunil. *Incarnations*	920
Lal, Ruby. *Empress*	B
Malhotra, Aanchal. *Remnants of Partition*	954.04
Richardson, Edmund. *The King's Shadow*	958.1
Satyamurti, Carole. *Mahabharata*	821

INDIAN OCEAN

Johnson, Steven. *Enemy of All Mankind*	910.4

INDIAN OCEAN TSUNAMI, 2004

Deraniyagala, Sonali. *Wave*	B

INDIAN PARTITION, 1947

Dutta, Sunil. *Stealing Green Mangoes*	973
Hajari, Nisid. *Midnight's Furies*	954.04
Malhotra, Aanchal. *Remnants of Partition*	954.04

INDIAN PEOPLE

Brierley, Saroo. *A Long Way Home*	B
Guha, Ramachandra. *Gandhi Before India*	B
Gupta, Prachi. ★*They Called Us Exceptional*	B
Magida, Arthur J. *Code Name Madeleine*	940.54
Nezhukumatathil, Aimee. *Bite by Bite*	641.3

INDIAN PEOPLE IN AFRICA

Guha, Ramachandra. *Gandhi Before India*	B

INDIAN PEOPLE IN GREAT BRITAIN

Guha, Ramachandra. *Gandhi Before India*	B

INDIAN PEOPLE IN THE UNITED STATES

Singh, Julietta. *The Breaks*	B
*The **Indian** World of George Washington*. Calloway, Colin G.	323.1197
★*Indian-ish*. Krishna, Priya	641.595

AUTHOR, TITLE, SERIES AND SUBJECT INDEX

INDIANA
    Buttigieg, Pete. *Shortest Way Home*   B
    Cox, Anna-Lisa. *The Bone and Sinew of the Land*   977
    Egan, Timothy. ★*A Fever in the Heartland*   322.4
    Ford, Ashley C. ★*Somebody's Daughter*   B
    Regan, Iliana. *Fieldwork*   B
    Schechter, Harold. *Hell's Princess*   B
    Scheeres, Julia. *Jesus Land*   B
Indianapolis. Vincent, Lynn   940.54
The Indifferent Stars Above. Brown, Daniel James   B

INDIGENOUS ACTIVISTS
    Alvarez, Noe. *Spirit Run*   796.42
    Bunnell, David. *Good Friday on the Rez*   B
    Hendricks, Steve. *The Unquiet Grave*   323.1197

INDIGENOUS ATHLETES
    Buford, Kate. *Native American Son*   B
    Colton, Larry. *Counting Coup*   796.323
    Crawford, Bill. ★*All American*   B
    Maraniss, David. ★*Path Lit by Lightning*   B

INDIGENOUS AUTHORS
    Harjo, Joy. *Crazy Brave*   B
    Harjo, Joy. ★*Poet Warrior*   B
    Hensley, William L. Iggiagruk. *Fifty Miles from Tomorrow*   B
    Hogan, Linda. *The Woman Who Watches Over the World*   B
    Metatawabin, Edmund. *Up Ghost River*   B
    Wagamese, Richard. *One Native Life*   B

INDIGENOUS CODE TALKERS
    Nez, Chester. *Code Talker*   B
★*Indigenous Continent*. Hamalainen, Pekka   970.004

INDIGENOUS FAMILIES
    Alexie, Sherman. *You Don't Have to Say You Love Me*   818
    Hyde, Anne Farrar. ★*Born of Lakes and Plains*   978

INDIGENOUS MEN
    Bitsui, Sherwin. *Dissolve*   811
    Jackson, Joe. *Black Elk*   978.004

INDIGENOUS OLYMPIC MEDAL WINNERS
    Crawford, Bill. ★*All American*   B

INDIGENOUS ORGANIZATIONS
    Hendricks, Steve. *The Unquiet Grave*   323.1197

INDIGENOUS PEOPLES
    Aguon, Julian. *No Country for Eight-Spot Butterflies*   305.89
    Alvarez, Noe. *Spirit Run*   796.42
    Clark, Doug Bock. *The Last Whalers*   639.2
    Diaz, Natalie. ★*Postcolonial Love Poem*   811
    DuVal, Kathleen. ★*Native Nations*   970.004
    Erdrich, Heid E. ★*Little Big Bully*   811
    Estes, Nick. *Our History Is the Future*   978.004
    Goodheart, Adam. *The Last Island*   954
    Hochschild, Adam. *King Leopold's Ghost*   967.51
    Keene, Adrienne. *Notable Native People*   920
    Kimmerer, Robin Wall. ★*Braiding Sweetgrass*   304.2
    Mojica Rodriguez, Prisca Dorcas. *For Brown Girls with Sharp Edges and Tender Hearts*   305.48
    Puglionesi, Alicia. *In Whose Ruins*   973
    Raff, Jennifer. *Origin*   576.5
    Roy, Arundhati. *Walking with the Comrades*   954
    Santos Perez, Craig. *From Unincorporated Territory [amot]*   811
    Sedgewick, Augustine. *Coffeeland*   338.4
    Sides, Hampton. ★*The Wide Wide Sea*   910.92
    Turvey, Samuel. ★*The Tomb of the Mili Mongga*   398.24
    Webb, Kinari. *Guardians of the Trees*   B

INDIGENOUS PEOPLES — LAND RIGHTS
    Warren, James A. *God, War, and Providence*   974.5

INDIGENOUS PEOPLES OF CENTRAL AMERICA
    Dodds Pennock, Caroline. ★*On Savage Shores*   970.004
    Mann, Charles C. ★*1491*   970.01
    Preston, Douglas J. ★*The Lost City of the Monkey God*   972.85

INDIGENOUS PEOPLES OF CENTRAL AMERICA — ANTIQUITIES
    Coe, Michael D. *The Maya*   972

INDIGENOUS PEOPLES OF MEXICO
    Cervantes, Fernando. *Conquistadores*   970.01
    Dodds Pennock, Caroline. ★*On Savage Shores*   970.004
    McDougall, Christopher. ★*Born to Run*   796.42
    Townsend, Richard F. *The Aztecs*   972

INDIGENOUS PEOPLES OF MEXICO — ANTIQUITIES
    Coe, Michael D. *The Maya*   972

INDIGENOUS PEOPLES OF MEXICO — HISTORY
    Restall, Matthew. *When Montezuma Met Cortes*   972

    Townsend, Richard F. *The Aztecs*   972

INDIGENOUS PEOPLES OF NORTH AMERICA
    Akins, Damon B. ★*We Are the Land*   978
    Alexie, Sherman. *You Don't Have to Say You Love Me*   818
    Alvarez, Noe. *Spirit Run*   796.42
    Belcourt, Billy-Ray. ★*A History of My Brief Body*   B
    Bellows, Amanda Brickell. *The Explorers*   910.92
    Bitsoie, Freddie. *New Native Kitchen*   641.59
    Black Elk. *Black Elk Speaks*   B
    Blackhawk, Ned. ★*The Rediscovery of America*   973.04
    Blum, Edward J. *The Color of Christ*   232
    Brooks, James. *Mesa of Sorrows*   979.1004
    Brown, Dee. ★*Bury My Heart at Wounded Knee*   978
    Buford, Kate. *Native American Son*   B
    Burns, Mike. *The Only One Living to Tell*   305.897
    Calloway, Colin G. *The Indian World of George Washington*   323.1197
    Calloway, Colin G. *One Vast Winter Count*   978
    Childs, Craig. *House of Rain*   978.9
    Colton, Larry. *Counting Coup*   796.323
    Connell, Evan S. *Son of the Morning Star*   973.8
    Cozzens, Peter. *A Brutal Reckoning*   973.5
    Crutchfield, James A. *Revolt at Taos*   972
    Curtis, Edward S. *Edward S. Curtis*   770.92
    Diaz, Natalie. ★*Postcolonial Love Poem*   811
    Dodds Pennock, Caroline. ★*On Savage Shores*   970.004
    Donovan, Jim. *A Terrible Glory*   973.8
    Drury, Bob. *The Heart of Everything That Is*   B
    Dunbar-Ortiz, Roxanne. ★*An Indigenous Peoples' History of the United States*   970.004
    DuVal, Kathleen. ★*Native Nations*   970.004
    Egan, Timothy. ★*Short Nights of the Shadow Catcher*   770.92
    Enss, Chris. *Mochi's War*   B
    Estes, Nick. *Our History Is the Future*   978.004
    Eustace, Nicole. ★*Covered with Night*   364.152
    Flores, Dan L. *Wild New World*   591.9709
    Frank, Lois Ellen. *Seed to Plate, Soil to Sky*   641.5
    Gardner, Mark L. *The Earth Is All That Lasts*   978.004
    Gayle, Caleb. *We Refuse to Forget*   975.004
    Grann, David. ★*Killers of the Flower Moon*   976.6004
    Grathwohl, Marya. *This Wheel of Rocks*   271
    Gulbrandsen, Don. *Edward Sheriff Curtis*   970.004
    Gwynne, S. C. *Empire of the Summer Moon*   B
    Hamalainen, Pekka. ★*Indigenous Continent*   970.004
    Harjo, Joy. *Catching the Light*   818
    Hogan, Linda. *The Woman Who Watches Over the World*   B
    Horn, James P. P. *A Kingdom Strange*   975.6
    Horn, James P. P. *Land as God Made It*   975.5
    Hutton, Paul Andrew. *The Apache Wars*   979
    Hyde, Anne Farrar. ★*Born of Lakes and Plains*   978
    Inskeep, Steve. *Jacksonland*   973.56
    Iverson, Peter. *Dine*   979.1004
    Jackson, Joe. *Black Elk*   978.004
    Jenkins, Peter. *Looking for Alaska*   979.8
    Johnson, Michael. *Encyclopedia of Native Tribes of North America*   970.00497
    Keene, Adrienne. *Notable Native People*   920
    Kimmerer, Robin Wall. ★*Braiding Sweetgrass*   304.2
    LaPointe, Sasha taqwseblu. *Thunder Song*   814
    Luger, Chelsey. ★*The Seven Circles*   610
    Mann, Charles C. ★*1491*   970.01
    Maraniss, David. ★*Path Lit by Lightning*   B
    Mays, Kyle. ★*An Afro-Indigenous History of the United States*   973
    McDonnell, Michael. *Masters of Empire*   977.4
    McMurtry, Larry. *Crazy Horse*   B
    McMurtry, Larry. *Custer*   B
    Metatawabin, Edmund. *Up Ghost River*   B
    Miranda, Deborah A. *Bad Indians*   305.8009794
    Momaday, N. Scott. ★*The Death of Sitting Bear*   811
    Momaday, N. Scott. *Earth Keeper*   814
    Mort, T. A. *Thieves' Road*   978.3
    Murdoch, Sierra Crane. ★*Yellow Bird*   364.152
    Myers, Leah. *Thinning Blood*   B
    Nelson, Megan Kate. *The Three-Cornered War*   978
    Nesteroff, Kliph. *We Had a Little Real Estate Problem*   970.004
    Neville, Aaron. *Tell It Like It Is*   B
    Nez, Chester. *Code Talker*   B
    Pasternak, Judy. *Yellow Dirt*   979.1004
    Philbrick, Nathaniel. ★*The Last Stand*   973.8

PUBLIC LIBRARY CORE COLLECTION: NONFICTION
Twentieth Edition

Pico, Tommy. *Junk*	811
Powell, Michael. ★*Canyon Dreams*	796.323
Powers, Thomas. *The Killing of Crazy Horse*	B
Price, David A. ★*Love and Hate in Jamestown*	975.5
Redniss, Lauren. ★*Oak Flat*	970.5
Roberts, David. *The Bears Ears*	979.2
Roberts, David. *Once They Moved Like the Wind*	B
Schultz, Eric B. *King Philip's War*	973.2
Sharfstein, Daniel J. ★*Thunder in the Mountains*	979.5
Sherman, Sean. ★*The Sioux Chef's Indigenous Kitchen*	641.59
Sides, Hampton. *Blood and Thunder*	978
Silverman, David J. ★*This Land Is Their Land*	974.4
Snyder, Christina. *Great Crossings*	976.9
Stiles, T. J. *Custer's Trials*	B
Streep, Abe. *Brothers on Three*	306.85
Taffa, Deborah Jackson. ★*Whiskey Tender*	B
Taylor, Alan. *The Divided Ground*	974.7
Thoreau, Henry David. *The Maine Woods*	917
Trask, Kerry A. *Black Hawk*	973.5
Utley, Robert M. ★*Geronimo*	B
Utley, Robert M. *Sitting Bull*	B
Wagamese, Richard. *For Joshua*	B
Wagamese, Richard. *One Native Life*	B
Ward, Geoffrey C. *The West*	978
Wilbur, Matika. *Project 562*	970.004

INDIGENOUS PEOPLES OF NORTH AMERICA — CIVIL RIGHTS

Hensley, William L. Iggiagruk. *Fifty Miles from Tomorrow*	B
Sharfstein, Daniel J. ★*Thunder in the Mountains*	979.5

INDIGENOUS PEOPLES OF NORTH AMERICA — FORCED REMOVAL

Berg, Scott W. ★*38 Nooses*	973.7
Brands, H. W. *The Last Campaign*	973.8
Enss, Chris. *Mochi's War*	B
Inskeep, Steve. *Jacksonland*	973.56
Saunt, Claudio. *Unworthy Republic*	323.1197
Wheelan, Joseph. ★*Terrible Swift Sword*	B

INDIGENOUS PEOPLES OF NORTH AMERICA — HISTORY

Black Elk. *Black Elk Speaks*	B
Brands, H. W. *Dreams of El Dorado*	978
Brooks, James. *Mesa of Sorrows*	979.1004
Brown, Dee. ★*Bury My Heart at Wounded Knee*	978
Bruchac, Joseph. *Our Stories Remember*	973.04
Bunnell, David. *Good Friday on the Rez*	B
Childs, Craig. *House of Rain*	978.9
Connell, Evan S. *Son of the Morning Star*	973.8
Cozzens, Peter. *Tecumseh and the Prophet*	920
Curtis, Edward S. *Edward S. Curtis*	770.92
Demos, John. *The Unredeemed Captive*	973.2
Duncan, Dayton. *Blood Memory*	599.64
Eckert, Allan W. *A Sorrow in Our Heart*	B
Hamalainen, Pekka. ★*Indigenous Continent*	970.004
Harjo, Joy. *An American Sunrise*	811
Hendricks, Steve. *The Unquiet Grave*	323.1197
Hyde, Anne Farrar. ★*Born of Lakes and Plains*	978
Inskeep, Steve. *Jacksonland*	973.56
Iverson, Peter. *Dine*	979.1004
Jackson, Joe. *Black Elk*	978.004
LaPointe, Sasha taqwseblu. *Red Paint*	B
Lepore, Jill. *The Name of War*	973.2
McLoughlin, William Gerald. *After the Trail of Tears*	973
Miranda, Deborah A. *Bad Indians*	305.8009794
Philbrick, Nathaniel. ★*Mayflower*	973.2
Roberts, David. *Once They Moved Like the Wind*	B
Schultz, Eric B. *King Philip's War*	973.2
Sides, Hampton. *Blood and Thunder*	978
Taylor, Alan. *The Divided Ground*	974.7
Trask, Kerry A. *Black Hawk*	973.5
Treuer, Anton. *Everything You Wanted to Know About Indians but Were Afraid to Ask*	970.1
Treuer, David. ★*The Heartbeat of Wounded Knee*	970.004
Utley, Robert M. *Sitting Bull*	B

INDIGENOUS PEOPLES OF NORTH AMERICA — LAND RIGHTS

Redniss, Lauren. ★*Oak Flat*	970.5
Saunt, Claudio. *Unworthy Republic*	323.1197

INDIGENOUS PEOPLES OF NORTH AMERICA — POLITICS AND GOVERNMENT

DuVal, Kathleen. ★*Native Nations*	970.004
McLoughlin, William Gerald. *After the Trail of Tears*	973

INDIGENOUS PEOPLES OF NORTH AMERICA — RELIGION

Black Elk. *Black Elk Speaks*	B
Brooks, James. *Mesa of Sorrows*	979.1004
Castaneda, Carlos. *The Teachings of Don Juan;*	299
Cozzens, Peter. *Tecumseh and the Prophet*	920
Jackson, Joe. *Black Elk*	978.004
Nabokov, Peter. *Where the Lightning Strikes*	299.7

INDIGENOUS PEOPLES OF NORTH AMERICA — RITES AND CEREMONIES

Erdrich, Louise. *Books and Islands in Ojibwe Country*	977

INDIGENOUS PEOPLES OF NORTH AMERICA — SOCIAL CONDITIONS

Colton, Larry. *Counting Coup*	796.323
Nesteroff, Kliph. *We Had a Little Real Estate Problem*	970.004

INDIGENOUS PEOPLES OF NORTH AMERICA — SOCIAL LIFE AND CUSTOMS

Bitsoie, Freddie. *New Native Kitchen*	641.59
Bruchac, Joseph. *Our Stories Remember*	973.04
Bunnell, David. *Good Friday on the Rez*	B
Gulbrandsen, Don. *Edward Sheriff Curtis*	970.004
Iverson, Peter. *Dine*	979.1004
Jenkins, Peter. *Looking for Alaska*	979.8
Kimmerer, Robin Wall. ★*Braiding Sweetgrass*	304.2
LaPointe, Sasha taqwseblu. *Red Paint*	B

INDIGENOUS PEOPLES OF NORTH AMERICA — WARS

Berg, Scott W. ★*38 Nooses*	973.7
Brands, H. W. *The Last Campaign*	973.8
Cozzens, Peter. *The Earth Is Weeping*	978
Cozzens, Peter. *Tecumseh and the Prophet*	920
Drury, Bob. *Blood and Treasure*	B
Eckert, Allan W. *A Sorrow in Our Heart*	B
Enss, Chris. *Mochi's War*	B
Gardner, Mark L. *The Earth Is All That Lasts*	978.004
Gwynne, S. C. *Empire of the Summer Moon*	B
Hogeland, William. *Autumn of the Black Snake*	970.004
Hutton, Paul Andrew. *The Apache Wars*	979
Lepore, Jill. *The Name of War*	973.2
McMurtry, Larry. *Custer*	B
Nelson, Megan Kate. *The Three-Cornered War*	978
Philbrick, Nathaniel. ★*The Last Stand*	973.8
Philbrick, Nathaniel. ★*Mayflower*	973.2
Roberts, David. *Once They Moved Like the Wind*	B
Sharfstein, Daniel J. ★*Thunder in the Mountains*	979.5
Sides, Hampton. *Blood and Thunder*	978
Utley, Robert M. ★*Geronimo*	B
Warren, James A. *God, War, and Providence*	974.5

INDIGENOUS PEOPLES OF NORTH AMERICA IN ART

Eisler, Benita. *The Red Man's Bones*	B

INDIGENOUS PEOPLES OF NORTH AMERICA IN POPULAR CULTURE

Parke, Henry C. *The Greatest Westerns Ever Made and the People Who Made Them*	791.43
Treuer, Anton. *Everything You Wanted to Know About Indians but Were Afraid to Ask*	970.1

INDIGENOUS PEOPLES OF NORTH AMERICA IN TEXTBOOKS

Powell, Nate. ★*Lies My Teacher Told Me*	741.5

INDIGENOUS PEOPLES OF NORTH AMERICA, TREATMENT OF

Blackhawk, Ned. ★*The Rediscovery of America*	973.04
Bunnell, David. *Good Friday on the Rez*	B
Dunbar-Ortiz, Roxanne. ★*An Indigenous Peoples' History of the United States*	970.004
Estes, Nick. *Our History Is the Future*	978.004
Long Soldier, Layli. ★*Whereas*	811
Miranda, Deborah A. *Bad Indians*	305.8009794
Sacco, Joe. ★*Paying the Land*	741.5
Saunt, Claudio. *Unworthy Republic*	323.1197
Treuer, David. ★*The Heartbeat of Wounded Knee*	970.004

INDIGENOUS PEOPLES OF SOUTH AMERICA

Bingham, Hiram. ★*Lost City of the Incas*	985
Cervantes, Fernando. *Conquistadores*	970.01
Dodds Pennock, Caroline. ★*On Savage Shores*	970.004
Heaney, Christopher. *Cradle of Gold*	B
Kars, Marjoleine. *Blood on the River*	306.3
Mann, Charles C. ★*1491*	970.01
Reel, Monte. *The Last of the Tribe*	981
Rojas Contreras, Ingrid. ★*The Man Who Could Move Clouds*	B
Wallace, Scott. *The Unconquered*	981

INDIGENOUS PEOPLES OF SOUTH AMERICA — ANTIQUITIES

Bingham, Hiram. ★*Lost City of the Incas*	985

AUTHOR, TITLE, SERIES AND SUBJECT INDEX

Heaney, Christopher. *Cradle of Gold* — B
INDIGENOUS PEOPLES OF SOUTH AMERICA — HISTORY
    Heaney, Christopher. *Cradle of Gold* — B
INDIGENOUS PEOPLES OF SOUTH AMERICA — SOCIAL CONDITIONS
    Reel, Monte. *The Last of the Tribe* — 981
INDIGENOUS PEOPLES OF SOUTH AMERICA — SOCIAL LIFE AND CUSTOMS
    Wallace, Scott. *The Unconquered* — 981
INDIGENOUS PEOPLES RELATIONS WITH MISSIONARIES, TRADERS, ETC.
    DuVal, Kathleen. ★*Native Nations* — 970.004
    Philbrick, Nathaniel. ★*Mayflower* — 973.2
    ★An **Indigenous** *Peoples' History of the United States*. Dunbar-Ortiz, Roxanne — 970.004

INDIGENOUS POETS
    Harjo, Joy. *Catching the Light* — 818
INDIGENOUS PRISONERS
    Enss, Chris. *Mochi's War* — B
INDIGENOUS RESERVATIONS
    Alexie, Sherman. *You Don't Have to Say You Love Me* — 818
    Bitsui, Sherwin. *Dissolve* — 811
    Bunnell, David. *Good Friday on the Rez* — B
    Estes, Nick. *Our History Is the Future* — 978.004
    Grathwohl, Marya. *This Wheel of Rocks* — 271
    Mailhot, Terese Marie. *Heart Berries* — B
    Murdoch, Sierra Crane. ★*Yellow Bird* — 364.152
    Powell, Michael. ★*Canyon Dreams* — 796.323
    Redniss, Lauren. ★*Oak Flat* — 970.5
    Streep, Abe. *Brothers on Three* — 306.85
    Taffa, Deborah Jackson. *Whiskey Tender* — B
INDIGENOUS RESIDENTIAL SCHOOLS
    Metatawabin, Edmund. *Up Ghost River* — B
    Sasakamoose, Fred. *Call Me Indian* — B
    Snyder, Christina. *Great Crossings* — 976.9
INDIGENOUS RESISTANCE AND REVOLTS
    Hendricks, Steve. *The Unquiet Grave* — 323.1197
    Philbrick, Nathaniel. ★*The Last Stand* — 973.8
    Treuer, David. ★*The Heartbeat of Wounded Knee* — 970.004
INDIGENOUS SOLDIERS
    Nez, Chester. *Code Talker* — B
    O'Donnell, Patrick K. *The Indispensables* — 973.3
    Taylor, Alan. *The Divided Ground* — 974.7
INDIGENOUS TEENAGERS
    Streep, Abe. *Brothers on Three* — 306.85
INDIGENOUS WOMEN
    Colton, Larry. *Counting Coup* — 796.323
    Harjo, Joy. *Catching the Light* — 818
    Hogan, Linda. *The Woman Who Watches Over the World* — B
    LaPointe, Sasha taqwseblu. *Thunder Song* — 814
    Mailhot, Terese Marie. *Heart Berries* — B
    McDiarmid, Jessica. *Highway of Tears* — 364.152
    Miles, Tiya. ★*Wild Girls* — 304.2
    Murdoch, Sierra Crane. ★*Yellow Bird* — 364.152
    Myers, Leah. *Thinning Blood* — B
INDIGENOUS WOMEN POETS
    Harjo, Joy. *Crazy Brave* — B
    Harjo, Joy. ★*Poet Warrior* — B
The **Indispensable** *Librarian*. Johnson, Doug — 025.1
The **Indispensables**. O'Donnell, Patrick K. — 973.3
INDIVIDUALISM
    Crawford, Matthew B. *The World Beyond Your Head* — 155.2
    Fukuyama, Francis. *Liberalism and Its Discontents* — 320.51
    Grayling, A. C. *The Age of Genius* — 940.2
    Kugel, James L. *The Great Shift* — 296.3
    Osnos, Evan. *Age of Ambition* — 951.06
    Quart, Alissa. *Bootstrapped* — 305.5
    Real, Terrence. *Us* — 646.7
    Storr, Will. *Selfie* — 155.2
INDIVIDUALITY
    Brown, Brene. *Braving the Wilderness* — 305.8
    Cargle, Rachel Elizabeth. *A Renaissance of Our Own* — B
    Gimenez Smith, Carmen. *Be Recorder* — 811
    Hankir, Zahra. *Eyeliner* — 391.6
    Shockley, Evie. *Suddenly We* — 811
INDIVIDUALIZED INSTRUCTION
    De Stefano, Cristina. *The Child Is the Teacher* — B
★**Indivisible**. Hamilton, Denise — 658.3
Indivisible. Paul, Joel R. — 973.5

INDOCHINA
    Logevall, Fredrik. *Embers of War* — 959.704
INDONESIA
    Clark, Doug Bock. *The Last Whalers* — 639.2
    Gilbert, Elizabeth. *Eat, Pray, Love* — B
    Turvey, Samuel. ★*The Tomb of the Mili Mongga* — 398.24
INDOOR CLIMBING
    Burgman, John. *High Drama* — 796.522
INDOOR GARDENING
    Durber, Sarah. *Make Your Own Indoor Garden* — 635
    Hay Hinsdale, Emily L. *What Is My Plant Telling Me?* — 635.9
    Isabel, Agatha. *Houseplant Hookups* — 635.9
    Martin, Tovah. *The Unexpected Houseplant* — 635.9
INDUSTRIAL DESIGN
    Ploszajski, Anna. *Handmade* — 620.1
INDUSTRIAL MANAGEMENT
    Herman, Arthur. *Freedom's Forge* — 940.53
    Washington, Ella F. *The Necessary Journey* — 658.3
    Wooldridge, Adrian. *Masters of Management* — 658
INDUSTRIAL MOBILIZATION
    Herman, Arthur. *Freedom's Forge* — 940.53
    Nelson, Craig. ★*V Is for Victory* — 973.917
INDUSTRIAL MUSIC
    Wiederhorn, Jon. *Louder Than Hell* — 781.6609
INDUSTRIAL POLICY
    Dikotter, Frank. *China After Mao* — 951.05
    Dikotter, Frank. *Mao's Great Famine* — 951.05
    Goldstein, Amy. *Janesville* — 330.9775
INDUSTRIAL PRODUCTIVITY
    Duhigg, Charles. *Smarter Faster Better* — 158
    Mueller, Jennifer. *Creative Change* — 658.4
INDUSTRIAL PSYCHOLOGY
    Economy, Peter. *Wait, I'm Working with Who?!?* — 650.1
    Edmondson, Amy C. *The Right Kind of Wrong* — 158.1
    Green, Alison. *Ask a Manager* — 650.1
    Webb, Caroline. *How to Have a Good Day* — 650.1
INDUSTRIAL REVOLUTION
    Ackroyd, Peter. *Revolution* — 941.07
    Baird, Julia. ★*Victoria the Queen* — B
    Farmer, Jared. *Elderflora* — 582.16
    Freeman, Joshua Benjamin. ★*Behemoth* — 338.6
    Merchant, Brian. *Blood in the Machine* — 303.48
    Satia, Priya. *Empire of Guns* — 330.941
INDUSTRIAL ROBOTS
    Merchant, Brian. *Blood in the Machine* — 303.48
INDUSTRIAL WASTES
    O'Brien, Keith. *Paradise Falls* — 363.738
INDUSTRIALISTS
    Baime, A. J. ★*Go Like Hell* — 796.7209
    Brinkley, Douglas. *Wheels for the World* — B
    Cannadine, David. ★*Mellon* — B
    Davenport, Christian. *The Space Barons* — 920
    Eisen, Norman L. *The Last Palace* — 920
    Hiltzik, Michael A. *Iron Empires* — 385.0973
    Krass, Peter. *Carnegie* — B
    Nasaw, David. *Andrew Carnegie* — B
    Rasenberger, Jim. *Revolver* — B
    Watts, Steven. *The People's Tycoon* — B
INDUSTRIALIZATION
    Freeman, Joshua Benjamin. ★*Behemoth* — 338.6
    Genoways, Ted. *This Blessed Earth* — 630.9
    Reiss, Benjamin. *Wild Nights* — 616.8
    Roy, Arundhati. *Walking with the Comrades* — 954
    Sanghera, Sathnam. *Empireworld* — 909
    Satia, Priya. *Empire of Guns* — 330.941
INDUSTRIES
    Arsenault, Kerri. *Mill Town* — B
    Goleman, Daniel. *Ecological Intelligence* — 333.7
    Green, Hardy. *The Company Town* — 307.76
    Haag, Pamela. ★*The Gunning of America* — 338.4
Indyk, Martin
    Master of the Game — 327.73
INEQUALITY
    Ayers, Edward L. *American Visions* — 973.5
    Berman, Ari. ★*Minority Rule* — 305.809
    Bogdanich, Walt. *When McKinsey Comes to Town* — 001
    Boo, Katherine. ★*Behind the Beautiful Forevers* — 305.5
    Bunnell, David. *Good Friday on the Rez* — B

PUBLIC LIBRARY CORE COLLECTION: NONFICTION
Twentieth Edition

Busby, Jill Louise. *Unfollow Me*	305.08
Chachra, Deb. *How Infrastructure Works*	363
Chomsky, Noam. *Global Discontents*	410.92
Davies, Richard. *Extreme Economies*	306.3
Duncan, Arne. *How Schools Work*	379
Edin, Kathryn. ★*The Injustice of Place*	339.4
Francis. *Let Us Dream*	282.092
Freeman, Andrea. ★*Ruin Their Crops on the Ground*	338.1
Garrett, Kent. *The Last Negroes at Harvard*	920
Gates, Henry Louis. ★*Stony the Road*	973
Gerald, Casey. *There Will Be No Miracles Here*	B
Gidla, Sujatha. *Ants Among Elephants*	305.5
Grant, Richard. *The Deepest South of All*	976.2
Hernandez, Daisy. *The Kissing Bug*	616.9
Herold, Benjamin. *Disillusioned*	307.76
Holton, Woody. *Liberty Is Sweet*	973.3
Honey, Michael K. *To the Promised Land*	323
Isen, Tajja. *Some of My Best Friends*	305.8
Kelley, Blair Murphy. *Black Folk*	331.6
Kim, Anne. ★*Poverty for Profit*	302.5
Kozol, Jonathan. *Fire in the Ashes*	362.77
Lemann, Nicholas. *Transaction Man*	330.973
Lichtman, Allan J. *The Embattled Vote in America*	324.6
Lim, Audrea. *Free the Land*	333.73
Lipman, Joanne. *That's What She Said*	305.30973
Livingston, Robert W. *The Conversation*	305.8
Lockhart, Chris. ★*Walking the Bowl*	362.7
Love, Bettina L. *Punished for Dreaming*	371.829
Luthra, Shefali. *Undue Burden*	362.1988
Mangino, Kate. ★*Equal Partners*	305.3
Markovits, Daniel. *The Meritocracy Trap*	305.5
Mask, Deirdre. *The Address Book*	388.1
McGhee, Heather C. ★*The Sum of Us*	305.8
McGrath, Tom. *Triumph of the Yuppies*	305.242
McLaughlin, Kathleen. *Blood Money*	362.17
Messenger, Tony. *Profit and Punishment*	362.5
Miller, Reuben Jonathan. *Halfway Home*	364.8
Murgia, Madhumita. *Code Dependent*	303.48
Noah, Timothy. *The Great Divergence*	339.2
O'Neil, Cathy. *Weapons of Math Destruction*	005.7
Osnos, Evan. *Wildland*	973.93
Otto, Mary. *Teeth*	617
Packer, George. *Last Best Hope*	973.93
Porter, Eduardo. *American Poison*	305.800973
Press, Eyal. ★*Dirty Work*	331.7
Prickett, Pamela J. ★*The Unclaimed*	363.7
Quart, Alissa. *Bootstrapped*	305.5
Ray, Victor. *On Critical Race Theory*	305.8
Richardson, Heather Cox. ★*How the South Won the Civil War*	306.20973
Samaha, Albert. *Concepcion*	929
Schwartz, Nelson. *The Velvet Rope Economy*	339.2
Sedgewick, Augustine. *Coffeeland*	338.4
Selingo, Jeffrey J. *Who Gets in and Why*	378.1
Sen, Amartya. *Home in the World*	B
Sexton, Jared Yates. *American Rule*	973
Singer, Jessie. *There Are No Accidents*	363.1
Smarsh, Sarah. ★*Heartland*	B
Smarsh, Sarah. *She Come by It Natural*	782.42164
Smith, Tracy K. ★*Wade in the Water*	811.6
Stiglitz, Joseph E. *The Price of Inequality*	305.50973
Taplin, Jonathan. *Move Fast and Break Things*	330.9
Taub, Jennifer. *Big Dirty Money*	364.16
Teachout, Zephyr. *Break 'Em Up*	338.8
Thrasher, Steven W. ★*The Viral Underclass*	362.1962
Tough, Paul. *The Years That Matter Most*	378.1
Valby, Karen. *The Swans of Harlem*	792.8
Villarosa, Linda. ★*Under the Skin*	362.1089
Winters, Mary-Frances. *Black Fatigue*	305.896
Wolf, Martin. ★*The Crisis of Democratic Capitalism*	330.12
Zygar, Mikhail. *The Empire Must Die*	947.08
★*The Inevitability of Tragedy*. Gewen, Barry	B
The Inevitable. Engelhart, Katie	179.7
The Inextinguishable Symphony. Goldsmith, Martin	
Infamous Scribblers. Burns, Eric	071
Infamy. Reeves, Richard	940.53
INFANTRY	
Dickson, Paul. *The Rise of the G.I. Army 1940-1941*	940.54
Edstrom, Erik. *Un-American*	B

Meyer, Dakota. *Into the Fire*	958.104
INFECTION	
Monosson, Emily. ★*Blight*	616.9
Inferior. Saini, Angela	305.4
The Infernal Library. Kalder, Daniel	321.9
The Infernal Machine. Johnson, Steven	335
Inferno. Hastings, Max	940.54
Inferno. Dante Alighieri	851
INFERTILITY	
Cobbs-Leonard, Tasha. *Do It Anyway*	241
Regan, Iliana. *Fieldwork*	B
★*Infidel*. Hirsi Ali, Ayaan	B
INFILTRATION (MILITARY SCIENCE)	
Fairweather, Jack. *The Volunteer*	B
The Infinite Book. Barrow, John D.	111
The Infinite Gift. Yang, Charles D.	401
Infinite Tuesday. Nesmith, Michael	B
Infinitesimal. Alexander, Amir R.	511
INFINITY	
Barrow, John D. *The Infinite Book*	111
Borges, Jorge Luis. *Selected Non-Fictions*	864
Infinity in the Palm of Your Hand. Chown, Marcus	523.1
The Inflamed Mind. Bullmore, Edward T.	616.85
INFLAMMATORY BOWEL DISEASE	
Scarlata, Kate. *Mind Your Gut*	616.3
INFLATION	
Bernanke, Ben. ★*21st Century Monetary Policy*	332.1
Ullrich, Volker. *Germany 1923*	943.085
Influence. Cialdini, Robert B.	153.8
INFLUENCE (LITERARY, ARTISTIC, ETC.)	
Alt, Matt. *Pure Invention*	306.0952
Basbanes, Nicholas A. ★*Cross of Snow*	B
Bate, Jonathan. *Radical Wordsworth*	B
Devantez, Chelsea. ★*I Shouldn't Be Telling You This*	B
Doty, Mark. *What Is the Grass*	811
Ferrante, Elena. *In the Margins*	809
Goldberg, Whoopi. *Bits and Pieces*	B
Goodall, Jane. ★*The Book of Hope*	128
Herzog, Werner. ★*Every Man for Himself and God Against All*	B
Kaye, Lenny. ★*Lightning Striking*	781.66
Lynskey, Dorian. *The Ministry of Truth*	823
Messud, Claire. *Kant's Little Prussian Head and Other Reasons Why I Write*	B
Moore, Marcus J. *The Butterfly Effect*	B
Morley, Paul. *The Age of Bowie*	B
Parini, Jay. *Borges and Me*	813
Peiffer, Prudence. *The Slip*	709.73
Reynolds, David S. ★*Abe*	B
Rioux, Anne Boyd. *Meg, Jo, Beth, Amy*	813
Rosen, Jeffrey. *The Pursuit of Happiness*	973.3
Ross, Alex. *Wagnerism*	B
Schwab, Tim. ★*The Bill Gates Problem*	361.7
Seidelman, Susan. *Desperately Seeking Something*	B
Shapiro, James. *Shakespeare in a Divided America*	822.33
Tallis, Frank. ★*Mortal Secrets*	B
Vargas Llosa, Mario. *The Call of the Tribe*	868
Waters, John. *Role Models*	B
Weiner, Eric. *Ben & Me*	B
INFLUENCE (PSYCHOLOGY)	
Austerlitz, Saul. *Kind of a Big Deal*	791.43
Ball, Molly. ★*Pelosi*	B
Bates, Laura. *Men Who Hate Women*	305.3
Bergstein, Rachelle. *The Genius of Judy*	813
Bialosky, Jill. *Poetry Will Save Your Life*	B
Borman, Tracy. *Anne Boleyn and Elizabeth I*	920
Boyle, Rebecca. *Our Moon*	523.3
Britt, Ryan. ★*The Spice Must Flow*	813
Chafkin, Max. *The Contrarian*	B
Cialdini, Robert B. *Influence*	153.8
Cohen, Jared. *Life After Power*	973.09
Cuddy, Amy. *Presence*	158.1
Dodds Pennock, Caroline. ★*On Savage Shores*	970.004
Dutton, Kevin. *Split-Second Persuasion*	153.8
Good, Cassandra A. *First Family*	920
Grinspan, Jon. *Wide Awake*	973.7
Hermes, Will. *Lou Reed*	B
Katz, Evan Ross. *Into Every Generation a Slayer Is Born*	791.45
Kenny, Glenn. *The World Is Yours*	791.43

AUTHOR, TITLE, SERIES AND SUBJECT INDEX

Lee, Julia Sun-Joo. *Biting the Hand*	B
Lorenz, Taylor. ★*Extremely Online*	302.23
Nicolson, Adam. *How to Be*	180
Obama, Michelle. ★*The Light We Carry*	B
Pomerantsev, Peter. ★*How to Win an Information War*	940.53
Ronald, Susan. *Hitler's Aristocrats*	940.53
Sanghera, Sathnam. *Empireworld*	909
Schafer, John R. *The Like Switch*	158.2
Silver, Alain. ★*From the Moment They Met It Was Murder*	791.43
Singer, Matt. *Opposable Thumbs*	791.43
Zanes, Warren. *Deliver Me from Nowhere*	782.42164
INFLUENCERS	
Darby, Seyward. ★*Sisters in Hate*	305.800973
DiResta, Renee. *Invisible Rulers*	320
Lorenz, Taylor. ★*Extremely Online*	302.23
Odell, Amy. *Anna*	B
The Influencing Machine. Gladstone, Brooke	741.5
INFLUENZA	
Barry, John M. ★*The Great Influenza*	614.5
Spinney, Laura. ★*Pale Rider*	614.5
INFLUENZA EPIDEMIC, 1918-1919	
Barry, John M. ★*The Great Influenza*	614.5
Honigsbaum, Mark. *The Pandemic Century*	614.4
Spinney, Laura. ★*Pale Rider*	614.5
The Information. Gleick, James	020.9
INFORMATION	
Chown, Marcus. *Infinity in the Palm of Your Hand*	523.1
Garfield, Simon. ★*All the Knowledge in the World*	030.9
Ritchie, Stuart. *Science Fictions*	500
Rosling, Hans. *Factfulness*	155.9
INFORMATION ACCESS	
Duncan, Dennis. *Index, a History of The*	025.3
INFORMATION LITERACY	
LaGarde, Jennifer. *Fact vs. Fiction*	370.15
Turnbow, Dominique. ★*Demystifying Online Instruction in Libraries*	028.7
INFORMATION MANAGEMENT	
Shapiro, Scott J. ★*Fancy Bear Goes Phishing*	364.16
Winchester, Simon. *Knowing What We Know*	306.4
Wright, Alex. *Cataloging the World*	020.9
INFORMATION ORGANIZATION	
Wright, Alex. *Cataloging the World*	020.9
INFORMATION SCIENCE	
Garfield, Simon. ★*All the Knowledge in the World*	030.9
Gladwell, Malcolm. *The Tipping Point*	302
Gleick, James. *The Information*	020.9
INFORMATION SERVICES	
Bignoli, Callan. ★*Responding to Rapid Change in Libraries*	020
Cassell, Kay Ann. ★*Reference and Information Services*	025.5
Wheelan, Charles J. *Naked Statistics*	519.5
INFORMATION SOCIETY	
Gleick, James. *The Information*	020.9
Lessig, Lawrence. *The Future of Ideas*	346.04
INFORMATION SUPERHIGHWAY	
Mitnick, Kevin D. *Ghost in the Wires*	B
INFORMATION TECHNOLOGY	
Bignoli, Callan. ★*Responding to Rapid Change in Libraries*	020
Brickman, Sophie. *Baby, Unplugged*	306.874
Copeland, B. Jack. *Turing*	B
Friedman, Thomas L. ★*Thank You for Being Late*	303.48
Kidder, Tracy. *A Truck Full of Money*	B
McCourt, Frank H. ★*Our Biggest Fight*	303.48
Schieffer, Bob. *Overload*	070.4
Thompson, Clive. *Coders*	005.1092
Wiggins, Christopher L. *How Data Happened*	310
Wu, Tim. *The Attention Merchants*	659.1
INFORMATION THEORY	
Soni, Jimmy. *A Mind at Play*	B
INFORMATION VISUALIZATION	
Cairo, Alberto. *How Charts Lie*	302.2
Page, Scott E. *The Model Thinker*	001.4
INFORMATION WARFARE	
Chertoff, Michael. *Exploding Data*	343.7309
Stengel, Richard. *Information Wars*	355.3
Information Wars. Stengel, Richard	355.3
The Informed Parent. Haelle, Tara	649
INFORMERS	
Carlo, Philip. *Gaspipe*	B
Figes, Orlando. ★*The Whisperers*	306.850947
Lauterbach, Preston. *Bluff City*	B
Mueller, Tom. *Crisis of Conscience*	364.16
Sherman, Casey. *Hunting Whitey*	B
INFRASTRUCTURE	
Blunt, Katherine. *California Burning*	333.793
Chachra, Deb. *How Infrastructure Works*	363
Denton, Sally. *The Profiteers*	B
Grabar, Henry. *Paved Paradise*	388.474
Humes, Edward. *Door to Door*	388.09
Winchester, Simon. *The Men Who United the States*	973
Ingall, Marjorie	
Sorry, Sorry, Sorry	158.2
Inge's War. O'Donnell, Svenja	943.086
Ingels, Darin	
The Lyme Solution	616.9
Inglis, Lucy	
Milk of Paradise	362.29
Ingrassia, Lawrence	
A Fatal Inheritance	616.99
INGRASSIA, LAWRENCE	
Ingrassia, Lawrence. *A Fatal Inheritance*	616.99
Ingrid Bergman. Thomson, David	B
★*Inheritance*. Shapiro, Dani	B
INHERITANCE AND SUCCESSION	
Beard, Mary. ★*Emperor of Rome*	937
Cooper, Anderson. *Vanderbilt*	920
Farley, Audrey Clare. *The Unfit Heiress*	B
Firdawsi. *Shahnameh*	891
Genoways, Ted. *This Blessed Earth*	630.9
Goldstone, Nancy Bazelon. *The Rival Queens*	944
Gristwood, Sarah. *Blood Sisters*	942.04092
Hubbard, Ben (Journalist). *Mbs*	B
Kaiser, Menachem. *Plunder*	940.53
Preszler, Trent. *Little and Often*	B
Sancton, Thomas. *The Bettencourt Affair*	B
Schiff, Stacy. ★*Cleopatra*	B
Singh, Julietta. *The Breaks*	B
Stewart, James B. *Unscripted*	658.1
Tallis, Nicola. *Crown of Blood*	B
Weir, Alison. *The Children of Henry VIII*	B
The Inheritance of Rome. Wickham, Chris	940.1
Initiated. Garcia, Amanda Yates	B
INITIATIONS (INTO TRADES, SOCIETIES, ETC.)	
Hechinger, John. ★*True Gentlemen*	371.85
INJURED ANIMALS	
Bragg, Rick. *The Speckled Beauty*	636.7
Montgomery, Sy. ★*Of Time and Turtles*	597.92
INJUSTICE	
Addario, Lynsey. *Of Love & War*	779
Ahmed, Sara. *The Feminist Killjoy Handbook*	305.42
Asgarian, Roxanna. *We Were Once a Family*	364.152
Barnett, Brittany K. ★*A Knock at Midnight*	B
Bazelon, Emily. ★*Charged*	345.73
Betts, Reginald Dwayne. ★*Redaction*	704.9
Burnham, Margaret A. ★*By Hands Now Known*	342.73
Canon, Dan. ★*Pleading Out*	345.73
Clifton, Lucille. *How to Carry Water*	811
Crawford, Lacy. *Notes on a Silencing*	B
Dunbar, Erica Armstrong. ★*Never Caught*	B
Fabricant, M. Chris. *Junk Science and the American Criminal Justice System*	363.25
Faleiro, Sonia. *The Good Girls*	364.152
Farmer, Paul. *Fevers, Feuds, and Diamonds*	614.5
Felix, Camonghne. *Build Yourself a Boat*	811
Fessler, Pam. *Carville's Cure*	362.19699
Geronimus, Arline T. ★*Weathering*	362.1089
Hagerty, Alexa. ★*Still Life with Bones*	599.9
Henning, Kristin. *The Rage of Innocence*	364.36
Henny, Ally. *I Won't Shut Up*	305.896
Hinton, Elizabeth Kai. ★*America on Fire*	305.800973
Hoja, Gulchehra. *A Stone Is Most Precious Where It Belongs*	B
Honig, Elie. *Untouchable*	364.1
Jacoby, Melissa B. ★*Unjust Debts*	346.73
Krakauer, Jon. *Missoula*	362.883
Lithwick, Dahlia. *Lady Justice*	345.73
Lorde, Audre. ★*The Selected Works of Audre Lorde*	814
Macy, Beth. ★*Truevine*	B
Mays, Kyle. ★*An Afro-Indigenous History of the United States*	973

PUBLIC LIBRARY CORE COLLECTION: NONFICTION
Twentieth Edition

Miller, Chanel. *Know My Name*	B
Miller, Reuben Jonathan. *Halfway Home*	364.8
Nusbaum, Eric. *Stealing Home*	796.357
Olivares, Efren C. *My Boy Will Die of Sorrow*	305.9
Packer, George. *Last Best Hope*	973.93
Petrosino, Kiki. *White Blood*	811
Reed, Justin Phillip. *The Malevolent Volume*	811
Rivlin, Gary. *Broke, Usa*	339.4
Rudolf, David S. *American Injustice*	345.73
Sentilles, Sarah. *Stranger Care*	B
Smith, Tracy K. ★*Such Color*	811
Smith, Zadie. *Intimations*	824
Sontag, Susan. *At the Same Time*	814
Souder, William. *Mad at the World*	813
Taibbi, Matt. *I Can't Breathe*	363.2
Taub, Jennifer. *Big Dirty Money*	364.16
Thrall, Nathan. ★*A Day in the Life of Abed Salama*	956.05
Walker, Alice. *The Cushion in the Road*	814
Wise, Tim J. *Dispatches from the Race War*	305.8
Wolff, Daniel J. *Grown-Up Anger*	920
Young, Kevin. *Brown*	811
Zucchino, David. *Wilmington's Lie*	305.8009756
★*The Injustice of Place.* Edin, Kathryn	339.4
The Injustice System. Smith, Clive Stafford	345.759
Ink & Paint. Johnson, Mindy	B
Inman, Matthew	
The Terrible and Wonderful Reasons Why I Run Long Distances	741.5
INNER CITY	
Fenn, Lisa. *Carry On*	B
Kozol, Jonathan. *Fire in the Ashes*	362.77
LeDuff, Charlie. *Detroit*	977.4
Samaha, Albert. *Never Ran, Never Will*	920
Westhoff, Ben. *Original Gangstas*	782.421649
INNER CITY CHILDREN	
Kamp, David. *Sunny Days*	791.4502
INNER CITY SCHOOLS	
Skelton, Marc. *Pounding the Rock*	796.323
INNER CITY VIOLENCE	
Bradbury, Rus. *All the Dreams We've Dreamed*	796.323
Leovy, Jill. *Ghettoside*	364.152
The Inner Coast. Hohn, Donovan	304.20973
★*The Inner Game of Tennis.* Gallwey, W. Timothy	796.342
INNOCENCE (LAW)	
Canon, Dan. ★*Pleading Out*	345.73
Dybdahl, Thomas L. *When Innocence Is Not Enough*	345.73
King, Gilbert. ★*Devil in the Grove*	305.896
McCloskey, Jim. *When Truth Is All You Have*	B
Morton, Michael. *Getting Life*	B
Rudolf, David S. *American Injustice*	345.73
Smith, Clive Stafford. *The Injustice System*	345.759
Turow, Scott. ★*Ultimate Punishment*	345.73
Viren, Sarah. *To Name the Bigger Lie*	B
Woodfox, Albert. *Solitary*	B
Zerwick, Phoebe. *Beyond Innocence*	347
Innovation. Ackroyd, Peter	942.082
★*The Innovators.* Isaacson, Walter	B
INQUISITION	
Downey, Kirstin. *Isabella*	B
Kamen, Henry. *The Spanish Inquisition*	272
Perez, Joseph. ★*The Spanish Inquisition*	272
INSANITY (LAW)	
Davis, Kevin. *The Brain Defense*	345.747
Moore, Kate. ★*The Woman They Could Not Silence*	B
INSANITY DEFENSE	
Davis, Kevin. *The Brain Defense*	345.747
INSCRIPTIONS	
Ferrara, Silvia. *The Greatest Invention*	411
INSECT BEHAVIOR	
Holldobler, Bert. *The Superorganism*	595.7
Nicholls, Steve. *Alien Worlds*	595.7
Sumner, Seirian. *Endless Forms*	595.79
Wilson, Edward O. *Tales from the Ant World*	595.79
INSECT PESTS	
Carson, Rachel. ★*Silent Spring*	363.738
Schmidt, Justin O. *The Sting of the Wild*	595.7
INSECT POLLINATORS	
Lavoipierre, Frederique. *Garden Allies*	635
Sumner, Seirian. *Endless Forms*	595.79
INSECT SOCIETIES	
Holldobler, Bert. *The Superorganism*	595.7
Nicholls, Steve. *Alien Worlds*	595.7
INSECTS	
Attenborough, David. *Life in the Undergrowth*	592
Balcombe, Jonathan P. *Super Fly*	595.77
Heinrich, Bernd. *A Naturalist at Large*	508
Hernandez, Daisy. *The Kissing Bug*	616.9
Lavoipierre, Frederique. *Garden Allies*	635
Lewis, Sara. *Silent Sparks*	595.76
MacNeal, David. *Bugged*	595.7
Milne, Lorus Johnson. ★*The Audubon Society Field Guide to North American Insects and Spiders*	595.7097
Nicholls, Steve. *Alien Worlds*	595.7
Schmidt, Justin O. *The Sting of the Wild*	595.7
Sumner, Seirian. *Endless Forms*	595.79
Sverdrup-Thygeson, Anne. *Buzz, Sting, Bite*	595.7
Waldbauer, Gilbert. *What Good Are Bugs?*	595.717
Williams, Wendy. *The Language of Butterflies*	595.78
Wilson, Edward O. *Tales from the Ant World*	595.79
INSECURITY	
Brown, Brene. *Braving the Wilderness*	305.8
Brown, Brene. *The Gifts of Imperfection*	158
Eyman, Scott. *Cary Grant*	B
Gill, Anton. *Art Lover*	B
Lancaster, Jen. *Welcome to the United States of Anxiety*	155.4
McDonald, Michael. ★*What a Fool Believes*	B
Insel, Thomas R.	
Healing	362.2
Inside Camp David. Giorgione, Michael	975.2
The Inside Game. Law, Keith	796.35764
Inside Money. Karabell, Zachary	332.1
★*Inside of a Dog.* Horowitz, Alexandra	636.7
Inside Out. Mason, Nick	B
Inside Scientology. Reitman, Janet	299
Inside The Kingdom. Lacey, Robert	953.805
Inside The Third Reich. Speer, Albert	B
Inside The Wave. Dunmore, Helen	821
Inside Vasubandhu's Yogacara. Connelly, Ben	294.3
INSIDER TRADING IN SECURITIES	
Kolhatkar, Sheelah. *Black Edge*	364.16
An Insider's Guide to the Un, 4th Ed. Fasulo, Linda M.	341.23
Inskeep, Steve	
Imperfect Union	B
Jacksonland	973.56
INSOMNIA	
Bond, Melissa. *Blood Orange Night*	616.8
Harvey, Samantha. *The Shapeless Unease*	B
Leschziner, Guy. *The Nocturnal Brain*	616.8
Macedo, Diane. *The Sleep Fix*	613.7
Mizrahi, Isaac. *I.M.*	B
Navab, Pedram. *Sleep Reimagined*	616.8
Pelayo, Rafael. ★*How to Sleep*	616.8
INSOMNIACS	
Bond, Melissa. *Blood Orange Night*	616.8
Harvey, Samantha. *The Shapeless Unease*	B
INSPIRATION	
Bass, Rick. *The Traveling Feast*	B
Brown, Tabitha. *I Did a New Thing*	158.1
Gabbert, Elisa. *Any Person Is the Only Self*	814
Gilbert, Elizabeth. ★*Big Magic*	153.3
Girzone, Joseph F. *Never Alone*	248.4
Gopnik, Adam. *All That Happiness Is*	158.1
Handler, Daniel. ★*And Then? and Then? What Else?*	813
Harjo, Joy. *Catching the Light*	818
Hecht, Jennifer Michael. ★*The Wonder Paradox*	808.1
Keltner, Dacher. ★*Awe*	152.4
Lewis, John. *Carry On*	328.73
Moss, Adam. ★*The Work of Art*	701
Mueller, Jennifer. *Creative Change*	658.4
Murakami, Haruki. ★*Novelist as a Vocation*	895.64
Nelson, Maggie. ★*Like Love*	814
Shapiro, James. *Shakespeare in a Divided America*	822.33
Steinem, Gloria. *The Truth Will Set You Free, but First It Will Piss You Off*	305.42
Tweedy, Jeff. *How to Write One Song*	782.42
Weinman, Sarah. *The Real Lolita*	362.88092
★*Inspire Your Home.* Merhi, Farah	747

2002

AUTHOR, TITLE, SERIES AND SUBJECT INDEX

The *Inspired* Houseplant. Stearns, Jen	635.9
Inspired Origami. Morin, John	736.982
Inspiring lives [Series]. Patrick, James	B
INSTALLATIONS (ART)	
Ai, Weiwei. *Ai Weiwei*	709.51
INSTANT MESSAGING	
Bilton, Nick. *Hatching Twitter*	006.7
Instill & Inspire. Stanislaus, Grace C.	704.03
INSTINCT	
Freud, Sigmund. *Civilization and Its Discontents*	150.19
Sapolsky, Robert M. *Behave*	612.8
INSTITUTIONAL CARE	
Leach, Samantha. ★*The Elissas*	362.73
INSTITUTIONAL CHILD ABUSE	
Kimmerle, Erin H. *We Carry Their Bones*	365
INSTITUTIONAL RACISM	
Alexander, Kwame. *Light for the World to See*	811.6
Cargle, Rachel Elizabeth. *A Renaissance of Our Own*	B
Flitter, Emily. *The White Wall*	332.0973
Geronimus, Arline T. ★*Weathering*	362.1089
Grant, Gail Milissa. *At the Elbows of My Elders*	B
Harris, Adam. ★*The State Must Provide*	379.2
Isen, Tajja. *Some of My Best Friends*	305.8
Jackson, Ted. ★*You Ought to Do a Story About Me*	B
Jacoby, Melissa B. ★*Unjust Debts*	346.73
Kim, Anne. ★*Poverty for Profit*	302.5
Mallory, Tamika D. *State of Emergency*	305.896
Malone, Sharon. *Grown Woman Talk*	362.1
Oluo, Ijeoma. ★*Be a Revolution*	305.8
Prescod, Danielle. *Token Black Girl*	B
Raymond, Edwin. *An Inconvenient Cop*	363.2
Rose, Tricia. ★*Metaracism*	305.8
Wilderson, Frank B. *Afropessimism*	B
Wilson, Jessica. *It's Always Been Ours*	613
Wingfield, Adia Harvey. *Gray Areas*	331.6
Winters, Mary-Frances. *Black Fatigue*	305.896
Wise, Tim J. *Dispatches from the Race War*	305.8
INSTITUTIONALIZED PEOPLE	
Larson, Kate Clifford. *Rosemary*	B
INSTRUCTIONAL MATERIALS CENTERS	
Hughes-Hassell, Sandra. ★*Collection Management for Youth*	025.2
Instrumental. Rhodes, James	B
INSULIN	
Taubes, Gary. ★*Rethinking Diabetes*	616.462
INSULTS	
Kohan, Rafi. ★*Trash Talk*	179
INSURANCE AGENTS	
Swafford, Jan. *Charles Ives*	B
INSURANCE COMPANIES	
Rosenthal, Elisabeth. *An American Sickness*	362.10973
INSURGENCY	
Abouzeid, Rania. *No Turning Back*	956.9104
Boot, Max. *Invisible Armies*	355.02
Crawford, Alan Pell. *This Fierce People*	975
Crutchfield, James A. *Revolt at Taos*	972
Dunn, Harry. *Standing My Ground*	B
Fairweather, Jack. *The Volunteer*	B
Fraser, Antonia. *Faith and Treason*	942.06
Kurlansky, Mark. *1968*	909.82
Lemmon, Gayle Tzemach. *The Daughters of Kobani*	956.9104
Loyn, David. *The Long War*	958.104
Maddow, Rachel. ★*Prequel*	320.53
Mazower, Mark. *The Greek Revolution*	949.5
Packer, George. *The Assassins' Gate*	956.7044
Roy, Arundhati. *Walking with the Comrades*	954
Ullrich, Volker. *Germany 1923*	943.085
Warren, James A. *Year of the Hawk*	959.704
INTEGRITY	
Davis, Seth. *Wooden*	B
Reynolds, David S. ★*Abe*	B
INTELLECTUAL FREEDOM	
Curran, Andrew S. *Diderot and the Art of Thinking Freely*	194
LaRue, James. ★*On Censorship*	025.2
Nafisi, Azar. *Read Dangerously*	809
Pinnell-Stephens, June. *Protecting Intellectual Freedom in Your Public Library*	025.2
INTELLECTUAL LIFE	
Abdurraqib, Hanif. ★*A Little Devil in America*	791.089
Anthony, Carl Sferrazza. *Camera Girl*	B
Bader, Philip. *African-American Writers*	810.9
Bartlett, Rosamund. ★*Tolstoy*	B
Barzun, Jacques. *From Dawn to Decadence*	940.2
Basbanes, Nicholas A. ★*Cross of Snow*	B
Bate, Jonathan. *Radical Wordsworth*	B
Benner, Erica. *Be Like the Fox*	B
Blumenthal, Sidney. *Wrestling with His Angel*	B
Bly, Robert. *Collected Poems*	811
Cheever, Susan. *American Bloomsbury*	920
Cheng, Nien. *Life and Death in Shanghai*	B
Coffin, Judith G. *Sex, Love, and Letters*	848
Cordery, Stacy A. *Alice*	B
Curran, Andrew S. *Diderot and the Art of Thinking Freely*	194
Dawkins, Richard. *Brief Candle in the Dark*	B
Di Cintio, Marcello. *Pay No Heed to the Rockets*	956.9405
Dinesen, Isak. *Out of Africa*	967.62
Ellis, Joseph J. *American Sphinx*	973.4
Ellison, Ralph. *The Selected Letters of Ralph Ellison*	813
Evans, William. *Black Nerd Problems*	814.6
Figes, Orlando. *The Europeans*	920
Frank, Joseph. ★*Dostoevsky*	B
Gabbert, Elisa. *Any Person Is the Only Self*	814
Gabriel, Mary. *Love and Capital*	920
Ginzberg, Lori D. *Elizabeth Cady Stanton*	B
Gluck, Louise. *American Originality*	814
Goodheart, Adam. *1861*	973.7
Gottlieb, Anthony. ★*The Dream of Enlightenment*	190
Grayling, A. C. *The Age of Genius*	940.2
Greenblatt, Stephen. ★*The Swerve*	940.2
Greenblatt, Stephen. ★*Will in the World*	B
Griffin, Farah Jasmine. *Read Until You Understand*	810.9
Gurdon, Meghan Cox. *The Enchanted Hour*	372.4
Harlan, Louis R. *Booker T. Washington*	B
Herman, Arthur. *How the Scots Invented the Modern World*	941.1
Hitchens, Christopher. *The Four Horsemen*	211
Hoffman, Adina. *Sacred Trash*	296.09
hooks, bell. *Remembered Rapture*	808
Housden, Roger. *Saved by Beauty*	955
Hughes, Bettany. ★*The Hemlock Cup*	B
Humez, Jean McMahon. *Harriet Tubman*	B
Hurston, Zora Neale. *Dust Tracks on a Road*	B
Joseph, Peniel E. *Waiting 'Til the Midnight Hour*	323.1196
Kaag, John J. *American Philosophy*	191
Kagan, Donald. *Thucydides*	938
Kamensky, Jane. *A Revolution in Color*	759.13
Khilnani, Sunil. *Incarnations*	920
King, Charles. *Midnight at the Pera Palace*	949.61
Lepore, Jill. ★*The Deadline*	814
Lester, Toby. *Da Vinci's Ghost*	741.092
Martin, Justin. *Rebel Souls*	920
Massie, Robert K. *Catherine the Great*	B
McCullough, David G. *The Greater Journey*	920
McHangama, Jacob. ★*Free Speech*	323.44
Menand, Louis. *The Free World*	306.0973
Meyerson, Michael. *Liberty's Blueprint*	342.7302
Mishra, Pankaj. *From the Ruins of Empire*	950.4
Nicolson, Adam. *How to Be*	180
Norrell, Robert J. *Up from History*	B
Nuland, Sherwin B. *Leonardo Da Vinci*	B
Nuttall, A. D. *Shakespeare the Thinker*	822.33
Penaluna, Regan. ★*How to Think Like a Woman*	190.82
Perry, Imani. *May We Forever Stand*	782.25
Pinckney, Darryl. *Come Back in September*	B
Poirier, Agnes. *Left Bank*	944
Rakove, Jack N. *Revolutionaries*	973.3
Ransby, Barbara. *Eslanda*	B
Rappaport, Helen. *After the Romanovs*	944
Robertson, Ritchie. *The Enlightenment*	190
Romano, Carlin. *America the Philosophical*	191
Russell, Bertrand. *The Problems of Philosophy*	110
Schell, Orville. *Wealth and Power*	920
Schlesinger, Arthur M. *A Life in the Twentieth Century*	B
Schwartz, David N. *The Last Man Who Knew Everything*	B
Showalter, Elaine. ★*A Jury of Her Peers*	810.9
Sigmund, Karl. *Exact Thinking in Demented Times*	920
Stewart, Jeffrey C. ★*The New Negro*	191
Tallis, Frank. ★*Mortal Secrets*	B

PUBLIC LIBRARY CORE COLLECTION: NONFICTION
Twentieth Edition

Twain, Mark. *Autobiography of Mark Twain*	B
Twain, Mark. ★*Autobiography of Mark Twain*	B
Twain, Mark. ★*Autobiography of Mark Twain*	B
Vargas Llosa, Mario. *The Call of the Tribe*	868
Walker, Alice. *Gathering Blossoms Under Fire*	B
Warren, Rosanna. *Max Jacob*	B
Watson, Peter. *The German Genius*	943
Whitaker, Mark. *Smoketown*	305.896
Wilson, Derek K. *A Magical World*	261.55
Wilson-Lee, Edward. ★*The Catalogue of Shipwrecked Books*	B
Wulf, Andrea. *Magnificent Rebels*	830.9
Zenith, Richard. *Pessoa*	B
Zygar, Mikhail. *The Empire Must Die*	947.08

INTELLECTUAL PROPERTY

Bellos, David. *Who Owns This Sentence?*	346.73
Lessig, Lawrence. *The Future of Ideas*	346.04
Lobel, Orly. *You Don't Own Me*	346.7304
Norwick, Kenneth P. *The Legal Guide for Writers, Artists and Other Creative People*	346.04
Taplin, Jonathan. *Move Fast and Break Things*	330.9

INTELLECTUAL PROPERTY INFRINGEMENT

Lobel, Orly. *You Don't Own Me*	346.7304

INTELLECTUALS

Bakewell, Sarah. *How to Live—Or—A Life of Montaigne*	B
Benner, Erica. *Be Like the Fox*	B
Chomsky, Noam. *Global Discontents*	410.92
Damrosch, Leopold. *The Club*	920
Eilenberger, Wolfram. *Time of the Magicians*	920
Ellis, Joseph J. *American Sphinx*	973.4
Gewen, Barry. ★*The Inevitability of Tragedy*	B
Gladwell, Malcolm. *Outliers*	302
Greenblatt, Stephen. ★*The Swerve*	940.2
Hardwick, Elizabeth. *The Dolphin Letters, 1970-1979*	811
Hester, Diarmuid. *Nothing Ever Just Disappears*	306.76
Hitchens, Christopher. *Hitch-22*	920
Kaag, John J. *American Philosophy*	191
Kaplan, Janice. *The Genius of Women*	920
Markovits, Daniel. *The Meritocracy Trap*	305.5
McCullough, David G. *The Greater Journey*	920
Meyerson, Michael. *Liberty's Blueprint*	342.7302
Miller, Jim. *Examined Lives*	B
Mishra, Pankaj. *From the Ruins of Empire*	950.4
Parkin, Simon. *The Island of Extraordinary Captives*	940.53
Poirier, Agnes. *Left Bank*	944
Prideaux, Sue. *I Am Dynamite!*	B
Ransby, Barbara. *Eslanda*	B
Rosenberg, Rosalind. ★*Jane Crow*	B
Schloss, Edith. *The Loft Generation*	700.9
Sen, Amartya. *Home in the World*	B
Shatz, Adam. *The Rebel's Clinic*	965
Sperber, Jonathan. *Karl Marx*	B
Strathern, Paul. *The Florentines*	945
Walls, Laura Dassow. ★*Henry David Thoreau*	B
Wheen, Francis. *Karl Marx*	B
Wilson-Lee, Edward. ★*The Catalogue of Shipwrecked Books*	B

INTELLIGENCE

Bloom, Paul. *Psych*	150
Brookwood, Marilyn. *The Orphans of Davenport*	305.231
Foster, Charles. *Being a Human*	155.7
Gould, Stephen Jay. *The Mismeasure of Man*	153.9
Hofstadter, Douglas R. *I Am a Strange Loop*	153
Kasparov, G. K. *Deep Thinking*	006.3
Murdoch, Stephen. *IQ*	153.9
Paul, Annie Murphy. *The Extended Mind*	128
Sagan, Carl. *Broca's Brain*	128
Sagan, Carl. *The Dragons of Eden*	153
Sarma, Sanjay E. *Grasp*	370.15
Schlanger, Zoe. ★*The Light Eaters*	571.2
Tough, Paul. ★*How Children Succeed*	372.210973

INTELLIGENCE OFFICERS

Anderson, Scott. ★*The Quiet Americans*	327.12
Boot, Max. ★*The Road Not Taken*	B
Conant, Jennet. *The Lotus Eaters*	940.54
Friedman, Matti. *Spies of No Country*	327.12
Helm, Sarah. *A Life in Secrets*	B
Henderson, Bruce B. *Sons and Soldiers*	940.53
Howley, Kerry. *Bottoms Up and the Devil Laughs*	352.37
Kix, Paul. *The Saboteur*	940.53

Purnell, Sonia. ★*A Woman of No Importance*	B
Wallace, Chris. *Countdown Bin Laden*	958.104
Waller, Douglas C. *Wild Bill Donovan*	B
Weiner, Tim. *Legacy of Ashes*	327.1273009

INTELLIGENCE SERVICE

Andrew, Christopher M. *The Secret World*	327.1209
Baker, Nicholson. *Baseless*	358
Berg, Raffi. *Red Sea Spies*	327.125694
Coker, Margaret. *The Spymaster of Baghdad*	956.7044
Conant, Jennet. *The Lotus Eaters*	940.54
Dean, Josh. *The Taking of K-129*	910.91
Fox, Amaryllis. *Life Undercover*	B
Friedman, Barry. ★*Unwarranted*	344.7305
Hastings, Max. *Operation Pedestal*	940.54
Hemming, Henry. *Agents of Influence*	940.54
Hillsberg, Christina. *License to Parent*	649.1
Hindley, Meredith. *Destination Casablanca*	940.54
Jacobsen, Annie. ★*Operation Paperclip*	940.54
Jacobsen, Annie. *Surprise, Kill, Vanish*	327.1273
Jacobson, Sidney. *The 9-11 Report*	741.5
Kershaw, Alex. *Avenue of Spies*	940.53
Lane, Charles. *Freedom's Detective*	B
Lisle, John. *The Dirty Tricks Department*	940.54
Macintyre, Ben. *Agent Zigzag*	B
Macintyre, Ben. ★*The Spy and the Traitor*	B
Magida, Arthur J. *Code Name Madeleine*	940.54
Manning, Chelsea. *Readme.Txt*	B
Maroney, Tyler. *The Modern Detective*	658.4
Mazzeo, Tilar J. *Sisters in Resistance*	945.091
McCoy, Alfred W. *A Question of Torture*	323.4
McKay, Sinclair. *The Secret Lives of Codebreakers*	940.54
Morley, Jefferson. *Scorpions' Dance*	973.924
Mundy, Liza. ★*The Sisterhood*	327.12
O'Neill, Tom. ★*Chaos*	364.152
Popkin, Jim. *Code Name Blue Wren*	327.12
Purnell, Sonia. ★*A Woman of No Importance*	B
Reynolds, Nicholas E. *Need to Know*	940.54
Risen, James. ★*The Last Honest Man*	973.92
Rose, Sarah. *D-Day Girls*	940.53
Scahill, Jeremy. *Dirty Wars*	355.00973
Scott-Clark, Cathy. *The Forever Prisoner*	364.6
Shakespeare, Nicholas. *Ian Fleming*	B
Talty, Stephan. *Agent Garbo*	940.5
Talty, Stephan. *The Good Assassin*	364.15
Vickers, Michael G. *By All Means Available*	355
Vogel, Steve. *Betrayal in Berlin*	327.1273043
Walder, Tracy. *The Unexpected Spy*	B
Waller, Douglas C. *Lincoln's Spies*	973.7
Waller, Douglas C. *Wild Bill Donovan*	B
Walton, Calder. *Spies*	327.1247
Weiner, Tim. *The Folly and the Glory*	327.73047
Weiner, Tim. *Legacy of Ashes*	327.1273009
Whipple, Chris. *The Spymasters*	920
Wiehl, Lis W. *A Spy in Plain Sight*	327.1247
Wilford, Hugh. *The CIA*	327.1273
Wright, Lawrence. ★*The Looming Tower*	973.931

INTELLIGENCE TESTS

Gould, Stephen Jay. *The Mismeasure of Man*	153.9
Murdoch, Stephen. *IQ*	153.9

*The **Intelligent** Investor.* Graham, Benjamin — 332.67

INTENSIVE CARE UNITS

Ely, Wes. *Every Deep-Drawn Breath*	616.02

INTERCLASS ROMANCE

Offerman, Nick. *The Greatest Love Story Ever Told*	B

INTERCONTINENTAL BALLISTIC MISSILES

Sheehan, Neil. *A Fiery Peace in a Cold War*	B

INTERCULTURAL COMMUNICATION

Fadiman, Anne. *The Spirit Catches You and You Fall Down*	306.4
Fischer, David Hackett. ★*African Founders*	973
Mukantabana, Yseult P. ★*Real Friends Talk About Race*	305.8
Oluo, Ijeoma. ★*So You Want to Talk About Race*	305.800973
Schweitzer, Sharon. *Access to Asia*	395.5
Tatum, Beverly Daniel. ★*"Why Are All the Black Kids Sitting Together in the Cafeteria?"*	305.800973
Tsu, Jing. *Kingdom of Characters*	495.111
Wagner, Alex. *Futureface*	B

INTERDEPENDENCE IN NATURE

Jabr, Ferris. ★*Becoming Earth*	570.1

AUTHOR, TITLE, SERIES AND SUBJECT INDEX

INTERDISCIPLINARY APPROACH IN EDUCATION
   Zinsser, William Knowlton. *Writing to Learn* — 808
INTEREST
   Keynes, John Maynard. ★*The General Theory of Employment, Interest, and Money* — 330.15
INTEREST GROUPS
   Leonard, Christopher. *Kochland* — 338.7
INTERETHNIC CONFLICT
   Blattman, Christopher. *Why We Fight* — 303.6
   Iyer, Pico. ★*The Half Known Life* — 203
   Matloff, Judith. *No Friends but the Mountains* — 355.009
   Mohan, Rohini. *The Seasons of Trouble* — 954.9303
   Peer, Basharat. *Curfewed Night* — B
   Platt, Stephen R. *Autumn in the Heavenly Kingdom* — 951
   Steinberg, Jonny. *A Man of Good Hope* — B
   Subramanian, Sammanth. *This Divided Island* — 954.9303
   Trebincevic, Kenan. *The Bosnia List* — B
INTERETHNIC FAMILIES
   Som, Brandon. *Tripas* — 811
   Wagner, Alex. *Futureface* — B
INTERETHNIC FRIENDSHIP
   Shehadeh, Raja. *Where the Line Is Drawn* — 956.9405
INTERETHNIC MARRIAGE
   Horn, James P. P. *A Kingdom Strange* — 975.6
INTERETHNIC RELATIONS
   Ackerman, Diane. ★*The Zookeeper's Wife* — 940.53
   Alexander, Michelle. *The New Jim Crow* — 364.973
   Ali, Wajahat. *Go Back to Where You Came From* — B
   Arce, Julissa. *You Sound Like a White Girl* — 303.48
   Armstrong, Karen. *Jerusalem* — 956.94
   Blum, Edward J. *The Color of Christ* — 232
   Carter, Jimmy. *Palestine* — 956.04
   Cozzens, Peter. *The Earth Is Weeping* — 978
   Curtis, Edward E. *Muslims in America* — 305.6
   Dalrymple, William. *White Mughals* — 954
   Dwork, Deborah. ★*Holocaust* — 940
   Edmonds, Chris. *No Surrender* — B
   Frank, Anne. ★*The Diary of a Young Girl* — 940.53
   Franklin, John Hope. ★*From Slavery to Freedom* — 973
   Fraser, Rebecca. *The Mayflower* — 974.4
   Freedman, Samuel G. *Jew vs. Jew* — 296
   Friedlander, Saul. *Nazi Germany and the Jews* — 940.53
   Fritzsche, Peter. *Life and Death in the Third Reich* — 943.086
   Gayle, Caleb. *We Refuse to Forget* — 975.004
   Gies, Miep. ★*Anne Frank Remembered* — B
   Gourevitch, Philip. *We Wish to Inform You That Tomorrow We Will Be Killed with Our Families* — 364.15
   Gross, Jan Tomasz. *Neighbors* — 940.53
   Hatzfeld, Jean. *Machete Season* — 967.57104
   Hayes, Peter. *Why?* — 940.53
   Izgil, Tahir Hamut. *Waiting to Be Arrested at Night* — B
   Kritzler, Ed. *Jewish Pirates of the Caribbean* — 972.9
   Lee, Erika. *The Making of Asian America* — 973
   Lindwer, Willy. *The Last Seven Months of Anne Frank* — B
   Maass, Peter. *Love Thy Neighbor* — 949.702
   Mazower, Mark. *The Balkans* — 949.6
   Ortiz, Paul. *An African American and Latinx History of the United States* — 305.8
   Pappe, Ilan. *The Biggest Prison on Earth* — 956.9405
   Peer, Basharat. *Curfewed Night* — B
   Platt, Stephen R. *Autumn in the Heavenly Kingdom* — 951
   Roberts, David. *Once They Moved Like the Wind* — B
   Sarna, Jonathan D. ★*American Judaism* — 296
   Sefarad, Mikhael. *The Wall and the Gate* — 341.48
   Shavit, Ari. *My Promised Land* — 956.05
   Steinberg, Jonny. *A Man of Good Hope* — B
   Taylor, Alan. *The Divided Ground* — 974.7
   Trebincevic, Kenan. *The Bosnia List* — B
   Treuer, Anton. *Everything You Wanted to Know About Indians but Were Afraid to Ask* — 970.1
INTERFAITH FAMILIES
   Mehra, Nishta. *Brown, White, Black* — 305.800973
INTERFAITH FRIENDSHIP
   AL Samawi, Mohammed. *The Fox Hunt* — 953
INTERFAITH RELATIONS
   Abdul Rauf, Feisal. *Moving the Mountain* — 297
   Akyol, Mustafa. *The Islamic Jesus* — 297.2
   Armstrong, Karen. *Jerusalem* — 956.94
   Asbridge, Thomas S. ★*The Crusades* — 909.07
   Carroll, James. *Constantine's Sword* — 261
   Cliff, Nigel. *Holy War* — 909
   Frankopan, Peter. *The First Crusade* — 956
   Griffith, R. Marie. *Moral Combat* — 261.8
   Griswold, Eliza. *The Tenth Parallel* — 297.2
   Jones, Dan. *Crusaders* — 909.07
   Kertzer, David I. *The Pope at War* — 940.53
   Lambert, Malcolm. *God's Armies* — 956
   Levine, Amy-Jill. *The Bible with and Without Jesus* — 220.6
   Rehman, Sabeeha. *Threading My Prayer Rug* — 305.8
   Sebag-Montefiore, Simon. *Jerusalem* — 956.94
   Taylor, Barbara Brown. *Holy Envy* — B
INTERGENERATIONAL COMMUNICATION
   Kline, Emily. ★*The School of Hard Talks* — 155.5
   Koh, EJ. *The Magical Language of Others* — 813
INTERGENERATIONAL FRIENDSHIP
   Frank, Michael. ★*One Hundred Saturdays* — B
   Von Drehle, David. ★*The Book of Charlie* — B
INTERGENERATIONAL RELATIONS
   Abdelmahmoud, Elamin. *Son of Elsewhere* — B
   Alexander, Kwame. *Why Fathers Cry at Night* — B
   Brand, Christo. *Mandela* — B
   Fishman, Boris. *Savage Feast* — B
   Hatzfeld, Jean. *Blood Papa* — 967.5710431
   Hulls, Tessa. ★*Feeding Ghosts* — 741.5
   Kan, Karoline. *Under Red Skies* — B
   Koh, EJ. *The Magical Language of Others* — 813
   McConville, Mark. *Failure to Launch* — 155.6
   Qu, Anna. *Made in China* — B
   Royster, Francesca T. *Choosing Family* — B
   Tanais. *In Sensorium* — B
   Tran, Paul. *All the Flowers Kneeling* — 811
   Twenge, Jean M. *Generations* — 305.2
INTERGENERATIONAL TRAUMA
   Alexander, Elizabeth. ★*The Trayvon Generation* — 305.896
   Asghar, Fatimah. *If They Come for Us* — 811
   Broome, Brian. ★*Punch Me up to the Gods* — B
   Buque, Mariel. *Break the Cycle* — 616.85
   Cain, Susan. ★*Bittersweet* — 155.2
   Choi, Franny. *The World Keeps Ending, and the World Goes On* — 811
   Davis, Viola. ★*Finding Me* — B
   Di Cintio, Marcello. *Pay No Heed to the Rockets* — 956.9405
   Foo, Stephanie. ★*What My Bones Know* — B
   Gerson, Merissa Nathan. *Forget Prayers, Bring Cake* — 155.9
   Gupta, Prachi. ★*They Called Us Exceptional* — B
   Hatzfeld, Jean. *Blood Papa* — 967.5710431
   Hempel, Jessi. *The Family Outing* — B
   Hernandez Castillo, Marcelo. *Children of the Land* — B
   Hill, Jemele. *Uphill* — B
   Hulls, Tessa. ★*Feeding Ghosts* — 741.5
   Nguyen, Viet Thanh. ★*A Man of Two Faces* — B
   Olivares, Efren C. *My Boy Will Die of Sorrow* — 305.9
   Potts, Monica. *The Forgotten Girls* — B
   Ralph, Laurence. *Sito* — 364.152
   Rojas Contreras, Ingrid. ★*The Man Who Could Move Clouds* — B
   Rosner, Elizabeth. *Survivor Cafe* — 940.53
   Shakur, Prince. *When They Tell You to Be Good* — B
   Streep, Abe. *Brothers on Three* — 306.85
   Tanais. *In Sensorium* — B
   Tran, Paul. *All the Flowers Kneeling* — 811
   Tyson, Cicely. ★*Just as I Am* — B
INTERIOR ARCHITECTURE
   Susanka, Sarah. *Creating the Not so Big House* — 728
   Susanka, Sarah. *Not so Big Solutions for Your Home* — 728
INTERIOR DECORATION
   Adams, Michael Henry. *Style and Grace* — 747
   Becker, Holly. *Decorate* — 747
   Blakeney, Justina. *Jungalow* — 747
   Blakeney, Justina. *The New Bohemians Handbook* — 747
   Boyd, Nikki. ★*Beautifully Organized* — 648
   Bradbury, Dominic. *The Iconic Interior* — 747
   Bradbury, Dominic. *Mountain Modern* — 728
   Bridges, Sheila. *Furnishing Forward* — 747
   Brits, Louisa Thomsen. *The Book of Hygge* — 747
   Carlson, Julie. *Remodelista* — 648
   Carter, Darryl. *The Collected Home* — 747
   Carter, Darryl. *The New Traditional* — 747

PUBLIC LIBRARY CORE COLLECTION: NONFICTION
Twentieth Edition

Carter, Hilton. *Wild Interiors*	747.98
Frisoni, Christine-Lea. *The Big Book of a Miniature House*	745.592
Gates, Erin T. ★*Elements of Family Style*	747
Gill, Shira. *Organized Living*	747
Gold, Jamie. *Taunton's New Bathroom Idea Book*	747.7
Grove, Kirsten. *Simply Styling*	747
Gura, Judith. *The Guide to Period Styles for Interiors*	747
Guralnick, Margot. *Remodelista*	747
Hays, Jeanine. *Remix*	747
Katz, Emily. *Modern Macrame*	746.42
Khemsurov, Monica. *How to Live with Objects*	747
Kotite, Erika. *She Sheds*	728
Lamb, Kelli. *Home with Rue*	747
Larson, Elsie. *A Beautiful Mess Happy Handmade Home*	745
Lee, Vinny. *Kitchenalia*	747.7
Linsley, Leslie. *Salvage Style*	747
McClain, John. *The Designer Within*	645
Merhi, Farah. ★*Inspire Your Home*	747
Moss, Charlotte. *Garden Inspirations*	747
Napier, Erin. *Heirloom Rooms*	747
Needleman, Deborah. *The Perfectly Imperfect Home*	747
Parrella-Van Den Berg, Janet. *White & Faded*	645
Petersik, Sherry. *Lovable Livable Home*	645
Spencer, Lara. *Flea Market Fabulous*	747
Tanov, Erica. *Design by Nature*	747
Taylor, Claude. *How to Zoom Your Room*	747
Wilhide, Elizabeth. *Scandinavian Home*	728

INTERIOR DECORATORS

Gaines, Joanna. *The Stories We Tell*	B
Gill, Shira. *Organized Living*	747
★*The Internal Enemy.* Taylor, Alan	975.5

INTERNAL SECURITY

Gopal, Anand. *No Good Men Among the Living*	920

INTERNATIONAL ADOPTION

Brierley, Saroo. *A Long Way Home*	B
Guida-Richards, Melissa. *What White Parents Should Know About Transracial Adoption*	362.734
Hayasaki, Erika. *Somewhere Sisters*	362.7

INTERNATIONAL BANKING

Enrich, David. *Dark Towers*	332.1
Michel, Casey. *American Kleptocracy*	364.16

INTERNATIONAL BUSINESSES

Bown, Stephen R. *Merchant Kings*	338.8
Elmore, Bartow J. *Citizen Coke*	338.7

INTERNATIONAL COMPETITION

Barr, James. *Lords of the Desert*	956
Brinkley, Douglas. ★*American Moonshot*	629.40973
Carter, Iain. *Golf Wars*	796.352
Dolnick, Edward. *The Writing of the Gods*	493
Donovan, Jim. ★*Shoot for the Moon*	629.45
Dugard, Martin. *Taking Berlin*	940.54
Ellsworth, Scott. *The World Beneath Their Feet*	796.522
Kurson, Robert. ★*Rocket Men*	629.45
Marshall, Tim. *The Power of Geography*	320.1
Miller, Chris. *Chip War*	338.4
Sherr, Lynn. *Sally Ride*	B
Shesol, Jeff. *Mercury Rising*	629.45
Shetterly, Margot Lee. ★*Hidden Figures*	510.92
Stone, Robert. *Chasing the Moon*	629.45
Walker, Stephen. *Beyond*	629.45
Walton, Calder. *Spies*	327.1247
Wilkinson, Toby A. H. *A World Beneath the Sands*	932

INTERNATIONAL COOKING

Bourdain, Anthony. ★*World Travel*	641.59
Hall, Carla. *Carla's Comfort Foods*	641.59
Hansen, Kim-Julie. *Best of Vegan*	641.5
Katzen, Mollie. *The Heart of the Plate*	641.5
Kimball, Christopher. *Christopher Kimball's Milk Street*	641.5
Kimball, Christopher. *Milk Street*	641.7
Lee, Edward. *Buttermilk Graffiti*	641.59
Pittman, Ann Taylor. *The Global Pantry Cookbook*	641.59
Rodriguez, Jessamyn Waldman. *The Hot Bread Kitchen Cookbook*	641.59
Rosenthal, Phil. ★*Somebody Feed Phil the Book*	641.59
Samuelsson, Marcus. *The Red Rooster Cookbook*	641.5974
Shepherd, Chris. *Cook Like a Local*	641.59
Snoop Dogg. *Goon with the Spoon*	641.59
Tandoh, Ruby. ★*Cook as You Are*	641.59

INTERNATIONAL COOPERATION

Burns, William J. *The Back Channel*	B
Cox, Joseph. *Dark Wire*	363.2
Gates, Bill. ★*How to Prevent the Next Pandemic*	614.5
Kershaw, Ian. *The Global Age*	940.55
Klare, Michael T. *All Hell Breaking Loose*	355.20973
Piketty, Thomas. ★*Capital and Ideology*	305
Scheyder, Ernest. *The War Below*	333.7

INTERNATIONAL CRIME

Greenberg, Andy. *Tracers in the Dark*	364.16
Nance, Malcolm W. *The Plot to Betray America*	973.933

INTERNATIONAL ECONOMIC INTEGRATION

Stiglitz, Joseph E. *Globalization and Its Discontents*	337

INTERNATIONAL ECONOMIC RELATIONS

Conway, Edmund. *The Summit*	337.09
Crowley, Roger. *City of Fortune*	945
Daunton, M. J. ★*The Economic Government of the World*	337

INTERNATIONAL FINANCE

Ahamed, Liaquat. *Lords of Finance*	920
Conway, Edmund. *The Summit*	337.09
Daunton, M. J. ★*The Economic Government of the World*	337
Goodman, Peter S. ★*How the World Ran Out of Everything*	658.7
Russell, Rupert. *Price Wars*	332.64
Steil, Benn. *The Battle of Bretton Woods*	339.5
Stiglitz, Joseph E. *Globalization and Its Discontents*	337

INTERNATIONAL INTRIGUE

Kix, Paul. *The Saboteur*	940.53
Maier, Thomas. *Mafia Spies*	364.1060973
McMeekin, Sean. *July 1914*	940.3
Walton, Calder. *Spies*	327.1247

INTERNATIONAL RELATIONS

Abrahamian, Ervand. *The Coup*	955.05
Ackerman, Spencer. *Reign of Terror*	973.931
Albright, Madeleine Korbel. *Hell and Other Destinations*	B
Ambinder, Marc. *The Brink*	355.5
Applebaum, Anne. *Iron Curtain*	947
Appy, Christian G. *American Reckoning*	959.704
Asbridge, Thomas S. ★*The Crusades*	909.07
Bacevich, Andrew J. *America's War for the Greater Middle East*	956.05
Baer, Daniel Brooks. *The Four Tests*	320.973
Baime, A. J. *The Accidental President*	B
Barr, James. *A Line in the Sand*	956
Barr, James. *Lords of the Desert*	956
Becker, Elizabeth. *Overbooked*	338.4
Bennis, Phyllis. *Understanding the Palestinian-Israeli Conflict*	956.9405
Beschloss, Michael R. *The Conquerors*	940.53
Bhutto, Benazir. *Reconciliation*	297.2
Bird, Kai. *The Outlier*	973.926
Black, George. ★*The Long Reckoning*	959.704
Blair, Tony. *A Journey*	B
Bouverie, Tim. *Appeasement*	327.41043
Bowden, Mark. *Guests of the Ayatollah*	955.05
Bowden, Mark. ★*Hue 1968*	959.704
Brands, H. W. *Woodrow Wilson*	B
Budiansky, Stephen. *Code Warriors*	327.73047
Burns, William J. *The Back Channel*	B
Capozzola, Christopher. *Bound by War*	355
Carlson, Peter. *K Blows Top*	947.085
Castro, Fidel. *Fidel Castro*	B
Chait, Jonathan. *Audacity*	973.932
Charter, David. *Royal Audience*	941.085
Chase, James. *Acheson*	B
Churchill, Winston. *The Grand Alliance*	940.53
Churchill, Winston. *Triumph and Tragedy*	940.53
Clarke, Thurston. *Honorable Exit*	959.704
Coleman, David G. *The Fourteenth Day*	973.922092
Coll, Steve. ★*The Achilles Trap*	956.7044
Coll, Steve. *The Bin Ladens*	920
Coll, Steve. *Directorate S*	958.104
Coll, Steve. ★*Ghost Wars*	958.104
Conant, Jennet. *Man of the Hour*	B
Conradi, Peter J. *Who Lost Russia?*	947.086
Cook, Jane Hampton. *American Phoenix*	973.5
Craig, William. *Yankee Come Home*	972.9107
Crowley, Roger. *1453*	949.61
Dallek, Robert. *Nixon and Kissinger*	B
Dalrymple, William. *The Return of a King*	958.1
Daunton, M. J. ★*The Economic Government of the World*	337

AUTHOR, TITLE, SERIES AND SUBJECT INDEX

Downey, Kirstin. *Isabella*	B
Draper, Robert. *To Start a War*	956.7044
Elnoury, Tamer. *American Radical*	B
Evans, Martin. *Algeria*	965
Farrow, Ronan. *War on Peace*	327.73
Fasulo, Linda M. *An Insider's Guide to the Un, 4th Ed.*	341.23
Ferguson, Niall. *Kissinger*	973.924
Fernandez-Armesto, Felipe. *Our America*	973
Ferreiro, Larrie D. *Brothers at Arms*	327.73
Ferrer, Ada. ★*Cuba*	972.91
Finn, Peter. *The Zhivago Affair*	891.73
Fisk, Robert. *The Great War for Civilisation*	956.04
FitzGerald, Frances. *Fire in the Lake*	959.704
Frank, Jeffrey. *The Trials of Harry S. Truman*	973.918
Friedman, Thomas L. ★*From Beirut to Jerusalem*	956.04
Friedman, Thomas L. ★*Thank You for Being Late*	303.48
Fullilove, Michael. *Rendezvous with Destiny*	973.917092
Galeotti, Mark. *A Short History of Russia*	947.086
Gans, John. *White House Warriors*	355
Gates, Robert Michael. *Exercise of Power*	973.929
Gewen, Barry. ★*The Inevitability of Tragedy*	B
Ghattas, Kim. *Black Wave*	955.05
Ghazvinian, John. *America and Iran*	327
Gomez, Laura E. ★*Inventing Latinos*	305.868
Gordin, Michael D. *Red Cloud at Dawn*	355.02
Grandin, Greg. *Kissinger's Shadow*	B
Gristwood, Sarah. *The Tudors in Love*	941.05
Hamilton, Nigel. *The Mantle of Command*	940.54
Harden, Blaine. *The Great Leader and the Fighter Pilot*	B
Harding, Luke. *Collusion*	324.70973
Harding, Luke. *Invasion*	947.7
Hastings, Max. *The Abyss*	972.9106
Herman, Arthur. *1917*	940.3
Hernandez, Kelly Lytle. ★*Bad Mexicans*	972
Hill, Fiona. *There Is Nothing for You Here*	327.2
Hindley, Meredith. *Destination Casablanca*	940.54
Hitchcock, William I. *The Age of Eisenhower*	973.921092
Hope, Bradley. *Blood and Oil*	B
Howe, Daniel Walker. *What Hath God Wrought*	973.5
Hoyer, Katja. *Blood and Iron*	943.08
Hvistendahl, Mara. ★*The Scientist and the Spy*	364.16
Indyk, Martin. *Master of the Game*	327.73
Isikoff, Michael. *Russian Roulette*	973.933
Jacobsen, Annie. *Surprise, Kill, Vanish*	327.1273
Jeppesen, Travis. *See You Again in Pyongyang*	951.93
Judt, Tony. *Postwar*	940.55
Kaplan, Robert D. *Warrior Politics*	320
Karabell, Zachary. *Inside Money*	332.1
Kasparov, Gary. *Winter Is Coming*	947.086
Kemper, Steve. *Our Man in Tokyo*	952.03
Kennedy, Robert F. *Thirteen Days*	327.73
Kertzer, David I. *The Pope at War*	940.53
Khan, Yasmin Sabina. *Enlightening the World*	974.7
Khodorkovsky, Mikhail. *The Russia Conundrum*	947.086
Kinzer, Stephen. ★*All the Shah's Men*	955.05
Kinzer, Stephen. ★*The True Flag*	327.73
Kurtz-Phelan, Daniel. *The China Mission*	951.04
Lieven, Anatol. *Pakistan*	954.9105
Logevall, Fredrik. *Embers of War*	959.704
Lovell, Julia. *Maoism*	335.43
Loyn, David. *The Long War*	958.104
Macy, Beth. ★*Factory Man*	338.7
Mahtani, Shibani. *Among the Braves*	951.25
Maier, Thomas. *Mafia Spies*	364.1060973
Manchester, William. *The Last Lion, Winston Spencer Churchill.*	B
Mann, Jim. *The Rebellion of Ronald Reagan*	973.927092
Marshall, Tim. *The Power of Geography*	320.1
McConahay, Mary Jo. *The Tango War*	940.53
McKean, David. *Watching Darkness Fall*	940.53
McMeekin, Sean. *July 1914*	940.3
McNamara, Kevin J. *Dreams of a Great Small Nation*	355.009437
Meacham, Jon. *Franklin and Winston*	940.53
Mead, Walter Russell. *The Arc of a Covenant*	327.73
Mendez, Antonio J. *Argo*	955.05
Merridale, Catherine. *Lenin on the Train*	B
Millard, Candice. ★*Hero of the Empire*	968.04
Miraldi, Robert. *Seymour Hersh*	B
Mirski, Sean A. *We May Dominate the World*	973.91
Mitter, Rana. *Forgotten Ally*	951.04
Moorhouse, Roger. *The Devils' Alliance*	940.53
Morris, Benny. *1948*	956.04
Morris, Ian. *Geography Is Destiny*	941
Nance, Malcolm W. *The Plot to Betray America*	973.933
Neu, Charles E. *Colonel House*	B
Newitz, Annalee. *Stories Are Weapons*	355.3
O'Toole, Patricia. *The Moralist*	B
Olson, Lynne. *Citizens of London*	940.54012
Olson, Lynne. *Those Angry Days*	940.53
Ortiz, Paul. *An African American and Latinx History of the United States*	305.8
Packer, George. *The Assassins' Gate*	956.7044
Pak, Jung H. *Becoming Kim Jong Un*	B
Pan, Philip P. *Out of Mao's Shadow*	306.20951
Phillips, Adrian. *Fighting Churchill, Appeasing Hitler*	327.41043
Platt, Stephen R. *Autumn in the Heavenly Kingdom*	951
Plokhy, Serhii. ★*Nuclear Folly*	972.9106
Plokhy, Serhii. *Yalta*	940.53
Preston, Diana. *Eight Days at Yalta*	940.53
Preston, Richard. *Crisis in the Red Zone*	614.5
Rasenberger, Jim. *The Brilliant Disaster*	972.9106
Reid, Stuart A. *The Lumumba Plot*	967.51
Ricks, Thomas E. *Fiasco*	956.7044
Risen, James. ★*The Last Honest Man*	973.92
Roll, David L. *George Marshall*	B
Ronald, Susan. *Hitler's Aristocrats*	940.53
Schama, Simon. *A History of Britain; 2*	941
Scharre, Paul. *Four Battlegrounds*	006.3
Schwartzel, Erich. *Red Carpet*	791.43
Service, Robert. *The End of the Cold War 1985-1991*	909.82
Shavit, Ari. *My Promised Land*	956.05
Shesol, Jeff. *Mercury Rising*	629.45
Shimer, David. *Rigged*	324.60973
Shlaim, Avi. *The Iron Wall*	956.04
Shuster, Simon. ★*The Showman*	B
Smith, Douglas. *The Russian Job*	947.084
Soyinka, Wole. *Of Africa*	960
Spicer, Charles. *Coffee with Hitler*	941.084
Stahr, Walter. *Seward*	B
Steil, Benn. ★*The Marshall Plan*	338.91
Stengel, Richard. *Information Wars*	355.3
Stephanopoulos, George. *The Situation Room*	973.09
Sullivan, Kevin. *Trump on Trial*	342.73
Taubman, William. *Khrushchev*	B
Thomas, Evan. *Ike's Bluff*	973.921092
Thompson, Nicholas. *The Hawk and the Dove*	973.92
Traub, James. *John Quincy Adams*	B
Trimble, Lee. *Beyond the Call*	940.54
Tuchman, Barbara W. *Stilwell and the American Experience in China, 1911-45*	B
Von Tunzelmann, Alex. *Blood and Sand*	909.82
Walker, Shaun. *The Long Hangover*	947.086
Warren, James A. *Year of the Hawk*	959.704
Warrick, Joby. *Red Line*	956.9104
Weiner, Tim. *The Folly and the Glory*	327.73047
Westad, Odd Arne. *The Cold War*	909.825
Whitlock, Craig. *The Afghanistan Papers*	958.104
Wiehl, Lis W. *A Spy in Plain Sight*	327.1247
Wong, Chun Han. *Party of One*	951.06
Wood, Michael. *The Story of China*	951
Yovanovitch, Marie. *Lessons from the Edge*	973.933

INTERNATIONAL SECURITY

Baer, Daniel Brooks. *The Four Tests*	320.973
Burns, William J. *The Back Channel*	B
Chomsky, Noam. *Global Discontents*	410.92
Coll, Steve. ★*The Achilles Trap*	956.7044
Guillemin, Jeanne. *Biological Weapons*	358
Stavridis, James. *Sea Power*	359
Wood, Graeme. *The Way of the Strangers*	363.325

INTERNATIONAL TRADE

Bown, Stephen R. *Merchant Kings*	338.8
Crowley, Roger. *City of Fortune*	945
De Long, J. Bradford. *Slouching Towards Utopia*	330.9
Goodman, Peter S. ★*How the World Ran Out of Everything*	658.7
Grandin, Greg. *The End of the Myth*	973
Hansen, Valerie. *The Year 1000*	909
Johnson, Steven. *Enemy of All Mankind*	910.4

PUBLIC LIBRARY CORE COLLECTION: NONFICTION
Twentieth Edition

Morris, Ian. *Geography Is Destiny* — 941
Platt, Stephen R. *Imperial Twilight* — 951
Roy, Arundhati. *Walking with the Comrades* — 954
Ujifusa, Steven. *Barons of the Sea* — 387.5
INTERNATIONAL TRADE REGULATION
  Stiglitz, Joseph E. *Globalization and Its Discontents* — 337
INTERNET
  Auletta, Ken. *Googled* — 338.7
  Bilton, Nick. *Hatching Twitter* — 006.7
  Chayka, Kyle. *Filterworld* — 306
  Chertoff, Michael. *Exploding Data* — 343.7309
  Cole, Samantha. *How the Internet Changed Sex and Sex Changed the Internet* — 306.7
  Ellis, Bret Easton. *White* — 814
  Evans, Claire Lisa. *Broad Band* — 920
  Galloway, Scott. *The Four* — 338.7
  Hale, Kathleen. ★*Slenderman* — 364.152
  Hayes, Dade. *Binge Times* — 384.55
  Lembke, Anna. *Dopamine Nation* — 152.4
  Lessig, Lawrence. *The Future of Ideas* — 346.04
  Levitin, Daniel J. ★*A Field Guide to Lies* — 153.4
  Lorenz, Taylor. ★*Extremely Online* — 302.23
  McCourt, Frank H. ★*Our Biggest Fight* — 303.48
  McHangama, Jacob. ★*Free Speech* — 323.44
  Mezrich, Ben. *Breaking Twitter* — 338.7
  Perkins, Nichole. *Sometimes I Trip on How Happy We Could Be* — B
  Quinn, Zoe. *Crash Override* — 794.8
  Ronson, Jon. *So You've Been Publicly Shamed* — 152.4
  Shapiro, Scott J. ★*Fancy Bear Goes Phishing* — 364.16
  Swisher, Kara. *Burn Book* — 303.48
  Taplin, Jonathan. *Move Fast and Break Things* — 330.9
  Taylor, Claude. *How to Zoom Your Room* — 747
  Tolentino, Jia. ★*Trick Mirror* — 973.93
  Turnbow, Dominique. ★*Demystifying Online Instruction in Libraries* — 028.7
  Ullman, Ellen. *Life in Code* — B
INTERNET ADDICTION
  Goodin, Tanya. *Stop Staring at Screens* — 004.67
  Linn, Susan. *Who's Raising the Kids?* — 649
INTERNET AND CHILDREN
  Brickman, Sophie. *Baby, Unplugged* — 306.874
  Goodin, Tanya. *Stop Staring at Screens* — 004.67
  Haidt, Jonathan. ★*The Anxious Generation* — 305.23
INTERNET AND IDENTITY
  Galloway, Scott. *The Four* — 338.7
INTERNET BROADCASTING
  Bergen, Mark. *Like, Comment, Subscribe* — 338.7
INTERNET FRAUD
  Ratliff, Evan. *The Mastermind* — B
INTERNET GAMES
  McGonigal, Jane. *Super Better* — 794.8
INTERNET INDUSTRY AND TRADE
  Auletta, Ken. *Googled* — 338.7
  Bergen, Mark. *Like, Comment, Subscribe* — 338.7
  Bilton, Nick. *Hatching Twitter* — 006.7
  Chang, Emily. *Brotopia* — 331.4
  Kidder, Tracy. *A Truck Full of Money* — B
  Pein, Corey. *Live Work Work Work Die* — 338.4
  Smith, Ben. *Traffic* — 070.4
INTERNET LITERACY
  McCourt, Frank H. ★*Our Biggest Fight* — 303.48
  Turnbow, Dominique. ★*Demystifying Online Instruction in Libraries* — 028.7
INTERNET MARKETING
  Vaynerchuk, Gary. *Crushing It!* — 650.1
INTERNET PERSONALITIES
  Bowen, Sesali. *Bad Fat Black Girl* — 305.42
  Brunson, Quinta. *She Memes Well* — B
  Busby, Jill Louise. *Unfollow Me* — 305.08
  Rainbow, Randy. *Playing with Myself* — B
  Wong, Carmen Rita. *Why Didn't You Tell Me?* — B
INTERNET PREDATORS
  Goldberg, Carrie. *Nobody's Victim* — 345.73
INTERNET SEARCHING
  Auletta, Ken. *Googled* — 338.7
  Lankford, Andrea. *Trail of the Lost* — 363.2
INTERNET SECURITY
  Howley, Kerry. *Bottoms Up and the Devil Laughs* — 352.37
  Mitnick, Kevin D. *The Art of Invisibility* — 005.8

INTERNET USERS
  Cole, Samantha. *How the Internet Changed Sex and Sex Changed the Internet* — 306.7
INTERNET VIDEOS
  Hayes, Dade. *Binge Times* — 384.55
  Hill, Marc Lamont. *Seen and Unseen* — 303.3
  Taylor, Claude. *How to Zoom Your Room* — 747
INTERNMENT CAMP INMATES
  Atria, Travis. *Better Days Will Come Again* — B
  Eisen, Max. *By Chance Alone* — 940.5318
  Haitiwaji, Gulbahar. *How I Survived a Chinese "Reeducation" Camp* — 305.8
  Pick-Goslar, Hannah Elizabeth. ★*My Friend Anne Frank* — B
  Wachsmann, Nikolaus. *Kl* — 940.53
  Weintraub, Robert. *No Better Friend* — 940.54
INTERNS
  Winder, Elizabeth. *Pain, Parties, Work* — B
INTERNS (MEDICINE)
  Stern, Adam. *Committed* — 616.89
INTERNSHIP PROGRAMS
  Winder, Elizabeth. *Pain, Parties, Work* — B
INTERPERSONAL ATTRACTION
  Carson, Anne. *Autobiography of Red* — 811
  Garcia, Mayte. *The Most Beautiful* — 920
  Offerman, Nick. *The Greatest Love Story Ever Told* — B
  Schafer, John R. *The Like Switch* — 158.2
  Smiler, Andrew P. *Dating and Sex* — 613.9071
INTERPERSONAL COMMUNICATION
  Alda, Alan. *If I Understood You, Would I Have This Look on My Face?* — 153.6
  Blyth, Catherine. *The Art of Conversation* — 395.5
  Brooks, David. ★*How to Know a Person* — 158.2
  Corrigan, Kelly. *Tell Me More* — 153.6
  Duhigg, Charles. ★*Supercommunicators* — 153.6
  Faber, Adele. ★*How to Talk so Kids Will Listen & Listen so Kids Will Talk* — 649
  Field, Andy. *Encounterism* — 302
  Fineman, Meredith. *Brag Better* — 650.1
  Gilliam, Fatimah. *Race Rules* — 305.8
  Gladwell, Malcolm. ★*Talking to Strangers* — 302
  Goodan, Chelsey. *Underestimated* — 305.235
  Gottman, Julie Schwartz. *Fight Right* — 616.89
  Headlee, Celeste Anne. *Speaking of Race* — 305.8
  Headlee, Celeste Anne. *We Need to Talk* — 153.6
  Kramer, Andrea S. *Breaking Through Bias* — 650.1
  Kross, Ethan. ★*Chatter* — 158.1
  Lieberman, David J. *Mindreader* — 401
  Mogel, Wendy. *Voice Lessons for Parents* — 649
  Murphy, Kate. *You're Not Listening* — 153.6
  Nowicki, Stephen. *Raising a Socially Successful Child* — 649
  Psaki, Jen. *Say More* — B
  Rakel, David. *The Compassionate Connection* — 610.1
  Roberts-Miller, Patricia. *Speaking of Race* — 305.8
  Rueckert, Veronica. *Outspoken* — 808.5
  Schein, Edgar H. *Humble Inquiry* — 302.2
  Seo, Bo. *Good Arguments* — 808.53
  Shlain, Tiffany. *24/6* — 158.1
  Stone, Douglas. *Difficult Conversations* — 158.2
INTERPERSONAL CONFLICT
  Browne, David. *Crosby, Stills, Nash and Young* — 920
  Duhigg, Charles. ★*Supercommunicators* — 153.6
  Economy, Peter. *Wait, I'm Working with Who?!?* — 650.1
  Gallo, Amy. *Getting Along* — 658.4
  Gilliam, Fatimah. *Race Rules* — 305.8
  Goulston, Mark. *Talking to Crazy* — 158.2
  Maupin, Armistead. *Logical Family* — B
  Real, Terrence. *Us* — 646.7
  Sutton, Robert I. *The Asshole Survival Guide* — 650.1
  Tierney, John. *The Power of Bad* — 158.1
  Twenge, Jean M. *Generations* — 305.2
INTERPERSONAL RELATIONS
  Abdurraqib, Hanif. *A Fortune for Your Disaster* — 811
  Alda, Alan. *If I Understood You, Would I Have This Look on My Face?* — 153.6
  Alderton, Dolly. *Everything I Know About Love* — B
  Andersen, Christopher P. *The Good Son* — B
  Bazelon, Emily. *Sticks and Stones* — 302.34
  Bell, Madison Smartt. *Child of Light* — B
  Bennett, Michael. *F*ck Feelings* — 158
  Berg, A. Scott. *Kate Remembered* — B
  Blaisdell, Robert. *Creating Anna Karenina* — 891.7

AUTHOR, TITLE, SERIES AND SUBJECT INDEX

Author/Title	Call #
Blyth, Catherine. *The Art of Conversation*	395.5
Bonner, Betsy. *The Book of Atlantis Black*	364.152
Bradbury, Ray. ★*Remembrance*	813
Bradford, Joy Harden. *Sisterhood Heals*	158.2
Brooks, David. ★*How to Know a Person*	158.2
Brous, Sharon. ★*The Amen Effect*	296.3
Brown, Brene. *Braving the Wilderness*	305.8
Brown, Carolyn. *Chance and Circumstance*	B
Burkus, David. *Friend of a Friend...*	650.1
Cacioppo, Stephanie. *Wired for Love*	616.8
Cain, Susan. ★*Bittersweet*	155.2
Cain, Susan. *Quiet*	155.2
Carroll, Rebecca. *Surviving the White Gaze*	B
Carson, Anne. *The Beauty of the Husband*	811
Carter, Jimmy. *Sharing Good Times*	973.926
Chapman, Gary D. *Love as a Way of Life*	241
Charter, David. *Royal Audience*	941.085
Chavez Perez, Inti. *Respect*	176
Citron, Danielle Keats. *The Fight for Privacy*	342.7308
Collins, Billy. *Whale Day*	811
Conyers, Jonathan. *I Wasn't Supposed to Be Here*	B
Copaken, Deborah. *Ladyparts*	B
Corrigan, Kelly. *Tell Me More*	153.6
Crawford, Robert. *Eliot After the Waste Land*	B
Crosley, Sloane. *Grief Is for People*	B
Cumming, Alan. *Baggage*	B
Dahl, Melissa. *Cringeworthy*	158.2
Daley, Tom. *Coming up for Air*	B
Dearborn, Mary V. *Carson McCullers*	B
DiAngelo, Robin J. *White Fragility*	305.8
Dietrich, Sean. *You Are My Sunshine*	B
Economy, Peter. *Wait, I'm Working with Who?!?*	650.1
Ellis, Bret Easton. *White*	814
Ellis, Helen. *Southern Lady Code*	814
Ellison, Ralph. *The Selected Letters of Ralph Ellison*	813
Ephron, Delia. *Left on Tenth*	B
Eyman, Scott. *Cary Grant*	B
Eyman, Scott. *Hank and Jim*	920
Faliveno, Melissa. *Tomboyland*	B
Febos, Melissa. *Girlhood*	818
Feiler, Bruce. *The First Love Story*	222
Felix, Camonghne. *Dyscalculia*	B
Ferrazzi, Keith. *Never Eat Alone*	658.4
Field, Andy. *Encounterism*	302
Forche, Carolyn. *In the Lateness of the World*	811
Franzen, Jonathan. *The End of the End of the Earth*	814
Gage, Beverly. *G-Man*	B
Gilliam, Fatimah. *Race Rules*	305.8
Gladwell, Malcolm. ★*Talking to Strangers*	302
Gless, Sharon. *Apparently There Were Complaints*	B
Goldstein, Meredith. *Can't Help Myself*	B
Goleman, Daniel. ★*Social Intelligence*	158.2
Gomez, Edgar. *High-Risk Homosexual*	B
Gottman, Julie Schwartz. *Fight Right*	616.89
Goulston, Mark. *Talking to Crazy*	158.2
Green, Alison. *Ask a Manager*	650.1
Greenfieldboyce, Nell. ★*Transient and Strange*	501
Griffin, Chante. *Loving Your Black Neighbor as Yourself*	261
Grue, Jan. *I Live a Life Like Yours*	B
Gunn, Thom. ★*The Letters of Thom Gunn*	821
Hagglund, Martin. *This Life*	110
Hanna, Kathleen. *Rebel Girl*	B
Hardwick, Elizabeth. *The Dolphin Letters, 1970-1979*	811
Hauser, CJ. *The Crane Wife*	B
Havrilesky, Heather. *What If This Were Enough?*	152.4
Hay, Matt. *Soundtrack of Silence*	B
Hayhoe, Katharine. *Saving Us*	304.2
Heath, Chip. *The Power of Moments*	128
Hermes, Will. *Lou Reed*	B
Highsmith, Patricia. ★*Patricia Highsmith's Diaries and Notebooks*	818
Hoffman, Damona. *F the Fairy Tale*	306.73
Holes, Paul. *Unmasked*	363.25
Hollis, Matthew. *The Waste Land*	821
Hubbard, Shanita. ★*Ride-Or-Die*	305.48
Iguodala, Andre. *The Sixth Man*	B
Imbler, Sabrina. *How Far the Light Reaches*	591.77
Isaacson, Walter. ★*Elon Musk*	B
Jackson, Danielle Bayard. *Fighting for Our Friendships*	302.34
James, Victoria. *Wine Girl*	B
Jamison, Leslie. ★*Make It Scream, Make It Burn*	814
Johnson, Graham. *Poulenc*	B
Kelly, Kevin. ★*Excellent Advice for Living*	158.1
Keltner, Dacher. *Born to Be Good*	155.2
Kennedy-Moore, Eileen. ★*Kid Confidence*	155.4
Kennicott, Philip. *Counterpoint*	B
Killam, Kasley. *The Art and Science of Connection*	302
King, Maxwell. *The Good Neighbor*	B
Kirtzman, Andrew. *Giuliani*	B
Kline, Emily. ★*The School of Hard Talks*	155.5
Kohan, Rafi. ★*Trash Talk*	179
Kozinn, Allan. *The McCartney Legacy*	B
LaPointe, Sasha taqwseblu. *Red Paint*	B
Laughlin, James. *The Luck of Friendship*	B
Lavery, Daniel M. *Dear Prudence*	170
Lekas Miller, Anna. *Love Across Borders*	323.6
Lemmon, Gayle Tzemach. *Ashley's War*	B
Lerner, Harriet Goldhor. ★*The Dance of Anger*	152.4
Lerner, Harriet Goldhor. *The Dance of Intimacy*	155.6
Lin, Jami Nakamura. *The Night Parade*	B
Lowery, Brian S. *Selfless*	155.2
Mann, William J. *Bogie & Bacall*	920
Mann, William J. *The Wars of the Roosevelts*	B
Mansel, Philip. *King of the World*	B
Marcum, Diana. *The Fallen Stones*	B
Marriott, Sue. *Secure Relating*	158.1
Martin, Wednesday. *Primates of Park Avenue*	974.7
McBride, Karyl. *Will I Ever Be Good Enough?*	616.85
McCartney, Paul. *The Lyrics*	782.42166
McCurdy, Jennette. ★*I'm Glad My Mom Died*	B
McDonald, Greg (Producer). *Elvis and the Colonel*	920
Miles, Tiya. ★*Night Flyer*	B
Minami, Jikisai. *It's Okay Not to Look for the Meaning of Life*	158.1
Morris, Mark. *Out Loud*	B
Myers, David G. *How Do We Know Ourselves?*	155.2
Nelson, Maggie. ★*The Argonauts*	B
Nelson, Willie. *It's a Long Story*	B
Newman, Paul. *The Extraordinary Life of an Ordinary Man*	B
Nordland, Rod. *Waiting for the Monsoon*	B
O'Donnell Heffington, Peggy. *Without Children*	306.85
Oakley, Charles. *The Last Enforcer*	B
Olds, Sharon. *Odes*	811
Oppedisano, Tony. *Sinatra and Me*	B
Owusu, Nadia. *Aftershocks*	B
Pearlman, Jeff. ★*Three-Ring Circus*	796.323
Peck, M. Scott. ★*The Road Less Traveled*	158.1
Pham, Larissa. *Pop Song*	709.2
Plath, Sylvia. *The Letters of Sylvia Plath*	811.54
Poehler, Amy. *Yes Please*	B
Porath, Christine Lynne. *Mastering Civility*	650.1
Power, Marianne. *Help Me!*	158.1
Prescod, Danielle. *Token Black Girl*	B
Prose, Francine. *1974*	B
Rakel, David. *The Compassionate Connection*	610.1
Raskin, Allison. *Overthinking About You*	646.7
Rawlence, Ben. *City of Thorns*	967.7305
Real, Terrence. *Us*	646.7
Rick, Scott. *Tightwads and Spendthrifts*	332.024
Ricketts, Rachel. ★*Do Better*	305.800973
Rigsby, Cody. ★*XOXO, Cody*	B
Robinson, Phoebe. *Please Don't Sit on My Bed in Your Outside Clothes*	818
Rollag, Keith. *What to Do When You're New*	158.2
Ronson, Jon. *So You've Been Publicly Shamed*	152.4
Ruhl, Sarah. *Smile*	B
Rushdie, Salman. *Joseph Anton*	B
Sale, Anna. ★*Let's Talk About Hard Things*	153.6
Schafer, John R. *The Like Switch*	158.2
Schein, Edgar H. *Humble Inquiry*	302.2
Schwalbe, Will. *We Should Not Be Friends*	B
Schwartz, David N. *The Last Man Who Knew Everything*	B
Sedaris, David. ★*The Best of Me*	818
Selleck, Tom. *You Never Know*	B
Shafrir, Doree. *Thanks for Waiting*	B
Shatner, William. *Boldly Go*	B
Shlain, Tiffany. *24/6*	158.1
Slice, Jessica. *Dateable*	646.7
Smith, Kenny. *Talk of Champions*	B

2009

PUBLIC LIBRARY CORE COLLECTION: NONFICTION
Twentieth Edition

Soep, Elisabeth. *Other People's Words*	155.9
Solnit, Rebecca. *The Faraway Nearby*	814
Sow, Aminatou. *Big Friendship*	177
Spears, Britney. *The Woman in Me*	B
Spiegel, Maura. *Sidney Lumet*	B
Stanley, Paul. *Backstage Pass*	B
Stern, Adam. *Committed*	616.89
Stewart, Chris. *Driving Over Lemons*	946
Stone, Douglas. *Difficult Conversations*	158.2
Stone, Lillian. ★*Everybody's Favorite*	814.6
Strings, Sabrina. *The End of Love*	155.3
Stryker, Kitty. *Ask*	302
Sutton, Robert I. *The Asshole Survival Guide*	650.1
Suvari, Mena. *The Great Peace*	B
Tate, Christie. *B.F.F.*	B
Thompson, Clive. *Coders*	005.1092
Tibble, Tayi. *Poukahangatus*	821
Tomlinson, Janis A. ★*Goya*	B
Van Zandt, Steve. *Unrequited Infatuations*	B
Vasquez-Lavado, Silvia. *In the Shadow of the Mountain*	B
Villarreal, Vanessa Anglica. *Magical/Realism*	814
Vitale, Tom. *In the Weeds*	B
Waldinger, Robert J. ★*The Good Life*	158.1
Walker, Alice. *Gathering Blossoms Under Fire*	B
Wallace, Christopher. *Twentieth-Century Man*	B
Wang, Jackie. *The Sunflower Cast a Spell to Save Us from the Void*	811
Waters, Alice. *Coming to My Senses*	B
Waxman, Jamye. *How to Break up with Anyone*	158.2
Weber, Charlotte Fox. *Tell Me What You Want*	153.8
Wert, Jeffry D. *Cavalryman of the Lost Cause*	B
Williams, Florence. *Heartbreak*	306.7
Winch, Guy. *How to Fix a Broken Heart*	155.9
Winkler, Henry. ★*Being Henry*	B
Womack, Kenneth. *All Things Must Pass Away*	781.66
Woolever, Laurie. *Bourdain*	B
Yong, Sable. *Die Hot with a Vengeance*	646.7
Zhu, Mimi. *Be Not Afraid of Love*	152.4
★*The Interpretation of Dreams.* Freud, Sigmund	154.6

INTERRACIAL ADOPTION

Carroll, Rebecca. *Surviving the White Gaze*	B
Chung, Nicole. *All You Can Ever Know*	B
Chung, Nicole. ★*A Living Remedy*	B
Guida-Richards, Melissa. *What White Parents Should Know About Transracial Adoption*	362.734
Harrison, Valerie I. *Do Right by Me*	649
Royster, Francesca T. *Choosing Family*	B
Samuelsson, Marcus. *Yes, Chef*	B
Scheeres, Julia. *Jesus Land*	B
Williams, Mary. *The Lost Daughter*	B

INTERRACIAL COMMUNICATION

Headlee, Celeste Anne. *Speaking of Race*	305.8

INTERRACIAL COUPLES

Sharma, Nina. *The Way You Make Me Feel*	B
Singh, Julietta. *The Breaks*	B

INTERRACIAL FAMILIES

Ball, Edward. *Slaves in the Family*	975.7
Carroll, Rebecca. *Surviving the White Gaze*	B
Cobbs-Leonard, Tasha. *Do It Anyway*	241
Greenidge, Kerri. ★*The Grimkes*	973.5
Guida-Richards, Melissa. *What White Parents Should Know About Transracial Adoption*	362.734
Harrison, Valerie I. *Do Right by Me*	649
Hyde, Anne Farrar. ★*Born of Lakes and Plains*	978
Jacob, Mira. *Good Talk*	741.5
Mehra, Nishta. *Brown, White, Black*	305.800973
Snyder, Christina. *Great Crossings*	976.9
Som, Brandon. *Tripas*	811
Trethewey, Natasha D. ★*Monument*	811

INTERRACIAL FRIENDSHIP

Brand, Christo. *Mandela*	B
Fumudoh, Ziwe. ★*Black Friend*	814
Margolick, David. *Elizabeth and Hazel*	379.2
Mukantabana, Yseult P. ★*Real Friends Talk About Race*	305.8
Painter, Nell Irvin. ★*Sojourner Truth*	B
Perron, Cam. ★*Comeback Season*	796.357
Sow, Aminatou. *Big Friendship*	177

INTERRACIAL MARRIAGE

Bernard, Emily. *Black Is the Body*	305.48

Brina, Elizabeth Miki. *Speak, Okinawa*	305.48
Locke, Tembi. ★*From Scratch*	B
McBride, James. *The Color of Water*	B
Royster, Francesca T. *Choosing Family*	B
Sharma, Nina. *The Way You Make Me Feel*	B

INTERRACIAL ROMANCE

Ward, Geoffrey C. *Unforgivable Blackness*	B

INTERSECTIONALITY

Adichie, Chimamanda Ngozi. *We Should All Be Feminists*	305.42
Alexander, Michelle. *The New Jim Crow*	364.973
Angelou, Maya. ★*I Know Why the Caged Bird Sings*	B
Baldwin, James. ★*Collected Essays*	814
Baldwin, James. ★*The Fire Next Time*	305.896
Beauvoir, Simone de. ★*The Second Sex*	305.4
Belcourt, Billy-Ray. ★*A History of My Brief Body*	B
Berry, Daina Ramey. ★*A Black Women's History of the United States*	305.48
Bowen, Sesali. *Bad Fat Black Girl*	305.42
Coates, Ta-Nehisi. ★*Between the World and Me*	305.800973
Cooper, Brittney C. *Eloquent Rage*	B
Copeland, Misty. ★*Life in Motion*	B
Cottom, Tressie McMillan. *Thick*	301
Du Bois, W. E. B. ★*The Souls of Black Folk*	973
Dunbar-Ortiz, Roxanne. ★*An Indigenous Peoples' History of the United States*	970.004
Ehrenreich, Barbara. ★*Nickel and Dimed*	B
Emezi, Akwaeke. ★*Dear Senthuran*	B
Faludi, Susan. *In the Darkroom*	B
Filipovic, Jill. *The H-Spot*	155.3
Fleming, Crystal Marie. *How to Be Less Stupid About Race*	305.800973
Gay, Roxane. *Bad Feminist*	814
Gerald, Casey. *There Will Be No Miracles Here*	B
Gilbert, Sandra M. ★*Still Mad*	810.9
Gordon, Kim. *Girl in a Band*	B
Haddish, Tiffany. *The Last Black Unicorn*	B
Hay, Carol. *Think Like a Feminist*	305.42
Hubbard, Shanita. ★*Ride-Or-Die*	305.48
Jackson, Jenn M. ★*Black Women Taught Us*	305.48
Jacobs, Harriet. ★*Incidents in the Life of a Slave Girl*	B
Jefferson, Margo. *Negroland*	305.896
Jerkins, Morgan. *Wandering in Strange Lands*	305.896
Jones, Saeed. *How We Fight for Our Lives*	B
Kendall, Mikki. *Hood Feminism*	305.420973
Khakpour, Porochista. *Brown Album*	304.8
Kristof, Nicholas D. *Half the Sky*	362.83
Lee, Erika. *The Making of Asian America*	973
Lehrer, Riva. *Golem Girl*	B
Lorde, Audre. ★*The Selected Works of Audre Lorde*	814
Lorde, Audre. *Sister Outsider*	814
Madden, T Kira. *Long Live the Tribe of Fatherless Girls*	814
Malone, Sharon. *Grown Woman Talk*	362.1
Mattlin, Ben. *Disability Pride*	323.3
McDiarmid, Jessica. *Highway of Tears*	364.152
Mehra, Nishta. *Brown, White, Black*	305.800973
Moran, Caitlin. *How to Be a Woman*	B
Muhammad, Ibtihaj. *Proud*	B
Ndopu, Eddie. *Sipping Dom Pérignon Through a Straw*	B
Neiman, Garrett. *Rich White Men*	305.5
Nelson, Maggie. ★*The Argonauts*	B
Oluo, Ijeoma. ★*So You Want to Talk About Race*	305.800973
Orenstein, Peggy. *Cinderella Ate My Daughter*	305.23082
Ortiz, Paul. *An African American and Latinx History of the United States*	305.8
Porter, Billy. ★*Unprotected*	B
Quinn, Bridget. *She Votes*	324.6
Ramesh, Jaya. *Parenting at the Intersections*	649
Rosenberg, Rosalind. ★*Jane Crow*	B
Schatz, Kate. *Rad Women Worldwide*	920
Schuller, Kyla. *The Trouble with White Women*	305.42
Smith, Danez. ★*Homie*	811
Smith, Mychal Denzel. *Invisible Man, Got the Whole World Watching*	305.242
Solnit, Rebecca. *Men Explain Things to Me*	305.42
Srinivasan, Amia. *The Right to Sex*	305.42
Steinem, Gloria. *My Life on the Road*	B
Stevenson, Bryan. *Just Mercy*	B
Talusan, Meredith. *Fairest*	305.30973
Tamblyn, Amber. ★*Era of Ignition*	B
Vogelstein, Rachel B. *Awakening*	305.42

AUTHOR, TITLE, SERIES AND SUBJECT INDEX

Walker, Alice. *The Cushion in the Road* — 814
Zakaria, Rafia. *Against White Feminism* — 305.42
INTERSEX PEOPLE
  Barnes, Katie. ★*Fair Play* — 796.082
  Semenya, Caster. *The Race to Be Myself* — B
  Weigel, Alicia Roth. *Inverse Cowgirl* — B
INTERSEXUALITY
  Semenya, Caster. *The Race to Be Myself* — B
The **Interstellar** *Age*. Bell, Jim — 919
INTERVENTION (INTERNATIONAL LAW)
  Bass, Gary Jonathan. *Freedom's Battle* — 341.5
  Olson, Lynne. *Those Angry Days* — 940.53
INTERVENTION (INTERNATIONAL RELATIONS)
  Abrahamian, Ervand. *The Coup* — 955.05
  Bacevich, Andrew J. *America's War for the Greater Middle East* — 956.05
  Bass, Gary Jonathan. *Freedom's Battle* — 341.5
  Dalrymple, William. *The Return of a King* — 958.1
  Mirski, Sean A. *We May Dominate the World* — 973.91
INTERVIEWING
  Currid-Halkett, Elizabeth. *The Overlooked Americans* — 307.76
  Ross, Catherine Sheldrick. *Conducting the Reference Interview* — 025.5
  Stern, Jessica. *My War Criminal* — 341.6
INTERVIEWS
  Baldwin, James. *I Am Not Your Negro* — 323.1196
  Chomsky, Noam. *Global Discontents* — 410.92
  Cott, Jonathan. *There's a Mystery There* — 813
  Dench, Judi. *Shakespeare* — 792
  Ellison, Ralph. ★*The Collected Essays of Ralph Ellison* — 814
  Fauci, Anthony S. *Expect the Unexpected* — 610.92
  Ferris, William R. *Give My Poor Heart Ease* — 781.643
  Ferriss, Timothy. *Tools of Titans* — 081
  Garrels, Anne. *Putin Country* — 947
  Garrett, Kent. *The Last Negroes at Harvard* — 920
  Gelwicks, Andrew. *The Queer Advantage* — 920
  Gillette, Michael L. *Lady Bird Johnson* — B
  Gooch, Brad. *Radiant* — B
  Han, Chenxing. *Be the Refuge* — 294.3
  Hatzfeld, Jean. *Blood Papa* — 967.5710431
  Hogan, William R. *Task Force Hogan* — 940.54
  Isaacson, Walter. ★*Steve Jobs* — B
  Jones, Dylan. *David Bowie* — B
  Le Guin, Ursula K. *Ursula K. Le Guin* — B
  Leavy, Jane. *Sandy Koufax* — B
  Max, D. T. *Finale* — 782.1
  Miller, Klancy. ★*For the Culture* — 641.59
  Newman, Paul. *The Extraordinary Life of an Ordinary Man* — B
  Patterson, James. *Walk in My Combat Boots* — 920
  Rapoport, Ron. *Let's Play Two* — B
  Raskin, Allison. *Overthinking About You* — 646.7
  Ratliff, Ben. *The Jazz Ear* — 781.6509
  Rees, Laurence. *Auschwitz* — 940.53
  Remnick, David. *Holding the Note* — 781.64
  Reston, James. *The Conviction of Richard Nixon* — 973.924092
  Rinzler, J. W. *The Making of Aliens* — 791.4372
  Robb, John. *Punk Rock* — 781.6609
  Robbins, Alexandra. ★*The Teachers* — 371.1
  Rubenstein, David M. *The American Story* — 973.07202
  Ruberg, Bonnie. ★*The Queer Games Avant-Garde* — 794.8
  Sanders, Chad. *Black Magic* — 305.896
  Seal, Mark. ★*Leave the Gun, Take the Cannoli* — 791.43
  Sisson, Gretchen E. ★*Relinquished* — 362.734
  Stanton, Brandon. *Humans* — 779
  Stevens, George, Jr. *Conversations at the American Film Institute with the Great Moviemakers* — 791.4302
  Terkel, Studs. *Hope Dies Last* — 920
  Turan, Kenneth. ★*Free for All* —
  Tye, Larry. ★*The Jazzmen* — 781.6509
  Walker, Hunter. *The Truce* — 324.2736
  Wiederhorn, Jon. *Louder Than Hell* — 781.6609
  Xuecun, Murong. *Deadly Quiet City* — 614.5
INTIMACY
  Flaherty, Meghan. *Tango Lessons* — 793.3
  Gerard, Sarah. *Sunshine State* — 814
  Heti, Sheila. *Alphabetical Diaries* — 818
  Lerner, Harriet Goldhor. *The Dance of Intimacy* — 155.6
  Mock, Janet. *Surpassing Certainty* — B
  Morgan, Abi. *This Is Not a Pity Memoir* — B
  Olds, Sally. ★*People Who Lunch* — 824

Phillips, Carl. ★*Then the War* — 811
Real, Terrence. *Us* — 646.7
Shockley, Evie. *Suddenly We* — 811
Taddeo, Lisa. *Three Women* — 306.7082
Zhu, Mimi. *Be Not Afraid of Love* — 152.4
The **Intimate** *Merton*. Merton, Thomas — B
Intimations. Smith, Zadie — 824
Into Every Generation a Slayer Is Born. Katz, Evan Ross — 791.45
Into *The Deep*. Ballard, Robert D. — 551.46092
Into *The Fire*. Meyer, Dakota — 958.104
Into *The Forest*. Frankel, Rebecca — 940.53
Into *The Raging Sea*. Slade, Rachel — 910.91
Into *The Silence*. Davis, Wade — B
Into *The Wild*. Krakauer, Jon — 917.9804
★**Into** *Thin Air*. Krakauer, Jon — 796.52
INTRIGUE
  Weir, Alison. *Queens of the Age of Chivalry* — 920
★**Introduction** *to Islam*. Ramadan, Tariq — 297
★**Introduction** *to Logic*. Copi, Irving M. — 160
INTROVERSION
  Cain, Susan. *Quiet* — 155.2
  Helgoe, Laurie A. *Introvert Power* — 155.2
Introvert Power. Helgoe, Laurie A. — 155.2
The **Introvert's** *Complete Career Guide*. Finkle, Jane — 650.14
INTROVERTS
  Cain, Susan. *Quiet* — 155.2
  Dahl, Melissa. *Cringeworthy* — 158.2
  Finkle, Jane. *The Introvert's Complete Career Guide* — 650.14
  Helgoe, Laurie A. *Introvert Power* — 155.2
  Pollak, Lindsey. *Recalculating* — 650.1
INTUITION
  Alda, Alan. *If I Understood You, Would I Have This Look on My Face?* — 153.6
  Gladwell, Malcolm. *Blink* — 153.4
  Kahneman, Daniel. ★*Thinking, Fast and Slow* — 153.4
Intuition *Pumps and Other Tools for Thinking*. Dennett, D. C. — 121
INUIT (NORTH AMERICAN PEOPLE)
  Ehrlich, Gretel. *This Cold Heaven* — 998.2
INUIT WOMEN
  Niven, Jennifer. *Ada Blackjack* — B
IÑUPIAT (NORTH AMERICAN PEOPLE)
  Hensley, William L. Iggiagruk. *Fifty Miles from Tomorrow* — B
Invasion. Harding, Luke — 947.7
Inventing Japan, 1853-1964. Buruma, Ian — 952.03
★*Inventing Latinos*. Gomez, Laura E. — 305.868
Inventing Wyatt Earp. Barra, Allen — B
The *Invention of Angela Carter*. Gordon, Edmund — B
The *Invention of Love*. Stoppard, Tom — 822
The *Invention of Nature*. Wulf, Andrea — B
INVENTIONS
  Agrawal, Roma. *Nuts and Bolts* — 609
  Aryee, Patrick. *30 Animals That Made Us Smarter* — 590
  Carlsen, Spike. *A Walk Around the Block* — 031
  Cline, Eric H. *After 1177 B.C.* — 937
  Doorley, Rachelle. *Tinkerlab* — 600
  Ducharme, Jamie. *Big Vape* — 338.7
  Hammack, William Scott. ★*Things We Make* — 620
  Harford, Tim. *50 Inventions That Shaped the Modern Economy* — 609
  Johnson, Steven. *Wonderland* — 790.1
  Marcal, Katrine. *Mother of Invention* — 604.82
  Rhodes, Richard. *Hedy's Folly* — B
  Wilkinson, Karen. *The Art of Tinkering* — 500
  Winchester, Simon. ★*The Perfectionists* — 620.009
Inventive Weaving on a Little Loom. Mitchell, Syne — 746.1
INVENTORS
  Bunker, Nick. *Young Benjamin Franklin* — B
  Carlson, W. Bernard. *Tesla* — B
  Fischer, Paul. *The Man Who Invented Motion Pictures* — 791.43
  Franklin, Benjamin. ★*The Autobiography of Benjamin Franklin* — B
  Gray, Charlotte. *Reluctant Genius* — 920
  Hazelgrove, William Elliott. *Wright Brothers, Wrong Story* — 920
  Isaacson, Walter. ★*Benjamin Franklin* — B
  Isaacson, Walter. ★*Elon Musk* — B
  Isaacson, Walter. ★*The Innovators* — B
  Kamkwamba, William. ★*The Boy Who Harnessed the Wind* — B
  Kurlansky, Mark. *Birdseye* — B
  Morris, Edmund. ★*Edison* — B
  Munson, Richard. *Tesla* — B
  Rasenberger, Jim. *Revolver* — B

PUBLIC LIBRARY CORE COLLECTION: NONFICTION
Twentieth Edition

    Rhodes, Richard. *Hedy's Folly* — B
    Rose, Alexander. *Empires of the Sky* — 920
Inverse Cowgirl. Weigel, Alicia Roth — B
INVERTEBRATES
    Attenborough, David. *Life in the Undergrowth* — 592
INVESTIGATIONS
    Miles, Kathryn. *Trailed* — 364.152
    Rear, Rachel. *Catch the Sparrow* — 364.152
    Weissmann, Andrew. ★*Where Law Ends* — 324.7
INVESTIGATIVE JOURNALISM
    Bernstein, Carl. ★*Chasing History* — B
    Blakinger, Keri. *Corrections in Ink* — B
    Bowden, Mark. *The Case of the Vanishing Blonde* — 364.10973
    Brokaw, Tom. *The Fall of Richard Nixon* — B
    Fagin, Dan. *Toms River* — 363.7209749
    Farrow, Ronan. ★*Catch and Kill* — 331.4
    Golay, Michael. *America 1933* — B
    Hersh, Seymour M. *Reporter* — B
    Johnson, Kirk W. *The Feather Thief* — 364.16
    Kantor, Jodi. *She Said* — 364.15
    Keefe, Patrick Radden. ★*Rogues* — 364.16
    Kroeger, Brooke. *Undaunted* — 070.4
    LeDuff, Charlie. *Detroit* — 977.4
    Marshall, McMillan. *Among the Bros* — 362.29
    McMillan, Tracie. *The American Way of Eating* — 338.4
    Mekhennet, Souad. *I Was Told to Come Alone* — 363.3250956
    Parks, Casey. *Diary of a Misfit* — B
    Todd, Kim. *Sensational* — 920
    Yaffa, Joshua. *Between Two Fires* — 920
INVESTIGATIVE JOURNALISTS
    Bauer, Shane. *American Prison* — 365
    Farrow, Ronan. ★*Catch and Kill* — 331.4
    Gellman, Barton. ★*Dark Mirror* — B
    Hersh, Seymour M. *Reporter* — B
    Kantor, Jodi. *She Said* — 364.15
    Miraldi, Robert. *Seymour Hersh* — B
    Mitchell, Jerry. ★*Race Against Time* — 364.152
    O'Neill, Tom. ★*Chaos* — 364.152
    Ressa, Maria. ★*How to Stand up to a Dictator* — 070.92
INVESTMENT ADVISERS
    Behar, Richard. *Madoff* — 364.16
    Fabre, Cin. *Wolf Hustle* — 332.6
    Thorp, Edward O. *A Man for All Markets* — B
INVESTMENT BANKERS
    Karabell, Zachary. *Inside Money* — 332.1
    Schroeder, Alice. *The Snowball* — B
    Schulman, Daniel. *The Money Kings* — 332.0973
INVESTMENT BANKING
    Enrich, David. *Dark Towers* — 332.1
    Hudson, Michael W. *The Monster* — 332.63
    Schroeder, Alice. *The Snowball* — B
INVESTMENTS
    Baer, Daniel Brooks. *The Four Tests* — 320.973
    Belfort, Jordan. ★*The Wolf of Investing* — 332.63
    Brown, Eliot. *The Cult of We* — 333.33
    Buffett, Mary. *Warren Buffett and the Art of Stock Arbitrage* — 332.645
    De Leon, Paco. *Finance for the People* — 332.024
    Fox, Justin. *The Myth of the Rational Market* — 332.64
    Graham, Benjamin. *The Intelligent Investor* — 332.67
    Hagstrom, Robert G. *The Warren Buffett Way* — 332.6
    Kolhatkar, Sheelah. *Black Edge* — 364.16
    Patterson, Scott. ★*Chaos Kings* — 338.5
    Quinn, Jane Bryant. ★*How to Make Your Money Last* — 332.024
    Scheyder, Ernest. *The War Below* — 333.7
    Simmons, Lauren. *Make Money Move* — 332.024
    Thorp, Edward O. *A Man for All Markets* — B
INVESTORS
    Fox, Justin. *The Myth of the Rational Market* — 332.64
    Gramm, Jeff. *Dear Chairman* — 659.2
    Hill, Kashmir. ★*Your Face Belongs to Us* — 006.2
    Schroeder, Alice. *The Snowball* — B
Invisible. Carter, Stephen L. — B
Invisible Americans. Madrick, Jeffrey G — 362.7086
Invisible Armies. Boot, Max — 355.02
The Invisible Bridge. Perlstein, Rick — 973.924
★*Invisible Child*. Elliott, Andrea — 362.7
★*The Invisible Kingdom*. O'Rourke, Meghan — 616
★*Invisible Labor*. Somerstein, Rachel — 618.8

Invisible Man, Got the Whole World Watching. Smith, Mychal Denzel — 305.242
Invisible Rulers. DiResta, Renee — 320
The Invisible Siege. Werb, Dan — 614.5
Invisible Storm. Kander, Jason — B
INVOLUNTARY STERILIZATION
    Cohen, Adam. ★*Imbeciles* — 344.7304
    Farley, Audrey Clare. *The Unfit Heiress* — B
    Okrent, Daniel. *The Guarded Gate* — 344.73
INVOLUNTARY TREATMENT
    Fessler, Pam. *Carville's Cure* — 362.19699
    Moore, Kate. ★*The Woman They Could Not Silence* — B
IOWA
    Brookwood, Marilyn. *The Orphans of Davenport* — 305.231
    Bryson, Bill. *The Life and Times of the Thunderbolt Kid* — B
    Cullen, Art. *Storm Lake* — 071.7
    Evans, R. Tripp. *Grant Wood* — B
    Myron, Vicki. ★*Dewey* — 636.80092
Iperen, Roxane van
    ★*The Sisters of Auschwitz* — 940.53
IPHONE (SMARTPHONE)
    Fagans, Michael. *iPhone Photography for Everybody* — 770
iPhone Photography for Everybody. Fagans, Michael — 770
IQ. Murdoch, Stephen — 153.9
Iran. Amanat, Abbas — 955
IRAN
    Abrahamian, Ervand. *The Coup* — 955.05
    Alikhani, Nasim. *Sofreh* — 641.595
    Alinizhad, Masih. *The Wind in My Hair* — B
    Amanat, Abbas. *Iran* — 955
    Azad. *Long Shot* — B
    Bowden, Mark. *Guests of the Ayatollah* — 955.05
    Cooper, Andrew Scott. *The Fall of Heaven* — B
    Firdawsi. *Shahnameh* — 891
    Follett, Ken. *On Wings of Eagles* — 955
    Ghattas, Kim. *Black Wave* — 955.05
    Ghazvinian, John. *America and Iran* — 327
    Housden, Roger. *Saved by Beauty* — 955
    Kinzer, Stephen. ★*All the Shah's Men* — 955.05
    Meltzer, Brad. ★*The Nazi Conspiracy* — 940.53
    Mendez, Antonio J. *Argo* — 955.05
    Nafisi, Azar. ★*Reading Lolita in Tehran* — B
    Nafisi, Azar. *Things I've Been Silent About* — B
    Navai, Ramita. *City of Lies* — 955
    Nemat, Marina. *Prisoner of Tehran* — B
    Orth, Stephan. *Couchsurfing in Iran* — 955.06
    Rezaian, Jason. *Prisoner* — B
    Satrapi, Marjane. *Chicken with Plums* — 741.5
    Satrapi, Marjane. ★*The Complete Persepolis* — 741.5
    Satrapi, Marjane. *Embroideries* — 741.5
    Setareh, Saghar. *Pomegranates & Artichokes* — 641.5
IRAN HOSTAGE CRISIS, 1979-1981
    Bowden, Mark. *Guests of the Ayatollah* — 955.05
    Follett, Ken. *On Wings of Eagles* — 955
    Mendez, Antonio J. *Argo* — 955.05
IRAN-IRAQ WAR, 1980-1988
    Satrapi, Marjane. ★*The Complete Persepolis* — 741.5
IRANIAN AMERICAN WOMEN
    Khakpour, Porochista. *Brown Album* — 304.8
IRANIAN AMERICANS
    Jobrani, Maziyar. *I'm Not a Terrorist, but I've Played One on TV* — B
    Rezaian, Jason. *Prisoner* — B
IRANIAN PEOPLE
    Ahdoot, Dan. *Undercooked* — 647.95
IRANIAN REVOLUTION, 1979-1997
    Ghattas, Kim. *Black Wave* — 955.05
    Nafisi, Azar. ★*Reading Lolita in Tehran* — B
    Satrapi, Marjane. ★*The Complete Persepolis* — 741.5
IRAQ
    Abdul-Ahad, Ghaith. *A Stranger in Your Own City* — 956.7044
    Ackerman, Elliot. *Places and Names* — B
    Bilal, Wafaa. *Shoot an Iraqi* — B
    Campbell, Deborah. *A Disappearance in Damascus* — 365
    Chandrasekaran, Rajiv. *Imperial Life in the Emerald City* — 956.7044
    Coker, Margaret. *The Spymaster of Baghdad* — 956.7044
    Coll, Steve. ★*The Achilles Trap* — 956.7044
    Fair, Eric. *Consequence* — B
    Findakly, Brigitte. *Poppies of Iraq* — 741.5
    Finkel, David. *The Good Soldiers* — 956.7044

Frederick, Jim. *Black Hearts*	956.7044
Gallego, Ruben. *They Called Us*	956.7044
Ghattas, Kim. *Black Wave*	955.05
Kriwaczek, Paul. *Babylon*	935
Mills, Dan. *Sniper One*	956.7044
Murad, Nadia. ★*The Last Girl*	B
Newton, Michael A. *Enemy of the State*	345.567
Nixon, John. *Debriefing the President*	956.7044
Packer, George. *The Assassins' Gate*	956.7044
Raddatz, Martha. *The Long Road Home*	B
Ricks, Thomas E. *Fiasco*	956.7044
Sabar, Ariel. *My Father's Paradise*	B
Saldana, Stephanie. *What We Remember Will Be Saved*	362.7
Seierstad, Asne. *A Hundred and One Days*	956.70443
Stewart, Rory. *The Prince of the Marshes*	956.7044
Van Agtmael, Peter. *Look at the USA*	070
Verini, James. *They Will Have to Die Now*	956.7044
Warren, W. Lee. *No Place to Hide*	B
Wright, Evan. *Generation Kill*	956.7044

IRAQ WAR VETERANS
Duckworth, Tammy. *Every Day Is a Gift*	B
Finkel, David. *An American Dreamer*	975.8
Frederick, Jim. *Black Hearts*	956.7044
Gallego, Ruben. *They Called Us*	956.7044
Kugler, Rob. *A Dog Named Beautiful*	B

IRAQ WAR, 2003-2011
Abdul-Ahad, Ghaith. *A Stranger in Your Own City*	956.7044
Ackerman, Elliot. *Places and Names*	B
Bergen, Peter L. *The Longest War*	909.83
Bilal, Wafaa. *Shoot an Iraqi*	B
Campbell, Deborah. *A Disappearance in Damascus*	365
Castner, Brian. *The Long Walk*	B
Chandrasekaran, Rajiv. *Imperial Life in the Emerald City*	956.7044
Chivers, C. J. *The Fighters*	920
Coll, Steve. ★*The Achilles Trap*	956.7044
Dower, John W. *Cultures of War*	355.00973
Draper, Robert. *To Start a War*	956.7044
Fair, Eric. *Consequence*	B
Filkins, Dexter. *The Forever War*	956.7044
Finkel, David. *The Good Soldiers*	956.7044
Finkel, David. *Thank You for Your Service*	920
Frederick, Jim. *Black Hearts*	956.7044
Gallego, Ruben. *They Called Us*	956.7044
Henderson, Artis. *Unremarried Widow*	B
Hennessey, Patrick. *The Junior Officers' Reading Club*	B
King, Charles Monroe. *A Journal for Jordan*	956.7044
Kugler, Rob. *A Dog Named Beautiful*	B
Luttrell, Marcus. *Service*	956.7044
Manning, Chelsea. *Readme.Txt*	B
Mills, Dan. *Sniper One*	956.7044
Murad, Nadia. ★*The Last Girl*	B
Nixon, John. *Debriefing the President*	956.7044
Packer, George. *The Assassins' Gate*	956.7044
Petraeus, David Howell. *Conflict*	355
Philipps, David. *Alpha*	956.7044
Poole, Robert M. *Section 60*	975.5
Raddatz, Martha. *The Long Road Home*	B
Ricks, Thomas E. *Fiasco*	956.7044
Seierstad, Asne. *A Hundred and One Days*	956.70443
Stewart, Rory. *The Prince of the Marshes*	956.7044
Van Agtmael, Peter. *Look at the USA*	070
Ward, Clarissa. *On All Fronts*	B
Warren, W. Lee. *No Place to Hide*	B
Wise, Beau. *Three Wise Men*	958.104
Wright, Evan. *Generation Kill*	956.7044

IRAQI PEOPLE
| Bilal, Wafaa. *Shoot an Iraqi* | B |
| Saldana, Stephanie. *What We Remember Will Be Saved* | 362.7 |

Irby, Samantha
| ★*Quietly Hostile* | 814 |
| *We Are Never Meeting in Real Life* | 814 |

IRBY, SAMANTHA
| Irby, Samantha. ★*Quietly Hostile* | 814 |
| Irby, Samantha. *We Are Never Meeting in Real Life* | 814 |

Iredale, Will
| *The Kamikaze Hunters* | 940.54 |

IRELAND
Boland, Eavan. *New Collected Poems*	821
Brown, Terence. *The Life of W.B. Yeats*	B
Cahill, Thomas. *How the Irish Saved Civilization*	941.501
Carroll, Rory. *There Will Be Fire*	363.325
Connell, John. *The Farmer's Son*	630.9
Dochartaigh, Kerri ni. *Cacophony of Bone*	B
Egan, Timothy. ★*The Immortal Irishman*	B
Ellmann, Richard. *Oscar Wilde*	B
Heaney, Seamus. *Human Chain*	821
Heaney, Seamus. *Opened Ground*	821
Moran, Rachel. *Paid For*	306.74082
Morris, Marc. *Castles*	728.81
O'Connell, Mark. *A Thread of Violence*	364.152
O'Toole, Fintan. ★*We Don't Know Ourselves*	941.7
Phelan, Tom. *We Were Rich and We Didn't Know It*	B
Puleo, Stephen. *Voyage of Mercy*	363.8
Sturgis, Matthew. *Oscar Wilde*	B
Toibin, Colm. *Mad, Bad, Dangerous to Know*	920
Wills, Clair. ★*Missing Persons*	929.2

Ireland, Tom
| *The Good Virus* | 579.2 |

Irena's Children. Mazzeo, Tilar J. | B
Iris. Conradi, Peter J. | B

IRISH AMERICAN MEN
| Schaap, Jeremy. *Cinderella Man* | B |

IRISH AMERICANS
Craughwell, Thomas J. *Stealing Lincoln's Body*	973.7092
Egan, Timothy. ★*The Immortal Irishman*	B
McCourt, Frank. ★*Angela's Ashes*	929
McCourt, Frank. *Teacher Man*	B
McCourt, Frank. *'Tis*	B
McCourt, Malachy. *A Monk Swimming*	B
McCourt, Malachy. *Singing My Him Song*	B

The Irish Assassins. Kavanagh, Julie | 941.5

IRISH HISTORY
Egan, Timothy. ★*The Immortal Irishman*	B
Gibney, John. *A Short History of Ireland, 1500-2000*	941.7
Kavanagh, Julie. *The Irish Assassins*	941.5
Kelly, John. *The Graves Are Walking*	941.5081

IRISH PEOPLE
Bowker, Gordon. ★*James Joyce*	B
Dochartaigh, Kerri ni. *Cacophony of Bone*	B
Ferguson, Jane. *No Ordinary Assignment*	B
Wills, Clair. ★*Missing Persons*	929.2

IRISH PEOPLE IN ENGLAND
| Wills, Clair. ★*Missing Persons* | 929.2 |

IRISH PEOPLE IN FOREIGN COUNTRIES
| Bowker, Gordon. ★*James Joyce* | B |

IRISH PEOPLE IN THE UNITED STATES
| Crouch, Gregory. *The Bonanza King* | B |

IRISH POTATO FAMINE (1845-1852)
Egan, Timothy. ★*The Immortal Irishman*	B
Kelly, John. *The Graves Are Walking*	941.5081
Puleo, Stephen. *Voyage of Mercy*	363.8

Irish, Lora S.
| *Basket Essentials* | 746.412 |

IRON
| Conway, Edmund. *Material World* | 333.7 |

Iron Ambition. Tyson, Mike | B
Iron Curtain. Applebaum, Anne | 947

IRON CURTAIN
Longo, Matthew. *The Picnic*	947.084
Moore, Tim. *The Cyclist Who Went Out in the Cold*	796.6
Phillips, Timothy. *Retracing the Iron Curtain*	909.82

Iron Empires. Hiltzik, Michael A. | 385.0973
Iron Horse. Robinson, Ray | B
★*Iron John*. Bly, Robert | 305.310973
Iron Tears. Weintraub, Stanley | 973.3
The Iron Wall. Shlaim, Avi | 956.04
Iron War. Fitzgerald, Matt | 796.42

IRONMAN TRIATHLONS
| Fitzgerald, Matt. *Iron War* | 796.42 |

IROQUOIS (HAUDENOSAUNEE) (NORTH AMERICAN PEOPLE)
| Taylor, Alan. *The Divided Ground* | 974.7 |

Irrational Man. Barrett, William | 142

IRRATIONALISM (PHILOSOPHY)
| Ariely, Dan. *Predictably Irrational* | 153.8 |
| Strevens, Michael. *The Knowledge Machine* | 500 |

PUBLIC LIBRARY CORE COLLECTION: NONFICTION
Twentieth Edition

IRRATIONALITY (PSYCHOLOGY)
    Montell, Amanda. ★*The Age of Magical Overthinking* — 153.4
    Pinker, Steven. *Rationality* — 153.4
IRRELIGION
    Ozment, Katherine. *Grace Without God* — 200.973
    Zuckerman, Phil. *Living the Secular Life* — 211
IRRIGATION
    Boccaletti, Giulio. *Water* — 909
Irritable Hearts. McClelland, Mac — B
IRVINE, ANDREW, 1902-1924
    Synnott, Mark. *The Third Pole* — 796.522
Irving, Apricot Anderson
    The Gospel of Trees — B
IRVING, APRICOT ANDERSON
    Irving, Apricot Anderson. *The Gospel of Trees* — B
IRVING, DAVID, 1938-
    Lipstadt, Deborah E. *History on Trial* — 940.53
IRVING, KYRIE, 1992-
    Sullivan, Matt. *Can't Knock the Hustle* — 796.323
Is Everyone Happier Than Me?. Bragg, Sarah — 248.4
★*Is Rape a Crime?*. Bowdler, Michelle — B
Is This a Cookbook?. Blumenthal, Heston — 641.5
Is This Anything?. Seinfeld, Jerry — 818
Is This Normal?. Brighten, Jolene — 618.1
Is, Is Not. Gallagher, Tess — 811
Isaacs, Ronald H.
    ★*Kosher Living* — 296.7
Isaacson, Walter
    ★*Benjamin Franklin* — B
    ★*The Code Breaker* — 576.5
    ★*Elon Musk* — B
    ★*The Innovators* — B
    ★*Leonardo Da Vinci* — B
    ★*Steve Jobs* — B
Isabel, Agatha
    Houseplant Hookups — 635.9
Isabella. Downey, Kirstin — B
ISABELLA I, QUEEN OF SPAIN, 1451-1504
    Downey, Kirstin. *Isabella* — B
ISABELLA, OF VALOIS, QUEEN, CONSORT OF RICHARD II, KING OF ENGLAND
    Weir, Alison. *Queens of the Age of Chivalry* — 920
ISABELLA, QUEEN, CONSORT OF EDWARD II, KING OF ENGLAND, 1292-1358
    Weir, Alison. *Queens of the Age of Chivalry* — 920
Isacoff, Stuart
    Musical Revolutions — 780.9
Isay, David
    Callings — 920
Isen, Tajja
    Some of My Best Friends — 305.8
ISEN, TAJJA
    Isen, Tajja. *Some of My Best Friends* — 305.8
Isenberg, Nancy
    The Problem of Democracy — 973.4
    White Trash — 305.5
Isenberg, Sheila
    Women Who Love Men Who Kill — 362.83
Ishi in Two Worlds. Kroeber, Theodora — B
ISHI, D.1916
    Kroeber, Theodora. *Ishi in Two Worlds* — B
ISHIDA, KENNETH N., 1977-1998
    Hsu, Hua. ★*Stay True* — B
Ishida, Sanae
    Sewing Happiness — 646.2
    Sewing Love — 646
ISHIDA, SANAE
    Ishida, Sanae. *Sewing Happiness* — 646.2
Ishikawa, Masaji
    ★*A River in Darkness* — B
ISHIKAWA, MASAJI
    Ishikawa, Masaji. ★*A River in Darkness* — B
Isikoff, Michael
    Russian Roulette — 973.933
★*Islam*. Armstrong, Karen — 297
Islam. Nasr, Seyyed Hossein — 297
ISLAM
    Abdul Rauf, Feisal. *Moving the Mountain* — 297
    Abou El Fadl, Khaled. *The Great Theft* — 297.09
    Akyol, Mustafa. *The Islamic Jesus* — 297.2
    Akyol, Mustafa. ★*Reopening Muslim Minds* — 297.09
    Ali-Karamali, Sumbul. *Demystifying Shariah* — 340.5
    Armstrong, Karen. *The Battle for God* — 200
    Armstrong, Karen. *A History of God* — 202
    Armstrong, Karen. ★*Islam* — 297
    Armstrong, Karen. *Jerusalem* — 956.94
    Armstrong, Karen. *Muhammad* — B
    Aslan, Reza. ★*No God but God* — 297
    Baker, Deborah. *The Convert* — B
    Ben Jelloun, Tahar. *Islam Explained* — 297
    Bhutto, Benazir. *Reconciliation* — 297.2
    Blanford, Nicholas. *Warriors of God* — 956.9204
    Bowden, Mark. *Guests of the Ayatollah* — 955.05
    Carter, Jimmy. *Palestine* — 956.04
    Cliff, Nigel. *Holy War* — 909
    Cook, M. A. *The Koran* — 297.122
    Curtis, Edward E. *Muslims in America* — 305.6
    Eteraz, Ali. *Children of Dust* — B
    Frankopan, Peter. *The First Crusade* — 956
    Ghobash, Omar Saif. *Letters to a Young Muslim* — 297.09
    Glasse, Cyril. *The New Encyclopedia of Islam* — 297.03
    Gordon, Matthew. *Understanding Islam* — 297
    Grieve, Paul. *A Brief Guide to Islam* — 297
    Griswold, Eliza. *The Tenth Parallel* — 297.2
    Hammer, Joshua. *The Bad-Ass Librarians of Timbuktu* — 025.8
    Harris, Sam. *Islam and the Future of Tolerance* — 297.2
    Hazleton, Lesley. *After the Prophet* — 297.8
    Hazleton, Lesley. *The First Muslim* — B
    Husain, Ed. ★*The House of Islam* — 297
    Jalal al-Din Rumi, Maulana. *Rumi* — 891
    Jebara, Mohamad. ★*The Life of the Qur'an* — 297.122
    Jebara, Mohamad. *Muhammad, the World-Changer* — B
    Jones, Dan. *Crusaders* — 909.07
    Kennedy, Hugh. ★*The Great Arab Conquests* — 297.09
    Kugle, Scott Alan. *Living Out Islam* — 297
    Lacey, Robert. *Inside the Kingdom* — 953.805
    Lambert, Malcolm. *God's Armies* — 956
    Mackintosh-Smith, Tim. *Arabs* — 909.04
    Manglik, Gauri. ★*Muslims in Story* — 809
    Marozzi, Justin. *Islamic Empires* — 909
    Mekhennet, Souad. *I Was Told to Come Alone* — 363.3250956
    Miles, Jack. *God in the Qur'an* — 297.2
    Moghul, Haroon. *How to Be a Muslim* — B
    Nasr, Seyyed Hossein. *Islam* — 297
    Power, Carla. *If the Oceans Were Ink* — B
    Qureshi, Saqib Iqbal. *Being Muslim Today* — 305.6
    Ramadan, Tariq. ★*Introduction to Islam* — 297
    Rashid, Ahmed. *Taliban* — 958.104
    Renard, John. *The Handy Islam Answer Book* — 297
    Roberts, Randy. *Blood Brothers* — 920
    Rushdie, Salman. *Joseph Anton* — B
    Sabar, Ariel. *My Father's Paradise* — B
    Sluglett, Peter. *Atlas of Islamic History* — 912.19
    Trofimov, Yaroslav. *The Siege of Mecca* — 953.805
    Warrick, Joby. *Black Flags* — 956.9104
    Wills, Garry. *What the Qur'an Meant and Why It Matters* — 297.1
    Wood, Graeme. *The Way of the Strangers* — 363.325
    Wright, Lawrence. ★*The Looming Tower* — 973.931
    Zafar, Harris. *Demystifying Islam* — 297
ISLAM AND ART
    Beard, Mary. ★*How Do We Look* — 704.9
ISLAM AND CULTURE
    Qureshi, Saqib Iqbal. *Being Muslim Today* — 305.6
ISLAM AND POLITICS
    Bhutto, Benazir. *Reconciliation* — 297.2
    Ghattas, Kim. *Black Wave* — 955.05
    Grieve, Paul. *A Brief Guide to Islam* — 297
    Nasr, Seyyed Vali Reza. *The Shia Revival* — 297.8
    Rashid, Ahmed. *Taliban* — 958.104
    Wills, Garry. *What the Qur'an Meant and Why It Matters* — 297.1
ISLAM AND SCIENCE
    Al-Khalili, Jim. *The House of Wisdom* — 509
ISLAM AND STATE
    Rashid, Ahmed. *Taliban* — 958.104
Islam and the Future of Tolerance. Harris, Sam — 297.2

AUTHOR, TITLE, SERIES AND SUBJECT INDEX

ISLAM AND WOMEN
- Brooks, Geraldine. *Nine Parts of Desire* — 305.48
- Wills, Garry. *What the Qur'an Meant and Why It Matters* — 297.1

ISLAM AND WORLD POLITICS
- Crowley, Roger. *1453* — 949.61

Islam Explained. Ben Jelloun, Tahar — 297
Islamic Art and Culture. Khalili, Nasser D. — 709.1

ISLAMIC COUNTRIES
- Ansary, Mir Tamim. *Games Without Rules* — 958.1
- Badkhen, Anna. *The World Is a Carpet* — 305.409581
- Marozzi, Justin. *Islamic Empires* — 909

ISLAMIC DOCTRINES
- Abou El Fadl, Khaled. *The Great Theft* — 297.09
- Ali-Karamali, Sumbul. *Demystifying Shariah* — 340.5
- Armstrong, Karen. *A History of God* — 202
- Ben Jelloun, Tahar. *Islam Explained* — 297
- Grieve, Paul. *A Brief Guide to Islam* — 297
- Mattson, Ingrid. ★*The Story of the Qur'an* — 297.122
- Nasr, Seyyed Hossein. *Islam* — 297
- Ramadan, Tariq. ★*Introduction to Islam* — 297
- Wills, Garry. *What the Qur'an Meant and Why It Matters* — 297.1
- Zafar, Harris. *Demystifying Islam* — 297

ISLAMIC EMPIRE
- Armstrong, Karen. ★*Islam* — 297
- Asbridge, Thomas S. ★*The Crusades* — 909.07
- Crowley, Roger. *1453* — 949.61
- Haag, Michael. *The Tragedy of the Templars* — 271.7913
- Kennedy, Hugh. ★*The Great Arab Conquests* — 297.09
- Khalili, Nasser D. *Islamic Art and Culture* — 709.1
- O'Kane, Bernard. *Treasures of Islam* — 709.1

Islamic Empires. Marozzi, Justin — 909
The Islamic Jesus. Akyol, Mustafa — 297.2

ISLAMIC LAW
- Ali-Karamali, Sumbul. *Demystifying Shariah* — 340.5
- Mattson, Ingrid. ★*The Story of the Qur'an* — 297.122
- Navai, Ramita. *City of Lies* — 955
- Wills, Garry. *What the Qur'an Meant and Why It Matters* — 297.1

ISLAMIC VALUES
- Mattson, Ingrid. ★*The Story of the Qur'an* — 297.122

ISLAMOPHOBIA
- Ali, Wajahat. *Go Back to Where You Came From* — B
- Ali-Karamali, Sumbul. *Demystifying Shariah* — 340.5
- Lehr, Dick. *White Hot Hate* — 363.325
- Power, Carla. *If the Oceans Were Ink* — B
- Qureshi, Saqib Iqbal. *Being Muslim Today* — 305.6

Island Infernos. McManus, John C. — 940.54

ISLAND LIFE
- DePalma, Anthony. *The Cubans* — 920
- Erdrich, Louise. *Books and Islands in Ojibwe Country* — 977
- Frank, Michael. ★*One Hundred Saturdays* — B
- Swift, Earl. *Chesapeake Requiem* — 639

The Island of Extraordinary Captives. Parkin, Simon — 940.53

ISLANDS
- Clark, Doug Bock. *The Last Whalers* — 639.2
- Diaz, Von. ★*Islas* — 641.59
- Ferrer, Ada. ★*Cuba* — 972.91
- Goodheart, Adam. *The Last Island* — 954
- Hastings, Max. *Operation Pedestal* — 940.54
- Sides, Hampton. ★*The Wide Wide Sea* — 910.92
- Swift, Earl. *Chesapeake Requiem* — 639
- Turvey, Samuel. ★*The Tomb of the Mili Mongga* — 398.24

★*Islands of Abandonment.* Flyn, Cal — 333.73
Islands of the Damned. Burgin, R. V. — B

ISLANDS OF THE INDIAN OCEAN
- Diaz, Von. ★*Islas* — 641.59

ISLANDS OF THE PACIFIC
- Clark, Doug Bock. *The Last Whalers* — 639.2
- Diaz, Von. ★*Islas* — 641.59
- Sides, Hampton. ★*The Wide Wide Sea* — 910.92
- Thompson, Christina. *Sea People* — 305.8994

★*Islas.* Diaz, Von — 641.59

ISLE OF MAN
- Parkin, Simon. *The Island of Extraordinary Captives* — 940.53

ISOLATIONISM
- Churchwell, Sarah Bartlett. *Behold, America* — 973.9
- Fifield, Anna. *The Great Successor* — B
- Jeppesen, Travis. *See You Again in Pyongyang* — 951.93
- Olson, Lynne. *Those Angry Days* — 940.53

Israel. Gordis, Daniel — 956.9405

ISRAEL
- Abuelaish, Izzeldin. *I Shall Not Hate* — B
- Armstrong, Karen. *The Battle for God* — 200
- Armstrong, Karen. ★*The Great Transformation* — 200.9
- Bascomb, Neal. *Hunting Eichmann* — 943.086
- Blanford, Nicholas. *Warriors of God* — 956.9204
- Burkett, Elinor. *Golda* — B
- Carter, Jimmy. *Palestine* — 956.04
- Century, Douglas. *Barney Ross* — B
- Ehrenreich, Ben. *The Way to the Spring* — 956.95
- Ephron, Dan. *Killing a King* — 956.9405
- Feldman, Noah. ★*To Be a Jew Today* — 296.3
- Friedman, Matti. *Spies of No Country* — 327.12
- Friedman, Thomas L. ★*From Beirut to Jerusalem* — 956.04
- Garfinkel, Yosef. *In the Footsteps of King David* — 933
- Glinert, Lewis. *The Story of Hebrew* — 492.4
- Goodman, Micah. *Catch-67* — 956.04
- Gordis, Daniel. *Impossible Takes Longer* — 956.94
- Gordis, Daniel. *Israel* — 956.9405
- Halevi, Yossi Klein. ★*Letters to My Palestinian Neighbor* — 956.94054
- Hoffman, Adina. ★*My Happiness Bears No Relation to Happiness* — B
- Kaufmann, Uri R. *Eighteen Days of October* — 956.04
- Keinan, Tal. *God Is in the Crowd* — 305.892
- Kershner, Isabel. *The Land of Hope and Fear* — 956.9405
- Klagsbrun, Francine. *Lioness* — B
- LeBor, Adam. *City of Oranges* — 956.94
- Mead, Walter Russell. *The Arc of a Covenant* — 327.73
- Mitchell, George J. *A Path to Peace* — 956.9405
- Morris, Benny. *1948* — 956.04
- Morris, Benny. *Righteous Victims* — 956
- Oren, Michael B. *Six Days of War* — 956.04
- Pappe, Ilan. *The Biggest Prison on Earth* — 956.9405
- Peres, Shimon. *No Room for Small Dreams* — B
- Pfeffer, Anshel. *Bibi* — B
- Qashu, Sayed. *Native* — 892.4
- Sefarad, Mikhael. *The Wall and the Gate* — 341.48
- Shavit, Ari. *My Promised Land* — 956.05
- Shehadeh, Raja. *Where the Line Is Drawn* — 956.9405
- Shlaim, Avi. *The Iron Wall* — 956.04
- Sokatch, Daniel. *Can We Talk About Israel?* — 956.9405
- Solomonov, Michael. *Israeli Soul* — 641.595
- Solomonov, Michael. *Zahav* — 641.595
- Talty, Stephan. *The Good Assassin* — 364.15
- Tolan, Sandy. *Children of the Stone* — 780

ISRAEL-ARAB WAR, 1948-1949
- Collins, Larry. *O Jerusalem!* — 956
- Friedman, Matti. *Spies of No Country* — 327.12
- Morris, Benny. *1948* — 956.04
- Petraeus, David Howell. *Conflict* — 355

ISRAEL-ARAB WAR, 1967
- Goodman, Micah. *Catch-67* — 956.04
- Kaufmann, Uri R. *Eighteen Days of October* — 956.04
- Oren, Michael B. *Six Days of War* — 956.04
- Petraeus, David Howell. *Conflict* — 355

ISRAEL-ARAB WAR, 1973
- Indyk, Martin. *Master of the Game* — 327.73
- Kaufmann, Uri R. *Eighteen Days of October* — 956.04
- Petraeus, David Howell. *Conflict* — 355
- Wright, Lawrence. *Thirteen Days in September* — 956.04

ISRAELI PEOPLE
- Carter, Jimmy. *Palestine* — 956.04
- Grossman, David. *The Yellow Wind* — 956.95
- Pick-Goslar, Hannah Elizabeth. ★*My Friend Anne Frank* — B
- Shavit, Ari. *My Promised Land* — 956.05
- Tolan, Sandy. ★*The Lemon Tree* — B

Israeli Soul. Solomonov, Michael — 641.595

ISRAELI WEST BANK BARRIER
- Ehrenreich, Ben. *The Way to the Spring* — 956.95
- Tolan, Sandy. *Children of the Stone* — 780

ISRAELI-OCCUPIED TERRITORIES
- Pappe, Ilan. *The Biggest Prison on Earth* — 956.9405
- Shehadeh, Raja. *Where the Line Is Drawn* — 956.9405

ISRAELI-PALESTINIAN RELATIONS
- Goodman, Micah. *Catch-67* — 956.04
- Grossman, David. *The Yellow Wind* — 956.95
- Hoffman, Adina. ★*My Happiness Bears No Relation to Happiness* — B
- Morris, Benny. *Righteous Victims* — 956

PUBLIC LIBRARY CORE COLLECTION: NONFICTION
Twentieth Edition

Pappe, Ilan. *The Biggest Prison on Earth*   956.9405
Peres, Shimon. *No Room for Small Dreams*   B
Sefarad, Mikhael. *The Wall and the Gate*   341.48
Tolan, Sandy. ★ *The Lemon Tree*   B
Issenberg, Sasha
    ★ *The Engagement*   346.7301
Isserman, Maurice
    Continental Divide   796.52
    The Winter Army   940.54
Istanbul. Hughes, Bettany   949.61
Istanbul. Madden, Thomas F.   949.61
Istanbul. Pamuk, Orhan   949.61
Istanbul & Beyond. Eckhardt, Robyn   641.595
ISTANBUL, TURKEY
    Crowley, Roger. *1453*   949.61
    Hughes, Bettany. *Istanbul*   949.61
    King, Charles. *Midnight at the Pera Palace*   949.61
    Madden, Thomas F. *Istanbul*   949.61
    Pamuk, Orhan. *Istanbul*   949.61
It Takes a Village. Clinton, Hillary Rodham   305.23
It Was All a Lie. Stevens, Stuart   324.2734
It Won't Be Easy. Rademacher, Tom   B
It's A Long Story. Nelson, Willie   B
It's All Easy. Paltrow, Gwyneth   641.5
It's All Relative. Jacobs, A. J.   929.1
It's Always Been Ours. Wilson, Jessica   613
It's Always Freezer Season. Christensen, Ashley   641.5
★ *It's Better to Be Feared*. Wickersham, Seth   796.332
It's Even Worse Than You Think. Johnston, David Cay   973.933
It's Great to Suck at Something. Rinaldi, Karen   158.1
★ *It's Hard for Me to Live with Me*. Chapman, Rex   B
It's Never Too Late to Begin Again. Cameron, Julia   155.67
★ *It's Not Hysteria*. Tang, Karen   618.2
It's Not yet Dark. Fitzmaurice, Simon   616.8
★ *It's Not You*. Durvasula, Ramani   155.2
It's Okay Not to Look for the Meaning of Life. Minami, Jikisai   158.1
It's What I Do. Addario, Lynsey   B
ITALIAN AMERICAN FAMILIES
    Hood, Ann. *Kitchen Yarns*   641.5
ITALIAN AMERICAN MEN
    DiMarco, Nyle. ★ *Deaf Utopia*   B
ITALIAN AMERICANS
    Carcaterra, Lorenzo. *Three Dreamers*   B
    Russell, Jan Jarboe. *The Train to Crystal City*   940.53
    Schwartz, David N. *The Last Man Who Knew Everything*   B
    Strang, Dean A. *Worse Than the Devil*   345.775
ITALIAN HISTORY
    Bailey, Catherine. *A Castle in Wartime*   943.086
    Benner, Erica. *Be Like the Fox*   B
    Bradford, Sarah. *Lucrezia Borgia*   B
    Crowley, Roger. *City of Fortune*   945
    Duggan, Christopher. *The Force of Destiny*   945
    Hale, Sheila. *Titian*   B
    Hales, Dianne R. *Mona Lisa*   B
    Hibbert, Christopher. *The Borgias and Their Enemies*   920
    Hibbert, Christopher. *The House of Medici*   920
    Holland, James. *Sicily '43*   940.54
    Kertzer, David I. *The Pope at War*   940.53
    King, Ross. *Brunelleschi's Dome*   726.6
    King, Ross. *Michelangelo & the Pope's Ceiling*   759.5
    Kneale, Matthew. *Rome*   945.6
    Lewis, Damien. *Churchill's Hellraisers*   940.54
    Madden, Thomas F. *Venice*   945
    Mazzeo, Tilar J. *Sisters in Resistance*   945.091
    McGregor, James H. *Rome from the Ground up*   711
    Meyer, G. J. *The Borgias*   920
    Moorehead, Caroline. *A House in the Mountains*   940.53
    Norwich, John Julius. *A History of Venice*   945
    Norwich, John Julius. *Sicily*   945.8
    Nuland, Sherwin B. *Leonardo Da Vinci*   B
    Parks, Tim. *The Hero's Way*   945
    Servadio, Gaia. *Rossini*   B
    Strathern, Paul. *The Borgias*   945.06
    Strathern, Paul. *The Florentines*   945
ITALIAN LANGUAGE
    Lahiri, Jhumpa. *In Other Words*   B
ITALIAN PEOPLE
    Hooper, John. *The Italians*   945.093

Levi, Primo. *The Reawakening*   B
★ *Italian Renaissance Art*. Adams, Laurie   709.45
Italian Ways. Parks, Tim   385
The Italians. Hooper, John   945.093
ITALY
    Atkinson, Rick. *The Day of Battle*   940.54
    Berendt, John. *The City of Falling Angels*   945
    Berger, William. *Puccini Without Excuses*   782.1
    Berger, William. *Verdi with a Vengeance*   B
    Butcher, Carmen Acevedo. *Man of Blessing*   B
    De Stefano, Cristina. *The Child Is the Teacher*   B
    Gilbert, Elizabeth. *Eat, Pray, Love*   B
    Hibbert, Christopher. *The Borgias and Their Enemies*   920
    Holland, James. *The Savage Storm*   940.53
    Hooper, John. *The Italians*   945.093
    Isserman, Maurice. *The Winter Army*   940.54
    Jacobs, Ryan McMahon. *The Truffle Underground*   381
    Kertzer, David I. *The Pope and Mussolini*   322
    King, Ross. *Bookseller of Florence*   381
    King, Ross. *Brunelleschi's Dome*   726.6
    King, Ross. *Michelangelo & the Pope's Ceiling*   759.5
    Koenig, Leah. *Portico*   641.5
    Lahiri, Jhumpa. *In Other Words*   B
    Levi, Primo. *The Periodic Table*   858
    Levi, Primo. ★ *Survival in Auschwitz*   B
    Lewis, Damien. *Churchill's Hellraisers*   940.54
    Mayes, Frances. *See You in the Piazza*   914.5
    Mazzeo, Tilar J. *Sisters in Resistance*   945.091
    Meyer, G. J. *The Borgias*   920
    Mohammadi, Kamin. *Bella Figura*   641.01
    Munno, Nadia Caterina. *The Pasta Queen*   641.82
    Norwich, John Julius. *A History of Venice*   945
    Parks, Tim. *The Hero's Way*   945
    Parks, Tim. *Italian Ways*   385
    Prose, Francine. *Caravaggio*   759.5
    Rowland, Ingrid D. *The Collector of Lives*   B
    Scarpaleggia, Giulia. ★ *Cucina Povera*   641.594
    Setareh, Saghar. *Pomegranates & Artichokes*   641.5
    Strathern, Paul. *The Borgias*   945.06
    Strathern, Paul. *The Florentines*   945
    Suchet, John. *Verdi*   782.1092
    Virgil. ★ *The Aeneid*   873
    Von Bremzen, Anya. *National Dish*   641.3
Itzkoff, Dave
    ★ *Robin*   B
Ivan's War. Merridale, Catherine   940.54
Iversen, Kristen
    Full Body Burden   363.17
IVERSEN, KRISTEN
    Iversen, Kristen. *Full Body Burden*   363.17
Iverson, Peter
    Diné   979.1004
IVES, CHARLES, 1874-1954
    Swafford, Jan. *Charles Ives*   B
IVORY POACHING
    Orenstein, Ronald I. *Ivory, Horn and Blood*   333.95
IVORY SMUGGLING
    Orenstein, Ronald I. *Ivory, Horn and Blood*   333.95
Ivory Vikings. Brown, Nancy Marie   736
Ivory, Horn and Blood. Orenstein, Ronald I.   333.95
IWO JIMA, BATTLE OF, 1945
    Bradley, James. *Flags of Our Fathers*   940.54
    Lucas, Jack. *Indestructible*   B
Iyengar, Sheena
    The Art of Choosing   153.8
Iyer, Pico
    A Beginner's Guide to Japan   952.05
    ★ *The Half Known Life*   203
    The Lady and the Monk   952
    The Open Road   B
IYER, PICO
    Iyer, Pico. *A Beginner's Guide to Japan*   952.05
    Iyer, Pico. *The Lady and the Monk*   952
Iyer, Raghavan
    Indian Cooking Unfolded   641.595
Izgil, Tahir Hamut
    Waiting to Be Arrested at Night   B

AUTHOR, TITLE, SERIES AND SUBJECT INDEX

IZGIL, TAHIR HAMUT, 1969-
    Izgil, Tahir Hamut. *Waiting to Be Arrested at Night*   B
Izzard, Eddie
    Believe Me   B
IZZARD, EDDIE
    Izzard, Eddie. *Believe Me*   B

J

J. M. Coetzee and the Life of Writing. Attwell, David   823
Jabbour, Niki
    ★*Groundbreaking Food Gardens*   635
    Growing Under Cover   635
    Niki Jabbour's Veggie Garden Remix   635
Jabr, Ferris
    ★*Becoming Earth*   570.1
Jack Be Nimble. O'Brien, Jack   B
JACK, THE RIPPER
    Cornwell, Patricia Daniels. *Ripper*   364.152
    Rubenhold, Hallie. ★*The Five*   362.88
JACK-O-LANTERNS
    Cupp, Lundy. *Realistic Pumpkin Carving*   745.5941646
★*Jackie*. Taraborrelli, J. Randy   B
Jackie Ormes. Goldstein, Nancy   B
Jackie's Girl. McKeon, Kathy   B
Jackie, Janet & Lee. Taraborrelli, J. Randy   920
Jackpot. Mechanic, Michael   305.5
Jackson family
    The Jacksons   782.421644
JACKSON FAMILY
    Jackson family. *The Jacksons*   782.421644
Jackson Pollock. Solomon, Deborah   B
JACKSON, ANARCHA, APPROXIMATELY 1821-1869
    Hallman, J. C. *Say Anarcha*   618.1
JACKSON, ANDREW, 1767-1845
    Brands, H. W. ★*Andrew Jackson, His Life and Times*   B
    Cozzens, Peter. *A Brutal Reckoning*   973.5
    Inskeep, Steve. *Jacksonland*   973.56
    Kilmeade, Brian. ★*Andrew Jackson and the Miracle of New Orleans*   973.5
    Meacham, Jon. ★*American Lion*   976.9
    Snyder, Christina. *Great Crossings*   976.9
Jackson, Angela
    A Surprised Queenhood in the New Black Sun   B
JACKSON, BO, 1962-
    Pearlman, Jeff. *The Last Folk Hero*   B
Jackson, Bruce
    Never Far from Home   B
JACKSON, BRUCE (LAWYER)
    Jackson, Bruce. *Never Far from Home*   B
Jackson, Curtis
    Hustle Harder, Hustle Smarter   B
JACKSON, CURTIS, 1975-
    Jackson, Curtis. *Hustle Harder, Hustle Smarter*   B
Jackson, Danielle Bayard
    Fighting for Our Friendships   302.34
Jackson, Jenn M.
    ★*Black Women Taught Us*   305.48
JACKSON, JENN M.
    Jackson, Jenn M. ★*Black Women Taught Us*   305.48
Jackson, Joe
    Black Elk   978.004
Jackson, Julian
    De Gaulle   B
Jackson, Kellie Carter
    We Refuse   323.1196
Jackson, Lawrence Patrick
    Chester B. Himes   B
Jackson, Major
    Razzle Dazzle   811
JACKSON, MICHAEL, 1958-2009
    Jefferson, Margo. *On Michael Jackson*   B
    Vogel, Joseph. *Man in the Music*   B
Jackson, Mitchell S.
    Survival Math   B
JACKSON, MITCHELL S.
    Jackson, Mitchell S. *Survival Math*   B

JACKSON, PHIL
    Pearlman, Jeff. ★*Three-Ring Circus*   796.323
Jackson, Regina
    White Women   305.8
Jackson, Shirley
    Let Me Tell You   818
    ★*The Letters of Shirley Jackson*   813
JACKSON, SHIRLEY, 1916-1965
    Franklin, Ruth. *Shirley Jackson*   B
    Jackson, Shirley. ★*The Letters of Shirley Jackson*   813
JACKSON, STONEWALL, 1824-1863
    Gwynne, S. C. *Rebel Yell*   B
    Robertson, James I. *Stonewall Jackson*   B
JACKSON, SUMNER WALDRON
    Kershaw, Alex. *Avenue of Spies*   940.53
Jackson, Ted
    ★*You Ought to Do a Story About Me*   B
JACKSON, TED
    Jackson, Ted. ★*You Ought to Do a Story About Me*   B
Jackson, Troy
    Becoming King   B
Jacksonland. Inskeep, Steve   973.56
The Jacksons. Jackson family   782.421644
JACOB, MAX, 1876-1944
    Warren, Rosanna. *Max Jacob*   B
Jacob, Mira
    Good Talk   741.5
JACOB, MIRA, 1973-
    Jacob, Mira. *Good Talk*   741.5
JACOBS FAMILY
    Jacobs, A. J. *It's All Relative*   929.1
Jacobs, A. J.
    It's All Relative   929.1
    The Puzzler   793.73
    ★*The Year of Living Constitutionally*   342.73
JACOBS, A. J., 1968-
    Jacobs, A. J. *It's All Relative*   929.1
    Jacobs, A. J. *The Puzzler*   793.73
    Jacobs, A. J. ★*The Year of Living Constitutionally*   342.73
Jacobs, Alan
    How to Think   153.4
    Original Sin   233
Jacobs, Alexandra
    Still Here   B
Jacobs, Harriet
    ★*Incidents in the Life of a Slave Girl*   B
JACOBS, HARRIET, 1818-1896
    Jacobs, Harriet. ★*Incidents in the Life of a Slave Girl*   B
JACOBS, JANE, 1916-2006
    Kanigel, Robert. *Eyes on the Street*   B
Jacobs, Laura
    ★*Celestial Bodies*   792.8
Jacobs, Ryan McMahon
    The Truffle Underground   381
Jacobs, Sally H.
    Althea   B
Jacobsen, Annie
    ★*Operation Paperclip*   940.54
    Phenomena   133.8
    Surprise, Kill, Vanish   327.1273
Jacobson, Sidney
    The 9-11 Report   741.5
    Anne Frank   741.5
Jacoby, Karl
    The Strange Career of William Ellis   B
Jacoby, Melissa B.
    ★*Unjust Debts*   346.73
Jacqueline Bouvier Kennedy Onassis. Leaming, Barbara   B
★*Jacques Pepin*. Pepin, Jacques   641.5
★*Jacques Pepin*. Pepin, Jacques   641.594
★*Jacques Pépin Cooking My Way*. Pepin, Jacques   641.5
JACQUET DE LA GUERRE, ELISABETH-CLAUDE, 1665-1729
    Porter, Cecelia Hopkins. *Five Lives in Music*   B
Jade, Holly
    The Essential Book of Vegan Bakes   641.5
Jadhav, Narendra
    Untouchables   305.5

PUBLIC LIBRARY CORE COLLECTION: NONFICTION
Twentieth Edition

JADHAV, NARENDRA, 1953-
   Jadhav, Narendra. *Untouchables* — 305.5
Jaffe, Sarah W.
   Wanting What's Best — 649
Jaffrey, Madhur
   ★*Madhur Jaffrey's Instantly Indian Cookbook* — 641.595
   Madhur Jaffrey's World Vegetarian. — 641.5
   Vegetarian India — 641.595
Jager, Eric
   Blood Royal — 944.026
JAGGER, BIANCA
   Winder, Elizabeth. *Parachute Women* — 782.42164
Jaher, David
   The Witch of Lime Street — B
Jahner, Harald
   ★*Aftermath* — 943.087
Jahren, Hope
   ★*Lab Girl* — B
JAHREN, HOPE
   Jahren, Hope. ★*Lab Girl* — B
The Jail Is Everywhere. Norton, Jack — 365
JAILS
   Fedderly, Eva. *These Walls* — 365
   Norton, Jack. *The Jail Is Everywhere* — 365
Jakes, T. D
   Destiny — 248.4
Jaku, Eddie
   ★*The Happiest Man on Earth* — B
JAKU, EDDIE
   Jaku, Eddie. ★*The Happiest Man on Earth* — B
JALAL AL-DIN RUMI, MAULANA, 1207-1273
   Housden, Roger. *Saved by Beauty* — 955
   Jalal al-Din Rumi, Maulana. *The Essential Rumi* — 891
   Jalal al-Din Rumi, Maulana. *Rumi* — 891
Jalal al-Din Rumi, Maulana
   The Essential Rumi — 891
   Rumi — 891
JAM BANDS
   Browne, David. *So Many Roads* — B
Jam Session. Goldstein, Joyce Esersky, author — 641.85
JAMAICA
   Grant, Colin. *The Natural Mystics* — B
JAMAICAN AMERICANS
   Chude-Sokei, Louis Onuorah. *Floating in a Most Peculiar Way* — 979.4
   Shakur, Prince. *When They Tell You to Be Good* — B
JAMAICAN PEOPLE
   Ashley, Maurice. *Move by Move* — 158
★*James Baldwin.* Mullen, Bill — B
JAMES BOND (FICTITIOUS CHARACTER)
   Shakespeare, Nicholas. *Ian Fleming* — B
James Dean. Gehring, Wes D. — B
James Herriot's Animal Stories. Herriot, James — B
James Herriot's Cat Stories. Herriot, James — 636.8
James Herriot's Dog Stories. Herriot, James — 636.7
James Herriot's Favorite Dog Stories. Herriot, James — 636.7
JAMES I, KING OF ENGLAND, 1566-1625
   Ackroyd, Peter. *Rebellion* — 941.06
   Woolley, Benjamin. *The King's Assassin* — B
★*James Joyce.* Bowker, Gordon — B
James Madison. Broadwater, Jeff — B
James Madison. Cheney, Lynne V. — B
James Madison. Wills, Garry — B
James Merrill. Hammer, Langdon — B
James Monroe. McGrath, Tim — B
James Patterson by James Patterson. Patterson, James — B
James Tiptree, Jr. Phillips, Julie — B
James Wright. Blunk, Jonathan — B
James, Henry
   Literary Criticism; Vol. 1 — 809
James, Jamie
   The Glamour of Strangeness — 700.1
JAMES, JESSE, 1847-1882
   Stiles, T. J. *Jesse James* — B
James, John W.
   ★*The Grief Recovery Handbook* — 155.9
James, Laura E.
   Odd Girl Out — B

James, Laura E.
   James, Laura E. *Odd Girl Out* — B
JAMES, LEBRON
   Babb, Valerie Melissa. *The Book of James* — B
   Benedict, Jeff. *Lebron* — B
   Windhorst, Brian. *Lebron, Inc.* — B
James, P. D.
   Talking About Detective Fiction — 823
James, Scott
   Trial by Fire — 363.3709745
James, Victoria
   Wine Girl — B
JAMES, VICTORIA
   James, Victoria. *Wine Girl* — B
James, William
   ★*The Varieties of Religious Experience* — 204
JAMES, WILLIAM, 1842-1910
   Blum, Deborah. *Ghost Hunters* — 133.9
   Richardson, Robert D. *William James* — B
Jameson, A. D.
   I Find Your Lack of Faith Disturbing — 791.43
JAMESTOWN, VIRGINIA
   Horn, James P. P. *Land as God Made It* — 975.5
   Kelly, Joseph. *Marooned* — 975.5
   Price, David A. ★*Love and Hate in Jamestown* — 975.5
Jamie, Poppy
   Happy Not Perfect — 158.1
Jamieson, Alexandra
   Women, Food, and Desire — 155.3
Jamieson, David
   Mint Condition — 796.357
Jamison, Kay Redfield
   Fires in the Dark — 616.89
JAMISON, KAY REDFIELD
   Jamison, Kay Redfield. *Fires in the Dark* — 616.89
Jamison, Leslie
   The Empathy Exams — 813
   ★*Make It Scream, Make It Burn* — 814
   ★*The Recovering* — B
JAMISON, LESLIE, 1983-
   Jamison, Leslie. *The Empathy Exams* — 813
   Jamison, Leslie. ★*Make It Scream, Make It Burn* — 814
   Jamison, Leslie. ★*The Recovering* — B
JAMMU AND KASHMIR (INDIA)
   Peer, Basharat. *Curfewed Night* — B
JAMS AND JELLIES
   Goldstein, Joyce Esersky, author. *Jam Session* — 641.85
Jane Austen, the Secret Radical. Kelly, Helena — 823
Jane Brody's Guide to the Great Beyond. Brody, Jane E. — 616
★*Jane Crow.* Rosenberg, Rosalind — B
JANE SEYMOUR, QUEEN, CONSORT OF HENRY VIII, KING OF ENGLAND, 1509?-1537
   Fraser, Antonia. ★*The Wives of Henry VIII* — 942.05
Janesville. Goldstein, Amy — 330.9775
Jang. Kang, Mingoo — 641.595
Jang, Jin-Sung
   Dear Leader — B
JANG, JIN-SUNG
   Jang, Jin-Sung. *Dear Leader* — B
Jang, Lucia
   Stars Between the Sun and Moon — 365.45092
JANG, LUCIA
   Jang, Lucia. *Stars Between the Sun and Moon* — 365.45092
★*Janis.* George-Warren, Holly — B
Jansen, Marius
   The Making of Modern Japan — 952
★*Janson's History of Art.* Janson, H. W. — 709
Janson, H. W.
   ★*Janson's History of Art* — 709
Jaouad, Suleika
   ★*Between Two Kingdoms* — B
JAOUAD, SULEIKA
   Jaouad, Suleika. ★*Between Two Kingdoms* — B
Japan. McClain, James — 952.03
JAPAN
   Alt, Matt. *Pure Invention* — 306.0952
   Barrett, David Dean. *140 Days to Hiroshima* — 940.54
   Bass, Gary Jonathan. ★*Judgment at Tokyo* — 952.04

AUTHOR, TITLE, SERIES AND SUBJECT INDEX

Bennett, Alexander. *Kendo*	796.86
Bix, Herbert P. *Hirohito and the Making of Modern Japan*	B
Blume, Lesley M. M. *Fallout*	940.54
Bradley, James. *Flags of Our Fathers*	940.54
Brotherton, Marcus. *A Bright and Blinding Sun*	940.54
Clements, Jonathan. *The Anime Encyclopedia*	791.43
Dower, John W. *Embracing Defeat*	952.04
Drabkin, Ronald. *Beverly Hills Spy*	940.54
Ellis, Richard. *Tuna*	333.95
Erwin, Jon. *Beyond Valor*	B
Finn, Adharanand. *The Way of the Runner*	796.42
Giangreco, D. M. *Hell to Pay*	940.54
Gladwell, Malcolm. ★*The Bomber Mafia*	940.54
Goulding, Matt. *Rice, Noodle, Fish*	394.1
Grayling, A. C. *Among the Dead Cities*	940.54
Hardacre, Helen. *Shinto*	299.5
Hastings, Max. *Retribution*	940.54
Hillenbrand, Laura. ★*Unbroken*	B
Hotta, Eri. *Japan 1941*	940.54
Iyer, Pico. *A Beginner's Guide to Japan*	952.05
Iyer, Pico. *The Lady and the Monk*	952
Johnson, Akemi. *Night in the American Village*	305.40952
Keene, Donald. *Emperor of Japan*	952.03
Keene, Donald. *The Pleasures of Japanese Literature*	895.6
Kemper, Steve. *Our Man in Tokyo*	952.03
Koh, EJ. *The Magical Language of Others*	813
Leong, Sonia. *101 Top Tips from Professional Manga Artists*	741.5
Lockley, Thomas. *African Samurai*	B
Lucas, Jack. *Indestructible*	B
Man, John. *Ninja*	355.5
Mitter, Rana. *Forgotten Ally*	951.04
Mizuki, Shigeru. *Showa 1926-1939*	741.5
Murakami, Haruki. *Underground*	364.15
Murakami, Haruki. *What I Talk About When I Talk About Running*	B
Perry, Mark. *The Most Dangerous Man in America*	B
Pilling, David. *Bending Adversity*	952.0512
Sherman, Anna. *The Bells of Old Tokyo*	952
Smith, Jim B. *The Last Mission*	940.54
Southard, Susan. *Nagasaki*	940.54
Stanley, Amy. *Stranger in the Shogun's City*	B
Von Bremzen, Anya. *National Dish*	641.3
Wallace, Chris. *Countdown 1945*	940.54
Yomota, Inuhiko. *What Is Japanese Cinema?*	791.43
Japan 1941. Hotta, Eri	940.54
JAPANESE AMERICAN FAMILIES	
Brown, Daniel James. ★*Facing the Mountain*	940.54
Sakamoto, Pamela Rotner. *Midnight in Broad Daylight*	940.53
JAPANESE AMERICAN FORCED REMOVAL AND INCARCERATION	
Cahan, Richard. *Un-American*	940.53
Daniels, Roger. *Prisoners Without Trial*	940.53
Henderson, Bruce B. *Bridge to the Sun*	940.53
Reeves, Richard. *Infamy*	940.53
Russell, Jan Jarboe. *The Train to Crystal City*	940.53
Sone, Monica Itoi. *Nisei Daughter*	979.7
JAPANESE AMERICAN WOMEN	
Brina, Elizabeth Miki. *Speak, Okinawa*	305.48
Hirono, Mazie. *Heart of Fire*	B
JAPANESE AMERICANS	
Brina, Elizabeth Miki. *Speak, Okinawa*	305.48
Brown, Daniel James. ★*Facing the Mountain*	940.54
Checkoway, Julie. *The Three-Year Swim Club*	797.2
Herrera, Hayden. *Listening to Stone*	B
Hsu, Hua. ★*Stay True*	B
Sakamoto, Pamela Rotner. *Midnight in Broad Daylight*	940.53
Sone, Monica Itoi. *Nisei Daughter*	979.7
Japanese Gardening. Chesshire, Charles	712
JAPANESE GARDENS	
Chesshire, Charles. *Japanese Gardening*	712
JAPANESE HISTORY	
Barrett, David Dean. *140 Days to Hiroshima*	940.54
Bix, Herbert P. *Hirohito and the Making of Modern Japan*	B
Blume, Lesley M. M. *Fallout*	940.54
Bruning, John R. *The Race of Aces*	940.54
Buruma, Ian. *Inventing Japan, 1853-1964*	952.03
Dower, John W. *Embracing Defeat*	952.04
Frank, Richard B. *Downfall*	940.54
Gordon, Andrew. *A Modern History of Japan*	952
Hardacre, Helen. *Shinto*	299.5
Hastings, Max. *Retribution*	940.54
Jansen, Marius. *The Making of Modern Japan*	952
Katsushika, Hokusai. *Hokusai*	769.92
Keene, Donald. *Emperor of Japan*	952.03
Lockley, Thomas. *African Samurai*	B
Man, John. *Ninja*	355.5
McClain, James. *Japan*	952.03
McManus, John C. *To the End of the Earth*	940.54
Mizuki, Shigeru. *Showa 1926-1939*	741.5
Parry, Richard Lloyd. *Ghosts of the Tsunami*	952.05
Pellegrino, Charles R. *To Hell and Back*	940.54
Pilling, David. *Bending Adversity*	952.0512
Scott, James. *Black Snow*	940.54
Sherman, Anna. *The Bells of Old Tokyo*	952
Stanley, Amy. *Stranger in the Shogun's City*	B
Wallace, Chris. *Countdown 1945*	940.54
Yomota, Inuhiko. *What Is Japanese Cinema?*	791.43
Japanese Home Cooking. Sakai, Sonoko	641.595
Japanese Knitting Stitch Bible. Shida, Hitomi	746.43
JAPANESE OCCUPATION, WORLD WAR II	
Alexander, Caroline. *Skies of Thunder*	940.54
Bruning, John R. *Indestructible*	B
Japanese Paper Flowers. Yamazaki, Hiromi	745.594
JAPANESE PEOPLE	
Kemper, Steve. *Our Man in Tokyo*	952.03
Rothenberg, Ben. *Naomi Osaka*	B
JAPANESE PEOPLE IN THE UNITED STATES	
Nimura, Janice P. *Daughters of the Samurai*	920
JAPANESE POETRY	
Rexroth, Kenneth. *One Hundred Poems from the Japanese*	895
Sato, Hiroaki. *On Haiku*	809.1
Japanese Stone Gardens. Mansfield, Stephen	712
Jarchow, Deborah	
The Weaving Explorer	746.1
Jarhead. Swofford, Anthony	956.7044
Jarnow, Jesse	
Big Day Coming	B
Jarrell, Randall	
★*The Complete Poems*	811
Jarrett, Valerie	
Finding My Voice	B
JARRETT, VALERIE, 1956-	
Jarrett, Valerie. *Finding My Voice*	B
Jauhar, Sandeep	
Heart	612.1
JAUHAR, SANDEEP, 1968-	
Jauhar, Sandeep. *Heart*	612.1
Jawando, Will	
★*My Seven Black Fathers*	B
JAWANDO, WILL, 1983-	
Jawando, Will. ★*My Seven Black Fathers*	B
Jaworksi, Ron	
The Games That Changed the Game	796.332
JAY, JOHN, 1745-1829	
Ellis, Joseph J. *The Quartet*	342.7302
JAY-Z, 1969-	
Greenburg, Zack O'Malley. *3 Kings*	782.421649
Jayapal, Pramila	
Use the Power You Have	B
JAYAPAL, PRAMILA, 1965-	
Jayapal, Pramila. *Use the Power You Have*	B
Jazz. Ward, Geoffrey C.	781.6509
Jazz. DeVeaux, Scott Knowles	781.65
The Jazz Ear. Ratliff, Ben	781.6509
JAZZ MUSIC	
Armstrong, Louis. *Louis Armstrong, in His Own Words*	B
Brothers, Thomas David. ★*Louis Armstrong, Master of Modernism*	B
Chinen, Nate. *Playing Changes*	781.6509
Cooke, Mervyn. *The Chronicle of Jazz*	781.6509
Crouch, Stanley. *Kansas City Lightning*	B
Dance, Stanley. ★*The World of Earl Hines*	B
DeVeaux, Scott Knowles. *Jazz*	781.65
Dregni, Michael. *Django*	B
Friedwald, Will. *Straighten up and Fly Right*	782.42164
Giddins, Gary. *Weather Bird*	781.6509
Gioia, Ted. *The History of Jazz*	781.6509
Kahn, Ashley. *The House That Trane Built*	781.6509
Kaplan, James. *3 Shades of Blue*	920

PUBLIC LIBRARY CORE COLLECTION: NONFICTION
Twentieth Edition

Kaplan, James. *Sinatra*	782.42164
Krist, Gary. *Empire of Sin*	976.3
Levy, Aidan. *Saxophone Colossus*	B
Marsalis, Wynton. *Moving to Higher Ground*	781.65
Morgenstern, Dan. *Living with Jazz*	781.65
Morton, Brian. ★*The Penguin Jazz Guide*	016
Murakami, Haruki. ★*Absolutely on Music*	784.2
Myers, Marc. *Why Jazz Happened*	781.65
Ratliff, Ben. *The Jazz Ear*	781.6509
Sandke, Randy. *Where the Dark and the Light Folks Meet*	781.6509
Teachout, Terry. *Duke*	B
Teachout, Terry. *Pops*	B
Torgoff, Martin. *Bop Apocalypse*	781.65
Tye, Larry. ★*The Jazzmen*	781.6509
Ward, Geoffrey C. *Jazz*	781.6509

JAZZ MUSIC COMPOSERS
Cooke, Mervyn. *The Chronicle of Jazz*	781.6509

JAZZ MUSICIANS
Armstrong, Louis. *Louis Armstrong, in His Own Words*	B
Atria, Travis. *Better Days Will Come Again*	B
Basie, Count. *Good Morning Blues*	B
Brothers, Thomas David. ★*Louis Armstrong, Master of Modernism*	B
Chinen, Nate. *Playing Changes*	781.6509
Cooke, Mervyn. *The Chronicle of Jazz*	781.6509
Crouch, Stanley. *Kansas City Lightning*	B
Dance, Stanley. ★*The World of Earl Hines*	B
Dregni, Michael. *Django*	B
Friedwald, Will. *Straighten up and Fly Right*	782.42164
Gabbard, Krin. *Better Git It in Your Soul*	B
Hayes, Elaine M. ★*Queen of Bebop*	B
Kaplan, James. *3 Shades of Blue*	920
Lees, Gene. *You Can't Steal a Gift*	B
Levy, Aidan. *Saxophone Colossus*	B
Myers, Marc. *Why Jazz Happened*	781.65
Ratliff, Ben. *The Jazz Ear*	781.6509
Teachout, Terry. *Pops*	B
Torgoff, Martin. *Bop Apocalypse*	781.65
Ward, Geoffrey C. *Jazz*	781.6509
Whitaker, Mark. *Smoketown*	305.896

JAZZ SINGERS
Alexander, Paul. *Bitter Crop*	B
Kaplan, James. *Sinatra*	782.42164

JAZZ TRUMPETERS
Kaplan, James. *3 Shades of Blue*	920
Teachout, Terry. *Pops*	B
★*The Jazzmen*. Tye, Larry	781.6509

Jeal, Tim
Explorers of the Nile	920

JEALOUSY
Homer. ★*The Iliad*	883
Mann, William J. *The Wars of the Roosevelts*	B
Peyser, Marc N. *Hissing Cousins*	B

Jebara, Mohamad
★*The Life of the Qur'an*	297.122
Muhammad, the World-Changer	B

Jeffers, Honorée Fanonne
The Age of Phillis	811

Jeffers, Robinson
The Selected Poetry of Robinson Jeffers	811

Jeffers, Susan J.
Feel the Fear— and Do It Anyway	152.4

Jefferson. Boles, John B. — B
Jefferson's Daughters. Kerrison, Catherine — 920

Jefferson, Margo
Negroland	305.896
On Michael Jackson	B

JEFFERSON, MARGO, 1947-
Jefferson, Margo. *Negroland*	305.896

Jefferson, Thomas
Writings	973.3

JEFFERSON, THOMAS, 1743-1826
Ambrose, Stephen E. ★*Undaunted Courage*	917.804
Boles, John B. *Jefferson*	B
Brands, H. W. ★*Founding Partisans*	973.3
Burstein, Andrew. *Madison and Jefferson*	973.4
Cheney, Lynne V. *The Virginia Dynasty*	B
Ellis, Joseph J. *American Sphinx*	973.4
Gordon-Reed, Annette. ★*The Hemingses of Monticello*	920
Gordon-Reed, Annette. ★*Most Blessed of the Patriarchs*	973.4
Groom, Winston. *The Patriots*	920
Gutzman, Kevin R. C. *The Jeffersonians*	973.5
Hitchens, Christopher. *Thomas Jefferson*	B
Jefferson, Thomas. *Writings*	973.3
Kerrison, Catherine. *Jefferson's Daughters*	920
Kilmeade, Brian. ★*Thomas Jefferson and the Tripoli Pirates*	973.4
Maier, Pauline. *American Scripture*	973.3
Meacham, Jon. ★*Thomas Jefferson*	B
Ricks, Thomas E. ★*First Principles*	973.09
Simon, James F. *What Kind of Nation*	342.73
White, Gayle Jessup. *Reclamation*	B
Wiencek, Henry. *Master of the Mountain*	973.4
Wood, Gordon S. *Friends Divided*	920

The Jeffersonians. Gutzman, Kevin R. C. — 973.5

JEHOVAH'S WITNESSES
Roy, Jessica. *American Girls*	305.48

The Jemima Code. Tipton-Martin, Toni — 641.59

Jena, Anupam B.
Random Acts of Medicine	616.0072

Jenkins, Jedidiah
To Shake the Sleeping Self	B

JENKINS, JEDIDIAH
Jenkins, Jedidiah. *To Shake the Sleeping Self*	B

Jenkins, Jessica D.
Exploring Women's Suffrage Through 50 Historic Treasures	324.6

Jenkins, Jessica Kerwin
All the Time in the World	390

Jenkins, Nancy Harmon
The New Mediterranean Diet Cookbook	641.59

Jenkins, Peter
Looking for Alaska	979.8
A Walk Across America	917.304

JENKINS, PETER, 1951-
Jenkins, Peter. *Looking for Alaska*	979.8
Jenkins, Peter. *A Walk Across America*	917.304

JENKINS, WAYNE, 1980-
Fenton, Justin. *We Own This City*	364.1

Jenkyns, Richard
Classical Literature	880.09

Jennifer's Way Kitchen. Esposito, Jennifer — 641.5

Jennings, Ken
★*100 Places to See After You Die*	202
Planet Funny	809.7

Jensen, Robert A.
Personal Effects	363.34

JENSEN, ROBERT A. (ROBERT ANDREW)
Jensen, Robert A. *Personal Effects*	363.34

Jeppesen, Travis
See You Again in Pyongyang	951.93

JEPPESEN, TRAVIS, 1979-
Jeppesen, Travis. *See You Again in Pyongyang*	951.93

JEREMIAH, THOMAS, D. 1775
Harris, J. William. *The Hanging of Thomas Jeremiah*	B

Jerkins, Morgan
Wandering in Strange Lands	305.896

JERKINS, MORGAN
Jerkins, Morgan. *Wandering in Strange Lands*	305.896

The Jersey Brothers. Freeman, Sally Mott — 920
Jerusalem. Armstrong, Karen — 956.94
★*Jerusalem*. Ottolenghi, Yotam — 641.5
Jerusalem. Sebag-Montefiore, Simon — 956.94

JERUSALEM, ISRAEL
Adunis. *Concerto Al-Quds*	892.7
Armstrong, Karen. *Jerusalem*	956.94
Collins, Larry. *O Jerusalem!*	956
Di Cintio, Marcello. *Pay No Heed to the Rockets*	956.9405
Lawler, Andrew. *Under Jerusalem*	956.94
Lipstadt, Deborah E. *The Eichmann Trial*	345.5694
Ottolenghi, Yotam. ★*Jerusalem*	641.5
Oz, Amos. *A Tale of Love and Darkness*	B
Sebag-Montefiore, Simon. *Jerusalem*	956.94
Stangneth, Bettina. *Eichmann Before Jerusalem*	B
Thrall, Nathan. ★*A Day in the Life of Abed Salama*	956.05

Jesse James. Stiles, T. J. — B
The Jesuit Guide to (Almost) Everything. Martin, James — 248.4

JESUIT MISSIONARIES
Lockley, Thomas. *African Samurai*	B

AUTHOR, TITLE, SERIES AND SUBJECT INDEX

Jesus and John Wayne. Du Mez, Kristin Kobes — 277.308
JESUS CHRIST
    Akyol, Mustafa. *The Islamic Jesus* — 297.2
    Blum, Edward J. *The Color of Christ* — 232
    Chittister, Joan. *Following the Path* — 248.4
    Francis. *Walking with Jesus* — 282.09
    Fredriksen, Paula. *Jesus of Nazareth, King of the Jews* — B
    Girzone, Joseph F. *A Portrait of Jesus* — 232.9
    Griffin, Chante. *Loving Your Black Neighbor as Yourself* — 261
    Levine, Amy-Jill. *Short Stories by Jesus* — 226.8
    Pagels, Elaine H. *Beyond Belief* — 229
    Price, Reynolds. *A Serious Way of Wondering* — 241
    Rohr, Richard. *The Universal Christ* — 232
    Villodas, Rich. *Good and Beautiful and Kind* — 232.9
Jesus Land. Scheeres, Julia — B
Jesus of Nazareth, King of the Jews. Fredriksen, Paula — B
Jesus Takes a Side. Rashid, Jonny — 261.7
JET PLANES
    Robison, Peter. ★*Flying Blind* — 338.7
Jeter Unfiltered. Jeter, Derek — B
Jeter, Derek
    Jeter Unfiltered — B
JETER, DEREK, 1974-
    Jeter, Derek. *Jeter Unfiltered* — B
JEUNE, CHIKA
    Albom, Mitch. *Finding Chika* — B
Jew vs. Jew. Freedman, Samuel G. — 296
Jew-Ish. Cohen, Jake — 641.5
Jewel
    Never Broken — 782.42164
JEWEL THIEVES
    Jobb, Dean. *A Gentleman and a Thief* — 364.16
JEWEL, 1974-
    Jewel. *Never Broken* — 782.42164
JEWELERS
    Brickell, Francesca Cartier. *The Cartiers* — B
JEWELRY MAKING
    Bluhm, Lisa. *Creative Soldered Jewelry & Accessories* — 745.594
    Brickell, Francesca Cartier. *The Cartiers* — B
    Codina, Carles. *The Complete Book of Jewelry Making* — 739.27
    Combs, Rebecca Ann. *Kumihimo* — 745.594
    Crowther, Janet. *Make a Statement* — 745.594
    DeCoster, Marcia. ★*Marcia Decoster's Beaded Opulence* — 739.27
    Gedeon, Jade. *Beautiful Bracelets by Hand* — 745.594
    Haab, Sherri. *The Art of Metal Clay* — 739.27
    Karon, Karen. *Advanced Chain Maille Jewelry Workshop* — 745.594
    Katz, Amy. *Seed Bead Chic* — 745.594
    Legenhausen, Courtney. *Fashion Jewelry* — 745.594
    Martin, Ann. *The Art of Quilling Paper Jewelry* — 745.54
    McGrath, Jinks. *The Complete Jewelry Making Course* — 739.27028
    Michaels, Chris Franchetti. *Teach Yourself Visually Jewelry Making & Beading* — 739.27
    Wiseman, Jill. *Jill Wiseman's Beautiful Beaded Ropes* — 745.594
    Young, Anastasia. *The Workbench Guide to Jewelry Techniques* — 739.27
JEWELRY THEFT
    Bilefsky, Dan. *The Last Job* — 364.16
    Ice-T. *Split Decision* — 920
    Jobb, Dean. *A Gentleman and a Thief* — 364.16
JEWISH AMERICAN FAMILIES
    Chernow, Ron. *The Warburgs* — B
    Louvish, Simon. *Monkey Business* — B
JEWISH AMERICAN MEN
    Greenfield, Martin. ★*Measure of a Man* — B
    Leavy, Jane. *Sandy Koufax* — B
    Louvish, Simon. *Monkey Business* — B
    Riesman, Abraham. *True Believer* — 741.5
    Spiegelman, Art. ★*Maus* — 741.5
JEWISH AMERICAN WOMEN
    Mann, William J. *Hello, Gorgeous* — B
    Streisand, Barbra. ★*My Name Is Barbra* — B
JEWISH AMERICANS
    Ashton, Dianne. *Hanukkah in America* — 296.4
    Chernow, Ron. *The Warburgs* — B
    Freedman, Samuel G. *Jew vs. Jew* — 296
    Kupperman, Michael. *All the Answers* — 741.5
    Leavy, Jane. *Sandy Koufax* — B
    Megdal, Howard. *The Baseball Talmud* — 796.357
    Novick, Peter. *The Holocaust in American Life* — 940.53

    Oppenheimer, Mark. *Squirrel Hill* — 364.152
    Rosenzweig, Laura B. *Hollywood's Spies* — 791.43
    Sarna, Jonathan D. ★*American Judaism* — 296
    Spiegelman, Art. ★*Maus* — 741.5
    Spiegelman, Art. *Metamaus* — B
    Turan, Kenneth. ★*Free for All* — B
    Weisman, Steven R. *The Chosen Wars* — 296.0973
JEWISH CHILDREN
    Chiger, Krystyna. *The Girl in the Green Sweater* — B
    Jacobson, Sidney. *Anne Frank* — 741.5
    Muller, Melissa. *Anne Frank* — B
    Pick-Goslar, Hannah Elizabeth. ★*My Friend Anne Frank* — B
    Pressman, Steven. *50 Children* — 940.53
Jewish Comedy. Dauber, Jeremy Asher — 809.7
JEWISH FAMILIES
    Albright, Madeleine Korbel. *Prague Winter* — 943.71
    Finkelstein, Daniel. *Two Roads Home* — 920
    Foer, Esther Safran. *I Want You to Know We're Still Here* — B
    Frankel, Rebecca. *Into the Forest* — 940.53
    Freeman, Hadley. *House of Glass* — B
    Fremont, Helen. *The Escape Artist* — B
    Glaser, Gabrielle. *American Baby* — B
    Kaufman, Jonathan. *The Last Kings of Shanghai* — 951
    Nathan, Joan. ★*My Life in Recipes* — 641.5
    Pogrebin, Abigail. *My Jewish Year* — 296.4
    Schindler, Meriel. *The Lost Cafe Schindler* — 943.64
    Sipress, David. *What's so Funny?* — B
    Van Wijk-Voskuijl, Joop. *The Last Secret of the Secret Annex* — 940.53
    Wiesel, Elie. ★*Night* — B
JEWISH HISTORY
    Chiger, Krystyna. *The Girl in the Green Sweater* — B
    Freedman, H. ★*The Talmud* — 296.1
    Gordis, Daniel. *Israel* — 956.9405
    Henderson, Bruce B. *Sons and Soldiers* — 940.53
    Schama, Simon. ★*The Story of the Jews; Volume One* — 909
    Schama, Simon. ★*The Story of the Jews; Volume Two* — 909
    Twitty, Michael. ★*Koshersoul* — 641.5
    Wiesel, Elie. *And the Sea Is Never Full* — B
JEWISH HOLIDAY COOKING
    Siva, Micah. *Nosh* — 641.5
JEWISH HOLIDAYS
    Pogrebin, Abigail. *My Jewish Year* — 296.4
JEWISH LEADERSHIP
    Telushkin, Joseph. *Rebbe* — 296.833
JEWISH MEN
    Bascomb, Neal. *Faster* — 796.7209
    Cohen-Solal, Annie. *Mark Rothko* — 759.13
    De Waal, Edmund. *The Hare with Amber Eyes* — B
    Ferguson, Niall. *Kissinger* — 973.924
    Freedland, Jonathan. ★*The Escape Artist* — 940.53
    Gay, Peter. *Freud* — B
    Gefter, Philip. *What Becomes a Legend Most* — B
    Jaku, Eddie. ★*The Happiest Man on Earth* — B
    Kolker, Robert Phillip. *Kubrick* — B
    Lansky, Aaron. *Outwitting History* — 002
    Levi, Primo. *The Periodic Table* — 858
    Nagorski, Andrew. *Saving Freud* — 940.53
    Rosenberg, Justus. *The Art of Resistance* — B
    Ross, Steve. *From Broken Glass* — B
    Roudinesco, Elisabeth. ★*Freud* — B
    Shapiro, Ari. ★*The Best Strangers in the World* — B
    Tallis, Frank. ★*Mortal Secrets* — B
JEWISH MOURNING CUSTOMS
    Wieseltier, Leon. *Kaddish* — 296.4
JEWISH PEOPLE
    Ackerman, Diane. ★*The Zookeeper's Wife* — 940.53
    Ahdoot, Dan. *Undercooked* — 647.95
    Aly, Gotz. *Europe Against the Jews* — 305.892
    Barton, John. *A History of the Bible* — 220.09
    Batalion, Judith. *The Light of Days* — 940.53
    Berg, Mary. *The Diary of Mary Berg* — B
    Berg, Raffi. *Red Sea Spies* — 327.125694
    Berr, Helene. *The Journal of Helene Berr* — B
    Blau, Magda Hellinger. *The Nazis Knew My Name* — 940.53
    Bronfman, Edgar M. *Why Be Jewish?* — 296
    Cadbury, Deborah. *The School That Escaped from the Nazis* — 940.53
    Carter, Jimmy. *Palestine* — 956.04
    Chernow, Ron. *The Warburgs* — B

PUBLIC LIBRARY CORE COLLECTION: NONFICTION
Twentieth Edition

Dauber, Jeremy Asher. *Jewish Comedy*	809.7
Debreczeni, Jozsef. *Cold Crematorium*	940.53
Diamant, Anita. *Pitching My Tent*	296.7
Dwork, Deborah. ★*Holocaust*	940
Edmonds, Chris. *No Surrender*	B
Eisen, Max. *By Chance Alone*	940.5318
Evans, Richard J. *The Third Reich in Power, 1933-1939*	943.086
Faludi, Susan. *In the Darkroom*	B
Feldman, Deborah. *Exodus*	B
Feldman, Deborah. *Unorthodox*	B
Feldman, Noah. ★*To Be a Jew Today*	296.3
Fersko, Diana. ★*We Need to Talk About Antisemitism*	305.892
Fishman, Boris. *Savage Feast*	B
Forgosh, Linda B. *Louis Bamberger*	B
Frank, Anne. ★*The Diary of a Young Girl*	940.53
Frank, Anne. *The Diary of Anne Frank*	B
Frankel, Rebecca. *Into the Forest*	940.53
Friedlander, Saul. *Nazi Germany and the Jews*	940.53
Friedlander, Saul. *Nazi Germany and the Jews*	940.53
Friedman, Thomas L. ★*From Beirut to Jerusalem*	956.04
Garrett, Leah. *X Troop*	940.54
Gies, Miep. ★*Anne Frank Remembered*	B
Glass, Sara. *Kissing Girls on Shabbat*	B
Goldsmith, Martin. *The Inextinguishable Symphony*	B
Golinkin, Lev. *A Backpack, a Bear, and Eight Crates of Vodka*	B
Greenfield, Martin. ★*Measure of a Man*	B
Grose, Peter. *A Good Place to Hide*	940.53
Gross, Jan Tomasz. *Neighbors*	940.53
Hayes, Peter. *Why?*	940.53
Hoffman, Adina. *Sacred Trash*	296.09
Hoffman, Bruce. *Anonymous Soldiers*	956.94
Horn, Dara. ★*People Love Dead Jews*	909
Hurowitz, Richard. *In the Garden of the Righteous*	940.53
Iperen, Roxane van. ★*The Sisters of Auschwitz*	940.53
Jacobson, Sidney. *Anne Frank*	741.5
Katin, Miriam. *We Are on Our Own*	741.5
Keinan, Tal. *God Is in the Crowd*	305.892
Kershner, Isabel. *The Land of Hope and Fear*	956.9405
Kertzer, David I. *The Pope at War*	940.53
King, Charles. *Odessa*	947.7
Kirsch, Adam. ★*The People and the Books*	809
Klemperer, Victor. *I Will Bear Witness*	B
Kramer, Clara. *Clara's War*	B
Kraus, Dita. *A Delayed Life*	B
Kritzler, Ed. *Jewish Pirates of the Caribbean*	972.9
Kurtz, Glenn. *Three Minutes in Poland*	947.7
LeBor, Adam. *City of Oranges*	956.94
Levi, Primo. *The Reawakening*	B
Lichtblau, Eric. *Return to the Reich*	B
Marton, Kati. *The Great Escape*	920
Mazzeo, Tilar J. *Irena's Children*	B
Muller, Melissa. *Anne Frank*	B
Nasaw, David. *The Last Million*	940.53
Neumann, Ariana. *When Time Stopped*	B
Paxson, Margaret. *The Plateau*	362.87
Pivnik, Sam. *Survivor*	940.5318
Rajchman, Chil. *The Last Jew of Treblinka*	940.53
Rees, Laurence. *Auschwitz*	940.53
Rees, Laurence. *The Holocaust*	940.53
Rosenberg, Justus. *The Art of Resistance*	B
Ross, Steven Joseph. ★*Hitler in Los Angeles*	979.4
Rynecki, Elizabeth. *Chasing Portraits*	B
Sabar, Ariel. *My Father's Paradise*	B
Salama, Jordan. ★*Stranger in the Desert*	982
Schindler, Meriel. *The Lost Cafe Schindler*	943.64
Schulman, Daniel. *The Money Kings*	332.0973
Sebag-Montefiore, Simon. *Jerusalem*	956.94
Shavit, Ari. *My Promised Land*	956.05
Shteyngart, Gary. ★*Little Failure*	B
Simon, Marie. *Underground in Berlin*	B
Snyder, Timothy. *Black Earth*	940.53
Spiegel, Renia. *Renia's Diary*	B
Streisand, Barbra. ★*My Name Is Barbra*	B
Sullivan, Rosemary. *The Betrayal of Anne Frank*	940.53
Talty, Stephan. *The Good Assassin*	364.15
Telushkin, Joseph. *Jewish Wisdom*	296.3
Van Es, Bart. *The Cut Out Girl*	B
White, Elizabeth B. ★*The Counterfeit Countess*	940.53

Jewish Pirates of the Caribbean. Kritzler, Ed	972.9
JEWISH PROPERTY	
Kaiser, Menachem. *Plunder*	940.53
JEWISH RESISTANCE AND REVOLTS	
Batalion, Judith. *The Light of Days*	940.53
Iperen, Roxane van. ★*The Sisters of Auschwitz*	940.53
Van De Perre, Selma. *My Name Is Selma*	940.53
White, Elizabeth B. ★*The Counterfeit Countess*	940.53
JEWISH TEENAGERS	
Frank, Anne. ★*The Diary of a Young Girl*	940.53
Gies, Miep. ★*Anne Frank Remembered*	B
Krimstein, Ken. *When I Grow Up*	741.5
Wiesel, Elie. ★*Night*	B
JEWISH WAY OF LIFE	
Bronfman, Edgar M. *Why Be Jewish?*	296
Epstein, Lawrence J. *The Basic Beliefs of Judaism*	296.3
Goldman, Ari L. *Being Jewish*	296.4
Haskell, Molly. *Steven Spielberg*	B
Held, Shai. ★*Judaism Is About Love*	296.3
Isaacs, Ronald H. ★*Kosher Living*	296.7
Keinan, Tal. *God Is in the Crowd*	305.892
Kirsch, Adam. ★*The People and the Books*	809
Koenig, Leah. *Portico*	641.5
Kushner, Harold S. *Who Needs God*	296.7
LeBor, Adam. *City of Oranges*	956.94
Nathan, Joan. *King Solomon's Table*	641.5
Ricanati, Elizabeth. *Braided*	B
The Jewish Wedding Now. Diamant, Anita	296.4
JEWISH WEDDINGS	
Diamant, Anita. *The Jewish Wedding Now*	296.4
Jewish Wisdom. Telushkin, Joseph	296.3
JEWISH WOMEN	
Batalion, Judith. *The Light of Days*	940.53
Diamant, Anita. *Pitching My Tent*	296.7
Feldman, Deborah. *Exodus*	B
Feldman, Deborah. *Unorthodox*	B
Foer, Esther Safran. *I Want You to Know We're Still Here*	B
Frank, Michael. ★*One Hundred Saturdays*	B
Frenkel, Francoise. *A Bookshop in Berlin*	B
Holden, Wendy. ★*Born Survivors*	940.53
Iperen, Roxane van. ★*The Sisters of Auschwitz*	940.53
Kalb, Bess. ★*Nobody Will Tell You This but Me*	306.874
Klagsbrun, Francine. *Lioness*	B
Koch, Bea. *Mad and Bad*	920
Macadam, Heather Dune. *999*	940.53
Markel, Howard. *The Secret of Life*	572.86
McBride, James. *The Color of Water*	B
Morton, Brian. *Tasha*	B
Mueller, Melissa. *Alice's Piano*	B
Nathan, Joan. ★*My Life in Recipes*	641.5
Ricanati, Elizabeth. *Braided*	B
Rodgers, Mary. *Shy*	B
Shapiro, Dani. ★*Inheritance*	B
Simon, Marie. *Underground in Berlin*	B
Streisand, Barbra. ★*My Name Is Barbra*	B
Van De Perre, Selma. *My Name Is Selma*	940.53
JEWISH-AMERICANS	
Grey, Joel. *Master of Ceremonies*	B
JEX-BLAKE, SOPHIA, 1840-1912	
Campbell, Olivia. *Women in White Coats*	610.92
★*JFK*. Logevall, Fredrik	B
JFK's Last Hundred Days. Clarke, Thurston	B
JIHAD	
Abouzeid, Rania. *No Turning Back*	956.9104
Bergen, Peter L. *The Rise and Fall of Osama Bin Laden*	958.104
Lambert, Malcolm. *God's Armies*	956
Mekhennet, Souad. *I Was Told to Come Alone*	363.3250956
Jill Wiseman's Beautiful Beaded Ropes. Wiseman, Jill	745.594
Jim Henson. Jones, Brian Jay	B
★*Jim* Trelease's Read-Aloud Handbook. Trelease, Jim	372.4
Jimenez, Stephen	
The Book of Matt	364.152
Jimmy Buffett. White, Ryan	782.42164
Jimmy Stewart. Smith, Starr	B
Jinich, Pati	
Mexican Today	641.5972
★*Treasures of the Mexican Table*	641.5972

2022

AUTHOR, TITLE, SERIES AND SUBJECT INDEX

JINNAH, MAHOMED ALI, 1876-1948
   Hajari, Nisid. *Midnight's Furies* — 954.04
JIU-JITSU
   Gracie, Rickson. *Breathe* — B
Jo Malone. Malone, Jo — B
Joan. Spoto, Donald — B
Joan Mitchell. Albers, Patricia — B
Joan of Arc. Castor, Helen — B
JOAN OF ARC, SAINT, 1412-1431
   Castor, Helen. *Joan of Arc* — B
   Shaw, Bernard. *Saint Joan* — 822
   Spoto, Donald. *Joan* — B
Job. Greenstein, Edward L. — 223
JOB APPLICATIONS
   Sandberg, Sheryl. *Lean In* — 658.4
JOB CREATION
   Taylor, Nick. *American Made* — 331.13
JOB HUNTING
   Alderton, Dolly. *Everything I Know About Love* — B
   Finkle, Jane. *The Introvert's Complete Career Guide* — 650.14
   Germer, Fawn. *Coming Back* — 650.14
   Louis, Matthew J. *Mission Transition* — 650.14
   Pollak, Lindsey. *Recalculating* — 650.1
   Sandberg, Sheryl. *Lean In* — 658.4
JOB SATISFACTION
   Godin, Seth. *The Practice* — 153.3
   Warzel, Charlie. *Out of Office* — 658.3
   Webb, Caroline. *How to Have a Good Day* — 650.1
JOB SECURITY
   Scott, Kevin. *Reprogramming the American Dream* — 338
JOB STRESS
   Robbins, Alexandra. ★*The Teachers* — 371.1
Jobb, Dean
   The Case of the Murderous Dr. Cream — 364.152
   A Gentleman and a Thief — 364.16
Jobrani, Maziyar
   I'm Not a Terrorist, but I've Played One on TV — B
JOBRANI, MAZIYAR, 1972-
   Jobrani, Maziyar. *I'm Not a Terrorist, but I've Played One on TV* — B
JOBS, STEVE, 1955-2011
   Isaacson, Walter. ★*Steve Jobs* — B
   Schlender, Brent. *Becoming Steve Jobs* — B
JOCKEYS
   Drape, Joe. *Black Maestro* — B
   Hillenbrand, Laura. ★*Seabiscuit* — 798.4
Joe Biden. Osnos, Evan — B
Joe DiMaggio. Cramer, Richard Ben — B
Joe Louis. Roberts, Randy — B
★*Johann Sebastian Bach*. Geck, Martin — 780.92
Johann Sebastian Bach. Wolff, Christoph — B
Johannes Brahms. Swafford, Jan — B
Johansen, Signe
   ★*How to Hygge* — 646.7
Johanson, Donald C.
   Lucy — 569
★*John Adams*. Grant, James — B
★*John Adams*. McCullough, David G. — B
John Ashbery. Ashbery, John — 811
John Brown, Abolitionist. Reynolds, David S. — B
John F. Kennedy. Brinkley, Alan — B
John Lennon. Norman, Philip — B
John Lewis. Arsenault, Raymond — B
John Marshall. Smith, Jean Edward — B
★*John Muir and the Ice That Started a Fire*. Heacox, Kim — 333.7209798
JOHN OF THE CROSS, SAINT, 1542-1591
   Gander, Forrest. ★*Be With* — 811
JOHN PAUL II, POPE, 1920-2005
   O'Connor, Garry. *Universal Father* — B
John Paul Jones. Morison, Samuel Eliot — B
★*John Paul Jones*. Thomas, Evan — B
John Quincy Adams. Kaplan, Fred — B
John Quincy Adams. Traub, James — B
John Tyler. May, Gary — B
John Wayne. Eyman, Scott — B
John Winthrop. Bremer, Francis J. — B
John, Elton
   ★*Me* — B

JOHN, ELTON
   John, Elton. ★*Me* — B
   Taupin, Bernie. *Scattershot* — B
JOHN, KING OF ENGLAND, 1167-1216
   Morris, Marc. *King John* — 942.033
★*Johnny Cash*. Hilburn, Robert — B
Johns Hopkins Press Health Book [Series]. Mace, Nancy L. — 616.8
Johnsen, Jan
   ★*Gardentopia* — 635.9
Johnson, Akemi
   Night in the American Village — 305.40952
JOHNSON, ANDREW, 1808-1875
   Cohen, Jared. *Accidental Presidents* — 973.09
   Gordon-Reed, Annette. *Andrew Johnson* — B
   Levine, Robert S. ★*The Failed Promise* — 973.8
   Wineapple, Brenda. *The Impeachers* — 973.8
Johnson, Brian
   The Lives of Brian — B
JOHNSON, BRIAN, 1947 OCTOBER 5-
   Johnson, Brian. *The Lives of Brian* — B
Johnson, Doug
   The Indispensable Librarian — 025.1
Johnson, Earl
   Finding Comfort During Hard Times — 155.9
Johnson, George
   Miss Leavitt's Stars — 522
Johnson, Graham
   Poulenc — B
Johnson, Ian
   The Souls of China — 200.951
Johnson, J. J.
   Between Harlem and Heaven — 641.59
JOHNSON, JACK, 1878-1946
   Ward, Geoffrey C. *Unforgivable Blackness* — B
Johnson, James Weldon
   Complete Poems — 811
JOHNSON, JAMES WELDON, 1871-1938
   Perry, Imani. *May We Forever Stand* — 782.25
   Swift, Earl. *Hell Put to Shame* — 364.15
JOHNSON, JOE, JR., 1926-2017
   Brotherton, Marcus. *A Bright and Blinding Sun* — 940.54
JOHNSON, JOHN ROSAMOND 1873-1954
   Perry, Imani. *May We Forever Stand* — 782.25
Johnson, Joyce
   The Voice Is All — B
Johnson, Katherine G.
   My Remarkable Journey — B
JOHNSON, KATHERINE G., 1918-2020
   Johnson, Katherine G. *My Remarkable Journey* — B
Johnson, Kirk W.
   The Feather Thief — 364.16
   The Fishermen and the Dragon — 976.4
JOHNSON, KIRK W.
   Johnson, Kirk W. *The Feather Thief* — 364.16
JOHNSON, LADY BIRD, 1912-2007
   Gillette, Michael L. *Lady Bird Johnson* — B
   Sweig, Julia. *Lady Bird Johnson* — B
Johnson, Lizzie
   ★*Paradise* — 363.37
Johnson, Lyndon B.
   Taking Charge — 973.923
JOHNSON, LYNDON B., 1908-1973
   Caro, Robert A. ★*The Passage of Power* — B
   Cohen, Jared. *Accidental Presidents* — 973.09
   Gillette, Michael L. *Lady Bird Johnson* — B
   Goodwin, Doris Kearns. ★*Leadership in Turbulent Times* — 973.09
   Johnson, Lyndon B. *Taking Charge* — 973.923
   Kotz, Nick. *Judgment Days* — 323
   Peters, Charles. *Lyndon B. Johnson* — B
   Sweig, Julia. *Lady Bird Johnson* — B
   Woods, Randall Bennett. *Prisoners of Hope* — 973.923
   Zeitz, Joshua. *Building the Great Society* — 973.923
Johnson, Michael
   Encyclopedia of Native Tribes of North America — 970.00497
Johnson, Mindy
   Ink & Paint — B
Johnson, Paul
   ★*Art* — 709

PUBLIC LIBRARY CORE COLLECTION: NONFICTION
Twentieth Edition

Churchill — B
Eisenhower — B
George Washington — B
Napoleon — B
Socrates — 183
Johnson, Peggy
  ★*Fundamentals of Collection Development and Management* — 025
JOHNSON, ROBERT UNDERWOOD, 1853-1937
  King, Dean. *Guardians of the Valley* — 333.72
JOHNSON, ROBERT, 1911-1938
  McCormick, Mack. *Biography of a Phantom* — 782.421643
  Patrick, James. *Robert Johnson* — B
  Wald, Elijah. ★*Escaping the Delta* — B
JOHNSON, SAMUEL, 1709-1784
  Boswell, James. ★*The Life of Samuel Johnson* — B
  Damrosch, Leopold. *The Club* — 920
  Moore, Peter. *Life, Liberty, and the Pursuit of Happiness* — 199
Johnson, Sarah Stewart
  The Sirens of Mars — 576.8
JOHNSON, SARAH STEWART
  Johnson, Sarah Stewart. *The Sirens of Mars* — 576.8
Johnson, Stephanie
  Tanqueray — B
JOHNSON, STEPHANIE (DANCER)
  Johnson, Stephanie. *Tanqueray* — B
Johnson, Steven
  Enemy of All Mankind — 910.4
  Extra Life — 362.1
  Farsighted — 153.8
  The Ghost Map — 614.5
  The Infernal Machine — 335
  Wonderland — 790.1
Johnson, Theodore R.
  When the Stars Begin to Fall — 305.800973
JOHNSON, THEODORE R.
  Johnson, Theodore R. *When the Stars Begin to Fall* — 305.800973
Johnson, Victoria
  ★*American Eden* — 580.973
Johnson, Walter
  Soul by Soul — 976.3
JOHNSON-SIRLEAF, ELLEN, 1938-
  Cooper, Helene. *Madame President* — 966.62
Johnston, Ann Dowsett
  Drink — 362.292
JOHNSTON, ANN DOWSETT
  Johnston, Ann Dowsett. *Drink* — 362.292
Johnston, David Cay
  The Big Cheat — 973.933
  It's Even Worse Than You Think — 973.933
Joint Libraries. Gunnels, Claire B. — 027.4
JOKES
  Dauber, Jeremy Asher. *Jewish Comedy* — 809.7
  Jennings, Ken. *Planet Funny* — 809.7
Jollett, Mikel
  ★*Hollywood Park* — B
JOLLETT, MIKEL
  Jollett, Mikel. ★*Hollywood Park* — B
Jones, Andrew
  Stickmaking Handbook — 736
Jones, Anna
  One — 641.5
Jones, Booker T.
  Time Is Tight — B
Jones, Brenda
  Alexandria Ocasio-Cortez — B
  Maxine Waters — B
Jones, Brian Jay
  ★*Becoming Dr. Seuss* — B
  George Lucas — B
  Jim Henson — B
Jones, Chip
  The Organ Thieves — 617.4
Jones, Chloe Cooper
  ★*Easy Beauty* — B
JONES, CHLOE COOPER
  Jones, Chloe Cooper. ★*Easy Beauty* — B
Jones, Dan
  Crusaders — 909.07

★*The Plantagenets* — 942.03092
The Templars — 271
★*The Wars of the Roses* — 942.04
Jones, Darryl N.
  The Birds at My Table — 598.072
Jones, Doug
  Bending Toward Justice — 323.1196
JONES, DOUG (G. DOUGLAS), 1954-
  Jones, Doug. *Bending Toward Justice* — 323.1196
Jones, Dylan
  David Bowie — B
JONES, E. H. (ELIAS HENRY), 1883-1942
  Fox, Margalit. *The Confidence Men* — 940.4
JONES, EDITH IRBY, 1927-2019
  Brown, Jasmine. *Twice as Hard* — 610.92
Jones, Faith
  Sex Cult Nun — B
JONES, FAITH
  Jones, Faith. *Sex Cult Nun* — B
JONES, GENEVIEVE (GENEVIEVE ESTELLE), 1847-1879
  Kiser, Joy M. *America's Other Audubon* — B
Jones, Gerard
  Men of Tomorrow — 741.5
Jones, Jacqueline
  Saving Savannah — 975.8
JONES, JIM, 1931-1978
  Guinn, Jeff. *The Road to Jonestown* — 289.9
JONES, JOHN PAUL, 1747-1792
  Morison, Samuel Eliot. *John Paul Jones* — B
  Thomas, Evan. ★*John Paul Jones* — B
Jones, Lucy
  ★*Matrescence* — 306.874
JONES, LUCY (JOURNALIST)
  Jones, Lucy. ★*Matrescence* — 306.874
Jones, Marie D.
  Celebrity Ghosts and Notorious Hauntings — 133.1
  Demons, the Devil, and Fallen Angels — 133.4
Jones, Michael K.
  The Black Prince — B
JONES, MICK
  Albertine, Viv. *Clothes, Clothes, Clothes. Music, Music, Music* — B
Jones, Nathaniel R.
  Answering the Call — B
JONES, NATHANIEL R., 1926-2020
  Jones, Nathaniel R. *Answering the Call* — B
Jones, Robert P.
  The Hidden Roots of White Supremacy — 305.8
  White Too Long — 277
JONES, ROBERT P. (ROBERT PATRICK)
  Jones, Robert P. *White Too Long* — 277
Jones, Saeed
  Alive at the End of the World — 811
  How We Fight for Our Lives — B
  Prelude to Bruise — 811
JONES, SAEED
  Jones, Saeed. *How We Fight for Our Lives* — B
JONES, SHARANDA
  Barnett, Brittany K. ★*A Knock at Midnight* — B
Jones, Sharon L.
  Critical Companion to Zora Neale Hurston — 813
Jones, Tom
  Space Shuttle Stories — 629.44
JONESTOWN MASS SUICIDE, JONESTOWN, GUYANA, 1978
  Guinn, Jeff. *The Road to Jonestown* — 289.9
Joo, Judy
  Korean Food Made Simple — 641.595
JOPLIN, JANIS, 1943-1970
  George-Warren, Holly. ★*Janis* — B
JOPLIN, SCOTT, 1868-1917
  Berlin, Edward A. *King of Ragtime* — B
JORDAN
  Noor. *Leap of Faith* — B
JORDAN, DAVID STARRR, 1851-1931
  Miller, Lulu. *Why Fish Don't Exist* — B
Jordan, Jonathan W.
  Brothers, Rivals, Victors — 940.54
Jordan, June
  ★*The Essential June Jordan* — 811

AUTHOR, TITLE, SERIES AND SUBJECT INDEX

Jordan, Mary
    The Art of Her Deal   B
Jordan, Michael
    Dictionary of Gods and Goddesses   202
Jordan, Wendy Adler
    Universal Design for the Home   728
Joseph Anton. Rushdie, Salman   B
JOSEPH, NEZ PERCE CHIEF, 1840-1904
    Sharfstein, Daniel J. ★*Thunder in the Mountains*   979.5
Joseph, Peniel E.
    The Sword and the Shield   B
    Waiting 'Til the Midnight Hour   323.1196
Josephine Tey. Thomson, Jennifer   823
JOSEPHINE, EMPRESS OF THE FRENCH, 1763-1814
    Williams, Kate. *Ambition and Desire*   B
JOTTER, LOIS
    Sevigny, Melissa L. ★*Brave the Wild River*   580.9
A Journal for Jordan. King, Charles Monroe   956.7044
The Journal of Helene Berr. Berr, Helene   B
JOURNALISM
    Blume, Lesley M. M. *Fallout*   940.54
    Burns, Eric. *Infamous Scribblers*   071
    Carpenter, Amanda B. *Gaslighting America*   973.933
    Chrisinger, David. *The Soldier's Truth*   940.54
    Cohen, Deborah. *Last Call at the Hotel Imperial*   070.92
    Cohen, Roger. *An Affirming Flame*   071
    Cullen, Art. *Storm Lake*   071.7
    Ebert, Roger. *Life Itself*   B
    Edwards, Bob. *Edward R. Murrow and the Birth of Broadcast Journalism*   B
    Fager, Jeffrey. *Fifty Years of 60 Minutes*   070.1
    Ferguson, Jane. *No Ordinary Assignment*   B
    Hartman, Darrell. *Battle of Ink and Ice*   998
    Hersh, Seymour M. *Reporter*   B
    Hunter-Gault, Charlayne. ★*My People*   305.48
    Jamison, Leslie. ★*Make It Scream, Make It Burn*   814
    Kluger, Richard. *Indelible Ink*   B
    Kristof, Nicholas D. ★*Chasing Hope*   B
    LaFollette, Marcel C. *Writing for Their Lives*   071.3
    Martinez Wood, Jamie. *Latino Writers and Journalists*   B
    McCraw, David Edward. *Truth in Our Times*   342.7308
    Miraldi, Robert. *Seymour Hersh*   B
    Mitchell, Elizabeth. *Lincoln's Lie*   973.7092
    Morris, James McGrath. *Pulitzer*   B
    Nagourney, Adam. *The Times*   071
    Napoli, Lisa. *Susan, Linda, Nina & Cokie*   920
    Nye, Naomi Shihab. *The Tiny Journalist*   811
    Ostertag, Bob. *People's Movements, People's Press*   071
    Ramos, Jorge. *Stranger*   325.73
    Roberts, Steven V. *Cokie*   B
    Schieffer, Bob. *Overload*   070.4
    Shapiro, Ari. ★*The Best Strangers in the World*   B
    Stelter, Brian. *Hoax*   070.4
    Sullivan, Margaret. *Newsroom Confidential*   070.92
    Thompson, Hunter S. *Fear and Loathing at Rolling Stone*   070.1
    Thompson, Hunter S. ★*Fear and Loathing in America*   B
    Tobin, James. *Ernie Pyle's War*   B
    Todd, Kim. *Sensational*   920
    Trillin, Calvin. *The Lede*   071
    Vargas Llosa, Mario. *Conversation at Princeton*   868
    Wainaina, Binyavanga. ★*How to Write About Africa*   814
    Zara, Christopher. *Uneducated*   B
JOURNALISTIC ETHICS
    Jamison, Leslie. ★*Make It Scream, Make It Burn*   814
    Morris, James McGrath. *Pulitzer*   B
    Stelter, Brian. *Hoax*   070.4
JOURNALISTS
    Adam, David. *The Man Who Couldn't Stop*   616.85
    Ali, Wajahat. *Go Back to Where You Came From*   B
    Arana, Marie. *American Chica*   B
    Auster, Paul. *Burning Boy*   B
    Baime, A. J. *White Lies*   B
    Baker, Billy. *We Need to Hang Out*   177
    Barbarisi, Daniel. *Chasing the Thrill*   796.1
    Barker, Elspeth. ★*Notes from the Henhouse*   828
    Baron, Martin. ★*Collision of Power*   070.4
    Bernstein, Carl. *Chasing History*   B
    Blume, Lesley M. M. *Fallout*   940.54
    Bogus, Carl T. *Buckley*   B
    Bowden, Mark. *The Last Stone*   363.25
    Brinkley, Alan. ★*The Publisher*   B
    Brinkley, Douglas. ★*Cronkite*   B
    Brokaw, Tom. *The Fall of Richard Nixon*   B
    Brown, Emma. *To Raise a Boy*   649
    Bruni, Frank. *The Beauty of Dusk*   B
    Butler, Brin-Jonathan. *The Domino Diaries*   796.83
    Caldwell, Gail. *Let's Take the Long Way Home*   B
    Campbell, Deborah. *A Disappearance in Damascus*   365
    Caro, Robert A. ★*Working*   B
    Carr, David. *The Night of the Gun*   B
    Carr, Erin Lee. *All That You Leave Behind*   B
    Chapin, Sasha. *All the Wrong Moves*   794.1092
    Cheung, Karen. *The Impossible City*   951.25
    Chrisinger, David. *The Soldier's Truth*   940.54
    Cohen, Deborah. *Last Call at the Hotel Imperial*   070.92
    Cohen, Rich. *The Sun and the Moon and the Rolling Stones*   782.42166
    Corcoran, Katherine. *In the Mouth of the Wolf*   364.152
    Cronkite, Walter. *Cronkite's War*   070.4
    Cronkite, Walter. *A Reporter's Life*   B
    Dearborn, Mary V. *Ernest Hemingway*   B
    Denevi, Timothy. *Freak Kingdom*   B
    Didion, Joan. ★*The Year of Magical Thinking*   B
    Doty, Cate. *Mergers and Acquisitions*   395.2
    Edwards, Bob. *Edward R. Murrow and the Birth of Broadcast Journalism*   B
    Eichenwald, Kurt. *A Mind Unraveled*   B
    Feldstein, Mark Avrom. *Poisoning the Press*   973.924092
    Foreman, Tom. *My Year of Running Dangerously*   B
    Fox, Porter. *The Last Winter*   363.738
    Gilliam, Dorothy Butler. *Trailblazer*   B
    Golay, Michael. *America 1933*   B
    Goodheart, Adam. *The Last Island*   954
    Grant, Will. *The Last Ride of the Pony Express*   917.804
    Green, Robin. *The Only Girl*   070.92
    Greenidge, Kerri. *Black Radical*   B
    Hari, Johann. ★*Magic Pill*   613.2
    Hemon, Aleksandar. *My Parents*   814
    Hendershot, Heather. *Open to Debate*   B
    Hersh, Seymour M. *Reporter*   B
    Hessler, Peter. *The Buried*   962.05
    Hiaasen, Carl. *The Downhill Lie*   B
    Hilsum, Lindsey. *In Extremis*   B
    Hitchens, Christopher. *Hitch-22*   920
    Hulls, Tessa. ★*Feeding Ghosts*   741.5
    Jacobs, A. J. *The Puzzler*   793.73
    Kan, Karoline. *Under Red Skies*   B
    Kois, Dan. *How to Be a Family*   910.4
    Kristof, Nicholas D. ★*Chasing Hope*   B
    Kurtz, Howard. *Media Madness*   973.933
    Lanzmann, Claude. *The Patagonian Hare*   B
    Lawson, Jenny. ★*Broken*   B
    LeDuff, Charlie. *Detroit*   977.4
    Lehr, Dick. ★*The Birth of a Nation*   305.800973
    Leland, Andrew. ★*The Country of the Blind*   B
    Lovato, Roberto. *Unforgetting*   B
    MacKrell, Judith. *The Correspondents*   070.4
    MacPherson, Myra. *All Governments Lie*   B
    McClelland, Mac. *Irritable Hearts*   B
    McGrath, Ben. *Riverman*   797.122
    McPhee, John. *Tabula Rasa; V.1*   818
    Millard, Candice. ★*Hero of the Empire*   968.04
    Miller, Christopher. *The War Came to Us*   947.7
    Miraldi, Robert. *Seymour Hersh*   B
    Mitchell, Elizabeth. *Lincoln's Lie*   973.7092
    Mitchell, Jerry. ★*Race Against Time*   364.152
    Moore, Michael Scott. *The Desert and the Sea*   364.15
    Morris, James McGrath. *Pulitzer*   B
    Page, Susan. ★*The Rulebreaker*   B
    Peer, Basharat. *Curfewed Night*   B
    Politkovskaya, Anna. *A Russian Diary*   947.086
    Pomerantsev, Peter. ★*How to Win an Information War*   940.53
    Popoff, Alexandra. *Vasily Grossman and the Soviet Century*   B
    Potts, Monica. *The Forgotten Girls*   B
    Rezaian, Jason. *Prisoner*   B
    Rinehart, Lorissa. *First to the Front*   B
    Roberts, Steven V. *Cokie*   B
    Rusbridger, Alan. ★*Play It Again*   B
    Russert, Luke. *Look for Me There*   B

Samaha, Albert. *Concepcion*	929
Schiavi, Michael R. *Celluloid Activist*	B
Schultz, Kevin Michael. *Buckley and Mailer*	920
Schwarz, Geraldine. *Those Who Forget*	940.53
Searcey, Dionne. *In Pursuit of Disobedient Women*	B
Seierstad, Asne. *A Hundred and One Days*	956.70443
Shakespeare, Nicholas. *Ian Fleming*	B
Shapiro, Ari. ★*The Best Strangers in the World*	B
Singer, Matt. *Opposable Thumbs*	791.43
Snyder, Rachel Louise. *Women We Buried, Women We Burned*	B
Soboroff, Jacob. ★*Separated*	325.73
Sullivan, Kevin. *Trump on Trial*	342.73
Swisher, Kara. *Burn Book*	303.48
Taylor, D. J. *Orwell*	B
Thomas, R. Eric. *Here for It*	B
Thompson, Hunter S. ★*Fear and Loathing in America*	B
Thompson, Juan F. *Stories I Tell Myself*	B
Tobin, James. *Ernie Pyle's War*	B
Todd, Kim. *Sensational*	920
Tomlinson, Tommy. *Dogland*	636.7
Trice, Dawn Turner. ★*Three Girls from Bronzeville*	977.311
Trillin, Calvin. *The Lede*	071
Vargas, Jose Antonio. *Dear America*	B
Von Drehle, David. ★*The Book of Charlie*	B
Vorobyov, Niko. *Dopeworld*	364.1
Wainaina, Binyavanga. *How to Write About Africa*	814
Wallace, Carvell. *Another Word for Love*	B
Welteroth, Elaine. *More Than Enough*	B
Wenner, Jann. *Like a Rolling Stone*	B
Williams, Florence. *Heartbreak*	306.7
Zara, Christopher. *Uneducated*	B
Journals, 1952-2000. Schlesinger, Arthur M.	973.91092
Journey. Adams, Simon	910.9
A Journey. Blair, Tony	B
Journey to the Edge of Reason. Budiansky, Stephen	B
JOY AND SORROW	
Bowler, Kate. *No Cure for Being Human*	B
Damasio, Antonio R. *Looking for Spinoza*	152.4
Gay, Ross. *The Book of (more) Delights*	814
Gay, Ross. *Inciting Joy*	814
Norris, Kathleen. *Acedia & Me*	248.8
Pipher, Mary Bray. *A Life in Light*	B
Risner, Vaneetha Rendall. *Walking Through Fire*	B
Tutu, Desmond. *Made for Goodness*	170
Joy Enough. McColl, Sarah	B
★*Joy of Cooking.* Rombauer, Irma S.	641.5973
★*Joy of Cooking.* Rombauer, Irma S.	641.5973
The Joy of Sweat. Everts, Sarah	612.7
Joyce, Anna	
Hand Dyed	746.6
Stamp Stencil Paint	745.7
JOYCE, JAMES, 1882-1941	
Bowker, Gordon. ★*James Joyce*	B
Toibin, Colm. *Mad, Bad, Dangerous to Know*	920
Joyce, Patrick	
Remembering Peasants	305.5
Joyce, Russell W.	
His Face Like Mine	248
Joyful Recollections of Trauma. Scheer, Paul	B
JOYNER FAMILY	
Emberton, Carole. *To Walk About in Freedom*	306.3
JOYNER, PRISCILLA, 1858-1944	
Emberton, Carole. *To Walk About in Freedom*	306.3
JUAN, DON, 1891-1973	
Castaneda, Carlos. *The Teachings of Don Juan;*	299
Juan, Li	
Winter Pasture	951.06
JUAN, LI	
Juan, Li. *Winter Pasture*	951.06
Juana Ines de la Cruz, Sister	
Selected Works	861
★*Jubilee.* Tipton-Martin, Toni	641.59
Judah, Hettie	
Lapidarium	553.8
JUDAIC DOCTRINES	
Armstrong, Karen. *A History of God*	202
Feldman, Deborah. *Unorthodox*	B
Freedman, H. ★*The Talmud*	296.1
Goodman, Martin. ★*A History of Judaism*	296.09
Leibovitz, Liel. ★*How the Talmud Can Change Your Life*	296.1
Ruttenberg, Danya. *On Repentance and Repair*	202
Weisman, Steven R. *The Chosen Wars*	296.0973
JUDAIC LAW	
Freedman, H. ★*The Talmud*	296.1
Leibovitz, Liel. ★*How the Talmud Can Change Your Life*	296.1
JUDAISM	
Akyol, Mustafa. *The Islamic Jesus*	297.2
Armstrong, Karen. *The Battle for God*	200
Armstrong, Karen. *A History of God*	202
Armstrong, Karen. *Jerusalem*	956.94
Ashton, Dianne. *Hanukkah in America*	296.4
Barton, John. *A History of the Bible*	220.09
Belser, Julia Watts. ★*Loving Our Own Bones*	296
Bernstein, Ellen. *Toward a Holy Ecology*	223
Bolsta, Hyla Shifra. *The Illuminated Kaddish*	296.4
Bronfman, Edgar M. *Why Be Jewish?*	296
Brous, Sharon. ★*The Amen Effect*	296.3
Carroll, James. *Constantine's Sword*	261
Carter, Jimmy. *Palestine*	956.04
Diamant, Anita. *Pitching My Tent*	296.7
Epstein, Lawrence J. *The Basic Beliefs of Judaism*	296.3
Feldman, Deborah. *Unorthodox*	B
Feldman, Noah. ★*To Be a Jew Today*	296.3
Freedman, H. ★*The Talmud*	296.1
Freedman, Samuel G. *Jew vs. Jew*	296
Goldman, Ari L. *Being Jewish*	296.4
Goodman, Martin. ★*A History of Judaism*	296.09
Grieve, Paul. *A Brief Guide to Islam*	297
Hoffman, Adina. *Sacred Trash*	296.09
Isaacs, Ronald H. ★*Kosher Living*	296.7
Keinan, Tal. *God Is in the Crowd*	305.892
Kertzer, David I. *The Pope at War*	940.53
Kirsch, Adam. *The Blessing and the Curse*	809
Kirsch, Adam. ★*The People and the Books*	809
Leibovitz, Liel. ★*How the Talmud Can Change Your Life*	296.1
Levine, Amy-Jill. *The Bible with and Without Jesus*	220.6
Pogrebin, Abigail. *My Jewish Year*	296.4
Ricanati, Elizabeth. *Braided*	B
Sabar, Ariel. *My Father's Paradise*	B
Sarna, Jonathan D. ★*American Judaism*	296
Schama, Simon. ★*The Story of the Jews; Volume One*	909
Schama, Simon. ★*The Story of the Jews; Volume Two*	909
Telushkin, Joseph. *Jewish Wisdom*	296.3
Telushkin, Joseph. *Rebbe*	296.833
Wagner, Jordan Lee. *The Synagogue Survival Kit*	296.4
Weisman, Steven R. *The Chosen Wars*	296.0973
Wieseltier, Leon. *Kaddish*	296.4
JUDAISM AND STATE	
Keinan, Tal. *God Is in the Crowd*	305.892
★*Judaism Is About Love.* Held, Shai	296.3
JUDGE, ONEY, 1773-1848	
Dunbar, Erica Armstrong. ★*Never Caught*	B
JUDGES	
Biskupic, Joan. ★*Nine Black Robes*	347.73
Brown-Nagin, Tomiko. *Civil Rights Queen*	B
Budiansky, Stephen. *Oliver Wendell Holmes*	B
Canellos, Peter S. *The Great Dissenter*	B
Carmon, Irin. *Notorious RBG*	B
Coyle, Marcia. *The Roberts Court*	347.73
De Hart, Jane Sherron. ★*Ruth Bader Ginsburg*	B
Gibson, Larry S. *Young Thurgood*	B
Ginsburg, Ruth Bader. ★*My Own Words*	347.73
Graetz, Michael J. *The Burger Court and the Rise of the Judicial Right*	347.73
Greenhouse, Linda. *Becoming Justice Blackmun*	B
Haygood, Wil. *Showdown*	B
Hirshman, Linda R. *Sisters in Law*	347.73
Jones, Nathaniel R. *Answering the Call*	B
Kaplan, David A. *The Most Dangerous Branch*	347.73
Leamer, Laurence. *The Price of Justice*	346.7302
Marshall, Thurgood. *Thurgood Marshall*	B
Murphy, Bruce Allen. *Scalia*	B
Olsen, Lise. *Code of Silence*	347.73
Paul, Joel R. ★*Without Precedent*	B
Robin, Corey. *The Enigma of Clarence Thomas*	347.73
Rosen, Jeffrey. *Conversations with RBG*	B

AUTHOR, TITLE, SERIES AND SUBJECT INDEX

Scalia, Antonin. *Scalia Speaks* — 081
Smith, Jean Edward. *John Marshall* — B
Sotomayor, Sonia. ★*My Beloved World* — B
Starks, Glenn L. *Thurgood Marshall* — B
Stevens, John Paul. *The Making of a Justice* — B
Toobin, Jeffrey. *The Nine* — 347.73
Totenberg, Nina. ★*Dinners with Ruth* — B
Urofsky, Melvin I. *Dissent and the Supreme Court* — 342.7302
Urofsky, Melvin I. *Louis D. Brandeis* — B
Williams, Juan. *Thurgood Marshall* — B

JUDGMENT
Bernstein, Gabrielle. *Judgment Detox* — 158
Bharara, Preet. *Doing Justice* — 347.73
Bolz-Weber, Nadia. *Shameless* — 261.8
Hortis, C. Alexander. *The Witch of New York* — 364.152
Oyler, Lauren. *No Judgment* — 814
Tuchman, Barbara W. *March of Folly* — 909.08
★*Judgment At Tokyo*. Bass, Gary Jonathan — 952.04
Judgment Days. Kotz, Nick — 323
Judgment Detox. Bernstein, Gabrielle — 158
The Judgment of Paris. King, Ross — 759.4

JUDICIAL CORRUPTION
Honig, Elie. *Untouchable* — 364.1
Leamer, Laurence. *The Price of Justice* — 346.7302
Olsen, Lise. *Code of Silence* — 347.73
Strang, Dean A. *Worse Than the Devil* — 345.775

JUDICIAL DISCRETION
Vladeck, Stephen I. *The Shadow Docket* — 347.73

JUDICIAL ERROR
Balko, Radley. ★*The Cadaver King and the Country Dentist* — 614
Barnett, Brittany K. ★*A Knock at Midnight* — B
Fabricant, M. Chris. *Junk Science and the American Criminal Justice System* — 363.25
Hinton, Anthony Ray. *The Sun Does Shine* — B
McCloskey, Jim. *When Truth Is All You Have* — B
McGarrahan, Ellen. *Two Truths and a Lie* — 364.152
Morton, Michael. *Getting Life* — B
Salaam, Yusef. *Better, Not Bitter* — B
Schneps, Leila. *Math on Trial* — 345
Smith, Clive Stafford. *The Injustice System* — 345.759
Woodfox, Albert. *Solitary* — B
Zerwick, Phoebe. *Beyond Innocence* — 347

JUDICIAL OPINIONS
Budiansky, Stephen. *Oliver Wendell Holmes* — B
Scalia, Antonin. *Scalia Speaks* — 081

JUDICIAL POWER
Berman, Ari. ★*Minority Rule* — 305.809
Breyer, Stephen G. *Making Our Democracy Work* — 347.73
Cohen, Adam. ★*Supreme Inequality* — 347.73
Driver, Justin. *The Schoolhouse Gate* — 344.73
Kaplan, David A. *The Most Dangerous Branch* — 347.73

JUDICIAL PROCESS
Foner, Eric. *The Second Founding* — 342.73
Friedman, Barry. *The Will of the People* — 347.73
O'Brien, David M. ★*Storm Center* — 347.73

JUDICIAL REVIEW
Breyer, Stephen G. ★*The Authority of the Court and the Peril of Politics* — 347.73
Breyer, Stephen G. *Making Our Democracy Work* — 347.73
Budiansky, Stephen. *Oliver Wendell Holmes* — B
Coyle, Marcia. *The Roberts Court* — 347.73
Driver, Justin. *The Schoolhouse Gate* — 344.73
Toobin, Jeffrey. *The Nine* — 347.73
Waldman, Michael. *The Supermajority* — 347.73

JUDICIAL SYSTEM
Barnett, Brittany K. ★*A Knock at Midnight* — B
Biskupic, Joan. ★*Nine Black Robes* — 347.73
Breyer, Stephen G. *Making Our Democracy Work* — 347.73
Coates, Laura Gayle. *Just Pursuit* — 345.73
Crump, Benjamin. *Open Season* — 364
Dybdahl, Thomas L. *When Innocence Is Not Enough* — 345.73
Friedman, Barry. *The Will of the People* — 347.73
Graetz, Michael J. *The Burger Court and the Rise of the Judicial Right* — 347.73
Miller, Reuben Jonathan. *Halfway Home* — 364.8
O'Connor, Sandra Day. ★*Out of Order* — 347.73
Prejean, Helen. *The Death of Innocents* — 364.66
Rapping, Jonathan. *Gideon's Promise* — 345.73

Rudolf, David S. *American Injustice* — 345.73
Scalia, Antonin. *Scalia Speaks* — 081
Shesol, Jeff. *Supreme Power* — 347.73
Van Meter, Matthew. *Deep Delta Justice* — 345.763
Waldman, Michael. *The Supermajority* — 347.73

JUDO
Gracie, Rickson. *Breathe* — B

Judson, Pieter M.
The Habsburg Empire — 943.6

Judt, Tony
Postwar — 940.55

Juke Joints, Jazz Clubs & Juice. Tipton-Martin, Toni — 641.87
Julia and Jacques Cooking at Home. Child, Julia — 641.594
★*Julian Bond's Time to Teach*. Bond, Julian — 323.0975
Julie and Julia. Powell, Julie — 641.5
Julius Chambers. Rosen, Richard A. — B

JULIUS II, POPE, 1443-1513
King, Ross. *Michelangelo & the Pope's Ceiling* — 759.5
July 1914. McMeekin, Sean — 940.3

Jun, Tasha
★*Tell Me the Dream Again* — 248

JUN, TASHA
Jun, Tasha. ★*Tell Me the Dream Again* — 248

JUNETEENTH
Taylor, Nicole A. ★*Watermelon & Red Birds* — 641.5

Jung, C. G.
★*The Basic Writings of C.G. Jung* — 150.19
Memories, Dreams, Reflections — 150.19

JUNG, C. G. (CARL GUSTAV), 1875-1961
Jung, C. G. *Memories, Dreams, Reflections* — 150.19

Jung, Kwan
Chinese Brush Painting — 751.4

Jungalow. Blakeney, Justina — 747

Junger, Sebastian
Fire — 909.82
★*In My Time of Dying* — 304.6
The Perfect Storm — 974.4
War — 958.104

JUNGER, SEBASTIAN
Junger, Sebastian. ★*In My Time of Dying* — 304.6

Jungle of Snakes. Arnold, James R. — 355.02
Jungle of Stone. Carlsen, William — B

JUNGLE SURVIVAL
Preston, Douglas J. ★*The Lost City of the Monkey God* — 972.85
Wallace, Scott. *The Unconquered* — 981

JUNGLE WARFARE
Holland, James. ★*Burma '44* — 940.54

JUNGLES
Preston, Douglas J. ★*The Lost City of the Monkey God* — 972.85

The Junior Officers' Reading Club. Hennessey, Patrick — B
Junk. Stewart, Alison — 616.85
Junk. Pico, Tommy — 811

JUNK FOOD
Schatzker, Mark. *The Dorito Effect* — 641.3

Junk Science and the American Criminal Justice System. Fabricant, M. Chris — 363.25

JURISPRUDENCE
De Hart, Jane Sherron. ★*Ruth Bader Ginsburg* — B
Urofsky, Melvin I. *Louis D. Brandeis* — B
★*A Jury of Her Peers*. Showalter, Elaine — 810.9

JURY TAMPERING
Gleeson, John. *The Gotti Wars* — 364.1

Just A Shot Away. Austerlitz, Saul — 781.66078
A Just and Generous Nation. Holzer, Harold — 973.7092
★*Just as I Am*. Tyson, Cicely — B
★*Just Kids*. Smith, Patti — B
Just Mercy. Stevenson, Bryan — B
Just Pursuit. Coates, Laura Gayle — 345.73
Just Ride. Petersen, Grant — 796.6
Just The Funny Parts. Scovell, Nell — B
★*Just Us*. Rankine, Claudia — 305.896

JUST WAR DOCTRINE
Brooks, Rosa. *How Everything Became War and the Military Became Everything* — 355
Justice. Sandel, Michael J. — 172

JUSTICE
Caruana Galizia, Paul. ★*A Death in Malta* — 364.15
Coates, Laura Gayle. *Just Pursuit* — 345.73

PUBLIC LIBRARY CORE COLLECTION: NONFICTION
Twentieth Edition

Cummings, Elijah. ★*We're Better Than This* — B
Ervin, Kristine S. *Rabbit Heart* — 364.152
Gleeson, John. *The Gotti Wars* — 364.1
Harjo, Joy. ★*Poet Warrior* — B
Herman, Judith Lewis. *Truth and Repair* — 362.883
Higham, Scott. *American Cartel* — 338.4
Jackson, Jenn M. ★*Black Women Taught Us* — 305.48
Kenneally, Christine. *Ghosts of the Orphanage* — 362.73
Kimmerle, Erin H. *We Carry Their Bones* — 365
Kinstler, Linda. *Come to This Court and Cry* — 940.53
Mandela, Nelson. *The Prison Letters of Nelson Mandela* — 968.06092
Mar, Alex. *Seventy Times Seven* — 362.88
McGarrahan, Ellen. *Two Truths and a Lie* — 364.152
Mills, Stephen Tukel. *Chosen* — B
Olsen, Lise. *Code of Silence* — 347.73
Pardlo, Gregory. *Spectral Evidence* — 811
Plant, Deborah G. *Of Greed and Glory* — 326
Plato. ★*The Republic* — 321
Pratt, Victoria. *The Power of Dignity* — 364.973
Rankine, Claudia. ★*Citizen* — 814
Rankine, Claudia. ★*Just Us* — 305.896
Rapping, Jonathan. *Gideon's Promise* — 345.73
Reilly, Ryan J. ★*Sedition Hunters* — 364.1
Sandel, Michael J. *Justice* — 172
Stevenson, Bryan. *Just Mercy* — B
Swift, Earl. *Hell Put to Shame* — 364.15
Talty, Stephan. *The Good Assassin* — 364.15
Toobin, Jeffrey. *True Crimes and Misdemeanors* — 973.933
Wade, Sabia. *Birthing Liberation* — 363.96

JUSTICE AND POLITICS
Purnell, Derecka. *Becoming Abolitionists* — 363.20973

JUTLAND, BATTLE OF, 1916
Massie, Robert K. *Castles of Steel* — 940.4

JUVENILE CORRECTIONAL INSTITUTIONS
Kimmerle, Erin H. *We Carry Their Bones* — 365

JUVENILE CORRECTIONS
Hobbs, Jeff. *Children of the State* — 364.36
Sweeney, Jennifer. *Literacy* — 027.62

JUVENILE DELINQUENCY
Hobbs, Jeff. *Children of the State* — 364.36

JUVENILE DELINQUENTS
Hale, Kathleen. ★*Slenderman* — 364.152
Hobbs, Jeff. *Children of the State* — 364.36
Manuel, Ian. *My Time Will Come* — B
Sweeney, Jennifer. *Literacy* — 027.62

JUVENILE DETENTION
Bergner, Daniel. ★*Sing for Your Life* — B

JUVENILE JUSTICE SYSTEM
Hobbs, Jeff. *Children of the State* — 364.36

K

K. Kepner, Tyler — 796.357
K Blows Top. Carlson, Peter — 947.085

K2 (MOUNTAIN), PAKISTAN
Conefrey, Mick. *The Ghosts of K2* — 796.522
Ellsworth, Scott. *The World Beneath Their Feet* — 796.522
Zuckerman, Peter. ★*Buried in the Sky* — 796.522

Kaag, John J.
  American Philosophy — 191
  Hiking with Nietzsche — 193

KAAG, JOHN J., 1979-
Kaag, John J. *American Philosophy* — 191

Kaba, Mariame
  No More Police — 363.2

KABUL, AFGHANISTAN
Lemmon, Gayle Tzemach. *The Dressmaker of Khair Khana* — B
Seierstad, Asne. *The Bookseller of Kabul* — 958.1

Kachka. Morales, Bonnie Frumkin — 641.594

KACZYNSKI, THEODORE JOHN, 1942-2023
Wiehl, Lis W. *Hunting the Unabomber* — 364.152

KADDISH
Bolsta, Hyla Shifra. *The Illuminated Kaddish* — 296.4
Wieseltier, Leon. *Kaddish* — 296.4

Kaddish. Wieseltier, Leon — 296.4

KADOORIE FAMILY
Kaufman, Jonathan. *The Last Kings of Shanghai* — 951

KADOORIE, ELLY, 1865-1944
Kaufman, Jonathan. *The Last Kings of Shanghai* — 951

Kadri, Sadakat
  The Trial — 345

Kael, Pauline
  ★*The Age of Movies* — 791.43

KAEPERNICK, COLIN, 1987-
Alexander, Kwame. *Light for the World to See* — 811.6

Kagan, Donald
  The Peloponnesian War — 938
  Thucydides — 938

Kahan, Paul
  Cheers to the Publican, Repast and Present — 641.594

Kahate, Ruta
  6 Spices 60 Dishes — 641.595

Kahlo, Frida
  The Diary of Frida Kahlo — B

KAHLO, FRIDA
Herrera, Hayden. *Frida* — B
Hesse, Maria. ★*Frida Kahlo* — B
Kahlo, Frida. *The Diary of Frida Kahlo* — B
Lozano, Luis-Martin. *Frida Kahlo* — 759.972
Stahr, Celia. *Frida in America* — B

Kahn, Ashley
  The House That Trane Built — 781.6509

Kahneman, Daniel
  ★*Thinking, Fast and Slow* — 153.4

KAHNEMAN, DANIEL, 1934-2024
Lewis, Michael. ★*The Undoing Project* — 920

KAISER FAMILY
Kaiser, Menachem. *Plunder* — 940.53

Kaiser, Charles
  The Cost of Courage — B

KAISER, MEIR MENACHEM, 1921-1977
Kaiser, Menachem. *Plunder* — 940.53

Kaiser, Menachem
  Plunder — 940.53

Kaiser, Robert G.
  Act of Congress — 346.73

Kakalios, James
  The Amazing Story of Quantum Mechanics — 530.12

Kaku, Michio
  ★*The Future of Humanity* — 629.45
  The God Equation — 523.1
  ★*Hyperspace* — 530.1
  Parallel Worlds — 523.1
  Quantum Supremacy — 006.3

Kakutani, Michiko
  Ex Libris — 028

KAKUTANI, MICHIKO
Kakutani, Michiko. *Ex Libris* — 028

Kalanithi, Paul
  ★*When Breath Becomes Air* — B

KALANITHI, PAUL
Kalanithi, Paul. ★*When Breath Becomes Air* — B

Kalb, Bess
  ★*Nobody Will Tell You This but Me* — 306.874

KALB, BESS, 1987-
Kalb, Bess. ★*Nobody Will Tell You This but Me* — 306.874

Kalb, Claudia
  Andy Warhol Was a Hoarder — 920

Kalder, Daniel
  The Infernal Library — 321.9

Kaling, Mindy
  Why Not Me? — B

KALING, MINDY
Kaling, Mindy. *Why Not Me?* — B

Kaltenegger, Lisa
  ★*Alien Earths* — 523.2

Kamen, Henry
  The Spanish Inquisition — 272

Kamenetz, Anya
  The Stolen Year — 306.43

Kamensky, Jane
  A Revolution in Color — 759.13

KAMENY, FRANK, 1925-2011
Cervini, Eric. *The Deviant's War* — B

The Kamikaze Hunters. Iredale, Will — 940.54

AUTHOR, TITLE, SERIES AND SUBJECT INDEX

Kaminsky, Ilya
   ★*Deaf Republic* — 811
Kamkwamba, William
   ★*The Boy Who Harnessed the Wind* — B
KAMKWAMBA, WILLIAM, 1987-
   Kamkwamba, William. ★*The Boy Who Harnessed the Wind* — B
KAMMAN, MADELEINE
   Sen, Mayukh. *Taste Makers* — 641.5092
Kamp, David
   Sunny Days — 791.4502
Kampen-O'Riley, Michael
   Art Beyond the West — 709
Kan, Karoline
   Under Red Skies — B
KAN, KAROLINE, 1989-
   Kan, Karoline. *Under Red Skies* — B
Kandel, Eric R.
   The Age of Insight — 154.2
   ★*The Disordered Mind* — 616.89
   In Search of Memory — B
KANDEL, ERIC R.
   Kandel, Eric R. *In Search of Memory* — B
Kander, Jason
   Invisible Storm — B
KANDER, JASON
   Kander, Jason. *Invisible Storm* — B
Kane, Cyndi
   Save-It-Forward Suppers — 641.5
Kanell, John
   Preppy Kitchen — 641.5
Kanfer, Stefan
   Tough Without a Gun — B
Kang, Lydia
   Patient Zero — 614.4
Kang, Mia
   Knockout — B
KANG, MIA
   Kang, Mia. *Knockout* — B
Kang, Mingoo
   Jang — 641.595
Kanigel, Robert
   Eyes on the Street — B
   The Man Who Knew Infinity — B
KANSAS
   Capote, Truman. ★*In Cold Blood* — 364.1
   Clavin, Thomas. *Dodge City* — 978.1
   Smarsh, Sarah. ★*Heartland* — B
Kansas City Lightning. Crouch, Stanley
KANSAS CITY, MISSOURI
   Crouch, Stanley. *Kansas City Lightning* — B
Kant's Little Prussian Head and Other Reasons Why I Write. Messud, Claire — B
Kant, Immanuel
   ★*Basic Writings of Kant* — 193
Kantor, Jodi
   She Said — 364.15
Kapilow, Robert
   ★*Listening for America* — 782.42164
Kaplan, Alice Yaeger
   Looking for the Stranger — B
Kaplan, David A.
   The Most Dangerous Branch — 347.73
Kaplan, Fred
   John Quincy Adams — B
   Lincoln and the Abolitionists — 973.7092
Kaplan, Fred M.
   The Bomb — 355.8
Kaplan, James
   3 Shades of Blue — 920
   Sinatra — 782.42164
Kaplan, Janice
   The Genius of Women — 920
Kaplan, Robert D.
   The Loom of Time — 327
   Warrior Politics — 320
Kaplan, Roberta A.
   Then Comes Marriage — 346.7301
KAPPUS, FRANZ XAVER, 1883-1966
   Rilke, Rainer Maria. ★*Letters to a Young Poet* — 831

Kara, Siddharth
   Cobalt Red — 338.2
Karabell, Zachary
   Inside Money — 332.1
Karachi Vice. Shackle, Samira — 954.91
KARACHI, PAKISTAN
   Shackle, Samira. *Karachi Vice* — 954.91
Karadsheh, Suzy
   ★*The Mediterranean Dish* — 641.59
KARADZIC, RADOVAN V., 1945-
   Stern, Jessica. *My War Criminal* — 341.6
KARAJAN, HERBERT VON
   Osborne, Richard. *Herbert Von Karajan* — B
Karbo, Karen
   In Praise of Difficult Women — 920
Kardas-Nelson, Mara
   We Are Not Able to Live in the Sky — 332.3
Karen, Dawnn
   Dress Your Best Life — 646
Kariko, Katalin
   Breaking Through — B
KARIKO, KATALIN
   Kariko, Katalin. *Breaking Through* — B
Karim-Cooper, Farah
   ★*The Great White Bard* — 822.33
Karl Marx. Sperber, Jonathan — B
Karl Marx. Wheen, Francis — B
Karl, Jonathan
   Betrayal — 973.933
   Front Row at the Trump Show — 973.933
   Tired of Winning — 973.933
KARL, JONATHAN, 1968-
   Karl, Jonathan. *Front Row at the Trump Show* — 973.933
Karlawish, Jason
   ★*The Problem of Alzheimer's* — 616.8
Karlsen, Carol F.
   ★*The Devil in the Shape of a Woman* — 133.4
Karnazes, Dean
   The Legend of Marathon — 796.42
Karnow, Stanley
   Vietnam, a History — 959.704
Karon, Jan
   Bathed in Prayer — 242
Karon, Karen
   Advanced Chain Maille Jewelry Workshop — 745.594
Karp, Josh
   Orson Welles's Last Movie — 791.43
Karr, Mary
   The Art of Memoir — B
   Tropic of Squalor — 811
Kars, Marjoleine
   Blood on the River — 306.3
Karski, Jan
   Story of a Secret State — 940.53
KARSKI, JAN, 1914-2000
   Karski, Jan. *Story of a Secret State* — 940.53
Kartes, Danielle
   Butter, Flour, Sugar, Joy — 641.86
Kartus, Lisa
   Knit Fix — 746.43
Kashner, Sam
   The Fabulous Bouvier Sisters — 920
   Furious Love — B
Kasischke, Laura
   Space, in Chains — 811
Kasparov, G. K.
   Deep Thinking — 006.3
KASPAROV, G. K. (GARRI KIMOVICH)
   Kasparov, G. K. *Deep Thinking* — 006.3
Kasparov, Gary
   Winter Is Coming — 947.086
Kassabova, Kapka
   Border — 949.9
Kassinger, Ruth
   ★*A Garden of Marvels* — 580.92
Kate. Mann, William J. — B
Kate Remembered. Berg, A. Scott — B
Katherine The Queen. Porter, Linda — B

PUBLIC LIBRARY CORE COLLECTION: NONFICTION
Twentieth Edition

Katin, Miriam
  We Are on Our Own — 741.5
KATLAMA, JACQUELINE BOULLOCHE, 1918-1994
  Kaiser, Charles. *The Cost of Courage* — B
Katrina. Rivlin, Gary — 976.3
Katsushika, Hokusai
  Hokusai — 769.92
KATSUSHIKA, HOKUSAI, 1760-1849
  Katsushika, Hokusai. *Hokusai* — 769.92
Kattan, Fadi
  ★*Bethlehem* — 641.59
KATYN FOREST MASSACRE, 1940
  Rogoyska, Jane. *Surviving Katyn* — 940.54
Katz, Amy
  Seed Bead Chic — 745.594
Katz, Catherine Grace
  The Daughters of Yalta — 920
Katz, David
  Barack Before Obama — B
Katz, Emily
  Modern Macrame — 746.42
Katz, Evan Ross
  Into Every Generation a Slayer Is Born — 791.45
KATZ, MARGARET ERLE
  Glaser, Gabrielle. *American Baby* — B
Katzen, Mollie
  The Heart of the Plate — 641.5
  ★*The Moosewood Cookbook* — 641.5
Katznelson, Ira
  Fear Itself — 973.917
Kauffman, Jonathan
  Hippie Food — 394.1
***Kaufman* Field Guide to Butterflies of North America**. Brock, James P. — 595.7
Kaufman, Amy
  Bachelor Nation — 791.45
Kaufman, Jonathan
  The Last Kings of Shanghai — 951
Kaufman, Kenn
  The Birds That Audubon Missed — 598
Kaufmann, Miranda
  Black Tudors — 941
Kaufmann, Uri R.
  Eighteen Days of October — 956.04
Kaur, Rupi
  Milk and Honey — 811
  The Sun and Her Flowers — 811.6
Kavanagh, Julie
  The Irish Assassins — 941.5
  Nureyev — B
KAVANAUGH, BRETT, 1965-
  Ford, Christine Blasey. *One Way Back* — B
KAVANAUGH, TIMOTHY (FICTITIOUS CHARACTER)
  Karon, Jan. *Bathed in Prayer* — 242
Kavin, Kim
  The Dog Merchants — 636.7
Kawa, Abraham
  Democracy — 741.5
Kawasaki, Guy
  The Art of the Start 2.0 — 658.1
***Kayak* Morning**. Rosenblatt, Roger — 155.9
Kayaking. Krauzer, Steven M. — 797.1
KAYAKING
  Krauzer, Steven M. *Kayaking* — 797.1
KAYAKS
  Krauzer, Steven M. *Kayaking* — 797.1
Kaye, Lenny
  ★*Lightning Striking* — 781.66
KAYE, LENNY
  Kaye, Lenny. ★*Lightning Striking* — 781.66
KAZAKHS
  Juan, Li. *Winter Pasture* — 951.06
Kazdin, Cole
  ★*What's Eating Us* — 616.85
KAZDIN, COLE
  Kazdin, Cole. ★*What's Eating Us* — 616.85
Kazin, Michael
  What It Took to Win — 324.2736

Kean, Sam
  The Bastard Brigade — 355.8
  Caesar's Last Breath — 551.51
  The Disappearing Spoon — 546
  The Icepick Surgeon — 509
  The Tale of the Dueling Neurosurgeons — 617.4
Kearney, Douglas
  Sho — 811
Kearse, Bettye
  The Other Madisons — 920
KEARSE, BETTYE
  Kearse, Bettye. *The Other Madisons* — 920
KEATON, BUSTER, 1895-1966
  Curtis, James. *Buster Keaton* — B
  Stevens, Dana. *Camera Man* — 791.4302
Keaton, Diane
  ★*Brother & Sister* — B
KEATON, DIANE
  Keaton, Diane. ★*Brother & Sister* — B
★***Keats***. Miller, Lucasta — 821
Keats, John
  ★*The Complete Poems of John Keats* — 821
  Poems — 821
KEATS, JOHN, 1795-1821
  Miller, Lucasta. ★*Keats* — 821
Keay, John
  India — 954
Keefe, Bob
  Clean Economy Now — 333.79
Keefe, Patrick Radden
  ★*Empire of Pain* — 338.7
  ★*Rogues* — 364.16
  ★*Say Nothing* — 364.152
Keegan, John
  The American Civil War — 973.7
  The First World War — 940.3
  The Second World War — 940.53
Keeling, Ida
  Can't Nothing Bring Me Down — B
KEELING, IDA, 1915-2021
  Keeling, Ida. *Can't Nothing Bring Me Down* — B
Keenan, Cody
  Grace — 973.932
KEENAN, CODY
  Keenan, Cody. *Grace* — 973.932
Keene, Adrienne
  Notable Native People — 920
KEENE, CAROLYN (PUBLISHER PSEUDONYM)
  Rehak, Melanie. *Girl Sleuth* — 813
Keene, Donald
  Emperor of Japan — 952.03
  The Pleasures of Japanese Literature — 895.6
Keene, John
  ★*Punks* — 811
Keene, Nancy
  Childhood Leukemia — 618.92
★***Keep* It Zesty**. Massih, Edy — 641.595
★***Keep* Sharp**. Gupta, Sanjay — 153.4
Keepers. Brennan, Kathy — 641.5973
Keepers. Schickel, Richard — 791.430973
***Keeping* an Eye Open**. Barnes, Julian — 709.04
***Keeping* Faith**. Carter, Jimmy — B
Keffer, Ken
  Earth Almanac — 508
Keflezighi, Meb
  26 Marathons — B
  Meb for Mortals — 796.4252
KEFLEZIGHI, MEB
  Keflezighi, Meb. *26 Marathons* — B
Keiler, Allan
  Marian Anderson — B
Keim, Brandon
  Meet the Neighbors — 591.5
Keinan, Tal
  God Is in the Crowd — 305.892
Keith, Philip A.
  All Blood Runs Red — B

AUTHOR, TITLE, SERIES AND SUBJECT INDEX

Keizer, Garret
   Getting Schooled … 373.1102
KEIZER, GARRET
   Keizer, Garret. *Getting Schooled* … 373.1102
Kelder, Diane
   The Great Book of French Impressionism … 759.4
Keller, Helen
   ★*The Story of My Life* … B
KELLER, HELEN, 1880-1968
   Gibson, William. ★*The Miracle Worker* … 812
   Herrmann, Dorothy. *Helen Keller* … B
   Keller, Helen. ★*The Story of My Life* … B
KELLER, JOE
   Dohrmann, George. ★*Play Their Hearts Out* … 796.323
Keller, Julia
   Quitting … 650.14
Keller, Thomas
   Bouchon Bakery … 641.594
   The French Laundry Cookbook … 641.5
Keller, Timothy J.
   The Reason for God … 239
Kelley, Blair Murphy
   Black Folk … 331.6
Kelley, Margot Anne
   A Gardener at the End of the World … 615.8
KELLEY, MARGOT ANNE
   Kelley, Margot Anne. *A Gardener at the End of the World* … 615.8
Kelly, Christopher R.
   Am I Dying?! … 362.1
Kelly, Donika
   The Renunciations … 811
Kelly, Helena
   Jane Austen, the Secret Radical … 823
Kelly, John
   The Graves Are Walking … 941.5081
   The Great Mortality … 614.5
Kelly, Joseph
   Marooned … 975.5
Kelly, Kate
   Ordinary Equality … 920
Kelly, Kevin
   ★*Excellent Advice for Living* … 158.1
Kelly, Minka
   ★*Tell Me Everything* … B
KELLY, R.
   DeRogatis, Jim. *Soulless* … B
Kelly, Scott
   ★*Endurance* … B
KELLY, SCOTT, 1964-
   Kelly, Scott. ★*Endurance* … B
Keltner, Dacher
   ★*Awe* … 152.4
   Born to Be Good … 155.2
Kemper, Ellie
   My Squirrel Days … B
KEMPER, ELLIE, 1980-
   Kemper, Ellie. *My Squirrel Days* … B
Kemper, Steve
   Our Man in Tokyo … 952.03
Kempner, Joanna
   Psychedelic Outlaws … 615.7
Kempowski, Walter
   Swansong 1945 … 940.54
Kempton, Beth
   The Way of the Fearless Writer … 808.02
Ken Schultz's Essentials of Fishing. Schultz, Ken … 799.1
Kenan, Randall
   Black Folk Could Fly … 813
KENAN, RANDALL
   Kenan, Randall. *Black Folk Could Fly* … 813
Kenda, Joe
   Killer Triggers … 364.152
KENDA, JOE
   Kenda, Joe. *Killer Triggers* … 364.152
Kendall, Mikki
   Hood Feminism … 305.420973
Kendall, Tim
   The Art of Robert Frost … 811

Kendi, Ibram X.
   ★*How to Be an Antiracist* … 305.8
   ★*How to Raise an Antiracist* … 649
   ★*Stamped from the Beginning* … 305.8
KENDI, IBRAM X.
   Kendi, Ibram X. ★*How to Be an Antiracist* … 305.8
   Kendi, Ibram X. ★*How to Raise an Antiracist* … 649
Kendo. Bennett, Alexander … 796.86
KENDO
   Bennett, Alexander. *Kendo* … 796.86
Kendrick, Kathleen M
   Official Guide to the Smithsonian National Museum of African American History & Culture … 975.3
Keneally, Thomas
   A Commonwealth of Thieves … 994
KENNAN, GEORGE F. (GEORGE FROST), 1904-2005
   Thompson, Nicholas. *The Hawk and the Dove* … 973.92
Kenneally, Christine
   Ghosts of the Orphanage … 362.73
Kennedy & Nixon. Matthews, Christopher … 973.922
Kennedy and King. Levingston, Steven … 920
KENNEDY FAMILY
   Andersen, Christopher P. *The Good Son* … B
   Byrne, Paula. *Kick* … B
   Farrell, John A. *Ted Kennedy* … B
   Gabler, Neal. *Catching the Wind* … B
   Larson, Kate Clifford. *Rosemary* … B
   Leamer, Laurence. *The Kennedy Men* … 920
   Leaming, Barbara. *Kick Kennedy* … B
   Logevall, Fredrik. ★*JFK* … B
   Mahoney, Richard D. *Sons & Brothers* … 920
   McKeon, Kathy. *Jackie's Girl* … B
   McNamara, Eileen. ★*Eunice* … B
   Nasaw, David. ★*The Patriarch* … B
   Taraborrelli, J. Randy. *After Camelot* … 920
   Taraborrelli, J. Randy. *The Kennedy Heirs* … 920
The Kennedy Heirs. Taraborrelli, J. Randy … 920
The Kennedy Men. Leamer, Laurence … 920
Kennedy's Avenger. Abrams, Dan … 973.922
Kennedy, David M.
   ★*Freedom from Fear* … 973.91
KENNEDY, EDWARD M. (EDWARD MOORE), 1932-2009
   Farrell, John A. *Ted Kennedy* … B
   Gabler, Neal. ★*Against the Wind* … B
   Gabler, Neal. *Catching the Wind* … B
Kennedy, Hugh
   ★*The Great Arab Conquests* … 297.09
Kennedy, John F.
   Profiles in Courage … 920
KENNEDY, JOHN F. (JOHN FITZGERALD), 1917-1963
   Abrams, Dan. *Kennedy's Avenger* … 973.922
   Baier, Bret. *Three Days in January* … B
   Brinkley, Alan. *John F. Kennedy* … B
   Brinkley, Douglas. ★*American Moonshot* … 629.40973
   Caro, Robert A. ★*The Passage of Power* … B
   Clarke, Thurston. *JFK's Last Hundred Days* … B
   Cohen, Andrew. *Two Days in June* … 973.922
   Coleman, David G. *The Fourteenth Day* … 973.922092
   Dallek, Robert. *Let Every Nation Know* … B
   Dallek, Robert. *An Unfinished Life* … B
   Hill, Clint. *Five Days in November* … 973.922092
   Leamer, Laurence. *The Kennedy Men* … 920
   Levingston, Steven. *Kennedy and King* … 920
   Logevall, Fredrik. ★*JFK* … B
   Mahoney, Richard D. *Sons & Brothers* … 920
   Maier, Thomas. *Mafia Spies* … 364.1060973
   Matthews, Christopher. *Kennedy & Nixon* … 973.922
   Minutaglio, Bill. *Dallas 1963* … 973.922092
   Oliphant, Thomas. ★*The Road to Camelot* … 973.922092
   Onassis, Jacqueline Kennedy. *Historic Conversations on Life with John F. Kennedy* … B
   Posner, Gerald L. *Case Closed* … 364.1
   Rasenberger, Jim. *The Brilliant Disaster* … 972.9106
   Sherman, Casey. *Above and Beyond* … 973.922092
   Sherwin, Martin J. *Gambling with Armageddon* … 972.9106
   Shesol, Jeff. *Mercury Rising* … 629.45
   Sorensen, Theodore C. *Counselor* … B
   Swanson, James L. *End of Days* … 973.922092

Zapruder, Alexandra. *Twenty-Six Seconds* 973.922092
KENNEDY, JOHN F. JR., 1960-1999
    Andersen, Christopher P. *The Good Son* .... B
    Gillon, Steven M. *America's Reluctant Prince* .... B
Kennedy, Jonathan
    Pathogenesis 614.4
KENNEDY, JOSEPH P. (JOSEPH PATRICK), 1888-1969
    Abrams, Dan. *Kennedy's Avenger* 973.922
    Leamer, Laurence. *The Kennedy Men* 920
    McKean, David. *Watching Darkness Fall* 940.53
    Nasaw, David. ★*The Patriarch* .... B
KENNEDY, KATHLEEN, 1920-1948
    Byrne, Paula. *Kick* .... B
    Leaming, Barbara. *Kick Kennedy* .... B
Kennedy, Kostya
    True .... B
Kennedy, Michael
    Richard Strauss .... B
Kennedy, Patrick J.
    ★*Profiles in Mental Health Courage* 362.29
Kennedy, Paul M.
    Engineers of Victory 940.54
    The Rise and Fall of the Great Powers 909.82
Kennedy, Robert F.
    Thirteen Days 327.73
Kennedy, Robert Francis
    RFK 973.92
KENNEDY, ROBERT FRANCIS, 1925-1968
    Clarke, Thurston, *The Last Campaign* .... B
    Dyson, Michael Eric. *What Truth Sounds Like* 305.800973
    Kennedy, Robert Francis. *RFK* 973.92
    Kurlansky, Mark. *1968* 909.82
    Mahoney, Richard D. *Sons & Brothers* 920
    Matthews, Christopher. *Bobby Kennedy* .... B
    Thomas, Evan. ★*Robert Kennedy* .... B
    Tye, Larry. ★*Bobby Kennedy* .... B
KENNEDY, ROSEMARY, 1918-2005
    Larson, Kate Clifford. *Rosemary* .... B
Kennedy-Moore, Eileen
    ★*Kid Confidence* 155.4
Kenner, Hugh
    The Pound Era 811
Kenner, Rob
    The Marathon Don't Stop .... B
Kenneth Clark. Stourton, James .... B
Kennicott, Philip
    Counterpoint .... B
KENNICOTT, PHILIP
    Kennicott, Philip. *Counterpoint* .... B
Kenny, Brian
    Ahead of the Curve 796.357
Kenny, Charles
    The Plague Cycle 614.4
Kenny, Glenn
    Made Men 791.43
    The World Is Yours 791.43
Kent State. Derf 741.5
KENT STATE SHOOTINGS, MAY 4, 1970
    Derf. *Kent State* 741.5
KENT, ENGLAND
    Cadbury, Deborah. *The School That Escaped from the Nazis* 940.53
KENTUCKY
    Drury, Bob. *Blood and Treasure* .... B
    Morgan, Robert. *Boone* .... B
    Snyder, Christina. *Great Crossings* 976.9
    Wilkinson, Crystal. *Praisesong for the Kitchen Ghosts* 641.5975
KENYA
    Anderson, David. *Histories of the Hanged* 967.62
    Dinesen, Isak. *Out of Africa* 967.62
    Huxley, Elspeth Joscelin Grant. *The Flame Trees of Thika* .... B
    Leng'ete, Nice. *The Girls in the Wild Fig Tree* .... B
    Maathai, Wangari. *Unbowed* .... B
    McCormick, Ty. *Beyond the Sand and Sea* 920
    Ngugi wa Thiong'o. *In the House of the Interpreter* .... B
    Obama, Barack. ★*Dreams from My Father* .... B
    Rawlence, Ben. *City of Thorns* 967.7305
    Wainaina, Binyavanga. ★*How to Write About Africa* 814
    Wainaina, Binyavanga. *One Day I Will Write About This Place* .... B

KENYAN PEOPLE
    Ngugi wa Thiong'o. *In the House of the Interpreter* .... B
    Wainaina, Binyavanga. ★*How to Write About Africa* 814
    Wainaina, Binyavanga. *One Day I Will Write About This Place* .... B
Keown, Damien
    ★*A Dictionary of Buddhism* 294.3
KEPLER, JOHANNES, 1571-1630
    Fauber, L. S. *Heaven on Earth* .... B
Kepner, Tyler
    K 796.357
KERENSKY, ALEXANDER, 1881-1970
    Figes, Orlando. *A People's Tragedy* 947.08
    Mieville, China. *October* 947.084
KERKORIAN, KIRK, 1917-2015
    Rempel, William C. *The Gambler* .... B
Kerner, Ian
    She Comes First 613.9
Kerouac, Jack
    Book of Blues 811
    Book of Sketches, 1952-57 818
    Scattered Poems 811
    Selected Letters, 1940-1956 813
    ★*Some of the Dharma* 294.3
KEROUAC, JACK, 1922-1969
    Johnson, Joyce. *The Voice Is All* .... B
    Kerouac, Jack. *Book of Sketches, 1952-57* 818
    Kerouac, Jack. *Selected Letters, 1940-1956* 813
Kerpen, Dave
    Likeable Social Media 658.8
Kerr, Christopher
    Death Is but a Dream 155.9
Kerrison, Catherine
    Jefferson's Daughters 920
Kerry, John
    Every Day Is Extra .... B
KERRY, JOHN, 1943-
    Kerry, John. *Every Day Is Extra* .... B
Kersey, Geoff
    Painting Successful Watercolours from Photographs 751.42
Kershaw, Alex
    Against All Odds 940.54
    Avenue of Spies 940.53
    The Few 940.54
    The First Wave 940.54
Kershaw, Ian
    The Global Age 940.55
    Hitler .... B
    Hitler .... B
Kershenbaum, Arik
    The Zoologist's Guide to the Galaxy 576.8
Kershner, Isabel
    The Land of Hope and Fear 956.9405
Kertzer, David I.
    The Pope and Mussolini 322
    The Pope at War 940.53
    The Pope Who Would Be King 282.092
Kesling, Ben
    Bravo Company 958.104
Kessler, David
    Finding Meaning 155.9
Kessler, Lauren
    Raising the Barre 792.8
KESSLER, LAUREN
    Kessler, Lauren. *Raising the Barre* 792.8
Kessler-Harris, Alice
    ★*Out to Work* 331.4
Ketchum, Richard M.
    Saratoga 973.3
Kethledge, Raymond Michael
    Lead Yourself First 658.4
KETOGENIC DIET
    Dada, Samah. *Dada Eats Love to Cook It* 641.5
Keville, Kathi
    The Aromatherapy Garden 635.9
Key, Keegan-Michael
    ★*The History of Sketch Comedy* 792.2
Keyes, Corey L. M.
    ★*Languishing* 152.1

AUTHOR, TITLE, SERIES AND SUBJECT INDEX

KEYES, ISRAEL
    Callahan, Maureen. *American Predator*   364.152
Keynes, John Maynard
    ★*The General Theory of Employment, Interest, and Money*   330.15
KEYNES, JOHN MAYNARD, 1883-1946
    Conway, Edmund. *The Summit*   337.09
    Steil, Benn. *The Battle of Bretton Woods*   339.5
KEYS, ANCEL BENJAMIN, 1904-2004
    Tucker, Todd. *The Great Starvation Experiment*   174.2
KGB AGENTS
    Macintyre, Ben. ★*The Spy and the Traitor*   B
Khakpour, Porochista
    Brown Album   304.8
KHAKPOUR, POROCHISTA
    Khakpour, Porochista. *Brown Album*   304.8
Khalaf, Farida
    The Girl Who Escaped Isis   B
KHALAF, FARIDA
    Khalaf, Farida. *The Girl Who Escaped Isis*   B
Khalidi, Rashid
    ★*The Hundred Years' War on Palestine*   956.9405
Khalili, Nasser D.
    Islamic Art and Culture   709.1
KHAN FAMILY
    Seierstad, Asne. *The Bookseller of Kabul*   958.1
Khan, Asma
    Ammu   641.595
Khan, Mahvish Rukhsana
    My Guantanamo Diary   973.931
KHAN, NASSER ALI
    Satrapi, Marjane. *Chicken with Plums*   741.5
KHAN, NOOR INAYAT, 1914-1944
    Magida, Arthur J. *Code Name Madeleine*   940.54
Khan, Yasmin
    Ripe Figs   641.595
    ★*Zaitoun*   641.595
Khan, Yasmin Sabina
    Enlightening the World   974.7
Khar, Erin
    Strung Out   B
KHAR, ERIN
    Khar, Erin. *Strung Out*   B
Khemsurov, Monica
    How to Live with Objects   747
Khilnani, Sunil
    Incarnations   920
Khlevniuk, Oleg V.
    Stalin   B
Khodorkovsky, Mikhail
    The Russia Conundrum   947.086
KHOMEINI, RUHOLLAH, 1902-1989
    Nafisi, Azar. ★*Reading Lolita in Tehran*   B
Khrushchev. Taubman, William   B
KHRUSHCHEV, NIKITA SERGEEVICH, 1894-1971
    Carlson, Peter. *K Blows Top*   947.085
    Coleman, David G. *The Fourteenth Day*   973.922092
    Taubman, William. *Khrushchev*   B
Kick. Byrne, Paula   B
Kick Kennedy. Leaming, Barbara   B
The Kid. Bradlee, Ben   B
★***Kid Confidence.*** Kennedy-Moore, Eileen   155.4
Kid in the Kitchen. Clark, Melissa   641.5
Kidder, Tracy
    Good Prose   808.02
    ★*Rough Sleepers*   362.5
    A Truck Full of Money   B
KIDDER, TRACY
    Kidder, Tracy. *Good Prose*   808.02
The Kidnap Years. Stout, David   364.15
KIDNAPPING
    Delisle, Guy. *Hostage*   741.5
    Keefe, Patrick Radden. ★*Say Nothing*   364.152
    Macy, Beth. ★*Truevine*
    Moore, Michael Scott. *The Desert and the Sea*   364.15
    Narayan, R. K. ★*The Ramayana*   294.5
    Oelhafen, Ingrid von. *Hitler's Stolen Children*
    Standiford, Les. *Bringing Adam Home*   364.15
    Stout, David. *The Kidnap Years*   364.15

    Weinman, Sarah. *The Real Lolita*   362.88092
KIDNAPPING INVESTIGATION
    Cross, Kim. *In Light of All Darkness*   363.25
KIDNAPPING VICTIMS
    Cross, Kim. *In Light of All Darkness*   363.25
    Delisle, Guy. *Hostage*   741.5
    Matar, Hisham. *The Return*   B
    Moore, Michael Scott. *The Desert and the Sea*   364.15
    Standiford, Les. *Bringing Adam Home*   364.15
    Weinman, Sarah. *The Real Lolita*   362.88092
The Kids in the Hall. Myers, Paul   920
Kids' Books and Maker Activities. Cox, Marge   372.41
Kieffer, Sarah
    100 Morning Treats   641.5
    ★*Baking for the Holidays*   641.5
Kierkegaard, Soren
    Fear and Trembling   248
KIERKEGAARD, SOREN, 1813-1855
    Carlisle, Clare. *Philosopher of the Heart*   B
Kiernan, Denise
    The Girls of Atomic City   976.8
    The Last Castle   975.6
KIKUYU (AFRICAN PEOPLE)
    Maathai, Wangari. *Unbowed*   B
    Ngugi wa Thiong'o. *In the House of the Interpreter*   B
Kildea, Paul Francis
    Chopin's Piano   B
Kill 'Em and Leave. McBride, James   B
Kill Shot. Dearen, Jason   616.8
Killam, Kasley
    The Art and Science of Connection   302
The Killer Across the Table. Douglas, John E.   B
A Killer by Design. Burgess, Ann Wolbert   364.3
Killer Triggers. Kenda, Joe   364.152
KILLER WHALE
    Neiwert, David A. *Of Orcas and Men*   599.53
★***Killers of the Flower Moon.*** Grann, David   976.6004
KILLING (ETHICS)
    Wood, David Bowne. ★*What Have We Done*   616.85
Killing A King. Ephron, Dan   956.9405
Killing King. Wexler, Stuart   323.092
The Killing of Crazy Horse. Powers, Thomas   B
Killing the SS. O'Reilly, Bill   940.53
Kilmeade, Brian
    ★*Andrew Jackson and the Miracle of New Orleans*   973.5
    ★*George Washington's Secret Six*   973.4
    ★*Thomas Jefferson and the Tripoli Pirates*   973.4
Kilo. Muse, Toby   363.4509861
A Kim Jong-Il Production. Fischer, Paul   791.43
Kim, Anne
    ★*Abandoned*   305.2350973
    ★*Poverty for Profit*   302.5
Kim, Bill
    Korean BBQ   641.595
KIM, CHONG-IL, 1942-2011
    Demick, Barbara. ★*Nothing to Envy*   920
    Fischer, Paul. *A Kim Jong-Il Production*   791.43
    Jang, Jin-Sung. *Dear Leader*   B
KIM, CHONG-UN, 1984-
    Fifield, Anna. *The Great Successor*   B
    Jeppesen, Travis. *See You Again in Pyongyang*   951.93
    Lankov, A. N. *The Real North Korea*   951.9304
    Lee, Sung-Yoon. *The Sister*   951.93
    Pak, Jung H. *Becoming Kim Jong Un*   B
Kim, Eric
    ★*Korean American*   641.595
Kim, Hooni
    My Korea   641.595
KIM, IL-SONG, 1912-1994
    Demick, Barbara. ★*Nothing to Envy*   920
    Harden, Blaine. *The Great Leader and the Fighter Pilot*   B
    Lankov, A. N. *The Real North Korea*   951.9304
Kim, John
    Single on Purpose   155.6
Kim, Suki
    Without You, There Is No Us   B
KIM, SUKI, 1970-
    Kim, Suki. *Without You, There Is No Us*   B

PUBLIC LIBRARY CORE COLLECTION: NONFICTION
Twentieth Edition

Kim, W. Chan
  Blue Ocean Shift — 658.8
KIM, YO-JONG
  Lee, Sung-Yoon. *The Sister* — 951.93
Kimball, Christopher
  Christopher Kimball's Milk Street — 641.5
  Christopher Kimball's Milk Street — 641.5
  ★*Milk Street 365* — 641.5
  Milk Street — 641.5
  Milk Street — 641.5
  Milk Street — 641.7
  Tuesday Nights Mediterranean — 641.59
Kimball, George
  Four Kings — B
Kimberley, Hannah
  A Woman's Place Is at the Top — B
Kimble, Megan
  ★*City Limits* — 388.1
Kimmerer, Robin Wall
  ★*Braiding Sweetgrass* — 304.2
KIMMERER, ROBIN WALL
  Kimmerer, Robin Wall. ★*Braiding Sweetgrass* — 304.2
Kimmerle, Erin H.
  We Carry Their Bones — 365
KIMMERLE, ERIN H.
  Kimmerle, Erin H. *We Carry Their Bones* — 365
Kimmerling, Baruch
  The Palestinian People — 956.94
Kinch, David
  At Home in the Kitchen — 641.5973
Kinch, Michael S.
  Between Hope and Fear — 614.4
Kind of a Big Deal. Austerlitz, Saul — 791.43
KINDNESS
  Asika, Uju. *Bringing up Race* — 155.4
  Carcaterra, Lorenzo. *Three Dreamers* — B
  Coombes, Joshua. *Do Something for Nothing* — 362.5
  Evans, Rachel Held. *Wholehearted Faith* — 248.4
  Gup, Ted. *A Secret Gift* — 977.1
  Lamott, Anne. ★*Hallelujah Anyway* — 241
  Lickona, Thomas. *How to Raise Kind Kids* — 649
  Parker, Kate T. *Strong Is the New Pretty* — 155.43
  Velasquez, Lizzie. *Dare to Be Kind* — 177
  Weir, Laura. *Cosy* — 646.7009
  Zamora, Javier. ★*Solito* — B
Kindred. Wragg Sykes, Rebecca — 569.9
Kindsvatter, Peter S.
  American Soldiers — 355
★*King*. Eig, Jonathan — B
The King and Queen of Malibu. Randall, David K. — B
King Con. Willetts, Paul — B
King Hedley II. Wilson, August — 812
King John. Morris, Marc — 942.033
King Leopold's Ghost. Hochschild, Adam — 967.51
King of Ragtime. Berlin, Edward A. — B
★*The King of Sports*. Easterbrook, Gregg — 796.332
King of the World. Mansel, Philip — B
King Philip's War. Schultz, Eric B. — 973.2
KING PHILIP'S WAR, 1675-1676
  Lepore, Jill. *The Name of War* — 973.2
  Schultz, Eric B. *King Philip's War* — 973.2
  Silverman, David J. ★*This Land Is Their Land* — 974.4
King Richard. Dobbs, Michael — 973.924
King Solomon's Table. Nathan, Joan — 641.5
The King's Assassin. Woolley, Benjamin — B
The King's Shadow. Richardson, Edmund — 958.1
KING, ALBERTA WILLIAMS, 1904-1974
  Tubbs, Anna Malaika. *The Three Mothers* — 306.874
King, B. B.
  ★*Blues All Around Me* — B
KING, B. B.
  King, B. B. ★*Blues All Around Me* — B
King, Billie Jean
  ★*All In* — B
KING, BILLIE JEAN, 1943-
  King, Billie Jean. ★*All In* — B
King, Charles
  ★*Gods of the Upper Air* — 920
  Midnight at the Pera Palace — 949.61
  Odessa — 947.7
King, Charles Monroe
  A Journal for Jordan — 956.7044
KING, CHARLES MONROE, D. 2006
  King, Charles Monroe. *A Journal for Jordan* — 956.7044
King, Chrissy
  The Body Liberation Project — 306.4
King, Coretta Scott
  ★*My Life, My Love, My Legacy* — B
KING, CORETTA SCOTT, 1927-2006
  King, Coretta Scott. ★*My Life, My Love, My Legacy* — B
King, David
  Death in the City of Light — 364.152
  Six Days in August — 364.15
  The Trial of Adolf Hitler — 345.43
King, Dean
  Guardians of the Valley — 333.72
KING, ERNEST JOSEPH, 1878-1956
  Borneman, Walter R. *The Admirals* — B
King, Gilbert
  Beneath a Ruthless Sun — B
  ★*Devil in the Grove* — 305.896
King, Greg
  The Assassination of the Archduke — B
  The Ghost Forest — 333.75
  Nothing but the Night — 364.152
  Twilight of Empire — 943.6
KING, GREG (JOURNALIST)
  King, Greg. *The Ghost Forest* — 333.75
King, Kaiser, Tsar. Clay, Catrine — B
King, Maren Ellingboe
  Fresh Midwest — 641.5977
King, Martin Luther
  The Autobiography of Martin Luther King, Jr. — B
  ★*A Testament of Hope* — 323.1
  "Thou, Dear God" — 242
  Why We Can't Wait — 305.8
KING, MARTIN LUTHER, JR., 1929-1968
  Boyd, Herb. *We Shall Overcome* — 323.1196
  Branch, Taylor. ★*At Canaan's Edge* — 323.1196
  Branch, Taylor. *Parting the Waters* — 973
  Branch, Taylor. ★*Pillar of Fire* — 323.1
  Eig, Jonathan. ★*King* — B
  Honey, Michael K. *To the Promised Land* — 323
  Jackson, Troy. *Becoming King* — B
  Joseph, Peniel E. *The Sword and the Shield* — B
  King, Coretta Scott. ★*My Life, My Love, My Legacy* — B
  King, Martin Luther. *The Autobiography of Martin Luther King, Jr.* — B
  Kix, Paul. ★*You Have to Be Prepared to Die Before You Can Begin to Live* — 976.1
  Kotz, Nick. *Judgment Days* — 323
  Kurlansky, Mark. *1968* — 909.82
  Levingston, Steven. *Kennedy and King* — 920
  Lewis, John. ★*March; Book One* — 741.5
  Rosenbloom, Joseph. *Redemption* — B
  Sides, Hampton. *Hellhound on His Trail* — 364.152
  Sokol, Jason. *The Heavens Might Crack* — 323.092
  Tubbs, Anna Malaika. *The Three Mothers* — 306.874
  West, Cornel. *Black Prophetic Fire* — 920
  Wexler, Stuart. *Killing King* — 323.092
King, Maxwell
  The Good Neighbor — B
King, Niloufer Ichaporia
  My Bombay Kitchen — 641.595
King, Ross
  Bookseller of Florence — 381
  Brunelleschi's Dome — 726.6
  Florence — 759.5
  The Judgment of Paris — 759.4
  ★*Leonardo and the Last Supper* — 759.5
  ★*Mad Enchantment* — 759.4
  Michelangelo & the Pope's Ceiling — 759.5
King, Stephen
  On Writing — B
KING, STEPHEN, 1947-
  King, Stephen. *On Writing* — B

AUTHOR, TITLE, SERIES AND SUBJECT INDEX

King, Vanessa
   10 Keys to Happier Living   158
***Kingdom** of Characters*. Tsu, Jing   495.111
KINGDOM OF GOD
   Augustine. *Concerning the City of God Against the Pagans*   239
***Kingdom** of Play*. Toomey, David   591.56
*The **Kingdom** of Speech*. Wolfe, Tom   401
*A **Kingdom** Strange*. Horn, James P. P.   975.6
*The **Kingdom**, The Power, and the Glory*. Alberta, Tim   270.8
Kingdon, Amorina
   ★*Sing Like Fish*   591.77
*The **Kings** of Big Spring*. Mealer, Bryan   B
Kingsley, Lisa
   Smithsonian American Table   641.5
Kingsolver, Barbara
   ★*Animal, Vegetable, Miracle*   641
KINGSOLVER, BARBARA
   Kingsolver, Barbara. ★*Animal, Vegetable, Miracle*   641
Kingston, Genevieve
   Did I Ever Tell You?   B
KINGSTON, GENEVIEVE
   Kingston, Genevieve. *Did I Ever Tell You?*   B
KINGSTON, JAMAICA
   Chevannes, Barry. *Rastafari*   299
Kingston, Maxine Hong
   The Woman Warrior   B
KINGSTON, MAXINE HONG
   Kingston, Maxine Hong. *The Woman Warrior*   B
Kinnell, Galway
   Collected Poems   811
   A New Selected Poems   811
   Strong Is Your Hold   811
KINSEY, ANGELA, 1971-
   Fischer, Jenna. *The Office BFFs*   791.45
KINSHIP
   Swarns, Rachel L. ★*American Tapestry*   B
KINSHIP-BASED SOCIETY
   Ansary, Mir Tamim. *Games Without Rules*   958.1
   Hyde, Anne Farrar. *Empires, Nations, and Families*   978
   Mackintosh-Smith, Tim. *Arabs*   909.04
   McDonnell, Michael. *Masters of Empire*   977.4
Kinstler, Linda
   Come to This Court and Cry   940.53
Kinzer, Stephen
   ★*All the Shah's Men*   955.05
   Poisoner in Chief   B
   ★*The True Flag*   327.73
Kinzler, Katherine D.
   How You Say It   302.2
KIOWA (NORTH AMERICAN PEOPLE)
   Momaday, N. Scott. *Earth Keeper*   814
Kiper, Dasha
   ★*Travelers to Unimaginable Lands*   616.8
Kipling, Rudyard
   Complete Verse   821
Kirigami Menagerie. Hayakawa, Hiroshi   736.98
Kirkby, Bruce
   Blue Sky Kingdom   954.96
KIRKBY, BRUCE, 1968-
   Kirkby, Bruce. *Blue Sky Kingdom*   954.96
Kirsch, Adam
   The Blessing and the Curse   809
   ★*The People and the Books*   809
Kirschbaum, Erik
   Soccer Without Borders   B
Kirshner, Jodie Adams
   ★*Broke*   336.3
Kirtzman, Andrew
   Giuliani   B
Kiser, Joy M.
   America's Other Audubon   B
Kishimi, Ichiro
   The Courage to Be Disliked   158
Kisor, Henry
   Traveling with Service Animals   362.4
*The **Kissing** Bug*. Hernandez, Daisy   616.9
***Kissing** Girls on Shabbat*. Glass, Sara   B
Kissinger. Ferguson, Niall   973.924

Kissinger's Shadow. Grandin, Greg   B
Kissinger, Henry
   Ending the Vietnam War   959.704
   Leadership   303.3
KISSINGER, HENRY, 1923-2023
   Dallek, Robert. *Nixon and Kissinger*   B
   Ferguson, Niall. *Kissinger*   973.924
   Gewen, Barry. ★*The Inevitability of Tragedy*   B
   Grandin, Greg. *Kissinger's Shadow*   B
   Indyk, Martin. *Master of the Game*   327.73
Kissinger, Meg
   While You Were Out   362.2
KISSINGER, MEG
   Kissinger, Meg. *While You Were Out*   362.2
Kistler, Vivian Carli
   The Complete Photo Guide to Framing and Displaying Artwork   749
Kitagawa, Kate
   The Secret Lives of Numbers   510.9
★*Kitchen Confidential*. Bourdain, Anthony   B
KITCHEN GARDENS
   Obama, Michelle. *American Grown*   635.09
   Stuckey, Maggie. *The Container Victory Garden*   635.9
   Watkins, Julia. *Simply Living Well*   640
   Webb, Leah M. *The Seven-Step Homestead*   635
*A **Kitchen** in France*. Thorisson, Mimi   641.594
*The **Kitchen** Shortcut Bible*. Weinstein, Bruce   641.555
KITCHEN UTENSILS
   McKoy, Bri. *The Cook's Book*   641.3
Kitchen Yarns. Hood, Ann   641.5
Kitchen, Denis
   The Art of Harvey Kurtzman   741.5
Kitchenalia. Lee, Vinny   747.7
KITCHENS
   Brennan, Kathy. *Keepers*   641.5973
   Lee, Vinny. *Kitchenalia*   747.7
   Sheehan, Jason. *Cooking Dirty*   B
Kitmacher, Gary
   Space Stations   629.44
Kix, Paul
   The Saboteur   940.53
   ★*You Have to Be Prepared to Die Before You Can Begin to Live*   976.1
Kizzia, Tom
   Pilgrim's Wilderness   B
Kl. Wachsmann, Nikolaus   940.53
KLAAS, POLLY HANNAH, 1981-1993
   Cross, Kim. *In Light of All Darkness*   363.25
Klagsbrun, Francine
   Lioness   B
KLALLAM (NORTH AMERICAN PEOPLE)
   Myers, Leah. *Thinning Blood*   B
Klan War. Bordewich, Fergus M.   973.8
Klare, Michael T.
   All Hell Breaking Loose   355.20973
Klarman, Michael J.
   The Framers' Coup   342.7302
Klass, Perri
   A Good Time to Be Born   362.19892
Klastorin, Michael
   Close Encounters of the Third Kind   791.43
Klay, Phil
   Uncertain Ground   359.9
KLAY, PHIL
   Klay, Phil. *Uncertain Ground*   359.9
Kleiman, Kathy
   Proving Ground   4.092
Klein, Cheryl B.
   The Magic Words   808.06
Klein, Dini
   Prep + Rally   641.5
Klein, Ezra
   ★*Why We're Polarized*   306.0973
Klein, Jessi
   I'll Show Myself Out   B
KLEIN, JESSI, 1975-
   Klein, Jessi. *I'll Show Myself Out*   B
Klein, Naomi
   ★*Doppelganger*   302.2

PUBLIC LIBRARY CORE COLLECTION: NONFICTION
Twentieth Edition

KLEIN, NAOMI, 1970-
   Klein, Naomi. ★*Doppelganger* — 302.2
Klein, Tovah P.
   How Toddlers Thrive — 305.232
Klemperer, Victor
   I Will Bear Witness — B
KLEMPERER, VICTOR, 1881-1960
   Klemperer, Victor. *I Will Bear Witness* — B
KLEZMER MUSIC
   Strom, Yale. *The Book of Klezmer* — 781.62
KLIMCHUK, A. B. (ALEKSANDR BORISOVICH)
   Tabor, James M. *Blind Descent* — 796.52
Kline, Emily
   ★*The School of Hard Talks* — 155.5
Kline, Fred R.
   Leonardo's Holy Child — 741.09
Klinenberg, Eric
   ★*2020* — 306
KLINGENSMITH, FLORENCE
   O'Brien, Keith. *Fly Girls* — 920
KLINSMANN, JURGEN
   Kirschbaum, Erik. *Soccer Without Borders* — B
Klobuchar, Amy
   ★*Antitrust* — 343.73
KLONDIKE RIVER VALLEY, YUKON TERRITORY
   Castner, Brian. *Stampede* — 971.9
Kloosterboer, Lorena
   Painting in Acrylics — 751.42
Klopotenko, Yevhen
   ★*The Authentic Ukrainian Kitchen* — 641.594
Klosterman, Chuck
   But What If We're Wrong — 909.83
   ★*The Nineties* — 306.0973
Kluger, Jeffrey
   ★*Apollo 8* — 629.45
   The Narcissist Next Door — 616.85
Kluger, Richard
   Indelible Ink — B
KNAPP, CAROLINE, 1959-2002
   Caldwell, Gail. *Let's Take the Long Way Home* — B
Knausgaard, Karl Ove
   So Much Longing in so Little Space — 759.81
   Spring — B
KNAUSGAARD, KARL OVE, 1968-
   Knausgaard, Karl Ove. *Spring* — B
Kneale, Matthew
   Rome — 945.6
Kneece, Mark
   The Art of Comic Book Writing — 741.5
Kneeland, Jessi
   Body Neutral — 306.4
KNICKERBOCKER, H. R. (HUBERT RENFRO), 1898-1949
   Cohen, Deborah. *Last Call at the Hotel Imperial* — 070.92
★*Knife*. Rushdie, Salman — B
KNIGHT, CHRISTOPHER THOMAS, 1965-
   Finkel, Michael. *The Stranger in the Woods* — B
Knight, Erika
   500 Crochet Stitches — 746.43
   750 Knitting Stitches — 746.43
Knight, Keltie
   Lady Secrets — 305.4
Knight, Molly
   The Best Team Money Can Buy — 796.357
Knight, Philip H.
   Shoe Dog — B
KNIGHT, PHILIP H., 1938-
   Knight, Philip H. *Shoe Dog* — B
Knight, Sam
   The Premonitions Bureau — 133.8
Knight, Sarah
   *The Life-Changing Magic of Not Giving a F*ck* — 818
KNIGHTS AND KNIGHTHOOD
   Ackroyd, Peter. *The Death of King Arthur* — 823
   Asbridge, Thomas S. *The Greatest Knight* — 942.03
   Jones, Michael K. *The Black Prince* — B
   Malory, Thomas. *Le Morte Darthur, Or, the Hoole Book of Kyng Arthur and of His Noble Knyghtes of the Rounde Table* — 823
Knit 2 Socks in 1. Talley, Safiyyah — 746.43

Knit Fix. Kartus, Lisa — 746.43
Knit Wear Love. Herzog, Amy — 746.43
★*The Knitter's Book of Knowledge*. Bliss, Debbie — 746.43
The Knitter's Book of Yarn. Parkes, Clara — 677
The Knitter's Companion. Square, Vicki — 746.432
The Knitter's Dictionary. Atherley, Kate — 746.43
The Knitter's Handy Book of Top-Down Sweaters. Budd, Ann — 746.43
KNITTERS
   Orenstein, Peggy. *Unraveling* — B
KNITTING
   Atherley, Kate. *The Knitter's Dictionary* — 746.43
   Bassetti, Amanda. *Arm Knitting* — 746.43
   Bernard, Wendy. *Up, Down, All-Around Stitch Dictionary* — 746.43
   Bestor, Leslie Ann. *Cast On, Bind Off* — 746.432
   Bliss, Debbie. ★*The Knitter's Book of Knowledge* — 746.43
   Budd, Ann. *The Knitter's Handy Book of Top-Down Sweaters* — 746.43
   Budd, Ann. *New Directions in Sock Knitting* — 746.43
   Budd, Ann. *Sock Knitting Master Class* — 746.43
   Corwin, Lena. *Lena Corwin's Made by Hand* — 746.6
   Dassau, Jennifer. *Knitting Short Rows* — 746.43
   Durant, Judith. *Cable Left, Cable Right* — 746.43
   Durant, Judith. *Increase, Decrease* — 746.43
   Epstein, Nicky. *Nicky Epstein, the Essential Edgings Collection* — 746.43
   Gaughan, Norah. *Norah Gaughan's Knitted Cable Sourcebook* — 746.43
   Herzog, Amy. *Knit Wear Love* — 746.43
   Herzog, Amy. *You Can Knit That* — 746.432
   Hiatt, June. *The Principles of Knitting* — 746.43
   Huff, Mary Scott. *The Mitten Handbook* — 746.43
   Impelen, Helgrid van. *Big Knits Big Needles* — 746.43
   Kartus, Lisa. *Knit Fix* — 746.43
   Knight, Erika. *750 Knitting Stitches* — 746.43
   Leapman, Melissa. *Mastering Color Knitting* — 746.43
   Ludwig, Frauke. *Essential Knit Sweaters* — 746.43
   Melville, Sally. *Knitting Pattern Essentials* — 746.43
   Newton, Deborah. *Finishing School* — 746.43
   Nico, Brooke. *More Lovely Knitted Lace* — 746.43
   Noldeke, Marisa. *50 Knitted Wraps and Shawls* — 746.43
   Orenstein, Peggy. *Unraveling* — B
   Parkes, Clara. *The Knitter's Book of Yarn* — 677
   Phelps, Isela. *Loom Knitting Primer* — 746.43
   Radcliffe, Margaret. *Circular Knitting Workshop* — 746.43
   Radcliffe, Margaret. *The Knitting Answer Book* — 746.43
   Radcliffe, Margaret. *The Knowledgeable Knitter* — 746.43
   Righetti, Maggie. *Knitting in Plain English* — 746.432
   Shida, Hitomi. *Japanese Knitting Stitch Bible* — 746.43
   Spainhower, Courtney. *Elemental Knits* — 746.43
   Square, Vicki. *The Knitter's Companion* — 746.432
   Stanfield, Lesley. *100 Flowers to Knit & Crochet* — 746.43
   Stoller, Debbie. *Stitch 'N Bitch Superstar Knitting* — 746.43
   Stoller, Debbie. ★*Stitch 'N Bitch* — 746.43
   Storey, Martin. *Easy Fair Isle Knitting* — 746.43
   Talley, Safiyyah. *Knit 2 Socks in 1* — 746.43
   Turner, Sharon. *Teach Yourself Visually Knitting* — 746.43
   Weil, Anne. *Knitting Without Needles* — 746.43
   Wood, Jennifer. *Refined Knits* — 746.43
   Zimmermann, Elizabeth. ★*Knitting Without Tears* — 746.4
The Knitting Answer Book. Radcliffe, Margaret — 746.43
Knitting in Plain English. Righetti, Maggie — 746.432
Knitting Pattern Essentials. Melville, Sally — 746.43
Knitting Short Rows. Dassau, Jennifer — 746.43
Knitting Without Needles. Weil, Anne — 746.43
★*Knitting Without Tears*. Zimmermann, Elizabeth — 746.4
★*A Knock At Midnight*. Barnett, Brittany K. — B
Knockout. Kang, Mia — B
Knoedelseder, William
   Bitter Brew — 338.7
Knoll, Debra J.
   Engaging Babies in the Library — 027.62
Knot Bad Amigurumi. Green-Hite, Vincent — 746.43
Know My Name. Miller, Chanel — B
Knowing What We Know. Winchester, Simon — 306.4
KNOWLEDGE
   Friedman, Ron. *Decoding Greatness* — 650.1
   Garfield, Simon. ★*All the Knowledge in the World* — 030.9
   Gladwell, Malcolm. *Blink* — 153.4
   Kalder, Daniel. *The Infernal Library* — 321.9
   Livio, Mario. *Why?* — 153.3
   Winchester, Simon. *Knowing What We Know* — 306.4

AUTHOR, TITLE, SERIES AND SUBJECT INDEX

Wright, Alex. *Cataloging the World* — 020.9
The ***Knowledge*** *Machine*. Strevens, Michael — 500
KNOWLEDGE MANAGEMENT
   Garfield, Simon. ★*All the Knowledge in the World* — 030.9
   Shapiro, Scott J. ★*Fancy Bear Goes Phishing* — 364.16
   Winchester, Simon. *Knowing What We Know* — 306.4
The ***Knowledgeable*** *Knitter*. Radcliffe, Margaret — 746.43
Koba *The Dread*. Amis, Martin — 947.084
Kobabe, Maia
   Gender Queer — 741.5
KOBABE, MAIA
   Kobabe, Maia. *Gender Queer* — 741.5
KOBER ALICE, 1906-1950
   Fox, Margalit. *The Riddle of the Labyrinth* — 920
Kobliner, Beth
   Make Your Kid a Money Genius (even If You're Not) — 332.024
Koch, Bea
   Mad and Bad — 920
KOCH, CHARLES G. (CHARLES DE GANAHL), 1935-
   Leonard, Christopher. *Kochland* — 338.7
   Mayer, Jane. ★*Dark Money* — 973.932
KOCH, DAVID H., 1940-2019
   Mayer, Jane. ★*Dark Money* — 973.932
Koch, Stephen
   The Modern Library Writer's Workshop — 808.3
Kochilas, Diane
   The Ikaria Way — 641.5
Kochland. Leonard, Christopher — 338.7
KOECHNER, KAREL
   Cunningham, Benjamin. *The Liar* — 327.1273
Koenig, Joan
   The Musical Child — 780.71
KOENIG, JOAN
   Koenig, Joan. *The Musical Child* — 780.71
Koenig, Leah
   Portico — 641.5
Koh, EJ
   The Magical Language of Others — 813
KOH, EJ, 1988-
   Koh, EJ. *The Magical Language of Others* — 813
Kohan, Rafi
   The Arena — 796.06
   ★*Trash Talk* — 179
Kohli, Sahaj Kaur
   ★*But What Will People Say?* — 616.89
Kois, Dan
   How to Be a Family — 910.4
KOIS, DAN
   Kois, Dan. *How to Be a Family* — 910.4
Kolata, Gina Bari
   Mercies in Disguise — 616
Kolbert, Elizabeth
   Field Notes from a Catastrophe — 363.738
   ★*Under a White Sky* — 304.2
Kolbert, Kathryn
   Controlling Women — 362.1988
Kolhatkar, Sheelah
   Black Edge — 364.16
KOLKATA, INDIA
   Brierley, Saroo. *A Long Way Home* — B
Kolker, Robert
   ★*Hidden Valley Road* — 920
Kolker, Robert Phillip
   Kubrick — B
Komunyakaa, Yusef
   The Chameleon Couch — 811
   ★*Everyday Mojo Songs of Earth* — 811
   Warhorses — 811
Kondo, Marie
   ★*The Life-Changing Magic of Tidying Up* — 648
   ★*Marie Kondo's Kurashi at Home* — 648
   ★*Spark Joy* — 648
KONDO, MARIE
   Knight, Sarah. *The Life-Changing Magic of Not Giving a F*ck* — 818
Kongtrul, Dzigar
   Peaceful Heart — 294.3
Konnikova, Maria
   The Biggest Bluff — 795.412

Mastermind — 153.4
KONNIKOVA, MARIA
   Konnikova, Maria. *The Biggest Bluff* — 795.412
Koones, Sheri
   Prefabulous Small Houses — 728
Kooser, Ted
   Delights & Shadows — 811
KOOTENAI (KTUNAXA) (NORTH AMERICAN PEOPLE)
   Streep, Abe. *Brothers on Three* — 306.85
Koppel, Lily
   The Astronaut Wives Club — 920
The ***Koran***. Cook, M. A. — 297.122
Korda, Michael
   Alone — 940.54
   Clouds of Glory — B
   Muse of Fire — 940.4
   With Wings Like Eagles — 940.54
KORDA, MICHAEL, 1933-
   Korda, Michael. *Alone* — 940.54
KOREA
   Hutton, Robin L. *Sgt. Reckless* — 951.904
   Kang, Mingoo. *Jang* — 641.595
   Sides, Hampton. *On Desperate Ground* — 951.904
   ★*Korean American*. Kim, Eric — 641.595
KOREAN AMERICAN CHILDREN
   Chung, Nicole. ★*A Living Remedy* — B
KOREAN AMERICAN FAMILIES
   Hong, Cathy Park. *Minor Feelings* — 305.48
KOREAN AMERICAN MEN
   Chee, Alexander. ★*How to Write an Autobiographical Novel* — B
KOREAN AMERICAN WOMEN
   Cho, Grace M. *Tastes Like War* — 305.48
   Chung, Nicole. *All You Can Ever Know* — B
KOREAN AMERICANS
   Chang, David. ★*Eat a Peach* — 641.5
   Gaines, Joanna. *The Stories We Tell* — B
   Hahn, Emanuel. *Koreatown Dreaming* — 979.4
   Howe, Ben Ryder. *My Korean Deli* — B
   Hu, Elise. *Flawless* — 646.7
   Jun, Tasha. ★*Tell Me the Dream Again* — 248
   Lee, Helie. *In the Absence of Sun* — B
   Zauner, Michelle. ★*Crying in H Mart* — B
   Korean BBQ. Kim, Bill — 641.595
   Korean Food Made Simple. Joo, Judy — 641.595
KOREAN PEOPLE
   Gaines, Joanna. *The Stories We Tell* — B
   Hahn, Emanuel. *Koreatown Dreaming* — 979.4
   Jun, Tasha. ★*Tell Me the Dream Again* — 248
   Sehee, Baek. *I Want to Die but I Want to Eat Tteokbokki* — B
   ★The ***Korean*** *Vegan Cookbook*. Lee Molinaro, Joanne — 641.595
The ***Korean*** *War*. Cumings, Bruce — 951.904
KOREAN WAR, 1950-1953
   Brady, James. *The Coldest War* — B
   Brands, H. W. *The General vs. the President* — 973.918092
   Choi, Don Mee. *DMZ Colony* — 818
   Cumings, Bruce. *The Korean War* — 951.904
   Halberstam, David. *The Coldest Winter* — 951.904
   Hutton, Robin L. *Sgt. Reckless* — 951.904
   Makos, Adam. *Devotion* — 920
   Petraeus, David Howell. *Conflict* — 355
   Roll, David L. *George Marshall* — B
   Sides, Hampton. *On Desperate Ground* — 951.904
   Koreatown. Hong, Deuki — 641.595
   Koreatown Dreaming. Hahn, Emanuel — 979.4
KORESH, DAVID, 1959-1993
   Cook, Kevin. *Waco Rising* — 299
Korkosz, Michal
   Fresh from Poland — 641.594
Kornacki, Steve
   The Red and the Blue — 306.20973
Kornfield, Jack
   The Wise Heart — 294.3
Kornhauser, Jacob
   The Cup of Coffee Club — 796.357
KORNILOV, LAVR GEORGIEVICH, 1870-1918
   Mieville, China. *October* — 947.084
KOSHER FOOD
   Apfelbaum, Chanie. ★*Totally Kosher* — 641.5

PUBLIC LIBRARY CORE COLLECTION: NONFICTION
Twentieth Edition

Guetta, Benedetta Jasmine. *Cooking Alla Giudia* — 641.5
Ricanati, Elizabeth. *Braided* — B
Roden, Claudia. ★*The Book of Jewish Food* — 641.5
Solomonov, Michael. *Israeli Soul* — 641.595
★*Kosher Living*. Isaacs, Ronald H. — 296.7
★*Koshersoul*. Twitty, Michael — 641.5
Kostigen, Thomas
  Hacking Planet Earth — 628
Kot, Greg
  I'll Take You There — B
Kotite, Erika
  She Sheds — 728
Kotkin, Stephen
  Stalin — B
  Stalin — B
Kotlikoff, Laurence J.
  Money Magic — 332.024
Kotz, Nick
  Judgment Days — 323
Kouchner, Camille
  The Familia Grande — B
KOUCHNER, CAMILLE, 1975-
  Kouchner, Camille. *The Familia Grande* — B
KOUFAX, SANDY, 1935-
  Leavy, Jane. *Sandy Koufax* — B
Kowal-Connelly, Suanne
  Parenting Through Puberty — 649
Kowalsky, Michelle
  Creating Inclusive Library Environments — 027.6
Kozinn, Allan
  The McCartney Legacy — B
KOZOL, HARRY L., 1906-2008
  Kozol, Jonathan. *The Theft of Memory* — B
Kozol, Jonathan
  ★*An End to Inequality* — 379.2
  Fire in the Ashes — 362.77
  Letters to a Young Teacher — 371.1
  Rachel and Her Children — 362.5
  The Theft of Memory — B
KOZOL, JONATHAN
  Kozol, Jonathan. *Letters to a Young Teacher* — 371.1
  Kozol, Jonathan. *The Theft of Memory* — B
KRAFT, ROBERT
  Benedict, Jeff. *The Dynasty* — 796.332
Krakauer, Jon
  Classic Krakauer — 814
  Into the Wild — 917.9804
  ★*Into Thin Air* — 796.52
  Missoula — 362.883
KRAKAUER, JON
  Krakauer, Jon. ★*Into Thin Air* — 796.52
Kram, Mark
  Smokin' Joe — B
Kramer, Andrea S.
  Breaking Through Bias — 650.1
Kramer, Clara
  Clara's War — B
KRAMER, CLARA
  Kramer, Clara. *Clara's War* — B
Kramer, Peter D.
  ★*Ordinarily Well* — 615.7
Kranish, Michael
  Trump Revealed — B
  The World's Fastest Man — B
Krass, Peter
  Carnegie — B
KRATZ, ERIK
  Brown, Tim. ★*The Tao of the Backup Catcher* — 796.357
Kraus, Dita
  A Delayed Life — B
KRAUS, DITA, 1929-
  Kraus, Dita. *A Delayed Life* — B
KRAUS, ELEANOR, 1903-1989
  Pressman, Steven. *50 Children* — 940.53
KRAUS, GILBERT, 1897-1975
  Pressman, Steven. *50 Children* — 940.53
Krause, Johannes
  A Short History of Humanity — 599.9

Krauss, Lawrence Maxwell
  The Greatest Story Ever Told—So Far — 530.01
Krauzer, Steven M.
  Kayaking — 797.1
Kraybill, Donald B.
  Concise Encyclopedia of Amish, Brethren, Hutterites, and Mennonites — 289.7
  ★*On the Backroad to Heaven* — 289.7
Krazy. Tisserand, Michael — 741.5
KRAZY KAT (COMIC STRIP)
  Tisserand, Michael. *Krazy* — 741.5
Kreeft, Peter
  ★*Philosophy 101 by Socrates* — 183
Kriegel, Mark
  Pistol — B
Krieger, Ellie
  You Have It Made! — 641.5
Krimstein, Ken
  When I Grow Up — 741.5
Krishna, Priya
  ★*Indian-ish* — 641.595
Kriss, Alexander
  Borderline — 616.85
KRISS, ALEXANDER
  Kriss, Alexander. *Borderline* — 616.85
Krist, Gary
  Empire of Sin — 976.3
  The Mirage Factory — 920
  The White Cascade — 979.7
KRISTALLNACHT, 1938
  Frenkel, Francoise. *A Bookshop in Berlin* — B
Kristof, Nicholas D.
  ★*Chasing Hope* — B
  Half the Sky — 362.83
  ★*Tightrope* — 306.0973
KRISTOF, NICHOLAS D., 1959-
  Kristof, Nicholas D. ★*Chasing Hope* — B
Kritzler, Ed
  Jewish Pirates of the Caribbean — 972.9
Kriwaczek, Paul
  Babylon — 935
Kroeber, Theodora
  Ishi in Two Worlds — B
Kroeger, Brooke
  Undaunted — 070.4
Kroger, Lisa
  Monster, She Wrote — 920
Kroll, Andy
  A Death on W Street — 364.152
Kross, Ethan
  ★*Chatter* — 158.1
Krouse, Erika
  ★*Tell Me Everything* — 363.25
KROUSE, ERIKA
  Krouse, Erika. ★*Tell Me Everything* — 363.25
Krug, Nora
  ★*Belonging* — 741.5
KRUG, NORA
  Krug, Nora. ★*Belonging* — 741.5
Krugman, Paul R.
  Arguing with Zombies — 330.973
Kruse, Kevin Michael
  Fault Lines — 973.92
Kruzan, Sara
  I Cried to Dream Again — B
KRUZAN, SARA, 1978-
  Kruzan, Sara. *I Cried to Dream Again* — B
KRZYZEWSKI, MIKE
  O'Connor, Ian. *Coach K* — B
Kubler-Ross, Elisabeth
  Life Lessons — 170
  ★*On Death and Dying* — 155.9
Kubrick. Kolker, Robert Phillip — B
KUBRICK, STANLEY
  Benson, Michael. *Space Odyssey* — 791.43
KUBRICK, STANLEY, 1928-1999
  D'Alessandro, Emilio. *Stanley Kubrick and Me* — 791.4302
  Kolker, Robert Phillip. *Kubrick* — B

AUTHOR, TITLE, SERIES AND SUBJECT INDEX

Kugel, James L.
   The Great Shift   296.3
Kugel, Seth
   Rediscovering Travel   306.4
KUGEL, SETH
   Kugel, Seth. *Rediscovering Travel*   306.4
Kugle, Scott Alan
   Living Out Islam   297
Kugler, Rob
   A Dog Named Beautiful   B
KUGLER, ROB
   Kugler, Rob. *A Dog Named Beautiful*   B
Kuhn, Cynthia
   Buzzed   362.29
Kulaga, Agatha
   Ovenly   641.81
Kumar, Priyanka
   Conversations with Birds   598
KUMAR, PRIYANKA, 1973-
   Kumar, Priyanka. *Conversations with Birds*   598
Kumihimo. Combs, Rebecca Ann   745.594
Kundera, Milan
   ★*The Curtain*   801
   Encounter   809
Kunetka, James W.
   The General and the Genius   355.8
KUNG FU
   Hendrix, Grady. *These Fists Break Bricks*   791
Kung, Hans
   Great Christian Thinkers   230
Kunitz, Stanley
   ★*The Collected Poems*   811
Kuo, Michelle
   Reading with Patrick   B
KUO, MICHELLE
   Kuo, Michelle. *Reading with Patrick*   B
KUPCHYNSKY, STEPHANIE
   Rear, Rachel. *Catch the Sparrow*   364.152
Kuper, Adam
   The Museum of Other People   305.8
Kuper, Simon
   Soccernomics   796.334
KUPPERMAN, JOEL
   Kupperman, Michael. *All the Answers*   741.5
Kupperman, Michael
   All the Answers   741.5
Kurcinka, Mary Sheedy
   Raising Your Spirited Baby   306.874
KURDS
   Azad. *Long Shot*   B
   Lemmon, Gayle Tzemach. *The Daughters of Kobani*   956.9104
   Sabar, Ariel. *My Father's Paradise*   B
KURITA, TAKEO, 1889-1977
   Thomas, Evan. *Sea of Thunder*   940.54
Kurkjian, Tim
   I'm Fascinated by Sacrifice Flies   796.357
Kurlansky, Mark
   1968   909.82
   The Basque History of the World   946
   Birdseye   B
   Cod   333.95
   The Eastern Stars   796.357
   Havana   972.91
   Milk!   637
   Paper   676
   Salt   553.6
KURLANSKY, MARK
   Kurlansky, Mark. *Havana*   972.91
Kurosawa, Akira
   Something Like an Autobiography   B
KUROSAWA, AKIRA, 1910-1998
   Kurosawa, Akira. *Something Like an Autobiography*   B
Kurson, Robert
   Pirate Hunters   910.91
   ★*Rocket Men*   629.45
Kurt Vonnegut. Vonnegut, Kurt   813
Kurtz, Glenn
   Three Minutes in Poland   947.7

KURTZ, GLENN
   Kurtz, Glenn. *Three Minutes in Poland*   947.7
Kurtz, Howard
   Media Madness   973.933
Kurtz-Phelan, Daniel
   The China Mission   951.04
KURTZMAN, HARVEY
   Kitchen, Denis. *The Art of Harvey Kurtzman*   741.5
Kurutz, Steven
   American Flannel   338.4
Kurzweil, Ray
   ★*The Singularity Is Near*   153.9
KUSHNER FAMILY
   Bernstein, Andrea. *American Oligarchs*   920
Kushner, Harold S.
   How Good Do We Have to Be?   296.7
   Overcoming Life's Disappointments   296.7
   When Bad Things Happen to Good People   296.3
   Who Needs God   296.7
Kushner, Jacob
   Look Away   305.9
KUSHNER, JARED, 1981-
   Bernstein, Andrea. *American Oligarchs*   920
Kushner, Tony
   Angels in America   812
KUSHNER, TONY
   Butler, Isaac. *The World Only Spins Forward*   812
Kwak, James
   Economism   330
Kweli, Talib
   Vibrate Higher   B
KWELI, TALIB
   Kweli, Talib. *Vibrate Higher*   B
Kyle, Taya
   American Spirit   B
KYLE, TAYA, 1974-
   Kyle, Taya. *American Spirit*   B
KYOTO, JAPAN
   Iyer, Pico. *The Lady and the Monk*   952
Kysar, Alana
   Aloha Kitchen   641.59969
Kytle, Ethan J.
   Denmark Vesey's Garden   975.7

L

Laar, Arnold van de
   Under the Knife   617
★*Lab Girl*. Jahren, Hope   B
A Lab of One's Own. Colwell, Rita R.   B
LABOR DISPUTES
   Berfield, Susan. *The Hour of Fate*   973.91
   Lobel, Orly. *You Don't Own Me*   346.7304
   Nolan, Hamilton. *The Hammer*   331.8
LABOR ECONOMICS
   Piketty, Thomas. ★*Capital in the Twenty-First Century*   332
LABOR EXPLOITATION
   Chang, Gordon H. *Ghosts of Gold Mountain*   331.6
   Ditmore, Melissa Hope. ★*Unbroken Chains*   306.74
   Hardy, Alyssa. *Worn Out*   338.4
   Sedgewick, Augustine. *Coffeeland*   338.4
   Sorvino, Chloe. *Raw Deal*   338.1
Labor in America. Dubofsky, Melvyn   331.880973
LABOR LAWS AND LEGISLATION
   McShane Wulfhart, Nell. *The Great Stewardess Rebellion*   331.4
   Nolan, Hamilton. *The Hammer*   331.8
   Sack, Steven Mitchell. *The Employee Rights Handbook*   344.7301
   Steingold, Fred S. *The Employer's Legal Handbook, 16th Ed.*   344.7301
   Von Drehle, Dave. ★*Triangle*   974.7
LABOR LEADERS
   Bradley, Mark A. *Blood Runs Coal*   B
   Nolan, Hamilton. *The Hammer*   331.8
   Pawel, Miriam. *The Crusades of Cesar Chavez*   B
LABOR MOVEMENT
   Dubofsky, Melvyn. *Labor in America*   331.880973
   Hochschild, Adam. *American Midnight*   973.91
   Johnson, Steven. *The Infernal Machine*   335

McAlevey, Jane. *A Collective Bargain*	331.890973
Monforton, Celeste. *On the Job*	331.1
Murolo, Priscilla. *From the Folks Who Brought You the Weekend*	331
Nolan, Hamilton. *The Hammer*	331.8
Pawel, Miriam. *The Crusades of Cesar Chavez*	B

LABOR ORGANIZERS
Berfield, Susan. *The Hour of Fate*	973.91
Monforton, Celeste. *On the Job*	331.1
Worley, Jennifer. *Neon Girls*	792.7

LABOR ORGANIZING
Monforton, Celeste. *On the Job*	331.1

LABOR POLICY
Monforton, Celeste. *On the Job*	331.1
Nolan, Hamilton. *The Hammer*	331.8
Senik, Troy. *A Man of Iron*	B

LABOR PRODUCTIVITY
Price, Devon. ★*Laziness Does Not Exist*	158.1
Warzel, Charlie. *Out of Office*	658.3
Zomorodi, Manoush. *Bored and Brilliant*	153.3

LABOR RIGHTS
Canellos, Peter S. *The Great Dissenter*	B

LABOR SUPPLY
Kelley, Blair Murphy. *Black Folk*	331.6

LABOR UNIONS
Bradley, Mark A. *Blood Runs Coal*	B
Bruck, Connie. *When Hollywood Had a King*	B
Dubofsky, Melvyn. *Labor in America*	331.880973
Hardy, Alyssa. *Worn Out*	338.4
Levy, Jonathan. *Ages of American Capitalism*	330.12
McAlevey, Jane. *A Collective Bargain*	331.890973
McShane Wulfhart, Nell. *The Great Stewardess Rebellion*	331.4
Monforton, Celeste. *On the Job*	331.1
Nolan, Hamilton. *The Hammer*	331.8
Pawel, Miriam. *The Crusades of Cesar Chavez*	B
Slade, Rachel. *American Hoodie*	338.4
Smith, Sam. *Hard Labor*	796.323
Worley, Jennifer. *Neon Girls*	792.7
Zieger, Robert H. *American Workers, American Unions, 4th Ed.*	331.88

LABOR-MANAGEMENT RELATIONS
Arsenault, Kerri. *Mill Town*	B
Green, Hardy. *The Company Town*	307.76
Wartzman, Rick. *Still Broke*	381

LABORATORIES
Schlosser, Eric. *Command and Control*	363.17

LABRADOR RETRIEVERS
Grogan, John. ★*Marley & Me*	636.752
Kugler, Rob. *A Dog Named Beautiful*	B

Labyrinth of Ice. Levy, Buddy — 910.91

LACE AND LACE MAKING
Wood, Jennifer. *Refined Knits*	746.43

Lacerda, Daniel
2,100 Asanas	613.7

Lacey, Robert
Great Tales from English History 1	941
Great Tales from English History 2	941
Great Tales from English History 3	941
Inside the Kingdom	953.805

LACEY, ROBERT
Lacey, Robert. *Inside the Kingdom*	953.805

LACKS, HENRIETTA, 1920-1951
Skloot, Rebecca. ★*The Immortal Life of Henrietta Lacks*	B

Lacovara, Kenneth
Why Dinosaurs Matter	567.9

LACROSSE
Hinkson, Jim. *Lacrosse for Dummies*	796.34

Lacrosse for Dummies. Hinkson, Jim — 796.34

Ladau, Emily
Demystifying Disability	305.9

Ladies Get Paid. Wasserman, Claire — 650.1
Ladies of Liberty. Roberts, Cokie — 920

LADIES-IN-WAITING
Glenconner, Anne. ★*Lady in Waiting*	B

Ladner, Mark
The Del Posto Cookbook	641.594

The Lady and Her Monsters. Montillo, Roseanne — 823
The Lady and the Monk. Iyer, Pico — 952
The Lady and the Panda. Croke, Vicki — 599.789
Lady Bird Johnson. Gillette, Michael L. — B
Lady Bird Johnson. Sweig, Julia — B
Lady Death. Pavlychenko, Liudmyla Mykhailivna — B
Lady First. Greenberg, Amy S. — B
The Lady from the Black Lagoon. O'Meara, Mallory — 921
The Lady in the Tower. Weir, Alison — B
★*Lady in Waiting*. Glenconner, Anne — B
Lady Justice. Lithwick, Dahlia — 345.73
Lady Romeo. Wojczuk, Tana — B
Lady Secrets. Knight, Keltie — 305.4
The Lady's Handbook for Her Mysterious Illness. Ramey, Sarah — B
Ladyparts. Copaken, Deborah — B

LAFAYETTE, MARIE JOSEPH PAUL YVES ROCH GILBERT DU MOTIER, MARQUIS DE, 1757-1834
Duncan, Michael. ★*Hero of Two Worlds*	B
Gaines, James R. *For Liberty and Glory*	B
Philbrick, Nathaniel. ★*In the Hurricane's Eye*	973.3

LaFollette, Marcel C.
Writing for Their Lives	071.3

LaGarde, Jennifer
Fact vs. Fiction	370.15

Lagasse, Emeril
Essential Emeril	641.5

Lagom. Dunne, Linnea — 158.1

Lahey, Jessica
The Addiction Inoculation	649
The Gift of Failure	649

Lahey, Jim
The Sullivan Street Bakery Cookbook	641.81

Lahiri, Jhumpa
In Other Words	B
Translating Myself and Others	418

LAHIRI, JHUMPA
Lahiri, Jhumpa. *In Other Words*	B
Lahiri, Jhumpa. *Translating Myself and Others*	418

Lahn, Bussho
Singing and Dancing Are the Voice of the Law	294.3

Lahti, Christine
True Stories from an Unreliable Eyewitness	B

LAHTI, CHRISTINE
Lahti, Christine. *True Stories from an Unreliable Eyewitness*	B

Laing, Olivia
Everybody	323
The Garden Against Time	635
★*The Lonely City*	700.1

LAING, OLIVIA
Laing, Olivia. *The Garden Against Time*	635
Laing, Olivia. ★*The Lonely City*	700.1

LAKE DISTRICT (ENGLAND)
Lear, Linda J. *Beatrix Potter*	B
Rebanks, James. *The Shepherd's Life*	942.7

LAKE ECOLOGY
Dennis, Jerry. *The Living Great Lakes*	977
Egan, Dan. ★*The Death and Life of the Great Lakes*	577.6

Lake Michigan. Borzutzky, Daniel — 811

Lake, Dianne
Member of the Family	364.152

LAKE, DIANNE
Lake, Dianne. *Member of the Family*	364.152

LAKES
Egan, Dan. ★*The Death and Life of the Great Lakes*	577.6

LAKOTA (NORTH AMERICAN PEOPLE)
Black Elk. *Black Elk Speaks*	B
Gardner, Mark L. *The Earth Is All That Lasts*	978.004
Jackson, Joe. *Black Elk*	978.004
Long Soldier, Layli. ★*Whereas*	811

Lakshmi, Padma
The Encyclopedia of Spices and Herbs	641.3
Love, Loss, and What We Ate	791.4502

LAKSHMI, PADMA
Lakshmi, Padma. *Love, Loss, and What We Ate*	791.4502

Lal, Ruby
Empress	B

Lalami, Laila
Conditional Citizens	323.60973

LALAMI, LAILA, 1968-
Lalami, Laila. *Conditional Citizens*	323.60973

Lalkhen, Abdul-Ghaaliq
An Anatomy of Pain	616

AUTHOR, TITLE, SERIES AND SUBJECT INDEX

LAMAR, KENDRICK, 1987-
   Moore, Marcus J. *The Butterfly Effect* — B
LAMAR, LACEY
   Ruffin, Amber. ★*The World Record Book of Racist Stories* — 305.896
   Ruffin, Amber. *You'll Never Believe What Happened to Lacey* — 305.896
LAMARR, HEDY, 1913-2000
   Rhodes, Richard. *Hedy's Folly* — B
   Shearer, Stephen Michael. *Beautiful* — B
Lamas, Daniela J.
   You Can Stop Humming Now — 616.02
Lamb, Christina
   House of Stone — 968.91
   Our Bodies, Their Battlefields — 341.6
Lamb, Kelli
   Home with Rue — 747
Lambert, David
   The Field Guide to Geology — 550
Lambert, Malcolm
   God's Armies — 956
Lambert, Miranda
   Y'all Eat Yet? — 641.5976
Lambert, Raymond
   Every Man a Hero — B
LAMBERT, RAYMOND, 1921-2021
   Lambert, Raymond. *Every Man a Hero* — B
LAMBS
   Connell, John. *The Farmer's Son* — 630.9
Lamott, Anne
   Almost Everything — 170
   Bird by Bird — 808
   ★*Dusk, Night, Dawn* — B
   ★*Hallelujah Anyway* — 241
   Small Victories — 248
   ★*Somehow* — 814
LAMOTT, ANNE
   Lamott, Anne. *Almost Everything* — 170
   Lamott, Anne. ★*Dusk, Night, Dawn* — B
   Lamott, Anne. *Small Victories* — 248
Lancaster, Bridget
   Cooking at Home with Bridget & Julia — 641.5
Lancaster, Jen
   Welcome to the United States of Anxiety — 155.4
LANCASTER, JEN, 1967-
   Lancaster, Jen. *Welcome to the United States of Anxiety* — 155.4
Lance, Rachel
   Chamber Divers — 940.54
   In the Waves — 973.7
LANCE, RACHEL
   Lance, Rachel. *In the Waves* — 973.7
Lanchester, John
   How to Speak Money — 330.1
***Land** as God Made It*. Horn, James P. P. — 975.5
LAND MINES
   Black, George. ★*The Long Reckoning* — 959.704
*The **Land** of Hope and Fear*. Kershner, Isabel — 956.9405
***Land** of Wondrous Cold*. Wood, Gillen D'Arcy — 919.89
LAND REFORM
   Berry, Wendell. *The Art of Loading Brush* — 338.10973
LAND SETTLEMENT
   Richardson, Heather Cox. ★*How the South Won the Civil War* — 306.20973
   Tobin, Jacqueline. *From Midnight to Dawn* — 973.7
LAND STEWARDSHIP
   Houston, Pam. *Deep Creek* — 814
   Ross, John F. *The Promise of the Grand Canyon* — 917.91
LAND TENURE
   Lamb, Christina. *House of Stone* — 968.91
   Linklater, Andro. *Owning the Earth* — 333.3
   Saunt, Claudio. *Unworthy Republic* — 323.1197
   Taylor, Alan. *The Divided Ground* — 974.7
LAND USE
   Fields, Micah. ★*We Hold Our Breath* — 976.4
   Franklin, Jonathan. *A Wild Idea* — B
   Lim, Audrea. *Free the Land* — 333.73
   Linklater, Andro. *Owning the Earth* — 333.3
★*The **Land** Where the Blues Began*. Lomax, Alan — 781.643
Land, Stephanie
   Maid — B
LAND, STEPHANIE
   Land, Stephanie. *Maid* — B
Landau, Herbert B.
   The Small Public Library Survival Guide — 025.1
Landdeck, Katherine Sharp
   The Women with Silver Wings — 920
LANDFILLS
   Roy, Saumya. *Castaway Mountain* — 363.72
LANDFORMS
   Marshall, Tim. *The Power of Geography* — 320.1
   Robinson, Kim Stanley. *The High Sierra* — 917.94
★***Landmark** Decisions of the United States Supreme Court*. Finkelman, Paul — 347.73
LANDOWNERS
   Lim, Audrea. *Free the Land* — 333.73
   Linklater, Andro. *Owning the Earth* — 333.3
   Swift, Earl. *Hell Put to Shame* — 364.15
LANDRUM, TOM, 1932-
   Wilkie, Curtis. *When Evil Lived in Laurel* — 305.8
LANDRY, TOM
   Ribowsky, Mark. *The Last Cowboy* — 796.332
***Lands** of Lost Borders*. Harris, Kate — 915.804
LANDSCAPE
   Dungy, Camille T. *Soil* — 635.0978
   Pennington, Emily. *Feral* — B
   Stewart, Rory. *The Marches* — 941.3
LANDSCAPE ARCHITECTS, AMERICAN
   Howard, Hugh. *Architects of an American Landscape* — 712.092
LANDSCAPE ARCHITECTURE
   Brenwall, Cynthia S. *The Central Park* — 974.7
   Gidding, John. *At Home with Nature* — 635.9
LANDSCAPE ASSESSMENT
   Farmer, Jared. *Elderflora* — 582.16
LANDSCAPE CHANGES
   Flyn, Cal. ★*Islands of Abandonment* — 333.73
LANDSCAPE GARDENING
   Bainbridge, David A. *Gardening with Less Water* — 635.9
   Baldwin, Debra Lee. *Succulents Simplified* — 635.9
   Buchanan, Rita. *Taylor's Master Guide to Landscaping* — 712
   Edwards, Adrienne L. *Firescaping Your Home* — 635.9
   Gidding, John. *At Home with Nature* — 635.9
   Holmes, Roger. *Midwest Home Landscaping* — 712
   Johnsen, Jan. ★*Gardentopia* — 635.9
   Schwartz, Bobbie. *Garden Renovation* — 635
   Silver, Johanna. ★*The Bold Dry Garden* — 635.9
LANDSCAPE PAINTERS
   Moyle, Franny. *Turner* — B
LANDSCAPE PAINTING
   Griffel, Lois. *Painting the Impressionist Landscape* — 751.45
   Kersey, Geoff. *Painting Successful Watercolours from Photographs* — 751.42
   Moyle, Franny. *Turner* — B
LANDSCAPE PHOTOGRAPHY
   Galassi, Peter. *Ansel Adams in Yosemite Valley* — 770.92
   Szarkowski, John. *Ansel Adams at 100* — B
   Watkins, Carleton E. *Carleton Watkins* — 778.9
LANDSCAPE PLANTS
   Edwards, Adrienne L. *Firescaping Your Home* — 635.9
LANDSCAPE PROTECTION
   Heacox, Kim. *Rhythm of the Wild* — 979.8
★***Landscape** Turned Red*. Sears, Stephen W. — 973.7
Landslide. Wolff, Michael — 973.933
LANDSLIDES
   Knight, Sam. *The Premonitions Bureau* — 133.8
Lane, Charles
   The Day Freedom Died — 976.3
   Freedom's Detective — B
Lane, Christina
   Dessert for Two — 641.86
   Phantom Lady — B
Lane, Stewart F.
   Black Broadway — 792.089
Lanegan, Mark
   Sing Backwards and Weep — B
LANEGAN, MARK
   Lanegan, Mark. *Sing Backwards and Weep* — B
Lang, Arne K.
   Sports Betting and Bookmaking — 798.4010973

PUBLIC LIBRARY CORE COLLECTION: NONFICTION
Twentieth Edition

LANG, JOSEPHINE, 1815-1880
   Porter, Cecelia Hopkins. *Five Lives in Music* — B
Lang, Kenneth R.
   The Cambridge Guide to the Solar System — 523.2
Lang, Maya
   What We Carry — B
LANG, MAYA
   Lang, Maya. *What We Carry* — B
Lang, Michael
   The Road to Woodstock — 781.66
LANG, MICHAEL, 1944-2022
   Lang, Michael. *The Road to Woodstock* — 781.66
LANGE, DOROTHEA, 1895-1965
   Gordon, Linda. *Dorothea Lange* — B
Langewiesche, William
   American Ground — 974.7
   The Atomic Bazaar — 355.02
Langguth, A. J.
   After Lincoln — 973.8
Langholtz, Gabrielle
   America — 641.5973
Langlands, Alex
   Cræft — 306.4
Langshur, Eric
   Start Here — 158
LANGUAGE ACQUISITION
   Pinker, Steven. *The Stuff of Thought* — 401
   Yang, Charles D. *The Infinite Gift* — 401
LANGUAGE AND CULTURE
   Deutscher, Guy. ★*Through the Language Glass* — 410
   Hessler, Peter. *Oracle Bones* — 951
   Hudes, Quiara Alegría. ★*My Broken Language* — B
   Lahiri, Jhumpa. *In Other Words* — B
   McWhorter, John H. *Talking Back, Talking Black* — 427
   Nuttall, Jennifer Anne. ★*Mother Tongue* — 422
   Ostler, Nicholas. *Ad Infinitum* — 470
   Pinker, Steven. *The Stuff of Thought* — 401
   Prothero, Stephen R. *The American Bible* — 973
   Wolfe, Tom. *The Kingdom of Speech* — 401
LANGUAGE AND HISTORY
   Nuttall, Jennifer Anne. ★*Mother Tongue* — 422
LANGUAGE AND LANGUAGES
   Akbar, Kaveh. *Pilgrim Bell* — 811
   Armantrout, Rae. *Wobble* — 811
   Bailey, Richard W. *Speaking American* — 427
   Bitsui, Sherwin. *Dissolve* — 811
   Clark, John Lee. *Touch the Future* — B
   Crystal, David. ★*How Language Works* — 410
   Crystal, David. *Spell It Out* — 421
   Crystal, David. ★*The Stories of English* — 427
   Crystal, David. *The Story of English in 100 Words* — 422
   Deutscher, Guy. ★*Through the Language Glass* — 410
   Dolnick, Edward. *The Writing of the Gods* — 493
   Dreyer, Benjamin. *Dreyer's English* — 808.02
   Everett, Daniel Leonard. *How Language Began* — 401
   Ferrante, Elena. *In the Margins* — 809
   Fox, Margalit. *The Riddle of the Labyrinth* — 920
   Fridland, Valerie. ★*Like, Literally, Dude* — 420.141
   Hitchings, Henry. *The Language Wars* — 420.9
   Jebara, Mohamad. ★*The Life of the Qur'an* — 297.122
   Kinzler, Katherine D. *How You Say It* — 302.2
   Lahiri, Jhumpa. *In Other Words* — B
   Lanchester, John. *How to Speak Money* — 330.1
   Long Soldier, Layli. ★*Whereas* — 811
   Mackintosh-Smith, Tim. *Arabs* — 909.04
   Marshall, Nate. *Finna* — 811
   McCrum, Robert. ★*The Story of English* — 420
   McWhorter, John H. *Talking Back, Talking Black* — 427
   Morrison, Toni. ★*The Source of Self-Regard* — 814
   Mustill, Tom. *How to Speak Whale* — 591.59
   Myers, Leah. *Thinning Blood* — B
   Nadeau, Jean-Benoit. ★*The Story of French* — 440
   Nadeau, Jean-Benoit. *The Story of Spanish* — 460
   Norris, Mary. *Between You and Me* — 428.2
   Nuttall, Jennifer Anne. ★*Mother Tongue* — 422
   Ogilvie, Sarah. *The Dictionary People* — 423
   Oliva, Alejandra. *Rivermouth* — 305.9
   Ostler, Nicholas. *Ad Infinitum* — 470
   Perlin, Ross. ★*Language City* — 306.44
   Pinker, Steven. *The Language Instinct* — 400
   Pinker, Steven. *The Stuff of Thought* — 401
   Pinker, Steven. *Words and Rules* — 415
   Rosenberg, Justus. *The Art of Resistance* — B
   Rushdie, Salman. *Languages of Truth* — 824
   Schor, Esther H. *Bridge of Words* — 499
   Sharif, Solmaz. *Customs* — 811
   Soep, Elisabeth. *Other People's Words* — 155.9
   Stamper, Kory. *Word by Word* — 413.028
   Truss, Lynne. *Eats, Shoots & Leaves* — 428.2
   Tsu, Jing. *Kingdom of Characters* — 495.111
   Watson, Cecelia. *Semicolon* — 428.2
   Winchester, Simon. *The Professor and the Madman* — 423
LANGUAGE AND POWER (SOCIAL SCIENCES)
   Kalder, Daniel. *The Infernal Library* — 321.9
LANGUAGE ARTS
   Leithauser, Brad. *Rhyme's Rooms* — 808.1
   McCrum, Robert. ★*The Story of English* — 420
   Orr, Gregory. *A Primer for Poets & Readers of Poetry* — 808.1
   Truss, Lynne. *Eats, Shoots & Leaves* — 428.2
LANGUAGE ARTS — GENERAL
   Espy, Willard R. *Words to Rhyme With* — 423
LANGUAGE ARTS — JOURNALISM
   Wenger, Debora Halpern. *Advancing the Story* — 070.1
LANGUAGE ARTS — WRITING AND RESEARCH
   Klein, Cheryl B. *The Magic Words* — 808.06
LANGUAGE ARTS — WRITING SKILLS
   Strunk, William. ★*The Elements of Style* — 808
LANGUAGE ARTS AND STUDIES — GENERAL
   Dresser, Norine. *Multicultural Manners* — 395
LANGUAGE ARTS AND STUDIES — JOURNALISM
   Baker, Nicholson. *The World on Sunday* — 071
LANGUAGE ARTS AND STUDIES — LINGUISTICS
   Crystal, David. ★*English as a Global Language* — 427
   Greenspan, Stanley I. *The First Idea* — 153.7
LANGUAGE ARTS AND STUDIES — PUBLIC SPEAKING
   Fish, Stanley Eugene. *Winning Arguments* — 808
   Gallo, Carmine. *Talk Like Ted* — 658.4
LANGUAGE ARTS AND STUDIES — READING SKILLS
   Maddigan, Beth. *Community Library Programs That Work* — 021.2
   Trelease, Jim. ★*Jim Trelease's Read-Aloud Handbook* — 372.4
LANGUAGE ARTS AND STUDIES — SIGN LANGUAGE
   Fouts, Roger. *Next of Kin* — 156
   Tennant, Richard A. *The American Sign Language Handshape Dictionary* — 419
LANGUAGE ARTS AND STUDIES — WRITING SKILLS
   Attenberg, Jami. *1000 Words* — 808.02
   Cameron, Julia. *Living the Artist's Way* — 153.3
   Damon-Moore, Laura C. *The Artist's Library* — 021.2
   Dufresne, John. *Storyville!* — 808.3
   Evans, Bec. *Written* — 808
   Fishman, Stephen. ★*The Copyright Handbook, 15th Ed.* — 346.7304
   Hult, Christine A. *The Handy English Grammar Answer Book* — 428.2
   Kempton, Beth. *The Way of the Fearless Writer* — 808.02
   Kneece, Mark. *The Art of Comic Book Writing* — 741.5
   Mosley, Walter. *Elements of Fiction* — 808.3
   Oliver, Mary. *A Poetry Handbook* — 808.1
   Orr, David. *You, Too, Could Write a Poem* — 808.1
   Sepetys, Ruta. ★*You* — 808.02
   Teicher, Craig Morgan. *We Begin in Gladness* — 808.1
   Turabian, Kate L. *Student's Guide to Writing College Papers* — 808.06
   Vogler, Christopher. ★*The Writer's Journey* — 808.2
★*Language City*. Perlin, Ross — 306.44
LANGUAGE DISORDERS
   Hendrickson, John. *Life on Delay* — B
   Preston, Katherine. *Out with It* — B
The Language Instinct. Pinker, Steven — 400
The Language of Butterflies. Williams, Wendy — 595.78
The Language of God. Collins, Francis S. — 215
LANGUAGE POLICY
   Perlin, Ross. ★*Language City* — 306.44
LANGUAGE REVIVAL
   Lansky, Aaron. *Outwitting History* — 002
   Perlin, Ross. ★*Language City* — 306.44
The Language Wars. Hitchings, Henry — 420.9
Languages of Truth. Rushdie, Salman — 824
★*Languishing*. Keyes, Corey L. M. — 152.1

AUTHOR, TITLE, SERIES AND SUBJECT INDEX

Lankford, Andrea
   Trail of the Lost   363.2
LANKFORD, ANDREA
   Lankford, Andrea. *Trail of the Lost*   363.2
Lankov, A. N.
   The Real North Korea   951.9304
LANSDALE, EDWARD GEARY, 1908-1987
   Anderson, Scott. ★*The Quiet Americans*   327.12
   Boot, Max. ★*The Road Not Taken*   B
Lansky, Aaron
   Outwitting History   002
LANSKY, AARON, 1955-
   Lansky, Aaron. *Outwitting History*   002
Lanterne Rouge. Leonard, Max   796.6
Lanterns. Edelman, Marian Wright   362.7
Lanza, Fabrizia
   The Food of Sicily   641.594
Lanzmann, Claude
   The Patagonian Hare   B
LANZMANN, CLAUDE
   Lanzmann, Claude. *The Patagonian Hare*   B
LAOS
   Hamilton, Lisa M. *The Hungry Season*   B
   Vang, Mai Der. *Afterland*   811
LAOTIAN PEOPLE
   Hamilton, Lisa M. *The Hungry Season*   B
Laperruque, Emma
   Food52 Big Little Recipes   641.5
Lapidarium. Judah, Hettie   553.8
Lapidus, Lenora M.
   ★*The Rights of Women*   346.7301
Lapierre, Corinne
   Folk Embroidered Felt Birds   746.0463
Lapierre, Dominique
   The City of Joy   954
LAPLANTE, EDGAR, 1888-1944
   Willetts, Paul. *King Con*   B
LaPointe, Sasha taqwseblu
   Red Paint   B
   Thunder Song   814
LAPOINTE, SASHA TAQWSEBLU
   LaPointe, Sasha taqwseblu. *Red Paint*   B
   LaPointe, Sasha taqwseblu. *Thunder Song*   814
LARGE HADRON COLLIDER (FRANCE AND SWITZERLAND)
   Cliff, Harry. *How to Make an Apple Pie from Scratch*   523.01
Larimer, Kevin
   The Poets & Writers Complete Guide to Being a Writer   808
Lark Jewelry & Beading Bead Inspirations [Series]. Katz, Amy   745.594
Larkin, Philip
   ★*Collected Poems*   821
   The Complete Poems   821
Larman, Alexander
   ★*Power and Glory*   941.085
   The Windsors at War   940.53
Larrington, Carolyne
   The Norse Myths   293
Larry McMurtry. Daugherty, Tracy   B
LARSEN, BOB
   Futterman, Matthew. *Running to the Edge*   796.42071
Larsen, Jeffrey
   ★*Gluten-Free Baking at Home*   641.5
Larson, Edward J.
   An Empire of Ice   919.8
   Evolution   576.8
   The Return of George Washington   B
Larson, Elsie
   A Beautiful Mess Happy Handmade Home   745
Larson, Erik
   ★*Dead Wake*   940.4
   ★*The Demon of Unrest*   973.7
   ★*The Devil in the White City*   364.15
   In the Garden of Beasts   B
   ★*The Splendid and the Vile*   940.54
Larson, Jeanette
   The Public Library Policy Writer   025.1
Larson, Kate Clifford
   Bound for the Promised Land   B
   Rosemary   B

Walk with Me   B
Larson, Kay
   Where the Heart Beats   700.1
LaRue, James
   ★*On Censorship*   025.2
LAS VEGAS, NEVADA
   Assael, Shaun. *The Murder of Sonny Liston*   B
   D'Agata, John. *About a Mountain*   979.3
   McManus, James. ★*Positively Fifth Street*   795.41
   Patterson, James. *What Really Happens in Vegas*   920
   Rempel, William C. *The Gambler*   B
Lasater, Judith
   Yoga Myths   613.7
Lasch, Christopher
   ★*The Revolt of the Elites*   306
Lashinsky, Adam
   Wild Ride   388.4
Laskas, Jeanne Marie
   Concussion   617.5
Laskin, David
   The Children's Blizzard   977
LASORDA, TOMMY
   Turbow, Jason. *They Bled Blue*   796.357
The Last Apocalypse. Reston, James   940.1
Last Best Hope. Packer, George   973.93
The Last Black Unicorn. Haddish, Tiffany   B
Last Boat Out of Shanghai. Zia, Helen   951.04
The Last Boy. Leavy, Jane   B
Last Call. Green, Elon   363.15
Last Call. Okrent, Daniel   363.4
Last Call at the Hotel Imperial. Cohen, Deborah   070.92
The Last Campaign. Brands, H. W.   973.8
The Last Campaign. Clarke, Thurston   B
The Last Castle. Kiernan, Denise   975.6
★*The Last Coach*. Barra, Allen   B
The Last Cowboy. Ribowsky, Mark   796.332
The Last Cowboys. Branch, John   920
★*Last Dance*. Feinstein, John   796.323
LAST DAYS
   Arthur, Alua. ★*Briefly Perfectly Human*   306.9
   Clarke, Rachel. *Dear Life*   B
   Volandes, Angelo E. *The Conversation*   616.02
The Last Days of the Dinosaurs. Black, Riley   576.8
The Last Empress. Pakula, Hannah   B
The Last Enforcer. Oakley, Charles   B
The Last Fire Season. Martin, Manjula   B
The Last Fisherman. Rotman, Jeffrey L.   778.7
The Last Folk Hero. Pearlman, Jeff   B
The Last Founding Father. Unger, Harlow G.   B
The Last Full Measure. Stephenson, Michael   305.9
The Last Giants. Wood, Levison   599.67
★*The Last Girl*. Murad, Nadia   B
Last Girl Before Freeway. Bennetts, Leslie   B
The Last Gun. Diaz, Tom   338.4
The Last Hero. Bryant, Howard   B
The Last Hill. Clavin, Tom   940.54
★*The Last Honest Man*. Risen, James   973.92
Last Hope Island. Olson, Lynne   940.53
The Last Island. Goodheart, Adam   954
The Last Jew of Treblinka. Rajchman, Chil   940.53
The Last Job. Bilefsky, Dan   364.16
The Last King of America. Roberts, Andrew   B
The Last Kings of Shanghai. Kaufman, Jonathan   951
Last lion (William Manchester) [Series]. Manchester, William   B
The Last Lion, Winston Spencer Churchill. Manchester, William   B
The Last Lion, Winston Spencer Churchill. Manchester, William   B
The Last Love Song. Daugherty, Tracy   B
The Last Man Who Knew Everything. Schwartz, David N.   B
The Last Million. Nasaw, David   940.53
The Last Mission. Smith, Jim B.   940.54
The Last Negroes at Harvard. Garrett, Kent   920
The Last of the Tribe. Reel, Monte   981
The Last Palace. Eisen, Norman L.   920
★*The Last Politician*. Foer, Franklin   973.934
The Last Republicans. Updegrove, Mark K.   973.928
The Last Ride of the Pony Express. Grant, Will   917.804
The Last Secret of the Secret Annex. Van Wijk-Voskuijl, Joop   940.53
The Last Seven Months of Anne Frank. Lindwer, Willy   B

PUBLIC LIBRARY CORE COLLECTION: NONFICTION
Twentieth Edition

The Last Slave Ship. Raines, Ben — 306.362
★*The Last Stand*. Philbrick, Nathaniel — 973.8
The Last Stargazers. Levesque, Emily — 520
The Last Stone. Bowden, Mark — 363.25
The Last Train to Zona Verde. Theroux, Paul — 916
The Last Whalers. Clark, Doug Bock — 639.2
The Last Winter. Fox, Porter — 363.738
Last Witnesses. Aleksievich, Svetlana — 940.53
Late Essays, 2006-2017. Coetzee, J. M. — 824
Later Poems. Rich, Adrienne — 811

LATIN AMERICA
    Anderson, Jon Lee. *Che Guevara* — B
    Bingham, Hiram. ★*Lost City of the Incas* — 985
    Cervantes, Fernando. *Conquistadores* — 970.01
    Chasteen, John Charles. *Americanos* — 980
    Chasteen, John Charles. *Born in Blood and Fire* — 980
    De Leon, Jason. ★*Soldiers and Kings* — 364.1
    Fernandez-Armesto, Felipe. *Our America* — 973
    Fuentes, Carlos. *The Buried Mirror* — 946
    Gomez, Laura E. ★*Inventing Latinos* — 305.868
    Grann, David. *The Lost City of Z* — 918.1
    Gutierrez, Sandra A. *Latinisimo* — 641.598
    Hagerty, Alexa. ★*Still Life with Bones* — 599.9
    McConahay, Mary Jo. *The Tango War* — 940.53
    Ortiz, Paul. *An African American and Latinx History of the United States* — 305.8
    Ruck, Rob. *Raceball* — 796.357
    Vargas Llosa, Mario. *Sabers and Utopias* — 980.03

LATIN AMERICAN PEOPLE
    Arana, Marie. ★*Latinoland* — 973
    Chasteen, John Charles. *Born in Blood and Fire* — 980
    Espada, Martin. ★*Floaters* — 811
    Luiselli, Valeria. *Tell Me How It Ends* — 305.23086
    Martin, Gerald. ★*Gabriel Garcia Marquez* — B
    Vargas Llosa, Mario. *Sabers and Utopias* — 980.03

LATIN AMERICAN POETRY
    Borges, Jorge Luis. ★*Selected Poems* — 861
    Neruda, Pablo. *All the Odes* — 861
    Neruda, Pablo. *Then Come Back* — 861
    Neruda, Pablo. ★*Twenty Love Poems and a Song of Despair* — 861
    Neruda, Pablo. *World's End* — 861

★*Latin for the Illiterati*. Stone, Jon R. — 473

LATIN LANGUAGE
    Ostler, Nicholas. *Ad Infinitum* — 470
    Stone, Jon R. ★*Latin for the Illiterati* — 473

Latino Writers and Journalists. Martinez Wood, Jamie — B
★*Latinoland*. Arana, Marie — 973
Latinos in the Arts. Otfinoski, Steven — 700.89
Latinisimo. Gutierrez, Sandra A. — 641.598

Lattin, Don
    The Harvard Psychedelic Club — 973.922092

LAUDOR, MICHAEL
    Rosen, Jonathan. ★*The Best Minds* — 616.89

LAUER, MATT, 1957-
    Farrow, Ronan. ★*Catch and Kill* — 331.4
    Stelter, Brian. *Top of the Morning* — 791.456

Laugh Lines. Zweibel, Alan — B
Laughing All the Way to the Mosque. Nawaz, Zarqa — 791.45028
★*Laughing At My Nightmare*. Burcaw, Shane — B

Laughlin, James
    The Luck of Friendship — B

LAUGHLIN, JAMES, 1914-1997
    Laughlin, James. *The Luck of Friendship* — B

Laughlin, Sara
    The Quality Library — 025.1

LAUGHTER
    Jennings, Ken. *Planet Funny* — 809.7

LAUNDRY
    Richardson, Patric. *Laundry Love* — 648

Laundry Love. Richardson, Patric — 648

Launius, Roger D.
    Apollo's Legacy — 629.45
    The Smithsonian History of Space Exploration — 629.4

Lauren, Jillian
    Behold the Monster — 364.152

LAURENS, HENRY, 1724-1792
    Harris, J. William. *The Hanging of Thomas Jeremiah* — B

Lauretta, D. S.
    The Asteroid Hunter — 523.44

Lauterbach, Preston
    Beale Street Dynasty — 976.8
    Bluff City — B

LAUTERPACHT, HERSCH, 1897-1960
    Sands, Philippe. *East West Street* — 345

Laux, Dorianne
    Only as the Day Is Long — 811

Lavelle, Christine
    How to Create a Wildlife Garden — 635

Lavender, Kenneth
    Book Repair — 025.8

Lavery, Daniel M.
    Dear Prudence — 170
    Something That May Shock and Discredit You — 814

Lavoipierre, Frederique
    Garden Allies — 635

LAW
    Amar, Akhil Reed. *The Words That Made Us* — 342.7302
    Auster, Paul. *Bloodbath Nation* — 363.33
    Bharara, Preet. *Doing Justice* — 347.73
    Biskupic, Joan. ★*Nine Black Robes* — 347.73
    Bowdler, Michelle. ★*Is Rape a Crime?* — B
    Burnham, Margaret A. ★*By Hands Now Known* — 342.73
    Cameron, Silver Donald. *Blood in the Water* — 364.152
    Dennie, Madiba K. *The Originalism Trap* — 342.73
    Ellis, Joseph J. ★*American Dialogue* — 973.3
    Lithwick, Dahlia. *Lady Justice* — 345.73
    Minow, Martha. *When Should Law Forgive?* — 345
    Murphy, Bruce Allen. *Scalia* — B
    Robb, Graham. *The Debatable Land* — 941.3
    Roffer, Michael H. *The Law Book* — 340.09
    Skach, C. L. *How to Be a Citizen* — 323.6
    Stone, Geoffrey R. ★*Sex and the Constitution* — 345.7302
    Tamanaha, Brian Z. *Failing Law Schools* — 340.071
    Tucker, Virginia. *Finding the Answers to Legal Questions* — 340.072
    Urofsky, Melvin I. *Dissent and the Supreme Court* — 342.7302
    Vladeck, Stephen I. *The Shadow Docket* — 347.73

LAW — CORPORATE, BUSINESS, AND FINANCE
    McKeever, Mike P. *How to Write a Business Plan* — 658.15
    O'Neill, Cara. *Chapter 13 Bankruptcy, 17th Ed.* — 346.7307
    Steingold, Fred S. *The Employer's Legal Handbook, 16th Ed.* — 344.7301

LAW — CRIMINAL LAW
    Trainum, James L. *How the Police Generate False Confessions* — 345.73

LAW — FAMILY LAW
    Green, Janice. ★*Divorce After 50* — 306.89

LAW — GENERAL
    Biskupic, Joan. ★*Nine Black Robes* — 347.73
    Finkelman, Paul. ★*Landmark Decisions of the United States Supreme Court* — 347.73
    Lapidus, Lenora M. ★*The Rights of Women* — 346.7301
    Maddex, Robert L. *The U.S. Constitution A to Z* — 342.730203
    Marshall, Thurgood. *Thurgood Marshall* — B
    Sanger, Carol. *About Abortion* — 179.7
    Tamanaha, Brian Z. *Failing Law Schools* — 340.071
    Tucker, Virginia. *Finding the Answers to Legal Questions* — 340.072

LAW — REAL ESTATE AND HOUSING
    Elias, Stephen. *The Foreclosure Survival Guide, 9th Ed.* — 346.7304

LAW — TRADEMARK, PATENT, AND INTELLECTUAL PROPERTY
    Butler, Rebecca P. ★*Copyright for Teachers & Librarians in the 21st Century* — 346.7304
    Crews, Kenneth D. ★*Copyright Law for Librarians and Educators* — 346.7304
    Fishman, Stephen. ★*The Copyright Handbook, 15th Ed.* — 346.7304
    Norwick, Kenneth P. *The Legal Guide for Writers, Artists and Other Creative People* — 346.04
    Russell, Carrie. *Complete Copyright for K-12 Librarians and Educators* — 346.73

LAW AND POLITICS
    Coyle, Marcia. *The Roberts Court* — 347.73
    Dennie, Madiba K. *The Originalism Trap* — 342.73
    Toobin, Jeffrey. *The Nine* — 347.73

LAW AND SOCIETY
    Farrell, John A. *Clarence Darrow* — B

The Law Book. Roffer, Michael H. — 340.09

LAW ENFORCEMENT
    Boessenecker, John. *Texas Ranger* — B
    Croke, Ken. *Riding with Evil* — 364.106

AUTHOR, TITLE, SERIES AND SUBJECT INDEX

Friedman, Barry. ★*Unwarranted*	344.7305
Gross, Neil. *Walk the Walk*	363.2
Hayes, Christopher. *A Colony in a Nation*	364.3
Horace, Matthew. *The Black and the Blue*	B
Johnson, Steven. *The Infernal Machine*	335
Rudolf, David S. *American Injustice*	345.73
Westhoff, Ben. *Fentanyl, Inc.*	362.29
LAW FIRMS	
Enrich, David. *Servants of the Damned*	340.023
Oller, John. *White Shoe*	346.73
Law Man. Hopwood, Shon	B
LAW REFORM	
Taub, Jennifer. *Big Dirty Money*	364.16
Urofsky, Melvin I. *Louis D. Brandeis*	B
LAW SCHOOLS	
Tamanaha, Brian Z. *Failing Law Schools*	340.071
LAW STUDENTS	
Marzano-Lesnevich, Alexandria. *The Fact of a Body*	364.152
Law, Keith	
The Inside Game	796.35764
Smart Baseball	796.357
Lawler, Andrew	
The Secret Token	975.6
Under Jerusalem	956.94
Lawrence in Arabia. Anderson, Scott	B
LAWRENCE, JOHN GEDDES	
Carpenter, Dale. *Flagrant Conduct*	342.7308
Lawrence, T. E.	
Seven Pillars of Wisdom	940.4
LAWRENCE, T. E. (THOMAS EDWARD), 1888-1935	
Anderson, Scott. *Lawrence in Arabia*	B
Lawrence, T. E. *Seven Pillars of Wisdom*	940.4
The Laws of Medicine. Mukherjee, Siddhartha	610.1
Lawson, Jenny	
★*Broken*	B
Furiously Happy	B
LAWSON, JENNY, 1973-	
Lawson, Jenny. ★*Broken*	B
Lawson, Jenny. *Furiously Happy*	B
Lawson, Nancy	
The Humane Gardener	577.5
Lawson, Nigella	
At My Table	641.59
★*Cook, Eat, Repeat*	641.5
★*Simply Nigella*	641.5
LAWSON, NIGELLA, 1960-	
Lawson, Nigella. ★*Cook, Eat, Repeat*	641.5
Lawton, Georgina	
Raceless	B
LAWTON, GEORGINA	
Lawton, Georgina. *Raceless*	B
LAWYERS	
Adams, Jarrett. *Redeeming Justice*	340.092
Addison, Corban. *Wastelands*	346.73
Ambroz, David. *A Place Called Home*	B
Barkan, Ady. *Eyes to the Wind*	B
Berman, Geoffrey. *Holding the Line*	345.73
Bilott, Robert. *Exposure*	344.04
Blumenthal, Sidney. *A Self-Made Man*	B
Blumenthal, Sidney. *Wrestling with His Angel*	B
Cenziper, Debbie. ★*Love Wins*	346.7301
Farrell, John A. *Clarence Darrow*	B
Glatt, John. *Tangled Vines*	364.152
Gleeson, John. *The Gotti Wars*	364.1
Guha, Ramachandra. *Gandhi Before India*	B
Guha, Ramachandra. *Gandhi*	B
Higham, Scott. *American Cartel*	338.4
Hopwood, Shon. *Law Man*	B
Jackson, Bruce. *Never Far from Home*	B
Jones, Doug. *Bending Toward Justice*	323.1196
Kirtzman, Andrew. *Giuliani*	B
Kouchner, Camille. *The Familia Grande*	B
Lane, Charles. *The Day Freedom Died*	976.3
Matney, Mandy. *Blood on Their Hands*	364.152
McCraw, David Edward. *Truth in Our Times*	342.7308
McCullough, David G. ★*John Adams*	B
McGinty, Brian. *Lincoln's Greatest Case*	346.7303
McPhee, Peter. *Robespierre*	B
Norgren, Jill. *Belva Lockwood*	B
Oller, John. *White Shoe*	346.73
Rudolf, David S. *American Injustice*	345.73
Shehadeh, Raja. ★*We Could Have Been Friends, My Father and I*	B
Sorensen, Theodore C. *Counselor*	B
Stevenson, Bryan. *Just Mercy*	B
Urofsky, Melvin I. *Louis D. Brandeis*	B
Lay Them to Rest. Norton, Laurah	363.25
Laymon, Kiese	
★*Heavy*	B
How to Slowly Kill Yourself and Others in America	814.6
The Lazarus Files. McGough, Matthew	364.152
LAZARUS, STEPHANIE	
McGough, Matthew. *The Lazarus Files*	364.152
LAZINESS	
Price, Devon. ★*Laziness Does Not Exist*	158.1
★*Laziness Does Not Exist*. Price, Devon	158.1
LAZOWSKI, PHILIP	
Frankel, Rebecca. *Into the Forest*	940.53
Le Carre, John	
The Pigeon Tunnel	B
LE CARRE, JOHN, 1931-2020	
Le Carre, John. *The Pigeon Tunnel*	B
LE CHAMBON-SUR-LIGNON, FRANCE	
Moorehead, Caroline. *Village of Secrets*	944
Paxson, Margaret. *The Plateau*	362.87
Le Guin, Ursula K.	
No Time to Spare	814
So Far so Good	811
Ursula K. Le Guin	811
Ursula K. Le Guin	B
Words Are My Matter	818
LE GUIN, URSULA K., 1929-2018	
Le Guin, Ursula K. *Ursula K. Le Guin*	B
Le Guin, Ursula K. *Words Are My Matter*	818
Le Morte Darthur, Or, the Hoole Book of Kyng Arthur and of His Noble Knyghtes of the Rounde Table. Malory, Thomas	823
LE PRINCE, LOUIS AIME AUGUSTIN, 1842-1890	
Fischer, Paul. *The Man Who Invented Motion Pictures*	791.43
LE ROUX, PAUL CALDER	
Ratliff, Evan. *The Mastermind*	B
Shannon, Elaine. *Hunting Leroux*	364.1
Le Sud. Peppler, Rebekah	641.594
Le, Mike	
That Noodle Life	641.82
LEACH, MIKE, 1961-	
Gwynne, S. C. *The Perfect Pass*	920
Leach, Samantha	
★*The Elissas*	362.73
LEAD CONTAMINATION	
Clark, Anna. *The Poisoned City*	363.6
Hanna-Attisha, Mona. *What the Eyes Don't See*	615.9
Lead from the Outside. Abrams, Stacey	B
Lead Yourself First. Kethledge, Raymond Michael	658.4
LEADBELLY, 1885-1949	
Wolfe, Charles K. ★*The Life and Legend of Leadbelly*	B
★*The Leader's Guide to Unconscious Bias*. Fuller, Pamela	658.3
Leader, Zachary	
The Life of Saul Bellow	B
Leadership. Kissinger, Henry	303.3
LEADERSHIP	
Arana, Marie. *Bolivar*	B
Baier, Bret. *To Rescue the Constitution*	973.4
Ball, Molly. ★*Pelosi*	B
Barsh, Joanna. *Grow Wherever You Work*	658.4
Beard, Mary. ★*Emperor of Rome*	937
Blair, Tony. *A Journey*	B
Blount, Roy. *Robert E. Lee*	B
Borman, Tracy. *Anne Boleyn and Elizabeth I*	920
Borman, Tracy. *Crown & Sceptre*	941
Borneman, Walter R. *The Admirals*	B
Borneman, Walter R. *Polk*	B
Branch, Taylor. *The Clinton Tapes*	973.929
Brown, Brene. ★*Dare to Lead*	658.4
Bunting, Josiah. ★*The Making of a Leader*	B
Burke, Monte. *Saban*	796.332
Castor, Helen. *Joan of Arc*	B
Cohen, Jared. *Life After Power*	973.09

PUBLIC LIBRARY CORE COLLECTION: NONFICTION
Twentieth Edition

Cole, Jason. *Elway*	B
Coles, Robert. *Lives of Moral Leadership*	170
Cooney, Kara. *When Women Ruled the World*	920
Cooper, Helene. *Madame President*	966.62
Covey, Stephen R. *The 8th Habit*	158
Cozzens, Peter. *A Brutal Reckoning*	973.5
Davis, William C. *Crucible of Command*	920
Downs, Paul. *Boss Life*	338.7
Dufu, Tiffany. *Drop the Ball*	650.1
Economy, Peter. *Wait, I'm the Boss?!?*	658
Eltahawy, Mona. *The Seven Necessary Sins for Women and Girls*	305.42
Everitt, Anthony. *Alexander the Great*	B
Fabritius, Friederike. *The Leading Brain*	158
Fauci, Anthony S. *Expect the Unexpected*	610.92
Fuller, Pamela. ★*The Leader's Guide to Unconscious Bias*	658.3
Gaddis, John Lewis. *On Grand Strategy*	355.4
Gallo, Carmine. *The Bezos Blueprint*	658.4
Gelwicks, Andrew. *The Queer Advantage*	920
Gentile, Mary C. *Giving Voice to Values*	174
Gessen, Masha. *Surviving Autocracy*	973.933
Gillard, Julia. ★*Women and Leadership*	158
Goleman, Daniel. *Primal Leadership*	658.4
Goodall, Amanda. *Credible*	658.4
Goodwin, Doris Kearns. ★*Team of Rivals*	B
Groom, Winston. *The Generals*	920
Guelzo, Allen C. *Robert E. Lee*	B
Harlan, Louis R. *Booker T. Washington*	B
Jebara, Mohamad. *Muhammad, the World-Changer*	B
Johnson, Paul. *Churchill*	B
Johnson, Paul. *George Washington*	B
Kaplan, Robert D. *Warrior Politics*	320
Kethledge, Raymond Michael. *Lead Yourself First*	658.4
Levy, Reynold. *They Told Me Not to Take That Job*	792.09
Lieven, Dominic. *In the Shadow of the Gods*	352.23
Mandela, Nelson. *Conversations with Myself*	B
Marton, Kati. ★*The Chancellor*	B
Massie, Robert K. *Catherine the Great*	B
Newkirk, Pamela. *Diversity, Inc.*	658.3
Palmieri, Jennifer. *Dear Madam President*	158
Perry, Mark. *The Most Dangerous Man in America*	B
Phillips, Collette A. M. *The Includers*	658.4
Pink, Daniel H. *Drive*	153.1
Rahmani, Niloofar. *Open Skies*	B
Randall, Willard Sterne. *George Washington*	B
Richards, Cecile. *Make Trouble*	B
Ricks, Thomas E. *Churchill and Orwell*	920
Ricks, Thomas E. ★*The Generals*	B
Ridley, Jane. *George V*	B
Riel, Jennifer. *Creating Great Choices*	658.4
Roberts, Andrew. ★*Churchill*	B
Roberts, Andrew. *Leadership in War*	920
Roll, David L. *Ascent to Power*	973.918
Rubenstein, David M. *The American Story*	973.07202
Sandberg, Sheryl. *Lean In*	658.4
Sandberg, Sheryl. *Lean In*	658.4
Sanders, Chad. *Black Magic*	305.896
Schiff, Stacy. ★*Cleopatra*	B
Schlender, Brent. *Becoming Steve Jobs*	B
Scott, Kim Malone. *Radical Candor*	658.4
Shah, Rajiv Janardan. *Big Bets*	303.4
Simmons, Ruth. ★*Up Home*	B
Smith, Sally Bedell. *Elizabeth the Queen*	920
Smith, Sally Bedell. *George VI and Elizabeth*	920
Stavridis, James. *To Risk It All*	359
Steinberg, Jonathan. *Bismarck*	B
Taylor, Jay. *The Generalissimo*	B
VanDuinkerken, Wyoma. *The Challenge of Library Management*	025.1
Voloj, Julian. *Ghetto Brother*	741.5
Wheelan, Joseph. ★*Terrible Swift Sword*	B
Wills, Garry. *Certain Trumpets*	303.3
Winters, Richard D. *Beyond Band of Brothers*	B

LEADERSHIP IN BUSINESS

Barsh, Joanna. *Grow Wherever You Work*	658.4
Boden, Anne. *Female Founders' Playbook*	658.4
Godin, Seth. *The Practice*	153.3
Kethledge, Raymond Michael. *Lead Yourself First*	658.4
Lipman, Joanne. *That's What She Said*	305.30973
Nadella, Satya. *Hit Refresh*	B
Nooyi, Indra. ★*My Life in Full*	B
Pink, Daniel H. *Drive*	153.1
Webb, Maynard. *Dear Founder*	658
★*Leadership in Turbulent Times*. Goodwin, Doris Kearns	973.09
Leadership in War. Roberts, Andrew	920
The Leading Brain. Fabritius, Friederike	158
Leading Inclusion. Cox, Gena	658.3
The League. Eisenberg, John	796.332
League of Denial. Fainaru-Wada, Mark	617.1
★*The League of Wives*. Lee, Heath Hardage	959.704

LEAHY, WILLIAM D.

Borneman, Walter R. *The Admirals*	B
O'Brien, Phillips Payson. *The Second Most Powerful Man in the World*	B

Leake, Lisa

100 Days of Real Food on a Budget	641.5
★*100 Days of Real Food*	641.5

Leakey, Richard E.

The Origin of Humankind	599.93

LEAKS (DISCLOSURE OF INFORMATION)

Horwitz, Jeff. ★*Broken Code*	302.3
Howley, Kerry. *Bottoms Up and the Devil Laughs*	352.37
Manning, Chelsea. *Readme.Txt*	B

Leal, Brigitte

The Ultimate Picasso	B

Leamer, Laurence

Hitchcock's Blondes	791.43
The Kennedy Men	920
The Price of Justice	346.7302

Leaming, Barbara

Jacqueline Bouvier Kennedy Onassis	B
Kick Kennedy	B
Mrs. Kennedy	B

Lean In. Sandberg, Sheryl	658.4
Lean In. Sandberg, Sheryl	658.4
Leap of Faith. Noor	B

Leapman, Melissa

Mastering Color Knitting	746.43
Lear. Bloom, Harold	822.33

Lear, Edward

The Complete Verse and Other Nonsense	821

LEAR, KING (LEGENDARY CHARACTER)

Bloom, Harold. *Lear*	822.33

Lear, Linda J.

Beatrix Potter	B

Lear, Norman

Even This I Get to Experience	B

LEAR, NORMAN

Lear, Norman. *Even This I Get to Experience*	B
Learn Better. Boser, Ulrich	153.1
Learn Calligraphy. Shepherd, Margaret	745.6
★*Learned Optimism*. Seligman, Martin E. P.	155.2

LEARNING

Burak, Asi. *Power Play*	794.8
Carey, Benedict. *How We Learn*	153.1
Christakis, Erika. *The Importance of Being Little*	372.21
Chu, Lenora. *Little Soldiers*	370
Eagleman, David. *Livewired*	612.8
Epstein, David J. ★*Range*	153.9
Foer, Joshua. *Moonwalking with Einstein*	153.1
Grant, Adam M. *Hidden Potential*	153.8
Livio, Mario. *Why?*	153.3
Preszler, Trent. *Little and Often*	B
Rademacher, Tom. *It Won't Be Easy*	B
Rubin, Rick. ★*The Creative Act*	153.3
Sarma, Sanjay E. *Grasp*	370.15
Seldin, Tim. *How to Raise an Amazing Child the Montessori Way*	649
Turnbow, Dominique. ★*Demystifying Online Instruction in Libraries*	028.7
Vanderbilt, Tom. ★*Beginners*	646.7
Young, Scott H. *Get Better at Anything*	650.1
★*Learning America*. Mufleh, Luma	371.826

LEARNING AND SCHOLARSHIP

Barzun, Jacques. *From Dawn to Decadence*	940.2
Cahill, Thomas. *How the Irish Saved Civilization*	941.501
Givens, Jarvis R. ★*School Clothes*	371.829

LEARNING BY DISCOVERY

Epstein, David J. ★*Range*	153.9
Robinson, Ken. *Creative Schools*	370.973

AUTHOR, TITLE, SERIES AND SUBJECT INDEX

LEARNING DISABILITIES
    Felix, Camonghne. *Dyscalculia* — B
    Flink, David. *Thinking Differently* — 371.9
The Learning Habit. Donaldson-Pressman, Stephanie — 371.30281
Learning Korean. Serpico, Peter — 641.595
Learning to Die in Miami. Eire, Carlos M. N. — B
★*Learning to Love Midlife.* Conley, Chip — 646.7
Learning to Pray. Martin, James — 248.3
Learning to See Creatively. Peterson, Bryan — 770
Learning to Speak Alzheimer's. Coste, Joanne Koenig — 362.1
LEARY, LEWIS SHERIDAN, 1835-1859
    Meyer, Eugene L. *Five for Freedom* — 973.7
LEARY, TIMOTHY, 1920-1996
    Lattin, Don. *The Harvard Psychedelic Club* — 973.922092
    Minutaglio, Bill. *The Most Dangerous Man in America* — B
★*The Least of Us.* Quinones, Sam — 362.29
LEATHERWORK
    Gethin, Rosanna Clare. *Sew Luxe Leather* — 745.53
★*Leave The Gun, Take the Cannoli.* Seal, Mark — 791.43
★*Leaves of Grass.* Whitman, Walt — 811
Leaving Before the Rains Come. Fuller, Alexandra — B
Leaving Isn't the Hardest Thing. Hough, Lauren — B
Leavitt, David
    The Man Who Knew Too Much — B
LEAVITT, HENRIETTA SWAN, 1868-1921
    Johnson, George. *Miss Leavitt's Stars* — 522
Leavy, Jane
    The Big Fella — B
    The Last Boy — B
    Sandy Koufax — B
LEBANON
    Blanford, Nicholas. *Warriors of God* — 956.9204
    Friedman, Matti. *Pumpkinflowers* — B
    Friedman, Matti. *Spies of No Country* — 327.12
    Friedman, Thomas L. ★*From Beirut to Jerusalem* — 956.04
    Shadid, Anthony. *House of Stone* — 306.0956
Lebo, Harlan
    ★*Citizen Kane* — 791.43
LeBor, Adam
    City of Oranges — 956.94
Lebovitz, David
    My Paris Kitchen — 641.594
LEBOVITZ, DAVID
    Lebovitz, David. *My Paris Kitchen* — 641.594
Lebron. Benedict, Jeff — B
Lebron, Christopher J
    The Making of Black Lives Matter — 305.896
Lebron, Inc. Windhorst, Brian — B
LECORGNE FAMILY
    Ball, Edward. *Life of a Klansman* — 305.8009763
LECORGNE, CONSTANT, 1832-1886
    Ball, Edward. *Life of a Klansman* — 305.8009763
Lecrae
    ★*I Am Restored* — B
LECRAE (MUSICIAN)
    Lecrae. ★*I Am Restored* — B
LECTURES AND LECTURING
    Borges, Jorge Luis. *Selected Non-Fictions* — 864
Led Zeppelin. Spitz, Bob — 782.42166
Ledbetter, James
    One Nation Under Gold — 332.4
The Lede. Trillin, Calvin — 071
Leder, Steven Z.
    The Beauty of What Remains — 306.9
LEDER, STEVEN Z.
    Leder, Steven Z. *The Beauty of What Remains* — 306.9
Lederer, Roger J.
    Beaks, Bones, and Bird Songs — 598
Ledger. Hirshfield, Jane — 811
The Ledger and the Chain. Rothman, Joshua D. — 306.362
LeDuff, Charlie
    Detroit — 977.4
LEDUFF, CHARLIE
    LeDuff, Charlie. *Detroit* — 977.4
Lee. Freeman, Douglas Southall — B
LEE FAMILY
    Lee, Helie. *In the Absence of Sun* — B
Lee Miller. Burke, Carolyn — B

Lee Molinaro, Joanne
    ★*The Korean Vegan Cookbook* — 641.595
LEE, BRUCE, 1940-1973
    Lee, Shannon. *Be Water, My Friend* — 796.8
    Polly, Matthew. ★*Bruce Lee* — B
Lee, Corky
    ★*Corky Lee's Asian America* — 770
LEE, CORKY, 1947-2021
    Lee, Corky. ★*Corky Lee's Asian America* — 770
Lee, Edward
    Buttermilk Graffiti — 641.59
LEE, EDWARD, 1972-
    Lee, Edward. *Buttermilk Graffiti* — 641.59
Lee, Erika
    America for Americans — 305.800973
    The Making of Asian America — 973
LEE, FRANCES GLESSNER, 1878-1962
    Goldfarb, Bruce. ★*18 Tiny Deaths* — B
LEE, GYPSY ROSE, 1914-1970
    Abbott, Karen. *American Rose* — B
LEE, HARPER
    Cep, Casey N. ★*Furious Hours* — 364.152
    Crespino, Joseph. *Atticus Finch* — B
Lee, Heath Hardage
    ★*The League of Wives* — 959.704
Lee, Helie
    In the Absence of Sun — B
Lee, Jennifer Tyler
    Half the Sugar, All the Love — 641.5
Lee, Julia Sun-Joo
    Biting the Hand — B
LEE, JULIA SUN-JOO, 1976-
    Lee, Julia Sun-Joo. *Biting the Hand* — B
Lee, Kai-Fu
    AI 2041 — 006.3
LEE, KUAN YEW, 1923-2015
    Kissinger, Henry. *Leadership* — 303.3
Lee, Lara
    A Splash of Soy — 641.595
Lee, Li-Young
    The Undressing — 811
Lee, Marshall
    Bookmaking — 686
LEE, RICHARD HENRY, 1732-1794
    Unger, Harlow G. *First Founding Father* — B
LEE, ROBERT E. (ROBERT EDWARD), 1807-1870
    Blount, Roy. *Robert E. Lee* — B
    Davis, William C. *Crucible of Command* — 920
    Fellman, Michael. *The Making of Robert E. Lee* — B
    Freeman, Douglas Southall. *Lee* — B
    Guelzo, Allen C. *Robert E. Lee* — B
    Gwynne, S. C. *Hymns of the Republic* — 973.7
    Korda, Michael. *Clouds of Glory* — B
    Seidule, Ty. *Robert E. Lee and Me* — 973.7
Lee, Shannon
    Be Water, My Friend — 796.8
Lee, Stan
    Stan Lee's How to Draw Comics — 741.5
LEE, STAN, 1922-2018
    Fingeroth, Danny. *A Marvelous Life* — 741.5
    Riesman, Abraham. *True Believer* — 741.5
Lee, Sung-Yoon
    The Sister — 951.93
Lee, Vinny
    Kitchenalia — 747.7
Leerhsen, Charles
    ★*Butch Cassidy* — B
Lees, Gene
    You Can't Steal a Gift — B
LEES, MICHAEL
    Lewis, Damien. *Churchill's Hellraisers* — 940.54
LEEUWENHOEK, ANTHONY VAN, 1632-1723
    Snyder, Laura J. *Eye of the Beholder* — 920
LeFavour, Cree
    Lights On, Rats Out — 616.85
LEFAVOUR, CREE
    LeFavour, Cree. *Lights On, Rats Out* — 616.85

PUBLIC LIBRARY CORE COLLECTION: NONFICTION
Twentieth Edition

LEFEVRE, DIDIER, 1957-2007
   Guibert, Emmanuel. *The Photographer* ... 741.5
Left Bank. Poirier, Agnes ... 944
LEFT BANK, PARIS FRANCE
   Poirier, Agnes. *Left Bank* ... 944
Left on Tenth. Ephron, Delia ... B
★*A Left-Handed Woman*. Thurman, Judith ... 814
Leg. Marshall, Greg ... B
LEGACIES
   Crasnianski, Tania. *The Children of Nazis* ... 943.086
   Giovanni, Nikki. *Make Me Rain* ... 811
   Posnanski, Joe. ★*The Life and Afterlife of Harry Houdini* ... 793.8
Legacy. Blackstock, Uche ... 610.92
Legacy of Ashes. Weiner, Tim ... 327.1273009
A Legacy of Liberation. Gevisser, Mark ... B
Legacy of Violence. Elkins, Caroline ... 909
LEGAL ASSISTANCE TO POOR PEOPLE
   Houppert, Karen. *Chasing Gideon* ... 345.73
   Rapping, Jonathan. *Gideon's Promise* ... 345.73
LEGAL DOCUMENTS
   Betts, Reginald Dwayne. ★*Redaction* ... 704.9
LEGAL ETHICS
   Lithwick, Dahlia. *Lady Justice* ... 345.73
The Legal Guide for Writers, Artists and Other Creative People. Norwick, Kenneth P. ... 346.04
LEGAL MALPRACTICE
   Dybdahl, Thomas L. *When Innocence Is Not Enough* ... 345.73
   King, Gilbert. *Beneath a Ruthless Sun* ... B
   Rudolf, David S. *American Injustice* ... 345.73
LEGAL RESEARCH
   Tucker, Virginia. *Finding the Answers to Legal Questions* ... 340.072
LEGAZPI, MIGUEL LOPEZ DE, 1510?-1572
   Resendez, Andres. *Conquering the Pacific* ... 959.9
The Legend of Marathon. Karnazes, Dean ... 796.42
LEGENDS
   Moore, Susanna. *Paradise of the Pacific* ... 996.9
★*The Legends Club*. Feinstein, John ... B
Legenhausen, Courtney
   Fashion Jewelry ... 745.594
LEGISLATION
   Andrews, Becca. ★*No Choice* ... 362.1988
   Barnett, Brittany K. ★*A Knock at Midnight* ... B
   Beard, Mary. ★*S.P.Q.R.* ... 937
   Brodsky, Alexandra. *Sexual Justice* ... 364.15
   Carpenter, Dale. *Flagrant Conduct* ... 342.7308
   Cenziper, Debbie. ★*Love Wins* ... 346.7301
   Cervini, Eric. *The Deviant's War* ... B
   Chertoff, Michael. *Exploding Data* ... 343.7309
   Cohn, Jonathan. *The Ten Year War* ... 368.38
   Crump, Benjamin. *Open Season* ... 364
   Davis, Lennard J. *Enabling Acts* ... 342.7308
   Delbanco, Andrew. *The War Before the War* ... 973.7
   Dufton, Emily. *Grass Roots* ... 362.29
   Feldman, Noah. *The Broken Constitution* ... 973.7
   Fieseler, Robert W. *Tinderbox* ... 364.152
   Freeberg, Ernest. *A Traitor to His Species* ... B
   Friedman, Barry. ★*Unwarranted* ... 344.7305
   Gergel, Richard. *Unexampled Courage* ... 323.1196
   Kaplan, Roberta A. *Then Comes Marriage* ... 346.7301
   Khan, Mahvish Rukhsana. *My Guantanamo Diary* ... 973.931
   Klobuchar, Amy. ★*Antitrust* ... 343.73
   Kotz, Nick. *Judgment Days* ... 323
   Lapidus, Lenora M. ★*The Rights of Women* ... 346.7301
   Leavitt, David. *The Man Who Knew Too Much* ... B
   Lessig, Lawrence. *The Future of Ideas* ... 346.04
   Luxenberg, Steve. ★*Separate* ... 342.7308
   Mandery, Evan J. *A Wild Justice* ... 345.73
   Marshall, Thurgood. *Thurgood Marshall*
   Masur, Kate. *Until Justice Be Done* ... 323.1196
   Murphy, Chris. ★*The Violence Inside Us* ... 303.60973
   Norwick, Kenneth P. *The Legal Guide for Writers, Artists and Other Creative People* ... 346.04
   O'Sullivan, Emer. *The Fall of the House of Wilde* ... B
   Prager, Joshua. *The Family Roe* ... 342.7308
   Prejean, Helen. *The Death of Innocents* ... 364.66
   Richards, Leonard L. *Who Freed the Slaves?* ... 342.7308
   Risen, Clay. *The Bill of the Century* ... 342.7308
   Roberts, Dorothy E. *Torn Apart* ... 362.7

   Sanger, Carol. *About Abortion* ... 179.7
   Shah, Meera. *You're the Only One I've Told* ... 362.1988
   Sohn, Amy. *The Man Who Hated Women* ... 363.28
   Urofsky, Melvin I. *The Affirmative Action Puzzle* ... 331.13
   Weiner, Mark Stuart. *Black Trials* ... 342.7308
   Wise, Steven M. *Though the Heavens May Fall* ... 342.42
LEGISLATIVE POWER
   Barron, David J. *Waging War* ... 342.73
LEGISLATORS
   Abrams, Stacey. *Lead from the Outside* ... B
   Biden, Joseph R. *Promise Me, Dad* ... B
   Blumenthal, Sidney. ★*All the Powers of Earth* ... B
   Bordewich, Fergus M. *Congress at War* ... 324.2734
   Clinton, Hillary Rodham. *Living History* ... B
   Cummings, Elijah. ★*We're Better Than This* ... B
   Farrell, John A. *Ted Kennedy* ... B
   Frank, Barney. *Frank* ... B
   Freeman, Joanne B. *The Field of Blood* ... 973.7
   Gabler, Neal. ★*Against the Wind* ... B
   Gabler, Neal. *Catching the Wind* ... B
   Gallego, Ruben. *They Called Us* ... 956.7044
   Hirono, Mazie. *Heart of Fire* ... B
   Jayapal, Pramila. *Use the Power You Have* ... B
   Jones, Brenda. *Alexandria Ocasio-Cortez* ... B
   Jones, Brenda. *Maxine Waters* ... B
   Katz, David. *Barack Before Obama* ... B
   Kennedy, John F. *Profiles in Courage* ... 920
   Kerry, John. *Every Day Is Extra* ... B
   Lewis, John. ★*Run; Book One* ... 741.5
   Lewis, John. *Walking with the Wind* ... B
   Logevall, Fredrik. ★*JFK* ... B
   Mahoney, Richard D. *Sons & Brothers* ... 920
   Matthews, Christopher. *Bobby Kennedy* ... B
   May, Gary. *John Tyler* ... B
   Obama, Barack. ★*The Audacity of Hope* ... B
   Obama, Barack. ★*Dreams from My Father* ... B
   Osnos, Evan. *Joe Biden* ... B
   Risen, James. ★*The Last Honest Man* ... 973.92
   Rumsfeld, Donald. *When the Center Held* ... 973.925092
   Sellers, Bakari. *My Vanishing Country* ... B
   Tester, Jon. *Grounded* ... B
   Thomas, Evan. ★*Robert Kennedy* ... B
   Tye, Larry. ★*Bobby Kennedy* ... B
   Tye, Larry. ★*Demagogue* ... B
   Zelizer, Julian E. *Burning Down the House* ... 328.73
Legitimating New Religions. Lewis, James R. ... 200
Legler, Casey
   ★*Godspeed* ... B
LEGLER, CASEY
   Legler, Casey. ★*Godspeed* ... B
LEGO TOYS
   Robertson, David C. *Brick by Brick* ... 338.7
   Still, Ben. *Particle Physics Brick by Brick* ... 539.7
Lehman, David
   A Fine Romance ... 781.64
LeHoullier, Craig
   Epic Tomatoes ... 635
Lehr, Dick
   ★*The Birth of a Nation* ... 305.800973
   White Hot Hate ... 363.325
Lehrer, Riva
   Golem Girl ... B
LEHRER, RIVA, 1958-
   Lehrer, Riva. *Golem Girl* ... B
Leibovitz, Annie
   A Photographer's Life, 1990-2005 ... 779
   Women ... 779
LEIBOVITZ, ANNIE, 1949-
   Leibovitz, Annie. *A Photographer's Life, 1990-2005* ... 779
   Leibovitz, Annie. *Women* ... 779
Leibovitz, Liel
   ★*How the Talmud Can Change Your Life* ... 296.1
Leinbach, Michael D.
   Bringing Columbia Home ... 363.12
LEISURE
   Biss, Eula. *Having and Being Had* ... 306.3
   Odell, Jenny. ★*Saving Time* ... 153.7
   Olds, Sally. ★*People Who Lunch* ... 824

AUTHOR, TITLE, SERIES AND SUBJECT INDEX

LEISURE CLASS
    Barr, Luke. *Ritz & Escoffier* — 920
    Veblen, Thorstein. ★*The Theory of the Leisure Class* — 305.5
Leithauser, Brad
    Rhyme's Rooms — 808.1
Lekas Miller, Anna
    Love Across Borders — 323.6
LEKAS MILLER, ANNA, 1990-
    Lekas Miller, Anna. *Love Across Borders* — 323.6
Leland, Andrew
    ★*The Country of the Blind* — B
LELAND, ANDREW
    Leland, Andrew. ★*The Country of the Blind* — B
Lemann, Nicholas
    Redemption — 975
    Transaction Man — 330.973
LEMAY, CURTIS E., 1906-1990
    Gladwell, Malcolm. ★*The Bomber Mafia* — 940.54
    Scott, James. *Black Snow* — 940.54
Lemay, Mimi
    What We Will Become — 306.874
LEMAY, MIMI
    Lemay, Mimi. *What We Will Become* — 306.874
Lembke, Anna
    Dopamine Nation — 152.4
LEMKIN, RAPHAEL, 1900-1959
    Sands, Philippe. *East West Street* — 345
Lemmon, Gayle Tzemach
    Ashley's War — B
    The Daughters of Kobani — 956.9104
    The Dressmaker of Khair Khana — B
    ★*The Lemon Tree*. Tolan, Sandy
Lemon, Don
    This Is the Fire — 305.896
LEMON, DON
    Lemon, Don. *This Is the Fire* — 305.896
LEMOND, GREG
    De Vise, Daniel. *The Comeback* — B
    Lena Corwin's Made by Hand. Corwin, Lena — 746.6
Lenburg, Jeff
    The Encyclopedia of Animated Cartoons — 791.43
Leng'ete, Nice
    The Girls in the Wild Fig Tree — B
LENG'ETE, NICE
    Leng'ete, Nice. *The Girls in the Wild Fig Tree* — B
    Leni Riefenstahl. Trimborn, Jurgen — B
    Lenin. Sebestyen, Victor — B
    Lenin on the Train. Merridale, Catherine — B
    Lenin's Tomb. Remnick, David — 947.085
LENIN, VLADIMIR IL'ICH, 1870-1924
    Figes, Orlando. *A People's Tragedy* — 947.08
    Herman, Arthur. *1917* — 940.3
    Merridale, Catherine. *Lenin on the Train* — B
    Mieville, China. *October* — 947.084
    Sebestyen, Victor. *Lenin* — B
    Service, Robert. *Lenin—A Biography* — B
    Lenin—A Biography. Service, Robert — B
    Leningrad. Moynahan, Brian — 780.92
    Leningrad. Reid, Anna — 940.54
LENNON, JOHN, 1940-1980
    Brown, Craig. *150 Glimpses of the Beatles* — 920
    Connolly, Ray. *Being John Lennon* — B
    Doggett, Peter. *You Never Give Me Your Money* — B
    Norman, Philip. *John Lennon* — B
LENNOX, MARGARET DOUGLAS, COUNTESS OF, 1515-1578
    Weir, Alison. *The Lost Tudor Princess* — B
LENZ, FRANK G
    Herlihy, David V. *The Lost Cyclist* — B
Lenzer, Jeanne
    The Danger Within Us — 338.4
Leon, Donna
    My Venice and Other Essays — 945
LEON, DONNA
    Leon, Donna. *My Venice and Other Essays* — 945
    ★*Leonard Bernstein*. Bernstein, Burton — B
    Leonard Woolf. Glendinning, Victoria — B
Leonard, Christopher
    Kochland — 338.7

Leonard, Max
    Lanterne Rouge — 796.6
LEONARD, SUGAR RAY, 1956-
    Kimball, George. *Four Kings* — B
    ★*Leonardo and the Last Supper*. King, Ross — 759.5
    Leonardo Da Vinci. Nuland, Sherwin B. — B
    Leonardo Da Vinci. Aquino, Lucia — 709.2
    ★*Leonardo Da Vinci*. Isaacson, Walter — B
    Leonardo's Holy Child. Kline, Fred R. — 741.09
LEONARDO, DA VINCI, 1452-1519
    Aquino, Lucia. *Leonardo Da Vinci* — 709.2
    Brewer, John. *The American Leonardo* — 759.5
    Hales, Dianne R. *Mona Lisa* — B
    Isaacson, Walter. ★*Leonardo Da Vinci* — B
    King, Ross. ★*Leonardo and the Last Supper* — 759.5
    Kline, Fred R. *Leonardo's Holy Child* — 741.09
    Lester, Toby. *Da Vinci's Ghost* — 741.092
    Nuland, Sherwin B. *Leonardo Da Vinci* — B
    Scotti, R. A. *Vanished Smile* — 759.5
    Strathern, Paul. *The Florentines* — 945
Leong, Sonia
    101 Top Tips from Professional Manga Artists — 741.5
Leonhardt, David
    ★*Ours Was the Shining Future* — 330.973
Leonnig, Carol
    I Alone Can Fix It — 973.933
LEOPOLD II, KING OF THE BELGIANS, 1835-1909
    Hochschild, Adam. *King Leopold's Ghost* — 967.51
Leopold, Aldo
    ★*A Sand County Almanac & Other Writings on Ecology and Conservation* — 814
LEOPOLD, ALDO, 1886-1948
    Freeman, Scott. *Saving Tarboo Creek* — 333.72
LEOPOLD, NATHAN FREUDENTHAL, 1904-1971
    King, Greg. *Nothing but the Night* — 364.152
Leovy, Jill
    Ghettoside — 364.152
LEPIDOPTERA
    Williams, Wendy. *The Language of Butterflies* — 595.78
Lepore, Jill
    Book of Ages — B
    ★*The Deadline* — 814
    The Name of War — 973.2
    New York Burning — 974.7
    ★*The Secret History of Wonder Woman* — 741.5
    ★*These Truths* — 973
LEPORE, JILL, 1966-
    Lepore, Jill. ★*The Deadline* — 814
LEPROSY
    Fessler, Pam. *Carville's Cure* — 362.19699
    White, Neil. *In the Sanctuary of Outcasts* — B
Lerner, Harriet Goldhor
    ★*The Dance of Anger* — 152.4
    The Dance of Intimacy — 155.6
    Les Fleurs Du Mal. Baudelaire, Charles — 841
LESBIAN ACTIVISTS
    Kugle, Scott Alan. *Living Out Islam* — 297
LESBIAN ATHLETES
    Howard, Johnette. *The Rivals* — B
LESBIAN AUTHORS
    Hagberg, Eva. *How to Be Loved* — 616.7
    Madden, T Kira. *Long Live the Tribe of Fatherless Girls* — 814
    Tea, Michelle. *Against Memoir* — B
LESBIAN COUPLES
    Asgarian, Roxanna. *We Were Once a Family* — 364.152
    Cenziper, Debbie. ★*Love Wins* — 346.7301
    Kaplan, Roberta A. *Then Comes Marriage* — 346.7301
LESBIAN CULTURE
    Possanza, Amelia. *Lesbian Love Story* — B
    Lesbian Love Story. Possanza, Amelia — B
LESBIAN MARRIAGE
    Becker, Jo. ★*Forcing the Spring* — 346.79401
LESBIAN MOTHERS
    Mehra, Nishta. *Brown, White, Black* — 305.800973
LESBIAN POETS
    Travisano, Thomas J. *Love Unknown* — B
LESBIAN TEENAGERS
    Bechdel, Alison. ★*Fun Home* — 741.5
    Cooper, Alex. *Saving Alex* — B

PUBLIC LIBRARY CORE COLLECTION: NONFICTION
Twentieth Edition

LESBIANISM
    Lorde, Audre. *Sister Outsider* — 814
LESBIANS
    Bechdel, Alison. ★*The Secret to Superhuman Strength* — 741.5
    Becker, Jo. ★*Forcing the Spring* — 346.79401
    Bronski, Michael. *A Queer History of the United States* — 306.76
    Butcher, Barbara. *What the Dead Know* — 614
    Carlile, Brandi. *Broken Horses* — B
    Carter, Alice A. *The Red Rose Girls* — B
    Carter, David. *Stonewall* — 306.76
    Cenziper, Debbie. ★*Love Wins* — 346.7301
    Cooper, Alex. *Saving Alex* — B
    Dais, Dawn. *The Sh!t No One Tells You About Divorce* — 306.89
    Diaz, Jaquira. *Ordinary Girls* — 818
    Doyle, Glennon. *Untamed* — B
    Etheridge, Melissa. *Talking to My Angels* — B
    Fagan, Kate. *All the Colors Came Out* — B
    Fremont, Helen. *The Escape Artist* — B
    Funk, Mason. *The Book of Pride* — 920
    Gadsby, Hannah. ★*Ten Steps to Nanette* — B
    Gaffney, Ginger. *Half Broke* — B
    Gelwicks, Andrew. *The Queer Advantage* — 920
    Glass, Sara. *Kissing Girls on Shabbat* — B
    Gutowitz, Jill. *Girls Can Kiss Now* — 814
    Hacker, Marilyn. *Selected Poems, 1965-1990* — 811
    Hempel, Jessi. *The Family Outing* — B
    Hester, Diarmuid. *Nothing Ever Just Disappears* — 306.76
    Highsmith, Patricia. ★*Patricia Highsmith's Diaries and Notebooks* — 818
    Irby, Samantha. ★*Quietly Hostile* — 814
    Kaplan, Roberta A. *Then Comes Marriage* — 346.7301
    King, Billie Jean. ★*All In* — B
    Koch, Bea. *Mad and Bad* — 920
    Kugle, Scott Alan. *Living Out Islam* — 297
    Machado, Carmen Maria. ★*In the Dream House* — B
    Moser, Benjamin. ★*Sontag* — B
    Mufleh, Luma. ★*Learning America* — 371.826
    Parks, Casey. *Diary of a Misfit* — B
    Possanza, Amelia. *Lesbian Love Story* — B
    Rapinoe, Megan. *One Life* — B
    Reang, Putsata. *Ma and Me* — B
    Regan, Iliana. *Fieldwork* — B
    Shapland, Jenn. *My Autobiography of Carson McCullers* — B
    Sherr, Lynn. *Sally Ride* — B
    Town, Caren J. *LGBTQ Young Adult Fiction* — 813.009
    Travisano, Thomas J. *Love Unknown* — B
    Wambach, Abby. *Forward* — B
    Windsor, Edie. *A Wild and Precious Life* — B
    Wojczuk, Tana. *Lady Romeo* — B
    Yoshino, Kenji. *Speak Now* — 346.79401
Leschziner, Guy
    The Nocturnal Brain — 616.8
The Less People Know About Us. Betz-Hamilton, Axton — 364.16
The Less You Know, the Better You Sleep. Satter, David — 947.086
LESSEPS, FERDINAND MARIE, COMTE DE, 1805-1894
    McCullough, David G. *The Path Between the Seas* — 972.87
Lessig, Lawrence
    The Future of Ideas — 346.04
    Remix — 346.7304
Lessing, Doris May
    Under My Skin — 823
LESSING, DORIS MAY, 1919-2013
    Lessing, Doris May. *Under My Skin* — 823
Lessons for Living. Stutz, Phil — 158.1
Lessons for Survival. Raboteau, Emily — 814
Lessons from a Dark Time. Hochschild, Adam — 909.82
Lessons from the Edge. Yovanovitch, Marie — 973.933
Lessons in Realistic Watercolor. Robinson, Mario Andres — 751.42
Lessons on Expulsion. Sanchez, Erika L. — 811
Lester, Toby
    Da Vinci's Ghost — 741.092
Let Every Nation Know. Dallek, Robert — B
Let Her Fly. Yousafzai, Ziauddin — B
Let History Judge. Medvedev, Roy Aleksandrovich — 947.084
Let Me Finish. Christie, Chris — B
Let Me Not Be Mad. Benjamin, A. K. — 612.8
Let Me Tell You. Jackson, Shirley — 818
★*Let Me Tell You What I Mean*. Didion, Joan — 814
★*Let The Lord Sort Them*. Chammah, Maurice — 364.66

Let Them Eat Dirt. Finlay, B. Brett — 616.9
★*Let Them See You*. Braswell, Porter — 650.1
Let Us Dream. Francis — 282.092
Let Us Now Praise Famous Men. Agee, James — 976.1
Let's Do It. Stanley, Bob — 781.64
Let's Eat. Pelosi, Dan — 641.5
Let's Go (so We Can Get Back). Tweedy, Jeff — B
Let's make (Graphic novel cookbooks) [Series]. Amano, Hugh — 741.5
★*Let's Make Bread!* Forkish, Ken — 741.5
Let's Make Dumplings! Amano, Hugh — 741.5
Let's Never Talk About This Again. Alterman, Sara Faith — 616.8
Let's Play Two. Rapoport, Ron — B
Let's Take the Long Way Home. Caldwell, Gail — B
★*Let's Talk About Hard Things*. Sale, Anna — 153.6
Let's Talk About Race in Storytimes. Bratt, Jessica Anne — 027.62
Letter to a Young Farmer. Logsdon, Gene — 338.10973
Letter to My Daughter. Angelou, Maya — 814
LETTER WRITING
    Adams, Abigail. *Abigail Adams* — 973.4
    Adichie, Chimamanda Ngozi. *Dear Ijeawele* — 649
    Bradbury, Ray. ★*Remembrance* — 813
    Cather, Willa. *The Selected Letters of Willa Cather* — B
    Coffin, Judith G. *Sex, Love, and Letters* — 848
    Ellison, Ralph. *The Selected Letters of Ralph Ellison* — 813
    Englund, Peter. *November 1942* — 940.53
    Fehrman, Craig. *Author in Chief* — 920
    Gunn, Thom. ★*The Letters of Thom Gunn* — 821
    Hardwick, Elizabeth. *The Dolphin Letters, 1970-1979* — 811
    Hemingway, Ernest. *Dear Papa* — 813
    Isenberg, Sheila. *Women Who Love Men Who Kill* — 362.83
    Jaouad, Suleika. ★*Between Two Kingdoms* — B
    Kingston, Genevieve. *Did I Ever Tell You?* — B
    Koh, EJ. *The Magical Language of Others* — 813
    Lepore, Jill. *Book of Ages* — B
    Porter, Carolyn. *Marcel's Letters* — 940.54
    Raban, Jonathan. *Father and Son* — B
    Reagan, Ronald. *Reagan* — B
    Shapland, Jenn. *My Autobiography of Carson McCullers* — B
    Thom, Kai Cheng. *Falling Back in Love with Being Human* — 811
    Wagamese, Richard. *For Joshua* — B
    Webb, Maynard. *Dear Founder* — 658
LETTERING
    Doh, Jenny. *Creative Lettering* — 745.6
    Flor, Martina. *The Golden Secrets of Lettering* — 745.6
    Glynn, Kathy. *Hand Lettering Step by Step* — 745.6
    Rodriguez, Dina. *The Big Awesome Book of Hand & Chalk Lettering* — 745.6
LETTERS
    Adams, John. *My Dearest Friend* — 973.4
    Beckett, Samuel. *The Letters of Samuel Beckett* — 848
    Bradbury, Ray. ★*Remembrance* — 813
    Coffin, Judith G. *Sex, Love, and Letters* — 848
    Cooper, Anderson. *The Rainbow Comes and Goes* — B
    Cronkite, Walter. *Cronkite's War* — 070.4
    Dyson, Freeman J. *Maker of Patterns* — B
    Ellison, Ralph. *The Selected Letters of Ralph Ellison* — 813
    Englund, Peter. *November 1942* — 940.53
    Ghobash, Omar Saif. *Letters to a Young Muslim* — 297.09
    Greene, Graham. *Graham Greene* — 823
    Gunn, Thom. ★*The Letters of Thom Gunn* — 821
    Halevi, Yossi Klein. ★*Letters to My Palestinian Neighbor* — 956.94054
    Hardwick, Elizabeth. *The Dolphin Letters, 1970-1979* — 811
    Hardy, Thomas. *The Collected Letters of Thomas Hardy* — 823
    Hemingway, Ernest. *Dear Papa* — 813
    Hogan, William R. *Task Force Hogan* — 940.54
    Hurston, Zora Neale. *Zora Neale Hurston* — B
    Jackson, Shirley. ★*The Letters of Shirley Jackson* — 813
    Jefferson, Thomas. *Writings* — 973.3
    Kempowski, Walter. *Swansong 1945* — 940.54
    Knausgaard, Karl Ove. *Spring* — B
    Koh, EJ. *The Magical Language of Others* — 813
    Laughlin, James. *The Luck of Friendship* — B
    Lowe, George. *Letters from Everest* — 796.522
    Mandela, Nelson. *The Prison Letters of Nelson Mandela* — 968.06092
    Moore, Marianne. *The Selected Letters of Marianne Moore* — B
    Olsen, Craig. *P.S. Burn This Letter Please* — 306.76
    Plath, Sylvia. *The Letters of Sylvia Plath* — 811.54
    Plath, Sylvia. *The Letters of Sylvia Plath* — 811.54
    Rilke, Rainer Maria. ★*Letters to a Young Poet* — 831

AUTHOR, TITLE, SERIES AND SUBJECT INDEX

Ruhl, Sarah. *Letters from Max*	811
Thompson, Hunter S. ★*Fear and Loathing in America*	B
Tyson, Neil deGrasse. *Letters from an Astrophysicist*	520.92
Vonnegut, Kurt. *Kurt Vonnegut*	813
Wagamese, Richard. *For Joshua*	B
Wilder, Laura Ingalls. *The Selected Letters of Laura Ingalls Wilder*	B
Wong, Ali. ★*Dear Girls*	B
Letters from an Astrophysicist. Tyson, Neil deGrasse	520.92
Letters from Everest. Lowe, George	796.522
Letters from Max. Ruhl, Sarah	811
The Letters of Samuel Beckett. Beckett, Samuel	848
Letters of Samuel Beckett [Series]. Beckett, Samuel	848
★*The Letters of Shirley Jackson*. Jackson, Shirley	813
The Letters of Sylvia Plath. Plath, Sylvia	811.54
The Letters of Sylvia Plath. Plath, Sylvia	811.54
★*The Letters of Thom Gunn*. Gunn, Thom	821
Letters to a Young Muslim. Ghobash, Omar Saif	297.09
★*Letters to a Young Poet*. Rilke, Rainer Maria	831
★*Letters to a Young Scientist*. Wilson, Edward O.	570.92
Letters to a Young Teacher. Kozol, Jonathan	371.1
Letters to a Young Writer. McCann, Colum	808.02
Letters to Malcolm. Lewis, C. S.	248.3
★*Letters to My Palestinian Neighbor*. Halevi, Yossi Klein	956.94054
Letters to My White Male Friends. Ross, Dax-Devlon	305.8
Letts, Elizabeth	
The Perfect Horse	940.54
★*The Ride of Her Life*	B
LEUKEMIA	
Jaouad, Suleika. ★*Between Two Kingdoms*	B
Mukherjee, Siddhartha. ★*The Emperor of All Maladies*	616.99
Leung, Bill	
★*The Woks of Life*	641.7
Lev, Arlene Istar	
The Complete Lesbian & Gay Parenting Guide	649
Levack, Brian P.	
The Devil Within	133.4
★*The Levantine Vegetarian*. Hage, Salma	641.595
LEVEES	
Horne, Jed. *Breach of Faith*	976.3
Level Up. Abrams, Stacey	658.4
Level Zero Heroes. Golembesky, Michael	958.104
Levels of the Game. McPhee, John	796.34
Leventon, Melissa	
What People Wore When	391.009
Lever, Evelyne	
Marie Antoinette	B
Levertov, Denise	
Selected Poems	811
Levesque, Emily	
The Last Stargazers	520
LEVESQUE, EMILY	
Levesque, Emily. *The Last Stargazers*	520
Levi, Heather	
The World of Lucha Libre	796.812
Levi, Primo	
★*The Drowned and the Saved*	940.53
The Periodic Table	858
The Reawakening	B
★*Survival in Auschwitz*	B
LEVI, PRIMO	
Levi, Primo. ★*The Drowned and the Saved*	940.53
Levi, Primo. *The Periodic Table*	858
Levi, Primo. *The Reawakening*	B
Levi, Primo. ★*Survival in Auschwitz*	B
Levi-Strauss, Claude	
★*The Savage Mind*	155.8
★*Leviathan*. Hobbes, Thomas	320.01
Levin, Daniel	
Proof of Life	956.9104
Levin, Daniel Barban	
Slonim Woods 9	B
LEVIN, DANIEL BARBAN	
Levin, Daniel Barban. *Slonim Woods 9*	B
LEVIN, DANIEL, 1963-	
Levin, Daniel. *Proof of Life*	956.9104
Levin, Gail	
Edward Hopper	759.13
Levin, Janna	
Black Hole Blues	539.7
Levin, Josh	
The Queen	364.16
Levine, Amy-Jill	
The Bible with and Without Jesus	220.6
Short Stories by Jesus	226.8
Levine, Bruce C.	
The Fall of the House of Dixie	973.7
Thaddeus Stevens	B
Levine, Madeline	
★*Ready or Not*	649
Levine, Philip	
The Simple Truth	811
Levine, Robert S.	
★*The Failed Promise*	973.8
Levingston, Steven	
Kennedy and King	920
Levinsohn, Florence Hamlish	
Looking for Farrakhan	B
Levitin, Daniel J.	
★*A Field Guide to Lies*	153.4
Levitt, Dan	
What's Gotten into You	539.7
Levitt, Steven D.	
★*Freakonomics*	330
Superfreakonomics	330
Levy, Aidan	
Saxophone Colossus	B
Levy, Buddy	
Labyrinth of Ice	910.91
Levy, Deborah	
The Cost of Living	B
★*Real Estate*	B
★*Things I Don't Want to Know*	B
LEVY, DEBORAH	
Levy, Deborah. *The Cost of Living*	B
Levy, Deborah. ★*Real Estate*	B
Levy, Jonathan	
Ages of American Capitalism	330.12
Levy, Reynold	
They Told Me Not to Take That Job	792.09
LEVY, REYNOLD	
Levy, Reynold. *They Told Me Not to Take That Job*	792.09
Levy, Shawn	
★*The Castle on Sunset*	647.95
★*In on the Joke*	792.7
Lewis, Anthony	
Gideon's Trumpet	345.73
Lewis, Bernard	
The Middle East	956
Lewis, C. S.	
★*A Grief Observed*	242
Letters to Malcolm	248.3
Mere Christianity	230
Miracles	231.7
★*The Screwtape Letters*	248.4
LEWIS, C. S. (CLIVE STAPLES), 1898-1963	
Lewis, C. S. ★*A Grief Observed*	242
Wilson, A. N. *C.S. Lewis*	823
LEWIS, CUDJO	
Hurston, Zora Neale. ★*Barracoon*	B
Lewis, Damien	
Agent Josephine	B
Churchill's Hellraisers	940.54
The Dog Who Could Fly	940.54
LEWIS, DAMIEN	
Lewis, Damien. *The Dog Who Could Fly*	940.54
Lewis, Daniel	
Twelve Trees	582.16
Lewis, David L.	
★*W.E.B. Du Bois*	B
Lewis, Edna	
In Pursuit of Flavor	641.5975
Lewis, James R.	
Legitimating New Religions	200
Lewis, Jenifer	
Walking in My Joy	B

PUBLIC LIBRARY CORE COLLECTION: NONFICTION
Twentieth Edition

LEWIS, JENIFER, 1957-
   Lewis, Jenifer. *Walking in My Joy* — B
Lewis, John
   Badass Vegan — 641.5
   Carry On — 328.73
   ★*March; Book One* — 741.5
   ★*March; Book Three* — 741.5
   ★*March; Book Two* — 741.5
   ★*Run; Book One* — 741.5
   Walking with the Wind — B
LEWIS, JOHN, 1940-2020
   Arsenault, Raymond. *John Lewis* — B
   Lewis, John. *Carry On* — 328.73
   Lewis, John. ★*March; Book One* — 741.5
   Lewis, John. ★*March; Book Three* — 741.5
   Lewis, John. ★*March; Book Two* — 741.5
   Lewis, John. ★*Run; Book One* — 741.5
   Lewis, John. *Walking with the Wind* — B
   Meacham, Jon. *His Truth Is Marching On* — B
LEWIS, MERIWETHER, 1774-1809
   Ambrose, Stephen E. ★*Undaunted Courage* — 917.804
Lewis, Michael
   The Big Short — 330.973
   The Blind Side — B
   ★*Going Infinite* — 305.5
   Moneyball — 796.357
   ★*The Premonition* — 614.5
   ★*The Undoing Project* — 920
Lewis, Oscar
   The Children of Sanchez — 306.85
Lewis, Robin Coste
   To the Realization of Perfect Helplessness — 811
Lewis, Sara
   Silent Sparks — 595.76
LEWIS, SINCLAIR, 1885-1951
   Nafisi, Azar. *The Republic of Imagination* — B
LEXICOGRAPHERS
   Boswell, James. ★*The Life of Samuel Johnson* — B
   Ogilvie, Sarah. *The Dictionary People* — 423
   Simpson, J. A. *The Word Detective* — B
   Stamper, Kory. *Word by Word* — 413.028
   Winchester, Simon. *The Professor and the Madman* — 423
LEXICOGRAPHY
   Curzan, Anne. ★*Says Who?* — 428
   Ogilvie, Sarah. *The Dictionary People* — 423
   Simpson, J. A. *The Word Detective* — B
   Stamper, Kory. *Word by Word* — 413.028
   Winchester, Simon. *The Professor and the Madman* — 423
LEXINGTON, BATTLE OF, 1775
   Fischer, David Hackett. *Paul Revere's Ride* — 973.3
   Norton, Mary Beth. *1774* — 973.3
   Phillips, Kevin. *1775* — 973.3
LEYTE GULF, BATTLE OF, 1944
   Thomas, Evan. *Sea of Thunder* — 940.54
LGBTQ Young Adult Fiction. Town, Caren J. — 813.009
★**LGBTQIA+** Books for Children and Teens. Breitenbach, Kathleen — 028.7
LGBTQIA+ CHILDREN
   Amer, Lindz. *Rainbow Parenting* — 649
   Berg, Ryan. *No House to Call My Home* — B
   Breitenbach, Kathleen. ★*LGBTQIA+ Books for Children and Teens* — 028.7
   Turban, Jack L. ★*Free to Be* — 616.85
LGBTQIA+ COMICS
   Bechdel, Alison. ★*Fun Home* — 741.5
   Kobabe, Maia. *Gender Queer* — 741.5
LGBTQIA+ PEOPLE
   Ali, Fatima. ★*Savor* — B
   Barnes, Katie. ★*Fair Play* — 796.082
   Belcher, Chris. *Pretty Baby* — B
   Belser, Julia Watts. ★*Loving Our Own Bones* — 296
   Blount, Tommye. *Fantasia for the Man in Blue* — 811
   Bowen, Sesali. *Bad Fat Black Girl* — 305.42
   Breitenbach, Kathleen. ★*LGBTQIA+ Books for Children and Teens* — 028.7
   Busby, Jill Louise. *Unfollow Me* — 305.08
   Carlile, Brandi. *Broken Horses* — B
   Chin, Curtis. *Everything I Learned, I Learned in a Chinese Restaurant* — B
   Corbett, Emily. *In Transition* — 809
   Corral, Eduardo C. *Guillotine* — 811.6
   Cumming, Alan. *Baggage* — B

Dais, Dawn. *The Sh!t No One Tells You About Divorce* — 306.89
Daley, Tom. *Coming up for Air* — B
Dearborn, Mary V. *Carson McCullers* — B
Dennison, Matthew. *Behind the Mask* — B
Emezi, Akwaeke. ★*Dear Senthuran* — B
Etheridge, Melissa. *Talking to My Angels* — B
Faliveno, Melissa. *Tomboyland* — B
Funk, Mason. *The Book of Pride* — 920
Gadsby, Hannah. ★*Ten Steps to Nanette* — B
Gelwicks, Andrew. *The Queer Advantage* — 920
Glass, Sara. *Kissing Girls on Shabbat* — B
Goetsch, Diana. *This Body I Wore* — B
Gomez, Edgar. *High-Risk Homosexual* — B
Gooch, Brad. *Radiant* — B
Goodman, Elyssa. *Glitter and Concrete* — 792.7
H, Lamya. ★*Hijab Butch Blues* — B
Hauser, CJ. *The Crane Wife* — B
Hays, Katie. *Family of Origin, Family of Choice* — 248.8086
Hempel, Jessi. *The Family Outing* — B
Hermes, Will. *Lou Reed* — B
Hester, Diarmuid. *Nothing Ever Just Disappears* — 306.76
Hewitt, Sean. *All Down Darkness Wide* — B
Hough, Lauren. *Leaving Isn't the Hardest Thing* — B
King, Billie Jean. ★*All In* — B
Kobabe, Maia. *Gender Queer* — 741.5
LaPointe, Sasha taqwseblu. *Thunder Song* — 814
Mans, Jasmine. *Black Girl, Call Home* — 811
Mock, Janet. *Surpassing Certainty* — B
Moss, Jeremiah. *Feral City* — B
Ndopu, Eddie. *Sipping Dom Pérignon Through a Straw* — B
Okporo, Edafe. *Asylum* — B
Possanza, Amelia. *Lesbian Love Story* — B
Regan, Iliana. *Fieldwork* — B
Royster, Francesca T. *Choosing Family* — B
RuPaul. ★*The House of Hidden Meanings* — B
Sabatini Sloan, Aisha. *Dreaming of Ramadi in Detroit* — 814
Sante, Lucy. *I Heard Her Call My Name* — B
Schneider, Amy. *In the Form of a Question* — B
Seligman, Craig. *Who Does That Bitch Think She Is?* — 792.02
Shapiro, Ari. ★*The Best Strangers in the World* — B
Singh, Julietta. *The Breaks* — B
Sjunneson, Elsa. *Being Seen* — 362.4
So, Anthony Veasna. *Songs on Endless Repeat* — 814
Specter, Emma. *More, Please* — 616.85
Velour, Sasha. ★*The Big Reveal* — 792.7
Viren, Sarah. *To Name the Bigger Lie* — B
Wallace, Carvell. *Another Word for Love* — B
Windsor, Edie. *A Wild and Precious Life* — B
Wojczuk, Tana. *Lady Romeo* — B
Wolf, Brandon J. *A Place for Us* — B
Yoshino, Kenji. *Say the Right Thing* — 305.3
LGBTQIA+ RIGHTS
   Becker, Jo. ★*Forcing the Spring* — 346.79401
   Black, Dustin Lance. *Mama's Boy* — B
   Butler, Isaac. *The World Only Spins Forward* — 812
   Carpenter, Dale. *Flagrant Conduct* — 342.7308
   Carter, David. *Stonewall* — 306.76
   Cenziper, Debbie. ★*Love Wins* — 346.7301
   Cervini, Eric. *The Deviant's War* — B
   Chee, Alexander. ★*How to Write an Autobiographical Novel* — B
   France, David. *How to Survive a Plague* — 362.196
   Funk, Mason. *The Book of Pride* — 920
   Kaplan, Roberta A. *Then Comes Marriage* — 346.7301
   Mullen, Bill. ★*James Baldwin* — B
   Nutt, Amy Ellis. *Becoming Nicole* — 920
   O'Connor, Garry. *Ian McKellen* — B
   Rashid, Jonny. *Jesus Takes a Side* — 261.7
   Velour, Sasha. ★*The Big Reveal* — 792.7
   Weigel, Alicia Roth. *Inverse Cowgirl* — B
   Willis, Raquel. *The Risk It Takes to Bloom* — B
   Windsor, Edie. *A Wild and Precious Life* — B
   Yoshino, Kenji. *Speak Now* — 346.79401
LGBTQIA+ TEENAGERS
   Berg, Ryan. *No House to Call My Home* — B
   Breitenbach, Kathleen. ★*LGBTQIA+ Books for Children and Teens* — 028.7
   Town, Caren J. *LGBTQ Young Adult Fiction* — 813.009
   Turban, Jack L. ★*Free to Be* — 616.85

AUTHOR, TITLE, SERIES AND SUBJECT INDEX

Li, Fei-Fei
   The Worlds I See   B
LI, FEI-FEI, 1976-
   Li, Fei-Fei. *The Worlds I See*   B
Li, Yiyun
   Dear Friend, from My Life I Write to You in Your Life   B
LI, YIYUN, 1972-
   Li, Yiyun. *Dear Friend, from My Life I Write to You in Your Life*   B
Li, Zhuqing
   Daughters of the Flower Fragrant Garden   951.04
Liao, Yiwu
   Bullets and Opium   951.05
   God Is Red   275
The Liar. Cunningham, Benjamin   327.1273
Liar's Circus. Hoffman, Carl   973.933
The Liar's Tale. Campbell, Jeremy   177
Liar, Temptress, Soldier, Spy. Abbott, Karen   920
LIBEL AND SLANDER
   Hortis, C. Alexander. *The Witch of New York*   364.152
   Kroll, Andy. *A Death on W Street*   364.152
   McCraw, David Edward. *Truth in Our Times*   342.7308
LIBERAL WRITING
   Ahmed, Sara. *The Feminist Killjoy Handbook*   305.42
   Barkan, Ady. *Eyes to the Wind*   B
   Bryant, Howard. *Full Dissidence*   306.20973
   Carpenter, Amanda B. *Gaslighting America*   973.933
   Chomsky, Noam. *Global Discontents*   410.92
   Clinton, Hillary Rodham. *Living History*   B
   Cohen, Adam. ★*Supreme Inequality*   347.73
   Cullen, Art. *Storm Lake*   071.7
   Cummings, Elijah. ★*We're Better Than This*   B
   DiFranco, Ani. *No Walls and the Recurring Dream*   782.42164
   Du Mez, Kristin Kobes. *Jesus and John Wayne*   277.308
   Frank, Barney. *Frank*   B
   Ganz, John. *When the Clock Broke*   320.52
   Gay, Roxane. ★*Opinions*   814
   Jones, Brenda. *Alexandria Ocasio-Cortez*   B
   Jones, Brenda. *Maxine Waters*   B
   Kaplan, David A. *The Most Dangerous Branch*   347.73
   Krugman, Paul R. *Arguing with Zombies*   330.973
   Kruse, Kevin Michael. *Fault Lines*   973.92
   Lithwick, Dahlia. *Lady Justice*   345.73
   Mogelson, Luke. *The Storm Is Here*   973.933
   Obama, Barack. ★*The Audacity of Hope*   B
   Plouffe, David. *A Citizen's Guide to Beating Donald Trump*   324.0973
   Sharpton, Al. *Rise Up*   973.933
   Solnit, Rebecca. *Call Them by Their True Names*   303.3
   Stelter, Brian. *Hoax*   070.4
   Tamblyn, Amber. ★*Era of Ignition*   B
   Theoharis, Jeanne. *A More Beautiful and Terrible History*   323.1196
   Toobin, Jeffrey. *True Crimes and Misdemeanors*   973.933
   Warren, Elizabeth. *This Fight Is Our Fight*   305.5
   Zinn, Howard. ★*A People's History of the United States*   973
LIBERALISM
   Busby, Jill Louise. *Unfollow Me*   305.08
   Coyle, Marcia. *The Roberts Court*   347.73
   Elkins, Caroline. *Legacy of Violence*   909
   Eyman, Scott. *Charlie Chaplin vs. America*   B
   Fukuyama, Francis. *Liberalism and Its Discontents*   320.51
   Gabler, Neal. *Catching the Wind*   B
   Peters, Charles. *Lyndon B. Johnson*   B
   Shorto, Russell. *Amsterdam*   949.2
   Woods, Randall Bennett. *Prisoners of Hope*   973.923
   Zeitz, Joshua. *Building the Great Society*   973.923
   Zygar, Mikhail. *The Empire Must Die*   947.08
Liberalism and Its Discontents. Fukuyama, Francis   320.51
LIBERALS
   Gabler, Neal. *Catching the Wind*   B
   Peters, Charles. *Lyndon B. Johnson*   B
   Spruill, Marjorie Julian. *Divided We Stand*   305.42
Liberation trilogy [Series]. Atkinson, Rick   940.54
LIBERIA
   Cooper, Helene. *The House at Sugar Beach*   921
   Cooper, Helene. *Madame President*   966.62
   Huffman, Alan. *Here I Am*   B
   Moore, Wayetu. *The Dragons, the Giant, the Women*   B
Libertarianism. Brennan, Jason   320.51

LIBERTARIANISM
   Brennan, Jason. *Libertarianism*   320.51
LIBERTARIANS
   Barlow, John Perry. *Mother American Night*   782.42164
Liberty Is Sweet. Holton, Woody   973.3
Liberty's Blueprint. Meyerson, Michael   342.7302
Librarian's Guide to Games and Gamers. Goodridge, Michelle   025.2
Librarian's Guide to Online Searching. Brown, Christopher C.   025.04
LIBRARIANS
   Bignoli, Callan. ★*Responding to Rapid Change in Libraries*   020
   Crews, Kenneth D. ★*Copyright Law for Librarians and Educators*   346.7304
   Crowley, Bill. *Defending Professionalism*   020.92
   Hammer, Joshua. *The Bad-Ass Librarians of Timbuktu*   025.8
   Harris, Lesley Ellen. *Licensing Digital Content*   346.7304
   Orlean, Susan. ★*The Library Book*   027.4
   Patterson, James. *The Secret Lives of Booksellers and Librarians*   381
   Russell, Carrie. *Complete Copyright for K-12 Librarians and Educators*   346.73
   Spence, Annie. *Dear Fahrenheit 451*   028.9
   Wright, Alex. *Cataloging the World*   020.9
LIBRARIES
   Anderson, Amelia. *Library Programming for Autistic Children and Teens*   027.6
   Anderson, Jimmeka. *Power Lines*   020
   Baez, Fernando. *Universal History of the Destruction of Books*   098
   Bignoli, Callan. ★*Responding to Rapid Change in Libraries*   020
   Boland, Becca. *Making the Most of Teen Library Volunteers*   023
   Bradford, Robin. ★*The Readers' Advisory Guide to Romance*   025.2
   Bratt, Jessica Anne. *Let's Talk About Race in Storytimes*   027.62
   Breitenbach, Kathleen. ★*LGBTQIA+ Books for Children and Teens*   028.7
   Curzon, Susan Carol. *What Every Library Director Should Know*   025.1
   Damon-Moore, Laura C. *The Artist's Library*   021.2
   Disher, Wayne. *Crash Course in Collection Development*   025.2
   Evans, G. Edward. *Collection Management Basics*   025.2
   Flaherty, Mary Grace. ★*The Disaster Planning Handbook for Libraries*   025.8
   Ghoting, Saroj Nadkarni. *Step into Storytime*   027.62
   Goodridge, Michelle. *Librarian's Guide to Games and Gamers*   025.2
   Hammer, Joshua. *The Bad-Ass Librarians of Timbuktu*   025.8
   Landau, Herbert B. *The Small Public Library Survival Guide*   025.1
   LaRue, James. ★*On Censorship*   025.2
   Maddigan, Beth. *Community Library Programs That Work*   021.2
   Myron, Vicki. *Dewey*   636.80092
   Orlean, Susan. ★*The Library Book*   027.4
   Pattee, Amy. *Developing Library Collections for Today's Young Adults*   027.62
   Pettegree, Andrew. *The Library*   027.4
   Phoenix, Jack. *Maximizing the Impact of Comics in Your Library*   026
   Reid, Rob. ★*200+ Original and Adapted Story Program Activities*   027.62
   Rogers-Whitehead, Carrie. ★*Serving Teens and Adults on the Autism Spectrum*   027.6
   Rydell, Anders. *The Book Thieves*   027
   Smith, G. Stevenson. *Cost Control for Nonprofits in Crisis*   025.1
   Snow, Jess. ★*Outreach Services for Teens*   027.4
   Spence, Annie. *Dear Fahrenheit 451*   028.9
   Spratford, Becky Siegel. *The Readers' Advisory Guide to Horror*   025.5
   Thenell, Jan. *The Library's Crisis Communications Planner*   021.7
   Thomson, Mike. *Syria's Secret Library*   956.9104
   Turnbow, Dominique. ★*Demystifying Online Instruction in Libraries*   028.7
   Verminski, Alana. ★*Fundamentals of Electronic Resources Management*   025.2
   Wilson-Lee, Edward. ★*The Catalogue of Shipwrecked Books*   B
LIBRARIES AND COMMUNITY
   Anderson, Jimmeka. *Power Lines*   020
   Damon-Moore, Laura C. *The Artist's Library*   021.2
   Farmer, Lesley S. J. ★*Impactful Community-Based Literacy Projects*   372.6
   Landau, Herbert B. *The Small Public Library Survival Guide*   025.1
   Maddigan, Beth. *Community Library Programs That Work*   021.2
   Snow, Jess. ★*Outreach Services for Teens*   027.4
LIBRARIES AND ELECTRONIC PUBLISHING
   Harris, Lesley Ellen. *Licensing Digital Content*   346.7304
   Verminski, Alana. ★*Fundamentals of Electronic Resources Management*   025.2
LIBRARIES AND SCHOOLS
   Anderson, Jimmeka. *Power Lines*   020
LIBRARIES AND SOCIETY
   Crowley, Bill. *Defending Professionalism*   020.92
   Thomson, Mike. *Syria's Secret Library*   956.9104

PUBLIC LIBRARY CORE COLLECTION: NONFICTION
Twentieth Edition

The Library. Pettegree, Andrew — 027.4
LIBRARY ADMINISTRATION
   Bignoli, Callan. ★*Responding to Rapid Change in Libraries* — 020
   Curzon, Susan Carol. *What Every Library Director Should Know* — 025.1
   Henry, Jo. *Cultivating Civility* — 023
   Laughlin, Sara. *The Quality Library* — 025.1
   McNeil, Beth. *Fundamentals of Library Supervision* — 023
   Smith, G. Stevenson. *Cost Control for Nonprofits in Crisis* — 025.1
   Tucker, Dennis C. *Crash Course in Library Supervision* — 023
   VanDuinkerken, Wyoma. *The Challenge of Library Management* — 025.1
   ★*The Library Book*. Orlean, Susan — 027.4
LIBRARY EMPLOYEES
   Henry, Jo. *Cultivating Civility* — 023
LIBRARY MATERIALS
   Bradford, Robin. ★*The Readers' Advisory Guide to Romance* — 025.2
   Breitenbach, Kathleen. ★*LGBTQIA+ Books for Children and Teens* — 028.7
   Dorr, Christina H. ★*Profiles in Resilience* — 028.5
   Flaherty, Mary Grace. ★*The Disaster Planning Handbook for Libraries* — 025.8
   Goodridge, Michelle. *Librarian's Guide to Games and Gamers* — 025.2
   Halsted, Deborah D. ★*Disaster Planning* — 025.8
   Johnson, Peggy. ★*Fundamentals of Collection Development and Management* — 025
   Spratford, Becky Siegel. *The Readers' Advisory Guide to Horror* — 025.5
The Library of America [Series]. Williams, Tennessee — 812
The library of America [Series]. Emerson, Ralph Waldo — 811
The library of Black America [Series]. Douglass, Frederick — 973.8
LIBRARY OUTREACH PROGRAMS
   Anderson, Jimmeka. *Power Lines* — 020
   Cole, Natalie. ★*Transforming Summer Programs at Your Library* — 028
   Rogers-Whitehead, Carrie. ★*Serving Teens and Adults on the Autism Spectrum* — 027.6
   Snow, Jess. ★*Outreach Services for Teens* — 027.4
LIBRARY PERSONNEL MANAGEMENT
   Henry, Jo. *Cultivating Civility* — 023
   McNeil, Beth. *Fundamentals of Library Supervision* — 023
   Newman, Bobbi L. ★*Fostering Wellness in the Workplace* — 023
   Stanley, Mary J. *Managing Library Employees* — 023
   Tucker, Dennis C. *Crash Course in Library Supervision* — 023
Library Programming for Autistic Children and Teens. Anderson, Amelia — 027.6
LIBRARY RESEARCH
   Brunsting, Karen. ★*Open Access Literature in Libraries* — 070.5
LIBRARY SCIENCE
   Berger, Sidney E. *The Dictionary of the Book* — 002.03
   Orlean, Susan. ★*The Library Book* — 027.4
LIBRARY USERS
   Bignoli, Callan. ★*Responding to Rapid Change in Libraries* — 020
   Damon-Moore, Laura C. *The Artist's Library* — 021.2
The Library's Crisis Communications Planner. Thenell, Jan — 021.7
LIBRETTOS
   Sondheim, Stephen. *Look, I Made a Hat* — 782.1
LIBYA
   Huffman, Alan. *Here I Am* — B
   Kilmeade, Brian. ★*Thomas Jefferson and the Tripoli Pirates* — 973.4
   Matar, Hisham. *The Return* — B
   Sattouf, Riad. *The Arab of the Future* — 741.5
License to Parent. Hillsberg, Christina — 649.1
Licensing Digital Content. Harris, Lesley Ellen — 346.7304
Lichtblau, Eric
   Return to the Reich — B
Lichtman, Allan J.
   The Embattled Vote in America — 324.6
Lickona, Thomas
   How to Raise Kind Kids — 649
LIDDELL, ERIC, 1902-1945
   Hamilton, Duncan. *For the Glory* — B
Liddell, Henry George
   A Greek-English Lexicon — 483
Lidia Cooks from the Heart of Italy. Bastianich, Lidia — 641.594
Lidia's. Bastianich, Lidia — 641.594
★*Lidia's A Pot, a Pan, and a Bowl*. Bastianich, Lidia — 641.82
Lidia's Commonsense Italian Cooking. Bastianich, Lidia — 641.594
Lidia's Family Table. Bastianich, Lidia — 641.594
Lidia's Favorite Recipes. Bastianich, Lidia — 641.594
★*Lidia's from Our Family Table to Yours*. Bastianich, Lidia — 641.594
Lidia's Mastering the Art of Italian Cuisine. Bastianich, Lidia — 641.594
Lieber, Ron
   The Opposite of Spoiled — 332.0240083

Lieberman, Daniel
   Exercised — 612.044
Lieberman, David J.
   Mindreader — 401
   Never Get Angry Again — 152.4
Lieberman, Jeffrey A.
   Malady of the Mind — 616.89
   Shrinks — 616.89
Liebling, A. J.
   ★*The Sweet Science* — 796.83
Liedman, Sven-Eric
   A World to Win — B
★*Lies My Teacher Told Me*. Powell, Nate — 741.5
Lieu, Susan
   ★*The Manicurist's Daughter* — B
LIEUTENANT GOVERNORS
   Hirono, Mazie. *Heart of Fire* — B
Lieven, Anatol
   Pakistan — 954.9105
Lieven, Dominic
   In the Shadow of the Gods — 352.23
Life. Francis — B
LIFE
   Bakewell, Sarah. *How to Live—Or—A Life of Montaigne* — B
   Becker, Ernest. ★*The Denial of Death* — 128
   Carroll, Sean M. *The Big Picture* — 577
   Chaput, Charles J. *Things Worth Dying For* — 248.4
   Cohen, Leonard. *The Flame* — 810
   Devantez, Chelsea. ★*I Shouldn't Be Telling You This* — B
   Dietrich, Sean. *You Are My Sunshine* — B
   Dillard, Annie. *The Abundance* — 814
   Dillard, Annie. *Teaching a Stone to Talk* — 508
   Egan, Kerry. *On Living* — 170
   Forche, Carolyn. *In the Lateness of the World* — 811
   Fusco, Daniel. *Crazy Happy* — 248.4
   Gay, Ross. *The Book of (more) Delights* — 814
   Gay, Ross. *Inciting Joy* — 814
   Gee, Henry. *A (Very) Short History of Life on Earth* — 576.8
   Godwin, Gail. *Getting to Know Death* — B
   Heughan, Sam. *Waypoints* — B
   Jabr, Ferris. ★*Becoming Earth* — 570.1
   Jenkins, Jessica Kerwin. *All the Time in the World* — 390
   Johansen, Signe. ★*How to Hygge* — 646.7
   Kubler-Ross, Elisabeth. *Life Lessons* — 170
   Lamott, Anne. *Almost Everything* — 170
   Lyons, Anna. *We All Know How This Ends* — 362.17
   Marcus Aurelius. ★*Meditations* — 188
   Notaro, Laurie. *Excuse Me While I Disappear* — B
   Pratchett, Terry. *A Slip of the Keyboard* — 824
   Randall, Lisa. *Dark Matter and the Dinosaurs* — 523.1
   Rothfeld, Becca. ★*All Things Are Too Small* — 814
   Rutherford, Adam. *The Complete Guide to Absolutely Everything* — 500
   Scottoline, Lisa. *I See Life Through Rose-Colored Glasses* — 813
   Seidel, Frederick. ★*Frederick Seidel Selected Poems* — 811
   Sharot, Tali. *Look Again* — 158.1
   Sharpe, Christina Elizabeth. *Ordinary Notes* — 305.896
   Sheldrake, Merlin. *Entangled Life* — 579.5
   Spong, John Shelby. *Eternal Life* — 236
   Steinem, Gloria. *The Truth Will Set You Free, but First It Will Piss You Off* — 305.42
   Tolentino, Jia. ★*Trick Mirror* — 973.93
   Tonelli, Guido. *Genesis* — 523.1
   Weber, Charlotte Fox. *Tell Me What You Want* — 153.8
LIFE (BIOLOGY)
   Dawkins, Richard. ★*The Ancestor's Tale* — 576.8
   Kaltenegger, Lisa. ★*Alien Earths* — 523.2
   Martinez Arias, Alfonso. *The Master Builder* — 571.6
   Zimmer, Carl. *Life's Edge* — 570
Life. Richards, Keith — B
Life 3.0. Tegmark, Max — 006.301
LIFE AFTER DEATH
   Dante Alighieri. *Inferno* — 851
   Dante Alighieri. *The Paradiso* — 851
   Dante Alighieri. *Paradiso* — 851
   Holloway, Richard. *Waiting for the Last Bus* — 202
   Jaher, David. *The Witch of Lime Street* — B
   Jennings, Ken. ★*100 Places to See After You Die* — 202
   Junger, Sebastian. ★*In My Time of Dying* — 304.6

AUTHOR, TITLE, SERIES AND SUBJECT INDEX

Manseau, Peter. *The Apparitionists*	B
Moody, Raymond A. *Life After Life*	133.9
Rasmussen, Christina. *Where Did You Go?*	133.9
Roach, Mary. ★*Spook*	129
Sogyal. *The Tibetan Book of Living and Dying*	294.3
Spong, John Shelby. *Eternal Life*	236
Terkel, Studs. *Will the Circle Be Unbroken?*	128
Turner, Alice K. *The History of Hell*	236
Wintz, Jack. *Will I See My Dog in Heaven?*	231.7
Life After Doom. McLaren, Brian D.	200.1
Life After Life. Moody, Raymond A.	133.9
Life After Power. Cohen, Jared	973.09
★*The Life and Afterlife of Harry Houdini*. Posnanski, Joe	793.8
Life and Death in Shanghai. Cheng, Nien	B
Life and Death in the Third Reich. Fritzsche, Peter	943.086
★*The Life and Legend of Leadbelly*. Wolfe, Charles K.	B
★*The Life and Times of Hannah Crafts*. Hecimovich, Gregg A.	B
The Life and Times of Little Richard. White, Charles	B
The Life and Times of the Thunderbolt Kid. Bryson, Bill	B
Life as We Do Not Know It. Ward, Peter Douglas	576.839
Life Between the Tides. Nicolson, Adam	577.69
The Life Brief. Wan, Bonnie	158.1

LIFE CHANGE EVENTS

Baskette, Molly Phinney. *How to Begin When Your World Is Ending*	248.8
Bergner, Daniel. ★*Sing for Your Life*	B
Boa, Kenneth D. *Recalibrate Your Life*	248.8
Bruni, Frank. *The Beauty of Dusk*	B
Chast, Roz. ★*Can't We Talk About Something More Pleasant?*	741.5
Dietrich, Sean. *You Are My Sunshine*	B
DiFelice, Bekah. *Almost There*	248.8
Elwood, Phil. *All the Worst Humans*	659.2
Feiler, Bruce. *Life Is in the Transitions*	392
Felton, Tom. ★*Beyond the Wand*	B
Francis. *Let Us Dream*	282.092
Hagberg, Eva. *How to Be Loved*	616.7
Hari, Daoud. *The Translator*	B
Harry. ★*Spare*	B
Hazzard, Kevin. *A Thousand Naked Strangers*	B
Heath, Chip. *The Power of Moments*	128
Hillenbrand, Laura. ★*Unbroken*	B
Kalanithi, Paul. ★*When Breath Becomes Air*	B
Keeling, Ida. *Can't Nothing Bring Me Down*	B
Klinenberg, Eric. ★*2020*	306
Krouse, Erika. ★*Tell Me Everything*	363.25
Lamas, Daniela J. *You Can Stop Humming Now*	616.02
Levy, Deborah. *The Cost of Living*	B
Lin, Amy. *Here After*	B
Makos, Adam. ★*A Higher Call*	940.54
Mariani, Mike. ★*What Doesn't Kill Us Makes Us*	155.9
May, Katherine. *Wintering*	155.9
McCloskey, Jim. *When Truth Is All You Have*	B
McInerny, Nora. *The Hot Young Widows Club*	155.9
Mitchell, Wendy. *Somebody I Used to Know*	B
Murray, Liz. *Breaking Night*	B
Nordland, Rod. *Waiting for the Monsoon*	B
O'Brien, Vanessa. *To the Greatest Heights*	B
Onwuachi, Kwame. ★*Notes from a Young Black Chef*	641.59
Orenstein, Peggy. *Unraveling*	B
Pennington, Emily. *Feral*	B
Phelan, Tom. *We Were Rich and We Didn't Know It*	B
Raban, Jonathan. *Father and Son*	B
Rakoff, Joanna Smith. *My Salinger Year*	B
Reichl, Ruth. *My Kitchen Year*	641.5
Rhodes, James. *Instrumental*	B
Rosenthal, Jason. *My Wife Said You May Want to Marry Me*	B
Rushdie, Salman. ★*Knife*	B
Schwalbe, Will. *We Should Not Be Friends*	B
Smith, Carol. *Crossing the River*	B
Smith, Patti. ★*Year of the Monkey*	B
Stone, Sharon. *The Beauty of Living Twice*	B
Stutz, Phil. *Lessons for Living*	158.1
Teege, Jennifer. *My Grandfather Would Have Shot Me*	929.2
Thi, Kim Phuc Phan. *Fire Road*	B
Trethewey, Natasha D. ★*Memorial Drive*	B
Weingarten, Gene. ★*One Day*	973
White, Neil. *In the Sanctuary of Outcasts*	B
Williams, Mary. *The Lost Daughter*	B
Winn, Raynor. ★*The Salt Path*	B

Wizenberg, Molly. *Fixed Stars*	B
Yousafzai, Malala. *I Am Malala*	B

LIFE CYCLES

Lavoipierre, Frederique. *Garden Allies*	635
Schlanger, Zoe. ★*The Light Eaters*	571.2
Wohlleben, Peter. *The Hidden Life of Trees*	582.16

LIFE EXPECTANCY

Ehrenreich, Barbara. *Natural Causes*	613.2
Geronimus, Arline T. ★*Weathering*	362.1089
Johnson, Steven. *Extra Life*	362.1
Kristof, Nicholas D. ★*Tightrope*	306.0973
Sinclair, David A. *Lifespan*	570
Life in a Medieval Castle. Gies, Joseph	940.1
Life in a Medieval Village. Gies, Frances	306
Life in Code. Ullman, Ellen	B
★*Life in Five Senses*. Rubin, Gretchen Craft	152.1
A Life in Light. Pipher, Mary Bray	B
★*Life in Motion*. Copeland, Misty	B
A Life in Secrets. Helm, Sarah	B
Life in the Garden. Lively, Penelope	B
Life in the Treetops. Lowman, Margaret	B
A Life in the Twentieth Century. Schlesinger, Arthur M.	B
Life in the Undergrowth. Attenborough, David	592
Life Is Hard. Setiya, Kieran	128
Life Is in the Transitions. Feiler, Bruce	392
Life Is Not an Accident. Williams, Jay	B
★*Life Is What You Bake It*. Lomas, Vallery	641.81
Life Isn't Everything. Carter, Ash	B
Life Itself. Ebert, Roger	B
Life Lessons. Kubler-Ross, Elisabeth	170
Life List. Gentile, Olivia	598.072
Life of a Klansman. Ball, Edward	305.8009763
A Life of Barbara Stanwyck. Wilson, Victoria	B
The Life of Birds. Attenborough, David	598.15
The Life of Charlotte Bronte. Gaskell, Elizabeth Cleghorn	B
The Life of Elizabeth I. Weir, Alison	B
Life of Fire. Martin, Pat	641.5
The Life of Langston Hughes. Rampersad, Arnold	B
★*The Life of Langston Hughes*. Rampersad, Arnold	B
★*The Life of Samuel Johnson*. Boswell, James	B
The Life of Saul Bellow. Leader, Zachary	B
The Life of the Automobile. Parissien, Steven	629.222
★*The Life of the Qur'an*. Jebara, Mohamad	297.122
The Life of W.B. Yeats. Brown, Terence	B
Life on Delay. Hendrickson, John	B
★*Life on Mars*. Smith, Tracy K.	811
Life on Other Planets. Shields, Aomawa L.	B

LIFE ON OTHER PLANETS

Green, Jaime. *The Possibility of Life*	576.8
Johnson, Sarah Stewart. *The Sirens of Mars*	576.8
Kaltenegger, Lisa. ★*Alien Earths*	523.2
Kershenbaum, Arik. *The Zoologist's Guide to the Galaxy*	576.8
Loeb, Abraham. *Extraterrestrial*	576.8
Scoles, Sarah. *They Are Already Here*	001.942
Stuart, Colin. *How to Live in Space*	629.45
Summers, Michael E. *Exoplanets*	523.2
Tyson, Neil deGrasse. *Letters from an Astrophysicist*	520.92
Ward, Peter Douglas. *Life as We Do Not Know It*	576.839
Whitehouse, David. *The Alien Perspective*	523.1
A Life on Our Planet. Attenborough, David	508
Life on the Line. Goldberg, Emma	362.1962
Life on the Mississippi. Buck, Rinker	917
Life Reimagined. Hagerty, Barbara Bradley	155.6

LIFE SCIENCES

Randall, Lisa. *Dark Matter and the Dinosaurs*	523.1
Wilson, David Sloan. *Evolution for Everyone*	576.801
Zimmer, Carl. *Life's Edge*	570
Life Sentence. Bowden, Mark	364.106

LIFE SKILLS

Bowers, Sharon. *Home Ec for Everyone*	640
Bried, Erin. *How to Sew a Button*	640
Carter, Jimmy. *Everything to Gain*	B
Greitens, Eric. *Resilience*	155.2
Hillsberg, Christina. *License to Parent*	649.1
Iggulden, Conn. *The Double Dangerous Book for Boys*	031.02
Rinaldi, Karen. *It's Great to Suck at Something*	158.1
Stryker, Kitty. *Ask*	302
Westheimer, Ruth. *The Doctor Is In*	B

PUBLIC LIBRARY CORE COLLECTION: NONFICTION
Twentieth Edition

Life Starts Now. Dokun, Chanel	248.8

LIFE STORIES — ARTS AND CULTURE

Acocella, Joan Ross. ★*The Bloodied Nightgown*	814
Addario, Lynsey. *It's What I Do*	B
Baker, Nicholson. *Finding a Likeness*	B
Begley, Adam. *The Great Nadar*	B
Bosker, Bianca. *Get the Picture*	701
English, Charlie. *The Gallery of Miracles and Madness*	709.04
Gill, Anton. *Art Lover*	B
Gorges, Eric. *A Craftsman's Legacy*	745.5
Griffin, Farah Jasmine. *Read Until You Understand*	810.9
Guralnick, Peter. ★*Sam Phillips*	B
Hester, Diarmuid. *Nothing Ever Just Disappears*	306.76
Kahlo, Frida. *The Diary of Frida Kahlo*	B
Laing, Olivia. ★*The Lonely City*	700.1
Lauterbach, Preston. *Bluff City*	B
Lucey, Donna M. *Sargent's Women*	920
Mann, Sally. ★*Hold Still*	B
Martin, Justin. *Rebel Souls*	920
Menand, Louis. *The Free World*	306.0973
Moss, Adam. ★*The Work of Art*	701
Obrist, Hans-Ulrich. *Ways of Curating*	707.5
Otfinoski, Steven. *Latinos in the Arts*	700.89
Patterson, James. *The Secret Lives of Booksellers and Librarians*	381
Perkins, Nichole. *Sometimes I Trip on How Happy We Could Be*	B
Poirier, Agnes. *Left Bank*	944
Porter, Carolyn. *Marcel's Letters*	940.54
Prescod, Danielle. *Token Black Girl*	B
Rempel, William C. *The Gambler*	B
Rusbridger, Alan. ★*Play It Again*	B
Sale, Anna. ★*Let's Talk About Hard Things*	153.6
Silver, Johanna. ★*The Bold Dry Garden*	635.9
Smyth, Adam. *The Book-Makers*	686.2
Stein, Judith E. *Eye of the Sixties*	B
Stourton, James. *Kenneth Clark*	B
Szerlip, Barbara. *The Man Who Designed the Future*	B
Tamblyn, Amber. ★*Era of Ignition*	B
Watling, Sarah. *Tomorrow Perhaps the Future*	946.081
Wulf, Andrea. *Magnificent Rebels*	830.9

LIFE STORIES — ARTS AND CULTURE — ARCHITECTS

Goldberger, Paul. *Building Art*	B
Howard, Hugh. *Architects of an American Landscape*	712.092
Huxtable, Ada Louise. ★*Frank Lloyd Wright*	B
Secrest, Meryle. *Frank Lloyd Wright*	B

LIFE STORIES — ARTS AND CULTURE — ARTISTS

Ai, Weiwei. *1000 Years of Joys and Sorrows*	709.2
Ai, Weiwei. *Zodiac*	741.5
Albers, Patricia. *Joan Mitchell*	B
Alinder, Mary Street. *Ansel Adams*	B
Anolik, Lili. *Hollywood's Eve*	B
Bair, Deirdre. *Saul Steinberg*	B
Beaton, Kate. ★*Ducks*	741.5
Bell, Julian. *Van Gogh*	B
Bigsby, Christopher William Edgar. *Arthur Miller*	B
Bilal, Wafaa. *Shoot an Iraqi*	B
Blom, Onno. *Young Rembrandt*	B
Burke, Carolyn. *Lee Miller*	B
Cohen-Solal, Annie. *Mark Rothko*	759.13
Crabapple, Molly. *Drawing Blood*	B
Cross, William R. *Winslow Homer*	759.13
Delisle, Guy. *Pyongyang*	741.5
DePastino, Todd. *Bill Mauldin*	B
Dery, Mark. *Born to Be Posthumous*	B
Doherty, Maggie. *The Equivalents*	920
Egan, Timothy. ★*Short Nights of the Shadow Catcher*	770.92
Eisler, Benita. *The Red Man's Bones*	B
Evans, R. Tripp. *Grant Wood*	B
Feaver, William. ★*The Lives of Lucian Freud*	B
Frey, Julia Bloch. *Toulouse-Lautrec*	B
Gabler, Neal. *Walt Disney*	B
Gabriel, Mary. *Ninth Street Women*	920
Gefter, Philip. *What Becomes a Legend Most*	B
Goldstein, Nancy. *Jackie Ormes*	B
Gooch, Brad. *Radiant*	B
Gopnik, Blake. ★*Warhol*	B
Gordon, Linda. *Dorothea Lange*	B
Graham-Dixon, Andrew. *Caravaggio*	B
Gruen, Bob. *Right Place, Right Time*	B
Hale, Sheila. *Titian*	B
Harryhausen, Ray. *The Art of Ray Harryhausen*	778
Herrera, Hayden. *Frida*	B
Herrera, Hayden. *Listening to Stone*	B
Hesse, Maria. ★*Frida Kahlo*	B
Hirst, Michael. *Michelangelo*	B
Hoban, Phoebe. *Alice Neel*	B
Holt, Nathalia. *The Queens of Animation*	920
Holzer, Harold. *Monument Man*	B
Hughes, Robert. *Goya*	B
Isaacson, Walter. ★*Leonardo Da Vinci*	B
Kamensky, Jane. *A Revolution in Color*	759.13
King, Ross. ★*Mad Enchantment*	759.4
Krug, Nora. ★*Belonging*	741.5
Lehrer, Riva. *Golem Girl*	B
Lozano, Luis-Martin. *Frida Kahlo*	759.972
Lubow, Arthur. *Diane Arbus*	B
Mankoff, Robert. *How About Never—Is Never Good for You?*	741.5
Manseau, Peter. *The Apparitionists*	B
Marks, Ann. *Vivian Maier Developed*	778.9
Marnham, Patrick. *Dreaming with His Eyes Open*	B
Michaelis, David. *Schulz and Peanuts*	B
Mordden, Ethan. *Ziegfeld*	B
Moyle, Franny. *Turner*	B
Naifeh, Steven W. *Van Gogh*	B
Nuland, Sherwin B. *Leonardo Da Vinci*	B
O'Meara, Mallory. *The Lady from the Black Lagoon*	921
Painter, Nell Irvin. *Old in Art School*	B
Peiffer, Prudence. *The Slip*	709.73
Perl, Jed. *Calder*	B
Perl, Jed. ★*Calder*	B
Pham, Larissa. *Pop Song*	709.2
Prideaux, Sue. *Edvard Munch*	B
Prose, Francine. *Caravaggio*	759.5
Rembert, Winfred. *Chasing Me to My Grave*	B
Riesman, Abraham. *True Believer*	741.5
Robinson, Roxana. *Georgia O'Keeffe*	B
Roe, Sue. *In Montmartre*	920
Roe, Sue. *The Private Lives of the Impressionists*	920
Rowland, Ingrid D. *The Collector of Lives*	B
Rynecki, Elizabeth. *Chasing Portraits*	B
Schloss, Edith. *The Loft Generation*	700.9
Schumacher, Michael. *Will Eisner*	741.5
Secrest, Meryle. *Modigliani*	B
Shaw, Jennifer Laurie. *Exist Otherwise*	709.2
Sipress, David. *What's so Funny?*	B
Smee, Sebastian. *The Art of Rivalry*	700.92
Smith, R. J. *American Witness*	B
Snyder, Laura J. *Eye of the Beholder*	920
Solomon, Deborah. *American Mirror*	B
Solomon, Deborah. *Jackson Pollock*	B
Spiegelman, Art. *Metamaus*	B
Spurling, Hilary. *Matisse the Master*	B
Stahr, Celia. *Frida in America*	B
Stevens, Norma. *Avedon*	B
Sykes, Christopher Simon. *David Hockney*	B
Sykes, Christopher Simon. *David Hockney*	B
Tisserand, Michael. *Krazy*	741.5
Tomine, Adrian. *The Loneliness of the Long-Distance Cartoonist*	741.5
Tomlinson, Janis A. ★*Goya*	B
Turan, Kenneth. ★*Free for All*	B
Unger, Miles. ★*Michelangelo*	B
Unger, Miles. *Picasso and the Painting That Shocked the World*	759.4
Ustvedt, Oystein. *Edvard Munch*	759.81
Van Haaften, Julia. ★*Berenice Abbott*	B
Volpe, Joseph. *The Toughest Show on Earth*	B
Wallace, Christopher. *Twentieth-Century Man*	B
Warren, Rosanna. *Max Jacob*	B
Wullschlager, Jackie. ★*Chagall*	B
Zhu, Mimi. *Be Not Afraid of Love*	152.4

LIFE STORIES — ARTS AND CULTURE — CULINARY ARTS

Bastianich, Lidia. *My American Dream*	B
Bertch, Jane. *The French Ingredient*	B
Birdsall, John. *The Man Who Ate Too Much*	B
Bourdain, Anthony. ★*Kitchen Confidential*	B
Bourdain, Anthony. *Medium Raw*	B
Buford, Bill. ★*Dirt*	B
Cailan, Alvin. *Amboy*	641.595

AUTHOR, TITLE, SERIES AND SUBJECT INDEX

Cecchi-Azzolina, Michael. *Your Table Is Ready*	647.95
Chang, David. ★*Eat a Peach*	641.5
Child, Julia. ★*My Life in France*	
Fall, Jeremy. *Falling Upwards*	158.1
Hamilton, Gabrielle. *Blood, Bones, and Butter*	B
Huang, Eddie. *Fresh off the Boat*	B
James, Victoria. *Wine Girl*	B
Lakshmi, Padma. *Love, Loss, and What We Ate*	791.4502
Lawson, Nigella. ★*Cook, Eat, Repeat*	641.5
Martinez, Rick. *Mi Cocina*	641.5972
Miller, Klancy. ★*For the Culture*	641.59
Nathan, Joan. ★*My Life in Recipes*	641.5
Nunn, Emily. *The Comfort Food Diaries*	641.5973
Onwuachi, Kwame. ★*Notes from a Young Black Chef*	641.59
Pepin, Jacques. *The Apprentice*	B
Pepin, Jacques. *Art of the Chicken*	641.665
Prud'homme, Alex. *The French Chef in America*	B
Reichl, Ruth. *Comfort Me with Apples*	B
Reichl, Ruth. *Garlic and Sapphires*	B
Reichl, Ruth. *My Kitchen Year*	641.5
Reichl, Ruth. ★*Save Me the Plums*	B
Ripert, Eric. *32 Yolks*	B
Samuelsson, Marcus. ★*The Rise*	641.59
Samuelsson, Marcus. *Yes, Chef*	B
Sanchez, Aaron. *Where I Come From*	641.5092
Solomonov, Michael. *Zahav*	641.595
Tucci, Stanley. ★*Taste*	B
Vitale, Tom. *In the Weeds*	B
Waters, Alice. *Coming to My Senses*	B
Woolever, Laurie. *Bourdain*	B

LIFE STORIES — ARTS AND CULTURE — FASHION

Brickell, Francesca Cartier. *The Cartiers*	B
Carter, Ruth E. ★*The Art of Ruth E. Carter*	746.9
Cleveland, Pat. *Walking with the Muses*	B
Crowe, Lauren Goldstein. *The Towering World of Jimmy Choo*	391.4
Cunningham, William J. ★*Fashion Climbing*	B
Day, Daniel R. *Dapper Dan*	B
De Courcy, Anne. *Chanel's Riviera*	944.9
Enninful, Edward. *A Visible Man*	B
Garelick, Rhonda K. *Mademoiselle*	B
Gucci, Patricia. *In the Name of Gucci*	B
Hilfiger, Tommy. *American Dreamer*	B
Kang, Mia. *Knockout*	B
Mizrahi, Isaac. *I.M.*	B
Ratajkowski, Emily. ★*My Body*	B
Richardson, Lance. *House of Nutter*	B
Secrest, Meryle. *Elsa Schiaparelli*	746.9
Talley, Andre Leon. *The Chiffon Trenches*	B
Thomas, Dana. *Gods and Kings*	920
Von Furstenberg, Diane. *The Woman I Wanted to Be*	B

LIFE STORIES — ARTS AND CULTURE — PERFORMING ARTS

Abdurraqib, Hanif. ★*A Little Devil in America*	791.089
Almond, Steve. *Rock and Roll Will Save Your Life*	781.6
Auletta, Ken. ★*Hollywood Ending*	791.43
Basinger, Jeanine. *Hollywood*	791.43
Coel, Michaela. ★*Misfits*	158.2
Courogen, Carrie. ★*Miss May Does Not Exist*	B
DiMarco, Nyle. ★*Deaf Utopia*	B
Evaristo, Bernardine. *Manifesto*	B
Fischer, Paul. *A Kim Jong-Il Production*	791.43
Haddish, Tiffany. *The Last Black Unicorn*	B
Hartigan, Patti. *August Wilson*	B
Hudes, Quiara Alegria. ★*My Broken Language*	B
Hytner, Nicholas. *Balancing Acts*	B
Ikpi, Bassey. *I'm Telling the Truth, but I'm Lying*	814
Imperioli, Michael. *Woke up This Morning*	791.45
Katz, Evan Ross. *Into Every Generation a Slayer Is Born*	791.45
Kenny, Glenn. *The World Is Yours*	791.43
Lanzmann, Claude. *The Patagonian Hare*	B
Lewis, Damien. *Agent Josephine*	B
McDonald, Greg (Producer). *Elvis and the Colonel*	920
McGilligan, Patrick. *Funny Man*	B
Nussbaum, Emily. *Cue the Sun!*	791.45
Osborne, Richard. *Herbert Von Karajan*	B
Otfinoski, Steven. *Latinos in the Arts*	700.89
Palmer, Amanda. ★*The Art of Asking*	782.42164
Parke, Henry C. *The Greatest Westerns Ever Made and the People Who Made Them*	791.43
Patterson, James. *What Really Happens in Vegas*	920
Porter, Billy. ★*Unprotected*	B
Porter, Cecelia Hopkins. *Five Lives in Music*	B
Purdum, Todd S. *Something Wonderful*	B
Ratajkowski, Emily. ★*My Body*	B
Riedel, Michael. *Singular Sensation*	792
Ruhl, Sarah. *Smile*	B
Scheer, Paul. *Joyful Recollections of Trauma*	B
Schulman, Michael. ★*Oscar Wars*	791.43
Shields, Charles J. *Lorraine Hansberry*	B
Silver, Alain. ★*From the Moment They Met It Was Murder*	791.43
Smith, Danyel. *Shine Bright*	782.42164
Suchet, John. *Beethoven*	B
Thomson, David. *The New Biographical Dictionary of Film*	791.4302
Thwaite, Ann. *Goodbye Christopher Robin*	B
Velasquez, Lizzie. *Dare to Be Kind*	177
Velour, Sasha. ★*The Big Reveal*	792.7
White, Charles. *The Life and Times of Little Richard*	B
Wilson, Robert. *Barnum*	B
Winder, Elizabeth. *Parachute Women*	782.42164
Yang, Jeff. *The Golden Screen*	791.43
Zucker, David. *Surely You Can't Be Serious*	791.43

LIFE STORIES — ARTS AND CULTURE — PERFORMING ARTS — ACTORS AND ACTRESSES

Ahdoot, Dan. *Undercooked*	647.95
Andrews, Julie. *Home Work*	B
Andrews, Julie. *Home*	B
Arkin, Alan. *An Improvised Life*	B
Armstrong, Jennifer Keishin. *When Women Invented Television*	791.45
Bacall, Lauren. *By Myself and Then Some*	B
Ball, Lucille. *Love, Lucy*	B
Beauvais, Garcelle. *Love Me as I Am*	B
Berg, A. Scott. *Kate Remembered*	B
Bertinelli, Valerie. *Enough Already*	B
Biskind, Peter. *Star*	B
Blair, Selma. *Mean Baby*	B
Brooks, Mel. ★*All About Me!*	B
Brower, Kate Andersen. *Elizabeth Taylor*	B
Caine, Michael. *Blowing the Bloody Doors Off*	B
Callow, Simon. ★*Orson Welles*	B
Carr, C. *Candy Darling*	B
Casillo, Charles. *Marilyn Monroe*	B
Chan, Jackie. *Never Grow Up*	B
Cumming, Alan. *Baggage*	B
Curtis, James. *Buster Keaton*	B
Curtis, James. *Spencer Tracy*	B
Davis, Geena. *Dying of Politeness*	B
Davis, Viola. ★*Finding Me*	B
De Vise, Daniel. ★*The Blues Brothers*	791.43
Dench, Judi. *Shakespeare*	792
Driver, Minnie. *Managing Expectations*	B
Dunne, Griffin. ★*The Friday Afternoon Club*	B
Elwes, Cary. *As You Wish*	791.43
Eyman, Scott. *Cary Grant*	B
Eyman, Scott. *Charlie Chaplin vs. America*	B
Eyman, Scott. *Hank and Jim*	920
Eyman, Scott. *John Wayne*	B
Felton, Tom. ★*Beyond the Wand*	B
Field, Sally. *In Pieces*	B
Fischer, Jenna. *The Office BFFs*	791.45
Fisher, Todd. *My Girls*	B
Foster, Sutton. *Hooked*	B
Fox, Michael J. *No Time Like the Future*	B
Foxx, Jamie. *Act Like You Got Some Sense*	B
Gehring, Wes D. *James Dean*	B
Gless, Sharon. *Apparently There Were Complaints*	B
Goessel, Tracey. *The First King of Hollywood*	B
Goldberg, Whoopi. *Bits and Pieces*	B
Goudsouzian, Aram. *Sidney Poitier*	B
Greenfield, Robert. *True West*	B
Grey, Jennifer. *Out of the Corner*	B
Grey, Joel. *Master of Ceremonies*	B
Harden, Marcia Gay. *The Seasons of My Mother*	B
Harris, Neil Patrick. *Neil Patrick Harris*	B
Henson, Taraji P. *Around the Way Girl*	B
Heughan, Sam. *Waypoints*	B
Howard, Ron. ★*The Boys*	B
Huang, Yunte. *Daughter of the Dragon*	B

PUBLIC LIBRARY CORE COLLECTION: NONFICTION
Twentieth Edition

Hussey, Olivia. *The Girl on the Balcony* — B
Huston, Anjelica. *Watch Me* — B
Itzkoff, Dave. ★*Robin* — B
Jacobs, Alexandra. *Still Here* — B
Kaling, Mindy. *Why Not Me?* — B
Kanfer, Stefan. *Tough Without a Gun* — B
Kashner, Sam. *Furious Love* — B
Keaton, Diane. ★*Brother & Sister* — B
Kelly, Minka. ★*Tell Me Everything* — B
Kemper, Ellie. *My Squirrel Days* — B
Lahti, Christine. *True Stories from an Unreliable Eyewitness* — B
Leamer, Laurence. *Hitchcock's Blondes* — 791.43
Lewis, Jenifer. *Walking in My Joy* — B
Lifford, Tina. *The Little Book of Big Lies* — 155.2
Liu, Simu. ★*We Were Dreamers* — B
Louvish, Simon. *Monkey Business* — B
Mann, William J. *Bogie & Bacall* — 920
Mann, William J. *The Contender* — B
Mann, William J. *Hello, Gorgeous* — B
Mann, William J. *Kate* — B
Margulies, Julianna. *Sunshine Girl* — B
Matzen, Robert. *Dutch Girl* — B
McCabe, John. *Cagney* — B
McConaughey, Matthew. *Greenlights* — B
McGowan, Rose. *Brave* — B
Merritt, Tyler. *I Take My Coffee Black* — 791.4302
Mills, Hayley. *Forever Young* — B
Mulgrew, Kate. *Born with Teeth* — 791.45028
Newman, Paul. *The Extraordinary Life of an Ordinary Man* — B
Nolte, Nick. *Rebel* — B
O'Connor, Garry. *Ian McKellen* — B
Odenkirk, Bob. *Comedy Comedy Comedy Drama* — B
Offerman, Nick. *The Greatest Love Story Ever Told* — B
Offerman, Nick. *Where the Deer and the Antelope Play* — 973.93
Orji, Yvonne. *Bamboozled by Jesus* — B
Page, Elliot. *Pageboy* — B
Penn, Kal. *You Can't Be Serious* — B
Perry, Matthew. *Friends, Lovers, and the Big Terrible Thing* — B
Plummer, Christopher. *In Spite of Myself* — B
Poitier, Sidney. *The Measure of a Man* — B
Polly, Matthew. ★*Bruce Lee* — B
Posey, Parker. *You're on an Airplane* — B
Rannells, Andrew. *Too Much Is Not Enough* — 792.02
Rannells, Andrew. *Uncle of the Year* — B
Retta. *So Close to Being the Sh*t, Y'all Don't Even Know* — B
Riley, Kathleen. *The Astaires* — B
Ripa, Kelly. *Live Wire* — B
Rogen, Seth. ★*Yearbook* — B
Rowe, Mickey. *Fearlessly Different* — B
Salisbury, Katie Gee. ★*Not Your China Doll* — B
Selleck, Tom. *You Never Know* — B
Shannon, Molly. ★*Hello, Molly!* — B
Shatner, William. *Boldly Go* — B
Shatner, William. *Live Long And—* — B
Shearer, Stephen Michael. *Beautiful* — B
Sinise, Gary. *Grateful American* — B
Slate, Jenny. *Little Weirds* — B
Smith, Jada Pinkett. *Worthy* — B
Smith, Starr. *Jimmy Stewart* — B
Smith, Will. ★*Will* — B
Spoto, Donald. *High Society* — B
Stamos, John. *If You Would Have Told Me* — B
Stevens, Dana. *Camera Man* — 791.4302
Stewart, Patrick. ★*Making It So* — B
Stone, Sharon. *The Beauty of Living Twice* — B
Streisand, Barbra. ★*My Name Is Barbra* — B
Suvari, Mena. *The Great Peace* — B
Taraborrelli, J. Randy. ★*The Secret Life of Marilyn Monroe* — B
Thompson, Kenan. *When I Was Your Age* — B
Thomson, David. *Bette Davis* — B
Thomson, David. *Ingrid Bergman* — B
Trejo, Danny. *Trejo* — B
Tyson, Cicely. ★*Just as I Am* — B
Union, Gabrielle. *We're Going to Need More Wine* — B
Union, Gabrielle. *You Got Anything Stronger?* — B
Van Zandt, Steve. *Unrequited Infatuations* — B
Ward, Maitland. *Rated X* — B
Warren, Louis S. *Buffalo Bill's America* — B

Washington, Kerry. *Thicker Than Water* — B
Wasson, Sam. *The Big Goodbye* — 791.43
Watts, Jill. *Hattie McDaniel* — B
Weller, Sheila. *Carrie Fisher* — B
Williams, Billy Dee. ★*What Have We Here* — B
Williams, Michael Kenneth. *Scenes from My Life* — B
Wilson, Rebel. *Rebel Rising* — B
Wilson, Victoria. *A Life of Barbara Stanwyck* — B
Winkler, Henry. ★*Being Henry* — B
Wojczuk, Tana. *Lady Romeo* — B
Wu, Constance. *Making a Scene* — B

LIFE STORIES — ARTS AND CULTURE — PERFORMING ARTS — DANCERS AND CHOREOGRAPHERS

Brown, Carolyn. *Chance and Circumstance* — B
Copeland, Misty. ★*Life in Motion* — B
Copeland, Misty. *The Wind at My Back* — B
Duncan, Isadora. *My Life* — B
Gottlieb, Robert. *George Balanchine* — B
Guillermoprieto, Alma. *Dancing with Cuba* — 972.9106
Hallberg, David. *A Body of Work* — B
Harss, Marina. *The Boy from Kyiv* — B
Johnson, Stephanie. *Tanqueray* — B
Kavanagh, Julie. *Nureyev* — B
Morris, Mark. *Out Loud* — B
Riley, Kathleen. *The Astaires* — B
Robb, Alice. ★*Don't Think, Dear* — 792.8
Teachout, Terry. ★*All in the Dances* — B
Valby, Karen. *The Swans of Harlem* — 792.8

LIFE STORIES — ARTS AND CULTURE — PERFORMING ARTS — DIRECTORS AND PRODUCERS

Brooks, Mel. ★*All About Me!* — B
Burrows, James. ★*Directed by James Burrows* — 791.4502
Callow, Simon. ★*Orson Welles* — B
Carter, Ash. *Life Isn't Everything* — B
D'Alessandro, Emilio. *Stanley Kubrick and Me* — 791.4302
Ebersol, Dick. *From Saturday Night to Sunday Night* — B
Else, Jon. *True South* — 305.800973
Eyman, Scott. *Empire of Dreams* — B
Fisher, Todd. *My Girls* — B
Harris, Mark. *Mike Nichols* — B
Haskell, Molly. *Steven Spielberg* — B
Herzog, Werner. ★*Every Man for Himself and God Against All* — B
Hirsch, Paul. *A Long Time Ago in a Cutting Room Far, Far Away* — B
Jones, Brian Jay. *George Lucas* — B
Kolker, Robert Phillip. *Kubrick* — B
Kurosawa, Akira. *Something Like an Autobiography* — B
Lane, Christina. *Phantom Lady* — B
Leamer, Laurence. *Hitchcock's Blondes* — 791.43
Lear, Norman. *Even This I Get to Experience* — B
Lebo, Harlan. ★*Citizen Kane* — 791.43
Lynch, David. *Room to Dream* — B
McGilligan, Patrick. *Oscar Micheaux* — B
McGilligan, Patrick. *Young Orson* — B
Nawaz, Zarqa. *Laughing All the Way to the Mosque* — 791.45028
O'Brien, Jack. *Jack Be Nimble* — B
Odenkirk, Bob. *Comedy Comedy Comedy Drama* — B
Rogen, Seth. ★*Yearbook* — B
Seidelman, Susan. *Desperately Seeking Something* — B
Shelton, Ron. *The Church of Baseball* — 791.43
Shone, Tom. *The Nolan Variations* — 791.4302
Soloway, Jill. *She Wants It* — B
Spiegel, Maura. *Sidney Lumet* — B
Spoto, Donald. *The Dark Side of Genius* — B
Streisand, Barbra. ★*My Name Is Barbra* — B
Szwed, John F. *Cosmic Scholar* — B
Tarantino, Quentin. *Cinema Speculation* — 791.43
Trimborn, Jurgen. *Leni Riefenstahl* — B
Wasson, Sam. *The Big Goodbye* — 791.43
Waters, John. *Mr. Know-It-All* — 814
Winkler, Henry. ★*Being Henry* — B
Zwick, Edward. ★*Hits, Flops, and Other Illusions* — B

LIFE STORIES — ARTS AND CULTURE — PERFORMING ARTS — ENTERTAINERS AND CELEBRITIES

Abbott, Karen. *American Rose* — B
Abramovic, Marina. *Walk Through Walls* — B
Ackroyd, Peter. *Charlie Chaplin* — B
Armstrong, Jennifer Keishin. *When Women Invented Television* — 791.45
Ball, Lucille. *Love, Lucy* — B

AUTHOR, TITLE, SERIES AND SUBJECT INDEX

Bamford, Maria. *Sure, I'll Join Your Cult*	B
Bennetts, Leslie. *Last Girl Before Freeway*	B
Black, Michael Ian. *A Better Man*	305.31
Branum, Guy. *My Life as a Goddess*	B
Brosh, Allie. ★*Hyperbole and a Half*	741.5
Brosh, Allie. ★*Solutions and Other Problems*	741.5
Brunson, Quinta. *She Memes Well*	B
Burnett, Carol. *In Such Good Company*	791.45
Carlin, Kelly. *A Carlin Home Companion*	B
Carlin, Peter Ames. *Bruce*	B
De Semlyen, Nick. *Wild and Crazy Guys*	920
Ditum, Sarah. *Toxic*	920.72
Duggar, Jill. *Counting the Cost*	B
Duran, Elvis. *Where Do I Begin?*	B
Eyman, Scott. *Charlie Chaplin vs. America*	B
Feast, Fancy. *Naked*	792.7
Fox, Julia. *Down the Drain*	B
Gabriel, Mary. *Madonna*	B
Gaines, Joanna. *The Stories We Tell*	B
Goodman, Elyssa. *Glitter and Concrete*	792.7
Graham, Ashley. *A New Model*	B
Gulman, Gary. *Misfit*	B
Hagan, Joe. *Sticky Fingers*	B
Hart, Hannah. *Buffering*	B
Hart, Kevin. *I Can't Make This Up*	B
Hendershot, Heather. *Open to Debate*	B
Hilton, Paris. *Paris*	B
Ice-T. *Split Decision*	920
Izzard, Eddie. *Believe Me*	B
Jacobs, Alexandra. *Still Here*	B
Jobrani, Maziyar. *I'm Not a Terrorist, but I've Played One on TV*	B
Johnson, Stephanie. *Tanqueray*	B
Jones, Brian Jay. *Jim Henson*	B
Kang, Mia. *Knockout*	B
King, Maxwell. *The Good Neighbor*	B
Levy, Shawn. ★*In on the Joke*	792.7
Maguire, James. *Impresario*	B
Mann, William J. *Hello, Gorgeous*	B
Martin, Steve. *Number One Is Walking*	B
Mooney, Paul. *Black Is the New White*	792.7
Moore, Susanna. *Miss Aluminum*	813
Myers, Paul. *The Kids in the Hall*	920
Nesteroff, Kliph. *We Had a Little Real Estate Problem*	970.004
Orji, Yvonne. *Bamboozled by Jesus*	B
Patterson, Pat. *Accepted*	B
Pellegrino, Danny. *How Do I Un-Remember This?*	B
Philipps, Busy. *This Will Only Hurt a Little*	B
Poehler, Amy. *Yes Please*	B
Pomerantsev, Peter. ★*How to Win an Information War*	940.53
Poole, W. Scott. *Vampira*	B
Posnanski, Joe. ★*The Life and Afterlife of Harry Houdini*	793.8
Rainbow, Randy. *Playing with Myself*	B
Ramsey, Franchesca. *Well, That Escalated Quickly*	B
Reynolds, Debbie. *Make 'Em Laugh*	B
Rigsby, Cody. ★*XOXO, Cody*	B
Ripa, Kelly. *Live Wire*	B
Robeson, Paul. *The Undiscovered Paul Robeson*	B
Robinson, Phoebe. *You Can't Touch My Hair and Other Things I Still Have to Explain*	792.7
RuPaul. ★*The House of Hidden Meanings*	B
Saul, Scott. ★*Becoming Richard Pryor*	B
Saunders, John. *Playing Hurt*	B
Schneider, Amy. *In the Form of a Question*	B
Segura, Tom. ★*I'd Like to Play Alone, Please*	B
Seinfeld, Jerry. *Is This Anything?*	818
Shannon, Molly. ★*Hello, Molly!*	B
Short, Martin. *I Must Say*	B
Spears, Britney. *The Woman in Me*	B
Spitz, Bob. ★*Dearie*	B
Staniforth, Nate. *Here Is Real Magic*	B
Stone, Alex. *Fooling Houdini*	B
Taraborrelli, J. Randy. ★*Jackie*	B
Thompson, Kenan. *When I Was Your Age*	B
Trebek, Alex. *The Answer Is ...*	791.4502
Vitale, Tom. *In the Weeds*	B
Wall, Duncan. *The Ordinary Acrobat*	B
Warren, Louis S. *Buffalo Bill's America*	B
Watts, Reggie. *Great Falls, MT*	B
Westheimer, Ruth. *The Doctor Is In*	B
Williams, Patricia. *Rabbit*	B
Wong, Ali. ★*Dear Girls*	B
Woolever, Laurie. *Bourdain*	B
Zoglin, Richard. *Hope*	B

LIFE STORIES — ARTS AND CULTURE — PERFORMING ARTS — MUSICIANS AND COMPOSERS

Abdurraqib, Hanif. *Go Ahead in the Rain*	782.421649
Adams, John. *Hallelujah Junction*	B
Ahmad, Aeham. *The Pianist from Syria*	B
Albertine, Viv. *Clothes, Clothes, Clothes. Music, Music, Music*	B
Alden, Ginger. *Elvis and Ginger*	B
Alekhina, Mariija. *Riot Days*	B
Alexander, Paul. *Bitter Crop*	B
Amos, Tori. *Resistance*	B
Armstrong, Louis. *Louis Armstrong, in His Own Words*	B
Atria, Travis. *Better Days Will Come Again*	B
Baraka, Sho. *He Saw That It Was Good*	261.5
Barlow, John Perry. *Mother American Night*	782.42164
Basie, Count. *Good Morning Blues*	B
Bego, Mark. *Aretha Franklin*	B
Belafonte, Harry. ★*My Song*	782.42164
Berger, William. *Puccini Without Excuses*	782.1
Berger, William. *Verdi with a Vengeance*	B
Bernstein, Burton. ★*Leonard Bernstein*	B
Black Thought. *The Upcycled Self*	B
Bogle, Donald. *Heat Wave*	782.42164
Bono. ★*Surrender*	B
Brothers, Thomas David. ★*Louis Armstrong, Master of Modernism*	B
Brown, Craig. *150 Glimpses of the Beatles*	920
Brown, Mick. ★*Tearing Down the Wall of Sound*	B
Browne, David. *Crosby, Stills, Nash and Young*	920
Broyles, Michael. ★*Revolutions in American Music*	780.9
Butler, Marcia. *The Skin Above My Knee*	B
Carlile, Brandi. *Broken Horses*	B
Cash, Rosanne. ★*Composed*	B
Chernaik, Judith. *Schumann*	B
Clapton, Eric. *Clapton*	B
Cohen, Rich. *The Sun and the Moon and the Rolling Stones*	782.42166
Cohodas, Nadine. *Princess Noire*	782.42164
Cole, Natalie. *Angel on My Shoulder*	B
Common. *One Day It'll All Make Sense*	B
Connolly, Ray. *Being Elvis*	B
Connolly, Ray. *Being John Lennon*	B
Costello, Elvis. *Unfaithful Music & Disappearing Ink*	B
Cross, Charles R. *Room Full of Mirrors*	B
Crouch, Stanley. *Kansas City Lightning*	B
Dance, Stanley. ★*The World of Earl Hines*	B
Davidson, Mark A. ★*Bob Dylan*	B
Davis, Stephen. *Gold Dust Woman*	B
DeCurtis, Anthony. *Lou Reed*	B
Dickinson, Bruce. *What Does This Button Do?*	B
DiFranco, Ani. *No Walls and the Recurring Dream*	782.42164
Doggett, Peter. *You Never Give Me Your Money*	B
Dolby, Thomas. *The Speed of Sound*	B
Dregni, Michael. *Django*	B
Dunaway, David King. ★*How Can I Keep from Singing?*	B
Duncan, Dayton. ★*Country Music*	781.642
Dylan, Bob. *Chronicles; Volume 1*	B
Eisler, Benita. ★*Chopin's Funeral*	B
Eliot, Marc. *The Hag*	B
Etheridge, Melissa. *Talking to My Angels*	B
Fernando, S. H., Jr. *From the Streets of Shaolin*	782.421
Fogerty, John. *Fortunate Son*	B
Friedwald, Will. ★*Sinatra! the Song Is You*	782.42164
Friedwald, Will. *Straighten up and Fly Right*	782.42164
Gabbard, Krin. *Better Git It in Your Soul*	B
Gabriel, Mary. *Madonna*	B
Gardiner, John Eliot. *Bach*	B
Garfunkel, Art. *What Is It All but Luminous*	782.42164
Gavin, James. ★*Stormy Weather*	782.42164
Gaye, Jan. *After the Dance*	B
Geck, Martin. ★*Johann Sebastian Bach*	780.92
George-Warren, Holly. ★*Janis*	B
Ghostface Killah. *Rise of a Killah*	B
Giddins, Gary. *Bing Crosby*	B
Giddins, Gary. *Bing Crosby*	B
Glass, Philip. *Words Without Music*	B

PUBLIC LIBRARY CORE COLLECTION: NONFICTION
Twentieth Edition

Goldsmith, Martin. *The Inextinguishable Symphony*	B
Gordon, Kim. *Girl in a Band*	B
Grandmaster Flash. *The Adventures of Grandmaster Flash*	B
Grant, Colin. *The Natural Mystics*	B
Gray, Michael. *Hand Me My Travelin' Shoes*	B
Greenman, Ben. *Dig If You Will the Picture*	B
Gutman, Robert W. *Mozart*	B
Hanna, Kathleen. *Rebel Girl*	B
Harris, Ellen T. *George Frideric Handel*	B
Harry, Debbie. *Face It*	B
Hayes, Elaine M. ★*Queen of Bebop*	B
Hemphill, Paul. *Lovesick Blues*	B
Hermes, Will. *Lou Reed*	B
Hilburn, Robert. ★*Johnny Cash*	B
Hilburn, Robert. ★*Paul Simon*	782.42164
Hopkins, Jerry. *No One Here Gets Out Alive*	B
Hopper, Jessica. *The First Collection of Criticism by a Living Female Rock Critic*	781.66
Hough, Stephen. *Rough Ideas*	786.2092
Hyden, Steven. *Long Road*	782.42166
Hyland, William G. *George Gershwin*	B
Iandoli, Kathy. *Baby Girl*	B
Iandoli, Kathy. *God Save the Queens*	782.421649
Isacoff, Stuart. *Musical Revolutions*	780.9
Jackson family. *The Jacksons*	782.421644
Jewel. *Never Broken*	782.42164
John, Elton. ★*Me*	B
Johnson, Brian. *The Lives of Brian*	B
Johnson, Graham. *Poulenc*	B
Jollett, Mikel. ★*Hollywood Park*	B
Jones, Booker T. *Time Is Tight*	B
Jones, Dylan. *David Bowie*	B
Kaplan, James. *3 Shades of Blue*	920
Kaplan, James. *Sinatra*	782.42164
Kaye, Lenny. ★*Lightning Striking*	781.66
Keiler, Allan. *Marian Anderson*	B
Kennedy, Michael. *Richard Strauss*	B
Kennicott, Philip. *Counterpoint*	B
Kildea, Paul Francis. *Chopin's Piano*	B
King, B. B. ★*Blues All Around Me*	B
Kot, Greg. *I'll Take You There*	B
Kozinn, Allan. *The McCartney Legacy*	B
Kweli, Talib. *Vibrate Higher*	B
Lambert, Miranda. *Y'all Eat Yet?*	641.5976
Lanegan, Mark. *Sing Backwards and Weep*	B
Larson, Kay. *Where the Heart Beats*	700.1
Lecrae. ★*I Am Restored*	B
Lehman, David. *A Fine Romance*	781.64
Levy, Aidan. *Saxophone Colossus*	B
Lloyd Webber, Andrew. *Unmasked*	B
Lockwood, Lewis. *Beethoven*	B
Louvin, Charlie. *Satan Is Real*	920
Lynn, Loretta. ★*Me & Patsy Kickin' up Dust*	B
Lynn, Loretta. *Still Woman Enough*	B
Mahon, Maureen. ★*Black Diamond Queens*	782.421
Mason, Nick. *Inside Out*	B
Max, D. T. *Finale*	782.1
McBride, James. *Kill 'Em and Leave*	B
McBrien, William. *Cole Porter*	B
McCartney, Paul. ★*1964*	782.42166
McCartney, Paul. *The Lyrics*	782.42166
McCormick, Mack. *Biography of a Phantom*	782.421643
McDonald, Michael. ★*What a Fool Believes*	B
McDonough, Jimmy. *Tammy Wynette*	B
Mehr, Bob. *Trouble Boys*	920
Moby. *Porcelain*	B
Moby. *Then It Fell Apart*	B
Momus. *Niche*	B
Moore, Marcus J. *The Butterfly Effect*	B
Moore, Thurston. *Sonic Life*	B
Morley, Paul. *The Age of Bowie*	B
Morris, Edmund. *Beethoven*	B
Moss, Marissa R. *Her Country*	781.642
Mueller, Melissa. *Alice's Piano*	B
Murakami, Haruki. ★*Absolutely on Music*	784.2
Murray, Charles Shaar. *Crosstown Traffic*	B
Nelson, Willie. *It's a Long Story*	B
Nesmith, Michael. *Infinite Tuesday*	B
Neville, Aaron. *Tell It Like It Is*	B
Newkey-Burden, Chas. *Taylor Swift*	B
Norman, Philip. *George Harrison*	B
Norman, Philip. *John Lennon*	B
Norman, Philip. ★*Wild Thing*	B
O'Connor, Sinead. ★*Rememberings*	B
Oppedisano, Tony. *Sinatra and Me*	B
Osbourne, Ozzy. *I Am Ozzy*	B
Parton, Dolly. ★*Behind the Seams*	B
Parton, Dolly. ★*Dolly Parton, Songteller*	B
Perry, Joe. *Rocks*	B
Phair, Liz. *Horror Stories*	B
Pollack, Howard. ★*George Gershwin*	B
Povey, Glenn. *Echoes*	782.42166
Powers, Ann. ★*Traveling*	B
Price, Margo. *Maybe We'll Make It*	B
Prince. *The Beautiful Ones*	B
Questlove. *Mo' Meta Blues*	782.42164
Quin, Tegan. ★*High School*	B
Remnick, David. *Holding the Note*	781.64
Rhodes, James. *Instrumental*	B
Ribowsky, Mark. *Dreams to Remember*	B
Ribowsky, Mark. *Signed, Sealed, and Delivered*	B
Richards, Keith. *Life*	B
Robertson, Robbie. ★*Testimony*	B
Robinson, Staci. ★*Tupac Shakur*	B
Rodgers, Mary. *Shy*	B
Ronstadt, Linda. *Feels Like Home*	B
Ross, Alex. *Wagnerism*	B
Santana, Carlos. *The Universal Tone*	B
Schemel, Patty. *Hit so Hard*	B
Schonberg, Harold C. ★*The Lives of the Great Composers*	780
Servadio, Gaia. *Rossini*	B
Shahidi, Afshin. *Prince*	B
Simmons, Nadirah. ★*First Things First*	782.42164
Simmons, Sylvie. *I'm Your Man*	B
Simon, Carly. ★*Boys in the Trees*	782.42164
Smarsh, Sarah. *She Come by It Natural*	782.42164
Smith, Patti. ★*Just Kids*	B
Smith, Patti. ★*M Train*	B
Smith, Patti. ★*Year of the Monkey*	B
Spears, Britney. *The Woman in Me*	B
Spera, Keith. *Groove Interrupted*	B
Spitz, Bob. ★*The Beatles*	B
Spitz, Bob. *Led Zeppelin*	782.42166
Springsteen, Bruce. ★*Born to Run*	B
Stanley, Bob. ★*The Story of the Bee Gees*	782.42164
Stanley, Paul. *Backstage Pass*	B
Stanley, Paul. *Face the Music*	B
Stone, Sly. *Thank You (Falettinme Be Mice Elf Agin)*	B
Streisand, Barbra. ★*My Name Is Barbra*	B
Suchet, John. *Mozart*	B
Suchet, John. *Verdi*	782.1092
Swafford, Jan. ★*Beethoven*	B
Swafford, Jan. *Charles Ives*	B
Swafford, Jan. *Johannes Brahms*	B
Swafford, Jan. *Mozart*	B
Taupin, Bernie. *Scattershot*	B
Teachout, Terry. *Duke*	B
Teachout, Terry. *Pops*	B
Thomson, Graeme. *George Harrison*	B
Threadgill, Henry. *Easily Slip into Another World*	B
Tolinski, Brad. *Light and Shade*	B
Travis, Randy. *Forever and Ever, Amen*	B
Turner, Tina. ★*Happiness Becomes You*	158.1
Tweedy, Jeff. *Let's Go (so We Can Get Back)*	B
Tye, Larry. ★*The Jazzmen*	781.6509
Van Zandt, Steve. *Unrequited Infatuations*	B
Vogel, Joseph. *Man in the Music*	B
Wald, Elijah. ★*Escaping the Delta*	B
Walsh, Stephen. ★*Debussy*	B
Warsaw-Fan Rauch, Arianna. ★*Declassified*	781.1
Weisman, Eliot. *The Way It Was*	782.42164
White, Richard Antoine. *I'm Possible*	B
White, Ryan. *Jimmy Buffett*	782.42164
Wilkinson, Alec. *The Protest Singer*	B
Williams, Lucinda. *Don't Tell Anybody the Secrets I Told You*	B
Williams, Michelle. *Checking In*	B

AUTHOR, TITLE, SERIES AND SUBJECT INDEX

Williams, Zach. *Rescue Story*	B
Wilson, Brian. *I Am Brian Wilson*	B
Wolfe, Charles K. ★*The Life and Legend of Leadbelly*	B
Wolff, Christoph. *Johann Sebastian Bach*	B
Wolff, Daniel J. *Grown-Up Anger*	920
Womack, Kenneth. *All Things Must Pass Away*	781.66
Wood, Damon. *Working for the Man, Playing in the Band*	782.42164
Yaffe, David. *Reckless Daughter*	782.42164
Young, Neil. *Waging Heavy Peace*	B
Zack, Ian. *Odetta*	B
Zanes, Warren. *Deliver Me from Nowhere*	782.42164
Zanes, Warren. *Petty*	B
Zauner, Michelle. ★*Crying in H Mart*	B
Zwonitzer, Mark. *Will You Miss Me When I'm Gone?*	920

LIFE STORIES — ARTS AND CULTURE — WRITING

Boswell, James. ★*The Life of Samuel Johnson*	B
Bram, Christopher. *Eminent Outlaws*	920
Briggs, Kate. *This Little Art*	418
Brinkley, Alan. ★*The Publisher*	B
Campbell, Hayley. *The Art of Neil Gaiman*	B
Carlson, Erin. *I'll Have What She's Having*	791.43
Cather, Willa. *The Selected Letters of Willa Cather*	B
Damrosch, Leopold. *The Club*	920
Darkshire, Oliver. *Once Upon a Tome*	B
De Hamel, Christopher. *The Manuscripts Club*	091
Franklin, Sara B. ★*The Editor*	B
Funder, Anna. *Wifedom*	B
Goldblatt, Duchess. *Becoming Duchess Goldblatt*	B
Greene, Graham. *Graham Greene*	823
Hardin, Lara Love. ★*The Many Lives of Mama Love*	B
Hartigan, Patti. *August Wilson*	B
Hartman, Darrell. *Battle of Ink and Ice*	998
Heyman, Stephen. *The Planter of Modern Life*	B
Hirshey, Gerri. *Not Pretty Enough*	B
Hodgman, John. *Medallion Status*	B
Hodgman, John. *Vacationland*	B
Hudes, Quiara Alegria. ★*My Broken Language*	B
Kakutani, Michiko. *Ex Libris*	028
Keenan, Cody. *Grace*	973.932
Kumar, Priyanka. *Conversations with Birds*	598
Lahiri, Jhumpa. *Translating Myself and Others*	418
Lepore, Jill. ★*The Deadline*	814
Maiklem, Lara. *Mudlark*	B
Mankoff, Robert. *How About Never—Is Never Good for You?*	741.5
Martinez Wood, Jamie. *Latino Writers and Journalists*	B
McPhee, John. *Tabula Rasa; V.1*	818
Mead, Rebecca. *My Life in Middlemarch*	823
Milch, David. *Life's Work*	B
Miller, Adrienne. *In the Land of Men*	070.5
Nafisi, Azar. *Read Dangerously*	809
Norris, Mary. *Between You and Me*	428.2
Odell, Amy. *Anna*	B
Pepys, Samuel. *The Diary of Samuel Pepys*	B
Popoff, Alexandra. *Vasily Grossman and the Soviet Century*	B
Raab, Nathan. *The Hunt for History*	790.1
Rakoff, Joanna Smith. *My Salinger Year*	B
Schultz, Kevin Michael. *Buckley and Mailer*	920
Shapiro, James. *The Year of Lear*	822.33
Simpson, J. A. *The Word Detective*	B
Thomson, Jennifer. *Josephine Tey*	823
Thwaite, Ann. *Goodbye Christopher Robin*	B
V. ★*Reckoning*	814
Wellman, Victoria. *Before You Say Anything*	808.5
Whyte, Kenneth. *The Uncrowned King*	B
Zweibel, Alan. *Laugh Lines*	B

LIFE STORIES — ARTS AND CULTURE — WRITING — AUTHORS

Achebe, Chinua. *The Education of a British-Protected Child*	B
Achebe, Chinua. *There Was a Country*	B
Alexie, Sherman. *You Don't Have to Say You Love Me*	818
Allende, Isabel. *My Invented Country*	B
Allende, Isabel. *The Sum of Our Days*	B
Anders, Charlie Jane. ★*Never Say You Can't Survive*	808.02
Andersen, Jens. *Astrid Lindgren*	B
Angelou, Maya. ★*I Know Why the Caged Bird Sings*	B
Angelou, Maya. *A Song Flung up to Heaven*	B
Attwell, David. *J. M. Coetzee and the Life of Writing*	823
Atwood, Margaret. *In Other Worlds*	813
Auster, Paul. *Burning Boy*	B

Banville, John. *Time Pieces*	914.1
Barker, Elspeth. ★*Notes from the Henhouse*	828
Bartlett, Rosamund. ★*Tolstoy*	B
Bass, Rick. *The Traveling Feast*	B
Bass, Rick. *Why I Came West*	333.78
Bechdel, Alison. ★*Fun Home*	741.5
Bell, Madison Smartt. *Child of Light*	B
Benner, Erica. *Be Like the Fox*	B
Bennett, Jackie. *The Writer's Garden*	920
Bergstein, Rachelle. *The Genius of Judy*	813
Berlin, Lucia. ★*Welcome Home*	B
Blaisdell, Robert. *Creating Anna Karenina*	891.7
Bowker, Gordon. ★*James Joyce*	B
Bradbury, Ray. ★*Remembrance*	813
Braitman, Laurel. *What Looks Like Bravery*	B
Briggs, Julia. *Virginia Woolf*	823
Broome, Brian. ★*Punch Me up to the Gods*	B
Brown, David S. *Paradise Lost*	813
Bryson, Bill. *Shakespeare*	B
Burroughs, Augusten. ★*Toil & Trouble*	B
Caldwell, Gail. *Let's Take the Long Way Home*	B
Calhoun, Ada. *Also a Poet*	B
Carcaterra, Lorenzo. *Three Dreamers*	B
Caro, Robert A. ★*Working*	B
Cep, Casey N. ★*Furious Hours*	364.152
Cercas, Javier. *Lord of All the Dead*	868
Chabon, Michael. *Manhood for Amateurs*	B
Chee, Alexander. ★*How to Write an Autobiographical Novel*	B
Cheever, Susan. *American Bloomsbury*	920
Cisneros, Sandra. *A House of My Own*	B
Cleage, Pearl. *Things I Should Have Told My Daughter*	B
Coffin, Judith G. *Sex, Love, and Letters*	848
Collins, Max Allan. *Spillane*	B
Conradi, Peter J. *Iris*	B
Conroy, Pat. *My Losing Season*	B
Cott, Jonathan. *There's a Mystery There*	813
Crespino, Joseph. *Atticus Finch*	B
Cusk, Rachel. *Coventry*	814
Daugherty, Tracy. *Larry McMurtry*	B
Daugherty, Tracy. *The Last Love Song*	B
Dawidziak, Mark. *A Mystery of Mysteries*	B
Dearborn, Mary V. *Carson McCullers*	B
Dearborn, Mary V. *Ernest Hemingway*	B
Dennison, Matthew. *Behind the Mask*	B
Dennison, Matthew. *The Man in the Willows*	B
Dery, Mark. *Born to Be Posthumous*	B
Diaz, Jaquira. *Ordinary Girls*	818
Didion, Joan. ★*Let Me Tell You What I Mean*	814
Dochartaigh, Kerri ni. *Cacophony of Bone*	B
Duberman, Martin B. *Andrea Dworkin*	B
Eade, Philip. *Evelyn Waugh*	B
Elledge, Scott. *E.B. White*	B
Ellison, Ralph. *The Selected Letters of Ralph Ellison*	813
Ellmann, Richard. *Oscar Wilde*	B
Emezi, Akwaeke. ★*Dear Senthuran*	B
Ephron, Delia. *Left on Tenth*	B
Ephron, Nora. *The Most of Nora Ephron*	814
Ernaux, Annie. ★*The Years*	B
Febos, Melissa. ★*Body Work*	808.06
Fehrman, Craig. *Author in Chief*	920
Feinstein, Adam. *Pablo Neruda*	B
Feldman, Deborah. *Unorthodox*	B
Ferrante, Elena. *In the Margins*	809
Fingeroth, Danny. *A Marvelous Life*	741.5
Frank, Joseph. ★*Dostoevsky*	B
Franklin, Ruth. *Shirley Jackson*	B
Fraser, Caroline. ★*Prairie Fires*	B
French, Patrick. *The World Is What It Is*	B
Gaiman, Neil. *The View from the Cheap Seats*	824
Garcia Marquez, Gabriel. *Living to Tell the Tale*	B
Garcia, Rodrigo. *A Farewell to Gabo and Mercedes*	B
Gary, Amy. *In the Great Green Room*	813
Gaskell, Elizabeth Cleghorn. *The Life of Charlotte Bronte*	B
Glaude, Eddie S. *Begin Again*	305.800973
Gomez, Edgar. *High-Risk Homosexual*	B
Gooch, Brad. ★*Flannery*	B
Gordon, Charlotte. *Romantic Outlaws*	920
Gordon, Edmund. *The Invention of Angela Carter*	B

PUBLIC LIBRARY CORE COLLECTION: NONFICTION
Twentieth Edition

Gorra, Michael Edward. *The Saddest Words*	813
Greenblatt, Stephen. ★*Will in the World*	B
Griffin, Susan. *Out of Silence, Sound. Out of Nothing, Something*	808.02
Guo, XIaolu. *Nine Continents*	B
Hamlin, Kimberly A. *Free Thinker*	B
Handler, Daniel. ★*And Then? and Then? What Else?*	813
Hardwick, Elizabeth. *The Dolphin Letters, 1970-1979*	811
Harlan, Elizabeth. *George Sand*	B
Harman, Claire. *Charlotte Bronte*	B
Harrison, Jim. *The Search for the Genuine*	814
Harvey, Samantha. *The Shapeless Unease*	B
Hastings, Selina. *The Secret Lives of Somerset Maugham*	B
Hauser, CJ. *The Crane Wife*	B
Havrilesky, Heather. *What If This Were Enough?*	152.4
Hecimovich, Gregg A. ★*The Life and Times of Hannah Crafts*	B
Hemingway, Ernest. *Dear Papa*	813
Hemon, Aleksandar. *My Parents*	814
Hensley, William L. Iggiagruk. *Fifty Miles from Tomorrow*	B
Herbert, Brian. *Dreamer of Dune*	B
Heti, Sheila. *Alphabetical Diaries*	818
Heughan, Sam. *Waypoints*	B
Highsmith, Patricia. ★*Patricia Highsmith's Diaries and Notebooks*	818
Hoffman, Adina. *My Happiness Bears No Relation to Happiness*	B
Hogan, Linda. *The Woman Who Watches Over the World*	B
hooks, bell. *Wounds of Passion*	B
Houston, Pam. *Deep Creek*	814
Hurston, Zora Neale. *Dust Tracks on a Road*	B
Hustvedt, Siri. *Mothers, Fathers, and Others*	814
Huxley, Elspeth Joscelin Grant. *The Flame Trees of Thika*	B
Iversen, Kristen. *Full Body Burden*	363.17
Jackson, Lawrence Patrick. *Chester B. Himes*	B
Jackson, Shirley. ★*The Letters of Shirley Jackson*	813
Jamison, Leslie. ★*Make It Scream, Make It Burn*	814
Johnson, Joyce. *The Voice Is All*	B
Jones, Brian Jay. ★*Becoming Dr. Seuss*	B
Kaplan, Alice Yaeger. *Looking for the Stranger*	B
Kenan, Randall. *Black Folk Could Fly*	813
King, Stephen. *On Writing*	B
Knausgaard, Karl Ove. *Spring*	B
Kroger, Lisa. *Monster, She Wrote*	920
Le Carre, John. *The Pigeon Tunnel*	B
Leader, Zachary. *The Life of Saul Bellow*	B
Lear, Linda J. *Beatrix Potter*	B
Leon, Donna. *My Venice and Other Essays*	945
Lessing, Doris May. *Under My Skin*	823
Levy, Deborah. *The Cost of Living*	B
Levy, Deborah. ★*Real Estate*	B
Levy, Deborah. ★*Things I Don't Want to Know*	B
Lippman, Laura. *My Life as a Villainess*	B
Lively, Penelope. *Life in the Garden*	B
Lynskey, Dorian. *The Ministry of Truth*	823
Mahjoub, Jamal. *A Line in the River*	962.404
Mantel, Hilary. *Mantel Pieces*	824.914
Martin, Gerald. ★*Gabriel Garcia Marquez*	B
Matteson, John. *Eden's Outcasts*	920
Maupin, Armistead. *Logical Family*	B
McCourt, Frank. *'Tis*	B
McCourt, Malachy. *Singing My Him Song*	B
McDowell, Marta. *The World of Laura Ingalls Wilder*	813
Messud, Claire. *Kant's Little Prussian Head and Other Reasons Why I Write*	B
Millet, Lydia. *We Loved It All*	813
Min, Anchee. *Red Azalea*	B
Montillo, Roseanne. *The Lady and Her Monsters*	823
Moore, Susanna. *Miss Aluminum*	813
Moore, Wayetu. *The Dragons, the Giant, the Women*	B
Morris, Jan. *A Writer's House in Wales*	942.9
Moser, Benjamin. ★*Sontag*	B
Moser, Benjamin. *Why This World*	B
Mullen, Bill. ★*James Baldwin*	B
Murakami, Haruki. ★*Novelist as a Vocation*	895.64
Murakami, Haruki. *What I Talk About When I Talk About Running*	B
Nayeri, Dina. ★*The Ungrateful Refugee*	362.87
Niven, Penelope. *Thornton Wilder*	B
O'Sullivan, Emer. *The Fall of the House of Wilde*	B
Okorafor, Nnedi. *Broken Places & Outer Spaces*	153.3
Orner, Peter. *Am I Alone Here?*	814
Oyler, Lauren. *No Judgment*	814
Palahniuk, Chuck. *Consider This*	B
Pamuk, Orhan. *Istanbul*	949.61
Parini, Jay. *Borges and Me*	813
Patchett, Ann. ★*These Precious Days*	814
Patterson, James. *James Patterson by James Patterson*	B
Phillips, Julie. *James Tiptree, Jr.*	B
Philpott, Mary Laura. *Bomb Shelter*	B
Pinckney, Darryl. *Come Back in September*	B
Pitzer, Andrea. *The Secret History of Vladimir Nabokov*	813
Pratchett, Terry. *A Slip of the Keyboard*	824
Prose, Francine. *1974*	B
Qashu, Sayed. *Native*	892.4
Quindlen, Anna. ★*Nanaville*	B
Rampersad, Arnold. ★*Ralph Ellison*	B
Richardson, Robert D. *Emerson*	814
Ricks, Thomas E. *Churchill and Orwell*	920
Rosnay, Tatiana de. *Manderley Forever*	B
Rushdie, Salman. *Joseph Anton*	B
Rushdie, Salman. ★*Knife*	B
Sabatini Sloan, Aisha. *Dreaming of Ramadi in Detroit*	814
Sacks, Oliver. *Gratitude*	306.9
Safranski, Rudiger. *Goethe*	B
Sampson, Fiona. *In Search of Mary Shelley*	B
Sanchez, Erika L. *Crying in the Bathroom*	B
Sartre, Jean-Paul. *We Have Only This Life to Live*	848
Schultz, Philip. *Comforts of the Abyss*	801
Scovell, Nell. *Just the Funny Parts*	B
Sedaris, David. ★*The Best of Me*	818
Sedaris, David. *Calypso*	814
Sedaris, David. ★*A Carnival of Snackery*	818
Sedaris, David. ★*Happy-Go-Lucky*	814
Sedaris, David. *Theft by Finding*	B
Seiple, Samantha. *Louisa on the Front Lines*	B
Shafrir, Doree. *Thanks for Waiting*	B
Shakespeare, Nicholas. *Ian Fleming*	B
Shapland, Jenn. *My Autobiography of Carson McCullers*	B
Shelden, Michael. *Mark Twain*	B
Sims, Michael. *Arthur and Sherlock*	B
Skal, David J. *Something in the Blood*	823
Slawenski, Kenneth. ★*Salinger*	B
Smith, Lee. *Dimestore*	975.5
Smith, Zadie. *Intimations*	824
Solnit, Rebecca. *Orwell's Roses*	B
Solnit, Rebecca. ★*Recollections of My Nonexistence*	B
Souder, William. *Mad at the World*	813
Spiegelman, Art. *Co-Mix*	741.5
Spurling, Hilary. *Anthony Powell*	B
Sturgis, Matthew. *Oscar Wilde*	B
Styron, William. *My Generation*	814
Tallent, Elizabeth. *Scratched*	B
Tan, Amy. ★*Where the Past Begins*	B
Taylor, D. J. *Orwell*	B
Teffi, N. A. *Memories*	B
Thompson, Juan F. *Stories I Tell Myself*	B
Todd, Olivier. *Albert Camus*	B
Toibin, Colm. *Mad, Bad, Dangerous to Know*	920
Tomalin, Claire. *Samuel Pepys*	B
Tomalin, Claire. *Thomas Hardy*	B
Tresch, John. *The Reason for the Darkness of the Night*	B
Twain, Mark. *Autobiography of Mark Twain*	B
Twain, Mark. ★*Autobiography of Mark Twain*	B
Twain, Mark. ★*Autobiography of Mark Twain*	B
Vargas Llosa, Mario. *The Call of the Tribe*	868
Verdelle, A. J. *Miss Chloe*	B
Vonnegut, Kurt. ★*A Man Without a Country*	818
Wagamese, Richard. *One Native Life*	B
Walker, Alice. *The Cushion in the Road*	814
Walker, Alice. *Gathering Blossoms Under Fire*	B
Wallace, Carvell. *Another Word for Love*	B
Walls, Laura Dassow. ★*Henry David Thoreau*	B
Watkins, D. *Black Boy Smile*	B
Watts, Steven. *Self-Help Messiah*	B
Weller, Sam. *The Bradbury Chronicles*	B
Weller, Sheila. *Carrie Fisher*	B
Welty, Eudora. *One Writer's Beginnings*	B
Wiesel, Elie. *And the Sea Is Never Full*	B
Wilder, Laura Ingalls. *Pioneer Girl*	B
Williamson, Edwin. *Borges*	B

AUTHOR, TITLE, SERIES AND SUBJECT INDEX

Wilson, A. N. *C.S. Lewis*	823
Wilson, A. N. *The Mystery of Charles Dickens*	823
Winkler, Elizabeth. *Shakespeare Was a Woman & Other Heresies*	822.33
Woolf, Virginia. *Moments of Being*	B
Worsley, Lucy. ★*Agatha Christie*	B
Wright, Richard. ★*Black Boy*	B

LIFE STORIES — ARTS AND CULTURE — WRITING — JOURNALISTS

Addario, Lynsey. *Of Love & War*	779
Alderton, Dolly. *Everything I Know About Love*	B
Arana, Marie. *American Chica*	B
Barnett, Erica C. *Quitter*	B
Baron, Martin. ★*Collision of Power*	070.4
Bernstein, Carl. ★*Chasing History*	B
Blakinger, Keri. *Corrections in Ink*	B
Blume, Lesley M. M. *Fallout*	940.54
Bogus, Carl T. *Buckley*	B
Brinkley, Douglas. ★*Cronkite*	B
Brokaw, Tom. *The Fall of Richard Nixon*	B
Brown, Tina. *The Vanity Fair Diaries*	B
Buck, Joe. *Lucky Bastard*	B
Butler, Brin-Jonathan. *The Domino Diaries*	796.83
Campbell, Deborah. *A Disappearance in Damascus*	365
Carr, David. *The Night of the Gun*	B
Carr, Erin Lee. *All That You Leave Behind*	B
Chrisinger, David. *The Soldier's Truth*	940.54
Cohen, Deborah. *Last Call at the Hotel Imperial*	070.92
Collins, Lauren. *When in French*	B
Couric, Katie. *Going There*	B
Crabapple, Molly. *Drawing Blood*	B
Cronkite, Walter. *A Reporter's Life*	B
Cullen, Art. *Storm Lake*	071.7
Dearborn, Mary V. *Ernest Hemingway*	B
Denevi, Timothy. *Freak Kingdom*	B
Dickinson, Amy. *Strangers Tend to Tell Me Things*	B
Doty, Cate. *Mergers and Acquisitions*	395.2
Ebert, Roger. *Life Itself*	B
Edwards, Bob. *Edward R. Murrow and the Birth of Broadcast Journalism*	B
Eichenwald, Kurt. *A Mind Unraveled*	B
Engel, Richard. *And Then All Hell Broke Loose*	956.05
Ferguson, Jane. *No Ordinary Assignment*	B
Garner, Dwight. *The Upstairs Delicatessen*	B
Gilliam, Dorothy Butler. *Trailblazer*	B
Gleiberman, Owen. *Movie Freak*	B
Goldstein, Meredith. *Can't Help Myself*	B
Green, Robin. *The Only Girl*	070.92
Greenidge, Kerri. *Black Radical*	B
Hersh, Seymour M. *Reporter*	B
Hessler, Peter. *The Buried*	962.05
Hill, Jemele. *Uphill*	B
Hilsum, Lindsey. *In Extremis*	B
Hinojosa, Maria. *Once I Was You*	B
Hitchens, Christopher. *Hitch-22*	920
Huffman, Alan. *Here I Am*	B
Kissinger, Meg. *While You Were Out*	362.2
Klein, Naomi. ★*Doppelganger*	302.2
Kluger, Ruth. *Indelible Ink*	B
Kristof, Nicholas D. ★*Chasing Hope*	B
Kroeger, Brooke. *Undaunted*	070.4
LaFollette, Marcel C. *Writing for Their Lives*	071.3
LeDuff, Charlie. *Detroit*	977.4
Lippman, Laura. *My Life as a Villainess*	B
MacKrell, Judith. *The Correspondents*	070.4
MacPherson, Myra. *All Governments Lie*	B
Mekhennet, Souad. *I Was Told to Come Alone*	363.3250956
Meltzer, Marisa. *This Is Big*	613.25
Miller, Lulu. *Why Fish Don't Exist*	B
Miraldi, Robert. *Seymour Hersh*	B
Mitchell, Jerry. ★*Race Against Time*	364.152
Mock, Janet. *Surpassing Certainty*	B
Morris, James McGrath. *Eye on the Struggle*	B
Morris, James McGrath. *Pulitzer*	B
Muse, Toby. *Kilo*	363.4509861
Nagourney, Adam. *The Times*	071
Napoli, Lisa. *Susan, Linda, Nina & Cokie*	920
Nussbaum, Emily. *I Like to Watch*	791.45
O'Toole, Fintan. ★*We Don't Know Ourselves*	941.7
Peer, Basharat. *Curfewed Night*	B
Pomerantsev, Peter. ★*How to Win an Information War*	940.53
Prothero, Stephen R. *God the Bestseller*	070.5
Quinn, Susan. *Eleanor and Hick*	B
Reed, Julia. *Dispatches from the Gilded Age*	B
Ribowsky, Mark. *Howard Cosell*	070.449796
Rinehart, Lorissa. *First to the Front*	B
Roberts, Steven V. *Cokie*	B
Searcey, Dionne. *In Pursuit of Disobedient Women*	B
Shapiro, Ari. ★*The Best Strangers in the World*	B
Singer, Matt. *Opposable Thumbs*	791.43
Snyder, Rachel Louise. *Women We Buried, Women We Burned*	B
Steinem, Gloria. *My Life on the Road*	B
Stelter, Brian. *Hoax*	070.4
Stuart, Amanda Mackenzie. *Empress of Fashion*	B
Sullivan, Margaret. *Newsroom Confidential*	070.92
Swisher, Kara. *Burn Book*	303.48
Taylor, D. J. *Orwell*	B
Thomas, R. Eric. *Here for It*	B
Thompson, Juan F. *Stories I Tell Myself*	B
Todd, Kim. *Sensational*	920
Tur, Katy. *Rough Draft*	B
Vargas, Jose Antonio. *Dear America*	B
Verini, James. *They Will Have to Die Now*	956.7044
Wainaina, Binyavanga. ★*How to Write About Africa*	814
Ward, Clarissa. *On All Fronts*	B
Ward, Jon. *Testimony*	277.308
Welteroth, Elaine. *More Than Enough*	B
Wenner, Jann. *Like a Rolling Stone*	B
Wilson, Robert. *Mathew Brady*	B

LIFE STORIES — ARTS AND CULTURE — WRITING — POETS

Ackmann, Martha. ★*These Fevered Days*	B
Basbanes, Nicholas A. ★*Cross of Snow*	B
Bate, Jonathan. *Radical Wordsworth*	B
Bialosky, Jill. *Poetry Will Save Your Life*	B
Binyon, T. J. *Pushkin*	B
Blanco, Richard. *The Prince of Los Cocuyos*	B
Blunk, Jonathan. *James Wright*	B
Boyer, Anne. *The Undying*	B
Brown, Molly McCully. *Places I've Taken My Body*	B
Brown, Terence. *The Life of W.B. Yeats*	B
Clark, Heather. ★*Red Comet*	B
Crawford, Robert. *Eliot After the Waste Land*	B
Crowther, Gail. *Three-Martini Afternoons at the Ritz*	920
Doty, Mark. *What Is the Grass*	811
Forche, Carolyn. *What You Have Heard Is True*	B
Gordon, Lyndall. ★*T.S. Eliot*	B
Gunn, Thom. ★*The Letters of Thom Gunn*	821
Hammer, Langdon. *James Merrill*	B
Hardwick, Elizabeth. *The Dolphin Letters, 1970-1979*	811
Harjo, Joy. *Catching the Light*	818
Harjo, Joy. *Crazy Brave*	B
Harjo, Joy. ★*Poet Warrior*	B
Hoffman, Adina. ★*My Happiness Bears No Relation to Happiness*	B
Hollis, Matthew. *The Waste Land*	821
Hong, Cathy Park. *Minor Feelings*	305.48
Hughes, Langston. ★*I Wonder as I Wander*	B
Izgil, Tahir Hamut. *Waiting to Be Arrested at Night*	B
Jackson, Angela. *A Surprised Queenhood in the New Black Sun*	B
Jang, Jin-Sung. *Dear Leader*	B
Johnson, Joyce. *The Voice Is All*	B
Korda, Michael. *Muse of Fire*	940.4
Milford, Nancy. *Savage Beauty*	B
Miller, Lucasta. ★*Keats*	821
Moody, Anthony David. *Ezra Pound*	B
Nicolson, Adam. *The Making of Poetry*	821.709
Parini, Jay. *Robert Frost*	B
Plath, Sylvia. *The Letters of Sylvia Plath*	811.54
Plath, Sylvia. *The Letters of Sylvia Plath*	811.54
Raffa, Guy P. *Dante's Bones*	851
Rampersad, Arnold. *The Life of Langston Hughes*	B
Rampersad, Arnold. ★*The Life of Langston Hughes*	B
Roffman, Karin. *The Songs We Know Best*	B
Rosenblitt, J. Alison. *The Beauty of Living*	B
Rundell, Katherine. ★*Super-Infinite*	B
Smith, Patti. ★*Just Kids*	B
Smith, Patti. ★*Year of the Monkey*	B
Travisano, Thomas J. *Love Unknown*	B
Waldstreicher, David. *The Odyssey of Phillis Wheatley*	B
Warren, Rosanna. *Max Jacob*	B

PUBLIC LIBRARY CORE COLLECTION: NONFICTION
Twentieth Edition

Wiman, Christian. *He Held Radical Light*	814
Winder, Elizabeth. *Pain, Parties, Work*	B
Zenith, Richard. *Pessoa*	B

LIFE STORIES — BUSINESS

Busby, Jill Louise. *Unfollow Me*	305.08
Ducharme, Jamie. *Big Vape*	338.7
Eggers, Dave. *The Monk of Mokha*	B
Fabre, Cin. *Wolf Hustle*	332.6
Kaufman, Jonathan. *The Last Kings of Shanghai*	951
Lemann, Nicholas. *Transaction Man*	330.973
Lewis, Michael. ★*Going Infinite*	305.5
Lima, Jamie Kern. *Believe It*	B
McDonald, Greg (Producer). *Elvis and the Colonel*	920
Norton, Hughes. ★*Rainmaker*	796.352
Rempel, William C. *The Gambler*	B
Schulman, Daniel. *The Money Kings*	332.0973
Sedgewick, Augustine. *Coffeeland*	338.4
Slade, Rachel. *American Hoodie*	338.4
Sun, Carrie. *Private Equity*	B
Thorp, Edward O. *A Man for All Markets*	B
Walton, Sam. *Sam Walton, Made in America*	B
Williams, Bari A. *Seen yet Unseen*	338.4

LIFE STORIES — BUSINESS — BUSINESS LEADERS

Ahamed, Liaquat. *Lords of Finance*	920
Au-Yeung, Angel. *Wonder Boy*	B
Auletta, Ken. *Media Man*	B
Barr, Luke. *Ritz & Escoffier*	920
Boden, Anne. *Female Founders' Playbook*	658.4
Brinkley, Douglas. *Wheels for the World*	B
Brown, Eliot. *The Cult of We*	333.33
Bruck, Connie. *When Hollywood Had a King*	B
Bundles, A'Lelia. *On Her Own Ground*	B
Cannadine, David. ★*Mellon*	B
Caro, Robert A. *The Power Broker*	B
Chafkin, Max. *The Contrarian*	B
Chernow, Ron. *The Warburgs*	B
Dennis, Felix. *How to Get Rich*	B
Downs, Paul. *Boss Life*	338.7
Dufu, Tiffany. *Drop the Ball*	650.1
Gabler, Neal. *Walt Disney*	B
Gelles, David. *The Man Who Broke Capitalism*	330.12
Gelwicks, Andrew. *The Queer Advantage*	920
Gotch, Jen. *The Upside of Being Down*	B
Greene, Joshua. *Unstoppable*	B
Harrison, Scott. *Thirst*	B
Hastings, Reed. *No Rules Rules*	384.55
Isaacson, Walter. ★*Elon Musk*	B
Isaacson, Walter. ★*Steve Jobs*	B
Jackson, Curtis. *Hustle Harder, Hustle Smarter*	B
Kidder, Tracy. *A Truck Full of Money*	B
Knight, Philip H. *Shoe Dog*	B
Kranish, Michael. *Trump Revealed*	B
Krass, Peter. *Carnegie*	B
Kurlansky, Mark. *Birdseye*	B
Leonard, Christopher. *Kochland*	338.7
Levy, Reynold. *They Told Me Not to Take That Job*	792.09
Mallaby, Sebastian. *The Man Who Knew*	B
Malone, Jo. *Jo Malone*	B
Marshall, Cynthia. *You've Been Chosen*	B
Mordden, Ethan. *Ziegfeld*	B
Nasaw, David. *Andrew Carnegie*	B
Nasaw, David. *The Chief*	B
Nooyi, Indra. ★*My Life in Full*	B
Orbanes, Philip. *The Game Makers*	338.7
Rathbone, John Paul. *The Sugar King of Havana*	B
Renehan, Edward. *Commodore*	B
Rubin, Robert Edward. *The Yellow Pad*	658.4
Sancton, Thomas. *The Bettencourt Affair*	B
Satow, Julie. *When Women Ran Fifth Avenue*	381.141
Schlender, Brent. *Becoming Steve Jobs*	B
Schroeder, Alice. *The Snowball*	B
Stewart, James B. *Unscripted*	658.1
Stiles, T. J. ★*The First Tycoon*	B
Watts, Steven. *The People's Tycoon*	B
White, Shane. *Prince of Darkness*	B
Wiedeman, Reeves. *Billion Dollar Loser*	333.33
Wilson, Robert. *Barnum*	B

LIFE STORIES — BUSINESS — WORKING LIFE

Ash, Lamorna. *Dark, Salt, Clear*	942.3
Butcher, Barbara. *What the Dead Know*	614
Chatelain, Marcia. ★*Franchise*	339
Doughty, Caitlin. *Smoke Gets in Your Eyes*	B
Elwood, Phil. *All the Worst Humans*	659.2
Flannery, Kate. *Strip Tees*	338.4
Howe, Ben Ryder. *My Korean Deli*	B
Jensen, Robert A. *Personal Effects*	363.34
Land, Stephanie. *Maid*	B
McShane Wulfhart, Nell. *The Great Stewardess Rebellion*	331.4
Melville, Wilma. ★*Hero Dogs*	636.7
Robbins, Alexandra. ★*The Teachers*	371.1
Sheehan, Jason. *Cooking Dirty*	B
Terkel, Studs. *Working*	920
Wassef, Nadia. *Shelf Life*	B
Wiener, Anna. ★*Uncanny Valley*	B
Wingfield, Adia Harvey. *Gray Areas*	331.6

LIFE STORIES — EDUCATION

Garrett, Kent. *The Last Negroes at Harvard*	920
Mitchell, Josh. *The Debt Trap*	378.3
Perkins, Anne Gardiner. *Yale Needs Women*	378
Seo, Bo. *Good Arguments*	808.53
Zara, Christopher. *Uneducated*	B

LIFE STORIES — EDUCATION — PHILOSOPHERS

Bakewell, Sarah. ★*At the Existentialist Cafe*	920
Bakewell, Sarah. *How to Live—Or—A Life of Montaigne*	B
Carlisle, Clare. *Philosopher of the Heart*	B
Coffin, Judith G. *Sex, Love, and Letters*	848
Curran, Andrew S. *Diderot and the Art of Thinking Freely*	194
Durant, Will. ★*The Story of Philosophy*	190
Eilenberger, Wolfram. *Time of the Magicians*	920
Hare, R. M. ★*Plato*	184
Hughes, Bettany. ★*The Hemlock Cup*	B
Johnson, Paul. *Socrates*	183
Liedman, Sven-Eric. *A World to Win*	B
Miller, Jim. *Examined Lives*	B
Nicolson, Adam. *How to Be*	180
Norman, Jesse. *Adam Smith*	B
Pearson, Roger. *Voltaire Almighty*	B
Penaluna, Regan. ★*How to Think Like a Woman*	190.82
Prideaux, Sue. *I Am Dynamite!*	B
Richardson, Robert D. *William James*	B
Sperber, Jonathan. *Karl Marx*	B
Stewart, Jeffrey C. ★*The New Negro*	191
Watson, Richard A. *Cogito Ergo Sum*	B
Wheen, Francis. *Karl Marx*	B
Wulf, Andrea. *Magnificent Rebels*	830.9

LIFE STORIES — EDUCATION — SCHOLARS AND EDUCATORS

Baker, Nicholson. *Substitute*	371.14
Biden, Jill. *Where the Light Enters*	B
Burger, Ariel. *Witness*	848
Cadbury, Deborah. *The School That Escaped from the Nazis*	940.53
Cook, Kevin. *The Burning Blue*	629.45
De Stefano, Cristina. *The Child Is the Teacher*	B
Dolnick, Edward. *The Writing of the Gods*	493
Fleming, Brandon P. *Miseducated*	B
Gates, Henry Louis. *Colored People*	B
Givens, Jarvis R. ★*School Clothes*	371.829
Glendinning, Victoria. *Leonard Woolf*	B
Hall, Rebecca. ★*Wake*	741.5
Harlan, Louis R. *Booker T. Washington*	B
Harlan, Louis R. *Booker T. Washington*	B
Kaag, John J. *American Philosophy*	191
Kagan, Donald. *Thucydides*	938
Kaplan, Janice. *The Genius of Women*	920
Keizer, Garret. *Getting Schooled*	373.1102
Kim, Suki. *Without You, There Is No Us*	B
King, Charles. ★*Gods of the Upper Air*	920
Kraus, Dita. *A Delayed Life*	B
Kuo, Michelle. *Reading with Patrick*	B
McCourt, Frank. *Teacher Man*	B
McGill, Joseph. *Sleeping with the Ancestors*	306.362
Miller, Lulu. *Why Fish Don't Exist*	B
Mufleh, Luma. ★*Learning America*	371.826
Nafisi, Azar. *The Republic of Imagination*	B
Norrell, Robert J. *Up from History*	B
Patterson, James. *The Secret Lives of Booksellers and Librarians*	381

AUTHOR, TITLE, SERIES AND SUBJECT INDEX

Rademacher, Tom. *It Won't Be Easy*		B
Rhodes, Richard. *Scientist*		B
Robbins, Alexandra. ★*The Teachers*		371.1
Rosenberg, Justus. *The Art of Resistance*		B
Seidule, Ty. *Robert E. Lee and Me*		973.7
Sen, Amartya. *Home in the World*		B
Shatz, Adam. *The Rebel's Clinic*		965
Simmons, Ruth. ★*Up Home*		B
Viren, Sarah. *To Name the Bigger Lie*		B
Washington, Booker T. ★*Up from Slavery*		B
Winchester, Simon. *The Professor and the Madman*		423
Yousafzai, Ziauddin. *Let Her Fly*		B

LIFE STORIES — FACING ADVERSITY

Alexie, Sherman. *You Don't Have to Say You Love Me*		818
Alvis-Walker, Marcie. *Everybody Come Alive*		B
Ambroz, David. *A Place Called Home*		B
Anthony, Carmelo. *Where Tomorrows Aren't Promised*		B
Arsenault, Kerri. *Mill Town*		B
Asher, Zain E. *Where the Children Take Us*		942.1
Barnes, Cinelle. *Monsoon Mansion*		B
Baskette, Molly Phinney. *How to Begin When Your World Is Ending*		248.8
Brown, Claude. *Manchild in the Promised Land*		B
Campoverdi, Alejandra. *First Gen*		B
Cobbs-Leonard, Tasha. *Do It Anyway*		241
Conyers, Jonathan. *I Wasn't Supposed to Be Here*		B
Cornejo Villavicencio, Karla. ★*The Undocumented Americans*		920
De Leon, Jason. ★*Soldiers and Kings*		364.1
Dubus, Andre. *Townie*		B
Eger, Edith Eva. *The Choice*		B
Elliott, Andrea. ★*Invisible Child*		362.7
Fleming, Brandon P. *Miseducated*		B
Flock, Elizabeth. ★*The Furies*		305.48
Foster, Craig. ★*Amphibious Soul*		155.9
Frangello, Gina. *Blow Your House Down*		813
Gaffney, Ginger. *Half Broke*		B
Georges, Gigi. *Downeast*		974.1
Gerald, Casey. *There Will Be No Miracles Here*		B
Glaser, Gabrielle. *American Baby*		B
Goldblatt, Duchess. *Becoming Duchess Goldblatt*		B
Gordon, Aubrey. *"You Just Need to Lose Weight"*		616.3
Goyal, Nikhil. ★*Live to See the Day*		305.5
Hall, Sands. ★*Flunk, Start*		B
Hamill, Kirkland. *Filthy Beasts*		B
Henderson, Rob Kim. *Troubled*		B
Hernandez Castillo, Marcelo. *Children of the Land*		B
Herold, Benjamin. *Disillusioned*		307.76
Hinton, Anthony Ray. *The Sun Does Shine*		B
Hough, Lauren. *Leaving Isn't the Hardest Thing*		B
Ignatieff, Michael. *On Consolation*		152.4
Jackson, Bruce. *Never Far from Home*		B
Jackson, Ted. ★*You Ought to Do a Story About Me*		B
Kelly, Minka. ★*Tell Me Everything*		B
Knight, Keltie. *Lady Secrets*		305.4
Kouchner, Camille. *The Familia Grande*		B
Kyle, Taya. *American Spirit*		B
Lockhart, Chris. ★*Walking the Bowl*		362.7
Lovato, Roberto. *Unforgetting*		B
Malone, Jo. *Jo Malone*		B
Mariani, Mike. ★*What Doesn't Kill Us Makes Us*		155.9
Markham, Lauren. ★*The Far Away Brothers*		920
Martin, Clancy W. *How Not to Kill Yourself*		362.28
May, Meredith. *The Honey Bus*		B
Meltzer, Marisa. *This Is Big*		613.25
Messenger, Alex. *The Twenty-Ninth Day*		B
Mizrahi, Isaac. *I.M.*		B
Moore, Kate. ★*The Woman They Could Not Silence*		B
Moran, Rachel. *Paid For*		306.74082
Nietfeld, Emi. *Acceptance*		B
Nyamayaro, Elizabeth. *I Am a Girl from Africa*		B
O'Farrell, Maggie. *I Am, I Am, I Am*		B
Oluseyi, Hakeem M. *A Quantum Life*		B
Osnos, Evan. *Joe Biden*		B
Porter, Billy. ★*Unprotected*		B
Potts, Monica. *The Forgotten Girls*		B
Price, Margo. *Maybe We'll Make It*		B
Qadiri, Humayra. *Dancing in the Mosque*		B
Rembert, Winfred. *Chasing Me to My Grave*		B
Ressa, Maria. ★*How to Stand up to a Dictator*		070.92
Rinder, Mike. ★*A Billion Years*		B
Roy, Saumya. *Castaway Mountain*		363.72
Samaha, Albert. *Concepcion*		929
Samaha, Albert. *Never Ran, Never Will*		920
Sandberg, Sheryl. *Option B*		155.9
Shackle, Samira. *Karachi Vice*		954.91
Shahani, Aarti Namdev. *Here We Are*		B
Smarsh, Sarah. *She Come by It Natural*		782.42164
Snyder, Rachel Louise. *Women We Buried, Women We Burned*		B
Sokolik, Vicki. ★*If You See Them*		362.5
Stone, Sharon. *The Beauty of Living Twice*		B
Taylor, Goldie. *The Love You Save*		B
Thomas, Joseph Earl. *Sink*		B
Toorpakai, Maria. *A Different Kind of Daughter*		B
Trejo, Danny. *Trejo*		B
Trethewey, Natasha D. ★*Memorial Drive*		B
Trice, Dawn Turner. ★*Three Girls from Bronzeville*		977.311
Umar, Ousman. *North to Paradise*		B
Vasquez, Karla Tatiana. ★*The Salvisoul Cookbook*		641.598
Wang, Qian Julie. ★*Beautiful Country*		B
Ward, Jesmyn. ★*Men We Reaped*		B
Watkins, D. *Black Boy Smile*		B
Wetherall, Tyler. *No Way Home*		B
White, Richard Antoine. *I'm Possible*		B
Wilkerson, Isabel. ★*The Warmth of Other Suns*		304.80973
Williams, Jay. *Life Is Not an Accident*		B
Wiman, Christian. *Zero at the Bone*		818
Wolf, Brandon J. *A Place for Us*		B
Xuecun, Murong. *Deadly Quiet City*		614.5
Yousafzai, Ziauddin. *Let Her Fly*		B
Zambreno, Kate. *The Light Room*		B

LIFE STORIES — FACING ADVERSITY — ABUSE SURVIVORS

Barr, John. *Start by Believing*		364.15
Butcher, Amy. *Mothertrucker*		B
Butler, Marcia. *The Skin Above My Knee*		B
Calcaterra, Regina. *Etched in Sand*		B
Calcaterra, Regina. *Girl Unbroken*		B
Crawford, Lacy. *Notes on a Silencing*		B
Diaz, Jaquira. *Ordinary Girls*		818
Ford, Ashley C. ★*Somebody's Daughter*		B
Freitas, Donna. *Consent*		364.158092
Grande, Reyna. ★*The Distance Between Us*		973
Harjo, Joy. *Crazy Brave*		B
Harjo, Joy. ★*Poet Warrior*		B
Hill, Anita. ★*Believing*		305.42
Horton, Michelle. *Dear Sister*		B
James, Victoria. *Wine Girl*		B
Jewel. *Never Broken*		782.42164
Jones, Faith. *Sex Cult Nun*		B
Krouse, Erika. ★*Tell Me Everything*		363.25
Kruzan, Sara. *I Cried to Dream Again*		B
Lake, Dianne. *Member of the Family*		364.152
Levin, Daniel Barban. *Slonim Woods 9*		B
Machado, Carmen Maria. ★*In the Dream House*		B
Marzano-Lesnevich, Alexandria. *The Fact of a Body*		364.152
Means, Brittany. *Hell If We Don't Change Our Ways*		B
Metatawabin, Edmund. *Up Ghost River*		B
Miller, Chanel. *Know My Name*		B
Mills, Stephen Tukel. *Chosen*		B
Qu, Anna. *Made in China*		B
Robison, John Elder. *Look Me in the Eye*		B
Selvaratnam, Tanya. *Assume Nothing*		B
Shorter, Frank. *My Marathon*		796.42
Sundberg, Kelly. *Goodbye, Sweet Girl*		B
Tjipombo, Tupa. *I Am Not Your Slave*		B
Tran, Phuc. ★*Sigh, Gone*		B
V. *The Apology*		818
V. ★*Reckoning*		814
Vasquez-Lavado, Silvia. *In the Shadow of the Mountain*		B
Wariner, Ruth. *The Sound of Gravel*		B
West, Cait. ★*Rift*		B
Westover, Tara. ★*Educated*		B
Wolff, Tobias. *This Boy's Life*		B
Young, Daniella Mestyanek. *Uncultured*		B
Zhu, Mimi. *Be Not Afraid of Love*		152.4

LIFE STORIES — FACING ADVERSITY — COPING WITH DEATH

Adichie, Chimamanda Ngozi. *Notes on Grief*		155.9
Alexander, Kwame. *Why Fathers Cry at Night*		B

PUBLIC LIBRARY CORE COLLECTION: NONFICTION
Twentieth Edition

Allende, Isabel. ★*Paula*	B
Arthur, Alua. ★*Briefly Perfectly Human*	306.9
Atleework, Kendra. *Miracle Country*	979.4
Bacall, Lauren. *By Myself and Then Some*	B
Biden, Joseph R. *Promise Me, Dad*	B
Bloom, Amy. *In Love*	B
Bonner, Betsy. *The Book of Atlantis Black*	364.152
Braitman, Laurel. *What Looks Like Bravery*	B
Carr, Erin Lee. *All That You Leave Behind*	B
Caruana Galizia, Paul. ★*A Death in Malta*	364.15
Cayton-Holland, Adam. *Tragedy Plus Time*	B
Chast, Roz. ★*Can't We Talk About Something More Pleasant?*	741.5
Chow, Kat. *Seeing Ghosts*	B
Chung, Nicole. ★*A Living Remedy*	B
Clarke, Rachel. *Dear Life*	B
Corrigan, Kelly. *Glitter and Glue*	B
Crosley, Sloane. *Grief Is for People*	B
Danticat, Edwidge. *The Art of Death*	809
Delaney, Rob. ★*A Heart That Works*	B
Deraniyagala, Sonali. *Wave*	B
Didion, Joan. ★*The Year of Magical Thinking*	B
Egan, Kerry. *On Living*	170
Ervin, Kristine S. *Rabbit Heart*	364.152
Etheridge, Melissa. *Talking to My Angels*	B
Fagan, Kate. *All the Colors Came Out*	B
Fuller, Alexandra. *Travel Light, Move Fast*	B
Garcia, Rodrigo. *A Farewell to Gabo and Mercedes*	B
Gerson, Merissa Nathan. *Forget Prayers, Bring Cake*	155.9
Godwin, Gail. *Getting to Know Death*	B
Granata, Vince. *Everything Is Fine*	B
Greene, Jayson. *Once More We Saw Stars*	155.9
Gupta, Prachi. ★*They Called Us Exceptional*	B
Hannig, Anita. *The Day I Die*	364.152
Henderson, Artis. *Unremarried Widow*	B
Hsu, Hua. ★*Stay True*	B
Jensen, Robert A. *Personal Effects*	363.34
Junger, Sebastian. ★*In My Time of Dying*	304.6
Kennicott, Philip. *Counterpoint*	B
Kessler, David. *Finding Meaning*	155.9
Leach, Samantha. ★*The Elissas*	362.73
Leder, Steven Z. *The Beauty of What Remains*	306.9
Lieu, Susan. ★*The Manicurist's Daughter*	B
Lin, Amy. *Here After*	B
Lin, Jami Nakamura. *The Night Parade*	B
Locke, Tembi. ★*From Scratch*	B
Maisel, Ivan. *I Keep Trying to Catch His Eye*	B
Mankell, Henning. *Quicksand*	B
McColl, Sarah. *Joy Enough*	B
McInerny, Nora. *The Hot Young Widows Club*	155.9
Ng, Fae Myenne. *Orphan Bachelors*	B
O'Hara, Maryanne. *Little Matches*	B
Pagels, Elaine H. ★*Why Religion?*	B
Preszler, Trent. *Little and Often*	B
Rehm, Diane. *On My Own*	B
Rehm, Diane. ★*When My Time Comes*	179.7
Riggs, Nina. *The Bright Hour*	B
Rosenthal, Jason. *My Wife Said You May Want to Marry Me*	B
Ruhl, Sarah. *Letters from Max*	811
Sacks, Oliver. *Gratitude*	306.9
Saint John, Bozoma. *The Urgent Life*	B
Schulz, Kathryn. ★*Lost & Found*	B
Schwalbe, Will. ★*The End of Your Life Book Club*	B
Seager, Sara. *The Smallest Lights in the Universe*	B
Smith, Carol. *Crossing the River*	B
Soep, Elisabeth. *Other People's Words*	155.9
Strayed, Cheryl. ★*Wild*	B
Taylor, Cory. *Dying*	B
Thomas, Elizabeth Marshall. *Growing Old*	305.26
Townsend, Alan R. ★*This Ordinary Stardust*	B
Yip-Williams, Julie. ★*The Unwinding of the Miracle*	973

LIFE STORIES — FACING ADVERSITY — DISASTERS AND TRAGEDIES

Albom, Mitch. *Finding Chika*	B
Asgarian, Roxanna. *We Were Once a Family*	364.152
Black Thought. *The Upcycled Self*	B
Deraniyagala, Sonali. *Wave*	B
Eggers, Dave. *Zeitoun*	305.892
Fields, Micah. ★*We Hold Our Breath*	976.4

Franklin, Jonathan. *438 Days*	910.91
Jensen, Robert A. *Personal Effects*	363.34
Johnson, Lizzie. ★*Paradise*	363.37
Krakauer, Jon. *Into the Wild*	917.9804
Niven, Jennifer. *Ada Blackjack*	B
Park, J. S. ★*As Long as You Need*	248.8
Roberts, David. *Alone on the Ice*	919.8904

LIFE STORIES — FACING ADVERSITY — MEDICAL ISSUES

B., David. *Epileptic*	741.5
Blair, Selma. *Mean Baby*	B
Cahalan, Susannah. *Brain on Fire*	616.8
Carpenter, Kyle. *You Are Worth It*	B
Clein, Emmeline. ★*Dead Weight*	616.85
Copaken, Deborah. *Ladyparts*	B
Davis, Patti. *Floating in the Deep End*	616.8
DiGregorio, Sarah. *Early*	618.92
Engelhart, Katie. *The Inevitable*	179.7
Fitzmaurice, Simon. *It's Not yet Dark*	616.8
Freeman, Hadley. *Good Girls*	616.85
Gregory, Rebekah. *Taking My Life Back*	B
Grey, Jennifer. *Out of the Corner*	B
Hari, Johann. ★*Magic Pill*	613.2
Harris, Taylor. *This Boy We Made*	B
Hitchens, Christopher. *Mortality*	304.6
Ingrassia, Lawrence. *A Fatal Inheritance*	616.99
Jones, Chloe Cooper. ★*Easy Beauty*	B
Joyce, Russell W. *His Face Like Mine*	248
Kang, Mia. *Knockout*	B
Lipska, Barbara K. *The Neuroscientist Who Lost Her Mind*	B
May, Katherine. *Wintering*	155.9
Nakazawa, Donna Jackson. *The Angel and the Assassin*	612.8
Newman, Magdalena. *Normal*	611
Okorafor, Nnedi. *Broken Places & Outer Spaces*	153.3
Patterson, James. *ER Nurses*	610.73
Preston, Katherine. *Out with It*	B
Ramey, Sarah. *The Lady's Handbook for Her Mysterious Illness*	B
Risner, Vaneetha Rendall. *Walking Through Fire*	B
Savage, Jodi M. *The Death of a Jaybird*	B
Senator, Susan. *Autism Adulthood*	616.85
Shah, Meera. *You're the Only One I've Told*	362.1988
Skloot, Rebecca. ★*The Immortal Life of Henrietta Lacks*	B
Somerstein, Rachel. ★*Invisible Labor*	618.8
Specter, Emma. *More, Please*	616.85
Tallent, Elizabeth. *Scratched*	B
Tammet, Daniel. *Born on a Blue Day*	B
Taylor, Jill Bolte. *My Stroke of Insight*	362.19681
Walton, Bill. *Back from the Dead*	B
Washington, Kate. ★*Already Toast*	649.8
Weller, Sheila. *Carrie Fisher*	B
Winn, Raynor. *The Wild Silence*	B

LIFE STORIES — FACING ADVERSITY — MEDICAL ISSUES — ADDICTION

Aron, Nina Renata. *Good Morning, Destroyer of Men's Souls*	B
Barnett, Erica C. *Quitter*	B
Biden, Robert Hunter. *Beautiful Things*	B
Blakinger, Keri. *Corrections in Ink*	B
Bond, Melissa. *Blood Orange Night*	616.8
Buhle, Kathleen. *If We Break*	B
Carr, David. *The Night of the Gun*	B
Carr, Erin Lee. *All That You Leave Behind*	B
Danler, Stephanie. *Stray*	B
Dresner, Amy. *My Fair Junkie*	B
Fisher, Carl Erik. ★*The Urge*	362.29
Hardin, Lara Love. ★*The Many Lives of Mama Love*	B
Hornbacher, Marya. *Wasted*	B
Jamison, Leslie. ★*The Recovering*	B
Johnston, Ann Dowsett. *Drink*	362.292
Kennedy, Patrick J. ★*Profiles in Mental Health Courage*	362.29
Khar, Erin. *Strung Out*	B
Lanegan, Mark. *Sing Backwards and Weep*	B
Leach, Samantha. ★*The Elissas*	362.73
Legler, Casey. ★*Godspeed*	B
Lembke, Anna. *Dopamine Nation*	152.4
Metatawabin, Edmund. *Up Ghost River*	B
Milch, David. *Life's Work*	B
Moby. *Then It Fell Apart*	B
Perry, Matthew. *Friends, Lovers, and the Big Terrible Thing*	B
Rao, Cheeni. *In Hanuman's Hands*	B

AUTHOR, TITLE, SERIES AND SUBJECT INDEX

Rieder, Travis. *In Pain*	362.29
Sabathia, CC. *Till the End*	796.357
Schemel, Patty. *Hit so Hard*	B
Smith, Freda Love. *I Quit Everything*	B
Stone, Sly. *Thank You (Falettinme Be Mice Elf Agin)*	B
Whitaker, Holly. ★*Quit Like a Woman*	616.86
Wilder-Taylor, Stefanie. ★*Drunk-Ish*	B
Williams, Zach. *Rescue Story*	B

LIFE STORIES — FACING ADVERSITY — MEDICAL ISSUES — LIVING WITH DISABILITIES

Ballard, Robert D. *Into the Deep*	551.46092
Belser, Julia Watts. ★*Loving Our Own Bones*	296
Blake, Melissa. *Beautiful People*	362.4
Brown, Molly McCully. *Places I've Taken My Body*	B
Bruni, Frank. *The Beauty of Dusk*	B
Chesney, Will. *No Ordinary Dog*	958.104
Clark, John Lee. *Touch the Future*	B
DiMarco, Nyle. ★*Deaf Utopia*	B
Dittrich, Luke. ★*Patient H.M.*	616.85
Fall, Jeremy. *Falling Upwards*	158.1
Fleming, Jory. *How to Be Human*	616.85
Girma, Haben. *Haben*	B
Grue, Jan. *I Live a Life Like Yours*	B
Hay, Matt. *Soundtrack of Silence*	B
Hendrickson, John. *Life on Delay*	B
Herrmann, Dorothy. *Helen Keller*	B
Heumann, Judith E. *Being Heumann*	B
James, Laura E. *Odd Girl Out*	B
Lehrer, Riva. *Golem Girl*	B
Leland, Andrew. ★*The Country of the Blind*	B
Marshall, Greg. *Leg*	B
Masters, Oksana. *The Hard Parts*	B
Mattlin, Ben. *Disability Pride*	323.3
McAnulty, Dara. *Diary of a Young Naturalist*	508.092
Melvin, Leland. *Chasing Space*	B
Mooney, Jonathan. *Normal Sucks*	B
Ndopu, Eddie. *Sipping Dom Pérignon Through a Straw*	B
Nerenberg, Jenara. *Divergent Mind*	616.89
O'Toole, Jennifer Cook. *Autism in Heels*	B
Quave, Cassandra Leah. *The Plant Hunter*	581.6
Roberts, Jason. *A Sense of the World*	B
Rodgers, Jodi. ★*How to Find a Four-Leaf Clover*	616.85
Rowe, Mickey. *Fearlessly Different*	B
Seager, Sara. *The Smallest Lights in the Universe*	B
Sjunneson, Elsa. *Being Seen*	362.4
Taussig, Rebekah. *Sitting Pretty*	B
Wong, Alice. ★*Year of the Tiger*	B

LIFE STORIES — FACING ADVERSITY — MEDICAL ISSUES — MENTAL ILLNESS

Adam, David. *The Man Who Couldn't Stop*	616.85
Aviv, Rachel. ★*Strangers to Ourselves*	616.89
Bailey, Lily. *Because We Are Bad*	B
Bamford, Maria. *Sure, I'll Join Your Cult*	B
Brosh, Allie. ★*Hyperbole and a Half*	741.5
Brosh, Allie. ★*Solutions and Other Problems*	741.5
Brownstein, Gabriel. ★*The Secret Mind of Bertha Pappenheim*	616.85
Carriere, Alice. *Everything/Nothing/Someone*	B
Chang, David. ★*Eat a Peach*	641.5
Chesney, Will. *No Ordinary Dog*	958.104
Cho, Grace M. *Tastes Like War*	305.48
Connell, John. *The Farmer's Son*	630.9
Crampton, Caroline. *A Body Made of Glass*	616.85
Cregan, Mary. *The Scar*	616.85
Farley, Audrey Clare. ★*Girls and Their Monsters*	306.875
Foo, Stephanie. ★*What My Bones Know*	B
Gagne, Patric. *Sociopath*	B
Gildiner, Catherine. *Good Morning, Monster*	616.89
Glass, Charles. *Soldiers Don't Go Mad*	616.85
Gotch, Jen. *The Upside of Being Down*	B
Gulman, Gary. *Misfit*	B
Gutman, Matt. ★*No Time to Panic*	616.85
Haig, Matt. *Notes on a Nervous Planet*	616.89
Harvey, Samantha. *The Shapeless Unease*	B
Hulls, Tessa. ★*Feeding Ghosts*	741.5
Hylton, Antonia. *Madness*	362.2
Ikpi, Bassey. *I'm Telling the Truth, but I'm Lying*	814
Kalb, Claudia. *Andy Warhol Was a Hoarder*	920
Kander, Jason. *Invisible Storm*	B
Kazdin, Cole. ★*What's Eating Us*	616.85
Keaton, Diane. ★*Brother & Sister*	B
Kennedy, Patrick J. ★*Profiles in Mental Health Courage*	362.29
Kiper, Dasha. ★*Travelers to Unimaginable Lands*	616.8
Kissinger, Meg. *While You Were Out*	362.2
Kolker, Robert. ★*Hidden Valley Road*	920
Kozol, Jonathan. *The Theft of Memory*	B
Kriss, Alexander. *Borderline*	616.85
Lawson, Jenny. ★*Broken*	B
Lawson, Jenny. *Furiously Happy*	B
Leaming, Barbara. *Jacqueline Bouvier Kennedy Onassis*	B
LeFavour, Cree. *Lights On, Rats Out*	616.85
Legler, Casey. ★*Godspeed*	B
Li, Yiyun. *Dear Friend, from My Life I Write to You in Your Life*	B
Lin, Jami Nakamura. *The Night Parade*	B
Mailhot, Terese Marie. *Heart Berries*	B
Mandel, Sarah. *Little Earthquakes*	B
McClelland, Mac. *Irritable Hearts*	B
Moe, John. *The Hilarious World of Depression*	616.85
Morris, David J. *The Evil Hours*	616.85
Nathan, Debbie. *Sybil Exposed*	B
Paperny, Anna Mehler. *Hello I Want to Die Please Fix Me*	362.2
Pentland, Jenny. *This Will Be Funny Later*	B
Petersen, Andrea. *On Edge*	616.85
Pritchett, Georgia. *My Mess Is a Bit of a Life*	B
Raskin, Allison. *Overthinking About You*	646.7
Rhodes, James. *Instrumental*	B
Riley, Alex. ★*A Cure for Darkness*	616.85
Rosen, Jonathan. ★*The Best Minds*	616.89
Sanchez, Erika L. *Crying in the Bathroom*	B
Sardy, Marin. *The Edge of Every Day*	B
Saunders, John. *Playing Hurt*	B
Schreiber, Flora Rheta. *Sybil*	616.85
Sehee, Baek. *I Want to Die but I Want to Eat Tteokbokki*	B
Stern, Amanda. *Little Panic*	616.8522
Thompson, J. M. *Running Is a Kind of Dreaming*	B
Waldman, Ayelet. *A Really Good Day*	B
Williams, Michelle. *Checking In*	B
Wilson, Brian. *I Am Brian Wilson*	B

LIFE STORIES — FACING ADVERSITY — MEDICAL ISSUES — PHYSICAL ILLNESS

Albom, Mitch. *Finding Chika*	B
Barkan, Ady. *Eyes to the Wind*	B
Berg, Elizabeth. *I'll Be Seeing You*	306.874
Billings, J. Todd. *Rejoicing in Lament*	248.8
Bowler, Kate. *No Cure for Being Human*	B
Boyer, Anne. *The Undying*	B
Brown, Theresa. *Healing*	616.99
Caldwell, Gail. *Let's Take the Long Way Home*	B
Case, Molly. *How to Treat People*	616.1
Cleghorn, Elinor. *Unwell Women*	613
Eichenwald, Kurt. *A Mind Unraveled*	B
Ephron, Delia. *Left on Tenth*	B
Fessler, Pam. *Carville's Cure*	362.19699
Fox, Michael J. *No Time Like the Future*	B
Gaffigan, Jeannie. *When Life Gives You Pears*	B
Gupta, Shalene. *The Cycle*	618.1
Hagberg, Eva. *How to Be Loved*	616.7
Harpham, Heather Elise. *Happiness*	B
Hawking, Stephen. *My Brief History*	B
Jaouad, Suleika. ★*Between Two Kingdoms*	B
Kalanithi, Paul. ★*When Breath Becomes Air*	B
Mandel, Sarah. *Little Earthquakes*	B
Marshall, Cynthia. *You've Been Chosen*	B
Milch, David. *Life's Work*	B
Mitchell, Wendy. *Somebody I Used to Know*	B
Mlodinow, Leonard. *Stephen Hawking*	B
Morgan, Abi. *This Is Not a Pity Memoir*	B
Nordland, Rod. *Waiting for the Monsoon*	B
Norman, Abby. *Ask Me About My Uterus*	618.1
O'Rourke, Meghan. ★*The Invisible Kingdom*	616
Parker, Lara. *Vagina Problems*	618.1
Pataki, Allison. *Beauty in the Broken Places*	B
Quinn, Tallu Schuyler. *What We Wish Were True*	B
Raban, Jonathan. *Father and Son*	B
Riggs, Nina. *The Bright Hour*	B
Roberts, David. *Limits of the Known*	B
Rubin, Kathy Kleiner. *A Light in the Dark*	364.152

PUBLIC LIBRARY CORE COLLECTION: NONFICTION
Twentieth Edition

Ruhl, Sarah. *Letters from Max* — 811
Ruhl, Sarah. *Smile* — B
Standefer, Katherine E. *Lightning Flowers* — B
Warraich, Haider. *The Song of Our Scars* — 616
Yousse, Bower. *Freddie Steinmark* — 796.332

LIFE STORIES — FACING ADVERSITY — PERSONAL TRANSFORMATION
Bergner, Daniel. ★*Sing for Your Life* — B
Brown, Jasmine. *Twice as Hard* — 610.92
Burton, Susan. *Becoming Ms. Burton* — B
Day, Daniel R. *Dapper Dan* — B
Dregni, Michael. *Django* — B
Fenn, Lisa. *Carry On* — B
Flaherty, Meghan. *Tango Lessons* — 793.3
Greenfield, Martin. ★*Measure of a Man* — B
Haddish, Tiffany. *The Last Black Unicorn* — B
Harjo, Joy. *Crazy Brave* — B
Hill, Fiona. *There Is Nothing for You Here* — 327.2
Hobbs, Jeff. ★*The Short and Tragic Life of Robert Peace* — B
Jadhav, Narendra. *Untouchables* — 305.5
LeFavour, Cree. *Lights On, Rats Out* — 616.85
Lewis, Michael. *The Blind Side* — B
Lifford, Tina. *The Little Book of Big Lies* — 155.2
Manuel, Ian. *My Time Will Come* — B
Moore, Wes. *The Other Wes Moore* — B
Moore, Wes. *The Work* — B
Murray, Liz. *Breaking Night* — B
Onwuachi, Kwame. ★*Notes from a Young Black Chef* — 641.59
Pace, Kristin Knight. *This Much Country* — B
Sasakamoose, Fred. *Call Me Indian* — B
Schultz, Howard. *From the Ground Up* — B
Smarsh, Sarah. ★*Heartland* — B
Travis, Randy. *Forever and Ever, Amen* — B
Winn, Raynor. ★*The Salt Path* — B

LIFE STORIES — FACING ADVERSITY — VICTIMS OF CRIME
Addison, Corban. *Wastelands* — 346.73
Ahmed, Azam. *Fear Is Just a Word* — 364.152
Belkin, Lisa. *Genealogy of a Murder* — 362.88
Betz-Hamilton, Axton. *The Less People Know About Us* — 364.16
Bowdler, Michelle. ★*Is Rape a Crime?* — B
Burke, Tarana. ★*Unbound* — B
Caruana Galizia, Paul. ★*A Death in Malta* — 364.15
Douglas, John E. *When a Killer Calls* — 364.152
Ford, Christine Blasey. *One Way Back* — B
Gerard, Sarah. *Carrie Carolyn Coco* — 364.152
Goldberg, Carrie. *Nobody's Victim* — 345.73
Hewlett, Sylvia Ann. *#metoo in the Corporate World* — 658.3
Hsu, Hua. ★*Stay True* — B
Kroll, Andy. *A Death on W Street* — 364.152
Lamb, Christina. *Our Bodies, Their Battlefields* — 341.6
McDiarmid, Jessica. *Highway of Tears* — 364.152
Norton, Laurah. *Lay Them to Rest* — 363.25
Olsen, Lise. *Code of Silence* — 347.73
Oppenheimer, Mark. *Squirrel Hill* — 364.152
Ralph, Laurence. *Sito* — 364.152
Rear, Rachel. *Catch the Sparrow* — 364.152
Roig-Debellis, Kaitlin. *Choosing Hope* — 371.7
Rubenhold, Hallie. ★*The Five* — 362.88
Rubin, Kathy Kleiner. *A Light in the Dark* — 364.152
Rushdie, Salman. ★*Knife* — B
Samuels, Robert. ★*His Name Is George Floyd* — B
Tjipombo, Tupa. *I Am Not Your Slave* — B
Tyson, Timothy B. *Blood Done Sign My Name* — 975.6
Vanasco, Jeannie. *Things We Didn't Talk About When I Was a Girl* — B
Williamson, Elizabeth. ★*Sandy Hook* — 364.152

LIFE STORIES — FACING ADVERSITY — VICTIMS OF CRIME — TERRORISM
Dunn, Harry. *Standing My Ground* — B
Graff, Garrett M. ★*The Only Plane in the Sky* — 973.931
Gregory, Rebekah. *Taking My Life Back* — B
Kushner, Jacob. *Look Away* — 305.9
Luckerson, Victor. *Built from the Fire* — 976.6
Pfeifer, Joseph. *Ordinary Heroes* — 973.931
Roy, Jessica. *American Girls* — 305.48
Williams, Kidada E. *I Saw Death Coming* — 973.8
Yousafzai, Malala. *I Am Malala* — B

LIFE STORIES — FACING ADVERSITY — WAR AND OPPRESSION
Abouzeid, Rania. *No Turning Back* — 956.9104
Abu Sayf, Atif. *The Drone Eats with Me* — B
Adayfi, Mansoor. *Don't Forget Us Here* — B
Ai, Weiwei. *Zodiac* — 741.5
Bailey, Catherine. *A Castle in Wartime* — 943.086
Bilal, Wafaa. *Shoot an Iraqi* — B
Branigan, Tania. *Red Memory* — 951.05
Chang, Jung. ★*Wild Swans* — B
Chen, Da. *Colors of the Mountain* — 951.05
Demick, Barbara. *Eat the Buddha* — 951
Demick, Barbara. ★*Nothing to Envy* — 920
Di Cintio, Marcello. *Pay No Heed to the Rockets* — 956.9405
Di Giovanni, Janine. *The Morning They Came for Us* — 956.9104
Dyson, Michael Eric. *Long Time Coming* — 305.800973
Eder, Mari K. *The Girls Who Stepped Out of Line* — 920
Enss, Chris. *Mochi's War* — B
Gidla, Sujatha. *Ants Among Elephants* — 305.5
Goodman, Simon. *The Orpheus Clock* — 940.53
Haitiwaji, Gulbahar. *How I Survived a Chinese "Reeducation" Camp* — 305.8
Harden, Blaine. *The Great Leader and the Fighter Pilot* — B
Hogan, William R. *Task Force Hogan* — 940.54
Hoja, Gulchehra. *A Stone Is Most Precious Where It Belongs* — B
Hurowitz, Richard. *In the Garden of the Righteous* — 940.53
Izgil, Tahir Hamut. *Waiting to Be Arrested at Night* — B
Jadhav, Narendra. *Untouchables* — 305.5
Keith, Philip A. *All Blood Runs Red* — B
Khan, Mahvish Rukhsana. *My Guantanamo Diary* — 973.931
Lamb, Christina. *Our Bodies, Their Battlefields* — 341.6
Li, Zhuqing. *Daughters of the Flower Fragrant Garden* — 951.04
Malek, Alia. *The Home That Was Our Country* — B
McCann, Colum. *American Mother* — 956.9104
Mikhaiil, Dunya. *The Beekeeper* — 956.7044
Min, Anchee. *Red Azalea* — B
Pang, Amelia. ★*Made in China* — 331.11
Rosenberg, Justus. *The Art of Resistance* — B
Rushdie, Salman. *Joseph Anton* — B
Sattouf, Riad. *The Arab of the Future 2* — 741.5
Sattouf, Riad. *The Arab of the Future* — 741.5
Seierstad, Asne. *The Bookseller of Kabul* — 958.1
Seierstad, Asne. *Two Sisters* — 956.9104
Shehadeh, Raja. ★*We Could Have Been Friends, My Father and I* — B
Siegal, Nina. *The Diary Keepers* — 940.54
Slahi, Mohamedou Ould. *The Mauritanian* — 958.104
Strauss, Gwen. *The Nine* — 940.53
Tamimi, Ahed. ★*They Called Me a Lioness* — B
Teffi, N. A. *Memories* — B
Thrall, Nathan. ★*A Day in the Life of Abed Salama* — 956.05
Warren, W. Lee. *No Place to Hide* — B
Wides-Munoz, Laura. *The Making of a Dream* — 920
Willner, Nina. *Forty Autumns* — B
Ypi, Lea. ★*Free* — B
Zuckoff, Mitchell. *The Secret Gate* — 958.104

LIFE STORIES — FACING ADVERSITY — WAR AND OPPRESSION — ENSLAVED PEOPLE
Blight, David W. ★*Frederick Douglass* — B
Blight, David W. *A Slave No More* — B
Carretta, Vincent. *Equiano, the African* — B
Clinton, Catherine. *Harriet Tubman* — B
Dunbar, Erica Armstrong. ★*She Came to Slay* — B
Durkin, Hannah. ★*The Survivors of the Clotilda* — 306.362
Emberton, Carole. *To Walk About in Freedom* — 306.3
Gordon-Reed, Annette. ★*The Hemingses of Monticello* — 920
Hallman, J. C. *Say Anarcha* — 618.1
Harris, J. William. *The Hanging of Thomas Jeremiah* — B
Hecimovich, Gregg A. ★*The Life and Times of Hannah Crafts* — B
Humez, Jean McMahon. *Harriet Tubman* — B
Jacobs, Harriet. ★*Incidents in the Life of a Slave Girl* — B
Larson, Kate Clifford. *Bound for the Promised Land* — B
Lineberry, Cate. *Be Free or Die* — B
Morgan-Owens, Jessie. *Girl in Black and White* — B
Northup, Solomon. *Twelve Years a Slave* — B
Raines, Ben. *The Last Slave Ship* — 306.362
Woo, Ilyon. ★*Master Slave Husband Wife* — 920

LIFE STORIES — FACING ADVERSITY — WAR AND OPPRESSION — HOLOCAUST
Asbrink, Elisabeth. *And in the Vienna Woods the Trees Remain* — B
Berr, Helene. *The Journal of Helene Berr* — B
Blau, Magda Hellinger. *The Nazis Knew My Name* — 940.53
Cadbury, Deborah. *The School That Escaped from the Nazis* — 940.53

AUTHOR, TITLE, SERIES AND SUBJECT INDEX

Debreczeni, Jozsef. *Cold Crematorium*	940.53
Edmonds, Chris. *No Surrender*	B
Eger, Edith Eva. *The Choice*	B
Eisen, Max. *By Chance Alone*	940.5318
Epstein, Franci. *Franci's War*	B
Finkelstein, Daniel. *Two Roads Home*	920
Frank, Michael. ★*One Hundred Saturdays*	B
Frankel, Rebecca. *Into the Forest*	940.53
Freeman, Hadley. *House of Glass*	B
Friedman, Tova. ★*The Daughter of Auschwitz*	B
Greene, Joshua. *Unstoppable*	B
Greenfield, Martin. ★*Measure of a Man*	B
Iperen, Roxane van. ★*The Sisters of Auschwitz*	940.53
Jaku, Eddie. ★*The Happiest Man on Earth*	B
Kaiser, Menachem. *Plunder*	940.53
Kramer, Clara. *Clara's War*	B
Kraus, Dita. *A Delayed Life*	B
Krimstein, Ken. *When I Grow Up*	741.5
Kurtz, Glenn. *Three Minutes in Poland*	947.7
Levi, Primo. *The Periodic Table*	858
Levi, Primo. *The Reawakening*	B
Lindwer, Willy. *The Last Seven Months of Anne Frank*	B
Mazzeo, Tilar J. *Irena's Children*	B
Neumann, Ariana. *When Time Stopped*	B
Pick-Goslar, Hannah Elizabeth. ★*My Friend Anne Frank*	B
Pivnik, Sam. *Survivor*	940.5318
Ross, Steve. *From Broken Glass*	B
Rynecki, Elizabeth. *Chasing Portraits*	B
Schindler, Meriel. *The Lost Cafe Schindler*	943.64
Simon, Marie. *Underground in Berlin*	B
Spiegel, Renia. *Renia's Diary*	B
Thomas, Gordon. *Defying Hitler*	920
Van De Perre, Selma. *My Name Is Selma*	940.53
Van Es, Bart. *The Cut Out Girl*	B
Wiesel, Elie. *All Rivers Run to the Sea*	B
Wiesel, Elie. *And the Sea Is Never Full*	B

LIFE STORIES — FACING ADVERSITY — WAR AND OPPRESSION — HOSTAGES AND POWS

Cheng, Nien. *Life and Death in Shanghai*	B
Chiger, Krystyna. *The Girl in the Green Sweater*	B
Clavin, Thomas. *Lightning Down*	940.54
Delisle, Guy. *Hostage*	741.5
Freeman, Sally Mott. *The Jersey Brothers*	920
Hillenbrand, Laura. ★*Unbroken*	B
Khalaf, Farida. *The Girl Who Escaped Isis*	B
Macintyre, Ben. ★*Prisoners of the Castle*	940.54
Mazzeo, Tilar J. *Sisters in Resistance*	945.091
Moore, Michael Scott. *The Desert and the Sea*	364.15
Nemat, Marina. *Prisoner of Tehran*	B
Parkin, Simon. *The Island of Extraordinary Captives*	940.53
Rezaian, Jason. *Prisoner*	B
Weintraub, Robert. *No Better Friend*	940.54

LIFE STORIES — FACING ADVERSITY — WAR AND OPPRESSION — REFUGEES

Ahmad, Aeham. *The Pianist from Syria*	B
AL Samawi, Mohammed. *The Fox Hunt*	953
Bittle, Jake. ★*The Great Displacement*	362.87
Chung, Vinh. *Where the Wind Leads*	B
Dogon, Mondiant. *Those We Throw Away Are Diamonds*	B
Dutta, Sunil. *Stealing Green Mangoes*	973
Fishman, Elly. *Refugee High*	370.8
Fleming, Melissa. *A Hope More Powerful Than the Sea*	956.9104
Garrett, Leah. *X Troop*	940.54
Golinkin, Lev. *A Backpack, a Bear, and Eight Crates of Vodka*	B
Hamilton, Lisa M. *The Hungry Season*	B
Hirsi Ali, Ayaan. ★*Infidel*	B
Hulls, Tessa. ★*Feeding Ghosts*	741.5
Ishikawa, Masaji. ★*A River in Darkness*	B
Jang, Jin-Sung. *Dear Leader*	B
Jang, Lucia. *Stars Between the Sun and Moon*	365.45092
Lieu, Susan. ★*The Manicurist's Daughter*	B
Malhotra, Aanchal. *Remnants of Partition*	954.04
Mardini, Yusra. *Butterfly*	B
McCormick, Ty. *Beyond the Sand and Sea*	920
Moore, Wayetu. *The Dragons, the Giant, the Women*	B
Mufleh, Luma. ★*Learning America*	371.826
Murad, Nadia. ★*The Last Girl*	B
Nayeri, Dina. ★*The Ungrateful Refugee*	362.87
Nguyen, Bich Minh. *Owner of a Lonely Heart*	B
Nguyen, Viet Thanh. ★*A Man of Two Faces*	B
O'Donnell, Svenja. *Inge's War*	943.086
Pablo Cruz, Rosayra. *The Book of Rosy*	B
Parkin, Simon. *The Island of Extraordinary Captives*	940.53
Passarlay, Gulwali. *The Lightless Sky*	B
Pearlman, Wendy. *We Crossed a Bridge and It Trembled*	956.9104
Pitzer, Andrea. *The Secret History of Vladimir Nabokov*	813
Saldana, Stephanie. *What We Remember Will Be Saved*	362.7
Samer. *The Raqqa Diaries*	956.9104
Slouka, Mark. *Nobody's Son*	B
Steinberg, Jonny. *A Man of Good Hope*	B
Taing, Mae Bunseng. *Under the Naga Tail*	B
Tolan, Sandy. *Children of the Stone*	780
Ung, Loung. *Lucky Child*	B
Yip-Williams, Julie. ★*The Unwinding of the Miracle*	973
Zamora, Javier. ★*Solito*	B
Zia, Helen. *Last Boat Out of Shanghai*	951.04

LIFE STORIES — FACING ADVERSITY — WAR AND OPPRESSION — WAR SURVIVORS

Abuelaish, Izzeldin. *I Shall Not Hate*	B
Akcam, Taner. *A Shameful Act*	956.6
Albright, Madeleine Korbel. *Prague Winter*	943.71
Atria, Travis. *Better Days Will Come Again*	B
Balakian, Peter. *The Burning Tigris*	956.6
Beah, Ishmael. ★*A Long Way Gone*	B
Black, George. ★*The Long Reckoning*	959.704
Burns, Mike. *The Only One Living to Tell*	305.897
Carpenter, Kyle. *You Are Worth It*	B
Chiger, Krystyna. *The Girl in the Green Sweater*	B
Cooper, Helene. *The House at Sugar Beach*	921
Edstrom, Erik. *Un-American*	B
Frenkel, Francoise. *A Bookshop in Berlin*	B
Ghafari, Zarifa. *Zarifa*	B
Gies, Miep. ★*Anne Frank Remembered*	B
Gopal, Anand. *No Good Men Among the Living*	920
Hari, Daoud. *The Translator*	B
Hatzfeld, Jean. *Blood Papa*	967.5710431
Jahner, Harald. ★*Aftermath*	943.087
Karski, Jan. *Story of a Secret State*	940.53
Katin, Miriam. *We Are on Our Own*	741.5
Kempowski, Walter. *Swansong 1945*	940.54
Lamb, Christina. *House of Stone*	968.91
Lemmon, Gayle Tzemach. *The Dressmaker of Khair Khana*	B
Loftis, Larry. ★*The Watchmaker's Daughter*	940.53
Mackeen, Dawn Anahid. *The Hundred-Year Walk*	956.6
Peer, Basharat. *Curfewed Night*	B
Raban, Jonathan. *Father and Son*	B
Spiegelman, Art. ★*Maus*	741.5
Thi, Kim Phuc Phan. *Fire Road*	B
Trebincevic, Kenan. *The Bosnia List*	B
Ung, Loung. *First They Killed My Father*	959.604
Weiss, Helga. *Helga's Diary*	B
Wiesel, Elie. ★*Night*	B

LIFE STORIES — GENERAL

Aguon, Julian. *No Country for Eight-Spot Butterflies*	305.89
Barbarisi, Daniel. *Chasing the Thrill*	796.1
Berg, Ryan. *No House to Call My Home*	B
Brennan, Thomas J. *Shooting Ghosts*	B
Chisholm, Edward. *A Waiter in Paris*	B
Coombes, Joshua. *Do Something for Nothing*	362.5
Crosley, Sloane. *I Was Told There'd Be Cake*	814
Crosley, Sloane. ★*Look Alive Out There*	814
DePalma, Anthony. *The Cubans*	920
Didion, Joan. *Where I Was from*	979.4
Eisenberg, Emma Copley. ★*The Third Rainbow Girl*	364.152
Erdman, Sarah. *Nine Hills to Nambonkaha*	966.68
Finkel, Michael. *The Stranger in the Woods*	B
Gay, Ross. *Inciting Joy*	814
Gerard, Sarah. *Sunshine State*	814
Green, Kristen. *Something Must Be Done About Prince Edward County*	379.2
Irby, Samantha. *We Are Never Meeting in Real Life*	814
Lang, Michael. *The Road to Woodstock*	781.66
McCalman, George. *Illustrated Black History*	920
McCourt, Malachy. *A Monk Swimming*	B
Mooallem, Jon. *Serious Face*	814
Morton, Michael. *Getting Life*	B
Nevins, Sheila. *You Don't Look Your Age*	B

PUBLIC LIBRARY CORE COLLECTION: NONFICTION
Twentieth Edition

Notaro, Laurie. *Excuse Me While I Disappear*	B
Reed, Shannon. *Why We Read*	028
Rocca, Mo. *Mobituaries*	920
Schell, Orville. *Wealth and Power*	920
Stanton, Brandon. *Humans*	779
Sullivan, Randall. *Graveyard of the Pacific*	979.7
Waldinger, Robert J. ★*The Good Life*	158.1
Walters, Billy. *Gambler*	796.092
Wiesenthal, Simon. ★*The Sunflower*	179.7
Zapruder, Alexandra. *Twenty-Six Seconds*	973.922092

LIFE STORIES — IDENTITY

Abdul-Ahad, Ghaith. *A Stranger in Your Own City*	956.7044
Alexander, Kwame. *Why Fathers Cry at Night*	B
Bee, Vanessa A. *Home Bound*	B
Berry, Erica. *Wolfish*	152.4
Blake, Melissa. *Beautiful People*	362.4
Bowen, Sesali. *Bad Fat Black Girl*	305.42
Bragg, Rick. *Where I Come From*	975
Broome, Brian. ★*Punch Me up to the Gods*	B
Busby, Jill Louise. *Unfollow Me*	305.08
Cargle, Rachel Elizabeth. *A Renaissance of Our Own*	B
Chaudry, Rabia. *Fatty Fatty Boom Boom*	B
Chin, Curtis. *Everything I Learned, I Learned in a Chinese Restaurant*	B
Cooper, Brittney C. *Eloquent Rage*	B
Cooper, Christian. *Better Living Through Birding*	B
Cottom, Tressie McMillan. *Thick*	301
Dubus, Andre. *Ghost Dogs*	814
Gadsby, Hannah. ★*Ten Steps to Nanette*	B
Gay, Roxane. ★*Opinions*	814
Geller, Danielle. *Dog Flowers*	B
Gerald, Casey. *There Will Be No Miracles Here*	B
Ghobash, Omar Saif. *Letters to a Young Muslim*	297.09
Hamilton, Lisa M. *The Hungry Season*	B
Hill, Jemele. *Uphill*	B
Ikpi, Bassey. *I'm Telling the Truth, but I'm Lying*	814
Imbler, Sabrina. *How Far the Light Reaches*	591.77
Irby, Samantha. ★*Quietly Hostile*	814
Isen, Tajja. *Some of My Best Friends*	305.8
Jones, Lucy. ★*Matrescence*	306.874
Kassabova, Kapka. *Border*	949.9
Klein, Naomi. ★*Doppelganger*	302.2
Krug, Nora. ★*Belonging*	741.5
Lavery, Daniel M. *Something That May Shock and Discredit You*	814
Lemay, Mimi. *What We Will Become*	306.874
Li, Zhuqing. *Daughters of the Flower Fragrant Garden*	951.04
Liu, Simu. ★*We Were Dreamers*	B
Mehra, Nishta. *Brown, White, Black*	305.800973
Miller, Kei. *Things I Have Withheld*	814
Miller, Michelle. *Belonging*	B
Moghul, Haroon. *How to Be a Muslim*	B
Moran, Joe. *Shrinking Violets*	155.2
Narayan, Shoba. *The Milk Lady of Bangalore*	390
Ndopu, Eddie. *Sipping Dom Pérignon Through a Straw*	B
Nooyi, Indra. ★*My Life in Full*	B
Oelhafen, Ingrid von. *Hitler's Stolen Children*	B
Owusu, Nadia. *Aftershocks*	B
Perry, Imani. ★*South to America*	917
Pham, Larissa. *Pop Song*	709.2
Phillips, Maya. *Nerd*	302.23
Sabatini Sloan, Aisha. *Dreaming of Ramadi in Detroit*	814
Samatar, Sofia. *The White Mosque*	B
Shapiro, Dani. ★*Inheritance*	B
So, Anthony Veasna. ★*Songs on Endless Repeat*	814
Talusan, Meredith. *Fairest*	305.30973
Tanais. *In Sensorium*	B
Taylor, Goldie. *The Love You Save*	B
Teege, Jennifer. *My Grandfather Would Have Shot Me*	929.2
Thomas, R. Eric. ★*Congratulations, the Best Is Over!*	B
Tometich, Annabelle. *The Mango Tree*	B
Tran, Ly. *House of Sticks*	B
Villarreal, Vanessa Anglica. *Magical/Realism*	814
Wainaina, Binyavanga. ★*How to Write About Africa*	814
Washington, Kerry. *Thicker Than Water*	B
Watkins, D. *Black Boy Smile*	B
Wong, Carmen Rita. *Why Didn't You Tell Me?*	B
Wright, Lawrence. *God Save Texas*	917.64
Wu, Simon. *Dancing on My Own*	700.1
Wynn-Grant, Rae. *Wild Life*	B
Yong, Sable. *Die Hot with a Vengeance*	646.7

LIFE STORIES — IDENTITY — GENDER

Addario, Lynsey. *It's What I Do*	B
Albertine, Viv. *Clothes, Clothes, Clothes. Music, Music, Music*	B
Barker, Nigel. *Models of Influence*	746.92092
Berry, Daina Ramey. ★*A Black Women's History of the United States*	305.48
Brown, Emma. *To Raise a Boy*	649
Campbell, Olivia. *Women in White Coats*	610.92
Coffin, Jaed. *Roughhouse Friday*	B
Cooke, Julia. *Come Fly the World*	387.7
Cooney, Kara. *When Women Ruled the World*	920
Copaken, Deborah. *Ladyparts*	B
Cornelius, Maria M. *The Final Season*	B
Darby, Seyward. ★*Sisters in Hate*	305.800973
Davis, Lisa Selin. *Tomboy*	305.409
Doherty, Maggie. *The Equivalents*	920
Faliveno, Melissa. *Tomboyland*	B
Febos, Melissa. *Girlhood*	818
Fitzgerald, Isaac. *Dirtbag, Massachusetts*	B
Flock, Elizabeth. ★*The Furies*	305.42
Frangello, Gina. *Blow Your House Down*	813
Gabriel, Mary. *Ninth Street Women*	920
Gilder, Ginny. *Course Correction*	797.12
Gilliam, Dorothy Butler. *Trailblazer*	B
Hegar, Mary Jennings. *Shoot Like a Girl*	B
Hickman, Katie. *Brave Hearted*	978
Hill, Katie. *She Will Rise*	305.42
Hirshey, Gerri. *Not Pretty Enough*	B
Hirsi Ali, Ayaan. ★*Infidel*	B
Hopper, Jessica. *The First Collection of Criticism by a Living Female Rock Critic*	781.66
Johnson, Akemi. *Night in the American Village*	305.40952
Jones, Brenda. *Alexandria Ocasio-Cortez*	B
Jones, Brenda. *Maxine Waters*	B
Kaplan, Janice. *The Genius of Women*	920
Kleiman, Kathy. *Proving Ground*	4.092
Knight, Keltie. *Lady Secrets*	305.4
Koch, Bea. *Mad and Bad*	920
Kroeger, Brooke. *Undaunted*	070.4
Levy, Deborah. *The Cost of Living*	B
Lithwick, Dahlia. *Lady Justice*	345.73
McNeur, Catherine. *Mischievous Creatures*	920
McShane Wulfhart, Nell. *The Great Stewardess Rebellion*	331.4
Messineo, Janet. *Casting into the Light*	799.1
Miller, Adrienne. *In the Land of Men*	070.5
Mojica Rodriguez, Prisca Dorcas. *For Brown Girls with Sharp Edges and Tender Hearts*	305.48
Moran, Caitlin. *How to Be a Woman*	B
Moran, Caitlin. *More Than a Woman*	B
Moss, Marissa R. *Her Country*	781.642
Muhammad, Ibtihaj. *Proud*	B
Nadeau, Barbie Latza. *The Godmother*	364.106
Penaluna, Regan. ★*How to Think Like a Woman*	190.82
Perkins, Nichole. *Sometimes I Trip on How Happy We Could Be*	B
Porizkova, Paulina. *No Filter*	B
Potts, Monica. *The Forgotten Girls*	B
Purnell, Sonia. ★*A Woman of No Importance*	B
Qadiri, Humayra. *Dancing in the Mosque*	B
Rahmani, Niloofar. *Open Skies*	B
Ratajkowski, Emily. ★*My Body*	B
Regan, Iliana. *Fieldwork*	B
Sante, Lucy. *I Heard Her Call My Name*	B
Sehee, Baek. *I Want to Die but I Want to Eat Tteokbokki*	B
Semenya, Caster. *The Race to Be Myself*	B
Shraya, Vivek. *I'm Afraid of Men*	813
Sinclair, Safiya. ★*How to Say Babylon*	B
Snyder, Rachel Louise. *Women We Buried, Women We Burned*	B
Solnit, Rebecca. ★*Recollections of My Nonexistence*	B
Somerstein, Rachel. ★*Invisible Labor*	618.8
Tamblyn, Amber. ★*Era of Ignition*	B
Teitel, Amy Shira. *Fighting for Space*	920
Turk, Katherine. *The Women of Now*	305.42
Walder, Tracy. *The Unexpected Spy*	B
Wassef, Nadia. *Shelf Life*	B
Watling, Sarah. *Tomorrow Perhaps the Future*	946.081
Winder, Elizabeth. *Parachute Women*	782.42164
Wright, Jennifer Ashley. ★*Madame Restell*	B

AUTHOR, TITLE, SERIES AND SUBJECT INDEX

LIFE STORIES — IDENTITY — IMMIGRANTS
Abdelmahmoud, Elamin. *Son of Elsewhere* — B
Ali, Wajahat. *Go Back to Where You Came From* — B
Arce, Julissa. *You Sound Like a White Girl* — 303.48
Asher, Zain E. *Where the Children Take Us* — 942.1
Barrett, Duncan. *GI Brides* — 920
Bobrow-Strain, Aaron. *The Death and Life of Aida Hernandez* — 972
Bui, Thi. ★*The Best We Could Do* — 741.5
Campoverdi, Alejandra. *First Gen* — B
Cho, Grace M. *Tastes Like War* — 305.48
Chude-Sokei, Louis Onuorah. *Floating in a Most Peculiar Way* — 979.4
Cornejo Villavicencio, Karla. ★*The Undocumented Americans* — 920
DeParle, Jason. ★*A Good Provider Is One Who Leaves* — 305.899
Fishman, Boris. *Savage Feast* — B
Gupta, Prachi. ★*They Called Us Exceptional* — B
Hakkakiyan, Ruya. *A Beginner's Guide to America* — 646.7
Hernandez Castillo, Marcelo. *Children of the Land* — B
Hinojosa, Maria. *Once I Was You* — B
Huang, Eddie. *Fresh off the Boat* — B
Iftin, Abdi Nor. *Call Me American* — 305.893
Jayapal, Pramila. *Use the Power You Have* — B
Khakpour, Porochista. *Brown Album* — 304.8
Lakshmi, Padma. *Love, Loss, and What We Ate* — 791.4502
Lalami, Laila. *Conditional Citizens* — 323.60973
Li, Fei-Fei. *The Worlds I See* — B
Lovato, Roberto. *Unforgetting* — B
Markham, Lauren. ★*The Far Away Brothers* — 920
Marton, Kati. *The Great Escape* — 920
McCormick, Ty. *Beyond the Sand and Sea* — 920
Mojica Rodriguez, Prisca Dorcas. *For Brown Girls with Sharp Edges and Tender Hearts* — 305.48
Nimura, Janice P. *Daughters of the Samurai* — 920
Oliva, Alejandra. *Rivermouth* — 305.9
Olivares, Efren C. *My Boy Will Die of Sorrow* — 305.9
Pablo Cruz, Rosayra. *The Book of Rosy* — B
Pham, Andrew X. ★*The Eaves of Heaven* — B
Qu, Anna. *Made in China* — B
Ramos, Jorge. *Stranger* — 325.73
Rehman, Sabeeha. *Threading My Prayer Rug* — 305.8
Samaha, Albert. *Concepcion* — 929
Shahani, Aarti Namdev. *Here We Are* — B
Shakur, Prince. *When They Tell You to Be Good* — B
Soboroff, Jacob. ★*Separated* — 325.73
Suarez, Ray. ★*We Are Home* — 325.73
Tobar, Hector. ★*Our Migrant Souls* — 305.868
Tran, Phuc. ★*Sigh, Gone* — B
Umar, Ousman. *North to Paradise* — B
Ung, Loung. *Lucky Child* — B
Velshi, Ali. *Small Acts of Courage* — B
Villarreal, Vanessa Anglica. *Magical/Realism* — 814
Wang, Qian Julie. ★*Beautiful Country* — B
Zamora, Javier. ★*Solito* — B

LIFE STORIES — IDENTITY — LGBTQIA+
Ali, Fatima. ★*Savor* — B
Bechdel, Alison. ★*The Secret to Superhuman Strength* — 741.5
Belcher, Chris. *Pretty Baby* — B
Belcourt, Billy-Ray. ★*A History of My Brief Body* — B
Berg, A. Scott. *Kate Remembered* — B
Black, Dustin Lance. *Mama's Boy* — B
Blanco, Richard. *The Prince of Los Cocuyos* — B
Bossiere, Zoe. *Cactus Country* — 306
Boylan, Jennifer Finney. *Good Boy* — B
Carlile, Brandi. *Broken Horses* — B
Carr, C. *Candy Darling* — B
Cervini, Eric. *The Deviant's War* — B
Chee, Alexander. ★*How to Write an Autobiographical Novel* — B
Clemmons, Francois S. *Officer Clemmons* — B
Cooper, Alex. *Saving Alex* — B
Daley, Tom. *Coming up for Air* — B
Dearborn, Mary V. *Carson McCullers* — B
Dennison, Matthew. *Behind the Mask* — B
Diaz, Jaquira. *Ordinary Girls* — 818
Doty, Mark. *What Is the Grass* — 811
Duberman, Martin B. *Hold Tight Gently* — 920
Emezi, Akwaeke. ★*Dear Senthuran* — B
Fagan, Kate. *All the Colors Came Out* — B
Faliveno, Melissa. *Tomboyland* — B
Faludi, Susan. *In the Darkroom* — B
Frank, Barney. *Frank* — B
Funk, Mason. *The Book of Pride* — 920
Gaffney, Ginger. *Half Broke* — B
Gehring, Wes D. *James Dean* — B
Gelwicks, Andrew. *The Queer Advantage* — 920
Glass, Sara. *Kissing Girls on Shabbat* — B
Goetsch, Diana. *This Body I Wore* — B
Gomez, Edgar. *High-Risk Homosexual* — B
Gunn, Thom. ★*The Letters of Thom Gunn* — 821
Gutowitz, Jill. *Girls Can Kiss Now* — 814
H, Lamya. ★*Hijab Butch Blues* — B
Hamill, Kirkland. *Filthy Beasts* — B
Hammer, Langdon. *James Merrill* — B
Hartke, Austen. *Transforming* — 277
Hays, Katie. *Family of Origin, Family of Choice* — 248.8086
Hempel, Jessi. *The Family Outing* — B
Hernandez, Daisy. *A Cup of Water Under My Bed* — B
Hester, Diarmuid. *Nothing Ever Just Disappears* — 306.76
Hewitt, Sean. *All Down Darkness Wide* — B
Hough, Lauren. *Leaving Isn't the Hardest Thing* — B
Jenkins, Jedidiah. *To Shake the Sleeping Self* — B
Jones, Saeed. *How We Fight for Our Lives* — B
King, Billie Jean. ★*All In* — B
Lehrer, Riva. *Golem Girl* — B
Mann, William J. *Kate* — B
Manning, Chelsea. *Readme.Txt* — B
Marshall, Greg. *Leg* — B
Maupin, Armistead. *Logical Family* — B
McBrien, William. *Cole Porter* — B
Mock, Janet. *Surpassing Certainty* — B
Moss, Jeremiah. *Feral City* — B
Nelson, Maggie. ★*The Argonauts* — B
Nutt, Amy Ellis. *Becoming Nicole* — 920
O'Connor, Garry. *Ian McKellen* — B
Okporo, Edafe. *Asylum* — B
Olsen, Craig. *P.S. Burn This Letter Please* — 306.76
Page, Elliot. *Pageboy* — B
Parks, Casey. *Diary of a Misfit* — B
Patterson, Pat. *Accepted* — B
Pellegrino, Danny. *How Do I Un-Remember This?* — B
Porter, Billy. ★*Unprotected* — B
Possanza, Amelia. *Lesbian Love Story* — B
Quin, Tegan. ★*High School* — B
Rannells, Andrew. *Uncle of the Year* — B
Rapinoe, Megan. *One Life* — B
Reang, Putsata. *Ma and Me* — B
Regan, Iliana. *Fieldwork* — B
Richardson, Lance. *House of Nutter* — B
Rigsby, Cody. ★*XOXO, Cody* — B
Rippon, Adam. *Beautiful on the Outside* — B
Rogers, Robbie. *Coming Out to Play* — B
Royster, Francesca T. *Choosing Family* — B
RuPaul. ★*The House of Hidden Meanings* — B
Sante, Lucy. *I Heard Her Call My Name* — B
Schiavi, Michael R. *Celluloid Activist* — B
Schneider, Amy. *In the Form of a Question* — B
Seligman, Craig. *Who Does That Bitch Think She Is?* — 792.02
Shakur, Prince. *When They Tell You to Be Good* — B
Shapiro, Ari. ★*The Best Strangers in the World* — B
Shapland, Jenn. *My Autobiography of Carson McCullers* — B
Shapland, Jenn. ★*Thin Skin* — 814
Singh, Julietta. *The Breaks* — B
Soloway, Jill. *She Wants It* — B
Tea, Michelle. *Against Memoir* — B
Thomas, R. Eric. *Here for It* — B
Tobia, Jacob. *Sissy* — 305.30973
Travisano, Thomas J. *Love Unknown* — B
Van Ness, Jonathan. *Love That Story* — 791.4502
Velour, Sasha. ★*The Big Reveal* — 792.7
Wambach, Abby. *Forward* — B
Weigel, Alicia Roth. *Inverse Cowgirl* — B
Whitney, Emerson. *Heaven* — B
Willis, Raquel. *The Risk It Takes to Bloom* — B
Windsor, Edie. *A Wild and Precious Life* — B
Wizenberg, Molly. *Fixed Stars* — B
Wojczuk, Tana. *Lady Romeo* — B
Wolf, Brandon J. *A Place for Us* — B

PUBLIC LIBRARY CORE COLLECTION: NONFICTION
Twentieth Edition

LIFE STORIES — IDENTITY — RACE AND ETHNICITY

Abdelmahmoud, Elamin. *Son of Elsewhere*	B
Alvarez, Noe. *Spirit Run*	796.42
Andrews-Dyer, Helena. *Reclaiming Her Time*	B
Arce, Julissa. *You Sound Like a White Girl*	303.48
Austin, Nefertiti. *Motherhood so White*	B
Babb, Valerie Melissa. *The Book of James*	B
Bailey, Issac J. *Why Didn't We Riot?*	305.800973
Baylor, Elgin. *Hang Time*	B
Belcourt, Billy-Ray. *A History of My Brief Body*	B
Bell, Darrin. ★*The Talk*	741.5
Bernard, Emily. *Black Is the Body*	305.48
Berry, Daina Ramey. *A Black Women's History of the United States*	305.48
Blain, Keisha N. *Until I Am Free*	B
Boykin, Keith. ★*Why Does Everything Have to Be About Race?*	305.8
Broom, Sarah M. *The Yellow House*	B
Brown, Austin Channing. ★*I'm Still Here*	B
Brown, Claude. *Manchild in the Promised Land*	B
Carroll, Rebecca. *Surviving the White Gaze*	B
Carruthers, Charlene A. *Unapologetic*	305.48
Chee, Alexander. ★*How to Write an Autobiographical Novel*	B
Chude-Sokei, Louis Onuorah. *Floating in a Most Peculiar Way*	979.4
Chung, Nicole. *All You Can Ever Know*	B
Chung, Nicole. ★*A Living Remedy*	B
Clemmons, Francois S. *Officer Clemmons*	B
Coates, Ta-Nehisi. *Between the World and Me*	305.800973
Coel, Michaela. ★*Misfits*	158.2
Cummings, Elijah. ★*We're Better Than This*	B
Dabiri, Emma. *Twisted*	391.5
Davis, Viola. ★*Finding Me*	B
Douglass, Frederick. *Narrative of the Life of Frederick Douglass, an American Slave*	B
Dungy, Camille T. *Soil*	635.0978
Eggers, Dave. *Zeitoun*	305.892
Emezi, Akwaeke. ★*Dear Senthuran*	B
Evaristo, Bernardine. *Manifesto*	B
Ford, Ashley C. ★*Somebody's Daughter*	B
Fumudoh, Ziwe. ★*Black Friend*	814
Garrett, Kent. *The Last Negroes at Harvard*	920
Garza, Alicia. *The Purpose of Power*	303.48
Gay, Ross. *The Book of (more) Delights*	814
Gayle, Caleb. *We Refuse to Forget*	975.004
Gilliam, Dorothy Butler. *Trailblazer*	B
Givens, Jarvis R. ★*School Clothes*	371.829
Gomez, Edgar. *High-Risk Homosexual*	B
Gregory, Dick. ★*The Essential Dick Gregory*	818
Griffin, Farah Jasmine. *Read Until You Understand*	810.9
Hall, Alvin D. *Driving the Green Book*	917.304
Harriot, Michael. ★*Black AF History*	973
Henderson, Bruce B. *Bridge to the Sun*	940.53
Henderson, Danielle. ★*The Ugly Cry*	B
Hernandez, Daisy. *A Cup of Water Under My Bed*	B
Hoja, Gulchehra. *A Stone Is Most Precious Where It Belongs*	B
Holley, Santi Elijah. *An Amerikan Family*	920
Hong, Cathy Park. *Minor Feelings*	305.48
Hsu, Hua. ★*Stay True*	B
Huang, Yunte. *Daughter of the Dragon*	B
Hudes, Quiara Alegria. ★*My Broken Language*	B
Hulls, Tessa. ★*Feeding Ghosts*	741.5
Hurston, Zora Neale. ★*You Don't Know Us Negroes and Other Essays*	814
Hylton, Antonia. *Madness*	362.2
Iguodala, Andre. *The Sixth Man*	B
Jacob, Mira. *Good Talk*	741.5
Jacobs, Sally H. *Althea*	B
Jacoby, Karl. *The Strange Career of William Ellis*	B
Jawando, Will. ★*My Seven Black Fathers*	B
Jefferson, Margo. *Negroland*	305.896
Jerkins, Morgan. *Wandering in Strange Lands*	305.896
Johnson, Akemi. *Night in the American Village*	305.40952
Johnson, Theodore R. *When the Stars Begin to Fall*	305.800973
Jones, Brenda. *Alexandria Ocasio-Cortez*	B
Jones, Brenda. *Maxine Waters*	B
Jones, Saeed. *How We Fight for Our Lives*	B
Jun, Tasha. ★*Tell Me the Dream Again*	248
Kearse, Bettye. *The Other Madisons*	920
Keene, Adrienne. *Notable Native People*	920
Kendi, Ibram X. ★*How to Raise an Antiracist*	649
Khakpour, Porochista. *Brown Album*	304.8
Kram, Mark. *Smokin' Joe*	B
Kranish, Michael. *The World's Fastest Man*	B
Kweli, Talib. *Vibrate Higher*	B
Lalami, Laila. *Conditional Citizens*	323.60973
LaPointe, Sasha taqwseblu. *Red Paint*	B
LaPointe, Sasha taqwseblu. *Thunder Song*	814
Lawton, Georgina. *Raceless*	B
Laymon, Kiese. ★*Heavy*	B
LeDuff, Charlie. *Detroit*	977.4
Lee, Julia Sun-Joo. *Biting the Hand*	B
Lemon, Don. *This Is the Fire*	305.896
Lewis, Robin Coste. *To the Realization of Perfect Helplessness*	811
Locke, Tembi. ★*From Scratch*	B
Luckerson, Victor. *Built from the Fire*	976.6
Mailhot, Terese Marie. *Heart Berries*	B
Marshall, Cynthia. *You've Been Chosen*	B
Mays, Willie. *24*	B
McBride, James. *The Color of Water*	B
McCauley, Esau. *How Far to the Promised Land*	B
Meacham, Jon. *His Truth Is Marching On*	B
Merritt, Tyler. *I Take My Coffee Black*	791.4302
Mock, Janet. *Surpassing Certainty*	B
Mojica Rodriguez, Prisca Dorcas. *For Brown Girls with Sharp Edges and Tender Hearts*	305.48
Moore, Wayetu. *The Dragons, the Giant, the Women*	B
Morgan-Owens, Jessie. *Girl in Black and White*	B
Mouton, Deborah D. E. E. P. *Black Chameleon*	B
Muhammad, Ibtihaj. *Proud*	B
Murad, Nadia. ★*The Last Girl*	B
Murdoch, Sierra Crane. ★*Yellow Bird*	364.152
Myers, Leah. *Thinning Blood*	B
Ng, Fae Myenne. *Orphan Bachelors*	B
Nguyen, Viet Thanh. ★*A Man of Two Faces*	B
Noah, Trevor. *Born a Crime*	B
Pablo Cruz, Rosayra. *The Book of Rosy*	B
Parker, Morgan. ★*You Get What You Pay For*	305.896
Paul, Richard. *We Could Not Fail*	920
Payne, Les. ★*The Dead Are Arising*	B
Perkins, Kendrick. *The Education of Kendrick Perkins*	B
Perkins, Nichole. *Sometimes I Trip on How Happy We Could Be*	B
Porter, Billy. ★*Unprotected*	B
Prescod, Danielle. *Token Black Girl*	B
Raboteau, Emily. *Lessons for Survival*	814
Rembert, Winfred. *Chasing Me to My Grave*	B
Robinson, Phoebe. *Please Don't Sit on My Bed in Your Outside Clothes*	818
Robinson, Phoebe. *You Can't Touch My Hair and Other Things I Still Have to Explain*	792.7
Rojas Contreras, Ingrid. ★*The Man Who Could Move Clouds*	B
Ronstadt, Linda. *Feels Like Home*	B
Royster, Francesca T. *Choosing Family*	B
Ruffin, Amber. ★*The World Record Book of Racist Stories*	305.896
Ruffin, Amber. *You'll Never Believe What Happened to Lacey*	305.896
Salisbury, Katie Gee. ★*Not Your China Doll*	B
Samaha, Albert. *Never Ran, Never Will*	920
Samuels, Robert. ★*His Name Is George Floyd*	B
Samuelsson, Marcus. ★*The Rise*	641.59
Sanchez, Erika L. *Crying in the Bathroom*	B
Sanders, Chad. *Black Magic*	305.896
Sasakamoose, Fred. *Call Me Indian*	B
Sattouf, Riad. *The Arab of the Future 2*	741.5
Sattouf, Riad. *The Arab of the Future*	741.5
Savage, Jodi M. *The Death of a Jaybird*	B
Shakur, Prince. *When They Tell You to Be Good*	B
Shane, Scott. ★*Flee North*	973.7
Sharma, Nina. *The Way You Make Me Feel*	B
Shih, David. *Chinese Prodigal*	B
Simmons, Ruth. ★*Up Home*	B
Smith, Clint. ★*How the Word Is Passed*	973
Smith, Mychal Denzel. *Invisible Man, Got the Whole World Watching*	305.242
Smith, Tracy K. ★*To Free the Captives*	818
Streep, Abe. *Brothers on Three*	306.85
Taffa, Deborah Jackson. ★*Whiskey Tender*	B
Talley, Andre Leon. *The Chiffon Trenches*	B
Thomas, R. Eric. *Here for It*	B
Thompson-Hernandez, Walter. *The Compton Cowboys*	920
Tisserand, Michael. *Krazy*	741.5
Tobar, Hector. ★*Our Migrant Souls*	305.868

AUTHOR, TITLE, SERIES AND SUBJECT INDEX

Tubbs, Michael. *The Deeper the Roots*	B
Valby, Karen. *The Swans of Harlem*	792.8
Wagamese, Richard. *For Joshua*	B
Wagner, Alex. *Futureface*	B
Wang, Connie. *Oh My Mother!*	B
Wang, Qian Julie. ★*Beautiful Country*	B
Ward, Jesmyn. *Men We Reaped*	B
Watts, Reggie. *Great Falls, MT*	B
West, Cornel. *Black Prophetic Fire*	920
White, Gayle Jessup. *Reclamation*	B
Wilbur, Matika. *Project 562*	970.004
Wilderson, Frank B. *Afropessimism*	B
Wilkerson, Isabel. ★*The Warmth of Other Suns*	304.80973
Wilson, A'ja. ★*Dear Black Girls*	158.1
Wilson, Chris. *The Master Plan*	B
Wong, Jane. ★*Meet Me Tonight in Atlantic City*	B
Young, Damon. *What Doesn't Kill You Makes You Blacker*	B
Young, R. J. *Requiem for the Massacre*	305.8
Zack, Ian. *Odetta*	B
Zauner, Michelle. ★*Crying in H Mart*	B

LIFE STORIES — LAW AND ORDER

Bowden, Mark. *The Case of the Vanishing Blonde*	364.10973
Burgess, Ann Wolbert. *A Killer by Design*	364.3
Butcher, Barbara. *What the Dead Know*	614
Cantu, Francisco. *The Line Becomes a River*	B
Cook, Kevin. *Waco Rising*	299
Dawson, Kate Winkler. *American Sherlock*	B
Fagone, Jason. *The Woman Who Smashed Codes*	B
Gage, Beverly. *G-Man*	B
Goldfarb, Bruce. ★*18 Tiny Deaths*	B
Hale, Grace Elizabeth. *In the Pines*	364.13
Higham, Scott. *American Cartel*	338.4
Hill, Clint. *Five Presidents*	B
Hill, Clint. *Mrs. Kennedy and Me*	973.922092
Hill, Clint. *My Travels with Mrs. Kennedy*	B
Holes, Paul. *Unmasked*	363.25
Hortis, C. Alexander. *The Witch of New York*	364.152
Krouse, Erika. ★*Tell Me Everything*	363.25
Levin, Daniel. *Proof of Life*	956.9104
Maroney, Tyler. *The Modern Detective*	658.4
Mueller, Tom. *Crisis of Conscience*	364.16
Murdoch, Sierra Crane. ★*Yellow Bird*	364.152
Van Meter, Matthew. *Deep Delta Justice*	345.763

LIFE STORIES — LAW AND ORDER — ARMED FORCES PERSONNEL

Abouzeid, Rania. *No Turning Back*	956.9104
Ackerman, Elliot. *Places and Names*	B
Albracht, William. *Abandoned in Hell*	959.704
Alexander, Larry. *Biggest Brother*	B
Ambrose, Stephen E. ★*Band of Brothers*	920
Arana, Marie. *Bolivar*	B
Asbridge, Thomas S. *The Greatest Knight*	942.03
Bird, Kai. *American Prometheus*	B
Bissinger, H. G. ★*The Mosquito Bowl*	796.332
Bradley, James. *Flags of Our Fathers*	940.54
Bradley, James. *Flyboys*	940.54
Brady, James. *The Coldest War*	B
Broadwater, Jeff. ★*George Mason*	B
Brokhausen, Nick. *Whispers in the Tall Grass*	959.704
Brotherton, Marcus. *A Bright and Blinding Sun*	940.54
Brown, Daniel James. ★*Facing the Mountain*	940.54
Bruning, John R. *Indestructible*	B
Bruning, John R. *The Race of Aces*	940.54
Burgin, R. V. *Islands of the Damned*	B
Caputo, Philip. *A Rumor of War*	959.704
Carpenter, Kyle. *You Are Worth It*	B
Carwardine, Richard. *Lincoln*	B
Castner, Brian. *The Long Walk*	B
Castor, Helen. *Joan of Arc*	B
Chesney, Will. *No Ordinary Dog*	958.104
Chivers, C. J. *The Fighters*	920
Cotton, Tom. *Sacred Duty*	355.6
Donald, David Herbert. *Lincoln*	B
Drury, Bob. *Lucky 666*	B
Eder, Mari K. *The Girls Who Stepped Out of Line*	920
Edstrom, Erik. *Un-American*	B
Erwin, Jon. *Beyond Valor*	B
Fair, Eric. *Consequence*	B
Finkel, David. *Thank You for Your Service*	920

Freeman, Sally Mott. *The Jersey Brothers*	920
Friedman, Matti. *Pumpkinflowers*	B
Fritz, Ian. *What the Taliban Told Me*	B
Gallego, Ruben. *They Called Us*	956.7044
Garrett, Leah. *X Troop*	940.54
Gerwarth, Robert. *Hitler's Hangman*	B
Gienapp, William E. *Abraham Lincoln and Civil War America*	B
Glass, Charles. *Soldiers Don't Go Mad*	616.85
Golembesky, Michael. *Level Zero Heroes*	958.104
Gonell, Aquilino. *American Shield*	B
Goodwin, Doris Kearns. *No Ordinary Time*	920
Grant, Ulysses S. *Memoirs and Selected Letters*	B
Greitens, Eric. *Resilience*	155.2
Groom, Winston. *The Aviators*	920
Grossi, Craig. *Craig & Fred*	B
Guibert, Emmanuel. *Alan's War*	741.5
Haffner, Sebastian. *Defying Hitler*	943.085
Hegar, Mary Jennings. *Shoot Like a Girl*	B
Henderson, Bruce B. *Bridge to the Sun*	940.53
Hennessey, Patrick. *The Junior Officers' Reading Club*	B
Hillenbrand, Laura. ★*Unbroken*	B
Holland, James. *Brothers in Arms*	940.54
Holland, James. *The Savage Storm*	940.53
Humphreys, Richard. *Under Pressure*	B
Kander, Jason. *Invisible Storm*	B
Kershaw, Alex. *Against All Odds*	940.54
Kershaw, Alex. *The First Wave*	940.54
King, Charles Monroe. *A Journal for Jordan*	956.7044
Klay, Phil. *Uncertain Ground*	359.9
Korda, Michael. *Muse of Fire*	940.4
Kunetka, James W. *The General and the Genius*	355.8
Lambert, Raymond. *Every Man a Hero*	B
Lance, Rachel. *Chamber Divers*	940.54
Landdeck, Katherine Sharp. *The Women with Silver Wings*	920
Lawrence, T. E. *Seven Pillars of Wisdom*	940.4
Lemmon, Gayle Tzemach. *Ashley's War*	B
Lemmon, Gayle Tzemach. *The Daughters of Kobani*	956.9104
Lewis, Damien. *The Dog Who Could Fly*	940.54
Longerich, Peter. *Hitler*	B
Luttrell, Marcus. *Lone Survivor*	958.104
Luttrell, Marcus. *Service*	956.7044
Makos, Adam. *Devotion*	920
Makos, Adam. *Spearhead*	B
Manchester, William. *Goodbye, Darkness*	B
Marozzi, Justin. *Tamerlane*	950.2
Maurer, Kevin. *Damn Lucky*	940.54
McLynn, Frank. *Genghis Khan*	950.2
McManus, John C. *Island Infernos*	940.54
McManus, John C. *To the End of the Earth*	940.54
Meyer, Dakota. *Into the Fire*	958.104
Miller, Scott. *The President and the Assassin*	973.8
Mills, Dan. *Sniper One*	956.7044
Mizuki, Shigeru. *Showa 1926-1939*	741.5
Murphy, Brian. *81 Days Below Zero*	940.54
O'Neill, Robert. *The Operator*	B
Owen, Mark. *No Easy Day*	B
Owen, Mark. *No Hero*	B
Paradis, Michel. *The Light of Battle*	940.54
Patterson, James. *Walk in My Combat Boots*	920
Patton, George S. *War as I Knew It*	B
Pavlychenko, Liudmyla Mykhailivna. *Lady Death*	B
Pham, Andrew X. ★*The Eaves of Heaven*	B
Philipps, David. *Alpha*	956.7044
Rahmani, Niloofar. *Open Skies*	B
Reiss, Tom. *The Black Count*	B
Sheehan, Neil. *A Bright Shining Lie*	959.704
Simms, Brendan. *The Silver Waterfall*	940.54
Smith, Starr. *Jimmy Stewart*	B
Swofford, Anthony. *Jarhead*	956.7044
Taylor, Stephen. *Commander*	B
Tobin, James. *Ernie Pyle's War*	B
Trimble, Lee. *Beyond the Call*	940.54
Ulander, Perry A. *Walking Point*	B
Wallace, Chris. *Countdown Bin Laden*	958.104
Warren, W. Lee. *No Place to Hide*	B
Weatherford, J. McIver. ★*Genghis Khan and the Making of the Modern World*	B
Wheelan, Joseph. ★*Terrible Swift Sword*	B

2073

PUBLIC LIBRARY CORE COLLECTION: NONFICTION
Twentieth Edition

White, Ronald C. *A. Lincoln*	B
Wills, Garry. *James Madison*	B
Winters, Richard D. *Beyond Band of Brothers*	
Wise, Beau. *Three Wise Men*	958.104
Wukovits, John F. *Lost at Sea*	940.54

LIFE STORIES — LAW AND ORDER — CRIMINALS AND LAW-BREAKERS

Alford, Terry. *Fortune's Fool*	B
Avrich, Paul. *Sasha and Emma*	920
Bair, Deirdre. *Al Capone*	B
Bardenwerper, William. *The Prisoner in His Palace*	956.7044
Barr, John. *Start by Believing*	364.15
Behar, Richard. *Madoff*	364.16
Bergen, Peter L. *The Rise and Fall of Osama Bin Laden*	958.104
Berman, Sarah. *Don't Call It a Cult*	361.4
Boessenecker, John. *Gentleman Bandit*	B
Brier, Bob. *The Murder of Tutankhamen*	B
Cannell, Michael T. *A Brotherhood Betrayed*	B
Carlo, Philip. *Gaspipe*	B
Cep, Casey N. ★*Furious Hours*	364.152
Cullen, Kevin. *Whitey Bulger*	B
Diamond, Cheryl. *Nowhere Girl*	B
Dolin, Eric Jay. *Black Flags, Blue Waters*	973.2
Dudley, Steven S. *MS-13*	364.106
Eig, Jonathan. *Get Capone*	364.1
Finkel, Michael. *The Art Thief*	364.1628
Fox, Margalit. *The Talented Mrs. Mandelbaum*	364.1
Garrison, Jessica. *The Devil's Harvest*	B
Glatt, John. *The Doomsday Mother*	364.152
Glatt, John. *Tangled Vines*	364.152
Greenberg, Andy. *Tracers in the Dark*	364.16
Guinn, Jeff. *Go Down Together*	B
Guinn, Jeff. ★*Manson*	B
Hill, David. *The Vapors*	976.7
Hopwood, Shon. *Law Man*	B
Howley, Kerry. *Bottoms Up and the Devil Laughs*	352.37
Ice-T. *Split Decision*	920
Jobb, Dean. *The Case of the Murderous Dr. Cream*	364.152
Jobb, Dean. *A Gentleman and a Thief*	364.16
Johnson, Kirk W. *The Feather Thief*	364.16
Keefe, Patrick Radden. ★*Rogues*	364.16
Kushner, Jacob. *Look Away*	305.9
Leerhsen, Charles. ★*Butch Cassidy*	B
Levin, Josh. *The Queen*	364.16
Maddow, Rachel. *Bag Man*	B
Manning, Chelsea. *Readme.Txt*	B
Marshall, McMillan. *Among the Bros*	362.29
Marwell, David G. *Mengele*	B
Matney, Mandy. *Blood on Their Hands*	364.152
McCracken, Patti. *The Angel Makers*	364.152
Muse, Toby. *Kilo*	363.4509861
Nadeau, Barbie Latza. *The Godmother*	364.106
O'Connell, Mark. *A Thread of Violence*	364.152
Ratliff, Evan. *The Mastermind*	B
Sands, Philippe. *The Ratline*	B
Schechter, Harold. *Hell's Princess*	B
Sebba, Anne. *Ethel Rosenberg*	B
Shannon, Elaine. *Hunting Leroux*	364.1
Sherman, Casey. *Hunting Whitey*	B
Sisman, Adam. *The Professor and the Parson*	364.16
Smith, Jeremy N. *Breaking and Entering*	B
Tetro, Tony. *Con/Artist*	B
Toobin, Jeffrey. ★*Homegrown*	363.325
Vorobyov, Niko. *Dopeworld*	364.1
Wallis, Michael. *Billy the Kid*	B
Weinman, Sarah. *Scoundrel*	364.152
Whitlock, Craig. ★*Fat Leonard*	364.16
Wiehl, Lis W. *Hunting the Unabomber*	364.152
Willetts, Paul. *King Con*	B
Wilson, Chris. *The Master Plan*	B
Yeebo, Yepoka. *Anansi's Gold*	364.16

LIFE STORIES — LAW AND ORDER — JUDGES AND LAWYERS

Adams, Jarrett. *Redeeming Justice*	340.092
Barnett, Brittany K. ★*A Knock at Midnight*	B
Berman, Geoffrey. *Holding the Line*	345.73
Bilott, Robert. *Exposure*	344.04
Brown-Nagin, Tomiko. *Civil Rights Queen*	B
Budiansky, Stephen. *Oliver Wendell Holmes*	B
Canellos, Peter S. *The Great Dissenter*	B
Carmon, Irin. *Notorious RBG*	B
Carter, Stephen L. *Invisible*	B
Chammah, Maurice. ★*Let the Lord Sort Them*	364.66
Coates, Laura Gayle. *Just Pursuit*	345.73
Crump, Benjamin. *Open Season*	364
De Hart, Jane Sherron. ★*Ruth Bader Ginsburg*	B
Farrell, John A. *Clarence Darrow*	B
Feige, David. *Indefensible*	B
Gibson, Larry S. *Young Thurgood*	B
Ginsburg, Ruth Bader. ★*My Own Words*	347.73
Gleeson, John. *The Gotti Wars*	364.1
Goldberg, Carrie. *Nobody's Victim*	345.73
Greenhouse, Linda. *Becoming Justice Blackmun*	B
Haygood, Wil. *Showdown*	B
Hirshman, Linda R. *Sisters in Law*	347.73
Jackson, Bruce. *Never Far from Home*	B
Jones, Nathaniel R. *Answering the Call*	B
Kaplan, David A. *The Most Dangerous Branch*	347.73
Kirtzman, Andrew. *Giuliani*	B
Lithwick, Dahlia. *Lady Justice*	345.73
Murphy, Bruce Allen. *Scalia*	B
Obama, Michelle. ★*Becoming*	B
Oller, John. *White Shoe*	346.73
Paul, Joel R. ★*Without Precedent*	B
Pratt, Victoria. *The Power of Dignity*	364.973
Rapping, Jonathan. *Gideon's Promise*	345.73
Robin, Corey. *The Enigma of Clarence Thomas*	347.73
Rosen, Jeffrey. *Conversations with RBG*	B
Rosen, Richard A. *Julius Chambers*	B
Smith, Jean Edward. *John Marshall*	B
Sorensen, Theodore C. *Counselor*	B
Sotomayor, Sonia. ★*My Beloved World*	B
Stevens, John Paul. *The Making of a Justice*	B
Stevenson, Bryan. *Just Mercy*	B
Thomas, Evan. ★*First*	B
Totenberg, Nina. ★*Dinners with Ruth*	B
Urofsky, Melvin I. *Louis D. Brandeis*	B
Williams, Juan. *Thurgood Marshall*	B

LIFE STORIES — LAW AND ORDER — MILITARY LEADERS

Ambrose, Stephen E. *The Victors*	940.54
Baier, Bret. *To Rescue the Constitution*	973.4
Blount, Roy. *Robert E. Lee*	B
Borneman, Walter R. *Macarthur at War*	B
Broers, Michael. *Napoleon*	B
Broers, Michael. *Napoleon*	944.05
Broers, Michael. *Napoleon*	B
Bunting, Josiah. ★*The Making of a Leader*	B
Chernow, Ron. ★*Grant*	B
Chernow, Ron. *Washington*	B
Clark, Lloyd. *The Commanders*	940.53
Crawford, Alan Pell. *This Fierce People*	975
Davis, William C. *Crucible of Command*	920
Drury, Bob. *Valley Forge*	973.3
Duncan, Michael. ★*Hero of Two Worlds*	B
Ellis, Joseph J. ★*His Excellency*	B
Everitt, Anthony. *Alexander the Great*	B
Fellman, Michael. *The Making of Robert E. Lee*	B
Ferling, John E. *Winning Independence*	973.3
Frank, Richard B. *Tower of Skulls*	940.54
Freeman, Douglas Southall. *Lee*	B
Gladwell, Malcolm. ★*The Bomber Mafia*	940.54
Goldsworthy, Adrian Keith. ★*Caesar*	B
Grant, Ulysses S. ★*The Annotated Memoirs of Ulysses S. Grant*	B
Groom, Winston. *The Allies*	940.5309
Groom, Winston. *The Generals*	920
Guelzo, Allen C. *Robert E. Lee*	B
Gwynne, S. C. *Rebel Yell*	B
Herman, Arthur. ★*Douglas Macarthur*	B
Hunt, Patrick. *Hannibal*	B
Jackson, Julian. *De Gaulle*	B
Johnson, Paul. *George Washington*	B
Johnson, Paul. *Napoleon*	B
Jones, Michael K. *The Black Prince*	B
Korda, Michael. *Clouds of Glory*	B
McDonough, James L. *William Tecumseh Sherman*	B
McMurtry, Larry. *Custer*	B
McRaven, William H. *Sea Stories*	B

AUTHOR, TITLE, SERIES AND SUBJECT INDEX

Morison, Samuel Eliot. *John Paul Jones*	B
Norris, Robert S. *Racing for the Bomb*	B
O'Connell, Robert L. *Revolutionary*	B
Perry, Mark. *The Most Dangerous Man in America*	B
Randall, Willard Sterne. *George Washington*	B
Roberts, Andrew. *Leadership in War*	920
Roberts, Andrew. ★*Napoleon*	B
Robertson, James I. *Stonewall Jackson*	B
Roll, David L. *George Marshall*	B
Sallah, Michael. *The Yankee Comandante*	972.91
Scott, James. *Black Snow*	940.54
Sears, Stephen W. *Lincoln's Lieutenants*	920
Stangneth, Bettina. *Eichmann Before Jerusalem*	B
Stewart, David O. *George Washington*	973.4
Stiles, T. J. *Custer's Trials*	B
Strauss, Barry S. ★*The War That Made the Roman Empire*	937
Thomas, Evan. ★*John Paul Jones*	B
Unger, Debi. *George Marshall*	B
Utley, Robert M. ★*Geronimo*	B
Varon, Elizabeth R. *Longstreet*	B
Wert, Jeffry D. *Cavalryman of the Lost Cause*	B
Wert, Jeffry D. *Custer*	B
White, Ronald C. *American Ulysses*	B
White, Ronald C. *On Great Fields*	B
Zambone, Albert Louis. *Daniel Morgan*	B
Zamoyski, Adam. *Napoleon*	B

LIFE STORIES — LAW AND ORDER — POLICE AND LAW OFFICERS

Barra, Allen. *Inventing Wyatt Earp*	B
Boessenecker, John. *Texas Ranger*	B
Clavin, Thomas. *Dodge City*	978.1
Clavin, Thomas. *Wild Bill*	B
Collins, Max Allan. *Eliot Ness and the Mad Butcher*	364.152
Croke, Ken. *Riding with Evil*	364.106
Douglas, John E. *The Killer Across the Table*	B
Douglas, John E. *When a Killer Calls*	364.152
Dunn, Harry. *Standing My Ground*	B
Greenberg, Andy. *Tracers in the Dark*	364.16
Hardy, Jason Matthew. ★*The Second Chance Club*	364.6
Hill, Clint. *Five Days in November*	973.922092
Horace, Matthew. *The Black and the Blue*	B
Kenda, Joe. *Killer Triggers*	364.152
Lane, Charles. *Freedom's Detective*	B
McGarrahan, Ellen. *Two Truths and a Lie*	364.152
Monroe, Jana. *Hearts of Darkness*	363.25
Navarro, Joe. *Three Minutes to Doomsday*	B
Patterson, James. *Walk the Blue Line*	920
Raymond, Edwin. *An Inconvenient Cop*	363.2
Stashower, Daniel. *American Demon*	364.152
Tefertiller, Casey. *Wyatt Earp*	B
Wiehl, Lis W. *Hunting the Unabomber*	364.152

LIFE STORIES — LAW AND ORDER — PRISONERS AND INMATES

Adams, Jarrett. *Redeeming Justice*	340.092
Austen, Ben. *Correction*	364.6
Blakinger, Keri. *Corrections in Ink*	B
Carlo, Philip. *Gaspipe*	B
Chammah, Maurice. ★*Let the Lord Sort Them*	364.66
Fabricant, M. Chris. *Junk Science and the American Criminal Justice System*	363.25
Fox, Margalit. *The Confidence Men*	940.4
Hardy, Jason Matthew. ★*The Second Chance Club*	364.6
Hinton, Anthony Ray. *The Sun Does Shine*	B
Hobbs, Jeff. *Children of the State*	364.36
Ice-T. *Split Decision*	920
Isenberg, Sheila. *Women Who Love Men Who Kill*	362.83
Manuel, Ian. *My Time Will Come*	B
Moore, Wes. *The Other Wes Moore*	B
Morton, Michael. *Getting Life*	B
Rudolf, David S. *American Injustice*	345.73
Sheff, David. *The Buddhist on Death Row*	B
White, Neil. *In the Sanctuary of Outcasts*	B
Woodfox, Albert. *Solitary*	B

LIFE STORIES — LAW AND ORDER — SPIES AND SECRET AGENTS

Abbott, Karen. *Liar, Temptress, Soldier, Spy*	920
Anderson, Scott. ★*The Quiet Americans*	327.12
Blum, Howard. *The Spy Who Knew Too Much*	327.12
Boot, Max. ★*The Road Not Taken*	B
Drabkin, Ronald. *Beverly Hills Spy*	940.54
Elnoury, Tamer. *American Radical*	B
Fox, Amaryllis. *Life Undercover*	B
Helm, Sarah. *A Life in Secrets*	B
Hillsberg, Christina. *License to Parent*	649.1
Hvistendahl, Mara. ★*The Scientist and the Spy*	364.16
Kershaw, Alex. *Avenue of Spies*	940.53
Kix, Paul. *The Saboteur*	940.53
Lauterbach, Preston. *Bluff City*	B
Lewis, Damien. *Agent Josephine*	B
Lichtblau, Eric. *Return to the Reich*	B
Loftis, Larry. *Code Name*	B
Macintyre, Ben. ★*Agent Sonya*	B
Macintyre, Ben. *Agent Zigzag*	B
Macintyre, Ben. *Double Cross*	940.54
Macintyre, Ben. *A Spy Among Friends*	B
Macintyre, Ben. ★*The Spy and the Traitor*	B
Magida, Arthur J. *Code Name Madeleine*	940.54
Mazzeo, Tilar J. *Sisters in Resistance*	945.091
Mulley, Clare. *The Spy Who Loved*	B
Olson, Lynne. ★*Madame Fourcade's Secret War*	B
Philipps, Roland. *A Spy Named Orphan*	B
Popkin, Jim. *Code Name Blue Wren*	327.12
Purnell, Sonia. ★*A Woman of No Importance*	B
Reynolds, Nicholas E. *Need to Know*	940.54
Ronald, Susan. *Hitler's Aristocrats*	940.53
Rose, Sarah. *D-Day Girls*	940.53
Talty, Stephan. *Agent Garbo*	940.5
Vickers, Michael G. *By All Means Available*	355
Vogel, Steve. *Betrayal in Berlin*	327.1273043
Walder, Tracy. *The Unexpected Spy*	B
Wallace, Chris. *Countdown Bin Laden*	958.104
Waller, Douglas C. *Wild Bill Donovan*	B
Whipple, Chris. *The Spymasters*	920
Wiehl, Lis W. *A Spy in Plain Sight*	327.1247

LIFE STORIES — NATURE AND OUTDOORS

Alexander, Jane. *Wild Things, Wild Places*	333.95
Attenborough, David. *Adventures of a Young Naturalist*	B
Auvinen, Karen. *Rough Beauty*	B
Bell, Laura. *Claiming Ground*	B
Cooper, Christian. *Better Living Through Birding*	B
Craig, Mya-Rose. *Birdgirl*	B
Darlington, Miriam. *Otter Country*	599.769
Delorme, Geoffroy. *Deer Man*	599.65
Dungy, Camille T. *Soil*	635.0978
Ehrlich, Gretel. *Unsolaced*	B
Foster, Craig. ★*Amphibious Soul*	155.9
Fowlds, Grant. *Saving the Last Rhinos*	599.66
Franklin, Jonathan. *A Wild Idea*	B
Freeman, Scott. *Saving Tarboo Creek*	333.72
Graham, Jasmin. *Sharks Don't Sink*	597.3
Grant, Will. *The Last Ride of the Pony Express*	917.804
Grylls, Bear. *Never Give Up*	B
Hargrove, Brantley. *The Man Who Caught the Storm*	B
Herriot, James. ★*All Creatures Great and Small*	B
Herriot, James. *All Things Wise and Wonderful*	B
Herriot, James. *Every Living Thing*	B
Herriot, James. *James Herriot's Animal Stories*	B
Herriot, James. *James Herriot's Cat Stories*	636.8
Herriot, James. *James Herriot's Dog Stories*	636.7
Herriot, James. *James Herriot's Favorite Dog Stories*	636.7
Heyman, Stephen. *The Planter of Modern Life*	B
Houston, Pam. *Deep Creek*	814
Kelley, Margot Anne. *A Gardener at the End of the World*	615.8
Kimberley, Hannah. *A Woman's Place Is at the Top*	B
King, Dean. *Guardians of the Valley*	333.72
King, Greg. *The Ghost Forest*	333.75
Kiser, Joy M. *America's Other Audubon*	B
Lankford, Andrea. *Trail of the Lost*	363.2
Lopez, Barry Holstun. *Horizon*	B
Magdalena, Carlos. *The Plant Messiah*	333.95
Malarkey, Tucker. *Stronghold*	639.2
Marcum, Diana. *The Fallen Stones*	B
Martin, Manjula. *The Last Fire Season*	B
May, Meredith. *The Honey Bus*	B
McGrath, Ben. *Riverman*	797.122
Messineo, Janet. *Casting into the Light*	799.1
Miles, Tiya. ★*Wild Girls*	304.2
Montgomery, Sy. *How to Be a Good Creature*	590
Montgomery, Sy. ★*Of Time and Turtles*	597.92

PUBLIC LIBRARY CORE COLLECTION: NONFICTION
Twentieth Edition

Mortimer, Frank. *Bee People and the Bugs They Love*	B
Muir, John. *The Story of My Boyhood and Youth*	B
Offerman, Nick. *Where the Deer and the Antelope Play*	973.93
Penniman, Leah. ★*Black Earth Wisdom*	333.72
Pennington, Emily. *Feral*	B
Rebanks, James. *The Shepherd's Life*	942.7
Regan, Iliana. *Fieldwork*	B
Renkl, Margaret. *The Comfort of Crows*	814.6
Renner, Rebecca. ★*Gator Country*	364.16
Robinson, Kim Stanley. *The High Sierra*	917.94
Ross, John F. *The Promise of the Grand Canyon*	917.91
Safina, Carl. ★*Alfie and Me*	598.9
Sevigny, Melissa L. ★*Brave the Wild River*	580.9
Shattuck, Ben. *Six Walks*	B
Simard, S. ★*Finding the Mother Tree*	582.16
Smith, Bren. *Eat Like a Fish*	338.3
Strøksnes, Morten Andreas. *Shark Drunk*	338.3
Van Hemert, Caroline. *The Sun Is a Compass*	979.8
Vasquez-Lavado, Silvia. *In the Shadow of the Mountain*	B
Wallace, Christopher. *Twentieth-Century Man*	B
Worster, Donald. *A Passion for Nature the Life of John Muir*	B
Wynn-Grant, Rae. *Wild Life*	B

LIFE STORIES — NATURE AND OUTDOORS — FARMERS AND RANCHERS

Branch, John. *The Last Cowboys*	920
Carter, Jimmy. *An Hour Before Daylight*	B
Connell, John. *The Farmer's Son*	630.9
Hamilton, Lisa M. *The Hungry Season*	B
Pawel, Miriam. *The Crusades of Cesar Chavez*	B
Thompson-Hernandez, Walter. *The Compton Cowboys*	920

LIFE STORIES — NATURE AND OUTDOORS — SIMPLE LIVING

Beavan, Colin. *No Impact Man*	B
Kingsolver, Barbara. ★*Animal, Vegetable, Miracle*	641

LIFE STORIES — PEOPLE IN HISTORY

Ball, Edward. *Life of a Klansman*	305.8009763
Bonanos, Christopher. *Flash*	B
Brands, H. W. ★*Our First Civil War*	973.3
Burrough, Bryan. *Forget the Alamo*	976.043
Caesar, Ed. *The Moth and the Mountain*	B
Cercas, Javier. *Lord of All the Dead*	868
Chin, Ava. ★*Mott Street*	974.7
Clavin, Thomas. *Dodge City*	978.1
Crouch, Gregory. *The Bonanza King*	B
De Courcy, Anne. *The Husband Hunters*	920
Dugard, Martin. *Taking Berlin*	940.54
Durkin, Hannah. ★*The Survivors of the Clotilda*	306.362
Emberton, Carole. *To Walk About in Freedom*	306.3
Farley, Audrey Clare. *The Unfit Heiress*	B
Figes, Orlando. *The Europeans*	920
Fischer, David Hackett. ★*African Founders*	973
Franklin, Benjamin. ★*Autobiography, Poor Richard, and Later Writings*	973.2
Franklin, John Hope. *In Search of the Promised Land*	929
Freedland, Jonathan. ★*The Escape Artist*	940.53
Gabriel, Mary. *Love and Capital*	920
Gallagher, Winifred. *New Women in the Old West*	978.02
Goldsworthy, Adrian Keith. *Antony and Cleopatra*	937
Gordon, Meryl. *Bunny Mellon*	B
Graff, Henry F. *Grover Cleveland*	B
Hales, Dianne R. *Mona Lisa*	B
Harrington, Joel F. *The Faithful Executioner*	B
Hecimovich, Gregg A. ★*The Life and Times of Hannah Crafts*	B
Hewitt, Catherine. *Renoir's Dancer*	B
Hibbert, Christopher. *The Borgias and Their Enemies*	920
Hill, Clint. *My Travels with Mrs. Kennedy*	B
Holton, Woody. *Liberty Is Sweet*	973.3
Howell, Georgina. *Gertrude Bell*	B
Hunt, Tristram. *Marx's General*	335.4092
Hurowitz, Richard. *In the Garden of the Righteous*	940.53
Jacoby, Karl. *The Strange Career of William Ellis*	B
Johnson, Victoria. ★*American Eden*	580.973
Joyce, Patrick. *Remembering Peasants*	305.5
Karbo, Karen. *In Praise of Difficult Women*	920
Kaufman, Jonathan. *The Last Kings of Shanghai*	951
Keneally, Thomas. *A Commonwealth of Thieves*	994
Kerrison, Catherine. *Jefferson's Daughters*	920
Khilnani, Sunil. *Incarnations*	920
Kimberley, Hannah. *A Woman's Place Is at the Top*	B
Koch, Bea. *Mad and Bad*	920
Krist, Gary. *The Mirage Factory*	920
Kroeber, Theodora. *Ishi in Two Worlds*	B
Larson, Kate Clifford. *Bound for the Promised Land*	B
Lepore, Jill. *Book of Ages*	B
Letts, Elizabeth. ★*The Ride of Her Life*	B
Lockley, Thomas. *African Samurai*	B
May, Gary. *John Tyler*	B
May, Gregory. *A Madman's Will*	973.5
Mealer, Bryan. *The Kings of Big Spring*	B
Mikanowski, Jacob. ★*Goodbye, Eastern Europe*	947
Minian, Ana Raquel. ★*In the Shadow of Liberty*	365
Moore, Peter. *Life, Liberty, and the Pursuit of Happiness*	199
Nicolson, Adam. *How to Be*	180
Norgren, Jill. *Belva Lockwood*	B
Oberman, Heiko Augustinus. *Luther*	B
Oelhafen, Ingrid von. *Hitler's Stolen Children*	B
Oller, John. *American Queen*	B
Rady, Martyn C. *The Middle Kingdoms*	943
Raines, Ben. *The Last Slave Ship*	306.362
Roberts, Jason. *A Sense of the World*	B
Ronald, Susan. *A Dangerous Woman*	B
Rosen, Richard A. *Julius Chambers*	B
Rosenberg, Justus. *The Art of Resistance*	B
Rothman, Joshua D. *The Ledger and the Chain*	306.362
Rousseau, Jean-Jacques. *Confessions*	B
Sakamoto, Pamela Rotner. *Midnight in Broad Daylight*	940.53
Schwarz, Geraldine. *Those Who Forget*	940.53
Smith, Clint. ★*How the Word Is Passed*	973
Sohn, Amy. *The Man Who Hated Women*	363.28
Stanley, Amy. *Stranger in the Shogun's City*	B
Tallis, Nicola. *Uncrowned Queen*	B
Ullrich, Volker. *Germany 1923*	943.085
Van Wijk-Voskuijl, Joop. *The Last Secret of the Secret Annex*	940.53
Varon, Elizabeth R. *Longstreet*	B
Wallach, Janet. *Desert Queen*	B
Weiner, Eric. *Ben & Me*	B
Weingarten, Gene. ★*One Day*	973
White, Elizabeth B. ★*The Counterfeit Countess*	940.53
White, Ralph. *Getting Out of Saigon*	959.704
Wills, Shomari. *Black Fortunes*	920
Womack, John. *Zapata and the Mexican Revolution*	B
Woo, Ilyon. ★*Master Slave Husband Wife*	920
Wright, Jennifer Ashley. ★*Madame Restell*	B
Wulf, Andrea. *The Brother Gardeners*	920

LIFE STORIES — PEOPLE IN HISTORY — EXPLORERS

Adams, Simon. *Journey*	910.9
Bellows, Amanda Brickell. *The Explorers*	910.92
Bergreen, Laurence. *In Search of a Kingdom*	B
Bergreen, Laurence. *Marco Polo*	B
Bound, Mensun. *The Ship Beneath the Ice*	919.8904
Cervantes, Fernando. *Conquistadores*	970.01
Croke, Vicki. *The Lady and the Panda*	599.789
Dana, Richard Henry. *Two Years Before the Mast*	910.4
Egan, Timothy. ★*Short Nights of the Shadow Catcher*	770.92
Ellsworth, Scott. *The World Beneath Their Feet*	796.522
Fernandez-Armesto, Felipe. ★*Amerigo*	B
Fiennes, Ranulph. *Shackleton*	B
Fischer, David Hackett. *Champlain's Dream*	B
Hartman, Darrell. *Battle of Ink and Ice*	998
Heacox, Kim. ★*John Muir and the Ice That Started a Fire*	333.7209798
Heaney, Christopher. *Cradle of Gold*	B
Jeal, Tim. *Explorers of the Nile*	920
Larson, Edward J. *An Empire of Ice*	919.8
Levy, Buddy. *Labyrinth of Ice*	910.91
Lowe, George. *Letters from Everest*	796.522
Millard, Candice. ★*River of the Gods*	916.204
Niven, Jennifer. *Ada Blackjack*	B
Resendez, Andres. *Conquering the Pacific*	959.9
Richardson, Edmund. *The King's Shadow*	958.1
Roberts, David. *Alone on the Ice*	919.8904
Ross, John F. *The Promise of the Grand Canyon*	917.91
Sancton, Julian. *Madhouse at the End of the Earth*	919.8904
Schmidt, Thomas. *The Saga of Lewis & Clark*	917.804
Sides, Hampton. ★*The Wide Wide Sea*	910.92
Synnott, Mark. *The Third Pole*	796.522
Wilkinson, Toby A. H. *A World Beneath the Sands*	932
Wilson-Lee, Edward. ★*The Catalogue of Shipwrecked Books*	B

AUTHOR, TITLE, SERIES AND SUBJECT INDEX

LIFE STORIES — PEOPLE IN HISTORY — FAMOUS FAMILIES
- Andersen, Christopher P. *The Good Son* — B
- Borman, Tracy. *The Private Lives of the Tudors* — 920
- Brickell, Francesca Cartier. *The Cartiers* — B
- Brown, Tina. ★*The Palace Papers* — 920
- Byrne, Paula. *Kick* — B
- Coll, Steve. *The Bin Ladens* — 920
- Cooper, Anderson. *Vanderbilt* — 920
- Cordery, Stacy A. *Alice* — B
- Edwards, Anne. *Matriarch* — B
- Gillon, Steven M. *America's Reluctant Prince* — B
- Good, Cassandra A. *First Family* — 920
- Hibbert, Christopher. *The Borgias and Their Enemies* — 920
- Hibbert, Christopher. *The House of Medici* — 920
- Keefe, Patrick Radden. ★*Empire of Pain* — 338.7
- Larson, Kate Clifford. *Rosemary* — B
- Leamer, Laurence. *The Kennedy Men* — 920
- Leaming, Barbara. *Kick Kennedy* — B
- Logevall, Fredrik. ★*JFK* — B
- Lovell, Mary S. *The Sisters* — 920.72
- Mahoney, Richard D. *Sons & Brothers* — 920
- Mann, William J. *The Wars of the Roosevelts* — B
- Meyer, G. J. *The Borgias* — 920
- Meyer, G. J. *The Tudors* — 920
- Pawel, Miriam. *The Browns of California* — 920
- Penn, Thomas. *The Brothers York* — 942.04
- Peyser, Marc N. *Hissing Cousins* — B
- Rappaport, Helen. *The Romanov Sisters* — 920
- Sancton, Thomas. *The Bettencourt Affair* — B
- Sankovitch, Nina. *American Rebels* — 920
- Saxton, Martha. *The Widow Washington* — B
- Sebag-Montefiore, Simon. ★*The World* — 929.7
- Shirley, Craig. *Mary Ball Washington* — B
- Shriver, Timothy P. *Fully Alive* — 796.087
- Snyder, Timothy. *The Red Prince* — B
- Strathern, Paul. *The Borgias* — 945.06
- Strathern, Paul. *The Medici* — 945.5
- Tallis, Nicola. *Crown of Blood* — B
- Taraborrelli, J. Randy. *After Camelot* — B
- Taraborrelli, J. Randy. *Jackie, Janet & Lee* — 920
- Taraborrelli, J. Randy. *The Kennedy Heirs* — 920
- Trump, Mary L. *Too Much and Never Enough* — B
- Weir, Alison. *The Lost Tudor Princess* — B
- White, Gayle Jessup. *Reclamation* — B

LIFE STORIES — PEOPLE IN HISTORY — INDIGENOUS PEOPLES
- Brands, H. W. *Dreams of El Dorado* — 978
- Buford, Kate. *Native American Son* — B
- Burns, Mike. *The Only One Living to Tell* — 305.897
- Cozzens, Peter. *Tecumseh and the Prophet* — 920
- Drury, Bob. *The Heart of Everything That Is* — B
- Egan, Timothy. ★*Short Nights of the Shadow Catcher* — 770.92
- Gardner, Mark L. *The Earth Is All That Lasts* — 978.004
- Hensley, William L. Iggiagruk. *Fifty Miles from Tomorrow* — B
- Jackson, Joe. *Black Elk* — 978.004
- Maraniss, David. ★*Path Lit by Lightning* — B
- McMurtry, Larry. *Crazy Horse* — B
- Myers, Leah. *Thinning Blood* — B
- Nesteroff, Kliph. *We Had a Little Real Estate Problem* — 970.004
- Utley, Robert M. ★*Geronimo* — B
- Utley, Robert M. *Sitting Bull* — B
- Wagamese, Richard. *One Native Life* — B
- Warren, James A. *God, War, and Providence* — 974.5
- Wilbur, Matika. *Project 562* — 970.004

LIFE STORIES — PEOPLE IN HISTORY — PIONEERS
- Brands, H. W. *Dreams of El Dorado* — 978
- Drury, Bob. *Blood and Treasure* — B
- Inskeep, Steve. *Imperfect Union* — B
- McCullough, David G. *The Pioneers* — 920
- McDowell, Marta. *The World of Laura Ingalls Wilder* — 813
- Morgan, Robert. *Boone* — B
- Murphy, Andrew R. *William Penn* — B
- Wilder, Laura Ingalls. *Pioneer Girl* — B

LIFE STORIES — PEOPLE IN HISTORY — WITNESS TO HISTORY
- Barrett, Duncan. *GI Brides* — 920
- Chang, Jung. *Big Sister, Little Sister, Red Sister* — B
- Chang, Jung. ★*Wild Swans* — B
- Cheung, Karen. *The Impossible City* — 951.25
- Crasnianski, Tania. *The Children of Nazis* — 943.086
- Cumming, Laura. ★*The Vanishing Velazquez* — 759.6
- Delany, Sarah Louise. *Having Our Say* — B
- Demick, Barbara. ★*Nothing to Envy* — 920
- Eisen, Norman L. *The Last Palace* — 920
- Englund, Peter. *November 1942* — 940.53
- Favro, Terri. *Generation Robot* — 006.3
- Finkel, David. *An American Dreamer* — 975.8
- Forche, Carolyn. *What You Have Heard Is True* — B
- Fraser, Rebecca. *The Mayflower* — 974.4
- Gortemaker, Heike B. *Eva Braun* — B
- Graff, Garrett M. ★*The Only Plane in the Sky* — 973.931
- Hatzfeld, Jean. *Blood Papa* — 967.5710431
- Hill, David. *The Vapors* — 976.7
- Jahner, Harald. ★*Aftermath* — 943.087
- Kan, Karoline. *Under Red Skies* — B
- Martin, Rachel Louise. *A Most Tolerant Little Town* — 379.2
- Matzen, Robert. *Dutch Girl* — B
- McKay, Sinclair. *The Fire and the Darkness* — 940.54
- McKean, David. *Watching Darkness Fall* — 940.53
- McKeon, Kathy. *Jackie's Girl* — B
- Miller, Marla. *Betsy Ross and the Making of America* — B
- Milton, Giles. *Soldier, Sailor, Frogman, Spy, Airman, Gangster, Kill or Die* — 940.54
- Min, Anchee. *Red Azalea* — B
- O'Donnell, Svenja. *Inge's War* — 943.086
- Porter, Carolyn. *Marcel's Letters* — 940.54
- Sharlet, Jeff. ★*The Undertow* — 322
- Sorensen, Theodore C. *Counselor* — B

LIFE STORIES — PERSONAL GROWTH
- Baker, Billy. *We Need to Hang Out* — 177
- Bauermeister, Erica. *House Lessons* — B
- Beavan, Colin. *No Impact Man* — B
- Bertinelli, Valerie. *Enough Already* — B
- Bosker, Bianca. *Cork Dork* — 641.2
- Butcher, Amy. *Mothertrucker* — B
- Cardwell, Diane. *Rockaway* — B
- Cargle, Rachel Elizabeth. *A Renaissance of Our Own* — B
- Chapin, Sasha. *All the Wrong Moves* — 794.1092
- Cobbs-Leonard, Tasha. *Do It Anyway* — 241
- Coel, Michaela. ★*Misfits* — 158.2
- Coffin, Jaed. *Roughhouse Friday* — B
- Conyers, Jonathan. *I Wasn't Supposed to Be Here* — B
- Corrigan, Kelly. *Tell Me More* — 153.6
- Davis, Viola. ★*Finding Me* — B
- Day, John D. *The Longevity Plan* — 612.6
- DiGiulian, Sasha. *Take the Lead* — B
- Doyne, Maggie. *Between the Mountain and the Sky* — B
- Fogg, B. J. *Tiny Habits* — 158
- Foreman, Tom. *My Year of Running Dangerously* — B
- Fremont, Helen. *The Escape Artist* — B
- Friedman, Rachel. ★*And Then We Grew Up* — 305.24
- Gaines, Joanna. *The Stories We Tell* — B
- Garcia, Amanda Yates. *Initiated* — B
- Gardner, Chris. ★*Permission to Dream* — 158.1
- Gay, Ross. *The Book of (more) Delights* — 814
- Gerson, Merissa Nathan. *Forget Prayers, Bring Cake* — 155.9
- Gilbert, Elizabeth. *Eat, Pray, Love* — B
- Gopnik, Adam. *All That Happiness Is* — 158.1
- Greitens, Eric. *Resilience* — 155.2
- Heminsley, Alexandra. *Running Like a Girl* — B
- Hempel, Jessi. *The Family Outing* — B
- Isay, David. *Callings* — 920
- Jacobs, A. J. *The Puzzler* — 793.73
- Jacobs, A. J. ★*The Year of Living Constitutionally* — 342.73
- Jenkins, Jedidiah. *To Shake the Sleeping Self* — B
- Kaag, John J. *American Philosophy* — 191
- Kessler, Lauren. *Raising the Barre* — 792.8
- Lecrae. ★*I Am Restored* — B
- Levy, Deborah. *The Cost of Living* — B
- Lifford, Tina. *The Little Book of Big Lies* — 155.2
- Lima, Jamie Kern. *Believe It* — B
- Loh, Sandra Tsing. *The Madwoman and the Roomba* — B
- Mann, Jen. ★*Midlife Bites* — 305.244
- May, Katherine. *Enchantment* — 158.1
- Mayes, Frances. *Under the Tuscan Sun* — 945
- Nunn, Emily. *The Comfort Food Diaries* — 641.5973
- Obama, Michelle. ★*The Light We Carry* — B
- Orenstein, Peggy. *Unraveling* — B

PUBLIC LIBRARY CORE COLLECTION: NONFICTION
Twentieth Edition

Pennington, Emily. *Feral*	B
Pittard, Hannah. *We Are Too Many*	B
Pogrebin, Abigail. *My Jewish Year*	296.4
Powell, Julie. *Julie and Julia*	641.5
Power, Marianne. *Help Me!*	158.1
Prescod, Danielle. *Token Black Girl*	B
Preszler, Trent. *Little and Often*	B
Proulx, Annie. *Bird Cloud*	B
Reichl, Ruth. *My Kitchen Year*	641.5
Riess, Jana. *Flunking Sainthood*	248.4
Rubin, Gretchen Craft. ★*Life in Five Senses*	152.1
Ruhl, Sarah. *Smile*	B
Rusbridger, Alan. ★*Play It Again*	B
Rush, Charaia. *Courageously Soft*	234
Sale, Anna. ★*Let's Talk About Hard Things*	153.6
Sherman, Anna. *The Bells of Old Tokyo*	952
Smith, Freda Love. *I Quit Everything*	B
Spears, Britney. *The Woman in Me*	B
Stone, Lillian. ★*Everybody's Favorite*	814.6
Tomlinson, Tommy. *The Elephant in the Room*	B
Toussaint, Alex. ★*Activate Your Greatness*	158.1
Van Ness, Jonathan. *Love That Story*	791.4502
Vanderbilt, Tom. ★*Beginners*	646.7
Von Drehle, David. ★*The Book of Charlie*	B
Weiner, Eric. *Ben & Me*	B
Winfrey, Oprah. *What Happened to You?*	616.85
Young, Daniella Mestyanek. *Uncultured*	B

LIFE STORIES — POLITICS

Arnsdorf, Isaac. ★*Finish What We Started*	320.52
Bakewell, Sarah. *How to Live—Or—A Life of Montaigne*	B
Biden Owens, Valerie. *Growing up Biden*	B
Biden, Jill. *Where the Light Enters*	B
Boucheron, Patrick. *Machiavelli*	320.1092
Bradford, Sarah. *Lucrezia Borgia*	B
Brands, H. W. ★*Our First Civil War*	973.3
Burns, William J. *The Back Channel*	B
Chase, James. *Acheson*	B
Conason, Joe. *The Longest Con*	320.52
Daniels, Stormy. *Full Disclosure*	B
Darby, Seyward. ★*Sisters in Hate*	305.800973
Dorey-Stein, Beck. *From the Corner of the Oval*	B
Draper, Robert. *To Start a War*	956.7044
Ford, Christine Blasey. *One Way Back*	B
Fried, Stephen. *Rush*	B
Gage, Beverly. *G-Man*	B
Ganz, John. *When the Clock Broke*	320.52
Goodwin, Doris Kearns. ★*An Unfinished Love Story*	B
Guerrero, Jean. *Hatemonger*	B
Guillermoprieto, Alma. *Dancing with Cuba*	972.9106
Hill, Clint. *Five Presidents*	B
Hill, Clint. *Mrs. Kennedy and Me*	973.922092
Hoffman, David E. *Give Me Liberty*	B
Hutchinson, Cassidy. *Enough*	B
Katz, Catherine Grace. *The Daughters of Yalta*	920
Keenan, Cody. *Grace*	973.932
Lee, Sung-Yoon. *The Sister*	951.93
Litt, David. *Thanks, Obama*	B
May, Gary. *John Tyler*	B
Mazzeo, Tilar J. ★*Eliza Hamilton*	B
Morley, Jefferson. *Scorpions' Dance*	973.924
Obama, Michelle. ★*The Light We Carry*	B
Page, Susan. ★*The Matriarch*	B
Prose, Francine. *1974*	B
Psaki, Jen. *Say More*	B
Rhodes, Benjamin J. *The World as It Is*	973.932
Rothkopf, David J. *American Resistance*	973.933
Rubin, Robert Edward. *The Yellow Pad*	658.4
Sebag-Montefiore, Simon. ★*The World*	929.7
Sorensen, Theodore C. *Counselor*	B
Stevens, Stuart. *The Conspiracy to End America*	324.2734
Strauss, Barry S. *The Death of Caesar*	937
Sullivan, Rosemary. *Stalin's Daughter*	B
Taraborrelli, J. Randy. ★*Jackie*	B
Tumulty, Karen. *The Triumph of Nancy Reagan*	B
Yaffa, Joshua. *Between Two Fires*	920

LIFE STORIES — POLITICS — ACTIVISTS AND REFORMERS

Ackerman, Diane. ★*The Zookeeper's Wife*	940.53
Ai, Weiwei. *Zodiac*	741.5

Alekhina, Mariija. *Riot Days*	B
Alinizhad, Masih. *The Wind in My Hair*	B
Ambroz, David. *A Place Called Home*	B
Anand, Anita. *The Patient Assassin*	B
Anderson, Jon Lee. *Che Guevara*	B
Ayers, Edward L. *American Visions*	973.5
Baime, A. J. *White Lies*	B
Barkan, Ady. *Eyes to the Wind*	B
Bell, Madison Smartt. *Toussaint Louverture*	B
Bell-Scott, Patricia. *The Firebrand and the First Lady*	920
Berry, Mary Frances. *My Face Is Black Is True*	B
Blain, Keisha N. *Until I Am Free*	B
Blight, David W. ★*Frederick Douglass*	B
Bono. ★*Surrender*	B
Brand, Christo. *Mandela*	B
Brands, H. W. ★*The Zealot and the Emancipator*	920
Brazile, Donna. *For Colored Girls Who Have Considered Politics*	328.73
Burke, Tarana. ★*Unbound*	B
Burton, Susan. *Becoming Ms. Burton*	B
Cervini, Eric. *The Deviant's War*	B
Chee, Alexander. ★*How to Write an Autobiographical Novel*	B
Cleaver, Eldridge. *Soul on Ice*	B
Clinton, Catherine. *Harriet Tubman*	B
De Stefano, Cristina. *The Child Is the Teacher*	B
Dennis, David J., Jr. *The Movement Made Us*	B
DiFranco, Ani. *No Walls and the Recurring Dream*	782.42164
Dilbeck, D. H. *Frederick Douglass*	B
Dogon, Mondiant. *Those We Throw Away Are Diamonds*	B
Donner, Rebecca. *All the Frequent Troubles of Our Days*	943
Douglass, Frederick. *My Bondage and My Freedom*	B
Doyne, Maggie. *Between the Mountain and the Sky*	B
Duberman, Martin B. *Andrea Dworkin*	B
Duberman, Martin B. *Howard Zinn*	B
Dunbar, Erica Armstrong. ★*She Came to Slay*	B
Edstrom, Erik. *Un-American*	B
Egan, Timothy. ★*The Immortal Irishman*	B
Eltahawy, Mona. *The Seven Necessary Sins for Women and Girls*	305.42
Fowlds, Grant. *Saving the Last Rhinos*	599.66
Gandhi. *An Autobiography*	B
Garza, Alicia. *The Purpose of Power*	303.48
Giddings, Paula. *Ida*	B
Ginzberg, Lori D. *Elizabeth Cady Stanton*	B
Goldfarb, Bruce. ★*18 Tiny Deaths*	B
Goodall, Jane. ★*The Book of Hope*	128
Greenidge, Kerri. ★*The Grimkes*	973.5
Gregory, Dick. ★*The Essential Dick Gregory*	818
Griffith, Elisabeth. *Formidable*	305.42
Guha, Ramachandra. *Gandhi Before India*	B
Guha, Ramachandra. *Gandhi*	B
Guha, Ramachandra. *Rebels Against the Raj*	954.03
Hamlin, Kimberly A. *Free Thinker*	B
Hanna-Attisha, Mona. *What the Eyes Don't See*	615.9
Harlan, Louis R. *Booker T. Washington*	B
Harrison, Scott. *Thirst*	B
Hennessy, Kate. *Dorothy Day*	B
Heumann, Judith E. *Being Heumann*	B
Hochschild, Adam. *Rebel Cinderella*	B
Holley, Santi Elijah. *An Amerikan Family*	920
Horwitz, Tony. ★*Midnight Rising*	973.7
Humez, Jean McMahon. *Harriet Tubman*	B
Jones, Brenda. *Alexandria Ocasio-Cortez*	B
Jones, Brenda. *Maxine Waters*	B
King, Coretta Scott. ★*My Life, My Love, My Legacy*	B
Larson, Kate Clifford. *Bound for the Promised Land*	B
Lekas Miller, Anna. *Love Across Borders*	323.6
Leng'ete, Nice. *The Girls in the Wild Fig Tree*	B
Lewis, John. ★*March; Book One*	741.5
Lewis, John. ★*March; Book Three*	741.5
Lewis, John. ★*March; Book Two*	741.5
Maathai, Wangari. *Unbowed*	B
Mallory, Tamika D. *State of Emergency*	305.896
Mandela, Nelson. *Dare Not Linger*	B
Mandela, Nelson. ★*Long Walk to Freedom*	B
Mandela, Nelson. *Mandela*	B
Mandela, Nelson. *The Prison Letters of Nelson Mandela*	968.06092
McAnulty, Dara. *Diary of a Young Naturalist*	508.092
McCloskey, Jim. *When Truth Is All You Have*	B
McCubbin, Lisa. *Betty Ford*	B

AUTHOR, TITLE, SERIES AND SUBJECT INDEX

McNamara, Eileen. ★*Eunice*	B
Miller, Char. *Gifford Pinchot and the Making of Modern Environmentalism*	B
Moore, Kate. ★*The Woman They Could Not Silence*	B
Morris, Edmund. ★*The Rise of Theodore Roosevelt*	B
Muir, John. *Nature Writings*	B
Norgren, Jill. *Belva Lockwood*	B
Nyamayaro, Elizabeth. *I Am a Girl from Africa*	B
O'Brien, Keith. *Paradise Falls*	363.738
O'Connor, Garry. *Ian McKellen*	B
Ohler, Norman. *The Bohemians*	940.53
Okporo, Edafe. *Asylum*	B
Pablo Cruz, Rosayra. *The Book of Rosy*	B
Painter, Nell Irvin. ★*Sojourner Truth*	B
Pawel, Miriam. *The Crusades of Cesar Chavez*	B
Paxson, Margaret. *The Plateau*	362.87
Perry, Imani. *Looking for Lorraine*	B
Peterson, Marlon. *Bird Uncaged*	B
Pryce, Jessica. ★*Broken*	362.7
Purnell, Derecka. *Becoming Abolitionists*	363.20973
Ransby, Barbara. *Eslanda*	B
Reid, Joy-Ann Lomena. ★*Medgar and Myrlie*	920
Reynolds, David S. *John Brown, Abolitionist*	B
Richards, Cecile. *Make Trouble*	B
Roberts, Randy. *Blood Brothers*	920
Rosenberg, Rosalind. ★*Jane Crow*	B
Rosenbloom, Joseph. *Redemption*	B
Rudd, Mark. *Underground*	378.1
Salaam, Yusef. *Better, Not Bitter*	B
Sarsour, Linda. *We Are Not Here to Be Bystanders*	B
Schiavi, Michael R. *Celluloid Activist*	B
Sen, Amartya. *Home in the World*	B
Shane, Scott. ★*Flee North*	973.7
Shatz, Adam. *The Rebel's Clinic*	965
Shields, Charles J. *Lorraine Hansberry*	B
Sjunneson, Elsa. *Being Seen*	362.4
Smith, David James. *Young Mandela*	B
Sokol, Jason. *The Heavens Might Crack*	323.092
Stauffer, John. *Picturing Fredrick Douglass*	B
Steinberg, Jonny. *Winnie and Nelson*	920
Steinem, Gloria. *My Life on the Road*	B
Tamimi, Ahed. ★*They Called Me a Lioness*	B
Theoharis, Jeanne. *The Rebellious Life of Mrs. Rosa Parks*	B
Thomas, Franklin A. *An Unplanned Life*	B
Tolokonnikova, Nadezhda. *Rules for Rulebreakers*	782.42166
Van Zandt, Steve. *Unrequited Infatuations*	B
Vargas, Jose Antonio. *Dear America*	B
Vella, Christina. *George Washington Carver*	B
Warren, James A. *God, War, and Providence*	974.5
Weigel, Alicia Roth. *Inverse Cowgirl*	B
West, Cornel. *Black Prophetic Fire*	920
Wexler, Stuart. *Killing King*	323.092
Wickenden, Dorothy. *The Agitators*	920
Williams, Juan. *Thurgood Marshall*	B
Willis, Raquel. *The Risk It Takes to Bloom*	B
Windsor, Edie. *A Wild and Precious Life*	B
Wong, Alice. ★*Year of the Tiger*	B
Worley, Jennifer. *Neon Girls*	792.7
Worster, Donald. *A Passion for Nature the Life of John Muir*	B
Yousafzai, Ziauddin. *Let Her Fly*	B

LIFE STORIES — POLITICS — ACTIVISTS AND REFORMERS — CIVIL RIGHTS LEADERS

Arsenault, Raymond. *John Lewis*	B
Bond, Julian. ★*Julian Bond's Time to Teach*	323.0975
Branch, Taylor. ★*At Canaan's Edge*	323.1196
Branch, Taylor. *Parting the Waters*	973
Branch, Taylor. ★*Pillar of Fire*	323.1
Brooks, Maegan Parker. *Fannie Lou Hamer*	B
Eig, Jonathan. ★*King*	B
Ford, Tanisha C. *Our Secret Society*	B
Greenidge, Kerri. *Black Radical*	B
Honey, Michael K. *To the Promised Land*	323
Jackson, Troy. *Becoming King*	B
Joseph, Peniel E. *The Sword and the Shield*	B
Kennedy, Kostya. *True*	B
King, Martin Luther. *The Autobiography of Martin Luther King, Jr.*	B
Kix, Paul. ★*You Have to Be Prepared to Die Before You Can Begin to Live*	976.1
Larson, Kate Clifford. *Walk with Me*	B
Levine, Robert S. ★*The Failed Promise*	973.8
Levingston, Steven. *Kennedy and King*	920
Lewis, David L. ★*W.E.B. Du Bois*	B
Lewis, John. *Carry On*	328.73
Lewis, John. *Walking with the Wind*	B
Malcolm X. ★*The Autobiography of Malcolm X*	B
Marable, Manning. ★*Malcolm X*	B
Meacham, Jon. *His Truth Is Marching On*	B
Payne, Les. ★*The Dead Are Arising*	B
Perry, Bruce. *Malcolm*	B
Person, Charles. *Buses Are a Comin'*	B
Roundtree, Dovey Johnson. ★*Mighty Justice*	B
Sharpton, Al. *Rise Up*	973.933
Swift, Earl. *Hell Put to Shame*	364.15
Whitaker, Mark. ★*Saying It Loud*	973.923
Zack, Ian. *Odetta*	B

LIFE STORIES — POLITICS — POLITICAL PRISONERS

Mandela, Nelson. *In His Own Words*	B
Matar, Hisham. *The Return*	B
Nemat, Marina. *Prisoner of Tehran*	B
Sallah, Michael. *The Yankee Comandante*	972.91

LIFE STORIES — POLITICS — POLITICIANS

Abrams, Dan. *Theodore Roosevelt for the Defense*	345.73
Albright, Madeleine Korbel. *Hell and Other Destinations*	B
Allen, Jonathan. *Lucky*	324.973
Allgor, Catherine. *A Perfect Union*	B
Alter, Jonathan. *His Very Best*	B
Andersen, Christopher P. *The Good Son*	B
Andrews-Dyer, Helena. *Reclaiming Her Time*	B
Anthony, Carl Sferrazza. *Camera Girl*	B
Anthony, Carl Sferrazza. *Nellie Taft*	B
Arana, Marie. *Bolivar*	B
Arsenault, Raymond. *John Lewis*	B
Avlon, John P. *Washington's Farewell*	973.4
Baier, Bret. *To Rescue the Constitution*	973.4
Baime, A. J. *The Accidental President*	B
Baker, Peter. *The Man Who Ran Washington*	B
Ball, Molly. ★*Pelosi*	B
Berg, A. Scott. ★*Wilson*	B
Bird, Kai. *The Outlier*	973.926
Blair, Tony. *A Journey*	B
Blumenthal, Sidney. ★*All the Powers of Earth*	B
Blumenthal, Sidney. *A Self-Made Man*	B
Blumenthal, Sidney. *Wrestling with His Angel*	B
Boles, John B. *Jefferson*	B
Bordewich, Fergus M. *Congress at War*	324.2734
Borman, Tracy. *Thomas Cromwell*	B
Borneman, Walter R. *Polk*	B
Brady, Patricia. *Martha Washington*	B
Branch, Taylor. *The Clinton Tapes*	973.929
Brand, Christo. *Mandela*	B
Brands, H. W. ★*Andrew Jackson, His Life and Times*	B
Brands, H. W. *The First American*	B
Brands, H. W. ★*Founding Partisans*	973.3
Brands, H. W. ★*The Man Who Saved the Union*	B
Brands, H. W. *Reagan*	B
Brands, H. W. *Traitor to His Class*	B
Brands, H. W. *Woodrow Wilson*	B
Brands, H. W. ★*The Zealot and the Emancipator*	920
Brazile, Donna. *For Colored Girls Who Have Considered Politics*	328.73
Bremer, Francis J. *John Winthrop*	B
Brinkley, Alan. *John F. Kennedy*	B
Brinkley, Douglas. *The Wilderness Warrior*	B
Broers, Michael. *Napoleon*	B
Broers, Michael. *Napoleon*	944.05
Broers, Michael. *Napoleon*	B
Brower, Kate Andersen. *First in Line*	920
Brower, Kate Andersen. *First Women*	920
Bunting, Josiah. *Ulysses S. Grant*	B
Burkett, Elinor. *Golda*	B
Burlingame, Michael. *Abraham Lincoln*	B
Burns, Eric. *Someone to Watch Over Me*	973.917092
Burstein, Andrew. *Madison and Jefferson*	973.4
Bush, George W. *41*	B
Bush, George W. *Decision Points*	B
Buttigieg, Pete. *Shortest Way Home*	B
Calloway, Colin G. *The Indian World of George Washington*	323.1197
Caro, Robert A. ★*The Passage of Power*	B

PUBLIC LIBRARY CORE COLLECTION: NONFICTION
Twentieth Edition

Carter, Jimmy. *A Full Life*	B
Carter, Jimmy. *An Hour Before Daylight*	B
Carter, Jimmy. *Keeping Faith*	B
Carter, Jimmy. *Sharing Good Times*	973.926
Carter, Jimmy. *White House Diary*	973.926
Carwardine, Richard. *Lincoln*	B
Castro, Fidel. *Fidel Castro*	B
Chang, Jung. *Mao*	B
Cheney, Liz. *Oath and Honor*	328.73
Cheney, Lynne V. *James Madison*	B
Chernow, Ron. ★*Alexander Hamilton*	B
Chernow, Ron. *Washington*	B
Chozick, Amy. *Chasing Hillary*	B
Christie, Chris. *Let Me Finish*	B
Clinton, Bill. *My Life*	B
Clinton, Hillary Rodham. *Living History*	B
Clinton, Hillary Rodham. *What Happened*	328.73
Coe, Alexis. ★*You Never Forget Your First*	B
Cohen, Andrew. *Two Days in June*	973.922
Cohen, Jared. *Life After Power*	973.09
Collins, Gail. *William Henry Harrison*	B
Coltman, Leycester. *The Real Fidel Castro*	B
Cook, Blanche Wiesen. *Eleanor Roosevelt; Volume 2*	B
Cook, Blanche Wiesen. ★*Eleanor Roosevelt; Volume 3*	B
Cook, Jane Hampton. *American Phoenix*	973.5
Cooper, Helene. *Madame President*	966.62
Cooper, John Milton. *Woodrow Wilson*	B
Cummings, Elijah. ★*We're Better Than This*	B
Dallek, Robert. ★*Franklin D. Roosevelt*	B
Dallek, Robert. *Let Every Nation Know*	B
Dallek, Robert. *An Unfinished Life*	B
Donald, Aida DiPace. *Citizen Soldier*	B
Donald, David Herbert. *Lincoln*	B
Duckworth, Tammy. *Every Day Is a Gift*	B
Duiker, William J. *Ho Chi Minh*	B
Edwards, Anne. *Matriarch*	B
Eizenstat, Stuart. ★*President Carter*	B
Ellis, Joseph J. ★*American Dialogue*	973.3
Ellis, Joseph J. *American Sphinx*	973.4
Ellis, Joseph J. ★*His Excellency*	B
Emanuel, Rahm. *The Nation City*	352.23
Erickson, Carolly. *Great Catherine*	B
Everitt, Anthony. *Cicero*	B
Everitt, Anthony. *Hadrian and the Triumph of Rome*	B
Farrell, John A. ★*Richard Nixon*	B
Farrell, John A. *Ted Kennedy*	B
Fehrman, Craig. *Author in Chief*	920
Feldman, Noah. *The Three Lives of James Madison*	B
Ferguson, Niall. *Kissinger*	973.924
Finkelman, Paul. *Millard Fillmore*	B
Fischer, Paul. *A Kim Jong-Il Production*	791.43
Flexner, James Thomas. *George Washington and the New Nation, 1783-1793*	973.4
Flexner, James Thomas. *George Washington*	B
Frank, Barney. *Frank*	B
Frank, Jeffrey. *The Trials of Harry S. Truman*	973.918
Franklin, Benjamin. ★*The Autobiography of Benjamin Franklin*	B
Franklin, Benjamin. *The Compleated Autobiography*	B
Gabler, Neal. ★*Against the Wind*	B
Gabler, Neal. *Catching the Wind*	B
Gallego, Ruben. *They Called Us*	956.7044
Garrow, David J. *Rising Star*	B
Gewen, Barry. ★*The Inevitability of Tragedy*	B
Gillette, Michael L. *Lady Bird Johnson*	B
Goldsworthy, Adrian Keith. ★*Caesar*	B
Goodwin, Doris Kearns. ★*Leadership in Turbulent Times*	973.09
Goodwin, Doris Kearns. *No Ordinary Time*	920
Goodyear, C. W. *President Garfield*	B
Gordon-Reed, Annette. *Andrew Johnson*	B
Gordon-Reed, Annette. ★*Most Blessed of the Patriarchs*	973.4
Graff, Henry F. *Grover Cleveland*	B
Grandin, Greg. *Kissinger's Shadow*	B
Grant, James. ★*John Adams*	B
Grant, Ulysses S. ★*The Annotated Memoirs of Ulysses S. Grant*	B
Greenberg, Amy S. *Lady First*	B
Groom, Winston. *The Allies*	940.5309
Groom, Winston. *The Patriots*	920
Gutzman, Kevin R. C. *The Jeffersonians*	973.5
Hager, Jenna Bush. *Sisters First*	B
Hennessey, Susan. *Unmaking the Presidency*	973.933
Hett, Benjamin Carter. *The Death of Democracy*	943.085
Hibbert, Christopher. *Edward VII*	B
Hill, Katie. *She Will Rise*	305.42
Hirono, Mazie. *Heart of Fire*	B
Hitchcock, William I. *The Age of Eisenhower*	973.921092
Hitchens, Christopher. *Thomas Jefferson*	B
Hitler, Adolf. *Mein Kampf*	B
Holton, Woody. *Abigail Adams*	B
Holzer, Harold. *Brought Forth on This Continent*	973.7
Holzer, Harold. *A Just and Generous Nation*	973.7092
Horn, Jonathan. *Washington's End*	B
Inskeep, Steve. *Imperfect Union*	B
Isaacson, Walter. ★*Benjamin Franklin*	B
Isenberg, Nancy. *The Problem of Democracy*	973.4
Jackson, Julian. *De Gaulle*	B
Jarrett, Valerie. *Finding My Voice*	B
Jayapal, Pramila. *Use the Power You Have*	B
Johnson, Paul. *Churchill*	B
Johnson, Paul. *Eisenhower*	B
Johnson, Paul. *Napoleon*	B
Jones, Brenda. *Alexandria Ocasio-Cortez*	B
Jones, Brenda. *Maxine Waters*	B
Jordan, Mary. *The Art of Her Deal*	B
Kaplan, Fred. *John Quincy Adams*	B
Katz, David. *Barack Before Obama*	B
Kennedy, John F. *Profiles in Courage*	920
Kerry, John. *Every Day Is Extra*	B
Kershaw, Ian. *Hitler*	B
Kershaw, Ian. *Hitler*	B
Khlevniuk, Oleg V. *Stalin*	B
King, David. *The Trial of Adolf Hitler*	345.43
Kirtzman, Andrew. *Giuliani*	B
Kissinger, Henry. *Leadership*	303.3
Klagsbrun, Francine. *Lioness*	B
Kotkin, Stephen. *Stalin*	B
Kotkin, Stephen. *Stalin*	B
Kranish, Michael. *Trump Revealed*	B
Larson, Edward J. *The Return of George Washington*	B
Larson, Erik. ★*The Demon of Unrest*	973.7
Larson, Erik. *In the Garden of Beasts*	B
Larson, Erik. ★*The Splendid and the Vile*	940.54
Leamer, Laurence. *The Kennedy Men*	920
Leaming, Barbara. *Jacqueline Bouvier Kennedy Onassis*	B
Leaming, Barbara. *Mrs. Kennedy*	B
Lever, Evelyne. *Marie Antoinette*	B
Levine, Bruce C. *Thaddeus Stevens*	B
Levingston, Steven. *Kennedy and King*	920
Lewis, John. *Carry On*	328.73
Lewis, John. ★*Run; Book One*	741.5
Lewis, John. *Walking with the Wind*	B
Logevall, Fredrik. ★*JFK*	B
Longerich, Peter. *Goebbels*	B
Lozada, Carlos. *The Washington Book*	320
MacCulloch, Diarmaid. *Thomas Cromwell*	B
Maddow, Rachel. *Bag Man*	B
Mahoney, Richard D. *Sons & Brothers*	920
Manchester, William. *The Last Lion, Winston Spencer Churchill.*	B
Manchester, William. *The Last Lion, Winston Spencer Churchill.*	B
Manchester, William. *The Last Lion, Winston Spencer Churchill.*	B
Mandela, Nelson. *Dare Not Linger*	B
Mandela, Nelson. ★*Long Walk to Freedom*	B
Mandela, Nelson. *Mandela*	B
Maraniss, David. ★*Barack Obama*	B
Marozzi, Justin. *Tamerlane*	950.2
Martini, Adrienne. *Somebody's Gotta Do It*	B
Marton, Kati. ★*The Chancellor*	B
Marvel, William. *Lincoln's Autocrat*	B
Matthews, Christopher. *Bobby Kennedy*	B
May, Gary. *John Tyler*	B
May, Gregory. *A Madman's Will*	973.5
McCarten, Anthony. *Darkest Hour*	941.084
McCullough, David G. ★*John Adams*	B
McCullough, David G. *Mornings on Horseback*	B
McCullough, David G. *Truman*	B
McDonough, Frank. *The Hitler Years*	943.086
McGinty, Brian. *Lincoln's Greatest Case*	346.7303

AUTHOR, TITLE, SERIES AND SUBJECT INDEX

McGrath, Tim. *James Monroe*	B
McKean, David. *Suspected of Independence*	B
McKean, David. *Watching Darkness Fall*	940.53
McMurtry, Larry. *Crazy Horse*	B
McPhee, Peter. *Robespierre*	B
McPherson, James M. ★*Abraham Lincoln*	B
Meacham, Jon. ★*American Lion*	B
Meacham, Jon. ★*And There Was Light*	B
Meacham, Jon. ★*Destiny and Power*	B
Meacham, Jon. *His Truth Is Marching On*	B
Meacham, Jon. ★*Thomas Jefferson*	B
Merry, Robert W. *A Country of Vast Designs*	B
Merry, Robert W. *President McKinley*	B
Michaelis, David. ★*Eleanor*	973.917
Millard, Candice. *Destiny of the Republic*	973.8
Millard, Candice. ★*Hero of the Empire*	968.04
Moore, Charles. *Margaret Thatcher*	941.085
Morris, Edmund. ★*Colonel Roosevelt*	B
Morris, Edmund. ★*The Rise of Theodore Roosevelt*	B
Morris, Edmund. ★*Theodore Rex*	973.911
Myers, Steven Lee. *The New Tsar*	B
Nasaw, David. ★*The Patriarch*	B
Neu, Charles E. *Colonel House*	B
O'Brien, Phillips Payson. *The Second Most Powerful Man in the World*	B
O'Toole, Patricia. *The Moralist*	B
Obama, Barack. ★*Dreams from My Father*	B
Obama, Barack. ★*A Promised Land*	B
Obama, Michelle. ★*Becoming*	B
Onassis, Jacqueline Kennedy. *Historic Conversations on Life with John F. Kennedy*	B
Osnos, Evan. *Joe Biden*	B
Packer, George. *Our Man*	B
Pak, Jung H. *Becoming Kim Jong Un*	B
Pakula, Hannah. *The Last Empress*	B
Pantsov, Alexander. *Mao*	B
Paradis, Michel. *The Light of Battle*	940.54
Paul, Joel R. *Indivisible*	973.5
Peters, Charles. *Lyndon B. Johnson*	B
Peyser, Marc N. *Hissing Cousins*	B
Pfeffer, Anshel. *Bibi*	B
Prud'homme, Alex. ★*Dinner with the President*	973
Pryor, Elizabeth Brown. *Six Encounters with Lincoln*	973.7092
Purnell, Sonia. *Clementine*	B
Quinn, Susan. *Eleanor and Hick*	B
Radzinskii, Edvard. *Stalin*	947.084
Reagan, Ronald. *Reagan*	B
Rees, Laurence. *Hitler and Stalin*	940.53
Remnick, David. *The Bridge*	B
Reynolds, David S. ★*Abe*	B
Rice, Condoleezza. *Extraordinary, Ordinary People*	B
Rice, Condoleezza. *No Higher Honor*	B
Ricks, Thomas E. *Churchill and Orwell*	920
Ricks, Thomas E. *First Principles*	973.09
Ridley, Jane. *The Heir Apparent*	B
Risen, James. ★*The Last Honest Man*	973.92
Roberts, Andrew. ★*Churchill*	B
Roberts, Andrew. *Leadership in War*	920
Roberts, Andrew. ★*Napoleon*	B
Rogers, Katie. ★*American Woman*	973.09
Roll, David L. *Ascent to Power*	973.918
Rumsfeld, Donald. *When the Center Held*	973.925092
Sandburg, Carl. *Abraham Lincoln*	B
Sankovitch, Nina. *American Rebels*	920
Sasakamoose, Fred. *Call Me Indian*	B
Sebag-Montefiore, Simon. *Stalin*	B
Sebag-Montefiore, Simon. *Young Stalin*	B
Sebestyen, Victor. *Lenin*	B
Sellers, Bakari. *My Vanishing Country*	B
Senik, Troy. *A Man of Iron*	B
Service, Robert. *Lenin—A Biography*	B
Shlaes, Amity. *Coolidge*	B
Short, Philip. *Putin*	B
Shuster, Simon. ★*The Showman*	B
Slevin, Peter. *Michelle Obama*	B
Smith, Jean Edward. *Bush*	973.931
Smith, Richard Norton. *On His Own Terms*	973.925092
Smith, Richard Norton. *An Ordinary Man*	B
Smith, Sally Bedell. *Elizabeth the Queen*	B
Southon, Emma. *Agrippina*	B
Souza, Pete. *Obama*	973.932
Souza, Pete. *Shade*	973.932
Souza, Pete. *The West Wing and Beyond*	917.53
Spitz, Bob. ★*Reagan*	B
Stahr, Walter. *Seward*	B
Stahr, Walter. ★*Stanton*	B
Stark, Peter. *Young Washington*	B
Steinberg, Jonathan. *Bismarck*	B
Steinberg, Jonny. *Winnie and Nelson*	920
Stern, Jessica. *My War Criminal*	341.6
Stewart, David O. *George Washington*	973.4
Stewart, David O. *Madison's Gift*	B
Stewart, Rory. *The Prince of the Marshes*	956.7044
Suny, Ronald Grigor. *Stalin*	B
Swarns, Rachel L. ★*American Tapestry*	B
Sweig, Julia. *Lady Bird Johnson*	B
Taubman, William. *Gorbachev*	B
Taubman, William. *Khrushchev*	B
Taylor, Jay. *The Generalissimo*	B
Tester, Jon. *Grounded*	B
Thomas, Evan. *Being Nixon*	B
Thomas, Evan. ★*Robert Kennedy*	B
Thomas, Louisa. *Louisa*	B
Traub, James. *John Quincy Adams*	B
Trump, Mary L. *Too Much and Never Enough*	B
Tubbs, Michael. *The Deeper the Roots*	B
Tye, Larry. ★*Bobby Kennedy*	B
Tye, Larry. ★*Demagogue*	B
Ullrich, Volker. *Hitler*	B
Ullrich, Volker. *Hitler*	B
Unger, Harlow G. *First Founding Father*	B
Unger, Harlow G. *The Last Founding Father*	B
Vargas Llosa, Mario. *The Call of the Tribe*	868
Vogel, Ezra F. *Deng Xlaoping and the Transformation of China*	B
Ward, Geoffrey C. ★*The Roosevelts*	B
Weber, Thomas. *Becoming Hitler*	B
Weiner, Tim. *One Man Against the World*	B
White, Ronald C. *A. Lincoln*	B
White, Ronald C. *Lincoln in Private*	B
White, Ronald C. *On Great Fields*	B
Whyte, Kenneth. *Hoover*	B
Widmer, Edward L. *Lincoln on the Verge*	B
Widmer, Edward L. *Martin Van Buren*	B
Wills, Garry. *James Madison*	B
Wong, Chun Han. *Party of One*	951.06
Wood, Gordon S. *Friends Divided*	920
Yovanovitch, Marie. *Lessons from the Edge*	973.933
Zamoyski, Adam. *Napoleon*	B
Zeitz, Joshua. *Building the Great Society*	973.923

LIFE STORIES — POLITICS — ROYALTY

Baird, Julia. ★*Victoria the Queen*	B
Beard, Mary. ★*Emperor of Rome*	937
Bix, Herbert P. *Hirohito and the Making of Modern Japan*	B
Blanning, T. C. W. *Frederick the Great*	B
Bordo, Susan. *The Creation of Anne Boleyn*	942.05
Borman, Tracy. *Anne Boleyn and Elizabeth I*	920
Borman, Tracy. *Crown & Sceptre*	941
Borman, Tracy. *Elizabeth's Women*	B
Borman, Tracy. *Henry VIII and the Men Who Made Him*	942.05
Borman, Tracy. *The Private Lives of the Tudors*	920
Brown, Craig. *Ninety-Nine Glimpses of Princess Margaret*	B
Brown, Tina. *The Diana Chronicles*	B
Brown, Tina. ★*The Palace Papers*	920
Cadbury, Deborah. *Princes at War*	920
Cadbury, Deborah. *Queen Victoria's Matchmaking*	941.081
Chang, Jung. *Empress Dowager Cixi*	B
Charter, David. *Royal Audience*	941.085
Cooney, Kara. *When Women Ruled the World*	920
Cooper, Andrew Scott. *The Fall of Heaven*	B
Darnton, Robert. *The Revolutionary Temper*	944
Downey, Kirstin. *Isabella*	B
Edwards, Anne. *Matriarch*	B
Foreman, Amanda. *Georgiana, Duchess of Devonshire*	B
Fraser, Antonia. *Love and Louis XIV*	B
Fraser, Antonia. *Marie Antoinette*	B
Fraser, Antonia. *Mary, Queen of Scots*	B
Fraser, Antonia. ★*The Wives of Henry VIII*	942.05

PUBLIC LIBRARY CORE COLLECTION: NONFICTION
Twentieth Edition

Glenconner, Anne. ★*Lady in Waiting*	B
Goldstone, Nancy Bazelon. *Daughters of the Winter Queen*	920
Goldstone, Nancy Bazelon. *In the Shadow of the Empress*	920
Goldstone, Nancy Bazelon. *The Rival Queens*	944
Goldsworthy, Adrian Keith. *Augustus*	B
Gristwood, Sarah. *The Tudors in Love*	941.05
Guy, John. *Hunting the Falcon*	B
Hadlow, Janice. *A Royal Experiment*	B
Hardman, Robert. *Queen of Our Times*	B
Hardman, Robert. *Queen of the World*	B
Harry. ★*Spare*	B
Hawksley, Lucinda. *Queen Victoria's Mysterious Daughter*	B
Hibbert, Christopher. *Edward VII*	B
Holmes, Elizabeth. *HRH*	941.085
Hope, Bradley. *Blood and Oil*	B
Hubbard, Ben (Journalist). *Mbs*	B
Jones, Michael K. *The Black Prince*	B
Keene, Donald. *Emperor of Japan*	952.03
King, Greg. *Twilight of Empire*	943.6
Lal, Ruby. *Empress*	B
Larman, Alexander. ★*Power and Glory*	941.085
Larman, Alexander. *The Windsors at War*	940.53
Lovell, Mary S. *Bess of Hardwick*	B
Lownie, Andrew. *Traitor King*	920
Mansel, Philip. *King of the World*	B
Massie, Robert K. *Catherine the Great*	B
Meyer, G. J. *The Tudors*	920
Morris, Marc. *A Great and Terrible King*	B
Morris, Marc. *King John*	942.033
Morton, Andrew. *Diana*	B
Morton, Andrew. *Wallis in Love*	B
Noor. *Leap of Faith*	B
Paranque, Estelle. *Blood, Fire & Gold*	920
Penn, Thomas. *The Brothers York*	942.04
Pitts, Mike. *Digging for Richard III*	942.046
Porter, Linda. *Katherine the Queen*	B
Puhak, Shelley. *The Dark Queens*	944
Rappaport, Helen. *The Romanov Sisters*	920
Ridley, Jane. *George V*	B
Ridley, Jane. *The Heir Apparent*	B
Roberts, Andrew. *The Last King of America*	B
Russell, Gareth. *Young and Damned and Fair*	B
Schiff, Stacy. ★*Cleopatra*	B
Shawcross, William. *The Queen Mother*	B
Smith, Sally Bedell. *Elizabeth the Queen*	B
Smith, Sally Bedell. *George VI and Elizabeth*	920
Smith, Sally Bedell. *Prince Charles*	B
Snyder, Timothy. *The Red Prince*	B
Spoto, Donald. *High Society*	B
Starkey, David. *Six Wives*	942.05
Strauss, Barry S. *Ten Caesars*	937
Tallis, Nicola. *Crown of Blood*	B
Tallis, Nicola. *Uncrowned Queen*	B
Weir, Alison. *Eleanor of Aquitaine*	B
Weir, Alison. *Henry VIII*	B
Weir, Alison. *The Lady in the Tower*	B
Weir, Alison. *The Life of Elizabeth I*	B
Weir, Alison. *Queens of the Age of Chivalry*	920
Williams, Kate. *Ambition and Desire*	B
Wilson, A. N. *Victoria*	B
Worsley, Lucy. *Queen Victoria*	B

LIFE STORIES — RELATIONSHIPS

Albom, Mitch. *Tuesdays with Morrie*	B
Bradbury, Ray. ★*Remembrance*	813
Brosh, Allie. *Hyperbole and a Half*	741.5
Brosh, Allie. ★*Solutions and Other Problems*	741.5
Brown, Brene. *The Gifts of Imperfection*	158
Carcaterra, Lorenzo. *Three Dreamers*	B
Charter, David. *Royal Audience*	941.085
Conyers, Jonathan. *I Wasn't Supposed to Be Here*	B
Cumming, Alan. *Baggage*	B
Dietrich, Sean. *You Are My Sunshine*	B
Dochartaigh, Kerri ni. *Cacophony of Bone*	B
Doyle, Glennon. *Untamed*	B
Edelman, Marian Wright. *Lanterns*	362.7
Ephron, Delia. *Left on Tenth*	B
Etheridge, Melissa. *Talking to My Angels*	B
Felix, Camonghne. *Dyscalculia*	B
Fennelly, Beth Ann. *Heating & Cooling*	B
Foo, Stephanie. ★*What My Bones Know*	B
Foster, Sutton. *Hooked*	B
Frangello, Gina. *Blow Your House Down*	813
Freitas, Donna. *Consent*	364.158092
Gerson, Merissa Nathan. *Forget Prayers, Bring Cake*	155.9
Goldstein, Meredith. *Can't Help Myself*	B
Greenfieldboyce, Nell. ★*Transient and Strange*	501
Hanna, Kathleen. *Rebel Girl*	B
Hauser, CJ. *The Crane Wife*	B
Hill, Clint. *Mrs. Kennedy and Me*	973.922092
Hill, Clint. *My Travels with Mrs. Kennedy*	B
Jamison, Leslie. *The Empathy Exams*	813
Lippman, Laura. *My Life as a Villainess*	B
Martin, Wednesday. *Primates of Park Avenue*	974.7
Maupin, Armistead. *Logical Family*	B
Millet, Lydia. *We Loved It All*	813
Obama, Michelle. ★*The Light We Carry*	B
Palmer, Amanda. ★*The Art of Asking*	782.42164
Parks, Casey. *Diary of a Misfit*	B
Patchett, Ann. ★*These Precious Days*	814
Philpott, Mary Laura. *Bomb Shelter*	B
Porizkova, Paulina. *No Filter*	B
Psaki, Jen. *Say More*	B
Quindlen, Anna. ★*Nanaville*	B
Radtke, Kristen. *Seek You*	741.5
Rannells, Andrew. *Uncle of the Year*	B
Robinson, Phoebe. *Please Don't Sit on My Bed in Your Outside Clothes*	818
Sale, Anna. ★*Let's Talk About Hard Things*	153.6
Schulz, Kathryn. ★*Lost & Found*	B
Sedaris, David. ★*Happy-Go-Lucky*	814
Skaife, Christopher. *The Ravenmaster*	B
Slate, Jenny. *Little Weirds*	B
Smith, Maggie. ★*You Could Make This Place Beautiful*	B
Soep, Elisabeth. *Other People's Words*	155.9
Teege, Jennifer. *My Grandfather Would Have Shot Me*	929.2
Tyson, Mike. *Iron Ambition*	B
Williams, Florence. *Heartbreak*	306.7
Winter, Molly Roden. *More*	B

LIFE STORIES — RELATIONSHIPS — COUPLES

Alden, Ginger. *Elvis and Ginger*	B
Bard, Elizabeth. *Lunch in Paris*	B
Bard, Elizabeth. *Picnic in Provence*	B
Bloom, Amy. *In Love*	B
Buhle, Kathleen. *If We Break*	B
Cacioppo, Stephanie. *Wired for Love*	616.8
Dais, Dawn. *The Sh!t No One Tells You About Divorce*	306.89
De Courcy, Anne. *The Husband Hunters*	920
Doty, Cate. *Mergers and Acquisitions*	395.2
Fuller, Alexandra. *Leaving Before the Rains Come*	B
Garcia, Mayte. *The Most Beautiful*	920
Gaye, Jan. *After the Dance*	B
Hardwick, Elizabeth. *The Dolphin Letters, 1970-1979*	811
Havrilesky, Heather. *Foreverland*	306.81
Isenberg, Sheila. *Women Who Love Men Who Kill*	362.83
Jordan, Mary. *The Art of Her Deal*	B
Machado, Carmen Maria. ★*In the Dream House*	B
Mann, William J. *Bogie & Bacall*	920
McClelland, Mac. *Irritable Hearts*	B
Morgan, Abi. *This Is Not a Pity Memoir*	B
Offerman, Nick. *The Greatest Love Story Ever Told*	B
Patchett, Ann. *This Is the Story of a Happy Marriage*	B
Pittard, Hannah. *We Are Too Many*	B
Rallo, Eli. *I Didn't Know I Needed This*	306.73
Reichl, Ruth. *Comfort Me with Apples*	B
Rosenthal, Jason. *My Wife Said You May Want to Marry Me*	B
Sharma, Nina. *The Way You Make Me Feel*	B
Steinberg, Jonny. *Winnie and Nelson*	920
Verant, Samantha. *Seven Letters from Paris*	B
Winn, Raynor. *The Wild Silence*	B

LIFE STORIES — RELATIONSHIPS — FAMILY

Alexander, Kwame. *Why Fathers Cry at Night*	B
Alterman, Sara Faith. *Let's Never Talk About This Again*	616.8
Barker, Elspeth. ★*Notes from the Henhouse*	828
Berg, Elizabeth. *I'll Be Seeing You*	306.874
Biden Owens, Valerie. *Growing up Biden*	B
Biden, Jill. *Where the Light Enters*	B
Bilger, Burkhard. *Fatherland*	B

AUTHOR, TITLE, SERIES AND SUBJECT INDEX

Bilton, Chrysta. *Normal Family*	B
Birbiglia, Mike. *The New One*	B
Bonner, Betsy. *The Book of Atlantis Black*	364.152
Brierley, Saroo. *A Long Way Home*	B
Brina, Elizabeth Miki. *Speak, Okinawa*	305.48
Carter, Jimmy. *Sharing Good Times*	973.926
Cayton-Holland, Adam. *Tragedy Plus Time*	B
Chan, Jackie. *Never Grow Up*	B
Chow, Kat. *Seeing Ghosts*	B
Chung, Nicole. *All You Can Ever Know*	B
Chung, Nicole. ★*A Living Remedy*	B
Cooper, Anderson. *The Rainbow Comes and Goes*	B
Crasnianski, Tania. *The Children of Nazis*	943.086
Dais, Dawn. *The Sh!t No One Tells You About Divorce*	306.89
Daley, Mark. *Safe*	B
Danler, Stephanie. *Stray*	B
Danticat, Edwidge. ★*Brother, I'm Dying*	B
Diamond, Cheryl. *Nowhere Girl*	B
Dunne, Griffin. ★*The Friday Afternoon Club*	B
Dutta, Sunil. *Stealing Green Mangoes*	973
Field, Sally. *In Pieces*	B
Finkelstein, Daniel. *Two Roads Home*	920
Fisher, Todd. *My Girls*	B
Foer, Esther Safran. *I Want You to Know We're Still Here*	B
Fremont, Helen. *The Escape Artist*	B
Garcia, Angela. ★*The Way That Leads Among the Lost*	362.29
Gates, Henry Louis. *Colored People*	B
Geller, Danielle. *Dog Flowers*	B
Goldberg, Whoopi. *Bits and Pieces*	B
Goldstone, Nancy Bazelon. *In the Shadow of the Empress*	920
Granata, Vince. *Everything Is Fine*	B
Gucci, Patricia. *In the Name of Gucci*	B
Gupta, Prachi. ★*They Called Us Exceptional*	B
Hale, Grace Elizabeth. *In the Pines*	364.13
Hamill, Kirkland. *Filthy Beasts*	B
Harry. ★*Spare*	B
Hayasaki, Erika. *Somewhere Sisters*	362.7
Hays, Katie. *Family of Origin, Family of Choice*	248.8086
Hempel, Jessi. *The Family Outing*	B
Hood, Ann. *Kitchen Yarns*	641.5
Horton, Michelle. *Dear Sister*	B
Howe, Ben Ryder. *My Korean Deli*	B
Hulls, Tessa. *Feeding Ghosts*	741.5
Hustvedt, Siri. *Mothers, Fathers, and Others*	814
Jackson family. *The Jacksons*	782.421644
Kalb, Bess. ★*Nobody Will Tell You This but Me*	306.874
Kan, Karoline. *Under Red Skies*	B
Kashner, Sam. *The Fabulous Bouvier Sisters*	920
Katz, Catherine Grace. *The Daughters of Yalta*	920
Kearse, Bettye. *The Other Madisons*	920
Keaton, Diane. ★*Brother & Sister*	B
Kirkby, Bruce. *Blue Sky Kingdom*	954.96
Kois, Dan. *How to Be a Family*	910.4
Kolker, Robert. ★*Hidden Valley Road*	920
Kouchner, Camille. *La Familia Grande*	B
Lewis, Oscar. *The Children of Sanchez*	306.85
Li, Zhuqing. *Daughters of the Flower Fragrant Garden*	951.04
Lockwood, Patricia. *Priestdaddy*	B
Louvin, Charlie. *Satan Is Real*	920
Madden, T Kira. *Long Live the Tribe of Fatherless Girls*	814
May, Katherine. *Wintering*	155.9
McCaulley, Esau. *How Far to the Promised Land*	B
McMillan, Tracie. *The White Bonus*	305.8
Mealer, Bryan. *The Kings of Big Spring*	B
Means, Brittany. *Hell If We Don't Change Our Ways*	B
Myers, Leah. *Thinning Blood*	B
Nelson, Maggie. ★*The Argonauts*	B
Nguyen, Viet Thanh. ★*A Man of Two Faces*	B
O'Reilly, Seamas. ★*Did Ye Hear Mammy Died?*	B
O'Sullivan, Emer. *The Fall of the House of Wilde*	B
Owusu, Nadia. *Aftershocks*	B
Pentland, Jenny. *This Will Be Funny Later*	B
Porter, Carolyn. *Marcel's Letters*	940.54
Raban, Jonathan. *Father and Son*	B
Rojas Contreras, Ingrid. ★*The Man Who Could Move Clouds*	B
Roy, Jessica. *American Girls*	305.48
Salama, Jordan. ★*Stranger in the Desert*	982
Sardy, Marin. *The Edge of Every Day*	B
Savage, Jodi M. *The Death of a Jaybird*	B
Scheeres, Julia. *Jesus Land*	B
Seierstad, Asne. *Two Sisters*	956.9104
Shapiro, Dani. ★*Inheritance*	B
Shih, David. *Chinese Prodigal*	B
Singh, Julietta. *The Breaks*	B
Sipress, David. *What's so Funny?*	B
Smith, Tracy K. ★*To Free the Captives*	818
Stewart, James B. *Unscripted*	658.1
Toibin, Colm. *Mad, Bad, Dangerous to Know*	920
Union, Gabrielle. *You Got Anything Stronger?*	B
Vance, J. D. *Hillbilly Elegy*	B
Wang, Connie. *Oh My Mother!*	B
Wilkinson, Crystal. *Praisesong for the Kitchen Ghosts*	641.5975
Williams, Marlena. *Night Mother*	791.43
Williams, Mary. *The Lost Daughter*	B
Wills, Clair. ★*Missing Persons*	929.2
Wilson, Katherine. *Only in Naples*	B
Wong, Carmen Rita. *Why Didn't You Tell Me?*	B
Wong, Jane. ★*Meet Me Tonight in Atlantic City*	B
Yancey, Philip. ★*Where the Light Fell*	B
Zauner, Michelle. ★*Crying in H Mart*	B

LIFE STORIES — RELATIONSHIPS — FRIENDSHIP

Abdul-Jabbar, Kareem. *Coach Wooden and Me*	B
Bass, Rick. *The Traveling Feast*	B
Burger, Ariel. *Witness*	848
Butcher, Amy. *Mothertrucker*	B
Caldwell, Gail. *Let's Take the Long Way Home*	B
Campbell, Deborah. *A Disappearance in Damascus*	365
Cohen, Rhaina. ★*The Other Significant Others*	177
Copeland, Misty. *The Wind at My Back*	B
Crosley, Sloane. *Grief Is for People*	B
Eyman, Scott. *Hank and Jim*	920
Feinstein, Michael. *The Gershwins and Me*	782.42164
Fenn, Lisa. *Carry On*	B
Fischer, Jenna. *The Office BFFs*	791.45
Gerard, Sarah. *Carrie Carolyn Coco*	364.152
Gorrindo, Simone. ★*The Wives*	B
Hagberg, Eva. *How to Be Loved*	616.7
Holloway, Kris. *Monique and the Mango Rains*	B
Hsu, Hua. ★*Stay True*	B
Jaouad, Suleika. ★*Between Two Kingdoms*	B
Laughlin, James. *The Luck of Friendship*	B
Lynn, Loretta. ★*Me & Patsy Kickin' up Dust*	B
Mlodinow, Leonard. *Stephen Hawking*	B
Patchett, Ann. *Truth & Beauty*	B
Pick-Goslar, Hannah Elizabeth. ★*My Friend Anne Frank*	B
Pinckney, Darryl. *Come Back in September*	B
Pittard, Hannah. *We Are Too Many*	B
Potts, Monica. *The Forgotten Girls*	B
Power, Carla. *If the Oceans Were Ink*	B
Quinn, Susan. *Eleanor and Hick*	B
Roberts, Randy. *Blood Brothers*	920
Rosen, Jonathan. ★*The Best Minds*	616.89
Schultz, Kevin Michael. *Buckley and Mailer*	920
Schwalbe, Will. *We Should Not Be Friends*	B
Sestero, Greg. *The Disaster Artist*	791.43
Smee, Sebastian. *The Art of Rivalry*	700.92
Sow, Aminatou. *Big Friendship*	177
Tate, Christie. *B.F.F.*	B
Tolan, Sandy. ★*The Lemon Tree*	B
Totenberg, Nina. ★*Dinners with Ruth*	B
Trice, Dawn Turner. ★*Three Girls from Bronzeville*	977.311
Verdelle, A. J. *Miss Chloe*	B
Von Drehle, David. ★*The Book of Charlie*	B
Wood, Gordon S. *Friends Divided*	920

LIFE STORIES — RELATIONSHIPS — GROWING UP

Al-Maria, Sophia. *The Girl Who Fell to Earth*	B
Alderton, Dolly. *Everything I Know About Love*	B
Arana, Marie. *American Chica*	B
Barnes, Cinelle. *Monsoon Mansion*	B
Bechdel, Alison. ★*Fun Home*	741.5
Bell, Darrin. ★*The Talk*	741.5
Black Thought. *The Upcycled Self*	B
Blair, Selma. *Mean Baby*	B
Blanco, Richard. *The Prince of Los Cocuyos*	B
Brina, Elizabeth Miki. *Speak, Okinawa*	305.48
Broom, Sarah M. *The Yellow House*	B

PUBLIC LIBRARY CORE COLLECTION: NONFICTION
Twentieth Edition

Broome, Brian. ★Punch Me up to the Gods	B
Bryson, Bill. The Life and Times of the Thunderbolt Kid	B
Bunnell, David. Good Friday on the Rez	B
Burton, Susan. Empty	B
Calcaterra, Regina. Etched in Sand	B
Calcaterra, Regina. Girl Unbroken	B
Carriere, Alice. Everything/Nothing/Someone	B
Carroll, Rebecca. Surviving the White Gaze	B
Carter, Jimmy. An Hour Before Daylight	B
Chaudry, Rabia. Fatty Fatty Boom Boom	B
Chin, Curtis. Everything I Learned, I Learned in a Chinese Restaurant	B
Coates, Ta-Nehisi. The Beautiful Struggle	B
Crais, Clifton C. History Lessons	B
Crowell, Rodney. Chinaberry Sidewalks	B
Devantez, Chelsea. ★I Shouldn't Be Telling You This	B
Diaz, Jaquira. Ordinary Girls	818
Dillard, Annie. An American Childhood	B
Edmundson, Mark. Why Football Matters	B
Eire, Carlos M. N. Learning to Die in Miami	B
Ellis, Helen. Southern Lady Code	814
Faliveno, Melissa. Tomboyland	B
Faust, Drew Gilpin. Necessary Trouble	B
Findakly, Brigitte. Poppies of Iraq	741.5
Fishman, Elly. Refugee High	370.8
Fitzgerald, Isaac. Dirtbag, Massachusetts	B
Ford, Ashley C. ★Somebody's Daughter	B
Ford, Richard. Between Them	B
Frank, Michael. ★One Hundred Saturdays	B
Fuller, Alexandra. Don't Let's Go to the Dogs Tonight	B
Gates, Henry Louis. Colored People	B
Georges, Gigi. Downeast	974.1
Grande, Reyna. ★The Distance Between Us	973
Grant, Gail Milissa. At the Elbows of My Elders	B
Gulman, Gary. Misfit	B
Guo, XIaolu. Nine Continents	B
Gutowitz, Jill. Girls Can Kiss Now	814
H, Lamya. ★Hijab Butch Blues	B
Hager, Jenna Bush. Sisters First	B
Hamill, Kirkland. Filthy Beasts	B
Henderson, Danielle. ★The Ugly Cry	B
Hobbs, Jeff. Children of the State	364.36
Hobbs, Jeff. Show Them You're Good	373
Howard, Ron. ★The Boys	B
Jawando, Will. ★My Seven Black Fathers	B
Jollett, Mikel. ★Hollywood Park	B
Jones, Saeed. How We Fight for Our Lives	B
Kim, Anne. ★Abandoned	305.2350973
Koh, EJ. The Magical Language of Others	813
Krimstein, Ken. When I Grow Up	741.5
Lakshmi, Padma. Love, Loss, and What We Ate	791.4502
Leach, Samantha. ★The Elissas	362.73
Legler, Casey. ★Godspeed	B
Lythcott-Haims, Julie. Your Turn	305.24
Madden, T Kira. Long Live the Tribe of Fatherless Girls	814
Marshall, Greg. Leg	B
McCourt, Frank. ★Angela's Ashes	929
McCurdy, Jennette. ★I'm Glad My Mom Died	B
Means, Brittany. Hell If We Don't Change Our Ways	B
Mouton, Deborah D. E. E. P. Black Chameleon	B
Mowat, Farley. Born Naked	B
Muir, John. Nature Writings	B
Nafisi, Azar. Things I've Been Silent About	B
Nawaz, Zarqa. Laughing All the Way to the Mosque	791.45028
Ngugi wa Thiong'o. In the House of the Interpreter	B
Nietfeld, Emi. Acceptance	B
O'Reilly, Seamas. ★Did Ye Hear Mammy Died?	B
Oz, Amos. A Tale of Love and Darkness	B
Pardlo, Gregory. Air Traffic	B
Pellegrino, Danny. How Do I Un-Remember This?	B
Pentland, Jenny. This Will Be Funny Later	B
Petrushevskaia, Liudmila. The Girl from the Metropol Hotel	B
Phelan, Tom. We Were Rich and We Didn't Know It	B
Pipher, Mary Bray. A Life in Light	B
Quin, Tegan. ★High School	B
Ronstadt, Linda. Feels Like Home	B
Rush, Chris. The Light Years	B
Satrapi, Marjane. ★The Complete Persepolis	741.5
Sattouf, Riad. The Arab of the Future 2	741.5
Sattouf, Riad. The Arab of the Future	741.5
Scheier, Liz. Never Simple	B
Schlesinger, Arthur M. A Life in the Twentieth Century	B
Shafrir, Doree. Thanks for Waiting	B
Shteyngart, Gary. ★Little Failure	B
Simmons, Ruth. ★Up Home	B
Sinclair, Safiya. ★How to Say Babylon	B
Sipress, David. What's so Funny?	B
Smith, Lee. Dimestore	975.5
Sone, Monica Itoi. Nisei Daughter	979.7
Stern, Amanda. Little Panic	616.8522
Stone, Lillian. ★Everybody's Favorite	814.6
Szczeszak-Brewer, Agata. The Hunger Book	B
Talusan, Meredith. Fairest	305.30973
Thomas, Joseph Earl. Sink	B
Thomas, R. Eric. Here for It	B
Tobia, Jacob. Sissy	305.30973
Tometich, Annabelle. The Mango Tree	B
Tran, Ly. House of Sticks	B
Tran, Phuc. ★Sigh, Gone	B
Wainaina, Binyavanga. One Day I Will Write About This Place	B
Walls, Jeannette. ★The Glass Castle	B
Wang, Qian Julie. ★Beautiful Country	B
Ward, Jesmyn. ★Men We Reaped	B
Wariner, Ruth. The Sound of Gravel	B
Whitney, Emerson. Heaven	B
Williams, Patricia. Rabbit	B
Wu, Simon. Dancing on My Own	700.1
Ypi, Lea. ★Free	B

LIFE STORIES — RELATIONSHIPS — PARENT AND CHILD

Albom, Mitch. Finding Chika	B
Alexie, Sherman. You Don't Have to Say You Love Me	818
Allende, Isabel. ★Paula	B
Andersen, Christopher P. The Good Son	B
Archibald, John. Shaking the Gates of Hell	B
Asher, Zain E. Where the Children Take Us	942.1
Austin, Nefertiti. Motherhood so White	B
Backman, Fredrik. Things My Son Needs to Know About the World	B
Bee, Vanessa A. Home Bound	B
Berger, Lynn. Second Thoughts	306.85
Biden, Joseph R. Promise Me, Dad	B
Black, Dustin Lance. Mama's Boy	B
Black, Michael Ian. A Better Man	305.31
Bragg, Rick. ★The Best Cook in the World	641.5975
Brickman, Sophie. Baby, Unplugged	306.874
Burns, Eric. Someone to Watch Over Me	973.917092
Calhoun, Ada. Also a Poet	B
Chabon, Michael. Pops	306.874
Cho, Grace M. Tastes Like War	305.48
Corrigan, Kelly. Glitter and Glue	B
Davis, Patti. Floating in the Deep End	616.8
Delaney, Rob. ★A Heart That Works	B
Dial, Roman. The Adventurer's Son	917.286
Fagan, Kate. All the Colors Came Out	B
Faludi, Susan. In the Darkroom	B
Foxx, Jamie. Act Like You Got Some Sense	B
Fuller, Alexandra. Travel Light, Move Fast	B
Gaffigan, Jim. Dad Is Fat	814
Garbes, Angela. Essential Labor	306.874
Garcia, Rodrigo. A Farewell to Gabo and Mercedes	B
Glaser, Gabrielle. American Baby	B
Harden, Marcia Gay. The Seasons of My Mother	B
Harpham, Heather Elise. Happiness	B
Harris, Taylor. This Boy We Made	B
Hemingway, Ernest. Dear Papa	813
Henderson, Danielle. ★The Ugly Cry	B
Hillsberg, Christina. License to Parent	649.1
Jones, Lucy. ★Matrescence	306.874
Kelly, Minka. ★Tell Me Everything	B
Kendi, Ibram X. ★How to Raise an Antiracist	649
Kingston, Genevieve. Did I Ever Tell You?	B
Klein, Jessi. I'll Show Myself Out	B
Koh, EJ. The Magical Language of Others	813
Kozol, Jonathan. The Theft of Memory	B
Kupperman, Michael. All the Answers	741.5
Lang, Maya. What We Carry	B
Lemay, Mimi. What We Will Become	306.874
Maisel, Ivan. I Keep Trying to Catch His Eye	B

AUTHOR, TITLE, SERIES AND SUBJECT INDEX

Matar, Hisham. *The Return*	B
McCurdy, Jennette. ★*I'm Glad My Mom Died*	B
Miller, Michelle. *Belonging*	B
Moorer, Allison. *I Dream He Talks to Me*	782.42164
Morton, Brian. *Tasha*	B
Newman, Magdalena. *Normal*	611
Nguyen, Bich Minh. *Owner of a Lonely Heart*	B
O'Hara, Maryanne. *Little Matches*	B
Qu, Anna. *Made in China*	B
Raboteau, Emily. *Lessons for Survival*	814
Reang, Putsata. *Ma and Me*	B
Rippon, Kelly. *Parent Up*	649
Rowe, Peggy. *About My Mother*	B
Russert, Luke. *Look for Me There*	B
Scheier, Liz. *Never Simple*	B
Schindler, Meriel. *The Lost Cafe Schindler*	943.64
Scottoline, Lisa. *I See Life Through Rose-Colored Glasses*	813
Sentilles, Sarah. *Stranger Care*	B
Shehadeh, Raja. ★*We Could Have Been Friends, My Father and I*	B
Slouka, Mark. *Nobody's Son*	B
Spiegelman, Nadja. ★*I'm Supposed to Protect You from All This*	741.5
Tallent, Elizabeth. *Scratched*	B
Taylor, Justin. *Riding with the Ghost*	B
Thompson, Juan F. *Stories I Tell Myself*	B
Tubbs, Anna Malaika. *The Three Mothers*	306.874
Union, Gabrielle. *You Got Anything Stronger?*	B
Wagamese, Richard. *For Joshua*	B
Wetherall, Tyler. *No Way Home*	B
Whippman, Ruth. ★*Boymom*	305.23
Wong, Ali. ★*Dear Girls*	B
Zambreno, Kate. *The Light Room*	B

LIFE STORIES — RELATIONSHIPS — PETS AND OWNERS

Achterberg, Cara Sue. *Another Good Dog*	636.7
Bailey, Elisabeth. *The Sound of a Wild Snail Eating*	594
Boylan, Jennifer Finney. *Good Boy*	B
Bragg, Rick. *The Speckled Beauty*	636.7
Charleson, Susannah. *Where the Lost Dogs Go*	636.7
Chesney, Will. *No Ordinary Dog*	958.104
Conaboy, Kelly. *The Particulars of Peter*	636.7
Fincham-Gray, Suzanne. *My Patients and Other Animals*	B
Gaffney, Ginger. *Half Broke*	B
Grossi, Craig. *Craig & Fred*	B
Halpern, Sue. *A Dog Walks into a Nursing Home*	B
Haupt, Lyanda Lynn. *Mozart's Starling*	B
Herriot, James. ★*All Creatures Great and Small*	B
Herriot, James. *All Things Wise and Wonderful*	B
Herriot, James. *Every Living Thing*	B
Herriot, James. *James Herriot's Animal Stories*	B
Herriot, James. *James Herriot's Dog Stories*	636.7
Horowitz, Alexandra. ★*The Year of the Puppy*	636.7
Hunger, Christina. *How Stella Learned to Talk*	636.7
Kugler, Rob. *A Dog Named Beautiful*	B
Lewis, Damien. *The Dog Who Could Fly*	940.54
McDougall, Christopher. *Running with Sherman*	636.1
Melville, Wilma. ★*Hero Dogs*	636.7
Montgomery, Sy. *The Good Good Pig*	636.4
Nir, Sarah Maslin. *Horse Crazy*	B
Orlean, Susan. *On Animals*	590
Sutherland, Amy. *Rescuing Penny Jane*	636.7
Tomlinson, Tommy. *Dogland*	636.7
Weintraub, Robert. *No Better Friend*	940.54

LIFE STORIES — RELIGION AND SPIRITUALITY

Alberta, Tim. *The Kingdom, the Power, and the Glory*	270.8
Archibald, John. *Shaking the Gates of Hell*	B
Carlile, Brandi. *Broken Horses*	B
Eddy, Mary Baker. ★*Mary Baker Eddy*	289.5
Girzone, Joseph F. *A Portrait of Jesus*	232.9
Han, Chenxing. *Be the Refuge*	294.3
Hays, Katie. *Family of Origin, Family of Choice*	248.8086
Hendrix, Scott H. *Martin Luther*	B
Oberman, Heiko Augustinus. *Luther*	B
Riess, Jana. *Flunking Sainthood*	248.4
Samatar, Sofia. *The White Mosque*	B
Turner, Tina. ★*Happiness Becomes You*	158.1
West, Cait. ★*Rift*	B

LIFE STORIES — RELIGION AND SPIRITUALITY — LEAVING RELIGION

Armstrong, Karen. *The Spiral Staircase*	B
Feldman, Deborah. *Exodus*	B
Glass, Sara. *Kissing Girls on Shabbat*	B
Jones, Faith. *Sex Cult Nun*	B
McCammon, Sarah. ★*The Exvangelicals*	277.308
Rinder, Mike. ★*A Billion Years*	B
Roberts, Matthias. *Holy Runaways*	262
Ward, Jon. *Testimony*	277.308
Young, Daniella Mestyanek. *Uncultured*	B

LIFE STORIES — RELIGION AND SPIRITUALITY — PERSONAL FAITH

Bailey, Jennifer. *To My Beloveds*	261.8
Baraka, Sho. *He Saw That It Was Good*	261.5
Belser, Julia Watts. ★*Loving Our Own Bones*	296
Bidwell, Duane R. *When One Religion Isn't Enough*	261.2
Billings, J. Todd. *Rejoicing in Lament*	248.8
Bolz-Weber, Nadia. *Accidental Saints*	284.1
Chittister, Joan. *Following the Path*	248.4
Chu, Jeff. *Does Jesus Really Love Me?*	261.8
Cobbs-Leonard, Tasha. *Do It Anyway*	241
DiFelice, Bekah. *Almost There*	248.8
Dilbeck, D. H. *Frederick Douglass*	B
Eteraz, Ali. *Children of Dust*	B
Evans, Rachel Held. *Wholehearted Faith*	248.4
Franklin, Missy. *Relentless Spirit*	B
Gaffigan, Jeannie. *When Life Gives You Pears*	B
Ghobash, Omar Saif. *Letters to a Young Muslim*	297.09
Grathwohl, Marya. *This Wheel of Rocks*	271
Guthrie, Savannah. *Mostly What God Does*	248.4
Hall, Sands. ★*Flunk, Start*	B
Harris, Dan. ★*10% Happier*	158.1
Hartke, Austen. *Transforming*	277
Haskell, Molly. *Steven Spielberg*	B
Henny, Ally. *I Won't Shut Up*	305.896
Jun, Tasha. ★*Tell Me the Dream Again*	248
Keeling, Ida. *Can't Nothing Bring Me Down*	B
Lamott, Anne. *Almost Everything*	170
Lamott, Anne. ★*Dusk, Night, Dawn*	B
Lamott, Anne. *Small Victories*	248
Loftis, Larry. ★*The Watchmaker's Daughter*	940.53
Moore, Beth. *All My Knotted-Up Life*	B
Orji, Yvonne. *Bamboozled by Jesus*	B
Pagels, Elaine H. ★*Why Religion?*	B
Pogrebin, Abigail. *My Jewish Year*	296.4
Poitier, Sidney. *The Measure of a Man*	B
Quinn, Tallu Schuyler. *What We Wish Were True*	B
Rao, Cheeni. *In Hanuman's Hands*	B
Roberts, Matthias. *Holy Runaways*	262
Rush, Charaia. *Courageously Soft*	234
Sagan, Sasha. *For Small Creatures Such as We*	390.09
Taylor, Barbara Brown. *Holy Envy*	B
Thi, Kim Phuc Phan. *Fire Road*	B
Thomas, R. Eric. *Here for It*	B
Wiman, Christian. *He Held Radical Light*	814

LIFE STORIES — RELIGION AND SPIRITUALITY — RELIGIOUS AND SPIRITUAL LEADERS

Armstrong, Karen. *Buddha*	B
Armstrong, Karen. *Muhammad*	B
Arrington, Leonard J. *Brigham Young*	B
Augustine. *Confessions*	B
Barry, John M. *Roger Williams and the Creation of the American Soul*	974.5
Barthel, Joan. *American Saint*	B
Baskette, Molly Phinney. *How to Begin When Your World Is Ending*	248.8
Black Elk. *Black Elk Speaks*	B
Butcher, Carmen Acevedo. *Man of Blessing*	B
Castor, Helen. *Joan of Arc*	B
Curry, Michael B. *Love Is the Way*	241
Dalai Lama. *Freedom in Exile*	B
Evanzz, Karl. *The Messenger*	B
Francis. *Let Us Dream*	282.092
Francis. *Life*	B
Fuhrmann, Joseph T. *Rasputin*	B
Guinn, Jeff. *The Road to Jonestown*	289.9
Harrington, Joel F. *Dangerous Mystic*	B
Hazleton, Lesley. *The First Muslim*	B
Hazleton, Lesley. *Mary*	B
Jebara, Mohamad. *Muhammad, the World-Changer*	B
Kertzer, David I. *The Pope at War*	940.53
Levinsohn, Florence Hamlish. *Looking for Farrakhan*	B
Marsh, Charles. *Strange Glory*	B

PUBLIC LIBRARY CORE COLLECTION: NONFICTION
Twentieth Edition

Martin, Valerie. *Salvation*	B
Massing, Michael. *Fatal Discord*	920
Merton, Thomas. ★*The Seven Storey Mountain*	B
Metaxas, Eric. *Martin Luther*	B
Moore, Beth. *All My Knotted-Up Life*	B
Newman, Richard S. *Freedom's Prophet*	B
Nhat Hanh. *The Art of Living*	294.3
O'Connor, Garry. *Universal Father*	B
Politi, Marco. *Pope Francis Among the Wolves*	282.092
Sawaki, Kodo. *Discovering the True Self*	294.3
Smith, Douglas. *Rasputin*	B
Spoto, Donald. *Joan*	B
Telushkin, Joseph. *Rebbe*	296.833
Tenzin Priyadarshi. *Running Toward Mystery*	B
Turner, John G. *Brigham Young, Pioneer Prophet*	B
Vallely, Paul. *Pope Francis*	B
Vaughn, Ellen Santilli. ★*Becoming Elisabeth Elliot*	B
Wacker, Grant. *America's Pastor*	B
Wills, Garry. *Saint Augustine*	B
Wilson, Derek. *Out of the Storm*	B

LIFE STORIES — RELIGION AND SPIRITUALITY — SPIRITUAL JOURNEYS

Baker, Deborah. *The Convert*	B
Bignon, Guillaume. *Confessions of a French Atheist*	239
Coldstream, Catherine. ★*Cloistered*	B
Duggar, Jill. *Counting the Cost*	B
Irving, Apricot Anderson. *The Gospel of Trees*	B
Lecrae. ★*I Am Restored*	B
McCloskey, Jim. *When Truth Is All You Have*	B
Merton, Thomas. *The Intimate Merton*	B
Panagore, Peter Baldwin. *Heaven Is Beautiful*	B
Power, Carla. *If the Oceans Were Ink*	B
Prejean, Helen. *River of Fire*	B
Risner, Vaneetha Rendall. *Walking Through Fire*	B
Sheff, David. *The Buddhist on Death Row*	B
Strobel, Lee. *The Case for Grace*	234
Tworkov, Helen. *Lotus Girl*	B
Williams, Michelle. *Checking In*	B
Yancey, Philip. ★*Where the Light Fell*	B

LIFE STORIES — SCIENCE, TECHNOLOGY AND MEDICINE

Imbler, Sabrina. *How Far the Light Reaches*	591.77

LIFE STORIES — SCIENCE, TECHNOLOGY AND MEDICINE — ASTRONAUTS AND PILOTS

Virts, Terry. *How to Astronaut*	629.45

LIFE STORIES — SCIENCE, TECHNOLOGY AND MEDICINE — SCIENTISTS AND INVENTORS

Seager, Sara. *The Smallest Lights in the Universe*	B

LIFE STORIES — SCIENCE, TECHNOLOGY, AND MEDICINE

Alexander, Brian. ★*The Hospital*	362.10973
Bhattacharya, Ananyo. *The Man from the Future*	B
Black, Alexandra. *Scientists Who Changed History*	509.22
Brooks, Michael. *The Art of More*	510.9
Brooks, Michael. *The Quantum Astrologer's Handbook*	B
Budiansky, Stephen. *Journey to the Edge of Reason*	B
Davenport, Christian. *The Space Barons*	920
Elliott, Carl. ★*The Occasional Human Sacrifice*	174.2
Evans, Claire Lisa. *Broad Band*	920
Ford, Elizabeth. *Sometimes Amazing Things Happen*	B
Gay, Peter. *A Godless Jew*	150.19
Greenfieldboyce, Nell. ★*Transient and Strange*	501
Hughes, Evan. *The Hard Sell*	338.4
Jung, C. G. *Memories, Dreams, Reflections*	150.19
Kanigel, Robert. *The Man Who Knew Infinity*	B
Kaplan, Janice. *The Genius of Women*	920
Kitagawa, Kate. *The Secret Lives of Numbers*	510.9
Kleiman, Kathy. *Proving Ground*	4.092
Mukherjee, Siddhartha. ★*The Song of the Cell*	571.6
Nadella, Satya. *Hit Refresh*	B
Nuila, Ricardo. *The People's Hospital*	362.1
Offit, Paul A. *You Bet Your Life*	615.5
Pauling, Linus. *Linus Pauling*	081
Popova, Maria. *Figuring*	920
Quammen, David. ★*Breathless*	614.5
Raffel, Dawn. *The Strange Case of Dr. Couney*	B
Shields, Aomawa L. *Life on Other Planets*	B
Sigmund, Karl. *Exact Thinking in Demented Times*	920
Smith, Jeremy N. *Breaking and Entering*	B
Ullman, Ellen. *Life in Code*	B
Wright, Alex. *Cataloging the World*	020.9

LIFE STORIES — SCIENCE, TECHNOLOGY, AND MEDICINE — ASTRONAUTS AND PILOTS

Ackmann, Martha. *The Mercury 13*	920
Aldrin, Buzz. *No Dream Is Too High*	B
Barbree, Jay. *Neil Armstrong*	B
Cook, Kevin. *The Burning Blue*	629.45
Grush, Loren. ★*The Six*	629.4
Jones, Tom. *Space Shuttle Stories*	629.44
Kelly, Scott. ★*Endurance*	B
Koppel, Lily. *The Astronaut Wives Club*	920
Markham, Beryl. *West with the Night*	B
McCullough, David G. ★*The Wright Brothers*	B
Melvin, Leland. *Chasing Space*	B
O'Brien, Keith. *Fly Girls*	920
Paul, Richard. *We Could Not Fail*	920
Rahmani, Niloofar. *Open Skies*	B
Sherr, Lynn. *Sally Ride*	B
Teitel, Amy Shira. *Fighting for Space*	920
Walker, Stephen. *Beyond*	629.45
Winters, Kathleen C. *Amelia Earhart*	B

LIFE STORIES — SCIENCE, TECHNOLOGY, AND MEDICINE — HEALTHCARE PROFESSIONALS

Aptowicz, Cristin O'Keefe. *Dr. Mutter's Marvels*	B
Attas, Amy. *Pets and the City*	B
Barnes, Julian. *The Man in the Red Coat*	B
Benjamin, A. K. *Let Me Not Be Mad*	612.8
Bjork, Daniel W. *B.F. Skinner*	B
Blackstock, Uche. *Legacy*	610.92
Bostridge, Mark. *Florence Nightingale*	B
Brenner, Marie. ★*The Desperate Hours*	362.1962
Brown, Jasmine. *Twice as Hard*	610.92
Brown, Theresa. *Healing*	616.99
Burgess, Ann Wolbert. *A Killer by Design*	364.3
Cahalan, Susannah. ★*The Great Pretender*	616.89
Campbell, Olivia. *Women in White Coats*	610.92
Clarke, Rachel. *Dear Life*	B
DiGregorio, Sarah. ★*Taking Care*	610.73
Ely, Wes. *Every Deep-Drawn Breath*	616.02
Engelhart, Katie. *The Inevitable*	179.7
Epstein, Mark. *The Zen of Therapy*	294.3
Fabes, Stephen. *Signs of Life*	B
Fauci, Anthony S. *Expect the Unexpected*	610.92
Fessler, Pam. *Carville's Cure*	362.19699
Fisher, Thomas. ★*The Emergency*	362.1089
Fitzharris, Lindsey. *The Butchering Art*	B
Fried, Stephen. *Rush*	B
Gay, Peter. *Freud*	B
Gildiner, Catherine. *Good Morning, Monster*	616.89
Goldberg, Emma. *Life on the Line*	362.1962
Gottlieb, Lori. ★*Maybe You Should Talk to Someone*	B
Green, Stefanie. *This Is Assisted Dying*	616.02
Guibert, Emmanuel. *The Photographer*	741.5
Hallman, J. C. *Say Anarcha*	618.1
Hanna-Attisha, Mona. *What the Eyes Don't See*	615.9
Hannig, Anita. *The Day I Die*	364.152
Harper, Michele. *The Beauty in Breaking*	B
Hazzard, Kevin. *A Thousand Naked Strangers*	B
Hazzard, Kevin M. *American Sirens*	362.18
Holloway, Kris. *Monique and the Mango Rains*	B
Jamison, Kay Redfield. *Fires in the Dark*	616.89
Jauhar, Sandeep. *Heart*	612.1
Kariko, Katalin. *Breaking Through*	B
Kidder, Tracy. ★*Rough Sleepers*	362.5
Leschziner, Guy. *The Nocturnal Brain*	616.8
Lewis, Michael. ★*The Premonition*	614.5
Lewis, Michael. ★*The Undoing Project*	920
Marsh, Henry. *Admissions*	B
Marsh, Henry. ★*Do No Harm*	B
Meyer, Robert. *Every Minute Is a Day*	362.1962
Mezrich, Joshua D. *When Death Becomes Life*	617.9
Minutaglio, Bill. *The Most Dangerous Man in America*	B
Nagorski, Andrew. *Saving Freud*	940.53
Nimura, Janice P. ★*The Doctors Blackwell*	610.92
Patterson, James. *ER Nurses*	610.73
Pipher, Mary Bray. *A Life in Light*	B
Raza, Azra. *The First Cell*	616.99
Ricanati, Elizabeth. *Braided*	B

AUTHOR, TITLE, SERIES AND SUBJECT INDEX

Rodgers, Jodi. ★*How to Find a Four-Leaf Clover*	616.85
Roudinesco, Elisabeth. ★*Freud*	B
Sacks, Oliver. *On the Move*	B
Schott, Philipp. *The Accidental Veterinarian*	B
Shah, Meera. *You're the Only One I've Told*	362.1988
Smilios, Maria. ★*The Black Angels*	610.73
Spofford, Tim. *What the Children Told Us*	150.92
Stern, Adam. *Committed*	616.89
Tallis, Frank. ★*Mortal Secrets*	B
Thompson, J. M. *Running Is a Kind of Dreaming*	B
Warraich, Haider. *The Song of Our Scars*	616
Webb, Kinari. *Guardians of the Trees*	B
Wellons, Jay. *All That Moves Us*	617.4
Weschler, Lawrence. *And How Are You, Dr. Sacks?*	B
Wilson, F. Perry. *How Medicine Works and When It Doesn't*	610.69
Wilson, Jessica. *It's Always Been Ours*	613

LIFE STORIES — SCIENCE, TECHNOLOGY, AND MEDICINE — SCIENTISTS AND INVENTORS

Ballard, Robert D. *Into the Deep*	551.46092
Berger, Eric. *Liftoff*	B
Beyer, Kurt. *Grace Hopper and the Invention of the Information Age*	B
Brands, H. W. *The First American*	B
Browne, E. J. *Charles Darwin*	B
Browne, E. J. *Charles Darwin*	B
Bunker, Nick. *Young Benjamin Franklin*	B
Byrne, Eugene. *Darwin*	741.5
Carlson, W. Bernard. *Tesla*	B
Colwell, Rita R. *A Lab of One's Own*	B
Conant, Jennet. *Man of the Hour*	B
Cooke, Lucy. *Bitch*	591.56
Copeland, B. Jack. *Turing*	B
Costa, James T. *Darwin's Backyard*	576.8
Costa, James T. *Radical by Nature*	B
Dawkins, Richard. *An Appetite for Wonder*	B
Dawkins, Richard. *Brief Candle in the Dark*	B
Dawson, Kate Winkler. ★*American Sherlock*	B
Dyson, Freeman J. *Maker of Patterns*	B
Eig, Jonathan. *The Birth of the Pill*	618.1
Essinger, James. *Ada's Algorithm*	B
Fauber, L. S. *Heaven on Earth*	B
Fischer, Paul. *The Man Who Invented Motion Pictures*	791.43
Fletcher, Seth. *Einstein's Shadow*	523.8
Forbes, Nancy. *Faraday, Maxwell, and the Electromagnetic Field*	B
Fox, Margalit. *The Riddle of the Labyrinth*	920
Frank, Lone. *The Pleasure Shock*	616.8
Franklin, Benjamin. ★*The Autobiography of Benjamin Franklin*	B
Goodall, Jane. ★*Beyond Innocence*	B
Goodall, Jane. ★*The Book of Hope*	128
Graham, Jasmin. *Sharks Don't Sink*	597.3
Gray, Charlotte. ★*Reluctant Genius*	920
Hagerty, Alexa. ★*Still Life with Bones*	599.9
Hawking, Stephen. *My Brief History*	B
Hazelgrove, William Elliott. *Wright Brothers, Wrong Story*	920
Heinrich, Bernd. *A Naturalist at Large*	508
Henig, Robin Marantz. *The Monk in the Garden*	B
Hickam, Homer H. ★*Rocket Boys*	B
Isaacson, Walter. ★*The Code Breaker*	576.5
Isaacson, Walter. ★*Elon Musk*	B
Isaacson, Walter. ★*Leonardo Da Vinci*	B
Jahren, Hope. ★*Lab Girl*	B
Johnson, George. *Miss Leavitt's Stars*	522
Johnson, Katherine G. *My Remarkable Journey*	B
Johnson, Sarah Stewart. *The Sirens of Mars*	576.8
Kamkwamba, William. ★*The Boy Who Harnessed the Wind*	B
Kandel, Eric R. *In Search of Memory*	B
Kaufman, Kenn. *The Birds That Audubon Missed*	598
Kinzer, Stephen. *Poisoner in Chief*	B
Knight, Sam. *The Premonitions Bureau*	133.8
Kunetka, James W. *The General and the Genius*	355.8
Lance, Rachel. *Chamber Divers*	940.54
Lance, Rachel. *In the Waves*	973.7
Levesque, Emily. *The Last Stargazers*	520
Levi, Primo. *The Periodic Table*	858
Li, Fei-Fei. *The Worlds I See*	B
Lowman, Margaret. *The Arbornaut*	581.7
Lowman, Margaret. *Life in the Treetops*	B
Maddox, Brenda. *Rosalind Franklin*	B
Markel, Howard. *Origin Story*	576.8
Markel, Howard. *The Secret of Life*	572.86
McNeur, Catherine. *Mischievous Creatures*	920
McWhirter, Cameron. *American Gun*	683.4
Miller, Lulu. *Why Fish Don't Exist*	B
Mlodinow, Leonard. *Stephen Hawking*	B
Morris, Edmund. ★*Edison*	B
Munson, Richard. *Tesla*	B
Norton, Laurah. *Lay Them to Rest*	363.25
Nuland, Sherwin B. *Leonardo Da Vinci*	B
Nye, Bill. *Everything All at Once*	153.4
Olson, Lynne. ★*Empress of the Nile*	B
Oluseyi, Hakeem M. *A Quantum Life*	B
Ottaviani, Jim. *Hawking*	741.5
Owens, Delia. *The Eye of the Elephant*	639.9
Quave, Cassandra Leah. *The Plant Hunter*	581.6
Rasenberger, Jim. *Revolver*	B
Reser, Anna. *Forces of Nature*	509.2
Rhodes, Richard. *Scientist*	B
Roberts, Jason. ★*Every Living Thing*	578
Rose, Alexander. *Empires of the Sky*	920
Ryckman, Pamela. *Candace Pert*	B
Sacks, Oliver. ★*Everything in Its Place*	B
Sacks, Oliver. *Gratitude*	306.9
Schwartz, David N. *The Last Man Who Knew Everything*	B
Sevigny, Melissa L. ★*Brave the Wild River*	580.9
Simard, S. ★*Finding the Mother Tree*	582.16
Snyder, Laura J. *Eye of the Beholder*	920
Sobel, Dava. *A More Perfect Heaven*	520.9
Soni, Jimmy. *A Mind at Play*	B
Souder, William. *On a Farther Shore*	B
Stanley, Matthew. *Einstein's War*	530
Stone, Daniel. *The Food Explorer*	B
Tegmark, Max. *Our Mathematical Universe*	523.1
Van Hemert, Caroline. *The Sun Is a Compass*	979.8
Vella, Christina. *George Washington Carver*	B
Widder, Edith. *Below the Edge of Darkness*	551.46092
Wilson, Edward O. *Tales from the Ant World*	595.79
Winchester, Simon. *The Map That Changed the World*	B
Wulf, Andrea. *The Invention of Nature*	B
Wynn-Grant, Rae. *Wild Life*	B
Zernike, Kate. *The Exceptions*	331.4

LIFE STORIES — SPORTS

Barbarisi, Daniel. *Dueling with Kings*	793.93
Berkow, Ira. *How Life Imitates Sports*	070.4
Bissinger, H. G. ★*The Mosquito Bowl*	796.332
Brady, Frank. *Endgame*	B
Butler, Brin-Jonathan. *The Domino Diaries*	796.83
Cardwell, Diane. *Rockaway*	B
Cole, Jason. *Elway*	B
Cornelius, Maria M. *The Final Season*	B
Coyne, Tom. *A Course Called Scotland*	796.352
DiGiulian, Sasha. *Take the Lead*	B
Dohrmann, George. *Switching Fields*	796.334
Edmundson, Mark. *Why Football Matters*	B
Fleshman, Lauren. ★*Good for a Girl*	B
Gessner, David. *Ultimate Glory*	796.2
Heminsley, Alexandra. *Running Like a Girl*	B
Konnikova, Maria. *The Biggest Bluff*	795.412
Lundquist, Verne. *Play by Play*	B
Manzione, Gianmarc. *Pin Action*	B
Montville, Leigh. *Tall Men, Short Shorts*	796.323
Norton, Hughes. ★*Rainmaker*	796.352
O'Brien, Keith. *Charlie Hustle*	796.357
Pennington, Bill. *Billy Martin*	B
Perron, Cam. ★*Comeback Season*	796.357
Pessah, Jon. *Yogi*	B
Smith, Kenny. *Talk of Champions*	B
Streep, Abe. *Brothers on Three*	306.85
Sullivan, Matt. *Can't Knock the Hustle*	796.323
Thompson, Wright. *The Cost of These Dreams*	B
Walton, Bill. *Back from the Dead*	B
Zimmerman, Paul. *Dr. Z*	B

LIFE STORIES — SPORTS — ATHLETES

Agassi, Andre. *Open*	B
Anthony, Carmelo. *Where Tomorrows Aren't Promised*	B
Askwith, Richard. *Unbreakable*	B
Babb, Valerie Melissa. *The Book of James*	B
Balf, Todd. *Major*	B

PUBLIC LIBRARY CORE COLLECTION: NONFICTION
Twentieth Edition

Bamberger, Michael. *The Second Life of Tiger Woods*	B
Barra, Allen. ★*The Last Coach*	B
Barra, Allen. ★*Yogi Berra*	B
Baylor, Elgin. *Hang Time*	B
Bella, Timothy. *Barkley*	B
Benedict, Jeff. *Lebron*	B
Benedict, Jeff. ★*Tiger Woods*	B
Bennett, Michael. *Things That Make White People Uncomfortable*	305.896
Blais, Madeleine. *Queen of the Court*	B
Bradlee, Ben. *The Kid*	B
Branch, John. *Boy on Ice*	B
Bryant, Howard. *The Last Hero*	B
Bryant, Howard. *Rickey*	B
Bryant, Kobe. *The Mamba Mentality*	B
Buford, Kate. *Native American Son*	B
Burgman, John. *High Drama*	796.522
Callahan, Tom. *Arnie*	B
Century, Douglas. *Barney Ross*	B
Chapman, Rex. ★*It's Hard for Me to Live with Me*	B
Clarey, Christopher. ★*The Master*	B
Clavin, Thomas. *The DiMaggios*	920
Cox, Lynne. *Swimming to Antarctica*	B
Cramer, Richard Ben. *Joe DiMaggio*	B
Crawford, Bill. ★*All American*	B
Creamer, Robert W. *Babe*	B
Creamer, Robert W. *Stengel*	796.357
Daley, Tom. *Coming up for Air*	B
Darling, Ron. *The Complete Game*	B
Davis, Jennifer Pharr. *The Pursuit of Endurance*	796.51
Davis, Seth. *Wooden*	B
De Vise, Daniel. *The Comeback*	B
Drape, Joe. *Black Maestro*	B
Dunnavant, Keith. *Montana*	B
Dykstra, Lenny. *House of Nails*	B
Eig, Jonathan. ★*Ali*	B
Engle, Charlie. *Running Man*	B
Epplin, Luke. *Our Team*	796.357
Eruzione, Mike. *The Making of a Miracle*	B
Fagan, Kate. *All the Colors Came Out*	B
Finn, Adharanand. *The Rise of the Ultra Runners*	B
Finnegan, William. *Barbarian Days*	B
Fitzgerald, Matt. *Iron War*	796.42
Foles, Nick. *Believe It*	B
Franklin, Missy. *Relentless Spirit*	B
Gehrig, Lou. *The Lost Memoir*	B
Gilder, Ginny. *Course Correction*	797.12
Gracie, Rickson. *Breathe*	B
Gretzky, Wayne. *99*	B
Hamilton, Duncan. *For the Glory*	B
Hamilton, Tyler. *The Secret Race*	796.62
Harig, Bob. *Drive*	796.352
Harris, David. *The Genius*	B
Haygood, Wil. ★*Sweet Thunder*	B
Hernandez, Keith. *I'm Keith Hernandez*	B
Hiaasen, Carl. *The Downhill Lie*	B
Hirsch, James S. *Willie Mays*	B
Honnold, Alex. *Alone on the Wall*	B
Iguodala, Andre. *The Sixth Man*	B
Jackson, Ted. ★*You Ought to Do a Story About Me*	B
Jacobs, Sally H. *Althea*	B
Jeter, Derek. *Jeter Unfiltered*	B
Keeling, Ida. *Can't Nothing Bring Me Down*	B
Keflezighi, Meb. *26 Marathons*	B
Kennedy, Kostya. *True*	B
King, Billie Jean. ★*All In*	B
Kornhauser, Jacob. *The Cup of Coffee Club*	796.357
Kram, Mark. *Smokin' Joe*	B
Kranish, Michael. *The World's Fastest Man*	B
Kriegel, Mark. *Pistol*	B
Leavy, Jane. *The Big Fella*	B
Leavy, Jane. *The Last Boy*	B
Leavy, Jane. *Sandy Koufax*	B
Lewis, Michael. *The Blind Side*	B
Lloyd, Carli. *When Nobody Was Watching*	B
Maraniss, Andrew. *Strong Inside*	B
Maraniss, David. *Clemente*	B
Maraniss, David. ★*Path Lit by Lightning*	B
Mardini, Yusra. *Butterfly*	B
Masters, Oksana. *The Hard Parts*	B
Mays, Willie. *24*	B
McCallum, Jack. *Dream Team*	796.323
Montgomery, Patrick. *Baseball's Great Expectations*	796.357
Montillo, Roseanne. *Fire on the Track*	B
Montville, Leigh. *Sting Like a Bee*	B
Moore, Colten. *Catching the Sky*	B
Muhammad, Ibtihaj. *Proud*	B
Namath, Joe Willie. ★*All the Way*	B
Nyad, Diana. *Find a Way*	B
O'Brien, Vanessa. *To the Greatest Heights*	B
O'Connor, Ian. *Belichick*	B
Oakley, Charles. *The Last Enforcer*	B
Ortiz, David. *Papi*	B
Palmer, Arnold. *A Golfer's Life*	B
Pappu, Sridhar. *The Year of the Pitcher*	920
Paulsen, Gary. *Winterdance*	B
Pearlman, Jeff. *Gunslinger*	B
Pearlman, Jeff. *The Last Folk Hero*	B
Pearlman, Jeff. *Sweetness*	B
Perkins, Kendrick. *The Education of Kendrick Perkins*	B
Phillips, Rowan Ricardo. *The Circuit*	796.342
Pippen, Scottie. *Unguarded*	B
Polly, Matthew. ★*Bruce Lee*	B
Posnanski, Joe. *The Baseball 100*	796.357
Posnanski, Joe. *The Soul of Baseball*	796.357
Prior-Palmer, Lara. *Rough Magic*	798.4
Rapinoe, Megan. *One Life*	B
Rapoport, Ron. *Let's Play Two*	B
Ravin, Idan. *The Hoops Whisperer*	796.323
Rippon, Adam. *Beautiful on the Outside*	B
Rivera, Mariano. *The Closer*	B
Roberts, David. *Limits of the Known*	B
Roberts, Randy. *Joe Louis*	B
Robinson, Ray. *Iron Horse*	B
Rogers, Robbie. *Coming Out to Play*	B
Rosen, Charles. *Sugar*	B
Rothenberg, Ben. *Naomi Osaka*	B
Sabathia, CC. *Till the End*	796.357
Sasakamoose, Fred. *Call Me Indian*	B
Schaap, Jeremy. *Cinderella Man*	B
Sharapova, Maria. *Unstoppable*	B
Shipnuck, Alan. *Phil*	B
Shorter, Frank. *My Marathon*	796.42
Sielski, Mike. *The Rise*	B
Stanton, Mike. ★*Unbeaten*	B
Stratton, W. K. *Floyd Patterson*	B
Stump, Al. *Cobb*	B
Summitt, Pat Head. *Sum It Up*	B
Toorpakai, Maria. *A Different Kind of Daughter*	B
Tye, Larry. *Satchel*	B
Tyson, Mike. *Iron Ambition*	B
Wade, Becky. *Run the World*	796.42
Wambach, Abby. *Forward*	B
Ward, Geoffrey C. *Unforgivable Blackness*	B
Wertheim, L. Jon. *Blood in the Cage*	796.815
West, Jerry. *West by West*	B
Williams, Jay. *Life Is Not an Accident*	B
Woods, Tiger. *The 1997 Masters*	B
Young, Steve. *QB*	B
Yousse, Bower. *Freddie Steinmark*	796.332

LIFE STORIES — SPORTS — COACHES, MANAGERS, AND OWNERS

Abdul-Jabbar, Kareem. *Coach Wooden and Me*	B
Auletta, Ken. *Media Man*	B
Barra, Allen. ★*The Last Coach*	B
Barra, Allen. ★*Yogi Berra*	B
Boeheim, Jim. *Bleeding Orange*	B
Burke, Monte. *Saban*	796.332
Creamer, Robert W. *Stengel*	796.357
Davis, Seth. *Wooden*	B
Futterman, Matthew. *Running to the Edge*	796.42071
Gwynne, S. C. *The Perfect Pass*	920
Harris, David. *The Genius*	B
Kirschbaum, Erik. *Soccer Without Borders*	B
O'Connor, Ian. *Belichick*	B
O'Connor, Ian. *Coach K*	B
Parcells, Bill. *Parcells*	B
Posnanski, Joe. *The Soul of Baseball*	796.357

AUTHOR, TITLE, SERIES AND SUBJECT INDEX

Ribowsky, Mark. *The Last Cowboy* — 796.332
Ribowsky, Mark. *Shula* — B
Skelton, Marc. *Pounding the Rock* — 796.323
Spurrier, Steve. *Head Ball Coach* — B
Summitt, Pat Head. *Sum It Up* — B
Torre, Joe. *The Yankee Years* — B
West, Jerry. *West by West* — B
Williams, Richard. *Black and White* — B
Life Strategies. McGraw, Phillip C. — 158
Life Undercover. Fox, Amaryllis
★*Life Upon These Shores*. Gates, Henry Louis — 973
Life Worth Living. Volf, Miroslav — 113
The Life You Long For. Nockels, Christy — 248.8
Life's Edge. Zimmer, Carl — 570
A Life's Work. Cusk, Rachel — 306.874
Life's Work. Milch, David
Life, Liberty, and the Pursuit of Happiness. Moore, Peter — 199
The Life-Changing Magic of Not Giving a F*ck. Knight, Sarah — 818
★*The Life-Changing Magic of Tidying Up*. Kondo, Marie — 648
LIFERS (PRISONERS)
Carlo, Philip. *Gaspipe* — B
King, Greg. *Nothing but the Night* — 364.152
Lauren, Jillian. *Behold the Monster* — 364.152
LIFESAVING
Gutman, Matt. *The Boys in the Cave* — 796.52
Lifespan. Sinclair, David A. — 570
LIFESTYLE CHANGE
Bosker, Bianca. *Cork Dork* — 641.2
Cardwell, Diane. *Rockaway* — B
James, Victoria. *Wine Girl* — B
Kim, Anne. ★*Abandoned* — 305.2350973
Phillips, Adam. *On Giving up* — 158.2
Reiss, Benjamin. *Wild Nights* — 616.8
LIFESTYLES
Beard, Mary. ★*Emperor of Rome* — 937
Lavery, Daniel M. *Dear Prudence* — 170
Levy, Deborah. *The Cost of Living* — B
McGrath, Tom. *Triumph of the Yuppies* — 305.242
Wilbur, Matika. *Project 562* — 970.004
LIFESTYLES AND HEALTH
Hamblin, James. *If Our Bodies Could Talk* — 613
Lifford, Tina
  The Little Book of Big Lies — 155.2
Lift Every Voice. Sullivan, Patricia — 973
Liftoff. Berger, Eric — B
LIGHT
Ananthaswamy, Anil. *Through Two Doors at Once* — 530.12
LIGHT AND DARKNESS
Eklof, Johan. *The Darkness Manifesto* — 363.7
Light and Shade. Tolinski, Brad — B
★*The Light Eaters*. Schlanger, Zoe — 571.2
Light for the World to See. Alexander, Kwame — 811.6
A Light in the Dark. Rubin, Kathy Kleiner — 364.152
The Light of Battle. Paradis, Michel — 940.54
The Light of Days. Batalion, Judith — 940.53
Light of the Stars. Frank, Adam — 523.1
LIGHT POLLUTION
Eklof, Johan. *The Darkness Manifesto* — 363.7
The Light Room. Zambreno, Kate — B
★*The Light We Carry*. Obama, Michelle — B
The Light Years. Rush, Chris — B
Light, Michael
  100 Suns — 779
★*Lighthead*. Hayes, Terrance — 811
The Lighthouse of Stalingrad. MacGregor, Iain — 940.54
The Lightless Sky. Passarlay, Gulwali — B
Lightman, Alan P.
  The Discoveries — 509
  Searching for Stars on an Island in Maine — 523.1
  The Transcendent Brain — 215
Lightner, Jill
  Cooking from Scratch — 641.5
Lightning Down. Clavin, Thomas — 940.54
Lightning Flowers. Standefer, Katherine E. — B
★*Lightning Striking*. Kaye, Lenny — 781.66
Lights On, Rats Out. LeFavour, Cree — 616.85
Lights Out. Gryta, Thomas — 338.7
Like A Rolling Stone. Wenner, Jann — B

★*Like Love*. Nelson, Maggie — 814
The Like Switch. Schafer, John R. — 158.2
Like, Comment, Subscribe. Bergen, Mark — 338.7
★*Like, Literally, Dude*. Fridland, Valerie — 420.141
Likeable Social Media. Kerpen, Dave — 658.8
Lillien, Lisa
  Hungry Girl 1-2-3 — 641.5
  Hungry Girl Simply 6 — 641.5
Lim, Audrea
  Free the Land — 333.73
Lim, Louisa
  Indelible City — 951.25
  The People's Republic of Amnesia — 951.05
Lima. Scenters-Zapico, Natalie — 811
Lima, Jamie Kern
  Believe It — B
LIMA, JAMIE KERN
  Lima, Jamie Kern. *Believe It* — B
LIMERICK, IRELAND
  McCourt, Frank. ★*Angela's Ashes* — 929
  McCourt, Malachy. *Singing My Him Song* — B
★*Limitless*. Smialek, Jeanna — 332.1
Limits of the Known. Roberts, David — B
Limon, Ada
  Bright Dead Things — 811
  ★*The Carrying* — 811
  ★*The Hurting Kind* — 811
Lin, Amy
  Here After — B
LIN, AMY
  Lin, Amy. *Here After* — B
Lin, Jami Nakamura
  The Night Parade — B
LIN, JAMI NAKAMURA
  Lin, Jami Nakamura. *The Night Parade* — B
Lincoff, Gary
  The Audubon Society Field Guide to North American Mushrooms — 579.6
Lincoln. Carwardine, Richard — B
Lincoln. Donald, David Herbert — B
Lincoln and Douglas. Guelzo, Allen C. — 973.6
Lincoln and His Admirals. Symonds, Craig L. — B
Lincoln and the Abolitionists. Kaplan, Fred — 973.7092
Lincoln and the Fight for Peace. Avlon, John P. — 973.7
Lincoln At Gettysburg. Wills, Garry — 973.7
The Lincoln Conspiracy. Meltzer, Brad — 973.7092
Lincoln in Private. White, Ronald C. — B
LINCOLN MEMORIAL, WASHINGTON, D.C.
  Holzer, Harold. *Monument Man* — B
The Lincoln Miracle. Achorn, Edward — 973.6
Lincoln on the Verge. Widmer, Edward L. — B
Lincoln's Autocrat. Marvel, William — B
Lincoln's Code. Witt, John Fabian — 343.73
Lincoln's Gamble. Brewster, Todd — 973.7
Lincoln's Greatest Case. McGinty, Brian — 346.7303
Lincoln's Lie. Mitchell, Elizabeth — 973.7092
Lincoln's Lieutenants. Sears, Stephen W. — 920
Lincoln's Spies. Waller, Douglas C. — 973.7
Lincoln, Abraham
  Speeches and Writings, 1832-1858 — 973.5
  Speeches and Writings, 1859-1865 — 973.6
LINCOLN, ABRAHAM, 1809-1865
  Achorn, Edward. *The Lincoln Miracle* — 973.6
  Alford, Terry. *Fortune's Fool* — B
  Avlon, John P. *Lincoln and the Fight for Peace* — 973.7
  Berg, Scott W. ★*38 Nooses* — 973.7
  Blumenthal, Sidney. ★*All the Powers of Earth* — 973.7
  Blumenthal, Sidney. *A Self-Made Man* — B
  Blumenthal, Sidney. *Wrestling with His Angel* — B
  Brands, H. W. ★*The Zealot and the Emancipator* — 920
  Brewster, Todd. *Lincoln's Gamble* — 973.7
  Burlingame, Michael. *Abraham Lincoln* — B
  Burlingame, Michael. *The Black Man's President* — 973.7
  Carwardine, Richard. *Lincoln* — B
  Craughwell, Thomas J. *Stealing Lincoln's Body* — 973.7092
  Donald, David Herbert. *Lincoln* — B
  Feldman, Noah. *The Broken Constitution* — 973.7
  Foner, Eric. *The Fiery Trial* — 973.7092
  Gienapp, William E. *Abraham Lincoln and Civil War America* — B

PUBLIC LIBRARY CORE COLLECTION: NONFICTION
Twentieth Edition

Goodwin, Doris Kearns. ★*Leadership in Turbulent Times*	973.09
Goodwin, Doris Kearns. ★*Team of Rivals*	B
Guelzo, Allen C. *Lincoln and Douglas*	973.6
Gwynne, S. C. *Hymns of the Republic*	973.7
Holzer, Harold. *Brought Forth on This Continent*	973.7
Holzer, Harold. *A Just and Generous Nation*	973.7092
Kaplan, Fred. *Lincoln and the Abolitionists*	973.7092
Larson, Erik. ★*The Demon of Unrest*	973.7
Lincoln, Abraham. *Speeches and Writings, 1832-1858*	973.5
Lowenstein, Roger. *Ways and Means*	973.7
Marvel, William. *Lincoln's Autocrat*	B
McGinty, Brian. *Lincoln's Greatest Case*	346.7303
McPherson, James M. ★*Abraham Lincoln*	B
McPherson, James M. *Drawn with the Sword*	973.7
McPherson, James M. ★*Tried by War*	973.7
Meacham, Jon. ★*And There Was Light*	B
Meltzer, Brad. *The Lincoln Conspiracy*	973.7092
Mitchell, Elizabeth. *Lincoln's Lie*	973.7092
Pryor, Elizabeth Brown. *Six Encounters with Lincoln*	973.7092
Reynolds, David S. ★*Abe*	B
Sandburg, Carl. *Abraham Lincoln*	B
Sears, Stephen W. *Lincoln's Lieutenants*	920
Stahr, Walter. ★*Stanton*	B
Symonds, Craig L. *Lincoln and His Admirals*	B
Waller, Douglas C. *Lincoln's Spies*	973.7
White, Ronald C. *A. Lincoln*	B
White, Ronald C. *Lincoln in Private*	B
Widmer, Edward L. *Lincoln on the Verge*	B
Wills, Garry. *Lincoln at Gettysburg*	973.7
Winik, Jay. *April 1865*	973.7
Witt, John Fabian. *Lincoln's Code*	343.73
Linda Goodman's Star Signs. Goodman, Linda	133.5
Linda Goodman's Sun Signs. Goodman, Linda	133.5
Lindbergh, Ben	
The Only Rule Is That It Has to Work	796.357
LINDBERGH, CHARLES A. (CHARLES AUGUSTUS), 1902-1974	
Groom, Winston. *The Aviators*	920
Olson, Lynne. *Those Angry Days*	940.53
Linden, Eugene	
Fire and Flood	304.2
LINDGREN, ASTRID, 1907-2002	
Andersen, Jens. *Astrid Lindgren*	B
LINDLEY, JOHN, 1799-1865	
Holway, Tatiana M. *The Flower of Empire*	727
Lindner, Dan	
★*A Guide to Federal Contracting, 2nd Ed.*	346.7302
Lindsay, Virginia Keleher	
Sewing to Sell	746
Lindwer, Willy	
The Last Seven Months of Anne Frank	B
The Line Becomes a River. Cantu, Francisco	B
A Line in the River. Mahjoub, Jamal	962.404
A Line in the Sand. Barr, James	956
Lineberry, Cate	
Be Free or Die	B
The Secret Rescue	940.54
Linett, Andrea	
The Cool Factor	746.9
LINGUISTIC CHANGE	
Kinzler, Katherine D. *How You Say It*	302.2
LINGUISTICS	
Crystal, David. ★*How Language Works*	410
Crystal, David. ★*The Stories of English*	427
Fox, Margalit. *The Riddle of the Labyrinth*	920
Fridland, Valerie. ★*Like, Literally, Dude*	420.141
Glinert, Lewis. *The Story of Hebrew*	492.4
Nadeau, Jean-Benoit. ★*The Story of French*	440
Nadeau, Jean-Benoit. *The Story of Spanish*	460
Nuttall, Jennifer Anne. ★*Mother Tongue*	422
Perlin, Ross. ★*Language City*	306.44
Yang, Charles D. *The Infinite Gift*	401
LINGUISTS	
Fair, Eric. *Consequence*	B
Linklater, Andro	
Owning the Earth	333.3
Linklater, Kristin	
Freeing the Natural Voice	808.5
Linn, Susan	
Who's Raising the Kids?	649
LINNÉ, CARL VON, 1707-1778	
Roberts, Jason. ★*Every Living Thing*	578
Linsley, Leslie	
Salvage Style	747
Lintott, Chris	
Accidental Astronomy	520
Linus Pauling. Pauling, Linus	081
The Lion in the Living Room. Tucker, Abigail	636.8
Lioness. Klagsbrun, Francine	B
Lions of the West. Morgan, Robert	978
LIPIZZANER HORSE	
Letts, Elizabeth. *The Perfect Horse*	940.54
Lipman, Joanne	
That's What She Said	305.30973
Lippman, Laura	
My Life as a Villainess	B
Lipska, Barbara K.	
The Neuroscientist Who Lost Her Mind	B
LIPSKA, BARBARA K.	
Lipska, Barbara K. *The Neuroscientist Who Lost Her Mind*	B
Lipsky, David	
★*The Parrot and the Igloo*	304.2
Lipstadt, Deborah E.	
The Eichmann Trial	345.5694
History on Trial	940.53
LIPSTADT, DEBORAH E., 1947-	
Lipstadt, Deborah E. *History on Trial*	940.53
Liquid Rules. Miodownik, Mark	530.4
LIQUIDS	
Miodownik, Mark. *Liquid Rules*	530.4
LIQUORS	
Rogers, Adam. *Proof*	663
Lisle, John	
The Dirty Tricks Department	940.54
LISPECTOR, CLARICE	
Moser, Benjamin. *Why This World*	B
LISTENING	
Alda, Alan. *If I Understood You, Would I Have This Look on My Face?*	153.6
Blyth, Catherine. *The Art of Conversation*	395.5
Brooks, David. ★*How to Know a Person*	158.2
Cameron, Julia. ★*The Listening Path*	153.6
Duhigg, Charles. ★*Supercommunicators*	153.6
Mauceri, John. *For the Love of Music*	781.1
Murphy, Kate. *You're Not Listening*	153.6
Rogers, Susan E. ★*This Is What It Sounds Like*	781.1
★*Listening for America.* Kapilow, Robert	782.42164
★*The Listening Path.* Cameron, Julia	153.6
Listening to Stone. Herrera, Hayden	B
Lister, Adrian	
Darwin's Fossils	576.8
LISTER, JOSEPH, BARON, 1827-1912	
Fitzharris, Lindsey. *The Butchering Art*	B
LISTON, SONNY, 1932-1970	
Assael, Shaun. *The Murder of Sonny Liston*	B
Literacy. Sweeney, Jennifer	027.62
LITERACY	
Cleaver, Samantha. *Raising an Active Reader*	372.4
Farmer, Lesley S. J. ★*Impactful Community-Based Literacy Projects*	372.6
Kuo, Michelle. *Reading with Patrick*	B
Mufleh, Luma. ★*Learning America*	371.826
Smart, Maya Payne. *Reading for Our Lives*	372.4
Sweeney, Jennifer. *Literacy*	027.62
LITERARY AGENTS	
Larimer, Kevin. *The Poets & Writers Complete Guide to Being a Writer*	808
Rakoff, Joanna Smith. *My Salinger Year*	B
LITERARY CRITICISM	
Acocella, Joan Ross. ★*The Bloodied Nightgown*	814
Alexander, Caroline. *The War That Killed Achilles*	883
Amar, Akhil Reed. *The Words That Made Us*	342.7302
Atwood, Margaret. *In Other Worlds*	813
Auster, Paul. *Burning Boy*	B
Bader, Philip. *African-American Writers*	810.9
Basbanes, Nicholas A. ★*Cross of Snow*	B
Bate, Jonathan. *Radical Wordsworth*	B
Bellos, David. *The Novel of the Century*	843
Berry, Wendell. *Imagination in Place*	814

AUTHOR, TITLE, SERIES AND SUBJECT INDEX

Bialosky, Jill. *Poetry Will Save Your Life*	B
Blaisdell, Robert. *Creating Anna Karenina*	891.7
Bloom, Harold. *The Western Canon*	809
Bly, Robert. *More Than True*	398.2
Brinkley, Alan. ★*The Publisher*	B
Britt, Ryan. ★*The Spice Must Flow*	813
Brown, David S. *Paradise Lost*	813
Browning, Robert. ★*Robert Browning's Poetry*	821
Burt, Stephanie. *Don't Read Poetry*	811
Campbell, Joseph. *The Masks of God*	201.3
Campbell, Joseph. *The Power of Myth*	201.3
Cart, Michael. *Young Adult Literature*	813.009
Chabon, Michael. *Bookends*	818
Coetzee, J. M. *Late Essays, 2006-2017*	824
Crase, Douglas. *On Autumn Lake*	809
Cusk, Rachel. *Coventry*	814
Damrosch, David. *Around the World in 80 Books*	809
Daugherty, Tracy. *Larry McMurtry*	B
Ellison, Ralph. ★*The Collected Essays of Ralph Ellison*	814
Ellison, Ralph. *The Selected Letters of Ralph Ellison*	813
Everitt, Anthony. *The Rise of Athens*	938
Favro, Terri. *Generation Robot*	006.3
Feder, Rachel. *The Darcy Myth*	823
Ferrante, Elena. *In the Margins*	809
Foster, Thomas C. *How to Read Poetry Like a Professor*	808.1
Gabbert, Elisa. *Any Person Is the Only Self*	814
Gates, Henry Louis. *The Black Box*	908
Ghosh, Amitav. *The Great Derangement*	809
Gilbert, Sandra M. ★*Still Mad*	810.9
Gorra, Michael Edward. *The Saddest Words*	813
Gosden, Chris. *Magic*	133.4
Greenblatt, Stephen. *The Rise and Fall of Adam and Eve*	233
Griffin, Farah Jasmine. ★*In Search of a Beautiful Freedom*	814
Griffin, Farah Jasmine. *Read Until You Understand*	810.9
Hart, James David. *The Oxford Companion to American Literature*	810.9
Hecht, Jennifer Michael. ★*The Wonder Paradox*	808.1
Hirsch, Edward. *How to Read a Poem*	808.1
Hirsch, Edward. *Poet's Choice*	808.81
hooks, bell. *Remembered Rapture*	808
Ignatieff, Michael. *On Consolation*	152.4
James, Henry. *Literary Criticism; Vol. 1*	809
James, P. D. *Talking About Detective Fiction*	823
Jenkyns, Richard. *Classical Literature*	880.09
Jennings, Ken. *Planet Funny*	809.7
Jones, Gerard. *Men of Tomorrow*	741.5
Kakutani, Michiko. *Ex Libris*	028
Karim-Cooper, Farah. ★*The Great White Bard*	822.33
Knausgaard, Karl Ove. *So Much Longing in so Little Space*	759.81
Kroger, Lisa. *Monster, She Wrote*	920
Kundera, Milan. *Encounter*	809
Le Guin, Ursula K. *Ursula K. Le Guin*	B
Le Guin, Ursula K. *Words Are My Matter*	818
Leithauser, Brad. *Rhyme's Rooms*	808.1
Lepore, Jill. ★*The Secret History of Wonder Woman*	741.5
Lynskey, Dorian. *The Ministry of Truth*	823
Manglik, Gauri. ★*Muslims in Story*	809
Mantel, Hilary. *Mantel Pieces*	824.914
McCloud, Scott. ★*Understanding Comics*	741.5
McDermott, Alice. *What About the Baby?*	814
Miller, Lucasta. ★*Keats*	821
Moore, Lorrie. *See What Can Be Done*	801
Morrison, Robert. *The Regency Years*	941.07
Morrison, Toni. ★*The Origin of Others*	809
Nabokov, Peter. *Where the Lightning Strikes*	299.7
Nafisi, Azar. *Read Dangerously*	809
Nesteroff, Kliph. *The Comedians*	792.7
Nesteroff, Kliph. *We Had a Little Real Estate Problem*	970.004
Nevala-Lee, Alec. *Astounding*	809.3
Nicolson, Adam. *The Making of Poetry*	821.709
Ozick, Cynthia. *Critics, Monsters, Fanatics, and Other Literary Essays*	801
Paglia, Camille. ★*Break, Blow, Burn*	821.009
Philbrick, Nathaniel. *Why Read Moby-Dick?*	813
Pitzer, Andrea. *The Secret History of Vladimir Nabokov*	813
Prose, Francine. *What to Read and Why*	028
Puchner, Martin. *The Written World*	809
Rehak, Melanie. *Girl Sleuth*	813
Ricks, Thomas E. ★*First Principles*	973.09
Rioux, Anne Boyd. *Meg, Jo, Beth, Amy*	813
Robinson, Marilynne. ★*Reading Genesis*	222
Row, Jess. *White Flights*	813
Sampson, Fiona. *In Search of Mary Shelley*	B
Schumacher, Michael. *Will Eisner*	741.5
Shales, Tom. *Live from New York*	791.45
Shattuck, Roger. *Proust's Way*	843
Showalter, Elaine. ★*A Jury of Her Peers*	810.9
Smith, Chris. *The Daily Show (the Book)*	791.45
Smith, Emma. *Portable Magic*	002
Sol, Adam. *How a Poem Moves*	808.1
Spiegelman, Art. *Co-Mix*	741.5
Spiegelman, Art. *Metamaus*	B
Tisserand, Michael. *Krazy*	741.5
Town, Caren J. *LGBTQ Young Adult Fiction*	813.009
Travisano, Thomas J. *Love Unknown*	B
Urofsky, Melvin I. *Dissent and the Supreme Court*	342.7302
Vargas Llosa, Mario. *Sabers and Utopias*	980.03
Watling, Sarah. *Tomorrow Perhaps the Future*	946.081
Weldon, Glen. ★*The Caped Crusade*	741.5
Weller, Sam. *The Bradbury Chronicles*	B
Wilson, A. N. *The Mystery of Charles Dickens*	823
Winkler, Elizabeth. *Shakespeare Was a Woman & Other Heresies*	822.33
Wolk, Douglas. ★*All of the Marvels*	741.5
Wood, James. *How Fiction Works*	808.3
Zenith, Richard. *Pessoa*	B
Literary Criticism; Vol. 1. James, Henry	809

LITERARY CURIOSITIES

Jenkins, Jessica Kerwin. *All the Time in the World*	390

LITERARY FORGERIES AND HOAXES

Shapiro, James. *Contested Will*	822.33

LITERARY FORM

Baldick, Chris. ★*The Oxford Dictionary of Literary Terms*	803

LITERARY JOURNALISM

Amis, Martin. *The Rub of Time*	824
Keefe, Patrick Radden. ★*Rogues*	364.16

LITERARY LANDMARKS

Cheever, Susan. *American Bloomsbury*	920
Heyman, Stephen. *The Planter of Modern Life*	B
Wright, Richard. ★*Black Boy*	B

LITERARY MOVEMENTS

Ginsberg, Allen. *Best Minds of My Generation*	810.9

LITERARY PRIZES

Leader, Zachary. *The Life of Saul Bellow*	B

LITERATURE

Appleman, Deborah. *Literature and the New Culture Wars*	807
Baldick, Chris. ★*The Oxford Dictionary of Literary Terms*	803
Borges, Jorge Luis. *Selected Non-Fictions*	864
Boyer, Anne. *The Undying*	B
Brewer, Ebenezer Cobham. ★*Brewer's Dictionary of Phrase & Fable*	423
Chabon, Michael. *Bookends*	818
Deutsch, Babette. *Poetry Handbook*	808.1
Figes, Orlando. *The Europeans*	920
Franzen, Jonathan. *Farther Away*	814
Glass, Charles. *Soldiers Don't Go Mad*	616.85
James, Henry. *Literary Criticism; Vol. 1*	809
Kakutani, Michiko. *Ex Libris*	028
Kundera, Milan. ★*The Curtain*	801
Lahiri, Jhumpa. *Translating Myself and Others*	418
Le Guin, Ursula K. *No Time to Spare*	814
Leader, Zachary. *The Life of Saul Bellow*	B
McCann, Colum. *Letters to a Young Writer*	808.02
McDermott, Alice. *What About the Baby?*	814
Messud, Claire. *Kant's Little Prussian Head and Other Reasons Why I Write*	B
Poe, Edgar Allan. *Essays and Reviews*	809
Prose, Francine. *What to Read and Why*	028
Prothero, Stephen R. *God the Bestseller*	070.5
Rakoff, Joanna Smith. *My Salinger Year*	B
Rosen, Jeffrey. *The Pursuit of Happiness*	973.3
Solnit, Rebecca. *The Faraway Nearby*	814
Sontag, Susan. *At the Same Time*	814
Thurman, Judith. ★*A Left-Handed Woman*	814
Vargas Llosa, Mario. *Conversation at Princeton*	868
Wood, James. *How Fiction Works*	808.3

LITERATURE AND HISTORY

Castleman, Michael. *The Untold Story of Books*	381
Norwich, John Julius. *Shakespeare's Kings*	822.33
Puchner, Martin. *The Written World*	809

PUBLIC LIBRARY CORE COLLECTION: NONFICTION
Twentieth Edition

Rosen, Jeffrey. *The Pursuit of Happiness*	973.3
Rosenblitt, J. Alison. *The Beauty of Living*	B
Severin, Timothy. *In Search of Robinson Crusoe*	996.1
LITERATURE AND SCIENCE	
Tresch, John. *The Reason for the Darkness of the Night*	B
LITERATURE AND SOCIETY	
Beard, Mary. ★*Women & Power*	305.409
Castillo, Elaine. ★*How to Read Now*	418
Di Cintio, Marcello. *Pay No Heed to the Rockets*	956.9405
Kelly, Helena. *Jane Austen, the Secret Radical*	823
Leader, Zachary. *The Life of Saul Bellow*	B
Morrison, Toni. ★*The Source of Self-Regard*	814
Nafisi, Azar. *The Republic of Imagination*	
Prothero, Stephen R. *The American Bible*	973
Puchner, Martin. *The Written World*	809
Rosen, Jeffrey. *The Pursuit of Happiness*	973.3
Shapiro, James. *Shakespeare in a Divided America*	822.33
Shapiro, James. *The Year of Lear*	822.33
Twain, Mark. *Autobiography of Mark Twain*	B
Twain, Mark. ★*Autobiography of Mark Twain*	B
Twain, Mark. ★*Autobiography of Mark Twain*	B
Wolk, Douglas. ★*All of the Marvels*	741.5
Literature and the New Culture Wars. Appleman, Deborah	807
LITHIUM	
Conway, Edmund. *Material World*	333.7
Lithwick, Dahlia	
Lady Justice	345.73
Litman, Laken	
Strong Like a Woman	796
Litt, David	
Democracy in One Book or Less	321.8
Thanks, Obama	B
LITT, DAVID, 1986-	
Litt, David. *Thanks, Obama*	B
Little and Often. Preszler, Trent	B
The Little Big Book of White Spells. Abrev, Ileana	133.4
★*Little Big Bully*. Erdrich, Heid E.	811
LITTLE BIGHORN, BATTLE OF THE, 1876	
Connell, Evan S. *Son of the Morning Star*	973.8
Donovan, Jim. *A Terrible Glory*	973.8
Gardner, Mark L. *The Earth Is All That Lasts*	978.004
McMurtry, Larry. *Custer*	B
Philbrick, Nathaniel. ★*The Last Stand*	973.8
Stiles, T. J. *Custer's Trials*	B
The Little Book of Big Lies. Lifford, Tina	155.2
Little Book of Book Making. Rivers, Charlotte	686
The Little Book of Hygge. Wiking, Meik	158.1
The Little Book of Lykke. Wiking, Meik	646.7
LITTLE CROW, DIED 1863	
Berg, Scott W. ★*38 Nooses*	973.7
★*A Little Devil in America*. Abdurraqib, Hanif	791.089
Little Earthquakes. Mandel, Sarah	B
★*Little Failure*. Shteyngart, Gary	B
A Little History of Poetry. Carey, John	809.1
LITTLE LEAGUE BASEBALL	
Geist, William. *Little League Confidential*	796.357
Little League Confidential. Geist, William	796.357
Little Matches. O'Hara, Maryanne	B
Little One-Yard Wonders. Yaker, Rebecca	646.2
Little Panic. Stern, Amanda	616.8522
The Little Red Book of Fly Fishing. Meyers, Charlie	799.12
LITTLE RICHARD, 1932-2020	
White, Charles. *The Life and Times of Little Richard*	B
LITTLE ROCK, ARKANSAS	
Margolick, David. *Elizabeth and Hazel*	379.2
Little Soldiers. Chu, Lenora	370
Little Weirds. Slate, Jenny	B
Little, Elbert L.	
The Audubon Society Field Guide to North American Trees	582.16097
LITTLE, LOUISE LANGDON, 1897-1989	
Tubbs, Anna Malaika. *The Three Mothers*	306.874
LITTLE, SAMUEL, 1940-2020	
Lauren, Jillian. *Behold the Monster*	364.152
Liu, Simu	
★*We Were Dreamers*	B
LIU, SIMU, 1989-	
Liu, Simu. ★*We Were Dreamers*	B
Live Cinema and Its Techniques. Coppola, Francis Ford	791.4302
Live from New York. Shales, Tom	791.45
Live Long And—. Shatner, William	B
★*Live to See the Day*. Goyal, Nikhil	305.5
Live Wire. Ripa, Kelly	B
Live Wires. Warner, Daniel	786.7
Live Work Work Work Die. Pein, Corey	338.4
Lively, Penelope	
Life in the Garden	B
LIVELY, PENELOPE, 1933-	
Lively, Penelope. *Life in the Garden*	B
Liverpool, Layal	
Systemic	362.1
The Lives of Brian. Johnson, Brian	B
★*The Lives of Lucian Freud*. Feaver, William	B
Lives of Moral Leadership. Coles, Robert	170
★*The Lives of the Great Composers*. Schonberg, Harold C.	780
Lives of the Popes. McBrien, Richard P.	B
Lives of the Stoics. Holiday, Ryan	188
The Lives of the Surrealists. Morris, Desmond	B
LIVESTOCK	
Baur, Gene. *Farm Sanctuary*	179
Faruqi, Sonia. *Project Animal Farm*	338.1
Foer, Jonathan Safran. ★*We Are the Weather*	636
Juan, Li. *Winter Pasture*	951.06
Rude, Emelyn. *Tastes Like Chicken*	338.1
Stewart, Tracey. *Do Unto Animals*	590
Livewired. Eagleman, David	612.8
LIVING ALONE	
Carr, Caleb. *My Beloved Monster*	B
The Living and the Dead. Hendrickson, Paul	959.704
The Living Fire. Hirsch, Edward	811
The Living Great Lakes. Dennis, Jerry	977
Living History. Clinton, Hillary Rodham	B
The Living Landscape. Darke, Rick	712
Living Lively. Thomas, Haile	641.5
Living Out Islam. Kugle, Scott Alan	297
★*A Living Remedy*. Chung, Nicole	B
Living The Artist's Way. Cameron, Julia	153.3
Living The Secular Life. Zuckerman, Phil	211
Living to Tell the Tale. Garcia Marquez, Gabriel	B
Living with Jazz. Morgenstern, Dan	781.65
Living Without Plastic. Allen, Brigette	640
Livingston, Jane	
The Paintings of Joan Mitchell	759.13
Livingston, Robert W.	
The Conversation	305.8
Livio, Mario	
Why?	153.3
Llewellyn's Complete Book of Chakras. Dale, Cyndi	131
LLOYD GEORGE, DAVID, 1863-1945	
MacMillan, Margaret. *Paris 1919*	940.3
Lloyd Webber, Andrew	
Unmasked	B
LLOYD WEBBER, ANDREW, 1948-	
Lloyd Webber, Andrew. *Unmasked*	B
Lloyd, Bobbie	
The Magnolia Bakery Handbook	641.86
Lloyd, Carli	
When Nobody Was Watching	B
LLOYD, CARLI, 1982-	
Lloyd, Carli. *When Nobody Was Watching*	B
Lloyd, Nick	
The Western Front	940.4
Lloyd, Seth	
Programming the Universe	530.12
Loades, Greg	
The Modern Cottage Garden	635
LOANS	
Hudson, Michael W. *The Monster*	332.63
LOBBYING	
Quigley, Fran. *Prescription for the People*	338.4
Winkler, Adam. *We the Corporations*	346.73
Lobel, Orly	
You Don't Own Me	346.7304
LOBO, JULIO, 1898-1983	
Rathbone, John Paul. *The Sugar King of Havana*	B
LOCAL ELECTIONS	
Martini, Adrienne. *Somebody's Gotta Do It*	B

AUTHOR, TITLE, SERIES AND SUBJECT INDEX

LOCAL FOODS
    Ackerman-Leist, Philip. *Rebuilding the Foodshed* — 338.1
    Batali, Mario. *Mario Batali Big American Cookbook* — 641.5973
    Hewitt, Ben. ★*The Town That Food Saved* — 338.1
    Howard, Vivian. *Deep Run Roots* — 641.5975
    Kochilas, Diane. *The Ikaria Way* — 641.5
    Terry, Bryant. *Vegan Soul Kitchen* — 641.5
    Waters, Alice. ★*We Are What We Eat* — 641.01

LOCAL GOVERNMENT
    Bordewich, Fergus M. *Washington* — 975.3
    LeDuff, Charlie. *Detroit* — 977.4
    Prickett, Pamela J. ★*The Unclaimed* — 363.7
    Rubinstein, Julian. ★*The Holly* — 364.106

LOCAL HISTORY
    Carlson, Brady. *Dead Presidents* — B
    Duncan, Dayton. *The National Parks* — 333.78
    Green, Matthew. *Shadowlands* — 941.03
    Hale, Grace Elizabeth. *In the Pines* — 364.13
    Lunenfeld, Peter. *City at the Edge of Forever* — 979.4
    Vowell, Sarah. *Assassination Vacation* — B

Local Visitations. Dunn, Stephen — 811

LOCKE, ALAIN LEROY, 1886-1954
    Stewart, Jeffrey C. ★*The New Negro* — 191

Locke, John
    An Essay Concerning Human Understanding — 121

Locke, Tembi
    ★*From Scratch* — B

LOCKE, TEMBI, 1970-
    Locke, Tembi. ★*From Scratch* — B

Lockhart, Chris
    ★*Walking the Bowl* — 362.7

Locking up Our Own. Forman, James — 364.973

Lockley, Thomas
    African Samurai — B

LOCKWOOD, BELVA ANN BENNETT, 1830-1917
    Norgren, Jill. *Belva Lockwood* — B

Lockwood, Lewis
    Beethoven — B

Lockwood, Patricia
    Priestdaddy — B

LOCKWOOD, PATRICIA
    Lockwood, Patricia. *Priestdaddy* — B

LOCOMOTIVES
    Solomon, Brian. *The Field Guide to Trains* — 625.2

LODGE, HENRY CABOT, 1902-1985
    Kinzer, Stephen. ★*The True Flag* — 327.73

Lodgings. Sosnowski, Andrzej — 891.8

The *Loeb* classical library [Series]. Horace — 874

Loeb, Abraham
    Extraterrestrial — 576.8

LOEB, RICHARD A., 1905-1936
    King, Greg. *Nothing but the Night* — 364.152

The *Loft Generation*. Schloss, Edith — 700.9

Loftis, Larry
    Code Name — B
    ★*The Watchmaker's Daughter* — 940.53

Loftus, Peter
    The Messenger — 338.4

Logan, M. David
    Mat, Mount, and Frame It Yourself — 749

Logan, William Bryant
    Sprout Lands — 582.16

Logevall, Fredrik
    Embers of War — 959.704
    ★*JFK* — B

LOGGING
    Thoreau, Henry David. *The Maine Woods* — 917

LOGIC
    Ariely, Dan. *Predictably Irrational* — 153.8
    Copi, Irving M. ★*Introduction to Logic* — 160
    Holt, Jim. ★*When Einstein Walked with Gödel* — 814
    Kershenbaum, Arik. *The Zoologist's Guide to the Galaxy* — 576.8
    Konnikova, Maria. *Mastermind* — 153.4
    Mlodinow, Leonard. *Emotional* — 152.4
    Novella, Steven. *The Skeptics' Guide to the Universe* — 500
    Pinker, Steven. *Rationality* — 153.4

Logical Family. Maupin, Armistead — B

LOGICIANS
    Budiansky, Stephen. *Journey to the Edge of Reason* — B

Logsdon, Gene
    Letter to a Young Farmer — 338.10973

Loh, Sandra Tsing
    The Madwoman and the Roomba — B

LOH, SANDRA TSING
    Loh, Sandra Tsing. *The Madwoman and the Roomba* — B

Lohman, Sarah
    ★*Endangered Eating* — 641.5973

LOKI (NORSE DEITY)
    Larrington, Carolyne. *The Norse Myths* — 293

Lomas, Vallery
    ★*Life Is What You Bake It* — 641.81

Lomax, Alan
    ★*The Land Where the Blues Began* — 781.643

London. Ackroyd, Peter — 942.1

The *London Scene*. Woolf, Virginia — 942.1

LONDON, ENGLAND
    Ackroyd, Peter. *London* — 942.1
    Asher, Zain E. *Where the Children Take Us* — 942.1
    Barnes, Julian. *The Man in the Red Coat* — B
    Benjamin, A. K. *Let Me Not Be Mad* — 612.8
    Bilefsky, Dan. *The Last Job* — 364.16
    Brickell, Francesca Cartier. *The Cartiers* — B
    Cronkite, Walter. *Cronkite's War* — 070.4
    Crowe, Lauren Goldstein. *The Towering World of Jimmy Choo* — 391.4
    Guha, Ramachandra. *Gandhi Before India* — B
    Jobb, Dean. *The Case of the Murderous Dr. Cream* — 364.152
    Lance, Rachel. *Chamber Divers* — 940.54
    Lipstadt, Deborah E. *History on Trial* — 940.53
    Maddox, Brenda. *Rosalind Franklin* — B
    Maiklem, Lara. *Mudlark* — B
    Nagorski, Andrew. *Saving Freud* — 940.53
    O'Sullivan, Emer. *The Fall of the House of Wilde* — B
    Russell, Gareth. ★*The Palace* — 942.1
    Skaife, Christopher. *The Ravenmaster* — B
    Tomalin, Claire. *Thomas Hardy* — B
    Woolf, Virginia. *The London Scene* — 942.1

LONDON, ENGLAND HISTORY
    Ackroyd, Peter. *London* — 942.1
    Cornwell, Patricia Daniels. *Ripper* — 364.152
    Damrosch, Leopold. *The Club* — 920
    Harman, Claire. *Murder by the Book* — 364.152
    Johnson, Steven. *The Ghost Map* — 614.5
    Larson, Erik. ★*The Splendid and the Vile* — 940.54
    Nicholl, Charles. *The Reckoning* — B
    Rubenhold, Hallie. ★*The Five* — 362.88
    Talty, Stephan. *Agent Garbo* — 940.5

LONDON, ONTARIO
    Brown, Vanessa. *The Forest City Killer* — 364.152

Lone Survivor. Luttrell, Marcus — 958.104

The *Loneliest Polar Bear*. Williams, Kale — 599.786

LONELINESS
    Baker, Billy. *We Need to Hang Out* — 177
    Brous, Sharon. ★*The Amen Effect* — 296.3
    Brown, Brene. *Braving the Wilderness* — 305.8
    Brownback, Lydia. *Finding God in My Loneliness* — 248.8
    DiFelice, Bekah. *Almost There* — 248.8
    Ehrlich, Gretel. *This Cold Heaven* — 998.2
    Henderson, Artis. *Unremarried Widow* — B
    Jamison, Leslie. ★*Make It Scream, Make It Burn* — 814
    Laing, Olivia. ★*The Lonely City* — 700.1
    Murthy, Vivek Hallegere. *Together* — 158.2
    Parker, Morgan. ★*You Get What You Pay For* — 305.896
    Prickett, Pamela J. ★*The Unclaimed* — 363.7
    Radtke, Kristen. *Seek You* — 741.5

LONELINESS IN TEENAGERS
    Legler, Casey. ★*Godspeed* — B

The *Loneliness of the Long-Distance Cartoonist*. Tomine, Adrian — 741.5

★The *Lonely City*. Laing, Olivia — 700.1

Lonely Planet Epic Surf Breaks of the World [Series]. Mackinnon, Al — 797.32

LONERS
    Laing, Olivia. ★*The Lonely City* — 700.1

LONG DISTANCE FRIENDSHIP
    Sow, Aminatou. *Big Friendship* — 177

LONG DISTANCE RUNNERS
    Alvarez, Noe. *Spirit Run* — 796.42

PUBLIC LIBRARY CORE COLLECTION: NONFICTION
Twentieth Edition

Davis, Jennifer Pharr. *The Pursuit of Endurance*	796.51
Engle, Charlie. *Running Man*	B
Finn, Adharanand. *The Rise of the Ultra Runners*	B
Foreman, Tom. *My Year of Running Dangerously*	B
The Long Hangover. Walker, Shaun	947.086
LONG ISLAND, NEW YORK	
Burns, Cherie. *The Great Hurricane—1938*	974.7
Calcaterra, Regina. *Etched in Sand*	B
Calcaterra, Regina. *Girl Unbroken*	B
Griswold, Mac K. *The Manor*	974.7
Hermes, Will. *Lou Reed*	B
Montillo, Roseanne. *Deliberate Cruelty*	364.152
Long Live the Tribe of Fatherless Girls. Madden, T Kira	814
★*The Long Reckoning*. Black, George	959.704
Long Road. Hyden, Steven	782.42166
The Long Road Home. Raddatz, Martha	B
Long Road to Hard Truth. Wilkins, Robert L.	069
Long Shot. Azad	B
Long Soldier, Layli	
★*Whereas*	811
The Long Summer. Fagan, Brian M.	551.6
A Long Time Ago in a Cutting Room Far, Far Away. Hirsch, Paul	B
Long Time Coming. Dyson, Michael Eric	305.800973
The Long Walk. Castner, Brian	B
★*Long Walk to Freedom*. Mandela, Nelson	B
The Long War. Loyn, David	958.104
★*A Long Way Gone*. Beah, Ishmael	B
A Long Way Home. Brierley, Saroo	B
LONG, BRECKINRIDGE, 1881-1958	
McKean, David. *Watching Darkness Fall*	940.53
LONG-DISTANCE RUNNING	
Engle, Charlie. *Running Man*	B
Finn, Adharanand. *The Rise of the Ultra Runners*	B
Finn, Adharanand. *The Way of the Runner*	796.42
Higdon, Hal. ★*Marathon*	796.42
Inman, Matthew. *The Terrible and Wonderful Reasons Why I Run Long Distances*	741.5
Keflezighi, Meb. *Meb for Mortals*	796.4252
Magill, Pete. *Build Your Running Body*	796.42
The Long-Distance Teammate. Eikenberry, Kevin	650.1
Longerich, Peter	
Goebbels	B
Hitler	B
The Longest Con. Conason, Joe	320.52
The Longest Fight. Gildea, William	B
The Longest Minute. Davenport, Matthew J.	979.4
The Longest War. Bergen, Peter L.	909.83
LONGEVITY	
Attia, Peter. ★*Outlive*	612.6
Crowley, Chris. *Younger Next Year*	613
Day, John D. *The Longevity Plan*	612.6
Ehrenreich, Barbara. *Natural Causes*	613.2
Esmonde-White, Miranda. *Aging Backwards*	613.7
Sinclair, David A. *Lifespan*	570
The Longevity Plan. Day, John D.	612.6
LONGFELLOW, HENRY WADSWORTH, 1807-1882	
Basbanes, Nicholas A. ★*Cross of Snow*	B
The Longing for Less. Chayka, Kyle	179.9
A Longing for the Light. Aleixandre, Vicente	861
Longitude. Sobel, Dava	526
LONGITUDE	
Sobel, Dava. *Longitude*	526
Longman, Jere	
Among the Heroes	974.8
Longo, Matthew	
The Picnic	947.084
LONGSTOCKING, PIPPI (FICTITIOUS CHARACTER)	
Andersen, Jens. *Astrid Lindgren*	B
Longstreet. Varon, Elizabeth R.	B
LONGSTREET, JAMES, 1821-1904	
Varon, Elizabeth R. *Longstreet*	B
LONGWORTH, ALICE ROOSEVELT, 1884-1980	
Cordery, Stacy A. *Alice*	B
Peyser, Marc N. *Hissing Cousins*	B
Longworth, Karina	
Seduction	B
Look. Sharif, Solmaz	811
Look Again. Sharot, Tali	158.1
Look Again. Ward, Ossian	750.1
★*Look Alive Out There*. Crosley, Sloane	814
Look at the USA. Van Agtmael, Peter	070
Look Away. Kushner, Jacob	305.9
Look Back in Anger. Osborne, John	822
Look for Me There. Russert, Luke	B
Look Me in the Eye. Robison, John Elder	B
The Look of Architecture. Rybczynski, Witold	721
Look, I Made a Hat. Sondheim, Stephen	782.1
Looking for Alaska. Jenkins, Peter	979.8
Looking for Farrakhan. Levinsohn, Florence Hamlish	B
Looking for Lorraine. Perry, Imani	B
Looking for Miss America. Mifflin, Margot	791.6
Looking for Spinoza. Damasio, Antonio R.	152.4
Looking for the Good War. Samet, Elizabeth D.	940.53
Looking for the Stranger. Kaplan, Alice Yaeger	B
Loom Knitting Primer. Phelps, Isela	746.43
The Loom of Time. Kaplan, Robert D.	327
★*The Looming Tower*. Wright, Lawrence	973.931
Loomis, Andrew	
Figure Drawing for All It's Worth	743.4
LOOMS	
Daly, Fiona. *Weaving on a Little Loom*	746.1
Mitchell, Syne. *Inventive Weaving on a Little Loom*	746.1
Phelps, Isela. *Loom Knitting Primer*	746.43
Loonshots. Bahcall, Safi	658.4
The Looting Machine. Burgis, Tom	338.2
Lopez, Barry Holstun	
Horizon	B
★*Of Wolves and Men*	599.773
LOPEZ, BARRY HOLSTUN, 1945-2020	
Lopez, Barry Holstun. *Horizon*	B
Lopez-Alt, J. Kenji	
The Food Lab	664
★*The Wok*	641.595
Lord of All the Dead. Cercas, Javier	868
Lord, Walter	
★*A Night to Remember*	910
Lorde, Audre	
★*The Selected Works of Audre Lorde*	814
Sister Outsider	814
Lords of Finance. Ahamed, Liaquat	920
Lords of the Desert. Barr, James	956
Lords of the Fly. Burke, Monte	799.124
Lorenz, Taylor	
★*Extremely Online*	302.23
Lorr, Benjamin	
The Secret Life of Groceries	381.4
Lorraine Hansberry. Shields, Charles J.	B
LOS ALAMOS, NEW MEXICO	
Kunetka, James W. *The General and the Genius*	355.8
LOS ANGELES, CALIFORNIA	
Brown, Mick. ★*Tearing Down the Wall of Sound*	B
Chude-Sokei, Louis Onuorah. *Floating in a Most Peculiar Way*	979.4
Dudley, Steven S. *MS-13*	364.106
Flannery, Kate. *Strip Tees*	338.4
Grande, Reyna. ★*The Distance Between Us*	973
Hahn, Emanuel. *Koreatown Dreaming*	979.4
Hirsch, Foster. ★*Hollywood and the Movies of the Fifties*	791.43
Hobbs, Jeff. *Show Them You're Good*	373
Jones, Brenda. *Maxine Waters*	B
Krist, Gary. *The Mirage Factory*	920
Leovy, Jill. *Ghettoside*	364.152
Lunenfeld, Peter. *City at the Edge of Forever*	979.4
McCourt, Malachy. *Singing My Him Song*	B
McGough, Matthew. *The Lazarus Files*	364.152
McKeen, William. *Everybody Had an Ocean*	781.6609
Meier, Richard. *Building the Getty*	727
Moore, Susanna. *Miss Aluminum*	813
Nusbaum, Eric. *Stealing Home*	796.357
Offerman, Nick. *The Greatest Love Story Ever Told*	B
Orlean, Susan. ★*The Library Book*	027.4
Pearlman, Jeff. ★*Three-Ring Circus*	796.323
Prickett, Pamela J. ★*The Unclaimed*	363.7
Rempel, William C. *The Gambler*	B
Rosenzweig, Laura B. *Hollywood's Spies*	791.43
Ross, Steven Joseph. ★*Hitler in Los Angeles*	979.4
Stein, Jean. *West of Eden*	979.4

AUTHOR, TITLE, SERIES AND SUBJECT INDEX

Turbow, Jason. *They Bled Blue*	796.357
Westhoff, Ben. *Original Gangstas*	782.421649
LOSERS	
Leonard, Max. *Lanterne Rouge*	796.6
Losing Earth. Rich, Nathaniel	363.738
★*Losing Our Minds.* Foulkes, Lucy	616.89
Losos, Jonathan B.	
The Cat's Meow	636.8
Improbable Destinies	576.8
LOSS	
Adichie, Chimamanda Ngozi. *Notes on Grief*	155.9
Alexander, Kwame. *Why Fathers Cry at Night*	B
Alterman, Sara Faith. *Let's Never Talk About This Again*	616.8
Alyan, Hala. *The Moon That Turns You Back*	811
Anthony, Carmelo. *Where Tomorrows Aren't Promised*	B
Atwood, Margaret. *Dearly*	811
Bailey, Jennifer. *To My Beloveds*	261.8
Baird, Julia. ★*Victoria the Queen*	B
Barker, Elspeth. ★*Notes from the Henhouse*	828
Barry, Harry. *Emotional Healing*	158.1
Berg, Elizabeth. *I'll Be Seeing You*	306.874
Bibbins, Mark. *13th Balloon*	813
Biden, Jill. *Where the Light Enters*	B
Biden, Joseph R. *Promise Me, Dad*	B
Biden, Robert Hunter. *Beautiful Things*	B
Bilton, Chrysta. *Normal Family*	B
Black Thought. *The Upcycled Self*	B
Bloom, Amy. *In Love*	B
Bowler, Kate. *No Cure for Being Human*	B
Braitman, Laurel. *What Looks Like Bravery*	B
Brown, Molly McCully. *Places I've Taken My Body*	B
Cacciatore, Joanne. *Bearing the Unbearable*	155.9
Caldwell, Gail. *Let's Take the Long Way Home*	B
Carr, Caleb. *My Beloved Monster*	B
Carr, Erin Lee. *All That You Leave Behind*	B
Cheng, Nien. *Life and Death in Shanghai*	B
Cho, Grace M. *Tastes Like War*	305.48
Chow, Kat. *Seeing Ghosts*	B
Crosley, Sloane. *Grief Is for People*	B
Danticat, Edwidge. *The Art of Death*	809
Delaney, Rob. ★*A Heart That Works*	B
Didion, Joan. ★*The Year of Magical Thinking*	B
Doyne, Maggie. *Between the Mountain and the Sky*	B
Driver, Minnie. *Managing Expectations*	B
Dugdale, Lydia S. *The Lost Art of Dying*	155.9
Dutta, Sunil. *Stealing Green Mangoes*	973
Edelman, Hope. *The Aftergrief*	155.9
Edelman, Hope. *Motherless Daughters*	155.9
Ephron, Delia. *Left on Tenth*	B
Etheridge, Melissa. *Talking to My Angels*	B
Fairbanks, Amanda M. *The Lost Boys of Montauk*	910.91
Faust, Drew Gilpin. *This Republic of Suffering*	973.7
Fields, Micah. ★*We Hold Our Breath*	976.4
Finkel, David. *An American Dreamer*	975.8
Foer, Esther Safran. *I Want You to Know We're Still Here*	B
Fox, Michael J. *No Time Like the Future*	B
Garcia, Angela. ★*The Way That Leads Among the Lost*	362.29
Garcia, Mayte. *The Most Beautiful*	920
Garcia, Rodrigo. *A Farewell to Gabo and Mercedes*	B
Gay, Ross. *Inciting Joy*	814
Geller, Danielle. *Dog Flowers*	B
Gerson, Merissa Nathan. *Forget Prayers, Bring Cake*	155.9
Geter, Hafizah. *Un-American*	811
Glass, Sara. *Kissing Girls on Shabbat*	B
Gluck, Louise. *Winter Recipes from the Collective*	811
Goldberg, Whoopi. *Bits and Pieces*	B
Gracie, Rickson. *Breathe*	B
Graham, Jorie. *To 2040*	811
Granata, Vince. *Everything Is Fine*	B
Greene, Jayson. *Once More We Saw Stars*	155.9
Grue, Jan. *I Live a Life Like Yours*	B
Gunn, Thom. ★*The Letters of Thom Gunn*	821
Hagerty, Alexa. ★*Still Life with Bones*	599.9
Harjo, Joy. ★*Poet Warrior*	B
Hass, Robert. *Summer Snow*	811.6
Hemon, Aleksandar. *My Parents*	814
Henderson, Artis. *Unremarried Widow*	B
Hesse, Maria. ★*Frida Kahlo*	B
Holloway, Richard. *Waiting for the Last Bus*	202
Hood, Ann. *Kitchen Yarns*	641.5
Hsu, Hua. ★*Stay True*	B
Irby, Samantha. ★*Quietly Hostile*	814
James, John W. ★*The Grief Recovery Handbook*	155.9
Katin, Miriam. *We Are on Our Own*	741.5
Kaur, Rupi. *The Sun and Her Flowers*	811.6
Kugler, Rob. *A Dog Named Beautiful*	B
Leach, Samantha. ★*The Elissas*	362.73
Leder, Steven Z. *The Beauty of What Remains*	306.9
Limon, Ada. *Bright Dead Things*	811
Limon, Ada. ★*The Hurting Kind*	811
Lin, Amy. *Here After*	B
Lin, Jami Nakamura. *The Night Parade*	B
Locke, Tembi. ★*From Scratch*	B
Lynn, Loretta. *Me & Patsy Kickin' up Dust*	B
Maisel, Ivan. *I Keep Trying to Catch His Eye*	B
Malhotra, Aanchal. *Remnants of Partition*	954.04
Mansbach, Adam. *I Had a Brother Once*	811
Masson, J. Moussaieff. *Lost Companions*	636.088
Matar, Hisham. *The Return*	B
McColl, Sarah. *Joy Enough*	B
McInerny, Nora. *The Hot Young Widows Club*	155.9
Miller, Michelle. *Belonging*	B
Moe, John. *The Hilarious World of Depression*	616.85
Morgan, Abi. *This Is Not a Pity Memoir*	B
Ng, Fae Myenne. *Orphan Bachelors*	B
O'Hara, Maryanne. *Little Matches*	B
O'Reilly, Seamas. ★*Did Ye Hear Mammy Died?*	B
Oates, Joyce Carol. *American Melancholy*	811
Olivares, Efren C. *My Boy Will Die of Sorrow*	305.9
Olivarez, Jose. *Promises of Gold = Promesas De Oro*	811
Ondaatje, Michael. *A Year of Last Things*	811
Pagels, Elaine H. ★*Why Religion?*	B
Park, J. S. ★*As Long as You Need*	248.8
Patterson, James. *Walk in My Combat Boots*	920
Petrosino, Kiki. *White Blood*	811
Peyser, Marc N. *Hissing Cousins*	B
Pittard, Hannah. *We Are Too Many*	B
Porizkova, Paulina. *No Filter*	B
Quinones, John. ★*One Year in Uvalde*	371.7
Rehm, Diane. *On My Own*	B
Reichl, Ruth. *My Kitchen Year*	641.5
Risbridger, Ella. *The Year of Miracles*	641.5
Risner, Vaneetha Rendall. *Walking Through Fire*	B
Roig-Debellis, Kaitlin. *Choosing Hope*	371.7
Rosenblatt, Roger. *Kayak Morning*	155.9
Rosenthal, Jason. *My Wife Said You May Want to Marry Me*	B
Rosner, Elizabeth. *Survivor Cafe*	940.53
Rushdie, Salman. ★*Knife*	B
Russert, Luke. *Look for Me There*	B
Sabathia, CC. *Till the End*	796.357
Saint John, Bozoma. *The Urgent Life*	B
Saldana, Stephanie. *What We Remember Will Be Saved*	362.7
Samuel, Julia. *Grief Works*	155.9
Sandberg, Sheryl. *Option B*	155.9
Sardy, Marin. *The Edge of Every Day*	B
Schulz, Kathryn. ★*Lost & Found*	B
Seager, Sara. *The Smallest Lights in the Universe*	B
Sedaris, David. ★*Happy-Go-Lucky*	814
Seierstad, Asne. *Angel of Grozny*	947.086
Shannon, Molly. ★*Hello, Molly!*	B
Sharpe, Christina Elizabeth. *Ordinary Notes*	305.896
Shattuck, Ben. *Six Walks*	B
Slate, Jenny. *Little Weirds*	B
Smith, Carol. *Crossing the River*	B
Smith, Patti. ★*M Train*	B
Smith, Patti. ★*Year of the Monkey*	B
Smith, Tracy K. ★*Such Color*	811
Soep, Elisabeth. *Other People's Words*	155.9
Stern, Adam. *Committed*	616.89
Strayed, Cheryl. ★*Wild*	B
Tan, Amy. ★*Where the Past Begins*	B
Taylor, Justin. *Riding with the Ghost*	B
Trejo, Danny. *Trejo*	B
Trice, Dawn Turner. ★*Three Girls from Bronzeville*	977.311
Turner, Tina. ★*Happiness Becomes You*	158.1
Vitale, Tom. *In the Weeds*	B

PUBLIC LIBRARY CORE COLLECTION: NONFICTION
Twentieth Edition

Vuong, Ocean. ★*Time Is a Mother*	811
Wiesel, Elie. ★*Night*	B
Williams, Florence. *Heartbreak*	306.7
Williamson, Elizabeth. ★*Sandy Hook*	364.152
Wolf, Brandon J. *A Place for Us*	B
Wolff, Daniel J. *Grown-Up Anger*	920
Young, Kevin. *Stones*	811
Zambreno, Kate. *The Light Room*	B
Zauner, Michelle. ★*Crying in H Mart*	B

LOSS IN CHILDREN
Emswiler, Mary Ann. *Guiding Your Child Through Grief*	155.9

LOSS IN TEENAGERS
Emswiler, Mary Ann. *Guiding Your Child Through Grief*	155.9
The Loss of a Pet. Sife, Wallace	155.9
★*Lost & Found*. Schulz, Kathryn	B
Lost and Stranded. Sprinkle, Timothy	613.6
The Lost Art of Dying. Dugdale, Lydia S.	155.9
The Lost Art of Scripture. Armstrong, Karen	208

LOST ARTICLES
Maiklem, Lara. *Mudlark*	B
Raab, Nathan. *The Hunt for History*	790.1
Satrapi, Marjane. *Chicken with Plums*	741.5
Lost At Sea. Wukovits, John F.	940.54
The Lost Bank. Grind, Kirsten	332.3
The Lost Book of Moses. Tigay, Chanan	098

LOST BOOKS
Davis, Margaret Leslie. *The Lost Gutenberg*	093
The Lost Boys of Montauk. Fairbanks, Amanda M.	910.91
The Lost Cafe Schindler. Schindler, Meriel	943.64
★*Lost City of the Incas*. Bingham, Hiram	985
★*The Lost City of the Monkey God*. Preston, Douglas J.	972.85
The Lost City of Z. Grann, David	918.1
Lost Companions. Masson, J. Moussaieff	636.088
The Lost Cyclist. Herlihy, David V.	B
The Lost Daughter. Williams, Mary	B

LOST DOGS
Charleson, Susannah. *Where the Lost Dogs Go*	636.7
The Lost Education of Horace Tate. Walker, Vanessa Siddle	370.92
The Lost Gutenberg. Davis, Margaret Leslie	093
Lost in Shangri-La. Zuckoff, Mitchell	940.54
Lost in the Dark. Weismann, Brad	791.43
Lost Kingdom. Plokhy, Serhii	947

LOST LOVE
Verant, Samantha. *Seven Letters from Paris*	B
The Lost Memoir. Gehrig, Lou	B
The Lost Spells. Macfarlane, Robert	811
Lost to the West. Brownworth, Lars	949.5
The Lost Tomb. Preston, Douglas J.	930.1
The Lost Tudor Princess. Weir, Alison	B

LOTHAIR II, KING OF LORRAINE, APPROXIMATELY 825-869
Winder, Simon. *Lotharingia*	944
Lotharingia. Winder, Simon	944
The Lotus Eaters. Conant, Jennet	940.54
Lotus Girl. Tworkov, Helen	B
Lou Reed. DeCurtis, Anthony	B
Lou Reed. Hermes, Will	B
Louder Than Hell. Wiederhorn, Jon	781.6609
Louis Armstrong, in His Own Words. Armstrong, Louis	B
★*Louis Armstrong, Master of Modernism*. Brothers, Thomas David	B
Louis Bamberger. Forgosh, Linda B.	B
Louis D. Brandeis. Urofsky, Melvin I.	B

LOUIS XIV, KING OF FRANCE, 1638-1715
DeJean, Joan E. *The Essence of Style*	391
DeJean, Joan E. *How Paris Became Paris*	944
Fraser, Antonia. *Love and Louis XIV*	B
Mansel, Philip. *King of the World*	944

LOUIS XV, KING OF FRANCE, 1710-1774
Darnton, Robert. *The Revolutionary Temper*	944

LOUIS XVI, KING OF FRANCE, 1754-1793
Darnton, Robert. *The Revolutionary Temper*	944
Schama, Simon. *Citizens*	944.04

LOUIS, JOE, 1914-1981
Roberts, Randy. *Joe Louis*	B

Louis, Matthew J.
Mission Transition	650.14
Louisa. Thomas, Louisa	B
Louisa on the Front Lines. Seiple, Samantha	B

LOUISE HOLLANDINE, COUNTESS PALATINE, ABBESS OF MAUBUISSON, 1622-1709
Goldstone, Nancy Bazelon. *Daughters of the Winter Queen*	920

LOUISE, PRINCESS OF GREAT BRITAIN, 1848-1939
Hawksley, Lucinda. *Queen Victoria's Mysterious Daughter*	B

LOUISIANA
Bauer, Shane. *American Prison*	365
Fessler, Pam. *Carville's Cure*	362.19699
Hardy, Jason Matthew. ★*The Second Chance Club*	364.6
Jackson, Ted. ★*You Ought to Do a Story About Me*	
Lambert, Miranda. *Y'all Eat Yet?*	641.5976
Northup, Solomon. *Twelve Years a Slave*	B
Van Meter, Matthew. *Deep Delta Justice*	345.763
Woodfox, Albert. *Solitary*	B

Louv, Richard
Our Wild Calling	615.8

Louvin, Charlie
Satan Is Real	920

LOUVIN, CHARLIE, 1927-2011
Louvin, Charlie. *Satan Is Real*	920

LOUVIN, IRA, 1924-1965
Louvin, Charlie. *Satan Is Real*	920

Louvish, Simon
Monkey Business	B
Lovable Livable Home. Petersik, Sherry	645

Lovato, Roberto
Unforgetting	B

LOVATO, ROBERTO
Lovato, Roberto. *Unforgetting*	B

LOVE
Abdurraqib, Hanif. ★*There's Always This Year*	796.323
Alderton, Dolly. *Everything I Know About Love*	B
Backman, Fredrik. *Things My Son Needs to Know About the World*	B
Belcourt, Billy-Ray. ★*A History of My Brief Body*	B
Bilton, Chrysta. *Normal Family*	B
Bloom, Amy. *In Love*	B
Boland, Eavan. *The Historians*	821
Braitman, Laurel. *What Looks Like Bravery*	B
Cacciatore, Joanne. *Bearing the Unbearable*	155.9
Caesar, Ed. *The Moth and the Mountain*	B
Carr, Caleb. *My Beloved Monster*	B
Chapman, Gary D. *Love as a Way of Life*	241
Coombes, Joshua. *Do Something for Nothing*	362.5
Curry, Michael B. *Love Is the Way*	241
Darling, Daniel. *Agents of Grace*	158.2
Dietrich, Sean. *You Are My Sunshine*	B
Doyne, Maggie. *Between the Mountain and the Sky*	B
Ephron, Delia. *Left on Tenth*	B
Feast, Fancy. *Naked*	792.7
Feiler, Bruce. *The First Love Story*	222
Felix, Camonghne. *Dyscalculia*	B
Fenn, Lisa. *Carry On*	B
Garcia, Mayte. *The Most Beautiful*	920
Goldstein, Meredith. *Can't Help Myself*	B
Gupta, Prachi. ★*They Called Us Exceptional*	B
Hagberg, Eva. *How to Be Loved*	616.7
Hay, Matt. *Soundtrack of Silence*	B
Hays, Katie. *Family of Origin, Family of Choice*	248.8086
Held, Shai. ★*Judaism Is About Love*	296.3
Hempel, Jessi. *The Family Outing*	B
Heughan, Sam. *Waypoints*	B
Jalal al-Din Rumi, Maulana. *Rumi*	891
Jordan, June. ★*The Essential June Jordan*	811
King, Billie Jean. ★*All In*	B
Kingston, Genevieve. *Did I Ever Tell You?*	B
Kohli, Sahaj Kaur. ★*But What Will People Say?*	616.89
Komunyakaa, Yusef. ★*Everyday Mojo Songs of Earth*	811
Kubler-Ross, Elisabeth. *Life Lessons*	170
Lamott, Anne. ★*Somehow*	814
Lekas Miller, Anna. *Love Across Borders*	323.6
Lin, Amy. *Here After*	B
Lorde, Audre. ★*The Selected Works of Audre Lorde*	814
Maisel, Ivan. *I Keep Trying to Catch His Eye*	B
Marshall, Nate. *Finna*	811
Miller, Michelle. *Belonging*	B
Moorer, Allison. *I Dream He Talks to Me*	782.42164
Morgan, Abi. *This Is Not a Pity Memoir*	B
Nelson, Maggie. ★*The Argonauts*	B

AUTHOR, TITLE, SERIES AND SUBJECT INDEX

Neruda, Pablo. ★*Twenty Love Poems and a Song of Despair*	861
Oates, Joyce Carol. *American Melancholy*	811
Olivarez, Jose. *Promises of Gold = Promesas De Oro*	811
Owens, Lama Rod. *Love and Rage*	152.4
Parks, Casey. *Diary of a Misfit*	B
Peck, M. Scott. ★*The Road Less Traveled*	158.1
Pham, Larissa. *Pop Song*	709.2
Poehler, Amy. *Yes Please*	B
Possanza, Amelia. *Lesbian Love Story*	B
Qadiri, Humayra. *Dancing in the Mosque*	B
Risbridger, Ella. *The Year of Miracles*	641.5
Rushdie, Salman. ★*Knife*	B
Saint John, Bozoma. *The Urgent Life*	B
Sanchez, Sonia. *Homegirls & Handgrenades*	811
Schulz, Kathryn. ★*Lost & Found*	B
Sharma, Nina. *The Way You Make Me Feel*	B
Shehadeh, Raja. ★*We Could Have Been Friends, My Father and I*	B
Smith, Tracy K. ★*Such Color*	811
Stern, Adam. *Committed*	616.89
Stone, Sharon. *The Beauty of Living Twice*	B
Strings, Sabrina. *The End of Love*	155.3
Tallis, Frank. *The Incurable Romantic*	152.4
Tanais. *In Sensorium*	B
Thom, Kai Cheng. *Falling Back in Love with Being Human*	811
Tran, Paul. *All the Flowers Kneeling*	811
Wallace, Carvell. *Another Word for Love*	B
Westheimer, Ruth. *The Doctor Is In*	B
Winch, Guy. *How to Fix a Broken Heart*	155.9
Winter, Molly Roden. *More*	B
Wolf, Brandon J. *A Place for Us*	B
Zhu, Mimi. *Be Not Afraid of Love*	152.4
★*Love & Lemons*. Donofrio, Jeanine	641.5
LOVE (CHRISTIANITY)	
Girzone, Joseph F. *Never Alone*	248.4
Griffin, Chante. *Loving Your Black Neighbor as Yourself*	261
Guthrie, Savannah. *Mostly What God Does*	248.4
Nagassar, Rohadi. *When We Belong*	254
Roberts, Matthias. *Holy Runaways*	262
Love Across Borders. Lekas Miller, Anna	323.6
Love and Capital. Gabriel, Mary	920
★*Love and Hate in Jamestown*. Price, David A.	975.5
Love and Louis XIV. Fraser, Antonia	B
Love and Rage. Owens, Lama Rod	152.4
Love as a Way of Life. Chapman, Gary D.	241
Love Child's Hotbed of Occasional Poetry. Finney, Nikky	811
Love Goes to Buildings on Fire. Hermes, Will	781.64
Love Hurts. Rinzler, Lodro	294.3
LOVE IN FILMS	
Carlson, Erin. *I'll Have What She's Having*	791.43
Love Is the Way. Curry, Michael B.	241
LOVE LETTER WRITING	
Verant, Samantha. *Seven Letters from Paris*	B
LOVE LETTERS	
Adams, John. *My Dearest Friend*	973.4
Cronkite, Walter. *Cronkite's War*	070.4
The Love Lives of Birds. Erickson, Laura	598.15
Love Me as I Am. Beauvais, Garcelle	B
Love Real Food. Taylor, Kathryne	641.5
Love That Story. Van Ness, Jonathan	791.4502
Love Thy Neighbor. Maass, Peter	949.702
LOVE TRIANGLES	
Ackroyd, Peter. *The Death of King Arthur*	823
Carson, Anne. *Autobiography of Red*	811
Figes, Orlando. *The Europeans*	920
McGough, Matthew. *The Lazarus Files*	364.152
Love Unknown. Travisano, Thomas J.	B
★*Love Wins*. Cenziper, Debbie	346.7301
The Love You Save. Taylor, Goldie	B
Love, Bettina L.	
Punished for Dreaming	371.829
Love, Henri. Nouwen, Henri J. M.	282.092
Love, Loss, and What We Ate. Lakshmi, Padma	791.4502
Love, Lucy. Ball, Lucille	B
Love, Susan M.	
★*Dr. Susan Love's Breast Book*	618.1
LOVELACE, ADA KING, COUNTESS OF, 1815-1852	
Essinger, James. *Ada's Algorithm*	B
Lovell, Julia	
Maoism	335.43
Lovell, Mary S.	
Bess of Hardwick	B
The Sisters	920.72
LOVELL, STANLEY P.	
Lisle, John. *The Dirty Tricks Department*	940.54
LOVERS	
Bibbins, Mark. *13th Balloon*	813
Lovesick Blues. Hemphill, Paul	B
★*Loving Our Own Bones*. Belser, Julia Watts	296
Loving Your Black Neighbor as Yourself. Griffin, Chante	261
Low Anthropology. Zahl, David	233
LOW-CALORIE DIET	
DiSpirito, Rocco. *Now Eat This!*	641.5
Gerard, Tieghan. *Half Baked Harvest Every Day*	641.5
Griffin, Brooke. *Skinny Suppers*	641.5
Homolka, Gina. *Skinnytaste Fast and Slow*	641.5
Homolka, Gina. *Skinnytaste One & Done*	641.5
Hunt, Lindsay Maitland. *Help Yourself*	641.5
Lillien, Lisa. *Hungry Girl 1-2-3*	641.5
Lillien, Lisa. *Hungry Girl Simply 6*	641.5
LOW-CARBOHYDRATE DIET	
Dada, Samah. *Dada Eats Love to Cook It*	641.5
Mullen, Seamus. *Real Food Heals*	641.5
Snodgrass, Alex. ★*The Defined Dish*	641.5
Urban, Melissa. *The Whole30 Friends & Family*	641.5
Wolf, Robb. *Wired to Eat*	641.5
LOW-COST COOKING	
Leake, Lisa. *100 Days of Real Food on a Budget*	641.5
Pepin, Jacques. ★*Jacques Pépin Cooking My Way*	641.5
LOW-FAT DIET	
Gerard, Tieghan. ★*Half Baked Harvest Every Day*	641.5
Jenkins, Nancy Harmon. *The New Mediterranean Diet Cookbook*	641.59
Lillien, Lisa. *Hungry Girl 1-2-3*	641.5
Lillien, Lisa. *Hungry Girl Simply 6*	641.5
Moskowitz, Isa Chandra. *Veganomicon*	641
LOW-INCOME HOUSING	
Desmond, Matthew. ★*Evicted*	339.4
Ross, Andrew. *Sunbelt Blues*	363.5
LOW-INTENSITY CONFLICTS (MILITARY SCIENCE)	
Junger, Sebastian. *Fire*	909.82
LOW-WAGE WORKERS	
Ehrenreich, Barbara. ★*Nickel and Dimed*	B
Freeman, Amanda. *Getting Me Cheap*	362.83
Land, Stephanie. *Maid*	B
Morgenson, Gretchen. ★*These Are the Plunderers*	332.6
Rivlin, Gary. *Broke, Usa*	339.4
Ross, Andrew. *Sunbelt Blues*	363.5
Lowe, George	
Letters from Everest	796.522
LOWE, GEORGE, 1924-2013	
Lowe, George. *Letters from Everest*	796.522
Lowe, Keith	
Prisoners of History	940.54
Savage Continent	940.55
Lowell, Amy	
Selected Poems	821
Lowell, Robert	
Collected Poems	811
LOWELL, ROBERT, 1917-1977	
Hardwick, Elizabeth. *The Dolphin Letters, 1970-1979*	811
Lowenstein, Roger	
America's Bank	332.1
Ways and Means	973.7
Lower Ed. Cottom, Tressie McMillan	378.73
Lower, Wendy	
Hitler's Furies	940.53
Lowery, Brian S.	
Selfless	155.2
LOWERY, EDDIE	
Frost, Mark. *The Match*	796.352
Lowery, Wesley	
★*American Whitelash*	305.8
Lowit, Roxanne	
Yves Saint Laurent	746.9
Lowman, Margaret	
The Arbornaut	581.7

Life in the Treetops	B
LOWMAN, MARGARET	
Lowman, Margaret. *The Arbornaut*	581.7
Lowman, Margaret. *Life in the Treetops*	B
Lownie, Andrew	
Traitor King	920
Lowry, Beverly	
Deer Creek Drive	364.152
Lowry, Erin	
★*Broke Millennial Talks Money*	332.024
Lowry, Melissa	
Vibrant Punch Needle Decor	746.44
Loxton, Daniel	
Abominable Science!	001.944
LOYALISTS (UNITED STATES HISTORY)	
Brands, H. W. ★*Our First Civil War*	973.3
Crawford, Alan Pell. *This Fierce People*	975
Kamensky, Jane. *A Revolution in Color*	759.13
Norton, Mary Beth. *1774*	973.3
LOYALTY	
Abdurraqib, Hanif. ★*There's Always This Year*	796.323
Jordan, Mary. *The Art of Her Deal*	B
Lewis, Damien. *The Dog Who Could Fly*	940.54
Rippon, Kelly. *Parent Up*	649
Taylor, Alan. *The Civil War of 1812*	973.5
Loyn, David	
In Afghanistan	958.1
The Long War	958.104
Lozada, Carlos	
The Washington Book	320
Lozano, Luis-Martin	
Frida Kahlo	759.972
LSD (DRUG)	
Kinzer, Stephen. *Poisoner in Chief*	B
Minutaglio, Bill. *The Most Dangerous Man in America*	B
Rush, Chris. *The Light Years*	B
LUBAVITCHER HASIDISM	
Telushkin, Joseph. *Rebbe*	296.833
Lubow, Arthur	
Diane Arbus	B
Lucado, Max	
Before Amen	248.3
Unshakable Hope	248.4
You Are Never Alone	248.4
LUCAS, GEORGE, 1944-	
Jones, Brian Jay. *George Lucas*	B
Lucas, Jack	
Indestructible	B
LUCAS, JACK, 1928-2008	
Lucas, Jack. *Indestructible*	B
LUCE, HENRY ROBINSON, 1898-1967	
Brinkley, Alan. ★*The Publisher*	B
Lucey, Donna M.	
Sargent's Women	920
LUCHA LIBRE	
Levi, Heather. *The World of Lucha Libre*	796.812
LUCIANO, LUCKY, 1897-1962	
Carter, Stephen L. *Invisible*	B
LUCID DREAMS	
Kerr, Christopher. *Death Is but a Dream*	155.9
LUCID, SHANNON, 1943-	
Grush, Loren. ★*The Six*	629.4
The Lucifer Effect. Zimbardo, Philip G.	155.9
The Luck of Friendship. Laughlin, James	B
LUCKADOO, JOHN, 1922-	
Maurer, Kevin. *Damn Lucky*	940.54
Luckerson, Victor	
Built from the Fire	976.6
Lucky. Allen, Jonathan	324.973
Lucky 666. Drury, Bob	B
Lucky Bastard. Buck, Joe	B
Lucky Child. Ung, Loung	B
Lucky Peach Presents 101 Easy Asian Recipes. Meehan, Peter	641.595
Lucretius Carus, Titus	
On the Nature of Things =	187
Lucrezia Borgia. Bradford, Sarah	B
Lucy. Johanson, Donald C.	569
LUDDITES	
Merchant, Brian. *Blood in the Machine*	303.48
LUDLOW, FITZ HUGH, 1836-1870	
Martin, Justin. *Rebel Souls*	920
Ludwig, David	
Always Hungry?	613.2
Ludwig, Frauke	
Essential Knit Sweaters	746.43
Ludwinski, Lisa	
Sister Pie	641.86
Luger, Chelsey	
★*The Seven Circles*	610
Luiselli, Valeria	
Tell Me How It Ends	305.23086
Lukacs, John	
Five Days in London, May 1940	940.53
Lukas, Albert	
★*Sweet Home Cafe Cookbook*	641.59
LUMBER INDUSTRY AND TRADE	
King, Greg. *The Ghost Forest*	333.75
Lumet, Sidney	
Making Movies	791.43
LUMET, SIDNEY, 1924-2011	
Spiegel, Maura. *Sidney Lumet*	B
The Lumumba Plot. Reid, Stuart A.	967.51
LUMUMBA, PATRICE, 1925-1961	
Reid, Stuart A. *The Lumumba Plot*	967.51
LUNAR ECLIPSES	
Nordgren, Tyler E. *Sun, Moon, Earth*	523.7
Lunardi, Joe	
★*Bracketology*	796.323
The Lunatic. Simic, Charles	811
Lunch in Paris. Bard, Elizabeth	B
Lunch Poems. O'Hara, Frank	811
LUNCHES	
Peters, Meike. *Noon*	641.5
Lundquist, Verne	
Play by Play	B
LUNDQUIST, VERNE	
Lundquist, Verne. *Play by Play*	B
Lunenfeld, Peter	
City at the Edge of Forever	979.4
LUNG CANCER	
Caldwell, Gail. *Let's Take the Long Way Home*	B
Kalanithi, Paul. ★*When Breath Becomes Air*	B
LUPUS	
Gooch, Brad. ★*Flannery*	B
Rubin, Kathy Kleiner. *A Light in the Dark*	364.152
Lusane, Clarence	
The Black History of the White House	975.3
Lustgarten, Abrahm	
★*On the Move*	363.7
Lustig, Robert H.	
Metabolical	616
Luther. Oberman, Heiko Augustinus	B
LUTHER, MARTIN, 1483-1546	
Hendrix, Scott H. *Martin Luther*	B
Massing, Michael. *Fatal Discord*	920
Metaxas, Eric. *Martin Luther*	B
Oberman, Heiko Augustinus. *Luther*	B
Wilson, Derek. *Out of the Storm*	B
LUTHERAN CHURCH	
Bolz-Weber, Nadia. *Accidental Saints*	284.1
Metaxas, Eric. *Martin Luther*	B
Luthra, Shefali	
★*Undue Burden*	362.1988
Luttrell, Marcus	
Lone Survivor	958.104
Service	956.7044
LUTTRELL, MARCUS	
Luttrell, Marcus. *Lone Survivor*	958.104
Luxenberg, Steve	
★*Separate*	342.7308
LUXURY	
Barr, Luke. *Ritz & Escoffier*	920
Brickell, Francesca Cartier. *The Cartiers*	B
Crowe, Lauren Goldstein. *The Towering World of Jimmy Choo*	391.4
Malone, Jo. *Jo Malone*	B

AUTHOR, TITLE, SERIES AND SUBJECT INDEX

Schwartz, Nelson. *The Velvet Rope Economy* — 339.2
Thomas, Dana. *Gods and Kings* — 920
Walvin, James. *Sugar* — 338.17361
Lyman, Monty
  The Remarkable Life of the Skin — 612.7
LYME DISEASE
  Ingels, Darin. *The Lyme Solution* — 616.9
The Lyme Solution. Ingels, Darin — 616.9
Lynas, Mark
  Six Degrees — 551.6
Lynch, David
  Room to Dream — B
LYNCH, DAVID, 1946-
  Lynch, David. *Room to Dream* — B
LYNCHING
  Cody, Anthony. *Borderland Apocrypha* — 811
  Dray, Philip. *At the Hands of Persons Unknown* — 364.1
  Giddings, Paula. *Ida* — B
  Morrison, Melanie. *Murder on Shades Mountain* — 345.761
  Phillips, Patrick. *Blood at the Root* — 305.8
  Rembert, Winfred. *Chasing Me to My Grave* — B
  Tyson, Timothy B. *The Blood of Emmett Till* — 364.1
Lyndon B. Johnson. Peters, Charles — B
Lynes, Barbara Buhler
  Georgia O'Keeffe Museum Collections — 759.13
Lynn, Loretta
  ★*Me & Patsy Kickin' up Dust* — B
  Still Woman Enough — B
LYNN, LORETTA
  Lynn, Loretta. ★*Me & Patsy Kickin' up Dust* — B
  Lynn, Loretta. *Still Woman Enough* — B
Lynskey, Dorian
  33 Revolutions per Minute — 782.42
  The Ministry of Truth — 823
LYON, FRANCE
  Buford, Bill. ★*Dirt* — B
Lyons, Anna
  We All Know How This Ends — 362.17
Lyons, Daniel
  STFU — 302.2
LYRIC WRITING
  Guesdon, Jean-Michel. *All the Songs* — 782.42166
  Sondheim, Stephen. *Look, I Made a Hat* — 782.1
The Lyrics. McCartney, Paul — 782.42166
Lysiak, Matthew
  Newtown — 371.7
Lythcott-Haims, Julie
  Your Turn — 305.24
Lyubomirsky, Sonja
  The How of Happiness — 158

M

★*M Train.* Smith, Patti — B
The M Word. Mansberg, Ginni — 612.6
Ma and Me. Reang, Putsata — B
Ma Rainey's Black Bottom. Wilson, August — 812
Maangchi
  Maangchi's Real Korean Cooking — 641.595
Maangchi's Real Korean Cooking. Maangchi — 641.595
MAASAI (AFRICAN PEOPLE)
  Leng'ete, Nice. *The Girls in the Wild Fig Tree* — B
Maass, Peter
  Crude World — 338.2
  Love Thy Neighbor — 949.702
MAASS, PETER, 1960-
  Maass, Peter. *Love Thy Neighbor* — 949.702
Maathai, Wangari
  Unbowed — B
MAATHAI, WANGARI
  Maathai, Wangari. *Unbowed* — B
Mabey, Richard
  The Cabaret of Plants — 580
Mac Sweeney, Naoise
  The West — 909
Macadam, Heather Dune
  999 — 940.53

MACARONS
  Greenspan, Dorie. *Baking Chez Moi* — 641.86
Macarthur At War. Borneman, Walter R. — B
MACARTHUR, DOUGLAS, 1880-1964
  Borneman, Walter R. *Macarthur at War* — B
  Brands, H. W. *The General vs. the President* — 973.918092
  Dower, John W. *Embracing Defeat* — 952.04
  Groom, Winston. *The Generals* — 920
  Herman, Arthur. ★*Douglas Macarthur* — B
  McManus, John C. *Fire and Fortitude* — 940.54
  McManus, John C. *Island Infernos* — 940.54
  Perry, Mark. *The Most Dangerous Man in America* — B
  Scott, James. *Rampage* — 940.54
  Toll, Ian W. *Twilight of the Gods* — 940.54
MACARTHUR, MALCOLM
  O'Connell, Mark. *A Thread of Violence* — 364.152
MACAULAY, CATHARINE, 1731-1791
  Moore, Peter. *Life, Liberty, and the Pursuit of Happiness* — 199
Macaulay, David
  The Way Things Work Now — 600
MACAWS
  Safina, Carl. ★*Becoming Wild* — 591.7
MacColl, Gail
  To Marry an English Lord — 974.7
MacCulloch, Diarmaid
  Christianity — 270
  The Reformation — 270.6
  Thomas Cromwell — B
Macdonald, Helen
  ★*Vesper Flights* — 508
MACDONALD, HELEN, 1970-
  Macdonald, Helen. ★*Vesper Flights* — 508
MACDONALD, JEFFREY R., 1943-
  McGinniss, Joe. *Fatal Vision* — B
Macdougall, J. D.
  Frozen Earth — 551.7
Mace, Nancy L.
  ★*The 36-Hour Day* — 616.8
Macedo, Diane
  The Sleep Fix — 613.7
MACEDONIA, ANCIENT GREECE
  Everitt, Anthony. *Alexander the Great* — B
Macfarlane, Robert
  The Lost Spells — 811
MacGillis, Alec
  Fulfillment — 381
MacGregor, Iain
  The Lighthouse of Stalingrad — 940.54
MacGregor, Neil
  Germany — 943
  A History of the World in 100 Objects — 930.1
Machado, Carmen Maria
  ★*In the Dream House* — B
Machete Season. Hatzfeld, Jean — 967.57104
Machiavelli. Boucheron, Patrick — 320.1092
Machiavelli for Women. Vanek Smith, Stacey — 650.1
Machiavelli, Niccolo
  ★*The Prince* — 320.1
MACHIAVELLI, NICCOLO, 1469-1527
  Benner, Erica. *Be Like the Fox* — B
  Boucheron, Patrick. *Machiavelli* — 320.1092
  Strathern, Paul. *The Florentines* — 945
  Vanek Smith, Stacey. *Machiavelli for Women* — 650.1
MACHINE LEARNING
  Roeder, Oliver. *Seven Games* — 794
  Wiggins, Christopher L. *How Data Happened* — 310
MACHINE QUILTING
  Gering, Jacquie. *Quilting Modern* — 746.46
  Gering, Jacquie. *Walk* — 746.46
  Goldsworthy, Lynne. *Quick & Easy Quilts* — 746.46
  Redford, Catherine. *Modern Machine Quilting* — 746.46
  Tomasson, Dara. *Walk, Jog, Run* — 746.46
  Walters, Angela. *Free-Motion Meandering* — 746.46
MACHINE SEWING
  Brandvig, Jera. *Quilt As-You-Go Made Vintage* — 746.46
  Ishida, Sanae. *Sewing Happiness* — 646.2
  Yaker, Rebecca. *Little One-Yard Wonders* — 646.2
  Yang, April. *DIY Thrift Flip* — 646.2

PUBLIC LIBRARY CORE COLLECTION: NONFICTION
Twentieth Edition

MACHINERY
   Macaulay, David. *The Way Things Work Now* — 600
MACHINES AND LABOR
   Merchant, Brian. *Blood in the Machine* — 303.48
   Tegmark, Max. *Life 3.0* — 006.301
MACHISMO
   Gomez, Edgar. *High-Risk Homosexual* — B
MACHU PICCHU, PERU
   Adams, Mark. *Turn Right at Machu Picchu* — 985
   Bingham, Hiram. ★*Lost City of the Incas* — 985
   Heaney, Christopher. *Cradle of Gold* — B
Macintyre, Ben
   ★*Agent Sonya* — B
   Agent Zigzag — B
   Double Cross — 940.54
   ★*Operation Mincemeat* — 940.54
   ★*Prisoners of the Castle* — 940.54
   ★*Rogue Heroes* — 940.54
   A Spy Among Friends — B
   ★*The Spy and the Traitor* — B
Mack, Katie
   The End of Everything — 523.1
Mackall, Joe
   Plain Secrets — 289.7
MACKAY, JOHN WILLIAM, 1831-1902
   Crouch, Gregory. *The Bonanza King* — B
Mackeen, Dawn Anahid
   The Hundred-Year Walk — 956.6
MACKEEN, DAWN ANAHID
   Mackeen, Dawn Anahid. *The Hundred-Year Walk* — 956.6
MacKellar, Pamela H.
   ★*Winning Grants* — 025.1
Mackenzie, Debora
   Covid-19 — 616.2
Mackey, Nathaniel
   Splay Anthem — 811
Mackinnon, Al
   Epic Surf Breaks of the World — 797.32
MacKinnon, J. B.
   ★*The Day the World Stops Shopping* — 339.4
Mackintosh-Smith, Tim
   Arabs — 909.04
MacKrell, Judith
   The Correspondents — 070.4
MACLEAN, DONALD DUART, 1913-1983
   Philipps, Roland. *A Spy Named Orphan* — B
MacLean, Harry N.
   Starkweather — 364.152
MacLean, Rory
   Berlin — 943.155
MACMILLAN, DONALD BAXTER, BORN 1874
   Welky, David. *A Wretched and Precarious Situation* — 910.911
MacMillan, Margaret
   Paris 1919 — 940.3
   War — 355.0209
MacMullan, Jackie
   ★*Basketball* — 796.323
MacNeal, David
   Bugged — 595.7
MacPhail, Theresa
   Allergic — 616.97
MacPhee, R. D. E.
   End of the Megafauna — 591.4
MacPherson, Myra
   All Governments Lie — B
Macrame. Zedenius, Fanny — 746.42
MACRAME
   Katz, Emily. *Modern Macrame* — 746.42
   Zedenius, Fanny. *Macrame* — 746.42
MACROECONOMICS
   Fowler, Corinne. ★*The Countryside* — 941
   Wheelan, Charles J. *Naked Economics* — 330
Macy, Beth
   ★*Dopesick* — 362.29
   ★*Factory Man* — 338.7
   ★*Raising Lazarus* — 362.29
   ★*Truevine* — B
Mad and Bad. Koch, Bea — 920

Mad At the World. Souder, William — 813
★*Mad Enchantment*. King, Ross — 759.4
Mad, Bad, Dangerous to Know. Toibin, Colm — 920
★*Madame Fourcade's Secret War*. Olson, Lynne — B
Madame President. Cooper, Helene — 966.62
★*Madame Restell*. Wright, Jennifer Ashley — B
MADDEN, OWNEY, 1891-1980
   Hill, David. *The Vapors* — 976.7
Madden, T Kira
   Long Live the Tribe of Fatherless Girls — 814
MADDEN, T KIRA
   Madden, T Kira. *Long Live the Tribe of Fatherless Girls* — 814
Madden, Thomas F.
   Istanbul — 949.61
   Venice — 945
Maddex, Robert L.
   The U.S. Constitution A to Z — 342.730203
Maddigan, Beth
   Community Library Programs That Work — 021.2
Maddow, Rachel
   Bag Man — B
   Blowout — 338.2
   ★*Prequel* — 320.53
Maddox, Brenda
   Rosalind Franklin — B
Made for Goodness. Tutu, Desmond — 170
★*Made in China*. Pang, Amelia — 331.11
Made in China. Qu, Anna — B
Made in India. Sodha, Meera — 641.595
Made Men. Kenny, Glenn — 791.43
Mademoiselle. Garelick, Rhonda K. — B
Madhouse At the End of the Earth. Sancton, Julian — 919.8904
★*Madhur Jaffrey's Instantly Indian Cookbook*. Jaffrey, Madhur — 641.595
Madhur Jaffrey's World Vegetarian. Jaffrey, Madhur — 641.5
Madigan, Tim
   The Burning — 976.6
Madison and Jefferson. Burstein, Andrew — 973.4
MADISON FAMILY
   Kearse, Bettye. *The Other Madisons* — 920
Madison's Gift. Stewart, David O. — B
Madison, Deborah
   In My Kitchen — 641.5
   Vegetable Literacy — 641.6
   Vegetarian Cooking for Everyone — 641.5
MADISON, DOLLEY, 1768-1849
   Allgor, Catherine. *A Perfect Union* — B
Madison, James
   ★*The Constitutional Convention* — 342.7302
MADISON, JAMES, 1751-1836
   Brands, H. W. ★*Founding Partisans* — 973.3
   Broadwater, Jeff. *James Madison* — B
   Burstein, Andrew. *Madison and Jefferson* — 973.4
   Cheney, Lynne V. *James Madison* — B
   Cheney, Lynne V. *The Virginia Dynasty* — B
   Ellis, Joseph J. *The Quartet* — 342.7302
   Feldman, Noah. *The Three Lives of James Madison* — B
   Gutzman, Kevin R. C. *The Jeffersonians* — 973.5
   Kearse, Bettye. *The Other Madisons* — 920
   Meyerson, Michael. *Liberty's Blueprint* — 342.7302
   Ricks, Thomas E. ★*First Principles* — 973.09
   Stewart, David O. *Madison's Gift* — B
   Wills, Garry. *James Madison* — B
MADISON, WISCONSIN
   Maraniss, David. *They Marched into Sunlight* — 959.704
A Madman's Will. May, Gregory — 973.5
Madness. Hylton, Antonia — 362.2
Madoff. Behar, Richard — 364.16
MADOFF, BERNARD L.
   Behar, Richard. *Madoff* — 364.16
Madonna. Gabriel, Mary — B
MADONNA, 1958-
   Gabriel, Mary. *Madonna* — B
Madrick, Jeffrey G
   Invisible Americans — 362.7086
The Madwoman and the Roomba. Loh, Sandra Tsing — B
Maestros and Their Music. Mauceri, John — 781.45
MAFIA
   Cannell, Michael T. *A Brotherhood Betrayed* — B

AUTHOR, TITLE, SERIES AND SUBJECT INDEX

Carlo, Philip. *Gaspipe* — B
Cramer, Richard Ben. *Joe DiMaggio* — B
Hill, David. *The Vapors* — 976.7
Maier, Thomas. *Mafia Spies* — 364.1060973
Nadeau, Barbie Latza. *The Godmother* — 364.106
Mafia Spies. Maier, Thomas — 364.1060973
MAFIA TRIALS
    Carter, Stephen L. *Invisible* — B
MAFIOSI
    Cannell, Michael T. *A Brotherhood Betrayed* — B
Magdalena. Davis, Wade — 986.1
Magdalena, Carlos
    The Plant Messiah — 333.95
MAGDALENA, CARLOS
    Magdalena, Carlos. *The Plant Messiah* — 333.95
Magee, Bryan
    The Story of Philosophy — 190
MAGEE, PATRICK, 1951-
    Carroll, Rory. *There Will Be Fire* — 363.325
MAGELLAN, FERDINAND, 1480?-1521
    Bergreen, Laurence. *Over the Edge of the World* — B
Maggot. Muldoon, Paul — 821
Magic. Gosden, Chris — 133.4
MAGIC
    Abrev, Ileana. *The Little Big Book of White Spells* — 133.4
    Ackroyd, Peter. *The Death of King Arthur* — 823
    Crosson, Monica. *The Magikal Family* — 299
    Dell, Christopher. *The Occult, Witchcraft & Magic* — 130
    Feldmann, Erica. *Hausmagick* — 133.4
    Garcia, Amanda Yates. *Initiated* — B
    Harkness, Deborah E. *The World of All Souls* — 813
    Rajchel, Diana. *Urban Magick* — 133.4
MAGIC LAMPS
    Seale, Yasmine. *Aladdin* — 398.2
The Magic of Math. Benjamin, Arthur — 510
★*The Magic of Thinking Big*. Schwartz, David Joseph — 158
★*Magic Pill*. Hari, Johann — 613.2
MAGIC SHOWS
    Owen, Oscar. *Mind-Blowing Magic Tricks for Everyone* — 793.8
MAGIC TRICKS
    Miles, Bryan. *101 Magic Tricks* — 793.8
    Owen, Oscar. *Mind-Blowing Magic Tricks for Everyone* — 793.8
    Posnanski, Joe. ★*The Life and Afterlife of Harry Houdini* — 793.8
    Staniforth, Nate. *Here Is Real Magic* — B
    Stone, Alex. *Fooling Houdini* — B
The Magic Words. Klein, Cheryl B. — 808.06
The Magical Language of Others. Koh, EJ — 813
Magical Mathematics. Diaconis, Persi — 793.8
Magical Negro. Parker, Morgan — 811
MAGICAL THINKING
    Gilbert, Elizabeth. ★*Big Magic* — 153.3
A Magical World. Wilson, Derek K. — 261.55
Magical/Realism. Villarreal, Vanessa Anglica — 814
MAGICIANS
    Fox, Margalit. *The Confidence Men* — 940.4
    Posnanski, Joe. ★*The Life and Afterlife of Harry Houdini* — 793.8
    Staniforth, Nate. *Here Is Real Magic* — B
    Stone, Alex. *Fooling Houdini* — B
Magida, Arthur J.
    Code Name Madeleine — 940.54
The Magikal Family. Crosson, Monica — 299
Magill, Pete
    Build Your Running Body — 796.42
Magner, Mike
    Poisoned Legacy — 338.7
MAGNETISM
    Forbes, Nancy. *Faraday, Maxwell, and the Electromagnetic Field* — B
Magnificent Minds. Goh, Suzanne — 618.92
Magnificent Rebels. Wulf, Andrea — 830.9
The Magnolia Bakery Handbook. Lloyd, Bobbie — 641.86
★*Magnolia Table*. Gaines, Joanna — 641.5975
★*Magritte*. Gohr, Siegfried — 759.9493
MAGRITTE, RENE, 1898-1967
    Gohr, Siegfried. ★*Magritte* — 759.9493
Magsamen, Susan
    Your Brain on Art — 111
Maguire, James
    Impresario — B

Mahabharata. Satyamurti, Carole — 821
Mahaffey, James A.
    Atomic Adventures — 333.792
MAHARAJ, KRIS
    Smith, Clive Stafford. *The Injustice System* — 345.759
Maher, Kris
    Desperate — 344
Mahjoub, Jamal
    A Line in the River — 962.404
MAHJOUB, JAMAL, 1960-
    Mahjoub, Jamal. *A Line in the River* — 962.404
MAHMOOD, AHLAM A.
    Campbell, Deborah. *A Disappearance in Damascus* — 365
Mahon, Maureen
    ★*Black Diamond Queens* — 782.421
Mahoney, Richard D.
    Sons & Brothers — 920
Mahtani, Shibani
    Among the Braves — 951.25
Maid. Land, Stephanie — B
Maier, Pauline
    American Scripture — 973.3
    Ratification — 342.7302
Maier, Thomas
    Mafia Spies — 364.1060973
MAIER, VIVIAN, 1926-2009
    Marks, Ann. *Vivian Maier Developed* — 778.9
Maiklem, Lara
    Mudlark — B
MAIKLEM, LARA, 1971-
    Maiklem, Lara. *Mudlark* — B
MAILER, NORMAN
    Schultz, Kevin Michael. *Buckley and Mailer* — 920
Mailhot, Terese Marie
    Heart Berries — B
MAILHOT, TERESE MARIE
    Mailhot, Terese Marie. *Heart Berries* — B
MAIMONIDES, 1135-1204
    Ruttenberg, Danya. *On Repentance and Repair* — 202
MAINE
    Arsenault, Kerri. *Mill Town* — B
    Bass, Amy. *One Goal* — 796.334
    Finkel, Michael. *The Stranger in the Woods* — B
    Georges, Gigi. *Downeast* — 974.1
    Iftin, Abdi Nor. *Call Me American* — 305.893
    Kelley, Margot Anne. *A Gardener at the End of the World* — 615.8
    Thoreau, Henry David. *The Maine Woods* — 917
The Maine Woods. Thoreau, Henry David — 917
MAINTENANCE AND REPAIR
    Bowers, Sharon. *Home Ec for Everyone* — 640
    Branson, Gary D. *Home, Water & Moisture Problems* — 643
    Byers, Charles T. *Ultimate Guide Home Repair and Improvement* — 643
    Milchtein, Chaya M. ★*Mechanic Shop Femme's Guide to Car Ownership* — 629.222
    Stewart, Martha. ★*The Martha Manual* — 640
    Weiss, Eben. ★*The Ultimate Bicycle Owner's Manual* — 796.6
    Wing, Charles. *How Your House Works* — 643
Maisel, Ivan
    I Keep Trying to Catch His Eye — B
MAISEL, IVAN, 1960-
    Maisel, Ivan. *I Keep Trying to Catch His Eye* — B
Maisonet, Illyanna
    ★*Diasporican* — 641.597295
MAJOLIE, BIANCA
    Ghez, Didier. *The Hidden Art of Disney's Golden Age* — 741.5
Major. Balf, Todd — B
Major Barbara. Shaw, Bernard — 822
★*Major Labels*. Sanneh, Kelefa — 781.64
Make 'Em Laugh. Reynolds, Debbie — B
Make A Statement. Crowther, Janet — 745.594
★*Make It Ahead*. Garten, Ina — 641.5
★*Make It Scream, Make It Burn*. Jamison, Leslie — 814
Make Me Rain. Giovanni, Nikki — 811
Make Money Move. Simmons, Lauren — 332.024
Make Space for Happiness. McCubbin, Tracy — 179
Make Trouble. Richards, Cecile — B
Make Your Kid a Money Genius (even If You're Not). Kobliner, Beth — 332.024
Make Your Own Indoor Garden. Durber, Sarah — 635

PUBLIC LIBRARY CORE COLLECTION: NONFICTION
Twentieth Edition

MAKE-AHEAD COOKING
   Christensen, Ashley. *It's Always Freezer Season* — 641.5
   Donofrio, Jeanine. ★*Love & Lemons* — 641.5
   Garten, Ina. ★*Go-To Dinners* — 641.5
   Garten, Ina. ★*Make It Ahead* — 641.5
   Hussain, Nadiya. *Time to Eat* — 641.5
   Kane, Cyndi. *Save-It-Forward Suppers* — 641.5
   Klein, Dini. *Prep + Rally* — 641.5
   Krieger, Ellie. *You Have It Made!* — 641.5
   Mullins, Brittany. *Mostly Veggies* — 641.5
   Ottolenghi, Yotam. *Ottolenghi Simple* — 641.59
   Pauline, Kathryn. ★*Piecemeal* — 641.5
Maker of Patterns. Dyson, Freeman J. — B
Making A Life. Falick, Melanie — 745.5
Making A Scene. Wu, Constance — B
Making Comics. McCloud, Scott — 741.5
★*Making Haste from Babylon*. Bunker, Nick — 974.4
★*Making It So*. Stewart, Patrick — B
Making Movies. Lumet, Sidney — 791.43
The Making of a Dream. Wides-Munoz, Laura — 920
The Making of a Justice. Stevens, John Paul — B
★*The Making of a Leader*. Bunting, Josiah — B
The Making of a Miracle. Eruzione, Mike — B
The Making of African America. Berlin, Ira — 973
The Making of Aliens. Rinzler, J. W. — 791.4372
The Making of Asian America. Lee, Erika — 973
The Making of Black Lives Matter. Lebron, Christopher J — 305.896
The Making of Modern Japan. Jansen, Marius — 952
The Making of Poetry. Nicolson, Adam — 821.709
The Making of Robert E. Lee. Fellman, Michael — B
Making Our Democracy Work. Breyer, Stephen G. — 347.73
Making Saints. Woodward, Kenneth L. — 235.24
Making Space, Clutter Free. McCubbin, Tracy — 648
Making the Most of Teen Library Volunteers. Boland, Becca — 023
Making Things Right. Thorstensen, Ole — 690
Making Work Work. Richards, Shola — 658.3
Makos, Adam
   Devotion — 920
   ★*A Higher Call* — 940.54
   Spearhead — B
Malady of the Mind. Lieberman, Jeffrey A. — 616.89
Malala, Justice
   The Plot to Save South Africa — 968.07
MALAN, FRIDA
   Moorehead, Caroline. *A House in the Mountains* — 940.53
MALARIA
   Woolley, Benjamin. *The King's Assassin* — B
Malarkey, Tucker
   Stronghold — 639.2
MALAWI
   Kamkwamba, William. ★*The Boy Who Harnessed the Wind* — B
MALAYSIAN PEOPLE
   Whitlock, Craig. ★*Fat Leonard* — 364.16
Malcolm. Perry, Bruce — B
Malcolm X
   ★*The Autobiography of Malcolm X* — B
   ★*Malcolm X*. Marable, Manning — B
MALCOLM X, 1925-1965
   Joseph, Peniel E. *The Sword and the Shield* — B
   Malcolm X. ★*The Autobiography of Malcolm X* — B
   Marable, Manning. ★*Malcolm X* — B
   Payne, Les. ★*The Dead Are Arising* — B
   Perry, Bruce. *Malcolm* — B
   Roberts, Randy. *Blood Brothers* — 920
   Tubbs, Anna Malaika. *The Three Mothers* — 306.874
   West, Cornel. *Black Prophetic Fire* — 920
Malcolm, Janet
   Reading Chekhov — 891.72
MALE DOMINATION (SOCIAL STRUCTURE)
   Hamilton, Lisa M. *The Hungry Season* — B
   Kroeger, Brooke. *Undaunted* — 070.4
   Marcal, Katrine. *Mother of Invention* — 604.82
   Oluo, Ijeoma. *Mediocre* — 305.310973
   Whitaker, Holly. ★*Quit Like a Woman* — 616.86
MALE FRIENDSHIP
   Baker, Billy. *We Need to Hang Out* — 177
   Guarnere, William. *Brothers in Battle, Best of Friends* — B
   Halberstam, David. *The Teammates* — B
   Hsu, Hua. ★*Stay True* — B
   Jackson, Ted. ★*You Ought to Do a Story About Me* — B
   Jordan, Jonathan W. *Brothers, Rivals, Victors* — 940.54
   Laughlin, James. *The Luck of Friendship* — B
   Lewis, Michael. ★*The Undoing Project* — 920
   Lowe, George. *Letters from Everest* — 796.522
   Murakami, Haruki. ★*Absolutely on Music* — 784.2
   Neu, Charles E. *Colonel House* — B
   Offerman, Nick. *Where the Deer and the Antelope Play* — 973.93
   Oppedisano, Tony. *Sinatra and Me* — B
   Palmer, Arnold. *A Golfer's Life* — B
   Roberts, Randy. *Blood Brothers* — 920
   Rosen, Jonathan. ★*The Best Minds* — 616.89
   Schwalbe, Will. *We Should Not Be Friends* — B
   Sestero, Greg. *The Disaster Artist* — 791.43
   Shehadeh, Raja. *Where the Line Is Drawn* — 956.9405
   Strøksnes, Morten Andreas. *Shark Drunk* — 338.3
   Watkins, D. *Black Boy Smile* — B
   Way, Niobe. *Rebels with a Cause* — 649
   Womack, Kenneth. *All Things Must Pass Away* — 781.66
   Wood, Gordon S. *Friends Divided* — 920
MALE IMPERSONATORS
   Nordberg, Jenny. *The Underground Girls of Kabul* — 305.3
Malek, Alia
   The Home That Was Our Country — B
MALEK, ALIA, 1974-
   Malek, Alia. *The Home That Was Our Country* — B
The Malevolent Volume. Reed, Justin Phillip — 811
Malhotra, Aanchal
   Remnants of Partition — 954.04
MALI
   Hammer, Joshua. *The Bad-Ass Librarians of Timbuktu* — 025.8
   Holloway, Kris. *Monique and the Mango Rains* — B
MALIBU, CALIFORNIA
   Randall, David K. *The King and Queen of Malibu* — B
MALICIOUS ACCUSATION
   Fabricant, M. Chris. *Junk Science and the American Criminal Justice System* — 363.25
   King, Gilbert. *Beneath a Ruthless Sun* — B
   King, Gilbert. ★*Devil in the Grove* — 305.896
   Rempel, William C. *The Gambler* — B
   Rezaian, Jason. *Prisoner* — B
   Rudolf, David S. *American Injustice* — 345.73
   Schiff, Stacy. *The Witches* — 345
   Stevenson, Bryan. *Just Mercy* — B
   Vincent, Lynn. *Indianapolis* — 940.54
Malinowski, Erik
   Betaball — 796.323
Mallaby, Sebastian
   The Man Who Knew — B
MALLORY, GEORGE, 1886-1924
   Davis, Wade. *Into the Silence* — B
Mallory, Tamika D.
   State of Emergency — 305.896
Malone, Jo
   Jo Malone — B
MALONE, JO
   Malone, Jo. *Jo Malone* — B
Malone, Sharon
   Grown Woman Talk — 362.1
MALONE, SHARON, 1959-
   Malone, Sharon. *Grown Woman Talk* — 362.1
Malone, Thomas W.
   Superminds — 005.7
MALONEY, ROSIE
   Calcaterra, Regina. *Girl Unbroken* — B
Malory, Thomas
   Le Morte Darthur, Or, the Hoole Book of Kyng Arthur and of His Noble Knyghtes of the Rounde Table — 823
MALORY, THOMAS, SIR, 15TH CENT
   Malory, Thomas. *Le Morte Darthur, Or, the Hoole Book of Kyng Arthur and of His Noble Knyghtes of the Rounde Table* — 823
MALTA
   Caruana Galizia, Paul. ★*A Death in Malta* — 364.15
   Hastings, Max. *Operation Pedestal* — 940.54
MALTESE PEOPLE
   Caruana Galizia, Paul. ★*A Death in Malta* — 364.15
Mama's Boy. Black, Dustin Lance — B

AUTHOR, TITLE, SERIES AND SUBJECT INDEX

★*Mama's* Last Hug. Waal, F. B. M. de 599.885
The *Mamba* Mentality. Bryant, Kobe B
Mamet, David
   True and False 792
MAMMALS
   Brusatte, Stephen. *The Rise and Reign of the Mammals* 569
   Drew, Liam. *I, Mammal* 599
   Nowak, Ronald M. *Walker's Mammals of the World.* 599
   Whitaker, John O. ★*National Audubon Society Field Guide to North American Mammals* 599.097
   Wood, Levison. *The Last Giants* 599.67
Man and Superman. Shaw, Bernard 822
A Man Called Intrepid. Stevenson, William 940.54
A Man for All Markets. Thorp, Edward O. B
A Man for All Seasons. Bolt, Robert 822
The Man from the Future. Bhattacharya, Ananyo B
Man in the Music. Vogel, Joseph B
The Man in the Red Coat. Barnes, Julian B
The Man in the Willows. Dennison, Matthew B
Man O' War. Ours, Dorothy 798.400929
Man of Blessing. Butcher, Carmen Acevedo B
A Man of Good Hope. Steinberg, Jonny B
A Man of Iron. Senik, Troy B
Man of the Hour. Conant, Jennet B
★*A Man of Two Faces*. Nguyen, Viet Thanh B
The Man Who Ate His Boots. Brandt, Anthony 910.91
The Man Who Ate Too Much. Birdsall, John B
The Man Who Broke Capitalism. Gelles, David 330.12
The Man Who Caught the Storm. Hargrove, Brantley B
★*The Man Who Could Move Clouds*. Rojas Contreras, Ingrid B
The Man Who Couldn't Stop. Adam, David 616.85
The Man Who Designed the Future. Szerlip, Barbara B
The Man Who Hated Women. Sohn, Amy 363.28
The Man Who Invented Motion Pictures. Fischer, Paul 791.43
The Man Who Knew. Mallaby, Sebastian B
The Man Who Knew Infinity. Kanigel, Robert B
The Man Who Knew Too Much. Leavitt, David B
The Man Who Mistook His Wife for a Hat and Other Clinical Tales. Sacks, Oliver 616.8
The Man Who Ran Washington. Baker, Peter B
★*The Man Who Saved the Union*. Brands, H. W. B
★*A Man Without a Country*. Vonnegut, Kurt 818
★*Man's Search for Meaning*. Frankl, Viktor E. B
Man, John
   Ninja 355.5
MANAGEMENT
   Brown, Brene. ★*Dare to Lead* 658.4
   Cox, Gena. *Leading Inclusion* 658.3
   Downs, Paul. *Boss Life* 338.7
   Economy, Peter. *Wait, I'm the Boss?!?* 658
   Goleman, Daniel. *Primal Leadership* 658.4
   Goodall, Amanda. *Credible* 658.4
   Horstman, Mark. *The Effective Manager* 658.4
   Knight, Molly. *The Best Team Money Can Buy* 796.357
   Lindsay, Virginia Keleher. *Sewing to Sell* 746
   Mattioli, Dana. ★*The Everything War* 381.142
   McNeil, Beth. *Fundamentals of Library Supervision* 023
   Peter, Laurence J. *The Peter Principle* 658
   Rice, Condoleezza. *Political Risk* 658.15
   Schweitzer, Sharon. *Access to Asia* 395.5
   Scott, Kim Malone. *Radical Candor* 658.4
   VanDuinkerken, Wyoma. *The Challenge of Library Management* 025.1
   Washington, Ella F. *The Necessary Journey* 658.3
Managing Expectations. Driver, Minnie B
Managing Library Employees. Stanley, Mary J. 023
Managing Prostate Cancer. Roth, Andrew J. 616.99
Manaugh, Geoff
   Until Proven Safe 614.4
Manchester, William
   Goodbye, Darkness B
   The Last Lion, Winston Spencer Churchill. B
   The Last Lion, Winston Spencer Churchill. B
   A World Lit Only by Fire 940.2
MANCHESTER, WILLIAM, 1922-2004
   Manchester, William. *Goodbye, Darkness* B
Manchild in the Promised Land. Brown, Claude B
Mandel, David
   Who's Who in the Jewish Bible B

Mandel, Sarah
   Little Earthquakes B
Mandela. Brand, Christo B
Mandela. Mandela, Nelson B
Mandela, Nelson
   Conversations with Myself B
   Dare Not Linger B
   In His Own Words B
   ★Long Walk to Freedom B
   Mandela B
   The Prison Letters of Nelson Mandela 968.06092
MANDELA, NELSON, 1918-2013
   Brand, Christo. *Mandela* B
   Carlin, John. *Playing the Enemy* 968.06
   Malala, Justice. *The Plot to Save South Africa* 968.07
   Mandela, Nelson. *Conversations with Myself* B
   Mandela, Nelson. *Dare Not Linger* B
   Mandela, Nelson. *In His Own Words* B
   Mandela, Nelson. ★*Long Walk to Freedom* B
   Mandela, Nelson. *Mandela* B
   Mandela, Nelson. *The Prison Letters of Nelson Mandela* 968.06092
   Smith, David James. *Young Mandela* B
   Steinberg, Jonny. *Winnie and Nelson* 920
MANDELBAUM, FREDERICKA, 1825-1894
   Fox, Margalit. *The Talented Mrs. Mandelbaum* 364.1
Manderley Forever. Rosnay, Tatiana de B
Mandery, Evan J.
   A Wild Justice 345.73
MANDY, ACTIVE 18TH CENTURY
   Kearse, Bettye. *The Other Madisons* 920
Manegold, Catherine S.
   Ten Hills Farm 974.4
MANET, EDOUARD, 1832-1883
   King, Ross. *The Judgment of Paris* 759.4
   Smee, Sebastian. *The Art of Rivalry* 700.92
MANGA
   Mizuki, Shigeru. *Showa 1926-1939* 741.5
Mangini, Cara
   The Vegetable Butcher 641.6
   ★The Vegetable Eater 641.6
Mangino, Kate
   ★Equal Partners 305.3
Manglik, Gauri
   ★Muslims in Story 809
The Mango Tree. Tometich, Annabelle B
MANGOES
   Tometich, Annabelle. *The Mango Tree* B
Manguel, Alberto
   The Dictionary of Imaginary Places 809
   Homer's the Iliad and the Odyssey 883
MANHATTAN, NEW YORK CITY
   Brown-Nagin, Tomiko. *Civil Rights Queen* B
   Greene, Jayson. *Once More We Saw Stars* 155.9
   Langewiesche, William. *American Ground* 974.7
   Miller, Donald L. *Supreme City* 974.7
   Moss, Jeremiah. *Feral City* B
   Reid, David. *The Brazen Age* 974.7
   Scheier, Liz. *Never Simple* B
Manheimer, Eric
   Twelve Patients 362.1109747
Manhood for Amateurs. Chabon, Michael B
Manhunt. Bergen, Peter L. 363.325
MANIA
   Summerscale, Kate. *The Book of Phobias and Manias* 616.85
★*The Manicurist's Daughter*. Lieu, Susan B
MANIFEST DESTINY
   Crutchfield, James A. *Revolt at Taos* 972
Manifesto. Evaristo, Bernardine B
MANILA, PHILIPPINES
   Scott, James. *Rampage* 940.54
MANIPULATION (SOCIAL SCIENCES)
   Berman, Sarah. *Don't Call It a Cult* 361.4
   Citron, Danielle Keats. *The Fight for Privacy* 342.7308
   Cutler, Max. *Cults* 364.15
   Goldstone, Nancy Bazelon. *The Rival Queens* 944
   Hasen, Richard L. *Election Meltdown* 324.973
   Jones, Faith. *Sex Cult Nun* B
   Lake, Dianne. *Member of the Family* 364.152

PUBLIC LIBRARY CORE COLLECTION: NONFICTION
Twentieth Edition

Leamer, Laurence. *Hitchcock's Blondes*	791.43
Moss, Michael. ★*Hooked*	613.2
Selvaratnam, Tanya. *Assume Nothing*	B
Southon, Emma. *Agrippina*	B
Trump, Mary L. *Too Much and Never Enough*	B
Weinman, Sarah. *Scoundrel*	364.152
Wu, Tim. *The Attention Merchants*	659.1
Zygar, Mikhail. *All the Kremlin's Men*	947.086

MANIPULATION BY MEN
Leamer, Laurence. *The Price of Justice*	346.7302
Levin, Daniel Barban. *Slonim Woods 9*	B

Mankell, Henning
Quicksand	B

MANKELL, HENNING, 1948-2015
Mankell, Henning. *Quicksand*	B

Mankoff, Robert
How About Never—Is Never Good for You?	741.5

MANKOFF, ROBERT
Mankoff, Robert. *How About Never—Is Never Good for You?*	741.5

Manly, Carla Marie
Aging Joyfully	305.26

Mann, Charles C.
★*1491*	970.01

Mann, Jen
★*Midlife Bites*	305.244

MANN, JEN
Mann, Jen. ★*Midlife Bites*	305.244

Mann, Jim
The Rebellion of Ronald Reagan	973.927092

Mann, Sally
★*Hold Still*	B

MANN, SALLY, 1951-
Mann, Sally. ★*Hold Still*	B

Mann, William J.
Bogie & Bacall	920
The Contender	B
Hello, Gorgeous	B
Kate	B
The Wars of the Roosevelts	B

Manning, Chandra
Troubled Refuge	973.7

Manning, Chelsea
Readme.Txt	B

MANNING, CHELSEA, 1987-
Manning, Chelsea. *Readme.Txt*	B

Manning, Ivy
Easy Soups from Scratch with Quick Breads to Match	641.81

MANNING, PEYTON
Myers, Gary. *Brady vs. Manning*	B

Mannix, Kathryn
With the End in Mind	304.6

The Manor. Griswold, Mac K. — 974.7

Mans, Jasmine
Black Girl, Call Home	811

Mansbach, Adam
I Had a Brother Once	811

Mansberg, Ginni
The M Word	612.6

Manseau, Peter
The Apparitionists	B
Objects of Devotion	277

Mansel, Philip
King of the World	B

Mansfield, Stephen
Japanese Stone Gardens	712

MANSIONS
Barnes, Cinelle. *Monsoon Mansion*	B
Eisen, Norman L. *The Last Palace*	920
Kiernan, Denise. *The Last Castle*	975.6

★*Manson*. Guinn, Jeff — B

MANSON, CHARLES, 1934-2017
Bugliosi, Vincent. ★*Helter Skelter*	364.1
Guinn, Jeff. ★*Manson*	B
Lake, Dianne. *Member of the Family*	364.152
O'Neill, Tom. ★*Chaos*	364.152
Wiehl, Lis W. *Hunting Charles Manson*	364.152

Manson, Mark
*Everything Is F*cked*	152.4
*The Subtle Art of Not Giving a F*ck*	158.1

Mantel Pieces. Mantel, Hilary — 824.914

Mantel, Hilary
Mantel Pieces	824.914

The Mantle of Command. Hamilton, Nigel — 940.54

MANTLE, MICKEY, 1931-1995
Leavy, Jane. *The Last Boy*	B

The Manual to Online Public Records. Sankey, Michael L. — 025.06

Manuel, Ian
My Time Will Come	B

MANUFACTURERS
Goldstein, Amy. *Janesville*	330.9775

MANUFACTURING INDUSTRY AND TRADE
Chang, Leslie T. *Factory Girls*	331.4
Cohan, William D. *Power Failure*	338.7
Goldstein, Amy. *Janesville*	330.9775
Herman, Arthur. *Freedom's Forge*	940.53
Kurutz, Steven. *American Flannel*	338.4
Pang, Amelia. ★*Made in China*	331.11
Satia, Priya. *Empire of Guns*	330.941

MANUFACTURING PROCESSES
Miodownik, Mark. *Stuff Matters*	620.1

MANUSCRIPTS
Cahill, Thomas. *How the Irish Saved Civilization*	941.501
Collins, Paul. *The Book of William*	016.8223
De Hamel, Christopher. ★*Meetings with Remarkable Manuscripts*	091
Hammer, Joshua. *The Bad-Ass Librarians of Timbuktu*	025.8
Hecimovich, Gregg A. ★*The Life and Times of Hannah Crafts*	B
Hoffman, Adina. *Sacred Trash*	296.09
King, Ross. *Bookseller of Florence*	381
Pettegree, Andrew. *The Library*	027.4
Raab, Nathan. *The Hunt for History*	790.1

The Manuscripts Club. De Hamel, Christopher — 091

MANUSCRIPTS, ENGLISH
Collins, Paul. *The Book of William*	016.8223

MANUSCRIPTS, MEDIEVAL
De Hamel, Christopher. *The Manuscripts Club*	091

★*The Many Lives of Mama Love*. Hardin, Lara Love — B
Many Things Under a Rock. Scheel, David — 594

Manzione, Gianmarc
Pin Action	B

Mao. Chang, Jung — B
Mao. Pantsov, Alexander — B
Mao's Great Famine. Dikotter, Frank — 951.05

Mao, Sally Wen
Oculus	811

MAO, ZEDONG, 1893-1976
Chang, Jung. *Mao*	B
Lovell, Julia. *Maoism*	335.43
Mitter, Rana. *Forgotten Ally*	951.04
Pantsov, Alexander. *Mao*	B

Maoism. Lovell, Julia — 335.43

MAORI (NEW ZEALAND PEOPLE)
Thompson, Christina. *Sea People*	305.8994

Map. Szymborska, Wislawa — 891.8
The Map as Art. Harmon, Katharine A. — 760
The Map That Changed the World. Winchester, Simon — B
A Map to the Next World. Harjo, Joy — 811

Maples, William R.
Dead Men Do Tell Tales	614

MAPLES, WILLIAM R., DIED 1997
Maples, William R. *Dead Men Do Tell Tales*	614

MAPPLETHORPE, ROBERT, 1946-1989
Smith, Patti. ★*Just Kids*	B

MAPS
Carballo, David M. *America*	912
Cheshire, James. *Where the Animals Go*	591.47
Garfield, Simon. *On the Map*	526.09
Hayes, Derek. *Historical Atlas of the American West*	911
Hayes, Derek. *Historical Atlas of the United States*	911
Marshall, Tim. *The Power of Geography*	320.1
Robb, Graham. *The Debatable Land*	941.3
Sluglett, Peter. *Atlas of Islamic History*	912.19

Maps and Legends. Chabon, Michael — 801

Mar, Alex
Seventy Times Seven	362.88
Witches of America	299

AUTHOR, TITLE, SERIES AND SUBJECT INDEX

MARA, TIM
   Eisenberg, John. *The League*   796.332
Marable, Manning
   ★*Malcolm X*   B
Maraniss, Andrew
   Strong Inside   B
Maraniss, David
   ★*Barack Obama*   B
   Clemente   B
   ★*Path Lit by Lightning*   B
   They Marched into Sunlight   959.704
★*Marathon*. Higdon, Hal   796.42
The Marathon Don't Stop. Kenner, Rob   B
MARATHON RUNNERS
   Karnazes, Dean. *The Legend of Marathon*   796.42
   Keflezighi, Meb. *26 Marathons*   B
   McDougall, Christopher. ★*Born to Run*   796.42
   Murakami, Haruki. *What I Talk About When I Talk About Running*   B
   Wade, Becky. *Run the World*   796.42
MARATHON RUNNING
   Foreman, Tom. *My Year of Running Dangerously*   B
   Karnazes, Dean. *The Legend of Marathon*   796.42
   Keflezighi, Meb. *26 Marathons*   B
   Keflezighi, Meb. *Meb for Mortals*   796.4252
   McDougall, Christopher. ★*Born to Run*   796.42
   McDougall, Christopher. *Natural Born Heroes*   940.53
   Murakami, Haruki. *What I Talk About When I Talk About Running*   B
   Nolan, Ali. *Master the Marathon*   796.42
   Shorter, Frank. *My Marathon*   796.42
   Wade, Becky. *Run the World*   796.42
MARATHON SWIMMING
   Cox, Lynne. *Swimming to Antarctica*   B
   Mortimer, Gavin. *The Great Swim*   B
   Nyad, Diana. *Find a Way*   B
MARATHON, BATTLE OF, GREECE, 490 B.C.E
   Karnazes, Dean. *The Legend of Marathon*   796.42
   McDougall, Christopher. *Natural Born Heroes*   940.53
MARATHONS
   Brooks, Amanda. *Run to the Finish*   613.7
   Higdon, Hal. ★*Marathon*   796.42
   Karnazes, Dean. *The Legend of Marathon*   796.42
   Keflezighi, Meb. *26 Marathons*   B
   Nolan, Ali. *Master the Marathon*   796.42
   Wade, Becky. *Run the World*   796.42
MARAVICH, PETE, 1947-1988
   Kriegel, Mark. *Pistol*   B
MARBLE, ALICE, 1913-1990
   Blais, Madeleine. *Queen of the Court*   B
Marcal, Katrine
   Mother of Invention   604.82
Marcel's Letters. Porter, Carolyn   940.54
March of Folly. Tuchman, Barbara W.   909.08
MARCH ON WASHINGTON FOR JOBS AND FREEDOM, 1963
   Branch, Taylor. ★*Pillar of Fire*   323.1
   Euchner, Charles C. *Nobody Turn Me Around*   975.3
A March to Madness. Feinstein, John   796.323
March [Series]. Lewis, John   741.5
★*March; Book One*. Lewis, John   741.5
★*March; Book Three*. Lewis, John   741.5
★*March; Book Two*. Lewis, John   741.5
Marchant, Jo
   Cure   616.89
   The Human Cosmos   523.1
The Marches. Stewart, Rory   941.3
★*Marcia Decoster's Beaded Opulence*. DeCoster, Marcia   739.27
MARCIANO, ROCKY, 1923-1969
   Stanton, Mike. ★*Unbeaten*   B
Marco Polo. Bergreen, Laurence   B
Marcum, Diana
   The Fallen Stones   B
MARCUM, DIANA
   Marcum, Diana. *The Fallen Stones*   B
Marcus Aurelius
   ★*Meditations*   188
Marcus off Duty. Samuelsson, Marcus   641.5
Marcus, Amy Dockser
   We the Scientists   618.92

Marcus, Leonard S.
   ★*Pictured Worlds*   741.6
Mardini, Yusra
   Butterfly   B
MARDINI, YUSRA
   Mardini, Yusra. *Butterfly*   B
MARESCA, PUPETTA, 1935-2021
   Nadeau, Barbie Latza. *The Godmother*   364.106
MARGARET OF ANJOU, QUEEN OF ENGLAND, 1430-1482
   Gristwood, Sarah. *Blood Sisters*   942.04092
   Jones, Dan. ★*The Wars of the Roses*   942.04
Margaret Thatcher. Moore, Charles   941.085
Margaret Thatcher [Series]. Moore, Charles   941.085
MARGARET, OF YORK, DUCHESS, CONSORT OF CHARLES THE BOLD, DUKE OF BURGUNDY, 1446-1503
   Gristwood, Sarah. *Blood Sisters*   942.04092
MARGARET, PRINCESS, COUNTESS OF SNOWDON, 1930-2002
   Brown, Craig. *Ninety-Nine Glimpses of Princess Margaret*   B
   Glenconner, Anne. ★*Lady in Waiting*   B
MARGARET, QUEEN, CONSORT OF EDWARD I, KING OF ENGLAND, 1279?-1318
   Weir, Alison. *Queens of the Age of Chivalry*   920
MARGERY, 1888-1941
   Jaher, David. *The Witch of Lime Street*   B
MARGINALIZED CHILDREN
   Conyers, Jonathan. *I Wasn't Supposed to Be Here*   B
   Elliott, Andrea. ★*Invisible Child*   362.7
   Emdin, Christopher. *Ratchetdemic*   370.1
   Fishman, Elly. *Refugee High*   370.8
   Henning, Kristin. *The Rage of Innocence*   364.36
   Lockhart, Chris. ★*Walking the Bowl*   362.7
   Mufleh, Luma. ★*Learning America*   371.826
   Ramesh, Jaya. *Parenting at the Intersections*   649
   White, Richard Antoine. *I'm Possible*   B
MARGINALIZED PEOPLE
   Abdurraqib, Hanif. ★*There's Always This Year*   796.323
   Adler, Kevin F. *When We Walk By*   362.5
   Ahmed, Sara. *The Feminist Killjoy Handbook*   305.42
   Alexander, Stephon. *Fear of a Black Universe*   523.1
   Anderson, Carol. ★*One Person, No Vote*   324.6
   Anderson, Jimmeka. *Power Lines*   020
   Arce, Julissa. *You Sound Like a White Girl*   303.48
   Armas, Kat. *Abuelita Faith*   248.8
   Ayers, Edward L. *American Visions*   973.5
   Berman, Ari. *Give Us the Ballot*   324.6
   Blake, Melissa. *Beautiful People*   362.4
   Bratt, Jessica Anne. *Let's Talk About Race in Storytimes*   027.62
   Campoverdi, Alejandra. *First Gen*   B
   Canellos, Peter S. *The Great Dissenter*   B
   Choi, Franny. *The World Keeps Ending, and the World Goes On*   811
   Cox, Gena. *Leading Inclusion*   658.3
   De Hart, Jane Sherron. ★*Ruth Bader Ginsburg*   B
   Dodds Pennock, Caroline. ★*On Savage Shores*   970.004
   Ellison, Ralph. ★*The Collected Essays of Ralph Ellison*   814
   Fisher, Thomas. ★*The Emergency*   362.1089
   Geronimus, Arline T. ★*Weathering*   362.1089
   Gilliam, Fatimah. *Race Rules*   305.8
   Goyal, Nikhil. ★*Live to See the Day*   305.5
   Graham, Jasmin. *Sharks Don't Sink*   597.3
   Gross, Rachel E. *Vagina Obscura*   618.1
   Hall, Alvin D. *Driving the Green Book*   917.304
   Hamilton, Denise. *Indivisible*   658.3
   Harriot, Michael. ★*Black AF History*   973
   Henry, Alan. *Seen, Heard, and Paid*   650.1
   Herold, Benjamin. *Disillusioned*   307.76
   Hoja, Gulchehra. *A Stone Is Most Precious Where It Belongs*   B
   Holton, Woody. *Liberty Is Sweet*   973.3
   Hunter-Gault, Charlayne. ★*My People*   305.48
   Hyde, Anne Farrar. ★*Born of Lakes and Plains*   978
   Izgil, Tahir Hamut. *Waiting to Be Arrested at Night*   B
   Jackson, Mitchell S. *Survival Math*   B
   Kirshner, Jodie Adams. ★*Broke*   336.3
   Kitagawa, Kate. *The Secret Lives of Numbers*   510.9
   Kohli, Sahaj Kaur. ★*But What Will People Say?*   616.89
   Kozol, Jonathan. *Fire in the Ashes*   362.77
   LaPointe, Sasha taqwseblu. *Thunder Song*   814
   Lee, Erika. *America for Americans*   305.800973
   Mattlin, Ben. *Disability Pride*   323.3

PUBLIC LIBRARY CORE COLLECTION: NONFICTION
Twentieth Edition

McMillan, Tracie. ★*The White Bonus* — 305.8
Moss, Jeremiah. *Feral City* — B
Nagassar, Rohadi. *When We Belong* — 254
Newkirk, Pamela. *Diversity, Inc.* — 658.3
Nguyen, Viet Thanh. ★*A Man of Two Faces* — B
Norton, Laurah. *Lay Them to Rest* — 363.25
Page, Elliot. *Pageboy* — B
Plant, Deborah G. *Of Greed and Glory* — 326
Ramsey, Donovan X. ★*When Crack Was King* — 362.29
Rose, Tricia. ★*Metaracism* — 305.8
Row, Jess. *White Flights* — 813
Salesses, Matthew. ★*Craft in the Real World* — 808.3
Smilios, Maria. ★*The Black Angels* — 610.73
Stevenson, Bryan. *Just Mercy* — B
Tamimi, Ahed. ★*They Called Me a Lioness* — B
Thrall, Nathan. ★*A Day in the Life of Abed Salama* — 956.05
Urofsky, Melvin I. *The Affirmative Action Puzzle* — 331.13
Villarosa, Linda. ★*Under the Skin* — 362.1089
Wade, Sabia. *Birthing Liberation* — 363.96
Wilderson, Frank B. *Afropessimism* — B
Willis, Raquel. *The Risk It Takes to Bloom* — B
Wise, Tim J. *Dispatches from the Race War* — 305.8

MARGINALIZED STUDENTS
Kozol, Jonathan. ★*An End to Inequality* — 379.2

MARGINALIZED TEENAGERS
Anderson, Jimmeka. *Power Lines* — 020
Fishman, Elly. *Refugee High* — 370.8

MARGINALIZED WOMEN
Evaristo, Bernardine. *Manifesto* — B
Flock, Elizabeth. ★*The Furies* — 305.48
Gaines, Joanna. *The Stories We Tell* — B
Gallagher, Winifred. *New Women in the Old West* — 978.02
Hamad, Ruby. *White Tears/Brown Scars* — 305.8
Harts, Minda. *Right Within* — 658.3
Hickman, Katie. *Brave Hearted* — 978
Kendall, Mikki. *Hood Feminism* — 305.420973
Koch, Bea. *Mad and Bad* — 920
McNeur, Catherine. *Mischievous Creatures* — 920
Mojica Rodriguez, Prisca Dorcas. *For Brown Girls with Sharp Edges and Tender Hearts* — 305.48
Schuller, Kyla. *The Trouble with White Women* — 305.42
Shields, Aomawa L. *Life on Other Planets* — B
Watling, Sarah. *Tomorrow Perhaps the Future* — 946.081
Young, Daniella Mestyanek. *Uncultured* — B
Zakaria, Rafia. *Against White Feminism* — 305.42

Margolick, David
Elizabeth and Hazel — 379.2

Margonelli, Lisa
Oil on the Brain — 338.2

Margotin, Philippe
The Rolling Stones — 782.42166

MARGUERITE, QUEEN, CONSORT OF HENRY IV, KING OF FRANCE, 1553-1615
Goldstone, Nancy Bazelon. *The Rival Queens* — 944

Margulies, Julianna
Sunshine Girl — B

MARGULIES, JULIANNA, 1966-
Margulies, Julianna. *Sunshine Girl* — B

Margulis, Lynn
Symbiotic Planet — 576.8

MARIA CAROLINA, QUEEN, CONSORT OF FERDINAND I, KING OF THE TWO SICILIES, 1752-1814
Goldstone, Nancy Bazelon. *In the Shadow of the Empress* — 920

MARIA CHRISTINE, CONSORT OF ALBRECHT KASIMIR, DUKE OF SAXE-TESCHEN, 1742-1798
Goldstone, Nancy Bazelon. *In the Shadow of the Empress* — 920

MARIA THERESA, EMPRESS OF AUSTRIA, 1717-1780
Goldstone, Nancy Bazelon. *In the Shadow of the Empress* — 920

Marian Anderson. Keiler, Allan — B

Mariani, Mike
★*What Doesn't Kill Us Makes Us* — 155.9

Marie Antoinette. Fraser, Antonia — B
Marie Antoinette. Lever, Evelyne — B

MARIE ANTOINETTE, QUEEN, CONSORT OF LOUIS XVI, KING OF FRANCE, 1755-1793
Fraser, Antonia. *Marie Antoinette* — B
Goldstone, Nancy Bazelon. *In the Shadow of the Empress* — 920
Lever, Evelyne. *Marie Antoinette* — B

★*Marie* Kondo's Kurashi at Home. Kondo, Marie — 648

Marie, Jane
★*Selling the Dream* — 658.8

MARIIA NIKOLAEVNA, GRAND DUCHESS, DAUGHTER OF NICHOLAS II, EMPEROR OF RUSSIA, 1899-1918
Massie, Robert K. *The Romanovs* — 947
Rappaport, Helen. *The Romanov Sisters* — 920

MARIJUANA
Berenson, Alex. ★*Tell Your Children* — 362.29
Dufton, Emily. *Grass Roots* — 362.29
Fine, Doug. *Too High to Fail* — 338.4
Ulander, Perry A. *Walking Point* — B

MARIJUANA ABUSE
Berenson, Alex. ★*Tell Your Children* — 362.29

MARIJUANA IN POPULAR CULTURE
Dufton, Emily. *Grass Roots* — 362.29

MARIJUANA TRAFFIC
Fine, Doug. *Too High to Fail* — 338.4

Marilyn Monroe. Casillo, Charles — B

MARINE ACCIDENTS
Franklin, Jonathan. *438 Days* — 910.91

MARINE ANIMALS
Carson, Rachel. *Under the Sea Wind* — 578.77
Ellis, Richard. ★*The Empty Ocean* — 577.7
Graham, Jasmin. *Sharks Don't Sink* — 597.3
Imbler, Sabrina. *How Far the Light Reaches* — 591.77
Kingdon, Amorina. ★*Sing Like Fish* — 591.77
Nestor, James. *Deep* — 797.2
Svensson, Patrik. *The Book of Eels* — 597
Widder, Edith. *Below the Edge of Darkness* — 551.46092

MARINE BIOLOGISTS
Ballard, Robert D. *Into the Deep* — 551.46092
Souder, William. *On a Farther Shore* — B
Widder, Edith. *Below the Edge of Darkness* — 551.46092

MARINE BIOLOGY
Bradley, James. *Deep Water* — 578.77
Carson, Rachel. *Under the Sea Wind* — 578.77
Casey, Susan. *The Underworld* — 551.46
Dennis, Jerry. *The Living Great Lakes* — 977
Ellis, Richard. ★*The Empty Ocean* — 577.7
Graham, Jasmin. *Sharks Don't Sink* — 597.3
Hoare, Philip. *The Whale* — 599.5
Imbler, Sabrina. *How Far the Light Reaches* — 591.77
Kingdon, Amorina. ★*Sing Like Fish* — 591.77
Nestor, James. *Deep* — 797.2
Pyenson, Nick. *Spying on Whales* — 599.5
Scheel, David. *Many Things Under a Rock* — 594
Widder, Edith. *Below the Edge of Darkness* — 551.46092

MARINE ECOLOGY
Barnett, Cynthia. ★*The Sound of the Sea* — 591.47
Bradley, James. *Deep Water* — 578.77
Carson, Rachel. *Under the Sea Wind* — 578.77
Casey, Susan. *The Underworld* — 551.46
Ellis, Richard. ★*The Empty Ocean* — 577.7
Nicolson, Adam. *The Seabird's Cry* — 598.177
Scales, Helen. *The Brilliant Abyss* — 551.46
Scales, Helen. *What the Wild Sea Can Be* — 577.7

MARINE INVERTEBRATES
Meinkoth, Norman August. *The Audubon Society Field Guide to North American Seashore Creatures* — 592
Nicolson, Adam. *Life Between the Tides* — 577.69

MARINE MAMMALS
Horwitz, Josh. *War of the Whales* — 333.95
Hoyt, Erich. *Encyclopedia of Whales, Dolphins and Porpoises* — 599.5
Pyenson, Nick. *Spying on Whales* — 599.5

MARINE ORGANISMS
Widder, Edith. *Below the Edge of Darkness* — 551.46092

MARINE PLANTS
Ellis, Richard. ★*The Empty Ocean* — 577.7

MARINE POLLUTION
Johnson, Kirk W. *The Fishermen and the Dragon* — 976.4
Scales, Helen. *What the Wild Sea Can Be* — 577.7

Marine, Carol
Daily Painting — 751.4

MARINES
Ackerman, Elliot. *Places and Names* — B
Bissinger, H. G. ★*The Mosquito Bowl* — 796.332
Bradley, James. *Flags of Our Fathers* — 940.54

AUTHOR, TITLE, SERIES AND SUBJECT INDEX

Brady, James. *The Coldest War*	B
Brennan, Thomas J. *Shooting Ghosts*	B
Burgin, R. V. *Islands of the Damned*	B
Caputo, Philip. *A Rumor of War*	959.704
Gallego, Ruben. *They Called Us*	956.7044
Golembesky, Michael. *Level Zero Heroes*	958.104
Grossi, Craig. *Craig & Fred*	B
Kindsvatter, Peter S. *American Soldiers*	355
Kugler, Rob. *A Dog Named Beautiful*	B
Lucas, Jack. *Indestructible*	B
Manchester, William. *Goodbye, Darkness*	B
Meyer, Dakota. *Into the Fire*	958.104
Nez, Chester. *Code Talker*	B
Sides, Hampton. *On Desperate Ground*	951.904
Swofford, Anthony. *Jarhead*	956.7044
Ventrone, Jillian. *From the Marine Corps to College*	378.1
Wheelan, Joseph. *Midnight in the Pacific*	940.54
Wright, Evan. *Generation Kill*	956.7044
Mario Batali Big American Cookbook. Batali, Mario	641.5973

MARITAL CONFLICT

Biden, Robert Hunter. *Beautiful Things*	B
Franklin, Ruth. *Shirley Jackson*	B
Garcia, Mayte. *The Most Beautiful*	920
Gordon, Kim. *Girl in a Band*	B
Hardwick, Elizabeth. *The Dolphin Letters, 1970-1979*	811
Koppel, Lily. *The Astronaut Wives Club*	920
McColl, Sarah. *Joy Enough*	B
Patchett, Ann. *This Is the Story of a Happy Marriage*	B
Steinberg, Jonny. *Winnie and Nelson*	920
Sundberg, Kelly. *Goodbye, Sweet Girl*	B
Thomas, Louisa. *Louisa*	B

MARJORY STONEMAN DOUGLAS HIGH SCHOOL SHOOTING, PARKLAND, FLORIDA, 2018

Cullen, David. *Parkland*	371.7
Mark Bittman's Kitchen Matrix. Bittman, Mark	641.5
Mark Rothko. Cohen-Solal, Annie	759.13
Mark Twain. Shelden, Michael	B
Marked for Death. Hamilton-Paterson, James	358.400941

Markel, Howard

Origin Story	576.8
The Secret of Life	572.86

MARKET INDICATORS

Nations, Scott. *A History of the United States in Five Crashes*	338.5

MARKET SEGMENTATION

Kim, W. Chan. *Blue Ocean Shift*	658.8

MARKETING

Ahuvia, Aaron. ★*The Things We Love*	790.1
Auletta, Ken. *Frenemies*	659.1
Capparell, Stephanie. *The Real Pepsi Challenge*	338.7
Chapin, Kari. ★*The Handmade Marketplace*	745.5
Fineman, Meredith. *Brag Better*	650.1
Haag, Pamela. ★*The Gunning of America*	338.4
Hardy, Alyssa. *Worn Out*	338.4
Hu, Elise. *Flawless*	646.7
Kerpen, Dave. *Likeable Social Media*	658.8
Landau, Herbert B. *The Small Public Library Survival Guide*	025.1
Marie, Jane. ★*Selling the Dream*	658.8
McDonald, Greg (Producer). *Elvis and the Colonel*	920
Oriard, Michael. *Brand NFL*	796.332
Raphael, Rina. *The Gospel of Wellness*	613
Shnayerson, Michael. *Boom*	701
Vaynerchuk, Gary. *Crushing It!*	650.1
Watkins, Alexandra. *Hello, My Name Is Awesome*	658.8
Windhorst, Brian. *Lebron, Inc.*	B
Wu, Tim. *The Attention Merchants*	659.1

MARKETS

Roth, Alvin E. *Who Gets What—And Why*	330.01

Markham, Beryl

West with the Night	B

MARKHAM, BERYL, 1902-1986

Markham, Beryl. *West with the Night*	B

Markham, Lauren

★*The Far Away Brothers*	920

Markovits, Daniel

The Meritocracy Trap	305.5

Marks, Ann

Vivian Maier Developed	778.9
★*Marley & Me*. Grogan, John	636.752

Marlowe, Christopher

The Complete Plays	822

MARLOWE, CHRISTOPHER, 1564-1593

Nicholl, Charles. *The Reckoning*	B

Marnham, Patrick

Dreaming with His Eyes Open	B

Maroney, Tyler

The Modern Detective	658.4

MARONEY, TYLER

Maroney, Tyler. *The Modern Detective*	658.4
Marooned. Kelly, Joseph	975.5

Marovich, Robert M.

A City Called Heaven	782.25

Marozzi, Justin

Islamic Empires	909
Tamerlane	950.2

MARRANOS

Kritzler, Ed. *Jewish Pirates of the Caribbean*	972.9

MARRIAGE

Alexander, Kwame. *Why Fathers Cry at Night*	B
Andrews, Julie. *Home Work*	B
Baer, Kate. *What Kind of Woman*	811
Bard, Elizabeth. *Lunch in Paris*	B
Bard, Elizabeth. *Picnic in Provence*	B
Berlin, Lucia. ★*Welcome Home*	B
Biden, Jill. *Where the Light Enters*	823
Binyon, T. J. *Pushkin*	B
Blaisdell, Robert. *Creating Anna Karenina*	891.7
Brown, Tina. ★*The Palace Papers*	920
Buhle, Kathleen. *If We Break*	B
Cadbury, Deborah. *Queen Victoria's Matchmaking*	941.081
Carson, Anne. *The Beauty of the Husband*	811
Chabon, Michael. *Manhood for Amateurs*	B
Cumming, Alan. *Baggage*	B
Cusk, Rachel. *Aftermath*	B
Cusk, Rachel. *Coventry*	814
Dearborn, Mary V. *Carson McCullers*	B
Didion, Joan. ★*The Year of Magical Thinking*	B
Doty, Cate. *Mergers and Acquisitions*	395.2
Dunn, Jancee. ★*How Not to Hate Your Husband After Kids*	646.7
Ellis, Helen. *Bring Your Baggage and Don't Pack Light*	814
Evans, Jimmy. *Strengths Based Marriage*	248.8
Feiler, Bruce. *The First Love Story*	222
Foster, Sutton. *Hooked*	B
Fuller, Alexandra. *Leaving Before the Rains Come*	B
Funder, Anna. *Wifedom*	B
Gaines, Joanna. *The Stories We Tell*	B
Garcia, Mayte. *The Most Beautiful*	920
Gaye, Jan. *After the Dance*	B
Goldstone, Nancy Bazelon. *In the Shadow of the Empress*	920
Goodwin, Doris Kearns. *No Ordinary Time*	920
Gorrindo, Simone. ★*The Wives*	B
Gristwood, Sarah. *The Tudors in Love*	941.05
Guy, John. *Hunting the Falcon*	B
Hardman, Robert. *Queen of Our Times*	B
Harry. ★*Spare*	B
Havrilesky, Heather. *Foreverland*	306.81
Hilfiger, Tommy. *American Dreamer*	B
Jackson, Shirley. ★*The Letters of Shirley Jackson*	813
Kelly, Donika. *The Renunciations*	811
Klein, Jessi. *I'll Show Myself Out*	B
Lessing, Doris May. *Under My Skin*	823
MacColl, Gail. *To Marry an English Lord*	974.7
Mann, William J. *Bogie & Bacall*	920
McBrien, William. *Cole Porter*	B
Mead, Rebecca. *My Life in Middlemarch*	823
Mendelson, Cheryl. ★*Vows*	203
Milch, David. *Life's Work*	B
Millwood, Molly. *To Have and to Hold*	306.874
Moran, Caitlin. *More Than a Woman*	B
Nasaw, David. *The Chief*	B
Nathan, Joan. ★*My Life in Recipes*	641.5
Newman, Paul. *The Extraordinary Life of an Ordinary Man*	B
Nooyi, Indra. ★*My Life in Full*	B
Olds, Sharon. *Stag's Leap*	811
Patchett, Ann. *This Is the Story of a Happy Marriage*	B
Plath, Sylvia. *The Letters of Sylvia Plath*	811.54
Plath, Sylvia. *The Letters of Sylvia Plath*	811.54

PUBLIC LIBRARY CORE COLLECTION: NONFICTION
Twentieth Edition

Porizkova, Paulina. *No Filter*	B
Powell, Julie. *Julie and Julia*	641.5
Quave, Cassandra Leah. *The Plant Hunter*	581.6
Ripa, Kelly. *Live Wire*	B
Risner, Vaneetha Rendall. *Walking Through Fire*	B
Robinson, Ray. *Iron Horse*	B
Rosnay, Tatiana de. *Manderley Forever*	B
Rowe, Mickey. *Fearlessly Different*	B
Rundell, Katherine. ★*Super-Infinite*	B
Rush, Charaia. *Courageously Soft*	234
Satrapi, Marjane. *Embroideries*	741.5
Schulz, Kathryn. ★*Lost & Found*	B
Smith, Jada Pinkett. *Worthy*	B
Smith, Maggie. ★*You Could Make This Place Beautiful*	B
Smith, Sally Bedell. *George VI and Elizabeth*	920
Spurling, Hilary. *Matisse the Master*	B
Steinberg, Jonny. *Winnie and Nelson*	920
Taraborrelli, J. Randy. *Jackie, Janet & Lee*	920
Tumulty, Karen. *The Triumph of Nancy Reagan*	B
Weir, Alison. *Queens of the Age of Chivalry*	920
Williams, Florence. *Heartbreak*	306.7
Wilson, A. N. *The Mystery of Charles Dickens*	823
Winter, Molly Roden. *More*	B
Xue, XInran. *The Book of Secrets*	951.05

MARRIAGE CUSTOMS AND RITES

Doty, Cate. *Mergers and Acquisitions*	395.2
Mendelson, Cheryl. ★*Vows*	203
Monger, George. *Marriage Customs of the World*	392.5
Marriage Customs of the World. Monger, George	392.5

MARRIAGE LAW

Cenziper, Debbie. ★*Love Wins*	346.7301
Kaplan, Roberta A. *Then Comes Marriage*	346.7301

MARRIAGES OF CELEBRITIES

Kashner, Sam. *Furious Love*	B

MARRIAGES OF ROYALTY AND NOBILITY

Fraser, Antonia. ★*The Wives of Henry VIII*	942.05
Larman, Alexander. ★*Power and Glory*	941.085
Morton, Andrew. *Wallis in Love*	B
Russell, Gareth. *Young and Damned and Fair*	B
Smith, Sally Bedell. *Prince Charles*	B
Starkey, David. *Six Wives*	942.05
Weir, Alison. *The Children of Henry VIII*	B
Weir, Alison. *The Six Wives of Henry VIII*	942.05

MARRIED MEN

Baker, Billy. *We Need to Hang Out*	177
Brown, David S. *Paradise Lost*	813
Chabon, Michael. *Manhood for Amateurs*	B
Kander, Jason. *Invisible Storm*	B
Leland, Andrew. ★*The Country of the Blind*	B
Mazzeo, Tilar J. *Sisters in Resistance*	945.091
Pittard, Hannah. *We Are Too Many*	B
Satrapi, Marjane. *Chicken with Plums*	741.5
Stiles, T. J. *Custer's Trials*	B
Thomas, R. Eric. *Here for It*	B

MARRIED PEOPLE

Adams, John. *My Dearest Friend*	973.4
Albee, Edward. ★*Who's Afraid of Virginia Woolf?*	812
Ellis, Joseph J. *First Family*	973.4
Glenconner, Anne. ★*Lady in Waiting*	B
Goodwin, Doris Kearns. ★*An Unfinished Love Story*	B
Jordan, Mary. *The Art of Her Deal*	B
Lockwood, Patricia. *Priestdaddy*	B
Millwood, Molly. *To Have and to Hold*	306.874
Ohler, Norman. *The Bohemians*	940.53
Real, Terrence. *Us*	646.7
Sundberg, Kelly. *Goodbye, Sweet Girl*	B
Washington, Kate. ★*Already Toast*	649.8
Williams, Tennessee. ★*A Streetcar Named Desire*	812

MARRIED WOMEN

Carcaterra, Lorenzo. *Three Dreamers*	B
Doyle, Glennon. *Untamed*	B
Franklin, Ruth. *Shirley Jackson*	B
Funder, Anna. *Wifedom*	B
Havrilesky, Heather. *Foreverland*	306.81
Koppel, Lily. *The Astronaut Wives Club*	920
Moore, Kate. ★*The Woman They Could Not Silence*	B
Pittard, Hannah. *We Are Too Many*	B
Rosnay, Tatiana de. *Manderley Forever*	B

Ruhl, Sarah. *Smile*	B
Schulz, Kathryn. ★*Lost & Found*	B
Sebba, Anne. *Ethel Rosenberg*	B
Weir, Alison. *The Six Wives of Henry VIII*	942.05
Wizenberg, Molly. *Fixed Stars*	B

Marriott, Sue

Secure Relating	158.1

MARS (PLANET)

Aldrin, Buzz. *Mission to Mars*	523.43
Johnson, Sarah Stewart. *The Sirens of Mars*	576.8

MARS PROBES

Aldrin, Buzz. *Mission to Mars*	523.43
Johnson, Sarah Stewart. *The Sirens of Mars*	576.8

MARS, FORREST, 1904-1999

Brenner, Joel Glenn. *The Emperors of Chocolate*	338.7

Mars, Roman

★*The 99% Invisible City*	720

Marsalis, Wynton

Moving to Higher Ground	781.65

Marschark, Marc

★*How Deaf Children Learn*	371.91

Marsh, Charles

Strange Glory	B

Marsh, Henry

Admissions	B
★*Do No Harm*	B

MARSH, HENRY

Marsh, Henry. *Admissions*	B
Marsh, Henry. ★*Do No Harm*	B
★*The Marshall Plan*. Steil, Benn	338.91

MARSHALL PLAN, 1948-1952

McCullough, David G. *Truman*	B
Roll, David L. *George Marshall*	B
Steil, Benn. ★*The Marshall Plan*	338.91
Unger, Debi. *George Marshall*	B

Marshall, Cynthia

You've Been Chosen	B

MARSHALL, CYNTHIA, 1959-

Marshall, Cynthia. *You've Been Chosen*	B

MARSHALL, GEORGE C. (GEORGE CATLETT), 1880-1959

Bunting, Josiah. ★*The Making of a Leader*	B
Kurtz-Phelan, Daniel. *The China Mission*	951.04
Roberts, Andrew. *Masters and Commanders*	940.5322
Roll, David L. *George Marshall*	B
Unger, Debi. *George Marshall*	B

MARSHALL, GEORGE C., (GEORGE CATLETT), 1880-1959

Groom, Winston. *The Generals*	920

MARSHALL, GEORGE PRESTON, 1896-1969

Eisenberg, John. *The League*	796.332

Marshall, Greg

Leg	B

MARSHALL, GREG (ESSAYIST)

Marshall, Greg. *Leg*	B

MARSHALL, JOHN, 1755-1835

Paul, Joel R. ★*Without Precedent*	B
Simon, James F. *What Kind of Nation*	342.73
Smith, Jean Edward. *John Marshall*	B

Marshall, McMillan

Among the Bros	362.29

Marshall, Nate

Finna	811

Marshall, Thurgood

Thurgood Marshall	B

MARSHALL, THURGOOD, 1908-1993

Gibson, Larry S. *Young Thurgood*	B
Haygood, Wil. *Showdown*	B
King, Gilbert. ★*Devil in the Grove*	305.896
Marshall, Thurgood. *Thurgood Marshall*	B
Starks, Glenn L. *Thurgood Marshall*	B
Williams, Juan. *Thurgood Marshall*	B

Marshall, Tim

The Power of Geography	320.1

MARSHES

Proulx, Annie. ★*Fen, Bog and Swamp*	551.41
Struzik, Edward. *Swamplands*	577.68

MARSTON, WILLIAM MOULTON, 1893-1947

Lepore, Jill. ★*The Secret History of Wonder Woman*	741.5
★*The Martha Manual*. Stewart, Martha	640

AUTHOR, TITLE, SERIES AND SUBJECT INDEX

★*Martha* Stewart's Baking Handbook. Stewart, Martha — 641.8
Martha Stewart's Cake Perfection. Stewart, Martha — 641.86
Martha Stewart's Cooking School. Stewart, Martha — 641.5
Martha Washington. Brady, Patricia — B
★*Martha's Flowers*. Stewart, Martha — 635.9
MARTIAL ARTISTS
    Chan, Jackie. *Never Grow Up* — B
    Gracie, Rickson. *Breathe* — B
    Man, John. *Ninja* — 355.5
    Polly, Matthew. ★*Bruce Lee* — B
    Wertheim, L. Jon. *Blood in the Cage* — 796.815
MARTIAL ARTS
    Bennett, Alexander. *Kendo* — 796.86
    Gracie, Rickson. *Breathe* — B
    Hendrix, Grady. *These Fists Break Bricks* — 791
    Lee, Shannon. *Be Water, My Friend* — 796.8
    Polly, Matthew. ★*Bruce Lee* — B
    Wertheim, L. Jon. *Blood in the Cage* — 796.815
MARTIAL ARTS FILMS
    Hendrix, Grady. *These Fists Break Bricks* — 791
Martin Luther. Hendrix, Scott H. — B
Martin Luther. Metaxas, Eric — B
Martin Van Buren. Widmer, Edward L. — B
Martin, Ann
    The Art of Quilling Paper Jewelry — 745.54
MARTIN, BILLY, 1928-1989
    Pennington, Bill. *Billy Martin* — B
Martin, Brett
    Difficult Men — 791.4509
Martin, Clancy W.
    How Not to Kill Yourself — 362.28
Martin, Gerald
    ★*Gabriel Garcia Marquez* — B
Martin, James
    The Jesuit Guide to (Almost) Everything — 248.4
    Learning to Pray — 248.3
Martin, Jonathan
    This Will Not Pass — 973.933
Martin, Justin
    Rebel Souls — 920
MARTIN, LOPE
    Resendez, Andres. *Conquering the Pacific* — 959.9
Martin, Manjula
    The Last Fire Season — B
Martin, Pat
    Life of Fire — 641.5
Martin, Rachel Louise
    A Most Tolerant Little Town — 379.2
Martin, Steve
    Number One Is Walking — B
MARTIN, STEVE, 1945-
    De Semlyen, Nick. *Wild and Crazy Guys* — 920
    Martin, Steve. *Number One Is Walking* — B
Martin, Tovah
    ★*The Indestructible Houseplant* — 635.9
    The New Terrarium — 635.9
    The Unexpected Houseplant — 635.9
MARTIN, TRAYVON, 1995-2012
    Alexander, Elizabeth. ★*The Trayvon Generation* — 305.896
Martin, Valerie
    Salvation — B
Martin, Wednesday
    Primates of Park Avenue — 974.7
MARTIN, WEDNESDAY
    Martin, Wednesday. *Primates of Park Avenue* — 974.7
Martina's Kitchen Mix. McBride, Martina — 641.5973
MARTINET, LOUIS A., 1849-1917
    Luxenberg, Steve. ★*Separate* — 342.7308
Martinez Arias, Alfonso
    The Master Builder — 571.6
Martinez Wood, Jamie
    Latino Writers and Journalists — B
MARTINEZ, JOSE MANUEL, 1962-
    Garrison, Jessica. *The Devil's Harvest* — B
MARTINEZ, REGINA
    Corcoran, Katherine. *In the Mouth of the Wolf* — 364.152
Martinez, Rick
    ★*Mi Cocina* — 641.5972

Martini, Adrienne
    Somebody's Gotta Do It — B
MARTINI, ADRIENNE, 1971-
    Martini, Adrienne. *Somebody's Gotta Do It* — B
Marton, Kati
    ★*The Chancellor* — B
    The Great Escape — 920
    Hidden Power — B
Marty, Martin E.
    Pilgrims in Their Own Land — 200
MARTYRDOM (CHRISTIANITY)
    Beam, Alex. *American Crucifixion* — B
    Rounding, Virginia. *The Burning Time* — 272
MARTYRS
    Rohr, Richard. *The Universal Christ* — 232
Marvel Comics. Howe, Sean — 741.5
Marvel, William
    Lincoln's Autocrat — B
A Marvelous Life. Fingeroth, Danny — 741.5
Marwell, David G.
    Mengele — B
Marx's General. Hunt, Tristram — 335.4092
MARX, JENNY, 1814-1881
    Gabriel, Mary. *Love and Capital* — 920
Marx, Karl
    ★*Capital* — 335.4
    ★*The Communist Manifesto* — 355.4
MARX, KARL, 1818-1883
    Gabriel, Mary. *Love and Capital* — 920
    Liedman, Sven-Eric. *A World to Win* — B
    Sperber, Jonathan. *Karl Marx* — B
    Wheen, Francis. *Karl Marx* — B
Marx, W. David
    ★*Status and Culture* — 305
MARXISM
    Brown, Archie. ★*The Rise and Fall of Communism* — 320.53
    Liedman, Sven-Eric. *A World to Win* — B
    McMeekin, Sean. *The Russian Revolution* — 947.084
    Pipes, Richard. *Communism* — 335.43
Mary. Hazleton, Lesley — B
★*Mary Baker Eddy*. Eddy, Mary Baker — 289.5
Mary Ball Washington. Shirley, Craig — B
MARY I, QUEEN OF ENGLAND, 1516-1558
    Rounding, Virginia. *The Burning Time* — 272
    Weir, Alison. *The Children of Henry VIII* — B
MARY II, QUEEN OF GREAT BRITAIN, 1662-1694
    Ackroyd, Peter. *Revolution* — 941.07
Mary Thomas's Dictionary of Embroidery Stitches. Eaton, Jan — 746.44
Mary Through the Centuries. Pelikan, Jaroslav — 232.91
MARY, BLESSED VIRGIN, SAINT
    Hazleton, Lesley. *Mary* — B
    Pelikan, Jaroslav. *Mary Through the Centuries* — 232.91
Mary, Queen of Scots. Fraser, Antonia — B
MARY, QUEEN OF SCOTS, 1542-1587
    Fraser, Antonia. *Mary, Queen of Scots* — B
    Weir, Alison. *The Lost Tudor Princess* — B
    Weir, Alison. *Mary, Queen of Scots, and the Murder of Lord Darnley* — 941.105
Mary, Queen of Scots, and the Murder of Lord Darnley. Weir, Alison — 941.105
MARY, QUEEN, CONSORT OF GEORGE V, KING OF GREAT BRITAIN, 1867-1953
    Edwards, Anne. *Matriarch* — B
    Ridley, Jane. *George V* — B
MARYLAND
    Cummings, Elijah. ★*We're Better Than This* — B
    Douglass, Frederick. *My Bondage and My Freedom* — B
    Hendrickson, John. *Life on Delay* — B
    Hylton, Antonia. *Madness* — 362.2
    Jawando, Will. ★*My Seven Black Fathers* — B
    Rudacille, Deborah. *Roots of Steel* — 338.4
    Snow, Peter. *When Britain Burned the White House* — 975.3
    Wilson, Chris. *The Master Plan* — B
Marzano-Lesnevich, Alexandria
    The Fact of a Body — 364.152
MARZANO-LESNEVICH, ALEXANDRIA
    Marzano-Lesnevich, Alexandria. *The Fact of a Body* — 364.152
Masciotra, David
    Exurbia Now — 320.973

PUBLIC LIBRARY CORE COLLECTION: NONFICTION
Twentieth Edition

MASCOTS
   Myron, Vicki. ★*Dewey* — 636.80092
MASCULINITY
   Austerlitz, Saul. *Kind of a Big Deal* — 791.43
   Black, Michael Ian. *A Better Man* — 305.31
   Bly, Robert. ★*Iron John* — 305.310973
   Bossiere, Zoe. *Cactus Country* — 306
   Brodeur, Michael Andor. ★*Swole* — 155.3
   Broome, Brian. ★*Punch Me up to the Gods* — B
   Brown, Emma. *To Raise a Boy* — 649
   Chabon, Michael. *Manhood for Amateurs* — B
   Coffin, Jaed. *Roughhouse Friday* — B
   Dearborn, Mary V. *Ernest Hemingway* — B
   Du Mez, Kristin Kobes. *Jesus and John Wayne* — 277.308
   Dubus, Andre. *Ghost Dogs* — 814
   Edmundson, Mark. *Why Football Matters* — B
   Fall, Jeremy. *Falling Upwards* — 158.1
   Fitzgerald, Isaac. *Dirtbag, Massachusetts* — B
   Hobbs, Jeff. *Show Them You're Good* — 373
   Merritt, Tyler. *I Take My Coffee Black* — 791.4302
   Moran, Caitlin. *What About Men?* — 155.3
   Orenstein, Peggy. ★*Boys & Sex* — 305.235
   Peterson, Marlon. *Bird Uncaged* — B
   Preszler, Trent. *Little and Often* — B
   Reiner, Andrew. *Better Boys, Better Men* — 155.43
   Scenters-Zapico, Natalie. *Lima* — 811
   Shraya, Vivek. *I'm Afraid of Men* — 813
   Strings, Sabrina. *The End of Love* — 155.3
   Watkins, D. *Black Boy Smile* — B
   Way, Niobe. *Rebels with a Cause* — 649
   Whippman, Ruth. ★*Boymom* — 305.23
MASHAM, DAMARIS, LADY, 1658-1708
   Penaluna, Regan. ★*How to Think Like a Woman* — 190.82
Mask, Deirdre
   The Address Book — 388.1
The Masks of God. Campbell, Joseph — 201.3
Maslon, Laurence
   ★*Broadway* — 782.1
MASON, GEORGE, 1725-1792
   Broadwater, Jeff. ★*George Mason* — B
Mason, Nick
   Inside Out — B
MASON, NICK
   Mason, Nick. *Inside Out* — B
MASON, SHIRLEY, 1923-1998
   Nathan, Debbie. *Sybil Exposed* — B
MASS (PHYSICS)
   Panek, Richard. *The Trouble with Gravity* — 531
MASS BURIALS
   Gessen, Masha. *Never Remember* — 365
   Hagerty, Alexa. ★*Still Life with Bones* — 599.9
MASS EXTINCTIONS
   Black, Riley. *The Last Days of the Dinosaurs* — 576.8
   Brannen, Peter. *The Ends of the World* — 576.8
MASS INCARCERATION
   Alexander, Michelle. *The New Jim Crow* — 364.973
   Austen, Ben. *Correction* — 364.6
   Bauer, Shane. *American Prison* — 365
   Bazelon, Emily. ★*Charged* — 345.73
   Betts, Reginald Dwayne. ★*Redaction* — 704.9
   Canon, Dan. ★*Pleading Out* — 345.73
   Miller, Reuben Jonathan. *Halfway Home* — 364.8
   Norton, Jack. *The Jail Is Everywhere* — 365
   Rapping, Jonathan. *Gideon's Promise* — 345.73
   Salaam, Yusef. *Better, Not Bitter* — B
   Sered, Danielle. *Until We Reckon* — 364.6
MASS MEDIA
   Appelman, J. Reuben. *While Idaho Slept* — 364.152
   Auletta, Ken. *Frenemies* — 659.1
   Austerlitz, Saul. *Kind of a Big Deal* — 791.43
   Carpenter, Amanda B. *Gaslighting America* — 973.933
   Coppola, Francis Ford. *Live Cinema and Its Techniques* — 791.4302
   Feldstein, Mark Avrom. *Poisoning the Press* — 973.924092
   Gladstone, Brooke. *The Influencing Machine* — 741.5
   Gladwell, Malcolm. *Talking to Strangers* — 302
   Hartman, Darrell. *Battle of Ink and Ice* — 998
   Hickey, Walt. ★*You Are What You Watch* — 791.4
   Kruse, Kevin Michael. *Fault Lines* — 973.92
   Kurtz, Howard. *Media Madness* — 973.933
   LaGarde, Jennifer. *Fact vs. Fiction* — 370.15
   Mitchell, Elizabeth. *Lincoln's Lie* — 973.7092
   Morris, James McGrath. *Pulitzer* — B
   Napoli, Lisa. *Up All Night* — 384.55
   Owens, Ernest. ★*The Case for Cancel Culture* — 303.3
   Poniewozik, James. *Audience of One* — 324.7
   Postman, Neil. *Amusing Ourselves to Death* — 302.2
   Ramsey, Franchesca. *Well, That Escalated Quickly* — B
   Schieffer, Bob. *Overload* — 070.4
   Schwartz, A. Brad. ★*Broadcast Hysteria* — 791.44
   Sepinwall, Alan. ★*TV (the Book)* — 791.45
   Smith, Ben. *Traffic* — 070.4
   Stelter, Brian. *Hoax* — 070.4
   Sullivan, Kevin. *Trump on Trial* — 342.73
   Woodward, Bob. *Shadow* — 973.92
   Wu, Tim. *The Attention Merchants* — 659.1
MASS MEDIA AND CULTURE
   Auletta, Ken. *Frenemies* — 659.1
   McNeil, Donald G. ★*The Wisdom of Plagues* — 614.4
   Wu, Tim. *The Attention Merchants* — 659.1
MASS MEDIA AND SPORTS
   Parry, John Weston. *The Burden of Sports* — 796.01
MASS MEDIA AND WORLD POLITICS
   Stengel, Richard. *Information Wars* — 355.3
MASS MEDIA BIAS
   Hinojosa, Maria. *Once I Was You* — B
   Kurtz, Howard. *Media Madness* — 973.933
   Levitin, Daniel J. ★*A Field Guide to Lies* — 153.4
   McNeil, Donald G. ★*The Wisdom of Plagues* — 614.4
   Stelter, Brian. *Hoax* — 070.4
MASS MEDIA EXECUTIVES
   Baron, Martin. ★*Collision of Power* — 070.4
   Biskind, Peter. *Pandora's Box* — 791.45
   Stewart, James B. *Unscripted* — 658.1
MASS MURDER
   Cullen, David. *Columbine* — 373
   Denton, Sally. *The Colony* — 364.152
   Fieseler, Robert W. *Tinderbox* — 364.152
   Hochschild, Adam. *King Leopold's Ghost* — 967.51
   Lysiak, Matthew. *Newtown* — 371.7
   Swift, Earl. *Hell Put to Shame* — 364.15
   Thompson, Jamie. *Standoff* — 364.152
   Williamson, Elizabeth. ★*Sandy Hook* — 364.152
   Wolff, Daniel J. *Grown-Up Anger* — 920
MASS MURDER INVESTIGATION
   Appelman, J. Reuben. *While Idaho Slept* — 364.152
   Wiehl, Lis W. *Hunting Charles Manson* — 364.152
MASS MURDERERS
   Guinn, Jeff. ★*Manson* — B
MASS PRODUCTION
   Brinkley, Douglas. *Wheels for the World* — B
   Goldstein, Amy. *Janesville* — 330.9775
   Parissien, Steven. *The Life of the Automobile* — 629.222
   Watts, Steven. *The People's Tycoon* — B
MASS SHOOTINGS
   Auster, Paul. *Bloodbath Nation* — 363.33
   Cox, John Woodrow. *Children Under Fire* — 371.7
   Cullen, David. *Columbine* — 373
   Cullen, David. *Parkland* — 371.7
   Hawes, Jennifer. *Grace Will Lead Us Home* — 364.152
   Keenan, Cody. *Grace* — 973.932
   Lysiak, Matthew. *Newtown* — 371.7
   McWhirter, Cameron. *American Gun* — 683.4
   Oppenheimer, Mark. *Squirrel Hill* — 364.152
   Quinones, John. ★*One Year in Uvalde* — 371.7
   Roig-Debellis, Kaitlin. *Choosing Hope* — 371.7
   Thompson, Jamie. *Standoff* — 364.152
   Williamson, Elizabeth. ★*Sandy Hook* — 364.152
MASSACHUSETTS
   Ackmann, Martha. ★*These Fevered Days* — B
   Bremer, Francis J. *John Winthrop* — B
   Bunker, Nick. ★*Making Haste from Babylon* — 974.4
   Demos, John. *The Unredeemed Captive* — 973.2
   Egerton, Douglas R. *Thunder at the Gates* — 973.7
   Fischer, David Hackett. *Paul Revere's Ride* — 973.3
   Frank, Barney. *Frank* — B
   Fraser, Rebecca. *The Mayflower* — 974.4

AUTHOR, TITLE, SERIES AND SUBJECT INDEX

Jeffers, Honorée Fanonne. *The Age of Phillis* — 811
Kidder, Tracy. ★*Rough Sleepers* — 362.5
Logevall, Fredrik. ★*JFK* — B
Manegold, Catherine S. *Ten Hills Farm* — 974.4
McCullough, David G. ★*John Adams* — B
Montgomery, Sy. ★*Of Time and Turtles* — 597.92
O'Donnell, Patrick K. *The Indispensables* — 973.3
Pestana, Carla Gardina. *The World of Plymouth Plantation* — 974.4
Philbrick, Nathaniel. ★*Bunker Hill* — 973.3
Philbrick, Nathaniel. ★*Mayflower* — 973.2
Phillips, Kevin. *1775* — 973.3
Prud'homme, Alex. *The French Chef in America* — B
Robertson, Cara. *The Trial of Lizzie Borden* — 345.744
Sankovitch, Nina. *American Rebels* — 920
Schiff, Stacy. *The Witches* — 345
Unger, Harlow G. *American Tempest* — 973.3
Watson, Bruce. *Sacco and Vanzetti* — 345.73
Whittock, Martyn. *Mayflower Lives* — 974.4
★*Massacre At Mountain Meadows*. Walker, Ronald W. — 979.2
MASSACRES
  Anand, Anita. *The Patient Assassin* — B
  Brooks, James. *Mesa of Sorrows* — 979.1004
  Chang, Iris. ★*The Rape of Nanking* — 951.04
  Enss, Chris. *Mochi's War* — B
  Hawes, Jennifer. *Grace Will Lead Us Home* — 364.152
  Keenan, Cody. *Grace* — 973.932
  Kurlansky, Mark. *1968* — 909.82
  Lane, Charles. *The Day Freedom Died* — 976.3
  Liao, Yiwu. *Bullets and Opium* — 951.05
  Rappaport, Helen. *The Race to Save the Romanovs* — 947.08
  Rogoyska, Jane. *Surviving Katyn* — 940.54
  Sacco, Joe. *Footnotes in Gaza* — 741.5
  Snyder, Timothy. ★*Bloodlands* — 940.54
  Walker, Ronald W. ★*Massacre at Mountain Meadows* — 979.2
  Young, R. J. *Requiem for the Massacre* — 305.8
  Zucchino, David. *Wilmington's Lie* — 305.8009756
MASSASOIT, WAMPANOAG CHIEF, 1590?-1661
  Philbrick, Nathaniel. ★*Mayflower* — 973.2
MASSERY, HAZEL BRYAN, 1942-
  Margolick, David. *Elizabeth and Hazel* — 379.2
Massie, Robert K.
  Castles of Steel — 940.4
  Catherine the Great — B
  Nicholas and Alexandra — B
  The Romanovs — 947
MASSIE, SUZANNE
  Mann, Jim. *The Rebellion of Ronald Reagan* — 973.927092
Massih, Edy
  ★*Keep It Zesty* — 641.595
Massing, Michael
  Fatal Discord — 920
MASSON, CHARLES, 1800-1853
  Richardson, Edmund. *The King's Shadow* — 958.1
Masson, J. Moussaieff
  Lost Companions — 636.088
Massov, Olga
  ★*Hot Sheet* — 641.82
MASTECTOMY
  Boyer, Anne. *The Undying* — B
  Brem, Rachel. *No Longer Radical* — 616.99
★*The Master*. Clarey, Christopher — B
The Master Builder. Martinez Arias, Alfonso — 571.6
★*Master Harold"—And the Boys*. Fugard, Athol — 822
Master of Ceremonies. Grey, Joel — B
Master of the Game. Indyk, Martin — 327.73
Master of the Mountain. Wiencek, Henry — 973.4
The Master Plan. Wilson, Chris — B
★*Master Slave Husband Wife*. Woo, Ilyon — 920
Master The Marathon. Nolan, Ali — 796.42
Mastering Civility. Porath, Christine Lynne — 650.1
Mastering Color Knitting. Leapman, Melissa — 746.43
Mastering Comics. Abel, Jessica — 741.5
Mastering Pizza. Vetri, Marc — 641.82
Mastering Stand-Up. Rosenfield, Stephen — 792.7
★*Mastering The Art of French Cooking*. Child, Julia — 641.594
Mastering The Art of Japanese Home Cooking. Morimoto, Masaharu — 641.595
Mastermind. Konnikova, Maria — 153.4
The Mastermind. Ratliff, Evan — B

Masterminds & Wingmen. Wiseman, Rosalind — 305.235
Masters and Commanders. Roberts, Andrew — 940.5322
Masters of Death. Rhodes, Richard — 940.53
Masters of Empire. McDonnell, Michael — 977.4
Masters of Management. Wooldridge, Adrian — 658
★*Masters of Modern Soccer*. Wahl, Grant — 796.334
★*Masters of the Air*. Miller, Donald L. — 940.54
Masters of the Planet. Tattersall, Ian — 599.93
MASTERS, JARVIS JAY, 1962-
  Sheff, David. *The Buddhist on Death Row* — B
Masters, Oksana
  The Hard Parts — B
MASTERS, OKSANA
  Masters, Oksana. *The Hard Parts* — B
MASTERS, PETER, 1922-2005
  Garrett, Leah. *X Troop* — 940.54
MASTERSON, BAT, 1853-1921
  Clavin, Thomas. *Dodge City* — 978.1
Masuno, Shunmy
  The Art of Simple Living — 294.3
Masur, Kate
  Until Justice Be Done — 323.1196
Masur, Louis P.
  The Civil War — 973.7
Mat, Mount, and Frame It Yourself. Logan, M. David — 749
Matar, Hisham
  The Return — B
MATAR, HISHAM, 1970-
  Matar, Hisham. *The Return* — B
The Match. Frost, Mark — 796.352
MATCHMAKING
  Cadbury, Deborah. *Queen Victoria's Matchmaking* — 941.081
MATE SELECTION
  De Courcy, Anne. *The Husband Hunters* — 920
  Monger, George. *Marriage Customs of the World* — 392.5
MATE SELECTION FOR WOMEN
  Isenberg, Sheila. *Women Who Love Men Who Kill* — 362.83
MATERIAL CULTURE
  Adams, Mark. *Turn Right at Machu Picchu* — 985
  Carlsen, Spike. *A Walk Around the Block* — 031
  De Hamel, Christopher. ★*Meetings with Remarkable Manuscripts* — 091
  Garfinkel, Yosef. *In the Footsteps of King David* — 933
  Langlands, Alex. *Craeft* — 306.4
  MacGregor, Neil. *A History of the World in 100 Objects* — 930.1
  Manseau, Peter. *Objects of Devotion* — 277
  Olson, Lynne. ★*Empress of the Nile* — B
  Rushin, Steve. *The 34-Ton Bat* — 796.357
  Tanais. *In Sensorium* — B
  Winder, Simon. *Lotharingia* — 944
Material World. Conway, Edmund — 333.7
MATERIALISM
  Howard, Jennifer. *Clutter* — 306.3
MATERIALS
  Conway, Edmund. *Material World* — 333.7
MATERIALS SCIENCE
  Conway, Edmund. *Material World* — 333.7
  Miodownik, Mark. *Liquid Rules* — 530.4
  Miodownik, Mark. *Stuff Matters* — 620.1
  Ploszajski, Anna. *Handmade* — 620.1
  Prasad, Aarathi. *Silk* — 677
MATERIALS SELECTION (LIBRARIES)
  Brunsting, Karen. ★*Open Access Literature in Libraries* — 070.5
  Disher, Wayne. *Crash Course in Collection Development* — 025.2
  Johnson, Peggy. ★*Fundamentals of Collection Development and Management* — 025
MATERNAL HEALTH SERVICES
  Holloway, Kris. *Monique and the Mango Rains* — B
  Somerstein, Rachel. ★*Invisible Labor* — 618.8
MATERNAL LOVE
  Jones, Lucy. ★*Matrescence* — 306.874
  Rippon, Kelly. *Parent Up* — 649
MATERNITY HOMES
  Wills, Clair. ★*Missing Persons* — 929.2
The Math Book. Pickover, Clifford A. — 510.9
The Math of Life and Death. Yates, Kit — 510
Math on Trial. Schneps, Leila — 345
MATHEMATICAL ABILITY
  Tammet, Daniel. *Born on a Blue Day* — B

PUBLIC LIBRARY CORE COLLECTION: NONFICTION
Twentieth Edition

MATHEMATICAL ANALYSIS
   Du Sautoy, Marcus. ★*Around the World in Eighty Games*   790.1
   Ellenberg, Jordan. ★*How Not to Be Wrong*   510
   Vincent, James. *Beyond Measure*   530.8
   Wheelan, Charles J. *Naked Statistics*   519.5

MATHEMATICAL MODELS
   Chayka, Kyle. *Filterworld*   306
   Du Sautoy, Marcus. ★*Around the World in Eighty Games*   790.1
   Lloyd, Seth. *Programming the Universe*   530.12
   O'Neil, Cathy. *Weapons of Math Destruction*   005.7
   Pontzen, Andrew. *The Universe in a Box*   523.1
   Thompson, Erica. *Escape from Model Land*   511

MATHEMATICAL PHYSICS
   Tegmark, Max. *Our Mathematical Universe*   523.1
   *The **Mathematical** Universe.* Dunham, William   510

MATHEMATICIANS
   Auburn, David. *Proof*   812
   Bhattacharya, Ananyo. *The Man from the Future*   B
   Brooks, Michael. *The Art of More*   510.9
   Brooks, Michael. *The Quantum Astrologer's Handbook*   B
   Budiansky, Stephen. *Journey to the Edge of Reason*   B
   Cheng, Eugenia. *How to Bake Pi*   510
   Copeland, B. Jack. *Turing*   B
   Dunham, William. *The Mathematical Universe*   510
   Essinger, James. *Ada's Algorithm*   B
   Fauber, L. S. *Heaven on Earth*   B
   Johnson, Katherine G. *My Remarkable Journey*   B
   Kanigel, Robert. *The Man Who Knew Infinity*   B
   Kitagawa, Kate. *The Secret Lives of Numbers*   510.9
   Leavitt, David. *The Man Who Knew Too Much*   B
   Singh, Simon. *Fermat's Enigma*   512
   Sobel, Dava. *A More Perfect Heaven*   520.9
   Soni, Jimmy. *A Mind at Play*   B
   Stewart, Ian. *Visions of Infinity*   510
   Thorp, Edward O. *A Man for All Markets*   B
   Watson, Richard A. *Cogito Ergo Sum*   B

MATHEMATICS
   Alexander, Amir R. *Infinitesimal*   511
   Barrow, John D. *The Infinite Book*   111
   Benjamin, Arthur. *The Magic of Math*   510
   Brooks, Michael. *The Art of More*   510.9
   Brooks, Michael. *The Quantum Astrologer's Handbook*   B
   Budiansky, Stephen. *Journey to the Edge of Reason*   B
   Cheng, Eugenia. *How to Bake Pi*   510
   Clegg, Brian. *Are Numbers Real?*   510
   Du Sautoy, Marcus. ★*Around the World in Eighty Games*   790.1
   Dunham, William. *The Mathematical Universe*   510
   Ellenberg, Jordan. ★*How Not to Be Wrong*   510
   Felix, Camonghne. *Dyscalculia*   B
   Fortnow, Lance. *The Golden Ticket*   511.3
   Holt, Jim. ★*When Einstein Walked with Godel*   814
   Kitagawa, Kate. *The Secret Lives of Numbers*   510.9
   Mazur, Joseph. *Fluke*   519.2
   Merzbach, Uta C. *A History of Mathematics*   510.9
   Parker, Matt. *Humble Pi*   510
   Pickover, Clifford A. *The Math Book*   510.9
   Rutherford, Adam. *The Complete Guide to Absolutely Everything*   500
   Seife, Charles. *Proofiness*   510
   Singh, Simon. *Fermat's Enigma*   512
   Smil, Vaclav. *Size*   153.7
   Stewart, Ian. *Professor Stewart's Casebook of Mathematical Mysteries*   793.74
   Stewart, Ian. *Visions of Infinity*   510
   Szpiro, George. *Poincare's Prize*   510.76
   Thompson, Erica. *Escape from Model Land*   511
   Wheelan, Charles J. *Naked Statistics*   519.5
   Yates, Kit. *The Math of Life and Death*   510

MATHEMATICS FUN
   Benjamin, Arthur. *The Magic of Math*   510
   Stewart, Ian. *Professor Stewart's Casebook of Mathematical Mysteries*   793.74

MATHEMATICS IN NATURE
   Mazur, Joseph. *Fluke*   519.2
   Mathew Brady. Wilson, Robert   B

MATHEW, THEOBALD, 1790-1856
   Puleo, Stephen. *Voyage of Mercy*   363.8

Mathewes-Green, Frederica
   Welcome to the Orthodox Church   281.9

Mathews, Daniel
   Trees in Trouble   634.9

Matisse The Master. Spurling, Hilary   B
Matisse, Henri
   Henri Matisse   709.2

MATISSE, HENRI, 1869-1954
   Matisse, Henri. *Henri Matisse*   709.2
   Roe, Sue. *In Montmartre*   920
   Smee, Sebastian. *The Art of Rivalry*   700.92
   Spurling, Hilary. *Matisse the Master*   B

Matloff, Judith
   No Friends but the Mountains   355.009

Matney, Mandy
   Blood on Their Hands   364.152

Matos, Michaelangelo
   The Underground Is Massive   781.648
   ★*Matrescence.* Jones, Lucy   306.874
   Matriarch. Edwards, Anne   B
   ★*The Matriarch.* Page, Susan   B

MATRIARCHS
   Hardman, Robert. *Queen of Our Times*   B
   Kearse, Bettye. *The Other Madisons*   920
   Page, Susan. ★*The Matriarch*   B
   Tallis, Nicola. *Uncrowned Queen*   B

Mattel, Trixie
   Working Girls   650.1

MATTER
   Cliff, Harry. *How to Make an Apple Pie from Scratch*   523.01
   Levitt, Dan. *What's Gotten into You*   539.7
   Miodownik, Mark. *Liquid Rules*   530.4
   Wilczek, Frank. *Fundamentals*   530.01
   *The **Matter** of Everything.* Sheehy, Suzie   539.7

Matteson, John
   Eden's Outcasts   920

Matthews, Christopher
   Bobby Kennedy   B
   Kennedy & Nixon   973.922

Matthews, Hannah
   You or Someone You Love   362.1988

Mattioli, Dana
   ★*The Everything War*   381.142

Mattlin, Ben
   Disability Pride   323.3

Mattson, Ingrid
   ★*The Story of the Qur'an*   297.122

Matzen, Robert
   Dutch Girl   B

MAU MAU MOVEMENT AND REVOLT, 1946-1960
   Anderson, David. *Histories of the Hanged*   967.62

Mauceri, John
   For the Love of Music   781.1
   Maestros and Their Music   781.45

MAUGHAM, W. SOMERSET (WILLIAM SOMERSET), 1874-1965
   Hastings, Selina. *The Secret Lives of Somerset Maugham*   B

Mauldin, Bill
   Willie & Joe   741.5

MAULDIN, WILLIAM HENRY, 1921-2003
   DePastino, Todd. *Bill Mauldin*   B

Maupin, Armistead
   Logical Family   B

MAUPIN, ARMISTEAD
   Maupin, Armistead. *Logical Family*   B

Maurer, Kevin
   Damn Lucky   940.54
   The Mauritanian. Slahi, Mohamedou Ould   958.104

Mauro, Jeff
   Come on Over   641.5
   ★*Maus.* Spiegelman, Art   741.5
   Max Jacob. Warren, Rosanna   B

Max, D. T.
   Finale   782.1
   Maximizing The Impact of Comics in Your Library. Phoenix, Jack   026

MAXIMS
   Miranda, Lin-Manuel. *Gmorning, Gnight!*   811
   Maximum City. Mehta, Suketu   954
   Maxine Waters. Jones, Brenda   B
   Maxwell's Handbook for Rda, Resource Description & Access. Maxwell, Robert L.   025.3

MAXWELL, JAMES CLARK, 1831-1879
   Forbes, Nancy. *Faraday, Maxwell, and the Electromagnetic Field*   B

AUTHOR, TITLE, SERIES AND SUBJECT INDEX

Maxwell, Lucas
   Podcasting with Youth 006.7
Maxwell, Robert L.
   Maxwell's Handbook for Rda, Resource Description & Access 025.3
Maxwell, Sarah
   Fearless with Fabric 746.46
MAXWELL, WILLIE
   Cep, Casey N. ★*Furious Hours* 364.152
May We Forever Stand. Perry, Imani 782.25
MAY, ELAINE, 1932-
   Courogen, Carrie. ★*Miss May Does Not Exist* . . . . B
May, Gary
   John Tyler . . . . B
May, Gregory
   A Madman's Will 973.5
May, Katherine
   Enchantment 158.1
   Wintering 155.9
MAY, KATHERINE
   May, Katherine. *Enchantment* 158.1
   May, Katherine. *Wintering* 155.9
May, Meredith
   The Honey Bus . . . . B
MAY, MEREDITH
   May, Meredith. *The Honey Bus* . . . . B
May, Rollo
   The Discovery of Being 150.19
MAYA (CENTRAL AMERICAN PEOPLE)
   Carlsen, William. *Jungle of Stone* . . . . B
   Coe, Michael D. *The Maya* 972
The Maya. Coe, Michael D. 972
Maybe We'll Make It. Price, Margo . . . . B
★*Maybe You Should Talk to Someone*. Gottlieb, Lori . . . . B
MAYER, FREDERICK, 1921-2016
   Lichtblau, Eric. *Return to the Reich* . . . . B
Mayer, Jane
   ★*Dark Money* 973.932
   The Dark Side 973.931
Mayes, Frances
   Bella Tuscany 945
   See You in the Piazza 914.5
   Under the Tuscan Sun 945
   A Year in the World . . . . B
MAYES, FRANCES
   Mayes, Frances. *Bella Tuscany* 945
   Mayes, Frances. *See You in the Piazza* 914.5
   Mayes, Frances. *Under the Tuscan Sun* 945
   Mayes, Frances. *A Year in the World* . . . . B
The Mayflower. Fraser, Rebecca 974.4
★*Mayflower*. Philbrick, Nathaniel 973.2
Mayflower Lives. Whittock, Martyn 974.4
Mayle, Peter
   Encore Provence 944
   My Twenty-Five Years in Provence 944.9
   Provence A-Z 944
   ★*A Year in Provence* 944
MAYLE, PETER
   Mayle, Peter. *Encore Provence* 944
   Mayle, Peter. ★*A Year in Provence* 944
Mayo Clinic Guide to Fibromyalgia. Abril, Andy 616.7
MAYORS
   Buttigieg, Pete. *Shortest Way Home* . . . . B
   Emanuel, Rahm. *The Nation City* 352.23
   Kirtzman, Andrew. *Giuliani* . . . . B
   Signer, Michael. *Cry Havoc* 305.800973
Mays, Kyle
   ★*An Afro-Indigenous History of the United States* 973
Mays, Willie
   24 . . . . B
MAYS, WILLIE, 1931-2024
   Hirsch, James S. *Willie Mays* . . . . B
   Mays, Willie. *24* . . . . B
Mazower, Mark
   The Balkans 949.6
   The Greek Revolution 949.5
   Hitler's Empire 940.53
   Salonica, City of Ghosts 949.5

Mazur, Joseph
   Fluke 519.2
Mazzeo, Tilar J.
   ★*Eliza Hamilton* . . . . B
   Irena's Children . . . . B
   The Secret of Chanel No. 5 . . . . 338.7
   Sisters in Resistance 945.091
Mazzucato, Mariana
   ★*The Big Con* 650.1
MBEKI, THABO
   Gevisser, Mark. *A Legacy of Liberation* . . . . B
Mbs. Hubbard, Ben (Journalist) . . . . B
McAfee, Andrew
   The Geek Way 658.3
McAfee, Richard
   Table Tennis 796.34
McAlester, Virginia
   A Field Guide to American Houses 728
McAlevey, Jane
   A Collective Bargain 331.890973
McAlister, Michael
   Taunton's Wiring Complete 621.3
McAlpine, Skye
   A Table Full of Love 641.5
McAnulty, Dara
   Diary of a Young Naturalist 508.092
MCANULTY, DARA
   McAnulty, Dara. *Diary of a Young Naturalist* 508.092
MCAULIFFE, CHRISTA, 1948-1986
   Cook, Kevin. *The Burning Blue* 629.45
McBride, James
   The Color of Water . . . . B
   Kill 'Em and Leave . . . . B
MCBRIDE, JAMES, 1957-
   McBride, James. *The Color of Water* . . . . B
McBride, Karyl
   Will I Ever Be Good Enough? 616.85
McBride, Martina
   Martina's Kitchen Mix 641.5973
MCBRIDE, PETER (PHOTOGRAPHER)
   Fedarko, Kevin. *A Walk in the Park* 917.91
MCBRIDE-JORDAN, RUTH, 1921-2010
   McBride, James. *The Color of Water* . . . . B
McBrien, Richard P.
   Lives of the Popes . . . . B
McBrien, William
   Cole Porter . . . . B
McCabe, John
   Cagney . . . . B
MCCAIN, JOHN, 1936-2018
   Balz, Daniel J. *The Battle for America, 2008* 973.932
McCallum, Jack
   Dream Team 796.323
   Golden Days 796.323
McCalman, George
   Illustrated Black History 920
McCalman, Iain
   Darwin's Armada 576.8
McCammon, Sarah
   ★*The Exvangelicals* 277.308
MCCANDLESS, CHRISTOPHER JOHNSON, 1968-1992
   Krakauer, Jon. *Into the Wild* 917.9804
McCann, Colum
   American Mother 956.9104
   Letters to a Young Writer 808.02
McCarten, Anthony
   Darkest Hour 941.084
McCarthy, Catherine
   Raising a Kid Who Can 649
MCCARTHY, JOSEPH, 1908-1957
   Conant, Jennet. *The Lotus Eaters* 940.54
   Tye, Larry. ★*Demagogue* . . . . B
MCCARTHY, MARY, 1912-1989
   Hardwick, Elizabeth. *The Dolphin Letters, 1970-1979* 811
MCCARTHYISM
   Bird, Kai. *American Prometheus* . . . . B
   Eyman, Scott. *Charlie Chaplin vs. America* . . . . B
The McCartney Legacy. Kozinn, Allan . . . . B

PUBLIC LIBRARY CORE COLLECTION: NONFICTION
Twentieth Edition

McCartney, Paul
  ★*1964*   782.42166
  The Lyrics   782.42166
MCCARTNEY, PAUL
  Brown, Craig. *150 Glimpses of the Beatles*   920
  Doggett, Peter. *You Never Give Me Your Money*   B
  Kozinn, Allan. *The McCartney Legacy*   B
  McCartney, Paul. *The Lyrics*   782.42166
McCaulley, Esau
  How Far to the Promised Land   B
MCCAULLEY, ESAU
  McCaulley, Esau. *How Far to the Promised Land*   B
McClain, James
  Japan   952.03
McClain, John
  The Designer Within   645
McClanahan, Paige
  The New Tourist   338.4
McClelland, Mac
  Irritable Hearts   B
MCCLELLAND, MAC
  McClelland, Mac. *Irritable Hearts*   B
McCloskey, Jim
  When Truth Is All You Have   B
MCCLOSKEY, JIM (MINISTER)
  McCloskey, Jim. *When Truth Is All You Have*   B
McCloud, Scott
  Making Comics   741.5
  Reinventing Comics   741.5
  ★*Understanding Comics*   741.5
McColl, Sarah
  Joy Enough   B
MCCOLL, SARAH
  McColl, Sarah. *Joy Enough*   B
McConahay, Mary Jo
  The Tango War   940.53
McConaughey, Matthew
  Greenlights   B
MCCONAUGHEY, MATTHEW, 1969-
  McConaughey, Matthew. *Greenlights*   B
McConnell, Patricia B.
  ★*The Other End of the Leash*   636.7
MCCONVILLE, JEAN
  Keefe, Patrick Radden. ★*Say Nothing*   364.152
McConville, Mark
  Failure to Launch   155.6
McCormick, Brad
  Extreme Sports   791.457
MCCORMICK, KATHERINE DEXTER, 1876-1967
  Eig, Jonathan. *The Birth of the Pill*   618.1
McCormick, Mack
  Biography of a Phantom   782.421643
MCCORMICK, MACK
  McCormick, Mack. *Biography of a Phantom*   782.421643
McCormick, Ty
  Beyond the Sand and Sea   920
MCCORVEY, NORMA, 1947-2017
  Prager, Joshua. *The Family Roe*   342.7308
MCCOURT FAMILY
  McCourt, Frank. ★*Angela's Ashes*   929
  McCourt, Frank. *'Tis*   B
McCourt, Frank
  ★*Angela's Ashes*   929
  Teacher Man   B
  'Tis   B
MCCOURT, FRANK
  McCourt, Frank. ★*Angela's Ashes*   929
  McCourt, Frank. *Teacher Man*   B
  McCourt, Frank. *'Tis*   B
McCourt, Frank H.
  ★*Our Biggest Fight*   303.48
McCourt, Malachy
  A Monk Swimming   B
  Singing My Him Song   B
MCCOURT, MALACHY, 1931-2024
  McCourt, Malachy. *A Monk Swimming*   B
  McCourt, Malachy. *Singing My Him Song*   B

McCoy, Alfred W.
  A Question of Torture   323.4
McCracken, Patti
  The Angel Makers   364.152
McCrae, Shane
  In the Language of My Captor   811
McCraw, David Edward
  Truth in Our Times   342.7308
MCCRAW, DAVID EDWARD
  McCraw, David Edward. *Truth in Our Times*   342.7308
McCraw, Thomas K.
  ★*The Founders and Finance*   330.973
McCrum, Robert
  ★*The Story of English*   420
McCubbin, Lisa
  Betty Ford   B
McCubbin, Tracy
  Make Space for Happiness   179
  Making Space, Clutter Free   648
MCCULLERS, CARSON, 1917-1967
  Dearborn, Mary V. *Carson McCullers*   B
  Nafisi, Azar. *The Republic of Imagination*   B
  Shapland, Jenn. *My Autobiography of Carson McCullers*   B
MCCULLOCH, BRUCE
  Myers, Paul. *The Kids in the Hall*   920
McCullough, David G.
  ★*1776*   973.3
  ★*The American Spirit*   973
  The Greater Journey   920
  ★*John Adams*   B
  Mornings on Horseback   B
  The Path Between the Seas   972.87
  The Pioneers   920
  Truman   B
  ★*The Wright Brothers*   B
McCumber, David
  Playing off the Rail   B
McCurdy, Jennette
  ★*I'm Glad My Mom Died*   B
MCCURDY, JENNETTE, 1992-
  McCurdy, Jennette. ★*I'm Glad My Mom Died*   B
McCurry, Steve
  The Iconic Photographs   779.092
MCDANIEL, HATTIE, 1895-1952
  Watts, Jill. *Hattie McDaniel*   B
McDermott, Alice
  What About the Baby?   814
McDermott, Kate
  ★*Art of the Pie*   641.86
McDiarmid, Jessica
  Highway of Tears   364.152
McDonald, Greg (Producer)
  Elvis and the Colonel   920
MCDONALD, KEVIN, 1961-
  Myers, Paul. *The Kids in the Hall*   920
McDonald, Michael
  ★*What a Fool Believes*   B
McDonnell, Michael
  Masters of Empire   977.4
McDonough, Frank
  The Hitler Years   943.086
McDonough, James L.
  William Tecumseh Sherman   B
McDonough, Jimmy
  Tammy Wynette   B
McDougall, Christopher
  ★*Born to Run*   796.42
  Natural Born Heroes   940.53
  Running with Sherman   636.1
MCDOUGALL, CHRISTOPHER, 1962-
  McDougall, Christopher. *Running with Sherman*   636.1
McDowell, Erin Jeanne
  ★*The Book on Pie*   641.86
  The Fearless Baker   641.81
McDowell, Marta
  The World of Laura Ingalls Wilder   813
McElya, Micki
  The Politics of Mourning   975.5

AUTHOR, TITLE, SERIES AND SUBJECT INDEX

McFadden, Joshua
   ★ *Grains for Every Season* — 641.3
   Six Seasons — 641.5
McGarrahan, Ellen
   Two Truths and a Lie — 364.152
MCGARRAHAN, ELLEN
   McGarrahan, Ellen. *Two Truths and a Lie* — 364.152
McGee, Harold
   ★ *Nose Dive* — 612.8
   ★ *On Food and Cooking* — 641.5
McGhee, Heather C.
   ★ *The Sum of Us* — 305.8
McGill, Joseph
   Sleeping with the Ancestors — 306.362
MCGILL, JOSEPH, JR
   McGill, Joseph. *Sleeping with the Ancestors* — 306.362
McGilligan, Patrick
   Funny Man — B
   Oscar Micheaux — B
   Young Orson — B
McGinnis, Patrick J.
   Fear of Missing Out — 153.8
McGinnis, Samuel M
   ★ *Peterson Field Guide to Western Reptiles and Amphibians* — 597.9
McGinniss, Joe
   Fatal Vision — B
McGinty, Brian
   Lincoln's Greatest Case — 346.7303
McGonigal, Jane
   Super Better — 794.8
McGough, Matthew
   The Lazarus Files — 364.152
McGovern, Anna
   Pottering — 158.1
MCGOVERN, GEORGE S., 1922-2012
   Ambrose, Stephen E. *The Wild Blue* — 940.54
McGowan, Rose
   Brave — B
MCGOWAN, ROSE, 1973-
   McGowan, Rose. *Brave* — B
McGrath, Ben
   Riverman — 797.122
McGrath, Campbell
   Nouns & Verbs — 811
McGrath, Jinks
   The Complete Jewelry Making Course — 739.27028
McGrath, Tim
   James Monroe — B
McGrath, Tom
   Triumph of the Yuppies — 305.242
McGraw, Phillip C.
   Life Strategies — 158
McGraw, Seamus
   The End of Country — 333.7909748
McGreal, Chris
   American Overdose — 362.29
McGreevy, John T.
   ★ *Catholicism* — 282.09
McGregor, Alyson J.
   Sex Matters — 613
McGregor, James H.
   Rome from the Ground up — 711
McGuckin, John Anthony
   ★ *The Eastern Orthodox Church* — 281.909
McHangama, Jacob
   ★ *Free Speech* — 323.44
McHargue, Mike
   You're a Miracle (and a Pain in the Ass) — 158.1
McHugh, Heather
   Muddy Matterhorn — 811
McIlwaine, Catherine
   Tolkien — 002.09
McIndoe, Andrew
   The Creative Shrub Garden — 635.9
McInerny, Nora
   The Hot Young Widows Club — 155.9
MCINERNY, NORA
   McInerny, Nora. *The Hot Young Widows Club* — 155.9

McIntire, Mike
   Champions Way — 796.043
McIntyre, Rick
   The Reign of Wolf 21 — 599.773
McKay, Matthew
   Self-Esteem — 155.2
McKay, Sinclair
   Berlin — 943
   The Fire and the Darkness — 940.54
   The Secret Lives of Codebreakers — 940.54
McKean, David
   Suspected of Independence — B
   Watching Darkness Fall — 940.53
MCKEAN, THOMAS, 1734-1817
   McKean, David. *Suspected of Independence* — B
McKee, Robert
   Dialogue — 809
McKeen, William
   Everybody Had an Ocean — 781.6609
McKeever, Mike P
   How to Write a Business Plan — 658.15
MCKELLEN, IAN
   O'Connor, Garry. *Ian McKellen* — B
McKenney, Sally
   ★ *Sally's Cookie Addiction* — 641.86
McKeon, Kathy
   Jackie's Girl — B
MCKEON, KATHY
   McKeon, Kathy. *Jackie's Girl* — B
McKeown, Greg
   Essentialism — 153.8
McKibben, Bill
   Falter — 909.83
McKinley, Richard
   Pastel Pointers — 741.2
MCKINLEY, WILLIAM, 1843-1901
   Creighton, Margaret S. *The Electrifying Fall of Rainbow City* — 607
   Merry, Robert W. *President McKinley* — B
   Miller, Scott. *The President and the Assassin* — 973.8
MCKINNEY, GAYLE
   Valby, Karen. *The Swans of Harlem* — 792.8
MCKINNEY, MARK, 1963-
   Myers, Paul. *The Kids in the Hall* — 920
McKinnon, Hetty
   ★ *Tenderheart* — 641.5
McKnight, Kent H.
   A Field Guide to Mushrooms, North America — 579.6
McKoy, Bri
   The Cook's Book — 641.3
MCLAIN, DENNY
   Pappu, Sridhar. *The Year of the Pitcher* — 920
McLaren, Brian D.
   Do I Stay Christian? — 270.8
   Faith After Doubt — 234
   Life After Doom — 200.1
McLaughlin, Chris
   The Good Garden — 635
McLaughlin, Kathleen
   Blood Money — 362.17
McLean, Bethany
   All the Devils Are Here — 330.973
McLeary, Susan
   Flowers for All — 745.92
McLoughlin, William Gerald
   After the Trail of Tears — 973
McLynn, Frank
   Genghis Khan — 950.2
McManus, James
   ★ *Positively Fifth Street* — 795.41
McManus, John C.
   Fire and Fortitude — 940.54
   Island Infernos — 940.54
   To the End of the Earth — 940.54
McMeekin, Sean
   July 1914 — 940.3
   The Russian Revolution — 947.084
   Stalin's War — 940.53

PUBLIC LIBRARY CORE COLLECTION: NONFICTION
Twentieth Edition

McMillan, John
   Reinventing the Bazaar — 330.12
McMillan, Tracie
   The American Way of Eating — 338.4
   ★*The White Bonus* — 305.8
McMurtry, Larry
   Crazy Horse — B
   Custer — B
MCMURTRY, LARRY, 1936-2021
   Daugherty, Tracy. *Larry McMurtry* — B
McNally, Dennis
   On Highway 61 — 781.64
McNamara, Eileen
   ★*Eunice* — B
McNamara, Kevin J.
   Dreams of a Great Small Nation — 355.009437
McNamara, Michelle
   I'll Be Gone in the Dark — 364.152
MCNAMARA, MICHELLE, 1970-2016
   McNamara, Michelle. *I'll Be Gone in the Dark* — 364.152
McNamara, Robert S.
   In Retrospect — 959.704
MCNAMARA, ROBERT S., 1916-2009
   Hendrickson, Paul. *The Living and the Dead* — 959.704
McNeil, Beth
   Fundamentals of Library Supervision — 023
McNeil, Donald G.
   ★*The Wisdom of Plagues* — 614.4
McNeur, Catherine
   Mischievous Creatures — 920
McPhee, John
   Levels of the Game — 796.34
   The Ransom of Russian Art — 709
   Tabula Rasa; V.1 — 818
   Uncommon Carriers — 388
MCPHEE, JOHN, 1931-
   McPhee, John. *Tabula Rasa; V.1* — 818
McPhee, Peter
   Robespierre — B
MCPHERSON, AIMEE SEMPLE, 1890-1944
   Krist, Gary. *The Mirage Factory* — 920
McPherson, James M.
   ★*Abraham Lincoln* — B
   Battle Cry of Freedom — 973.7
   Drawn with the Sword — 973.7
   For Cause and Comrades — 973.7
   Hallowed Ground — 973.7
   ★*Tried by War* — 973.7
MCQUEEN, ALEXANDER, 1969-2010
   Thomas, Dana. *Gods and Kings* — 920
McRaven, William H.
   Sea Stories — B
MCRAVEN, WILLIAM H. (WILLIAM HARRY), 1955-
   McRaven, William H. *Sea Stories* — B
   Wallace, Chris. *Countdown Bin Laden* — 958.104
McShane Wulfhart, Nell
   The Great Stewardess Rebellion — 331.4
McSwane, J. David
   ★*Pandemic, Inc.* — 362.1962
MCTELL, BLIND WILLIE, 1901-1959
   Gray, Michael. *Hand Me My Travelin' Shoes* — B
McTier, Moiya
   The Milky Way — 523.1
★*McU*. Robinson, Joanna — 791.43
MCVAY, CHARLES BUTLER, III, 1898-1968
   Vincent, Lynn. *Indianapolis* — 940.54
MCVEIGH, TIMOTHY, 1968-2001
   Toobin, Jeffrey. ★*Homegrown* — 363.325
McWhirter, Cameron
   American Gun — 683.4
McWhorter, Diane
   Carry Me Home — 976.1
McWhorter, John H.
   Talking Back, Talking Black — 427
★*Me*. John, Elton — B
★*Me & Patsy Kickin' up Dust*. Lynn, Loretta — B
★*Me and White Supremacy*. Saad, Layla F. — 305.809

ME TOO MOVEMENT
   Amos, Tori. *Resistance* — B
   Bravo, Reah. ★*Complicit* — 331.4
   Burke, Tarana. ★*Unbound* — B
   Farrow, Ronan. ★*Catch and Kill* — 331.4
   Hewlett, Sylvia Ann. *#metoo in the Corporate World* — 658.3
   Hirshman, Linda R. *Reckoning* — 305.420973
   Kantor, Jodi. *She Said* — 364.15
   Vanasco, Jeannie. *Things We Didn't Talk About When I Was a Girl* — B
   Vogelstein, Rachel B. *Awakening* — 305.42
Meacham, Jon
   ★*American Lion* — B
   ★*And There Was Light* — B
   ★*Destiny and Power* — B
   Franklin and Winston — 940.53
   His Truth Is Marching On — B
   Songs of America — 782.42
   ★*The Soul of America* — 973
   ★*Thomas Jefferson* — B
Mead, Corey
   The Hidden History of the White House — 975.3
Mead, Margaret
   Coming of Age in Samoa — 306
Mead, Rebecca
   My Life in Middlemarch — 823
MEAD, REBECCA
   Mead, Rebecca. *My Life in Middlemarch* — 823
Mead, Walter Russell
   The Arc of a Covenant — 327.73
MEAGHER, THOMAS FRANCIS, 1823-1867
   Egan, Timothy. ★*The Immortal Irishman* — B
Mealer, Bryan
   The Kings of Big Spring — B
MEALER, BRYAN
   Mealer, Bryan. *The Kings of Big Spring* — B
Meals, Music, and Muses. Smalls, Alexander — 641.59
Meals, Roy A.
   Bones — 599.9
   Muscle — 612.7
Mean Baby. Blair, Selma — B
The Meaning of Birds. Barnes, Simon — 598
The Meaning of Human Existence. Wilson, Edward O. — 128
★*The Meaning of It All*. Feynman, Richard P. — 500
The Meaning of Relativity. Einstein, Albert — 530.11
★*Means of Control*. Tau, Byron — 363.25
Means, Brittany
   Hell If We Don't Change Our Ways — B
MEANS, BRITTANY
   Means, Brittany. *Hell If We Don't Change Our Ways* — B
Means, Howard B.
   ★*Splash!* — 797.2
Mearns, David L.
   The Shipwreck Hunter — 910.452
MEARNS, DAVID L.
   Mearns, David L. *The Shipwreck Hunter* — 910.452
MEASLES
   Wadman, Meredith. *The Vaccine Race* — 614.5
★*Measure of a Man*. Greenfield, Martin — B
The Measure of a Man. Poitier, Sidney — B
MEASUREMENT
   Sobel, Dava. *Longitude* — 526
   Stone, Deborah A. *Counting* — 001.4
   Vincent, James. *Beyond Measure* — 530.8
MEAT
   Danforth, Adam. *Butchering Poultry, Rabbit, Lamb, Goat, and Pork* — 664
   Williams, Wyatt. *Springer Mountain* — 394.1
MEAT CUTTING
   Danforth, Adam. *Butchering Poultry, Rabbit, Lamb, Goat, and Pork* — 664
Meat Eater. Rinella, Steven — B
MEAT INDUSTRY AND TRADE
   Foer, Jonathan Safran. *Eating Animals* — 641.3
   Genoways, Ted. *The Chain* — 338.7
   Sorvino, Chloe. *Raw Deal* — 338.1
Meat on the Side. Dinki, Nikki — 641.3
MEAT SUBSTITUTES
   Headley, Brooks. *Superiority Burger Cookbook* — 641.5
   Schinner, Miyoko Nishimoto. *The Vegan Meat Cookbook* — 641.5
   Sorvino, Chloe. *Raw Deal* — 338.1

AUTHOR, TITLE, SERIES AND SUBJECT INDEX

★*Meathead*. Goldwyn, Meathead	641.7
Meb for Mortals. Keflezighi, Meb	796.4252
Mecham, Jesse	
You Need a Budget	332.024
★*Mechanic Shop Femme's Guide to Car Ownership*. Milchtein, Chaya M.	629.222
Mechanic, Michael	
Jackpot	305.5
MECHANICS	
Cox, Brian. *The Quantum Universe*	530.12
Kakalios, James. *The Amazing Story of Quantum Mechanics*	530.12
Macaulay, David. *The Way Things Work Now*	600
Meckler, Laura	
★*Dream Town*	305.8
MECOM, JANE, 1712-1794	
Lepore, Jill. *Book of Ages*	B
MEDAD, JACOB, 1919-2012	
Talty, Stephan. *The Good Assassin*	364.15
MEDAL OF HONOR	
Erwin, Jon. *Beyond Valor*	B
Kershaw, Alex. *Against All Odds*	940.54
MEDAL OF HONOR RECIPIENTS	
Carpenter, Kyle. *You Are Worth It*	B
Kershaw, Alex. *Against All Odds*	940.54
Medallion Status. Hodgman, John	B
Meder, Danielle	
Draw Fashion Now	741.6
★*Medgar and Myrlie*. Reid, Joy-Ann Lomena	920
MEDIA FANDOM	
Evans, William. *Black Nerd Problems*	814.6
Goetz, Kevin. *Audienceology*	791.43
Nussbaum, Emily. *I Like to Watch*	791.45
Phillips, Maya. *Nerd*	302.23
MEDIA LITERACY	
Anderson, Jimmeka. *Power Lines*	020
Media Madness. Kurtz, Howard	973.933
Media Man. Auletta, Ken	B
MEDIA TIE-INS	
Alterman, Sara Faith. *Let's Never Talk About This Again*	616.8
Attenborough, David. *Life in the Undergrowth*	592
Attenborough, David. *The Life of Birds*	598.15
Baldwin, James. *I Am Not Your Negro*	323.1196
Bennett, Roger. *Men in Blazers Present Encyclopedia Blazertannica*	796.334
Boilen, Bob. *Your Song Changed My Life*	780.92
Dasal, Jennifer. *Artcurious*	709
Doran, Peter B. *Breaking Rockefeller*	338.7
Douglas, John E. *When a Killer Calls*	364.152
Duncan, Dayton. ★*Country Music*	781.642
Eagleman, David. *The Brain*	612.8
Garcia, Amanda Yates. *Initiated*	B
Gates, Henry Louis. *And Still I Rise*	305.896
Gates, Henry Louis. ★*Stony the Road*	973
Grossman, Pam. *Waking the Witch*	133.4
Longworth, Karina. *Seduction*	B
Maddow, Rachel. *Bag Man*	B
Mars, Roman. ★*The 99% Invisible City*	720
Moe, John. *The Hilarious World of Depression*	616.85
Nashawaty, Chris. *Caddyshack*	791.43
Novella, Steven. *The Skeptics' Guide to the Universe*	500
Palin, Michael. *North Korea Journal*	951.9305
Pesca, Mike. *Upon Further Review*	796
Pressman, Steven. *50 Children*	940.53
Rehm, Diane. *When My Time Comes*	179.7
Rinzler, J. W. *The Making of Aliens*	791.4372
Rocca, Mo. *Mobituaries*	920
Rosenthal, Phil. ★*Somebody Feed Phil the Book*	641.59
Schama, Simon. ★*The Story of the Jews; Volume One*	909
Schama, Simon. ★*The Story of the Jews; Volume Two*	909
Sloan, Nate. *Switched on Pop*	781.64
Smith, Richard MacLean. *Unexplained*	130
Sow, Aminatou. *Big Friendship*	177
Stone, Robert. *Chasing the Moon*	629.45
Tippett, Krista. ★*Becoming Wise*	158.1
Toler, Pamela D. *Heroines of Mercy Street*	973.7
Tyson, Neil deGrasse. *Cosmic Queries*	523.1
Wald, Elijah. *American Epic*	781.64
Ward, Geoffrey C. ★*The Roosevelts*	B
Ward, Geoffrey C. ★*The Vietnam War*	959.704
Zambone, Albert Louis. *Daniel Morgan*	B
MEDIATION	
Voloj, Julian. *Ghetto Brother*	741.5
MEDICAL ACCOUNTABILITY	
Lenzer, Jeanne. *The Danger Within Us*	338.4
MEDICAL CARE	
Abramson, John. *Sickening*	338.4
Alexander, Brian. ★*The Hospital*	362.10973
Allen, Marshall. ★*Never Pay the First Bill*	610.28
Aptowicz, Cristin O'Keefe. *Dr. Mutter's Marvels*	B
Aronson, Louise. *Elderhood*	362.60973
Blackstock, Uche. *Legacy*	610.92
Block, Jennifer. *Everything Below the Waist*	613
Boyer, Anne. *The Undying*	B
Brown, Theresa. *Healing*	616.99
Campbell, Olivia. *Women in White Coats*	610.92
Castro, M. Regina. ★*The Essential Diabetes Book*	616.4
Christakis, Nicholas A. *Apollo's Arrow*	362.1962
Cleghorn, Elinor. *Unwell Women*	613
Cohn, Jonathan. *The Ten Year War*	368.38
Comen, Elizabeth. ★*All in Her Head*	613
Cornelius, Maria M. *The Final Season*	B
Coste, Joanne Koenig. *Learning to Speak Alzheimer's*	362.1
Coyle, Marcia. *The Roberts Court*	347.73
Dakwar, Elias. *The Captive Imagination*	616.85
DiGregorio, Sarah. ★*Taking Care*	610.73
Eichenwald, Kurt. *A Mind Unraveled*	B
Ely, Wes. *Every Deep-Drawn Breath*	616.02
Fabes, Stephen. *Signs of Life*	B
Fadiman, Anne. *The Spirit Catches You and You Fall Down*	306.4
Fisher, Thomas. ★*The Emergency*	362.1089
Fox, Michael J. *No Time Like the Future*	B
Glass, Charles. *Soldiers Don't Go Mad*	616.85
Goldberg, Emma. *Life on the Line*	362.1962
Guibert, Emmanuel. *The Photographer*	741.5
Gupta, Shalene. *The Cycle*	618.1
Hamblin, James. *If Our Bodies Could Talk*	613
Harper, Michele. *The Beauty in Breaking*	B
Harris, Taylor. *This Boy We Made*	B
Hazzard, Kevin M. *American Sirens*	362.18
Hernandez, Daisy. *The Kissing Bug*	616.9
Hongoltz-Hetling, Matthew. *If It Sounds Like a Quack*	615.8
Jamison, Leslie. *The Empathy Exams*	813
Jena, Anupam B. *Random Acts of Medicine*	616.0072
Johnson, Steven. *Extra Life*	362.1
Jones, Chip. *The Organ Thieves*	617.4
Keefe, Patrick Radden. ★*Empire of Pain*	338.7
Kempner, Joanna. *Psychedelic Outlaws*	615.7
Kissinger, Meg. *While You Were Out*	362.2
Klass, Perri. *A Good Time to Be Born*	362.19892
Lenzer, Jeanne. *The Danger Within Us*	338.4
Lewis, Michael. ★*The Premonition*	614.5
Liverpool, Layal. *Systemic*	362.1
Malone, Sharon. *Grown Woman Talk*	362.1
Mannix, Kathryn. *With the End in Mind*	304.6
Marsh, Henry. *Admissions*	B
McGregor, Alyson J. *Sex Matters*	613
Mukherjee, Siddhartha. *The Laws of Medicine*	610.1
Mukherjee, Siddhartha. ★*The Song of the Cell*	571.6
Nimura, Janice P. ★*The Doctors Blackwell*	610.92
Norman, Elizabeth M. *We Band of Angels*	940.54
Nuila, Ricardo. *The People's Hospital*	362.1
O'Rourke, Meghan. ★*The Invisible Kingdom*	616
Otto, Mary. *Teeth*	617
Patterson, James. *ER Nurses*	610.73
Porter, Roy. *The Greatest Benefit to Mankind*	610
Powell, Tia. *Dementia Reimagined*	616.8
Pratt, Misty. *All in Her Head*	616.89
Quinones, Sam. *Dreamland*	362.29
Ramey, Sarah. *The Lady's Handbook for Her Mysterious Illness*	B
Rankin, Lauren. *Bodies on the Line*	362.1988
Rosenthal, Elisabeth. *An American Sickness*	362.10973
Rutkow, Ira M. *Empire of the Scalpel*	617
Sacks, Oliver. *The Man Who Mistook His Wife for a Hat and Other Clinical Tales*	616.8
Savage, Jodi M. *The Death of a Jaybird*	B
Shah, Meera. *You're the Only One I've Told*	362.1988
Snyder, Timothy. ★*Our Malady*	362.10973

PUBLIC LIBRARY CORE COLLECTION: NONFICTION
Twentieth Edition

Somerstein, Rachel. ★*Invisible Labor* — 618.8
Standefer, Katherine E. *Lightning Flowers* — B
Tabery, James. ★*Tyranny of the Gene* — 572.8
Toler, Pamela D. *Heroines of Mercy Street* — 973.7
Turban, Jack L. ★*Free to Be* — 616.85
Tweedy, Damon. *Facing the Unseen* — 362.2
Villarosa, Linda. ★*Under the Skin* — 362.1089
Wade, Sabia. *Birthing Liberation* — 363.96
Warraich, Haider. *The Song of Our Scars* — 616
Washington, Kate. ★*Already Toast* — 649.8
Wilson, F. Perry. *How Medicine Works and When It Doesn't* — 610.69
Wright, Jennifer Ashley. ★*Madame Restell* — B
Wright, Lawrence. ★*The Plague Year* — 614.5
Yurkiewicz, Ilana. *Fragmented* — 362.1
Zaitchik, Alexander. *Owning the Sun* — 362.1

MEDICAL CARE REFORM
Cohn, Jonathan. *The Ten Year War* — 368.38
Ely, Wes. *Every Deep-Drawn Breath* — 616.02
Insel, Thomas R. *Healing* — 362.2
Moore, Kate. ★*The Woman They Could Not Silence* — B
Quigley, Fran. *Prescription for the People* — 338.4
Snyder, Timothy. ★*Our Malady* — 362.10973
Tweedy, Damon. *Facing the Unseen* — 362.2
Yurkiewicz, Ilana. *Fragmented* — 362.1

MEDICAL CARE SERVICES
Eichenwald, Kurt. *A Mind Unraveled* — B
Ford, Elizabeth. *Sometimes Amazing Things Happen* — B
Liverpool, Layal. *Systemic* — 362.1
Nuila, Ricardo. *The People's Hospital* — 362.1
Owen, David. *Volume Control* — 617.8
Rosenthal, Elisabeth. *An American Sickness* — 362.10973

MEDICAL COVER-UPS
Lieu, Susan. ★*The Manicurist's Daughter* — B

MEDICAL EMERGENCIES
Patterson, James. *ER Nurses* — 610.73

MEDICAL EQUIPMENT
Lenzer, Jeanne. *The Danger Within Us* — 338.4

MEDICAL ERRORS
Allen, Marshall. ★*Never Pay the First Bill* — 610.28
Gawande, Atul. *Complications* — B

MEDICAL ETHICS
DiGregorio, Sarah. *Early* — 618.92
Dittrich, Luke. ★*Patient H.M.* — 616.85
Elliott, Carl. ★*The Occasional Human Sacrifice* — 174.2
Frank, Lone. *The Pleasure Shock* — 616.8
Gawande, Atul. *Complications* — B
Hallman, J. C. *Say Anarcha* — 618.1
Hughes, Evan. *The Hard Sell* — 338.4
Jones, Chip. *The Organ Thieves* — 617.4
Kinzer, Stephen. *Poisoner in Chief* — B
Kolata, Gina Bari. *Mercies in Disguise* — 616
Lenzer, Jeanne. *The Danger Within Us* — 338.4
Lisle, John. *The Dirty Tricks Department* — 940.54
Reverby, Susan M. *Examining Tuskegee* — 174.2
Rutherford, Adam. *Control* — 363.9
Skloot, Rebecca. ★*The Immortal Life of Henrietta Lacks* — B
Volandes, Angelo E. *The Conversation* — 616.02

MEDICAL FRAUD
Lenzer, Jeanne. *The Danger Within Us* — 338.4

MEDICAL GENETICS
Castro, M. Regina. ★*The Essential Diabetes Book* — 616.4
Gooch, Brad. ★*Flannery* — B
Ingrassia, Lawrence. *A Fatal Inheritance* — 616.99
Jones, Chloe Cooper. ★*Easy Beauty* — B
Kolata, Gina Bari. *Mercies in Disguise* — 616
Marcus, Amy Dockser. *We the Scientists* — 618.92
Newman, Magdalena. *Normal* — 611
Piore, Adam. *The Body Builders* — 660.6
Taraborrelli, J. Randy. ★*The Secret Life of Marilyn Monroe* — B

MEDICAL INNOVATIONS
Aptowicz, Cristin O'Keefe. *Dr. Mutter's Marvels* — B
DiGregorio, Sarah. *Early* — 618.92
Lieberman, Jeffrey A. *Malady of the Mind* — 616.89
Mukherjee, Siddhartha. ★*The Song of the Cell* — 571.6
Nakazawa, Donna Jackson. *The Angel and the Assassin* — 612.8
Offit, Paul A. *You Bet Your Life* — 615.5
Owen, David. *Volume Control* — 617.8

MEDICAL MALPRACTICE
Carriere, Alice. *Everything/Nothing/Someone* — B
Cleghorn, Elinor. *Unwell Women* — 613
Elliott, Carl. ★*The Occasional Human Sacrifice* — 174.2
Fink, Sheri. *Five Days at Memorial* — 362.1109763
Jones, Chip. *The Organ Thieves* — 617.4

MEDICAL MARIJUANA
Dufton, Emily. *Grass Roots* — 362.29

MEDICAL MICROBIOLOGY
Finlay, B. Brett. *Let Them Eat Dirt* — 616.9
Ireland, Tom. *The Good Virus* — 579.2

MEDICAL MISCONCEPTIONS
Harrison, Christy. *The Wellness Trap* — 613

MEDICAL PERSONNEL
Brenner, Marie. ★*The Desperate Hours* — 362.1962
Cahalan, Susannah. ★*The Great Pretender* — 616.89
Conyers, Jonathan. *I Wasn't Supposed to Be Here* — B
Goldberg, Emma. *Life on the Line* — 362.1962
Patterson, James. *ER Nurses* — 610.73

MEDICAL RESEARCH
Borrell, Brendan. *The First Shots* — 615.3
Dittrich, Luke. ★*Patient H.M.* — 616.85
Eagleman, David. *The Brain* — 612.8
Elliott, Carl. ★*The Occasional Human Sacrifice* — 174.2
Goldacre, Ben. *Bad Science* — 500
Ingrassia, Lawrence. *A Fatal Inheritance* — 616.99
Karlawish, Jason. ★*The Problem of Alzheimer's* — 616.8
Kempner, Joanna. *Psychedelic Outlaws* — 615.7
Klass, Perri. *A Good Time to Be Born* — 362.19892
Kolata, Gina Bari. *Mercies in Disguise* — 616
Marcus, Amy Dockser. *We the Scientists* — 618.92
McGregor, Alyson J. *Sex Matters* — 613
Mukherjee, Siddhartha. ★*The Song of the Cell* — 571.6
Nakazawa, Donna Jackson. *The Angel and the Assassin* — 612.8
Pollan, Michael. *How to Change Your Mind* — 615.7
Pratchett, Terry. *A Slip of the Keyboard* — 824
Reverby, Susan M. *Examining Tuskegee* — 174.2
Roach, Mary. ★*Stiff* — 611
Schama, Simon. *Foreign Bodies* — 614.4
Skloot, Rebecca. ★*The Immortal Life of Henrietta Lacks* — B
Stanger, Ben. *From One Cell* — 571.6
Wilson, F. Perry. *How Medicine Works and When It Doesn't* — 610.69

MEDICAL SCIENTISTS
Kandel, Eric R. *In Search of Memory* — B

MEDICAL STUDENTS
Stern, Adam. *Committed* — 616.89

MEDICAL TECHNOLOGY
Rutkow, Ira M. *Empire of the Scalpel* — 617
Standefer, Katherine E. *Lightning Flowers* — B

MEDICALLY UNINSURED PEOPLE
Nuila, Ricardo. *The People's Hospital* — 362.1
Rosenthal, Elisabeth. *An American Sickness* — 362.10973

The Medici. Strathern, Paul — 945.5

MEDICI, HOUSE OF
Hibbert, Christopher. *The House of Medici* — 920
Strathern, Paul. *The Medici* — 945.5

MEDICINAL PLANTS
Chevallier, Andrew. *Encyclopedia of Herbal Medicine* — 615.3
Davis, Wade. *One River* — 581.6
Quave, Cassandra Leah. *The Plant Hunter* — 581.6

MEDICINE
Balakrishnan, Chris. *How to Win Friends and Influence Fungi* — 502
Barry, John M. ★*The Great Influenza* — 614.5
Comen, Elizabeth. ★*All in Her Head* — 613
Crosby, Molly Caldwell. *The American Plague* — 614.5
Ely, Wes. *Every Deep-Drawn Breath* — 616.02
English, Camper. *Doctors and Distillers* — 615.7
Fitzharris, Lindsey. *The Butchering Art* — B
Gawande, Atul. *Complications* — B
Harrington, Anne. *Mind Fixers* — 616.89
Kempner, Joanna. *Psychedelic Outlaws* — 615.7
Laar, Arnold van de. *Under the Knife* — 617
Lamas, Daniela J. *You Can Stop Humming Now* — 616.02
Lenzer, Jeanne. *The Danger Within Us* — 338.4
Mezrich, Joshua D. *When Death Becomes Life* — 617.9
Monosson, Emily. ★*Blight* — 616.9
Mukherjee, Siddhartha. *The Laws of Medicine* — 610.1
Offit, Paul A. *You Bet Your Life* — 615.5

AUTHOR, TITLE, SERIES AND SUBJECT INDEX

Porter, Roy. *The Greatest Benefit to Mankind*	610
Rutkow, Ira M. *Empire of the Scalpel*	617
Ryckman, Pamela. *Candace Pert*	B
Senthilingam, Meera. *Outbreaks and Epidemics*	614.4
Servan-Schreiber, David. *Anticancer*	616.99
Sheldrake, Rupert. *Science and Spiritual Practices*	201
Slater, Lauren. *Blue Dreams*	615.7
Tweedy, Damon. *Facing the Unseen*	362.2

MEDICINE PEOPLE (INDIGENOUS RELIGIONS)

Gardner, Mark L. *The Earth Is All That Lasts*	978.004

MEDIEVAL ARCHITECTURE

Morris, Marc. *Castles*	728.81

MEDIEVAL MILITARY HISTORY

Gies, Joseph. *Life in a Medieval Castle*	940.1

MEDIEVAL PERIOD (476-1492)

Ackroyd, Peter. *Foundation*	942
Asbridge, Thomas S. ★*The Crusades*	909.07
Asbridge, Thomas S. *The Greatest Knight*	942.03
Barker, Juliet R. V. *Agincourt*	944
Borman, Tracy. *Thomas Cromwell*	B
Brown, Nancy Marie. *The Abacus and the Cross*	
Brown, Nancy Marie. *Ivory Vikings*	736
Brown, Nancy Marie. *The Real Valkyrie*	948
Brown, Peter. *Through the Eye of a Needle*	270.2
Brownworth, Lars. *Lost to the West*	949.5
Bryson, Bill. *Notes from a Small Island*	914
Bryson, Bill. *The Road to Little Dribbling*	914
Cahill, Thomas. *How the Irish Saved Civilization*	941.501
Cantor, Norman F. *In the Wake of the Plague*	614.5
Castor, Helen. *Joan of Arc*	B
Charles-Edwards, T. M. *Wales and the Britons, 350-1064*	942.901
Crowley, Roger. *1453*	949.61
Crowley, Roger. *City of Fortune*	945
Davies, Brian. *The Thought of Thomas Aquinas*	230
De Hamel, Christopher. *The Manuscripts Club*	091
De Hamel, Christopher. ★*Meetings with Remarkable Manuscripts*	091
Ehrman, Bart D. *The Triumph of Christianity*	270.1
Frankopan, Peter. *The First Crusade*	956
Gibbon, Edward. ★*The Decline and Fall of the Roman Empire*	937
Gies, Frances. *Life in a Medieval Village*	306
Gies, Joseph. *Life in a Medieval Castle*	940.1
Gristwood, Sarah. *Blood Sisters*	942.04092
Haag, Michael. *The Tragedy of the Templars*	271.7913
Herrin, Judith. *Byzantium*	949.5
Jager, Eric. *Blood Royal*	944.026
Jones, Dan. *Crusaders*	909.07
Jones, Dan. ★*The Plantagenets*	942.03092
Jones, Dan. *The Templars*	271
Kelly, John. *The Great Mortality*	614.5
Lacey, Robert. *Great Tales from English History 1*	941
Lacey, Robert. *Great Tales from English History 2*	941
Manchester, William. *A World Lit Only by Fire*	940.2
Morris, Marc. ★*The Anglo-Saxons*	942.01
Morris, Marc. *Castles*	728.81
Morris, Marc. *King John*	942.033
Morris, Marc. *The Norman Conquest*	942.02
Morrison, Robert. *The Regency Years*	941.07
Norwich, John Julius. *Byzantium*	949.5
Norwich, John Julius. *Byzantium*	949.5
Norwich, John Julius. *Byzantium*	949.5
Norwich, John Julius. *Shakespeare's Kings*	822.33
Norwich, John Julius. *A Short History of Byzantium*	949.5
Puhak, Shelley. *The Dark Queens*	944
Ramirez, Janina. *Femina*	940.1
Reston, James. *The Last Apocalypse*	940.1
Robb, Graham. *The Debatable Land*	941.3
Strathern, Paul. *The Florentines*	945
Tuchman, Barbara W. ★*A Distant Mirror*	944
Weir, Alison. *Eleanor of Aquitaine*	B
Weir, Alison. *Queens of the Conquest*	920
Weir, Alison. *The Wars of the Roses*	942.04
Wickham, Chris. *The Inheritance of Rome*	940.1
Winder, Simon. *Lotharingia*	944
Winroth, Anders. *The Age of the Vikings*	948

MEDIEVAL SCIENCE

Weinberg, Steven. *To Explain the World*	509

Medina, John

Brain Rules	153

Medini, Shari

Parenting While Working from Home	650.1
Mediocre. Oluo, Ijeoma	305.310973

MEDIOCRITY

Oluo, Ijeoma. *Mediocre*	305.310973
Meditate Your Weight. Cruikshank, Tiffany	613.2

MEDITATION

Epstein, Mark. *The Zen of Therapy*	294.3
Fletcher, Emily. *Stress Less, Accomplish More*	155.9
Goleman, Daniel. *Why We Meditate*	158.1
Gunaratana, Henepola. *Start Here, Start Now*	294.3
Harris, Dan. ★*10% Happier*	158.1
Harris, Dan. *Meditation for Fidgety Skeptics*	158.1
Hase, Craig. *How Not to Be a Hot Mess*	158.1
Heller, Rick. *Secular Meditation*	158.1
Lahn, Bussho. *Singing and Dancing Are the Voice of the Law*	294.3
Nhat Hanh. *The Art of Living*	294.3
Sheff, David. *The Buddhist on Death Row*	B
Sheldrake, Rupert. *Science and Spiritual Practices*	201
Shumsky, Susan G. *Earth Energy Meditations*	133.8
Siegel, Daniel J. *Aware*	158.1
Siff, Jason. *Thoughts Are Not the Enemy*	294.3
Suzuki, Shunryu. *Zen Mind, Beginner's Mind*	294.3
Zorn, Justin. *Golden*	128
Meditation for Fidgety Skeptics. Harris, Dan	158.1

MEDITATIONS

Angelou, Maya. *Wouldn't Take Nothing for My Journey Now*	814
★*Meditations*. Marcus Aurelius	188
★*The Mediterranean Dish*. Karadsheh, Suzy	641.59

MEDITERRANEAN REGION

Cline, Eric H. *After 1177 B.C.*	937
Crowley, Roger. *City of Fortune*	945
Kassabova, Kapka. *Border*	949.9
Setareh, Saghar. *Pomegranates & Artichokes*	641.5

MEDITERRANEAN SEA

Hastings, Max. *Operation Pedestal*	940.54
Medium Raw. Bourdain, Anthony	B

Medvedev, Roy Aleksandrovich

Let History Judge	947.084

Meehan, Peter

Lucky Peach Presents 101 Easy Asian Recipes	641.595
★*Meet Me Tonight in Atlantic City*. Wong, Jane	B
Meet The Neighbors. Keim, Brandon	591.5

MEETINGS

Taylor, Claude. *How to Zoom Your Room*	747
★*Meetings with Remarkable Manuscripts*. De Hamel, Christopher	091
Meg, Jo, Beth, Amy. Rioux, Anne Boyd	813

MEGALITHIC MONUMENTS

Parker Pearson, Michael. *Stonehenge*	936.2
Pryor, Francis. ★*Stonehenge*	936.2

Megdal, Howard

The Baseball Talmud	796.357

MEGHAN, DUCHESS OF SUSSEX, 1981-

Holmes, Elizabeth. *HRH*	941.085

Mehr, Bob

Trouble Boys	920

Mehra, Nishta

Brown, White, Black	305.800973

MEHRA, NISHTA

Mehra, Nishta. *Brown, White, Black*	305.800973

Mehta, Suketu

Maximum City	954

MEHTA, SUKETU

Mehta, Suketu. *Maximum City*	954

Meiburg, Jonathan

A Most Remarkable Creature	598.9

Meier, Richard

Building the Getty	727

MEIJI, EMPEROR OF JAPAN, 1852-1912

Jansen, Marius. *The Making of Modern Japan*	952
Keene, Donald. *Emperor of Japan*	952.03
Mein Kampf. Hitler, Adolf	B

Meinkoth, Norman August

The Audubon Society Field Guide to North American Seashore Creatures	592

MEIR, GOLDA, 1898-1978

Burkett, Elinor. *Golda*	B
Klagsbrun, Francine. *Lioness*	B

PUBLIC LIBRARY CORE COLLECTION: NONFICTION
Twentieth Edition

MEIRHOFER, DAVID, 1949-1974
   Franscell, Ron. *Shadowman* — 362.88
MEISSONIER, JEAN LOUIS ERNEST, 1815-1891
   King, Ross. *The Judgment of Paris* — 759.4
Mekhennet, Souad
   I Was Told to Come Alone — 363.3250956
MEKHENNET, SOUAD
   Mekhennet, Souad. *I Was Told to Come Alone* — 363.3250956
MELANCHOLY
   Cain, Susan. ★*Bittersweet* — 155.2
   Norris, Kathleen. *Acedia & Me* — 248.8
   ★*Melba's American Comfort*. Wilson, Melba — 641.5973
MELENDEZ, BENJY
   Voloj, Julian. *Ghetto Brother* — 741.5
MELHBERG, JOSEPHINE JANINA, 1905-1969
   White, Elizabeth B. ★*The Counterfeit Countess* — 940.53
★*Mellon*. Cannadine, David
MELLON, ANDREW W. (ANDREW WILLIAM), 1855-1937
   Cannadine, David. ★*Mellon* — B
MELLON, PAUL, MRS
   Gordon, Meryl. *Bunny Mellon* — B
MELLON, TAMARA, 1967-
   Crowe, Lauren Goldstein. *The Towering World of Jimmy Choo* — 391.4
Meltzer, Allan H.
   A History of the Federal Reserve — 332.1
Meltzer, Brad
   ★*The First Conspiracy* — 973.4
   The Lincoln Conspiracy — 973.7092
   ★*The Nazi Conspiracy* — 940.53
Meltzer, Marisa
   This Is Big — 613.25
MELTZER, MARISA, 1977-
   Meltzer, Marisa. *This Is Big* — 613.25
Melville, Herman
   Complete Poems — 811
MELVILLE, HERMAN, 1819-1891
   Philbrick, Nathaniel. *Why Read Moby-Dick?* — 813
Melville, Sally
   Knitting Pattern Essentials — 746.43
Melville, Wilma
   ★*Hero Dogs* — 636.7
MELVILLE, WILMA
   Melville, Wilma. ★*Hero Dogs* — 636.7
Melvin, Leland
   Chasing Space — B
MELVIN, LELAND
   Melvin, Leland. *Chasing Space* — B
***Member** of the Family*. Lake, Dianne — 364.152
MEMETICS
   Gladwell, Malcolm. *The Tipping Point* — 302
***Memoirs** and Selected Letters*. Grant, Ulysses S. — B
MEMORIAL DAY
   Poole, Robert M. *Section 60* — 975.5
★*Memorial Drive*. Trethewey, Natasha D. — B
MEMORIALIZATION
   Cotton, Tom. *Sacred Duty* — 355.6
   Gerard, Sarah. *Carrie Carolyn Coco* — 364.152
   Lowe, Keith. *Prisoners of History* — 940.54
   Poole, Robert M. *Section 60* — 975.5
   Thompson, Erin L. *Smashing Statues* — 725
MEMORIALS
   Cotton, Tom. *Sacred Duty* — 355.6
   Holzer, Harold. *Monument Man* — B
   McElya, Micki. *The Politics of Mourning* — 975.5
   Soep, Elisabeth. *Other People's Words* — 155.9
Memories. Teffi, N. A. — B
MEMORIES
   Albright, Madeleine Korbel. *Prague Winter* — 943.71
   Alexie, Sherman. *You Don't Have to Say You Love Me* — 818
   Angelou, Maya. *Great Food, All Day Long* — 641.5973
   Atwood, Margaret. *Dearly* — 811
   Bonner, Betsy. *The Book of Atlantis Black* — 364.152
   Cercas, Javier. *Lord of All the Dead* — 868
   Chin, Curtis. *Everything I Learned, I Learned in a Chinese Restaurant* — B
   Chow, Kat. *Seeing Ghosts* — B
   Crawford, Lacy. *Notes on a Silencing* — B
   Crosley, Sloane. *Grief Is for People* — B
   Dial, Roman. *The Adventurer's Son* — 917.286

   Ernaux, Annie. ★*The Years* — B
   Finney, Nikky. *Love Child's Hotbed of Occasional Poetry* — 811
   Fisher, Todd. *My Girls* — B
   Foer, Joshua. *Moonwalking with Einstein* — 153.1
   Frank, Michael. ★*One Hundred Saturdays* — B
   Garcia Marquez, Gabriel. *Living to Tell the Tale* — B
   Gessen, Masha. *Never Remember* — 365
   Giovanni, Nikki. *Make Me Rain* — 811
   Godwin, Gail. *Getting to Know Death* — B
   Greenfieldboyce, Nell. ★*Transient and Strange* — 501
   Gulman, Gary. *Misfit* — B
   Harvilla, Rob. *60 Songs That Explain the '90s* — 782.42164
   Hemon, Aleksandar. *My Parents* — 814
   Hood, Ann. *Kitchen Yarns* — 641.5
   Imperioli, Michael. *Woke up This Morning* — 791.45
   Kattan, Fadi. ★*Bethlehem* — 641.59
   Lanzmann, Claude. *The Patagonian Hare* — B
   Limon, Ada. *Bright Dead Things* — 811
   Lynn, Loretta. ★*Me & Patsy Kickin' up Dust* — B
   Malhotra, Aanchal. *Remnants of Partition* — 954.04
   McCartney, Paul. *The Lyrics* — 782.42166
   Nezhukumatathil, Aimee. *Bite by Bite* — 641.3
   Ng, Fae Myenne. *Orphan Bachelors* — B
   Parker, James. ★*Get Me Through the Next Five Minutes* — 158.1
   Pataki, Allison. *Beauty in the Broken Places* — B
   Pipher, Mary Bray. *A Life in Light* — B
   Posnanski, Joe. ★*Why We Love Baseball* — 796.357
   Ranganath, Charan. ★*Why We Remember* — 153.1
   Rembert, Winfred. *Chasing Me to My Grave* — B
   Renkl, Margaret. *The Comfort of Crows* — 814.6
   Rojas Contreras, Ingrid. ★*The Man Who Could Move Clouds* — B
   Ronstadt, Linda. *Feels Like Home* — B
   Schacter, Daniel L. *The Seven Sins of Memory* — 153.1
   Smith, Patti. ★*M Train* — B
   Smith, Tracy K. ★*To Free the Captives* — 818
   Villarreal, Vanessa Anglica. *Magical/Realism* — 814
   Wiking, Meik. *The Art of Making Memories* — 153.1
   Woolever, Laurie. *Bourdain* — B
   Zwick, Edward. ★*Hits, Flops, and Other Illusions* — B
***Memories**, Dreams, Reflections*. Jung, C. G. — 150.19
MEMORY
   Alyan, Hala. *The Moon That Turns You Back* — 811
   Bailey, Jennifer. *To My Beloveds* — 261.8
   Boland, Eavan. *The Historians* — 821
   Branigan, Tania. *Red Memory* — 951.05
   Burnett, Dean. *Idiot Brain* — 612.8
   Cahalan, Susannah. *Brain on Fire* — 616.8
   Carey, Benedict. *How We Learn* — 153.1
   Clark, Tiana. *I Can't Talk About the Trees Without the Blood* — 811
   Dittrich, Luke. ★*Patient H.M.* — 616.85
   Ehrlich, Gretel. *Unsolaced* — B
   Foer, Joshua. *Moonwalking with Einstein* — 153.1
   Fogler, Janet. *Improving Your Memory* — 153.1
   Gluck, Louise. *Winter Recipes from the Collective* — 811
   Gorman, Amanda. ★*Call Us What We Carry* — 811
   Harari, Yuval N. ★*Sapiens* — 909
   Harvey, Samantha. *The Shapeless Unease* — B
   Hatzfeld, Jean. *Blood Papa* — 967.5710431
   Hay, Matt. *Soundtrack of Silence* — B
   Hudes, Quiara Alegria. ★*My Broken Language* — B
   Kandel, Eric R. *In Search of Memory* — B
   Karr, Mary. *The Art of Memoir* — B
   Kelly, Donika. *The Renunciations* — 811
   Kinstler, Linda. *Come to This Court and Cry* — 940.53
   Kundera, Milan. *Encounter* — 809
   Kytle, Ethan J. *Denmark Vesey's Garden* — 975.7
   Le Guin, Ursula K. *So Far so Good* — 811
   Levi, Primo. *The Periodic Table* — 858
   Levy, Deborah. ★*Things I Don't Want to Know* — B
   Macdonald, Helen. ★*Vesper Flights* — 508
   Mansbach, Adam. *I Had a Brother Once* — 811
   Nguyen, Viet Thanh. *Nothing Ever Dies* — 959.704
   Oates, Joyce Carol. *American Melancholy* — 811
   Ondaatje, Michael. *A Year of Last Things* — 811
   Pittard, Hannah. *We Are Too Many* — B
   Puglionesi, Alicia. *In Whose Ruins* — 973
   Ranganath, Charan. ★*Why We Remember* — 153.1
   Saldana, Stephanie. *What We Remember Will Be Saved* — 362.7

AUTHOR, TITLE, SERIES AND SUBJECT INDEX

Samet, Elizabeth D. *Looking for the Good War*	940.53
Savage, Jodi M. *The Death of a Jaybird*	B
Schacter, Daniel L. *The Seven Sins of Memory*	153.1
Schwarz, Geraldine. *Those Who Forget*	940.53
Sepetys, Ruta. ★*You*	808.02
Siegal, Nina. *The Diary Keepers*	940.54
Smith, Maggie. ★*You Could Make This Place Beautiful*	B
Soep, Elisabeth. *Other People's Words*	155.9
Thomas, Elizabeth Marshall. *Growing Old*	305.26
Thomson, Helen. *Unthinkable*	612.8
Vuong, Ocean. ★*Time Is a Mother*	811
Wiking, Meik. *The Art of Making Memories*	153.1
Wiman, Christian. *He Held Radical Light*	814
Wolff, Daniel J. *Grown-Up Anger*	920
Young, R. J. *Requiem for the Massacre*	305.8
Zadra, Antonio. *When Brains Dream*	613.7
Zapruder, Alexandra. *Twenty-Six Seconds*	973.922092

MEMORY DISORDERS

Mitchell, Wendy. *Somebody I Used to Know*	B
Morgan, Abi. *This Is Not a Pity Memoir*	B
Schacter, Daniel L. *The Seven Sins of Memory*	153.1
★*Memory Rose into Threshold Speech*. Celan, Paul	831

MEMPHIS, TENNESSEE

Crosby, Molly Caldwell. *The American Plague*	614.5
Jones, Booker T. *Time Is Tight*	B
Lauterbach, Preston. *Beale Street Dynasty*	976.8

MEN

Albom, Mitch. *Tuesdays with Morrie*	B
Barkan, Ady. *Eyes to the Wind*	B
Bercovici, Jeff. *Play On*	613.7
Black, Michael Ian. *A Better Man*	305.31
Blair, Gabrielle Stanley. ★*Ejaculate Responsibly*	362.1988
Bloom, Amy. *In Love*	B
Bly, Robert. ★*Iron John*	305.310973
Bragg, Rick. *Where I Come From*	975
Braitman, Laurel. *What Looks Like Bravery*	B
Brown, Mick. ★*Tearing Down the Wall of Sound*	B
Caesar, Ed. *The Moth and the Mountain*	B
Cott, Jonathan. *There's a Mystery There*	813
Dearborn, Mary V. *Ernest Hemingway*	B
DiMarco, Nyle. ★*Deaf Utopia*	B
Eyman, Scott. *Cary Grant*	B
Fairweather, Jack. *The Volunteer*	B
Fine, Cordelia. *Testosterone Rex*	155.3
Gomez, Edgar. *High-Risk Homosexual*	B
Gracie, Rickson. *Breathe*	B
Guha, Ramachandra. *Gandhi Before India*	B
Hamilton, Tyler. *The Secret Race*	796.62
Harrington, Joel F. *The Faithful Executioner*	B
Hitchens, Christopher. *Mortality*	304.6
Hughes, Robert. *Goya*	B
Ishikawa, Masaji. ★*A River in Darkness*	B
Itzkoff, Dave. ★*Robin*	B
Kander, Jason. *Invisible Storm*	B
Kidder, Tracy. *A Truck Full of Money*	B
McGrath, Ben. *Riverman*	797.122
Melvin, Leland. *Chasing Space*	B
Miller, Kei. *Things I Have Withheld*	814
Moby. *Then It Fell Apart*	B
Moghul, Haroon. *How to Be a Muslim*	B
Moran, Caitlin. *What About Men?*	155.3
Morris, Edmund. *Beethoven*	B
Namath, Joe Willie. ★*All the Way*	B
O'Connell, Robert L. *Revolutionary*	B
Osbourne, Ozzy. *I Am Ozzy*	B
Preszler, Trent. *Little and Often*	B
Prideaux, Sue. *I Am Dynamite!*	B
Rapoport, Ron. *Let's Play Two*	B
Roth, Andrew J. *Managing Prostate Cancer*	616.99
Ruhl, Sarah. *Letters from Max*	811
Satrapi, Marjane. *Chicken with Plums*	741.5
Sawaki, Kodo. *Discovering the True Self*	294.3
Servadio, Gaia. *Rossini*	B
Stahl, Jerry. *Nein, Nein, Nein!*	B
Strings, Sabrina. *The End of Love*	155.3
Thomas, R. Eric. *Here for It*	B
Thomson, Graeme. *George Harrison*	B
Tomine, Adrian. *The Loneliness of the Long-Distance Cartoonist*	741.5
Walker, Stephen. *Beyond*	629.45
Washington, Kate. ★*Already Toast*	649.8

MEN AND BIRDS

Skaife, Christopher. *The Ravenmaster*	B

MEN AND CATS

Carr, Caleb. *My Beloved Monster*	B

MEN AND DOGS

Grogan, John. ★*Marley & Me*	636.752
Grossi, Craig. *Craig & Fred*	B
Steinbeck, John. *Travels with Charley*	B

MEN AND HORSES

Hillenbrand, Laura. ★*Seabiscuit*	798.4

MEN AND NATURE

Ehrlich, Gretel. *This Cold Heaven*	998.2
Heinrich, Bernd. *A Naturalist at Large*	508
Kaag, John J. *Hiking with Nietzsche*	193
Krakauer, Jon. *Classic Krakauer*	814
Krakauer, Jon. *Into the Wild*	917.9804
Shattuck, Ben. *Six Walks*	B
Wohlleben, Peter. *The Hidden Life of Trees*	582.16

MEN AND PETS

Steinbeck, John. *Travels with Charley*	B

MEN AND SUCCESS

Dearborn, Mary V. *Ernest Hemingway*	B
Hart, Kevin. *I Can't Make This Up*	B
McGilligan, Patrick. *Young Orson*	B
Shatner, William. *Live Long And—*	B
Springsteen, Bruce. ★*Born to Run*	B

MEN BALLET DANCERS

Hallberg, David. *A Body of Work*	B

MEN DANCERS

Rigsby, Cody. ★*XOXO, Cody*	B
Men Explain Things to Me. Solnit, Rebecca	305.42
Men in Blazers Present Encyclopedia Blazertannica. Bennett, Roger	796.334
Men of Tomorrow. Jones, Gerard	741.5

MEN RECLUSES

Zenith, Richard. *Pessoa*	B
★*Men We Reaped*. Ward, Jesmyn	B
Men Who Hate Women. Bates, Laura	305.3
The Men Who United the States. Winchester, Simon	973

MEN-MEN RELATIONS

Hewitt, Sean. *All Down Darkness Wide*	B
Mizrahi, Isaac. *I.M.*	B
Thomas, R. Eric. *Here for It*	B

MEN-WOMEN COMMUNICATION

Rueckert, Veronica. *Outspoken*	808.5

MEN-WOMEN RELATIONS

Alden, Ginger. *Elvis and Ginger*	B
Alderton, Dolly. *Everything I Know About Love*	B
Allgor, Catherine. *A Perfect Union*	B
Auburn, David. *Proof*	812
Bard, Elizabeth. *Lunch in Paris*	B
Binyon, T. J. *Pushkin*	B
Brooks, David. *The Social Animal*	305.5
Caesar, Ed. *The Moth and the Mountain*	B
Carcaterra, Lorenzo. *Three Dreamers*	B
Chavez Perez, Inti. *Respect*	176
Clavin, Thomas. *Wild Bill*	B
Cook, Blanche Wiesen. *Eleanor Roosevelt; Volume 2*	B
Cook, Blanche Wiesen. ★*Eleanor Roosevelt; Volume 3*	B
Cramer, Richard Ben. *Joe DiMaggio*	B
Curtis, James. *Spencer Tracy*	B
Dalrymple, William. *White Mughals*	954
Dickinson, Amy. *Strangers Tend to Tell Me Things*	B
Doty, Cate. *Mergers and Acquisitions*	395.2
Ellis, Joseph J. ★*His Excellency*	B
Ephron, Delia. *Left on Tenth*	B
Feiler, Bruce. *The First Love Story*	222
Fennelly, Beth Ann. *Heating & Cooling*	B
Fraser, Antonia. *Love and Louis XIV*	B
Garfunkel, Art. *What Is It All but Luminous*	782.42164
Gaye, Jan. *After the Dance*	B
Glenconner, Anne. ★*Lady in Waiting*	B
Goethe, Johann Wolfgang von. *Goethe's Faust*	832
Goodwin, Doris Kearns. *No Ordinary Time*	920
Gristwood, Sarah. *The Tudors in Love*	941.05
Hesse, Maria. ★*Frida Kahlo*	B
Homer. ★*The Iliad*	883

PUBLIC LIBRARY CORE COLLECTION: NONFICTION
Twentieth Edition

Isenberg, Sheila. *Women Who Love Men Who Kill*	362.83
Kerouac, Jack. *Book of Sketches, 1952-57*	818
King, Greg. *The Assassination of the Archduke*	B
Laux, Dorianne. *Only as the Day Is Long*	811
Leaming, Barbara. *Mrs. Kennedy*	B
Lessing, Doris May. *Under My Skin*	823
Mann, William J. *Kate*	B
Mansel, Philip. *King of the World*	B
Margulies, Julianna. *Sunshine Girl*	B
Marnham, Patrick. *Dreaming with His Eyes Open*	B
McBrien, William. *Cole Porter*	B
McClelland, Mac. *Irritable Hearts*	B
Miller, Adrienne. *In the Land of Men*	070.5
Mock, Janet. *Surpassing Certainty*	B
Mordden, Ethan. *Ziegfeld*	B
Nasaw, David. *Andrew Carnegie*	B
Nasaw, David. *The Chief*	B
Nelson, Willie. *It's a Long Story*	B
Noor. *Leap of Faith*	B
Offerman, Nick. *The Greatest Love Story Ever Told*	B
Palmer, Arnold. *A Golfer's Life*	B
Pittard, Hannah. *We Are Too Many*	B
Powell, Julie. *Julie and Julia*	641.5
Rakoff, Joanna Smith. *My Salinger Year*	B
Rallo, Eli. *I Didn't Know I Needed This*	306.73
Raskin, Allison. *Overthinking About You*	646.7
Simmons, Sylvie. *I'm Your Man*	B
Solnit, Rebecca. *Men Explain Things to Me*	305.42
Spurling, Hilary. *Matisse the Master*	B
Taddeo, Lisa. *Three Women*	306.7082
Taraborrelli, J. Randy. ★*The Secret Life of Marilyn Monroe*	B
Tate, Christie. ★*Group*	B
Tyson, Cicely. ★*Just as I Am*	B
Williams, Florence. *Heartbreak*	306.7
Zimmerman, Jess. *Women and Other Monsters*	155.3

Menand, Louis
The Free World	306.0973

Mend It, Wear It, Love It! Edwards, Zoe — 646

MENDEL, GREGOR, 1822-1884
Henig, Robin Marantz. *The Monk in the Garden*	B

Mendelson, Cheryl
★*Home Comforts*	640
★*Vows*	203

Mendelson, Zoe
Pussypedia	612.6

Mendez, Antonio J.
Argo	955.05

MENDEZ, ANTONIO J.
Mendez, Antonio J. *Argo*	955.05

Mending Life. Montenegro, Sonya — 646
Mending with Love. Misumi, Noriko — 646.6
Mengele. Marwell, David G. — B

MENGELE, JOSEF, 1911-1979
Marwell, David G. *Mengele*	B

MENINGITIS
Dearen, Jason. *Kill Shot*	616.8

MENKEN, ADAH ISAACS, 1839?-1868
Martin, Justin. *Rebel Souls*	920

MENNONITES
Samatar, Sofia. *The White Mosque*	B

MENOPAUSE
Allmen, Tara. *Menopause Confidential*	618.1
Corinna, Heather. *What Fresh Hell Is This?*	618.1
Dunn, Jancee. *Hot and Bothered*	618.1
Gunter, Jen. *The Menopause Manifesto*	618.175
Haver, Mary Claire. ★*The New Menopause*	618.1
Mansberg, Ginni. *The M Word*	612.6

Menopause Confidential. Allmen, Tara — 618.1
The Menopause Manifesto. Gunter, Jen — 618.175

MENSTRUATION
Brighten, Jolene. *Is This Normal?*	618.1
Diamant, Anita. ★*Period. End of Sentence*	612.6
Gunter, Jen. ★*Blood*	612.6
Gupta, Shalene. *The Cycle*	618.1

MENSTRUATION DISORDERS
Gupta, Shalene. *The Cycle*	618.1

MENTAL DISCIPLINE
Morin, Amy. *13 Things Mentally Strong Women Don't Do*	158.1

Willink, Jocko. *Discipline Equals Freedom*	158.1

MENTAL HEALTH
Albright, Mary Beth. ★*Eat & Flourish*	612.3
Applebaum, Allison. *Stand by Me*	649.8
Bamberger, Michael. *The Second Life of Tiger Woods*	B
Bamford, Maria. *Sure, I'll Join Your Cult*	B
Benjamin, A. K. *Let Me Not Be Mad*	612.8
Berenson, Alex. ★*Tell Your Children*	362.29
Blumenthal, Brett. *52 Small Changes for the Mind*	616.89
Bullmore, Edward T. *The Inflamed Mind*	616.85
Buque, Mariel. *Break the Cycle*	616.85
Calhoun, Ada. *Why We Can't Sleep*	305.244
Campoverdi, Alejandra. *First Gen*	B
Carriere, Alice. *Everything/Nothing/Someone*	B
Common. ★*And Then We Rise*	613
Crampton, Caroline. *A Body Made of Glass*	616.85
Dooner, Caroline. *Tired as F*ck*	152.1
Fall, Jeremy. *Falling Upwards*	158.1
Farley, Audrey Clare. ★*Girls and Their Monsters*	306.875
Felix, Camonghne. *Dyscalculia*	B
Foster, Sutton. *Hooked*	B
Foulkes, Lucy. ★*Losing Our Minds*	616.89
Ghostface Killah. *Rise of a Killah*	B
Glass, Charles. *Soldiers Don't Go Mad*	616.85
Gless, Sharon. *Apparently There Were Complaints*	B
Golbeck, Jennifer. *The Purest Bond*	636.7
Gutman, Matt. ★*No Time to Panic*	616.85
Hackman, Rose. ★*Emotional Labor*	155.3
Haidt, Jonathan. ★*The Anxious Generation*	305.23
Hari, Johann. ★*Magic Pill*	613.2
Harvey, Samantha. *The Shapeless Unease*	B
Hazan, Jack. *Mind Over Batter*	641.81
Hibbs, B. Janet. *The Stressed Years of Their Lives*	616.8900835
Ikpi, Bassey. *I'm Telling the Truth, but I'm Lying*	814
Insel, Thomas R. *Healing*	362.2
Jamie, Poppy. *Happy Not Perfect*	158.1
Jefferson, Margo. *On Michael Jackson*	B
Kandel, Eric R. ★*The Disordered Mind*	616.89
Kazdin, Cole. ★*What's Eating Us*	616.85
Keltner, Dacher. ★*Awe*	152.4
Kennedy, Patrick J. ★*Profiles in Mental Health Courage*	362.29
Keyes, Corey L. M. ★*Languishing*	152.1
King, Vanessa. *10 Keys to Happier Living*	158
Kissinger, Meg. *While You Were Out*	362.2
Kohli, Sahaj Kaur. ★*But What Will People Say?*	616.89
Kramer, Peter D. ★*Ordinarily Well*	615.7
Langshur, Eric. *Start Here*	158
Lifford, Tina. *The Little Book of Big Lies*	155.2
Magsamen, Susan. *Your Brain on Art*	111
Marriott, Sue. *Secure Relating*	158.1
Moe, John. *The Hilarious World of Depression*	616.85
Morris, David J. *The Evil Hours*	616.85
Murthy, Vivek Hallegere. *Together*	158.2
Nerenberg, Jenara. *Divergent Mind*	616.89
Nietfeld, Emi. *Acceptance*	B
Northrup, Christiane. *Dodging Energy Vampires*	155.2
Page, Elliot. *Pageboy*	B
Paperny, Anna Mehler. *Hello I Want to Die Please Fix Me*	362.2
Parker, Morgan. ★*You Get What You Pay For*	305.896
Parry, John Weston. *The Burden of Sports*	796.01
Petersen, Andrea. *On Edge*	616.85
Pipher, Mary Bray. *A Life in Light*	B
Pratt, Misty. *All in Her Head*	616.89
Ralph, Laurence. *Sito*	364.152
Raskin, Allison. *Overthinking About You*	646.7
Rauch, Jonathan. *The Happiness Curve*	155.6
Ripley, Amanda. *The Unthinkable*	155.9
Ronson, Jon. ★*The Psychopath Test*	616.85
Rothenberg, Ben. *Naomi Osaka*	B
Saul, Richard. *ADHD Does Not Exist*	618.92
Sehee, Baek. *I Want to Die but I Want to Eat Tteokbokki*	B
Shange, Ntozake. ★*Sing a Black Girl's Song*	818
Sharma, Nina. *The Way You Make Me Feel*	B
Slater, Lauren. *Blue Dreams*	615.7
Smith, Freda Love. *I Quit Everything*	B
Tallent, Elizabeth. *Scratched*	B
Turban, Jack L. ★*Free to Be*	616.85
Tweedy, Damon. *Facing the Unseen*	362.2

AUTHOR, TITLE, SERIES AND SUBJECT INDEX

Way, Niobe. *Rebels with a Cause*	649
Williams, Michelle. *Checking In*	B
Wilson, Sarah. *First, We Make the Beast Beautiful*	616.85
Winters, Mary-Frances. *Black Fatigue*	305.896
Wray, Britt. *Generation Dread*	155.9
Zimbardo, Philip G. *The Lucifer Effect*	155.9

MENTAL HEALTH LAWS
Moore, Kate. ★*The Woman They Could Not Silence*	B

MENTAL HEALTH POLICY
Hylton, Antonia. *Madness*	362.2
Insel, Thomas R. *Healing*	362.2

MENTAL HEALTH SERVICES
Cahalan, Susannah. ★*The Great Pretender*	616.89
Insel, Thomas R. *Healing*	362.2
Riley, Alex. ★*A Cure for Darkness*	616.85
Sardy, Marin. *The Edge of Every Day*	B
Sederer, Lloyd I. *The Family Guide to Mental Health Care*	616.89
Tweedy, Damon. *Facing the Unseen*	362.2

MENTAL ILLNESS
Au-Yeung, Angel. *Wonder Boy*	B
Aviv, Rachel. ★*Strangers to Ourselves*	616.89
Bailey, Lily. *Because We Are Bad*	B
Benjamin, A. K. *Let Me Not Be Mad*	612.8
Bering, Jesse. *Suicidal*	362.2
Bonner, Betsy. *The Book of Atlantis Black*	364.152
Braitman, Laurel. *Animal Madness*	591.5
Cahalan, Susannah. ★*The Great Pretender*	616.89
Carriere, Alice. *Everything/Nothing/Someone*	B
Chernaik, Judith. *Schumann*	B
Crais, Clifton C. *History Lessons*	B
Crampton, Caroline. *A Body Made of Glass*	616.85
Crowther, Gail. *Three-Martini Afternoons at the Ritz*	920
Deisseroth, Karl. *Projections*	616.89
Diaz, Jaquira. *Ordinary Girls*	818
Foulkes, Lucy. ★*Losing Our Minds*	616.89
Frank, Lone. *The Pleasure Shock*	616.8
Fremont, Helen. *The Escape Artist*	B
Gagne, Patric. *Sociopath*	B
Granata, Vince. *Everything Is Fine*	B
Grinker, Roy Richard. *Nobody's Normal*	616.89
Haig, Matt. *Notes on a Nervous Planet*	616.89
Hale, Kathleen. ★*Slenderman*	364.152
Harrington, Anne. *Mind Fixers*	616.89
Harvey, Samantha. *The Shapeless Unease*	B
Hewitt, Sean. *All Down Darkness Wide*	B
Hylton, Antonia. *Madness*	362.2
Ikpi, Bassey. *I'm Telling the Truth, but I'm Lying*	814
Insel, Thomas R. *Healing*	362.2
Jamison, Kay Redfield. *Fires in the Dark*	616.89
Kalb, Claudia. *Andy Warhol Was a Hoarder*	920
Kander, Jason. *Invisible Storm*	B
Keaton, Diane. ★*Brother & Sister*	B
Kennedy, Patrick J. ★*Profiles in Mental Health Courage*	362.29
Kissinger, Meg. *While You Were Out*	362.2
Lawson, Jenny. ★*Broken*	B
Lawson, Jenny. *Furiously Happy*	B
Lieberman, Jeffrey A. *Malady of the Mind*	616.89
Lieberman, Jeffrey A. *Shrinks*	616.89
Lin, Jami Nakamura. *The Night Parade*	B
Lipska, Barbara K. *The Neuroscientist Who Lost Her Mind*	B
Nesse, Randolph M. *Good Reasons for Bad Feelings*	616.89
O'Connor, Sinead. ★*Rememberings*	B
Paperny, Anna Mehler. *Hello I Want to Die Please Fix Me*	362.2
Perkins, Nichole. *Sometimes I Trip on How Happy We Could Be*	B
Pollan, Michael. *How to Change Your Mind*	615.7
Pratt, Misty. *All in Her Head*	616.89
Raskin, Allison. *Overthinking About You*	646.7
Rhodes, James. *Instrumental*	B
Ronson, Jon. ★*The Psychopath Test*	616.85
Rosen, Jonathan. ★*The Best Minds*	616.89
Sardy, Marin. *The Edge of Every Day*	B
Scheier, Liz. *Never Simple*	B
Sederer, Lloyd I. *The Family Guide to Mental Health Care*	616.89
Sehee, Baek. *I Want to Die but I Want to Eat Tteokbokki*	B
Solomon, Deborah. *American Mirror*	B
Tallis, Frank. *The Incurable Romantic*	152.4
Taraborrelli, J. Randy. ★*The Secret Life of Marilyn Monroe*	B
Waldman, Ayelet. *A Really Good Day*	B
Williams, Michelle. *Checking In*	B

MENTAL SUGGESTION
Clark, Andy. *The Experience Machine*	153

MENTORING
Abdul-Jabbar, Kareem. *Coach Wooden and Me*	B
Bradbury, Ray. ★*Remembrance*	813
Copeland, Misty. *The Wind at My Back*	B
Edelman, Marian Wright. *Lanterns*	362.7
Gillard, Julia. ★*Women and Leadership*	158
Smith, Kenny. *Talk of Champions*	B
Tenzin Priyadarshi. *Running Toward Mystery*	B

MENTORS
Bass, Rick. *The Traveling Feast*	B
Conyers, Jonathan. *I Wasn't Supposed to Be Here*	B
Copeland, Misty. *The Wind at My Back*	B
Fleshman, Lauren. ★*Good for a Girl*	B
Freitas, Donna. *Consent*	364.158092
Jawando, Will. ★*My Seven Black Fathers*	B
Konnikova, Maria. *The Biggest Bluff*	795.412
McKeon, Kathy. *Jackie's Girl*	B
Tenzin Priyadarshi. *Running Toward Mystery*	B
Tyson, Mike. *Iron Ambition*	B

MENU PLANNING
Hartwig, Melissa. *The Whole30 Slow Cooker*	641.5
Merchant, Jessica. *Everyday Dinners*	641.82
Mullins, Brittany. *Mostly Veggies*	641.5

Menuez, Doug
Fearless Genius	979.4

MENUS
Bayless, Rick. ★*Fiesta at Rick's*	641.5972
Brennan, Kathy. *Keepers*	641.5973
Garten, Ina. *Barefoot Contessa at Home*	641.5
Pulde, Alona. ★*The Forks Over Knives Plan*	641.5

Merchant Kings. Bown, Stephen R.   338.8

MERCHANT MARINE
Slade, Rachel. *Into the Raging Sea*	910.91

MERCHANT SHIPS
Bown, Stephen R. *Merchant Kings*	338.8
Crowley, Roger. *City of Fortune*	945
Hastings, Max. *Operation Pedestal*	940.54
Johnson, Steven. *Enemy of All Mankind*	910.4

Merchant, Brian
Blood in the Machine	303.48

Merchant, Jessica
Everyday Dinners	641.82

MERCHANTS
Bown, Stephen R. *Merchant Kings*	338.8
Crowley, Roger. *City of Fortune*	945
Ronald, Susan. *The Pirate Queen*	B

Merchants of Doubt. Oreskes, Naomi   174
Mercies in Disguise. Kolata, Gina Bari   616
The Mercury 13. Ackmann, Martha   920
Mercury Rising. Shesol, Jeff   629.45
Mercy. Clifton, Lucille   811

MERCY
Francis. *The Church of Mercy*	252
Francis. *Happiness in This Life*	248.4
Lamott, Anne. ★*Hallelujah Anyway*	241
Stevenson, Bryan. *Just Mercy*	B

Mere Christianity. Lewis, C. S.   230

Meredith, Martin
The Fortunes of Africa	960

Mergers and Acquisitions. Doty, Cate   395.2

Merhi, Farah
★*Inspire Your Home*	747

The Meritocracy Trap. Markovits, Daniel   305.5

MERKEL, ANGELA, 1954–
Marton, Kati. ★*The Chancellor*	B

MERLIN (LEGENDARY CHARACTER)
Ackroyd, Peter. *The Death of King Arthur*	823

★*Merriam-Webster's Visual Dictionary.* Corbeil, Jean-Claude   423

Merridale, Catherine
Ivan's War	940.54
Lenin on the Train	B

MERRILL, JAMES INGRAM
Hammer, Langdon. *James Merrill*	B

Merriman, Helena
★*Tunnel 29*	943

Merritt, Tyler
   I Take My Coffee Black — 791.4302
Merry, Robert W.
   A Country of Vast Designs — B
   President McKinley — B
Mertens, Maggie
   Better Faster Farther — 796.42
Merton, Thomas
   The Intimate Merton — B
   ★*The Seven Storey Mountain* — B
MERTON, THOMAS, 1915-1968
   Merton, Thomas. *The Intimate Merton* — B
   Merton, Thomas. ★*The Seven Storey Mountain* — B
Mertz, Barbara
   Temples, Tombs, & Hieroglyphs — 932
Merwin, W. S.
   The Shadow of Sirius — 811
Merzbach, Uta C.
   A History of Mathematics — 510.9
***Mesa** of Sorrows*. Brooks, James — 979.1004
Meslow, Scott
   From Hollywood with Love — 791.43
MESOPOTAMIA
   Kriwaczek, Paul. *Babylon* — 935
*A **Message** from Ukraine*. Zelensky, Volodymyr — 947.7
*The **Messenger***. Evanzz, Karl — B
*The **Messenger***. Loftus, Peter — 338.4
Messenger, Alex
   The Twenty-Ninth Day — B
MESSENGER, ALEX
   Messenger, Alex. *The Twenty-Ninth Day* — B
Messenger, Tony
   Profit and Punishment — 362.5
MESSIAHS
   Telushkin, Joseph. *Rebbe* — 296.833
Messineo, Janet
   Casting into the Light — 799.1
MESSINEO, JANET
   Messineo, Janet. *Casting into the Light* — 799.1
Messud, Claire
   Kant's Little Prussian Head and Other Reasons Why I Write — B
MESSUD, CLAIRE, 1966-
   Messud, Claire. *Kant's Little Prussian Head and Other Reasons Why I Write* — B
Messy. Harford, Tim — 153.3
Metabolical. Lustig, Robert H. — 616
METABOLISM
   Cruikshank, Tiffany. *Meditate Your Weight* — 613.2
   Ludwig, David. *Always Hungry?* — 613.2
Metahuman. Chopra, Deepak — 204
METAL INDUSTRY AND TRADE
   Rudacille, Deborah. *Roots of Steel* — 338.4
METAL-WORK
   Gorges, Eric. *A Craftsman's Legacy* — 745.5
   Haab, Sherri. *The Art of Metal Clay* — 739.27
   Karon, Karen. *Advanced Chain Maille Jewelry Workshop* — 745.594
METALS
   Scheyder, Ernest. *The War Below* — 333.7
Metamaus. Spiegelman, Art — B
METAMORPHOSIS
   Ovid. *Tales from Ovid* — 873
METAPHOR
   Powers, Ann. *Good Booty* — 781.64
METAPHYSICS
   Barrow, John D. *The Infinite Book* — 111
   Heidegger, Martin. ★*Being and Time* — 111
   Rovelli, Carlo. *There Are Places in the World Where Rules Are Less Important Than Kindness* — 500
   Watson, Richard A. *Cogito Ergo Sum* — B
★***Metaracism***. Rose, Tricia — 305.8
Metatawabin, Edmund
   Up Ghost River — B
METATAWABIN, EDMUND, 1947-
   Metatawabin, Edmund. *Up Ghost River* — B
Metaxas, Eric
   Martin Luther — B
METEOROLOGY
   Dolin, Eric Jay. *A Furious Sky* — 363.34
   Hargrove, Brantley. *The Man Who Caught the Storm* — B
   Redniss, Lauren. *Thunder & Lightning* — 741.5
   Williams, Jack. ★*The Ams Weather Book* — 551.5
METHAMPHETAMINE
   Jimenez, Stephen. *The Book of Matt* — 364.152
   Quinones, Sam. ★*The Least of Us* — 362.29
*The **Method***. Butler, Isaac — 792.02
METHOD ACTING
   Butler, Isaac. *The Method* — 792.02
   Moore, Sonia. *The Stanislavski System* — 792
   Stanislavsky, Konstantin. *An Actor's Work* — 792.02
***Metoo** in the Corporate World*. Hewlett, Sylvia Ann — 658.3
METROPOLITAN AREAS
   Anderson, Jimmeka. *Power Lines* — 020
METROPOLITAN GOVERNMENT
   Bordewich, Fergus M. *Washington* — 975.3
Mettler, Suzanne
   Degrees of Inequality — 378.73
Metzl, Jonathan M.
   ★*What We've Become* — 364.152
MEXICAN AMERICAN MEN
   Trejo, Danny. *Trejo* — B
MEXICAN AMERICAN TEENAGERS
   Davis, Joshua. *Spare Parts* — 629.8
MEXICAN AMERICAN WOMEN
   Campoverdi, Alejandra. *First Gen* — B
   Cisneros, Sandra. *A House of My Own* — B
   Grande, Reyna. ★*The Distance Between Us* — 973
   Sanchez, Erika L. *Crying in the Bathroom* — B
MEXICAN AMERICANS
   Cantu, Francisco. *The Line Becomes a River* — B
   Cisneros, Sandra. *A House of My Own* — B
   Grande, Reyna. ★*The Distance Between Us* — 973
   Hernandez Castillo, Marcelo. *Children of the Land* — B
   Hernandez, Kelly Lytle. ★*Bad Mexicans* — 972
   Hinojosa, Maria. *Once I Was You* — B
   Nusbaum, Eric. *Stealing Home* — 796.357
   Olivarez, Jose. *Promises of Gold = Promesas De Oro* — 811
   Ronstadt, Linda. *Feels Like Home* — B
   Sanchez, Aaron. *Where I Come From* — 641.5092
   Santana, Carlos. *The Universal Tone* — B
   Villarreal, Vanessa Anglica. *Magical/Realism* — 814
***Mexican** Everyday*. Bayless, Rick — 641.5972
MEXICAN HISTORY
   Diaz del Castillo, Bernal. *The Discovery and Conquest of Mexico, 1517-1521* — 972
   Foster, Lynn V. *A Brief History of Mexico* — 972
   Guinn, Jeff. ★*War on the Border* — 972.08
   Hernandez, Kelly Lytle. ★*Bad Mexicans* — 972
   Marnham, Patrick. *Dreaming with His Eyes Open* — B
   Restall, Matthew. *When Montezuma Met Cortes* — 972
   Taylor, Alan. *American Civil Wars* — 973.7
   Womack, John. *Zapata and the Mexican Revolution* — B
***Mexican** Ice Cream*. Gerson, Fany — 641.86
MEXICAN PEOPLE
   Corcoran, Katherine. *In the Mouth of the Wolf* — 364.152
MEXICAN PEOPLE IN THE UNITED STATES
   Bobrow-Strain, Aaron. *The Death and Life of Aida Hernandez* — 972
MEXICAN REVOLUTION (1910-1920)
   Guinn, Jeff. ★*War on the Border* — 972.08
***Mexican** Today*. Jinich, Pati — 641.5972
MEXICAN-AMERICAN BORDER REGION
   Bobrow-Strain, Aaron. *The Death and Life of Aida Hernandez* — 972
   Cantu, Francisco. *The Line Becomes a River* — B
   Gander, Forrest. ★*Be With* — 811
   Guinn, Jeff. ★*War on the Border* — 972.08
   Hernandez, Kelly Lytle. ★*Bad Mexicans* — 972
   Jacoby, Karl. *The Strange Career of William Ellis* — B
   Ronstadt, Linda. *Feels Like Home* — B
   Soboroff, Jacob. ★*Separated* — 325.73
   Theroux, Paul. *On the Plain of Snakes* — 917
   Urrea, Luis Alberto. *The Devil's Highway* — 304.8
MEXICAN-AMERICAN WAR, 1846-1848
   Crutchfield, James A. *Revolt at Taos* — 972
MEXICO
   Ahmed, Azam. *Fear Is Just a Word* — 364.152
   Alvarez, Noe. *Spirit Run* — 796.42
   Cisneros, Sandra. *A House of My Own* — B

AUTHOR, TITLE, SERIES AND SUBJECT INDEX

Coe, Michael D. *The Maya* — 972
De Leon, Jason. ★*Soldiers and Kings* — 364.1
Denton, Sally. *The Colony* — 364.152
Garcia, Angela. ★*The Way That Leads Among the Lost* — 362.29
Gerson, Fany. *Mexican Ice Cream* — 641.86
Gerson, Fany. *My Sweet Mexico* — 641.5972
Grande, Reyna. ★*The Distance Between Us* — 973
Hernandez Castillo, Marcelo. *Children of the Land* — B
Hernandez, Kelly Lytle. ★*Bad Mexicans* — 972
Herrera, Hayden. *Frida* — B
Levi, Heather. *The World of Lucha Libre* — 796.812
Marnham, Patrick. *Dreaming with His Eyes Open* — B
McDougall, Christopher. ★*Born to Run* — 796.42
Quinones, Sam. *Dreamland* — 362.29
Resendez, Andres. *Conquering the Pacific* — 959.9
Theroux, Paul. *On the Plain of Snakes* — 917
Townsend, Richard F. *The Aztecs* — 972
Urrea, Luis Alberto. *The Devil's Highway* — 304.8
Von Bremzen, Anya. *National Dish* — 641.3
Wariner, Ruth. *The Sound of Gravel* — B
Womack, John. *Zapata and the Mexican Revolution* — B

MEXICO CITY, MEXICO
Camara, Gabriela. *My Mexico City Kitchen* — 641.5972
Garcia, Angela. ★*The Way That Leads Among the Lost* — 362.29
Lewis, Oscar. *The Children of Sanchez* — 306.85
Marnham, Patrick. *Dreaming with His Eyes Open* — B

Meyaard-Schaap, Kyle
Following Jesus in a Warming World — 241

Meyer, Dakota
Into the Fire — 958.104

Meyer, Eugene L.
Five for Freedom — 973.7

Meyer, G. J.
The Borgias — 920
The Tudors — 920

Meyer, Joyce
Seize the Day — 248.4

Meyer, Robert
Every Minute Is a Day — 362.1962

MEYER, ROBERT (ROBERT H.)
Meyer, Robert. *Every Minute Is a Day* — 362.1962

Meyers, Charlie
The Little Red Book of Fly Fishing — 799.12

Meyerson, Michael
Liberty's Blueprint — 342.7302

Mezoff, Rebecca
★*The Art of Tapestry Weaving* — 746.7

Mezrich, Ben
The 37th Parallel — 001.942
Breaking Twitter — 338.7

Mezrich, Joshua D.
When Death Becomes Life — 617.9

MEZRICH, JOSHUA D.
Mezrich, Joshua D. *When Death Becomes Life* — 617.9
★*Mi Cocina*. Martinez, Rick — 641.5972

MIAMI, FLORIDA
Diaz, Jaquira. *Ordinary Girls* — 818
Eire, Carlos M. N. *Learning to Die in Miami* — B
Michael Symon's Playing with Fire. Symon, Michael — 641.7

Michaelis, David
★*Eleanor* — 973.917
Schulz and Peanuts — B

Michaels, Chris Franchetti
Teach Yourself Visually Jewelry Making & Beading — 739.27

Michaud-Skog, Summer
Fat Girls Hiking — 796.51

MICHEAUX, OSCAR, 1884-1951
McGilligan, Patrick. *Oscar Micheaux* — B

Michel, Casey
American Kleptocracy — 364.16
★*Michelangelo*. Unger, Miles — B
Michelangelo & the Pope's Ceiling. King, Ross — 759.5

MICHELANGELO BUONARROTI, 1475-1564
Hirst, Michael. *Michelangelo*. — B
King, Ross. *Michelangelo & the Pope's Ceiling* — 759.5
Unger, Miles. ★*Michelangelo* — B
Michelangelo. Hirst, Michael — B
Michelle Obama. Slevin, Peter — B

Michener, James A.
The Bridge at Andau — 943.9

MICHIGAN
Clark, Anna. *The Poisoned City* — 363.6
Hanna-Attisha, Mona. *What the Eyes Don't See* — 615.9
Kirshner, Jodie Adams. ★*Broke* — 336.3
Regan, Iliana. *Fieldwork* — B

MICKELSON, PHIL, 1970-
Shipnuck, Alan. *Phil* — B

MICKEY FREE
Hutton, Paul Andrew. *The Apache Wars* — 979

Micklethwait, John
The Company — 338.7

Micklewright, Keith
Drawing — 741.2

MICROAGGRESSIONS
Brown, Austin Channing. ★*I'm Still Here* — B
Harper, Michele. *The Beauty in Breaking* — B
Harts, Minda. *Right Within* — 658.3
Liverpool, Layal. *Systemic* — 362.1
Oluo, Ijeoma. ★*So You Want to Talk About Race* — 305.800973

MICROBIOLOGY
Collen, Alanna. *10% Human* — 612.3
Ireland, Tom. *The Good Virus* — 579.2
Kinch, Michael S. *Between Hope and Fear* — 614.4
Nelson, Bryn. *Flush* — 612.3

MICROCHIPS
Miller, Chris. *Chip War* — 338.4

MICROCOMPUTERS
Lloyd, Seth. *Programming the Universe* — 530.12

MICROECONOMICS
Davies, Richard. *Extreme Economies* — 306.3
Wheelan, Charles J. *Naked Economics* — 330

MICROLENDING
Kardas-Nelson, Mara. *We Are Not Able to Live in the Sky* — 332.3

MICROORGANISMS
Collen, Alanna. *10% Human* — 612.3

MIDDLE AGE
Bertinelli, Valerie. *Enough Already* — B
Boa, Kenneth D. *Recalibrate Your Life* — 248.8
Crawford, Robert. *Eliot After the Waste Land* — B
Crosley, Sloane. ★*Look Alive Out There* — 814
Gunter, Jen. *The Menopause Manifesto* — 618.175
Hagerty, Barbara Bradley. *Life Reimagined* — 155.6
Klein, Jessi. *I'll Show Myself Out* — B
Notaro, Laurie. *Excuse Me While I Disappear* — B
Rauch, Jonathan. *The Happiness Curve* — 155.6
Thomas, R. Eric. ★*Congratulations, the Best Is Over!* — B
The Middle Ages in 50 Objects. Gertsman, Elina — 909.07

MIDDLE CLASS
Gelles, David. *The Man Who Broke Capitalism* — 330.12
Goldstein, Amy. *Janesville* — 330.9775
Lemann, Nicholas. *Transaction Man* — 330.973
Markovits, Daniel. *The Meritocracy Trap* — 305.5
Morgenson, Gretchen. ★*These Are the Plunderers* — 332.6
Packer, George. ★*The Unwinding* — 973.924
Putnam, Robert D. *Our Kids* — 305.5
Quart, Alissa. *Squeezed* — 305.5
Reeves, Richard V. *Dream Hoarders* — 305.5
Schwartz, Nelson. *The Velvet Rope Economy* — 339.2
Servon, Lisa J. *The Unbanking of America* — 332.10973
Warren, Elizabeth. *This Fight Is Our Fight* — 305.5

MIDDLE CLASS AFRICAN AMERICAN FAMILIES
Grant, Gail Milissa. *At the Elbows of My Elders* — B
Jefferson, Margo. *Negroland* — 305.896

MIDDLE CLASS AFRICAN AMERICANS
Harlan, Louis R. *Booker T. Washington* — B
Jefferson, Margo. *Negroland* — 305.896

MIDDLE EARTH (IMAGINARY PLACE)
McIlwaine, Catherine. *Tolkien* — 002.09
The Middle East. Lewis, Bernard — 956
The Middle Kingdoms. Rady, Martyn C. — 943
The Middle of Everywhere. Pipher, Mary Bray — 305.9

MIDDLE SCHOOL EDUCATION
Fagell, Phyllis L. ★*Middle School Matters* — 373.236
★*Middle School Matters*. Fagell, Phyllis L. — 373.236

MIDDLE SCHOOL STUDENTS
Fagell, Phyllis L. ★*Middle School Matters* — 373.236

PUBLIC LIBRARY CORE COLLECTION: NONFICTION
Twentieth Edition

MIDDLE WEST
    Egan, Timothy. *The Worst Hard Time* — 978
    Goldstein, Amy. *Janesville* — 330.9775
    Holmes, Roger. *Midwest Home Landscaping* — 712
    King, Maren Ellingboe. *Fresh Midwest* — 641.5977
    Laskin, David. *The Children's Blizzard* — 977
    McDowell, Marta. *The World of Laura Ingalls Wilder* — 813

MIDDLE-AGED MEN
    Tomlinson, Tommy. *The Elephant in the Room* — B

MIDDLE-AGED PEOPLE
    Conley, Chip. ★*Learning to Love Midlife* — 646.7
    Green, Janice. ★*Divorce After 50* — 306.89
    Notaro, Laurie. *Excuse Me While I Disappear* — B

MIDDLE-AGED WOMEN
    Allmen, Tara. *Menopause Confidential* — 618.1
    Calhoun, Ada. *Why We Can't Sleep* — 305.244
    Doust, Kelly. *The Power Age* — 305.244
    Ellis, Helen. *Bring Your Baggage and Don't Pack Light* — 814
    Frangello, Gina. *Blow Your House Down* — 813
    Hagerty, Barbara Bradley. *Life Reimagined* — 155.6
    Haver, Mary Claire. ★*The New Menopause* — 618.1
    Levy, Deborah. *The Cost of Living* — B
    Loh, Sandra Tsing. *The Madwoman and the Roomba* — B
    Mann, Jen. ★*Midlife Bites* — 305.244
    Notaro, Laurie. *Excuse Me While I Disappear* — B
    Philpott, Mary Laura. *Bomb Shelter* — B
    Smith, Maggie. ★*You Could Make This Place Beautiful* — B

Middlekauff, Robert
    The Glorious Cause — 973.3

MIDGLEY, PETER, 1921-1991
    Parkin, Simon. *The Island of Extraordinary Captives* — 940.53

★*Midlife Bites*. Mann, Jen — 305.244

MIDLIFE CRISIS
    Calhoun, Ada. *Why We Can't Sleep* — 305.244
    Hagerty, Barbara Bradley. *Life Reimagined* — 155.6
    Mann, Jen. ★*Midlife Bites* — 305.244
    Rauch, Jonathan. *The Happiness Curve* — 155.6

Midnight At the Pera Palace. King, Charles — 949.61
Midnight in Broad Daylight. Sakamoto, Pamela Rotner — 940.53
★*Midnight in Chernobyl*. Higginbotham, Adam — 363.17
Midnight in Siberia. Greene, David — 914
Midnight in the Garden of Good and Evil. Berendt, John — 975.8
Midnight in the Pacific. Wheelan, Joseph — 940.54
★*Midnight Rising*. Horwitz, Tony — 973.7
Midnight's Furies. Hajari, Nisid — 954.04

MIDWAY ISLANDS
    Symonds, Craig L. *The Battle of Midway* — 940.54

MIDWAY, BATTLE OF, 1942
    Simms, Brendan. *The Silver Waterfall* — 940.54
    Symonds, Craig L. *The Battle of Midway* — 940.54

MIDWEST (UNITED STATES) HISTORY
    Laskin, David. *The Children's Blizzard* — 977
Midwest Home Landscaping. Holmes, Roger — 712
★*Midwest Made*. Sever, Shauna — 641.5977

MIDWIFERY
    Holloway, Kris. *Monique and the Mango Rains* — B

MIDWIVES
    Holloway, Kris. *Monique and the Mango Rains* — B
    McCracken, Patti. *The Angel Makers* — 364.152

Mieville, China
    October — 947.084

Mifflin, Margot
    Looking for Miss America — 791.6

Mightier Than the Sword. Reynolds, David S. — 813
★*Mighty Justice*. Roundtree, Dovey Johnson — B

Miglore, Kristen
    Food52 Genius Desserts — 641.86
    ★*Food52 Genius Recipes* — 641.5
    ★*Food52 Simply Genius* — 641.5

MIGRANT WORKERS
    Bruder, Jessica. ★*Nomadland* — 331.3
    Chang, Leslie T. *Factory Girls* — 331.4
    De Leon, Jason. ★*Soldiers and Kings* — 364.1
    Kurlansky, Mark. *The Eastern Stars* — 796.357

MIGRATION, INTERNAL
    Berlin, Ira. *The Making of African America* — 973
    Bittle, Jake. ★*The Great Displacement* — 362.87
    Brands, H. W. *The Age of Gold* — 979.4
    Lustgarten, Abrahm. ★*On the Move* — 363.7
    Nelson, Megan Kate. *The Three-Cornered War* — 978
    Rushdie, Salman. *Languages of Truth* — 824
    Santos Perez, Craig. *From Unincorporated Territory [amot]* — 811
    Vince, Gaia. *Nomad Century* — 362.87
    Wilkerson, Isabel. ★*The Warmth of Other Suns* — 304.80973

MIGRATORY ANIMALS
    Weidensaul, Scott. *A World on the Wing* — 598.156

Mikanowski, Jacob
    ★*Goodbye, Eastern Europe* — 947

MIKANOWSKI, JACOB
    Mikanowski, Jacob. ★*Goodbye, Eastern Europe* — 947

MIKE D, 1965-
    Mike D. *Beastie Boys Book* — 782.42164

Mike D.
    Beastie Boys Book — 782.42164

Mike Nichols. Harris, Mark — B

Mikhaiil, Dunya
    The Beekeeper — 956.7044

Mikhail, Alan
    God's Shadow — B

MILAN, ITALY
    Brooks, Michael. *The Quantum Astrologer's Handbook* — B

Milanovic, Branko
    The Have and the Have-Nots — 339.2

Milch, David
    Life's Work — B

MILCH, DAVID, 1945-
    Milch, David. *Life's Work* — B

Milchtein, Chaya M.
    ★*Mechanic Shop Femme's Guide to Car Ownership* — 629.222

Miles, Bryan
    101 Magic Tricks — 793.8

Miles, Jack
    God in the Qur'an — 297.2
    Religion as We Know It — 200.9

Miles, Jonathan
    St. Petersburg — 947

Miles, Kathryn
    Trailed — 364.152

Miles, Tiya
    The Dawn of Detroit — 977.4
    ★*Night Flyer* — B
    ★*Wild Girls* — 304.2

MILETICH, PATRICK JAY, 1968-
    Wertheim, L. Jon. *Blood in the Cage* — 796.815

Milford, Nancy
    Savage Beauty — B

MILITANTS
    Blanford, Nicholas. *Warriors of God* — 956.9204
    Horwitz, Tony. ★*Midnight Rising* — 973.7
    Meyer, Eugene L. *Five for Freedom* — 973.7
    Reynolds, David S. *John Brown, Abolitionist* — B
    Wright, Lawrence. ★*The Looming Tower* — 973.931

MILITARISM
    Brooks, Rosa. *How Everything Became War and the Military Became Everything* — 355
    Grinspan, Jon. *Wide Awake* — 973.7
    McDonough, Frank. *The Hitler Years* — 943.086
    McMeekin, Sean. *July 1914* — 940.3
    Santos Perez, Craig. *From Unincorporated Territory [amot]* — 811

MILITARY AIRCRAFT
    Hamilton-Paterson, James. *Marked for Death* — 358.400941
    Hampton, Dan. *Chasing the Demon* — 629.132
    Holland, James. *Big Week* — 940.54
    Kershaw, Alex. *The Few* — 940.54
    Mulley, Clare. *The Women Who Flew for Hitler* — 920
    Simms, Brendan. *The Silver Waterfall* — 940.54

MILITARY ART AND SCIENCE
    Bennett, Alexander. *Kendo* — 796.86
    Boot, Max. ★*War Made New* — 355.0209
    Cotterell, Arthur. *Chariot* — 357
    Emery, Theo. *Hellfire Boys* — 358
    France, John. *Perilous Glory* — 355
    Gaddis, John Lewis. *On Grand Strategy* — 355.4
    Kneale, Matthew. *Rome* — 945.6
    Macintyre, Ben. ★*Rogue Heroes* — 940.54
    Roach, Mary. ★*Grunt* — 355

AUTHOR, TITLE, SERIES AND SUBJECT INDEX

Tyson, Neil deGrasse. *Accessory to War*   355.001
MILITARY ATTACHES
    Tuchman, Barbara W. *Stilwell and the American Experience in China, 1911-45*   B

MILITARY AVIATION
    Bruning, John R. *Indestructible*   B
    Groom, Winston. *The Aviators*   920
    Hamilton-Paterson, James. *Marked for Death*   358.400941
    Hampton, Dan. *Chasing the Demon*   629.132
    Hastings, Max. *Operation Chastise*   940.54
    Holland, James. *Big Week*   940.54
    Sheehan, Neil. *A Fiery Peace in a Cold War*   B
    Sherman, Casey. *Above and Beyond*   973.922092

MILITARY BASES, AMERICAN
    Johnson, Akemi. *Night in the American Village*   305.40952

MILITARY CAMPAIGNS
    Alexander, Caroline. *Skies of Thunder*   940.54
    Alexander, Larry. *Biggest Brother*   B
    Allport, Alan. *Britain at Bay*   940.53
    Ambrose, Stephen E. ★*Band of Brothers*   920
    Ambrose, Stephen E. *Citizen Soldiers*   940.54
    Ambrose, Stephen E. *D-Day, June 6, 1944*   940.54
    Ambrose, Stephen E. *The Victors*   940.54
    Anderson, Scott. *Lawrence in Arabia*   B
    Ash, Stephen V. *Firebrand of Liberty*   973.7
    Atkinson, Rick. *An Army at Dawn*   940.54
    Atkinson, Rick. *The Day of Battle*   940.54
    Atkinson, Rick. *The Guns at Last Light*   940.54
    Beevor, Antony. *The Battle of Arnhem*   940.54
    Beevor, Antony. *D-Day*   940.54
    Blount, Roy. *Robert E. Lee*   B
    Boot, Max. ★*The Road Not Taken*   B
    Bowden, Mark. ★*Hue 1968*   959.704
    Bradley, James. *Flags of Our Fathers*   940.54
    Brighton, Terry. *Patton, Montgomery, Rommel*   B
    Brown, Daniel James. ★*Facing the Mountain*   940.54
    Burgin, R. V. *Islands of the Damned*   B
    Caddick-Adams, Peter. *Sand and Steel*   940.54
    Campbell, James. *The Ghost Mountain Boys*   940.53
    Churchill, Winston. *The Grand Alliance*   940.53
    Churchill, Winston. *Their Finest Hour*   940.53
    Churchill, Winston. *Triumph and Tragedy*   940.53
    Clark, Lloyd. *The Commanders*   940.2
    Cornwell, Bernard. *Waterloo*   940.4
    Davenport, Matthew J. *First Over There*   940.54
    Dimbleby, Jonathan. *The Battle of the Atlantic*   940.54
    Drury, Bob. *Valley Forge*   973.3
    Dugard, Martin. *Taking Berlin*   940.54
    Dugard, Martin. *Taking Paris*   940.54
    Egerton, Douglas R. *Thunder at the Gates*   973.7
    Ferling, John E. *Winning Independence*   973.3
    Finkel, David. *The Good Soldiers*   956.7044
    Fischer, David Hackett. *Washington's Crossing*   973.3
    Frank, Richard B. *Downfall*   940.54
    Gallego, Ruben. *They Called Us*   956.7044
    Garrett, Leah. *X Troop*   940.54
    Giangreco, D. M. *Hell to Pay*   940.54
    Graff, Garrett M. ★*When the Sea Came Alive*   940.54
    Grant, Ulysses S. ★*The Annotated Memoirs of Ulysses S. Grant*   B
    Groom, Winston. *The Generals*   920
    Groom, Winston. *Shiloh, 1862*   973.7
    Guarnere, William. *Brothers in Battle, Best of Friends*   B
    Guibert, Emmanuel. *Alan's War*   741.5
    Guinn, Jeff. ★*War on the Border*   972.08
    Hastings, Max. *Armageddon*   940.54
    Hastings, Max. *Operation Chastise*   940.54
    Hastings, Max. *Overlord*   940.54
    Hastings, Max. *Retribution*   940.54
    Hervieux, Linda. *Forgotten*   940.54
    Hillenbrand, Laura. ★*Unbroken*   B
    Hindley, Meredith. *Destination Casablanca*   940.54
    Hogan, William R. *Task Force Hogan*   940.54
    Holland, James. *Big Week*   940.54
    Holland, James. *Brothers in Arms*   940.54
    Holland, James. ★*Burma '44*   940.54
    Holland, James. *Normandy '44*   940.54
    Holland, James. *The Savage Storm*   940.53
    Holland, James. *Sicily '43*   940.54

Hornfischer, James D. *Neptune's Inferno*   940.54
Horwitz, Tony. *Confederates in the Attic*   973.7
Hunt, Patrick. *Hannibal*   B
Hutton, Robin L. *Sgt. Reckless*   951.904
Isserman, Maurice. *The Winter Army*   940.54
Jordan, Jonathan W. *Brothers, Rivals, Victors*   940.54
Junger, Sebastian. *War*   958.104
Keegan, John. *The American Civil War*   973.7
Keegan, John. *The First World War*   940.3
Kershaw, Alex. *Against All Odds*   940.54
Kershaw, Alex. *The First Wave*   940.54
Kesling, Ben. *Bravo Company*   958.104
Ketchum, Richard M. *Saratoga*   973.3
Kilmeade, Brian. ★*Andrew Jackson and the Miracle of New Orleans*   973.5
Kneale, Matthew. *Rome*   945.6
Lambert, Raymond. *Every Man a Hero*   B
Lawrence, T. E. *Seven Pillars of Wisdom*   940.4
Lewis, Damien. *Churchill's Hellraisers*   940.54
Lloyd, Nick. *The Western Front*   940.4
Loyn, David. *The Long War*   958.104
Luttrell, Marcus. *Lone Survivor*   958.104
Macintyre, Ben. *Double Cross*   940.54
Makos, Adam. *Spearhead*   B
Maurer, Kevin. *Damn Lucky*   940.54
McCarten, Anthony. *Darkest Hour*   941.084
McDonough, Frank. *The Hitler Years*   943.086
McDonough, James L. *William Tecumseh Sherman*   B
McManus, John C. *Fire and Fortitude*   940.54
McManus, John C. *Island Infernos*   940.54
McManus, John C. *To the End of the Earth*   940.54
McPherson, James M. *Battle Cry of Freedom*   973.7
McPherson, James M. *Hallowed Ground*   973.7
Merridale, Catherine. *Ivan's War*   940.54
Miller, Donald L. ★*Masters of the Air*   940.54
Milton, Giles. *Soldier, Sailor, Frogman, Spy, Airman, Gangster, Kill or Die*   940.54
Moore, Harold G. *We Are Soldiers Still*   959.704
O'Connell, Robert L. *The Ghosts of Cannae*   937
O'Keeffe, Paul. *Waterloo*   940.2
Paradis, Michel. *The Light of Battle*   940.54
Patton, George S. *War as I Knew It*   B
Perry, Mark. *The Most Dangerous Man in America*   B
Plokhy, Serhii. ★*The Russo-Ukrainian War*   947.7
Roberts, Andrew. *The Storm of War*   940.54
Romesha, Clinton. *Red Platoon*   958.104
Sears, Stephen W. ★*Chancellorsville*   973.7
Sears, Stephen W. *Gettysburg*   973.7
Sears, Stephen W. ★*Landscape Turned Red*   973.7
Sides, Hampton. ★*Ghost Soldiers*   940.54
Sides, Hampton. *On Desperate Ground*   951.904
Smith, Starr. *Jimmy Stewart*   B
Snow, Peter. *When Britain Burned the White House*   975.3
Stanton, Doug. *The Odyssey of Echo Company*   959.704
Strauss, Barry S. ★*The War That Made the Roman Empire*   937
Thomas, Evan. *Sea of Thunder*   940.54
Toll, Ian W. *The Conquering Tide*   940.54
Toll, Ian W. *Pacific Crucible*   940.54
Toll, Ian W. *Twilight of the Gods*   940.54
Tuchman, Barbara W. ★*The Guns of August*   940.4
Ullrich, Volker. *Hitler*   B
Varon, Elizabeth R. *Longstreet*   B
Wert, Jeffry D. *Cavalryman of the Lost Cause*   B
Wheelan, Joseph. *Midnight in the Pacific*   940.54
Whitlock, Craig. *The Afghanistan Papers*   958.104
Winters, Richard D. *Beyond Band of Brothers*   B

MILITARY CAPITULATIONS
    Kempowski, Walter. *Swansong 1945*   940.54
    McManus, John C. *To the End of the Earth*   940.54

MILITARY CEMETERIES
    Cotton, Tom. *Sacred Duty*   355.6
    Poole, Robert M. *Section 60*   975.5

MILITARY COVER-UPS
    Blume, Lesley M. M. *Fallout*   940.54
    Horwitz, Josh. *War of the Whales*   333.95

MILITARY DECEPTION
    Macintyre, Ben. ★*Operation Mincemeat*   940.54

MILITARY DEFEAT
    Beevor, Antony. *The Battle of Arnhem*   940.54

PUBLIC LIBRARY CORE COLLECTION: NONFICTION
Twentieth Edition

Broers, Michael. *Napoleon*	944.05
Dalrymple, William. *The Return of a King*	958.1
Drury, Bob. *Valley Forge*	973.3
Kempowski, Walter. *Swansong 1945*	940.54

MILITARY DEPENDENTS

Finkel, David. *Thank You for Your Service*	920

MILITARY DESERTION

Azad. *Long Shot*	B

MILITARY DISCIPLINE

Drury, Bob. *Valley Forge*	973.3
Philipps, David. *Alpha*	956.7044

MILITARY EDUCATION

Bunting, Josiah. ★*The Making of a Leader*	B
Dickson, Paul. *The Rise of the G.I. Army 1940-1941*	940.54

MILITARY ENGINEERING

Emery, Theo. *Hellfire Boys*	358
Glatthaar, Joseph T. *The American Military*	355.00973
Kunetka, James W. *The General and the Genius*	355.8
Lloyd, Nick. *The Western Front*	940.4
Miller, Chris. *Chip War*	338.4
Norris, Robert S. *Racing for the Bomb*	B
Scharre, Paul. *Four Battlegrounds*	006.3
Sheehan, Neil. *A Fiery Peace in a Cold War*	B
Simms, Brendan. *The Silver Waterfall*	940.54
Tyson, Neil deGrasse. *Accessory to War*	355.001

MILITARY ETHICS

O'Connell, Robert L. *Revolutionary*	B

MILITARY GOVERNMENT

Abouzeid, Rania. *No Turning Back*	956.9104
Taing, Mae Bunseng. *Under the Naga Tail*	B

MILITARY HISTORY

Alexander, Larry. *Biggest Brother*	B
Ambrose, Stephen E. *D-Day, June 6, 1944*	940.54
Anderson, Fred. *The Dominion of War*	973
Armitage, David. *Civil Wars*	355.02
Arnold, James R. *Jungle of Snakes*	355.02
Ash, Stephen V. *Firebrand of Liberty*	973.7
Atkinson, Rick. *An Army at Dawn*	940.54
Atkinson, Rick. ★*The British Are Coming*	973.3
Atkinson, Rick. *The Day of Battle*	940.54
Atkinson, Rick. *The Guns at Last Light*	940.54
Bacevich, Andrew J. *America's War for the Greater Middle East*	956.05
Barker, Juliet R. V. *Agincourt*	944
Beevor, Antony. *Ardennes 1944*	940.54
Beevor, Antony. *D-Day*	940.54
Beschloss, Michael R. ★*Presidents of War*	355.00973
Bissinger, H. G. ★*The Mosquito Bowl*	796.332
Boot, Max. ★*War Made New*	355.0209
Borneman, Walter R. *Macarthur at War*	B
Bradley, James. *Flags of Our Fathers*	940.54
Bradley, James. *Flyboys*	940.54
Brighton, Terry. *Patton, Montgomery, Rommel*	B
Brooks, Rosa. *How Everything Became War and the Military Became Everything*	355
Brown, Daniel James. ★*Facing the Mountain*	940.54
Bruning, John R. *The Race of Aces*	940.54
Burke, Edmund. *Reflections on the Revolution in France*	944.04
Campbell, James. *The Ghost Mountain Boys*	940.54
Capozzola, Christopher. *Bound by War*	355
Chamberlin, Paul Thomas. *The Cold War's Killing Fields*	355.009
Chivers, C. J. *The Fighters*	920
Clavin, Tom. *The Last Hill*	940.54
Cohen, Eliot A. *Conquered into Liberty*	355.009747
Cornwell, Bernard. *Waterloo*	940.2
Cotton, Tom. *Sacred Duty*	355.6
Crowley, Roger. *City of Fortune*	945
Davis, William C. *Crucible of Command*	920
Dickson, Paul. *The Rise of the G.I. Army 1940-1941*	940.54
Donovan, Jim. *A Terrible Glory*	973.8
Dower, John W. *Cultures of War*	355.00973
Drury, Bob. *Valley Forge*	973.3
Englund, Peter. *The Beauty and the Sorrow*	940.309
Erwin, Jon. *Beyond Valor*	B
Evans, Richard J. *The Third Reich at War*	940.53
Feifer, Gregory. *The Great Gamble*	958.104
Ferling, John E. *Winning Independence*	973.3
Fisk, Robert. *The Great War for Civilisation*	956.04
Follett, Ken. *On Wings of Eagles*	955
France, John. *Perilous Glory*	355
Frank, Richard B. *Tower of Skulls*	940.54
Gardner, Mark L. *Rough Riders*	973.911
Giangreco, D. M. *Hell to Pay*	940.54
Gies, Joseph. *Life in a Medieval Castle*	940.1
Gilbert, Martin. *The Second World War*	940.53
Glatthaar, Joseph T. *The American Military*	355.00973
Goldsworthy, Adrian Keith. *Pax Romana*	937
Goodheart, Adam. *1861*	973.7
Graff, Garrett M. ★*When the Sea Came Alive*	940.54
Grayling, A. C. *Among the Dead Cities*	940.54
Groom, Winston. *The Aviators*	920
Groom, Winston. *The Generals*	920
Hanson, Victor Davis. *The Father of Us All*	355.0209
Hanson, Victor Davis. *The Soul of Battle*	355
Harden, Blaine. *The Great Leader and the Fighter Pilot*	B
Hastings, Max. *Catastrophe 1914*	940.3
Hastings, Max. *Operation Chastise*	940.54
Hastings, Max. *Overlord*	940.54
Hastings, Max. *Retribution*	940.54
Hastings, Max. ★*Vietnam*	959.704
Hedges, Chris. *War Is a Force That Gives Us Meaning*	355.02
Henderson, Bruce B. *Bridge to the Sun*	940.53
Herman, Arthur. ★*Douglas Macarthur*	B
Hervieux, Linda. *Forgotten*	940.54
Hillenbrand, Laura. ★*Unbroken*	B
Hogan, William R. *Task Force Hogan*	940.54
Hogeland, William. *Autumn of the Black Snake*	970.004
Holland, James. *Battle of Britain*	940.54
Holland, James. *Brothers in Arms*	940.54
Holland, James. *The Savage Storm*	940.53
Holland, James. *Sicily '43*	940.54
Hornfischer, James D. *Neptune's Inferno*	940.54
Iredale, Will. *The Kamikaze Hunters*	940.54
Isserman, Maurice. *The Winter Army*	940.54
Jones, Dan. *Crusaders*	909.07
Jordan, Jonathan W. *Brothers, Rivals, Victors*	940.54
Kagan, Donald. *The Peloponnesian War*	938
Kaufmann, Uri R. *Eighteen Days of October*	956.04
Keegan, John. *The American Civil War*	973.7
Keegan, John. *The Second World War*	940.53
Kershaw, Alex. *Against All Odds*	940.54
Kershaw, Alex. *Avenue of Spies*	940.53
Kneale, Matthew. *Rome*	945.6
Korda, Michael. *Clouds of Glory*	B
Korda, Michael. *With Wings Like Eagles*	940.54
Larson, Erik. ★*Dead Wake*	940.4
Loyn, David. *In Afghanistan*	958.1
Lucas, Jack. *Indestructible*	B
Lukacs, John. *Five Days in London, May 1940*	940.53
Macintyre, Ben. *Double Cross*	940.54
Macintyre, Ben. ★*Rogue Heroes*	940.54
MacMillan, Margaret. *War*	355.0209
Makos, Adam. *Spearhead*	B
Mazower, Mark. *The Greek Revolution*	949.5
McElya, Micki. *The Politics of Mourning*	975.5
McLynn, Frank. *Genghis Khan*	950.2
McManus, John C. *Fire and Fortitude*	940.54
McManus, John C. *Island Infernos*	940.54
McNamara, Robert S. *In Retrospect*	959.704
McPherson, James M. *Battle Cry of Freedom*	973.7
McPherson, James M. *Drawn with the Sword*	973.7
McPherson, James M. *For Cause and Comrades*	973.7
McPherson, James M. *Hallowed Ground*	973.7
Merridale, Catherine. *Ivan's War*	940.54
Moore, Harold G. *We Are Soldiers Still*	959.704
Moore, Harold G. *We Were Soldiers Once—And Young*	959.704
Morris, Benny. *1948*	956.04
Nelson, Craig. *Pearl Harbor*	940.54
Nelson, Megan Kate. *The Three-Cornered War*	978
Nez, Chester. *Code Talker*	B
Nolan, Cathal J. *The Allure of Battle*	355.409
Norman, Michael. *Tears in the Darkness*	940.54
Norris, Robert S. *Racing for the Bomb*	B
O'Connell, Robert L. *The Ghosts of Cannae*	937
O'Donnell, Patrick K. *The Indispensables*	973.3
Olson, Lynne. *Citizens of London*	940.54012
Patton, George S. *War as I Knew It*	B

AUTHOR, TITLE, SERIES AND SUBJECT INDEX

Petraeus, David Howell. *Conflict*	355
Philbrick, Nathaniel. ★*Bunker Hill*	973.3
Philbrick, Nathaniel. ★*In the Hurricane's Eye*	973.3
Philbrick, Nathaniel. ★*Valiant Ambition*	B
Plokhy, Serhii. ★*The Russo-Ukrainian War*	947.7
Plokhy, Serhii. *Yalta*	940.53
Preston, Diana. *Eight Days at Yalta*	940.53
Raines, Howell. *Silent Cavalry*	973.7
Ricks, Thomas E. ★*The Generals*	B
Roberts, Andrew. *Leadership in War*	920
Roberts, Andrew. *Masters and Commanders*	940.5322
Rogan, Eugene L. *The Fall of the Ottomans*	940.3
Rohde, David. *Endgame*	949.703
Roll, David L. *George Marshall*	B
Rosbottom, Ronald C. *When Paris Went Dark*	944.0816
Scahill, Jeremy. *Dirty Wars*	355.00973
Schlosser, Eric. *Command and Control*	363.17
Scott, James. *Target Tokyo*	940.54
Sears, Stephen W. *Lincoln's Lieutenants*	920
Sheinkin, Steve. *Bomb*	623.4
Sides, Hampton. *Blood and Thunder*	978
Sides, Hampton. ★*Ghost Soldiers*	940.54
Sides, Hampton. *On Desperate Ground*	951.904
Snow, Peter. *When Britain Burned the White House*	975.3
Stanton, Doug. *12 Strong*	958.104
Stargardt, Nicholas. *The German War*	940.53
Stark, Peter. *Young Washington*	B
Stavridis, James. *To Risk It All*	359
Stephenson, Michael. *The Last Full Measure*	305.9
Talty, Stephan. *Saving Bravo*	959.704
Thomas, Evan. *Sea of Thunder*	940.54
Toll, Ian W. *The Conquering Tide*	940.54
Toll, Ian W. *Twilight of the Gods*	940.54
Ward, Geoffrey C. *The Civil War*	973.7
Ward, Geoffrey C. ★*The Vietnam War*	959.704
Weale, Adrian. *Army of Evil*	940.54
Wert, Jeffry D. *Cavalryman of the Lost Cause*	B
Zambone, Albert Louis. *Daniel Morgan*	B
MILITARY INTELLIGENCE	
Andrew, Christopher M. *The Secret World*	327.1209
Boot, Max. ★*The Road Not Taken*	B
Copeland, B. Jack. *Turing*	B
Drabkin, Ronald. *Beverly Hills Spy*	940.54
Draper, Robert. *To Start a War*	956.7044
Fagone, Jason. *The Woman Who Smashed Codes*	B
Fairweather, Jack. *The Volunteer*	B
Fritz, Ian. *What the Taliban Told Me*	B
Garrett, Leah. *X Troop*	940.54
Hastings, Max. *The Secret War*	940.54
Henderson, Bruce B. *Bridge to the Sun*	940.53
Macintyre, Ben. ★*Operation Mincemeat*	940.54
Macintyre, Ben. ★*Prisoners of the Castle*	940.54
Manning, Chelsea. *Readme.Txt*	B
McKay, Sinclair. *The Secret Lives of Codebreakers*	940.54
Meltzer, Brad. ★*The First Conspiracy*	973.4
Navarro, Joe. *Three Minutes to Doomsday*	B
Ohler, Norman. *The Bohemians*	940.53
Price, David A. *Geniuses at War*	940.54
Reynolds, Nicholas E. *Need to Know*	940.54
Soufan, Ali H. *The Black Banners Declassified*	363.325
Stephanopoulos, George. ★*The Situation Room*	973.09
Trimble, Lee. *Beyond the Call*	940.54
Walton, Calder. *Spies*	327.1247
Xue, XInran. *The Book of Secrets*	951.05
MILITARY INTELLIGENCE OFFICERS	
Willner, Nina. *Forty Autumns*	B
MILITARY INTERROGATION	
Fair, Eric. *Consequence*	B
Henderson, Bruce B. *Sons and Soldiers*	940.53
McCoy, Alfred W. *A Question of Torture*	323.4
Nixon, John. *Debriefing the President*	956.7044
Scott-Clark, Cathy. *The Forever Prisoner*	364.6
MILITARY JOURNALISM	
MacKrell, Judith. *The Correspondents*	070.4
MILITARY LAW	
Witt, John Fabian. *Lincoln's Code*	343.73
MILITARY LIFE	
Chrisinger, David. *The Soldier's Truth*	940.54
Fritz, Ian. *What the Taliban Told Me*	B
Glatthaar, Joseph T. *The American Military*	355.00973
Gorrindo, Simone. ★*The Wives*	B
MILITARY MISSIONS	
Geroux, William. *The Ghost Ships of Archangel*	940.54
Owen, Mark. *No Hero*	B
Trimble, Lee. *Beyond the Call*	940.54
MILITARY NURSES	
Seiple, Samantha. *Louisa on the Front Lines*	B
MILITARY NURSING	
Seiple, Samantha. *Louisa on the Front Lines*	B
MILITARY OCCUPATION	
Alexander, Caroline. *Skies of Thunder*	940.54
Ansary, Mir Tamim. *Games Without Rules*	958.1
Askwith, Richard. *Unbreakable*	B
Dower, John W. *Embracing Defeat*	952.04
Dugard, Martin. *Taking Paris*	940.54
Feifer, Gregory. *The Great Gamble*	958.104
Frank, Richard B. *Tower of Skulls*	940.54
Harding, Luke. *Invasion*	947.7
Kaiser, Charles. *The Cost of Courage*	B
Kaminsky, Ilya. ★*Deaf Republic*	811
Khalidi, Rashid. ★*The Hundred Years' War on Palestine*	956.9405
Lewis, Damien. *Churchill's Hellraisers*	940.54
Loyn, David. *In Afghanistan*	958.1
Loyn, David. *The Long War*	958.104
MacGregor, Iain. *The Lighthouse of Stalingrad*	940.54
McKean, David. *Watching Darkness Fall*	940.53
Oren, Michael B. *Six Days of War*	956.04
Pappe, Ilan. *The Biggest Prison on Earth*	956.9405
Rosbottom, Ronald C. *When Paris Went Dark*	944.0816
Scott, James. *Rampage*	940.54
Shehadeh, Raja. *Where the Line Is Drawn*	956.9405
Tamimi, Ahed. ★*They Called Me a Lioness*	B
Thrall, Nathan. ★*A Day in the Life of Abed Salama*	956.05
Trofimov, Yaroslav. ★*Our Enemies Will Vanish*	947.7
Verini, James. *They Will Have to Die Now*	956.7044
Warren, James A. *Year of the Hawk*	959.704
White, Ralph. *Getting Out of Saigon*	959.704
MILITARY OFFICERS	
Bass, Gary Jonathan. ★*Judgment at Tokyo*	952.04
Groom, Winston. *The Generals*	920
Hogan, William R. *Task Force Hogan*	940.54
Katz, Catherine Grace. *The Daughters of Yalta*	920
Sears, Stephen W. *Lincoln's Lieutenants*	920
Weintraub, Stanley. *Iron Tears*	973.3
MILITARY PILOTS	
Bascomb, Neal. *The Escape Artists*	940.4
Bradley, James. *Flyboys*	940.54
Groom, Winston. *The Aviators*	920
Hastings, Max. *Operation Chastise*	940.54
Keith, Philip A. *All Blood Runs Red*	B
Kershaw, Alex. *Avenue of Spies*	940.53
Kershaw, Alex. *The Few*	940.54
Landdeck, Katherine Sharp. *The Women with Silver Wings*	920
Lee, Heath Hardage. ★*The League of Wives*	959.704
Lewis, Damien. *The Dog Who Could Fly*	940.54
Murphy, Brian. *81 Days Below Zero*	940.54
Sherman, Casey. *Above and Beyond*	973.922092
Wallace, Chris. *Countdown 1945*	940.54
MILITARY PLANNING	
Caddick-Adams, Peter. *Sand and Steel*	940.54
Graff, Garrett M. *Raven Rock*	363.350973
Holland, James. *Normandy '44*	940.54
Hotta, Eri. *Japan 1941*	940.54
Tyson, Neil deGrasse. *Accessory to War*	355.001
MILITARY POLICY	
Ackerman, Spencer. *Reign of Terror*	973.931
Bacevich, Andrew J. *America's War for the Greater Middle East*	956.05
Brands, H. W. *The General vs. the President*	973.918092
Brands, H. W. *Woodrow Wilson*	B
Brooks, Rosa. *How Everything Became War and the Military Became Everything*	355
Capozzola, Christopher. *Bound by War*	355
Donovan, Jim. *A Terrible Glory*	973.8
Dower, John W. *Cultures of War*	355.00973
Draper, Robert. *To Start a War*	956.7044
Edstrom, Erik. *Un-American*	B

PUBLIC LIBRARY CORE COLLECTION: NONFICTION
Twentieth Edition

Gans, John. *White House Warriors*	355
Gates, Robert Michael. ★*Exercise of Power*	973.929
Gopal, Anand. *No Good Men Among the Living*	920
Halberstam, David. *The Best and the Brightest*	973.92
Halberstam, David. *The Coldest Winter*	951.904
Hendrickson, Paul. *The Living and the Dead*	959.704
Hotta, Eri. *Japan 1941*	940.54
Kaplan, Fred M. *The Bomb*	355.8
Klare, Michael T. *All Hell Breaking Loose*	355.20973
Klay, Phil. *Uncertain Ground*	359.9
Loyn, David. *The Long War*	958.104
McNamara, Robert S. *In Retrospect*	959.704
Mirski, Sean A. *We May Dominate the World*	973.91
Nelson, Megan Kate. *The Three-Cornered War*	978
Olson, Lynne. *Those Angry Days*	940.53
Packer, George. *The Assassins' Gate*	956.7044
Warren, James A. *Year of the Hawk*	959.704

MILITARY POWER
Chomsky, Noam. *Who Rules the World?*	327.73
Hanson, Victor Davis. *The Second World Wars*	940.54
Toll, Ian W. ★*Six Frigates*	359.00973

MILITARY PRISONS
Bardenwerper, William. *The Prisoner in His Palace*	956.7044
Khan, Mahvish Rukhsana. *My Guantanamo Diary*	973.931

MILITARY RECONNAISSANCE
Stanton, Doug. *The Odyssey of Echo Company*	959.704

MILITARY RECRUITING AND ENLISTMENT
Young, Daniella Mestyanek. *Uncultured*	B

MILITARY RELIGIOUS ORDERS
Haag, Michael. *The Tragedy of the Templars*	271.7913
Jones, Dan. *The Templars*	271

MILITARY RESEARCH
Jacobsen, Annie. ★*Operation Paperclip*	940.54
Jacobsen, Annie. *Phenomena*	133.8
Kiernan, Denise. *The Girls of Atomic City*	976.8
Lance, Rachel. *Chamber Divers*	940.54
Roach, Mary. ★*Grunt*	355

MILITARY SECRETS
Baker, Nicholson. *Baseless*	358
Coll, Steve. ★*The Achilles Trap*	956.7044
Graff, Garrett M. *Raven Rock*	363.350973
Horwitz, Josh. *War of the Whales*	333.95
Manning, Chelsea. *Readme.Txt*	B
Whitlock, Craig. ★*Fat Leonard*	364.16

MILITARY SERVICE
Cotton, Tom. *Sacred Duty*	355.6
Henderson, Rob Kim. *Troubled*	B
Luttrell, Marcus. *Service*	956.7044
McElya, Micki. *The Politics of Mourning*	975.5
Patterson, James. *Walk in My Combat Boots*	920
Wise, Beau. *Three Wise Men*	958.104

MILITARY SPOUSES
DiFelice, Bekah. *Almost There*	248.8
Gorrindo, Simone. ★*The Wives*	B
Henderson, Artis. *Unremarried Widow*	B
Lee, Heath Hardage. ★*The League of Wives*	959.704

MILITARY STRATEGY
Ackerman, Elliot. *The Fifth Act*	958.104
Barker, Juliet R. V. *Agincourt*	944
Barrett, David Dean. *140 Days to Hiroshima*	940.54
Beevor, Antony. *The Battle of Arnhem*	940.54
Beschloss, Michael R. ★*Presidents of War*	355.00973
Boot, Max. *Invisible Armies*	355.02
Borneman, Walter R. *Macarthur at War*	B
Bowden, Mark. *Black Hawk Down*	967.7305
Brands, H. W. *The Last Campaign*	973.8
Brooks, Rosa. *How Everything Became War and the Military Became Everything*	355
Churchill, Winston. *Their Finest Hour*	940.53
Cohen, Eliot A. *Conquered into Liberty*	355.009747
Davis, William C. *Crucible of Command*	920
Dower, John W. *Cultures of War*	355.00973
Ferling, John E. *Winning Independence*	973.3
Fischer, David Hackett. *Washington's Crossing*	973.3
France, John. *Perilous Glory*	355
Gans, John. *White House Warriors*	355
Gladwell, Malcolm. ★*The Bomber Mafia*	940.54
Groom, Winston. *The Allies*	940.5309
Groom, Winston. *The Generals*	920
Gwynne, S. C. *Hymns of the Republic*	973.7
Hastings, Max. *Operation Chastise*	940.54
Holland, James. *Sicily '43*	940.54
Keegan, John. *The American Civil War*	973.7
Keegan, John. *The Second World War*	940.53
Kennedy, Paul. *Engineers of Victory*	940.54
Kneale, Matthew. *Rome*	945.6
Massie, Robert K. *Castles of Steel*	940.4
McCarten, Anthony. *Darkest Hour*	941.084
McManus, John C. *Fire and Fortitude*	940.54
McManus, John C. *Island Infernos*	940.54
Morris, Marc. *A Great and Terrible King*	B
Newitz, Annalee. *Stories Are Weapons*	355.3
O'Connell, Robert L. *The Ghosts of Cannae*	937
Parkin, Simon. *A Game of Birds and Wolves*	940.54
Patton, George S. *War as I Knew It*	B
Ricks, Thomas E. *Fiasco*	956.7044
Roberts, Andrew. *Leadership in War*	920
Roberts, Andrew. *The Storm of War*	940.54
Stavridis, James. *To Risk It All*	359
Symonds, Craig L. *Lincoln and His Admirals*	B
Toll, Ian W. *The Conquering Tide*	940.54
Toll, Ian W. *Twilight of the Gods*	940.54
Weintraub, Stanley. *Iron Tears*	973.3
Wert, Jeffry D. *Cavalryman of the Lost Cause*	B
Wheelan, Joseph. ★*Terrible Swift Sword*	B
Winters, Richard D. *Beyond Band of Brothers*	B
Woolf, Greg. *Rome*	937
Yergin, Daniel. ★*The Prize*	338.2
Yergin, Daniel. *The Quest*	333.79

MILITARY SUPPLIES
Geroux, William. *The Ghost Ships of Archangel*	940.54

MILITARY TACTICS
Atkinson, Rick. *The Guns at Last Light*	940.54
Hanson, Victor Davis. *The Soul of Battle*	355
Kennedy, Paul. *Engineers of Victory*	940.54
Lloyd, Nick. *The Western Front*	940.4
Philbrick, Nathaniel. ★*Bunker Hill*	973.3

MILITARY-INDUSTRIAL COMPLEX
Edstrom, Erik. *Un-American*	B
Tyson, Neil deGrasse. *Accessory to War*	355.001

MILITIA MOVEMENT
Cook, Kevin. *Waco Rising*	299
Lehr, Dick. *White Hot Hate*	363.325

MILITIAS AND IRREGULAR ARMIES
Atkinson, Rick. ★*The British Are Coming*	973.3
Azad. *Long Shot*	B
Crawford, Alan Pell. *This Fierce People*	975
Flock, Elizabeth. ★*The Furies*	305.48
McCullough, David G. ★*1776*	973.3

MILK
Kurlansky, Mark. *Milk!*	637
Narayan, Shoba. *The Milk Lady of Bangalore*	390
Milk and Honey. Kaur, Rupi	811
The Milk Lady of Bangalore. Narayan, Shoba	390
Milk of Paradise. Inglis, Lucy	362.29
Milk Street. Kimball, Christopher	641.5
Milk Street. Kimball, Christopher	641.5
Milk Street. Kimball, Christopher	641.7
★*Milk Street 365*. Kimball, Christopher	641.5
Milk! Kurlansky, Mark	637

MILK-FREE DIET
Cavallari, Kristin. *True Roots*	641.5
Moskowitz, Isa Chandra. *Veganomicon*	641
Walker, Danielle. *Danielle Walker's Against All Grain*	641.5
The Milky Way. McTier, Moiya	523.1

MILKY WAY
McTier, Moiya. *The Milky Way*	523.1
Mill Town. Arsenault, Kerri	B

MILL TOWNS
Rudacille, Deborah. *Roots of Steel*	338.4
Millard Fillmore. Finkelman, Paul	B

Millard, Candice
Destiny of the Republic	973.8
★*Hero of the Empire*	968.04
River of Doubt	918.1
★*River of the Gods*	916.204

AUTHOR, TITLE, SERIES AND SUBJECT INDEX

Millay, Edna St. Vincent
   Collected Poems   811
   Selected Poems   811
MILLAY, EDNA ST. VINCENT, 1892-1950
   Milford, Nancy. *Savage Beauty*   B
MILLENNIALS
   Arceneaux, Michael. *I Finally Bought Some Jordans*   306.76
   Lowry, Erin. ★*Broke Millennial Talks Money*   332.024
   Petersen, Anne Helen. *Can't Even*   305.242
MILLENNIUM (CHRISTIAN ESCHATOLOGY)
   Hansen, Valerie. *The Year 1000*   909
Miller's Arts & Crafts. Miller, Judith   745.409034
Miller, Adrienne
   In the Land of Men   070.5
MILLER, ADRIENNE
   Miller, Adrienne. *In the Land of Men*   070.5
MILLER, ARTHUR, 1915-2005
   Bigsby, Christopher William Edgar. *Arthur Miller*   B
MILLER, BODE, 1977-
   Vinton, Nathaniel. *The Fall Line*   796.93
Miller, Caroline Adams
   Creating Your Best Life   158.1
Miller, Chanel
   Know My Name   B
MILLER, CHANEL
   Miller, Chanel. *Know My Name*   B
Miller, Char
   Gifford Pinchot and the Making of Modern Environmentalism   B
Miller, Chris
   Chip War   338.4
Miller, Christopher
   The War Came to Us   947.7
MILLER, CHRISTOPHER
   Miller, Christopher. *The War Came to Us*   947.7
Miller, Donald L.
   City of the Century   977.311
   ★*Masters of the Air*   940.54
   Supreme City   974.7
   Vicksburg   973.7
Miller, Jim
   Examined Lives   B
Miller, Judith
   Furniture   749
   Miller's Arts & Crafts   745.409034
Miller, Kei
   Things I Have Withheld   814
MILLER, KEI
   Miller, Kei. *Things I Have Withheld*   814
Miller, Kenneth R.
   The Human Instinct   155.7
Miller, Klancy
   ★*For the Culture*   641.59
MILLER, LEE, 1907-1977
   Burke, Carolyn. *Lee Miller*   B
Miller, Lucasta
   ★*Keats*   821
Miller, Lulu
   Why Fish Don't Exist   B
MILLER, LULU
   Miller, Lulu. *Why Fish Don't Exist*   B
Miller, Marla
   Betsy Ross and the Making of America   B
Miller, Max
   ★*Tasting History*   641.509
Miller, Megan
   ★*The Ultimate Unofficial Encyclopedia for Minecrafters*   794.8
Miller, Michelle
   Belonging   B
Miller, Pat
   ★*The Power of Positive Dog Training*   636.7
Miller, Reuben Jonathan
   Halfway Home   364.8
Miller, Scott
   The President and the Assassin   973.8
MILLER, STEPHEN (POLITICAL ADVISOR)
   Guerrero, Jean. *Hatemonger*   B
Miller, Susan
   Planets and Possibilities   133.5

Miller, T. Christian
   A False Report   364.15
Millet, Lydia
   We Loved It All   813
MILLET, LYDIA, 1968-
   Millet, Lydia. *We Loved It All*   813
Milliken, Kirsten
   PLAYDHD   616.85
MILLIONAIRES
   Isaacson, Walter. ★*Steve Jobs*   B
   Jacoby, Karl. *The Strange Career of William Ellis*   B
   Stiles, T. J. ★*The First Tycoon*   B
   Walton, Sam. *Sam Walton, Made in America*   B
   Wills, Shomari. *Black Fortunes*   920
MILLS AND MILLWORK
   Rudacille, Deborah. *Roots of Steel*   338.4
Mills, Dan
   Sniper One   956.7044
MILLS, DAN, 1968-
   Mills, Dan. *Sniper One*   956.7044
Mills, Hayley
   Forever Young   B
MILLS, HAYLEY, 1946-
   Mills, Hayley. *Forever Young*   B
Mills, Stephen Tukel
   Chosen   B
MILLS, STEPHEN TUKEL
   Mills, Stephen Tukel. *Chosen*   B
Millwood, Molly
   To Have and to Hold   306.874
MILNE, A. A. (ALAN ALEXANDER), 1882-1956
   Thwaite, Ann. *Goodbye Christopher Robin*   B
MILNE, CHRISTOPHER, 1920-1996
   Thwaite, Ann. *Goodbye Christopher Robin*   B
Milne, Lorus Johnson
   ★*The Audubon Society Field Guide to North American Insects and Spiders*   595.7097
Milner, Greg
   Perfecting Sound Forever   781.49
MILOSEVIC, SLOBODAN, 1941-2006
   Maass, Peter. *Love Thy Neighbor*   949.702
★*Milosz's ABC's*. Milosz, Czeslaw   891.8
Milosz, Czeslaw
   ★*Milosz's ABC's*   891.8
MILOSZ, CZESLAW
   Milosz, Czeslaw. ★*Milosz's ABC's*   891.8
Milton, Giles
   Checkmate in Berlin   943
   Churchill's Ministry of Ungentlemanly Warfare   940.54
   Soldier, Sailor, Frogman, Spy, Airman, Gangster, Kill or Die   940.54
MILWAUKEE, WISCONSIN
   Desmond, Matthew. ★*Evicted*   339.4
   Strang, Dean A. *Worse Than the Devil*   345.775
MIMICRY (BIOLOGY)
   Forbes, Peter. *Dazzled and Deceived*   578.4
Min, Anchee
   Red Azalea   B
MIN, ANCHEE, 1957-
   Min, Anchee. *Red Azalea*   B
Minami, Jikisai
   It's Okay Not to Look for the Meaning of Life   158.1
MIND AND BODY
   Chopra, Deepak. *Metahuman*   204
   Clegg, Brian. *Extra Sensory*   133.8
   Common. ★*And Then We Rise*   613
   Daley-Ward, Yrsa. *The How*   158.1
   Damasio, Antonio R. *The Feeling of What Happens*   153
   Denworth, Lydia. *Friendship*   158.2
   Fleming, Renee. ★*Music and Mind*   615.8
   Foo, Stephanie. ★*What My Bones Know*   B
   Goleman, Daniel. *Why We Meditate*   158.1
   Harris, Dan. ★*10% Happier*   158.1
   Hotz, Julia. ★*The Connection Cure*   610
   Jamie, Poppy. *Happy Not Perfect*   158.1
   Kandel, Eric R. ★*The Disordered Mind*   616.89
   Kempton, Beth. *The Way of the Fearless Writer*   808.02
   Lee, Shannon. *Be Water, My Friend*   796.8
   Marchant, Jo. *Cure*   616.89

PUBLIC LIBRARY CORE COLLECTION: NONFICTION
Twentieth Edition

Nakazawa, Donna Jackson. *The Angel and the Assassin* — 612.8
O'Sullivan, Suzanne. *The Sleeping Beauties* — 616.85
Rakel, David. *The Compassionate Connection* — 610.1
Teng, Tara. ★*Your Body Is a Revolution* — 306.4
MIND AND BODY THERAPIES
    Fleming, Renee. ★*Music and Mind* — 615.8
    Marchant, Jo. *Cure* — 616.89
    Stanley, Jessamyn. ★*Yoke* — 613.7
    Taylor, Madisyn. *Unmedicated* — 615.8
A Mind At Play. Soni, Jimmy — B
MIND CONTROL
    Bugliosi, Vincent. ★*Helter Skelter* — 364.1
    Kinzer, Stephen. *Poisoner in Chief* — B
    Simon, Matt. *Plight of the Living Dead* — 591.6
Mind Fixers. Harrington, Anne — 616.89
Mind Over Batter. Hazan, Jack — 641.81
Mind Over Meds. Weil, Andrew — 362.29
Mind Over Money. Hammond, Claudia — 332.401
A Mind Unraveled. Eichenwald, Kurt — B
Mind Your Gut. Scarlata, Kate — 616.3
Mind-Blowing Magic Tricks for Everyone. Owen, Oscar — 793.8
Minden, Eliza Gaynor
    The Ballet Companion — 792.8
MINDFULNESS
    Allen, Cory. *Now Is the Way* — 158.1
    Armstrong, Karen. *Twelve Steps to a Compassionate Life* — 177
    Cameron, Julia. ★*The Listening Path* — 153.6
    Goleman, Daniel. *Why We Meditate* — 158.1
    Harris, Dan. ★*10% Happier* — 158.1
    Hase, Craig. *How Not to Be a Hot Mess* — 158.1
    Jamie, Poppy. *Happy Not Perfect* — 158.1
    Kempton, Beth. *The Way of the Fearless Writer* — 808.02
    Morin, John. *Inspired Origami* — 736.982
    Nhat Hanh. *The Art of Living* — 294.3
    Rubin, Gretchen Craft. ★*Life in Five Senses* — 152.1
    Siegel, Daniel J. *Aware* — 158.1
    Smith, James K. A. *How to Inhabit Time* — 223
    Zorn, Justin. *Golden* — 128
Mindreader. Lieberman, David J. — 401
★*Mindset.* Dweck, Carol S. — 153.8
Mindware. Nisbett, Richard E. — 153.4
MINECRAFT (GAME)
    Miller, Megan. ★*The Ultimate Unofficial Encyclopedia for Minecrafters* — 794.8
MINERAL INDUSTRY AND TRADE
    Kara, Siddharth. *Cobalt Red* — 338.2
MINERALS
    Bjornerud, Marcia. *Geopedia* — 551
MINERS
    Hamby, Chris. *Soul Full of Coal Dust* — 363.11
    Kara, Siddharth. *Cobalt Red* — 338.2
MINES AND MINERAL RESOURCES
    Beaton, Kate. ★*Ducks* — 741.5
    Biggers, Jeff. *Reckoning at Eagle Creek* — 333.73
    Brands, H. W. *The Age of Gold* — 979.4
    Castner, Brian. *Stampede* — 971.9
    Conway, Edmund. *Material World* — 333.7
    Crouch, Gregory. *The Bonanza King* — B
    Hunt, Will. *Underground* — 624.1
    Judah, Hettie. *Lapidarium* — 553.8
    Kara, Siddharth. *Cobalt Red* — 338.2
    Kurlansky, Mark. *Salt* — 553.6
    Leamer, Laurence. *The Price of Justice* — 346.7302
    Maher, Kris. *Desperate* — 344
    Mort, T. A. *Thieves' Road* — 978.3
    Pasternak, Judy. *Yellow Dirt* — 979.1004
    Prendergast, John. *Congo Stories* — 967.5103
    Redniss, Lauren. ★*Oak Flat* — 970.5
    Roy, Arundhati. *Walking with the Comrades* — 954
    Sacco, Joe. ★*Paying the Land* — 741.5
    Scheyder, Ernest. *The War Below* — 333.7
    Vaillant, John. ★*Fire Weather* — 363.37
MINGUS, CHARLES, 1922-1979
    Gabbard, Krin. *Better Git It in Your Soul* — B
Mini Amigurumi Animals. Abbondio, Sarah — 746.43
Mini Crochet Creatures. Bergstrom, Lauren — 746.43
Mini Makers. Minter, Laura — 745.5

Minian, Ana Raquel
    ★*In the Shadow of Liberty* — 365
MINIATURE CRAFT
    Frisoni, Christine-Lea. *The Big Book of a Miniature House* — 745.592
    Garfield, Simon. *In Miniature* — 745.5928
MINIATURE OBJECTS
    Garfield, Simon. *In Miniature* — 745.5928
    Smith, Sally J. *Fairy Houses* — 745.592
The Minimalist Home. Becker, Joshua — 241
MINIMUM WAGE
    Ehrenreich, Barbara. ★*Nickel and Dimed* — B
    Freeman, Amanda. *Getting Me Cheap* — 362.83
    Guendelsberger, Emily. *On the Clock* — 331.0973
MINING CORPORATIONS
    Conway, Edmund. *Material World* — 333.7
The Ministry of Truth. Lynskey, Dorian — 823
MINNEAPOLIS, MINNESOTA
    Carr, David. *The Night of the Gun* — B
MINNESOTA
    Berg, Elizabeth. *I'll Be Seeing You* — 306.874
    Erdrich, Louise. *Books and Islands in Ojibwe Country* — 977
    Jones, Robert P. *The Hidden Roots of White Supremacy* — 305.8
    King, Maren Ellingboe. *Fresh Midwest* — 641.5977
    Porter, Carolyn. *Marcel's Letters* — 940.54
Minois, Georges
    The Atheist's Bible — 200
Minor Feelings. Hong, Cathy Park — 305.48
MINOR LEAGUE BASEBALL
    Barry, Dan. *Bottom of the 33rd* — 796.357
    Feinstein, John. *Where Nobody Knows Your Name* — 796.357
    Kornhauser, Jacob. *The Cup of Coffee Club* — 796.357
    Lindbergh, Ben. *The Only Rule Is That It Has to Work* — 796.357
    Shelton, Ron. *The Church of Baseball* — 791.43
MINOR LEAGUE BASEBALL PLAYERS
    Feinstein, John. *Where Nobody Knows Your Name* — 796.357
MINOR LEAGUE BASEBALL TEAMS
    Lindbergh, Ben. *The Only Rule Is That It Has to Work* — 796.357
A Minor Revolution. Benforado, Adam — 362.7
MINOR, WILLIAM CHESTER, 1834-1920
    Winchester, Simon. *The Professor and the Madman* — 423
★*Minority Rule.* Berman, Ari — 305.809
Minow, Martha
    When Should Law Forgive? — 345
MINSTREL SHOWS
    Lane, Stewart F. *Black Broadway* — 792.089
Mint Condition. Jamieson, David — 796.357
Minter, Adam
    Secondhand — 381
Minter, Laura
    Mini Makers — 745.5
Minutaglio, Bill
    Dallas 1963 — 973.922092
    The Most Dangerous Man in America — B
Miodownik, Mark
    Liquid Rules — 530.4
    Stuff Matters — 620.1
Miracle Country. Atleework, Kendra — 979.4
★*Miracle in the Andes.* Parrado, Nando — 982
★*The Miracle Worker.* Gibson, William — 812
Miracles. Lewis, C. S. — 231.7
MIRACLES
    Lewis, C. S. *Miracles* — 231.7
    Woodward, Kenneth L. *The Book of Miracles* — 231.7
The Mirage Factory. Krist, Gary — 920
Miraldi, Robert
    Seymour Hersh — B
Miranda, Deborah A.
    Bad Indians — 305.8009794
Miranda, Lin-Manuel
    Gmorning, Gnight! — 811
    Hamilton — 782.1
MIRANDA, LIN-MANUEL, 1980-
    Miranda, Lin-Manuel. *Hamilton* — 782.1
Mirski, Sean A.
    We May Dominate the World — 973.91
MISADVENTURES
    Alford, Henry. *And Then We Danced* — 792.8
    Bass, Rick. *The Traveling Feast* — B

AUTHOR, TITLE, SERIES AND SUBJECT INDEX

Crosley, Sloane. ★*Look Alive Out There*	814
Irby, Samantha. *We Are Never Meeting in Real Life*	814
Kugel, Seth. *Rediscovering Travel*	306.4
Weiner, Tim. *Legacy of Ashes*	327.1273009

MISANTHROPY

Souder, William. *Mad at the World*	813
Misbehaving. Thaler, Richard H.	330.01

MISBEHAVIOR

Bragg, Rick. *The Speckled Beauty*	636.7

MISCARRIAGE

Stahr, Celia. *Frida in America*	B
White, Kate. *Your Guide to Miscarriage & Pregnancy Loss*	618.3

MISCHIEF

Grogan, John. ★*Marley & Me*	636.752
Mischievous Creatures. McNeur, Catherine	920

MISCONCEPTIONS

Ali-Karamali, Sumbul. *Demystifying Shariah*	340.5
Cooke, Lucy. *The Truth About Animals*	590.2
Heine, Steven J. *DNA Is Not Destiny*	572.8
Krugman, Paul R. *Arguing with Zombies*	330.973
Montero, David. ★*The Stolen Wealth of Slavery*	381
Pinker, Steven. *Rationality*	153.4
Richardson, Heather Cox. *Democracy Awakening*	320.473
Schulz, Kathryn. *Being Wrong*	121
Stone, Deborah A. *Counting*	001.4

MISCONDUCT IN OFFICE

Bade, Rachael. ★*Unchecked*	342.73
Johnston, David Cay. *The Big Cheat*	973.933
Rothkopf, David J. *American Resistance*	973.933
Toobin, Jeffrey. *True Crimes and Misdemeanors*	973.933
Wolff, Michael. *Landslide*	973.933

Miseducated. Fleming, Brandon P.	B
Misfit. Gulman, Gary	B
★*Misfits*. Coel, Michaela	158.2

MISFITS (PEOPLE)

Coel, Michaela. ★*Misfits*	158.2
Nye, Bill. *Everything All at Once*	153.4
Porter, Billy. ★*Unprotected*	B
Satrapi, Marjane. ★*The Complete Persepolis*	741.5
Sestero, Greg. *The Disaster Artist*	791.43
Thomas, Joseph Earl. *Sink*	B
Tran, Phuc. ★*Sigh, Gone*	B
Watts, Reggie. *Great Falls, MT*	B

Mishra, Pankaj

Age of Anger	909.8
From the Ruins of Empire	950.4

MISINFORMATION

Ali-Karamali, Sumbul. *Demystifying Shariah*	340.5
Bates, Laura. *Men Who Hate Women*	305.3
Beres, Derek. *Conspirituality*	001.9
Bowlin, Ben. *Stuff They Don't Want You to Know*	001.9
Boykin, Keith. ★*Why Does Everything Have to Be About Race?*	305.8
Cairo, Alberto. *How Charts Lie*	302.2
Christakis, Nicholas A. *Apollo's Arrow*	362.1962
DiResta, Renee. *Invisible Rulers*	320
Goldacre, Ben. *Bad Science*	500
Harriot, Michael. ★*Black AF History*	973
Harrison, Christy. *The Wellness Trap*	613
Hartman, Darrell. *Battle of Ink and Ice*	998
Hongoltz-Hetling, Matthew. *If It Sounds Like a Quack*	615.8
Kroll, Andy. *A Death on W Street*	364.152
Levitin, Daniel J. ★*A Field Guide to Lies*	153.4
Newitz, Annalee. *Stories Are Weapons*	355.3
Pomerantsev, Peter. ★*How to Win an Information War*	940.53
Smith, Erin Geiger. ★*Thank You for Voting*	324.973
Stelter, Brian. *Hoax*	070.4
van der Linden, Sander. ★*Foolproof*	302.3
Yates, Kit. *The Math of Life and Death*	510

MISKJIAN, STEPAN, 1886-1974

Mackeen, Dawn Anahid. *The Hundred-Year Walk*	956.6
The Mismeasure of Man. Gould, Stephen Jay	153.9

MISOGYNY

Bates, Laura. *Men Who Hate Women*	305.3
Beard, Mary. ★*Women & Power*	305.409
Cleghorn, Elinor. *Unwell Women*	613
D'Antonio, Michael. *The Hunting of Hillary*	B
Erdrich, Heid E. ★*Little Big Bully*	811
Flannery, Kate. *Strip Tees*	338.4

Flock, Elizabeth. ★*The Furies*	305.48
Frangello, Gina. *Blow Your House Down*	813
Gibson, Marion. *Witchcraft*	133.4
Gillard, Julia. ★*Women and Leadership*	158
Greenblatt, Stephen. *The Rise and Fall of Adam and Eve*	233
Hallman, J. C. *Say Anarcha*	618.1
Hill, Katie. *She Will Rise*	305.42
Hortis, C. Alexander. *The Witch of New York*	364.152
Hustvedt, Siri. *Mothers, Fathers, and Others*	814
Jackson, Regina. *White Women*	305.8
McShane Wulfhart, Nell. *The Great Stewardess Rebellion*	331.4
Miller, T. Christian. *A False Report*	364.15
Penaluna, Regan. ★*How to Think Like a Woman*	190.82
Peters, Rebecca Todd. *Trust Women*	362.1988
Qadiri, Humayra. *Dancing in the Mosque*	B
Quinn, Zoe. *Crash Override*	794.8
Ratajkowski, Emily. ★*My Body*	B
Selvaratnam, Tanya. *Assume Nothing*	B
Sharlet, Jeff. ★*The Undertow*	322
Solnit, Rebecca. *Recollections of My Nonexistence*	B
V. ★*Reckoning*	814
Walder, Tracy. *The Unexpected Spy*	B
Wassef, Nadia. *Shelf Life*	B
West, Lindy. *The Witches Are Coming*	305.420973
Zimmerman, Jess. *Women and Other Monsters*	155.3
Miss Aluminum. Moore, Susanna	813
Miss Chloe. Verdelle, A. J.	B
Miss Leavitt's Stars. Johnson, George	522
★*Miss May Does Not Exist*. Courogen, Carrie	B

MISSILE SILOS

Schlosser, Eric. *Command and Control*	363.17

MISSILES

Coleman, David G. *The Fourteenth Day*	973.922092
Hastings, Max. *The Abyss*	972.9106
Sorensen, Theodore C. *Counselor*	B

MISSING CHILDREN

Bowden, Mark. *The Last Stone*	363.25
Cross, Kim. *In Light of All Darkness*	363.25
Douglas, John E. *When a Killer Calls*	364.152
McDiarmid, Jessica. *Highway of Tears*	364.152

MISSING IN ACTION

Freeman, Sally Mott. *The Jersey Brothers*	920
Helm, Sarah. *A Life in Secrets*	B
Lee, Heath Hardage. ★*The League of Wives*	959.704
Zuckoff, Mitchell. *Lost in Shangri-La*	940.54

MISSING MEN

Dial, Roman. *The Adventurer's Son*	917.286
Lankford, Andrea. *Trail of the Lost*	363.2
Levin, Daniel. *Proof of Life*	956.9104
McGrath, Ben. *Riverman*	797.122
Murdoch, Sierra Crane. ★*Yellow Bird*	364.152
Missing Microbes. Blaser, Martin J.	615.7
★*Missing Persons*. Wills, Clair	929.2

MISSING PERSONS

Diamond, Cheryl. *Nowhere Girl*	B
Fischer, Paul. *The Man Who Invented Motion Pictures*	791.43
Herlihy, David V. *The Lost Cyclist*	B
Hoffman, Carl. ★*Savage Harvest*	995.1
Levin, Daniel. *Proof of Life*	956.9104
Matar, Hisham. *The Return*	B
Stout, David. *The Kidnap Years*	364.15

MISSING PERSONS INVESTIGATION

Bowden, Mark. *The Last Stone*	363.25
Lankford, Andrea. *Trail of the Lost*	363.2
Levin, Daniel. *Proof of Life*	956.9104
Murdoch, Sierra Crane. ★*Yellow Bird*	364.152

MISSING WOMEN

Bonner, Betsy. *The Book of Atlantis Black*	364.152
McDiarmid, Jessica. *Highway of Tears*	364.152
Mission in a Bottle. Goldman, Seth	741.5
Mission to Mars. Aldrin, Buzz	523.43
Mission Transition. Louis, Matthew J.	650.14
Mission Vegan. Bowien, Danny	641.5

MISSIONARIES

Bellows, Amanda Brickell. *The Explorers*	910.92
Hamilton, Duncan. *For the Glory*	B
Irving, Apricot Anderson. *The Gospel of Trees*	B
Loftis, Larry. ★*The Watchmaker's Daughter*	940.53

PUBLIC LIBRARY CORE COLLECTION: NONFICTION
Twentieth Edition

MISSISSIPPI
  Balko, Radley. ★*The Cadaver King and the Country Dentist*   614
  Blain, Keisha N. *Until I Am Free*   B
  Hale, Grace Elizabeth. *In the Pines*   364.13
  Jones, Robert P. *The Hidden Roots of White Supremacy*   305.8
  Laymon, Kiese. ★*Heavy*   B
  Laymon, Kiese. *How to Slowly Kill Yourself and Others in America*   814.6
  Lowry, Beverly. *Deer Creek Drive*   364.152
  McCormick, Mack. *Biography of a Phantom*   782.421643
  Miller, Donald L. *Vicksburg*   973.7
  Mitchell, Jerry. ★*Race Against Time*   364.152
  Oshinsky, David M. *Worse Than Slavery*   365
  Trethewey, Natasha D. ★*Memorial Drive*
  Trethewey, Natasha D. ★*Monument*   811
  Tyson, Timothy B. *The Blood of Emmett Till*   364.1
  Ward, Jesmyn. ★*Men We Reaped*
  Watson, Bruce. *Freedom Summer*   323.1196
  Welty, Eudora. *One Time, One Place*   976.2
  Welty, Eudora. *One Writer's Beginnings*   B
  Wilkie, Curtis. *When Evil Lived in Laurel*   305.8
  Wright, Richard. ★*Black Boy*   B

MISSISSIPPI RIVER
  Barry, John M. *Rising Tide*   977
  Buck, Rinker. *Life on the Mississippi*   917

MISSISSIPPI VALLEY
  Barry, John M. *Rising Tide*   977

Missoula. Krakauer, Jon   362.883

MISSOURI
  Cooper, Sean Patrick. *The Shooter at Midnight*   363.25
  Stiles, T. J. *Jesse James*   B

MISTAKEN IDENTITY
  Hinton, Anthony Ray. *The Sun Does Shine*   B
  Klein, Naomi. ★*Doppelganger*   302.2

MISTRESSES
  Chang, Jung. *Empress Dowager Cixi*   B
  Daniels, Stormy. *Full Disclosure*   B
  Gortemaker, Heike B. *Eva Braun*   B
  King, Greg. *Twilight of Empire*   943.6

Misumi, Noriko
  Mending with Love   646.6
★*Misunderstood Vegetables*. Selengut, Becky   641.6
Mitchell, Andie
  Eating in the Middle   641.3
Mitchell, Elizabeth
  Lincoln's Lie   973.7092
Mitchell, George J.
  A Path to Peace   956.9405
Mitchell, Jerry
  ★*Race Against Time*   364.152

MITCHELL, JERRY
  Mitchell, Jerry. ★*Race Against Time*   364.152

MITCHELL, JOAN, 1926-1992
  Albers, Patricia. *Joan Mitchell*   B
  Livingston, Jane. *The Paintings of Joan Mitchell*   759.13

MITCHELL, JOHN W., 1914-1995
  Hampton, Dan. *Operation Vengeance*   940.54

MITCHELL, JONI, 1943-
  Powers, Ann. ★*Traveling*   B
  Yaffe, David. *Reckless Daughter*   782.42164

Mitchell, Josh
  The Debt Trap   378.3

MITCHELL, MARIA, 1818-1889
  Baron, David. *American Eclipse*   523.7

Mitchell, Ryan
  Tiny House Living   728.37
Mitchell, Syne
  Inventive Weaving on a Little Loom   746.1
Mitchell, Wendy
  Somebody I Used to Know   B

MITCHELL, WENDY, 1969-
  Mitchell, Wendy. *Somebody I Used to Know*   B

MITFORD FAMILY
  Lovell, Mary S. *The Sisters*   920.72
Mitford years [Series]. Karon, Jan   242
Mitford, Jessica
  ★*The American Way of Death Revisited*   338.4

MITFORD, JESSICA, 1917-1996
  Lovell, Mary S. *The Sisters*   920.72

Mitford, Jessica. ★*The American Way of Death Revisited*   338.4

MITFORD, NANCY, 1904-1973
  Lovell, Mary S. *The Sisters*   920.72

MITFORD, NORTH CAROLINA (IMAGINARY PLACE)
  Karon, Jan. *Bathed in Prayer*   242

MITFORD, UNITY, 1914-1948
  Lovell, Mary S. *The Sisters*   920.72

Mitnick, Kevin D.
  The Art of Invisibility   005.8
  Ghost in the Wires   B

MITNICK, KEVIN D. (KEVIN DAVID), 1963-
  Mitnick, Kevin D. *Ghost in the Wires*   B

The Mitten Handbook. Huff, Mary Scott   746.43

MITTENS
  Huff, Mary Scott. *The Mitten Handbook*   746.43

Mitter, Rana
  Forgotten Ally   951.04

MIXED MARTIAL ARTS
  Gracie, Rickson. *Breathe*   B
  Wertheim, L. Jon. *Blood in the Cage*   796.815

MIXTAPES
  Mike D. *Beastie Boys Book*   782.42164

Mizrahi, Isaac
  I.M.   B

MIZRAHI, ISAAC
  Mizrahi, Isaac. *I.M.*   B

Mizuki, Shigeru
  Showa 1926-1939   741.5

Mlodinow, Leonard
  Emotional   152.4
  Stephen Hawking   B

MLODINOW, LEONARD, 1954-
  Mlodinow, Leonard. *Stephen Hawking*   B

MNEMONICS
  Foer, Joshua. *Moonwalking with Einstein*   153.1
  Fogler, Janet. *Improving Your Memory*   153.1

Mo' Meta Blues. Questlove   782.42164

MOBILE, ALABAMA
  Durkin, Hannah. ★*The Survivors of the Clotilda*   306.362
  Tabor, Nick. *Africatown*   976.1

Mobituaries. Rocca, Mo   920

Moby
  Porcelain   B
  Then It Fell Apart   B

MOBY
  Moby. *Porcelain*   B
  Moby. *Then It Fell Apart*   B

Mochi's War. Enss, Chris   B

MOCHI, APPROXIMATELY 1841-1881
  Enss, Chris. *Mochi's War*   B

Mock, Janet
  Surpassing Certainty   B

MOCK, JANET, 1983-
  Mock, Janet. *Surpassing Certainty*   B

MODEL T AUTOMOBILE
  Brinkley, Douglas. *Wheels for the World*   B

The Model Thinker. Page, Scott E   001.4

MODELS AND MODEL MAKING
  Garfield, Simon. *In Miniature*   745.5928
  Thompson, Erica. *Escape from Model Land*   511

Models of Influence. Barker, Nigel   746.92092

MODERATION
  Walker, Hunter. *The Truce*   324.2736

Modern Architecture Since 1900. Curtis, William J. R.   724

MODERN ART
  Arnason, H. Harvard. ★*History of Modern Art*   709.04
  Barnes, Julian. *Keeping an Eye Open*   709.04
  Gompertz, Will. *What Are You Looking At?*   709
  Herrera, Hayden. *Listening to Stone*
  Knausgaard, Karl Ove. *So Much Longing in so Little Space*   759.81
  Naifeh, Steven W. *Van Gogh*   B
  Salle, David. *How to See*   709.04
  Shnayerson, Michael. *Boom*   701
  Smee, Sebastian. *The Art of Rivalry*   700.92
  Sykes, Christopher Simon. *David Hockney*   B
  Sykes, Christopher Simon. *David Hockney*   B
  Tomlinson, Janis A. ★*Goya*   B
  Unger, Miles. *Picasso and the Painting That Shocked the World*   759.4

AUTHOR, TITLE, SERIES AND SUBJECT INDEX

MODERN ARTS
   Morris, Desmond. *The Lives of the Surrealists*   B
   Morrison, Robert. *The Regency Years*   941.07
Modern Calligraphy. Thorpe, Molly Suber   745.6
Modern Calligraphy Workshop. Owen, Imogen   745.6
★*Modern Comfort Food.* Garten, Ina   641.5
The *Modern Cottage Garden.* Loades, Greg   635
MODERN DANCE
   Duncan, Isadora. *My Life*   B
   Fuhrer, Margaret. ★*American Dance*   792.809
   Guillermoprieto, Alma. *Dancing with Cuba*   972.9106
Modern Death. Warraich, Haider   179.7
The *Modern Detective.* Maroney, Tyler   658.4
Modern Fabric. Gilchrist, Abby   746.092
MODERN HISTORY
   Dyson, Freeman J. *Maker of Patterns*   B
   French, Howard W. *Born in Blackness*   960
   Kennedy, Paul M. *The Rise and Fall of the Great Powers*   909.82
   Kurlansky, Mark. *1968*   909.82
   MacGregor, Neil. *A History of the World in 100 Objects*   930.1
   Tuchman, Barbara W. *March of Folly*   909.08
   Tuchman, Barbara W. *The Proud Tower*   909.82
   Winchester, Simon. ★*The Perfectionists*   620.009
A Modern History of Japan. Gordon, Andrew   952
Modern Jewish Comfort Food. Sarna, Shannon   641.5
The *Modern* Library classics [Series]. Aristotle   185
The *Modern Library Writer's Workshop.* Koch, Stephen   808.3
MODERN LITERATURE
   Kundera, Milan. *Encounter*   809
   Mantel, Hilary. *Mantel Pieces*   824.914
   Moore, Lorrie. *See What Can Be Done*   801
   Spiegelman, Art. *Metamaus*   B
Modern Machine Quilting. Redford, Catherine   746.46
Modern Macrame. Katz, Emily   746.42
MODERN MUSIC
   Swafford, Jan. *Charles Ives*   B
Modern Patchwork. Hartman, Elizabeth   746.46
Modern Quilt Magic. Wolfe, Victoria Findlay   746.46
MODERNISM (AESTHETICS)
   English, Charlie. *The Gallery of Miracles and Madness*   709.04
   Perl, Jed. *Calder*   B
   Perl, Jed. ★*Calder*   B
MODERNISM (ART)
   English, Charlie. *The Gallery of Miracles and Madness*   709.04
   Roe, Sue. *In Montmartre*   920
   Secrest, Meryle. *Modigliani*   B
   Ustvedt, Oystein. *Edvard Munch*   759.81
   Warren, Rosanna. *Max Jacob*   B
MODERNISM (LITERATURE)
   Bowker, Gordon. ★*James Joyce*   B
MODERNIZATION (SOCIAL SCIENCES)
   Ansary, Mir Tamim. *Games Without Rules*   958.1
   Hoyer, Katja. ★*Beyond the Wall*   943.087
   Mazower, Mark. *The Greek Revolution*   949.5
Modigliani. Secrest, Meryle   B
MODIGLIANI, AMEDEO, 1884-1920
   Roe, Sue. *In Montmartre*   920
   Secrest, Meryle. *Modigliani*   B
Moe, John
   The Hilarious World of Depression   616.85
MOE, JOHN
   Moe, John. *The Hilarious World of Depression*   616.85
MOGADISHU, SOMALIA
   Bowden, Mark. *Black Hawk Down*   967.7305
Mogel, Wendy
   Voice Lessons for Parents   649
Mogelson, Luke
   The Storm Is Here   973.933
MOGELSON, LUKE
   Mogelson, Luke. *The Storm Is Here*   973.933
Moghul, Haroon
   How to Be a Muslim   B
MOGHUL, HAROON
   Moghul, Haroon. *How to Be a Muslim*   B
Mohammadi, Kamin
   Bella Figura   641.01
MOHAMMADI, KAMIN
   Mohammadi, Kamin. *Bella Figura*   641.01

MOHAMMED BIN SALMAN, CROWN PRINCE OF SAUDI ARABIA, 1985-
   Hubbard, Ben (Journalist). *Mbs*   B
MOHAMMED REZA PAHLAVI, SHAH OF IRAN, 1919-1980
   Cooper, Andrew Scott. *The Fall of Heaven*   B
Mohan, Rohini
   The Seasons of Trouble   954.9303
MOHAWK (NORTH AMERICAN PEOPLE)
   Demos, John. *The Unredeemed Captive*   973.2
Mojica Rodriguez, Prisca Dorcas
   For Brown Girls with Sharp Edges and Tender Hearts   305.48
MOJICA RODRIGUEZ, PRISCA DORCAS, 1985-
   Mojica Rodriguez, Prisca Dorcas. *For Brown Girls with Sharp Edges and Tender Hearts*   305.48
MOLECULAR BIOLOGISTS
   Maddox, Brenda. *Rosalind Franklin*   B
MOLECULAR BIOLOGY
   Cech, Thomas. *The Catalyst*   572.8
Molecules. Gray, Theodore W.   541
MOLECULES
   Gray, Theodore W. *Molecules*   541
   Gray, Theodore W. *Reactions*   530
   Miodownik, Mark. *Liquid Rules*   530.4
MOLES (ANIMALS)
   Catania, Kenneth. *Great Adaptations*   576.8
MOLES (SPIES)
   Vogel, Steve. *Betrayal in Berlin*   327.1273043
   Wiehl, Lis W. *A Spy in Plain Sight*   327.1247
MOLLUSKS
   Barnett, Cynthia. ★*The Sound of the Sea*   591.47
   Nicolson, Adam. *Life Between the Tides*   577.69
   Prasad, Aarathi. *Silk*   677
Molnar, Petra
   The Walls Have Eyes   363.28
The *Mom 100 Cookbook.* Workman, Katie   641.5
Mom Milestones. Farris, Grace   306.87
★*Mom Rage.* Dubin, Minna   306.874
Momaday, N. Scott
   ★*The Death of Sitting Bear*   811
   Earth Keeper   814
★*The Moment of Lift.* Gates, Melinda   305.42
Moments. Buell, Hal   070.4
Moments of Being. Woolf, Virginia   B
Momfluenced. Petersen, Sara   306.87
★*Mommy Burnout.* Ziegler, Sheryl   646.7
Momus
   Niche   B
MOMUS, 1960-
   Momus. *Niche*   B
Mona Lisa. Hales, Dianne R.   B
MONA LISA (PAINTING)
   Hales, Dianne R. *Mona Lisa*   B
MONACO
   Spoto, Donald. *High Society*   B
MONARCHY
   Borman, Tracy. *Anne Boleyn and Elizabeth I*   920
   Borman, Tracy. *Crown & Sceptre*   941
   Borman, Tracy. *The Private Lives of the Tudors*   920
   Brown, Tina. ★*The Palace Papers*   920
   Cadbury, Deborah. *Princes at War*   920
   Charter, David. *Royal Audience*   941.085
   Fraser, Antonia. *Mary, Queen of Scots*   B
   Fraser, Antonia. ★*The Wives of Henry VIII*   942.05
   Hardman, Robert. *Queen of Our Times*   B
   Hardman, Robert. *Queen of the World*   B
   Hibbert, Christopher. *Edward VII*   B
   Larman, Alexander. ★*Power and Glory*   941.085
   Meyer, G. J. *The Tudors*   920
   Paine, Thomas. ★*Rights of Man*   320.5
   Pakula, Hannah. *The Last Empress*   B
   Ridley, Jane. *George V*   B
   Ridley, Jane. *The Heir Apparent*   B
   Russell, Gareth. *Young and Damned and Fair*   B
   Sebag-Montefiore, Simon. *The Romanovs*   947
   Shawcross, William. *The Queen Mother*   B
   Smith, Sally Bedell. *Elizabeth the Queen*   B
   Worsley, Lucy. *Queen Victoria*   B
The *Monarchy of Fear.* Nussbaum, Martha Craven   306.20973

MONARCHY, FRENCH
    Fraser, Antonia. *Love and Louis XIV* — B
    Fraser, Antonia. *Marie Antoinette* — B
    Mansel, Philip. *King of the World* — B
MONASTERIES
    Iyer, Pico. *The Lady and the Monk* — 952
    Norris, Kathleen. *The Cloister Walk* — 255
The Monastic Heart. Chittister, Joan — 248.8
MONASTICISM AND RELIGIOUS ORDERS
    Chittister, Joan. *The Monastic Heart* — 248.8
    Norris, Kathleen. *Acedia & Me* — 248.8
    Norris, Kathleen. *The Cloister Walk* — 255
MONASTICISM AND RELIGIOUS ORDERS FOR WOMEN
    Coldstream, Catherine. ★*Cloistered* — B
Monbiot, George
    ★*Regenesis* — 338.1
Monet. Shackelford, George T. M. — 759.4
MONET, CLAUDE, 1840-1926
    King, Ross. ★*Mad Enchantment* — 759.4
    Shackelford, George T. M. *Monet* — 759.4
MONETARY POLICY
    Bernanke, Ben. ★*21st Century Monetary Policy* — 332.1
    Conway, Edmund. *The Summit* — 337.09
    Dikotter, Frank. *China After Mao* — 951.05
    Goldstein, Jacob. *Money* — 332.4
    Keynes, John Maynard. ★*The General Theory of Employment, Interest, and Money* — 330.15
    Ledbetter, James. *One Nation Under Gold* — 332.4
    Lowenstein, Roger. *Ways and Means* — 973.7
    Mallaby, Sebastian. *The Man Who Knew* — B
    McCraw, Thomas K. ★*The Founders and Finance* — 330.973
    Senik, Troy. *A Man of Iron* — B
    Smialek, Jeanna. ★*Limitless* — 332.1
    Steil, Benn. *The Battle of Bretton Woods* — 339.5
    Wessel, David. *In Fed We Trust* — 332.1
Money. Goldstein, Jacob — 332.4
MONEY
    Ariely, Dan. *Dollars and Sense* — 332.024
    Burrough, Bryan. *The Big Rich* — 338.2
    De Leon, Paco. *Finance for the People* — 332.024
    Goldstein, Jacob. *Money* — 332.4
    Hammond, Claudia. *Mind Over Money* — 332.401
    Hansberry, Lorraine. ★*A Raisin in the Sun* — 812
    Keynes, John Maynard. ★*The General Theory of Employment, Interest, and Money* — 330.15
    Lanchester, John. *How to Speak Money* — 330.1
    Lieber, Ron. *The Opposite of Spoiled* — 332.0240083
    McMillan, Tracie. ★*The White Bonus* — 305.8
    O'Connell, Mark. *A Thread of Violence* — 364.152
    Rosen, Charles. *Sugar* — B
    Sale, Anna. ★*Let's Talk About Hard Things* — 153.6
    Simmons, Lauren. *Make Money Move* — 332.024
    Sowell, Thomas. *Basic Economics* — 330
    Wenner, Jann. *Like a Rolling Stone* — B
    Yergin, Daniel. *The Quest* — 333.79
Money for Nothing. Austerlitz, Saul — 780.26
The Money Kings. Schulman, Daniel — 332.0973
MONEY LAUNDERING
    Bensinger, Ken. ★*Red Card* — 796.334
    Bullough, Oliver. *Moneyland* — 364.1
    Conn, David. *The Fall of the House of FIFA* — 796.334
    Michel, Casey. *American Kleptocracy* — 364.16
    Small, Zachary. ★*Token Supremacy* — 332.4
Money Magic. Kotlikoff, Laurence J. — 332.024
★*Moneyball*. Lewis, Michael — 796.357
Moneyland. Bullough, Oliver — 364.1
Monforton, Celeste
    On the Job — 331.1
Monger, George
    Marriage Customs of the World — 392.5
MONGOLIA
    McLynn, Frank. *Genghis Khan* — 950.2
    Prior-Palmer, Lara. *Rough Magic* — 798.4
    Weatherford, J. McIver. *Genghis Khan and the Quest for God* — 323.44
MONGOLS
    Marozzi, Justin. *Tamerlane* — 950.2
    McLynn, Frank. *Genghis Khan* — 950.2

    Weatherford, J. McIver. ★*Genghis Khan and the Making of the Modern World* — B
Monique and the Mango Rains. Holloway, Kris — B
The Monk in the Garden. Henig, Robin Marantz — B
The Monk of Mokha. Eggers, Dave — B
A Monk Swimming. McCourt, Malachy — B
Monkey Business. Louvish, Simon — B
Monks of New Skete
    The Art of Raising a Puppy — 636.7
MONOPOLIES
    Bown, Stephen R. *Merchant Kings* — 338.8
    Doran, Peter B. *Breaking Rockefeller* — 338.7
    Klobuchar, Amy. ★*Antitrust* — 343.73
    Mattioli, Dana. ★*The Everything War* — 381.142
    Neiman, Garrett. *Rich White Men* — 305.5
    Taplin, Jonathan. *Move Fast and Break Things* — 330.9
    Teachout, Zephyr. *Break 'Em Up* — 338.8
    Zaitchik, Alexander. *Owning the Sun* — 362.1
Monopolized. Dayen, David — 338.8
Monosson, Emily
    ★*Blight* — 616.9
MONOTHEISM
    Armstrong, Karen. *The Case for God* — 211
    Armstrong, Karen. ★*The Great Transformation* — 200.9
    Armstrong, Karen. *A History of God* — 202
    Armstrong, Karen. ★*Islam* — 297
    Armstrong, Karen. *Jerusalem* — 956.94
    Aslan, Reza. *God* — 211
    Darnell, John Coleman. *Egypt's Golden Couple* — 932
    Husain, Ed. ★*The House of Islam* — 297
MONROE DOCTRINE
    Kaplan, Fred. *John Quincy Adams* — B
MONROE, JAMES, 1758-1831
    Cheney, Lynne V. *The Virginia Dynasty* — B
    Gutzman, Kevin R. C. *The Jeffersonians* — 973.5
    McGrath, Tim. *James Monroe* — B
    Unger, Harlow G. *The Last Founding Father* — B
Monroe, Jana
    Hearts of Darkness — 363.25
MONROE, JANA
    Monroe, Jana. *Hearts of Darkness* — 363.25
MONROE, MARILYN, 1926-1962
    Casillo, Charles. *Marilyn Monroe* — B
    Cramer, Richard Ben. *Joe DiMaggio* — B
    Taraborrelli, J. Randy. ★*The Secret Life of Marilyn Monroe* — B
Monsoon Mansion. Barnes, Cinelle — B
The Monster. Hudson, Michael W. — 332.63
MONSTER FILMS
    O'Meara, Mallory. *The Lady from the Black Lagoon* — 921
    Weismann, Brad. *Lost in the Dark* — 791.43
Monster, She Wrote. Kroger, Lisa — 920
★*Monsters*. Dederer, Claire — 700.1
MONSTERS
    Braudy, Leo. *Haunted* — 398.45
    Carson, Anne. *Autobiography of Red* — 811
    Carson, Anne. *Red Doc* — 811
    Feder, Rachel. *The Darcy Myth* — 823
    Homer. *Odyssey* — 883
    O'Connor, John. *The Secret History of Bigfoot* — 001.944
    Zimmerman, Jess. *Women and Other Monsters* — 155.3
MONSTERS IN LITERATURE
    Montillo, Roseanne. *The Lady and Her Monsters* — 823
MONTAGU, EWEN, 1901-1985
    Macintyre, Ben. ★*Operation Mincemeat* — 940.54
MONTAIGNE, MICHEL DE, 1533-1592
    Bakewell, Sarah. *How to Live—Or—A Life of Montaigne* — B
    Frampton, Saul. *When I Am Playing with My Cat, How Do I Know She Is Not Playing with Me?* — 844
Montana. Dunnavant, Keith — B
MONTANA
    Bass, Rick. *Why I Came West* — 333.78
    Colton, Larry. *Counting Coup* — 796.323
    Connell, Evan S. *Son of the Morning Star* — 973.8
    Egan, Timothy. ★*The Big Burn* — 973.911
    Franscell, Ron. *Shadowman* — 362.88
    Grathwohl, Marya. *This Wheel of Rocks* — 271
    Philbrick, Nathaniel. ★*The Last Stand* — 973.8
    Raban, Jonathan. *Bad Land* — 978

AUTHOR, TITLE, SERIES AND SUBJECT INDEX

Streep, Abe. *Brothers on Three* — 306.85
Watts, Reggie. *Great Falls, MT* — B
MONTANA, JOE, 1956-
   Dunnavant, Keith. *Montana* — B
MONTAUK, NEW YORK
   Fairbanks, Amanda M. *The Lost Boys of Montauk* — 910.91
Montell, Amanda
   ★ *The Age of Magical Overthinking* — 153.4
Montenegro, Sonya
   Mending Life — 646
Montero, David
   ★ *The Stolen Wealth of Slavery* — 381
MONTES, ANA
   Popkin, Jim. *Code Name Blue Wren* — 327.12
★ *The Montessori Method.* Montessori, Maria — 372
MONTESSORI METHOD OF EDUCATION
   Alvarez, Celine. *The Natural Laws of Children* — 372.21
   Davies, Simone. *The Montessori Toddler* — 371.39
   De Stefano, Cristina. *The Child Is the Teacher* — B
   Montessori, Maria. ★ *The Montessori Method* — 372
   Seldin, Tim. *How to Raise an Amazing Child the Montessori Way* — 649
The Montessori Toddler. Davies, Simone — 371.39
Montessori, Maria
   ★ *The Montessori Method* — 372
MONTESSORI, MARIA, 1870-1952
   De Stefano, Cristina. *The Child Is the Teacher* — B
MONTEZUMA II, EMPEROR OF MEXICO, CA. 1480-1520
   Restall, Matthew. *When Montezuma Met Cortes* — 972
MONTGOMERY OF ALAMEIN, BERNARD LAW MONTGOMERY, VISCOUNT, 1887-1976
   Brighton, Terry. *Patton, Montgomery, Rommel* — B
   Clark, Lloyd. *The Commanders* — 940.53
MONTGOMERY, ALABAMA
   Jackson, Troy. *Becoming King* — B
   Theoharis, Jeanne. *The Rebellious Life of Mrs. Rosa Parks* — B
Montgomery, David R.
   What Your Food Ate — 631.4
Montgomery, Patrick
   Baseball's Great Expectations — 796.357
Montgomery, Sy
   The Good Good Pig — 636.4
   The Hawk's Way — 598.9
   How to Be a Good Creature — 590
   The Hummingbirds' Gift — 598.7
   ★ *Of Time and Turtles* — 597.92
MONTGOMERY, SY
   Montgomery, Sy. *The Good Good Pig* — 636.4
★ *The Month-By-Month Gardening Guide.* Bohmig, Franz — 635
MONTHS
   Englund, Peter. *November 1942* — 940.53
Montillo, Roseanne
   Deliberate Cruelty — 364.152
   Fire on the Track
   The Lady and Her Monsters — 823
MONTMARTRE, PARIS, FRANCE
   Roe, Sue. *In Montmartre* — 920
Montville, Leigh
   Sting Like a Bee — B
   Tall Men, Short Shorts — 796.323
MONTVILLE, LEIGH
   Montville, Leigh. *Tall Men, Short Shorts* — 796.323
★ *Monument.* Trethewey, Natasha D. — 811
Monument Man. Holzer, Harold — B
MONUMENTS
   Carlson, Brady. *Dead Presidents* — B
   Khan, Yasmin Sabina. *Enlightening the World* — 974.7
   Pryor, Francis. ★ *Stonehenge* — 936.2
   Thompson, Bob. *Revolutionary Roads* — 973.3
   Thompson, Erin L. *Smashing Statues* — 725
The Monuments Men. Edsel, Robert M. — 940.53
Mooallem, Jon
   Serious Face — 814
   Wild Ones — 333.95
MOOALLEM, JON
   Mooallem, Jon. *Wild Ones* — 333.95
Moody, Anne
   The Children Money Can Buy — 362.73

Moody, Anthony David
   Ezra Pound — B
Moody, Raymond A.
   Life After Life — 133.9
MOON
   Boyle, Rebecca. *Our Moon* — 523.3
   Brinkley, Douglas. ★ *American Moonshot* — 629.40973
   Donovan, Jim. ★ *Shoot for the Moon* — 629.45
   Fishman, Charles. ★ *One Giant Leap* — 629.45
   Nordgren, Tyler E. *Sun, Moon, Earth* — 523.7
The Moon That Turns You Back. Alyan, Hala — 811
MOON, MOLLIE
   Ford, Tanisha C. *Our Secret Society* — B
Mooncakes + Milk Bread. Cho, Kristina — 641.595
Mooney, Jonathan
   Normal Sucks — B
MOONEY, JONATHAN
   Mooney, Jonathan. *Normal Sucks* — B
Mooney, Paul
   Black Is the New White — 792.7
MOONEY, PAUL, 1941-2021
   Mooney, Paul. *Black Is the New White* — 792.7
MOONVES, LESLIE
   Stewart, James B. *Unscripted* — 658.1
Moonwalking with Einstein. Foer, Joshua — 153.1
Moore, Beth
   All My Knotted-Up Life — B
MOORE, BETH, 1957-
   Moore, Beth. *All My Knotted-Up Life* — B
Moore, Charles
   Margaret Thatcher — 941.085
Moore, Colten
   Catching the Sky — B
MOORE, COLTEN
   Moore, Colten. *Catching the Sky* — B
Moore, Harold G.
   We Are Soldiers Still — 959.704
   We Were Soldiers Once—And Young — 959.704
MOORE, HAROLD G., 1922-2017
   Moore, Harold G. *We Are Soldiers Still* — 959.704
Moore, Kate
   The Radium Girls — 363.17
   ★ *The Woman They Could Not Silence* — B
Moore, Kathleen Dean
   Earth's Wild Music — 576.8
Moore, Lorrie
   See What Can Be Done — 801
Moore, Marcus J.
   The Butterfly Effect — B
Moore, Marianne
   New Collected Poems — 811
   The Selected Letters of Marianne Moore — B
MOORE, MARIANNE, 1887-1972
   Moore, Marianne. *The Selected Letters of Marianne Moore* — B
Moore, Matt
   Serial Griller — 641.7
Moore, Michael Scott
   The Desert and the Sea — 364.15
MOORE, MICHAEL SCOTT
   Moore, Michael Scott. *The Desert and the Sea* — 364.15
Moore, Peter
   Life, Liberty, and the Pursuit of Happiness — 199
Moore, Rachel
   The Artist's Compass — 791
Moore, Sonia
   The Stanislavski System — 792
Moore, Susanna
   Miss Aluminum — 813
   Paradise of the Pacific — 996.9
MOORE, SUSANNA
   Moore, Susanna. *Miss Aluminum* — 813
Moore, Thomas
   Ageless Soul — 155.67
Moore, Thurston
   Sonic Life — B
MOORE, THURSTON
   Moore, Thurston. *Sonic Life* — B

PUBLIC LIBRARY CORE COLLECTION: NONFICTION
Twentieth Edition

Moore, Tim
   The Cyclist Who Went Out in the Cold — 796.6
MOORE, TIM, 1964-
   Moore, Tim. *The Cyclist Who Went Out in the Cold* — 796.6
Moore, Wayetu
   The Dragons, the Giant, the Women — B
MOORE, WAYETU
   Moore, Wayetu. *The Dragons, the Giant, the Women* — B
Moore, Wendy
   No Man's Land — 940.4
Moore, Wes
   ★*Five Days* — 363.32
   The Other Wes Moore — B
   The Work — B
MOORE, WES, 1975-
   Moore, Wes. *The Other Wes Moore* — B
MOORE, WES, 1978-
   Moore, Wes. *The Other Wes Moore* — B
   Moore, Wes. *The Work* — B
Moorehead, Caroline
   A House in the Mountains — 940.53
   A Train in Winter — 940.53
   Village of Secrets — 944
Moorer, Allison
   I Dream He Talks to Me — 782.42164
MOORER, ALLISON
   Moorer, Allison. *I Dream He Talks to Me* — 782.42164
Moorhouse, Roger
   Berlin at War — 943
   The Devils' Alliance — 940.53
   The Forgers — 940.53
★*The Moosewood Cookbook*. Katzen, Mollie — 641.5
Moral Combat. Griffith, R. Marie — 261.8
MORAL CONDITIONS
   Barber, William J. *We Are Called to Be a Movement* — 261.8
   Callahan, David. *The Cheating Culture* — 174
   Holland, Tom. *Dominion* — 261
   Sohn, Amy. *The Man Who Hated Women* — 363.28
MORAL DEVELOPMENT
   Hawthorne, Britt. ★*Raising Antiracist Children* — 649
The Moral Lives of Animals. Peterson, Dale — 156
MORALE
   Korda, Michael. *Alone* — 940.54
Morales, Bonnie Frumkin
   Kachka — 641.594
The Moralist. O'Toole, Patricia — B
Moran, Caitlin
   How to Be a Woman — B
   More Than a Woman — B
   What About Men? — 155.3
MORAN, CAITLIN, 1975-
   Moran, Caitlin. *How to Be a Woman* — B
   Moran, Caitlin. *More Than a Woman* — B
Moran, Joe
   Shrinking Violets — 155.2
Moran, Rachel
   Paid For — 306.74082
MORAN, RACHEL
   Moran, Rachel. *Paid For* — 306.74082
Mordden, Ethan
   Anything Goes — 782.1
   Ziegfeld — B
Morduch, Jonathan
   The Financial Diaries — 332.024
More. Winter, Molly Roden — B
A More Beautiful and Terrible History. Theoharis, Jeanne — 323.1196
More Lovely Knitted Lace. Nico, Brooke — 746.43
★*More Mexican Everyday*. Bayless, Rick — 641.5972
The More of Less. Becker, Joshua — 241
More of You. Beck, Amanda Martinez — 613
A More Perfect Heaven. Sobel, Dava — 520.9
A More Perfect Reunion. Baker, Calvin — 305.800973
More Than a Woman. Moran, Caitlin — B
More Than Enough. Welteroth, Elaine — B
More Than True. Bly, Robert — 398.2
More, Please. Specter, Emma — 616.85
MORE, THOMAS, SAINT, 1478-1535
   Bolt, Robert. *A Man for All Seasons* — 822

Morgan, Abi
   This Is Not a Pity Memoir — B
MORGAN, ABI
   Morgan, Abi. *This Is Not a Pity Memoir* — B
MORGAN, DANIEL, 1736-1802
   Crawford, Alan Pell. *This Fierce People* — 975
   Zambone, Albert Louis. *Daniel Morgan* — B
Morgan, Genevieve
   Undecided — 331.702
MORGAN, JOHN PIERPONT, 1837-1913
   Berfield, Susan. *The Hour of Fate* — 973.91
Morgan, Robert
   Boone — B
   Lions of the West — 978
Morgan, Wesley
   The Hardest Place — 958.104
MORGAN, WILLIAM, 1928-1961
   Sallah, Michael. *The Yankee Comandante* — 972.91
Morgan-Owens, Jessie
   Girl in Black and White — B
Morgenson, Gretchen
   ★*These Are the Plunderers* — 332.6
Morgenstern, Dan
   Living with Jazz — 781.65
Morgenstern, Julie
   Time to Parent — 649
MORGENTHAU, HENRY, 1891-1967
   Beschloss, Michael R. *The Conquerors* — 940.53
Morgue. Di Maio, Vincent J. M. — B
Morimoto, Masaharu
   Mastering the Art of Japanese Home Cooking — 641.595
Morin, Amy
   13 Things Mentally Strong Parents Don't Do — 649
   13 Things Mentally Strong Women Don't Do — 158.1
Morin, John
   Inspired Origami — 736.982
Morison, Samuel Eliot
   John Paul Jones — B
Morley, Jefferson
   Scorpions' Dance — 973.924
Morley, Paul
   The Age of Bowie — B
MORMON POLYGAMY
   Beam, Alex. *American Crucifixion* — B
MORMON THEOLOGY
   Brown, Samuel Morris. *In Heaven as It Is on Earth* — 289.3
   Bushman, Richard L. *Mormonism* — 289.3
   Park, Benjamin E. *American Zion* — 289.3
   Wariner, Ruth. *The Sound of Gravel* — B
MORMON WOMEN
   Wariner, Ruth. *The Sound of Gravel* — B
Mormonism. Bushman, Richard L. — 289.3
MORMONS
   Arrington, Leonard J. *Brigham Young* — B
   Beam, Alex. *American Crucifixion* — B
   Black, Dustin Lance. *Mama's Boy* — B
   Cooper, Alex. *Saving Alex* — B
   Denton, Sally. *The Colony* — 364.152
   Glatt, John. *The Doomsday Mother* — 364.152
   Gutjahr, Paul C. *The Book of Mormon* — 289.3
   Kushner, Tony. *Angels in America* — 812
   Park, Benjamin E. *American Zion* — 289.3
   Turner, John G. *Brigham Young, Pioneer Prophet* — B
   Walker, Ronald W. ★*Massacre at Mountain Meadows* — 979.2
   Wariner, Ruth. *The Sound of Gravel* — B
   Young, Steve. *QB* — B
The Morning They Came for Us. Di Giovanni, Janine — 956.9104
Mornings on Horseback. McCullough, David G. — B
Mornu, Nathalie
   Embroider Your Life — 746.44
MOROCCO
   Hindley, Meredith. *Destination Casablanca* — 940.54
MORPHINE ADDICTION
   Milford, Nancy. *Savage Beauty* — B
Morris, Benny
   1948 — 956.04
   Righteous Victims — 956

AUTHOR, TITLE, SERIES AND SUBJECT INDEX

Morris, Bonnie J.
   ★*The Feminist Revolution*   305.4209
Morris, David J.
   The Evil Hours   616.85
MORRIS, DAVID J., 1971-
   Morris, David J. *The Evil Hours*   616.85
Morris, Desmond
   The Lives of the Surrealists   B
Morris, Edmund
   Beethoven   B
   ★*Colonel Roosevelt*   B
   ★*Edison*   B
   The Rise of Theodore Roosevelt   B
   ★*Theodore Rex*   973.911
MORRIS, ELIZABETH CARRINGTON, 1795-1865
   McNeur, Catherine. *Mischievous Creatures*   920
Morris, Errol
   Believing Is Seeing   770.9
Morris, Ian
   Geography Is Destiny   941
Morris, James McGrath
   Eye on the Struggle   B
   Pulitzer   B
Morris, Jan
   A Writer's House in Wales   942.9
MORRIS, JAN, 1926-2020
   Morris, Jan. *A Writer's House in Wales*   942.9
Morris, Jim
   ★*The Cancer Factory*   658.3
Morris, Marc
   ★*The Anglo-Saxons*   942.01
   Castles   728.81
   A Great and Terrible King   B
   King John   942.033
   The Norman Conquest   942.02
MORRIS, MARGARETTA HARE, 1797-1867
   McNeur, Catherine. *Mischievous Creatures*   920
Morris, Mark
   Out Loud   B
MORRIS, MARK, 1956-
   Morris, Mark. *Out Loud*   B
MORRISON, JIM, 1943-1971
   Hopkins, Jerry. *No One Here Gets Out Alive*   B
Morrison, Melanie
   Murder on Shades Mountain   345.761
Morrison, Robert
   The Regency Years   941.07
Morrison, Simon Alexander
   Bolshoi Confidential   792.8
Morrison, Toni
   ★*The Origin of Others*   809
   Playing in the Dark   810.9
   ★*The Source of Self-Regard*   814
MORRISON, TONI, 1931-2019
   Gillespie, Carmen. *Critical Companion to Toni Morrison*   813
   Verdelle, A. J. *Miss Chloe*   B
Morrissey, Sinead
   Parallax   821
Mort, T. A.
   Thieves' Road   978.3
★*Mortal Secrets*. Tallis, Frank   B
MORTALITY
   Ali, Fatima. ★*Savor*   B
   Arthur, Alua. ★*Briefly Perfectly Human*   306.9
   Becker, Ernest. ★*The Denial of Death*   128
   Bowler, Kate. *No Cure for Being Human*   B
   Boyer, Anne. *The Undying*   B
   Collins, Billy. *Whale Day*   811
   Doughty, Caitlin. *From Here to Eternity*   393
   Doughty, Caitlin. *Will My Cat Eat My Eyeballs?*   306.9
   Fox, Michael J. *No Time Like the Future*   B
   Gluck, Louise. *Winter Recipes from the Collective*   811
   Graham, Jorie. *To 2040*   811
   Hitchens, Christopher. *Mortality*   304.6
   Kerr, Christopher. *Death Is but a Dream*   155.9
   Leder, Steven Z. *The Beauty of What Remains*   306.9
   Limon, Ada. *Bright Dead Things*   811
   McPhee, John. *Tabula Rasa; V.1*   818

   Ritvo, Max. *The Final Voicemails*   811
   Ruhl, Sarah. *Letters from Max*   811
   Seidel, Frederick. ★*Frederick Seidel Selected Poems*   811
   Shanahan, Charif. *Trace Evidence*   811
   Solnit, Rebecca. *The Faraway Nearby*   814
   Thomas, Elizabeth Marshall. *Growing Old*   305.26
   Vuong, Ocean. ★*Time Is a Mother*   811
   Williams, C. K. *Falling Ill*   811
   Yalom, Irvin D. *Staring at the Sun*   155.9
Mortality. Hitchens, Christopher   304.6
MORTGAGE BACKED SECURITIES
   Hudson, Michael W. *The Monster*   332.63
   McLean, Bethany. *All the Devils Are Here*   330.973
MORTGAGE LOANS
   Elias, Stephen. *The Foreclosure Survival Guide, 9th Ed.*   346.7304
The Mortgage Wars. Howard, Timothy   332.7
MORTGAGES
   Dayen, David. *Chain of Title*   330.973
   Howard, Timothy. *The Mortgage Wars*   332.7
   Hudson, Michael W. *The Monster*   332.63
   McLean, Bethany. *All the Devils Are Here*   330.973
Mortimer, Frank
   Bee People and the Bugs They Love   B
MORTIMER, FRANK
   Mortimer, Frank. *Bee People and the Bugs They Love*   B
Mortimer, Gavin
   The Great Swim   B
Mortimer, Ian
   The Time Traveler's Guide to Elizabethan England   942.05
   The Time Traveler's Guide to Restoration Britain   941.06
MORTIMER, KATHLEEN LANIER HARRIMAN, 1917-2011
   Katz, Catherine Grace. *The Daughters of Yalta*   920
Morton, Andrew
   17 Carnations   941.084
   Diana   B
   Wallis in Love   B
Morton, Brian
   ★*The Penguin Jazz Guide*   016
   Tasha   B
MORTON, BRIAN, 1955-
   Morton, Brian. *Tasha*   B
Morton, Lisa
   Trick or Treat   394.2646
Morton, Michael
   Getting Life   B
MOSADDEQ, MOHAMMAD, 1880-1967
   Kinzer, Stephen. ★*All the Shah's Men*   955.05
Mosaic Garden Projects. Brody, Mark   712
MOSAICS
   Brody, Mark. *Mosaic Garden Projects*   712
MOSCOW, RUSSIA
   Alekhina, Mariija. *Riot Days*   B
   Petrushevskaia, Liudmila. *The Girl from the Metropol Hotel*   B
   Slezkine, Yuri. *The House of Government*   947.084
Moser, Benjamin
   ★*Sontag*   B
   Why This World   B
MOSER, JOSEPH F.
   Clavin, Thomas. *Lightning Down*   940.54
MOSES (BIBLICAL LEADER)
   Kushner, Harold S. *Overcoming Life's Disappointments*   296.7
MOSES, ROBERT, 1888-1981
   Caro, Robert A. *The Power Broker*   B
Moskowitz, Isa Chandra
   The Superfun Times Vegan Holiday Cookbook   651.56
   Veganomicon   641
Mosley, Walter
   Elements of Fiction   808.3
MOSQUES
   Trofimov, Yaroslav. *The Siege of Mecca*   953.805
★*The Mosquito Bowl*. Bissinger, H. G.   796.332
Moss, Adam
   ★*The Work of Art*   701
Moss, Charlotte
   Garden Inspirations   747
Moss, Gabrielle
   Paperback Crush   813.009

PUBLIC LIBRARY CORE COLLECTION: NONFICTION
Twentieth Edition

Moss, Jeremiah
   Feral City — B
MOSS, JEREMIAH, 1971-
   Moss, Jeremiah. *Feral City* — B
Moss, Marissa R.
   Her Country — 781.642
Moss, Michael
   ★*Hooked* — 613.2
   Salt, Sugar, Fat — 613.2
MOSSAD AGENTS
   Friedman, Matti. *Spies of No Country* — 327.12
   Talty, Stephan. *The Good Assassin* — 364.15
The Most Beautiful. Garcia, Mayte — 920
★*Most Blessed of the Patriarchs.* Gordon-Reed, Annette — 973.4
The Most Dangerous Branch. Kaplan, David A. — 347.73
The Most Dangerous Man in America. Minutaglio, Bill — B
The Most Dangerous Man in America. Perry, Mark — B
A Most Improbable Journey. Alvarez, Walter — 550
The Most of Nora Ephron. Ephron, Nora — 814
A Most Remarkable Creature. Meiburg, Jonathan — 598.9
A Most Tolerant Little Town. Martin, Rachel Louise — 379.2
Mostly Veggies. Mullins, Brittany — 641.5
Mostly What God Does. Guthrie, Savannah — 248.4
MOSUL, IRAQ
   Findakly, Brigitte. *Poppies of Iraq* — 741.5
   Philipps, David. *Alpha* — 956.7044
   Verini, James. *They Will Have to Die Now* — 956.7044
The Moth and the Mountain. Caesar, Ed — B
Mother American Night. Barlow, John Perry — 782.42164
MOTHER AND ADULT DAUGHTER
   Allende, Isabel. ★*Paula* — B
   Lang, Maya. *What We Carry* — B
MOTHER AND ADULT SON
   Cooper, Anderson. *The Rainbow Comes and Goes* — B
   Schwalbe, Will. ★*The End of Your Life Book Club* — B
MOTHER AND BABY
   Brickman, Sophie. *Baby, Unplugged* — 306.874
MOTHER AND CHILD
   Brickman, Sophie. *Baby, Unplugged* — 306.874
   Casares, Whitney. *The Working Mom Blueprint* — 306.8743
   Farris, Grace. *Mom Milestones* — 306.87
   Fennelly, Beth Ann. *Heating & Cooling* — B
   Fisher, Todd. *My Girls* — B
   Harris, Taylor. *This Boy We Made* — B
   Pablo Cruz, Rosayra. *The Book of Rosy* — B
   Philpott, Mary Laura. *Bomb Shelter* — B
   Shaughnessy, Brenda. *The Octopus Museum* — 811
   Singh, Julietta. *The Breaks* — B
   Whitney, Emerson. *Heaven* — B
Mother Brain. Conaboy, Chelsea — 306.874
The Mother of All Questions. Solnit, Rebecca — 305.42
Mother of Invention. Marcal, Katrine — 604.82
★*Mother Tongue.* Nuttall, Jennifer Anne — 422
MOTHER-DESERTED CHILDREN
   Koh, EJ. *The Magical Language of Others* — 813
MOTHER-SEPARATED CHILDREN
   Edelman, Hope. *Motherless Daughters* — 155.9
   Glaser, Gabrielle. *American Baby* — B
   Henderson, Danielle. ★*The Ugly Cry* — B
   Nguyen, Bich Minh. *Owner of a Lonely Heart* — B
MOTHER-SEPARATED TEENAGERS
   Haddish, Tiffany. *The Last Black Unicorn* — B
MOTHERHOOD
   Baer, Kate. *What Kind of Woman* — 811
   Barker, Elspeth. ★*Notes from the Henhouse* — 828
   Beauvais, Garcelle. *Love Me as I Am* — B
   Berg, Anastasia. ★*What Are Children For?* — 306.87
   Berger, Lynn. *Second Thoughts* — 306.85
   Casares, Whitney. *The Working Mom Blueprint* — 306.8743
   Chang, Tina. *Hybrida* — 811
   Cleage, Pearl. *Things I Should Have Told My Daughter* — B
   Clifton, Lucille. *How to Carry Water* — 811
   Conaboy, Chelsea. *Mother Brain* — 306.874
   Corrigan, Kelly. *Glitter and Glue* — B
   Cusk, Rachel. *Coventry* — 814
   Cusk, Rachel. *A Life's Work* — 306.874
   Driver, Minnie. *Managing Expectations* — B
   Dubin, Minna. ★*Mom Rage* — 306.874
   Dungy, Camille T. *Soil* — 635.0978
   Farris, Grace. *Mom Milestones* — 306.87
   Field, Sally. *In Pieces* — B
   Frangello, Gina. *Blow Your House Down* — 813
   Franklin, Ruth. *Shirley Jackson* — B
   Gaines, Joanna. *The Stories We Tell* — B
   Garbes, Angela. *Essential Labor* — 306.874
   Glenconner, Anne. ★*Lady in Waiting* — B
   Grose, Jessica. *Screaming on the Inside* — 306.874
   Harjo, Joy. *Catching the Light* — 818
   Harris, Taylor. *This Boy We Made* — B
   Hatmaker, Jen. *Of Mess and Moxie* — 248.8
   Hazleton, Lesley. *Mary* — B
   Jamison, Leslie. ★*Make It Scream, Make It Burn* — 814
   Jones, Chloe Cooper. ★*Easy Beauty* — B
   Jones, Lucy. ★*Matrescence* — 306.874
   Khar, Erin. *Strung Out* — B
   Klein, Jessi. *I'll Show Myself Out* — B
   Lemay, Mimi. *What We Will Become* — 306.874
   Levy, Deborah. ★*Things I Don't Want to Know* — B
   Lippman, Laura. *My Life as a Villainess* — B
   Lowman, Margaret. *Life in the Treetops* — B
   Mehra, Nishta. *Brown, White, Black* — 305.800973
   Millwood, Molly. *To Have and to Hold* — 306.874
   Nathan, Joan. ★*My Life in Recipes* — 641.5
   Nezhukumatathil, Aimee. *World of Wonders* — 590
   Nguyen, Bich Minh. *Owner of a Lonely Heart* — B
   Nooyi, Indra. ★*My Life in Full* — B
   O'Donnell Heffington, Peggy. *Without Children* — 306.85
   O'Hara, Maryanne. *Little Matches* — B
   Peters, Rebecca Todd. *Trust Women* — 362.1988
   Petersen, Sara. *Momfluenced* — 306.87
   Plath, Sylvia. *The Letters of Sylvia Plath* — 811.54
   Porizkova, Paulina. *No Filter* — B
   Psaki, Jen. *Say More* — B
   Qadiri, Humayra. *Dancing in the Mosque* — B
   Quave, Cassandra Leah. *The Plant Hunter* — 581.6
   Reichl, Ruth. *Comfort Me with Apples* — B
   Reynolds, Debbie. *Make 'Em Laugh* — B
   Ricanati, Elizabeth. *Braided* — B
   Rodgers, Mary. *Shy* — B
   Rush, Charaia. *Courageously Soft* — 234
   Sanchez, Erika L. *Crying in the Bathroom* — B
   Shields, Aomawa L. *Life on Other Planets* — B
   Sisson, Gretchen E. ★*Relinquished* — 362.734
   Southon, Emma. *Agrippina* — B
   Spears, Britney. *The Woman in Me* — B
   Szczeszak-Brewer, Agata. *The Hunger Book* — B
   Tubbs, Anna Malaika. *The Three Mothers* — 306.874
   Union, Gabrielle. *You Got Anything Stronger?* — B
   Warner, Judith. *Perfect Madness* — 306.874
   Winter, Molly Roden. *More* — B
   Worsley, Lucy. *Queen Victoria* — B
   Zambreno, Kate. *The Light Room* — B
   Ziegler, Sheryl. ★*Mommy Burnout* — 646.7
Motherhood so White. Austin, Nefertiti — B
MOTHERING
   Saxton, Martha. *The Widow Washington* — B
   Shirley, Craig. *Mary Ball Washington* — B
   Singh, Julietta. *The Breaks* — B
Motherless Daughters. Edelman, Hope — 155.9
The Motherlode. Hope, Clover — 920
MOTHERS
   Ahmed, Azam. *Fear Is Just a Word* — 364.152
   Blair, Selma. *Mean Baby* — B
   Bond, Melissa. *Blood Orange Night* — 616.8
   Carcaterra, Lorenzo. *Three Dreamers* — B
   Cusk, Rachel. *A Life's Work* — 306.874
   DiGregorio, Sarah. *Early* — 618.92
   Ervin, Kristine S. *Rabbit Heart* — 364.152
   Farris, Grace. *Mom Milestones* — 306.87
   Gaffigan, Jeannie. *When Life Gives You Pears* — B
   Garbes, Angela. *Essential Labor* — 306.874
   Glass, Sara. *Kissing Girls on Shabbat* — B
   Goldberg, Whoopi. *Bits and Pieces* — B
   Grose, Jessica. *Screaming on the Inside* — 306.874
   Jones, Lucy. ★*Matrescence* — 306.874
   Martin, Wednesday. *Primates of Park Avenue* — 974.7

AUTHOR, TITLE, SERIES AND SUBJECT INDEX

McBride, James. *The Color of Water*	B
McCann, Colum. *American Mother*	956.9104
Millwood, Molly. *To Have and to Hold*	306.874
Moore, Wayetu. *The Dragons, the Giant, the Women*	B
Obama, Michelle. ★*The Light We Carry*	B
Petersen, Sara. *Momfluenced*	306.87
Pritchett, Georgia. *My Mess Is a Bit of a Life*	B
Qadiri, Humayra. *Dancing in the Mosque*	B
Raboteau, Emily. *Lessons for Survival*	814
Riggs, Nina. *The Bright Hour*	B
Ruhl, Sarah. *Smile*	B
Sardy, Marin. *The Edge of Every Day*	B
Smith, Carol. *Crossing the River*	B
Tometich, Annabelle. *The Mango Tree*	B
Tubbs, Anna Malaika. *The Three Mothers*	306.874
Warner, Judith. *Perfect Madness*	306.874
Willner, Nina. *Forty Autumns*	B
Zauner, Michelle. ★*Crying in H Mart*	B
Ziegler, Sheryl. ★*Mommy Burnout*	646.7

MOTHERS AND DAUGHTERS

Berg, Elizabeth. *I'll Be Seeing You*	306.874
Borman, Tracy. *Anne Boleyn and Elizabeth I*	920
Brown, Tina. *The Diana Chronicles*	B
Chang, Jung. ★*Wild Swans*	B
Cho, Grace M. *Tastes Like War*	305.48
Corrigan, Kelly. *Glitter and Glue*	B
Craig, Mya-Rose. *Birdgirl*	B
Didion, Joan. ★*The Year of Magical Thinking*	B
Edelman, Hope. *Motherless Daughters*	155.9
Erdrich, Louise. *Books and Islands in Ojibwe Country*	977
Field, Sally. *In Pieces*	B
Geller, Danielle. *Dog Flowers*	B
Goldstone, Nancy Bazelon. *In the Shadow of the Empress*	920
Goldstone, Nancy Bazelon. *The Rival Queens*	944
Gordon, Charlotte. *Romantic Outlaws*	920
Hacker, Marilyn. *Selected Poems, 1965-1990*	811
Harden, Marcia Gay. *The Seasons of My Mother*	B
Hulls, Tessa. ★*Feeding Ghosts*	741.5
Kelly, Minka. ★*Tell Me Everything*	B
Kingston, Genevieve. *Did I Ever Tell You?*	B
Koh, EJ. *The Magical Language of Others*	813
Lang, Maya. *What We Carry*	B
Laux, Dorianne. *Only as the Day Is Long*	811
Loh, Sandra Tsing. *The Madwoman and the Roomba*	B
Lowry, Beverly. *Deer Creek Drive*	364.152
Mailhot, Terese Marie. *Heart Berries*	B
Margulies, Julianna. *Sunshine Girl*	B
McBride, Karyl. *Will I Ever Be Good Enough?*	616.85
McColl, Sarah. *Joy Enough*	B
Means, Brittany. *Hell If We Don't Change Our Ways*	B
Milford, Nancy. *Savage Beauty*	B
Miller, Michelle. *Belonging*	B
Mulgrew, Kate. *Born with Teeth*	791.45028
Myers, Leah. *Thinning Blood*	B
Nguyen, Bich Minh. *Owner of a Lonely Heart*	B
Nguyen, Hoa. *A Thousand Times You Lose Your Treasure*	811
O'Hara, Maryanne. *Little Matches*	B
Orenstein, Peggy. *Cinderella Ate My Daughter*	305.23082
Qu, Anna. *Made in China*	B
Reang, Putsata. *Ma and Me*	B
Rojas Contreras, Ingrid. ★*The Man Who Could Move Clouds*	B
Rowe, Peggy. *About My Mother*	B
Scheier, Liz. *Never Simple*	B
Scottoline, Lisa. *I See Life Through Rose-Colored Glasses*	813
Solnit, Rebecca. *The Faraway Nearby*	814
Spiegelman, Nadja. ★*I'm Supposed to Protect You from All This*	741.5
Szczeszak-Brewer, Agata. *The Hunger Book*	B
Taraborrelli, J. Randy. *Jackie, Janet & Lee*	920
Taraborrelli, J. Randy. ★*The Secret Life of Marilyn Monroe*	B
Wang, Connie. *Oh My Mother!*	B
Williams, Marlena. *Night Mother*	791.43
Wong, Ali. ★*Dear Girls*	B
Zauner, Michelle. ★*Crying in H Mart*	B

MOTHERS AND SONS

Alexie, Sherman. *You Don't Have to Say You Love Me*	818
Andersen, Christopher P. *The Good Son*	B
Black, Dustin Lance. *Mama's Boy*	B
Bragg, Rick. ★*The Best Cook in the World*	641.5975
Caruana Galizia, Paul. ★*A Death in Malta*	364.15
Cooper, Anderson. *The Rainbow Comes and Goes*	B
Fraser, Antonia. *Love and Louis XIV*	B
Hamill, Kirkland. *Filthy Beasts*	B
Jacob, Mira. *Good Talk*	741.5
Jones, Saeed. *How We Fight for Our Lives*	B
Laymon, Kiese. ★*Heavy*	B
McBride, James. *The Color of Water*	B
McCann, Colum. *American Mother*	956.9104
Mizrahi, Isaac. *I.M.*	B
Morton, Brian. *Tasha*	B
Newman, Magdalena. *Normal*	611
Noah, Trevor. *Born a Crime*	B
Qadiri, Humayra. *Dancing in the Mosque*	B
Robinson, Staci. ★*Tupac Shakur*	B
Sanchez, Aaron. *Where I Come From*	641.5092
Saxton, Martha. *The Widow Washington*	B
Shirley, Craig. *Mary Ball Washington*	B
Slouka, Mark. *Nobody's Son*	B
Tubbs, Anna Malaika. *The Three Mothers*	306.874
Vuong, Ocean. ★*Time Is a Mother*	811
Whippman, Ruth. ★*Boymom*	305.23
Wolff, Tobias. *This Boy's Life*	B
Yancey, Philip. ★*Where the Light Fell*	B
Zuckoff, Mitchell. *The Secret Gate*	958.104
Mothers of Invention. Faust, Drew Gilpin	973.7
Mothers, Fathers, and Others. Hustvedt, Siri	814

MOTHERS-IN-LAW

Wilson, Katherine. *Only in Naples*	B
Mothertrucker. Butcher, Amy	B

MOTHS

Prasad, Aarathi. *Silk*	677

MOTIVATION

Bargh, John A. *Before You Know It*	154.2
Becker, Ernest. ★*The Denial of Death*	128
Duhigg, Charles. *Smarter Faster Better*	158
Ehrenreich, Barbara. *Bright-Sided*	155.2
Fogg, B. J. *Tiny Habits*	158
Grant, Adam M. *Give and Take*	158.2
Grant, Adam M. *Hidden Potential*	153.8
Grover, Joanna. *The Choice Point*	158.1
Hansen, Morten T. *Great at Work*	650.1
Hanson, Victor Davis. *The Soul of Battle*	355
Keyes, Corey L. M. ★*Languishing*	152.1
Kline, Emily. ★*The School of Hard Talks*	155.5
Miranda, Lin-Manuel. *Gmorning, Gnight!*	811
Mueller, Jennifer. *Creative Change*	658.4
Peterson, Dale. *The Moral Lives of Animals*	156
Pink, Daniel H. *Drive*	153.1
Rinaldi, Karen. *It's Great to Suck at Something*	158.1
Sincero, Jen. *You Are a Badass Every Day*	158.1
Wojcicki, Esther. *How to Raise Successful People*	649

MOTLEY, CONSTANCE BAKER, 1921-2005

Brown-Nagin, Tomiko. *Civil Rights Queen*	B

MOTORCYCLE ACCIDENTS

Williams, Jay. *Life Is Not an Accident*	B

MOTORCYCLE GANGS

Croke, Ken. *Riding with Evil*	364.106
★*Motown*. White, Adam	781.644
★*Mott Street*. Chin, Ava	974.7

MOUA, IA

Hamilton, Lisa M. *The Hungry Season*	B

Moulton, Sara

Sara Moulton's Home Cooking 101	641.5973

MOULY, FRANCOISE

Spiegelman, Nadja. ★*I'm Supposed to Protect You from All This*	741.5

MOUNT DENALI (ALASKA)

Hall, Andy. *Denali's Howl*	796.522

MOUNT EVEREST

Bukreev, Anatolii Nikolaevich. *The Climb*	796.52
Caesar, Ed. *The Moth and the Mountain*	B
Coburn, Broughton. *Everest*	796.5
Davis, Wade. *Into the Silence*	B
Ellsworth, Scott. *The World Beneath Their Feet*	796.522
Krakauer, Jon. ★*Into Thin Air*	796.52
Lowe, George. *Letters from Everest*	796.522
Synnott, Mark. *The Third Pole*	796.522
Vasquez-Lavado, Silvia. *In the Shadow of the Mountain*	B

PUBLIC LIBRARY CORE COLLECTION: NONFICTION
Twentieth Edition

MOUNT EVEREST EXPEDITION, 1924
  Davis, Wade. *Into the Silence* — B
  Synnott, Mark. *The Third Pole* — 796.522
MOUNT EVEREST EXPEDITION, 1953
  Lowe, George. *Letters from Everest* — 796.522
MOUNT EVEREST EXPEDITION, 1996
  Bukreev, Anatolii Nikolaevich. *The Climb* — 796.52
  Krakauer, Jon. ★*Into Thin Air* — 796.52
MOUNT VERNON
  Dunbar, Erica Armstrong. ★*Never Caught* — B
MOUNTAIN LIFE
  Auvinen, Karen. *Rough Beauty* — B
  Biggers, Jeff. *Reckoning at Eagle Creek* — 333.73
  Matloff, Judith. *No Friends but the Mountains* — 355.009
MOUNTAIN MEADOWS MASSACRE, 1857
  Walker, Ronald W. ★*Massacre at Mountain Meadows* — 979.2
Mountain Modern. Bradbury, Dominic — 728
MOUNTAIN WARFARE
  Isserman, Maurice. *The Winter Army* — 940.54
MOUNTAINEERING
  Caesar, Ed. *The Moth and the Mountain* — B
  Conefrey, Mick. *The Ghosts of K2* — 796.522
  Cordes, Kelly. *The Tower* — 796.522
  Davis, Wade. *Into the Silence* — B
  Eichar, Donnie. *Dead Mountain* — 914
  Ellsworth, Scott. *The World Beneath Their Feet* — 796.522
  Hall, Andy. *Denali's Howl* — 796.522
  Isserman, Maurice. *Continental Divide* — 796.52
  Kaag, John J. *Hiking with Nietzsche* — 193
  Kimberley, Hannah. *A Woman's Place Is at the Top* — B
  Krakauer, Jon. *Classic Krakauer* — 814
  Lowe, George. *Letters from Everest* — 796.522
  O'Brien, Vanessa. *To the Greatest Heights* — B
  Roberts, David. *Limits of the Known* — B
  Synnott, Mark. *The Third Pole* — 796.522
  Taylor, Joseph E. *Pilgrims of the Vertical* — 796.52
  Zuckerman, Peter. ★*Buried in the Sky* — 796.522
MOUNTAINEERING ACCIDENTS
  Bukreev, Anatolii Nikolaevich. *The Climb* — 796.52
  Coburn, Broughton. *Everest* — 796.5
  Eichar, Donnie. *Dead Mountain* — 914
  Hall, Andy. *Denali's Howl* — 796.522
  Krakauer, Jon. ★*Into Thin Air* — 796.52
  Zuckerman, Peter. ★*Buried in the Sky* — 796.522
MOUNTAINEERS
  Cordes, Kelly. *The Tower* — 796.522
  Davis, Wade. *Into the Silence* — B
  Ellsworth, Scott. *The World Beneath Their Feet* — 796.522
  Kimberley, Hannah. *A Woman's Place Is at the Top* — B
  Krakauer, Jon. *Classic Krakauer* — 814
  Krakauer, Jon. ★*Into Thin Air* — 796.52
  Lowe, George. *Letters from Everest* — 796.522
  Synnott, Mark. *The Third Pole* — 796.522
  Taylor, Joseph E. *Pilgrims of the Vertical* — 796.52
  Vasquez-Lavado, Silvia. *In the Shadow of the Mountain* — B
  Zuckerman, Peter. ★*Buried in the Sky* — 796.522
MOUNTAINS
  Conefrey, Mick. *The Ghosts of K2* — 796.522
  Cordes, Kelly. *The Tower* — 796.522
  Kirkby, Bruce. *Blue Sky Kingdom* — 954.96
  Matloff, Judith. *No Friends but the Mountains* — 355.009
  Robinson, Kim Stanley. *The High Sierra* — 917.94
MOURNING CUSTOMS
  Doughty, Caitlin. *From Here to Eternity* — 393
  Gilbert, Sandra M. *Death's Door* — 155.9
Mouton, Deborah D. E. E. P.
  Black Chameleon — B
MOUTON, DEBORAH D. E. E. P.
  Mouton, Deborah D. E. E. P. *Black Chameleon* — B
Move by Move. Ashley, Maurice — 158
Move Fast and Break Things. Taplin, Jonathan — 330.9
The Movement Made Us. Dennis, David J., Jr — B
Movie Freak. Gleiberman, Owen — B
Moving The Mountain. Abdul Rauf, Feisal — 297
MOVING TO A NEW CITY
  Flannery, Kate. *Strip Tees* — 338.4
  Guo, XIaolu. *Nine Continents* — B

MOVING TO A NEW COUNTRY
  Bertch, Jane. *The French Ingredient* — B
  Buford, Bill. ★*Dirt* — B
  Hakkakiyan, Ruya. *A Beginner's Guide to America* — 646.7
  Mayle, Peter. ★*A Year in Provence* — 944
MOVING TO A NEW HOME
  Betz-Hamilton, Axton. *The Less People Know About Us* — 364.16
  Burton, Susan. *Empty* — B
  DiFelice, Bekah. *Almost There* — 248.8
  Dochartaigh, Kerri ni. *Cacophony of Bone* — B
  Mayle, Peter. ★*A Year in Provence* — 944
  Wenzke, Ali. ★*The Art of Happy Moving* — 648
MOVING TO A NEW STATE
  Rush, Chris. *The Light Years* — B
Moving to Higher Ground. Marsalis, Wynton — 781.65
Movsesian, Sona
  The World's Worst Assistant — 791.4302
MOVSESIAN, SONA
  Movsesian, Sona. *The World's Worst Assistant* — 791.4302
Mowat, Farley
  Born Naked — B
MOWAT, FARLEY
  Mowat, Farley. *Born Naked* — B
Moyle, Franny
  Turner — B
Moynahan, Brian
  Leningrad — 780.92
MOZAMBIQUE
  Hanes, Stephanie. *White Man's Game* — 333.95
  Wilson, Edward O. *A Window on Eternity* — 333.95
Mozart. Gutman, Robert W. — B
Mozart. Suchet, John — B
Mozart. Swafford, Jan — B
Mozart's Starling. Haupt, Lyanda Lynn — B
MOZART, WOLFGANG AMADEUS, 1756-1791
  Gutman, Robert W. *Mozart* — B
  Haupt, Lyanda Lynn. *Mozart's Starling* — B
  Rosen, Charles. *The Classical Style* — 780.9
  Shaffer, Peter. *Peter Shaffer's Amadeus* — 822
  Suchet, John. *Mozart* — B
  Swafford, Jan. *Mozart* — B
Mr. Know-It-All. Waters, John — 814
Mr. President. Raphael, Ray — 352.230973
Mrs. Kennedy. Leaming, Barbara — B
Mrs. Kennedy and Me. Hill, Clint — 973.922092
MS-13. Dudley, Steven S. — 364.106
Mubarak, Heather
  Stuffed — 641.86
MUD
  Maiklem, Lara. *Mudlark* — B
Muddy Matterhorn. McHugh, Heather — 811
MUDGETT, HERMAN W., 1861-1896
  Larson, Erik. ★*The Devil in the White City* — 364.15
Mudlark. Maiklem, Lara — B
Mueller, Jennifer
  Creative Change — 658.4
Mueller, Melissa
  Alice's Piano — B
MUELLER, ROBERT S., III, 1944-
  Weissmann, Andrew. ★*Where Law Ends* — 324.7
Mueller, Tom
  Crisis of Conscience — 364.16
Mufleh, Luma
  ★*Learning America* — 371.826
MUFLEH, LUMA
  Mufleh, Luma. ★*Learning America* — 371.826
  St. John, Warren. *Outcasts United* — B
MUGHAL EMPIRE
  Dalrymple, William. ★*The Anarchy* — 954.03
Muhammad. Armstrong, Karen — B
Muhammad, Ibtihaj
  Proud — B
MUHAMMAD, IBTIHAJ, 1985-
  Muhammad, Ibtihaj. *Proud* — B
Muhammad, Khalil Gibran
  The Condemnation of Blackness — 364.2
MUHAMMAD, PROPHET, D. 632
  Armstrong, Karen. *Muhammad* — B

AUTHOR, TITLE, SERIES AND SUBJECT INDEX

Ben Jelloun, Tahar. *Islam Explained*	297
Hazleton, Lesley. *After the Prophet*	297.8
Hazleton, Lesley. *The First Muslim*	B
Jebara, Mohamad. *Muhammad, the World-Changer*	B
Zafar, Harris. *Demystifying Islam*	297
Muhammad, *The World-Changer.* Jebara, Mohamad	B
Muir, John	
Nature Writings	B
The Story of My Boyhood and Youth	B
The Yosemite	979.4
Muir, John Kenneth	
The Encyclopedia of Superheroes on Film and Television	791.43
MUIR, JOHN, 1838-1914	
Heacox, Kim. ★*John Muir and the Ice That Started a Fire*	333.7209798
King, Dean. *Guardians of the Valley*	333.72
Muir, John. *Nature Writings*	B
Muir, John. *The Story of My Boyhood and Youth*	B
Worster, Donald. *A Passion for Nature the Life of John Muir*	B
Mukantabana, Yseult P.	
★*Real Friends Talk About Race*	305.8
Mukherjee, Siddhartha	
★*The Emperor of All Maladies*	616.99
★*The Gene*	616
The Laws of Medicine	610.1
★*The Song of the Cell*	571.6
Mulac, Carolyn	
Fundamentals of Reference	025.5
MULALLY, ALAN R.	
DeBord, Matthew. *Return to Glory*	338.4
Mulcahy, Diane	
The Gig Economy	650.1
Muldoon, Paul	
Maggot	821
Selected Poems 1968-2014	821
Mulgrew, Kate	
Born with Teeth	791.45028
MULGREW, KATE, 1955-	
Mulgrew, Kate. *Born with Teeth*	791.45028
MULHOLLAND, WILLIAM, 1855-1935	
Krist, Gary. *The Mirage Factory*	920
Mullainathan, Sendhil	
Scarcity	338.5
MULLALLY, MEGAN	
Offerman, Nick. *The Greatest Love Story Ever Told*	B
Mullen, Bill	
★*James Baldwin*	B
Mullen, Marissa	
That Cheese Plate Wants to Party	641.6
Mullen, Michelle	
Bowling Fundamentals	794.6
Mullen, Seamus	
Real Food Heals	641.5
Muller, Kristin	
The Potter's Studio Handbook	738.1
Muller, Melissa	
Anne Frank	B
Mullett-Bowlsby, Shannon	
★*Complete Crochet Course*	746.43
Mulley, Clare	
The Spy Who Loved	B
The Women Who Flew for Hitler	920
Mullins, Brittany	
Mostly Veggies	641.5
Mullins, Edwin	
The Four Roads to Heaven	263
MULTICULTURAL EDUCATION	
Bratt, Jessica Anne. *Let's Talk About Race in Storytimes*	027.62
***Multicultural** Manners.* Dresser, Norine	395
MULTICULTURALISM	
Bagby, Meredith E. *The New Guys*	305
Braswell, Porter. ★*Let Them See You*	650.1
Chin, Curtis. *Everything I Learned, I Learned in a Chinese Restaurant*	B
Cox, Gena. *Leading Inclusion*	658.3
DiAngelo, Robin J. *White Fragility*	305.8
Dohrmann, George. *Switching Fields*	796.334
Dresser, Norine. *Multicultural Manners*	395
Dungy, Camille T. *Soil*	635.0978
Dusoulier, Clotilde. *Tasting Paris*	641.594
Eddo-Lodge, Reni. *Why I'm No Longer Talking to White People About Race*	305.8
Faloyin, Dipo. ★*Africa Is Not a Country*	960.33
Fuller, Pamela. ★*The Leader's Guide to Unconscious Bias*	658.3
Ghobash, Omar Saif. *Letters to a Young Muslim*	297.09
Guerrero, Jean. *Hatemonger*	B
Hamilton, Denise. ★*Indivisible*	658.3
Harts, Minda. *Right Within*	658.3
Headlee, Celeste Anne. *Speaking of Race*	305.8
Henry, Alan. *Seen, Heard, and Paid*	650.1
Johnson, Theodore R. *When the Stars Begin to Fall*	305.800973
King, Charles. *Odessa*	947.7
McGreevy, John T. ★*Catholicism*	282.09
Mikanowski, Jacob. ★*Goodbye, Eastern Europe*	947
Nagassar, Rohadi. *When We Belong*	254
Newkirk, Pamela. *Diversity, Inc.*	658.3
Phillips, Collette A. M. *The Includers*	658.4
Proenza-Coles, Christina. *American Founders*	973
Reiss, Tom. *The Black Count*	B
Ronstadt, Linda. *Feels Like Home*	B
Rushdie, Salman. *Languages of Truth*	824
Samuelsson, Marcus. ★*The Rise*	641.59
Sanghera, Sathnam. ★*Empireland*	941
Sarsour, Linda. *We Are Not Here to Be Bystanders*	B
Scott, Andy. *One Kiss or Two?*	395.4
Sharpton, Al. *Rise Up*	973.933
Stanley, Brian. *Christianity in the Twentieth Century*	270.8
Tobar, Hector. ★*Our Migrant Souls*	305.868
Washington, Ella F. *The Necessary Journey*	658.3
Williams, Bari A. *Seen yet Unseen*	338.4
Zakaria, Rafia. *Against White Feminism*	305.42
MULTINATIONAL CORPORATIONS	
Chandler, Adam. *Drive-Thru Dreams*	647.95
Clark, Taylor. *Starbucked*	338
MULTIPLE INTELLIGENCES	
Epstein, David J. ★*Range*	153.9
MULTIRACIAL CHILDREN	
Arana, Marie. *American Chica*	B
Bell, Darrin. ★*The Talk*	741.5
Chang, Tina. *Hybrida*	811
Jacob, Mira. *Good Talk*	741.5
Kerrison, Catherine. *Jefferson's Daughters*	920
Morgan-Owens, Jessie. *Girl in Black and White*	B
MULTIRACIAL MEN	
Coffin, Jaed. *Roughhouse Friday*	B
Dove, Rita. *Sonata Mulattica*	811
Hutton, Paul Andrew. *The Apache Wars*	979
Jawando, Will. ★*My Seven Black Fathers*	B
Lauterbach, Preston. *Beale Street Dynasty*	976.8
Reiss, Tom. *The Black Count*	B
Resendez, Andres. *Conquering the Pacific*	959.9
Robertson, Robbie. ★*Testimony*	B
Watts, Reggie. *Great Falls, MT*	B
MULTIRACIAL PEOPLE	
Gay, Ross. *Inciting Joy*	814
Gordon-Reed, Annette. ★*The Hemingses of Monticello*	920
Hyde, Anne Farrar. ★*Born of Lakes and Plains*	978
Jun, Tasha. ★*Tell Me the Dream Again*	248
Kearse, Bettye. *The Other Madisons*	920
McBride, James. *The Color of Water*	B
Mock, Janet. *Surpassing Certainty*	B
Myers, Leah. *Thinning Blood*	B
Obama, Barack. ★*Dreams from My Father*	B
Obama, Barack. ★*A Promised Land*	B
Owusu, Nadia. *Aftershocks*	B
Remnick, David. *The Bridge*	B
Rothenberg, Ben. *Naomi Osaka*	B
Shanahan, Charif. *Trace Evidence*	811
Wolf, Brandon J. *A Place for Us*	B
MULTIRACIAL WOMEN	
Cho, Grace M. *Tastes Like War*	305.48
Diaz, Jaquira. *Ordinary Girls*	818
Duckworth, Tammy. *Every Day Is a Gift*	B
Emberton, Carole. *To Walk About in Freedom*	306.3
Evaristo, Bernardine. *Manifesto*	B
Hudes, Quiara Alegría. ★*My Broken Language*	B
Isen, Tajja. *Some of My Best Friends*	305.8
Kang, Mia. *Knockout*	B

PUBLIC LIBRARY CORE COLLECTION: NONFICTION
Twentieth Edition

Lawton, Georgina. *Raceless* — B
Madden, T Kira. *Long Live the Tribe of Fatherless Girls* — 814
Miller, Michelle. *Belonging* — B
Owusu, Nadia. *Aftershocks* — B
Perry, Imani. ★*South to America* — 917
Sabatini Sloan, Aisha. *Dreaming of Ramadi in Detroit* — 814
Teege, Jennifer. *My Grandfather Would Have Shot Me* — 929.2
Trethewey, Natasha D. ★*Memorial Drive* — B
Washington, Kerry. *Thicker Than Water* — B
Welteroth, Elaine. *More Than Enough* — B
Wong, Carmen Rita. *Why Didn't You Tell Me?* — B

MUMBAI, INDIA
Boo, Katherine. ★*Behind the Beautiful Forevers* — 305.5
Mehta, Suketu. *Maximum City* — 954
Roy, Saumya. *Castaway Mountain* — 363.72

Mumford, Lewis
The City in History — 307.76

MUMLER, WILLIAM H.
Manseau, Peter. *The Apparitionists* — B

MUMME, HAL
Gwynne, S. C. *The Perfect Pass* — 920

MUMMIES
Pringle, Heather Anne. *The Mummy Congress* — 393
The Mummy Congress. Pringle, Heather Anne — 393

MUNCH, EDVARD, 1863-1944
Dolnick, Edward. *The Rescue Artist* — 364.16
Knausgaard, Karl Ove. *So Much Longing in so Little Space* — 759.81
Prideaux, Sue. *Edvard Munch* — B
Ustvedt, Oystein. *Edvard Munch* — 759.81

Mundy, Liza
Code Girls — 940.54
★*The Sisterhood* — 327.12

MUNICIPAL ENGINEERING
Chachra, Deb. *How Infrastructure Works* — 363

MUNICIPAL GOVERNMENT
Berg, Scott W. *The Burning of the World* — 977.311
Bordewich, Fergus M. *Washington* — 975.3
Clark, Anna. *The Poisoned City* — 363.6
Emanuel, Rahm. *The Nation City* — 352.23
Hanna-Attisha, Mona. *What the Eyes Don't See* — 615.9
Nusbaum, Eric. *Stealing Home* — 796.357
Tubbs, Michael. *The Deeper the Roots* — B

MUNICIPAL SERVICES
Emanuel, Rahm. *The Nation City* — 352.23
Phillips-Fein, Kim. *Fear City* — 330.9747

Munno, Nadia Caterina
The Pasta Queen — 641.82

Munroe, Randall
How To — 500
Thing Explainer — 500
What If? 2 — 500
★*What If?* — 500

Munson, Richard
Tesla — B

Murad, Nadia
★*The Last Girl* — B

MURAD, NADIA
Murad, Nadia. ★*The Last Girl* — B

Murad, Noor
★*Ottolenghi Test Kitchen* — 641.3
Ottolenghi Test Kitchen — 641.5

Murakami, Haruki
★*Absolutely on Music* — 784.2
★*Novelist as a Vocation* — 895.64
Underground — 364.15
What I Talk About When I Talk About Running — B

MURAKAMI, HARUKI, 1949-
Murakami, Haruki. ★*Novelist as a Vocation* — 895.64
Murakami, Haruki. *What I Talk About When I Talk About Running* — B

MURAL PAINTING AND DECORATION
Ganz, Nicholas. ★*Graffiti World* — 751.7

MURAL PAINTING AND DECORATION, ITALIAN
King, Ross. ★*Leonardo and the Last Supper* — 759.5
King, Ross. *Michelangelo & the Pope's Ceiling* — 759.5

MURAL PAINTING AND DECORATION, RENAISSANCE (EUROPE)
King, Ross. *Michelangelo & the Pope's Ceiling* — 759.5

MURALS
Ganz, Nicholas. ★*Graffiti World* — 751.7

Marnham, Patrick. *Dreaming with His Eyes Open* — B

MURDAUGH, ALEX (RICHARD ALEXANDER), 1968-
Glatt, John. *Tangled Vines* — 364.152
Matney, Mandy. *Blood on Their Hands* — 364.152

MURDER
Ahmed, Azam. *Fear Is Just a Word* — 364.152
Appelman, J. Reuben. *While Idaho Slept* — 364.152
Assael, Shaun. *The Murder of Sonny Liston* — B
Austerlitz, Saul. *Just a Shot Away* — 781.66078
Berendt, John. *Midnight in the Garden of Good and Evil* — 975.8
Bowden, Mark. *The Case of the Vanishing Blonde* — 364.10973
Bugliosi, Vincent. ★*Helter Skelter* — 364.1
Cameron, Silver Donald. *Blood in the Water* — 364.152
Cannell, Michael T. *A Brotherhood Betrayed* — B
Capote, Truman. ★*In Cold Blood* — 364.1
Corcoran, Katherine. *In the Mouth of the Wolf* — 364.152
Cornwell, Patricia Daniels. *Ripper* — 364.152
Cross, Kim. *In Light of All Darkness* — 363.25
Eisenberg, Emma Copley. ★*The Third Rainbow Girl* — 364.152
English, Charlie. *The Gallery of Miracles and Madness* — 709.04
English, T. J. *The Corporation* — 364.106089
Ervin, Kristine S. *Rabbit Heart* — 364.152
Eustace, Nicole. ★*Covered with Night* — 364.152
Frederick, Jim. *Black Hearts* — 956.7044
Fuhrmann, Joseph T. *Rasputin* — B
Glatt, John. ★*The Perfect Father* — 364.152
Glatt, John. *Tangled Vines* — 364.152
Grann, David. ★*The Wager* — 910.91
Green, Elon. *Last Call* — 363.15
Guinn, Jeff. ★*Manson* — 364.152
Guinn, Jeff. *The Road to Jonestown* — 289.9
Hale, Grace Elizabeth. *In the Pines* — 364.13
Harman, Claire. *Murder by the Book* — 364.152
Horton, Michelle. *Dear Sister* — B
Humes, Edward. *The Forever Witness* — 363.25
Jimenez, Stephen. *The Book of Matt* — 364.152
Kavanagh, Julie. *The Irish Assassins* — 941.5
Keefe, Patrick Radden. ★*Say Nothing* — 364.152
Kenda, Joe. *Killer Triggers* — 364.152
King, Greg. *Nothing but the Night* — 364.152
Krist, Gary. *Empire of Sin* — 976.3
Larson, Erik. ★*The Devil in the White City* — 364.15
Leovy, Jill. *Ghettoside* — 364.152
Lowe, Keith. *Savage Continent* — 940.55
Lowry, Beverly. *Deer Creek Drive* — 364.152
MacLean, Harry N. *Starkweather* — 364.152
Maier, Thomas. *Mafia Spies* — 364.1060973
Malhotra, Aanchal. *Remnants of Partition* — 954.04
Mar, Alex. *Seventy Times Seven* — 362.88
Marshall, McMillan. *Among the Bros* — 362.29
Matney, Mandy. *Blood on Their Hands* — 364.152
McGinniss, Joe. *Fatal Vision* — B
McGough, Matthew. *The Lazarus Files* — 364.152
McNamara, Kevin J. *Dreams of a Great Small Nation* — 355.009437
Miles, Kathryn. *Trailed* — 364.152
Mitchell, Jerry. ★*Race Against Time* — 364.152
Nelson, David B. *Boys Enter the House* — 364.152
Nicholl, Charles. *The Reckoning* — B
O'Connell, Mark. *A Thread of Violence* — 364.152
Phillips, Patrick. *Blood at the Root* — 305.8
Rappaport, Helen. *The Race to Save the Romanovs* — 947.08
Rear, Rachel. *Catch the Sparrow* — 364.152
Robertson, Cara. *The Trial of Lizzie Borden* — 345.744
Rose, Jacqueline. *On Violence and on Violence Against Women* — 362.88
Rosen, Jonathan. ★*The Best Minds* — 616.89
Rule, Ann. *The Stranger Beside Me* — B
Schechter, Harold. *Murderabilia* — 364.152
Signer, Michael. *Cry Havoc* — 305.800973
Smith, Clive Stafford. *The Injustice System* — 345.759
Sullivan, Randall. *The Devil's Best Trick* — 235
Tyson, Timothy B. *Blood Done Sign My Name* — 975.6
Weinman, Sarah. *Scoundrel* — 364.152
Weinman, Sarah. ★*Unspeakable Acts* — 364.1
Weir, Alison. *Mary, Queen of Scots, and the Murder of Lord Darnley* — 941.105
White, Richard. *Who Killed Jane Stanford?* — 364.152
Wiehl, Lis W. *Hunting Charles Manson* — 364.152
Woolley, Benjamin. *The King's Assassin* — B

AUTHOR, TITLE, SERIES AND SUBJECT INDEX

MURDER AND GUNS
    Diaz, Tom. *The Last Gun* — 338.4
Murder by the Book. Harman, Claire — 364.152
MURDER IN LITERATURE
    Harman, Claire. *Murder by the Book* — 364.152
MURDER IN MASS MEDIA
    Hortis, C. Alexander. *The Witch of New York* — 364.152
    Kroll, Andy. *A Death on W Street* — 364.152
MURDER INVESTIGATION
    Bonner, Betsy. *The Book of Atlantis Black* — 364.152
    Bowden, Mark. *The Case of the Vanishing Blonde* — 364.10973
    Capote, Truman. ★*In Cold Blood* — 364.1
    Collins, Max Allan. *Eliot Ness and the Mad Butcher* — 364.152
    Cooper, Becky. *We Keep the Dead Close* — 364.152
    Cooper, Sean Patrick. *The Shooter at Midnight* — 363.25
    Egan, Timothy. ★*A Fever in the Heartland* — 322.4
    Eisenberg, Emma Copley. ★*The Third Rainbow Girl* — 364.152
    Eustace, Nicole. ★*Covered with Night* — 364.152
    Glatt, John. *The Doomsday Mother* — 364.152
    Glatt, John. ★*The Perfect Father* — 364.152
    Goldfarb, Bruce. ★*18 Tiny Deaths* — B
    Grann, David. ★*Killers of the Flower Moon* — 976.6004
    Jager, Eric. *Blood Royal* — 944.026
    Kavanagh, Julie. *The Irish Assassins* — 941.5
    Lockhart, Chris. ★*Walking the Bowl* — 362.7
    McGarrahan, Ellen. *Two Truths and a Lie* — 364.152
    Mitchell, Jerry. ★*Race Against Time* — 364.152
    O'Neill, Tom. ★*Chaos* — 364.152
    Ratliff, Evan. *The Mastermind* — B
    Shannon, Elaine. *Hunting Leroux* — 364.1
    Standiford, Les. *Bringing Adam Home* — 364.15
    Stashower, Daniel. *American Demon* — 364.152
The Murder of Sonny Liston. Assael, Shaun — B
The Murder of Tutankhamen. Brier, Bob — B
Murder on Shades Mountain. Morrison, Melanie — 345.761
MURDER SUSPECTS
    Harman, Claire. *Murder by the Book* — 364.152
    Kuo, Michelle. *Reading with Patrick* — B
    Levin, Josh. *The Queen* — 364.16
    O'Neill, Tom. ★*Chaos* — 364.152
    Robertson, Cara. *The Trial of Lizzie Borden* — 345.744
MURDER VICTIMS
    Belkin, Lisa. *Genealogy of a Murder* — 362.88
    Butcher, Barbara. *What the Dead Know* — 614
    Capote, Truman. ★*In Cold Blood* — 364.1
    Caruana Galizia, Paul. ★*A Death in Malta* — 364.15
    Cooper, Becky. *We Keep the Dead Close* — 364.152
    Corcoran, Katherine. *In the Mouth of the Wolf* — 364.152
    Cross, Kim. *In Light of All Darkness* — 363.25
    Harman, Claire. *Murder by the Book* — 364.152
    Herman, Eleanor. *The Royal Art of Poison* — 364.152
    Hsu, Hua. ★*Stay True* — B
    Kimmerle, Erin H. *We Carry Their Bones* — 365
    Kroll, Andy. *A Death on W Street* — 364.152
    Lockhart, Chris. ★*Walking the Bowl* — 362.7
    Mar, Alex. *Seventy Times Seven* — 362.88
    Montillo, Roseanne. *Deliberate Cruelty* — 364.152
    Mulley, Clare. *The Spy Who Loved* — B
    Nelson, David B. *Boys Enter the House* — 364.152
    Nicholl, Charles. *The Reckoning* — B
    Norton, Laurah. *Lay Them to Rest* — 363.25
    Samuels, Robert. ★*His Name Is George Floyd* — B
    Sherman, Casey. *Hunting Whitey* — B
    Stashower, Daniel. *American Demon* — 364.152
Murderabilia. Schechter, Harold — 364.152
MURDERERS
    Berendt, John. *Midnight in the Garden of Good and Evil* — 975.8
    Bugliosi, Vincent. ★*Helter Skelter* — 364.1
    Callahan, Maureen. *American Predator* — 364.152
    Carlo, Philip. *Gaspipe* — B
    Cornwell, Patricia Daniels. *Ripper* — 364.152
    Cullen, Kevin. *Whitey Bulger* — B
    Garrison, Jessica. *The Devil's Harvest* — 363.25
    Humes, Edward. *The Forever Witness* — 363.25
    Isenberg, Sheila. *Women Who Love Men Who Kill* — 362.83
    Kenda, Joe. *Killer Triggers* — 364.152
    Leovy, Jill. *Ghettoside* — 364.152
    McGinniss, Joe. *Fatal Vision* — B

    Miles, Kathryn. *Trailed* — 364.152
    Montillo, Roseanne. *Deliberate Cruelty* — 364.152
    Nelson, David B. *Boys Enter the House* — 364.152
    Rule, Ann. *The Stranger Beside Me* — B
    Schechter, Harold. *Murderabilia* — 364.152
    Schechter, Harold. ★*Ripped from the Headlines!* — 791.43
    Sides, Hampton. *Hellhound on His Trail* — 364.152
    Weinman, Sarah. *Scoundrel* — 364.152
    Weinman, Sarah. ★*Unspeakable Acts* — 364.1
    Wiehl, Lis W. *Hunting Charles Manson* — 364.152
MURDOCH, IRIS
    Conradi, Peter J. *Iris* — B
Murdoch, Sierra Crane
    ★*Yellow Bird* — 364.152
Murdoch, Stephen
    IQ — 153.9
Murgia, Madhumita
    Code Dependent — 303.48
Murie, Olaus J.
    ★*A Field Guide to Animal Tracks* — 599
Murkoff, Heidi Eisenberg
    What to Expect the First Year — 305.232
    ★*What to Expect the Second Year* — 649
    ★*What to Expect When You're Expecting* — 618.2
Murolo, Priscilla
    From the Folks Who Brought You the Weekend — 331
Murphy, Andrew R.
    William Penn — B
MURPHY, AUDIE, 1924-1971
    Kershaw, Alex. *Against All Odds* — 940.54
Murphy, Brian
    81 Days Below Zero — 940.54
Murphy, Bruce Allen
    Scalia — B
Murphy, Chris
    ★*The Violence Inside Us* — 303.60973
Murphy, Cullen
    The Word According to Eve — 220.8
MURPHY, EDDIE, 1961-
    De Semlyen, Nick. *Wild and Crazy Guys* — 920
Murphy, Emily
    Grow Now — 635
Murphy, Kate
    You're Not Listening — 153.6
Murphy, Marilyn
    Woven to Wear — 746.1
MURRAY, BILL, 1950 SEPTEMBER 21-
    De Semlyen, Nick. *Wild and Crazy Guys* — 920
Murray, Charles A.
    Coming Apart — 305.8
Murray, Charles Shaar
    Crosstown Traffic — B
MURRAY, JAMES A. H., 1837-1915
    Ogilvie, Sarah. *The Dictionary People* — 423
    Winchester, Simon. *The Professor and the Madman* — 423
Murray, Liz
    Breaking Night — B
MURRAY, LIZ, 1980-
    Murray, Liz. *Breaking Night* — B
MURRAY, PAULI, 1910-1985
    Bell-Scott, Patricia. *The Firebrand and the First Lady* — 920
    Rosenberg, Rosalind. ★*Jane Crow* — B
MURROW, EDWARD R., 1908-1965
    Edwards, Bob. *Edward R. Murrow and the Birth of Broadcast Journalism* — B
    Olson, Lynne. *Citizens of London* — 940.54012
Murthy, Vivek Hallegere
    Together — 158.2
Muscle. Meals, Roy A. — 612.7
MUSCLE STRENGTH
    Current, Austin. *Science of Strength Training* — 613.7
    Meals, Roy A. *Muscle* — 612.7
MUSCLES
    Current, Austin. *Science of Strength Training* — 613.7
    Meals, Roy A. *Muscle* — 612.7
MUSCULAR DYSTROPHY
    Wong, Alice. ★*Year of the Tiger* — B
MUSCULOSKELETAL SYSTEM
    Meals, Roy A. *Muscle* — 612.7

PUBLIC LIBRARY CORE COLLECTION: NONFICTION
Twentieth Edition

Muse of Fire. Korda, Michael — 940.4
Muse, Toby
  Kilo — 363.4509861
MUSE, TOBY
  Muse, Toby. *Kilo* — 363.4509861
MUSES (PEOPLE)
  Burke, Carolyn. *Lee Miller* — B
MUSEUM CURATORS
  Obrist, Hans-Ulrich. *Ways of Curating* — 707.5
  Stourton, James. *Kenneth Clark* — B
MUSEUM EXHIBITS
  Kuper, Adam. *The Museum of Other People* — 305.8
  The Museum of Other People. Kuper, Adam — 305.8
  A Museum of Their Own. Holladay, Wilhelmina Cole — 704
MUSEUM THEFTS
  Dolnick, Edward. *The Rescue Artist* — 364.16
MUSEUMS
  Conniff, Richard. *House of Lost Worlds* — 069
  Holladay, Wilhelmina Cole. *A Museum of Their Own* — 704
  Obrist, Hans-Ulrich. *Ways of Curating* — 707.5
  Wilkins, Robert L. *Long Road to Hard Truth* — 069
MUSHERS
  Paulsen, Gary. *Winterdance* — B
Mushrooming. Borsato, Diane — 579.6
MUSHROOMS
  Borsato, Diane. *Mushrooming* — 579.6
  Jacobs, Ryan McMahon. *The Truffle Underground* — 381
  Kempner, Joanna. *Psychedelic Outlaws* — 615.7
  Lincoff, Gary. *The Audubon Society Field Guide to North American Mushrooms* — 579.6
  McKnight, Kent H. *A Field Guide to Mushrooms, North America* — 579.6
  Regan, Iliana. *Fieldwork* — B
Music. Gioia, Ted — 780.9
MUSIC
  Adams, John. *Hallelujah Junction* — B
  Ahmad, Aeham. *The Pianist from Syria* — B
  Austerlitz, Saul. *Money for Nothing* — 780.26
  Black Thought. *The Upcycled Self* — B
  Broyles, Michael. ★*Revolutions in American Music* — 780.9
  Burton-Hill, Clemency. ★*Year of Wonder* — 780.9
  Carlile, Brandi. *Broken Horses* — B
  Cash, Rosanne. ★*Composed* — B
  Chernaik, Judith. *Schumann* — B
  Cohodas, Nadine. *Princess Noire* — 782.42164
  Crawford, Richard. *America's Musical Life* — 780
  Cross, Charles R. *Here We Are Now* — 782.42166
  Doggett, Peter. *Electric Shock* — 781.64
  Feinstein, Michael. *The Gershwins and Me* — 782.42164
  Figes, Orlando. *The Europeans* — 920
  Garnice, Michael. *The Ultimate Guide to Great Reggae* — 781.646
  Gasser, Nolan. *Why You Like It* — 781.1
  Gioia, Ted. *Music* — 780.9
  Glass, Philip. *Words Without Music* — B
  Guralnick, Peter. ★*Sam Phillips* — B
  Hay, Matt. *Soundtrack of Silence* — B
  Hermes, Will. *Love Goes to Buildings on Fire* — 781.64
  Hoffman, Miles. *The NPR Classical Music Companion* — 780.3
  Houghton, Mick. *Becoming Elektra* — 781.64
  Koenig, Joan. *The Musical Child* — 780.71
  Lynskey, Dorian. *33 Revolutions per Minute* — 782.42
  Marsalis, Wynton. *Moving to Higher Ground* — 781.65
  Mauceri, John. *For the Love of Music* — 781.1
  McNally, Dennis. *On Highway 61* — 781.64
  Meacham, Jon. *Songs of America* — 782.42
  Milner, Greg. *Perfecting Sound Forever* — 781.49
  Moore, Kathleen Dean. *Earth's Wild Music* — 576.8
  Moore, Thurston. *Sonic Life* — B
  Morley, Paul. *The Age of Bowie* — B
  Neville, Aaron. *Tell It Like It Is* — B
  Newkey-Burden, Chas. *Taylor Swift* — B
  Piston, Walter. *Orchestration* — 781.63
  Pollack, Howard. ★*George Gershwin* — B
  Popova, Maria. *Figuring* — 920
  Powers, Ann. ★*Traveling* — B
  Rapkin, Mickey. *Pitch Perfect* — 782.5
  Ratliff, Ben. *The Jazz Ear* — 781.6509
  Rhodes, James. *Instrumental* — B
  Ribowsky, Mark. *The Supremes* — B
  Rogers, Susan E. ★*This Is What It Sounds Like* — 781.1
  Ronstadt, Linda. *Feels Like Home* — B
  Ross, Alex. *Wagnerism* — B
  Sachs, Harvey. *The Ninth* — 784.2
  Sandke, Randy. *Where the Dark and the Light Folks Meet* — 781.6509
  Servadio, Gaia. *Rossini* — B
  Smith, Patti. ★*Just Kids* — B
  Taupin, Bernie. *Scattershot* — B
  Threadgill, Henry. *Easily Slip into Another World* — B
  Tinsley, Omise'eke Natasha. *Beyonce in Formation* — 782.42164
  Tunstall, Tricia. *Changing Lives* — 780.71
  Wald, Elijah. *American Epic* — 781.64
  Wald, Elijah. *Dylan Goes Electric!* — 782.42164
  Wald, Elijah. *How the Beatles Destroyed Rock 'N' Roll* — 781.64
  Warner, Daniel. *Live Wires* — 786.7
  Wenner, Jann. *Like a Rolling Stone* — B
  Westhoff, Ben. *Dirty South* — 782.421649
  Whitney, Craig R. *All the Stops* — 786.5
  Wilkinson, Alec. *The Protest Singer* — B
  Williams, Lucinda. *Don't Tell Anybody the Secrets I Told You* — B
  Wilson, Brian. *I Am Brian Wilson* — B
MUSIC AGENTS
  McDonald, Greg (Producer). *Elvis and the Colonel* — 920
MUSIC AND LITERATURE
  Ross, Alex. *Wagnerism* — B
  ★*Music and Mind*. Fleming, Renee — 615.8
MUSIC AND RACE (SOCIAL SCIENCES)
  Mahon, Maureen. ★*Black Diamond Queens* — 782.421
  Torgoff, Martin. *Bop Apocalypse* — 781.65
MUSIC AND SOCIETY
  Abrams, Jonathan P. D. ★*The Come Up* — 782.421649
  Amos, Tori. *Resistance* — B
  Ashon, Will. *Chamber Music* — 782.421649
  Chang, Jeff. *Can't Stop, Won't Stop* — 306.4
  Isacoff, Stuart. *Musical Revolutions* — 780.9
  Marsalis, Wynton. *Moving to Higher Ground* — 781.65
  Matos, Michaelangelo. *The Underground Is Massive* — 781.648
  Questlove. *Music Is History* — 782.42164
  Sachs, Harvey. *The Ninth* — 784.2
  Stanley, Bob. *Let's Do It* — 781.64
  Thomas, Richard F. ★*Why Bob Dylan Matters* — 782.42164
  Tolan, Sandy. *Children of the Stone* — 780
  Torgoff, Martin. *Bop Apocalypse* — 781.65
MUSIC AND TECHNOLOGY
  Dolby, Thomas. *The Speed of Sound* — B
  Fleming, Renee. ★*Music and Mind* — 615.8
MUSIC APPRECIATION
  Burton-Hill, Clemency. ★*Year of Wonder* — 780.9
  Gasser, Nolan. *Why You Like It* — 781.1
  Marsalis, Wynton. *Moving to Higher Ground* — 781.65
  Mauceri, John. *For the Love of Music* — 781.1
  Powers, Ann. ★*Traveling* — B
  Questlove. *Mo' Meta Blues* — 782.42164
  Rogers, Susan E. ★*This Is What It Sounds Like* — 781.1
  Tweedy, Jeff. *How to Write One Song* — 782.42
  Warsaw-Fan Rauch, Arianna. ★*Declassified* — 781.1
MUSIC CRITICS
  Hopper, Jessica. *The First Collection of Criticism by a Living Female Rock Critic* — 781.66
MUSIC FESTIVALS
  Lang, Michael. *The Road to Woodstock* — 781.66
MUSIC HISTORY AND CRITICISM
  Abrams, Jonathan P. D. ★*The Come Up* — 782.421649
  Albertine, Viv. *Clothes, Clothes, Clothes. Music, Music, Music* — B
  Armstrong, Louis. *Louis Armstrong, in His Own Words* — B
  Boilen, Bob. *Your Song Changed My Life* — 780.92
  Bostridge, Ian. *Schubert's Winter Journey* — 782.4
  Breihan, Tom. ★*The Number Ones* — 782.42164
  Brothers, Thomas David. ★*Louis Armstrong, Master of Modernism* — B
  Broyles, Michael. ★*Revolutions in American Music* — 780.9
  Buckland, Gail. *Who Shot Rock & Roll* — 779
  Bullock, Darryl W. *David Bowie Made Me Gay* — 780
  Chang, Jeff. *Can't Stop, Won't Stop* — 306.4
  Chinen, Nate. *Playing Changes* — 781.6509
  Chuck D. *Chuck D Presents This Day in Rap and Hip-Hop History* — 782.421649
  Cooke, Mervyn. *The Chronicle of Jazz* — 781.6509
  Crawford, Richard. *America's Musical Life* — 780

AUTHOR, TITLE, SERIES AND SUBJECT INDEX

Cross, Charles R. *Here We Are Now* — 782.42166
Davidson, Mark A. ★*Bob Dylan* — B
Day, Timothy. ★*A Century of Recorded Music* — 780
DeVeaux, Scott Knowles. *Jazz* — 781.65
Doggett, Peter. *You Never Give Me Your Money* — B
Dregni, Michael. *Django* — B
Duncan, Dayton. ★*Country Music* — 781.642
Dylan, Bob. ★*The Philosophy of Modern Song* — 782.42
Edwards, Paul. *The Concise Guide to Hip-Hop Music* — 782.421649
Feinstein, Michael. *The Gershwins and Me* — 782.42164
Ferris, William R. *Give My Poor Heart Ease* — 781.643
Geck, Martin. ★*Johann Sebastian Bach* — 780.92
Giddins, Gary. *Weather Bird* — 781.6509
Gioia, Ted. *The History of Jazz* — 781.6509
Guesdon, Jean-Michel. *All the Songs* — 782.42166
Harvilla, Rob. *60 Songs That Explain the '90s* — 782.42164
Heller, Jason. *Strange Stars* — 781.6609
Hepworth, David. *Uncommon People* — B
Hermes, Will. *Love Goes to Buildings on Fire* — 781.64
Hilburn, Robert. ★*Johnny Cash* — B
Horowitz, Joseph. ★*Classical Music in America* — 781.6
Houghton, Mick. *Becoming Elektra* — 781.64
Hyden, Steven. *Long Road* — 782.42166
Hyden, Steven. *Twilight of the Gods* — 781.6609
Iandoli, Kathy. *God Save the Queens* — 782.421649
Isacoff, Stuart. *Musical Revolutions* — 780.9
Johnson, Graham. *Poulenc* — B
Kahn, Ashley. *The House That Trane Built* — 781.6509
Kapilow, Robert. ★*Listening for America* — 782.42164
Kaplan, James. *3 Shades of Blue* — 920
Kaye, Lenny. ★*Lightning Striking* — 781.66
Kennicott, Philip. *Counterpoint* — B
Kundera, Milan. *Encounter* — 809
Lang, Michael. *The Road to Woodstock* — 781.66
Lehman, David. *A Fine Romance* — 781.64
Lomax, Alan. ★*The Land Where the Blues Began* — 781.643
Lynskey, Dorian. *33 Revolutions per Minute* — 782.42
Mahon, Maureen. ★*Black Diamond Queens* — 782.421
Marovich, Robert M. *A City Called Heaven* — 782.25
Mauceri, John. *For the Love of Music* — 781.1
McCartney, Paul. *The Lyrics* — 782.42166
McCormick, Mack. *Biography of a Phantom* — 782.421643
McKeen, William. *Everybody Had an Ocean* — 781.6609
McNally, Dennis. *On Highway 61* — 781.64
Meacham, Jon. *Songs of America* — 782.42
Milner, Greg. *Perfecting Sound Forever* — 781.49
Morgenstern, Dan. *Living with Jazz* — 781.65
Morton, Brian. ★*The Penguin Jazz Guide* — 016
Moss, Marissa R. *Her Country* — 781.642
Murakami, Haruki. *Absolutely on Music* — 784.2
Myers, Marc. *Why Jazz Happened* — 781.65
Norman, Philip. *George Harrison* — B
Philip, Robert. *The Classical Music Lover's Companion to Orchestral Music* — 784.2
Polenberg, Richard. *Hear My Sad Story* — 782.42162
Povey, Glenn. *Echoes* — 782.42166
Powers, Ann. ★*Traveling* — B
Questlove. ★*Hip-Hop Is History* — 782.421649
Questlove. *Music Is History* — 782.42164
Remnick, David. *Holding the Note* — 781.64
Reynolds, Simon. *Shock and Awe* — 781.6609
Ribowsky, Mark. *Signed, Sealed, and Delivered* — B
Ribowsky, Mark. *The Supremes* — B
Robb, John. *Punk Rock* — 781.6609
Rose, Michael. *The Birth of an Opera* — 782.1
Rosen, Charles. *The Classical Style* — 780.9
Ross, Alex. *Wagnerism* — B
Row, Jess. *White Flights* — 813
Russell, Tony. *Country Music Originals* — B
Sachs, Harvey. *The Ninth* — 784.2
Sachs, Harvey. *Ten Masterpieces of Music* — 780.9
Sandburg, Carl. *The American Songbag* — 782.42162
Sandke, Randy. *Where the Dark and the Light Folks Meet* — 781.6509
Sanneh, Kelefa. ★*Major Labels* — 781.64
Servadio, Gaia. *Rossini* — B
Sloan, Nate. *Switched on Pop* — 781.64
Smith, Danyel. *Shine Bright* — 782.42164
Spera, Keith. *Groove Interrupted* — B

Spitzer, Michael. *The Musical Human* — 780.9
Stempel, Larry. ★*Showtime* — 792.609
Swafford, Jan. ★*Beethoven* — B
Thomas, Richard F. ★*Why Bob Dylan Matters* — 782.42164
Thomson, Graeme. *George Harrison* — B
Torgoff, Martin. *Bop Apocalypse* — 781.65
Tye, Larry. ★*The Jazzmen* — 781.6509
Viertel, Jack. *The Secret Life of the American Musical* — 792.609
Waksman, Steve. *This Ain't the Summer of Love* — 781.66
Wald, Elijah. *Dylan Goes Electric!* — 782.42164
Wald, Elijah. ★*Escaping the Delta* — B
Ward, Geoffrey C. *Jazz* — 781.6509
Warner, Daniel. *Live Wires* — 786.7
Westhoff, Ben. *Dirty South* — 782.421649
White, Adam. ★*Motown* — 781.644
Whitney, Craig R. *All the Stops* — 786.5
Wiederhorn, Jon. *Louder Than Hell* — 781.6609
Womack, Kenneth. *All Things Must Pass Away* — 781.66
Young, Rob. *Electric Eden* — 781.62
Zwonitzer, Mark. *Will You Miss Me When I'm Gone?* — 920

MUSIC INDUSTRY AND TRADE
Broyles, Michael. ★*Revolutions in American Music* — 780.9
Calamar, Gary. *Record Store Days* — 780.26
Carlin, Peter Ames. *Bruce* — B
Charnas, Dan. *The Big Payback* — 306.4
Common. *One Day It'll All Make Sense* — B
DeRogatis, Jim. *Soulless* — B
Dolby, Thomas. *The Speed of Sound* — B
Dylan, Bob. ★*The Philosophy of Modern Song* — 782.42
Fernando, S. H., Jr. *From the Streets of Shaolin* — 782.421
Guralnick, Peter. ★*Sam Phillips* — B
Harvilla, Rob. *60 Songs That Explain the '90s* — 782.42164
McDonald, Greg (Producer). *Elvis and the Colonel* — 920
Mike D. *Beastie Boys Book* — 782.42164
Moss, Marissa R. *Her Country* — 781.642
Myers, Marc. *Why Jazz Happened* — 781.65
Powers, Ann. ★*Traveling* — B
Price, Margo. *Maybe We'll Make It* — B
Sanneh, Kelefa. ★*Major Labels* — 781.64
Stanley, Bob. *Let's Do It* — 781.64
Van Zandt, Steve. *Unrequited Infatuations* — B
Warsaw-Fan Rauch, Arianna. ★*Declassified* — 781.1
Westhoff, Ben. *Original Gangstas* — 782.421649
Williams, Lucinda. *Don't Tell Anybody the Secrets I Told You* — B
Winder, Elizabeth. *Parachute Women* — 782.42164
Music Is History. Questlove — 782.42164

MUSIC STORES
Calamar, Gary. *Record Store Days* — 780.26

MUSIC TEACHERS
Koenig, Joan. *The Musical Child* — 780.71

MUSIC THEORY
Kennicott, Philip. *Counterpoint* — B

MUSIC THERAPY
Butler, Marcia. *The Skin Above My Knee* — B
Fleming, Renee. ★*Music and Mind* — 615.8

MUSIC VIDEOS
Austerlitz, Saul. *Money for Nothing* — 780.26
Nesmith, Michael. *Infinite Tuesday* — B

MUSIC, AMERICAN
Bernstein, Burton. ★*Leonard Bernstein* — B
Crawford, Richard. *America's Musical Life* — 780
Gaddy, K. R. ★*Well of Souls* — 787
Kaplan, James. *3 Shades of Blue* — 920
Lomax, Alan. ★*The Land Where the Blues Began* — 781.643
Marsalis, Wynton. *Moving to Higher Ground* — 781.65
Powers, Ann. *Good Booty* — 781.64
Questlove. *Music Is History* — 782.42164
Threadgill, Henry. *Easily Slip into Another World* — B
Zwonitzer, Mark. *Will You Miss Me When I'm Gone?* — 920

Music, Carla Lalli
That Sounds so Good — 641.5
Where Cooking Begins — 641.5

MUSIC, GERMAN
Geck, Martin. ★*Johann Sebastian Bach* — 780.92
Swafford, Jan. ★*Beethoven* — B

MUSIC, JEWISH
Strom, Yale. *The Book of Klezmer* — 781.62

PUBLIC LIBRARY CORE COLLECTION: NONFICTION
Twentieth Edition

MUSIC, LATIN AMERICAN
   Santana, Carlos. *The Universal Tone* — B
MUSICAL ABILITY
   Spitzer, Michael. *The Musical Human* — 780.9
   The Musical Child. Koenig, Joan — 780.71
MUSICAL FILMS
   Santopietro, Tom. *The Sound of Music Story* — 791.43
   The Musical Human. Spitzer, Michael — 780.9
MUSICAL INSTRUMENTS
   Gaddy, K. R. ★*Well of Souls* — 787
   Whitney, Craig R. *All the Stops* — 786.5
MUSICAL PERFORMANCE
   Etheridge, Melissa. *Talking to My Angels* — B
   Hough, Stephen. *Rough Ideas* — 786.2092
   Mauceri, John. *For the Love of Music* — 781.1
   Mauceri, John. *Maestros and Their Music* — 781.45
   Musical Revolutions. Isacoff, Stuart — 780.9
MUSICAL STYLE
   Gasser, Nolan. *Why You Like It* — 781.1
MUSICALS
   Andrews, Julie. *Home Work* — B
   Bloom, Ken. *Broadway Musicals* — 792.6
   Butler, Isaac. *The World Only Spins Forward* — 812
   Hischak, Thomas S. *The Oxford Companion to the American Musical* — 782.1
   Kapilow, Robert. ★*Listening for America* — 782.42164
   Lane, Stewart F. *Black Broadway* — 792.089
   Lloyd Webber, Andrew. *Unmasked* — B
   Maslon, Laurence. ★*Broadway* — 782.1
   Max, D. T. *Finale* — 782.1
   Merritt, Tyler. *I Take My Coffee Black* — 791.4302
   Miranda, Lin-Manuel. *Hamilton* — 782.1
   Mordden, Ethan. *Anything Goes* — 782.1
   Purdum, Todd S. *Something Wonderful*
   Riedel, Michael. *Razzle Dazzle* — 792.09
   Riedel, Michael. *Singular Sensation* — 792
   Rodgers, Mary. *Shy*
   Santopietro, Tom. *The Sound of Music Story* — 791.43
   Sondheim, Stephen. *Look, I Made a Hat* — 782.1
   Stempel, Larry. ★*Showtime* — 792.609
   Viertel, Jack. *The Secret Life of the American Musical* — 792.609
MUSICIANS
   Amos, Tori. *Resistance* — B
   Barlow, John Perry. *Mother American Night* — 782.42164
   Bernstein, Burton. ★*Leonard Bernstein* — B
   Boilen, Bob. *Your Song Changed My Life* — 780.92
   Bono. ★*Surrender* — B
   Bullock, Darryl W. *David Bowie Made Me Gay* — 780
   Butler, Marcia. *The Skin Above My Knee* — B
   Carlin, Peter Ames. *Bruce* — B
   Chernaik, Judith. *Schumann* — B
   Clapton, Eric. *Clapton* — B
   Connolly, Ray. *Being John Lennon* — B
   Costello, Elvis. *Unfaithful Music & Disappearing Ink* — B
   Crouch, Stanley. *Kansas City Lightning* — B
   DeRogatis, Jim. *Soulless* — B
   Dove, Rita. *Sonata Mulattica* — 811
   Feinstein, Michael. *The Gershwins and Me* — 782.42164
   Goldsmith, Martin. *The Inextinguishable Symphony* — B
   Greenman, Ben. *Dig If You Will the Picture* — B
   Haupt, Lyanda Lynn. *Mozart's Starling* — B
   Hyden, Steven. *Twilight of the Gods* — 781.6609
   Isacoff, Stuart. *Musical Revolutions* — 780.9
   Jones, Booker T. *Time Is Tight* — B
   Levy, Aidan. *Saxophone Colossus* — B
   McBride, James. *Kill 'Em and Leave* — B
   McKeen, William. *Everybody Had an Ocean* — 781.6609
   Moby. *Porcelain* — B
   Momus. *Niche* — B
   Morris, Edmund. *Beethoven* — B
   Moss, Adam. ★*The Work of Art* — 701
   Moynahan, Brian. *Leningrad* — 780.92
   Nesmith, Michael. *Infinite Tuesday* — B
   Norman, Philip. *George Harrison* — B
   Oppedisano, Tony. *Sinatra and Me* — B
   Palmer, Amanda. ★*The Art of Asking* — 782.42164
   Porter, Cecelia Hopkins. *Five Lives in Music* — B
   Powers, Ann. *Good Booty* — 781.64
   Powers, Ann. ★*Traveling* — B

   Prince. *The Beautiful Ones* — B
   Questlove. *Mo' Meta Blues* — 782.42164
   Quin, Tegan. ★*High School* — B
   Ratliff, Ben. *The Jazz Ear* — 781.6509
   Remnick, David. *Holding the Note* — 781.64
   Ribowsky, Mark. *Dreams to Remember* — B
   Satrapi, Marjane. *Chicken with Plums* — 741.5
   Simmons, Sylvie. *I'm Your Man* — B
   Smith, Patti. ★*A Book of Days* — 779
   Smith, Patti. ★*Just Kids* — B
   Spera, Keith. *Groove Interrupted* — B
   Stanley, Bob. ★*The Story of the Bee Gees* — 782.42164
   Suchet, John. *Mozart* — B
   Swafford, Jan. *Mozart* — B
   Teachout, Terry. *Pops* — B
   Thomson, Graeme. *George Harrison* — B
   Threadgill, Henry. *Easily Slip into Another World* — B
   Vogel, Joseph. *Man in the Music* — B
   Watts, Reggie. *Great Falls, MT* — B
   Williams, Lucinda. *Don't Tell Anybody the Secrets I Told You* — B
   Williams, Zach. *Rescue Story* — B
   Wolff, Daniel J. *Grown-Up Anger* — 920
   Womack, Kenneth. *All Things Must Pass Away* — 781.66
   Wood, Damon. *Working for the Man, Playing in the Band* — 782.42164
   Young, Neil. *Waging Heavy Peace* — B
   Zanes, Warren. *Deliver Me from Nowhere* — 782.42164
   Zanes, Warren. *Petty* — B
MUSICIANS' SPOUSES
   Gaye, Jan. *After the Dance* — B
MUSICOLOGISTS
   McCormick, Mack. *Biography of a Phantom* — 782.421643
MUSICOLOGY
   Gasser, Nolan. *Why You Like It* — 781.1
   Sloan, Nate. *Switched on Pop* — 781.64
MUSK, ELON
   Berger, Eric. *Liftoff* — B
   Davenport, Christian. *The Space Barons* — 920
   Higgins, Tim. *Power Play* — 338.7
   Isaacson, Walter. ★*Elon Musk* — B
   Mezrich, Ben. *Breaking Twitter* — 338.7
MUSLIM AMERICANS
   Moghul, Haroon. *How to Be a Muslim* — B
MUSLIM FAMILIES
   Hoja, Gulchehra. *A Stone Is Most Precious Where It Belongs* — B
MUSLIM MEN
   AL Samawi, Mohammed. *The Fox Hunt* — 953
   Elnoury, Tamer. *American Radical* — B
   Moghul, Haroon. *How to Be a Muslim* — B
MUSLIM WOMEN
   Baker, Deborah. *The Convert* — B
   Brooks, Geraldine. *Nine Parts of Desire* — 305.48
   Goudeau, Jessica. ★*After the Last Border* — 362.83
   Hirsi Ali, Ayaan. ★*Infidel* — B
   Lal, Ruby. *Empress* — B
   Lalami, Laila. *Conditional Citizens* — 323.60973
   Lemmon, Gayle Tzemach. *The Dressmaker of Khair Khana* — B
   Muhammad, Ibtihaj. *Proud* — B
   Nafisi, Azar. *Things I've Been Silent About* — B
   Nawaz, Zarqa. *Laughing All the Way to the Mosque* — 791.45028
   Power, Carla. *If the Oceans Were Ink* — B
   Rehman, Sabeeha. *Threading My Prayer Rug* — 305.8
   Sarsour, Linda. *We Are Not Here to Be Bystanders* — B
   Zoepf, Katherine. *Excellent Daughters* — 305.42
MUSLIM WOMEN'S RIGHTS
   Hirsi Ali, Ayaan. ★*Infidel* — B
MUSLIM YOUTH
   Ghobash, Omar Saif. *Letters to a Young Muslim* — 297.09
MUSLIMS
   Abdul Rauf, Feisal. *Moving the Mountain* — 297
   Akyol, Mustafa. ★*Reopening Muslim Minds* — 297.09
   Ali-Karamali, Sumbul. *Demystifying Shariah* — 340.5
   Armstrong, Karen. ★*Islam* — 297
   Armstrong, Karen. *Muhammad* — B
   Baker, Deborah. *The Convert* — B
   Blanford, Nicholas. *Warriors of God* — 956.9204
   Carranca, Adriana. *Soul by Soul* — 230
   Carter, Jimmy. *Palestine* — 956.04
   Curtis, Edward E. *Muslims in America* — 305.6

AUTHOR, TITLE, SERIES AND SUBJECT INDEX

Eggers, Dave. *Zeitoun*	305.892
Eteraz, Ali. *Children of Dust*	B
Geter, Hafizah. *Un-American*	811
H, Lamya. ★*Hijab Butch Blues*	B
Hirsi Ali, Ayaan. ★*Infidel*	B
Husain, Ed. ★*The House of Islam*	297
Iftin, Abdi Nor. *Call Me American*	305.893
Kugle, Scott Alan. *Living Out Islam*	297
Maass, Peter. *Love Thy Neighbor*	949.702
Manglik, Gauri. ★*Muslims in Story*	809
Marable, Manning. ★*Malcolm X*	B
Mattson, Ingrid. ★*The Story of the Qur'an*	297.122
Moghul, Haroon. *How to Be a Muslim*	B
Muhammad, Ibtihaj. *Proud*	B
Nasr, Seyyed Hossein. *Islam*	297
Nawaz, Zarqa. *Laughing All the Way to the Mosque*	791.45028
Qureshi, Saqib Iqbal. *Being Muslim Today*	305.6
Ramadan, Tariq. ★*Introduction to Islam*	297
Rashid, Ahmed. *Taliban*	958.104
Rehman, Sabeeha. *Threading My Prayer Rug*	305.8
Satrapi, Marjane. ★*The Complete Persepolis*	741.5
Seierstad, Asne. *Two Sisters*	956.9104
Tanais. *In Sensorium*	B
Trebincevic, Kenan. *The Bosnia List*	B
Velshi, Ali. *Small Acts of Courage*	B
Muslims in America. Curtis, Edward E.	305.6
★*Muslims in Story.* Manglik, Gauri	809
MUSSOLINI, BENITO, 1883-1945	
Kertzer, David I. *The Pope and Mussolini*	322
Mustich, James	
★*1,000 Books to Read*	028
Mustill, Tom	
How to Speak Whale	591.59
MUSTILL, TOM	
Mustill, Tom. *How to Speak Whale*	591.59
MUTINY	
Alexander, Caroline. *The Bounty*	996.1
Grann, David. ★*The Wager*	910.91
Johnson, Steven. *Enemy of All Mankind*	910.4
Rediker, Marcus. *The Amistad Rebellion*	326.0973
Young, Kevin. *Ardency*	811
MUTTER, THOMAS D. (THOMAS DENT), 1811-1859	
Aptowicz, Cristin O'Keefe. *Dr. Mutter's Marvels*	B
MUTUAL FUNDS	
Belfort, Jordan. ★*The Wolf of Investing*	332.63
Mutual Rescue. Novello, Carol	636.088
MUTUALISM	
Brooks, David. ★*How to Know a Person*	158.2
My American Dream. Bastianich, Lidia	B
My Autobiography of Carson McCullers. Shapland, Jenn	B
My Beloved Monster. Carr, Caleb	B
★*My Beloved World.* Sotomayor, Sonia	B
★*My Body.* Ratajkowski, Emily	B
My Bombay Kitchen. King, Niloufer Ichaporia	641.595
My Bondage and My Freedom. Douglass, Frederick	B
My Boy Will Die of Sorrow. Olivares, Efren C.	305.9
My Brief History. Hawking, Stephen	B
★*My Broken Language.* Hudes, Quiara Alegria	B
★*My Child Is Trans, Now What?.* Greene, Benjamin	649
My Cubs. Simon, Scott	796.357
My Dearest Friend. Adams, John	973.4
My Face Is Black Is True. Berry, Mary Frances	B
My Fair Junkie. Dresner, Amy	B
My Father's Paradise. Sabar, Ariel	B
My Fellow Soldiers. Carroll, Andrew	940.4
★*My Friend Anne Frank.* Pick-Goslar, Hannah Elizabeth	B
My Generation. Styron, William	814
My Girls. Fisher, Todd	B
My Grandfather Would Have Shot Me. Teege, Jennifer	929.2
My Guantanamo Diary. Khan, Mahvish Rukhsana	973.931
★*My Happiness Bears No Relation to Happiness.* Hoffman, Adina	B
My Invented Country. Allende, Isabel	B
My Jewish Year. Pogrebin, Abigail	296.4
My Kitchen Year. Reichl, Ruth	641.5
My Korea. Kim, Hooni	641.595
My Korean Deli. Howe, Ben Ryder	B
My Life. Duncan, Isadora	B
My Life. Clinton, Bill	B

My Life as a Goddess. Branum, Guy	B
My Life as a Villainess. Lippman, Laura	B
★*My Life in France.* Child, Julia	B
★*My Life in Full.* Nooyi, Indra	B
My Life in Middlemarch. Mead, Rebecca	823
★*My Life in Recipes.* Nathan, Joan	641.5
My Life on the Road. Steinem, Gloria	B
★*My Life, My Love, My Legacy.* King, Coretta Scott	B
My Losing Season. Conroy, Pat	B
My Marathon. Shorter, Frank	796.42
My Master Recipes. Wells, Patricia	641.5
My Mess Is a Bit of a Life. Pritchett, Georgia	B
My Mexico City Kitchen. Camara, Gabriela	641.5972
★*My Name Is Barbra.* Streisand, Barbra	B
My Name Is Selma. Van De Perre, Selma	940.53
★*My Own Words.* Ginsburg, Ruth Bader	347.73
My Parents. Hemon, Aleksandar	814
My Paris Kitchen. Lebovitz, David	641.594
My Patients and Other Animals. Fincham-Gray, Suzanne	B
★*My People.* Hunter-Gault, Charlayne	305.48
My Promised Land. Shavit, Ari	956.05
My Remarkable Journey. Johnson, Katherine G.	B
My Salinger Year. Rakoff, Joanna Smith	B
★*My Seven Black Fathers.* Jawando, Will	B
★*My Song.* Belafonte, Harry	782.42164
My Squirrel Days. Kemper, Ellie	B
My Stroke of Insight. Taylor, Jill Bolte	362.19681
My Sweet Mexico. Gerson, Fany	641.5972
My Time Will Come. Manuel, Ian	B
My Travels with Mrs. Kennedy. Hill, Clint	B
My Twenty-Five Years in Provence. Mayle, Peter	944.9
My Vanishing Country. Sellers, Bakari	B
My Venice and Other Essays. Leon, Donna	945
My Vocabulary Did This to Me. Spicer, Jack	811
My War Criminal. Stern, Jessica	341.6
My Wife Said You May Want to Marry Me. Rosenthal, Jason	B
My Year of Running Dangerously. Foreman, Tom	B
MYCOLOGY	
Monosson, Emily. ★*Blight*	616.9
Sheldrake, Merlin. *Entangled Life*	579.5
Myers, Amy	
The Autoimmune Solution Cookbook	641.5
★*The Autoimmune Solution*	616.97
Myers, David G.	
How Do We Know Ourselves?	155.2
MYERS, ELSIE PALMER, 1872-1955	
Lucey, Donna M. *Sargent's Women*	920
Myers, Gary	
Brady vs. Manning	B
The Catch	796.332
Myers, Isabel Briggs	
Gifts Differing	155.2
Myers, Leah	
Thinning Blood	B
MYERS, LEAH	
Myers, Leah. *Thinning Blood*	B
Myers, Marc	
Why Jazz Happened	781.65
Myers, Paul	
The Kids in the Hall	920
Myers, Steven Lee	
The New Tsar	B
Myles, Eileen	
I Must Be Living Twice	811.54
Myron, Vicki	
★*Dewey*	636.80092
MYSTERIES	
Rehak, Melanie. *Girl Sleuth*	813
Mysteries of nature trilogy [Series]. Wohlleben, Peter	582.16
Mysteries of the Mall. Rybczynski, Witold	720
MYSTERY AUTHORS	
Collins, Max Allan. *Spillane*	B
James, P. D. *Talking About Detective Fiction*	823
Sims, Michael. *Arthur and Sherlock*	B
The Mystery of Charles Dickens. Wilson, A. N.	823
A Mystery of Mysteries. Dawidziak, Mark	B
MYSTERY WRITING	
Collins, Max Allan. *Spillane*	B

James, P. D. *Talking About Detective Fiction*	823
Worsley, Lucy. ★*Agatha Christie*	B

MYSTICISM

Bly, Robert. *Collected Poems*	811
Gibran, Kahlil. *And the Prophet Said*	811
Harrington, Joel F. *Dangerous Mystic*	B
Husain, Ed. ★*The House of Islam*	297
Jalal al-Din Rumi, Maulana. *Rumi*	891

MYSTICS

Fuhrmann, Joseph T. *Rasputin*	B
Harrington, Joel F. *Dangerous Mystic*	B
Smith, Douglas. *Rasputin*	B
The Myth of Sisyphus and Other Essays. Camus, Albert	844
The Myth of the Rational Market. Fox, Justin	332.64

MYTHICAL CREATURES

Jennings, Ken. ★*100 Places to See After You Die*	202
Larrington, Carolyne. *The Norse Myths*	293
Loxton, Daniel. *Abominable Science!*	001.944
O'Connor, John. *The Secret History of Bigfoot*	001.944
★*Mythology.* Hamilton, Edith	292.1

MYTHOLOGY

Alexander, Caroline. *The War That Killed Achilles*	883
Armstrong, Karen. ★*A Short History of Myth*	201
Becker, Ernest. ★*The Denial of Death*	128
Brewer, Ebenezer Cobham. ★*Brewer's Dictionary of Phrase & Fable*	423
Campbell, Joseph. *The Masks of God*	201.3
Campbell, Joseph. *The Power of Myth*	201.3
Carroll, Georgie. *The Mythology Book*	201
Everitt, Anthony. *The Rise of Athens*	938
Gosden, Chris. *Magic*	133.4
Lin, Jami Nakamura. *The Night Parade*	B
Mouton, Deborah D. E. E. P. *Black Chameleon*	
Nabokov, Peter. *Where the Lightning Strikes*	299.7
O'Connor, John. *The Secret History of Bigfoot*	001.944

MYTHOLOGY — CLASSICAL — GREEK

Homer. *The Iliad*	883
Homer. *Iliad*	883
The Mythology Book. Carroll, Georgie	201

MYTHOLOGY IN LITERATURE

Hughes, Bettany. *Venus and Aphrodite*	292
Judah, Hettie. *Lapidarium*	553.8
Vogler, Christopher. ★*The Writer's Journey*	808.2

MYTHOLOGY, CHINESE

Yang, Lihui. ★*Handbook of Chinese Mythology*	299.5

MYTHOLOGY, EGYPTIAN

Wilkinson, Richard H. ★*The Complete Gods and Goddesses of Ancient Egypt*	299

MYTHOLOGY, FOLKLORE, AND LEGENDS

Carroll, Georgie. *The Mythology Book*	201
Hamilton, Edith. ★*Mythology*	292.1
Larrington, Carolyne. *The Norse Myths*	293
Pullman, Philip. ★*Fairy Tales from the Brothers Grimm*	398.2
Schonwerth, Franz Xaver von. *The Turnip Princess*	398.2
Seale, Yasmine. *Aladdin*	398.2
Wilkinson, Richard H. ★*The Complete Gods and Goddesses of Ancient Egypt*	299
Zimmerman, Jess. *Women and Other Monsters*	155.3

MYTHOLOGY, GREEK

Zimmerman, Jess. *Women and Other Monsters*	155.3

MYTHOLOGY, JAPANESE

Lin, Jami Nakamura. *The Night Parade*	B

MYTHOLOGY, NORSE

Brown, Nancy Marie. *The Real Valkyrie*	948
Larrington, Carolyne. *The Norse Myths*	293

N

Nabokov, Peter	
Where the Lightning Strikes	299.7

NABOKOV, VLADIMIR VLADIMIROVICH, 1899-1977

Pitzer, Andrea. *The Secret History of Vladimir Nabokov*	813
Pyle, Robert Michael. *Nature Matrix*	508
Weinman, Sarah. *The Real Lolita*	362.88092

NADAR, FELIX, 1820-1910

Begley, Adam. *The Great Nadar*	B
Nadeau, Barbie Latza	
The Godmother	364.106

Nadeau, Jean-Benoit	
★*The Story of French*	440
The Story of Spanish	460
Nadella, Satya	
Hit Refresh	B
★*Nadiya Bakes.* Hussain, Nadiya	641.81
★*Nadiya's Everyday Baking.* Hussain, Nadiya	641.5
Nafisi, Azar	
Read Dangerously	809
★*Reading Lolita in Tehran*	B
The Republic of Imagination	B
Things I've Been Silent About	B

NAFISI, AZAR

Nafisi, Azar. *Read Dangerously*	809
Nafisi, Azar. ★*Reading Lolita in Tehran*	B
Nafisi, Azar. *Things I've Been Silent About*	B
Nagasaki. Southard, Susan	940.54

NAGASAKI, JAPAN

Barrett, David Dean. *140 Days to Hiroshima*	940.54
Ham, Paul. *Hiroshima Nagasaki*	940.54
Smith, Jim B. *The Last Mission*	940.54
Southard, Susan. *Nagasaki*	940.54
Wallace, Chris. *Countdown 1945*	940.54
Nagassar, Rohadi	
When We Belong	254
Nagorski, Andrew	
Saving Freud	940.53
Nagourney, Adam	
The Times	071
Naifeh, Steven W.	
Van Gogh	B

NAIPAUL, V. S. (VIDIADHAR SURAJPRASAD), 1932-2018

French, Patrick. *The World Is What It Is*	B
Nakazawa, Donna Jackson	
The Angel and the Assassin	612.8

NAKAZAWA, DONNA JACKSON

Nakazawa, Donna Jackson. *The Angel and the Assassin*	612.8
Naked. Feast, Fancy	792.7
Naked Economics. Wheelan, Charles J.	330
Naked Statistics. Wheelan, Charles J.	519.5
Namath, Joe Willie	
★*All the Way*	B

NAMATH, JOE WILLIE, 1943-

Namath, Joe Willie. ★*All the Way*	B
The Name of War. Lepore, Jill	973.2

NAME-BRAND PRODUCTS

Knoedelseder, William. *Bitter Brew*	338.7
Windhorst, Brian. *Lebron, Inc.*	B
★*Nanaville.* Quindlen, Anna	B
Nance, Malcolm W.	
The Plot to Betray America	973.933

NANKING MASSACRE, NANJING, JIANGSU SHENG, CHINA, 1937

Chang, Iris. ★*The Rape of Nanking*	951.04
Mitter, Rana. *Forgotten Ally*	951.04
Mizuki, Shigeru. *Showa 1926-1939*	741.5

NANNIES

Corrigan, Kelly. *Glitter and Glue*	B
Marks, Ann. *Vivian Maier Developed*	778.9
McKeon, Kathy. *Jackie's Girl*	B

NANOTECHNOLOGY

Kurzweil, Ray. ★*The Singularity Is Near*	153.9
Naomi Osaka. Rothenberg, Ben	B
Napier, Erin	
Heirloom Rooms	747

NAPLES, ITALY

Wilson, Katherine. *Only in Naples*	B
Napoleon. Broers, Michael	B
Napoleon. Broers, Michael	944.05
Napoleon. Broers, Michael	B
★*Napoleon.* Roberts, Andrew	B
Napoleon. Zamoyski, Adam	B
Napoleon. Johnson, Paul	B
Napoleon (Michael Broers) [Series]. Broers, Michael	B

NAPOLEON I, EMPEROR OF THE FRENCH, 1769-1821

Broers, Michael. *Napoleon*	B
Broers, Michael. *Napoleon*	944.05
Broers, Michael. *Napoleon*	B
Cornwell, Bernard. *Waterloo*	940.2

AUTHOR, TITLE, SERIES AND SUBJECT INDEX

Johnson, Paul. *Napoleon* .... B
Roberts, Andrew. ★*Napoleon* .... B
Williams, Kate. *Ambition and Desire* .... B
Zamoyski, Adam. *Napoleon* .... B
NAPOLEONIC WARS, 1800-1815
    Ackroyd, Peter. *Revolution* 941.07
    Broers, Michael. *Napoleon* 944.05
    Cornwell, Bernard. *Waterloo* 940.2
    O'Keeffe, Paul. *Waterloo* 940.2
    Zamoyski, Adam. *Napoleon* .... B
Napoli, Lisa
    Susan, Linda, Nina & Cokie 920
    Up All Night 384.55
Narayan, R. K.
    ★*The Ramayana* 294.5
Narayan, Shoba
    The Milk Lady of Bangalore 390
NARAYAN, SHOBA
    Narayan, Shoba. *The Milk Lady of Bangalore* 390
NARCISSISM
    Durvasula, Ramani. ★*It's Not You* 155.2
    Kluger, Jeffrey. *The Narcissist Next Door* 616.85
    McBride, Karyl. *Will I Ever Be Good Enough?* 616.85
    Sisman, Adam. *The Professor and the Parson* 364.16
The Narcissist Next Door. Kluger, Jeffrey 616.85
NARCOLEPSY
    Leschziner, Guy. *The Nocturnal Brain* 616.8
NARCOTICS
    Inglis, Lucy. *Milk of Paradise* 362.29
    Quinones, Sam. *Dreamland* 362.29
NARCOTICS INVESTIGATION
    Ratliff, Evan. *The Mastermind* .... B
NARRAGANSETT (NORTH AMERICAN PEOPLE)
    Warren, James A. *God, War, and Providence* 974.5
NARRATION (RHETORIC)
    Le Guin, Ursula K. *Words Are My Matter* 818
    Vogler, Christopher. ★*The Writer's Journey* 808.2
NARRATIVE NONFICTION FOR KIDS AND TEENS
    Burcaw, Shane. ★*Laughing at My Nightmare* .... B
    Sheinkin, Steve. *Bomb* 623.4
Narrative of the Life of Frederick Douglass, an American Slave. Douglass, Frederick .... B
The Narrow Corridor. Acemoglu, Daron 320.01
Nasaw, David
    Andrew Carnegie .... B
    The Chief .... B
    The Last Million 940.53
    ★*The Patriarch* .... B
Nashawaty, Chris
    Caddyshack 791.43
NASHVILLE, TENNESSEE
    Franklin, John Hope. *In Search of the Promised Land* 929
    Halberstam, David. ★*The Children* 323.1
    Moss, Marissa R. *Her Country* 781.642
Nasr, Seyyed Hossein
    Islam 297
Nasr, Seyyed Vali Reza
    The Shia Revival 297.8
NASSAR, LARRY
    Barr, John. *Start by Believing* 364.15
The Nasty Bits. Bourdain, Anthony 641.5092
NATCHEZ, MISSISSIPPI
    Grant, Richard. *The Deepest South of All* 976.2
Nathan, Debbie
    Sybil Exposed .... B
Nathan, Joan
    King Solomon's Table 641.5
    ★*My Life in Recipes* 641.5
NATHAN, JOAN
    Nathan, Joan. ★*My Life in Recipes* 641.5
Nathans, Sydney
    To Free a Family .... B
NATION BUILDING
    Amar, Akhil Reed. *The Words That Made Us* 342.7302
    Peres, Shimon. *No Room for Small Dreams* .... B
The Nation City. Emanuel, Rahm 352.23
A Nation Under Our Feet. Hahn, Steven 975

NATION-BUILDING
    Brands, H. W. ★*Heirs of the Founders* 973.5
    Hoyer, Katja. ★*Beyond the Wall* 943.087
    Kelly, John. *The Graves Are Walking* 941.5081
    Lepore, Jill. ★*These Truths* 973
    Proenza-Coles, Christina. *American Founders* 973
    Rakove, Jack N. *Revolutionaries* 973.3
★*National Audubon Society Field Guide to Fishes*. Gilbert, Carter Rowell 597
★*The National Audubon Society Field Guide to North American Birds*. Bull, John L. 598.097
★*National Audubon Society Field Guide to North American Mammals*. Whitaker, John O. 599.097
NATIONAL CEMETERIES
    Cotton, Tom. *Sacred Duty* 355.6
    McElya, Micki. *The Politics of Mourning* 975.5
    Poole, Robert M. *Section 60* 975.5
NATIONAL CHARACTERISTICS
    Booth, Michael. *The Almost Nearly Perfect People* 948.071
    Faloyin, Dipo. ★*Africa Is Not a Country* 960.33
    Mikanowski, Jacob. ★*Goodbye, Eastern Europe* ... 947
    Paul, Joel R. *Indivisible* 973.5
    Smith, Helmut Walser. *Germany, a Nation in Its Time* 943
    Trentmann, Frank. *Out of the Darkness* 943.08
NATIONAL CHARACTERISTICS, AMERICAN
    Anderson, Fred. *The Dominion of War* 973
    Avlon, John P. *Washington's Farewell* 973.4
    Blanco, Richard. *How to Love a Country* 811
    Boorstin, Daniel J. *The Americans* 973
    Brookhiser, Richard. *Give Me Liberty* 320.540973
    Cheever, Susan. *Drinking in America* 394.1
    Churchwell, Sarah Bartlett. *Behold, America* 973.9
    Didion, Joan. *Where I Was from* 979.4
    Ellis, Joseph J. *American Creation* 973.3
    Grandin, Greg. *The End of the Myth* 973
    Hakkakiyan, Ruya. *A Beginner's Guide to America* 646.7
    Holzer, Harold. *Monument Man* .... B
    Klosterman, Chuck. *But What If We're Wrong* 909.83
    Kushner, Tony. *Angels in America* 812
    Lee, Erika. *America for Americans* 305.800973
    Lohman, Sarah. ★*Endangered Eating* 641.5973
    McCullough, David G. ★*The American Spirit* 973
    Meacham, Jon. ★*The Soul of America* 973
    Nafisi, Azar. *The Republic of Imagination* .... B
    Obama, Barack. ★*The Audacity of Hope* .... B
    Offerman, Nick. *Where the Deer and the Antelope Play* 973.93
    Oluo, Ijeoma. *Mediocre* 305.310973
    Packer, George. *Last Best Hope* 973.93
    Packer, George. ★*The Unwinding* 973.924
    Prothero, Stephen R. *The American Bible* 973
    Prothero, Stephen R. *God the Bestseller* 070.5
    Puglionesi, Alicia. *In Whose Ruins* 973
    Rather, Dan. *What Unites Us* 323.6
    Samet, Elizabeth D. *Looking for the Good War* 940.53
    Sexton, Jared Yates. *American Rule* 973
NATIONAL CHARACTERISTICS, AUSTRALIAN
    Bryson, Bill. *In a Sunburned Country* 919
NATIONAL CHARACTERISTICS, BRITISH
    Bryson, Bill. *Notes from a Small Island* 914
    Bryson, Bill. *The Road to Little Dribbling* 914
    Tombs, Robert. *The English and Their History* 942
NATIONAL CHARACTERISTICS, CHINESE
    Theroux, Paul. *Riding the Iron Rooster* 915
NATIONAL CHARACTERISTICS, ENGLISH
    Morrison, Robert. *The Regency Years* 941.07
NATIONAL CHARACTERISTICS, FRENCH
    Sciolino, Elaine. *The Seine* 944
NATIONAL CHARACTERISTICS, GERMAN
    MacGregor, Neil. *Germany* 943
NATIONAL CHARACTERISTICS, ITALIAN
    Hooper, John. *The Italians* 945.093
    Raffa, Guy P. *Dante's Bones* 851
NATIONAL CHARACTERISTICS, JAPANESE
    Finn, Adharanand. *The Way of the Runner* 796.42
    Pilling, David. *Bending Adversity* 952.0512
NATIONAL CHARACTERISTICS, SCOTTISH
    Herman, Arthur. *How the Scots Invented the Modern World* 941.1
National Dish. Von Bremzen, Anya 641.3
National Geographic Atlas of Beer. Hoalst-Pullen, Nancy 663

PUBLIC LIBRARY CORE COLLECTION: NONFICTION
Twentieth Edition

National Geographic Atlas of the National Parks. Waterman, Jonathan — 917.304
National Geographic Birding Essentials. Alderfer, Jonathan K. — 598.072
National Geographic Complete Guide to Pet Health, Behavior, and Happiness.
    Weitzman, Gary — 636.088
National Geographic the National Parks. Heacox, Kim — 363.6
NATIONAL HEALTH INSURANCE
    Cohn, Jonathan. *The Ten Year War* — 368.38
NATIONAL LIBERATION MOVEMENTS
    Anand, Anita. *The Patient Assassin* — B
    Arana, Marie. *Bolivar* — B
    Chasteen, John Charles. *Americanos* — 980
    Guha, Ramachandra. *Rebels Against the Raj* — 954.03
    Hoffman, David E. *Give Me Liberty* — B
    Mohan, Rohini. *The Seasons of Trouble* — 954.9303
NATIONAL MONUMENTS
    Smith, Clint. ★*How the Word Is Passed* — 973
The National Parks. Duncan, Dayton — 333.78
NATIONAL PARKS AND RESERVES
    Black, George. *Empire of Shadows* — 978.7
    Duncan, Dayton. *The National Parks* — 333.78
    Egan, Timothy. ★*The Big Burn* — 973.911
    Galassi, Peter. *Ansel Adams in Yosemite Valley* — 770.92
    Heacox, Kim. *National Geographic the National Parks* — 363.6
    Heacox, Kim. *Rhythm of the Wild* — 979.8
    King, Dean. *Guardians of the Valley* — 333.72
    McIntyre, Rick. *The Reign of Wolf 21* — 599.773
    Pennington, Emily. *Feral* — B
    Roberts, David. *The Bears Ears* — 979.2
    Ross, John F. *The Promise of the Grand Canyon* — 917.91
    Waterman, Jonathan. *National Geographic Atlas of the National Parks* — 917.304
NATIONAL SECURITY
    Ackerman, Spencer. *Reign of Terror* — 973.931
    Boghosian, Heidi. *"i Have Nothing to Hide"* — 363.1
    Brooks, Rosa. *How Everything Became War and the Military Became Everything* — 355
    Farmer, John J. *The Ground Truth* — 973.931
    Gage, Beverly. *G-Man* — B
    Gans, John. *White House Warriors* — 355
    Graff, Garrett M. *Raven Rock* — 363.350973
    Greenberg, Andy. *Sandworm* — 364.16
    Hill, Clint. *Five Presidents* — B
    Jacobsen, Annie. *Phenomena* — 133.8
    Jacobson, Sidney. *The 9-11 Report* — 741.5
    Kaplan, Fred M. *The Bomb* — 355.8
    Klare, Michael T. *All Hell Breaking Loose* — 355.20973
    Manning, Chelsea. *Readme.Txt* — B
    Mayer, Jane. *The Dark Side* — 973.931
    Risen, James. ★*The Last Honest Man* — 973.92
    Scharre, Paul. *Four Battlegrounds* — 006.3
    Stone, Geoffrey R. *Perilous Times* — 323.44
    Thomas, Evan. *Ike's Bluff* — 973.921092
    Thompson, Nicholas. *The Hawk and the Dove* — 973.92
    Vickers, Michael G. *By All Means Available* — 355
    Whitlock, Craig. ★*Fat Leonard* — 364.16
    Woodward, Bob. *Peril* — 973.933
NATIONAL SECURITY ADVISORS
    Ferguson, Niall. *Kissinger* — 973.924
NATIONAL SONGS
    Clague, Mark. *O Say Can You Hear?* — 782.42
NATIONAL TERRITORY
    Grandin, Greg. *The End of the Myth* — 973
    Kassabova, Kapka. *Border* — 949.9
    Shehadeh, Raja. *Where the Line Is Drawn* — 956.9405
    Taylor, Alan. *The Civil War of 1812* — 973.5
NATIONALISM
    Alberta, Tim. *The Kingdom, the Power, and the Glory* — 270.8
    Aly, Gotz. *Europe Against the Jews* — 305.892
    Applebaum, Anne. *Twilight of Democracy* — 321.9
    Appy, Christian G. *American Reckoning* — 959.704
    Askwith, Richard. *Unbreakable* — B
    Brookhiser, Richard. *Give Me Liberty* — 320.540973
    Churchwell, Sarah Bartlett. *Behold, America* — 973.9
    Cotton, Tom. *Sacred Duty* — 355.6
    Daunton, M. J. ★*The Economic Government of the World* — 337
    Duiker, William J. *Ho Chi Minh* — B
    Erdozain, Dominic. *One Nation Under Guns* — 363.33
    Feldman, Noah. ★*To Be a Jew Today* — 296.3

Figes, Orlando. ★*The Whisperers* — 306.850947
Foroohar, Rana. *Homecoming* — 338.6
Frank, Richard B. *Tower of Skulls* — 940.54
Galeotti, Mark. *A Short History of Russia* — 947.086
Grandin, Greg. *The End of the Myth* — 973
Hedges, Chris. *War Is a Force That Gives Us Meaning* — 355.02
Judson, Pieter M. *The Habsburg Empire* — 943.6
King, David. *The Trial of Adolf Hitler* — 345.43
Kinzer, Stephen. ★*The True Flag* — 327.73
Lee, Erika. *America for Americans* — 305.800973
Lepore, Jill. ★*These Truths* — 973
MacMillan, Margaret. *Paris 1919* — 940.3
McElya, Micki. *The Politics of Mourning* — 975.5
Mishra, Pankaj. *Age of Anger* — 909.8
Mohan, Rohini. *The Seasons of Trouble* — 954.9303
Neiwert, David A. ★*The Age of Insurrection* — 303.48
Nusseibeh, Sari. *Once Upon a Country* — B
O'Donnell, Svenja. *Inge's War* — 943.086
Paul, Joel R. *Indivisible* — 973.5
Plokhy, Serhii. *Lost Kingdom* — 947
Prothero, Stephen R. *The American Bible* — 973
Satter, David. *The Less You Know, the Better You Sleep* — 947.086
Sattouf, Riad. *The Arab of the Future 2* — 741.5
Sattouf, Riad. *The Arab of the Future* — 741.5
Schama, Simon. *Citizens* — 944.04
Schama, Simon. *The Embarrassment of Riches* — 949.2
Smith, Helmut Walser. *Germany, a Nation in Its Time* — 943
Snyder, Timothy. *The Red Prince* — B
Soyinka, Wole. *Of Africa* — 960
Stanley, Jason. *How Fascism Works* — 321.9
Stevens, Stuart. *It Was All a Lie* — 324.2734
Taylor, Alan. *The Civil War of 1812* — 973.5
Taylor, Jay. *The Generalissimo* — B
Van Agtmael, Peter. *Look at the USA* — 070
Von Bremzen, Anya. *National Dish* — 641.3
Wallis, Jim. *The False White Gospel* — 261.7
Wertheim, L. Jon. *This Is Your Brain on Sports* — 796.01
Zakaria, Fareed. *Age of Revolutions* — 303.6
NATIONALISTS
    Gandhi. *An Autobiography* — B
    Snyder, Timothy. *The Red Prince* — B
Nations, Scott
    A History of the United States in Five Crashes — 338.5
Native. Qashu, Sayed — 892.4
Native American Son. Buford, Kate — B
★*Native Guard*. Trethewey, Natasha D. — 811
NATIVE HAWAIIANS
    Keene, Adrienne. *Notable Native People* — 920
NATIVE LANGUAGE
    Crystal, David. *The Story of English in 100 Words* — 422
★*Native Nations*. DuVal, Kathleen — 970.004
★*Native North American Art*. Berlo, Janet Catherine — 704.03
NATIVE PLANTS
    Edwards, Adrienne L. *Firescaping Your Home* — 635.9
    Gidding, John. *At Home with Nature* — 635.9
NATIVE PLANTS FOR CULTIVATION
    Branhagen, Alan. *Native Plants of the Midwest* — 635.9
    Tallamy, Douglas W. ★*Nature's Best Hope* — 635.9
Native Plants of the Midwest. Branhagen, Alan — 635.9
NATIVISM
    Ackerman, Spencer. *Reign of Terror* — 973.931
    Okrent, Daniel. *The Guarded Gate* — 344.73
Natterson, Cara Familian
    ★*Decoding Boys* — 649
NATURAL AREAS
    Black, George. *Empire of Shadows* — 978.7
    Duncan, Dayton. *The National Parks* — 333.78
    Hiss, Tony. ★*Rescuing the Planet* — 333.75
    Proulx, Annie. *Bird Cloud* — B
    Steelquist, Robert. *The Northwest Coastal Explorer* — 508
Natural Born Heroes. McDougall, Christopher — 940.53
Natural Causes. Ehrenreich, Barbara — 613.2
Natural Color. Duerr, Sasha — 746.6
NATURAL DISASTERS
    Aktipis, Athena. ★*A Field Guide to the Apocalypse* — 155.2
    Bittle, Jake. ★*The Great Displacement* — 362.87
    Blunt, Katherine. *California Burning* — 333.793
    Burns, Cherie. *The Great Hurricane—1938* — 974.7

AUTHOR, TITLE, SERIES AND SUBJECT INDEX

Davenport, Matthew J. *The Longest Minute*	979.4
Deraniyagala, Sonali. *Wave*	B
Dolin, Eric Jay. *A Furious Sky*	363.34
Edwards, Adrienne L. *Firescaping Your Home*	635.9
Fagan, Brian M. *Climate Chaos*	304.2
Ferguson, Niall. *Doom*	362.1962
Fields, Micah. ★*We Hold Our Breath*	976.4
Johnson, Lizzie. ★*Paradise*	363.37
Junger, Sebastian. *The Perfect Storm*	974.4
Kneale, Matthew. *Rome*	945.6
Martin, Manjula. *The Last Fire Season*	B
Melville, Wilma. ★*Hero Dogs*	636.7
Neufeld, Josh. *A.D.*	741.5
Parry, Richard Lloyd. *Ghosts of the Tsunami*	952.05
Pilling, David. *Bending Adversity*	952.0512
Rivlin, Gary. *Katrina*	976.3
Roker, Al. *Ruthless Tide*	974.8
Roripaugh, Lee Ann. *Tsunami vs. the Fukushima 50*	811
Rush, Elizabeth A. *Rising*	551.45
Winchester, Simon. *A Crack in the Edge of the World*	979.4

NATURAL FOODS

Barber, Dan. *The Third Plate*	641.3
Chaplin, Amy. *Whole Food Cooking Every Day*	641.3
Flanagan, Shalane. *Run Fast, Cook Fast, Eat Slow*	641.5
Hill, McKel. *Nutrition Stripped*	641.3
Kauffman, Jonathan. *Hippie Food*	394.1
Kingsolver, Barbara. ★*Animal, Vegetable, Miracle*	641
Nguyen, Andrea Quynhgiao. *Ever-Green Vietnamese*	641.595
Pollan, Michael. *The Omnivore's Dilemma*	394.1
Pulde, Alona. *The Forks Over Knives Plan*	641.5
Robinson, Jo. *Eating on the Wild Side*	641.3

NATURAL GAS

McGraw, Seamus. *The End of Country*	333.7909748
Zuckerman, Gregory. *The Frackers*	B

NATURAL GAS INDUSTRY AND TRADE

Zuckerman, Gregory. *The Frackers*	B

NATURAL GAS SUPPLY

McGraw, Seamus. *The End of Country*	333.7909748

NATURAL HEALING

May, Katherine. *Wintering*	155.9

NATURAL HISTORY

Attenborough, David. *Life in the Undergrowth*	592
Attenborough, David. *A Life on Our Planet*	508
Barnett, Cynthia. ★*The Sound of the Sea*	591.47
Black, Riley. *The Last Days of the Dinosaurs*	576.8
Browne, E. J. *Charles Darwin*	B
Browne, E. J. *Charles Darwin*	B
Brusatte, Stephen. *The Rise and Reign of the Mammals*	569
Bryson, Bill. ★*A Walk in the Woods*	917
Byrne, Eugene. *Darwin*	741.5
Childs, Craig. *Atlas of a Lost World*	551.7
Darwin, Charles. ★*The Voyage of the Beagle*	508
Dennis, Jerry. *The Living Great Lakes*	977
Douglas, Marjory Stoneman. *The Everglades*	975.9
Drew, Liam. *I, Mammal*	599
Duncan, Dayton. *Blood Memory*	599.64
Dunn, Jon L. *The Glitter in the Green*	598.7
Farmer, Jared. *Elderflora*	582.16
Flannery, Tim F. *Europe*	508.4
Gould, Stephen Jay. *The Richness of Life*	508
Halliday, Thomas. ★*Otherlands*	560
Heacox, Kim. *Rhythm of the Wild*	979.8
Heinrich, Bernd. *A Naturalist at Large*	508
Hunt, Will. *Underground*	624.1
Johnson, Kirk W. *The Feather Thief*	364.16
Keffer, Ken. *Earth Almanac*	508
Lopez, Barry Holstun. *Horizon*	B
Mabey, Richard. *The Cabaret of Plants*	580
McAnulty, Dara. *Diary of a Young Naturalist*	508.092
Meiburg, Jonathan. *A Most Remarkable Creature*	598.9
Millard, Candice. *River of Doubt*	918.1
Muir, John. *Nature Writings*	B
Neiwert, David A. *Of Orcas and Men*	599.53
Nicolson, Adam. *Sea Room*	941.1
Nye, Bill. *Undeniable*	576.8
Offerman, Nick. *Where the Deer and the Antelope Play*	973.93
Peck, Robert McCracken. *A Glorious Enterprise*	508
Preston, Diana. *The Evolution of Charles Darwin*	508
Proulx, Annie. ★*Fen, Bog and Swamp*	551.41
Pyle, Robert Michael. *Nature Matrix*	508
Rinella, Steven. ★*Outdoor Kids in an Inside World*	649
Robinson, Kim Stanley. *The High Sierra*	917.94
Sanders, Ella Frances. *Eating the Sun*	520
Spira, Timothy P. *Waterfalls and Wildflowers in the Southern Appalachians*	796.5109756
Stark, Lizzie. ★*Egg*	641.3
Steelquist, Robert. *The Northwest Coastal Explorer*	508
Strycker, Noah K. *The Thing with Feathers*	598.072
Thoreau, Henry David. *The Maine Woods*	917
Thoreau, Henry David. ★*Walden, Or, Life in the Woods*	813
Wilson, Edward O. *Tales from the Ant World*	595.79
Wilson, Edward O. *A Window on Eternity*	333.95
Wohlforth, Charles P. *The Fate of Nature*	304.209798

NATURAL HISTORY MUSEUMS

Conniff, Richard. *House of Lost Worlds*	069
Johnson, Kirk W. *The Feather Thief*	364.16
A Natural History of the Senses. Ackerman, Diane	152.1

NATURAL LANDSCAPING

Darke, Rick. *The Living Landscape*	712
Gidding, John. *At Home with Nature*	635.9
Tallamy, Douglas W. ★*Nature's Best Hope*	635.9

NATURAL LAW

Cicero, Marcus Tullius. ★*The Republic*	320.1
Will, George F. *The Conservative Sensibility*	320.520973
The Natural Laws of Children. Alvarez, Celine	372.21
The Natural Mystics. Grant, Colin	B

NATURAL RESOURCES

Boccaletti, Giulio. *Water*	909
Solomon, Steven. *Water*	553.7
Zuckerman, Gregory. *The Frackers*	B

NATURAL SELECTION

Costa, James T. *Darwin's Backyard*	576.8
Costa, James T. *Radical by Nature*	B
Darwin, Charles. *Charles Darwin*	576.8
Darwin, Charles. ★*The Origin of Species by Means of Natural Selection, Or, the Preservation of Favored Races in the Struggle for Life*	575
Dennett, D. C. *Darwin's Dangerous Idea*	146
Losos, Jonathan B. *Improbable Destinies*	576.8
Markel, Howard. *Origin Story*	576.8
McIntyre, Rick. *The Reign of Wolf 21*	599.773
Miller, Kenneth R. *The Human Instinct*	155.7
Pinker, Steven. *How the Mind Works*	153
Preston, Diana. *The Evolution of Charles Darwin*	508
Schilthuizen, Menno. *Darwin Comes to Town*	577.5
Simon, Matt. *The Wasp That Brainwashed the Caterpillar*	578.4

NATURALISM

Carroll, Sean M. *The Big Picture*	577
A Naturalist At Large. Heinrich, Bernd	508

NATURALISTS

Browne, E. J. *Charles Darwin*	B
Browne, E. J. *Charles Darwin*	B
Byrne, Eugene. *Darwin*	741.5
Costa, James T. *Darwin's Backyard*	576.8
Darwin, Charles. *Charles Darwin*	576.8
Haupt, Lyanda Lynn. *Mozart's Starling*	B
Johnson, Kirk W. *The Feather Thief*	364.16
Kaufman, Kenn. *The Birds That Audubon Missed*	598
King, Dean. *Guardians of the Valley*	333.72
McAnulty, Dara. *Diary of a Young Naturalist*	508.092
McCalman, Iain. *Darwin's Armada*	576.8
Miller, Lulu. *Why Fish Don't Exist*	B
Muir, John. *Nature Writings*	B
Muir, John. *The Story of My Boyhood and Youth*	B
Preston, Diana. *The Evolution of Charles Darwin*	508
Pyle, Robert Michael. *Nature Matrix*	508
Rhodes, Richard. *Scientist*	B
Roberts, Jason. ★*Every Living Thing*	578
Robinson, Kim Stanley. *The High Sierra*	917.94
Ross, John F. *The Promise of the Grand Canyon*	917.91
Souder, William. *On a Farther Shore*	B
Stott, Rebecca. ★*Darwin's Ghosts*	576.8
Wallace, Christopher. *Twentieth-Century Man*	B
Walls, Laura Dassow. ★*Henry David Thoreau*	B
Wilson, Edward O. ★*Letters to a Young Scientist*	570.92
Worster, Donald. *A Passion for Nature the Life of John Muir*	B
Wulf, Andrea. *The Invention of Nature*	B

NATURALIZATION
- Lalami, Laila. *Conditional Citizens* — 323.60973
- Luiselli, Valeria. *Tell Me How It Ends* — 305.23086
- *Naturally* Nourished. Britton, Sarah — 641.5

NATURE
- Aryee, Patrick. *30 Animals That Made Us Smarter* — 590
- Atwood, Margaret. *Dearly* — 811
- Ball, Philip. *Patterns in Nature* — 500.201
- Bernstein, Ellen. *Toward a Holy Ecology* — 223
- Berry, Wendell. *A Timbered Choir* — 811
- Birkhead, Tim. *Birds and Us* — 598
- Bishop, Elizabeth. ★*Poems* — 811
- Boccaletti, Giulio. *Water* — 909
- Carlsen, Spike. *A Walk Around the Block* — 031
- Carson, Rachel. *The Edge of the Sea* — 578.769
- Cooper, Christian. *Better Living Through Birding* — B
- Cousteau, Jacques Yves. *The Human, the Orchid, and the Octopus* — B
- Dawkins, Richard. *Science in the Soul* — 500
- Delorme, Geoffroy. *Deer Man* — 599.65
- Dickie, Gloria. *Eight Bears* — 599.78
- Dillard, Annie. *The Abundance* — 814
- Dillard, Annie. *Pilgrim at Tinker Creek* — 508
- Dillard, Annie. *Teaching a Stone to Talk* — 508
- Dochartaigh, Kerri ni. *Cacophony of Bone* — B
- Douglas, Marjory Stoneman. *The Everglades* — 975.9
- Dungy, Camille T. *Soil* — 635.0978
- Ehrlich, Gretel. *Unsolaced* — B
- Eklof, Johan. *The Darkness Manifesto* — 363.7
- Foster, Craig. ★*Amphibious Soul* — 155.9
- Gay, Ross. *Inciting Joy* — 814
- Goodall, Jane. ★*The Book of Hope* — 128
- Graham, Jasmin. *Sharks Don't Sink* — 597.3
- Graham, Jorie. *From the New World* — 811
- Graham, Jorie. *To 2040* — 811
- Grylls, Bear. *Never Give Up* — B
- Harrison, Jim. *The Search for the Genuine* — 814
- Hass, Robert. *Summer Snow* — 811.6
- Houston, Pam. *Deep Creek* — 814
- Imbler, Sabrina. *How Far the Light Reaches* — 591.77
- Jabr, Ferris. ★*Becoming Earth* — 570.1
- Kaag, John J. *Hiking with Nietzsche* — 193
- Kaufman, Kenn. *The Birds That Audubon Missed* — 598
- Kelley, Margot Anne. *A Gardener at the End of the World* — 615.8
- Kimmerer, Robin Wall. ★*Braiding Sweetgrass* — 304.2
- Krakauer, Jon. *Into the Wild* — 917.9804
- Kumar, Priyanka. *Conversations with Birds* — 598
- Lewis, Daniel. *Twelve Trees* — 582.16
- Limon, Ada. ★*The Hurting Kind* — 811
- Logsdon, Gene. *Letter to a Young Farmer* — 338.10973
- Lopez, Barry Holstun. ★*Of Wolves and Men* — 599.773
- Louv, Richard. *Our Wild Calling* — 615.8
- Mabey, Richard. *The Cabaret of Plants* — 580
- Macdonald, Helen. ★*Vesper Flights* — 508
- Macfarlane, Robert. *The Lost Spells* — 811
- Marcum, Diana. *The Fallen Stones* — B
- McAnulty, Dara. *Diary of a Young Naturalist* — 508.092
- Momaday, N. Scott. *Earth Keeper* — 814
- Montgomery, Sy. *How to Be a Good Creature* — 590
- Moore, Kathleen Dean. *Earth's Wild Music* — 576.6
- Nezhukumatathil, Aimee. *Oceanic* — 811
- Nezhukumatathil, Aimee. *World of Wonders* — 590
- Oliver, Mary. ★*Devotions* — 811
- Oliver, Mary. ★*Upstream* — 814
- Pearce, Fred. *A Trillion Trees* — 577.3
- Penniman, Leah. ★*Black Earth Wisdom* — 333.72
- Quave, Cassandra Leah. *The Plant Hunter* — 581.6
- Renkl, Margaret. *The Comfort of Crows* — 814.6
- Rich, Nathaniel. *Second Nature* — 304.2
- Rinella, Steven. *Meat Eater* — 641
- Rinella, Steven. ★*Outdoor Kids in an Inside World* — 649
- Roberts, Jason. ★*Every Living Thing* — 578
- Rogers, Pattiann. *Quickening Fields* — 811
- Safina, Carl. ★*Alfie and Me* — 598.9
- Sagan, Sasha. *For Small Creatures Such as We* — 390.09
- Scales, Helen. *The Brilliant Abyss* — 551.46
- Scales, Helen. *What the Wild Sea Can Be* — 577.7
- Schilthuizen, Menno. *Darwin Comes to Town* — 577.5
- Shatner, William. *Boldly Go* — B
- Shattuck, Ben. *Six Walks* — B
- Solnit, Rebecca. *Orwell's Roses* — B
- Szczeszak-Brewer, Agata. *The Hunger Book* — B
- Tan, Amy. ★*The Backyard Bird Chronicles* — 598
- Thoreau, Henry David. *The Maine Woods* — 917
- Vigliotti, Jonathan. *Before It's Gone* — 577
- Wallace, Christopher. *Twentieth-Century Man* — B
- Welz, Adam. *The End of Eden* — 577.2
- Williams, Florence. *The Nature Fix* — 155.9
- Wohlleben, Peter. *Forest Walking* — 582.16
- Wohlleben, Peter. *The Heartbeat of Trees* — 582.16
- Wohlleben, Peter. *The Hidden Life of Trees* — 582.16
- Woolfson, Esther. *Between Light and Storm* — 599.93
- Worster, Donald. *A Passion for Nature the Life of John Muir* — B
- Wulf, Andrea. *The Invention of Nature* — B
- Wynn-Grant, Rae. *Wild Life* — B

NATURE (AESTHETICS)
- Bate, Jonathan. *Radical Wordsworth* — B
- Nicolson, Adam. *The Making of Poetry* — 821.709

NATURE AND CIVILIZATION
- Roripaugh, Lee Ann. *Tsunami vs. the Fukushima 50* — 811

NATURE AND CULTURE
- Bernstein, Ellen. *Toward a Holy Ecology* — 223
- Grathwohl, Marya. *This Wheel of Rocks* — 271
- Macdonald, Helen. ★*Vesper Flights* — 508
- Oliver, Mary. ★*Upstream* — 814
- Wohlleben, Peter. *The Heartbeat of Trees* — 582.16

NATURE CONSERVATION
- Ackerman, Jennifer. ★*What an Owl Knows* — 598.9
- Brinkley, Douglas. *Rightful Heritage* — B
- Brinkley, Douglas. *The Wilderness Warrior* — B
- Cousteau, Jacques Yves. *The Human, the Orchid, and the Octopus* — B
- Davis, Jack E. *An Everglades Providence* — B
- Duncan, Dayton. *The National Parks* — 333.78
- Egan, Timothy. ★*The Big Burn* — 973.911
- Farmer, Jared. *Elderflora* — 582.16
- Flyn, Cal. ★*Islands of Abandonment* — 333.73
- Heacox, Kim. ★*John Muir and the Ice That Started a Fire* — 333.7209798
- Heacox, Kim. *Rhythm of the Wild* — 979.8
- Hiss, Tony. ★*Rescuing the Planet* — 333.75
- King, Dean. *Guardians of the Valley* — 333.72
- Leopold, Aldo. ★*A Sand County Almanac & Other Writings on Ecology and Conservation* — 814
- Offerman, Nick. *Where the Deer and the Antelope Play* — 973.93
- Proulx, Annie. ★*Fen, Bog and Swamp* — 551.41
- Redniss, Lauren. ★*Oak Flat* — 970.5
- Robinson, Kim Stanley. *The High Sierra* — 917.94
- Ross, John F. *The Promise of the Grand Canyon* — 917.91
- Welz, Adam. *The End of Eden* — 577.2
- Williams, Terry Tempest. *Erosion* — 814
- Wilson, Edward O. *The Future of Life* — 333.95
- Wilson, Edward O. *A Window on Eternity* — 333.95

NATURE CRAFT
- Isabel, Agatha. *Houseplant Hookups* — 635.9
- Ploszajski, Anna. *Handmade* — 620.1
- Smith, Sally J. *Fairy Houses* — 745.592
- *The Nature Fix*. Williams, Florence — 155.9

NATURE IN LITERATURE
- Dennison, Matthew. *The Man in the Willows* — B
- McDowell, Marta. *The World of Laura Ingalls Wilder* — 813
- *Nature Matrix*. Pyle, Robert Michael — 508
- *The Nature of Space and Time*. Hawking, Stephen — 530.1

NATURE PHOTOGRAPHY
- Alinder, Mary Street. *Ansel Adams* — B
- *Nature Play at Home*. Striniste, Nancy — 796.083
- *Nature Poem*. Pico, Tommy — 811

NATURE SOUNDS
- Kingdon, Amorina. ★*Sing Like Fish* — 591.77

NATURE STUDY
- Attenborough, David. *Adventures of a Young Naturalist* — B
- Johnson, Victoria. ★*American Eden* — 580.973
- Pyle, Robert Michael. *Nature Matrix* — 508
- Striniste, Nancy. *Nature Play at Home* — 796.083

NATURE WALKS
- Offerman, Nick. *Where the Deer and the Antelope Play* — 973.93

NATURE WRITING
- Greenfieldboyce, Nell. ★*Transient and Strange* — 501

AUTHOR, TITLE, SERIES AND SUBJECT INDEX

NATURE WRITING — ANIMAL STUDIES
Aryee, Patrick. *30 Animals That Made Us Smarter* — 590
Attenborough, David. *Adventures of a Young Naturalist* — B
Attenborough, David. *Life in the Undergrowth* — 592
Balcombe, Jonathan P. *Super Fly* — 595.77
Baur, Gene. *Farm Sanctuary* — 179
Beers, Diane L. ★*For the Prevention of Cruelty* — 179
Black, Scott Hoffman. *Gardening for Butterflies* — 638
Blakeslee, Nate. *American Wolf* — 599.773
Bradshaw, John. ★*Cat Sense* — 636.8
Bradshaw, John. ★*Dog Sense* — 636.7
Braitman, Laurel. *Animal Madness* — 591.5
Brand, Adele. *The Hidden World of the Fox* — 599.775
Brock, James P. *Kaufman Field Guide to Butterflies of North America* — 595.7
Brown, Sarah L. *The Hidden Language of Cats* — 636.8
Brusatte, Stephen. *The Rise and Reign of the Mammals* — 569
Busch, Robert. *The Wolf Almanac* — 599.773
Carr, Caleb. *My Beloved Monster* — B
Carson, Rachel. *The Edge of the Sea* — 578.769
Carson, Rachel. *Under the Sea Wind* — 578.77
Castello, Jose R. *Bovids of the World* — 599.64
Catania, Kenneth. *Great Adaptations* — 576.8
Cheshire, James. *Where the Animals Go* — 591.47
Connell, John. *The Farmer's Son* — 630.9
Cooke, Lucy. *Bitch* — 591.56
Cooke, Lucy. *The Truth About Animals* — 590.2
Cranshaw, Whitney. *Garden Insects of North America* — 635
Darlington, Miriam. *Otter Country* — 599.769
Dickey, Bronwen. *Pit Bull* — 636.755
Dickie, Gloria. *Eight Bears* — 599.78
Duncan, Dayton. *Blood Memory* — 599.64
Durrani, Matin. *Furry Logic* — 591.5
Emlen, Douglas John. *Animal Weapons* — 591.47
Flottum, Kim. *The Backyard Beekeeper* — 638
Gaffney, Ginger. *Half Broke* — B
Goldfarb, Ben. *Eager* — 333.95
Goodall, Jane. ★*The Ten Trusts* — 333.95
Graham, Jasmin. *Sharks Don't Sink* — 597.3
Grandin, Temple. ★*Animals in Translation* — 591.5
Grandin, Temple. ★*Animals Make Us Human* — 636.08
Grandin, Temple. *Temple Grandin's Guide to Working with Farm Animals* — 636
Greek, C. Ray. *Sacred Cows and Golden Geese* — 179
Habib, Rodney. ★*The Forever Dog* — 636.7
Hanson, Thor. *Hurricane Lizards and Plastic Squid* — 577.2
Herriot, James. ★*All Creatures Great and Small* — B
Herriot, James. *All Things Wise and Wonderful* — B
Herriot, James. *Every Living Thing* — B
Herriot, James. *James Herriot's Animal Stories* — B
Higgins, Jackie. *Sentient* — 573.8
Hoare, Philip. *The Whale* — 599.5
Holldobler, Bert. *The Superorganism* — 595.7
Horowitz, Alexandra. ★*Being a Dog* — 636.7
Horowitz, Alexandra. ★*Inside of a Dog* — 636.7
Horowitz, Alexandra. *Our Dogs, Ourselves* — 636.7
Horowitz, Alexandra. ★*The Year of the Puppy* — 636.7
Howsare, Erika. *The Age of Deer* — 599.65
Hoyt, Erich. *Encyclopedia of Whales, Dolphins and Porpoises* — 599.5
Hunger, Christina. *How Stella Learned to Talk* — 636.7
Keim, Brandon. *Meet the Neighbors* — 591.5
Lawson, Nancy. *The Humane Gardener* — 577.5
Letts, Elizabeth. *The Perfect Horse* — 940.54
Lewis, Sara. *Silent Sparks* — 595.76
Lopez, Barry Holstun. ★*Of Wolves and Men* — 599.773
Losos, Jonathan B. *The Cat's Meow* — 636.8
Louv, Richard. *Our Wild Calling* — 615.8
MacPhee, R. D. E. *End of the Megafauna* — 591.4
May, Meredith. *The Honey Bus* — B
McDougall, Christopher. *Running with Sherman* — 636.1
McGinnis, Samuel M. ★*Peterson Field Guide to Western Reptiles and Amphibians* — 597.9
Meinkoth, Norman August. *The Audubon Society Field Guide to North American Seashore Creatures* — 592
Milne, Lorus Johnson. ★*The Audubon Society Field Guide to North American Insects and Spiders* — 595.7097
Montgomery, Sy. *How to Be a Good Creature* — 590
Montgomery, Sy. ★*Of Time and Turtles* — 597.92
Mooallem, Jon. *Wild Ones* — 333.95

Mortimer, Frank. *Bee People and the Bugs They Love* — B
Murie, Olaus J. ★*A Field Guide to Animal Tracks* — 599
Mustill, Tom. *How to Speak Whale* — 591.59
Nicholls, Steve. *Alien Worlds* — 595.7
Nicolson, Adam. *Life Between the Tides* — 577.69
Nordhaus, Hannah. *The Beekeeper's Lament* — 638
Nowak, Ronald M. *Walker's Mammals of the World* — 599
Orlean, Susan. *On Animals* — 590
Orlean, Susan. *Rin Tin Tin* — 636.737
Owens, Delia. *The Eye of the Elephant* — 639.9
Page, Lawrence M. ★*Peterson Field Guide to Freshwater Fishes of North America North of Mexico* — 597.176
Paul, Gregory S. *The Princeton Field Guide to Dinosaurs* — 567.9
Paulson, Dennis. *Dragonflies & Damselflies* — 595.7
Peterson, Dale. *Giraffe Reflections* — 599.638
Peterson, Dale. *The Moral Lives of Animals* — 156
Prasad, Aarathi. *Silk* — 677
Renner, Rebecca. ★*Gator Country* — 364.16
Roach, Mary. ★*Fuzz* — 591.5
Roberts, Jason. ★*Every Living Thing* — 578
Roman, Joe. *Eat, Poop, Die* — 577
Safina, Carl. ★*Becoming Wild* — 591.7
Safina, Carl. *Beyond Words* — 591.56
Scales, Helen. *What the Wild Sea Can Be* — 577.7
Scheel, David. *Many Things Under a Rock* — 594
Schmidt, Justin O. *The Sting of the Wild* — 595.7
Schott, Philipp. *The Accidental Veterinarian* — B
Schutt, Bill. *Cannibalism* — 394
Simon, Matt. *Plight of the Living Dead* — 591.6
Simon, Matt. *The Wasp That Brainwashed the Caterpillar* — 578.4
Singer, Peter. ★*Animal Liberation* — 179
Skomal, Gregory. *Chasing Shadows* — 597.3
Stewart, Tracey. *Do Unto Animals* — 590
Strøksnes, Morten Andreas. *Shark Drunk* — 338.3
Suddendorf, Thomas. *The Gap* — 156
Sumner, Seirian. *Endless Forms* — 595.79
Taylor, Marianne. *Bats* — 599.4
Tomlinson, Tommy. *Dogland* — 636.7
Toomey, David. *Kingdom of Play* — 591.56
Waal, F. B. M. de. ★*Mama's Last Hug* — 599.885
Waldbauer, Gilbert. *What Good Are Bugs?* — 595.717
Ward, Ashley. *The Social Lives of Animals* — 591.7
Wasik, Bill. ★*Our Kindred Creatures* — 179
Weitzman, Gary. *National Geographic Complete Guide to Pet Health, Behavior, and Happiness* — 636.088
Welz, Adam. *The End of Eden* — 577.2
Whitaker, John O. ★*National Audubon Society Field Guide to North American Mammals* — 599.097
Williams, Jim. *Path of the Puma* — 599.75
Williams, Wendy. *The Language of Butterflies* — 595.78
Wilson, Edward O. *Tales from the Ant World* — 595.79
Wilson, Joseph S. *The Bees in Your Backyard* — 595.79
Woolfson, Esther. *Between Light and Storm* — 599.93
Wynne, Clive D. L. ★*Dog Is Love* — 636.7
Yong, Ed. ★*An Immense World* — 591.5

NATURE WRITING — ANIMAL STUDIES — BIRDS AND BIRDING
Ackerman, Jennifer. *The Bird Way* — 598.15
Ackerman, Jennifer. ★*What an Owl Knows* — 598.9
Alderfer, Jonathan K. *National Geographic Birding Essentials* — 598.072
Attenborough, David. *The Life of Birds* — 598.15
Barker, Margaret A. *Audubon Birdhouse Book* — 728
Barnes, Simon. *The Meaning of Birds* — 598
Birkhead, T. R. *Bird Sense* — 598
Birkhead, Tim. *Birds and Us* — 598
Bull, John L. ★*The National Audubon Society Field Guide to North American Birds* — 598.097
Burton, Robert. *Audubon North American Birdfeeder Guide* — 598
Cooper, Christian. *Better Living Through Birding* — B
Craig, Mya-Rose. *Birdgirl* — B
Davies, N. B. *Cuckoo* — 598.7
Davis, Jack E. *The Bald Eagle* — 598.9
Duncan, James R. *Owls of the World* — 598.9
Dunn, Jon L. *The Glitter in the Green* — 598.7
Erickson, Laura. ★*100 Plants to Feed the Birds* — 635
Erickson, Laura. *The Love Lives of Birds* — 598.15
Floyd, Ted. *How to Know the Birds* — 598.072
Floyd, Ted. *Smithsonian Field Guide to the Birds of North America* — 598.097
Gentile, Olivia. *Life List* — 598.072

PUBLIC LIBRARY CORE COLLECTION: NONFICTION
Twentieth Edition

Gyllenhaal, Anders. *A Wing and a Prayer*	639.97
Hammer, Joshua. *The Falcon Thief*	364.16
Haupt, Lyanda Lynn. *Mozart's Starling*	B
Heinrich, Bernd. *White Feathers*	598.8
Hirschfeld, Erik. *The World's Rarest Birds*	333.95822
Johnson, Kirk W. *The Feather Thief*	364.16
Jones, Darryl N. *The Birds at My Table*	598.072
Kaufman, Kenn. *The Birds That Audubon Missed*	598
Kumar, Priyanka. *Conversations with Birds*	598
Lederer, Roger J. *Beaks, Bones, and Bird Songs*	598
Meiburg, Jonathan. *A Most Remarkable Creature*	598.9
Montgomery, Sy. *The Hawk's Way*	598.9
Montgomery, Sy. *The Hummingbirds' Gift*	598.7
Nicolson, Adam. *The Seabird's Cry*	598.177
Peterson, Roger Tory. *Peterson Field Guide to Birds of Eastern and Central North America*	598.097
Peterson, Roger Tory. *Peterson Field Guide to Birds of Western North America*	598.097
Robbins, Jim. *The Wonder of Birds*	598
Safina, Carl. ★*Alfie and Me*	598.9
Shunk, Stephen A. *Peterson Reference Guide to Woodpeckers of North America*	598.7
Sibley, David. *Sibley Birds East*	598.097
Sibley, David. ★*Sibley Birds West*	598.097
Sibley, David. *The Sibley Guide to Birds*	598.097
Sibley, David. ★*Sibley's Birding Basics*	598
Slaght, Jonathan C. *Owls of the Eastern Ice*	598.9
Stokes, Donald W. *The New Stokes Field Guide to Birds.*	598
Strycker, Noah K. *The Thing with Feathers*	598.072
Tan, Amy. ★*The Backyard Bird Chronicles*	598
Tougias, Robert. *Birder on Berry Lane*	598.072
Weidensaul, Scott. *A World on the Wing*	598.156
Zickefoose, Julie. *Baby Birds*	751.42

NATURE WRITING — ANIMAL STUDIES — ENDANGERED SPECIES

Barrow, Mark V. *Nature's Ghosts*	333.95
Croke, Vicki. *The Lady and the Panda*	599.789
Dunn, Jon L. *The Glitter in the Green*	598.7
Ellis, Richard. ★*The Empty Ocean*	577.7
Flores, Dan L. *Wild New World*	591.9709
Fowlds, Grant. *Saving the Last Rhinos*	599.66
Goldfarb, Ben. *Crossings*	333.77
Hirschfeld, Erik. *The World's Rarest Birds*	333.95822
McIntyre, Rick. *The Reign of Wolf 21*	599.773
Neiwert, David A. *Of Orcas and Men*	599.53
O'Connor, Maura R. *Resurrection Science*	591.68
Orenstein, Ronald I. *Ivory, Horn and Blood*	333.95
Pittman, Craig. *Cat Tale*	599.75
Preston, Christopher J. *Tenacious Beasts*	591.68
Pyenson, Nick. *Spying on Whales*	599.5
Rinella, Steven. *American Buffalo*	599.64
Sartore, Joel. ★*The Photo Ark*	779
Vaillant, John. *The Tiger*	599.756
Williams, Kale. *The Loneliest Polar Bear*	599.786
Wilson, Edward O. *The Future of Life*	333.95
Wood, Levison. *The Last Giants*	599.67

NATURE WRITING — ANIMAL STUDIES — FISH AND FISHING

Ash, Lamorna. *Dark, Salt, Clear*	942.3
Balcombe, Jonathan P. *What a Fish Knows*	597.15
Barnett, Cynthia. ★*The Sound of the Sea*	591.47
Burke, Monte. *Lords of the Fly*	799.124
Ellis, Richard. *Tuna*	333.95
Gierach, John. *All Fishermen Are Liars*	799.12
Gierach, John. *Dumb Luck and the Kindness of Strangers*	799.124
Gierach, John. *A Fly Rod of Your Own*	799.12
Gilbert, Carter Rowell. ★*National Audubon Society Field Guide to Fishes.*	597
Greenberg, Paul. *Four Fish*	333.95
Hilborn, Ray. *Overfishing*	338.3
Horwitz, Josh. *War of the Whales*	333.95
Kingdon, Amorina. ★*Sing Like Fish*	591.77
Malarkey, Tucker. *Stronghold*	639.2
Svensson, Patrik. *The Book of Eels*	597

NATURE WRITING — ANIMAL STUDIES — PET CARE

Sife, Wallace. *The Loss of a Pet*	155.9
Weitzman, Gary. *National Geographic Complete Guide to Pet Health, Behavior, and Happiness*	636.088

NATURE WRITING — ANIMAL STUDIES — PET CARE — CATS

Galaxy, Jackson. ★*Total Cat Mojo*	636.8
Schotz, Susanne. *The Secret Language of Cats*	636.8

NATURE WRITING — ANIMAL STUDIES — PET CARE — DOGS

Coile, D. Caroline. *Encyclopedia of Dog Breeds*	636.7
Friedman, Elias Weiss. *The Dogist*	779
Miller, Pat. ★*The Power of Positive Dog Training*	636.7
Monks of New Skete. *The Art of Raising a Puppy*	636.7
Nichols, Kerry. *Puppy Brain*	636.7

NATURE WRITING — ANIMAL STUDIES — PRIMATES

Fossey, Dian. ★*Gorillas in the Mist*	599.884
Fouts, Roger. *Next of Kin*	156
Goodall, Jane. ★*Beyond Innocence*	B
Goodall, Jane. ★*In the Shadow of Man*	599.8
Waal, F. B. M. de. *Bonobo*	599.88
Waal, F. B. M. de. *Our Inner Ape*	156

NATURE WRITING — ENVIRONMENTAL ISSUES

Ackerman, Diane. *The Human Age*	304.2
Addison, Corban. *Wastelands*	346.73
Aguon, Julian. *No Country for Eight-Spot Butterflies*	305.89
Allen, Brigette. *Living Without Plastic*	640
Arsenault, Kerri. *Mill Town*	B
Atleework, Kendra. *Miracle Country*	979.4
Attenborough, David. *A Life on Our Planet*	508
Barnett, Cynthia. ★*The Sound of the Sea*	591.47
Beavan, Colin. *No Impact Man*	B
Bell, Alice R. *Our Biggest Experiment*	363.738
Berry, Wendell. *The Art of Loading Brush*	338.10973
Berry, Wendell. ★*The World-Ending Fire*	818
Bilott, Robert. *Exposure*	344.04
Bittle, Jake. ★*The Great Displacement*	362.87
Boccaletti, Giulio. *Water*	909
Bradley, James. *Deep Water*	578.77
Briody, Blaire. *The New Wild West*	338.2
Carson, Rachel. ★*Silent Spring*	363.738
Cousteau, Jacques Yves. *The Human, the Orchid, and the Octopus*	B
Davis, Jack E. *An Everglades Providence*	B
Davis, Jack E. ★*The Gulf*	909
Diamond, Jared M. *Collapse*	304.2
Dolin, Eric Jay. *A Furious Sky*	363.34
Douglas, Marjory Stoneman. *The Everglades*	975.9
Egan, Dan. ★*The Death and Life of the Great Lakes*	577.6
Ehrlich, Gretel. *Unsolaced*	B
Eklof, Johan. *The Darkness Manifesto*	363.7
Estes, Nick. *Our History Is the Future*	978.004
Fagan, Brian M. *Climate Chaos*	304.2
Fagan, Brian M. *The Long Summer*	551.6
Fagin, Dan. *Toms River*	363.7209749
Fields, Micah. ★*We Hold Our Breath*	976.4
Flyn, Cal. ★*Islands of Abandonment*	333.73
Fox, Porter. *The Last Winter*	363.738
Franklin-Wallis, Oliver. ★*Wasteland*	363.72
Frankopan, Peter. *The Earth Transformed*	304.2
Freeman, Scott. *Saving Tarboo Creek*	333.72
Ghosh, Amitav. *The Great Derangement*	809
Gleick, Peter H. *The Three Ages of Water*	333.91
Goldfarb, Ben. *Crossings*	333.77
Goodell, Jeff. *The Heat Will Kill You First*	363.738
Goodell, Jeff. *The Water Will Come*	551.45
Gyllenhaal, Anders. *A Wing and a Prayer*	639.97
Hanson, Thor. *Hurricane Lizards and Plastic Squid*	577.2
Hayhoe, Katharine. *Saving Us*	304.2
Hiss, Tony. ★*Rescuing the Planet*	333.75
Holthaus, Eric. *The Future Earth*	363.738
Horn, Miriam. *Rancher, Farmer, Fisherman*	B
Humes, Edward. ★*Total Garbage*	628.4
Iversen, Kristen. *Full Body Burden*	363.17
Jabr, Ferris. ★*Becoming Earth*	570.1
Johnson, Kirk W. *The Fishermen and the Dragon*	976.4
King, Greg. *The Ghost Forest*	333.75
Klare, Michael T. *All Hell Breaking Loose*	355.20973
Kolbert, Elizabeth. *Field Notes from a Catastrophe*	363.738
Kolbert, Elizabeth. ★*Under a White Sky*	304.2
Kumar, Priyanka. *Conversations with Birds*	598
Lacovara, Kenneth. *Why Dinosaurs Matter*	567.9
Linden, Eugene. *Fire and Flood*	304.2
Lipsky, David. ★*The Parrot and the Igloo*	304.2
Lopez, Barry Holstun. *Horizon*	B
Lustgarten, Abrahm. ★*On the Move*	363.7
Lynas, Mark. *Six Degrees*	551.6

AUTHOR, TITLE, SERIES AND SUBJECT INDEX

Macdougall, J. D. *Frozen Earth*	551.7
MacPhail, Theresa. *Allergic*	616.97
Maher, Kris. *Desperate*	344
Malarkey, Tucker. *Stronghold*	639.2
Martin, Manjula. *The Last Fire Season*	B
Mathews, Daniel. *Trees in Trouble*	634.9
McGraw, Seamus. *The End of Country*	333.7909748
Meyaard-Schaap, Kyle. *Following Jesus in a Warming World*	241
Miller, Char. *Gifford Pinchot and the Making of Modern Environmentalism*	B
Millet, Lydia. *We Loved It All*	813
Momaday, N. Scott. *Earth Keeper*	814
Monbiot, George. ★*Regenesis*	338.1
Montgomery, David R. *What Your Food Ate*	631.4
Moore, Kathleen Dean. *Earth's Wild Music*	576.8
Neiwert, David A. *Of Orcas and Men*	599.53
Nordhaus, Hannah. *The Beekeeper's Lament*	638
O'Brien, Keith. *Paradise Falls*	363.738
Owens, Jay. *Dust*	551.51
Park, Chris C. *A Dictionary of Environment and Conservation*	333.703
Pearce, Fred. *A Trillion Trees*	577.3
Penniman, Leah. ★*Black Earth Wisdom*	333.72
Pollack, H. N. *A World Without Ice*	551.31
Proulx, Annie. ★*Fen, Bog and Swamp*	551.41
Rawlence, Ben. *The Treeline*	577.3
Reid, John W. *Ever Green*	634.9
Rich, Nathaniel. *Losing Earth*	363.738
Rich, Nathaniel. *Second Nature*	304.2
Ritchie, Hannah. *Not the End of the World*	338.9
Roman, Joe. *Eat, Poop, Die*	577
Ross, John F. *The Promise of the Grand Canyon*	917.91
Roy, Saumya. *Castaway Mountain*	363.72
Scales, Helen. *What the Wild Sea Can Be*	577.7
Scheyder, Ernest. *The War Below*	333.7
Schilthuizen, Menno. *Darwin Comes to Town*	577.5
Smith, Bren. *Eat Like a Fish*	338.3
Solomon, Steven. *Water*	553.7
Souder, William. *On a Farther Shore*	B
Struzik, Edward. *Swamplands*	577.68
Swift, Earl. *Chesapeake Requiem*	639
Tallamy, Douglas W. ★*Nature's Best Hope*	635.9
Thunberg, Greta. ★*The Climate Book*	363.738
Vaillant, John. ★*Fire Weather*	363.37
Vaillant, John. *The Tiger*	599.756
Vigliotti, Jonathan. *Before It's Gone*	577
Vince, Gaia. *Nomad Century*	362.87
Vollmann, William T. *No Immediate Danger*	333.79
Wallace-Wells, David. *The Uninhabitable Earth*	304.2
Webb, Kinari. *Guardians of the Trees*	B
Welz, Adam. *The End of Eden*	577.2
Williams, Terry Tempest. *Erosion*	814
Wilson, Edward O. *In Search of Nature*	113
Wohlforth, Charles P. *The Fate of Nature*	304.209798
Woolfson, Esther. *Between Light and Storm*	599.93
Wray, Britt. *Generation Dread*	155.9
Zuckerman, Jocelyn C. *Planet Palm*	633.8

NATURE WRITING — FLOWERS AND PLANTS

Borsato, Diane. *Mushrooming*	579.6
Brown, George E. *Essential Pruning Techniques*	635.9
Chace, Teri Dunn. *Seeing Seeds*	581.4
Crary, Calvert. *The Encyclopedia of Cut Flowers*	745.92
Darcey, Cheralyn. *Flowerpaedia*	580
Dickinson, Richard. *Weeds of North America*	632
Drori, Jonathan. *Around the World in 80 Trees*	582.16
Erickson, Laura. ★*100 Plants to Feed the Birds*	635
Hay Hinsdale, Emily L. *What Is My Plant Telling Me?*	635.9
Isabel, Agatha. *Houseplant Hookups*	635.9
Lincoff, Gary. *The Audubon Society Field Guide to North American Mushrooms*	579.6
Little, Elbert L. *The Audubon Society Field Guide to North American Trees*	582.16097
McKnight, Kent H. *A Field Guide to Mushrooms, North America*	579.6
Petrides, George A. *A Field Guide to Western Trees*	582.16
Rodd, Tony. *Trees*	582.16
Sibley, David. ★*The Sibley Guide to Trees*	582.16097

NATURE WRITING — GARDENS

Bainbridge, David A. *Gardening with Less Water*	635.9
Bennett, Jackie. *The Writer's Garden*	920
Brenwall, Cynthia S. *The Central Park*	974.7
Brown, George E. *Essential Pruning Techniques*	635.9
Dungy, Camille T. *Soil*	635.0978
Gidding, John. *At Home with Nature*	635.9
Holway, Tatiana M. *The Flower of Empire*	727
Johnson, Victoria. ★*American Eden*	580.973
Kassinger, Ruth. ★*A Garden of Marvels*	580.92
Kelley, Margot Anne. *A Gardener at the End of the World*	615.8
Laing, Olivia. *The Garden Against Time*	635
Lavelle, Christine. *How to Create a Wildlife Garden*	635
Lavoipierre, Frederique. *Garden Allies*	635
Lawson, Nancy. *The Humane Gardener*	577.5
Lively, Penelope. *Life in the Garden*	B
Logsdon, Gene. *Letter to a Young Farmer*	338.10973
McDowell, Marta. *The World of Laura Ingalls Wilder*	813
McLaughlin, Chris. *The Good Garden*	635
Murphy, Emily. *Grow Now*	635
Obama, Michelle. *American Grown*	635.09
Pleasant, Barbara. ★*Starter Vegetable Gardens*	635
Roach, Margaret. ★*A Way to Garden*	635
Schlanger, Zoe. ★*The Light Eaters*	571.2
Simard, S. ★*Finding the Mother Tree*	582.16
Solnit, Rebecca. *Orwell's Roses*	B
Stuckey, Maggie. *The Container Victory Garden*	635.9
Webb, Leah M. *The Seven-Step Homestead*	635
Wulf, Andrea. *The Brother Gardeners*	920

NATURE WRITING — GENERAL

Ackerman-Leist, Philip. *Rebuilding the Foodshed*	338.1
Anthony, Leslie. *The Aliens Among Us*	578.6
Ball, Philip. *Patterns in Nature*	500.201
Barnett, Cynthia. *Rain*	551.57
Bernstein, Ellen. *Toward a Holy Ecology*	223
Brinkley, Douglas. *Rightful Heritage*	B
Brinkley, Douglas. *The Wilderness Warrior*	B
Brookshire, Bethany. *Pests*	590
Dawkins, Richard. *Science in the Soul*	500
Drori, Jonathan. *Around the World in 80 Plants*	581.63
Egan, Timothy. ★*The Big Burn*	973.911
Franklin, Jonathan. *A Wild Idea*	B
Genoways, Ted. *This Blessed Earth*	630.9
Hugo, Nancy R. *Seeing Trees*	582.16
Keffer, Ken. *Earth Almanac*	508
Kimmerer, Robin Wall. ★*Braiding Sweetgrass*	304.2
Krakauer, Jon. *Classic Krakauer*	814
Leopold, Aldo. ★*A Sand County Almanac & Other Writings on Ecology and Conservation*	814
Lewis, Daniel. *Twelve Trees*	582.16
Lowman, Margaret. *The Arbornaut*	581.7
McAnulty, Dara. *Diary of a Young Naturalist*	508.092
Muir, John. *Nature Writings*	814
Newitz, Annalee. *Scatter, Adapt, and Remember*	576.8
Nezhukumatathil, Aimee. *World of Wonders*	590
Rehder, Harald Alfred. *The Audubon Society Field Guide to North American Seashells*	594
Rhodes, Richard. *Scientist*	B
Rinella, Steven. ★*Outdoor Kids in an Inside World*	649
Sprinkle, Timothy. *Lost and Stranded*	613.6
Steelquist, Robert. *The Northwest Coastal Explorer*	508
Stewart, Amy. *Wicked Plants*	581.6
Sverdrup-Thygeson, Anne. *Buzz, Sting, Bite*	595.7
Taylor, Joseph E. *Pilgrims of the Vertical*	796.52
Thoreau, Henry David. ★*Walden, Or, Life in the Woods*	813
Tsui, Bonnie. *Why We Swim*	797.2
Wilson, Edward O. *In Search of Nature*	113
Wilson, Edward O. ★*Letters to a Young Scientist*	570.92
Wilson, Edward O. *A Window on Eternity*	333.95
Wohlleben, Peter. *The Heartbeat of Trees*	582.16
Wohlleben, Peter. *The Secret Wisdom of Nature*	508
Worster, Donald. *A Passion for Nature the Life of John Muir*	B
Wulf, Andrea. *The Invention of Nature*	B
Wynn-Grant, Rae. *Wild Life*	B

NATURE WRITING — NATURAL DISASTER

Barry, John M. *Rising Tide*	977
Brannen, Peter. *The Ends of the World*	576.8
Brinkley, Douglas. *The Great Deluge*	976.3
Bukreev, Anatolii Nikolaevich. *The Climb*	796.52
Burns, Cherie. *The Great Hurricane—1938*	974.7
Dyson, Michael Eric. *Come Hell or High Water*	976.3
Gee, Alastair. *Fire in Paradise*	363.37

PUBLIC LIBRARY CORE COLLECTION: NONFICTION
Twentieth Edition

Horne, Jed. *Breach of Faith* — 976.3
Johnson, Lizzie. ★*Paradise* — 363.37
Junger, Sebastian. *The Perfect Storm* — 974.4
Krist, Gary. *The White Cascade* — 979.7
Lustgarten, Abraham. ★*On the Move* — 363.7
Martin, Manjula. *The Last Fire Season* — B
Neufeld, Josh. *A.D.* — 741.5
Parry, Richard Lloyd. *Ghosts of the Tsunami* — 952.05
Roker, Al. *Ruthless Tide* — 974.8
Slade, Rachel. *Into the Raging Sea* — 910.91
Vaillant, John. ★*Fire Weather* — 363.37
Winchester, Simon. *A Crack in the Edge of the World* — 979.4

NATURE WRITING — NATURAL LANDSCAPES
Baszile, Natalie. *We Are Each Other's Harvest* — 630.89
Black, George. *Empire of Shadows* — 978.7
Casey, Susan. *The Underworld* — 551.46
Chamberlin, Silas. *On the Trail* — 796.510973
Czerski, Helen. *The Blue Machine* — 551.46
Darwin, Charles. ★*The Voyage of the Beagle* — 508
Davis, Wade. *Magdalena* — 986.1
Davis, Wade. *One River* — 581.6
Dennis, Jerry. *The Living Great Lakes* — 977
Douglas, Marjory Stoneman. *The Everglades* — 975.9
Doyle, Martin. *The Source* — 333.91
Duncan, Dayton. *The National Parks* — 333.78
Farmer, Jared. *Elderflora* — 582.16
Fedarko, Kevin. *A Walk in the Park* — 917.91
Flyn, Cal. ★*Islands of Abandonment* — 333.73
Heacox, Kim. *Rhythm of the Wild* — 979.8
Hunt, Will. *Underground* — 624.1
Jabr, Ferris. ★*Becoming Earth* — 570.1
King, Dean. *Guardians of the Valley* — 333.72
Lankford, Andrea. *Trail of the Lost* — 363.2
Logan, William Bryant. *Sprout Lands* — 582.16
Maiklem, Lara. *Mudlark* — B
McDowell, Marta. *The World of Laura Ingalls Wilder* — 813
Muir, John. *The Yosemite* — 979.4
Nicolson, Adam. *Life Between the Tides* — 577.69
Owen, David. *Where the Water Goes* — 917.91
Preston, Richard. *The Wild Trees* — 585
Proulx, Annie. ★*Fen, Bog and Swamp* — 551.41
Roberts, David. *The Bears Ears* — 979.2
Robinson, Kim Stanley. *The High Sierra* — 917.94
Roman, Joe. *Eat, Poop, Die* — 577
Ross, John F. *The Promise of the Grand Canyon* — 917.91
Rotman, Jeffrey L. *The Last Fisherman* — 778.7
Scales, Helen. *The Brilliant Abyss* — 551.46
Shattuck, Ben. *Six Walks* — B
Struzik, Edward. *Swamplands* — 577.68
Waterman, Jonathan. *National Geographic Atlas of the National Parks* — 917.304
Williams, Terry Tempest. *Erosion* — 814
Wohlleben, Peter. *Forest Walking* — 582.16
Wood, Gillen D'Arcy. *Land of Wondrous Cold* — 919.89

NATURE WRITING — PERSONAL RESPONSES
Alexander, Jane. *Wild Things, Wild Places* — 333.95
Atleework, Kendra. *Miracle Country* — 979.4
Attenborough, David. *A Life on Our Planet* — 508
Bailey, Elisabeth. *The Sound of a Wild Snail Eating* — 594
Bell, Laura. *Claiming Ground* — B
Berry, Erica. *Wolfish* — 152.4
Bryson, Bill. ★*A Walk in the Woods* — 917
Delorme, Geoffroy. *Deer Man* — 599.65
Dillard, Annie. *Pilgrim at Tinker Creek* — 508
Ehrlich, Gretel. *Unsolaced* — B
Greenfieldboyce, Nell. ★*Transient and Strange* — 501
Grylls, Bear. *Never Give Up* — B
Heacox, Kim. *Rhythm of the Wild* — 979.8
Heinrich, Bernd. *A Naturalist at Large* — 508
Houston, Pam. *Deep Creek* — 814
Howsare, Erika. *The Age of Deer* — 599.65
Johnson, Sarah Stewart. *The Sirens of Mars* — 576.8
Kassinger, Ruth. ★*A Garden of Marvels* — 580.92
Kelley, Margot Anne. *A Gardener at the End of the World* — 615.8
Logan, William Bryant. *Sprout Lands* — 582.16
Macdonald, Helen. ★*Vesper Flights* — 508
Magdalena, Carlos. *The Plant Messiah* — 333.95
Marcum, Diana. *The Fallen Stones* — B

Miles, Tiya. ★*Wild Girls* — 304.2
Momaday, N. Scott. *Earth Keeper* — 814
Moore, Kathleen Dean. *Earth's Wild Music* — 576.8
Oliver, Mary. ★*Upstream* — 814
Pyle, Robert Michael. *Nature Matrix* — 508
Renkl, Margaret. *The Comfort of Crows* — 814.6
Roach, Margaret. ★*A Way to Garden* — 635
Robinson, Kim Stanley. *The High Sierra* — 917.94
Shattuck, Ben. *Six Walks* — B
Simard, S. ★*Finding the Mother Tree* — 582.16
Solnit, Rebecca. *Wanderlust* — 796.51
Tan, Amy. ★*The Backyard Bird Chronicles* — 598
Thoreau, Henry David. *The Maine Woods* — 917
Van Hemert, Caroline. *The Sun Is a Compass* — 979.8
Williams, Florence. *The Nature Fix* — 155.9
Williams, Terry Tempest. *Erosion* — 814
Wohlleben, Peter. *The Hidden Life of Trees* — 582.16
Nature Writings. Muir, John — B
★*Nature's Best Hope*. Tallamy, Douglas W. — 635.9
Nature's Ghosts. Barrow, Mark V. — 333.95

NATUROPATHY
Ingels, Darin. *The Lyme Solution* — 616.9

Naumburg, Carla
★*You Are Not a Sh*tty Parent* — 649

Navab, Pedram
Sleep Reimagined — 616.8

Navai, Ramita
City of Lies — 955

NAVAJO (DINÉ) (NORTH AMERICAN PEOPLE)
Bitsui, Sherwin. *Dissolve* — 811
Geller, Danielle. *Dog Flowers* — B
Iverson, Peter. *Dine* — 979.1004
Nelson, Megan Kate. *The Three-Cornered War* — 978
Nez, Chester. *Code Talker* — B
Pasternak, Judy. *Yellow Dirt* — 979.1004
Powell, Michael. ★*Canyon Dreams* — 796.323
Sides, Hampton. *Blood and Thunder* — 978
Tapahonso, Luci. *A Radiant Curve* — 811

NAVAJO (DINÉ) CODE TALKERS
Nez, Chester. *Code Talker* — B

NAVAJO RESERVATION
Pasternak, Judy. *Yellow Dirt* — 979.1004

NAVAL ART AND SCIENCE
Borneman, Walter R. *The Admirals* — B
Symonds, Craig L. *World War II at Sea* — 940.54

NAVAL BATTLES
Dimbleby, Jonathan. *The Battle of the Atlantic* — 940.54
Hastings, Max. *Operation Pedestal* — 940.54
Hornfischer, James D. *Neptune's Inferno* — 940.54
Kilmeade, Brian. ★*Thomas Jefferson and the Tripoli Pirates* — 973.4
Philbrick, Nathaniel. ★*In the Hurricane's Eye* — 973.3
Simms, Brendan. *The Silver Waterfall* — 940.54
Strauss, Barry S. ★*The War That Made the Roman Empire* — 937
Sullivan, James. *Unsinkable* — 940.54
Symonds, Craig L. *The Battle of Midway* — 940.54
Symonds, Craig L. *Lincoln and His Admirals* — B
Taylor, Stephen. *Commander* — B
Thomas, Evan. *Sea of Thunder* — 940.54
Toll, Ian W. *The Conquering Tide* — 940.54
Toll, Ian W. *Pacific Crucible* — 940.54
Toll, Ian W. *Twilight of the Gods* — 940.54
Wheelan, Joseph. *Midnight in the Pacific* — 940.54

NAVAL CONVOYS
Geroux, William. *The Ghost Ships of Archangel* — 940.54
Hastings, Max. *Operation Pedestal* — 940.54

NAVAL HISTORY
Bergreen, Laurence. *In Search of a Kingdom* — B
Crowley, Roger. *City of Fortune* — 945
Dolin, Eric Jay. ★*Rebels at Sea* — 973.3
Hornfischer, James D. *Who Can Hold the Sea* — 359.00973
Larson, Erik. ★*Dead Wake* — 940.4
Massie, Robert K. *Castles of Steel* — 940.4
Resendez, Andres. *Conquering the Pacific* — 959.9
Ronald, Susan. *The Pirate Queen* — B
Stanton, Doug. *In Harm's Way* — 940.54
Stavridis, James. *Sea Power* — 359
Symonds, Craig L. *Lincoln and His Admirals* — B
Symonds, Craig L. *World War II at Sea* — 940.54

AUTHOR, TITLE, SERIES AND SUBJECT INDEX

Taylor, Stephen. *Commander* — B
Toll, Ian W. *The Conquering Tide* — 940.54
Toll, Ian W. ★*Six Frigates* — 359.00973
Toll, Ian W. *Twilight of the Gods* — 940.54
Whitlock, Craig. ★*Fat Leonard* — 364.16

NAVAL OPERATIONS
Borneman, Walter R. *The Admirals* — B
Budiansky, Stephen. *Blackett's War* — 940.54
Geroux, William. *The Ghost Ships of Archangel* — 940.54
Graff, Garrett M. ★*When the Sea Came Alive* — 940.54
Hastings, Max. *Operation Pedestal* — 940.54
Lance, Rachel. *In the Waves* — 973.7
Larson, Erik. ★*Dead Wake* — 940.4
Massie, Robert K. *Castles of Steel* — 940.4
Morison, Samuel Eliot. *John Paul Jones* — B
Stanton, Doug. *In Harm's Way* — 940.54
Symonds, Craig L. *The Battle of Midway* — 940.54
Symonds, Craig L. *Lincoln and His Admirals* — B
Symonds, Craig L. *World War II at Sea* — 940.54
Thomas, Evan. ★*John Paul Jones* — B
Vincent, Lynn. *Indianapolis* — 940.54

NAVAL POWER
Madden, Thomas F. *Venice* — 945

NAVAL TACTICS
Budiansky, Stephen. *Blackett's War* — 940.54
Toll, Ian W. *The Conquering Tide* — 940.54
Toll, Ian W. *Pacific Crucible* — 940.54

Navarro, Joe
Three Minutes to Doomsday — B

NAVARRO, JOE, 1953-
Navarro, Joe. *Three Minutes to Doomsday* — B

Navigating Autism. Grandin, Temple — 618.92

NAVIGATION
Alexander, Caroline. *The Bounty* — 996.1
Ellard, Colin. *You Are Here* — 153.7
Geroux, William. *The Ghost Ships of Archangel* — 940.54
Graham, Ian. *Fifty Ships That Changed the Course of History* — 387.2
Stavridis, James. *Sea Power* — 359

NAVRATILOVA, MARTINA, 1956-
Howard, Johnette. *The Rivals* — B

NAVY SEALS
Chesney, Will. *No Ordinary Dog* — 958.104
Couch, Dick. *The Warrior Elite* — 359.9
Denver, Rorke. *Worth Dying For* — 359.9
Luttrell, Marcus. *Lone Survivor* — 958.104
Luttrell, Marcus. *Service* — 956.7044
O'Neill, Robert. *The Operator* — B
Owen, Mark. *No Easy Day* — B
Owen, Mark. *No Hero* — B
Wallace, Chris. *Countdown Bin Laden* — 958.104

Nawaz, Zarqa
Laughing All the Way to the Mosque — 791.45028

NAWAZ, ZARQA
Nawaz, Zarqa. *Laughing All the Way to the Mosque* — 791.45028

Nayeri, Dina
★*The Ungrateful Refugee* — 362.87

NAYERI, DINA
Nayeri, Dina. ★*The Ungrateful Refugee* — 362.87

NAZI COLLABORATORS
Gross, Jan Tomasz. *Neighbors* — 940.53
Kershaw, Alex. *Avenue of Spies* — 940.53
Matzen, Robert. *Dutch Girl* — B
Ronald, Susan. *A Dangerous Woman* — B
Ronald, Susan. *Hitler's Aristocrats* — 940.53
Rosbottom, Ronald C. *When Paris Went Dark* — 944.0816
Sullivan, Rosemary. *The Betrayal of Anne Frank* — 940.53
Trimborn, Jurgen. *Leni Riefenstahl* — B
★*The Nazi Conspiracy*. Meltzer, Brad — 940.53

NAZI FUGITIVES
Marwell, David G. *Mengele* — B
Nazi Germany and the Jews. Friedlander, Saul — 940.53
Nazi Germany and the Jews. Friedlander, Saul — 940.53

NAZI HUNTERS
Marwell, David G. *Mengele* — B
O'Reilly, Bill. *Killing the SS* — 940.53

NAZI PLUNDER
Edsel, Robert M. *The Monuments Men* — 940.53
Goodman, Simon. *The Orpheus Clock* — 940.53

Kaiser, Menachem. *Plunder* — 940.53
Rydell, Anders. *The Book Thieves* — 027

NAZI PROPAGANDA
King, David. *The Trial of Adolf Hitler* — 345.43
Letts, Elizabeth. *The Perfect Horse* — 940.54
Longerich, Peter. *Goebbels* — B
Ronald, Susan. *Hitler's Aristocrats* — 940.53
Trimborn, Jurgen. *Leni Riefenstahl* — B

NAZI-SOVIET PACT, 1939
Moorhouse, Roger. *The Devils' Alliance* — 940.53
Sebag-Montefiore, Simon. *Stalin* — B

NAZIS
Askwith, Richard. *Unbreakable* — B
Bascomb, Neal. *Hunting Eichmann* — 943.086
Cadbury, Deborah. *The School That Escaped from the Nazis* — 940.53
Childers, Thomas. *The Third Reich* — 943.086
Crasnianski, Tania. *The Children of Nazis* — 943.086
Dwork, Deborah. ★*Holocaust* — 940
Fishman, David E. *The Book Smugglers* — 940.53
Gerwarth, Robert. *Hitler's Hangman* — B
Goodman, Simon. *The Orpheus Clock* — 940.53
Grose, Peter. *A Good Place to Hide* — 940.53
Hitler, Adolf. *Mein Kampf* — B
Holland, James. *The Rise of Germany, 1939-1941; Vol. 1* — 940.54
Jacobsen, Annie. ★*Operation Paperclip* — 940.54
Katin, Miriam. *We Are on Our Own* — 741.5
Kean, Sam. *The Bastard Brigade* — 355.8
Kershaw, Ian. *Hitler* — B
Kershaw, Ian. *Hitler* — B
Lineberry, Cate. *The Secret Rescue* — 940.54
Loftis, Larry. *Code Name* — B
Longerich, Peter. *Goebbels* — B
MacGregor, Iain. *The Lighthouse of Stalingrad* — 940.54
Matzen, Robert. *Dutch Girl* — B
Mazower, Mark. *Hitler's Empire* — 940.53
Meltzer, Brad. ★*The Nazi Conspiracy* — 940.53
Morton, Andrew. *17 Carnations* — 941.084
O'Reilly, Bill. *Killing the SS* — 940.53
Petropoulos, Jonathan. *The Faustian Bargain* — 709
Pressman, Steven. *50 Children* — 940.53
Rashke, Richard. *Useful Enemies* — 341.69
Rees, Laurence. *Auschwitz* — 940.53
Rose, Sarah. *D-Day Girls* — 940.53
Ross, Steven Joseph. ★*Hitler in Los Angeles* — 979.4
Ryback, Timothy W. *Hitler's Private Library* — 027
Rydell, Anders. *The Book Thieves* — 027
Sands, Philippe. *The Ratline* — B
Simon, Marie. *Underground in Berlin* — B
Speer, Albert. *Inside the Third Reich* — B
Spicer, Charles. *Coffee with Hitler* — 941.084
Stangneth, Bettina. *Eichmann Before Jerusalem* — B
Talty, Stephan. *The Good Assassin* — 364.15
Teege, Jennifer. *My Grandfather Would Have Shot Me* — 929.2
Ullrich, Volker. ★*Eight Days in May* — 943.086
Weber, Thomas. *Becoming Hitler* — B
The Nazis Knew My Name. Blau, Magda Hellinger — 940.53

NAZISM
Allert, Tilman. *Heil Hitler* — 395.4
Bascomb, Neal. *Faster* — 796.7209
Eisner, Peter. *The Pope's Last Crusade* — 282.092
English, Charlie. *The Gallery of Miracles and Madness* — 709.04
Evans, Richard J. *The Coming of the Third Reich* — 943.08
Evans, Richard J. *The Third Reich in Power, 1933-1939* — 943.086
Fritzsche, Peter. *Life and Death in the Third Reich* — 943.086
Goldhagen, Daniel Jonah. *Hitler's Willing Executioners* — 940.53
Haffner, Sebastian. *Defying Hitler* — 943.085
Hett, Benjamin Carter. *The Death of Democracy* — 943.085
Hitler, Adolf. *Mein Kampf* — B
Kershaw, Alex. *Avenue of Spies* — 940.53
Kershaw, Ian. *Hitler* — B
Kershaw, Ian. *Hitler* — B
Larson, Erik. *In the Garden of Beasts* — B
Longerich, Peter. *Goebbels* — B
Longerich, Peter. *Hitler* — B
Lower, Wendy. *Hitler's Furies* — 940.53
Maddow, Rachel. ★*Prequel* — 320.53
Mazower, Mark. *Hitler's Empire* — 940.53
McDonough, Frank. *The Hitler Years* — 943.086

PUBLIC LIBRARY CORE COLLECTION: NONFICTION
Twentieth Edition

Oelhafen, Ingrid von. *Hitler's Stolen Children*   B
Okrent, Daniel. *The Guarded Gate*   344.73
Pressman, Steven. *50 Children*   940.53
Read, Anthony. *The Fall of Berlin*   940.54
Ronald, Susan. *Hitler's Aristocrats*   940.53
Roth, Joseph. *What I Saw*   943
Schindler, Meriel. *The Lost Cafe Schindler*   943.64
Shirer, William L. ★*The Rise and Fall of the Third Reich*   943.086
Spicer, Charles. *Coffee with Hitler*   941.084
Thomas, Gordon. *Defying Hitler*   920
Trimborn, Jurgen. *Leni Riefenstahl*   B
Ullrich, Volker. *Hitler*   B
Ullrich, Volker. *Hitler*   B
Urwand, Ben. *The Collaboration*   791.430973
Weale, Adrian. *Army of Evil*   940.54
Weber, Thomas. *Becoming Hitler*   B
Ndopu, Eddie
   Sipping Dom Pérignon Through a Straw   B
NDOPU, EDDIE
   Ndopu, Eddie. *Sipping Dom Pérignon Through a Straw*   B
NEANDERTHALS
   Flannery, Tim F. *Europe*   508.4
   Pattison, Kermit. *Fossil Men*   569.9
   Tattersall, Ian. *Masters of the Planet*   599.93
   Wragg Sykes, Rebecca. *Kindred*   569.9
NEAR-DEATH EXPERIENCE
   Junger, Sebastian. ★*In My Time of Dying*   304.6
   Moody, Raymond A. *Life After Life*   133.9
   O'Farrell, Maggie. *I Am, I Am, I Am*   B
   Panagore, Peter Baldwin. *Heaven Is Beautiful*   B
   Roach, Mary. ★*Spook*   129
NEATNESS AND MESSINESS
   Harford, Tim. *Messy*   153.3
NEBRASKA
   Genoways, Ted. *This Blessed Earth*   630.9
   Hopwood, Shon. *Law Man*   B
   MacLean, Harry N. *Starkweather*   364.152
   Pipher, Mary Bray. *The Middle of Everywhere*   305.9
The Necessary Journey. Washington, Ella F.   658.3
Necessary Trouble. Faust, Drew Gilpin   B
Nederlanden, Elisabet der
   ★*Holiday Cookies*   641.86
NEED
   Shapland, Jenn. ★*Thin Skin*   814
Need to Know. Reynolds, Nicholas E.   940.54
Needle Felting. Adams, Liza   746
Needleman, Deborah
   The Perfectly Imperfect Home   747
   ★*The Needlepoint Book.* Christensen, Jo Ippolito   746.44
NEEDLEWORK
   Brasfield, Hope. *Satisfying Stitches*   746.44
   Galbraith, Melissa. *How to Embroider Texture and Pattern*   746.44
   Ganderton, Lucinda. ★*Embroidery*   746.44
   Montenegro, Sonya. *Mending Life*   646
   Mornu, Nathalie. *Embroider Your Life*   746.44
NEEL, ALICE, 1900-1984
   Hoban, Phoebe. *Alice Neel*   B
NEFERTITI, QUEEN OF EGYPT, 14TH CENT. B.C.E
   Darnell, John Coleman. *Egypt's Golden Couple*   932
NEGATIVISM
   Tierney, John. *The Power of Bad*   158.1
NEGLIGENCE
   Ritchie, Stuart. *Science Fictions*   500
NEGOTIATION
   Baker, Peter. *The Man Who Ran Washington*   B
   Barrett, David Dean. *140 Days to Hiroshima*   940.54
   Davidds, Yasmin. *Your Own Terms*   658.4
   Ferguson, Niall. *Kissinger*   973.924
   Fisher, Roger. ★*Getting to Yes*   158
   Lowry, Erin. ★*Broke Millennial Talks Money*   332.024
   Sally, David. *One Step Ahead*   658.4
   Smith, Sam. *Hard Labor*   796.323
   Vanek Smith, Stacey. *Machiavelli for Women*   650.1
NEGOTIATION IN BUSINESS
   Davidds, Yasmin. *Your Own Terms*   658.4
   Pessah, Jon. *The Game*   796.357
   Sally, David. *One Step Ahead*   658.4

NEGOTIATORS
   Levin, Daniel. *Proof of Life*   956.9104
NEGRO LEAGUES
   Posnanski, Joe. *The Soul of Baseball*   796.357
   Tye, Larry. *Satchel*   B
NEGRO LEAGUES PLAYERS
   Perron, Cam. ★*Comeback Season*   796.357
   Tye, Larry. *Satchel*   B
Negroland. Jefferson, Margo   305.896
NEHRU, JAWAHARLAL, 1889-1964
   Hajari, Nisid. *Midnight's Furies*   954.04
Neifert, Marianne R.
   The Essential Guide to Breastfeeding   649
NEIGHBORHOODS
   Chin, Curtis. *Everything I Learned, I Learned in a Chinese Restaurant*   B
   DePalma, Anthony. *The Cubans*   920
   Hirsch, James S. *Riot and Remembrance*   976.6
   Kanigel, Robert. *Eyes on the Street*   B
   Madigan, Tim. *The Burning*   976.6
   Nusbaum, Eric. *Stealing Home*   796.357
   Oppenheimer, Mark. *Squirrel Hill*   364.152
   Schmitz, Rob. *Street of Eternal Happiness*   951
Neighbors. Gross, Jan Tomasz   940.53
NEIGHBORS
   Addison, Corban. *Wastelands*   346.73
   Pick-Goslar, Hannah Elizabeth. ★*My Friend Anne Frank*   B
Neighbors, Joy
   The Family Tree Cemetery Field Guide   929
Neil Armstrong. Barbree, Jay   B
Neil Patrick Harris. Harris, Neil Patrick   B
Neiman, Garrett
   Rich White Men   305.5
Neiman, Ophelie
   Wine Isn't Rocket Science   641.2
Nein, Nein, Nein! Stahl, Jerry   B
Neiwert, David A.
   ★*The Age of Insurrection*   303.48
   Of Orcas and Men   599.53
Nellie Taft. Anthony, Carl Sferrazza   B
Nelson, Bryn
   Flush   612.3
Nelson, Candace
   The Sprinkles Baking Book   641.81
Nelson, Craig
   Pearl Harbor   940.54
   Rocket Men   629.45
   ★*V Is for Victory*   973.917
Nelson, David B.
   Boys Enter the House   364.152
Nelson, Glenn C.
   Ceramics   738
Nelson, Kim
   Daisy Cakes Bakes   641.86
Nelson, Maggie
   ★*The Argonauts*   B
   ★*Like Love*   814
NELSON, MAGGIE, 1973-
   Nelson, Maggie. ★*The Argonauts*   B
   Nelson, Maggie. ★*Like Love*   814
Nelson, Megan Kate
   The Three-Cornered War   978
NELSON, SARA, 1973-
   Nolan, Hamilton. *The Hammer*   331.8
Nelson, Willie
   It's a Long Story   B
NELSON, WILLIE, 1933-
   Nelson, Willie. *It's a Long Story*   B
Nemat, Marina
   Prisoner of Tehran   B
NEMAT, MARINA
   Nemat, Marina. *Prisoner of Tehran*   B
Nemiroff, Robert
   To Be Young, Gifted, and Black   B
Neon Girls. Worley, Jennifer   792.7
NEONATAL INTENSIVE CARE
   DiGregorio, Sarah. *Early*   618.92
   Raffel, Dawn. *The Strange Case of Dr. Couney*   B

AUTHOR, TITLE, SERIES AND SUBJECT INDEX

NEOPAGANISM
    Adler, Margot. *Drawing Down the Moon* — 299
    Hutton, Ronald. *The Triumph of the Moon* — 133.4
    Mar, Alex. *Witches of America* — 299
    Rajchel, Diana. *Urban Magick* — 133.4

NEPAL
    Doyne, Maggie. *Between the Mountain and the Sky* — B
    Krakauer, Jon. ★*Into Thin Air* — 796.52

Neptune's Inferno. Hornfischer, James D. — 940.54

Nerd. Phillips, Maya — 302.23

Nerenberg, Jenara
    Divergent Mind — 616.89

NERENBERG, JENARA
    Nerenberg, Jenara. *Divergent Mind* — 616.89

NERO EMPEROR OF ROME 37-68
    Southon, Emma. *Agrippina* — B

Neruda, Pablo
    All the Odes — 861
    Then Come Back — 861
    ★*Twenty Love Poems and a Song of Despair* — 861
    World's End — 861

NERUDA, PABLO, 1904-1973
    Feinstein, Adam. *Pablo Neruda* — B
    Neruda, Pablo. *All the Odes* — 861
    Neruda, Pablo. *Then Come Back* — 861
    Neruda, Pablo. *World's End* — 861

NERVOUS BREAKDOWN
    Eade, Philip. *Evelyn Waugh* — B

NERVOUS SYSTEM
    Dittrich, Luke. ★*Patient H.M.* — 616.85
    Kolata, Gina Bari. *Mercies in Disguise* — 616
    Lalkhen, Abdul-Ghaaliq. *An Anatomy of Pain* — 616
    Ruhl, Sarah. *Smile* — B

Nesmith, Michael
    Infinite Tuesday — B

NESMITH, MICHAEL
    Nesmith, Michael. *Infinite Tuesday* — B

NESS, ELIOT
    Collins, Max Allan. *Eliot Ness and the Mad Butcher* — 364.152
    Stashower, Daniel. *American Demon* — 364.152

Nesse, Randolph M.
    Good Reasons for Bad Feelings — 616.89

Nesteroff, Kliph
    The Comedians — 792.7
    We Had a Little Real Estate Problem — 970.004

Nestor, James
    Deep — 797.2

NESTS
    Hammer, Joshua. *The Falcon Thief* — 364.16

NETANYAHU, BINYAMIN
    Pfeffer, Anshel. *Bibi* — B

NETHERLANDS
    Beevor, Antony. *The Battle of Arnhem* — 940.54
    Bell, Julian. *Van Gogh* — B
    Blom, Onno. *Young Rembrandt* — B
    Finkelstein, Daniel. *Two Roads Home* — 920
    Gies, Miep. ★*Anne Frank Remembered* — B
    Goodrich, Frances. *The Diary of Anne Frank* — 812
    Hirsi Ali, Ayaan. ★*Infidel* — B
    Iperen, Roxane van. ★*The Sisters of Auschwitz* — 940.53
    Jacobson, Sidney. *Anne Frank* — 741.5
    Lindwer, Willy. *The Last Seven Months of Anne Frank* — B
    Matzen, Robert. *Dutch Girl* — B
    Muller, Melissa. *Anne Frank* — B
    Schama, Simon. *The Embarrassment of Riches* — 949.2
    Siegal, Nina. *The Diary Keepers* — 940.54
    Snyder, Laura J. *Eye of the Beholder* — 920
    Sullivan, Rosemary. *The Betrayal of Anne Frank* — 940.53
    Van De Perre, Selma. *My Name Is Selma* — 940.53
    Van Es, Bart. *The Cut Out Girl* — B
    Van Wijk-Voskuijl, Joop. *The Last Secret of the Secret Annex* — 940.53
    Winder, Simon. *Lotharingia* — 944

NETWORKING
    Burkus, David. *Friend of a Friend...* — 650.1

NETWORKS
    Burkus, David. *Friend of a Friend...* — 650.1

Neu, Charles E.
    Colonel House — B

Neuburger, Emily K.
    Show Me a Story — 745.5083

Neufeld, Josh
    A.D. — 741.5

NEUMANN, ADAM, 1979-
    Brown, Eliot. *The Cult of We* — 333.33
    Wiedeman, Reeves. *Billion Dollar Loser* — 333.33

Neumann, Ariana
    When Time Stopped — B

NEUMANN, ARIANA
    Neumann, Ariana. *When Time Stopped* — B

NEUMANN, HANUS STANISLAV, 1921-2001
    Neumann, Ariana. *When Time Stopped* — B

NEUROBIOLOGY
    Eagleman, David. *Livewired* — 612.8
    Kandel, Eric R. *In Search of Memory* — B
    Marriott, Sue. *Secure Relating* — 158.1
    Sapolsky, Robert M. *Behave* — 612.8

NEUROCHEMISTRY
    Harrington, Anne. *Mind Fixers* — 616.89
    Slater, Lauren. *Blue Dreams* — 615.7

NEURODIVERGENT PEOPLE
    Donvan, John. *In a Different Key* — 616.85
    Fall, Jeremy. *Falling Upwards* — 158.1
    Felix, Camonghne. *Dyscalculia* — B
    Fleming, Jory. *How to Be Human* — 616.85
    Gadsby, Hannah. ★*Ten Steps to Nanette* — B
    Grandin, Temple. ★*Animals in Translation* — 591.5
    James, Laura E. *Odd Girl Out* — B
    Kirkby, Bruce. *Blue Sky Kingdom* — 954.96
    Legler, Casey. ★*Godspeed* — B
    Malone, Jo. *Jo Malone* — B
    McAnulty, Dara. *Diary of a Young Naturalist* — 508.092
    Moorer, Allison. *I Dream He Talks to Me* — 782.42164
    Nerenberg, Jenara. *Divergent Mind* — 616.89
    Nigg, Joel T. *Getting Ahead of ADHD* — 618.92
    O'Toole, Jennifer Cook. *Autism in Heels* — B
    Ramesh, Jaya. *Parenting at the Intersections* — 649
    Robison, John Elder. *Look Me in the Eye* — B
    Rodgers, Jodi. ★*How to Find a Four-Leaf Clover* — 616.85
    Rowe, Mickey. *Fearlessly Different* — B
    Ruthsatz, Joanne. *The Prodigy's Cousin* — 155.45
    Schwarz, Alan. *ADHD Nation* — 618.92
    Seager, Sara. *The Smallest Lights in the Universe* — B
    Tammet, Daniel. *Born on a Blue Day* — B
    Winkler, Henry. ★*Being Henry* — B

NEUROLOGISTS
    Eichenwald, Kurt. *A Mind Unraveled* — B
    Kandel, Eric R. *In Search of Memory* — B
    Kozol, Jonathan. *The Theft of Memory* — B
    Sacks, Oliver. ★*Everything in Its Place* — B
    Sacks, Oliver. *Gratitude* — 306.9
    Sacks, Oliver. *The Man Who Mistook His Wife for a Hat and Other Clinical Tales* — 616.8
    Sacks, Oliver. *On the Move* — B
    Weschler, Lawrence. *And How Are You, Dr. Sacks?* — B

NEUROLOGY
    Eagleman, David. *Incognito* — 153
    Kean, Sam. *The Tale of the Dueling Neurosurgeons* — 617.4
    Sacks, Oliver. *The Man Who Mistook His Wife for a Hat and Other Clinical Tales* — 616.8
    Shermer, Michael. *The Believing Brain* — 153.4
    Wertheim, L. Jon. *This Is Your Brain on Sports* — 796.01

NEUROMUSCULAR DISEASES
    Burcaw, Shane. ★*Laughing at My Nightmare* — B
    Grue, Jan. *I Live a Life Like Yours* — B

NEUROPHYSIOLOGY
    Sapolsky, Robert M. *Behave* — 612.8

NEUROPLASTICITY
    Eagleman, David. *Livewired* — 612.8

NEUROPSYCHIATRY
    Deisseroth, Karl. *Projections* — 616.89
    Harrington, Anne. *Mind Fixers* — 616.89

NEUROPSYCHOLOGY
    Benjamin, A. K. *Let Me Not Be Mad* — 612.8
    Damasio, Antonio R. *Looking for Spinoza* — 152.4
    Denworth, Lydia. *Friendship* — 158.2
    Fine, Cordelia. *Testosterone Rex* — 155.3

PUBLIC LIBRARY CORE COLLECTION: NONFICTION
Twentieth Edition

Fleming, Renee. ★*Music and Mind*   615.8
Hoffman, Donald D. *Visual Intelligence*   152.14
Lewis, Michael. ★*The Undoing Project*   920
Mooney, Jonathan. *Normal Sucks*   B
Nerenberg, Jenara. *Divergent Mind*   616.89
O'Sullivan, Suzanne. *The Sleeping Beauties*   616.85
Pinker, Steven. *How the Mind Works*   153
Provine, Robert R. *Curious Behavior*   152.3
Waldman, Ayelet. *A Really Good Day*   B
Webb, Caroline. *How to Have a Good Day*   650.1
NEUROSCIENCE
  Barrett, Lisa Feldman. ★*How Emotions Are Made*   152.4
  Bullmore, Edward T. *The Inflamed Mind*   616.85
  Burnett, Dean. *Idiot Brain*   612.8
  Cacioppo, Stephanie. *Wired for Love*   616.8
  Clark, Andy. *The Experience Machine*   153
  Conaboy, Chelsea. *Mother Brain*   306.874
  Crais, Clifton C. *History Lessons*   B
  Dakwar, Elias. *The Captive Imagination*   616.85
  Damasio, Antonio R. *The Feeling of What Happens*   153
  Dittrich, Luke. ★*Patient H.M.*   616.85
  Eagleman, David. *The Brain*   612.8
  Eagleman, David. *Incognito*   153
  Foer, Joshua. *Moonwalking with Einstein*   153.1
  Goleman, Daniel. ★*Social Intelligence*   158.2
  Guyenet, Stephan J. *The Hungry Brain*   616.85
  Hammond, Claudia. *Mind Over Money*   332.401
  Higgins, Jackie. *Sentient*   573.8
  Kandel, Eric R. *The Age of Insight*   154.2
  Kandel, Eric R. ★*The Disordered Mind*   616.89
  Kandel, Eric R. *In Search of Memory*   B
  Kean, Sam. *The Tale of the Dueling Neurosurgeons*   617.4
  Koenig, Joan. *The Musical Child*   780.71
  Leschziner, Guy. *The Nocturnal Brain*   616.8
  Lewis, Michael. ★*The Undoing Project*   920
  Li, Fei-Fei. *The Worlds I See*   B
  Livio, Mario. *Why?*   153.3
  Magsamen, Susan. *Your Brain on Art*   111
  Mlodinow, Leonard. *Emotional*   152.4
  Nigg, Joel T. *Getting Ahead of ADHD*   618.92
  Paul, Annie Murphy. *The Extended Mind*   128
  Petersen, Andrea. *On Edge*   616.85
  Ranganath, Charan. ★*Why We Remember*   153.1
  Rogers, Susan E. ★*This Is What It Sounds Like*   781.1
  Simon, Matt. *Plight of the Living Dead*   591.6
  Thomson, Helen. *Unthinkable*   612.8
  Ward, Ashley. *Where We Meet the World*   612.8
  Wiking, Meik. *The Art of Making Memories*   153.1
  Wolf, Maryanne. *Reader, Come Home*   418
  Yong, Ed. ★*An Immense World*   591.5
  Zadra, Antonio. *When Brains Dream*   613.7
The Neuroscientist Who Lost Her Mind. Lipska, Barbara K.   B
NEUROSCIENTISTS
  Lipska, Barbara K. *The Neuroscientist Who Lost Her Mind*   B
  Ryckman, Pamela. *Candace Pert*   B
  Taylor, Jill Bolte. *My Stroke of Insight*   362.19681
NEUROSES
  Crampton, Caroline. *A Body Made of Glass*   616.85
NEUROSURGEONS
  Dittrich, Luke. ★*Patient H.M.*   616.85
  Kalanithi, Paul. ★*When Breath Becomes Air*   B
  Marsh, Henry. *Admissions*   B
  Marsh, Henry. ★*Do No Harm*   B
  Wellons, Jay. *All That Moves Us*   617.4
Neus, Nora
  24 Hours in Charlottesville   973.933
NEVADA
  Patterson, James. *What Really Happens in Vegas*   920
Nevala-Lee, Alec
  Astounding   809.3
Never Alone. Girzone, Joseph F.   248.4
Never Broken. Jewel   782.42164
★*Never Caught*. Dunbar, Erica Armstrong   B
Never Eat Alone. Ferrazzi, Keith   658.4
Never Far from Home. Jackson, Bruce   B
Never Get Angry Again. Lieberman, David J   152.4
Never Give Up. Grylls, Bear   B
Never Grow Up. Chan, Jackie   B

★*Never Pay the First Bill*. Allen, Marshall   610.28
Never Ran, Never Will. Samaha, Albert   920
Never Remember. Gessen, Masha   365
★*Never Say You Can't Survive*. Anders, Charlie Jane   808.02
Never Simple. Scheier, Liz   B
Neville, Aaron
  Tell It Like It Is   B
NEVILLE, AARON, 1941-
  Neville, Aaron. *Tell It Like It Is*   B
Nevins, Sheila
  You Don't Look Your Age   B
NEVINS, SHEILA
  Nevins, Sheila. *You Don't Look Your Age*   B
New & Selected Poems. Dunn, Stephen   811
NEW AGE
  Beres, Derek. *Conspirituality*   001.9
New and Collected Poems, 1964-2007. Reed, Ishmael   811
New and Selected Poems. Simic, Charles   811
New and Selected Poems,; Vol. 1. Oliver, Mary   811
The New Basics Cookbook. Rosso, Julee   641.5
The New Biographical Dictionary of Film. Thomson, David   791.4302
The New Black. Shockley, Evie   811
The New Bohemians Handbook. Blakeney, Justina   747
NEW BUSINESSES
  Berger, Eric. *Liftoff*   B
  Bertch, Jane. *The French Ingredient*   B
  Brown, Eliot. *The Cult of We*   333.33
  Carreyrou, John. ★*Bad Blood*   338.7
  Downs, Paul. *Boss Life*   338.7
  Gotch, Jen. *The Upside of Being Down*   B
  Kawasaki, Guy. *The Art of the Start 2.0*   658.1
  Lima, Jamie Kern. *Believe It*   B
  McKeever, Mike P. *How to Write a Business Plan*   658.15
  Pein, Corey. *Live Work Work Work Die*   338.4
  Webb, Maynard. *Dear Founder*   658
  Wiener, Anna. ★*Uncanny Valley*   B
  Yunus, Muhammad. *A World of Three Zeros*   330
New Collected Poems. Moore, Marianne   811
New Collected Poems. Boland, Eavan   821
New Collected Poems. Berry, Wendell   811
NEW DEAL, 1933-1939
  Brands, H. W. *Traitor to His Class*   B
  Brinkley, Douglas. *Rightful Heritage*   B
  Katznelson, Ira. *Fear Itself*   973.917
  Kennedy, David M. ★*Freedom from Fear*   973.91
  Shlaes, Amity. *The Forgotten Man*   973.91
  Simon, James F. *FDR and Chief Justice Hughes*   973.917092
New Directions in Sock Knitting. Budd, Ann   746.43
New Directions paperbook [Series]. Transtromer, Tomas   839.71
The New Encyclopedia of Islam. Glasse, Cyril   297.03
NEW ENGLAND
  Albee, Edward. ★*Who's Afraid of Virginia Woolf?*   812
  Karlsen, Carol F. ★*The Devil in the Shape of a Woman*   133.4
  Shattuck, Ben. *Six Walks*   B
  Skomal, Gregory. *Chasing Shadows*   597.3
NEW ENGLAND HISTORY
  Burns, Cherie. *The Great Hurricane—1938*   974.7
  Cook, Blanche Wiesen. *Eleanor Roosevelt; Volume 2*   B
  Cook, Blanche Wiesen. ★*Eleanor Roosevelt; Volume 3*   B
  Schultz, Eric B. *King Philip's War*   973.2
  Shlaes, Amity. *Coolidge*   B
  Warren, James A. *God, War, and Providence*   974.5
NEW ENGLAND HURRICANE, 1938
  Burns, Cherie. *The Great Hurricane—1938*   974.7
NEW FRANCE (1534-1763)
  Fischer, David Hackett. *Champlain's Dream*   B
New German Cooking. Nolen, Jeremy   641.594
NEW GUINEA
  Hoffman, Carl. ★*Savage Harvest*   995.1
  Zuckoff, Mitchell. *Lost in Shangri-La*   940.54
The New Guys. Bagby, Meredith E.   305
NEW HAMPSHIRE
  Carroll, Rebecca. *Surviving the White Gaze*   B
  Crawford, Lacy. *Notes on a Silencing*   B
  Montgomery, Sy. *The Good Good Pig*   636.4
  Wilder, Thornton. *Our Town*   812
NEW HAVEN, CONNECTICUT
  Hobbs, Jeff. ★*The Short and Tragic Life of Robert Peace*   B

AUTHOR, TITLE, SERIES AND SUBJECT INDEX

    Perkins, Anne Gardiner. *Yale Needs Women* — 378
NEW JERSEY
    Christie, Chris. *Let Me Finish* — B
    Fagin, Dan. *Toms River* — 363.7209749
    Fischer, David Hackett. *Washington's Crossing* — 973.3
    Mortimer, Frank. *Bee People and the Bugs They Love* — B
    Weinman, Sarah. *Scoundrel* — 364.152
    Williams, William Carlos. *Paterson* — 811
The New Jim Crow. Alexander, Michelle — 364.973
The New Joys of Yiddish. Rosten, Leo — 422
The New Map. Yergin, Daniel — 333.79
The New Mediterranean Diet Cookbook. Jenkins, Nancy Harmon — 641.59
★*The New Menopause.* Haver, Mary Claire — 618.1
NEW MEXICO
    Childs, Craig. *House of Rain* — 978.9
    Crutchfield, James A. *Revolt at Taos* — 972
    Gaffney, Ginger. *Half Broke* — B
    Taffa, Deborah Jackson. ★*Whiskey Tender* — B
NEW MEXICO (TERRITORY)
    Nelson, Megan Kate. *The Three-Cornered War* — 978
The New Mind of the South. Thompson, Tracy — 305.800975
A New Model. Graham, Ashley — B
NEW MOTHERS
    Cusk, Rachel. *A Life's Work* — 306.874
    Millwood, Molly. *To Have and to Hold* — 306.874
New Native Kitchen. Bitsoie, Freddie — 641.59
★*The New Negro.* Stewart, Jeffrey C. — 191
NEW NEIGHBORS
    Von Drehle, David. ★*The Book of Charlie* — B
The New Normal. Ashton, Jennifer — 613
The New One. Birbiglia, Mike — B
★*The New Organic Grower.* Coleman, Eliot — 635
NEW ORLEANS, BATTLE OF, 1815
    Kilmeade, Brian. ★*Andrew Jackson and the Miracle of New Orleans* — 973.5
NEW ORLEANS, LOUISIANA
    Armstrong, Louis. *Louis Armstrong, in His Own Words* — B
    Ball, Edward. *Life of a Klansman* — 305.8009763
    Baum, Dan. *Nine Lives* — B
    Berry, Jason. *City of a Million Dreams* — 976.3
    Brinkley, Douglas. *The Great Deluge* — 976.3
    Broom, Sarah M. *The Yellow House* — B
    Brothers, Thomas David. ★*Louis Armstrong, Master of Modernism* — B
    Crais, Clifton C. *History Lessons* — B
    Eggers, Dave. *Zeitoun* — 305.892
    Fieseler, Robert W. *Tinderbox* — 364.152
    Fink, Sheri. *Five Days at Memorial* — 362.1109763
    Hereford, Mason. *Turkey and the Wolf* — 641.5976
    Horne, Jed. *Breach of Faith* — 976.3
    Jackson, Ted. ★*You Ought to Do a Story About Me* — B
    Johnson, Walter. *Soul by Soul* — 976.3
    Kilmeade, Brian. ★*Andrew Jackson and the Miracle of New Orleans* — 973.5
    Krist, Gary. *Empire of Sin* — 976.3
    Neufeld, Josh. *A.D.* — 741.5
    Rasmussen, Daniel. *American Uprising* — 976.3
    Rivlin, Gary. *Katrina* — 976.3
    Sanchez, Aaron. *Where I Come From* — 641.5092
    Spera, Keith. *Groove Interrupted* — B
    Tisserand, Michael. *Krazy* — 741.5
    Varon, Elizabeth R. *Longstreet* — B
A New Path to the Waterfall. Carver, Raymond — 811
New Poems. Rilke, Rainer Maria — 831
NEW PRODUCTS
    Grant, Adam M. *Originals* — 153.3
    Kim, W. Chan. *Blue Ocean Shift* — 658.8
The New Religious Intolerance. Nussbaum, Martha Craven — 201.723
NEW RIGHT
    Alberta, Tim. *The Kingdom, the Power, and the Glory* — 270.8
    Applebaum, Anne. *Twilight of Democracy* — 321.9
    Berman, Ari. ★*Minority Rule* — 305.809
    Du Mez, Kristin Kobes. *Jesus and John Wayne* — 277.308
    Ganz, John. *When the Clock Broke* — 320.52
    Spencer, Kyle. *Raising Them Right* — 320.5
    Stelter, Brian. *Hoax* — 070.4
    Wallis, Jim. *The False White Gospel* — 261.7
A New Selected Poems. Kinnell, Galway — 811
The New Shade Garden. Druse, Kenneth — 635.9
The New Stokes Field Guide to Birds. Stokes, Donald W. — 598

The New Strong's Expanded Exhaustive Concordance of the Bible. Strong, James — 220.5
A New Take on Cake. Byrn, Anne — 641.86
The New Terrarium. Martin, Tovah — 635.9
The New Tourist. McClanahan, Paige — 338.4
The New Traditional. Carter, Darryl — 747
The New Tsar. Myers, Steven Lee — B
NEW WAVE MUSIC
    Gordon, Kim. *Girl in a Band* — B
    Harry, Debbie. *Face It* — B
    Moore, Thurston. *Sonic Life* — B
NEW WAVE MUSICIANS
    Harry, Debbie. *Face It* — B
The New Wild West. Briody, Blaire — 338.2
New Women in the Old West. Gallagher, Winifred — 978.02
A New World Begins. Popkin, Jeremy D. — 944.04
NEW YORK (STATE)
    Ambroz, David. *A Place Called Home* — B
    Attas, Amy. *Pets and the City* — B
    Blum, Deborah. *The Poisoner's Handbook* — 614
    Brina, Elizabeth Miki. *Speak, Okinawa* — 305.48
    Cardwell, Diane. *Rockaway* — B
    Cohen, Eliot A. *Conquered into Liberty* — 355.009747
    Daughan, George C. *Revolution on the Hudson* — 974.7
    Delany, Sarah Louise. *Having Our Say* — B
    Elliott, Andrea. ★*Invisible Child* — 362.7
    Fairbanks, Amanda M. *The Lost Boys of Montauk* — 910.91
    Fedderly, Eva. *These Walls* — 365
    Fox, Margalit. *The Talented Mrs. Mandelbaum* — 364.1
    France, David. *How to Survive a Plague* — 362.196
    Griswold, Mac K. *The Manor* — 974.7
    Ketchum, Richard M. *Saratoga* — 973.3
    Kilmeade, Brian. ★*George Washington's Secret Six* — 973.4
    Levin, Daniel Barban. *Slonim Woods 9* — B
    Martini, Adrienne. *Somebody's Gotta Do It* — B
    McCourt, Malachy. *Singing My Him Song* — B
    Morris, Edmund. ★*The Rise of Theodore Roosevelt* — B
    O'Brien, Keith. *Paradise Falls* — 363.738
    Peiffer, Prudence. *The Slip* — 709.73
    Perlin, Ross. ★*Language City* — 306.44
    Phillips-Fein, Kim. *Fear City* — 330.9747
    Pinckney, Darryl. *Come Back in September* — B
    Raboteau, Emily. *Lessons for Survival* — 814
    Rayman, Graham. ★*Rikers* — 365
    Rosen, Jonathan. ★*The Best Minds* — 616.89
    Salaam, Yusef. *Better, Not Bitter* — B
    Samuelsson, Marcus. *The Red Rooster Cookbook* — 641.5974
    Satow, Julie. *When Women Ran Fifth Avenue* — 381.141
    Sipress, David. *What's so Funny?* — B
    Stahr, Walter. *Seward* — B
    Taylor, Alan. *The Divided Ground* — 974.7
    Thompson, Heather Ann. *Blood in the Water* — 365
    Wayland-Smith, Ellen. *Oneida* — 307.77
    Wickenden, Dorothy. *The Agitators* — 920
    Wright, Jennifer Ashley. ★*Madame Restell* — B
New York Burning. Lepore, Jill — 974.7
NEW YORK CITY
    Abrams, Jonathan P. D. ★*The Come Up* — 782.421649
    Adams, Michael Henry. *Style and Grace* — 747
    Ambroz, David. *A Place Called Home* — B
    Anbinder, Tyler. ★*City of Dreams* — 974.7
    Ashon, Will. *Chamber Music* — 782.421649
    Attas, Amy. *Pets and the City* — B
    Belfort, Jordan. ★*The Wolf of Investing* — 332.63
    Bourdain, Anthony. ★*Kitchen Confidential* — B
    Bourdain, Anthony. *Medium Raw* — B
    Brickell, Francesca Cartier. *The Cartiers* — B
    Brown, Claude. *Manchild in the Promised Land* — B
    Brown, Tina. *The Vanity Fair Diaries* — B
    Butcher, Barbara. *What the Dead Know* — 614
    Calhoun, Ada. *Also a Poet* — B
    Cannell, Michael T. *A Brotherhood Betrayed* — B
    Carlo, Philip. *Gaspipe* — B
    Carr, David. *The Night of the Gun* — B
    Carter, David. *Stonewall* — 306.76
    Carter, Stephen L. *Invisible* — B
    Cecchi-Azzolina, Michael. *Your Table Is Ready* — 647.95
    Crouch, Stanley. *Kansas City Lightning* — B

PUBLIC LIBRARY CORE COLLECTION: NONFICTION
Twentieth Edition

Cunningham, William J. ★*Fashion Climbing*	B
Day, Daniel R. *Dapper Dan*	B
Dubus, Andre. *Ghost Dogs*	814
Dwyer, Jim. *102 Minutes*	974.7
Elliott, Andrea. ★*Invisible Child*	362.7
Eyman, Scott. *Hank and Jim*	920
Feldman, Deborah. *Unorthodox*	B
Flaherty, Meghan. *Tango Lessons*	793.3
Fox, Margalit. *The Talented Mrs. Mandelbaum*	364.1
Frankel, Glenn. *Shooting Midnight Cowboy*	791.43
Friend, David. *Watching the World Change*	974.7
Gabriel, Mary. *Ninth Street Women*	920
Gage, Beverly. *The Day Wall Street Exploded*	974.7
Gehrig, Lou. *The Lost Memoir*	B
Glaser, Gabrielle. *American Baby*	B
Gleeson, John. *The Gotti Wars*	364.1
Gooch, Brad. *Radiant*	B
Graff, Garrett M. ★*The Only Plane in the Sky*	973.931
Green, Elon. *Last Call*	363.15
Greene, Jayson. *Once More We Saw Stars*	155.9
Grey, Joel. *Master of Ceremonies*	B
Hamill, Kirkland. *Filthy Beasts*	B
Hamilton, Gabrielle. *Blood, Bones, and Butter*	B
Harry, Debbie. *Face It*	B
Healy, Thomas. *The Great Dissent*	342.7308
Hermes, Will. *Lou Reed*	B
Hermes, Will. *Love Goes to Buildings on Fire*	781.64
Hernandez, Daisy. *A Cup of Water Under My Bed*	B
Hochschild, Adam. *Rebel Cinderella*	B
Hortis, C. Alexander. *The Witch of New York*	364.152
Howe, Ben Ryder. *My Korean Deli*	B
Ikpi, Bassey. *I'm Telling the Truth, but I'm Lying*	814
Jacobs, Alexandra. *Still Here*	B
Johnson, Stephanie. *Tanqueray*	B
Johnson, Steven. *The Infernal Machine*	335
Jones, Brenda. *Alexandria Ocasio-Cortez*	B
Kanigel, Robert. *Eyes on the Street*	B
Kirtzman, Andrew. *Giuliani*	B
Lane, Stewart F. *Black Broadway*	792.089
Langewiesche, William. *American Ground*	974.7
Lepore, Jill. *New York Burning*	974.7
Louvish, Simon. *Monkey Business*	B
MacColl, Gail. *To Marry an English Lord*	974.7
Manzione, Gianmarc. *Pin Action*	B
Martin, Justin. *Rebel Souls*	920
Martin, Wednesday. *Primates of Park Avenue*	974.7
Maslon, Laurence. ★*Broadway*	782.1
McBride, James. *The Color of Water*	B
McCourt, Frank. *Teacher Man*	B
McCourt, Frank. *'Tis*	B
McCourt, Malachy. *A Monk Swimming*	B
McMillan, Tracie. *The American Way of Eating*	338.4
Meyer, Robert. *Every Minute Is a Day*	362.1962
Miller, Adrienne. *In the Land of Men*	070.5
Miller, Donald L. *Supreme City*	974.7
Moby. *Porcelain*	B
Moby. *Then It Fell Apart*	B
Morris, Mark. *Out Loud*	B
Moss, Jeremiah. *Feral City*	B
Murray, Liz. *Breaking Night*	B
Oller, John. *White Shoe*	346.73
Olsen, Craig. *P.S. Burn This Letter Please*	306.76
Oshinsky, David M. *Bellevue*	362.1109747
Peiffer, Prudence. *The Slip*	709.73
Perlin, Ross. ★*Language City*	306.44
Peterson, Marlon. *Bird Uncaged*	B
Pfeifer, Joseph. *Ordinary Heroes*	973.931
Phillips-Fein, Kim. *Fear City*	330.9747
Pinckney, Darryl. *Come Back in September*	B
Purdum, Todd S. *Something Wonderful*	B
Qu, Anna. *Made in China*	B
Rakoff, Joanna Smith. *My Salinger Year*	B
Rannells, Andrew. *Too Much Is Not Enough*	792.02
Raymond, Edwin. *An Inconvenient Cop*	363.2
Riedel, Michael. *Singular Sensation*	792
Ruffin, Amber. *You'll Never Believe What Happened to Lacey*	305.896
Salaam, Yusef. *Better, Not Bitter*	B
Sanchez, Aaron. *Where I Come From*	641.5092
Sandler, Lauren. *This Is All I Got*	B
Satow, Julie. *When Women Ran Fifth Avenue*	381.141
Savage, Jodi M. *The Death of a Jaybird*	B
Shahani, Aarti Namdev. *Here We Are*	B
Sipress, David. *What's so Funny?*	B
Skelton, Marc. *Pounding the Rock*	796.323
Smilios, Maria. ★*The Black Angels*	610.73
Smith, Patti. ★*Just Kids*	B
Spiegelman, Art. *In the Shadow of No Towers*	741.5
Stahr, Celia. *Frida in America*	B
Stern, Amanda. *Little Panic*	616.8522
Stewart, Jeffrey C. ★*The New Negro*	191
Stewart, Nikita. *Troop 6000*	369
Stille, Alexander. *The Sullivanians*	307.77
Streisand, Barbra. ★*My Name Is Barbra*	B
Taibbi, Matt. *I Can't Breathe*	363.2
Torre, Joe. *The Yankee Years*	B
Tran, Ly. *House of Sticks*	B
Voloj, Julian. *Ghetto Brother*	741.5
Volpe, Joseph. *The Toughest Show on Earth*	B
Von Drehle, Dave. ★*Triangle*	974.7
Winder, Elizabeth. *Pain, Parties, Work*	B
Wright, Jennifer Ashley. ★*Madame Restell*	B

NEW YORK CITY HISTORY

Brenner, Marie. ★*The Desperate Hours*	362.1962
Cannato, Vincent. *American Passage*	325.73
Caro, Robert A. *The Power Broker*	B
Carter, David. *Stonewall*	306.76
Gage, Beverly. *The Day Wall Street Exploded*	974.7
Gill, Jonathan. *Harlem*	974.7
Goldberg, Emma. *Life on the Line*	362.1962
Goodman, Elyssa. *Glitter and Concrete*	792.7
Goodman, Matthew. *The City Game*	796.323
Hortis, C. Alexander. *The Witch of New York*	364.152
Johnson, Steven. *The Infernal Machine*	335
Khan, Yasmin Sabina. *Enlightening the World*	974.7
Kluger, Richard. *Indelible Ink*	B
Lepore, Jill. *New York Burning*	974.7
Miller, Donald L. *Supreme City*	974.7
Nasaw, David. *The Chief*	B
Reid, David. *The Brazen Age*	974.7
Satow, Julie. *The Plaza*	917.47
Von Drehle, Dave. ★*Triangle*	974.7
Wallace, Mike. *Greater Gotham*	974.7
Whyte, Kenneth. *The Uncrowned King*	B
★*The New York Times Cooking No-Recipe Recipes*. Sifton, Sam	641.5

NEW ZEALAND

Lowe, George. *Letters from Everest*	796.522
Tibble, Tayi. *Poukahangatus*	821

NEW ZEALAND LITERATURE

Lowe, George. *Letters from Everest*	796.522
McCarten, Anthony. *Darkest Hour*	941.084

NEW ZEALAND POETRY

Tibble, Tayi. *Poukahangatus*	821

NEWARK, NEW JERSEY

Hobbs, Jeff. ★*The Short and Tragic Life of Robert Peace*	B

NEWBORN BABIES

Harpham, Heather Elise. *Happiness*	B

NEWBORN BABY CARE

DiGregorio, Sarah. *Early*	618.92

NEWBY, DANGERFIELD, 1815-1859

Meyer, Eugene L. *Five for Freedom*	973.7
The Newcomers. Thorpe, Helen	373.18

Newitz, Annalee

Scatter, Adapt, and Remember	576.8
Stories Are Weapons	355.3

Newkey-Burden, Chas

Taylor Swift	B

Newkirk, Pamela

Diversity, Inc.	658.3

NEWMAN FAMILY

Neumann, Ariana. *When Time Stopped*	B

Newman, Bobbi L.

★*Fostering Wellness in the Workplace*	023

Newman, Magdalena

Normal	611

NEWMAN, MAGDALENA

Newman, Magdalena. *Normal*	611

AUTHOR, TITLE, SERIES AND SUBJECT INDEX

NEWMAN, MAX
   Price, David A. *Geniuses at War* — 940.54
NEWMAN, NATHANIEL
   Newman, Magdalena. *Normal* — 611
Newman, Paul
   The Extraordinary Life of an Ordinary Man — B
NEWMAN, PAUL, 1925-2008
   Newman, Paul. *The Extraordinary Life of an Ordinary Man* — B
Newman, Richard S.
   Freedom's Prophet — B
NEWS AGENCIES
   Trillin, Calvin. *The Lede* — 071
NEWS MEDIA
   Cullen, David. *Columbine* — 373
   Nagourney, Adam. *The Times* — 071
   Smith, Ben. *Traffic* — 070.4
   Todd, Kim. *Sensational* — 920
NEWSPAPER COMIC STRIPS
   Wood, Lawrence. *Your Caption Has Been Selected* — 741.5
NEWSPAPER EDITORS
   Baron, Martin. ★*Collision of Power* — 070.4
   Nagourney, Adam. *The Times* — 071
   Rusbridger, Alan. ★*Play It Again* — B
NEWSPAPER PUBLISHERS AND PUBLISHING
   Hartman, Darrell. *Battle of Ink and Ice* — 998
   Morris, James McGrath. *Pulitzer* — B
   Nasaw, David. *The Chief* — B
   Whyte, Kenneth. *The Uncrowned King* — B
NEWSPAPERS
   Baron, Martin. ★*Collision of Power* — 070.4
   Burns, Eric. *Infamous Scribblers* — 071
   Cullen, Art. *Storm Lake* — 071.7
   Gladstone, Brooke. *The Influencing Machine* — 741.5
   Hartman, Darrell. *Battle of Ink and Ice* — 998
   Knight, Sam. *The Premonitions Bureau* — 133.8
   Luckerson, Victor. *Built from the Fire* — 976.6
   McCraw, David Edward. *Truth in Our Times* — 342.7308
   Nagourney, Adam. *The Times* — 071
   Ostertag, Bob. *People's Movements, People's Press* — 071
   Todd, Kim. *Sensational* — 920
   Whyte, Kenneth. *The Uncrowned King* — B
Newsroom Confidential. Sullivan, Margaret — 070.92
Newton, Deborah
   Finishing School — 746.43
Newton, Michael A.
   Enemy of the State — 345.567
Newtown. Lysiak, Matthew — 371.7
The Next Millionaire Next Door. Stanley, Thomas J. — 332.024
Next of Kin. Fouts, Roger — 156
Neyer, Rob
   Power Ball — 796.357
NEZ PERCE (NIMÍIPUU) (NORTH AMERICAN PEOPLE)
   Sharfstein, Daniel J. ★*Thunder in the Mountains* — 979.5
Nez, Chester
   Code Talker — B
NEZ, CHESTER
   Nez, Chester. *Code Talker* — B
Nezhukumatathil, Aimee
   Bite by Bite — 641.3
   Oceanic — 811
   World of Wonders — 590
NEZHUKUMATATHIL, AIMEE
   Nezhukumatathil, Aimee. *Bite by Bite* — 641.3
   Nezhukumatathil, Aimee. *World of Wonders* — 590
Nfl Century. Horrigan, Joe — 796.332
Ng, Fae Myenne
   Orphan Bachelors — B
NG, FAE MYENNE, 1956-
   Ng, Fae Myenne. *Orphan Bachelors* — B
Ngugi wa Thiong'o
   In the House of the Interpreter — B
NGUGI WA THIONG'O, 1938-
   Ngugi wa Thiong'o. *In the House of the Interpreter* — B
Nguyen, Andrea Quynhgiao
   Ever-Green Vietnamese — 641.595
   The Pho Cookbook — 641.595
   ★*Vietnamese Food Any Day* — 641.595

Nguyen, Bich Minh
   Owner of a Lonely Heart — B
NGUYEN, BICH MINH
   Nguyen, Bich Minh. *Owner of a Lonely Heart* — B
Nguyen, Diana Khoi
   Ghost of — 811
Nguyen, Hieu Minh
   Not Here — 811
Nguyen, Hoa
   A Thousand Times You Lose Your Treasure — 811
Nguyen, Viet Thanh
   ★*A Man of Two Faces* — B
   Nothing Ever Dies — 959.704
NGUYEN, VIET THANH, 1971-
   Nguyen, Viet Thanh. ★*A Man of Two Faces* — B
Nhat Hanh
   The Art of Living — 294.3
   Zen and the Art of Saving the Planet — 294.3
NHAT HANH, THICH 1926-2022
   Nhat Hanh. *The Art of Living* — 294.3
NICARAGUAN PEOPLE
   Mojica Rodriguez, Prisca Dorcas. *For Brown Girls with Sharp Edges and Tender Hearts* — 305.48
Niche. Momus — B
Nicholas and Alexandra. Massie, Robert K. — B
NICHOLAS II, EMPEROR OF RUSSIA, 1868-1918
   Carter, Miranda. *George, Nicholas and Wilhelm* — 940.3
   Clay, Catrine. *King, Kaiser, Tsar* — B
   Massie, Robert K. *Nicholas and Alexandra* — B
   Massie, Robert K. *The Romanovs* — 947
   Rappaport, Helen. *The Romanov Sisters* — 920
Nicholas, Kristin
   Crafting a Patterned Home — 745.5
Nicholl, Charles
   The Reckoning — B
Nicholls, Steve
   Alien Worlds — 595.7
Nichols, Kerry
   Puppy Brain — 636.7
NICHOLS, MIKE
   Carter, Ash. *Life Isn't Everything* — B
   Harris, Mark. *Mike Nichols* — B
NICHOLS, RUTH, 1901-1960
   O'Brien, Keith. *Fly Girls* — 920
NICHOLSON, JACK, 1937-
   Huston, Anjelica. *Watch Me* — B
   Wasson, Sam. *The Big Goodbye* — 791.43
Nichtern, David
   Creativity, Spirituality & Making a Buck — 294.3
★*Nickel and Dimed*. Ehrenreich, Barbara — B
NICKS, STEVIE, 1948-
   Davis, Stephen. *Gold Dust Woman* — B
Nicky Epstein, the Essential Edgings Collection. Epstein, Nicky — 746.43
Nico, Brooke
   More Lovely Knitted Lace — 746.43
Nicolson, Adam
   How to Be — 180
   Life Between the Tides — 577.69
   The Making of Poetry — 821.709
   Sea Room — 941.1
   The Seabird's Cry — 598.177
   Why Homer Matters — 883
NICOLSON, ADAM, 1957-
   Nicolson, Adam. *Sea Room* — 941.1
Nicolson, Juliet
   The Great Silence — 941.083
★*Nicomachean Ethics*. Aristotle — 171
NICOTINE ADDICTION
   Ducharme, Jamie. *Big Vape* — 338.7
   Etter, Lauren. ★*The Devil's Playbook* — 338.7
NIDETCH, JEAN
   Meltzer, Marisa. *This Is Big* — 613.25
Nielsen, Kim E.
   A Disability History of the United States — 362.40973
Nietfeld, Emi
   Acceptance — B
NIETFELD, EMI
   Nietfeld, Emi. *Acceptance* — B

PUBLIC LIBRARY CORE COLLECTION: NONFICTION
Twentieth Edition

Nietzsche, Friedrich Wilhelm
  ★*Basic Writings of Nietzsche*   193
  ★*Thus Spoke Zarathustra*   193
  The Will to Power   193
NIETZSCHE, FRIEDRICH WILHELM, 1844-1900
  Kaag, John J. *Hiking with Nietzsche*   193
  Prideaux, Sue. *I Am Dynamite!*   B
NIGERIA
  Achebe, Chinua. *The Education of a British-Protected Child*   B
  Achebe, Chinua. *There Was a Country*   B
  Adichie, Chimamanda Ngozi. *Notes on Grief*   155.9
  Chude-Sokei, Louis Onuorah. *Floating in a Most Peculiar Way*   979.4
  Ikpi, Bassey. *I'm Telling the Truth, but I'm Lying*   814
  Okporo, Edafe. *Asylum*   B
  Onwuachi, Kwame. ★*Notes from a Young Black Chef*   641.59
NIGERIAN AMERICANS
  Chude-Sokei, Louis Onuorah. *Floating in a Most Peculiar Way*   979.4
  Jawando, Will. ★*My Seven Black Fathers*   B
  Oyeneyin, Tunde. *Speak*   158.1
NIGERIAN PEOPLE IN FOREIGN COUNTRIES
  Asher, Zain E. *Where the Children Take Us*   942.1
Nigg, Joel T.
  Getting Ahead of ADHD   618.92
NIGHT
  Ekirch, A. Roger. ★*At Day's Close*   306.4
  Eklof, Johan. *The Darkness Manifesto*   363.7
★*Night*. Wiesel, Elie   B
★*Night Flyer*. Miles, Tiya   B
Night in the American Village. Johnson, Akemi   305.40952
Night Mother. Williams, Marlena   791.43
The Night of the Gun. Carr, David   B
The Night Parade. Lin, Jami Nakamura   B
★*A Night to Remember*. Lord, Walter   910
NIGHTCLUB OWNERS
  Abrams, Dan. *Kennedy's Avenger*   973.922
NIGHTCLUBS
  Fall, Jeremy. *Falling Upwards*   158.1
  James, Scott. *Trial by Fire*   363.3709745
  Worley, Jennifer. *Neon Girls*   792.7
Nightingale. Rekdal, Paisley   811
NIGHTINGALE, FLORENCE, 1820-1910
  Bostridge, Mark. *Florence Nightingale*   B
NIGHTMARES
  Leschziner, Guy. *The Nocturnal Brain*   616.8
Niki Jabbour's Veggie Garden Remix. Jabbour, Niki   635
The Nile. Wilkinson, Toby A. H.   962
NILE RIVER
  Jeal, Tim. *Explorers of the Nile*   920
  Millard, Candice. ★*River of the Gods*   916.204
  Wilkinson, Toby A. H. *The Nile*   962
NILE VALLEY
  Wilkinson, Toby A. H. *A World Beneath the Sands*   932
NILES, BLAIR
  Zanglein, Jayne E. *The Girl Explorers*   B
Nilsson, Lennart
  A Child Is Born   612.6
NIMITZ, CHESTER W. (CHESTER WILLIAM), 1885-1966
  Borneman, Walter R. *The Admirals*   B
Nimura, Janice P.
  Daughters of the Samurai   920
  ★*The Doctors Blackwell*   610.92
The Nine. Strauss, Gwen   940.53
The Nine. Toobin, Jeffrey   347.73
★*Nine Black Robes*. Biskupic, Joan   347.73
Nine Continents. Guo, Xlaolu   B
Nine Hills to Nambonkaha. Erdman, Sarah   966.68
Nine Lives. Baum, Dan   B
Nine Lives. Dalrymple, William   294
The Nine Lives of Pakistan. Walsh, Declan   954.91
Nine Parts of Desire. Brooks, Geraldine   305.48
Nine Pints. George, Rose   612.1
NINE-YEAR-OLD BOYS
  Zamora, Javier. ★*Solito*   B
★*The Nineties*. Klosterman, Chuck   306.0973
Ninety-Nine Glimpses of Princess Margaret. Brown, Craig   B
Ninja. Man, John   355.5
NINJA
  Man, John. *Ninja*   355.5

NINJUTSU
  Man, John. *Ninja*   355.5
NINTENDO VIDEO GAMES
  Harris, Blake J. *Console Wars*   338.7
The Ninth. Sachs, Harvey   784.2
Ninth Street Women. Gabriel, Mary   920
Nir, Sarah Maslin
  Horse Crazy   B
NIR, SARAH MASLIN, 1983-
  Nir, Sarah Maslin. *Horse Crazy*   B
Nisbett, Richard E.
  Mindware   153.4
Nisei Daughter. Sone, Monica Itoi   979.7
Nistisima. Hayden, Georgina   641.5
NITZE, PAUL H.
  Thompson, Nicholas. *The Hawk and the Dove*   973.92
Niven, Jennifer
  Ada Blackjack   B
Niven, Penelope
  Thornton Wilder   B
Nixon and Kissinger. Dallek, Robert   B
The Nixon Defense. Dean, John W.   973.924092
Nixon, John
  Debriefing the President   956.7044
NIXON, JOHN (MIDDLE EAST EXPERT)
  Nixon, John. *Debriefing the President*   956.7044
NIXON, RICHARD M. (RICHARD MILHOUS), 1913-1994
  Brokaw, Tom. *The Fall of Richard Nixon*   B
  Dallek, Robert. *Nixon and Kissinger*   B
  Dean, John W. *The Nixon Defense*   973.924092
  Denevi, Timothy. *Freak Kingdom*   B
  Dobbs, Michael. *King Richard*   973.924
  Farrell, John A. ★*Richard Nixon*   B
  Feldstein, Mark Avrom. *Poisoning the Press*   973.924092
  Graff, Garrett M. *Watergate*   973.924
  Kissinger, Henry. *Leadership*   303.3
  Maddow, Rachel. *Bag Man*   B
  Mann, Jim. *The Rebellion of Ronald Reagan*   973.927092
  Matthews, Christopher. *Kennedy & Nixon*   973.922
  Morley, Jefferson. *Scorpions' Dance*   973.924
  Perlstein, Rick. *The Invisible Bridge*   973.924
  Perlstein, Rick. ★*Nixonland*   973.924
  Reston, James. *The Conviction of Richard Nixon*   973.924092
  Thomas, Evan. *Being Nixon*   B
  Weiner, Tim. *One Man Against the World*   B
  Woodward, Bob. *The Final Days*   B
  Woodward, Bob. *Shadow*   973.92
★*Nixonland*. Perlstein, Rick   973.924
No Better Friend. Weintraub, Robert   940.54
★*No Choice*. Andrews, Becca   362.1988
No Country for Eight-Spot Butterflies. Aguon, Julian   305.89
No Crueler Tyrannies. Rabinowitz, Dorothy   345.73
No Cure for Being Human. Bowler, Kate   B
No Dream Is Too High. Aldrin, Buzz   B
No Easy Day. Owen, Mark   B
★*No Exit, and Three Other Plays*. Sartre, Jean-Paul   842
No Filter. Porizkova, Paulina   B
No Friends but the Mountains. Matloff, Judith   355.009
★*No God but God*. Aslan, Reza   297
No Good Men Among the Living. Gopal, Anand   920
No Hero. Owen, Mark   B
No Higher Honor. Rice, Condoleezza   B
No House to Call My Home. Berg, Ryan   B
No Immediate Danger. Vollmann, William T.   333.79
No Impact Man. Beavan, Colin   B
No Judgment. Oyler, Lauren   814
No Longer Radical. Brem, Rachel   616.99
No Man's Land. Moore, Wendy   940.4
No More Police. Kaba, Mariame   363.2
No Nature. Snyder, Gary   811
No One at the Wheel. Schwartz, Samuel I.   629.2
No One Here Gets Out Alive. Hopkins, Jerry   B
No Ordinary Assignment. Ferguson, Jane   B
No Ordinary Dog. Chesney, Will   958.104
No Ordinary Time. Goodwin, Doris Kearns   920
No Place to Hide. Warren, W. Lee   B
No Room for Small Dreams. Peres, Shimon   B
No Rules Rules. Hastings, Reed   384.55

AUTHOR, TITLE, SERIES AND SUBJECT INDEX

No Scrap Left Behind. Nyberg, Amanda Jean — 746.46
No Surrender. Edmonds, Chris — B
★*No Time Like the Future*. Fox, Michael J. — B
★*No Time to Panic*. Gutman, Matt — 616.85
No Time to Spare. Le Guin, Ursula K. — 814
No Turning Back. Abouzeid, Rania — 956.9104
No Visible Bruises. Snyder, Rachel Louise — 362.82
No Walls and the Recurring Dream. DiFranco, Ani — 782.42164
No Way Home. Wetherall, Tyler — B

NO, KUM-SOK
   Harden, Blaine. *The Great Leader and the Fighter Pilot* — B

The No-Fuss Family Cookbook. Scott, Ryan — 641.5

Noah, Timothy
   The Great Divergence — 339.2

Noah, Trevor
   Born a Crime — B

NOAH, TREVOR, 1984-
   Noah, Trevor. *Born a Crime* — B

NOBEL PRIZE WINNERS
   Attwell, David. *J. M. Coetzee and the Life of Writing* — 823
   Bunting, Josiah. ★*The Making of a Leader* — B
   French, Patrick. *The World Is What It Is* — B
   Isaacson, Walter. ★*The Code Breaker* — 576.5
   Kandel, Eric R. *In Search of Memory* — B
   Lewis, Michael. ★*The Undoing Project* — 920
   Maathai, Wangari. *Unbowed* — B
   Mandela, Nelson. *In His Own Words* — B
   Martin, Gerald. ★*Gabriel Garcia Marquez* — B
   Morris, Edmund. ★*The Rise of Theodore Roosevelt* — B
   Morris, Edmund. ★*Theodore Rex* — 973.911
   Schwartz, David N. *The Last Man Who Knew Everything* — B

NOBEL PRIZES
   Kandel, Eric R. *In Search of Memory* — B

NOBILITY
   Borman, Tracy. *Elizabeth's Women* — B
   Borman, Tracy. *The Private Lives of the Tudors* — 920
   Bradford, Sarah. *Lucrezia Borgia* — B
   Foreman, Amanda. *Georgiana, Duchess of Devonshire* — B
   Hardman, Robert. *Queen of the World* — B
   Harman, Claire. *Murder by the Book* — 364.152
   Hawksley, Lucinda. *Queen Victoria's Mysterious Daughter* — B
   Hibbert, Christopher. *The Borgias and Their Enemies* — 920
   Lovell, Mary S. *Bess of Hardwick* — B
   MacColl, Gail. *To Marry an English Lord* — 974.7
   Massie, Robert K. *Catherine the Great* — B
   Massie, Robert K. *Nicholas and Alexandra* — B
   Meyer, G. J. *The Borgias* — 920
   Morton, Andrew. *Wallis in Love* — B
   Snyder, Timothy. *The Red Prince* — B
   Strathern, Paul. *The Borgias* — 945.06
   Tallis, Nicola. *Uncrowned Queen* — B
   Weir, Alison. *The Lost Tudor Princess* — B

Nobody Turn Me Around. Euchner, Charles C. — 975.3
★*Nobody Will Tell You This but Me*. Kalb, Bess — 306.874
Nobody's Normal. Grinker, Roy Richard — 616.89
Nobody's Son. Slouka, Mark — B
Nobody's Victim. Goldberg, Carrie — 345.73

Nocera, Joseph
   The Big Fail — 362.1962
   Indentured — 796.04

Nockels, Christy
   The Life You Long For — 248.8

NOCTURNAL ANIMALS
   Ackerman, Jennifer. ★*What an Owl Knows* — 598.9

The Nocturnal Brain. Leschziner, Guy — 616.8

NOGUCHI, ISAMU, 1904-1988
   Herrera, Hayden. *Listening to Stone* — B

NOISE
   Kingdon, Amorina. ★*Sing Like Fish* — 591.77
   Zorn, Justin. *Golden* — 128

The Nolan Variations. Shone, Tom — 791.4302

Nolan, Ali
   Master the Marathon — 796.42

Nolan, Cathal J.
   The Allure of Battle — 355.409

NOLAN, CHRISTOPHER, 1970-
   Shone, Tom. *The Nolan Variations* — 791.4302

Nolan, Hamilton
   The Hammer — 331.8

Noldeke, Marisa
   50 Knitted Wraps and Shawls — 746.43

Nolen, Jeremy
   New German Cooking — 641.594

Nolte, Nick
   Rebel — B

NOLTE, NICK
   Nolte, Nick. *Rebel* — B

The Noma Guide to Fermentation. Redzepi, Rene — 664
Nomad Century. Vince, Gaia — 362.87
★*Nomadland*. Bruder, Jessica — 331.3

NOMADS
   Juan, Li. *Winter Pasture* — 951.06
   Mackintosh-Smith, Tim. *Arabs* — 909.04

NON-INDUSTRIAL SOCIETIES
   King, Charles. ★*Gods of the Upper Air* — 920
   Zuckoff, Mitchell. *Lost in Shangri-La* — 940.54

NONAGENARIANS
   Frank, Michael. ★*One Hundred Saturdays* — B

NONALCOHOLIC DRINKS
   Ramirez, Elva. *Zero Proof* — 641.87

NONBINARY PEOPLE
   Bongiovanni, Archie. *A Quick & Easy Guide to They/Them Pronouns* — 741.5
   Davis, Lisa Selin. *Tomboy* — 305.409
   Kobabe, Maia. *Gender Queer* — 741.5
   Soloway, Jill. *She Wants It* — B
   Tobia, Jacob. *Sissy* — 305.30973
   Whitney, Emerson. *Heaven* — B

NONCONFORMISTS
   Fuller, Alexandra. *Travel Light, Move Fast* — B
   Gabriel, Mary. *Ninth Street Women* — 920
   Gopnik, Blake. ★*Warhol* — B
   Lockwood, Patricia. *Priestdaddy* — B
   Waters, John. *Mr. Know-It-All* — 814

NONCONFORMITY
   Shaw, Julia. *Bi* — 306.76

None of My Business. O'Rourke, P. J. — 332

NONFICTION THAT READS LIKE FICTION
   Ackmann, Martha. ★*These Fevered Days* — B
   Addison, Corban. *Wastelands* — 346.73
   Anderson, Scott. *Lawrence in Arabia* — B
   Au-Yeung, Angel. *Wonder Boy* — B
   Barbarisi, Daniel. *Chasing the Thrill* — 796.1
   Berendt, John. *Midnight in the Garden of Good and Evil* — 975.8
   Blum, Howard. *The Spy Who Knew Too Much* — 327.12
   Boo, Katherine. ★*Behind the Beautiful Forevers* — 305.5
   Brewer, John. *The American Leonardo* — 759.5
   Brotherton, Marcus. *A Bright and Blinding Sun* — 940.54
   Brown, Daniel James. ★*The Boys in the Boat* — 797.12
   Bryson, Bill. *In a Sunburned Country* — 919
   Bryson, Bill. *The Life and Times of the Thunderbolt Kid* — B
   Bryson, Bill. ★*A Walk in the Woods* — 917
   Bugliosi, Vincent. ★*Helter Skelter* — 364.1
   Capote, Truman. ★*In Cold Blood* — 364.1
   Carreyrou, John. ★*Bad Blood* — 338.7
   Chang, Emily. *Brotopia* — 331.4
   Coker, Margaret. *The Spymaster of Baghdad* — 956.7044
   Croke, Ken. *Riding with Evil* — 364.106
   Cumming, Laura. ★*The Vanishing Velazquez* — 759.6
   Dawson, Kate Winkler. ★*American Sherlock* — B
   De Leon, Jason. ★*Soldiers and Kings* — 364.1
   Demick, Barbara. ★*Nothing to Envy* — 920
   Drabkin, Ronald. *Beverly Hills Spy* — 940.54
   Drury, Bob. *Lucky 666* — B
   Ehrenreich, Barbara. ★*Nickel and Dimed* — B
   Ellsworth, Scott. *The World Beneath Their Feet* — 796.522
   Evangelista, Patricia. ★*Some People Need Killing* — 364.4
   Finkel, David. *An American Dreamer* — 975.8
   Finkel, Michael. *The Art Thief* — 364.1628
   Finkel, Michael. *The Stranger in the Woods* — B
   Follett, Ken. *On Wings of Eagles* — 955
   Fox, Amaryllis. *Life Undercover* — B
   Fox, Margalit. *The Confidence Men* — 940.4
   Freeman, Sally Mott. *The Jersey Brothers* — 920
   Funder, Anna. *Wifedom* — B
   Gagne, Patric. *Sociopath* — B

PUBLIC LIBRARY CORE COLLECTION: NONFICTION
Twentieth Edition

Gilbert, Elizabeth. *Eat, Pray, Love*	B
Graff, Garrett M. *Watergate*	973.924
Grann, David. ★*Killers of the Flower Moon*	976.6004
Grann, David. *The Lost City of Z*	918.1
Grant, Richard. *The Deepest South of All*	976.2
Greenberg, Andy. *Tracers in the Dark*	364.16
Groom, Winston. *The Generals*	920
Guinn, Jeff. ★*War on the Border*	972.08
Guo, XIaolu. *Nine Continents*	B
Gwynne, S. C. *Empire of the Summer Moon*	B
Halberstam, David. *The Teammates*	B
Harris, Mark. *Mike Nichols*	B
Hartman, Darrell. *Battle of Ink and Ice*	998
Hastings, Max. *Operation Pedestal*	940.54
Hersh, Seymour M. *Reporter*	B
Hill, David. *The Vapors*	976.7
Hillenbrand, Laura. ★*Seabiscuit*	798.4
Hillenbrand, Laura. ★*Unbroken*	B
Hoffman, David E. *Give Me Liberty*	B
Hughes, Evan. *The Hard Sell*	338.4
Hutton, Paul Andrew. *The Apache Wars*	979
Hvistendahl, Mara. ★*The Scientist and the Spy*	364.16
Jang, Jin-Sung. *Dear Leader*	B
Johnson, Steven. *The Infernal Machine*	335
Junger, Sebastian. *The Perfect Storm*	974.4
Kaiser, Menachem. *Plunder*	940.53
Katz, Catherine Grace. *The Daughters of Yalta*	920
Keith, Philip A. *All Blood Runs Red*	B
Kinzer, Stephen. ★*All the Shah's Men*	955.05
Kix, Paul. ★*You Have to Be Prepared to Die Before You Can Begin to Live*	976.1
Kizzia, Tom. *Pilgrim's Wilderness*	B
Kleiman, Kathy. *Proving Ground*	4.092
Kolata, Gina Bari. *Mercies in Disguise*	616
Krakauer, Jon. *Into the Wild*	917.9804
Krakauer, Jon. *Into Thin Air*	796.52
Larson, Erik. ★*Dead Wake*	940.4
Larson, Erik. ★*The Devil in the White City*	364.15
Larson, Erik. *In the Garden of Beasts*	B
Larson, Erik. ★*The Splendid and the Vile*	940.54
Lemmon, Gayle Tzemach. *The Dressmaker of Khair Khana*	B
Lichtblau, Eric. *Return to the Reich*	B
Loftis, Larry. *Code Name*	B
Lord, Walter. ★*A Night to Remember*	910
Macintyre, Ben. *Agent Zigzag*	B
Macintyre, Ben. ★*The Spy and the Traitor*	B
Macy, Beth. ★*Factory Man*	338.7
Mann, William J. *Hello, Gorgeous*	B
Manseau, Peter. *The Apparitionists*	B
Marzano-Lesnevich, Alexandria. *The Fact of a Body*	364.152
Massie, Robert K. *Catherine the Great*	B
Mayle, Peter. ★*A Year in Provence*	944
McCourt, Frank. ★*Angela's Ashes*	929
McCullough, David G. ★*John Adams*	B
McNamara, Michelle. *I'll Be Gone in the Dark*	364.152
Mezrich, Ben. *Breaking Twitter*	338.7
Millard, Candice. *Destiny of the Republic*	973.8
Millard, Candice. *River of Doubt*	918.1
Mitchell, Jerry. ★*Race Against Time*	364.152
Moore, Peter. *Life, Liberty, and the Pursuit of Happiness*	199
Moore, Wayetu. *The Dragons, the Giant, the Women*	B
Myron, Vicki. ★*Dewey*	636.80092
Nimura, Janice P. ★*The Doctors Blackwell*	610.92
Parkin, Simon. *A Game of Birds and Wolves*	940.54
Penn, Thomas. *The Brothers York*	942.04
Petrushevskaia, Liudmila. *The Girl from the Metropol Hotel*	B
Plokhy, Serhii. ★*Nuclear Folly*	972.9106
Posner, Gerald L. *God's Bankers*	364.16
Preston, Richard. *The Hot Zone*	614.5
Preston, Richard. *The Wild Trees*	585
Price, David A. *Geniuses at War*	940.54
Raines, Ben. *The Last Slave Ship*	306.362
Rakoff, Joanna Smith. *My Salinger Year*	B
Reiss, Tom. *The Black Count*	B
Richardson, Edmund. *The King's Shadow*	958.1
Riedel, Michael. *Razzle Dazzle*	792.09
Risen, James. ★*The Last Honest Man*	973.92
Roach, Mary. ★*Stiff*	611
Roberts, Jason. *A Sense of the World*	B
Roker, Al. *Ruthless Tide*	974.8
Rosnay, Tatiana de. *Manderley Forever*	B
Rynecki, Elizabeth. *Chasing Portraits*	B
Sancton, Julian. *Madhouse at the End of the Earth*	919.8904
Schindler, Meriel. *The Lost Cafe Schindler*	943.64
Seiple, Samantha. *Louisa on the Front Lines*	B
Sevigny, Melissa L. ★*Brave the Wild River*	580.9
Shane, Scott. ★*Flee North*	973.7
Skloot, Rebecca. ★*The Immortal Life of Henrietta Lacks*	B
Smilios, Maria. ★*The Black Angels*	610.73
Smith, Jeremy N. *Breaking and Entering*	B
Spitz, Bob. ★*Reagan*	B
Standiford, Les. ★*Battle for the Big Top*	791.3
Taylor, Goldie. *The Love You Save*	B
Ujifusa, Steven. *Barons of the Sea*	387.5
Vanderbes, Jennifer. ★*Wonder Drug*	615
Viren, Sarah. *To Name the Bigger Lie*	B
Von Furstenberg, Diane. *The Woman I Wanted to Be*	B
Von Tunzelmann, Alex. *Blood and Sand*	909.82
Walls, Jeannette. ★*The Glass Castle*	B
Ward, Geoffrey C. *A Disposition to Be Rich*	B
Warrick, Joby. *Red Line*	956.9104
Wasson, Sam. *Fifth Avenue, 5 A.M.*	791.43
Weir, Alison. *The Six Wives of Henry VIII*	942.05
Westover, Tara. ★*Educated*	B
Wiedeman, Reeves. *Billion Dollar Loser*	333.33
Wilkerson, Isabel. ★*The Warmth of Other Suns*	304.80973
Willner, Nina. *Forty Autumns*	B
Winchester, Simon. *The Professor and the Madman*	423
Winter, Molly Roden. *More*	B
Wolfe, Tom. ★*The Right Stuff*	629.4
Woo, Ilyon. ★*Master Slave Husband Wife*	920
Yeebo, Yepoka. *Anansi's Gold*	364.16
Zuckerman, Gregory. *The Frackers*	B

NONFICTION WRITING

Booth, Wayne C. *The Craft of Research*	001.4
Kidder, Tracy. *Good Prose*	808.02

NONPRESCRIPTION DRUGS

Wright, Jennifer Ashley. ★*Madame Restell*	B

NONPROFIT ORGANIZATIONS

Adler, Kevin F. *When We Walk By*	362.5
Burak, Asi. *Power Play*	794.8
Harrison, Scott. *Thirst*	B
Smith, G. Stevenson. *Cost Control for Nonprofits in Crisis*	025.1
Webb, Kinari. *Guardians of the Trees*	B

NONTRADITIONAL FAMILIES

Lepore, Jill. ★*The Secret History of Wonder Woman*	741.5

NONVERBAL COMMUNICATION

Nowicki, Stephen. *Raising a Socially Successful Child*	649

NONVIOLENCE

Arsenault, Raymond. *John Lewis*	
Branch, Taylor. ★*At Canaan's Edge*	323.1196
Gandhi. ★*Gandhi on Non-Violence*	179.7
Halberstam, David. ★*The Children*	323.1
King, Martin Luther. *Why We Can't Wait*	305.8
Lewis, John. ★*March; Book One*	741.5
Lewis, John. ★*March; Book Three*	741.5
Lewis, John. ★*March; Book Two*	741.5
Voloj, Julian. *Ghetto Brother*	741.5

★*Noodles, Rice, and Everything Spice*. Witte, Christina De 641.595
Noon. Peters, Meike 641.5
Noor
  Leap of Faith B
NOOR, QUEEN, CONSORT OF HUSSEIN, KING OF JORDAN, 1951-
  Noor. *Leap of Faith* B
Nooyi, Indra
  ★*My Life in Full* B
NOOYI, INDRA, 1955-
  Nooyi, Indra. ★*My Life in Full* B
Norah Gaughan's Knitted Cable Sourcebook. Gaughan, Norah 746.43
Nordberg, Jenny
  The Underground Girls of Kabul 305.3
Nordgren, Tyler E.
  Sun, Moon, Earth 523.7
Nordhaus, Hannah
  The Beekeeper's Lament 638

AUTHOR, TITLE, SERIES AND SUBJECT INDEX

Nordland, Rod
   Waiting for the Monsoon — B
NORDLAND, ROD
   Nordland, Rod. *Waiting for the Monsoon* — B
Norgren, Jill
   Belva Lockwood — B
Normal. Newman, Magdalena — 611
Normal Family. Bilton, Chrysta — B
Normal Sucks. Mooney, Jonathan — B
NORMALITY (PSYCHOLOGY)
   Mooney, Jonathan. *Normal Sucks* — B
The Norman Conquest. Morris, Marc — 942.02
NORMAN PERIOD (1066-1154)
   Asbridge, Thomas S. *The Greatest Knight* — 942.03
   Gies, Frances. *Life in a Medieval Village* — 306
   Lacey, Robert. *Great Tales from English History 2* — 941
   Morris, Marc. *The Norman Conquest* — 942.02
   Weir, Alison. *Queens of the Conquest* — 920
Norman, Abby
   Ask Me About My Uterus — 618.1
NORMAN, ABBY
   Norman, Abby. *Ask Me About My Uterus* — 618.1
Norman, Elizabeth M.
   We Band of Angels — 940.54
Norman, Jesse
   Adam Smith — B
Norman, Michael
   Haunted America — 133.1
   Tears in the Darkness — 940.54
Norman, Philip
   George Harrison — B
   John Lennon — B
   ★*Wild Thing* — B
NORMANDY
   Ambrose, Stephen E. *D-Day, June 6, 1944* — 940.54
   Beevor, Antony. *D-Day* — 940.54
   Caddick-Adams, Peter. *Sand and Steel* — 940.54
   Graff, Garrett M. ★*When the Sea Came Alive* — 940.54
   Hastings, Max. *Overlord* — 940.54
   Hervieux, Linda. *Forgotten* — 940.54
   Holland, James. *Normandy '44* — 940.54
   Lambert, Raymond. *Every Man a Hero* — B
   Macintyre, Ben. *Double Cross* — 940.54
   Paradis, Michel. *The Light of Battle* — 940.54
Normandy '44. Holland, James
NORMANDY INVASION, JUNE 6, 1944
   Ambrose, Stephen E. ★*Band of Brothers* — 920
   Ambrose, Stephen E. *D-Day, June 6, 1944* — 940.54
   Atkinson, Rick. *The Guns at Last Light* — 940.54
   Beevor, Antony. *D-Day* — 940.54
   Caddick-Adams, Peter. *Sand and Steel* — 940.54
   Graff, Garrett M. ★*When the Sea Came Alive* — 940.54
   Hastings, Max. *Overlord* — 940.54
   Hervieux, Linda. *Forgotten* — 940.54
   Holland, James. *Big Week* — 940.54
   Holland, James. *Brothers in Arms* — 940.54
   Holland, James. *Normandy '44* — 940.54
   Kershaw, Alex. *The First Wave* — 940.54
   Lambert, Raymond. *Every Man a Hero* — B
   Lance, Rachel. *Chamber Divers* — 940.54
   Milton, Giles. *Soldier, Sailor, Frogman, Spy, Airman, Gangster, Kill or Die* — 940.54
   Paradis, Michel. *The Light of Battle* — 940.54
   Sullivan, James. *Unsinkable* — 940.54
NORMANS
   Morris, Marc. *The Norman Conquest* — 942.02
Norrell, Robert J.
   Up from History — B
Norris, Kathleen
   Acedia & Me — 248.8
   The Cloister Walk — 255
NORRIS, KATHLEEN, 1947-
   Norris, Kathleen. *Acedia & Me* — 248.8
   Norris, Kathleen. *The Cloister Walk* — 255
Norris, Mary
   Between You and Me — 428.2
NORRIS, MARY (EDITOR)
   Norris, Mary. *Between You and Me* — 428.2

Norris, Michele
   ★*Our Hidden Conversations* — 305
Norris, Robert S.
   Racing for the Bomb — B
The Norse Myths. Larrington, Carolyne — 293
NORTH AMERICA
   Alvarez, Noe. *Spirit Run* — 796.42
   Anderson, Fred. *The Dominion of War* — 973
   Berlo, Janet Catherine. ★*Native North American Art* — 704.03
   Black, Riley. *The Last Days of the Dinosaurs* — 576.8
   Bohl, Loree. *Fearless Gardening* — 712
   Borsato, Diane. *Mushrooming* — 579.6
   Brock, James P. *Kaufman Field Guide to Butterflies of North America* — 595.7
   Brockman, Christian Frank. *Trees of North America* — 582.16097
   Bull, John L. ★*The National Audubon Society Field Guide to North American Birds* — 598.097
   Burton, Robert. *Audubon North American Birdfeeder Guide* — 598
   Carballo, David M. *America* — 912
   Childs, Craig. *Atlas of a Lost World* — 551.7
   DuVal, Kathleen. ★*Native Nations* — 970.004
   Flores, Dan L. *Wild New World* — 591.9709
   Floyd, Ted. *Smithsonian Field Guide to the Birds of North America* — 598.097
   Goldfarb, Ben. *Eager* — 333.95
   Horwitz, Tony. ★*A Voyage Long and Strange* — 970.01
   Keffer, Ken. *Earth Almanac* — 508
   Kiser, Joy M. *America's Other Audubon* — B
   Lepore, Jill. *The Name of War* — 973.2
   Luger, Chelsey. ★*The Seven Circles* — 610
   McKnight, Kent H. *A Field Guide to Mushrooms, North America* — 579.6
   Milne, Lorus Johnson. ★*The Audubon Society Field Guide to North American Insects and Spiders* — 595.7097
   Momaday, N. Scott. *Earth Keeper* — 814
   Murie, Olaus J. ★*A Field Guide to Animal Tracks* — 599
   Peterson, Roger Tory. *Peterson Field Guide to Birds of Eastern and Central North America* — 598.097
   Raff, Jennifer. *Origin* — 576.5
   Rehder, Harald Alfred. *The Audubon Society Field Guide to North American Seashells* — 594
   Shunk, Stephen A. *Peterson Reference Guide to Woodpeckers of North America* — 598.7
   Sibley, David. *Sibley Birds East* — 598.097
   Sibley, David. *The Sibley Guide to Birds* — 598.097
   Sides, Hampton. ★*The Wide Wide Sea* — 910.92
   Stokes, Donald W. *The New Stokes Field Guide to Birds* — 598
   Utley, Robert M. *Sitting Bull* — B
   Whitaker, John O. ★*National Audubon Society Field Guide to North American Mammals* — 599.097
NORTH AMERICAN HISTORY
   Brandt, Anthony. *The Man Who Ate His Boots* — 910.91
   De Leon, Jason. ★*Soldiers and Kings* — 364.1
   Dodds Pennock, Caroline. ★*On Savage Shores* — 970.004
   Ellis, Joseph J. *The Cause* — 973.3
   Guinn, Jeff. ★*War on the Border* — 972.08
   Hernandez, Kelly Lytle. ★*Bad Mexicans* — 972
   Kluger, Richard. *Indelible Ink* — B
   Taylor, Alan. *American Civil Wars* — 973.7
NORTH AMERICAN PEOPLE
   Ahdoot, Dan. *Undercooked* — 647.95
   Alexander, Kwame. *Why Fathers Cry at Night* — B
   Babb, Valerie Melissa. *The Book of James* — B
   Baier, Bret. *To Rescue the Constitution* — 973.4
   Bell, Darrin. ★*The Talk* — 741.5
   Black Thought. *The Upcycled Self* — B
   Blair, Gabrielle Stanley. ★*Ejaculate Responsibly* — 362.1988
   Bradbury, Ray. ★*Remembrance* — 813
   Braitman, Laurel. *What Looks Like Bravery* — B
   Bunting, Josiah. ★*The Making of a Leader* — B
   Butcher, Barbara. *What the Dead Know* — 614
   Cecchi-Azzolina, Michael. *Your Table Is Ready* — 647.95
   Cheney, Liz. *Oath and Honor* — 328.73
   Chin, Curtis. *Everything I Learned, I Learned in a Chinese Restaurant* — B
   Chrisinger, David. *The Soldier's Truth* — 940.54
   Chung, Nicole. ★*A Living Remedy* — B
   Cohen, Jared. *Life After Power* — 973.09
   Conyers, Jonathan. *I Wasn't Supposed to Be Here* — B
   Cooper, Christian. *Better Living Through Birding* — B
   Crosley, Sloane. *Grief Is for People* — B
   Daley, Mark. *Safe* — B

PUBLIC LIBRARY CORE COLLECTION: NONFICTION
Twentieth Edition

Daugherty, Tracy. *Larry McMurtry*	B
Duggar, Jill. *Counting the Cost*	B
Dunn, Harry. *Standing My Ground*	B
Etheridge, Melissa. *Talking to My Angels*	B
Eyman, Scott. *Charlie Chaplin vs. America*	B
Fall, Jeremy. *Falling Upwards*	158.1
Finkel, David. *An American Dreamer*	975.8
Flannery, Kate. *Strip Tees*	338.4
Fleshman, Lauren. ★*Good for a Girl*	B
Foer, Franklin. ★*The Last Politician*	973.934
Ford, Tanisha C. *Our Secret Society*	B
Fox, Julia. *Down the Drain*	B
Fumudoh, Ziwe. *Black Friend*	814
Gabriel, Mary. *Madonna*	B
Gage, Beverly. *G-Man*	B
Gaines, Joanna. *The Stories We Tell*	B
Garner, Dwight. *The Upstairs Delicatessen*	B
Gonell, Aquilino. *American Shield*	B
Greenidge, Kerri. ★*The Grimkes*	973.5
Grush, Loren. ★*The Six*	629.4
Gulman, Gary. *Misfit*	B
Gupta, Prachi. ★*They Called Us Exceptional*	B
Gutzman, Kevin R. C. *The Jeffersonians*	973.5
Hallman, J. C. *Say Anarcha*	618.1
Hamilton, Lisa M. *The Hungry Season*	B
Hansberry, Lorraine. ★*A Raisin in the Sun*	812
Harry. ★*Spare*	B
Harss, Marina. *The Boy from Kyiv*	B
Henderson, Rob Kim. *Troubled*	B
Hermes, Will. *Lou Reed*	B
Heti, Sheila. *Alphabetical Diaries*	818
Hobbs, Jeff. *Children of the State*	364.36
Hoja, Gulchehra. *A Stone Is Most Precious Where It Belongs*	B
Holley, Santi Elijah. *An Amerikan Family*	920
Horton, Michelle. *Dear Sister*	B
Isaacson, Walter. ★*Elon Musk*	B
Jacobs, Sally H. *Althea*	B
Jun, Tasha. ★*Tell Me the Dream Again*	248
Kemper, Steve. *Our Man in Tokyo*	952.03
Kissinger, Meg. *While You Were Out*	362.2
Lewis, Robin Coste. *To the Realization of Perfect Helplessness*	811
Li, Fei-Fei. *The Worlds I See*	B
Mann, William J. *Bogie & Bacall*	920
Marshall, Greg. *Leg*	B
Masters, Oksana. *The Hard Parts*	B
Mattlin, Ben. *Disability Pride*	323.3
Max, D. T. *Finale*	782.1
McCormick, Mack. *Biography of a Phantom*	782.421643
McDonald, Greg (Producer). *Elvis and the Colonel*	920
McNeur, Catherine. *Mischievous Creatures*	920
Means, Brittany. *Hell If We Don't Change Our Ways*	B
Miles, Tiya. ★*Wild Girls*	304.2
Monroe, Jana. *Hearts of Darkness*	363.25
Moore, Beth. *All My Knotted-Up Life*	B
Moore, Thurston. *Sonic Life*	B
Morgenson, Gretchen. ★*These Are the Plunderers*	332.6
Myers, Leah. *Thinning Blood*	B
Neiman, Garrett. *Rich White Men*	305.5
Ng, Fae Myenne. *Orphan Bachelors*	B
Nguyen, Bich Minh. *Owner of a Lonely Heart*	B
Nguyen, Viet Thanh. ★*A Man of Two Faces*	B
Norris, Michele. ★*Our Hidden Conversations*	305
Obama, Michelle. ★*The Light We Carry*	B
Page, Elliot. *Pageboy*	B
Pepin, Jacques. *Art of the Chicken*	641.665
Pittard, Hannah. *We Are Too Many*	B
Popkin, Jim. *Code Name Blue Wren*	327.12
Quinones, John. ★*One Year in Uvalde*	371.7
Raban, Jonathan. *Father and Son*	B
Regan, Iliana. *Fieldwork*	B
Renkl, Margaret. *The Comfort of Crows*	814.6
Risen, James. ★*The Last Honest Man*	973.92
Roy, Jessica. *American Girls*	305.48
Royster, Francesca T. *Choosing Family*	B
Ruffin, Amber. ★*The World Record Book of Racist Stories*	305.896
Schneider, Amy. *In the Form of a Question*	B
Shane, Scott. ★*Flee North*	973.7
Shapiro, Ari. ★*The Best Strangers in the World*	B
Simmons, Ruth. ★*Up Home*	B
Singer, Matt. *Opposable Thumbs*	791.43
Sisson, Gretchen E. ★*Relinquished*	362.734
Smith, Freda Love. *I Quit Everything*	B
Smith, Jada Pinkett. *Worthy*	B
Smith, Richard Norton. *An Ordinary Man*	B
Sokolik, Vicki. ★*If You See Them*	362.5
Sole-Smith, Virginia. ★*Fat Talk*	649.1
Spears, Britney. *The Woman in Me*	B
Stamos, John. *If You Would Have Told Me*	B
Stone, Sly. *Thank You (Falettinme Be Mice Elf Agin)*	B
Streisand, Barbra. ★*My Name Is Barbra*	B
Sun, Carrie. *Private Equity*	B
Taraborrelli, J. Randy. ★*Jackie*	B
Tate, Christie. *B.F.F.*	B
Toobin, Jeffrey. ★*Homegrown*	363.325
Velour, Sasha. ★*The Big Reveal*	792.7
Wagamese, Richard. *For Joshua*	B
Ward, Jon. *Testimony*	277.308
Washington, Kerry. *Thicker Than Water*	B
Watts, Reggie. *Great Falls, MT*	B
Weigel, Alicia Roth. *Inverse Cowgirl*	B
White, Ralph. *Getting Out of Saigon*	959.704
White, Ronald C. *On Great Fields*	B
Williams, Billy Dee. ★*What Have We Here*	B
Williams, Marlena. *Night Mother*	791.43
Wilson, A'ja. ★*Dear Black Girls*	158.1
Winkler, Henry. ★*Being Henry*	B
Zwick, Edward. ★*Hits, Flops, and Other Illusions*	B

NORTH ATLANTIC OCEAN

Butler, Daniel Allen. *"Unsinkable"*	910
Fairbanks, Amanda M. *The Lost Boys of Montauk*	910.91
Henry, John. *Great White Fleet*	387.243
Junger, Sebastian. *The Perfect Storm*	974.4
Kurlansky, Mark. *Cod*	333.95
Larson, Erik. ★*Dead Wake*	940.4
Lord, Walter. ★*A Night to Remember*	910

NORTH ATLANTIC REGION

Henry, John. *Great White Fleet*	387.243

NORTH CAROLINA

Addison, Corban. *Wastelands*	346.73
Blight, David W. *A Slave No More*	B
Chansky, Art. *Blue Blood II*	796.323
Delany, Sarah Louise. *Having Our Say*	B
Emberton, Carole. *To Walk About in Freedom*	306.3
Howard, Vivian. *Deep Run Roots*	641.5975
Jacobs, Harriet. ★*Incidents in the Life of a Slave Girl*	B
Kiernan, Denise. *The Last Castle*	975.6
Lawler, Andrew. *The Secret Token*	975.6
McGinniss, Joe. *Fatal Vision*	B
Nathans, Sydney. *To Free a Family*	B
Rosen, Richard A. *Julius Chambers*	B
Zerwick, Phoebe. *Beyond Innocence*	347
Zucchino, David. *Wilmington's Lie*	305.8009756

NORTH DAKOTA

Briody, Blaire. *The New Wild West*	338.2
Murdoch, Sierra Crane. ★*Yellow Bird*	364.152
Raban, Jonathan. *Bad Land*	978
Rao, Maya. *Great American Outpost*	338.2

NORTH KOREA

Delisle, Guy. *Pyongyang*	741.5
Demick, Barbara. ★*Nothing to Envy*	920
Fifield, Anna. *The Great Successor*	B
Fischer, Paul. *A Kim Jong-Il Production*	791.43
Harden, Blaine. *The Great Leader and the Fighter Pilot*	B
Ishikawa, Masaji. ★*A River in Darkness*	B
Jang, Jin-Sung. *Dear Leader*	B
Jang, Lucia. *Stars Between the Sun and Moon*	365.45092
Jeppesen, Travis. *See You Again in Pyongyang*	951.93
Kim, Suki. *Without You, There Is No Us*	B
Lankov, A. N. *The Real North Korea*	951.9304
Lee, Helie. *In the Absence of Sun*	B
Lee, Sung-Yoon. *The Sister*	951.93
Oberdorfer, Don. *The Two Koreas 3rd Ed.*	951.904
Pak, Jung H. *Becoming Kim Jong Un*	B
Palin, Michael. *North Korea Journal*	951.9305
Tudor, Daniel. *North Korea Confidential*	951.93
North *Korea Confidential*. Tudor, Daniel	951.93

AUTHOR, TITLE, SERIES AND SUBJECT INDEX

North Korea Journal. Palin, Michael — 951.9305
NORTH PACIFIC OCEAN
   Steelquist, Robert. *The Northwest Coastal Explorer* — 508
NORTH POLE
   Hartman, Darrell. *Battle of Ink and Ice* — 998
   Welky, David. ★*A Wretched and Precarious Situation* — 910.911
NORTH POLE EXPEDITIONS
   Hartman, Darrell. *Battle of Ink and Ice* — 998
NORTH SEA
   Massie, Robert K. *Castles of Steel* — 940.4
North to Paradise. Umar, Ousman — B
NORTH-SOUTH ECONOMIC RELATIONS
   Mishra, Pankaj. *Age of Anger* — 909.8
NORTH-SOUTH RELATIONS
   Mishra, Pankaj. *Age of Anger* — 909.8
NORTHEASTERN STATES
   Junger, Sebastian. *The Perfect Storm* — 974.4
NORTHERN BOUNDARY OF THE UNITED STATES
   Taylor, Alan. *The Civil War of 1812* — 973.5
NORTHERN CALIFORNIA
   Preston, Richard. *The Wild Trees* — 585
NORTHERN EUROPE
   Larrington, Carolyne. *The Norse Myths* — 293
NORTHERN IRELAND
   Carroll, Rory. *There Will Be Fire* — 363.325
   Keefe, Patrick Radden. ★*Say Nothing* — 364.152
   McAnulty, Dara. *Diary of a Young Naturalist* — 508.092
   O'Toole, Fintan. ★*We Don't Know Ourselves* — 941.7
NORTHMEN AND NORTHWOMEN
   Herman, Arthur. *The Viking Heart* — 948
   Price, Neil S. ★*Children of Ash and Elm* — 948
   Winroth, Anders. *The Age of the Vikings* — 948
Northrup, Christiane
   Dodging Energy Vampires — 155.2
Northup, Solomon
   Twelve Years a Slave — B
NORTHUP, SOLOMON, 1808-1863?
   Northup, Solomon. *Twelve Years a Slave* — B
The **Northwest** *Coastal Explorer*. Steelquist, Robert — 508
NORTHWEST PASSAGE
   Watson, Paul. *Ice Ghosts* — 917
Norton, Hughes
   ★*Rainmaker* — 796.352
NORTON, HUGHES
   Norton, Hughes. ★*Rainmaker* — 796.352
Norton, Jack
   The Jail Is Everywhere — 365
Norton, Laurah
   Lay Them to Rest — 363.25
NORTON, LAURAH
   Norton, Laurah. *Lay Them to Rest* — 363.25
Norton, Mary Beth
   1774 — 973.3
Norton, Michael
   ★*The Ritual Effect* — 650.1
NORWAY
   Bascomb, Neal. *The Winter Fortress* — 940.54
   Booth, Michael. *The Almost Nearly Perfect People* — 948.071
   Dolnick, Edward. *The Rescue Artist* — 364.16
   Grue, Jan. *I Live a Life Like Yours* — B
   Seierstad, Asne. *Two Sisters* — 956.9104
   Strøksnes, Morten Andreas. *Shark Drunk* — 338.3
Norwich. Crouse, Karen — 796
Norwich, John Julius
   Byzantium — 949.5
   Byzantium — 949.5
   Byzantium — 949.5
   A History of France — 944
   A History of Venice — 945
   Shakespeare's Kings — 822.33
   A Short History of Byzantium — 949.5
   Sicily — 945.8
Norwich, Kenneth P.
   The Legal Guide for Writers, Artists and Other Creative People — 346.04
★*Nose* Dive. McGee, Harold — 612.8
Nosh. Siva, Micah — 641.5
Nosrat, Samin
   ★*Salt, Fat, Acid, Heat* — 641.5

NOSTALGIA
   Brown, David S. *Paradise Lost* — 813
   Favro, Terri. *Generation Robot* — 006.3
   Macdonald, Helen. ★*Vesper Flights* — 508
   Villarreal, Vanessa Anglica. *Magical/Realism* — 814
   Wiking, Meik. *The Art of Making Memories* — 153.1
Not Here. Nguyen, Hieu Minh — 811
Not Pretty Enough. Hirshey, Gerri — B
Not so Big Solutions for Your Home. Susanka, Sarah — 728
Not The End of the World. Ritchie, Hannah — 338.9
Not to Be Missed. Turan, Kenneth — 791.43
★*Not Your China Doll*. Salisbury, Katie Gee — B
Notable Native People. Keene, Adrienne — 920
Notaro, Laurie
   Excuse Me While I Disappear — B
NOTARO, LAURIE
   Notaro, Laurie. *Excuse Me While I Disappear* — B
NOTEBOOKS
   Kerouac, Jack. *Book of Sketches, 1952-57* — 818
Notes from a Small Island. Bryson, Bill — 914
★*Notes from a Young Black Chef*. Onwuachi, Kwame — 641.59
Notes from the Air. Ashbery, John — 811
★*Notes from the Henhouse*. Barker, Elspeth — 828
★*Notes of a Native Son*. Baldwin, James — 305.8
Notes on a Nervous Planet. Haig, Matt — 616.89
Notes on a Silencing. Crawford, Lacy — B
Notes on Grief. Adichie, Chimamanda Ngozi — 155.9
NOTHING
   McGovern, Anna. *Pottering* — 158.1
Nothing but the Night. King, Greg — 364.152
Nothing Ever Dies. Nguyen, Viet Thanh — 959.704
Nothing Ever Just Disappears. Hester, Diarmuid — 306.76
★*Nothing Fancy*. Roman, Alison — 642
Nothing Is Wrong and Here Is Why. Petri, Alexandra — 973.933
Nothing Like It in the World. Ambrose, Stephen E. — 385
★*Nothing* to Envy. Demick, Barbara — 920
Notley, Alice
   Certain Magical Acts — 811
NOTORIOUS B.I.G., 1972-1997
   Westhoff, Ben. *Original Gangstas* — 782.421649
Notorious RBG. Carmon, Irin — B
Nouns & Verbs. McGrath, Campbell — 811
Nourse, Victoria F.
   In Reckless Hands — 344.7304
NOUVEAUX RICHES
   De Courcy, Anne. *The Husband Hunters* — 920
   MacColl, Gail. *To Marry an English Lord* — 974.7
Nouwen, Henri J. M.
   Love, Henri — 282.092
NOUWEN, HENRI J. M.
   Nouwen, Henri J. M. *Love, Henri* — 282.092
NOVA SCOTIA
   Cameron, Silver Donald. *Blood in the Water* — 364.152
The Novel of the Century. Bellos, David — 843
★*Novelist as a Vocation*. Murakami, Haruki — 895.64
Novella, Steven
   The Skeptics' Guide to the Universe — 500
Novello, Carol
   Mutual Rescue — 636.088
NOVELS IN VERSE
   Carson, Anne. *Autobiography of Red* — 811
November 1942. Englund, Peter — 940.53
Novick, Peter
   The Holocaust in American Life — 940.53
Now & Again. Turshen, Julia — 641.5
Now Eat This! DiSpirito, Rocco — 641.5
Now Is the Way. Allen, Cory — 158.1
Nowak, Ronald M.
   Walker's Mammals of the World — 599
Nowhere Girl. Diamond, Cheryl — B
Nowicki, Stephen
   Raising a Socially Successful Child — 649
Noyes, Brian
   The Red Truck Bakery Farmhouse Cookbook — 641.5973
The NPR Classical Music Companion. Hoffman, Miles — 780.3
NUCLEAR ACCIDENTS
   Higginbotham, Adam. ★*Midnight in Chernobyl* — 363.17
   Schlosser, Eric. *Command and Control* — 363.17

Vollmann, William T. *No Immediate Danger*   333.79
NUCLEAR ARMS CONTROL
    Gordin, Michael D. *Red Cloud at Dawn*   355.02
Nuclear Energy. Ferguson, Charles D.   333.792
NUCLEAR EXPLOSIONS
    Berman, Bob. *Earth-Shattering*   523.1
NUCLEAR FISSION
    Preston, Diana. *Before the Fallout*   303.48
    ★*Nuclear Folly.* Plokhy, Serhii   972.9106
NUCLEAR NONPROLIFERATION
    Langewiesche, William. *The Atomic Bazaar*   355.02
NUCLEAR PHYSICISTS
    Schwartz, David N. *The Last Man Who Knew Everything*   B
    Wallace, Chris. *Countdown 1945*   940.54
NUCLEAR PHYSICS
    Mahaffey, James A. *Atomic Adventures*   333.792
NUCLEAR POWER
    Higginbotham, Adam. ★*Midnight in Chernobyl*   363.17
    Vollmann, William T. *No Immediate Danger*   333.79
NUCLEAR POWER INDUSTRY AND TRADE
    Vollmann, William T. *No Immediate Danger*   333.79
NUCLEAR POWER PLANTS
    Higginbotham, Adam. ★*Midnight in Chernobyl*   363.17
    Roripaugh, Lee Ann. *Tsunami vs. the Fukushima 50*   811
NUCLEAR POWER RESEARCH
    Sheinkin, Steve. *Bomb*   623.4
NUCLEAR REACTORS
    Higginbotham, Adam. ★*Midnight in Chernobyl*   363.17
NUCLEAR SUBMARINES
    Humphreys, Richard. *Under Pressure*   B
NUCLEAR WARFARE
    Ambinder, Marc. *The Brink*   355.5
    Barrett, David Dean. *140 Days to Hiroshima*   940.54
    Blume, Lesley M. M. *Fallout*   940.54
    Brands, H. W. *The General vs. the President*   973.918092
    Dean, Josh. *The Taking of K-129*   910.91
    Graff, Garrett M. *Raven Rock*   363.350973
    Ham, Paul. *Hiroshima Nagasaki*   940.54
    Hersey, John. ★*Hiroshima*   940.54
    Kaplan, Fred M. *The Bomb*   355.8
    Pellegrino, Charles R. *To Hell and Back*   940.54
    Plokhy, Serhii. ★*Nuclear Folly*   972.9106
    Preston, Diana. *Before the Fallout*   303.48
    Sakamoto, Pamela Rotner. *Midnight in Broad Daylight*   940.53
    Sherwin, Martin J. *Gambling with Armageddon*   972.9106
    Smith, Jim B. *The Last Mission*   940.54
    Southard, Susan. *Nagasaki*   940.54
    Thomas, Evan. *Ike's Bluff*   973.921092
    Wallace, Chris. *Countdown 1945*   940.54
NUCLEAR WARFARE FACILITIES
    Iversen, Kristen. *Full Body Burden*   363.17
NUCLEAR WEAPONS
    Barrett, David Dean. *140 Days to Hiroshima*   940.54
    Blume, Lesley M. M. *Fallout*   940.54
    Coleman, David G. *The Fourteenth Day*   973.922092
    Gordin, Michael D. *Red Cloud at Dawn*   355.02
    Ham, Paul. *Hiroshima Nagasaki*   940.54
    Hersey, John. ★*Hiroshima*   940.54
    Kaplan, Fred M. *The Bomb*   355.8
    Kean, Sam. *The Bastard Brigade*   355.8
    Langewiesche, William. *The Atomic Bazaar*   355.02
    Light, Michael. *100 Suns*   779
    Macintyre, Ben. ★*Agent Sonya*   B
    Mahaffey, James A. *Atomic Adventures*   333.792
    Norris, Robert S. *Racing for the Bomb*   B
    Pak, Jung H. *Becoming Kim Jong Un*   B
    Pellegrino, Charles R. *To Hell and Back*   940.54
    Preston, Diana. *Before the Fallout*   303.48
    Roll, David L. *Ascent to Power*   973.918
    Sakamoto, Pamela Rotner. *Midnight in Broad Daylight*   940.53
    Schlosser, Eric. *Command and Control*   363.17
    Sheehan, Neil. *A Fiery Peace in a Cold War*   B
    Sherman, Casey. *Above and Beyond*   973.922092
    Smith, Jim B. *The Last Mission*   940.54
    Southard, Susan. *Nagasaki*   940.54
    Thomas, Evan. *Ike's Bluff*   973.921092
    Wallace, Chris. *Countdown 1945*   940.54

NUCLEAR WEAPONS DEVELOPMENT
    Preston, Diana. *Before the Fallout*   303.48
NUCLEAR WEAPONS POLICY
    Blume, Lesley M. M. *Fallout*   940.54
Nuila, Ricardo
    The People's Hospital   362.1
Nuland, Sherwin B.
    Leonardo Da Vinci   B
NUMBER CONCEPT
    Clegg, Brian. *Are Numbers Real?*   510
    Number One Is Walking. Martin, Steve   B
    ★*The Number Ones.* Breihan, Tom   782.42164
NUMBER THEORY
    Clegg, Brian. *Are Numbers Real?*   510
    Conway, John Horton. *The Book of Numbers*   512
NUMBERS
    Vincent, James. *Beyond Measure*   530.8
    The Numbers Game. Anderson, Christopher   796.334
NUMEROLOGY
    Crawford, Saffi. *The Power of Birthdays, Stars & Numbers*   133.5
Nunn, Emily
    The Comfort Food Diaries   641.5973
NUNN, EMILY
    Nunn, Emily. *The Comfort Food Diaries*   641.5973
NUNS
    Barthel, Joan. *American Saint*   B
    Coldstream, Catherine. ★*Cloistered*   B
    Grathwohl, Marya. *This Wheel of Rocks*   271
    Prejean, Helen. *River of Fire*   B
    Shanley, John Patrick. *Doubt*   812
NUR JAHAN, EMPRESS, CONSORT OF JAHANGIR, EMPEROR OF HINDUSTAN, D. 1645
    Lal, Ruby. *Empress*   B
NUREMBERG WAR CRIME TRIALS, 1946-1949
    Sands, Philippe. *East West Street*   345
NUREMBERG, GERMANY
    Harrington, Joel F. *The Faithful Executioner*   B
Nureyev. Kavanagh, Julie   B
NUREYEV, RUDOLF, 1938-1993
    Kavanagh, Julie. *Nureyev*   B
NURSES
    Bostridge, Mark. *Florence Nightingale*   B
    Brenner, Marie. ★*The Desperate Hours*   362.1962
    Brown, Theresa. *Healing*   616.99
    Case, Molly. *How to Treat People*   616.1
    DiGregorio, Sarah. ★*Taking Care*   610.73
    Lineberry, Cate. *The Secret Rescue*   940.54
    Mitchell, Wendy. *Somebody I Used to Know*   B
    Norman, Elizabeth M. *We Band of Angels*   940.54
    Patterson, James. *ER Nurses*   610.73
    Smilios, Maria. ★*The Black Angels*   610.73
    Toler, Pamela D. *Heroines of Mercy Street*   973.7
NURSING
    Case, Molly. *How to Treat People*   616.1
    DiGregorio, Sarah. ★*Taking Care*   610.73
    Patterson, James. *ER Nurses*   610.73
NURSING HOME PATIENTS
    Berg, Elizabeth. *I'll Be Seeing You*   306.874
NURSING HOMES
    Halpern, Sue. *A Dog Walks into a Nursing Home*   B
    ★*The Nursing Mother's Companion.* Huggins, Kathleen   649
Nusbaum, Eric
    Stealing Home   796.357
Nussbaum, Emily
    Cue the Sun!   791.45
    I Like to Watch   791.45
NUSSBAUM, EMILY, 1966-
    Nussbaum, Emily. *I Like to Watch*   791.45
Nussbaum, Martha Craven
    The Monarchy of Fear   306.20973
    The New Religious Intolerance   201.723
Nusseibeh, Sari
    Once Upon a Country   B
NUSSEIBEH, SARI
    Nusseibeh, Sari. *Once Upon a Country*   B
NUTRITION
    Albright, Mary Beth. ★*Eat & Flourish*   612.3
    Altmann, Tanya Remer. *What to Feed Your Baby*   649

AUTHOR, TITLE, SERIES AND SUBJECT INDEX

Attia, Peter. ★*Outlive*	612.6
Barrett, Pearl. *Trim Healthy Mama Trim Healthy Table*	613.2
Bittman, Mark. *A Bone to Pick*	338.10973
Britton, Sarah. *Naturally Nourished*	641.5
Campbell, T. Colin. *The China Study*	613.2
Common. ★*And Then We Rise*	613
Curry, Kevin. *Fit Men Cook*	641.5
DiSpirito, Rocco. *Rocco's Healthy+Delicious*	641.3
Fuhrman, Joel. *Eat to Live Quick & Easy Cookbook*	641.5
Hartwig, Melissa. *The Whole30 Fast & Easy*	641.5
Hartwig, Melissa. *The Whole30 Slow Cooker*	641.5
Hunt, Lindsay Maitland. *Help Yourself*	641.5
Jamieson, Alexandra. *Women, Food, and Desire*	155.3
Lee, Jennifer Tyler. *Half the Sugar, All the Love*	641.5
McGee, Harold. ★*On Food and Cooking*	641.5
McMillan, Tracie. *The American Way of Eating*	338.4
Mitchell, Andie. *Eating in the Middle*	641.3
Moss, Michael. ★*Hooked*	613.2
Moss, Michael. *Salt, Sugar, Fat*	613.2
Nigg, Joel T. *Getting Ahead of ADHD*	618.92
Obama, Michelle. *American Grown*	635.09
Olmsted, Larry. *Real Food/Fake Food*	641.3
Porto, Anthony. *The Pediatrician's Guide to Feeding Babies & Toddlers*	618.92
Price, Catherine. *Vitamania*	612.3
Pulde, Alona. *Forks Over Knives Family*	641.5
Sanfilippo, Diane. *Practical Paleo*	613.2
Schatzker, Mark. *The Dorito Effect*	641.3
Smith, Michelle. *The Whole Smiths Good Food Cookbook*	641.5
Taubes, Gary. ★*Rethinking Diabetes*	616.462
Wilson, Bee. *The Way We Eat Now*	641.01
Nutrition Stripped. Hill, McKel	641.3
NUTRITIONAL THERAPY	
Hartwig, Melissa. *The Whole30 Fast & Easy*	641.5
Hartwig, Melissa. *The Whole30 Slow Cooker*	641.5
Mullen, Seamus. *Real Food Heals*	641.5
Myers, Amy. *The Autoimmune Solution Cookbook*	641.5
Scarlata, Kate. *Mind Your Gut*	616.3
Smith, Michelle. *The Whole Smiths Good Food Cookbook*	641.5
NUTRITIONALLY INDUCED DISEASES	
Campbell, T. Colin. *The China Study*	613.2
Price, Catherine. *Vitamania*	612.3
Nuts and Bolts. Agrawal, Roma	609
Nutt, Amy Ellis	
Becoming Nicole	920
Nuttall, A. D.	
Shakespeare the Thinker	822.33
Nuttall, Jennifer Anne	
★*Mother Tongue*	422
NUTTER, TOMMY, 1943-1992	
Richardson, Lance. *House of Nutter*	B
Nyad, Diana	
Find a Way	B
NYAD, DIANA	
Nyad, Diana. *Find a Way*	B
Nyamayaro, Elizabeth	
I Am a Girl from Africa	B
NYAMAYARO, ELIZABETH	
Nyamayaro, Elizabeth. *I Am a Girl from Africa*	B
Nyberg, Amanda Jean	
No Scrap Left Behind	746.46
Nye, Bill	
Everything All at Once	153.4
Undeniable	576.8
NYE, BILL	
Nye, Bill. *Everything All at Once*	153.4
Nye, Naomi Shihab	
The Tiny Journalist	811
You & Yours	811

O

O Jerusalem! Collins, Larry	956
O Say Can You Hear?. Clague, Mark	782.42
O'Brady, Colin	
★*The Impossible First*	919.8904

O'BRADY, COLIN	
O'Brady, Colin. ★*The Impossible First*	919.8904
O'BRIEN, CONAN	
Movsesian, Sona. *The World's Worst Assistant*	791.4302
O'Brien, David M	
★*Storm Center*	347.73
O'Brien, Jack	
Jack Be Nimble	B
O'BRIEN, JACK, 1939-	
O'Brien, Jack. *Jack Be Nimble*	B
O'Brien, Keith	
Charlie Hustle	796.357
Fly Girls	920
Paradise Falls	363.738
O'Brien, Phillips Payson	
The Second Most Powerful Man in the World	B
O'Brien, Vanessa	
To the Greatest Heights	B
O'BRIEN, VANESSA, 1964-	
O'Brien, Vanessa. *To the Greatest Heights*	B
O'Connell, Mark	
A Thread of Violence	364.152
O'Connell, Robert L.	
The Ghosts of Cannae	937
Revolutionary	B
O'Connor, Birgit	
Watercolor Essentials	751.42
O'CONNOR, FLANNERY	
Gooch, Brad. ★*Flannery*	B
O'Connor, Garry	
Ian McKellen	B
Universal Father	B
O'Connor, Ian	
Belichick	B
Coach K	B
O'Connor, John	
The Secret History of Bigfoot	001.944
O'Connor, Maura R.	
Resurrection Science	591.68
O'Connor, Sandra Day	
★*Out of Order*	347.73
O'CONNOR, SANDRA DAY, 1930-2023	
Hirshman, Linda R. *Sisters in Law*	347.73
Thomas, Evan. ★*First*	B
O'Connor, Sinead	
★*Rememberings*	B
O'CONNOR, SINEAD. 1966-2023	
O'Connor, Sinead. ★*Rememberings*	B
O'Donnell Heffington, Peggy	
Without Children	306.85
O'DONNELL, FRANCIS	
Belliveau, Denis. *In the Footsteps of Marco Polo*	915
O'Donnell, Patrick K.	
The Indispensables	973.3
The Unvanquished	973.7
O'Donnell, Svenja	
Inge's War	943.086
O'Farrell, Maggie	
I Am, I Am, I Am	B
O'FARRELL, MAGGIE, 1972-	
O'Farrell, Maggie. *I Am, I Am, I Am*	B
O'Gieblyn, Meghan	
God, Human, Animal, Machine	814
O'GIEBLYN, MEGHAN	
O'Gieblyn, Meghan. *God, Human, Animal, Machine*	814
O'Hara, Frank	
Lunch Poems.	811
O'HARA, FRANK, 1926-1966	
Calhoun, Ada. *Also a Poet*	B
O'Hara, Maryanne	
Little Matches	B
O'HARA, MARYANNE	
O'Hara, Maryanne. *Little Matches*	B
O'Kane, Bernard	
Treasures of Islam	709.1
O'KEEFFE, GEORGIA, 1887-1986	
Lynes, Barbara Buhler. *Georgia O'Keeffe Museum Collections*	759.13
Robinson, Roxana. *Georgia O'Keeffe*	B

PUBLIC LIBRARY CORE COLLECTION: NONFICTION
Twentieth Edition

O'Keeffe, Paul
   Waterloo — 940.2
O'Meara, Mallory
   Girly Drinks — 641.2
   The Lady from the Black Lagoon — 921
O'MEARA, MALLORY
   O'Meara, Mallory. *The Lady from the Black Lagoon* — 921
O'NEAL, SHAQUILLE, 1972-
   Pearlman, Jeff. ★*Three-Ring Circus* — 796.323
O'NEIL, BUCK, 1911-2006
   Posnanski, Joe. *The Soul of Baseball* — 796.357
O'Neil, Cathy
   The Shame Machine — 152.4
   Weapons of Math Destruction — 005.7
O'NEIL, CATHY
   O'Neil, Cathy. *The Shame Machine* — 152.4
O'Neil, Dennis
   The DC Comics Guide to Writing Comics — 808
O'Neill, Cara
   Chapter 13 Bankruptcy, 17th Ed. — 346.7307
O'Neill, Robert
   The Operator — B
O'NEILL, ROBERT, 1976-
   O'Neill, Robert. *The Operator* — B
O'Neill, Tom
   ★*Chaos* — 364.152
O'NEILL, TOM
   O'Neill, Tom. ★*Chaos* — 364.152
O'Reilly, Bill
   Killing the SS — 940.53
O'REILLY, FINBARR
   Brennan, Thomas J. *Shooting Ghosts* — B
O'Reilly, Seamas
   ★*Did Ye Hear Mammy Died?* — B
O'Rourke, Meghan
   ★*The Invisible Kingdom* — 616
O'ROURKE, MEGHAN
   O'Rourke, Meghan. ★*The Invisible Kingdom* — 616
O'Rourke, P. J.
   None of My Business — 332
O'Sullivan, Emer
   The Fall of the House of Wilde — B
O'Sullivan, Suzanne
   The Sleeping Beauties — 616.85
O'Toole, Fintan
   ★*We Don't Know Ourselves* — 941.7
O'TOOLE, FINTAN, 1958-
   O'Toole, Fintan. ★*We Don't Know Ourselves* — 941.7
O'Toole, Jennifer Cook
   Autism in Heels — B
O'TOOLE, JENNIFER COOK
   O'Toole, Jennifer Cook. *Autism in Heels* — B
O'Toole, Patricia
   The Moralist — B
★*Oak Flat*. Redniss, Lauren — 970.5
OAK RIDGE, TENNESSEE
   Kiernan, Denise. *The Girls of Atomic City* — 976.8
Oakes, James
   Freedom National — 973.7
Oakes, John G. H.
   ★*The Fast* — 613.2
OAKLAND, CALIFORNIA
   Markham, Lauren. ★*The Far Away Brothers* — 920
Oakley, Charles
   The Last Enforcer — B
OAKLEY, CHARLES, 1963-
   Oakley, Charles. *The Last Enforcer* — B
OAKLEY, VIOLET, 1874-
   Carter, Alice A. *The Red Rose Girls* — B
Oates, Joyce Carol
   American Melancholy — 811
Oath and Honor. Cheney, Liz — 328.73
The Oath and the Office. Brettschneider, Corey Lang — 342.73
Obama. Souza, Pete — 973.932
Obama, Barack
   ★*The Audacity of Hope* — B
   ★*Dreams from My Father* — B
   ★*A Promised Land* — B

OBAMA, BARACK
   Alexander, Kwame. *Light for the World to See* — 811.6
   Balz, Daniel J. *The Battle for America, 2008* — 973.932
   Chait, Jonathan. *Audacity* — 973.932
   Coates, Ta-Nehisi. ★*We Were Eight Years in Power* — 305.896
   Dyson, Michael Eric. *The Black Presidency* — 305.800973
   Garrow, David J. *Rising Star* — B
   Jarrett, Valerie. *Finding My Voice* — B
   Katz, David. *Barack Before Obama* — B
   Keenan, Cody. *Grace* — 973.932
   Maraniss, David. ★*Barack Obama* — B
   Obama, Barack. ★*The Audacity of Hope* — B
   Obama, Barack. ★*Dreams from My Father* — B
   Obama, Barack. ★*A Promised Land* — B
   Remnick, David. *The Bridge* — B
   Smith, Michael S. *Designing History* — 975.3
   Souza, Pete. *Obama* — 973.932
   Souza, Pete. *Shade* — 973.932
   Souza, Pete. *The West Wing and Beyond* — 917.53
Obama, Michelle
   American Grown — 635.09
   ★*Becoming* — B
   ★*The Light We Carry* — B
OBAMA, MICHELLE, 1964-
   Obama, Michelle. ★*Becoming* — B
   Obama, Michelle. ★*The Light We Carry* — B
   Slevin, Peter. *Michelle Obama* — B
   Smith, Michael S. *Designing History* — 975.3
   Swarns, Rachel L. ★*American Tapestry* — B
Oberdorfer, Don
   The Two Koreas 3rd Ed. — 951.904
OBERHOLTZER, MADGE, 1896-1925
   Egan, Timothy. ★*A Fever in the Heartland* — 322.4
Oberman, Heiko Augustinus
   Luther — B
OBESITY
   Gordon, Aubrey. *"You Just Need to Lose Weight"* — 616.3
   Guyenet, Stephan J. *The Hungry Brain* — 616.85
   Laymon, Kiese. ★*Heavy* — B
   Moss, Michael. ★*Hooked* — 613.2
   Sole-Smith, Virginia. ★*Fat Talk* — 649.1
   Tomlinson, Tommy. *The Elephant in the Room* — B
   Tulleken, Chris van. *Ultra-Processed People* — 664
Obit. Chang, Victoria — 811
OBITUARIES
   Chang, Victoria. *Obit* — 811
   Rocca, Mo. *Mobituaries* — 920
OBJECTIFICATION (SOCIAL PSYCHOLOGY)
   Ratajkowski, Emily. ★*My Body* — B
   Ruhl, Sarah. *Smile* — B
OBJECTIVISM (PHILOSOPHY)
   Rand, Ayn. ★*The Virtue of Selfishness* — 149
OBJECTIVITY
   Bawer, Bruce. *The Victims' Revolution* — 320.973
   Tobin, James. *Ernie Pyle's War* — B
Objects of Devotion. Manseau, Peter — 277
Obrist, Hans-Ulrich
   Ways of Curating — 707.5
OBRIST, HANS-ULRICH
   Obrist, Hans-Ulrich. *Ways of Curating* — 707.5
OBSCENITY (LAW)
   Stone, Geoffrey R. ★*Sex and the Constitution* — 345.7302
OBSERVATION (PSYCHOLOGY)
   Franzen, Jonathan. *The End of the End of the Earth* — 814
   Herman, Amy. *Visual Intelligence* — 152.14
   Kerouac, Jack. *Book of Sketches, 1952-57* — 818
OBSERVING THINGS
   Hoffman, Donald D. *The Case Against Reality* — 121
   Ridpath, Ian. *Stars & Planets* — 520
   Sedaris, David. ★*A Carnival of Snackery* — 818
   Sharot, Tali. *Look Again* — 158.1
   Vincent, James. *Beyond Measure* — 530.8
OBSESSION
   Ahdoot, Dan. *Undercooked* — 647.95
   Aron, Nina Renata. *Good Morning, Destroyer of Men's Souls* — B
   Barbarisi, Daniel. *Chasing the Thrill* — 796.1
   Bosker, Bianca. *Get the Picture* — 701
   Chapin, Sasha. *All the Wrong Moves* — 794.1092

AUTHOR, TITLE, SERIES AND SUBJECT INDEX

Conaboy, Kelly. *The Particulars of Peter*	636.7
Finnegan, William. *Barbarian Days*	B
Gerard, Sarah. *Sunshine State*	814
Grann, David. *The White Darkness*	B
Gristwood, Sarah. *The Tudors in Love*	941.05
Hammer, Joshua. *The Falcon Thief*	364.16
Kang, Mia. *Knockout*	B
Kean, Sam. *The Icepick Surgeon*	509
Leamer, Laurence. *Hitchcock's Blondes*	791.43
Mortimer, Frank. *Bee People and the Bugs They Love*	
Pham, Larissa. *Pop Song*	709.2
Raphael, Rina. *The Gospel of Wellness*	613
Stone, Daniel. *Sinkable*	910.91
Summerscale, Kate. *The Book of Phobias and Manias*	616.85
Tallis, Frank. *The Incurable Romantic*	152.4

OBSTETRICIANS

Abuelaish, Izzeldin. *I Shall Not Hate*	B

OBSTETRICS

DiGregorio, Sarah. *Early*	618.92
Fisher, Susan J. *Taking Charge of Your Pregnancy*	618.2

OBSTINACY

De Stefano, Cristina. *The Child Is the Teacher*	B
McGilligan, Patrick. *Funny Man*	B

OCASIO-CORTEZ, ALEXANDRIA, 1989-

Jones, Brenda. *Alexandria Ocasio-Cortez*	B
★*The Occasional Human Sacrifice*. Elliott, Carl	174.2
The Occult, Witchcraft & Magic. Dell, Christopher	130

OCCULTISM

Abrev, Ileana. *The Little Big Book of White Spells*	133.4
Crosson, Monica. *The Magikal Family*	299
Dell, Christopher. *The Occult, Witchcraft & Magic*	130
Dickey, Colin. *The Unidentified*	130
Feldmann, Erica. *Hausmagick*	133.4
Garcia, Amanda Yates. *Initiated*	B
Gosden, Chris. *Magic*	133.4
Grossman, Pam. *Waking the Witch*	133.4
Jamison, Kay Redfield. *Fires in the Dark*	616.89
Jones, Marie D. *Demons, the Devil, and Fallen Angels*	133.4
Rajchel, Diana. *Urban Magick*	133.4
Rojas Contreras, Ingrid. ★*The Man Who Could Move Clouds*	B
Stone, Alex. *Fooling Houdini*	B

OCCUPATIONAL HEALTH AND SAFETY

Genoways, Ted. *The Chain*	338.7
Monforton, Celeste. *On the Job*	331.1
Moore, Kate. *The Radium Girls*	363.17
Morris, Jim. ★*The Cancer Factory*	658.3

OCCUPATIONS

De Botton, Alain. *The Pleasures and Sorrows of Work*	306.3
Harrington, Joel F. *The Faithful Executioner*	B
Morgan, Genevieve. *Undecided*	331.702
Press, Eyal. ★*Dirty Work*	331.7
Terkel, Studs. *Working*	920

OCD

Adam, David. *The Man Who Couldn't Stop*	616.85
Bailey, Lily. *Because We Are Bad*	B
Fall, Jeremy. *Falling Upwards*	158.1
Freeman, Hadley. *Good Girls*	616.85
Hornbacher, Marya. *Wasted*	B
Raskin, Allison. *Overthinking About You*	646.7
Shaffer, Peter. ★*Equus*	822
Solomon, Deborah. *American Mirror*	B
Williams, Lucinda. *Don't Tell Anybody the Secrets I Told You*	B

OCD IN TEENAGERS

Stone, Lillian. ★*Everybody's Favorite*	814.6

OCEAN BOTTOM

Casey, Susan. *The Underworld*	551.46

OCEAN TRAVEL

Bergreen, Laurence. *Over the Edge of the World*	B
Homer. ★*The Odyssey*	883
Johnson, Steven. *Enemy of All Mankind*	910.4
Preston, Diana. *Paradise in Chains*	996.18
Roberts, Jason. *A Sense of the World*	B
Stark, Peter. *Astoria*	979.5
Thomson, Keith. *Born to Be Hanged*	910.4
Ujifusa, Steven. *Barons of the Sea*	387.5

OCEANIA

Alexander, Caroline. *The Bounty*	996.1
Thompson, Christina. *Sea People*	305.8994

Oceanic. Nezhukumatathil, Aimee	811

OCEANOGRAPHERS

Ballard, Robert D. *Into the Deep*	551.46092
Cousteau, Jacques Yves. *The Human, the Orchid, and the Octopus*	B
Mearns, David L. *The Shipwreck Hunter*	910.452

OCEANOGRAPHY

Ballard, Robert D. *Into the Deep*	551.46092
Bradley, James. *Deep Water*	578.77
Casey, Susan. *The Underworld*	551.46
Czerski, Helen. *The Blue Machine*	551.46
Mearns, David L. *The Shipwreck Hunter*	910.452
Scales, Helen. *The Brilliant Abyss*	551.46

OCEANS

Ballard, Robert D. *Into the Deep*	551.46092
Bradley, James. *Deep Water*	578.77
Casey, Susan. *The Underworld*	551.46
Czerski, Helen. *The Blue Machine*	551.46
Ellis, Richard. ★*The Empty Ocean*	577.7
Nicolson, Adam. *The Seabird's Cry*	598.177
Scales, Helen. *The Brilliant Abyss*	551.46
Scales, Helen. *What the Wild Sea Can Be*	577.7
Smith, Bren. *Eat Like a Fish*	338.3
Stavridis, James. *Sea Power*	359
Strøksnes, Morten Andreas. *Shark Drunk*	338.3
Winchester, Simon. *Atlantic*	551.46
Winchester, Simon. *Pacific*	909

Ockwell-Smith, Sarah

Ready, Set, Go!	649
October. Mieville, China	947.084

OCTOGENARIANS

Esty, Katharaine C. *Eightysomethings*	612.6
The Octopus Museum. Shaughnessy, Brenda	811

OCTOPUSES

Scheel, David. *Many Things Under a Rock*	594
Oculus. Mao, Sally Wen	811

ODA, NOBUNAGA, 1534-1582

Lockley, Thomas. *African Samurai*	B

ODAWA (NORTH AMERICAN PEOPLE)

McDonnell, Michael. *Masters of Empire*	977.4
Odd Girl Out. James, Laura E.	B
Odd Girl Out. Simmons, Rachel	302.5

Odell, Amy

Anna	B

Odell, Jenny

★*Saving Time*	153.7

Odenkirk, Bob

Comedy Comedy Comedy Drama	B

ODENKIRK, BOB, 1962-

Odenkirk, Bob. *Comedy Comedy Comedy Drama*	B
Odes. Olds, Sharon	811
Odes and Epodes. Horace	874
Odessa. King, Charles	947.7
Odetta. Zack, Ian	B

ODETTA, 1930-2008

Zack, Ian. *Odetta*	B

ODETTE, 1912-1995

Loftis, Larry. *Code Name*	B
Rose, Sarah. *D-Day Girls*	940.53

ODIN (NORSE DEITY)

Larrington, Carolyne. *The Norse Myths*	293

ODORS

Mazzeo, Tilar J. *The Secret of Chanel No. 5*	338.7
McGee, Harold. ★*Nose Dive*	612.8
Tanais. *In Sensorium*	B

ODYSSEUS (GREEK MYTHOLOGY)

Homer. *The Odyssey*	883
Homer. *The Odyssey*	883
Homer. *Odyssey*	883
Homer. ★*The Odyssey*	883

ODYSSEUS, KING OF ITHACA (MYTHOLOGICAL CHARACTER)

Manguel, Alberto. *Homer's the Iliad and the Odyssey*	883
The Odyssey. Homer	883
The Odyssey. Homer	883
Odyssey. Homer	883
★*The Odyssey*. Homer	883
The Odyssey. Homer	883
The Odyssey of Echo Company. Stanton, Doug	959.704
The Odyssey of Phillis Wheatley. Waldstreicher, David	B

Oelhafen, Ingrid von
  Hitler's Stolen Children — B
OELHAFEN, INGRID VON
  Oelhafen, Ingrid von. *Hitler's Stolen Children* — B
Of Africa. Soyinka, Wole — 960
Of All That Ends. Grass, Gunter — 838
Of Arms and Artists. Staiti, Paul J. — B
Of Greed and Glory. Plant, Deborah G. — 326
Of Ice and Men. Hogge, Fred — 338.4
Of Love & War. Addario, Lynsey — 779
Of Mess and Moxie. Hatmaker, Jen — 248.8
Of Orcas and Men. Neiwert, David A. — 599.53
★*Of Time and Turtles.* Montgomery, Sy — 597.92
★*Of Wolves and Men.* Lopez, Barry Holstun — 599.773
Off The Edge. Weill, Kelly — 001.9
Offerman, Nick
  The Greatest Love Story Ever Told — B
  Where the Deer and the Antelope Play — 973.93
OFFERMAN, NICK, 1970-
  Offerman, Nick. *The Greatest Love Story Ever Told* — B
  Offerman, Nick. *Where the Deer and the Antelope Play* — 973.93
The Office. Greene, Andy — 791.45
The Office BFFs. Fischer, Jenna — 791.45
OFFICE ENVIRONMENT
  Hamilton, Denise. ★*Indivisible* — 658.3
OFFICE POLITICS
  Williams, Joan. *What Works for Women at Work* — 650.1
OFFICE ROMANCE
  Dorey-Stein, Beck. *From the Corner of the Oval* — B
Officer Clemmons. Clemmons, Francois S. — B
Official Guide to the Smithsonian National Museum of African American History & Culture. Kendrick, Kathleen M — 975.3
Offit, Paul A.
  You Bet Your Life — 615.5
Offolter, Enid
  Welcome to the Jungle — 635.9
Ogilvie, Sarah
  The Dictionary People — 423
OGLALA (NORTH AMERICAN PEOPLE)
  Black Elk. *Black Elk Speaks* — B
  Bunnell, David. *Good Friday on the Rez* — B
  Drury, Bob. *The Heart of Everything That Is* — B
  Jackson, Joe. *Black Elk* — 978.004
  McMurtry, Larry. *Crazy Horse* — B
  Powers, Thomas. *The Killing of Crazy Horse* — B
Ogura, Yoshiko
  The Complete Guide to Drawing for Beginners — 740
Oh My Mother! Wang, Connie — B
Oh, Scrap! Alexander, Lissa — 746.46
OHER, MICHAEL
  Lewis, Michael. *The Blind Side* — B
OHIO
  Abdurraqib, Hanif. ★*There's Always This Year* — 796.323
  Alexander, Brian. ★*The Hospital* — 362.10973
  Cox, Anna-Lisa. *The Bone and Sinew of the Land* — 977
  Derf. *Kent State* — 741.5
  Heyman, Stephen. *The Planter of Modern Life* — B
  Mackall, Joe. *Plain Secrets* — 289.7
  Meckler, Laura. ★*Dream Town* — 305.8
  Schwartzman, Nancy. *Roll Red Roll* — 364.15
  Williams, Kale. *The Loneliest Polar Bear* — 599.786
OHIO RIVER VALLEY
  Cozzens, Peter. *Tecumseh and the Prophet* — 920
  McCullough, David G. *The Pioneers* — 920
Ohler, Norman
  The Bohemians — 940.53
Ohrenstein, Dora
  The Crocheter's Skill-Building Workshop — 746.43
OIL
  Beaton, Kate. ★*Ducks* — 741.5
  Conway, Edmund. *Material World* — 333.7
  Magner, Mike. *Poisoned Legacy* — 338.7
  Margonelli, Lisa. *Oil on the Brain* — 338.2
OIL EXECUTIVES
  Maddow, Rachel. *Blowout* — 338.2
OIL INDUSTRY AND TRADE
  Abrahamian, Ervand. *The Coup* — 955.05
  Barr, James. *Lords of the Desert* — 956
  Beaton, Kate. ★*Ducks* — 741.5
  Briody, Blaire. *The New Wild West* — 338.2
  Burrough, Bryan. *The Big Rich* — 338.2
  Coll, Steve. *Private Empire* — 338.7
  Doran, Peter B. *Breaking Rockefeller* — 338.7
  Estes, Nick. *Our History Is the Future* — 978.004
  Fields, Micah. ★*We Hold Our Breath* — 976.4
  Hope, Bradley. *Blood and Oil* — B
  Kershaw, Ian. *The Global Age* — 940.55
  Maass, Peter. *Crude World* — 338.2
  Maddow, Rachel. *Blowout* — 338.2
  Magner, Mike. *Poisoned Legacy* — 338.7
  Margonelli, Lisa. *Oil on the Brain* — 338.2
  Mealer, Bryan. *The Kings of Big Spring* — B
  Murdoch, Sierra Crane. ★*Yellow Bird* — 364.152
  Rao, Maya. *Great American Outpost* — 338.2
  Rich, Nathaniel. *Losing Earth* — 363.738
  Vaillant, John. ★*Fire Weather* — 363.37
  Yergin, Daniel. ★*The Prize* — 338.2
  Yergin, Daniel. *The Quest* — 333.79
  Zuckerman, Gregory. *The Frackers* — B
Oil on the Brain. Margonelli, Lisa — 338.2
OIL PRODUCTION
  Maass, Peter. *Crude World* — 338.2
OIL SPILLS
  Johnson, Kirk W. *The Fishermen and the Dragon* — 976.4
OIL SUPPLY
  Maass, Peter. *Crude World* — 338.2
OIL WELLS
  Grann, David. ★*Killers of the Flower Moon* — 976.6004
OIL WORKERS
  Glatt, John. ★*The Perfect Father* — 364.152
  Magner, Mike. *Poisoned Legacy* — 338.7
  Murdoch, Sierra Crane. ★*Yellow Bird* — 364.152
  Rao, Maya. *Great American Outpost* — 338.2
OJIBWE (NORTH AMERICAN PEOPLE)
  Erdrich, Louise. *Books and Islands in Ojibwe Country* — 977
  Treuer, Anton. *Everything You Wanted to Know About Indians but Were Afraid to Ask* — 970.1
  Wagamese, Richard. *For Joshua* — B
  Wagamese, Richard. *One Native Life* — B
OKINAWA
  Bissinger, H. G. ★*The Mosquito Bowl* — 796.332
  Brina, Elizabeth Miki. *Speak, Okinawa* — 305.48
  Johnson, Akemi. *Night in the American Village* — 305.40952
OKLAHOMA
  Ellsworth, Scott. *The Ground Breaking* — 976.6
  Ervin, Kristine S. *Rabbit Heart* — 364.152
  Grann, David. ★*Killers of the Flower Moon* — 976.6004
  Ikpi, Bassey. *I'm Telling the Truth, but I'm Lying* — 814
  Jones, Robert P. *The Hidden Roots of White Supremacy* — 305.8
  Nourse, Victoria F. *In Reckless Hands* — 344.7304
OKLAHOMA CITY BOMBING, APRIL 19, 1995
  Toobin, Jeffrey. ★*Homegrown* — 363.325
OKLAHOMA CITY, OKLAHOMA
  Anderson, Sam. *Boom Town* — 976.6
Okorafor, Nnedi
  Broken Places & Outer Spaces — 153.3
Okporo, Edafe
  Asylum — B
Okrent, Daniel
  The Guarded Gate — 344.73
  Last Call — 363.4
OLD AGE ASSISTANCE
  Thomas, Elizabeth Marshall. *Growing Old* — 305.26
OLD GROWTH FOREST CONSERVATION
  Farmer, Jared. *Elderflora* — 582.16
OLD GROWTH FORESTS
  Farmer, Jared. *Elderflora* — 582.16
Old in Art School. Painter, Nell Irvin — B
OLD ORDER MENNONITES
  Kraybill, Donald B. ★*On the Backroad to Heaven* — 289.7
Olds, Sally
  ★*People Who Lunch* — 824
Olds, Sharon
  Arias — 811
  Odes — 811
  Stag's Leap — 811

AUTHOR, TITLE, SERIES AND SUBJECT INDEX

OLGA, GRAND DUCHESS OF RUSSIA, 1895-1918
   Massie, Robert K. *The Romanovs*   947
   Rappaport, Helen. *The Romanov Sisters*   920
Oliphant, Thomas
   ★*The Road to Camelot*   973.922092
Oliva, Alejandra
   Rivermouth   305.9
OLIVA, ALEJANDRA
   Oliva, Alejandra. *Rivermouth*   305.9
Olivares, Efren C.
   My Boy Will Die of Sorrow   305.9
OLIVARES, EFREN C.
   Olivares, Efren C. *My Boy Will Die of Sorrow*   305.9
Olivarez, Jose
   Promises of Gold = Promesas De Oro   811
Oliver Wendell Holmes. Budiansky, Stephen   B
Oliver, Jamie
   Together   641.5
Oliver, Joan Duncan
   Buddhism   294.3
Oliver, Mary
   ★*Devotions*   811
   Dream Work   811
   New and Selected Poems,; Vol. 1   811
   A Poetry Handbook   808.1
   A Thousand Mornings   811
   ★*Upstream*   814
OLIVER, MARY, 1935-2019
   Oliver, Mary. ★*Upstream*   814
Olives, Lemons & Za'atar. Bishara, Rawia   641.59
Oller, John
   American Queen   B
   White Shoe   346.73
Ollestad, Norman
   Crazy for the Storm   B
OLLESTAD, NORMAN
   Ollestad, Norman. *Crazy for the Storm*   B
OLLESTAD, NORMAN, 1935-1979
   Ollestad, Norman. *Crazy for the Storm*   B
Ollivier, Bernard
   Out of Istanbul   B
OLLIVIER, BERNARD
   Ollivier, Bernard. *Out of Istanbul*   B
OLMECS (MEXICAN PEOPLE)
   Beard, Mary. ★*How Do We Look*   704.9
OLMSTED, FREDERICK LAW, 1822-1903
   Horwitz, Tony. *Spying on the South*   917
   Howard, Hugh. *Architects of an American Landscape*   712.092
Olmsted, Larry
   Real Food/Fake Food   641.3
Olsen, Craig
   P.S. Burn This Letter Please   306.76
Olsen, Lise
   Code of Silence   347.73
Olson, Carl
   Historical Dictionary of Buddhism   294.3
Olson, Lynne
   Citizens of London   940.54012
   ★*Empress of the Nile*   B
   Last Hope Island   940.53
   ★*Madame Fourcade's Secret War*   B
   Those Angry Days   940.53
   Troublesome Young Men   941.084
Olson, Roger E.
   ★*Handbook of Denominations in the United States*   200.973
Oluo, Ijeoma
   ★*Be a Revolution*   305.8
   Mediocre   305.310973
   ★*So You Want to Talk About Race*   305.800973
Oluseyi, Hakeem M.
   A Quantum Life   B
OLUSEYI, HAKEEM M. (HAKEEM MUATA)
   Oluseyi, Hakeem M. *A Quantum Life*   B
OLYMPIC ATHLETES
   Brown, Daniel James. ★*The Boys in the Boat*   797.12
   Coffey, Wayne R. ★*The Boys of Winter*   796.962
   Crouse, Karen. *Norwich*   796
   Daley, Tom. *Coming up for Air*   B

   Eruzione, Mike. *The Making of a Miracle*   B
   Franklin, Missy. *Relentless Spirit*   B
   Hamilton, Duncan. *For the Glory*   B
   Hart, Matt. *Win at All Costs*   338.7
   Iguodala, Andre. *The Sixth Man*   B
   Legler, Casey. ★*Godspeed*   B
   Mardini, Yusra. *Butterfly*   B
   Masters, Oksana. *The Hard Parts*   B
OLYMPIC GAMES
   Brown, Daniel James. ★*The Boys in the Boat*   797.12
   Checkoway, Julie. *The Three-Year Swim Club*   797.2
   Crawford, Bill. ★*All American*   B
   Ebersol, Dick. *From Saturday Night to Sunday Night*   B
   Goldblatt, David. *The Games*   796.4809
   Halberstam, David. *The Amateurs*   B
   Means, Howard B. ★*Splash!*   797.2
OLYMPIC GAMES (ANCIENT)
   Means, Howard B. ★*Splash!*   797.2
OLYMPIC MEDAL WINNERS
   Eruzione, Mike. *The Making of a Miracle*   B
   Keflezighi, Meb. *26 Marathons*   B
   Masters, Oksana. *The Hard Parts*   B
   Pippen, Scottie. *Unguarded*   B
   Rippon, Adam. *Beautiful on the Outside*   B
   Shorter, Frank. *My Marathon*   796.42
OMAHA, NEBRASKA
   Ruffin, Amber. *You'll Never Believe What Happened to Lacey*   305.896
OMALU, BENNET I. (BENNET IFEAKANDU)
   Laskas, Jeanne Marie. *Concussion*   617.5
Omar Khayyam
   Rubaiyat of Omar Khayyam   891
Omeros. Walcott, Derek   811
The Omnivore's Dilemma. Pollan, Michael   394.1
OMNIVORES
   Pollan, Michael. *The Omnivore's Dilemma*   394.1
On A Farther Shore. Souder, William   B
On Account of Race. Goldstone, Lawrence   342.7308
On All Fronts. Ward, Clarissa   B
On Animals. Orlean, Susan   590
On Architecture. Huxtable, Ada Louise   724
On Autumn Lake. Crase, Douglas   809
On Becoming Baby Wise. Ezzo, Gary   649
★*On Censorship*. LaRue, James   025.2
On Consolation. Ignatieff, Michael   152.4
On Critical Race Theory. Ray, Victor   305.8
★*On Death and Dying*. Kubler-Ross, Elisabeth   155.9
On Democracy's Doorstep. Smith, J. Douglas   342.73
On Desperate Ground. Sides, Hampton   951.904
On Edge. Petersen, Andrea   616.85
★*On Food and Cooking*. McGee, Harold   641.5
On Garden Style. Williams, Bunny   712
On Giving up. Phillips, Adam   158.2
On Grand Strategy. Gaddis, John Lewis   355.4
On Great Fields. White, Ronald C.   B
On Haiku. Sato, Hiroaki   809.1
On Her Own Ground. Bundles, A'Lelia   B
On Highway 61. McNally, Dennis   781.64
On Hinduism. Doniger, Wendy   294.5
On His Own Terms. Smith, Richard Norton   973.925092
On Living. Egan, Kerry   170
On Michael Jackson. Jefferson, Margo   B
On My Country and the World. Gorbachev, Mikhail   947.085
On My Own. Rehm, Diane   B
On Paper. Basbanes, Nicholas A.   676
On Politics. Ryan, Alan   320.01
On Repentance and Repair. Ruttenberg, Danya   202
★*On Savage Shores*. Dodds Pennock, Caroline   970.004
On The Air. Dunning, John   791.44
★*On The Backroad to Heaven*. Kraybill, Donald B.   289.7
On The Brink. Paulson, Henry M.   330.973
On The Clock. Guendelsberger, Emily   331.0973
On The Job. Monforton, Celeste   331.1
On The Map. Garfield, Simon   526.09
★*On The Move*. Lustgarten, Abrahm   363.7
On The Move. Sacks, Oliver   B
On The Nature of Things =. Lucretius Carus, Titus   187
On The Plain of Snakes. Theroux, Paul   917
On The Rim of the Caribbean. Pressly, Paul M.   975.8

PUBLIC LIBRARY CORE COLLECTION: NONFICTION
Twentieth Edition

On The Spectrum of Possible Deaths. Perillo, Lucia — 811
On The Trail. Chamberlin, Silas — 796.510973
On Ugliness. Eco, Umberto — 111
On Vegetables. Fox, Jeremy — 641.6
On Violence and on Violence Against Women. Rose, Jacqueline — 362.88
On Wings of Eagles. Follett, Ken — 955
On Writing. King, Stephen — B
Onassis, Jacqueline Kennedy
    Historic Conversations on Life with John F. Kennedy — B
ONASSIS, JACQUELINE KENNEDY, 1929-1994
    Andersen, Christopher P. *The Good Son* — B
    Anthony, Carl Sferrazza. *Camera Girl* — B
    Hill, Clint. *Five Days in November* — 973.922092
    Hill, Clint. *Mrs. Kennedy and Me* — 973.922092
    Hill, Clint. *My Travels with Mrs. Kennedy* — B
    Kashner, Sam. *The Fabulous Bouvier Sisters* — 920
    Leaming, Barbara. *Jacqueline Bouvier Kennedy Onassis* — B
    Leaming, Barbara. *Mrs. Kennedy* — B
    McKeon, Kathy. *Jackie's Girl* — B
    Onassis, Jacqueline Kennedy. *Historic Conversations on Life with John F. Kennedy* — B
    Taraborrelli, J. Randy. *Jackie, Janet & Lee* — 920
    Taraborrelli, J. Randy. ★*Jackie* — B
Once I Was You. Hinojosa, Maria — B
Once More We Saw Stars. Greene, Jayson — 155.9
Once They Moved Like the Wind. Roberts, David — B
Once Upon a Car. Vlasic, Bill — 338.4
Once Upon a Country. Nusseibeh, Sari — B
Once Upon a Tome. Darkshire, Oliver — B
ONCOLOGISTS
    Raza, Azra. *The First Cell* — 616.99
ONCOLOGY
    Mukherjee, Siddhartha. ★*The Emperor of All Maladies* — 616.99
ONCOLOGY NURSES
    Brown, Theresa. *Healing* — 616.99
Ondaatje, Michael
    A Year of Last Things — 811
Ondra, Nancy J
    Container Theme Gardens — 635.9
One. Jones, Anna — 641.5
★*One Day*. Weingarten, Gene — 973
One Day I Will Write About This Place. Wainaina, Binyavanga — B
One Day I'll Work for Myself. Waterhouse, Benjamin C. — 338
One Day It'll All Make Sense. Common — B
One Dough, Ten Breads. Black, Sarah — 641.81
★*One* Giant Leap. Fishman, Charles — 629.45
One Goal. Bass, Amy — 796.334
One Hundred Poems from the Japanese. Rexroth, Kenneth — 895
★*One* Hundred Saturdays. Frank, Michael — B
One Kiss or Two?. Scott, Andy — 395.4
One Life. Rapinoe, Megan — B
One Man Against the World. Weiner, Tim — B
★*One* Mighty and Irresistible Tide. Yang, Jia Lynn — 325.73
One Nation Under Gold. Ledbetter, James — 332.4
One Nation Under Guns. Erdozain, Dominic — 363.33
One Native Life. Wagamese, Richard — B
★*One* Person, No Vote. Anderson, Carol — 324.6
One Person, One Vote. Seabrook, Nicholas R. — 328.3
One River. Davis, Wade — 581.6
One Step Ahead. Sally, David — 658.4
One Summer. Bryson, Bill — 973.91
One Time, One Place. Welty, Eudora — 976.2
One Vast Winter Count. Calloway, Colin G. — 978
One Way Back. Ford, Christine Blasey — B
One with Others. Wright, C. D. — 811
One Writer's Beginnings. Welty, Eudora — B
★*One* Year in Uvalde. Quinones, John — 371.7
One-Block Wonders of the World. Rosenthal, Maxine — 746.46
The *One-Cent* Magenta. Barron, James — 769.569
ONE-DISH MEALS
    Bastianich, Lidia. ★*Lidia's Pot, a Pan, and a Bowl* — 641.82
    Byrn, Anne. *Skillet Love* — 641.7
    Clark, Melissa. ★*Dinner in One* — 641.82
    Henry, Diana. *From the Oven to the Table* — 641.82
    Homolka, Gina. *Skinnytaste One & Done* — 641.5
    Jones, Anna. *One* — 641.5
    Massov, Olga. ★*Hot Sheet* — 641.82
    Shumski, Daniel. *How to Instant Pot* — 641.5

Volger, Lukas. *Bowl* — 641.81
The *One-Percent* Edge. Solovic, Susan Wilson — 658.4
Oneida. Wayland-Smith, Ellen — 307.77
ONLINE DATING
    Cole, Samantha. *How the Internet Changed Sex and Sex Changed the Internet* — 306.7
    Isenberg, Sheila. *Women Who Love Men Who Kill* — 362.83
ONLINE ETIQUETTE
    Post, Lizzie. *Emily Post's Etiquette* — 395
    Post, Lizzie. *Emily Post's Etiquette* — 395
ONLINE FRIENDSHIP
    AL Samawi, Mohammed. *The Fox Hunt* — 953
ONLINE HATE SPEECH
    Bates, Laura. *Men Who Hate Women* — 305.3
ONLINE IDENTITIES
    Irby, Samantha. *We Are Never Meeting in Real Life* — 814
ONLINE JOURNALISM
    Levitin, Daniel J. ★*A Field Guide to Lies* — 153.4
    Nagourney, Adam. *The Times* — 071
ONLINE SHOPPING
    Del Rey, Jason. *Winner Sells All* — 381
ONLINE SOCIAL NETWORKS
    Bergen, Mark. *Like, Comment, Subscribe* — 338.7
    Bilton, Nick. *Hatching Twitter* — 006.7
    Ellis, Bret Easton. *White* — 814
    Ferrazzi, Keith. *Never Eat Alone* — 658.4
    Kerpen, Dave. *Likeable Social Media* — 658.8
Only as the Day Is Long. Laux, Dorianne — 811
The *Only* Girl. Green, Robin — 070.92
Only in Naples. Wilson, Katherine — B
The *Only* One Living to Tell. Burns, Mike — 305.897
★The *Only* Plane in the Sky. Graff, Garrett M. — 973.931
The *Only* Rule Is That It Has to Work. Lindbergh, Ben — 796.357
The *Only* Street in Paris. Sciolino, Elaine — 944
Only Yesterday. Allen, Frederick Lewis — 973.9
ONTARIO
    Brown, Vanessa. *The Forest City Killer* — 364.152
    Erdrich, Louise. *Books and Islands in Ojibwe Country* — 977
    Holmes, Roger. *Midwest Home Landscaping* — 712
    Metatawabin, Edmund. *Up Ghost River* — B
    Taylor, Alan. *The Civil War of 1812* — 973.5
    Taylor, Alan. *The Divided Ground* — 974.7
    Tobin, Jacqueline. *From Midnight to Dawn* — 973.7
ONTOLOGY
    Bakewell, Sarah. ★*At the Existentialist Cafe* — 920
    Heidegger, Martin. ★*Being and Time* — 111
    Tillich, Paul. ★*The Courage to Be* — 179
Onwuachi, Kwame
    ★*Notes from a Young Black Chef* — 641.59
ONWUACHI, KWAME
    Onwuachi, Kwame. ★*Notes from a Young Black Chef* — 641.59
Open. Agassi, Andre — B
Open Access. Suber, Peter — 070.5
★*Open* Access Literature in Libraries. Brunsting, Karen — 070.5
Open Closed Open. Amichai, Yehuda — 892.4
OPEN MARRIAGE
    Dennison, Matthew. *Behind the Mask* — B
    Winter, Molly Roden. *More* — B
The *Open* Road. Campany, David — 770
The *Open* Road. Iyer, Pico — B
Open Season. Crump, Benjamin — 364
Open Skies. Rahmani, Niloofar — B
OPEN SOURCE (SOFTWARE)
    Burak, Asi. *Power Play* — 794.8
Open to Debate. Hendershot, Heather — B
Opened Ground. Heaney, Seamus — 821
Opening The Qur'an. Wagner, Walter H. — 297.1
OPERA HOUSES
    Berendt, John. *The City of Falling Angels* — 945
OPERA PRODUCERS AND DIRECTORS
    Volpe, Joseph. *The Toughest Show on Earth* — B
OPERA SINGERS
    Bergner, Daniel. ★*Sing for Your Life* — B
    Figes, Orlando. *The Europeans* — 920
OPERAS
    Berger, William. *Puccini Without Excuses* — 782.1
    Rose, Michael. *The Birth of an Opera* — 782.1
    Ross, Alex. *Wagnerism* — B

AUTHOR, TITLE, SERIES AND SUBJECT INDEX

Servadio, Gaia. *Rossini* — B
OPERATION BARBAROSSA
  Beevor, Antony. *Stalingrad* — 940.54
  Reid, Anna. *Leningrad* — 940.54
Operation Chastise. Hastings, Max — 940.54
★*Operation Mincemeat*. Macintyre, Ben — 940.54
Operation Nemesis. Bogosian, Eric — 956.62
OPERATION NEPTUNE
  Lambert, Raymond. *Every Man a Hero* — B
OPERATION OVERLORD
  Caddick-Adams, Peter. *Sand and Steel* — 940.54
  Holland, James. *Normandy '44* — 940.54
★*Operation Paperclip*. Jacobsen, Annie — 940.54
Operation Pedestal. Hastings, Max — 940.54
OPERATION RESTORE HOPE, 1992-1993
  Bowden, Mark. *Black Hawk Down* — 967.7305
Operation Vengeance. Hampton, Dan — 940.54
The Operator. O'Neill, Robert — B
★*Opinions*. Gay, Roxane — 814
OPIOID ABUSE
  Eyre, Eric. *Death in Mud Lick* — 362.29
  Higham, Scott. *American Cartel* — 338.4
  Inglis, Lucy. *Milk of Paradise* — 362.29
  Khar, Erin. *Strung Out* — B
  Leach, Samantha. ★*The Elissas* — 362.73
  Macy, Beth. ★*Dopesick* — 362.29
  Macy, Beth. ★*Raising Lazarus* — 362.29
  McGreal, Chris. *American Overdose* — 362.29
  Quinones, Sam. ★*The Least of Us* — 362.29
  Rieder, Travis. *In Pain* — 362.29
  Westhoff, Ben. *Fentanyl, Inc.* — 362.29
OPIOID EPIDEMIC
  Eyre, Eric. *Death in Mud Lick* — 362.29
  Higham, Scott. *American Cartel* — 338.4
  Hughes, Evan. *The Hard Sell* — 338.4
  Macy, Beth. ★*Dopesick* — 362.29
  Macy, Beth. ★*Raising Lazarus* — 362.29
  McGreal, Chris. *American Overdose* — 362.29
  Posner, Gerald L. ★*Pharma* — 338.4
  Quinones, Sam. ★*The Least of Us* — 362.29
  Rieder, Travis. *In Pain* — 362.29
  Westhoff, Ben. *Fentanyl, Inc.* — 362.29
OPIOIDS
  Eyre, Eric. *Death in Mud Lick* — 362.29
  Hughes, Evan. *The Hard Sell* — 338.4
  Inglis, Lucy. *Milk of Paradise* — 362.29
  Keefe, Patrick Radden. ★*Empire of Pain* — 338.7
  Macy, Beth. ★*Dopesick* — 362.29
  Macy, Beth. ★*Raising Lazarus* — 362.29
  Rieder, Travis. *In Pain* — 362.29
OPIUM
  Inglis, Lucy. *Milk of Paradise* — 362.29
  Pollan, Michael. ★*This Is Your Mind on Plants* — 581.6
OPIUM ADDICTION
  Inglis, Lucy. *Milk of Paradise* — 362.29
  Rieder, Travis. *In Pain* — 362.29
OPIUM INDUSTRY AND TRADE
  Inglis, Lucy. *Milk of Paradise* — 362.29
  Platt, Stephen R. *Imperial Twilight* — 951
  Ujifusa, Steven. *Barons of the Sea* — 387.5
Oppedisano, Tony
  Sinatra and Me — B
OPPEDISANO, TONY
  Oppedisano, Tony. *Sinatra and Me* — B
Oppenheimer, Betty
  The Candlemaker's Companion — 745.593
OPPENHEIMER, J. ROBERT, 1904-1967
  Bird, Kai. *American Prometheus* — B
  Kunetka, James W. *The General and the Genius* — 355.8
Oppenheimer, Mark
  Squirrel Hill — 364.152
Opposable Thumbs. Singer, Matt — 791.43
The Opposite of *Spoiled*. Lieber, Ron — 332.0240083
OPPOSITION (POLITICAL SCIENCE)
  Anderson, Carol. ★*White Rage* — 305.800973
  Brands, H. W. ★*Our First Civil War* — 973.3
  Levine, Robert S. *The Failed Promise* — 973.8
  Lithwick, Dahlia. *Lady Justice* — 345.73

Richardson, Heather Cox. *Democracy Awakening* — 320.473
Scheyder, Ernest. *The War Below* — 333.7
Taylor, Fred. *The Berlin Wall* — 943
OPPRESSION (PSYCHOLOGY)
  Cwiklik, Robert. *Sheridan's Secret Mission* — 973.8
  Davis, Angela Y. *Abolition* — 364.6
  Erdrich, Heid E. ★*Little Big Bully* — 811
  Feldman, Deborah. *Unorthodox* — B
  Freud, Sigmund. *Civilization and Its Discontents* — 150.19
  Izgil, Tahir Hamut. *Waiting to Be Arrested at Night* — B
  Kristof, Nicholas D. *Half the Sky* — 362.83
  Oluo, Ijeoma. ★*Be a Revolution* — 305.8
  Plant, Deborah G. *Of Greed and Glory* — 326
  Postel, Charles. *Equality* — 305.50973
  Sattouf, Riad. *The Arab of the Future 2* — 741.5
  Sattouf, Riad. *The Arab of the Future* — 741.5
  Toorpakai, Maria. *A Different Kind of Daughter* — B
  West, Cait. ★*Rift* — B
OPTIMISM
  Ehrenreich, Barbara. *Bright-Sided* — 155.2
  Fox, Michael J. *No Time Like the Future* — B
  Manson, Mark. *Everything Is F*cked* — 152.4
  Philpott, Mary Laura. *Bomb Shelter* — B
  Plantinga, Cornelius. *Gratitude* — 179
  Ridley, Matt. *The Rational Optimist* — 339.2
  Seligman, Martin E. P. ★*Learned Optimism* — 155.2
  Shriver, Maria. *I've Been Thinking ...* — 170
  Tough, Paul. ★*How Children Succeed* — 372.210973
  Tutu, Desmond. *Made for Goodness* — 170
  Van Ness, Jonathan. *Love That Story* — 791.4502
  Westheimer, Ruth. *The Doctor Is In* — B
Option B. Sandberg, Sheryl — 155.9
OPTIONS, ALTERNATIVES, CHOICES
  Berg, Anastasia. ★*What Are Children For?* — 306.87
  Bidwell, Duane R. *When One Religion Isn't Enough* — 261.2
  Blackstone, Amy. *Childfree by Choice* — 306.874
  Bloom, Amy. *In Love* — B
  Davis, Pete. *Dedicated* — 158.1
  Forche, Carolyn. *What You Have Heard Is True* — B
  Georges, Gigi. *Downeast* — 974.1
  Grover, Joanna. *The Choice Point* — 158.1
  Ice-T. *Split Decision* — 920
  Iyengar, Sheena. *The Art of Choosing* — 153.8
  McKeown, Greg. *Essentialism* — 153.8
  Pesca, Mike. *Upon Further Review* — 796
  Potts, Monica. *The Forgotten Girls* — B
  Rosling, Hans. *Factfulness* — 155.9
  Russert, Luke. *Look for Me There* — B
  Sapolsky, Robert M. *Determined* — 123
  Scheyder, Ernest. *The War Below* — 333.7
  Sharot, Tali. *Look Again* — 158.1
  Vanderbilt, Tom. *You May Also Like* — 153.8
  Vollmer, Becky. *You Are Not Stuck* — 158.1
Oracle Bones. Hessler, Peter — 951
ORACLES, GREEK
  Homer. ★*The Iliad* — 883
ORAL COMMUNICATION
  Blyth, Catherine. *The Art of Conversation* — 395.5
  Everett, Daniel Leonard. *How Language Began* — 401
  Fridland, Valerie. ★*Like, Literally, Dude* — 420.141
  Wolfe, Tom. *The Kingdom of Speech* — 401
ORAL CONTRACEPTIVES
  Eig, Jonathan. *The Birth of the Pill* — 618.1
ORAL HISTORIES
  Abrams, Jonathan P. D. ★*The Come Up* — 782.421649
  Aleksievich, Svetlana. ★*Secondhand Time* — 947.086
  Basinger, Jeanine. *Hollywood* — 791.43
  Bingham, Clara. *Witness to the Revolution* — 303.48
  Branigan, Tania. *Red Memory* — 951.05
  Graff, Garrett M. ★*The Only Plane in the Sky* — 973.931
  Greene, Andy. *The Office* — 791.45
  Hays, Katie. *Family of Origin, Family of Choice* — 248.8086
  Imperioli, Michael. *Woke up This Morning* — 791.45
  Isay, David. *Callings* — 920
  Jones, Dylan. *David Bowie* — B
  Jones, Tom. *Space Shuttle Stories* — 629.44
  Katz, Evan Ross. *Into Every Generation a Slayer Is Born* — 791.45
  Longo, Matthew. *The Picnic* — 947.084

PUBLIC LIBRARY CORE COLLECTION: NONFICTION
Twentieth Edition

MacMullan, Jackie. ★*Basketball*	796.323
Malhotra, Aanchal. *Remnants of Partition*	954.04
Moore, Wes. ★*Five Days*	363.32
Rayman, Graham. ★*Rikers*	365
Rembert, Winfred. *Chasing Me to My Grave*	B
Robb, John. *Punk Rock*	781.6609
Smith, Chris. *The Daily Show (the Book)*	791.45
Suarez, Ray. ★*We Are Home*	325.73
Terkel, Studs. *The Good War*	940.54
Terkel, Studs. ★*Hard Times*	973.91
Terkel, Studs. *Hope Dies Last*	920
Terkel, Studs. *Will the Circle Be Unbroken?*	128
Vitale, Tom. *In the Weeds*	B
Westhoff, Ben. *Original Gangstas*	782.421649
Wiederhorn, Jon. *Louder Than Hell*	781.6609
Wilbur, Matika. *Project 562*	970.004
Woolever, Laurie. *Bourdain*	B
Zucker, David. *Surely You Can't Be Serious*	791.43

ORAL HISTORY PROJECTS
Kearse, Bettye. *The Other Madisons*	920
Stein, Jean. *West of Eden*	979.4

ORAL INTERPRETATION OF POETRY
Pinsky, Robert. *The Sounds of Poetry*	808.5

ORAL SEX
Kerner, Ian. *She Comes First*	613.9

ORAL TRADITION
Saldana, Stephanie. *What We Remember Will Be Saved*	362.7

ORATORY
Blight, David W. ★*Frederick Douglass*	B

Orbanes, Philip
The Game Makers	338.7

ORBITS
Boyle, Rebecca. *Our Moon*	523.3

ORCHESTRAL MUSIC
Johnson, Graham. *Poulenc*	B
Mauceri, John. *Maestros and Their Music*	781.45
Philip, Robert. *The Classical Music Lover's Companion to Orchestral Music*	784.2
Piston, Walter. *Orchestration*	781.63

ORCHESTRAS
Mauceri, John. *Maestros and Their Music*	781.45
Orchestration. Piston, Walter	781.63
The Orchid and the Dandelion. Boyce, W. Thomas	649

ORDER (PHILOSOPHY)
Fukuyama, Francis. *Political Order and Political Decay*	320.1
Wilson, Edward O. *Consilience*	121
The Order of Time. Rovelli, Carlo	530.11

ORDERLINESS
Becker, Joshua. *The Minimalist Home*	241
Carlson, Julie. *Remodelista*	648
Casazza, Allie. *Declutter Like a Mother*	648
Davis, KC. ★*How to Keep House While Drowning*	648
Ewer, Cynthia Townley. *Cut the Clutter*	648
Gill, Shira. *Organized Living*	747
Howard, Jennifer. *Clutter*	306.3
Kondo, Marie. ★*The Life-Changing Magic of Tidying Up*	648
Kondo, Marie. ★*Spark Joy*	648
McCubbin, Tracy. *Make Space for Happiness*	179
McCubbin, Tracy. *Making Space, Clutter Free*	648
Rubin, Gretchen. *Outer Order, Inner Calm*	158
Shearer, Clea. ★*The Home Edit Life*	648
White, Dana. *How to Manage Your Home Without Losing Your Mind*	648

ORDERS OF KNIGHTHOOD AND CHIVALRY
Haag, Michael. *The Tragedy of the Templars*	271.7913
★*Ordinarily Well*. Kramer, Peter D.	615.7
The Ordinary Acrobat. Wall, Duncan	B
Ordinary Equality. Kelly, Kate	920
Ordinary Girls. Diaz, Jaquira	818
Ordinary Heroes. Pfeifer, Joseph	973.931
An Ordinary Man. Smith, Richard Norton	B
Ordinary Notes. Sharpe, Christina Elizabeth	305.896

ORDINATION OF WOMEN
Wills, Garry. *The Future of the Catholic Church with Pope Francis*	282.09

OREGON
Chung, Nicole. ★*A Living Remedy*	B
Edwards, Adrienne L. *Firescaping Your Home*	635.9
Lankford, Andrea. *Trail of the Lost*	363.2
Malarkey, Tucker. *Stronghold*	639.2

Oren, Michael B.
Six Days of War	956.04

Orenstein, Peggy
★*Boys & Sex*	305.235
Cinderella Ate My Daughter	305.23082
Don't Call Me Princess	305.42
Unraveling	B

ORENSTEIN, PEGGY
Orenstein, Peggy. *Unraveling*	B

Orenstein, Ronald I.
Ivory, Horn and Blood	333.95

Oreskes, Naomi
Merchants of Doubt	174
The Oresteia. Aeschylus	882

ORESTES (GREEK MYTHOLOGY)
Aeschylus. *The Oresteia*	882

ORGAN DONORS
Mezrich, Joshua D. *When Death Becomes Life*	617.9

ORGAN MUSIC
Whitney, Craig R. *All the Stops*	786.5
The Organ Thieves. Jones, Chip	617.4
Organic Beauty. Godas, Maru	646.7

ORGANIC COMPOUNDS
Gray, Theodore W. *Molecules*	541

ORGANIC FARMING
Coleman, Eliot. ★*The New Organic Grower*	635
Faruqi, Sonia. *Project Animal Farm*	338.1

ORGANIC GARDENING
Coleman, Eliot. ★*The New Organic Grower*	635
Cowden, Meg McAndrews. ★*Plant Grow Harvest Repeat*	635.9
Deardorff, David C. *What's Wrong with My Houseplant?*	635.9
McLaughlin, Chris. *The Good Garden*	635
Murphy, Emily. *Grow Now*	635
Smith, Edward C. *The Vegetable Gardener's Bible*	635
Webb, Leah M. *The Seven-Step Homestead*	635
Whitman, John. *Fresh from the Garden*	635.9

ORGANIC LIFESTYLE
Godas, Maru. *Organic Beauty*	646.7

ORGANISM INTRODUCTION
Egan, Dan. ★*The Death and Life of the Great Lakes*	577.6

ORGANISMS
Jabr, Ferris. ★*Becoming Earth*	570.1
Martinez Arias, Alfonso. *The Master Builder*	571.6
Sheldrake, Merlin. *Entangled Life*	579.5

ORGANISTS
Whitney, Craig R. *All the Stops*	786.5

ORGANIZATION
Howard, Jennifer. *Clutter*	306.3

ORGANIZATIONAL BEHAVIOR
Duhigg, Charles. ★*The Power of Habit*	158.1
Henry, Jo. *Cultivating Civility*	023
Porath, Christine Lynne. *Mastering Civility*	650.1
Rapping, Jonathan. *Gideon's Promise*	345.73
Schein, Edgar H. *Humble Inquiry*	302.2
Solovic, Susan Wilson. *The One-Percent Edge*	658.4
Sutton, Robert I. *The Asshole Survival Guide*	650.1
Tracy, Brian. *Full Engagement!*	658.3
Yoshino, Kenji. *Say the Right Thing*	305.3

ORGANIZATIONAL CHANGE
Bignoli, Callan. ★*Responding to Rapid Change in Libraries*	020
Cox, Gena. *Leading Inclusion*	658.3
Economy, Peter. *Wait, I'm the Boss?!?*	658
Grant, Adam M. *Originals*	153.3
Nooyi, Indra. ★*My Life in Full*	B
Phillips, Collette A. M. *The Includers*	658.4
Solovic, Susan Wilson. *The One-Percent Edge*	658.4
VanDuinkerken, Wyoma. *The Challenge of Library Management*	025.1
Webb, Maynard. *Dear Founder*	658
Weitzman, Yaron. *Tanking to the Top*	796.323
Wingfield, Adia Harvey. *Gray Areas*	331.6

ORGANIZATIONAL EFFECTIVENESS
Tracy, Brian. *Full Engagement!*	658.3

ORGANIZED CRIME
Abrams, Dan. *Kennedy's Avenger*	973.922
Assael, Shaun. *The Murder of Sonny Liston*	B
Bair, Deirdre. *Al Capone*	B
Bowden, Mark. *Life Sentence*	364.106
Bullough, Oliver. *Moneyland*	364.1

AUTHOR, TITLE, SERIES AND SUBJECT INDEX

Cannell, Michael T. *A Brotherhood Betrayed*	B
Carlo, Philip. *Gaspipe*	B
Carter, David. *Stonewall*	306.76
Carter, Stephen L. *Invisible*	B
Cox, Joseph. *Dark Wire*	363.2
Croke, Ken. *Riding with Evil*	364.106
Cullen, Kevin. *Whitey Bulger*	B
Dudley, Steven S. *MS-13*	364.106
Eig, Jonathan. *Get Capone*	364.1
English, T. J. *The Corporation*	364.106089
Fenton, Justin. *We Own This City*	364.1
Fox, Margalit. *The Talented Mrs. Mandelbaum*	364.1
Gleeson, John. *The Gotti Wars*	364.1
Goodman, Matthew. *The City Game*	796.323
Greenberg, Andy. *Tracers in the Dark*	364.16
Hill, David. *The Vapors*	976.7
Krist, Gary. *Empire of Sin*	976.3
Maier, Thomas. *Mafia Spies*	364.1060973
Manzione, Gianmarc. *Pin Action*	B
Nadeau, Barbie Latza. *The Godmother*	364.106
Risen, James. ★*The Last Honest Man*	973.92
Shackle, Samira. *Karachi Vice*	954.91
Shannon, Elaine. *Hunting Leroux*	364.1
Sherman, Casey. *Hunting Whitey*	B
Vorobyov, Niko. *Dopeworld*	364.1
ORGANIZED CRIME INVESTIGATION	
Cox, Joseph. *Dark Wire*	363.2
Organized Living. Gill, Shira	747
ORGANS (ANATOMY)	
Hazard, Leah. *Womb*	612.6
ORGASM	
Roach, Mary. *Bonk*	612.6
ORGASM, FEMALE	
Kerner, Ian. *She Comes First*	613.9
Roach, Mary. *Bonk*	612.6
Oriard, Michael	
Brand NFL	796.332
ORIENTATION	
Sobel, Dava. *Longitude*	526
ORIGAMI	
Baard, Nelliana van den. *Better Living Through Origami*	736.982
Hayakawa, Hiroshi. *Kirigami Menagerie*	736.98
Morin, John. *Inspired Origami*	736.982
Origin. Raff, Jennifer	576.5
The Origin of Humankind. Leakey, Richard E.	599.93
★*The Origin of Others*. Morrison, Toni	809
The Origin of Satan. Pagels, Elaine H.	235
★*The Origin of Species by Means of Natural Selection, Or, the Preservation of Favored Races in the St.* Darwin, Charles	575
Origin Story. Christian, David	909
Origin Story. Markel, Howard	576.8
Original Gangstas. Westhoff, Ben	782.421649
Original Sin. Jacobs, Alan	233
ORIGINAL SIN (CHRISTIAN THEOLOGY)	
Jacobs, Alan. *Original Sin*	233
ORIGINAL SPANISH-LANGUAGE MATERIALS	
Castro, M. Regina. ★*The Essential Diabetes Book*	616.4
The Originalism Trap. Dennie, Madiba K.	342.73
ORIGINALITY	
Ellenhorn, Ross D. ★*Purple Crayons*	153.3
Originals. Grant, Adam M.	153.3
The Origins of Totalitarianism. Arendt, Hannah	320.53
Orji, Yvonne	
Bamboozled by Jesus	B
ORJI, YVONNE	
Orji, Yvonne. *Bamboozled by Jesus*	B
Orkin, Ivan	
The Gaijin Cookbook	641.595
Orlando Furioso =. Ariosto, Lodovico	851
Orlean, Susan	
★*The Library Book*	027.4
On Animals	590
Rin Tin Tin	636.737
ORLEANS, LOUIS, DUC D', 1372-1407	
Jager, Eric. *Blood Royal*	944.026
Orman, Suze	
★*The Ultimate Retirement Guide for 50+*	306.3
Women & Money	332.0240082
ORMES, JACKIE, 1911-1985	
Goldstein, Nancy. *Jackie Ormes*	B
ORNAMENTAL PLANTS	
Williams, Bunny. *On Garden Style*	712
Orner, Peter	
Am I Alone Here?	814
ORNER, PETER	
Orner, Peter. *Am I Alone Here?*	814
ORNITHOLOGISTS	
Johnson, Kirk W. *The Feather Thief*	364.16
Kaufman, Kenn. *The Birds That Audubon Missed*	598
Kiser, Joy M. *America's Other Audubon*	B
ORNITHOLOGY	
Ackerman, Jennifer. *The Bird Way*	598.15
Attenborough, David. *The Life of Birds*	598.15
Davies, N. B. *Cuckoo*	598.7
Erickson, Laura. *The Love Lives of Birds*	598.15
Kaufman, Kenn. *The Birds That Audubon Missed*	598
Nicolson, Adam. *The Seabird's Cry*	598.177
Orphan Bachelors. Ng, Fae Myenne	B
ORPHANAGES	
Brookwood, Marilyn. *The Orphans of Davenport*	305.231
Doyne, Maggie. *Between the Mountain and the Sky*	B
Kenneally, Christine. *Ghosts of the Orphanage*	362.73
ORPHANS	
Albom, Mitch. *Finding Chika*	B
Black Thought. *The Upcycled Self*	B
Burns, Mike. *The Only One Living to Tell*	305.897
Kenneally, Christine. *Ghosts of the Orphanage*	362.73
Parkin, Simon. *The Island of Extraordinary Captives*	940.53
Sawaki, Kodo. *Discovering the True Self*	294.3
Saxton, Martha. *The Widow Washington*	B
Seierstad, Asne. *Angel of Grozny*	947.086
Steinberg, Jonny. *A Man of Good Hope*	B
The Orphans of Davenport. Brookwood, Marilyn	305.231
Orpheus. Wroe, Ann	398.2093802
ORPHEUS (GREEK MYTHOLOGY)	
Wroe, Ann. *Orpheus*	398.2093802
The Orpheus Clock. Goodman, Simon	940.53
Orr, Cynthia	
★*Crash Course in Readers' Advisory*	025.5
Orr, David	
You, Too, Could Write a Poem	808.1
Orr, Gregory	
A Primer for Poets & Readers of Poetry	808.1
★*Orson Welles*. Callow, Simon	B
Orson Welles (Simon Callow) [Series]. Callow, Simon	B
Orson Welles's Last Movie. Karp, Josh	791.43
Ortega Y Gasset, Jose	
What Is Philosophy?	101
Orth, Stephan	
Couchsurfing in Iran	955.06
ORTHODOX JEWISH MEN	
Mizrahi, Isaac. *I.M.*	B
ORTHODOX JEWS	
Lemay, Mimi. *What We Will Become*	306.874
ORTHODOX JUDAISM	
Armstrong, Karen. *The Battle for God*	200
Ephron, Dan. *Killing a King*	956.9405
Freedman, Samuel G. *Jew vs. Jew*	296
Glass, Sara. *Kissing Girls on Shabbat*	B
Telushkin, Joseph. *Rebbe*	296.833
Ortiz, David	
Papi	B
ORTIZ, DAVID, 1975-	
Ortiz, David. *Papi*	B
Ortiz, Paul	
An African American and Latinx History of the United States	305.8
The Orvis Fly-Fishing Guide. Rosenbauer, Tom	799.12
Orwell. Taylor, D. J.	B
Orwell's Roses. Solnit, Rebecca	B
Orwell, George	
Diaries	828
ORWELL, GEORGE, 1903-1950	
Funder, Anna. *Wifedom*	B
Lynskey, Dorian. *The Ministry of Truth*	823
Orwell, George. *Diaries*	828
Ricks, Thomas E. *Churchill and Orwell*	920

Solnit, Rebecca. *Orwell's Roses* — B
Taylor, D. J. *Orwell* — B
OSAGE (NORTH AMERICAN PEOPLE)
  Grann, David. ★*Killers of the Flower Moon* — 976.6004
OSAKA, NAOMI, 1997-
  Rothenberg, Ben. *Naomi Osaka* — B
Osborne, John
  Look Back in Anger — 822
Osborne, Richard
  Herbert Von Karajan — B
Osborne, Robert
  85 Years of the Oscar — 791.43079
Osbourne, Ozzy
  I Am Ozzy — B
OSBOURNE, OZZY, 1948-
  Osbourne, Ozzy. *I Am Ozzy* — B
Oscar Micheaux. McGilligan, Patrick — B
★*Oscar Wars*. Schulman, Michael — 791.43
Oscar Wilde. Sturgis, Matthew — B
Oscar Wilde. Ellmann, Richard — B
Oshinsky, David M.
  Bellevue — 362.1109747
  ★*Polio* — 614.5
  Worse Than Slavery — 365
OSLER, WILLIAM, SIR, 1849-1919
  Jamison, Kay Redfield. *Fires in the Dark* — 616.89
OSLO ACCORDS, 1993
  Morris, Benny. *Righteous Victims* — 956
OSMAN I, SULTAN OF THE TURKS, 1258-1326
  Finkel, Caroline. *Osman's Dream* — 956.1
Osman's Dream. Finkel, Caroline — 956.1
Osnos, Evan
  Age of Ambition — 951.06
  Joe Biden — B
  Wildland — 973.93
OSNOS, EVAN, 1976-
  Osnos, Evan. *Wildland* — 973.93
Osteen, Joel
  The Power of I Am — 248.4
Oster, Emily
  ★*Cribsheet* — 618.2
  ★*The Unexpected* — 618.2
OSTER, HANS
  Thomas, Gordon. *Defying Hitler* — 920
Ostertag, Bob
  People's Movements, People's Press — 071
Ostler, Nicholas
  Ad Infinitum — 470
OSTRACISM
  Crawford, Lacy. *Notes on a Silencing* — B
  Fessler, Pam. *Carville's Cure* — 362.19699
  Porter, Billy. ★*Unprotected* — B
Oswald, Alice
  Falling Awake — 821
OSWALD, LEE HARVEY, 1939-1963
  Abrams, Dan. *Kennedy's Avenger* — 973.922
  Posner, Gerald L. *Case Closed* — 364.1
Otfinoski, Steven
  Latinos in the Arts — 700.89
★*The Other End of the Leash*. McConnell, Patricia B. — 636.7
The Other Madisons. Kearse, Bettye — 920
Other People's Words. Soep, Elisabeth — 155.9
Other Rivers. Hessler, Peter — 378.1
★*The Other Significant Others*. Cohen, Rhaina — 177
The Other Wes Moore. Moore, Wes — B
★*Otherlands*. Halliday, Thomas — 560
OTLET, PAUL, 1868-1944
  Wright, Alex. *Cataloging the World* — 020.9
Ottaviani, Jim
  Hawking — 741.5
Ottemiller's Index to Plays in Collections. Ottemiller, John H. — 016
Ottemiller, John H.
  Ottemiller's Index to Plays in Collections — 016
Otter Country. Darlington, Miriam — 599.769
OTTERS
  Darlington, Miriam. *Otter Country* — 599.769
Otto, Mary
  Teeth — 617

Ottolenghi. Ottolenghi, Yotam — 641.59
Ottolenghi Simple. Ottolenghi, Yotam — 641.59
★*Ottolenghi Test Kitchen*. Murad, Noor — 641.3
Ottolenghi Test Kitchen. Murad, Noor — 641.5
Ottolenghi, Yotam
  ★*Jerusalem* — 641.5
  Ottolenghi Simple — 641.59
  Ottolenghi — 641.59
  ★*Plenty More* — 641.6
  Plenty — 641.6
  Sweet — 641.86
OTTOMAN EMPIRE (1299-1922)
  Crowley, Roger. *1453* — 949.61
  Finkel, Caroline. *Osman's Dream* — 956.1
  Madden, Thomas F. *Istanbul* — 949.61
  Mikhail, Alan. *God's Shadow* — B
  Pamuk, Orhan. *Istanbul* — 949.61
  Rogan, Eugene L. *The Fall of the Ottomans* — 940.3
★*Our America*. Burns, Ken — 973
Our America. Fernandez-Armesto, Felipe — 973
Our Biggest Experiment. Bell, Alice R. — 363.738
★*Our Biggest Fight*. McCourt, Frank H. — 303.48
Our Bodies, Their Battlefields. Lamb, Christina — 341.6
Our Dogs, Ourselves. Horowitz, Alexandra — 636.7
★*Our Enemies Will Vanish*. Trofimov, Yaroslav — 947.7
★*Our First Civil War*. Brands, H. W. — 973.3
★*Our Hidden Conversations*. Norris, Michele — 305
Our History Is the Future. Estes, Nick — 978.004
Our Inner Ape. Waal, F. B. M. de — 156
Our Kids. Putnam, Robert D. — 305.5
★*Our Kindred Creatures*. Wasik, Bill — 179
Our Lives, Our Fortunes and Our Sacred Honor. Beeman, Richard R. — 973.3
★*Our Malady*. Snyder, Timothy — 362.10973
Our Man. Packer, George — B
Our Man in Tokyo. Kemper, Steve — 952.03
Our Mathematical Universe. Tegmark, Max — 523.1
★*Our Migrant Souls*. Tobar, Hector — 305.868
Our Moon. Boyle, Rebecca — 523.3
Our Mothers' War. Yellin, Emily — 940.53
Our Secret Society. Ford, Tanisha C. — B
Our Stories Remember. Bruchac, Joseph — 973.04
Our Team. Epplin, Luke — 796.357
Our Time Is Now. Abrams, Stacey — 324.60973
Our Town. Wilder, Thornton — 812
Our Towns. Fallows, James M. — 306.0973
Our Wild Calling. Louv, Richard — 615.8
★*Ours Was the Shining Future*. Leonhardt, David — 330.973
Ours, Dorothy
  Man O' War — 798.400929
Out Loud. Morris, Mark — B
Out of Africa. Dinesen, Isak — 967.62
Out of Istanbul. Ollivier, Bernard — B
Out of Mao's Shadow. Pan, Philip P. — 306.20951
Out of Office. Warzel, Charlie — 658.3
★*Out of Order*. O'Connor, Sandra Day — 347.73
Out of Silence, Sound. Out of Nothing, Something. Griffin, Susan — 808.02
Out of the Corner. Grey, Jennifer — B
Out of the Darkness. Trentmann, Frank — 943.08
Out of the Storm. Wilson, Derek — B
★*Out to Work*. Kessler-Harris, Alice — 331.4
Out with It. Preston, Katherine — B
Outbreaks and Epidemics. Senthilingam, Meera — 614.4
Outcasts United. St. John, Warren — B
OUTDOOR COOKING
  Anthony, Jason C. *Hoosh* — 394.1
  Kim, Bill. *Korean BBQ* — 641.595
  Moore, Matt. *Serial Griller* — 641.7
  Purviance, Jamie. *Weber's Greatest Hits* — 641.5
  Purviance, Jamie. *Weber's Ultimate Grilling* — 641.5
  Rodriguez, Ashley. *Rooted Kitchen* — 641.5
OUTDOOR GAMES
  Gessner, David. *Ultimate Glory* — 796.2
★*Outdoor Kids in an Inside World*. Rinella, Steven — 649
OUTDOOR LIFE
  Canterbury, Dave. *Bushcraft 101* — 613.6
  McGrath, Ben. *Riverman* — 797.122
  Michaud-Skog, Summer. *Fat Girls Hiking* — 796.51
  Miles, Tiya. ★*Wild Girls* — 304.2

AUTHOR, TITLE, SERIES AND SUBJECT INDEX

Robinson, Kim Stanley. *The High Sierra*	917.94
Sprinkle, Timothy. *Lost and Stranded*	613.6
White, Dan. *Under the Stars*	796.54
OUTDOOR LIVING SPACES	
Kotite, Erika. *She Sheds*	728
Slatalla, Michelle. *Gardenista*	635
OUTDOOR RECREATION	
Burgman, John. *High Drama*	796.522
Canterbury, Dave. *Bushcraft 101*	613.6
Michaud-Skog, Summer. *Fat Girls Hiking*	796.51
Offerman, Nick. *Where the Deer and the Antelope Play*	973.93
Sprinkle, Timothy. *Lost and Stranded*	613.6
OUTDOOR RECREATION FOR CHILDREN	
Citro, Asia. *150+ Screen-Free Activities for Kids*	796.5
Striniste, Nancy. *Nature Play at Home*	796.083
Outer Order, Inner Calm. Rubin, Gretchen	158
OUTFIELDERS (BASEBALL)	
Cramer, Richard Ben. *Joe DiMaggio*	B
Leavy, Jane. *The Last Boy*	B
Outlander Kitchen. Carle-Sanders, Theresa	641.5
OUTLAWS	
Boessenecker, John. *Gentleman Bandit*	B
Clavin, Thomas. *Dodge City*	978.1
Diamond, Cheryl. *Nowhere Girl*	B
Leerhsen, Charles. ★*Butch Cassidy*	B
Stiles, T. J. *Jesse James*	B
Wallis, Michael. *Billy the Kid*	B
The Outlier. Bird, Kai	973.926
Outliers. Gladwell, Malcolm	302
★*Outlive*. Attia, Peter	612.6
Outrageous Acts and Everyday Rebellions. Steinem, Gloria	305.42
★*Outreach* Services for Teens. Snow, Jess	027.4
OUTSIDER ART	
Rembert, Winfred. *Chasing Me to My Grave*	B
Outsmarting The Sociopath Next Door. Stout, Martha	155.2
Outspoken. Rueckert, Veronica	808.5
Outwitting History. Lansky, Aaron	002
Ovenly. Kulaga, Agatha	641.81
Over The Edge of the World. Bergreen, Laurence	B
Overbooked. Becker, Elizabeth	338.4
Overcoming Life's Disappointments. Kushner, Harold S.	296.7
OVERDOING THINGS	
Jones, Dylan. *David Bowie*	B
Wiener, Anna. ★*Uncanny Valley*	B
OVEREATING	
Guyenet, Stephan J. *The Hungry Brain*	616.85
Overfishing. Hilborn, Ray	338.3
OVERFISHING	
Barnett, Cynthia. ★*The Sound of the Sea*	591.47
Ellis, Richard. *Tuna*	333.95
Hilborn, Ray. *Overfishing*	338.3
Rotman, Jeffrey L. *The Last Fisherman*	778.7
OVERLAND JOURNEYS TO THE PACIFIC	
Ambrose, Stephen E. ★*Undaunted Courage*	917.804
Brown, Daniel James. *The Indifferent Stars Above*	B
Letts, Elizabeth. ★*The Ride of Her Life*	B
Stark, Peter. *Astoria*	979.5
Wallis, Michael. *The Best Land Under Heaven*	978
Overload. Schieffer, Bob	070.4
The Overlooked Americans. Currid-Halkett, Elizabeth	307.76
Overlord. Graham, Jorie	811
Overlord. Hastings, Max	940.54
OVERPOPULATION	
Shackle, Samira. *Karachi Vice*	954.91
OVERPROTECTIVENESS IN PARENTS	
Lahey, Jessica. *The Gift of Failure*	649
Oversize Fashion Crochet. Baca, Salena	746.43
Overthinking About You. Raskin, Allison	646.7
Overy, R. J.	
Why the Allies Won	940.53
Ovid	
Tales from Ovid	873
Owen, David	
Volume Control	617.8
Where the Water Goes	917.91
OWEN, DAVID, 1955-	
Owen, David. *Where the Water Goes*	917.91
Owen, Imogen	
Modern Calligraphy Workshop	745.6
Owen, Mark	
No Easy Day	B
No Hero	B
OWEN, MARK	
Owen, Mark. *No Easy Day*	B
Owen, Mark. *No Hero*	B
Owen, Oscar	
Mind-Blowing Magic Tricks for Everyone	793.8
OWEN, WILFRED, 1893-1918	
Glass, Charles. *Soldiers Don't Go Mad*	616.85
Owens, Delia	
The Eye of the Elephant	639.9
OWENS, DELIA	
Owens, Delia. *The Eye of the Elephant*	639.9
Owens, Ernest	
★*The Case for Cancel Culture*	303.3
Owens, Jay	
Dust	551.51
Owens, Lama Rod	
Love and Rage	152.4
OWENS, MARK	
Owens, Delia. *The Eye of the Elephant*	639.9
OWLS	
Ackerman, Jennifer. ★*What an Owl Knows*	598.9
Duncan, James R. *Owls of the World*	598.9
Safina, Carl. ★*Alfie and Me*	598.9
Slaght, Jonathan C. *Owls of the Eastern Ice*	598.9
Owls of the Eastern Ice. Slaght, Jonathan C.	598.9
Owls of the World. Duncan, James R.	598.9
Owner of a Lonely Heart. Nguyen, Bich Minh	B
OWNERSHIP	
Mezrich, Ben. *Breaking Twitter*	338.7
Morris, James McGrath. *Pulitzer*	B
Small, Zachary. ★*Token Supremacy*	332.4
Waterhouse, Benjamin C. *One Day I'll Work for Myself*	338
Whyte, Kenneth. *The Uncrowned King*	B
Owning The Earth. Linklater, Andro	333.3
Owning The Sun. Zaitchik, Alexander	362.1
Owusu, Nadia	
Aftershocks	B
OWUSU, NADIA, 1981-	
Owusu, Nadia. *Aftershocks*	B
Oxenham, Gwendolyn	
Under the Lights and in the Dark	796.334
The Oxford Companion to American Literature. Hart, James David	810.9
The Oxford Companion to the American Musical. Hischak, Thomas S.	782.1
The Oxford Dictionary of Dance. Craine, Debra	792.8
★*The Oxford* Dictionary of Literary Terms. Baldick, Chris	803
The Oxford Dictionary of Philosophy. Blackburn, Simon	103
The Oxford Dictionary of Saints. Farmer, David Hugh	270
The Oxford W.E.B. Du Bois Reader. Du Bois, W. E. B.	305.896
Oxford world's classics (Oxford University Press) [Series]. Augustine	B
OXYCODONE	
Quinones, Sam. *Dreamland*	362.29
Oyeneyin, Tunde	
Speak	158.1
OYENEYIN, TUNDE	
Oyeneyin, Tunde. *Speak*	158.1
Oyler, Lauren	
No Judgment	814
OYLER, LAUREN	
Oyler, Lauren. *No Judgment*	814
OYSTERS	
Greenberg, Paul. *American Catch*	333.95
Oz, Amos	
A Tale of Love and Darkness	B
OZ, AMOS	
Oz, Amos. *A Tale of Love and Darkness*	B
Oz, Daphne	
The Happy Cook	641.5
OZARK MOUNTAIN REGION	
Potts, Monica. *The Forgotten Girls*	B
OZAWA, SEIJI, 1935-2024	
Murakami, Haruki. ★*Absolutely on Music*	784.2
Ozick, Cynthia	
Critics, Monsters, Fanatics, and Other Literary Essays	801

PUBLIC LIBRARY CORE COLLECTION: NONFICTION
Twentieth Edition

Ozment, Katherine
   Grace Without God — 200.973

P

P.S. Burn This Letter Please. Olsen, Craig — 306.76
Pablo Cruz, Rosayra
   The Book of Rosy — B
PABLO CRUZ, ROSAYRA
   Pablo Cruz, Rosayra. *The Book of Rosy* — B
   Pablo Neruda. Feinstein, Adam
Pace, Kristin Knight
   This Much Country — B
PACE, KRISTIN KNIGHT
   Pace, Kristin Knight. *This Much Country* — B
Pacific. Winchester, Simon — 909
PACIFIC AREA
   Bass, Gary Jonathan. ★*Judgment at Tokyo* — 952.04
   Bradley, James. *Flags of Our Fathers* — 940.54
   Burgin, R. V. *Islands of the Damned* — B
   Capozzola, Christopher. *Bound by War* — 355
   Frank, Richard B. *Tower of Skulls* — 940.54
   Hastings, Max. *Retribution* — 940.54
   Hillenbrand, Laura. ★*Unbroken* — B
   Iredale, Will. *The Kamikaze Hunters* — 940.54
   McManus, John C. *Fire and Fortitude* — 940.54
   McManus, John C. *Island Infernos* — 940.54
   McManus, John C. *To the End of the Earth* — 940.54
   Toll, Ian W. *The Conquering Tide* — 940.54
   Toll, Ian W. *Twilight of the Gods* — 940.54
   Wukovits, John F. *Lost at Sea* — 940.54
PACIFIC COAST (NORTH AMERICA)
   Steelquist, Robert. *The Northwest Coastal Explorer* — 508
PACIFIC CREST TRAIL
   Lankford, Andrea. *Trail of the Lost* — 363.2
   Strayed, Cheryl. ★*Wild* — B
Pacific Crucible. Toll, Ian W. — 940.54
PACIFIC ISLANDER PEOPLE
   Aguon, Julian. *No Country for Eight-Spot Butterflies* — 305.89
PACIFIC NORTHWEST
   Jackson, Mitchell S. *Survival Math* — B
   O'Connor, John. *The Secret History of Bigfoot* — 001.944
PACIFIC OCEAN
   Frank, Richard B. *Tower of Skulls* — 940.54
   Manchester, William. *Goodbye, Darkness* — B
   McManus, John C. *Fire and Fortitude* — 940.54
   McManus, John C. *Island Infernos* — 940.54
   Resendez, Andres. *Conquering the Pacific* — 959.9
   Sides, Hampton. ★*The Wide Wide Sea* — 910.92
   Simms, Brendan. *The Silver Waterfall* — 940.54
   Stanton, Doug. *In Harm's Way* — 940.54
   Symonds, Craig L. *The Battle of Midway* — 940.54
   Thomas, Evan. *Sea of Thunder* — 940.54
   Thompson, Christina. *Sea People* — 305.8994
   Tobin, James. *Ernie Pyle's War* — B
   Toll, Ian W. *Pacific Crucible* — 940.54
   Winchester, Simon. *Pacific* — 909
PACIFIC SALMON
   Malarkey, Tucker. *Stronghold* — 639.2
PACIFISM
   Guha, Ramachandra. *Gandhi Before India* — B
PACKARD, E. P. W. (ELIZABETH PARSONS WARE), 1816-1897
   Moore, Kate. ★*The Woman They Could Not Silence* — B
Packer, George
   The Assassins' Gate — 956.7044
   Last Best Hope — 973.93
   Our Man — B
   ★*The Unwinding* — 973.924
Packing for Mars. Roach, Mary — 571.0919
Padgett, Ron
   Collected Poems — 811
PAGANISM
   Adler, Margot. *Drawing Down the Moon* — 299
   Mar, Alex. *Witches of America* — 299
   Pagels, Elaine H. *The Origin of Satan* — 235
PAGE TO SCREEN
   Ackerman, Diane. ★*The Zookeeper's Wife* — 940.53

Albom, Mitch. *Tuesdays with Morrie* — B
Alderton, Dolly. *Everything I Know About Love* — B
Ambrose, Stephen E. ★*Band of Brothers* — 920
Ariely, Dan. *Predictably Irrational* — 153.8
Berendt, John. *Midnight in the Garden of Good and Evil* — 975.8
Bernstein, Carl. ★*All the President's Men* — 364.1
Bilott, Robert. *Exposure* — 344.04
Bird, Kai. *American Prometheus* — B
Bissinger, H. G. ★*Friday Night Lights* — 796.332
Bissonnette, Zac. *The Great Beanie Baby Bubble* — 338.7
Blackmon, Douglas A. *Slavery by Another Name* — 305.896
Borrell, Brendan. *The First Shots* — 615.3
Bowden, Mark. *Black Hawk Down* — 967.7305
Bradley, James. *Flags of Our Fathers* — 940.54
Brandt, Anthony K. *The Runaway Species* — 153.3
Brierley, Saroo. *A Long Way Home* — B
Brown, Daniel James. ★*The Boys in the Boat* — 797.12
Brown, Dee. ★*Bury My Heart at Wounded Knee* — 978
Bruder, Jessica. ★*Nomadland* — 331.3
Bryson, Bill. ★*A Walk in the Woods* — 917
Bugliosi, Vincent. ★*Helter Skelter* — 364.1
Bundles, A'Lelia. *On Her Own Ground* — B
Capote, Truman. ★*In Cold Blood* — 364.1
Carlin, John. *Playing the Enemy* — 968.06
Chandrasekaran, Rajiv. *Imperial Life in the Emerald City* — 956.7044
Connell, Evan S. *Son of the Morning Star* — 973.8
Davis, Michael. *Street Gang* — 791.43
Dinesen, Isak. *Out of Africa* — 967.62
Ebert, Roger. *Life Itself* — B
Edsel, Robert M. *The Monuments Men* — 940.53
Eig, Jonathan. ★*King* — B
Ellmann, Richard. *Oscar Wilde* — B
Fallows, James M. *Our Towns* — 306.0973
Faust, Drew Gilpin. *This Republic of Suffering* — 973.7
Feldman, Deborah. *Unorthodox* — B
Fenton, Justin. *We Own This City* — 364.1
Fink, Sheri. *Five Days at Memorial* — 362.1109763
Finkel, David. *Thank You for Your Service* — 920
Foer, Jonathan Safran. *Eating Animals* — 641.3
Foreman, Amanda. *Georgiana, Duchess of Devonshire* — B
Fossey, Dian. ★*Gorillas in the Mist* — 599.884
Frank, Anne. ★*The Diary of a Young Girl* — 940.53
Gates, Henry Louis. ★*The Black Church* — 277
Gibran, Kahlil. ★*The Prophet* — 811
Gilbert, Elizabeth. *Eat, Pray, Love* — B
Goodwin, Doris Kearns. ★*Team of Rivals* — B
Grann, David. ★*Killers of the Flower Moon* — 976.6004
Grann, David. *The Lost City of Z* — 918.1
Grogan, John. ★*Marley & Me* — 636.752
Harris, Jessica B. *High on the Hog* — 641.59
Herrera, Hayden. *Frida*
Herriot, James. ★*All Creatures Great and Small* — B
Herriot, James. *All Things Wise and Wonderful* — B
Hickam, Homer H. ★*Rocket Boys* — B
Hillenbrand, Laura. ★*Seabiscuit* — 798.4
Hillenbrand, Laura. ★*Unbroken* — B
Homer. *The Iliad* — 883
Homer. ★*The Iliad* — 883
Homer. *The Odyssey* — 883
Homer. *The Odyssey* — 883
Homer. *Odyssey* — 883
Homer. ★*The Odyssey* — 883
Huang, Eddie. *Fresh off the Boat* — B
Hughes, Evan. *The Hard Sell* — 338.4
Huxley, Elspeth Joscelin Grant. *The Flame Trees of Thika* — B
Jaouad, Suleika. ★*Between Two Kingdoms* — B
Junger, Sebastian. *The Perfect Storm* — 974.4
Kamkwamba, William. ★*The Boy Who Harnessed the Wind* — B
Kantor, Jodi. *She Said* — 364.15
Kavanagh, Julie. *Nureyev* — B
Kendi, Ibram X. ★*Stamped from the Beginning* — 305.8
Koppel, Lily. *The Astronaut Wives Club* — 920
Krakauer, Jon. *Into the Wild* — 917.9804
Kristof, Nicholas D. *Half the Sky* — 362.83
Land, Stephanie. *Maid* — B
Lapierre, Dominique. *The City of Joy* — 954
Laskas, Jeanne Marie. *Concussion* — 617.5
Lawrence, T. E. *Seven Pillars of Wisdom* — 940.4

AUTHOR, TITLE, SERIES AND SUBJECT INDEX

Levin, Daniel Barban. *Slonim Woods 9* — B
Levitt, Steven D. ★*Freakonomics* — 330
Lewis, Michael. *The Blind Side* — B
Lewis, Michael. ★*Moneyball* — 796.357
Lipstadt, Deborah E. *History on Trial* — 940.53
Locke, Tembi. ★*From Scratch* — B
Lord, Walter. ★*A Night to Remember* — 910
Luttrell, Marcus. *Lone Survivor* — 958.104
Macintyre, Ben. ★*Operation Mincemeat* — 940.54
Macintyre, Ben. *A Spy Among Friends* — B
Macy, Beth. ★*Dopesick* — 362.29
Makos, Adam. *Devotion* — 920
Malcolm X. ★*The Autobiography of Malcolm X* — B
Mandela, Nelson. ★*Long Walk to Freedom* — 945
Manson, Mark. *The Subtle Art of Not Giving a F*ck* — 158.1
Mayes, Frances. *Under the Tuscan Sun* — 945
McCarten, Anthony. *Darkest Hour* — 941.084
McCourt, Frank. ★*Angela's Ashes* — 929
McCullough, David G. ★*John Adams* — B
McNamara, Michelle. *I'll Be Gone in the Dark* — 364.152
Mendez, Antonio J. *Argo* — 955.05
Miller, Donald L. ★*Masters of the Air* — 940.54
Miller, T. Christian. *A False Report* — 364.15
Moore, Harold G. *We Were Soldiers Once—And Young* — 959.704
Northup, Solomon. *Twelve Years a Slave* — B
Nosrat, Samin. ★*Salt, Fat, Acid, Heat* — 641.5
Nyad, Diana. *Find a Way* — B
Oz, Amos. *A Tale of Love and Darkness* — B
Pollan, Michael. *How to Change Your Mind* — 615.7
Powell, Julie. *Julie and Julia* — 641.5
Quin, Tegan. ★*High School* — B
Rakoff, Joanna Smith. *My Salinger Year* — B
Ralston, Aron. *Between a Rock and a Hard Place* — 796.522
Rapkin, Mickey. *Pitch Perfect* — 782.5
Read, Piers Paul. ★*Alive* — 982
Ruffin, Amber. *You'll Never Believe What Happened to Lacey* — 305.896
Rule, Ann. *The Stranger Beside Me* — B
Satrapi, Marjane. *Chicken with Plums* — 741.5
Scahill, Jeremy. *Dirty Wars* — 355.00973
Schreiber, Flora Rheta. *Sybil* — 616.85
Sestero, Greg. *The Disaster Artist* — 791.43
Shetterly, Margot Lee. ★*Hidden Figures* — 510.92
Shilts, Randy. ★*And the Band Played On* — 362.196
Skloot, Rebecca. ★*The Immortal Life of Henrietta Lacks* — B
Sobel, Dava. *Longitude* — 526
Sorkin, Andrew Ross. *Too Big to Fail* — 330.973
Stanton, Doug. *12 Strong* — 958.104
Stelter, Brian. *Top of the Morning* — 791.456
Stevenson, Bryan. *Just Mercy* — B
Strayed, Cheryl. ★*Wild* — B
Sweig, Julia. *Lady Bird Johnson* — B
Swofford, Anthony. *Jarhead* — 956.7044
Thompson, Hunter S. ★*Fear and Loathing in America* — B
Vance, J. D. *Hillbilly Elegy* — B
Walls, Jeannette. ★*The Glass Castle* — B
West, Lindy. *Shrill* — 818
Wilkerson, Isabel. ★*Caste* — 305.5
Wolfe, Tom. ★*The Right Stuff* — 629.4
Wolff, Tobias. *This Boy's Life* — B
Woolley, Benjamin. *The King's Assassin* — B
Wright, Lawrence. *Going Clear* — 299
Wright, Lawrence. ★*The Looming Tower* — 973.931

Page, Elliot
  Pageboy — B
PAGE, ELLIOT, 1987-
  Page, Elliot. *Pageboy* — B
PAGE, JIMMY
  Tolinski, Brad. *Light and Shade* — B
Page, Karen
  The Flavor Bible — 641.5
Page, Lawrence M.
  ★*Peterson Field Guide to Freshwater Fishes of North America North of Mexico* — 597.176
Page, Scott E
  The Model Thinker — 001.4
Page, Susan
  ★*The Matriarch* — B
  ★*The Rulebreaker* — B

Pageboy. Page, Elliot — B
Pagels, Elaine H.
  Beyond Belief — 229
  ★*The Gnostic Gospels* — 273
  The Origin of Satan — 235
  ★*Why Religion?* — B
PAGELS, ELAINE H., 1943-
  Pagels, Elaine H. ★*Why Religion?* — B
Paglia, Camille
  ★*Break, Blow, Burn* — 821.009
Paid For. Moran, Rachel — 306.74082
PAIGE, SATCHEL, 1906-1982
  Epplin, Luke. *Our Team* — 796.357
  Tye, Larry. *Satchel* — B
PAIN
  Gorman, Amanda. ★*Call Us What We Carry* — 811
  Gupta, Shalene. *The Cycle* — 618.1
  Hughes, Evan. *The Hard Sell* — 338.4
  Jamison, Leslie. *The Empathy Exams* — 813
  Jones, Saeed. *Alive at the End of the World* — 811
  Lalkhen, Abdul-Ghaaliq. *An Anatomy of Pain* — 616
  Lembke, Anna. *Dopamine Nation* — 152.4
  Limon, Ada. ★*The Hurting Kind* — 811
  Ramey, Sarah. *The Lady's Handbook for Her Mysterious Illness* — 362.29
  Rieder, Travis. *In Pain* — 362.29
  Rosner, Elizabeth. *Survivor Cafe* — 940.53
  Sauls, Scott. *Beautiful People Don't Just Happen* — 248.8
  Standefer, Katherine E. *Lightning Flowers* — B
  Warraich, Haider. *The Song of Our Scars* — 616
PAIN CONTROL
  Kempner, Joanna. *Psychedelic Outlaws* — 615.7
  Lalkhen, Abdul-Ghaaliq. *An Anatomy of Pain* — 616
  McGreal, Chris. *American Overdose* — 362.29
  Rieder, Travis. *In Pain* — 362.29
Pain, Parties, Work. Winder, Elizabeth — B
Paine, Thomas
  ★*Rights of Man* — 320.5
PAINE, THOMAS, 1737-1809
  Moore, Peter. *Life, Liberty, and the Pursuit of Happiness* — 199
  Phillips, Kevin. *1775* — 973.3
Painter, Nell Irvin
  ★*I Just Keep Talking* — 814
  Old in Art School — B
  ★*Sojourner Truth* — B
PAINTER, NELL IRVIN
  Painter, Nell Irvin. *Old in Art School* — B
PAINTERS
  Albers, Patricia. *Joan Mitchell* — B
  Bell, Julian. *Van Gogh* — B
  Blom, Onno. *Young Rembrandt* — B
  Cohen-Solal, Annie. *Mark Rothko* — 759.13
  Cross, William R. *Winslow Homer* — 759.13
  Eisler, Benita. *The Red Man's Bones* — B
  Evans, R. Tripp. *Grant Wood* — B
  Feaver, William. ★*The Lives of Lucian Freud* — B
  Graham-Dixon, Andrew. *Caravaggio* — B
  Hale, Sheila. *Titian* — B
  Herdrich, Stephanie L. ★*Sargent* — 759.13
  Herrera, Hayden. *Frida* — B
  Hewitt, Catherine. *Renoir's Dancer* — B
  Kahlo, Frida. *The Diary of Frida Kahlo* — B
  Kamensky, Jane. *A Revolution in Color* — 759.13
  King, Ross. *The Judgment of Paris* — 759.4
  King, Ross. ★*Mad Enchantment* — 759.4
  Knausgaard, Karl Ove. *So Much Longing in so Little Space* — 759.81
  Marnham, Patrick. *Dreaming with His Eyes Open* — B
  Moyle, Franny. *Turner* — B
  Naifeh, Steven W. *Van Gogh* — B
  Prideaux, Sue. *Edvard Munch* — B
  Prose, Francine. *Caravaggio* — 759.5
  Roe, Sue. *The Private Lives of the Impressionists* — 920
  Secrest, Meryle. *Modigliani* — B
  Snyder, Laura J. *Eye of the Beholder* — 920
  Solomon, Deborah. *American Mirror* — B
  Solomon, Deborah. *Jackson Pollock* — B
  Spurling, Hilary. *Matisse the Master* — B
  Staiti, Paul J. *Of Arms and Artists* — B
  Tomlinson, Janis A. ★*Goya* — B

PUBLIC LIBRARY CORE COLLECTION: NONFICTION
Twentieth Edition

Unger, Miles. *Picasso and the Painting That Shocked the World*	759.4
Ustvedt, Oystein. *Edvard Munch*	759.81
Wullschlager, Jackie. ★*Chagall*	B

PAINTING

Baker, Nicholson. *Finding a Likeness*	B
Blair, Barb. *Furniture Makeovers*	684.1
Graham-Dixon, Andrew. *Caravaggio*	B
Herdrich, Stephanie L. ★*Sargent*	759.13
Joyce, Anna. *Stamp Stencil Paint*	745.7
Jung, Kwan. *Chinese Brush Painting*	751.4
Katsushika, Hokusai. *Hokusai*	769.92
Kersey, Geoff. *Painting Successful Watercolours from Photographs*	751.42
Kiser, Joy M. *America's Other Audubon*	B
Kundera, Milan. *Encounter*	809
Prideaux, Sue. *Edvard Munch*	B
Scotti, R. A. *Vanished Smile*	759.5
Self, Caroline. *Chinese Brush Painting*	751.4
Seuss, Diane. *Still Life with Two Dead Peacocks and a Girl*	811.6
Sloan, Annie. *Color Recipes for Painted Furniture and More*	745.7
Stahr, Celia. *Frida in America*	B
Staiti, Paul J. *Of Arms and Artists*	B
Unger, Miles. *Picasso and the Painting That Shocked the World*	759.4
Ustvedt, Oystein. *Edvard Munch*	759.81
Ward, Ossian. *Look Again*	750.1
Wullschlager, Jackie. ★*Chagall*	B
Painting in Acrylics. Kloosterboer, Lorena	751.42
Painting Successful Watercolours from Photographs. Kersey, Geoff	751.42

PAINTING TECHNIQUE

Barnes, Julian. *Keeping an Eye Open*	709.04
Crilley, Mark. *The Realism Challenge*	751.4
Evans, R. Tripp. *Grant Wood*	B
Griffel, Lois. *Painting the Impressionist Landscape*	751.45
Jung, Kwan. *Chinese Brush Painting*	751.4
Kersey, Geoff. *Painting Successful Watercolours from Photographs*	751.42
Kloosterboer, Lorena. *Painting in Acrylics*	751.42
Marine, Carol. *Daily Painting*	751.4
O'Connor, Birgit. *Watercolor Essentials*	751.42
Robinson, Mario Andres. *Lessons in Realistic Watercolor*	751.42
Self, Caroline. *Chinese Brush Painting*	751.4
Painting The Impressionist Landscape. Griffel, Lois	751.45
Painting with Pastels. Price, Maggie	741.2

PAINTING, AMERICAN

Gerdts, William H. *American Impressionism*	759.13

PAINTING, DUTCH

Blom, Onno. *Young Rembrandt*	B

PAINTING, FRENCH

Kelder, Diane. *The Great Book of French Impressionism*	759.4
King, Ross. *The Judgment of Paris*	759.4
King, Ross. ★*Mad Enchantment*	759.4
Spurling, Hilary. *Matisse the Master*	B

PAINTING, ITALIAN

Hale, Sheila. *Titian*	B
King, Ross. *Florence*	759.5
King, Ross. ★*Leonardo and the Last Supper*	759.5

PAINTING, MODERN

Pepin, Jacques. ★*Jacques Pépin Cooking My Way*	641.5
Tomlinson, Janis A. ★*Goya*	B

PAINTING, RENAISSANCE (EUROPE)

Brewer, John. *The American Leonardo*	759.5
Hale, Sheila. *Titian*	B
King, Ross. *Florence*	759.5

PAINTING, SPANISH

Tomlinson, Janis A. ★*Goya*	B
The Paintings of Joan Mitchell. Livingston, Jane	759.13

Pak, Jung H.

Becoming Kim Jong Un	B
Pakistan. Lieven, Anatol	954.9105

PAKISTAN

Baker, Deborah. *The Convert*	B
Bhutto, Benazir. *Reconciliation*	297.2
Carney, Scott. *The Vortex*	954.92
Coll, Steve. *Directorate S*	958.104
Eteraz, Ali. *Children of Dust*	B
Hajari, Nisid. *Midnight's Furies*	954.04
Langewiesche, William. *The Atomic Bazaar*	355.02
Lieven, Anatol. *Pakistan*	954.9105
Malhotra, Aanchal. *Remnants of Partition*	954.04
Toorpakai, Maria. *A Different Kind of Daughter*	B
Wallace, Chris. *Countdown Bin Laden*	958.104
Walsh, Declan. *The Nine Lives of Pakistan*	954.91
Yousafzai, Malala. *I Am Malala*	B

PAKISTANI AMERICANS

Ali, Fatima. ★*Savor*	B
Ali, Wajahat. *Go Back to Where You Came From*	B
Chaudry, Rabia. *Fatty Fatty Boom Boom*	B
Rehman, Sabeeha. *Threading My Prayer Rug*	305.8

PAKISTANI PEOPLE IN THE UNITED STATES

Eteraz, Ali. *Children of Dust*	B

Pakula, Hannah

The Last Empress	B
★*The Palace*. Russell, Gareth	942.1
★*The Palace* Papers. Brown, Tina	920

PALACES

Eisen, Norman L. *The Last Palace*	920
Russell, Gareth. ★*The Palace*	942.1

Palahniuk, Chuck

Consider This	B

PALAHNIUK, CHUCK

Palahniuk, Chuck. *Consider This*	B
Pale Blue Dot. Sagan, Carl	919
★*Pale Rider*. Spinney, Laura	614.5

PALEO-INDIGENOUS PEOPLES OF NORTH AMERICA

Childs, Craig. *Atlas of a Lost World*	551.7

PALEOBIOLOGY

Halliday, Thomas. ★*Otherlands*	560

PALEOCLIMATOLOGY

Fagan, Brian M. *Climate Chaos*	304.2
Macdougall, J. D. *Frozen Earth*	551.7

PALEOECOLOGY

Childs, Craig. *Atlas of a Lost World*	551.7
Halliday, Thomas. ★*Otherlands*	560

PALEOGRAPHY

Porter, Carolyn. *Marcel's Letters*	940.54

PALEONTOLOGY

Brusatte, Stephen. ★*The Rise and Fall of the Dinosaurs*	567.9
Flannery, Tim F. *Europe*	508.4
Lacovara, Kenneth. *Why Dinosaurs Matter*	567.9
Larson, Edward J. *Evolution*	576.8
MacPhee, R. D. E. *End of the Megafauna*	591.4
Pattison, Kermit. *Fossil Men*	569.9
Raff, Jennifer. *Origin*	576.5
Yi, Sang-Hui. *Close Encounters with Humankind*	599.93
Palestine. Carter, Jimmy	956.04

PALESTINE

Ahmad, Aeham. *The Pianist from Syria*	B
Carter, Jimmy. *Palestine*	956.04
Friedman, Matti. *Spies of No Country*	327.12
Hoffman, Adina. ★*My Happiness Bears No Relation to Happiness*	B
Hoffman, Bruce. *Anonymous Soldiers*	956.94
Kattan, Fadi. ★*Bethlehem*	641.59
Khalidi, Rashid. ★*The Hundred Years' War on Palestine*	956.9405
Khan, Yasmin. ★*Zaitoun*	641.595
Mitchell, George J. *A Path to Peace*	956.9405
Morris, Benny. *1948*	956.04
Morris, Benny. *Righteous Victims*	956
Nusseibeh, Sari. *Once Upon a Country*	B
Nye, Naomi Shihab. *The Tiny Journalist*	811
Sefarad, Mikhael. *The Wall and the Gate*	341.48
Shehadeh, Raja. *Where the Line Is Drawn*	956.9405
Sokatch, Daniel. *Can We Talk About Israel?*	956.9405
Tamimi, Sami. *Falastin*	641.595

PALESTINIAN AMERICANS

Sarsour, Linda. *We Are Not Here to Be Bystanders*	B

PALESTINIAN MEN

Shehadeh, Raja. ★*We Could Have Been Friends, My Father and I*	B
Thrall, Nathan. ★*A Day in the Life of Abed Salama*	956.05
The Palestinian People. Kimmerling, Baruch	956.94

PALESTINIAN PEOPLE

Abu Sayf, Atif. *The Drone Eats with Me*	B
Abuelaish, Izzeldin. *I Shall Not Hate*	B
Di Cintio, Marcello. *Pay No Heed to the Rockets*	956.9405
Ehrenreich, Ben. *The Way to the Spring*	956.95
Friedman, Thomas L. ★*From Beirut to Jerusalem*	956.04
Grossman, David. *The Yellow Wind*	956.95
Halevi, Yossi Klein. ★*Letters to My Palestinian Neighbor*	956.94054
Kattan, Fadi. ★*Bethlehem*	641.59

AUTHOR, TITLE, SERIES AND SUBJECT INDEX

Kimmerling, Baruch. *The Palestinian People*	956.94
Nusseibeh, Sari. *Once Upon a Country*	B
Nye, Naomi Shihab. *The Tiny Journalist*	811
Pappe, Ilan. *The Biggest Prison on Earth*	956.9405
Qashu, Sayed. *Native*	892.4
Sacco, Joe. *Footnotes in Gaza*	741.5
Sefarad, Mikhael. *The Wall and the Gate*	341.48
Shehadeh, Raja. ★*We Could Have Been Friends, My Father and I*	B
Tamimi, Ahed. ★*They Called Me a Lioness*	B
Tolan, Sandy. ★*The Lemon Tree*	B

Palin, Michael
   North Korea Journal   951.9305

PALIN, MICHAEL
   Palin, Michael. *North Korea Journal*   951.9305

PALLENBERG, ANITA
   Winder, Elizabeth. *Parachute Women*   782.42164

PALLIATIVE TREATMENT
Brody, Jane E. *Jane Brody's Guide to the Great Beyond*	616
Clarke, Rachel. *Dear Life*	B
Speerstra, Karen. *The Divine Art of Dying*	202
Volandes, Angelo E. *The Conversation*	616.02

Palmer, Amanda
   ★*The Art of Asking*   782.42164

PALMER, AMANDA, 1976-
   Palmer, Amanda. ★*The Art of Asking*   782.42164

Palmer, Arnold
   A Golfer's Life   B

PALMER, ARNOLD, 1929-2016
Callahan, Tom. *Arnie*	B
Palmer, Arnold. *A Golfer's Life*	B

Palmieri, Jennifer
Dear Madam President	158
She Proclaims	305.42

Paltrow, Gwyneth
   It's All Easy   641.5

Pamuk, Orhan
   Istanbul   949.61

PAMUK, ORHAN, 1952-
   Pamuk, Orhan. *Istanbul*   949.61

Pan, Philip P.
   Out of Mao's Shadow   306.20951

Panagore, Peter Baldwin
   Heaven Is Beautiful   B

PANAGORE, PETER BALDWIN
   Panagore, Peter Baldwin. *Heaven Is Beautiful*   B

PANAMA
McCullough, David G. *The Path Between the Seas*	972.87
Thomson, Keith. *Born to Be Hanged*	910.4

PANAMA CANAL
McCullough, David G. *The Path Between the Seas*	972.87
Morris, Edmund. ★*Theodore Rex*	973.911
Parker, Matthew. *Panama Fever*	972.87

Panama Fever. Parker, Matthew   972.87

PANCREATIC CANCER
   Schwalbe, Will. ★*The End of Your Life Book Club*   B

The Pandemic Century. Honigsbaum, Mark   614.4
★*Pandemic, Inc.* McSwane, J. David   362.1962
Pandora's Box. Biskind, Peter   791.45

Panek, Richard
   The Trouble with Gravity   531

PANETTA, LEON E., 1938-
   Wallace, Chris. *Countdown Bin Laden*   958.104

Pang, Amelia
   ★*Made in China*   331.11

Pang, Kevin
   A Very Chinese Cookbook   641.595

PANIC
Hoffman, Liz. *Crash Landing*	330
Zia, Helen. *Last Boat Out of Shanghai*	951.04

PANIC ATTACKS
Gutman, Matt. ★*No Time to Panic*	616.85
Haig, Matt. *Notes on a Nervous Planet*	616.89

PANIC DISORDERS
Gutman, Matt. ★*No Time to Panic*	616.85
Stern, Amanda. *Little Panic*	616.8522

★*The Panic of 1907, 2nd Ed.* Bruner, Robert F.   330.973

Pansino, Rosanna
   Baking All Year Round   641.86

PANTHERS
   Pittman, Craig. *Cat Tale*   599.75

Pantsov, Alexander
   Mao   B

PAPACY
Duffy, Eamon. *Saints & Sinners*	262
Kertzer, David I. *The Pope and Mussolini*	322
Kertzer, David I. *The Pope Who Would Be King*	282.092
McBrien, Richard P. *Lives of the Popes*	B
McGreevy, John T. ★*Catholicism*	282.09

Papenfuss, Mary
   American Huckster   B

Paper. Kurlansky, Mark   676

PAPER
Basbanes, Nicholas A. *On Paper*	676
Kurlansky, Mark. *Paper*	676

PAPER FLOWERS
Cetti, Livia. *The Exquisite Book of Paper Flowers*	745.594
Thuss, Rebecca. *Paper to Petal*	745.54
Turner, Tiffanie. *The Fine Art of Paper Flowers*	745.92
Yamazaki, Hiromi. *Japanese Paper Flowers*	745.594

PAPER INDUSTRY AND TRADE
Basbanes, Nicholas A. *On Paper*	676
Kurlansky, Mark. *Paper*	676

PAPER MILLS
   Arsenault, Kerri. *Mill Town*   B

PAPER MONEY
   Lowenstein, Roger. *Ways and Means*   973.7

The Paper Playhouse. Rodabaugh, Katrina   745.5

PAPER PRODUCTS
   Basbanes, Nicholas A. *On Paper*   676

Paper to Petal. Thuss, Rebecca   745.54

PAPER WORK
Basbanes, Nicholas A. *On Paper*	676
Descamps, Ghylenn. *Beginner's Guide to Kirigami*	745.54
Gilleland, Diane. *All Points Patchwork*	746.46
Watanabe, Judi. *The Complete Photo Guide to Cardmaking*	745.594

Paperback Crush. Moss, Gabrielle   813.009

PAPERMAKING
Basbanes, Nicholas A. *On Paper*	676
Kurlansky, Mark. *Paper*	676

Paperny, Anna Mehler
   Hello I Want to Die Please Fix Me   362.2

PAPERNY, ANNA MEHLER
   Paperny, Anna Mehler. *Hello I Want to Die Please Fix Me*   362.2

Papi. Ortiz, David   B

PAPP, JOSEPH, 1921-1991
   Turan, Kenneth. ★*Free for All*   B

Pappe, Ilan
   The Biggest Prison on Earth   956.9405

PAPPENHEIM, BERTHA, 1859-1936
   Brownstein, Gabriel. ★*The Secret Mind of Bertha Pappenheim*   616.85

Pappu, Sridhar
   The Year of the Pitcher   920

PAPUA NEW GUINEA
   Campbell, James. *The Ghost Mountain Boys*   940.54

PARACHUTE TROOPS
Beevor, Antony. *The Battle of Arnhem*	940.54
Lewis, Damien. *Churchill's Hellraisers*	940.54

Parachute Women. Winder, Elizabeth   782.42164

Paradis, Michel
   The Light of Battle   940.54

★*Paradise*. Johnson, Lizzie   363.37

PARADISE
Dante Alighieri. *The Paradiso*	851
Dante Alighieri. *Paradiso*	851
Iyer, Pico. ★*The Half Known Life*	203
Laing, Olivia. *The Garden Against Time*	635

A Paradise Built in Hell. Solnit, Rebecca   303.48
Paradise Falls. O'Brien, Keith   363.738
Paradise in Chains. Preston, Diana   996.18
Paradise Lost. Brown, David S.   813
A Paradise of Small Houses. Podemski, Max   363.5
Paradise of the Pacific. Moore, Susanna   996.9
The Paradiso. Dante Alighieri   851
Paradiso. Dante Alighieri   851
Parallax. Morrissey, Sinead   821

PUBLIC LIBRARY CORE COLLECTION: NONFICTION
Twentieth Edition

PARALLEL UNIVERSES
- Kaku, Michio. *Parallel Worlds* — 523.1
- Tegmark, Max. *Our Mathematical Universe* — 523.1
- *Parallel Worlds*. Kaku, Michio — 523.1

PARALYSIS
- Okorafor, Nnedi. *Broken Places & Outer Spaces* — 153.3
- Raban, Jonathan. *Father and Son* — B

PARAMEDICS
- Hazzard, Kevin. *A Thousand Naked Strangers* — B
- Hazzard, Kevin M. *American Sirens* — 362.18
- Lambert, Raymond. *Every Man a Hero* — B

PARAMILITARY FORCES
- Ackerman, Elliot. *The Fifth Act* — 958.104
- Jacobsen, Annie. *Surprise, Kill, Vanish* — 327.1273

PARAMOURS
- Fraser, Antonia. *Love and Louis XIV* — B
- Gortemaker, Heike B. *Eva Braun* — B

PARANOIA
- Betz-Hamilton, Axton. *The Less People Know About Us* — 364.16
- Kim, Suki. *Without You, There Is No Us* — B

PARANORMAL PHENOMENA
- Aykroyd, Peter. *A History of Ghosts* — 133.1
- Blum, Deborah. *Ghost Hunters* — 133.9
- Braudy, Leo. *Haunted* — 398.45
- Clegg, Brian. *Extra Sensory* — 133.8
- Dickey, Colin. *Ghostland* — 133.1
- Dickey, Colin. *The Unidentified* — 130
- Guiley, Rosemary. *The Encyclopedia of Demons and Demonology* — 133.4
- Jacobsen, Annie. *Phenomena* — 133.8
- Manseau, Peter. *The Apparitionists* — B
- Mezrich, Ben. *The 37th Parallel* — 001.942
- Prothero, Donald R. *UFOs, Chemtrails, and Aliens* — 001.94
- Roach, Mary. ★*Spook* — 129
- Smith, Richard MacLean. *Unexplained* — 130

Paranque, Estelle
- *Blood, Fire & Gold* — 920

PARASITES
- Simon, Matt. *Plight of the Living Dead* — 591.6

PARASITISM
- Simon, Matt. *The Wasp That Brainwashed the Caterpillar* — 578.4

Parcells. Parcells, Bill — B

Parcells, Bill
- *Parcells* — B

PARCELLS, BILL, 1941-
- Parcells, Bill. *Parcells* — B

Pardlo, Gregory
- *Air Traffic* — B
- *Spectral Evidence* — 811

PARDLO, GREGORY
- Pardlo, Gregory. *Air Traffic* — B

PARDON
- Manning, Chelsea. *Readme.Txt* — B
- Minow, Martha. *When Should Law Forgive?* — 345

PARENT AND ADULT CHILD
- Chast, Roz. ★*Can't We Talk About Something More Pleasant?* — 741.5
- Hibbs, B. Janet. *You're Not Done Yet* — 649
- Kline, Emily. ★*The School of Hard Talks* — 155.5
- Lockwood, Patricia. *Priestdaddy* — B
- McConville, Mark. *Failure to Launch* — 155.6
- Satrapi, Marjane. ★*The Complete Persepolis* — 741.5

PARENT AND BABY
- Bryson, Tina Payne. *The Bottom Line for Baby* — 618.92
- Ezzo, Gary. *On Becoming Baby Wise* — 649
- Kurcinka, Mary Sheedy. *Raising Your Spirited Baby* — 306.874

PARENT AND CHILD
- Airton, Lee. ★*Gender* — 305.3
- Arment, Ainsley. *The Wild + Free Family* — 649
- Bechdel, Alison. ★*Fun Home* — 741.5
- Birbiglia, Mike. *The New One* — B
- Bond, Melissa. *Blood Orange Night* — 616.8
- Brookwood, Marilyn. *The Orphans of Davenport* — 305.231
- Brown, Noah. *Reading Together* — 028.5
- Carey, Tanith. *What's My Child Thinking?* — 155.4
- Ford, Richard. *Between Them* — B
- Franklin, Missy. *Relentless Spirit* — B
- Gaffigan, Jim. *Dad Is Fat* — 814
- Gopnik, Alison. *The Gardener and the Carpenter* — 155.4
- Harpham, Heather Elise. *Happiness* — B

- Jollett, Mikel. ★*Hollywood Park* — B
- Lieber, Ron. *The Opposite of Spoiled* — 332.0240083
- Marschark, Marc. ★*How Deaf Children Learn* — 371.91
- McCarthy, Catherine. *Raising a Kid Who Can* — 649
- Mogel, Wendy. *Voice Lessons for Parents* — 649
- Morton, Brian. *Tasha* — B
- Natterson, Cara Familian. ★*Decoding Boys* — 649
- Perry, Philippa. ★*The Book You Wish Your Parents Had Read* — 649
- Pressman, Aliza. *The 5 Principles of Parenting* — 649.1
- Pullman, Philip. ★*Fairy Tales from the Brothers Grimm* — 398.2
- Rippon, Kelly. *Parent Up* — 649
- Rowe, Peggy. *About My Mother* — B
- Saline, Sharon. *What Your ADHD Child Wishes You Knew* — 618.92
- Senior, Jennifer. *All Joy and No Fun* — 306.874
- Siegel, Daniel J. *Parenting from the Inside Out* — 649
- Siegel, Daniel J. *The Power of Showing Up* — 649
- Solomon, Andrew. *Far from the Tree* — 362.4083
- Stern, Amanda. *Little Panic* — 616.8522
- Stixrud, William R. ★*What Do You Say?* — 155.4
- Van't Hul, Jean. *The Artful Parent* — 745.5083
- Vlock, Deborah. *Parenting Children with Mental Health Challenges* — 618.92
- Wong, Ali. ★*Dear Girls* — B

PARENT AND TEENAGER
- Apter, T. E. *The Teen Interpreter* — 306.874
- Damour, Lisa. *The Emotional Lives of Teenagers* — 155.5
- Galinsky, Ellen. ★*The Breakthrough Years* — 649
- Kline, Emily. ★*The School of Hard Talks* — 155.5
- Kowal-Connelly, Suanne. *Parenting Through Puberty* — 649
- Vernacchio, Al. *For Goodness Sex* — 613.9071
- Wiseman, Rosalind. *Masterminds & Wingmen* — 305.235

PARENT CAREGIVERS FOR PEOPLE WITH DISABILITIES
- Senator, Susan. *Autism Adulthood* — 616.85
- *Parent Up*. Rippon, Kelly — 649

PARENT-SEPARATED CHILDREN
- Horton, Michelle. *Dear Sister* — B
- Pryce, Jessica. ★*Broken* — 362.7
- Soboroff, Jacob. ★*Separated* — 325.73

PARENTAL BEHAVIOR IN ANIMALS
- Erickson, Laura. *The Love Lives of Birds* — 598.15

PARENTAL KIDNAPPING
- Calcaterra, Regina. *Girl Unbroken* — B

PARENTAL LOVE
- Rowe, Peggy. *About My Mother* — B

PARENTHOOD
- Barker, Elspeth. ★*Notes from the Henhouse* — 828
- Berg, Anastasia. ★*What Are Children For?* — 306.874
- Berger, Lynn. *Second Thoughts* — 306.85
- Brickman, Sophie. *Baby, Unplugged* — 306.874
- Conaboy, Chelsea. *Mother Brain* — 306.874
- Duggar, Jill. *Counting the Cost* — B
- Gaffigan, Jim. *Dad Is Fat* — 814
- Haelle, Tara. *The Informed Parent* — 649
- Jaffe, Sarah W. *Wanting What's Best* — 649
- Klein, Jessi. *I'll Show Myself Out* — B
- Milch, David. *Life's Work* — B
- Millwood, Molly. *To Have and to Hold* — 306.874
- Oster, Emily. ★*Cribsheet* — 618.2
- Philpott, Mary Laura. *Bomb Shelter* — B
- Poehler, Amy. *Yes Please* — B
- Rowe, Mickey. *Fearlessly Different* — B
- Tuama, Padraig O. ★*Poetry Unbound* — 808.1

PARENTING
- Airton, Lee. ★*Gender* — 305.3
- Amer, Lindz. *Rainbow Parenting* — 649
- Apter, T. E. *The Teen Interpreter* — 306.874
- Arment, Ainsley. *The Wild + Free Family* — 649
- Asika, Uju. *Bringing up Race* — 155.4
- Bauer, Susan Wise. *Rethinking School* — 371.19
- Baxley, Traci. *Social Justice Parenting* — 649
- Berger, Lynn. *Second Thoughts* — 306.85
- Birbiglia, Mike. *The New One* — B
- Boyce, W. Thomas. *The Orchid and the Dandelion* — 649
- Brown, Maressa. *Raising Baby by the Stars* — 133.5
- Brown, Noah. *Reading Together* — 028.5
- Carey, Tanith. *What's My Child Thinking?* — 155.4
- Casares, Whitney. *The Working Mom Blueprint* — 306.8743
- Clinton, Hillary Rodham. *It Takes a Village* — 305.23
- Cusk, Rachel. *A Life's Work* — 306.874

AUTHOR, TITLE, SERIES AND SUBJECT INDEX

Davies, Simone. *The Montessori Toddler*	371.39
Donaldson-Pressman, Stephanie. *The Learning Habit*	371.30281
Dunn, Jancee. ★*How Not to Hate Your Husband After Kids*	646.7
Faber, Adele. ★*How to Talk so Kids Will Listen & Listen so Kids Will Talk*	649
Fagell, Phyllis L. ★*Middle School Matters*	373.236
Foxx, Jamie. *Act Like You Got Some Sense*	B
Fradin, Kelly. *Advanced Parenting*	649
Galanti, Regine. ★*Parenting Anxious Kids*	155.4
Galinsky, Ellen. ★*The Breakthrough Years*	649
Garbes, Angela. *Essential Labor*	306.874
Goh, Suzanne. *Magnificent Minds*	618.92
Gopnik, Alison. *The Gardener and the Carpenter*	155.4
Grandin, Temple. ★*Visual Thinking*	152.14
Greene, Benjamin. ★*My Child Is Trans, Now What?*	649
Harris, Taylor. *This Boy We Made*	B
Hawthorne, Britt. ★*Raising Antiracist Children*	649
Hibbs, B. Janet. *You're Not Done Yet*	649
Hillsberg, Christina. *License to Parent*	649.1
Jaffe, Sarah W. *Wanting What's Best*	649
Kelly, Kevin. ★*Excellent Advice for Living*	158.1
Kendi, Ibram X. ★*How to Raise an Antiracist*	649
Kennedy-Moore, Eileen. ★*Kid Confidence*	155.4
Kline, Emily. ★*The School of Hard Talks*	155.5
Kobliner, Beth. *Make Your Kid a Money Genius (even If You're Not)*	332.024
Lahey, Jessica. *The Addiction Inoculation*	649
Lahey, Jessica. *The Gift of Failure*	649
Lev, Arlene Istar. *The Complete Lesbian & Gay Parenting Guide*	649
Levine, Madeline. ★*Ready or Not*	649
Lickona, Thomas. *How to Raise Kind Kids*	649
Lieber, Ron. *The Opposite of Spoiled*	332.0240083
Linn, Susan. *Who's Raising the Kids?*	649
McCarthy, Catherine. *Raising a Kid Who Can*	649
Medini, Shari. *Parenting While Working from Home*	650.1
Mogel, Wendy. *Voice Lessons for Parents*	649
Moorer, Allison. *I Dream He Talks to Me*	782.42164
Moran, Caitlin. *More Than a Woman*	B
Morgenstern, Julie. *Time to Parent*	649
Morin, Amy. *13 Things Mentally Strong Parents Don't Do*	649
Natterson, Cara Familian. ★*Decoding Boys*	649
Naumburg, Carla. ★*You Are Not a Sh*tty Parent*	649
Orenstein, Peggy. *Cinderella Ate My Daughter*	305.23082
Oster, Emily. ★*Cribsheet*	618.2
Perry, Philippa. ★*The Book You Wish Your Parents Had Read*	649
Petersen, Anne Helen. *Can't Even*	305.242
Petersen, Sara. *Momfluenced*	306.87
Phelan, Thomas W. *1-2-3 Magic*	649
Pressman, Aliza. *The 5 Principles of Parenting*	649.1
Raboteau, Emily. *Lessons for Survival*	814
Ramesh, Jaya. *Parenting at the Intersections*	649
Rippon, Kelly. *Parent Up*	649
Senior, Jennifer. *All Joy and No Fun*	306.874
Sentilles, Sarah. *Stranger Care*	B
Siegel, Daniel J. *Parenting from the Inside Out*	649
Siegel, Daniel J. *The Power of Showing Up*	649
Siegel, Daniel J. ★*The Yes Brain*	155.4
Singh, Julietta. *The Breaks*	B
Sisson, Gretchen E. ★*Relinquished*	362.734
Smart, Maya Payne. *Reading for Our Lives*	372.4
Smith, Maggie. ★*You Could Make This Place Beautiful*	B
Sole-Smith, Virginia. ★*Fat Talk*	649.1
Stanley, Paul. *Backstage Pass*	B
Stixrud, William R. *The Self-Driven Child*	155.4
Thomas, Joseph Earl. *Sink*	B
Thompson, Kenan. *When I Was Your Age*	B
Traig, Jennifer. *Act Natural*	306.874
Turban, Jack L. ★*Free to Be*	616.85
Wallace, Carvell. *Another Word for Love*	B
Wojcicki, Esther. *How to Raise Successful People*	649
★*Parenting Anxious Kids*. Galanti, Regine	155.4
Parenting At the Intersections. Ramesh, Jaya	649
PARENTING BY SIBLINGS	
Calcaterra, Regina. *Etched in Sand*	B
Parenting Children with Mental Health Challenges. Vlock, Deborah	618.92
Parenting from the Inside Out. Siegel, Daniel J.	649
Parenting Through Puberty. Kowal-Connelly, Suanne	649
Parenting While Working from Home. Medini, Shari	650.1
PARENTS	
Brown, Emma. *To Raise a Boy*	649
Delaney, Rob. ★*A Heart That Works*	B
Greenblatt, Stephen. *The Rise and Fall of Adam and Eve*	233
Millwood, Molly. *To Have and to Hold*	306.874
Tur, Katy. *Rough Draft*	B
PARENTS OF AUTISTIC CHILDREN	
Goh, Suzanne. *Magnificent Minds*	618.92
Grandin, Temple. *Navigating Autism*	618.92
Moorer, Allison. *I Dream He Talks to Me*	782.42164
Senator, Susan. *Autism Adulthood*	616.85
PARENTS OF TRANSGENDER CHILDREN	
Greene, Benjamin. ★*My Child Is Trans, Now What?*	649
Lemay, Mimi. *What We Will Become*	306.874
PARIAHS	
Eyman, Scott. *Charlie Chaplin vs. America*	B
Gidla, Sujatha. *Ants Among Elephants*	305.5
O'Brien, Keith. *Charlie Hustle*	796.357
Parini, Jay	
The Art of Teaching	378.1
Borges and Me	813
Robert Frost	B
PARINI, JAY	
Parini, Jay. *The Art of Teaching*	378.1
Parini, Jay. *Borges and Me*	813
Paris. Hilton, Paris	B
Paris 1919. MacMillan, Margaret	940.3
PARIS, FRANCE	
Bard, Elizabeth. *Lunch in Paris*	B
Barnes, Julian. *The Man in the Red Coat*	B
Begley, Adam. *The Great Nadar*	B
Bertch, Jane. *The French Ingredient*	B
Brickell, Francesca Cartier. *The Cartiers*	B
Child, Julia. ★*My Life in France*	B
Chisholm, Edward. *A Waiter in Paris*	B
De Waal, Edmund. *The Hare with Amber Eyes*	B
DeJean, Joan E. *How Paris Became Paris*	944
Downie, David. *A Taste of Paris*	394.1
Dusoulier, Clotilde. *Tasting Paris*	641.594
Kershaw, Alex. *Avenue of Spies*	940.53
Kildea, Paul Francis. *Chopin's Piano*	B
Lebovitz, David. *My Paris Kitchen*	641.594
McCullough, David G. *The Greater Journey*	920
O'Donnell, Svenja. *Inge's War*	943.086
Poirier, Agnes. *Left Bank*	944
Rappaport, Helen. *After the Romanovs*	944
Ripert, Eric. *32 Yolks*	B
Roe, Sue. *In Montmartre*	920
Ronald, Susan. *A Dangerous Woman*	B
Sancton, Thomas. *The Bettencourt Affair*	B
Sciolino, Elaine. *The Seine*	944
Scotti, R. A. *Vanished Smile*	759.5
Secrest, Meryle. *Modigliani*	B
Todd, Olivier. *Albert Camus*	B
Verant, Samantha. *Seven Letters from Paris*	B
Warren, Rosanna. *Max Jacob*	B
White, Edmund. *The Flaneur*	944
PARIS, FRANCE HISTORY	
Atria, Travis. *Better Days Will Come Again*	B
Berr, Helene. *The Journal of Helene Berr*	B
DeJean, Joan E. *How Paris Became Paris*	944
Dugard, Martin. *Taking Paris*	940.54
Horne, Alistair. *Seven Ages of Paris*	944
King, Ross. *The Judgment of Paris*	759.4
MacMillan, Margaret. *Paris 1919*	940.3
Robb, Graham. *Parisians*	944
Sciolino, Elaine. *The Seine*	944
Parisians. Robb, Graham	944
Parissien, Steven	
The Life of the Automobile	629.222
PARK RANGERS	
Lankford, Andrea. *Trail of the Lost*	363.2
Park, Benjamin E.	
American Zion	289.3
Park, Chris C.	
A Dictionary of Environment and Conservation	333.703
Park, J. S.	
★*As Long as You Need*	248.8

PUBLIC LIBRARY CORE COLLECTION: NONFICTION
Twentieth Edition

PARK, J. S. (HOSPITAL CHAPLAIN)
   Park, J. S. ★*As Long as You Need* — 248.8
Parke, Henry C.
   The Greatest Westerns Ever Made and the People Who Made Them — 791.43
Parker Pearson, Michael
   Stonehenge — 936.2
PARKER, BONNIE, 1910-1934
   Boessenecker, John. *Texas Ranger* — B
   Guinn, Jeff. *Go Down Together* — B
PARKER, CHARLIE, 1920-1955
   Crouch, Stanley. *Kansas City Lightning* — B
Parker, James
   ★*Get Me Through the Next Five Minutes* — 158.1
Parker, Kate T.
   Strong Is the New Pretty — 155.43
Parker, Lara
   Vagina Problems — 618.1
PARKER, LARA (WRITER AND EDITOR)
   Parker, Lara. *Vagina Problems* — 618.1
Parker, Matt
   Humble Pi — 510
Parker, Matthew
   Panama Fever — 972.87
Parker, Meghan
   Teaching Artfully — 741.5
PARKER, MEGHAN
   Parker, Meghan. *Teaching Artfully* — 741.5
Parker, Morgan
   Magical Negro — 811
   There Are More Beautiful Things Than Beyonce — 811
   ★*You Get What You Pay For* — 305.896
PARKER, MORGAN
   Parker, Morgan. ★*You Get What You Pay For* — 305.896
PARKER, QUANAH, COMANCHE CHIEF, 1847-1911
   Gwynne, S. C. *Empire of the Summer Moon* — B
PARKER, TOM, 1909-1997
   McDonald, Greg (Producer). *Elvis and the Colonel* — 920
Parker, Vergil R.
   Pickleball 101 — 796.34
Parkes, Clara
   The Knitter's Book of Yarn — 677
Parkin, Simon
   A Game of Birds and Wolves — 940.54
   An Illustrated History of 151 Video Games — 794.8
   The Island of Extraordinary Captives — 940.53
PARKING LOTS
   Grabar, Henry. *Paved Paradise* — 388.474
Parkland. Cullen, David — 371.7
PARKS
   Duncan, Dayton. *The National Parks* — 333.78
   Howard, Hugh. *Architects of an American Landscape* — 712.092
Parks, Carrie
   Secrets to Drawing Realistic Faces — 743.4
Parks, Casey
   Diary of a Misfit — B
PARKS, CASEY
   Parks, Casey. *Diary of a Misfit* — B
PARKS, ROSA, 1913-2005
   Theoharis, Jeanne. *The Rebellious Life of Mrs. Rosa Parks* — B
Parks, Stella
   ★*Bravetart* — 641.86
Parks, Tim
   The Hero's Way — 945
   Italian Ways — 385
PARKS, TIM
   Parks, Tim. *The Hero's Way* — 945
   Parks, Tim. *Italian Ways* — 385
Parla, Katie
   Tasting Rome — 641.59
PAROLE
   Austen, Ben. *Correction* — 364.6
   Hardy, Jason Matthew. ★*The Second Chance Club* — 364.6
PAROLE OFFICERS
   Hardy, Jason Matthew. ★*The Second Chance Club* — 364.6
PAROLEES
   Austen, Ben. *Correction* — 364.6
   Belkin, Lisa. *Genealogy of a Murder* — 362.88
   Hardy, Jason Matthew. ★*The Second Chance Club* — 364.6

Parrado, Nando
   ★*Miracle in the Andes* — 982
PARRADO, NANDO, 1949-
   Parrado, Nando. ★*Miracle in the Andes* — 982
Parrella-Van Den Berg, Janet
   White & Faded — 645
PARRICIDE
   Granata, Vince. *Everything Is Fine* — B
Parrish, Thomas D.
   The Submarine — 359.9
★*The Parrot and the Igloo*. Lipsky, David — 304.2
Parry, John Weston
   The Burden of Sports — 796.01
Parry, Richard Lloyd
   Ghosts of the Tsunami — 952.05
PART-TIME EMPLOYMENT
   Mulcahy, Diane. *The Gig Economy* — 650.1
PARTICLE ACCELERATORS
   Sheehy, Suzie. *The Matter of Everything* — 539.7
Particle Physics Brick by Brick. Still, Ben — 539.7
PARTICLES (NUCLEAR PHYSICS)
   Cliff, Harry. *How to Make an Apple Pie from Scratch* — 523.01
   Mahaffey, James A. *Atomic Adventures* — 333.792
   Prescod-Weinstein, Chanda. *The Disordered Cosmos* — 523.01
   Sheehy, Suzie. *The Matter of Everything* — 539.7
   Still, Ben. *Particle Physics Brick by Brick* — 539.7
   Tonelli, Guido. *Genesis* — 523.1
The Particulars of Peter. Conaboy, Kelly — 636.7
PARTIES
   Hudson, Kate. *Pretty Fun* — 642
   Moss, Jeremiah. *Feral City* — B
   Mullen, Marissa. *That Cheese Plate Wants to Party* — 641.6
   Zizka, Maria. *The Hostess Handbook* — 642
Parting The Waters. Branch, Taylor — 973
PARTITION, TERRITORIAL
   Malhotra, Aanchal. *Remnants of Partition* — 954.04
PARTNER ABUSE
   Butcher, Amy. *Mothertrucker* — B
   Means, Brittany. *Hell If We Don't Change Our Ways* — B
   Selvaratnam, Tanya. *Assume Nothing* — B
   Snyder, Rachel Louise. *No Visible Bruises* — 362.82
   Zhu, Mimi. *Be Not Afraid of Love* — 152.4
Parton, Dolly
   ★*Behind the Seams* — B
   ★*Dolly Parton, Songteller* — B
PARTON, DOLLY, 1946-
   Parton, Dolly. ★*Behind the Seams* — B
   Parton, Dolly. ★*Dolly Parton, Songteller* — B
   Smarsh, Sarah. *She Come by It Natural* — 782.42164
Party of One. Wong, Chun Han — 951.06
Parwana. Ayubi, Durkhanai — 641.595
Pashman, Dan
   Anything's Pastable — 641.82
★*The Passage of Power*. Caro, Robert A. — B
Passan, Jeff
   The Arm — 796.3576
Passarlay, Gulwali
   The Lightless Sky — B
PASSARLAY, GULWALI
   Passarlay, Gulwali. *The Lightless Sky* — B
PASSENGER SHIPS
   Henry, John. *Great White Fleet* — 387.243
   Larson, Erik. ★*Dead Wake* — 940.4
PASSING (IDENTITY)
   Baime, A. J. *White Lies* — B
   Jacoby, Karl. *The Strange Career of William Ellis* — B
   Kushner, Tony. *Angels in America* — 812
   Morgan-Owens, Jessie. *Girl in Black and White* — B
   Talusan, Meredith. *Fairest* — 305.30973
   Tisserand, Michael. *Krazy* — 741.5
   Toorpakai, Maria. *A Different Kind of Daughter* — B
   Woo, Ilyon. ★*Master Slave Husband Wife* — 920
PASSION
   Gopnik, Adam. *All That Happiness Is* — 158.1
   Neruda, Pablo. ★*Twenty Love Poems and a Song of Despair* — 861
The Passion Economy. Davidson, Adam — 330.9
A Passion for Nature the Life of John Muir. Worster, Donald — B

AUTHOR, TITLE, SERIES AND SUBJECT INDEX

PASSIVE RESISTANCE
    Guha, Ramachandra. *Gandhi*   B
PASSPORTS
    Lekas Miller, Anna. *Love Across Borders*   323.6
PASTA
    Lanza, Fabrizia. *The Food of Sicily*   641.594
    Pashman, Dan. *Anything's Pastable*   641.82
    Roddy, Rachel. ★*An A-Z of Pasta*   641.82
    Williams, Odette. ★*Simple Pasta*   641.822
The **Pasta** *Queen*. Munno, Nadia Caterina   641.82
Pastel *Painting Atelier*. Eagle, Ellen   741.2
Pastel *Pointers*. McKinley, Richard   741.2
PASTERNAK, BORIS LEONIDOVICH, 1890-1960
    Finn, Peter. *The Zhivago Affair*   891.73
Pasternak, Judy
    Yellow Dirt   979.1004
PASTORAL POETRY
    Virgil. *The Eclogues of Virgil*   871
PASTRY
    Barrow, Cathy. ★*Pie Squared*   641.86
    Behan, Ren. ★*The Sweet Polish Kitchen*   641.594
    Beranbaum, Rose Levy. ★*Rose's Baking Basics*   641.81
    Chang, Joanne. *Pastry Love*   641.86
    Greenspan, Dorie. *Baking Chez Moi*   641.86
    Lloyd, Bobbie. *The Magnolia Bakery Handbook*   641.86
    Ludwinski, Lisa. *Sister Pie*   641.86
    Ottolenghi, Yotam. *Sweet*   641.86
    Pfeiffer, Jacquy. *The Art of French Pastry*   641.86
    Weller, Melissa. *A Good Bake*   641.86
Pastry *Love*. Chang, Joanne   641.86
PATAGONIA (ARGENTINA AND CHILE)
    Grann, David. ★*The Wager*   910.91
The **Patagonian** *Hare*. Lanzmann, Claude   B
Pataki, Allison
    Beauty in the Broken Places   B
PATAKI, ALLISON
    Pataki, Allison. *Beauty in the Broken Places*   B
Patchett, Ann
    ★*These Precious Days*   814
    This Is the Story of a Happy Marriage   B
    Truth & Beauty   B
PATCHETT, ANN
    Patchett, Ann. ★*These Precious Days*   814
    Patchett, Ann. *This Is the Story of a Happy Marriage*   B
    Patchett, Ann. *Truth & Beauty*   B
PATCHWORK
    Alexander, Lissa. *Oh, Scrap!*   746.46
    Belyea, Patricia. *East-Meets-West Quilts*   746.46
    Beyer, Jinny. *A Quilter's Album of Patchwork Patterns*   746.46
    Brandvig, Jera. *Quilt As-You-Go Made Vintage*   746.46
    Doughty, Kathy. *Adding Layers*   746.46
    Gering, Jacquie. *Quilting Modern*   746.46
    Gilleland, Diane. *All Points Patchwork*   746.46
    Goertzen, Vanessa. ★*Charm School*   746.46
    Goldsworthy, Lynne. *Quick & Easy Quilts*   746.46
    Hunter, Bonnie K. *String Frenzy*   746.46
    Nyberg, Amanda Jean. *No Scrap Left Behind*   746.46
    Redford, Catherine. *Modern Machine Quilting*   746.46
    Rosenthal, Maxine. *One-Block Wonders of the World*   746.46
    Stocker, Blair. *Wise Craft Quilts*   746.46
    Wolfe, Victoria Findlay. *Modern Quilt Magic*   746.46
PATCHWORK QUILTS
    Brandvig, Jera. *Quilt As-You-Go Made Vintage*   746.46
    Goertzen, Vanessa. ★*Charm School*   746.46
    Goldsworthy, Lynne. *Quick & Easy Quilts*   746.46
    Grisham, Candyce Copp. *Dresden Quilt Blocks Reimagined*   746.46
    Hartman, Elizabeth. *Modern Patchwork*   746.46
    Stocker, Blair. *Wise Craft Quilts*   746.46
Patel, Palak
    Food Is Love   641.595
PATENT LAWS AND LEGISLATION
    Zaitchik, Alexander. *Owning the Sun*   362.1
PATENTS
    Fischer, Paul. *The Man Who Invented Motion Pictures*   791.43
PATERNITY
    Shapiro, Dani. ★*Inheritance*   B
Paterson. Williams, William Carlos   811
The **Path** *Between the Seas*. McCullough, David G.   972.87

★**Path** *Lit by Lightning*. Maraniss, David   B
Path *of the Puma*. Williams, Jim   599.75
A **Path** *to Peace*. Mitchell, George J.   956.9405
Pathogenesis. Kennedy, Jonathan   614.4
PATHOGENIC MICROORGANISMS
    Finlay, B. Brett. *Let Them Eat Dirt*   616.9
    Monosson, Emily. ★*Blight*   616.9
    Zaman, Muhammad H. *Biography of Resistance*   616.9
PATHOLOGISTS
    Di Maio, Vincent J. M. *Morgue*   B
PATHOLOGY
    Aptowicz, Cristin O'Keefe. *Dr. Mutter's Marvels*   B
PATIENCE
    Kongtrul, Dzigar. *Peaceful Heart*   294.3
    Moss, Adam. ★*The Work of Art*   701
    Park, J. S. ★*As Long as You Need*   248.8
PATIENT ADVOCACY
    Allen, Marshall. ★*Never Pay the First Bill*   610.28
    Brown, Theresa. *Healing*   616.99
    Elliott, Carl. ★*The Occasional Human Sacrifice*   174.2
    Fox, Michael J. *No Time Like the Future*   B
    Karlawish, Jason. ★*The Problem of Alzheimer's*   616.8
    Malone, Sharon. *Grown Woman Talk*   362.1
    McGregor, Alyson J. *Sex Matters*   613
    Tang, Karen. ★*It's Not Hysteria*   618.2
The **Patient** *Assassin*. Anand, Anita   B
★**Patient** *H.M.* Dittrich, Luke   616.85
Patient *Zero*. Kang, Lydia   614.4
PATIENTS
    Alexander, Brian. ★*The Hospital*   362.10973
    Applebaum, Allison. *Stand by Me*   649.8
    Elliott, Carl. ★*The Occasional Human Sacrifice*   174.2
    Hari, Johann. ★*Magic Pill*   613.2
    Hutton, Andrea. *Bald Is Better with Earrings*   362.19699
    Ingrassia, Lawrence. *A Fatal Inheritance*   616.99
    Kriss, Alexander. *Borderline*   616.85
    Lamas, Daniela J. *You Can Stop Humming Now*   616.02
    Nuila, Ricardo. *The People's Hospital*   362.1
    Wilson, F. Perry. *How Medicine Works and When It Doesn't*   610.69
PATIENTS' RIGHTS
    Fessler, Pam. *Carville's Cure*   362.19699
★*The* **Patriarch**. Nasaw, David   B
PATRIARCHS
    Cooper, Anderson. *Vanderbilt*   920
PATRIARCHY
    Amos, Tori. *Resistance*   B
    Campbell, Olivia. *Women in White Coats*   610.92
    Cleghorn, Elinor. *Unwell Women*   613
    Cooney, Kara. *When Women Ruled the World*   920
    Eltahawy, Mona. *The Seven Necessary Sins for Women and Girls*   305.42
    Garcia, Amanda Yates. *Initiated*   B
    Herman, Judith Lewis. *Truth and Repair*   362.883
    Hustvedt, Siri. *Mothers, Fathers, and Others*   814
    Jones, Faith. *Sex Cult Nun*   B
    Marcal, Katrine. *Mother of Invention*   604.82
    McGregor, Alyson J. *Sex Matters*   613
    Miller, Adrienne. *In the Land of Men*   070.5
    Moore, Kate. ★*The Woman They Could Not Silence*   B
    O'Meara, Mallory. *Girly Drinks*   641.2
    Palmieri, Jennifer. *She Proclaims*   305.42
    Sinclair, Safiya. ★*How to Say Babylon*   B
    Way, Niobe. *Rebels with a Cause*   649
    West, Cait. ★*Rift*   B
★**Patricia** *Highsmith's Diaries and Notebooks*. Highsmith, Patricia   818
Patrick, James
    Robert Johnson   B
Patrick, Jane
    The Weaver's Idea Book   746.1
PATRICK, MILICENT, 1915-1998
    O'Meara, Mallory. *The Lady from the Black Lagoon*   921
Patrick, Vanessa M.
    The Power of Saying No   158.1
PATRIOTIC MUSIC
    Meacham, Jon. *Songs of America*   782.42
PATRIOTIC MUSIC, AMERICAN
    Clague, Mark. *O Say Can You Hear?*   782.42
PATRIOTISM
    Coker, Margaret. *The Spymaster of Baghdad*   956.7044

PUBLIC LIBRARY CORE COLLECTION: NONFICTION
Twentieth Edition

Duckworth, Tammy. *Every Day Is a Gift*	B
McCullough, David G. ★*The American Spirit*	973
Miller, Marla. *Betsy Ross and the Making of America*	B
Neiwert, David A. ★*The Age of Insurrection*	303.48
Rather, Dan. *What Unites Us*	323.6
Smith, Mychal Denzel. *Stakes Is High*	973.933
The *Patriots*. Groom, Winston	920
Pattee, Amy	
Developing Library Collections for Today's Young Adults	027.62
Patterns in Nature. Ball, Philip	500.201
PATTERSON, FLOYD	
Stratton, W. K. *Floyd Patterson*	B
Patterson, James	
ER Nurses	610.73
James Patterson by James Patterson	B
The Secret Lives of Booksellers and Librarians	381
Walk in My Combat Boots	920
Walk the Blue Line	920
What Really Happens in Vegas	920
PATTERSON, JAMES, 1947-	
Patterson, James. *James Patterson by James Patterson*	B
Patterson, Pat	
Accepted	B
PATTERSON, PAT	
Patterson, Pat. *Accepted*	B
Patterson, Scott	
★*Chaos Kings*	338.5
Pattison, Kermit	
Fossil Men	569.9
Patton, George S.	
War as I Knew It	B
PATTON, GEORGE S., 1885-1945	
Brighton, Terry. *Patton, Montgomery, Rommel*	B
Clark, Lloyd. *The Commanders*	940.53
Groom, Winston. *The Generals*	920
Hanson, Victor Davis. *The Soul of Battle*	355
Jordan, Jonathan W. *Brothers, Rivals, Victors*	940.54
Letts, Elizabeth. *The Perfect Horse*	940.54
Patton, George S. *War as I Knew It*	B
Patton, Montgomery, Rommel. Brighton, Terry	B
Patton, Sharon F.	
African-American Art	704.03
Paul Revere's Ride. Fischer, David Hackett	973.3
★*Paul Simon*. Hilburn, Robert	782.42164
Paul, Annie Murphy	
The Extended Mind	128
Paul, Gregory S.	
The Princeton Field Guide to Dinosaurs	567.9
Paul, Joel R.	
Indivisible	973.5
★*Without Precedent*	B
PAUL, LES, 1915-2009	
Port, Ian S. *The Birth of Loud*	787.87
Paul, Pamela	
★*How to Raise a Reader*	649
Paul, Richard	
We Could Not Fail	920
★*Paula*. Allende, Isabel	B
Pauline, Kathryn	
A Dish for All Seasons	641.5
★*Piecemeal*	641.5
Pauling, Linus	
Linus Pauling	081
PAULING, LINUS, 1901-1994	
Markel, Howard. *The Secret of Life*	572.86
Pauling, Linus. *Linus Pauling*	081
Paulsen, Gary	
Winterdance	B
PAULSEN, GARY, 1939-2021	
Paulsen, Gary. *Winterdance*	B
Paulsen, Michael Stokes	
The Constitution	342.7302
Paulson, Dennis	
Dragonflies & Damselflies	595.7
Paulson, Henry M.	
On the Brink	330.973
Paved Paradise. Grabar, Henry	388.474
Pavelka, Lisa	
The Complete Book of Polymer Clay	738.1
Pavlychenko, Liudmyla Mykhailivna	
Lady Death	B
PAVLYCHENKO, LIUDMYLA MYKHAILIVNA, 1916-1974	
Pavlychenko, Liudmyla Mykhailivna. *Lady Death*	B
Pawel, Miriam	
The Browns of California	920
The Crusades of Cesar Chavez	B
PAWNBROKING	
Rivlin, Gary. *Broke, Usa*	339.4
Pawuk, Michael	
Graphic Novels	016.74
Pax Romana. Goldsworthy, Adrian Keith	937
Paxson, Margaret	
The Plateau	362.87
PAXSON, MARGARET	
Paxson, Margaret. *The Plateau*	362.87
Paxton, Robert O.	
The Anatomy of Fascism	320.53
PAY EQUITY	
Rivlin, Gary. *Broke, Usa*	339.4
Pay No Heed to the Rockets. Di Cintio, Marcello	956.9405
PAYA, OSWALDO, 1952-2012	
Hoffman, David E. *Give Me Liberty*	B
★*Paying The Land*. Sacco, Joe	741.5
Paying The Price. Goldrick-Rab, Sara	378.3
PAYNE, ETHEL L.	
Morris, James McGrath. *Eye on the Struggle*	B
Payne, Les	
★*The Dead Are Arising*	B
PAYTON, WALTER, 1954-1999	
Pearlman, Jeff. *Sweetness*	B
Paz, Octavio	
★*The Collected Poems of Octavio Paz, 1957-1987*	861
The Poems of Octavio Paz	861
PAZ, OCTAVIO, 1914-1998	
Paz, Octavio. ★*The Collected Poems of Octavio Paz, 1957-1987*	861
Paz, Octavio. *The Poems of Octavio Paz*	861
PEACE	
Avlon, John P. *Lincoln and the Fight for Peace*	973.7
Blattman, Christopher. *Why We Fight*	303.6
Carter, Jimmy. *Palestine*	956.04
Chodron, Pema. *Practicing Peace*	294.3
Dalai Lama. *How to Be Compassionate*	294.3
Davis, William C. *Crucible of Command*	920
Einstein, Albert. *Ideas and Opinions*	081
Kershaw, Ian. *The Global Age*	940.55
MacMillan, Margaret. *Paris 1919*	940.3
Malala, Justice. *The Plot to Save South Africa*	968.07
Mitchell, George J. *A Path to Peace*	956.9405
Plokhy, Serhii. *Yalta*	940.53
Preston, Diana. *Eight Days at Yalta*	940.53
Winik, Jay. *April 1865*	973.7
PEACE ACTIVISTS	
Gandhi. *An Autobiography*	B
PEACE MOVEMENTS	
Bingham, Clara. *Witness to the Revolution*	303.48
Carter, Jimmy. *Palestine*	956.04
Lang, Michael. *The Road to Woodstock*	781.66
Purnell, Derecka. *Becoming Abolitionists*	363.20973
Wilkinson, Alec. *The Protest Singer*	B
PEACE OF MIND	
Chodron, Pema. *Practicing Peace*	294.3
Kerr, Christopher. *Death Is but a Dream*	155.9
Winkler, Kyle. *Permission to Be Imperfect*	170
PEACE OFFICERS	
Barra, Allen. *Inventing Wyatt Earp*	B
Clavin, Thomas. *Dodge City*	978.1
Clavin, Thomas. *Wild Bill*	B
Tefertiller, Casey. *Wyatt Earp*	B
PEACE, ROBERT, 1980-2010	
Hobbs, Jeff. ★*The Short and Tragic Life of Robert Peace*	B
PEACE-BUILDING	
Blattman, Christopher. *Why We Fight*	303.6
Dalai Lama. *An Appeal to the World*	170
Gopal, Anand. *No Good Men Among the Living*	920
Roll, David L. *Ascent to Power*	973.918

AUTHOR, TITLE, SERIES AND SUBJECT INDEX

Peaceful Heart. Kongtrul, Dzigar   294.3
Peak. Ericsson, K. Anders   153.9
Peak Performance. Stulberg, Brad   158.1
PEALE, CHARLES WILLSON, 1741-1827
   Staiti, Paul J. *Of Arms and Artists*   B
PEANUTS
   Vella, Christina. *George Washington Carver*   B
PEANUTS (COMIC STRIP)
   Michaelis, David. *Schulz and Peanuts*   B
Pearce, Fred
   A Trillion Trees   577.3
Pearl Harbor. Nelson, Craig   940.54
PEARL HARBOR, ATTACK ON, 1941
   Bass, Gary Jonathan. ★*Judgment at Tokyo*   952.04
   Drabkin, Ronald. *Beverly Hills Spy*   940.54
   Harmon, Mark. *Ghosts of Honolulu*   940.54
   Hotta, Eri. *Japan 1941*   940.54
   Nelson, Craig. *Pearl Harbor*   940.54
   Prange, Gordon W. *At Dawn We Slept*   940.54
   Sakamoto, Pamela Rotner. *Midnight in Broad Daylight*   940.53
   Twomey, Steve. *Countdown to Pearl Harbor*   940.54
PEARL HARBOR, HAWAII
   Harmon, Mark. *Ghosts of Honolulu*   940.54
Pearlman, Jeff
   Boys Will Be Boys   796.332
   Football for a Buck   796.332
   Gunslinger   B
   The Last Folk Hero   B
   Sweetness   B
   ★*Three-Ring Circus*   796.323
Pearlman, Wendy
   We Crossed a Bridge and It Trembled   956.9104
Pearson, Roger
   Voltaire Almighty   B
PEARY, ROBERT E. (ROBERT EDWIN), 1856-1920
   Hartman, Darrell. *Battle of Ink and Ice*   998
PEASANTRY
   Gies, Frances. *Life in a Medieval Village*   306
   Joyce, Patrick. *Remembering Peasants*   305.5
   McMeekin, Sean. *The Russian Revolution*   947.084
Pease, Allan
   The Definitive Book of Body Language   153.6
PECK, ANNIE S. (ANNIE SMITH), 1850-1935
   Kimberley, Hannah. *A Woman's Place Is at the Top*   B
Peck, M. Scott
   ★*The Road Less Traveled*   158.1
Peck, Robert McCracken
   A Glorious Enterprise   508
PECKINPAH, SAM, 1925-1984
   Stratton, W. K. *The Wild Bunch*   791.43
PECORA, FERDINAND, 1882-1971
   Perino, Michael A. *The Hellhound of Wall Street*   330.973
A Peculiar Indifference. Currie, Elliott   305.800973
PEDIATRIC SURGEONS
   Wellons, Jay. *All That Moves Us*   617.4
The Pediatrician's Guide to Feeding Babies & Toddlers. Porto, Anthony   618.92
PEER PRESSURE
   Zimbardo, Philip G. *The Lucifer Effect*   155.9
Peer, Basharat
   Curfewed Night   B
PEER, BASHARAT, 1977-
   Peer, Basharat. *Curfewed Night*   B
Peiffer, Prudence
   The Slip   709.73
Pein, Corey
   Live Work Work Work Die   338.4
Peisner, David
   Homey Don't Play That!   791.45
Pelaez, Ana Sofia
   The Cuban Table   641.597291
Pelayo, Rafael
   ★*How to Sleep*   616.8
Pelikan, Jaroslav
   Mary Through the Centuries   232.91
PELKE, BILL
   Mar, Alex. *Seventy Times Seven*   362.88
PELKE, RUTH
   Mar, Alex. *Seventy Times Seven*   362.88

Pellegrino, Charles R.
   To Hell and Back   940.54
Pellegrino, Danny
   How Do I Un-Remember This?   B
PELLEGRINO, DANNY
   Pellegrino, Danny. *How Do I Un-Remember This?*   B
The Peloponnesian War. Kagan, Donald   938
PELOPONNESIAN WAR, 431-404 B.C.E
   Kagan, Donald. *The Peloponnesian War*   938
   Kagan, Donald. *Thucydides*   938
   Roberts, Jennifer Tolbert. *The Plague of War*   938
★*Pelosi.* Ball, Molly   B
Pelosi, Dan
   Let's Eat   641.5
PELOSI, NANCY, 1940-
   Ball, Molly. ★*Pelosi*   B
Pember, Mat
   DIY Garden Projects   712
PEMBROKE, WILLIAM MARSHAL, EARL OF, 1144?-1219
   Asbridge, Thomas S. *The Greatest Knight*   942.03
Pen to Thread. Watson, Sarah   746.44
PENAL COLONIES
   Hughes, Robert. *The Fatal Shore*   994
   Keneally, Thomas. *A Commonwealth of Thieves*   994
Penaluna, Regan
   ★*How to Think Like a Woman*   190.82
PENALUNA, REGAN
   Penaluna, Regan. ★*How to Think Like a Woman*   190.82
The Penguin American library [Series]. Douglass, Frederick   B
★*The Penguin Jazz Guide.* Morton, Brian   016
Penguin poets [Series]. Hayes, Terrance   811
Penick, Pam
   The Water-Saving Garden   635.9
Penn, Kal
   You Can't Be Serious   B
PENN, KAL, 1977-
   Penn, Kal. *You Can't Be Serious*   B
Penn, Thomas
   The Brothers York   942.04
PENN, WILLIAM, 1644-1718
   Murphy, Andrew R. *William Penn*   B
Pennavaria, Katherine
   Genealogy for Beginners   929.1
Penniman, Leah
   ★*Black Earth Wisdom*   333.72
Pennington, Bill
   Billy Martin   B
Pennington, Emily
   Feral   B
PENNSYLVANIA
   Bradley, Mark A. *Blood Runs Coal*   B
   Drury, Bob. *Valley Forge*   973.3
   Fischer, David Hackett. *Washington's Crossing*   973.3
   McDougall, Christopher. *Running with Sherman*   636.1
   McGraw, Seamus. *The End of Country*   333.7909748
   Miller, Marla. *Betsy Ross and the Making of America*   B
   Murphy, Andrew R. *William Penn*   B
   Price, S. L. *Playing Through the Whistle*   796.332
   Roker, Al. *Ruthless Tide*   974.8
   Sears, Stephen W. *Gettysburg*   973.7
   Tran, Phuc. ★*Sigh, Gone*   B
PENTAGON PAPERS CASE
   Prose, Francine. *1974*   B
PENTECOSTALS
   Means, Brittany. *Hell If We Don't Change Our Ways*   B
Pentland, Jenny
   This Will Be Funny Later   B
PENTLAND, JENNY
   Pentland, Jenny. *This Will Be Funny Later*   B
PEONAGE
   Swift, Earl. *Hell Put to Shame*   364.15
★*The People and the Books.* Kirsch, Adam   809
A People Betrayed. Preston, Paul   946
★*People Love Dead Jews.* Horn, Dara   909
PEOPLE WHO ARE BLIND
   Clark, John Lee. *Touch the Future*   B
   Fenn, Lisa. *Carry On*   B
   Gray, Michael. *Hand Me My Travelin' Shoes*   B

PUBLIC LIBRARY CORE COLLECTION: NONFICTION
Twentieth Edition

Keller, Helen. ★ *The Story of My Life*	B
Leland, Andrew. ★ *The Country of the Blind*	B
Sjunneson, Elsa. *Being Seen*	362.4

PEOPLE WHO ARE BLIND AND DEAF
Girma, Haben. *Haben*	B
Herrmann, Dorothy. *Helen Keller*	B
Keller, Helen. ★ *The Story of My Life*	B
Sjunneson, Elsa. *Being Seen*	362.4

PEOPLE WHO ARE DEAF
Clark, John Lee. *Touch the Future*	B
DiMarco, Nyle. ★ *Deaf Utopia*	B
Hay, Matt. *Soundtrack of Silence*	B
Hughes, Robert. *Goya*	B
Keller, Helen. ★ *The Story of My Life*	B
Marschark, Marc. ★ *How Deaf Children Learn*	371.91
Melvin, Leland. *Chasing Space*	B
Morris, Edmund. *Beethoven*	B
Sjunneson, Elsa. *Being Seen*	362.4

PEOPLE WHO HAVE HAD AMPUTATIONS
Gregory, Rebekah. *Taking My Life Back*	B

PEOPLE WHO HAVE HAD STROKES
Dearborn, Mary V. *Carson McCullers*	B
Pataki, Allison. *Beauty in the Broken Places*	B
Raban, Jonathan. *Father and Son*	B
Stone, Sharon. *The Beauty of Living Twice*	B
Taylor, Jill Bolte. *My Stroke of Insight*	362.19681
Travis, Randy. *Forever and Ever, Amen*	B
★ *People Who Lunch*. Olds, Sally	824

PEOPLE WITH AIDS
Duberman, Martin B. *Hold Tight Gently*	920
France, David. *How to Survive a Plague*	362.196
Schiavi, Michael R. *Celluloid Activist*	B

PEOPLE WITH ALLERGIES
MacPhail, Theresa. *Allergic*	616.97

PEOPLE WITH ALZHEIMER'S DISEASE
Alterman, Sara Faith. *Let's Never Talk About This Again*	616.8
Berg, Elizabeth. *I'll Be Seeing You*	306.874
Cornelius, Maria M. *The Final Season*	B
Coste, Joanne Koenig. *Learning to Speak Alzheimer's*	362.1
Davis, Patti. *Floating in the Deep End*	616.8
Garcia, Rodrigo. *A Farewell to Gabo and Mercedes*	B
Harden, Marcia Gay. *The Seasons of My Mother*	B
Karlawish, Jason. ★ *The Problem of Alzheimer's*	616.8
Kiper, Dasha. ★ *Travelers to Unimaginable Lands*	616.8
Kozol, Jonathan. *The Theft of Memory*	B
Lang, Maya. *What We Carry*	B
Milch, David. *Life's Work*	B
Mitchell, Wendy. *Somebody I Used to Know*	B
Mulgrew, Kate. *Born with Teeth*	791.45028
Powell, Tia. *Dementia Reimagined*	616.8
Pratchett, Terry. *A Slip of the Keyboard*	824
Summitt, Pat Head. *Sum It Up*	B

PEOPLE WITH AMNESIA
Rojas Contreras, Ingrid. ★ *The Man Who Could Move Clouds*	B

PEOPLE WITH AMYOTROPHIC LATERAL SCLEROSIS
Albom, Mitch. *Tuesdays with Morrie*	B
Barkan, Ady. *Eyes to the Wind*	B
Fitzmaurice, Simon. *It's Not yet Dark*	616.8
Hawking, Stephen. *My Brief History*	B
Mlodinow, Leonard. *Stephen Hawking*	B
Ottaviani, Jim. *Hawking*	741.5
Robinson, Ray. *Iron Horse*	B

PEOPLE WITH ANOREXIA
Hornbacher, Marya. *Wasted*	B

PEOPLE WITH BIPOLAR DISORDER
Casillo, Charles. *Marilyn Monroe*	B
Chang, David. ★ *Eat a Peach*	641.5
Craig, Mya-Rose. *Birdgirl*	B
Gotch, Jen. *The Upside of Being Down*	B
Ikpi, Bassey. *I'm Telling the Truth, but I'm Lying*	814
Kidder, Tracy. *A Truck Full of Money*	B
Lewis, Jenifer. *Walking in My Joy*	B
Lin, Jami Nakamura. *The Night Parade*	B
Mailhot, Terese Marie. *Heart Berries*	B
Moghul, Haroon. *How to Be a Muslim*	B
Waldman, Ayelet. *A Really Good Day*	B

PEOPLE WITH BRAIN TUMORS
Gaffigan, Jeannie. *When Life Gives You Pears*	B

PEOPLE WITH BREAST CANCER
Malone, Jo. *Jo Malone*	B
Riggs, Nina. *The Bright Hour*	B
Savage, Jodi M. *The Death of a Jaybird*	B

PEOPLE WITH CANCER
Arsenault, Kerri. *Mill Town*	B
Billings, J. Todd. *Rejoicing in Lament*	248.8
Bowler, Kate. *No Cure for Being Human*	B
Boyer, Anne. *The Undying*	B
Brem, Rachel. *No Longer Radical*	616.99
Brown, Theresa. *Healing*	616.99
Cacioppo, Stephanie. *Wired for Love*	616.8
Chow, Kat. *Seeing Ghosts*	B
Hagberg, Eva. *How to Be Loved*	616.7
Hitchens, Christopher. *Mortality*	304.6
Jaouad, Suleika. ★ *Between Two Kingdoms*	B
Kalanithi, Paul. ★ *When Breath Becomes Air*	B
Mankell, Henning. *Quicksand*	B
Morgan, Abi. *This Is Not a Pity Memoir*	B
Mukherjee, Siddhartha. ★ *The Emperor of All Maladies*	616.99
Patchett, Ann. *Truth & Beauty*	B
Pearlman, Jeff. *Sweetness*	B
Quinn, Tallu Schuyler. *What We Wish Were True*	B
Raza, Azra. *The First Cell*	616.99
Richtel, Matt. ★ *An Elegant Defense*	616.07
Roberts, David. *Limits of the Known*	B
Ruhl, Sarah. *Letters from Max*	811
Sacks, Oliver. *Gratitude*	306.9
Schwalbe, Will. ★ *The End of Your Life Book Club*	B
Servan-Schreiber, David. *Anticancer*	616.99
Simard, S. ★ *Finding the Mother Tree*	582.16
Skloot, Rebecca. ★ *The Immortal Life of Henrietta Lacks*	B
Stump, Al. *Cobb*	B
Townsend, Alan R. ★ *This Ordinary Stardust*	B
Von Furstenberg, Diane. *The Woman I Wanted to Be*	B
Washington, Kate. ★ *Already Toast*	649.8
Wiman, Christian. *He Held Radical Light*	814
Yip-Williams, Julie. ★ *The Unwinding of the Miracle*	973

PEOPLE WITH CEREBRAL PALSY
Marshall, Greg. *Leg*	B

PEOPLE WITH CHRONIC ILLNESSES
Hagberg, Eva. *How to Be Loved*	616.7
O'Rourke, Meghan. ★ *The Invisible Kingdom*	616
Slice, Jessica. *Dateable*	646.7

PEOPLE WITH CRITICAL ILLNESSES
Ely, Wes. *Every Deep-Drawn Breath*	616.02

PEOPLE WITH CYSTIC FIBROSIS
O'Hara, Maryanne. *Little Matches*	B

PEOPLE WITH DEMENTIA
Davis, Patti. *Floating in the Deep End*	616.8
Kiper, Dasha. ★ *Travelers to Unimaginable Lands*	616.8
Mitchell, Wendy. *Somebody I Used to Know*	B
Morton, Brian. *Tasha*	B

PEOPLE WITH DEPRESSION
Armstrong, Karen. *The Spiral Staircase*	B
Brosh, Allie. ★ *Hyperbole and a Half*	741.5
Brosh, Allie. ★ *Solutions and Other Problems*	741.5
Butcher, Barbara. *What the Dead Know*	614
Calhoun, Ada. *Why We Can't Sleep*	305.244
Chrisinger, David. *The Soldier's Truth*	940.54
Clark, Heather. ★ *Red Comet*	B
Cobbs-Leonard, Tasha. *Do It Anyway*	241
Cregan, Mary. *The Scar*	616.85
Gulman, Gary. *Misfit*	B
Hamilton, Tyler. *The Secret Race*	796.62
Itzkoff, Dave. ★ *Robin*	B
Kander, Jason. *Invisible Storm*	B
Lawson, Jenny. ★ *Broken*	B
Lawson, Jenny. *Furiously Happy*	B
Li, Yiyun. *Dear Friend, from My Life I Write to You in Your Life*	B
Mizrahi, Isaac. *I.M.*	B
Moby. *Then It Fell Apart*	B
Moe, John. *The Hilarious World of Depression*	616.85
Paperny, Anna Mehler. *Hello I Want to Die Please Fix Me*	362.2
Rapoport, Ron. *Let's Play Two*	B
Riley, Alex. ★ *A Cure for Darkness*	616.85
Sanchez, Erika L. *Crying in the Bathroom*	B
Satrapi, Marjane. *Chicken with Plums*	741.5

AUTHOR, TITLE, SERIES AND SUBJECT INDEX

Saunders, John. *Playing Hurt*	B
Sehee, Baek. *I Want to Die but I Want to Eat Tteokbokki*	B
Servadio, Gaia. *Rossini*	B
Stahl, Jerry. *Nein, Nein, Nein!*	B
Taylor, Justin. *Riding with the Ghost*	B
Thompson, J. M. *Running Is a Kind of Dreaming*	B
Waldman, Ayelet. *A Really Good Day*	B
Williams, Michelle. *Checking In*	B

PEOPLE WITH DEVELOPMENTAL DISABILITIES

Brown, Molly McCully. *The Virginia State Colony for Epileptics and Feebleminded*	811
King, Gilbert. *Beneath a Ruthless Sun*	B
Larson, Kate Clifford. *Rosemary*	B
Senator, Susan. *Autism Adulthood*	616.85
Shriver, Timothy P. *Fully Alive*	796.087

PEOPLE WITH DISABILITIES

Anderson, Amelia. *Library Programming for Autistic Children and Teens*	027.6
Belser, Julia Watts. ★*Loving Our Own Bones*	296
Blake, Melissa. *Beautiful People*	362.4
Brookwood, Marilyn. *The Orphans of Davenport*	305.231
Burcaw, Shane. ★*Laughing at My Nightmare*	B
Chesney, Will. *No Ordinary Dog*	958.104
Davis, Lennard J. *Enabling Acts*	342.7308
Donvan, John. *In a Different Key*	616.85
Duckworth, Tammy. *Every Day Is a Gift*	B
Erwin, Jon. *Beyond Valor*	B
Fenn, Lisa. *Carry On*	B
Grue, Jan. *I Live a Life Like Yours*	B
Hawking, Stephen. *My Brief History*	B
Hay, Matt. *Soundtrack of Silence*	B
Heumann, Judith E. *Being Heumann*	B
Kisor, Henry. *Traveling with Service Animals*	362.4
Ladau, Emily. *Demystifying Disability*	305.9
Lehrer, Riva. *Golem Girl*	B
Leland, Andrew. ★*The Country of the Blind*	B
Mattlin, Ben. *Disability Pride*	323.3
Mlodinow, Leonard. *Stephen Hawking*	B
Mooney, Jonathan. *Normal Sucks*	B
Ndopu, Eddie. *Sipping Dom Pérignon Through a Straw*	B
Nielsen, Kim E. *A Disability History of the United States*	362.40973
Quave, Cassandra Leah. *The Plant Hunter*	581.6
Ramey, Sarah. *The Lady's Handbook for Her Mysterious Illness*	B
Rogers-Whitehead, Carrie. ★*Serving Teens and Adults on the Autism Spectrum*	027.6
Shriver, Timothy P. *Fully Alive*	796.087
Sinise, Gary. *Grateful American*	B
Sjunneson, Elsa. *Being Seen*	362.4
Slice, Jessica. *Dateable*	646.7
Taussig, Rebekah. *Sitting Pretty*	B
Wong, Alice. ★*Year of the Tiger*	B
Yoshino, Kenji. *Say the Right Thing*	305.3

PEOPLE WITH DISFIGUREMENTS

Patchett, Ann. *Truth & Beauty*	B

PEOPLE WITH DISSOCIATIVE IDENTITY DISORDER

Nathan, Debbie. *Sybil Exposed*	B

PEOPLE WITH DYSLEXIA

Malone, Jo. *Jo Malone*	B

PEOPLE WITH EATING DISORDERS

Burton, Susan. *Empty*	B
Clein, Emmeline. ★*Dead Weight*	616.85
Couric, Katie. *Going There*	B
Freeman, Hadley. *Good Girls*	616.85
Kazdin, Cole. ★*What's Eating Us*	616.85

PEOPLE WITH EMOTIONAL ILLNESSES

Taraborrelli, J. Randy. ★*The Secret Life of Marilyn Monroe*	B

PEOPLE WITH EPILEPSY

B., David. *Epileptic*	741.5
Brown, Molly McCully. *The Virginia State Colony for Epileptics and Feebleminded*	811
Eichenwald, Kurt. *A Mind Unraveled*	B

PEOPLE WITH HIV

Duberman, Martin B. *Hold Tight Gently*	920
France, David. *How to Survive a Plague*	362.196
Gooch, Brad. *Radiant*	B
Holt, Nathalia. *Cured*	614.5

PEOPLE WITH LEPROSY

Fessler, Pam. *Carville's Cure*	362.19699

PEOPLE WITH LUNG CANCER

Caldwell, Gail. *Let's Take the Long Way Home*	B

PEOPLE WITH MENTAL ILLNESSES

Aviv, Rachel. ★*Strangers to Ourselves*	616.89
Bamford, Maria. *Sure, I'll Join Your Cult*	B
Deisseroth, Karl. *Projections*	616.89
English, Charlie. *The Gallery of Miracles and Madness*	709.04
Ford, Elizabeth. *Sometimes Amazing Things Happen*	B
Grinker, Roy Richard. *Nobody's Normal*	616.89
Hulls, Tessa. ★*Feeding Ghosts*	741.5
Kennedy, Patrick J. ★*Profiles in Mental Health Courage*	362.29
Kissinger, Meg. *While You Were Out*	362.2
Kolker, Robert. ★*Hidden Valley Road*	920
Kriss, Alexander. *Borderline*	616.85
Lawson, Jenny. *Furiously Happy*	B
Lieberman, Jeffrey A. *Shrinks*	616.89
McGrath, Ben. *Riverman*	797.122
Nathan, Debbie. *Sybil Exposed*	B
Paperny, Anna Mehler. *Hello I Want to Die Please Fix Me*	362.2
Prideaux, Sue. *I Am Dynamite!*	B
Sardy, Marin. *The Edge of Every Day*	B
Scheier, Liz. *Never Simple*	B
Schreiber, Flora Rheta. *Sybil*	616.85
Stryker, Kitty. *Ask*	302
Tallis, Frank. *The Incurable Romantic*	152.4
Taraborrelli, J. Randy. ★*The Secret Life of Marilyn Monroe*	B
Tweedy, Damon. *Facing the Unseen*	362.2
Wilson, Brian. *I Am Brian Wilson*	B

PEOPLE WITH MULTIPLE SCLEROSIS

Blair, Selma. *Mean Baby*	B

PEOPLE WITH PARAPLEGIA

Okorafor, Nnedi. *Broken Places & Outer Spaces*	153.3
Taussig, Rebekah. *Sitting Pretty*	B

PEOPLE WITH PARKINSON'S DISEASE

Fox, Michael J. *No Time Like the Future*	B
Rehm, Diane. *On My Own*	B

PEOPLE WITH POLIOMYELITIS

Heumann, Judith E. *Being Heumann*	B
Risner, Vaneetha Rendall. *Walking Through Fire*	B

PEOPLE WITH POST-TRAUMATIC STRESS DISORDER

Kander, Jason. *Invisible Storm*	B
Leaming, Barbara. *Jacqueline Bouvier Kennedy Onassis*	B
Mailhot, Terese Marie. *Heart Berries*	B

PEOPLE WITH SCHIZOPHRENIA

Granata, Vince. *Everything Is Fine*	B
Kolker, Robert. ★*Hidden Valley Road*	920
Lieberman, Jeffrey A. *Malady of the Mind*	616.89
Rosen, Jonathan. ★*The Best Minds*	616.89
Sardy, Marin. *The Edge of Every Day*	B

PEOPLE WITH SPINAL CORD INJURIES

Walton, Bill. *Back from the Dead*	B

PEOPLE WITH TERMINAL ILLNESSES

Albom, Mitch. *Tuesdays with Morrie*	B
Ali, Fatima. ★*Savor*	B
Arthur, Alua. ★*Briefly Perfectly Human*	306.9
Bailey, Elisabeth. *The Sound of a Wild Snail Eating*	594
Barkan, Ady. *Eyes to the Wind*	B
Biden, Joseph R. *Promise Me, Dad*	B
Bloom, Amy. *In Love*	B
Braitman, Laurel. *What Looks Like Bravery*	B
Danticat, Edwidge. *The Art of Death*	809
Engelhart, Katie. *The Inevitable*	179.7
Fagan, Kate. *All the Colors Came Out*	B
Hitchens, Christopher. *Mortality*	304.6
Kerr, Christopher. *Death Is but a Dream*	155.9
Kubler-Ross, Elisabeth. *On Death and Dying*	155.9
Preszler, Trent. *Little and Often*	B
Quinn, Tallu Schuyler. *What We Wish Were True*	B
Riggs, Nina. *The Bright Hour*	B
Ruhl, Sarah. *Letters from Max*	811
Schwalbe, Will. ★*The End of Your Life Book Club*	B
Taylor, Cory. *Dying*	B
Winn, Raynor. ★*The Salt Path*	B
Winn, Raynor. *The Wild Silence*	B
Zauner, Michelle. ★*Crying in H Mart*	B

PEOPLE WITH TUBERCULOSIS

Secrest, Meryle. *Modigliani*	B
Smilios, Maria. ★*The Black Angels*	610.73

PUBLIC LIBRARY CORE COLLECTION: NONFICTION
Twentieth Edition

PEOPLE WITH VISUAL DISABILITIES
    Bruni, Frank. *The Beauty of Dusk* — B
A People's History of the American Revolution. Raphael, Ray — 973.3
★*A People's* History of the United States. Zinn, Howard — 973
The *People's* Hospital. Nuila, Ricardo — 362.1
People's Movements, People's Press. Ostertag, Bob — 071
The *People's* Republic of Amnesia. Lim, Louisa — 951.05
A People's Tragedy. Figes, Orlando — 947.08
The *People's* Tycoon. Watts, Steven — B
The *People,* No. Frank, Thomas — 320.56
Pepin, Jacques
    The Apprentice — B
    Art of the Chicken — 641.665
    Essential Pepin — 641.594
    ★*Jacques Pepin* — 641.5
    ★*Jacques Pepin* — 641.594
    ★*Jacques Pepin Cooking My Way* — 641.5
PEPIN, JACQUES, 1935-
    Child, Julia. *Julia and Jacques Cooking at Home* — 641.594
    Pepin, Jacques. *The Apprentice* — B
    Pepin, Jacques. *Art of the Chicken* — 641.665
The *Pepper* Thai Cookbook. Teigen, Pepper (Vilailuck) — 641.595
PEPPERS
    Kang, Mingoo. *Jang* — 641.595
Peppler, Rebekah
    Le Sud — 641.594
Pepys, Samuel
    The Diary of Samuel Pepys — B
PEPYS, SAMUEL, 1633-1703
    Pepys, Samuel. *The Diary of Samuel Pepys* — B
    Tomalin, Claire. *Samuel Pepys* — B
PERCEPTION
    Bloom, Paul. *Psych* — 150
    Bordo, Susan. *The Creation of Anne Boleyn* — 942.05
    Cole, Teju. *Blind Spot* — 770
    Currid-Halkett, Elizabeth. *The Overlooked Americans* — 307.76
    Higgins, Jackie. *Sentient* — 573.8
    Hoffman, Donald D. *The Case Against Reality* — 121
    Kandel, Eric R. *The Age of Insight* — 154.2
    Kinzler, Katherine D. *How You Say It* — 302.2
    Livio, Mario. *Why?* — 153.3
    Medina, John. *Brain Rules* — 153
    Rogers, Adam. *Full Spectrum* — 152.14
    Rubin, Gretchen Craft. ★*Life in Five Senses* — 152.1
    Smith, Richard MacLean. *Unexplained* — 130
    Stone, Deborah A. *Counting* — 001.4
    Strevens, Michael. *The Knowledge Machine* — 500
    Ward, Ashley. *Where We Meet the World* — 612.8
PERCY FAMILY
    Barry, John M. *Rising Tide* — 977
Percy, Benjamin
    Thrill Me — 808.3
Perelman, Deb
    ★*The Smitten Kitchen Cookbook* — 641.5
    ★*Smitten Kitchen Every Day* — 641.5
    ★*Smitten Kitchen Keepers* — 641.5
PERELMAN, GRIGORI, 1966-
    Szpiro, George. *Poincare's Prize* — 510.76
Perennial. Forsythe, Kelly — 811
Peres, Shimon
    No Room for Small Dreams — B
PERESTROIKA
    Remnick, David. *Lenin's Tomb* — 947.085
    Taubman, William. *Gorbachev* — B
PERETTI, JONAH
    Smith, Ben. *Traffic* — 070.4
Perez, Joseph
    ★*The Spanish Inquisition* — 272
★*The Perfect* Father. Glatt, John — 364.152
The *Perfect* Horse. Letts, Elizabeth — 940.54
Perfect Madness. Warner, Judith — 306.874
Perfect Pan Pizza. Reinhart, Peter — 641.82
The *Perfect* Pass. Gwynne, S. C. — 920
The *Perfect* Storm. Junger, Sebastian — 974.4
A Perfect Union. Allgor, Catherine — B
Perfecting Sound Forever. Milner, Greg — 781.49
PERFECTION
    Kushner, Harold S. *How Good Do We Have to Be?* — 296.7

Preston, Katherine. *Out with It* — B
Riess, Jana. *Flunking Sainthood* — 248.4
Stone, Lillian. ★*Everybody's Favorite* — 814.6
The *Perfection* Deception. Bluestein, Jane — 155.2
PERFECTIONISM
    Bluestein, Jane. *The Perfection Deception* — 155.2
    Gaines, Joanna. *The Stories We Tell* — B
    Hu, Elise. *Flawless* — 646.7
    Leader, Zachary. *The Life of Saul Bellow* — B
    Prescod, Danielle. *Token Black Girl* — B
    Storr, Will. *Selfie* — 155.2
    Tallent, Elizabeth. *Scratched* — B
    ★*The Perfectionists.* Winchester, Simon — 620.009
The *Perfectly* Imperfect Home. Needleman, Deborah — 747
PERFORMANCE
    Duhigg, Charles. *Smarter Faster Better* — 158
    Ericsson, K. Anders. *Peak* — 153.9
    Fabritius, Friederike. *The Leading Brain* — 158
    Fox, Dan. *Pretentiousness* — 700
    Friedman, Ron. *Decoding Greatness* — 650.1
    Hansen, Morten T. *Great at Work* — 650.1
    Kessler, Lauren. *Raising the Barre* — 792.8
    Mueller, Jennifer. *Creative Change* — 658.4
    Rainbow, Randy. *Playing with Myself* — B
    Segura, Tom. ★*I'd Like to Play Alone, Please* — B
    Tracy, Brian. *Full Engagement!* — 658.3
    Webb, Caroline. *How to Have a Good Day* — 650.1
PERFORMANCE ART
    Abramovic, Marina. *Walk Through Walls* — B
    Mauceri, John. *For the Love of Music* — 781.1
PERFORMANCE ARTISTS
    Abramovic, Marina. *Walk Through Walls* — B
PERFORMANCE IN CHILDREN
    Shankar, Shalini. *Beeline* — 155.4
The *Performance* of Becoming Human. Borzutzky, Daniel — 811
PERFORMING ARTS
    Abdurraqib, Hanif. ★*A Little Devil in America* — 791.089
    Butler, Isaac. *The Method* — 792.02
    Giddins, Gary. *Weather Bird* — 781.6509
    Levy, Reynold. *They Told Me Not to Take That Job* — 792.09
    Madden, Thomas F. *Venice* — 945
    Moore, Rachel. *The Artist's Compass* — 791
    Mordden, Ethan. *Ziegfeld* — B
    Posnanski, Joe. ★*The Life and Afterlife of Harry Houdini* — 793.8
    RuPaul. ★*The House of Hidden Meanings* — B
PERFORMING ARTS FESTIVALS
    Lang, Michael. *The Road to Woodstock* — 781.66
PERFUMES
    Mazzeo, Tilar J. *The Secret of Chanel No. 5* — 338.7
    Tanais. *In Sensorium* — B
PERFUMES INDUSTRY AND TRADE
    Malone, Jo. *Jo Malone* — B
    Mazzeo, Tilar J. *The Secret of Chanel No. 5* — 338.7
Peril. Woodward, Bob — 973.933
Perillo, Lucia
    On the Spectrum of Possible Deaths — 811
    Time Will Clean the Carcass Bones — 811
Perilous Glory. France, John — 355
Perilous Times. Stone, Geoffrey R. — 323.44
Perino, Michael A.
    The Hellhound of Wall Street — 330.973
★*Period.* End of Sentence. Diamant, Anita — 612.6
PERIODIC LAW
    Challoner, Jack. *The Elements* — 546
    Gray, Theodore W. ★*The Elements* — 546
    Kean, Sam. *The Disappearing Spoon* — 546
The *Periodic* Table. Levi, Primo — 858
PERIODIC TABLE OF THE ELEMENTS
    Levi, Primo. *The Periodic Table* — 858
PERIODICAL EDITORS
    Hirshey, Gerri. *Not Pretty Enough* — B
    King, Dean. *Guardians of the Valley* — 333.72
    Mankoff, Robert. *How About Never—Is Never Good for You?* — 741.5
    Miller, Adrienne. *In the Land of Men* — 070.5
    Prescod, Danielle. *Token Black Girl* — B
PERIODICAL PUBLISHERS AND PUBLISHING
    Brunsting, Karen. ★*Open Access Literature in Libraries* — 070.5
    Gillon, Steven M. *America's Reluctant Prince* — B

AUTHOR, TITLE, SERIES AND SUBJECT INDEX

PERIODICAL WRITERS
   Roach, Margaret. ★*A Way to Garden* — 635
PERIODICAL WRITING
   Gay, Roxane. ★*Opinions* — 814
   Harrison, Jim. *The Search for the Genuine* — 814
   Lepore, Jill. ★*The Deadline* — 814
   Thompson, Hunter S. *Fear and Loathing at Rolling Stone* — 070.1
   Welteroth, Elaine. *More Than Enough* — B
PERIODICALS
   Brinkley, Alan. ★*The Publisher* — B
   Green, Robin. *The Only Girl* — 070.92
   Miller, Adrienne. *In the Land of Men* — 070.5
   Winder, Elizabeth. *Pain, Parties, Work* — B
Perkins, Anne Gardiner
   Yale Needs Women — 378
Perkins, Kendrick
   The Education of Kendrick Perkins — B
PERKINS, KENDRICK, 1984-
   Perkins, Kendrick. *The Education of Kendrick Perkins* — B
Perkins, Nichole
   Sometimes I Trip on How Happy We Could Be — B
PERKINS, NICHOLE
   Perkins, Nichole. *Sometimes I Trip on How Happy We Could Be* — B
Perl, Jed
   Calder — B
   ★*Calder* — B
Perlin, Ross
   ★*Language City* — 306.44
Perlmutter, David
   The Grain Brain Cookbook — 651.56
Perlstein, Rick
   The Invisible Bridge — 973.924
   ★*Nixonland* — 973.924
   ★*Reaganland* — 973.926
Permission to Be Imperfect. Winkler, Kyle — 170
★*Permission to Dream.* Gardner, Chris — 158.1
Permission to Feel. Brackett, Marc A — 152.4
PEROT, H. ROSS, 1930-2019
   Follett, Ken. *On Wings of Eagles* — 955
Perron, Cam
   ★*Comeback Season* — 796.357
PERRON, CAM, 1994-
   Perron, Cam. ★*Comeback Season* — 796.357
Perry Lang, Adam
   Serious Barbecue — 641.5
Perry, Bruce
   Malcolm — B
Perry, Dawn
   Ready, Set, Cook — 641.5
Perry, Imani
   Looking for Lorraine — B
   May We Forever Stand — 782.25
   ★*South to America* — 917
PERRY, IMANI, 1972-
   Perry, Imani. ★*South to America* — 917
Perry, Joe
   Rocks — B
PERRY, JOE
   Perry, Joe. *Rocks* — B
PERRY, KRISTIN
   Yoshino, Kenji. *Speak Now* — 346.79401
Perry, Mark
   The Most Dangerous Man in America — B
Perry, Matthew
   Friends, Lovers, and the Big Terrible Thing — B
PERRY, MATTHEW, 1969-2023
   Perry, Matthew. *Friends, Lovers, and the Big Terrible Thing* — B
Perry, Philippa
   ★*The Book You Wish Your Parents Had Read* — 649
PERSECUTION BY NAZIS
   Bascomb, Neal. *Faster* — 796.7209
   Hayes, Peter. *Why?* — 940.53
   Macadam, Heather Dune. *999* — 940.53
   Olson, Lynne. *Last Hope Island* — 940.53
   Rees, Laurence. *The Holocaust* — 940.53
PERSEPHONE (GREEK DEITY)
   Gluck, Louise. *Averno* — 811

PERSHING, JOHN JOSEPH, 1860-1948
   Carroll, Andrew. *My Fellow Soldiers* — 940.4
   Guinn, Jeff. ★*War on the Border* — 972.08
PERSIAN GULF WAR, 1991
   Petraeus, David Howell. *Conflict* — 355
   Swofford, Anthony. *Jarhead* — 956.7044
PERSIAN WARS, 500-449 B.C.E
   Herodotus. *The Histories* — 938
Persico, Joseph E.
   Franklin and Lucy — 973.917092
PERSISTENCE
   Alter, Adam L. *Anatomy of a Breakthrough* — 158.1
   Brenner, Marie. ★*The Desperate Hours* — 362.1962
   Brown, Jasmine. *Twice as Hard* — 610.92
   Clinton, Hillary Rodham. *The Book of Gutsy Women* — 920
   Cobbs-Leonard, Tasha. *Do It Anyway* — 241
   Copeland, Misty. *The Wind at My Back* — B
   DiGiulian, Sasha. *Take the Lead* — B
   Duckworth, Angela. *Grit* — 158.1
   Goodall, Jane. ★*The Book of Hope* — 128
   Keller, Julia. *Quitting* — 650.14
   Levine, Madeline. ★*Ready or Not* — 649
   Marshall, Cynthia. *You've Been Chosen* — B
   Miller, Lulu. *Why Fish Don't Exist* — B
   Moss, Marissa R. *Her Country* — 781.642
   Price, Margo. *Maybe We'll Make It* — B
   Rowe, Mickey. *Fearlessly Different* — B
   Rusbridger, Alan. ★*Play It Again* — B
   Samaha, Albert. *Never Ran, Never Will* — 920
   Schacter, Daniel L. *The Seven Sins of Memory* — 153.1
   Tough, Paul. ★*How Children Succeed* — 372.210973
   Tran, Paul. *All the Flowers Kneeling* — 811
Person, Charles
   Buses Are a Comin' — B
PERSON, CHARLES
   Person, Charles. *Buses Are a Comin'* — B
PERSONAL ASSISTANTS
   McKeon, Kathy. *Jackie's Girl* — B
   Movsesian, Sona. *The World's Worst Assistant* — 791.4302
PERSONAL BELONGINGS
   Becker, Joshua. *The Minimalist Home* — 241
   Saldana, Stephanie. *What We Remember Will Be Saved* — 362.7
PERSONAL CONDUCT
   Abdul-Jabbar, Kareem. *Coach Wooden and Me* — B
   Ariely, Dan. *The Honest Truth About Dishonesty* — 177
   Ariely, Dan. *Predictably Irrational* — 153.8
   Arthur, Alua. ★*Briefly Perfectly Human* — 306.9
   Ashley, Maurice. *Move by Move* — 158
   Asprey, Dave. *Game Changers* — 158.1
   Bamberger, Michael. *The Second Life of Tiger Woods* — B
   Bass, Diana Butler. *Grateful* — 241
   Bialosky, Jill. *Poetry Will Save Your Life* — B
   Black, Michael Ian. *A Better Man* — 305.31
   Bly, Robert. *More Than True* — 398.2
   Blyth, Catherine. *The Art of Conversation* — 395.5
   Bragg, Sarah. *Is Everyone Happier Than Me?* — 248.4
   Brenner, Andrea. *How to College* — 378.1
   Brooks, David. ★*The Second Mountain* — 302
   Brosh, Allie. ★*Hyperbole and a Half* — 741.5
   Brosh, Allie. ★*Solutions and Other Problems* — 741.5
   Brown, Brene. *Braving the Wilderness* — 305.8
   Brown, Mick. ★*Tearing Down the Wall of Sound* — B
   Browne, Mahogany L. ★*Black Girl Magic* — 811.6
   Bruni, Frank. *The Beauty of Dusk* — B
   Cargle, Rachel Elizabeth. *A Renaissance of Our Own* — B
   Carter, Jimmy. *Everything to Gain* — B
   Carter, Jimmy. *Sharing Good Times* — 973.926
   Chittister, Joan. *The Gift of Years* — 200
   Christakis, Erika. *The Importance of Being Little* — 372.21
   Clear, James. ★*Atomic Habits* — 155.24
   Clemmons, Francois S. *Officer Clemmons* — B
   Coel, Michaela. ★*Misfits* — 158.2
   Cohen, Rhaina. ★*The Other Significant Others* — 177
   Coles, Robert. *Lives of Moral Leadership* — 170
   Conley, Chip. ★*Learning to Love Midlife* — 646.7
   Corrigan, Kelly. *Tell Me More* — 153.6
   Covey, Stephen R. ★*The 7 Habits of Highly Effective People* — 158
   Cramer, Richard Ben. *Joe DiMaggio* — B

PUBLIC LIBRARY CORE COLLECTION: NONFICTION
Twentieth Edition

Crawford, Matthew B. *The World Beyond Your Head*	155.2
Dabiri, Emma. *Twisted*	391.5
Davis, Geena. *Dying of Politeness*	B
Day, John D. *The Longevity Plan*	612.6
De Botton, Alain. *The Pleasures and Sorrows of Work*	306.3
Dederer, Claire. ★*Monsters*	700.1
Doyle, Glennon. *Untamed*	B
Edelman, Marian Wright. *Lanterns*	362.7
Feiler, Bruce. *Life Is in the Transitions*	392
Feiler, Bruce. ★*The Search*	306.3
Ferriss, Timothy. *Tools of Titans*	081
Fitzmaurice, Simon. *It's Not yet Dark*	616.8
Fleming, Brandon P. *Miseducated*	B
Friedman, Rachel. ★*And Then We Grew Up*	305.24
Fumudoh, Ziwe. ★*Black Friend*	814
Gilbert, Elizabeth. ★*Big Magic*	153.3
Gladwell, Malcolm. *Outliers*	302
Gladwell, Malcolm. ★*Talking to Strangers*	302
Goldblatt, Duchess. *Becoming Duchess Goldblatt*	B
Greitens, Eric. *Resilience*	155.2
Guo, XIaolu. *Nine Continents*	B
Haig, Matt. *Notes on a Nervous Planet*	616.89
Hart, Hannah. *Buffering*	B
Hase, Craig. *How Not to Be a Hot Mess*	158.1
Havrilesky, Heather. *What If This Were Enough?*	152.4
Hazzard, Kevin. *A Thousand Naked Strangers*	B
Heath, Chip. *The Power of Moments*	128
Hechinger, John. ★*True Gentlemen*	371.85
Held, Shai. ★*Judaism Is About Love*	296.3
Hodgman, John. *Vacationland*	B
Holiday, Ryan. *Ego Is the Enemy*	158.1
Ignatieff, Michael. *On Consolation*	152.4
Ingall, Marjorie. *Sorry, Sorry, Sorry*	158.2
Isay, David. *Callings*	920
Jones, Brian Jay. ★*Becoming Dr. Seuss*	B
Kalanithi, Paul. ★*When Breath Becomes Air*	B
Karbo, Karen. *In Praise of Difficult Women*	920
Keeling, Ida. *Can't Nothing Bring Me Down*	B
Kelly, Kevin. ★*Excellent Advice for Living*	158.1
Keltner, Dacher. *Born to Be Good*	155.2
Kim, John. *Single on Purpose*	155.6
King, Maxwell. *The Good Neighbor*	B
Kishimi, Ichiro. *The Courage to Be Disliked*	158
Knausgaard, Karl Ove. *Spring*	B
Kohli, Sahaj Kaur. ★*But What Will People Say?*	616.89
Kubler-Ross, Elisabeth. *Life Lessons*	170
Lamott, Anne. ★*Hallelujah Anyway*	241
Lamott, Anne. ★*Somehow*	814
Lapierre, Dominique. *The City of Joy*	954
Lavery, Daniel M. *Dear Prudence*	170
Le Guin, Ursula K. *No Time to Spare*	814
Leder, Steven Z. *The Beauty of What Remains*	306.9
Lee, Shannon. *Be Water, My Friend*	796.8
LeFavour, Cree. *Lights On, Rats Out*	616.85
Levy, Deborah. *The Cost of Living*	B
Loh, Sandra Tsing. *The Madwoman and the Roomba*	B
Lyons, Daniel. *STFU*	302.2
Lythcott-Haims, Julie. *Your Turn*	305.24
Mankell, Henning. *Quicksand*	B
Manson, Mark. *The Subtle Art of Not Giving a F*ck*	158.1
Mattel, Trixie. *Working Girls*	650.1
Mays, Willie. *24*	B
McConaughey, Matthew. *Greenlights*	B
McDonough, James L. *William Tecumseh Sherman*	B
McGovern, Anna. *Pottering*	158.1
Miranda, Lin-Manuel. *Gmorning, Gnight!*	811
Mojica Rodriguez, Prisca Dorcas. *For Brown Girls with Sharp Edges and Tender Hearts*	305.48
Mooallem, Jon. *Serious Face*	814
Moore, Wes. *The Other Wes Moore*	B
Nevins, Sheila. *You Don't Look Your Age*	B
Nicolson, Adam. *How to Be*	180
Notaro, Laurie. *Excuse Me While I Disappear*	B
O'Connell, Robert L. *Revolutionary*	B
Orner, Peter. *Am I Alone Here?*	814
Osbourne, Ozzy. *I Am Ozzy*	B
Pardlo, Gregory. *Air Traffic*	B
Patchett, Ann. ★*These Precious Days*	814
Patrick, Vanessa M. *The Power of Saying No*	158.1
Pearlman, Jeff. *Boys Will Be Boys*	796.332
Phillips, Adam. *On Giving up*	158.2
Post, Lizzie. *Emily Post's Etiquette*	395
Post, Lizzie. *Emily Post's Etiquette*	395
Psaki, Jen. *Say More*	B
Quinn, Tallu Schuyler. *What We Wish Were True*	B
Radtke, Kristen. *Seek You*	741.5
Reiner, Andrew. *Better Boys, Better Men*	155.43
Retta. *So Close to Being the Sh*t, Y'all Don't Even Know*	B
Rhodes, James. *Instrumental*	B
Ricketts, Rachel. ★*Do Better*	305.800973
Riggs, Nina. *The Bright Hour*	B
Rothfeld, Becca. ★*All Things Are Too Small*	814
Saad, Layla F. ★*Me and White Supremacy*	305.809
Sandel, Michael J. *Justice*	172
Saunders, John. *Playing Hurt*	B
Schultz, Howard. *From the Ground Up*	B
Sedaris, David. ★*A Carnival of Snackery*	818
Sedaris, David. *Theft by Finding*	B
Setiya, Kieran. *Life Is Hard*	128
Shachtman, Tom. ★*Rumspringa*	305.235
Shatner, William. *Live Long And—*	B
Shipnuck, Alan. *Phil*	B
Sullivan, Meghan. *The Good Life Method*	170
Thompson, Kenan. *When I Was Your Age*	B
Tierney, John. *The Power of Bad*	158.1
Tippett, Krista. ★*Becoming Wise*	158.1
Toussaint, Alex. ★*Activate Your Greatness*	158.1
Volf, Miroslav. *Life Worth Living*	113
Wan, Bonnie. *The Life Brief*	158.1
Weber, Charlotte Fox. *Tell Me What You Want*	153.8
Welteroth, Elaine. *More Than Enough*	B
West, Lindy. *Shrill*	818
Westheimer, Ruth. *The Doctor Is In*	B
Wiking, Meik. *The Little Book of Hygge*	158.1
Williams, Patricia. *Rabbit*	B
Wilson, Chris. *The Master Plan*	B
Winkler, Kyle. *Permission to Be Imperfect*	170
Wong, Ali. ★*Dear Girls*	B
Wright, Robert. *Why Buddhism Is True*	294.3
Zuckerman, Phil. *Living the Secular Life*	211

PERSONAL DIARIES

Berg, Mary. *The Diary of Mary Berg*	B
Carroll, Ryder. ★*The Bullet Journal Method*	640
Carter, Jimmy. *White House Diary*	973.926
Dana, Richard Henry. *Two Years Before the Mast*	910.4
Ernaux, Annie. ★*The Years*	B
Harrington, Joel F. *The Faithful Executioner*	B
Kemper, Steve. *Our Man in Tokyo*	952.03
Klemperer, Victor. *I Will Bear Witness*	B
Merton, Thomas. *The Intimate Merton*	B
Reagan, Ronald. *The Reagan Diaries*	B
Schlesinger, Arthur M. *Journals, 1952-2000*	973.91092
Siegal, Nina. *The Diary Keepers*	940.54
Spiegel, Renia. *Renia's Diary*	B
Thomson, Keith. *Born to Be Hanged*	910.4
Walker, Alice. *Gathering Blossoms Under Fire*	B

Personal Effects. Jensen, Robert A. — 363.34

PERSONAL FINANCE

Allen, Marshall. ★*Never Pay the First Bill*	610.28
Ariely, Dan. *Dollars and Sense*	332.024
Calhoun, Ada. *Why We Can't Sleep*	305.244
Davenport, Anthony. *Your Score*	332.7
De Leon, Paco. *Finance for the People*	332.024
Fagan, Chelsea. *The Financial Diet*	332.024
Halpern, Jake. *Bad Paper*	332.7
Hammond, Claudia. *Mind Over Money*	332.401
Kardas-Nelson, Mara. *We Are Not Able to Live in the Sky*	332.3
Kobliner, Beth. *Make Your Kid a Money Genius (even If You're Not)*	332.024
Kotlikoff, Laurence J. *Money Magic*	332.024
Lanchester, John. *How to Speak Money*	330.1
Lieber, Ron. *The Opposite of Spoiled*	332.0240083
Lowry, Erin. ★*Broke Millennial Talks Money*	332.024
Mecham, Jesse. *You Need a Budget*	332.024
Morduch, Jonathan. *The Financial Diaries*	332.024
Orman, Suze. ★*The Ultimate Retirement Guide for 50+*	306.3
Orman, Suze. *Women & Money*	332.0240082

AUTHOR, TITLE, SERIES AND SUBJECT INDEX

Power, Marianne. *Help Me!*	158.1
Quart, Alissa. *Squeezed*	305.5
Quinn, Jane Bryant. ★*How to Make Your Money Last*	332.024
Ramsey, Dave. *The Total Money Makeover*	332.024
Rick, Scott. *Tightwads and Spendthrifts*	332.024
Sabatier, Grant. *Financial Freedom*	332.024
Servon, Lisa J. *The Unbanking of America*	332.10973
Simmons, Lauren. *Make Money Move*	332.024
Stanley, Thomas J. *The Next Millionaire Next Door*	332.024
Tu, Vivian. *Rich Af*	332.024

PERSONAL LETTERS
Gooch, Brad. ★*Flannery*	B
Lewis, C. S. ★*The Screwtape Letters*	248.4

PERSONAL SPACE
Dabiri, Emma. *Twisted*	391.5

PERSONAL TRAINERS
Rigsby, Cody. ★*XOXO, Cody*	B
Toussaint, Alex. ★*Activate Your Greatness*	158.1

PERSONALITY
Crawford, Saffi. *The Power of Birthdays, Stars & Numbers*	133.5
Duckworth, Angela. *Grit*	158.1
Gimenez Smith, Carmen. *Be Recorder*	811
Goldschneider, Gary. ★*The Secret Language of Birthdays*	133.5
Horowitz, Alexandra. ★*The Year of the Puppy*	636.7
Rogers, Susan E. ★*This Is What It Sounds Like*	781.1
Ullrich, Volker. *Hitler*	B

PERSONALITY AND POLITICS
Hoffman, Carl. *Liar's Circus*	973.933

PERSONALITY DEVELOPMENT
Wegner, Bobbi. *Raising Feminist Boys*	305.23
Whippman, Ruth. ★*Boymom*	305.23

PERSONALITY DISORDERS
Kriss, Alexander. *Borderline*	616.85
Nathan, Debbie. *Sybil Exposed*	B
Ronson, Jon. ★*The Psychopath Test*	616.85

PERSONALITY TESTS
Gould, Stephen Jay. *The Mismeasure of Man*	153.9

PERSONNEL MANAGEMENT
Braswell, Porter. ★*Let Them See You*	650.1
Economy, Peter. *Wait, I'm the Boss?!?*	658
Fuller, Pamela. ★*The Leader's Guide to Unconscious Bias*	658.3
Gallo, Amy. *Getting Along*	658.4
Scott, Kim Malone. *Radical Candor*	658.4
Smith, Clint. *How to Hire*	658.3

PERSPECTIVE
Brehm, Matthew T. *Drawing Perspective*	742
Chelsea, David. *Perspective in Action*	741.5
Jackson, Major. *Razzle Dazzle*	811
Tyson, Neil deGrasse. *Starry Messenger*	901
Perspective in Action. Chelsea, David	741.5

PERSPECTIVE, PERSONAL
Kethledge, Raymond Michael. *Lead Yourself First*	658.4
★*The Persuaders.* Giridharadas, Anand	320.973

PERSUASION (PSYCHOLOGY)
Cialdini, Robert B. *Influence*	153.8
Dutton, Kevin. *Split-Second Persuasion*	153.8
Giridharadas, Anand. ★*The Persuaders*	320.973
Seo, Bo. *Good Arguments*	808.53

PERSUASION (RHETORIC)
Fish, Stanley Eugene. *Winning Arguments*	808

PERT, CANDACE B., 1946-2013
Ryckman, Pamela. *Candace Pert*	B

PERU
Adams, Mark. *Turn Right at Machu Picchu*	985
Arana, Marie. *American Chica*	B
Bingham, Hiram. ★*Lost City of the Incas*	985
Heaney, Christopher. *Cradle of Gold*	B

PERUVIAN PEOPLE
Vargas Llosa, Mario. *The Call of the Tribe*	868

Pesca, Mike
Upon Further Review	796

PESKY, JOHNNY, 1919-2012
Halberstam, David. *The Teammates*	B

Pessah, Jon
The Game	796.357
Yogi	B
Pessoa. Zenith, Richard	B

PESSOA, FERNANDO, 1888-1935
Zenith, Richard. *Pessoa*	B

Pestana, Carla Gardina
The World of Plymouth Plantation	974.4

Pester, Sophie
Homemade Holiday	745.594
Supercraft	745.5

PESTICIDES
Carson, Rachel. ★*Silent Spring*	363.738
Souder, William. *On a Farther Shore*	B
Pests. Brookshire, Bethany	590

PESTS
Brookshire, Bethany. *Pests*	590

PET ADOPTION
Carr, Caleb. *My Beloved Monster*	B
Novello, Carol. *Mutual Rescue*	636.088

PET CARE
Schott, Philipp. *The Accidental Veterinarian*	B

PET INDUSTRY AND TRADE
Kavin, Kim. *The Dog Merchants*	636.7

PET OWNERS
Masson, J. Moussaieff. *Lost Companions*	636.088
Montgomery, Sy. *The Good Good Pig*	636.4
Orlean, Susan. *On Animals*	590
Sife, Wallace. *The Loss of a Pet*	155.9

PET THERAPY
Halpern, Sue. *A Dog Walks into a Nursing Home*	B
Louv, Richard. *Our Wild Calling*	615.8

Peta, Joe
Trading Bases	796.357
The Peter Principle. Peter, Laurence J.	658
Peter Shaffer's Amadeus. Shaffer, Peter	822

Peter, Laurence J.
The Peter Principle	658

Peters, Charles
Lyndon B. Johnson	B

Peters, Meike
Noon	641.5

Peters, Rebecca Todd
Trust Women	362.1988

PETERS, ROBERT PARKINS
Sisman, Adam. *The Professor and the Parson*	364.16

Petersen, Andrea
On Edge	616.85

PETERSEN, ANDREA
Petersen, Andrea. *On Edge*	616.85

Petersen, Anne Helen
Can't Even	305.242

Petersen, Grant
Just Ride	796.6

Petersen, Sara
Momfluenced	306.87

Petersik, Sherry
Lovable Livable Home	645
The *Peterson* field guide series [Series]. McKnight, Kent H.	579.6
Peterson Field Guide to Birds of Eastern and Central North America. Peterson, Roger Tory	598.097
Peterson Field Guide to Birds of Western North America. Peterson, Roger Tory	598.097
★*Peterson Field Guide to Freshwater Fishes of North America North of Mexico.* Page, Lawrence M.	597.176
★*Peterson Field Guide to Western Reptiles and Amphibians.* McGinnis, Samuel M	597.9
Peterson Reference Guide to Woodpeckers of North America. Shunk, Stephen A.	598.7

Peterson, Bryan
Learning to See Creatively	770
Understanding Exposure	771

Peterson, Dale
Giraffe Reflections	599.638
The Moral Lives of Animals	156

Peterson, Eugene H.
This Hallelujah Banquet	228

Peterson, James
Sauces	641.81

Peterson, Marlon
Bird Uncaged	B

PETERSON, MARLON
   Peterson, Marlon. *Bird Uncaged* — B
Peterson, Roger Tory
   Peterson Field Guide to Birds of Eastern and Central North America — 598.097
   Peterson Field Guide to Birds of Western North America — 598.097
PETERSON, WILLIE, 1896-1940
   Morrison, Melanie. *Murder on Shades Mountain* — 345.761
PETIOT, MARCEL
   King, David. *Death in the City of Light* — 364.152
Petraeus, David Howell
   Conflict — 355
Petri, Alexandra
   Alexandra Petri's US History — 817
   Nothing Is Wrong and Here Is Why — 973.933
Petrides, George A.
   A Field Guide to Western Trees — 582.16
Petropoulos, Jonathan
   The Faustian Bargain — 709
Petrosino, Kiki
   White Blood — 811
Petrushevskaia, Liudmila
   The Girl from the Metropol Hotel — B
PETRUSHEVSKAIA, LIUDMILA
   Petrushevskaia, Liudmila. *The Girl from the Metropol Hotel* — B
PETS
   Attas, Amy. *Pets and the City* — B
   Habib, Rodney. ★*The Forever Dog* — 636.7
   Montgomery, Sy. *The Good Good Pig* — 636.4
   Myron, Vicki. ★*Dewey* — 636.80092
   Orlean, Susan. *On Animals* — 590
   Stewart, Tracey. *Do Unto Animals* — 590
   Weitzman, Gary. *National Geographic Complete Guide to Pet Health, Behavior, and Happiness* — 636.088
Pets and the City. Attas, Amy — B
Pettegree, Andrew
   The Book in the Renaissance — 070.5
   The Library — 027.4
Petty. Zanes, Warren — B
PETTY, TOM
   Zanes, Warren. *Petty* — B
Peyser, Marc N.
   Hissing Cousins — B
Pfeffer, Anshel
   Bibi — B
Pfeifer, Joseph
   Ordinary Heroes — 973.931
PFEIFER, JOSEPH, 1956-
   Pfeifer, Joseph. *Ordinary Heroes* — 973.931
Pfeiffer, Jacquy
   The Art of French Pastry — 641.86
Phair, Liz
   Horror Stories — B
PHAIR, LIZ
   Phair, Liz. *Horror Stories* — B
Pham, Andrew X.
   ★*The Eaves of Heaven* — B
Pham, Larissa
   Pop Song — 709.2
PHAM, LARISSA
   Pham, Larissa. *Pop Song* — 709.2
PHAM, THONG VAN
   Pham, Andrew X. ★*The Eaves of Heaven* — B
Phantom Lady. Lane, Christina — B
★*Pharma.* Posner, Gerald L. — 338.4
PHARMACEUTICAL RESEARCH
   Slater, Lauren. *Blue Dreams* — 615.7
PHARMACOLOGISTS
   Ryckman, Pamela. *Candace Pert* — B
Phasers on Stun! Britt, Ryan — 791.45
PHEIDIPPIDES, FL. 490 B.C.E
   Karnazes, Dean. *The Legend of Marathon* — 796.42
   McDougall, Christopher. *Natural Born Heroes* — 940.53
Phelan, Thomas W.
   1-2-3 Magic — 649
Phelan, Tom
   We Were Rich and We Didn't Know It — B
Phelps, Isela
   Loom Knitting Primer — 746.43

PHENOLOGY
   Keffer, Ken. *Earth Almanac* — 508
Phenomena. Jacobsen, Annie — 133.8
PHENOMENOLOGY
   Eilenberger, Wolfram. *Time of the Magicians* — 920
Phil. Shipnuck, Alan — B
PHILADELPHIA, PENNSYLVANIA
   Black Thought. *The Upcycled Self* — B
   Dunbar, Erica Armstrong. ★*Never Caught* — B
   Goyal, Nikhil. ★*Live to See the Day* — 305.5
   Greenidge, Kerri. ★*The Grimkes* — 973.5
   Hudes, Quiara Alegria. ★*My Broken Language* — B
   Solomonov, Michael. *Israeli Soul* — 641.595
   Solomonov, Michael. *Zahav* — 641.595
PHILANTHROPISTS
   Cannadine, David. ★*Mellon* — B
   Cargle, Rachel Elizabeth. *A Renaissance of Our Own* — B
   Forgosh, Linda B. *Louis Bamberger* — B
   Gordon, Meryl. *Bunny Mellon* — B
   Hanes, Stephanie. *White Man's Game* — 333.95
   Kidder, Tracy. *A Truck Full of Money* — B
   Krass, Peter. *Carnegie* — B
   McNamara, Eileen. ★*Eunice* — B
   Nasaw, David. *Andrew Carnegie* — B
   Newman, Paul. *The Extraordinary Life of an Ordinary Man* — B
   Ronald, Susan. *A Dangerous Woman* — B
   Schwab, Tim. ★*The Bill Gates Problem* — 361.7
   Smith, Richard Norton. *On His Own Terms* — 973.925092
   Thomas, Franklin A. *An Unplanned Life* — B
   Watts, Steven. *The People's Tycoon* — B
PHILANTHROPY
   Doyne, Maggie. *Between the Mountain and the Sky* — B
   Ford, Tanisha C. *Our Secret Society* — B
   Hanes, Stephanie. *White Man's Game* — 333.95
Philbrick, Nathaniel
   ★*Bunker Hill* — 973.3
   ★*In the Hurricane's Eye* — 973.3
   ★*The Last Stand* — 973.8
   ★*Mayflower* — 973.2
   Travels with George — 973.4
   ★*Valiant Ambition* — B
   Why Read Moby-Dick? — 813
PHILBRICK, NATHANIEL
   Philbrick, Nathaniel. *Travels with George* — 973.4
PHILBY, KIM, 1912-1988
   Macintyre, Ben. *A Spy Among Friends* — B
PHILIP, PRINCE, CONSORT OF ELIZABETH II, QUEEN OF GREAT BRITAIN, 1921-2021
   Larman, Alexander. ★*Power and Glory* — 941.085
Philip, Robert
   The Classical Music Lover's Companion to Orchestral Music — 784.2
PHILIPPA, QUEEN, CONSORT OF EDWARD III, KING OF ENGLAND, -1369
   Weir, Alison. *Queens of the Age of Chivalry* — 920
PHILIPPINES
   Barnes, Cinelle. *Monsoon Mansion* — B
   Brotherton, Marcus. *A Bright and Blinding Sun* — 940.54
   Bruning, John R. *Indestructible* — B
   Capozzola, Christopher. *Bound by War* — 355
   Evangelista, Patricia. ★*Some People Need Killing* — 364.4
   Freeman, Sally Mott. *The Jersey Brothers* — 920
   Immerwahr, Daniel. *How to Hide an Empire* — 973
   Morris, Edmund. ★*Theodore Rex* — 973.911
   Norman, Elizabeth M. *We Band of Angels* — 940.54
   Resendez, Andres. *Conquering the Pacific* — 959.9
   Ressa, Maria. ★*How to Stand up to a Dictator* — 070.92
   Samaha, Albert. *Concepcion* — 929
   Scott, James. *Rampage* — 940.54
   Thomas, Evan. *Sea of Thunder* — 940.54
Philipps, Busy
   This Will Only Hurt a Little — B
PHILIPPS, BUSY, 1979-
   Philipps, Busy. *This Will Only Hurt a Little* — B
Philipps, David
   Alpha — 956.7044
Philipps, Roland
   A Spy Named Orphan — B

AUTHOR, TITLE, SERIES AND SUBJECT INDEX

PHILLIP, ARTHUR, 1738-1814
 Keneally, Thomas. *A Commonwealth of Thieves*   994
Phillips, Adam
 On Giving up   158.2
Phillips, Adrian
 Fighting Churchill, Appeasing Hitler   327.41043
Phillips, Carl
 ★ *Then the War*   811
Phillips, Collette A. M.
 The Includers   658.4
PHILLIPS, IRNA, 1901-1973
 Armstrong, Jennifer Keishin. *When Women Invented Television*   791.45
Phillips, Julie
 James Tiptree, Jr.   B
Phillips, Kevin
 1775   973.3
Phillips, Maya
 Nerd   302.23
PHILLIPS, MAYA, 1990-
 Phillips, Maya. *Nerd*   302.23
Phillips, Patrick
 Blood at the Root   305.8
Phillips, Rowan Ricardo
 The Circuit   796.342
PHILLIPS, SAM, 1923-2003
 Guralnick, Peter. ★ *Sam Phillips*   B
Phillips, Timothy
 Retracing the Iron Curtain   909.82
PHILLIPS, TIMOTHY
 Phillips, Timothy. *Retracing the Iron Curtain*   909.82
Phillips-Fein, Kim
 Fear City   330.9747
PHILOLOGISTS
 Klemperer, Victor. *I Will Bear Witness*   B
***Philosopher** of the Heart*. Carlisle, Clare   B
PHILOSOPHERS
 Bakewell, Sarah. ★ *At the Existentialist Cafe*   920
 Blight, David W. ★ *Frederick Douglass*   B
 Carlisle, Clare. *Philosopher of the Heart*   B
 Conradi, Peter J. *Iris*   B
 Curran, Andrew S. *Diderot and the Art of Thinking Freely*   194
 Durant, Will. ★ *The Story of Philosophy*   190
 Eilenberger, Wolfram. *Time of the Magicians*   920
 Frampton, Saul. *When I Am Playing with My Cat, How Do I Know She Is Not Playing with Me?*   844
 Grayling, A. C. *The History of Philosophy*   109
 Hagglund, Martin. *This Life*   110
 Hughes, Bettany. ★ *The Hemlock Cup*   B
 Ignatieff, Michael. *On Consolation*   152.4
 Johnson, Paul. *Socrates*   183
 Kaplan, Alice Yaeger. *Looking for the Stranger*   B
 Liedman, Sven-Eric. *A World to Win*   B
 Miller, Jim. *Examined Lives*   B
 Moore, Peter. *Life, Liberty, and the Pursuit of Happiness*   199
 Prideaux, Sue. *I Am Dynamite!*   B
 Richardson, Robert D. *William James*   B
 Ruttenberg, Danya. *On Repentance and Repair*   202
 Soep, Elisabeth. *Other People's Words*   155.9
 Sperber, Jonathan. *Karl Marx*   B
 Stone, I. F. *The Trial of Socrates*   183
 Vanek Smith, Stacey. *Machiavelli for Women*   650.1
 Watson, Richard A. *Cogito Ergo Sum*   B
 Wulf, Andrea. *Magnificent Rebels*   830.9
PHILOSOPHICAL ANTHROPOLOGY
 Wilson, Edward O. *The Meaning of Human Existence*   128
PHILOSOPHY
 Aptowicz, Cristin O'Keefe. *Dr. Mutter's Marvels*   B
 Aristotle. ★ *The Basic Works of Aristotle*   185
 Aristotle. ★ *Politics, 2nd Ed*   320
 Bakewell, Sarah. ★ *At the Existentialist Cafe*   920
 Bakewell, Sarah. *How to Live—Or—A Life of Montaigne*   B
 Bari, Shahidha K. *Dressed*   391
 Barra, Allen. ★ *The Last Coach*   B
 Beard, Mary. ★ *S.P.Q.R.*   937
 Black Elk. *Black Elk Speaks*   B
 Blackburn, Simon. *The Oxford Dictionary of Philosophy*   103
 Blackburn, Simon. *Think*   100
 Boucheron, Patrick. *Machiavelli*   320.1092

 Brown, Archie. ★ *The Rise and Fall of Communism*   320.53
 Budiansky, Stephen. *Journey to the Edge of Reason*   B
 Carroll, Sean M. *The Big Picture*   577
 Crawford, Matthew B. *The World Beyond Your Head*   155.2
 Dawkins, Richard. ★ *The Ancestor's Tale*   576.8
 De Bres, Helena. *How to Be Multiple*   155.44
 Delaney, Brigid. *Reasons Not to Worry*   158.1
 Dennett, D. C. *Darwin's Dangerous Idea*   146
 Dennett, D. C. *Intuition Pumps and Other Tools for Thinking*   121
 Descartes, Rene. ★ *Descartes*   194
 Durant, Will. ★ *The Story of Philosophy*   190
 Eco, Umberto. *History of Beauty*   111
 Einstein, Albert. *Ideas and Opinions*   081
 Ellis, Joseph J. ★ *American Dialogue*   973.3
 Fletcher, Seth. *Einstein's Shadow*   523.8
 Foer, Jonathan Safran. *Eating Animals*   641.3
 Foulkes, Lucy. ★ *Losing Our Minds*   616.89
 Fukuyama, Francis. *Liberalism and Its Discontents*   320.51
 Gay, Peter. *The Enlightenment*   190
 Gay, Peter. *The Enlightenment*   190
 Gewen, Barry. ★ *The Inevitability of Tragedy*   B
 Gottlieb, Anthony. ★ *The Dream of Enlightenment*   190
 Gottlieb, Anthony. *The Dream of Reason*   180
 Graeber, David. *The Dawn of Everything*   901
 Grayling, A. C. *The History of Philosophy*   109
 Greene, B. *Until the End of Time*   523.1
 Gutting, Gary. *What Philosophy Can Do*   100
 Harman, Oren Solomon. *Evolutions*   201
 Hawking, Stephen. ★ *Black Holes and Baby Universes and Other Essays*   530.1
 Hayek, Friedrich A. von. *The Road to Serfdom*   330.1
 Heidegger, Martin. ★ *Being and Time*   111
 Hitchens, Christopher. *The Four Horsemen*   211
 Hobbes, Thomas. ★ *Leviathan*   320.01
 Holiday, Ryan. *Lives of the Stoics*   188
 Holt, Jim. *Why Does the World Exist?*   113
 Hunt, Tristram. *Marx's General*   335.4092
 Ignatieff, Michael. *On Consolation*   152.4
 Isenberg, Nancy. *The Problem of Democracy*   973.4
 Johnson, Paul. *Socrates*   183
 Junger, Sebastian. ★ *In My Time of Dying*   304.6
 Kaag, John J. *American Philosophy*   191
 Kaag, John J. *Hiking with Nietzsche*   193
 Kant, Immanuel. ★ *Basic Writings of Kant*   193
 Kawa, Abraham. *Democracy*   741.5
 Kimmerer, Robin Wall. ★ *Braiding Sweetgrass*   304.2
 Kishimi, Ichiro. *The Courage to Be Disliked*   158
 Kreeft, Peter. ★ *Philosophy 101 by Socrates*   183
 Kundera, Milan. ★ *The Curtain*   801
 Larson, Edward J. *Evolution*   576.8
 Lee, Shannon. *Be Water, My Friend*   796.8
 Liedman, Sven-Eric. *A World to Win*   B
 Lightman, Alan P. *Searching for Stars on an Island in Maine*   523.1
 Magee, Bryan. *The Story of Philosophy*   190
 Martin, Clancy W. *How Not to Kill Yourself*   362.28
 McLaren, Brian D. *Do I Stay Christian?*   270.8
 Miller, Jim. *Examined Lives*   B
 Moore, Kathleen Dean. *Earth's Wild Music*   576.8
 Mukherjee, Siddhartha. *The Laws of Medicine*   610.1
 Nietzsche, Friedrich Wilhelm. ★ *Basic Writings of Nietzsche*   193
 Nietzsche, Friedrich Wilhelm. ★ *Thus Spoke Zarathustra*   193
 Norman, Jesse. *Adam Smith*   B
 Novella, Steven. *The Skeptics' Guide to the Universe*   500
 O'Giebyln, Meghan. *God, Human, Animal, Machine*   814
 Obama, Barack. ★ *The Audacity of Hope*   B
 Odell, Jenny. ★ *Saving Time*   153.7
 Ortega Y Gasset, Jose. *What Is Philosophy?*   101
 Parker, Meghan. *Teaching Artfully*   741.5
 Pinker, Steven. *The Stuff of Thought*   401
 Pinn, Anthony B. *The Black Practice of Disbelief*   211
 Prideaux, Sue. *I Am Dynamite!*   B
 Rand, Ayn. *The Voice of Reason*   191
 Ricks, Thomas E. ★ *First Principles*   973.09
 Robertson, Ritchie. *The Enlightenment*   190
 Rohr, Richard. *The Universal Christ*   232
 Romano, Carlin. *America the Philosophical*   191
 Rousseau, Jean-Jacques. ★ *The Social Contract*   320.1
 Rovelli, Carlo. *The Order of Time*   530.11

PUBLIC LIBRARY CORE COLLECTION: NONFICTION
Twentieth Edition

Rovelli, Carlo. *There Are Places in the World Where Rules Are Less Important Than Kindness* — 500
Rubin, Rick. ★*The Creative Act* — 153.3
Russell, Bertrand. *A History of Western Philosophy, and Its Connection with Political and Social Circumstances from the Earliest Times to the Present Day* — 109
Russell, Bertrand. *The Problems of Philosophy* — 110
Ruttenberg, Danya. *On Repentance and Repair* — 202
Sagan, Carl. *Broca's Brain* — 128
Sapolsky, Robert M. *Determined* — 123
Setiya, Kieran. *Life Is Hard* — 128
Shahvisi, Arianne. *Arguing for a Better World* — 170
Shapiro, Scott J. ★*Fancy Bear Goes Phishing* — 364.16
Shepard, Jim. *The Tunnel at the End of the Light* — 791.43
Sigmund, Karl. *Exact Thinking in Demented Times* — 920
Srinivasan, Amia. *The Right to Sex* — 305.42
Stanley, Jason. *How Fascism Works* — 321.9
Strevens, Michael. *The Knowledge Machine* — 500
Thorstensen, Ole. *Making Things Right* — 690
Truss, Lynne. *Eats, Shoots & Leaves* — 428.2
Vanek Smith, Stacey. *Machiavelli for Women* — 650.1
Viren, Sarah. *To Name the Bigger Lie* — B
Volf, Miroslav. *Life Worth Living* — 113
Watson, Richard A. *Cogito Ergo Sum* — B
Weiner, Eric. *The Socrates Express* — 100
Wilson, Derek K. *A Magical World* — 261.55
Wilson, Edward O. *Consilience* — 121
Wilson, Edward O. *Half-Earth* — 333.95
Wilson, Edward O. *In Search of Nature* — 113
Wilson, Edward O. *The Meaning of Human Existence* — 128
Wilson, Edward O. ★*The Social Conquest of Earth* — 599.93
Wilson, Ellen Judy. *Encyclopedia of the Enlightenment* — 940.2
Wulf, Andrea. *Magnificent Rebels* — 830.9
Zorn, Justin. *Golden* — 128
★*Philosophy 101 by Socrates*. Kreeft, Peter — 183

PHILOSOPHY AND RELIGION
Aslan, Reza. *God* — 211
James, William. ★*The Varieties of Religious Experience* — 204
Teilhard de Chardin, Pierre. ★*The Divine Milieu* — 233
Wright, Lawrence. *Going Clear* — 299

PHILOSOPHY AND SCIENCE
Wilson, Edward O. *Consilience* — 121

PHILOSOPHY OF MIND
Hoffman, Donald D. *The Case Against Reality* — 121
★*The Philosophy of Modern Song*. Dylan, Bob — 782.42

PHILOSOPHY OF NATURE
Kimmerer, Robin Wall. ★*Braiding Sweetgrass* — 304.2
Nezhukumatathil, Aimee. *World of Wonders* — 590
Wilson, Edward O. *In Search of Nature* — 113

PHILOSOPHY, ANCIENT
Armstrong, Karen. ★*The Great Transformation* — 200.9
Cahill, Thomas. *Sailing the Wine-Dark Sea* — 909
Gottlieb, Anthony. *The Dream of Reason* — 180
Grayling, A. C. *The History of Philosophy* — 109
Hare, R. M. ★*Plato* — 184
Johnson, Paul. *Socrates* — 183
Lucretius Carus, Titus. *On the Nature of Things =* — 187
Nicolson, Adam. *How to Be* — 180
Plato. ★*The Collected Dialogues of Plato, Including the Letters* — 184
Ricks, Thomas E. ★*First Principles* — 973.09

PHILOSOPHY, ASIAN
Grayling, A. C. *The History of Philosophy* — 109

PHILOSOPHY, BUDDHIST
Dalai Lama. *An Appeal to the World* — 170
Kempton, Beth. *The Way of the Fearless Writer* — 808.02
Wright, Robert. *Why Buddhism Is True* — 294.3

PHILOSOPHY, FRENCH
Descartes, Rene. ★*Descartes* — 194

PHILOSOPHY, INDIGENOUS
Kimmerer, Robin Wall. ★*Braiding Sweetgrass* — 304.2
Luger, Chelsey. ★*The Seven Circles* — 610

PHILOSOPHY, JEWISH
Levine, Amy-Jill. *Short Stories by Jesus* — 226.8

PHILOSOPHY, MEDIEVAL
Grayling, A. C. *The History of Philosophy* — 109

PHILOSOPHY, MODERN
Beauvoir, Simone de. ★*The Second Sex* — 305.4
Carlisle, Clare. *Philosopher of the Heart* — B

Eilenberger, Wolfram. *Time of the Magicians* — 920
Gottlieb, Anthony. ★*The Dream of Enlightenment* — 190
Grayling, A. C. *The History of Philosophy* — 109
May, Rollo. *The Discovery of Being* — 150.19
Purnell, Carolyn. *The Sensational Past* — 152.109
Romano, Carlin. *America the Philosophical* — 191

PHILOSOPHY, WESTERN
Gottlieb, Anthony. *The Dream of Reason* — 180
Grayling, A. C. *The History of Philosophy* — 109

Philpott, Mary Laura
Bomb Shelter — B

PHILPOTT, MARY LAURA
Philpott, Mary Laura. *Bomb Shelter* — B

PHLEBOTOMY
George, Rose. *Nine Pints* — 612.1
The Pho Cookbook. Nguyen, Andrea Quynhgiao — 641.595

PHOBIAS
Gardner, Dan. *The Science of Fear* — 152.4
Lawson, Jenny. *Furiously Happy* — B
Summerscale, Kate. *The Book of Phobias and Manias* — 616.85

PHOENIX, ARIZONA
Davis, Joshua. *Spare Parts* — 629.8

Phoenix, Jack
Maximizing the Impact of Comics in Your Library — 026
★*The Photo Ark*. Sartore, Joel — 779
The Photographer. Guibert, Emmanuel — 741.5
A Photographer's Life, 1990-2005. Leibovitz, Annie — 779
The Photographer's Mind. Freeman, Michael — 770

PHOTOGRAPHERS
Alinder, Mary Street. *Ansel Adams* — B
Alinder, Mary Street. *Group F.64* — 770.92
Begley, Adam. *The Great Nadar* — B
Bonanos, Christopher. *Flash* — B
Burke, Carolyn. *Lee Miller* — B
Carson, Anne. *Autobiography of Red* — 811
Cunningham, William J. ★*Fashion Climbing* — B
Curtis, Edward S. *Edward S. Curtis* — 770.92
Delorme, Geoffroy. *Deer Man* — 599.65
Egan, Timothy. ★*Short Nights of the Shadow Catcher* — 770.92
Galassi, Peter. *Ansel Adams in Yosemite Valley* — 770.92
Gefter, Philip. *What Becomes a Legend Most* — B
Gordon, Linda. *Dorothea Lange* — B
Grey, Joel. *Master of Ceremonies* — B
Gruen, Bob. *Right Place, Right Time* — B
Huffman, Alan. *Here I Am* — B
Lubow, Arthur. *Diane Arbus* — B
Mann, Sally. ★*Hold Still* — B
Manseau, Peter. *The Apparitionists* — B
Marks, Ann. *Vivian Maier Developed* — 778.9
Richardson, Lance. *House of Nutter* — B
Shahidi, Afshin. *Prince* — B
Smith, Patti. ★*A Book of Days* — 779
Smith, Patti. ★*Just Kids* — B
Smith, R. J. *American Witness* — B
Stevens, Norma. *Avedon* — B
Van Haaften, Julia. ★*Berenice Abbott* — B
Wallace, Christopher. *Twentieth-Century Man* — B
Wilson, Robert. *Mathew Brady* — B

PHOTOGRAPHS
Alexander, Caroline. *The Endurance* — 919.8
Bradley, James. *Flags of Our Fathers* — 940.54
Davidson, Mark A. ★*Bob Dylan* — B
Gordon, Linda. *Dorothea Lange* — B
Gruen, Bob. *Right Place, Right Time* — B
Lewis, Robin Coste. *To the Realization of Perfect Helplessness* — 811
McCartney, Paul. ★*1964* — 782.42166
Morgan-Owens, Jessie. *Girl in Black and White* — B
Waal, F. B. M. de. *Bonobo* — 599.88
White, Marco Pierre. *White Heat* — 641.594
Photography. Ang, Tom — 770.9

PHOTOGRAPHY
Alinder, Mary Street. *Group F.64* — 770.92
Ang, Tom. *Digital Photographer's Handbook* — 771
Ang, Tom. *Digital Photography Masterclass* — 770
Ang, Tom. *Photography* — 770.9
Burns, Ken. ★*Our America* — 973
Cole, Teju. *Blind Spot* — 770
Curtis, Edward S. *Edward S. Curtis* — 770.92

AUTHOR, TITLE, SERIES AND SUBJECT INDEX

Fagans, Michael. *iPhone Photography for Everybody*	770
Finkelstein, Elizabeth. *Cheap Old Houses*	643
Fischer, Paul. *The Man Who Invented Motion Pictures*	791.43
Fordham, Demetrius. ★*If You're Bored with Your Camera Read This Book*	770.23
Freeman, Michael. *The Photographer's Mind*	770
Gatcum, Chris. ★*The Beginner's Photography Guide*	770
Gefter, Philip. *What Becomes a Legend Most*	B
Gordon, Linda. *Dorothea Lange*	B
Horenstein, Henry. *Digital Photography*	770
Leibovitz, Annie. *Women*	779
Mann, Sally. ★*Hold Still*	B
Manseau, Peter. *The Apparitionists*	B
Morris, Errol. *Believing Is Seeing*	770.9
Peterson, Bryan. *Learning to See Creatively*	770
Peterson, Bryan. *Understanding Exposure*	771
Rinehart, Lorissa. *First to the Front*	B
Smith, Patti. ★*A Book of Days*	779
Souza, Pete. *The West Wing and Beyond*	917.53
Stanton, Brandon. *Humans*	779
Stevens, Norma. *Avedon*	B
Taylor, David. *Digital Photography Complete Course*	770
Van Agtmael, Peter. *Look at the USA*	070
Van Haaften, Julia. ★*Berenice Abbott*	B
Willis, Deborah. ★*The Black Civil War Soldier*	973.7
Willis, Deborah. *Reflections in Black*	770
Wilson, Robert. *Mathew Brady*	B

PHOTOGRAPHY OF ANIMALS
Sartore, Joel. ★*The Photo Ark*	779

PHOTOGRAPHY OF CHILDREN
Bethencourt, Kahran. *Glory*	779.2

PHOTOGRAPHY OF DOGS
Friedman, Elias Weiss. *The Dogist*	779

PHOTOJOURNALISM
Buell, Hal. *Moments*	070.4
Morris, Errol. *Believing Is Seeing*	770.9
Rinehart, Lorissa. *First to the Front*	B
Van Agtmael, Peter. *Look at the USA*	070
Wilson, Robert. *Mathew Brady*	B

PHOTOJOURNALISTS
Addario, Lynsey. *It's What I Do*	B
Addario, Lynsey. *Of Love & War*	779
Bonanos, Christopher. *Flash*	B
Burke, Carolyn. *Lee Miller*	B
Copaken, Deborah. *Ladyparts*	B
Guibert, Emmanuel. *The Photographer*	741.5
Huffman, Alan. *Here I Am*	B
Lauterbach, Preston. *Bluff City*	B
Rinehart, Lorissa. *First to the Front*	B
Wilson, Robert. *Mathew Brady*	B

PHOTOSYNTHESIS
Sanders, Ella Frances. *Eating the Sun*	520

PHYSICAL ANTHROPOLOGISTS
Maples, William R. *Dead Men Do Tell Tales*	614

PHYSICAL ANTHROPOLOGY
Maples, William R. *Dead Men Do Tell Tales*	614
Pattison, Kermit. *Fossil Men*	569.9
Pringle, Heather Anne. *The Mummy Congress*	393

PHYSICAL CHEMISTRY
Maddox, Brenda. *Rosalind Franklin*	B

PHYSICAL DISABILITIES
Heumann, Judith E. *Being Heumann*	B
Jones, Chloe Cooper. ★*Easy Beauty*	B

PHYSICAL EDUCATION AND TRAINING
Afremow, James A. *The Champion's Mind*	796.01
Aschwanden, Christie. *Good to Go*	617.1
Lieberman, Daniel. *Exercised*	612.044

PHYSICAL FITNESS
Bechdel, Alison. ★*The Secret to Superhuman Strength*	741.5
Common. ★*And Then We Rise*	613
Esmonde-White, Miranda. *Aging Backwards*	613.7
Ferriss, Timothy. *Tools of Titans*	081
Futterman, Matthew. *Running to the Edge*	796.42071
Hayes, Bill. *Sweat*	613.7
Lieberman, Daniel. *Exercised*	612.044
Rountree, Sage. *The Athlete's Guide to Recovery*	617.1
Stanley, Jessamyn. *Every Body Yoga*	613.7

PHYSICAL FITNESS FOR WOMEN
Green, Louise. *Big Fit Girl*	613.7

PHYSICAL GEOGRAPHY
Barnett, Cynthia. *Rain*	551.57

PHYSICAL LAWS
Carroll, Sean M. *The Big Picture*	577

PHYSICAL SCIENCES
Carroll, Sean M. *From Eternity to Here*	530.11

PHYSICAL THERAPY
Carpenter, Kyle. *You Are Worth It*	B

PHYSICIAN AND PATIENT
Brown, Theresa. *Healing*	616.99
Ely, Wes. *Every Deep-Drawn Breath*	616.02
Goldberg, Sana. *How to Be a Patient*	610.69
Harper, Michele. *The Beauty in Breaking*	B
Kidder, Tracy. ★*Rough Sleepers*	362.5
Mannix, Kathryn. *With the End in Mind*	304.6
Marsh, Henry. ★*Do No Harm*	B
Offit, Paul A. *You Bet Your Life*	615.5
Raza, Azra. *The First Cell*	616.99
Roth, Andrew J. *Managing Prostate Cancer*	616.99
Sacks, Oliver. *The Man Who Mistook His Wife for a Hat and Other Clinical Tales*	616.8
Volandes, Angelo E. *The Conversation*	616.02
Wellons, Jay. *All That Moves Us*	617.4
Wilson, F. Perry. *How Medicine Works and When It Doesn't*	610.69
Yurkiewicz, Ilana. *Fragmented*	362.1

PHYSICIAN-ASSISTED SUICIDE
Bloom, Amy. *In Love*	B
Engelhart, Katie. *The Inevitable*	179.7
Hannig, Anita. *The Day I Die*	364.152

PHYSICIANS
Abuelaish, Izzeldin. *I Shall Not Hate*	B
Alexander, Brian. ★*The Hospital*	362.10973
Aptowicz, Cristin O'Keefe. *Dr. Mutter's Marvels*	B
Barr, John. *Start by Believing*	364.15
Belkin, Lisa. *Genealogy of a Murder*	362.88
Blackstock, Uche. *Legacy*	610.92
Bond, Melissa. *Blood Orange Night*	616.8
Brenner, Marie. ★*The Desperate Hours*	362.1962
Brooks, Michael. *The Quantum Astrologer's Handbook*	B
Clarke, Rachel. *Dear Life*	B
Egan, Kerry. *On Living*	170
Fabes, Stephen. *Signs of Life*	B
Fauci, Anthony S. *Expect the Unexpected*	610.92
Fitzharris, Lindsey. *The Butchering Art*	B
Frank, Lone. *The Pleasure Shock*	616.8
Fried, Stephen. *Rush*	B
Goldberg, Emma. *Life on the Line*	362.1962
Hari, Johann. ★*Magic Pill*	613.2
Hughes, Evan. *The Hard Sell*	338.4
Jacobsen, Annie. ★*Operation Paperclip*	940.54
Jamison, Kay Redfield. *Fires in the Dark*	616.89
Jena, Anupam B. *Random Acts of Medicine*	616.0072
Jobb, Dean. *The Case of the Murderous Dr. Cream*	364.152
Johnson, Victoria. ★*American Eden*	580.973
Kean, Sam. *The Tale of the Dueling Neurosurgeons*	617.4
Kershaw, Alex. *Avenue of Spies*	940.53
Kidder, Tracy. ★*Rough Sleepers*	362.5
King, David. *Death in the City of Light*	364.152
Lamas, Daniela J. *You Can Stop Humming Now*	616.02
Lewis, Michael. ★*The Premonition*	614.5
Mannix, Kathryn. *With the End in Mind*	304.6
Marwell, David G. *Mengele*	B
McCullough, David G. *The Greater Journey*	920
Mukherjee, Siddhartha. *The Laws of Medicine*	610.1
Mukherjee, Siddhartha. ★*The Song of the Cell*	571.6
Nuila, Ricardo. *The People's Hospital*	362.1
Sacks, Oliver. *On the Move*	B
Sagan, Carl. *Broca's Brain*	128
Tweedy, Damon. *Facing the Unseen*	362.2
Warraich, Haider. *The Song of Our Scars*	616
Wellons, Jay. *All That Moves Us*	617.4
Wilson, F. Perry. *How Medicine Works and When It Doesn't*	610.69
Yurkiewicz, Ilana. *Fragmented*	362.1

PHYSICIANS AND NURSES
Wright, Lawrence. ★*The Plague Year*	614.5

PUBLIC LIBRARY CORE COLLECTION: NONFICTION
Twentieth Edition

PHYSICISTS
- Becker, Adam. *What Is Real?* — 920
- Bird, Kai. *American Prometheus* — B
- Cliff, Harry. *How to Make an Apple Pie from Scratch* — 523.01
- Dyson, Freeman J. *Maker of Patterns* — B
- Einstein, Albert. ★*A Stubbornly Persistent Illusion* — 530.092
- Feynman, Richard P. ★*The Meaning of It All* — 500
- Forbes, Nancy. *Faraday, Maxwell, and the Electromagnetic Field* — B
- Hawking, Stephen. ★*Black Holes and Baby Universes and Other Essays* — 530.1
- Hawking, Stephen. *My Brief History* — B
- Kunetka, James W. *The General and the Genius* — 355.8
- Mack, Katie. *The End of Everything* — 523.1
- Mlodinow, Leonard. *Stephen Hawking* — B
- Oluseyi, Hakeem M. *A Quantum Life* — B
- Ottaviani, Jim. *Hawking* — 741.5
- Panek, Richard. *The Trouble with Gravity* — .531
- Schwartz, David N. *The Last Man Who Knew Everything* — B

PHYSICS
- Alexander, Stephon. *Fear of a Black Universe* — 523.1
- Ananthaswamy, Anil. *Through Two Doors at Once* — 530.12
- Becker, Adam. *What Is Real?* — 920
- Bird, Kai. *American Prometheus* — B
- Carroll, Sean M. *The Biggest Ideas in the Universe* — 530.11
- Carroll, Sean M. *From Eternity to Here* — 530.11
- Carroll, Sean M. *Something Deeply Hidden* — 530.12
- Cliff, Harry. *How to Make an Apple Pie from Scratch* — 523.01
- Cox, Brian. *The Quantum Universe* — 530.12
- Crease, Robert P. *The Quantum Moment* — 530.12
- Czerski, Helen. *The Blue Machine* — 551.46
- Czerski, Helen. *Storm in a Teacup* — 530
- Durrani, Matin. *Furry Logic* — 591.5
- Einstein, Albert. ★*The Evolution of Physics* — 530
- Einstein, Albert. *Ideas and Opinions* — 081
- Einstein, Albert. ★*A Stubbornly Persistent Illusion* — 530.092
- Feynman, Richard P. ★*Six Easy Pieces* — 530
- Fletcher, Seth. *Einstein's Shadow* — 523.8
- Greene, B. ★*The Elegant Universe* — 539.7
- Greene, B. *The Fabric of the Cosmos* — 523.1
- Greene, B. ★*The Hidden Reality* — 530.12
- Greene, B. *Until the End of Time* — 523.1
- Hawking, Stephen. ★*Black Holes and Baby Universes and Other Essays* — 530.1
- Hawking, Stephen. *A Brief History of Time* — 523.1
- Hawking, Stephen. ★*The Grand Design* — 530.14
- Hawking, Stephen. *My Brief History* — B
- Hawking, Stephen. ★*The Universe in a Nutshell* — 530.12
- Impey, Chris. *Einstein's Monsters* — 523.8
- Kakalios, James. *The Amazing Story of Quantum Mechanics* — 530.12
- Kaku, Michio. *The God Equation* — 523.1
- Kaku, Michio. ★*Hyperspace* — 530.1
- Krauss, Lawrence Maxwell. *The Greatest Story Ever Told—So Far* — 530.01
- Li, Fei-Fei. *The Worlds I See* — 523.1
- McTier, Moiya. *The Milky Way* — 523.1
- Miodownik, Mark. *Liquid Rules* — 530.4
- Mlodinow, Leonard. *Stephen Hawking* — B
- Ottaviani, Jim. *Hawking* — 741.5
- Panek, Richard. *The Trouble with Gravity* — 531
- Pontzen, Andrew. *The Universe in a Box* — 523.1
- Rogers, Adam. *Full Spectrum* — 152.14
- Rovelli, Carlo. *Helgoland* — 530.12
- Rovelli, Carlo. *Reality Is Not What It Seems* — 530.14
- Rovelli, Carlo. ★*Seven Brief Lessons on Physics* — 530
- Rovelli, Carlo. *There Are Places in the World Where Rules Are Less Important Than Kindness* — 500
- Sanders, Ella Frances. *Eating the Sun* — 520
- Sapolsky, Robert M. *Determined* — 123
- Schwartz, David N. *The Last Man Who Knew Everything* — B
- Sheehy, Suzie. *The Matter of Everything* — 539.7
- Smil, Vaclav. *Size* — 153.7
- Still, Ben. *Particle Physics Brick by Brick* — 539.7
- Tyson, Neil deGrasse. *Cosmic Queries* — 523.1
- Weatherall, James Owen. *The Physics of Wall Street* — 332.63
- Wilczek, Frank. *Fundamentals* — 530.01
- *The Physics of Wall Street.* Weatherall, James Owen — 332.63

PHYSIOGNOMY
- Dimitrius, Jo-Ellan. *Reading People* — 155.2

PHYSIOLOGY
- Aschwanden, Christie. *Good to Go* — 617.1
- Bohannon, Cat. ★*Eve* — 613
- Deisseroth, Karl. *Projections* — 616.89
- Diamant, Anita. ★*Period. End of Sentence* — 612.6
- Enright, Lynn. *Vagina* — 612.6
- Harari, Yuval N. ★*Sapiens* — 909
- Hickey, Walt. ★*You Are What You Watch* — 791.4
- Kean, Sam. *The Tale of the Dueling Neurosurgeons* — 617.4
- Lyman, Monty. *The Remarkable Life of the Skin* — 612.7
- Rawlence, Ben. *The Treeline* — 577.3
- Rountree, Sage. *The Athlete's Guide to Recovery* — 617.1
- Sapolsky, Robert M. *Behave* — 612.8
- Wolf, Maryanne. *Reader, Come Home* — 418
- Yong, Ed. ★*An Immense World* — 591.5

PIAGET, JEAN, 1896-1980
- Bloom, Paul. *Psych* — 150

The Pianist from Syria. Ahmad, Aeham — B

PIANISTS
- Ahmad, Aeham. *The Pianist from Syria* — B
- Eisler, Benita. ★*Chopin's Funeral* — B
- Friedwald, Will. *Straighten up and Fly Right* — 782.42164
- Hafner, Katie. *A Romance on Three Legs* — 786.2092
- Haupt, Lyanda Lynn. *Mozart's Starling* — B
- Hough, Stephen. *Rough Ideas* — 786.2092
- Kennicott, Philip. *Counterpoint* — B
- Mueller, Melissa. *Alice's Piano* — B
- Pollack, Howard. ★*George Gershwin* — B
- Rhodes, James. *Instrumental* — B
- Rusbridger, Alan. ★*Play It Again* — B

PIANO
- Hafner, Katie. *A Romance on Three Legs* — 786.2092
- Rusbridger, Alan. ★*Play It Again* — B

The Piano Lesson. Wilson, August — 812

PIANO MUSIC
- Ahmad, Aeham. *The Pianist from Syria* — B
- Walsh, Stephen. ★*Debussy* — B

PIANOS
- Kildea, Paul Francis. *Chopin's Piano* — B

★*Picasso and American Art.* FitzGerald, Michael C. — 709.73
Picasso and the Painting That Shocked the World. Unger, Miles — 759.4

PICASSO, PABLO, 1881-1973
- FitzGerald, Michael C. ★*Picasso and American Art* — 709.73
- Leal, Brigitte. *The Ultimate Picasso* — B
- Roe, Sue. *In Montmartre* — 920
- Smee, Sebastian. *The Art of Rivalry* — 700.92
- Unger, Miles. *Picasso and the Painting That Shocked the World* — 759.4

Pick-Goslar, Hannah Elizabeth
- ★*My Friend Anne Frank* — B

PICK-GOSLAR, HANNAH ELIZABETH, 1928-2022
- Pick-Goslar, Hannah Elizabeth. ★*My Friend Anne Frank* — B

Pickleball 101. Parker, Vergil R. — 796.34
Pickleball for All. Simon, Rachel — 796.34
Pickleball Mindset. Gingrich, Dayne — 796.34

Pickover, Clifford A.
- *The Math Book* — 510.9

The Picnic. Longo, Matthew — 947.084
Picnic in Provence. Bard, Elizabeth — B

PICNICKING
- Longo, Matthew. *The Picnic* — 947.084

Pico, Tommy
- *Feed* — 811
- *Junk* — 811
- *Nature Poem* — 811

Picower, Bree
- *Reading, Writing, and Racism* — 371.829

PICTURE BOOKS FOR ADULTS
- Lozano, Luis-Martin. *Frida Kahlo* — 759.972
- Szarkowski, John. *Ansel Adams at 100* — B

PICTURE DICTIONARIES
- Corbeil, Jean-Claude. ★*Merriam-Webster's Visual Dictionary* — 423

PICTURE FRAMES AND FRAMING
- Kistler, Vivian Carli. *The Complete Photo Guide to Framing and Displaying Artwork* — 749
- Logan, M. David. *Mat, Mount, and Frame It Yourself* — 749

★*Picture This.* Bang, Molly — 741.6
★*Pictured Worlds.* Marcus, Leonard S. — 741.6
Pictures At a Revolution. Harris, Mark — 791.43

2204

AUTHOR, TITLE, SERIES AND SUBJECT INDEX

Picturing Fredrick Douglass. Stauffer, John	B
★*Pie Squared*. Barrow, Cathy	641.86
★*Piecemeal*. Pauline, Kathryn	641.5
Pierce, D.	
The Accessible Home	728
Piercy, Marge	
So You Want to Write	808.3
Pierson, Joy	
Vegan Holiday Cooking from Candle Cafe	641.5
PIES	
Barrow, Cathy. ★*Pie Squared*	641.86
Beranbaum, Rose Levy. ★*Rose's Baking Basics*	641.81
Day, Cheryl. *Back in the Day Bakery, Made with Love*	641.81
Hussain, Nadiya. ★*Nadiya Bakes*	641.81
Larsen, Jeffrey. ★*Gluten-Free Baking at Home*	641.5
Ludwinski, Lisa. *Sister Pie*	641.86
McDermott, Kate. ★*Art of the Pie*	641.86
McDowell, Erin Jeanne. ★*The Book on Pie*	641.86
Roman, Alison. *Sweet Enough*	641.86
Weller, Melissa. *A Good Bake*	641.86
PIG FARMING	
Addison, Corban. *Wastelands*	346.73
The **Pigeon** *Tunnel*. Le Carre, John	B
PIGS	
Montgomery, Sy. *The Good Good Pig*	636.4
PIGS AS PETS	
Montgomery, Sy. *The Good Good Pig*	636.4
Pigza, Jessica	
Bibliocraft	745.5
Piketty, Thomas	
A Brief History of Equality	305.09
★*Capital and Ideology*	305
★*Capital in the Twenty-First Century*	332
The Economics of Inequality	339.2
PILECKI, WITOLD, 1901-1948	
Fairweather, Jack. *The Volunteer*	B
Pilgrim At Tinker Creek. Dillard, Annie	508
Pilgrim Bell. Akbar, Kaveh	811
Pilgrim's Wilderness. Kizzia, Tom	B
A Pilgrimage to Eternity. Egan, Timothy	263
PILGRIMS (NEW ENGLAND SETTLERS)	
Bunker, Nick. ★*Making Haste from Babylon*	974.4
Fraser, Rebecca. *The Mayflower*	974.4
Pestana, Carla Gardina. *The World of Plymouth Plantation*	974.4
Philbrick, Nathaniel. ★*Mayflower*	973.2
Silverman, David J. ★*This Land Is Their Land*	974.4
Whittock, Martyn. *Mayflower Lives*	974.4
PILGRIMS AND PILGRIMAGES	
Egan, Timothy. *A Pilgrimage to Eternity*	263
Feiler, Bruce. *Walking the Bible*	915
Mullins, Edwin. *The Four Roads to Heaven*	263
PILGRIMS AND PILGRIMAGES, CHRISTIAN	
Melville, Herman. *Complete Poems*	811
Pilgrims in Their Own Land. Marty, Martin E.	200
Pilgrims of the Vertical. Taylor, Joseph E.	796.52
PILLAGE	
Beevor, Antony. *The Fall of Berlin, 1945*	940.54
Edsel, Robert M. *The Monuments Men*	940.53
Hammer, Joshua. *The Bad-Ass Librarians of Timbuktu*	025.8
Hoock, Holger. *Scars of Independence*	973.3
Kaiser, Menachem. *Plunder*	940.53
Rydell, Anders. *The Book Thieves*	027
★*Pillar of Fire*. Branch, Taylor	323.1
PILLARS OF ISLAM	
Ramadan, Tariq. ★*Introduction to Islam*	297
Pilling, David	
Bending Adversity	952.0512
PILOTS	
Barbree, Jay. *Neil Armstrong*	B
Bruning, John R. *Indestructible*	B
Chivers, C. J. *The Fighters*	920
Drabkin, Ronald. *Beverly Hills Spy*	940.54
Groom, Winston. *The Aviators*	920
Hampton, Dan. *Chasing the Demon*	629.132
Makos, Adam. ★*A Higher Call*	940.54
Markham, Beryl. *West with the Night*	B
Rahmani, Niloofar. *Open Skies*	B
Vanhoenacker, Mark. *Imagine a City*	629.13
Winters, Kathleen C. *Amelia Earhart*	B
Pim, Keiron	
Dinosaurs the Grand Tour	567.9
Pin Action. Manzione, Gianmarc	B
PINCHOT, GIFFORD, 1865-1946	
Egan, Timothy. ★*The Big Burn*	973.911
Miller, Char. *Gifford Pinchot and the Making of Modern Environmentalism*	B
Pinckney, Darryl	
Busted in New York and Other Essays	305.800973
Come Back in September	B
PINCKNEY, DARRYL, 1953-	
Pinckney, Darryl. *Come Back in September*	B
Pincus, Edward	
The Filmmaker's Handbook	777
PINCUS, GREGORY, 1903-1967	
Eig, Jonathan. *The Birth of the Pill*	618.1
PINE RIDGE INDIAN RESERVATION, SOUTH DAKOTA	
Bunnell, David. *Good Friday on the Rez*	B
Pink Brain, Blue Brain. Eliot, Lise	612.6
Pink, Daniel H.	
Drive	153.1
When	153.7
Pinker, Steven	
The Blank Slate	155.2
★*Enlightenment Now*	303.44
How the Mind Works	153
The Language Instinct	400
Rationality	153.4
The Stuff of Thought	401
Words and Rules	415
PINKERTON, ALLAN, 1819-1884	
Meltzer, Brad. *The Lincoln Conspiracy*	973.7092
Waller, Douglas C. *Lincoln's Spies*	973.7
Pinn, Anthony B.	
The Black Practice of Disbelief	211
Pinnell-Stephens, June	
Protecting Intellectual Freedom in Your Public Library	025.2
Pinsky, Robert	
The Figured Wheel	811
Singing School	808.1
The Sounds of Poetry	808.5
PIONEER FAMILIES	
McCullough, David G. *The Pioneers*	920
Pioneer Girl. Wilder, Laura Ingalls	B
★*The Pioneer Woman Cooks*. Drummond, Ree	641.5
PIONEER WOMEN	
Brown, Daniel James. *The Indifferent Stars Above*	B
Fraser, Caroline. ★*Prairie Fires*	B
Gallagher, Winifred. *New Women in the Old West*	978.02
Inskeep, Steve. *Imperfect Union*	B
McDowell, Marta. *The World of Laura Ingalls Wilder*	813
Wilder, Laura Ingalls. *Pioneer Girl*	B
The Pioneers. McCullough, David G.	920
PIONEERS	
Brands, H. W. *Dreams of El Dorado*	978
Brown, Daniel James. *The Indifferent Stars Above*	B
Brown, Dee. *The American West*	978
Castner, Brian. *Stampede*	971.9
Drury, Bob. *Blood and Treasure*	B
Hyde, Anne Farrar. *Empires, Nations, and Families*	978
Inskeep, Steve. *Imperfect Union*	B
Laskin, David. *The Children's Blizzard*	977
McCullough, David G. *The Pioneers*	920
Morgan, Robert. *Boone*	B
Morgan, Robert. *Lions of the West*	978
Murphy, Andrew R. *William Penn*	B
Wallis, Michael. *The Best Land Under Heaven*	978
Ward, Geoffrey C. *The West*	978
Warren, Louis S. *Buffalo Bill's America*	B
Piore, Adam	
The Body Builders	660.6
Pipes, Richard	
Communism	335.43
A Concise History of the Russian Revolution	947.084
The Russian Revolution	947.084
Pipher, Mary Bray	
A Life in Light	B
The Middle of Everywhere	305.9

Women Rowing North 305.26
PIPHER, MARY BRAY
   Pipher, Mary Bray. *A Life in Light* B
Pippen, Scottie
   Unguarded B
PIPPEN, SCOTTIE
   Pippen, Scottie. *Unguarded* B
PIRACY
   Cordingly, David. *Under the Black Flag* 910.4
   Dolin, Eric Jay. *Black Flags, Blue Waters* 973.2
   Johnson, Steven. *Enemy of All Mankind* 910.4
   Kilmeade, Brian. ★*Thomas Jefferson and the Tripoli Pirates* 973.4
   Ronald, Susan. *The Pirate Queen* B
   Thomson, Keith. *Born to Be Hanged* 910.4
Pirate Hunters. Kurson, Robert 910.91
The Pirate Queen. Ronald, Susan B
PIRATE SHIPS
   Cordingly, David. *Under the Black Flag* 910.4
   Kurson, Robert. *Pirate Hunters* 910.91
PIRATES
   Cordingly, David. *Under the Black Flag* 910.4
   Dolin, Eric Jay. *Black Flags, Blue Waters* 973.2
   Johnson, Steven. *Enemy of All Mankind* 910.4
   Kilmeade, Brian. ★*Thomas Jefferson and the Tripoli Pirates* 973.4
   Kritzler, Ed. *Jewish Pirates of the Caribbean* 972.9
   Moore, Michael Scott. *The Desert and the Sea* 364.15
   Thomson, Keith. *Born to Be Hanged* 910.4
   Toll, Ian W. ★*Six Frigates* 359.00973
PIRZIO-BIROLI, DETALMO, 1916-
   Bailey, Catherine. *A Castle in Wartime* 943.086
Pistol. Kriegel, Mark B
Piston, Walter
   Orchestration 781.63
Pit Bull. Dickey, Bronwen 636.755
PIT BULL TERRIERS
   Dickey, Bronwen. *Pit Bull* 636.755
Pitch Perfect. Rapkin, Mickey 782.5
PITCHERS (BASEBALL)
   Darling, Ron. *The Complete Game* B
   Kepner, Tyler. *K* 796.357
   Leavy, Jane. *Sandy Koufax* B
   Pappu, Sridhar. *The Year of the Pitcher* 920
   Passan, Jeff. *The Arm* 796.3576
   Rivera, Mariano. *The Closer* B
   Turbow, Jason. *They Bled Blue* 796.357
   Tye, Larry. *Satchel* B
PITCHING (BASEBALL)
   Darling, Ron. *The Complete Game* B
   Kepner, Tyler. *K* 796.357
   Pappu, Sridhar. *The Year of the Pitcher* 920
   Passan, Jeff. *The Arm* 796.3576
Pitching My Tent. Diamant, Anita 296.7
PITMAN, HENRY
   Severin, Timothy. *In Search of Robinson Crusoe* 996.1
Pittard, Hannah
   We Are Too Many B
PITTARD, HANNAH
   Pittard, Hannah. *We Are Too Many* B
Pittman, Ann Taylor
   The Global Pantry Cookbook 641.59
Pittman, Craig
   Cat Tale 599.75
Pitts, Mike
   Digging for Richard III 942.046
PITTSBURGH, PENNSYLVANIA
   Dillard, Annie. *An American Childhood* B
   Hazzard, Kevin M. *American Sirens* 362.18
   Oppenheimer, Mark. *Squirrel Hill* 364.152
   Whitaker, Mark. *Smoketown* 305.896
   Young, Damon. ★*What Doesn't Kill You Makes You Blacker* B
Pitzer, Andrea
   The Secret History of Vladimir Nabokov 813
PIUS IX, POPE, 1792-1878
   Kertzer, David I. *The Pope Who Would Be King* 282.092
PIUS XI, POPE, 1857-1939
   Eisner, Peter. *The Pope's Last Crusade* 282.092
   Kertzer, David I. *The Pope and Mussolini* 322

PIUS XII, POPE, 1876-1958
   Cornwell, John. *Hitler's Pope* B
   Kertzer, David I. *The Pope at War* 940.53
Pivnik, Sam
   Survivor 940.5318
PIVNIK, SAM, 1926-2017
   Pivnik, Sam. *Survivor* 940.5318
PIZZA
   Bianco, Chris. *Bianco* 641.5
   Forkish, Ken. *Flour Water Salt Yeast* 641.81
   Lanza, Fabrizia. *The Food of Sicily* 641.594
   Reinhart, Peter. *Perfect Pan Pizza* 641.82
   Vetri, Marc. *Mastering Pizza* 641.82
PLACE (PHILOSOPHY)
   Hester, Diarmuid. *Nothing Ever Just Disappears* 306.76
   Heughan, Sam. *Waypoints* B
   Krug, Nora. ★*Belonging* 741.5
   Ondaatje, Michael. *A Year of Last Things* 811
A Place Called Home. Ambroz, David B
A Place for Us. Wolf, Brandon J. B
PLACEBO (MEDICINE)
   Goldacre, Ben. *Bad Science* 500
   Marchant, Jo. *Cure* 616.89
PLACES
   Young, Kevin. *Stones* 811
Places and Names. Ackerman, Elliot B
Places I've Taken My Body. Brown, Molly McCully B
PLAGUE
   Barry, John M. ★*The Great Influenza* 614.5
   Cantor, Norman F. *In the Wake of the Plague* 614.5
   Christakis, Nicholas A. *Apollo's Arrow* 362.1962
   Kelly, John. *The Great Mortality* 614.5
   Kennedy, Jonathan. *Pathogenesis* 614.4
   Kenny, Charles. *The Plague Cycle* 614.4
   McNeil, Donald G. ★*The Wisdom of Plagues* 614.4
   Price, Polly J. *Plagues in the Nation* 614.4
   Randall, David K. *Black Death at the Golden Gate* 616.9
   Senthilingam, Meera. *Outbreaks and Epidemics* 614.4
The Plague Cycle. Kenny, Charles 614.4
The Plague of War. Roberts, Jennifer Tolbert 938
★*The Plague Year*. Wright, Lawrence 614.5
Plagues in the Nation. Price, Polly J. 614.4
PLAIN PEOPLE
   Kraybill, Donald B. ★*On the Backroad to Heaven* 289.7
Plain Secrets. Mackall, Joe 289.7
★*Plain, Honest Men*. Beeman, Richard R. 342.7302
Plait, Philip C.
   Under Alien Skies 520
Planet Funny. Jennings, Ken 809.7
Planet Palm. Zuckerman, Jocelyn C. 633.8
PLANETARY THEORY
   Lauretta, D. S. *The Asteroid Hunter* 523.44
PLANETOLOGY
   Lauretta, D. S. *The Asteroid Hunter* 523.44
PLANETS
   Bell, Jim. *The Interstellar Age* 919
   Fauber, L. S. *Heaven on Earth* B
   Johnson, Sarah Stewart. *The Sirens of Mars* 576.8
   Plait, Philip C. *Under Alien Skies* 520
   Ridpath, Ian. *Stars & Planets* 520
   Summers, Michael E. *Exoplanets* 523.2
   Trefil, James. *Space Atlas* 520
   Tyson, Neil deGrasse. *To Infinity and Beyond* 520
   Tyson, Neil deGrasse. *Welcome to the Universe* 523.1
Planets and Possibilities. Miller, Susan 133.5
Plankton. Sardet, Christian 578.77
PLANNING
   Bordewich, Fergus M. *Washington* 975.3
   McKeever, Mike P. *How to Write a Business Plan* 658.15
   Quinn, Jane Bryant. ★*How to Make Your Money Last* 332.024
PLANT CLOSINGS
   Goldstein, Amy. *Janesville* 330.9775
PLANT COLLECTING
   Wulf, Andrea. *The Brother Gardeners* 920
PLANT COLLECTORS
   Wulf, Andrea. *The Brother Gardeners* 920
PLANT CONSERVATION
   Magdalena, Carlos. *The Plant Messiah* 333.95

AUTHOR, TITLE, SERIES AND SUBJECT INDEX

PLANT ECOLOGY
    Drori, Jonathan. *Around the World in 80 Plants* — 581.63
PLANT GEOGRAPHY
    Stone, Daniel. *The Food Explorer* — B
★*Plant Grow Harvest Repeat*. Cowden, Meg McAndrews — 635.9
PLANT GROWTH
    Roach, Margaret. ★*A Way to Garden* — 635
    Schlanger, Zoe. ★*The Light Eaters* — 571.2
The Plant Hunter. Quave, Cassandra Leah — 581.6
PLANT INTRODUCTION
    Stone, Daniel. *The Food Explorer* — B
The Plant Messiah. Magdalena, Carlos — 333.95
Plant Parenting. Halleck, Leslie F. — 631.5
Plant Partners. Walliser, Jessica — 635
PLANT PHYSIOLOGY
    Schlanger, Zoe. ★*The Light Eaters* — 571.2
PLANT PROPAGATION
    Gough, Robert E. *The Complete Guide to Saving Seeds* — 631.5
    Halleck, Leslie F. *Plant Parenting* — 631.5
Plant, Deborah G.
    Of Greed and Glory — 326
PLANTAGENET PERIOD (1154-1485)
    Asbridge, Thomas S. *The Greatest Knight* — 942.03
    Gies, Frances. *Life in a Medieval Village* — 306
    Gristwood, Sarah. *Blood Sisters* — 942.04092
    Jones, Dan. ★*The Plantagenets* — 942.03092
    Jones, Dan. ★*The Wars of the Roses* — 942.04
    Lacey, Robert. *Great Tales from English History 2* — 941
    Morris, Marc. *A Great and Terrible King* — B
    Morris, Marc. *King John* — 942.033
    Penn, Thomas. *The Brothers York* — 942.04
    Tallis, Nicola. *Uncrowned Queen* — B
    Weir, Alison. *Eleanor of Aquitaine* — B
    Weir, Alison. *Queens of the Age of Chivalry* — 920
    Weir, Alison. *Queens of the Conquest* — 920
    Weir, Alison. *The Wars of the Roses* — 942.04
PLANTAGENET, HOUSE OF
    Gristwood, Sarah. *Blood Sisters* — 942.04092
    Jones, Dan. ★*The Plantagenets* — 942.03092
    Jones, Dan. ★*The Wars of the Roses* — 942.04
    Weir, Alison. *Queens of the Age of Chivalry* — 920
    Weir, Alison. *Queens of the Conquest* — 920
★*The Plantagenets*. Jones, Dan — 942.03092
PLANTATION LIFE
    Ball, Edward. *Slaves in the Family* — 975.7
    Deetz, Kelley Fanto. *Bound to the Fire* — 641.59
    Douglass, Frederick. *My Bondage and My Freedom* — B
    Griswold, Mac K. *The Manor* — 974.7
    Levine, Bruce C. *The Fall of the House of Dixie* — 973.7
    Northup, Solomon. *Twelve Years a Slave* — B
    Taylor, Alan. ★*The Internal Enemy* — 975.5
    Wiencek, Henry. *Master of the Mountain* — 973.4
PLANTATION OWNERS
    Griswold, Mac K. *The Manor* — 974.7
    Sedgewick, Augustine. *Coffeeland* — 338.4
PLANTATIONS
    Griswold, Mac K. *The Manor* — 974.7
    Pressly, Paul M. *On the Rim of the Caribbean* — 975.8
    Zuckerman, Jocelyn C. *Planet Palm* — 633.8
The Planter of Modern Life. Heyman, Stephen — B
Plantinga, Cornelius
    Gratitude — 179
The Plantpower Way. Roll, Rich — 641.5
PLANTS
    Chapman, Baylor. ★*Decorating with Plants* — 635.9
    Drori, Jonathan. *Around the World in 80 Plants* — 581.63
    Dungy, Camille T. *Soil* — 635.0978
    Erickson, Laura. ★*100 Plants to Feed the Birds* — 635
    Godas, Maru. *Organic Beauty* — 646.7
    Jahren, Hope. ★*Lab Girl* — B
    Kassinger, Ruth. ★*A Garden of Marvels* — 580.92
    Lewis, Daniel. *Twelve Trees* — 582.16
    Loades, Greg. *The Modern Cottage Garden* — 635
    Lowman, Margaret. *The Arbornaut* — 581.7
    Mabey, Richard. *The Cabaret of Plants* — 580
    Nezhukumatathil, Aimee. *World of Wonders* — 590
    Offolter, Enid. *Welcome to the Jungle* — 635.9
    Pollan, Michael. ★*This Is Your Mind on Plants* — 581.6

    Schlanger, Zoe. ★*The Light Eaters* — 571.2
    Sevigny, Melissa L. ★*Brave the Wild River* — 580.9
    Stewart, Amy. *Wicked Plants* — 581.6
    Walliser, Jessica. *Plant Partners* — 635
    Wohlleben, Peter. *The Heartbeat of Trees* — 582.16
    Ziegler, Lisa Mason. *Vegetables Love Flowers* — 635
PLANTS IN ART
    Borsato, Diane. *Mushrooming* — 579.6
PLASTIC BAG POLLUTION
    Allen, Brigette. *Living Without Plastic* — 640
PLASTIC BOTTLES
    Allen, Brigette. *Living Without Plastic* — 640
PLASTIC MARINE DEBRIS
    Allen, Brigette. *Living Without Plastic* — 640
PLASTIC SCRAP
    Allen, Brigette. *Living Without Plastic* — 640
PLASTIC SURGERY
    Lieu, Susan. ★*The Manicurist's Daughter* — B
    Satrapi, Marjane. *Embroideries* — 741.5
PLASTICS
    Allen, Brigette. *Living Without Plastic* — 640
    Humes, Edward. ★*Total Garbage* — 628.4
The Plateau. Paxson, Margaret — 362.87
Plath, Sylvia
    ★*Ariel* — 811
    ★*The Collected Poems* — 811
    The Letters of Sylvia Plath — 811.54
    The Letters of Sylvia Plath — 811.54
PLATH, SYLVIA
    Clark, Heather. ★*Red Comet* — B
    Crowther, Gail. *Three-Martini Afternoons at the Ritz* — 920
    Plath, Sylvia. ★*Ariel* — 811
    Plath, Sylvia. *The Letters of Sylvia Plath* — 811.54
    Plath, Sylvia. *The Letters of Sylvia Plath* — 811.54
    Winder, Elizabeth. *Pain, Parties, Work* — B
Plato
    ★*The Collected Dialogues of Plato, Including the Letters* — 184
    ★*The Republic* — 321
★*Plato*. Hare, R. M. — 184
PLATO, 428-347 B.C.E
    Hare, R. M. ★*Plato* — 184
    Kreeft, Peter. ★*Philosophy 101 by Socrates* — 183
Platonic. Franco, Marisa G. — 302.34
PLATONIC LOVE
    Cohen, Rhaina. ★*The Other Significant Others* — 177
Platt, Stephen R.
    Autumn in the Heavenly Kingdom — 951
    Imperial Twilight — 951
PLAY
    Elkind, David. *The Power of Play* — 155.4
    Fletcher, Susan A. *Exploring the History of Childhood and Play Through 50 Historic Treasures* — 790
    Rinaldi, Karen. *It's Great to Suck at Something* — 158.1
    Striniste, Nancy. *Nature Play at Home* — 796.083
    Ticktin, Allie. *Play to Progress* — 370.15
    Toomey, David. *Kingdom of Play* — 591.56
PLAY BEHAVIOR IN ANIMALS
    Toomey, David. *Kingdom of Play* — 591.56
Play by Play. Lundquist, Verne — B
★*Play It Again*. Rusbridger, Alan — B
Play On. Bercovici, Jeff — 613.7
Play Poker Like the Pros. Hellmuth, Phil — 795.41
★*Play Their Hearts Out*. Dohrmann, George — 796.323
Play to Progress. Ticktin, Allie — 370.15
★*Play Your Best Straight Pool*. Capelle, Philip B. — 790
★*The Playbook*. Shapiro, James — 792
PLAYDHD. Milliken, Kirsten — 616.85
PLAYING CARDS
    Ho, Oliver. *The Ultimate Book of Family Card Games* — 795.4
Playing Changes. Chinen, Nate — 781.6509
Playing Hurt. Saunders, John — B
Playing in the Dark. Morrison, Toni — 810.9
Playing off the Rail. McCumber, David — B
Playing The Enemy. Carlin, John — 968.06
Playing Through the Whistle. Price, S. L. — 796.332
Playing with Myself. Rainbow, Randy — B
Playlist for the Apocalypse. Dove, Rita — 811
Plays, 1937-1955. Williams, Tennessee — 812

PUBLIC LIBRARY CORE COLLECTION: NONFICTION
Twentieth Edition

Plays, 1957-1980. Williams, Tennessee — 812
PLAYWRIGHTS
  Ali, Wajahat. *Go Back to Where You Came From* — B
  Greenfield, Robert. *True West* — B
  Hartigan, Patti. *August Wilson* — B
  Hudes, Quiara Alegria. ★*My Broken Language* — B
  Purdum, Todd S. *Something Wonderful* — B
  Shields, Charles J. *Lorraine Hansberry* — B
  Thomas, R. Eric. *Here for It* — B
PLAYWRIGHTS, AMERICAN
  Bigsby, Christopher William Edgar. *Arthur Miller* — B
  Hartigan, Patti. *August Wilson* — B
  Niven, Penelope. *Thornton Wilder* — B
  Perry, Imani. *Looking for Lorraine* — B
  Ruhl, Sarah. *Smile* — B
  Shields, Charles J. *Lorraine Hansberry* — B
PLAYWRIGHTS, ENGLISH
  Bryson, Bill. *Shakespeare* — B
  Greenblatt, Stephen. ★*Will in the World* — B
  Nicholl, Charles. *The Reckoning* — B
  Winkler, Elizabeth. *Shakespeare Was a Woman & Other Heresies* — 822.33
PLAYWRIGHTS, IRISH
  Ellmann, Richard. *Oscar Wilde* — B
PLAYWRITING
  McKee, Robert. *Dialogue* — 809
The Plaza. Satow, Julie — 917.47
PLEA BARGAINING
  Canon, Dan. ★*Pleading Out* — 345.73
★*Pleading Out.* Canon, Dan — 345.73
Pleasant, Barbara
  The Complete Compost Gardening Guide — 631.8
  The Complete Houseplant Survival Manual — 635.9
  Homegrown Pantry — 635
  ★*Starter Vegetable Gardens* — 635
Please Don't Sit on My Bed in Your Outside Clothes. Robinson, Phoebe — 818
Please, Sorry, Thanks. Batterson, Mark — 179
PLEASURE
  Lembke, Anna. *Dopamine Nation* — 152.4
  Nezhukumatathil, Aimee. *Bite by Bite* — 641.3
The Pleasure Shock. Frank, Lone — 616.8
The Pleasures and Sorrows of Work. De Botton, Alain — 306.3
The Pleasures of Japanese Literature. Keene, Donald — 895.6
Plenty. Ottolenghi, Yotam — 641.6
★*Plenty More.* Ottolenghi, Yotam — 641.6
PLESSY CASE, 1896
  Canellos, Peter S. *The Great Dissenter* — B
PLESSY, HOMER ADOLPH
  Luxenberg, Steve. ★*Separate* — 342.7308
Plight of the Living Dead. Simon, Matt — 591.6
Plokhy, Serhii
  ★*The Gates of Europe* — 947.7
  Lost Kingdom — 947
  ★*Nuclear Folly* — 972.9106
  ★*The Russo-Ukrainian War* — 947.7
  Yalta — 940.53
Ploszajski, Anna
  Handmade — 620.1
The Plot to Betray America. Nance, Malcolm W. — 973.933
The Plot to Save South Africa. Malala, Justice — 968.07
Plouffe, David
  A Citizen's Guide to Beating Donald Trump — 324.0973
PLOWMAN, TIMOTHY
  Davis, Wade. *One River* — 581.6
Plummer, Christopher
  In Spite of Myself — B
PLUMMER, CHRISTOPHER. 1929-2021
  Plummer, Christopher. *In Spite of Myself* — B
  Santopietro, Tom. *The Sound of Music Story* — 791.43
Plunder. Kaiser, Menachem — 940.53
PLURALISM (SOCIAL SCIENCES)
  Bidwell, Duane R. *When One Religion Isn't Enough* — 261.2
  Nussbaum, Martha Craven. *The Monarchy of Fear* — 306.20973
  Richardson, Heather Cox. *Democracy Awakening* — 320.473
Pluriverse. Cardenal, Ernesto — 861
PLUTO (DWARF PLANET)
  Stern, Alan. *Chasing New Horizons* — 629.43
PLUTOCRACY
  Frank, Thomas. *The People, No* — 320.56

PLUTONIUM
  Iversen, Kristen. *Full Body Burden* — 363.17
PLYMOUTH, MASSACHUSETTS
  Bunker, Nick. ★*Making Haste from Babylon* — 974.4
  Philbrick, Nathaniel. ★*Mayflower* — 973.2
  Silverman, David J. ★*This Land Is Their Land* — 974.4
  Whittock, Martyn. *Mayflower Lives* — 974.4
POACHING
  Fowlds, Grant. *Saving the Last Rhinos* — 599.66
  Orenstein, Ronald I. *Ivory, Horn and Blood* — 333.95
  Renner, Rebecca. ★*Gator Country* — 364.16
  Vaillant, John. *The Tiger* — 599.756
POCAHONTAS, D. 1617
  Price, David A. ★*Love and Hate in Jamestown* — 975.5
PODCASTERS
  Alterman, Sara Faith. *Let's Never Talk About This Again* — 616.8
  Hodgman, John. *Medallion Status* — B
  Knight, Keltie. *Lady Secrets* — 305.4
  Norton, Laurah. *Lay Them to Rest* — 363.25
  Pellegrino, Danny. *How Do I Un-Remember This?* — B
  Perkins, Nichole. *Sometimes I Trip on How Happy We Could Be* — B
  Roach, Margaret. ★*A Way to Garden* — 635
  Sale, Anna. ★*Let's Talk About Hard Things* — 153.6
  Shafrir, Doree. *Thanks for Waiting* — B
  Wallace, Carvell. *Another Word for Love* — B
PODCASTING
  Maxwell, Lucas. *Podcasting with Youth* — 006.7
Podcasting with Youth. Maxwell, Lucas — 006.7
PODCASTS
  Evans, William. *Black Nerd Problems* — 814.6
  Imperioli, Michael. *Woke up This Morning* — 791.45
  Sale, Anna. ★*Let's Talk About Hard Things* — 153.6
  Weinman, Sarah. ★*Unspeakable Acts* — 364.1
Podemski, Max
  A Paradise of Small Houses — 363.5
PODLIASKY, HÉLÈNE, 1920-2012
  Strauss, Gwen. *The Nine* — 940.53
Poe, Edgar Allan
  Complete Poems — 810
  Essays and Reviews — 809
  ★*Poetry and Tales* — 818
POE, EDGAR ALLAN, 1809-1849
  Dawidziak, Mark. *A Mystery of Mysteries* — B
  Tresch, John. *The Reason for the Darkness of the Night* — B
Poehler, Amy
  Yes Please — B
POEHLER, AMY, 1971-
  Poehler, Amy. *Yes Please* — B
Poems. Akhmatova, Anna Andreevna — 891.71
Poems. Keats, John — 821
Poems. Tennyson, Alfred — 821
★*Poems.* Bishop, Elizabeth — 811
Poems. Baudelaire, Charles — 841
★*Poems 1962-2012.* Gluck, Louise — 811
★*Poems and Translations.* Pound, Ezra — 811
The Poems of Catullus. Catullus, Gaius Valerius — 874
The Poems of Dylan Thomas. Thomas, Dylan — 821
The Poems of Francois Villon. Villon, Francois — 841
The Poems of Octavio Paz. Paz, Octavio — 861
The Poems of Phillis Wheatley. Wheatley, Phillis — 811
Poet in New York. Garcia Lorca, Federico — 861
★*Poet Warrior.* Harjo, Joy — B
Poet's Choice. Hirsch, Edward — 808.81
A Poet's Glossary. Hirsch, Edward — 808.1
POETRY
  Hafiz. ★*The Gift* — 891
  Abdurraqib, Hanif. *A Fortune for Your Disaster* — 811
  Adunis. *Concerto Al-Quds* — 892.7
  Aguon, Julian. *No Country for Eight-Spot Butterflies* — 305.89
  Akbar, Kaveh. *Calling a Wolf a Wolf* — 811
  Akbar, Kaveh. *Pilgrim Bell* — 811
  Akhmatova, Anna Andreevna. ★*The Complete Poems of Anna Akhmatova* — 891.71
  Akhmatova, Anna Andreevna. *Poems* — 891.71
  Aleixandre, Vicente. *A Longing for the Light* — 861
  Alexander, Elizabeth. *Crave Radiance* — 811
  Alexander, Kwame. *Light for the World to See* — 811.6
  Alexander, Will. *Refractive Africa* — 811

AUTHOR, TITLE, SERIES AND SUBJECT INDEX

Alvarez, Julia. *The Woman I Kept to Myself*	811
Alyan, Hala. *The Moon That Turns You Back*	811
Amichai, Yehuda. *Open Closed Open*	892.4
Angelou, Maya. *The Complete Poetry*	811
Ariosto, Lodovico. *Orlando Furioso =*	851
Armantrout, Rae. *Versed*	811
Armantrout, Rae. *Wobble*	811
Asghar, Fatimah. *If They Come for Us*	811
Ashbery, John. *Commotion of the Birds*	811
Ashbery, John. *John Ashbery*	811
Ashbery, John. *Notes from the Air*	811
Ashbery, John. *Selected Poems*	811
Atwood, Margaret. *Dearly*	811
Auden, W. H. *Collected Poems*	811
Auden, W. H. *Selected Poems*	821
Baca, Jimmy Santiago. *Selected Poems*	811
Baer, Kate. *What Kind of Woman*	811
Bailey, Desiree C. *What Noise Against the Cane*	811
Bang, Mary Jo. *The Bride of E*	811
Bang, Mary Jo. *A Doll for Throwing*	811
Bang, Mary Jo. *Elegy*	811
Baraka, Amiri. *S O S*	811
Barot, Rick. *The Galleons*	811
Baudelaire, Charles. *Les Fleurs Du Mal*	841
Baudelaire, Charles. *Poems*	841
Beckett, Samuel. *Collected Poems in English and French*	841
Berry, Wendell. *New Collected Poems*	811
Berry, Wendell. *A Timbered Choir*	811
Berryman, John. *Collected Poems, 1937-1971*	811
Berssenbrugge, Mei-Mei. *A Treatise on Stars*	811
Betts, Reginald Dwayne. *Felon*	811
Betts, Reginald Dwayne. ★*Redaction*	704.9
Bibbins, Mark. *13th Balloon*	813
Bidart, Frank. ★*Half-Light*	811
Bishop, Elizabeth. ★*Poems*	811
Bitsui, Sherwin. *Dissolve*	811
Blanco, Richard. *How to Love a Country*	811
Blount, Tommye. *Fantasia for the Man in Blue*	811
Bly, Robert. *Collected Poems*	811
Boland, Eavan. *The Historians*	821
Boland, Eavan. *New Collected Poems*	821
Boland, Eavan. *A Woman Without a Country*	821
Borges, Jorge Luis. ★*Selected Poems*	861
Boruch, Marianne. *Eventually One Dreams the Real Thing*	811
Borzutzky, Daniel. *Lake Michigan*	811
Borzutzky, Daniel. *The Performance of Becoming Human*	811
Brock-Broido, Lucie. *Stay, Illusion*	811
Brooks, Gwendolyn. ★*The Essential Gwendolyn Brooks*	811
Brooks, Gwendolyn. *In Montgomery, and Other Poems*	811
Brown, Jericho. ★*The Tradition*	811
Brown, Molly McCully. *The Virginia State Colony for Epileptics and Feebleminded*	811
Browne, Mahogany L. ★*Black Girl Magic*	811.6
Browning, Robert. ★*Robert Browning's Poetry*	821
Browning, Robert. *Robert Browning*	821.8
Bunting, Basil. *Complete Poems*	821
Burns, Robert. *Burns*	821
Byas, Taylor. *I Done Clicked My Heels Three Times*	811
Byron, George Gordon Byron. *Selected Poetry of Lord Byron*	821
Cardenal, Ernesto. *Pluriverse*	861
Carey, John. *A Little History of Poetry*	809.1
Carson, Anne. *The Beauty of the Husband*	811
Carson, Anne. *Decreation*	818
Carson, Anne. *Red Doc*	811
Carver, Raymond. *All of Us*	811
Carver, Raymond. *A New Path to the Waterfall*	811
Cavafy, Constantine. *The Collected Poems*	889
Celan, Paul. *Breathturn into Timestead*	831
Celan, Paul. ★*Memory Rose into Threshold Speech*	831
Chang, Tina. *Hybrida*	811
Chang, Victoria. *Obit*	811
Charles, Jos. *Feeld*	811
Choi, Don Mee. *DMZ Colony*	818
Choi, Don Mee. *Hardly War*	811
Choi, Franny. *The World Keeps Ending, and the World Goes On*	811
Clark, Tiana. *I Can't Talk About the Trees Without the Blood*	811
Clifton, Lucille. *How to Carry Water*	811
Clifton, Lucille. *Mercy*	811
Codjoe, Ama. *Bluest Nude*	811
Cody, Anthony. *Borderland Apocrypha*	811
Cohen, Leonard. *The Flame*	810
Coleridge, Samuel Taylor. *The Complete Poems*	821
Collins, Billy. *Aimless Love*	811
Collins, Billy. *Sailing Alone Around the Room*	811
Collins, Billy. *The Trouble with Poetry and Other Poems*	811
Collins, Billy. *Whale Day*	811
Collins, Martha. *Admit One*	811
Corral, Eduardo C. *Guillotine*	811.6
Cummings, E. E. ★*Complete Poems, 1904-1962*	811
Daley-Ward, Yrsa. *The How*	158.1
Dante Alighieri. ★*The Divine Comedy*	851
Dante Alighieri. *Inferno*	851
Dante Alighieri. *The Paradiso*	851
Dante Alighieri. *Paradiso*	851
Dante Alighieri. *Purgatorio*	851
Darwish, Mamoud. *If I Were Another*	892.7
Darwish, Mamoud. ★*Unfortunately, It Was Paradise*	892
Day-Lewis, Cecil. *The Complete Poems of C. Day Lewis*	821
Derricotte, Toi. *I*	811
Diaz, Natalie. ★*Postcolonial Love Poem*	811
Dickinson, Emily. ★*The Complete Poems.*	811.4
Dickinson, Emily. *Dickinson*	811
Doty, Mark. *Deep Lane*	811
Doty, Mark. *Fire to Fire*	811
Dove, Rita. *Playlist for the Apocalypse*	811
Dove, Rita. ★*Selected Poems*	811
Dove, Rita. *Sonata Mulattica*	811
Duncan, Robert. *Selected Poems*	811
Dunmore, Helen. *Inside the Wave*	821
Dunn, Stephen. *Local Visitations*	811
Dunn, Stephen. *New & Selected Poems*	811
Eliot, T. S. *Collected Poems, 1909-1962.*	821.912
Eliot, T. S. ★*Complete Poems and Plays.*	810
Ellis, Thomas Sayers. *Skin, Inc.*	811
Emerson, Ralph Waldo. ★*Collected Poems and Translations*	811
Erdrich, Heid E. ★*Little Big Bully*	811
Espada, Martin. ★*Floaters*	811
Evans, William. *We Inherit What the Fires Left*	811
Ewing, Eve L. *1919*	811
Faizullah, Tarfia. *Registers of Illuminated Villages*	811
Felix, Camonghne. *Build Yourself a Boat*	811
Fenton, James. *Selected Poems*	821
Ferlinghetti, Lawrence. *These Are My Rivers*	811
Finney, Nikky. *Love Child's Hotbed of Occasional Poetry*	811
Flynn, Nick. *The Captain Asks for a Show of Hands*	811
Forche, Carolyn. *Blue Hour*	811
Forche, Carolyn. *In the Lateness of the World*	811
Forsythe, Kelly. *Perennial*	811
Foster, Thomas C. *How to Read Poetry Like a Professor*	808.1
Gallagher, Tess. *Dear Ghosts*	811
Gallagher, Tess. *Is, Is Not*	811
Gander, Forrest. ★*Be With*	811
Garcia Lorca, Federico. *Collected Poems*	861
Garcia Lorca, Federico. *Poet in New York*	861
Gay, Ross. ★*Catalog of Unabashed Gratitude*	811
Geter, Hafizah. *Un-American*	811
Gibran, Kahlil. *And the Prophet Said*	811
Gibran, Kahlil. *The Collected Works*	811
Gibran, Kahlil. ★*The Prophet*	811
Gilbert, Jack. *Collected Poems*	811
Gimenez Smith, Carmen. *Be Recorder*	811
Ginsberg, Allen. ★*Howl*	811.54
Gioia, Dana. *99 Poems*	811
Giovanni, Nikki. ★*The Collected Poetry of Nikki Giovanni, 1968-1998*	811
Giovanni, Nikki. *A Good Cry*	811
Giovanni, Nikki. *Make Me Rain*	811
Giovanni, Nikki. *Quilting the Black-Eyed Pea*	811
Girmay, Aracelis. *The Black Maria*	811
Gluck, Louise. *Averno*	811
Gluck, Louise. ★*Poems 1962-2012*	811
Gluck, Louise. *Winter Recipes from the Collective*	811
Goethe, Johann Wolfgang von. *Selected Poetry*	831
Gorman, Amanda. ★*Call Us What We Carry*	811
Graham, Jorie. *The Dream of the Unified Field*	811
Graham, Jorie. *Fast*	811
Graham, Jorie. *From the New World*	811

PUBLIC LIBRARY CORE COLLECTION: NONFICTION
Twentieth Edition

Graham, Jorie. *Overlord*	811
Graham, Jorie. *To 2040*	811
Grass, Gunter. *Of All That Ends*	838
greathouse, torrin a. *Wound from the Mouth of a Wound*	811
Gregg, Linda. *All of It Singing*	811.54
Gunn, Thom. *Boss Cupid*	821
H. D. *Collected Poems, 1912-1944*	811
Hacker, Marilyn. *Selected Poems, 1965-1990*	811
Hacker, Marilyn. *A Stranger's Mirror*	811
Hall, Donald. *The Back Chamber*	811
Hall, Donald. *The Selected Poems of Donald Hall.*	811
Hall, Donald. *White Apples and the Taste of Stone*	811
Hardy, Thomas. *Thomas Hardy*	821
Harjo, Joy. *An American Sunrise*	811
Harjo, Joy. *A Map to the Next World*	811
Harjo, Joy. ★*Poet Warrior*	B
Harrison, Jim. *The Essential Poems of Jim Harrison*	811
Harrison, Jim. *Songs of Unreason*	811
Harrison, Leslie. *The Book of Endings*	811
Hass, Robert. *The Apple Trees at Olema*	811
Hass, Robert. *Summer Snow*	811.6
Hayden, Robert. *Collected Poems*	811
Hayes, Terrance. ★*American Sonnets for My Past and Future Assassin*	811
Hayes, Terrance. *How to Be Drawn*	811
Hayes, Terrance. ★*Lighthead*	811
Hayes, Terrance. *So to Speak*	811
Heaney, Seamus. *District and Circle*	821
Heaney, Seamus. *Human Chain*	821
Heaney, Seamus. *Opened Ground*	821
Herbert, Zbigniew. *The Collected Poems, 1956-1998*	891.8
Herrera, Juan Felipe. *Every Day We Get More Illegal*	811
Hesiod. *Works and Days and Theogony*	881
Higginson, William J. *The Haiku Handbook*	808.1
Hill, DaMaris B. *Breath Better Spent*	811
Hill, Geoffrey. *Selected Poems*	821
Hirsch, Edward. *Gabriel*	811
Hirsch, Edward. *The Living Fire*	811
Hirsch, Edward. *Special Orders*	811
Hirsch, Edward. *Stranger by Night*	811
Hirshfield, Jane. *After*	811
Hirshfield, Jane. *The Beauty*	811
Hirshfield, Jane. *Ledger*	811
Hoagland, Tony. *Priest Turned Therapist Treats Fear of God*	811
Hoagland, Tony. *Unincorporated Persons in the Late Honda Dynasty*	811
Homer. *The Iliad*	883
Homer. *The Iliad*	883
Homer. *Iliad*	883
Homer. ★*The Iliad*	883
Homer. *The Odyssey*	883
Homer. *The Odyssey*	883
Homer. *Odyssey*	883
Homer. ★*The Odyssey*	883
Homer. *The Odyssey*	883
Hong, Cathy Park. *Engine Empire*	811
Horace. *Odes and Epodes*	874
Howe, Fanny. *Second Childhood*	811
Hutchinson, Ishion. *House of Lords and Commons*	811
Jackson, Major. *Razzle Dazzle*	811
Jalal al-Din Rumi, Maulana. *The Essential Rumi*	891
Jalal al-Din Rumi, Maulana. *Rumi*	891
Jarrell, Randall. ★*The Complete Poems*	811
Jeffers, Honorée Fanonne. *The Age of Phillis*	811
Jeffers, Robinson. *The Selected Poetry of Robinson Jeffers*	811
Johnson, James Weldon. *Complete Poems*	811
Jones, Saeed. *Alive at the End of the World*	811
Jones, Saeed. *Prelude to Bruise*	811
Jordan, June. ★*The Essential June Jordan*	811
Juana Ines de la Cruz, Sister. *Selected Works*	861
Kaminsky, Ilya. ★*Deaf Republic*	811
Karr, Mary. *Tropic of Squalor*	811
Kasischke, Laura. *Space, in Chains*	811
Kaur, Rupi. *Milk and Honey*	811
Kaur, Rupi. *The Sun and Her Flowers*	811.6
Kearney, Douglas. *Sho*	811
Keats, John. ★*The Complete Poems of John Keats*	821
Keats, John. *Poems*	821
Keene, John. ★*Punks*	811
Kelly, Donika. *The Renunciations*	811
Kendall, Tim. *The Art of Robert Frost*	811
Kerouac, Jack. *Book of Blues*	811
Kerouac, Jack. *Book of Sketches, 1952-57*	818
Kerouac, Jack. *Scattered Poems*	811
Kinnell, Galway. *Collected Poems*	811
Kinnell, Galway. *A New Selected Poems*	811
Kinnell, Galway. *Strong Is Your Hold*	811
Kipling, Rudyard. *Complete Verse*	821
Komunyakaa, Yusef. *The Chameleon Couch*	811
Komunyakaa, Yusef. ★*Everyday Mojo Songs of Earth*	811
Komunyakaa, Yusef. *Warhorses*	811
Kooser, Ted. *Delights & Shadows*	811
Kunitz, Stanley. ★*The Collected Poems*	811
Larkin, Philip. ★*Collected Poems*	821
Larkin, Philip. *The Complete Poems*	821
Laux, Dorianne. *Only as the Day Is Long*	811
Le Guin, Ursula K. *So Far so Good*	811
Le Guin, Ursula K. *Ursula K. Le Guin*	811
Lear, Edward. *The Complete Verse and Other Nonsense*	821
Levertov, Denise. *Selected Poems*	811
Levine, Philip. *The Simple Truth*	811
Lewis, Robin Coste. *To the Realization of Perfect Helplessness*	811
Limon, Ada. *Bright Dead Things*	811
Limon, Ada. ★*The Carrying*	811
Limon, Ada. ★*The Hurting Kind*	811
Long Soldier, Layli. ★*Whereas*	811
Lorde, Audre. ★*The Selected Works of Audre Lorde*	814
Lowell, Amy. *Selected Poems*	821
Lowell, Robert. *Collected Poems*	811
Macfarlane, Robert. *The Lost Spells*	811
Mackey, Nathaniel. *Splay Anthem*	811
Manguel, Alberto. *Homer's the Iliad and the Odyssey*	883
Mans, Jasmine. *Black Girl, Call Home*	811
Mansbach, Adam. *I Had a Brother Once*	811
Mao, Sally Wen. *Oculus*	811
Marshall, Nate. *Finna*	811
McCrae, Shane. *In the Language of My Captor*	811
McGrath, Campbell. *Nouns & Verbs*	811
McHugh, Heather. *Muddy Matterhorn*	811
Melville, Herman. *Complete Poems*	811
Merwin, W. S. *The Shadow of Sirius*	811
Millay, Edna St. Vincent. *Collected Poems*	811
Millay, Edna St. Vincent. *Selected Poems*	811
Momaday, N. Scott. ★*The Death of Sitting Bear*	811
Moore, Marianne. *New Collected Poems*	811
Morrissey, Sinead. *Parallax*	821
Muldoon, Paul. *Maggot*	821
Muldoon, Paul. *Selected Poems 1968-2014*	821
Myles, Eileen. *I Must Be Living Twice*	811.54
Neruda, Pablo. *All the Odes*	861
Neruda, Pablo. *Then Come Back*	861
Neruda, Pablo. ★*Twenty Love Poems and a Song of Despair*	861
Neruda, Pablo. *World's End*	861
Nezhukumatathil, Aimee. *Oceanic*	811
Nguyen, Diana Khoi. *Ghost of*	811
Nguyen, Hieu Minh. *Not Here*	811
Nguyen, Hoa. *A Thousand Times You Lose Your Treasure*	811
Nicolson, Adam. *The Making of Poetry*	821.709
Notley, Alice. *Certain Magical Acts*	811
Nye, Naomi Shihab. *The Tiny Journalist*	811
Nye, Naomi Shihab. *You & Yours*	811
O'Hara, Frank. *Lunch Poems.*	811
Oates, Joyce Carol. *American Melancholy*	811
Olds, Sharon. *Arias*	811
Olds, Sharon. *Odes*	811
Olds, Sharon. *Stag's Leap*	811
Olivarez, Jose. *Promises of Gold = Promesas De Oro*	811
Oliver, Mary. ★*Devotions*	811
Oliver, Mary. *Dream Work*	811
Oliver, Mary. *New and Selected Poems,; Vol. 1*	811
Oliver, Mary. *A Thousand Mornings*	811
Omar Khayyam. *Rubaiyat of Omar Khayyam*	891
Ondaatje, Michael. *A Year of Last Things*	811
Orr, David. *You, Too, Could Write a Poem*	808.1
Oswald, Alice. *Falling Awake*	821
Ovid. *Tales from Ovid*	873
Padgett, Ron. *Collected Poems*	811
Paglia, Camille. ★*Break, Blow, Burn*	821.009

AUTHOR, TITLE, SERIES AND SUBJECT INDEX

Pardlo, Gregory. *Spectral Evidence*	811
Parker, Morgan. *Magical Negro*	811
Parker, Morgan. *There Are More Beautiful Things Than Beyonce*	811
Paz, Octavio. ★*The Collected Poems of Octavio Paz, 1957-1987*	861
Paz, Octavio. *The Poems of Octavio Paz*	861
Perillo, Lucia. *On the Spectrum of Possible Deaths*	811
Perillo, Lucia. *Time Will Clean the Carcass Bones*	811
Petrosino, Kiki. *White Blood*	811
Phillips, Carl. ★*Then the War*	811
Pico, Tommy. *Feed*	811
Pico, Tommy. *Junk*	811
Pico, Tommy. *Nature Poem*	811
Pinsky, Robert. *The Figured Wheel*	811
Plath, Sylvia. ★*Ariel*	811
Plath, Sylvia. ★*The Collected Poems*	811
Poe, Edgar Allan. *Complete Poems*	810
Pope, Alexander. *Selected Poetry*	821
Pound, Ezra. ★*Poems and Translations*	811
Powell, D. A. *Useless Landscape*	811
Pushkin, Aleksandr Sergeevich. *Eugene Onegin*	891.71
Rankine, Claudia. ★*Citizen*	814
Rankine, Claudia. ★*Just Us*	305.896
Rasmussen, Matt. *Black Aperture*	811
Reed, Ishmael. *New and Collected Poems, 1964-2007*	811
Reed, Justin Phillip. *Indecency*	811
Reed, Justin Phillip. *The Malevolent Volume*	811
Rekdal, Paisley. *Nightingale*	811
Rekdal, Paisley. *West*	811
Rich, Adrienne. *Collected Early Poems, 1950-1970*	811
Rich, Adrienne. *Collected Poems*	811
Rich, Adrienne. *Later Poems*	811
Rich, Adrienne. *The School Among the Ruins*	811
Rilke, Rainer Maria. *Ahead of All Parting*	831
Rilke, Rainer Maria. ★*Duino Elegies*	831
Rilke, Rainer Maria. *New Poems*	831
Rilke, Rainer Maria. ★*Sonnets to Orpheus*	831
Rimbaud, Arthur. *The Illuminations*	841
Ritvo, Max. *The Final Voicemails*	811
Ritvo, Max. *Four Reincarnations*	811
Roethke, Theodore. *The Collected Poems of Theodore Roethke*	811
Rogers, Pattiann. *Quickening Fields*	811
Roripaugh, Lee Ann. *Tsunami vs. the Fukushima 50*	811
Rossetti, Christina Georgina. *Christina Rossetti*	821.8
Ruefle, Mary. *Dunce*	811
Ruefle, Mary. *Selected Poems*	811
Rukeyser, Muriel. *Selected Poems*	811
Ryan, Kay. *The Best of It*	811
Salter, Mary Jo. *The Surveyors*	811
Sanchez, Erika L. *Lessons on Expulsion*	811
Sanchez, Sonia. *Homegirls & Handgrenades*	811
Sandburg, Carl. ★*The Complete Poems of Carl Sandburg*	811
Santos Perez, Craig. *From Unincorporated Territory [amot]*	811
Sappho. *If Not, Winter*	884
Sarton, May. *Selected Poems of May Sarton*	811
Satyamurti, Carole. *Mahabharata*	821
Scenters-Zapico, Natalie. *Lima*	811
Schiff, Robyn. *A Woman of Property*	811
Schuyler, James. *Collected Poems*	811
Seidel, Frederick. ★*Frederick Seidel Selected Poems*	811
Seuss, Diane. ★*Frank*	811
Seuss, Diane. *Still Life with Two Dead Peacocks and a Girl*	811.6
Sexton, Anne. *Selected Poems of Anne Sexton*	811
Shanahan, Charif. *Trace Evidence*	811
Shange, Ntozake. ★*Sing a Black Girl's Song*	818
Shapiro, Karl. *Selected Poems*	811
Sharif, Solmaz. *Customs*	811
Sharif, Solmaz. *Look*	811
Shaughnessy, Brenda. *The Octopus Museum*	811
Shelley, Percy Bysshe. *Shelley's Poetry and Prose*	821
Shelley, Percy Bysshe. *Shelley*	821
Shockley, Evie. *The New Black*	811
Shockley, Evie. *Semiautomatic*	811
Shockley, Evie. *Suddenly We*	811
Simic, Charles. *Come Closer and Listen*	811
Simic, Charles. *The Lunatic*	811
Simic, Charles. *New and Selected Poems*	811
Simic, Charles. *The Voice at 3*	811
Sinclair, Safiya. *Cannibal*	811
Skaja, Emily. *Brute*	811.6
Smith, Clint. ★*Above Ground*	811
Smith, Danez. ★*Don't Call Us Dead*	811.6
Smith, Danez. ★*Homie*	811
Smith, Patricia. *Blood Dazzler*	811
Smith, Patricia. ★*Incendiary Art*	811.54
Smith, Patricia. *Shoulda Been Jimi Savannah*	811
Smith, Patricia. *Unshuttered*	811
Smith, Tracy K. *Duende*	811
Smith, Tracy K. ★*Life on Mars*	811
Smith, Tracy K. ★*Such Color*	811
Smith, Tracy K. ★*Wade in the Water*	811.6
Snyder, Gary. *No Nature*	811
Som, Brandon. *Tripas*	811
Sosnowski, Andrzej. *Lodgings*	891.8
Spicer, Jack. *My Vocabulary Did This to Me*	811
Stanford, Frank. *What About This*	811
Stevens, Wallace. *Collected Poetry and Prose*	811
Strand, Mark. *Collected Poems*	811
Swenson, May. *Collected Poems*	811
Sze, Arthur. *Sight Lines*	811
Szymborska, Wislawa. *Here*	891.8
Szymborska, Wislawa. *Map*	891.8
Tagore, Rabindranath. *Selected Poems*	891
Tapahonso, Luci. *A Radiant Curve*	811
Tennyson, Alfred. *Poems*	821
Thom, Kai Cheng. *Falling Back in Love with Being Human*	811
Thomas, Dylan. *The Poems of Dylan Thomas*	821
Thoreau, Henry David. ★*Collected Essays and Poems*	818
Tibble, Tayi. *Poukahangatus*	821
Tran, Paul. *All the Flowers Kneeling*	811
Transtromer, Tomas. *The Great Enigma*	839.71
Trethewey, Natasha D. ★*Monument*	811
Trethewey, Natasha D. ★*Native Guard*	811
Tsvetaeva, Marina. *Selected Poems*	891.71
Tuama, Padraig O. ★*Poetry Unbound*	808.1
Valentine, Jean. *Door in the Mountain*	811
Vang, Mai Der. *Afterland*	811
Villon, Francois. *The Poems of Francois Villon*	841
Virgil. ★*The Aeneid*	873
Virgil. *The Aeneid*	873
Virgil. *The Eclogues of Virgil*	871
Vuong, Ocean. ★*Time Is a Mother*	811
Walcott, Derek. *Omeros*	811
Walcott, Derek. *The Poetry of Derek Walcott 1948-2013*	811
Waldrop, Keith. *Transcendental Studies*	811
Walker, Alice. *Hard Times Require Furious Dancing*	811
Wang, Jackie. *The Sunflower Cast a Spell to Save Us from the Void*	811
Wheatley, Phillis. *The Poems of Phillis Wheatley*	811
Whitman, Walt. ★*Leaves of Grass*	811
Whitman, Walt. ★*Poetry and Prose*	811
Whitman, Walt. ★*Selected Poems*	811
Wicker, Marcus. *Silencer*	811
Wilbur, Richard. *Anterooms*	811
Wilbur, Richard. ★*Collected Poems, 1943-2004*	811
Williams, C. K. ★*Collected Poems*	811
Williams, C. K. *Falling Ill*	811
Williams, William Carlos. *Paterson*	811
Wiman, Christian. *Zero at the Bone*	818
Wright, C. D. *One with Others*	811
Wright, James Arlington. *Above the River*	811
XIe, Jenny. *Eye Level*	811
Yeats, W. B. *The Collected Poems of W.B. Yeats*	821
Youn, Monica. *Blackacre*	811.6
Young, Kevin. *Ardency*	811
Young, Kevin. ★*The Art of Losing*	811
Young, Kevin. *Book of Hours*	811
Young, Kevin. *Brown*	811
Young, Kevin. *Stones*	811
Zagajewski, Adam. *Eternal Enemies*	891.8
Zapruder, Matthew. *Come on All You Ghosts*	811

POETRY — AFRICAN AMERICAN AUTHORS

Alexander, Elizabeth. *Crave Radiance*	811
Baraka, Amiri. *S O S*	811
Brooks, Gwendolyn. ★*The Essential Gwendolyn Brooks*	811
Brooks, Gwendolyn. *In Montgomery, and Other Poems*	811
Dove, Rita. ★*Selected Poems*	811
Dove, Rita. *Sonata Mulattica*	811

PUBLIC LIBRARY CORE COLLECTION: NONFICTION
Twentieth Edition

Ferlinghetti, Lawrence. *These Are My Rivers* — 811
Giovanni, Nikki. *A Good Cry* — 811
Hughes, Langston. ★*Selected Poems of Langston Hughes* — 811
Hutchinson, Ishion. *House of Lords and Commons* — 811
Johnson, James Weldon. *Complete Poems* — 811
Mackey, Nathaniel. *Splay Anthem* — 811
Smith, Patricia. ★*Incendiary Art* — 811.54
Walker, Alice. *Hard Times Require Furious Dancing* — 811

POETRY — ARAB AMERICAN AUTHORS
Sharif, Solmaz. *Look* — 811

POETRY — ASIAN AMERICAN AUTHORS
Choi, Don Mee. *Hardly War* — 811
Hong, Cathy Park. *Engine Empire* — 811
Lee, Li-Young. *The Undressing* — 811
Nezhukumatathil, Aimee. *Oceanic* — 811
Nguyen, Diana Khoi. *Ghost of* — 811
Nguyen, Hieu Minh. *Not Here* — 811
Youn, Monica. *Blackacre* — 811.6

POETRY — COLLECTIONS
Hirsch, Edward. *Poet's Choice* — 808.81
Pinsky, Robert. *Singing School* — 808.1
Rexroth, Kenneth. *One Hundred Poems from the Japanese* — 895

POETRY — HISPANIC AMERICAN
Sanchez, Erika L. *Lessons on Expulsion* — 811

POETRY — LGBTQIA
Jones, Saeed. *Prelude to Bruise* — 811
Myles, Eileen. *I Must Be Living Twice* — 811.54
Nguyen, Hieu Minh. *Not Here* — 811
Pico, Tommy. *Feed* — 811
Pico, Tommy. *Nature Poem* — 811
Reed, Justin Phillip. *Indecency* — 811

POETRY — NATIVE AMERICAN AUTHORS
Harjo, Joy. *A Map to the Next World* — 811
Pico, Tommy. *Feed* — 811
Pico, Tommy. *Nature Poem* — 811
★*Poetry and Prose*. Whitman, Walt — 811

POETRY AND SOCIETY
Hecht, Jennifer Michael. ★*The Wonder Paradox* — 808.1
Hirsch, Edward. *Poet's Choice* — 808.81
★*Poetry and Tales*. Poe, Edgar Allan — 818
Poetry Handbook. Deutsch, Babette — 808.1
A Poetry Handbook. Oliver, Mary — 808.1
The Poetry of Derek Walcott 1948-2013. Walcott, Derek — 811

POETRY OF PLACES
Berssenbrugge, Mei-Mei. *A Treatise on Stars* — 811
Boruch, Marianne. *Eventually One Dreams the Real Thing* — 811
Forsythe, Kelly. *Perennial* — 811
Graham, Jorie. *From the New World* — 811
Hirsch, Edward. *Stranger by Night* — 811
Nezhukumatathil, Aimee. *Oceanic* — 811
Wicker, Marcus. *Silencer* — 811
Williams, William Carlos. *Paterson* — 811
★*Poetry Unbound*. Tuama, Padraig O. — 808.1
Poetry Will Save Your Life. Bialosky, Jill — B

POETRY WRITING
Basbanes, Nicholas A. ★*Cross of Snow* — B
Bate, Jonathan. *Radical Wordsworth* — B
Burt, Stephanie. *Don't Read Poetry* — 811
Crase, Douglas. *On Autumn Lake* — 809
Deutsch, Babette. *Poetry Handbook* — 808.1
Doty, Mark. *What Is the Grass* — 811
Foster, Thomas C. *How to Read Poetry Like a Professor* — 808.1
Garfunkel, Art. *What Is It All but Luminous* — 782.42164
Gluck, Louise. *American Originality* — 814
Harjo, Joy. *Catching the Light* — 818
Hass, Robert. *Summer Snow* — 811.6
Higginson, William J. *The Haiku Handbook* — 808.1
Hirsch, Edward. *How to Read a Poem* — 808.1
Hirsch, Edward. *A Poet's Glossary* — 808.1
Hoffman, Adina. ★*My Happiness Bears No Relation to Happiness* — B
Hollis, Matthew. *The Waste Land* — 821
Korda, Michael. *Muse of Fire* — 940.4
Larimer, Kevin. *The Poets & Writers Complete Guide to Being a Writer* — 808
Leithauser, Brad. *Rhyme's Rooms* — 808.1
Miller, Lucasta. ★*Keats* — 821
Nicolson, Adam. *The Making of Poetry* — 821.709
Oliver, Mary. *A Poetry Handbook* — 808.1
Orr, David. *You, Too, Could Write a Poem* — 808.1
Orr, Gregory. *A Primer for Poets & Readers of Poetry* — 808.1
Paglia, Camille. ★*Break, Blow, Burn* — 821.009
Pinsky, Robert. *Singing School* — 808.1
Sato, Hiroaki. *On Haiku* — 809.1
Sol, Adam. *How a Poem Moves* — 808.1
Travisano, Thomas J. *Love Unknown* — B
Warren, Rosanna. *Max Jacob* — B
Wiman, Christian. *He Held Radical Light* — 814
Zenith, Richard. *Pessoa* — B

POETS
Auvinen, Karen. *Rough Beauty* — B
Belcourt, Billy-Ray. ★*A History of My Brief Body* — B
Blanco, Richard. *The Prince of Los Cocuyos* — B
Boyer, Anne. *The Undying* — B
Broome, Brian. ★*Punch Me up to the Gods* — B
Clark, Heather. ★*Red Comet* — B
Damrosch, David. *Around the World in 80 Books* — 809
Di Cintio, Marcello. *Pay No Heed to the Rockets* — 956.9405
Forche, Carolyn. *What You Have Heard Is True* — B
Glass, Charles. *Soldiers Don't Go Mad* — 616.85
Gluck, Louise. *American Originality* — 814
Hardwick, Elizabeth. *The Dolphin Letters, 1970-1979* — 811
Heaney, Seamus. *District and Circle* — 821
Hecht, Jennifer Michael. ★*The Wonder Paradox* — 808.1
Izgil, Tahir Hamut. *Waiting to Be Arrested at Night* — B
Jang, Jin-Sung. *Dear Leader* — B
Korda, Michael. *Muse of Fire* — 940.4
Larimer, Kevin. *The Poets & Writers Complete Guide to Being a Writer* — 808
Le Guin, Ursula K. *So Far so Good* — 811
Moss, Adam. ★*The Work of Art* — 701
Moss, Jeremiah. *Feral City* — B
Nicolson, Adam. *Why Homer Matters* — 883
Oliver, Mary. ★*Upstream* — 814
Rilke, Rainer Maria. ★*Letters to a Young Poet* — 831
Robinson, Staci. ★*Tupac Shakur* — B
Ruhl, Sarah. *Letters from Max* — 811
Sampson, Fiona. *In Search of Mary Shelley* — B
Thomas, Dylan. *A Child's Christmas in Wales* — B
Wiman, Christian. *He Held Radical Light* — 814
Wong, Jane. ★*Meet Me Tonight in Atlantic City* — B
Wulf, Andrea. *Magnificent Rebels* — 830.9
Zenith, Richard. *Pessoa* — B
The Poets & Writers Complete Guide to Being a Writer. Larimer, Kevin — 808

POETS, AMERICAN
Ackmann, Martha. ★*These Fevered Days* — B
Basbanes, Nicholas A. ★*Cross of Snow* — B
Bialosky, Jill. *Poetry Will Save Your Life* — B
Blunk, Jonathan. *James Wright* — B
Calhoun, Ada. *Also a Poet* — B
Clark, Heather. ★*Red Comet* — B
Crase, Douglas. *On Autumn Lake* — 809
Crawford, Robert. *Eliot After the Waste Land* — B
Crowther, Gail. *Three-Martini Afternoons at the Ritz* — 920
Doty, Mark. *What Is the Grass* — 811
Ginsberg, Allen. *Best Minds of My Generation* — 810.9
Goetsch, Diana. *This Body I Wore* — B
Gordon, Lyndall. ★*T.S. Eliot* — B
Hammer, Langdon. *James Merrill* — B
Hartigan, Patti. *August Wilson* — B
Hong, Cathy Park. *Minor Feelings* — 305.48
Hughes, Langston. ★*I Wonder as I Wander* — B
Jackson, Angela. *A Surprised Queenhood in the New Black Sun* — B
Milford, Nancy. *Savage Beauty* — B
Moody, Anthony David. *Ezra Pound* — B
Moore, Marianne. *The Selected Letters of Marianne Moore* — B
Parini, Jay. *Robert Frost* — B
Rampersad, Arnold. *The Life of Langston Hughes* — B
Rampersad, Arnold. ★*The Life of Langston Hughes* — B
Roffman, Karin. *The Songs We Know Best* — B
Rosenblitt, J. Alison. *The Beauty of Living* — B
Schultz, Philip. *Comforts of the Abyss* — 801
Smith, Patti. ★*Just Kids* — B
Smith, Patti. ★*Year of the Monkey* — B
Travisano, Thomas J. *Love Unknown* — B
Tresch, John. *The Reason for the Darkness of the Night* — B
Waldstreicher, David. *The Odyssey of Phillis Wheatley* — B
Winder, Elizabeth. *Pain, Parties, Work* — B

AUTHOR, TITLE, SERIES AND SUBJECT INDEX

POETS, ENGLISH
   Bate, Jonathan. *Radical Wordsworth* — B
   Greenblatt, Stephen. ★*Will in the World* — B
   Gunn, Thom. *The Letters of Thom Gunn* — 821
   Miller, Lucasta. ★*Keats* — 821
   Nicolson, Adam. *The Making of Poetry* — 821.709
   Rundell, Katherine. ★*Super-Infinite* — B

POETS, FRENCH
   Baudelaire, Charles. *Les Fleurs Du Mal* — 841
   Baudelaire, Charles. *Poems* — 841
   Rimbaud, Arthur. *The Illuminations* — 841
   Warren, Rosanna. *Max Jacob* — B

POETS, GERMAN
   Rilke, Rainer Maria. ★*Letters to a Young Poet* — 831

POETS, IRISH
   Beckett, Samuel. *Collected Poems in English and French* — 841
   Boland, Eavan. *New Collected Poems* — 821
   Brown, Terence. *The Life of W.B. Yeats* — B
   Ellmann, Richard. *Oscar Wilde* — B
   Heaney, Seamus. *Human Chain* — 821
   Hollis, Matthew. *The Waste Land* — 821
   Muldoon, Paul. *Maggot* — 821
   Toibin, Colm. *Mad, Bad, Dangerous to Know* — 920
   Yeats, W. B. *The Collected Poems of W.B. Yeats* — 821

POETS, RUSSIAN
   Binyon, T. J. *Pushkin* — B

Pogrebin, Abigail
   My Jewish Year — 296.4

POGREBIN, ABIGAIL
   Pogrebin, Abigail. *My Jewish Year* — 296.4

Pohlman, Dean
   Yoga Fitness for Men — 613.7

Poincare's Prize. Szpiro, George — 510.76

POINTER (DOG BREED)
   Weintraub, Robert. *No Better Friend* — 940.54

Poirier, Agnes
   Left Bank — 944

The Poisoned City. Clark, Anna — 363.6
Poisoned Legacy. Magner, Mike — 338.7
Poisoner in Chief. Kinzer, Stephen — B
The Poisoner's Handbook. Blum, Deborah — 614

POISONERS
   Blum, Deborah. *The Poisoner's Handbook* — 614
   Bradbury, Neil. *A Taste for Poison* — 615.9

POISONING
   Blum, Deborah. *The Poisoner's Handbook* — 614
   Bradbury, Neil. *A Taste for Poison* — 615.9
   Guinn, Jeff. *The Road to Jonestown* — 289.9
   Herman, Eleanor. *The Royal Art of Poison* — 364.152
   Kinzer, Stephen. *Poisoner in Chief* — B
   White, Richard. *Who Killed Jane Stanford?* — 364.152
   Woolley, Benjamin. *The King's Assassin* — B

Poisoning The Press. Feldstein, Mark Avrom — 973.924092

POISONOUS GASES
   Preston, Diana. *A Higher Form of Killing* — 940.4

POISONOUS INSECTS
   Schmidt, Justin O. *The Sting of the Wild* — 595.7

POISONOUS PLANTS
   Borsato, Diane. *Mushrooming* — 579.6
   Stewart, Amy. *Wicked Plants* — 581.6

POISONS
   Bradbury, Neil. *A Taste for Poison* — 615.9
   Carson, Rachel. ★*Silent Spring* — 363.738
   Herman, Eleanor. *The Royal Art of Poison* — 364.152

Poitier, Sidney
   The Measure of a Man — B

POITIER, SIDNEY
   Goudsouzian, Aram. *Sidney Poitier* — B
   Poitier, Sidney. *The Measure of a Man* — B

POKER
   Hellmuth, Phil. *Play Poker Like the Pros* — 795.41
   Konnikova, Maria. *The Biggest Bluff* — 795.412
   McManus, James. ★*Positively Fifth Street* — 795.41

POKER PLAYERS
   Konnikova, Maria. *The Biggest Bluff* — 795.412
   McManus, James. ★*Positively Fifth Street* — 795.41

POLAND
   Ackerman, Diane. ★*The Zookeeper's Wife* — 940.53
   Allen, Arthur. ★*The Fantastic Laboratory of Dr. Weigl* — 614.5
   Batalion, Judith. *The Light of Days* — 940.53
   Behan, Ren. *The Sweet Polish Kitchen* — 641.594
   Berg, Mary. *The Diary of Mary Berg* — B
   Finkelstein, Daniel. *Two Roads Home* — 920
   Foer, Esther Safran. *I Want You to Know We're Still Here* — B
   Greenfield, Martin. ★*Measure of a Man* — B
   Gross, Jan Tomasz. *Neighbors* — 940.53
   Kaiser, Menachem. *Plunder* — 940.53
   Karski, Jan. *Story of a Secret State* — 940.53
   Kramer, Clara. *Clara's War* — B
   Kurtz, Glenn. *Three Minutes in Poland* — 947.7
   Macadam, Heather Dune. *999* — 940.53
   Marwell, David G. *Mengele* — B
   Mazzeo, Tilar J. *Irena's Children* — B
   Milosz, Czeslaw. ★*Milosz's ABC's* — 891.8
   Moorhouse, Roger. *The Forgers* — 940.53
   Rajchman, Chil. *The Last Jew of Treblinka* — 940.53
   Rees, Laurence. *Auschwitz* — 940.53
   Rhodes, Richard. *Masters of Death* — 940.53
   Sobel, Dava. *A More Perfect Heaven* — 520.9
   Spiegel, Renia. *Renia's Diary* — B
   Spiegelman, Art. ★*Maus* — 741.5
   Stahl, Jerry. *Nein, Nein, Nein!* — B
   Szczeszak-Brewer, Agata. *The Hunger Book* — B
   White, Elizabeth B. ★*The Counterfeit Countess* — 940.53

POLANSKI, ROMAN
   Wasson, Sam. *The Big Goodbye* — 791.43

POLAR BEAR
   Mooallem, Jon. *Wild Ones* — 333.95
   Williams, Kale. *The Loneliest Polar Bear* — 599.786

POLAR BEAR CUBS
   Williams, Kale. *The Loneliest Polar Bear* — 599.786

POLAR EXPEDITIONS
   Sancton, Julian. *Madhouse at the End of the Earth* — 919.8904
   Sides, Hampton. ★*In the Kingdom of Ice* — 910.4
   Wood, Gillen D'Arcy. *Land of Wondrous Cold* — 919.89

POLAR REGIONS
   Levy, Buddy. *Labyrinth of Ice* — 910.91
   Sancton, Julian. *Madhouse at the End of the Earth* — 919.8904
   Turney, Chris. *1912* — 998

POLARIZATION (SOCIAL SCIENCES)
   Alberta, Tim. *American Carnage* — 324.2734
   Alberta, Tim. *The Kingdom, the Power, and the Glory* — 270.8
   Brands, H. W. ★*Founding Partisans* — 973.3
   Caldwell, Christopher. *The Age of Entitlement* — 305.240973
   DiResta, Renee. *Invisible Rulers* — 320
   Finkel, David. *An American Dreamer* — 975.8
   Freeman, Joanne B. *The Field of Blood* — 973.7
   Giridharadas, Anand. ★*The Persuaders* — 320.973
   Hayhoe, Katharine. *Saving Us* — 304.2
   Kershner, Isabel. *The Land of Hope and Fear* — 956.9405
   Klein, Ezra. ★*Why We're Polarized* — 306.0973
   Klein, Naomi. ★*Doppelganger* — 302.2
   Kruse, Kevin Michael. *Fault Lines* — 973.92
   Lasch, Christopher. ★*The Revolt of the Elites* — 306
   Martin, Jonathan. *This Will Not Pass* — 973.933
   Masciotra, David. *Exurbia Now* — 320.973
   McWhirter, Cameron. *American Gun* — 683.4
   Mezrich, Ben. *Breaking Twitter* — 338.7
   Mogelson, Luke. *The Storm Is Here* — 973.933
   Nussbaum, Martha Craven. *The Monarchy of Fear* — 306.20973
   Osnos, Evan. *Wildland* — 973.93
   Owens, Ernest. ★*The Case for Cancel Culture* — 303.3
   Sharlet, Jeff. ★*The Undertow* — 322
   Skach, C. L. *How to Be a Citizen* — 323.6
   Stanley, Jason. *How Fascism Works* — 321.9
   Turchin, Peter. *End Times* — 320.01
   Tyson, Neil deGrasse. *Starry Messenger* — 901
   Waldman, Michael. *The Supermajority* — 347.73
   Walker, Hunter. *The Truce* — 324.2736

Polenberg, Richard
   Hear My Sad Story — 782.42162

Poliafito, Renato
   ★*Dolci!* — 641.81

POLICE
   Belkin, Lisa. *Genealogy of a Murder* — 362.88
   Bilefsky, Dan. *The Last Job* — 364.16

PUBLIC LIBRARY CORE COLLECTION: NONFICTION
Twentieth Edition

Boessenecker, John. *Texas Ranger*	B
Butler, Paul. *Chokehold*	363.2
Dunn, Harry. *Standing My Ground*	B
Dutta, Sunil. *Stealing Green Mangoes*	973
Gross, Neil. *Walk the Walk*	363.2
Henning, Kristin. *The Rage of Innocence*	364.36
Hinton, Elizabeth Kai. ★*America on Fire*	305.800973
Horace, Matthew. *The Black and the Blue*	B
Johnson, Steven. *The Infernal Machine*	335
Kaba, Mariame. *No More Police*	363.2
King, David. *Six Days in August*	364.15
McGough, Matthew. *The Lazarus Files*	364.152
Patterson, James. *Walk the Blue Line*	920
Raymond, Edwin. *An Inconvenient Cop*	363.2
Rushdie, Salman. *Joseph Anton*	B
Schwartz, Joanna C. ★*Shielded*	344.7305
Taibbi, Matt. *I Can't Breathe*	363.2
Thompson, Jamie. *Standoff*	364.152

POLICE AND AFRICAN AMERICANS
Hinton, Elizabeth Kai. ★*America on Fire*	305.800973
Moore, Wes. ★*Five Days*	363.32
Rubinstein, Julian. ★*The Holly*	364.106

POLICE BRUTALITY
Alexander, Kwame. *Light for the World to See*	811.6
Bailey, Issac J. *Why Didn't We Riot?*	305.800973
Barron, Justine. *They Killed Freddie Gray*	363.32
Bell, Darrin. ★*The Talk*	741.5
Butler, Paul. *Chokehold*	363.2
Carruthers, Charlene A. *Unapologetic*	305.48
Chemerinsky, Erwin. *Presumed Guilty*	344.7305
Cross, Tiffany D. ★*Say It Louder!*	324.6
Crump, Benjamin. *Open Season*	364
Dyson, Michael Eric. *Tears We Cannot Stop*	305.800973
Evangelista, Patricia. ★*Some People Need Killing*	364.4
Gergel, Richard. *Unexampled Courage*	323.1196
Hinton, Elizabeth Kai. ★*America on Fire*	305.800973
Horace, Matthew. *The Black and the Blue*	B
Jordan, June. ★*The Essential June Jordan*	811
Kaba, Mariame. *No More Police*	363.2
Kix, Paul. ★*You Have to Be Prepared to Die Before You Can Begin to Live*	976.1
Moore, Wes. ★*Five Days*	363.32
Purnell, Derecka. *Becoming Abolitionists*	363.20973
Samuels, Robert. ★*His Name Is George Floyd*	B
Smith, Zadie. *Intimations*	824
Taibbi, Matt. *I Can't Breathe*	363.2
Thompson, Heather Ann. *Blood in the Water*	365
Thompson, Jamie. *Standoff*	364.152

POLICE CHARGES
Karl, Jonathan. *Tired of Winning*	973.933
Miller, T. Christian. *A False Report*	364.15

POLICE CHIEFS
Krist, Gary. *Empire of Sin*	976.3

POLICE CORRUPTION
Bowden, Mark. *The Case of the Vanishing Blonde*	364.10973
Carlo, Philip. *Gaspipe*	B
Cooper, Sean Patrick. *The Shooter at Midnight*	363.25
Fenton, Justin. *We Own This City*	364.1
Greenberg, Andy. *Tracers in the Dark*	364.16
McGough, Matthew. *The Lazarus Files*	364.152
Raymond, Edwin. *An Inconvenient Cop*	363.2
Thompson, Heather Ann. *Blood in the Water*	365

POLICE COVER-UPS
Assael, Shaun. *The Murder of Sonny Liston*	B
Barron, Justine. *They Killed Freddie Gray*	363.32
Hale, Grace Elizabeth. *In the Pines*	364.13
O'Neill, Tom. ★*Chaos*	364.152

POLICE ETHICS
Kaba, Mariame. *No More Police*	363.2

POLICE MISCONDUCT
Butler, Paul. *Chokehold*	363.2
Carlo, Philip. *Gaspipe*	B
Chemerinsky, Erwin. *Presumed Guilty*	344.7305
Fenton, Justin. *We Own This City*	364.1
King, Gilbert. *Beneath a Ruthless Sun*	B
Moore, Wes. ★*Five Days*	363.32
O'Neill, Tom. ★*Chaos*	364.152
Raymond, Edwin. *An Inconvenient Cop*	363.2

Schwartz, Joanna C. ★*Shielded*	344.7305
Smith, Mychal Denzel. *Stakes Is High*	973.933
Thompson, Heather Ann. *Blood in the Water*	365

POLICE MURDERS
Thompson, Jamie. *Standoff*	364.152

POLICE QUESTIONING
Trainum, James L. *How the Police Generate False Confessions*	345.73

POLICE SURVEILLANCE
Johnson, Steven. *The Infernal Machine*	335

POLICY SCIENCES
Baer, Daniel Brooks. *The Four Tests*	320.973
Tyson, Neil deGrasse. *Accessory to War*	355.001
★*Polio*. Oshinsky, David M.	614.5

POLIOMYELITIS
Oshinsky, David M. ★*Polio*	614.5

POLISH PEOPLE
Ackerman, Diane. ★*The Zookeeper's Wife*	940.53
Batalion, Judith. *The Light of Days*	940.53
Berg, Mary. *The Diary of Mary Berg*	B
Chiger, Krystyna. *The Girl in the Green Sweater*	B
Finkelstein, Daniel. *Two Roads Home*	920
Frankel, Rebecca. *Into the Forest*	940.53
Gross, Jan Tomasz. *Neighbors*	940.53
Kramer, Clara. *Clara's War*	B
Kurtz, Glenn. *Three Minutes in Poland*	947.7
Mazzeo, Tilar J. *Irena's Children*	B
Pivnik, Sam. *Survivor*	940.5318
Rosenberg, Justus. *The Art of Resistance*	B
Spiegel, Renia. *Renia's Diary*	B
Szczeszak-Brewer, Agata. *The Hunger Book*	B
White, Elizabeth B. ★*The Counterfeit Countess*	940.53

Politi, Marco
Pope Francis Among the Wolves	282.092

POLITICAL ACTION COMMITTEES
Spencer, Kyle. *Raising Them Right*	320.5

POLITICAL ACTIVISTS
Ai, Weiwei. *Zodiac*	741.5
Ali, Wajahat. *Go Back to Where You Came From*	B
Anderson, Carol. ★*One Person, No Vote*	324.6
Avrich, Paul. *Sasha and Emma*	920
Barkan, Ady. *Eyes to the Wind*	B
Barlow, John Perry. *Mother American Night*	782.42164
Becker, Jo. ★*Forcing the Spring*	346.79401
Carter, Stephen L. *Invisible*	B
Duberman, Martin B. *Howard Zinn*	B
Forche, Carolyn. *What You Have Heard Is True*	B
Ghafari, Zarifa. *Zarifa*	B
Gregory, Dick. ★*The Essential Dick Gregory*	818
Hitchens, Christopher. *Hitch-22*	920
Hochschild, Adam. *Lessons from a Dark Time*	909.82
Holley, Santi Elijah. *An Amerikan Family*	920
Izgil, Tahir Hamut. *Waiting to Be Arrested at Night*	B
Jackson, Jenn M. ★*Black Women Taught Us*	305.48
Joseph, Peniel E. *The Sword and the Shield*	B
Kimberley, Hannah. *A Woman's Place Is at the Top*	B
Mahtani, Shibani. *Among the Braves*	951.25
Payne, Les. ★*The Dead Are Arising*	B
Prose, Francine. *1974*	B
Roberts, Randy. *Blood Brothers*	920
Robeson, Paul. *The Undiscovered Paul Robeson*	B
Rosenzweig, Laura B. *Hollywood's Spies*	791.43
Sen, Amartya. *Home in the World*	B
Shehadeh, Raja. ★*We Could Have Been Friends, My Father and I*	B
Shehadeh, Raja. *Where the Line Is Drawn*	956.9405
Sontag, Susan. *At the Same Time*	814
Thomas, Etan. *We Matter*	796.08
Union, Gabrielle. *You Got Anything Stronger?*	B
Van Zandt, Steve. *Unrequited Infatuations*	B
Vargas, Jose Antonio. *Dear America*	B
Wainaina, Binyavanga. ★*How to Write About Africa*	814
Weigel, Alicia Roth. *Inverse Cowgirl*	B
West, Cornel. *Black Prophetic Fire*	B
Yoshino, Kenji. *Speak Now*	346.79401
Yousafzai, Ziauddin. *Let Her Fly*	B

POLITICAL ATROCITIES
Medvedev, Roy Aleksandrovich. *Let History Judge*	947.084

POLITICAL CAMPAIGNS
Allen, Jonathan. *Lucky*	324.973

AUTHOR, TITLE, SERIES AND SUBJECT INDEX

Allen, Jonathan. *Shattered*	324.973
Balz, Daniel J. *The Battle for America, 2008*	973.932
Bender, Michael C. *"Frankly, We Did Win This Election"*	973.933
Biden Owens, Valerie. *Growing up Biden*	B
Brazile, Donna. *For Colored Girls Who Have Considered Politics*	328.73
Carpenter, Amanda B. *Gaslighting America*	973.933
Chozick, Amy. *Chasing Hillary*	B
Clinton, Hillary Rodham. *What Happened*	328.73
Collins, Gail. *William Henry Harrison*	B
Denevi, Timothy. *Freak Kingdom*	B
Graff, Garrett M. *Watergate*	973.924
Karl, Jonathan. *Tired of Winning*	973.933
Lewis, John. ★*Run; Book One*	741.5
Martini, Adrienne. *Somebody's Gotta Do It*	B
Oliphant, Thomas. ★*The Road to Camelot*	973.922092
Plouffe, David. *A Citizen's Guide to Beating Donald Trump*	324.0973
Schieffer, Bob. *Overload*	070.4
Weissmann, Andrew. ★*Where Law Ends*	324.7
Wilson, Rick. *Running Against the Devil*	973.933

POLITICAL CONSULTANTS

Albright, Madeleine Korbel. *Hell and Other Destinations*	B
Arnsdorf, Isaac. ★*Finish What We Started*	320.52
Biden Owens, Valerie. *Growing up Biden*	B
Brown, Robert J. *You Can't Go Wrong Doing Right*	B
Conason, Joe. *The Longest Con*	320.52
Elwood, Phil. *All the Worst Humans*	659.2
Ganz, John. *When the Clock Broke*	320.52
Goodwin, Doris Kearns. ★*Team of Rivals*	B
Guerrero, Jean. *Hatemonger*	B
Jarrett, Valerie. *Finding My Voice*	B
Kroll, Andy. *A Death on W Street*	364.152
Rothkopf, David J. *American Resistance*	973.933
Sorensen, Theodore C. *Counselor*	B
Stevens, Stuart. *The Conspiracy to End America*	324.2734
Zygar, Mikhail. *All the Kremlin's Men*	947.086

POLITICAL CORRECTNESS (CONCEPT)

Gold, Judy. *Yes I Can Say That*	792.7

POLITICAL CORRUPTION

Abrams, Dan. *Theodore Roosevelt for the Defense*	345.73
Berman, Geoffrey. *Holding the Line*	345.73
Bernstein, Carl. ★*All the President's Men*	364.1
Bowden, Mark. *The Steal*	973.933
Bryant, Howard. *Full Dissidence*	306.20973
Bullough, Oliver. *Moneyland*	364.1
Caro, Robert A. *The Power Broker*	B
Caruana Galizia, Paul. ★*A Death in Malta*	364.15
Chandrasekaran, Rajiv. *Imperial Life in the Emerald City*	956.7044
Coll, Steve. ★*The Achilles Trap*	956.7044
Collins, Max Allan. *Eliot Ness and the Mad Butcher*	364.152
Cooper, Helene. *Madame President*	966.62
Cooper, Sean Patrick. *The Shooter at Midnight*	363.25
Cullen, Kevin. *Whitey Bulger*	B
Dean, John W. *The Nixon Defense*	973.924092
Dobbs, Michael. *King Richard*	973.924
Enrich, David. *Servants of the Damned*	340.023
Feldstein, Mark Avrom. *Poisoning the Press*	973.924092
Foner, Eric. ★*Reconstruction*	973.8
Gidla, Sujatha. *Ants Among Elephants*	305.5
Graff, Garrett M. *Watergate*	973.924
Harding, Luke. *Collusion*	324.70973
Hasen, Richard L. *Election Meltdown*	324.973
Higginbotham, Adam. ★*Midnight in Chernobyl*	363.17
Hill, David. *The Vapors*	976.7
Isikoff, Michael. *Russian Roulette*	973.933
Johnston, David Cay. *The Big Cheat*	973.933
Kelly, John. *The Graves Are Walking*	941.5081
Khodorkovsky, Mikhail. *The Russia Conundrum*	947.086
Krist, Gary. *Empire of Sin*	976.3
Leamer, Laurence. *The Price of Justice*	346.7302
LeDuff, Charlie. *Detroit*	977.4
Leonnig, Carol. *I Alone Can Fix It*	973.933
Maddow, Rachel. *Bag Man*	B
Maddow, Rachel. ★*Prequel*	320.53
McSwane, J. David. ★*Pandemic, Inc.*	362.1962
Millard, Candice. *Destiny of the Republic*	973.8
Mueller, Tom. *Crisis of Conscience*	364.16
Nance, Malcolm W. *The Plot to Betray America*	973.933
Penn, Thomas. *The Brothers York*	942.04
Petri, Alexandra. *Nothing Is Wrong and Here Is Why*	973.933
Politkovskaya, Anna. *A Russian Diary*	947.086
Preston, Paul. *A People Betrayed*	946
Rawlence, Ben. *City of Thorns*	967.7305
Ressa, Maria. ★*How to Stand up to a Dictator*	070.92
Risen, James. ★*The Last Honest Man*	973.92
Rothkopf, David J. *American Resistance*	973.933
Schmidt, Michael S. ★*Donald Trump v. The United States*	973.933
Shimer, David. *Rigged*	324.60973
Stengel, Richard. *Information Wars*	355.3
Stevens, Stuart. *The Conspiracy to End America*	324.2734
Strathern, Paul. *The Borgias*	945.06
Taylor, Alan. *American Civil Wars*	973.7
Thant Myint-U. *The Hidden History of Burma*	959.105
Toobin, Jeffrey. *True Crimes and Misdemeanors*	973.933
van der Linden, Sander. ★*Foolproof*	302.3
Weintraub, Stanley. *Iron Tears*	973.3
Weissmann, Andrew. ★*Where Law Ends*	324.7
Woodward, Bob. *The Final Days*	B
Woodward, Bob. *Peril*	973.933
Yaffa, Joshua. *Between Two Fires*	920

POLITICAL CRIMES AND OFFENSES

Meltzer, Brad. *The Lincoln Conspiracy*	973.7092

POLITICAL CULTURE

Alberta, Tim. *American Carnage*	324.2734
Alberta, Tim. *The Kingdom, the Power, and the Glory*	270.8
Applebaum, Anne. *Iron Curtain*	947
Appleman, Deborah. *Literature and the New Culture Wars*	807
Appy, Christian G. *American Reckoning*	959.704
Blanco, Richard. *How to Love a Country*	811
Boykin, Keith. *Race Against Time*	305.8
Brands, H. W. ★*Andrew Jackson, His Life and Times*	B
Brands, H. W. ★*Founding Partisans*	973.3
Brands, H. W. *Traitor to His Class*	B
Branigan, Tania. *Red Memory*	951.05
Brill, Steven. *Tailspin*	306.0973
Bryant, Howard. *Full Dissidence*	306.20973
Caldwell, Christopher. *The Age of Entitlement*	305.240973
Chang, Jung. *Big Sister, Little Sister, Red Sister*	B
Cheney, Liz. *Oath and Honor*	328.73
Conradi, Peter J. *Who Lost Russia?*	947.086
Cottom, Tressie McMillan. *Thick*	301
Damrosch, Leopold. *The Club*	920
DiResta, Renee. *Invisible Rulers*	320
Dorey-Stein, Beck. *From the Corner of the Oval*	B
Dyson, Michael Eric. *The Black Presidency*	305.800973
Ellis, Joseph J. *American Creation*	973.3
Ellis, Joseph J. ★*American Dialogue*	973.3
Everitt, Anthony. *The Rise of Rome*	937
Feldstein, Mark Avrom. *Poisoning the Press*	973.924092
Figes, Orlando. ★*The Story of Russia*	947
Finkel, David. *An American Dreamer*	975.8
Fitzpatrick, Cara. *The Death of Public School*	379.73
Foer, Franklin. ★*The Last Politician*	973.934
Frank, Barney. *Frank*	B
Frank, Thomas. *The People, No*	320.56
Frum, David. *Trumpocracy*	973.933
Garrels, Anne. *Putin Country*	947
Gay, Roxane. ★*Opinions*	814
Gessen, Masha. *Surviving Autocracy*	973.933
Giridharadas, Anand. ★*The Persuaders*	320.973
Goodman, Micah. *Catch-67*	956.04
Goodwin, Doris Kearns. ★*Leadership in Turbulent Times*	973.09
Griffin, Farah Jasmine. ★*In Search of a Beautiful Freedom*	814
Harding, Luke. *Collusion*	324.70973
Herrera, Juan Felipe. *Every Day We Get More Illegal*	811
Hoffman, Carl. *Liar's Circus*	973.933
Hustvedt, Siri. *Mothers, Fathers, and Others*	814
Johnston, David Cay. *It's Even Worse Than You Think*	973.933
Katznelson, Ira. *Fear Itself*	973.917
Kelly, John. *The Graves Are Walking*	941.5081
Kershner, Isabel. *The Land of Hope and Fear*	956.9405
Khakpour, Porochista. *Brown Album*	304.8
Klein, Ezra. ★*Why We're Polarized*	306.0973
Kruse, Kevin Michael. *Fault Lines*	973.92
Kurtz, Howard. *Media Madness*	973.933
Lankov, A. N. *The Real North Korea*	951.9304
LaRue, James. ★*On Censorship*	025.2

PUBLIC LIBRARY CORE COLLECTION: NONFICTION
Twentieth Edition

Lepore, Jill. ★*The Deadline*	814
Lowery, Wesley. ★*American Whitelash*	305.8
Lynskey, Dorian. *The Ministry of Truth*	823
Manson, Mark. *Everything Is F*cked*	152.4
Masciotra, David. *Exurbia Now*	320.973
Mayer, Jane. ★*Dark Money*	973.932
Meacham, Jon. ★*American Lion*	B
Mogelson, Luke. *The Storm Is Here*	973.933
Moore, Lorrie. *See What Can Be Done*	801
Newitz, Annalee. *Stories Are Weapons*	355.3
Olson, Lynne. *Those Angry Days*	940.53
Osnos, Evan. *Wildland*	973.93
Owens, Ernest. ★*The Case for Cancel Culture*	303.3
Phillips, Adrian. *Fighting Churchill, Appeasing Hitler*	327.41043
Purdum, Todd S. *An Idea Whose Time Has Come*	342.7308
Rashid, Jonny. *Jesus Takes a Side*	261.7
Rhodes, Benjamin J. *The World as It Is*	973.932
Richardson, Heather Cox. ★*How the South Won the Civil War*	306.20973
Rohde, David. *In Deep*	973.933
Rovelli, Carlo. *There Are Places in the World Where Rules Are Less Important Than Kindness*	500
Scenters-Zapico, Natalie. *Lima*	811
Sharfstein, Daniel J. ★*Thunder in the Mountains*	979.5
Sharlet, Jeff. ★*The Undertow*	322
Shimer, David. *Rigged*	324.60973
Smith, Patti. ★*Year of the Monkey*	B
Smith, Zadie. ★*Feel Free*	824
Snyder, Christina. *Great Crossings*	976.9
Solnit, Rebecca. *Call Them by Their True Names*	303.3
Stevens, Stuart. *It Was All a Lie*	324.2734
Tamblyn, Amber. ★*Era of Ignition*	B
Tocqueville, Alexis de. ★*Democracy in America*	320.973
Toobin, Jeffrey. ★*Homegrown*	363.325
Ullrich, Volker. *Germany 1923*	943.085
Walker, Shaun. *The Long Hangover*	947.086
Waterhouse, Benjamin C. *One Day I'll Work for Myself*	338
Whipple, Chris. *The Gatekeepers*	973.92092
Williams, Terry Tempest. *Erosion*	814
Wolff, Michael. *Fire and Fury*	973.933
Woodward, Bob. *Fear*	973.933
Woodward, Bob. *Peril*	973.933
Yaffa, Joshua. *Between Two Fires*	920
Yang, Jisheng. *The World Turned Upside Down*	951.05
Zakaria, Fareed. *Age of Revolutions*	303.6
Zelizer, Julian E. *Burning Down the House*	328.73

POLITICAL ETHICS

Blair, Tony. *A Journey*	B
Boucheron, Patrick. *Machiavelli*	320.1092
Brands, H. W. *Woodrow Wilson*	B
Gabler, Neal. *Catching the Wind*	B
Kaplan, Robert D. *Warrior Politics*	320
Machiavelli, Niccolo. ★*The Prince*	320.1
Rousseau, Jean-Jacques. ★*The Social Contract*	320.1
Wood, David Bowne. ★*What Have We Done*	616.85

POLITICAL FORECASTING

Marshall, Tim. *The Power of Geography*	320.1

POLITICAL INSTITUTIONS

Tocqueville, Alexis de. ★*Democracy in America*	320.973

POLITICAL INTRIGUE

Barr, James. *Lords of the Desert*	956
Greenberg, Amy S. *Lady First*	B
Gristwood, Sarah. *The Tudors in Love*	941.05
Hindley, Meredith. *Destination Casablanca*	940.54
Jager, Eric. *Blood Royal*	944.026
Maier, Thomas. *Mafia Spies*	364.1060973
McConahay, Mary Jo. *The Tango War*	940.53
McMeekin, Sean. *July 1914*	940.3
Miles, Jonathan. *St. Petersburg*	947
Morley, Jefferson. *Scorpions' Dance*	973.924
Norwich, John Julius. *A History of France*	944
Sallah, Michael. *The Yankee Comandante*	972.91
Southon, Emma. *Agrippina*	B
Waller, Douglas C. *Lincoln's Spies*	973.7
Wolff, Michael. *Fire and Fury*	973.933
Wolff, Michael. *Landslide*	973.933
Woodward, Bob. *Fear*	973.933
Woodward, Bob. *Peril*	973.933

POLITICAL JOURNALISM

Balz, Daniel J. *The Battle for America, 2008*	973.932
Baron, Martin. ★*Collision of Power*	070.4
Denevi, Timothy. *Freak Kingdom*	B
Freeman, Joanne B. *The Field of Blood*	973.7
Schieffer, Bob. *Overload*	070.4
Thompson, Hunter S. ★*Fear and Loathing in America*	B

POLITICAL JOURNALISTS

Hitchens, Christopher. *Hitch-22*	920
Karl, Jonathan. *Front Row at the Trump Show*	973.933

POLITICAL LEADERSHIP

Abrams, Stacey. *Lead from the Outside*	B
Alter, Jonathan. *His Very Best*	B
Ambinder, Marc. *The Brink*	355.5
Avlon, John P. *Washington's Farewell*	973.4
Baer, Daniel Brooks. *The Four Tests*	320.973
Baime, A. J. *The Accidental President*	B
Baker, Peter. *The Divider*	973.933
Beschloss, Michael R. ★*Presidents of War*	355.00973
Blumenthal, Sidney. *A Self-Made Man*	B
Brands, H. W. ★*Andrew Jackson, His Life and Times*	B
Brands, H. W. *The First American*	B
Brands, H. W. *Traitor to His Class*	B
Brands, H. W. *Woodrow Wilson*	B
Brazile, Donna. *For Colored Girls Who Have Considered Politics*	328.73
Brewster, Todd. *Lincoln's Gamble*	973.7
Burlingame, Michael. *Abraham Lincoln*	B
Carter, Jimmy. *White House Diary*	973.926
Chait, Jonathan. *Audacity*	973.932
Chernow, Ron. *Washington*	B
Clarke, Thurston. *JFK's Last Hundred Days*	B
Coe, Alexis. ★*You Never Forget Your First*	B
Cummings, Elijah. ★*We're Better Than This*	B
Dallek, Robert. ★*Franklin D. Roosevelt*	B
Dikotter, Frank. *The Cultural Revolution*	951.056
Duiker, William J. *Ho Chi Minh*	B
Egan, Timothy. ★*The Big Burn*	973.911
Eizenstat, Stuart. ★*President Carter*	B
Emanuel, Rahm. *The Nation City*	352.23
Feldman, Noah. *The Three Lives of James Madison*	B
Ferguson, Niall. *Doom*	362.1962
Frank, Jeffrey. *The Trials of Harry S. Truman*	973.918
Gevisser, Mark. *A Legacy of Liberation*	B
Goodwin, Doris Kearns. ★*Leadership in Turbulent Times*	973.09
Goodwin, Doris Kearns. ★*Team of Rivals*	B
Groom, Winston. *The Allies*	940.5309
Hennessey, Susan. *Unmaking the Presidency*	973.933
Hitchens, Christopher. *Thomas Jefferson*	B
Kasparov, Gary. *Winter Is Coming*	947.086
Khlevniuk, Oleg V. *Stalin*	B
Kinzer, Stephen. ★*All the Shah's Men*	955.05
Kissinger, Henry. *Leadership*	303.3
Kurtz-Phelan, Daniel. *The China Mission*	951.04
Leonnig, Carol. *I Alone Can Fix It*	973.933
Lozada, Carlos. *The Washington Book*	320
Malala, Justice. *The Plot to Save South Africa*	968.07
Mann, Jim. *The Rebellion of Ronald Reagan*	973.927092
Marton, Kati. ★*The Chancellor*	B
Mazower, Mark. *Hitler's Empire*	940.53
McPherson, James M. ★*Abraham Lincoln*	B
McPherson, James M. ★*Tried by War*	973.7
Meacham, Jon. ★*American Lion*	B
Meacham, Jon. *Franklin and Winston*	940.53
Moore, Charles. *Margaret Thatcher*	941.085
Morris, Marc. *A Great and Terrible King*	B
Morris, Marc. *King John*	942.033
Myers, Steven Lee. *The New Tsar*	B
Newton, Michael A. *Enemy of the State*	345.567
O'Toole, Patricia. *The Moralist*	B
Pak, Jung H. *Becoming Kim Jong Un*	B
Pakula, Hannah. *The Last Empress*	B
Pantsov, Alexander. *Mao*	B
Raphael, Ray. *Mr. President*	352.230973
Rappleye, Charles. *Herbert Hoover in the White House*	B
Rees, Laurence. *Hitler and Stalin*	940.53
Reynolds, David S. ★*Abe*	B
Ricks, Thomas E. *Churchill and Orwell*	920
Roberts, Andrew. ★*Napoleon*	B

AUTHOR, TITLE, SERIES AND SUBJECT INDEX

Roll, David L. *George Marshall*	B
Ryback, Timothy W. *Hitler's Private Library*	027
Shesol, Jeff. *Supreme Power*	347.73
Short, Philip. *Putin*	B
Smith, Richard Norton. *An Ordinary Man*	B
Souza, Pete. *Shade*	973.932
Stephanopoulos, George. ★*The Situation Room*	973.09
Stewart, David O. *George Washington*	973.4
Thomas, Evan. *Being Nixon*	B
Traub, James. *John Quincy Adams*	B
Von Tunzelmann, Alex. *Blood and Sand*	909.82
Whipple, Chris. *The Fight of His Life*	973.934
White, Ronald C. *A. Lincoln*	B
Wills, Garry. *James Madison*	B
Wills, Garry. *Lincoln at Gettysburg*	973.7
Winik, Jay. *1944*	940.53
Wolff, Michael. *Fire and Fury*	973.933
Wolff, Michael. *Landslide*	973.933
Wong, Chun Han. *Party of One*	951.06
Woodward, Bob. *Fear*	973.933
Woodward, Bob. *Peril*	973.933
Yaffa, Joshua. *Between Two Fires*	920
Zelensky, Volodymyr. *A Message from Ukraine*	947.7
Zelizer, Julian E. *Burning Down the House*	328.73

POLITICAL OBLIGATION

Johnson, Theodore R. *When the Stars Begin to Fall*	305.800973
Litt, David. *Democracy in One Book or Less*	321.8
Sunstein, Cass R. *Impeachment*	342.73

POLITICAL ORATORY

Blight, David W. ★*Frederick Douglass*	B
Blumenthal, Sidney. ★*All the Powers of Earth*	B
Blumenthal, Sidney. *Wrestling with His Angel*	B
Cohen, Andrew. *Two Days in June*	973.922
Political Order and Political Decay. Fukuyama, Francis	320.1

POLITICAL PARTICIPATION

Abrams, Stacey. *Lead from the Outside*	B
Abrams, Stacey. *Our Time Is Now*	324.60973
Ahmed, Sara. *The Feminist Killjoy Handbook*	305.42
Bailey, Issac J. *Why Didn't We Riot?*	305.800973
Barkan, Ady. *Eyes to the Wind*	B
Boykin, Keith. *Race Against Time*	305.8
Brazile, Donna. *For Colored Girls Who Have Considered Politics*	328.73
Cadava, Geraldo L. *The Hispanic Republican*	324.2734089
Carruthers, Charlene A. *Unapologetic*	305.48
Chee, Alexander. ★*How to Write an Autobiographical Novel*	B
Collins-Dexter, Brandi. *Black Skinhead*	324.2734
D'Antonio, Michael. *The Hunting of Hillary*	B
Derf. *Kent State*	741.5
Foner, Eric. ★*Reconstruction*	973.8
Garza, Alicia. *The Purpose of Power*	303.48
Gates, Henry Louis. ★*The Black Church*	277
Gillette, Michael L. *Lady Bird Johnson*	B
Giridharadas, Anand. ★*The Persuaders*	320.973
Gordon-Reed, Annette. ★*Most Blessed of the Patriarchs*	973.4
Gray, Emma. *A Girl's Guide to Joining the Resistance*	303.48
Greenidge, Kerri. *Black Radical*	B
Griffith, R. Marie. *Moral Combat*	261.8
Guha, Ramachandra. *Rebels Against the Raj*	954.03
Gunst, Kathy. *Rage Baking*	641.86
Hahn, Steven. *A Nation Under Our Feet*	975
Hill, Katie. *She Will Rise*	305.42
Joseph, Peniel E. *Waiting 'Til the Midnight Hour*	323.1196
Klein, Ezra. ★*Why We're Polarized*	306.0973
Leonard, Christopher. *Kochland*	338.7
Litt, David. *Democracy in One Book or Less*	321.8
Marton, Kati. *Hidden Power*	B
Masur, Kate. *Until Justice Be Done*	323.1196
Meyaard-Schaap, Kyle. *Following Jesus in a Warming World*	241
Mullen, Bill. ★*James Baldwin*	B
Palmieri, Jennifer. *She Proclaims*	305.42
Perkins, Kendrick. *The Education of Kendrick Perkins*	B
Plouffe, David. *A Citizen's Guide to Beating Donald Trump*	324.0973
Quigley, Fran. *Prescription for the People*	338.4
Roberts, Cokie. *Capital Dames*	920
Roberts, Cokie. *Founding Mothers*	920
Roberts, Cokie. *Ladies of Liberty*	920
Rosenfeld, Seth. *Subversives*	378.1
Rosenzweig, Laura B. *Hollywood's Spies*	791.43

Sage, Sami. *Democracy in Retrograde*	324
Searcey, Dionne. *In Pursuit of Disobedient Women*	B
Sellers, Bakari. *My Vanishing Country*	B
Spencer, Kyle. *Raising Them Right*	320.5
Steinhauer, Jennifer. *The Firsts*	320.082
Sweig, Julia. *Lady Bird Johnson*	B
Tamimi, Ahed. ★*They Called Me a Lioness*	B
Thomas, Etan. *We Matter*	796.08
Tolokonnikova, Nadezhda. *Rules for Rulebreakers*	782.42166
Traister, Rebecca. *Good and Mad*	305.420973
Turk, Katherine. *The Women of Now*	305.42
Volf, Miroslav. *Public Faith in Action*	261.7
Worley, Jennifer. *Neon Girls*	792.7

POLITICAL PARTIES

Avlon, John P. *Washington's Farewell*	973.4
Bade, Rachael. ★*Unchecked*	342.73
Balz, Daniel J. *The Battle for America, 2008*	973.932
Bowden, Mark. *The Steal*	973.933
Brands, H. W. ★*Founding Partisans*	973.3
Cercas, Javier. *Lord of All the Dead*	868
Conason, Joe. *The Longest Con*	320.52
Horn, Jonathan. *Washington's End*	B
Kaplan, David A. *The Most Dangerous Branch*	347.73
Karl, Jonathan. *Tired of Winning*	973.933
Kazin, Michael. *What It Took to Win*	324.2736
Klein, Ezra. ★*Why We're Polarized*	306.0973
Kornacki, Steve. *The Red and the Blue*	306.20973
Kruse, Kevin Michael. *Fault Lines*	973.92
Nussbaum, Martha Craven. *The Monarchy of Fear*	306.20973
Stevens, Stuart. *The Conspiracy to End America*	324.2734
Stevens, Stuart. *It Was All a Lie*	324.2734
Tocqueville, Alexis de. ★*Democracy in America*	320.973
Walker, Hunter. *The Truce*	324.2736
Wilson, Rick. *Running Against the Devil*	973.933
Wong, Chun Han. *Party of One*	951.06
Wood, Gordon S. *Friends Divided*	920

POLITICAL PERSECUTION

Amis, Martin. *Koba the Dread*	947.084
Applebaum, Anne. *Iron Curtain*	947
Bird, Kai. *American Prometheus*	B
Branigan, Tania. *Red Memory*	951.05
Demick, Barbara. *Eat the Buddha*	951
Gessen, Masha. *The Future Is History*	947.086
Gessen, Masha. *Never Remember*	365
Hochschild, Adam. *Lessons from a Dark Time*	909.82
Hoja, Gulchehra. *A Stone Is Most Precious Where It Belongs*	
Hulls, Tessa. ★*Feeding Ghosts*	741.5
Ishikawa, Masaji. ★*A River in Darkness*	B
Kavanagh, Julie. *The Irish Assassins*	941.5
Kraus, Dita. *A Delayed Life*	B
Kristof, Nicholas D. *Half the Sky*	362.83
Liao, Yiwu. *Bullets and Opium*	951.05
Molnar, Petra. *The Walls Have Eyes*	363.28
Nafisi, Azar. *Read Dangerously*	809
Navai, Ramita. *City of Lies*	955
Pitzer, Andrea. *The Secret History of Vladimir Nabokov*	813
Rees, Laurence. *The Holocaust*	940.53
Stanley, Matthew. *Einstein's War*	530
Stone, Geoffrey R. *Perilous Times*	323.44
Yaffa, Joshua. *Between Two Fires*	920
Ypi, Lea. ★*Free*	B

POLITICAL PLANNING

Brazile, Donna. *For Colored Girls Who Have Considered Politics*	328.73

POLITICAL PRISONERS

Brand, Christo. *Mandela*	B
Campbell, Deborah. *A Disappearance in Damascus*	365
Cheng, Nien. *Life and Death in Shanghai*	B
Gessen, Masha. *Never Remember*	365
Guha, Ramachandra. *Rebels Against the Raj*	954.03
Liao, Yiwu. *Bullets and Opium*	951.05
Mandela, Nelson. *In His Own Words*	B
Matar, Hisham. *The Return*	B
Mazzeo, Tilar J. *Sisters in Resistance*	945.091
Nasaw, David. *The Last Million*	940.53
Nemat, Marina. *Prisoner of Tehran*	B
Pang, Amelia. ★*Made in China*	331.11
Rezaian, Jason. *Prisoner*	B
Sallah, Michael. *The Yankee Comandante*	972.91

PUBLIC LIBRARY CORE COLLECTION: NONFICTION
Twentieth Edition

Smith, David James. *Young Mandela*	B
Solzhenitsyn, Aleksandr Isaevich. ★*The Gulag Archipelago 1918-1956*	365
Solzhenitsyn, Aleksandr Isaevich. ★*The Gulag Archipelago, 1918-1956*	365
Steinberg, Jonny. *Winnie and Nelson*	920
Van De Perre, Selma. *My Name Is Selma*	940.53
Weir, Alison. *The Lady in the Tower*	B

POLITICAL PSYCHOLOGY
Newitz, Annalee. *Stories Are Weapons*	355.3

POLITICAL PURGES
Slezkine, Yuri. *The House of Government*	947.084

POLITICAL QUESTIONS AND JUDICIAL POWER
Biskupic, Joan. ★*Nine Black Robes*	347.73
Brettschneider, Corey Lang. *The Oath and the Office*	342.73
Breyer, Stephen G. ★*The Authority of the Court and the Peril of Politics*	347.73
Breyer, Stephen G. *Making Our Democracy Work*	347.73
Cohen, Adam. ★*Supreme Inequality*	347.73
Coyle, Marcia. *The Roberts Court*	347.73
Graetz, Michael J. *The Burger Court and the Rise of the Judicial Right*	347.73
O'Brien, David M. ★*Storm Center*	347.73
Robin, Corey. *The Enigma of Clarence Thomas*	347.73
Shesol, Jeff. *Supreme Power*	347.73
Simon, James F. *FDR and Chief Justice Hughes*	973.917092
Simon, James F. *What Kind of Nation*	342.73
Toobin, Jeffrey. *The Nine*	347.73

POLITICAL REFORM
Blair, Tony. *A Journey*	B

POLITICAL REFUGEES
Haitiwaji, Gulbahar. *How I Survived a Chinese "Reeducation" Camp*	305.8
Jang, Jin-Sung. *Dear Leader*	B
Jang, Lucia. *Stars Between the Sun and Moon*	365.45092
Longo, Matthew. *The Picnic*	947.084
Nasaw, David. *The Last Million*	940.53
Oliva, Alejandra. *Rivermouth*	305.9
Olson, Lynne. *Last Hope Island*	940.53
Rappaport, Helen. *After the Romanovs*	944
Zia, Helen. *Last Boat Out of Shanghai*	951.04

POLITICAL RIGHTS
Chemerinsky, Erwin. *Closing the Courthouse Door*	347.73
DuBois, Ellen Carol. *Suffrage*	324.6
Murphy, Chris. ★*The Violence Inside Us*	303.60973
Watson, Bruce. *Freedom Summer*	323.1196
Political Risk. Rice, Condoleezza	658.15

POLITICAL SCIENCE
Abrams, Stacey. *Our Time Is Now*	324.60973
Allitt, Patrick. *The Conservatives*	320.520973
Aristotle. ★*Politics*	320
Aristotle. ★*Politics, 2nd Ed*	320
Balz, Daniel J. *The Battle for America, 2008*	973.932
Berry, Wendell. *The Art of Loading Brush*	338.10973
Blattman, Christopher. *Why We Fight*	303.6
Blumenthal, Sidney. *Wrestling with His Angel*	B
Boucheron, Patrick. *Machiavelli*	320.1092
Brands, H. W. *Traitor to His Class*	B
Brazile, Donna. *For Colored Girls Who Have Considered Politics*	328.73
Brown, Archie. ★*The Rise and Fall of Communism*	320.53
Buttigieg, Pete. *Shortest Way Home*	B
Christie, Chris. *Let Me Finish*	B
Cicero, Marcus Tullius. ★*The Republic*	320.1
Collins-Dexter, Brandi. *Black Skinhead*	324.2734
Cross, Tiffany D. ★*Say It Louder!*	324.6
Dalai Lama. *An Appeal to the World*	170
Dallek, Robert. ★*Franklin D. Roosevelt*	B
Davis, Angela Y. *Abolition*	364.6
Didion, Joan. ★*Let Me Tell You What I Mean*	814
Ellis, Joseph J. ★*American Dialogue*	973.3
Emanuel, Rahm. *The Nation City*	352.23
Farmer, John J. *The Ground Truth*	973.931
Fukuyama, Francis. *Liberalism and Its Discontents*	320.51
Fukuyama, Francis. *Political Order and Political Decay*	320.1
Hayek, Friedrich A. von. *The Road to Serfdom*	330.1
Hobbes, Thomas. ★*Leviathan*	320.01
Hoffman, Bruce. *Anonymous Soldiers*	956.94
Hunt, Tristram. *Marx's General*	335.4092
Jordan, Mary. *The Art of Her Deal*	B
Kawa, Abraham. *Democracy*	741.5
Kazin, Michael. *What It Took to Win*	324.2736
Kissinger, Henry. *Leadership*	303.3
Kornacki, Steve. *The Red and the Blue*	306.20973
Ledbetter, James. *One Nation Under Gold*	332.4
Levingston, Steven. *Kennedy and King*	920
Liedman, Sven-Eric. *A World to Win*	B
Litt, David. *Democracy in One Book or Less*	321.8
Machiavelli, Niccolo. ★*The Prince*	320.1
Marshall, Tim. *The Power of Geography*	320.1
Martin, Jonathan. *This Will Not Pass*	973.933
Marx, Karl. ★*The Communist Manifesto*	355.4
Mieville, China. *October*	947.084
Moore, Peter. *Life, Liberty, and the Pursuit of Happiness*	199
Oates, Joyce Carol. *American Melancholy*	811
Obama, Barack. ★*The Audacity of Hope*	B
Painter, Nell Irvin. ★*I Just Keep Talking*	814
Paulsen, Michael Stokes. *The Constitution*	342.7302
Peres, Shimon. *No Room for Small Dreams*	B
Phillips, Adrian. *Fighting Churchill, Appeasing Hitler*	327.41043
Plato. ★*The Republic*	321
Popkin, Jeremy D. *A New World Begins*	944.04
Rand, Ayn. *The Voice of Reason*	191
Raphael, Ray. *Constitutional Myths*	342.7302
Rhodes, Benjamin J. *The World as It Is*	973.932
Ricks, Thomas E. ★*First Principles*	973.09
Rousseau, Jean-Jacques. ★*The Social Contract*	320.1
Runciman, David. *The Confidence Trap*	321.8
Ryan, Alan. *On Politics*	320.01
Schell, Orville. *Wealth and Power*	920
Sharma, Ruchir. *The Rise and Fall of Nations*	330.9
Shavit, Ari. *My Promised Land*	956.05
Stanley, Brian. *Christianity in the Twentieth Century*	270.8
Stanley, Jason. *How Fascism Works*	321.9
Thurman, Judith. ★*A Left-Handed Woman*	814
Tocqueville, Alexis de. ★*Democracy in America*	320.973
Wehle, Kim. *What You Need to Know About Voting and Why*	324.60973
Whitby, Andrew. *The Sum of the People*	001.4
Will, George F. *The Conservative Sensibility*	320.520973
Wilson, Rick. *Running Against the Devil*	973.933
Wong, Chun Han. *Party of One*	951.06

POLITICAL SCIENTISTS
Benner, Erica. *Be Like the Fox*	B
Boucheron, Patrick. *Machiavelli*	320.1092
Glendinning, Victoria. *Leonard Woolf*	B
Ryan, Alan. *On Politics*	320.01
Ypi, Lea. ★*Free*	B

POLITICAL STABILITY
Merridale, Catherine. *Lenin on the Train*	B
Turchin, Peter. *End Times*	320.01
Ullrich, Volker. *Germany 1923*	943.085
Ypi, Lea. ★*Free*	B

POLITICAL SURVEILLANCE
Connelly, Matthew James. *The Declassification Engine*	352.3
Friedman, Barry. ★*Unwarranted*	344.73035
Molnar, Petra. *The Walls Have Eyes*	363.28
Risen, James. ★*The Last Honest Man*	973.92

POLITICAL VALUES
Alberta, Tim. *American Carnage*	324.2734
Gordon-Reed, Annette. ★*Most Blessed of the Patriarchs*	973.4
Lepore, Jill. ★*These Truths*	973

POLITICAL VIOLENCE
Acemoglu, Daron. *The Narrow Corridor*	320.01
Branigan, Tania. *Red Memory*	951.05
Burrough, Bryan. *Days of Rage*	303.48
Dagher, Sam. *Assad or We Burn the Country*	956.9104
Di Giovanni, Janine. *The Morning They Came for Us*	956.9104
Ephron, Dan. *Killing a King*	956.9405
Evangelista, Patricia. ★*Some People Need Killing*	364.4
Gonell, Aquilino. *American Shield*	B
Hagerty, Alexa. ★*Still Life with Bones*	599.9
Hernandez, Kelly Lytle. ★*Bad Mexicans*	972
Hochschild, Adam. *American Midnight*	973.91
Hoock, Holger. *Scars of Independence*	973.3
Kaminsky, Ilya. ★*Deaf Republic*	811
Keefe, Patrick Radden. ★*Say Nothing*	364.152
Kurlansky, Mark. *1968*	909.82
Mogelson, Luke. *The Storm Is Here*	973.933
Pearlman, Wendy. *We Crossed a Bridge and It Trembled*	956.9104
Popkin, Jeremy D. *A New World Begins*	944.04

AUTHOR, TITLE, SERIES AND SUBJECT INDEX

Rappaport, Helen. *The Race to Save the Romanovs*	947.08
Reilly, Ryan J. ★*Sedition Hunters*	364.1
Toobin, Jeffrey. ★*Homegrown*	363.325
Wainaina, Binyavanga. *One Day I Will Write About This Place*	B

POLITICIANS

Abrams, Dan. *Theodore Roosevelt for the Defense*	345.73
Abrams, Stacey. *Lead from the Outside*	B
Allen, Jonathan. *Shattered*	324.973
Allitt, Patrick. *The Conservatives*	320.520973
Baier, Bret. *Three Days in January*	B
Baier, Bret. *To Rescue the Constitution*	973.4
Baker, Peter. *The Man Who Ran Washington*	B
Barrett, David Dean. *140 Days to Hiroshima*	940.54
Beeman, Richard R. *Our Lives, Our Fortunes and Our Sacred Honor*	973.3
Benner, Erica. *Be Like the Fox*	B
Berg, A. Scott. ★*Wilson*	B
Bernstein, Carl. ★*All the President's Men*	364.1
Blair, Tony. *A Journey*	B
Blumenthal, Sidney. ★*All the Powers of Earth*	B
Boles, John B. *Jefferson*	B
Borman, Tracy. *Thomas Cromwell*	B
Borneman, Walter R. *Polk*	B
Branch, Taylor. *The Clinton Tapes*	973.929
Brands, H. W. ★*Andrew Jackson, His Life and Times*	B
Brands, H. W. *The First American*	B
Brands, H. W. ★*Heirs of the Founders*	973.5
Brazile, Donna. *For Colored Girls Who Have Considered Politics*	328.73
Brinkley, Alan. *John F. Kennedy*	B
Broadwater, Jeff. ★*George Mason*	B
Broadwater, Jeff. *James Madison*	B
Broers, Michael. *Napoleon*	B
Broers, Michael. *Napoleon*	B
Brower, Kate Andersen. *First in Line*	920
Burlingame, Michael. *Abraham Lincoln*	B
Burstein, Andrew. *Madison and Jefferson*	973.4
Bush, George W. *Decision Points*	B
Buttigieg, Pete. *Shortest Way Home*	B
Cannadine, David. ★*Mellon*	B
Caro, Robert A. ★*The Passage of Power*	B
Carter, Jimmy. *A Full Life*	B
Carter, Jimmy. *White House Diary*	973.926
Chase, James. *Acheson*	B
Cheney, Lynne V. *James Madison*	B
Cheney, Lynne V. *The Virginia Dynasty*	B
Chernow, Ron. ★*Alexander Hamilton*	B
Chozick, Amy. *Chasing Hillary*	B
Christie, Chris. *Let Me Finish*	B
Clinton, Bill. *My Life*	B
Clinton, Hillary Rodham. *Living History*	B
Collins, Gail. *William Henry Harrison*	B
Conason, Joe. *The Longest Con*	320.52
Cooper, Helene. *Madame President*	966.62
Cooper, John Milton. *Woodrow Wilson*	B
Cummings, Elijah. ★*We're Better Than This*	B
Dallek, Robert. ★*Franklin D. Roosevelt*	B
Dallek, Robert. *Harry S. Truman*	B
Dallek, Robert. *Nixon and Kissinger*	B
Dallek, Robert. *An Unfinished Life*	B
Denevi, Timothy. *Freak Kingdom*	B
Donald, David Herbert. *Lincoln*	B
Duckworth, Tammy. *Every Day Is a Gift*	B
Duiker, William J. *Ho Chi Minh*	B
Duncan, Michael. ★*Hero of Two Worlds*	B
Ellis, Joseph J. *American Creation*	973.3
Ellis, Joseph J. *American Sphinx*	973.4
Ellis, Joseph J. *Founding Brothers*	973.4
Ellis, Joseph J. ★*His Excellency*	B
Ellis, Joseph J. ★*Revolutionary Summer*	973.3
Elwood, Phil. *All the Worst Humans*	659.2
Everitt, Anthony. *Cicero*	B
Farrell, John A. ★*Richard Nixon*	B
Farrell, John A. *Ted Kennedy*	B
Farris, Scott. *Almost President*	324.973
Fehrman, Craig. *Author in Chief*	920
Feldman, Noah. *The Three Lives of James Madison*	B
Ferguson, Niall. *Kissinger*	973.924
Finkelman, Paul. *Millard Fillmore*	B
Foner, Eric. *The Fiery Trial*	973.7092
Frank, Barney. *Frank*	B
Franklin, Benjamin. ★*The Autobiography of Benjamin Franklin*	B
Franklin, Benjamin. ★*Autobiography, Poor Richard, and Later Writings*	973.2
Franklin, Benjamin. *The Compleated Autobiography*	B
Freeman, Joanne B. *The Field of Blood*	973.7
Gabler, Neal. ★*Against the Wind*	B
Gabler, Neal. *Catching the Wind*	B
Gaines, James R. *For Liberty and Glory*	B
Gandhi. *An Autobiography*	B
Ganz, John. *When the Clock Broke*	320.52
Gewen, Barry. ★*The Inevitability of Tragedy*	B
Goldsworthy, Adrian Keith. *Antony and Cleopatra*	937
Goldsworthy, Adrian Keith. ★*Caesar*	B
Goodwin, Doris Kearns. ★*An Unfinished Love Story*	B
Goodyear, C. W. *President Garfield*	B
Gordon-Reed, Annette. *Andrew Johnson*	B
Groom, Winston. *The Patriots*	920
Guelzo, Allen C. *Lincoln and Douglas*	973.6
Halberstam, David. *The Best and the Brightest*	973.92
Hett, Benjamin Carter. *The Death of Democracy*	943.085
Hirsi Ali, Ayaan. ★*Infidel*	B
Hitchens, Christopher. *Thomas Jefferson*	B
Inskeep, Steve. *Imperfect Union*	B
Isaacson, Walter. ★*Benjamin Franklin*	B
Johnson, Paul. *Churchill*	B
Johnson, Paul. *Napoleon*	B
Kander, Jason. *Invisible Storm*	B
Katz, David. *Barack Before Obama*	B
Kennedy, John F. *Profiles in Courage*	920
Kennedy, Robert Francis. *RFK*	973.92
Kerry, John. *Every Day Is Extra*	B
Kershaw, Ian. *Hitler*	B
Kethledge, Raymond Michael. *Lead Yourself First*	658.4
King, David. *The Trial of Adolf Hitler*	345.43
Klarman, Michael J. *The Framers' Coup*	342.7302
Kornacki, Steve. *The Red and the Blue*	306.20973
Kurtz, Howard. *Media Madness*	973.933
Larson, Erik. *In the Garden of Beasts*	B
Leamer, Laurence. *The Kennedy Men*	920
Levingston, Steven. *Kennedy and King*	920
Lewis, John. ★*March; Book One*	741.5
Lewis, John. ★*March; Book Three*	741.5
Lewis, John. ★*March; Book Two*	741.5
Lewis, John. ★*Run; Book One*	741.5
Lozada, Carlos. *The Washington Book*	320
MacCulloch, Diarmaid. *Thomas Cromwell*	B
Maddow, Rachel. ★*Prequel*	320.53
Manchester, William. *The Last Lion, Winston Spencer Churchill.*	B
Manchester, William. *The Last Lion, Winston Spencer Churchill.*	B
Manchester, William. *The Last Lion, Winston Spencer Churchill.*	B
Mandela, Nelson. *Conversations with Myself*	B
Mandela, Nelson. *Dare Not Linger*	B
Mandela, Nelson. *In His Own Words*	B
Mandela, Nelson. ★*Long Walk to Freedom*	B
Mandela, Nelson. *Mandela*	B
Mandela, Nelson. *The Prison Letters of Nelson Mandela*	968.06092
Martini, Adrienne. *Somebody's Gotta Do It*	B
Marvel, William. *Lincoln's Autocrat*	B
Matthews, Christopher. *Bobby Kennedy*	B
McCourt, Malachy. *Singing My Him Song*	B
McCullough, David G. ★*John Adams*	B
McCullough, David G. *Truman*	B
McGrath, Tim. *James Monroe*	B
McKean, David. *Suspected of Independence*	B
McMeekin, Sean. *July 1914*	940.3
McPhee, Peter. *Robespierre*	B
McPherson, James M. ★*Abraham Lincoln*	B
Meacham, Jon. ★*Destiny and Power*	B
Meacham, Jon. *Franklin and Winston*	940.53
Meacham, Jon. ★*Thomas Jefferson*	B
Merry, Robert W. *A Country of Vast Designs*	B
Millard, Candice. ★*Hero of the Empire*	968.04
Miller, Char. *Gifford Pinchot and the Making of Modern Environmentalism*	B
Moore, Peter. *Life, Liberty, and the Pursuit of Happiness*	199
Morris, Edmund. ★*Colonel Roosevelt*	B
Morris, Edmund. ★*The Rise of Theodore Roosevelt*	B
Morris, Edmund. ★*Theodore Rex*	973.911

PUBLIC LIBRARY CORE COLLECTION: NONFICTION
Twentieth Edition

Nasaw, David. ★*The Patriarch*	B
Neu, Charles E. *Colonel House*	B
Norwich, John Julius. *A History of France*	944
Oller, John. *American Queen*	B
Packer, George. *Our Man*	B
Pantsov, Alexander. *Mao*	B
Paul, Joel R. *Indivisible*	973.5
Peters, Charles. *Lyndon B. Johnson*	B
Pfeffer, Anshel. *Bibi*	B
Philbrick, Nathaniel. ★*Valiant Ambition*	B
Rakove, Jack N. *Revolutionaries*	973.3
Raphael, Ray. *Mr. President*	352.230973
Reagan, Ronald. *The Reagan Diaries*	B
Remnick, David. *The Bridge*	B
Richards, Leonard L. *Who Freed the Slaves?*	342.7308
Ricks, Thomas E. *Churchill and Orwell*	920
Ricks, Thomas E. ★*First Principles*	973.09
Roberts, Andrew. ★*Churchill*	B
Rogers, Katie. ★*American Woman*	973.09
Rohde, David. *In Deep*	973.933
Roll, David L. *George Marshall*	B
Rumsfeld, Donald. *When the Center Held*	973.925092
Sedgwick, John. *War of Two*	973.4
Shuster, Simon. ★*The Showman*	B
Smith, Richard Norton. *On His Own Terms*	973.925092
Snyder, Timothy. *The Red Prince*	B
Sorensen, Theodore C. *Counselor*	B
Stahr, Walter. *Seward*	B
Stahr, Walter. ★*Stanton*	B
Stark, Peter. *Young Washington*	B
Steinberg, Jonathan. *Bismarck*	B
Steinberg, Jonny. *Winnie and Nelson*	920
Stewart, David O. *Madison's Gift*	B
Sullivan, Kevin. *Trump on Trial*	342.73
Thomas, Evan. *Being Nixon*	B
Thomas, Evan. ★*Robert Kennedy*	B
Traub, James. *John Quincy Adams*	B
Tye, Larry. ★*Bobby Kennedy*	B
Tye, Larry. ★*Demagogue*	B
Unger, Debi. *George Marshall*	B
Unger, Harlow G. *First Founding Father*	B
Unger, Harlow G. *The Last Founding Father*	B
Updegrove, Mark K. *The Last Republicans*	973.928
Vogel, Ezra F. *Deng Xlaoping and the Transformation of China*	B
Weiner, Eric. *Ben & Me*	B
Weiner, Tim. *One Man Against the World*	B
Weintraub, Stanley. *Iron Tears*	973.3
Weissmann, Andrew. ★*Where Law Ends*	324.7
White, Ronald C. *A. Lincoln*	B
Whyte, Kenneth. *Hoover*	B
Wills, Garry. *James Madison*	B
Wise, Steven M. *Though the Heavens May Fall*	342.42
Wood, Gordon S. *Empire of Liberty*	973.4
Wood, Gordon S. *Friends Divided*	920
Woodward, Bob. *The Final Days*	B
Woodward, Bob. *Shadow*	973.92
Zamoyski, Adam. *Napoleon*	B
Zelizer, Julian E. *Burning Down the House*	328.73

POLITICIANS' FAMILIES

Garrow, David J. *Rising Star*	B
Maraniss, David. ★*Barack Obama*	B
Taraborrelli, J. Randy. *The Kennedy Heirs*	920

POLITICIANS' SPOUSES

Biden, Jill. *Where the Light Enters*	B
Inskeep, Steve. *Imperfect Union*	B
Mazzeo, Tilar J. ★*Eliza Hamilton*	B
Slevin, Peter. *Michelle Obama*	B
★*Politics*. Aristotle	320

POLITICS AND CULTURE

Arendt, Hannah. *The Origins of Totalitarianism*	320.53
Berkshire, Jennifer. *The Education Wars*	371.01
Burstein, Andrew. *Madison and Jefferson*	973.4
Friedman, George. *Flashpoints*	940.56
Hahn, Steven. *A Nation Under Our Feet*	975
Lebron, Christopher J. *The Making of Black Lives Matter*	305.896
Lieven, Anatol. *Pakistan*	954.9105
Lovell, Julia. *Maoism*	335.43
Pan, Philip P. *Out of Mao's Shadow*	306.20951
Schlesinger, Arthur M. *Journals, 1952-2000*	973.91092

POLITICS AND EDUCATION

Berkshire, Jennifer. *The Education Wars*	371.01
Duncan, Arne. *How Schools Work*	379

POLITICS AND GLOBAL AFFAIRS — CIVIL AND HUMAN RIGHTS

Abrams, Stacey. *Lead from the Outside*	B
Achorn, Edward. *The Lincoln Miracle*	973.6
Adayfi, Mansoor. *Don't Forget Us Here*	B
Addario, Lynsey. *Of Love & War*	779
Alexander, Kwame. *Light for the World to See*	811.6
Anderson, Carol. ★*The Second*	344.7305
Andrews, Becca. ★*No Choice*	362.1988
Baker, Calvin. *A More Perfect Reunion*	305.800973
Barnett, Brittany K. ★*A Knock at Midnight*	B
Becker, Jo. ★*Forcing the Spring*	346.79401
Berman, Ari. *Give Us the Ballot*	324.6
Bharara, Preet. *Doing Justice*	347.73
Boghosian, Heidi. *"i Have Nothing to Hide"*	363.1
Bookman, Marc. *A Descending Spiral*	345.73
Boschert, Sherry. *37 Words*	344.73
Brodsky, Alexandra. *Sexual Justice*	364.15
Bryant, Howard. *Full Dissidence*	306.20973
Burnham, Margaret A. ★*By Hands Now Known*	342.73
Butler, Paul. *Chokehold*	363.2
Canon, Dan. ★*Pleading Out*	345.73
Carruthers, Charlene A. *Unapologetic*	305.48
Cenziper, Debbie. ★*Love Wins*	346.7301
Chemerinsky, Erwin. *Presumed Guilty*	344.7305
Citron, Danielle Keats. *The Fight for Privacy*	342.7308
Collins-Dexter, Brandi. *Black Skinhead*	324.2734
Dennie, Madiba K. *The Originalism Trap*	342.73
Derf. *Kent State*	741.5
Erdozain, Dominic. *One Nation Under Guns*	363.33
Finan, Christopher M. *How Free Speech Saved Democracy*	342.73
Friedman, Barry. ★*Unwarranted*	344.7305
Fukuyama, Francis. *Liberalism and Its Discontents*	320.51
Funk, Mason. *The Book of Pride*	920
Garza, Alicia. *The Purpose of Power*	303.48
Gates, Melinda. ★*The Moment of Lift*	305.42
Gessen, Masha. *Never Remember*	365
Goldstone, Lawrence. *On Account of Race*	342.7308
Hayes, Christopher. *A Colony in a Nation*	364.3
Hill, Anita. ★*Believing*	305.42
Hill, Kashmir. ★*Your Face Belongs to Us*	006.2
Hochschild, Adam. *Lessons from a Dark Time*	909.82
Jackson, Kellie Carter. *We Refuse*	323.1196
Kaplan, Roberta A. *Then Comes Marriage*	346.7301
Kara, Siddharth. *Cobalt Red*	338.2
King, Martin Luther. *"Thou, Dear God"*	242
Kluger, Richard. *Indelible Ink*	B
Kolbert, Kathryn. *Controlling Women*	362.1988
Lamb, Christina. *Our Bodies, Their Battlefields*	341.6
LaRue, James. ★*On Censorship*	025.2
Lebron, Christopher J. *The Making of Black Lives Matter*	305.896
Liao, Yiwu. *Bullets and Opium*	951.05
Lithwick, Dahlia. *Lady Justice*	345.73
Mahtani, Shibani. *Among the Braves*	951.25
Mallory, Tamika D. *State of Emergency*	305.896
Manning, Chelsea. *Readme.Txt*	B
McHangama, Jacob. ★*Free Speech*	323.44
Metzl, Jonathan M. ★*What We've Become*	364.152
Molnar, Petra. *The Walls Have Eyes*	363.28
Morrison, Toni. ★*The Source of Self-Regard*	814
Murad, Nadia. ★*The Last Girl*	B
Nafisi, Azar. *Read Dangerously*	809
Oluo, Ijeoma. *Mediocre*	305.310973
Paine, Thomas. ★*Rights of Man*	320.5
Porter, Eduardo. *American Poison*	305.800973
Postel, Charles. *Equality*	305.50973
Prager, Joshua. *The Family Roe*	342.7308
Richardson, Heather Cox. *Democracy Awakening*	320.473
Rosenberg, Ian. *The Fight for Free Speech*	342.73
Sacco, Joe. ★*Paying the Land*	741.5
Searcey, Dionne. *In Pursuit of Disobedient Women*	B
Signer, Michael. *Cry Havoc*	305.800973
Strossen, Nadine. *Hate*	342.7308
Taibbi, Matt. *I Can't Breathe*	363.2
Toorpakai, Maria. *A Different Kind of Daughter*	B

AUTHOR, TITLE, SERIES AND SUBJECT INDEX

Urofsky, Melvin I. *The Affirmative Action Puzzle* — 331.13
Van Meter, Matthew. *Deep Delta Justice* — 345.763
Vogelstein, Rachel B. *Awakening* — 305.42
Wehle, Kim. *What You Need to Know About Voting and Why* — 324.60973
Winkler, Adam. *We the Corporations* — 346.73
Worth, Robert Forsyth. ★*A Rage for Order* — 909
Yoshino, Kenji. *Speak Now* — 346.79401
Zuckerman, Jocelyn C. *Planet Palm* — 633.8

POLITICS AND GLOBAL AFFAIRS — ELECTIONS

Abrams, Stacey. *Lead from the Outside* — B
Abrams, Stacey. *Our Time Is Now* — 324.60973
Allen, Jonathan. *Lucky* — 324.973
Allen, Jonathan. *Shattered* — 324.973
Anderson, Carol. ★*One Person, No Vote* — 324.6
Arnsdorf, Isaac. ★*Finish What We Started* — 320.52
Balz, Daniel J. *The Battle for America, 2008* — 973.932
Bender, Michael C. *"Frankly, We Did Win This Election"* — 973.933
Berman, Ari. ★*Minority Rule* — 305.809
Bowden, Mark. *The Steal* — 973.933
Brazile, Donna. *For Colored Girls Who Have Considered Politics* — 328.73
Chozick, Amy. *Chasing Hillary* — B
Clinton, Hillary Rodham. *What Happened* — 328.73
Cross, Tiffany D. ★*Say It Louder!* — 324.6
Harding, Luke. *Collusion* — 324.70973
Hasen, Richard L. *Election Meltdown* — 324.973
Hoffman, Carl. *Liar's Circus* — 973.933
Isikoff, Michael. *Russian Roulette* — 973.933
Karl, Jonathan. *Tired of Winning* — 973.933
Lichtman, Allan J. *The Embattled Vote in America* — 324.6
Martin, Jonathan. *This Will Not Pass* — 973.933
Martini, Adrienne. *Somebody's Gotta Do It* — B
Plouffe, David. *A Citizen's Guide to Beating Donald Trump* — 324.0973
Seabrook, Nicholas R. *One Person, One Vote* — 328.3
Shimer, David. *Rigged* — 324.60973
Smith, Erin Geiger. ★*Thank You for Voting* — 324.973
Steinhauer, Jennifer. *The Firsts* — 320.082
Stevens, Stuart. *It Was All a Lie* — 324.2734
Wehle, Kim. *What You Need to Know About Voting and Why* — 324.60973
Wilson, Rick. *Running Against the Devil* — 973.933

POLITICS AND GLOBAL AFFAIRS — ENVIRONMENTAL ISSUES AND POLICIES

Berners-Lee, Mike. *The Carbon Footprint of Everything* — 363.738
Berry, Wendell. *The Art of Loading Brush* — 338.10973
Bittle, Jake. ★*The Great Displacement* — 362.87
Chachra, Deb. *How Infrastructure Works* — 363
Cullen, Art. *Storm Lake* — 071.7
Flowers, Catherine Coleman. *Waste* — 363.72
Foer, Jonathan Safran. ★*We Are the Weather* — 636
Gee, Alastair. *Fire in Paradise* — 363.37
Ghosh, Amitav. *The Great Derangement* — 809
Grabar, Henry. *Paved Paradise* — 388.474
Hayhoe, Katharine. *Saving Us* — 304.2
Holthaus, Eric. *The Future Earth* — 363.738
Johnson, Lizzie. ★*Paradise* — 363.37
Keefe, Bob. *Clean Economy Now* — 333.79
Klare, Michael T. *All Hell Breaking Loose* — 355.20973
Linden, Eugene. *Fire and Flood* — 304.2
Lustgarten, Abrahm. ★*On the Move* — 363.7
Maher, Kris. *Desperate* — 344
McKibben, Bill. *Falter* — 909.83
Monbiot, George. ★*Regenesis* — 338.1
Moore, Kathleen Dean. *Earth's Wild Music* — 576.8
Morris, Jim. ★*The Cancer Factory* — 658.4
Redniss, Lauren. ★*Oak Flat* — 970.5
Rush, Elizabeth A. *Rising* — 551.45
Sachs, Jeffrey. *The Age of Sustainable Development* — 338.9
Scheyder, Ernest. *The War Below* — 333.7
Smil, Vaclav. *How the World Really Works* — 500
Thunberg, Greta. ★*The Climate Book* — 363.738
Vollmann, William T. *No Immediate Danger* — 333.79
Yergin, Daniel. *The New Map* — 333.79
Zuckerman, Gregory. *The Frackers* — B

POLITICS AND GLOBAL AFFAIRS — GENERAL

Austen, Ben. *Correction* — 364.6
Auster, Paul. *Bloodbath Nation* — 363.33
Baer, Daniel Brooks. *The Four Tests* — 320.973
Barkan, Ady. *Eyes to the Wind* — B
Boykin, Keith. *Race Against Time* — 305.8
Brettschneider, Corey Lang. *The Oath and the Office* — 342.73
Caldwell, Christopher. *The Age of Entitlement* — 305.240973
Chafkin, Max. *The Contrarian* — B
Chammah, Maurice. ★*Let the Lord Sort Them* — 364.66
Chomsky, Noam. *Global Discontents* — 410.92
Churchwell, Sarah Bartlett. *Behold, America* — 973.9
Clinton, Hillary Rodham. *It Takes a Village* — 305.23
Dayen, David. *Chain of Title* — 330.973
DiResta, Renee. *Invisible Rulers* — 320
Emanuel, Rahm. *The Nation City* — 352.23
Ferguson, Niall. *Doom* — 362.1962
Finkelman, Paul. ★*Landmark Decisions of the United States Supreme Court* — 347.73
Fitzpatrick, Cara. *The Death of Public School* — 379.73
Foner, Eric. *The Second Founding* — 342.73
Giridharadas, Anand. *The Persuaders* — 320.973
Gray, Emma. *A Girl's Guide to Joining the Resistance* — 303.48
Hutchinson, Cassidy. *Enough* — B
Jacobs, A. J. ★*The Year of Living Constitutionally* — 342.73
Jacoby, Melissa B. ★*Unjust Debts* — 346.73
Keenan, Cody. *Grace* — 973.932
Kim, Anne. ★*Poverty for Profit* — 302.5
Klobuchar, Amy. ★*Antitrust* — 343.73
Kruse, Kevin Michael. *Fault Lines* — 973.92
Leonard, Christopher. *Kochland* — 338.7
Litt, David. *Democracy in One Book or Less* — 321.8
Marx, Karl. ★*Capital* — 335.4
Masciotra, David. *Exurbia Now* — 320.973
Michel, Casey. *American Kleptocracy* — 364.16
Mogelson, Luke. *The Storm Is Here* — 973.933
Murolo, Priscilla. *From the Folks Who Brought You the Weekend* — 331
O'Brien, David M. ★*Storm Center* — 347.73
O'Neil, Cathy. *Weapons of Math Destruction* — 005.7
Osnos, Evan. *Wildland* — 973.93
Plato. ★*The Republic* — 321
Reilly, Ryan J. ★*Sedition Hunters* — 364.1
Richardson, Heather Cox. ★*How the South Won the Civil War* — 306.20973
Roffer, Michael H. *The Law Book* — 340.09
Rohde, David. *In Deep* — 973.933
Ross, Andrew. *Sunbelt Blues* — 363.5
Rubin, Robert Edward. *The Yellow Pad* — 658.4
Sage, Sami. *Democracy in Retrograde* — 324
Sanghera, Sathnam. *Empireworld* — 909
Schneier, Bruce. *A Hacker's Mind* — 364.16
Schwab, Tim. ★*The Bill Gates Problem* — 361.7
Sharpton, Al. *Rise Up* — 973.933
Singer, Jessie. *There Are No Accidents* — 363.1
Smith, Mychal Denzel. *Stakes Is High* — 973.933
Smith, Zadie. ★*Feel Free* — 824
Solnit, Rebecca. *Call Them by Their True Names* — 303.3
Sommer, Will. ★*Trust the Plan* — 973.933
Sontag, Susan. *At the Same Time* — 814
Souza, Pete. *Obama* — 973.932
Sunstein, Cass R. *Impeachment* — 342.73
Tau, Byron. ★*Means of Control* — 363.25
Teachout, Zephyr. *Break 'Em Up* — 338.8
Tester, Jon. *Grounded* — B
Turchin, Peter. *End Times* — 320.01
Whitby, Andrew. *The Sum of the People* — 001.4
Zakaria, Fareed. *Age of Revolutions* — 303.6

POLITICS AND GLOBAL AFFAIRS — IMMIGRATION

Blitzer, Jonathan. *Everyone Who Is Gone Is Here* — 305.9
Bobrow-Strain, Aaron. *The Death and Life of Aida Hernandez* — 972
Goudeau, Jessica. ★*After the Last Border* — 362.83
Guerrero, Jean. *Hatemonger* — B
Hinojosa, Maria. *Once I Was You* — B
Lalami, Laila. *Conditional Citizens* — 323.60973
Lekas Miller, Anna. *Love Across Borders* — 323.6
Markham, Lauren. ★*The Far Away Brothers* — 920
Molnar, Petra. *The Walls Have Eyes* — 363.28
Olivares, Efren C. *My Boy Will Die of Sorrow* — 305.9
Soboroff, Jacob. ★*Separated* — 325.73
Vargas, Jose Antonio. *Dear America* — B
Wides-Munoz, Laura. *The Making of a Dream* — 920

POLITICS AND GLOBAL AFFAIRS — JUDICIAL POLITICS

Amar, Akhil Reed. *The Constitution Today* — 342.73
Berman, Geoffrey. *Holding the Line* — 345.73

PUBLIC LIBRARY CORE COLLECTION: NONFICTION
Twentieth Edition

Breyer, Stephen G. ★ *The Authority of the Court and the Peril of Politics*	347.73
Chemerinsky, Erwin. *Closing the Courthouse Door*	347.73
Chemerinsky, Erwin. *Presumed Guilty*	344.7305
Cohen, Adam. ★ *Supreme Inequality*	347.73
Coyle, Marcia. *The Roberts Court*	347.73
Dennie, Madiba K. *The Originalism Trap*	342.73
Driver, Justin. *The Schoolhouse Gate*	344.73
Kaplan, David A. *The Most Dangerous Branch*	347.73
O'Connor, Sandra Day. ★ *Out of Order*	347.73
Olsen, Lise. *Code of Silence*	347.73
Robin, Corey. *The Enigma of Clarence Thomas*	347.73
Rosen, Jeffrey. *Conversations with RBG*	B
Rosenberg, Ian. *The Fight for Free Speech*	342.73
Scalia, Antonin. *Scalia Speaks*	081
Smith, J. Douglas. *On Democracy's Doorstep*	342.73
Stone, Geoffrey R. ★ *Sex and the Constitution*	345.7302
Toobin, Jeffrey. *The Nine*	347.73
Tribe, Laurence H. *Uncertain Justice*	342.73
Urofsky, Melvin I. *Dissent and the Supreme Court*	342.7302
Vladeck, Stephen I. *The Shadow Docket*	347.73
Waldman, Michael. *The Supermajority*	347.73

POLITICS AND GLOBAL AFFAIRS — MASS MEDIA AND POLITICS

Baron, Martin. ★ *Collision of Power*	070.4
Carpenter, Amanda B. *Gaslighting America*	973.933
Cross, Tiffany D. ★ *Say It Louder!*	324.6
Elwood, Phil. *All the Worst Humans*	659.2
Gold, Judy. *Yes I Can Say That*	792.7
Kroll, Andy. *A Death on W Street*	364.152
McCraw, David Edward. *Truth in Our Times*	342.7308
Napoli, Lisa. *Up All Night*	384.55
Owens, Ernest. ★ *The Case for Cancel Culture*	303.3
Poniewozik, James. *Audience of One*	324.7
Ressa, Maria. ★ *How to Stand up to a Dictator*	070.92
Schieffer, Bob. *Overload*	070.4
Stelter, Brian. *Hoax*	070.4
Stengel, Richard. *Information Wars*	355.3
Sullivan, Kevin. *Trump on Trial*	342.73
van der Linden, Sander. ★ *Foolproof*	302.3

POLITICS AND GLOBAL AFFAIRS — NATIONAL SECURITY

Ackerman, Spencer. *Reign of Terror*	973.931
Baker, Nicholson. *Baseless*	358
Boghosian, Heidi. *"i Have Nothing to Hide"*	363.1
Brooks, Rosa. *How Everything Became War and the Military Became Everything*	355
Chertoff, Michael. *Exploding Data*	343.7309
Connelly, Matthew James. *The Declassification Engine*	352.3
Dunn, Harry. *Standing My Ground*	B
Friedman, Barry. ★ *Unwarranted*	344.7305
Gellman, Barton. ★ *Dark Mirror*	B
Graff, Garrett M. *Raven Rock*	363.350973
Greenberg, Andy. *Sandworm*	364.16
Howley, Kerry. *Bottoms Up and the Devil Laughs*	352.37
Kaplan, Fred M. *The Bomb*	355.8
Manning, Chelsea. *Readme.Txt*	B
Mundy, Liza. ★ *The Sisterhood*	327.12
Nance, Malcolm W. *The Plot to Betray America*	973.933
Scharre, Paul. *Four Battlegrounds*	006.3
Stengel, Richard. *Information Wars*	355.3
Stephanopoulos, George. ★ *The Situation Room*	973.09
Walton, Calder. *Spies*	327.1247
Wilford, Hugh. *The CIA*	327.1273

POLITICS AND GLOBAL AFFAIRS — POLITICAL FIGURES

Achorn, Edward. *The Lincoln Miracle*	973.6
Andrews-Dyer, Helena. *Reclaiming Her Time*	B
Bade, Rachael. ★ *Unchecked*	342.73
Baker, Peter. *The Divider*	973.933
Ball, Molly. ★ *Pelosi*	B
Bender, Michael C. *"Frankly, We Did Win This Election"*	973.933
Bernstein, Andrea. *American Oligarchs*	920
Biden Owens, Valerie. *Growing up Biden*	B
Bird, Kai. *The Outlier*	973.926
Brettschneider, Corey Lang. *The Presidents and the People*	342.73
Chait, Jonathan. *Audacity*	973.932
Cheney, Liz. *Oath and Honor*	328.73
Christie, Chris. *Let Me Finish*	B
Clinton, Hillary Rodham. *Living History*	B
Cummings, Elijah. ★ *We're Better Than This*	B
D'Antonio, Michael. *The Hunting of Hillary*	B
Dyson, Michael Eric. *The Black Presidency*	305.800973
Elwood, Phil. *All the Worst Humans*	659.2
Evangelista, Patricia. ★ *Some People Need Killing*	364.4
Farrell, John A. *Ted Kennedy*	B
Foer, Franklin. ★ *The Last Politician*	973.934
Ganz, John. *When the Clock Broke*	320.52
Gessen, Masha. *Surviving Autocracy*	973.933
Gillard, Julia. ★ *Women and Leadership*	158
Goodwin, Doris Kearns. ★ *Leadership in Turbulent Times*	973.09
Goodyear, C. W. *President Garfield*	B
Graff, Garrett M. *Watergate*	973.924
Guerrero, Jean. *Hatemonger*	B
Harding, Luke. *Invasion*	947.7
Hennessey, Susan. *Unmaking the Presidency*	973.933
Hill, Fiona. *There Is Nothing for You Here*	327.2
Hope, Bradley. *Blood and Oil*	B
Johnston, David Cay. *The Big Cheat*	973.933
Jones, Brenda. *Alexandria Ocasio-Cortez*	B
Jones, Brenda. *Maxine Waters*	B
Jordan, Mary. *The Art of Her Deal*	B
Karl, Jonathan. *Betrayal*	973.933
Karl, Jonathan. *Tired of Winning*	973.933
Kirtzman, Andrew. *Giuliani*	B
Kissinger, Henry. *Leadership*	303.3
Kranish, Michael. *Trump Revealed*	B
Leonnig, Carol. *I Alone Can Fix It*	973.933
Lozada, Carlos. *The Washington Book*	320
Malala, Justice. *The Plot to Save South Africa*	968.07
Martin, Jonathan. *This Will Not Pass*	973.933
Marton, Kati. ★ *The Chancellor*	B
Obama, Barack. ★ *The Audacity of Hope*	B
Osnos, Evan. *Joe Biden*	B
Pfeffer, Anshel. *Bibi*	B
Poniewozik, James. *Audience of One*	324.7
Psaki, Jen. *Say More*	B
Remnick, David. *The Bridge*	B
Rothkopf, David J. *American Resistance*	973.933
Rumsfeld, Donald. *When the Center Held*	973.925092
Schmidt, Michael S. ★ *Donald Trump v. The United States*	973.933
Smith, Richard Norton. *An Ordinary Man*	B
Steinhauer, Jennifer. *The Firsts*	320.082
Stelter, Brian. *Hoax*	070.4
Sullivan, Kevin. *Trump on Trial*	342.73
Toobin, Jeffrey. *True Crimes and Misdemeanors*	973.933
Tubbs, Michael. *The Deeper the Roots*	B
Whipple, Chris. *The Fight of His Life*	973.934
Wolff, Michael. *Fire and Fury*	973.934
Wolff, Michael. *Landslide*	973.933
Woodward, Bob. *Peril*	973.933
Yaffa, Joshua. *Between Two Fires*	920
Zelensky, Volodymyr. *A Message from Ukraine*	947.7
Zelizer, Julian E. *Burning Down the House*	328.73
Zygar, Mikhail. *All the Kremlin's Men*	947.086

POLITICS AND GLOBAL AFFAIRS — POLITICAL PARTIES

Alberta, Tim. *American Carnage*	324.2734
Arnsdorf, Isaac. ★ *Finish What We Started*	320.52
Bade, Rachael. ★ *Unchecked*	342.73
Berman, Ari. ★ *Minority Rule*	305.809
Brennan, Jason. *Libertarianism*	320.51
Cadava, Geraldo L. *The Hispanic Republican*	324.2734089
Conason, Joe. *The Longest Con*	320.52
Hendershot, Heather. *Open to Debate*	B
Kazin, Michael. *What It Took to Win*	324.2736
Klein, Ezra. ★ *Why We're Polarized*	306.0973
Kornacki, Steve. *The Red and the Blue*	306.20973
Martin, Jonathan. *This Will Not Pass*	973.933
Mayer, Jane. ★ *Dark Money*	973.932
Seabrook, Nicholas R. *One Person, One Vote*	328.3
Sharlet, Jeff. ★ *The Undertow*	322
Spencer, Kyle. *Raising Them Right*	320.5
Stevens, Stuart. *The Conspiracy to End America*	324.2734
Stevens, Stuart. *It Was All a Lie*	324.2734
Vladeck, Stephen I. *The Shadow Docket*	347.73
Walker, Hunter. *The Truce*	324.2736
Will, George F. *The Conservative Sensibility*	320.520973
Wilson, Rick. *Running Against the Devil*	973.933
Zelizer, Julian E. *Burning Down the House*	328.73

AUTHOR, TITLE, SERIES AND SUBJECT INDEX

POLITICS AND GLOBAL AFFAIRS — POLITICAL PHILOSOPHY
Acemoglu, Daron. *The Narrow Corridor*	320.01
Amar, Akhil Reed. ★*America's Constitution*	342.7302
Applebaum, Anne. *Twilight of Democracy*	321.9
Arendt, Hannah. *The Origins of Totalitarianism*	320.53
Aristotle. ★*Politics*	320
Aristotle. ★*Politics, 2nd Ed*	320
Bakewell, Sarah. *How to Live—Or—A Life of Montaigne*	B
Boucheron, Patrick. *Machiavelli*	320.1092
Bregman, Rutger. *Utopia for Realists*	335
Brown, Archie. ★*The Rise and Fall of Communism*	320.53
Cicero, Marcus Tullius. ★*The Republic*	320.1
Ellis, Joseph J. ★*American Dialogue*	973.3
Frank, Thomas. *The People, No*	320.56
Fukuyama, Francis. *Liberalism and Its Discontents*	320.51
Fukuyama, Francis. *Political Order and Political Decay*	320.1
Gandhi. ★*Gandhi on Non-Violence*	179.7
Gewen, Barry. ★*The Inevitability of Tragedy*	B
Ghodsee, Kristen Rogheh. *Everyday Utopia*	335
Hennessey, Jonathan. *The United States Constitution*	741.5
Hobbes, Thomas. ★*Leviathan*	320.01
Kaplan, Robert D. *Warrior Politics*	320
Kawa, Abraham. *Democracy*	741.5
Lasch, Christopher. ★*The Revolt of the Elites*	306
Liedman, Sven-Eric. *A World to Win*	B
Lovell, Julia. *Maoism*	335.43
Machiavelli, Niccolo. ★*The Prince*	320.1
Mahtani, Shibani. *Among the Braves*	951.25
Marx, Karl. ★*The Communist Manifesto*	355.4
McAlevey, Jane. *A Collective Bargain*	331.890973
McHangama, Jacob. ★*Free Speech*	323.44
Minow, Martha. *When Should Law Forgive?*	345
Neiwert, David A. ★*The Age of Insurrection*	303.48
Nussbaum, Martha Craven. *The Monarchy of Fear*	306.20973
Paxton, Robert O. *The Anatomy of Fascism*	320.53
Piketty, Thomas. ★*Capital and Ideology*	305
Randall, Willard Sterne. *The Founders' Fortunes*	973.3
Ressa, Maria. ★*How to Stand up to a Dictator*	070.92
Ricks, Thomas E. ★*First Principles*	973.09
Rousseau, Jean-Jacques. ★*The Social Contract*	320.1
Ryan, Alan. *On Politics*	320.01
Skach, C. L. *How to Be a Citizen*	323.6
Stanley, Jason. *How Fascism Works*	321.9
Stevens, Stuart. *It Was All a Lie*	324.2734
Szablowski, Witold. *Dancing Bears*	947.086
Tocqueville, Alexis de. ★*Democracy in America*	320.973
Westad, Odd Arne. *The Cold War*	909.825
Will, George F. *The Conservative Sensibility*	320.520973

POLITICS AND GLOBAL AFFAIRS — PUBLIC HEALTH
Alexander, Brian. ★*The Hospital*	362.10973
Allen, Marshall. ★*Never Pay the First Bill*	610.28
Beres, Derek. *Conspirituality*	001.9
Block, Jennifer. *Everything Below the Waist*	613
Borrell, Brendan. *The First Shots*	615.3
Christakis, Nicholas A. *Apollo's Arrow*	362.1962
Clark, Anna. *The Poisoned City*	363.6
Cohn, Jonathan. *The Ten Year War*	368.38
Foster, Diana Greene. *The Turnaway Study*	362.1988
Geronimus, Arline T. ★*Weathering*	362.1089
Hanna-Attisha, Mona. *What the Eyes Don't See*	615.9
Insel, Thomas R. *Healing*	362.2
Lewis, Michael. ★*The Premonition*	614.5
Liverpool, Layal. *Systemic*	362.1
Mackenzie, Debora. *Covid-19*	616.2
McNeil, Donald G. ★*The Wisdom of Plagues*	614.4
Nocera, Joseph. *The Big Fail*	362.1962
Nuila, Ricardo. *The People's Hospital*	362.1
Price, Polly J. *Plagues in the Nation*	614.4
Quigley, Fran. *Prescription for the People*	338.4
Rosenthal, Elisabeth. *An American Sickness*	362.10973
Snyder, Timothy. ★*Our Malady*	362.10973
Tabery, James. ★*Tyranny of the Gene*	572.8
Westhoff, Ben. *Fentanyl, Inc.*	362.29
Wright, Lawrence. ★*The Plague Year*	614.5

POLITICS AND GLOBAL AFFAIRS — RELIGION AND POLITICS
Alberta, Tim. *The Kingdom, the Power, and the Glory*	270.8
Bhutto, Benazir. *Reconciliation*	297.2
Du Mez, Kristin Kobes. *Jesus and John Wayne*	277.308
FitzGerald, Frances. *The Evangelicals*	277
Ghattas, Kim. *Black Wave*	955.05
Griffith, R. Marie. *Moral Combat*	261.8
Husain, Ed. ★*The House of Islam*	297
Liao, Yiwu. *God Is Red*	275
Peters, Rebecca Todd. *Trust Women*	362.1988
Rashid, Jonny. *Jesus Takes a Side*	261.7
Seierstad, Asne. *Two Sisters*	956.9104
Wallis, Jim. *The False White Gospel*	261.7

POLITICS AND GLOBAL AFFAIRS — SOCIAL ISSUES AND POLICIES
Greene, Jamal. *How Rights Went Wrong*	342.7308
Luthra, Shefali. ★*Undue Burden*	362.1988
Nolan, Hamilton. *The Hammer*	331.8
Wiggins, Christopher L. *How Data Happened*	310

POLITICS AND GLOBAL AFFAIRS — TERRORISM
Bergen, Peter L. *The Longest War*	909.83
Bergen, Peter L. *Manhunt*	363.325
Bergen, Peter L. *The Rise and Fall of Osama Bin Laden*	958.104
Coker, Margaret. *The Spymaster of Baghdad*	956.7044
Coll, Steve. *Directorate S*	958.104
Filkins, Dexter. *The Forever War*	956.7044
Jacobsen, Annie. *Surprise, Kill, Vanish*	327.1273
Johnson, Steven. *The Infernal Machine*	335
Lehr, Dick. *White Hot Hate*	363.325
Matloff, Judith. *No Friends but the Mountains*	355.009
Mayer, Jane. *The Dark Side*	973.931
Mekhennet, Souad. *I Was Told to Come Alone*	363.3250956
Moore, Michael Scott. *The Desert and the Sea*	364.15
Murakami, Haruki. *Underground*	364.15
Neiwert, David A. ★*The Age of Insurrection*	303.48
Neus, Nora. *24 Hours in Charlottesville*	973.933
Rashid, Ahmed. *Taliban*	958.104
Scahill, Jeremy. *Dirty Wars*	355.00973
Seierstad, Asne. *Two Sisters*	956.9104
Stengel, Richard. *Information Wars*	355.3
Toobin, Jeffrey. ★*Homegrown*	363.325
Verini, James. *They Will Have to Die Now*	956.7044
Vickers, Michael G. *By All Means Available*	355
Warrick, Joby. *Black Flags*	956.9104
Wood, Graeme. *The Way of the Strangers*	363.325

POLITICS AND GLOBAL AFFAIRS — WORLD POLITICS
Albright, Madeleine Korbel. *Hell and Other Destinations*	B
Applebaum, Anne. *Twilight of Democracy*	321.9
Bennis, Phyllis. *Understanding the Palestinian-Israeli Conflict*	956.9405
Bhutto, Benazir. *Reconciliation*	297.2
Blattman, Christopher. *Why We Fight*	303.6
Dalai Lama. *An Appeal to the World*	170
Friedman, Thomas L. ★*Thank You for Being Late*	303.48
Gates, Robert Michael. ★*Exercise of Power*	973.929
Gillard, Julia. ★*Women and Leadership*	158
Harari, Yuval N. ★*21 Lessons for the 21st Century*	909.82
Hill, Fiona. *There Is Nothing for You Here*	327.2
Hochschild, Adam. *Lessons from a Dark Time*	909.82
Kissinger, Henry. *Leadership*	303.3
Maddow, Rachel. *Blowout*	338.2
Marshall, Tim. *The Power of Geography*	320.1
Mishra, Pankaj. *Age of Anger*	909.8
Rice, Condoleezza. *Political Risk*	658.15
Scharre, Paul. *Four Battlegrounds*	006.3
Walton, Calder. *Spies*	327.1247
Weiner, Tim. *The Folly and the Glory*	327.73047
Wolf, Martin. ★*The Crisis of Democratic Capitalism*	330.12
Yergin, Daniel. *The New Map*	333.79

POLITICS AND GLOBAL AFFAIRS — WORLD POLITICS — AFRICA
Faloyin, Dipo. ★*Africa Is Not a Country*	960.33
Hammer, Joshua. *The Bad-Ass Librarians of Timbuktu*	025.8
Holloway, Kris. *Monique and the Mango Rains*	B
Malala, Justice. *The Plot to Save South Africa*	968.07
Prendergast, John. *Congo Stories*	967.5103
Reid, Stuart A. *The Lumumba Plot*	967.51
Searcey, Dionne. *In Pursuit of Disobedient Women*	B
Wainaina, Binyavanga. ★*How to Write About Africa*	814

POLITICS AND GLOBAL AFFAIRS — WORLD POLITICS — ASIA
Bhutto, Benazir. *Reconciliation*	297.2
Cheung, Karen. *The Impossible City*	951.25
Dikotter, Frank. *China After Mao*	951.05
Evangelista, Patricia. ★*Some People Need Killing*	364.4
Fifield, Anna. *The Great Successor*	B

PUBLIC LIBRARY CORE COLLECTION: NONFICTION
Twentieth Edition

Jang, Jin-Sung. *Dear Leader*	B
Jeppesen, Travis. *See You Again in Pyongyang*	951.93
Kaplan, Robert D. *The Loom of Time*	327
Langewiesche, William. *The Atomic Bazaar*	355.02
Lankov, A. N. *The Real North Korea*	951.9304
Lieven, Anatol. *Pakistan*	954.9105
Lim, Louisa. *Indelible City*	951.25
Loyn, David. *The Long War*	958.104
Osnos, Evan. *Age of Ambition*	951.06
Pang, Amelia. ★*Made in China*	331.11
Parry, Richard Lloyd. *Ghosts of the Tsunami*	952.05
Pilling, David. *Bending Adversity*	952.0512
Roy, Arundhati. *Walking with the Comrades*	954
Schell, Orville. *Wealth and Power*	920
Strittmatter, Kai. *We Have Been Harmonized*	323.44
Thant Myint-U. *The Hidden History of Burma*	959.105
Tudor, Daniel. *North Korea Confidential*	951.93
Whitlock, Craig. *The Afghanistan Papers*	958.104
Wood, Michael. *The Story of China*	951
Xue, XInran. *The Book of Secrets*	951.05

POLITICS AND GLOBAL AFFAIRS — WORLD POLITICS — EUROPE

Conradi, Peter J. *Who Lost Russia?*	947.086
Friedman, George. *Flashpoints*	940.56
Galeotti, Mark. *A Short History of Russia*	947.086
Garrels, Anne. *Putin Country*	947
Gessen, Masha. *The Future Is History*	947.086
Gessen, Masha. *Never Remember*	365
Harding, Luke. *Invasion*	947.7
Kasparov, Gary. *Winter Is Coming*	947.086
Kershaw, Ian. *The Global Age*	940.55
Khodorkovsky, Mikhail. *The Russia Conundrum*	947.086
Marton, Kati. ★*The Chancellor*	B
Miller, Christopher. *The War Came to Us*	947.7
Morris, Ian. *Geography Is Destiny*	941
Myers, Steven Lee. *The New Tsar*	B
Plokhy, Serhii. ★*The Gates of Europe*	947.7
Plokhy, Serhii. ★*The Russo-Ukrainian War*	947.7
Politkovskaya, Anna. *A Russian Diary*	947.086
Trentmann, Frank. *Out of the Darkness*	943.08
Walker, Shaun. *The Long Hangover*	947.086
Yaffa, Joshua. *Between Two Fires*	920
Zelensky, Volodymyr. *A Message from Ukraine*	947.7
Zygar, Mikhail. *All the Kremlin's Men*	947.086

POLITICS AND GLOBAL AFFAIRS — WORLD POLITICS — LATIN AMERICA

Vargas Llosa, Mario. *Sabers and Utopias*	980.03

POLITICS AND GLOBAL AFFAIRS — WORLD POLITICS — SOUTHWEST ASIA AND NORTH AFRICA (MIDDLE EAST)

Abou El Fadl, Khaled. *The Great Theft*	297.09
Abouzeid, Rania. *No Turning Back*	956.9104
Barr, James. *Lords of the Desert*	956
Coll, Steve. ★*The Achilles Trap*	956.7044
Dagher, Sam. *Assad or We Burn the Country*	956.9104
Engel, Richard. *And Then All Hell Broke Loose*	956.05
Ghattas, Kim. *Black Wave*	955.05
Ghazvinian, John. *America and Iran*	327
Hessler, Peter. *The Buried*	962.05
Hope, Bradley. *Blood and Oil*	B
Kaplan, Robert D. *The Loom of Time*	327
Kershner, Isabel. *The Land of Hope and Fear*	956.9405
Malek, Alia. *The Home That Was Our Country*	B
Murad, Nadia. ★*The Last Girl*	B
Nasr, Seyyed Vali Reza. *The Shia Revival*	297.8
Nixon, John. *Debriefing the President*	956.7044
Samer. *The Raqqa Diaries*	956.9104
Walsh, Declan. *The Nine Lives of Pakistan*	954.91
Warrick, Joby. *Black Flags*	956.9104
Warrick, Joby. *Red Line*	956.9104
Worth, Robert Forsyth. ★*A Rage for Order*	909
Zuckoff, Mitchell. *The Secret Gate*	958.104

POLITICS AND GLOBAL AFFAIRS — WORLD POLITICS — SOUTHWEST ASIA AND NORTH AFRICA (MIDDLE EAST) — ISRAEL AND PALESTINE

Abu Sayf, Atif. *The Drone Eats with Me*	B
Abuelaish, Izzeldin. *I Shall Not Hate*	B
Carter, Jimmy. *Palestine*	956.04
Goodman, Micah. *Catch-67*	956.04
Gordis, Daniel. *Impossible Takes Longer*	956.94
Halevi, Yossi Klein. ★*Letters to My Palestinian Neighbor*	956.94054
Khalidi, Rashid. ★*The Hundred Years' War on Palestine*	956.9405
Mitchell, George J. *A Path to Peace*	956.9405
Nusseibeh, Sari. *Once Upon a Country*	B
Pfeffer, Anshel. *Bibi*	B
Qashu, Sayed. *Native*	892.4
Sefarad, Mikhael. *The Wall and the Gate*	341.48
Shehadeh, Raja. *Where the Line Is Drawn*	956.9405
Sokatch, Daniel. *Can We Talk About Israel?*	956.9405
Tamimi, Ahed. ★*They Called Me a Lioness*	B

POLITICS AND GLOBAL AFFAIRS — WORLD POLITICS — UNITED STATES

Ackerman, Spencer. *Reign of Terror*	973.931
Alberta, Tim. *American Carnage*	324.2734
Bergen, Peter L. *The Rise and Fall of Osama Bin Laden*	958.104
Brill, Steven. *Tailspin*	306.0973
Burns, William J. *The Back Channel*	B
Cadava, Geraldo L. *The Hispanic Republican*	324.2734089
Chertoff, Michael. *Exploding Data*	343.7309
Chomsky, Noam. *Who Rules the World?*	327.73
Cohen, Roger. *An Affirming Flame*	071
Diaz, Tom. *The Last Gun*	338.4
Edstrom, Erik. *Un-American*	B
Enrich, David. *Servants of the Damned*	340.023
Farrow, Ronan. *War on Peace*	327.73
Frum, David. *Trumpocracy*	973.933
Gans, John. *White House Warriors*	355
Gellman, Barton. ★*Dark Mirror*	B
Ghazvinian, John. *America and Iran*	327
Graff, Garrett M. *Raven Rock*	363.350973
Immerwahr, Daniel. *How to Hide an Empire*	973
Jayapal, Pramila. *Use the Power You Have*	B
Johnston, David Cay. *It's Even Worse Than You Think*	973.933
Kaiser, Robert G. *Act of Congress*	346.73
Karl, Jonathan. *Front Row at the Trump Show*	973.933
Kennedy, Robert Francis. *RFK*	973.92
Kurtz, Howard. *Media Madness*	973.933
McAlevey, Jane. *A Collective Bargain*	331.890973
Mead, Walter Russell. *The Arc of a Covenant*	327.73
Murphy, Chris. ★*The Violence Inside Us*	303.60973
Nance, Malcolm W. *The Plot to Betray America*	973.933
Newitz, Annalee. *Stories Are Weapons*	355.3
Obama, Barack. ★*The Audacity of Hope*	B
Obama, Barack. ★*A Promised Land*	B
Packer, George. *Last Best Hope*	973.93
Packer, George. ★*The Unwinding*	973.924
Putnam, Robert D. *Our Kids*	305.5
Rather, Dan. *What Unites Us*	323.6
Reid, T. R. *A Fine Mess*	336.200973
Rothschild, Mike. *The Storm Is Upon Us*	973.933
Sexton, Jared Yates. *American Rule*	973
Sowell, Thomas. *Wealth, Poverty and Politics*	330.1
Spruill, Marjorie Julian. *Divided We Stand*	305.42
Stephanopoulos, George. ★*The Situation Room*	973.09
Tribe, Laurence H. *Uncertain Justice*	342.73
Trump, Mary L. *Too Much and Never Enough*	B
Warren, Elizabeth. *This Fight Is Our Fight*	305.5
Will, George F. *The Conservative Sensibility*	320.520973
Woodward, Bob. *Fear*	973.933

POLITICS AND GOVERNMENT

Abrams, Stacey. *Our Time Is Now*	324.60973
Abu Sayf, Atif. *The Drone Eats with Me*	B
Abuelaish, Izzeldin. *I Shall Not Hate*	B
Achorn, Edward. *The Lincoln Miracle*	973.6
Ackerman, Spencer. *Reign of Terror*	973.931
Alberta, Tim. *American Carnage*	324.2734
Allen, Jonathan. *Lucky*	324.973
Allen, Jonathan. *Shattered*	324.973
Allgor, Catherine. *A Perfect Union*	B
Allitt, Patrick. *The Conservatives*	320.520973
Allport, Alan. *Britain at Bay*	940.53
Amar, Akhil Reed. ★*America's Constitution*	342.7302
Amis, Martin. *Koba the Dread*	947.084
Anderson, Carol. ★*One Person, No Vote*	324.6
Applebaum, Anne. ★*Gulag*	365
Applebaum, Anne. *Iron Curtain*	947
Armstrong, Karen. *Jerusalem*	956.94
Arnsdorf, Isaac. ★*Finish What We Started*	320.52

AUTHOR, TITLE, SERIES AND SUBJECT INDEX

Ayers, Edward L. *American Visions*	973.5
Bade, Rachael. ★*Unchecked*	342.73
Baer, Daniel Brooks. *The Four Tests*	320.973
Baier, Bret. *Three Days in January*	B
Baime, A. J. *The Accidental President*	B
Baker, Peter. *The Divider*	973.933
Baker, Peter. *The Man Who Ran Washington*	B
Ball, Molly. ★*Pelosi*	B
Balz, Daniel J. *The Battle for America, 2008*	973.932
Baron, Martin. ★*Collision of Power*	070.4
Barr, James. *A Line in the Sand*	956
Barron, David J. *Waging War*	342.73
Beeman, Richard R. *Our Lives, Our Fortunes and Our Sacred Honor*	973.3
Bender, Michael C. *"Frankly, We Did Win This Election"*	973.933
Berg, A. Scott. ★*Wilson*	B
Berman, Ari. ★*Minority Rule*	305.809
Berman, Geoffrey. *Holding the Line*	345.73
Beschloss, Michael R. *The Conquerors*	940.53
Bharara, Preet. *Doing Justice*	347.73
Bhutto, Benazir. *Reconciliation*	297.2
Bird, Kai. *The Outlier*	973.926
Bix, Herbert P. *Hirohito and the Making of Modern Japan*	B
Bogus, Carl T. *Buckley*	B
Boles, John B. *Jefferson*	B
Bordewich, Fergus M. *America's Great Debate*	973.6
Bordewich, Fergus M. *Congress at War*	324.2734
Borman, Tracy. *Henry VIII and the Men Who Made Him*	942.05
Borneman, Walter R. *Polk*	B
Bouverie, Tim. *Appeasement*	327.41043
Bowden, Mark. *The Steal*	973.933
Boykin, Keith. *Race Against Time*	305.8
Branch, Taylor. *The Clinton Tapes*	973.929
Brand, Christo. *Mandela*	B
Brands, H. W. ★*Andrew Jackson, His Life and Times*	B
Brands, H. W. *The First American*	B
Brands, H. W. ★*Founding Partisans*	973.3
Brands, H. W. ★*Heirs of the Founders*	973.5
Brands, H. W. ★*Our First Civil War*	973.3
Brands, H. W. *Reagan*	B
Brands, H. W. *Traitor to His Class*	B
Brands, H. W. *Woodrow Wilson*	B
Brazile, Donna. *For Colored Girls Who Have Considered Politics*	328.73
Brennan, Jason. *Libertarianism*	320.51
Brettschneider, Corey Lang. *The Oath and the Office*	342.73
Brettschneider, Corey Lang. *The Presidents and the People*	342.73
Brewster, Todd. *Lincoln's Gamble*	973.7
Brill, Steven. *Class Warfare*	371.010973
Brill, Steven. *Tailspin*	306.0973
Brinkley, Alan. *John F. Kennedy*	B
Broadwater, Jeff. *James Madison*	B
Broers, Michael. *Napoleon*	B
Broers, Michael. *Napoleon*	B
Brokaw, Tom. *The Fall of Richard Nixon*	B
Brookhiser, Richard. *Give Me Liberty*	320.540973
Brower, Kate Andersen. *First in Line*	920
Brown, Peter. *Through the Eye of a Needle*	270.1
Bryant, Howard. *Full Dissidence*	306.20973
Bunting, Josiah. *Ulysses S. Grant*	B
Burke, Edmund. *Reflections on the Revolution in France*	944.04
Burlingame, Michael. *Abraham Lincoln*	B
Burstein, Andrew. *Madison and Jefferson*	973.4
Bush, George W. *Decision Points*	B
Caldwell, Christopher. *The Age of Entitlement*	305.240973
Camus, Albert. *Resistance, Rebellion, and Death*	844
Cannadine, David. ★*Mellon*	B
Carlin, John. *Playing the Enemy*	968.06
Carlson, Brady. *Dead Presidents*	B
Caro, Robert A. ★*The Passage of Power*	B
Carpenter, Amanda B. *Gaslighting America*	973.933
Carroll, Rory. *There Will Be Fire*	363.325
Carruthers, Charlene A. *Unapologetic*	305.48
Carter, Jimmy. *A Full Life*	B
Carter, Jimmy. *Keeping Faith*	B
Carter, Jimmy. *White House Diary*	973.926
Carter, Miranda. *George, Nicholas and Wilhelm*	940.3
Caruana Galizia, Paul. ★*A Death in Malta*	364.15
Carwardine, Richard. *Lincoln*	B
Chait, Jonathan. *Audacity*	973.932
Chammah, Maurice. ★*Let the Lord Sort Them*	364.66
Chandrasekaran, Rajiv. *Imperial Life in the Emerald City*	956.7044
Chang, Jung. *Empress Dowager Cixi*	B
Charter, David. *Royal Audience*	941.085
Cheney, Liz. *Oath and Honor*	328.73
Cheney, Lynne V. *James Madison*	B
Cheney, Lynne V. *The Virginia Dynasty*	B
Chernow, Ron. ★*Alexander Hamilton*	B
Chernow, Ron. ★*Grant*	B
Chertoff, Michael. *Exploding Data*	343.7309
Childers, Thomas. *The Third Reich*	943.086
Chomsky, Noam. *Who Rules the World?*	327.73
Chozick, Amy. *Chasing Hillary*	B
Christie, Chris. *Let Me Finish*	B
Cicero, Marcus Tullius. ★*The Republic*	320.1
Clarke, Thurston. *JFK's Last Hundred Days*	B
Clarke, Thurston. *The Last Campaign*	B
Clinton, Bill. *My Life*	B
Clinton, Hillary Rodham. *Living History*	B
Clinton, Hillary Rodham. *What Happened*	328.73
Coates, Ta-Nehisi. ★*We Were Eight Years in Power*	305.896
Cohen, Adam. ★*Supreme Inequality*	347.73
Cohen, Andrew. *Two Days in June*	973.922
Cohen, Jared. *Life After Power*	973.09
Coleman, David G. *The Fourteenth Day*	973.922092
Coll, Steve. ★*The Achilles Trap*	956.7044
Coll, Steve. ★*Ghost Wars*	958.104
Coll, Steve. *Private Empire*	338.7
Collins, Gail. *William Henry Harrison*	B
Collins-Dexter, Brandi. *Black Skinhead*	324.2734
Conason, Joe. *The Longest Con*	320.52
Connelly, Matthew James. *The Declassification Engine*	352.3
Cooper, John Milton. *Woodrow Wilson*	B
Cornwell, John. *Hitler's Pope*	B
Cummings, Elijah. ★*We're Better Than This*	B
D'Antonio, Michael. *The Hunting of Hillary*	B
Dagher, Sam. *Assad or We Burn the Country*	956.9104
Dallek, Robert. ★*Franklin D. Roosevelt*	B
Dallek, Robert. *Harry S. Truman*	B
Dallek, Robert. *Let Every Nation Know*	B
Dallek, Robert. *An Unfinished Life*	B
Darnton, Robert. *The Revolutionary Temper*	944
Denevi, Timothy. *Freak Kingdom*	B
Dikotter, Frank. *China After Mao*	951.05
Dobbs, Michael. *King Richard*	973.924
Donald, Aida DiPace. *Citizen Soldier*	B
Dorey-Stein, Beck. *From the Corner of the Oval*	B
Dower, John W. *Embracing Defeat*	952.04
Draper, Robert. *To Start a War*	956.7044
Dray, Philip. *Capitol Men*	973.8
Driver, Justin. *The Schoolhouse Gate*	344.73
DuBois, Ellen Carol. *Suffrage*	324.6
Duckworth, Tammy. *Every Day Is a Gift*	B
Duiker, William J. *Ho Chi Minh*	B
Dunn, Harry. *Standing My Ground*	B
DuVal, Kathleen. ★*Native Nations*	970.004
Dwork, Deborah. ★*Holocaust*	940
Eisner, Peter. *The Pope's Last Crusade*	282.092
Eizenstat, Stuart. ★*President Carter*	B
Elkins, Caroline. *Legacy of Violence*	909
Ellis, Joseph J. *American Creation*	973.3
Ellis, Joseph J. ★*American Dialogue*	973.3
Ellis, Joseph J. *American Sphinx*	973.4
Ellis, Joseph J. *The Cause*	973.3
Ellis, Joseph J. *First Family*	973.4
Ellis, Joseph J. *Founding Brothers*	973.4
Ellis, Joseph J. *The Quartet*	342.7302
Emanuel, Rahm. *The Nation City*	352.23
Engel, Richard. *And Then All Hell Broke Loose*	956.05
English, Charlie. *The Gallery of Miracles and Madness*	709.04
Ephron, Dan. *Killing a King*	956.9405
Evangelista, Patricia. ★*Some People Need Killing*	364.4
Evans, Richard J. *The Pursuit of Power*	940.2
Evans, Richard J. *The Third Reich in Power, 1933-1939*	943.086
Everitt, Anthony. *Cicero*	B
Everitt, Anthony. *Hadrian and the Triumph of Rome*	B
Fallows, James M. *Our Towns*	306.0973
Faloyin, Dipo. ★*Africa Is Not a Country*	960.33

PUBLIC LIBRARY CORE COLLECTION: NONFICTION
Twentieth Edition

Farrell, John A. *Clarence Darrow*	B
Farrell, John A. ★*Richard Nixon*	B
Farrell, John A. *Ted Kennedy*	B
Farris, Scott. *Almost President*	324.973
Feldman, Noah. *The Broken Constitution*	973.7
Feldman, Noah. *The Three Lives of James Madison*	B
Feldstein, Mark Avrom. *Poisoning the Press*	973.924092
Fifield, Anna. *The Great Successor*	B
Filkins, Dexter. *The Forever War*	956.7044
Finan, Christopher M. *How Free Speech Saved Democracy*	342.73
Finkelman, Paul. *Millard Fillmore*	B
Finn, Peter. *The Zhivago Affair*	891.73
Fishman, Charles. ★*One Giant Leap*	629.45
Flexner, James Thomas. *George Washington and the New Nation, 1783-1793*	973.4
Flexner, James Thomas. *George Washington*	B
Foer, Franklin. ★*The Last Politician*	973.934
Foner, Eric. *The Fiery Trial*	973.7092
Foner, Eric. *Forever Free*	973.8
Foner, Eric. ★*Reconstruction*	973.8
Forche, Carolyn. *What You Have Heard Is True*	B
Frank, Barney. *Frank*	B
Frank, Jeffrey. *The Trials of Harry S. Truman*	973.918
Frank, Thomas. *The People, No*	320.56
Franklin, Benjamin. ★*Autobiography, Poor Richard, and Later Writings*	973.2
Franklin, Benjamin. *The Compleated Autobiography*	B
Fraser, Antonia. *Faith and Treason*	942.06
Fraser, Steve. *The Age of Acquiescence*	973.91
Freeman, Joanne B. *The Field of Blood*	973.7
Friedman, Barry. ★*Unwarranted*	344.7305
Friedman, Barry. *The Will of the People*	347.73
Friedman, George. *Flashpoints*	940.56
Friedman, Thomas L. ★*From Beirut to Jerusalem*	956.04
Friedman, Thomas L. ★*Thank You for Being Late*	303.48
Fritzsche, Peter. *Life and Death in the Third Reich*	943.086
Frum, David. *Trumpocracy*	973.933
Gabler, Neal. ★*Against the Wind*	B
Gabler, Neal. *Catching the Wind*	B
Gage, Beverly. *G-Man*	B
Galeotti, Mark. *A Short History of Russia*	947.086
Gandhi. *An Autobiography*	B
Ganz, John. *When the Clock Broke*	320.52
Garrow, David J. *Rising Star*	B
Gates, Robert Michael. ★*Exercise of Power*	973.929
Gellman, Barton. ★*Dark Mirror*	B
Gerwarth, Robert. *Hitler's Hangman*	B
Gessen, Masha. *The Future Is History*	947.086
Gessen, Masha. *Never Remember*	365
Gessen, Masha. *Surviving Autocracy*	973.933
Gevisser, Mark. *A Legacy of Liberation*	B
Gienapp, William E. *Abraham Lincoln and Civil War America*	B
Gillette, Michael L. *Lady Bird Johnson*	B
Giridharadas, Anand. ★*The Persuaders*	320.973
Goldsworthy, Adrian Keith. *Antony and Cleopatra*	937
Goldsworthy, Adrian Keith. *Augustus*	B
Goldsworthy, Adrian Keith. ★*Caesar*	B
Goodheart, Adam. *1861*	973.7
Goodwin, Doris Kearns. ★*The Bully Pulpit*	973.91
Goodwin, Doris Kearns. ★*Leadership in Turbulent Times*	973.09
Goodwin, Doris Kearns. ★*Team of Rivals*	B
Gordon-Reed, Annette. *Andrew Johnson*	B
Gordon-Reed, Annette. ★*Most Blessed of the Patriarchs*	973.4
Gourevitch, Philip. *We Wish to Inform You That Tomorrow We Will Be Killed with Our Families*	364.15
Graff, Garrett M. *Raven Rock*	363.350973
Graff, Garrett M. *Watergate*	973.924
Greenberg, Amy S. *Lady First*	B
Gristwood, Sarah. *The Tudors in Love*	941.05
Groom, Winston. *The Patriots*	920
Guelzo, Allen C. *Lincoln and Douglas*	973.6
Guerrero, Jean. *Hatemonger*	B
Guevara, Che. *Diary of a Combatant*	972.91063
Gutzman, Kevin R. C. *The Jeffersonians*	973.5
Hahn, Steven. *A Nation Under Our Feet*	975
Halberstam, David. *The Best and the Brightest*	973.92
Halberstam, David. *The Fifties*	973.92
Halevi, Yossi Klein. ★*Letters to My Palestinian Neighbor*	956.94054
Hardacre, Helen. *Shinto*	299.5
Hasen, Richard L. *Election Meltdown*	324.973
Hayek, Friedrich A. von. *The Road to Serfdom*	330.1
Haygood, Wil. *Showdown*	B
Healey, Jonathan. *The Blazing World*	941.06
Hendrickson, Paul. *The Living and the Dead*	959.704
Hennessey, Jonathan. *The United States Constitution*	741.5
Hennessey, Susan. *Unmaking the Presidency*	973.933
Hessler, Peter. *The Buried*	962.05
Hill, Clint. *Five Presidents*	B
Hill, Katie. *She Will Rise*	305.42
Hirono, Mazie. *Heart of Fire*	B
Hirshman, Linda R. *Sisters in Law*	347.73
Hitchens, Christopher. *Thomas Jefferson*	B
Hitler, Adolf. *Mein Kampf*	B
Hochschild, Adam. *American Midnight*	973.91
Hochschild, Adam. *King Leopold's Ghost*	967.51
Hochschild, Adam. *Rebel Cinderella*	B
Hochschild, Adam. *Spain in Our Hearts*	946.081
Hoffman, Bruce. *Anonymous Soldiers*	956.94
Hoffman, Carl. *Liar's Circus*	973.933
Hoffman, David E. *Give Me Liberty*	B
Hogeland, William. *Declaration*	973.3
Holzer, Harold. *Brought Forth on This Continent*	973.7
Holzer, Harold. *A Just and Generous Nation*	973.7092
Hope, Bradley. *Blood and Oil*	B
Horn, Jonathan. *Washington's End*	B
Howe, Daniel Walker. *What Hath God Wrought*	973.5
Hubbard, Ben (Journalist). *Mbs*	B
Hunt, Patrick. *Hannibal*	B
Hutchinson, Cassidy. *Enough*	B
Inskeep, Steve. *Jacksonland*	973.56
Isaacson, Walter. ★*Benjamin Franklin*	B
Isenberg, Nancy. *The Problem of Democracy*	973.4
Ishikawa, Masaji. ★*A River in Darkness*	B
Jackson, Julian. *De Gaulle*	B
Jackson, Kellie Carter. *We Refuse*	323.1196
Jacobsen, Annie. *Phenomena*	133.8
Jang, Jin-Sung. *Dear Leader*	B
Jayapal, Pramila. *Use the Power You Have*	B
Jefferson, Thomas. *Writings*	973.3
Jeppesen, Travis. *See You Again in Pyongyang*	951.93
Johnson, Lyndon B. *Taking Charge*	973.923
Johnson, Paul. *Churchill*	B
Johnson, Paul. *Eisenhower*	B
Johnson, Paul. *George Washington*	B
Johnson, Paul. *Napoleon*	B
Johnston, David Cay. *It's Even Worse Than You Think*	973.933
Jones, Brenda. *Alexandria Ocasio-Cortez*	B
Jones, Brenda. *Maxine Waters*	B
Judt, Tony. *Postwar*	940.55
Kaiser, Robert G. *Act of Congress*	346.73
Kaplan, Robert D. *The Loom of Time*	327
Karl, Jonathan. *Betrayal*	973.933
Karl, Jonathan. *Front Row at the Trump Show*	973.933
Karl, Jonathan. *Tired of Winning*	973.933
Katznelson, Ira. *Fear Itself*	973.917
Kazin, Michael. *What It Took to Win*	324.2736
Kennedy, John F. *Profiles in Courage*	920
Kerry, John. *Every Day Is Extra*	B
Kershaw, Ian. *Hitler*	B
Kershaw, Ian. *Hitler*	B
Kershner, Isabel. *The Land of Hope and Fear*	956.9405
Kertzer, David I. *The Pope Who Would Be King*	282.092
Khlevniuk, Oleg V. *Stalin*	B
Khodorkovsky, Mikhail. *The Russia Conundrum*	947.086
King, Greg. *Twilight of Empire*	943.6
Kinzer, Stephen. ★*The True Flag*	327.73
Kirtzman, Andrew. *Giuliani*	B
Klagsbrun, Francine. *Lioness*	B
Klare, Michael T. *All Hell Breaking Loose*	355.20973
Klay, Phil. *Uncertain Ground*	359.9
Klein, Ezra. ★*Why We're Polarized*	306.0973
Klobuchar, Amy. ★*Antitrust*	343.73
Korda, Michael. *Clouds of Glory*	B
Kornacki, Steve. *The Red and the Blue*	306.20973
Kotz, Nick. *Judgment Days*	323
Kranish, Michael. *Trump Revealed*	B

AUTHOR, TITLE, SERIES AND SUBJECT INDEX

Krugman, Paul R. *Arguing with Zombies*	330.973
Kurtz, Howard. *Media Madness*	973.933
Lamb, Christina. *House of Stone*	968.91
Langewiesche, William. *The Atomic Bazaar*	355.02
Langguth, A. J. *After Lincoln*	973.8
Lankov, A. N. *The Real North Korea*	951.9304
Larman, Alexander. *The Windsors at War*	940.53
Larson, Edward J. *The Return of George Washington*	B
Lasch, Christopher. ★*The Revolt of the Elites*	306
Lawler, Andrew. *Under Jerusalem*	956.94
Leaming, Barbara. *Mrs. Kennedy*	B
Lee, Corky. ★*Corky Lee's Asian America*	770
Lee, Heath Hardage. ★*The League of Wives*	959.704
Lee, Sung-Yoon. *The Sister*	951.93
Lemann, Nicholas. *Redemption*	975
Lemann, Nicholas. *Transaction Man*	330.973
Leonnig, Carol. *I Alone Can Fix It*	973.933
Levine, Bruce C. *Thaddeus Stevens*	B
Levine, Robert S. ★*The Failed Promise*	973.8
Lewis, John. ★*Run; Book One*	741.5
Lewis, Michael. ★*The Premonition*	614.5
Liao, Yiwu. *Bullets and Opium*	951.05
Lichtman, Allan J. *The Embattled Vote in America*	324.6
Lim, Louisa. *Indelible City*	951.25
Lim, Louisa. *The People's Republic of Amnesia*	951.05
Lincoln, Abraham. *Speeches and Writings, 1832-1858*	973.5
Lincoln, Abraham. *Speeches and Writings, 1859-1865*	973.6
Lithwick, Dahlia. *Lady Justice*	345.73
Litt, David. *Democracy in One Book or Less*	321.8
Litt, David. *Thanks, Obama*	B
Logevall, Fredrik. ★*JFK*	B
Longerich, Peter. *Goebbels*	B
Longerich, Peter. *Hitler*	B
Lowenstein, Roger. *Ways and Means*	973.7
Loyn, David. *In Afghanistan*	958.1
Lukacs, John. *Five Days in London, May 1940*	940.53
Macintyre, Ben. *Double Cross*	940.54
Maddow, Rachel. *Bag Man*	B
Mahjoub, Jamal. *A Line in the River*	962.404
Mahoney, Richard D. *Sons & Brothers*	920
Mahtani, Shibani. *Among the Braves*	951.25
Maier, Pauline. *American Scripture*	973.3
Maier, Pauline. *Ratification*	342.7302
Malala, Justice. *The Plot to Save South Africa*	968.07
Manchester, William. *The Last Lion, Winston Spencer Churchill.*	B
Manchester, William. *The Last Lion, Winston Spencer Churchill.*	B
Manchester, William. *The Last Lion, Winston Spencer Churchill.*	B
Mandela, Nelson. *Dare Not Linger*	B
Mandela, Nelson. *In His Own Words*	B
Mandela, Nelson. ★*Long Walk to Freedom*	B
Mandela, Nelson. *Mandela*	B
Mandela, Nelson. *The Prison Letters of Nelson Mandela*	968.06092
Maraniss, David. ★*Barack Obama*	B
Maraniss, David. *They Marched into Sunlight*	959.704
Martin, Jonathan. *This Will Not Pass*	973.933
Martini, Adrienne. *Somebody's Gotta Do It*	B
Marton, Kati. ★*The Chancellor*	B
Marton, Kati. *Hidden Power*	B
Matthews, Christopher. *Bobby Kennedy*	B
Matthews, Christopher. *Kennedy & Nixon*	973.922
May, Gary. *John Tyler*	B
Mayer, Jane. ★*Dark Money*	973.932
Mayer, Jane. *The Dark Side*	973.931
Mazzeo, Tilar J. *Sisters in Resistance*	945.091
McCoy, Alfred W. *A Question of Torture*	323.4
McCraw, David Edward. *Truth in Our Times*	342.7308
McCraw, Thomas K. ★*The Founders and Finance*	330.973
McCullough, David G. ★*John Adams*	B
McCullough, David G. *Truman*	B
McDonough, Frank. *The Hitler Years*	943.086
McGrath, Tim. *James Monroe*	B
McNamara, Robert S. *In Retrospect*	959.704
McPhee, Peter. *Robespierre*	B
McPherson, James M. ★*Tried by War*	973.7
Meacham, Jon. ★*American Lion*	B
Meacham, Jon. ★*And There Was Light*	B
Meacham, Jon. ★*Destiny and Power*	B
Meacham, Jon. ★*The Soul of America*	973
Meacham, Jon. ★*Thomas Jefferson*	B
Mead, Walter Russell. *The Arc of a Covenant*	327.73
Medvedev, Roy Aleksandrovich. *Let History Judge*	947.084
Merry, Robert W. *A Country of Vast Designs*	B
Merry, Robert W. *President McKinley*	B
Miller, Scott. *The President and the Assassin*	973.8
Minutaglio, Bill. *The Most Dangerous Man in America*	B
Miraldi, Robert. *Seymour Hersh*	B
Mitchell, George J. *A Path to Peace*	956.9405
Mogelson, Luke. *The Storm Is Here*	973.933
Moore, Charles. *Margaret Thatcher*	941.085
Morley, Jefferson. *Scorpions' Dance*	973.924
Morris, Benny. *1948*	956.04
Morris, Edmund. ★*Colonel Roosevelt*	B
Morris, Edmund. ★*The Rise of Theodore Roosevelt*	B
Morris, Edmund. ★*Theodore Rex*	973.911
Murphy, Andrew R. *William Penn*	B
Murphy, Bruce Allen. *Scalia*	B
Murphy, Chris. ★*The Violence Inside Us*	303.60973
Myers, Steven Lee. *The New Tsar*	B
Nasr, Seyyed Vali Reza. *The Shia Revival*	297.8
Navai, Ramita. *City of Lies*	955
Neiwert, David A. ★*The Age of Insurrection*	303.48
Nelson, Craig. ★*V Is for Victory*	973.917
Nemat, Marina. *Prisoner of Tehran*	B
Neu, Charles E. *Colonel House*	B
Newton, Michael A. *Enemy of the State*	345.567
Nixon, John. *Debriefing the President*	956.7044
Nussbaum, Martha Craven. *The Monarchy of Fear*	306.20973
Nusseibeh, Sari. *Once Upon a Country*	B
Obama, Barack. ★*The Audacity of Hope*	B
Obama, Barack. ★*A Promised Land*	B
Obama, Michelle. ★*Becoming*	B
Oliphant, Thomas. ★*The Road to Camelot*	973.922092
Oller, John. *American Queen*	B
Olson, Lynne. *Last Hope Island*	940.53
Olson, Lynne. *Those Angry Days*	940.53
Olson, Lynne. *Troublesome Young Men*	941.084
Oren, Michael B. *Six Days of War*	956.04
Osnos, Evan. *Age of Ambition*	951.06
Osnos, Evan. *Joe Biden*	B
Osnos, Evan. *Wildland*	973.93
Packer, George. *The Assassins' Gate*	956.7044
Packer, George. *Last Best Hope*	973.93
Packer, George. *Our Man*	B
Packer, George. ★*The Unwinding*	973.924
Page, Susan. ★*The Matriarch*	B
Paine, Thomas. ★*Rights of Man*	320.5
Pak, Jung H. *Becoming Kim Jong Un*	B
Pantsov, Alexander. *Mao*	B
Paul, Joel R. *Indivisible*	973.5
Paulsen, Michael Stokes. *The Constitution*	342.7302
Peres, Shimon. *No Room for Small Dreams*	B
Perlstein, Rick. ★*Reaganland*	973.926
Peters, Charles. *Lyndon B. Johnson*	B
Petri, Alexandra. *Nothing Is Wrong and Here Is Why*	973.933
Pfeffer, Anshel. *Bibi*	B
Philbrick, Nathaniel. *Travels with George*	973.4
Phillips, Adrian. *Fighting Churchill, Appeasing Hitler*	327.41043
Phillips, Kevin. *1775*	973.3
Pilling, David. *Bending Adversity*	952.0512
Plokhy, Serhii. ★*The Russo-Ukrainian War*	947.7
Politkovskaya, Anna. *A Russian Diary*	947.086
Prejean, Helen. *The Death of Innocents*	364.66
Preston, Paul. *A People Betrayed*	946
Preston, Paul. *The Spanish Holocaust*	946.081
Price, Polly J. *Plagues in the Nation*	614.4
Psaki, Jen. *Say More*	B
Purdum, Todd S. *An Idea Whose Time Has Come*	342.7308
Rakove, Jack N. *Revolutionaries*	973.3
Randall, Willard Sterne. *The Founders' Fortunes*	973.3
Raphael, Ray. *Mr. President*	352.230973
Rappleye, Charles. *Herbert Hoover in the White House*	B
Reagan, Ronald. *The Reagan Diaries*	B
Reagan, Ronald. *Reagan*	B
Reid, Stuart A. *The Lumumba Plot*	967.51
Reilly, Ryan J. ★*Sedition Hunters*	364.1
Remnick, David. *The Bridge*	B

PUBLIC LIBRARY CORE COLLECTION: NONFICTION
Twentieth Edition

Remnick, David. *Lenin's Tomb*	947.085
Reston, James. *The Conviction of Richard Nixon*	973.924092
Reynolds, David S. ★*Abe*	B
Rezaian, Jason. *Prisoner*	B
Rhodes, Benjamin J. *The World as It Is*	973.932
Rice, Condoleezza. *No Higher Honor*	B
Richardson, Heather Cox. *Democracy Awakening*	320.473
Richardson, Heather Cox. ★*How the South Won the Civil War*	306.20973
Ricks, Thomas E. ★*First Principles*	973.09
Risen, Clay. *The Bill of the Century*	342.7308
Roberts, Andrew. ★*Churchill*	B
Roberts, Andrew. *The Last King of America*	B
Roberts, Andrew. *Napoleon*	B
Robin, Corey. *The Enigma of Clarence Thomas*	347.73
Rohde, David. *In Deep*	973.933
Roll, David L. *George Marshall*	B
Rosenberg, Ian. *The Fight for Free Speech*	342.73
Rosenfeld, Seth. *Subversives*	378.1
Roth, Joseph. *What I Saw*	943
Rothkopf, David J. *American Resistance*	973.933
Rothschild, Mike. *The Storm Is Upon Us*	973.933
Roy, Arundhati. *Walking with the Comrades*	954
Rubenstein, David M. *The American Experiment*	973
Rumsfeld, Donald. *When the Center Held*	973.925092
Sage, Sami. *Democracy in Retrograde*	324
Sarotte, M. E. *The Collapse*	943.087
Satter, David. *The Less You Know, the Better You Sleep*	947.086
Schell, Orville. *Wealth and Power*	920
Schlesinger, Arthur M. *Journals, 1952-2000*	973.91092
Schmidt, Michael S. ★*Donald Trump v. The United States*	973.933
Schulman, Bruce J. *The Seventies*	973.92
Scott-Clark, Cathy. *The Forever Prisoner*	364.6
Seabrook, Nicholas R. *One Person, One Vote*	328.3
Searcey, Dionne. *In Pursuit of Disobedient Women*	B
Sebestyen, Victor. *Lenin*	B
Sebestyen, Victor. *Revolution 1989*	947.085
Sedgwick, John. *War of Two*	973.4
Self, Robert O. *All in the Family*	320.50973
Service, Robert. *Lenin—A Biography*	B
Sexton, Jared Yates. *American Rule*	973
Sharpton, Al. *Rise Up*	973.933
Shavit, Ari. *My Promised Land*	956.05
Shesol, Jeff. *Supreme Power*	347.73
Short, Philip. *Putin*	B
Shultz, Richard H. *The Secret War Against Hanoi*	959.704
Shuster, Simon. ★*The Showman*	B
Signer, Michael. *Cry Havoc*	305.800973
Simon, James F. *Eisenhower vs. Warren*	347.73
Simon, James F. *FDR and Chief Justice Hughes*	973.917092
Simon, James F. *What Kind of Nation*	342.73
Slahi, Mohamedou Ould. *The Mauritanian*	958.104
Slezkine, Yuri. *The House of Government*	947.084
Smith, David James. *Young Mandela*	B
Smith, Douglas. *Rasputin*	B
Smith, J. Douglas. *On Democracy's Doorstep*	342.73
Smith, Jean Edward. *Bush*	973.931
Smith, Jim B. *The Last Mission*	940.54
Smith, Mychal Denzel. *Stakes Is High*	973.933
Smith, Richard Norton. *On His Own Terms*	973.925092
Smith, Richard Norton. *An Ordinary Man*	B
Sokatch, Daniel. *Can We Talk About Israel?*	956.9405
Sommer, Will. ★*Trust the Plan*	973.933
Sontag, Susan. *At the Same Time*	814
Sorensen, Theodore C. *Counselor*	B
Soufan, Ali H. *The Black Banners Declassified*	363.325
Southon, Emma. *Agrippina*	B
Speer, Albert. *Inside the Third Reich*	B
Spencer, Kyle. *Raising Them Right*	320.5
Spitz, Bob. ★*Reagan*	B
Spruill, Marjorie Julian. *Divided We Stand*	305.42
Stahr, Walter. *Seward*	B
Stargardt, Nicholas. *The German War*	940.53
Steinberg, Jonathan. *Bismarck*	B
Steinberg, Jonny. *Winnie and Nelson*	920
Steinhauer, Jennifer. *The Firsts*	320.082
Stephanopoulos, George. ★*The Situation Room*	973.09
Stevens, Stuart. *The Conspiracy to End America*	324.2734
Stevens, Stuart. *It Was All a Lie*	324.2734
Stewart, David O. *George Washington*	973.4
Stiglitz, Joseph E. *Globalization and Its Discontents*	337
Strauss, Barry S. *The Death of Caesar*	937
Strauss, Barry S. *Ten Caesars*	937
Strittmatter, Kai. *We Have Been Harmonized*	323.44
Suetonius. ★*The Twelve Caesars*	B
Sullivan, Kevin. *Trump on Trial*	342.73
Swanson, James L. *End of Days*	973.922092
Sweig, Julia. *Lady Bird Johnson*	B
Taibbi, Matt. *I Can't Breathe*	363.2
Talty, Stephan. *Agent Garbo*	940.5
Tau, Byron. ★*Means of Control*	363.25
Taubman, William. *Gorbachev*	B
Taubman, William. *Khrushchev*	B
Taylor, Fred. *1939*	940.53
Taylor, Fred. *The Berlin Wall*	943
Taylor, Nick. *American Made*	331.13
Tester, Jon. *Grounded*	B
Thomas, Evan. *Being Nixon*	B
Thomas, Gordon. *Defying Hitler*	920
Tocqueville, Alexis de. ★*Democracy in America*	320.973
Toobin, Jeffrey. *True Crimes and Misdemeanors*	973.933
Traub, James. *John Quincy Adams*	B
Trentmann, Frank. *Out of the Darkness*	943.08
Tribe, Laurence H. *Uncertain Justice*	342.73
Trump, Mary L. *Too Much and Never Enough*	B
Tuchman, Barbara W. *Stilwell and the American Experience in China, 1911-45*	B
Tumulty, Karen. *The Triumph of Nancy Reagan*	B
Turchin, Peter. *End Times*	320.01
Tye, Larry. ★*Demagogue*	B
Ullrich, Volker. ★*Eight Days in May*	943.086
Ullrich, Volker. *Hitler*	B
Ung, Loung. *First They Killed My Father*	959.604
Unger, Harlow G. *The Last Founding Father*	B
Updegrove, Mark K. *The Last Republicans*	973.928
Urofsky, Melvin I. *Dissent and the Supreme Court*	342.7302
Urofsky, Melvin I. *Louis D. Brandeis*	B
Vargas Llosa, Mario. *Sabers and Utopias*	980.03
Verini, James. *They Will Have to Die Now*	956.7044
Vladeck, Stephen I. *The Shadow Docket*	347.73
Vogel, Ezra F. *Deng XIaoping and the Transformation of China*	B
Vonnegut, Kurt. ★*A Man Without a Country*	818
Waldman, Michael. *The Supermajority*	347.73
Walker, Hunter. *The Truce*	324.2736
Walker, Shaun. *The Long Hangover*	947.086
Walsh, Declan. *The Nine Lives of Pakistan*	954.91
Ward, Geoffrey C. ★*The Roosevelts*	B
Warren, Elizabeth. *This Fight Is Our Fight*	305.5
Warrick, Joby. *Black Flags*	956.9104
Weale, Adrian. *Army of Evil*	940.54
Weber, Thomas. *Becoming Hitler*	B
Wehle, Kim. *What You Need to Know About Voting and Why*	324.60973
Weiner, Tim. *One Man Against the World*	B
Westad, Odd Arne. *The Cold War*	909.825
Whipple, Chris. *The Fight of His Life*	973.934
Whipple, Chris. *The Gatekeepers*	973.92092
White, Ronald C. *A. Lincoln*	B
White, Ronald C. ★*American Ulysses*	B
White, Ronald C. *Lincoln in Private*	B
Whitlock, Craig. *The Afghanistan Papers*	958.104
Whyte, Kenneth. *Hoover*	B
Widmer, Edward L. *Martin Van Buren*	B
Will, George F. *The Conservative Sensibility*	320.520973
Wills, Garry. *James Madison*	B
Wilson, Rick. *Running Against the Devil*	973.933
Wineapple, Brenda. *The Impeachers*	973.8
Wolff, Michael. *Landslide*	973.933
Wong, Chun Han. *Party of One*	951.06
Wood, Gordon S. *Empire of Liberty*	973.4
Wood, Gordon S. *Friends Divided*	920
Woods, Randall Bennett. *Prisoners of Hope*	973.923
Woodward, Bob. *Fear*	973.933
Woodward, Bob. *The Final Days*	B
Woodward, Bob. *Peril*	973.933
Woodward, Bob. *Shadow*	973.92
Woodward, C. Vann. *The Strange Career of Jim Crow*	305.896
Worth, Robert Forsyth. ★*A Rage for Order*	909

AUTHOR, TITLE, SERIES AND SUBJECT INDEX

Wright, Lawrence. *God Save Texas* — 917.64
Yaffa, Joshua. *Between Two Fires* — 920
Young, Ralph F. *Dissent* — 303.48
Yovanovitch, Marie. *Lessons from the Edge* — 973.933
Zamoyski, Adam. *Napoleon* — B
Zeitz, Joshua. *Building the Great Society* — 973.923
Zelensky, Volodymyr. *A Message from Ukraine* — 947.7
Zelizer, Julian E. *Burning Down the House* — 328.73
Zucchino, David. *Wilmington's Lie* — 305.8009756
Zygar, Mikhail. *All the Kremlin's Men* — 947.086
Zygar, Mikhail. *The Empire Must Die* — 947.08

POLITICS AND LITERATURE
Finn, Peter. *The Zhivago Affair* — 891.73
Nafisi, Azar. *Read Dangerously* — 809
Poirier, Agnes. *Left Bank* — 944
Shapiro, James. ★*The Playbook* — 792
Shapiro, James. *Shakespeare in a Divided America* — 822.33
Vargas Llosa, Mario. *Conversation at Princeton* — 868

POLITICS AND WAR
Barron, David J. *Waging War* — 342.73
Lambert, Malcolm. *God's Armies* — 956
The Politics of Mourning. McElya, Micki — 975.5
★*Politics*, 2nd Ed. Aristotle — 320

Politkovskaya, Anna
A Russian Diary — 947.086

POLITKOVSKAYA, ANNA
Igort. *The Ukrainian and Russian Notebooks* — 741.5

Polk. Borneman, Walter R. — B

POLK, JAMES K. (JAMES KNOX), 1795-1849
Borneman, Walter R. *Polk* — B
Greenberg, Amy S. *Lady First* — B
Merry, Robert W. *A Country of Vast Designs* — B

POLK, SARAH CHILDRESS, 1803-1891
Greenberg, Amy S. *Lady First* — B

Pollack, H. N.
A World Without Ice — 551.31

Pollack, Howard
★*George Gershwin* — B

Pollak, Lindsey
Recalculating — 650.1

The Pollan Family Table. Pollan, Corky — 641.5

Pollan, Corky
The Pollan Family Table — 641.5

Pollan, Michael
Cooked — 641.5
How to Change Your Mind — 615.7
The Omnivore's Dilemma — 394.1
★*This Is Your Mind on Plants* — 581.6

POLLAN, MICHAEL
Pollan, Michael. ★*This Is Your Mind on Plants* — 581.6

POLLINATION
Nordhaus, Hannah. *The Beekeeper's Lament* — 638

POLLOCK, JACKSON, 1912-1956
Smee, Sebastian. *The Art of Rivalry* — 700.92
Solomon, Deborah. *Jackson Pollock* — B

POLLUTION
Attenborough, David. *A Life on Our Planet* — 508
Atwood, Margaret. *Dearly* — 811
Bilott, Robert. *Exposure* — 344.04
Fagan, Brian M. *Climate Chaos* — 304.2
Fagin, Dan. *Toms River* — 363.7209749
Fields, Micah. ★*We Hold Our Breath* — 976.4
Kimble, Megan. ★*City Limits* — 388.1
O'Brien, Keith. *Paradise Falls* — 363.738
Owens, Jay. *Dust* — 551.51
Pasternak, Judy. *Yellow Dirt* — 979.1004
Rich, Nathaniel. *Second Nature* — 304.2

POLLUTION CONTROL
Miller, Char. *Gifford Pinchot and the Making of Modern Environmentalism* — B

POLLUTION PREVENTION
Allen, Brigette. *Living Without Plastic* — 640

Polly, Matthew
★*Bruce Lee* — B

POLO, MARCO, 1254-1323?
Belliveau, Denis. *In the Footsteps of Marco Polo* — 915
Bergreen, Laurence. *Marco Polo* — B

POLYGAMY
Beam, Alex. *American Crucifixion* — B

Denton, Sally. *The Colony* — 364.152
Jones, Faith. *Sex Cult Nun* — B
Wariner, Ruth. *The Sound of Gravel* — B

POLYMER CLAY SCULPTURE
Heaser, Sue. *The Polymer Clay Techniques Book* — 731.4
Pavelka, Lisa. *The Complete Book of Polymer Clay* — 738.1
Stone, Francesca. *Easy Homemade Pottery* — 738.1
The Polymer Clay Techniques Book. Heaser, Sue — 731.4

POLYNESIA
Thompson, Christina. *Sea People* — 305.8994

POLYNESIANS
Thompson, Christina. *Sea People* — 305.8994

POLYTHEISM
Doniger, Wendy. *On Hinduism* — 294.5

Pomegranates & Artichokes. Setareh, Saghar — 641.5

Pomerantsev, Peter
★*How to Win an Information War* — 940.53

POMPEII (EXTINCT CITY)
Beard, Mary. *The Fires of Vesuvius* — 937
Berry, Joanne. *The Complete Pompeii* — 937

Poniewozik, James
Audience of One — 324.7

PONS, SILVIA, 1919-1958
Moorehead, Caroline. *A House in the Mountains* — 940.53

Ponseca, Nicole
I Am a Filipino and This Is How We Cook — 641.595

Pontzen, Andrew
The Universe in a Box — 523.1

PONY EXPRESS
Grant, Will. *The Last Ride of the Pony Express* — 917.804

PONZI SCHEMES
Behar, Richard. *Madoff* — 364.16
Ward, Geoffrey C. *A Disposition to Be Rich* — B
Zuckoff, Mitchell. *Ponzi's Scheme* — B

Ponzi's Scheme. Zuckoff, Mitchell — B

PONZI, CHARLES
Zuckoff, Mitchell. *Ponzi's Scheme* — B

POODLES
Steinbeck, John. *Travels with Charley* — B

POOL (GAME)
Capelle, Philip B. ★*Play Your Best Straight Pool* — 790
McCumber, David. *Playing off the Rail* — B

POOL PLAYERS
McCumber, David. *Playing off the Rail* — B

Poole, Robert M.
Section 60 — 975.5

Poole, W. Scott
Vampira — B

POOR AFRICAN AMERICANS
Watkins, D. *Black Boy Smile* — B

POOR CHILDREN
Checkoway, Julie. *The Three-Year Swim Club* — 797.2
Dorr, Christina H. ★*Profiles in Resilience* — 028.5
Kozol, Jonathan. *Fire in the Ashes* — 362.77
Madrick, Jeffrey G. *Invisible Americans* — 362.7086
Tunstall, Tricia. *Changing Lives* — 780.71

POOR FAMILIES
Agee, James. ★*Cotton Tenants* — 976.1
Desmond, Matthew. ★*Evicted* — 339.4
Hansberry, Lorraine. ★*A Raisin in the Sun* — 812
Kozol, Jonathan. *Fire in the Ashes* — 362.77
McCourt, Frank. ★*Angela's Ashes* — 929
Phelan, Tom. *We Were Rich and We Didn't Know It* — B
Roy, Saumya. *Castaway Mountain* — 363.72
Smarsh, Sarah. ★*Heartland* — B
Vance, J. D. *Hillbilly Elegy* — B
Yancey, Philip. ★*Where the Light Fell* — B

POOR PEOPLE
Agee, James. ★*Cotton Tenants* — 976.1
Barber, William J. *We Are Called to Be a Movement* — 261.8
Boo, Katherine. ★*Behind the Beautiful Forevers* — 305.5
Brown, Claude. *Manchild in the Promised Land* — B
Bruder, Jessica. ★*Nomadland* — 331.3
Dorr, Christina H. ★*Profiles in Resilience* — 028.5
Dyson, Michael Eric. *Come Hell or High Water* — 976.3
Edin, Kathryn. *$2.00 a Day* — 339.4
Edin, Kathryn. ★*The Injustice of Place* — 339.4
Ehrenreich, Barbara. ★*Nickel and Dimed* — B

PUBLIC LIBRARY CORE COLLECTION: NONFICTION
Twentieth Edition

Freeman, Amanda. *Getting Me Cheap*	362.83
Goyal, Nikhil. ★*Live to See the Day*	305.5
Hedges, Chris. *Days of Destruction, Days of Revolt*	741.5
Houppert, Karen. *Chasing Gideon*	345.73
Isenberg, Nancy. *White Trash*	305.5
Kim, Anne. ★*Poverty for Profit*	302.5
Kozol, Jonathan. *Rachel and Her Children*	362.5
Lewis, Oscar. *The Children of Sanchez*	306.85
Lockhart, Chris. ★*Walking the Bowl*	362.7
Madrick, Jeffrey G. *Invisible Americans*	362.7086
Marie, Jane. ★*Selling the Dream*	658.8
McCaulley, Esau. *How Far to the Promised Land*	B
Messenger, Tony. *Profit and Punishment*	362.5
Mettler, Suzanne. *Degrees of Inequality*	378.73
Milanovic, Branko. *The Have and the Have-Nots*	339.2
Potts, Monica. *The Forgotten Girls*	
Pryce, Jessica. ★*Broken*	362.7
Rivlin, Gary. *Broke, Usa*	339.4
Walls, Jeannette. ★*The Glass Castle*	B

POOR WOMEN
Freeman, Amanda. *Getting Me Cheap*	362.83
Smarsh, Sarah. *She Come by It Natural*	782.42164

POP ART
Gopnik, Blake. ★*Warhol*	B
Sykes, Christopher Simon. *David Hockney*	B
Sykes, Christopher Simon. *David Hockney*	B

POP ARTISTS
Gopnik, Blake. ★*Warhol*	B

POP MUSICIANS
Breihan, Tom. ★*The Number Ones*	782.42164
John, Elton. ★*Me*	B

Pop Song. Pham, Larissa	709.2
The Pope and Mussolini. Kertzer, David I.	322
The Pope At War. Kertzer, David I.	940.53
Pope Francis. Vallely, Paul	B
Pope Francis Among the Wolves. Politi, Marco	282.092
The Pope Who Would Be King. Kertzer, David I.	282.092
The Pope's Last Crusade. Eisner, Peter	282.092

Pope, Alexander
Selected Poetry	821

POPES
Brown, Nancy Marie. *The Abacus and the Cross*	B
Douthat, Ross Gregory. *To Change the Church*	230
Duffy, Eamon. *Saints & Sinners*	262
Eisner, Peter. *The Pope's Last Crusade*	282.092
Francis. *Life*	B
Kertzer, David I. *The Pope at War*	940.53
Kertzer, David I. *The Pope Who Would Be King*	282.092
McBrien, Richard P. *Lives of the Popes*	B
Minois, Georges. *The Atheist's Bible*	200
O'Connor, Garry. *Universal Father*	B
Politi, Marco. *Pope Francis Among the Wolves*	282.092
Strathern, Paul. *The Borgias*	945.06
Vallely, Paul. *Pope Francis*	B
Wills, Garry. *The Future of the Catholic Church with Pope Francis*	282.09

Popkin, Jeremy D.
A New World Begins	944.04

Popkin, Jim
Code Name Blue Wren	327.12

Popoff, Alexandra
Vasily Grossman and the Soviet Century	B

Popova, Maria
Figuring	920

POPPER, KARL, 1902-1994
Edmonds, David. *Wittgenstein's Poker*	192

Poppies of Iraq. Findakly, Brigitte	741.5
Pops. Chabon, Michael	306.874
Pops. Teachout, Terry	B

POPULAR CULTURE
Abrams, Jonathan P. D. ★*The Come Up*	782.421649
Albertine, Viv. *Clothes, Clothes, Clothes. Music, Music, Music*	B
Alt, Matt. *Pure Invention*	306.0952
Appy, Christian G. *American Reckoning*	959.704
Armstrong, Jennifer Keishin. *Seinfeldia*	791.45
Armstrong, Jennifer Keishin. *Sex and the City and Us*	791.45
Armstrong, Jennifer Keishin. *When Women Invented Television*	791.45
Bergen, Mark. *Like, Comment, Subscribe*	338.7
Biskind, Peter. *Pandora's Box*	791.45

Bissell, Tom. *Extra Lives*	794.8
Blay, Zeba. *Carefree Black Girls*	305.48
Bordo, Susan. *The Creation of Anne Boleyn*	942.05
Branum, Guy. *My Life as a Goddess*	B
Britt, Ryan. *Phasers on Stun!*	791.45
Britt, Ryan. ★*The Spice Must Flow*	813
Brown, Carolyn. *Chance and Circumstance*	B
Brown, Craig. *150 Glimpses of the Beatles*	920
Bryson, Bill. *The Life and Times of the Thunderbolt Kid*	B
Bryson, Bill. *One Summer*	973.91
Bullock, Darryl W. *David Bowie Made Me Gay*	780
Carlin, Peter Ames. *Bruce*	B
Chuck D. *Chuck D Presents This Day in Rap and Hip-Hop History*	782.421649
Clavin, Thomas. *The DiMaggios*	920
Clein, Emmeline. ★*Dead Weight*	616.85
Connolly, Ray. *Being John Lennon*	B
Crease, Robert P. *The Quantum Moment*	530.12
Davis, Michael. *Street Gang*	791.43
Ditum, Sarah. *Toxic*	920.72
Doggett, Peter. *Electric Shock*	781.64
Doggett, Peter. *You Never Give Me Your Money*	B
Ellis, Helen. *Southern Lady Code*	814
Ernaux, Annie. ★*The Years*	B
Evans, William. *Black Nerd Problems*	814.6
Eyman, Scott. *John Wayne*	B
Favro, Terri. *Generation Robot*	006.3
Feder, Rachel. *The Darcy Myth*	823
Feiler, Bruce. *The First Love Story*	222
Feinstein, Michael. *The Gershwins and Me*	782.42164
Felisbret, Eric. *Graffiti New York*	751.7
Felton, Tom. ★*Beyond the Wand*	B
Fernando, S. H., Jr. *From the Streets of Shaolin*	782.421
Fox, Jesse David. *Comedy Book*	792.7
Fumudoh, Ziwe. ★*Black Friend*	814
Gerber, Robin. *Barbie and Ruth*	B
Giddins, Gary. *Bing Crosby*	B
Giddins, Gary. *Bing Crosby*	B
Gioia, Ted. *Music*	780.9
Gitlin, Marty. *A Celebration of Animation*	741.5
Gooch, Brad. *Radiant*	B
Green, Jaime. *The Possibility of Life*	576.8
Green, Robin. *The Only Girl*	070.92
Greene, Andy. *The Office*	791.45
Greenman, Ben. *Dig If You Will the Picture*	B
Gutowitz, Jill. *Girls Can Kiss Now*	814
Hagan, Joe. *Sticky Fingers*	B
Halberstam, David. *The Fifties*	973.92
Harvilla, Rob. *60 Songs That Explain the '90s*	782.42164
Heller, Jason. *Strange Stars*	781.6609
Hermes, Will. *Love Goes to Buildings on Fire*	781.64
Hickey, Walt. ★*You Are What You Watch*	791.4
Holway, Tatiana M. *The Flower of Empire*	727
Howe, Sean. *Marvel Comics*	741.5
Hsu, Hua. ★*Stay True*	B
Hubbard, Shanita. ★*Ride-Or-Die*	305.48
Hyden, Steven. *Long Road*	782.42166
Hyden, Steven. *Twilight of the Gods*	781.6609
Iandoli, Kathy. *Baby Girl*	B
Irby, Samantha. ★*Quietly Hostile*	814
Jameson, A. D. *I Find Your Lack of Faith Disturbing*	791.43
Jamieson, David. *Mint Condition*	796.357
Jefferson, Margo. *On Michael Jackson*	B
Jennings, Ken. ★*100 Places to See After You Die*	202
Jones, Dylan. *David Bowie*	B
Kapilow, Robert. ★*Listening for America*	782.42164
Kaufman, Amy. *Bachelor Nation*	791.45
Kavanagh, Julie. *Nureyev*	B
Kenny, Glenn. *Made Men*	791.43
Kenny, Glenn. *The World Is Yours*	791.43
Klosterman, Chuck. *But What If We're Wrong*	909.83
Klosterman, Chuck. ★*The Nineties*	306.0973
Kornacki, Steve. *The Red and the Blue*	306.20973
Lavery, Daniel M. *Something That May Shock and Discredit You*	814
Lepore, Jill. ★*The Secret History of Wonder Woman*	741.5
Louvin, Charlie. *Satan Is Real*	920
Lunenfeld, Peter. *City at the Edge of Forever*	979.4
Lynskey, Dorian. *33 Revolutions per Minute*	782.42

AUTHOR, TITLE, SERIES AND SUBJECT INDEX

Mamet, David. *True and False*	792
Martin, Brett. *Difficult Men*	791.4509
McKeen, William. *Everybody Had an Ocean*	781.6609
Menand, Louis. *The Free World*	306.0973
Meslow, Scott. *From Hollywood with Love*	791.43
Mike D. *Beastie Boys Book*	782.42164
Miranda, Lin-Manuel. *Hamilton*	782.1
Mizrahi, Isaac. *I.M.*	B
Momus. *Niche*	B
Moss, Gabrielle. *Paperback Crush*	813.009
Norman, Philip. *George Harrison*	B
Nussbaum, Emily. *I Like to Watch*	791.45
O'Connor, John. *The Secret History of Bigfoot*	001.944
Olds, Sharon. *Arias*	811
Orenstein, Peggy. *Cinderella Ate My Daughter*	305.23082
Pardlo, Gregory. *Spectral Evidence*	811
Perkins, Nichole. *Sometimes I Trip on How Happy We Could Be*	B
Phillips, Maya. *Nerd*	302.23
Pico, Tommy. *Junk*	811
Pratchett, Terry. *A Slip of the Keyboard*	824
Reed, Justin Phillip. *The Malevolent Volume*	811
Ribowsky, Mark. *Signed, Sealed, and Delivered*	B
Richardson, Lance. *House of Nutter*	741.5
Riesman, Abraham. *True Believer*	B
Robb, John. *Punk Rock*	781.6609
Robinson, Joanna. ★*McU*	791.43
Robinson, Staci. ★*Tupac Shakur*	B
Sanneh, Kelefa. ★*Major Labels*	781.64
Santana, Carlos. *The Universal Tone*	B
Savage, Jon. ★*1966*	781.6609
Schechter, Harold. ★*Ripped from the Headlines!*	791.43
Schickel, Richard. *Keepers*	791.430973
Scovell, Nell. *Just the Funny Parts*	B
Seidelman, Susan. *Desperately Seeking Something*	791.45
Sepinwall, Alan. ★*TV (the Book)*	B
Sharma, Nina. *The Way You Make Me Feel*	B
Smith, Patti. ★*A Book of Days*	779
So, Anthony Veasna. ★*Songs on Endless Repeat*	814
Spitz, Bob. ★*The Beatles*	B
Springsteen, Bruce. ★*Born to Run*	B
Stein, Jean. *West of Eden*	979.4
Tarantino, Quentin. *Cinema Speculation*	791.43
Thomas, Richard F. ★*Why Bob Dylan Matters*	782.42164
Thomson, David. *The Fatal Alliance*	791.43
Thomson, David. ★*How to Watch a Movie*	791.43
Tibble, Tayi. *Poukahangatus*	821
Tolinski, Brad. *Light and Shade*	B
Trebek, Alex. *The Answer Is ...*	791.4502
Tye, Larry. ★*The Jazzmen*	781.6509
Villarreal, Vanessa Anglica. *Magical/Realism*	814
Wasson, Sam. ★*Improv Nation*	792.02
Waterhouse, Benjamin C. *One Day I'll Work for Myself*	338
Weinman, Sarah. *Unspeakable Acts*	364.1
Weldon, Glen. ★*The Caped Crusade*	741.5
Westhoff, Ben. *Original Gangstas*	782.421649
Wiederhorn, Jon. *Louder Than Hell*	781.6609
Wilson, Robert. *Barnum*	B
Wolk, Douglas. ★*All of the Marvels*	741.5
Yang, Jeff. *The Golden Screen*	791.43
Yang, Jeff. ★*Rise*	973
Yong, Sable. *Die Hot with a Vengeance*	646.7
Young, Damon. *The Art of Reading*	028.9
POPULAR MUSIC	
Austerlitz, Saul. *Money for Nothing*	780.26
Boilen, Bob. *Your Song Changed My Life*	780.92
Breihan, Tom. ★*The Number Ones*	782.42164
Broyles, Michael. ★*Revolutions in American Music*	780.9
Carlin, Peter Ames. *Bruce*	B
Doggett, Peter. *Electric Shock*	781.64
Dylan, Bob. ★*The Philosophy of Modern Song*	782.42
Feinstein, Michael. *The Gershwins and Me*	782.42164
Friedwald, Will. *The Great Jazz and Pop Vocal Albums*	016.78
Gabriel, Mary. *Madonna*	B
Garnice, Michael. *The Ultimate Guide to Great Reggae*	781.646
Gasser, Nolan. *Why You Like It*	781.1
Greenman, Ben. *Dig If You Will the Picture*	B
Guesdon, Jean-Michel. *All the Songs*	782.42166
Harvilla, Rob. *60 Songs That Explain the '90s*	782.42164
Hay, Matt. *Soundtrack of Silence*	B
Hayes, Elaine M. ★*Queen of Bebop*	B
Heller, Jason. *Strange Stars*	781.6609
Hermes, Will. *Love Goes to Buildings on Fire*	781.64
Houghton, Mick. *Becoming Elektra*	781.64
Hyden, Steven. *Twilight of the Gods*	781.6609
Jackson family. *The Jacksons*	782.421644
Jefferson, Margo. *On Michael Jackson*	B
John, Elton. ★*Me*	B
Kapilow, Robert. ★*Listening for America*	782.42164
Kaye, Lenny. ★*Lightning Striking*	781.66
Lanegan, Mark. *Sing Backwards and Weep*	B
Lehman, David. *A Fine Romance*	781.64
Lynskey, Dorian. *33 Revolutions per Minute*	782.42
Marovich, Robert M. *A City Called Heaven*	782.25
McCartney, Paul. *The Lyrics*	782.42166
McKeen, William. *Everybody Had an Ocean*	781.6609
McNally, Dennis. *On Highway 61*	781.64
Milner, Greg. *Perfecting Sound Forever*	781.49
Newkey-Burden, Chas. *Taylor Swift*	B
Port, Ian S. *The Birth of Loud*	787.87
Powers, Ann. *Good Booty*	781.64
Ribowsky, Mark. *Signed, Sealed, and Delivered*	B
Ribowsky, Mark. *The Supremes*	B
Russell, Tony. *Country Music Originals*	B
Sanneh, Kelefa. ★*Major Labels*	781.64
Savage, Jon. ★*1966*	781.6609
Simon, Carly. ★*Boys in the Trees*	782.42164
Sloan, Nate. *Switched on Pop*	781.64
Smith, Danyel. *Shine Bright*	782.42164
Spears, Britney. *The Woman in Me*	B
Stanley, Bob. *Let's Do It*	781.64
Stanley, Bob. *The Story of the Bee Gees*	782.42164
Streisand, Barbra. ★*My Name Is Barbra*	B
Thomas, Richard F. ★*Why Bob Dylan Matters*	782.42164
Thomson, Graeme. *George Harrison*	B
Tweedy, Jeff. *Let's Go (so We Can Get Back)*	B
Vogel, Joseph. *Man in the Music*	B
Wald, Elijah. *Dylan Goes Electric!*	782.42164
Wald, Elijah. *How the Beatles Destroyed Rock 'N' Roll*	781.64
Westhoff, Ben. *Dirty South*	782.421649
White, Adam. ★*Motown*	781.644
Wolff, Daniel J. *Grown-Up Anger*	920
Zanes, Warren. *Deliver Me from Nowhere*	782.42164
POPULAR MUSIC (VOCAL)	
Dylan, Bob. ★*The Philosophy of Modern Song*	782.42
POPULAR MUSIC COMPOSERS	
Greenman, Ben. *Dig If You Will the Picture*	B
Remnick, David. *Holding the Note*	781.64
POPULAR MUSIC INDUSTRY AND TRADE	
Breihan, Tom. ★*The Number Ones*	782.42164
Dylan, Bob. ★*The Philosophy of Modern Song*	782.42
POPULARITY	
Shlaes, Amity. *Coolidge*	B
POPULATION	
Anderson, Sam. *Boom Town*	976.6
Briody, Blaire. *The New Wild West*	338.2
Sciubba, Jennifer Dabbs. *8 Billion and Counting*	304.6
POPULISM	
Frank, Thomas. *The People, No*	320.56
Ganz, John. *When the Clock Broke*	320.52
Grandin, Greg. *The End of the Myth*	973
Hill, Fiona. *There Is Nothing for You Here*	327.2
Isenberg, Nancy. *The Problem of Democracy*	973.4
Lasch, Christopher. ★*The Revolt of the Elites*	306
Zakaria, Fareed. *Age of Revolutions*	303.6
Porath, Christine Lynne	
Mastering Civility	650.1
Porcelain. Moby	B
PORCHES	
Cory, Steve. *Ultimate Guide*	690
Porizkova, Paulina	
No Filter	B
PORIZKOVA, PAULINA	
Porizkova, Paulina. *No Filter*	B
PORK INDUSTRY AND TRADE	
Addison, Corban. *Wastelands*	346.73

PUBLIC LIBRARY CORE COLLECTION: NONFICTION
Twentieth Edition

PORNOGRAPHIC FILM INDUSTRY AND TRADE
   Burke, Kelsy. *The Pornography Wars*   306.77
   Ward, Maitland. *Rated X*   B
PORNOGRAPHIC FILMS
   Daniels, Stormy. *Full Disclosure*   B
   Ward, Maitland. *Rated X*   B
PORNOGRAPHY
   Burke, Kelsy. *The Pornography Wars*   306.77
   Sohn, Amy. *The Man Who Hated Women*   363.28
PORNOGRAPHY AND SOCIETY
   Burke, Kelsy. *The Pornography Wars*   306.77
*The **Pornography** Wars*. Burke, Kelsy   306.77
Porowski, Antoni
   Antoni   641.5
Port, Ian S
   The Birth of Loud   787.87
*The **Portable** Frederick Douglass*. Douglass, Frederick   973.8
Portable Magic. Smith, Emma   002
Porter, Billy
   ★*Unprotected*   B
PORTER, BILLY
   Porter, Billy. ★*Unprotected*   B
Porter, Carolyn
   Marcel's Letters   940.54
PORTER, CAROLYN
   Porter, Carolyn. *Marcel's Letters*   940.54
Porter, Cecelia Hopkins
   Five Lives in Music   B
PORTER, COLE, 1891-1964
   McBrien, William. *Cole Porter*   B
Porter, Eduardo
   American Poison   305.800973
Porter, Linda
   Katherine the Queen   B
Porter, Roy
   The Greatest Benefit to Mankind   610
Portico. Koenig, Leah   641.5
PORTLAND, OREGON
   Jackson, Mitchell S. *Survival Math*   B
Porto, Anthony
   The Pediatrician's Guide to Feeding Babies & Toddlers   618.92
*A **Portrait** of Jesus*. Girzone, Joseph F.   232.9
PORTRAIT PAINTERS
   Feaver, William. ★*The Lives of Lucian Freud*   B
   Hoban, Phoebe. *Alice Neel*   B
   Tomlinson, Janis A. ★*Goya*   B
PORTRAIT PAINTING
   Cumming, Laura. ★*The Vanishing Velazquez*   759.6
   Hoban, Phoebe. *Alice Neel*   B
PORTRAIT PHOTOGRAPHY
   Begley, Adam. *The Great Nadar*   B
   Cunningham, William J. ★*Fashion Climbing*   B
   Hahn, Emanuel. *Koreatown Dreaming*   979.4
   Lee, Corky. ★*Corky Lee's Asian America*   770
   Leibovitz, Annie. *A Photographer's Life, 1990-2005*   779
   McCurry, Steve. *The Iconic Photographs*   779.092
   Stanton, Brandon. *Humans*   779
   Wilbur, Matika. *Project 562*   970.004
PORTRAITS
   Barnes, Julian. *The Man in the Red Coat*   B
   Curtis, Edward S. *Edward S. Curtis*   770.92
   Egan, Timothy. ★*Short Nights of the Shadow Catcher*   770.92
   Gulbrandsen, Don. *Edward Sheriff Curtis*   970.004
   Lucey, Donna M. *Sargent's Women*   920
   Willis, Deborah. ★*The Black Civil War Soldier*   973.7
★*Portraits and Observations*. Capote, Truman   814
PORTUGUESE PEOPLE
   Zenith, Richard. *Pessoa*   B
Posey, Parker
   You're on an Airplane   B
POSEY, PARKER, 1968-
   Posey, Parker. *You're on an Airplane*   B
POSITIVE PSYCHOLOGY
   Fredrickson, Barbara. *Positivity*   158.1
   Goldsmith, Marshall. *Triggers*   155.2
★*Positively Fifth Street*. McManus, James   795.41
Positivity. Fredrickson, Barbara   158.1

Posnanski, Joe
   The Baseball 100   796.357
   ★*The Life and Afterlife of Harry Houdini*   793.8
   The Soul of Baseball   796.357
   ★*Why We Love Baseball*   796.357
POSNANSKI, JOE
   Posnanski, Joe. *The Soul of Baseball*   796.357
Posner, Gerald L.
   Case Closed   364.1
   God's Bankers   364.16
   ★*Pharma*   338.4
Possanza, Amelia
   Lesbian Love Story   B
POSSANZA, AMELIA
   Possanza, Amelia. *Lesbian Love Story*   B
*The **Possessed***. Batuman, Elif   891.7
POSSIBILITIES
   Rosling, Hans. *Factfulness*   155.9
*The **Possibility** of Life*. Green, Jaime   576.8
POST TRAUMATIC STRESS DISORDER
   Grossi, Craig. *Craig & Fred*   B
Post, Lizzie
   Emily Post's Etiquette   395
   Emily Post's Etiquette   395
POST-COMMUNISM
   Aleksievich, Svetlana. ★*Secondhand Time*   947.086
   Szablowski, Witold. *Dancing Bears*   947.086
   Walker, Shaun. *The Long Hangover*   947.086
   Ypi, Lea. ★*Free*   B
POST-TRAUMATIC STRESS DISORDER
   Brennan, Thomas J. *Shooting Ghosts*   B
   Chesney, Will. *No Ordinary Dog*   958.104
   Eger, Edith Eva. *The Choice*   B
   Finkel, David. *Thank You for Your Service*   920
   Foo, Stephanie. ★*What My Bones Know*   B
   Gallego, Ruben. *They Called Us*   956.7044
   Glass, Charles. *Soldiers Don't Go Mad*   616.85
   Gonell, Aquilino. *American Shield*   B
   Greitens, Eric. *Resilience*   155.2
   Hillenbrand, Laura. ★*Unbroken*   B
   Kander, Jason. *Invisible Storm*   B
   Mailhot, Terese Marie. *Heart Berries*   B
   McClelland, Mac. *Irritable Hearts*   B
   Metatawabin, Edmund. *Up Ghost River*   B
   Morris, David J. *The Evil Hours*   616.85
   Thompson-Hernandez, Walter. *The Compton Cowboys*   920
   Van der Kolk, Bessel A. *The Body Keeps the Score*   616.85
   Zerwick, Phoebe. *Beyond Innocence*   347
POSTAGE STAMPS
   Barron, James. *The One-Cent Magenta*   769.569
POSTAL INSPECTORS
   Sohn, Amy. *The Man Who Hated Women*   363.28
★*Postcolonial Love Poem*. Diaz, Natalie   811
POSTCOLONIALISM
   Barot, Rick. *The Galleons*   811
   Carlin, John. *Playing the Enemy*   968.06
   Dangarembga, Tsitsi. *Black and Female*   305.48
   Sanghera, Sathnam. ★*Empireland*   941
   Soyinka, Wole. *Of Africa*   960
   Taylor, Alan. *American Revolutions*   973.3
Postel, Charles
   Equality   305.50973
POSTHUMANISM
   O'Gieblyn, Meghan. *God, Human, Animal, Machine*   814
Postman, Neil
   Amusing Ourselves to Death   302.2
POSTMODERNISM
   Larson, Kay. *Where the Heart Beats*   700.1
POSTNATAL CARE
   Murkoff, Heidi Eisenberg. ★*What to Expect When You're Expecting*   618.2
   Serrallach, Oscar. *The Postnatal Depletion Cure*   618.6
*The **Postnatal** Depletion Cure*. Serrallach, Oscar   618.6
POSTPARTUM
   Millwood, Molly. *To Have and to Hold*   306.874
POSTPARTUM DEPRESSION
   Fox Starr, Rebecca. *Beyond the Baby Blues*   618.7
   Lang, Maya. *What We Carry*   B
Postwar. Judt, Tony   940.55

AUTHOR, TITLE, SERIES AND SUBJECT INDEX

POSTWAR LIFE
   Ayers, Edward L. ★*The Thin Light of Freedom* — 975.5
   Black, George. ★*The Long Reckoning* — 959.704
   Coffin, Judith G. *Sex, Love, and Letters* — 848
   Crasnianski, Tania. *The Children of Nazis* — 943.086
   Eder, Mari K. *The Girls Who Stepped Out of Line* — 920
   Eyman, Scott. *Charlie Chaplin vs. America* — B
   Feigel, Lara. *The Bitter Taste of Victory* — 320.943
   Gallego, Ruben. *They Called Us* — 956.7044
   Hatzfeld, Jean. *Blood Papa* — 967.5710431
   Hirsch, Foster. ★*Hollywood and the Movies of the Fifties* — 791.43
   Jahner, Harald. ★*Aftermath* — 943.087
   Judt, Tony. *Postwar* — 940.55
   Kesling, Ben. *Bravo Company* — 958.104
   Kraus, Dita. *A Delayed Life* — B
   Menand, Louis. *The Free World* — 306.0973
   Nez, Chester. *Code Talker* — B
   Roll, David L. *Ascent to Power* — 973.918
   Samet, Elizabeth D. *Looking for the Good War* — 940.53
   Schloss, Edith. *The Loft Generation* — 700.9
   Schwarz, Geraldine. *Those Who Forget* — 940.53
   Stanton, Doug. *The Odyssey of Echo Company* — 959.704
   Yancey, Philip. ★*Where the Light Fell* — B

POSTWAR RECONSTRUCTION
   Chandrasekaran, Rajiv. *Imperial Life in the Emerald City* — 956.7044
   Jahner, Harald. ★*Aftermath* — 943.087

POTATOES
   Frank, Lois Ellen. *Seed to Plate, Soil to Sky* — 641.5

POTAWATOMI (NORTH AMERICAN PEOPLE)
   Kimmerer, Robin Wall. ★*Braiding Sweetgrass* — 304.2

The Potter's Studio Handbook. Muller, Kristin — 738.1

POTTER, BEATRIX, 1866-1943
   Lear, Linda J. *Beatrix Potter* — B

Pottering. McGovern, Anna — 158.1

POTTERY
   Burnett, Jason Bige. *Graphic Clay* — 738.1
   Muller, Kristin. *The Potter's Studio Handbook* — 738.1
   Stone, Francesca. *Easy Homemade Pottery* — 738.1

Potts, Monica
   The Forgotten Girls — B

Pough, Frederick H.
   ★*A Field Guide to Rocks and Minerals* — 549

Poukahangatus. Tibble, Tayi — 821

Poulenc. Johnson, Graham

POULENC, FRANCIS, 1899-1963
   Johnson, Graham. *Poulenc* — B

The Pound Era. Kenner, Hugh — 811

Pound, Ezra
   ★*Poems and Translations* — 811

POUND, EZRA, 1885-1972
   Kenner, Hugh. *The Pound Era* — 811
   Moody, Anthony David. *Ezra Pound* — B

Pounding The Rock. Skelton, Marc — 796.323

Pourny, Christophe
   ★*The Furniture Bible* — 684.1

POVERTY
   Agee, James. ★*Cotton Tenants* — 976.1
   Agee, James. *Let Us Now Praise Famous Men* — 976.1
   Alexie, Sherman. *You Don't Have to Say You Love Me* — 818
   Ambroz, David. *A Place Called Home* — B
   Anthony, Carmelo. *Where Tomorrows Aren't Promised* — B
   Asher, Zain E. *Where the Children Take Us* — 942.1
   Badkhen, Anna. *The World Is a Carpet* — 305.409581
   Barber, William J. *We Are Called to Be a Movement* — 261.8
   Bellos, David. *The Novel of the Century* — 843
   Bergner, Daniel. ★*Sing for Your Life* — B
   Bono. ★*Surrender* — B
   Boo, Katherine. ★*Behind the Beautiful Forevers* — 305.5
   Bowden, Mark. *Life Sentence* — 364.106
   Brown, Claude. *Manchild in the Promised Land* — B
   Chung, Nicole. ★*A Living Remedy* — B
   Copaken, Deborah. *Ladyparts* — B
   Cornejo Villavicencio, Karla. ★*The Undocumented Americans* — 920
   Crais, Clifton C. *History Lessons* — B
   DePalma, Anthony. *The Cubans* — 920
   Desmond, Matthew. ★*Evicted* — 339.4
   Desmond, Matthew. ★*Poverty, by America* — 362.5
   Dorr, Christina H. ★*Profiles in Resilience* — 028.5
   Edin, Kathryn. *$2.00 a Day* — 339.4
   Edin, Kathryn. ★*The Injustice of Place* — 339.4
   Ehrenreich, Barbara. ★*Nickel and Dimed* — B
   Elliott, Andrea. ★*Invisible Child* — 362.7
   Felix, Camonghne. *Build Yourself a Boat* — 811
   Fitzgerald, Isaac. *Dirtbag, Massachusetts* — B
   Forche, Carolyn. *What You Have Heard Is True* — B
   Francis. *The Church of Mercy* — 252
   Freeman, Amanda. *Getting Me Cheap* — 362.83
   Freeman, Andrea. ★*Ruin Their Crops on the Ground* — 338.1
   Georges, Gigi. *Downeast* — 974.1
   Gerald, Casey. *There Will Be No Miracles Here* — B
   Geronimo, Arline T. ★*Weathering* — 362.1089
   Gidla, Sujatha. *Ants Among Elephants* — 305.5
   Golay, Michael. *America 1933* — B
   Goyal, Nikhil. ★*Live to See the Day* — 305.5
   Hamill, Kirkland. *Filthy Beasts* — B
   Hansberry, Lorraine. ★*A Raisin in the Sun* — 812
   Henderson, Rob Kim. *Troubled* — B
   Hickel, Jason. *The Divide* — 330.9
   Jackson, Ted. ★*You Ought to Do a Story About Me* — B
   Johnson, Brian. *The Lives of Brian* — B
   Jollett, Mikel. ★*Hollywood Park* — B
   Kim, Anne. ★*Abandoned* — 305.2350973
   Kim, Anne. ★*Poverty for Profit* — 302.5
   Kirshner, Jodie Adams. ★*Broke* — 336.3
   Kozol, Jonathan. *Fire in the Ashes* — 362.77
   Kozol, Jonathan. *Rachel and Her Children* — 362.5
   Kristof, Nicholas D. ★*Tightrope* — 306.0973
   Land, Stephanie. *Maid* — B
   Lewis, Oscar. *The Children of Sanchez* — 306.85
   Lockhart, Chris. ★*Walking the Bowl* — 362.7
   Lovato, Roberto. *Unforgetting* — B
   Madrick, Jeffrey G. *Invisible Americans* — 362.7086
   McCaulley, Esau. *How Far to the Promised Land* — B
   McCourt, Frank. ★*Angela's Ashes* — 929
   McCourt, Malachy. *A Monk Swimming* — B
   McMillan, Tracie. *The American Way of Eating* — 338.4
   Messenger, Tony. *Profit and Punishment* — 362.5
   Milanovic, Branko. *The Have and the Have-Nots* — 339.2
   Mullainathan, Sendhil. *Scarcity* — 338.5
   Muse, Toby. *Kilo* — 363.4509861
   Noah, Timothy. *The Great Divergence* — 339.2
   Noah, Trevor. *Born a Crime* — B
   Nyamayaro, Elizabeth. *I Am a Girl from Africa* — B
   Oates, Joyce Carol. *American Melancholy* — 811
   Oluseyi, Hakeem M. *A Quantum Life* — B
   Otto, Mary. *Teeth* — 617
   Parks, Casey. *Diary of a Misfit* — B
   Peterson, Marlon. *Bird Uncaged* — B
   Phelan, Tom. *We Were Rich and We Didn't Know It* — B
   Potts, Monica. *The Forgotten Girls* — B
   Price, Margo. *Maybe We'll Make It* — B
   Rivlin, Gary. *Broke, Usa* — 339.4
   Samaha, Albert. *Never Ran, Never Will* — 920
   Sandler, Lauren. *This Is All I Got* — B
   Sedgewick, Augustine. *Coffeeland* — 338.4
   Sen, Amartya. *Home in the World* — B
   Smarsh, Sarah. ★*Heartland* — B
   Sokolik, Vicki. ★*If You See Them* — 362.5
   Sowell, Thomas. *Wealth, Poverty and Politics* — 330.1
   Stevenson, Bryan. *Just Mercy* — B
   Streep, Abe. *Brothers on Three* — 306.85
   Tubbs, Michael. *The Deeper the Roots* — B
   Ullrich, Volker. *Germany 1923* — 943.085
   Vallely, Paul. *Pope Francis* — B
   Vance, J. D. *Hillbilly Elegy* — B
   Wang, Qian Julie. ★*Beautiful Country* — B
   Williams, Mary. *The Lost Daughter* — B
   Williams, Patricia. *Rabbit* — B

★*Poverty for Profit*. Kim, Anne — 302.5
★*Poverty, by America*. Desmond, Matthew — 362.5

Povey, Glenn
   Echoes — 782.42166

POWELL, ANTHONY, 1905-2000
   Spurling, Hilary. *Anthony Powell* — B

Powell, D. A.
   Useless Landscape — 811

PUBLIC LIBRARY CORE COLLECTION: NONFICTION
Twentieth Edition

POWELL, JOHN WESLEY, 1834-1902
   Ross, John F. *The Promise of the Grand Canyon*   917.91
Powell, Julie
   Julie and Julia   641.5
POWELL, JULIE
   Powell, Julie. *Julie and Julia*   641.5
Powell, Michael
   The Acting Bible   792.02
   ★*Canyon Dreams*   796.323
Powell, Nate
   ★*Lies My Teacher Told Me*   741.5
Powell, Tia
   Dementia Reimagined   616.8
POWER
   Acemoglu, Daron. *The Narrow Corridor*   320.01
   Akbar, Kaveh. *Pilgrim Bell*   811
   Asim, Jabari. *We Can't Breathe*   305.896
   Auletta, Ken. ★*Hollywood Ending*   791.43
   Ayers, Edward L. *American Visions*   973.5
   Baer, Kate. *What Kind of Woman*   811
   Baker, Peter. *The Man Who Ran Washington*   B
   Baron, Martin. ★*Collision of Power*   070.4
   Beard, Mary. ★*Emperor of Rome*   937
   Beard, Mary. ★*Women & Power*   305.409
   Belcher, Chris. *Pretty Baby*   B
   Benner, Erica. *Be Like the Fox*   B
   Borman, Tracy. *Henry VIII and the Men Who Made Him*   942.05
   Brettschneider, Corey Lang. *The Oath and the Office*   342.73
   Brettschneider, Corey Lang. *The Presidents and the People*   342.73
   Bryant, Howard. *Full Dissidence*   306.20973
   Cadbury, Deborah. *Queen Victoria's Matchmaking*   941.081
   Cameron, Silver Donald. *Blood in the Water*   364.152
   Chafkin, Max. *The Contrarian*   B
   Christie, Chris. *Let Me Finish*   B
   Cohen, Jared. *Life After Power*   973.09
   Cox, Josie. *Women Money Power*   330.082
   Crawford, Lacy. *Notes on a Silencing*   B
   Darnton, Robert. *The Revolutionary Temper*   944
   Egan, Timothy. ★*A Fever in the Heartland*   322.4
   Elwood, Phil. *All the Worst Humans*   659.2
   Farrell, John A. ★*Richard Nixon*   B
   Fraser, Steve. *The Age of Acquiescence*   973.91
   Friedan, Betty. ★*The Feminine Mystique*   305.42
   Gage, Beverly. *G-Man*   B
   Garbes, Angela. *Essential Labor*   306.874
   Gewen, Barry. ★*The Inevitability of Tragedy*   B
   Glatt, John. *Tangled Vines*   364.152
   Good, Cassandra A. *First Family*   920
   Greenberg, Amy S. *Lady First*   B
   Gristwood, Sarah. *The Tudors in Love*   941.05
   Hemon, Aleksandar. *My Parents*   814
   Herman, Eleanor. *The Royal Art of Poison*   364.152
   Hirsch, Jennifer S. *Sexual Citizens*   371.7
   Honig, Elie. *Untouchable*   364.1
   Hubbard, Ben (Journalist). *Mbs*   B
   Hughes, Bettany. *Venus and Aphrodite*   292
   Kaplan, David A. *The Most Dangerous Branch*   347.73
   Kertzer, David I. *The Pope Who Would Be King*   282.092
   Kissinger, Henry. *Leadership*   303.3
   Lee, Sung-Yoon. *The Sister*   951.93
   Lorenz, Taylor. ★*Extremely Online*   302.23
   Lozada, Carlos. *The Washington Book*   320
   Mann, William J. *The Wars of the Roosevelts*   B
   Mansel, Philip. *King of the World*   B
   Marton, Kati. *Hidden Power*   B
   Matney, Mandy. *Blood on Their Hands*   364.152
   Mattioli, Dana. ★*The Everything War*   381.142
   McHangama, Jacob. ★*Free Speech*   323.44
   McPhee, Peter. *Robespierre*   B
   Meacham, Jon. ★*Thomas Jefferson*   B
   Montell, Amanda. ★*The Age of Magical Overthinking*   153.4
   Morris, Ian. *Geography Is Destiny*   941
   Morrison, Toni. ★*The Source of Self-Regard*   814
   Myers, Steven Lee. *The New Tsar*   B
   Neiman, Garrett. *Rich White Men*   305.5
   Odell, Amy. *Anna*   B
   Oller, John. *American Queen*   B
   Oluo, Ijeoma. *Mediocre*   305.310973
   Packer, George. *Our Man*   B
   Pak, Jung H. *Becoming Kim Jong Un*   B
   Peyser, Marc N. *Hissing Cousins*   B
   Platt, Stephen R. *Imperial Twilight*   951
   Raphael, Ray. *Mr. President*   352.230973
   Rose, Jacqueline. *On Violence and on Violence Against Women*   362.88
   Ryan, Maureen. *Burn It Down*   791.43
   Scharre, Paul. *Four Battlegrounds*   006.3
   Schmidt, Michael S. ★*Donald Trump v. The United States*   973.933
   Schneier, Bruce. *A Hacker's Mind*   364.16
   Schwab, Tim. ★*The Bill Gates Problem*   361.7
   Schwartzman, Nancy. *Roll Red Roll*   364.15
   Sebag-Montefiore, Simon. ★*The World*   929.7
   Singer, Jessie. *There Are No Accidents*   363.1
   Southon, Emma. *Agrippina*   B
   Stevens, Stuart. *The Conspiracy to End America*   324.2734
   Stewart, James B. *Unscripted*   658.1
   Strathern, Paul. *The Borgias*   945.06
   Strathern, Paul. *The Medici*   945.5
   Stryker, Kitty. *Ask*   302
   Suleyman, Mustafa. *The Coming Wave*   303.48
   Taylor, Alan. *American Civil Wars*   973.7
   Tuchman, Barbara W. *March of Folly*   909.08
   Turchin, Peter. *End Times*   320.01
   Ullrich, Volker. *Hitler*   B
   Union, Gabrielle. *We're Going to Need More Wine*   B
   Vanek Smith, Stacey. *Machiavelli for Women*   650.1
   Vladeck, Stephen I. *The Shadow Docket*   347.73
   Whitaker, Mark. ★*Saying It Loud*   973.923
   Wiggins, Christopher L. *How Data Happened*   310
   Wilkerson, Isabel. ★*Caste*   305.5
   Wills, Garry. *Certain Trumpets*   303.3
   Wong, Chun Han. *Party of One*   951.06
   Yaffa, Joshua. *Between Two Fires*   920
   Zakaria, Rafia. *Against White Feminism*   305.42
   Zelizer, Julian E. *Burning Down the House*   328.73
The Power Age. Doust, Kelly   305.244
★*Power and Glory*. Larman, Alexander   941.085
Power and Progress. Acemoglu, Daron   303.48
Power Ball. Neyer, Rob   796.357
The Power Broker. Caro, Robert A.   B
Power Failure. Cohan, William D.   338.7
POWER FAILURES
   Bakke, Gretchen Anna. *The Grid*   333.793
Power Lines. Anderson, Jimmeka   020
The Power of Art. Schama, Simon   709
The Power of Bad. Tierney, John   158.1
The Power of Birthdays, Stars & Numbers. Crawford, Saffi   133.5
The Power of Dignity. Pratt, Victoria   364.973
The Power of Geography. Marshall, Tim   320.1
★*The Power of Habit*. Duhigg, Charles   158.1
The Power of I Am. Osteen, Joel   248.4
★*The Power of Intention*. Dyer, Wayne W.   158.1
The Power of Moments. Heath, Chip   128
The Power of Myth. Campbell, Joseph   201.3
The Power of Play. Elkind, David   155.4
★*The Power of Positive Dog Training*. Miller, Pat   636.7
The Power of Saying No. Patrick, Vanessa M.   158.1
The Power of Showing Up. Siegel, Daniel J.   649
The Power of Us. Van Bavel, Jay J.   155.2
The Power of Writing It Down. Fallon, Allison   158.1
Power Play. Burak, Asi   794.8
Power Play. Higgins, Tim   338.7
Power, Carla
   If the Oceans Were Ink   B
POWER, CARLA
   Power, Carla. *If the Oceans Were Ink*   B
Power, Marianne
   Help Me!   158.1
POWER, MARIANNE
   Power, Marianne. *Help Me!*   158.1
Power, Thomas J.
   If Your Adolescent Has ADHD   616.85
Powers, Ann
   Good Booty   781.64
   ★*Traveling*   B
Powers, Thomas
   The Killing of Crazy Horse   B

AUTHOR, TITLE, SERIES AND SUBJECT INDEX

POWHATAN (NORTH AMERICAN PEOPLE)
   Horn, James P. P. *Land as God Made It* — 975.5
   Price, David A. ★*Love and Hate in Jamestown* — 975.5
POZZI, SAMUEL, 1846-1918
   Barnes, Julian. *The Man in the Red Coat* — B
***Practical** Paleo.* Sanfilippo, Diane — 613.2
PRACTICAL POLITICS
   Balz, Daniel J. *The Battle for America, 2008* — 973.932
   Litt, David. *Democracy in One Book or Less* — 321.8
   Plouffe, David. *A Citizen's Guide to Beating Donald Trump* — 324.0973
PRACTICAL REASON
   Ariely, Dan. *Predictably Irrational* — 153.8
   Ridley, Matt. *The Rational Optimist* — 339.2
*The **Practice**.* Godin, Seth — 153.3
PRACTICE OF LAW
   Urofsky, Melvin I. *Louis D. Brandeis* — B
***Practicing** Peace.* Chodron, Pema — 294.3
Prager, Joshua
   The Family Roe — 342.7308
***Prague** Winter.* Albright, Madeleine Korbel — 943.71
PRAGUE, CZECH REPUBLIC
   Albright, Madeleine Korbel. *Prague Winter* — 943.71
   Eisen, Norman L. *The Last Palace* — 920
   Epstein, Franci. *Franci's War* — B
   Weiss, Helga. *Helga's Diary* — B
★***Prairie** Fires.* Fraser, Caroline — B
PRAIRIE LIFE
   Raban, Jonathan. *Bad Land* — 978
PRAIRIES
   Laskin, David. *The Children's Blizzard* — 977
***Praisesong** for the Kitchen Ghosts.* Wilkinson, Crystal — 641.5975
Prange, Gordon W.
   At Dawn We Slept — 940.54
Prasad, Aarathi
   Silk — 677
Pratchett, Terry
   A Slip of the Keyboard — 824
PRATCHETT, TERRY
   Pratchett, Terry. *A Slip of the Keyboard* — 824
Pratt, Misty
   All in Her Head — 616.89
Pratt, Victoria
   The Power of Dignity — 364.973
PRATT, VICTORIA
   Pratt, Victoria. *The Power of Dignity* — 364.973
PRAYER
   Brownback, Lydia. *Finding God in My Loneliness* — 248.8
   Guthrie, Savannah. *Mostly What God Does* — 248.4
   Tutu, Desmond. *Made for Goodness* — 170
PRAYER (CHRISTIANITY)
   Lewis, C. S. *Letters to Malcolm* — 248.3
   Lucado, Max. *Before Amen* — 248.3
   Martin, James. *Learning to Pray* — 248.3
PRAYER (JUDAISM)
   Wagner, Jordan Lee. *The Synagogue Survival Kit* — 296.4
PRAYERS
   Karon, Jan. *Bathed in Prayer* — 242
   King, Martin Luther. *"Thou, Dear God"* — 242
   Martin, James. *Learning to Pray* — 248.3
PRECIOUS STONES
   Judah, Hettie. *Lapidarium* — 553.8
PRECOGNITION
   Burroughs, Augusten. ★*Toil & Trouble* — B
   Jacobsen, Annie. *Phenomena* — 133.8
   Knight, Sam. *The Premonitions Bureau* — 133.8
PREDATION (BIOLOGY)
   Simon, Matt. *Plight of the Living Dead* — 591.6
   Simon, Matt. *The Wasp That Brainwashed the Caterpillar* — 578.4
PREDATORY ANIMALS
   Berry, Erica. *Wolfish* — 152.4
   Brand, Adele. *The Hidden World of the Fox* — 599.775
   McIntyre, Rick. *The Reign of Wolf 21* — 599.773
   Sumner, Seirian. *Endless Forms* — 595.79
***Predictably** Irrational.* Ariely, Dan — 153.8
PREDICTION (PSYCHOLOGY)
   Clark, Andy. *The Experience Machine* — 153
   Patterson, Scott. ★*Chaos Kings* — 338.5
***Prefabulous** Small Houses.* Koones, Sheri — 728

PREGNANCY
   Berg, Anastasia. ★*What Are Children For?* — 306.87
   Berger, Lynn. *Second Thoughts* — 306.85
   Bhattacharya, Shaoni. *The Baby Book* — 649.1
   Birbiglia, Mike. *The New One* — B
   Curtis, Glade B. *Your Pregnancy Week by Week* — 618.2
   Dochartaigh, Kerri ni. *Cacophony of Bone* — B
   Fisher, Susan J. *Taking Charge of Your Pregnancy* — 618.2
   Haelle, Tara. *The Informed Parent* — 649
   Harshe, January. *Birth Without Fear* — 618.2
   Jones, Lucy. ★*Matrescence* — 306.874
   Murkoff, Heidi Eisenberg. ★*What to Expect When You're Expecting* — 618.2
   Nelson, Maggie. ★*The Argonauts* — B
   Nilsson, Lennart. *A Child Is Born* — 612.6
   Oster, Emily. ★*Cribsheet* — 618.2
   Oster, Emily. ★*The Unexpected* — 618.2
   Rope, Kate. *Strong as a Mother* — 618.2
   Somerstein, Rachel. ★*Invisible Labor* — 618.8
   Zernicka-Goetz, Magdalena. *The Dance of Life* — 591.56
PREGNANCY COMPLICATIONS
   Oster, Emily. ★*The Unexpected* — 618.2
PREGNANT WOMEN
   Foster, Diana Greene. *The Turnaway Study* — 362.1988
   Glatt, John. ★*The Perfect Father* — 364.152
   Harshe, January. *Birth Without Fear* — 618.2
   Herriot, James. *All Things Wise and Wonderful* — B
   Holden, Wendy. ★*Born Survivors* — 940.53
   Mandel, Sarah. *Little Earthquakes* — B
   Nguyen, Bich Minh. *Owner of a Lonely Heart* — B
   Oster, Emily. ★*Cribsheet* — 618.2
   Oster, Emily. ★*The Unexpected* — 618.2
   Rope, Kate. *Strong as a Mother* — 618.2
PREHISTORIC ANIMALS
   Brusatte, Stephen. *The Rise and Reign of the Mammals* — 569
   Flannery, Tim F. *Europe* — 508.4
PREHISTORIC ERA (CENOZOIC, PLEISTOCENE)
   MacPhee, R. D. E. *End of the Megafauna* — 591.4
PREHISTORIC ERA (STONE AGE)
   Childs, Craig. *Atlas of a Lost World* — 551.7
   Johanson, Donald C. *Lucy* — 569
   Leakey, Richard E. *The Origin of Humankind* — 599.93
   Parker Pearson, Michael. *Stonehenge* — 936.2
   Pattison, Kermit. *Fossil Men* — 569.9
   Wrangham, Richard W. *Catching Fire* — 394.1
PREHISTORIC HUMANS
   Bohannon, Cat. ★*Eve* — 613
   Bohme, Madelaine. *Ancient Bones* — 599.93
   Childs, Craig. *Atlas of a Lost World* — 551.7
   Fagan, Brian M. *The Long Summer* — 551.6
   Flannery, Tim F. *Europe* — 508.4
   Johanson, Donald C. *Lucy* — 569
   Krause, Johannes. *A Short History of Humanity* — 599.9
   Leakey, Richard E. *The Origin of Humankind* — 599.93
   Pattison, Kermit. *Fossil Men* — 569.9
   Pryor, Francis. ★*Stonehenge* — 936.2
   Sanfilippo, Diane. *Practical Paleo* — 613.2
   Tattersall, Ian. *Masters of the Planet* — 599.93
   Wragg Sykes, Rebecca. *Kindred* — 569.9
   Wrangham, Richard W. *Catching Fire* — 394.1
   Yi, Sang-Hui. *Close Encounters with Humankind* — 599.93
PREHISTORIC RELIGION
   Robb, Graham. *The Discovery of France* — 944
Prejean, Helen
   The Death of Innocents — 364.66
   River of Fire — B
PREJEAN, HELEN
   Prejean, Helen. *River of Fire* — B
PREJUDICE
   Adichie, Chimamanda Ngozi. *We Should All Be Feminists* — 305.42
   Agarwal, Pragya. *Sway* — 177
   Alexander, Michelle. *The New Jim Crow* — 364.973
   Applewhite, Ashton. *This Chair Rocks* — 155.67
   Austin, Nefertiti. *Motherhood so White* — B
   Baker, Calvin. *A More Perfect Reunion* — 305.800973
   Baxley, Traci. *Social Justice Parenting* — 649
   Betts, Reginald Dwayne. *Felon* — 811
   Branch, Taylor. *Parting the Waters* — 973
   Cohen, Adam. ★*Imbeciles* — 344.7304

PUBLIC LIBRARY CORE COLLECTION: NONFICTION
Twentieth Edition

Currid-Halkett, Elizabeth. *The Overlooked Americans*	307.76
Eberhardt, Jennifer L. ★*Biased*	303.3
Espada, Martin. ★*Floaters*	811
Fuller, Pamela. ★*The Leader's Guide to Unconscious Bias*	658.3
Gates, Henry Louis. *And Still I Rise*	305.896
Gates, Henry Louis. ★*Stony the Road*	973
Holzer, Harold. *Brought Forth on This Continent*	973.7
Horace, Matthew. *The Black and the Blue*	B
Isen, Tajja. *Some of My Best Friends*	305.8
Jacobs, Sally H. *Althea*	B
Jawando, Will. ★*My Seven Black Fathers*	B
Kinzler, Katherine D. *How You Say It*	302.2
Lane, Charles. *Freedom's Detective*	B
Laymon, Kiese. ★*Heavy*	B
Levin, Josh. *The Queen*	364.16
McWhorter, Diane. *Carry Me Home*	976.1
Nussbaum, Martha Craven. *The New Religious Intolerance*	201.723
Okrent, Daniel. *The Guarded Gate*	344.73
Oluo, Ijeoma. ★*Be a Revolution*	305.8
Oluo, Ijeoma. ★*So You Want to Talk About Race*	305.800973
Pablo Cruz, Rosayra. *The Book of Rosy*	B
Phillips, Patrick. *Blood at the Root*	305.8
Qashu, Sayed. *Native*	892.4
Rudolf, David S. *American Injustice*	345.73
Ryan, Maureen. *Burn It Down*	791.43
Saad, Layla F. ★*Me and White Supremacy*	305.809
Smith, Danez. ★*Homie*	811
Tobar, Hector. ★*Our Migrant Souls*	305.868
Wingfield, Adia Harvey. *Gray Areas*	331.6
Prelude to Bruise. Jones, Saeed	811

PREMATURE BABIES
DiGregorio, Sarah. *Early*	618.92
Raffel, Dawn. *The Strange Case of Dr. Couney*	B

PREMATURE BABY CARE
DiGregorio, Sarah. *Early*	618.92

PREMATURE LABOR
DiGregorio, Sarah. *Early*	618.92

PREMENSTRUAL SYNDROME
Gupta, Shalene. *The Cycle*	618.1
★*The Premonition*. Lewis, Michael	614.5
The Premonitions Bureau. Knight, Sam	133.8

PRENATAL CARE
Fisher, Susan J. *Taking Charge of Your Pregnancy*	618.2
Oster, Emily. ★*The Unexpected*	618.2

Prendergast, John
Congo Stories	967.5103
Prep + *Rally*. Klein, Dini	641.5

PREPAREDNESS
Aktipis, Athena. ★*A Field Guide to the Apocalypse*	155.2
Christakis, Nicholas A. *Apollo's Arrow*	362.1962
Ripley, Amanda. *The Unthinkable*	155.9
Preppy Kitchen. Kanell, John	641.5
★*Prequel*. Maddow, Rachel	320.53

PRESBYTERIAN CHURCH
King, Maxwell. *The Good Neighbor*	B

PRESCHOOL CHILDREN
Christakis, Erika. *The Importance of Being Little*	372.21
Ghoting, Saroj Nadkarni. *Step into Storytime*	027.62
Reid, Rob. ★*200+ Original and Adapted Story Program Activities*	027.62
Santomero, Angela C. *Preschool Clues*	305.233
Preschool Clues. Santomero, Angela C	305.233

PRESCHOOL EDUCATION
Christakis, Erika. *The Importance of Being Little*	372.21

Prescod, Danielle
Token Black Girl	B

PRESCOD, DANIELLE
Prescod, Danielle. *Token Black Girl*	B

Prescod-Weinstein, Chanda
The Disordered Cosmos	523.01

Prescott, Matthew
Food Is the Solution	613.2

PRESCRIPTION DRUG ABUSE
Bond, Melissa. *Blood Orange Night*	616.8
Eyre, Eric. *Death in Mud Lick*	362.29
Macy, Beth. ★*Dopesick*	362.29
Macy, Beth. ★*Raising Lazarus*	362.29
McGreal, Chris. *American Overdose*	362.29
Rieder, Travis. *In Pain*	362.29
Tweedy, Jeff. *Let's Go (so We Can Get Back)*	B

PRESCRIPTION DRUG ABUSERS
Tweedy, Jeff. *Let's Go (so We Can Get Back)*	B

PRESCRIPTION DRUGS
Abramson, John. *Sickening*	338.4
Eyre, Eric. *Death in Mud Lick*	362.29
Hari, Johann. ★*Magic Pill*	613.2
Keefe, Patrick Radden. ★*Empire of Pain*	338.7
Macy, Beth. ★*Dopesick*	362.29
McGreal, Chris. *American Overdose*	362.29
Posner, Gerald L. ★*Pharma*	338.4
Prescription for the People. Quigley, Fran	338.4

PRESCRIPTION PRICING
Quigley, Fran. *Prescription for the People*	338.4
Presence. Cuddy, Amy	158.1
The President and the Assassin. Miller, Scott	973.8
★*President Carter*. Eizenstat, Stuart	B
President Garfield. Goodyear, C. W.	B
President McKinley. Merry, Robert W.	B

PRESIDENTIAL CANDIDATES
Allen, Jonathan. *Lucky*	324.973
Allen, Jonathan. *Shattered*	324.973
Arnsdorf, Isaac. ★*Finish What We Started*	320.52
Balz, Daniel J. *The Battle for America, 2008*	973.932
Bowden, Mark. *The Steal*	973.933
Chozick, Amy. *Chasing Hillary*	B
Christie, Chris. *Let Me Finish*	B
D'Antonio, Michael. *The Hunting of Hillary*	B
Farris, Scott. *Almost President*	324.973
Katz, David. *Barack Before Obama*	B
Kerry, John. *Every Day Is Extra*	B
Kranish, Michael. *Trump Revealed*	B
Lozada, Carlos. *The Washington Book*	320
Oliphant, Thomas. ★*The Road to Camelot*	973.922092
Osnos, Evan. *Joe Biden*	B

PRESIDENTIAL ELECTION, 1860
Achorn, Edward. *The Lincoln Miracle*	973.6
Grinspan, Jon. *Wide Awake*	973.7

PRESIDENTIAL ELECTION, 1948
McCullough, David G. *Truman*	B

PRESIDENTIAL ELECTION, 1960
Oliphant, Thomas. ★*The Road to Camelot*	973.922092

PRESIDENTIAL ELECTION, 1964
Sweig, Julia. *Lady Bird Johnson*	B

PRESIDENTIAL ELECTION, 1968
Clarke, Thurston. *The Last Campaign*	B

PRESIDENTIAL ELECTION, 2008
Balz, Daniel J. *The Battle for America, 2008*	973.932
Slevin, Peter. *Michelle Obama*	B

PRESIDENTIAL ELECTION, 2016
Alberta, Tim. *American Carnage*	324.2734
Allen, Jonathan. *Shattered*	324.973
Carpenter, Amanda B. *Gaslighting America*	973.933
Chozick, Amy. *Chasing Hillary*	B
Clinton, Hillary Rodham. *What Happened*	328.73
Gessen, Masha. *Surviving Autocracy*	973.933
Glaude, Eddie S. *Begin Again*	305.800973
Gunst, Kathy. *Rage Baking*	641.86
Harding, Luke. *Collusion*	324.70973
Howley, Kerry. *Bottoms Up and the Devil Laughs*	352.37
Jacob, Mira. *Good Talk*	741.5
Karl, Jonathan. *Front Row at the Trump Show*	973.933
Kranish, Michael. *Trump Revealed*	B
Nussbaum, Martha Craven. *The Monarchy of Fear*	306.20973
Schieffer, Bob. *Overload*	070.4
Shimer, David. *Rigged*	324.60973
Weiner, Tim. *The Folly and the Glory*	327.73047
Weissmann, Andrew. ★*Where Law Ends*	324.7

PRESIDENTIAL ELECTION, 2020
Abrams, Stacey. *Our Time Is Now*	324.60973
Bender, Michael C. *"Frankly, We Did Win This Election"*	973.933
Biden Owens, Valerie. *Growing up Biden*	B
Bowden, Mark. *The Steal*	973.933
Dunn, Harry. *Standing My Ground*	B
Hasen, Richard L. *Election Meltdown*	324.973
Klinenberg, Eric. ★*2020*	306
Martin, Jonathan. *This Will Not Pass*	973.933
Plouffe, David. *A Citizen's Guide to Beating Donald Trump*	324.0973

AUTHOR, TITLE, SERIES AND SUBJECT INDEX

Reilly, Ryan J. ★*Sedition Hunters* — 364.1
Shimer, David. *Rigged* — 324.60973
Wilson, Rick. *Running Against the Devil* — 973.933

PRESIDENTIAL ELECTIONS
Collins, Gail. *William Henry Harrison* — B
Denevi, Timothy. *Freak Kingdom* — B
Farris, Scott. *Almost President* — 324.973
Guelzo, Allen C. *Lincoln and Douglas* — 973.6
Lowery, Wesley. ★*American Whitelash* — 305.8
Wehle, Kim. *What You Need to Know About Voting and Why* — 324.60973
Whyte, Kenneth. *The Uncrowned King* — B

PRESIDENTIAL STAFF
Daniels, Stormy. *Full Disclosure* — B
Dorey-Stein, Beck. *From the Corner of the Oval* — B
Guerrero, Jean. *Hatemonger* — B
Litt, David. *Thanks, Obama* — B
O'Brien, Phillips Payson. *The Second Most Powerful Man in the World* — B
Psaki, Jen. *Say More* — B
Rhodes, Benjamin J. *The World as It Is* — 973.932
Rice, Condoleezza. *No Higher Honor* — B
Whipple, Chris. *The Gatekeepers* — 973.92092

PRESIDENTIAL TAPES
Brokaw, Tom. *The Fall of Richard Nixon* — B
Dobbs, Michael. *King Richard* — 973.924

PRESIDENTS
Abrams, Dan. *Kennedy's Avenger* — 973.922
Adams, John. *My Dearest Friend* — 973.4
Allen, Jonathan. *Lucky* — 324.973
Alter, Jonathan. *His Very Best* — B
Arnsdorf, Isaac. ★*Finish What We Started* — 320.52
Avlon, John P. *Washington's Farewell* — 973.4
Bade, Rachael. ★*Unchecked* — 342.73
Baier, Bret. *Three Days in January* — B
Baier, Bret. *To Rescue the Constitution* — 973.4
Baime, A. J. *The Accidental President* — B
Baker, Peter. *The Divider* — 973.933
Baron, Martin. ★*Collision of Power* — 070.4
Barron, David J. *Waging War* — 342.73
Bender, Michael C. *"Frankly, We Did Win This Election"* — 973.933
Berfield, Susan. *The Hour of Fate* — 973.91
Berg, A. Scott. ★*Wilson* — B
Bernstein, Carl. ★*All the President's Men* — 364.1
Beschloss, Michael R. ★*Presidents of War* — 355.00973
Biden Owens, Valerie. *Growing up Biden* — B
Bird, Kai. *The Outlier* — 973.926
Blumenthal, Sidney. *A Self-Made Man* — B
Blumenthal, Sidney. *Wrestling with His Angel* — B
Boles, John B. *Jefferson* — B
Borneman, Walter R. *Polk* — B
Boykin, Keith. *Race Against Time* — 305.8
Branch, Taylor. *The Clinton Tapes* — 973.929
Brand, Christo. *Mandela* — B
Brands, H. W. *Andrew Jackson, His Life and Times* — B
Brands, H. W. *The General vs. the President* — 973.918092
Brands, H. W. ★*The Man Who Saved the Union* — B
Brands, H. W. *Reagan* — B
Brands, H. W. *Traitor to His Class* — B
Brands, H. W. *Woodrow Wilson* — B
Brands, H. W. ★*The Zealot and the Emancipator* — 920
Brettschneider, Corey Lang. *The Oath and the Office* — 342.73
Brettschneider, Corey Lang. *The Presidents and the People* — 342.73
Brewster, Todd. *Lincoln's Gamble* — 973.7
Brinkley, Alan. *John F. Kennedy* — B
Brinkley, Douglas. ★*American Moonshot* — 629.40973
Brinkley, Douglas. *Rightful Heritage* — B
Brinkley, Douglas. *The Wilderness Warrior* — B
Broadwater, Jeff. *James Madison* — B
Brokaw, Tom. *The Fall of Richard Nixon* — B
Brower, Kate Andersen. *First in Line* — 920
Brower, Kate Andersen. *The Residence* — 975.3
Bunting, Josiah. *Ulysses S. Grant* — B
Burlingame, Michael. *Abraham Lincoln* — B
Burstein, Andrew. *Madison and Jefferson* — 973.4
Bush, George. *All the Best, George Bush* — 973.928
Bush, George W. *41* — B
Bush, George W. *Decision Points* — B
Byrne, Paula. *Kick* — B
Calloway, Colin G. *The Indian World of George Washington* — 323.1197

Carlin, John. *Playing the Enemy* — 968.06
Carlson, Brady. *Dead Presidents* — B
Caro, Robert A. ★*The Passage of Power* — B
Carter, Jimmy. *Everything to Gain* — B
Carter, Jimmy. *A Full Life* — B
Carter, Jimmy. *An Hour Before Daylight* — B
Carter, Jimmy. *Keeping Faith* — B
Carter, Jimmy. *Sharing Good Times* — 973.926
Carter, Jimmy. *White House Diary* — 973.926
Carwardine, Richard. *Lincoln* — B
Chait, Jonathan. *Audacity* — 973.932
Charter, David. *Royal Audience* — 941.085
Cheney, Lynne V. *James Madison* — B
Cheney, Lynne V. *The Virginia Dynasty* — B
Chernow, Ron. ★*Grant* — B
Chernow, Ron. *Washington* — B
Clarke, Thurston. *JFK's Last Hundred Days* — B
Clinton, Bill. *My Life* — B
Coe, Alexis. ★*You Never Forget Your First* — B
Cohen, Andrew. *Two Days in June* — 973.922
Cohen, Jared. *Accidental Presidents* — 973.09
Cohen, Jared. *Life After Power* — 973.09
Cook, Jane Hampton. *American Phoenix* — 973.5
Cooper, John Milton. *Woodrow Wilson* — B
Craughwell, Thomas J. *Stealing Lincoln's Body* — 973.7092
Dallek, Robert. ★*Franklin D. Roosevelt* — B
Dallek, Robert. *Harry S. Truman* — B
Dallek, Robert. *Let Every Nation Know* — B
Dallek, Robert. *Nixon and Kissinger* — B
Dallek, Robert. *An Unfinished Life* — B
Dean, John W. *The Nixon Defense* — 973.924092
Donald, Aida DiPace. *Citizen Soldier* — B
Donald, David Herbert. *Lincoln* — B
Draper, Robert. *To Start a War* — 956.7044
Duiker, William J. *Ho Chi Minh* — B
Dunbar, Erica Armstrong. ★*Never Caught* — B
Dyson, Michael Eric. *The Black Presidency* — 305.800973
Egan, Timothy. ★*The Big Burn* — 973.911
Eizenstat, Stuart. ★*President Carter* — B
Ellis, Joseph J. *American Sphinx* — 973.4
Ellis, Joseph J. *First Family* — 973.4
Ellis, Joseph J. *Founding Brothers* — 973.4
Ellis, Joseph J. ★*His Excellency* — B
Evangelista, Patricia. ★*Some People Need Killing* — 364.4
Farrell, John A. ★*Richard Nixon* — B
Fehrman, Craig. *Author in Chief* — 920
Feldman, Noah. *The Three Lives of James Madison* — B
Feldstein, Mark Avrom. *Poisoning the Press* — 973.924092
Finkelman, Paul. *Millard Fillmore* — B
Flexner, James Thomas. *George Washington and the New Nation, 1783-1793* — 973.4
Flexner, James Thomas. *George Washington* — B
Foer, Franklin. ★*The Last Politician* — 973.934
Foner, Eric. *The Fiery Trial* — 973.7092
Frank, Jeffrey. *The Trials of Harry S. Truman* — 973.918
Gaines, James R. *For Liberty and Glory* — B
Garrow, David J. *Rising Star* — B
Gevisser, Mark. *A Legacy of Liberation* — B
Gienapp, William E. *Abraham Lincoln and Civil War America* — B
Giorgione, Michael. *Inside Camp David* — 975.2
Good, Cassandra A. *First Family* — 920
Goodwin, Doris Kearns. ★*The Bully Pulpit* — 973.91
Goodwin, Doris Kearns. ★*Leadership in Turbulent Times* — 973.09
Goodwin, Doris Kearns. *No Ordinary Time* — 920
Goodwin, Doris Kearns. ★*Team of Rivals* — B
Goodyear, C. W. *President Garfield* — B
Gordon-Reed, Annette. *Andrew Johnson* — B
Gordon-Reed, Annette. ★*Most Blessed of the Patriarchs* — 973.4
Graff, Garrett M. *Watergate* — 973.924
Graff, Henry F. *Grover Cleveland* — B
Grant, James. ★*John Adams* — B
Grant, Ulysses S. ★*The Annotated Memoirs of Ulysses S. Grant* — B
Grant, Ulysses S. *Memoirs and Selected Letters* — B
Grinspan, Jon. *Wide Awake* — 973.7
Gutzman, Kevin R. C. *The Jeffersonians* — 973.5
Hager, Jenna Bush. *Sisters First* — B
Halberstam, David. *The Best and the Brightest* — 973.92
Hennessey, Susan. *Unmaking the Presidency* — 973.933

PUBLIC LIBRARY CORE COLLECTION: NONFICTION
Twentieth Edition

Hill, Clint. *Five Days in November*	973.922092
Hill, Clint. *Five Presidents*	B
Hitchcock, William I. *The Age of Eisenhower*	973.921092
Hitchens, Christopher. *Thomas Jefferson*	B
Holzer, Harold. *Brought Forth on This Continent*	973.7
Horn, Jonathan. *Washington's End*	B
Hutchinson, Cassidy. *Enough*	B
Isenberg, Nancy. *The Problem of Democracy*	973.4
Jackson, Julian. *De Gaulle*	B
Jacobsen, Annie. *Surprise, Kill, Vanish*	327.1273
Jarrett, Valerie. *Finding My Voice*	B
Johnson, Lyndon B. *Taking Charge*	973.923
Johnson, Paul. *Eisenhower*	B
Johnson, Paul. *George Washington*	B
Johnston, David Cay. *The Big Cheat*	973.933
Johnston, David Cay. *It's Even Worse Than You Think*	973.933
Kaplan, Fred. *John Quincy Adams*	B
Kaplan, Fred. *Lincoln and the Abolitionists*	973.7092
Karl, Jonathan. *Betrayal*	973.933
Karl, Jonathan. *Front Row at the Trump Show*	973.933
Kearse, Bettye. *The Other Madisons*	920
Keenan, Cody. *Grace*	973.932
Kornacki, Steve. *The Red and the Blue*	306.20973
Kurtz, Howard. *Media Madness*	973.933
Larson, Edward J. *The Return of George Washington*	B
Larson, Erik. *The Demon of Unrest*	973.7
Leaming, Barbara. *Kick Kennedy*	B
Leonnig, Carol. *I Alone Can Fix It*	973.933
Levine, Robert S. ★*The Failed Promise*	973.8
Levingston, Steven. *Kennedy and King*	920
Lithwick, Dahlia. *Lady Justice*	345.73
Logevall, Fredrik. ★*JFK*	B
Lowenstein, Roger. *Ways and Means*	973.7
Lozada, Carlos. *The Washington Book*	320
Lusane, Clarence. *The Black History of the White House*	975.3
Mahoney, Richard D. *Sons & Brothers*	920
Mandela, Nelson. *Dare Not Linger*	B
Mandela, Nelson. *In His Own Words*	B
Mandela, Nelson. ★*Long Walk to Freedom*	B
Mandela, Nelson. *Mandela*	B
Mandela, Nelson. *The Prison Letters of Nelson Mandela*	968.06092
Mann, Jim. *The Rebellion of Ronald Reagan*	973.927092
Maraniss, David. ★*Barack Obama*	B
Martin, Jonathan. *This Will Not Pass*	973.933
Marton, Kati. *Hidden Power*	B
May, Gary. *John Tyler*	B
Mayer, Jane. *The Dark Side*	973.931
McCullough, David G. ★*John Adams*	B
McCullough, David G. *Mornings on Horseback*	B
McCullough, David G. *Truman*	B
McGinty, Brian. *Lincoln's Greatest Case*	346.7303
McGrath, Tim. *James Monroe*	B
McKean, David. *Watching Darkness Fall*	940.53
McPherson, James M. ★*Abraham Lincoln*	B
McPherson, James M. ★*Tried by War*	973.7
Meacham, Jon. ★*American Lion*	B
Meacham, Jon. ★*And There Was Light*	B
Meacham, Jon. ★*Destiny and Power*	B
Meacham, Jon. ★*The Soul of America*	973
Meacham, Jon. ★*Thomas Jefferson*	B
Meltzer, Brad. ★*The First Conspiracy*	973.4
Meltzer, Brad. *The Lincoln Conspiracy*	973.7092
Merry, Robert W. *A Country of Vast Designs*	B
Merry, Robert W. *President McKinley*	B
Millard, Candice. *Destiny of the Republic*	973.8
Millard, Candice. *River of Doubt*	918.1
Miller, Scott. *The President and the Assassin*	973.8
Minutaglio, Bill. *Dallas 1963*	973.922092
Mitchell, Elizabeth. *Lincoln's Lie*	973.7092
Morgan, Robert. *Lions of the West*	978
Morley, Jefferson. *Scorpions' Dance*	973.924
Morris, Edmund. ★*Colonel Roosevelt*	B
Morris, Edmund. ★*The Rise of Theodore Roosevelt*	B
Morris, Edmund. ★*Theodore Rex*	973.911
Myers, Steven Lee. *The New Tsar*	B
O'Toole, Patricia. *The Moralist*	B
Obama, Barack. ★*A Promised Land*	B
Onassis, Jacqueline Kennedy. *Historic Conversations on Life with John F. Kennedy*	B
Page, Susan. ★*The Matriarch*	B
Peres, Shimon. *No Room for Small Dreams*	B
Perlstein, Rick. *The Invisible Bridge*	973.924
Perlstein, Rick. ★*Nixonland*	973.924
Perlstein, Rick. ★*Reaganland*	973.926
Persico, Joseph E. *Franklin and Lucy*	973.917092
Peters, Charles. *Lyndon B. Johnson*	B
Petri, Alexandra. *Nothing Is Wrong and Here Is Why*	973.933
Philbrick, Nathaniel. *Travels with George*	973.4
Poniewozik, James. *Audience of One*	324.7
Posner, Gerald L. *Case Closed*	364.1
Prud'homme, Alex. ★*Dinner with the President*	973
Randall, Willard Sterne. *George Washington*	B
Raphael, Ray. *Mr. President*	352.230973
Rappleye, Charles. *Herbert Hoover in the White House*	B
Reagan, Ronald. *The Reagan Diaries*	B
Reagan, Ronald. *Reagan*	B
Remnick, David. *The Bridge*	B
Reston, James. *The Conviction of Richard Nixon*	973.924092
Reynolds, David S. ★*Abe*	B
Ricks, Thomas E. ★*First Principles*	973.09
Rohde, David. *In Deep*	973.933
Roll, David L. *Ascent to Power*	973.918
Rothkopf, David J. *American Resistance*	973.933
Rubenstein, David M. *The American Story*	973.07202
Rumsfeld, Donald. *When the Center Held*	973.925092
Sandburg, Carl. *Abraham Lincoln*	B
Saxton, Martha. *The Widow Washington*	B
Schmidt, Michael S. ★*Donald Trump v. The United States*	973.933
Senik, Troy. *A Man of Iron*	B
Sherman, Casey. *Above and Beyond*	973.922092
Shesol, Jeff. *Supreme Power*	347.73
Shirley, Craig. *Mary Ball Washington*	B
Shlaes, Amity. *Coolidge*	B
Short, Philip. *Putin*	B
Smith, Jean Edward. *Bush*	973.931
Smith, Jean Edward. *FDR*	B
Smith, Michael S. *Designing History*	975.3
Smith, Richard Norton. *An Ordinary Man*	B
Sorensen, Theodore C. *Counselor*	B
Souza, Pete. *Obama*	973.932
Souza, Pete. *Shade*	973.932
Souza, Pete. *The West Wing and Beyond*	917.53
Spitz, Bob. ★*Reagan*	B
Stark, Peter. *Young Washington*	B
Steinberg, Jonny. *Winnie and Nelson*	920
Stelter, Brian. *Hoax*	070.4
Stephanopoulos, George. ★*The Situation Room*	973.09
Stewart, David O. *George Washington*	973.4
Stewart, David O. *Madison's Gift*	B
Sullivan, Kevin. *Trump on Trial*	342.73
Sunstein, Cass R. *Impeachment*	342.73
Swanson, James L. *End of Days*	973.922092
Symonds, Craig L. *Lincoln and His Admirals*	B
Taubman, William. *Gorbachev*	B
Taylor, Jay. *The Generalissimo*	B
Thomas, Evan. *Being Nixon*	B
Thomas, Evan. *Ike's Bluff*	973.921092
Toobin, Jeffrey. *True Crimes and Misdemeanors*	973.933
Traub, James. *John Quincy Adams*	B
Trump, Mary L. *Too Much and Never Enough*	B
Unger, Harlow G. *The Last Founding Father*	B
Updegrove, Mark K. *The Last Republicans*	973.928
Van Doren, Adam. *The House Tells the Story*	728
Von Tunzelmann, Alex. *Blood and Sand*	909.82
Vowell, Sarah. *Assassination Vacation*	B
Walker, Shaun. *The Long Hangover*	947.086
Wallace, Chris. *Countdown 1945*	940.54
Ward, Geoffrey C. ★*The Roosevelts*	B
Weiner, Tim. *One Man Against the World*	B
Whipple, Chris. *The Fight of His Life*	973.934
Whipple, Chris. *The Spymasters*	920
White, Gayle Jessup. *Reclamation*	B
White, Ronald C. *A. Lincoln*	B
White, Ronald C. ★*American Ulysses*	B
Whitlock, Craig. *The Afghanistan Papers*	958.104

AUTHOR, TITLE, SERIES AND SUBJECT INDEX

Whyte, Kenneth. *Hoover*	B
Widmer, Edward L. *Lincoln on the Verge*	B
Widmer, Edward L. *Martin Van Buren*	B
Wills, Garry. *James Madison*	B
Wills, Garry. *Lincoln at Gettysburg*	973.7
Winik, Jay. *1944*	940.53
Wolff, Michael. *Fire and Fury*	973.933
Wolff, Michael. *Landslide*	973.933
Wood, Gordon S. *Empire of Liberty*	973.4
Wood, Gordon S. *Friends Divided*	920
Woodward, Bob. *Fear*	973.933
Woodward, Bob. *The Final Days*	B
Woodward, Bob. *Peril*	973.933
Woodward, Bob. *Shadow*	973.92
Yaffa, Joshua. *Between Two Fires*	920
Zeitz, Joshua. *Building the Great Society*	973.923
Zelensky, Volodymyr. *A Message from Ukraine*	947.7
The **Presidents** and the People. Brettschneider, Corey Lang	342.73
★**Presidents** of War. Beschloss, Michael R.	355.00973

PRESIDENTS' SPOUSES

Adams, Abigail. *Abigail Adams*	973.4
Adams, John. *My Dearest Friend*	973.4
Allgor, Catherine. *A Perfect Union*	B
Anthony, Carl Sferrazza. *Camera Girl*	B
Anthony, Carl Sferrazza. *Nellie Taft*	B
Bell-Scott, Patricia. *The Firebrand and the First Lady*	920
Brady, Patricia. *Martha Washington*	B
Brower, Kate Andersen. *First Women*	920
Brower, Kate Andersen. *The Residence*	975.3
Burns, Eric. *Someone to Watch Over Me*	973.917092
Carter, Jimmy. *Everything to Gain*	B
Clinton, Hillary Rodham. *It Takes a Village*	305.23
Clinton, Hillary Rodham. *Living History*	B
Cook, Blanche Wiesen. *Eleanor Roosevelt; Volume 2*	B
Cook, Blanche Wiesen. ★*Eleanor Roosevelt; Volume 3*	B
Cook, Jane Hampton. *American Phoenix*	973.5
Ellis, Joseph J. *First Family*	973.4
Gillette, Michael L. *Lady Bird Johnson*	B
Goodwin, Doris Kearns. *No Ordinary Time*	920
Greenberg, Amy S. *Lady First*	B
Hill, Clint. *Mrs. Kennedy and Me*	973.922092
Hill, Clint. *My Travels with Mrs. Kennedy*	B
Holton, Woody. *Abigail Adams*	B
Jordan, Mary. *The Art of Her Deal*	B
Kashner, Sam. *The Fabulous Bouvier Sisters*	920
Leaming, Barbara. *Jacqueline Bouvier Kennedy Onassis*	B
Leaming, Barbara. *Mrs. Kennedy*	B
Marton, Kati. *Hidden Power*	B
McCubbin, Lisa. *Betty Ford*	B
McKeon, Kathy. *Jackie's Girl*	B
Michaelis, David. ★*Eleanor*	973.917
Obama, Michelle. ★*Becoming*	B
Obama, Michelle. ★*The Light We Carry*	B
Onassis, Jacqueline Kennedy. *Historic Conversations on Life with John F. Kennedy*	B
Page, Susan. ★*The Matriarch*	B
Pakula, Hannah. *The Last Empress*	B
Persico, Joseph E. *Franklin and Lucy*	973.917092
Peyser, Marc N. *Hissing Cousins*	B
Quinn, Susan. *Eleanor and Hick*	973.09
Rogers, Katie. ★*American Woman*	973.09
Slevin, Peter. *Michelle Obama*	B
Steinberg, Jonny. *Winnie and Nelson*	920
Swarns, Rachel L. ★*American Tapestry*	B
Sweig, Julia. *Lady Bird Johnson*	B
Taraborrelli, J. Randy. *Jackie, Janet & Lee*	920
Taraborrelli, J. Randy. ★*Jackie*	B
Thomas, Louisa. *Louisa*	B
Tumulty, Karen. *The Triumph of Nancy Reagan*	B
Ward, Geoffrey C. ★*The Roosevelts*	B
Presilla, Maricel E.	
Gran Cocina Latina	641.5972

PRESLEY, ELVIS, 1935-1977

Alden, Ginger. *Elvis and Ginger*	B
Connolly, Ray. *Being Elvis*	B
McDonald, Greg (Producer). *Elvis and the Colonel*	920

PRESS

Burns, Eric. *Infamous Scribblers*	071
Didion, Joan. ★*Let Me Tell You What I Mean*	814
LaFollette, Marcel C. *Writing for Their Lives*	071.3

PRESS AND POLITICS

Baron, Martin. ★*Collision of Power*	070.4
Brokaw, Tom. *The Fall of Richard Nixon*	B
Carpenter, Amanda B. *Gaslighting America*	973.933
Elwood, Phil. *All the Worst Humans*	659.2
Feldstein, Mark Avrom. *Poisoning the Press*	973.924092
Goodwin, Doris Kearns. ★*The Bully Pulpit*	973.91
Karl, Jonathan. *Front Row at the Trump Show*	973.933
Kroll, Andy. *A Death on W Street*	364.152
McCraw, David Edward. *Truth in Our Times*	342.7308
Mitchell, Elizabeth. *Lincoln's Lie*	973.7092
Schieffer, Bob. *Overload*	070.4

PRESS LAW

McCraw, David Edward. *Truth in Our Times*	342.7308

Press, Eyal	
★*Dirty Work*	331.7
Press, Joy	
Stealing the Show	791.45
Pressly, Paul M.	
On the Rim of the Caribbean	975.8
Pressman, Aliza	
The 5 Principles of Parenting	649.1
Pressman, Steven	
50 Children	940.53

PRESSURE COOKING

Clark, Melissa. *Comfort in an Instant*	641.5
Conner, Polly. ★*From Freezer to Cooker*	641.6
Hartwig, Melissa. *The Whole30 Slow Cooker*	641.5
Jaffrey, Madhur. ★*Madhur Jaffrey's Instantly Indian Cookbook*	641.595
Shumski, Daniel. *How to Instant Pot*	641.5
Weinstein, Bruce. *The Great Big Pressure Cooker Book*	641.5

Preston, Christopher J.	
Tenacious Beasts	591.68
Preston, Diana	
Before the Fallout	303.48
Eight Days at Yalta	940.53
The Evolution of Charles Darwin	508
A Higher Form of Killing	940.4
Paradise in Chains	996.18
Preston, Douglas J.	
★*The Lost City of the Monkey God*	972.85
The Lost Tomb	930.1

PRESTON, DOUGLAS J.

Preston, Douglas J. ★*The Lost City of the Monkey God*	972.85
Preston, Douglas J. *The Lost Tomb*	930.1

Preston, Katherine	
Out with It	B

PRESTON, KATHERINE, 1984-

Preston, Katherine. *Out with It*	B

Preston, Paul	
A People Betrayed	946
The Spanish Holocaust	946.081
Preston, Richard	
Crisis in the Red Zone	614.5
The Hot Zone	614.5
The Wild Trees	585
Presumed Guilty. Chemerinsky, Erwin	344.7305
Preszler, Trent	
Little and Often	B

PRESZLER, TRENT

Preszler, Trent. *Little and Often*	B
Pretentiousness. Fox, Dan	700
Pretty Baby. Belcher, Chris	B
Pretty Fun. Hudson, Kate	642
Preventing The Next Pandemic. Hotez, Peter J.	362.1969

PREVENTIVE MEDICINE

Barry, John M. ★*The Great Influenza*	614.5
Benson, Herbert. *The Relaxation Response*	155.9
Brem, Rachel. *No Longer Radical*	616.99
Deer, Brian. *The Doctor Who Fooled the World*	610.92
Esmonde-White, Miranda. *Aging Backwards*	613.7
Funk, Kristi. *Breasts*	616.99
Gates, Bill. ★*How to Prevent the Next Pandemic*	614.5
Gupta, Sanjay. ★*Keep Sharp*	153.4
Holt, Nathalia. *Cured*	614.5
Hotez, Peter J. *Preventing the Next Pandemic*	362.1969

PUBLIC LIBRARY CORE COLLECTION: NONFICTION
Twentieth Edition

Lieberman, Jeffrey A. *Malady of the Mind*	616.89
Mackenzie, Debora. *Covid-19*	616.2
Nakazawa, Donna Jackson. *The Angel and the Assassin*	612.8
Randall, David K. *Black Death at the Golden Gate*	616.9
Raza, Azra. *The First Cell*	616.99
Servan-Schreiber, David. *Anticancer*	616.99
The *Price* of Inequality. Stiglitz, Joseph E.	305.50973
The *Price* of Justice. Leamer, Laurence	346.7302
PRICE POLICY	
Russell, Rupert. *Price Wars*	332.64
Price Wars. Russell, Rupert	332.64
Price, Catherine	
Vitamania	612.3
Price, David A.	
Geniuses at War	940.54
★*Love and Hate in Jamestown*	975.5
Price, Devon	
★*Laziness Does Not Exist*	158.1
Price, Maggie	
Painting with Pastels	741.2
Price, Margo	
Maybe We'll Make It	B
PRICE, MARGO, 1983-	
Price, Margo. *Maybe We'll Make It*	B
Price, Neil S.	
★*Children of Ash and Elm*	948
Price, Polly J.	
Plagues in the Nation	614.4
Price, Reynolds	
A Serious Way of Wondering	241
Price, S. L.	
Playing Through the Whistle	796.332
PRICES	
Derks, Scott. *The Value of a Dollar*	338.5
Derks, Scott. *The Value of a Dollar*	338.5
Prickett, Pamela J.	
★*The Unclaimed*	363.7
PRIDE AND VANITY	
Perry, Mark. *The Most Dangerous Man in America*	B
Yong, Sable. *Die Hot with a Vengeance*	646.7
Prideaux, Sue	
Edvard Munch	B
I Am Dynamite!	B
PRIEST IMPERSONATORS	
Sisman, Adam. *The Professor and the Parson*	364.16
Priest Turned Therapist Treats Fear of God. Hoagland, Tony	811
Priestdaddy. Lockwood, Patricia	B
PRIESTHOOD	
Phelan, Tom. *We Were Rich and We Didn't Know It*	B
PRIESTS	
Lockwood, Patricia. *Priestdaddy*	B
Rundell, Katherine. ★*Super-Infinite*	B
Primal Leadership. Goleman, Daniel	658.4
PRIMARY EDUCATION	
De Stefano, Cristina. *The Child Is the Teacher*	B
PRIMATES	
Martin, Wednesday. *Primates of Park Avenue*	974.7
Primates of Park Avenue. Martin, Wednesday	974.7
PRIMATOLOGISTS	
Fouts, Roger. *Next of Kin*	156
Goodall, Jane. ★*Beyond Innocence*	B
Goodall, Jane. ★*In the Shadow of Man*	599.8
Waal, F. B. M. de. *Bonobo*	599.88
PRIME MINISTERS	
Blair, Tony. *A Journey*	B
Borman, Tracy. *Thomas Cromwell*	B
Burkett, Elinor. *Golda*	B
Johnson, Paul. *Churchill*	B
Larson, Erik. ★*The Splendid and the Vile*	940.54
Manchester, William. *The Last Lion, Winston Spencer Churchill.*	B
Manchester, William. *The Last Lion, Winston Spencer Churchill.*	B
Manchester, William. *The Last Lion, Winston Spencer Churchill.*	B
Moore, Charles. *Margaret Thatcher*	941.085
Pfeffer, Anshel. *Bibi*	B
Roberts, Andrew. ★*Churchill*	B
PRIME MINISTERS' SPOUSES	
Purnell, Sonia. *Clementine*	B
A *Primer* for Poets & Readers of Poetry. Orr, Gregory	808.1

Prince	
The Beautiful Ones	B
Prince. Shahidi, Afshin	B
PRINCE	
Garcia, Mayte. *The Most Beautiful*	920
Greenman, Ben. *Dig If You Will the Picture*	B
Prince. *The Beautiful Ones*	B
Shahidi, Afshin. *Prince*	B
★*The Prince.* Machiavelli, Niccolo	320.1
Prince Charles. Smith, Sally Bedell	B
Prince of Darkness. White, Shane	B
The *Prince* of Los Cocuyos. Blanco, Richard	B
The *Prince* of the Marshes. Stewart, Rory	956.7044
PRINCES	
Barnes, Julian. *The Man in the Red Coat*	B
Cadbury, Deborah. *Princes at War*	920
Gill, Gillian. *We Two*	941.081
Grant, Richard. *The Deepest South of All*	976.2
Harry. ★*Spare*	B
Hope, Bradley. *Blood and Oil*	B
Hubbard, Ben (Journalist). *Mbs*	B
Jones, Michael K. *The Black Prince*	B
King, Greg. *The Assassination of the Archduke*	B
King, Greg. *Twilight of Empire*	943.6
Smith, Sally Bedell. *Prince Charles*	B
Snyder, Timothy. *The Red Prince*	B
Stoppard, Tom. ★*Rosencrantz & Guildenstern Are Dead*	822
Woolley, Benjamin. *The King's Assassin*	B
Princes At War. Cadbury, Deborah	920
Princess Noire. Cohodas, Nadine	782.42164
PRINCESSES	
Brown, Craig. *Ninety-Nine Glimpses of Princess Margaret*	B
Brown, Tina. *The Diana Chronicles*	B
Goldstone, Nancy Bazelon. *Daughters of the Winter Queen*	920
Hawksley, Lucinda. *Queen Victoria's Mysterious Daughter*	B
Holmes, Elizabeth. *HRH*	941.085
King, Greg. *The Assassination of the Archduke*	B
Morton, Andrew. *Diana*	B
Rappaport, Helen. *The Romanov Sisters*	920
Spoto, Donald. *High Society*	B
Thomson, Keith. *Born to Be Hanged*	910.4
The *Princeton* Dictionary of Ancient Egypt. Shaw, Ian	932
The *Princeton* Field Guide to Dinosaurs. Paul, Gregory S.	567.9
The *Principles* of Knitting. Hiatt, June	746.43
Pringle, Heather Anne	
The Mummy Congress	393
Print, Pattern, Sew. Hewett, Jen	646.4
PRINTERS	
Brands, H. W. *The First American*	B
Bunker, Nick. *Young Benjamin Franklin*	B
Franklin, Benjamin. ★*The Autobiography of Benjamin Franklin*	B
Isaacson, Walter. ★*Benjamin Franklin*	B
PRINTING	
Houston, Keith. *The Book*	002.09
Kluger, Richard. *Indelible Ink*	B
Kurlansky, Mark. *Paper*	676
Pettegree, Andrew. *The Book in the Renaissance*	070.5
Printing by Hand. Corwin, Lena	745.5
PRINTING INDUSTRY AND TRADE	
Smyth, Adam. *The Book-Makers*	686.2
Printing on Fabric. Swearington, Jen	746.6
PRINTING PRESSES	
Castleman, Michael. *The Untold Story of Books*	381
PRINZHORN, HANS, 1886-1933	
English, Charlie. *The Gallery of Miracles and Madness*	709.04
Prior-Palmer, Lara	
Rough Magic	798.4
PRIOR-PALMER, LARA	
Prior-Palmer, Lara. *Rough Magic*	798.4
PRIORITIES	
Bruni, Frank. *The Beauty of Dusk*	B
PRISON CORRUPTION	
Bauer, Shane. *American Prison*	365
Davis, Angela Y. *Abolition*	364.6
PRISON GUARDS	
Bardenwerper, William. *The Prisoner in His Palace*	956.7044
Bauer, Shane. *American Prison*	365
Brand, Christo. *Mandela*	B

AUTHOR, TITLE, SERIES AND SUBJECT INDEX

PRISON INDUSTRY AND TRADE
    Bauer, Shane. *American Prison* — 365
    Davis, Angela Y. *Abolition* — 364.6
    Ford, Elizabeth. *Sometimes Amazing Things Happen* — B
*The **Prison** Letters of Nelson Mandela*. Mandela, Nelson — 968.06092
PRISON LIBRARIES
    Hopwood, Shon. *Law Man* — B
    Sweeney, Jennifer. *Literacy* — 027.62
PRISON REFORM
    Blakinger, Keri. *Corrections in Ink* — B
    Burton, Susan. *Becoming Ms. Burton* — B
    Hobbs, Jeff. *Children of the State* — 364.36
    Norton, Jack. *The Jail Is Everywhere* — 365
    Peterson, Marlon. *Bird Uncaged* — B
    Salaam, Yusef. *Better, Not Bitter* — B
    Sered, Danielle. *Until We Reckon* — 364.6
PRISON RIOTS
    Thompson, Heather Ann. *Blood in the Water* — 365
PRISON SENTENCES
    Canon, Dan. ★*Pleading Out* — 345.73
    King, David. *The Trial of Adolf Hitler* — 345.43
    Manning, Chelsea. *Readme.Txt* — B
PRISON-INDUSTRIAL COMPLEX
    Bauer, Shane. *American Prison* — 365
    Betts, Reginald Dwayne. *Felon* — 811
    Ford, Elizabeth. *Sometimes Amazing Things Happen* — B
Prisoner. Rezaian, Jason
PRISONER ABUSE
    Adayfi, Mansoor. *Don't Forget Us Here* — B
    Khan, Mahvish Rukhsana. *My Guantanamo Diary* — 973.931
    Thompson, Heather Ann. *Blood in the Water* — 365
*The **Prisoner** in His Palace*. Bardenwerper, William — 956.7044
***Prisoner** of Tehran*. Nemat, Marina — B
PRISONER OF WAR CAMPS
    Bruning, John R. *Indestructible* — B
    Fox, Margalit. *The Confidence Men* — 940.4
PRISONER-OF-WAR ESCAPES
    Fox, Margalit. *The Confidence Men* — 940.4
    Macintyre, Ben. ★*Prisoners of the Castle* — 940.54
    Strauss, Gwen. *The Nine* — 940.53
PRISONERS
    Adayfi, Mansoor. *Don't Forget Us Here* — B
    Austen, Ben. *Correction* — 364.6
    Bailey, Catherine. *A Castle in Wartime* — 943.086
    Bardenwerper, William. *The Prisoner in His Palace* — 956.7044
    Barnett, Brittany K. ★*A Knock at Midnight* — B
    Bauer, Shane. *American Prison* — 365
    Belkin, Lisa. *Genealogy of a Murder* — 362.88
    Betts, Reginald Dwayne. ★*Redaction* — 704.9
    Blakinger, Keri. *Corrections in Ink* — B
    Bowden, Mark. *The Last Stone* — 363.25
    Egan, Timothy. ★*The Immortal Irishman* — B
    Fabricant, M. Chris. *Junk Science and the American Criminal Justice System* — 363.25
    Fairweather, Jack. *The Volunteer* — B
    Fedderly, Eva. *These Walls* — 365
    Ford, Elizabeth. *Sometimes Amazing Things Happen* — B
    Gaffney, Ginger. *Half Broke* — B
    Guinn, Jeff. ★*Manson* — B
    Isenberg, Sheila. *Women Who Love Men Who Kill* — 362.83
    Jobb, Dean. *A Gentleman and a Thief* — 364.16
    Keneally, Thomas. *A Commonwealth of Thieves* — 994
    Khan, Mahvish Rukhsana. *My Guantanamo Diary* — 973.931
    King, David. *The Trial of Adolf Hitler* — 345.43
    Kuo, Michelle. *Reading with Patrick* — B
    Lauren, Jillian. *Behold the Monster* — 364.152
    Moore, Wes. *The Other Wes Moore* — B
    Morton, Michael. *Getting Life* — B
    O'Connell, Mark. *A Thread of Violence* — 364.152
    Oshinsky, David M. *Worse Than Slavery* — 365
    Pang, Amelia. ★*Made in China* — 331.11
    Prejean, Helen. *The Death of Innocents* — 364.66
    Preston, Diana. *Paradise in Chains* — 996.18
    Rayman, Graham. ★*Rikers* — 365
    Rudolf, David S. *American Injustice* — 345.73
    Salaam, Yusef. *Better, Not Bitter* — B
    Scott-Clark, Cathy. *The Forever Prisoner* — 364.6
    Sheff, David. *The Buddhist on Death Row* — B

    Thompson, Heather Ann. *Blood in the Water* — 365
    Toobin, Jeffrey. ★*Homegrown* — 363.325
    White, Neil. *In the Sanctuary of Outcasts* — B
    Woodfox, Albert. *Solitary* — B
***Prisoners** of History*. Lowe, Keith — 940.54
***Prisoners** of Hope*. Woods, Randall Bennett — 973.923
★***Prisoners** of the Castle*. Macintyre, Ben — 940.54
PRISONERS OF WAR
    Adayfi, Mansoor. *Don't Forget Us Here* — B
    Bascomb, Neal. *The Escape Artists* — 940.4
    Bradley, James. *Flyboys* — 940.54
    Brotherton, Marcus. *A Bright and Blinding Sun* — 940.54
    Bruning, John R. *Indestructible* — B
    Clavin, Thomas. *Lightning Down* — 940.54
    Edmonds, Chris. *No Surrender* — B
    Englund, Peter. *November 1942* — 940.53
    Enss, Chris. *Mochi's War* — B
    Fox, Margalit. *The Confidence Men* — 940.4
    Freeman, Sally Mott. *The Jersey Brothers* — 920
    Hamilton, Duncan. *For the Glory* — B
    Henderson, Bruce B. *Bridge to the Sun* — 940.53
    Khan, Mahvish Rukhsana. *My Guantanamo Diary* — 973.931
    Lichtblau, Eric. *Return to the Reich* — B
    Macintyre, Ben. ★*Prisoners of the Castle* — 940.54
    Millard, Candice. ★*Hero of the Empire* — 968.04
    Nasaw, David. *The Last Million* — 940.53
    Norman, Elizabeth M. *We Band of Angels* — 940.54
    Norman, Michael. *Tears in the Darkness* — 940.54
    Parkin, Simon. *The Island of Extraordinary Captives* — 940.53
    Russell, Jan Jarboe. *The Train to Crystal City* — 940.53
    Slahi, Mohamedou Ould. *The Mauritanian* — 958.104
    Trimble, Lee. *Beyond the Call* — 940.54
    Weintraub, Robert. *No Better Friend* — 940.54
PRISONERS OF WAR, AMERICAN
    Clavin, Thomas. *Lightning Down* — 940.54
    Hillenbrand, Laura. ★*Unbroken* — B
    Lee, Heath Hardage. ★*The League of Wives* — 959.704
    Sides, Hampton. ★*Ghost Soldiers* — 940.54
PRISONERS OF WAR, BRITISH
    Sides, Hampton. ★*Ghost Soldiers* — 940.54
PRISONERS OF WAR, FRENCH
    Humbert, Agnes. *Resistance* — B
PRISONERS OF WAR, GERMAN
    Strauss, Gwen. *The Nine* — 940.53
PRISONERS OF WAR, JAPANESE
    Hillenbrand, Laura. ★*Unbroken* — B
PRISONERS OF WAR, POLISH
    Karski, Jan. *Story of a Secret State* — 940.53
    Rogoyska, Jane. *Surviving Katyn* — 940.54
***Prisoners** Without Trial*. Daniels, Roger — 940.53
PRISONERS' FAMILIES
    Ford, Ashley C. ★*Somebody's Daughter* — B
    Shahani, Aarti Namdev. *Here We Are* — B
PRISONS
    Applebaum, Anne. ★*Gulag* — 365
    Austen, Ben. *Correction* — 364.6
    Bauer, Shane. *American Prison* — 365
    Betts, Reginald Dwayne. *Felon* — 811
    Blau, Magda Hellinger. *The Nazis Knew My Name* — 940.53
    Borzutzky, Daniel. *Lake Michigan* — 811
    Bradley, James. *Flyboys* — 940.54
    Clavin, Thomas. *Lightning Down* — 940.54
    Davis, Angela Y. *Abolition* — 364.6
    Dudley, Steven S. *MS-13* — 364.106
    Edmonds, Chris. *No Surrender* — B
    Gilliard, Dominique Dubois. *Rethinking Incarceration* — 261.8
    Hillenbrand, Laura. ★*Unbroken* — B
    Humbert, Agnes. *Resistance* — B
    Khan, Mahvish Rukhsana. *My Guantanamo Diary* — 973.931
    Lee, Heath Hardage. ★*The League of Wives* — 959.704
    Love, Bettina L. *Punished for Dreaming* — 371.829
    Macintyre, Ben. ★*Prisoners of the Castle* — 940.54
    Magida, Arthur J. *Code Name Madeleine* — 940.54
    Norman, Elizabeth M. *We Band of Angels* — 940.54
    Norman, Michael. *Tears in the Darkness* — 940.54
    Rezaian, Jason. *Prisoner* — B
    Rogoyska, Jane. *Surviving Katyn* — 940.54
    Russell, Jan Jarboe. *The Train to Crystal City* — 940.53

PUBLIC LIBRARY CORE COLLECTION: NONFICTION
Twentieth Edition

Sered, Danielle. *Until We Reckon*	364.6
Sides, Hampton. ★*Ghost Soldiers*	940.54
Smith, Mychal Denzel. *Stakes Is High*	973.933
Solzhenitsyn, Aleksandr Isaevich. ★*The Gulag Archipelago 1918-1956*	365
Solzhenitsyn, Aleksandr Isaevich. ★*The Gulag Archipelago, 1918-1956*	365
Strauss, Gwen. *The Nine*	940.53
Trimble, Lee. *Beyond the Call*	940.54
Wachsmann, Nikolaus. *Kl*	940.53
Weintraub, Robert. *No Better Friend*	940.54

PRISONS FOR WOMEN

Blakinger, Keri. *Corrections in Ink*	B

Pritchett, Georgia

My Mess Is a Bit of a Life	B

PRITCHETT, GEORGIA

Pritchett, Georgia. *My Mess Is a Bit of a Life*	B

PRIVACY

Citron, Danielle Keats. *The Fight for Privacy*	342.7308
Friedman, Barry. ★*Unwarranted*	344.7305
Gellman, Barton. *Dark Mirror*	
Hill, Kashmir. ★*Your Face Belongs to Us*	006.2
Humes, Edward. *The Forever Witness*	363.25
Waldman, Michael. *The Supermajority*	347.73

PRIVACY RIGHTS

Boghosian, Heidi. *"i Have Nothing to Hide"*	363.1
Chertoff, Michael. *Exploding Data*	343.7309
Cole, Samantha. *How the Internet Changed Sex and Sex Changed the Internet*	306.7
Cox, Joseph. *Dark Wire*	363.2
Friedman, Barry. ★*Unwarranted*	344.7305
Mitnick, Kevin D. *The Art of Invisibility*	005.8
Strittmatter, Kai. *We Have Been Harmonized*	323.44
Wiggins, Christopher L. *How Data Happened*	310
Private Empire. Coll, Steve	338.7
Private Equity. Sun, Carrie	B

PRIVATE EQUITY

Morgenson, Gretchen. ★*These Are the Plunderers*	332.6
Romeo, Nick. *The Alternative*	174

PRIVATE INVESTIGATORS

Bowden, Mark. *The Case of the Vanishing Blonde*	364.10973
Maroney, Tyler. *The Modern Detective*	658.4
The Private Lives of the Impressionists. Roe, Sue	920
The Private Lives of the Tudors. Borman, Tracy	920

PRIVATE SCHOOLS

Crawford, Lacy. *Notes on a Silencing*	B
Fitzpatrick, Cara. *The Death of Public School*	379.73

PRIVATEERING

Bergreen, Laurence. *In Search of a Kingdom*	B
Dolin, Eric Jay. ★*Rebels at Sea*	973.3
Thomson, Keith. *Born to Be Hanged*	910.4

PRIVATEERS

Dolin, Eric Jay. ★*Rebels at Sea*	973.3
Ronald, Susan. *The Pirate Queen*	B

PRIVATIZATION

Bauer, Shane. *American Prison*	365
Vance, Ashlee. *When the Heavens Went on Sale*	621.43

PRIVILEGE (SOCIAL PSYCHOLOGY)

Blakinger, Keri. *Corrections in Ink*	B
Dubus, Andre. *Ghost Dogs*	814
Henderson, Rob Kim. *Troubled*	B
Jaffe, Sarah W. *Wanting What's Best*	649
Leach, Samantha. ★*The Elissas*	362.73
Marshall, McMillan. *Among the Bros*	362.29
Miller, Kei. *Things I Have Withheld*	814
Oluo, Ijeoma. *Mediocre*	305.310973

Prizant, Barry M.

★*Uniquely Human*	618.92
★*The Prize*. Yergin, Daniel	338.2

PRO-CHOICE MOVEMENT

Andrews, Becca. ★*No Choice*	362.1988
Prager, Joshua. *The Family Roe*	342.7308
Rankin, Lauren. *Bodies on the Line*	362.1988

PRO-LIFE MOVEMENT

Prager, Joshua. *The Family Roe*	342.7308
Shah, Meera. *You're the Only One I've Told*	362.1988

PROBABILITIES

Brooks, Michael. *The Quantum Astrologer's Handbook*	B
Pinker, Steven. *Rationality*	153.4
Schneps, Leila. *Math on Trial*	345

Thorp, Edward O. *A Man for All Markets*	B
Wheelan, Charles J. *Naked Statistics*	519.5

PROBATION

Hardy, Jason Matthew. ★*The Second Chance Club*	364.6
★*The Problem of Alzheimer's*. Karlawish, Jason	616.8
The Problem of Democracy. Isenberg, Nancy	973.4

PROBLEM SOLVING

Bennett, Michael. *F*ck Feelings*	158
Christian, Brian. *Algorithms to Live By*	153.4
Du Sautoy, Marcus. ★*Around the World in Eighty Games*	790.1
Duhigg, Charles. ★*Supercommunicators*	153.6
Eberhardt, Jennifer L. ★*Biased*	303.3
Goldfarb, Ben. *Crossings*	333.77
Kaku, Michio. *Quantum Supremacy*	006.3
Nelson, Bryn. *Flush*	612.3
Riel, Jennifer. *Creating Great Choices*	658.4
The Problems of Philosophy. Russell, Bertrand	110

PROCESSED FOODS

Freeman, Andrea. ★*Ruin Their Crops on the Ground*	338.1
Moss, Michael. ★*Hooked*	613.2
Tulleken, Chris van. *Ultra-Processed People*	664

PROCRASTINATION

Gilkey, Charlie. *Start Finishing*	658.4
The Prodigy's Cousin. Ruthsatz, Joanne	155.45

PRODUCT MANAGEMENT

Kerpen, Dave. *Likeable Social Media*	658.8

PRODUCT SAFETY

Etter, Lauren. ★*The Devil's Playbook*	338.7

PRODUCTS

Hammack, William Scott. ★*Things We Make*	620
Pang, Amelia. ★*Made in China*	331.11

Proenza-Coles, Christina

American Founders	973

PROFESSIONAL ATHLETES

Babb, Valerie Melissa. *The Book of James*	B
Bella, Timothy. *Barkley*	B
Bennett, Michael. *Things That Make White People Uncomfortable*	305.896
Bryant, Kobe. *The Mamba Mentality*	B
Chapman, Rex. ★*It's Hard for Me to Live with Me*	B
Clarke, Gemma. *Soccerwomen*	796.334
Feinstein, John. *Quarterback*	B
Hernandez, Keith. *I'm Keith Hernandez*	B
Lloyd, Carli. *When Nobody Was Watching*	B
Ortiz, David. *Papi*	B
Oxenham, Gwendolyn. *Under the Lights and in the Dark*	796.334
Rapinoe, Megan. *One Life*	B
Rogers, Robbie. *Coming Out to Play*	B
Rosen, Charles. *Sugar*	B
Smith, Sam. *Hard Labor*	796.323
Wertheim, L. Jon. *This Is Your Brain on Sports*	796.01

PROFESSIONAL BASEBALL

Brown, Tim. ★*The Tao of the Backup Catcher*	796.357
Bryant, Howard. *The Last Hero*	B
Bryant, Howard. *Rickey*	B
Clavin, Thomas. *The DiMaggios*	920
Cook, Kevin. *Ten Innings at Wrigley*	796.357
Diamond, Jared M. *Swing Kings*	796.357
Dykstra, Lenny. *House of Nails*	B
Eisenberg, John. *The Streak*	796.357
Halberstam, David. *Summer of '49*	796.357
Halberstam, David. *The Teammates*	B
Hample, Zack. *The Baseball*	796.357
Hirsch, James S. *Willie Mays*	B
Law, Keith. *The Inside Game*	796.35764
Leavy, Jane. *The Big Fella*	B
Mays, Willie. *24*	B
Megdal, Howard. *The Baseball Talmud*	796.357
Neyer, Rob. *Power Ball*	796.357
Perron, Cam. ★*Comeback Season*	796.357
Pessah, Jon. *The Game*	796.357
Rapp, David. *Tinker to Evers to Chance*	796.357
Reiter, Ben. *Astroball*	796.357
Simon, Scott. *My Cubs*	796.357
Stout, Glenn. *Fenway 1912*	796.357
Svrluga, Barry. *The Grind*	796.357

PROFESSIONAL BASEBALL MANAGERS

Creamer, Robert W. *Stengel*	796.357
Pennington, Bill. *Billy Martin*	B

2242

AUTHOR, TITLE, SERIES AND SUBJECT INDEX

PROFESSIONAL BASEBALL PLAYERS
    Bryant, Howard. *The Last Hero* — B
    Bryant, Howard. *Rickey* — B
    Clavin, Thomas. *The DiMaggios* — 920
    Cook, Kevin. *Ten Innings at Wrigley* — 796.357
    Diamond, Jared M. *Swing Kings* — 796.357
    Dykstra, Lenny. *House of Nails* — B
    Eisenberg, John. *The Streak* — 796.357
    Halberstam, David. *The Teammates* — B
    Hample, Zack. *The Baseball* — 796.357
    Hernandez, Keith. *I'm Keith Hernandez* — B
    Hirsch, James S. *Willie Mays* — B
    Kepner, Tyler. *K* — 796.357
    Knight, Molly. *The Best Team Money Can Buy* — 796.357
    Maraniss, David. *Clemente* — B
    Mays, Willie. *24* — B
    Montgomery, Patrick. *Baseball's Great Expectations* — 796.357
    Posnanski, Joe. *The Baseball 100* — 796.357
    Rapp, David. *Tinker to Evers to Chance* — 796.357
    Robinson, Jackie. *I Never Had It Made* — B
    Santiago, Wilfred. *"21"* — 741.5
    Turbow, Jason. *They Bled Blue* — 796.357

PROFESSIONAL BASEBALL SCOUTING
    Lewis, Michael. ★*Moneyball* — 796.357
    Lindbergh, Ben. *The Only Rule Is That It Has to Work* — 796.357

PROFESSIONAL BASEBALL SCOUTS
    Posnanski, Joe. *The Soul of Baseball* — 796.357

PROFESSIONAL BASEBALL TEAMS
    Cohen, Rich. *The Chicago Cubs* — 796.357
    Halberstam, David. *Summer of '49* — 796.357
    Knight, Molly. *The Best Team Money Can Buy* — 796.357
    Pennington, Bill. *Billy Martin* — B
    Simon, Scott. *My Cubs* — 796.357
    Stout, Glenn. *Fenway 1912* — 796.357
    Turbow, Jason. *They Bled Blue* — 796.357

PROFESSIONAL BASKETBALL
    Baylor, Elgin. *Hang Time* — B
    Glockner, Andy. *Chasing Perfection* — 796.323
    Kriegel, Mark. *Pistol* — B
    MacMullan, Jackie. ★*Basketball* — 796.323
    Malinowski, Erik. *Betaball* — 796.323
    McCallum, Jack. *Golden Days* — 796.323
    Pearlman, Jeff. ★*Three-Ring Circus* — 796.323
    Pippen, Scottie. *Unguarded* — B
    Simmons, Bill. *The Book of Basketball* — 796.323
    Weitzman, Yaron. *Tanking to the Top* — 796.323
    West, Jerry. *West by West* — B
    Williams, Jay. *Life Is Not an Accident* — B

PROFESSIONAL BASKETBALL PLAYERS
    Anthony, Carmelo. *Where Tomorrows Aren't Promised* — B
    Bella, Timothy. *Barkley* — B
    Benedict, Jeff. *Lebron* — B
    Bryant, Kobe. *The Mamba Mentality* — B
    Glockner, Andy. *Chasing Perfection* — 796.323
    Iguodala, Andre. *The Sixth Man* — B
    Kriegel, Mark. *Pistol* — B
    McCallum, Jack. *Golden Days* — 796.323
    Oakley, Charles. *The Last Enforcer* — B
    Pearlman, Jeff. ★*Three-Ring Circus* — 796.323
    Pippen, Scottie. *Unguarded* — B
    Sielski, Mike. *The Rise* — B
    Smith, Sam. *Hard Labor* — 796.323
    Weitzman, Yaron. *Tanking to the Top* — 796.323
    Windhorst, Brian. *Lebron, Inc.* — B

PROFESSIONAL BASKETBALL TEAMS
    Simmons, Bill. *The Book of Basketball* — 796.323

PROFESSIONAL EMPLOYEES
    Wingfield, Adia Harvey. *Gray Areas* — 331.6

PROFESSIONAL ETHICS
    Callahan, David. *The Cheating Culture* — 174

PROFESSIONAL FOOTBALL
    Cole, Jason. *Elway* — B
    Dawidoff, Nicholas. *Collision Low Crossers* — 796.332
    Easterbrook, Gregg. ★*The King of Sports* — 796.332
    Eatman, Nicholas. *Friday, Saturday, Sunday in Texas* — 796.332
    Eisenberg, John. *The League* — 796.332
    Fainaru-Wada, Mark. *League of Denial* — 617.1
    Feinstein, John. *Quarterback* — B

    Harris, David. *The Genius* — B
    Horrigan, Joe. *NFL Century* — 796.332
    Jaworksi, Ron. *The Games That Changed the Game* — 796.332
    Laskas, Jeanne Marie. *Concussion* — 617.5
    Myers, Gary. *Brady vs. Manning* — B
    Myers, Gary. *The Catch* — 796.332
    Oriard, Michael. *Brand NFL* — 796.332
    Pearlman, Jeff. *Boys Will Be Boys* — 796.332
    Pearlman, Jeff. *Football for a Buck* — 796.332
    Ribowsky, Mark. *The Last Cowboy* — 796.332
    Rice, Jerry. *America's Game* — 796.332
    Sando, Mike. *The Football 100* — 796.332
    Wickersham, Seth. ★*It's Better to Be Feared* — 796.332

PROFESSIONAL FOOTBALL COACHES
    Parcells, Bill. *Parcells* — B
    Pearlman, Jeff. *Boys Will Be Boys* — 796.332
    Ribowsky, Mark. *The Last Cowboy* — 796.332
    Ribowsky, Mark. *Shula* — B

PROFESSIONAL FOOTBALL PLAYERS
    Eatman, Nicholas. *Friday, Saturday, Sunday in Texas* — 796.332
    Feinstein, John. *Quarterback* — B
    Myers, Gary. *Brady vs. Manning* — B
    Oriard, Michael. *Brand NFL* — 796.332
    Pearlman, Jeff. *Boys Will Be Boys* — 796.332
    Pearlman, Jeff. *Football for a Buck* — 796.332
    Pearlman, Jeff. *Gunslinger* — B
    Ribowsky, Mark. *Shula* — B
    Sando, Mike. *The Football 100* — 796.332
    Wickersham, Seth. ★*It's Better to Be Feared* — 796.332

PROFESSIONAL FOOTBALL TEAMS
    Parcells, Bill. *Parcells* — B
    Pearlman, Jeff. *Boys Will Be Boys* — 796.332

PROFESSIONAL GOLF
    Carter, Iain. *Golf Wars* — 796.352
    Shipnuck, Alan. *Phil* — B

PROFESSIONAL GOLFERS
    Callahan, Tom. *Arnie* — B
    Carter, Iain. *Golf Wars* — 796.352
    Norton, Hughes. ★*Rainmaker* — 796.352
    Shipnuck, Alan. *Phil* — B
    Woods, Tiger. *The 1997 Masters* — B

PROFESSIONAL HOCKEY
    Gretzky, Wayne. *99* — B

PROFESSIONAL HOCKEY PLAYERS
    Gretzky, Wayne. *99* — B

PROFESSIONAL MATERIALS — COLLECTION DEVELOPMENT
    Alabaster, Carol. *Developing an Outstanding Core Collection* — 025.2
    Bartlett, Wendy K. *Floating Collections* — 025.2
    Breitenbach, Kathleen. ★*LGBTQIA+ Books for Children and Teens* — 028.7
    Cart, Michael. *Young Adult Literature* — 813.009
    Chance, Rosemary. *Young Adult Literature in Action* — 011.62
    Disher, Wayne. *Crash Course in Collection Development* — 025.2
    Dorr, Christina H. ★*Profiles in Resilience* — 028.5
    Evans, G. Edward. *Collection Management Basics* — 025.2
    Hughes-Hassell, Sandra. ★*Collection Management for Youth* — 025.2
    Johnson, Peggy. ★*Fundamentals of Collection Development and Management* — 025
    Manglik, Gauri. ★*Muslims in Story* — 809
    Orr, Cynthia. ★*Crash Course in Readers' Advisory* — 025.5
    Pattee, Amy. *Developing Library Collections for Today's Young Adults* — 027.62
    Pawuk, Michael. *Graphic Novels* — 016.74
    Phoenix, Jack. *Maximizing the Impact of Comics in Your Library* — 026
    Vnuk, Rebecca. *The Weeding Handbook* — 025.2
    Wilkinson, Frances C. *The Complete Guide to Acquisitions Management* — 025.2

PROFESSIONAL MATERIALS — GENERAL
    Berger, Sidney E. *The Dictionary of the Book* — 002.03
    Bignoli, Callan. ★*Responding to Rapid Change in Libraries* — 020
    Boland, Becca. *Making the Most of Teen Library Volunteers* — 023
    Brown, Christopher C. *Librarian's Guide to Online Searching* — 025.04
    Brunsting, Karen. ★*Open Access Literature in Libraries* — 070.5
    Butler, Rebecca P. ★*Copyright for Teachers & Librarians in the 21st Century* — 346.7304
    Cassell, Kay Ann. ★*Reference and Information Services* — 025.5
    Cole, Natalie. ★*Transforming Summer Programs at Your Library* — 028
    Crews, Kenneth D. ★*Copyright Law for Librarians and Educators* — 346.7304
    Damon-Moore, Laura C. *The Artist's Library* — 021.2

PUBLIC LIBRARY CORE COLLECTION: NONFICTION
Twentieth Edition

Farmer, Lesley S. J. ★*Impactful Community-Based Literacy Projects*	372.6
Flowers, Sarah. *Evaluating Teen Services and Programs*	027.62
Gasaway, Laura N. *Copyright Questions and Answers for Information Professionals*	346.7304
Ghoting, Saroj Nadkarni. *Step into Storytime*	027.62
Goldsmith, Francisca. *Crash Course in Contemporary Reference*	025.5
Gunnels, Claire B. *Joint Libraries*	027.4
Hernon, Peter. *Assessing Service Quality*	025.5
Landau, Herbert B. *The Small Public Library Survival Guide*	025.1
Laughlin, Sara. *The Quality Library*	025.1
Lavender, Kenneth. *Book Repair*	025.8
Maxwell, Robert L. *Maxwell's Handbook for Rda, Resource Description & Access*	025.3
Mulac, Carolyn. *Fundamentals of Reference*	025.5
Pinnell-Stephens, June. *Protecting Intellectual Freedom in Your Public Library*	025.2
Reid, Rob. ★*200+ Original and Adapted Story Program Activities*	027.62
Ross, Catherine Sheldrick. *Conducting the Reference Interview*	025.5
Russell, Carrie. *Complete Copyright for K-12 Librarians and Educators*	346.73
Smith, G. Stevenson. *Cost Control for Nonprofits in Crisis*	025.1
Stanley, Mary J. *Managing Library Employees*	023
Suber, Peter. *Open Access*	070.5
Sweeney, Jennifer. *Literacy*	027.62
Tucker, Dennis C. *Crash Course in Library Supervision*	023
Tucker, Virginia. *Finding the Answers to Legal Questions*	340.072
VanDuinkerken, Wyoma. *The Challenge of Library Management*	025.1

PROFESSIONAL MATERIALS — LIBRARY MANAGEMENT

Crowley, Bill. *Defending Professionalism*	020.92
Curzon, Susan Carol. *What Every Library Director Should Know*	025.1
Flaherty, Mary Grace. ★*The Disaster Planning Handbook for Libraries*	025.8
Halsted, Deborah D. ★*Disaster Planning*	025.8
Harris, Lesley Ellen. *Licensing Digital Content*	346.7304
Henry, Jo. *Cultivating Civility*	023
Johnson, Doug. *The Indispensable Librarian*	025.1
Kowalsky, Michelle. *Creating Inclusive Library Environments*	027.6
Larson, Jeanette. *The Public Library Policy Writer*	025.1
MacKellar, Pamela H. ★*Winning Grants*	025.1
Maddigan, Beth. *Community Library Programs That Work*	021.2
McNeil, Beth. *Fundamentals of Library Supervision*	023
Newman, Bobbi L. ★*Fostering Wellness in the Workplace*	023
Verminski, Alana. ★*Fundamentals of Electronic Resources Management*	025.2
Wilkinson, Frances C. *The Complete Guide to Acquisitions Management*	025.2

PROFESSIONAL MATERIALS — PROGRAMMING

Anderson, Amelia. *Library Programming for Autistic Children and Teens*	027.6
Anderson, Jimmeka. *Power Lines*	020
Bratt, Jessica Anne. *Let's Talk About Race in Storytimes*	027.62
Cox, Marge. *Kids' Books and Maker Activities*	372.41
Del Negro, Janice. *Folktales Aloud*	027.62
Maxwell, Lucas. *Podcasting with Youth*	006.7
Phoenix, Jack. *Maximizing the Impact of Comics in Your Library*	026
Rogers-Whitehead, Carrie. ★*Serving Teens and Adults on the Autism Spectrum*	027.6
Snow, Jess. ★*Outreach Services for Teens*	027.4
Trelease, Jim. ★*Jim Trelease's Read-Aloud Handbook*	372.4

PROFESSIONAL MATERIALS — READERS' ADVISORY

Bradford, Robin. ★*The Readers' Advisory Guide to Romance*	025.2
Dorr, Christina H. ★*Profiles in Resilience*	028.5
Goldsmith, Francisca. *The Readers' Advisory Guide to Graphic Novels*	025.2
Manglik, Gauri. ★*Muslims in Story*	809
Orr, Cynthia. ★*Crash Course in Readers' Advisory*	025.5
Pawuk, Michael. *Graphic Novels*	016.74
Spratford, Becky Siegel. *The Readers' Advisory Guide to Horror*	025.5

PROFESSIONAL MATERIALS — SCHOOL MEDIA CENTERS

Cox, Marge. *Kids' Books and Maker Activities*	372.41
Del Negro, Janice. *Folktales Aloud*	027.62
Johnson, Doug. *The Indispensable Librarian*	025.1
Knoll, Debra J. *Engaging Babies in the Library*	027.62

PROFESSIONAL MATERIALS — TECHNOLOGY

Turnbow, Dominique. ★*Demystifying Online Instruction in Libraries*	028.7

PROFESSIONAL SOCCER

Abbot, Sebastian. *The Away Game*	796.334
Clarke, Gemma. *Soccerwomen*	796.334
Conn, David. *The Fall of the House of FIFA*	796.334
Cox, Michael. *Zonal Marking*	796
Dohrmann, George. *Switching Fields*	796.334

PROFESSIONAL SPORTS

Dohrmann, George. *Switching Fields*	796.334
Gehrig, Lou. *The Lost Memoir*	B
Law, Keith. *The Inside Game*	796.35764
Lundquist, Verne. *Play by Play*	B
Schoenfeld, Bruce. ★*Game of Edges*	796.04
Simmons, Bill. *The Book of Basketball*	796.323
Thompson, Wright. *The Cost of These Dreams*	B
Wertheim, L. Jon. *Glory Days*	796.09
Wertheim, L. Jon. *This Is Your Brain on Sports*	796.01

PROFESSIONAL SPORTS TEAMS

Lewis, Michael. ★*Moneyball*	796.357
Malinowski, Erik. *Betaball*	796.323
Pessah, Jon. *The Game*	796.357

PROFESSIONAL TENNIS

Agassi, Andre. *Open*	B
Fisher, Marshall Jon. *A Terrible Splendor*	796.342
Phillips, Rowan Ricardo. *The Circuit*	796.342

PROFESSIONAL TENNIS PLAYERS

Agassi, Andre. *Open*	B
Clarey, Christopher. ★*The Master*	B
Fisher, Marshall Jon. *A Terrible Splendor*	796.342
King, Billie Jean. ★*All In*	B
McPhee, John. *Levels of the Game*	796.34

PROFESSIONAL WRESTLERS

Patterson, Pat. *Accepted*	B

PROFESSIONAL WRESTLING

Patterson, Pat. *Accepted*	B

PROFESSIONAL-CLIENT RELATIONS

Elwood, Phil. *All the Worst Humans*	659.2
The Professor and the Madman. Winchester, Simon	423
The Professor and the Parson. Sisman, Adam	364.16
Professor Stewart's Casebook of Mathematical Mysteries. Stewart, Ian	793.74
Profiles in Courage. Kennedy, John F.	920
★*Profiles in Mental Health Courage*. Kennedy, Patrick J.	362.29
★*Profiles in Resilience*. Dorr, Christina H.	028.5

PROFIT

Citron, Danielle Keats. *The Fight for Privacy*	342.7308
Gelles, David. *The Man Who Broke Capitalism*	330.12
Johnston, David Cay. *The Big Cheat*	973.933
Profit and Punishment. Messenger, Tony	362.5

PROFITEERING

Blunt, Katherine. *California Burning*	333.793
The Profiteers. Denton, Sally	B

PROGRAM EVALUATION IN EDUCATION

Ravitch, Diane. *The Death and Life of the Great American School System*	379.1
Programming The Universe. Lloyd, Seth	530.12

PROGRESS

Acemoglu, Daron. *Power and Progress*	303.48
Winchester, Simon. *The Men Who United the States*	973

PROGRESSIVE ROCK MUSIC

Povey, Glenn. *Echoes*	782.42166
Reynolds, Simon. *Shock and Awe*	781.6609

PROGRESSIVISM (UNITED STATES POLITICS)

Caldwell, Christopher. *The Age of Entitlement*	305.240973
Farrell, John A. *Clarence Darrow*	B
Ford, Tanisha C. *Our Secret Society*	B
Frank, Thomas. *The People, No*	320.56
Goodwin, Doris Kearns. ★*The Bully Pulpit*	973.91
Hochschild, Adam. *Rebel Cinderella*	B
Jayapal, Pramila. *Use the Power You Have*	B
Jones, Brenda. *Alexandria Ocasio-Cortez*	B
Morris, Edmund. ★*Colonel Roosevelt*	B
Sharpton, Al. *Rise Up*	973.933
Tubbs, Michael. *The Deeper the Roots*	B
Walker, Hunter. *The Truce*	324.2736

PROHIBITION

Bair, Deirdre. *Al Capone*	B
Eig, Jonathan. *Get Capone*	364.1
Okrent, Daniel. *Last Call*	363.4
Stout, David. *The Kidnap Years*	364.15
Project 562. Wilbur, Matika	970.004
Project Animal Farm. Faruqi, Sonia	338.1

PROJECT MERCURY

Ackmann, Martha. *The Mercury 13*	920

AUTHOR, TITLE, SERIES AND SUBJECT INDEX

Shesol, Jeff. *Mercury Rising* — 629.45
PROJECT VOYAGER
  Bell, Jim. *The Interstellar Age* — 919
Projections. Deisseroth, Karl — 616.89
Promise Me, Dad. Biden, Joseph R. — B
The Promise of the Grand Canyon. Ross, John F. — 917.91
★*A Promised Land*. Obama, Barack — B
PROMISES
  Dietrich, Sean. *You Are My Sunshine* — B
  Mendelson, Cheryl. ★*Vows* — 203
Promises of Gold = Promesas De Oro. Olivarez, Jose — 811
PROMOTION OF SPECIAL EVENTS
  Lang, Michael. *The Road to Woodstock* — 781.66
PRONOUNS
  Baron, Dennis E. *What's Your Pronoun?* — 425.55
Proof. Auburn, David — 812
Proof. Rogers, Adam — 663
Proof of Life. Levin, Daniel — 956.9104
Proofiness. Seife, Charles — 510
PROPAGANDA
  Cairo, Alberto. *How Charts Lie* — 302.2
  Churchwell, Sarah Bartlett. *Behold, America* — 973.9
  Deer, Brian. *The Doctor Who Fooled the World* — 610.92
  Fischer, Paul. *A Kim Jong-Il Production* — 791.43
  Hasen, Richard L. *Election Meltdown* — 324.973
  Hemming, Henry. *Agents of Influence* — 940.54
  Huxley, Aldous. ★*Brave New World Revisited* — 823
  Jang, Jin-Sung. *Dear Leader* — B
  Kalder, Daniel. *The Infernal Library* — 321.9
  King, David. *The Trial of Adolf Hitler* — 345.43
  Kroll, Andy. *A Death on W Street* — 364.152
  Kupperman, Michael. *All the Answers* — 741.5
  Levitin, Daniel J. ★*A Field Guide to Lies* — 153.4
  Maddow, Rachel. ★*Prequel* — 320.53
  Marie, Jane. ★*Selling the Dream* — 658.8
  Newitz, Annalee. *Stories Are Weapons* — 355.3
  Pomerantsev, Peter. ★*How to Win an Information War* — 940.53
  Stelter, Brian. *Hoax* — 070.4
  Stengel, Richard. *Information Wars* — 355.3
  Strittmatter, Kai. *We Have Been Harmonized* — 323.44
  Trimborn, Jurgen. *Leni Riefenstahl* — B
  Weiner, Tim. *The Folly and the Glory* — 327.73047
  Wilkman, Jon. *Screening Reality* — 070.1
PROPERTY
  Piketty, Thomas. ★*Capital and Ideology* — 305
PROPERTY RIGHTS
  Linklater, Andro. *Owning the Earth* — 333.3
  Taylor, Alan. *The Divided Ground* — 974.7
PROPHECY
  Gibran, Kahlil. *And the Prophet Said* — 811
  Gibran, Kahlil. ★*The Prophet* — 811
★*The Prophet*. Gibran, Kahlil — 811
PROPHETS
  Akyol, Mustafa. *The Islamic Jesus* — 297.2
  Gibran, Kahlil. *And the Prophet Said* — 811
  Gibran, Kahlil. ★*The Prophet* — 811
  Hazleton, Lesley. *The First Muslim* — B
  Jebara, Mohamad. ★*The Life of the Qur'an* — 297.122
  Jebara, Mohamad. *Muhammad, the World-Changer* — B
PROPOSAL WRITING FOR GRANTS
  MacKellar, Pamela H. ★*Winning Grants* — 025.1
Prose, Francine
  1974 — B
  Caravaggio — 759.5
  What to Read and Why — 028
PROSE, FRANCINE, 1947-
  Prose, Francine. *1974* — B
PROSECUTION
  Bazelon, Emily. ★*Charged* — 345.73
PROSLAVERY MOVEMENTS
  Meltzer, Brad. *The Lincoln Conspiracy* — 973.7092
PROSPECTING
  Crouch, Gregory. *The Bonanza King* — B
PROSPECTORS
  Brands, H. W. *The Age of Gold* — 979.4
  Crouch, Gregory. *The Bonanza King* — B
PROSPERITY
  Acemoglu, Daron. *Power and Progress* — 303.48

Kenny, Charles. *The Plague Cycle* — 614.4
Kershaw, Ian. *The Global Age* — 940.55
Ridley, Matt. *The Rational Optimist* — 339.2
Shlaes, Amity. *Coolidge* — B
Stiglitz, Joseph E. *The Price of Inequality* — 305.50973
PROSTATE CANCER
  Roth, Andrew J. *Managing Prostate Cancer* — 616.99
  Walsh, Patrick C. *Dr. Patrick Walsh's Guide to Surviving Prostate Cancer* — 616.99
PROSTITUTES
  Brotherton, Marcus. *A Bright and Blinding Sun* — 940.54
  Moran, Rachel. *Paid For* — 306.74082
PROSTITUTION
  Ditmore, Melissa Hope. ★*Unbroken Chains* — 306.74
  Hill, David. *The Vapors* — 976.7
  Johnson, Akemi. *Night in the American Village* — 305.40952
  Krist, Gary. *Empire of Sin* — 976.3
  Moran, Rachel. *Paid For* — 306.74082
Protecting Intellectual Freedom in Your Public Library. Pinnell-Stephens, June — 025.2
PROTECTIVE CLOTHING
  Herbertson, Angie. *Sewing Face Masks, Scrub Caps, Arm Slings, and More* — 646.4
PROTECTIVENESS
  Bell, Darrin. ★*The Talk* — 741.5
  Glass, Sara. *Kissing Girls on Shabbat* — B
  McIntyre, Rick. *The Reign of Wolf 21* — 599.773
  Raboteau, Emily. *Lessons for Survival* — 814
PROTEST MOVEMENTS
  Alekhina, Mariija. *Riot Days* — B
  Bingham, Clara. *Witness to the Revolution* — 303.48
  Dagher, Sam. *Assad or We Burn the Country* — 956.9104
  Derf. *Kent State* — 741.5
  Dyson, Michael Eric. *Long Time Coming* — 305.800973
  Fraser, Steve. *The Age of Acquiescence* — 973.91
  Kurlansky, Mark. *1968* — 909.82
  Lebron, Christopher J. *The Making of Black Lives Matter* — 305.896
  Lim, Louisa. *Indelible City* — 951.25
  Maraniss, David. *They Marched into Sunlight* — 959.704
  Pearlman, Wendy. *We Crossed a Bridge and It Trembled* — 956.9104
  Rudd, Mark. *Underground* — 378.1
  Young, Ralph F. *Dissent* — 303.48
  Zinn, Howard. ★*A People's History of the United States* — 973
The Protest Singer. Wilkinson, Alec — B
PROTEST SONGS
  Lynskey, Dorian. *33 Revolutions per Minute* — 782.42
  Meacham, Jon. *Songs of America* — 782.42
PROTESTANT CHURCHES
  Griffith, R. Marie. *Moral Combat* — 261.8
PROTESTANTISM
  FitzGerald, Frances. *The Evangelicals* — 277
  Friedman, Benjamin M. *Religion and the Rise of Capitalism* — 330.12
  MacCulloch, Diarmaid. *The Reformation* — 270.6
  Metaxas, Eric. *Martin Luther* — B
  Ryrie, Alec. *Protestants* — 280
Protestants. Ryrie, Alec — 280
PROTESTS, DEMONSTRATIONS, VIGILS, ETC.
  Ahmed, Sara. *The Feminist Killjoy Handbook* — 305.42
  Alexander, Kwame. *Light for the World to See* — 811.6
  Arsenault, Raymond. *John Lewis* — B
  Barber, William J. *We Are Called to Be a Movement* — 261.8
  Bingham, Clara. *Witness to the Revolution* — 303.48
  Cheung, Karen. *The Impossible City* — 951.25
  Estes, Nick. *Our History Is the Future* — 978.004
  Ewing, Eve L. *Ghosts in the Schoolyard* — 370.89
  Grinspan, Jon. *Wide Awake* — 973.7
  Hinton, Elizabeth Kai. ★*America on Fire* — 305.800973
  Hochschild, Adam. *Rebel Cinderella* — B
  Hoffman, David E. *Give Me Liberty* — B
  Kix, Paul. ★*You Have to Be Prepared to Die Before You Can Begin to Live* — 976.1
  Lewis, John. ★*March; Book One* — 741.5
  Lewis, John. ★*March; Book Three* — 741.5
  Lewis, John. ★*March; Book Two* — 741.5
  Martin, Rachel Louise. *A Most Tolerant Little Town* — 379.2
  Merchant, Brian. *Blood in the Machine* — 303.48
  Mogelson, Luke. *The Storm Is Here* — 973.933
  Moss, Jeremiah. *Feral City* — B

PUBLIC LIBRARY CORE COLLECTION: NONFICTION
Twentieth Edition

Nye, Naomi Shihab. *The Tiny Journalist*	811
Owens, Ernest. ★*The Case for Cancel Culture*	303.3
Sharpton, Al. *Rise Up*	973.933
Signer, Michael. *Cry Havoc*	305.800973
Tamimi, Ahed. ★*They Called Me a Lioness*	B
Thompson, Jamie. *Standoff*	364.152
Unger, Harlow G. *American Tempest*	973.3
Weiss, Elaine F. *The Woman's Hour*	324.6
Prothero, Donald R.	
UFOs, Chemtrails, and Aliens	001.94
Prothero, Stephen R.	
The American Bible	973
God Is Not One	200
God the Bestseller	070.5
Religious Literacy	200.71
Proud. Muhammad, Ibtihaj	B
The Proud Tower. Tuchman, Barbara W.	909.82
Proulx, Annie	
Bird Cloud	B
★*Fen, Bog and Swamp*	551.41
PROULX, ANNIE	
Proulx, Annie. *Bird Cloud*	B
Proust's Way. Shattuck, Roger	843
PROUST, MARCEL, 1871-1922	
Shattuck, Roger. *Proust's Way*	843
Provence A-Z. Mayle, Peter	944
PROVENCE, FRANCE	
Bard, Elizabeth. *Picnic in Provence*	B
Mayle, Peter. *Encore Provence*	944
Mayle, Peter. *My Twenty-Five Years in Provence*	944.9
Mayle, Peter. *Provence A-Z*	944
Mayle, Peter. ★*A Year in Provence*	944
Peppler, Rebekah. *Le Sud*	641.594
PROVERBS	
Miranda, Lin-Manuel. *Gmorning, Gnight!*	811
PROVIDENCE AND GOVERNMENT OF GOD (JUDAISM)	
Kushner, Harold S. *When Bad Things Happen to Good People*	296.3
PROVIDENCE, RHODE ISLAND	
Hood, Ann. *Kitchen Yarns*	641.5
Provine, Robert R.	
Curious Behavior	152.3
Proving Ground. Kleiman, Kathy	4.092
PROZAC	
Slater, Lauren. *Blue Dreams*	615.7
Prud'homme, Alex	
★*Dinner with the President*	973
The French Chef in America	B
Prune. Hamilton, Gabrielle	641.3
PRUNING	
Bradley, Steve. *Pruning Simplified*	631.5
Brown, George E. *Essential Pruning Techniques*	635.9
Logan, William Bryant. *Sprout Lands*	582.16
Pruning Simplified. Bradley, Steve	631.5
PRUSSIA	
Blanning, T. C. W. *Frederick the Great*	B
Pryce, Jessica	
★*Broken*	362.7
PRYCE, JESSICA	
Pryce, Jessica. ★*Broken*	362.7
Pryor, Elizabeth Brown	
Six Encounters with Lincoln	973.7092
Pryor, Francis	
★*Stonehenge*	936.2
Pryor, Karen	
★*Don't Shoot the Dog*	153.8
PRYOR, RICHARD	
Saul, Scott. ★*Becoming Richard Pryor*	B
Psaki, Jen	
Say More	B
PSAKI, JEN	
Psaki, Jen. *Say More*	B
PSEUDOSCIENCE	
Andersen, Kurt. ★*Fantasyland*	973
Goldacre, Ben. *Bad Science*	500
Loxton, Daniel. *Abominable Science!*	001.944
Novella, Steven. *The Skeptics' Guide to the Universe*	500
Prothero, Donald R. *UFOs, Chemtrails, and Aliens*	001.94
Raphael, Rina. *The Gospel of Wellness*	613
Seife, Charles. *Proofiness*	510
Shermer, Michael. *Why People Believe Weird Things*	133
Weill, Kelly. *Off the Edge*	001.9
Psych. Bloom, Paul	150
PSYCHEDELIC EXPERIENCE	
Pollan, Michael. *How to Change Your Mind*	615.7
Psychedelic Outlaws. Kempner, Joanna	615.7
PSYCHEDELIC ROCK MUSIC	
Norman, Philip. ★*Wild Thing*	B
Povey, Glenn. *Echoes*	782.42166
PSYCHIATRIC HOSPITAL PATIENTS	
Aviv, Rachel. ★*Strangers to Ourselves*	616.89
Benjamin, A. K. *Let Me Not Be Mad*	612.8
Cahalan, Susannah. ★*The Great Pretender*	616.89
Hylton, Antonia. *Madness*	362.2
Winchester, Simon. *The Professor and the Madman*	423
PSYCHIATRIC HOSPITALS	
Benjamin, A. K. *Let Me Not Be Mad*	612.8
Cahalan, Susannah. ★*The Great Pretender*	616.89
Cregan, Mary. *The Scar*	616.85
Hylton, Antonia. *Madness*	362.2
LeFavour, Cree. *Lights On, Rats Out*	616.85
Moore, Kate. ★*The Woman They Could Not Silence*	B
PSYCHIATRIC NURSES	
Burgess, Ann Wolbert. *A Killer by Design*	364.3
PSYCHIATRIST AND PATIENT	
Brownstein, Gabriel. ★*The Secret Mind of Bertha Pappenheim*	616.85
Deisseroth, Karl. *Projections*	616.89
Harrington, Anne. *Mind Fixers*	616.89
PSYCHIATRISTS	
English, Charlie. *The Gallery of Miracles and Madness*	709.04
Fisher, Carl Erik. ★*The Urge*	362.29
Knight, Sam. *The Premonitions Bureau*	133.8
LeFavour, Cree. *Lights On, Rats Out*	616.85
Shatz, Adam. *The Rebel's Clinic*	965
Stern, Adam. *Committed*	616.89
PSYCHIATRY	
Aviv, Rachel. ★*Strangers to Ourselves*	616.89
Bullmore, Edward T. *The Inflamed Mind*	616.85
Cahalan, Susannah. ★*The Great Pretender*	616.89
Foulkes, Lucy. ★*Losing Our Minds*	616.89
Grinker, Roy Richard. *Nobody's Normal*	616.89
Harrington, Anne. *Mind Fixers*	616.89
Kohli, Sahaj Kaur. ★*But What Will People Say?*	616.89
Lieberman, Jeffrey A. *Malady of the Mind*	616.89
Lieberman, Jeffrey A. *Shrinks*	616.89
Nesse, Randolph M. *Good Reasons for Bad Feelings*	616.89
Stern, Adam. *Committed*	616.89
Tweedy, Damon. *Facing the Unseen*	362.2
PSYCHIC ABILITY	
Clegg, Brian. *Extra Sensory*	133.8
Knight, Sam. *The Premonitions Bureau*	133.8
Rojas Contreras, Ingrid. ★*The Man Who Could Move Clouds*	B
Shumsky, Susan G. *Earth Energy Meditations*	133.8
PSYCHIC HEALING	
Harper, Michele. *The Beauty in Breaking*	B
PSYCHIC TRAUMA	
Alexander, Elizabeth. ★*The Trayvon Generation*	305.896
Ambroz, David. *A Place Called Home*	B
Beaton, Kate. ★*Ducks*	741.5
Black, George. ★*The Long Reckoning*	959.704
Blair, Selma. *Mean Baby*	B
Bowdler, Michelle. ★*Is Rape a Crime?*	B
Branigan, Tania. *Red Memory*	951.05
Buque, Mariel. *Break the Cycle*	616.85
Carriere, Alice. *Everything/Nothing/Someone*	B
Coel, Michaela. ★*Misfits*	158.2
Crais, Clifton C. *History Lessons*	B
Crawford, Lacy. *Notes on a Silencing*	B
Cumming, Alan. *Baggage*	B
Danler, Stephanie. *Stray*	B
Diamond, Cheryl. *Nowhere Girl*	B
Diamond, Jared M. *Upheaval*	303.48
Dunn, Harry. *Standing My Ground*	B
Eger, Edith Eva. *The Choice*	B
Erdrich, Heid E. ★*Little Big Bully*	811
Farley, Audrey Clare. ★*Girls and Their Monsters*	306.875
Febos, Melissa. ★*Body Work*	808.06

AUTHOR, TITLE, SERIES AND SUBJECT INDEX

Felix, Camonghne. *Dyscalculia*	B
Fitzgerald, Isaac. *Dirtbag, Massachusetts*	B
Flaherty, Meghan. *Tango Lessons*	793.3
Fleming, Brandon P. *Miseducated*	B
Foo, Stephanie. ★ *What My Bones Know*	B
Fremont, Helen. *The Escape Artist*	B
Gildiner, Catherine. *Good Morning, Monster*	616.89
Glass, Charles. *Soldiers Don't Go Mad*	616.85
Gottlieb, Lori. ★ *Maybe You Should Talk to Someone*	B
Hagerty, Alexa. ★ *Still Life with Bones*	599.9
Hatzfeld, Jean. *Blood Papa*	967.5710431
Hawes, Jennifer. *Grace Will Lead Us Home*	364.152
Hempel, Jessi. *The Family Outing*	B
Herman, Judith Lewis. *Truth and Repair*	362.883
Hernandez Castillo, Marcelo. *Children of the Land*	B
Hill, DaMaris B. *Breath Better Spent*	811
Jamison, Kay Redfield. *Fires in the Dark*	616.89
Johnson, Earl. *Finding Comfort During Hard Times*	155.9
Jones, Saeed. *Alive at the End of the World*	811
Kelly, Donika. *The Renunciations*	811
Kenneally, Christine. *Ghosts of the Orphanage*	362.73
Kohli, Sahaj Kaur. ★ *But What Will People Say?*	616.89
LaPointe, Sasha taqwseblu. *Red Paint*	B
Lecrae. ★ *I Am Restored*	B
Lovato, Roberto. *Unforgetting*	B
Machado, Carmen Maria. ★ *In the Dream House*	B
Mandel, Sarah. *Little Earthquakes*	B
Mariani, Mike. ★ *What Doesn't Kill Us Makes Us*	155.9
Marzano-Lesnevich, Alexandria. *The Fact of a Body*	364.152
McCauley, Esau. *How Far to the Promised Land*	B
Means, Brittany. *Hell If We Don't Change Our Ways*	B
Mohan, Rohini. *The Seasons of Trouble*	954.9303
Monroe, Jana. *Hearts of Darkness*	363.25
Morgan, Abi. *This Is Not a Pity Memoir*	B
O'Donnell, Svenja. *Inge's War*	943.086
Owusu, Nadia. *Aftershocks*	B
Parks, Casey. *Diary of a Misfit*	B
Pham, Larissa. *Pop Song*	709.2
Pipher, Mary Bray. *A Life in Light*	B
Prescod, Danielle. *Token Black Girl*	B
Pryce, Jessica. ★ *Broken*	362.7
Reang, Putsata. *Ma and Me*	B
Rhodes, James. *Instrumental*	B
Rosner, Elizabeth. *Survivor Cafe*	940.53
Rush, Charaia. *Courageously Soft*	234
Sasakamoose, Fred. *Call Me Indian*	B
Shanahan, Charif. *Trace Evidence*	811
Shange, Ntozake. ★ *Sing a Black Girl's Song*	818
Stahl, Jerry. *Nein, Nein, Nein!*	B
Steinberg, Jonny. *Winnie and Nelson*	920
Stone, Sharon. *The Beauty of Living Twice*	B
Streep, Abe. *Brothers on Three*	306.85
Sullivan, Randall. *Graveyard of the Pacific*	979.7
Szczeszak-Brewer, Agata. *The Hunger Book*	B
Taylor, Goldie. *The Love You Save*	B
Tesfamariam, Rahiel. ★ *Imagine Freedom*	305.896
Thompson, J. M. *Running Is a Kind of Dreaming*	B
Tran, Paul. *All the Flowers Kneeling*	811
V. ★ *Reckoning*	814
Vasquez-Lavado, Silvia. *In the Shadow of the Mountain*	B
Vuong, Ocean. ★ *Time Is a Mother*	811
West, Cait. ★ *Rift*	B
Williams, Kidada E. *I Saw Death Coming*	973.8
Williams, Lucinda. *Don't Tell Anybody the Secrets I Told You*	B
Winfrey, Oprah. *What Happened to You?*	616.85
Yancey, Philip. *Where the Light Fell*	B

PSYCHIC TRAUMA IN CHILDREN
Burke Harris, Nadine. *The Deepest Well*	618.92
Travisano, Thomas J. *Love Unknown*	B

PSYCHICS
Jacobsen, Annie. *Phenomena*	133.8
Manseau, Peter. *The Apparitionists*	B

PSYCHOANALYSIS
Brownstein, Gabriel. ★ *The Secret Mind of Bertha Pappenheim*	616.85
Freud, Sigmund. ★ *The Basic Writings of Sigmund Freud*	150.19
Freud, Sigmund. *Civilization and Its Discontents*	150.19
Freud, Sigmund. ★ *The Interpretation of Dreams*	154.6
Gay, Peter. *Freud*	B
Jung, C. G. ★ *The Basic Writings of C.G. Jung*	150.19
Phillips, Adam. *On Giving up*	158.2
Tallis, Frank. ★ *Mortal Secrets*	B

PSYCHOANALYSIS AND RELIGION
Gay, Peter. *A Godless Jew*	150.19

PSYCHOANALYSTS
Gay, Peter. *Freud*	B
Jung, C. G. *Memories, Dreams, Reflections*	150.19
Laing, Olivia. *Everybody*	323
Nagorski, Andrew. *Saving Freud*	940.53
Roudinesco, Elisabeth. ★ *Freud*	B
Tallis, Frank. ★ *Mortal Secrets*	B

PSYCHOKINESIS
Jacobsen, Annie. *Phenomena*	133.8

PSYCHOLINGUISTICS
Everett, Daniel Leonard. *How Language Began*	401
Lieberman, David J. *Mindreader*	401

PSYCHOLOGICAL GROWTH
Bradford, Joy Harden. *Sisterhood Heals*	158.2
Brown, Brene. ★ *Dare to Lead*	658.4
Canfield, Jack. *The Success Principles*	158
Coggan, Philip. *Surviving the Daily Grind*	658.3
Delaney, Brigid. *Reasons Not to Worry*	158.1
Franco, Marisa G. *Platonic*	302.34
Gildiner, Catherine. *Good Morning, Monster*	616.89
Golbeck, Jennifer. *The Purest Bond*	636.7
Iyer, Pico. ★ *The Half Known Life*	203
Kaur, Rupi. *Milk and Honey*	811
Lamott, Anne. ★ *Somehow*	814
Lee, Shannon. *Be Water, My Friend*	796.8
Manson, Mark. *The Subtle Art of Not Giving a F*ck*	158.1
McBride, Karyl. *Will I Ever Be Good Enough?*	616.85
McGraw, Phillip C. *Life Strategies*	158
McLaren, Brian D. *Faith After Doubt*	234
Parker, James. ★ *Get Me Through the Next Five Minutes*	158.1
Peck, M. Scott. ★ *The Road Less Traveled*	158.1
Pink, Daniel H. *Drive*	153.1
Pritchett, Georgia. *My Mess Is a Bit of a Life*	B
Risbridger, Ella. *The Year of Miracles*	641.5
Robbins, Anthony. *Unlimited Power*	158.1
Sheff, David. *The Buddhist on Death Row*	B
Smith, Carol. *Crossing the River*	B
Stern, Adam. *Committed*	616.89
Suvari, Mena. *The Great Peace*	B
Thompson, Kenan. *When I Was Your Age*	B
Tippett, Krista. ★ *Becoming Wise*	158.1
Wiking, Meik. *The Art of Making Memories*	153.1
Winter, Molly Roden. *More*	B

PSYCHOLOGICAL RESEARCH
Farley, Audrey Clare. ★ *Girls and Their Monsters*	306.875

PSYCHOLOGICAL WARFARE
Newitz, Annalee. *Stories Are Weapons*	355.3
Shultz, Richard H. *The Secret War Against Hanoi*	959.704

PSYCHOLOGIST AND PATIENT
Benjamin, A. K. *Let Me Not Be Mad*	612.8
Wilson, Brian. *I Am Brian Wilson*	B

PSYCHOLOGISTS
Benjamin, A. K. *Let Me Not Be Mad*	612.8
Bjork, Daniel W. *B.F. Skinner*	B
Eger, Edith Eva. *The Choice*	B
Frankl, Viktor E. ★ *Man's Search for Meaning*	B
Gildiner, Catherine. *Good Morning, Monster*	616.89
Jamison, Kay Redfield. *Fires in the Dark*	616.89
Konnikova, Maria. *The Biggest Bluff*	795.412
Kriss, Alexander. *Borderline*	616.85
Lewis, Michael. ★ *The Undoing Project*	920
Minutaglio, Bill. *The Most Dangerous Man in America*	B
Spofford, Tim. *What the Children Told Us*	150.92

PSYCHOLOGY
Alexander, Elizabeth. ★ *The Trayvon Generation*	305.896
Ariely, Dan. *The Honest Truth About Dishonesty*	177
Bass, Ellen. ★ *The Courage to Heal*	616.85
Billings, J. Todd. *Rejoicing in Lament*	248.8
Bjork, Daniel W. *B.F. Skinner*	B
Bloom, Paul. *Psych*	150
Bluestein, Jane. *The Perfection Deception*	155.2
Bly, Robert. ★ *Iron John*	305.310973
Boyer, Anne. *The Undying*	B

PUBLIC LIBRARY CORE COLLECTION: NONFICTION
Twentieth Edition

Bradshaw, John. ★*Cat Sense*	636.8
Bradshaw, John. ★*Dog Sense*	636.7
Brooks, David. ★*How to Know a Person*	158.2
Brown, Emma. *To Raise a Boy*	649
Burgess, Ann Wolbert. *A Killer by Design*	364.3
Calhoun, Ada. *Why We Can't Sleep*	305.244
Chittister, Joan. *The Gift of Years*	200
Cleaver, Eldridge. *Soul on Ice*	B
Cott, Jonathan. *There's a Mystery There*	813
Cuddy, Amy. *Presence*	158.1
Cullen, David. *Columbine*	373
Dahl, Melissa. *Cringeworthy*	158.2
Dakwar, Elias. *The Captive Imagination*	616.86
Damour, Lisa. ★*Under Pressure*	155.5
Damour, Lisa. *Untangled*	305.235
Dearborn, Mary V. *Ernest Hemingway*	B
Douglas, John E. *The Killer Across the Table*	B
Dubin, Minna. ★*Mom Rage*	306.874
Eberhardt, Jennifer L. ★*Biased*	303.3
Edmondson, Amy C. *The Right Kind of Wrong*	158.1
Epstein, Mark. *Advice Not Given*	294.3
Filipovic, Jill. *The H-Spot*	155.3
Franco, Marisa G. *Platonic*	302.34
Frederick, Jim. *Black Hearts*	956.7044
Friedan, Betty. ★*The Feminine Mystique*	305.42
Gaiman, Neil. *The View from the Cheap Seats*	824
Gardner, Dan. *The Science of Fear*	152.4
Gilbert, Daniel Todd. ★*Stumbling on Happiness*	158
Glasser, William. *Choice Theory*	150
Goldhagen, Daniel Jonah. *Hitler's Willing Executioners*	940.53
Gottman, Julie Schwartz. *Fight Right*	616.89
Guendelsberger, Emily. *On the Clock*	331.0973
Guida-Richards, Melissa. *What White Parents Should Know About Transracial Adoption*	362.734
Hackman, Rose. ★*Emotional Labor*	155.3
Hari, Johann. ★*Magic Pill*	613.2
Herman, Judith Lewis. *Truth and Repair*	362.883
Hibbs, B. Janet. *The Stressed Years of Their Lives*	616.8900835
Hickey, Walt. ★*You Are What You Watch*	791.4
Hofstadter, Douglas R. *Surfaces and Essences*	169
Horowitz, Alexandra. ★*Inside of a Dog*	636.7
Horowitz, Alexandra. ★*The Year of the Puppy*	636.7
Iyengar, Sheena. *The Art of Choosing*	153.8
Jamieson, Alexandra. *Women, Food, and Desire*	155.3
Jones, Lucy. ★*Matrescence*	306.874
Killam, Kasley. *The Art and Science of Connection*	302
Kishimi, Ichiro. *The Courage to Be Disliked*	158
Kohli, Sahaj Kaur. ★*But What Will People Say?*	616.89
Konnikova, Maria. *The Biggest Bluff*	795.412
Kornfield, Jack. *The Wise Heart*	294.3
Kubler-Ross, Elisabeth. ★*On Death and Dying*	155.9
Laing, Olivia. ★*The Lonely City*	700.1
Lerner, Harriet Goldhor. ★*The Dance of Anger*	152.4
Lerner, Harriet Goldhor. *The Dance of Intimacy*	155.6
Lythcott-Haims, Julie. *Your Turn*	305.24
Manly, Carla Marie. *Aging Joyfully*	305.26
Marriott, Sue. *Secure Relating*	158.1
Masson, J. Moussaieff. *Lost Companions*	636.088
Mead, Margaret. *Coming of Age in Samoa*	306
Millwood, Molly. *To Have and to Hold*	306.874
Monroe, Jana. *Hearts of Darkness*	363.25
Montell, Amanda. ★*The Age of Magical Overthinking*	153.4
Morris, David J. *The Evil Hours*	616.85
Moss, Adam. ★*The Work of Art*	701
Mullainathan, Sendhil. *Scarcity*	338.5
Myers, David G. *How Do We Know Ourselves?*	155.2
Naifeh, Steven W. *Van Gogh*	B
Natterson, Cara Familian. ★*Decoding Boys*	649
O'Connell, Robert L. *Revolutionary*	B
Orenstein, Peggy. *Cinderella Ate My Daughter*	305.23082
Parker, Kate T. *Strong Is the New Pretty*	155.43
Pinker, Steven. *How the Mind Works*	153
Pinker, Steven. *Rationality*	153.4
Pipher, Mary Bray. *Women Rowing North*	305.26
Power, Marianne. *Help Me!*	158.1
Price, Devon. ★*Laziness Does Not Exist*	158.1
Pryor, Karen. ★*Don't Shoot the Dog*	153.8
Rauch, Jonathan. *The Happiness Curve*	155.6
Real, Terrence. *Us*	646.7
Reiner, Andrew. *Better Boys, Better Men*	155.43
Roiphe, Katie. *The Violet Hour*	809
Rosling, Hans. *Factfulness*	155.9
Rotella, Robert J. *How Champions Think*	796.01
Rubin, Gretchen Craft. ★*Life in Five Senses*	152.1
Rubin, Rick. ★*The Creative Act*	153.3
Sandberg, Sheryl. *Option B*	155.9
Sante, Lucy. *I Heard Her Call My Name*	B
Schulz, Kathryn. *Being Wrong*	121
Shatz, Adam. *The Rebel's Clinic*	965
Sife, Wallace. *The Loss of a Pet*	155.9
Simmons, Rachel. ★*Enough as She Is*	155.5
Simmons, Rachel. *Odd Girl Out*	302.5
Smee, Sebastian. *The Art of Rivalry*	700.92
Stone, Deborah A. *Counting*	001.4
Strings, Sabrina. *The End of Love*	155.3
Suddendorf, Thomas. *The Gap*	156
Summerscale, Kate. *The Book of Phobias and Manias*	616.85
Tallis, Frank. *The Incurable Romantic*	152.4
Taraborrelli, J. Randy. ★*The Secret Life of Marilyn Monroe*	B
Tweedy, Damon. *Facing the Unseen*	362.2
Updike, John. *Always Looking*	700
Van Buren, Mark. *A Fool's Guide to Actual Happiness*	294.3
Vedantam, Shankar. *Useful Delusions*	153.4
Waldinger, Robert J. ★*The Good Life*	158.1
Warner, Judith. *Perfect Madness*	306.874
Washington, Kate. ★*Already Toast*	649.8
Weber, Charlotte Fox. *Tell Me What You Want*	153.8
Weitzman, Gary. *National Geographic Complete Guide to Pet Health, Behavior, and Happiness*	636.088
Whippman, Ruth. ★*Boymom*	305.23
Whitefield-Madrano, Autumn. *Face Value*	111
Williams, Florence. *Heartbreak*	306.7
Wilson, A. N. *The Mystery of Charles Dickens*	823
Wiseman, Rosalind. *Masterminds & Wingmen*	305.235
Wright, Evan. *Generation Kill*	956.7044
Wynne, Clive D. L. ★*Dog Is Love*	636.7
Ziegler, Sheryl. ★*Mommy Burnout*	646.7
★*The Psychopath Test.* Ronson, Jon	616.85

PSYCHOPATHOLOGY

Ronson, Jon. ★*The Psychopath Test*	616.85
Sullivan, Randall. *The Devil's Best Trick*	235

PSYCHOPATHS

Gagne, Patric. *Sociopath*	B
Schechter, Harold. ★*Ripped from the Headlines!*	791.43
Stout, Martha. *Outsmarting the Sociopath Next Door*	155.2

PSYCHOPHARMACOLOGY

Cahalan, Susannah. ★*The Great Pretender*	616.89

PSYCHOSOMATIC DISORDERS

O'Sullivan, Suzanne. *The Sleeping Beauties*	616.85

PSYCHOSURGERY

Larson, Kate Clifford. *Rosemary*	B

PSYCHOTHERAPIST AND PATIENT

Epstein, Mark. *The Zen of Therapy*	294.3
Gildiner, Catherine. *Good Morning, Monster*	616.89
Gottlieb, Lori. ★*Maybe You Should Talk to Someone*	B
Lembke, Anna. *Dopamine Nation*	152.4
Shaffer, Peter. ★*Equus*	822
Weber, Charlotte Fox. *Tell Me What You Want*	153.8

PSYCHOTHERAPISTS

Epstein, Mark. *The Zen of Therapy*	294.3
Glass, Sara. *Kissing Girls on Shabbat*	B
Gottlieb, Lori. ★*Maybe You Should Talk to Someone*	B
LeFavour, Cree. *Lights On, Rats Out*	616.85
Tate, Christie. ★*Group*	B

PSYCHOTHERAPY

Brownstein, Gabriel. ★*The Secret Mind of Bertha Pappenheim*	616.85
Epstein, Mark. *Advice Not Given*	294.3
Epstein, Mark. *The Zen of Therapy*	294.3
Fall, Jeremy. *Falling Upwards*	158.1
Gildiner, Catherine. *Good Morning, Monster*	616.89
Gottman, Julie Schwartz. *Fight Right*	616.89
Jamison, Kay Redfield. *Fires in the Dark*	616.89
Kander, Jason. *Invisible Storm*	B
Kriss, Alexander. *Borderline*	616.85
LeFavour, Cree. *Lights On, Rats Out*	616.85
Mandel, Sarah. *Little Earthquakes*	B

AUTHOR, TITLE, SERIES AND SUBJECT INDEX

May, Rollo. *The Discovery of Being*	150.19
McCurdy, Jennette. ★*I'm Glad My Mom Died*	B
Riley, Alex. ★*A Cure for Darkness*	616.85
Stille, Alexander. *The Sullivanians*	307.77
Weber, Charlotte Fox. *Tell Me What You Want*	153.8

PSYCHOTHERAPY PATIENTS

Aviv, Rachel. ★*Strangers to Ourselves*	616.89
Epstein, Mark. *The Zen of Therapy*	294.3
Gildiner, Catherine. *Good Morning, Monster*	616.89
Kennedy, Patrick J. ★*Profiles in Mental Health Courage*	362.29

PSYCHOTROPIC DRUGS

Harrington, Anne. *Mind Fixers*	616.89
Kramer, Peter D. ★*Ordinarily Well*	615.7
Slater, Lauren. *Blue Dreams*	615.7

PTOLEMY, ACTIVE 2ND CENTURY

Robb, Graham. *The Debatable Land*	941.3

PUBERTY

Bergstein, Rachelle. *The Genius of Judy*	813
Kowal-Connelly, Suanne. *Parenting Through Puberty*	649
Natterson, Cara Familian. ★*Decoding Boys*	649

PUBLIC ADMINISTRATION

Connelly, Matthew James. *The Declassification Engine*	352.3

PUBLIC ART

Ganz, Nicholas. ★*Graffiti World*	751.7

PUBLIC DEBT

Jacoby, Melissa B. ★*Unjust Debts*	346.73

PUBLIC DEFENDERS

Feige, David. *Indefensible*	B
Rapping, Jonathan. *Gideon's Promise*	345.73

PUBLIC EDUCATION

Appleman, Deborah. *Literature and the New Culture Wars*	807
Chu, Lenora. *Little Soldiers*	370
Emdin, Christopher. *Ratchetdemic*	370.1
Fitzpatrick, Cara. *The Death of Public School*	379.73
Hessler, Peter. *Other Rivers*	378.1
Hixenbaugh, Michael. ★*They Came for the Schools*	371.9
Ravitch, Diane. *Slaying Goliath*	371.010973
Robbins, Alexandra. ★*The Teachers*	371.1
Skelton, Marc. *Pounding the Rock*	796.323
Public Faith in Action. Volf, Miroslav	261.7

PUBLIC FINANCE

McCraw, Thomas K. ★*The Founders and Finance*	330.973
Reid, T. R. *A Fine Mess*	336.200973

PUBLIC HEALTH

Alexander, Brian. ★*The Hospital*	362.10973
Ashton, Jennifer. *The New Normal*	613
Beres, Derek. *Conspirituality*	001.9
Block, Jennifer. *Everything Below the Waist*	613
Borrell, Brendan. *The First Shots*	615.3
Christakis, Nicholas A. *Apollo's Arrow*	362.1962
Clark, Anna. *The Poisoned City*	363.6
Cohn, Jonathan. *The Ten Year War*	368.38
DiGregorio, Sarah. ★*Taking Care*	610.73
Farmer, Paul. *Fevers, Feuds, and Diamonds*	614.5
Fauci, Anthony S. *Expect the Unexpected*	610.92
Flowers, Catherine Coleman. *Waste*	363.72
Hanna-Attisha, Mona. *What the Eyes Don't See*	615.9
Harrington, Anne. *Mind Fixers*	616.89
Hendrickson, Debra. ★*The Air They Breathe*	363.7
Hongoltz-Hetling, Matthew. *If It Sounds Like a Quack*	615.8
Honigsbaum, Mark. *The Pandemic Century*	614.4
Hotez, Peter J. *Preventing the Next Pandemic*	362.1969
Insel, Thomas R. *Healing*	362.2
Johnson, Steven. *Extra Life*	362.1
Johnson, Steven. *The Ghost Map*	614.5
Kenny, Charles. *The Plague Cycle*	614.4
Klass, Perri. *A Good Time to Be Born*	362.19892
Lewis, Michael. ★*The Premonition*	614.5
Mackenzie, Debora. *Covid-19*	616.2
Macy, Beth. ★*Raising Lazarus*	362.29
Matthews, Hannah. *You or Someone You Love*	362.1988
McNeil, Donald G. ★*The Wisdom of Plagues*	614.4
Metzl, Jonathan M. ★*What We've Become*	364.152
Murthy, Vivek Hallegere. *Together*	158.2
Nocera, Joseph. *The Big Fail*	362.1962
Preston, Richard. *Crisis in the Red Zone*	614.5
Price, Polly J. *Plagues in the Nation*	614.4
Quammen, David. ★*Breathless*	614.5
Quammen, David. ★*Spillover*	614.4
Quinones, Sam. ★*The Least of Us*	362.29
Schama, Simon. *Foreign Bodies*	614.4
Senthilingam, Meera. *Outbreaks and Epidemics*	614.4
Snyder, Rachel Louise. *No Visible Bruises*	362.82
Tabery, James. ★*Tyranny of the Gene*	572.8
Wright, Lawrence. ★*The Plague Year*	614.5
Zaitchik, Alexander. *Owning the Sun*	362.1
Zaman, Muhammad H. *Biography of Resistance*	616.9

PUBLIC HOSPITALS

Manheimer, Eric. *Twelve Patients*	362.1109747
Oshinsky, David M. *Bellevue*	362.1109747

PUBLIC INTEREST

Zapruder, Alexandra. *Twenty-Six Seconds*	973.922092

PUBLIC LIBRARIES

Alabaster, Carol. *Developing an Outstanding Core Collection*	025.2
Anderson, Jimmeka. *Power Lines*	020
Bartlett, Wendy K. *Floating Collections*	025.2
Bignoli, Callan. ★*Responding to Rapid Change in Libraries*	020
Landau, Herbert B. *The Small Public Library Survival Guide*	025.1
Larson, Jeanette. *The Public Library Policy Writer*	025.1
Pettegree, Andrew. *The Library*	027.4
Pinnell-Stephens, June. *Protecting Intellectual Freedom in Your Public Library*	025.2
Vnuk, Rebecca. *The Weeding Handbook*	025.2
The Public Library Policy Writer. Larson, Jeanette	025.1

PUBLIC OFFICIALS

Collins, Max Allan. *Eliot Ness and the Mad Butcher*	364.152
Graff, Garrett M. ★*The Only Plane in the Sky*	973.931
Rothkopf, David J. *American Resistance*	973.933

PUBLIC OPINION

Adichie, Chimamanda Ngozi. *We Should All Be Feminists*	305.42
Andersen, Kurt. ★*Fantasyland*	973
Applewhite, Ashton. *This Chair Rocks*	155.67
Babb, Valerie Melissa. *The Book of James*	B
Barron, David J. *Waging War*	342.73
Bingham, Clara. *Witness to the Revolution*	303.48
Blume, Lesley M. M. *Fallout*	940.54
Breyer, Stephen G. ★*The Authority of the Court and the Peril of Politics*	347.73
Brokaw, Tom. *The Fall of Richard Nixon*	B
Burke, Edmund. *Reflections on the Revolution in France*	944.04
Butler, Isaac. *The World Only Spins Forward*	812
Chammah, Maurice. ★*Let the Lord Sort Them*	364.66
Coffin, Judith G. *Sex, Love, and Letters*	848
Eyman, Scott. *Charlie Chaplin vs. America*	B
Fallows, James M. *Our Towns*	306.0973
Friedman, Barry. *The Will of the People*	347.73
Ghosh, Amitav. *The Great Derangement*	809
Heine, Steven J. *DNA Is Not Destiny*	572.8
Hemming, Henry. *Agents of Influence*	940.54
Holzer, Harold. *Brought Forth on This Continent*	973.7
Hortis, C. Alexander. *The Witch of New York*	364.152
Karl, Jonathan. *Tired of Winning*	973.933
Kempowski, Walter. *Swansong 1945*	940.54
Klein, Naomi. ★*Doppelganger*	302.2
Koppel, Lily. *The Astronaut Wives Club*	920
Launius, Roger D. *Apollo's Legacy*	629.45
Lawler, Andrew. *The Secret Token*	975.6
Levin, Josh. *The Queen*	364.16
Markel, Howard. *Origin Story*	576.8
Nagourney, Adam. *The Times*	071
Novick, Peter. *The Holocaust in American Life*	940.53
O'Sullivan, Emer. *The Fall of the House of Wilde*	B
Owens, Ernest. ★*The Case for Cancel Culture*	303.3
Peters, Rebecca Todd. *Trust Women*	362.1988
Ramos, Jorge. *Stranger*	325.73
Saini, Angela. *Inferior*	305.4
Sanneh, Kelefa. ★*Major Labels*	781.64
Scheyder, Ernest. *The War Below*	333.7
Shlaes, Amity. *Coolidge*	B
Taylor, Fred. *1939*	940.53
Thompson, Erin L. *Smashing Statues*	725
Vanderbilt, Tom. *You May Also Like*	153.8
Weintraub, Stanley. *Iron Tears*	973.3
West, Lindy. *The Witches Are Coming*	305.420973
Wides-Munoz, Laura. *The Making of a Dream*	920
Wiesel, Elie. *And the Sea Is Never Full*	B

Williams, David. *Bitterly Divided*	973.7
Yaffa, Joshua. *Between Two Fires*	920
PUBLIC PROSECUTORS	
Bazelon, Emily. ★*Charged*	345.73
Berman, Geoffrey. *Holding the Line*	345.73
Carter, Stephen L. *Invisible*	B
Chammah, Maurice. ★*Let the Lord Sort Them*	364.66
Gleeson, John. *The Gotti Wars*	364.1
O'Neill, Tom. ★*Chaos*	364.152
PUBLIC PROSECUTORS' MISCONDUCT	
Bazelon, Emily. ★*Charged*	345.73
Dybdahl, Thomas L. *When Innocence Is Not Enough*	345.73
Rudolf, David S. *American Injustice*	345.73
PUBLIC RADIO	
Napoli, Lisa. *Susan, Linda, Nina & Cokie*	920
PUBLIC RECORDS	
Sankey, Michael L. *The Manual to Online Public Records*	025.06
PUBLIC RELATIONS	
Butler, Paul. *Chokehold*	363.2
Elwood, Phil. *All the Worst Humans*	659.2
Ferrazzi, Keith. *Never Eat Alone*	658.4
Henning, Kristin. *The Rage of Innocence*	364.36
Thompson, Jamie. *Standoff*	364.152
PUBLIC RELATIONS AND POLITICS	
Elwood, Phil. *All the Worst Humans*	659.2
PUBLIC SAFETY	
Collins, Max Allan. *Eliot Ness and the Mad Butcher*	364.152
Kaba, Mariame. *No More Police*	363.2
Purnell, Derecka. *Becoming Abolitionists*	363.20973
Rubinstein, Julian. ★*The Holly*	364.106
Signer, Michael. *Cry Havoc*	305.800973
PUBLIC SCHOOLS	
Berkshire, Jennifer. *The Education Wars*	371.01
Brill, Steven. *Class Warfare*	371.010973
Driver, Justin. *The Schoolhouse Gate*	344.73
Duncan, Arne. *How Schools Work*	379
Ewing, Eve L. *Ghosts in the Schoolyard*	370.89
Fitzpatrick, Cara. *The Death of Public School*	379.73
Givens, Jarvis R. ★*School Clothes*	371.829
Goldstein, Dana. *The Teacher Wars*	371.1020973
Herold, Benjamin. *Disillusioned*	307.76
Keizer, Garret. *Getting Schooled*	373.1102
Love, Bettina L. *Punished for Dreaming*	371.829
Picower, Bree. *Reading, Writing, and Racism*	371.829
Ravitch, Diane. *The Death and Life of the Great American School System*	379.1
Ravitch, Diane. *Slaying Goliath*	371.010973
Reese, William J. *Testing Wars in the Public Schools*	371.260973
Robbins, Alexandra. ★*The Teachers*	371.1
PUBLIC SHAMING	
Ronson, Jon. *So You've Been Publicly Shamed*	152.4
PUBLIC SPACES	
Howard, Hugh. *Architects of an American Landscape*	712.092
Moss, Jeremiah. *Feral City*	B
PUBLIC SPEAKING	
Gallo, Carmine. *Talk Like Ted*	658.4
Wellman, Victoria. *Before You Say Anything*	808.5
PUBLIC TRANSPORTATION	
Zoellner, Tom. *Train*	385.09
PUBLIC WORKS	
Caro, Robert A. *The Power Broker*	B
Chachra, Deb. *How Infrastructure Works*	363
Clark, Anna. *The Poisoned City*	363.6
Hanna-Attisha, Mona. *What the Eyes Don't See*	615.9
Mars, Roman. ★*The 99% Invisible City*	720
PUBLICITY	
Hartman, Darrell. *Battle of Ink and Ice*	998
Hortis, C. Alexander. *The Witch of New York*	364.152
PUBLICITY STUNTS	
Begley, Adam. *The Great Nadar*	B
★*The Publisher*. Brinkley, Alan	B
PUBLISHERS AND PUBLISHING	
Brinkley, Alan. ★*The Publisher*	B
Brunsting, Karen. ★*Open Access Literature in Libraries*	070.5
Castleman, Michael. *The Untold Story of Books*	381
Corbett, Emily. *In Transition*	809
Duncan, Dennis. *Index, a History of The*	025.3
Fingeroth, Danny. *A Marvelous Life*	741.5
Franklin, Sara B. ★*The Editor*	B
Glendinning, Victoria. *Leonard Woolf*	B
Hagan, Joe. *Sticky Fingers*	B
Harman, Claire. *Murder by the Book*	364.152
Houston, Keith. *The Book*	002.09
Howe, Sean. *Marvel Comics*	741.5
Isen, Tajja. *Some of My Best Friends*	305.8
Larimer, Kevin. *The Poets & Writers Complete Guide to Being a Writer*	808
Laughlin, James. *The Luck of Friendship*	B
Miller, Adrienne. *In the Land of Men*	070.5
Nagourney, Adam. *The Times*	071
Nasaw, David. *The Chief*	B
Odell, Amy. *Anna*	B
Prothero, Stephen R. *God the Bestseller*	070.5
Rakoff, Joanna Smith. *My Salinger Year*	B
Rehak, Melanie. *Girl Sleuth*	813
Riesman, Abraham. *True Believer*	741.5
Smith, Emma. *Portable Magic*	002
Verdelle, A. J. *Miss Chloe*	B
Whyte, Kenneth. *The Uncrowned King*	B
Puccini Without Excuses. Berger, William	782.1
PUCCINI, GIACOMO, 1858-1924	
Berger, William. *Puccini Without Excuses*	782.1
Puchner, Martin	
The Written World	809
PUEBLO (NORTH AMERICAN PEOPLE)	
Brooks, James. *Mesa of Sorrows*	979.1004
Childs, Craig. *House of Rain*	978.9
Taffa, Deborah Jackson. ★*Whiskey Tender*	B
PUEBLO REVOLT, 1680	
Brooks, James. *Mesa of Sorrows*	979.1004
PUERTO RICAN PEOPLE IN THE UNITED STATES	
Maraniss, David. *Clemente*	B
Santiago, Wilfred. *"21"*	741.5
PUERTO RICO	
Diaz, Jaquira. *Ordinary Girls*	818
Immerwahr, Daniel. *How to Hide an Empire*	973
PUFFINS	
Nicolson, Adam. *The Seabird's Cry*	598.177
PUGET SOUND	
Neiwert, David A. *Of Orcas and Men*	599.53
Puglionesi, Alicia	
In Whose Ruins	973
Puhak, Shelley	
The Dark Queens	944
PUJOL, JUAN	
Talty, Stephan. *Agent Garbo*	940.5
Pukui, Mary Kawena	
Hawaiian Dictionary	499
Pulde, Alona	
Forks Over Knives Family	641.5
★*The Forks Over Knives Plan*	641.5
Puleo, Stephen	
Voyage of Mercy	363.8
Pulitzer. Morris, James McGrath	B
PULITZER PRIZES	
Buell, Hal. *Moments*	070.4
PULITZER, JOSEPH, 1847-1911	
Morris, James McGrath. *Pulitzer*	B
Pull up a Chair. Thiessen, Tiffani	641.5
Pullman, Philip	
★*Fairy Tales from the Brothers Grimm*	398.2
Pulp. Berens, Abra	641.6
PULP PERIODICALS	
Kakalios, James. *The Amazing Story of Quantum Mechanics*	530.12
PUMA	
Williams, Jim. *Path of the Puma*	599.75
Pump. Schutt, Bill	612.1
PUMPKIN	
Cupp, Lundy. *Realistic Pumpkin Carving*	745.5941646
Pumpkinflowers. Friedman, Matti	B
★*Punch Me up to the Gods*. Broome, Brian	B
PUNCTUATION	
Brandreth, Gyles Daubeney. *Have You Eaten Grandma?*	428
Dreyer, Benjamin. *Dreyer's English*	808.02
Hazrat, Florence. *An Admirable Point*	411
Houston, Keith. *Shady Characters*	411
Watson, Cecelia. *Semicolon*	428.2

AUTHOR, TITLE, SERIES AND SUBJECT INDEX

PUNIC WARS, 264-146 B.C.E
    Hunt, Patrick. *Hannibal* — B
    O'Connell, Robert L. *The Ghosts of Cannae* — 937
Punished for Dreaming. Love, Bettina L. — 371.829
PUNISHMENT
    Austen, Ben. *Correction* — 364.6
    Bazelon, Emily. ★*Charged* — 345.73
    Belkin, Lisa. *Genealogy of a Murder* — 362.88
    Bharara, Preet. *Doing Justice* — 347.73
    Elkins, Caroline. *Legacy of Violence* — 909
    Henning, Kristin. *The Rage of Innocence* — 364.36
    Miller, Reuben Jonathan. *Halfway Home* — 364.8
    Minow, Martha. *When Should Law Forgive?* — 345
    Olivares, Efren C. *My Boy Will Die of Sorrow* — 305.9
    Seréd, Danielle. *Until We Reckon* — 364.6
PUNK CULTURE
    Hanna, Kathleen. *Rebel Girl* — B
    LaPointe, Sasha taqwseblu. *Red Paint* — B
    LaPointe, Sasha taqwseblu. *Thunder Song* — 814
Punk Rock. Robb, John — 781.6609
PUNK ROCK MUSIC
    Albertine, Viv. *Clothes, Clothes, Clothes. Music, Music, Music* — B
    Hanna, Kathleen. *Rebel Girl* — B
    Harry, Debbie. *Face It* — B
    Robb, John. *Punk Rock* — 781.6609
    Tolokonnikova, Nadezhda. *Rules for Rulebreakers* — 782.42166
    Tran, Phuc. ★*Sigh, Gone* — B
    Waksman, Steve. *This Ain't the Summer of Love* — 781.66
PUNK ROCK MUSICIANS
    Albertine, Viv. *Clothes, Clothes, Clothes. Music, Music, Music* — B
    Alekhina, Mariija. *Riot Days* — B
    Robb, John. *Punk Rock* — 781.6609
    Tolokonnikova, Nadezhda. *Rules for Rulebreakers* — 782.42166
★*Punks*. Keene, John — 811
PUPPET THEATERS
    Blumenthal, Eileen. *Puppetry* — 791.5
PUPPETEERS
    Blumenthal, Eileen. *Puppetry* — 791.5
    Jones, Brian Jay. *Jim Henson* — B
Puppetry. Blumenthal, Eileen — 791.5
PUPPETRY
    Blumenthal, Eileen. *Puppetry* — 791.5
PUPPETS
    Blumenthal, Eileen. *Puppetry* — 791.5
PUPPIES
    Horowitz, Alexandra. ★*The Year of the Puppy* — 636.7
    Monks of New Skete. *The Art of Raising a Puppy* — 636.7
    Nichols, Kerry. *Puppy Brain* — 636.7
Puppy Brain. Nichols, Kerry — 636.7
PUPPY CARE
    Nichols, Kerry. *Puppy Brain* — 636.7
Purdum, Todd S.
    An Idea Whose Time Has Come — 342.7308
    Something Wonderful — B
Pure Invention. Alt, Matt — 306.0952
Pure Skin Care. Tourles, Stephanie L. — 646.7
The Purest Bond. Golbeck, Jennifer — 636.7
Purgatorio. Dante Alighieri — 851
PURGATORY
    Dante Alighieri. *Purgatorio* — 851
PURITANISM
    Schiff, Stacy. *The Witches* — 345
PURITANS
    Bremer, Francis J. *John Winthrop* — B
    Schiff, Stacy. *The Witches* — 345
    Warren, James A. *God, War, and Providence* — 974.5
Purnell, Carolyn
    The Sensational Past — 152.109
Purnell, Derecka
    Becoming Abolitionists — 363.20973
PURNELL, DERECKA
    Purnell, Derecka. *Becoming Abolitionists* — 363.20973
Purnell, Sonia
    Clementine — B
    ★*A Woman of No Importance* — B
★*Purple Crayons*. Ellenhorn, Ross D. — 153.3
PURPOSE IN LIFE
    Albom, Mitch. *Tuesdays with Morrie* — B
    Arthur, Alua. ★*Briefly Perfectly Human* — 306.9
    Beck, Martha Nibley. *The Way of Integrity* — 158.1
    Boa, Kenneth D. *Recalibrate Your Life* — 248.8
    Bowler, Kate. *No Cure for Being Human* — B
    Braitman, Laurel. *What Looks Like Bravery* — B
    Brooks, David. ★*The Second Mountain* — 302
    Chaput, Charles J. *Things Worth Dying For* — 248.4
    Chittister, Joan. *Following the Path* — 248.4
    Dakwar, Elias. *The Captive Imagination* — 616.85
    Derricotte, Toi. *I* — 811
    Frankl, Viktor E. *Yes to Life* — 150.19
    Godwin, Gail. *Getting to Know Death* — B
    Gorges, Eric. *A Craftsman's Legacy* — 745.5
    Gottlieb, Lori. ★*Maybe You Should Talk to Someone* — B
    Gracie, Rickson. *Breathe* — B
    Greene, B. *Until the End of Time* — 523.1
    Gupta, Suneel. *Everyday Dharma* — 158.1
    Hagglund, Martin. *This Life* — 110
    Hecht, Jennifer Michael. ★*The Wonder Paradox* — 808.1
    Hilton, Paris. *Paris* — B
    Hitchens, Christopher. *The Four Horsemen* — 211
    Kalanithi, Paul. ★*When Breath Becomes Air* — B
    Kessler, David. *Finding Meaning* — 155.9
    Knight, Sam. *The Premonitions Bureau* — 133.8
    Kois, Dan. *How to Be a Family* — 910.4
    Kyle, Taya. *American Spirit* — B
    Levi, Primo. *The Periodic Table* — 858
    McConville, Mark. *Failure to Launch* — 155.6
    Moore, Wes. *The Work* — B
    Nicolson, Adam. *How to Be* — 180
    Patchett, Ann. ★*These Precious Days* — 814
    Pham, Larissa. *Pop Song* — 709.2
    Philpott, Mary Laura. *Bomb Shelter* — B
    Popova, Maria. *Figuring* — 920
    Rannells, Andrew. *Uncle of the Year* — B
    Riggs, Nina. *The Bright Hour* — B
    Roberts, David. *Limits of the Known* — B
    Russo, Richard. *The Destiny Thief* — 814
    Sacks, Jonathan. *The Great Partnership* — 201
    Shankle, Melanie. *Church of the Small Things* — 248.8
    Shields, Aomawa L. *Life on Other Planets* — B
    Shriver, Maria. *I've Been Thinking ...* — 170
    Thomas, R. Eric. ★*Congratulations, the Best Is Over!* — B
    Volf, Miroslav. *Life Worth Living* — 113
    Von Drehle, David. ★*The Book of Charlie* — B
    Waldinger, Robert J. ★*The Good Life* — 158.1
    Weber, Charlotte Fox. *Tell Me What You Want* — 153.8
    Weiner, Eric. *Ben & Me* — B
    Weiner, Eric. *The Socrates Express* — 100
    Wilson, Chris. *The Master Plan* — B
The Purpose of Power. Garza, Alicia — 303.48
The Pursuit of Endurance. Davis, Jennifer Pharr — 796.51
The Pursuit of Happiness. Rosen, Jeffrey — 973.3
The Pursuit of Power. Evans, Richard J. — 940.2
Purviance, Jamie
    Weber's Greatest Hits — 641.5
    Weber's Ultimate Grilling — 641.5
PURWIN, HILDE, 1919-2010
    Mazzeo, Tilar J. *Sisters in Resistance* — 945.091
Pushkin. Binyon, T. J. — B
Pushkin, Aleksandr Sergeevich
    Eugene Onegin — 891.71
PUSHKIN, ALEKSANDR SERGEEVICH, 1799-1837
    Binyon, T. J. *Pushkin* — B
Pussypedia. Mendelson, Zoe — 612.6
Putin. Short, Philip — 947
Putin Country. Garrels, Anne — 947
PUTIN, VLADIMIR VLADIMIROVICH, 1952-
    Garrels, Anne. *Putin Country* — 947
    Gessen, Masha. *Never Remember* — 365
    Harding, Luke. *Invasion* — 947.7
    Isikoff, Michael. *Russian Roulette* — 973.933
    Kasparov, Gary. *Winter Is Coming* — 947.086
    Khodorkovsky, Mikhail. *The Russia Conundrum* — 947.086
    Myers, Steven Lee. *The New Tsar* — B
    Nance, Malcolm W. *The Plot to Betray America* — 973.933
    Plokhy, Serhii. ★*The Russo-Ukrainian War* — 947.7
    Politkovskaya, Anna. *A Russian Diary* — 947.086

PUBLIC LIBRARY CORE COLLECTION: NONFICTION
Twentieth Edition

Short, Philip. *Putin* — B
Walker, Shaun. *The Long Hangover* — 947.086
Weiner, Tim. *The Folly and the Glory* — 327.73047
Yaffa, Joshua. *Between Two Fires* — 920
Zygar, Mikhail. *All the Kremlin's Men* — 947.086
Putnam, Robert D.
  Our Kids — 305.5
PUZO, MARIO, 1920-1999
  Seal, Mark. ★*Leave the Gun, Take the Cannoli* — 791.43
The Puzzler. Jacobs, A. J. — 793.73
PUZZLES
  Jacobs, A. J. *The Puzzler* — 793.73
Pyenson, Nick
  Spying on Whales — 599.5
★*Pygmalion.* Shaw, Bernard — 822
PYLE, ERNIE, 1900-1945
  Chrisinger, David. *The Soldier's Truth* — 940.54
  Tobin, James. *Ernie Pyle's War* — B
Pyle, Robert Michael
  Nature Matrix — 508
PYLE, ROBERT MICHAEL
  Pyle, Robert Michael. *Nature Matrix* — 508
Pyongyang. Delisle, Guy — 741.5

Q

QADDAFI, MUAMMAR
  Sattouf, Riad. *The Arab of the Future* — 741.5
Qadiri, Humayra
  Dancing in the Mosque — B
QADIRI, HUMAYRA, 1979 OR 1980-
  Qadiri, Humayra. *Dancing in the Mosque* — B
  Zuckoff, Mitchell. *The Secret Gate* — 958.104
Qashu, Sayed
  Native — 892.4
QASHU, SAYED, 1975-
  Qashu, Sayed. *Native* — 892.4
QB. Young, Steve — B
QING DYNASTY (1644-1912)
  Platt, Stephen R. *Autumn in the Heavenly Kingdom* — 951
  Platt, Stephen R. *Imperial Twilight* — 951
  Spence, Jonathan D. *The Search for Modern China* — 951
Qu, Anna
  Made in China — B
QU, ANNA
  Qu, Anna. *Made in China* — B
QUACKS AND QUACKERY
  Hongoltz-Hetling, Matthew. *If It Sounds Like a Quack* — 615.8
QUADRUPLETS
  Farley, Audrey Clare. ★*Girls and Their Monsters* — 306.875
QUAKER WOMEN
  Greenidge, Kerri. ★*The Grimkes* — 973.5
QUAKERS
  Hamm, Thomas D. ★*The Quakers in America* — 289.6
  Murphy, Andrew R. *William Penn* — B
★*The Quakers in America.* Hamm, Thomas D. — 289.6
The Quality Library. Laughlin, Sara — 025.1
QUALITY OF LIFE
  Angelou, Maya. *Letter to My Daughter* — 814
  Biss, Eula. *Having and Being Had* — 306.3
  Clarke, Rachel. *Dear Life* — B
  Crawford, Matthew B. *The World Beyond Your Head* — 155.2
  Currid-Halkett, Elizabeth. *The Overlooked Americans* — 307.76
  Ellison, Ralph. ★*The Collected Essays of Ralph Ellison* — 814
  Esty, Katharaine C. *Eightysomethings* — 612.6
  Gawande, Atul. ★*Being Mortal* — 362.17
  Geronimus, Arline T. ★*Weathering* — 362.1089
  Johnson, Steven. *Extra Life* — 362.1
  Karbo, Karen. *In Praise of Difficult Women* — 920
  Karlawish, Jason. ★*The Problem of Alzheimer's* — 616.8
  Lim, Audrea. *Free the Land* — 333.7
  McGovern, Anna. *Pottering* — 158.1
  Pinker, Steven. ★*Enlightenment Now* — 303.44
  Reeves, Richard V. *Dream Hoarders* — 305.5
  Shatner, William. *Live Long And—* — B
  Shlain, Tiffany. *24/6* — 158.1

Skach, C. L. *How to Be a Citizen* — 323.6
Volandes, Angelo E. *The Conversation* — 616.02
Warraich, Haider. *Modern Death* — 179.7
Weir, Laura. *Cosy* — 646.7009
Westheimer, Ruth. *The Doctor Is In* — B
Wiking, Meik. *The Little Book of Lykke* — 646.7
QUALITY OF WORK LIFE
  Barsh, Joanna. *Grow Wherever You Work* — 658.4
  Coggan, Philip. *Surviving the Daily Grind* — 658.3
  Feiler, Bruce. ★*The Search* — 306.3
  Mulcahy, Diane. *The Gig Economy* — 650.1
  Robbins, Alexandra. ★*The Teachers* — 371.1
Quammen, David
  ★*Breathless* — 614.5
  ★*Spillover* — 614.4
The Quantum Astrologer's Handbook. Brooks, Michael — B
QUANTUM COMPUTERS
  Kaku, Michio. *Quantum Supremacy* — 006.3
  Lloyd, Seth. *Programming the Universe* — 530.12
QUANTUM GRAVITY
  Rovelli, Carlo. *Reality Is Not What It Seems* — 530.14
A Quantum Life. Oluseyi, Hakeem M. — B
The Quantum Moment. Crease, Robert P. — 530.12
Quantum Supremacy. Kaku, Michio — 006.3
QUANTUM THEORY
  Alexander, Stephon. *Fear of a Black Universe* — 523.1
  Ananthaswamy, Anil. *Through Two Doors at Once* — 530.12
  Becker, Adam. *What Is Real?* — 920
  Brooks, Michael. *The Quantum Astrologer's Handbook* — B
  Carroll, Sean M. *Something Deeply Hidden* — 530.12
  Cox, Brian. *The Quantum Universe* — 530.12
  Crease, Robert P. *The Quantum Moment* — 530.12
  Dyson, Freeman J. *Maker of Patterns* — B
  Einstein, Albert. ★*The Evolution of Physics* — 530
  Einstein, Albert. ★*A Stubbornly Persistent Illusion* — 530.092
  Greene, B. ★*The Elegant Universe* — 539.7
  Greene, B. ★*The Hidden Reality* — 530.12
  Greene, B. *Until the End of Time* — 523.1
  Hawking, Stephen. ★*The Grand Design* — 530.14
  Hawking, Stephen. *The Nature of Space and Time* — 530.1
  Hawking, Stephen. ★*The Universe in a Nutshell* — 530.12
  Holt, Jim. ★*When Einstein Walked with Godel* — 814
  Kakalios, James. *The Amazing Story of Quantum Mechanics* — 530.12
  Kaku, Michio. *The God Equation* — 523.1
  Kaku, Michio. *Quantum Supremacy* — 006.3
  Krauss, Lawrence Maxwell. *The Greatest Story Ever Told—So Far* — 530.01
  Lloyd, Seth. *Programming the Universe* — 530.12
  Mack, Katie. *The End of Everything* — 523.1
  Pontzen, Andrew. *The Universe in a Box* — 523.1
  Rovelli, Carlo. *Helgoland* — 530.12
  Schwartz, David N. *The Last Man Who Knew Everything* — B
  Still, Ben. *Particle Physics Brick by Brick* — 539.7
The Quantum Universe. Cox, Brian — 530.12
QUARANTINE
  Mackenzie, Debora. *Covid-19* — 616.2
  Manaugh, Geoff. *Until Proven Safe* — 614.4
  Randall, David K. *Black Death at the Golden Gate* — 616.9
  Xuecun, Murong. *Deadly Quiet City* — 614.5
QUARRELING
  Pearlman, Jeff. ★*Three-Ring Circus* — 796.323
Quart, Alissa
  Bootstrapped — 305.5
  Squeezed — 305.5
Quarterback. Feinstein, John — B
QUARTERBACKS (FOOTBALL)
  Benedict, Jeff. *The Dynasty* — 796.332
  Cole, Jason. *Elway* — B
  Dunnavant, Keith. *Montana* — B
  Feinstein, John. *Quarterback* — B
  Foles, Nick. *Believe It* — B
  Myers, Gary. *Brady vs. Manning* — B
  Namath, Joe Willie. ★*All the Way* — B
  Pearlman, Jeff. *Gunslinger* — B
  Young, Steve. *QB* — B
The Quartet. Ellis, Joseph J. — 342.7302
Quave, Cassandra Leah
  The Plant Hunter — 581.6

AUTHOR, TITLE, SERIES AND SUBJECT INDEX

QUAVE, CASSANDRA LEAH
   Quave, Cassandra Leah. *The Plant Hunter* — 581.6
QUEBEC (PROVINCE)
   Fischer, David Hackett. *Champlain's Dream* — B
QUECHAN (NORTH AMERICAN PEOPLE)
   Taffa, Deborah Jackson. ★*Whiskey Tender* — B
The Queen. Levin, Josh — 364.16
The Queen Mother. Shawcross, William — B
★*Queen of Bebop*. Hayes, Elaine M. — B
Queen of Our Times. Hardman, Robert — B
Queen of the Court. Blais, Madeleine — B
Queen of the World. Hardman, Robert — B
The Queen V. Walters, Jacqueline — 612.6
Queen Victoria. Worsley, Lucy — B
Queen Victoria's Matchmaking. Cadbury, Deborah — 941.081
Queen Victoria's Mysterious Daughter. Hawksley, Lucinda — B
The Queens of Animation. Holt, Nathalia — 920
Queens of the Age of Chivalry. Weir, Alison — 920
Queens of the Conquest. Weir, Alison — 920
QUEENS, NEW YORK CITY
   Shteyngart, Gary. ★*Little Failure* — B
The Queer Advantage. Gelwicks, Andrew — 920
★*The Queer Games Avant-Garde*. Ruberg, Bonnie — 794.8
A Queer History of the United States. Bronski, Michael — 306.76
QUEER THEORY
   Edman, Elizabeth M. *Queer Virtue* — 230
   Hester, Diarmuid. *Nothing Ever Just Disappears* — 306.76
   Lorde, Audre. ★*The Selected Works of Audre Lorde* — 814
   Nelson, Maggie. ★*Like Love* — 814
   Ruberg, Bonnie. ★*The Queer Games Avant-Garde* — 794.8
   Singh, Julietta. *The Breaks* — B
   Town, Caren J. *LGBTQ Young Adult Fiction* — 813.009
Queer Virtue. Edman, Elizabeth M. — 230
The Quest. Yergin, Daniel — 333.79
A Question and Answer Guide to Astronomy. Christian, Carol — 520
A Question of Torture. McCoy, Alfred W. — 323.4
QUESTIONING
   Bowden, Mark. *The Last Stone* — 363.25
   Cox, Brian. *Universal* — 523.1
   Evans, Rachel Held. *Wholehearted Faith* — 248.4
   Grant, Adam M. ★*Think Again* — 153.4
QUESTIONING (SEXUAL OR GENDER IDENTITY)
   Wizenberg, Molly. *Fixed Stars* — B
QUESTIONS AND ANSWERS
   Ben Jelloun, Tahar. *Islam Explained* — 297
   Carlsen, Spike. *A Walk Around the Block* — 031
   Gerard, Sarah. *Carrie Carolyn Coco* — 364.152
   Hawking, Stephen. ★*Brief Answers to the Big Questions* — 500
   Munroe, Randall. *What If? 2* — 500
   Munroe, Randall. ★*What If?* — 500
   Rutherford, Adam. *The Complete Guide to Absolutely Everything* — 500
   Serrano, Shea. *Basketball (and Other Things)* — 796.323
   Volf, Miroslav. *Life Worth Living* — 113
Questlove
   ★*Hip-Hop Is History* — 782.421649
   Mo' Meta Blues — 782.42164
   Music Is History — 782.42164
QUESTLOVE (MUSICIAN)
   Questlove. *Mo' Meta Blues* — 782.42164
QUESTS
   Ackroyd, Peter. *The Death of King Arthur* — 823
   O'Brady, Colin. ★*The Impossible First* — 919.8904
   Satrapi, Marjane. *Chicken with Plums* — 741.5
A Quick & Easy Guide to They/Them Pronouns. Bongiovanni, Archie — 741.5
Quick & Easy Quilts. Goldsworthy, Lynne — 746.46
★*Quick and Delicious*. Ramsay, Gordon — 641.5
QUICK AND EASY COOKING
   Acheson, Hugh. *The Chef and the Slow Cooker* — 641.5
   Anderson, Pam. *How to Cook Without a Book* — 641.5
   Bastianich, Lidia. ★*Lidia's a Pot, a Pan, and a Bowl* — 641.82
   Bastianich, Lidia. ★*Lidia's from Our Family Table to Yours* — 641.594
   Baz, Molly. *Cook This Book* — 641.5
   Ben-Ishay, Melissa. *Come Hungry* — 641.5
   Berg, Meliz. *Dinner Tonight* — 641.595
   Bittman, Mark. ★*Dinner for Everyone* — 641.5
   Bittman, Mark. *How to Cook Everything Fast* — 641.5
   Bittman, Mark. *How to Cook Everything* — 641.5
   Brennan, Kathy. *Keepers* — 641.5973
   Cayne, Alison. *The Haven's Kitchen Cooking School* — 641.5
   Clark, Melissa. *Comfort in an Instant* — 641.5
   Clark, Melissa. ★*Dinner in an Instant* — 641.5
   Clark, Melissa. ★*Dinner in One* — 641.82
   Clark, Melissa. *Dinner* — 641.5
   Comerford, Hope. *Fix-It and Forget-It Healthy 5-Ingredient Cookbook* — 641.5
   Conner, Polly. ★*From Freezer to Cooker* — 641.6
   Coscarelli, Chloe. *Chloe Flavor* — 641.5
   Donofrio, Jeanine. ★*Love & Lemons* — 641.5
   Drummond, Ree. ★*The Pioneer Woman Cooks* — 641.5
   Fuentes, Laura. *The Best Homemade Kids' Snacks on the Planet* — 641.5
   Garten, Ina. ★*Go-To Dinners* — 641.5
   Garten, Ina. ★*Make It Ahead* — 641.5
   Gerard, Tieghan. ★*Half Baked Harvest Every Day* — 641.5
   Good, Phyllis Pellman. *Fix-It and Forget-It New Cookbook* — 641.5
   Greenspan, Eric. *The Great Grilled Cheese Book* — 641.6
   Griffin, Brooke. *Skinny Suppers* — 641.5
   Hartwig, Melissa. *The Whole30 Fast & Easy* — 641.5
   Hartwig, Melissa. *The Whole30 Slow Cooker* — 641.5
   Hayden, Georgina. *Greekish* — 641.594
   Henry, Diana. *From the Oven to the Table* — 641.82
   Heuck, Lidey. ★*Cooking in Real Life* — 641.5
   Homolka, Gina. *Skinnytaste Fast and Slow* — 641.5
   Homolka, Gina. *Skinnytaste One & Done* — 641.5
   Howard, Vivian. *This Will Make It Taste Good* — 641.5
   Hussain, Nadiya. *Time to Eat* — 641.5
   Kane, Cyndi. *Save-It-Forward Suppers* — 641.5
   Kimball, Christopher. *Christopher Kimball's Milk Street* — 641.5
   Kimball, Christopher. *Tuesday Nights Mediterranean* — 641.59
   Kinch, David. *At Home in the Kitchen* — 641.5973
   Klein, Dini. *Prep + Rally* — 641.5
   Laperruque, Emma. *Food52 Big Little Recipes* — 641.5
   Lawson, Nigella. *At My Table* — 641.59
   Leake, Lisa. *100 Days of Real Food on a Budget* — 641.5
   Lee, Lara. *A Splash of Soy* — 641.595
   Lillien, Lisa. *Hungry Girl 1-2-3* — 641.5
   Lillien, Lisa. *Hungry Girl Simply 6* — 641.5
   Meehan, Peter. *Lucky Peach Presents 101 Easy Asian Recipes* — 641.595
   Merchant, Jessica. *Everyday Dinners* — 641.82
   Miglore, Kristen. ★*Food52 Simply Genius* — 641.5
   Mullins, Brittany. *Mostly Veggies* — 641.5
   Music, Carla Lalli. *That Sounds so Good* — 641.5
   Nelson, Kim. *Daisy Cakes Bakes* — 641.86
   Nguyen, Andrea Quynhgiao. ★*Vietnamese Food Any Day* — 641.595
   Oliver, Jamie. *Together* — 641.5
   Ottolenghi, Yotam. *Ottolenghi Simple* — 641.59
   Oz, Daphne. *The Happy Cook* — 641.5
   Paltrow, Gwyneth. *It's All Easy* — 641.5
   Pauline, Kathryn. ★*Piecemeal* — 641.5
   Perry, Dawn. *Ready, Set, Cook* — 641.5
   Peters, Meike. *Noon* — 641.5
   Porowski, Antoni. *Antoni* — 641.5
   Ramsay, Gordon. ★*Quick and Delicious* — 641.5
   Roman, Alison. ★*Nothing Fancy* — 642
   Rosen, Ali. *Bring It!* — 641.5973
   Saffitz, Claire. ★*What's for Dessert* — 641.86
   Sakai, Sonoko. *Japanese Home Cooking* — 641.595
   Saltz, Joanna. *Delish* — 641.5
   Scott, Ryan. *The No-Fuss Family Cookbook* — 641.5
   Serpico, Peter. *Learning Korean* — 641.595
   Sheehan, Jessie. ★*Snackable Bakes* — 641.7
   Shumski, Daniel. *How to Instant Pot* — 641.5
   Sifton, Sam. ★*The New York Times Cooking No-Recipe Recipes* — 641.5
   Snodgrass, Alex. ★*The Defined Dish* — 641.5
   Snodgrass, Alex. *Dinner Tonight* — 641.5
   Snyder, Sabrina. *Dinner Then Dessert* — 641.5
   Stone, Robyn. *Add a Pinch Cookbook* — 641.5975
   Tam, Michelle. *Ready or Not!* — 641.5
   Tandoh, Ruby. ★*Cook as You Are* — 641.59
   Teigen, Chrissy. *Cravings* — 641.5
   Tosi, Christina. *All About Cake* — 641.86
   Walch, Aubry. *The Herbivorous Butcher Cookbook* — 641.5
   Walker, Danielle. *Danielle Walker's Healthy in a Hurry* — 641.5
   Weil, Andrew. *Fast Food, Good Food* — 641.3
   Weinstein, Bruce. *The Great Big Pressure Cooker Book* — 641.5
   Weinstein, Bruce. *The Kitchen Shortcut Bible* — 641.555
   Westerhausen, Shelly. *Every Season Is Soup Season* — 641.81
   Workman, Katie. *The Mom 100 Cookbook* — 641.5

Yearwood, Trisha. *Trisha's Kitchen* — 641.5
Quickening Fields. Rogers, Pattiann — 811
Quicksand. Mankell, Henning — B
Quiet. Cain, Susan — 155.2
★*The Quiet Americans.* Anderson, Scott — 327.12
Quiet Beauty. Brown, Kendall H. — 712.09
★*Quietly Hostile.* Irby, Samantha — 814
Quigley, Fran
   Prescription for the People — 338.4
Quilt As-You-Go Made Vintage. Brandvig, Jera — 746.46
A Quilter's Album of Patchwork Patterns. Beyer, Jinny — 746.46
QUILTING
   Alexander, Lissa. *Oh, Scrap!* — 746.46
   Belyea, Patricia. *East-Meets-West Quilts* — 746.46
   Beyer, Jinny. *A Quilter's Album of Patchwork Patterns* — 746.46
   Doughty, Kathy. *Adding Layers* — 746.46
   Gering, Jacquie. *Quilting Modern* — 746.46
   Gilleland, Diane. *All Points Patchwork* — 746.46
   Glass, Alison. *Alison Glass Applique.* — 746.44
   Goertzen, Vanessa. ★*Charm School* — 746.46
   Goldsworthy, Lynne. *Quick & Easy Quilts* — 746.46
   Grisham, Candyce Copp. *Dresden Quilt Blocks Reimagined* — 746.46
   Hartman, Elizabeth. *Modern Patchwork* — 746.46
   Hunter, Bonnie K. *String Frenzy* — 746.46
   Maxwell, Sarah. *Fearless with Fabric* — 746.46
   Nyberg, Amanda Jean. *No Scrap Left Behind* — 746.46
   Redford, Catherine. *Modern Machine Quilting* — 746.46
   Rosenthal, Maxine. *One-Block Wonders of the World* — 746.46
   Wolfe, Victoria Findlay. *Modern Quilt Magic* — 746.46
   Wood, Sherri. *The Improv Handbook for Modern Quilters* — 746.46
Quilting Modern. Gering, Jacquie — 746.46
Quilting The Black-Eyed Pea. Giovanni, Nikki — 811
QUILTS
   Shaw, Robert. *American Quilts* — 746.46
QUIN, SARA, 1980-
   Quin, Tegan. ★*High School* — B
Quin, Tegan
   ★*High School* — B
QUIN, TEGAN, 1980-
   Quin, Tegan. ★*High School* — B
QUINCY FAMILY
   Sankovitch, Nina. *American Rebels* — 920
QUINCY, JOSIAH, 1744-1775
   Sankovitch, Nina. *American Rebels* — 920
Quindlen, Anna
   ★*Nanaville* — B
QUINDLEN, ANNA
   Quindlen, Anna. ★*Nanaville* — B
Quindt, Svetlana
   The Costume Making Guide — 646.4
Quinn, Bridget
   Broad Strokes — 920
   She Votes — 324.6
Quinn, Jane Bryant
   ★*How to Make Your Money Last* — 332.024
Quinn, Susan
   Eleanor and Hick — B
Quinn, Tallu Schuyler
   What We Wish Were True — B
QUINN, TALLU SCHUYLER
   Quinn, Tallu Schuyler. *What We Wish Were True* — B
Quinn, Zoe
   Crash Override — 794.8
Quinones, John
   ★*One Year in Uvalde* — 371.7
Quinones, Sam
   Dreamland — 362.29
   ★*The Least of Us* — 362.29
★*Quit Like a Woman.* Whitaker, Holly — 616.86
Quitter. Barnett, Erica C. — B
Quitting. Keller, Julia — 650.14
QUIZ SHOWS
   Trebek, Alex. *The Answer Is ...* — 791.4502
QUMRAN COMMUNITY
   Schiffman, Lawrence H. *Reclaiming the Dead Sea Scrolls* — 296.1
QUOTATIONS
   Bartlett, John. *Bartlett's Familiar Quotations, 19th Ed.* — 808.88

Steinem, Gloria. *The Truth Will Set You Free, but First It Will Piss You Off* — 305.42
Telushkin, Joseph. *Jewish Wisdom* — 296.3
★*The Qur'an.* Haleem, M. A. S. Abdel — 297.122
Qureshi, Saqib Iqbal
   Being Muslim Today — 305.6

R

R. Crumb. Crumb, R. — 741.6
Raab, Nathan
   The Hunt for History — 790.1
RAAB, NATHAN, 1978-
   Raab, Nathan. *The Hunt for History* — 790.1
Raban, Jonathan
   Bad Land — 978
   Father and Son — B
RABAN, JONATHAN
   Raban, Jonathan. *Father and Son* — B
RABAN, PETER, 1918-1996
   Raban, Jonathan. *Father and Son* — B
Rabban, David M.
   Free Speech in Its Forgotten Years — 342.73
RABBIS
   Leder, Steven Z. *The Beauty of What Remains* — 306.9
   Telushkin, Joseph. *Rebbe* — 296.833
Rabbit. Williams, Patricia — B
Rabbit Heart. Ervin, Kristine S. — 364.152
RABE, JOHN, 1882-1950
   Chang, Iris. ★*The Rape of Nanking* — 951.04
Rabid. Wasik, Bill — 614.5
RABIES
   Wasik, Bill. *Rabid* — 614.5
RABIN, YITZHAK, 1922-1995
   Ephron, Dan. *Killing a King* — 956.9405
RABINOWITZ FAMILY
   Frankel, Rebecca. *Into the Forest* — 940.53
Rabinowitz, Dorothy
   No Crueler Tyrannies — 345.73
RABINOWITZ, MIRIAM DWORETSKY, 1908-1981
   Frankel, Rebecca. *Into the Forest* — 940.53
RABINOWITZ, MORRIS, 1906-1982
   Frankel, Rebecca. *Into the Forest* — 940.53
Raboteau, Emily
   Lessons for Survival — 814
RABOTEAU, EMILY
   Raboteau, Emily. *Lessons for Survival* — 814
RACE (BIOLOGY)
   Young, Kevin. *Bunk* — 177
RACE (SOCIAL SCIENCES)
   Abdelmahmoud, Elamin. *Son of Elsewhere* — B
   Anderson, Carol. ★*White Rage* — 305.800973
   Baime, A. J. *White Lies* — B
   Boykin, Keith. ★*Why Does Everything Have to Be About Race?* — 305.8
   Bratt, Jessica Anne. *Let's Talk About Race in Storytimes* — 027.62
   Brown, Austin Channing. ★*I'm Still Here* — B
   Brown, Jericho. ★*The Tradition* — 811
   Clark, Tiana. *I Can't Talk About the Trees Without the Blood* — 811
   Coates, Ta-Nehisi. ★*Between the World and Me* — 305.800973
   Coates, Ta-Nehisi. ★*We Were Eight Years in Power* — 305.896
   Copeland, Misty. *The Wind at My Back* — B
   Dangarembga, Tsitsi. *Black and Female* — 305.48
   Dungy, Camille T. *Soil* — 635.0978
   Dyson, Michael Eric. *The Black Presidency* — 305.800973
   Dyson, Michael Eric. *Tears We Cannot Stop* — 305.800973
   Dyson, Michael Eric. *What Truth Sounds Like* — 305.800973
   Else, Jon. *True South* — 305.800973
   Evans, William. *Black Nerd Problems* — 814.6
   Felix, Camonghne. *Build Yourself a Boat* — 811
   Freeman, Andrea. ★*Ruin Their Crops on the Ground* — 338.1
   Gay, Roxane. ★*Opinions* — 814
   Gayle, Caleb. *We Refuse to Forget* — 975.004
   Gregory, Dick. *Defining Moments in Black History* — 973
   Griffin, Farah Jasmine. ★*In Search of a Beautiful Freedom* — 814
   Griffith, Elisabeth. *Formidable* — 305.42
   Haddish, Tiffany. *The Last Black Unicorn* — B
   Han, Chenxing. *Be the Refuge* — 294.3

AUTHOR, TITLE, SERIES AND SUBJECT INDEX

Haygood, Wil. ★*Colorization*	791.43
Headlee, Celeste Anne. *Speaking of Race*	305.8
Hobbs, Jeff. *Show Them You're Good*	373
Hunter-Gault, Charlayne. *My People*	305.48
Hurston, Zora Neale. ★*You Don't Know Us Negroes and Other Essays*	814
Hylton, Antonia. *Madness*	362.2
Imani, Blair. *Read This to Get Smarter*	303.3
Imbler, Sabrina. *How Far the Light Reaches*	591.77
Karim-Cooper, Farah. ★*The Great White Bard*	822.33
Kenan, Randall. *Black Folk Could Fly*	813
Kendi, Ibram X. ★*How to Raise an Antiracist*	649
Kozol, Jonathan. *Fire in the Ashes*	362.77
Lawton, Georgina. *Raceless*	B
Lee, Julia Sun-Joo. *Biting the Hand*	B
Lemon, Don. *This Is the Fire*	305.896
Lorde, Audre. ★*The Selected Works of Audre Lorde*	814
Mans, Jasmine. *Black Girl, Call Home*	811
Moore, Wayetu. *The Dragons, the Giant, the Women*	B
Morrison, Toni. *Playing in the Dark*	810.9
Morrison, Toni. ★*The Source of Self-Regard*	814
Mukantabana, Yseult P. ★*Real Friends Talk About Race*	305.8
Nezhukumatathil, Aimee. *World of Wonders*	590
Phillips, Maya. *Nerd*	302.23
Pinckney, Darryl. *Busted in New York and Other Essays*	305.800973
Powers, Ann. *Good Booty*	781.64
Questlove. *Mo' Meta Blues*	782.42164
Raboteau, Emily. *Lessons for Survival*	814
Ray, Victor. *On Critical Race Theory*	305.8
Reed, Justin Phillip. *The Malevolent Volume*	811
Roberts-Miller, Patricia. *Speaking of Race*	305.8
Robinson, Phoebe. *Please Don't Sit on My Bed in Your Outside Clothes*	818
Rosen, Richard A. *Julius Chambers*	B
Row, Jess. *White Flights*	813
Sabatini Sloan, Aisha. *Dreaming of Ramadi in Detroit*	814
Savage, Jodi M. *The Death of a Jaybird*	B
Sharma, Nina. *The Way You Make Me Feel*	B
Smith, Clint. ★*Above Ground*	811
Tisserand, Michael. *Krazy*	741.5
Wingfield, Adia Harvey. *Gray Areas*	331.6
Wong, Carmen Rita. *Why Didn't You Tell Me?*	B
Race Against Time. Boykin, Keith	305.8
★*Race Against Time*. Mitchell, Jerry	364.152

RACE AWARENESS

Bayoumi, Moustafa. *How Does It Feel to Be a Problem?*	305.892
Bell, Darrin. ★*The Talk*	741.5
Broome, Brian. ★*Punch Me up to the Gods*	B
Busby, Jill Louise. *Unfollow Me*	305.08
Dyson, Michael Eric. *The Black Presidency*	305.800973
Fleming, Crystal Marie. *How to Be Less Stupid About Race*	305.800973
Gates, Henry Louis. *And Still I Rise*	305.896
Gilliam, Fatimah. *Race Rules*	305.8
Kendi, Ibram X. ★*How to Raise an Antiracist*	649
Lemon, Don. *This Is the Fire*	305.896
McWhorter, John H. *Talking Back, Talking Black*	427
Parker, Morgan. ★*You Get What You Pay For*	305.896
Porter, Eduardo. *American Poison*	305.800973
Ross, Dax-Devlon. *Letters to My White Male Friends*	305.8
Row, Jess. *White Flights*	813
Tatum, Beverly Daniel. ★ " *Why Are All the Black Kids Sitting Together in the Cafeteria?* "	305.800973

RACE AWARENESS IN CHILDREN

Asika, Uju. *Bringing up Race*	155.4
Baxley, Traci. *Social Justice Parenting*	649
Carroll, Rebecca. *Surviving the White Gaze*	B
Guida-Richards, Melissa. *What White Parents Should Know About Transracial Adoption*	362.734
Harrison, Valerie I. *Do Right by Me*	649
Ramesh, Jaya. *Parenting at the Intersections*	649

RACE HORSE TRAINERS

Markham, Beryl. *West with the Night*	B

RACE HORSES

Drape, Joe. *American Pharoah*	798.40092
Hillenbrand, Laura. ★*Seabiscuit*	798.4
Ours, Dorothy. *Man O' War*	798.400929
The Race of Aces. Bruning, John R.	940.54

RACE RELATIONS

Abdurraqib, Hanif. ★*A Little Devil in America*	791.089
Agarwal, Pragya. *Sway*	177

Alexander, Elizabeth. ★*The Trayvon Generation*	305.896
Alexander, Kwame. *Light for the World to See*	811.6
Alexander, Michelle. *The New Jim Crow*	364.973
Alvis-Walker, Marcie. *Everybody Come Alive*	B
Anderson, Carol. ★*The Second*	344.7305
Anderson, Carol. ★*White Rage*	305.800973
Archibald, John. *Shaking the Gates of Hell*	B
Arsenault, Raymond. *John Lewis*	B
Asim, Jabari. *We Can't Breathe*	305.896
Avlon, John P. *Lincoln and the Fight for Peace*	973.7
Bailey, Issac J. *Why Didn't We Riot?*	305.800973
Baime, A. J. *White Lies*	B
Baker, Calvin. *A More Perfect Reunion*	305.800973
Baldwin, James. ★*Collected Essays*	814
Baldwin, James. ★*The Fire Next Time*	305.896
Baldwin, James. *I Am Not Your Negro*	323.1196
Baldwin, James. ★*Notes of a Native Son*	305.8
Ball, Edward. *Life of a Klansman*	305.8009763
Ball, Edward. *Slaves in the Family*	975.7
Barry, John M. *Rising Tide*	977
Bass, Amy. *One Goal*	796.334
Bayoumi, Moustafa. *How Does It Feel to Be a Problem?*	305.892
Bell, W. Kamau. ★*Do the Work!*	305.8
Bennett, Michael. *Things That Make White People Uncomfortable*	305.896
Berlin, Ira. *The Making of African America*	973
Berman, Ari. *Give Us the Ballot*	324.6
Bernard, Emily. *Black Is the Body*	305.48
Berry, Daina Ramey. ★*A Black Women's History of the United States*	305.48
Blackmon, Douglas A. *Slavery by Another Name*	305.896
Blum, Edward J. *The Color of Christ*	232
Bordewich, Fergus M. *Klan War*	973.8
Boyd, Herb. *We Shall Overcome*	323.1196
Boykin, Keith. *Race Against Time*	305.8
Boykin, Keith. ★*Why Does Everything Have to Be About Race?*	305.8
Boyle, Kevin. *Arc of Justice*	345.73
Boyle, Kevin. *The Shattering*	973.923
Bradburd, Rus. *All the Dreams We've Dreamed*	796.323
Branch, Taylor. ★*Pillar of Fire*	323.1
Brands, H. W. *The Last Campaign*	973.8
Braswell, Porter. ★*Let Them See You*	650.1
Brennan, Chad. *Faithful Antiracism*	277.308
Brown, Austin Channing. ★*I'm Still Here*	B
Broyles, Michael. ★*Revolutions in American Music*	780.9
Bryant, Howard. *The Last Hero*	B
Burnham, Margaret A. ★*By Hands Now Known*	342.73
Butler, Paul. *Chokehold*	363.2
Calloway, Colin G. *One Vast Winter Count*	978
Cargle, Rachel Elizabeth. *A Renaissance of Our Own*	B
Carlin, John. *Playing the Enemy*	968.06
Carruthers, Charlene A. *Unapologetic*	305.48
Cep, Casey N. ★*Furious Hours*	364.152
Chang, Tina. *Hybrida*	811
Cleaver, Eldridge. *Soul on Ice*	B
Coates, Ta-Nehisi. ★*Between the World and Me*	305.800973
Coates, Ta-Nehisi. ★*We Were Eight Years in Power*	305.896
Collins-Dexter, Brandi. *Black Skinhead*	324.2734
Cox, Anna-Lisa. *The Bone and Sinew of the Land*	977
Cozzens, Peter. *A Brutal Reckoning*	973.5
Cozzens, Peter. *The Earth Is Weeping*	978
Crump, Benjamin. *Open Season*	364
Currie, Elliott. *A Peculiar Indifference*	305.800973
Darby, Seyward. ★*Sisters in Hate*	305.800973
Deetz, Kelley Fanto. *Bound to the Fire*	641.59
Delany, Sarah Louise. *Having Our Say*	B
Delmont, Matthew F. *Half American*	940.54
Dennis, David J., Jr. *The Movement Made Us*	B
DiAngelo, Robin J. *White Fragility*	305.8
Dray, Philip. *At the Hands of Persons Unknown*	364.1
Dray, Philip. *Capitol Men*	973.8
Du Bois, W. E. B. *The Oxford W.E.B. Du Bois Reader*	305.896
Du Bois, W. E. B. ★*The Souls of Black Folk*	973
Dyson, Michael Eric. *The Black Presidency*	305.800973
Dyson, Michael Eric. *Come Hell or High Water*	976.3
Dyson, Michael Eric. *Long Time Coming*	305.800973
Dyson, Michael Eric. *Tears We Cannot Stop*	305.800973
Dyson, Michael Eric. *What Truth Sounds Like*	305.800973
Eberhardt, Jennifer L. ★*Biased*	303.3

PUBLIC LIBRARY CORE COLLECTION: NONFICTION
Twentieth Edition

Eddo-Lodge, Reni. *Why I'm No Longer Talking to White People About Race*	305.8
Eig, Jonathan. ★*Ali*	B
Eig, Jonathan. ★*King*	B
Ellison, Ralph. ★*The Collected Essays of Ralph Ellison*	814
Ellsworth, Scott. *The Ground Breaking*	976.6
Enss, Chris. *Mochi's War*	B
Epplin, Luke. *Our Team*	796.357
Faust, Drew Gilpin. *Necessary Trouble*	B
Fleming, Crystal Marie. *How to Be Less Stupid About Race*	305.800973
Foner, Eric. *The Fiery Trial*	973.7092
Foner, Eric. *Forever Free*	973.8
Foner, Eric. *The Second Founding*	342.73
Ford, Tanisha C. *Dressed in Dreams*	391
Forman, James. *Locking up Our Own*	364.973
Francois, Willie Dwayne. *Silencing White Noise*	277
Franklin, John Hope. *In Search of the Promised Land*	929
Fugard, Athol. ★*"master Harold"—And the Boys*	822
Fuller, Alexandra. *Don't Let's Go to the Dogs Tonight*	B
Fumudoh, Ziwe. ★*Black Friend*	814
Gardner, Mark L. *The Earth Is All That Lasts*	978.004
Garrett, Kent. *The Last Negroes at Harvard*	920
Gates, Henry Louis. *100 Amazing Facts About the Negro*	973
Gates, Henry Louis. *And Still I Rise*	305.896
Gates, Henry Louis. *The Black Box*	908
Gates, Henry Louis. *The Future of the Race*	305.896
Gates, Henry Louis. ★*Stony the Road*	973
Gay, Roxane. *Bad Feminist*	814
Gayle, Caleb. *We Refuse to Forget*	975.004
Gevisser, Mark. *A Legacy of Liberation*	B
Giddings, Paula. *Ida*	B
Gildea, William. *The Longest Fight*	B
Gilliam, Dorothy Butler. *Trailblazer*	B
Gilliam, Fatimah. *Race Rules*	305.8
Glaude, Eddie S. *Begin Again*	305.800973
Gomez, Laura E. ★*Inventing Latinos*	305.868
Goodman, Matthew. *The City Game*	796.323
Gordon-Reed, Annette. *Andrew Johnson*	B
Gorra, Michael Edward. *The Saddest Words*	813
Grant, Gail Milissa. *At the Elbows of My Elders*	B
Grant, Richard. *The Deepest South of All*	976.2
Green, Kristen. *Something Must Be Done About Prince Edward County*	379.2
Greenidge, Kerri. *Black Radical*	B
Greenidge, Kerri. ★*The Grimkes*	973.5
Gregory, Dick. *Defining Moments in Black History*	973
Griffin, Chante. *Loving Your Black Neighbor as Yourself*	261
Griffin, Farah Jasmine. *Read Until You Understand*	810.9
Gwynne, S. C. *Empire of the Summer Moon*	B
Hahn, Steven. *A Nation Under Our Feet*	975
Halberstam, David. ★*The Children*	323.1
Hall, Alvin D. *Driving the Green Book*	917.304
Hamad, Ruby. *White Tears/Brown Scars*	305.8
Hamalainen, Pekka. ★*Indigenous Continent*	970.004
Hansberry, Lorraine. ★*A Raisin in the Sun*	812
Hardwick, Lamar. *How Ableism Fuels Racism*	261.8
Harris, Adam. ★*The State Must Provide*	379.2
Harris, J. William. *The Hanging of Thomas Jeremiah*	B
Harrison, Valerie I. *Do Right by Me*	649
Hawes, Jennifer. *Grace Will Lead Us Home*	364.152
Hayes, Christopher. *A Colony in a Nation*	364.3
Haygood, Wil. ★*Colorization*	791.43
Hazzard, Kevin M. *American Sirens*	362.18
Headlee, Celeste Anne. *Speaking of Race*	305.8
Herold, Benjamin. *Disillusioned*	307.76
Hervieux, Linda. *Forgotten*	940.54
Hill, DaMaris B. *Breath Better Spent*	811
Hill, Marc Lamont. *Seen and Unseen*	303.3
Hinton, Elizabeth Kai. *America on Fire*	305.800973
Hirsch, James S. *Riot and Remembrance*	976.6
Hochschild, Adam. *King Leopold's Ghost*	967.51
Hong, Cathy Park. *Minor Feelings*	305.48
Horace, Matthew. *The Black and the Blue*	B
Horn, James P. P. *Land as God Made It*	975.5
Horwitz, Tony. *Spying on the South*	917
Huang, Eddie. *Fresh off the Boat*	B
Hunter-Gault, Charlayne. ★*My People*	305.48
Hurston, Zora Neale. ★*You Don't Know Us Negroes and Other Essays*	814
Inskeep, Steve. *Jacksonland*	973.56
Jackson, Jenn M. ★*Black Women Taught Us*	305.48
Jackson, Kellie Carter. *We Refuse*	323.1196
Jackson, Lawrence Patrick. *Chester B. Himes*	B
Jackson, Major. *Razzle Dazzle*	811
Jackson, Mitchell S. *Survival Math*	B
Jackson, Regina. *White Women*	305.8
Jackson, Troy. *Becoming King*	B
Jacoby, Karl. *The Strange Career of William Ellis*	B
Johnson, Katherine G. *My Remarkable Journey*	B
Johnson, Theodore R. *When the Stars Begin to Fall*	305.800973
Johnson, Walter. *Soul by Soul*	976.3
Jones, Doug. *Bending Toward Justice*	323.1196
Jones, Jacqueline. *Saving Savannah*	975.8
Joseph, Peniel E. *The Sword and the Shield*	B
Joseph, Peniel E. *Waiting 'Til the Midnight Hour*	323.1196
Kamp, David. *Sunny Days*	791.4502
Kaplan, Fred. *Lincoln and the Abolitionists*	973.7092
Kelley, Blair Murphy. *Black Folk*	331.6
Kendi, Ibram X. ★*How to Be an Antiracist*	305.8
Kendi, Ibram X. *How to Raise an Antiracist*	649
Kendi, Ibram X. ★*Stamped from the Beginning*	305.8
Kennedy, Kostya. *True*	B
King, Coretta Scott. ★*My Life, My Love, My Legacy*	B
King, Gilbert. ★*Devil in the Grove*	305.896
King, Martin Luther. ★*A Testament of Hope*	323.1
Kotz, Nick. *Judgment Days*	323
Krist, Gary. *Empire of Sin*	976.3
Kuo, Michelle. *Reading with Patrick*	B
Lamb, Christina. *House of Stone*	968.91
Lane, Charles. *The Day Freedom Died*	976.3
Lauterbach, Preston. *Beale Street Dynasty*	976.8
Laymon, Kiese. ★*Heavy*	B
Laymon, Kiese. *How to Slowly Kill Yourself and Others in America*	814.6
Lebron, Christopher J. *The Making of Black Lives Matter*	305.896
Lee, Erika. *America for Americans*	305.800973
Lee, Erika. *The Making of Asian America*	973
Lee, Julia Sun-Joo. *Biting the Hand*	B
Lees, Gene. *You Can't Steal a Gift*	B
Lehr, Dick. ★*The Birth of a Nation*	305.800973
Lemann, Nicholas. *Redemption*	975
Lemon, Don. *This Is the Fire*	305.896
Lepore, Jill. *New York Burning*	974.7
Levine, Robert S. ★*The Failed Promise*	973.8
Lewis, John. ★*March; Book One*	741.5
Lewis, John. ★*March; Book Three*	741.5
Lewis, John. ★*March; Book Two*	741.5
Lewis, Robin Coste. *To the Realization of Perfect Helplessness*	811
Lim, Audrea. *Free the Land*	333.73
Lowery, Wesley. ★*American Whitelash*	305.8
Lowry, Beverly. *Deer Creek Drive*	364.152
Lusane, Clarence. *The Black History of the White House*	975.3
Luxenberg, Steve. ★*Separate*	342.7308
Macy, Beth. ★*Truevine*	B
Madigan, Tim. *The Burning*	976.6
Malala, Justice. *The Plot to Save South Africa*	968.07
Mallory, Tamika D. *State of Emergency*	305.896
Mandela, Nelson. *In His Own Words*	B
Manegold, Catherine S. *Ten Hills Farm*	974.4
Maraniss, Andrew. *Strong Inside*	B
Markham, Beryl. *West with the Night*	B
Martin, Rachel Louise. *A Most Tolerant Little Town*	379.2
Masur, Kate. *Until Justice Be Done*	323.1196
Mays, Kyle. ★*An Afro-Indigenous History of the United States*	973
McCormick, Ty. *Beyond the Sand and Sea*	920
McDonnell, Michael. *Masters of Empire*	977.4
McGhee, Heather C. ★*The Sum of Us*	305.8
McGilligan, Patrick. *Oscar Micheaux*	B
McMillan, Tracie. ★*The White Bonus*	305.8
McMurtry, Larry. *Crazy Horse*	B
McNally, Dennis. *On Highway 61*	781.64
McWhorter, Diane. *Carry Me Home*	976.1
Meacham, Jon. ★*And There Was Light*	B
Meckler, Laura. ★*Dream Town*	305.8
Mehra, Nishta. *Brown, White, Black*	305.800973
Merritt, Tyler. *I Take My Coffee Black*	791.4302
Meyer, Eugene L. *Five for Freedom*	973.7
Miles, Tiya. *The Dawn of Detroit*	977.4
Miranda, Deborah A. *Bad Indians*	305.8009794

AUTHOR, TITLE, SERIES AND SUBJECT INDEX

Mojica Rodriguez, Prisca Dorcas. *For Brown Girls with Sharp Edges and Tender Hearts*   305.48
Moore, Wes. ★*Five Days*   363.32
Moore, Wes. *The Other Wes Moore*   B
Morgan-Owens, Jessie. *Girl in Black and White*   B
Morrison, Melanie. *Murder on Shades Mountain*   345.761
Morrison, Toni. *Playing in the Dark*   810.9
Mort, T. A. *Thieves' Road*   978.3
Muhammad, Khalil Gibran. *The Condemnation of Blackness*   364.2
Mukantabana, Yseult P. ★*Real Friends Talk About Race*   305.8
Neiman, Garrett. *Rich White Men*   305.5
Neus, Nora. *24 Hours in Charlottesville*   973.933
Noah, Trevor. *Born a Crime*   B
Norris, Michele. ★*Our Hidden Conversations*   305
Obama, Barack. ★*Dreams from My Father*   B
Okrent, Daniel. *The Guarded Gate*   344.73
Oluo, Ijeoma. ★*Be a Revolution*   305.8
Oluo, Ijeoma. *Mediocre*   305.310973
Oluo, Ijeoma. ★*So You Want to Talk About Race*   305.800973
Ortiz, Paul. *An African American and Latinx History of the United States*   305.8
Painter, Nell Irvin. ★*I Just Keep Talking*   814
Parker, Morgan. ★*You Get What You Pay For*   305.896
Pawel, Miriam. *The Crusades of Cesar Chavez*   B
Payne, Les. ★*The Dead Are Arising*   B
Perry, Bruce. *Malcolm*   B
Perry, Imani. *May We Forever Stand*   782.25
Perry, Imani. ★*South to America*   917
Person, Charles. *Buses Are a Comin'*   B
Phillips, Patrick. *Blood at the Root*   305.8
Pinckney, Darryl. *Busted in New York and Other Essays*   305.800973
Plant, Deborah G. *Of Greed and Glory*   326
Porter, Eduardo. *American Poison*   305.800973
Postel, Charles. *Equality*   305.50973
Powell, Michael. ★*Canyon Dreams*   796.323
Price, David A. ★*Love and Hate in Jamestown*   975.5
Price, S. L. *Playing Through the Whistle*   796.332
Proenza-Coles, Christina. *American Founders*   973
Raboteau, Emily. *Lessons for Survival*   814
Raines, Ben. *The Last Slave Ship*   306.362
Ralph, Laurence. *Sito*   364.152
Ramsey, Franchesca. *Well, That Escalated Quickly*   B
Rankine, Claudia. ★*Citizen*   814
Rankine, Claudia. ★*Just Us*   305.896
Rankine, Claudia. *The White Card*   812
Rapoport, Ron. *Let's Play Two*   B
Rasmussen, Daniel. *American Uprising*   976.3
Ray, Victor. *On Critical Race Theory*   305.8
Rembert, Winfred. *Chasing Me to My Grave*   B
Rice, Condoleezza. *Extraordinary, Ordinary People*   B
Ricketts, Rachel. ★*Do Better*   305.800973
Risen, Clay. *The Bill of the Century*   342.7308
Rose, Tricia. ★*Metaracism*   305.8
Rosen, Richard A. *Julius Chambers*   B
Ross, Dax-Devlon. *Letters to My White Male Friends*   305.8
Rothstein, Richard. ★*The Color of Law*   305.800973
Row, Jess. *White Flights*   813
Royster, Francesca T. *Choosing Family*   B
Rubinstein, Julian. ★*The Holly*   364.106
Ruffin, Amber. ★*The World Record Book of Racist Stories*   305.896
Ruffin, Amber. *You'll Never Believe What Happened to Lacey*   305.896
Runstedtler, Theresa. *Black Ball*   796.323
Saad, Layla F. ★*Me and White Supremacy*   305.809
Samuels, Robert. ★*His Name Is George Floyd*   B
Seidule, Ty. *Robert E. Lee and Me*   973.7
Shakur, Prince. *When They Tell You to Be Good*   B
Sharfstein, Daniel J. ★*Thunder in the Mountains*   979.5
Sharma, Nina. *The Way You Make Me Feel*   B
Shetterly, Margot Lee. ★*Hidden Figures*   510.92
Shih, David. *Chinese Prodigal*   B
Signer, Michael. *Cry Havoc*   305.800973
Simon, James F. *Eisenhower vs. Warren*   347.73
Smith, Clint. ★*Above Ground*   811
Smith, Danez. ★*Don't Call Us Dead*   811.6
Smith, Mychal Denzel. *Invisible Man, Got the Whole World Watching*   305.242
Smith, Tracy K. ★*To Free the Captives*   818
Smith, Tracy K. ★*Wade in the Water*   811.6

Smith, Zadie. ★*Feel Free*   824
Snyder, Christina. *Great Crossings*   976.9
Sorin, Gretchen Sullivan. *Driving While Black*   323.1196
Stevens, Stuart. *It Was All a Lie*   324.2734
Sullivan, Matt. *Can't Knock the Hustle*   796.323
Sullivan, Patricia. *Lift Every Voice*   973
Takaki, Ronald T. *Double Victory*   940.53
Tatum, Beverly Daniel. ★*"Why Are All the Black Kids Sitting Together in the Cafeteria?"*   305.800973
Taylor, Alan. *American Republics*   973.3
Theoharis, Jeanne. *A More Beautiful and Terrible History*   323.1196
Theoharis, Jeanne. *The Rebellious Life of Mrs. Rosa Parks*   B
Thomas, Etan. *We Matter*   796.08
Thomas, Franklin A. *An Unplanned Life*   B
Thompson, Tracy. *The New Mind of the South*   305.800975
Tobar, Hector. ★*Our Migrant Souls*   305.868
Trethewey, Natasha D. ★*Monument*   811
Treuer, Anton. *Everything You Wanted to Know About Indians but Were Afraid to Ask*   970.1
Tubbs, Anna Malaika. *The Three Mothers*   306.874
Tyson, Timothy B. *Blood Done Sign My Name*   975.6
Tyson, Timothy B. *The Blood of Emmett Till*   364.1
Utley, Robert M. ★*Geronimo*   B
Walker, Vanessa Siddle. *The Lost Education of Horace Tate*   370.92
Ward, Geoffrey C. *The Civil War*   973.7
Ward, Jesmyn. ★*The Fire This Time*   305.896
Washington, Booker T. ★*Up from Slavery*   B
Watson, Bruce. *Freedom Summer*   323.1196
Watts, Jill. *Hattie McDaniel*   B
Weiner, Mark Stuart. *Black Trials*   342.7308
Whitaker, Mark. ★*Saying It Loud*   973.923
White, Gayle Jessup. *Reclamation*   B
White, Shane. *Prince of Darkness*   B
Wilder, Craig Steven. *Ebony and Ivy*   379.2
Wilkerson, Isabel. ★*Caste*   305.5
Wilkerson, Isabel. ★*The Warmth of Other Suns*   304.80973
Wilkie, Curtis. *When Evil Lived in Laurel*   305.8
Wilkins, Robert L. *Long Road to Hard Truth*   069
Williams, Bari A. *Seen yet Unseen*   338.4
Williams, David. *Bitterly Divided*   973.7
Williams, Juan. *Eyes on the Prize*   323.4
Williams, Mary. *The Lost Daughter*   B
Williams, Sophie. *Anti-Racist Ally*   305.8
Willis, Deborah. ★*The Black Civil War Soldier*   973.7
Wills, Shomari. *Black Fortunes*   920
Wise, Tim J. *Dispatches from the Race War*   305.8
Woodward, C. Vann. *The Strange Career of Jim Crow*   305.896
Yacovone, Donald. ★*Teaching White Supremacy*   370.89
Young, Damon. ★*What Doesn't Kill You Makes You Blacker*   B
Young, Kevin. *Brown*   811
Zeitz, Joshua. *Building the Great Society*   973.923
Zucchino, David. *Wilmington's Lie*   305.8009756

RACE RELATIONS IN LITERATURE
Gorra, Michael Edward. *The Saddest Words*   813

RACE RELATIONS IN SPORTS
Carlin, John. *Playing the Enemy*   968.06
Iguodala, Andre. *The Sixth Man*   B
Kennedy, Kostya. *True*   B
Tye, Larry. *Satchel*   B

RACE RIOTS
Ewing, Eve L. *1919*   811
Hirsch, James S. *Riot and Remembrance*   976.6
Madigan, Tim. *The Burning*   976.6
Tyson, Timothy B. *Blood Done Sign My Name*   975.6
Young, R. J. *Requiem for the Massacre*   305.8

Race Rules. Gilliam, Fatimah   305.8
The Race to Be Myself. Semenya, Caster   B
The Race to Save the Romanovs. Rappaport, Helen   947.08
Raceball. Ruck, Rob   796.357
Raceless. Lawton, Georgina   B
Rachel and Her Children. Kozol, Jonathan   362.5

RACIAL PROFILING
Anderson, Carol. ★*The Second*   344.7305
Crump, Benjamin. *Open Season*   364
Dyson, Michael Eric. *Long Time Coming*   305.800973
Henning, Kristin. *The Rage of Innocence*   364.36

Racing for the Bomb. Norris, Robert S.   B

PUBLIC LIBRARY CORE COLLECTION: NONFICTION
Twentieth Edition

RACISM

Abdurraqib, Hanif. *A Fortune for Your Disaster*	811
Abrams, Stacey. *Our Time Is Now*	324.60973
Agarwal, Pragya. *Sway*	177
Alexander, Elizabeth. ★*The Trayvon Generation*	305.896
Alexander, Kwame. *Light for the World to See*	811.6
Alexander, Michelle. *The New Jim Crow*	364.973
Ali, Wajahat. *Go Back to Where You Came From*	B
Aly, Gotz. *Europe Against the Jews*	305.892
Anderson, Carol. ★*One Person, No Vote*	324.6
Anderson, Carol. ★*The Second*	344.7305
Anderson, Carol. ★*White Rage*	305.800973
Angyal, Chloe. *Turning Pointe*	792.8
Asher, Zain E. *Where the Children Take Us*	942.1
Asim, Jabari. *We Can't Breathe*	305.896
Austerlitz, Saul. *Just a Shot Away*	781.66078
Austin, Nefertiti. *Motherhood so White*	B
Ayers, Edward L. *American Visions*	973.5
Babb, Valerie Melissa. *The Book of James*	B
Bailey, Issac J. *Why Didn't We Riot?*	305.800973
Bailey, Jennifer. *To My Beloveds*	261.8
Baker, Calvin. *A More Perfect Reunion*	305.800973
Baldwin, James. ★*Collected Essays*	814
Baldwin, James. ★*The Fire Next Time*	305.896
Baldwin, James. *I Am Not Your Negro*	323.1196
Baldwin, James. ★*Notes of a Native Son*	305.8
Ball, Edward. *Life of a Klansman*	305.8009763
Baylor, Elgin. *Hang Time*	B
Bell, Darrin. ★*The Talk*	741.5
Bell, W. Kamau. ★*Do the Work!*	305.8
Bennett, Michael. *Things That Make White People Uncomfortable*	305.896
Berg, Scott W. *The Burning of the World*	977.311
Bergner, Daniel. ★*Sing for Your Life*	B
Berman, Ari. ★*Minority Rule*	305.809
Berry, Daina Ramey. ★*A Black Women's History of the United States*	305.48
Blackstock, Uche. *Legacy*	610.92
Blum, Edward J. *The Color of Christ*	232
Bossiere, Zoe. *Cactus Country*	306
Boyd, Herb. *We Shall Overcome*	323.1196
Boykin, Keith. *Race Against Time*	305.8
Boykin, Keith. ★*Why Does Everything Have to Be About Race?*	305.8
Boyle, Kevin. *Arc of Justice*	345.73
Branch, Taylor. *Parting the Waters*	973
Brennan, Chad. *Faithful Antiracism*	277.308
Broom, Sarah M. *The Yellow House*	B
Broome, Brian. ★*Punch Me up to the Gods*	B
Brothers, Thomas David. ★*Louis Armstrong, Master of Modernism*	B
Brown, Austin Channing. ★*I'm Still Here*	B
Brown, Daniel James. ★*Facing the Mountain*	940.54
Bryant, Howard. *The Last Hero*	B
Burnham, Margaret A. ★*By Hands Now Known*	342.73
Butler, Paul. *Chokehold*	363.2
Carroll, Rebecca. *Surviving the White Gaze*	B
Chin, Ava. ★*Mott Street*	974.7
Clifton, Lucille. *How to Carry Water*	811
Coates, Ta-Nehisi. ★*Between the World and Me*	305.800973
Coates, Ta-Nehisi. ★*We Were Eight Years in Power*	305.896
Collins, Martha. *Admit One*	811
Copeland, Misty. *The Wind at My Back*	B
Cox, Anna-Lisa. *The Bone and Sinew of the Land*	977
Cross, Tiffany D. ★*Say It Louder!*	324.6
Crump, Benjamin. *Open Season*	364
Currie, Elliott. *A Peculiar Indifference*	305.800973
Cwiklik, Robert. *Sheridan's Secret Mission*	973.8
Dabiri, Emma. *Twisted*	391.5
Dangarembga, Tsitsi. *Black and Female*	305.48
Darby, Seyward. ★*Sisters in Hate*	305.800973
Davis, Thomas J. *History of African Americans*	973
Delmont, Matthew F. *Half American*	940.54
DiAngelo, Robin J. *White Fragility*	305.8
Dray, Philip. *Capitol Men*	973.8
Du Bois, W. E. B. ★*The Souls of Black Folk*	973
Dyson, Michael Eric. *The Black Presidency*	305.800973
Dyson, Michael Eric. *Come Hell or High Water*	976.3
Dyson, Michael Eric. *Long Time Coming*	305.800973
Dyson, Michael Eric. *Tears We Cannot Stop*	305.800973
Dyson, Michael Eric. *What Truth Sounds Like*	305.800973
Eberhardt, Jennifer L. ★*Biased*	303.3
Eddo-Lodge, Reni. *Why I'm No Longer Talking to White People About Race*	305.8
Egan, Timothy. ★*A Fever in the Heartland*	322.4
Eggers, Dave. *Zeitoun*	305.892
Ellsworth, Scott. *The Ground Breaking*	976.6
Erdozain, Dominic. *One Nation Under Guns*	363.33
Espada, Martin. ★*Floaters*	811
Evaristo, Bernardine. *Manifesto*	B
Ewing, Eve L. *1919*	811
Fishman, Elly. *Refugee High*	370.8
Fleming, Crystal Marie. *How to Be Less Stupid About Race*	305.800973
Flitter, Emily. *The White Wall*	332.0973
Foner, Eric. *The Fiery Trial*	973.7092
Ford, Richard T. *Rights Gone Wrong*	342.7308
Francois, Willie Dwayne. *Silencing White Noise*	277
Fuller, Alexandra. *Don't Let's Go to the Dogs Tonight*	B
Fumudoh, Ziwe. ★*Black Friend*	814
Gage, Beverly. *G-Man*	B
Garrett, Kent. *The Last Negroes at Harvard*	920
Gates, Henry Louis. *100 Amazing Facts About the Negro*	973
Gates, Henry Louis. *And Still I Rise*	305.896
Gates, Henry Louis. *The Black Box*	908
Gates, Henry Louis. *Colored People*	B
Gates, Henry Louis. ★*Stony the Road*	973
Gayle, Caleb. *We Refuse to Forget*	975.004
Gergel, Richard. *Unexampled Courage*	323.1196
Geter, Hafizah. *Un-American*	811
Gilliam, Fatimah. *Race Rules*	305.8
Giovanni, Nikki. *Make Me Rain*	811
Givens, Jarvis R. ★*School Clothes*	371.829
Glaude, Eddie S. *Begin Again*	305.800973
Gomez, Laura E. ★*Inventing Latinos*	305.868
Grann, David. ★*Killers of the Flower Moon*	976.6004
Grant, Richard. *The Deepest South of All*	976.2
Greenidge, Kerri. ★*The Grimkes*	973.5
Gregory, Dick. *Defining Moments in Black History*	973
Guerrero, Jean. *Hatemonger*	B
Hale, Grace Elizabeth. *In the Pines*	364.13
Hall, Alvin D. *Driving the Green Book*	917.304
Han, Chenxing. *Be the Refuge*	294.3
Hansberry, Lorraine. ★*A Raisin in the Sun*	812
Hardwick, Lamar. *How Ableism Fuels Racism*	261.8
Harper, Michele. *The Beauty in Breaking*	B
Harriot, Michael. ★*Black AF History*	973
Harris, Adam. ★*The State Must Provide*	379.2
Harrison, Valerie I. *Do Right by Me*	649
Hayes, Christopher. *A Colony in a Nation*	364.3
Hayes, Elaine M. ★*Queen of Bebop*	B
Haygood, Wil. ★*Colorization*	791.43
Headlee, Celeste Anne. *Speaking of Race*	305.8
Hechinger, John. ★*True Gentlemen*	371.85
Henny, Ally. *I Won't Shut Up*	305.896
Hill, Jemele. *Uphill*	B
Hill, Marc Lamont. *Seen and Unseen*	303.3
Hinojosa, Maria. *Once I Was You*	B
Hirsch, James S. *Riot and Remembrance*	976.6
Hixenbaugh, Michael. ★*They Came for the Schools*	371.9
Horace, Matthew. *The Black and the Blue*	B
Hunter-Gault, Charlayne. ★*My People*	305.48
Hurston, Zora Neale. ★*You Don't Know Us Negroes and Other Essays*	814
Jackson, Kellie Carter. *We Refuse*	323.1196
Jackson, Lawrence Patrick. *Chester B. Himes*	B
Jackson, Regina. *White Women*	305.8
Jackson, Ted. ★*You Ought to Do a Story About Me*	B
Jacob, Mira. *Good Talk*	741.5
Jawando, Will. ★*My Seven Black Fathers*	B
Jefferson, Margo. *Negroland*	305.896
Jerkins, Morgan. *Wandering in Strange Lands*	305.896
Johnson, Katherine G. *My Remarkable Journey*	B
Johnson, Kirk W. *The Fishermen and the Dragon*	976.4
Johnson, Theodore R. *When the Stars Begin to Fall*	305.800973
Jones, Chip. *The Organ Thieves*	617.4
Jones, Doug. *Bending Toward Justice*	323.1196
Jones, Robert P. *The Hidden Roots of White Supremacy*	305.8
Jones, Robert P. *White Too Long*	277
Jones, Saeed. *Alive at the End of the World*	811
Jordan, June. ★*The Essential June Jordan*	811
Joseph, Peniel E. *The Sword and the Shield*	B

AUTHOR, TITLE, SERIES AND SUBJECT INDEX

Karim-Cooper, Farah. ★*The Great White Bard*	822.33
Kearse, Bettye. *The Other Madisons*	920
Keenan, Cody. *Grace*	973.932
Keiler, Allan. *Marian Anderson*	B
Kelley, Blair Murphy. *Black Folk*	331.6
Kendi, Ibram X. ★*How to Be an Antiracist*	305.8
Kendi, Ibram X. ★*How to Raise an Antiracist*	649
Kendi, Ibram X. ★*Stamped from the Beginning*	305.8
Kimmerle, Erin H. *We Carry Their Bones*	365
King, Chrissy. *The Body Liberation Project*	306.4
King, Greg. *The Ghost Forest*	333.75
Kirshner, Jodie Adams. ★*Broke*	336.3
Kix, Paul. ★*You Have to Be Prepared to Die Before You Can Begin to Live*	976.1
Komunyakaa, Yusef. ★*Everyday Mojo Songs of Earth*	811
Kram, Mark. *Smokin' Joe*	B
Kranish, Michael. *The World's Fastest Man*	B
Kruse, Kevin Michael. *Fault Lines*	973.92
Kuo, Michelle. *Reading with Patrick*	B
Kuper, Adam. *The Museum of Other People*	305.8
Kushner, Jacob. *Look Away*	305.9
Lalami, Laila. *Conditional Citizens*	323.60973
Lane, Charles. *The Day Freedom Died*	976.3
Lawton, Georgina. *Raceless*	B
Laymon, Kiese. ★*Heavy*	B
Laymon, Kiese. *How to Slowly Kill Yourself and Others in America*	814.6
Lebron, Christopher J. *The Making of Black Lives Matter*	305.896
Lee, Erika. *America for Americans*	305.800973
Lee, Erika. *The Making of Asian America*	973
Lee, Julia Sun-Joo. *Biting the Hand*	B
Lehr, Dick. ★*The Birth of a Nation*	305.800973
Lehr, Dick. *White Hot Hate*	363.325
Lemann, Nicholas. *Redemption*	975
Lemon, Don. *This Is the Fire*	305.896
Levin, Josh. *The Queen*	364.16
Levine, Robert S. ★*The Failed Promise*	973.8
Levy, Jonathan. *Ages of American Capitalism*	330.12
Lewis, Jenifer. *Walking in My Joy*	B
Lewis, John. ★*March; Book One*	741.5
Lewis, John. ★*March; Book Three*	741.5
Lewis, John. ★*March; Book Two*	741.5
Liverpool, Layal. *Systemic*	362.1
Livingston, Robert W. *The Conversation*	305.8
Lorde, Audre. ★*The Selected Works of Audre Lorde*	814
Lorde, Audre. *Sister Outsider*	814
Lowery, Wesley. ★*American Whitelash*	305.8
Luxenberg, Steve. ★*Separate*	342.7308
Macy, Beth. ★*Truevine*	B
Madigan, Tim. *The Burning*	976.6
Madrick, Jeffrey G. *Invisible Americans*	362.7086
Mallory, Tamika D. *State of Emergency*	305.896
Mandela, Nelson. *Dare Not Linger*	B
Margolick, David. *Elizabeth and Hazel*	379.2
Marshall, Nate. *Finna*	811
Marshall, Thurgood. *Thurgood Marshall*	B
Mays, Kyle. ★*An Afro-Indigenous History of the United States*	973
Mays, Willie. *24*	B
McCauley, Esau. *How Far to the Promised Land*	B
McDiarmid, Jessica. *Highway of Tears*	364.152
McGhee, Heather C. ★*The Sum of Us*	305.8
McMillan, Tracie. ★*The White Bonus*	305.8
McWhorter, Diane. *Carry Me Home*	976.1
McWhorter, John H. *Talking Back, Talking Black*	427
Merritt, Tyler. *I Take My Coffee Black*	791.4302
Miller, Kei. *Things I Have Withheld*	814
Mojica Rodriguez, Prisca Dorcas. *For Brown Girls with Sharp Edges and Tender Hearts*	305.48
Moore, Wes. ★*Five Days*	363.32
Morgan-Owens, Jessie. *Girl in Black and White*	B
Morrison, Melanie. *Murder on Shades Mountain*	345.761
Morrison, Toni. ★*The Origin of Others*	809
Muhammad, Ibtihaj. *Proud*	B
Muhammad, Khalil Gibran. *The Condemnation of Blackness*	364.2
Mukantabana, Yseult P. ★*Real Friends Talk About Race*	305.8
Mullen, Bill. ★*James Baldwin*	B
Neus, Nora. *24 Hours in Charlottesville*	973.933
Neville, Aaron. *Tell It Like It Is*	B
Ng, Fae Myenne. *Orphan Bachelors*	B
Norris, Michele. ★*Our Hidden Conversations*	305
Nusbaum, Eric. *Stealing Home*	796.357
Oates, Joyce Carol. *American Melancholy*	811
Obama, Barack. ★*Dreams from My Father*	B
Okorafor, Nnedi. *Broken Places & Outer Spaces*	153.3
Okrent, Daniel. *The Guarded Gate*	344.73
Oluo, Ijeoma. ★*Be a Revolution*	305.8
Oluo, Ijeoma. *Mediocre*	305.310973
Oluo, Ijeoma. ★*So You Want to Talk About Race*	305.800973
Oluseyi, Hakeem M. *A Quantum Life*	B
Painter, Nell Irvin. ★*I Just Keep Talking*	814
Painter, Nell Irvin. *Old in Art School*	B
Pardlo, Gregory. *Spectral Evidence*	811
Parker, Morgan. *Magical Negro*	811
Paul, Richard. *We Could Not Fail*	920
Perkins, Kendrick. *The Education of Kendrick Perkins*	B
Phillips, Patrick. *Blood at the Root*	305.8
Picower, Bree. *Reading, Writing, and Racism*	371.829
Pinckney, Darryl. *Busted in New York and Other Essays*	305.800973
Porter, Billy. ★*Unprotected*	B
Porter, Eduardo. *American Poison*	305.800973
Powell, Nate. ★*Lies My Teacher Told Me*	741.5
Prescod, Danielle. *Token Black Girl*	B
Prescod-Weinstein, Chanda. *The Disordered Cosmos*	523.01
Pryce, Jessica. ★*Broken*	362.7
Ramos, Jorge. *Stranger*	325.73
Randall, David K. *Black Death at the Golden Gate*	616.9
Rankine, Claudia. ★*Citizen*	814
Rankine, Claudia. ★*Just Us*	305.896
Rembert, Winfred. *Chasing Me to My Grave*	B
Rice, Condoleezza. *Extraordinary, Ordinary People*	B
Ricketts, Rachel. ★*Do Better*	305.800973
Risen, Clay. *The Bill of the Century*	342.7308
Roberts, Dorothy E. *Torn Apart*	362.7
Roberts-Miller, Patricia. *Speaking of Race*	305.8
Robin, Corey. *The Enigma of Clarence Thomas*	347.73
Robinson, Phoebe. *You Can't Touch My Hair and Other Things I Still Have to Explain*	792.7
Rose, Tricia. ★*Metaracism*	305.8
Ross, Dax-Devlon. *Letters to My White Male Friends*	305.8
Rothstein, Richard. ★*The Color of Law*	305.800973
Roundtree, Dovey Johnson. ★*Mighty Justice*	B
Ruffin, Amber. ★*The World Record Book of Racist Stories*	305.896
Ruffin, Amber. *You'll Never Believe What Happened to Lacey*	305.896
Rutherford, Adam. *Control*	363.9
Saad, Layla F. ★*Me and White Supremacy*	305.809
Sacco, Joe. ★*Paying the Land*	741.5
Salisbury, Katie Gee. ★*Not Your China Doll*	B
Samuels, Robert. ★*His Name Is George Floyd*	B
Sanghera, Sathnam. ★*Empireland*	941
Sasakamoose, Fred. *Call Me Indian*	B
Scheeres, Julia. *Jesus Land*	B
Schuller, Kyla. *The Trouble with White Women*	305.42
Seidule, Ty. *Robert E. Lee and Me*	973.7
Sellers, Bakari. *My Vanishing Country*	B
Shahani, Aarti Namdev. *Here We Are*	B
Sharpe, Christina Elizabeth. *Ordinary Notes*	305.896
Shatz, Adam. *The Rebel's Clinic*	965
Shih, David. *Chinese Prodigal*	B
Signer, Michael. *Cry Havoc*	305.800973
Siler, Julia Flynn. *The White Devil's Daughters*	306.3
Singh, Julietta. *The Breaks*	B
Smilios, Maria. ★*The Black Angels*	610.73
Smith, Danez. ★*Don't Call Us Dead*	811.6
Smith, Danez. ★*Homie*	811
Smith, Mychal Denzel. *Invisible Man, Got the Whole World Watching*	305.242
Smith, Mychal Denzel. *Stakes Is High*	973.933
Smith, Tracy K. ★*Such Color*	811
Smith, Zadie. *Intimations*	824
Snyder, Christina. *Great Crossings*	976.9
Stevens, Stuart. *It Was All a Lie*	324.2734
Streep, Abe. *Brothers on Three*	306.85
Strings, Sabrina. *The End of Love*	155.3
Swift, Earl. *Hell Put to Shame*	364.15
Taibbi, Matt. *I Can't Breathe*	363.2
Takaki, Ronald T. *Double Victory*	940.53
Talley, Andre Leon. *The Chiffon Trenches*	B

PUBLIC LIBRARY CORE COLLECTION: NONFICTION
Twentieth Edition

Taylor, Goldie. *The Love You Save*	B
Tobar, Hector. ★*Our Migrant Souls*	305.868
Tran, Ly. *House of Sticks*	B
Tran, Phuc. ★*Sigh, Gone*	B
Trice, Dawn Turner. ★*Three Girls from Bronzeville*	977.311
Tubbs, Anna Malaika. *The Three Mothers*	306.874
Tyson, Timothy B. *The Blood of Emmett Till*	364.1
Umar, Ousman. *North to Paradise*	B
Union, Gabrielle. *We're Going to Need More Wine*	B
Valby, Karen. *The Swans of Harlem*	792.8
Van Meter, Matthew. *Deep Delta Justice*	345.763
Villarosa, Linda. ★*Under the Skin*	362.1089
Wade, Sabia. *Birthing Liberation*	363.96
Wainaina, Binyavanga. ★*How to Write About Africa*	814
Wang, Qian Julie. ★*Beautiful Country*	B
Ward, Jesmyn. *The Fire This Time*	305.896
Wilderson, Frank B. *Afropessimism*	B
Williams, Billy Dee. ★*What Have We Here*	B
Williams, Kidada E. *I Saw Death Coming*	973.8
Williams, Sophie. *Anti-Racist Ally*	305.8
Wilson, A'ja. ★*Dear Black Girls*	158.1
Wilson, Jessica. *It's Always Been Ours*	613
Winters, Mary-Frances. *Black Fatigue*	305.896
Wise, Tim J. *Dispatches from the Race War*	305.8
Woodfox, Albert. *Solitary*	B
Woodward, C. Vann. *The Strange Career of Jim Crow*	305.896
Wright, Richard. ★*Black Boy*	B
Yacovone, Donald. ★*Teaching White Supremacy*	370.89
Yancey, Philip. ★*Where the Light Fell*	B
Yang, Jia Lynn. ★*One Mighty and Irresistible Tide*	325.73
Young, Damon. ★*What Doesn't Kill You Makes You Blacker*	B
Young, Kevin. *Brown*	811
Young, R. J. *Requiem for the Massacre*	305.8
Zack, Ian. *Odetta*	B
Zerwick, Phoebe. *Beyond Innocence*	347
Zucchino, David. *Wilmington's Lie*	305.8009756

RACISM IN BASEBALL
Epplin, Luke. *Our Team*	796.357
Perron, Cam. ★*Comeback Season*	796.357
Robinson, Jackie. *I Never Had It Made*	B

RACISM IN CHRISTIANITY
Nagassar, Rohadi. *When We Belong*	254

RACISM IN CRIMINOLOGY
Butler, Paul. *Chokehold*	363.2

RACISM IN EDUCATION
Emdin, Christopher. *Ratchetdemic*	370.1
Ewing, Eve L. *Ghosts in the Schoolyard*	370.89
Kendi, Ibram X. ★*How to Raise an Antiracist*	649
Kozol, Jonathan. *An End to Inequality*	379.2
Love, Bettina L. *Punished for Dreaming*	371.829
Martin, Rachel Louise. *A Most Tolerant Little Town*	379.2
Picower, Bree. *Reading, Writing, and Racism*	371.829
Walker, Vanessa Siddle. *The Lost Education of Horace Tate*	370.92

RACISM IN EMPLOYMENT
Cox, Gena. *Leading Inclusion*	658.3
Fuller, Pamela. ★*The Leader's Guide to Unconscious Bias*	658.3
Livingston, Robert W. *The Conversation*	305.8
Shetterly, Margot Lee. ★*Hidden Figures*	510.92

RACISM IN ENVIRONMENTAL POLICY
Flowers, Catherine Coleman. *Waste*	363.72
Penniman, Leah. ★*Black Earth Wisdom*	333.72

RACISM IN LAW
Delbanco, Andrew. *The War Before the War*	973.7

RACISM IN LAW ENFORCEMENT
Chemerinsky, Erwin. *Presumed Guilty*	344.7305
Dyson, Michael Eric. *Long Time Coming*	305.800973
Forman, James. *Locking up Our Own*	364.973
Henning, Kristin. *The Rage of Innocence*	364.36
Hill, Marc Lamont. *Seen and Unseen*	303.3
Hinton, Elizabeth Kai. ★*America on Fire*	305.800973
Horace, Matthew. *The Black and the Blue*	B
Purnell, Derecka. *Becoming Abolitionists*	363.20973
Ralph, Laurence. *Sito*	364.152
Rubinstein, Julian. ★*The Holly*	364.106
Thompson, Jamie. *Standoff*	364.152
Zerwick, Phoebe. *Beyond Innocence*	347

RACISM IN LITERATURE
Castillo, Elaine. ★*How to Read Now*	418

Morrison, Toni. ★*The Origin of Others*	809

RACISM IN MEDICAL CARE
Blackstock, Uche. *Legacy*	610.92
Fisher, Thomas. ★*The Emergency*	362.1089
Goldberg, Emma. *Life on the Line*	362.1962
Hallman, J. C. *Say Anarcha*	618.1
Hernandez, Daisy. *The Kissing Bug*	616.9
Hylton, Antonia. *Madness*	362.2
Jones, Chip. *The Organ Thieves*	617.4
Liverpool, Layal. *Systemic*	362.1
Reverby, Susan M. *Examining Tuskegee*	174.2
Smilios, Maria. ★*The Black Angels*	610.73
Villarosa, Linda. ★*Under the Skin*	362.1089
Wade, Sabia. *Birthing Liberation*	363.96

RACISM IN POLITICS AND GOVERNMENT
Kaplan, Fred. *Lincoln and the Abolitionists*	973.7092
Shetterly, Margot Lee. ★*Hidden Figures*	510.92

RACISM IN POPULAR CULTURE
Gates, Henry Louis. ★*Stony the Road*	973
Mifflin, Margot. *Looking for Miss America*	791.6

RACISM IN SPORTS
Babb, Valerie Melissa. *The Book of James*	B
Baylor, Elgin. *Hang Time*	B
Jacobs, Sally H. *Althea*	B
Kranish, Michael. *The World's Fastest Man*	B
Maraniss, Andrew. *Strong Inside*	B
Perkins, Kendrick. *The Education of Kendrick Perkins*	B
Perron, Cam. ★*Comeback Season*	796.357
Rapoport, Ron. *Let's Play Two*	B
Rhoden, William C. *$40 Million Slaves*	796
Robinson, Jackie. *I Never Had It Made*	B
Ruck, Rob. *Raceball*	796.357

RACISM IN THE CRIMINAL JUSTICE SYSTEM
Adams, Jarrett. *Redeeming Justice*	340.092
Balko, Radley. ★*The Cadaver King and the Country Dentist*	614
Barnett, Brittany K. ★*A Knock at Midnight*	B
Chammah, Maurice. ★*Let the Lord Sort Them*	364.66
Chemerinsky, Erwin. *Presumed Guilty*	344.7305
Coates, Laura Gayle. *Just Pursuit*	345.73
Crump, Benjamin. *Open Season*	364
Fabricant, M. Chris. *Junk Science and the American Criminal Justice System*	363.25
Forman, James. *Locking up Our Own*	364.973
Hale, Grace Elizabeth. *In the Pines*	364.13
Hayes, Christopher. *A Colony in a Nation*	364.3
Henning, Kristin. *The Rage of Innocence*	364.36
King, Gilbert. ★*Devil in the Grove*	305.896
Manuel, Ian. *My Time Will Come*	B
Miller, Reuben Jonathan. *Halfway Home*	364.8
Muhammad, Khalil Gibran. *The Condemnation of Blackness*	364.2
Salaam, Yusef. *Better, Not Bitter*	B
Samuels, Robert. ★*His Name Is George Floyd*	B
Shahani, Aarti Namdev. *Here We Are*	B
Van Meter, Matthew. *Deep Delta Justice*	345.763
Zerwick, Phoebe. *Beyond Innocence*	347

RACISM IN THE JUDICIAL SYSTEM
Forman, James. *Locking up Our Own*	364.973
Horace, Matthew. *The Black and the Blue*	B
Miller, Reuben Jonathan. *Halfway Home*	364.8
Muhammad, Khalil Gibran. *The Condemnation of Blackness*	364.2

RACISM IN THE MILITARY
Delmont, Matthew F. *Half American*	940.54
Makos, Adam. *Devotion*	920
McManus, John C. *Island Infernos*	940.54

RACISM IN THE PERFORMING ARTS
Penn, Kal. *You Can't Be Serious*	B

RACISM IN UNIVERSITIES AND COLLEGES
Harris, Adam. ★*The State Must Provide*	379.2

RACKET GAMES
Gingrich, Dayne. *Pickleball Mindset*	796.34
Parker, Vergil R. *Pickleball 101*	796.34
Simon, Rachel. *Pickleball for All*	796.34

Rad Women Worldwide. Schatz, Kate 920

RADAR
Budiansky, Stephen. *Blackett's War*	940.54

Radcliffe, Margaret
Circular Knitting Workshop	746.43
The Knitting Answer Book	746.43

AUTHOR, TITLE, SERIES AND SUBJECT INDEX

The Knowledgeable Knitter	746.43
Raddatz, Martha	
The Long Road Home	B
Rademacher, Tom	
It Won't Be Easy	B
RADEMACHER, TOM, 1981-	
Rademacher, Tom. *It Won't Be Easy*	B
Radiant. Gooch, Brad	B
A Radiant Curve. Tapahonso, Luci	811
RADIATION	
Moore, Kate. *The Radium Girls*	363.17
Pasternak, Judy. *Yellow Dirt*	979.1004
RADIATION INJURIES	
Higginbotham, Adam. ★*Midnight in Chernobyl*	363.17
RADIATION VICTIMS	
Pasternak, Judy. *Yellow Dirt*	979.1004
Pellegrino, Charles R. *To Hell and Back*	940.54
Southard, Susan. *Nagasaki*	940.54
RADICAL ART	
Ganz, Nicholas. ★*Graffiti World*	751.7
Radical by Nature. Costa, James T.	B
Radical Candor. Scott, Kim Malone	658.4
RADICAL JOURNALISTS	
Kurtz, Howard. *Media Madness*	973.933
RADICAL ORGANIZATIONS	
Burrough, Bryan. *Days of Rage*	303.48
Stille, Alexander. *The Sullivanians*	307.77
Radical Wordsworth. Bate, Jonathan	B
RADICALISM	
Ahmed, Sara. *The Feminist Killjoy Handbook*	305.42
Bawer, Bruce. *The Victims' Revolution*	320.973
Bingham, Clara. *Witness to the Revolution*	303.48
Brands, H. W. *Traitor to His Class*	B
Burrough, Bryan. *Days of Rage*	303.48
Butterworth, Alex. *The World That Never Was*	335
Johnson, Steven. *The Infernal Machine*	335
Jones, Faith. *Sex Cult Nun*	B
Kelly, Helena. *Jane Austen, the Secret Radical*	823
Kurlansky, Mark. *1968*	909.82
Marable, Manning. ★*Malcolm X*	B
Mayer, Jane. ★*Dark Money*	973.932
Minutaglio, Bill. *The Most Dangerous Man in America*	B
Moser, Benjamin. ★*Sontag*	B
Roy, Jessica. *American Girls*	305.48
Seierstad, Asne. *Two Sisters*	956.9104
Sommer, Will. ★*Trust the Plan*	973.933
Spencer, Kyle. *Raising Them Right*	320.5
Spruill, Marjorie Julian. *Divided We Stand*	305.42
Whitaker, Mark. ★*Saying It Loud*	973.923
Wright, Lawrence. ★*The Looming Tower*	973.931
RADICALS	
Duberman, Martin B. *Howard Zinn*	B
Neiwert, David A. ★*The Age of Insurrection*	303.48
Rudd, Mark. *Underground*	378.1
RADIO	
Napoli, Lisa. *Susan, Linda, Nina & Cokie*	920
RADIO ASTRONOMY	
Fletcher, Seth. *Einstein's Shadow*	523.8
RADIO BROADCASTERS	
Carlin, Kelly. *A Carlin Home Companion*	B
Duran, Elvis. *Where Do I Begin?*	B
Iftin, Abdi Nor. *Call Me American*	305.893
Rehm, Diane. *On My Own*	B
RADIO BROADCASTING	
Schwartz, A. Brad. ★*Broadcast Hysteria*	791.44
RADIO INDUSTRY AND TRADE	
Duran, Elvis. *Where Do I Begin?*	B
RADIO JOURNALISM	
Shapiro, Ari. ★*The Best Strangers in the World*	B
RADIO JOURNALISTS	
Shahani, Aarti Namdev. *Here We Are*	B
Shapiro, Ari. ★*The Best Strangers in the World*	B
RADIO OPERATORS	
Magida, Arthur J. *Code Name Madeleine*	940.54
RADIO PERSONALITIES	
Duran, Elvis. *Where Do I Begin?*	B
Pomerantsev, Peter. ★*How to Win an Information War*	940.53
RADIO PRODUCERS AND DIRECTORS	
McGilligan, Patrick. *Young Orson*	B
RADIO PROGRAMS	
Burton, Susan. *Empty*	B
Dunning, John. *On the Air*	791.44
Duran, Elvis. *Where Do I Begin?*	B
Giddins, Gary. *Bing Crosby*	B
Giddins, Gary. *Bing Crosby*	B
Napoli, Lisa. *Susan, Linda, Nina & Cokie*	920
RADIO TALK SHOWS	
Duran, Elvis. *Where Do I Begin?*	B
Shapiro, Ari. ★*The Best Strangers in the World*	B
RADIO TELESCOPES	
Fletcher, Seth. *Einstein's Shadow*	523.8
RADIOACTIVE FALLOUT	
Blume, Lesley M. M. *Fallout*	940.54
Higginbotham, Adam. ★*Midnight in Chernobyl*	363.17
Owens, Jay. *Dust*	551.51
RADIOACTIVE POLLUTION	
Higginbotham, Adam. ★*Midnight in Chernobyl*	363.17
Iversen, Kristen. *Full Body Burden*	363.17
Moore, Kate. *The Radium Girls*	363.17
RADIOACTIVE WASTE SITES	
D'Agata, John. *About a Mountain*	979.3
Iversen, Kristen. *Full Body Burden*	363.17
RADIOACTIVE WASTES	
D'Agata, John. *About a Mountain*	979.3
RADIOACTIVITY	
Higginbotham, Adam. ★*Midnight in Chernobyl*	363.17
Mahaffey, James A. *Atomic Adventures*	333.792
Preston, Diana. *Before the Fallout*	303.48
RADIUM	
Moore, Kate. *The Radium Girls*	363.17
The Radium Girls. Moore, Kate	363.17
Radke, Heather	
Butts	611
RADKE, HEATHER	
Radke, Heather. *Butts*	611
Radtke, Kristen	
Seek You	741.5
Rady, Martyn C.	
The Middle Kingdoms	943
Radzinskii, Edvard	
Stalin	947.084
RADZIWILL, LEE BOUVIER, 1933-2019	
Kashner, Sam. *The Fabulous Bouvier Sisters*	920
Taraborrelli, J. Randy. *Jackie, Janet & Lee*	920
Rae, Noel	
★*The Great Stain*	306.3
Rae-Venter, Barbara	
I Know Who You Are	364.152
Raff, Jennifer	
Origin	576.5
Raffa, Guy P.	
Dante's Bones	851
Raffel, Dawn	
The Strange Case of Dr. Couney	B
Rage Baking. Gunst, Kathy	641.86
Rage Becomes Her. Chemaly, Soraya L.	155.3
★*A Rage for Order*. Worth, Robert Forsyth	909
The Rage of Innocence. Henning, Kristin	364.36
RAGPICKERS	
Roy, Saumya. *Castaway Mountain*	363.72
Rahmani, Niloofar	
Open Skies	B
RAHMANI, NILOOFAR	
Rahmani, Niloofar. *Open Skies*	B
RAHR, GUIDO	
Malarkey, Tucker. *Stronghold*	639.2
Raichlen, Steven	
The Brisket Chronicles	641.6
How to Grill Vegetables	641.6
RAIDS (MILITARY SCIENCE)	
Atkinson, Rick. ★*The British Are Coming*	973.3
Caddick-Adams, Peter. *Sand and Steel*	940.54
Cook, Kevin. *Waco Rising*	299
Fields-Black, Edda L. *Combee*	973.7
Holland, James. *Normandy '44*	940.54

PUBLIC LIBRARY CORE COLLECTION: NONFICTION
Twentieth Edition

Johnson, Steven. *Enemy of All Mankind* — 910.4
Lewis, Damien. *Churchill's Hellraisers* — 940.54
McRaven, William H. *Sea Stories* — B
Milton, Giles. *Soldier, Sailor, Frogman, Spy, Airman, Gangster, Kill or Die* — 940.54
Wallace, Chris. *Countdown Bin Laden* — 958.104

Raiford, Matthew
  Bress 'N' Nyam — 641.59

RAIFORD, MATTHEW
  Raiford, Matthew. *Bress 'N' Nyam* — 641.59

RAILROAD ACCIDENTS
  Krist, Gary. *The White Cascade* — 979.7

RAILROAD OWNERS
  Cooper, Anderson. *Vanderbilt* — 920

RAILROAD TRAVEL
  Figes, Orlando. *The Europeans* — 920
  Greene, David. *Midnight in Siberia* — 914
  Krist, Gary. *The White Cascade* — 979.7
  Parks, Tim. *Italian Ways* — 385
  Theroux, Paul. *The Great Railway Bazaar* — 915
  Theroux, Paul. *Riding the Iron Rooster* — 915
  Widmer, Edward L. *Lincoln on the Verge* — B
  Zoellner, Tom. *Train* — 385.09

RAILROAD WORKERS
  Ambrose, Stephen E. *Nothing Like It in the World* — 385
  Chang, Gordon H. *Ghosts of Gold Mountain* — 331.6
  Rekdal, Paisley. *West* — 811

RAILROADS
  Ambrose, Stephen E. *Nothing Like It in the World* — 385
  Chang, Gordon H. *Ghosts of Gold Mountain* — 331.6
  Hiltzik, Michael A. *Iron Empires* — 385.0973
  McGinty, Brian. *Lincoln's Greatest Case* — 346.7303
  Renehan, Edward. *Commodore* — B
  Shaughnessy, Jim. *The Call of Trains* — 779
  Standage, Tom. *A Brief History of Motion* — 388
  Stiles, T. J. ★*The First Tycoon*
  Theroux, Paul. *The Great Railway Bazaar* — 915
  Zoellner, Tom. *Train* — 385.09

Rain. Barnett, Cynthia — 551.57

RAIN AND RAINFALL
  Barnett, Cynthia. *Rain* — 551.57
  Redniss, Lauren. *Thunder & Lightning* — 741.5

RAIN FOREST ECOLOGY
  Lowman, Margaret. *The Arbornaut* — 581.7
  Lowman, Margaret. *Life in the Treetops* — B

RAIN FORESTS
  Dial, Roman. *The Adventurer's Son* — 917.286
  Kars, Marjoleine. *Blood on the River* — 306.3
  Millard, Candice. *River of Doubt* — 918.1
  Preston, Douglas J. ★*The Lost City of the Monkey God* — 972.85
  Wallace, Scott. *The Unconquered* — 981
  Webb, Kinari. *Guardians of the Trees* — B

The Rainbow Comes and Goes. Cooper, Anderson — B
Rainbow Parenting. Amer, Lindz — 649

Rainbow, Randy
  Playing with Myself — B

RAINBOW, RANDY, 1981-
  Rainbow, Randy. *Playing with Myself* — B

Raines, Abigail Sotto
  Rice. Noodles. Yum. — 641.595

Raines, Ben
  The Last Slave Ship — 306.362

Raines, Howell
  Silent Cavalry — 973.7

★*Rainmaker*. Norton, Hughes — 796.352
★*A Raisin in the Sun*. Hansberry, Lorraine — 812
Raising A Kid Who Can. McCarthy, Catherine — 649
Raising A Socially Successful Child. Nowicki, Stephen — 649
Raising an Active Reader. Cleaver, Samantha — 372.4
★*Raising Antiracist Children*. Hawthorne, Britt — 649
Raising Baby by the Stars. Brown, Maressa — 133.5
Raising Feminist Boys. Wegner, Bobbi — 305.23
★*Raising Lazarus*. Macy, Beth — 362.29
Raising The Barre. Kessler, Lauren — 792.8
Raising Them Right. Spencer, Kyle — 320.5
Raising Your Spirited Baby. Kurcinka, Mary Sheedy — 306.874

Rajchel, Diana
  Urban Magick — 133.4

Rajchman, Chil
  The Last Jew of Treblinka — 940.53

Rakel, David
  The Compassionate Connection — 610.1

Rakoff, Joanna Smith
  My Salinger Year — B

RAKOFF, JOANNA SMITH, 1972-
  Rakoff, Joanna Smith. *My Salinger Year* — B

Rakove, Jack N.
  Revolutionaries — 973.3

Rallo, Eli
  I Didn't Know I Needed This — 306.73

RALLO, ELI
  Rallo, Eli. *I Didn't Know I Needed This* — 306.73

★*Ralph Ellison*. Rampersad, Arnold — B

Ralph, Ann
  Grow a Little Fruit Tree — 634

Ralph, Laurence
  Sito — 364.152

Ralston, Aron
  Between a Rock and a Hard Place — 796.522

RALSTON, ARON
  Ralston, Aron. *Between a Rock and a Hard Place* — 796.522

RAM DASS
  Lattin, Don. *The Harvard Psychedelic Club* — 973.922092

RAMA (HINDU DEITY)
  Narayan, R. K. ★*The Ramayana* — 294.5

Ramadan, Tariq
  ★*Introduction to Islam* — 297

RAMANUJAN AIYANGAR, SRINIVASA, 1887-1920
  Kanigel, Robert. *The Man Who Knew Infinity* — B

★*The Ramayana*. Narayan, R. K. — 294.5

RAMEN
  Goulding, Matt. *Rice, Noodle, Fish* — 394.1

Ramesh, Jaya
  Parenting at the Intersections — 649

Ramey, Sarah
  The Lady's Handbook for Her Mysterious Illness — B

RAMEY, SARAH
  Ramey, Sarah. *The Lady's Handbook for Her Mysterious Illness* — B

Ramirez, Elva
  Zero Proof — 641.87

Ramirez, Janina
  Femina — 940.1

Ramos, Jorge
  Stranger — 325.73

RAMOS, JORGE, 1958-
  Ramos, Jorge. *Stranger* — 325.73

Rampage. Scott, James — 940.54

Rampersad, Arnold
  The Life of Langston Hughes — B
  ★*The Life of Langston Hughes* — B
  ★*Ralph Ellison* — B

Ramsay, Gordon
  ★*Quick and Delicious* — 641.5

Ramsey, Dave
  The Total Money Makeover — 332.024

Ramsey, Donovan X.
  ★*When Crack Was King* — 362.29

Ramsey, Franchesca
  Well, That Escalated Quickly — B

RAMSEY, FRANCHESCA, 1983-
  Ramsey, Franchesca. *Well, That Escalated Quickly* — B

Ramsland, Katherine M.
  Ghost — 133.1

RAMSLAND, KATHERINE M., 1953-
  Ramsland, Katherine M. *Ghost* — 133.1

RANCH LIFE
  Bell, Laura. *Claiming Ground* — B
  Genoways, Ted. *This Blessed Earth* — 630.9
  Thompson-Hernandez, Walter. *The Compton Cowboys* — 920

Rancher, Farmer, Fisherman. Horn, Miriam — B

RANCHERS
  Branch, John. *The Last Cowboys* — 920
  Genoways, Ted. *This Blessed Earth* — 630.9
  Horn, Miriam. *Rancher, Farmer, Fisherman* — B
  Leerhsen, Charles. ★*Butch Cassidy* — B

AUTHOR, TITLE, SERIES AND SUBJECT INDEX

RANCHES
    Bell, Laura. *Claiming Ground* — B
    Brown, Dee. *The American West* — 978
    Houston, Pam. *Deep Creek* — 814
RANCHING
    Bell, Laura. *Claiming Ground* — B
Rand, Ayn
    ★*The Virtue of Selfishness* — 149
    The Voice of Reason — 191
RAND, AYN
    Rand, Ayn. *The Voice of Reason* — 191
Randall, David K.
    Black Death at the Golden Gate — 616.9
    The King and Queen of Malibu — B
Randall, Lisa
    Dark Matter and the Dinosaurs — 523.1
Randall, Willard Sterne
    The Founders' Fortunes — 973.3
    George Washington — B
RANDOLPH, JOHN
    May, Gregory. *A Madman's Will* — 973.5
RANDOLPH, MARTHA JEFFERSON, 1772-1836
    Kerrison, Catherine. *Jefferson's Daughters* — 920
Random Acts of Medicine. Jena, Anupam B. — 616.0072
Ranganath, Charan
    ★*Why We Remember* — 153.1
★*Range*. Epstein, David J. — 153.9
RANIERE, KEITH
    Berman, Sarah. *Don't Call It a Cult* — 361.4
Rankin, Lauren
    Bodies on the Line — 362.1988
Rankine, Claudia
    ★*Citizen* — 814
    ★*Just Us* — 305.896
    The White Card — 812
Rannells, Andrew
    Too Much Is Not Enough — 792.02
    Uncle of the Year — B
RANNELLS, ANDREW
    Rannells, Andrew. *Too Much Is Not Enough* — 792.02
    Rannells, Andrew. *Uncle of the Year* — B
Ransby, Barbara
    Eslanda — B
RANSOM
    Craughwell, Thomas J. *Stealing Lincoln's Body* — 973.7092
    King, Greg. *Nothing but the Night* — 364.152
The Ransom of Russian Art. McPhee, John — 709
The Ransomware Hunting Team. Dudley, Renee — 363.25
Rao, Cheeni
    In Hanuman's Hands — B
RAO, CHEENI
    Rao, Cheeni. *In Hanuman's Hands* — B
Rao, Maya
    Great American Outpost — 338.2
RAP MUSIC
    Abdurraqib, Hanif. *Go Ahead in the Rain* — 782.421649
    Abrams, Jonathan P. D. ★*The Come Up* — 782.421649
    Ashon, Will. *Chamber Music* — 782.421649
    Black Thought. *The Upcycled Self* — B
    Chang, Jeff. *Can't Stop, Won't Stop* — 306.4
    Charnas, Dan. *The Big Payback* — 306.4
    Chuck D. *Chuck D Presents This Day in Rap and Hip-Hop History* — 782.421649
    Edwards, Paul. *The Concise Guide to Hip-Hop Music* — 782.421649
    Fernando, S. H., Jr. *From the Streets of Shaolin* — 782.421
    Ghostface Killah. *Rise of a Killah* — B
    Greenburg, Zack O'Malley. *3 Kings* — 782.421649
    Harvilla, Rob. *60 Songs That Explain the '90s* — 782.42164
    Hope, Clover. *The Motherlode* — 920
    Iandoli, Kathy. *God Save the Queens* — 782.421649
    Kweli, Talib. *Vibrate Higher* — B
    Mike D. *Beastie Boys Book* — 782.42164
    Moore, Marcus J. *The Butterfly Effect* — B
    Questlove. ★*Hip-Hop Is History* — 782.421649
    Robinson, Staci. ★*Tupac Shakur* — B
    Simmons, Nadirah. ★*First Things First* — 782.42164
    Westhoff, Ben. *Dirty South* — 782.421649

RAP MUSIC INDUSTRY AND TRADE
    Charnas, Dan. *The Big Payback* — 306.4
    Chuck D. *Chuck D Presents This Day in Rap and Hip-Hop History* — 782.421649
    Ghostface Killah. *Rise of a Killah* — B
    Kweli, Talib. *Vibrate Higher* — B
    Simmons, Nadirah. ★*First Things First* — 782.42164
    Westhoff, Ben. *Original Gangstas* — 782.421649
RAP MUSICIANS
    Abdurraqib, Hanif. *Go Ahead in the Rain* — 782.421649
    Abrams, Jonathan P. D. ★*The Come Up* — 782.421649
    Ashon, Will. *Chamber Music* — 782.421649
    Baraka, Sho. *He Saw That It Was Good* — 261.5
    Black Thought. *The Upcycled Self* — B
    Common. *One Day It'll All Make Sense* — B
    Dyson, Michael Eric. *Holler If You Hear Me* — B
    Edwards, Paul. *The Concise Guide to Hip-Hop Music* — 782.421649
    Fernando, S. H., Jr. *From the Streets of Shaolin* — 782.421
    Ghostface Killah. *Rise of a Killah* — B
    Grandmaster Flash. *The Adventures of Grandmaster Flash* — B
    Greenburg, Zack O'Malley. *3 Kings* — 782.421649
    Hope, Clover. *The Motherlode* — 920
    Ice-T. *Split Decision* — 920
    Jackson, Curtis. *Hustle Harder, Hustle Smarter* — B
    Kenner, Rob. *The Marathon Don't Stop* — B
    Kweli, Talib. *Vibrate Higher* — B
    Lecrae. ★*I Am Restored* — B
    Mike D. *Beastie Boys Book* — 782.42164
    Moore, Marcus J. *The Butterfly Effect* — B
    Robinson, Staci. ★*Tupac Shakur* — B
    Simmons, Nadirah. ★*First Things First* — 782.42164
    Smith, Will. ★*Will* — B
    Westhoff, Ben. *Dirty South* — 782.421649
    Westhoff, Ben. *Original Gangstas* — 782.421649
RAPE
    Abdulali, Sohaila. *What We Talk About When We Talk About Rape* — 364.15
    Bowdler, Michelle. ★*Is Rape a Crime?* — B
    Crawford, Lacy. *Notes on a Silencing* — B
    Frederick, Jim. *Black Hearts* — 956.7044
    Grigoriadis, Vanessa. *Blurred Lines* — 371.7
    Hirsch, Jennifer S. *Sexual Citizens* — 371.7
    King, Gilbert. *Beneath a Ruthless Sun* — B
    King, Gilbert. ★*Devil in the Grove* — 305.896
    Krakauer, Jon. *Missoula* — 362.883
    Krouse, Erika. ★*Tell Me Everything* — 363.25
    Lamb, Christina. *Our Bodies, Their Battlefields* — 341.6
    Miller, T. Christian. *A False Report* — 364.15
    Moore, Susanna. *Miss Aluminum* — 813
    Rhodes, James. *Instrumental* — B
    Rose, Jacqueline. *On Violence and on Violence Against Women* — 362.88
    Schwartzman, Nancy. *Roll Red Roll* — 364.15
    Taylor, Goldie. *The Love You Save* — B
    Tjipombo, Tupa. *I Am Not Your Slave* — B
    Vanasco, Jeannie. *Things We Didn't Talk About When I Was a Girl* — B
    Williams, Tennessee. ★*A Streetcar Named Desire* — 812
RAPE CASE PROSECUTION
    Grigoriadis, Vanessa. *Blurred Lines* — 371.7
    Krakauer, Jon. *Missoula* — 362.883
RAPE CULTURE
    Hirsch, Jennifer S. *Sexual Citizens* — 371.7
    Schwartzman, Nancy. *Roll Red Roll* — 364.15
    Tuerkheimer, Deborah. *Credible* — 363.25
RAPE IN UNIVERSITIES AND COLLEGES
    McIntire, Mike. *Champions Way* — 796.043
    Miller, Chanel. *Know My Name* — B
RAPE IN WAR
    Hoock, Holger. *Scars of Independence* — 973.3
RAPE INVESTIGATION
    Bowdler, Michelle. ★*Is Rape a Crime?* — B
    Miller, T. Christian. *A False Report* — 364.15
★*The Rape of Nanking*. Chang, Iris — 951.04
RAPE OF TEENAGERS
    Schwartzman, Nancy. *Roll Red Roll* — 364.15
RAPE SUSPECTS
    Hale, Grace Elizabeth. *In the Pines* — 364.13
RAPE VICTIMS
    Abdulali, Sohaila. *What We Talk About When We Talk About Rape* — 364.15
    Bowdler, Michelle. ★*Is Rape a Crime?* — B

PUBLIC LIBRARY CORE COLLECTION: NONFICTION
Twentieth Edition

Burke, Tarana. ★*Unbound*	B
Ford, Ashley C. ★*Somebody's Daughter*	B
Grigoriadis, Vanessa. *Blurred Lines*	371.7
James, Victoria. *Wine Girl*	B
Krakauer, Jon. *Missoula*	362.883
Lamb, Christina. *Our Bodies, Their Battlefields*	341.6
Miller, Chanel. *Know My Name*	B
Miller, T. Christian. *A False Report*	364.15
Mulgrew, Kate. *Born with Teeth*	791.45028
Rhodes, James. *Instrumental*	B
Tjipombo, Tupa. *I Am Not Your Slave*	B
Union, Gabrielle. *We're Going to Need More Wine*	B
Vanasco, Jeannie. *Things We Didn't Talk About When I Was a Girl*	B
Raphael, Ray	
Constitutional Myths	342.7302
Mr. President	352.230973
A People's History of the American Revolution	973.3
Raphael, Rina	
The Gospel of Wellness	613
RAPIER FAMILY	
Franklin, John Hope. *In Search of the Promised Land*	929
Rapinoe, Megan	
One Life	B
RAPINOE, MEGAN, 1985-	
Rapinoe, Megan. *One Life*	B
RAPISTS	
Egan, Timothy. ★*A Fever in the Heartland*	322.4
Miller, Chanel. *Know My Name*	B
Rae-Venter, Barbara. *I Know Who You Are*	364.152
Schwartzman, Nancy. *Roll Red Roll*	364.15
Rapkin, Mickey	
Pitch Perfect	782.5
Rapoport, Adam	
The Grilling Book	641.7
Rapoport, Ron	
Let's Play Two	B
Rapp, David	
Tinker to Evers to Chance	796.357
Rappaport, Helen	
After the Romanovs	944
Caught in the Revolution	355.00947
The Race to Save the Romanovs	947.08
The Romanov Sisters	920
Rapping, Jonathan	
Gideon's Promise	345.73
RAPPING, JONATHAN	
Rapping, Jonathan. *Gideon's Promise*	345.73
Rappleye, Charles	
Herbert Hoover in the White House	B
The Raqqa Diaries. Samer	956.9104
RARE AND ENDANGERED ANIMALS	
Alexander, Jane. *Wild Things, Wild Places*	333.95
Barrow, Mark V. *Nature's Ghosts*	333.95
Blakeslee, Nate. *American Wolf*	599.773
Croke, Vicki. *The Lady and the Panda*	599.789
Ellis, Richard. ★*The Empty Ocean*	577.7
Flores, Dan L. *Wild New World*	591.9709
Lopez, Barry Holstun. ★*Of Wolves and Men*	599.773
Mooallem, Jon. *Wild Ones*	333.95
Nicolson, Adam. *The Seabird's Cry*	598.177
O'Connor, Maura R. *Resurrection Science*	591.68
Orenstein, Ronald I. *Ivory, Horn and Blood*	333.95
Pittman, Craig. *Cat Tale*	599.75
Pyenson, Nick. *Spying on Whales*	599.5
Saladino, Dan. *Eating to Extinction*	641.3
Sartore, Joel. ★*The Photo Ark*	779
Williams, Kale. *The Loneliest Polar Bear*	599.786
Wilson, Edward O. *The Future of Life*	333.95
Wood, Levison. *The Last Giants*	599.67
RARE AND ENDANGERED BIRDS	
Craig, Mya-Rose. *Birdgirl*	B
Dunn, Jon L. *The Glitter in the Green*	598.7
Gyllenhaal, Anders. *A Wing and a Prayer*	639.97
Hammer, Joshua. *The Falcon Thief*	364.16
Hirschfeld, Erik. *The World's Rarest Birds*	333.95822
Meiburg, Jonathan. *A Most Remarkable Creature*	598.9
Slaght, Jonathan C. *Owls of the Eastern Ice*	598.9
RARE AND ENDANGERED FISHES	
Ellis, Richard. *Tuna*	333.95
RARE AND ENDANGERED INSECTS	
Mooallem, Jon. *Wild Ones*	333.95
RARE AND ENDANGERED MAMMALS	
McIntyre, Rick. *The Reign of Wolf 21*	599.773
RARE AND ENDANGERED PLANTS	
Barrow, Mark V. *Nature's Ghosts*	333.95
Ellis, Richard. ★*The Empty Ocean*	577.7
Magdalena, Carlos. *The Plant Messiah*	333.95
Saladino, Dan. *Eating to Extinction*	641.3
Wilson, Edward O. *The Future of Life*	333.95
RARE BOOKS	
Collins, Paul. *The Book of William*	016.8223
Darkshire, Oliver. *Once Upon a Tome*	B
Davis, Margaret Leslie. *The Lost Gutenberg*	093
Kaag, John J. *American Philosophy*	191
Pettegree, Andrew. *The Library*	027.4
RARE DISEASES	
Marcus, Amy Dockser. *We the Scientists*	618.92
Rasenberger, Jim	
The Brilliant Disaster	972.9106
Revolver	B
Rashid, Ahmed	
Taliban	958.104
Rashid, Jonny	
Jesus Takes a Side	261.7
Rashke, Richard	
Useful Enemies	341.69
Raskin, Allison	
Overthinking About You	646.7
Rasmussen, Christina	
Where Did You Go?	133.9
Rasmussen, Daniel	
American Uprising	976.3
RASMUSSEN, KNUD JOHAN VICTOR, 1879-1933	
Ehrlich, Gretel. *This Cold Heaven*	998.2
Rasmussen, Matt	
Black Aperture	811
RASMUSSEN, SHERRI	
McGough, Matthew. *The Lazarus Files*	364.152
Rasputin. Fuhrmann, Joseph T.	B
Rasputin. Smith, Douglas	B
RASPUTIN, GRIGORI EFIMOVICH, 1869-1916	
Fuhrmann, Joseph T. *Rasputin*	B
Smith, Douglas. *Rasputin*	B
Rastafari. Chevannes, Barry	299
RASTAFARI MOVEMENT	
Sinclair, Safiya. ★*How to Say Babylon*	B
RASTAFARIANS	
Chevannes, Barry. *Rastafari*	299
Grant, Colin. *The Natural Mystics*	
Sinclair, Safiya. ★*How to Say Babylon*	B
Ratajkowski, Emily	
★*My Body*	B
RATAJKOWSKI, EMILY, 1991-	
Ratajkowski, Emily. ★*My Body*	B
Ratchetdemic. Emdin, Christopher	370.1
Rated X. Ward, Maitland	B
Rathbone, John Paul	
The Sugar King of Havana	B
Rather, Dan	
What Unites Us	323.6
Ratification. Maier, Pauline	342.7302
Ratio. Ruhlman, Michael	641.5
RATIO AND PROPORTION	
Ruhlman, Michael. *Ratio*	641.5
The Rational Optimist. Ridley, Matt	339.2
RATIONALISM	
Dawkins, Richard. *Science in the Soul*	500
Minois, Georges. *The Atheist's Bible*	200
Rationality. Pinker, Steven	153.4
RATIONING	
Moorhouse, Roger. *Berlin at War*	943
Ratliff, Ben	
The Jazz Ear	781.6509
Ratliff, Evan	
The Mastermind	B

AUTHOR, TITLE, SERIES AND SUBJECT INDEX

The **Ratline**. Sands, Philippe — B
RATMANSKII, ALEKSEI, 1968-
   Harss, Marina. *The Boy from Kyiv* — B
Rauch, Jonathan
   The Happiness Curve — 155.6
Raven Rock. Graff, Garrett M. — 363.350973
The **Ravenmaster**. Skaife, Christopher — B
RAVENS
   Skaife, Christopher. *The Ravenmaster* — B
Ravensbruck. Helm, Sarah — 940.53
RAVES
   Matos, Michaelangelo. *The Underground Is Massive* — 781.648
Ravin, Idan
   The Hoops Whisperer — 796.323
RAVIN, IDAN
   Ravin, Idan. *The Hoops Whisperer* — 796.323
Ravitch, Diane
   The Death and Life of the Great American School System — 379.1
   Slaying Goliath — 371.010973
Raw Deal. Sorvino, Chloe — 338.1
Rawlence, Ben
   City of Thorns — 967.7305
   The Treeline — 577.3
Rawles, James Wesley
   Tools for Survival — 613.6
RAY, JAMES EARL, 1928-1998
   Sides, Hampton. *Hellhound on His Trail* — 364.152
   Wexler, Stuart. *Killing King* — 323.092
RAY, LARRY (LAWRENCE), 1960-
   Levin, Daniel Barban. *Slonim Woods 9* — B
Ray, Rachael
   Everyone Is Italian on Sunday — 641.594
   ★*This Must Be the Place* — 641.5
RAY, RACHAEL
   Ray, Rachael. ★*This Must Be the Place* — 641.5
Ray, Victor
   On Critical Race Theory — 305.8
Rayman, Graham
   ★*Rikers* — 365
Raymond, Edwin
   An Inconvenient Cop — 363.2
RAYMOND, EDWIN, 1986-
   Raymond, Edwin. *An Inconvenient Cop* — 363.2
Raza, Azra
   The First Cell — 616.99
RAZA, AZRA
   Raza, Azra. *The First Cell* — 616.99
Razzle Dazzle. Jackson, Major — 811
Razzle Dazzle. Riedel, Michael — 792.09
RDZOGS-CHEN
   Thondup. *Enlightened Journey* — 294.3
Reactions. Gray, Theodore W. — 530
Read Dangerously. Nafisi, Azar — 809
Read This to Get Smarter. Imani, Blair — 303.3
Read Until You Understand. Griffin, Farah Jasmine — 810.9
Read, Anthony
   The Fall of Berlin — 940.54
Read, Piers Paul
   ★*Alive* — 982
Reader, Come Home. Wolf, Maryanne — 418
READERS
   Batuman, Elif. *The Possessed* — 891.7
   Chabon, Michael. *Maps and Legends* — 801
   Mead, Rebecca. *My Life in Middlemarch* — 823
   Reed, Shannon. *Why We Read* — 028
The **Readers'** *Advisory Guide to Graphic Novels*. Goldsmith, Francisca — 025.2
The **Readers'** *Advisory Guide to Horror*. Spratford, Becky Siegel — 025.5
★*The* **Readers'** *Advisory Guide to Romance*. Bradford, Robin — 025.2
READING
   Batuman, Elif. *The Possessed* — 891.7
   Briggs, Kate. *This Little Art* — 418
   Brown, Noah. *Reading Together* — 028.5
   Dehaene, Stanislas. *Reading in the Brain* — 418
   Ferrante, Elena. *In the Margins* — 809
   Gurdon, Meghan Cox. *The Enchanted Hour* — 372.4
   Houston, Keith. *The Book* — 002.09
   Kakutani, Michiko. *Ex Libris* — 028
   Mead, Rebecca. *My Life in Middlemarch* — 823

   Prose, Francine. *What to Read and Why* — 028
   Reed, Shannon. *Why We Read* — 028
   Reynolds, David S. *Mightier Than the Sword* — 813
   Spence, Annie. *Dear Fahrenheit 451* — 028.9
   Young, Damon. *The Art of Reading* — 028.9
READING (ELEMENTARY)
   Cox, Marge. *Kids' Books and Maker Activities* — 372.41
   Smart, Maya Payne. *Reading for Our Lives* — 372.4
READING ALOUD
   Gurdon, Meghan Cox. *The Enchanted Hour* — 372.4
   Paul, Pamela. ★*How to Raise a Reader* — 649
   Smart, Maya Payne. *Reading for Our Lives* — 372.4
   Trelease, Jim. ★*Jim Trelease's Read-Aloud Handbook* — 372.4
Reading Chekhov. Malcolm, Janet — 891.72
READING COMPREHENSION
   Cleaver, Samantha. *Raising an Active Reader* — 372.4
Reading for Our Lives. Smart, Maya Payne — 372.4
★*Reading Genesis*. Robinson, Marilynne — 222
Reading in the Brain. Dehaene, Stanislas — 418
READING INTERESTS
   Young, Damon. *The Art of Reading* — 028.9
★*Reading Lolita in Tehran*. Nafisi, Azar — B
Reading People. Dimitrius, Jo-Ellan — 155.2
READING PROGRAMS
   Farmer, Lesley S. J. ★*Impactful Community-Based Literacy Projects* — 372.6
READING PROMOTION
   Cole, Natalie. ★*Transforming Summer Programs at Your Library* — 028
   Young, Damon. *The Art of Reading* — 028.9
Reading Together. Brown, Noah — 028.5
Reading with Patrick. Kuo, Michelle — B
Reading, Writing, and Racism. Picower, Bree — 371.829
Readme.Txt. Manning, Chelsea — B
★*Ready or Not*. Levine, Madeline — 649
Ready or Not! Tam, Michelle — 641.5
Ready, Set, Cook. Perry, Dawn — 641.5
Ready, Set, Go! Ockwell-Smith, Sarah — 649
Reagan. Brands, H. W. — B
Reagan. Reagan, Ronald — B
★*Reagan*. Spitz, Bob — B
The **Reagan** *Diaries*. Reagan, Ronald — B
REAGAN FAMILY
   Tumulty, Karen. *The Triumph of Nancy Reagan* — B
REAGAN, NANCY, 1921-2016
   Tumulty, Karen. *The Triumph of Nancy Reagan* — B
Reagan, Ronald
   The Reagan Diaries — B
   Reagan — B
REAGAN, RONALD
   Ambinder, Marc. *The Brink* — 355.5
   Brands, H. W. *Reagan* — B
   Davis, Patti. *Floating in the Deep End* — 616.8
   Mann, Jim. *The Rebellion of Ronald Reagan* — 973.927092
   Perlstein, Rick. *The Invisible Bridge* — 973.924
   Perlstein, Rick. ★*Reaganland* — 973.926
   Reagan, Ronald. *The Reagan Diaries* — B
   Reagan, Ronald. *Reagan* — B
   Rosenfeld, Seth. *Subversives* — 378.1
   Spitz, Bob. ★*Reagan* — B
   Stevens, Stuart. *It Was All a Lie* — 324.2734
   Tumulty, Karen. *The Triumph of Nancy Reagan* — B
   Woodward, Bob. *Shadow* — 973.92
★*Reaganland*. Perlstein, Rick — 973.926
★*Real Estate*. Levy, Deborah — B
REAL ESTATE
   Podemski, Max. *A Paradise of Small Houses* — 363.5
REAL ESTATE BUSINESS
   Brown, Eliot. *The Cult of We* — 333.33
   Wiedeman, Reeves. *Billion Dollar Loser* — 333.33
REAL ESTATE DEVELOPERS
   Bernstein, Andrea. *American Oligarchs* — 920
REAL ESTATE INVESTMENT
   Ross, Andrew. *Sunbelt Blues* — 363.5
The **Real** *Fidel Castro*. Coltman, Leycester — B
Real Food Heals. Mullen, Seamus — 641.5
Real Food/Fake Food. Olmsted, Larry — 641.3
★*Real Friends Talk About Race*. Mukantabana, Yseult P. — 305.8
The **Real** *Lolita*. Weinman, Sarah — 362.88092
The **Real** *North Korea*. Lankov, A. N. — 951.9304

PUBLIC LIBRARY CORE COLLECTION: NONFICTION
Twentieth Edition

The Real Pepsi Challenge. Capparell, Stephanie	338.7
The Real Valkyrie. Brown, Nancy Marie	948
The Real Work. Gopnik, Adam	153.9
Real, Terrence	
Us	646.7
REALISM	
Levin, Gail. *Edward Hopper*	759.13
The Realism Challenge. Crilley, Mark	751.4
REALISM IN ART	
Barnes, Julian. *Keeping an Eye Open*	709.04
Levin, Gail. *Edward Hopper*	759.13
Robinson, Mario Andres. *Lessons in Realistic Watercolor*	751.42
Realistic Pumpkin Carving. Cupp, Lundy	745.5941646
REALITY	
Ananthaswamy, Anil. *Through Two Doors at Once*	530.12
Andersen, Kurt. ★*Fantasyland*	973
Atwood, Margaret. *Dearly*	811
Carroll, Sean M. *Something Deeply Hidden*	530.12
Dakwar, Elias. *The Captive Imagination*	616.85
Hoffman, Donald D. *The Case Against Reality*	121
Rovelli, Carlo. *Helgoland*	530.12
Smith, Patti. ★*M Train*	B
Wilczek, Frank. *Fundamentals*	530.01
Reality Is Not What It Seems. Rovelli, Carlo	530.14
REALITY TELEVISION PROGRAMS	
Chang, David. ★*Eat a Peach*	641.5
Duggar, Jill. *Counting the Cost*	B
Nussbaum, Emily. *Cue the Sun!*	791.45
Poniewozik, James. *Audience of One*	324.7
Tolentino, Jia. ★*Trick Mirror*	973.93
A Really Good Day. Waldman, Ayelet	B
Reang, Putsata	
Ma and Me	B
REANG, PUTSATA	
Reang, Putsata. *Ma and Me*	B
Rear, Rachel	
Catch the Sparrow	364.152
REAR, RACHEL	
Rear, Rachel. *Catch the Sparrow*	364.152
REASON	
Ariely, Dan. *Predictably Irrational*	153.8
Dawkins, Richard. *Science in the Soul*	500
Gardner, Dan. *The Science of Fear*	152.4
Johnson, Steven. *Farsighted*	153.8
Mlodinow, Leonard. *Emotional*	152.4
Pinker, Steven. *Rationality*	153.4
Robertson, Ritchie. *The Enlightenment*	190
Tyson, Neil deGrasse. *Starry Messenger*	901
Watson, Richard A. *Cogito Ergo Sum*	B
The Reason for God. Keller, Timothy J.	239
The Reason for the Darkness of the Night. Tresch, John	B
REASONING	
Hecht, Jennifer Michael. *Doubt*	121
Hofstadter, Douglas R. *Surfaces and Essences*	169
Jacobs, Alan. *How to Think*	153.4
Kahneman, Daniel. ★*Thinking, Fast and Slow*	153.4
Konnikova, Maria. *Mastermind*	153.4
Levitin, Daniel J. ★*A Field Guide to Lies*	153.4
Nisbett, Richard E. *Mindware*	153.4
Raphael, Ray. *Mr. President*	352.230973
Reasons Not to Worry. Delaney, Brigid	158.1
The Reawakening. Levi, Primo	B
Rebanks, James	
The Shepherd's Life	942.7
REBANKS, JAMES	
Rebanks, James. *The Shepherd's Life*	942.7
Rebbe. Telushkin, Joseph	296.833
★*Rebecca Ringquist's Embroidery Workshops.* Ringquist, Rebecca	746.44
The Rebel. Camus, Albert	303.6
Rebel. Nolte, Nick	B
Rebel Cinderella. Hochschild, Adam	B
Rebel Girl. Hanna, Kathleen	B
Rebel Rising. Wilson, Rebel	B
Rebel Souls. Martin, Justin	920
Rebel Yell. Gwynne, S. C.	B
The Rebel's Clinic. Shatz, Adam	965
Rebellion. Ackroyd, Peter	941.06
The Rebellion of Ronald Reagan. Mann, Jim	973.927092

The Rebellious Life of Mrs. Rosa Parks. Theoharis, Jeanne	B
REBELS	
Bartlett, Rosamund. ★*Tolstoy*	B
Fraser, Antonia. *Faith and Treason*	942.06
Keefe, Patrick Radden. ★*Rogues*	364.16
McCullough, David G. ★*1776*	973.3
Mieville, China. *October*	947.084
Rebels Against the Raj. Guha, Ramachandra	954.03
★*Rebels At Sea.* Dolin, Eric Jay	973.3
Rebels on the Backlot. Waxman, Sharon	791.4302
Rebels with a Cause. Way, Niobe	649
REBIRTH (PSYCHOLOGY)	
Terkel, Studs. *Will the Circle Be Unbroken?*	128
Rebuilding The Foodshed. Ackerman-Leist, Philip	338.1
Recalculating. Pollak, Lindsey	650.1
Recalibrate Your Life. Boa, Kenneth D.	248.8
RECEIVING STOLEN GOODS	
Fox, Margalit. *The Talented Mrs. Mandelbaum*	364.1
RECESSION (ECONOMICS)	
Alt, Matt. *Pure Invention*	306.0952
Hoffman, Liz. *Crash Landing*	330
Katznelson, Ira. *Fear Itself*	973.917
Krugman, Paul R. *Arguing with Zombies*	330.973
Leonnig, Carol. *I Alone Can Fix It*	973.933
Lowe, Keith. *Savage Continent*	940.55
Murdoch, Sierra Crane. ★*Yellow Bird*	364.152
Nations, Scott. *A History of the United States in Five Crashes*	338.5
Small, Zachary. ★*Token Supremacy*	332.4
RECIDIVISM	
Hardy, Jason Matthew. ★*The Second Chance Club*	364.6
RECIPES	
Adams, Jocelyn Delk. *Grandbaby Cakes*	641.86
Adarme, Adrianna. *The Year of Cozy*	641.3
Alexander, Kwame. *Why Fathers Cry at Night*	B
Allibhoy, Omar. *Spanish Made Simple*	641.594
Anderson, Pam. *How to Cook Without a Book*	641.5
Andres, Jose. *Vegetables Unleashed*	641.5
Anthony, Michael. *V Is for Vegetables*	641.6
Aron, Jules. *Vegan Cheese*	641.5
Bard, Elizabeth. *Lunch in Paris*	B
Bard, Elizabeth. *Picnic in Provence*	B
Barrett, Pearl. *Trim Healthy Mama Trim Healthy Table*	613.2
Barrow, Cathy. ★*Pie Squared*	641.86
Bastianich, Lidia. *Felidia*	641.594
Bastianich, Lidia. *Lidia Cooks from the Heart of Italy*	641.594
Bastianich, Lidia. *Lidia's Commonsense Italian Cooking*	641.594
Bastianich, Lidia. *Lidia's Family Table*	641.594
Bastianich, Lidia. *Lidia's Favorite Recipes*	641.594
Bastianich, Lidia. *Lidia's Mastering the Art of Italian Cuisine*	641.594
Bastianich, Lidia. *Lidia's*	641.594
Batali, Mario. *Mario Batali Big American Cookbook*	641.5973
Bayless, Rick. *Authentic Mexican*	641.5972
Bayless, Rick. ★*Fiesta at Rick's*	641.5972
Bayless, Rick. *Mexican Everyday*	641.5972
Bayless, Rick. ★*More Mexican Everyday*	641.5972
Bayless, Rick. *Rick Bayless Mexico One Plate at a Time*	641.5972
Belsinger, Susan. *Grow Your Own Herbs*	635
Beranbaum, Rose Levy. ★*Rose's Baking Basics*	641.81
Beranbaum, Rose Levy. *Rose's Ice Cream Bliss*	641.86
Berry, Mary. *Cooking with Mary Berry.*	641.5
Bianco, Chris. *Bianco*	641.5
Bittman, Mark. ★*Dinner for Everyone*	641.5
Bittman, Mark. ★*How to Bake Everything*	641.81
Bittman, Mark. ★*How to Cook Everything Vegetarian*	641.5
Bittman, Mark. ★*How to Cook Everything*	641.5
Bittman, Mark. *How to Cook Everything*	641.5
Bittman, Mark. ★*How to Grill Everything*	641.7
Bittman, Mark. *Mark Bittman's Kitchen Matrix*	641.5
Bittman, Mark. *The VB6 Cookbook*	641.5
Bjork, Katrin. *From the North*	641.594
Black, Sarah. *One Dough, Ten Breads*	641.81
Bourdain, Anthony. ★*Appetites*	641.5
Bracken, Peg. *The I Hate to Cook Book*	641.5
Brennan, Kathy. *Keepers*	641.5973
Brock, Sean. *South*	641.5975
Brown, Leanne. ★*Good and Cheap*	641.5
Byrn, Anne. ★*American Cake*	641.86
Byrn, Anne. ★*American Cookie*	641.86

AUTHOR, TITLE, SERIES AND SUBJECT INDEX

Byrn, Anne. *Skillet Love*	641.7
Cailan, Alvin. *Amboy*	641.595
Camara, Gabriela. *My Mexico City Kitchen*	641.5972
Carle-Sanders, Theresa. *Outlander Kitchen*	641.5
Cavallari, Kristin. *True Roots*	641.5
Cayne, Alison. *The Haven's Kitchen Cooking School*	641.5
Centeno, Josef. *Ama*	641.5979
Chang, Joanne. *Pastry Love*	641.86
Chaplin, Amy. *Whole Food Cooking Every Day*	641.3
Child, Julia. *Julia and Jacques Cooking at Home*	641.594
Child, Julia. ★*Mastering the Art of French Cooking*	641.594
Clark, Melissa. *Comfort in an Instant*	641.5
Clark, Melissa. ★*Dinner in an Instant*	641.5
Clark, Melissa. *Dinner in French*	641.594
Conner, Polly. ★*From Freezer to Cooker*	641.6
Conners, Rachel. *Bakerita*	641.81
Coscarelli, Chloe. *Chloe Flavor*	641.5
Crocker, Betty. ★*Betty Crocker Cookbook*	641.5
Curl, Jami. *Candy Is Magic*	641.85
Curry, Kevin. *Fit Men Cook*	641.5
Danford, Natalie. *How to Eataly*	641.594
Danforth, Adam. *Butchering Poultry, Rabbit, Lamb, Goat, and Pork*	664
David, Laurie. *The Family Cooks*	641.3
Day, Cheryl. *Back in the Day Bakery, Made with Love*	641.81
De Laurentiis, Giada. ★*Giada's Italy*	641.594
De Laurentiis, Giada. *Giada's Kitchen*	641.594
DiGregorio, Sarah. *Adventures in Slow Cooking*	641.5
Disbrowe, Paula. *Thank You for Smoking*	641.5
DiSpirito, Rocco. *Now Eat This!*	641.5
DiSpirito, Rocco. *Rocco's Healthy+Delicious*	641.3
Drummond, Ree. ★*The Pioneer Woman Cooks*	641.5
Dusoulier, Clotilde. *Tasting Paris*	641.594
El-Waylly, Sohla. ★*Start Here*	641.3
Emberling, Amy. *Zingerman's Bakehouse*	641.81
Esposito, Jennifer. *Jennifer's Way Kitchen*	641.5
Falk, Daina. *The Hungry Fan's Game Day Cookbook*	641.5973
Fearnley-Whittingstall, Hugh. *River Cottage Veg*	641.5
Fishman, Boris. *Savage Feast*	B
Flanagan, Shalane. *Run Fast, Cook Fast, Eat Slow*	641.5
Flay, Bobby. *Bobby at Home*	641.5
Forkish, Ken. *Flour Water Salt Yeast*	641.81
Forte, Sara. *The Sprouted Kitchen*	641.3
Francois, Zoe. *Holiday and Celebration Bread in Five Minutes a Day*	641.81
Franklin, Aaron. *Franklin Barbecue*	641.7
Fuentes, Laura. *The Best Homemade Kids' Snacks on the Planet*	641.5
Fuhrman, Joel. *Eat to Live Quick & Easy Cookbook*	641.5
Gaines, Joanna. ★*Magnolia Table*	641.5975
Ganeshram, Ramin. *Future Chefs*	641.3
Garten, Ina. *Barefoot Contessa at Home*	641.5
Garten, Ina. *Barefoot Contessa Family Style*	641.5
Garten, Ina. ★*Barefoot Contessa, How Easy Is That?*	641.5
Garten, Ina. ★*Cook Like a Pro*	641.5
Gerson, Fany. *Mexican Ice Cream*	641.86
Gerson, Fany. *My Sweet Mexico*	641.5972
Goldman, Duff. *Duff Bakes*	641.81
Good, Phyllis Pellman. *Fix-It and Forget-It New Cookbook*	641.5
Greenspan, Dorie. *Around My French Table*	641.594
Greenspan, Dorie. *Baking Chez Moi*	641.86
Greenspan, Dorie. *Baking with Julia*	641.8
Greenspan, Dorie. *Baking*	641.8
Greenspan, Dorie. ★*Dorie's Cookies*	641.86
Greenspan, Eric. *The Great Grilled Cheese Book*	641.6
Griffin, Brooke. *Skinny Suppers*	641.5
Guarnaschelli, Alex. *The Home Cook*	641.5973
Gunst, Kathy. *Rage Baking*	641.86
Guy, Jerrelle. *Black Girl Baking*	641.59
Hall, Carla. *Carla Hall's Soul Food*	641.5975
Hall, Carla. *Carla's Comfort Foods*	641.59
Hamilton, Gabrielle. *Prune*	641.3
Hamshaw, Gena. *Food 52 Vegan*	641.5
Hartwig, Melissa. *The Whole30 Fast & Easy*	641.5
Hassan, Hawa. *In Bibi's Kitchen*	641.596
Hazan, Marcella. ★*Essentials of Classic Italian Cooking*	641.594
Headley, Brooks. *Superiority Burger Cookbook*	641.5
Helou, Anissa. *Feast*	641.595
Hesser, Amanda. ★*The Essential New York Times Cook Book*	641.5
Hill, McKel. *Nutrition Stripped*	641.3
Homolka, Gina. *Skinnytaste Fast and Slow*	641.5
Hong, Deuki. *Koreatown*	641.595
Hood, Ann. *Kitchen Yarns*	641.5
Howard, Vivian. *Deep Run Roots*	641.5975
Howard, Vivian. *This Will Make It Taste Good*	641.5
Hudson, Kate. *Pretty Fun*	642
Huff, Mary Scott. *The Mitten Handbook*	746.43
Hunt, Lindsay Maitland. *Healthyish*	641.5
Hunt, Lindsay Maitland. *Help Yourself*	641.5
Hussain, Nadiya. ★*Nadiya's Everyday Baking*	641.5
Iyer, Raghavan. *Indian Cooking Unfolded*	641.595
Jaffrey, Madhur. ★*Madhur Jaffrey's Instantly Indian Cookbook*	641.595
Jaffrey, Madhur. *Madhur Jaffrey's World Vegetarian*.	641.5
Jaffrey, Madhur. *Vegetarian India*	641.595
Jenkins, Nancy Harmon. *The New Mediterranean Diet Cookbook*	641.59
Jinich, Pati. *Mexican Today*	641.5972
Kahan, Paul. *Cheers to the Publican, Repast and Present*	641.594
Kattan, Fadi. ★*Bethlehem*	641.59
Katzen, Mollie. *The Heart of the Plate*	641.5
Khan, Yasmin. ★*Zaitoun*	641.595
Kim, Hooni. *My Korea*	641.595
Kimball, Christopher. *Christopher Kimball's Milk Street*	641.5
Kimball, Christopher. *Milk Street*	641.5
Korkosz, Michal. *Fresh from Poland*	641.594
Krieger, Ellie. *You Have It Made!*	641.5
Krishna, Priya. ★*Indian-ish*	641.595
Kulaga, Agatha. *Ovenly*	641.81
Kysar, Alana. *Aloha Kitchen*	641.59969
Lagasse, Emeril. *Essential Emeril*	641.5
Lahey, Jim. *The Sullivan Street Bakery Cookbook*	641.81
Lancaster, Bridget. *Cooking at Home with Bridget & Julia*	641.5
Lane, Christina. *Dessert for Two*	641.86
Langholtz, Gabrielle. *America*	641.5973
Larsen, Jeffrey. ★*Gluten-Free Baking at Home*	641.5
Lawson, Nigella. *At My Table*	641.59
Leake, Lisa. *100 Days of Real Food on a Budget*	641.5
Leake, Lisa. ★*100 Days of Real Food*	641.5
Lebovitz, David. *My Paris Kitchen*	641.594
Lightner, Jill. *Cooking from Scratch*	641.5
Lillien, Lisa. *Hungry Girl 1-2-3*	641.5
Ludwig, David. *Always Hungry?*	613.2
Lukas, Albert. ★*Sweet Home Cafe Cookbook*	641.59
Madison, Deborah. *In My Kitchen*	641.5
Madison, Deborah. *Vegetable Literacy*	641.6
Madison, Deborah. *Vegetarian Cooking for Everyone*	641.5
Mangini, Cara. *The Vegetable Butcher*	641.6
Manning, Ivy. *Easy Soups from Scratch with Quick Breads to Match*	641.81
Mayes, Frances. *See You in the Piazza*	914.5
McBride, Martina. *Martina's Kitchen Mix*	641.5973
McDermott, Kate. ★*Art of the Pie*	641.86
McFadden, Joshua. *Six Seasons*	641.5
McKenney, Sally. ★*Sally's Cookie Addiction*	641.86
Meehan, Peter. *Lucky Peach Presents 101 Easy Asian Recipes*	641.595
Merchant, Jessica. *Everyday Dinners*	641.82
Miglore, Kristen. *Food52 Genius Desserts*	641.86
Miglore, Kristen. ★*Food52 Genius Recipes*	641.5
Miller, Klancy. ★*For the Culture*	641.59
Miller, Max. ★*Tasting History*	641.509
Mitchell, Andie. *Eating in the Middle*	641.3
Moore, Matt. *Serial Griller*	641.7
Morales, Bonnie Frumkin. *Kachka*	641.594
Moskowitz, Isa Chandra. *The Superfun Times Vegan Holiday Cookbook*	651.56
Moskowitz, Isa Chandra. *Veganomicon*	641
Moulton, Sara. *Sara Moulton's Home Cooking 101*	641.5973
Mullen, Seamus. *Real Food Heals*	641.5
Music, Carla Lalli. *Where Cooking Begins*	641.5
Myers, Amy. *The Autoimmune Solution Cookbook*	641.5
Nederlanden, Elisabet der. ★*Holiday Cookies*	641.86
Neiman, Ophelie. *Wine Isn't Rocket Science*	641.2
Nelson, Candace. *The Sprinkles Baking Book*	641.81
Nelson, Kim. *Daisy Cakes Bakes*	641.86
Nguyen, Andrea Quynhgiao. ★*Vietnamese Food Any Day*	641.595
Nolen, Jeremy. *New German Cooking*	641.594
Orkin, Ivan. *The Gaijin Cookbook*	641.595
Ottolenghi, Yotam. ★*Jerusalem*	641.5
Ottolenghi, Yotam. ★*Plenty More*	641.6
Ottolenghi, Yotam. *Plenty*	641.6
Oz, Daphne. *The Happy Cook*	641.5

PUBLIC LIBRARY CORE COLLECTION: NONFICTION
Twentieth Edition

Paltrow, Gwyneth. *It's All Easy*	641.5
Pansino, Rosanna. *Baking All Year Round*	641.86
Parks, Stella. ★*Bravetart*	641.86
Parla, Katie. *Tasting Rome*	641.59
Pelaez, Ana Sofia. *The Cuban Table*	641.597291
Pepin, Jacques. *Art of the Chicken*	641.665
Pepin, Jacques. *Essential Pepin*	641.594
Pepin, Jacques. ★*Jacques Pepin*	641.594
Perelman, Deb. ★*The Smitten Kitchen Cookbook*	641.5
Perelman, Deb. ★*Smitten Kitchen Every Day*	641.5
Perlmutter, David. *The Grain Brain Cookbook*	651.56
Perry Lang, Adam. *Serious Barbecue*	641.5
Peterson, James. *Sauces*	641.81
Pierson, Joy. *Vegan Holiday Cooking from Candle Cafe*	641.5
Pollan, Corky. *The Pollan Family Table*	641.5
Ponseca, Nicole. *I Am a Filipino and This Is How We Cook*	641.595
Powell, Julie. *Julie and Julia*	641.5
Prescott, Matthew. *Food Is the Solution*	613.2
Presilla, Maricel E. *Gran Cocina Latina*	641.5972
Pulde, Alona. ★*The Forks Over Knives Plan*	641.5
Purviance, Jamie. *Weber's Greatest Hits*	641.5
Purviance, Jamie. *Weber's Ultimate Grilling*	641.5
Raines, Abigail Sotto. *Rice. Noodles. Yum.*	641.595
Ramirez, Elva. *Zero Proof*	641.87
Ray, Rachael. *Everyone Is Italian on Sunday*	641.594
Redzepi, Rene. *The Noma Guide to Fermentation*	664
Reichl, Ruth. *Comfort Me with Apples*	B
Reichl, Ruth. *My Kitchen Year*	641.5
Richards, Todd. *Soul*	641.59296073
Rinella, Steven. *The Complete Guide to Hunting, Butchering, and Cooking Wild Game; Volume 2*	799.2
Risbridger, Ella. *The Year of Miracles*	641.5
Risen, Clay. *American Whiskey, Bourbon, & Rye*	641.2
Roden, Claudia. ★*The Book of Jewish Food*	641.5
Rodriguez, Jessamyn Waldman. *The Hot Bread Kitchen Cookbook*	641.59
Roll, Rich. *The Plantpower Way*	641.5
Rondinelli-Hamilton, Lara. *The Diabetes Cookbook*	641.5
Rosen, Ali. *Bring It!*	641.5973
Rosenstrach, Jenny. *How to Celebrate Everything*	641.5
Rosso, Julee. *The Silver Palate Cookbook*	641.5
Ruhlman, Michael. *Ratio*	641.5
Saltz, Joanna. *Delish*	641.5
Samuelsson, Marcus. *Marcus off Duty*	641.5
Samuelsson, Marcus. ★*The Rise*	641.59
Sarno, Chad. *The Wicked Healthy Cookbook*	651.56
Sever, Shauna. ★*Midwest Made*	641.5977
Shepherd, Chris. *Cook Like a Local*	641.59
Sherman, Sean. ★*The Sioux Chef's Indigenous Kitchen*	641.59
Shumski, Daniel. *How to Instant Pot*	641.5
Sifton, Sam. ★*See You on Sunday*	641.5
Sifton, Sam. *Thanksgiving*	641.5
Smalls, Alexander. *Meals, Music, and Muses*	641.59
Smith, Michelle. *The Whole Smiths Good Food Cookbook*	641.5
Smith, R. Garth. *Asd, the Complete Autism Spectrum Disorder Health & Diet Guide*	616.85
Snodgrass, Alex. ★*The Defined Dish*	641.5
Sodha, Meera. *Made in India*	641.595
Solomonov, Michael. *Israeli Soul*	641.595
Solomonov, Michael. *Zahav*	641.595
Stewart, Martha. ★*Martha Stewart's Baking Handbook*	641.8
Stewart, Martha. *Martha Stewart's Cooking School*	641.5
Symon, Michael. ★*Fix It with Food*	641.5
Symon, Michael. *Michael Symon's Playing with Fire*	641.7
Tam, Michelle. *Ready or Not!*	641.5
Tamimi, Sami. *Falastin*	641.595
Taylor, Kathryne. *Love Real Food*	641.5
Teigen, Chrissy. *Cravings*	641.5
Terry, Bryant. *Afro-Vegan*	641.59
Terry, Bryant. ★*Vegetable Kingdom*	641.5
Thiessen, Tiffani. *Pull up a Chair*	641.5
Thomas, Anna. *Vegan Vegetarian Omnivore*	641.5
Thomas, Haile. *Living Lively*	641.5
Thorisson, Mimi. *A Kitchen in France*	641.594
Tila, Jet. *101 Asian Dishes You Need to Cook Before You Die*	641.595
Tipton-Martin, Toni. *The Jemima Code*	641.59
Tipton-Martin, Toni. ★*Jubilee*	641.59
Tosi, Christina. *All About Cake*	641.86
Trejo, Danny. *Trejo's Tacos*	641.5979
Turshen, Julia. *Feed the Resistance*	641.5
Turshen, Julia. *Small Victories*	641.5
Twitty, Michael. ★*Koshersoul*	641.5
Urban, Melissa. *The Whole30 Friends & Family*	641.5
Van't Hul, Jean. *The Artful Year*	745.594
Vasquez, Karla Tatiana. ★*The Salvisoul Cookbook*	641.598
Vicenzino, Cettina. *The Sicily Cookbook*	641.59458
Volger, Lukas. *Bowl*	641.81
Walker, Danielle. *Danielle Walker's Against All Grain*	641.5
Wang, Jason. *XI'an Famous Foods*	641.595
Wangler, Justin. *Season*	641.5979
Waters, Alice. *Coming to My Senses*	B
Weil, Andrew. *Fast Food, Good Food*	641.3
Weinstein, Bruce. *The Kitchen Shortcut Bible*	641.555
Weiss, Luisa. *Classic German Baking*	641.594
Wells, Patricia. *My Master Recipes*	641.5
West, Kevin. *Saving the Season*	641.4
Wilkinson, Crystal. *Praisesong for the Kitchen Ghosts*	641.5975
Williams, Odette. *Simple Cake*	641.86
Witte, Christina De. ★*Noodles, Rice, and Everything Spice*	641.595
Wolf, Robb. *Wired to Eat*	641.5
Workman, Katie. *Dinner Solved!*	641.5
Workman, Katie. *The Mom 100 Cookbook*	641.5
Wright, Caroline. *Cake Magic!*	641.86
Zanini De Vita, Oretta. *Encyclopedia of Pasta*	641.822
Reckless Daughter. Yaffe, David	782.42164
Reckoning. Hirshman, Linda R.	305.420973
The Reckoning. Nicholl, Charles	B
★**Reckoning**. V	814
Reckoning At Eagle Creek. Biggers, Jeff	333.73
Reclaiming Her Time. Andrews-Dyer, Helena	B
Reclaiming The Dead Sea Scrolls. Schiffman, Lawrence H.	296.1
Reclamation. White, Gayle Jessup	B

RECLUSES

Dery, Mark. *Born to Be Posthumous*	B
Finkel, Michael. *The Stranger in the Woods*	B
Keaton, Diane. ★*Brother & Sister*	B
★**Recollections** of My Nonexistence. Solnit, Rebecca	B
Reconciliation. Bhutto, Benazir	297.2

RECONCILIATION

Blum, Howard. *The Spy Who Knew Too Much*	327.12
Calhoun, Ada. *Also a Poet*	B
Griffin, Chante. *Loving Your Black Neighbor as Yourself*	261
Preszler, Trent. *Little and Often*	B
Raines, Ben. *The Last Slave Ship*	306.362
Ruttenberg, Danya. *On Repentance and Repair*	202
Sale, Anna. ★*Let's Talk About Hard Things*	153.6
Tutu, Desmond. *The Book of Forgiving*	179
Williams, Mary. *The Lost Daughter*	B
★**Reconstruction**. Foner, Eric	973.8

RECONSTRUCTION (1939-1951)

Beschloss, Michael R. *The Conquerors*	940.53
Brands, H. W. *The General vs. the President*	973.918092
Feigel, Lara. *The Bitter Taste of Victory*	320.943
Lowe, Keith. *Savage Continent*	940.55

RECONSTRUCTION (UNITED STATES HISTORY)

Ayers, Edward L. ★*The Thin Light of Freedom*	975.5
Ball, Edward. *Life of a Klansman*	305.8009763
Bordewich, Fergus M. *Klan War*	973.8
Cwiklik, Robert. *Sheridan's Secret Mission*	973.8
Dray, Philip. *Capitol Men*	973.8
Foner, Eric. *Forever Free*	973.8
Foner, Eric. ★*Reconstruction*	973.8
Foner, Eric. *The Second Founding*	342.73
Gates, Henry Louis. ★*Stony the Road*	973
Jacoby, Karl. *The Strange Career of William Ellis*	B
Lane, Charles. *The Day Freedom Died*	976.3
Lane, Charles. *Freedom's Detective*	B
Langguth, A. J. *After Lincoln*	973.8
Lemann, Nicholas. *Redemption*	975
Levine, Bruce C. *Thaddeus Stevens*	B
Levine, Robert S. ★*The Failed Promise*	973.8
Marvel, William. *Lincoln's Autocrat*	B
Postel, Charles. *Equality*	305.50973
Sinha, Manisha. ★*The Rise and Fall of the Second American Republic*	973.8
Stahr, Walter. ★*Stanton*	B
Varon, Elizabeth R. *Longstreet*	B
Williams, Kidada E. *I Saw Death Coming*	973.8

AUTHOR, TITLE, SERIES AND SUBJECT INDEX

Wineapple, Brenda. *Ecstatic Nation*	973.6
Wineapple, Brenda. *The Impeachers*	973.8
Woodward, C. Vann. *The Strange Career of Jim Crow*	305.896

RECORD INDUSTRY AND TRADE
Grandmaster Flash. *The Adventures of Grandmaster Flash*	B
Record Makers and Breakers. Broven, John	B

RECORD SETTING
Eisenberg, John. *The Streak*	796.357
Hawley, Sam. *Speed Duel*	796.72
Record Store Days. Calamar, Gary	780.26

RECORDS, PHONOGRAPH
Calamar, Gary. *Record Store Days*	780.26
★*The Recovering*. Jamison, Leslie	B

RECOVERING ADDICTS
Carr, Erin Lee. *All That You Leave Behind*	B
John, Elton. ★*Me*	B
Kennedy, Patrick J. ★*Profiles in Mental Health Courage*	362.29

RECOVERING ALCOHOLICS
Biden, Robert Hunter. *Beautiful Things*	B
Jamison, Leslie. ★*The Recovering*	B
Namath, Joe Willie. ★*All the Way*	B
Wilder-Taylor, Stefanie. ★*Drunk-Ish*	B

RECOVERING DRUG ABUSERS
Biden, Robert Hunter. *Beautiful Things*	B

RECOVERY MOVEMENT
Fisher, Carl Erik. ★*The Urge*	362.29

RECREATION
Carlsen, Spike. *A Walk Around the Block*	031
Ho, Oliver. *The Ultimate Book of Family Card Games*	795.4
Iggulden, Conn. *The Double Dangerous Book for Boys*	031.02
St. John, Warren. *Outcasts United*	B

RECREATION INDUSTRY AND TRADE
Becker, Elizabeth. *Overbooked*	338.4
Kugel, Seth. *Rediscovering Travel*	306.4

RECYCLING (WASTE, ETC.)
Nelson, Bryn. *Flush*	612.3
Tonti, Lucianne. *Sundressed*	746.9
Yang, April. *DIY Thrift Flip*	646.2

RED (COLOR)
Carson, Anne. *Autobiography of Red*	811
The Red and the Blue. Kornacki, Steve	306.20973
Red Azalea. Min, Anchee	B
★*Red Card*. Bensinger, Ken	796.334
Red Carpet. Schwartzel, Erich	791.43
Red Cloud at Dawn. Gordin, Michael D.	355.02

RED CLOUD'S WAR, 1866-1867
Drury, Bob. *The Heart of Everything That Is*	B

RED CLOUD, 1822-1909
Drury, Bob. *The Heart of Everything That Is*	B
★*Red Comet*. Clark, Heather	B
Red Doc. Carson, Anne	811
★*Red Famine*. Applebaum, Anne	947.708
Red Line. Warrick, Joby	956.9104
The Red Man's Bones. Eisler, Benita	B
Red Memory. Branigan, Tania	951.05
Red Paint. LaPointe, Sasha taqwseblu	B
Red Platoon. Romesha, Clinton	958.104

RED POWER
Hendricks, Steve. *The Unquiet Grave*	323.1197
The Red Prince. Snyder, Timothy	B
The Red Rooster Cookbook. Samuelsson, Marcus	641.5974
The Red Rose Girls. Carter, Alice A.	B
Red Sea Spies. Berg, Raffi	327.125694
The Red Truck Bakery Farmhouse Cookbook. Noyes, Brian	641.5973
★*Redaction*. Betts, Reginald Dwayne	704.9

REDDING, OTIS, 1941-1967
Ribowsky, Mark. *Dreams to Remember*	B
Redeeming Justice. Adams, Jarrett	340.092
Redemption. Lemann, Nicholas	975
Redemption. Rosenbloom, Joseph	B

REDEMPTION
Black, George. ★*The Long Reckoning*	959.704
Blum, Howard. *The Spy Who Knew Too Much*	327.12
Brotherton, Marcus. *A Bright and Blinding Sun*	940.54
Dykstra, Lenny. *House of Nails*	B
Hardin, Lara Love. ★*The Many Lives of Mama Love*	B
Hopwood, Shon. *Law Man*	B
Manuel, Ian. *My Time Will Come*	B
Novello, Carol. *Mutual Rescue*	636.088
Rao, Cheeni. *In Hanuman's Hands*	B
Risner, Vaneetha Rendall. *Walking Through Fire*	B
Shannon, Molly. ★*Hello, Molly!*	B
Stevenson, Bryan. *Just Mercy*	B
Suvari, Mena. *The Great Peace*	B
Trejo, Danny. *Trejo*	B

Redford, Catherine
Modern Machine Quilting	746.46

Rediker, Marcus
The Amistad Rebellion	326.0973
Rediscovering Travel. Kugel, Seth	306.4
★*The Rediscovery of America*. Blackhawk, Ned	973.04

REDNECKS (SOUTHERN UNITED STATES)
Isenberg, Nancy. *White Trash*	305.5

Redniss, Lauren
★*Oak Flat*	970.5
Thunder & Lightning	741.5

REDSTONE, SHARI
Stewart, James B. *Unscripted*	658.1

REDSTONE, SUMNER
Stewart, James B. *Unscripted*	658.1

REDWOOD
Preston, Richard. *The Wild Trees*	585

Redzepi, Rene
The Noma Guide to Fermentation	664

Reed, Ishmael
New and Collected Poems, 1964-2007	811

Reed, John
Ten Days That Shook the World	947.084

Reed, Julia
Dispatches from the Gilded Age	B

REED, JULIA
Reed, Julia. *Dispatches from the Gilded Age*	B

Reed, Justin Phillip
Indecency	811
The Malevolent Volume	811

REED, LOU, 1942-2013
DeCurtis, Anthony. *Lou Reed*	B
Hermes, Will. *Lou Reed*	B

Reed, Shannon
Why We Read	028

REED, SHANNON
Reed, Shannon. *Why We Read*	028

Reel, Monte
The Last of the Tribe	981

REENGINEERING (MANAGEMENT)
Wooldridge, Adrian. *Masters of Management*	658

Rees, Darrel
How to Be an Illustrator	741.6

Rees, Laurence
Auschwitz	940.53
Hitler and Stalin	940.53
The Holocaust	940.53

Reese, Anney
★*Stuff Mom Never Told You*	305.42

Reese, William J.
Testing Wars in the Public Schools	371.260973

Reeves, Richard
Infamy	940.53

Reeves, Richard V.
Dream Hoarders	305.5

REFERENCE — ATLASES
Carballo, David M. *America*	912
Hayes, Derek. *Historical Atlas of the American West*	911
Sluglett, Peter. *Atlas of Islamic History*	912.19
Trefil, James. *Space Atlas*	520
Waterman, Jonathan. *National Geographic Atlas of the National Parks*	917.304

REFERENCE — BIBLIOGRAPHIES AND INDEXES
Bradford, Robin. ★*The Readers' Advisory Guide to Romance*	025.2
Cart, Michael. *Young Adult Literature*	813.009
Dorr, Christina H. ★*Profiles in Resilience*	028.5
Mulac, Carolyn. *Fundamentals of Reference*	025.5
Ottemiller, John H. *Ottemiller's Index to Plays in Collections*	016
Spratford, Becky Siegel. *The Readers' Advisory Guide to Horror*	025.5
Town, Caren J. *LGBTQ Young Adult Fiction*	813.009

PUBLIC LIBRARY CORE COLLECTION: NONFICTION
Twentieth Edition

REFERENCE — BIOGRAPHICAL DICTIONARIES
Hart, James David. *The Oxford Companion to American Literature* — 810.9
Martinez Wood, Jamie. *Latino Writers and Journalists* — B
Thomson, David. *The New Biographical Dictionary of Film* — 791.4302
Trahair, R. C. S. *Encyclopedia of Cold War Espionage, Spies, and Secret Operations 3rd Ed.* — 327.12

REFERENCE — BUSINESS
Derks, Scott. *The Value of a Dollar* — 338.5
Derks, Scott. *The Value of a Dollar* — 338.5
Gallo, Carmine. *Talk Like Ted* — 658.4
Siegel, Joel G. *Accounting Handbook.* — 657

REFERENCE — CONSUMER GUIDES
Milchtein, Chaya M. ★*Mechanic Shop Femme's Guide to Car Ownership* — 629.222

REFERENCE — DICTIONARIES
Ammer, Christine. *The American Heritage Dictionary of Idioms* — 423
Berger, Sidney E. *The Dictionary of the Book* — 002.03
Blackburn, Simon. *The Oxford Dictionary of Philosophy* — 103
Brewer, Ebenezer Cobham. ★*Brewer's Dictionary of Phrase & Fable* — 423
Corbeil, Jean-Claude. ★*Merriam-Webster's Visual Dictionary* — 423
Garner, Bryan A. *Garner's Modern English Usage* — 423
Hirsch, Edward. *A Poet's Glossary* — 808.1
Hischak, Thomas S. *The Oxford Companion to the American Musical* — 782.1
Hoffman, Miles. *The NPR Classical Music Companion* — 780.3
Holder, R. W. *How Not to Say What You Mean* — 427
Jordan, Michael. *Dictionary of Gods and Goddesses* — 202
Keown, Damien. ★*A Dictionary of Buddhism* — 294.3
Liddell, Henry George. *A Greek-English Lexicon* — 483
Manguel, Alberto. *The Dictionary of Imaginary Places* — 809
Olson, Carl. *Historical Dictionary of Buddhism* — 294.3
Shaw, Ian. *The Princeton Dictionary of Ancient Egypt* — 932
Stone, Jon R. ★*Latin for the Illiterati* — 473
Winter, Ruth. *A Consumer's Dictionary of Food Additives* — 664

REFERENCE — ENCYCLOPEDIAS
Carroll, Georgie. *The Mythology Book* — 201
Chevallier, Andrew. *Encyclopedia of Herbal Medicine* — 615.3
Clements, Jonathan. *The Anime Encyclopedia* — 791.43
Coile, D. Caroline. *Encyclopedia of Dog Breeds* — 636.7
Crary, Calvert. *The Encyclopedia of Cut Flowers* — 745.92
Glasse, Cyril. *The New Encyclopedia of Islam* — 297.03
Guiley, Rosemary. ★*The Encyclopedia of Ghosts and Spirits* — 133.1
Guiley, Rosemary. *The Encyclopedia of Witches, Witchcraft and Wicca* — 133.4
Johnson, Michael. *Encyclopedia of Native Tribes of North America* — 970.00497
Kraybill, Donald B. *Concise Encyclopedia of Amish, Brethren, Hutterites, and Mennonites* — 289.7
Miller, Judith. *Furniture* — 749
Monger, George. *Marriage Customs of the World* — 392.5
Muir, John Kenneth. *The Encyclopedia of Superheroes on Film and Television* — 791.43
Schultz, David A. *Encyclopedia of the United States Constitution* — 342.730203
Snodgrass, Mary Ellen. *The Underground Railroad* — 973.7
Zanini De Vita, Oretta. *Encyclopedia of Pasta* — 641.822

REFERENCE — GENEALOGY
Neighbors, Joy. *The Family Tree Cemetery Field Guide* — 929
Pennavaria, Katherine. *Genealogy for Beginners* — 929.1

REFERENCE — GENERAL
Berger, Karen. *America's Great Hiking Trails* — 796.510973
Bowlin, Ben. *Stuff They Don't Want You to Know* — 001.9
Busch, Robert. *The Wolf Almanac* — 599.773
Coile, D. Caroline. *Encyclopedia of Dog Breeds* — 636.7
Cranshaw, Whitney. *Garden Insects of North America* — 635
Dresser, Norine. *Multicultural Manners* — 395
Farmer, David Hugh. *The Oxford Dictionary of Saints* — 270
Formosa, Dan. *Baseball Field Guide* — 796.357
Forni, Pier Massimo. *The Civility Solution* — 395
Galaxy, Jackson. ★*Total Cat Mojo* — 636.8
Glass, Brent D. *50 Great American Places* — 973
Koch, Stephen. *The Modern Library Writer's Workshop* — 808.3
Miller, Megan. ★*The Ultimate Unofficial Encyclopedia for Minecrafters* — 794.8
Paul, Gregory S. *The Princeton Field Guide to Dinosaurs* — 567.9
Post, Lizzie. *Emily Post's Etiquette* — 395
Sibley, David. ★*Sibley Birds West* — 598.097
Sibley, David. ★*Sibley's Birding Basics* — 598
Spira, Timothy P. *Waterfalls and Wildflowers in the Southern Appalachians* — 796.5109756
Taylor, Marianne. *Bats* — 599.4

Thursby, Jacqueline S. *Critical Companion to Maya Angelou* — 818
Tower, Jeremiah. ★*Table Manners* — 395.5
Weitzman, Gary. *National Geographic Complete Guide to Pet Health, Behavior, and Happiness* — 636.088
Wilson, Joseph S. *The Bees in Your Backyard* — 595.79

REFERENCE — HEALTH
Mendelson, Zoe. *Pussypedia* — 612.6

REFERENCE — INSTRUCTIONAL MATERIALS
Brown, Amanda. ★*Spruce* — 747
Edwards, Adrienne L. *Firescaping Your Home* — 635.9
Edwards, Betty. *Drawing on the Right Side of the Brain* — 741.2
Godas, Maru. *Organic Beauty* — 646.7
Katz, Emily. *Modern Macrame* — 746.42
Oster, Emily. ★*Cribsheet* — 618.2
Rawles, James Wesley. *Tools for Survival* — 613.6
Schultz, Ken. *Ken Schultz's Essentials of Fishing* — 799.1
Zedenius, Fanny. *Macrame* — 746.42

REFERENCE — LANGUAGE LEARNING
Liddell, Henry George. *A Greek-English Lexicon* — 483
Pukui, Mary Kawena. *Hawaiian Dictionary* — 499
Stone, Jon R. ★*Latin for the Illiterati* — 473

REFERENCE — QUOTATIONS
Bartlett, John. *Bartlett's Familiar Quotations, 19th Ed.* — 808.88
Einstein, Albert. *The Ultimate Quotable Einstein* — 530.092

REFERENCE — TRAVEL GUIDES
Fili, Louise. *The Cognoscenti's Guide to Florence* — 381
Glass, Brent D. *50 Great American Places* — 973
McAlester, Virginia. *A Field Guide to American Houses* — 728
Spira, Timothy P. *Waterfalls and Wildflowers in the Southern Appalachians* — 796.5109756
Steelquist, Robert. *The Northwest Coastal Explorer* — 508
Waterman, Jonathan. *National Geographic Atlas of the National Parks* — 917.304

REFERENCE — VOCATIONAL GUIDANCE
Congdon, Lisa. *Art Inc.* — 702

REFERENCE — WEDDINGS
Diamant, Anita. *The Jewish Wedding Now* — 296.4
Monger, George. *Marriage Customs of the World* — 392.5

REFERENCE — WRITING
Booth, Wayne C. *The Craft of Research* — 001.4
Dufresne, John. *Storyville!* — 808.3
Elster, Charles Harrington. *How to Tell Fate from Destiny* — 428.1
Garner, Bryan A. *The Chicago Guide to Grammar, Usage, and Punctuation* — 428.2
Garner, Bryan A. *Garner's Modern English Usage* — 423
McKee, Robert. *Dialogue* — 809
Mosley, Walter. *Elements of Fiction* — 808.3
Oliver, Mary. *A Poetry Handbook* — 808.1
Turabian, Kate L. *Student's Guide to Writing College Papers* — 808.06
Yager, Jan. *How to Self Publish Your Book* — 070.5
★*Reference and Information Services*. Cassell, Kay Ann — 025.5

REFERENCE BOOKS
Alderfer, Jonathan K. *National Geographic Birding Essentials* — 598.072
Aronson, Joseph. *The Encyclopedia of Furniture* — 749
Brock, James P. *Kaufman Field Guide to Butterflies of North America* — 595.7
Darcey, Cheralyn. *Flowerpaedia* — 580
Davies, Simone. *The Montessori Toddler* — 371.39
Espy, Willard R. *Words to Rhyme With* — 423
Fischer, Jenna. *The Actor's Life* — 792.02
Hirschfeld, Erik. *The World's Rarest Birds* — 333.95822
Hoffman, Maggie. *Batch Cocktails* — 641.87
Howcroft, Heidi. *Garden Design* — 712
Hoyt, Erich. *Encyclopedia of Whales, Dolphins and Porpoises* — 599.5
Kampen-O'Riley, Michael. *Art Beyond the West* — 709
Kelly, Christopher R. *Am I Dying?!* — 362.1
Klein, Cheryl B. *The Magic Words* — 808.06
Lawson, Nancy. *The Humane Gardener* — 577.5
Lenburg, Jeff. *The Encyclopedia of Animated Cartoons* — 791.43
Lincoff, Gary. *The Audubon Society Field Guide to North American Mushrooms* — 579.6
Little, Elbert L. *The Audubon Society Field Guide to North American Trees* — 582.16097
Maddex, Robert L. *The U.S. Constitution A to Z* — 342.730203
McGinnis, Samuel M. ★*Peterson Field Guide to Western Reptiles and Amphibians* — 597.9
McKnight, Kent H. *A Field Guide to Mushrooms, North America* — 579.6
Meinkoth, Norman August. *The Audubon Society Field Guide to North American Seashore Creatures* — 592

AUTHOR, TITLE, SERIES AND SUBJECT INDEX

Milne, Lorus Johnson. ★ *The Audubon Society Field Guide to North American Insects and Spiders*	595.7097
Murie, Olaus J. ★ *A Field Guide to Animal Tracks*	599
Murkoff, Heidi Eisenberg. *What to Expect the First Year*	305.232
Page, Lawrence M. ★ *Peterson Field Guide to Freshwater Fishes of North America North of Mexico*	597.176
Petrides, George A. *A Field Guide to Western Trees*	582.16
Piercy, Marge. *So You Want to Write*	808.3
Rehder, Harald Alfred. *The Audubon Society Field Guide to North American Seashells*	594
Sibley, David. ★ *The Sibley Guide to Trees*	582.16097
Stokes, Donald W. *The New Stokes Field Guide to Birds.*	598
Tucker, Dennis C. *Crash Course in Library Supervision*	023
Weiss, Eben. ★ *The Ultimate Bicycle Owner's Manual*	796.6
Wilson, Ellen Judy. *Encyclopedia of the Enlightenment*	940.2
Yang, Lihui. ★ *Handbook of Chinese Mythology*	299.5
Zinsser, William Knowlton. *Writing to Learn*	808
REFERENCE BOOKS — DIRECTORIES	
Sankey, Michael L. *The Manual to Online Public Records*	025.06
REFERENCE BOOKS — ENCYCLOPEDIAS	
Znamierowski, Alfred. *The World Encyclopedia of Flags*	903
REFERENCE BOOKS — HANDBOOKS, MANUALS, ETC.	
Byers, Charles T. *Ultimate Guide Home Repair and Improvement*	643
Canterbury, Dave. *Bushcraft 101*	613.6
Cumming, Robert. *Art*	700
Green, Janice. ★ *Divorce After 50*	306.89
Horwood, Roger. *Woodworker's Handbook*	684
Jones, Sharon L. *Critical Companion to Zora Neale Hurston*	813
MacKellar, Pamela H. ★ *Winning Grants*	025.1
Magill, Pete. *Build Your Running Body*	796.42
McAlister, Michael. *Taunton's Wiring Complete*	621.3
Minden, Eliza Gaynor. *The Ballet Companion*	792.8
Neighbors, Joy. *The Family Tree Cemetery Field Guide*	929
Petersen, Grant. *Just Ride*	796.6
Pincus, Edward. *The Filmmaker's Handbook*	777
Powell, Michael. *The Acting Bible*	792.02
Siegel, Joel G. *Accounting Handbook.*	657
Sleight, Steve. *The Complete Sailing Manual*	797.1
Stanley, Mary J. *Managing Library Employees*	023
Thenell, Jan. *The Library's Crisis Communications Planner*	021.7
Townsend, Chris. *The Backpacker's Handbook*	796.51
Vnuk, Rebecca. *The Weeding Handbook*	025.2
Wayne, Tiffany K. *Critical Companion to Ralph Waldo Emerson*	814
REFERENCE BOOKS — HISTORY	
Grant, R. G. *World War I*	940.3
Grun, Bernard. ★ *The Timetables of History*	902
Tuchman, Barbara W. *March of Folly*	909.08
REFERENCE BOOKS — HUMANITIES	
Blackburn, Simon. *The Oxford Dictionary of Philosophy*	103
REFERENCE BOOKS — LANGUAGE LEARNING	
Rosten, Leo. *The New Joys of Yiddish*	422
REFERENCE BOOKS — LIBRARY SCIENCE	
Del Negro, Janice. *Folktales Aloud*	027.62
REFERENCE BOOKS — LITERATURE	
Baldick, Chris. ★ *The Oxford Dictionary of Literary Terms*	803
Hart, James David. *The Oxford Companion to American Literature*	810.9
Manguel, Alberto. *The Dictionary of Imaginary Places*	809
Wayne, Tiffany K. *Critical Companion to Ralph Waldo Emerson*	814
REFERENCE BOOKS — MEDICINE	
Kuhn, Cynthia. *Buzzed*	362.29
REFERENCE BOOKS — PERFORMING ARTS	
Barr, Patricia. *Ultimate Star Wars*	791.43
Craine, Debra. *The Oxford Dictionary of Dance*	792.8
Fischer, Jenna. *The Actor's Life*	792.02
Hischak, Thomas S. *The Oxford Companion to the American Musical*	782.1
Hoffman, Miles. *The NPR Classical Music Companion*	780.3
Muir, John Kenneth. *The Encyclopedia of Superheroes on Film and Television*	791.43
Osborne, Robert. *85 Years of the Oscar*	791.43079
Pincus, Edward. *The Filmmaker's Handbook*	777
Schonberg, Harold C. ★ *The Lives of the Great Composers*	780
Thomson, David. *The New Biographical Dictionary of Film*	791.4302
REFERENCE BOOKS — PSYCHOLOGY	
Sederer, Lloyd I. *The Family Guide to Mental Health Care*	616.89
REFERENCE BOOKS — RELIGION	
Mandel, David. *Who's Who in the Jewish Bible*	B
McBrien, Richard P. *Lives of the Popes*	B
Olson, Carl. *Historical Dictionary of Buddhism*	294.3
Strong, James. *The New Strong's Expanded Exhaustive Concordance of the Bible*	220.5
REFERENCE BOOKS — SCIENCE	
Gates, Alexander E. *Encyclopedia of Earthquakes and Volcanoes*	551.2
Tirion, Wil. *The Cambridge Star Atlas*	523.8
REFERENCE BOOKS — SPORTS	
Canterbury, Dave. *Bushcraft 101*	613.6
Geist, William. *Little League Confidential*	796.357
Magill, Pete. *Build Your Running Body*	796.42
Sleight, Steve. *The Complete Sailing Manual*	797.1
REFERENCE BOOKS — STUDY GUIDES	
Fiske, Edward B. *Fiske Guide to Getting into the Right College*	378.1
REFERENCE SERVICES (LIBRARIES)	
Cassell, Kay Ann. ★ *Reference and Information Services*	025.5
Goldsmith, Francisca. *Crash Course in Contemporary Reference*	025.5
Mulac, Carolyn. *Fundamentals of Reference*	025.5
Ross, Catherine Sheldrick. *Conducting the Reference Interview*	025.5
REFERENCE SOURCES	
Cassell, Kay Ann. ★ *Reference and Information Services*	025.5
Mulac, Carolyn. *Fundamentals of Reference*	025.5
Refined Knits. Wood, Jennifer	746.43
Reflections in Black. Willis, Deborah	770
Reflections on the Revolution in France. Burke, Edmund	944.04
REFORM JUDAISM	
Freedman, Samuel G. *Jew vs. Jew*	296
REFORMATION	
Ackroyd, Peter. *Tudors*	942.05
Borman, Tracy. *Thomas Cromwell*	B
Hendrix, Scott H. *Martin Luther*	B
MacCulloch, Diarmaid. *The Reformation*	270.6
Metaxas, Eric. *Martin Luther*	B
Oberman, Heiko Augustinus. *Luther*	B
Pettegree, Andrew. *The Book in the Renaissance*	070.5
Ryrie, Alec. *Protestants*	280
The Reformation. MacCulloch, Diarmaid	270.6
Refractive Africa. Alexander, Will	811
REFRIGERATION AND REFRIGERATING MACHINERY	
Hogge, Fred. *Of Ice and Men*	338.4
Twilley, Nicola. ★ *Frostbite*	621
REFRIGERATORS	
Twilley, Nicola. ★ *Frostbite*	621
REFUGEE CAMPS	
Ackerman, Elliot. *Places and Names*	B
Dogon, Mondiant. *Those We Throw Away Are Diamonds*	B
Hamilton, Lisa M. *The Hungry Season*	B
McCormick, Ty. *Beyond the Sand and Sea*	920
Nayeri, Dina. ★ *The Ungrateful Refugee*	362.87
Rawlence, Ben. *City of Thorns*	967.7305
Saldana, Stephanie. *What We Remember Will Be Saved*	362.7
Refugee High. Fishman, Elly	370.8
REFUGEE POLICY	
Goudeau, Jessica. ★ *After the Last Border*	362.83
REFUGEES	
Addario, Lynsey. *Of Love & War*	779
Alyan, Hala. *The Moon That Turns You Back*	811
Asbrink, Elisabeth. *And in the Vienna Woods the Trees Remain*	B
Bastianich, Lidia. *My American Dream*	B
Bittle, Jake. ★ *The Great Displacement*	362.87
Campbell, Deborah. *A Disappearance in Damascus*	365
Chung, Vinh. *Where the Wind Leads*	B
Clarke, Thurston. *Honorable Exit*	959.704
Dogon, Mondiant. *Those We Throw Away Are Diamonds*	B
Dudley, Steven S. *MS-13*	364.106
Dutta, Sunil. *Stealing Green Mangoes*	973
Eder, Mari K. *The Girls Who Stepped Out of Line*	920
Fleming, Melissa. *A Hope More Powerful Than the Sea*	956.9104
Gatrell, Peter. *The Unsettling of Europe*	304.8
Gewen, Barry. ★ *The Inevitability of Tragedy*	B
Girma, Haben. *Haben*	B
Hamilton, Lisa M. *The Hungry Season*	B
Henderson, Bruce B. *Sons and Soldiers*	940.53
Johnson, Kirk W. *The Fishermen and the Dragon*	976.4
Kassabova, Kapka. *Border*	949.9
Khakpour, Porochista. *Brown Album*	304.8
Khan, Yasmin. *Ripe Figs*	641.595
Klare, Michael T. *All Hell Breaking Loose*	355.20973
Lapierre, Dominique. *The City of Joy*	954
Li, Zhuqing. *Daughters of the Flower Fragrant Garden*	951.04

PUBLIC LIBRARY CORE COLLECTION: NONFICTION
Twentieth Edition

Lichtblau, Eric. *Return to the Reich*	B
Malhotra, Aanchal. *Remnants of Partition*	954.04
Mardini, Yusra. *Butterfly*	B
McCormick, Ty. *Beyond the Sand and Sea*	920
Merriman, Helena. ★*Tunnel 29*	943
Mohan, Rohini. *The Seasons of Trouble*	954.9303
Molnar, Petra. *The Walls Have Eyes*	363.28
Moore, Wayetu. *The Dragons, the Giant, the Women*	B
Mufleh, Luma. ★*Learning America*	371.826
Nasaw, David. *The Last Million*	940.53
Nayeri, Dina. ★*The Ungrateful Refugee*	362.87
Nguyen, Bich Minh. *Owner of a Lonely Heart*	B
Nguyen, Viet Thanh. ★*A Man of Two Faces*	B
O'Donnell, Svenja. *Inge's War*	943.086
Pablo Cruz, Rosayra. *The Book of Rosy*	B
Passarlay, Gulwali. *The Lightless Sky*	B
Paxson, Margaret. *The Plateau*	362.87
Pearlman, Wendy. *We Crossed a Bridge and It Trembled*	956.9104
Pham, Andrew X. ★*The Eaves of Heaven*	B
Pipher, Mary Bray. *The Middle of Everywhere*	305.9
Pitzer, Andrea. *The Secret History of Vladimir Nabokov*	813
Saldana, Stephanie. *What We Remember Will Be Saved*	362.7
Schindler, Meriel. *The Lost Cafe Schindler*	943.64
Slouka, Mark. *Nobody's Son*	B
Taing, Mae Bunseng. *Under the Naga Tail*	B
Thant Myint-U. *The Hidden History of Burma*	959.105
Tran, Phuc. ★*Sigh, Gone*	B
Trebincevic, Kenan. *The Bosnia List*	B
Ung, Loung. *First They Killed My Father*	959.604
Ung, Loung. *Lucky Child*	B
Vang, Mai Der. *Afterland*	811
Zia, Helen. *Last Boat Out of Shanghai*	951.04

REFUGEES, AFGHAN
Passarlay, Gulwali. *The Lightless Sky*	B

REFUGEES, AFRICAN
St. John, Warren. *Outcasts United*	B

REFUGEES, ARMENIAN
Bogosian, Eric. *Operation Nemesis*	956.62
Mackeen, Dawn Anahid. *The Hundred-Year Walk*	956.6

REFUGEES, BOSNIAN
Hemon, Aleksandar. *My Parents*	814

REFUGEES, CAMBODIAN
Ung, Loung. *First They Killed My Father*	959.604

REFUGEES, HUNGARIAN
Michener, James A. *The Bridge at Andau*	943.9

REFUGEES, JEWISH
Asbrink, Elisabeth. *And in the Vienna Woods the Trees Remain*	B
Finkelstein, Daniel. *Two Roads Home*	920
Freeman, Hadley. *House of Glass*	B
Frenkel, Francoise. *A Bookshop in Berlin*	B
Garrett, Leah. *X Troop*	940.54
Golinkin, Lev. *A Backpack, a Bear, and Eight Crates of Vodka*	B
Hochschild, Adam. *Rebel Cinderella*	B
Katin, Miriam. *We Are on Our Own*	741.5
Marton, Kati. *The Great Escape*	920
Nasaw, David. *The Last Million*	940.53
Parkin, Simon. *The Island of Extraordinary Captives*	940.53
Pick-Goslar, Hannah Elizabeth. ★*My Friend Anne Frank*	B

REFUGEES, PALESTINIAN
Ahmad, Aeham. *The Pianist from Syria*	B
Tolan, Sandy. *Children of the Stone*	780

REFUGEES, RWANDAN
Dogon, Mondiant. *Those We Throw Away Are Diamonds*	B

REFUGEES, SALVADORAN
Zamora, Javier. ★*Solito*	B

REFUGEES, SOMALI
Hirsi Ali, Ayaan. ★*Infidel*	B
Rawlence, Ben. *City of Thorns*	967.7305
Steinberg, Jonny. *A Man of Good Hope*	B

REFUGEES, SUDANESE
Deng, Alephonsion. *They Poured Fire on Us from the Sky*	B

REFUGEES, SYRIAN
Fleming, Melissa. *A Hope More Powerful Than the Sea*	956.9104
Samer. *The Raqqa Diaries*	956.9104

REFUGEES, TIBETAN
Demick, Barbara. *Eat the Buddha*	951

REFUGEES, VIETNAMESE
Lieu, Susan. ★*The Manicurist's Daughter*	B

Tran, Phuc. ★*Sigh, Gone*	B
Yip-Williams, Julie. ★*The Unwinding of the Miracle*	973

Regan, Iliana
Fieldwork	B

REGENCY PERIOD (1811-1820)
Koch, Bea. *Mad and Bad*	920
Morrison, Robert. *The Regency Years*	941.07
The Regency Years. Morrison, Robert	941.07
★*Regenesis*. Monbiot, George	338.1

REGGAE MUSIC
Garnice, Michael. *The Ultimate Guide to Great Reggae*	781.646
Grant, Colin. *The Natural Mystics*	B

REGGAE MUSICIANS
Garnice, Michael. *The Ultimate Guide to Great Reggae*	781.646
Grant, Colin. *The Natural Mystics*	B

REGICIDE
Ackroyd, Peter. *Rebellion*	941.06
Jager, Eric. *Blood Royal*	944.026

REGIME CHANGE
Foer, Franklin. ★*The Last Politician*	973.934
Karl, Jonathan. *Betrayal*	973.933
Popkin, Jeremy D. *A New World Begins*	944.04

REGIONALISM
Fischer, David Hackett. ★*African Founders*	973
Foroohar, Rana. *Homecoming*	338.6
Mikanowski, Jacob. ★*Goodbye, Eastern Europe*	947
Perry, Imani. ★*South to America*	917
Podemski, Max. *A Paradise of Small Houses*	363.5
Registers of Illuminated Villages. Faizullah, Tarfia	811

REGRESSION (CIVILIZATION)
Harper, Kyle. *The Fate of Rome*	937

REGRET
Egan, Kerry. *On Living*	170
Keaton, Diane. ★*Brother & Sister*	B
Peyser, Marc N. *Hissing Cousins*	B
Satrapi, Marjane. *Embroideries*	741.5
Sauls, Scott. *Beautiful People Don't Just Happen*	248.8
Shehadeh, Raja. ★*We Could Have Been Friends, My Father and I*	B

REHABILITATION
Akbar, Kaveh. *Calling a Wolf a Wolf*	811
Belkin, Lisa. *Genealogy of a Murder*	362.88
Burton, Susan. *Becoming Ms. Burton*	B
Canfield, Jack. *The 30 Day Sobriety Solution*	616.89
Dresner, Amy. *My Fair Junkie*	B
Fisher, Carl Erik. ★*The Urge*	362.29
Gaffney, Ginger. *Half Broke*	B
Hardy, Jason Matthew. ★*The Second Chance Club*	364.6
Johnston, Ann Dowsett. *Drink*	362.292
Raban, Jonathan. *Father and Son*	B
Rao, Cheeni. *In Hanuman's Hands*	B
Sweeney, Jennifer. *Literacy*	027.62
Wilson, Chris. *The Master Plan*	B

Rehak, Melanie
Girl Sleuth	813

Rehder, Harald Alfred
The Audubon Society Field Guide to North American Seashells	594

Rehm, Diane
On My Own	B
★*When My Time Comes*	179.7

REHM, DIANE
Rehm, Diane. *On My Own*	B

REHM, JOHN B.
Rehm, Diane. *On My Own*	B

Rehman, Sabeeha
Threading My Prayer Rug	305.8

REHMAN, SABEEHA
Rehman, Sabeeha. *Threading My Prayer Rug*	305.8

REICH, WILHELM, 1897-1957
Laing, Olivia. *Everybody*	323

Reichl, Ruth
Comfort Me with Apples	B
Garlic and Sapphires	B
My Kitchen Year	641.5
★*Save Me the Plums*	B

REICHL, RUTH
Reichl, Ruth. *Comfort Me with Apples*	B
Reichl, Ruth. *Garlic and Sapphires*	B
Reichl, Ruth. *My Kitchen Year*	641.5

AUTHOR, TITLE, SERIES AND SUBJECT INDEX

Reichl, Ruth. ★*Save Me the Plums* — B
Reid, Anna
  Leningrad — 940.54
Reid, David
  The Brazen Age — 974.7
Reid, John W.
  Ever Green — 634.9
Reid, Joy-Ann Lomena
  ★*Medgar and Myrlie* — 920
Reid, Rob
  ★*200+ Original and Adapted Story Program Activities* — 027.62
Reid, Stuart A.
  The Lumumba Plot — 967.51
Reid, T. R.
  A Fine Mess — 336.200973
Reign of Terror. Ackerman, Spencer — 973.931
The *Reign* of Wolf 21. McIntyre, Rick — 599.773
Reilly, Ryan J.
  ★*Sedition Hunters* — 364.1
Reimagining Death. Herring, Lucinda — 393
Reiner, Andrew
  Better Boys, Better Men — 155.43
REINHARDT, DJANGO, 1910-1953
  Dregni, Michael. *Django* — B
Reinhart, Peter
  Perfect Pan Pizza — 641.82
Reinventing Comics. McCloud, Scott — 741.5
Reinventing The Bazaar. McMillan, John — 330.12
Reiss, Benjamin
  Wild Nights — 616.8
Reiss, Mike
  Springfield Confidential — 791.45
Reiss, Tom
  The Black Count — B
Reiter, Ben
  Astroball — 796.357
Reitman, Janet
  Inside Scientology — 299
REITSCH, HANNAH
  Mulley, Clare. *The Women Who Flew for Hitler* — 920
REJECTION
  Corral, Eduardo C. *Guillotine* — 811.6
  Preszler, Trent. *Little and Often* — B
  Wilson, Rebel. *Rebel Rising* — B
Rejoicing in Lament. Billings, J. Todd — 248.8
REJUVENATION
  Esmonde-White, Miranda. *Aging Backwards* — 613.7
Rekdal, Paisley
  Nightingale — 811
  West — 811
RELATIONSHIPS BETWEEN YOUNG WOMEN AND OLDER MEN
  Alden, Ginger. *Elvis and Ginger* — B
  Eyman, Scott. *Charlie Chaplin vs. America* — B
  Mann, William J. *Bogie & Bacall* — 920
RELATIVITY (PHYSICS)
  Einstein, Albert. ★*The Evolution of Physics* — 530
  Einstein, Albert. *The Meaning of Relativity* — 530.11
  Einstein, Albert. ★*A Stubbornly Persistent Illusion* — 530.092
  Fletcher, Seth. *Einstein's Shadow* — 523.8
  Greene, B. ★*The Elegant Universe* — 539.7
  Greene, B. ★*The Hidden Reality* — 530.12
  Hawking, Stephen. ★*The Universe in a Nutshell* — 530.12
  Rovelli, Carlo. ★*Seven Brief Lessons on Physics* — 530
  Sanders, Ella Frances. *Eating the Sun* — 520
  Stanley, Matthew. *Einstein's War* — 530
  Tyson, Neil deGrasse. *Welcome to the Universe* — 523.1
RELAXATION
  Benson, Herbert. *The Relaxation Response* — 155.9
  Grossman, Gail Boorstein. *Restorative Yoga for Life* — 613.7
  Heller, Rick. *Secular Meditation* — 158.1
  McGovern, Anna. *Pottering* — 158.1
The *Relaxation* Response. Benson, Herbert — 155.9
Relentless Spirit. Franklin, Missy — B
RELES, ABE, 1906-1941
  Cannell, Michael T. *A Brotherhood Betrayed* — B
RELIABILITY
  Morris, Errol. *Believing Is Seeing* — 770.9

RELICS
  Raffa, Guy P. *Dante's Bones* — 851
RELIEF PITCHERS (BASEBALL)
  Rivera, Mariano. *The Closer* — B
RELIGION AND CIVILIZATION
  Holland, Tom. *Dominion* — 261
  Stanley, Brian. *Christianity in the Twentieth Century* — 270.8
RELIGION AND CULTURE
  Abdul Rauf, Feisal. *Moving the Mountain* — 297
  Armstrong, Karen. *The Lost Art of Scripture* — 208
  Holland, Tom. *Dominion* — 261
  Kennedy, Hugh. ★*The Great Arab Conquests* — 297.09
  Kugel, James L. *The Great Shift* — 296.3
  Miles, Jack. *Religion as We Know It* — 200.9
  Nasr, Seyyed Hossein. *Islam* — 297
  Orth, Stephan. *Couchsurfing in Iran* — 955.06
  Rohr, Richard. *The Universal Christ* — 232
  Sebag-Montefiore, Simon. *Jerusalem* — 956.94
  Stanley, Brian. *Christianity in the Twentieth Century* — 270.8
  Weatherford, J. McIver. *Genghis Khan and the Quest for God* — 323.44
  Weisman, Steven R. *The Chosen Wars* — 296.0973
RELIGION AND HOMOSEXUALITY
  Thomas, R. Eric. *Here for It* — B
RELIGION AND LITERATURE
  Greenblatt, Stephen. *The Rise and Fall of Adam and Eve* — 233
RELIGION AND POLITICS
  Berkshire, Jennifer. *The Education Wars* — 371.01
  Cornwell, John. *Hitler's Pope* — B
  Douthat, Ross Gregory. *To Change the Church* — 230
  Du Mez, Kristin Kobes. *Jesus and John Wayne* — 277.308
  Eisner, Peter. *The Pope's Last Crusade* — 282.092
  FitzGerald, Frances. *The Evangelicals* — 277
  Fraser, Antonia. *Faith and Treason* — 942.06
  Ghattas, Kim. *Black Wave* — 955.05
  Griffith, R. Marie. *Moral Combat* — 261.8
  McCammon, Sarah. ★*The Exvangelicals* — 277.308
  Mead, Walter Russell. *The Arc of a Covenant* — 327.73
  Soyinka, Wole. *Of Africa* — 960
  Wallis, Jim. *The False White Gospel* — 261.7
  Ward, Jon. *Testimony* — 277.308
  Weatherford, J. McIver. *Genghis Khan and the Quest for God* — 323.44
  Wills, Garry. *The Future of the Catholic Church with Pope Francis* — 282.09
  Woolf, Greg. *Rome* — 937
RELIGION AND SCIENCE
  Al-Khalili, Jim. *The House of Wisdom* — 509
  Alexander, Amir R. *Infinitesimal* — 511
  Brown, Nancy Marie. *The Abacus and the Cross* — B
  Collins, Francis S. *The Language of God* — 215
  Dolnick, Edward. *Seeds of Life* — 612.6
  Feynman, Richard P. ★*The Meaning of It All* — 500
  Grant, Edward. *Science and Religion, 400 B.C. To A.D. 1550* — 201
  Lightman, Alan P. *Searching for Stars on an Island in Maine* — 523.1
  Lightman, Alan P. *The Transcendent Brain* — 215
  Markel, Howard. *Origin Story* — 576.8
  Nye, Bill. *Undeniable* — 576.8
  Roach, Mary. ★*Spook* — 129
  Sacks, Jonathan. *The Great Partnership* — 201
  Sheldrake, Rupert. *Science and Spiritual Practices* — 201
  Townsend, Alan R. *This Ordinary Stardust* — B
  Wilson, Derek K. *A Magical World* — 261.55
RELIGION AND SOCIAL PROBLEMS
  Ricketts, Rachel. ★*Do Better* — 305.800973
RELIGION AND STATE
  Weatherford, J. McIver. *Genghis Khan and the Quest for God* — 323.44
Religion and the Rise of Capitalism. Friedman, Benjamin M. — 330.12
Religion as We Know It. Miles, Jack — 200.9
Religion for Atheists. De Botton, Alain — 200
RELIGION IN THE PUBLIC SCHOOLS
  Prothero, Stephen R. *Religious Literacy* — 200.71
RELIGIONS
  Abdul Rauf, Feisal. *Moving the Mountain* — 297
  Akyol, Mustafa. *The Islamic Jesus* — 297.2
  Alexander, Amir R. *Infinitesimal* — 511
  Ali-Karamali, Sumbul. *Demystifying Shariah* — 340.5
  Armstrong, Karen. *The Bible* — 220.09
  Armstrong, Karen. ★*The Great Transformation* — 200.9
  Armstrong, Karen. *A History of God* — 202
  Armstrong, Karen. ★*Islam* — 297

PUBLIC LIBRARY CORE COLLECTION: NONFICTION
Twentieth Edition

Armstrong, Karen. *Jerusalem*	956.94
Armstrong, Karen. *The Lost Art of Scripture*	208
Aslan, Reza. *God*	211
Augustine. *Confessions*	B
Belser, Julia Watts. ★*Loving Our Own Bones*	296
Bidwell, Duane R. *When One Religion Isn't Enough*	261.2
Bignon, Guillaume. *Confessions of a French Atheist*	239
Blum, Edward J. *The Color of Christ*	232
Brooks, Geraldine. *Nine Parts of Desire*	305.48
Campbell, Joseph. *The Masks of God*	201.3
Campbell, Joseph. *The Power of Myth*	201.3
Chevannes, Barry. *Rastafari*	299
Chittister, Joan. *Following the Path*	248.4
Collins, Francis S. *The Language of God*	215
Curtis, Edward E. *Muslims in America*	305.6
Dalai Lama. *The Second Dalai Lama*	294.3
Dennett, D. C. *Breaking the Spell*	200
Doniger, Wendy. *On Hinduism*	294.5
Du Mez, Kristin Kobes. *Jesus and John Wayne*	277.308
Ehrman, Bart D. *The Triumph of Christianity*	270.1
Francis. *Life*	B
Friedman, Benjamin M. *Religion and the Rise of Capitalism*	330.12
Gates, Henry Louis. ★*The Black Church*	277
Gerard, Sarah. *Sunshine State*	814
Goldberg, Philip. *American Veda*	294.509
Goodman, Martin. ★*A History of Judaism*	296.09
Gosden, Chris. *Magic*	133.4
Grieve, Paul. *A Brief Guide to Islam*	297
Griffith, R. Marie. *Moral Combat*	261.8
Griswold, Eliza. *The Tenth Parallel*	297.2
Hardacre, Helen. *Shinto*	299.5
Harrington, Joel F. *Dangerous Mystic*	B
Hecht, Jennifer Michael. *Doubt*	121
Heidegger, Martin. ★*Being and Time*	111
Hexham, Irving. *Understanding World Religions*	200
Hitchens, Christopher. *The Four Horsemen*	211
Holifield, E. Brooks. *Theology in America*	230
Hughes, Bettany. *Istanbul*	949.61
Hutton, Ronald. *The Triumph of the Moon*	133.4
Ignatieff, Michael. *On Consolation*	152.4
James, William. ★*The Varieties of Religious Experience*	204
Jamison, Kay Redfield. *Fires in the Dark*	616.89
Jennings, Ken. ★*100 Places to See After You Die*	202
Johnson, Ian. *The Souls of China*	200.951
Kamen, Henry. *The Spanish Inquisition*	272
Kennedy, Hugh. ★*The Great Arab Conquests*	297.09
Kugel, James L. *The Great Shift*	296.3
Lambert, Malcolm. *God's Armies*	956
Lattin, Don. *The Harvard Psychedelic Club*	973.922092
Levine, Amy-Jill. *The Bible with and Without Jesus*	220.6
Lewis, James R. *Legitimating New Religions*	200
Liao, Yiwu. *God Is Red*	275
Mackall, Joe. *Plain Secrets*	289.7
Manseau, Peter. *Objects of Devotion*	277
Marty, Martin E. *Pilgrims in Their Own Land*	200
McLaren, Brian D. *Do I Stay Christian?*	270.8
Miles, Jack. *God in the Qur'an*	297.2
Miles, Jack. *Religion as We Know It*	200.9
Nagassar, Rohadi. *When We Belong*	254
Olson, Roger E. ★*Handbook of Denominations in the United States*	200.973
Ozment, Katherine. *Grace Without God*	200.973
Peters, Rebecca Todd. *Trust Women*	362.1988
Phillips, Maya. *Nerd*	302.23
Popova, Maria. *Figuring*	920
Power, Carla. *If the Oceans Were Ink*	B
Prothero, Stephen R. *God Is Not One*	200
Prothero, Stephen R. *God the Bestseller*	070.5
Prothero, Stephen R. *Religious Literacy*	200.71
Rady, Martyn C. *The Middle Kingdoms*	943
Reitman, Janet. *Inside Scientology*	299
Rohr, Richard. *The Universal Christ*	232
Sarna, Jonathan D. ★*American Judaism*	296
Sengupta, Hindol. *Being Hindu*	294.5
Shachtman, Tom. ★*Rumspringa*	305.235
Spence, Jonathan D. *God's Chinese Son*	951
Stanley, Brian. *Christianity in the Twentieth Century*	270.8
Taylor, Barbara Brown. *Holy Envy*	B
Tickle, Phyllis. *The Great Emergence*	270.8
Volf, Miroslav. *Life Worth Living*	113
Waldman, Steven. *Sacred Liberty*	341.4
Weatherford, J. McIver. *Genghis Khan and the Quest for God*	323.44
Weisman, Steven R. *The Chosen Wars*	296.0973
Wilkinson, Richard H. ★*The Complete Gods and Goddesses of Ancient Egypt*	299
Wilkinson, Toby A. H. *The Nile*	962
Williams, Juan. *This Far by Faith*	200
Wilson, Derek. *Out of the Storm*	B
Wiman, Christian. *He Held Radical Light*	814
Wintz, Jack. *Will I See My Dog in Heaven?*	231.7
Wray, T. J. *The Birth of Satan*	235
Wright, Lawrence. *Going Clear*	299
Zuckerman, Phil. *Living the Secular Life*	211

RELIGIOUS ADHERENTS

Bidwell, Duane R. *When One Religion Isn't Enough*	261.2

RELIGIOUS ART AND SYMBOLISM

Beard, Mary. ★*How Do We Look*	704.9

RELIGIOUS ARTICLES

Manseau, Peter. *Objects of Devotion*	277

RELIGIOUS COMMUNITIES

Fersko, Diana. ★*We Need to Talk About Antisemitism*	305.892
Wayland-Smith, Ellen. *Oneida*	307.77

RELIGIOUS CONVERSION

Cervantes, Fernando. *Conquistadores*	970.01
James, William. ★*The Varieties of Religious Experience*	204

RELIGIOUS CONVERTS

Carranca, Adriana. *Soul by Soul*	230

RELIGIOUS CORRUPTION

Posner, Gerald L. *God's Bankers*	364.16

RELIGIOUS DISCRIMINATION

Berkshire, Jennifer. *The Education Wars*	371.01
Fersko, Diana. ★*We Need to Talk About Antisemitism*	305.892
Muhammad, Ibtihaj. *Proud*	B
Nussbaum, Martha Craven. *The New Religious Intolerance*	201.723

RELIGIOUS EDUCATION

Prothero, Stephen R. *Religious Literacy*	200.71

RELIGIOUS ETHICS

Archibald, John. *Shaking the Gates of Hell*	B
Price, Reynolds. *A Serious Way of Wondering*	241

RELIGIOUS FANATICISM

Glatt, John. *The Doomsday Mother*	364.152
Roy, Jessica. *American Girls*	305.48
Sharlet, Jeff. ★*The Undertow*	322

RELIGIOUS HOLIDAYS

Goldman, Ari L. *Being Jewish*	296.4

RELIGIOUS LEADERS

Armstrong, Karen. *Muhammad*	B
Arrington, Leonard J. *Brigham Young*	B
Brown, Nancy Marie. *The Abacus and the Cross*	B
Hazleton, Lesley. *The First Muslim*	B
Iyer, Pico. *The Open Road*	B
Jebara, Mohamad. *Muhammad, the World-Changer*	B
Metaxas, Eric. *Martin Luther*	B
Telushkin, Joseph. *Rebbe*	296.833
Wilson, Derek. *Out of the Storm*	B

RELIGIOUS LIFE

Akyol, Mustafa. ★*Reopening Muslim Minds*	297.09
Armstrong, Karen. *The Case for God*	211
Armstrong, Karen. *The Spiral Staircase*	B
Curtis, Edward E. *Muslims in America*	305.6
Dalrymple, William. *Nine Lives*	294
De Botton, Alain. *Religion for Atheists*	200
DeSteno, David. *How God Works*	200.1
Dokun, Chanel. *Life Starts Now*	248.8
Downey, Kirstin. *Isabella*	B
Girzone, Joseph F. *Never Alone*	248.4
Guha, Ramachandra. *Gandhi Before India*	B
Hays, Katie. *Family of Origin, Family of Choice*	248.8086
Masuno, Shunmy. *The Art of Simple Living*	294.3
Moore, Thomas. *Ageless Soul*	155.67
Namath, Joe Willie. ★*All the Way*	B
Nockels, Christy. *The Life You Long For*	248.8
Oakes, John G. H. ★*The Fast*	613.2
Pinn, Anthony B. *The Black Practice of Disbelief*	211
Rowan, Barry L. *The Spiritual Art of Business*	261.8
Sogyal. *The Tibetan Book of Living and Dying*	294.3
Taylor, Barbara Brown. *Holy Envy*	B

AUTHOR, TITLE, SERIES AND SUBJECT INDEX

Telushkin, Joseph. *Rebbe*	296.833
Wright, Lawrence. *Going Clear*	299
Religious Literacy. Prothero, Stephen R.	200.71

RELIGIOUS PERSECUTION

AL Samawi, Mohammed. *The Fox Hunt*	953
Aly, Gotz. *Europe Against the Jews*	305.892
Dwork, Deborah. ★*Holocaust*	940
Evans, Richard J. *The Third Reich in Power, 1933-1939*	943.086
Frank, Anne. ★*The Diary of a Young Girl*	940.53
Friedlander, Saul. *Nazi Germany and the Jews*	940.53
Friedlander, Saul. *Nazi Germany and the Jews*	940.53
Gies, Miep. ★*Anne Frank Remembered*	B
Grose, Peter. *A Good Place to Hide*	940.53
Gross, Jan Tomasz. *Neighbors*	940.53
Hayes, Peter. *Why?*	940.53
Kertzer, David I. *The Pope at War*	940.53
Kramer, Clara. *Clara's War*	B
Mahjoub, Jamal. *A Line in the River*	962.404
Morris, Marc. *A Great and Terrible King*	B
Murphy, Andrew R. *William Penn*	B
Pearlman, Wendy. *We Crossed a Bridge and It Trembled*	956.9104
Rees, Laurence. *Auschwitz*	940.53
Rees, Laurence. *The Holocaust*	940.53
Rounding, Virginia. *The Burning Time*	272
Schindler, Meriel. *The Lost Cafe Schindler*	943.64
Shapiro, James. *The Year of Lear*	822.33
Simon, Marie. *Underground in Berlin*	B
Talty, Stephan. *The Good Assassin*	364.15
Walker, Ronald W. ★*Massacre at Mountain Meadows*	979.2

RELIGIOUS PLURALISM

Lewis, James R. *Legitimating New Religions*	200
Prothero, Stephen R. *God the Bestseller*	070.5

RELIGIOUS POETRY

Hafiz. ★*The Gift*	891
Jall al-Dn Rm. *Rumi*	891
Karr, Mary. *Tropic of Squalor*	811
Wicker, Marcus. *Silencer*	811

RELIGIOUS PSYCHOLOGY

DeSteno, David. *How God Works*	200.1
Hagglund, Martin. *This Life*	110
James, William. ★*The Varieties of Religious Experience*	204
Lewis, James R. *Legitimating New Religions*	200
Moore, Thomas. *Ageless Soul*	155.67
West, Cait. ★*Rift*	B

RELIGIOUS REFORMERS

Massing, Michael. *Fatal Discord*	920
Metaxas, Eric. *Martin Luther*	B

RELIGIOUS TERRORISM

Armstrong, Karen. *Fields of Blood*	201
Murakami, Haruki. *Underground*	364.15

RELIGIOUS THOUGHT

Friedman, Benjamin M. *Religion and the Rise of Capitalism*	330.12

RELIGIOUS TOLERANCE

Asbridge, Thomas S. ★*The Crusades*	909.07
Nussbaum, Martha Craven. *The New Religious Intolerance*	201.723
Weatherford, J. McIver. *Genghis Khan and the Quest for God*	323.44
★*Relinquished*. Sisson, Gretchen E.	362.734
★*Reluctant Genius*. Gray, Charlotte	920
The Remarkable Life of the Skin. Lyman, Monty	612.7

REMARRIAGE

Crawford, Robert. *Eliot After the Waste Land*	B
Mayes, Frances. *Bella Tuscany*	945
Patchett, Ann. *This Is the Story of a Happy Marriage*	B
Reichl, Ruth. *Comfort Me with Apples*	B

Rembert, Winfred

Chasing Me to My Grave	B

REMBERT, WINFRED

Rembert, Winfred. *Chasing Me to My Grave*	B

REMBRANDT HARMENSZOON VAN RIJN, 1606-1669

Blom, Onno. *Young Rembrandt*	B
Remembered Rapture. hooks, bell	808
Remembering Peasants. Joyce, Patrick	305.5
★*Rememberings*. O'Connor, Sinead	B
★*Remembrance*. Bradbury, Ray	813

REMINISCING IN OLD AGE

Angelou, Maya. *Wouldn't Take Nothing for My Journey Now*	814
McPhee, John. *Tabula Rasa; V.1*	818
Ondaatje, Michael. *A Year of Last Things*	811

Von Drehle, David. ★*The Book of Charlie*	B
Remix. Hays, Jeanine	747
Remix. Lessig, Lawrence	346.7304
Remnants of Partition. Malhotra, Aanchal	954.04

Remnick, David

The Bridge	B
Holding the Note	781.64
Lenin's Tomb	947.085
Remodelista. Carlson, Julie	648
Remodelista. Guralnick, Margot	747

REMORSE

Ingall, Marjorie. *Sorry, Sorry, Sorry*	158.2

REMOTELY OPERATED SUBMERSIBLES

Davis, Joshua. *Spare Parts*	629.8

Rempel, William C.

The Gambler	B

RENAISSANCE (1300-1600)

Benner, Erica. *Be Like the Fox*	B
Bergreen, Laurence. *In Search of a Kingdom*	B
Bergreen, Laurence. *Marco Polo*	B
Bergreen, Laurence. *Over the Edge of the World*	B
Borman, Tracy. *Elizabeth's Women*	B
Borman, Tracy. *The Private Lives of the Tudors*	920
Bradford, Sarah. *Lucrezia Borgia*	B
Downey, Kirstin. *Isabella*	B
Fauber, L. S. *Heaven on Earth*	B
Frampton, Saul. *When I Am Playing with My Cat, How Do I Know She Is Not Playing with Me?*	844
Fraser, Antonia. *Faith and Treason*	942.06
Fraser, Antonia. *Mary, Queen of Scots*	B
Fraser, Antonia. ★*The Wives of Henry VIII*	942.05
Goldstone, Nancy Bazelon. *The Rival Queens*	944
Goodman, Ruth. *How to Be a Tudor*	942.05
Greenblatt, Stephen. ★*The Swerve*	940.2
Greenblatt, Stephen. ★*Will in the World*	B
Guy, John. *Hunting the Falcon*	B
Hibbert, Christopher. *The Borgias and Their Enemies*	920
Hibbert, Christopher. *The House of Medici*	920
Isaacson, Walter. ★*Leonardo Da Vinci*	B
Kamen, Henry. *The Spanish Inquisition*	272
Kaufmann, Miranda. *Black Tudors*	941
King, Ross. *Bookseller of Florence*	381
King, Ross. *Brunelleschi's Dome*	726.6
King, Ross. *Michelangelo & the Pope's Ceiling*	759.5
Lester, Toby. *Da Vinci's Ghost*	741.092
Lovell, Mary S. *Bess of Hardwick*	B
MacCulloch, Diarmaid. *The Reformation*	270.6
Manchester, William. *A World Lit Only by Fire*	940.2
Massing, Michael. *Fatal Discord*	920
Metaxas, Eric. *Martin Luther*	B
Meyer, G. J. *The Borgias*	920
Mortimer, Ian. *The Time Traveler's Guide to Elizabethan England*	942.05
Norwich, John Julius. *A History of Venice*	945
Norwich, John Julius. *Shakespeare's Kings*	822.33
Nuland, Sherwin B. *Leonardo Da Vinci*	B
Paranque, Estelle. *Blood, Fire & Gold*	920
Pettegree, Andrew. *The Book in the Renaissance*	070.5
Porter, Linda. *Katherine the Queen*	B
Ronald, Susan. *The Pirate Queen*	B
Rounding, Virginia. *The Burning Time*	272
Russell, Gareth. *Young and Damned and Fair*	B
Spoto, Donald. *Joan*	B
Starkey, David. *Six Wives*	942.05
Strathern, Paul. *The Borgias*	945.06
Strathern, Paul. *The Florentines*	945
Strathern, Paul. *The Medici*	945.5
Tallis, Nicola. *Crown of Blood*	B
Weir, Alison. *The Children of Henry VIII*	B
Weir, Alison. *Henry VIII*	B
Weir, Alison. *The Lady in the Tower*	B
Weir, Alison. *The Life of Elizabeth I*	B
Weir, Alison. *The Lost Tudor Princess*	B
Weir, Alison. *Mary, Queen of Scots, and the Murder of Lord Darnley*	941.105
Weir, Alison. *The Six Wives of Henry VIII*	942.05
Weir, Alison. *The Wars of the Roses*	942.04
Wilson, Derek. *Out of the Storm*	B
Wilson, Derek K. *A Magical World*	261.55
Wilson-Lee, Edward. ★*The Catalogue of Shipwrecked Books*	B

PUBLIC LIBRARY CORE COLLECTION: NONFICTION
Twentieth Edition

A Renaissance of Our Own. Cargle, Rachel Elizabeth — B
RENAISSANCE SCIENCE
   Alexander, Amir R. *Infinitesimal* — 511
   Fauber, L. S. *Heaven on Earth* — B
Renard, John
   The Handy Islam Answer Book — 297
Rendezvous with Destiny. Fullilove, Michael — 973.917092
Rendgen, Sandra
   Understanding the World — 741.6
Renehan, Edward
   Commodore — B
RENEWABLE ENERGY INDUSTRY AND TRADE
   Keefe, Bob. *Clean Economy Now* — 333.79
RENEWABLE ENERGY SOURCES
   Humes, Edward. ★*Total Garbage* — 628.4
   Keefe, Bob. *Clean Economy Now* — 333.79
   Miller, Char. *Gifford Pinchot and the Making of Modern Environmentalism* — B
   Sachs, Jeffrey. *The Age of Sustainable Development* — 338.9
   Scheyder, Ernest. *The War Below* — 333.7
   Yergin, Daniel. *The New Map* — 333.79
   Yunus, Muhammad. *A World of Three Zeros* — 330
RENEWABLE RESOURCE MANAGEMENT
   Sachs, Jeffrey. *The Age of Sustainable Development* — 338.9
Renia's Diary. Spiegel, Renia — B
Renkl, Margaret
   The Comfort of Crows — 814.6
RENKL, MARGARET
   Renkl, Margaret. *The Comfort of Crows* — 814.6
Renner, Rebecca
   ★*Gator Country* — 364.16
Renoir's Dancer. Hewitt, Catherine — B
RENOVATION (ARCHITECTURE)
   Finkelstein, Elizabeth. *Cheap Old Houses* — 643
   Mayes, Frances. *Under the Tuscan Sun* — 945
RENT AND RENTING
   Ehrenreich, Barbara. ★*Nickel and Dimed* — B
The Renunciations. Kelly, Donika — 811
★*Reopening* Muslim Minds. Akyol, Mustafa — 297.09
Reorganized Religion. Smietana, Bob — 262.001
REPARATIONS
   Berry, Mary Frances. *My Face Is Black Is True* — B
   Ellsworth, Scott. *The Ground Breaking* — 976.6
   Kaiser, Menachem. *Plunder* — 940.53
   MacMillan, Margaret. *Paris 1919* — 940.3
REPARATIONS FOR HISTORICAL INJUSTICES
   Montero, David. ★*The Stolen Wealth of Slavery* — 381
REPATRIATION
   Ishikawa, Masaji. ★*A River in Darkness* — B
REPENTANCE
   Dante Alighieri. *Purgatorio* — 851
   Ruttenberg, Danya. *On Repentance and Repair* — 202
Report from Ground Zero. Smith, Dennis — 974.7
REPORT WRITING
   Strunk, William. ★*The Elements of Style* — 808
   Turabian, Kate L. *Student's Guide to Writing College Papers* — 808.06
Reporter. Hersh, Seymour M.
A Reporter's Life. Cronkite, Walter — B
REPRESENTATION (PHILOSOPHY)
   Han, Chenxing. *Be the Refuge* — 294.3
REPRESENTATIVE GOVERNMENT AND REPRESENTATION
   Acemoglu, Daron. *The Narrow Corridor* — 320.01
   Linklater, Andro. *Owning the Earth* — 333.3
REPRESSION (PSYCHOLOGY)
   Laing, Olivia. *Everybody* — 323
REPRODUCTIVE HEALTH
   Block, Jennifer. *Everything Below the Waist* — 613
   Brighten, Jolene. *Is This Normal?* — 618.1
   Matthews, Hannah. *You or Someone You Love* — 362.1988
   Schrock, Leslie. *Fertility Rules* — 613.9
   Tang, Karen. ★*It's Not Hysteria* — 618.2
REPRODUCTIVE RIGHTS
   Andrews, Becca. ★*No Choice* — 362.1988
   Dennie, Madiba K. *The Originalism Trap* — 342.73
   Farley, Audrey Clare. *The Unfit Heiress* — B
   Foster, Diana Greene. *The Turnaway Study* — 362.1988
   Kolbert, Kathryn. *Controlling Women* — 362.1988
   Luthra, Shefali. ★*Undue Burden* — 362.1988
   Matthews, Hannah. *You or Someone You Love* — 362.1988

Prager, Joshua. *The Family Roe* — 342.7308
Shah, Meera. *You're the Only One I've Told* — 362.1988
Sisson, Gretchen E. ★*Relinquished* — 362.734
Sohn, Amy. *The Man Who Hated Women* — 363.28
Wade, Sabia. *Birthing Liberation* — 363.96
Wright, Jennifer Ashley. ★*Madame Restell* — B
Reprogramming The American Dream. Scott, Kevin — 338
REPTILES
   McGinnis, Samuel M. ★*Peterson Field Guide to Western Reptiles and Amphibians* — 597.9
   Montgomery, Sy. ★*Of Time and Turtles* — 597.92
★*The Republic*. Cicero, Marcus Tullius — 320.1
★*The Republic*. Plato — 321
The Republic of Imagination. Nafisi, Azar — B
REPUBLICANISM
   Anderson, Fred. *The Dominion of War* — 973
   Gutzman, Kevin R. C. *The Jeffersonians* — 973.5
REPUBLICANS
   Alberta, Tim. *American Carnage* — 324.2734
   Bush, George W. *Decision Points* — B
   Cheney, Liz. *Oath and Honor* — 328.73
   Reagan, Ronald. *The Reagan Diaries* — B
   Shlaes, Amity. *Coolidge* — B
   Smith, Richard Norton. *On His Own Terms* — 973.925092
   Sommer, Will. ★*Trust the Plan* — 973.933
   Stahr, Walter. *Seward* — B
REPUTATION
   Brown, Craig. *Ninety-Nine Glimpses of Princess Margaret* — B
Requiem for the Massacre. Young, R. J. — 305.8
The Rescue Artist. Dolnick, Edward — 364.16
RESCUE DOGS
   Melville, Wilma. ★*Hero Dogs* — 636.7
Rescue Story. Williams, Zach — B
RESCUE WORK
   Bowden, Mark. *Black Hawk Down* — 967.7305
   Dwyer, Jim. *102 Minutes* — 974.7
   Eggers, Dave. *Zeitoun* — 305.892
   Smith, Dennis. *Report from Ground Zero* — 974.7
RESCUES
   Ackerman, Diane. ★*The Zookeeper's Wife* — 940.53
   Bruning, John R. *Indestructible* — B
   Clarke, Thurston. *Honorable Exit* — 959.704
   Fields, Micah. ★*We Hold Our Breath* — 976.4
   Grose, Peter. *A Good Place to Hide* — 940.53
   Levy, Buddy. *Labyrinth of Ice* — 910.91
   Mazzeo, Tilar J. *Irena's Children* — B
   Moorhouse, Roger. *The Forgers* — 940.53
   Pressman, Steven. *50 Children* — 940.53
   Rappaport, Helen. *The Race to Save the Romanovs* — 947.08
   Thomson, Keith. *Born to Be Hanged* — 910.4
   Trimble, Lee. *Beyond the Call* — 940.54
   White, Ralph. *Getting Out of Saigon* — 959.704
Rescuing Penny Jane. Sutherland, Amy — 636.7
★*Rescuing* The Planet. Hiss, Tony — 333.75
RESEARCH
   Alexander, Stephon. *Fear of a Black Universe* — 523.1
   Barrett, Lisa Feldman. ★*How Emotions Are Made* — 152.4
   Bell, Alice R. *Our Biggest Experiment* — 363.738
   Booth, Wayne C. *The Craft of Research* — 001.4
   Brunsting, Karen. ★*Open Access Literature in Libraries* — 070.5
   Deisseroth, Karl. *Projections* — 616.89
   Dittrich, Luke. ★*Patient H.M.* — 616.85
   Forbes, Nancy. *Faraday, Maxwell, and the Electromagnetic Field* — B
   Fox, Margalit. *The Riddle of the Labyrinth* — 920
   Frank, Lone. *The Pleasure Shock* — 616.8
   Henig, Robin Marantz. *The Monk in the Garden* — B
   Kaku, Michio. ★*Hyperspace* — 530.1
   Kean, Sam. *The Bastard Brigade* — 355.8
   Kean, Sam. *The Icepick Surgeon* — 509
   Kiernan, Denise. *The Girls of Atomic City* — 976.8
   Kinzer, Stephen. *Poisoner in Chief* — B
   Lattin, Don. *The Harvard Psychedelic Club* — 973.922092
   Levesque, Emily. *The Last Stargazers* — 520
   Lightman, Alan P. *The Discoveries* — 509
   Lisle, John. *The Dirty Tricks Department* — 940.54
   Lowman, Margaret. *The Arbornaut* — 581.7
   Lowman, Margaret. *Life in the Treetops* — B
   Mahaffey, James A. *Atomic Adventures* — 333.792

AUTHOR, TITLE, SERIES AND SUBJECT INDEX

Ritchie, Stuart. *Science Fictions* — 500
Roach, Mary. ★*Spook* — 129
Sagan, Carl. *Broca's Brain* — 128
Saini, Angela. *Inferior* — 305.4
Servan-Schreiber, David. *Anticancer* — 616.99
Slater, Lauren. *Blue Dreams* — 615.7
Taubes, Gary. ★*Rethinking Diabetes* — 616.462
Tyson, Neil deGrasse. *Accessory to War* — 355.001
Waldinger, Robert J. ★*The Good Life* — 158.1
Ward, Peter Douglas. *Life as We Do Not Know It* — 576.839
Zadra, Antonio. *When Brains Dream* — 613.7

RESEARCH INSTITUTES
Sarma, Sanjay E. *Grasp* — 370.15

Resendez, Andres
Conquering the Pacific — 959.9

Reser, Anna
Forces of Nature — 509.2

The Residence. Brower, Kate Andersen — 975.3

RESIDENTS (MEDICINE)
Goldberg, Emma. *Life on the Line* — 362.1962
Stern, Adam. *Committed* — 616.89

Resilience. Greitens, Eric — 155.2

RESILIENCE
Addario, Lynsey. *Of Love & War* — 779
Aktipis, Athena. ★*A Field Guide to the Apocalypse* — 155.2
Ali, Fatima. ★*Savor* — B
Ashton, Jennifer. *The New Normal* — 613
Asim, Jabari. *We Can't Breathe* — 305.896
Baskette, Molly Phinney. *How to Begin When Your World Is Ending* — 248.8
Black, Dustin Lance. *Mama's Boy* — B
Clinton, Hillary Rodham. *The Book of Gutsy Women* — 920
Coombes, Joshua. *Do Something for Nothing* — 362.5
Copeland, Misty. *The Wind at My Back* — B
Crais, Clifton C. *History Lessons* — B
Curry, Michael B. *Love Is the Way* — 241
DePalma, Anthony. *The Cubans* — 920
Edmondson, Amy C. *The Right Kind of Wrong* — 158.1
Ellenhorn, Ross D. ★*Purple Crayons* — 153.3
Evaristo, Bernardine. *Manifesto* — B
Fleming, Melissa. *A Hope More Powerful Than the Sea* — 956.9104
Fox, Margalit. *The Talented Mrs. Mandelbaum* — 364.1
Fox, Michael J. *No Time Like the Future* — B
Frankl, Viktor E. *Yes to Life* — 150.19
Frenkel, Francoise. *A Bookshop in Berlin* — B
Gelwicks, Andrew. *The Queer Advantage* — 920
Goodwin, Doris Kearns. ★*Leadership in Turbulent Times* — 973.09
Greitens, Eric. *Resilience* — 155.2
Grey, Jennifer. *Out of the Corner* — B
Harding, Luke. *Invasion* — 947.7
Hatmaker, Jen. *Of Mess and Moxie* — 248.8
Hemon, Aleksandar. *My Parents* — 814
Hickman, Katie. *Brave Hearted* — 978
Hill, Jemele. *Uphill* — B
Ignatieff, Michael. *On Consolation* — 152.4
Izgil, Tahir Hamut. *Waiting to Be Arrested at Night* — B
James, Victoria. *Wine Girl* — B
Kang, Mia. *Knockout* — B
Kelly, Donika. *The Renunciations* — 811
Kelly, Minka. ★*Tell Me Everything* — B
Kyle, Taya. *American Spirit* — B
LaPointe, Sasha taqwseblu. *Red Paint* — B
Levy, Shawn. ★*In on the Joke* — 792.7
Luckerson, Victor. *Built from the Fire* — 976.6
Mardini, Yusra. *Butterfly* — B
Mariani, Mike. ★*What Doesn't Kill Us Makes Us* — 155.9
Marshall, Greg. *Leg* — B
McGonigal, Jane. *Super Better* — 794.8
McLaren, Brian D. *Life After Doom* — 200.1
Means, Brittany. *Hell If We Don't Change Our Ways* — B
Mooallem, Jon. *Serious Face* — 814
Moorer, Allison. *I Dream He Talks to Me* — 782.42164
Nietfeld, Emi. *Acceptance* — B
Obama, Michelle. ★*The Light We Carry* — B
Oppenheimer, Mark. *Squirrel Hill* — 364.152
Osnos, Evan. *Joe Biden* — B
Parker, Kate T. *Strong Is the New Pretty* — 155.43
Pennington, Emily. *Feral* — B
Pfeifer, Joseph. *Ordinary Heroes* — 973.931

Pipher, Mary Bray. *A Life in Light* — B
Raban, Jonathan. *Father and Son* — B
Ramsey, Donovan X. ★*When Crack Was King* — 362.29
Reang, Putsata. *Ma and Me* — B
Rinaldi, Karen. *It's Great to Suck at Something* — 158.1
Rinder, Mike. ★*A Billion Years* — B
Ripley, Amanda. *The Unthinkable* — 155.9
Rojas Contreras, Ingrid. ★*The Man Who Could Move Clouds* — B
Rush, Charaia. *Courageously Soft* — 234
Rushdie, Salman. ★*Knife* — B
Sabathia, CC. *Till the End* — 796.357
Saldana, Stephanie. *What We Remember Will Be Saved* — 362.7
Sandberg, Sheryl. *Option B* — 155.9
Sasakamoose, Fred. *Call Me Indian* — B
Semenya, Caster. *The Race to Be Myself* — B
Shannon, Molly. ★*Hello, Molly!* — B
Snyder, Rachel Louise. *Women We Buried, Women We Burned* — B
Stone, Sharon. *The Beauty of Living Twice* — B
Stutz, Phil. *Lessons for Living* — 158.1
Szczeszak-Brewer, Agata. *The Hunger Book* — B
Thompson, J. M. *Running Is a Kind of Dreaming* — B
Thomson, Mike. *Syria's Secret Library* — 956.9104
Tran, Paul. *All the Flowers Kneeling* — 811
Trice, Dawn Turner. ★*Three Girls from Bronzeville* — 977.311
Tuama, Padraig O. ★*Poetry Unbound* — 808.1
Vasquez-Lavado, Silvia. *In the Shadow of the Mountain* — B
Vaughn, Ellen Santilli. ★*Becoming Elisabeth Elliot* — B
Wang, Qian Julie. ★*Beautiful Country* — B
Wariner, Ruth. *The Sound of Gravel* — B
Williams, Kidada E. *I Saw Death Coming* — 973.8
Willner, Nina. *Forty Autumns* — B
Wilson, Robert. *Barnum* — B
Winfrey, Oprah. *What Happened to You?* — 616.85
Wolf, Brandon J. *A Place for Us* — B
Zia, Helen. *Last Boat Out of Shanghai* — 951.04

RESILIENCE IN CHILDREN
McCarthy, Catherine. *Raising a Kid Who Can* — 649
Siegel, Daniel J. ★*The Yes Brain* — 155.4

Resistance. Amos, Tori — B
Resistance. Humbert, Agnes — B

RESISTANCE (PSYCHOLOGY)
Givens, Jarvis R. ★*School Clothes* — 371.829
Goodheart, Adam. *The Last Island* — 954
Nafisi, Azar. *Read Dangerously* — 809

RESISTANCE TO GOVERNMENT
Ackroyd, Peter. *Rebellion* — 941.06
Alekhina, Mariija. *Riot Days* — B
Cozzens, Peter. *Tecumseh and the Prophet* — 920
Demick, Barbara. *Eat the Buddha* — 951
Estes, Nick. *Our History Is the Future* — 978.004
Forche, Carolyn. *What You Have Heard Is True* — B
Gardner, Mark L. *The Earth Is All That Lasts* — 978.004
Gies, Miep. ★*Anne Frank Remembered* — B
Guha, Ramachandra. *Rebels Against the Raj* — 954.03
Jackson, Kellie Carter. *We Refuse* — 323.1196
Kaminsky, Ilya. ★*Deaf Republic* — 811
Lithwick, Dahlia. *Lady Justice* — 345.73
Ngugi wa Thiong'o. *In the House of the Interpreter* — B
Olson, Lynne. *Last Hope Island* — 940.53
Paxson, Margaret. *The Plateau* — 362.87
Preston, Paul. *The Spanish Holocaust* — 946.081
Rothkopf, David J. *American Resistance* — 973.933
Tamimi, Ahed. ★*They Called Me a Lioness* — B
Zinn, Howard. ★*A People's History of the United States* — 973

RESISTANCE TO MILITARY OCCUPATION
Allen, Arthur. ★*The Fantastic Laboratory of Dr. Weigl* — 614.5
Bailey, Catherine. *A Castle in Wartime* — 943.086
Bascomb, Neal. *The Winter Fortress* — 940.54
Batalion, Judith. *The Light of Days* — 940.53
Donner, Rebecca. *All the Frequent Troubles of Our Days* — 943
Dugard, Martin. *Taking Paris* — 940.54
Dumbach, Annette E. *Sophie Scholl and the White Rose* — 943.086
Iperen, Roxane van. ★*The Sisters of Auschwitz* — 940.53
Kershaw, Alex. *Avenue of Spies* — 940.53
Lichtblau, Eric. *Return to the Reich* — B
Magida, Arthur J. *Code Name Madeleine* — 940.54
McManus, John C. *To the End of the Earth* — 940.54
Miller, Christopher. *The War Came to Us* — 947.7

PUBLIC LIBRARY CORE COLLECTION: NONFICTION
Twentieth Edition

Moorehead, Caroline. *A House in the Mountains*	940.53
Moorehead, Caroline. *A Train in Winter*	940.53
Ohler, Norman. *The Bohemians*	940.53
Pomerantsev, Peter. ★*How to Win an Information War*	940.53
Rosenberg, Justus. *The Art of Resistance*	B
Siegal, Nina. *The Diary Keepers*	940.54
Stiles, T. J. *Jesse James*	B
Strauss, Gwen. *The Nine*	940.53
White, Elizabeth B. ★*The Counterfeit Countess*	940.53
Zelensky, Volodymyr. *A Message from Ukraine*	947.7
Resistance, Rebellion, and Death. Camus, Albert	844

RESNIK, JUDITH, 1949-1986
Grush, Loren. ★*The Six*	629.4

RESORT TOWNS
Hill, David. *The Vapors*	976.7

RESOURCE ALLOCATION
Piketty, Thomas. ★*Capital in the Twenty-First Century*	332
Piketty, Thomas. *The Economics of Inequality*	339.2

RESOURCEFULNESS
McGovern, Anna. *Pottering*	158.1
Price, David A. ★*Love and Hate in Jamestown*	975.5
Sonenshein, Scott. *Stretch*	153.3
Respect. Chavez Perez, Inti	176

RESPECT
Berman, Lea. *Treating People Well*	395
Brooks, David. ★*How to Know a Person*	158.2
Brown, Emma. *To Raise a Boy*	649
Chavez Perez, Inti. *Respect*	176
Patrick, Vanessa M. *The Power of Saying No*	158.1
Pratt, Victoria. *The Power of Dignity*	364.973
Yoshino, Kenji. *Say the Right Thing*	305.3
★*Respect for Acting.* Hagen, Uta	792.02
★*Responding to Rapid Change in Libraries.* Bignoli, Callan	020

RESPONSIBILITY
Brooks, David. ★*The Second Mountain*	302
McConville, Mark. *Failure to Launch*	155.6
Morrison, Toni. ★*The Source of Self-Regard*	814
Ruttenberg, Danya. *On Repentance and Repair*	202
Ryan, Maureen. *Burn It Down*	791.43
Senior, Jennifer. *All Joy and No Fun*	306.874
Sered, Danielle. *Until We Reckon*	364.6
Sunstein, Cass R. *Impeachment*	342.73
Tester, Jon. *Grounded*	B

Ressa, Maria
★*How to Stand up to a Dictator*	070.92

REST
May, Katherine. *Wintering*	155.9
Nockels, Christy. *The Life You Long For*	248.8
Shlain, Tiffany. *24/6*	158.1
Shulevitz, Judith. *The Sabbath World*	296.4

Restall, Matthew
When Montezuma Met Cortes	972

RESTAURANT CRITICS
Garner, Dwight. *The Upstairs Delicatessen*	B
Reichl, Ruth. *Garlic and Sapphires*	B
Reichl, Ruth. ★*Save Me the Plums*	B

RESTAURANT WORKERS
Cecchi-Azzolina, Michael. *Your Table Is Ready*	647.95

RESTAURANTS
Bourdain, Anthony. ★*Kitchen Confidential*	B
Bourdain, Anthony. *Medium Raw*	B
Bourdain, Anthony. *The Nasty Bits*	641.5092
Cailan, Alvin. *Amboy*	641.595
Cecchi-Azzolina, Michael. *Your Table Is Ready*	647.95
Fall, Jeremy. *Falling Upwards*	158.1
Fili, Louise. *The Cognoscenti's Guide to Florence*	381
Friedman, Andrew. *The Dish*	647.95
Keller, Thomas. *The French Laundry Cookbook*	641.5
Koenig, Leah. *Portico*	641.5
Ladner, Mark. *The Del Posto Cookbook*	641.594
Miller, Klancy. ★*For the Culture*	641.59
Schindler, Meriel. *The Lost Cafe Schindler*	943.64
Sheehan, Jason. *Cooking Dirty*	B
Waters, Alice. *Coming to My Senses*	B
White, Marco Pierre. *White Heat*	641.594

RESTAURATEURS
Cecchi-Azzolina, Michael. *Your Table Is Ready*	647.95
Chang, David. ★*Eat a Peach*	641.5

Chatelain, Marcia. ★*Franchise*	339
Chin, Curtis. *Everything I Learned, I Learned in a Chinese Restaurant*	B
Fall, Jeremy. *Falling Upwards*	158.1
Hamilton, Gabrielle. *Blood, Bones, and Butter*	B
Huang, Eddie. *Fresh off the Boat*	B
Jacobs, Ryan McMahon. *The Truffle Underground*	381
Lee, Edward. *Buttermilk Graffiti*	641.59
Onwuachi, Kwame. ★*Notes from a Young Black Chef*	641.59
Regan, Iliana. *Fieldwork*	B
Ripert, Eric. *32 Yolks*	B
Solomonov, Michael. *Zahav*	641.595
Wang, Jason. *XI'an Famous Foods*	641.595
Waters, Alice. *Coming to My Senses*	B

RESTELL, MADAME, 1811-1878
Wright, Jennifer Ashley. ★*Madame Restell*	B

Reston, James
The Conviction of Richard Nixon	973.924092
The Last Apocalypse	940.1

RESTON, JAMES, JR., 1941-2023
Reston, James. *The Conviction of Richard Nixon*	973.924092

RESTORATION
Parrella-Van Den Berg, Janet. *White & Faded*	645
Pourny, Christophe. ★*The Furniture Bible*	684.1

RESTORATION ECOLOGY
Flyn, Cal. ★*Islands of Abandonment*	333.73
Maathai, Wangari. *Unbowed*	B
Wilson, Edward O. *A Window on Eternity*	333.95

RESTORATION ENGLAND (1660-1688)
Mortimer, Ian. *The Time Traveler's Guide to Restoration Britain*	941.06
Tomalin, Claire. *Samuel Pepys*	B

RESTORATIVE JUSTICE
Manuel, Ian. *My Time Will Come*	B
Sered, Danielle. *Until We Reckon*	364.6
Restorative Yoga for Life. Grossman, Gail Boorstein	613.7
Resurrection Science. O'Connor, Maura R.	591.68

RETAIL INDUSTRY AND TRADE
Del Rey, Jason. *Winner Sells All*	381
Wartzman, Rick. *Still Broke*	381
★*Rethinking Diabetes.* Taubes, Gary	616.462
Rethinking Incarceration. Gilliard, Dominique Dubois	261.8
Rethinking School. Bauer, Susan Wise	371.19

RETIREES
Bruder, Jessica. ★*Nomadland*	331.3
Orman, Suze. ★*The Ultimate Retirement Guide for 50+*	306.3
Quinn, Jane Bryant. ★*How to Make Your Money Last*	332.024

RETIREMENT
Bruder, Jessica. ★*Nomadland*	331.3
Cohen, Jared. *Life After Power*	973.09
Horn, Jonathan. *Washington's End*	B

RETIREMENT INCOME
Quinn, Jane Bryant. ★*How to Make Your Money Last*	332.024
Retracing The Iron Curtain. Phillips, Timothy	909.82

RETREAT CENTERS
Giorgione, Michael. *Inside Camp David*	975.2
Retribution. Hastings, Max	940.54

Retta
So Close to Being the Sh*t, Y'all Don't Even Know	B

RETTA
Retta. *So Close to Being the Sh*t, Y'all Don't Even Know*	B

Rettke, Amanda
Homestead Recipes	641.5977
The Return. Matar, Hisham	B
The Return of a King. Dalrymple, William	958.1
The Return of George Washington. Larson, Edward J.	B
Return to Glory. DeBord, Matthew	338.4
Return to the Reich. Lichtblau, Eric	B

Reuben, Steven Carr
★*Becoming Jewish*	296.7

REUNIONS
Charleson, Susannah. *Where the Lost Dogs Go*	636.7
Nguyen, Bich Minh. *Owner of a Lonely Heart*	B
Pick-Goslar, Hannah Elizabeth. ★*My Friend Anne Frank*	B
Verant, Samantha. *Seven Letters from Paris*	B

REVENGE
Ahmed, Azam. *Fear Is Just a Word*	364.152
Anand, Anita. *The Patient Assassin*	B
Bogosian, Eric. *Operation Nemesis*	956.62
Cameron, Silver Donald. *Blood in the Water*	364.152

AUTHOR, TITLE, SERIES AND SUBJECT INDEX

Enss, Chris. *Mochi's War*	B
Flock, Elizabeth. ★*The Furies*	305.48
Mort, T. A. *Thieves' Road*	978.3
Stoppard, Tom. ★*Rosencrantz & Guildenstern Are Dead*	822
Tutu, Desmond. *The Book of Forgiving*	179
Reverby, Susan M.	
Examining Tuskegee	174.2
REVERE, PAUL, 1735-1818	
Fischer, David Hackett. *Paul Revere's Ride*	973.3
***Revolt** At Taos*. Crutchfield, James A.	972
★*The **Revolt** of the Elites*. Lasch, Christopher	306
Revolution. Ackroyd, Peter	941.07
***Revolution** 1989*. Sebestyen, Victor	947.085
*A **Revolution** in Color*. Kamensky, Jane	759.13
***Revolution** on the Hudson*. Daughan, George C.	974.7
Revolutionaries. Rakove, Jack N.	973.3
REVOLUTIONARIES	
Anand, Anita. *The Patient Assassin*	B
Anderson, Jon Lee. *Che Guevara*	B
Arana, Marie. *Bolivar*	B
Atkinson, Rick. ★*The British Are Coming*	973.3
Baier, Bret. *To Rescue the Constitution*	973.4
Beeman, Richard R. *Our Lives, Our Fortunes and Our Sacred Honor*	973.3
Bell, Madison Smartt. *Toussaint Louverture*	B
Bobrick, Benson. *Angel in the Whirlwind*	973.3
Brands, H. W. ★*Our First Civil War*	973.3
Burrough, Bryan. *Days of Rage*	303.48
Butterworth, Alex. *The World That Never Was*	335
Castro, Fidel. *Fidel Castro*	B
Egan, Timothy. ★*The Immortal Irishman*	B
Ellis, Joseph J. *The Cause*	973.3
Ellis, Joseph J. *Founding Brothers*	973.4
Figes, Orlando. *A People's Tragedy*	947.08
Fischer, David Hackett. *Paul Revere's Ride*	973.3
Fried, Stephen. *Rush*	B
Gabriel, Mary. *Love and Capital*	920
Gidla, Sujatha. *Ants Among Elephants*	305.5
Groom, Winston. *The Patriots*	920
Guinn, Jeff. ★*War on the Border*	972.08
Hernandez, Kelly Lytle. ★*Bad Mexicans*	972
Hogeland, William. *Declaration*	973.3
McCullough, David G. ★*1776*	973.3
McPhee, Peter. *Robespierre*	B
Merridale, Catherine. *Lenin on the Train*	B
Mieville, China. *October*	947.084
Miller, Marla. *Betsy Ross and the Making of America*	B
Ngugi wa Thiong'o. *In the House of the Interpreter*	B
Parks, Tim. *The Hero's Way*	945
Popkin, Jeremy D. *A New World Begins*	944.04
Preston, Paul. *The Spanish Holocaust*	946.081
Rakove, Jack N. *Revolutionaries*	973.3
Sallah, Michael. *The Yankee Comandante*	972.91
Sankovitch, Nina. *American Rebels*	920
Schama, Simon. *Citizens*	944.04
Scurr, Ruth. *Fatal Purity*	B
Sebestyen, Victor. *Lenin*	B
Service, Robert. *Lenin—A Biography*	B
Shatz, Adam. *The Rebel's Clinic*	965
Unger, Harlow G. *American Tempest*	973.3
West, Cornel. *Black Prophetic Fire*	920
Womack, John. *Zapata and the Mexican Revolution*	B
Revolutionary. O'Connell, Robert L.	B
REVOLUTIONARY AMERICA (1775-1783)	
Adams, Abigail. *Abigail Adams*	973.4
Adams, John. *My Dearest Friend*	973.4
Atkinson, Rick. ★*The British Are Coming*	973.3
Baier, Bret. *To Rescue the Constitution*	973.4
Beeman, Richard R. *Our Lives, Our Fortunes and Our Sacred Honor*	973.3
Bobrick, Benson. *Angel in the Whirlwind*	973.3
Boles, John B. *Jefferson*	B
Brands, H. W. ★*Our First Civil War*	973.3
Broadwater, Jeff. ★*George Mason*	B
Calloway, Colin G. *The Indian World of George Washington*	323.1197
Cozzens, Peter. *Tecumseh and the Prophet*	920
Crawford, Alan Pell. *This Fierce People*	975
Daughan, George C. *Revolution on the Hudson*	974.7
Dolin, Eric Jay. ★*Rebels at Sea*	973.3
Drury, Bob. *Blood and Treasure*	B
Drury, Bob. *Valley Forge*	973.3
Duncan, Michael. ★*Hero of Two Worlds*	B
Ellis, Joseph J. *American Creation*	973.3
Ellis, Joseph J. *The Cause*	973.3
Ellis, Joseph J. ★*His Excellency*	B
Ellis, Joseph J. *The Quartet*	342.7302
Ellis, Joseph J. ★*Revolutionary Summer*	973.3
Ferling, John E. *Winning Independence*	973.3
Ferreiro, Larrie D. *Brothers at Arms*	327.73
Fischer, David Hackett. *Paul Revere's Ride*	973.3
Fischer, David Hackett. *Washington's Crossing*	973.3
Gaines, James R. *For Liberty and Glory*	B
Groom, Winston. *The Patriots*	920
Hogeland, William. *Declaration*	973.3
Holton, Woody. *Liberty Is Sweet*	973.3
Hoock, Holger. *Scars of Independence*	973.3
Johnson, Paul. *George Washington*	B
Kamensky, Jane. *A Revolution in Color*	759.13
Ketchum, Richard M. *Saratoga*	973.3
Kilmeade, Brian. ★*George Washington's Secret Six*	973.4
Maier, Pauline. *American Scripture*	973.3
McCraw, Thomas K. ★*The Founders and Finance*	330.973
McCullough, David G. ★*1776*	973.3
McKean, David. *Suspected of Independence*	B
Meltzer, Brad. ★*The First Conspiracy*	973.4
Middlekauff, Robert. *The Glorious Cause*	973.3
Miller, Marla. *Betsy Ross and the Making of America*	B
Morison, Samuel Eliot. *John Paul Jones*	B
Norton, Mary Beth. *1774*	973.3
O'Connell, Robert L. *Revolutionary*	B
O'Donnell, Patrick K. *The Indispensables*	973.3
Philbrick, Nathaniel. ★*Bunker Hill*	973.3
Philbrick, Nathaniel. ★*In the Hurricane's Eye*	973.3
Philbrick, Nathaniel. ★*Valiant Ambition*	B
Phillips, Kevin. *1775*	973.3
Rakove, Jack N. *Revolutionaries*	973.3
Randall, Willard Sterne. *The Founders' Fortunes*	973.3
Raphael, Ray. *A People's History of the American Revolution*	973.3
Roberts, Andrew. *The Last King of America*	B
Roberts, Cokie. *Founding Mothers*	920
Rosen, Jeffrey. *The Pursuit of Happiness*	973.3
Sankovitch, Nina. *American Rebels*	920
Saxton, Martha. *The Widow Washington*	B
Shirley, Craig. *Mary Ball Washington*	B
Staiti, Paul J. *Of Arms and Artists*	B
Stewart, David O. *George Washington*	973.4
Taylor, Alan. *American Revolutions*	973.3
Taylor, Alan. *The Divided Ground*	974.7
Thomas, Evan. ★*John Paul Jones*	B
Thompson, Bob. *Revolutionary Roads*	973.3
Unger, Harlow G. *American Tempest*	973.3
Unger, Harlow G. *First Founding Father*	B
Zambone, Albert Louis. *Daniel Morgan*	B
REVOLUTIONARY FRANCE (1789-1799)	
Burke, Edmund. *Reflections on the Revolution in France*	944.04
Davidson, Ian. *The French Revolution*	944.04
Duncan, Michael. ★*Hero of Two Worlds*	B
Gaines, James R. *For Liberty and Glory*	B
Lever, Evelyne. *Marie Antoinette*	B
McPhee, Peter. *Robespierre*	B
Paine, Thomas. ★*Rights of Man*	320.5
Popkin, Jeremy D. *A New World Begins*	944.04
Schama, Simon. *Citizens*	944.04
Scurr, Ruth. *Fatal Purity*	B
***Revolutionary** Roads*. Thompson, Bob	973.3
★***Revolutionary** Summer*. Ellis, Joseph J.	973.3
*The **Revolutionary** Temper*. Darnton, Robert	944
REVOLUTIONS	
Abouzeid, Rania. *No Turning Back*	956.9104
Adams, John. *My Dearest Friend*	973.4
Ai, Weiwei. *Zodiac*	741.5
Anderson, Jon Lee. *Che Guevara*	B
Arana, Marie. *Bolivar*	B
Beevor, Antony. *Russia*	947.084
Bell, Madison Smartt. *Toussaint Louverture*	B
Bobrick, Benson. *Angel in the Whirlwind*	973.3
Boles, John B. *Jefferson*	B
Branigan, Tania. *Red Memory*	951.05

PUBLIC LIBRARY CORE COLLECTION: NONFICTION
Twentieth Edition

Broadwater, Jeff. ★*George Mason*	B
Burke, Edmund. *Reflections on the Revolution in France*	944.04
Burrough, Bryan. *Forget the Alamo*	976.043
Camus, Albert. *The Rebel*	303.6
Carney, Scott. *The Vortex*	954.92
Cheng, Nien. *Life and Death in Shanghai*	B
Darnton, Robert. *The Revolutionary Temper*	944
Daughan, George C. *Revolution on the Hudson*	974.7
Dikotter, Frank. *The Cultural Revolution*	951.056
Dolin, Eric Jay. ★*Rebels at Sea*	973.3
Ellis, Joseph J. *American Creation*	973.3
Ellis, Joseph J. ★*His Excellency*	B
Ellis, Joseph J. *The Quartet*	342.7302
Evans, Martin. *Algeria*	965
Ferling, John E. *Winning Independence*	973.3
Ferrer, Ada. ★*Cuba*	972.91
Figes, Orlando. *A People's Tragedy*	947.08
Fischer, David Hackett. *Paul Revere's Ride*	973.3
Fischer, David Hackett. *Washington's Crossing*	973.3
Gaines, James R. *For Liberty and Glory*	B
Goldstone, Nancy Bazelon. *In the Shadow of the Empress*	920
Guillermoprieto, Alma. *Dancing with Cuba*	972.9106
Hernandez, Kelly Lytle. ★*Bad Mexicans*	972
Hessler, Peter. *The Buried*	962.05
Hochschild, Adam. *Spain in Our Hearts*	946.081
Hogeland, William. *Declaration*	973.3
Holton, Woody. *Liberty Is Sweet*	973.3
Johnson, Paul. *George Washington*	B
Ketchum, Richard M. *Saratoga*	973.3
Lemmon, Gayle Tzemach. *The Daughters of Kobani*	956.9104
Maier, Pauline. *American Scripture*	973.3
Mazower, Mark. *The Greek Revolution*	949.5
McCraw, Thomas K. ★*The Founders and Finance*	330.973
McCullough, David G. ★*1776*	973.3
McMeekin, Sean. *The Russian Revolution*	947.084
Merridale, Catherine. *Lenin on the Train*	B
Michener, James A. *The Bridge at Andau*	943.9
Middlekauff, Robert. *The Glorious Cause*	973.3
Miller, Marla. *Betsy Ross and the Making of America*	B
Min, Anchee. *Red Azalea*	B
Morison, Samuel Eliot. *John Paul Jones*	B
Norton, Mary Beth. *1774*	973.3
Pantsov, Alexander. *Mao*	B
Phillips, Kevin. *1775*	973.3
Pipes, Richard. *A Concise History of the Russian Revolution*	947.084
Popkin, Jeremy D. *A New World Begins*	944.04
Preston, Paul. *The Spanish Holocaust*	946.081
Rakove, Jack N. *Revolutionaries*	973.3
Raphael, Ray. *A People's History of the American Revolution*	973.3
Rappaport, Helen. *Caught in the Revolution*	355.00947
Rappaport, Helen. *The Race to Save the Romanovs*	947.08
Rasmussen, Daniel. *American Uprising*	976.3
Ridley, Jane. *George V*	B
Roberts, Cokie. *Founding Mothers*	920
Rudd, Mark. *Underground*	378.1
Sallah, Michael. *The Yankee Comandante*	972.91
Schama, Simon. *Citizens*	944.04
Spence, Jonathan D. *God's Chinese Son*	951
Taing, Mae Bunseng. *Under the Naga Tail*	B
Taylor, Alan. *American Revolutions*	973.3
Taylor, Alan. *The Divided Ground*	974.7
Thomas, Evan. ★*John Paul Jones*	B
Thompson, Bob. *Revolutionary Roads*	973.3
Tuchman, Barbara W. *Stilwell and the American Experience in China, 1911-45*	B
Turchin, Peter. *End Times*	320.01
Unger, Harlow G. *American Tempest*	973.3
Unger, Harlow G. *First Founding Father*	B
Weintraub, Stanley. *Iron Tears*	973.3
Whitaker, Mark. ★*Saying It Loud*	973.923
Yang, Jisheng. *The World Turned Upside Down*	951.05
Zakaria, Fareed. *Age of Revolutions*	303.6
★*Revolutions* in American Music. Broyles, Michael	780.9
Revolver. Rasenberger, Jim	B
REVOLVERS	
Rasenberger, Jim. *Revolver*	B
Rexroth, Kenneth	
One Hundred Poems from the Japanese	895
Reynolds, David S.	
★*Abe*	B
John Brown, Abolitionist	B
Mightier Than the Sword	813
Reynolds, Debbie	
Make 'Em Laugh	B
REYNOLDS, DEBBIE	
Fisher, Todd. *My Girls*	B
Reynolds, Debbie. *Make 'Em Laugh*	B
REYNOLDS, JOEL	
Horwitz, Josh. *War of the Whales*	333.95
Reynolds, Nicholas E.	
Need to Know	940.54
Reynolds, Simon	
Shock and Awe	781.6609
Rezaian, Jason	
Prisoner	B
REZAIAN, JASON	
Rezaian, Jason. *Prisoner*	B
RFK. Kennedy, Robert Francis	973.92
RHATICUS, GEORG JOACHIM, 1514-1576	
Sobel, Dava. *A More Perfect Heaven*	520.9
RHETORIC	
Everitt, Anthony. *Cicero*	B
Fish, Stanley Eugene. *Winning Arguments*	808
Prothero, Stephen R. *The American Bible*	973
Wills, Garry. *Lincoln at Gettysburg*	973.7
Woods, Geraldine. *25 Great Sentences and How They Got That Way*	808
Zelizer, Julian E. *Burning Down the House*	328.73
RHINOCEROS	
Fowlds, Grant. *Saving the Last Rhinos*	599.66
Orenstein, Ronald I. *Ivory, Horn and Blood*	333.95
RHODE ISLAND	
Barry, John M. *Roger Williams and the Creation of the American Soul*	974.5
James, Scott. *Trial by Fire*	363.3709745
Rhoden, William C.	
$40 Million Slaves	796
Rhodes, Benjamin J.	
The World as It Is	973.932
RHODES, BENJAMIN J., 1977-	
Rhodes, Benjamin J. *The World as It Is*	973.932
Rhodes, James	
Instrumental	B
RHODES, JAMES, 1975-	
Rhodes, James. *Instrumental*	B
Rhodes, Richard	
★*Energy*	333.7909
Hedy's Folly	B
Masters of Death	940.53
Scientist	B
Rhyme's Rooms. Leithauser, Brad	808.1
RHYTHM AND BLUES MUSIC	
De Vise, Daniel. ★*The Blues Brothers*	791.43
Harvilla, Rob. *60 Songs That Explain the '90s*	782.42164
Neville, Aaron. *Tell It Like It Is*	B
Ribowsky, Mark. *Signed, Sealed, and Delivered*	B
RHYTHM AND BLUES MUSICIANS	
Coleman, Rick. ★*Blue Monday*	B
De Vise, Daniel. ★*The Blues Brothers*	791.43
Iandoli, Kathy. *Baby Girl*	B
Ribowsky, Mark. *Signed, Sealed, and Delivered*	B
Stone, Sly. *Thank You (Falettinme Be Mice Elf Agin)*	B
Rhythm of the Wild. Heacox, Kim	979.8
Riasanovsky, Nicholas V.	
A History of Russia	947
Ribowsky, Mark	
Dreams to Remember	B
Howard Cosell	070.449796
The Last Cowboy	796.332
Shula	B
Signed, Sealed, and Delivered	B
The Supremes	B
Ricanati, Elizabeth	
Braided	B
RICANATI, ELIZABETH	
Ricanati, Elizabeth. *Braided*	B
RICE FARMERS	
Hamilton, Lisa M. *The Hungry Season*	B

AUTHOR, TITLE, SERIES AND SUBJECT INDEX

Rice, Condoleezza
   Extraordinary, Ordinary People   B
   No Higher Honor   B
   Political Risk   658.15
RICE, CONDOLEEZZA, 1954-
   Rice, Condoleezza. *Extraordinary, Ordinary People*   B
   Rice, Condoleezza. *No Higher Honor*   B
Rice, Jerry
   America's Game   796.332
Rice, *Noodle*, *Fish*. Goulding, Matt   394.1
Rice. *Noodles*. *Yum*. Raines, Abigail Sotto   641.595
Rich Af. Tu, Vivian   332.024
RICH AFRICAN AMERICANS
   Jefferson, Margo. *Negroland*   305.896
RICH CONSUMERS
   Schwartz, Nelson. *The Velvet Rope Economy*   339.2
RICH FAMILIES
   Barnes, Cinelle. *Monsoon Mansion*   B
   Barthel, Joan. *American Saint*   B
   Bernstein, Andrea. *American Oligarchs*   920
   Brickell, Francesca Cartier. *The Cartiers*   B
   Cooper, Anderson. *Vanderbilt*   920
   Hamill, Kirkland. *Filthy Beasts*   B
   Kaufman, Jonathan. *The Last Kings of Shanghai*   951
   Keefe, Patrick Radden. ★*Empire of Pain*   338.7
   Mann, William J. *The Wars of the Roosevelts*   B
   Plummer, Christopher. *In Spite of Myself*   B
   Stewart, James B. *Unscripted*   658.1
   Taraborrelli, J. Randy. *Jackie, Janet & Lee*   920
   Taraborrelli, J. Randy. *The Kennedy Heirs*   920
RICH MEN
   De Waal, Edmund. *The Hare with Amber Eyes*   B
   Gup, Ted. *A Secret Gift*   977.1
   Nasaw, David. *Andrew Carnegie*   B
   Rathbone, John Paul. *The Sugar King of Havana*   B
RICH PEOPLE
   Barr, Luke. *Ritz & Escoffier*   920
   Bernstein, Andrea. *American Oligarchs*   920
   Honig, Elie. *Untouchable*   364.1
   Kiernan, Denise. *The Last Castle*   975.6
   Mealer, Bryan. *The Kings of Big Spring*   B
   Mechanic, Michael. *Jackpot*   305.5
   Milanovic, Branko. *The Have and the Have-Nots*   339.2
   Neiman, Garrett. *Rich White Men*   305.5
   Sancton, Thomas. *The Bettencourt Affair*   B
   Taraborrelli, J. Randy. *After Camelot*   B
   Taub, Jennifer. *Big Dirty Money*   364.16
   Wills, Shomari. *Black Fortunes*   920
Rich White Men. Neiman, Garrett   305.5
RICH WOMEN
   Gill, Anton. *Art Lover*   B
   Greenberg, Amy S. *Lady First*   B
Rich, Adrienne
   Collected Early Poems, 1950-1970   811
   Collected Poems   811
   Essential Essays   814
   Later Poems   811
   The School Among the Ruins   811
RICH, ADRIENNE, 1929-2012
   Hardwick, Elizabeth. *The Dolphin Letters, 1970-1979*   811
Rich, Chris
   Stained Glass Basics   748.5
Rich, Nathaniel
   Losing Earth   363.738
   Second Nature   304.2
RICHARD II, KING OF ENGLAND, 1367-1400
   Weir, Alison. *The Wars of the Roses*   942.04
RICHARD III, KING OF ENGLAND, 1452-1485
   Penn, Thomas. *The Brothers York*   942.04
   Pitts, Mike. *Digging for Richard III*   942.046
★*Richard Nixon*. Farrell, John A.   B
Richard Strauss. Kennedy, Michael   B
Richards, Cecile
   Make Trouble   B
RICHARDS, CECILE
   Richards, Cecile. *Make Trouble*   B
Richards, Keith
   Life   B

RICHARDS, KEITH, 1943-
   Richards, Keith. *Life*   B
Richards, Leonard L.
   Who Freed the Slaves?   342.7308
Richards, Shola
   Making Work Work   658.3
Richards, Todd
   Soul   641.59296073
Richardson, Edmund
   The King's Shadow   958.1
Richardson, Heather Cox
   Democracy Awakening   320.473
   ★*How the South Won the Civil War*   306.20973
RICHARDSON, HENRY HOBSON, 1838-1886
   Howard, Hugh. *Architects of an American Landscape*   712.092
Richardson, Lance
   House of Nutter   B
RICHARDSON, MICHEAL RAY
   Rosen, Charles. *Sugar*   B
Richardson, Patric
   Laundry Love   648
Richardson, Robert D.
   Emerson   814
   William James   B
RICHMOND, VIRGINIA
   Winik, Jay. *April 1865*   973.7
The Richness of Life. Gould, Stephen Jay   508
Richtel, Matt
   ★*An Elegant Defense*   616.07
Rick Bayless Mexico One Plate at a Time. Bayless, Rick   641.5972
Rick, Scott
   Tightwads and Spendthrifts   332.024
RICKENBACKER, EDDIE, 1890-1973
   Groom, Winston. *The Aviators*   920
   Wukovits, John F. *Lost at Sea*   940.54
Ricketts, Rachel
   ★*Do Better*   305.800973
Rickey. Bryant, Howard   B
Ricks, Thomas E.
   Churchill and Orwell   920
   Fiasco   956.7044
   ★*First Principles*   973.09
   ★*The Generals*   B
The Riddle of the Labyrinth. Fox, Margalit   920
★*The Ride of Her Life*. Letts, Elizabeth   B
RIDE, SALLY
   Grush, Loren. ★*The Six*   629.4
   Sherr, Lynn. *Sally Ride*   B
★*Ride-Or-Die*. Hubbard, Shanita   305.48
RIDESHARING
   Lashinsky, Adam. *Wild Ride*   388.4
RIDGE, MAJOR, APPROXIMATELY 1771-1839
   Sedgwick, John. *Blood Moon*   975.004
Riding The Iron Rooster. Theroux, Paul   915
Riding with Evil. Croke, Ken   364.106
Riding with the Ghost. Taylor, Justin   B
Ridley, Jane
   George V   B
   The Heir Apparent   B
Ridley, Matt
   The Rational Optimist   339.2
Ridpath, Ian
   Stars & Planets   520
Riedel, Michael
   Razzle Dazzle   792.09
   Singular Sensation   792
Rieder, Travis
   In Pain   362.29
RIEDER, TRAVIS
   Rieder, Travis. *In Pain*   362.29
RIEFENSTAHL, LENI
   Trimborn, Jurgen. *Leni Riefenstahl*   B
Riel, Jennifer
   Creating Great Choices   658.4
Riesman, Abraham
   True Believer   741.5
Riess, Jana
   Flunking Sainthood   248.4

PUBLIC LIBRARY CORE COLLECTION: NONFICTION
Twentieth Edition

RIESS, JANA
   Riess, Jana. *Flunking Sainthood* — 248.4
RIFLES
   McWhirter, Cameron. *American Gun* — 683.4
★*Rift*. West, Cait — B
Rigged. Shimer, David — 324.60973
Riggs, Nina
   The Bright Hour — B
RIGGS, NINA
   Riggs, Nina. *The Bright Hour* — B
Righetti, Maggie
   Crocheting in Plain English — 746.43
   Knitting in Plain English — 746.432
RIGHT AND LEFT (POLITICAL SCIENCE)
   Berkshire, Jennifer. *The Education Wars* — 371.01
   Berman, Ari. ★*Minority Rule* — 305.809
   Caldwell, Christopher. *The Age of Entitlement* — 305.240973
   Frank, Barney. *Frank* — B
   Fukuyama, Francis. *Liberalism and Its Discontents* — 320.51
   Hendershot, Heather. *Open to Debate* — B
   Klein, Ezra. ★*Why We're Polarized* — 306.0973
   Kruse, Kevin Michael. *Fault Lines* — 973.92
   Kushner, Jacob. *Look Away* — 305.9
   Minutaglio, Bill. *Dallas 1963* — 973.922092
   Neiwert, David A. ★*The Age of Insurrection* — 303.48
   Perlstein, Rick. ★*Reaganland* — 973.926
   Zakaria, Fareed. *Age of Revolutions* — 303.6
RIGHT AND WRONG
   Schulz, Kathryn. *Being Wrong* — 121
RIGHT FIELDERS (BASEBALL)
   Maraniss, David. *Clemente* — B
   Santiago, Wilfred. *"21"* — 741.5
The Right Kind of Wrong. Edmondson, Amy C. — 158.1
Right Place, Right Time. Gruen, Bob — B
★*The Right Stuff*. Wolfe, Tom — 629.4
RIGHT TO BEAR ARMS
   Anderson, Carol. ★*The Second* — 344.7305
   Erdozain, Dominic. *One Nation Under Guns* — 363.33
   McWhirter, Cameron. *American Gun* — 683.4
   Murphy, Chris. ★*The Violence Inside Us* — 303.60973
RIGHT TO COUNSEL
   Houppert, Karen. *Chasing Gideon* — 345.73
   Lewis, Anthony. *Gideon's Trumpet* — 345.73
   Rapping, Jonathan. *Gideon's Promise* — 345.73
RIGHT TO DIE
   Engelhart, Katie. *The Inevitable* — 179.7
   Hannig, Anita. *The Day I Die* — 364.152
   Rehm, Diane. ★*When My Time Comes* — 179.7
   Wanzer, Sidney H. ★*To Die Well* — 179.7
   Warraich, Haider. *Modern Death* — 179.7
The Right to Sex. Srinivasan, Amia — 305.42
Right Within. Harts, Minda — 658.3
The Right—And Wrong—Stuff. Cast, Carter — 650.1
RIGHT-WING EXTREMISTS
   Arnsdorf, Isaac. ★*Finish What We Started* — 320.52
   Darby, Seyward. ★*Sisters in Hate* — 305.800973
   Ephron, Dan. *Killing a King* — 956.9405
   Hitler, Adolf. *Mein Kampf* — B
   Kushner, Jacob. *Look Away* — 305.9
   Maddow, Rachel. ★*Prequel* — 320.53
   Neiwert, David A. ★*The Age of Insurrection* — 303.48
   Neus, Nora. *24 Hours in Charlottesville* — 973.933
   Rothschild, Mike. *The Storm Is Upon Us* — 973.933
   Sharlet, Jeff. ★*The Undertow* — 322
   Spencer, Kyle. *Raising Them Right* — 320.5
   Toobin, Jeffrey. ★*Homegrown* — 363.325
   Ullrich, Volker. *Germany 1923* — 943.085
   Weber, Thomas. *Becoming Hitler* — B
RIGHTEOUS GENTILES IN THE HOLOCAUST
   Ackerman, Diane. ★*The Zookeeper's Wife* — 940.53
   Edmonds, Chris. *No Surrender* — B
   Gies, Miep. ★*Anne Frank Remembered* — B
   Hurowitz, Richard. *In the Garden of the Righteous* — 940.53
   Loftis, Larry. ★*The Watchmaker's Daughter* — 940.53
   Marsh, Charles. *Strange Glory* — B
   Mazzeo, Tilar J. *Irena's Children* — B
   Moorehead, Caroline. *Village of Secrets* — 944
Righteous Victims. Morris, Benny — 956

Rightful Heritage. Brinkley, Douglas — B
Rights Gone Wrong. Ford, Richard T. — 342.7308
★*Rights of Man*. Paine, Thomas — 320.5
★*The Rights of Women*. Lapidus, Lenora M. — 346.7301
Rigsby, Cody
   ★*XOXO, Cody* — B
RIGSBY, CODY
   Rigsby, Cody. ★*XOXO, Cody* — B
★*Rikers*. Rayman, Graham — 365
RIKERS ISLAND (N.Y.)
   Fedderly, Eva. *These Walls* — 365
   Rayman, Graham. ★*Rikers* — 365
Riley, Alex
   ★*A Cure for Darkness* — 616.85
RILEY, ALEX
   Riley, Alex. ★*A Cure for Darkness* — 616.85
Riley, Gregory J.
   The River of God — 270.1
Riley, Kathleen
   The Astaires — B
Rilke, Rainer Maria
   Ahead of All Parting — 831
   ★*Duino Elegies* — 831
   ★*Letters to a Young Poet* — 831
   New Poems — 831
   ★*Sonnets to Orpheus* — 831
RILKE, RAINER MARIA, 1875-1926
   Rilke, Rainer Maria. *Ahead of All Parting* — 831
   Rilke, Rainer Maria. ★*Duino Elegies* — 831
   Rilke, Rainer Maria. ★*Letters to a Young Poet* — 831
Rimbaud, Arthur
   The Illuminations — 841
RIMBAUD, ARTHUR, 1854-1891
   Rimbaud, Arthur. *The Illuminations* — 841
Rin Tin Tin. Orlean, Susan — 636.737
RIN-TIN-TIN (DOG)
   Orlean, Susan. *Rin Tin Tin* — 636.737
Rinaldi, Karen
   It's Great to Suck at Something — 158.1
Rinder, Mike
   ★*A Billion Years* — B
RINDER, MIKE
   Rinder, Mike. ★*A Billion Years* — B
Rinehart, Lorissa
   First to the Front — B
Rinella, Steven
   American Buffalo — 599.64
   The Complete Guide to Hunting, Butchering, and Cooking Wild Game — 799.2
   Meat Eater — B
   ★*Outdoor Kids in an Inside World* — 649
RINELLA, STEVEN
   Rinella, Steven. *American Buffalo* — 599.64
   Rinella, Steven. *Meat Eater* — B
RINGLING FAMILY
   Standiford, Les. ★*Battle for the Big Top* — 791.3
RINGLING, JOHN, 1866-1936
   Standiford, Les. ★*Battle for the Big Top* — 791.3
Ringquist, Rebecca
   ★*Rebecca Ringquist's Embroidery Workshops* — 746.44
Rinzler, J. W.
   The Making of Aliens — 791.4372
Rinzler, Lodro
   The Buddha Walks into a Bar — 294.3
   Love Hurts — 294.3
Riot and Remembrance. Hirsch, James S. — 976.6
Riot Days. Alekhina, Mariija — B
RIOT GRRRL MOVEMENT
   Hanna, Kathleen. *Rebel Girl* — B
RIOTS
   Gonell, Aquilino. *American Shield* — B
   Hinton, Elizabeth Kai. ★*America on Fire* — 305.800973
   Hirsch, James S. *Riot and Remembrance* — 976.6
   Madigan, Tim. *The Burning* — 976.6
   Reilly, Ryan J. ★*Sedition Hunters* — 364.1
   Signer, Michael. *Cry Havoc* — 305.800973
   Smith, Zadie. *Intimations* — 824
   Tyson, Timothy B. *Blood Done Sign My Name* — 975.6

AUTHOR, TITLE, SERIES AND SUBJECT INDEX

Rioux, Anne Boyd
   Meg, Jo, Beth, Amy — 813
Ripa, Kelly
   Live Wire — B
RIPA, KELLY
   Ripa, Kelly. *Live Wire* — B
Ripe Figs. Khan, Yasmin — 641.595
Ripert, Eric
   32 Yolks — B
   Seafood Simple — 641.6
RIPERT, ERIC
   Ripert, Eric. *32 Yolks* — B
Ripken, Bill
   State of Play — 796.357
RIPKEN, CAL, JR., 1960-
   Eisenberg, John. *The Streak* — 796.357
Ripley, Amanda
   The Unthinkable — 155.9
★*Ripped from the Headlines!* Schechter, Harold — 791.43
Ripper. Cornwell, Patricia Daniels — 364.152
Rippon, Adam
   Beautiful on the Outside — B
RIPPON, ADAM, 1989-
   Rippon, Adam. *Beautiful on the Outside* — B
   Rippon, Kelly. *Parent Up* — 649
Rippon, Kelly
   Parent Up — 649
RIPPON, KELLY
   Rippon, Kelly. *Parent Up* — 649
Risbridger, Ella
   The Year of Miracles — 641.5
★*The Rise.* Samuelsson, Marcus — 641.59
The Rise. Sielski, Mike — B
★*Rise.* Yang, Jeff — 973
The Rise and Fall of Adam and Eve. Greenblatt, Stephen — 233
★*The Rise and Fall of American Growth.* Gordon, Robert J. — 339.4
★*The Rise and Fall of Ancient Egypt.* Wilkinson, Toby A. H. — 932
★*The Rise and Fall of Communism.* Brown, Archie — 320.53
The Rise and Fall of Nations. Sharma, Ruchir — 330.9
The Rise and Fall of Osama Bin Laden. Bergen, Peter L. — 958.104
★*The Rise and Fall of the Dinosaurs.* Brusatte, Stephen — 567.9
The Rise and Fall of the Great Powers. Kennedy, Paul M. — 909.82
★*The Rise and Fall of the Second American Republic.* Sinha, Manisha — 973.8
★*The Rise and Fall of the Third Reich.* Shirer, William L. — 943.086
Rise and Fire. Fury, Shawn — 796.323
The Rise and Reign of the Mammals. Brusatte, Stephen — 569
Rise of a Killah. Ghostface Killah — B
The Rise of Athens. Everitt, Anthony — 938
The Rise of Germany, 1939-1941; Vol. 1. Holland, James — 940.54
The Rise of Rome. Everitt, Anthony — 937
The Rise of the G.I. Army 1940-1941. Dickson, Paul — 940.54
★*Rise of the Rocket Girls.* Holt, Nathalia — 629.4
The Rise of the Ultra Runners. Finn, Adharanand — B
★*The Rise of Theodore Roosevelt.* Morris, Edmund — B
Rise Up. Sharpton, Al — 973.933
Risen, Clay
   American Whiskey, Bourbon, & Rye — 641.2
   The Bill of the Century — 342.7308
Risen, James
   ★*The Last Honest Man* — 973.92
Rising. Rush, Elizabeth A. — 551.45
Rising Star. Garrow, David J. — B
Rising Tide. Barry, John M. — 977
RISK
   Elliott, Carl. ★*The Occasional Human Sacrifice* — 174.2
   Gardner, Dan. *The Science of Fear* — 152.4
   Hari, Johann. ★*Magic Pill* — 613.2
   Offit, Paul A. *You Bet Your Life* — 615.5
RISK ANALYSIS
   Gardner, Dan. *The Science of Fear* — 152.4
   Rice, Condoleezza. *Political Risk* — 658.15
   Ripley, Amanda. *The Unthinkable* — 155.9
   Russell, Stuart J. *Human Compatible* — 006.301
   Stavridis, James. *To Risk It All* — 359
The Risk It Takes to Bloom. Willis, Raquel — B
RISK MANAGEMENT
   Rice, Condoleezza. *Political Risk* — 658.15
   Ripley, Amanda. *The Unthinkable* — 155.9

Russell, Stuart J. *Human Compatible* — 006.301
RISK-TAKING
   Chan, Jackie. *Never Grow Up* — B
   Krakauer, Jon. *Classic Krakauer* — 814
   McCormick, Brad. *Extreme Sports* — 791.457
   Patterson, Scott. ★*Chaos Kings* — 338.5
   Rempel, William C. *The Gambler* — B
   Stavridis, James. *To Risk It All* — 359
Risner, Vaneetha Rendall
   Walking Through Fire — B
RISNER, VANEETHA RENDALL, 1964-
   Risner, Vaneetha Rendall. *Walking Through Fire* — B
RIST, EDWIN
   Johnson, Kirk W. *The Feather Thief* — 364.16
Ritchie, Hannah
   Not the End of the World — 338.9
Ritchie, Stuart
   Science Fictions — 500
RITES AND CEREMONIES
   Allert, Tilman. *Heil Hitler* — 395.4
   Bolsta, Hyla Shifra. *The Illuminated Kaddish* — 296.4
   Clark, Doug Bock. *The Last Whalers* — 639.2
   Doughty, Caitlin. *From Here to Eternity* — 393
   Gaddy, K. R. ★*Well of Souls* — 787
   Garcia, Amanda Yates. *Initiated* — B
   Goldman, Ari L. *Being Jewish* — 296.4
   Hardacre, Helen. *Shinto* — 299.5
   Jamison, Kay Redfield. *Fires in the Dark* — 616.89
   Oakes, John G. H. ★*The Fast* — 613.2
   Pogrebin, Abigail. *My Jewish Year* — 296.4
   Rajchel, Diana. *Urban Magick* — 133.4
   Ricanati, Elizabeth. *Braided* — B
   Sagan, Sasha. *For Small Creatures Such as We* — 390.09
   Wieseltier, Leon. *Kaddish* — 296.4
★*The Ritual Effect.* Norton, Michael — 650.1
Ritvo, Max
   The Final Voicemails — 811
   Four Reincarnations — 811
RITVO, MAX, 1990-2016
   Ruhl, Sarah. *Letters from Max* — 811
Ritz & Escoffier. Barr, Luke — 920
RITZ, CESAR, 1850-1918
   Barr, Luke. *Ritz & Escoffier* — 920
The Rival Queens. Goldstone, Nancy Bazelon — 944
The Rivals. Howard, Johnette — B
River Cottage Veg. Fearnley-Whittingstall, Hugh — 641.5
★*A River in Darkness.* Ishikawa, Masaji — B
RIVER LIFE
   Davis, Wade. *Magdalena* — 986.1
   Doyle, Martin. *The Source* — 333.91
   Sciolino, Elaine. *The Seine* — 944
River of Doubt. Millard, Candice — 918.1
River of Fire. Prejean, Helen — B
The River of God. Riley, Gregory J. — 270.1
★*River of the Gods.* Millard, Candice — 916.204
RIVER TRAVEL
   Davis, Wade. *Magdalena* — 986.1
RIVERA, DIEGO, 1886-1957
   Marnham, Patrick. *Dreaming with His Eyes Open* — B
   Stahr, Celia. *Frida in America* — B
Rivera, Mariano
   The Closer — B
RIVERA, MARIANO, 1969-
   Rivera, Mariano. *The Closer* — B
Riverman. McGrath, Ben — 797.122
Rivermouth. Oliva, Alejandra — 305.9
RIVERS
   Buck, Rinker. *Life on the Mississippi* — 917
   Davis, Wade. *Magdalena* — 986.1
   Doyle, Martin. *The Source* — 333.91
   Maiklem, Lara. *Mudlark* — B
   McGrath, Ben. *Riverman* — 797.122
   Millard, Candice. ★*River of the Gods* — 916.204
   Sciolino, Elaine. *The Seine* — 944
   Wilkinson, Toby A. H. *The Nile* — 962
Rivers of Gold. Thomas, Hugh — 980
Rivers, Charlotte
   Little Book of Book Making — 686

PUBLIC LIBRARY CORE COLLECTION: NONFICTION
Twentieth Edition

RIVERS, JOAN
    Bennetts, Leslie. *Last Girl Before Freeway* — B
RIVERS, W. H. R. (WILLIAM HALSE RIVERS), 1864-1922
    Jamison, Kay Redfield. *Fires in the Dark* — 616.89
Rivlin, Gary
    Broke, Usa — 339.4
    Katrina — 976.3
Roach, Margaret
    ★*A Way to Garden* — 635
ROACH, MARGARET
    Roach, Margaret. ★*A Way to Garden* — 635
Roach, Mary
    Bonk — 612.6
    ★*Fuzz* — 591.5
    ★*Grunt* — 355
    Gulp — 612.3
    Packing for Mars — 571.0919
    ★*Spook* — 129
    ★*Stiff* — 611
★*The Road Less Traveled.* Peck, M. Scott — 158.1
ROAD MANAGERS
    Weisman, Eliot. *The Way It Was* — 782.42164
★*The Road Not Taken.* Boot, Max — B
★*The Road to Camelot.* Oliphant, Thomas — 973.922092
The Road to Jonestown. Guinn, Jeff — 289.9
The Road to Little Dribbling. Bryson, Bill — 914
The Road to Serfdom. Hayek, Friedrich A. von — 330.1
The Road to Woodstock. Lang, Michael — 781.66
ROADS
    Caro, Robert A. *The Power Broker* — B
    Goldfarb, Ben. *Crossings* — 333.77
    Kimble, Megan. ★*City Limits* — 388.1
    McDiarmid, Jessica. *Highway of Tears* — 364.152
    Thubron, Colin. *Shadow of the Silk Road* — 915
    Wallis, Michael. *Route 66* — 917.804
Roads to Quoz. Heat Moon, William Least — 917.3
ROANOKE COLONY
    Horn, James P. P. *A Kingdom Strange* — 975.6
    Lawler, Andrew. *The Secret Token* — 975.6
ROANOKE ISLAND, NORTH CAROLINA
    Horn, James P. P. *A Kingdom Strange* — 975.6
    Lawler, Andrew. *The Secret Token* — 975.6
Robb, Alice
    ★*Don't Think, Dear* — 792.8
ROBB, ALICE
    Robb, Alice. ★*Don't Think, Dear* — 792.8
Robb, Graham
    The Debatable Land — 941.3
    The Discovery of France — 944
    France — 944
    Parisians — 944
ROBB, GRAHAM, 1958-
    Robb, Graham. *The Debatable Land* — 941.3
    Robb, Graham. *France* — 944
Robb, John
    Punk Rock — 781.6609
ROBBERY
    Belkin, Lisa. *Genealogy of a Murder* — 362.88
ROBBERY INVESTIGATION
    Dolnick, Edward. *The Rescue Artist* — 364.16
Robbins, Alexandra
    ★*The Teachers* — 371.1
Robbins, Anthony
    Unlimited Power — 158.1
Robbins, Jim
    The Wonder of Birds — 598
Robert Browning. Browning, Robert — 821.8
★*Robert Browning's Poetry.* Browning, Robert — 821
Robert E. Lee. Guelzo, Allen C. — B
Robert E. Lee. Blount, Roy — B
Robert E. Lee and Me. Seidule, Ty — 973.7
Robert Frost. Parini, Jay — B
Robert Johnson. Patrick, James — B
★*Robert Kennedy.* Thomas, Evan — B
The Roberts Court. Coyle, Marcia — 347.73
Roberts, Andrew
    ★*Churchill* — B
    The Last King of America — B
    Leadership in War — 920
    Masters and Commanders — 940.5322
    ★*Napoleon* — B
    The Storm of War — 940.54
Roberts, Cokie
    Capital Dames — 920
    Founding Mothers — 920
    Ladies of Liberty — 920
ROBERTS, COKIE, 1943-2019
    Napoli, Lisa. *Susan, Linda, Nina & Cokie* — 920
    Roberts, Steven V. *Cokie* — B
Roberts, David
    Alone on the Ice — 919.8904
    The Bears Ears — 979.2
    Limits of the Known — B
    Once They Moved Like the Wind — B
ROBERTS, DAVID, 1943-
    Roberts, David. *The Bears Ears* — 979.2
    Roberts, David. *Limits of the Known* — B
Roberts, Dorothy E.
    Torn Apart — 362.7
Roberts, Jason
    ★*Every Living Thing* — 578
    A Sense of the World — B
Roberts, Jennifer Tolbert
    The Plague of War — 938
ROBERTS, JOHN G., 1955-
    Coyle, Marcia. *The Roberts Court* — 347.73
Roberts, Julius
    The Farm Table — 641.594
Roberts, Matthias
    Holy Runaways — 262
ROBERTS, MATTHIAS
    Roberts, Matthias. *Holy Runaways* — 262
Roberts, Randy
    Blood Brothers — 920
    Joe Louis — B
Roberts, Steven V.
    Cokie — B
Roberts-Miller, Patricia
    Speaking of Race — 305.8
Robertson, Cara
    The Trial of Lizzie Borden — 345.744
Robertson, David C.
    Brick by Brick — 338.7
Robertson, James I.
    Stonewall Jackson — B
Robertson, Ritchie
    The Enlightenment — 190
Robertson, Robbie
    ★*Testimony* — B
ROBERTSON, ROBBIE
    Robertson, Robbie. ★*Testimony* — B
ROBESON, ESLANDA GOODE, 1896-1965
    Ransby, Barbara. *Eslanda* — B
Robeson, Paul
    Here I Stand — B
    The Undiscovered Paul Robeson — B
ROBESON, PAUL, 1898-1976
    Ransby, Barbara. *Eslanda* — B
    Robeson, Paul. *Here I Stand* — B
    Robeson, Paul. *The Undiscovered Paul Robeson* — B
Robespierre. McPhee, Peter — B
ROBESPIERRE, MAXIMILIEN, 1758-1794
    McPhee, Peter. *Robespierre* — B
    Scurr, Ruth. *Fatal Purity* — B
★*Robin.* Itzkoff, Dave — B
Robin, Corey
    The Enigma of Clarence Thomas — 347.73
Robins, Gay
    The Art of Ancient Egypt — 709
ROBINSON, BETTY, 1911-1999
    Montillo, Roseanne. *Fire on the Track* — B
Robinson, Jackie
    I Never Had It Made — B
ROBINSON, JACKIE, 1919-1972
    Kennedy, Kostya. *True* — B
    Robinson, Jackie. *I Never Had It Made* — B

AUTHOR, TITLE, SERIES AND SUBJECT INDEX

Robinson, Jo
  Eating on the Wild Side — 641.3
Robinson, Joanna
  ★*McU* — 791.43
Robinson, Ken
  Creative Schools — 370.973
Robinson, Kim Stanley
  The High Sierra — 917.94
ROBINSON, KIM STANLEY
  Robinson, Kim Stanley. *The High Sierra* — 917.94
Robinson, Marilynne
  ★*Reading Genesis* — 222
Robinson, Mario Andres
  Lessons in Realistic Watercolor — 751.42
Robinson, Phoebe
  Please Don't Sit on My Bed in Your Outside Clothes — 818
  You Can't Touch My Hair and Other Things I Still Have to Explain — 792.7
ROBINSON, PHOEBE
  Robinson, Phoebe. *Please Don't Sit on My Bed in Your Outside Clothes* — 818
  Robinson, Phoebe. *You Can't Touch My Hair and Other Things I Still Have to Explain* — 792.7
Robinson, Ray
  Iron Horse — B
Robinson, Roxana
  Georgia O'Keeffe — B
Robinson, Staci
  ★*Tupac Shakur* — B
ROBINSON, SUGAR RAY, 1920-1989
  Haygood, Wil. ★*Sweet Thunder* — B
Robison, John Elder
  Look Me in the Eye — B
ROBISON, JOHN ELDER
  Robison, John Elder. *Look Me in the Eye* — B
Robison, Peter
  ★*Flying Blind* — 338.7
ROBOTICS
  Davis, Joshua. *Spare Parts* — 629.8
  Kasparov, G. K. *Deep Thinking* — 006.3
  Kurzweil, Ray. ★*The Singularity Is Near* — 153.9
  Tegmark, Max. *Life 3.0* — 006.301
ROBOTS
  Davis, Joshua. *Spare Parts* — 629.8
  Waldman, Jonathan. *Sam* — 629.8
Robson, Deborah
  The Field Guide to Fleece — 677
Rocca, Mo
  Mobituaries — 920
Rocco's Healthy+Delicious. DiSpirito, Rocco — 641.3
Rock and Roll Will Save Your Life. Almond, Steve — 781.6
ROCK CLIMBERS
  Burgman, John. *High Drama* — 796.522
  Honnold, Alex. *Alone on the Wall* — B
  Taylor, Joseph E. *Pilgrims of the Vertical* — 796.52
ROCK CLIMBING
  Burgman, John. *High Drama* — 796.522
  DiGiulian, Sasha. *Take the Lead* — B
  Honnold, Alex. *Alone on the Wall* — B
  Ralston, Aron. *Between a Rock and a Hard Place* — 796.522
  Taylor, Joseph E. *Pilgrims of the Vertical* — 796.52
ROCK CLIMBING ACCIDENTS
  Ralston, Aron. *Between a Rock and a Hard Place* — 796.522
ROCK CONCERTS
  Austerlitz, Saul. *Just a Shot Away* — 781.66078
  James, Scott. *Trial by Fire* — 363.3709745
  Lang, Michael. *The Road to Woodstock* — 781.66
Rock Gardening. Tychonievich, Joseph — 635.9
ROCK GARDENS
  Tychonievich, Joseph. *Rock Gardening* — 635.9
ROCK GROUPS
  Browne, David. *Crosby, Stills, Nash and Young* — 920
  Cohen, Rich. *The Sun and the Moon and the Rolling Stones* — 782.42166
  Cross, Charles R. *Here We Are Now* — 782.42166
  Davis, Stephen. *Gold Dust Woman* — B
  Dickinson, Bruce. *What Does This Button Do?* — B
  Gordon, Kim. *Girl in a Band* — B
  Hyden, Steven. *Long Road* — 782.42166
  Johnson, Brian. *The Lives of Brian* — B
  Mehr, Bob. *Trouble Boys* — 920

Moore, Thurston. *Sonic Life* — B
Richards, Keith. *Life* — B
Robertson, Robbie. ★*Testimony* — B
Schemel, Patty. *Hit so Hard* — B
Spitz, Bob. *Led Zeppelin* — 782.42166
Stanley, Bob. ★*The Story of the Bee Gees* — 782.42164
Stanley, Paul. *Backstage Pass* — B
Stanley, Paul. *Face the Music* — B
Thomson, Graeme. *George Harrison* — B
Wald, Elijah. *How the Beatles Destroyed Rock 'N' Roll* — 781.64
Zanes, Warren. *Petty* — B
ROCK MUSIC
  Alden, Ginger. *Elvis and Ginger* — B
  Almond, Steve. *Rock and Roll Will Save Your Life* — 781.6
  Austerlitz, Saul. *Just a Shot Away* — 781.66078
  Broven, John. *Record Makers and Breakers* — B
  Brown, Craig. *150 Glimpses of the Beatles* — 920
  Browne, David. *Crosby, Stills, Nash and Young* — 920
  Browne, David. *So Many Roads* — B
  Buckland, Gail. *Who Shot Rock & Roll* — 779
  Carlin, Peter Ames. *Bruce* — B
  Connolly, Ray. *Being Elvis* — B
  Costello, Elvis. *Unfaithful Music & Disappearing Ink* — B
  Cross, Charles R. *Here We Are Now* — 782.42166
  Doggett, Peter. *You Never Give Me Your Money* — B
  Gordon, Kim. *Girl in a Band* — B
  Gruen, Bob. *Right Place, Right Time* — B
  Guesdon, Jean-Michel. *All the Songs* — 782.42166
  Hagan, Joe. *Sticky Fingers* — B
  Harvilla, Rob. *60 Songs That Explain the '90s* — 782.42164
  Hepworth, David. *Uncommon People* — B
  Hermes, Will. *Lou Reed* — B
  Hopper, Jessica. *The First Collection of Criticism by a Living Female Rock Critic* — 781.66
  Hyden, Steven. *Long Road* — 782.42166
  Hyden, Steven. *Twilight of the Gods* — 781.6609
  Jarnow, Jesse. *Big Day Coming* — B
  John, Elton. ★*Me* — B
  Jollett, Mikel. ★*Hollywood Park* — B
  Jones, Dylan. *David Bowie* — B
  Kaye, Lenny. ★*Lightning Striking* — 781.66
  Kozinn, Allan. *The McCartney Legacy* — B
  Mahon, Maureen. ★*Black Diamond Queens* — 782.421
  Margotin, Philippe. *The Rolling Stones* — 782.42166
  McDonald, Michael. ★*What a Fool Believes* — B
  McKeen, William. *Everybody Had an Ocean* — 781.6609
  Moore, Thurston. *Sonic Life* — B
  Morley, Paul. *The Age of Bowie* — B
  Norman, Philip. *George Harrison* — B
  Norman, Philip. *John Lennon* — B
  Norman, Philip. ★*Wild Thing* — B
  O'Connor, Sinead. ★*Rememberings* — B
  Osbourne, Ozzy. *I Am Ozzy* — B
  Phair, Liz. *Horror Stories* — B
  Port, Ian S. *The Birth of Loud* — 787.87
  Povey, Glenn. *Echoes* — 782.42166
  Prince. *The Beautiful Ones* — B
  Reynolds, Simon. *Shock and Awe* — 781.6609
  Richards, Keith. *Life* — B
  Robb, John. *Punk Rock* — 781.6609
  Robertson, Robbie. ★*Testimony* — B
  Smith, Patti. *Collected Lyrics* — 782
  Spitz, Bob. *Led Zeppelin* — 782.42166
  Springsteen, Bruce. ★*Born to Run* — B
  Stanley, Paul. *Backstage Pass* — B
  Stanley, Paul. *Face the Music* — B
  Thomas, Richard F. ★*Why Bob Dylan Matters* — 782.42164
  Thomson, Graeme. *George Harrison* — B
  Wald, Elijah. *How the Beatles Destroyed Rock 'N' Roll* — 781.64
  White, Ryan. *Jimmy Buffett* — 782.42164
  Winder, Elizabeth. *Parachute Women* — 782.42164
  Womack, Kenneth. *All Things Must Pass Away* — 781.66
  Young, Neil. *Waging Heavy Peace* — B
  Zanes, Warren. *Deliver Me from Nowhere* — 782.42164
  Zanes, Warren. *Petty* — B
ROCK MUSIC INDUSTRY AND TRADE
  Gruen, Bob. *Right Place, Right Time* — B

PUBLIC LIBRARY CORE COLLECTION: NONFICTION
Twentieth Edition

ROCK MUSICIANS
Alden, Ginger. *Elvis and Ginger* — B
Almond, Steve. *Rock and Roll Will Save Your Life* — 781.6
Bono. ★*Surrender* — B
Browne, David. *Crosby, Stills, Nash and Young* — 920
Browne, David. *So Many Roads* — B
Buckland, Gail. *Who Shot Rock & Roll* — 779
Carlin, Peter Ames. *Bruce* — B
Clapton, Eric. *Clapton* — B
Cohen, Rich. *The Sun and the Moon and the Rolling Stones* — 782.42166
Coleman, Rick. ★*Blue Monday* — B
Connolly, Ray. *Being Elvis* — B
Connolly, Ray. *Being John Lennon* — B
Costello, Elvis. *Unfaithful Music & Disappearing Ink* — B
Cross, Charles R. *Here We Are Now* — 782.42166
Cross, Charles R. *Room Full of Mirrors* — B
Davidson, Mark A. ★*Bob Dylan* — B
Davis, Stephen. *Gold Dust Woman* — B
DeCurtis, Anthony. *Lou Reed* — B
Dickinson, Bruce. *What Does This Button Do?* — B
Doggett, Peter. *You Never Give Me Your Money* — B
Fogerty, John. *Fortunate Son* — B
Garcia, Mayte. *The Most Beautiful* — 920
George-Warren, Holly. ★*Janis* — B
Greenman, Ben. *Dig If You Will the Picture* — B
Gruen, Bob. *Right Place, Right Time* — B
Hepworth, David. *Uncommon People* — B
Hermes, Will. *Lou Reed* — B
Hilburn, Robert. ★*Paul Simon* — 782.42164
Hopkins, Jerry. *No One Here Gets Out Alive* — B
Hopper, Jessica. *The First Collection of Criticism by a Living Female Rock Critic* — 781.66
Hyden, Steven. *Long Road* — 782.42166
Hyden, Steven. *Twilight of the Gods* — 781.6609
Jarnow, Jesse. *Big Day Coming* — B
John, Elton. ★*Me* — B
Johnson, Brian. *The Lives of Brian* — B
Jollett, Mikel. ★*Hollywood Park* — B
Jones, Dylan. *David Bowie* — B
Kaye, Lenny. ★*Lightning Striking* — 781.66
Kozinn, Allan. *The McCartney Legacy* — B
Lanegan, Mark. *Sing Backwards and Weep* — B
Mahon, Maureen. ★*Black Diamond Queens* — 782.421
Mason, Nick. *Inside Out* — B
McCartney, Paul. *The Lyrics* — 782.42166
McDonald, Greg (Producer). *Elvis and the Colonel* — 920
McDonald, Michael. ★*What a Fool Believes* — B
McKeen, William. *Everybody Had an Ocean* — 781.6609
Mehr, Bob. *Trouble Boys* — 920
Moby. *Then It Fell Apart* — B
Moore, Thurston. *Sonic Life* — B
Morley, Paul. *The Age of Bowie* — B
Murray, Charles Shaar. *Crosstown Traffic* — B
Norman, Philip. *George Harrison* — B
Norman, Philip. *John Lennon* — B
Norman, Philip. ★*Wild Thing* — B
O'Connor, Sinead. ★*Rememberings* — B
Osbourne, Ozzy. *I Am Ozzy* — B
Perry, Joe. *Rocks* — B
Phair, Liz. *Horror Stories* — B
Povey, Glenn. *Echoes* — 782.42166
Reynolds, Simon. *Shock and Awe* — 781.6609
Richards, Keith. *Life* — B
Robb, John. *Punk Rock* — 781.6609
Robertson, Robbie. ★*Testimony* — B
Santana, Carlos. *The Universal Tone* — B
Shahidi, Afshin. *Prince* — B
Spitz, Bob. ★*The Beatles* — B
Spitz, Bob. *Led Zeppelin* — 782.42166
Springsteen, Bruce. ★*Born to Run* — B
Stanley, Paul. *Backstage Pass* — B
Stanley, Paul. *Face the Music* — B
Stone, Sly. *Thank You (Falettinme Be Mice Elf Agin)* — B
Thomas, Richard F. ★*Why Bob Dylan Matters* — 782.42164
Thomson, Graeme. *George Harrison* — B
Tolokonnikova, Nadezhda. *Rules for Rulebreakers* — 782.42166
Turner, Tina. ★*Happiness Becomes You* — 158.1
Van Zandt, Steve. *Unrequited Infatuations* — B
White, Charles. *The Life and Times of Little Richard* — B
White, Ryan. *Jimmy Buffett* — 782.42164
Wilson, Brian. *I Am Brian Wilson* — B
Womack, Kenneth. *All Things Must Pass Away* — 781.66
Young, Neil. *Waging Heavy Peace* — B
Zanes, Warren. *Petty* — B
Zauner, Michelle. ★*Crying in H Mart* — B

ROCK, JOHN, 1890-1984
Eig, Jonathan. *The Birth of the Pill* — 618.1
Rockaway. Cardwell, Diane — B

ROCKEFELLER, JOHN D. (JOHN DAVISON), 1839-1937
Doran, Peter B. *Breaking Rockefeller* — 338.7

ROCKEFELLER, MICHAEL CLARK
Hoffman, Carl. ★*Savage Harvest* — 995.1

ROCKEFELLER, NELSON ALDRICH, 1908-1979
Smith, Richard Norton. *On His Own Terms* — 973.925092
★*Rocket Boys*. Hickam, Homer H.
★*Rocket Men*. Kurson, Robert — 629.45
Rocket Men. Nelson, Craig — 629.45

ROCKETRY
Berger, Eric. *Liftoff* — B

ROCKETS (AVIATION)
Berger, Eric. *Liftoff* — B
Vance, Ashlee. *When the Heavens Went on Sale* — 621.43
Rocks. Perry, Joe — B

ROCKS
Bjornerud, Marcia. *Geopedia* — 551
Pough, Frederick H. ★*A Field Guide to Rocks and Minerals* — 549

ROCKWELL, NORMAN, 1894-1978
Solomon, Deborah. *American Mirror* — B

ROCKY MOUNTAINS
Auvinen, Karen. *Rough Beauty* — B
Barbarisi, Daniel. *Chasing the Thrill* — 796.1
Houston, Pam. *Deep Creek* — 814

Rodabaugh, Katrina
The Paper Playhouse — 745.5

Rodale, Maria
Scratch — 641.3

Rodd, Tony
Trees — 582.16

Roddy, Rachel
★*An A-Z of Pasta* — 641.82

Roden, Claudia
Arabesque — 641.59
★*The Book of Jewish Food* — 641.5

RODEO PERFORMERS
Branch, John. *The Last Cowboys* — 920

RODEOS
Branch, John. *The Last Cowboys* — 920

Rodgers, Jodi
★*How to Find a Four-Leaf Clover* — 616.85

Rodgers, Mary
Shy — B

RODGERS, MARY, 1931-2014
Rodgers, Mary. *Shy* — B

RODGERS, RICHARD, 1902-1979
Purdum, Todd S. *Something Wonderful* — B
★*Rodney Scott's World of BBQ*. Scott, Rodney — 641.7

Rodriguez, Ashley
Rooted Kitchen — 641.5

Rodriguez, Dina
The Big Awesome Book of Hand & Chalk Lettering — 745.6

Rodriguez, Jessamyn Waldman
The Hot Bread Kitchen Cookbook — 641.59

Rodsky, Eve
Find Your Unicorn Space — 158.1

Roe, Sue
In Montmartre — 920
The Private Lives of the Impressionists — 920

Roeder, Oliver
Seven Games — 794

Roethke, Theodore
The Collected Poems of Theodore Roethke — 811

Roffer, Michael H.
The Law Book — 340.09

Roffman, Karin
The Songs We Know Best — B

AUTHOR, TITLE, SERIES AND SUBJECT INDEX

Rogan, Eugene L.
   The Fall of the Ottomans   940.3
Rogen, Seth
   ★ *Yearbook*   B
ROGEN, SETH, 1982-
   Rogen, Seth. ★ *Yearbook*   B
Roger Williams and the Creation of the American Soul. Barry, John M.   974.5
Rogers, Adam
   Full Spectrum   152.14
   Proof   663
ROGERS, FRED
   Clemmons, Francois S. *Officer Clemmons*   B
   King, Maxwell. *The Good Neighbor*   B
Rogers, Katie
   ★ *American Woman*   973.09
Rogers, Pattiann
   Quickening Fields   811
Rogers, Robbie
   Coming Out to Play   B
ROGERS, ROBBIE
   Rogers, Robbie. *Coming Out to Play*   B
Rogers, Susan E.
   ★ *This Is What It Sounds Like*   781.1
ROGERS, SUSAN E.
   Rogers, Susan E. ★ *This Is What It Sounds Like*   781.1
Rogers-Whitehead, Carrie
   ★ *Serving Teens and Adults on the Autism Spectrum*   027.6
Rogoyska, Jane
   Surviving Katyn   940.54
★ *Rogue Heroes*. Macintyre, Ben   940.54
★ *Rogues*. Keefe, Patrick Radden   364.16
Rogues' Gallery. Hook, Philip   709.2
ROHAN, SHEILA
   Valby, Karen. *The Swans of Harlem*   792.8
Rohde, David
   Endgame   949.703
   In Deep   973.933
ROHINGYA (BURMESE PEOPLE)
   Thant Myint-U. *The Hidden History of Burma*   959.105
Rohr, Richard
   The Universal Christ   232
Roig-Debellis, Kaitlin
   Choosing Hope   371.7
ROIG-DEBELLIS, KAITLIN
   Roig-Debellis, Kaitlin. *Choosing Hope*   371.7
Roiphe, Katie
   The Violet Hour   809
Rojas Contreras, Ingrid
   ★ *The Man Who Could Move Clouds*   B
ROJAS CONTRERAS, INGRID
   Rojas Contreras, Ingrid. ★ *The Man Who Could Move Clouds*   B
Roker, Al
   Ruthless Tide   974.8
ROLAND (LEGENDARY CHARACTER)
   Ariosto, Lodovico. *Orlando Furioso =*   851
ROLE MODELS
   Boden, Anne. *Female Founders' Playbook*   658.4
   Carcaterra, Lorenzo. *Three Dreamers*   B
   Coles, Robert. *Lives of Moral Leadership*   170
   Gillard, Julia. ★ *Women and Leadership*   158
   Jawando, Will. ★ *My Seven Black Fathers*   B
   Obama, Michelle. ★ *The Light We Carry*   B
   Smarsh, Sarah. *She Come by It Natural*   782.42164
   Thomas, Louisa. *Louisa*   B
   Tubbs, Michael. *The Deeper the Roots*   B
Role Models. Waters, John   B
ROLE PLAYING GAMES
   Goodridge, Michelle. *Librarian's Guide to Games and Gamers*   025.2
Roll Red Roll. Schwartzman, Nancy   364.15
Roll, David L.
   Ascent to Power   973.918
   George Marshall   B
Roll, Jordan, Roll. Genovese, Eugene D.   975
Roll, Rich
   The Plantpower Way   641.5
Rollag, Keith
   What to Do When You're New   158.2

Rollich, Christiaan
   Bar Chef   641.87
The Rolling Stones. Margotin, Philippe   782.42166
ROLLINS, SONNY, 1930-
   Levy, Aidan. *Saxophone Colossus*   B
ROMAN BRITAIN (55 B.C.E.-449 C.E.)
   Higgins, Charlotte. *Under Another Sky*   936
   Robb, Graham. *The Debatable Land*   941.3
ROMAN EMPERORS
   Beard, Mary. ★ *Emperor of Rome*   937
   Everitt, Anthony. *Hadrian and the Triumph of Rome*   B
   Goldsworthy, Adrian Keith. *Augustus*   B
   Southon, Emma. *Agrippina*   B
   Strauss, Barry S. *Ten Caesars*   937
   Suetonius. ★ *The Twelve Caesars*   B
   Woolf, Greg. *Rome*   937
ROMAN EMPIRE (27 B.C.E.-476 C.E.)
   Beard, Mary. ★ *Emperor of Rome*   937
   Brown, Peter. *Through the Eye of a Needle*   270.2
   Everitt, Anthony. *Hadrian and the Triumph of Rome*   B
   Everitt, Anthony. *The Rise of Rome*   937
   Gibbon, Edward. ★ *The Decline and Fall of the Roman Empire*   937
   Goldsworthy, Adrian Keith. *Augustus*   B
   Goldsworthy, Adrian Keith. *Pax Romana*   937
   Harper, Kyle. *The Fate of Rome*   937
   Southon, Emma. *Agrippina*   B
   Strauss, Barry S. *Ten Caesars*   937
   Suetonius. ★ *The Twelve Caesars*   B
   Woolf, Greg. *Rome*   937
ROMAN PEOPLE IN GREAT BRITAIN
   Higgins, Charlotte. *Under Another Sky*   936
ROMAN REPUBLIC (509-27 B.C.E.)
   Everitt, Anthony. *Cicero*   B
   Goldsworthy, Adrian Keith. *Antony and Cleopatra*   937
   Goldsworthy, Adrian Keith. ★ *Caesar*   937
   Hunt, Patrick. *Hannibal*   B
   O'Connell, Robert L. *The Ghosts of Cannae*   937
   Strauss, Barry S. *The Death of Caesar*   937
   Strauss, Barry S. ★ *The War That Made the Roman Empire*   937
Roman, Alison
   Dining In   641.5
   ★ *Nothing Fancy*   642
   Sweet Enough   641.86
Roman, Joe
   Eat, Poop, Die   577
ROMANCE AUTHORS
   Bradford, Robin. ★ *The Readers' Advisory Guide to Romance*   025.2
   Feder, Rachel. *The Darcy Myth*   823
A Romance on Three Legs. Hafner, Katie   786.2092
ROMANIES
   Dregni, Michael. *Django*   B
Romano, Carlin
   America the Philosophical   191
ROMANOV DYNASTY (1613-1917)
   Beevor, Antony. *Russia*   947.084
   Carter, Miranda. *George, Nicholas and Wilhelm*   940.3
   Clay, Catrine. *King, Kaiser, Tsar*   B
   Erickson, Carolly. *Great Catherine*   B
   Figes, Orlando. *A People's Tragedy*   947.08
   Fuhrmann, Joseph T. *Rasputin*   B
   Massie, Robert K. *Catherine the Great*   B
   Massie, Robert K. *Nicholas and Alexandra*   B
   Massie, Robert K. *The Romanovs*   947
   Pipes, Richard. *A Concise History of the Russian Revolution*   947.084
   Pipes, Richard. *The Russian Revolution*   947.084
   Rappaport, Helen. *Caught in the Revolution*   355.00947
   Rappaport, Helen. *The Romanov Sisters*   920
   Smith, Douglas. *Rasputin*   B
   Zygar, Mikhail. *The Empire Must Die*   947.08
The Romanov Sisters. Rappaport, Helen   920
ROMANOV, HOUSE OF
   Massie, Robert K. *Nicholas and Alexandra*   B
   Massie, Robert K. *The Romanovs*   947
   Rappaport, Helen. *The Race to Save the Romanovs*   947.08
   Rappaport, Helen. *The Romanov Sisters*   920
   Sebag-Montefiore, Simon. *The Romanovs*   947
   Smith, Douglas. *Rasputin*   B
   Zygar, Mikhail. *The Empire Must Die*   947.08

Romanov, Nicholas S.
   The Running Revolution — 796.42
The *Romanovs*. Massie, Robert K. — 947
The *Romanovs*. Sebag-Montefiore, Simon — 947
ROMANS
   Beard, Mary. ★*S.P.Q.R.* — 937
   Everitt, Anthony. *The Rise of Rome* — 937
   Goldsworthy, Adrian Keith. *Antony and Cleopatra* — 937
ROMANTIC LOVE
   Cacioppo, Stephanie. *Wired for Love* — 616.8
   Carson, Anne. *The Beauty of the Husband* — 811
   Etheridge, Melissa. *Talking to My Angels* — B
   Feiler, Bruce. *The First Love Story* — 222
   Hauser, CJ. *The Crane Wife* — B
   Havrilesky, Heather. *Foreverland* — 306.81
   Hoffman, Damona. *F the Fairy Tale* — 306.73
   Homer. *Odyssey* — 883
   Isenberg, Sheila. *Women Who Love Men Who Kill* — 362.83
   Jobb, Dean. *A Gentleman and a Thief* — 364.16
   Jones, Saeed. *Prelude to Bruise* — 811
   Komunyakaa, Yusef. *Warhorses* — 811
   Locke, Tembi. ★*From Scratch* — B
   Mendelson, Cheryl. ★*Vows* — 203
   Neruda, Pablo. ★*Twenty Love Poems and a Song of Despair* — 861
   Nguyen, Hieu Minh. *Not Here* — 811
   Pico, Tommy. *Feed* — 811
   Pico, Tommy. *Junk* — 811
   Reed, Justin Phillip. *Indecency* — 811
   Salter, Mary Jo. *The Surveyors* — 811
Romantic Outlaws. Gordon, Charlotte — 920
ROMANTICISM
   Holmes, Richard. *The Age of Wonder* — 509
   Kildea, Paul Francis. *Chopin's Piano* — B
   Wulf, Andrea. *Magnificent Rebels* — 830.9
ROMANTICISM IN ART
   Barnes, Julian. *Keeping an Eye Open* — 709.04
   Bate, Jonathan. *Radical Wordsworth* — B
   Wulf, Andrea. *Magnificent Rebels* — 830.9
ROMANTICISM IN POETRY
   Coleridge, Samuel Taylor. *The Complete Poems* — 821
   Keats, John. *Poems* — 821
   Nicolson, Adam. *The Making of Poetry* — 821.709
Rombauer, Irma S.
   ★*Joy of Cooking* — 641.5973
   ★*Joy of Cooking* — 641.5973
Rome. Hughes, Robert — 945.6
Rome. Kneale, Matthew — 945.6
Rome. Woolf, Greg — 937
Rome from the Ground up. McGregor, James H. — 711
ROME, ITALY
   Hughes, Robert. *Rome* — 945.6
   Kneale, Matthew. *Rome* — 945.6
   Koenig, Leah. *Portico* — 641.5
   McGregor, James H. *Rome from the Ground up* — 711
Romeo, Nick
   The Alternative — 174
Romer, John
   A History of Ancient Egypt — 932
Romesha, Clinton
   Red Platoon — 958.104
ROMESHA, CLINTON
   Romesha, Clinton. *Red Platoon* — 958.104
ROMMEL, ERWIN, 1891-1944
   Brighton, Terry. *Patton, Montgomery, Rommel* — B
   Clark, Lloyd. *The Commanders* — 940.53
Ronald, Susan
   A Dangerous Woman — B
   Hitler's Aristocrats — 940.53
   The Pirate Queen — B
Rondinelli-Hamilton, Lara
   The Diabetes Cookbook — 641.5
Ronson, Jon
   ★*The Psychopath Test* — 616.85
   So You've Been Publicly Shamed — 152.4
Ronstadt, Linda
   Feels Like Home — B
RONSTADT, LINDA, 1946-
   Ronstadt, Linda. *Feels Like Home* — B

Room Full of Mirrors. Cross, Charles R. — B
Room to Dream. Lynch, David — B
ROOMMATES
   Gerard, Sarah. *Carrie Carolyn Coco* — 364.152
ROOMS
   Bryson, Bill. ★*At Home* — 643
ROONEY, ART, 1901-1988
   Eisenberg, John. *The League* — 796.332
ROOSEVELT FAMILY
   Mann, William J. *The Wars of the Roosevelts* — B
   Peyser, Marc N. *Hissing Cousins* — B
ROOSEVELT, ANNA, 1906-1975
   Katz, Catherine Grace. *The Daughters of Yalta* — 920
ROOSEVELT, ELEANOR, 1884-1962
   Bell-Scott, Patricia. *The Firebrand and the First Lady* — 920
   Burns, Eric. *Someone to Watch Over Me* — 973.917092
   Cook, Blanche Wiesen. *Eleanor Roosevelt; Volume 2* — B
   Cook, Blanche Wiesen. ★*Eleanor Roosevelt; Volume 3* — B
   Goodwin, Doris Kearns. *No Ordinary Time* — 920
   Mann, William J. *The Wars of the Roosevelts* — B
   Michaelis, David. ★*Eleanor* — 973.917
   Persico, Joseph E. *Franklin and Lucy* — 973.917092
   Peyser, Marc N. *Hissing Cousins* — B
   Quinn, Susan. *Eleanor and Hick* — B
   Ward, Geoffrey C. ★*The Roosevelts* — B
ROOSEVELT, ELLIOT BULLOCH, 1860-1894
   Burns, Eric. *Someone to Watch Over Me* — 973.917092
ROOSEVELT, FRANKLIN D. (FRANKLIN DELANO), 1882-1945
   Beschloss, Michael R. *The Conquerors* — 940.53
   Brands, H. W. *Traitor to His Class* — B
   Brinkley, Douglas. *Rightful Heritage* — B
   Cook, Blanche Wiesen. *Eleanor Roosevelt; Volume 2* — B
   Cook, Blanche Wiesen. ★*Eleanor Roosevelt; Volume 3* — B
   Dallek, Robert. ★*Franklin D. Roosevelt* — B
   Fullilove, Michael. *Rendezvous with Destiny* — 973.917092
   Goodwin, Doris Kearns. ★*Leadership in Turbulent Times* — 973.09
   Goodwin, Doris Kearns. *No Ordinary Time* — 920
   Groom, Winston. *The Allies* — 940.5309
   Hamilton, Nigel. *The Mantle of Command* — 940.54
   Katznelson, Ira. *Fear Itself* — 973.917
   Mann, William J. *The Wars of the Roosevelts* — B
   McKean, David. *Watching Darkness Fall* — 940.53
   Meacham, Jon. *Franklin and Winston* — 940.53
   Meltzer, Brad. ★*The Nazi Conspiracy* — 940.53
   Michaelis, David. ★*Eleanor* — 973.917
   Nelson, Craig. ★*V Is for Victory* — 973.917
   Olson, Lynne. *Those Angry Days* — 940.53
   Persico, Joseph E. *Franklin and Lucy* — 973.917092
   Preston, Diana. *Eight Days at Yalta* — 940.53
   Roberts, Andrew. *Masters and Commanders* — 940.5322
   Shesol, Jeff. *Supreme Power* — 347.73
   Simon, James F. *FDR and Chief Justice Hughes* — 973.917092
   Smith, Jean Edward. *FDR* — B
   Ward, Geoffrey C. ★*The Roosevelts* — B
   Winik, Jay. *1944* — 940.53
ROOSEVELT, THEODORE, 1858-1919
   Abrams, Dan. *Theodore Roosevelt for the Defense* — 345.73
   Berfield, Susan. *The Hour of Fate* — 973.91
   Brinkley, Douglas. *The Wilderness Warrior* — B
   Cohen, Jared. *Accidental Presidents* — 973.09
   Cordery, Stacy A. *Alice* — B
   Egan, Timothy. ★*The Big Burn* — 973.911
   Gardner, Mark L. *Rough Riders* — 973.911
   Goodwin, Doris Kearns. ★*The Bully Pulpit* — 973.91
   Goodwin, Doris Kearns. ★*Leadership in Turbulent Times* — 973.09
   Kinzer, Stephen. ★*The True Flag* — 327.73
   Klobuchar, Amy. ★*Antitrust* — 343.73
   Mann, William J. *The Wars of the Roosevelts* — B
   McCullough, David G. *Mornings on Horseback* — B
   McCullough, David G. *The Path Between the Seas* — 972.87
   Millard, Candice. *River of Doubt* — 918.1
   Morris, Edmund. ★*Colonel Roosevelt* — B
   Morris, Edmund. ★*The Rise of Theodore Roosevelt* — B
   Morris, Edmund. ★*Theodore Rex* — 973.911
   Ward, Geoffrey C. ★*The Roosevelts* — B
★*The Roosevelts*. Ward, Geoffrey C.
Rooted Kitchen. Rodriguez, Ashley — 641.5
Roots of Steel. Rudacille, Deborah — 338.4

AUTHOR, TITLE, SERIES AND SUBJECT INDEX

Rope, Kate
  Strong as a Mother — 618.2
Roripaugh, Lee Ann
  Tsunami vs. the Fukushima 50 — 811
Rosalind Franklin. Maddox, Brenda — B
Rosbottom, Ronald C.
  When Paris Went Dark — 944.0816
★*Rose's Baking Basics.* Beranbaum, Rose Levy — 641.81
Rose's Ice Cream Bliss. Beranbaum, Rose Levy — 641.86
Rose, Alexander
  Empires of the Sky — 920
Rose, Jacqueline
  On Violence and on Violence Against Women — 362.88
Rose, Michael
  The Birth of an Opera — 782.1
Rose, Mike
  Back to School — 374
ROSE, PETE, 1941-2024
  O'Brien, Keith. *Charlie Hustle* — 796.357
Rose, Reginald
  Twelve Angry Men — 812
Rose, Sarah
  D-Day Girls — 940.53
Rose, Tricia
  ★*Metaracism* — 305.8
Rosemary. Larson, Kate Clifford — B
Rosen, Ali
  Bring It! — 641.5973
Rosen, Charles
  The Classical Style — 780.9
  Sugar — B
Rosen, Ilene
  Saladish — 641.83
Rosen, Jeffrey
  Conversations with RBG — B
  The Pursuit of Happiness — 973.3
Rosen, Jody
  Two Wheels Good — 629.227
Rosen, Jonathan
  ★*The Best Minds* — 616.89
ROSEN, JONATHAN, 1963-
  Rosen, Jonathan. ★*The Best Minds* — 616.89
Rosen, Michael
  Alphabetical — 421
Rosen, Richard A.
  Julius Chambers — B
Rosenbauer, Tom
  The Orvis Fly-Fishing Guide — 799.12
Rosenbaum, Jonathan
  ★*Essential Cinema* — 791.43
ROSENBERG, DAVID, 1961-2014
  Glaser, Gabrielle. *American Baby* — B
ROSENBERG, ETHEL, 1915-1953
  Sebba, Anne. *Ethel Rosenberg* — B
Rosenberg, Ian
  The Fight for Free Speech — 342.73
Rosenberg, Justus
  The Art of Resistance — B
ROSENBERG, JUSTUS, 1921-2021
  Rosenberg, Justus. *The Art of Resistance* — B
Rosenberg, Rosalind
  ★*Jane Crow* — B
Rosenblatt, Roger
  Kayak Morning — 155.9
Rosenblitt, J. Alison
  The Beauty of Living — B
Rosenbloom, Joseph
  Redemption — B
★*Rosencrantz & Guildenstern Are Dead.* Stoppard, Tom — 822
Rosenfeld, Seth
  Subversives — 378.1
Rosenfield, Stephen
  Mastering Stand-Up — 792.7
ROSENHAN, DAVID L.
  Cahalan, Susannah. ★*The Great Pretender* — 616.89
Rosenstrach, Jenny
  How to Celebrate Everything — 641.5
  ★*The Weekday Vegetarians* — 641.5

ROSENTHAL, AMY KROUSE
  Rosenthal, Jason. *My Wife Said You May Want to Marry Me* — B
Rosenthal, Elisabeth
  An American Sickness — 362.10973
Rosenthal, Jason
  My Wife Said You May Want to Marry Me — B
ROSENTHAL, JASON
  Rosenthal, Jason. *My Wife Said You May Want to Marry Me* — B
ROSENTHAL, JOE, 1911-2006
  Bradley, James. *Flags of Our Fathers* — 940.54
Rosenthal, Maxine
  One-Block Wonders of the World — 746.46
Rosenthal, Phil
  ★*Somebody Feed Phil the Book* — 641.59
ROSENTHAL, PHIL, 1960-
  Rosenthal, Phil. ★*Somebody Feed Phil the Book* — 641.59
Rosenzweig, Laura B.
  Hollywood's Spies — 791.43
ROSES
  Solnit, Rebecca. *Orwell's Roses* — B
ROSH HA-SHANAH
  Pogrebin, Abigail. *My Jewish Year* — 296.4
Rosling, Hans
  Factfulness — 155.9
Rosnay, Tatiana de
  Manderley Forever — B
Rosner, Elizabeth
  Survivor Cafe — 940.53
Ross, Alex
  Wagnerism — B
Ross, Andrew
  Sunbelt Blues — 363.5
ROSS, BARNEY, 1909-1967
  Century, Douglas. *Barney Ross* — B
Ross, Catherine Sheldrick
  Conducting the Reference Interview — 025.5
Ross, Dax-Devlon
  Letters to My White Male Friends — 305.8
ROSS, DAX-DEVLON
  Ross, Dax-Devlon. *Letters to My White Male Friends* — 305.8
ROSS, ELIZABETH GRISCOM, 1752-1836
  Miller, Marla. *Betsy Ross and the Making of America* — B
Ross, John F.
  The Promise of the Grand Canyon — 917.91
ROSS, JOHN, 1790-1866
  Inskeep, Steve. *Jacksonland* — 973.56
  Sedgwick, John. *Blood Moon* — 975.004
Ross, Steve
  From Broken Glass — B
ROSS, STEVE, (GRAPHIC NOVELIST)
  Ross, Steve. *From Broken Glass* — B
Ross, Steven Joseph
  ★*Hitler in Los Angeles* — 979.4
ROSSELLI, JOHNNY, 1905-1976
  Maier, Thomas. *Mafia Spies* — 364.1060973
Rossetti, Christina Georgina
  Christina Rossetti — 821.8
Rossini. Servadio, Gaia — B
ROSSINI, GIOACCHINO, 1792-1868
  Servadio, Gaia. *Rossini* — B
Rosso, Julee
  The New Basics Cookbook — 641.5
  The Silver Palate Cookbook — 641.5
Rosten, Leo
  The New Joys of Yiddish — 422
Rotella, Robert J.
  Golf Is Not a Game of Perfect — 796.352
  How Champions Think — 796.01
Roth, Alvin E.
  Who Gets What—And Why — 330.01
Roth, Andrew J.
  Managing Prostate Cancer — 616.99
Roth, Harold
  The Witching Herbs — 133.4
Roth, Joseph
  What I Saw — 943
Roth, Robert
  Strength in Stillness — 158.1

Rothenberg, Ben
  Naomi Osaka — B
Rothfeld, Becca
  ★*All Things Are Too Small* — 814
Rothko. Rothko, Mark — 759.13
Rothko, Mark
  Rothko — 759.13
ROTHKO, MARK, 1903-1970
  Cohen-Solal, Annie. *Mark Rothko* — 759.13
  Rothko, Mark. *Rothko* — 759.13
Rothkopf, David J.
  American Resistance — 973.933
Rothman, Joshua D.
  The Ledger and the Chain — 306.362
Rothschild, Mike
  The Storm Is Upon Us — 973.933
Rothstein, Richard
  ★*The Color of Law* — 305.800973
Rotman, Jeffrey L.
  The Last Fisherman — 778.7
ROTMAN, JEFFREY L.
  Rotman, Jeffrey L. *The Last Fisherman* — 778.7
Rott, Ira
  Crochet Animal Rugs — 746.7
Roudinesco, Elisabeth
  ★*Freud* — B
Rough *Beauty.* Auvinen, Karen — B
Rough *Draft.* Tur, Katy — B
Rough *Ideas.* Hough, Stephen — 786.2092
Rough *Magic.* Prior-Palmer, Lara — 798.4
Rough *Riders.* Gardner, Mark L. — 973.911
★***Rough*** *Sleepers.* Kidder, Tracy — 362.5
The ***Roughest*** *Riders.* Tuccille, Jerome — 973.8
Roughhouse *Friday.* Coffin, Jaed — B
Rounding, Virginia
  The Burning Time — 272
Roundtree, Dovey Johnson
  ★*Mighty Justice* — B
ROUNDTREE, DOVEY JOHNSON, 1914-2018
  Roundtree, Dovey Johnson. ★*Mighty Justice* — B
Rountree, Sage
  The Athlete's Guide to Recovery — 617.1
Rousseau, Jean-Jacques
  Confessions — B
  ★*The Social Contract* — 320.1
ROUSSEAU, JEAN-JACQUES, 1712-1778
  Rousseau, Jean-Jacques. *Confessions* — B
Route *66.* Wallis, Michael — 917.804
Rovelli, Carlo
  Helgoland — 530.12
  The Order of Time — 530.11
  Reality Is Not What It Seems — 530.14
  ★*Seven Brief Lessons on Physics* — 530
  There Are Places in the World Where Rules Are Less Important Than Kindness — 500
Row, Jess
  White Flights — 813
ROW, JESS
  Row, Jess. *White Flights* — 813
Rowan, Barry L.
  The Spiritual Art of Business — 261.8
Rowe, Mickey
  Fearlessly Different — B
ROWE, MICKEY, 1988-
  Rowe, Mickey. *Fearlessly Different* — B
Rowe, Peggy
  About My Mother — B
ROWE, PEGGY
  Rowe, Peggy. *About My Mother* — B
ROWE, THELMA
  Rowe, Peggy. *About My Mother* — B
ROWERS
  Brown, Daniel James. ★*The Boys in the Boat* — 797.12
  Gilder, Ginny. *Course Correction* — 797.12
  Halberstam, David. *The Amateurs* — B
ROWING
  Brown, Daniel James. ★*The Boys in the Boat* — 797.12
  Gilder, Ginny. *Course Correction* — 797.12

  Halberstam, David. *The Amateurs* — B
Rowland, Ingrid D.
  The Collector of Lives — B
ROWLANDSON, MARY WHITE, APPROXIMATELY 1635-1711
  Silverman, David J. ★*This Land Is Their Land* — 974.4
Roy, Arundhati
  Walking with the Comrades — 954
Roy, Jessica
  American Girls — 305.48
Roy, Saumya
  Castaway Mountain — 363.72
The ***Royal*** *Art of Poison.* Herman, Eleanor — 364.152
Royal *Audience.* Charter, David — 941.085
A ***Royal*** *Experiment.* Hadlow, Janice — B
ROYAL HOUSES
  Ackroyd, Peter. *Innovation* — 942.082
  Ackroyd, Peter. *Rebellion* — 941.06
  Ackroyd, Peter. *Revolution* — 941.07
  Ackroyd, Peter. *Tudors* — 942.05
  Borman, Tracy. *Crown & Sceptre* — 941
  Borman, Tracy. *Elizabeth's Women* — B
  Borman, Tracy. *Henry VIII and the Men Who Made Him* — 942.05
  Borman, Tracy. *The Private Lives of the Tudors* — 920
  Brown, Tina. ★*The Palace Papers* — 920
  Cadbury, Deborah. *Princes at War* — 920
  Cadbury, Deborah. *Queen Victoria's Matchmaking* — 941.081
  Edwards, Anne. *Matriarch* — B
  Goldstone, Nancy Bazelon. *In the Shadow of the Empress* — 920
  Goldstone, Nancy Bazelon. *The Rival Queens* — 944
  Hadlow, Janice. *A Royal Experiment* — B
  Hardman, Robert. *Queen of Our Times* — B
  Hardman, Robert. *Queen of the World* — B
  Harry. ★*Spare* — B
  Hawksley, Lucinda. *Queen Victoria's Mysterious Daughter* — B
  Hope, Bradley. *Blood and Oil* — B
  Jones, Dan. ★*The Plantagenets* — 942.03092
  King, Greg. *Twilight of Empire* — 943.6
  Lacey, Robert. *Inside the Kingdom* — 953.805
  Larman, Alexander. ★*Power and Glory* — 941.085
  Larman, Alexander. *The Windsors at War* — 940.53
  Massie, Robert K. *Nicholas and Alexandra* — B
  Massie, Robert K. *The Romanovs* — 947
  Meyer, G. J. *The Tudors* — 920
  Morton, Andrew. *17 Carnations* — 941.084
  Pakula, Hannah. *The Last Empress* — B
  Penn, Thomas. *The Brothers York* — 942.04
  Porter, Linda. *Katherine the Queen* — B
  Rappaport, Helen. *The Race to Save the Romanovs* — 947.08
  Rappaport, Helen. *The Romanov Sisters* — 920
  Ridley, Jane. *George V* — B
  Sebag-Montefiore, Simon. *The Romanovs* — 947
  Sebag-Montefiore, Simon. ★*The World* — 929.7
  Smith, Sally Bedell. *Elizabeth the Queen* — B
  Smith, Sally Bedell. *George VI and Elizabeth* — 920
  Weir, Alison. *The Children of Henry VIII* — B
ROYAL PRETENDERS
  Massie, Robert K. *The Romanovs* — 947
ROYAL WEDDINGS
  Cadbury, Deborah. *Queen Victoria's Matchmaking* — 941.081
Royster, Francesca T.
  Choosing Family — B
The ***Rub*** *of Time.* Amis, Martin — 824
Rubaiyat *of Omar Khayyam.* Omar Khayyam — 891
Rubber *Band Engineer.* Akiyama, Lance — 745.57
RUBBER STAMPING
  Corwin, Lena. *Printing by Hand* — 745.5
Rubenhold, Hallie
  ★*The Five* — 362.88
Rubenstein, David M.
  The American Experiment — 973
  The American Story — 973.07202
Ruberg, Bonnie
  ★*The Queer Games Avant-Garde* — 794.8
Rubin, Daniel Joshua
  27 Essential Principles of Story — 808.02
Rubin, Gretchen
  Outer Order, Inner Calm — 158

AUTHOR, TITLE, SERIES AND SUBJECT INDEX

Rubin, Gretchen Craft
   ★*Life in Five Senses*   152.1
RUBIN, GRETCHEN CRAFT
   Rubin, Gretchen Craft. ★*Life in Five Senses*   152.1
Rubin, Kathy Kleiner
   A Light in the Dark   364.152
Rubin, Rick
   ★*The Creative Act*   153.3
Rubin, Robert Edward
   The Yellow Pad   658.4
RUBIN, ROBERT EDWARD, 1938-
   Rubin, Robert Edward. *The Yellow Pad*   658.4
Rubinstein, Julian
   ★*The Holly*   364.106
RUBY, JACK, 1911-1967
   Abrams, Dan. *Kennedy's Avenger*   973.922
Ruck, Rob
   Raceball   796.357
Rudacille, Deborah
   Roots of Steel   338.4
Rudd, Mark
   Underground   378.1
RUDD, MARK
   Rudd, Mark. *Underground*   378.1
Rude, Emelyn
   Tastes Like Chicken   338.1
Ruden, Sarah
   The Face of Water   220.5
RUDENESS
   Kohan, Rafi. ★*Trash Talk*   179
RUDOLF, CROWN PRINCE OF AUSTRIA, 1858-1889
   King, Greg. *Twilight of Empire*   943.6
Rudolf, David S.
   American Injustice   345.73
RUDOLF, DAVID S.
   Rudolf, David S. *American Injustice*   345.73
Rueckert, Veronica
   Outspoken   808.5
Ruefle, Mary
   Dunce   811
   Selected Poems   811
Ruffage. Berens, Abra   641.5
Ruffin, Amber
   ★*The World Record Book of Racist Stories*   305.896
   You'll Never Believe What Happened to Lacey   305.896
RUFFIN, AMBER
   Ruffin, Amber. ★*The World Record Book of Racist Stories*   305.896
   Ruffin, Amber. *You'll Never Believe What Happened to Lacey*   305.896
RUGBY FOOTBALL
   Carlin, John. *Playing the Enemy*   968.06
RUGBY FOOTBALL PLAYERS
   Parrado, Nando. ★*Miracle in the Andes*   982
   Read, Piers Paul. ★*Alive*   982
RUGS
   Rott, Ira. *Crochet Animal Rugs*   746.7
Ruhl, Sarah
   Letters from Max   811
   Smile   B
RUHL, SARAH, 1974-
   Ruhl, Sarah. *Letters from Max*   811
   Ruhl, Sarah. *Smile*   B
Ruhlman, Michael
   Ratio   641.5
★*Ruin Their Crops on the Ground*. Freeman, Andrea   338.1
Rukeyser, Muriel
   Selected Poems   811
RULE OF LAW
   Breyer, Stephen G. ★*The Authority of the Court and the Peril of Politics*   347.73
Rule, Ann
   The Stranger Beside Me   B
★*The Rulebreaker*. Page, Susan   B
RULERS
   Ackroyd, Peter. *The Death of King Arthur*   823
   Ackroyd, Peter. *Innovation*   942.082
   Aristotle. ★*Politics, 2nd Ed*   320
   Beard, Mary. ★*Emperor of Rome*   937
   Bix, Herbert P. *Hirohito and the Making of Modern Japan*   B
   Blanning, T. C. W. *Frederick the Great*   B
   Borman, Tracy. *Crown & Sceptre*   941
   Borman, Tracy. *Elizabeth's Women*   B
   Borman, Tracy. *Henry VIII and the Men Who Made Him*   942.05
   Borman, Tracy. *The Private Lives of the Tudors*   920
   Brands, H. W. *The Last Campaign*   973.8
   Brier, Bob. *The Murder of Tutankhamen*   B
   Broers, Michael. *Napoleon*   B
   Broers, Michael. *Napoleon*   944.05
   Broers, Michael. *Napoleon*   B
   Cadbury, Deborah. *Princes at War*   920
   Carter, Miranda. *George, Nicholas and Wilhelm*   940.3
   Castor, Helen. *She-Wolves*   942
   Clay, Catrine. *King, Kaiser, Tsar*   B
   Cooney, Kara. *When Women Ruled the World*   920
   Dagher, Sam. *Assad or We Burn the Country*   956.9104
   Dalrymple, William. *The Return of a King*   958.1
   Darnell, John Coleman. *Egypt's Golden Couple*   932
   Darnton, Robert. *The Revolutionary Temper*   944
   Everitt, Anthony. *Alexander the Great*   B
   Finkel, Caroline. *Osman's Dream*   956.1
   Firdawsi. *Shahnameh*   891
   Fraser, Antonia. *Love and Louis XIV*   B
   Fraser, Antonia. *Marie Antoinette*   B
   Goldstone, Nancy Bazelon. *The Rival Queens*   944
   Gristwood, Sarah. *Blood Sisters*   942.04092
   Gristwood, Sarah. *The Tudors in Love*   941.05
   Hansen, Valerie. *The Year 1000*   909
   Hardman, Robert. *Queen of the World*   B
   Herman, Eleanor. *The Royal Art of Poison*   364.152
   Hibbert, Christopher. *Edward VII*   B
   Johnson, Paul. *Napoleon*   B
   Jones, Dan. ★*The Plantagenets*   942.03092
   Keene, Donald. *Emperor of Japan*   952.03
   Larman, Alexander. ★*Power and Glory*   941.085
   Larman, Alexander. *The Windsors at War*   940.53
   Lieven, Dominic. *In the Shadow of the Gods*   352.23
   Lownie, Andrew. *Traitor King*   920
   MacCulloch, Diarmaid. *Thomas Cromwell*   B
   Malory, Thomas. *Le Morte Darthur, Or, the Hoole Book of Kyng Arthur and of His Noble Knyghtes of the Rounde Table*   823
   Mansel, Philip. *King of the World*   B
   Marozzi, Justin. *Tamerlane*   950.2
   Massie, Robert K. *Catherine the Great*   B
   Massie, Robert K. *Nicholas and Alexandra*   B
   McLynn, Frank. *Genghis Khan*   950.2
   Meyer, G. J. *The Tudors*   920
   Morris, Marc. *A Great and Terrible King*   B
   Morris, Marc. *King John*   942.033
   Noor. *Leap of Faith*   B
   Norwich, John Julius. *A History of France*   944
   Penn, Thomas. *The Brothers York*   942.04
   Pitts, Mike. *Digging for Richard III*   942.046
   Porter, Linda. *Katherine the Queen*   B
   Powers, Thomas. *The Killing of Crazy Horse*   B
   Puhak, Shelley. *The Dark Queens*   944
   Ridley, Jane. *George V*   B
   Ridley, Jane. *The Heir Apparent*   B
   Roberts, Andrew. *The Last King of America*   B
   Roberts, Andrew. ★*Napoleon*   B
   Satyamurti, Carole. *Mahabharata*   821
   Sebag-Montefiore, Simon. *The Romanovs*   947
   Sebag-Montefiore, Simon. ★*The World*   929.7
   Smith, Sally Bedell. *Elizabeth the Queen*   B
   Smith, Sally Bedell. *George VI and Elizabeth*   920
   Strauss, Barry S. *The Death of Caesar*   937
   Strauss, Barry S. *Ten Caesars*   937
   Suetonius. ★*The Twelve Caesars*   937
   Tallis, Nicola. *Crown of Blood*   B
   Weatherford, J. McIver. ★*Genghis Khan and the Making of the Modern World*   B
   Weatherford, J. McIver. *Genghis Khan and the Quest for God*   323.44
   Weir, Alison. *The Children of Henry VIII*   B
   Weir, Alison. *Henry VIII*   B
   Weir, Alison. *The Lady in the Tower*   B
   Weir, Alison. *Queens of the Conquest*   920
   Winder, Simon. *Lotharingia*   944
   Woolf, Greg. *Rome*   937

PUBLIC LIBRARY CORE COLLECTION: NONFICTION
Twentieth Edition

Worsley, Lucy. *Queen Victoria* — B
Zamoyski, Adam. *Napoleon* — B
RULERS' SPOUSES
  Bordo, Susan. *The Creation of Anne Boleyn* — 942.05
RULES
  Formosa, Dan. *Baseball Field Guide* — 796.357
  Gilliam, Fatimah. *Race Rules* — 305.8
  Parker, Vergil R. *Pickleball 101* — 796.34
  Turbow, Jason. *The Baseball Codes* — 796.357
Rules for Rulebreakers. Tolokonnikova, Nadezhda — 782.42166
Rumi. Jalal al-Din Rumi, Maulana — 891
RUMOR
  DiResta, Renee. *Invisible Rulers* — 320
  Kroll, Andy. *A Death on W Street* — 364.152
A *Rumor* of War. Caputo, Philip — 959.704
Rumsfeld, Donald
  When the Center Held — 973.925092
RUMSFELD, DONALD, 1932-2021
  Rumsfeld, Donald. *When the Center Held* — 973.925092
  ★*Rumspringa*. Shachtman, Tom — 305.235
RUMSPRINGA
  Mackall, Joe. *Plain Secrets* — 289.7
  Shachtman, Tom. ★*Rumspringa* — 305.235
Run (John Lewis) [Series]. Lewis, John — 741.5
Run Fast, Cook Fast, Eat Slow. Flanagan, Shalane — 641.5
Run The World. Wade, Becky — 796.42
Run to the Finish. Brooks, Amanda — 613.7
★*Run*; Book One. Lewis, John — 741.5
RUNAWAY CHILDREN
  Murray, Liz. *Breaking Night* — B
RUNAWAY MOTHERS
  Sullivan, Rosemary. *Stalin's Daughter* — B
The *Runaway* Species. Brandt, Anthony K. — 153.3
RUNAWAY TEENAGERS
  Snyder, Rachel Louise. *Women We Buried, Women We Burned* — B
RUNAWAYS
  Seierstad, Asne. *Two Sisters* — 956.9104
Runciman, David
  The Confidence Trap — 321.8
Rundell, Katherine
  ★*Super-Infinite* — B
RUNNERS
  Brooks, Amanda. *Run to the Finish* — 613.7
  Engle, Charlie. *Running Man* — B
  Finn, Adharanand. *The Rise of the Ultra Runners* — B
  Finn, Adharanand. *The Way of the Runner* — 796.42
  Futterman, Matthew. *Running to the Edge* — 796.42071
  Hamilton, Duncan. *For the Glory* — B
  Hart, Matt. *Win at All Costs* — 338.7
  Heminsley, Alexandra. *Running Like a Girl* — B
  Inman, Matthew. *The Terrible and Wonderful Reasons Why I Run Long Distances* — 741.5
  Keeling, Ida. *Can't Nothing Bring Me Down* — B
  Keflezighi, Meb. *26 Marathons* — B
  McDougall, Christopher. ★*Born to Run* — 796.42
  Mertens, Maggie. *Better Faster Farther* — 796.42
  Shorter, Frank. *My Marathon* — 796.42
  Thompson, J. M. *Running Is a Kind of Dreaming* — B
  Wade, Becky. *Run the World* — 796.42
RUNNING
  Alvarez, Noe. *Spirit Run* — 796.42
  Brooks, Amanda. *Run to the Finish* — 613.7
  Davis, Jennifer Pharr. *The Pursuit of Endurance* — 796.51
  Engle, Charlie. *Running Man* — B
  Finn, Adharanand. *The Rise of the Ultra Runners* — B
  Finn, Adharanand. *The Way of the Runner* — 796.42
  Futterman, Matthew. *Running to the Edge* — 796.42071
  Heminsley, Alexandra. *Running Like a Girl* — B
  Higdon, Hal. ★*Marathon* — 796.42
  Inman, Matthew. *The Terrible and Wonderful Reasons Why I Run Long Distances* — 741.5
  Keeling, Ida. *Can't Nothing Bring Me Down* — B
  Magill, Pete. *Build Your Running Body* — 796.42
  McDougall, Christopher. ★*Born to Run* — 796.42
  McDougall, Christopher. *Natural Born Heroes* — 940.53
  McDougall, Christopher. *Running with Sherman* — 636.1
  Mertens, Maggie. *Better Faster Farther* — 796.42
  Montillo, Roseanne. *Fire on the Track* — B

Romanov, Nicholas S. *The Running Revolution* — 796.42
Thompson, J. M. *Running Is a Kind of Dreaming* — B
Wade, Becky. *Run the World* — 796.42
Running Against the Devil. Wilson, Rick — 973.933
RUNNING FOR WOMEN
  Heminsley, Alexandra. *Running Like a Girl* — B
Running Is a Kind of Dreaming. Thompson, J. M. — B
Running Like a Girl. Heminsley, Alexandra — B
Running Man. Engle, Charlie — B
RUNNING RACES
  Davis, Jennifer Pharr. *The Pursuit of Endurance* — 796.51
  Futterman, Matthew. *Running to the Edge* — 796.42071
  Hamilton, Duncan. *For the Glory* — B
  Heminsley, Alexandra. *Running Like a Girl* — B
  McDougall, Christopher. *Running with Sherman* — 636.1
  Wade, Becky. *Run the World* — 796.42
The *Running* Revolution. Romanov, Nicholas S. — 796.42
Running to the Edge. Futterman, Matthew — 796.42071
Running Toward Mystery. Tenzin Priyadarshi — B
Running with Sherman. McDougall, Christopher — 636.1
Runstedtler, Theresa
  Black Ball — 796.323
RuPaul
  ★*The House of Hidden Meanings* — B
RUPAUL, 1960-
  RuPaul. ★*The House of Hidden Meanings* — B
RURAL AFRICAN AMERICANS
  Sellers, Bakari. *My Vanishing Country* — B
RURAL CHILDREN
  Lewis, John. ★*March; Book One* — 741.5
RURAL CONDITIONS
  Agee, James. *Let Us Now Praise Famous Men* — 976.1
RURAL CRIMES
  Cep, Casey N. ★*Furious Hours* — 364.152
RURAL DEVELOPMENT
  Briody, Blaire. *The New Wild West* — 338.2
RURAL FAMILIES
  Agee, James. ★*Cotton Tenants* — 976.1
  Badkhen, Anna. *The World Is a Carpet* — 305.409581
  Heaney, Seamus. *District and Circle* — 821
  Juan, Li. *Winter Pasture* — 951.06
  Phelan, Tom. *We Were Rich and We Didn't Know It* — B
RURAL HEALTH SERVICES
  Fabes, Stephen. *Signs of Life* — B
RURAL LANDS
  Fowler, Corinne. ★*The Countryside* — 941
RURAL LIFE
  Agee, James. ★*Cotton Tenants* — 976.1
  Barker, Elspeth. *Notes from the Henhouse* — 828
  Bennett, Jackie. *The Writer's Garden* — 920
  Berry, Wendell. ★*The World-Ending Fire* — 818
  Bitsui, Sherwin. *Dissolve* — 811
  Carter, Jimmy. *An Hour Before Daylight* — B
  Cep, Casey N. ★*Furious Hours* — 364.152
  Cullen, Art. *Storm Lake* — 071.7
  Currid-Halkett, Elizabeth. *The Overlooked Americans* — 307.76
  Dennison, Matthew. *The Man in the Willows* — B
  Dinesen, Isak. *Out of Africa* — 967.62
  Eisenberg, Emma Copley. ★*The Third Rainbow Girl* — 364.152
  Georges, Gigi. *Downeast* — 974.1
  Heaney, Seamus. *District and Circle* — 821
  Huxley, Elspeth Joscelin Grant. *The Flame Trees of Thika* — B
  Kelley, Margot Anne. *A Gardener at the End of the World* — 615.8
  Kingsolver, Barbara. ★*Animal, Vegetable, Miracle* — 641
  Locke, Tembi. ★*From Scratch* — B
  Logsdon, Gene. *Letter to a Young Farmer* — 338.10973
  Masciotra, David. *Exurbia Now* — 320.973
  Mayle, Peter. *My Twenty-Five Years in Provence* — 944.9
  Miles, Tiya. ★*Wild Girls* — 304.2
  Offerman, Nick. *Where the Deer and the Antelope Play* — 973.93
  Parks, Casey. *Diary of a Misfit* — B
  Phelan, Tom. *We Were Rich and We Didn't Know It* — B
  Potts, Monica. *The Forgotten Girls* — B
  Rao, Maya. *Great American Outpost* — 338.2
  Rebanks, James. *The Shepherd's Life* — 942.7
  Sellers, Bakari. *My Vanishing Country* — B
  Simmons, Ruth. ★*Up Home* — B
  Stewart, Chris. *Driving Over Lemons* — 946

AUTHOR, TITLE, SERIES AND SUBJECT INDEX

Tester, Jon. *Grounded*	B
Vigliotti, Jonathan. *Before It's Gone*	577
Westover, Tara. ★*Educated*	B
Wilkinson, Crystal. *Praisesong for the Kitchen Ghosts*	641.5975
Winn, Raynor. ★*The Salt Path*	B

RURAL POOR PEOPLE
Scott, Kevin. *Reprogramming the American Dream*	338
Ward, Jesmyn. ★*Men We Reaped*	B

RURAL POVERTY
Edin, Kathryn. ★*The Injustice of Place*	339.4

RURAL SOCIOLOGY
Masciotra, David. *Exurbia Now*	320.973
Scott, Kevin. *Reprogramming the American Dream*	338

RURAL-URBAN MIGRATION
Wilkerson, Isabel. ★*The Warmth of Other Suns*	304.80973

Rusbridger, Alan
★*Play It Again*	B

RUSBRIDGER, ALAN
Rusbridger, Alan. ★*Play It Again*	B

Rush. Fried, Stephen

RUSH, BENJAMIN, 1746-1813
Fried, Stephen. *Rush*	B

Rush, Charaia
Courageously Soft	234

RUSH, CHARAIA, 1991-
Rush, Charaia. *Courageously Soft*	234

Rush, Chris
The Light Years	B

RUSH, CHRIS, 1956-
Rush, Chris. *The Light Years*	B

Rush, Elizabeth A.
Rising	551.45

RUSH, ELIZABETH A.
Rush, Elizabeth A. *Rising*	551.45

Rushdie, Salman
Joseph Anton	B
★*Knife*	B
Languages of Truth	824

RUSHDIE, SALMAN
Rushdie, Salman. *Joseph Anton*	B
Rushdie, Salman. ★*Knife*	B
Rushdie, Salman. *Languages of Truth*	824

Rushin, Steve
The 34-Ton Bat	796.357

Russell, Bertrand
A History of Western Philosophy, and Its Connection with Political and Social Circumstances from the Earliest Times to the Present Day	109
The Problems of Philosophy	110

RUSSELL, BILL, 1934-2022
Montville, Leigh. *Tall Men, Short Shorts*	796.323

Russell, Carrie
Complete Copyright for K-12 Librarians and Educators	346.73

Russell, Gareth
★*The Palace*	942.1
The Ship of Dreams	910.91
Young and Damned and Fair	B

Russell, Jan Jarboe
The Train to Crystal City	940.53

Russell, Rupert
Price Wars	332.64

Russell, Stuart J.
Human Compatible	006.301

Russell, Tony
Country Music Originals	B

RUSSELL, WILLIAM, LORD, 1767-1840
Harman, Claire. *Murder by the Book*	364.152

Russert, Luke
Look for Me There	B

RUSSERT, LUKE
Russert, Luke. *Look for Me There*	B

Russia. Beevor, Antony — 947.084

RUSSIA
Aleksievich, Svetlana. ★*Secondhand Time*	947.086
Beevor, Antony. *Russia*	947.084
Conradi, Peter J. *Who Lost Russia?*	947.086
Cook, Jane Hampton. *American Phoenix*	973.5
Erickson, Carolly. *Great Catherine*	B
Figes, Orlando. ★*The Story of Russia*	947
Frank, Joseph. ★*Dostoevsky*	B
Galeotti, Mark. *A Short History of Russia*	947.086
Garrels, Anne. *Putin Country*	947
Gessen, Masha. *The Future Is History*	947.086
Gessen, Masha. *Never Remember*	365
Greene, David. *Midnight in Siberia*	914
Harding, Luke. *Collusion*	324.70973
Harding, Luke. *Invasion*	947.7
Isikoff, Michael. *Russian Roulette*	973.933
Kasparov, Gary. *Winter Is Coming*	947.086
Kavanagh, Julie. *Nureyev*	B
Khodorkovsky, Mikhail. *The Russia Conundrum*	947.086
Malarkey, Tucker. *Stronghold*	639.2
Malcolm, Janet. *Reading Chekhov*	891.72
Massie, Robert K. *Catherine the Great*	B
Merridale, Catherine. *Lenin on the Train*	B
Morrison, Simon Alexander. *Bolshoi Confidential*	792.8
Myers, Steven Lee. *The New Tsar*	B
Nance, Malcolm W. *The Plot to Betray America*	973.933
Phillips, Timothy. *Retracing the Iron Curtain*	909.82
Plokhy, Serhii. *Lost Kingdom*	947
Politkovskaya, Anna. *A Russian Diary*	947.086
Rappaport, Helen. *The Romanov Sisters*	920
Riasanovsky, Nicholas V. *A History of Russia*	947
Rogoyska, Jane. *Surviving Katyn*	940.54
Satter, David. *The Less You Know, the Better You Sleep*	947.086
Sebag-Montefiore, Simon. *The Romanovs*	947
Sebestyen, Victor. *Lenin*	B
Service, Robert. *Lenin—A Biography*	B
Shimer, David. *Rigged*	324.60973
Short, Philip. *Putin*	B
Slaght, Jonathan C. *Owls of the Eastern Ice*	598.9
Slezkine, Yuri. *The House of Government*	947.084
Smith, Douglas. *Rasputin*	B
Stengel, Richard. *Information Wars*	355.3
Trofimov, Yaroslav. ★*Our Enemies Will Vanish*	947.7
Vaillant, John. *The Tiger*	599.756
Walker, Shaun. *The Long Hangover*	947.086
Walton, Calder. *Spies*	327.1247
Weiner, Tim. *The Folly and the Glory*	327.73047
Wiehl, Lis W. *A Spy in Plain Sight*	327.1247
Wullschlager, Jackie. ★*Chagall*	B
Yaffa, Joshua. *Between Two Fires*	920
Zygar, Mikhail. *All the Kremlin's Men*	947.086
Zygar, Mikhail. *The Empire Must Die*	947.08

The Russia Conundrum. Khodorkovsky, Mikhail — 947.086
A Russian Diary. Politkovskaya, Anna — 947.086

RUSSIAN HISTORY
Bartlett, Rosamund. ★*Tolstoy*	B
Beevor, Antony. *Russia*	947.084
Carter, Miranda. *George, Nicholas and Wilhelm*	940.3
Clay, Catrine. *King, Kaiser, Tsar*	B
Erickson, Carolly. *Great Catherine*	B
Figes, Orlando. *A People's Tragedy*	947.08
Frank, Joseph. ★*Dostoevsky*	B
Fuhrmann, Joseph T. *Rasputin*	B
Galeotti, Mark. *A Short History of Russia*	947.086
Gorbachev, Mikhail. *On My Country and the World*	947.085
Igort. *The Ukrainian and Russian Notebooks*	741.5
Kotkin, Stephen. *Stalin*	B
Kotkin, Stephen. *Stalin*	B
Massie, Robert K. *Catherine the Great*	B
Massie, Robert K. *Nicholas and Alexandra*	B
Massie, Robert K. *The Romanovs*	947
Mieville, China. *October*	947.084
Miles, Jonathan. *St. Petersburg*	947
Pipes, Richard. *A Concise History of the Russian Revolution*	947.084
Pipes, Richard. *The Russian Revolution*	947.084
Plokhy, Serhii. *Lost Kingdom*	947
Plokhy, Serhii. ★*The Russo-Ukrainian War*	947.7
Popoff, Alexandra. *Vasily Grossman and the Soviet Century*	B
Rappaport, Helen. *Caught in the Revolution*	355.00947
Rappaport, Helen. *The Romanov Sisters*	920
Riasanovsky, Nicholas V. *A History of Russia*	947
Sebag-Montefiore, Simon. *The Romanovs*	947
Sebag-Montefiore, Simon. *Young Stalin*	B
Seierstad, Asne. *Angel of Grozny*	947.086
Smith, Douglas. *Rasputin*	B

PUBLIC LIBRARY CORE COLLECTION: NONFICTION
Twentieth Edition

Zygar, Mikhail. *The Empire Must Die*	947.08
*The **Russian** Job*. Smith, Douglas	947.084
RUSSIAN PEOPLE	
Akhmatova, Anna Andreevna. ★*The Complete Poems of Anna Akhmatova*	
	891.71
Golinkin, Lev. *A Backpack, a Bear, and Eight Crates of Vodka*	B
Harss, Marina. *The Boy from Kyiv*	B
Loyn, David. *In Afghanistan*	958.1
MacGregor, Iain. *The Lighthouse of Stalingrad*	940.54
Shteyngart, Gary. ★*Little Failure*	B
Thubron, Colin. *In Siberia*	957
RUSSIAN PEOPLE IN FOREIGN COUNTRIES	
Rappaport, Helen. *After the Romanovs*	944
RUSSIAN PEOPLE IN THE UNITED STATES	
Carlson, Peter. *K Blows Top*	947.085
Shteyngart, Gary. ★*Little Failure*	B
*The **Russian** Revolution*. McMeekin, Sean	947.084
*The **Russian** Revolution*. Pipes, Richard	947.084
RUSSIAN REVOLUTION AND CIVIL WAR (1917-1921)	
Beevor, Antony. *Russia*	947.084
Figes, Orlando. *A People's Tragedy*	947.08
Herman, Arthur. *1917*	940.3
Kotkin, Stephen. *Stalin*	B
McMeekin, Sean. *The Russian Revolution*	947.084
McNamara, Kevin J. *Dreams of a Great Small Nation*	355.009437
Merridale, Catherine. *Lenin on the Train*	B
Mieville, China. *October*	947.084
Pipes, Richard. *A Concise History of the Russian Revolution*	947.084
Pipes, Richard. *The Russian Revolution*	947.084
Rappaport, Helen. *After the Romanovs*	944
Rappaport, Helen. *Caught in the Revolution*	355.00947
Reed, John. *Ten Days That Shook the World*	947.084
Teffi, N. A. *Memories*	B
Zygar, Mikhail. *The Empire Must Die*	947.08
***Russian** Roulette*. Isikoff, Michael	973.933
RUSSO, ANTHONY J. (ANTHONY JOSEPH)	
Prose, Francine. *1974*	B
Russo, Richard	
The Destiny Thief	814
RUSSO, VITO	
Schiavi, Michael R. *Celluloid Activist*	B
★*The **Russo**-Ukrainian War*. Plokhy, Serhii	947.7
RUSSO-UKRAINIAN WAR, 2014-	
Harding, Luke. *Invasion*	947.7
Miller, Christopher. *The War Came to Us*	947.7
Petraeus, David Howell. *Conflict*	355
Plokhy, Serhii. ★*The Russo-Ukrainian War*	947.7
Stengel, Richard. *Information Wars*	355.3
Trofimov, Yaroslav. ★*Our Enemies Will Vanish*	947.7
Zelensky, Volodymyr. *A Message from Ukraine*	947.7
★***Ruth** Bader Ginsburg*. De Hart, Jane Sherron	B
RUTH, BABE, 1895-1948	
Creamer, Robert W. *Babe*	B
Leavy, Jane. *The Big Fella*	B
Rutherford, Adam	
The Complete Guide to Absolutely Everything	500
Control	363.9
Humanimal	599.93
RUTHERFURD, LUCY MERCER	
Persico, Joseph E. *Franklin and Lucy*	973.917092
***Ruthless** Tide*. Roker, Al	974.8
RUTHLESSNESS	
Farrell, John A. ★*Richard Nixon*	B
Mann, William J. *The Wars of the Roosevelts*	B
McPhee, Peter. *Robespierre*	B
Zelizer, Julian E. *Burning Down the House*	328.73
Ruthsatz, Joanne	
The Prodigy's Cousin	155.45
Rutkow, Ira M.	
Empire of the Scalpel	617
RUTLAND, FREDERICK, 1887-1949	
Drabkin, Ronald. *Beverly Hills Spy*	940.54
Ruttenberg, Danya	
On Repentance and Repair	202
RWANDA	
Gourevitch, Philip. *We Wish to Inform You That Tomorrow We Will Be Killed with Our Families*	364.15
Hatzfeld, Jean. *Blood Papa*	967.5710431
Hatzfeld, Jean. *Machete Season*	967.57104
RWANDAN CIVIL WAR, 1994	
Hatzfeld, Jean. *Blood Papa*	967.5710431
Hatzfeld, Jean. *Machete Season*	967.57104
Ryan, Alan	
On Politics	320.01
RYAN, GEORGE H.	
Turow, Scott. ★*Ultimate Punishment*	345.73
Ryan, Kay	
The Best of It	811
Ryan, Maureen	
Burn It Down	791.43
Ryback, Timothy W.	
Hitler's Private Library	027
Takeover	943.086
Rybczynski, Witold	
The Look of Architecture	721
Mysteries of the Mall	720
Ryckman, Pamela	
Candace Pert	B
Rydell, Anders	
The Book Thieves	027
RYDER CUP (GOLF)	
Feinstein, John. *The First Major*	796.352
Ryder, Anthony	
The Artist's Complete Guide to Figure Drawing	743.4
Rynecki, Elizabeth	
Chasing Portraits	B
RYNECKI, MOSHE, 1881-1943	
Rynecki, Elizabeth. *Chasing Portraits*	B
Ryrie, Alec	
Protestants	280

S

S O S. Baraka, Amiri	811
★*S.P.Q.R.* Beard, Mary	937
Saad, Layla F.	
★*Me and White Supremacy*	305.809
Sababa. Sussman, Adeena	641.5
Saban. Burke, Monte	796.332
SABAN, NICK	
Burke, Monte. *Saban*	796.332
Sabar, Ariel	
My Father's Paradise	B
SABAR, ARIEL	
Sabar, Ariel. *My Father's Paradise*	B
SABAR, YONA	
Sabar, Ariel. *My Father's Paradise*	B
Sabathia, CC	
Till the End	796.357
SABATHIA, CC (CARSTEN CHARLES)	
Sabathia, CC. *Till the End*	796.357
Sabatier, Grant	
Financial Freedom	332.024
Sabatini Sloan, Aisha	
Dreaming of Ramadi in Detroit	814
SABATINI SLOAN, AISHA	
Sabatini Sloan, Aisha. *Dreaming of Ramadi in Detroit*	814
SABBATH	
Shulevitz, Judith. *The Sabbath World*	296.4
SABBATH (JUDAISM)	
Sussman, Adeena. ★*Shabbat*	641.5
*The **Sabbath** World*. Shulevitz, Judith	296.4
***Sabers** and Utopias*. Vargas Llosa, Mario	980.03
SABOTAGE	
Bascomb, Neal. *The Winter Fortress*	940.54
Batalion, Judith. *The Light of Days*	940.53
Friedman, Matti. *Spies of No Country*	327.12
Kean, Sam. *The Bastard Brigade*	355.8
Kix, Paul. *The Saboteur*	940.53
Macintyre, Ben. ★*Rogue Heroes*	940.54
*The **Saboteur***. Kix, Paul	940.53
***Sacco** and Vanzetti*. Watson, Bruce	345.73
Sacco, Joe	
Footnotes in Gaza	741.5
★*Paying the Land*	741.5

AUTHOR, TITLE, SERIES AND SUBJECT INDEX

SACCO, NICOLA, 1891-1927
   Watson, Bruce. *Sacco and Vanzetti* — 345.73
SACCO-VANZETTI CASE
   Watson, Bruce. *Sacco and Vanzetti* — 345.73
Sachs, Harvey
   The Ninth — 784.2
   Ten Masterpieces of Music — 780.9
Sachs, Jeffrey
   The Age of Sustainable Development — 338.9
Sack, Steven Mitchell
   The Employee Rights Handbook — 344.7301
SACKLER FAMILY
   Keefe, Patrick Radden. ★*Empire of Pain* — 338.7
SACKLER, ARTHUR M.
   Keefe, Patrick Radden. ★*Empire of Pain* — 338.7
Sacks, Jonathan
   The Great Partnership — 201
Sacks, Oliver
   ★*Everything in Its Place* — B
   Gratitude — 306.9
   The Man Who Mistook His Wife for a Hat and Other Clinical Tales — 616.8
   On the Move — B
SACKS, OLIVER, 1933-2015
   Sacks, Oliver. ★*Everything in Its Place* — B
   Sacks, Oliver. *Gratitude* — 306.9
   Sacks, Oliver. *On the Move* — B
   Weschler, Lawrence. *And How Are You, Dr. Sacks?* — B
SACKVILLE-WEST, V. (VICTORIA), 1892-1962
   Dennison, Matthew. *Behind the Mask* — B
SACRAMENTS
   Francis. *Walking with Jesus* — 282.09
SACRED BOOKS
   Armstrong, Karen. *The Lost Art of Scripture* — 208
   Husain, Ed. ★*The House of Islam* — 297
   Jebara, Mohamad. ★*The Life of the Qur'an* — 297.122
Sacred Cows and Golden Geese. Greek, C. Ray — 179
Sacred Duty. Cotton, Tom — 355.6
Sacred Liberty. Waldman, Steven — 341.4
SACRED SPACE
   Lambert, Malcolm. *God's Armies* — 956
   Mort, T. A. *Thieves' Road* — 978.3
   Nabokov, Peter. *Where the Lightning Strikes* — 299.7
   Redniss, Lauren. ★*Oak Flat* — 970.5
   Roberts, David. *The Bears Ears* — 979.2
Sacred Trash. Hoffman, Adina — 296.09
SADAT, ANWAR, 1918-1981
   Kissinger, Henry. *Leadership* — 303.3
   Wright, Lawrence. *Thirteen Days in September* — 956.04
The Saddest Words. Gorra, Michael Edward — 813
SADISM
   Rees, Laurence. *Auschwitz* — 940.53
SADNESS
   Cain, Susan. ★*Bittersweet* — 155.2
   Edelman, Hope. *The Aftergrief* — 155.9
Safe. Daley, Mark — B
SAFETY
   Aktipis, Athena. ★*A Field Guide to the Apocalypse* — 155.2
   Easterbrook, Gregg. ★*The King of Sports* — 796.332
   Flaherty, Mary Grace. ★*The Disaster Planning Handbook for Libraries* — 025.8
   H, Lamya. ★*Hijab Butch Blues* — B
   Haidt, Jonathan. ★*The Anxious Generation* — 305.23
   Hill, Clint. *Five Presidents* — B
   Metzl, Jonathan M. ★*What We've Become* — 364.152
   Parker, Morgan. ★*You Get What You Pay For* — 305.896
   Sprinkle, Timothy. *Lost and Stranded* — 613.6
   Von Drehle, Dave. ★*Triangle* — 974.7
Saffitz, Claire
   ★*What's for Dessert* — 641.86
Safina, Carl
   ★*Alfie and Me* — 598.9
   ★*Becoming Wild* — 591.7
   Beyond Words — 591.56
SAFINA, CARL, 1955-
   Safina, Carl. ★*Alfie and Me* — 598.9
Safranski, Rudiger
   Goethe — B
The Saga of Lewis & Clark. Schmidt, Thomas — 917.804

Sagan, Carl
   Billions and Billions — 500
   Broca's Brain — 128
   Cosmos — 520
   The Dragons of Eden — 153
   Pale Blue Dot — 919
Sagan, Sasha
   For Small Creatures Such as We — 390.09
SAGAN, SASHA (ALEXANDRA RACHEL DRUYAN)
   Sagan, Sasha. *For Small Creatures Such as We* — 390.09
Sage, Sami
   Democracy in Retrograde — 324
The Sagrada Familia. Van Hensbergen, Gijs — 726.5
Sahadi Whelan, Christine
   Flavors of the Sun — 641.595
SAHNI, JULIE
   Sen, Mayukh. *Taste Makers* — 641.5092
SAILING
   Melville, Herman. *Complete Poems* — 811
   Sleight, Steve. *The Complete Sailing Manual* — 797.1
   Strøksnes, Morten Andreas. *Shark Drunk* — 338.3
   Thomas, Evan. ★*John Paul Jones* — B
Sailing Alone Around the Room. Collins, Billy — 811
Sailing The Wine-Dark Sea. Cahill, Thomas — 909
SAILORS
   Dana, Richard Henry. *Two Years Before the Mast* — 910.4
   Grann, David. ★*The Wager* — 910.91
   Humphreys, Richard. *Under Pressure* — B
   O'Donnell, Patrick K. *The Indispensables* — 973.3
   Resendez, Andres. *Conquering the Pacific* — 959.9
   Roberts, Jason. *A Sense of the World* — B
   Slade, Rachel. *Into the Raging Sea* — 910.91
   Symonds, Craig L. *World War II at Sea* — 940.54
   Wheelan, Joseph. *Midnight in the Pacific* — 940.54
Saini, Angela
   Inferior — 305.4
Saint Augustine. Wills, Garry — B
Saint Joan. Shaw, Bernard — 822
Saint John, Bozoma
   The Urgent Life — B
SAINT JOHN, BOZOMA
   Saint John, Bozoma. *The Urgent Life* — B
SAINT LAURENT, YVES, 1936-2008
   Lowit, Roxanne. *Yves Saint Laurent* — 746.9
SAINTS
   Farmer, David Hugh. *The Oxford Dictionary of Saints* — 270
Saints & Sinners. Duffy, Eamon — 262
Sakai, Sonoko
   Japanese Home Cooking — 641.595
Sakamoto, Pamela Rotner
   Midnight in Broad Daylight — 940.53
Sakepedia. Cioletti, Jeff — 663
SAKHAROV, ANDREI, 1921-1989
   Remnick, David. *Lenin's Tomb* — 947.085
Salaam, Yusef
   Better, Not Bitter — B
SALAAM, YUSEF, 1974-
   Salaam, Yusef. *Better, Not Bitter* — B
Salad Freak. Damuck, Jess — 641.83
The Salad Lab. Schrijver, Darlene — 641.83
SALADIN, SULTAN OF EGYPT AND SYRIA, 1137-1193
   Haag, Michael. *The Tragedy of the Templars* — 271.7913
Saladino, Dan
   Eating to Extinction — 641.3
Saladish. Rosen, Ilene — 641.83
SALADS
   Damuck, Jess. *Salad Freak* — 641.83
   Rosen, Ilene. *Saladish* — 641.83
   Schrijver, Darlene. *The Salad Lab* — 641.83
SALAMA, ABED
   Thrall, Nathan. ★*A Day in the Life of Abed Salama* — 956.05
Salama, Jordan
   ★*Stranger in the Desert* — 982
SALAMA, JORDAN
   Salama, Jordan. ★*Stranger in the Desert* — 982
SALAZAR, ALBERTO, 1958-
   Hart, Matt. *Win at All Costs* — 338.7

PUBLIC LIBRARY CORE COLLECTION: NONFICTION
Twentieth Edition

Saldana, Stephanie
   What We Remember Will Be Saved   362.7
Sale, Anna
   ★*Let's Talk About Hard Things*   153.6
SALE, ANNA ★
   Sale, Anna. ★*Let's Talk About Hard Things*   153.6
SALEM, MASSACHUSETTS
   Schiff, Stacy. *The Witches*   345
SALES
   Marie, Jane. ★*Selling the Dream*   658.8
SALES PERSONNEL
   Marie, Jane. ★*Selling the Dream*   658.8
Salesses, Matthew
   ★*Craft in the Real World*   808.3
Salguero, C. Pierce
   ★*Buddhish*   294.3
SALIERI, ANTONIO, 1750-1825
   Shaffer, Peter. *Peter Shaffer's Amadeus*   822
Saline, Sharon
   What Your ADHD Child Wishes You Knew   618.92
★*Salinger*. Slawenski, Kenneth   B
SALINGER, J. D. (JEROME DAVID), 1919-2010
   Rakoff, Joanna Smith. *My Salinger Year*   B
   Slawenski, Kenneth. ★*Salinger*   B
Salisbury, Katie Gee
   ★*Not Your China Doll*   B
SALISH (NORTH AMERICAN PEOPLE)
   Streep, Abe. *Brothers on Three*   306.85
SALISHAN WOMEN
   LaPointe, Sasha taqwseblu. *Red Paint*   B
   LaPointe, Sasha taqwseblu. *Thunder Song*   814
SALK, JONAS, 1914-1995
   Oshinsky, David M. ★*Polio*   614.5
Sallah, Michael
   The Yankee Comandante   972.91
Salle, David
   How to See   709.04
Sally Ride. Sherr, Lynn   B
★*Sally's Cookie Addiction*. McKenney, Sally   641.86
Sally, David
   One Step Ahead   658.4
SALMON
   Greenberg, Paul. *Four Fish*   333.95
   Malarkey, Tucker. *Stronghold*   639.2
SALMON FISHERIES
   Greenberg, Paul. *American Catch*   333.95
Salonica, City of Ghosts. Mazower, Mark   949.5
SALONS
   Coffin, Judith G. *Sex, Love, and Letters*   848
Salt. Kurlansky, Mark   553.6
SALT
   Conway, Edmund. *Material World*   333.7
   Kurlansky, Mark. *Salt*   553.6
   Moss, Michael. *Salt, Sugar, Fat*   613.2
   ★*The Salt Path*. Winn, Raynor   B
★*Salt, Fat, Acid, Heat*. Nosrat, Samin   641.5
Salt, Sugar, Fat. Moss, Michael   613.2
SALT-WATER FISHING
   Fagan, Brian M. *Fishing*   338.3
   Messineo, Janet. *Casting into the Light*   799.1
Salter, James
   Don't Save Anything   818
Salter, Mary Jo
   The Surveyors   811
Saltz, Joanna
   ★*Delish Insane Sweets*   641.81
   Delish   641.5
SALUTATIONS
   Allert, Tilman. *Heil Hitler*   395.4
   Miranda, Lin-Manuel. *Gmorning, Gnight!*   811
   Scott, Andy. *One Kiss or Two?*   395.4
SALVADORAN AMERICANS
   Dudley, Steven S. *MS-13*   364.106
   Markham, Lauren. ★*The Far Away Brothers*   920
   Vasquez, Karla Tatiana. ★*The Salvisoul Cookbook*   641.598
   Zamora, Javier. ★*Solito*   B
SALVAGE
   Watson, Paul. *Ice Ghosts*   917

Salvage Style. Linsley, Leslie   747
Salvation. Martin, Valerie   B
SALVATION
   Dante Alighieri. *Purgatorio*   851
★*The Salvisoul Cookbook*. Vasquez, Karla Tatiana   641.598
Sam. Waldman, Jonathan   629.8
★*Sam Phillips*. Guralnick, Peter   B
Sam Walton, Made in America. Walton, Sam   B
Samaha, Albert
   Concepcion   929
   Never Ran, Never Will   920
SAMAHA, ALBERT
   Samaha, Albert. *Concepcion*   929
SAMARAS, TIM
   Hargrove, Brantley. *The Man Who Caught the Storm*   B
Samatar, Sofia
   The White Mosque   B
SAMATAR, SOFIA
   Samatar, Sofia. *The White Mosque*   B
SAME-SEX MARRIAGE
   Cenziper, Debbie. ★*Love Wins*   346.7301
   Issenberg, Sasha. ★*The Engagement*   346.7301
   Kaplan, Roberta A. *Then Comes Marriage*   346.7301
Samer
   The Raqqa Diaries   956.9104
SAMER, 1992 OR 1993-
   Samer. *The Raqqa Diaries*   956.9104
Samet, Elizabeth D.
   Looking for the Good War   940.53
SAMOAN ISLANDS
   Mead, Margaret. *Coming of Age in Samoa*   306
SAMOAN PEOPLE
   Mead, Margaret. *Coming of Age in Samoa*   306
Sampson, Fiona
   In Search of Mary Shelley   B
Samuel Pepys. Tomalin, Claire   B
Samuel, Julia
   Grief Works   155.9
SAMUEL, MARCUS, 1853-1927
   Doran, Peter B. *Breaking Rockefeller*   338.7
Samuell, Kristine
   A Year of Gingerbread Houses   745.5
Samuels, Robert
   ★*His Name Is George Floyd*   B
Samuelsson, Marcus
   Marcus off Duty   641.5
   The Red Rooster Cookbook   641.5974
   ★*The Rise*   641.59
   Yes, Chef   B
SAMUELSSON, MARCUS
   Samuelsson, Marcus. *Marcus off Duty*   641.5
   Samuelsson, Marcus. *Yes, Chef*   B
SAMURAI
   Lockley, Thomas. *African Samurai*   B
   Stanley, Amy. *Stranger in the Shogun's City*   B
SAN ANTONIO, TEXAS
   Burrough, Bryan. *Forget the Alamo*   976.043
SAN FRANCISCO BAY AREA
   Hsu, Hua. ★*Stay True*   B
SAN FRANCISCO EARTHQUAKE AND FIRE, CALIF., 1906
   Davenport, Matthew J. *The Longest Minute*   979.4
   Miller, Lulu. *Why Fish Don't Exist*   B
   Winchester, Simon. *A Crack in the Edge of the World*   979.4
SAN FRANCISCO, CALIFORNIA
   Davenport, Matthew J. *The Longest Minute*   979.4
   Dougherty, Conor. *Golden Gates*   363.509794
   Lovato, Roberto. *Unforgetting*   B
   Nasaw, David. *The Chief*   B
   Ng, Fae Myenne. *Orphan Bachelors*   B
   Ralph, Laurence. *Sito*   364.152
   Randall, David K. *Black Death at the Golden Gate*   616.9
   Samaha, Albert. *Concepcion*   929
   Siler, Julia Flynn. *The White Devil's Daughters*   306.3
   Solnit, Rebecca. ★*Recollections of My Nonexistence*   B
   Stahr, Celia. *Frida in America*   B
   Winchester, Simon. *A Crack in the Edge of the World*   979.4
   Worley, Jennifer. *Neon Girls*   792.7

AUTHOR, TITLE, SERIES AND SUBJECT INDEX

SAN JOSE, CALIFORNIA
   Nguyen, Viet Thanh. ★*A Man of Two Faces*   B
Sanchez, Aaron
   Where I Come From   641.5092
SANCHEZ, AARON
   Sanchez, Aaron. *Where I Come From*   641.5092
Sanchez, Erika L.
   Crying in the Bathroom   B
   Lessons on Expulsion   811
SANCHEZ, ERIKA L.
   Sanchez, Erika L. *Crying in the Bathroom*   B
Sanchez, Sonia
   Homegirls & Handgrenades   811
Sancton, Julian
   Madhouse at the End of the Earth   919.8904
Sancton, Thomas
   The Bettencourt Affair   B
SAND
   Conway, Edmund. *Material World*   333.7
Sand and Steel. Caddick-Adams, Peter   940.54
★*A Sand County Almanac & Other Writings on Ecology and Conservation*.
   Leopold, Aldo   814
SAND CREEK MASSACRE, NOVEMBER 29, 1864
   Enss, Chris. *Mochi's War*   B
SAND, GEORGE, 1804-1876
   Eisler, Benita. ★*Chopin's Funeral*   B
   Harlan, Elizabeth. *George Sand*   B
Sandberg, Sheryl
   Lean In   658.4
   Lean In   658.4
   Option B   155.9
SANDBERG, SHERYL
   Sandberg, Sheryl. *Lean In*   658.4
Sandburg, Carl
   Abraham Lincoln   B
   The American Songbag   782.42162
   ★*The Complete Poems of Carl Sandburg*   811
Sandel, Michael J.
   Justice   172
   What Money Can't Buy   174
Sanders, Chad
   Black Magic   305.896
SANDERS, CHAD
   Sanders, Chad. *Black Magic*   305.896
Sanders, Ella Frances
   Eating the Sun   520
Sandke, Randy
   Where the Dark and the Light Folks Meet   781.6509
Sandler, Lauren
   This Is All I Got   B
Sando, Mike
   The Football 100   796.332
Sands, Philippe
   East West Street   345
   The Ratline   B
SANDWICHES
   Barrow, Cathy. *Bagels, Schmears, and a Nice Piece of Fish*   641.81
   Greenspan, Eric. *The Great Grilled Cheese Book*   641.6
Sandworm. Greenberg, Andy   364.16
★*Sandy Hook*. Williamson, Elizabeth   364.152
SANDY HOOK ELEMENTARY SCHOOL SHOOTING, NEWTOWN, CONN., 2012
   Lysiak, Matthew. *Newtown*   371.7
   Roig-Debellis, Kaitlin. *Choosing Hope*   371.7
   Williamson, Elizabeth. ★*Sandy Hook*   364.152
Sandy Koufax. Leavy, Jane   B
Sanfilippo, Diane
   Practical Paleo   613.2
Sanger, Carol
   About Abortion   179.7
SANGER, MARGARET, 1879-1966
   Eig, Jonathan. *The Birth of the Pill*   618.1
Sanghera, Sathnam
   ★*Empireland*   941
   Empireworld   909
SANITATION
   Flowers, Catherine Coleman. *Waste*   363.72
   Klass, Perri. *A Good Time to Be Born*   362.19892

   Randall, David K. *Black Death at the Golden Gate*   616.9
Sankey, Michael L.
   The Manual to Online Public Records   025.06
Sankovitch, Nina
   American Rebels   920
Sanneh, Kelefa
   ★*Major Labels*   781.64
SANTA CLARA VALLEY, CALIFORNIA
   Menuez, Doug. *Fearless Genius*   979.4
Santana, Carlos
   The Universal Tone   B
SANTANA, CARLOS
   Santana, Carlos. *The Universal Tone*   B
Sante, Lucy
   I Heard Her Call My Name   B
SANTE, LUCY, 1954-
   Sante, Lucy. *I Heard Her Call My Name*   B
Santiago, Wilfred
   "21"   741.5
SANTIDEVA, ACTIVE 7TH CENTURY
   Kongtrul, Dzigar. *Peaceful Heart*   294.3
Santomero, Angela C
   Preschool Clues   305.233
Santopietro, Tom
   The Sound of Music Story   791.43
Santos Perez, Craig
   From Unincorporated Territory [amot]   811
★*Sapiens*. Harari, Yuval N.   909
Sapolsky, Robert M.
   Behave   612.8
   Determined   123
Sappho
   If Not, Winter   884
Sara Moulton's Home Cooking 101. Moulton, Sara   641.5973
SARAJEVO (BOSNIA AND HERCEGOVINA)
   Hemon, Aleksandar. *My Parents*   814
SARAO, NAVINDER SINGH
   Vaughan, Liam. *Flash Crash*   B
Saratoga. Ketchum, Richard M.   973.3
SARATOGA CAMPAIGN, 1777
   Ketchum, Richard M. *Saratoga*   973.3
SARATOGA SPRINGS, NEW YORK
   Ketchum, Richard M. *Saratoga*   973.3
Sardet, Christian
   Plankton   578.77
Sardy, Marin
   The Edge of Every Day   B
SARDY, MARIN
   Sardy, Marin. *The Edge of Every Day*   B
★*Sargent*. Herdrich, Stephanie L   759.13
Sargent's Women. Lucey, Donna M.   920
SARGENT, JOHN SINGER, 1856-1925
   Herdrich, Stephanie L. ★*Sargent*   759.13
   Lucey, Donna M. *Sargent's Women*   920
SARKOZY, NICOLAS, 1955-
   Sancton, Thomas. *The Bettencourt Affair*   B
Sarma, Sanjay E.
   Grasp   370.15
Sarna, Jonathan D.
   ★*American Judaism*   296
Sarna, Shannon
   Modern Jewish Comfort Food   641.5
Sarno, Chad
   The Wicked Healthy Cookbook   651.56
Sarotte, M. E
   The Collapse   943.087
SARS (DISEASE)
   Honigsbaum, Mark. *The Pandemic Century*   614.4
Sarsour, Linda
   We Are Not Here to Be Bystanders   B
SARSOUR, LINDA, 1980-
   Sarsour, Linda. *We Are Not Here to Be Bystanders*   B
Sarton, May
   Selected Poems of May Sarton   811
Sartore, Joel
   ★*The Photo Ark*   779
Sartre, Jean-Paul
   ★*Being and Nothingness*   111

PUBLIC LIBRARY CORE COLLECTION: NONFICTION
Twentieth Edition

Existentialism and Human Emotions	111
★*No Exit, and Three Other Plays*	842
We Have Only This Life to Live	848
SARTRE, JEAN-PAUL, 1905-1980	
Sartre, Jean-Paul. ★*No Exit, and Three Other Plays*	842
Sartre, Jean-Paul. *We Have Only This Life to Live*	848
Sasakamoose, Fred	
Call Me Indian	B
SASAKAMOOSE, FRED, 1933-2020	
Sasakamoose, Fred. *Call Me Indian*	B
Sasha and Emma. Avrich, Paul	920
SASKATCHEWAN	
Sasakamoose, Fred. *Call Me Indian*	B
SASQUATCH	
O'Connor, John. *The Secret History of Bigfoot*	001.944
SASSOON FAMILY	
Kaufman, Jonathan. *The Last Kings of Shanghai*	951
SASSOON, DAVID, 1792-1864	
Kaufman, Jonathan. *The Last Kings of Shanghai*	951
SASSOON, SIEGFRIED, 1886-1967	
Glass, Charles. *Soldiers Don't Go Mad*	616.85
Satan Is Real. Louvin, Charlie	920
SATANISM	
Sullivan, Randall. *The Devil's Best Trick*	235
Satchel. Tye, Larry	B
SATELLITES	
Boyle, Rebecca. *Our Moon*	523.3
Satia, Priya	
Empire of Guns	330.941
SATIRE AND PARODIES	
Petri, Alexandra. *Nothing Is Wrong and Here Is Why*	973.933
SATIRICAL COMICS	
Inman, Matthew. *The Terrible and Wonderful Reasons Why I Run Long Distances*	741.5
SATIRISTS	
Wainaina, Binyavanga. ★*How to Write About Africa*	814
Satisfying Stitches. Brasfield, Hope	746.44
Sato, Hiroaki	
On Haiku	809.1
Satow, Julie	
The Plaza	917.47
When Women Ran Fifth Avenue	381.141
Satrapi, Marjane	
Chicken with Plums	741.5
★*The Complete Persepolis*	741.5
Embroideries	741.5
SATRAPI, MARJANE, 1969-	
Satrapi, Marjane. ★*The Complete Persepolis*	741.5
Satrapi, Marjane. *Embroideries*	741.5
Satter, David	
The Less You Know, the Better You Sleep	947.086
Sattouf, Riad	
The Arab of the Future 2	741.5
The Arab of the Future	741.5
SATTOUF, RIAD	
Sattouf, Riad. *The Arab of the Future 2*	741.5
Sattouf, Riad. *The Arab of the Future*	741.5
Satyamurti, Carole	
Mahabharata	821
Sauces. Peterson, James	641.81
SAUCES	
Kang, Mingoo. *Jang*	641.595
Murad, Noor. ★*Ottolenghi Test Kitchen*	641.3
Peterson, James. *Sauces*	641.81
SAUDI ARABIA	
Carter, Iain. *Golf Wars*	796.352
Coll, Steve. *The Bin Ladens*	920
Ghattas, Kim. *Black Wave*	955.05
Hope, Bradley. *Blood and Oil*	B
Hubbard, Ben (Journalist). *Mbs*	B
Lacey, Robert. *Inside the Kingdom*	953.805
SAUK (NORTH AMERICAN PEOPLE)	
Trask, Kerry A. *Black Hawk*	973.5
Saul Steinberg. Bair, Deirdre	B
Saul, Richard	
ADHD Does Not Exist	618.92
Saul, Scott	
★*Becoming Richard Pryor*	B
Sauls, Scott	
Beautiful People Don't Just Happen	248.8
Saunders, George	
★*A Swim in a Pond in the Rain*	891.7
Saunders, John	
Playing Hurt	B
SAUNDERS, JOHN, 1955-2016	
Saunders, John. *Playing Hurt*	B
Saunt, Claudio	
Unworthy Republic	323.1197
Savage Beauty. Milford, Nancy	B
Savage Continent. Lowe, Keith	940.55
Savage Feast. Fishman, Boris	B
★*Savage Harvest*. Hoffman, Carl	995.1
★*The Savage Mind*. Levi-Strauss, Claude	155.8
The Savage Storm. Holland, James	940.53
Savage, Jodi M.	
The Death of a Jaybird	B
SAVAGE, JODI M., 1978-	
Savage, Jodi M. *The Death of a Jaybird*	B
Savage, Jon	
★*1966*	781.6609
Savage, Phil	
4th and Goal Every Day	796.332
SAVANNAH, GEORGIA	
Berendt, John. *Midnight in the Garden of Good and Evil*	975.8
Jones, Jacqueline. *Saving Savannah*	975.8
SAVANT SYNDROME	
Ruthsatz, Joanne. *The Prodigy's Cousin*	155.45
Tammet, Daniel. *Born on a Blue Day*	B
★*Save Me the Plums*. Reichl, Ruth	B
Save-It-Forward Suppers. Kane, Cyndi	641.5
Saved by Beauty. Housden, Roger	955
Saving Alex. Cooper, Alex	B
SAVING AND INVESTMENT	
Tu, Vivian. *Rich Af*	332.024
SAVING AND THRIFT	
De Leon, Paco. *Finance for the People*	332.024
Saxton, Martha. *The Widow Washington*	B
Shirley, Craig. *Mary Ball Washington*	B
Saving Bravo. Talty, Stephan	959.704
Saving Freud. Nagorski, Andrew	940.53
Saving Savannah. Jones, Jacqueline	975.8
Saving Tarboo Creek. Freeman, Scott	333.72
Saving The Last Rhinos. Fowlds, Grant	599.66
Saving The Season. West, Kevin	641.4
★*Saving Time*. Odell, Jenny	153.7
Saving Us. Hayhoe, Katharine	304.2
★*Savor*. Ali, Fatima	B
Sawaki, Kodo	
Discovering the True Self	294.3
SAWAKI, KODO, 1880-1965	
Sawaki, Kodo. *Discovering the True Self*	294.3
Sawchik, Travis	
Big Data Baseball	796.357
SAWYER, DIANE, 1945-	
Stelter, Brian. *Top of the Morning*	791.456
Saxophone Colossus. Levy, Aidan	B
SAXOPHONISTS	
Crouch, Stanley. *Kansas City Lightning*	B
Levy, Aidan. *Saxophone Colossus*	B
Threadgill, Henry. *Easily Slip into Another World*	B
Saxton, Martha	
The Widow Washington	B
Say Anarcha. Hallman, J. C.	618.1
★*Say It Louder!* Cross, Tiffany D.	324.6
Say More. Psaki, Jen	B
★*Say Nothing*. Keefe, Patrick Radden	364.152
Say The Right Thing. Yoshino, Kenji	305.3
★*Saying It Loud*. Whitaker, Mark	973.923
★*Says Who?*. Curzan, Anne	428
Scahill, Jeremy	
Dirty Wars	355.00973
Scales, Helen	
The Brilliant Abyss	551.46
What the Wild Sea Can Be	577.7
Scalia. Murphy, Bruce Allen	B
Scalia Speaks. Scalia, Antonin	081

AUTHOR, TITLE, SERIES AND SUBJECT INDEX

Scalia, Antonin
  Scalia Speaks   081
SCALIA, ANTONIN, 1936-2016
  Murphy, Bruce Allen. *Scalia*   B
  Scalia, Antonin. *Scalia Speaks*   081
Scalzi, John
  Don't Live for Your Obituary   808.02
SCANDALS
  Bamberger, Michael. *The Second Life of Tiger Woods*   B
  Bensinger, Ken. ★*Red Card*   796.334
  Bernstein, Andrea. *American Oligarchs*   920
  Brown, Eliot. *The Cult of We*   333.33
  Brown, Tina. ★*The Palace Papers*   920
  Cadbury, Deborah. *Queen Victoria's Matchmaking*   941.081
  Caruana Galizia, Paul. ★*A Death in Malta*   364.15
  Conn, David. *The Fall of the House of FIFA*   796.334
  Creighton, Margaret S. *The Electrifying Fall of Rainbow City*   607
  Daniels, Stormy. *Full Disclosure*   B
  Dobbs, Michael. *King Richard*   973.924
  Elliott, Carl. ★*The Occasional Human Sacrifice*   174.2
  Enrich, David. *Dark Towers*   332.1
  Flannery, Kate. *Strip Tees*   338.4
  Goodman, Matthew. *The City Game*   796.323
  Graff, Garrett M. *Watergate*   973.924
  Guinn, Jeff. *The Road to Jonestown*   289.9
  Hanna-Attisha, Mona. *What the Eyes Don't See*   615.9
  Hortis, C. Alexander. *The Witch of New York*   364.152
  King, Greg. *The Assassination of the Archduke*   B
  King, Greg. *Twilight of Empire*   943.6
  Kirtzman, Andrew. *Giuliani*   B
  Levy, Shawn. ★*The Castle on Sunset*   647.95
  Lownie, Andrew. *Traitor King*   920
  Mann, William J. *The Wars of the Roosevelts*   B
  McGreevy, John T. ★*Catholicism*   282.09
  Mead, Corey. *The Hidden History of the White House*   975.3
  Minois, Georges. *The Atheist's Bible*   200
  Montillo, Roseanne. *Deliberate Cruelty*   364.152
  Nagourney, Adam. *The Times*   071
  Norton, Hughes. ★*Rainmaker*   796.352
  Oller, John. *American Queen*   B
  Pearlman, Jeff. *Boys Will Be Boys*   796.332
  Rempel, William C. *The Gambler*   B
  Robison, Peter. ★*Flying Blind*   338.7
  Ryan, Maureen. *Burn It Down*   791.43
  Sancton, Thomas. *The Bettencourt Affair*   B
  Senik, Troy. *A Man of Iron*   B
  Smith, Douglas. *Rasputin*   B
  Stewart, James B. *Unscripted*   658.1
  Toobin, Jeffrey. *True Crimes and Misdemeanors*   973.933
  Woodward, Bob. *Shadow*   973.92
  Zminda, Don. *Double Plays and Double Crosses*   796.357
SCANDINAVIA
  Booth, Michael. *The Almost Nearly Perfect People*   948.071
  Brown, Nancy Marie. *The Real Valkyrie*   948
  Herman, Arthur. *The Viking Heart*   948
  Johansen, Signe. ★*How to Hygge*   646.7
  Larrington, Carolyne. *The Norse Myths*   293
  Wilhide, Elizabeth. *Scandinavian Home*   728
SCANDINAVIAN AMERICANS
  Herman, Arthur. *The Viking Heart*   948
Scandinavian Home. Wilhide, Elizabeth   728
The Scar. Cregan, Mary   616.85
Scarcity. Mullainathan, Sendhil   338.5
SCARCITY
  Gleick, Peter H. *The Three Ages of Water*   333.91
  Goodman, Peter S. ★*How the World Ran Out of Everything*   658.7
  Miller, Chris. *Chip War*   338.4
  Mullainathan, Sendhil. *Scarcity*   338.5
  Solomon, Steven. *Water*   553.7
  Turchin, Peter. *End Times*   320.01
Scarlata, Kate
  Mind Your Gut   616.3
Scarpaleggia, Giulia
  ★*Cucina Povera*   641.594
SCARS
  Joyce, Russell W. *His Face Like Mine*   248
  LeFavour, Cree. *Lights On, Rats Out*   616.85
Scars of Independence. Hoock, Holger   973.3

Scatter, Adapt, and Remember. Newitz, Annalee   576.8
Scattered Poems. Kerouac, Jack   811
Scattershot. Taupin, Bernie   B
SCAVENGING
  Maiklem, Lara. *Mudlark*   B
  Roy, Saumya. *Castaway Mountain*   363.72
Scenes from My Life. Williams, Michael Kenneth   B
Scenters-Zapico, Natalie
  Lima   811
Schaap, Jeremy
  Cinderella Man   B
Schacter, Daniel L.
  The Seven Sins of Memory   153.1
Schafer, John R.
  The Like Switch   158.2
Schama, Simon
  Citizens   944.04
  The Embarrassment of Riches   949.2
  Foreign Bodies   614.4
  A History of Britain; 2   941
  The Power of Art   709
  ★*The Story of the Jews; Volume One*   909
  ★*The Story of the Jews; Volume Two*   909
Scharre, Paul
  Four Battlegrounds   006.3
Schatz, Kate
  Rad Women Worldwide   920
Schatzker, Mark
  The Dorito Effect   641.3
Schechter, Harold
  Hell's Princess   B
  Murderabilia   364.152
  ★*Ripped from the Headlines!*   791.43
Scheel, David
  Many Things Under a Rock   594
Scheer, Paul
  Joyful Recollections of Trauma   B
SCHEER, PAUL, 1976-
  Scheer, Paul. *Joyful Recollections of Trauma*   B
Scheeres, Julia
  Jesus Land   B
SCHEERES, JULIA
  Scheeres, Julia. *Jesus Land*   B
Scheier, Liz
  Never Simple   B
SCHEIER, LIZ
  Scheier, Liz. *Never Simple*   B
SCHEIN, ANN, 1939-
  Porter, Cecelia Hopkins. *Five Lives in Music*   B
Schein, Edgar H.
  Humble Inquiry   302.2
Scheinberger, Felix
  Dare to Sketch   741.2
SCHELL, LUCY
  Bascomb, Neal. *Faster*   796.7209
Schell, Orville
  Wealth and Power   920
Schemel, Patty
  Hit so Hard   B
SCHEMEL, PATTY, 1967-
  Schemel, Patty. *Hit so Hard*   B
Scheyder, Ernest
  The War Below   333.7
SCHIAPARELLI, ELSA, 1890-1973
  Secrest, Meryle. *Elsa Schiaparelli*   746.9
Schiavi, Michael R.
  Celluloid Activist   B
Schickel, Richard
  Keepers   791.430973
Schieffer, Bob
  Overload   070.4
Schiff, Robyn
  A Woman of Property   811
Schiff, Stacy
  ★*Cleopatra*   B
  The Witches   345
Schiffman, Lawrence H.
  Reclaiming the Dead Sea Scrolls   296.1

PUBLIC LIBRARY CORE COLLECTION: NONFICTION
Twentieth Edition

Schilthuizen, Menno
   Darwin Comes to Town — 577.5
SCHINDLER FAMILY
   Schindler, Meriel. *The Lost Cafe Schindler* — 943.64
SCHINDLER, HUGO, 1888-1952
   Schindler, Meriel. *The Lost Cafe Schindler* — 943.64
SCHINDLER, KURT, 1925-2017
   Schindler, Meriel. *The Lost Cafe Schindler* — 943.64
Schindler, Meriel
   The Lost Cafe Schindler — 943.64
SCHINDLER, MERIEL, 1964-
   Schindler, Meriel. *The Lost Cafe Schindler* — 943.64
Schinner, Miyoko Nishimoto
   The Vegan Meat Cookbook — 641.5
SCHIZOPHRENIA
   Cho, Grace M. *Tastes Like War* — 305.48
   Farley, Audrey Clare. ★*Girls and Their Monsters* — 306.875
   Granata, Vince. *Everything Is Fine* — B
   Hale, Kathleen. ★*Slenderman* — 364.152
   Kolker, Robert. ★*Hidden Valley Road* — 920
   Lieberman, Jeffrey A. *Malady of the Mind* — 616.89
   Rosen, Jonathan. ★*The Best Minds* — 616.89
   Sardy, Marin. *The Edge of Every Day* — B
   Torrey, E. Fuller. *Surviving Schizophrenia* — 616.89
SCHJELDAHL, PETER
   Calhoun, Ada. *Also a Poet* — B
Schlanger, Zoe
   ★*The Light Eaters* — 571.2
SCHLEGLE, ERNIE
   Manzione, Gianmarc. *Pin Action* — B
Schlender, Brent
   Becoming Steve Jobs — B
Schlesinger, Arthur M.
   Journals, 1952-2000 — 973.91092
   A Life in the Twentieth Century — B
SCHLESINGER, ARTHUR M. (ARTHUR MEIER), 1917-2007
   Schlesinger, Arthur M. *Journals, 1952-2000* — 973.91092
   Schlesinger, Arthur M. *A Life in the Twentieth Century* — B
Schloss, Edith
   The Loft Generation — 700.9
SCHLOSS, EDITH, 1919-2011
   Schloss, Edith. *The Loft Generation* — 700.9
Schlosser, Eric
   Command and Control — 363.17
SCHMIDT, FRANZ, D. 1634
   Harrington, Joel F. *The Faithful Executioner* — B
Schmidt, Justin O.
   The Sting of the Wild — 595.7
Schmidt, Michael S.
   ★*Donald Trump v. The United States* — 973.933
Schmidt, Thomas
   The Saga of Lewis & Clark — 917.804
Schmitz, Rob
   Street of Eternal Happiness — 951
SCHNEERSON, MENACHEM MENDEL, 1902-1994
   Telushkin, Joseph. *Rebbe* — 296.833
Schneider, Amy
   In the Form of a Question — B
SCHNEIDER, AMY, 1979-
   Schneider, Amy. *In the Form of a Question* — B
SCHNEIDERMAN, ERIC T., 1954-
   Selvaratnam, Tanya. *Assume Nothing* — B
Schneier, Bruce
   A Hacker's Mind — 364.16
Schneps, Leila
   Math on Trial — 345
Schoenfeld, Bruce
   ★*Game of Edges* — 796.04
SCHOLARLY COVER-UPS
   Crawford, Lacy. *Notes on a Silencing* — B
SCHOLARS AND ACADEMICS
   Dolnick, Edward. *The Writing of the Gods* — 493
   Eilenberger, Wolfram. *Time of the Magicians* — 920
   Kaag, John J. *American Philosophy* — 191
   Lovato, Roberto. *Unforgetting* — B
   Ndopu, Eddie. *Sipping Dom Pérignon Through a Straw* — B
   Rundell, Katherine. ★*Super-Infinite* — B
   Seo, Bo. *Good Arguments* — 808.53

Telushkin, Joseph. *Rebbe* — 296.833
Tenzin Priyadarshi. *Running Toward Mystery* — B
SCHOLARSHIPS AND FELLOWSHIPS
   Doherty, Maggie. *The Equivalents* — 920
SCHOLL, SOPHIE, 1921-1943
   Dumbach, Annette E. *Sophie Scholl and the White Rose* — 943.086
   Thomas, Gordon. *Defying Hitler* — 920
SCHOMBURGK, ROBERT H. (ROBERT HERMANN), SIR, 1804-1865
   Holway, Tatiana M. *The Flower of Empire* — 727
Schonberg, Harold C.
   ★*The Lives of the Great Composers* — 780
Schonwerth, Franz Xaver von
   The Turnip Princess — 398.2
SCHOOL ADMINISTRATORS
   Crawford, Lacy. *Notes on a Silencing* — B
The School Among the Ruins. Rich, Adrienne — 811
SCHOOL CHILDREN
   Quinones, John. ★*One Year in Uvalde* — 371.7
SCHOOL CHOICE
   Fitzpatrick, Cara. *The Death of Public School* — 379.73
   Love, Bettina L. *Punished for Dreaming* — 371.829
   Ravitch, Diane. *The Death and Life of the Great American School System* — 379.1
SCHOOL CLOSINGS
   Ewing, Eve L. *Ghosts in the Schoolyard* — 370.89
   Kimmerle, Erin H. *We Carry Their Bones* — 365
★*School Clothes*. Givens, Jarvis R. — 371.829
SCHOOL DESEGREGATION DECISION, 1954
   Green, Kristen. *Something Must Be Done About Prince Edward County* — 379.2
   Williams, Juan. *Thurgood Marshall* — B
The School for Scandal and Other Plays. Sheridan, Richard Brinsley — 822
SCHOOL IMPROVEMENT PROGRAMS
   Brill, Steven. *Class Warfare* — 371.010973
SCHOOL INTEGRATION
   Green, Kristen. *Something Must Be Done About Prince Edward County* — 379.2
   Kozol, Jonathan. ★*An End to Inequality* — 379.2
   Margolick, David. *Elizabeth and Hazel* — 379.2
   Martin, Rachel Louise. *A Most Tolerant Little Town* — 379.2
   Meckler, Laura. ★*Dream Town* — 305.8
   Simon, James F. *Eisenhower vs. Warren* — 347.73
   Zeitz, Joshua. *Building the Great Society* — 973.923
SCHOOL LIBRARIANS
   Hughes-Hassell, Sandra. ★*Collection Management for Youth* — 025.2
   Johnson, Doug. *The Indispensable Librarian* — 025.1
SCHOOL LIBRARIES
   Hughes-Hassell, Sandra. ★*Collection Management for Youth* — 025.2
   Johnson, Doug. *The Indispensable Librarian* — 025.1
   Russell, Carrie. *Complete Copyright for K-12 Librarians and Educators* — 346.73

★*The School of Hard Talks*. Kline, Emily — 155.5
SCHOOL PRINCIPALS
   Cadbury, Deborah. *The School That Escaped from the Nazis* — 940.53
SCHOOL READINESS
   Smart, Maya Payne. *Reading for Our Lives* — 372.4
SCHOOL SHOOTINGS
   Cox, John Woodrow. *Children Under Fire* — 371.7
   Cullen, David. *Columbine* — 373
   Cullen, David. *Parkland* — 371.7
   Lysiak, Matthew. *Newtown* — 371.7
   Quinones, John. ★*One Year in Uvalde* — 371.7
   Roig-Debellis, Kaitlin. *Choosing Hope* — 371.7
   Williamson, Elizabeth. ★*Sandy Hook* — 364.152
SCHOOL SPORTS
   Powell, Michael. ★*Canyon Dreams* — 796.323
The School That Escaped from the Nazis. Cadbury, Deborah — 940.53
The Schoolhouse Gate. Driver, Justin — 344.73
SCHOOLS
   Bazelon, Emily. *Sticks and Stones* — 302.34
   Cadbury, Deborah. *The School That Escaped from the Nazis* — 940.53
   Duncan, Arne. *How Schools Work* — 379
   Gulman, Gary. *Misfit* — B
   Mufleh, Luma. ★*Learning America* — 371.826
   Robinson, Ken. *Creative Schools* — 370.973
SCHOOLS AND GUNS
   Cullen, David. *Parkland* — 371.7
Schor, Esther H.
   Bridge of Words — 499

AUTHOR, TITLE, SERIES AND SUBJECT INDEX

Schott, Philipp
   The Accidental Veterinarian — B
SCHOTT, PHILIPP
   Schott, Philipp. *The Accidental Veterinarian* — B
Schotz, Susanne
   The Secret Language of Cats — 636.8
Schreiber, Flora Rheta
   Sybil — 616.85
SCHREIBER, FLORA RHETA, 1918-1988
   Schreiber, Flora Rheta. *Sybil* — 616.85
SCHRIEVER, BERNARD A.
   Sheehan, Neil. *A Fiery Peace in a Cold War* — B
Schrijver, Darlene
   The Salad Lab — 641.83
Schrock, Leslie
   Fertility Rules — 613.9
Schroeder, Alice
   The Snowball — B
Schubert's Winter Journey. Bostridge, Ian — 782.4
SCHUBERT, FRANZ, 1797-1828
   Bostridge, Ian. *Schubert's Winter Journey* — 782.4
Schuller, Kyla
   The Trouble with White Women — 305.42
Schulman, Bruce J.
   The Seventies — 973.92
Schulman, Daniel
   The Money Kings — 332.0973
Schulman, Michael
   ★*Oscar Wars* — 791.43
SCHULTES, RICHARD EVANS, 1915-2001
   Davis, Wade. *One River* — 581.6
Schultz, David A.
   Encyclopedia of the United States Constitution — 342.730203
Schultz, Eric B.
   King Philip's War — 973.2
Schultz, Howard
   From the Ground Up — B
SCHULTZ, HOWARD
   Schultz, Howard. *From the Ground Up* — B
Schultz, Ken
   Ken Schultz's Essentials of Fishing — 799.1
Schultz, Kevin Michael
   Buckley and Mailer — 920
Schultz, Philip
   Comforts of the Abyss — 801
SCHULTZ, PHILIP
   Schultz, Philip. *Comforts of the Abyss* — 801
Schulz and Peanuts. Michaelis, David — B
SCHULZ, CHARLES M. (CHARLES MONROE), 1922-2000
   Michaelis, David. *Schulz and Peanuts* — B
Schulz, Kathryn
   Being Wrong — 121
   ★*Lost & Found* — B
SCHULZ, KATHRYN
   Schulz, Kathryn. ★*Lost & Found* — B
SCHULZE-BOYSEN, HARRO, 1909-1942
   Ohler, Norman. *The Bohemians* — 940.53
   Thomas, Gordon. *Defying Hitler* — 920
SCHULZE-BOYSEN, LIBERTAS, 1913-1942
   Ohler, Norman. *The Bohemians* — 940.53
Schumacher, E. F.
   Small Is Beautiful — 330
Schumacher, Michael
   Will Eisner — 741.5
Schumann. Chernaik, Judith — B
SCHUMANN, ROBERT, 1810-1856
   Chernaik, Judith. *Schumann* — B
Schumer, Amy
   The Girl with the Lower Back Tattoo — B
SCHUMER, AMY
   Schumer, Amy. *The Girl with the Lower Back Tattoo* — B
Schutt, Bill
   Cannibalism — 394
   Pump — 612.1
Schuyler, James
   Collected Poems — 811
Schwab, Tim
   ★*The Bill Gates Problem* — 361.7

Schwalbe, Will
   ★*The End of Your Life Book Club* — B
   We Should Not Be Friends — B
Schwartz, A. Brad
   ★*Broadcast Hysteria* — 791.44
Schwartz, Bobbie
   Garden Renovation — 635
Schwartz, David Joseph
   ★*The Magic of Thinking Big* — 158
Schwartz, David N.
   The Last Man Who Knew Everything — B
Schwartz, Joanna C.
   ★*Shielded* — 344.7305
SCHWARTZ, MORRIS S.
   Albom, Mitch. *Tuesdays with Morrie* — B
Schwartz, Nelson
   The Velvet Rope Economy — 339.2
Schwartz, Samuel I.
   No One at the Wheel — 629.2
Schwartzel, Erich
   Red Carpet — 791.43
Schwartzman, Nancy
   Roll Red Roll — 364.15
SCHWARZ FAMILY
   Schwarz, Geraldine. *Those Who Forget* — 940.53
Schwarz, Alan
   ADHD Nation — 618.92
Schwarz, Geraldine
   Those Who Forget — 940.53
SCHWARZ, GERALDINE
   Schwarz, Geraldine. *Those Who Forget* — 940.53
Schweitzer, Sharon
   Access to Asia — 395.5
SCIENCE
   Al-Khalili, Jim. *The House of Wisdom* — 509
   Alexander, Amir R. *Infinitesimal* — 511
   Alvarez, Walter. *A Most Improbable Journey* — 550
   Balakrishnan, Chris. *How to Win Friends and Influence Fungi* — 502
   Baron, David. *American Eclipse* — 523.7
   Bell, Alice R. *Our Biggest Experiment* — 363.738
   Bignon, Guillaume. *Confessions of a French Atheist* — 239
   Bird, Kai. *American Prometheus* — B
   Boyle, Rebecca. *Our Moon* — 523.3
   Brockman, John. *This Idea Is Brilliant* — 500
   Bryson, Bill. ★*A Short History of Nearly Everything* — 500
   Carroll, Sean M. *The Biggest Ideas in the Universe* — 530.11
   Catania, Kenneth. *Great Adaptations* — 576.8
   Cham, Jorge. *Frequently Asked Questions About the Universe* — 523.1
   Chown, Marcus. *Infinity in the Palm of Your Hand* — 523.1
   Christian, David. *Origin Story* — 909
   Conniff, Richard. *House of Lost Worlds* — 069
   Costa, James T. *Darwin's Backyard* — 576.8
   Cox, Brian. *Universal* — 523.1
   Czerski, Helen. *Storm in a Teacup* — 530
   Dawkins, Richard. *The Greatest Show on Earth* — 576.8
   Dawkins, Richard. *Science in the Soul* — 500
   Dolnick, Edward. *Seeds of Life* — 612.6
   Du Sautoy, Marcus. *The Great Unknown* — 500
   Einstein, Albert. *Ideas and Opinions* — 081
   Einstein, Albert. ★*A Stubbornly Persistent Illusion* — 530.092
   Fauber, L. S. *Heaven on Earth* — B
   Feynman, Richard P. ★*The Meaning of It All* — 500
   Feynman, Richard P. ★*Six Easy Pieces* — 530
   Frank, Lone. *The Pleasure Shock* — 616.8
   Gleick, Peter H. *The Three Ages of Water* — 333.91
   Goldacre, Ben. *Bad Science* — 500
   Green, Jaime. *The Possibility of Life* — 576.8
   Harman, Oren Solomon. *Evolutions* — 201
   Hawking, Stephen. ★*Black Holes and Baby Universes and Other Essays* — 530.1
   Hawking, Stephen. ★*Brief Answers to the Big Questions* — 500
   Heine, Steven J. *DNA Is Not Destiny* — 572.8
   Heinrich, Bernd. *A Naturalist at Large* — 508
   Holmes, Richard. *The Age of Wonder* — 509
   Judah, Hettie. *Lapidarium* — 553.8
   Junger, Sebastian. ★*In My Time of Dying* — 304.6
   Kang, Lydia. *Patient Zero* — 614.4
   Kean, Sam. *The Icepick Surgeon* — 509

PUBLIC LIBRARY CORE COLLECTION: NONFICTION
Twentieth Edition

Levitt, Dan. *What's Gotten into You*	539.7
Lightman, Alan P. *The Discoveries*	509
Lightman, Alan P. *The Transcendent Brain*	215
Lipsky, David. ★ *The Parrot and the Igloo*	304.2
Macaulay, David. *The Way Things Work Now*	600
Mahaffey, James A. *Atomic Adventures*	333.792
McAfee, Andrew. *The Geek Way*	658.3
Miodownik, Mark. *Liquid Rules*	530.4
Mukherjee, Siddhartha. *The Laws of Medicine*	610.1
Munroe, Randall. *How To*	500
Munroe, Randall. *Thing Explainer*	500
Munroe, Randall. *What If? 2*	500
Munroe, Randall. ★ *What If?*	500
Nordgren, Tyler E. *Sun, Moon, Earth*	523.7
Novella, Steven. *The Skeptics' Guide to the Universe*	500
Nuland, Sherwin B. *Leonardo Da Vinci*	B
Nye, Bill. *Everything All at Once*	153.4
Pauling, Linus. *Linus Pauling*	081
Preston, Diana. *Before the Fallout*	303.48
Reser, Anna. *Forces of Nature*	509.2
Ritchie, Stuart. *Science Fictions*	500
Rogers, Adam. *Full Spectrum*	152.14
Rovelli, Carlo. *Reality Is Not What It Seems*	530.14
Rovelli, Carlo. ★ *Seven Brief Lessons on Physics*	530
Rovelli, Carlo. *There Are Places in the World Where Rules Are Less Important Than Kindness*	500
Rutherford, Adam. *The Complete Guide to Absolutely Everything*	500
Sacks, Jonathan. *The Great Partnership*	201
Sacks, Oliver. ★ *Everything in Its Place*	B
Sagan, Carl. *Billions and Billions*	500
Sagan, Carl. *Broca's Brain*	128
Sagan, Carl. *Cosmos*	520
Sagan, Sasha. *For Small Creatures Such as We*	390.09
Saini, Angela. *Inferior*	305.4
Shermer, Michael. *Why People Believe Weird Things*	133
Sigmund, Karl. *Exact Thinking in Demented Times*	509
Slater, Lauren. *Blue Dreams*	615.7
Smil, Vaclav. *How the World Really Works*	500
Snyder, Laura J. *Eye of the Beholder*	920
Stanley, Matthew. *Einstein's War*	530
Stott, Rebecca. ★ *Darwin's Ghosts*	576.8
Strevens, Michael. *The Knowledge Machine*	500
Tesoriero, Heather Won. *The Class*	507.1
Tresch, John. *The Reason for the Darkness of the Night*	B
Tyson, Neil deGrasse. *Accessory to War*	355.001
Tyson, Neil deGrasse. *Letters from an Astrophysicist*	520.92
Tyson, Neil deGrasse. *Starry Messenger*	901
Vincent, James. *Beyond Measure*	530.8
Weinberg, Steven. *To Explain the World*	509
Wilson, Derek K. *A Magical World*	261.55
Wilson, Edward O. ★ *Letters to a Young Scientist*	570.92
Woodford, Chris. *Atoms Under the Floorboards*	500
SCIENCE — BIOLOGY — GENETICS	
Isaacson, Walter. ★ *The Code Breaker*	576.5
SCIENCE — CHEMISTRY — ATOMS AND MOLECULES	
Gray, Theodore W. *Molecules*	541
SCIENCE — CHEMISTRY — ELEMENTS AND COMPOUNDS	
Gray, Theodore W. ★ *The Elements*	546
SCIENCE — GENERAL	
Christian, David. *Origin Story*	909
SCIENCE — HUMAN BODY — NERVOUS SYSTEM	
Hallinan, Joseph T. *Why We Make Mistakes*	153
SCIENCE — PHYSICS AND PHYSICAL SCIENCE	
Still, Ben. *Particle Physics Brick by Brick*	539.7
SCIENCE — PLANTS — TREES	
Brockman, Christian Frank. *Trees of North America*	582.16097
SCIENCE — TECHNOLOGY	
Macaulay, David. *The Way Things Work Now*	600
SCIENCE AND ART	
Kandel, Eric R. *The Age of Insight*	154.2
Snyder, Laura J. *Eye of the Beholder*	920
SCIENCE AND PARANORMAL PHENOMENA	
Clegg, Brian. *Extra Sensory*	133.8
Science and Religion, 400 B.C. To A.D. 1550. Grant, Edward	201
Science and Spiritual Practices. Sheldrake, Rupert	201
SCIENCE FAIR EXPERIMENTS	
Tesoriero, Heather Won. *The Class*	507.1

SCIENCE FAIRS	
Tesoriero, Heather Won. *The Class*	507.1
SCIENCE FICTION	
Atwood, Margaret. *In Other Worlds*	813
Favro, Terri. *Generation Robot*	006.3
Le Guin, Ursula K. *Words Are My Matter*	818
Nevala-Lee, Alec. *Astounding*	809.3
Weller, Sam. *The Bradbury Chronicles*	B
SCIENCE FICTION AUTHORS	
Bradbury, Ray. ★ *Remembrance*	813
Britt, Ryan. ★ *The Spice Must Flow*	813
Kroger, Lisa. *Monster, She Wrote*	920
Okorafor, Nnedi. *Broken Places & Outer Spaces*	153.3
Scalzi, John. *Don't Live for Your Obituary*	808.02
SCIENCE FICTION FANDOM	
Jameson, A. D. *I Find Your Lack of Faith Disturbing*	791.43
SCIENCE FICTION FILMS	
Benson, Michael. *Space Odyssey*	791.43
Britt, Ryan. ★ *The Spice Must Flow*	813
Klastorin, Michael. *Close Encounters of the Third Kind*	791.43
Rinzler, J. W. *The Making of Aliens*	791.4372
SCIENCE FICTION WRITING	
Atwood, Margaret. *In Other Worlds*	813
Britt, Ryan. ★ *The Spice Must Flow*	813
Herbert, Brian. *Dreamer of Dune*	B
Le Guin, Ursula K. *Words Are My Matter*	818
Nevala-Lee, Alec. *Astounding*	809.3
Scalzi, John. *Don't Live for Your Obituary*	808.02
Weller, Sam. *The Bradbury Chronicles*	B
Science Fictions. Ritchie, Stuart	500
SCIENCE IN MASS MEDIA	
Goldacre, Ben. *Bad Science*	500
SCIENCE IN POPULAR CULTURE	
Kakalios, James. *The Amazing Story of Quantum Mechanics*	530.12
Science in the Soul. Dawkins, Richard	500
SCIENCE JOURNALISM	
Greenfieldboyce, Nell. ★ *Transient and Strange*	501
LaFollette, Marcel C. *Writing for Their Lives*	071.3
SCIENCE MUSEUMS	
Kuper, Adam. *The Museum of Other People*	305.8
SCIENCE NEWS	
Oreskes, Naomi. *Merchants of Doubt*	174
The Science of Fear. Gardner, Dan	152.4
Science of Strength Training. Current, Austin	613.7
SCIENCE POLICY	
McNeil, Donald G. ★ *The Wisdom of Plagues*	614.4
SCIENCE PROJECTS	
Tesoriero, Heather Won. *The Class*	507.1
SCIENCE TEACHERS	
Tesoriero, Heather Won. *The Class*	507.1
SCIENCE WRITERS	
Souder, William. *On a Farther Shore*	B
SCIENCE WRITING	
Owen, David. *Volume Control*	617.8
SCIENCE WRITING — ASTRONOMY	
Christian, Carol. *A Question and Answer Guide to Astronomy*	520
Kaltenegger, Lisa. ★ *Alien Earths*	523.2
Lang, Kenneth R. *The Cambridge Guide to the Solar System*	523.2
Lauretta, D. S. *The Asteroid Hunter*	523.44
Lintott, Chris. *Accidental Astronomy*	520
McTier, Moiya. *The Milky Way*	523.1
Pontzen, Andrew. *The Universe in a Box*	523.1
Ridpath, Ian. *Stars & Planets*	520
Shore, Linda. *The Total Skywatcher's Manual*	523
Trefil, James. *Space Atlas*	520
Tyson, Neil deGrasse. *Starry Messenger*	901
SCIENCE WRITING — BIOLOGY	
Ackerman, Diane. *A Natural History of the Senses*	152.1
Ackerman, Jennifer. ★ *What an Owl Knows*	598.9
Anthony, Leslie. *The Aliens Among Us*	578.6
Aryee, Patrick. *30 Animals That Made Us Smarter*	590
Balcombe, Jonathan P. *Super Fly*	595.77
Bercovici, Jeff. *Play On*	613.7
Black, Riley. *The Last Days of the Dinosaurs*	576.8
Bohannon, Cat. ★ *Eve*	613
Bohme, Madelaine. *Ancient Bones*	599.93
Bradbury, Neil. *A Taste for Poison*	615.9
Browne, E. J. *Charles Darwin*	B

AUTHOR, TITLE, SERIES AND SUBJECT INDEX

Browne, E. J. *Charles Darwin*	B
Brusatte, Stephen. *The Rise and Reign of the Mammals*	569
Bryson, Bill. *The Body*	612
Burnett, Dean. *Idiot Brain*	612.8
Byrne, Eugene. *Darwin*	741.5
Cacioppo, Stephanie. *Wired for Love*	616.8
Carson, Rachel. *The Edge of the Sea*	578.769
Casey, Susan. *The Underworld*	551.46
Catania, Kenneth. *Great Adaptations*	576.8
Cech, Thomas. *The Catalyst*	572.8
Chace, Teri Dunn. *Seeing Seeds*	581.4
Collen, Alanna. *10% Human*	612.3
Colwell, Rita R. *A Lab of One's Own*	B
Cooke, Lucy. *Bitch*	591.56
Costa, James T. *Darwin's Backyard*	576.8
Costa, James T. *Radical by Nature*	B
Crystal, David. ★*How Language Works*	410
Czerski, Helen. *The Blue Machine*	551.46
Damasio, Antonio R. *The Feeling of What Happens*	153
Damasio, Antonio R. *Looking for Spinoza*	152.4
Darwin, Charles. *Charles Darwin*	576.8
Dawkins, Richard. ★*The Ancestor's Tale*	576.8
Dawkins, Richard. *An Appetite for Wonder*	B
Dawkins, Richard. *Brief Candle in the Dark*	B
Dawkins, Richard. *The Greatest Show on Earth*	576.8
Dehaene, Stanislas. *Reading in the Brain*	418
Deisseroth, Karl. *Projections*	616.89
Dennett, D. C. *Darwin's Dangerous Idea*	146
Denworth, Lydia. *Friendship*	158.2
Desilva, Jeremy. *First Steps*	599.93
Dettmer, Philipp. *Immune*	616.07
Dickinson, Richard. *Weeds of North America*	632
Dolnick, Edward. *Seeds of Life*	612.6
Doughty, Caitlin. *Will My Cat Eat My Eyeballs?*	306.9
Drew, Liam. *I, Mammal*	599
Dunbar, R. I. M. *Human Evolution*	155.7
Eagleman, David. *The Brain*	612.8
Eagleman, David. *Incognito*	153
Eagleman, David. *Livewired*	612.8
Eldredge, Niles. *Why We Do It*	155.3
Elmore, Bartow J. *Seed Money*	338.7
Emera, Deena. *A Brief History of the Female Body*	612.6
Everts, Sarah. *The Joy of Sweat*	612.7
Farmer, Jared. *Elderflora*	582.16
Fine, Cordelia. *Testosterone Rex*	155.3
Finkel, Elizabeth. *The Genome Generation*	599.93
Finlay, B. Brett. *Let Them Eat Dirt*	616.9
Flyn, Cal. ★*Islands of Abandonment*	333.73
Foer, Joshua. *Moonwalking with Einstein*	153.1
Forbes, Peter. *Dazzled and Deceived*	578.4
Foster, Charles. *Being a Human*	155.7
Gardner, Dan. *The Science of Fear*	152.4
Gee, Henry. *A (Very) Short History of Life on Earth*	576.8
George, Rose. *Nine Pints*	612.1
Gould, Stephen Jay. *The Mismeasure of Man*	153.9
Gould, Stephen Jay. *The Richness of Life*	508
Gould, Stephen Jay. *The Structure of Evolutionary Theory*	576.8
Grabbe, Lester L. *Faith and Fossils*	231.7
Gray, Theodore W. *Reactions*	530
Gross, Rachel E. *Vagina Obscura*	618.1
Guyenet, Stephan J. *The Hungry Brain*	616.85
Halliday, Thomas. ★*Otherlands*	560
Hanson, Thor. *Feathers*	598.147
Hanson, Thor. *Hurricane Lizards and Plastic Squid*	577.2
Harari, Yuval N. *Homo Deus*	909.83
Harari, Yuval N. ★*Sapiens*	909
Hazard, Leah. *Womb*	612.6
Henig, Robin Marantz. *The Monk in the Garden*	B
Higgins, Jackie. *Sentient*	573.8
Hoffman, Donald D. *The Case Against Reality*	121
Hoffman, Donald D. *Visual Intelligence*	152.14
Holmes, Bob. *Flavor*	612.8
Hoyt, Erich. *Encyclopedia of Whales, Dolphins and Porpoises*	599.5
Imbler, Sabrina. *How Far the Light Reaches*	591.77
Ireland, Tom. *The Good Virus*	579.2
Jabr, Ferris. ★*Becoming Earth*	570.1
Jahren, Hope. ★*Lab Girl*	B
Johanson, Donald C. *Lucy*	569
Johnson, Steven. *Extra Life*	362.1
Kandel, Eric R. *The Age of Insight*	154.2
Kandel, Eric R. ★*The Disordered Mind*	616.89
Kandel, Eric R. *In Search of Memory*	B
Keltner, Dacher. *Born to Be Good*	155.2
Kershenbaum, Arik. *The Zoologist's Guide to the Galaxy*	576.8
Kingdon, Amorina. ★*Sing Like Fish*	591.77
Konnikova, Maria. *Mastermind*	153.4
Kurzweil, Ray. ★*The Singularity Is Near*	153.9
Larson, Edward J. *Evolution*	576.8
Leakey, Richard E. *The Origin of Humankind*	599.93
Lederer, Roger J. *Beaks, Bones, and Bird Songs*	598
Leschziner, Guy. *The Nocturnal Brain*	616.8
Levitt, Dan. *What's Gotten into You*	539.7
Lewis, Michael. ★*The Undoing Project*	920
Lister, Adrian. *Darwin's Fossils*	576.8
Losos, Jonathan B. *Improbable Destinies*	576.8
Lowman, Margaret. *The Arbornaut*	581.7
Lowman, Margaret. *Life in the Treetops*	B
Lyman, Monty. *The Remarkable Life of the Skin*	612.7
MacPhee, R. D. E. *End of the Megafauna*	591.4
Maddox, Brenda. *Rosalind Franklin*	B
Magsamen, Susan. *Your Brain on Art*	111
Margulis, Lynn. *Symbiotic Planet*	576.8
Markel, Howard. *Origin Story*	576.8
Markel, Howard. *The Secret of Life*	572.86
Martinez Arias, Alfonso. *The Master Builder*	571.6
McCalman, Iain. *Darwin's Armada*	576.8
McGee, Harold. ★*Nose Dive*	612.8
McIntyre, Rick. *The Reign of Wolf 21*	599.773
McNeur, Catherine. *Mischievous Creatures*	920
Meals, Roy A. *Bones*	599.9
Meals, Roy A. *Muscle*	612.7
Meiburg, Jonathan. *A Most Remarkable Creature*	598.9
Miller, Kenneth R. *The Human Instinct*	155.7
Monosson, Emily. ★*Blight*	616.9
Montgomery, David R. *What Your Food Ate*	631.4
Mukherjee, Siddhartha. ★*The Gene*	616
Mukherjee, Siddhartha. ★*The Song of the Cell*	571.6
Nakazawa, Donna Jackson. *The Angel and the Assassin*	612.8
Nelson, Bryn. *Flush*	612.3
Nestor, James. *Deep*	797.2
Newitz, Annalee. *Scatter, Adapt, and Remember*	576.8
Nicholls, Steve. *Alien Worlds*	595.7
Nowak, Ronald M. *Walker's Mammals of the World.*	599
Nye, Bill. *Undeniable*	576.8
O'Connor, Maura R. *Resurrection Science*	591.68
Pattison, Kermit. *Fossil Men*	569.9
Paul, Annie Murphy. *The Extended Mind*	128
Paulson, Dennis. *Dragonflies & Damselflies*	595.7
Peck, Robert McCracken. *A Glorious Enterprise*	508
Peterson, Dale. *Giraffe Reflections*	599.638
Peterson, Roger Tory. *Peterson Field Guide to Birds of Eastern and Central North America*	598.097
Peterson, Roger Tory. *Peterson Field Guide to Birds of Western North America*	598.097
Pinker, Steven. *The Blank Slate*	155.2
Pinker, Steven. *How the Mind Works*	153
Pinker, Steven. *The Language Instinct*	400
Pinker, Steven. *Rationality*	153.4
Pinker, Steven. *The Stuff of Thought*	401
Pinker, Steven. *Words and Rules*	415
Piore, Adam. *The Body Builders*	660.6
Pollan, Michael. ★*This Is Your Mind on Plants*	581.6
Preston, Diana. *The Evolution of Charles Darwin*	508
Provine, Robert R. *Curious Behavior*	152.3
Radke, Heather. *Butts*	611
Rhodes, Richard. *Scientist*	B
Roach, Mary. *Bonk*	612.6
Roach, Mary. *Gulp*	612.3
Roach, Mary. ★*Stiff*	611
Roberts, Jason. ★*Every Living Thing*	578
Roman, Joe. *Eat, Poop, Die*	577
Rutherford, Adam. *Control*	363.9
Rutherford, Adam. *Humanimal*	599.93
Sagan, Carl. *The Dragons of Eden*	153
Sanders, Ella Frances. *Eating the Sun*	520
Sapolsky, Robert M. *Behave*	612.8

PUBLIC LIBRARY CORE COLLECTION: NONFICTION
Twentieth Edition

Author. Title	Dewey
Sapolsky, Robert M. *Determined*	123
Sardet, Christian. *Plankton*	578.77
Sarma, Sanjay E. *Grasp*	370.15
Scales, Helen. *What the Wild Sea Can Be*	577.7
Scheel, David. *Many Things Under a Rock*	594
Schilthuizen, Menno. *Darwin Comes to Town*	577.5
Schlanger, Zoe. ★*The Light Eaters*	571.2
Schutt, Bill. *Cannibalism*	394
Schutt, Bill. *Pump*	612.1
Sheldrake, Merlin. *Entangled Life*	579.5
Shermer, Michael. *The Believing Brain*	153.4
Sinclair, David A. *Lifespan*	570
Skloot, Rebecca. ★*The Immortal Life of Henrietta Lacks*	B
Smil, Vaclav. *Size*	153.7
Souder, William. *On a Farther Shore*	B
Stanger, Ben. *From One Cell*	571.6
Stott, Rebecca. ★*Darwin's Ghosts*	576.8
Struzik, Edward. *Swamplands*	577.68
Suddendorf, Thomas. *The Gap*	156
Sumner, Seirian. *Endless Forms*	595.79
Sverdrup-Thygeson, Anne. *Buzz, Sting, Bite*	595.7
Switek, Brian. *Skeleton Keys*	611
Tattersall, Ian. *Masters of the Planet*	599.93
Taylor, Jill Bolte. *My Stroke of Insight*	362.19681
Taylor, Marianne. *Bats*	599.4
Thomson, Helen. *Unthinkable*	612.8
Toomey, David. *Kingdom of Play*	591.56
Tougias, Robert. *Birder on Berry Lane*	598.072
Vince, Gaia. *Transcendence*	599.93
Ward, Ashley. *Where We Meet the World*	612.8
Webb, Kinari. *Guardians of the Trees*	B
Welz, Adam. *The End of Eden*	577.2
Whitehouse, David. *The Alien Perspective*	523.1
Widder, Edith. *Below the Edge of Darkness*	551.46092
Wiking, Meik. *The Art of Making Memories*	153.1
Williams, Florence. *Heartbreak*	306.7
Wilson, David Sloan. *Evolution for Everyone*	576.801
Wilson, Edward O. *The Diversity of Life*	333.95
Wilson, Edward O. *Genesis*	591.5
Wilson, Edward O. *Half-Earth*	333.95
Wilson, Edward O. ★*The Social Conquest of Earth*	599.93
Wilson, Edward O. *Tales from the Ant World*	595.79
Wohlleben, Peter. *Forest Walking*	582.16
Wohlleben, Peter. *The Heartbeat of Trees*	582.16
Wohlleben, Peter. *The Hidden Life of Trees*	582.16
Wohlleben, Peter. *The Secret Wisdom of Nature*	508
Wolf, Maryanne. *Reader, Come Home*	418
Yi, Sang-Hui. *Close Encounters with Humankind*	599.93
Yong, Ed. ★*An Immense World*	591.5
Zadra, Antonio. *When Brains Dream*	613.7
Zernicka-Goetz, Magdalena. *The Dance of Life*	591.56
Zimmer, Carl. *Life's Edge*	570
Zimmer, Carl. *She Has Her Mother's Laugh*	576.5

SCIENCE WRITING — CHEMISTRY

Author. Title	Dewey
Bodanis, David. *Electric Universe*	537
Challoner, Jack. *The Elements*	546
Gray, Theodore W. *Reactions*	530
Kean, Sam. *Caesar's Last Breath*	551.51
Kean, Sam. *The Disappearing Spoon*	546
Miodownik, Mark. *Liquid Rules*	530.4
Miodownik, Mark. *Stuff Matters*	620.1
Nelson, Bryn. *Flush*	612.3
Ploszajski, Anna. *Handmade*	620.1

SCIENCE WRITING — COMPUTING, THE INTERNET, AND TECHNOLOGY

Author. Title	Dewey
Auletta, Ken. *Googled*	338.7
Beyer, Kurt. *Grace Hopper and the Invention of the Information Age*	B
Bilton, Nick. *Hatching Twitter*	006.7
Bissell, Tom. *Extra Lives*	794.8
Burak, Asi. *Power Play*	794.8
Chayka, Kyle. *Filterworld*	306
Chertoff, Michael. *Exploding Data*	343.7309
Cole, Samantha. *How the Internet Changed Sex and Sex Changed the Internet*	306.7
Copeland, B. Jack. *Turing*	B
Cox, Joseph. *Dark Wire*	363.2
Dudley, Renee. *The Ransomware Hunting Team*	363.25
Dyson, George. *Turing's Cathedral*	004
Essinger, James. *Ada's Algorithm*	B
Fagans, Michael. *iPhone Photography for Everybody*	770
Favro, Terri. *Generation Robot*	006.3
Fortnow, Lance. *The Golden Ticket*	511.3
Galloway, Scott. *The Four*	338.7
Gleick, James. *The Information*	020.9
Greenberg, Andy. *Sandworm*	364.16
Greenberg, Andy. *Tracers in the Dark*	364.16
Hill, Kashmir. ★*Your Face Belongs to Us*	006.2
Howley, Kerry. *Bottoms Up and the Devil Laughs*	352.37
Isaacson, Walter. ★*The Innovators*	B
Kaku, Michio. *Quantum Supremacy*	006.3
Kasparov, G. K. *Deep Thinking*	006.3
Kleiman, Kathy. *Proving Ground*	4.092
Leavitt, David. *The Man Who Knew Too Much*	B
Lee, Kai-Fu. *AI 2041*	006.3
Lessig, Lawrence. *The Future of Ideas*	346.04
Levitin, Daniel J. ★*A Field Guide to Lies*	153.4
Li, Fei-Fei. *The Worlds I See*	B
Lloyd, Seth. *Programming the Universe*	530.12
Malone, Thomas W. *Superminds*	005.7
McCourt, Frank H. ★*Our Biggest Fight*	303.48
McKibben, Bill. *Falter*	909.83
Merchant, Brian. *Blood in the Machine*	303.48
Miller, Chris. *Chip War*	338.4
Mitnick, Kevin D. *The Art of Invisibility*	005.8
Mitnick, Kevin D. *Ghost in the Wires*	B
Mustill, Tom. *How to Speak Whale*	591.59
Nadella, Satya. *Hit Refresh*	B
O'Gieblyn, Meghan. *God, Human, Animal, Machine*	814
Page, Scott E. *The Model Thinker*	001.4
Rhodes, Richard. ★*Energy*	333.7909
Russell, Stuart J. *Human Compatible*	006.301
Schwartz, Samuel I. *No One at the Wheel*	629.2
Scott, Kevin. *Reprogramming the American Dream*	338
Shapiro, Scott J. ★*Fancy Bear Goes Phishing*	364.16
Soni, Jimmy. *A Mind at Play*	B
Taylor, Claude. *How to Zoom Your Room*	747
Tegmark, Max. *Life 3.0*	006.301
Thompson, Clive. *Coders*	005.1092
Ullman, Ellen. *Life in Code*	B
Waldman, Jonathan. *Sam*	629.8
Williams, Richard. *The Animator's Survival Kit*	778

SCIENCE WRITING — COMPUTING, THE INTERNET, AND TECHNOLOGY — ARTIFICIAL INTELLIGENCE AND MACHINE LE

Author. Title	Dewey
Murgia, Madhumita. *Code Dependent*	303.48
Wiggins, Christopher L. *How Data Happened*	310

SCIENCE WRITING — COMPUTING, THE INTERNET, AND TECHNOLOGY — INTERNET

Author. Title	Dewey
Kerpen, Dave. *Likeable Social Media*	658.8

SCIENCE WRITING — GENERAL

Author. Title	Dewey
Agrawal, Roma. *Nuts and Bolts*	609
Al-Khalili, Jim. *The House of Wisdom*	509
Alvarez, Walter. *A Most Improbable Journey*	550
Ariely, Dan. *The Honest Truth About Dishonesty*	177
Ball, Philip. *Patterns in Nature*	500.201
Bell, Alice R. *Our Biggest Experiment*	363.738
Black, Alexandra. *Scientists Who Changed History*	509.22
Bradley, James. *Deep Water*	578.77
Brands, H. W. *The First American*	B
Brockman, John. *This Idea Is Brilliant*	500
Brown, Nancy Marie. *The Abacus and the Cross*	B
Bryson, Bill. ★*A Short History of Nearly Everything*	500
Burdick, Alan. *Why Time Flies*	529
Cain, Susan. *Quiet*	155.2
Carroll, Sean M. *From Eternity to Here*	530.11
Cassidy, Cody. *And Then You're Dead*	612
Chown, Marcus. *Infinity in the Palm of Your Hand*	523.1
Coleman, Eliot. ★*The New Organic Grower*	635
Danforth, Adam. *Butchering Poultry, Rabbit, Lamb, Goat, and Pork*	664
Darwin, Charles. ★*The Origin of Species by Means of Natural Selection, Or, the Preservation of Favored Races in the Struggle for Life*	575
Davis, Kevin. *The Brain Defense*	345.747
Dawkins, Richard. *Science in the Soul*	500
Druse, Kenneth. *The New Shade Garden*	635.9
Du Sautoy, Marcus. *The Great Unknown*	500
Duhigg, Charles. ★*The Power of Habit*	158.1
Egan, Dan. ★*The Death and Life of the Great Lakes*	577.6

AUTHOR, TITLE, SERIES AND SUBJECT INDEX

Einstein, Albert. *Ideas and Opinions*	081
Ellard, Colin. *You Are Here*	153.7
Fabricant, M. Chris. *Junk Science and the American Criminal Justice System*	363.25
Ferguson, Charles D. *Nuclear Energy*	333.792
Flottum, Kim. *The Backyard Beekeeper*	638
Frey, Kate. *The Bee-Friendly Garden*	595.79
Gleick, James. *Time Travel*	530.11
Goldfarb, Ben. *Crossings*	333.77
Goodin, Tanya. *Stop Staring at Screens*	004.67
Grant, Edward. *Science and Religion, 400 B.C. To A.D. 1550*	201
Gray, Theodore W. *Reactions*	530
Greenfieldboyce, Nell. ★*Transient and Strange*	501
Gryta, Thomas. *Lights Out*	338.7
Hagerty, Barbara Bradley. *Life Reimagined*	155.6
Hammack, William Scott. ★*Things We Make*	620
Harman, Oren Solomon. *Evolutions*	201
Hawking, Stephen. ★*Brief Answers to the Big Questions*	500
Herman, Amy. *Visual Intelligence*	152.14
Heyman, Stephen. *The Planter of Modern Life*	B
Higginbotham, Adam. ★*Midnight in Chernobyl*	363.17
Hilborn, Ray. *Overfishing*	338.3
Hofstadter, Douglas R. *Surfaces and Essences*	169
Hogge, Fred. *Of Ice and Men*	338.4
Holmes, Richard. *The Age of Wonder*	509
Holt, Jim. ★*When Einstein Walked with Godel*	814
Holt, Jim. *Why Does the World Exist?*	113
Humes, Edward. ★*Total Garbage*	628.4
Isaacson, Walter. ★*Benjamin Franklin*	B
Johnson, Steven. *Farsighted*	153.8
Johnson, Steven. *Wonderland*	790.1
Junger, Sebastian. ★*In My Time of Dying*	304.6
Kaku, Michio. ★*The Future of Humanity*	629.45
Kean, Sam. *The Icepick Surgeon*	509
Kolbert, Elizabeth. ★*Under a White Sky*	304.2
Lightman, Alan P. *The Discoveries*	509
Lightman, Alan P. *Searching for Stars on an Island in Maine*	523.1
Lightman, Alan P. *The Transcendent Brain*	215
Lipsky, David. ★*The Parrot and the Igloo*	304.2
Livio, Mario. *Why?*	153.3
Medina, John. *Brain Rules*	153
Munroe, Randall. *How To*	500
Munroe, Randall. *Thing Explainer*	500
Munroe, Randall. *What If? 2*	500
Munroe, Randall. ★*What If?*	500
Norton, Laurah. *Lay Them to Rest*	363.25
Novella, Steven. *The Skeptics' Guide to the Universe*	500
Nuland, Sherwin B. *Leonardo Da Vinci*	B
Oreskes, Naomi. *Merchants of Doubt*	174
Owens, Jay. *Dust*	551.51
Paulson, Dennis. *Dragonflies & Damselflies*	595.7
Ploszajski, Anna. *Handmade*	620.1
Prasad, Aarathi. *Silk*	677
Prescott, Matthew. *Food Is the Solution*	613.2
Prothero, Donald R. *UFOs, Chemtrails, and Aliens*	001.94
Reser, Anna. *Forces of Nature*	509.2
Ritchie, Stuart. *Science Fictions*	500
Roach, Mary. ★*Fuzz*	591.5
Roach, Mary. ★*Grunt*	355
Roach, Mary. ★*Spook*	129
Rogers, Adam. *Full Spectrum*	152.14
Rogers, Adam. *Proof*	663
Rovelli, Carlo. *The Order of Time*	530.11
Rutherford, Adam. *The Complete Guide to Absolutely Everything*	500
Sacks, Jonathan. *The Great Partnership*	201
Sacks, Oliver. ★*Everything in Its Place*	B
Sagan, Carl. *Billions and Billions*	500
Sagan, Carl. *Broca's Brain*	128
Sagan, Sasha. *For Small Creatures Such as We*	390.09
Saini, Angela. *Inferior*	305.4
Sheldrake, Rupert. *Science and Spiritual Practices*	201
Shermer, Michael. *Why People Believe Weird Things*	133
Sigmund, Karl. *Exact Thinking in Demented Times*	920
Smil, Vaclav. *Size*	153.7
Strevens, Michael. *The Knowledge Machine*	500
Tesoriero, Heather Won. *The Class*	507.1
Tourles, Stephanie L. *Pure Skin Care*	646.7
Townsend, Alan R. ★*This Ordinary Stardust*	B
Tresch, John. *The Reason for the Darkness of the Night*	B
Vincent, James. *Beyond Measure*	530.8
Weill, Kelly. *Off the Edge*	001.9
Weinberg, Steven. *To Explain the World*	509
Wilson, Edward O. *In Search of Nature*	113
Wilson, Edward O. ★*Letters to a Young Scientist*	570.92
Winchester, Simon. ★*The Perfectionists*	620.009
Woodford, Chris. *Atoms Under the Floorboards*	500
Wragg Sykes, Rebecca. *Kindred*	569.9
Yang, Charles D. *The Infinite Gift*	401

SCIENCE WRITING — GEOGRAPHY

Hayes, Derek. *Historical Atlas of the United States*	911

SCIENCE WRITING — GEOLOGY

Ball, Philip. *Patterns in Nature*	500.201
Bjornerud, Marcia. *Geopedia*	551
Dean, Cornelia. *Against the Tide*	333.91
Gates, Alexander E. *Encyclopedia of Earthquakes and Volcanoes*	551.2
Gee, Henry. *A (Very) Short History of Life on Earth*	576.8
Gleick, Peter H. *The Three Ages of Water*	333.91
Jabr, Ferris. ★*Becoming Earth*	570.1
Judah, Hettie. *Lapidarium*	553.8
Pough, Frederick H. ★*A Field Guide to Rocks and Minerals*	549
Turney, Chris. *1912*	998
Winchester, Simon. *The Map That Changed the World*	B

SCIENCE WRITING — GREAT ENGINEERING FEATS

Berger, Eric. *Liftoff*	B
Blockley, David. *Bridges*	725
Carlsen, Spike. *A Walk Around the Block*	031
Carlson, W. Bernard. *Tesla*	B
Gray, Charlotte. ★*Reluctant Genius*	920
Kaku, Michio. *Quantum Supremacy*	006.3
Kostigen, Thomas. *Hacking Planet Earth*	628
Li, Fei-Fei. *The Worlds I See*	B
Morris, Edmund. ★*Edison*	B
Parker, Matthew. *Panama Fever*	972.87
Rose, Alexander. *Empires of the Sky*	920
Sobel, Dava. *Longitude*	526
Standage, Tom. *A Brief History of Motion*	388
Vance, Ashlee. *When the Heavens Went on Sale*	621.43

SCIENCE WRITING — MATHEMATICS

Alexander, Amir R. *Infinitesimal*	511
Anderson, Christopher. *The Numbers Game*	796.334
Barrow, John D. *The Infinite Book*	111
Benjamin, Arthur. *The Magic of Math*	510
Bhattacharya, Ananyo. *The Man from the Future*	B
Brooks, Michael. *The Art of More*	510.9
Brooks, Michael. *The Quantum Astrologer's Handbook*	B
Budiansky, Stephen. *Journey to the Edge of Reason*	B
Cairo, Alberto. *How Charts Lie*	302.2
Cheng, Eugenia. *How to Bake Pi*	510
Christian, Brian. *Algorithms to Live By*	153.4
Clegg, Brian. *Are Numbers Real?*	510
Conway, John Horton. *The Book of Numbers*	512
Diaconis, Persi. *Magical Mathematics*	793.8
Du Sautoy, Marcus. ★*Around the World in Eighty Games*	790.1
Dunham, William. *The Mathematical Universe*	510
Ellenberg, Jordan. ★*How Not to Be Wrong*	510
Fortnow, Lance. *The Golden Ticket*	511.3
Johnson, Katherine G. *My Remarkable Journey*	B
Kanigel, Robert. *The Man Who Knew Infinity*	B
Kitagawa, Kate. *The Secret Lives of Numbers*	510.9
Law, Keith. *Smart Baseball*	796.357
Mazur, Joseph. *Fluke*	519.2
Merzbach, Uta C. *A History of Mathematics*	510.9
Page, Scott E. *The Model Thinker*	001.4
Parker, Matt. *Humble Pi*	510
Pickover, Clifford A. *The Math Book*	510.9
Sawchik, Travis. *Big Data Baseball*	796.357
Schneps, Leila. *Math on Trial*	345
Seife, Charles. *Proofiness*	510
Singh, Simon. *Fermat's Enigma*	512
Stewart, Ian. *Professor Stewart's Casebook of Mathematical Mysteries*	793.74
Stewart, Ian. *Visions of Infinity*	510
Stone, Deborah A. *Counting*	001.4
Szpiro, George. *Poincare's Prize*	510.76
Tegmark, Max. *Our Mathematical Universe*	523.1
Thompson, Erica. *Escape from Model Land*	511
Tufte, Edward R. *The Visual Display of Quantitative Information*	001.4

PUBLIC LIBRARY CORE COLLECTION: NONFICTION
Twentieth Edition

Wheelan, Charles J. *Naked Statistics*	519.5
Yates, Kit. *The Math of Life and Death*	510
SCIENCE WRITING — MEDICINE AND HEALTH	
Allmen, Tara. *Menopause Confidential*	618.1
Applebaum, Allison. *Stand by Me*	649.8
Aronson, Louise. *Elderhood*	362.60973
Asprey, Dave. *Game Changers*	158.1
Barrett, Lisa Feldman. ★*How Emotions Are Made*	152.4
Bechdel, Alison. ★*The Secret to Superhuman Strength*	741.5
Block, Jennifer. *Everything Below the Waist*	613
Cassidy, Cody. *And Then You're Dead*	612
Cech, Thomas. *The Catalyst*	572.8
Clark, Andy. *The Experience Machine*	153
Cleghorn, Elinor. *Unwell Women*	613
Comen, Elizabeth. ★*All in Her Head*	613
Conaboy, Chelsea. *Mother Brain*	306.874
Coste, Joanne Koenig. *Learning to Speak Alzheimer's*	362.1
Curry, Kevin. *Fit Men Cook*	641.5
Dearen, Jason. *Kill Shot*	616.8
Dettmer, Philipp. *Immune*	616.07
Dolnick, Edward. *Seeds of Life*	612.6
Elliott, Carl. ★*The Occasional Human Sacrifice*	174.2
Emera, Deena. *A Brief History of the Female Body*	612.6
Engelhart, Katie. *The Inevitable*	179.7
Epstein, Mark. *The Zen of Therapy*	294.3
Gawande, Atul. ★*Being Mortal*	362.17
Goldacre, Ben. *Bad Science*	500
Goldberg, Sana. *How to Be a Patient*	610.69
Green, Stefanie. *This Is Assisted Dying*	616.02
Gross, Rachel E. *Vagina Obscura*	618.1
Gunter, Jen. ★*Blood*	612.6
Gunter, Jen. *The Vagina Bible*	612.6
Gupta, Shalene. *The Cycle*	618.1
Hamblin, James. *If Our Bodies Could Talk*	613
Hannig, Anita. *The Day I Die*	364.152
Hari, Johann. ★*Magic Pill*	613.2
Heine, Steven J. *DNA Is Not Destiny*	572.8
Hendrickson, Debra. ★*The Air They Breathe*	363.7
Hongoltz-Hetling, Matthew. *If It Sounds Like a Quack*	615.8
Hotz, Julia. ★*The Connection Cure*	610
Hughes, Evan. *The Hard Sell*	338.4
Isaacson, Walter. ★*The Code Breaker*	576.5
Jamieson, Alexandra. *Women, Food, and Desire*	155.9
Jena, Anupam B. *Random Acts of Medicine*	616.0072
Jones, Chip. *The Organ Thieves*	617.4
Kempner, Joanna. *Psychedelic Outlaws*	615.7
Kerr, Christopher. *Death Is but a Dream*	155.9
Lalkhen, Abdul-Ghaaliq. *An Anatomy of Pain*	616
Lamas, Daniela J. *You Can Stop Humming Now*	616.02
Lieberman, Daniel. *Exercised*	612.044
Luthra, Shefali. ★*Undue Burden*	362.1988
Malone, Sharon. *Grown Woman Talk*	362.1
Manheimer, Eric. *Twelve Patients*	362.1109747
Marchant, Jo. *Cure*	616.89
Marschark, Marc. ★*How Deaf Children Learn*	371.91
McGregor, Alyson J. *Sex Matters*	613
Meals, Roy A. *Muscle*	612.7
Mukherjee, Siddhartha. *The Laws of Medicine*	610.1
Mukherjee, Siddhartha. ★*The Song of the Cell*	571.6
Nigg, Joel T. *Getting Ahead of ADHD*	618.92
Nuila, Ricardo. *The People's Hospital*	362.1
Oakes, John G. H. ★*The Fast*	613.2
Oshinsky, David M. *Bellevue*	362.1109747
Owen, David. *Volume Control*	617.8
Porter, Roy. *The Greatest Benefit to Mankind*	610
Powell, Tia. *Dementia Reimagined*	616.8
Preston, Katherine. *Out with It*	B
Price, Catherine. *Vitamania*	612.3
Pulde, Alona. ★*The Forks Over Knives Plan*	641.5
Quave, Cassandra Leah. *The Plant Hunter*	581.6
Raffel, Dawn. *The Strange Case of Dr. Couney*	B
Randall, David K. *Black Death at the Golden Gate*	616.9
Raphael, Rina. *The Gospel of Wellness*	613
Reiss, Benjamin. *Wild Nights*	616.8
Roth, Andrew J. *Managing Prostate Cancer*	616.99
Rutkow, Ira M. *Empire of the Scalpel*	617
Ryckman, Pamela. *Candace Pert*	B
Sacks, Oliver. *The Man Who Mistook His Wife for a Hat and Other Clinical Tales*	616.8
Snyder, Timothy. ★*Our Malady*	362.10973
Specter, Emma. *More, Please*	616.85
Standefer, Katherine E. *Lightning Flowers*	B
Tabery, James. ★*Tyranny of the Gene*	572.8
Tang, Karen. ★*It's Not Hysteria*	618.2
Tulleken, Chris van. *Ultra-Processed People*	664
Turban, Jack L. ★*Free to Be*	616.85
Vernacchio, Al. *For Goodness Sex*	613.9071
Villarosa, Linda. ★*Under the Skin*	362.1089
Volandes, Angelo E. *The Conversation*	616.02
Wade, Sabia. *Birthing Liberation*	363.96
Warraich, Haider. *Modern Death*	179.7
Webb, Kinari. *Guardians of the Trees*	B
Weil, Andrew. *Mind Over Meds*	362.29
Wiking, Meik. *The Little Book of Hygge*	158.1
Wiking, Meik. *The Little Book of Lykke*	646.7
Williams, Florence. *The Nature Fix*	155.9
Wilson, Jessica. *It's Always Been Ours*	613
Xuecun, Murong. *Deadly Quiet City*	614.5
Yurkiewicz, Ilana. *Fragmented*	362.1
Zaman, Muhammad H. *Biography of Resistance*	616.9
Zuckerman, Gregory. *A Shot to Save the World*	614.5
SCIENCE WRITING — MEDICINE AND HEALTH — ADDICTION	
Carr, David. *The Night of the Gun*	B
Fisher, Carl Erik. ★*The Urge*	362.29
Hornbacher, Marya. *Wasted*	B
Johnston, Ann Dowsett. *Drink*	362.292
McGreal, Chris. *American Overdose*	362.29
Rieder, Travis. *In Pain*	362.29
Whitaker, Holly. ★*Quit Like a Woman*	616.86
SCIENCE WRITING — MEDICINE AND HEALTH — AGING AND LONGEVITY	
Attia, Peter. ★*Outlive*	612.6
Crowley, Chris. *Younger Next Year*	613
Esmonde-White, Miranda. *Aging Backwards*	613.7
Gupta, Sanjay. ★*Keep Sharp*	153.4
Hecht, M. E. *Two Old Broads*	613
SCIENCE WRITING — MEDICINE AND HEALTH — ALLERGIES	
Sears, Robert W. *The Allergy Book*	618.92
SCIENCE WRITING — MEDICINE AND HEALTH — ALTERNATIVE MEDICINE	
Chevallier, Andrew. *Encyclopedia of Herbal Medicine*	615.3
Cruikshank, Tiffany. *Meditate Your Weight*	613.2
Grossman, Gail Boorstein. *Restorative Yoga for Life*	613.7
Ingels, Darin. *The Lyme Solution*	616.9
Keville, Kathi. *The Aromatherapy Garden*	635.9
Kornfield, Jack. *The Wise Heart*	294.3
Myers, Amy. ★*The Autoimmune Solution*	616.97
Pohlman, Dean. *Yoga Fitness for Men*	613.7
Stanley, Jessamyn. *Every Body Yoga*	613.7
Taillac, Victoire de. *An Atlas of Natural Beauty*	646.7
Taylor, Madisyn. *Unmedicated*	615.8
Tourles, Stephanie L. *Pure Skin Care*	646.7
Van der Kolk, Bessel A. *The Body Keeps the Score*	616.85
Wayne, Peter. *The Harvard Medical School Guide to Tai Chi*	613.7
Weil, Andrew. *Mind Over Meds*	362.29
SCIENCE WRITING — MEDICINE AND HEALTH — BRAIN FUNCTION AND MEMORY	
Fleming, Renee. ★*Music and Mind*	615.8
Mace, Nancy L. ★*The 36-Hour Day*	616.8
Willeumier, Kristen. ★*Biohack Your Brain*	612.8
SCIENCE WRITING — MEDICINE AND HEALTH — CHILDREN'S HEALTH	
Altmann, Tanya Remer. *What to Feed Your Baby*	649
Bhattacharya, Shaoni. *The Baby Book*	649.1
Finlay, B. Brett. *Let Them Eat Dirt*	616.9
Fradin, Kelly. *Advanced Parenting*	649
Galanti, Regine. ★*Parenting Anxious Kids*	155.4
Goh, Suzanne. *Magnificent Minds*	618.92
Keene, Nancy. *Childhood Leukemia*	618.92
Porto, Anthony. *The Pediatrician's Guide to Feeding Babies & Toddlers*	618.92
Power, Thomas J. *If Your Adolescent Has ADHD*	616.85
Sears, Robert W. *The Allergy Book*	618.92

AUTHOR, TITLE, SERIES AND SUBJECT INDEX

SCIENCE WRITING — MEDICINE AND HEALTH — DIET AND NUTRITION
Altmann, Tanya Remer. *What to Feed Your Baby* — 649
Bittman, Mark. *The VB6 Cookbook* — 641.5
Campbell, T. Colin. *The China Study* — 613.2
Copeland, Misty. ★*Ballerina Body* — 792.8
Cruikshank, Tiffany. *Meditate Your Weight* — 613.2
Harrison, Christy. *The Wellness Trap* — 613
Ludwig, David. *Always Hungry?* — 613.2
Lustig, Robert H. *Metabolical* — 616
Myers, Amy. ★*The Autoimmune Solution* — 616.97
Porto, Anthony. *The Pediatrician's Guide to Feeding Babies & Toddlers* — 618.92
Pulde, Alona. ★*The Forks Over Knives Plan* — 641.5
Robinson, Jo. *Eating on the Wild Side* — 641.3
Sanfilippo, Diane. *Practical Paleo* — 613.2
Scarlata, Kate. *Mind Your Gut* — 616.3
Winter, Ruth. *A Consumer's Dictionary of Food Additives* — 664
Wolf, Robb. *Wired to Eat* — 641.5

SCIENCE WRITING — MEDICINE AND HEALTH — DIET AND NUTRITION — WEIGHT LOSS
Curry, Kevin. *Fit Men Cook* — 641.5
Greger, Michael. ★*The How Not to Diet Cookbook* — 641.5
Griffin, Brooke. *Skinny Suppers* — 641.5
Sanfilippo, Diane. *Practical Paleo* — 613.2
Wolf, Robb. *Wired to Eat* — 641.5

SCIENCE WRITING — MEDICINE AND HEALTH — DISABILITIES AND DISORDERS
Belser, Julia Watts. ★*Loving Our Own Bones* — 296
Blake, Melissa. *Beautiful People* — 362.4
Bruni, Frank. *The Beauty of Dusk* — B
Donvan, John. *In a Different Key* — 616.85
Goh, Suzanne. *Magnificent Minds* — 618.92
Grandin, Temple. ★*Animals in Translation* — 591.5
Grandin, Temple. *Navigating Autism* — 618.92
Grandin, Temple. ★*Visual Thinking* — 152.14
Hawking, Stephen. *My Brief History* — B
Herrmann, Dorothy. *Helen Keller* — B
Jones, Chloe Cooper. ★*Easy Beauty* — B
Ladau, Emily. *Demystifying Disability* — 305.9
Leland, Andrew. ★*The Country of the Blind* — B
Marcus, Amy Dockser. *We the Scientists* — 618.92
Mattlin, Ben. *Disability Pride* — 323.3
Nielsen, Kim E. *A Disability History of the United States* — 362.40973
Robison, John Elder. *Look Me in the Eye* — B
Rodgers, Jodi. *How to Find a Four-Leaf Clover* — 616.85
Ruthsatz, Joanne. *The Prodigy's Cousin* — 155.45
Schwarz, Alan. *ADHD Nation* — 618.92
Senator, Susan. *Autism Adulthood* — 616.85
Tammet, Daniel. *Born on a Blue Day* — B
Taussig, Rebekah. *Sitting Pretty* — B
Taylor, Jill Bolte. *My Stroke of Insight* — 362.19681

SCIENCE WRITING — MEDICINE AND HEALTH — DOCTORS AND NURSES
Aptowicz, Cristin O'Keefe. *Dr. Mutter's Marvels* — B
Blackstock, Uche. *Legacy* — 610.92
Bostridge, Mark. *Florence Nightingale* — B
Brenner, Marie. ★*The Desperate Hours* — 362.1962
Brown, Jasmine. *Twice as Hard* — 610.92
Brown, Theresa. *Healing* — 616.99
Campbell, Olivia. *Women in White Coats* — 610.92
DiGregorio, Sarah. ★*Taking Care* — 610.73
Ely, Wes. *Every Deep-Drawn Breath* — 616.02
Fauci, Anthony S. *Expect the Unexpected* — 610.92
Fisher, Thomas. ★*The Emergency* — 362.1089
Fitzharris, Lindsey. *The Butchering Art* — B
Gawande, Atul. *Complications* — B
Gildiner, Catherine. *Good Morning, Monster* — 616.89
Goldberg, Emma. *Life on the Line* — 362.1962
Harper, Michele. *The Beauty in Breaking* — B
Kinzer, Stephen. *Poisoner in Chief* — B
Marsh, Henry. *Admissions* — B
Marsh, Henry. ★*Do No Harm* — B
Meyer, Robert. *Every Minute Is a Day* — 362.1962
Nimura, Janice P. ★*The Doctors Blackwell* — 610.92
Patterson, James. *ER Nurses* — 610.73
Smilios, Maria. ★*The Black Angels* — 610.73
Spofford, Tim. *What the Children Told Us* — 150.92

Stern, Adam. *Committed* — 616.89
Tweedy, Damon. *Facing the Unseen* — 362.2
Wellons, Jay. *All That Moves Us* — 617.4
Wilson, F. Perry. *How Medicine Works and When It Doesn't* — 610.69

SCIENCE WRITING — MEDICINE AND HEALTH — EXERCISE
Clements, Carol. *Better Balance for Life* — 617
Copeland, Misty. ★*Ballerina Body* — 792.8
Current, Austin. *Science of Strength Training* — 613.7
Esmonde-White, Miranda. *Aging Backwards* — 613.7
Fishman, Loren. *Yoga for Arthritis* — 616.7
Green, Louise. *Big Fit Girl* — 613.7
Lacerda, Daniel. *2,100 Asanas* — 613.7
Pohlman, Dean. *Yoga Fitness for Men* — 613.7
Rountree, Sage. *The Athlete's Guide to Recovery* — 617.1
Streets, Annabel. *52 Ways to Walk* — 796.51
Weiss, Eben. ★*The Ultimate Bicycle Owner's Manual* — 796.6

SCIENCE WRITING — MEDICINE AND HEALTH — FERTILITY AND SEXUAL HEALTH
Brighten, Jolene. *Is This Normal?* — 618.1
Schrock, Leslie. *Fertility Rules* — 613.9

SCIENCE WRITING — MEDICINE AND HEALTH — HYGIENE AND BEAUTY
Bowe, Whitney. *The Beauty of Dirty Skin* — 646.7
Hamblin, James. *Clean* — 613
Linett, Andrea. *The Cool Factor* — 746.9
Taillac, Victoire de. *An Atlas of Natural Beauty* — 646.7
Thomas, Mathilde. *The French Beauty Solution* — 646.7
Tourles, Stephanie L. *Pure Skin Care* — 646.7

SCIENCE WRITING — MEDICINE AND HEALTH — ILLNESS AND DISEASE
Abril, Andy. *Mayo Clinic Guide to Fibromyalgia* — 616.7
Alterman, Sara Faith. *Let's Never Talk About This Again* — 616.8
Ashton, Jennifer. *The New Normal* — 613
B., David. *Epileptic* — 741.5
Barry, John M. ★*The Great Influenza* — 614.5
Blaser, Martin J. *Missing Microbes* — 615.7
Borrell, Brendan. *The First Shots* — 615.3
Brem, Rachel. *No Longer Radical* — 616.99
Cahalan, Susannah. *Brain on Fire* — 616.8
Castro, M. Regina. ★*The Essential Diabetes Book* — 616.4
Christakis, Nicholas A. *Apollo's Arrow* — 362.1962
Crosby, Molly Caldwell. *The American Plague* — 614.5
Deer, Brian. *The Doctor Who Fooled the World* — 610.92
Eichenwald, Kurt. *A Mind Unraveled* — B
Fadiman, Anne. *The Spirit Catches You and You Fall Down* — 306.4
Fainaru-Wada, Mark. *League of Denial* — 617.1
Farmer, Paul. *Fevers, Feuds, and Diamonds* — 614.5
Fessler, Pam. *Carville's Cure* — 362.19699
Fishman, Loren. *Yoga for Arthritis* — 616.7
Fung, Jason. ★*The Cancer Code* — 616.99
Funk, Kristi. *Breasts* — 616.99
Gates, Bill. ★*How to Prevent the Next Pandemic* — 614.5
Goldberg, Emma. *Life on the Line* — 362.1962
Granata, Vince. *Everything Is Fine* — B
Hagberg, Eva. *How to Be Loved* — 616.7
Hitchens, Christopher. *Mortality* — 304.6
Holt, Nathalia. *Cured* — 614.5
Honigsbaum, Mark. *The Pandemic Century* — 614.4
Hotez, Peter J. *Preventing the Next Pandemic* — 362.1969
Hutton, Andrea. *Bald Is Better with Earrings* — 362.19699
Ingels, Darin. *The Lyme Solution* — 616.9
Johnson, Steven. *The Ghost Map* — 614.5
Kang, Lydia. *Patient Zero* — 614.4
Karlawish, Jason. ★*The Problem of Alzheimer's* — 616.8
Keene, Nancy. *Childhood Leukemia* — 618.92
Kelly, Christopher R. *Am I Dying?!* — 362.1
Kelly, John. *The Great Mortality* — 614.5
Kenny, Charles. *The Plague Cycle* — 614.4
Kinch, Michael S. *Between Hope and Fear* — 614.4
Kiper, Dasha. ★*Travelers to Unimaginable Lands* — 616.8
Kolata, Gina Bari. *Mercies in Disguise* — 616
Laskas, Jeanne Marie. *Concussion* — 617.5
Leschziner, Guy. *The Nocturnal Brain* — 616.8
Lewis, Michael. ★*The Premonition* — 614.5
Lieberman, Jeffrey A. *Malady of the Mind* — 616.89
Lipska, Barbara K. *The Neuroscientist Who Lost Her Mind* — B
Love, Susan M. ★*Dr. Susan Love's Breast Book* — 618.1
Mackenzie, Debora. *Covid-19* — 616.2

PUBLIC LIBRARY CORE COLLECTION: NONFICTION
Twentieth Edition

MacPhail, Theresa. *Allergic*	616.97
Meyer, Robert. *Every Minute Is a Day*	362.1962
Monosson, Emily. ★*Blight*	616.9
Moss, Michael. ★*Hooked*	613.2
Mukherjee, Siddhartha. ★*The Emperor of All Maladies*	616.99
Myers, Amy. ★*The Autoimmune Solution*	616.97
Nakazawa, Donna Jackson. *The Angel and the Assassin*	612.8
O'Rourke, Meghan. ★*The Invisible Kingdom*	616
Oshinsky, David M. ★*Polio*	614.5
Powell, Tia. *Dementia Reimagined*	616.8
Preston, Richard. *Crisis in the Red Zone*	614.5
Preston, Richard. *The Hot Zone*	614.5
Quammen, David. ★*Breathless*	614.5
Quammen, David. ★*Spillover*	614.4
Raza, Azra. *The First Cell*	616.99
Reverby, Susan M. *Examining Tuskegee*	174.2
Richtel, Matt. ★*An Elegant Defense*	616.07
Roth, Andrew J. *Managing Prostate Cancer*	616.99
Scarlata, Kate. *Mind Your Gut*	616.3
Schacter, Daniel L. *The Seven Sins of Memory*	153.1
Schwalbe, Will. ★*The End of Your Life Book Club*	B
Senthilingam, Meera. *Outbreaks and Epidemics*	614.4
Servan-Schreiber, David. *Anticancer*	616.99
Shilts, Randy. ★*And the Band Played On*	362.196
Spinney, Laura. ★*Pale Rider*	614.5
Swartz, Mimi. *Ticker*	617.4
Taubes, Gary. ★*Rethinking Diabetes*	616.462
Warraich, Haider. *The Song of Our Scars*	616
Washington, Kate. ★*Already Toast*	649.8
Wasik, Bill. *Rabid*	614.5
Werb, Dan. *The Invisible Siege*	614.5
Wright, Lawrence. ★*The Plague Year*	614.5

SCIENCE WRITING — MEDICINE AND HEALTH — ILLNESS AND DISEASE — VACCINATION

Davidson, Tish. *The Vaccine Debate*	615.3

SCIENCE WRITING — MEDICINE AND HEALTH — MEDICAL BREAKTHROUGHS

Aschwanden, Christie. *Good to Go*	617.1
Deer, Brian. *The Doctor Who Fooled the World*	610.92
DiGregorio, Sarah. *Early*	618.92
Graeber, Charles. *The Breakthrough*	616.99
Ingrassia, Lawrence. *A Fatal Inheritance*	616.99
Kariko, Katalin. *Breaking Through*	B
Kean, Sam. *The Tale of the Dueling Neurosurgeons*	617.4
Kinch, Michael S. *Between Hope and Fear*	614.4
Klass, Perri. *A Good Time to Be Born*	362.19892
Kolata, Gina Bari. *Mercies in Disguise*	616
Laar, Arnold van de. *Under the Knife*	617
Nakazawa, Donna Jackson. *The Angel and the Assassin*	612.8
Offit, Paul A. *You Bet Your Life*	615.5
Quammen, David. ★*Breathless*	614.5
Wadman, Meredith. *The Vaccine Race*	614.5

SCIENCE WRITING — MEDICINE AND HEALTH — MEN'S HEALTH

Chavez Perez, Inti. *Respect*	176
Crowley, Chris. *Younger Next Year*	613
Pohlman, Dean. *Yoga Fitness for Men*	613.7
Roth, Andrew J. *Managing Prostate Cancer*	616.99
Schrock, Leslie. *Fertility Rules*	613.9
Walsh, Patrick C. *Dr. Patrick Walsh's Guide to Surviving Prostate Cancer*	616.99

SCIENCE WRITING — MEDICINE AND HEALTH — MENTAL HEALTH

Albright, Mary Beth. ★*Eat & Flourish*	612.3
Aviv, Rachel. ★*Strangers to Ourselves*	616.89
Benjamin, A. K. *Let Me Not Be Mad*	612.8
Bullmore, Edward T. *The Inflamed Mind*	616.85
Cahalan, Susannah. ★*The Great Pretender*	616.89
Clein, Emmeline. ★*Dead Weight*	616.85
Crampton, Caroline. *A Body Made of Glass*	616.85
Cregan, Mary. *The Scar*	616.85
Damasio, Antonio R. *Looking for Spinoza*	152.4
Deisseroth, Karl. *Projections*	616.89
Dittrich, Luke. ★*Patient H.M.*	616.85
Fall, Jeremy. *Falling Upwards*	158.1
Farley, Audrey Clare. ★*Girls and Their Monsters*	306.875
Foo, Stephanie. ★*What My Bones Know*	B
Foulkes, Lucy. ★*Losing Our Minds*	616.89
Frank, Lone. *The Pleasure Shock*	616.8
Freud, Sigmund. *Civilization and Its Discontents*	150.19
Gagne, Patric. *Sociopath*	B
Gay, Peter. *Freud*	B
Goleman, Daniel. *Focus*	153.7
Grinker, Roy Richard. *Nobody's Normal*	616.89
Gutman, Matt. ★*No Time to Panic*	616.85
Haidt, Jonathan. ★*The Anxious Generation*	305.23
Harrington, Anne. *Mind Fixers*	616.89
Harvey, Samantha. *The Shapeless Unease*	B
Hylton, Antonia. *Madness*	362.2
Insel, Thomas R. *Healing*	362.2
Jamison, Kay Redfield. *Fires in the Dark*	616.89
Kahneman, Daniel. ★*Thinking, Fast and Slow*	153.4
Kalb, Claudia. *Andy Warhol Was a Hoarder*	920
Kazdin, Cole. ★*What's Eating Us*	616.85
Keltner, Dacher. ★*Awe*	152.4
Kennedy, Patrick J. ★*Profiles in Mental Health Courage*	362.29
Kissinger, Meg. *While You Were Out*	362.2
Kohli, Sahaj Kaur. ★*But What Will People Say?*	616.89
Kolker, Robert. ★*Hidden Valley Road*	920
Kramer, Peter D. ★*Ordinarily Well*	615.7
Kriss, Alexander. *Borderline*	616.85
Kubler-Ross, Elisabeth. ★*On Death and Dying*	155.9
Laing, Olivia. *Everybody*	323
Lawson, Jenny. ★*Broken*	B
Lawson, Jenny. *Furiously Happy*	B
Lieberman, Jeffrey A. *Malady of the Mind*	616.89
Lieberman, Jeffrey A. *Shrinks*	616.89
Lin, Jami Nakamura. *The Night Parade*	B
Mlodinow, Leonard. *Emotional*	152.4
Moore, Kate. ★*The Woman They Could Not Silence*	B
Morris, David J. *The Evil Hours*	616.85
Mullainathan, Sendhil. *Scarcity*	338.5
Murthy, Vivek Hallegere. *Together*	158.2
Nagorski, Andrew. *Saving Freud*	940.53
Nathan, Debbie. *Sybil Exposed*	B
Nerenberg, Jenara. *Divergent Mind*	616.89
Nesse, Randolph M. *Good Reasons for Bad Feelings*	616.89
O'Sullivan, Suzanne. *The Sleeping Beauties*	616.85
Paperny, Anna Mehler. *Hello I Want to Die Please Fix Me*	362.2
Parry, John Weston. *The Burden of Sports*	796.01
Pollan, Michael. *How to Change Your Mind*	615.7
Pollan, Michael. ★*This Is Your Mind on Plants*	581.6
Pratt, Misty. *All in Her Head*	616.89
Ranganath, Charan. ★*Why We Remember*	153.1
Rauch, Jonathan. *The Happiness Curve*	155.6
Riley, Alex. ★*A Cure for Darkness*	616.85
Ripley, Amanda. *The Unthinkable*	155.9
Ronson, Jon. ★*The Psychopath Test*	616.85
Rosen, Jonathan. ★*The Best Minds*	616.89
Satrapi, Marjane. *Chicken with Plums*	741.5
Saul, Richard. *ADHD Does Not Exist*	618.92
Schreiber, Flora Rheta. *Sybil*	616.85
Schulz, Kathryn. *Being Wrong*	121
Sehee, Baek. *I Want to Die but I Want to Eat Tteokbokki*	B
Slater, Lauren. *Blue Dreams*	615.7
Tallis, Frank. ★*Mortal Secrets*	B
Taraborrelli, J. Randy. ★*The Secret Life of Marilyn Monroe*	B
Thompson, J. M. *Running Is a Kind of Dreaming*	B
Tweedy, Damon. *Facing the Unseen*	362.2
Waldinger, Robert J. ★*The Good Life*	158.1
Waldman, Ayelet. *A Really Good Day*	B
Yalom, Irvin D. *Staring at the Sun*	155.9
Zimbardo, Philip G. *The Lucifer Effect*	155.9

SCIENCE WRITING — MEDICINE AND HEALTH — PSYCHOLOGY

Bass, Ellen. ★*The Courage to Heal*	616.85
Bennett, Michael. *F*ck Feelings*	158
Boser, Ulrich. *Learn Better*	153.1
Boyes, Alice. *The Anxiety Toolkit*	616.85
Brackett, Marc A. *Permission to Feel*	152.4
Breggin, Peter Roger. *Guilt, Shame, and Anxiety*	152.4
Buque, Mariel. *Break the Cycle*	616.85
Burke Harris, Nadine. *The Deepest Well*	618.92
Cacciatore, Joanne. *Bearing the Unbearable*	155.9
Carey, Tanith. *What's My Child Thinking?*	155.4
Carnegie, Dale. ★*How to Win Friends and Influence People*	158
Cialdini, Robert B. *Influence*	153.8
Dimitrius, Jo-Ellan. *Reading People*	155.2
Dobelli, Rolf. *The Art of Thinking Clearly*	153.4

AUTHOR, TITLE, SERIES AND SUBJECT INDEX

Duke, Annie. *Thinking in Bets*	658.4
Dweck, Carol S. ★*Mindset*	153.8
Elkind, David. *The Power of Play*	155.4
Epstein, Mark. *Advice Not Given*	294.3
Ericsson, K. Anders. *Peak*	153.9
Fabritius, Friederike. *The Leading Brain*	158
Frankl, Viktor E. *Yes to Life*	150.19
Fredrickson, Barbara. *Positivity*	158.1
Freud, Sigmund. ★*The Basic Writings of Sigmund Freud*	150.19
Freud, Sigmund. ★*The Interpretation of Dreams*	154.6
Galanti, Regine. ★*Parenting Anxious Kids*	155.4
Glasser, William. *Choice Theory*	150
Goleman, Daniel. *Emotional Intelligence*	152.4
Goulston, Mark. *Talking to Crazy*	158.2
Greenspan, Stanley I. *The First Idea*	153.7
Hibbs, B. Janet. *The Stressed Years of Their Lives*	616.8900835
Johnson, Earl. *Finding Comfort During Hard Times*	155.9
Jung, C. G. ★*The Basic Writings of C.G. Jung*	150.19
Jung, C. G. *Memories, Dreams, Reflections*	150.19
Karen, Dawnn. *Dress Your Best Life*	646
Keyes, Corey L. M. ★*Languishing*	152.1
Killam, Kasley. *The Art and Science of Connection*	302
Klein, Tovah P. *How Toddlers Thrive*	305.232
Kluger, Jeffrey. *The Narcissist Next Door*	616.85
Kornfield, Jack. *The Wise Heart*	294.3
Lerner, Harriet Goldhor. *The Dance of Intimacy*	155.6
Lickona, Thomas. *How to Raise Kind Kids*	649
Lieberman, David J. *Never Get Angry Again*	152.4
Lieberman, David J. *Mindreader*	401
Lyubomirsky, Sonja. *The How of Happiness*	158
Manly, Carla Marie. *Aging Joyfully*	305.26
Marriott, Sue. *Secure Relating*	158.1
McGonigal, Jane. *Super Better*	794.8
Milliken, Kirsten. *PLAYDHD*	616.85
Moran, Joe. *Shrinking Violets*	155.2
Myers, Isabel Briggs. *Gifts Differing*	155.2
Perry, Philippa. ★*The Book You Wish Your Parents Had Read*	649
Powell, Tia. *Dementia Reimagined*	616.8
Power, Thomas J. *If Your Adolescent Has ADHD*	616.85
Prizant, Barry M. ★*Uniquely Human*	618.92
Saline, Sharon. *What Your ADHD Child Wishes You Knew*	618.92
Schein, Edgar H. *Humble Inquiry*	302.2
Sederer, Lloyd I. *The Family Guide to Mental Health Care*	616.89
Seligman, Martin E. P. ★*Learned Optimism*	155.2
Siegel, Daniel J. *Aware*	158.1
Siegel, Daniel J. ★*The Yes Brain*	155.4
Simmons, Rachel. *Odd Girl Out*	302.5
Stixrud, William R. *The Self-Driven Child*	155.4
Stout, Martha. *Outsmarting the Sociopath Next Door*	155.2
Stulberg, Brad. *Peak Performance*	158.1
Torrey, E. Fuller. *Surviving Schizophrenia*	616.89
Van der Kolk, Bessel A. *The Body Keeps the Score*	616.85
Vlock, Deborah. *Parenting Children with Mental Health Challenges*	618.92
Webb, Caroline. *How to Have a Good Day*	650.1
Wiseman, Rosalind. *Masterminds & Wingmen*	305.235
SCIENCE WRITING — MEDICINE AND HEALTH — SLEEP	
Freud, Sigmund. ★*The Interpretation of Dreams*	154.6
Macedo, Diane. *The Sleep Fix*	613.7
Navab, Pedram. *Sleep Reimagined*	616.8
Pelayo, Rafael. ★*How to Sleep*	616.8
SCIENCE WRITING — MEDICINE AND HEALTH — WOMEN'S HEALTH	
Allmen, Tara. *Menopause Confidential*	618.1
Brighten, Jolene. *Is This Normal?*	618.1
Fox Starr, Rebecca. *Beyond the Baby Blues*	618.7
Funk, Kristi. *Breasts*	616.99
Green, Louise. *Big Fit Girl*	613.7
Harshe, January. *Birth Without Fear*	618.2
Hecht, M. E. *Two Old Broads*	613
Hutton, Andrea. *Bald Is Better with Earrings*	362.19699
Jamieson, Alexandra. *Women, Food, and Desire*	155.3
Manly, Carla Marie. *Aging Joyfully*	305.26
Mansberg, Ginni. *The M Word*	612.6
Nolan, Ali. *Master the Marathon*	796.42
Schrock, Leslie. *Fertility Rules*	613.9
Serrallach, Oscar. *The Postnatal Depletion Cure*	618.6
Walters, Jacqueline. *The Queen V*	612.6
SCIENCE WRITING — MEDICINE AND HEALTH — WOMEN'S HEALTH — MENOPAUSE	
Corinna, Heather. *What Fresh Hell Is This?*	618.1
Dunn, Jancee. *Hot and Bothered*	618.1
Gunter, Jen. *The Menopause Manifesto*	618.175
Haver, Mary Claire. ★*The New Menopause*	618.1
Mansberg, Ginni. *The M Word*	612.6
Walters, Jacqueline. *The Queen V*	612.6
SCIENCE WRITING — MEDICINE AND HEALTH — WOMEN'S HEALTH — PREGNANCY AND CHILDBIRTH	
Curtis, Glade B. *Your Pregnancy Week by Week*	618.2
Fisher, Susan J. *Taking Charge of Your Pregnancy*	618.2
Fox Starr, Rebecca. *Beyond the Baby Blues*	618.7
Haelle, Tara. *The Informed Parent*	649
Harshe, January. *Birth Without Fear*	618.2
Huggins, Kathleen. ★*The Nursing Mother's Companion*	649
Murkoff, Heidi Eisenberg. ★*What to Expect When You're Expecting*	618.2
Neifert, Marianne R. *The Essential Guide to Breastfeeding*	649
Nilsson, Lennart. *A Child Is Born*	612.6
Oster, Emily. ★*The Unexpected*	618.2
Rope, Kate. *Strong as a Mother*	618.2
Serrallach, Oscar. *The Postnatal Depletion Cure*	618.6
Walters, Jacqueline. *The Queen V*	612.6
White, Kate. *Your Guide to Miscarriage & Pregnancy Loss*	618.3
SCIENCE WRITING — PALEONTOLOGY	
Black, Riley. *The Last Days of the Dinosaurs*	576.8
Bohannon, Cat. ★*Eve*	613
Brusatte, Stephen. ★*The Rise and Fall of the Dinosaurs*	567.9
Brusatte, Stephen. *The Rise and Reign of the Mammals*	569
Flannery, Tim F. *Europe*	508.4
Halliday, Thomas. ★*Otherlands*	560
Lacovara, Kenneth. *Why Dinosaurs Matter*	567.9
Larson, Edward J. *Evolution*	576.8
MacPhee, R. D. E. *End of the Megafauna*	591.4
Pattison, Kermit. *Fossil Men*	569.9
Paul, Gregory S. *The Princeton Field Guide to Dinosaurs*	567.9
Pim, Keiron. *Dinosaurs the Grand Tour*	567.9
Raff, Jennifer. *Origin*	576.5
Thompson, Ida. ★*The Audubon Society Field Guide to North American Fossils*	560
Yi, Sang-Hui. *Close Encounters with Humankind*	599.93
SCIENCE WRITING — PHYSICS	
Alexander, Stephon. *Fear of a Black Universe*	523.1
Ananthaswamy, Anil. *Through Two Doors at Once*	530.12
Becker, Adam. *What Is Real?*	920
Berman, Bob. *Earth-Shattering*	523.1
Bird, Kai. *American Prometheus*	B
Blackburn, Simon. *Think*	100
Carroll, Sean M. *The Biggest Ideas in the Universe*	530.11
Carroll, Sean M. *The Big Picture*	577
Carroll, Sean M. *Something Deeply Hidden*	530.12
Cliff, Harry. *How to Make an Apple Pie from Scratch*	523.01
Conway, Edmund. *Material World*	333.7
Cox, Brian. *The Quantum Universe*	530.12
Cox, Brian. *Universal*	523.1
Crease, Robert P. *The Quantum Moment*	530.12
Czerski, Helen. *The Blue Machine*	551.46
Czerski, Helen. *Storm in a Teacup*	530
Einstein, Albert. ★*The Evolution of Physics*	530
Einstein, Albert. *The Meaning of Relativity*	530.11
Einstein, Albert. ★*A Stubbornly Persistent Illusion*	530.092
Feynman, Richard P. ★*The Meaning of It All*	500
Feynman, Richard P. ★*Six Easy Pieces*	530
Fletcher, Seth. *Einstein's Shadow*	523.8
Forbes, Nancy. *Faraday, Maxwell, and the Electromagnetic Field*	B
Frank, Adam. *Light of the Stars*	523.1
Greene, B. ★*The Elegant Universe*	539.7
Greene, B. *The Fabric of the Cosmos*	523.1
Greene, B. ★*The Hidden Reality*	530.12
Greene, B. *Until the End of Time*	523.1
Hawking, Stephen. *A Brief History of Time*	523.1
Hawking, Stephen. ★*A Briefer History of Time*	523.1
Hawking, Stephen. ★*The Grand Design*	530.14
Hawking, Stephen. *My Brief History*	B
Hawking, Stephen. ★*The Universe in a Nutshell*	530.12
Hickam, Homer H. ★*Rocket Boys*	B
Impey, Chris. *Einstein's Monsters*	523.8
Kakalios, James. *The Amazing Story of Quantum Mechanics*	530.12

Kaku, Michio. *The God Equation*	523.1
Kaku, Michio. ★*Hyperspace*	530.1
Kaku, Michio. *Parallel Worlds*	523.1
Krauss, Lawrence Maxwell. *The Greatest Story Ever Told—So Far*	530.01
Levin, Janna. *Black Hole Blues*	539.7
Light, Michael. *100 Suns*	779
Mack, Katie. *The End of Everything*	523.1
Mahaffey, James A. *Atomic Adventures*	333.792
Munroe, Randall. *How To*	500
Norris, Robert S. *Racing for the Bomb*	B
Oluseyi, Hakeem M. *A Quantum Life*	B
Ottaviani, Jim. *Hawking*	741.5
Panek, Richard. *The Trouble with Gravity*	531
Ploszajski, Anna. *Handmade*	620.1
Pontzen, Andrew. *The Universe in a Box*	523.1
Prescod-Weinstein, Chanda. *The Disordered Cosmos*	523.01
Preston, Diana. *Before the Fallout*	303.48
Randall, Lisa. *Dark Matter and the Dinosaurs*	523.1
Rovelli, Carlo. *Helgoland*	530.12
Rovelli, Carlo. *Reality Is Not What It Seems*	530.14
Rovelli, Carlo. ★*Seven Brief Lessons on Physics*	530
Rovelli, Carlo. *There Are Places in the World Where Rules Are Less Important Than Kindness*	500
Sapolsky, Robert M. *Determined*	123
Schlosser, Eric. *Command and Control*	363.17
Sheehy, Suzie. *The Matter of Everything*	539.7
Smil, Vaclav. *Size*	153.7
Sobel, Dava. *A More Perfect Heaven*	520.9
Tonelli, Guido. *Genesis*	523.1
Tucker, Wallace H. *Chandra's Cosmos*	523.1
Tyson, Neil deGrasse. *Accessory to War*	355.001
Tyson, Neil deGrasse. ★*Astrophysics for People in a Hurry*	523.01
Tyson, Neil deGrasse. *Cosmic Queries*	523.1
Tyson, Neil deGrasse. *Letters from an Astrophysicist*	520.92
Tyson, Neil deGrasse. *Welcome to the Universe*	523.1
Wilczek, Frank. *Fundamentals*	530.01

SCIENCE WRITING — SPACE AND FLIGHT

Ackmann, Martha. *The Mercury 13*	920
Aldrin, Buzz. *Mission to Mars*	523.43
Bagby, Meredith E. *The New Guys*	305
Barbree, Jay. *Neil Armstrong*	B
Bell, Jim. *The Interstellar Age*	919
Berger, Eric. *Liftoff*	B
Berman, Bob. *Earth-Shattering*	523.1
Boyle, Rebecca. *Our Moon*	523.3
Brinkley, Douglas. ★*American Moonshot*	629.40973
Carroll, Sean M. *The Biggest Ideas in the Universe*	530.11
Cham, Jorge. *Frequently Asked Questions About the Universe*	523.1
Cook, Kevin. *The Burning Blue*	629.45
Cox, Brian. *Universal*	523.1
Davenport, Christian. *The Space Barons*	920
Donovan, Jim. ★*Shoot for the Moon*	629.45
Fauber, L. S. *Heaven on Earth*	B
Fletcher, Seth. *Einstein's Shadow*	523.8
Frank, Adam. *Light of the Stars*	523.1
Green, Jaime. *The Possibility of Life*	576.8
Grush, Loren. ★*The Six*	629.4
Guthrie, Julian. *How to Make a Spaceship*	629.47
Hawking, Stephen. ★*Black Holes and Baby Universes and Other Essays*	530.1
Hawking, Stephen. *The Nature of Space and Time*	530.1
Hawking, Stephen. ★*The Universe in a Nutshell*	530.12
Hickam, Homer H. ★*Rocket Boys*	B
Higginbotham, Adam. ★*Challenger*	629.45
Holmes, Richard. *Falling Upwards*	387.7
Holt, Nathalia. ★*Rise of the Rocket Girls*	629.4
Impey, Chris. *Einstein's Monsters*	523.8
Johnson, George. *Miss Leavitt's Stars*	522
Johnson, Sarah Stewart. *The Sirens of Mars*	576.8
Jones, Tom. *Space Shuttle Stories*	629.44
Kaku, Michio. ★*Hyperspace*	530.1
Kaltenegger, Lisa. ★*Alien Earths*	523.2
Kershenbaum, Arik. *The Zoologist's Guide to the Galaxy*	576.8
Kitmacher, Gary. *Space Stations*	629.44
Krauss, Lawrence Maxwell. *The Greatest Story Ever Told—So Far*	530.01
Kurson, Robert. ★*Rocket Men*	629.45
Launius, Roger D. *The Smithsonian History of Space Exploration*	629.4
Launius, Roger D. *Apollo's Legacy*	629.45
Levesque, Emily. *The Last Stargazers*	520
Levin, Janna. *Black Hole Blues*	539.7
Loeb, Abraham. *Extraterrestrial*	576.8
Marchant, Jo. *The Human Cosmos*	523.1
McCullough, David G. ★*The Wright Brothers*	B
McTier, Moiya. *The Milky Way*	523.1
Nelson, Craig. *Rocket Men*	629.45
Nordgren, Tyler E. *Sun, Moon, Earth*	523.7
Oluseyi, Hakeem M. *A Quantum Life*	B
Plait, Philip C. *Under Alien Skies*	520
Prescod-Weinstein, Chanda. *The Disordered Cosmos*	523.01
Roach, Mary. *Packing for Mars*	571.0919
Rose, Alexander. *Empires of the Sky*	920
Sagan, Carl. *Cosmos*	520
Sagan, Carl. *Pale Blue Dot*	919
Sanders, Ella Frances. *Eating the Sun*	520
Seager, Sara. *The Smallest Lights in the Universe*	B
Sherr, Lynn. *Sally Ride*	B
Shesol, Jeff. *Mercury Rising*	629.45
Shetterly, Margot Lee. ★*Hidden Figures*	510.92
Shields, Aomawa L. *Life on Other Planets*	B
Sobel, Dava. *A More Perfect Heaven*	520.9
Stern, Alan. *Chasing New Horizons*	629.43
Stone, Robert. *Chasing the Moon*	629.45
Stuart, Colin. *How to Live in Space*	629.45
Summers, Michael E. *Exoplanets*	523.2
Swift, Earl. *Across the Airless Wilds*	629.45
Tirion, Wil. *The Cambridge Star Atlas*	523.8
Tonelli, Guido. *Genesis*	523.1
Trefil, James. *Space Atlas*	520
Tucker, Wallace H. *Chandra's Cosmos*	523.1
Tyson, Neil deGrasse. *Accessory to War*	355.001
Tyson, Neil deGrasse. *Cosmic Queries*	523.1
Tyson, Neil deGrasse. *Space Chronicles*	629.40973
Tyson, Neil deGrasse. *Startalk*	523.1
Tyson, Neil deGrasse. *To Infinity and Beyond*	520
Tyson, Neil deGrasse. *Welcome to the Universe*	523.1
Vance, Ashlee. *When the Heavens Went on Sale*	621.43
Virts, Terry. *How to Astronaut*	629.45
Walker, Stephen. *Beyond*	629.45
Ward, Peter Douglas. *Life as We Do Not Know It*	576.839
Weinersmith, Kelly. ★*A City on Mars*	629.4
Whitehouse, David. *The Alien Perspective*	523.1
Winters, Kathleen C. *Amelia Earhart*	B
Wohlforth, Charles P. *Beyond Earth*	629.45
Wolfe, Tom. ★*The Right Stuff*	629.4

SCIENCE WRITING — WEATHER

Barnett, Cynthia. *Rain*	551.57
Dolin, Eric Jay. *A Furious Sky*	363.34
Fagan, Brian M. *Climate Chaos*	304.2
Fox, Porter. *The Last Winter*	363.738
Hargrove, Brantley. *The Man Who Caught the Storm*	B
Kostigen, Thomas. *Hacking Planet Earth*	628
Lambert, David. *The Field Guide to Geology*	550
Lustgarten, Abrahm. ★*On the Move*	363.7
Redniss, Lauren. *Thunder & Lightning*	741.5
Rich, Nathaniel. *Losing Earth*	363.738
Williams, Jack. ★*The Ams Weather Book*	551.5

SCIENCE WRITING — WEIRD SCIENCE

Aykroyd, Peter. *A History of Ghosts*	133.1
Blum, Deborah. *Ghost Hunters*	133.9
Braudy, Leo. *Haunted*	398.45
Clegg, Brian. *Extra Sensory*	133.8
Dickey, Colin. *Ghostland*	133.1
Dickey, Colin. *The Unidentified*	130
Graff, Garrett M. *UFO*	001.942
Knight, Sam. *The Premonitions Bureau*	133.8
Loxton, Daniel. *Abominable Science!*	001.944
Mezrich, Ben. *The 37th Parallel*	001.942
Novella, Steven. *The Skeptics' Guide to the Universe*	500
O'Connor, John. *The Secret History of Bigfoot*	001.944
Scoles, Sarah. *They Are Already Here*	001.942
Smith, Richard MacLean. *Unexplained*	130
Whitmer, Jamie Davis. *America's Most Haunted Hotels*	133.1

SCIENTIFIC DISCOVERIES

Bohme, Madelaine. *Ancient Bones*	599.93
Carroll, Sean M. *The Big Picture*	577
Christian, David. *Origin Story*	909

AUTHOR, TITLE, SERIES AND SUBJECT INDEX

Costa, James T. *Radical by Nature*	B
Dolnick, Edward. *Seeds of Life*	612.6
Du Sautoy, Marcus. *The Great Unknown*	500
Dyson, Freeman J. *Maker of Patterns*	B
Holmes, Richard. *The Age of Wonder*	509
Holway, Tatiana M. *The Flower of Empire*	727
Kaufman, Kenn. *The Birds That Audubon Missed*	598
Lightman, Alan P. *The Discoveries*	509
Lintott, Chris. *Accidental Astronomy*	520
Maddox, Brenda. *Rosalind Franklin*	B
McCalman, Iain. *Darwin's Armada*	576.8
Miodownik, Mark. *Stuff Matters*	620.1
Pattison, Kermit. *Fossil Men*	569.9
Reser, Anna. *Forces of Nature*	509.2
Rutherford, Adam. *The Complete Guide to Absolutely Everything*	500
Ryckman, Pamela. *Candace Pert*	B
Sheehy, Suzie. *The Matter of Everything*	539.7
Skloot, Rebecca. ★*The Immortal Life of Henrietta Lacks*	B
Tonelli, Guido. *Genesis*	523.1
Woodford, Chris. *Atoms Under the Floorboards*	500
Wragg Sykes, Rebecca. *Kindred*	569.9

SCIENTIFIC ERRORS
Fabricant, M. Chris. *Junk Science and the American Criminal Justice System*	363.25
Goldacre, Ben. *Bad Science*	500
Novella, Steven. *The Skeptics' Guide to the Universe*	500
Ritchie, Stuart. *Science Fictions*	500
Weill, Kelly. *Off the Edge*	001.9

SCIENTIFIC EXPEDITIONS
Larson, Edward J. *An Empire of Ice*	919.8

SCIENTIFIC FORECASTING
Cech, Thomas. *The Catalyst*	572.8
Favro, Terri. *Generation Robot*	006.3
Kaku, Michio. ★*The Future of Humanity*	629.45
Pontzen, Andrew. *The Universe in a Box*	523.1
Whitehouse, David. *The Alien Perspective*	523.1

Scientist. Rhodes, Richard | B
★*The Scientist and the Spy*. Hvistendahl, Mara | 364.16

SCIENTISTS
Allen, Arthur. ★*The Fantastic Laboratory of Dr. Weigl*	614.5
Berger, Eric. *Liftoff*	B
Black, Alexandra. *Scientists Who Changed History*	509.22
Black, George. ★*The Long Reckoning*	959.704
Brands, H. W. *The First American*	B
Budiansky, Stephen. *Blackett's War*	940.54
Bunker, Nick. *Young Benjamin Franklin*	B
Colwell, Rita R. *A Lab of One's Own*	B
Conant, Jennet. *Man of the Hour*	B
Costa, James T. *Radical by Nature*	B
Dawkins, Richard. *An Appetite for Wonder*	B
Dawkins, Richard. *Brief Candle in the Dark*	B
Dolnick, Edward. *Seeds of Life*	612.6
Dyson, Freeman J. *Maker of Patterns*	B
Fishman, Charles. ★*One Giant Leap*	629.45
Forbes, Nancy. *Faraday, Maxwell, and the Electromagnetic Field*	B
Fox, Porter. *The Last Winter*	363.738
Franklin, Benjamin. ★*The Autobiography of Benjamin Franklin*	B
Henig, Robin Marantz. *The Monk in the Garden*	B
Holmes, Richard. *The Age of Wonder*	509
Ignotofsky, Rachel. *Women in Science*	920
Isaacson, Walter. ★*Benjamin Franklin*	B
Isaacson, Walter. ★*Leonardo Da Vinci*	B
Jacobsen, Annie. ★*Operation Paperclip*	940.54
Kean, Sam. *The Bastard Brigade*	355.8
Kean, Sam. *The Disappearing Spoon*	546
Kean, Sam. *The Icepick Surgeon*	509
Kinzer, Stephen. *Poisoner in Chief*	B
Lance, Rachel. *Chamber Divers*	940.54
Levi, Primo. *The Periodic Table*	858
Levy, Buddy. *Labyrinth of Ice*	910.91
Lewis, Michael. ★*The Premonition*	614.5
Lightman, Alan P. *The Discoveries*	509
Lisle, John. *The Dirty Tricks Department*	940.54
Mahaffey, James A. *Atomic Adventures*	333.792
Markel, Howard. *The Secret of Life*	572.86
Mlodinow, Leonard. *Stephen Hawking*	B
Montillo, Roseanne. *The Lady and Her Monsters*	823
Nuland, Sherwin B. *Leonardo Da Vinci*	B
Okrent, Daniel. *The Guarded Gate*	344.73
Oreskes, Naomi. *Merchants of Doubt*	174
Ottaviani, Jim. *Hawking*	741.5
Pauling, Linus. *Linus Pauling*	081
Ploszajski, Anna. *Handmade*	620.1
Popova, Maria. *Figuring*	920
Quammen, David. ★*Breathless*	614.5
Ritchie, Stuart. *Science Fictions*	500
Roberts, Jason. ★*Every Living Thing*	578
Snyder, Laura J. *Eye of the Beholder*	920
Stanley, Matthew. *Einstein's War*	530
Stott, Rebecca. ★*Darwin's Ghosts*	576.8
Swift, Earl. *Across the Airless Wilds*	629.45
Weschler, Lawrence. *And How Are You, Dr. Sacks?*	B
Wilson, Edward O. ★*Letters to a Young Scientist*	570.92
Wulf, Andrea. *The Invention of Nature*	B
Scientists Who Changed History. Black, Alexandra	509.22

SCIENTOLOGISTS
Hall, Sands. ★*Flunk, Start*	B
Rinder, Mike. ★*A Billion Years*	B
Wright, Lawrence. *Going Clear*	299

Sciolino, Elaine
The Only Street in Paris	944
The Seine	944

SCIOLINO, ELAINE
Sciolino, Elaine. *The Seine*	944

SCIPIO, AFRICANUS 236?-183 B.C.E
O'Connell, Robert L. *The Ghosts of Cannae*	937

Sciubba, Jennifer Dabbs
8 Billion and Counting	304.6

Scoles, Sarah
They Are Already Here	001.942

SCOLIOSIS
Okorafor, Nnedi. *Broken Places & Outer Spaces*	153.3

Scorpions' Dance. Morley, Jefferson | 973.924
Scorsese by Ebert. Ebert, Roger | B

SCORSESE, MARTIN, 1942-
Ebert, Roger. *Scorsese by Ebert*	B

SCOTLAND
Brown, Nancy Marie. *Ivory Vikings*	736
Coyne, Tom. *A Course Called Scotland*	796.352
Herman, Arthur. *How the Scots Invented the Modern World*	941.1
Heughan, Sam. *Waypoints*	B
Nicolson, Adam. *Life Between the Tides*	577.69
Nicolson, Adam. *Sea Room*	941.1
Parini, Jay. *Borges and Me*	813
Stewart, Rory. *The Marches*	941.3
Weir, Alison. *Mary, Queen of Scots, and the Murder of Lord Darnley*	941.105

Scott, Andy
One Kiss or Two?	395.4

Scott, Chris
Homage	641.5

SCOTT, DAVE
Fitzgerald, Matt. *Iron War*	796.42

SCOTT, HAZEL
Armstrong, Jennifer Keishin. *When Women Invented Television*	791.45

Scott, James
Black Snow	940.54
Rampage	940.54
Target Tokyo	940.54

Scott, Jonathan
★*Dream Home*	643

Scott, Kevin
Reprogramming the American Dream	338

Scott, Kim Malone
Radical Candor	658.4

SCOTT, ROBERT FALCON, 1868-1912
Larson, Edward J. *An Empire of Ice*	919.8

Scott, Rodney
★*Rodney Scott's World of BBQ*	641.7

Scott, Ryan
The No-Fuss Family Cookbook	641.5

Scott-Clark, Cathy
The Forever Prisoner	364.6

Scotti, R. A.
Vanished Smile	759.5

SCOTTISH BORDERS (ENGLAND AND SCOTLAND)
Robb, Graham. *The Debatable Land*	941.3

2311

PUBLIC LIBRARY CORE COLLECTION: NONFICTION
Twentieth Edition

SCOTTISH HISTORY
    Fraser, Antonia. *Mary, Queen of Scots* — B
    Robb, Graham. *The Debatable Land* — 941.3
    Weir, Alison. *Mary, Queen of Scots, and the Murder of Lord Darnley* — 941.105

SCOTTISH PEOPLE
    Barker, Elspeth. ★*Notes from the Henhouse* — 828
    Heughan, Sam. *Waypoints* — B
    Smith, Sally Bedell. *George VI and Elizabeth* — 920

SCOTTISH PEOPLE IN FOREIGN COUNTRIES
    Herman, Arthur. *How the Scots Invented the Modern World* — 941.1

SCOTTISH STEWART PERIOD (1371-1603)
    Fraser, Antonia. *Mary, Queen of Scots* — B
    Weir, Alison. *Mary, Queen of Scots, and the Murder of Lord Darnley* — 941.105

Scottoline, Lisa
    I See Life Through Rose-Colored Glasses — 813

Scoundrel. Weinman, Sarah — 364.152

Scovell, Nell
    Just the Funny Parts — B

SCOVELL, NELL
    Scovell, Nell. *Just the Funny Parts* — B

SCOVILLE, WILLIAM BEECHER, 1906-1984
    Dittrich, Luke. ★*Patient H.M.* — 616.85

Scratch. Rodale, Maria — 641.3
Scratched. Tallent, Elizabeth — B
Screaming on the Inside. Grose, Jessica — 306.874
Screening Reality. Wilkman, Jon — 070.1

SCREENPLAY WRITING
    Frankel, Glenn. *High Noon* — 791.43
    Goldman, William. *Adventures in the Screen Trade* — 384
    McKee, Robert. *Dialogue* — 809
    Vogler, Christopher. ★*The Writer's Journey* — 808.2
    Wasson, Sam. *The Big Goodbye* — 791.43

SCREENWRITERS
    Armstrong, Jennifer Keishin. *Seinfeldia* — 791.45
    Armstrong, Jennifer Keishin. *Sex and the City and Us* — 791.45
    Austerlitz, Saul. *Kind of a Big Deal* — 791.43
    Black, Dustin Lance. *Mama's Boy* — B
    Courogen, Carrie. ★*Miss May Does Not Exist* — B
    Daugherty, Tracy. *Larry McMurtry* — B
    Dickinson, Bruce. *What Does This Button Do?* — B
    Frankel, Glenn. *High Noon* — 791.43
    Goldman, William. *Adventures in the Screen Trade* — 384
    Rogen, Seth. ★*Yearbook* — B
    Schechter, Harold. ★*Ripped from the Headlines!* — 791.43
    Shelton, Ron. *The Church of Baseball* — 791.43
    Shone, Tom. *The Nolan Variations* — 791.4302
    Silver, Alain. ★*From the Moment They Met It Was Murder* — 791.43
    Waters, John. *Role Models* — B
    Zucker, David. *Surely You Can't Be Serious* — 791.43

★*The Screwtape Letters*. Lewis, C. S. — 248.4

SCUBA DIVING
    Graver, Dennis. *Scuba Diving* — 797.2

Scuba Diving. Graver, Dennis — 797.2

SCULPTORS
    Hawksley, Lucinda. *Queen Victoria's Mysterious Daughter* — B
    Herrera, Hayden. *Listening to Stone* — B
    Holzer, Harold. *Monument Man* — B
    Khan, Yasmin Sabina. *Enlightening the World* — 974.7
    Perl, Jed. *Calder* — B
    Perl, Jed. ★*Calder* — B

SCULPTURE
    Beard, Mary. ★*How Do We Look* — 704.9
    Herrera, Hayden. *Listening to Stone* — B

Scurr, Ruth
    Fatal Purity — B

SEA BIRDS
    Carson, Rachel. *Under the Sea Wind* — 578.77
    Nicolson, Adam. *The Seabird's Cry* — 598.177

SEA LEVEL
    Goodell, Jeff. *The Water Will Come* — 551.45
    Rush, Elizabeth A. *Rising* — 551.45
    Swift, Earl. *Chesapeake Requiem* — 639

Sea of Thunder. Thomas, Evan — 940.54
Sea People. Thompson, Christina — 305.8994
Sea Power. Stavridis, James — 359

SEA POWER
    Crowley, Roger. *City of Fortune* — 945
    Hornfischer, James D. *Who Can Hold the Sea* — 359.00973

Sea Room. Nicolson, Adam — 941.1
Sea Stories. McRaven, William H. — B

SEA SURVIVAL
    Franklin, Jonathan. *438 Days* — 910.91
    Preston, Diana. *Paradise in Chains* — 996.18

SEA-POWER
    Stavridis, James. *Sea Power* — 359
    Toll, Ian W. ★*Six Frigates* — 359.00973

The Seabird's Cry. Nicolson, Adam — 598.177
★*Seabiscuit*. Hillenbrand, Laura — 798.4

SEABISCUIT (RACE HORSE)
    Hillenbrand, Laura. ★*Seabiscuit* — 798.4

Seabrook, Nicholas R.
    One Person, One Vote — 328.3

SEAFARING LIFE
    Clark, Liz. *Swell* — B
    Cordingly, David. *Under the Black Flag* — 910.4
    Dana, Richard Henry. *Two Years Before the Mast* — 910.4
    Homer. ★*The Odyssey* — 883
    Humphreys, Richard. *Under Pressure* — B
    Nicolson, Adam. *How to Be* — 180
    Roberts, Jason. *A Sense of the World* — B
    Taylor, Stephen. *Commander* — B
    Thomson, Keith. *Born to Be Hanged* — 910.4

SEAFOOD
    Greenberg, Paul. *American Catch* — 333.95
    Ripert, Eric. *Seafood Simple* — 641.6

SEAFOOD INDUSTRY AND TRADE
    Greenberg, Paul. *American Catch* — 333.95

Seafood Simple. Ripert, Eric — 641.6

Seager, Sara
    The Smallest Lights in the Universe — B

SEAGER, SARA
    Seager, Sara. *The Smallest Lights in the Universe* — B

Seal, Mark
    ★*Leave the Gun, Take the Cannoli* — 791.43

Seale, Yasmine
    Aladdin — 398.2

SEAMSTRESSES
    Miller, Marla. *Betsy Ross and the Making of America* — B

Searcey, Dionne
    In Pursuit of Disobedient Women — B

SEARCEY, DIONNE
    Searcey, Dionne. *In Pursuit of Disobedient Women* — B

★*The Search*. Feiler, Bruce — 306.3

SEARCH AND RESCUE OPERATIONS
    Bukreev, Anatolii Nikolaevich. *The Climb* — 796.52
    Charleson, Susannah. *Where the Lost Dogs Go* — 636.7
    Graff, Garrett M. ★*The Only Plane in the Sky* — 973.931
    Gutman, Matt. *The Boys in the Cave* — 796.52
    Hall, Andy. *Denali's Howl* — 796.522
    Makos, Adam. *Devotion* — 920
    Melville, Wilma. ★*Hero Dogs* — 636.7
    Pfeifer, Joseph. *Ordinary Heroes* — 973.931
    Talty, Stephan. *Saving Bravo* — 959.704
    Wukovits, John F. *Lost at Sea* — 940.54
    Zuckoff, Mitchell. *Frozen in Time* — 998.2
    Zuckoff, Mitchell. *Lost in Shangri-La* — 940.54

SEARCH DOGS
    Charleson, Susannah. *Where the Lost Dogs Go* — 636.7
    Melville, Wilma. ★*Hero Dogs* — 636.7

The Search for Modern China. Spence, Jonathan D. — 951
The Search for the Genuine. Harrison, Jim — 814

SEARCHES AND SEIZURES
    Chemerinsky, Erwin. *Presumed Guilty* — 344.7305
    Friedman, Barry. ★*Unwarranted* — 344.7305

SEARCHING
    Barbarisi, Daniel. *Chasing the Thrill* — 796.1
    Bonner, Betsy. *The Book of Atlantis Black* — 364.152
    Dial, Roman. *The Adventurer's Son* — 917.286
    Lankford, Andrea. *Trail of the Lost* — 363.2
    McNamara, Michelle. *I'll Be Gone in the Dark* — 364.152

Searching for Stars on an Island in Maine. Lightman, Alan P. — 523.1

Sears, Robert W.
    The Allergy Book — 618.92

Sears, Stephen W.
    ★*Chancellorsville* — 973.7
    Gettysburg — 973.7

AUTHOR, TITLE, SERIES AND SUBJECT INDEX

★*Landscape Turned Red*	973.7
Lincoln's Lieutenants	920

SEASHORE
Carson, Rachel. *The Edge of the Sea*	578.769

SEASHORE ANIMALS
Carson, Rachel. *The Edge of the Sea*	578.769
Nicolson, Adam. *Life Between the Tides*	577.69

SEASHORE BIOLOGY
Carson, Rachel. *The Edge of the Sea*	578.769

SEASHORE ECOLOGY
Carson, Rachel. *The Edge of the Sea*	578.769
Nicolson, Adam. *Life Between the Tides*	577.69
Season. Wangler, Justin	641.5979
Season of Saturdays. Weinreb, Michael	796.332

SEASONAL COOKING
Barber, Dan. *The Third Plate*	641.3
Bayless, Rick. ★*More Mexican Everyday*	641.5972
Brock, Sean. *South*	641.5975
Cayne, Alison. *The Haven's Kitchen Cooking School*	641.5
Clark, Melissa. *Dinner in French*	641.594
Dissen, William Stark. *Thoughtful Cooking*	641.5975
Feinberg, Andrew. *Franny's*	641.594
Gaines, Joanna. ★*Magnolia Table*	641.5975
Goldstein, Joyce Esersky, author. *Jam Session*	641.85
Holland, Tanya. ★*Tanya Holland's California Soul*	641.59
Kanell, John. *Preppy Kitchen*	641.5
Lightner, Jill. *Cooking from Scratch*	641.5
Mangini, Cara. ★*The Vegetable Eater*	641.6
McBride, Martina. *Martina's Kitchen Mix*	641.5973
McFadden, Joshua. *Six Seasons*	641.5
Pauline, Kathryn. *A Dish for All Seasons*	641.5
Pepin, Jacques. ★*Jacques Pépin Cooking My Way*	641.5
Roberts, Julius. *The Farm Table*	641.594
Rodale, Maria. *Scratch*	641.3
Rodriguez, Ashley. *Rooted Kitchen*	641.5
Roll, Rich. *The Plantpower Way*	641.5
Roman, Alison. ★*Nothing Fancy*	642
Rosen, Ali. *Bring It!*	641.5973
Sussman, Adeena. *Sababa*	641.5
Terry, Bryant. *Vegan Soul Kitchen*	641.5
Thorisson, Mimi. *A Kitchen in France*	641.594
Van't Hul, Jean. *The Artful Year*	745.594
Wangler, Justin. *Season*	641.5979
Waters, Alice. *The Art of Simple Food*	641.5
Waters, Alice. *Coming to My Senses*	B
West, Kevin. *Saving the Season*	641.4
★*Seasonal Flower Arranging*. Chezar, Ariella	635.9

SEASONS
Dillard, Annie. *Pilgrim at Tinker Creek*	508
McAnulty, Dara. *Diary of a Young Naturalist*	508.092
Phillips, Rowan Ricardo. *The Circuit*	796.342
Renkl, Margaret. *The Comfort of Crows*	814.6
Theroux, Paul. *Deep South*	975
Thorisson, Mimi. *A Kitchen in France*	641.594
Tougias, Robert. *Birder on Berry Lane*	598.072
The Seasons of My Mother. Harden, Marcia Gay	B
The Seasons of Trouble. Mohan, Rohini	954.9303

SEATTLE, WASHINGTON
Grind, Kirsten. *The Lost Bank*	332.3
Lanegan, Mark. *Sing Backwards and Weep*	B
Lightner, Jill. *Cooking from Scratch*	641.5
Newman, Magdalena. *Normal*	611
Sone, Monica Itoi. *Nisei Daughter*	979.7
Wong, Jane. ★*Meet Me Tonight in Atlantic City*	B

SEAWEED
Smith, Bren. *Eat Like a Fish*	338.3

Sebag-Montefiore, Simon
Jerusalem	956.94
The Romanovs	947
Stalin	B
★*The World*	929.7
Young Stalin	B

Sebba, Anne
Ethel Rosenberg	B

Sebestyen, Victor
Budapest	943.912
Lenin	B
Revolution 1989	947.085

SECESSION
Larson, Erik. ★*The Demon of Unrest*	973.7
Widmer, Edward L. *Lincoln on the Verge*	B
Williams, David. *Bitterly Divided*	973.7
★*The Second*. Anderson, Carol	344.7305
★*The Second Chance Club*. Hardy, Jason Matthew	364.6

SECOND CHANCES
Lamas, Daniela J. *You Can Stop Humming Now*	616.02
Second Childhood. Howe, Fanny	811
The Second Dalai Lama. Dalai Lama	294.3
The Second Founding. Foner, Eric	342.73

SECOND LANGUAGE ACQUISITION
Kinzler, Katherine D. *How You Say It*	302.2
The Second Life of Tiger Woods. Bamberger, Michael	B
The Second Most Powerful Man in the World. O'Brien, Phillips Payson	B
★*The Second Mountain*. Brooks, David	302
Second Nature. Rich, Nathaniel	304.2
★*The Second Sex*. Beauvoir, Simone de	305.4
Second Thoughts. Berger, Lynn	306.85
The Second World War. Gilbert, Martin	940.53
The Second World War. Keegan, John	940.53
The Second World War. Beevor, Antony	940.54

SECOND WORLD WAR ERA (1939-1945)
Albright, Madeleine Korbel. *Prague Winter*	943.71
Aleksievich, Svetlana. *Last Witnesses*	940.53
Aleksievich, Svetlana. ★*The Unwomanly Face of War*	940.53
Alexander, Caroline. *Skies of Thunder*	940.54
Allport, Alan. *Britain at Bay*	940.53
Ambrose, Stephen E. *Citizen Soldiers*	940.54
Andrews, Lena S. ★*Valiant Women*	940.53
Asbrink, Elisabeth. *And in the Vienna Woods the Trees Remain*	B
Askwith, Richard. *Unbreakable*	B
Atria, Travis. *Better Days Will Come Again*	B
Barrett, David Dean. *140 Days to Hiroshima*	940.54
Batalion, Judith. *The Light of Days*	940.53
Beevor, Antony. *The Battle of Arnhem*	940.54
Beschloss, Michael R. *The Conquerors*	940.53
Bissinger, H. G. ★*The Mosquito Bowl*	796.332
Blume, Lesley M. M. *Fallout*	940.54
Bradley, James. *Flags of Our Fathers*	940.54
Brown, Daniel James. ★*Facing the Mountain*	940.54
Bruning, John R. *The Race of Aces*	940.54
Budiansky, Stephen. *Blackett's War*	940.54
Cahan, Richard. *Un-American*	940.53
Childers, Thomas. *The Third Reich*	943.086
Daniels, Roger. *Prisoners Without Trial*	940.53
Dickson, Paul. *The Rise of the G.I. Army 1940-1941*	940.54
Dower, John W. *Embracing Defeat*	952.04
Drabkin, Ronald. *Beverly Hills Spy*	940.54
Dugard, Martin. *Taking Berlin*	940.54
Edwards, Bob. *Edward R. Murrow and the Birth of Broadcast Journalism*	B
Englund, Peter. *November 1942*	940.53
Epstein, Franci. *Franci's War*	B
Erwin, Jon. *Beyond Valor*	B
Evans, Richard J. *The Third Reich at War*	940.53
Frank, Richard B. *Downfall*	940.54
Freeman, Sally Mott. *The Jersey Brothers*	920
Fullilove, Michael. *Rendezvous with Destiny*	973.917092
Giangreco, D. M. *Hell to Pay*	940.54
Gladwell, Malcolm. ★*The Bomber Mafia*	940.54
Graff, Garrett M. ★*When the Sea Came Alive*	940.54
Grayling, A. C. *Among the Dead Cities*	940.54
Groom, Winston. *The Generals*	920
Ham, Paul. *Hiroshima Nagasaki*	940.54
Hampton, Dan. *Operation Vengeance*	940.54
Hanson, Victor Davis. *The Second World Wars*	940.53
Harmon, Mark. *Ghosts of Honolulu*	940.54
Hastings, Max. *Operation Chastise*	940.54
Hemming, Henry. *Agents of Influence*	940.54
Henderson, Bruce B. *Bridge to the Sun*	940.53
Henderson, Bruce B. *Sons and Soldiers*	940.53
Hersey, John. ★*Hiroshima*	940.54
Hogan, William R. *Task Force Hogan*	940.54
Holland, James. *Big Week*	940.54
Holland, James. ★*Burma '44*	940.54
Holland, James. *The Savage Storm*	940.53
Holland, James. *Sicily '43*	940.54
Iperen, Roxane van. ★*The Sisters of Auschwitz*	940.53

PUBLIC LIBRARY CORE COLLECTION: NONFICTION
Twentieth Edition

Isserman, Maurice. *The Winter Army*   940.54
Kemper, Steve. *Our Man in Tokyo*   952.03
Kix, Paul. *The Saboteur*   940.53
Lambert, Raymond. *Every Man a Hero*   B
Lance, Rachel. *Chamber Divers*   940.54
Landdeck, Katherine Sharp. *The Women with Silver Wings*   920
Larson, Erik. ★*The Splendid and the Vile*   940.54
Levi, Primo. *The Periodic Table*   858
Lewis, Damien. *Churchill's Hellraisers*   940.54
Lisle, John. *The Dirty Tricks Department*   940.54
Lowe, Keith. *Prisoners of History*   940.54
Lucas, Jack. *Indestructible*   B
Macadam, Heather Dune. *999*   940.53
MacGregor, Iain. *The Lighthouse of Stalingrad*   940.54
Macintyre, Ben. ★*Rogue Heroes*   940.54
MacKrell, Judith. *The Correspondents*   070.4
Maddow, Rachel. ★*Prequel*   320.53
McKay, Sinclair. *The Fire and the Darkness*   940.54
McKean, David. *Watching Darkness Fall*   940.53
McManus, John C. *Fire and Fortitude*   940.54
McMeekin, Sean. *Stalin's War*   940.53
Milton, Giles. *Soldier, Sailor, Frogman, Spy, Airman, Gangster, Kill or Die*   940.54
Moorehead, Caroline. *A House in the Mountains*   940.53
Moorhouse, Roger. *The Forgers*   940.53
Mulley, Clare. *The Women Who Flew for Hitler*   920
Nelson, Craig. ★*V Is for Victory*   973.917
Norman, Elizabeth M. *We Band of Angels*   940.54
O'Donnell, Svenja. *Inge's War*   943.086
Ohler, Norman. *The Bohemians*   940.53
Olson, Lynne. *Those Angry Days*   940.53
Parkin, Simon. *A Game of Birds and Wolves*   940.54
Parkin, Simon. *The Island of Extraordinary Captives*   940.53
Pellegrino, Charles R. *To Hell and Back*   940.54
Pomerantsev, Peter. ★*How to Win an Information War*   940.53
Porter, Carolyn. *Marcel's Letters*   940.54
Preston, Diana. *Before the Fallout*   303.48
Price, David A. *Geniuses at War*   940.54
Purnell, Sonia. ★*A Woman of No Importance*   B
Raban, Jonathan. *Father and Son*   B
Reeves, Richard. *Infamy*   940.53
Ricks, Thomas E. *Churchill and Orwell*   920
Roberts, Andrew. *The Storm of War*   940.54
Ross, Steve. *From Broken Glass*   B
Ross, Steven Joseph. ★*Hitler in Los Angeles*   979.4
Russell, Jan Jarboe. *The Train to Crystal City*   940.53
Sakamoto, Pamela Rotner. *Midnight in Broad Daylight*   940.53
Sands, Philippe. *The Ratline*   B
Scott, James. *Rampage*   940.54
Scott, James. *Target Tokyo*   940.54
Sheinkin, Steve. *Bomb*   623.4
Siegal, Nina. *The Diary Keepers*   940.54
Smith, Jim B. *The Last Mission*   940.54
Sone, Monica Itoi. *Nisei Daughter*   979.7
Southard, Susan. *Nagasaki*   940.54
Stone, Dan. ★*The Holocaust*   940.53
Strauss, Gwen. *The Nine*   940.53
Sullivan, James. *Unsinkable*   940.54
Terkel, Studs. *The Good War*   940.54
Trimble, Lee. *Beyond the Call*   940.54
Twomey, Steve. *Countdown to Pearl Harbor*   940.54
Ullrich, Volker. ★*Eight Days in May*   943.086
Ullrich, Volker. *Hitler*   B
Wallace, Chris. *Countdown 1945*   940.54
Wheelan, Joseph. *Midnight in the Pacific*   940.54
White, Elizabeth B. ★*The Counterfeit Countess*   940.53
The Second World Wars. Hanson, Victor Davis   940.54

SECOND-BORN CHILDREN
Berger, Lynn. *Second Thoughts*   306.85

SECONDARY EDUCATION
Appleman, Deborah. *Literature and the New Culture Wars*   807
Fishman, Elly. *Refugee High*   370.8
Powell, Nate. ★*Lies My Teacher Told Me*   741.5
Thorpe, Helen. *The Newcomers*   373.18
Secondhand. Minter, Adam   381

SECONDHAND INDUSTRY AND TRADE
Minter, Adam. *Secondhand*   381
★*Secondhand Time*. Aleksievich, Svetlana   947.086

SECRECY
Eyre, Eric. *Death in Mud Lick*   362.29
Hemming, Henry. *Agents of Influence*   940.54
Kiernan, Denise. *The Girls of Atomic City*   976.8
Morton, Andrew. *17 Carnations*   941.084
Mueller, Tom. *Crisis of Conscience*   364.16
Neumann, Ariana. *When Time Stopped*   B
Rushdie, Salman. *Joseph Anton*   B
Vladeck, Stephen I. *The Shadow Docket*   347.73
White, Richard. *Who Killed Jane Stanford?*   364.152

SECRECY IN GOVERNMENT
Baker, Nicholson. *Baseless*   358
Connelly, Matthew James. *The Declassification Engine*   352.3
Gellman, Barton. ★*Dark Mirror*   B
Graff, Garrett M. *Raven Rock*   363.350973
Higginbotham, Adam. ★*Midnight in Chernobyl*   363.17
Howley, Kerry. *Bottoms Up and the Devil Laughs*   352.37
Iversen, Kristen. *Full Body Burden*   363.17
Jacobsen, Annie. *Phenomena*   133.8
Rohde, David. *In Deep*   973.933
Trimble, Lee. *Beyond the Call*   940.54
Weiner, Tim. *The Folly and the Glory*   327.73047
Weiner, Tim. *Legacy of Ashes*   327.1273009

Secrest, Meryle
  Elsa Schiaparelli   746.9
  Frank Lloyd Wright   B
  Modigliani   B

The Secret Gate. Zuckoff, Mitchell   958.104
A Secret Gift. Gup, Ted   977.1
The Secret History of Bigfoot. O'Connor, John   001.944
The Secret History of Food. Siegel, Matt   641.3
The Secret History of Vladimir Nabokov. Pitzer, Andrea   813
★*The Secret History of Wonder Woman*. Lepore, Jill   741.5

SECRET IDENTITY
Richardson, Edmund. *The King's Shadow*   958.1
Woo, Ilyon. ★*Master Slave Husband Wife*   920
★*The Secret Language of Birthdays*. Goldschneider, Gary   133.5
The Secret Language of Cats. Schotz, Susanne   636.8
The Secret Life of Groceries. Lorr, Benjamin   381.4
★*The Secret Life of Marilyn Monroe*. Taraborrelli, J. Randy   B
The Secret Life of the American Musical. Viertel, Jack   792.609
The Secret Lives of Booksellers and Librarians. Patterson, James   381
The Secret Lives of Buildings. Hollis, Edward   720.9
The Secret Lives of Codebreakers. McKay, Sinclair   940.54
The Secret Lives of Numbers. Kitagawa, Kate   510.9
The Secret Lives of Somerset Maugham. Hastings, Selina   B
★*The Secret Mind of Bertha Pappenheim*. Brownstein, Gabriel   616.85
The Secret of Chanel No. 5. Mazzeo, Tilar J.   338.7
The Secret of Life. Markel, Howard   572.86
The Secret Race. Hamilton, Tyler   796.62
The Secret Rescue. Lineberry, Cate   940.54

SECRET SERVICE
Bascomb, Neal. *Hunting Eichmann*   943.086
Conant, Jennet. *The Lotus Eaters*   940.54
Donner, Rebecca. *All the Frequent Troubles of Our Days*   943
Garrett, Leah. *X Troop*   940.54
Hastings, Max. *The Secret War*   940.54
Helm, Sarah. *A Life in Secrets*   B
Hill, Clint. *Five Days in November*   973.922092
Hill, Clint. *Five Presidents*   B
Hill, Clint. *Mrs. Kennedy and Me*   973.922092
Hill, Clint. *My Travels with Mrs. Kennedy*   B
Kilmeade, Brian. ★*George Washington's Secret Six*   973.4
Lewis, Damien. *Agent Josephine*   B
Loftis, Larry. *Code Name*   B
Macintyre, Ben. *Agent Zigzag*   B
Macintyre, Ben. *Double Cross*   940.54
Macintyre, Ben. ★*Operation Mincemeat*   940.54
Macintyre, Ben. *A Spy Among Friends*   B
Mulley, Clare. *The Spy Who Loved*   B
O'Donnell, Patrick K. *The Unvanquished*   973.7
Olson, Lynne. ★*Madame Fourcade's Secret War*   B
Philipps, Roland. *A Spy Named Orphan*   B
Rhodes, Richard. *Masters of Death*   940.53
Rose, Sarah. *D-Day Girls*   940.53
Stevenson, William. *A Man Called Intrepid*   940.54
Talty, Stephan. *Agent Garbo*   940.5
Waller, Douglas C. *Wild Bill Donovan*   B

AUTHOR, TITLE, SERIES AND SUBJECT INDEX

SECRET SOCIETIES
    Berman, Sarah. *Don't Call It a Cult*   361.4
    Haag, Michael. *The Tragedy of the Templars*   271.7913
    Jones, Dan. *The Templars*   271
★ *The Secret to Superhuman Strength*. Bechdel, Alison   741.5
The Secret Token. Lawler, Andrew   975.6
The Secret War. Hastings, Max   940.54
The Secret War Against Hanoi. Shultz, Richard H.   959.704
The Secret Wisdom of Nature. Wohlleben, Peter   508
The Secret World. Andrew, Christopher M.   327.1209
SECRETS
    Bilger, Burkhard. *Fatherland*   B
    Bilton, Chrysta. *Normal Family*   B
    Buhle, Kathleen. *If We Break*   B
    Devantez, Chelsea. ★ *I Shouldn't Be Telling You This*   B
    Frangello, Gina. *Blow Your House Down*   813
    Glatt, John. ★ *The Perfect Father*   364.152
    Hempel, Jessi. *The Family Outing*   B
    Hilton, Paris. *Paris*   B
    Horton, Michelle. *Dear Sister*   B
    Howley, Kerry. *Bottoms Up and the Devil Laughs*   352.37
    Kershaw, Alex. *Avenue of Spies*   940.53
    Kimmerle, Erin H. *We Carry Their Bones*   365
    Knight, Keltie. *Lady Secrets*   305.4
    Marshall, McMillan. *Among the Bros*   362.29
    Morley, Jefferson. *Scorpions' Dance*   973.924
    O'Donnell, Svenja. *Inge's War*   943.086
    Reitman, Janet. *Inside Scientology*   299
    Schwalbe, Will. *We Should Not Be Friends*   B
    Tetro, Tony. *Con/Artist*   B
    Thomson, Mike. *Syria's Secret Library*   956.9104
    Weigel, Alicia Roth. *Inverse Cowgirl*   B
    Wong, Carmen Rita. *Why Didn't You Tell Me?*   B
    Wright, Lawrence. *Going Clear*   299
    Xue, XInran. *The Book of Secrets*   951.05
Secrets to Drawing Realistic Faces. Parks, Carrie   743.4
Section 60. Poole, Robert M.   975.5
SECTS
    Olson, Roger E. ★ *Handbook of Denominations in the United States*   200.973
SECULAR HUMANISM
    Pinn, Anthony B. *The Black Practice of Disbelief*   211
    Zuckerman, Phil. *Living the Secular Life*   211
Secular Meditation. Heller, Rick   158.1
SECULARISM
    Hagglund, Martin. *This Life*   110
    Harris, Sam. *Islam and the Future of Tolerance*   297.2
    Heller, Rick. *Secular Meditation*   158.1
    Sagan, Sasha. *For Small Creatures Such as We*   390.09
    Zuckerman, Phil. *Living the Secular Life*   211
Secure Relating. Marriott, Sue   158.1
SECURITIES
    Belfort, Jordan. ★ *The Wolf of Investing*   332.63
    Graham, Benjamin. *The Intelligent Investor*   332.67
    Patterson, Scott. ★ *Chaos Kings*   338.5
SECURITIES INDUSTRY AND TRADE
    Belfort, Jordan. ★ *The Wolf of Investing*   332.63
    Kolhatkar, Sheelah. *Black Edge*   364.16
    Weatherall, James Owen. *The Physics of Wall Street*   332.63
    White, Shane. *Prince of Darkness*   B
SECURITY
    Aktipis, Athena. ★ *A Field Guide to the Apocalypse*   155.2
SECURITY CLASSIFICATION (GOVERNMENT DOCUMENTS)
    Connelly, Matthew James. *The Declassification Engine*   352.3
    Howley, Kerry. *Bottoms Up and the Devil Laughs*   352.37
Sedaris, David
    ★ *The Best of Me*   818
    Calypso   814
    ★ *A Carnival of Snackery*   818
    ★ *Happy-Go-Lucky*   814
    Theft by Finding   B
SEDARIS, DAVID
    Sedaris, David. ★ *The Best of Me*   818
    Sedaris, David. *Calypso*   814
    Sedaris, David. ★ *A Carnival of Snackery*   818
    Sedaris, David. ★ *Happy-Go-Lucky*   814
    Sedaris, David. *Theft by Finding*   B
SEDDON, RHEA
    Grush, Loren. ★ *The Six*   629.4

Sederer, Lloyd I.
    The Family Guide to Mental Health Care   616.89
Sedgewick, Augustine
    Coffeeland   338.4
Sedgwick, John
    Blood Moon   975.004
    War of Two   973.4
★ *Sedition Hunters*. Reilly, Ryan J.   364.1
Seduction. Longworth, Karina   B
See What Can Be Done. Moore, Lorrie   801
See You Again in Pyongyang. Jeppesen, Travis   951.93
See You in the Piazza. Mayes, Frances   914.5
★ *See You on Sunday*. Sifton, Sam   641.5
Seed Bead Chic. Katz, Amy   745.594
SEED INDUSTRY AND TRADE
    Elmore, Bartow J. *Seed Money*   338.7
Seed Money. Elmore, Bartow J.   338.7
Seed to Plate, Soil to Sky. Frank, Lois Ellen   641.5
SEEDS
    Chace, Teri Dunn. *Seeing Seeds*   581.4
    Gough, Robert E. *The Complete Guide to Saving Seeds*   631.5
    Kelley, Margot Anne. *A Gardener at the End of the World*   615.8
Seeds of Life. Dolnick, Edward   612.6
Seeger, Pete
    How to Play the 5-String Banjo   787
SEEGER, PETE, 1919-2014
    Dunaway, David King. ★ *How Can I Keep from Singing?*   B
    Wilkinson, Alec. *The Protest Singer*   B
Seeing Gender. Gottlieb, Iris   305.3
Seeing Ghosts. Chow, Kat   B
Seeing Seeds. Chace, Teri Dunn   581.4
Seeing Trees. Hugo, Nancy R.   582.16
Seek You. Radtke, Kristen   741.5
Seen and Unseen. Hill, Marc Lamont   303.3
Seen yet Unseen. Williams, Bari A.   338.4
Seen, Heard, and Paid. Henry, Alan   650.1
Sefarad, Mikhael
    The Wall and the Gate   341.48
Segnit, Niki
    ★ *The Flavor Thesaurus*   641.5
SEGREGATION
    Carlin, John. *Playing the Enemy*   968.06
    Fuller, Alexandra. *Don't Let's Go to the Dogs Tonight*   B
    Gates, Henry Louis. *Colored People*   B
    Gates, Henry Louis. ★ *Stony the Road*   973
    Grant, Gail Milissa. *At the Elbows of My Elders*   B
    Hall, Alvin D. *Driving the Green Book*   917.304
    Hylton, Antonia. *Madness*   362.2
    Kimble, Megan. ★ *City Limits*   388.1
    Lemann, Nicholas. *Redemption*   975
    Lewis, John. ★ *March; Book One*   741.5
    Lewis, John. ★ *March; Book Three*   741.5
    Lewis, John. ★ *March; Book Two*   741.5
    Luxenberg, Steve. ★ *Separate*   342.7308
    Neiman, Garrett. *Rich White Men*   305.5
    Person, Charles. *Buses Are a Comin'*   B
    Rapoport, Ron. *Let's Play Two*   B
    Risen, Clay. *The Bill of the Century*   342.7308
    Rothstein, Richard. ★ *The Color of Law*   305.800973
    Roundtree, Dovey Johnson. ★ *Mighty Justice*   B
    Row, Jess. *White Flights*   813
    Sorin, Gretchen Sullivan. *Driving While Black*   323.1196
    Spofford, Tim. *What the Children Told Us*   150.92
    Sullivan, Patricia. *Lift Every Voice*   973
    Woodward, C. Vann. *The Strange Career of Jim Crow*   305.896
SEGREGATION IN EDUCATION
    Kozol, Jonathan. ★ *An End to Inequality*   379.2
    McWhorter, Diane. *Carry Me Home*   976.1
    Walker, Vanessa Siddle. *The Lost Education of Horace Tate*   370.92
SEGREGATION IN TRANSPORTATION
    Jackson, Troy. *Becoming King*   B
    Luxenberg, Steve. ★ *Separate*   342.7308
    Sorin, Gretchen Sullivan. *Driving While Black*   323.1196
    Theoharis, Jeanne. *The Rebellious Life of Mrs. Rosa Parks*   B
Segura, Tom
    ★ *I'd Like to Play Alone, Please*   B
SEGURA, TOM
    Segura, Tom. ★ *I'd Like to Play Alone, Please*   B

PUBLIC LIBRARY CORE COLLECTION: NONFICTION
Twentieth Edition

Sehee, Baek
   I Want to Die but I Want to Eat Tteokbokki   B
SEHEE, BAEK
   Sehee, Baek. *I Want to Die but I Want to Eat Tteokbokki*   B
SEIDEL, ERIK, 1959-
   Konnikova, Maria. *The Biggest Bluff*   795.412
Seidel, Frederick
   ★*Frederick Seidel Selected Poems*   811
Seidelman, Susan
   Desperately Seeking Something   B
SEIDELMAN, SUSAN
   Seidelman, Susan. *Desperately Seeking Something*   B
Seidule, Ty
   Robert E. Lee and Me   973.7
SEIDULE, TY
   Seidule, Ty. *Robert E. Lee and Me*   973.7
Seierstad, Asne
   Angel of Grozny   947.086
   The Bookseller of Kabul   958.1
   A Hundred and One Days   956.70443
   Two Sisters   956.9104
SEIERSTAD, ASNE, 1970-
   Seierstad, Asne. *The Bookseller of Kabul*   958.1
   Seierstad, Asne. *A Hundred and One Days*   956.70443
Seife, Charles
   Proofiness   510
Seiffert, Amy
   Starved   248
The Seine. Sciolino, Elaine   944
SEINE RIVER
   Sciolino, Elaine. *The Seine*   944
Seinfeld, Jerry
   Is This Anything?   818
SEINFELD, JERRY
   Armstrong, Jennifer Keishin. *Seinfeldia*   791.45
   Seinfeld, Jerry. *Is This Anything?*   818
Seinfeldia. Armstrong, Jennifer Keishin   791.45
Seiple, Samantha
   Louisa on the Front Lines   B
Seitz, Matt Zoller
   The Sopranos Sessions   791.45
Seize The Day. Meyer, Joyce   248.4
SELDEN, GEORGE BALDWIN, 1846-1922
   Goldstone, Lawrence. *Drive!*   338.4
Seldin, Tim
   How to Raise an Amazing Child the Montessori Way   649
The Selected Letters of Laura Ingalls Wilder. Wilder, Laura Ingalls   B
The Selected Letters of Marianne Moore. Moore, Marianne   B
The Selected Letters of Ralph Ellison. Ellison, Ralph   813
The Selected Letters of Willa Cather. Cather, Willa   B
Selected Letters, 1940-1956. Kerouac, Jack   813
Selected Non-Fictions. Borges, Jorge Luis   864
Selected Poems. Baca, Jimmy Santiago   811
★*Selected Poems*. Borges, Jorge Luis   861
Selected Poems. Ruefle, Mary   811
Selected Poems. Ashbery, John   811
Selected Poems. Duncan, Robert   811
Selected Poems. Auden, W. H.   821
Selected Poems. Tsvetaeva, Marina   891.71
Selected Poems. Millay, Edna St. Vincent   811
Selected Poems. Shapiro, Karl   811
★*Selected Poems*. Whitman, Walt   811
Selected Poems. Rukeyser, Muriel   811
Selected Poems. Hill, Geoffrey   821
★*Selected Poems*. Dove, Rita   811
Selected Poems. Lowell, Amy   821
Selected Poems. Fenton, James   821
Selected Poems. Levertov, Denise   811
Selected Poems. Tagore, Rabindranath   891
Selected Poems 1968-2014. Muldoon, Paul   821
Selected Poems of Anne Sexton. Sexton, Anne   811
The Selected Poems of Donald Hall. Hall, Donald   811
★*Selected Poems of Langston Hughes*. Hughes, Langston   811
Selected Poems of May Sarton. Sarton, May   811
Selected Poems, 1965-1990. Hacker, Marilyn   811
Selected Poetry. Pope, Alexander   821
Selected Poetry. Goethe, Johann Wolfgang von   831
Selected Poetry of Lord Byron. Byron, George Gordon Byron   821

The Selected Poetry of Robinson Jeffers. Jeffers, Robinson   811
Selected Works. Cicero, Marcus Tullius   875
Selected Works. Juana Ines de la Cruz, Sister   861
★*The Selected Works of Audre Lorde*. Lorde, Audre   814
Selected Writings. Thomas   230
Selengut, Becky
   ★*Misunderstood Vegetables*   641.6
SELF
   Bossiere, Zoe. *Cactus Country*   306
   Dahl, Melissa. *Cringeworthy*   158.2
   De Bres, Helena. *How to Be Multiple*   155.44
   Febos, Melissa. *Girlhood*   818
   Franzen, Jonathan. *Farther Away*   814
   Gimenez Smith, Carmen. *Be Recorder*   811
   Hardy, Benjamin. *Willpower Doesn't Work*   158
   Hofstadter, Douglas R. *I Am a Strange Loop*   153
   Kaag, John J. *Hiking with Nietzsche*   193
   Kandel, Eric R. ★*The Disordered Mind*   616.89
   Klein, Jessi. *I'll Show Myself Out*   B
   Le Guin, Ursula K. *So Far so Good*   811
   Minami, Jikisai. *It's Okay Not to Look for the Meaning of Life*   158.1
   Myers, David G. *How Do We Know Ourselves?*   155.2
   Nordland, Rod. *Waiting for the Monsoon*   B
   Russert, Luke. *Look for Me There*   B
   Sawaki, Kodo. *Discovering the True Self*   294.3
   Shapland, Jenn. ★*Thin Skin*   814
   Sinclair, Safiya. ★*How to Say Babylon*   B
   Storr, Will. *Selfie*   155.2
   Winter, Molly Roden. *More*   B
   Wu, Simon. *Dancing on My Own*   700.1
   Wulf, Andrea. *Magnificent Rebels*   830.9
SELF IN LITERATURE
   Briggs, Julia. *Virginia Woolf*   823
Self, Caroline
   Chinese Brush Painting   751.4
Self, Robert O.
   All in the Family   320.50973
SELF-ACCEPTANCE
   Agassi, Andre. *Open*   B
   Alderton, Dolly. *Everything I Know About Love*   B
   Baer, Kate. *What Kind of Woman*   811
   Bertinelli, Valerie. *Enough Already*   B
   Bowen, Sesali. *Bad Fat Black Girl*   305.42
   Boylan, Jennifer Finney. *Good Boy*   B
   Branum, Guy. *My Life as a Goddess*   B
   Brown, Brene. *The Gifts of Imperfection*   158
   Chang, David. ★*Eat a Peach*   641.5
   Cooper, Christian. *Better Living Through Birding*   B
   Cumming, Alan. *Baggage*   B
   Davis, Viola. ★*Finding Me*   B
   Eger, Edith Eva. *The Choice*   B
   Fitzgerald, Isaac. *Dirtbag, Massachusetts*   B
   Ford, Ashley C. ★*Somebody's Daughter*   B
   Gerson, Merissa Nathan. *Forget Prayers, Bring Cake*   155.9
   Glass, Sara. *Kissing Girls on Shabbat*   B
   Goodan, Chelsey. *Underestimated*   305.235
   Gordon, Aubrey. *"You Just Need to Lose Weight"*   616.3
   Graham, Ashley. *A New Model*   B
   Guthrie, Savannah. *Mostly What God Does*   248.4
   Gutowitz, Jill. *Girls Can Kiss Now*   814
   Hatmaker, Jen. *Of Mess and Moxie*   248.8
   Hewitt, Sean. *All Down Darkness Wide*   B
   Hillenbrand, Laura. ★*Seabiscuit*   798.4
   Hogan, Linda. *The Woman Who Watches Over the World*   B
   hooks, bell. *Wounds of Passion*   B
   Kang, Mia. *Knockout*   B
   Kazdin, Cole. ★*What's Eating Us*   616.85
   King, Chrissy. *The Body Liberation Project*   306.4
   Lamott, Anne. ★*Dusk, Night, Dawn*   B
   Lawson, Jenny. *Furiously Happy*   B
   Lifford, Tina. *The Little Book of Big Lies*   155.2
   May, Katherine. *Wintering*   155.9
   McBride, Karyl. *Will I Ever Be Good Enough?*   616.85
   McCourt, Frank. *Teacher Man*   B
   McCourt, Frank. *'Tis*   B
   McHargue, Mike. *You're a Miracle (and a Pain in the Ass)*   158.1
   Naumburg, Carla. ★*You Are Not a Sh*tty Parent*   649
   Rigsby, Cody. ★*XOXO, Cody*   B

AUTHOR, TITLE, SERIES AND SUBJECT INDEX

Rinaldi, Karen. *It's Great to Suck at Something*	158.1
Ruhl, Sarah. *Smile*	B
Scheer, Paul. *Joyful Recollections of Trauma*	B
Stone, Lillian. ★*Everybody's Favorite*	814.6
Stryker, Kitty. *Ask*	302
Tallent, Elizabeth. *Scratched*	B
Teng, Tara. ★*Your Body Is a Revolution*	306.4
Tobia, Jacob. *Sissy*	305.30973
Tuama, Padraig O. ★*Poetry Unbound*	808.1
Weigel, Alicia Roth. *Inverse Cowgirl*	B
Welteroth, Elaine. *More Than Enough*	B
Wu, Constance. *Making a Scene*	B

SELF-ACTUALIZATION

Alter, Adam L. *Anatomy of a Breakthrough*	158.1
Bennett, Michael. *F*ck Feelings*	158
Bernstein, Gabrielle. *Judgment Detox*	158
Brown, Tabitha. *I Did a New Thing*	158.1
Cameron, Julia. *Living the Artist's Way*	153.3
Dais, Dawn. *The Sh!t No One Tells You About Divorce*	306.89
Dokun, Chanel. *Life Starts Now*	248.8
Dunne, Linnea. *Lagom*	158.1
Fenet, Lydia. *Claim Your Confidence*	158.1
Ferriss, Timothy. *Tools of Titans*	081
Gawain, Shakti. ★*Creative Visualization*	153.3
Grant, Adam M. *Hidden Potential*	153.8
Grover, Joanna. *The Choice Point*	158.1
Gupta, Suneel. *Everyday Dharma*	158.1
Holmes, Cassie. *Happier Hour*	158.1
Jamieson, Alexandra. *Women, Food, and Desire*	155.3
Kennedy-Moore, Eileen. ★*Kid Confidence*	155.4
Kishimi, Ichiro. *The Courage to Be Disliked*	158
Marriott, Sue. *Secure Relating*	158.1
May, Katherine. *Enchantment*	158.1
Miller, Caroline Adams. *Creating Your Best Life*	158.1
Minami, Jikisai. *It's Okay Not to Look for the Meaning of Life*	158.1
Norton, Michael. ★*The Ritual Effect*	650.1
Oyeneyin, Tunde. *Speak*	B
Richards, Shola. *Making Work Work*	658.3
Rubin, Gretchen. *Outer Order, Inner Calm*	158
Siegel, Daniel J. *Aware*	158.1
Sincero, Jen. *You Are a Badass*	158.1
Stulberg, Brad. *Peak Performance*	158.1
Tatum, Scott. *Friendly Reminders*	158.1
Wan, Bonnie. *The Life Brief*	158.1
Wiking, Meik. *The Little Book of Hygge*	158.1

SELF-AWARENESS

Epstein, Mark. *The Zen of Therapy*	294.3
Eteraz, Ali. *Children of Dust*	B
Febos, Melissa. *Girlhood*	818
Gotch, Jen. *The Upside of Being Down*	B
Griffin, Susan. *Out of Silence, Sound. Out of Nothing, Something*	808.02
Hofstadter, Douglas R. *I Am a Strange Loop*	153
Lifford, Tina. *The Little Book of Big Lies*	155.2
Weber, Charlotte Fox. *Tell Me What You Want*	153.8

SELF-CARE

Applebaum, Allison. *Stand by Me*	649.8
Beattie, Melody. *Codependent No More*	616.86
Castro, M. Regina. ★*The Essential Diabetes Book*	616.4
Common. ★*And Then We Rise*	613
Dooner, Caroline. *Tired as F*ck*	152.1
Falter, Suzanne. *The Extremely Busy Woman's Guide to Self-Care*	613
Gerson, Merissa Nathan. *Forget Prayers, Bring Cake*	155.9
Harper, Michele. *The Beauty in Breaking*	B
Harrison, Christy. *The Wellness Trap*	613
Hartwig, Melissa. *The Whole30 Fast & Easy*	641.5
Hartwig, Melissa. *The Whole30 Slow Cooker*	641.5
Hazan, Jack. *Mind Over Batter*	641.81
Hubbard, Shanita. ★*Ride-Or-Die*	305.48
Kelly, Christopher R. *Am I Dying?!*	362.1
Killam, Kasley. *The Art and Science of Connection*	302
Lifford, Tina. *The Little Book of Big Lies*	155.2
Ludwig, David. *Always Hungry?*	613.2
Luger, Chelsey. *The Seven Circles*	610
Mann, Jen. ★*Midlife Bites*	305.244
May, Katherine. *Enchantment*	158.1
McGregor, Alyson J. *Sex Matters*	613
Oakes, John G. H. ★*The Fast*	613.2
Raphael, Rina. *The Gospel of Wellness*	613
Slate, Jenny. *Little Weirds*	B
Smith, Michelle. *The Whole Smiths Good Food Cookbook*	641.5
Thomas, Mathilde. *The French Beauty Solution*	646.7

SELF-CONFIDENCE

Beck, Martha Nibley. *The Way of Integrity*	158.1
Clark, Lloyd. *The Commanders*	940.53
Cuddy, Amy. *Presence*	158.1
Ehrenreich, Barbara. *Bright-Sided*	155.2
Fenet, Lydia. *Claim Your Confidence*	158.1
Graham, Ashley. *A New Model*	B
Lima, Jamie Kern. *Believe It*	B
Osteen, Joel. *The Power of I Am*	248.4
Rippon, Kelly. *Parent Up*	649
Rollag, Keith. *What to Do When You're New*	158.2
Schneider, Amy. *In the Form of a Question*	B
Tough, Paul. ★*How Children Succeed*	372.210973
Williams, Billy Dee. ★*What Have We Here*	B

SELF-CONFIDENCE IN CHILDREN

Morin, Amy. *13 Things Mentally Strong Parents Don't Do*	649
Parker, Kate T. *Strong Is the New Pretty*	155.43

SELF-CONSCIOUSNESS

Tomine, Adrian. *The Loneliness of the Long-Distance Cartoonist*	741.5

SELF-CONTROL

Goleman, Daniel. *Focus*	153.7
Oakes, John G. H. ★*The Fast*	613.2
Tough, Paul. ★*How Children Succeed*	372.210973
Willink, Jocko. *Discipline Equals Freedom*	158.1

SELF-DECEPTION

Tolentino, Jia. ★*Trick Mirror*	973.93
Vedantam, Shankar. *Useful Delusions*	153.4

SELF-DEFENSE

Flock, Elizabeth. ★*The Furies*	305.48
Wertheim, L. Jon. *Blood in the Cage*	796.815

SELF-DESTRUCTIVE BEHAVIOR

Blakinger, Keri. *Corrections in Ink*	B
Casillo, Charles. *Marilyn Monroe*	B
Fleming, Brandon P. *Miseducated*	B
Leach, Samantha. ★*The Elissas*	362.73
Martin, Clancy W. *How Not to Kill Yourself*	362.28
Milch, David. *Life's Work*	B
Moby. *Then It Fell Apart*	B
Moe, John. *The Hilarious World of Depression*	616.85
O'Sullivan, Emer. *The Fall of the House of Wilde*	B
Stern, Amanda. *Little Panic*	616.8522

SELF-DISCOVERY

Agassi, Andre. *Open*	B
Alvarez, Noe. *Spirit Run*	796.42
Baraka, Sho. *He Saw That It Was Good*	261.5
Bechdel, Alison. ★*The Secret to Superhuman Strength*	741.5
Branum, Guy. *My Life as a Goddess*	B
Byas, Taylor. *I Done Clicked My Heels Three Times*	811
Cahalan, Susannah. *Brain on Fire*	616.8
Cardwell, Diane. *Rockaway*	B
Cargle, Rachel Elizabeth. *A Renaissance of Our Own*	B
Clark, Liz. *Swell*	B
Coel, Michaela. ★*Misfits*	158.2
Coffin, Jaed. *Roughhouse Friday*	B
Conyers, Jonathan. *I Wasn't Supposed to Be Here*	B
Davis, Jennifer Pharr. *Called Again*	B
Davis, Viola. ★*Finding Me*	B
Diaz, Jaquira. *Ordinary Girls*	818
Doyle, Glennon. *Untamed*	B
Driver, Minnie. *Managing Expectations*	B
Epstein, David J. ★*Range*	153.9
Feldman, Deborah. *Unorthodox*	B
Felix, Camonghne. *Dyscalculia*	B
Flaherty, Meghan. *Tango Lessons*	793.3
Frank, Michael. ★*One Hundred Saturdays*	B
Friedman, Rachel. ★*And Then We Grew Up*	305.24
Fuller, Alexandra. *Leaving Before the Rains Come*	B
Garcia, Amanda Yates. *Initiated*	B
Geller, Danielle. *Dog Flowers*	B
Gilbert, Elizabeth. *Eat, Pray, Love*	B
Gottlieb, Lori. ★*Maybe You Should Talk to Someone*	B
Guo, XIaolu. *Nine Continents*	B
Harjo, Joy. *Crazy Brave*	B
Hauser, CJ. *The Crane Wife*	B
Hempel, Jessi. *The Family Outing*	B

PUBLIC LIBRARY CORE COLLECTION: NONFICTION
Twentieth Edition

Heughan, Sam. *Waypoints*	B
Jenkins, Jedidiah. *To Shake the Sleeping Self*	B
Jerkins, Morgan. *Wandering in Strange Lands*	305.896
Jollett, Mikel. ★*Hollywood Park*	B
Jun, Tasha. ★*Tell Me the Dream Again*	248
Kugel, Seth. *Rediscovering Travel*	306.4
Lee, Julia Sun-Joo. *Biting the Hand*	B
Mahjoub, Jamal. *A Line in the River*	962.404
May, Katherine. *Enchantment*	158.1
May, Rollo. *The Discovery of Being*	150.19
McDonald, Michael. ★*What a Fool Believes*	B
Miles, Tiya. ★*Wild Girls*	304.2
Mock, Janet. *Surpassing Certainty*	B
Moore, Beth. *All My Knotted-Up Life*	B
Moore, Susanna. *Miss Aluminum*	813
Nafisi, Azar. ★*Reading Lolita in Tehran*	B
Orenstein, Peggy. *Unraveling*	B
Page, Elliot. *Pageboy*	B
Palmer, Amanda. ★*The Art of Asking*	782.42164
Pataki, Allison. *Beauty in the Broken Places*	B
Pellegrino, Danny. *How Do I Un-Remember This?*	B
Pennington, Emily. *Feral*	B
Phillips, Carl. *Then the War*	811
Porter, Billy. ★*Unprotected*	B
Reichl, Ruth. *My Kitchen Year*	641.5
Remnick, David. *The Bridge*	B
Rubin, Rick. ★*The Creative Act*	153.3
Russert, Luke. *Look for Me There*	B
Salama, Jordan. ★*Stranger in the Desert*	982
Sawaki, Kodo. *Discovering the True Self*	294.3
Schulz, Kathryn. ★*Lost & Found*	B
Shafrir, Doree. *Thanks for Waiting*	B
Shakur, Prince. *When They Tell You to Be Good*	B
Skaja, Emily. *Brute*	811.6
Talusan, Meredith. *Fairest*	305.30973
Tate, Christie. *B.F.F.*	B
Tesfamariam, Rahiel. ★*Imagine Freedom*	305.896
Tran, Phuc. ★*Sigh, Gone*	B
Wagamese, Richard. *For Joshua*	B
Wang, Connie. *Oh My Mother!*	B
Washington, Kerry. *Thicker Than Water*	B
Whitney, Emerson. *Heaven*	B
Williams, Patricia. *Rabbit*	B
Wilson, Rebel. *Rebel Rising*	B
Wolf, Brandon J. *A Place for Us*	B
Wu, Simon. *Dancing on My Own*	700.1
Yancey, Philip. ★*Where the Light Fell*	B
Yong, Sable. *Die Hot with a Vengeance*	646.7

SELF-DISCOVERY IN CHILDREN

May, Meredith. *The Honey Bus*	B

SELF-DOUBT

Didion, Joan. ★*Let Me Tell You What I Mean*	814
Lima, Jamie Kern. *Believe It*	B
Tur, Katy. *Rough Draft*	B
The Self-Driven Child. Stixrud, William R.	155.4

SELF-EMPLOYMENT

Marie, Jane. ★*Selling the Dream*	658.8
Self-Esteem. McKay, Matthew	155.2

SELF-ESTEEM

Albertine, Viv. *Clothes, Clothes, Clothes. Music, Music, Music*	B
Beck, Amanda Martinez. *More of You*	613
Cameron, Silver Donald. *Blood in the Water*	364.152
Chaudry, Rabia. *Fatty Fatty Boom Boom*	B
Doust, Kelly. *The Power Age*	305.244
Hubbard, Shanita. ★*Ride-Or-Die*	305.48
Kang, Mia. *Knockout*	B
Kneeland, Jessi. *Body Neutral*	306.4
Kushner, Harold S. *How Good Do We Have to Be?*	296.7
Lamott, Anne. *Almost Everything*	170
Lifford, Tina. *The Little Book of Big Lies*	155.2
McKay, Matthew. *Self-Esteem*	155.2
Meltzer, Marisa. *This Is Big*	613.25
Miranda, Lin-Manuel. *Gmorning, Gnight!*	811
Preston, Katherine. *Out with It*	B
Sehee, Baek. *I Want to Die but I Want to Eat Tteokbokki*	B
Tate, Christie. *B.F.F.*	B
Wilson, A'ja. ★*Dear Black Girls*	158.1
Zimmerman, Jess. *Women and Other Monsters*	155.3

SELF-ESTEEM IN CHILDREN

Kennedy-Moore, Eileen. ★*Kid Confidence*	155.4
Sole-Smith, Virginia. ★*Fat Talk*	649.1

SELF-EVALUATION

Boa, Kenneth D. *Recalibrate Your Life*	248.8
Tate, Christie. *B.F.F.*	B

SELF-FULFILLMENT

Bechdel, Alison. ★*The Secret to Superhuman Strength*	741.5
Blackstone, Amy. *Childfree by Choice*	306.874
Boone, Matthew S. *Stop Avoiding Stuff*	152.4
Braitman, Laurel. *What Looks Like Bravery*	B
Branum, Guy. *My Life as a Goddess*	B
Brooks, Arthur C. *Build the Life You Want*	158.1
Brooks, David. ★*How to Know a Person*	158.2
Burnett, William. *Designing Your Life*	650.1
Calhoun, Ada. *Why We Can't Sleep*	305.244
Cargle, Rachel Elizabeth. *A Renaissance of Our Own*	B
Chittister, Joan. *Following the Path*	248.4
Chopra, Deepak. *Metahuman*	204
Cleage, Pearl. *Things I Should Have Told My Daughter*	B
Covey, Stephen R. ★*The 7 Habits of Highly Effective People*	158
Covey, Stephen R. *The 8th Habit*	158
Daley-Ward, Yrsa. *The How*	158.1
Doherty, Maggie. *The Equivalents*	920
Doyle, Glennon. *Untamed*	B
Emdin, Christopher. *Ratchetdemic*	370.1
Ferriss, Timothy. *Tools of Titans*	081
Friedman, Rachel. ★*And Then We Grew Up*	305.24
Fuller, Alexandra. *Leaving Before the Rains Come*	B
Gaines, Joanna. *The Stories We Tell*	B
Gardner, Chris. ★*Permission to Dream*	158.1
Gentile, Olivia. *Life List*	598.072
Goldstein, Meredith. *Can't Help Myself*	B
Gopnik, Adam. *All That Happiness Is*	158.1
Jenkins, Peter. *A Walk Across America*	917.304
Kaur, Rupi. *Milk and Honey*	811
Kaur, Rupi. *The Sun and Her Flowers*	811.6
Kim, John. *Single on Purpose*	155.6
Kondo, Marie. ★*Marie Kondo's Kurashi at Home*	648
Kushner, Harold S. *Overcoming Life's Disappointments*	296.7
Loh, Sandra Tsing. *The Madwoman and the Roomba*	B
Lythcott-Haims, Julie. *Your Turn*	305.24
Manson, Mark. *The Subtle Art of Not Giving a F*ck*	158.1
McConaughey, Matthew. *Greenlights*	B
McCurdy, Jennette. ★*I'm Glad My Mom Died*	B
McHargue, Mike. *You're a Miracle (and a Pain in the Ass)*	158.1
Miller, Caroline Adams. *Creating Your Best Life*	158.1
Owens, Lama Rod. *Love and Rage*	152.4
Palmieri, Jennifer. *She Proclaims*	305.42
Parks, Casey. *Diary of a Misfit*	B
Peck, M. Scott. ★*The Road Less Traveled*	158.1
Pipher, Mary Bray. *Women Rowing North*	305.26
Power, Marianne. *Help Me!*	158.1
Rinaldi, Karen. *It's Great to Suck at Something*	158.1
Roberts, Matthias. *Holy Runaways*	262
Rodsky, Eve. *Find Your Unicorn Space*	158.1
Rodgers, Mary. *Shy*	B
Rubin, Gretchen Craft. ★*Life in Five Senses*	152.1
Sante, Lucy. *I Heard Her Call My Name*	B
Seligman, Martin E. P. ★*Learned Optimism*	155.2
Shafrir, Doree. *Thanks for Waiting*	B
Sharot, Tali. *Look Again*	158.1
Smith, Jada Pinkett. *Worthy*	B
Solnit, Rebecca. ★*Recollections of My Nonexistence*	B
Stamos, John. *If You Would Have Told Me*	B
Storr, Will. *Selfie*	155.2
Streisand, Barbra. ★*My Name Is Barbra*	B
Suh, Krista. *DIY Rules for a WTF World*	158.1
Talusan, Meredith. *Fairest*	305.30973
Tatum, Scott. *Friendly Reminders*	158.1
Van Ness, Jonathan. *Love That Story*	791.4502
Vanderbilt, Tom. ★*Beginners*	646.7
Volf, Miroslav. *Life Worth Living*	113
Vollmer, Becky. *You Are Not Stuck*	158.1
Wan, Bonnie. *The Life Brief*	158.1
Waxman, Jamye. *How to Break up with Anyone*	158.2
Wilson, Chris. *The Master Plan*	B

AUTHOR, TITLE, SERIES AND SUBJECT INDEX

Yalom, Irvin D. *Staring at the Sun*	155.9
SELF-FULFILLMENT IN CHILDREN	
Crouse, Karen. *Norwich*	796
SELF-HARM	
Carriere, Alice. *Everything/Nothing/Someone*	B
LeFavour, Cree. *Lights On, Rats Out*	616.85
SELF-HATE	
LeFavour, Cree. *Lights On, Rats Out*	616.85
Tate, Christie. ★*Group*	B
SELF-HELP — CAREER AND FINANCIAL SUCCESS	
Braswell, Porter. ★*Let Them See You*	650.1
Casares, Whitney. *The Working Mom Blueprint*	306.8743
De Leon, Paco. *Finance for the People*	332.024
Economy, Peter. *Wait, I'm the Boss?!?*	658
Economy, Peter. *Wait, I'm Working with Who?!?*	650.1
Eikenberry, Kevin. *The Long-Distance Teammate*	650.1
Finkle, Jane. *The Introvert's Complete Career Guide*	650.14
Gallo, Carmine. *Talk Like Ted*	658.4
Germer, Fawn. *Coming Back*	650.14
Harts, Minda. *Right Within*	658.3
Kotlikoff, Laurence J. *Money Magic*	332.024
Louis, Matthew J. *Mission Transition*	650.14
Lowry, Erin. ★*Broke Millennial Talks Money*	332.024
Medini, Shari. *Parenting While Working from Home*	650.1
Orman, Suze. ★*The Ultimate Retirement Guide for 50+*	306.3
Orman, Suze. *Women & Money*	332.0240082
Pollak, Lindsey. *Recalculating*	650.1
Ramsey, Dave. *The Total Money Makeover*	332.024
Rick, Scott. *Tightwads and Spendthrifts*	332.024
Simmons, Lauren. *Make Money Move*	332.024
Tu, Vivian. *Rich Af*	332.024
Wasserman, Claire. *Ladies Get Paid*	650.1
Young, Scott H. *Get Better at Anything*	650.1
SELF-HELP — DIET AND NUTRITION	
Hunt, Lindsay Maitland. *Help Yourself*	641.5
SELF-HELP — GENERAL	
Applebaum, Allison. *Stand by Me*	649.8
Bass, Ellen. ★*The Courage to Heal*	616.85
Belasco, Andrew. *The Enlightened College Applicant*	378.1
Benson, Herbert. *The Relaxation Response*	155.9
Blumenthal, Brett. *52 Small Changes for the Mind*	616.89
Cilley, Marla. *The Chaos* Cure*	648
Clear, James. *Atomic Habits*	155.24
Dunne, Linnea. *Lagom*	158.1
Falter, Suzanne. *The Extremely Busy Woman's Guide to Self-Care*	613
Haver, Mary Claire. ★*The New Menopause*	618.1
Ingall, Marjorie. *Sorry, Sorry, Sorry*	158.2
Knight, Sarah. *The Life-Changing Magic of Not Giving a F*ck*	818
Lieberman, David J. *Mindreader*	401
McGovern, Anna. *Pottering*	158.1
Morgenstern, Julie. *Time to Parent*	649
Northrup, Christiane. *Dodging Energy Vampires*	155.2
Piercy, Marge. *So You Want to Write*	808.3
Pryor, Karen. ★*Don't Shoot the Dog*	153.8
Richardson, Patric. *Laundry Love*	648
Sage, Sami. *Democracy in Retrograde*	324
Stout, Martha. *Outsmarting the Sociopath Next Door*	155.2
Wiking, Meik. *The Little Book of Lykke*	646.7
Ziegler, Sheryl. ★*Mommy Burnout*	646.7
SELF-HELP — MENTAL HEALTH	
Breggin, Peter Roger. *Guilt, Shame, and Anxiety*	152.4
Davis, KC. ★*How to Keep House While Drowning*	648
Dooner, Caroline. *Tired as F*ck*	152.1
Durvasula, Ramani. ★*It's Not You*	155.2
Hazan, Jack. *Mind Over Batter*	641.81
Johnson, Earl. *Finding Comfort During Hard Times*	155.9
Keyes, Corey L. M. ★*Languishing*	152.1
May, Rollo. *The Discovery of Being*	150.19
Navab, Pedram. *Sleep Reimagined*	616.8
SELF-HELP — MENTAL HEALTH — ADDICTION	
Beattie, Melody. *Codependent No More*	616.86
Canfield, Jack. *The 30 Day Sobriety Solution*	616.89
Lahey, Jessica. *The Addiction Inoculation*	649
SELF-HELP — MENTAL HEALTH — ANGER	
Lerner, Harriet Goldhor. ★*The Dance of Anger*	152.4
Lieberman, David J. *Never Get Angry Again*	152.4
Owens, Lama Rod. *Love and Rage*	152.4
SELF-HELP — MENTAL HEALTH — ANXIETY AND STRESS	
Allen, Cory. *Now Is the Way*	158.1
Boyes, Alice. *The Anxiety Toolkit*	616.85
SELF-HELP — MENTAL HEALTH — DEPRESSION	
Lucado, Max. *Unshakable Hope*	248.4
Taylor, Madisyn. *Unmedicated*	615.8
SELF-HELP — MENTAL HEALTH — GRIEF AND LOSS	
Barry, Harry. *Emotional Healing*	158.1
Brody, Jane E. *Jane Brody's Guide to the Great Beyond*	616
Butler, Katy. *The Art of Dying Well*	616.02
Cacciatore, Joanne. *Bearing the Unbearable*	155.9
Dugdale, Lydia S. *The Lost Art of Dying*	155.9
Edelman, Hope. *The Aftergrief*	155.9
Fersko-Weiss, Henry. *Caring for the Dying*	616.02
Herring, Lucinda. *Reimagining Death*	393
James, John W. ★*The Grief Recovery Handbook*	155.9
Lyons, Anna. *We All Know How This Ends*	362.17
Rasmussen, Christina. *Where Did You Go?*	133.9
Wanzer, Sidney H. ★*To Die Well*	179.7
White, Kate. *Your Guide to Miscarriage & Pregnancy Loss*	618.3
SELF-HELP — MENTAL HEALTH — POST-TRAUMATIC STRESS DISORDER	
Buque, Mariel. *Break the Cycle*	616.85
SELF-HELP — PERSONAL GROWTH	
Asprey, Dave. *Game Changers*	158.1
Batterson, Mark. *Please, Sorry, Thanks*	179
Blumenthal, Brett. *52 Small Changes for the Mind*	616.89
Boone, Matthew S. *Stop Avoiding Stuff*	152.4
Boser, Ulrich. *Learn Better*	153.1
Brown, Robert J. *You Can't Go Wrong Doing Right*	B
Burnett, William. *Designing Your Life*	650.1
Canfield, Jack. *The 30 Day Sobriety Solution*	616.89
Canfield, Jack. *The Success Principles*	158
Carnegie, Dale. ★*How to Win Friends and Influence People*	158
Carroll, Ryder. ★*The Bullet Journal Method*	640
Coggan, Philip. *Surviving the Daily Grind*	658.3
Common. ★*And Then We Rise*	613
Davis, Pete. *Dedicated*	158.1
Ellenhorn, Ross D. ★*Purple Crayons*	153.3
Ericsson, K. Anders. *Peak*	153.9
Evans, Bec. *Written*	808
Fagan, Chelsea. *The Financial Diet*	332.024
Fallon, Allison. *The Power of Writing It Down*	158.1
Fenet, Lydia. *Claim Your Confidence*	158.1
Ferriss, Timothy. *Tools of Titans*	081
Fletcher, Emily. *Stress Less, Accomplish More*	155.9
Fogler, Janet. *Improving Your Memory*	153.1
Gilkey, Charlie. *Start Finishing*	658.4
Goldsmith, Marshall. *Triggers*	155.2
Goodman, Linda. *Linda Goodman's Star Signs*	133.5
Goodman, Linda. *Linda Goodman's Sun Signs*	133.5
Hardy, Benjamin. *Willpower Doesn't Work*	158
Harris, Dan. *Meditation for Fidgety Skeptics*	158.1
Headlee, Celeste Anne. *We Need to Talk*	153.6
Helgoe, Laurie A. *Introvert Power*	155.2
Herman, Amy. *Visual Intelligence*	152.14
Herring, Lucinda. *Reimagining Death*	393
Hill, Napoleon. *Think and Grow Rich*	650.1
Holiday, Ryan. *Ego Is the Enemy*	158.1
Holiday, Ryan. *Lives of the Stoics*	188
Holmes, Cassie. *Happier Hour*	158.1
Howes, Molly. *A Good Apology*	158.2
Jamie, Poppy. *Happy Not Perfect*	158.1
Jeffers, Susan J. *Feel the Fear— and Do It Anyway*	152.4
Johansen, Signe. ★*How to Hygge*	646.7
Kelly, Kevin. ★*Excellent Advice for Living*	158.1
Kim, John. *Single on Purpose*	155.6
King, Chrissy. *The Body Liberation Project*	306.4
Lyons, Daniel. *STFU*	302.2
Marriott, Sue. *Secure Relating*	158.1
McGraw, Phillip C. *Life Strategies*	158
McKeown, Greg. *Essentialism*	153.8
Milliken, Kirsten. *PLAYDHD*	616.85
Minami, Jikisai. *It's Okay Not to Look for the Meaning of Life*	158.1
Moody, Raymond A. *Life After Life*	133.9
Moore, Rachel. *The Artist's Compass*	791
Northrup, Christiane. *Dodging Energy Vampires*	155.2
Norton, Michael. ★*The Ritual Effect*	650.1

PUBLIC LIBRARY CORE COLLECTION: NONFICTION
Twentieth Edition

Patrick, Vanessa M. *The Power of Saying No*	158.1
Perry, Philippa. ★*The Book You Wish Your Parents Had Read*	649
Prescott, Matthew. *Food Is the Solution*	613.2
Richards, Shola. *Making Work Work*	658.3
Rinzler, Lodro. *Love Hurts*	294.3
Robbins, Anthony. *Unlimited Power*	158.1
Rotella, Robert J. *How Champions Think*	796.01
Roth, Robert. *Strength in Stillness*	158.1
Rubin, Gretchen. *Outer Order, Inner Calm*	158
Sabatier, Grant. *Financial Freedom*	332.024
Schafer, John R. *The Like Switch*	158.2
Schwartz, David Joseph. ★*The Magic of Thinking Big*	158
Shapiro, Susan. *The Forgiveness Tour*	158.2
Siegel, Daniel J. *Aware*	158.1
Sonenshein, Scott. *Stretch*	153.3
Steib, Mike. *The Career Manifesto*	650.1
Stulberg, Brad. *Peak Performance*	158.1
Stutz, Phil. *Lessons for Living*	158.1
Thom, Kai Cheng. *Falling Back in Love with Being Human*	811
Wan, Bonnie. *The Life Brief*	158.1
Waxman, Jamye. *How to Break up with Anyone*	158.2
Williamson, Marianne. *Tears to Triumph*	299
Willink, Jocko. *Discipline Equals Freedom*	158.1

SELF-HELP — PERSONAL GROWTH — AGING

Attia, Peter. ★*Outlive*	612.6
Cameron, Julia. *It's Never Too Late to Begin Again*	155.67
Clements, Carol. *Better Balance for Life*	617
Conley, Chip. ★*Learning to Love Midlife*	646.7
Corinna, Heather. *What Fresh Hell Is This?*	618.1
Doust, Kelly. *The Power Age*	305.244
Hecht, M. E. *Two Old Broads*	613
Manly, Carla Marie. *Aging Joyfully*	305.26

SELF-HELP — PERSONAL GROWTH — CREATIVITY

Adarme, Adrianna. *The Year of Cozy*	641.3
Attenberg, Jami. *1000 Words*	808.02
Cameron, Julia. *It's Never Too Late to Begin Again*	155.67
Cameron, Julia. ★*The Listening Path*	153.6
Cameron, Julia. *Living the Artist's Way*	153.3
Crispin, Jessa. ★*The Creative Tarot*	133.3
Gilbert, Elizabeth. ★*Big Magic*	153.3
Greenberg, Sarah Stein. *Creative Acts for Curious People*	153.3
Kempton, Beth. *The Way of the Fearless Writer*	808.02
Marine, Carol. *Daily Painting*	751.4
Nichtern, David. *Creativity, Spirituality & Making a Buck*	294.3
Rodsky, Eve. *Find Your Unicorn Space*	158.1
Scheinberger, Felix. *Dare to Sketch*	741.2
Sincero, Jen. *You Are a Badass Every Day*	158.
Suh, Krista. *DIY Rules for a WTF World*	158.1
Zomorodi, Manoush. *Bored and Brilliant*	153.3

SELF-HELP — PERSONAL GROWTH — DIET AND NUTRITION

Bittman, Mark. *VB6*	641.5
David, Laurie. *The Family Cooks*	641.3
Fuhrman, Joel. *Eat to Live Quick & Easy Cookbook*	641.5
Harrison, Christy. *The Wellness Trap*	613
Mullen, Seamus. *Real Food Heals*	641.5
Myers, Amy. *The Autoimmune Solution Cookbook*	641.5
Smith, Michelle. *The Whole Smiths Good Food Cookbook*	641.5

SELF-HELP — PERSONAL GROWTH — FASHION AND STYLE

Dunne, Linnea. *Lagom*	158.1
Karen, Dawnn. *Dress Your Best Life*	646
Linett, Andrea. *The Cool Factor*	746.9
Mohammadi, Kamin. *Bella Figura*	641.01
Taillac, Victoire de. *An Atlas of Natural Beauty*	646.7

SELF-HELP — PERSONAL GROWTH — HAPPINESS

Allen, Cory. *Now Is the Way*	158.1
Asprey, Dave. *Game Changers*	158.1
Beck, Martha Nibley. *The Way of Integrity*	158.1
Becker, Joshua. *The Minimalist Home*	241
Bennett, Michael. *F*ck Feelings*	158
Bernstein, Gabrielle. *Judgment Detox*	158
Blumenthal, Brett. *52 Small Changes for the Mind*	616.89
Bragg, Sarah. *Is Everyone Happier Than Me?*	248.4
Brits, Louisa Thomsen. *The Book of Hygge*	747
Brooks, Arthur C. *Build the Life You Want*	158.1
Conley, Chip. ★*Learning to Love Midlife*	646.7
Dokun, Chanel. *Life Starts Now*	248.8
Dweck, Carol S. ★*Mindset*	153.8
Emet, Joseph. *Finding the Blue Sky*	294.3
Falter, Suzanne. *The Extremely Busy Woman's Guide to Self-Care*	613
Fusco, Daniel. *Crazy Happy*	248.4
Goleman, Daniel. *Why We Meditate*	158.1
Gupta, Suneel. *Everyday Dharma*	158.1
Hardy, Benjamin. *Willpower Doesn't Work*	158
Harris, Dan. *Meditation for Fidgety Skeptics*	158.1
Hase, Craig. *How Not to Be a Hot Mess*	158.1
Hotz, Julia. ★*The Connection Cure*	610
Hutton, Andrea. *Bald Is Better with Earrings*	362.19699
Jamieson, Alexandra. *Women, Food, and Desire*	155.3
Keller, Julia. *Quitting*	650.14
Killam, Kasley. *The Art and Science of Connection*	302
King, Vanessa. *10 Keys to Happier Living*	158
Kishimi, Ichiro. *The Courage to Be Disliked*	158
Knight, Sarah. *The Life-Changing Magic of Not Giving a F*ck*	818
Kondo, Marie. ★*Marie Kondo's Kurashi at Home*	648
Langshur, Eric. *Start Here*	158
Lerner, Harriet Goldhor. ★*The Dance of Anger*	152.4
Luger, Chelsey. ★*The Seven Circles*	610
Masuno, Shunmy. *The Art of Simple Living*	294.3
McCubbin, Tracy. *Make Space for Happiness*	179
McCubbin, Tracy. *Making Space, Clutter Free*	648
McGinnis, Patrick J. *Fear of Missing Out*	153.8
McGonigal, Jane. *Super Better*	794.8
McHargue, Mike. *You're a Miracle (and a Pain in the Ass)*	158.1
Miller, Caroline Adams. *Creating Your Best Life*	158.1
Mohammadi, Kamin. *Bella Figura*	641.01
Morin, Amy. *13 Things Mentally Strong Women Don't Do*	158.1
Rubin, Gretchen. *Outer Order, Inner Calm*	158
Seligman, Martin E. P. ★*Learned Optimism*	155.2
Setiya, Kieran. *Life Is Hard*	128
Sincero, Jen. *You Are a Badass*	158.1
Van Buren, Mark. *A Fool's Guide to Actual Happiness*	294.3
Vollmer, Becky. *You Are Not Stuck*	158.1
Wenzke, Ali. ★*The Art of Happy Moving*	648
Wiking, Meik. *The Little Book of Hygge*	158.1
Wiking, Meik. *The Little Book of Lykke*	646.7
Ziegler, Sheryl. ★*Mommy Burnout*	646.7

SELF-HELP — PERSONAL GROWTH — MEDITATION

Allen, Cory. *Now Is the Way*	158.1
Chodron, Pema. *Practicing Peace*	294.3
Cruikshank, Tiffany. *Meditate Your Weight*	613.2
Gawain, Shakti. ★*Creative Visualization*	153.3
Goleman, Daniel. *Why We Meditate*	158.1
Harris, Dan. *Meditation for Fidgety Skeptics*	158.1
Heller, Rick. *Secular Meditation*	158.1
Roth, Robert. *Strength in Stillness*	158.1

SELF-HELP — PERSONAL GROWTH — MOTIVATION

Abrams, Stacey. *Lead from the Outside*	B
Allen, David. ★*Getting Things Done*	646.7
Alter, Adam L. *Anatomy of a Breakthrough*	158.1
Ashley, Maurice. *Move by Move*	158
Becker, Joshua. *The Minimalist Home*	241
Becker, Joshua. *The More of Less*	241
Bernstein, Gabrielle. *Judgment Detox*	158
Brits, Louisa Thomsen. *The Book of Hygge*	747
Brown, Tabitha. *I Did a New Thing*	158.1
Canfield, Jack. *The 30 Day Sobriety Solution*	616.89
Canfield, Jack. *The Success Principles*	158
Casazza, Allie. *Declutter Like a Mother*	648
Chopra, Deepak. *Metahuman*	204
Falter, Suzanne. *The Extremely Busy Woman's Guide to Self-Care*	613
Gilbert, Elizabeth. ★*Big Magic*	153.3
Gill, Shira. *Organized Living*	747
Green, Louise. *Big Fit Girl*	613.7
Grover, Joanna. *The Choice Point*	158.1
Hardy, Benjamin. *Willpower Doesn't Work*	158
Hendricks, Gay. *Conscious Luck*	158.1
Holiday, Ryan. *Ego Is the Enemy*	158.1
Keller, Julia. *Quitting*	650.14
Kondo, Marie. ★*The Life-Changing Magic of Tidying Up*	648
Kondo, Marie. ★*Marie Kondo's Kurashi at Home*	648
Kondo, Marie. ★*Spark Joy*	648
Linett, Andrea. *The Cool Factor*	746.9
Lucado, Max. *Unshakable Hope*	248.4
Macedo, Diane. *The Sleep Fix*	613.7
McCubbin, Tracy. *Making Space, Clutter Free*	648
McHargue, Mike. *You're a Miracle (and a Pain in the Ass)*	158.1

AUTHOR, TITLE, SERIES AND SUBJECT INDEX

Orman, Suze. *Women & Money*	332.0240082
Oyeneyin, Tunde. *Speak*	158.1
Rotella, Robert J. *How Champions Think*	796.01
Sincero, Jen. *You Are a Badass*	158.1
Sincero, Jen. *You Are a Badass Every Day*	158.1
Streets, Annabel. *52 Ways to Walk*	796.51
Toussaint, Alex. ★*Activate Your Greatness*	158.1
Vaynerchuk, Gary. *Crushing It!*	650.1
Velasquez, Lizzie. *Dare to Be Kind*	177
Willink, Jocko. *Discipline Equals Freedom*	158.1

SELF-HELP — PERSONAL GROWTH — SELF-ESTEEM

Beck, Amanda Martinez. *More of You*	613
Bluestein, Jane. *The Perfection Deception*	155.2
Daley-Ward, Yrsa. *The How*	158.1
Kennedy-Moore, Eileen. ★*Kid Confidence*	155.4
Kishimi, Ichiro. *The Courage to Be Disliked*	158
Kneeland, Jessi. *Body Neutral*	306.4
McKay, Matthew. *Self-Esteem*	155.2
Naumburg, Carla. ★*You Are Not a Sh*tty Parent*	649
Stanley, Jessamyn. ★*Yoke*	613.7
Suh, Krista. *DIY Rules for a WTF World*	158.1
Tatum, Scott. *Friendly Reminders*	158.1
Teng, Tara. ★*Your Body Is a Revolution*	306.4
Vollmer, Becky. *You Are Not Stuck*	158.1

SELF-HELP — PERSONAL GROWTH — SEX

Mendelson, Zoe. *Pussypedia*	612.6

SELF-HELP — PERSONAL GROWTH — SPIRITUALITY

Brownback, Lydia. *Finding God in My Loneliness*	248.8
Chittister, Joan. *The Monastic Heart*	248.8
Chopra, Deepak. *Metahuman*	204
Das, Gaur Gopal. *The Way of the Monk*	294.5
Luger, Chelsey. ★*The Seven Circles*	610
Martin, James. *Learning to Pray*	248.3
Nockels, Christy. *The Life You Long For*	248.8
Seiffert, Amy. *Starved*	248
Williamson, Marianne. *Tears to Triumph*	299
Winkler, Kyle. *Permission to Be Imperfect*	170

SELF-HELP — RELATIONSHIPS

Beattie, Melody. *Codependent No More*	616.86
Gottman, Julie Schwartz. *Fight Right*	616.89
Goulston, Mark. *Talking to Crazy*	158.2
Hoffman, Damona. *F the Fairy Tale*	306.73
Howes, Molly. *A Good Apology*	158.2
Jackson, Danielle Bayard. *Fighting for Our Friendships*	302.34
Marriott, Sue. *Secure Relating*	158.1
Medini, Shari. *Parenting While Working from Home*	650.1
Mogel, Wendy. *Voice Lessons for Parents*	649
Mukantabana, Yseult P. ★*Real Friends Talk About Race*	305.8
Murphy, Kate. *You're Not Listening*	153.6
Rakel, David. *The Compassionate Connection*	610.1
Rick, Scott. *Tightwads and Spendthrifts*	332.024
Slice, Jessica. *Dateable*	646.7
Stixrud, William R. ★*What Do You Say?*	155.4
Self-Help Messiah. Watts, Steven	B

SELF-HELP PSYCHOLOGY

Dooner, Caroline. *Tired as F*ck*	152.1
Goodman, Linda. *Linda Goodman's Star Signs*	133.5
Goodman, Linda. *Linda Goodman's Sun Signs*	133.5
Manson, Mark. *Everything Is F*cked*	152.4
Manson, Mark. *The Subtle Art of Not Giving a F*ck*	158.1
McKay, Matthew. *Self-Esteem*	155.2
Power, Marianne. *Help Me!*	158.1
Wilder-Taylor, Stefanie. *Drunk-Ish*	B

SELF-HELP TECHNIQUES

Bennett, Michael. *F*ck Feelings*	158
Bluestein, Jane. *The Perfection Deception*	155.2
Greitens, Eric. *Resilience*	155.2
Jamie, Poppy. *Happy Not Perfect*	158.1
Knight, Sarah. *The Life-Changing Magic of Not Giving a F*ck*	818
Sincero, Jen. *You Are a Badass*	158.1
Sonenshein, Scott. *Stretch*	153.3
Tatum, Scott. *Friendly Reminders*	158.1
Waxman, Jamye. *How to Break up with Anyone*	158.2

SELF-IMPROVEMENT

Fogg, B. J. *Tiny Habits*	158
Hu, Elise. *Flawless*	646.7
Kethledge, Raymond Michael. *Lead Yourself First*	658.4
Power, Marianne. *Help Me!*	158.1
Smith, Freda Love. *I Quit Everything*	B
Stanley, Paul. *Backstage Pass*	B
Stone, Lillian. ★*Everybody's Favorite*	814.6

SELF-INCRIMINATION

Trainum, James L. *How the Police Generate False Confessions*	345.73

SELF-INJURIOUS BEHAVIOR

LeFavour, Cree. *Lights On, Rats Out*	616.85
A Self-Made Man. Blumenthal, Sidney	B

SELF-MANAGEMENT

Allen, David. ★*Getting Things Done*	646.7
Hansen, Morten T. *Great at Work*	650.1
McHargue, Mike. *You're a Miracle (and a Pain in the Ass)*	158.1
Tierney, John. *The Power of Bad*	158.1

SELF-PERCEPTION

Bertinelli, Valerie. *Enough Already*	B
Codjoe, Ama. *Bluest Nude*	811
Dahl, Melissa. *Cringeworthy*	158.2
Gill, Anton. *Art Lover*	B
Graham, Ashley. *A New Model*	B
Lima, Jamie Kern. *Believe It*	B
Meltzer, Marisa. *This Is Big*	613.25
Prescod, Danielle. *Token Black Girl*	B
Preston, Katherine. *Out with It*	B
Robb, Alice. ★*Don't Think, Dear*	792.8
Ruhl, Sarah. *Smile*	B
Siegel, Daniel J. *Parenting from the Inside Out*	649
Skaja, Emily. *Brute*	811.6
Whitefield-Madrano, Autumn. *Face Value*	111
The Self-Portrait. Hall, James	704.9

SELF-PORTRAITS

Hall, James. *The Self-Portrait*	704.9

SELF-PRESERVATION

Dwyer, Jim. *102 Minutes*	974.7
Keller, Julia. *Quitting*	650.14

SELF-PUBLISHERS AND PUBLISHING

Castleman, Michael. *The Untold Story of Books*	381

SELF-RELIANCE

Didion, Joan. *Where I Was from*	979.4
Ellenhorn, Ross D. ★*Purple Crayons*	153.3
Grandin, Greg. *The End of the Myth*	973
Hillsberg, Christina. *License to Parent*	649.1
Keller, Julia. *Quitting*	650.14
Pennington, Emily. *Feral*	B
Quart, Alissa. *Bootstrapped*	305.5
Storr, Will. *Selfie*	155.2
Waterhouse, Benjamin C. *One Day I'll Work for Myself*	338

SELF-RELIANCE IN CHILDREN

Lahey, Jessica. *The Gift of Failure*	649
Stixrud, William R. *The Self-Driven Child*	155.4
Stixrud, William R. ★*What Do You Say?*	155.4

SELF-SACRIFICE

Carpenter, Kyle. *You Are Worth It*	B
Goldberg, Emma. *Life on the Line*	362.1962
Hogan, William R. *Task Force Hogan*	940.54
Patterson, James. *Walk in My Combat Boots*	920
Phillips, Adam. *On Giving up*	158.2
Qadiri, Humayra. *Dancing in the Mosque*	B
Vaughn, Ellen Santilli. ★*Becoming Elisabeth Elliot*	B

SELF-SUFFICIENCY

Cox, Josie. *Women Money Power*	330.082

SELF-TALK

Kross, Ethan. ★*Chatter*	158.1
Osteen, Joel. *The Power of I Am*	248.4
Selfie. Storr, Will	155.2

SELFISHNESS

Rand, Ayn. ★*The Virtue of Selfishness*	149
Selfless. Lowery, Brian S.	155.2

Seligman, Craig

Who Does That Bitch Think She Is?	792.02

Seligman, Martin E. P.

★*Learned Optimism*	155.2

SELIM I, SULTAN OF THE TURKS, 1470-1520

Mikhail, Alan. *God's Shadow*	B

Selingo, Jeffrey J.

College (un)bound	378
Who Gets in and Why	378.1

SELKIRK, ALEXANDER, 1676-1721

Severin, Timothy. *In Search of Robinson Crusoe*	996.1

PUBLIC LIBRARY CORE COLLECTION: NONFICTION
Twentieth Edition

Selleck, Tom
  You Never Know — B
SELLECK, TOM, 1945-
  Selleck, Tom. *You Never Know* — B
Sellers, Bakari
  My Vanishing Country — B
SELLERS, BAKARI, 1984-
  Sellers, Bakari. *My Vanishing Country* — B
SELLING
  Chapin, Kari. ★*The Handmade Marketplace* — 745.5
  Lindsay, Virginia Keleher. *Sewing to Sell* — 746
  ★*Selling The Dream*. Marie, Jane — 658.8
SELLS, MARCIA LYNN
  Valby, Karen. *The Swans of Harlem* — 792.8
Selvaratnam, Tanya
  Assume Nothing — B
SELVARATNAM, TANYA
  Selvaratnam, Tanya. *Assume Nothing* — B
SEMANTICS
  Armstrong, Karen. *The Lost Art of Scripture* — 208
  Carroll, Sean M. *The Big Picture* — 577
  Falick, Melanie. *Making a Life* — 745.5
  Hagglund, Martin. *This Life* — 110
  Wilson, Edward O. *Consilience* — 121
Semenya, Caster
  The Race to Be Myself — B
SEMENYA, CASTER, 1991-
  Semenya, Caster. *The Race to Be Myself* — B
Semiautomatic. Shockley, Evie — 811
Semicolon. Watson, Cecelia — 428.2
SEMIOTICS
  Eilenberger, Wolfram. *Time of the Magicians* — 920
  Everett, Daniel Leonard. *How Language Began* — 401
Sen, Amartya
  The Argumentative Indian — 954
  Home in the World — B
SEN, AMARTYA
  Sen, Amartya. *Home in the World* — B
Sen, Mayukh
  Taste Makers — 641.5092
Senator, Susan
  Autism Adulthood — 616.85
SENDAK, MAURICE
  Cott, Jonathan. *There's a Mystery There* — 813
SENDLEROWA, IRENA, 1910-2008
  Mazzeo, Tilar J. *Irena's Children* — B
SENEGAL
  Searcey, Dionne. *In Pursuit of Disobedient Women* — B
Seneviratne, Samantha
  Bake Smart — 641.81
Sengupta, Hindol
  Being Hindu — 294.5
Senik, Troy
  A Man of Iron — B
SENIOR ARTISTS
  Painter, Nell Irvin. *Old in Art School* — B
SENIOR MEN
  Leader, Zachary. *The Life of Saul Bellow* — B
  Von Drehle, David. ★*The Book of Charlie* — B
SENIOR WOMEN
  Delany, Sarah Louise. *Having Our Say* — B
  Doust, Kelly. *The Power Age* — 305.244
  Godwin, Gail. *Getting to Know Death* — B
  Hecht, M. E. *Two Old Broads* — 613
  Letts, Elizabeth. ★*The Ride of Her Life* — B
  Pipher, Mary Bray. *Women Rowing North* — 305.26
  Sancton, Thomas. *The Bettencourt Affair* — B
Senior, Jennifer
  All Joy and No Fun — 306.874
SENIORS
  Applewhite, Ashton. *This Chair Rocks* — 155.67
  Aronson, Louise. *Elderhood* — 362.60973
  Bilefsky, Dan. *The Last Job* — 364.16
  Bruder, Jessica. ★*Nomadland* — 331.3
  Chast, Roz. ★*Can't We Talk About Something More Pleasant?* — 741.5
  Chittister, Joan. *The Gift of Years* — 200
  Delany, Sarah Louise. *Having Our Say* — B
  Esty, Katharaine C. *Eightysomethings* — 612.6
  Halpern, Sue. *A Dog Walks into a Nursing Home* — B
  Moore, Thomas. *Ageless Soul* — 155.67
  Remnick, David. *Holding the Note* — 781.64
  Smith, Michael. *Cabin Fever* — 614.5
  Thomas, Elizabeth Marshall. *Growing Old* — 305.26
SENIORS' MEMORY
  Fogler, Janet. *Improving Your Memory* — 153.1
Sensational. Todd, Kim — 920
The Sensational Past. Purnell, Carolyn — 152.109
SENSATIONALISM IN JOURNALISM
  Todd, Kim. *Sensational* — 920
  Whyte, Kenneth. *The Uncrowned King* — B
SENSATIONALISM IN NEWSPAPERS
  Todd, Kim. *Sensational* — 920
A Sense of the World. Roberts, Jason — B
SENSE OF WONDER
  Catania, Kenneth. *Great Adaptations* — 576.8
  Hecht, Jennifer Michael. ★*The Wonder Paradox* — 808.1
  Keltner, Dacher. ★*Awe* — 152.4
  Limon, Ada. ★*The Hurting Kind* — 811
  Macfarlane, Robert. *The Lost Spells* — 811
  Marchant, Jo. *The Human Cosmos* — 523.1
  May, Katherine. *Enchantment* — 158.1
  Smith, Clint. ★*Above Ground* — 811
  Staniforth, Nate. *Here Is Real Magic* — B
SENSES AND SENSATION
  Ackerman, Diane. *A Natural History of the Senses* — 152.1
  Birkhead, T. R. *Bird Sense* — 598
  Bosker, Bianca. *Cork Dork* — 641.2
  Easto, Jessica. *How to Taste Coffee* — 663
  Ellard, Colin. *You Are Here* — 153.7
  Foster, Charles. *Being a Human* — 155.7
  Grandin, Temple. ★*Animals in Translation* — 591.5
  Higgins, Jackie. *Sentient* — 573.8
  Holmes, Bob. *Flavor* — 612.8
  Lalkhen, Abdul-Ghaaliq. *An Anatomy of Pain* — 616
  Medina, John. *Brain Rules* — 153
  Purnell, Carolyn. *The Sensational Past* — 152.109
  Rubin, Gretchen Craft. ★*Life in Five Senses* — 152.1
  Ward, Ashley. *Where We Meet the World* — 612.8
  Wohlleben, Peter. *Forest Walking* — 582.16
  Yong, Ed. ★*An Immense World* — 591.5
SENSES AND SENSATION IN CHILDREN
  Ticktin, Allie. *Play to Progress* — 370.15
SENSITIVITY (PERSONAL QUALITY)
  Nerenberg, Jenara. *Divergent Mind* — 616.89
  Northrup, Christiane. *Dodging Energy Vampires* — 155.2
SENSORY STIMULATION
  Grandin, Temple. ★*Animals in Translation* — 591.5
  Ticktin, Allie. *Play to Progress* — 370.15
★*Sensual Faith*. Briggs, Lyvonne — 204
SENTENCES (CRIMINAL PROCEDURE)
  Bazelon, Emily. ★*Charged* — 345.73
SENTENCES (GRAMMAR)
  Woods, Geraldine. *25 Great Sentences and How They Got That Way* — 808
Senthilingam, Meera
  Outbreaks and Epidemics — 614.4
Sentient. Higgins, Jackie — 573.8
Sentilles, Sarah
  Stranger Care — B
SENTILLES, SARAH
  Sentilles, Sarah. *Stranger Care* — B
Seo, Bo
  Good Arguments — 808.53
SEO, BO
  Seo, Bo. *Good Arguments* — 808.53
SEOUL, KOREA
  Hu, Elise. *Flawless* — 646.7
★*Separate*. Luxenberg, Steve — 342.7308
★*Separated*. Soboroff, Jacob — 325.73
SEPARATED COUPLES
  Harpham, Heather Elise. *Happiness* — B
SEPARATED FRIENDS, RELATIVES, ETC.
  Guerrero, Jean. *Hatemonger* — B
  Hernandez Castillo, Marcelo. *Children of the Land* — B
  Nguyen, Bich Minh. *Owner of a Lonely Heart* — B
  Olivares, Efren C. *My Boy Will Die of Sorrow* — 305.9
  Pablo Cruz, Rosayra. *The Book of Rosy* — B

AUTHOR, TITLE, SERIES AND SUBJECT INDEX

Pick-Goslar, Hannah Elizabeth. ★*My Friend Anne Frank*	B
Soboroff, Jacob. ★*Separated*	325.73
Wagamese, Richard. *For Joshua*	B
Wiesel, Elie. ★*Night*	B
Willner, Nina. *Forty Autumns*	B
Zamora, Javier. ★*Solito*	B

SEPARATION
Steinberg, Jonny. *Winnie and Nelson*	920
Williams, Florence. *Heartbreak*	306.7

SEPARATION OF POWERS
Bade, Rachael. ★*Unchecked*	342.73
Beeman, Richard R. ★*Plain, Honest Men*	342.7302
Brettschneider, Corey Lang. *The Oath and the Office*	342.73
Brettschneider, Corey Lang. *The Presidents and the People*	342.73
Breyer, Stephen G. *Making Our Democracy Work*	347.73
Kaplan, David A. *The Most Dangerous Branch*	347.73
Raphael, Ray. *Mr. President*	352.230973
Rohde, David. *In Deep*	973.933
Stevens, Stuart. *The Conspiracy to End America*	324.2734
Vladeck, Stephen I. *The Shadow Docket*	347.73
Will, George F. *The Conservative Sensibility*	320.520973

Sepetys, Ruta
★*You*	808.02

Sepinwall, Alan
★*TV (the Book)*	791.45

SEPTEMBER 11 TERRORIST ATTACKS, 2001
Ackerman, Spencer. *Reign of Terror*	973.931
Addario, Lynsey. *It's What I Do*	B
Allende, Isabel. *My Invented Country*	B
Bergen, Peter L. *The Rise and Fall of Osama Bin Laden*	958.104
Chomsky, Noam. *Who Rules the World?*	327.73
Coll, Steve. *The Bin Ladens*	920
Dower, John W. *Cultures of War*	355.00973
Draper, Robert. *To Start a War*	956.7044
Dwyer, Jim. *102 Minutes*	974.7
Farmer, John J. *The Ground Truth*	973.931
Friend, David. *Watching the World Change*	974.7
Graff, Garrett M. ★*The Only Plane in the Sky*	973.931
Jacobson, Sidney. *The 9-11 Report*	741.5
Langewiesche, William. *American Ground*	974.7
Longman, Jere. *Among the Heroes*	974.8
Pfeifer, Joseph. *Ordinary Heroes*	973.931
Smith, Dennis. *Report from Ground Zero*	974.7
Soufan, Ali H. *The Black Banners Declassified*	363.325
Spiegelman, Art. *In the Shadow of No Towers*	741.5
Wright, Lawrence. ★*The Looming Tower*	973.931
Zuckoff, Mitchell. ★*Fall and Rise*	973.931

SERBIA
Debreczeni, Jozsef. *Cold Crematorium*	940.53

SERBIAN AMERICANS
Munson, Richard. *Tesla*	B

SERBIAN PEOPLE
Maass, Peter. *Love Thy Neighbor*	949.702

Sered, Danielle
Until We Reckon	364.6

SERGEANT RECKLESS (WAR HORSE), APPROXIMATELY 1948-1968
Hutton, Robin L. *Sgt. Reckless*	951.904

Serial Griller. Moore, Matt | 641.7

SERIAL MURDER INVESTIGATION
Brown, Vanessa. *The Forest City Killer*	364.152
Burgess, Ann Wolbert. *A Killer by Design*	364.3
Callahan, Maureen. *American Predator*	364.152
Collins, Max Allan. *Eliot Ness and the Mad Butcher*	364.152
Douglas, John E. *The Killer Across the Table*	B
Douglas, John E. *When a Killer Calls*	364.152
Franscell, Ron. *Shadowman*	362.88
Lauren, Jillian. *Behold the Monster*	364.152
Wiehl, Lis W. *Hunting the Unabomber*	364.152

SERIAL MURDERERS
Burgess, Ann Wolbert. *A Killer by Design*	364.3
Callahan, Maureen. *American Predator*	364.152
Cep, Casey N. ★*Furious Hours*	364.152
Collins, Max Allan. *Eliot Ness and the Mad Butcher*	364.152
Cornwell, Patricia Daniels. *Ripper*	364.152
Douglas, John E. *The Killer Across the Table*	B
Douglas, John E. *When a Killer Calls*	364.152
Franscell, Ron. *Shadowman*	362.88
Green, Elon. *Last Call*	363.15
Jobb, Dean. *The Case of the Murderous Dr. Cream*	364.152
King, David. *Death in the City of Light*	364.152
Larson, Erik. ★*The Devil in the White City*	364.15
Lauren, Jillian. *Behold the Monster*	364.152
MacLean, Harry N. *Starkweather*	364.152
McCracken, Patti. *The Angel Makers*	364.152
Monroe, Jana. *Hearts of Darkness*	363.25
Nelson, David B. *Boys Enter the House*	364.152
Rae-Venter, Barbara. *I Know Who You Are*	364.152
Rubin, Kathy Kleiner. *A Light in the Dark*	364.152
Rule, Ann. *The Stranger Beside Me*	B
Schechter, Harold. *Murderabilia*	364.152

SERIAL MURDERS
Brown, Vanessa. *The Forest City Killer*	364.152
Cornwell, Patricia Daniels. *Ripper*	364.152
Garrison, Jessica. *The Devil's Harvest*	B
Grann, David. ★*Killers of the Flower Moon*	976.6004
Jobb, Dean. *The Case of the Murderous Dr. Cream*	364.152
King, David. *Death in the City of Light*	364.152
Larson, Erik. ★*The Devil in the White City*	364.15
Lauren, Jillian. *Behold the Monster*	364.152
MacLean, Harry N. *Starkweather*	364.152
McCracken, Patti. *The Angel Makers*	364.152
McNamara, Michelle. *I'll Be Gone in the Dark*	364.152
Nelson, David B. *Boys Enter the House*	364.152
Rubin, Kathy Kleiner. *A Light in the Dark*	364.152
Rule, Ann. *The Stranger Beside Me*	B
Schechter, Harold. *Hell's Princess*	B
Schechter, Harold. *Murderabilia*	364.152
Stashower, Daniel. *American Demon*	364.152

SERIAL RAPISTS
Lauren, Jillian. *Behold the Monster*	364.152
McNamara, Michelle. *I'll Be Gone in the Dark*	364.152
Miller, T. Christian. *A False Report*	364.15

Serious Barbecue. Perry Lang, Adam | 641.5
Serious Face. Mooallem, Jon | 814
A *Serious* Way of Wondering. Price, Reynolds | 241

SERMONS, AMERICAN
Karon, Jan. *Bathed in Prayer*	242

Serpico, Peter
Learning Korean	641.595

Serrallach, Oscar
The Postnatal Depletion Cure	618.6

Serrano, Shea
Basketball (and Other Things)	796.323

Servadio, Gaia
Rossini	B

Servan-Schreiber, David
Anticancer	616.99

Servants of the Damned. Enrich, David | 340.023
Service. Luttrell, Marcus | 956.7044

SERVICE DOGS
Chesney, Will. *No Ordinary Dog*	958.104

SERVICE INDUSTRY AND TRADE
Guendelsberger, Emily. *On the Clock*	331.0973

SERVICE INDUSTRY AND TRADE WORKERS
Guendelsberger, Emily. *On the Clock*	331.0973

Service, Robert
The End of the Cold War 1985-1991	909.82
Lenin—A Biography	B

★*Serving* Teens and Adults on the Autism Spectrum. Rogers-Whitehead, Carrie | 027.6

Servon, Lisa J.
The Unbanking of America	332.10973

Sestero, Greg
The Disaster Artist	791.43

SESTERO, GREG, 1978-
Sestero, Greg. *The Disaster Artist*	791.43

SET DESIGNERS
Essin, Christin. *Stage Designers in Early Twentieth-Century America*	792.02

Setareh, Saghar
Pomegranates & Artichokes	641.5

Setiya, Kieran
Life Is Hard	128

SETON, ELIZABETH ANN, SAINT, 1774-1821
Barthel, Joan. *American Saint*	B

Seuss, Diane
★*Frank*	811

Still Life with Two Dead Peacocks and a Girl 811.6
SEUSS, DR
    Jones, Brian Jay. ★*Becoming Dr. Seuss* B
Seven Ages of Paris. Horne, Alistair 944
★*Seven Brief Lessons on Physics.* Rovelli, Carlo 530
★*The Seven Circles.* Luger, Chelsey 610
Seven Games. Roeder, Oliver 794
Seven Letters from Paris. Verant, Samantha B
The Seven Necessary Sins for Women and Girls. Eltahawy, Mona 305.42
Seven Pillars of Wisdom. Lawrence, T. E. 940.4
The Seven Sins of Memory. Schacter, Daniel L. 153.1
★*The Seven Storey Mountain.* Merton, Thomas B
The Seven-Step Homestead. Webb, Leah M. 635
SEVEN-YEAR-OLD GIRLS
    Nye, Naomi Shihab. *The Tiny Journalist* 811
The Seventies. Schulman, Bruce J. 973.92
Seventy Times Seven. Mar, Alex 362.88
Sever, Shauna
    ★*Midwest Made* 641.5977
Severin, Timothy
    In Search of Robinson Crusoe 996.1
Sevigny, Melissa L.
    ★*Brave the Wild River* 580.9
Sew Luxe Leather. Gethin, Rosanna Clare 745.53
SEWAGE DISPOSAL
    Flowers, Catherine Coleman. *Waste* 363.72
Seward. Stahr, Walter B
SEWARD, FRANCES ADELINE, 1805-1865
    Wickenden, Dorothy. *The Agitators* 920
SEWARD, WILLIAM HENRY, 1801-1872
    Goodwin, Doris Kearns. ★*Team of Rivals* B
    Stahr, Walter. *Seward* B
Sewell, Darrel
    Thomas Eakins 759.13
SEWING
    Alicia, Anna. *Bags* 646.4
    Chanin, Natalie. ★*The Geometry of Hand-Sewing* 746.44
    Conahan, Gillian. *The Hero's Closet* 646.2
    Corwin, Lena. *Lena Corwin's Made by Hand* 746.6
    Edwards, Zoe. *Mend It, Wear It, Love It!* 646
    Goldsmith, Becky. *The Ultimate Thread Guide* 677
    Herbertson, Angie. *Sewing Face Masks, Scrub Caps, Arm Slings, and More* 646.4
    Ishida, Sanae. *Sewing Love* 646
    Misumi, Noriko. *Mending with Love* 646.6
Sewing Face Masks, Scrub Caps, Arm Slings, and More. Herbertson, Angie 646.4
Sewing Happiness. Ishida, Sanae 646.2
Sewing Love. Ishida, Sanae 646
Sewing to Sell. Lindsay, Virginia Keleher 746
SEX (BIOLOGY)
    Eldredge, Niles. *Why We Do It* 155.3
    Fine, Cordelia. *Testosterone Rex* 155.3
    Roach, Mary. *Bonk* 612.6
SEX (PSYCHOLOGY)
    Parks, Casey. *Diary of a Misfit* B
Sex and the City and Us. Armstrong, Jennifer Keishin 791.45
★*Sex and the Constitution.* Stone, Geoffrey R. 345.7302
SEX COUNSELORS AND THERAPISTS
    Westheimer, Ruth. *The Doctor Is In* B
SEX CRIME INVESTIGATION
    Krouse, Erika. ★*Tell Me Everything* 363.25
SEX CRIMES
    Auletta, Ken. ★*Hollywood Ending* 791.43
    Barr, John. *Start by Believing* 364.15
    Bravo, Reah. *Complicit* 331.4
    Farrow, Ronan. ★*Catch and Kill* 331.4
    Ford, Christine Blasey. *One Way Back* B
    Goldberg, Carrie. *Nobody's Victim* 345.73
    Harry, Debbie. *Face It* B
    Herman, Judith Lewis. *Truth and Repair* 362.883
    Hirshman, Linda R. *Reckoning* 305.420973
    Johnson, Akemi. *Night in the American Village* 305.40952
    Kantor, Jodi. *She Said* 364.15
    Ratajkowski, Emily. ★*My Body* B
    Roy, Jessica. *American Girls* 305.4
    Vanasco, Jeannie. *Things We Didn't Talk About When I Was a Girl* B
    Viren, Sarah. *To Name the Bigger Lie* B

Yeung, Bernice. *In a Day's Work* 362.88086
Sex Cult Nun. Jones, Faith B
SEX CUSTOMS
    Hamlin, Kimberly A. *Free Thinker* B
    Krist, Gary. *Empire of Sin* 976.3
    Roach, Mary. *Bonk* 612.6
SEX DIFFERENCES
    Bohannon, Cat. ★*Eve* 613
    Brown, Jericho. ★*The Tradition* 811
    Cooke, Lucy. *Bitch* 591.56
    Eliot, Lise. *Pink Brain, Blue Brain* 612.6
    Emera, Deena. *A Brief History of the Female Body* 612.6
    Fine, Cordelia. *Testosterone Rex* 155.3
    Hartley, Gemma. *Fed Up* 155.3
    Nerenberg, Jenara. *Divergent Mind* 616.89
    Pease, Allan. *The Definitive Book of Body Language* 153.6
    Saini, Angela. *Inferior* 305.4
SEX DISCRIMINATION
    Ackmann, Martha. *The Mercury 13* 920
    Adichie, Chimamanda Ngozi. *We Should All Be Feminists* 305.42
    Agarwal, Pragya. *Sway* 177
    Bolz-Weber, Nadia. *Shameless* 261.8
    Brooks, Geraldine. *Nine Parts of Desire* 305.48
    Chemaly, Soraya L. *Rage Becomes Her* 155.3
    Colwell, Rita R. *A Lab of One's Own* B
    Hamad, Ruby. *White Tears/Brown Scars* 305.8
    Hu, Elise. *Flawless* 646.7
    Kramer, Andrea S. *Breaking Through Bias* 650.1
    Traister, Rebecca. *Good and Mad* 305.420973
SEX DISCRIMINATION AGAINST WOMEN
    Barnes, Katie. ★*Fair Play* 796.082
    Boschert, Sherry. *37 Words* 344.73
    Brodsky, Alexandra. *Sexual Justice* 364.15
    Brooks, Geraldine. *Nine Parts of Desire* 305.48
    Chang, Emily. *Brotopia* 331.4
    Cooper, Helene. *Madame President* 966.62
    Cox, Josie. *Women Money Power* 330.082
    De Stefano, Cristina. *The Child Is the Teacher* B
    Fleshman, Lauren. ★*Good for a Girl* B
    Grush, Loren. ★*The Six* 629.4
    Hegar, Mary Jennings. *Shoot Like a Girl* B
    McShane Wulfhart, Nell. *The Great Stewardess Rebellion* 331.4
    Scovell, Nell. *Just the Funny Parts* B
    Thomas, Gillian. *Because of Sex* 344.7301
SEX DISCRIMINATION IN EMPLOYMENT
    Auletta, Ken. ★*Hollywood Ending* 791.43
    Chang, Emily. *Brotopia* 331.4
    Farrow, Ronan. ★*Catch and Kill* 331.4
    Thomas, Gillian. *Because of Sex* 344.7301
    Wasserman, Claire. *Ladies Get Paid* 650.1
SEX DISCRIMINATION IN SPORTS
    Allred, Alexandra Powe. *When Women Stood* 796.082
    Barnes, Katie. ★*Fair Play* 796.082
    Fleshman, Lauren. ★*Good for a Girl* B
    Rapinoe, Megan. *One Life* B
SEX EDUCATION FOR ADULTS
    Kerner, Ian. *She Comes First* 613.9
    Vernacchio, Al. *For Goodness Sex* 613.9071
SEX EDUCATION FOR CHILDREN
    Orenstein, Peggy. ★*Boys & Sex* 305.235
SEX EDUCATION FOR TEENAGERS
    Smiler, Andrew P. *Dating and Sex* 613.9071
SEX IN MASS MEDIA
    Blay, Zeba. *Carefree Black Girls* 305.48
SEX INDUSTRY AND TRADE
    Burke, Kelsy. *The Pornography Wars* 306.77
    Feast, Fancy. *Naked* 792.7
SEX LAWS
    Stone, Geoffrey R. ★*Sex and the Constitution* 345.7302
    Thomas, Gillian. *Because of Sex* 344.7301
Sex Matters. McGregor, Alyson J. 613
SEX SCANDALS
    Mazzeo, Tilar J. ★*Eliza Hamilton* B
SEX SYMBOLISM
    Selleck, Tom. *You Never Know* B
Sex, Love, and Letters. Coffin, Judith G. 848
SEXISM
    Ackmann, Martha. *The Mercury 13* 920

AUTHOR, TITLE, SERIES AND SUBJECT INDEX

Angyal, Chloe. *Turning Pointe*	792.8
Austerlitz, Saul. *Kind of a Big Deal*	791.43
Ayers, Edward L. *American Visions*	973.5
Bates, Laura. *Men Who Hate Women*	305.3
Beard, Mary. ★*Women & Power*	305.409
Berry, Daina Ramey. ★*A Black Women's History of the United States*	305.48
Block, Jennifer. *Everything Below the Waist*	613
Bossiere, Zoe. *Cactus Country*	306
Bravo, Reah. ★*Complicit*	331.4
Brooks, Geraldine. *Nine Parts of Desire*	305.48
Brown, Nancy Marie. *The Real Valkyrie*	948
Chang, Emily. *Brotopia*	331.4
Chemaly, Soraya L. *Rage Becomes Her*	155.3
Colwell, Rita R. *A Lab of One's Own*	B
Couric, Katie. *Going There*	B
D'Antonio, Michael. *The Hunting of Hillary*	B
Ditum, Sarah. *Toxic*	920.72
Dubin, Minna. ★*Mom Rage*	306.874
Feldman, Deborah. *Unorthodox*	B
Flannery, Kate. *Strip Tees*	338.4
Friedan, Betty. ★*The Feminine Mystique*	305.42
Gidla, Sujatha. *Ants Among Elephants*	305.5
Gillard, Julia. ★*Women and Leadership*	158
Glenconner, Anne. ★*Lady in Waiting*	B
Grush, Loren. ★*The Six*	629.4
Gupta, Prachi. ★*They Called Us Exceptional*	B
Hamad, Ruby. *White Tears/Brown Scars*	305.8
Hartley, Gemma. *Fed Up*	155.3
Hay, Carol. *Think Like a Feminist*	305.42
Holt, Nathalia. *The Queens of Animation*	920
Huang, Yunte. *Daughter of the Dragon*	B
Iandoli, Kathy. *God Save the Queens*	782.421649
James, Victoria. *Wine Girl*	B
Johnson, Katherine G. *My Remarkable Journey*	B
Kleiman, Kathy. *Proving Ground*	4.092
Krakauer, Jon. *Missoula*	362.883
LaFollette, Marcel C. *Writing for Their Lives*	071.3
Lalami, Laila. *Conditional Citizens*	323.60973
Landdeck, Katherine Sharp. *The Women with Silver Wings*	920
Lorde, Audre. *Sister Outsider*	814
Lynn, Loretta. ★*Me & Patsy Kickin' up Dust*	B
Mangino, Kate. ★*Equal Partners*	305.3
Marcal, Katrine. *Mother of Invention*	604.82
Mifflin, Margot. *Looking for Miss America*	791.6
Miller, Adrienne. *In the Land of Men*	070.5
Miller, Kei. *Things I Have Withheld*	814
Miller, T. Christian. *A False Report*	364.15
Muhammad, Ibtihaj. *Proud*	B
Napoli, Lisa. *Susan, Linda, Nina & Cokie*	920
O'Meara, Mallory. *Girly Drinks*	641.2
O'Meara, Mallory. *The Lady from the Black Lagoon*	921
Oluo, Ijeoma. *Mediocre*	305.310973
Peters, Rebecca Todd. *Trust Women*	362.1988
Price, Margo. *Maybe We'll Make It*	B
Quinn, Zoe. *Crash Override*	794.8
Rahmani, Niloofar. *Open Skies*	B
Raphael, Rina. *The Gospel of Wellness*	613
Rapinoe, Megan. *One Life*	B
Rodgers, Mary. *Shy*	B
Scovell, Nell. *Just the Funny Parts*	B
Shange, Ntozake. ★*Sing a Black Girl's Song*	818
Sherr, Lynn. *Sally Ride*	B
Simard, S. ★*Finding the Mother Tree*	582.16
Smarsh, Sarah. *She Come by It Natural*	782.42164
Strings, Sabrina. *The End of Love*	155.3
Thomas, Evan. ★*First*	B
Traister, Rebecca. *Good and Mad*	305.420973
Tran, Ly. *House of Sticks*	B
Union, Gabrielle. *We're Going to Need More Wine*	B
V. ★*Reckoning*	814
Vogelstein, Rachel B. *Awakening*	305.42
Walder, Tracy. *The Unexpected Spy*	B
West, Lindy. *The Witches Are Coming*	305.420973
Wills, Garry. *The Future of the Catholic Church with Pope Francis*	282.09
Wilson, A'ja. ★*Dear Black Girls*	158.1
Winder, Elizabeth. *Parachute Women*	782.42164
Zack, Ian. *Odetta*	B
Zernike, Kate. *The Exceptions*	331.4

SEXISM IN BUSINESS
Marcal, Katrine. *Mother of Invention*	604.82

SEXISM IN EDUCATION
Perkins, Anne Gardiner. *Yale Needs Women*	378
Zernike, Kate. *The Exceptions*	331.4

SEXISM IN EMPLOYMENT
Beaton, Kate. ★*Ducks*	741.5
Chang, Emily. *Brotopia*	331.4
Colwell, Rita R. *A Lab of One's Own*	B
Cox, Gena. *Leading Inclusion*	658.3
Fuller, Pamela. ★*The Leader's Guide to Unconscious Bias*	658.3
Green, Robin. *The Only Girl*	070.92
Miller, Adrienne. *In the Land of Men*	070.5
Monroe, Jana. *Hearts of Darkness*	363.25
O'Meara, Mallory. *The Lady from the Black Lagoon*	921
Thomas, Gillian. *Because of Sex*	344.7301
Vanek Smith, Stacey. *Machiavelli for Women*	650.1
Worley, Jennifer. *Neon Girls*	792.7

SEXISM IN MEDICINE
Brownstein, Gabriel. ★*The Secret Mind of Bertha Pappenheim*	616.85
Campbell, Olivia. *Women in White Coats*	610.92
Cleghorn, Elinor. *Unwell Women*	613
DiGregorio, Sarah. ★*Taking Care*	610.73
Gunter, Jen. ★*Blood*	612.6
Gupta, Shalene. *The Cycle*	618.1
McGregor, Alyson J. *Sex Matters*	613
Nerenberg, Jenara. *Divergent Mind*	616.89
Nimura, Janice P. ★*The Doctors Blackwell*	610.92
Norman, Abby. *Ask Me About My Uterus*	618.1
Parker, Lara. *Vagina Problems*	618.1
Pratt, Misty. *All in Her Head*	616.89
Ramey, Sarah. *The Lady's Handbook for Her Mysterious Illness*	B
Ryckman, Pamela. *Candace Pert*	B
Tang, Karen. ★*It's Not Hysteria*	618.2

SEXISM IN POLITICS AND GOVERNMENT
D'Antonio, Michael. *The Hunting of Hillary*	B

SEXISM IN SCIENCE
Ackmann, Martha. *The Mercury 13*	920
Cooke, Lucy. *Bitch*	591.56
Marcal, Katrine. *Mother of Invention*	604.82
McNeur, Catherine. *Mischievous Creatures*	920
Prescod-Weinstein, Chanda. *The Disordered Cosmos*	523.01
Saini, Angela. *Inferior*	305.4
Zernike, Kate. *The Exceptions*	331.4

SEXISM IN SPORTS
King, Billie Jean. ★*All In*	B
Montillo, Roseanne. *Fire on the Track*	B

SEXISM IN THE MILITARY
Hegar, Mary Jennings. *Shoot Like a Girl*	B

SEXISM IN UNIVERSITIES AND COLLEGES
Freitas, Donna. *Consent*	364.158092
Grigoriadis, Vanessa. *Blurred Lines*	371.7
Krakauer, Jon. *Missoula*	362.883
Penaluna, Regan. ★*How to Think Like a Woman*	190.82
Perkins, Anne Gardiner. *Yale Needs Women*	378

Sexton, Anne
Selected Poems of Anne Sexton	811

SEXTON, ANNE, 1928-1974
Crowther, Gail. *Three-Martini Afternoons at the Ritz*	920

Sexton, Jared Yates
American Rule	973

Sexual Citizens. Hirsch, Jennifer S. | 371.7

SEXUAL CONSENT
Freitas, Donna. *Consent*	364.158092

SEXUAL ETHICS
Blair, Gabrielle Stanley. ★*Ejaculate Responsibly*	362.1988
Srinivasan, Amia. *The Right to Sex*	305.42
Vernacchio, Al. *For Goodness Sex*	613.9071

SEXUAL EXCITEMENT
Roach, Mary. *Bonk*	612.6

SEXUAL FREEDOM
Bolz-Weber, Nadia. *Shameless*	261.8
Wayland-Smith, Ellen. *Oneida*	307.77
Winter, Molly Roden. *More*	B

SEXUAL HARASSMENT
Beaton, Kate. ★*Ducks*	741.5
Bravo, Reah. ★*Complicit*	331.4
Brodsky, Alexandra. *Sexual Justice*	364.15

PUBLIC LIBRARY CORE COLLECTION: NONFICTION
Twentieth Edition

Colwell, Rita R. *A Lab of One's Own*	B
Farrow, Ronan. ★*Catch and Kill*	331.4
Flannery, Kate. *Strip Tees*	338.4
Freitas, Donna. *Consent*	364.158092
Goldberg, Carrie. *Nobody's Victim*	345.73
Hewlett, Sylvia Ann. *#metoo in the Corporate World*	658.3
Kantor, Jodi. *She Said*	364.15
Longworth, Karina. *Seduction*	B
McGowan, Rose. *Brave*	B
McShane Wulfhart, Nell. *The Great Stewardess Rebellion*	331.4
Yeung, Bernice. *In a Day's Work*	362.88086

SEXUAL HARASSMENT IN THE MILITARY
Hegar, Mary Jennings. *Shoot Like a Girl*	B

SEXUAL HARASSMENT IN UNIVERSITIES AND COLLEGES
Krouse, Erika. ★*Tell Me Everything*	363.25

SEXUAL HARASSMENT OF WOMEN
Auletta, Ken. ★*Hollywood Ending*	791.43
Burke, Tarana. ★*Unbound*	B
Farrow, Ronan. ★*Catch and Kill*	331.4
Hill, Anita. ★*Believing*	305.42
Hirshman, Linda R. *Reckoning*	305.420973
Kantor, Jodi. *She Said*	364.15
Olsen, Lise. *Code of Silence*	347.73
Vanasco, Jeannie. *Things We Didn't Talk About When I Was a Girl*	B

SEXUAL HEALTH
Brighten, Jolene. *Is This Normal?*	618.1
Gunter, Jen. *The Vagina Bible*	612.6
Mendelson, Zoe. *Pussypedia*	612.6
Tang, Karen. ★*It's Not Hysteria*	618.2
Walters, Jacqueline. *The Queen V*	612.6
Sexual Justice. Brodsky, Alexandra	364.15

SEXUAL ORIENTATION
Gottlieb, Iris. *Seeing Gender*	305.3
Kushner, Tony. *Angels in America*	812
Shaw, Julia. *Bi*	306.76

SEXUAL SLAVERY
Berman, Sarah. *Don't Call It a Cult*	361.4
Mikhaiil, Dunya. *The Beekeeper*	956.7044
Murad, Nadia. ★*The Last Girl*	B
Tjipombo, Tupa. *I Am Not Your Slave*	B

SEXUAL VIOLENCE
Abdulali, Sohaila. *What We Talk About When We Talk About Rape*	364.15
Bowdler, Michelle. ★*Is Rape a Crime?*	B
Brown, Emma. *To Raise a Boy*	649
Hay, Carol. *Think Like a Feminist*	305.42
Hill, Anita. ★*Believing*	305.42
Hirsch, Jennifer S. *Sexual Citizens*	371.7
Johnson, Akemi. *Night in the American Village*	305.40952
Lamb, Christina. *Our Bodies, Their Battlefields*	341.6
Mans, Jasmine. *Black Girl, Call Home*	811
Rekdal, Paisley. *Nightingale*	811
Rose, Jacqueline. *On Violence and on Violence Against Women*	362.88
Schwartzman, Nancy. *Roll Red Roll*	364.15
Srinivasan, Amia. *The Right to Sex*	305.42
Tanais. *In Sensorium*	B
Tjipombo, Tupa. *I Am Not Your Slave*	B
Tran, Paul. *All the Flowers Kneeling*	811
Tuerkheimer, Deborah. *Credible*	363.25
V. ★*Reckoning*	814
Vanasco, Jeannie. *Things We Didn't Talk About When I Was a Girl*	B
Wu, Constance. *Making a Scene*	B

SEXUAL VIOLENCE VICTIMS
Barr, John. *Start by Believing*	364.15
Brodsky, Alexandra. *Sexual Justice*	364.15
Burke, Tarana. ★*Unbound*	B
Coel, Michaela. ★*Misfits*	158.2
Diaz, Jaquira. *Ordinary Girls*	818
Faleiro, Sonia. *The Good Girls*	364.152
Farrow, Ronan. ★*Catch and Kill*	331.4
Ford, Christine Blasey. *One Way Back*	B
Harry, Debbie. *Face It*	B
Herman, Judith Lewis. *Truth and Repair*	362.883
Hewlett, Sylvia Ann. *#metoo in the Corporate World*	658.3
Hill, Anita. ★*Believing*	305.42
Miller, Chanel. *Know My Name*	B
Olsen, Lise. *Code of Silence*	347.73
Page, Elliot. *Pageboy*	B
Rhodes, James. *Instrumental*	B
Tuerkheimer, Deborah. *Credible*	363.25
Yeung, Bernice. *In a Day's Work*	362.88086

SEXUALITY
Ali, Fatima. ★*Savor*	B
Baer, Kate. *What Kind of Woman*	811
Beauvoir, Simone de. ★*The Second Sex*	305.4
Belcher, Chris. *Pretty Baby*	B
Blair, Gabrielle Stanley. ★*Ejaculate Responsibly*	362.1988
Block, Jennifer. *Everything Below the Waist*	613
Bolz-Weber, Nadia. *Shameless*	261.8
Briggs, Lyvonne. ★*Sensual Faith*	204
Brighten, Jolene. *Is This Normal?*	618.1
Brown, Emma. *To Raise a Boy*	649
Brown, Jericho. ★*The Tradition*	811
Butler, Judith. ★*Who's Afraid of Gender?*	305.3
Byas, Taylor. *I Done Clicked My Heels Three Times*	811
Cole, Samantha. *How the Internet Changed Sex and Sex Changed the Internet*	306.7
Davis, Lisa Selin. *Tomboy*	305.409
Diaz, Natalie. ★*Postcolonial Love Poem*	811
Duncan, Isadora. *My Life*	B
Ellmann, Richard. *Oscar Wilde*	B
Evaristo, Bernardine. *Manifesto*	B
Eyman, Scott. *Charlie Chaplin vs. America*	B
Faliveno, Melissa. *Tomboyland*	B
Feast, Fancy. *Naked*	792.7
Febos, Melissa. *Girlhood*	818
Fraser, Antonia. *Love and Louis XIV*	B
Gay, Roxane. ★*Opinions*	814
Gill, Anton. *Art Lover*	B
Gomez, Edgar. *High-Risk Homosexual*	B
Gunn, Thom. ★*The Letters of Thom Gunn*	821
Hall, Jake. *The Art of Drag*	792.8
Highsmith, Patricia. ★*Patricia Highsmith's Diaries and Notebooks*	818
Hirsch, Jennifer S. *Sexual Citizens*	371.7
Howard, Johnette. *The Rivals*	B
Hughes, Bettany. *Venus and Aphrodite*	292
Iandoli, Kathy. *God Save the Queens*	782.421649
Imbler, Sabrina. *How Far the Light Reaches*	591.77
King, Billie Jean. ★*All In*	B
Laing, Olivia. *Everybody*	323
Lehrer, Riva. *Golem Girl*	B
Mann, William J. *Kate*	B
Milford, Nancy. *Savage Beauty*	B
Moran, Caitlin. *More Than a Woman*	B
Olds, Sharon. *Odes*	811
Orenstein, Peggy. ★*Boys & Sex*	305.235
Orenstein, Peggy. *Don't Call Me Princess*	305.42
Perkins, Nichole. *Sometimes I Trip on How Happy We Could Be*	B
Powers, Ann. *Good Booty*	781.64
Roach, Mary. *Bonk*	612.6
Satrapi, Marjane. *Embroideries*	741.5
Shaw, Julia. *Bi*	306.76
Slice, Jessica. *Dateable*	646.7
Smiler, Andrew P. *Dating and Sex*	613.9071
Sohn, Amy. *The Man Who Hated Women*	363.28
Srinivasan, Amia. *The Right to Sex*	305.42
Stille, Alexander. *The Sullivanians*	307.77
Stone, Geoffrey R. ★*Sex and the Constitution*	345.7302
Suvari, Mena. *The Great Peace*	B
Taddeo, Lisa. *Three Women*	306.7082
Tinsley, Omise'eke Natasha. *Beyonce in Formation*	782.42164
Vasquez-Lavado, Silvia. *In the Shadow of the Mountain*	B
Wilson, A. N. *The Mystery of Charles Dickens*	823
Winter, Molly Roden. *More*	B
Wizenberg, Molly. *Fixed Stars*	B

SEXUALITY AND POWER (SOCIAL SCIENCES)
Longworth, Karina. *Seduction*	B
Srinivasan, Amia. *The Right to Sex*	305.42

SEXUALLY ABUSED CHILDREN
DeRogatis, Jim. *Soulless*	B
Jones, Faith. *Sex Cult Nun*	B
Mills, Stephen Tukel. *Chosen*	B
V. *The Apology*	818

SEXUALLY ABUSED TEENAGERS
DeRogatis, Jim. *Soulless*	B
Seymour Hersh. Miraldi, Robert	B
Sgt. Reckless. Hutton, Robin L.	951.904

AUTHOR, TITLE, SERIES AND SUBJECT INDEX

The Sh!t No One Tells You About Divorce. Dais, Dawn	306.89
★*Shabbat*. Sussman, Adeena	641.5
Shachtman, Tom	
★*Rumspringa*	305.235
Shackelford, George T. M.	
Monet	759.4
Shackle, Samira	
Karachi Vice	954.91
Shackleton. Fiennes, Ranulph	B
SHACKLETON, ERNEST HENRY, SIR, 1874-1922	
Alexander, Caroline. *The Endurance*	919.8
Bound, Mensun. *The Ship Beneath the Ice*	919.8904
Fiennes, Ranulph. *Shackleton*	B
Grann, David. *The White Darkness*	B
Larson, Edward J. *An Empire of Ice*	919.8
Shade. Souza, Pete	973.932
Shadid, Anthony	
House of Stone	306.0956
Shadow. Woodward, Bob	973.92
The Shadow Docket. Vladeck, Stephen I.	347.73
The Shadow of Sirius. Merwin, W. S.	811
Shadow of the Silk Road. Thubron, Colin	915
SHADOW THEATERS	
Blumenthal, Eileen. *Puppetry*	791.5
Shadowlands. Green, Matthew	941.03
Shadowman. Franscell, Ron	362.88
Shady Characters. Houston, Keith	411
Shaffer, Peter	
★*Equus*	822
Peter Shaffer's Amadeus	822
Shafrir, Doree	
Thanks for Waiting	B
SHAFRIR, DOREE	
Shafrir, Doree. *Thanks for Waiting*	B
SHAH SHUJA, AMIR OF AFGHANISTAN, 1780?-1842	
Dalrymple, William. *The Return of a King*	958.1
Shah, Meera	
You're the Only One I've Told	362.1988
SHAH, MEERA	
Shah, Meera. *You're the Only One I've Told*	362.1988
Shah, Rajiv Janardan	
Big Bets	303.4
Shahani, Aarti Namdev	
Here We Are	B
SHAHANI, AARTI NAMDEV	
Shahani, Aarti Namdev. *Here We Are*	B
Shahidi, Afshin	
Prince	B
Shahnameh. Firdawsi	891
Shahvisi, Arianne	
Arguing for a Better World	170
The Shaker Experience in America. Stein, Stephen J.	289
Shakespeare. Bloom, Harold	822.33
Shakespeare. Bryson, Bill	B
Shakespeare. Dench, Judi	792
Shakespeare in a Divided America. Shapiro, James	822.33
Shakespeare The Thinker. Nuttall, A. D.	822.33
Shakespeare Was a Woman & Other Heresies. Winkler, Elizabeth	822.33
Shakespeare's Kings. Norwich, John Julius	822.33
Shakespeare, Nicholas	
Ian Fleming	B
Shakespeare, William	
★*The Complete Works*	822.33
SHAKESPEARE, WILLIAM, 1564-1616	
Bloom, Harold. *Lear*	822.33
Bloom, Harold. *Shakespeare*	822.33
Bryson, Bill. *Shakespeare*	B
Collins, Paul. *The Book of William*	016.8223
Dench, Judi. *Shakespeare*	792
Dromgoole, Dominic. *Hamlet Globe to Globe*	792.9
Greenblatt, Stephen. ★*Will in the World*	B
Hatchard, Gurinder Kaur. *Hooked on Shakespeare*	746.43
Karim-Cooper, Farah. ★*The Great White Bard*	822.33
Norwich, John Julius. *Shakespeare's Kings*	822.33
Nuttall, A. D. *Shakespeare the Thinker*	822.33
Shapiro, James. *Contested Will*	822.33
Shapiro, James. *Shakespeare in a Divided America*	822.33
Shapiro, James. *The Year of Lear*	822.33
Smith, Emma. *This Is Shakespeare*	822.33
Winkler, Elizabeth. *Shakespeare Was a Woman & Other Heresies*	822.33
Shaking The Gates of Hell. Archibald, John	B
SHAKUR FAMILY	
Holley, Santi Elijah. *An Amerikan Family*	920
SHAKUR, AFENI	
Holley, Santi Elijah. *An Amerikan Family*	920
SHAKUR, LUMUMBA ABDUL, 1943-1985	
Holley, Santi Elijah. *An Amerikan Family*	920
Shakur, Prince	
When They Tell You to Be Good	B
SHAKUR, TUPAC, 1971-1996	
Dyson, Michael Eric. *Holler If You Hear Me*	B
Holley, Santi Elijah. *An Amerikan Family*	920
Robinson, Staci. ★*Tupac Shakur*	B
Westhoff, Ben. *Original Gangstas*	782.421649
SHAKYA, LALLI	
Faleiro, Sonia. *The Good Girls*	364.152
SHAKYA, PADMA	
Faleiro, Sonia. *The Good Girls*	364.152
Shales, Tom	
Live from New York	791.45
The Shambhala Guide to Sufism. Ernst, Carl W.	297.4
SHAME	
Bolz-Weber, Nadia. *Shameless*	261.8
Breggin, Peter Roger. *Guilt, Shame, and Anxiety*	152.4
Cercas, Javier. *Lord of All the Dead*	868
Coombes, Joshua. *Do Something for Nothing*	362.5
Crawford, Lacy. *Notes on a Silencing*	B
Dubin, Minna. ★*Mom Rage*	306.874
Freeman, Hadley. *Good Girls*	616.85
Hardin, Lara Love. ★*The Many Lives of Mama Love*	B
Harrington, Joel F. *The Faithful Executioner*	B
Knight, Keltie. *Lady Secrets*	305.4
Kouchner, Camille. *The Familia Grande*	B
O'Neil, Cathy. *The Shame Machine*	152.4
Ronson, Jon. *So You've Been Publicly Shamed*	152.4
The Shame Machine. O'Neil, Cathy	152.4
A Shameful Act. Akcam, Taner	956.6
Shameless. Bolz-Weber, Nadia	261.8
Shanahan, Charif	
Trace Evidence	811
Shane, Scott	
★*Flee North*	973.7
Shange, Ntozake	
★*Sing a Black Girl's Song*	818
SHANGE, NTOZAKE	
Shange, Ntozake. ★*Sing a Black Girl's Song*	818
SHANGHAI, CHINA	
Chu, Lenora. *Little Soldiers*	370
Kaufman, Jonathan. *The Last Kings of Shanghai*	951
Schmitz, Rob. *Street of Eternal Happiness*	951
Zia, Helen. *Last Boat Out of Shanghai*	951.04
Shankar, Shalini	
Beeline	155.4
Shankle, Melanie	
Church of the Small Things	248.8
SHANKLE, MELANIE	
Shankle, Melanie. *Church of the Small Things*	248.8
Shanley, John Patrick	
Doubt	812
SHANNON, CLAUDE ELWOOD, 1916-2001	
Soni, Jimmy. *A Mind at Play*	B
Shannon, Elaine	
Hunting Leroux	364.1
Shannon, Molly	
★*Hello, Molly!*	B
SHANNON, MOLLY, 1964-	
Shannon, Molly. ★*Hello, Molly!*	B
The Shapeless Unease. Harvey, Samantha	B
SHAPES	
Nico, Brooke. *More Lovely Knitted Lace*	746.43
SHAPIRA, MOZES VILHELM, 1830?-1884	
Tigay, Chanan. *The Lost Book of Moses*	098
Shapiro, Ari	
★*The Best Strangers in the World*	B
SHAPIRO, ARI, 1978-	
Shapiro, Ari. ★*The Best Strangers in the World*	B

Shapiro, Dani
  ★*Inheritance* — B
SHAPIRO, DANI
  Shapiro, Dani. ★*Inheritance* — B
Shapiro, James
  Contested Will — 822.33
  ★*The Playbook* — 792
  Shakespeare in a Divided America — 822.33
  The Year of Lear — 822.33
Shapiro, Karl
  Selected Poems — 811
Shapiro, Scott J.
  ★*Fancy Bear Goes Phishing* — 364.16
Shapiro, Susan
  The Forgiveness Tour — 158.2
SHAPIRO, SUSAN
  Shapiro, Susan. *The Forgiveness Tour* — 158.2
Shapland, Jenn
  My Autobiography of Carson McCullers — B
  ★*Thin Skin* — 814
SHAPLAND, JENN, 1987-
  Shapland, Jenn. *My Autobiography of Carson McCullers* — B
  Shapland, Jenn. ★*Thin Skin* — 814
Sharapova, Maria
  Unstoppable — B
SHARAPOVA, MARIA, 1987-
  Sharapova, Maria. *Unstoppable* — B
SHARECROPPERS
  Agee, James. ★*Cotton Tenants* — 976.1
SHARECROPPING
  Agee, James. ★*Cotton Tenants* — 976.1
Sharfstein, Daniel J.
  ★*Thunder in the Mountains* — 979.5
SHARIA (ISLAMIC RELIGIOUS PRACTICE)
  Ali-Karamali, Sumbul. *Demystifying Shariah* — 340.5
  Navai, Ramita. *City of Lies* — 955
Sharif, Solmaz
  Customs — 811
  Look — 811
SHARING
  Carter, Jimmy. *Sharing Good Times* — 973.926
  Knight, Keltie. *Lady Secrets* — 305.4
  Vasquez, Karla Tatiana. ★*The Salvisoul Cookbook* — 641.598
Sharing Good Times. Carter, Jimmy — 973.926
SHARK ATTACKS
  Skomal, Gregory. *Chasing Shadows* — 597.3
Shark Drunk. Strøksnes, Morten Andreas — 338.3
SHARKS
  Graham, Jasmin. *Sharks Don't Sink* — 597.3
Sharks Don't Sink. Graham, Jasmin — 597.3
Sharlet, Jeff
  ★*The Undertow* — 322
Sharma, Nik
  Veg-Table — 641.6
Sharma, Nina
  The Way You Make Me Feel — B
Sharma, Ruchir
  The Rise and Fall of Nations — 330.9
Sharot, Tali
  Look Again — 158.1
Sharpe, Christina Elizabeth
  Ordinary Notes — 305.896
SHARPE, GEORGE H. (GEORGE HENRY), 1828-1900
  Waller, Douglas C. *Lincoln's Spies* — 973.7
Sharpton, Al
  Rise Up — 973.933
SHARPTON, AL
  Sharpton, Al. *Rise Up* — 973.933
Shatner, William
  Boldly Go — B
  Live Long And— — B
SHATNER, WILLIAM
  Shatner, William. *Boldly Go* — B
  Shatner, William. *Live Long And—* — B
Shattered. Allen, Jonathan — 324.973
The Shattering. Boyle, Kevin — 973.923
Shattuck, Ben
  Six Walks — B

SHATTUCK, BEN, 1984-
  Shattuck, Ben. *Six Walks* — B
Shattuck, Roger
  Proust's Way — 843
Shatz, Adam
  The Rebel's Clinic — 965
Shaughnessy, Brenda
  The Octopus Museum — 811
Shaughnessy, Jim
  The Call of Trains — 779
Shavit, Ari
  My Promised Land — 956.05
Shaw, Bernard
  Heartbreak House — 822
  Major Barbara — 822
  Man and Superman — 822
  ★*Pygmalion* — 822
  Saint Joan — 822
Shaw, Ian
  The Princeton Dictionary of Ancient Egypt — 932
Shaw, Jennifer Laurie
  Exist Otherwise — 709.2
Shaw, Julia
  Bi — 306.76
Shaw, Robert
  American Quilts — 746.46
Shawcross, William
  The Queen Mother — B
SHAWLS
  Noldeke, Marisa. *50 Knitted Wraps and Shawls* — 746.43
SHAWNEE (NORTH AMERICAN PEOPLE)
  Cozzens, Peter. *Tecumseh and the Prophet* — 920
  Eckert, Allan W. *A Sorrow in Our Heart* — B
★*She Came to Slay*. Dunbar, Erica Armstrong — B
She Come by It Natural. Smarsh, Sarah — 782.42164
She Comes First. Kerner, Ian — 613.9
She Has Her Mother's Laugh. Zimmer, Carl — 576.5
She Memes Well. Brunson, Quinta — B
She Proclaims. Palmieri, Jennifer — 305.42
She Said. Kantor, Jodi — 364.15
She Sheds. Kotite, Erika — 728
She Votes. Quinn, Bridget — 324.6
She Wants It. Soloway, Jill — B
She Will Rise. Hill, Katie — 305.42
She-Wolves. Castor, Helen — 942
Shearer, Clea
  ★*The Home Edit Life* — 648
Shearer, Stephen Michael
  Beautiful — B
SHEDS
  Kotite, Erika. *She Sheds* — 728
SHEEAN, VINCENT, 1899-1975
  Cohen, Deborah. *Last Call at the Hotel Imperial* — 070.92
Sheehan, Jason
  Cooking Dirty — B
SHEEHAN, JASON
  Sheehan, Jason. *Cooking Dirty* — B
Sheehan, Jessie
  ★*Snackable Bakes* — 641.7
Sheehan, Neil
  A Bright Shining Lie — 959.704
  A Fiery Peace in a Cold War — B
Sheehy, Suzie
  The Matter of Everything — 539.7
SHEEP
  Connell, John. *The Farmer's Son* — 630.9
SHEEP RANCHES
  Stewart, Chris. *Driving Over Lemons* — 946
Sheet Cake. Dodge, Abigail Johnson — 641.86
Sheff, David
  The Buddhist on Death Row — B
SHEHADEH, AZIZ
  Shehadeh, Raja. ★*We Could Have Been Friends, My Father and I* — B
Shehadeh, Raja
  ★*We Could Have Been Friends, My Father and I* — B
  Where the Line Is Drawn — 956.9405
SHEHADEH, RAJA, 1951-
  Shehadeh, Raja. ★*We Could Have Been Friends, My Father and I* — B

AUTHOR, TITLE, SERIES AND SUBJECT INDEX

Shehadeh, Raja. *Where the Line Is Drawn*	956.9405
Sheinkin, Steve	
Bomb	623.4
SHELBY, CARROLL, 1923-2012	
Baime, A. J. ★*Go Like Hell*	796.7209
Shelden, Michael	
Mark Twain	B
Sheldrake, Merlin	
Entangled Life	579.5
Sheldrake, Rupert	
Science and Spiritual Practices	201
Shelf Life. Wassef, Nadia	B
Shelley. Shelley, Percy Bysshe	821
Shelley's Poetry and Prose. Shelley, Percy Bysshe	821
SHELLEY, MARY WOLLSTONECRAFT, 1797-1851	
Gordon, Charlotte. *Romantic Outlaws*	920
Montillo, Roseanne. *The Lady and Her Monsters*	823
Sampson, Fiona. *In Search of Mary Shelley*	B
Shelley, Percy Bysshe	
Shelley's Poetry and Prose	821
Shelley	821
SHELLEY, PERCY BYSSHE, 1792-1822	
Shelley, Percy Bysshe. *Shelley's Poetry and Prose*	821
SHELLFISH	
Barnett, Cynthia. ★*The Sound of the Sea*	591.47
Smith, Bren. *Eat Like a Fish*	338.3
SHELLS	
Barnett, Cynthia. ★*The Sound of the Sea*	591.47
Rehder, Harald Alfred. *The Audubon Society Field Guide to North American Seashells*	594
SHELTERS FOR THE HOMELESS	
Elliott, Andrea. ★*Invisible Child*	362.7
Sokolik, Vicki. ★*If You See Them*	362.5
Stewart, Nikita. *Troop 6000*	369
SHELTON, KARLYA	
Valby, Karen. *The Swans of Harlem*	792.8
Shelton, Ron	
The Church of Baseball	791.43
SHELTON, RON, 1945-	
Shelton, Ron. *The Church of Baseball*	791.43
Shepard, Jim	
The Tunnel at the End of the Light	791.43
SHEPARD, MATTHEW, 1976-1998	
Jimenez, Stephen. *The Book of Matt*	364.152
SHEPARD, SAM, 1943-2017	
Greenfield, Robert. *True West*	B
The Shepherd's Life. Rebanks, James	942.7
Shepherd, Chris	
Cook Like a Local	641.59
Shepherd, Margaret	
Learn Calligraphy	745.6
SHEPHERDS	
Bell, Laura. *Claiming Ground*	B
Rebanks, James. *The Shepherd's Life*	942.7
Sheridan's Secret Mission. Cwiklik, Robert	973.8
SHERIDAN, PHILIP HENRY, 1831-1888	
Cwiklik, Robert. *Sheridan's Secret Mission*	973.8
Wheelan, Joseph. ★*Terrible Swift Sword*	B
Sheridan, Richard Brinsley	
The School for Scandal and Other Plays	822
SHERIFFS	
Hale, Grace Elizabeth. *In the Pines*	364.13
Patterson, James. *Walk the Blue Line*	920
Sherman's March. Davis, Burke	973.7
SHERMAN'S MARCH THROUGH THE CAROLINAS	
Davis, Burke. *Sherman's March*	973.7
SHERMAN'S MARCH TO THE SEA	
Davis, Burke. *Sherman's March*	973.7
Sherman, Anna	
The Bells of Old Tokyo	952
SHERMAN, ANNA (ANNE KATHERINE), 1970-	
Sherman, Anna. *The Bells of Old Tokyo*	952
Sherman, Casey	
Above and Beyond	973.922092
Hunting Whitey	B
Sherman, Sean	
★*The Sioux Chef's Indigenous Kitchen*	641.59
SHERMAN, WILLIAM TECUMSEH, 1820-1891	
Brands, H. W. *The Last Campaign*	973.8
Davis, Burke. *Sherman's March*	973.7
Hanson, Victor Davis. *The Soul of Battle*	355
McDonough, James L. *William Tecumseh Sherman*	B
Shermer, Michael	
The Believing Brain	153.4
Why People Believe Weird Things	133
SHERPA (NEPALESE PEOPLE)	
Zuckerman, Peter. ★*Buried in the Sky*	796.522
Sherr, Lynn	
Sally Ride	B
Sherwin, Martin J.	
Gambling with Armageddon	972.9106
Shesol, Jeff	
Mercury Rising	629.45
Supreme Power	347.73
Shetterly, Margot Lee	
★*Hidden Figures*	510.92
The Shia Revival. Nasr, Seyyed Vali Reza	297.8
SHIAH ISLAM	
Blanford, Nicholas. *Warriors of God*	956.9204
Hazleton, Lesley. *After the Prophet*	297.8
Husain, Ed. ★*The House of Islam*	297
Shida, Hitomi	
Japanese Knitting Stitch Bible	746.43
★*Shielded*. Schwartz, Joanna C.	344.7305
Shields, Aomawa L.	
Life on Other Planets	B
SHIELDS, AOMAWA L.	
Shields, Aomawa L. *Life on Other Planets*	B
Shields, Charles J.	
Lorraine Hansberry	B
Shields, Christopher John	
Aristotle	185
Shih, David	
Chinese Prodigal	B
SHIH, DAVID, 1970-	
Shih, David. *Chinese Prodigal*	B
SHIITES	
Ghattas, Kim. *Black Wave*	955.05
Nasr, Seyyed Vali Reza. *The Shia Revival*	297.8
Shiloh, 1862. Groom, Winston	973.7
SHILOH, BATTLE OF, 1862	
Groom, Winston. *Shiloh, 1862*	973.7
Shilts, Randy	
★*And the Band Played On*	362.196
Shimer, David	
Rigged	324.60973
Shimoda, Naoko	
Artfully Embroidered	746.44
Shine Bright. Smith, Danyel	782.42164
Shinto. Hardacre, Helen	299.5
SHINTO	
Hardacre, Helen. *Shinto*	299.5
The Ship Beneath the Ice. Bound, Mensun	919.8904
SHIP CAPTAINS	
Grann, David. ★*The Wager*	910.91
Lineberry, Cate. *Be Free or Die*	B
Raines, Ben. *The Last Slave Ship*	306.362
Sides, Hampton. ★*The Wide Wide Sea*	910.92
Taylor, Stephen. *Commander*	B
The Ship of Dreams. Russell, Gareth	910.91
SHIP PASSENGERS	
Russell, Gareth. *The Ship of Dreams*	910.91
Smith, Michael. *Cabin Fever*	614.5
SHIPBUILDERS	
Fabey, Michael. *Heavy Metal*	338.4
Ujifusa, Steven. *Barons of the Sea*	387.5
Shipnuck, Alan	
Phil	B
SHIPPING	
Larson, Erik. ★*Dead Wake*	940.4
Ujifusa, Steven. *Barons of the Sea*	387.5
SHIPPING INDUSTRY AND TRADE	
Montero, David. ★*The Stolen Wealth of Slavery*	381
Slade, Rachel. *Into the Raging Sea*	910.91
Ujifusa, Steven. *Barons of the Sea*	387.5

PUBLIC LIBRARY CORE COLLECTION: NONFICTION
Twentieth Edition

SHIPS
- Bound, Mensun. *The Ship Beneath the Ice* — 919.8904
- Graham, Ian. *Fifty Ships That Changed the Course of History* — 387.2
- Sancton, Julian. *Madhouse at the End of the Earth* — 919.8904
- Slade, Rachel. *Into the Raging Sea* — 910.91
- Smith, Michael. *Cabin Fever* — 614.5
- Ujifusa, Steven. *Barons of the Sea* — 387.5

*The **Shipwreck** Hunter*. Mearns, David L. — 910.452

SHIPWRECK VICTIMS
- Grann, David. ★*The Wager* — 910.91

SHIPWRECKS
- Ballard, Robert D. *Into the Deep* — 551.46092
- Bound, Mensun. *The Ship Beneath the Ice* — 919.8904
- Butler, Daniel Allen. *"Unsinkable"* — 910
- Fairbanks, Amanda M. *The Lost Boys of Montauk* — 910.91
- Franklin, Jonathan. *438 Days* — 910.91
- Gibbins, David J. L. *A History of the World in Twelve Shipwrecks* — 909
- Grann, David. ★*The Wager* — 910.91
- Junger, Sebastian. *The Perfect Storm* — 974.4
- Lance, Rachel. *In the Waves* — 973.7
- Larson, Erik. ★*Dead Wake* — 940.4
- Lord, Walter. ★*A Night to Remember* — 910
- Mearns, David L. *The Shipwreck Hunter* — 910.452
- Raines, Ben. *The Last Slave Ship* — 306.362
- Russell, Gareth. *The Ship of Dreams* — 910.91
- Sides, Hampton. ★*In the Kingdom of Ice* — 910.4
- Slade, Rachel. *Into the Raging Sea* — 910.91
- Stanton, Doug. *In Harm's Way* — 940.54
- Stone, Daniel. *Sinkable* — 910.91
- Sullivan, Randall. *Graveyard of the Pacific* — 979.7
- Vincent, Lynn. *Indianapolis* — 940.54
- Watson, Paul. *Ice Ghosts* — 917

SHIPYARD WORKERS
- Fabey, Michael. *Heavy Metal* — 338.4

Shirer, William L.
- ★*The Rise and Fall of the Third Reich* — 943.086

Shirley Jackson. Franklin, Ruth — B

Shirley, Craig
- *Mary Ball Washington* — B

Shlaes, Amity
- *Coolidge* — B
- *The Forgotten Man* — 973.91

Shlaim, Avi
- *The Iron Wall* — 956.04

Shlain, Tiffany
- *24/6* — 158.1

Shnayerson, Michael
- *Boom* — 701

Sho. Kearney, Douglas — 811

Shock and Awe. Reynolds, Simon — 781.6609

Shockley, Evie
- *The New Black* — 811
- *Semiautomatic* — 811
- *Suddenly We* — 811

Shoe Dog. Knight, Philip H. — B

SHOE INDUSTRY AND TRADE
- Au-Yeung, Angel. *Wonder Boy* — B
- Knight, Philip H. *Shoe Dog* — B

SHOES
- Knight, Philip H. *Shoe Dog* — B

Shone, Tom
- *The Nolan Variations* — 791.4302

Shoot an Iraqi. Bilal, Wafaa

★*Shoot for the Moon*. Donovan, Jim — 629.45

Shoot Like a Girl. Hegar, Mary Jennings — B

The Shooter At Midnight. Cooper, Sean Patrick — 363.25

Shooting Ghosts. Brennan, Thomas J. — B

Shooting Midnight Cowboy. Frankel, Glenn — 791.43

SHOPPING
- Barnes, Julian. *The Man in the Red Coat* — B
- Cline, Elizabeth L. *The Conscious Closet* — 646
- Del Rey, Jason. *Winner Sells All* — 381
- Fili, Louise. *The Cognoscenti's Guide to Florence* — 381

Shore, Linda
- *The Total Skywatcher's Manual* — 523

★*The Short and Tragic Life of Robert Peace*. Hobbs, Jeff

A Short History of Byzantium. Norwich, John Julius — 949.5

A Short History of Film. Dixon, Wheeler W. — 791.43

A Short History of Humanity. Krause, Johannes — 599.9

A Short History of Ireland, 1500-2000. Gibney, John — 941.7

★*A Short History of Myth*. Armstrong, Karen — 201

★*A Short History of Nearly Everything*. Bryson, Bill — 500

A Short History of Russia. Galeotti, Mark — 947.086

★*Short Nights of the Shadow Catcher*. Egan, Timothy — 770.92

SHORT STORIES
- Jackson, Shirley. *Let Me Tell You* — 818
- Saunders, George. ★*A Swim in a Pond in the Rain* — 891.7

Short Stories by Jesus. Levine, Amy-Jill — 226.8

SHORT STORY WRITING
- Gooch, Brad. ★*Flannery* — B
- Saunders, George. ★*A Swim in a Pond in the Rain* — 891.7

Short, Martin
- *I Must Say* — B

SHORT, MARTIN, 1950-
- Short, Martin. *I Must Say* — B

Short, Philip
- *Putin* — B

Shorter, Frank
- *My Marathon* — 796.42

SHORTER, FRANK, 1947-
- Shorter, Frank. *My Marathon* — 796.42

The Shortest History of Europe. Hirst, J. B — 940

Shortest Way Home. Buttigieg, Pete — B

Shorto, Russell
- *Amsterdam* — 949.2

SHORTSTOPS (BASEBALL PLAYERS)
- Eisenberg, John. *The Streak* — 796.357

SHOSTAKOVICH, DMITRII DMITRIEVICH, 1906-1975
- Moynahan, Brian. *Leningrad* — 780.92

Shot Down. Snyder, Steve — 940.54

A Shot to Save the World. Zuckerman, Gregory — 614.5

Shoulda Been Jimi Savannah. Smith, Patricia — 811

SHOW DOGS
- Tomlinson, Tommy. *Dogland* — 636.7

Show Me a Story. Neuburger, Emily K. — 745.5083

Show Them You're Good. Hobbs, Jeff — 373

Showa [Series]. Mizuki, Shigeru — 741.5

Showa 1926-1939. Mizuki, Shigeru — 741.5

SHOWA PERIOD (1926-1989)
- Bix, Herbert P. *Hirohito and the Making of Modern Japan* — B
- Mizuki, Shigeru. *Showa 1926-1939* — 741.5

Showalter, Elaine
- ★*A Jury of Her Peers* — 810.9

Showdown. Haygood, Wil — B

★*The Showman*. Shuster, Simon — B

★*Showtime*. Stempel, Larry — 792.609

Shraya, Vivek
- *I'm Afraid of Men* — 813

SHRAYA, VIVEK, 1981-
- Shraya, Vivek. *I'm Afraid of Men* — 813

SHREWS
- Catania, Kenneth. *Great Adaptations* — 576.8

SHREWSBURY, ELIZABETH HARDWICK TALBOT, COUNTESS OF, 1527?-1608
- Lovell, Mary S. *Bess of Hardwick* — B

Shrill. West, Lindy — 818

SHRINKING CITIES
- Goldstein, Amy. *Janesville* — 330.9775

Shrinking Violets. Moran, Joe — 155.2

Shrinks. Lieberman, Jeffrey A. — 616.89

SHRIVER FAMILY
- Shriver, Timothy P. *Fully Alive* — 796.087

SHRIVER, EUNICE KENNEDY
- McNamara, Eileen. ★*Eunice* — B

Shriver, Maria
- *I've Been Thinking ...* — 170

Shriver, Timothy P.
- *Fully Alive* — 796.087

SHRIVER, TIMOTHY P.
- Shriver, Timothy P. *Fully Alive* — 796.087

SHRUBS
- Bradley, Steve. *Pruning Simplified* — 631.5
- Brown, George E. *Essential Pruning Techniques* — 635.9
- McIndoe, Andrew. *The Creative Shrub Garden* — 635.9

Shteyngart, Gary
- ★*Little Failure* — B

AUTHOR, TITLE, SERIES AND SUBJECT INDEX

SHTEYNGART, GARY, 1972-
   Shteyngart, Gary. ★*Little Failure* — B
Shuk. Admony, Einat — 641.595
Shula. Ribowsky, Mark — B
SHULA, DON, 1930-2020
   Ribowsky, Mark. *Shula* — B
Shulevitz, Judith
   The Sabbath World — 296.4
SHULEVITZ, JUDITH, 1963-
   Shulevitz, Judith. *The Sabbath World* — 296.4
Shultz, Richard H.
   The Secret War Against Hanoi — 959.704
Shumski, Daniel
   How to Instant Pot — 641.5
Shumsky, Susan G.
   Earth Energy Meditations — 133.8
Shunk, Stephen A.
   Peterson Reference Guide to Woodpeckers of North America — 598.7
Shuster, Simon
   ★*The Showman* — B
SHUTTLESWORTH, FRED L., 1922-2011
   Kix, Paul. ★*You Have to Be Prepared to Die Before You Can Begin to Live* — 976.1
Shy. Rodgers, Mary — B
SHYNESS
   Dahl, Melissa. *Cringeworthy* — 158.2
   Thomson, Graeme. *George Harrison* — B
SIBERIA
   Frazier, Ian. *Travels in Siberia* — 957
   Thubron, Colin. *In Siberia* — 957
SIBERIAN TIGERS
   Vaillant, John. *The Tiger* — 599.756
Sibley Birds East. Sibley, David — 598.097
★*Sibley* Birds West. Sibley, David — 598.097
The Sibley Guide to Birds. Sibley, David — 598.097
★*The Sibley Guide to Trees*. Sibley, David — 582.16097
★*Sibley's Birding Basics*. Sibley, David — 598
Sibley, David
   Sibley Birds East — 598.097
   ★*Sibley Birds West* — 598.097
   The Sibley Guide to Birds — 598.097
   ★*The Sibley Guide to Trees* — 582.16097
   ★*Sibley's Birding Basics* — 598
SIBLING RIVALRY
   Berger, Lynn. *Second Thoughts* — 306.85
   Cooper, Anderson. *Vanderbilt* — 920
   Kashner, Sam. *The Fabulous Bouvier Sisters* — 920
   Mann, William J. *The Wars of the Roosevelts* — B
SIBLINGS
   Alexie, Sherman. *You Don't Have to Say You Love Me* — 818
   Berger, Lynn. *Second Thoughts* — 306.85
   Biden Owens, Valerie. *Growing up Biden* — B
   Bilton, Chrysta. *Normal Family* — B
   Byrne, Paula. *Kick* — B
   Calcaterra, Regina. *Etched in Sand* — B
   Cayton-Holland, Adam. *Tragedy Plus Time* — B
   Fisher, Todd. *My Girls* — B
   Keaton, Diane. ★*Brother & Sister* — B
   Lepore, Jill. *Book of Ages* — B
   O'Reilly, Seamas. ★*Did Ye Hear Mammy Died?* — B
   Riley, Kathleen. *The Astaires* — B
   Scheeres, Julia. *Jesus Land* — B
   Sedaris, David. ★*The Best of Me* — 818
   Seierstad, Asne. *Two Sisters* — 956.9104
   Strathern, Paul. *The Borgias* — 945.06
   Wariner, Ruth. *The Sound of Gravel* — B
SICHEL, PETER M. F.
   Anderson, Scott. ★*The Quiet Americans* — 327.12
Sicily '43. Holland, James — 940.54
Sicily. Norwich, John Julius — 945.8
The Sicily Cookbook. Vicenzino, Cettina — 641.59458
SICILY, ITALY
   Holland, James. *Sicily '43* — 940.54
   Lanza, Fabrizia. *The Food of Sicily* — 641.594
   Locke, Tembi. ★*From Scratch* — B
   Norwich, John Julius. *Sicily* — 945.8
SICK ANIMALS
   Montgomery, Sy. ★*Of Time and Turtles* — 597.92

SICK CHILDREN
   Harris, Taylor. *This Boy We Made* — B
SICK MEN
   Morgan, Abi. *This Is Not a Pity Memoir* — B
SICK PEOPLE
   Brenner, Marie. ★*The Desperate Hours* — 362.1962
   Carr, Caleb. *My Beloved Monster* — B
   Eichenwald, Kurt. *A Mind Unraveled* — B
   Goldberg, Emma. *Life on the Line* — 362.1962
   Markel, Howard. *Origin Story* — 576.8
   O'Farrell, Maggie. *I Am, I Am, I Am* — B
   O'Rourke, Meghan. ★*The Invisible Kingdom* — 616
   Richtel, Matt. ★*An Elegant Defense* — 616.07
   Sacks, Oliver. *Gratitude* — 306.9
   Spinney, Laura. ★*Pale Rider* — 614.5
SICK WOMEN
   Cleghorn, Elinor. *Unwell Women* — 613
Sickening. Abramson, John — 338.4
SICKERT, WALTER RICHARD, 1860-1942
   Cornwell, Patricia Daniels. *Ripper* — 364.152
Sides, Hampton
   Blood and Thunder — 978
   ★*Ghost Soldiers* — 940.54
   Hellhound on His Trail — 364.152
   ★*In the Kingdom of Ice* — 910.4
   On Desperate Ground — 951.904
   ★*The Wide Wide Sea* — 910.92
SIDESHOW PERFORMERS
   Macy, Beth. ★*Truevine* — B
SIDESHOWS
   Macy, Beth. ★*Truevine* — B
   Raffel, Dawn. *The Strange Case of Dr. Couney* — B
Sidney Lumet. Spiegel, Maura — B
Sidney Poitier. Goudsouzian, Aram — B
Siegal, Nina
   The Diary Keepers — 940.54
The Siege of Mecca. Trofimov, Yaroslav — 953.805
SIEGE WARFARE
   Philbrick, Nathaniel. ★*Bunker Hill* — 973.3
   Reid, Anna. *Leningrad* — 940.54
Siegel, Daniel J.
   Aware — 158.1
   Brainstorm — 155.5
   Parenting from the Inside Out — 649
   The Power of Showing Up — 649
   ★*The Yes Brain* — 155.4
Siegel, Joel G.
   Accounting Handbook — 657
Siegel, Matt
   The Secret History of Food — 641.3
SIEGES
   Donovan, Jim. *The Blood of Heroes* — 976.4
   Hemon, Aleksandar. *My Parents* — 814
   Miller, Donald L. *Vicksburg* — 973.7
   Moorhouse, Roger. *Berlin at War* — 943
   Moynahan, Brian. *Leningrad* — 780.92
   Reid, Anna. *Leningrad* — 940.54
Sielski, Mike
   The Rise — B
SIERRA LEONE
   Beah, Ishmael. ★*A Long Way Gone* — B
   Kardas-Nelson, Mara. *We Are Not Able to Live in the Sky* — 332.3
SIERRA MADRE MOUNTAINS, MEXICO
   Matloff, Judith. *No Friends but the Mountains* — 355.009
SIERRA NEVADA MOUNTAINS
   Atleework, Kendra. *Miracle Country* — 979.4
   Brown, Daniel James. *The Indifferent Stars Above* — B
   Robinson, Kim Stanley. *The High Sierra* — 917.94
Sife, Wallace
   The Loss of a Pet — 155.9
Siff, Jason
   Thoughts Are Not the Enemy — 294.3
Sifton, Sam
   ★*The New York Times Cooking No-Recipe Recipes* — 641.5
   ★*See You on Sunday* — 641.5
   Thanksgiving — 641.5
★*Sigh, Gone*. Tran, Phuc — B
Sight Lines. Sze, Arthur — 811

PUBLIC LIBRARY CORE COLLECTION: NONFICTION
Twentieth Edition

Sigmund, Karl
   Exact Thinking in Demented Times   920
SIGN LANGUAGE
   Kaminsky, Ilya. ★*Deaf Republic*   811
***Signed**, Sealed, and Delivered*. Ribowsky, Mark   B
Signer, Michael
   Cry Havoc   305.800973
SIGNER, MICHAEL
   Signer, Michael. *Cry Havoc*   305.800973
SIGNS AND SYMBOLS
   Ferrara, Silvia. *The Greatest Invention*   411
   Gimenez Smith, Carmen. *Be Recorder*   811
   Houston, Keith. *Shady Characters*   411
   Stark, Lizzie. ★*Egg*   641.3
***Signs** of Life*. Fabes, Stephen   B
***Signs** of the Zodiac*. Snodgrass, Mary Ellen   133.5
SILENCE AND SILENT THINGS
   Lyons, Daniel. *STFU*   302.2
   Zorn, Justin. *Golden*   128
Silencer. Wicker, Marcus   811
***Silencing** White Noise*. Francois, Willie Dwayne   277
***Silent** Cavalry*. Raines, Howell   973.7
SILENT FILM INDUSTRY AND TRADE
   Eyman, Scott. *Empire of Dreams*   B
SILENT FILMS
   Goessel, Tracey. *The First King of Hollywood*   B
   Stevens, Dana. *Camera Man*   791.4302
***Silent** Sparks*. Lewis, Sara   595.76
★***Silent** Spring*. Carson, Rachel   363.738
Siler, Julia Flynn
   The White Devil's Daughters   306.3
SILICON
   Kean, Sam. *The Disappearing Spoon*   546
SILICON VALLEY, CALIFORNIA
   Chafkin, Max. *The Contrarian*   B
   Chang, Emily. *Brotopia*   331.4
   Pein, Corey. *Live Work Work Work Die*   338.4
   Stone, Brad. *The Upstarts*   338.04
   Swisher, Kara. *Burn Book*   303.48
   Wiener, Anna. ★*Uncanny Valley*   B
   Williams, Bari A. *Seen yet Unseen*   338.4
Silk. Prasad, Aarathi   677
SILK
   Prasad, Aarathi. *Silk*   677
SILK INDUSTRY AND TRADE
   Ollivier, Bernard. *Out of Istanbul*   B
   Prasad, Aarathi. *Silk*   677
SILK ROAD
   Frankopan, Peter. *The Silk Roads*   909
   Hansen, Valerie. *The Year 1000*   909
   Harris, Kate. *Lands of Lost Borders*   915.804
   Ollivier, Bernard. *Out of Istanbul*   B
   Samatar, Sofia. *The White Mosque*   B
   Thubron, Colin. *Shadow of the Silk Road*   915
*The **Silk** Roads*. Frankopan, Peter   909
SILKWORMS
   Prasad, Aarathi. *Silk*   677
*The **Silver** Palate Cookbook*. Rosso, Julee   641.5
*The **Silver** Waterfall*. Simms, Brendan   940.54
Silver, Alain
   ★*From the Moment They Met It Was Murder*   791.43
Silver, Johanna
   ★*The Bold Dry Garden*   635.9
Silverman, David J.
   ★*This Land Is Their Land*   974.4
Silverton, Nancy
   ★*The Cookie That Changed My Life*   641.81
Simard, S.
   ★*Finding the Mother Tree*   582.16
SIMARD, S. (SUZANNE)
   Simard, S. ★*Finding the Mother Tree*   582.16
Simeon, Sheldon
   Cook Real Hawai?i   641.59969
Simic, Charles
   Come Closer and Listen   811
   The Lunatic   811
   New and Selected Poems   811
   The Voice at 3   811

Simmons, Bill
   The Book of Basketball   796.323
Simmons, Lauren
   Make Money Move   332.024
Simmons, Nadirah
   ★*First Things First*   782.42164
Simmons, Rachel
   ★*Enough as She Is*   155.5
   Odd Girl Out   302.5
Simmons, Ruth
   ★*Up Home*   B
SIMMONS, RUTH, 1945-
   Simmons, Ruth. ★*Up Home*   B
Simmons, Sylvie
   I'm Your Man   B
Simms, Brendan
   The Silver Waterfall   940.54
Simon, Carly
   ★*Boys in the Trees*   782.42164
SIMON, CARLY
   Simon, Carly. ★*Boys in the Trees*   782.42164
Simon, James F.
   Eisenhower vs. Warren   347.73
   FDR and Chief Justice Hughes   973.917092
   What Kind of Nation   342.73
Simon, Marie
   Underground in Berlin   B
SIMON, MARIE, 1922-1998
   Simon, Marie. *Underground in Berlin*   B
Simon, Matt
   Plight of the Living Dead   591.6
   The Wasp That Brainwashed the Caterpillar   578.4
SIMON, PAUL, 1941-
   Hilburn, Robert. ★*Paul Simon*   782.42164
Simon, Rachel
   Pickleball for All   796.34
Simon, Scott
   My Cubs   796.357
SIMON, SCOTT
   Simon, Scott. *My Cubs*   796.357
SIMONE, NINA, 1933-2003
   Cohodas, Nadine. *Princess Noire*   782.42164
***Simple** Cake*. Williams, Odette   641.86
SIMPLE LIFE
   Sundeen, Mark. *The Unsettlers*   640
★***Simple** Pasta*. Williams, Odette   641.822
*The **Simple** Truth*. Levine, Philip   811
SIMPLICITY
   Becker, Joshua. *The Minimalist Home*   241
   Becker, Joshua. *The More of Less*   241
   Chayka, Kyle. *The Longing for Less*   179.9
   Masuno, Shunmy. *The Art of Simple Living*   294.3
   McCubbin, Tracy. *Make Space for Happiness*   179
   Shankle, Melanie. *Church of the Small Things*   248.8
***Simply** Julia*. Turshen, Julia   641.3
***Simply** Living Well*. Watkins, Julia   640
★***Simply** Nigella*. Lawson, Nigella   641.5
***Simply** Styling*. Grove, Kirsten   747
★***Simply** Tomato*. Holmberg, Martha   641.6
Simpson, J. A.
   The Word Detective   B
SIMPSON, J. A., 1953-
   Simpson, J. A. *The Word Detective*   B
SIMS, J. MARION (JAMES MARION), 1813-1883
   Hallman, J. C. *Say Anarcha*   618.1
Sims, Michael
   Arthur and Sherlock   B
SIN
   Dante Alighieri. *Purgatorio*   851
   Jacobs, Alan. *Original Sin*   233
   Zahl, David. *Low Anthropology*   233
SIN, SANG-OK, 1926-2006
   Fischer, Paul. *A Kim Jong-Il Production*   791.43
Sinatra. Kaplan, James   782.42164
***Sinatra** and Me*. Oppedisano, Tony   B
★***Sinatra!** The Song Is You*. Friedwald, Will   782.42164
SINATRA, FRANK, 1915-1998
   Friedwald, Will. ★*Sinatra! the Song Is You*   782.42164

AUTHOR, TITLE, SERIES AND SUBJECT INDEX

Kaplan, James. *Sinatra*	782.42164
Oppedisano, Tony. *Sinatra and Me*	B
Weisman, Eliot. *The Way It Was*	782.42164
Sincero, Jen	
You Are a Badass	158.1
You Are a Badass Every Day	158.1
Sinclair, David A.	
Lifespan	570
Sinclair, Safiya	
Cannibal	811
★*How to Say Babylon*	B
SINCLAIR, SAFIYA	
Sinclair, Safiya. ★*How to Say Babylon*	B
★*Sing A Black Girl's Song.* Shange, Ntozake	818
Sing Backwards and Weep. Lanegan, Mark	B
★*Sing for Your Life.* Bergner, Daniel	B
★*Sing Like Fish.* Kingdon, Amorina	591.77
Singer, Jessie	
There Are No Accidents	363.1
Singer, Matt	
Opposable Thumbs	791.43
Singer, Peter	
★*Animal Liberation*	179
SINGERS	
Alden, Ginger. *Elvis and Ginger*	B
Andrews, Julie. *Home*	B
Belafonte, Harry. ★*My Song*	782.42164
Bogle, Donald. *Heat Wave*	782.42164
Carlile, Brandi. *Broken Horses*	B
Carlin, Peter Ames. *Bruce*	B
Cash, Rosanne. ★*Composed*	B
Cohen, Leonard. *The Flame*	810
Cohodas, Nadine. *Princess Noire*	782.42164
Cole, Natalie. *Angel on My Shoulder*	B
Connolly, Ray. *Being Elvis*	B
Davis, Stephen. *Gold Dust Woman*	B
DeCurtis, Anthony. *Lou Reed*	B
Dickinson, Bruce. *What Does This Button Do?*	B
DiFranco, Ani. *No Walls and the Recurring Dream*	782.42164
Dylan, Bob. *Chronicles; Volume 1*	B
Friedwald, Will. *The Great Jazz and Pop Vocal Albums*	016.78
Friedwald, Will. ★*Sinatra! the Song Is You*	782.42164
Gavin, James. ★*Stormy Weather*	782.42164
Gaye, Jan. *After the Dance*	B
Giddins, Gary. *Bing Crosby*	B
Giddins, Gary. *Bing Crosby*	B
Harris, Neil Patrick. *Neil Patrick Harris*	B
Hermes, Will. *Lou Reed*	B
Jewel. *Never Broken*	782.42164
Kaplan, James. *Sinatra*	782.42164
Lanegan, Mark. *Sing Backwards and Weep*	B
McCartney, Paul. *The Lyrics*	782.42166
McDonald, Greg (Producer). *Elvis and the Colonel*	920
Moorer, Allison. *I Dream He Talks to Me*	782.42164
Neville, Aaron. *Tell It Like It Is*	B
Newkey-Burden, Chas. *Taylor Swift*	B
O'Connor, Sinead. ★*Rememberings*	B
Oppedisano, Tony. *Sinatra and Me*	B
Parton, Dolly. ★*Behind the Seams*	B
Parton, Dolly. ★*Dolly Parton, Songteller*	B
Phair, Liz. *Horror Stories*	B
Porter, Billy. ★*Unprotected*	B
Powers, Ann. *Good Booty*	781.64
Powers, Ann. ★*Traveling*	B
Quin, Tegan. ★*High School*	B
Rainbow, Randy. *Playing with Myself*	B
Rannells, Andrew. *Uncle of the Year*	B
Robeson, Paul. *The Undiscovered Paul Robeson*	B
Santopietro, Tom. *The Sound of Music Story*	791.43
Simon, Carly. ★*Boys in the Trees*	782.42164
Smith, Patti. ★*A Book of Days*	779
Streisand, Barbra. ★*My Name Is Barbra*	B
White, Ryan. *Jimmy Buffett*	782.42164
Williams, Lucinda. *Don't Tell Anybody the Secrets I Told You*	B
Zanes, Warren. *Petty*	B
Zauner, Michelle. ★*Crying in H Mart*	B
Singh, Julietta	
The Breaks	B
SINGH, JULIETTA, 1976-	
Singh, Julietta. *The Breaks*	B
Singh, Simon	
Fermat's Enigma	512
SINGING	
Neville, Aaron. *Tell It Like It Is*	B
Singing and Dancing Are the Voice of the Law. Lahn, Bussho	294.3
Singing My Him Song. McCourt, Malachy	B
Singing School. Pinsky, Robert	808.1
SINGLE FATHERS	
Rosenthal, Jason. *My Wife Said You May Want to Marry Me*	B
SINGLE MOTHERS	
Asher, Zain E. *Where the Children Take Us*	942.1
Feldman, Deborah. *Exodus*	B
Fessler, Ann. *The Girls Who Went Away*	362.82
Henson, Taraji P. *Around the Way Girl*	B
Hill, David. *The Vapors*	976.7
Kelly, Minka. ★*Tell Me Everything*	B
Land, Stephanie. *Maid*	B
O'Donnell, Svenja. *Inge's War*	943.086
Pablo Cruz, Rosayra. *The Book of Rosy*	B
Sandler, Lauren. *This Is All I Got*	B
Scheier, Liz. *Never Simple*	B
Wills, Clair. ★*Missing Persons*	929.2
Single on Purpose. Kim, John	155.6
SINGLE PEOPLE	
Cohen, Rhaina. ★*The Other Significant Others*	177
Kim, John. *Single on Purpose*	155.6
SINGLE WOMEN	
Gerson, Merissa Nathan. *Forget Prayers, Bring Cake*	155.9
Macadam, Heather Dune. *999*	940.53
Moore, Marianne. *The Selected Letters of Marianne Moore*	B
SINGLE-HANDED SAILING	
Clark, Liz. *Swell*	B
SINGLE-PARENT FAMILIES	
Ford, Ashley C. ★*Somebody's Daughter*	B
O'Reilly, Seamas. ★*Did Ye Hear Mammy Died?*	B
Rippon, Kelly. *Parent Up*	649
Singular Sensation. Riedel, Michael	792
★*The Singularity Is Near.* Kurzweil, Ray	153.9
Sinha, Manisha	
★*The Rise and Fall of the Second American Republic*	973.8
The Slave's Cause	326
Sinise, Gary	
Grateful American	B
SINISE, GARY	
Sinise, Gary. *Grateful American*	B
Sink. Thomas, Joseph Earl	B
Sinkable. Stone, Daniel	910.91
SINO-JAPANESE CONFLICT, 1937-1945	
Chang, Iris. ★*The Rape of Nanking*	951.04
Mitter, Rana. *Forgotten Ally*	951.04
★*The Sioux Chef's Indigenous Kitchen.* Sherman, Sean	641.59
Sipping Dom Pérignon Through a Straw. Ndopu, Eddie	B
Sipress, David	
What's so Funny?	B
SIPRESS, DAVID	
Sipress, David. *What's so Funny?*	B
The Sirens of Mars. Johnson, Sarah Stewart	576.8
SISKEL, GENE	
Singer, Matt. *Opposable Thumbs*	791.43
Sisman, Adam	
The Professor and the Parson	364.16
Sisson, Gretchen E.	
★*Relinquished*	362.734
Sissy. Tobia, Jacob	305.30973
The Sister. Lee, Sung-Yoon	951.93
Sister Outsider. Lorde, Audre	814
Sister Pie. Ludwinski, Lisa	641.86
★*The Sisterhood.* Mundy, Liza	327.12
SISTERHOOD	
Bradford, Joy Harden. *Sisterhood Heals*	158.2
Kashner, Sam. *The Fabulous Bouvier Sisters*	920
Trice, Dawn Turner. ★*Three Girls from Bronzeville*	977.311
Valby, Karen. *The Swans of Harlem*	792.8
Sisterhood Heals. Bradford, Joy Harden	158.2
The Sisters. Lovell, Mary S.	920.72

PUBLIC LIBRARY CORE COLLECTION: NONFICTION
Twentieth Edition

SISTERS
    Alvarez, Julia. *The Woman I Kept to Myself*   811
    Bonner, Betsy. *The Book of Atlantis Black*   364.152
    Calcaterra, Regina. *Girl Unbroken*   B
    Chang, Jung. *Big Sister, Little Sister, Red Sister*   B
    Farley, Audrey Clare. ★*Girls and Their Monsters*   306.875
    Goldstone, Nancy Bazelon. *In the Shadow of the Empress*   920
    Hayasaki, Erika. *Somewhere Sisters*   362.7
    Horton, Michelle. *Dear Sister*   B
    Iperen, Roxane van. ★*The Sisters of Auschwitz*   940.53
    Kashner, Sam. *The Fabulous Bouvier Sisters*   920
    Li, Zhuqing. *Daughters of the Flower Fragrant Garden*   951.04
    Lovell, Mary S. *The Sisters*   920.72
    McNeur, Catherine. *Mischievous Creatures*   920
    Milford, Nancy. *Savage Beauty*   B
    Nimura, Janice P. ★*The Doctors Blackwell*   610.92
    Popkin, Jim. *Code Name Blue Wren*   327.12
    Rappaport, Helen. *The Romanov Sisters*   920
    Roy, Jessica. *American Girls*   305.48
    Ruffin, Amber. ★*The World Record Book of Racist Stories*   305.896
    Ruffin, Amber. *You'll Never Believe What Happened to Lacey*   305.896
    Ung, Loung. *Lucky Child*   B
    Williams, Tennessee. ★*A Streetcar Named Desire*   812
Sisters First. Hager, Jenna Bush
★*Sisters in Hate*. Darby, Seyward   305.800973
Sisters in Law. Hirshman, Linda R.   347.73
SISTERS IN LAW
    Puhak, Shelley. *The Dark Queens*   944
Sisters in Resistance. Mazzeo, Tilar J.   945.091
★*The Sisters of Auschwitz*. Iperen, Roxane van   940.53
Sito. Ralph, Laurence   364.152
SITTING BEAR KIOWA CHIEF, 1810-1871
    Momaday, N. Scott. ★*The Death of Sitting Bear*   811
Sitting Bull. Utley, Robert M.   B
SITTING BULL, 1831-1890
    Gardner, Mark L. *The Earth Is All That Lasts*   978.004
    Philbrick, Nathaniel. ★*The Last Stand*   973.8
    Utley, Robert M. *Sitting Bull*
Sitting Pretty. Taussig, Rebekah   B
★*The Situation Room*. Stephanopoulos, George   973.09
Siva, Micah
    Nosh   641.5
★*The Six*. Grush, Loren   629.4
Six Days in August. King, David   364.15
Six Days of War. Oren, Michael B.   956.04
Six Degrees. Lynas, Mark   551.6
★*Six Easy Pieces*. Feynman, Richard P.   530
Six Encounters with Lincoln. Pryor, Elizabeth Brown   973.7092
★*Six Frigates*. Toll, Ian W.   359.00973
Six Seasons. McFadden, Joshua   641.5
Six Walks. Shattuck, Ben   B
Six Wives. Starkey, David   942.05
The Six Wives of Henry VIII. Weir, Alison   942.05
SIXTEEN-YEAR-OLD GIRLS
    Capote, Truman. ★*In Cold Blood*   364.1
The Sixth Man. Iguodala, Andre   B
Size. Smil, Vaclav   153.7
SIZE
    Smil, Vaclav. *Size*   153.7
Sjunneson, Elsa
    Being Seen   362.4
SJUNNESON, ELSA, 1985-
    Sjunneson, Elsa. *Being Seen*   362.4
Skach, C. L.
    How to Be a Citizen   323.6
Skaife, Christopher
    The Ravenmaster   B
SKAIFE, CHRISTOPHER, 1965-
    Skaife, Christopher. *The Ravenmaster*   B
Skaja, Emily
    Brute   811.6
Skal, David J.
    Something in the Blood   823
SKARBEK, KRYSTYNA, 1908-1952
    Mulley, Clare. *The Spy Who Loved*   B
SKATEBOARDERS
    Tran, Phuc. ★*Sigh, Gone*   B

SKELETON
    Bass, William M. *Death's Acre*   614
    Meals, Roy A. *Bones*   599.9
    Switek, Brian. *Skeleton Keys*   611
Skeleton Keys. Switek, Brian   611
Skelton, Marc
    Pounding the Rock   796.323
SKELTON, MARC, 1974-
    Skelton, Marc. *Pounding the Rock*   796.323
SKEPTICISM
    Hecht, Jennifer Michael. *Doubt*   121
    Keller, Timothy J. *The Reason for God*   239
    Knight, Sam. *The Premonitions Bureau*   133.8
    Manseau, Peter. *The Apparitionists*   B
    Novella, Steven. *The Skeptics' Guide to the Universe*   500
    Nye, Bill. *Everything All at Once*   153.4
    Pinn, Anthony B. *The Black Practice of Disbelief*   211
SKEPTICS
    Ghosh, Amitav. *The Great Derangement*   809
    Jaher, David. *The Witch of Lime Street*   B
The Skeptics' Guide to the Universe. Novella, Steven   500
Skidmore, Thomas E.
    Brazil   981
SKIERS
    Vinton, Nathaniel. *The Fall Line*   796.93
Skies of Thunder. Alexander, Caroline   940.54
SKIING
    Isserman, Maurice. *The Winter Army*   940.54
    Ollestad, Norman. *Crazy for the Storm*   B
    Vinton, Nathaniel. *The Fall Line*   796.93
Skillet Love. Byrn, Anne   641.7
SKILLS
    Cast, Carter. *The Right—And Wrong—Stuff*   650.1
    Crawford, Matthew B. *The World Beyond Your Head*   155.2
    Epstein, David J. ★*Range*   153.9
    Gopnik, Adam. *The Real Work*   153.9
    Levine, Madeline. ★*Ready or Not*   649
    Vanderbilt, Tom. ★*Beginners*   646.7
SKIN
    Bowe, Whitney. *The Beauty of Dirty Skin*   646.7
    Lyman, Monty. *The Remarkable Life of the Skin*   612.7
    Thomas, Mathilde. *The French Beauty Solution*   646.7
    Tourles, Stephanie L. *Pure Skin Care*   646.7
The Skin Above My Knee. Butler, Marcia   B
SKIN CARE
    Godas, Maru. *Organic Beauty*   646.7
    Hamblin, James. *Clean*   613
    Lyman, Monty. *The Remarkable Life of the Skin*   612.7
SKIN DISEASES
    Fessler, Pam. *Carville's Cure*   362.19699
    Lyman, Monty. *The Remarkable Life of the Skin*   612.7
SKIN DIVING
    Nestor, James. *Deep*   797.2
Skin, Inc. Ellis, Thomas Sayers   811
SKINNER, B. F., 1904-1990
    Bjork, Daniel W. *B.F. Skinner*   B
    Bloom, Paul. *Psych*   150
SKINNER, JACK T., D.1977
    Nourse, Victoria F. *In Reckless Hands*   344.7304
Skinny Suppers. Griffin, Brooke   641.5
Skinnytaste Fast and Slow. Homolka, Gina   641.5
Skinnytaste One & Done. Homolka, Gina   641.5
SKIS
    Vinton, Nathaniel. *The Fall Line*   796.93
Skloot, Rebecca
    ★*The Immortal Life of Henrietta Lacks*   B
Skomal, Gregory
    Chasing Shadows   597.3
SKOMAL, GREGORY
    Skomal, Gregory. *Chasing Shadows*   597.3
SKYSCRAPERS
    Cornille, Didier. *Who Built That?*   720
    Langewiesche, William. *American Ground*   974.7
Slade, Rachel
    American Hoodie   338.4
    Into the Raging Sea   910.91
Slaght, Jonathan C.
    Owls of the Eastern Ice   598.9

AUTHOR, TITLE, SERIES AND SUBJECT INDEX

SLAGHT, JONATHAN C.
   Slaght, Jonathan C. *Owls of the Eastern Ice* — 598.9
Slahi, Mohamedou Ould
   The Mauritanian — 958.104
SLAHI, MOHAMEDOU OULD
   Slahi, Mohamedou Ould. *The Mauritanian* — 958.104
SLANG
   Fridland, Valerie. ★*Like, Literally, Dude* — 420.141
Slatalla, Michelle
   Gardenista — 635
Slate, Jenny
   Little Weirds — B
SLATE, JENNY
   Slate, Jenny. *Little Weirds* — B
Slater, Lauren
   Blue Dreams — 615.7
SLATTER, HOPE H. (HOPE HULL), 1790-1853
   Shane, Scott. ★*Flee North* — 973.7
SLAUGHTER-HOUSES AND SLAUGHTERING
   Danforth, Adam. *Butchering Poultry, Rabbit, Lamb, Goat, and Pork* — 664
A Slave No More. Blight, David W. — B
SLAVE SHIPS
   Durkin, Hannah. ★*The Survivors of the Clotilda* — 306.362
SLAVE TRADE
   Berlin, Ira. *The Making of African America* — 973
   Carretta, Vincent. *Equiano, the African* — B
   Durkin, Hannah. ★*The Survivors of the Clotilda* — 306.362
   French, Howard W. *Born in Blackness* — 960
   Gaddy, K. R. ★*Well of Souls* — 787
   Hochschild, Adam. *Bury the Chains* — 326
   Hurston, Zora Neale. ★*Barracoon* — B
   Johnson, Walter. *Soul by Soul* — 976.3
   Kars, Marjoleine. *Blood on the River* — 306.3
   Manegold, Catherine S. *Ten Hills Farm* — 974.4
   Miles, Tiya. *The Dawn of Detroit* — 977.4
   Montero, David. ★*The Stolen Wealth of Slavery* — 381
   Rae, Noel. ★*The Great Stain* — 306.3
   Raines, Ben. *The Last Slave Ship* — 306.362
   Rediker, Marcus. *The Amistad Rebellion* — 326.0973
   Rothman, Joshua D. *The Ledger and the Chain* — 306.362
   Shane, Scott. ★*Flee North* — 973.7
   Young, Kevin. *Ardency* — 811
SLAVE TRADERS
   Raines, Ben. *The Last Slave Ship* — 306.362
   Rothman, Joshua D. *The Ledger and the Chain* — 306.362
The Slave's Cause. Sinha, Manisha — 326
SLAVEHOLDERS
   Ball, Edward. *Slaves in the Family* — 975.7
   Ford, Lacy K. *Deliver Us from Evil* — 973.7
   Good, Cassandra A. *First Family* — 920
   Gordon-Reed, Annette. ★*The Hemingses of Monticello* — 920
   Greenberg, Amy S. *Lady First* — B
   Hurston, Zora Neale. ★*Barracoon* — B
   Johnson, Walter. *Soul by Soul* — 976.3
   May, Gregory. *A Madman's Will* — 973.5
   Rae, Noel. ★*The Great Stain* — 306.3
   Saxton, Martha. *The Widow Washington* — B
   Shirley, Craig. *Mary Ball Washington* — B
   Swarns, Rachel L. *The 272* — 975.2
SLAVERY
   Ayers, Edward L. *American Visions* — 973.5
   Beckert, Sven. *Empire of Cotton* — 338.4
   Blackmon, Douglas A. *Slavery by Another Name* — 305.896
   Blumenthal, Sidney. ★*All the Powers of Earth* — B
   Bordewich, Fergus M. *America's Great Debate* — 973.6
   Bordewich, Fergus M. *Congress at War* — 324.2734
   Burlingame, Michael. *The Black Man's President* — 973.7
   Burrough, Bryan. *Forget the Alamo* — 976.043
   Delbanco, Andrew. *The War Before the War* — 973.7
   Dodds Pennock, Caroline. ★*On Savage Shores* — 970.004
   Dunbar, Erica Armstrong. ★*Never Caught* — B
   Ellis, Joseph J. *The Cause* — 973.3
   Feldman, Noah. *The Broken Constitution* — 973.7
   Ferrer, Ada. ★*Cuba* — 972.91
   Fischer, David Hackett. ★*African Founders* — 973
   Foner, Eric. *The Fiery Trial* — 973.7092
   Foner, Eric. ★*Gateway to Freedom* — 973.7
   Ford, Lacy K. *Deliver Us from Evil* — 973.7
   Fowler, Corinne. ★*The Countryside* — 941
   Franklin, John Hope. ★*From Slavery to Freedom* — 973
   Franklin, John Hope. *In Search of the Promised Land* — 929
   Freeman, Joanne B. *The Field of Blood* — 973.7
   Genovese, Eugene D. *Roll, Jordan, Roll* — 975
   Goodheart, Adam. *1861* — 973.7
   Gordon-Reed, Annette. ★*The Hemingses of Monticello* — 920
   Grant, Richard. *The Deepest South of All* — 976.2
   Greenidge, Kerri. ★*The Grimkes* — 973.5
   Grinspan, Jon. *Wide Awake* — 973.7
   Griswold, Mac K. *The Manor* — 974.7
   Hahn, Steven. *A Nation Under Our Feet* — 975
   Hall, Rebecca. ★*Wake* — 741.5
   Harris, J. William. *The Hanging of Thomas Jeremiah* — B
   Hochschild, Adam. *Bury the Chains* — 326
   Hochschild, Adam. *King Leopold's Ghost* — 967.51
   Holton, Woody. *Liberty Is Sweet* — 973.3
   Hoock, Holger. *Scars of Independence* — 973.3
   Hurston, Zora Neale. ★*Barracoon* — B
   Hylton, Antonia. *Madness* — 362.2
   Jacobs, Harriet. ★*Incidents in the Life of a Slave Girl* — B
   Jeffers, Honorée Fanonne. *The Age of Phillis* — 811
   Jones, Jacqueline. *Saving Savannah* — 975.8
   Jones, Robert P. *The Hidden Roots of White Supremacy* — 305.8
   Kaplan, Fred. *Lincoln and the Abolitionists* — 973.7092
   Kars, Marjoleine. *Blood on the River* — 306.3
   Kytle, Ethan J. *Denmark Vesey's Garden* — 975.7
   Lepore, Jill. ★*These Truths* — 973
   Levine, Bruce C. *The Fall of the House of Dixie* — 973.7
   Lineberry, Cate. *Be Free or Die* — B
   Lusane, Clarence. *The Black History of the White House* — 975.3
   Manegold, Catherine S. *Ten Hills Farm* — 974.4
   May, Gregory. *A Madman's Will* — 973.5
   Mays, Kyle. ★*An Afro-Indigenous History of the United States* — 973
   McGill, Joseph. *Sleeping with the Ancestors* — 306.362
   Meacham, Jon. ★*And There Was Light* — B
   Meyer, Eugene L. *Five for Freedom* — 973.7
   Miles, Tiya. *The Dawn of Detroit* — 977.4
   Montero, David. ★*The Stolen Wealth of Slavery* — 381
   Morgan-Owens, Jessie. *Girl in Black and White* — B
   Morrison, Toni. ★*The Origin of Others* — 809
   Northup, Solomon. *Twelve Years a Slave* — B
   Oakes, James. *Freedom National* — 973.7
   Petrosino, Kiki. *White Blood* — 811
   Plant, Deborah G. *Of Greed and Glory* — 326
   Rae, Noel. ★*The Great Stain* — 306.3
   Raines, Ben. *The Last Slave Ship* — 306.362
   Rasmussen, Daniel. *American Uprising* — 976.3
   Rediker, Marcus. *The Amistad Rebellion* — 326.0973
   Richards, Leonard L. *Who Freed the Slaves?* — 342.7308
   Rothman, Joshua D. *The Ledger and the Chain* — 306.362
   Sanghera, Sathnam. *Empireworld* — 909
   Seidule, Ty. *Robert E. Lee and Me* — 973.7
   Sinha, Manisha. *The Slave's Cause* — 326
   Smith, Clint. ★*How the Word Is Passed* — 973
   Smith, Patricia. *Unshuttered* — 811
   Snodgrass, Mary Ellen. *The Underground Railroad* — 973.7
   Snyder, Christina. *Great Crossings* — 976.9
   Stuart, Andrea. *Sugar in the Blood* — 338.1
   Swarns, Rachel L. *The 272* — 975.2
   Tabor, Nick. *Africatown* — 976.1
   Taylor, Alan. *American Revolutions* — 973.3
   Taylor, Alan. ★*The Internal Enemy* — 975.5
   Tjipombo, Tupa. *I Am Not Your Slave* — B
   Walvin, James. *Sugar* — 338.17361
   Ward, Geoffrey C. *The Civil War* — 973.7
   Weiner, Mark Stuart. *Black Trials* — 342.7308
   White, Gayle Jessup. *Reclamation* — B
   Wiencek, Henry. *Master of the Mountain* — 973.4
   Wilder, Craig Steven. *Ebony and Ivy* — 379.2
   Wineapple, Brenda. *Ecstatic Nation* — 973.6
   Wise, Steven M. *Though the Heavens May Fall* — 342.42
   Woo, Ilyon. ★*Master Slave Husband Wife* — 920
Slavery by Another Name. Blackmon, Douglas A. — 305.896
Slaves in the Family. Ball, Edward — 975.7
★*The Slaves' War*. Ward, Andrew — 973.7
Slawenski, Kenneth
   ★*Salinger* — B

PUBLIC LIBRARY CORE COLLECTION: NONFICTION
Twentieth Edition

Slaying Goliath. Ravitch, Diane — 371.010973
SLED DOG RACING
  Pace, Kristin Knight. *This Much Country* — B
SLED DOGS
  Pace, Kristin Knight. *This Much Country* — B
SLEEP
  Ezzo, Gary. *On Becoming Baby Wise* — 649
  Harvey, Samantha. *The Shapeless Unease* — B
  Leschziner, Guy. *The Nocturnal Brain* — 616.8
  Macedo, Diane. *The Sleep Fix* — 613.7
  Navab, Pedram. *Sleep Reimagined* — 616.8
  Nigg, Joel T. *Getting Ahead of ADHD* — 618.92
  Pelayo, Rafael. ★*How to Sleep* — 616.8
  Reiss, Benjamin. *Wild Nights* — 616.8
  Zadra, Antonio. *When Brains Dream* — 613.7
SLEEP APNEA
  Leschziner, Guy. *The Nocturnal Brain* — 616.8
SLEEP DEPRIVATION
  Harvey, Samantha. *The Shapeless Unease* — B
  Leschziner, Guy. *The Nocturnal Brain* — 616.8
SLEEP DISORDERS
  Leschziner, Guy. *The Nocturnal Brain* — 616.8
  Macedo, Diane. *The Sleep Fix* — 613.7
  Pelayo, Rafael. ★*How to Sleep* — 616.8
  Reiss, Benjamin. *Wild Nights* — 616.8
  Zadra, Antonio. *When Brains Dream* — 613.7
The Sleep Fix. Macedo, Diane — 613.7
Sleep Reimagined. Navab, Pedram — 616.8
SLEEP-WAKE CYCLE
  Reiss, Benjamin. *Wild Nights* — 616.8
The Sleeping Beauties. O'Sullivan, Suzanne — 616.85
SLEEPING CUSTOMS
  Reiss, Benjamin. *Wild Nights* — 616.8
Sleeping with the Ancestors. McGill, Joseph — 306.362
SLEEPWALKING
  Leschziner, Guy. *The Nocturnal Brain* — 616.8
Sleight, Steve
  The Complete Sailing Manual — 797.1
★*Slenderman*. Hale, Kathleen — 364.152
Slevin, Peter
  Michelle Obama — B
Slezkine, Yuri
  The House of Government — 947.084
Slice, Jessica
  Dateable — 646.7
The Slip. Peiffer, Prudence — 709.73
A Slip of the Keyboard. Pratchett, Terry — 824
Sloan, Annie
  Color Recipes for Painted Furniture and More — 745.7
Sloan, Nate
  Switched on Pop — 781.64
SLOGANS
  Churchwell, Sarah Bartlett. *Behold, America* — 973.9
Slonim Woods 9. Levin, Daniel Barban — B
SLOTHS
  Cooke, Lucy. *The Truth About Animals* — 590.2
Slouching Towards Utopia. De Long, J. Bradford — 330.9
Slouka, Mark
  Nobody's Son — B
SLOUKA, MARK
  Slouka, Mark. *Nobody's Son* — B
SLOVAKIA
  Blau, Magda Hellinger. *The Nazis Knew My Name* — 940.53
  Macadam, Heather Dune. *999* — 940.53
  McNamara, Kevin J. *Dreams of a Great Small Nation* — 355.009437
SLOW FOOD MOVEMENT
  Waters, Alice. ★*We Are What We Eat* — 641.01
Sluglett, Peter
  Atlas of Islamic History — 912.19
Small Acts of Courage. Velshi, Ali — B
SMALL BUSINESS
  Abrams, Stacey. *Level Up* — 658.4
  Downs, Paul. *Boss Life* — 338.7
  Hahn, Emanuel. *Koreatown Dreaming* — 979.4
  Lindsay, Virginia Keleher. *Sewing to Sell* — 746
  McKeever, Mike P. *How to Write a Business Plan* — 658.15
  Thorstensen, Ole. *Making Things Right* — 690
  Yunus, Muhammad. *A World of Three Zeros* — 330

SMALL FARMS
  Logsdon, Gene. *Letter to a Young Farmer* — 338.10973
SMALL HOUSES
  Koones, Sheri. *Prefabulous Small Houses* — 728
  Mitchell, Ryan. *Tiny House Living* — 728.37
  Podemski, Max. *A Paradise of Small Houses* — 363.5
Small Is Beautiful. Schumacher, E. F. — 330
The Small Public Library Survival Guide. Landau, Herbert B. — 025.1
SMALL TOWN LIFE
  Bard, Elizabeth. *Picnic in Provence* — B
  Bass, Amy. *One Goal* — 796.334
  Biggers, Jeff. *Reckoning at Eagle Creek* — 333.73
  Bissinger, H. G. ★*Friday Night Lights* — 796.332
  Capote, Truman. ★*In Cold Blood* — 364.1
  Currid-Halkett, Elizabeth. *The Overlooked Americans* — 307.76
  Dubus, Andre. *Townie* — B
  Finkel, David. *An American Dreamer* — 975.8
  Heat Moon, William Least. *Roads to Quoz* — 917.3
  Hewitt, Ben. ★*The Town That Food Saved* — 338.1
  Hickam, Homer H. ★*Rocket Boys* — B
  Mayle, Peter. *My Twenty-Five Years in Provence* — 944.9
SMALL TOWNS
  Alexander, Brian. ★*The Hospital* — 362.10973
  Arsenault, Kerri. *Mill Town* — B
  Ash, Lamorna. *Dark, Salt, Clear* — 942.3
  Bass, Amy. *One Goal* — 796.334
  Cameron, Silver Donald. *Blood in the Water* — 364.152
  Cullen, Art. *Storm Lake* — 071.7
  Douglas, John E. *When a Killer Calls* — 364.152
  Eyre, Eric. *Death in Mud Lick* — 362.29
  Faleiro, Sonia. *The Good Girls* — 364.152
  Garcia Marquez, Gabriel. *Living to Tell the Tale* — B
  Goldstein, Amy. *Janesville* — 330.9775
  Hale, Grace Elizabeth. *In the Pines* — 364.13
  Heat Moon, William Least. *Roads to Quoz* — 917.3
  Henderson, Danielle. ★*The Ugly Cry* — B
  Hill, David. *The Vapors* — 976.7
  Kimmerle, Erin H. *We Carry Their Bones* — 365
  Kurtz, Glenn. *Three Minutes in Poland* — 947.7
  Lehr, Dick. *White Hot Hate* — 363.325
  Martin, Rachel Louise. *A Most Tolerant Little Town* — 379.2
  Masciotra, David. *Exurbia Now* — 320.973
  McGraw, Seamus. *The End of Country* — 333.7909748
  Parks, Casey. *Diary of a Misfit* — B
  Streep, Abe. *Brothers on Three* — 306.85
  Vigliotti, Jonathan. *Before It's Gone* — 577
  Watts, Reggie. *Great Falls, MT* — B
Small Victories. Lamott, Anne — 248
Small Victories. Turshen, Julia — 641.5
Small, Zachary
  ★*Token Supremacy* — 332.4
Small-Space Vegetable Gardens. Bellamy, Andrea — 635
The Smallest Lights in the Universe. Seager, Sara — B
Smalls, Alexander
  Meals, Music, and Muses — 641.59
SMALLS, ROBERT, 1839-1915
  Lineberry, Cate. *Be Free or Die* — B
SMALLWOOD, THOMAS, 1801-1883
  Shane, Scott. ★*Flee North* — 973.7
Smarsh, Sarah
  ★*Heartland* — B
  She Come by It Natural — 782.42164
SMARSH, SARAH
  Smarsh, Sarah. ★*Heartland* — B
  Smarsh, Sarah. *She Come by It Natural* — 782.42164
Smart Baseball. Law, Keith — 796.357
Smart, Maya Payne
  Reading for Our Lives — 372.4
Smarter Faster Better. Duhigg, Charles — 158
SMARTPHONES
  Haidt, Jonathan. ★*The Anxious Generation* — 305.23
  Linn, Susan. *Who's Raising the Kids?* — 649
Smashing Statues. Thompson, Erin L. — 725
Smee, Sebastian
  The Art of Rivalry — 700.92
SMELL
  Ackerman, Diane. *A Natural History of the Senses* — 152.1
  Easto, Jessica. *How to Taste Coffee* — 663

AUTHOR, TITLE, SERIES AND SUBJECT INDEX

Horowitz, Alexandra. ★*Being a Dog*	636.7
McGee, Harold. ★*Nose Dive*	612.8
Tanais. *In Sensorium*	B
Smialek, Jeanna	
★*Limitless*	332.1
Smietana, Bob	
Reorganized Religion	262.001
Smil, Vaclav	
How the World Really Works	500
Size	153.7
Smile. Ruhl, Sarah	B
Smiler, Andrew P.	
Dating and Sex	613.9071
Smiley, Jane	
Thirteen Ways of Looking at the Novel	B
SMILEY, JANE	
Smiley, Jane. *Thirteen Ways of Looking at the Novel*	B
Smilios, Maria	
★*The Black Angels*	610.73
Smith, Adam	
★*The Wealth of Nations*	330.15
SMITH, ADAM, 1723-1790	
Norman, Jesse. *Adam Smith*	B
Smith, Ben	
Traffic	070.4
Smith, Bren	
Eat Like a Fish	338.3
SMITH, BREN	
Smith, Bren. *Eat Like a Fish*	338.3
SMITH, BUSTER, 1904-1991	
Crouch, Stanley. *Kansas City Lightning*	B
Smith, Carol	
Crossing the River	B
Smith, Chris	
The Daily Show (the Book)	791.45
Smith, Clint	
★*Above Ground*	811
★*How the Word Is Passed*	973
How to Hire	658.3
Smith, Clive Stafford	
The Injustice System	345.759
Smith, Danez	
★*Don't Call Us Dead*	811.6
★*Homie*	811
Smith, Danyel	
Shine Bright	782.42164
Smith, David James	
Young Mandela	B
Smith, Dennis	
Report from Ground Zero	974.7
Smith, Douglas	
Rasputin	B
The Russian Job	947.084
SMITH, EDGAR, 1934-2017	
Weinman, Sarah. *Scoundrel*	364.152
Smith, Edward C.	
The Vegetable Gardener's Bible	635
The Vegetable Gardener's Container Bible	635
Smith, Emma	
Portable Magic	002
This Is Shakespeare	822.33
Smith, Erin Geiger	
★*Thank You for Voting*	324.973
Smith, Freda Love	
I Quit Everything	B
SMITH, FREDA LOVE	
Smith, Freda Love. *I Quit Everything*	B
Smith, G. Stevenson	
Cost Control for Nonprofits in Crisis	025.1
SMITH, HARRY EVERETT, 1923-1991	
Szwed, John F. *Cosmic Scholar*	B
Smith, Helmut Walser	
Germany, a Nation in Its Time	943
SMITH, HUSTON, 1919-2016	
Lattin, Don. *The Harvard Psychedelic Club*	973.922092
Smith, J. Douglas	
On Democracy's Doorstep	342.73
Smith, Jada Pinkett	
Worthy	B
SMITH, JADA PINKETT, 1971-	
Smith, Jada Pinkett. *Worthy*	B
Smith, James K. A.	
How to Inhabit Time	223
Smith, Jean Edward	
Bush	973.931
FDR	B
John Marshall	B
Smith, Jeremy N.	
Breaking and Entering	B
SMITH, JESSIE WILLCOX, 1863-1935	
Carter, Alice A. *The Red Rose Girls*	B
Smith, Jim B.	
The Last Mission	940.54
Smith, Joel	
Edward Steichen	779
SMITH, JOHN, 1580-1631	
Horn, James P. P. *Land as God Made It*	975.5
Price, David A. ★*Love and Hate in Jamestown*	975.5
SMITH, JOSEPH 1805-1844	
Beam, Alex. *American Crucifixion*	B
SMITH, JOSEPH, 1805-1844	
Brown, Samuel Morris. *In Heaven as It Is on Earth*	289.3
Gutjahr, Paul C. *The Book of Mormon*	289.3
Smith, Kenny	
Talk of Champions	B
SMITH, KENNY, 1965 MARCH 8-	
Smith, Kenny. *Talk of Champions*	B
Smith, Lee	
Dimestore	975.5
SMITH, LEE, 1944-	
Smith, Lee. *Dimestore*	975.5
Smith, Maggie	
★*You Could Make This Place Beautiful*	B
SMITH, MAGGIE, 1977-	
Smith, Maggie. ★*You Could Make This Place Beautiful*	B
Smith, Michael	
Cabin Fever	614.5
Smith, Michael S.	
Designing History	975.3
Smith, Michelle	
The Whole Smiths Good Food Cookbook	641.5
Smith, Mychal Denzel	
Invisible Man, Got the Whole World Watching	305.242
Stakes Is High	973.933
SMITH, MYCHAL DENZEL, 1986-	
Smith, Mychal Denzel. *Invisible Man, Got the Whole World Watching*	305.242
Smith, Nathan	
Color Concrete Garden Projects	721
Smith, Patricia	
Blood Dazzler	811
★*Incendiary Art*	811.54
Shoulda Been Jimi Savannah	811
Unshuttered	811
Smith, Patti	
★*A Book of Days*	779
Collected Lyrics	782
★*Just Kids*	B
★*M Train*	B
★*Year of the Monkey*	B
SMITH, PATTI	
Smith, Patti. ★*Just Kids*	B
Smith, Patti. ★*M Train*	B
Smith, Patti. ★*Year of the Monkey*	B
SMITH, PERRY EDWARD, 1928-1965	
Capote, Truman. ★*In Cold Blood*	364.1
Smith, R. Garth	
Asd, the Complete Autism Spectrum Disorder Health & Diet Guide	616.85
Smith, R. J.	
American Witness	B
Smith, Richard MacLean	
Unexplained	130
Smith, Richard Norton	
On His Own Terms	973.925092
An Ordinary Man	B

PUBLIC LIBRARY CORE COLLECTION: NONFICTION
Twentieth Edition

Smith, Sally Bedell
  Elizabeth the Queen — B
  George VI and Elizabeth — 920
  Prince Charles — B
Smith, Sally J.
  Fairy Houses — 745.592
Smith, Sam
  Hard Labor — 796.323
Smith, Starr
  Jimmy Stewart — B
Smith, Tracy K.
  Duende — 811
  ★*Life on Mars* — 811
  ★*Such Color* — 811
  ★*To Free the Captives* — 818
  ★*Wade in the Water* — 811.6
Smith, Will
  ★*Will* — B
SMITH, WILL, 1968-
  Smith, Will. ★*Will* — B
SMITH, WILLIAM, 1769-1839
  Winchester, Simon. *The Map That Changed the World* — B
Smith, Zadie
  ★*Feel Free* — 824
  Intimations — 824
SMITH, ZADIE
  Smith, Zadie. *Intimations* — 824
Smithsonian [Series]. Carballo, David M. — 912
Smithsonian American Table. Kingsley, Lisa — 641.5
Smithsonian Baseball. Wong, Stephen — 796.357
Smithsonian Field Guide to the Birds of North America. Floyd, Ted — 598.097
The Smithsonian History of Space Exploration. Launius, Roger D — 629.4
★*The Smitten Kitchen Cookbook*. Perelman, Deb — 641.5
★*Smitten Kitchen Every Day*. Perelman, Deb — 641.5
★*Smitten Kitchen Keepers*. Perelman, Deb — 641.5
SMOG
  Owens, Jay. *Dust* — 551.51
SMOKE
  Owens, Jay. *Dust* — 551.51
Smoke Gets in Your Eyes. Doughty, Caitlin — B
SMOKERS
  Ducharme, Jamie. *Big Vape* — 338.7
Smoketown. Whitaker, Mark — 305.896
Smokin' Joe. Kram, Mark — B
SMOKING
  Ducharme, Jamie. *Big Vape* — 338.7
  Etter, Lauren. ★*The Devil's Playbook* — 338.7
SMOYER, CLARENCE, 1923-2022
  Makos, Adam. *Spearhead* — B
SMUGGLERS
  De Leon, Jason. ★*Soldiers and Kings* — 364.1
  Hammer, Joshua. *The Falcon Thief* — 364.16
SMUGGLING
  De Leon, Jason. ★*Soldiers and Kings* — 364.1
  Jacobs, Ryan McMahon. *The Truffle Underground* — 381
Smyth, Adam
  The Book-Makers — 686.2
Smyth, Katharine
  All the Lives We Ever Lived — B
SMYTH, KATHARINE, 1981-
  Smyth, Katharine. *All the Lives We Ever Lived* — B
SNACK FOODS
  Fuentes, Laura. *The Best Homemade Kids' Snacks on the Planet* — 641.5
★*Snackable Bakes*. Sheehan, Jessie — 641.7
Snacking Cakes. Arefi, Yossy — 641.86
SNAILS
  Bailey, Elisabeth. *The Sound of a Wild Snail Eating* — 594
SNAKES
  Catania, Kenneth. *Great Adaptations* — 576.8
SNARE, JOHN
  Cumming, Laura. ★*The Vanishing Velazquez* — 759.6
SNEAKERS
  Knight, Philip H. *Shoe Dog* — B
SNETSINGER, PHOEBE, 1931-1999
  Gentile, Olivia. *Life List* — 598.072
Sniper One. Mills, Dan — 956.7044
SNIPERS
  Azad. *Long Shot* — B
  Meyer, Dakota. *Into the Fire* — 958.104
  Mills, Dan. *Sniper One* — 956.7044
  Pavlychenko, Liudmyla Mykhailivna. *Lady Death* — B
  Swofford, Anthony. *Jarhead* — 956.7044
Snodgrass, Alex
  ★*The Defined Dish* — 641.5
  Dinner Tonight — 641.5
Snodgrass, Mary Ellen
  Signs of the Zodiac — 133.5
  The Underground Railroad — 973.7
Snoop Dogg
  Goon with the Spoon — 641.59
SNOW
  Fox, Porter. *The Last Winter* — 363.738
  Redniss, Lauren. *Thunder & Lightning* — 741.5
SNOW AND ICE CLIMBING
  Panagore, Peter Baldwin. *Heaven Is Beautiful* — B
Snow, Jess
  ★*Outreach Services for Teens* — 027.4
Snow, Peter
  When Britain Burned the White House — 975.3
Snow, Richard
  Disney's Land — 791.06
Snow, Shane
  Dream Teams — 658.4
The Snowball. Schroeder, Alice — B
SNOWDEN, EDWARD J., 1983-
  Gellman, Barton. ★*Dark Mirror* — B
SNOWMOBILES
  Moore, Colten. *Catching the Sky* — B
Snyder, Brad
  A Well-Paid Slave — B
Snyder, Christina
  Great Crossings — 976.9
Snyder, Gary
  No Nature — 811
SNYDER, HOWARD, 1915-2007
  Snyder, Steve. *Shot Down* — 940.54
Snyder, Laura J.
  Eye of the Beholder — 920
Snyder, Rachel Louise
  No Visible Bruises — 362.82
  Women We Buried, Women We Burned — B
SNYDER, RACHEL LOUISE
  Snyder, Rachel Louise. *Women We Buried, Women We Burned* — B
Snyder, Sabrina
  Dinner Then Dessert — 641.5
Snyder, Steve
  Shot Down — 940.54
Snyder, Timothy
  Black Earth — 940.53
  ★*Bloodlands* — 940.54
  ★*Our Malady* — 362.10973
  The Red Prince — B
*So Close to Being the Sh*t, Y'all Don't Even Know*. Retta — B
So Far so Good. Le Guin, Ursula K. — 811
So Many Roads. Browne, David — B
So Much Longing in so Little Space. Knausgaard, Karl Ove — 759.81
So to Speak. Hayes, Terrance — 811
★*So You Want to Talk About Race*. Oluo, Ijeoma — 305.800973
So You Want to Write. Piercy, Marge — 808.3
So You've Been Publicly Shamed. Ronson, Jon — 152.4
So, Anthony Veasna
  ★*Songs on Endless Repeat* — 814
SO, ANTHONY VEASNA, 1992-2020
  So, Anthony Veasna. ★*Songs on Endless Repeat* — 814
Sobel, Dava
  Longitude — 526
  A More Perfect Heaven — 520.9
SOBOL, RICHARD B.
  Van Meter, Matthew. *Deep Delta Justice* — 345.763
Soboroff, Jacob
  ★*Separated* — 325.73
Sobremesa. Villasuso, Susana — 641.5972
SOBRIETY
  Barnett, Erica C. *Quitter* — B
  Biden, Robert Hunter. *Beautiful Things* — B
  Butcher, Barbara. *What the Dead Know* — 614

AUTHOR, TITLE, SERIES AND SUBJECT INDEX

Carr, Erin Lee. *All That You Leave Behind*	B
Jamison, Leslie. ★*The Recovering*	B
Khar, Erin. *Strung Out*	B
Milch, David. *Life's Work*	B
Schemel, Patty. *Hit so Hard*	B
Smith, Freda Love. *I Quit Everything*	B
Stamos, John. *If You Would Have Told Me*	B
Stone, Sly. *Thank You (Falettinme Be Mice Elf Agin)*	B
Whitaker, Holly. ★*Quit Like a Woman*	616.86
Wilder-Taylor, Stefanie. ★*Drunk-Ish*	B

SOCCER
Abbot, Sebastian. *The Away Game*	796.334
Anderson, Christopher. *The Numbers Game*	796.334
Bass, Amy. *One Goal*	796.334
Bennett, Roger. *Men in Blazers Present Encyclopedia Blazertannica*	796.334
Bensinger, Ken. ★*Red Card*	796.334
Conn, David. *The Fall of the House of FIFA*	796.334
Cox, Michael. *Zonal Marking*	796
Dohrmann, George. *Switching Fields*	796.334
Galeano, Eduardo. *Soccer in Sun and Shadow*	796.334
Goldblatt, David. ★*The Age of Football*	796.334
Honigstein, Raphael. *DAS Reboot*	796.334
Hopcraft, Arthur. *The Football Man*	796.334
Kirschbaum, Erik. *Soccer Without Borders*	B
Kuper, Simon. *Soccernomics*	796.334
Lloyd, Carli. *When Nobody Was Watching*	B
Oxenham, Gwendolyn. *Under the Lights and in the Dark*	796.334
Papenfuss, Mary. *American Huckster*	B
Rapinoe, Megan. *One Life*	B
Vecsey, George. *Eight World Cups*	796.334
Villoro, Juan. *God Is Round*	796.334
Wahl, Grant. ★*Masters of Modern Soccer*	796.334
Wambach, Abby. *Forward*	B

SOCCER COACHES
Kirschbaum, Erik. *Soccer Without Borders*	B
St. John, Warren. *Outcasts United*	B

SOCCER COACHING
Dohrmann, George. *Switching Fields*	796.334

SOCCER FOR CHILDREN
Dohrmann, George. *Switching Fields*	796.334

SOCCER FOR WOMEN
Clarke, Gemma. *Soccerwomen*	796.334
Soccer in Sun and Shadow. Galeano, Eduardo	796.334

SOCCER PLAYERS
Bennett, Roger. *Men in Blazers Present Encyclopedia Blazertannica*	796.334
Clarke, Gemma. *Soccerwomen*	796.334
Cox, Michael. *Zonal Marking*	796
Galeano, Eduardo. *Soccer in Sun and Shadow*	796.334
Lloyd, Carli. *When Nobody Was Watching*	B
Rogers, Robbie. *Coming Out to Play*	B
Vecsey, George. *Eight World Cups*	796.334
Villoro, Juan. *God Is Round*	796.334
Wahl, Grant. ★*Masters of Modern Soccer*	796.334
Wambach, Abby. *Forward*	B

SOCCER TEAMS
Cox, Michael. *Zonal Marking*	796
Gutman, Matt. *The Boys in the Cave*	796.52
Lloyd, Carli. *When Nobody Was Watching*	B
Mufleh, Luma. ★*Learning America*	371.826

SOCCER TOURNAMENTS
Conn, David. *The Fall of the House of FIFA*	796.334
Soccer Without Borders. Kirschbaum, Erik	
Soccernomics. Kuper, Simon	796.334
Soccerwomen. Clarke, Gemma	796.334

SOCIAL ACCEPTANCE
Blake, Melissa. *Beautiful People*	362.4
Clein, Emmeline. ★*Dead Weight*	616.85
Ellis, Bret Easton. *White*	814
George-Warren, Holly. ★*Janis*	B
Tammet, Daniel. *Born on a Blue Day*	B

SOCIAL ACTION
Abrams, Stacey. *Lead from the Outside*	B
Barber, William J. *We Are Called to Be a Movement*	261.8
Eltahawy, Mona. *The Seven Necessary Sins for Women and Girls*	305.42
Estes, Nick. *Our History Is the Future*	978.004
Farmer, Lesley S. J. ★*Impactful Community-Based Literacy Projects*	372.6
Gray, Emma. *A Girl's Guide to Joining the Resistance*	303.48
Shah, Rajiv Janardan. *Big Bets*	303.4

Sharpton, Al. *Rise Up*	973.933
Sokolik, Vicki. ★*If You See Them*	362.5
Terkel, Studs. *Hope Dies Last*	920

SOCIAL ADVOCACY
Adler, Kevin F. *When We Walk By*	362.5
Akins, Damon B. ★*We Are the Land*	978
Alexander, Kwame. *Light for the World to See*	811.6
Alter, Jonathan. *His Very Best*	B
Amos, Tori. *Resistance*	B
Avlon, John P. *Lincoln and the Fight for Peace*	973.7
Babb, Valerie Melissa. *The Book of James*	B
Belser, Julia Watts. ★*Loving Our Own Bones*	296
Black, Dustin Lance. *Mama's Boy*	B
Blais, Madeleine. *Queen of the Court*	B
Bookman, Marc. *A Descending Spiral*	345.73
Brownstein, Gabriel. ★*The Secret Mind of Bertha Pappenheim*	616.85
Canellos, Peter S. *The Great Dissenter*	B
Citron, Danielle Keats. *The Fight for Privacy*	342.7308
Clark, Anna. *The Poisoned City*	363.6
Cooper, Christian. *Better Living Through Birding*	B
Craig, Mya-Rose. *Birdgirl*	B
Cullen, Art. *Storm Lake*	071.7
Daley, Mark. *Safe*	B
Desmond, Matthew. ★*Poverty, by America*	362.5
Farrell, John A. *Clarence Darrow*	B
Fried, Stephen. *Rush*	B
Gabriel, Mary. *Madonna*	B
Gregory, Dick. *Defining Moments in Black History*	973
Griffith, Elisabeth. *Formidable*	305.42
Hamilton, Denise. ★*Indivisible*	658.3
Hardy, Alyssa. *Worn Out*	338.4
Hennessy, Kate. *Dorothy Day*	B
Henny, Ally. *I Won't Shut Up*	305.896
Hill, Anita. ★*Believing*	305.42
Hirshman, Linda R. *Reckoning*	305.420973
Hochschild, Adam. *Lessons from a Dark Time*	909.82
Hoja, Gulchehra. *A Stone Is Most Precious Where It Belongs*	B
Ice-T. *Split Decision*	920
Jaffe, Sarah W. *Wanting What's Best*	649
Jarrett, Valerie. *Finding My Voice*	B
Kimble, Megan. ★*City Limits*	388.1
Klein, Naomi. ★*Doppelganger*	302.2
LaPointe, Sasha taqwseblu. *Thunder Song*	814
Lithwick, Dahlia. *Lady Justice*	345.73
McGowan, Rose. *Brave*	B
Mikhaiil, Dunya. *The Beekeeper*	956.7044
Mojica Rodriguez, Prisca Dorcas. *For Brown Girls with Sharp Edges and Tender Hearts*	305.48
Mufleh, Luma. ★*Learning America*	371.826
Murad, Nadia. ★*The Last Girl*	B
Nyamayaro, Elizabeth. *I Am a Girl from Africa*	B
Oluo, Ijeoma. ★*Be a Revolution*	305.8
Page, Elliot. *Pageboy*	B
Page, Susan. ★*The Matriarch*	B
Prejean, Helen. *River of Fire*	B
Pryce, Jessica. ★*Broken*	362.7
Purnell, Derecka. *Becoming Abolitionists*	363.20973
Quinones, John. ★*One Year in Uvalde*	371.7
Ricketts, Rachel. ★*Do Better*	305.800973
Ryan, Maureen. *Burn It Down*	791.43
Shehadeh, Raja. ★*We Could Have Been Friends, My Father and I*	B
Sokolik, Vicki. ★*If You See Them*	362.5
Tamblyn, Amber. ★*Era of Ignition*	B
Thomas, Etan. *We Matter*	796.08
Tolokonnikova, Nadezhda. *Rules for Rulebreakers*	782.42166
Washington, Kerry. *Thicker Than Water*	B
Weigel, Alicia Roth. *Inverse Cowgirl*	B
Wilbur, Matika. *Project 562*	970.004
Williams, Sophie. *Anti-Racist Ally*	305.8

SOCIAL ADVOCATES
Ai, Weiwei. *1000 Years of Joys and Sorrows*	709.2
Alinizhad, Masih. *The Wind in My Hair*	B
Avlon, John P. *Lincoln and the Fight for Peace*	973.7
Baime, A. J. *White Lies*	B
Blain, Keisha N. *Until I Am Free*	B
Bono. ★*Surrender*	B
Brooks, Maegan Parker. *Fannie Lou Hamer*	B
Clark, John Lee. *Touch the Future*	B

PUBLIC LIBRARY CORE COLLECTION: NONFICTION
Twentieth Edition

Dayen, David. *Chain of Title*	330.973
Diamant, Anita. ★*Period. End of Sentence*	612.6
DiMarco, Nyle. ★*Deaf Utopia*	B
Evaristo, Bernardine. *Manifesto*	B
Goodall, Jane. ★*The Book of Hope*	128
Guha, Ramachandra. *Gandhi Before India*	B
Guha, Ramachandra. *Gandhi*	B
Guha, Ramachandra. *Rebels Against the Raj*	954.03
Hamlin, Kimberly A. *Free Thinker*	B
Harrison, Scott. *Thirst*	B
Heumann, Judith E. *Being Heumann*	B
Hoffman, David E. *Give Me Liberty*	B
Jackson, Lawrence Patrick. *Chester B. Himes*	B
Joseph, Peniel E. *The Sword and the Shield*	B
Keith, Philip A. *All Blood Runs Red*	B
Kelly, Kate. *Ordinary Equality*	920
King, Greg. *The Ghost Forest*	333.75
Kruzan, Sara. *I Cried to Dream Again*	B
Larson, Kate Clifford. *Walk with Me*	B
Mandela, Nelson. *Conversations with Myself*	B
Mandela, Nelson. *Dare Not Linger*	B
Mandela, Nelson. ★*Long Walk to Freedom*	B
Mandela, Nelson. *Mandela*	B
Mandela, Nelson. *The Prison Letters of Nelson Mandela*	968.06092
McCloskey, Jim. *When Truth Is All You Have*	B
Peterson, Marlon. *Bird Uncaged*	B
Prose, Francine. *1974*	B
Rapinoe, Megan. *One Life*	B
Rodgers, Jodi. ★*How to Find a Four-Leaf Clover*	616.85
Ross, Steve. *From Broken Glass*	B
Rothenberg, Ben. *Naomi Osaka*	B
Roundtree, Dovey Johnson. ★*Mighty Justice*	B
Rudd, Mark. *Underground*	378.1
Sen, Amartya. *Home in the World*	B
Sokolik, Vicki. ★*If You See Them*	362.5
Spofford, Tim. *What the Children Told Us*	150.92
Stevenson, Bryan. *Just Mercy*	B
Washington, Booker T. ★*Up from Slavery*	B
Wiesel, Elie. *And the Sea Is Never Full*	B
Williams, Michelle. *Checking In*	B
Windsor, Edie. *A Wild and Precious Life*	B
Wolf, Brandon J. *A Place for Us*	B
Wong, Alice. ★*Year of the Tiger*	B
The Social Animal. Brooks, David	305.5

SOCIAL BEHAVIOR

Brooks, David. ★*How to Know a Person*	158.2
Hammond, Claudia. *Mind Over Money*	332.401
Pinker, Steven. ★*Enlightenment Now*	303.44
Pryor, Elizabeth Brown. *Six Encounters with Lincoln*	973.7092
Zimbardo, Philip G. *The Lucifer Effect*	155.9

SOCIAL BEHAVIOR IN ANIMALS

Ackerman, Jennifer. ★*What an Owl Knows*	598.9
Goodall, Jane. ★*In the Shadow of Man*	599.8
Holldobler, Bert. *The Superorganism*	595.7
Safina, Carl. ★*Becoming Wild*	591.7
Sumner, Seirian. *Endless Forms*	595.79
Toomey, David. *Kingdom of Play*	591.56
Ward, Ashley. *The Social Lives of Animals*	591.7
Wood, Levison. *The Last Giants*	599.67

SOCIAL BEHAVIOR IN CHIMPANZEES

Goodall, Jane. ★*In the Shadow of Man*	599.8

SOCIAL BEHAVIOR IN INSECTS

Holldobler, Bert. *The Superorganism*	595.7

SOCIAL CHANGE

Abrams, Stacey. *Lead from the Outside*	B
Abrams, Stacey. *Our Time Is Now*	324.60973
Adichie, Chimamanda Ngozi. *We Should All Be Feminists*	305.42
Ahmed, Sara. *The Feminist Killjoy Handbook*	305.42
Alberta, Tim. *The Kingdom, the Power, and the Glory*	270.8
Amos, Tori. *Resistance*	B
Atwood, Margaret. *Burning Questions*	814
Ayers, Edward L. *American Visions*	973.5
Benjamin, Ruha. ★*Imagination*	302
Bidwell, Duane R. *When One Religion Isn't Enough*	261.2
Blanning, T. C. W. *Frederick the Great*	B
Bordewich, Fergus M. *Congress at War*	324.2734
Boykin, Keith. *Race Against Time*	305.8
Brands, H. W. *The Age of Gold*	979.4
Brands, H. W. *Traitor to His Class*	B
Brill, Steven. *Tailspin*	306.0973
Brown, Emma. *To Raise a Boy*	649
Broyles, Michael. ★*Revolutions in American Music*	780.9
Burak, Asi. *Power Play*	794.8
Caldwell, Christopher. *The Age of Entitlement*	305.240973
Chemaly, Soraya L. *Rage Becomes Her*	155.3
Churchwell, Sarah Bartlett. *Behold, America*	973.9
Cross, Tiffany D. ★*Say It Louder!*	324.6
Curzan, Anne. ★*Says Who?*	428
Darnell, John Coleman. *Egypt's Golden Couple*	932
De Long, J. Bradford. *Slouching Towards Utopia*	330.9
Demick, Barbara. *Eat the Buddha*	951
Dennis, David J., Jr. *The Movement Made Us*	B
Diamond, Jared M. *Collapse*	304.2
Diamond, Jared M. *Upheaval*	303.48
Douthat, Ross Gregory. *To Change the Church*	230
Dubin, Minna. ★*Mom Rage*	306.874
Dyson, Michael Eric. *What Truth Sounds Like*	305.800973
Eilenberger, Wolfram. *Time of the Magicians*	920
Ernaux, Annie. ★*The Years*	B
Ferrer, Ada. ★*Cuba*	972.91
Figes, Orlando. *A People's Tragedy*	947.08
Finan, Christopher M. *How Free Speech Saved Democracy*	342.73
Finkel, David. *An American Dreamer*	975.8
Francis. *Life*	B
Frank, Barney. *Frank*	B
Friedman, Thomas L. ★*Thank You for Being Late*	303.48
Gabriel, Mary. *Ninth Street Women*	920
Garbes, Angela. *Essential Labor*	306.874
Garza, Alicia. *The Purpose of Power*	303.48
Gessen, Masha. *Surviving Autocracy*	973.933
Ghobash, Omar Saif. *Letters to a Young Muslim*	297.09
Giridharadas, Anand. ★*The Persuaders*	320.973
Givhan, Robin. *The Battle of Versailles*	746.9
Gladwell, Malcolm. *The Tipping Point*	302
Gopnik, Blake. ★*Warhol*	B
Gray, Emma. *A Girl's Guide to Joining the Resistance*	303.48
Gregory, Dick. *Defining Moments in Black History*	973
Griffith, Elisabeth. *Formidable*	305.42
Guha, Ramachandra. *Gandhi*	B
Hamilton, Denise. ★*Indivisible*	658.3
Hardman, Robert. *Queen of Our Times*	B
Hardwick, Lamar. *How Ableism Fuels Racism*	261.8
Henny, Ally. *I Won't Shut Up*	305.896
Herman, Arthur. *1917*	940.3
Hessler, Peter. *The Buried*	962.05
Hessler, Peter. *Other Rivers*	378.1
Hochschild, Adam. *Spain in Our Hearts*	946.081
Holzer, Harold. *Brought Forth on This Continent*	973.7
Howe, Daniel Walker. *What Hath God Wrought*	973.5
Hubbard, Shanita. *Ride-Or-Die*	305.48
Issenberg, Sasha. ★*The Engagement*	346.7301
Jahner, Harald. ★*Aftermath*	943.087
Kan, Karoline. *Under Red Skies*	B
Kelly, Helena. *Jane Austen, the Secret Radical*	823
Kennedy, Robert Francis. *RFK*	973.92
King, Charles. *Midnight at the Pera Palace*	949.61
King, Charles. *Odessa*	947.7
Klosterman, Chuck. ★*The Nineties*	306.0973
Lankov, A. N. *The Real North Korea*	951.9304
Lee, Julia Sun-Joo. *Biting the Hand*	B
Levine, Bruce C. *The Fall of the House of Dixie*	973.7
Lunenfeld, Peter. *City at the Edge of Forever*	979.4
Mallory, Tamika D. *State of Emergency*	305.896
Martin, Rachel Louise. *A Most Tolerant Little Town*	379.2
McGreevy, John T. ★*Catholicism*	282.09
McMeekin, Sean. *The Russian Revolution*	947.084
Moore, Lorrie. *See What Can Be Done*	801
Moore, Susanna. *Paradise of the Pacific*	996.9
Moss, Jeremiah. *Feral City*	B
Nagourney, Adam. *The Times*	071
Nhat Hanh. *Zen and the Art of Saving the Planet*	294.3
Nicolson, Juliet. *The Great Silence*	941.083
Nye, Bill. *Everything All at Once*	153.4
O'Rourke, P. J. *None of My Business*	332
Oates, Joyce Carol. *American Melancholy*	811
Osnos, Evan. *Age of Ambition*	951.06

AUTHOR, TITLE, SERIES AND SUBJECT INDEX

Owens, Ernest. ★*The Case for Cancel Culture* — 303.3
Owens, Lama Rod. *Love and Rage* — 152.4
Perry, Imani. *May We Forever Stand* — 782.25
Phillips, Collette A. M. *The Includers* — 658.4
Piketty, Thomas. ★*Capital and Ideology* — 305
Popkin, Jeremy D. *A New World Begins* — 944.04
Postel, Charles. *Equality* — 305.50973
Preston, Paul. *The Spanish Holocaust* — 946.081
Prose, Francine. *1974* — B
Rappaport, Helen. *Caught in the Revolution* — 355.00947
Reeves, Richard V. *Dream Hoarders* — 305.5
Reiss, Benjamin. *Wild Nights* — 616.8
Ridley, Jane. *George V* — B
Rubenstein, David M. *The American Experiment* — 973
Russell, Gareth. *The Ship of Dreams* — 910.91
Ryan, Maureen. *Burn It Down* — 791.43
Sage, Sami. *Democracy in Retrograde* — 324
Sandel, Michael J. *Justice* — 172
Savage, Jon. ★*1966* — 781.6609
Sciubba, Jennifer Dabbs. *8 Billion and Counting* — 304.6
Shah, Rajiv Janardan. *Big Bets* — 303.4
Shahvisi, Arianne. *Arguing for a Better World* — 170
Sharma, Ruchir. *The Rise and Fall of Nations* — 330.9
Simon, James F. *Eisenhower vs. Warren* — 347.73
Sjunneson, Elsa. *Being Seen* — 362.4
Smith, Mychal Denzel. *Stakes Is High* — 973.933
Sorin, Gretchen Sullivan. *Driving While Black* — 323.1196
St. John, Warren. *Outcasts United* — B
Stanley, Brian. *Christianity in the Twentieth Century* — 270.8
Szablowski, Witold. *Dancing Bears* — 947.086
Taubman, William. *Gorbachev* — B
Tesfamariam, Rahiel. ★*Imagine Freedom* — 305.896
Tolentino, Jia. ★*Trick Mirror* — 973.93
Totenberg, Nina. ★*Dinners with Ruth* — B
Traister, Rebecca. *Good and Mad* — 305.420973
Trentmann, Frank. *Out of the Darkness* — 943.08
Turchin, Peter. *End Times* — 320.01
Tye, Larry. ★*The Jazzmen* — 781.6509
Ullrich, Volker. *Germany 1923* — 943.085
V. ★*Reckoning* — 814
Warzel, Charlie. *Out of Office* — 658.3
Weisman, Steven R. *The Chosen Wars* — 296.0973
Whitby, Andrew. *The Sum of the People* — 001.4
Wills, Garry. *The Future of the Catholic Church with Pope Francis* — 282.09
Wolf, Martin. ★*The Crisis of Democratic Capitalism* — 330.12
Wolff, Daniel J. *Grown-Up Anger* — 920
Woods, Randall Bennett. *Prisoners of Hope* — 973.923
Yancey, Philip. ★*Where the Light Fell* — B
Ypi, Lea. ★*Free* — B
Zakaria, Fareed. *Age of Revolutions* — 303.6
Zeitz, Joshua. *Building the Great Society* — 973.923
Zoepf, Katherine. *Excellent Daughters* — 305.42

SOCIAL CLASSES

Baldwin, James. ★*Notes of a Native Son* — 305.8
Beard, Mary. ★*Women & Power* — 305.409
Bee, Vanessa A. *Home Bound* — B
Belcher, Chris. *Pretty Baby* — B
Berg, Scott W. *The Burning of the World* — 977.311
Biss, Eula. *Having and Being Had* — 306.3
Bossiere, Zoe. *Cactus Country* — 306
Brands, H. W. *Traitor to His Class* — B
Brown, David S. *Paradise Lost* — 813
Bruni, Frank. *Where You Go Is Not Who You'll Be* — 378.1
Eddo-Lodge, Reni. *Why I'm No Longer Talking to White People About Race* — 305.8
Evaristo, Bernardine. *Manifesto* — B
Everitt, Anthony. *The Rise of Rome* — 937
Fowler, Corinne. ★*The Countryside* — 941
Gerald, Casey. *There Will Be No Miracles Here* — B
Goldstein, Dana. *The Teacher Wars* — 371.1020973
Goodman, Matthew. *The City Game* — 796.323
Haddish, Tiffany. *The Last Black Unicorn* — B
Hedges, Chris. *Days of Destruction, Days of Revolt* — 741.5
Henderson, Rob Kim. *Troubled* — B
Hobbs, Jeff. *Show Them You're Good* — 373
Imani, Blair. *Read This to Get Smarter* — 303.3
Isenberg, Nancy. *White Trash* — 305.5
Jones, Jacqueline. *Saving Savannah* — 975.8

Joyce, Patrick. *Remembering Peasants* — 305.5
Kelly, Joseph. *Marooned* — 975.5
Laing, Olivia. *The Garden Against Time* — 635
Levine, Bruce C. *The Fall of the House of Dixie* — 973.7
Levy, Jonathan. *Ages of American Capitalism* — 330.12
Mahjoub, Jamal. *A Line in the River* — 962.404
Martin, Wednesday. *Primates of Park Avenue* — 974.7
Mask, Deirdre. *The Address Book* — 388.1
McGrath, Tom. *Triumph of the Yuppies* — 305.242
McLaughlin, Kathleen. *Blood Money* — 362.17
McMeekin, Sean. *The Russian Revolution* — 947.084
Mechanic, Michael. *Jackpot* — 305.5
Miles, Jonathan. *St. Petersburg* — 947
Murray, Charles A. *Coming Apart* — 305.8
Neiman, Garrett. *Rich White Men* — 305.5
Nicolson, Juliet. *The Great Silence* — 941.083
Norris, Michele. ★*Our Hidden Conversations* — 305
Piketty, Thomas. *A Brief History of Equality* — 305.09
Piketty, Thomas. *The Economics of Inequality* — 339.2
Plummer, Christopher. *In Spite of Myself* — B
Postel, Charles. *Equality* — 305.50973
Rivlin, Gary. *Broke, USA* — 339.4
Russell, Gareth. *The Ship of Dreams* — 910.91
Servon, Lisa J. *The Unbanking of America* — 332.10973
Smarsh, Sarah. *She Come by It Natural* — 782.42164
Smith, Tracy K. ★*Wade in the Water* — 811.6
Taub, Jennifer. *Big Dirty Money* — 364.16
Trice, Dawn Turner. ★*Three Girls from Bronzeville* — 977.311
Turchin, Peter. *End Times* — 320.01
Wainaina, Binyavanga. ★*How to Write About Africa* — 814
Wilkerson, Isabel. ★*Caste* — 305.5
Williams, David. *Bitterly Divided* — 973.7
Wu, Simon. *Dancing on My Own* — 700.1
Zara, Christopher. *Uneducated* — B

SOCIAL CLASSES AND FAMILY

Faliveno, Melissa. *Tomboyland* — B
Jefferson, Margo. *Negroland* — 305.896
McMillan, Tracie. ★*The White Bonus* — 305.8

SOCIAL CONFLICT

Blattman, Christopher. *Why We Fight* — 303.6
Brands, H. W. ★*Our First Civil War* — 973.3
Caldwell, Christopher. *The Age of Entitlement* — 305.240973
Crawford, Alan Pell. *This Fierce People* — 975
DiResta, Renee. *Invisible Rulers* — 320
Fraser, Steve. *The Age of Acquiescence* — 973.91
Ghattas, Kim. *Black Wave* — 955.05
Gladwell, Malcolm. ★*Talking to Strangers* — 302
Grinspan, Jon. *Wide Awake* — 973.7
Hirsch, James S. *Riot and Remembrance* — 976.6
Jackson, Major. *Razzle Dazzle* — 811
Kelly, John. *The Graves Are Walking* — 941.5081
Kershner, Isabel. *The Land of Hope and Fear* — 956.9405
Martin, Rachel Louise. *A Most Tolerant Little Town* — 379.2
Matloff, Judith. *No Friends but the Mountains* — 355.009
Mays, Kyle. ★*An Afro-Indigenous History of the United States* — 973
Mogelson, Luke. *The Storm Is Here* — 973.933
Nasr, Seyyed Vali Reza. *The Shia Revival* — 297.8
Price, Polly J. *Plagues in the Nation* — 614.4
Shackle, Samira. *Karachi Vice* — 954.91
Smith, Tracy K. ★*To Free the Captives* — 818
Theoharis, Jeanne. *A More Beautiful and Terrible History* — 323.1196
Tyson, Neil deGrasse. *Starry Messenger* — 901
Williams, David. *Bitterly Divided* — 973.7
★*The Social Conquest of Earth*. Wilson, Edward O. — 599.93

SOCIAL CONTRACT

Marx, Karl. ★*The Communist Manifesto* — 355.4
Rousseau, Jean-Jacques. ★*The Social Contract* — 320.1
★*The Social Contract*. Rousseau, Jean-Jacques — 320.1

SOCIAL CONTROL

Branigan, Tania. *Red Memory* — 951.05
Chayka, Kyle. *Filterworld* — 306
Hessler, Peter. *Other Rivers* — 378.1
Hoja, Gulchehra. *A Stone Is Most Precious Where It Belongs* — B
Hope, Bradley. *Blood and Oil* — B
McHangama, Jacob. ★*Free Speech* — 323.44
Molnar, Petra. *The Walls Have Eyes* — 363.28
Moore, Kate. ★*The Woman They Could Not Silence* — B
O'Neil, Cathy. *The Shame Machine* — 152.4

PUBLIC LIBRARY CORE COLLECTION: NONFICTION
Twentieth Edition

Peters, Rebecca Todd. *Trust Women*	362.1988
Ronson, Jon. *So You've Been Publicly Shamed*	152.4
Rutherford, Adam. *Control*	363.9
Stille, Alexander. *The Sullivanians*	307.77
Whitaker, Holly. ★*Quit Like a Woman*	616.86
Whitby, Andrew. *The Sum of the People*	001.4

SOCIAL CRITICISM
Evans, William. *Black Nerd Problems*	814.6
Gay, Roxane. ★*Opinions*	814
Gessen, Masha. *Surviving Autocracy*	973.933
Griffin, Farah Jasmine. ★*In Search of a Beautiful Freedom*	814
Hurston, Zora Neale. ★*You Don't Know Us Negroes and Other Essays*	814
Isen, Tajja. *Some of My Best Friends*	305.8
Nelson, Maggie. ★*Like Love*	814
Oyler, Lauren. *No Judgment*	814
Penaluna, Regan. ★*How to Think Like a Woman*	190.82
Phillips, Maya. *Nerd*	302.23
Sedaris, David. ★*Happy-Go-Lucky*	814
Sjunneson, Elsa. *Being Seen*	362.4
Wainaina, Binyavanga. ★*How to Write About Africa*	814

SOCIAL DARWINISM
Levy, Jonathan. *Ages of American Capitalism*	330.12

SOCIAL DRINKING
Cheever, Susan. *Drinking in America*	394.1

SOCIAL ETHICS
Callahan, David. *The Cheating Culture*	174
Dederer, Claire. ★*Monsters*	700.1
Standefer, Katherine E. *Lightning Flowers*	B

SOCIAL EVOLUTION
Diamond, Jared M. *Guns, Germs, and Steel*	303.4
Diamond, Jared M. *Upheaval*	303.48
Graeber, David. *The Dawn of Everything*	901
Wilson, Edward O. *Half-Earth*	333.95
Wilson, Edward O. *The Meaning of Human Existence*	128
Wilson, Edward O. ★*The Social Conquest of Earth*	599.93

SOCIAL FORECASTING
Bregman, Rutger. *Utopia for Realists*	335
Burak, Asi. *Power Play*	794.8
Christakis, Nicholas A. *Apollo's Arrow*	362.1962
Francis. *Life*	B
Lankov, A. N. *The Real North Korea*	951.9304
Lee, Kai-Fu. *AI 2041*	006.3
Turchin, Peter. *End Times*	320.01

SOCIAL GROUPS
Bahcall, Safi. *Loonshots*	658.4
Lowery, Brian S. *Selfless*	155.2
Maupin, Armistead. *Logical Family*	B
Scott, Andy. *One Kiss or Two?*	395.4
Thompson, Clive. *Coders*	005.1092

SOCIAL HISTORY
Anderson, Sam. *Boom Town*	976.6
Dabiri, Emma. *Twisted*	391.5
Diamond, Jared M. *Collapse*	304.2
Diamond, Jared M. *Upheaval*	303.48
DuVal, Kathleen. ★*Native Nations*	970.004
Ekirch, A. Roger. ★*At Day's Close*	306.4
Ernaux, Annie. ★*The Years*	B
Finney, Nikky. *Love Child's Hotbed of Occasional Poetry*	811
Gibson, Marion. *Witchcraft*	133.4
Goldblatt, David. *The Games*	796.4809
Graeber, David. *The Dawn of Everything*	901
Greenberg, Amy S. *Lady First*	B
Haag, Pamela. ★*The Gunning of America*	338.4
Hankir, Zahra. *Eyeliner*	391.6
Henaut, Stephane. *A Bite-Sized History of France*	394.1
Holton, Woody. *Liberty Is Sweet*	973.3
Hughes, Bettany. *Istanbul*	949.61
Inglis, Lucy. *Milk of Paradise*	362.29
Isenberg, Nancy. *White Trash*	305.5
Jennings, Ken. *Planet Funny*	809.7
Joyce, Patrick. *Remembering Peasants*	305.5
Kelley, Blair Murphy. *Black Folk*	331.6
Kimble, Megan. ★*City Limits*	388.1
Klinenberg, Eric. ★*2020*	306
Krist, Gary. *The Mirage Factory*	920
Lee, Corky. ★*Corky Lee's Asian America*	770
MacGregor, Neil. *A History of the World in 100 Objects*	930.1
McCourt, Frank H. ★*Our Biggest Fight*	303.48

McGill, Joseph. *Sleeping with the Ancestors*	306.362
McKeen, William. *Everybody Had an Ocean*	781.6609
Mertens, Maggie. *Better Faster Farther*	796.42
Nielsen, Kim E. *A Disability History of the United States*	362.40973
Olsen, Craig. *P.S. Burn This Letter Please*	306.76
Parker, Morgan. ★*You Get What You Pay For*	305.896
Pinckney, Darryl. *Busted in New York and Other Essays*	305.800973
Qureshi, Saqib Iqbal. *Being Muslim Today*	305.6
Rehak, Melanie. *Girl Sleuth*	813
Robb, Graham. *Parisians*	944
Rosner, Elizabeth. *Survivor Cafe*	940.53
Rothfeld, Becca. ★*All Things Are Too Small*	814
Savage, Jon. ★*1966*	781.6609
Sides, Hampton. *Hellhound on His Trail*	364.152
Snyder, Christina. *Great Crossings*	976.9
Stark, Lizzie. ★*Egg*	641.3
Tietjen, Jill S. *Hollywood, Her Story*	791.43
Tipton-Martin, Toni. *The Jemima Code*	641.59
Traig, Jennifer. *Act Natural*	306.874
Tsui, Bonnie. *Why We Swim*	797.2
Tuchman, Barbara W. *The Proud Tower*	909.82
Weisman, Steven R. *The Chosen Wars*	296.0973
Weldon, Glen. ★*The Caped Crusade*	741.5
Wills, Clair. ★*Missing Persons*	929.2
Wolfe, Tom. *The Kingdom of Speech*	401

SOCIAL INDICATORS
Currid-Halkett, Elizabeth. *The Overlooked Americans*	307.76
O'Neil, Cathy. *Weapons of Math Destruction*	005.7
Pinker, Steven. ★*Enlightenment Now*	303.44

SOCIAL INFLUENCE
Petersen, Sara. *Momfluenced*	306.87
Purnell, Carolyn. *The Sensational Past*	152.109
Sullivan, Matt. *Can't Knock the Hustle*	796.323

SOCIAL INTEGRATION
Baker, Calvin. *A More Perfect Reunion*	305.800973
Brookhiser, Richard. *Give Me Liberty*	320.540973
Nagassar, Rohadi. *When We Belong*	254
Rodgers, Jodi. ★*How to Find a Four-Leaf Clover*	616.85
Yoshino, Kenji. *Say the Right Thing*	305.3
Zakaria, Rafia. *Against White Feminism*	305.42
★*Social Intelligence*. Goleman, Daniel	158.2

SOCIAL INTELLIGENCE
Goleman, Daniel. ★*Social Intelligence*	158.2

SOCIAL INTERACTION
Baker, Billy. *We Need to Hang Out*	177
Denworth, Lydia. *Friendship*	158.2
Duhigg, Charles. ★*Supercommunicators*	153.6
Field, Andy. *Encounterism*	302
Hotz, Julia. ★*The Connection Cure*	610
Killam, Kasley. *The Art and Science of Connection*	302
Lancaster, Jen. *Welcome to the United States of Anxiety*	155.4
Ruffin, Amber. ★*The World Record Book of Racist Stories*	305.896
Ruffin, Amber. *You'll Never Believe What Happened to Lacey*	305.896
Skach, C. L. *How to Be a Citizen*	323.6

SOCIAL INTERACTION IN CHILDREN
Nowicki, Stephen. *Raising a Socially Successful Child*	649

SOCIAL ISOLATION
Adler, Kevin F. *When We Walk By*	362.5
Bell, Laura. *Claiming Ground*	B
Betz-Hamilton, Axton. *The Less People Know About Us*	364.16
Christakis, Nicholas A. *Apollo's Arrow*	362.1962
Dochartaigh, Kerri ni. *Cacophony of Bone*	B
Farley, Audrey Clare. ★*Girls and Their Monsters*	306.875
Fessler, Pam. *Carville's Cure*	362.19699
Laing, Olivia. ★*The Lonely City*	700.1
Manaugh, Geoff. *Until Proven Safe*	614.4
Matloff, Judith. *No Friends but the Mountains*	355.009
Parker, Morgan. ★*You Get What You Pay For*	305.896
Prickett, Pamela J. ★*The Unclaimed*	363.7
Radtke, Kristen. *Seek You*	741.5
Smith, Freda Love. *I Quit Everything*	B
Smith, Zadie. *Intimations*	824
Tate, Christie. *B.F.F.*	B
Zambreno, Kate. *The Light Room*	B

SOCIAL ISSUES — EDUCATION
Burger, Ariel. *Witness*	848
Powell, Nate. ★*Lies My Teacher Told Me*	741.5

AUTHOR, TITLE, SERIES AND SUBJECT INDEX

SOCIAL ISSUES — ENVIRONMENT — CONSERVATION
Cline, Elizabeth L. *The Conscious Closet* ... 646
SOCIAL ISSUES — HUMAN RIGHTS — LGBTQIA+
Bongiovanni, Archie. *A Quick & Easy Guide to They/Them Pronouns* ... 741.5
Gottlieb, Iris. *Seeing Gender* ... 305.3
SOCIAL ISSUES — HUMAN RIGHTS — RACE AND ETHNICITY
Powell, Nate. ★*Lies My Teacher Told Me* ... 741.5
SOCIAL JUSTICE
Abdulali, Sohaila. *What We Talk About When We Talk About Rape* ... 364.15
Adams, Jarrett. *Redeeming Justice* ... 340.092
Aguon, Julian. *No Country for Eight-Spot Butterflies* ... 305.89
Alexander, Elizabeth. ★*The Trayvon Generation* ... 305.896
Andrews-Dyer, Helena. *Reclaiming Her Time* ... B
Archibald, John. *Shaking the Gates of Hell* ... B
Arsenault, Raymond. *John Lewis* ... B
Asika, Uju. *Bringing up Race* ... 155.4
Baldwin, James. *I Am Not Your Negro* ... 323.1196
Baraka, Sho. *He Saw That It Was Good* ... 261.5
Barber, William J. *We Are Called to Be a Movement* ... 261.8
Baxley, Traci. *Social Justice Parenting* ... 649
Belcourt, Billy-Ray. ★*A History of My Brief Body* ... B
Bell, Darrin. ★*The Talk* ... 741.5
Bell, W. Kamau. ★*Do the Work!* ... 305.8
Bell-Scott, Patricia. *The Firebrand and the First Lady* ... 920
Benjamin, Ruha. ★*Imagination* ... 302
Bennett, Michael. *Things That Make White People Uncomfortable* ... 305.896
Berry, Daina Ramey. ★*A Black Women's History of the United States* ... 305.48
Bharara, Preet. *Doing Justice* ... 347.73
Blake, Melissa. *Beautiful People* ... 362.4
Bowdler, Michelle. *Is Rape a Crime?* ... B
Boykin, Keith. *Race Against Time* ... 305.8
Boykin, Keith. ★*Why Does Everything Have to Be About Race?* ... 305.8
Brennan, Chad. *Faithful Antiracism* ... 277.308
Brown-Nagin, Tomiko. *Civil Rights Queen* ... B
Canellos, Peter S. *The Great Dissenter* ... B
Cervini, Eric. *The Deviant's War* ... B
Cox, Josie. *Women Money Power* ... 330.082
Currie, Elliott. *A Peculiar Indifference* ... 305.800973
Dennis, David J., Jr. *The Movement Made Us* ... B
Diamant, Anita. ★*Period. End of Sentence* ... 612.6
Dray, Philip. *Capitol Men* ... 973.8
Dyson, Michael Eric. *Long Time Coming* ... 305.800973
Ehrenreich, Barbara. *Had I Known* ... 814
Else, Jon. *True South* ... 305.800973
Espada, Martin. ★*Floaters* ... 811
Fersko, Diana. ★*We Need to Talk About Antisemitism* ... 305.892
Finan, Christopher M. *How Free Speech Saved Democracy* ... 342.73
Fisher, Thomas. ★*The Emergency* ... 362.1089
Ford, Richard T. *Rights Gone Wrong* ... 342.7308
Ford, Tanisha C. *Our Secret Society* ... B
Forman, James. *Locking up Our Own* ... 364.973
Francis. *Let Us Dream* ... 282.092
Garcia, Damon. *The God Who Riots* ... 269
Giridharadas, Anand. ★*The Persuaders* ... 320.973
Gordon, Aubrey. *"You Just Need to Lose Weight"* ... 616.3
Greenidge, Kerri. *Black Radical* ... B
Griffin, Farah Jasmine. *Read Until You Understand* ... 810.9
Hill, Marc Lamont. *Seen and Unseen* ... 303.3
Hochschild, Adam. *Lessons from a Dark Time* ... 909.82
Honey, Michael K. *To the Promised Land* ... 323
Imani, Blair. *Read This to Get Smarter* ... 303.3
Jackson, Jenn M. ★*Black Women Taught Us* ... 305.48
Jackson, Major. *Razzle Dazzle* ... 811
Jackson, Regina. *White Women* ... 305.8
Jones, Brenda. *Alexandria Ocasio-Cortez* ... B
Jones, Brenda. *Maxine Waters* ... B
Kaba, Mariame. *No More Police* ... 363.2
Kennedy, Robert Francis. *RFK* ... 973.92
King, Billie Jean. ★*All In* ... B
King, Chrissy. *The Body Liberation Project* ... 306.4
King, Martin Luther. *Why We Can't Wait* ... 305.8
Krouse, Erika. ★*Tell Me Everything* ... 363.25
LeDuff, Charlie. *Detroit* ... 977.4
Lemon, Don. *This Is the Fire* ... 305.896
Lewis, Jenifer. *Walking in My Joy* ... B
Lewis, John. *Carry On* ... 328.73
Lim, Audrea. *Free the Land* ... 333.73
Lorde, Audre. *Sister Outsider* ... 814

Love, Bettina L. *Punished for Dreaming* ... 371.829
Mallory, Tamika D. *State of Emergency* ... 305.896
McCloskey, Jim. *When Truth Is All You Have* ... B
McDiarmid, Jessica. *Highway of Tears* ... 364.152
Meacham, Jon. *His Truth Is Marching On* ... B
Mullen, Bill. ★*James Baldwin* ... B
Nafisi, Azar. *Read Dangerously* ... 809
Nagassar, Rohadi. *When We Belong* ... 254
Neiman, Garrett. *Rich White Men* ... 305.5
Norton, Jack. *The Jail Is Everywhere* ... 365
Nye, Naomi Shihab. *The Tiny Journalist* ... 811
Oluo, Ijeoma. ★*Be a Revolution* ... 305.8
Oluo, Ijeoma. ★*So You Want to Talk About Race* ... 305.800973
Ostertag, Bob. *People's Movements, People's Press* ... 071
Pablo Cruz, Rosayra. *The Book of Rosy* ... B
Penniman, Leah. ★*Black Earth Wisdom* ... 333.72
Perkins, Kendrick. *The Education of Kendrick Perkins* ... B
Peterson, Marlon. *Bird Uncaged* ... B
Picower, Bree. *Reading, Writing, and Racism* ... 371.829
Piketty, Thomas. *A Brief History of Equality* ... 305.09
Prejean, Helen. *River of Fire* ... B
Purnell, Derecka. *Becoming Abolitionists* ... 363.20973
Raboteau, Emily. *Lessons for Survival* ... 814
Ramesh, Jaya. *Parenting at the Intersections* ... 649
Ramsey, Franchesca. *Well, That Escalated Quickly* ... B
Rapinoe, Megan. *One Life* ... B
Ray, Victor. *On Critical Race Theory* ... 305.8
Richards, Cecile. *Make Trouble* ... B
Ricketts, Rachel. ★*Do Better* ... 305.800973
Romeo, Nick. *The Alternative* ... 174
Rosenberg, Rosalind. ★*Jane Crow* ... B
Rothenberg, Ben. *Naomi Osaka* ... B
Ruttenberg, Danya. *On Repentance and Repair* ... 202
Salaam, Yusef. *Better, Not Bitter* ... B
Samuels, Robert. ★*His Name Is George Floyd* ... B
Sen, Amartya. *Home in the World* ... B
Shahvisi, Arianne. *Arguing for a Better World* ... 170
Smith, Mychal Denzel. *Stakes Is High* ... 973.933
Sole-Smith, Virginia. ★*Fat Talk* ... 649.1
Solnit, Rebecca. *The Mother of All Questions* ... 305.42
Sontag, Susan. *At the Same Time* ... 814
Steinberg, Jonny. *Winnie and Nelson* ... 920
Stiglitz, Joseph E. *The Price of Inequality* ... 305.50973
Sullivan, Matt. *Can't Knock the Hustle* ... 796.323
Tamimi, Ahed. ★*They Called Me a Lioness* ... B
Tubbs, Michael. *The Deeper the Roots* ... B
Van Meter, Matthew. *Deep Delta Justice* ... 345.763
Van Zandt, Steve. *Unrequited Infatuations* ... B
Velshi, Ali. *Small Acts of Courage* ... B
Walker, Vanessa Siddle. *The Lost Education of Horace Tate* ... 370.92
Washington, Ella F. *The Necessary Journey* ... 658.3
Whitaker, Mark. ★*Saying It Loud* ... 973.923
Winters, Mary-Frances. *Black Fatigue* ... 305.896
Wise, Tim J. *Dispatches from the Race War* ... 305.8
Wolf, Brandon J. *A Place for Us* ... B
Yoshino, Kenji. *Say the Right Thing* ... 305.3
Zakaria, Rafia. *Against White Feminism* ... 305.42
Social Justice Parenting. Baxley, Traci ... 649
SOCIAL LIFE AND CUSTOMS
Abdurraqib, Hanif. ★*There's Always This Year* ... 796.323
Ackerman, Diane. *A Natural History of the Senses* ... 152.1
Ackroyd, Peter. *Innovation* ... 942.082
Ackroyd, Peter. *London* ... 942.1
Adams, John. *Hallelujah Junction* ... B
Albom, Mitch. *Tuesdays with Morrie* ... B
Alford, Henry. *And Then We Danced* ... 792.8
Alkon, Amy. *Good Manners for Nice People* ... 395
Anderson, Lars. *Carlisle vs. Army* ... 796.332
Angelou, Maya. ★*I Know Why the Caged Bird Sings* ... B
Angelou, Maya. *A Song Flung up to Heaven* ... B
Anolik, Lili. *Hollywood's Eve* ... B
Arceneaux, Michael. *I Finally Bought Some Jordans* ... 306.76
Armstrong, Jennifer Keishin. *Seinfeldia* ... 791.45
Armstrong, Jennifer Keishin. *Sex and the City and Us* ... 791.45
Armstrong, Louis. *Louis Armstrong, in His Own Words* ... B
Arsenault, Kerri. *Mill Town* ... B
Ash, Lamorna. *Dark, Salt, Clear* ... 942.3
Ashon, Will. *Chamber Music* ... 782.421649

PUBLIC LIBRARY CORE COLLECTION: NONFICTION
Twentieth Edition

Auletta, Ken. *Media Man*	B
Baker, Billy. *We Need to Hang Out*	177
Ball, Lucille. *Love, Lucy*	B
Bard, Elizabeth. *Lunch in Paris*	B
Barra, Allen. ★*The Last Coach*	B
Barra, Allen. ★*Yogi Berra*	B
Basinger, Jeanine. *The Star Machine*	384
Bauer, Shane. *American Prison*	365
Baum, Dan. *Nine Lives*	B
Beard, Mary. ★*Emperor of Rome*	937
Beard, Mary. *The Fires of Vesuvius*	937
Bell, Julian. *Van Gogh*	B
Bell, Laura. *Claiming Ground*	B
Berendt, John. *The City of Falling Angels*	945
Berendt, John. *Midnight in the Garden of Good and Evil*	975.8
Berg, A. Scott. *Kate Remembered*	B
Berger, William. *Puccini Without Excuses*	782.1
Berger, William. *Verdi with a Vengeance*	B
Berry, Wendell. ★*The World-Ending Fire*	818
Bigsby, Christopher William Edgar. *Arthur Miller*	B
Bilal, Wafaa. *Shoot an Iraqi*	B
Bissinger, H. G. ★*Friday Night Lights*	796.332
Blom, Onno. *Young Rembrandt*	B
Boorstin, Daniel J. *The Americans*	973
Bourdain, Anthony. ★*Kitchen Confidential*	B
Bourdain, Anthony. *Medium Raw*	B
Bragg, Rick. *Where I Come From*	975
Briggs, Julia. *Virginia Woolf*	823
Bronski, Michael. *A Queer History of the United States*	306.76
Brooks, Mel. ★*All About Me!*	B
Broven, John. *Record Makers and Breakers*	B
Brown, Carolyn. *Chance and Circumstance*	B
Brown, Mick. ★*Tearing Down the Wall of Sound*	B
Brownworth, Lars. *Lost to the West*	949.5
Bryson, Bill. *One Summer*	973.91
Bryson, Bill. *Shakespeare*	B
Buckland, Gail. *Who Shot Rock & Roll*	779
Burke, Kelsy. *The Pornography Wars*	306.77
Burns, Eric. *Infamous Scribblers*	071
Burns, Ken. ★*Our America*	973
Byrne, Paula. *Kick*	B
Campany, David. *The Open Road*	770
Capote, Truman. ★*Portraits and Observations*	814
Capparell, Stephanie. *The Real Pepsi Challenge*	338.7
Carr, David. *The Night of the Gun*	B
Century, Douglas. *Barney Ross*	B
Chandler, Adam. *Drive-Thru Dreams*	647.95
Cheung, Karen. *The Impossible City*	951.25
Chisholm, Edward. *A Waiter in Paris*	B
Cho, Grace M. *Tastes Like War*	305.48
Clark, Taylor. *Starbucked*	338
Cleaver, Eldridge. *Soul on Ice*	B
Coates, Ta-Nehisi. *The Beautiful Struggle*	B
Cohen, Deborah. *Last Call at the Hotel Imperial*	070.92
Collins, Lauren. *When in French*	B
Common. *One Day It'll All Make Sense*	B
Conradi, Peter J. *Iris*	B
Cooke, Alistair. *The American Home Front, 1941-1942*	940.53
Cottom, Tressie McMillan. *Lower Ed*	378.73
Cottom, Tressie McMillan. *Thick*	301
Coyle, Marcia. *The Roberts Court*	347.73
Crampton, Caroline. *A Body Made of Glass*	616.85
Crawford, Bill. ★*All American*	B
Creamer, Robert W. *Stengel*	796.357
Cross, William R. *Winslow Homer*	759.13
Crowe, Lauren Goldstein. *The Towering World of Jimmy Choo*	391.4
Curran, Andrew S. *Diderot and the Art of Thinking Freely*	194
D'Agata, John. *About a Mountain*	979.3
Dalrymple, William. *Nine Lives*	294
Dalrymple, William. *White Mughals*	954
Darnton, Robert. *The Revolutionary Temper*	944
Davis, Michael. *Street Gang*	791.43
Day, John D. *The Longevity Plan*	612.6
De Courcy, Anne. *Chanel's Riviera*	944.9
De Hamel, Christopher. *The Manuscripts Club*	091
De Hamel, Christopher. ★*Meetings with Remarkable Manuscripts*	091
DeJean, Joan E. *The Essence of Style*	391
DeJean, Joan E. *How Paris Became Paris*	944
Dery, Mark. *Born to Be Posthumous*	B
Dickinson, Bruce. *What Does This Button Do?*	B
Dillard, Annie. *An American Childhood*	B
Dillard, Annie. *The Writing Life*	B
Dinesen, Isak. *Out of Africa*	967.62
Doggett, Peter. *You Never Give Me Your Money*	B
Dorey-Stein, Beck. *From the Corner of the Oval*	B
Doughty, Caitlin. *Smoke Gets in Your Eyes*	B
Dower, John W. *Embracing Defeat*	952.04
Drape, Joe. *Black Maestro*	B
Duncan, Dayton. ★*Country Music*	781.642
Ebert, Roger. *Life Itself*	B
Edwards, Bob. *Edward R. Murrow and the Birth of Broadcast Journalism*	B
Elledge, Scott. *E.B. White*	B
Ellis, Helen. *Southern Lady Code*	814
Ellis, Richard. *Tuna*	333.95
Ellison, Ralph. ★*The Collected Essays of Ralph Ellison*	814
Eteraz, Ali. *Children of Dust*	B
Faloyin, Dipo. ★*Africa Is Not a Country*	960.33
Faust, Drew Gilpin. *Necessary Trouble*	B
Feinstein, Adam. *Pablo Neruda*	B
Figes, Orlando. *The Europeans*	920
Finkel, David. *Thank You for Your Service*	920
Flanders, Judith. *The Victorian City*	942.1
Fletcher, Susan A. *Exploring the History of Childhood and Play Through 50 Historic Treasures*	790
Foreman, Amanda. *Georgiana, Duchess of Devonshire*	B
Frazier, Ian. *Travels in Siberia*	957
Frederick, Jim. *Black Hearts*	956.7044
Frey, Julia Bloch. *Toulouse-Lautrec*	B
Friedwald, Will. ★*Sinatra! the Song Is You*	782.42164
Gabriel, Mary. *Ninth Street Women*	920
Gaddy, K. R. ★*Well of Souls*	787
Galeano, Eduardo. *Soccer in Sun and Shadow*	796.334
Gallagher, Winifred. *New Women in the Old West*	978.02
Garelick, Rhonda K. *Mademoiselle*	B
Garrels, Anne. *Putin Country*	947
Garrett, Kent. *The Last Negroes at Harvard*	920
Gaskell, Elizabeth Cleghorn. *The Life of Charlotte Bronte*	B
Gavin, James. ★*Stormy Weather*	782.42164
Gefter, Philip. *What Becomes a Legend Most*	B
Gehring, Wes D. *James Dean*	B
Gentile, Olivia. *Life List*	598.072
Gibson, Larry S. *Young Thurgood*	B
Giddins, Gary. *Bing Crosby*	B
Giddins, Gary. *Bing Crosby*	B
Gies, Frances. *Life in a Medieval Village*	306
Gill, A. A. *To America with Love*	973.93
Gill, Anton. *Art Lover*	B
Gooch, Brad. ★*Flannery*	B
Goodman, Ruth. *How to Be a Tudor*	942.05
Goodman, Ruth. *How to Be a Victorian*	941.08
Goodman, Ruth. *How to Behave Badly in Elizabethan England*	942.05
Gopnik, Blake. ★*Warhol*	B
Gordon, Linda. *Dorothea Lange*	B
Gottlieb, Robert. *George Balanchine*	B
Goulding, Matt. *Grape, Olive, Pig*	394.1
Grant, Colin. *The Natural Mystics*	B
Gray, Charlotte. ★*Reluctant Genius*	920
Gray, Michael. *Hand Me My Travelin' Shoes*	B
Greenburg, Zack O'Malley. *3 Kings*	782.421649
Greene, Andy. *The Office*	791.45
Guha, Ramachandra. *India After Gandhi*	954.04
Guibert, Emmanuel. *Alan's War*	741.5
Guinn, Jeff. ★*Manson*	B
Hahn, Emanuel. *Koreatown Dreaming*	979.4
Hakkakiyan, Ruya. *A Beginner's Guide to America*	646.7
Halberstam, David. *The Fifties*	973.92
Halberstam, David. *Summer of '49*	796.357
Hardacre, Helen. *Shinto*	299.5
Harding, Thomas. *The House by the Lake*	943
Harlan, Elizabeth. *George Sand*	B
Harrington, Joel F. *The Faithful Executioner*	B
Harris, Mark. *Pictures at a Revolution*	791.43
Hastings, Selina. *The Secret Lives of Somerset Maugham*	B
Hayes, Christopher. *A Colony in a Nation*	364.3
Hechinger, John. ★*True Gentlemen*	371.85
Henaut, Stephane. *A Bite-Sized History of France*	394.1

AUTHOR, TITLE, SERIES AND SUBJECT INDEX

Hensley, William L. Iggiagruk. *Fifty Miles from Tomorrow*	B
Hermes, Will. *Love Goes to Buildings on Fire*	781.64
Herrera, Hayden. *Frida*	B
Herriot, James. ★*All Creatures Great and Small*	B
Herriot, James. *All Things Wise and Wonderful*	B
Herriot, James. *James Herriot's Dog Stories*	636.7
Hessler, Peter. *The Buried*	962.05
Hessler, Peter. *Oracle Bones*	951
Hiaasen, Carl. *The Downhill Lie*	B
Hickam, Homer H. ★*Rocket Boys*	B
Hilfiger, Tommy. *American Dreamer*	B
Hitchens, Christopher. *Hitch-22*	920
Hoffman, Adina. ★*My Happiness Bears No Relation to Happiness*	B
Hornbacher, Marya. *Wasted*	B
Horwitz, Tony. *Spying on the South*	917
Housden, Roger. *Saved by Beauty*	955
Howard, Johnette. *The Rivals*	B
Howard, Vivian. *Deep Run Roots*	641.5975
Howe, Ben Ryder. *My Korean Deli*	B
Hurston, Zora Neale. *Dust Tracks on a Road*	B
Huxley, Elspeth Joscelin Grant. *The Flame Trees of Thika*	B
Isaacson, Walter. ★*Steve Jobs*	B
Iyer, Pico. *A Beginner's Guide to Japan*	952.05
Jacobs, Alexandra. *Still Here*	B
Jadhav, Narendra. *Untouchables*	305.5
Jenkins, Jessica Kerwin. *All the Time in the World*	390
Jenkins, Peter. *Looking for Alaska*	979.8
Johnson, George. *Miss Leavitt's Stars*	522
Johnson, Joyce. *The Voice Is All*	B
Johnson, Katherine G. *My Remarkable Journey*	B
Jones, Gerard. *Men of Tomorrow*	741.5
Judt, Tony. *Postwar*	940.55
Kahn, Ashley. *The House That Trane Built*	781.6509
Kaku, Michio. ★*Hyperspace*	530.1
Kamp, David. *Sunny Days*	791.4502
Kan, Karoline. *Under Red Skies*	B
Kanigel, Robert. *The Man Who Knew Infinity*	B
Kashner, Sam. *Furious Love*	B
Kattan, Fadi. ★*Bethlehem*	641.59
Keay, John. *India*	954
Kenan, Randall. *Black Folk Could Fly*	813
Kennedy, Michael. *Richard Strauss*	B
Kershner, Isabel. *The Land of Hope and Fear*	956.9405
Khan, Yasmin. ★*Zaitoun*	641.595
Khilnani, Sunil. *Incarnations*	920
Kimball, George. *Four Kings*	B
Kingsley, Lisa. *Smithsonian American Table*	641.5
Kingsolver, Barbara. ★*Animal, Vegetable, Miracle*	641
Klosterman, Chuck. ★*The Nineties*	306.0973
Koch, Bea. *Mad and Bad*	920
Koppel, Lily. *The Astronaut Wives Club*	920
Kozol, Jonathan. *Letters to a Young Teacher*	371.1
Kriegel, Mark. *Pistol*	B
Krimstein, Ken. *When I Grow Up*	741.5
Lacey, Robert. *Great Tales from English History 3*	941
Laing, Olivia. *The Garden Against Time*	635
Lancaster, Jen. *Welcome to the United States of Anxiety*	155.4
Law, Keith. *The Inside Game*	796.35764
Leaming, Barbara. *Kick Kennedy*	B
Leavy, Jane. *The Last Boy*	B
Leavy, Jane. *Sandy Koufax*	B
Lebovitz, David. *My Paris Kitchen*	641.594
Leng'ete, Nice. *The Girls in the Wild Fig Tree*	B
Lessig, Lawrence. *Remix*	346.7304
Levi, Heather. *The World of Lucha Libre*	796.812
Levitt, Steven D. ★*Freakonomics*	330
Levitt, Steven D. *Superfreakonomics*	330
Levy, Shawn. ★*In on the Joke*	792.7
Litt, David. *Thanks, Obama*	B
Lohman, Sarah. ★*Endangered Eating*	641.5973
Louvish, Simon. *Monkey Business*	B
Lunenfeld, Peter. *City at the Edge of Forever*	979.4
Lynn, Loretta. *Still Woman Enough*	B
MacColl, Gail. *To Marry an English Lord*	974.7
Mahjoub, Jamal. *A Line in the River*	962.404
Mann, William J. *The Contender*	B
Mann, William J. *Hello, Gorgeous*	B
Maraniss, Andrew. *Strong Inside*	B
Maraniss, David. *Clemente*	B
Margonelli, Lisa. *Oil on the Brain*	338.2
Martin, Wednesday. *Primates of Park Avenue*	974.7
Matteson, John. *Eden's Outcasts*	920
Mayes, Frances. *Bella Tuscany*	945
Mayes, Frances. *Under the Tuscan Sun*	945
Mayle, Peter. *Encore Provence*	944
Mayle, Peter. *Provence A-Z*	944
Mayle, Peter. ★*A Year in Provence*	944
McBride, James. *Kill 'Em and Leave*	B
McCourt, Frank. *Teacher Man*	B
McCourt, Malachy. *Singing My Him Song*	B
McGilligan, Patrick. *Funny Man*	B
McGilligan, Patrick. *Oscar Micheaux*	B
Mead, Corey. *The Hidden History of the White House*	975.3
Mehta, Suketu. *Maximum City*	954
Mendelson, Cheryl. ★*Vows*	203
Meredith, Martin. *The Fortunes of Africa*	960
Meslow, Scott. *From Hollywood with Love*	791.43
Michaelis, David. *Schulz and Peanuts*	B
Milford, Nancy. *Savage Beauty*	B
Miller, Donald L. *Supreme City*	974.7
Mishra, Pankaj. *From the Ruins of Empire*	950.4
Montgomery, Sy. *The Good Good Pig*	636.4
Mooney, Paul. *Black Is the New White*	792.7
Mordden, Ethan. *Ziegfeld*	B
Morgan, Robert. *Boone*	B
Morris, Jan. *A Writer's House in Wales*	942.9
Morrison, Robert. *The Regency Years*	941.07
Mortimer, Ian. *The Time Traveler's Guide to Elizabethan England*	942.05
Moss, Gabrielle. *Paperback Crush*	813.009
Murakami, Haruki. *What I Talk About When I Talk About Running*	B
Murgia, Madhumita. *Code Dependent*	303.48
Myron, Vicki. ★*Dewey*	636.80092
Nafisi, Azar. ★*Reading Lolita in Tehran*	B
Nafisi, Azar. *The Republic of Imagination*	B
Narayan, Shoba. *The Milk Lady of Bangalore*	390
Navai, Ramita. *City of Lies*	955
Nelson, Willie. *It's a Long Story*	B
Norman, Philip. *John Lennon*	B
O'Connor, Ian. *Belichick*	B
O'Meara, Mallory. *Girly Drinks*	641.2
Olds, Sharon. *Arias*	811
Oller, John. *American Queen*	B
Olsen, Craig. *P.S. Burn This Letter Please*	306.76
Ostertag, Bob. *People's Movements, People's Press*	071
Ours, Dorothy. *Man O' War*	798.400929
Parini, Jay. *Robert Frost*	B
Parks, Tim. *Italian Ways*	385
Parry, John Weston. *The Burden of Sports*	796.01
Patterson, James. *What Really Happens in Vegas*	920
Pearlman, Jeff. *Boys Will Be Boys*	796.332
Pearson, Roger. *Voltaire Almighty*	B
Peiffer, Prudence. *The Slip*	709.73
Pepys, Samuel. *The Diary of Samuel Pepys*	B
Perry, Imani. ★*South to America*	917
Plummer, Christopher. *In Spite of Myself*	B
Posnanski, Joe. ★*The Life and Afterlife of Harry Houdini*	793.8
Posnanski, Joe. *The Soul of Baseball*	796.357
Post, Lizzie. *Emily Post's Etiquette*	395
Post, Lizzie. *Emily Post's Etiquette*	395
Prose, Francine. *Caravaggio*	759.5
Prud'homme, Alex. *The French Chef in America*	B
Rampersad, Arnold. ★*Ralph Ellison*	B
Ratliff, Ben. *The Jazz Ear*	781.6509
Reed, Julia. *Dispatches from the Gilded Age*	B
Reichl, Ruth. *My Kitchen Year*	641.5
Reynolds, David S. ★*Abe*	B
Rhoden, William C. *$40 Million Slaves*	796
Rhodes, Benjamin J. *The World as It Is*	973.932
Riasanovsky, Nicholas V. *A History of Russia*	947
Ribowsky, Mark. *Howard Cosell*	070.449796
Ribowsky, Mark. *Signed, Sealed, and Delivered*	B
Richardson, Robert D. *Emerson*	814
Richardson, Robert D. *William James*	B
Robertson, Robbie. ★*Testimony*	B
Robinson, Ray. *Iron Horse*	B
Robison, John Elder. *Look Me in the Eye*	B

PUBLIC LIBRARY CORE COLLECTION: NONFICTION
Twentieth Edition

Rocca, Mo. *Mobituaries*	920
Roth, Joseph. *What I Saw*	943
Russell, Gareth. ★*The Palace*	942.1
Sandel, Michael J. *Justice*	172
Satrapi, Marjane. *Chicken with Plums*	741.5
Satrapi, Marjane. ★*The Complete Persepolis*	741.5
Satrapi, Marjane. *Embroideries*	741.5
Schaap, Jeremy. *Cinderella Man*	B
Schlesinger, Arthur M. *Journals, 1952-2000*	973.91092
Schulman, Bruce J. *The Seventies*	973.92
Schumacher, Michael. *Will Eisner*	741.5
Scott, Andy. *One Kiss or Two?*	395.4
Sen, Amartya. *The Argumentative Indian*	954
Sharif, Solmaz. *Customs*	811
Sherman, Anna. *The Bells of Old Tokyo*	952
Slice, Jessica. *Dateable*	646.7
Smietana, Bob. *Reorganized Religion*	262.001
Smith, Emma. *This Is Shakespeare*	822.33
Sohn, Amy. *The Man Who Hated Women*	363.28
Solomon, Deborah. *Jackson Pollock*	B
Solomonov, Michael. *Israeli Soul*	641.595
Solomonov, Michael. *Zahav*	641.595
Southon, Emma. *Agrippina*	B
Spencer, Kyle. *Raising Them Right*	320.5
Spitz, Bob. ★*Dearie*	B
Spoto, Donald. *High Society*	B
St. John, Warren. *Outcasts United*	B
Stanley, Amy. *Stranger in the Shogun's City*	B
Stanley, Paul. *Backstage Pass*	B
Stanley, Paul. *Face the Music*	B
Stein, Jean. *West of Eden*	979.4
Stewart, Chris. *Driving Over Lemons*	946
Stone, I. F. *The Trial of Socrates*	183
Stuart, Amanda Mackenzie. *Empress of Fashion*	B
Sturgis, Matthew. *Oscar Wilde*	B
Styron, William. *My Generation*	814
Taddeo, Lisa. *Three Women*	306.7082
Tammet, Daniel. *Born on a Blue Day*	B
Teachout, Terry. ★*All in the Dances*	B
Terkel, Studs. *Hope Dies Last*	920
Theroux, Paul. *Deep South*	975
Theroux, Paul. *On the Plain of Snakes*	917
Thomas, Dylan. *A Child's Christmas in Wales*	B
Thomas, Elizabeth Marshall. *Growing Old*	305.26
Thubron, Colin. *In Siberia*	957
Tibble, Tayi. *Poukahangatus*	821
Tinsley, Omise'eke Natasha. *Beyonce in Formation*	782.42164
Tipton-Martin, Toni. *Juke Joints, Jazz Clubs & Juice*	641.87
Tomalin, Claire. *Samuel Pepys*	B
Tomalin, Claire. *Thomas Hardy*	B
Toobin, Jeffrey. *The Nine*	347.73
Torre, Joe. *The Yankee Years*	B
Tremlett, Giles. *Ghosts of Spain*	946.08
Trimborn, Jurgen. *Leni Riefenstahl*	B
Twenge, Jean M. *Generations*	305.2
Twitty, Michael. ★*The Cooking Gene*	641.59
Updike, John. *Always Looking*	700
Volpe, Joseph. *The Toughest Show on Earth*	B
Vonnegut, Kurt. *Kurt Vonnegut*	813
Wagamese, Richard. *One Native Life*	B
Wald, Elijah. *Dylan Goes Electric!*	782.42164
Wald, Elijah. *How the Beatles Destroyed Rock 'N' Roll*	781.64
Walker, Alice. *Gathering Blossoms Under Fire*	B
Walls, Laura Dassow. ★*Henry David Thoreau*	B
Wasson, Sam. ★*Improv Nation*	792.02
Watson, Bruce. *Sacco and Vanzetti*	345.73
Weingarten, Gene. ★*One Day*	973
Weir, Laura. *Cosy*	646.7009
Weller, Sam. *The Bradbury Chronicles*	B
Welty, Eudora. *One Writer's Beginnings*	B
Wenner, Jann. *Like a Rolling Stone*	B
Wertheim, L. Jon. *Blood in the Cage*	796.815
Westhoff, Ben. *Dirty South*	782.421649
Whippman, Ruth. ★*Boymom*	305.23
White, Edmund. *The Flaneur*	944
Wilkinson, Alec. *The Protest Singer*	B
Williamson, Edwin. *Borges*	B
Wilson, Katherine. *Only in Naples*	B
Wilson, Victoria. *A Life of Barbara Stanwyck*	B
Witte, Christina De. ★*Noodles, Rice, and Everything Spice*	641.595
Wolff, Daniel J. *Grown-Up Anger*	920
Woolf, Virginia. *The London Scene*	942.1
Worley, Jennifer. *Neon Girls*	792.7
Wragg Sykes, Rebecca. *Kindred*	569.9
Wrangham, Richard W. *Catching Fire*	394.1
Wright, Lawrence. *God Save Texas*	917.64
Wullschlager, Jackie. ★*Chagall*	B
Yang, Jeff. ★*Rise*	973
Zimmerman, Paul. *Dr. Z*	B
The Social Lives of Animals. Ward, Ashley	591.7

SOCIAL MARGINALITY

Belser, Julia Watts. ★*Loving Our Own Bones*	296
Currie, Elliott. *A Peculiar Indifference*	305.800973
Desmond, Matthew. ★*Poverty, by America*	362.5
Espada, Martin. ★*Floaters*	811
Finney, Nikky. *Love Child's Hotbed of Occasional Poetry*	811
Garbes, Angela. *Essential Labor*	306.874
Gerald, Casey. *There Will Be No Miracles Here*	B
Goodman, Elyssa. *Glitter and Concrete*	792.7
Hester, Diarmuid. *Nothing Ever Just Disappears*	306.76
Hurston, Zora Neale. ★*You Don't Know Us Negroes and Other Essays*	814
Jun, Tasha. ★*Tell Me the Dream Again*	248
Marshall, Nate. *Finna*	811
Miles, Tiya. ★*Wild Girls*	304.2
Nagassar, Rohadi. *When We Belong*	254
Prickett, Pamela J. ★*The Unclaimed*	363.7
Sabatini Sloan, Aisha. *Dreaming of Ramadi in Detroit*	814
Sanchez, Erika L. *Crying in the Bathroom*	B
Sjunneson, Elsa. *Being Seen*	362.4
Solnit, Rebecca. ★*Recollections of My Nonexistence*	B

SOCIAL MEDIA

AL Samawi, Mohammed. *The Fox Hunt*	953
Arceneaux, Michael. *I Finally Bought Some Jordans*	306.76
Busby, Jill Louise. *Unfollow Me*	305.08
Carpenter, Amanda B. *Gaslighting America*	973.933
DiGiulian, Sasha. *Take the Lead*	B
DiResta, Renee. *Invisible Rulers*	320
Ellis, Bret Easton. *White*	814
Galloway, Scott. *The Four*	338.7
Goldblatt, Duchess. *Becoming Duchess Goldblatt*	B
Haidt, Jonathan. ★*The Anxious Generation*	305.23
Horwitz, Jeff. ★*Broken Code*	302.3
Irby, Samantha. ★*Quietly Hostile*	814
Klein, Naomi. *Doppelganger*	302.2
Lancaster, Jen. *Welcome to the United States of Anxiety*	155.4
Lankford, Andrea. *Trail of the Lost*	363.2
Lorenz, Taylor. ★*Extremely Online*	302.23
Lyons, Daniel. *STFU*	302.2
McCourt, Frank H. ★*Our Biggest Fight*	303.48
Mezrich, Ben. *Breaking Twitter*	338.7
Murgia, Madhumita. *Code Dependent*	303.48
Owens, Ernest. ★*The Case for Cancel Culture*	303.3
Perkins, Nichole. *Sometimes I Trip on How Happy We Could Be*	B
Petersen, Anne Helen. *Can't Even*	305.242
Petersen, Sara. *Momfluenced*	306.87
Ramsey, Franchesca. *Well, That Escalated Quickly*	B
Ressa, Maria. ★*How to Stand up to a Dictator*	070.92
Ronson, Jon. *So You've Been Publicly Shamed*	152.4
Schwartzman, Nancy. *Roll Red Roll*	364.15
Seierstad, Asne. *Two Sisters*	956.9104
Smith, Erin Geiger. ★*Thank You for Voting*	324.973
Smith, Freda Love. *I Quit Everything*	B
Smith, Patti. ★*A Book of Days*	779
Smith, Zadie. ★*Feel Free*	824
Stengel, Richard. *Information Wars*	355.3
Tolentino, Jia. ★*Trick Mirror*	973.93
Vanderbilt, Tom. *You May Also Like*	153.8
Vaynerchuk, Gary. *Crushing It!*	650.1

SOCIAL MEDICINE

Fisher, Thomas. ★*The Emergency*	362.1089
Honigsbaum, Mark. *The Pandemic Century*	614.4
Liverpool, Layal. *Systemic*	362.1
Porter, Roy. *The Greatest Benefit to Mankind*	610

SOCIAL MOBILITY

Biss, Eula. *Having and Being Had*	306.3
Brooks, David. *The Social Animal*	305.5

AUTHOR, TITLE, SERIES AND SUBJECT INDEX

Holzer, Harold. *A Just and Generous Nation*	973.7092
Murray, Charles A. *Coming Apart*	305.8
Nietfeld, Emi. *Acceptance*	B
Putnam, Robert D. *Our Kids*	305.5
Reeves, Richard V. *Dream Hoarders*	305.5
Sorin, Gretchen Sullivan. *Driving While Black*	323.1196
Tough, Paul. *The Years That Matter Most*	378.1
Vance, J. D. *Hillbilly Elegy*	B

SOCIAL MOVEMENTS

Arendt, Hannah. *The Origins of Totalitarianism*	320.53
Barber, William J. *We Are Called to Be a Movement*	261.8
Bingham, Clara. *Witness to the Revolution*	303.48
Burak, Asi. *Power Play*	794.8
Carruthers, Charlene A. *Unapologetic*	305.48
Darby, Seyward. ★ *Sisters in Hate*	305.800973
Dennis, David J., Jr. *The Movement Made Us*	
Frank, Thomas. *The People, No*	320.56
Garza, Alicia. *The Purpose of Power*	303.48
Griffith, Elisabeth. *Formidable*	305.42
Heumann, Judith E. *Being Heumann*	B
Kaba, Mariame. *No More Police*	363.2
Lee, Corky. ★ *Corky Lee's Asian America*	770
Lim, Louisa. *Indelible City*	951.25
Meacham, Jon. *His Truth Is Marching On*	B
Merchant, Brian. *Blood in the Machine*	303.48
Montero, David. ★ *The Stolen Wealth of Slavery*	381
Postel, Charles. *Equality*	305.50973
Purnell, Derecka. *Becoming Abolitionists*	363.20973
Richardson, Heather Cox. *Democracy Awakening*	320.473
Rutherford, Adam. *Control*	363.9
Saad, Layla F. ★ *Me and White Supremacy*	305.809
Sommer, Will. ★ *Trust the Plan*	973.933
Theoharis, Jeanne. *A More Beautiful and Terrible History*	323.1196
Vogelstein, Rachel B. *Awakening*	305.42
Wides-Munoz, Laura. *The Making of a Dream*	920
Worth, Robert Forsyth. *A Rage for Order*	909
Zakaria, Fareed. *Age of Revolutions*	303.6
Zinn, Howard. ★ *A People's History of the United States*	973

SOCIAL NETWORKS

Bilton, Nick. *Hatching Twitter*	006.7
Burkus, David. *Friend of a Friend...*	650.1
Kerpen, Dave. *Likeable Social Media*	658.8
Tolentino, Jia. ★ *Trick Mirror*	973.93
van der Linden, Sander. ★ *Foolproof*	302.3

SOCIAL NORMS

Cohen, Rhaina. ★ *The Other Significant Others*	177
Corbett, Emily. *In Transition*	809
Davis, Lisa Selin. *Tomboy*	305.409
Filipovic, Jill. *The H-Spot*	155.3
Martin, Brett. *Difficult Men*	791.4509
Shafrir, Doree. *Thanks for Waiting*	B
Wojczuk, Tana. *Lady Romeo*	B

SOCIAL PARTICIPATION

Thomas, Etan. *We Matter*	796.08
Thunberg, Greta. ★ *The Climate Book*	363.738
Wills, Garry. *Certain Trumpets*	303.3

SOCIAL PERCEPTION

Betts, Reginald Dwayne. *Felon*	811

SOCIAL PHILOSOPHY

Jarrett, Valerie. *Finding My Voice*	B

SOCIAL PHOBIA

Dahl, Melissa. *Cringeworthy*	158.2

SOCIAL POLICY

Booth, Michael. *The Almost Nearly Perfect People*	948.071
Currie, Elliott. *A Peculiar Indifference*	305.800973
Garza, Alicia. *The Purpose of Power*	303.48
Geronimus, Arline T. ★ *Weathering*	362.1089
Kim, Anne. ★ *Poverty for Profit*	302.5
Markovits, Daniel. *The Meritocracy Trap*	305.5
Phillips-Fein, Kim. *Fear City*	330.9747
Porter, Eduardo. *American Poison*	305.800973
Putnam, Robert D. *Our Kids*	305.5
Self, Robert O. *All in the Family*	320.50973
Stone, Deborah A. *Counting*	001.4
Warren, Elizabeth. *This Fight Is Our Fight*	305.5
Woods, Randall Bennett. *Prisoners of Hope*	973.923

SOCIAL PREDICTION

Friedman, George. *Flashpoints*	940.56

SOCIAL PRESSURE

Havrilesky, Heather. *What If This Were Enough?*	152.4
Leach, Samantha. ★ *The Elissas*	362.73

SOCIAL PROBLEMS

Applewhite, Ashton. *This Chair Rocks*	155.67
Bellos, David. *The Novel of the Century*	843
Davis, Angela Y. *Abolition*	364.6
Francis. *Let Us Dream*	282.092
Grandin, Greg. *The End of the Myth*	973
Herold, Benjamin. *Disillusioned*	307.76
Imani, Blair. *Read This to Get Smarter*	303.3
Kelly, Helena. *Jane Austen, the Secret Radical*	823
O'Neil, Cathy. *The Shame Machine*	152.4
Ostertag, Bob. *People's Movements, People's Press*	071
Packer, George. ★ *The Unwinding*	973.924
Price, S. L. *Playing Through the Whistle*	796.332
Prickett, Pamela J. ★ *The Unclaimed*	363.7
Rivlin, Gary. *Broke, Usa*	339.4
Ross, Andrew. *Sunbelt Blues*	363.5
Rubin, Robert Edward. *The Yellow Pad*	658.4
Solnit, Rebecca. *Call Them by Their True Names*	303.3
Stiglitz, Joseph E. *The Price of Inequality*	305.50973
Taub, Jennifer. *Big Dirty Money*	364.16
Young, Ralph F. *Dissent*	303.48

SOCIAL PSYCHOLOGY

Baker, Billy. *We Need to Hang Out*	177
Bering, Jesse. *Suicidal*	362.2
Brandt, Anthony K. *The Runaway Species*	153.3
Brooks, David. ★ *How to Know a Person*	158.2
De Bres, Helena. *How to Be Multiple*	155.44
Duhigg, Charles. ★ *The Power of Habit*	158.1
Duhigg, Charles. ★ *Supercommunicators*	153.6
Fraser, Steve. *The Age of Acquiescence*	973.91
Gladwell, Malcolm. ★ *Talking to Strangers*	302
Gladwell, Malcolm. *The Tipping Point*	302
Grant, Adam M. *Give and Take*	158.2
Grant, Adam M. ★ *Think Again*	153.4
Grinker, Roy Richard. *Nobody's Normal*	616.89
Hammond, Claudia. *Mind Over Money*	332.401
Hawes, Jennifer. *Grace Will Lead Us Home*	364.152
Heine, Steven J. *DNA Is Not Destiny*	572.8
Hoffman, Carl. *Liar's Circus*	973.933
Kinzler, Katherine D. *How You Say It*	302.2
Livingston, Robert W. *The Conversation*	305.8
Lowery, Brian S. *Selfless*	155.2
Pinker, Steven. ★ *Enlightenment Now*	303.44
Price, Devon. ★ *Laziness Does Not Exist*	158.1
Rothschild, Mike. *The Storm Is Upon Us*	973.933
Scott, Andy. *One Kiss or Two?*	395.4
Van Bavel, Jay J. *The Power of Us*	155.2
van der Linden, Sander. ★ *Foolproof*	302.3
Way, Niobe. *Rebels with a Cause*	649
Wood, Wendy. *Good Habits, Bad Habits*	152.3
Yoshino, Kenji. *Say the Right Thing*	305.3
Young, Daniella Mestyanek. *Uncultured*	B
Zimbardo, Philip G. *The Lucifer Effect*	155.9

SOCIAL REFORMERS

Ayers, Edward L. *American Visions*	973.5
DiFranco, Ani. *No Walls and the Recurring Dream*	782.42164
Grant, James. ★ *John Adams*	B
Guha, Ramachandra. *Gandhi Before India*	B
Guha, Ramachandra. *Gandhi*	B
Hennessy, Kate. *Dorothy Day*	B
King, Coretta Scott. ★ *My Life, My Love, My Legacy*	B
Painter, Nell Irvin. ★ *Sojourner Truth*	B
Rosenberg, Rosalind. ★ *Jane Crow*	B
Rubenstein, David M. *The American Story*	973.07202
Walker, Alice. *Gathering Blossoms Under Fire*	B
Young, Ralph F. *Dissent*	303.48
Yousafzai, Ziauddin. *Let Her Fly*	B

SOCIAL RESPONSIBILITY

Brodsky, Alexandra. *Sexual Justice*	364.15
Emanuel, Rahm. *The Nation City*	352.23
Hirsch, Jennifer S. *Sexual Citizens*	371.7
Hirshfield, Jane. *Ledger*	811
Jaffe, Sarah W. *Wanting What's Best*	649
Linklater, Andro. *Owning the Earth*	333.3
Nooyi, Indra. ★ *My Life in Full*	B

PUBLIC LIBRARY CORE COLLECTION: NONFICTION
Twentieth Edition

O'Neil, Cathy. *The Shame Machine*	152.4
Owens, Ernest. ★*The Case for Cancel Culture*	303.3
Ruttenberg, Danya. *On Repentance and Repair*	202
Schultz, Howard. *From the Ground Up*	B
Schwarz, Geraldine. *Those Who Forget*	940.53
Sharpton, Al. *Rise Up*	973.933
Skach, C. L. *How to Be a Citizen*	323.6

SOCIAL SCIENCES

Blattman, Christopher. *Why We Fight*	303.6

SOCIAL SECRETARIES

Persico, Joseph E. *Franklin and Lucy*	973.917092

SOCIAL SECURITY

Krugman, Paul R. *Arguing with Zombies*	330.973
Orman, Suze. ★*The Ultimate Retirement Guide for 50+*	306.3

SOCIAL SKILLS

Berman, Lea. *Treating People Well*	395

SOCIAL SKILLS IN CHILDREN

Goh, Suzanne. *Magnificent Minds*	618.92

SOCIAL STATUS

Brooks, David. *The Social Animal*	305.5
Marx, W. David. ★*Status and Culture*	305
Thrasher, Steven W. ★*The Viral Underclass*	362.1962

SOCIAL STRUCTURE

Nicolson, Juliet. *The Great Silence*	941.083
Servon, Lisa J. *The Unbanking of America*	332.10973

SOCIAL SUCCESS

Marx, W. David. ★*Status and Culture*	305

SOCIAL SURVEYS

Fallows, James M. *Our Towns*	306.0973

SOCIAL VALUES

Berkshire, Jennifer. *The Education Wars*	371.01
Creighton, Margaret S. *The Electrifying Fall of Rainbow City*	607
DiGregorio, Sarah. ★*Taking Care*	610.73
Hagglund, Martin. *This Life*	110
Harford, Tim. *Messy*	153.3
Hayhoe, Katharine. *Saving Us*	304.2
Lepore, Jill. ★*These Truths*	973
Self, Robert O. *All in the Family*	320.50973
Westheimer, Ruth. *The Doctor Is In*	B

SOCIAL WORK

Roberts, Dorothy E. *Torn Apart*	362.7
Siler, Julia Flynn. *The White Devil's Daughters*	306.3

SOCIAL WORKERS

Prickett, Pamela J. ★*The Unclaimed*	363.7
Pryce, Jessica. ★*Broken*	362.7

SOCIALISM

Kotkin, Stephen. *Stalin*	B
Kotkin, Stephen. *Stalin*	B
Marx, Karl. ★*The Communist Manifesto*	355.4
Piketty, Thomas. ★*Capital and Ideology*	305
Sebestyen, Victor. *Revolution 1989*	947.085
Westad, Odd Arne. *The Cold War*	909.825
Ypi, Lea. ★*Free*	B

SOCIALISTS

Gabriel, Mary. *Love and Capital*	920
Glendinning, Victoria. *Leonard Woolf*	B
Guinn, Jeff. *The Road to Jonestown*	289.9
Mieville, China. *October*	947.084

SOCIALITES

Bascomb, Neal. *Faster*	796.7209
Boessenecker, John. *Gentleman Bandit*	B
Byrne, Paula. *Kick*	B
De Courcy, Anne. *Chanel's Riviera*	944.9
Farley, Audrey Clare. *The Unfit Heiress*	B
Ford, Tanisha C. *Our Secret Society*	B
Hilton, Paris. *Paris*	B
Leaming, Barbara. *Kick Kennedy*	B
Montillo, Roseanne. *Deliberate Cruelty*	364.152
O'Connell, Mark. *A Thread of Violence*	364.152
Oller, John. *American Queen*	B
Ronald, Susan. *A Dangerous Woman*	B
Wallace, Christopher. *Twentieth-Century Man*	B

SOCIETY AND CULTURE — ANTHROPOLOGY

Cicero, Marcus Tullius. *Selected Works*	875
Kuper, Adam. *The Museum of Other People*	305.8
Treister, Kenneth. *Easter Island's Silent Sentinels*	996.18

SOCIETY AND CULTURE — CHILDREN'S STUDIES

Brackett, Marc A. *Permission to Feel*	152.4

Burke Harris, Nadine. *The Deepest Well*	618.92

SOCIETY AND CULTURE — EDUCATION

Appleman, Deborah. *Literature and the New Culture Wars*	807
Baker, Nicholson. *Substitute*	371.14
Bazelon, Emily. *Sticks and Stones*	302.34
Berens, Kimberly Nix. *Blind Spots*	370.15
Berkshire, Jennifer. *The Education Wars*	371.01
Boyce, W. Thomas. *The Orchid and the Dandelion*	649
Brill, Steven. *Class Warfare*	371.010973
Carey, Benedict. *How We Learn*	153.1
Christakis, Erika. *The Importance of Being Little*	372.21
Chu, Lenora. *Little Soldiers*	370
Cushman, Kathleen. *Fires in Our Lives*	373.1102
Davis, Joshua. *Spare Parts*	629.8
De Stefano, Cristina. *The Child Is the Teacher*	B
Driver, Justin. *The Schoolhouse Gate*	344.73
Duncan, Arne. *How Schools Work*	379
Easterbrook, Gregg. ★*The King of Sports*	796.332
Emdin, Christopher. *Ratchetdemic*	370.1
Ewing, Eve L. *Ghosts in the Schoolyard*	370.89
Fishman, Elly. *Refugee High*	370.8
Fitzpatrick, Cara. *The Death of Public School*	379.73
Givens, Jarvis R. ★*School Clothes*	371.829
Goldstein, Dana. *The Teacher Wars*	371.1020973
Grandin, Temple. ★*Visual Thinking*	152.14
Herold, Benjamin. *Disillusioned*	307.76
Hessler, Peter. *Other Rivers*	378.1
Hixenbaugh, Michael. ★*They Came for the Schools*	371.9
Hobbs, Jeff. *Show Them You're Good*	373
Kamenetz, Anya. *The Stolen Year*	306.43
Keizer, Garret. *Getting Schooled*	373.1102
Koenig, Joan. *The Musical Child*	780.71
Kozol, Jonathan. ★*An End to Inequality*	379.2
Kozol, Jonathan. *Fire in the Ashes*	362.77
Kozol, Jonathan. *Letters to a Young Teacher*	371.1
Love, Bettina L. *Punished for Dreaming*	371.829
Meckler, Laura. ★*Dream Town*	305.8
Mooney, Jonathan. *Normal Sucks*	B
Mufleh, Luma. ★*Learning America*	371.826
Murdoch, Stephen. *IQ*	153.9
Nye, Bill. *Undeniable*	576.8
Picower, Bree. *Reading, Writing, and Racism*	371.829
Rademacher, Tom. *It Won't Be Easy*	B
Ravitch, Diane. *The Death and Life of the Great American School System*	379.1
Ravitch, Diane. *Slaying Goliath*	371.010973
Reese, William J. *Testing Wars in the Public Schools*	371.260973
Robbins, Alexandra. ★*The Teachers*	371.1
Robinson, Ken. *Creative Schools*	370.973
Sarma, Sanjay E. *Grasp*	370.15
Seo, Bo. *Good Arguments*	808.53
Shankar, Shalini. *Beeline*	155.4
Skelton, Marc. *Pounding the Rock*	796.323
Smart, Maya Payne. *Reading for Our Lives*	372.4
Tesoriero, Heather Won. *The Class*	507.1
Thorpe, Helen. *The Newcomers*	373.18
Tolan, Sandy. *Children of the Stone*	780
Tough, Paul. ★*How Children Succeed*	372.210973
Wilder, Craig Steven. *Ebony and Ivy*	379.2
Yacovone, Donald. ★*Teaching White Supremacy*	370.89
Yousafzai, Malala. *I Am Malala*	B
Yousafzai, Ziauddin. *Let Her Fly*	B

SOCIETY AND CULTURE — EDUCATION — HIGHER EDUCATION

Bain, Ken. *What the Best College Students Do*	378.1
Bawer, Bruce. *The Victims' Revolution*	320.973
Bok, Derek Curtis. *The Struggle to Reform Our Colleges*	378.73
Bruni, Frank. *Where You Go Is Not Who You'll Be*	378.1
Cooper, Becky. *We Keep the Dead Close*	364.152
Cottom, Tressie McMillan. *Lower Ed*	378.73
Garrett, Kent. *The Last Negroes at Harvard*	920
Gaul, Gilbert M. *Billion-Dollar Ball*	796.332
Goldrick-Rab, Sara. *Paying the Price*	378.3
Grigoriadis, Vanessa. *Blurred Lines*	371.7
Harris, Adam. ★*The State Must Provide*	379.2
Hechinger, John. ★*True Gentlemen*	371.85
Hirsch, Jennifer S. *Sexual Citizens*	371.7
Krakauer, Jon. *Missoula*	362.883
Marshall, McMillan. *Among the Bros*	362.29

2348

AUTHOR, TITLE, SERIES AND SUBJECT INDEX

McIntire, Mike. *Champions Way*	796.043
Mettler, Suzanne. *Degrees of Inequality*	378.73
Mitchell, Josh. *The Debt Trap*	378.3
Perkins, Anne Gardiner. *Yale Needs Women*	378
Rose, Mike. *Back to School*	374
Selingo, Jeffrey J. *College (un)bound*	378
Selingo, Jeffrey J. *Who Gets in and Why*	378.1
Tough, Paul. *The Years That Matter Most*	378.1
Wilder, Craig Steven. *Ebony and Ivy*	379.2

SOCIETY AND CULTURE — ETHNIC STUDIES

Alt, Matt. *Pure Invention*	306.0952
Alvarez, Noe. *Spirit Run*	796.42
Arana, Marie. ★*Latinoland*	973
Arce, Julissa. *You Sound Like a White Girl*	303.48
Bader, Philip. *African-American Writers*	810.9
Badkhen, Anna. *The World Is a Carpet*	305.409581
Belcourt, Billy-Ray. ★*A History of My Brief Body*	B
Bethencourt, Kahran. *Glory*	779.2
Bitsoie, Freddie. *New Native Kitchen*	641.59
Bragg, Rick. *Where I Come From*	975
Bunnell, David. *Good Friday on the Rez*	B
Cadava, Geraldo L. *The Hispanic Republican*	324.2734089
Cahan, Richard. *Un-American*	940.53
Clark, Doug Bock. *The Last Whalers*	639.2
Davis, Thomas J. *History of African Americans*	973
Demick, Barbara. *Eat the Buddha*	951
Douglass, Frederick. *The Portable Frederick Douglass*	973.8
Faloyin, Dipo. ★*Africa Is Not a Country*	960.33
Feldman, Noah. ★*To Be a Jew Today*	296.3
Ferris, William R. *Give My Poor Heart Ease*	781.643
Fersko, Diana. ★*We Need to Talk About Antisemitism*	305.892
Garcia, Angela. ★*The Way That Leads Among the Lost*	362.29
Gayle, Caleb. *We Refuse to Forget*	975.004
Gidla, Sujatha. *Ants Among Elephants*	305.5
Glinert, Lewis. *The Story of Hebrew*	492.4
Goodheart, Adam. *The Last Island*	954
Guida-Richards, Melissa. *What White Parents Should Know About Transracial Adoption*	362.734
Hahn, Emanuel. *Koreatown Dreaming*	979.4
Harris, M. A. *The Black Book*	920
Held, Shai. ★*Judaism Is About Love*	296.3
Hoja, Gulchehra. *A Stone Is Most Precious Where It Belongs*	B
Horn, Dara. ★*People Love Dead Jews*	909
Jerkins, Morgan. *Wandering in Strange Lands*	305.896
Jobrani, Maziyar. *I'm Not a Terrorist, but I've Played One on TV*	B
Joyce, Patrick. *Remembering Peasants*	305.5
King, Charles. ★*Gods of the Upper Air*	920
King, Martin Luther. ★*A Testament of Hope*	323.1
Kuper, Adam. *The Museum of Other People*	305.8
LaPointe, Sasha taqwseblu. *Red Paint*	B
LaPointe, Sasha taqwseblu. *Thunder Song*	814
Lee, Erika. *The Making of Asian America*	973
Mackintosh-Smith, Tim. *Arabs*	909.04
Mays, Kyle. ★*An Afro-Indigenous History of the United States*	973
Mikanowski, Jacob. ★*Goodbye, Eastern Europe*	947
Robeson, Paul. *Here I Stand*	B
Rojas Contreras, Ingrid. ★*The Man Who Could Move Clouds*	B
Salama, Jordan. ★*Stranger in the Desert*	982
Saldana, Stephanie. *What We Remember Will Be Saved*	362.7
Samaha, Albert. *Concepcion*	929
Sarna, Jonathan D. ★*American Judaism*	296
Schmitz, Rob. *Street of Eternal Happiness*	951
Shankar, Shalini. *Beeline*	155.4
Shockley, Evie. *The New Black*	811
Treuer, David. ★*The Heartbeat of Wounded Knee*	970.004
Wagner, Alex. *Futureface*	B
Wilbur, Matika. *Project 562*	970.004
Wilkerson, Isabel. ★*Caste*	305.5
Williams, Juan. *I'll Find a Way or Make One*	378.73
Yang, Jeff. *The Golden Screen*	791.43
Yang, Jeff. ★*Rise*	973
Zakaria, Rafia. *Against White Feminism*	305.42

SOCIETY AND CULTURE — GENDER

Airton, Lee. ★*Gender*	305.3
Baron, Dennis E. *What's Your Pronoun?*	425.55
Bravo, Reah. ★*Complicit*	331.4
Butler, Judith. ★*Who's Afraid of Gender?*	305.3
Chang, Leslie T. ★*Egyptian Made*	331.4
Corbett, Emily. *In Transition*	809
Cox, Gena. *Leading Inclusion*	658.3
Cox, Josie. *Women Money Power*	330.082
Dangarembga, Tsitsi. *Black and Female*	305.48
Davis, Lisa. ★*Housewife*	331.4
Davis, Lisa Selin. *Tomboy*	305.409
Eliot, Lise. *Pink Brain, Blue Brain*	612.6
Feiler, Bruce. *The First Love Story*	222
Fine, Cordelia. *Testosterone Rex*	155.3
Freeman, Amanda. *Getting Me Cheap*	362.83
Hewlett, Sylvia Ann. *#metoo in the Corporate World*	658.3
Isen, Tajja. *Some of My Best Friends*	305.8
LaRue, James. ★*On Censorship*	025.2
Longworth, Karina. *Seduction*	B
Mangino, Kate. ★*Equal Partners*	305.3
Mehra, Nishta. *Brown, White, Black*	305.800973
Olsen, Craig. *P.S. Burn This Letter Please*	306.76
Oluo, Ijeoma. *Mediocre*	305.310973
Reese, Anney. ★*Stuff Mom Never Told You*	305.42
Rose, Jacqueline. *On Violence and on Violence Against Women*	362.88
Ruberg, Bonnie. ★*The Queer Games Avant-Garde*	794.8
Shraya, Vivek. *I'm Afraid of Men*	813
Talusan, Meredith. *Fairest*	305.30973
Tobia, Jacob. *Sissy*	305.30973
Tuerkheimer, Deborah. *Credible*	363.25
Turban, Jack L. ★*Free to Be*	616.85
Yousafzai, Ziauddin. *Let Her Fly*	B

SOCIETY AND CULTURE — GENDER — MEN

Baker, Billy. *We Need to Hang Out*	177
Bates, Laura. *Men Who Hate Women*	305.3
Black, Michael Ian. *A Better Man*	305.31
Bly, Robert. ★*Iron John*	305.310973
Brodeur, Michael Andor. ★*Swole*	155.3
Brown, Emma. *To Raise a Boy*	649
Hobbs, Jeff. *Show Them You're Good*	373
Moran, Caitlin. *What About Men?*	155.3
Neiman, Garrett. *Rich White Men*	305.5
Orenstein, Peggy. ★*Boys & Sex*	305.235
Reiner, Andrew. *Better Boys, Better Men*	155.43
Taylor, Justin. *Riding with the Ghost*	B
Walsh, Patrick C. *Dr. Patrick Walsh's Guide to Surviving Prostate Cancer*	616.99
Way, Niobe. *Rebels with a Cause*	649

SOCIETY AND CULTURE — GENDER — WOMEN

Abdulali, Sohaila. *What We Talk About When We Talk About Rape*	364.15
Adichie, Chimamanda Ngozi. *Dear Ijeawele*	649
Adichie, Chimamanda Ngozi. *We Should All Be Feminists*	305.42
Ahmed, Sara. *The Feminist Killjoy Handbook*	305.42
Alinizhad, Masih. *The Wind in My Hair*	B
Allred, Alexandra Powe. *When Women Stood*	796.082
Beard, Mary. ★*Women & Power*	305.409
Beauvoir, Simone de. ★*The Second Sex*	305.4
Berg, Anastasia. ★*What Are Children For?*	306.87
Blay, Zeba. *Carefree Black Girls*	305.48
Block, Jennifer. *Everything Below the Waist*	613
Bohannon, Cat. ★*Eve*	613
Bowen, Sesali. *Bad Fat Black Girl*	305.42
Brem, Rachel. *No Longer Radical*	616.99
Briggs, Lyvonne. ★*Sensual Faith*	204
Cahn, Naomi R. ★*Fair Shake*	331.4
Calhoun, Ada. *Why We Can't Sleep*	305.244
Chang, Emily. *Brotopia*	331.4
Chang, Leslie T. *Factory Girls*	331.4
Chemaly, Soraya L. *Rage Becomes Her*	155.3
Cleghorn, Elinor. *Unwell Women*	613
Clein, Emmeline. ★*Dead Weight*	616.85
Clinton, Hillary Rodham. *The Book of Gutsy Women*	920
Comen, Elizabeth. ★*All in Her Head*	613
Cooke, Julia. *Come Fly the World*	387.7
Cooper, Becky. *We Keep the Dead Close*	364.152
Cooper, Brittney C. *Eloquent Rage*	B
Copaken, Deborah. *Ladyparts*	B
Cottom, Tressie McMillan. *Thick*	301
Darby, Seyward. ★*Sisters in Hate*	305.800973
Diamant, Anita. ★*Period. End of Sentence*	612.6
Ditum, Sarah. *Toxic*	920.72
Dubin, Minna. ★*Mom Rage*	306.874
Eltahawy, Mona. *The Seven Necessary Sins for Women and Girls*	305.42

PUBLIC LIBRARY CORE COLLECTION: NONFICTION
Twentieth Edition

Emera, Deena. *A Brief History of the Female Body*	612.6
Enright, Lynn. *Vagina*	612.6
Faleiro, Sonia. *The Good Girls*	364.152
Faust, Drew Gilpin. *Mothers of Invention*	973.7
Febos, Melissa. *Girlhood*	818
Felder, Deborah G. *The American Women's Almanac*	305.40973
Filipovic, Jill. *The H-Spot*	155.3
Fleshman, Lauren. ★*Good for a Girl*	B
Flock, Elizabeth. ★*The Furies*	305.48
Friedan, Betty. ★*The Feminine Mystique*	305.42
Garbes, Angela. *Essential Labor*	306.874
Garcia, Amanda Yates. *Initiated*	B
Gates, Melinda. *The Moment of Lift*	305.42
Gay, Roxane. *Bad Feminist*	814
Georges, Gigi. *Downeast*	974.1
Gilbert, Sandra M. ★*Still Mad*	810.9
Gillard, Julia. ★*Women and Leadership*	158
Gilliam, Dorothy Butler. *Trailblazer*	B
Goodan, Chelsey. *Underestimated*	305.235
Griffin, Farah Jasmine. ★*In Search of a Beautiful Freedom*	814
Griffith, Elisabeth. *Formidable*	305.42
Grose, Jessica. *Screaming on the Inside*	306.874
Gross, Rachel E. *Vagina Obscura*	618.1
Grossman, Pam. *Waking the Witch*	133.4
Gunter, Jen. ★*Blood*	612.6
Gunter, Jen. *The Menopause Manifesto*	618.175
Gunter, Jen. *The Vagina Bible*	612.6
Gupta, Shalene. *The Cycle*	618.1
Hackman, Rose. ★*Emotional Labor*	155.3
Hamad, Ruby. *White Tears/Brown Scars*	305.8
Hartley, Gemma. *Fed Up*	155.3
Hay, Carol. *Think Like a Feminist*	305.42
Henny, Ally. *I Won't Shut Up*	305.896
Hill, Katie. *She Will Rise*	305.42
Hirshman, Linda R. *Reckoning*	305.420973
Hirsi Ali, Ayaan. ★*Infidel*	B
Horton, Michelle. *Dear Sister*	B
Hubbard, Shanita. ★*Ride-Or-Die*	305.48
Hustvedt, Siri. *Mothers, Fathers, and Others*	814
Iandoli, Kathy. *God Save the Queens*	782.421649
Jackson, Jenn M. ★*Black Women Taught Us*	305.48
Jackson, Regina. *White Women*	305.8
Jones, Lucy. ★*Matrescence*	306.874
Kantor, Jodi. *She Said*	364.15
Kaplan, Janice. *The Genius of Women*	920
Karbo, Karen. *In Praise of Difficult Women*	920
Kazdin, Cole. ★*What's Eating Us*	616.85
Kendall, Mikki. *Hood Feminism*	305.420973
King, Chrissy. *The Body Liberation Project*	306.4
Kristof, Nicholas D. *Half the Sky*	362.83
Lahti, Christine. *True Stories from an Unreliable Eyewitness*	B
Lemmon, Gayle Tzemach. *The Dressmaker of Khair Khana*	B
Leng'ete, Nice. *The Girls in the Wild Fig Tree*	B
Levy, Deborah. ★*Real Estate*	B
Malone, Sharon. *Grown Woman Talk*	362.1
Mann, Jen. ★*Midlife Bites*	305.244
Marcal, Katrine. *Mother of Invention*	604.82
McDiarmid, Jessica. *Highway of Tears*	364.152
McGregor, Alyson J. *Sex Matters*	613
Mendelson, Zoe. *Pussypedia*	612.6
Mifflin, Margot. *Looking for Miss America*	791.6
Miles, Tiya. ★*Wild Girls*	304.2
Miller, Adrienne. *In the Land of Men*	070.5
Moran, Caitlin. *How to Be a Woman*	B
Moran, Caitlin. *More Than a Woman*	B
Morin, Amy. *13 Things Mentally Strong Women Don't Do*	158.1
Morris, Bonnie J. ★*The Feminist Revolution*	305.4209
Moss, Marissa R. *Her Country*	781.642
Mundy, Liza. *Code Girls*	940.54
Nerenberg, Jenara. *Divergent Mind*	616.89
Nevins, Sheila. *You Don't Look Your Age*	B
Nordberg, Jenny. *The Underground Girls of Kabul*	305.3
Norman, Abby. *Ask Me About My Uterus*	618.1
O'Donnell Heffington, Peggy. *Without Children*	306.85
O'Meara, Mallory. *Girly Drinks*	641.2
Orenstein, Peggy. *Cinderella Ate My Daughter*	305.23082
Orenstein, Peggy. *Don't Call Me Princess*	305.42
Palmieri, Jennifer. *She Proclaims*	305.42
Parker, Lara. *Vagina Problems*	618.1
Penaluna, Regan. ★*How to Think Like a Woman*	190.82
Perkins, Anne Gardiner. *Yale Needs Women*	378
Pipher, Mary Bray. *Women Rowing North*	305.26
Press, Joy. *Stealing the Show*	791.45
Radke, Heather. *Butts*	611
Ramey, Sarah. *The Lady's Handbook for Her Mysterious Illness*	B
Raphael, Rina. *The Gospel of Wellness*	613
Ratajkowski, Emily. ★*My Body*	B
Richards, Cecile. *Make Trouble*	B
Rueckert, Veronica. *Outspoken*	808.5
Saini, Angela. *Inferior*	305.4
Schuller, Kyla. *The Trouble with White Women*	305.42
Scovell, Nell. *Just the Funny Parts*	B
Searcey, Dionne. *In Pursuit of Disobedient Women*	B
Semenya, Caster. *The Race to Be Myself*	B
Simmons, Rachel. ★*Enough as She Is*	155.5
Smarsh, Sarah. *She Come by It Natural*	782.42164
Snyder, Rachel Louise. *No Visible Bruises*	362.82
Sollee, Kristen J. *Witch Hunt*	133
Solnit, Rebecca. *Men Explain Things to Me*	305.42
Solnit, Rebecca. *The Mother of All Questions*	305.42
Solnit, Rebecca. ★*Recollections of My Nonexistence*	B
Somerstein, Rachel. ★*Invisible Labor*	618.8
Spruill, Marjorie Julian. *Divided We Stand*	305.42
Srinivasan, Amia. *The Right to Sex*	305.42
Steinem, Gloria. *Outrageous Acts and Everyday Rebellions*	305.42
Steinem, Gloria. *The Truth Will Set You Free, but First It Will Piss You Off*	305.42
Taddeo, Lisa. *Three Women*	306.7082
Tamblyn, Amber. ★*Era of Ignition*	B
Tang, Karen. ★*It's Not Hysteria*	618.2
Tatar, Maria. *The Heroine with 1001 Faces*	809
Tea, Michelle. *Against Memoir*	B
Tietjen, Jill S. *Hollywood, Her Story*	791.43
Tinsley, Omise'eke Natasha. *Beyonce in Formation*	782.42164
Toorpakai, Maria. *A Different Kind of Daughter*	B
Traister, Rebecca. *Good and Mad*	305.420973
Turk, Katherine. *The Women of Now*	305.42
Union, Gabrielle. *We're Going to Need More Wine*	B
V. ★*Reckoning*	814
Vanasco, Jeannie. *Things We Didn't Talk About When I Was a Girl*	B
Vanek Smith, Stacey. *Machiavelli for Women*	650.1
Vogelstein, Rachel B. *Awakening*	305.42
Warner, Judith. *Perfect Madness*	306.874
Wasson, Sam. *Fifth Avenue, 5 A.M.*	791.43
West, Lindy. *Shrill*	818
West, Lindy. *The Witches Are Coming*	305.420973
Whitefield-Madrano, Autumn. *Face Value*	111
Williams, Marlena. *Night Mother*	791.43
Yeung, Bernice. *In a Day's Work*	362.88086
Yousafzai, Malala. *I Am Malala*	B
Zakaria, Rafia. *Against White Feminism*	305.42
Zimmerman, Jess. *Women and Other Monsters*	155.3
Zoepf, Katherine. *Excellent Daughters*	305.42

SOCIETY AND CULTURE — GENDER — WOMEN — REPRODUCTIVE RIGHTS

Andrews, Becca. ★*No Choice*	362.1988
Blackstone, Amy. *Childfree by Choice*	306.874
Blair, Gabrielle Stanley. ★*Ejaculate Responsibly*	362.1988
Foster, Diana Greene. *The Turnaway Study*	362.1988
Gross, Rachel E. *Vagina Obscura*	618.1
Kolbert, Kathryn. *Controlling Women*	362.1988
Luthra, Shefali. ★*Undue Burden*	362.1988
Matthews, Hannah. *You or Someone You Love*	362.1988
Peters, Rebecca Todd. *Trust Women*	362.1988
Petersen, Sara. *Momfluenced*	306.87
Prager, Joshua. *The Family Roe*	342.7308
Rankin, Lauren. *Bodies on the Line*	362.1988
Sanger, Carol. *About Abortion*	179.7
Shah, Meera. *You're the Only One I've Told*	362.1988
Sisson, Gretchen E. ★*Relinquished*	362.734

SOCIETY AND CULTURE — GENERAL

Ackerman-Leist, Philip. *Rebuilding the Foodshed*	338.1
Agarwal, Pragya. *Sway*	177
Alkon, Amy. *Good Manners for Nice People*	395
Amar, Akhil Reed. *The Constitution Today*	342.73
Amis, Martin. *The Rub of Time*	824

AUTHOR, TITLE, SERIES AND SUBJECT INDEX

Amos, Tori. *Resistance*	B
Applewhite, Ashton. *This Chair Rocks*	155.67
Atwood, Margaret. *Burning Questions*	814
Auerbach, Annie. *Flex*	331.25
Bagby, Meredith E. *The New Guys*	305
Baraka, Sho. *He Saw That It Was Good*	261.5
Baron, Dennis E. *What's Your Pronoun?*	425.55
Berry, Wendell. ★*The World-Ending Fire*	818
Blake, Melissa. *Beautiful People*	362.4
Bowlin, Ben. *Stuff They Don't Want You to Know*	001.9
Brady, Amy. *Ice*	553.7
Caldwell, Christopher. *The Age of Entitlement*	305.240973
Campbell, Hayley. *All the Living and the Dead*	363.7
Carballo, David M. *America*	912
Castaneda, Carlos. *The Teachings of Don Juan;*	299
Castleman, Michael. *The Untold Story of Books*	381
Chomsky, Noam. *Global Discontents*	410.92
Churchwell, Sarah Bartlett. *Behold, America*	973.9
Cohen, Rhaina. ★*The Other Significant Others*	177
Crosley, Sloane. ★*Look Alive Out There*	814
Curzan, Anne. ★*Says Who?*	428
Cutler, Max. *Cults*	364.15
Daley, Mark. *Safe*	B
Dederer, Claire. ★*Monsters*	700.1
Desmond, Matthew. ★*Poverty, by America*	362.5
Dillard, Annie. *The Abundance*	814
Doughty, Caitlin. *From Here to Eternity*	393
Ehrenreich, Barbara. *Had I Known*	814
Ellison, Ralph. ★*The Collected Essays of Ralph Ellison*	814
Everett, Daniel Leonard. *How Language Began*	401
Ferguson, Niall. *Doom*	362.1962
Figes, Orlando. *The Europeans*	920
Frazier, Ian. *Hogs Wild*	814
Fridland, Valerie. ★*Like, Literally, Dude*	420.141
Garfield, Simon. ★*All the Knowledge in the World*	030.9
Gay, Roxane. ★*Opinions*	814
Genoways, Ted. *The Chain*	338.7
Graeber, David. *The Dawn of Everything*	901
Hammack, William Scott. ★*Things We Make*	620
Hankir, Zahra. *Eyeliner*	391.6
Havrilesky, Heather. *What If This Were Enough?*	152.4
Hayasaki, Erika. *Somewhere Sisters*	362.7
Hayhoe, Katharine. *Saving Us*	304.2
Hillstrom, Laurie Collier. *The Thanksgiving Book*	394.2649
Hough, Stephen. *Rough Ideas*	786.2092
Imani, Blair. *Read This to Get Smarter*	303.3
Jamison, Leslie. ★*Make It Scream, Make It Burn*	814
Jebara, Mohamad. ★*The Life of the Qur'an*	297.122
Johnson, Akemi. *Night in the American Village*	305.40952
Kelly, Helena. *Jane Austen, the Secret Radical*	823
Kisor, Henry. *Traveling with Service Animals*	362.4
Kohan, Rafi. ★*Trash Talk*	179
Kruse, Kevin Michael. *Fault Lines*	973.92
Kuo, Michelle. *Reading with Patrick*	B
Le Guin, Ursula K. *Ursula K. Le Guin*	B
Leach, Samantha. ★*The Elissas*	362.73
Leland, Andrew. ★*The Country of the Blind*	B
Levi-Strauss, Claude. ★*The Savage Mind*	155.8
Lorde, Audre. *Sister Outsider*	814
Mannix, Kathryn. *With the End in Mind*	304.6
Mariani, Mike. ★*What Doesn't Kill Us Makes Us*	155.9
McCullough, David G. ★*The American Spirit*	973
McGrath, Tom. *Triumph of the Yuppies*	305.242
McLaughlin, Kathleen. *Blood Money*	362.17
McWhorter, John H. *Talking Back, Talking Black*	427
Mead, Margaret. *Coming of Age in Samoa*	306
Monger, George. *Marriage Customs of the World*	392.5
Mooallem, Jon. *Serious Face*	814
Moody, Anne. *The Children Money Can Buy*	362.73
Nadeau, Jean-Benoit. ★*The Story of French*	440
Nelson, Maggie. ★*Like Love*	814
Offerman, Nick. *Where the Deer and the Antelope Play*	973.93
Olds, Sally. ★*People Who Lunch*	824
Oyler, Lauren. *No Judgment*	814
Ozment, Katherine. *Grace Without God*	200.973
Pein, Corey. *Live Work Work Work Die*	338.4
Petersen, Anne Helen. *Can't Even*	305.242
Petri, Alexandra. *Nothing Is Wrong and Here Is Why*	973.933
Pollan, Michael. ★*This Is Your Mind on Plants*	581.6
Post, Lizzie. *Emily Post's Etiquette*	395
Post, Lizzie. *Emily Post's Etiquette*	395
Pryce, Jessica. ★*Broken*	362.7
Ramesh, Jaya. *Parenting at the Intersections*	649
Rich, Adrienne. *Essential Essays*	814
Robinson, Jo. *Eating on the Wild Side*	641.3
Rothfeld, Becca. ★*All Things Are Too Small*	814
Russo, Richard. *The Destiny Thief*	814
Samet, Elizabeth D. *Looking for the Good War*	940.53
Sciubba, Jennifer Dabbs. *8 Billion and Counting*	304.6
Shah, Rajiv Janardan. *Big Bets*	303.4
Shapland, Jenn. ★*Thin Skin*	814
Sharlet, Jeff. ★*The Undertow*	322
Sjunneson, Elsa. *Being Seen*	362.4
Smith, Clint. ★*How the Word Is Passed*	973
Smith, Zadie. ★*Feel Free*	824
Soep, Elisabeth. *Other People's Words*	155.9
Solnit, Rebecca. *A Paradise Built in Hell*	303.48
Sommer, Will. ★*Trust the Plan*	973.933
Specter, Emma. *More, Please*	616.85
Stamper, Kory. *Word by Word*	413.028
Stanton, Brandon. *Humans*	779
Strings, Sabrina. *The End of Love*	155.3
Sundeen, Mark. *The Unsettlers*	640
Szablowski, Witold. *Dancing Bears*	947.086
Thomson, Mike. *Syria's Secret Library*	956.9104
Thurman, Judith. ★*A Left-Handed Woman*	814
Tulleken, Chris van. *Ultra-Processed People*	664
Turchin, Peter. *End Times*	320.01
Twenge, Jean M. *Generations*	305.2
Tyson, Neil deGrasse. *Starry Messenger*	901
Van Ness, Jonathan. *Love That Story*	791.4502
Vince, Gaia. *Nomad Century*	362.87
Wainaina, Binyavanga. ★*How to Write About Africa*	814
Warzel, Charlie. *Out of Office*	658.3
Weingarten, Gene. ★*One Day*	973
Wides-Munoz, Laura. *The Making of a Dream*	920
Wilson, Bee. *The Way We Eat Now*	641.01
Wilson, Jessica. *It's Always Been Ours*	613

SOCIETY AND CULTURE — ILLNESS AND DISEASE

Arthur, Alua. ★*Briefly Perfectly Human*	306.9
Blaser, Martin J. *Missing Microbes*	615.7
Boyer, Anne. *The Undying*	B
Davis, Lennard J. *Enabling Acts*	342.7308
Dearen, Jason. *Kill Shot*	616.8
Dufton, Emily. *Grass Roots*	362.29
Ehrenreich, Barbara. *Natural Causes*	613.2
Fabes, Stephen. *Signs of Life*	B
Fisher, Thomas. ★*The Emergency*	362.1089
Gawande, Atul. ★*Being Mortal*	362.17
Geronimus, Arline T. ★*Weathering*	362.1089
Grinker, Roy Richard. *Nobody's Normal*	616.89
Gupta, Shalene. *The Cycle*	618.1
Hendrickson, Debra. ★*The Air They Breathe*	363.7
Hernandez, Daisy. *The Kissing Bug*	616.9
Heumann, Judith E. *Being Heumann*	B
Hotz, Julia. ★*The Connection Cure*	610
Ikpi, Bassey. *I'm Telling the Truth, but I'm Lying*	814
Johnson, Steven. *Extra Life*	362.1
Kang, Lydia. *Patient Zero*	614.4
Karlawish, Jason. ★*The Problem of Alzheimer's*	616.8
Lehrer, Riva. *Golem Girl*	B
Lieberman, Daniel. *Exercised*	612.044
MacPhail, Theresa. *Allergic*	616.97
Morris, Jim. ★*The Cancer Factory*	658.3
Norman, Abby. *Ask Me About My Uterus*	618.1
Otto, Mary. *Teeth*	617
Parker, Lara. *Vagina Problems*	618.1
Quammen, David. ★*Spillover*	614.4
Ramey, Sarah. *The Lady's Handbook for Her Mysterious Illness*	B
Schama, Simon. *Foreign Bodies*	614.4
Tabery, James. ★*Tyranny of the Gene*	572.8
Thrasher, Steven W. ★*The Viral Underclass*	362.1962
Tweedy, Damon. *Facing the Unseen*	362.2
Warraich, Haider. *Modern Death*	179.7
Yurkiewicz, Ilana. *Fragmented*	362.1
Zaitchik, Alexander. *Owning the Sun*	362.1

PUBLIC LIBRARY CORE COLLECTION: NONFICTION
Twentieth Edition

SOCIETY AND CULTURE — ILLNESS AND DISEASE — ADDICTION

Berenson, Alex. ★*Tell Your Children*	362.29
Bond, Melissa. *Blood Orange Night*	616.8
Clein, Emmeline. ★*Dead Weight*	616.85
Dakwar, Elias. *The Captive Imagination*	616.85
Etter, Lauren. ★*The Devil's Playbook*	338.7
Eyre, Eric. *Death in Mud Lick*	362.29
Fisher, Carl Erik. ★*The Urge*	362.29
Johnston, Ann Dowsett. *Drink*	362.292
Kazdin, Cole. ★*What's Eating Us*	616.85
Khar, Erin. *Strung Out*	B
Lahey, Jessica. *The Addiction Inoculation*	649
Lembke, Anna. *Dopamine Nation*	152.4
Macy, Beth. ★*Dopesick*	362.29
Macy, Beth. ★*Raising Lazarus*	362.29
McGreal, Chris. *American Overdose*	362.29
Moss, Michael. ★*Hooked*	613.2
Quinones, Sam. *Dreamland*	362.29
Quinones, Sam. ★*The Least of Us*	362.29
Rieder, Travis. *In Pain*	362.29
Schemel, Patty. *Hit so Hard*	B
Smith, Freda Love. *I Quit Everything*	B
Westhoff, Ben. *Fentanyl, Inc.*	362.29
Whitaker, Holly. ★*Quit Like a Woman*	616.86

SOCIETY AND CULTURE — ILLNESS AND DISEASE — EPIDEMICS

Ashton, Jennifer. *The New Normal*	613
Borrell, Brendan. *The First Shots*	615.3
Brenner, Marie. ★*The Desperate Hours*	362.1962
Christakis, Nicholas A. *Apollo's Arrow*	362.1962
Farmer, Paul. *Fevers, Feuds, and Diamonds*	614.5
France, David. *How to Survive a Plague*	362.196
Gates, Bill. ★*How to Prevent the Next Pandemic*	614.5
Goldberg, Emma. *Life on the Line*	362.1962
Holt, Nathalia. *Cured*	614.5
Kennedy, Jonathan. *Pathogenesis*	614.4
Kenny, Charles. *The Plague Cycle*	614.4
Klinenberg, Eric. ★*2020*	306
Lewis, Michael. ★*The Premonition*	614.5
Mackenzie, Debora. *Covid-19*	616.2
Manaugh, Geoff. *Until Proven Safe*	614.4
McNeil, Donald G. ★*The Wisdom of Plagues*	614.4
Meyer, Robert. *Every Minute Is a Day*	362.1962
Moss, Jeremiah. *Feral City*	B
Nocera, Joseph. *The Big Fail*	362.1962
Preston, Richard. *Crisis in the Red Zone*	614.5
Price, Polly J. *Plagues in the Nation*	614.4
Quammen, David. ★*Spillover*	614.4
Senthilingam, Meera. *Outbreaks and Epidemics*	614.4
Shilts, Randy. ★*And the Band Played On*	362.196
Smith, Michael. *Cabin Fever*	614.5
Smith, Zadie. *Intimations*	824
Werb, Dan. *The Invisible Siege*	614.5
Wright, Lawrence. ★*The Plague Year*	614.5
Xuecun, Murong. *Deadly Quiet City*	614.5

SOCIETY AND CULTURE — IMMIGRATION

Bass, Amy. *One Goal*	796.334
Blitzer, Jonathan. *Everyone Who Is Gone Is Here*	305.9
Bobrow-Strain, Aaron. *The Death and Life of Aida Hernandez*	972
Cantu, Francisco. *The Line Becomes a River*	B
Chang, Leslie T. *Factory Girls*	331.4
Cornejo Villavicencio, Karla. ★*The Undocumented Americans*	920
DeParle, Jason. ★*A Good Provider Is One Who Leaves*	305.899
Fishman, Elly. *Refugee High*	370.8
Fleming, Melissa. *A Hope More Powerful Than the Sea*	956.9104
Gatrell, Peter. *The Unsettling of Europe*	304.8
Gonzalez, Karen. *Beyond Welcome*	261.8
Goudeau, Jessica. ★*After the Last Border*	362.83
Grandin, Greg. *The End of the Myth*	973
Hakkakiyan, Ruya. *A Beginner's Guide to America*	646.7
Hernandez Castillo, Marcelo. *Children of the Land*	B
Hinojosa, Maria. *Once I Was You*	B
Khakpour, Porochista. *Brown Album*	304.8
Lee, Erika. *America for Americans*	305.800973
Lekas Miller, Anna. *Love Across Borders*	323.6
Luiselli, Valeria. *Tell Me How It Ends*	305.23086
Minian, Ana Raquel. ★*In the Shadow of Liberty*	365
Molnar, Petra. *The Walls Have Eyes*	363.28
Mufleh, Luma. ★*Learning America*	371.826
Ng, Fae Myenne. *Orphan Bachelors*	B
Okrent, Daniel. *The Guarded Gate*	344.73
Oliva, Alejandra. *Rivermouth*	305.9
Olivares, Efren C. *My Boy Will Die of Sorrow*	305.9
Perlin, Ross. ★*Language City*	306.44
Ramos, Jorge. *Stranger*	325.73
Samaha, Albert. *Concepcion*	929
Shahani, Aarti Namdev. *Here We Are*	B
Suarez, Ray. ★*We Are Home*	325.73
Vargas, Jose Antonio. *Dear America*	B
Yang, Jia Lynn. ★*One Mighty and Irresistible Tide*	325.73
Zamora, Javier. ★*Solito*	B

SOCIETY AND CULTURE — LGBTQIA+

Airton, Lee. ★*Gender*	305.3
Barnes, Katie. ★*Fair Play*	796.082
Becker, Jo. ★*Forcing the Spring*	346.79401
Belcourt, Billy-Ray. ★*A History of My Brief Body*	B
Berg, Ryan. *No House to Call My Home*	B
Bowen, Sesali. *Bad Fat Black Girl*	305.42
Bram, Christopher. *Eminent Outlaws*	920
Bronski, Michael. *A Queer History of the United States*	306.76
Butler, Isaac. *The World Only Spins Forward*	812
Carruthers, Charlene A. *Unapologetic*	305.48
Carter, David. *Stonewall*	306.76
Cenziper, Debbie. ★*Love Wins*	346.7301
Chu, Jeff. *Does Jesus Really Love Me?*	261.8
Cooper, Alex. *Saving Alex*	B
Davis, Lisa Selin. *Tomboy*	305.409
Duberman, Martin B. *Hold Tight Gently*	920
Edman, Elizabeth M. *Queer Virtue*	230
Fieseler, Robert W. *Tinderbox*	364.152
France, David. *How to Survive a Plague*	362.196
Funk, Mason. *The Book of Pride*	920
Gelwicks, Andrew. *The Queer Advantage*	920
Goodman, Elyssa. *Glitter and Concrete*	792.7
Gutowitz, Jill. *Girls Can Kiss Now*	814
Hall, Jake. *The Art of Drag*	792.8
Hartke, Austen. *Transforming*	277
Hester, Diarmuid. *Nothing Ever Just Disappears*	306.76
Kaplan, Roberta A. *Then Comes Marriage*	346.7301
Kugle, Scott Alan. *Living Out Islam*	297
Lemay, Mimi. *What We Will Become*	306.874
Manning, Chelsea. *Readme.Txt*	B
Mattel, Trixie. *Working Girls*	650.1
Nutt, Amy Ellis. *Becoming Nicole*	920
Olsen, Craig. *P.S. Burn This Letter Please*	306.76
Page, Elliot. *Pageboy*	B
Ruberg, Bonnie. ★*The Queer Games Avant-Garde*	794.8
Schiavi, Michael R. *Celluloid Activist*	B
Seligman, Craig. *Who Does That Bitch Think She Is?*	792.02
Shapland, Jenn. *My Autobiography of Carson McCullers*	B
Shaw, Julia. *Bi*	306.76
Tea, Michelle. *Against Memoir*	B
Tobia, Jacob. *Sissy*	305.30973
Velour, Sasha. ★*The Big Reveal*	792.7
Weigel, Alicia Roth. *Inverse Cowgirl*	B
Windsor, Edie. *A Wild and Precious Life*	B
Yoshino, Kenji. *Speak Now*	346.79401

SOCIETY AND CULTURE — MEDIA AND TECHNOLOGY

Bergen, Mark. *Like, Comment, Subscribe*	338.7
Boghosian, Heidi. *"i Have Nothing to Hide"*	363.1
Brickman, Sophie. *Baby, Unplugged*	306.874
Cairo, Alberto. *How Charts Lie*	302.2
Chayka, Kyle. *Filterworld*	306
Citron, Danielle Keats. *The Fight for Privacy*	342.7308
Cole, Samantha. *How the Internet Changed Sex and Sex Changed the Internet*	306.7
Cross, Tiffany D. ★*Say It Louder!*	324.6
DiResta, Renee. *Invisible Rulers*	320
Dixon, Wheeler W. *A Short History of Film*	791.43
Ellis, Bret Easton. *White*	814
Evans, Claire Lisa. *Broad Band*	920
Friedman, Thomas L. ★*Thank You for Being Late*	303.48
Galloway, Scott. *The Four*	338.7
Gladwell, Malcolm. ★*Talking to Strangers*	302
Goldblatt, Duchess. *Becoming Duchess Goldblatt*	B
Greenberg, Andy. *Sandworm*	364.16
Haidt, Jonathan. ★*The Anxious Generation*	305.23

AUTHOR, TITLE, SERIES AND SUBJECT INDEX

Hill, Marc Lamont. *Seen and Unseen*	303.3
Horwitz, Jeff. ★*Broken Code*	302.3
Howley, Kerry. *Bottoms Up and the Devil Laughs*	352.37
Kaku, Michio. *Quantum Supremacy*	006.3
Klein, Naomi. ★*Doppelganger*	302.2
Kurtz, Howard. *Media Madness*	973.933
Lancaster, Jen. *Welcome to the United States of Anxiety*	155.4
Lavery, Daniel M. *Dear Prudence*	170
Lee, Kai-Fu. *AI 2041*	006.3
Lessig, Lawrence. *Remix*	346.7304
Linn, Susan. *Who's Raising the Kids?*	649
Lorenz, Taylor. ★*Extremely Online*	302.23
Malone, Thomas W. *Superminds*	005.7
McCourt, Frank H. ★*Our Biggest Fight*	303.48
Merchant, Brian. *Blood in the Machine*	303.48
Mitchell, Elizabeth. *Lincoln's Lie*	973.7092
Mitnick, Kevin D. *The Art of Invisibility*	005.8
Molnar, Petra. *The Walls Have Eyes*	363.28
Murgia, Madhumita. *Code Dependent*	303.48
Napoli, Lisa. *Up All Night*	384.55
O'Gieblyn, Meghan. *God, Human, Animal, Machine*	814
O'Neil, Cathy. *Weapons of Math Destruction*	005.7
Owens, Ernest. *The Case for Cancel Culture*	303.3
Peisner, David. *Homey Don't Play That!*	791.45
Poniewozik, James. *Audience of One*	324.7
Quinn, Zoe. *Crash Override*	794.8
Ramsey, Franchesca. *Well, That Escalated Quickly*	B
Russell, Stuart J. *Human Compatible*	006.301
Schieffer, Bob. *Overload*	070.4
Schneier, Bruce. *A Hacker's Mind*	364.16
Schwartz, A. Brad. ★*Broadcast Hysteria*	791.44
Shlain, Tiffany. *24/6*	158.1
Small, Zachary. ★*Token Supremacy*	332.4
Smith, Ben. *Traffic*	070.4
Suleyman, Mustafa. *The Coming Wave*	303.48
Swisher, Kara. *Burn Book*	303.48
Taplin, Jonathan. *Move Fast and Break Things*	330.9
Tegmark, Max. *Life 3.0*	006.301
Thompson, Clive. *Coders*	005.1092
Tolentino, Jia. ★*Trick Mirror*	973.93
Trillin, Calvin. *The Lede*	071
van der Linden, Sander. ★*Foolproof*	302.3
Wiggins, Christopher L. *How Data Happened*	310

SOCIETY AND CULTURE — PHILOSOPHY

Adler, Mortimer Jerome. *Aristotle for Everybody*	185
Aristotle. ★*The Basic Works of Aristotle*	185
Aristotle. ★*Nicomachean Ethics*	171
Bakewell, Sarah. ★*At the Existentialist Cafe*	920
Barrett, William. *Irrational Man*	142
Bregman, Rutger. *Utopia for Realists*	335
Brooks, David. ★*The Second Mountain*	302
Campbell, Jeremy. *The Liar's Tale*	177
Camus, Albert. *The Myth of Sisyphus and Other Essays*	844
Camus, Albert. *The Rebel*	303.6
Carlisle, Clare. *Philosopher of the Heart*	B
Carroll, Sean M. *The Big Picture*	577
Copi, Irving M. ★*Introduction to Logic*	160
De Bres, Helena. *How to Be Multiple*	155.44
Delaney, Brigid. *Reasons Not to Worry*	158.1
Descartes, Rene. ★*Descartes*	194
Durant, Will. ★*The Story of Philosophy*	190
Eilenberger, Wolfram. *Time of the Magicians*	920
Gandhi. ★*Gandhi on Non-Violence*	179.7
Gay, Peter. *The Enlightenment*	190
Ghodsee, Kristen Rogheh. *Everyday Utopia*	335
Gopnik, Adam. *All That Happiness Is*	158.1
Gottlieb, Anthony. ★*The Dream of Enlightenment*	190
Gottlieb, Anthony. *The Dream of Reason*	180
Grayling, A. C. *The History of Philosophy*	109
Gutting, Gary. *What Philosophy Can Do*	100
Hagglund, Martin. *This Life*	110
Harari, Yuval N. *Homo Deus*	909.83
Hare, R. M. ★*Plato*	184
Harman, Oren Solomon. *Evolutions*	201
Hay, Carol. *Think Like a Feminist*	305.42
Heidegger, Martin. *Basic Writings*	193
Heidegger, Martin. ★*Being and Time*	111
Hitchens, Christopher. *The Four Horsemen*	211
Holiday, Ryan. *Lives of the Stoics*	188
Ignatieff, Michael. *On Consolation*	152.4
Johnson, Paul. *Socrates*	183
Kaag, John J. *American Philosophy*	191
Kaag, John J. *Hiking with Nietzsche*	193
Kierkegaard, Soren. *Fear and Trembling*	248
Le Guin, Ursula K. *No Time to Spare*	814
Lee, Shannon. *Be Water, My Friend*	796.8
Lightman, Alan P. *Searching for Stars on an Island in Maine*	523.1
Livio, Mario. *Why?*	153.3
Lowery, Brian S. *Selfless*	155.2
McLaren, Brian D. *Do I Stay Christian?*	270.8
Mendelson, Cheryl. ★*Vows*	203
Nhat Hanh. *Zen and the Art of Saving the Planet*	294.3
Nicolson, Adam. *How to Be*	180
Nietzsche, Friedrich Wilhelm. *The Will to Power*	193
Nye, Bill. *Everything All at Once*	153.4
Ortega Y Gasset, Jose. *What Is Philosophy?*	101
Penaluna, Regan. ★*How to Think Like a Woman*	190.82
Phillips, Adam. *On Giving up*	158.2
Pinn, Anthony B. *The Black Practice of Disbelief*	211
Plato. ★*The Collected Dialogues of Plato, Including the Letters*	184
Prideaux, Sue. *I Am Dynamite!*	B
Purnell, Carolyn. *The Sensational Past*	152.109
Rand, Ayn. *The Voice of Reason*	191
Rovelli, Carlo. *There Are Places in the World Where Rules Are Less Important Than Kindness*	500
Russell, Bertrand. *A History of Western Philosophy, and Its Connection with Political and Social Circumstances from the Earliest Times to the Present Day*	109
Russell, Bertrand. *The Problems of Philosophy*	110
Ruttenberg, Danya. *On Repentance and Repair*	202
Sapolsky, Robert M. *Determined*	155.2
Sartre, Jean-Paul. ★*Being and Nothingness*	111
Sartre, Jean-Paul. *Existentialism and Human Emotions*	111
Setiya, Kieran. *Life Is Hard*	128
Shahvisi, Arianne. *Arguing for a Better World*	170
Shields, Christopher John. *Aristotle*	185
Skach, C. L. *How to Be a Citizen*	323.6
Srinivasan, Amia. *The Right to Sex*	305.42
Sullivan, Meghan. *The Good Life Method*	170
Sullivan, Randall. *The Devil's Best Trick*	235
Tillich, Paul. ★*The Courage to Be*	179
Vanek Smith, Stacey. *Machiavelli for Women*	650.1
Volf, Miroslav. *Life Worth Living*	113
Weiner, Eric. *The Socrates Express*	100
Wilson, Edward O. *Consilience*	121
Wilson, Edward O. *The Meaning of Human Existence*	128
Wright, Robert. *Why Buddhism Is True*	294.3
Wulf, Andrea. *Magnificent Rebels*	830.9
Zuckerman, Phil. *Living the Secular Life*	211

SOCIETY AND CULTURE — POP CULTURE

Abdurraqib, Hanif. *Go Ahead in the Rain*	782.421649
Alt, Matt. *Pure Invention*	306.0952
Armstrong, Jennifer Keishin. *Seinfeldia*	791.45
Armstrong, Jennifer Keishin. *Sex and the City and Us*	791.45
Baum, Dan. *Nine Lives*	B
Bechdel, Alison. ★*The Secret to Superhuman Strength*	741.5
Blay, Zeba. *Carefree Black Girls*	305.48
Braudy, Leo. *Haunted*	398.45
Breihan, Tom. ★*The Number Ones*	782.42164
Britt, Ryan. *Phasers on Stun!*	791.45
Callahan, David. *The Cheating Culture*	174
Dickey, Colin. *The Unidentified*	130
Ditum, Sarah. *Toxic*	920.72
Doggett, Peter. *Electric Shock*	781.64
Dylan, Bob. ★*The Philosophy of Modern Song*	782.42
Ellis, Bret Easton. *White*	814
Evans, William. *Black Nerd Problems*	814.6
Favro, Terri. *Generation Robot*	006.3
Felisbret, Eric. *Graffiti New York*	751.7
Fox, Dan. *Pretentiousness*	700
Fox, Jesse David. *Comedy Book*	792.7
Graham, Ashley. *A New Model*	B
Green, Jaime. *The Possibility of Life*	576.8
Greene, Andy. *The Office*	791.45
Gross, Edward. *The Fifty Year Mission*	791.45
Grossman, Pam. *Waking the Witch*	133.4

PUBLIC LIBRARY CORE COLLECTION: NONFICTION
Twentieth Edition

Gutowitz, Jill. *Girls Can Kiss Now*	814
Hickey, Walt. ★*You Are What You Watch*	791.4
Howard, Jennifer. *Clutter*	306.3
Hu, Elise. *Flawless*	646.7
Hyden, Steven. *Twilight of the Gods*	781.6609
Jameson, A. D. *I Find Your Lack of Faith Disturbing*	791.43
Jennings, Ken. ★*100 Places to See After You Die*	202
Jennings, Ken. *Planet Funny*	809.7
Kamp, David. *Sunny Days*	791.4502
Klosterman, Chuck. *But What If We're Wrong*	909.83
Klosterman, Chuck. ★*The Nineties*	306.0973
Kroger, Lisa. *Monster, She Wrote*	920
Lorenz, Taylor. ★*Extremely Online*	302.23
Lowery, Brian S. *Selfless*	155.2
Marx, W. David. ★*Status and Culture*	305
Mike D. *Beastie Boys Book*	782.42164
Montell, Amanda. ★*The Age of Magical Overthinking*	153.4
Moss, Gabrielle. *Paperback Crush*	813.009
Norman, Philip. *George Harrison*	B
Nussbaum, Emily. *I Like to Watch*	791.45
O'Connor, John. *The Secret History of Bigfoot*	001.944
Perkins, Nichole. *Sometimes I Trip on How Happy We Could Be*	B
Phillips, Maya. *Nerd*	302.23
Prothero, Donald R. *UFOs, Chemtrails, and Aliens*	001.94
Questlove. *Music Is History*	782.42164
Radke, Heather. *Butts*	611
Robinson, Joanna. ★*McU*	791.43
Ryan, Maureen. *Burn It Down*	791.43
Sanneh, Kelefa. *Major Labels*	781.64
Shone, Tom. *The Nolan Variations*	791.4302
Sloan, Nate. *Switched on Pop*	781.64
Smith, Ben. *Traffic*	070.4
Smith, Danyel. *Shine Bright*	782.42164
Smith, Patti. ★*A Book of Days*	779
Snodgrass, Mary Ellen. *Signs of the Zodiac*	133.5
Steinem, Gloria. *The Truth Will Set You Free, but First It Will Piss You Off*	305.42
Stewart, Alison. *Junk*	616.85
Tatar, Maria. *The Heroine with 1001 Faces*	809
Tolentino, Jia. ★*Trick Mirror*	973.93
Traig, Jennifer. *Act Natural*	306.874
Tye, Larry. ★*The Jazzmen*	781.6509
Villarreal, Vanessa Anglica. *Magical/Realism*	814
Weldon, Glen. ★*The Caped Crusade*	741.5
Westhoff, Ben. *Original Gangstas*	782.421649
Wolk, Douglas. ★*All of the Marvels*	741.5
Yang, Jeff. ★*Rise*	973
Yang, Lihui. ★*Handbook of Chinese Mythology*	299.5
Yong, Sable. *Die Hot with a Vengeance*	646.7
Young, Kevin. *Bunk*	177

SOCIETY AND CULTURE — PSYCHOLOGY AND HUMAN BEHAVIOR

Ahuvia, Aaron. ★*The Things We Love*	790.1
Alda, Alan. *If I Understood You, Would I Have This Look on My Face?*	153.6
Andersen, Kurt. ★*Fantasyland*	973
Ariely, Dan. *The Honest Truth About Dishonesty*	177
Baker, Billy. *We Need to Hang Out*	177
Bargh, John A. *Before You Know It*	154.2
Bering, Jesse. *Suicidal*	362.2
Blattman, Christopher. *Why We Fight*	303.6
Bloom, Paul. *Psych*	150
Bradford, Joy Harden. *Sisterhood Heals*	158.2
Brandt, Anthony K. *The Runaway Species*	153.3
Brooks, David. ★*How to Know a Person*	158.2
Brooks, David. *The Social Animal*	305.5
Brookwood, Marilyn. *The Orphans of Davenport*	305.231
Brotherton, Rob. *Suspicious Minds*	153.4
Brown, Brene. *Braving the Wilderness*	305.8
Brown, Brene. ★*Dare to Lead*	658.4
Brown, Brene. *The Gifts of Imperfection*	158
Brownstein, Gabriel. ★*The Secret Mind of Bertha Pappenheim*	616.85
Cain, Susan. ★*Bittersweet*	155.2
Calhoun, Ada. *Why We Can't Sleep*	305.244
Christian, Brian. *Algorithms to Live By*	153.4
Clark, Andy. *The Experience Machine*	153
Corrigan, Kelly. *Tell Me More*	153.6
Crouse, Karen. *Norwich*	796
Cuddy, Amy. *Presence*	158.1
Dahl, Melissa. *Cringeworthy*	158.2
Dakwar, Elias. *The Captive Imagination*	616.85
Davis, Lisa Selin. *Tomboy*	305.409
Denworth, Lydia. *Friendship*	158.2
Diamond, Jared M. *Upheaval*	303.48
Duckworth, Angela. *Grit*	158.1
Duhigg, Charles. ★*Supercommunicators*	153.6
Durvasula, Ramani. ★*It's Not You*	155.2
Eberhardt, Jennifer L. ★*Biased*	303.3
Edmondson, Amy C. *The Right Kind of Wrong*	158.1
Ehrenreich, Barbara. *Bright-Sided*	155.2
Epstein, David J. ★*Range*	153.9
Epstein, Mark. *The Zen of Therapy*	294.3
Esty, Katharaine C. *Eightysomethings*	612.6
Feiler, Bruce. *Life Is in the Transitions*	392
Feiler, Bruce. ★*The Search*	306.3
Field, Andy. *Encounterism*	302
Fogg, B. J. *Tiny Habits*	158
Foster, Charles. *Being a Human*	155.7
Franco, Marisa G. *Platonic*	302.34
Friedman, Ron. *Decoding Greatness*	650.1
Gallagher, Richard E. *Demonic Foes*	133.42
Gibson, Marion. *Witchcraft*	133.4
Gilbert, Daniel Todd. ★*Stumbling on Happiness*	158
Gilliam, Fatimah. *Race Rules*	305.8
Gladwell, Malcolm. *David and Goliath*	155.2
Gladwell, Malcolm. ★*Talking to Strangers*	302
Gladwell, Malcolm. *The Tipping Point*	302
Goleman, Daniel. ★*Social Intelligence*	158.2
Gopnik, Adam. *The Real Work*	153.9
Gopnik, Alison. *The Gardener and the Carpenter*	155.4
Gordon, Aubrey. *"You Just Need to Lose Weight"*	616.3
Gosden, Chris. *Magic*	133.4
Gottlieb, Lori. ★*Maybe You Should Talk to Someone*	B
Grandin, Temple. ★*Visual Thinking*	152.14
Grant, Adam M. *Hidden Potential*	153.8
Grant, Adam M. ★*Think Again*	153.4
Greene, B. *Until the End of Time*	523.1
Gurdon, Meghan Cox. *The Enchanted Hour*	372.4
Hagglund, Martin. *This Life*	110
Haidt, Jonathan. ★*The Anxious Generation*	305.23
Haig, Matt. *Notes on a Nervous Planet*	616.89
Hammond, Claudia. *Mind Over Money*	332.401
Harari, Yuval N. ★*Sapiens*	909
Heath, Chip. *The Power of Moments*	128
Herman, Judith Lewis. *Truth and Repair*	362.883
Hofstadter, Douglas R. *Surfaces and Essences*	169
Howard, Jennifer. *Clutter*	306.3
Hubbard, Shanita. ★*Ride-Or-Die*	305.48
Ingall, Marjorie. *Sorry, Sorry, Sorry*	158.2
Iyengar, Sheena. *The Art of Choosing*	153.8
Jacobs, Alan. *How to Think*	153.4
Keltner, Dacher. ★*Awe*	152.4
Killam, Kasley. *The Art and Science of Connection*	302
King, David. *Six Days in August*	364.15
Kinzler, Katherine D. *How You Say It*	302.2
Kohli, Sahaj Kaur. ★*But What Will People Say?*	616.89
Konnikova, Maria. *The Biggest Bluff*	795.412
Kriss, Alexander. *Borderline*	616.85
Kross, Ethan. ★*Chatter*	158.1
Laing, Olivia. *Everybody*	323
Lavery, Daniel M. *Dear Prudence*	170
Lembke, Anna. *Dopamine Nation*	152.4
Lifford, Tina. *The Little Book of Big Lies*	155.2
Livio, Mario. *Why?*	153.3
Lowery, Brian S. *Selfless*	155.2
McConville, Mark. *Failure to Launch*	155.6
McInerny, Nora. *The Hot Young Widows Club*	155.9
Miller, Kenneth R. *The Human Instinct*	155.7
Miranda, Lin-Manuel. *Gmorning, Gnight!*	811
Mlodinow, Leonard. *Emotional*	152.4
Montell, Amanda. ★*The Age of Magical Overthinking*	153.4
Mooney, Jonathan. *Normal Sucks*	B
Morrison, Toni. ★*The Origin of Others*	809
Mullainathan, Sendhil. *Scarcity*	338.5
Myers, David G. *How Do We Know Ourselves?*	155.2
Nisbett, Richard E. *Mindware*	153.4
Nussbaum, Martha Craven. *The Monarchy of Fear*	306.20973
O'Neil, Cathy. *The Shame Machine*	152.4

AUTHOR, TITLE, SERIES AND SUBJECT INDEX

O'Sullivan, Suzanne. *The Sleeping Beauties*	616.85
Odell, Jenny. ★*Saving Time*	153.7
Paul, Annie Murphy. *The Extended Mind*	128
Petersen, Sara. *Momfluenced*	306.87
Phillips, Adam. *On Giving up*	158.2
Pink, Daniel H. *Drive*	153.1
Pinker, Steven. ★*Enlightenment Now*	303.44
Pinker, Steven. *Rationality*	153.4
Pipher, Mary Bray. *Women Rowing North*	305.26
Price, Devon. ★*Laziness Does Not Exist*	158.1
Pryor, Karen. ★*Don't Shoot the Dog*	153.8
Radtke, Kristen. *Seek You*	741.5
Ranganath, Charan. ★*Why We Remember*	153.1
Raskin, Allison. *Overthinking About You*	646.7
Rauch, Jonathan. *The Happiness Curve*	155.6
Real, Terrence. *Us*	646.7
Riley, Alex. ★*A Cure for Darkness*	616.85
Rinaldi, Karen. *It's Great to Suck at Something*	158.1
Rogers, Susan E. ★*This Is What It Sounds Like*	781.1
Ronson, Jon. *So You've Been Publicly Shamed*	152.4
Rosling, Hans. *Factfulness*	155.9
Rubin, Gretchen Craft. ★*Life in Five Senses*	152.1
Rubin, Rick. ★*The Creative Act*	153.3
Sale, Anna. ★*Let's Talk About Hard Things*	153.6
Sandberg, Sheryl. *Option B*	155.9
Sapolsky, Robert M. *Behave*	612.8
Sapolsky, Robert M. *Determined*	123
Schulz, Kathryn. *Being Wrong*	121
Schutt, Bill. *Cannibalism*	394
Scott, Andy. *One Kiss or Two?*	395.4
Sharot, Tali. *Look Again*	158.1
Siegel, Daniel J. *Brainstorm*	155.5
Smil, Vaclav. *Size*	153.7
Sole-Smith, Virginia. ★*Fat Talk*	649.1
Sow, Aminatou. *Big Friendship*	177
Spofford, Tim. *What the Children Told Us*	150.92
Stewart, Alison. *Junk*	616.85
Stone, Deborah A. *Counting*	001.4
Storr, Will. *Selfie*	155.2
Stryker, Kitty. *Ask*	302
Summerscale, Kate. *The Book of Phobias and Manias*	616.85
Tallis, Frank. *The Incurable Romantic*	152.4
Tallis, Frank. ★*Mortal Secrets*	B
Thompson, J. M. *Running Is a Kind of Dreaming*	B
Tierney, John. *The Power of Bad*	158.1
Van Bavel, Jay J. *The Power of Us*	155.2
Vanderbilt, Tom. ★*Beginners*	646.7
Vedantam, Shankar. *Useful Delusions*	153.4
Visser, Margaret. *The Gift of Thanks*	394
Volf, Miroslav. *Life Worth Living*	113
Waal, F. B. M. de. ★*Mama's Last Hug*	599.885
Waldinger, Robert J. ★*The Good Life*	158.1
Walker, Sam. *The Captain Class*	796.07
Way, Niobe. *Rebels with a Cause*	649
Weber, Charlotte Fox. *Tell Me What You Want*	153.8
Weir, Laura. *Cosy*	646.7009
Wertheim, L. Jon. *This Is Your Brain on Sports*	796.01
Wiking, Meik. *The Art of Making Memories*	153.1
Wilson, Sarah. *First, We Make the Beast Beautiful*	616.85
Winch, Guy. *How to Fix a Broken Heart*	155.9
Winfrey, Oprah. *What Happened to You?*	616.85
Wolfe, Tom. *The Kingdom of Speech*	401
Wood, Wendy. *Good Habits, Bad Habits*	152.3
Wray, Britt. *Generation Dread*	155.9
Wright, Robert. *Why Buddhism Is True*	294.3
Yates, Kit. *The Math of Life and Death*	510
Yoshino, Kenji. *Say the Right Thing*	305.3
Zorn, Justin. *Golden*	128

SOCIETY AND CULTURE — RACE

Abdelmahmoud, Elamin. *Son of Elsewhere*	B
Abdurraqib, Hanif. ★*A Little Devil in America*	791.089
Abrams, Stacey. *Our Time Is Now*	324.60973
Adams, Jarrett. *Redeeming Justice*	340.092
Akins, Damon B. ★*We Are the Land*	978
Alexander, Elizabeth. ★*The Trayvon Generation*	305.896
Alexander, Kwame. *Light for the World to See*	811.6
Alexander, Michelle. *The New Jim Crow*	364.973
Alvis-Walker, Marcie. *Everybody Come Alive*	B
Anderson, Carol. ★*The Second*	344.7305
Anderson, Carol. ★*White Rage*	305.800973
Asika, Uju. *Bringing up Race*	155.4
Asim, Jabari. *We Can't Breathe*	305.896
Austin, Nefertiti. *Motherhood so White*	B
Babb, Valerie Melissa. *The Book of James*	B
Bailey, Issac J. *Why Didn't We Riot?*	305.800973
Baker, Calvin. *A More Perfect Reunion*	305.800973
Baszile, Natalie. *We Are Each Other's Harvest*	630.89
Baxley, Traci. *Social Justice Parenting*	649
Bayoumi, Moustafa. *How Does It Feel to Be a Problem?*	305.892
Bell, Darrin. ★*The Talk*	741.5
Bell, W. Kamau. ★*Do the Work!*	305.8
Bennett, Michael. *Things That Make White People Uncomfortable*	305.896
Bergner, Daniel. ★*Sing for Your Life*	B
Bernard, Emily. *Black Is the Body*	305.48
Blay, Zeba. *Carefree Black Girls*	305.48
Blum, Edward J. *The Color of Christ*	232
Bond, Julian. ★*Julian Bond's Time to Teach*	323.0975
Bowen, Sesali. *Bad Fat Black Girl*	305.42
Boyd, Herb. *We Shall Overcome*	323.1196
Boykin, Keith. *Race Against Time*	305.8
Boykin, Keith. ★*Why Does Everything Have to Be About Race?*	305.8
Bradburd, Rus. *All the Dreams We've Dreamed*	796.323
Brennan, Chad. *Faithful Antiracism*	277.308
Brothers, Thomas David. ★*Louis Armstrong, Master of Modernism*	B
Brown, Austin Channing. ★*I'm Still Here*	B
Busby, Jill Louise. *Unfollow Me*	305.08
Butler, Paul. *Chokehold*	363.2
Cadava, Geraldo L. *The Hispanic Republican*	324.2734089
Carruthers, Charlene A. *Unapologetic*	305.48
Castillo, Elaine. ★*How to Read Now*	418
Chatelain, Marcia. ★*Franchise*	339
Choy, Catherine Ceniza. ★*Asian American Histories of the United States*	973
Chung, Nicole. *All You Can Ever Know*	B
Coates, Ta-Nehisi. ★*Between the World and Me*	305.800973
Coates, Ta-Nehisi. ★*We Were Eight Years in Power*	305.896
Collins-Dexter, Brandi. *Black Skinhead*	324.2734
Cooper, Brittney C. *Eloquent Rage*	B
Cottom, Tressie McMillan. *Thick*	301
Cox, Anna-Lisa. *The Bone and Sinew of the Land*	977
Cox, Gena. *Leading Inclusion*	658.3
Cross, Tiffany D. ★*Say It Louder!*	324.6
Crump, Benjamin. *Open Season*	364
Dabiri, Emma. *Twisted*	391.5
Dangarembga, Tsitsi. *Black and Female*	305.48
Darby, Seyward. ★*Sisters in Hate*	305.800973
Delmont, Matthew F. *Half American*	940.54
DiAngelo, Robin J. *White Fragility*	305.8
Dunbar-Ortiz, Roxanne. ★*An Indigenous Peoples' History of the United States*	970.004
Durkin, Hannah. ★*The Survivors of the Clotilda*	306.362
Dyson, Michael Eric. *The Black Presidency*	305.800973
Dyson, Michael Eric. *Long Time Coming*	305.800973
Dyson, Michael Eric. *Tears We Cannot Stop*	305.800973
Dyson, Michael Eric. *What Truth Sounds Like*	305.800973
Eberhardt, Jennifer L. ★*Biased*	303.3
Eddo-Lodge, Reni. *Why I'm No Longer Talking to White People About Race*	305.8
Ellison, Ralph. ★*The Collected Essays of Ralph Ellison*	814
Ellsworth, Scott. *The Ground Breaking*	976.6
Else, Jon. *True South*	305.800973
Emdin, Christopher. *Ratchetdemic*	370.1
Evans, William. *Black Nerd Problems*	814.6
Evaristo, Bernardine. *Manifesto*	B
Ewing, Eve L. *Ghosts in the Schoolyard*	370.89
Fersko, Diana. ★*We Need to Talk About Antisemitism*	305.892
Fisher, Thomas. ★*The Emergency*	362.1089
Fleming, Crystal Marie. *How to Be Less Stupid About Race*	305.800973
Flitter, Emily. *The White Wall*	332.0973
Ford, Richard T. *Rights Gone Wrong*	342.7308
Forman, James. *Locking up Our Own*	364.973
Francois, Willie Dwayne. *Silencing White Noise*	277
French, Howard W. *Born in Blackness*	960
Fumudoh, Ziwe. ★*Black Friend*	814
Garrett, Kent. *The Last Negroes at Harvard*	920
Garza, Alicia. *The Purpose of Power*	303.48
Gates, Henry Louis. *100 Amazing Facts About the Negro*	973

PUBLIC LIBRARY CORE COLLECTION: NONFICTION
Twentieth Edition

Gates, Henry Louis. *And Still I Rise*	305.896
Gates, Henry Louis. *The Black Box*	908
Gates, Henry Louis. ★*The Black Church*	277
Gates, Henry Louis. *Colored People*	B
Gates, Henry Louis. ★*Stony the Road*	973
Gayle, Caleb. *We Refuse to Forget*	975.004
Geronimus, Arline T. ★*Weathering*	362.1089
Gilliam, Dorothy Butler. *Trailblazer*	B
Gilliam, Fatimah. *Race Rules*	305.8
Gilliard, Dominique Dubois. *Rethinking Incarceration*	261.8
Glaude, Eddie S. *Begin Again*	305.800973
Gomez, Laura E. ★*Inventing Latinos*	305.868
Gorra, Michael Edward. *The Saddest Words*	813
Grant, Richard. *The Deepest South of All*	976.2
Green, Kristen. *Something Must Be Done About Prince Edward County*	379.2
Greenidge, Kerri. ★*The Grimkes*	973.5
Gregory, Dick. *Defining Moments in Black History*	973
Griffin, Chante. *Loving Your Black Neighbor as Yourself*	261
Griffin, Farah Jasmine. ★*In Search of a Beautiful Freedom*	814
Guida-Richards, Melissa. *What White Parents Should Know About Transracial Adoption*	362.734
Hale, Grace Elizabeth. *In the Pines*	364.13
Hamad, Ruby. *White Tears/Brown Scars*	305.8
Han, Chenxing. *Be the Refuge*	294.3
Hardwick, Lamar. *How Ableism Fuels Racism*	261.8
Harriot, Michael. *Black AF History*	973
Harris, Adam. ★*The State Must Provide*	379.2
Harrison, Valerie I. *Do Right by Me*	649
Harts, Minda. *Right Within*	658.3
Hawes, Jennifer. *Grace Will Lead Us Home*	364.152
Hayes, Christopher. *A Colony in a Nation*	364.3
Hazzard, Kevin M. *American Sirens*	362.18
Headlee, Celeste Anne. *Speaking of Race*	305.8
Henning, Kristin. *The Rage of Innocence*	364.36
Henny, Ally. *I Won't Shut Up*	305.896
Herold, Benjamin. *Disillusioned*	307.76
Hill, Marc Lamont. *Seen and Unseen*	303.3
Hinton, Elizabeth Kai. ★*America on Fire*	305.800973
Hirsch, James S. *Riot and Remembrance*	976.6
Hobbs, Jeff. ★*The Short and Tragic Life of Robert Peace*	B
Holley, Santi Elijah. *An Amerikan Family*	920
Hong, Cathy Park. *Minor Feelings*	305.48
Horace, Matthew. *The Black and the Blue*	B
Hubbard, Shanita. ★*Ride-Or-Die*	305.48
Hunter-Gault, Charlayne. ★*My People*	305.48
Hurston, Zora Neale. ★*You Don't Know Us Negroes and Other Essays*	814
Hylton, Antonia. *Madness*	362.2
Iguodala, Andre. *The Sixth Man*	B
Isen, Tajja. *Some of My Best Friends*	305.8
Jackson, Jenn M. ★*Black Women Taught Us*	305.48
Jackson, Kellie Carter. *We Refuse*	323.1196
Jackson, Mitchell S. *Survival Math*	B
Jackson, Regina. *White Women*	305.8
Jacob, Mira. *Good Talk*	741.5
Jefferson, Margo. *Negroland*	305.896
Jerkins, Morgan. *Wandering in Strange Lands*	305.896
Johnson, Kirk W. *The Fishermen and the Dragon*	976.4
Johnson, Theodore R. *When the Stars Begin to Fall*	305.800973
Jones, Chip. *The Organ Thieves*	617.4
Jones, Robert P. *The Hidden Roots of White Supremacy*	305.8
Jones, Robert P. *White Too Long*	277
Joseph, Peniel E. *The Sword and the Shield*	B
Jun, Tasha. ★*Tell Me the Dream Again*	248
Karim-Cooper, Farah. ★*The Great White Bard*	822.33
Kelley, Blair Murphy. *Black Folk*	331.6
Kenan, Randall. *Black Folk Could Fly*	813
Kendi, Ibram X. ★*How to Be an Antiracist*	305.8
Kendi, Ibram X. ★*How to Raise an Antiracist*	649
Kendi, Ibram X. ★*Stamped from the Beginning*	305.8
Khakpour, Porochista. *Brown Album*	304.8
Kimmerle, Erin H. *We Carry Their Bones*	365
King, Chrissy. *The Body Liberation Project*	306.4
King, Martin Luther. *The Autobiography of Martin Luther King, Jr.*	B
King, Martin Luther. *Why We Can't Wait*	305.8
Kozol, Jonathan. ★*An End to Inequality*	379.2
Kozol, Jonathan. *Fire in the Ashes*	362.77
Laymon, Kiese. *How to Slowly Kill Yourself and Others in America*	814.6
Lebron, Christopher J. *The Making of Black Lives Matter*	305.896
Lee, Corky. ★*Corky Lee's Asian America*	770
Lee, Erika. *America for Americans*	305.800973
Lemon, Don. *This Is the Fire*	305.896
Leovy, Jill. *Ghettoside*	364.152
Levin, Josh. *The Queen*	364.16
Lewis, John. ★*March; Book One*	741.5
Lewis, John. ★*March; Book Three*	741.5
Lewis, John. ★*March; Book Two*	741.5
Lewis, Robin Coste. *To the Realization of Perfect Helplessness*	811
Liverpool, Layal. *Systemic*	362.1
Livingston, Robert W. *The Conversation*	305.8
Love, Bettina L. *Punished for Dreaming*	371.829
Lowery, Wesley. ★*American Whitelash*	305.8
Mallory, Tamika D. *State of Emergency*	305.896
Malone, Sharon. *Grown Woman Talk*	362.1
Maraniss, Andrew. *Strong Inside*	B
Mays, Kyle. ★*An Afro-Indigenous History of the United States*	973
McDiarmid, Jessica. *Highway of Tears*	364.152
McGhee, Heather C. ★*The Sum of Us*	305.8
McWhorter, John H. *Talking Back, Talking Black*	427
Meckler, Laura. ★*Dream Town*	305.8
Mehra, Nishta. *Brown, White, Black*	305.800973
Miller, Reuben Jonathan. *Halfway Home*	364.8
Moore, Wes. ★*Five Days*	363.32
Morrison, Melanie. *Murder on Shades Mountain*	345.761
Morrison, Toni. ★*The Origin of Others*	809
Mukantabana, Yseult P. ★*Real Friends Talk About Race*	305.8
Nagassar, Rohadi. *When We Belong*	254
Neus, Nora. *24 Hours in Charlottesville*	973.933
Newkirk, Pamela. *Diversity, Inc.*	658.3
Ng, Fae Myenne. *Orphan Bachelors*	B
Norris, Michele. ★*Our Hidden Conversations*	305
Obama, Barack. ★*Dreams from My Father*	B
Okrent, Daniel. *The Guarded Gate*	344.73
Oluo, Ijeoma. ★*Be a Revolution*	305.8
Oluo, Ijeoma. *Mediocre*	305.310973
Oluo, Ijeoma. ★*So You Want to Talk About Race*	305.800973
Ortiz, Paul. *An African American and Latinx History of the United States*	305.8
Parker, Morgan. ★*You Get What You Pay For*	305.896
Paul, Richard. *We Could Not Fail*	920
Peisner, David. *Homey Don't Play That!*	791.45
Perry, Imani. *May We Forever Stand*	782.25
Phillips, Collette A. M. *The Includers*	658.4
Phillips, Patrick. *Blood at the Root*	305.8
Picower, Bree. *Reading, Writing, and Racism*	371.829
Pinckney, Darryl. *Busted in New York and Other Essays*	305.800973
Pinn, Anthony B. *The Black Practice of Disbelief*	211
Plant, Deborah G. *Of Greed and Glory*	326
Porter, Eduardo. *American Poison*	305.800973
Powell, Michael. ★*Canyon Dreams*	796.323
Powers, Ann. *Good Booty*	781.64
Prescod, Danielle. *Token Black Girl*	B
Proenza-Coles, Christina. *American Founders*	973
Ralph, Laurence. *Sito*	364.152
Ramsey, Donovan X. ★*When Crack Was King*	362.29
Rankine, Claudia. ★*Citizen*	814
Rankine, Claudia. ★*Just Us*	305.896
Ray, Victor. *On Critical Race Theory*	305.8
Redniss, Lauren. ★*Oak Flat*	970.5
Reynolds, David S. *Mightier Than the Sword*	813
Ricketts, Rachel. ★*Do Better*	305.800973
Roberts, Dorothy E. *Torn Apart*	362.7
Roberts-Miller, Patricia. *Speaking of Race*	305.8
Rose, Tricia. ★*Metaracism*	305.8
Ross, Dax-Devlon. *Letters to My White Male Friends*	305.8
Rothstein, Richard. ★*The Color of Law*	305.800973
Row, Jess. *White Flights*	813
Rubinstein, Julian. ★*The Holly*	364.106
Ruck, Rob. *Raceball*	796.357
Ruffin, Amber. ★*The World Record Book of Racist Stories*	305.896
Ruffin, Amber. *You'll Never Believe What Happened to Lacey*	305.896
Saad, Layla F. ★*Me and White Supremacy*	305.809
Sabatini Sloan, Aisha. *Dreaming of Ramadi in Detroit*	814
Salaam, Yusef. *Better, Not Bitter*	B
Samuels, Robert. ★*His Name Is George Floyd*	B
Sanders, Chad. *Black Magic*	305.896
Seidule, Ty. *Robert E. Lee and Me*	973.7

AUTHOR, TITLE, SERIES AND SUBJECT INDEX

Shange, Ntozake. ★*Sing a Black Girl's Song*	818
Sharma, Nina. *The Way You Make Me Feel*	B
Sharpe, Christina Elizabeth. *Ordinary Notes*	305.896
Signer, Michael. *Cry Havoc*	305.800973
Smith, Danyel. *Shine Bright*	782.42164
Smith, Mychal Denzel. *Invisible Man, Got the Whole World Watching*	305.242
Smith, Mychal Denzel. *Stakes Is High*	973.933
Smith, Zadie. *Intimations*	824
Sorin, Gretchen Sullivan. *Driving While Black*	323.1196
Stevens, Stuart. *It Was All a Lie*	324.2734
Taibbi, Matt. *I Can't Breathe*	363.2
Tatum, Beverly Daniel. ★*"Why Are All the Black Kids Sitting Together in the Cafeteria?"*	305.800973
Tesfamariam, Rahiel. ★*Imagine Freedom*	305.896
Theoharis, Jeanne. *A More Beautiful and Terrible History*	323.1196
Thomas, Etan. *We Matter*	796.08
Thompson, Jamie. *Standoff*	364.152
Thompson, Tracy. *The New Mind of the South*	305.800975
Tinsley, Omise'eke Natasha. *Beyonce in Formation*	782.42164
Tobar, Hector. ★*Our Migrant Souls*	305.868
Treuer, Anton. *Everything You Wanted to Know About Indians but Were Afraid to Ask*	970.1
Villarosa, Linda. ★*Under the Skin*	362.1089
Wade, Sabia. *Birthing Liberation*	363.96
Ward, Jesmyn. ★*The Fire This Time*	305.896
West, Cornel. *Black Prophetic Fire*	920
White, Gayle Jessup. *Reclamation*	B
Wilder, Craig Steven. *Ebony and Ivy*	379.2
Wilderson, Frank B. *Afropessimism*	B
Wilkerson, Isabel. ★*Caste*	305.5
Williams, Bari A. *Seen yet Unseen*	338.4
Williams, Mary. *The Lost Daughter*	B
Williams, Sophie. *Anti-Racist Ally*	305.8
Willis, Deborah. ★*The Black Civil War Soldier*	973.7
Wingfield, Adia Harvey. *Gray Areas*	331.6
Winters, Mary-Frances. *Black Fatigue*	305.896
Wise, Tim J. *Dispatches from the Race War*	305.8
Yacovone, Donald. ★*Teaching White Supremacy*	370.89
Young, Damon. ★*What Doesn't Kill You Makes You Blacker*	B
Young, Kevin. *Bunk*	177
Young, R. J. *Requiem for the Massacre*	305.8
Zakaria, Rafia. *Against White Feminism*	305.42
Zerwick, Phoebe. *Beyond Innocence*	347

SOCIETY AND CULTURE — SEX AND SEXUALITY

Belcher, Chris. *Pretty Baby*	B
Blair, Gabrielle Stanley. ★*Ejaculate Responsibly*	362.1988
Bolz-Weber, Nadia. *Shameless*	261.8
Brodsky, Alexandra. *Sexual Justice*	364.15
Eig, Jonathan. *The Birth of the Pill*	618.1
Gunter, Jen. ★*Blood*	612.6
Hirsch, Jennifer S. *Sexual Citizens*	371.7
Orenstein, Peggy. ★*Boys & Sex*	305.235
Powers, Ann. *Good Booty*	781.64
Raskin, Allison. *Overthinking About You*	646.7
Shaw, Julia. *Bi*	306.76
Srinivasan, Amia. *The Right to Sex*	305.42
Stone, Geoffrey R. ★*Sex and the Constitution*	345.7302
Taddeo, Lisa. *Three Women*	306.7082
Winter, Molly Roden. *More*	B

SOCIETY AND CULTURE — SEX AND SEXUALITY — SEX INDUSTRY

Burke, Kelsy. *The Pornography Wars*	306.77
Feast, Fancy. *Naked*	792.7
Moran, Rachel. *Paid For*	306.74082
Worley, Jennifer. *Neon Girls*	792.7

SOCIETY AND CULTURE — SOCIAL ACTIVISM AND PHILANTHROPY

Adler, Kevin F. *When We Walk By*	362.5
Ahmed, Sara. *The Feminist Killjoy Handbook*	305.42
Alvarez, Noe. *Spirit Run*	796.42
Avlon, John P. *Lincoln and the Fight for Peace*	973.7
Barkan, Ady. *Eyes to the Wind*	B
Benforado, Adam. *A Minor Revolution*	362.7
Benjamin, Ruha. ★*Imagination*	302
Bowdler, Michelle. ★*Is Rape a Crime?*	B
Burak, Asi. *Power Play*	794.8
Chemaly, Soraya L. *Rage Becomes Her*	155.3
Craig, Mya-Rose. *Birdgirl*	B
Cullen, Art. *Storm Lake*	071.7

Cullen, David. *Parkland*	371.7
Eltahawy, Mona. *The Seven Necessary Sins for Women and Girls*	305.42
Estes, Nick. *Our History Is the Future*	978.004
Freeberg, Ernest. *A Traitor to His Species*	B
Giridharadas, Anand. ★*The Persuaders*	320.973
Griffith, Elisabeth. *Formidable*	305.42
Hamilton, Denise. ★*Indivisible*	658.3
Hanna-Attisha, Mona. *What the Eyes Don't See*	615.9
Heumann, Judith E. *Being Heumann*	B
Hochschild, Adam. *Lessons from a Dark Time*	909.82
Ice-T. *Split Decision*	920
Jaffe, Sarah W. *Wanting What's Best*	649
Kardas-Nelson, Mara. *We Are Not Able to Live in the Sky*	332.3
Mallory, Tamika D. *State of Emergency*	305.896
Mattlin, Ben. *Disability Pride*	323.3
McCloskey, Jim. *When Truth Is All You Have*	B
McGraw, Seamus. *The End of Country*	333.7909748
Mojica Rodriguez, Prisca Dorcas. *For Brown Girls with Sharp Edges and Tender Hearts*	305.48
Ndopu, Eddie. *Sipping Dom Pérignon Through a Straw*	B
Nyamayaro, Elizabeth. *I Am a Girl from Africa*	B
Owens, Ernest. ★*The Case for Cancel Culture*	303.3
Paxson, Margaret. *The Plateau*	362.87
Prejean, Helen. *River of Fire*	B
Prendergast, John. *Congo Stories*	967.5103
Purnell, Derecka. *Becoming Abolitionists*	363.20973
Rapinoe, Megan. *One Life*	B
Roberts, Dorothy E. *Torn Apart*	362.7
Roy, Arundhati. *Walking with the Comrades*	954
Saad, Layla F. ★*Me and White Supremacy*	305.809
Sarsour, Linda. *We Are Not Here to Be Bystanders*	B
Schwab, Tim. ★*The Bill Gates Problem*	361.7
Shahvisi, Arianne. *Arguing for a Better World*	170
Solnit, Rebecca. *Call Them by Their True Names*	303.3
Tamblyn, Amber. ★*Era of Ignition*	B
Theoharis, Jeanne. *A More Beautiful and Terrible History*	323.1196
Tolokonnikova, Nadezhda. *Rules for Rulebreakers*	782.42166
Tunstall, Tricia. *Changing Lives*	780.71
V. ★*Reckoning*	814
Walker, Alice. *The Cushion in the Road*	814

SOCIETY AND CULTURE — SOCIOLOGY

Durkheim, Emile. ★*Suicide*	394.8
Gray, Emma. *A Girl's Guide to Joining the Resistance*	303.48
Hillstrom, Laurie Collier. *The Thanksgiving Book*	394.2649
Murphy, Kate. *You're Not Listening*	153.6
Tufte, Edward R. *The Visual Display of Quantitative Information*	001.4
Veblen, Thorstein. ★*The Theory of the Leisure Class*	305.5

SOCIETY AND CULTURE — URBAN AND REGIONAL STUDIES

Alexander, Brian. ★*The Hospital*	362.10973
Anderson, Sam. *Boom Town*	976.6
Arsenault, Kerri. *Mill Town*	B
Ash, Lamorna. *Dark, Salt, Clear*	942.3
Chachra, Deb. *How Infrastructure Works*	363
Clark, Anna. *The Poisoned City*	363.6
Cullen, Art. *Storm Lake*	071.7
Currid-Halkett, Elizabeth. *The Overlooked Americans*	307.76
D'Agata, John. *About a Mountain*	979.3
Demick, Barbara. *Eat the Buddha*	951
Didion, Joan. *Where I Was from*	979.4
Dougherty, Conor. *Golden Gates*	363.509794
Edin, Kathryn. ★*The Injustice of Place*	339.4
Emanuel, Rahm. *The Nation City*	352.23
Emdin, Christopher. *Ratchetdemic*	370.1
Ewing, Eve L. *Ghosts in the Schoolyard*	370.89
Fields, Micah. ★*We Hold Our Breath*	976.4
Gee, Alastair. *Fire in Paradise*	363.7
Georges, Gigi. *Downeast*	974.1
Goldhagen, Sarah Williams. *Welcome to Your World*	720.1
Grabar, Henry. *Paved Paradise*	388.474
Hessler, Peter. *The Buried*	962.05
Hobbs, Jeff. ★*The Short and Tragic Life of Robert Peace*	B
Hoyer, Katja. ★*Beyond the Wall*	943.087
Jackson, Mitchell S. *Survival Math*	B
Johnson, Lizzie. ★*Paradise*	363.37
Joyce, Patrick. *Remembering Peasants*	305.5
Kershner, Isabel. *The Land of Hope and Fear*	956.9405
Kimble, Megan. ★*City Limits*	388.1
Kirshner, Jodie Adams. ★*Broke*	336.3

PUBLIC LIBRARY CORE COLLECTION: NONFICTION
Twentieth Edition

Klinenberg, Eric. ★ *2020*	306
LeDuff, Charlie. *Detroit*	977.4
Lim, Audrea. *Free the Land*	333.73
Lunenfeld, Peter. *City at the Edge of Forever*	979.4
Maher, Kris. *Desperate*	344
Mars, Roman. ★ *The 99% Invisible City*	720
Masciotra, David. *Exurbia Now*	320.973
Mask, Deirdre. *The Address Book*	388.1
Minter, Adam. *Secondhand*	381
Moss, Jeremiah. *Feral City*	B
Nolan, Hamilton. *The Hammer*	331.8
Oppenheimer, Mark. *Squirrel Hill*	364.152
Osnos, Evan. *Wildland*	973.93
Perlin, Ross. ★ *Language City*	306.44
Perry, Imani. ★ *South to America*	917
Podemski, Max. *A Paradise of Small Houses*	363.5
Prickett, Pamela J. ★ *The Unclaimed*	363.7
Rajchel, Diana. *Urban Magick*	133.4
Ramsey, Donovan X. ★ *When Crack Was King*	362.29
Rao, Maya. *Great American Outpost*	338.2
Roach, Mary. ★ *Fuzz*	591.5
Ronstadt, Linda. *Feels Like Home*	B
Ross, Andrew. *Sunbelt Blues*	363.5
Roy, Saumya. *Castaway Mountain*	363.72
Rybczynski, Witold. *Mysteries of the Mall*	720
Samaha, Albert. *Never Ran, Never Will*	920
Schilthuizen, Menno. *Darwin Comes to Town*	577.5
Sciolino, Elaine. *The Only Street in Paris*	944
Shackle, Samira. *Karachi Vice*	954.91
Sokolik, Vicki. ★ *If You See Them*	362.5
Stewart, Nikita. *Troop 6000*	369
Streep, Abe. *Brothers on Three*	306.85
Swift, Earl. *Chesapeake Requiem*	639
Vigliotti, Jonathan. *Before It's Gone*	577

SOCIETY AND CULTURE — VIOLENCE AND CRIME

Abdulali, Sohaila. *What We Talk About When We Talk About Rape*	364.15
Auletta, Ken. ★ *Hollywood Ending*	791.43
Auster, Paul. *Bloodbath Nation*	363.33
Blattman, Christopher. *Why We Fight*	303.6
Bowden, Mark. *Life Sentence*	364.106
Bradburd, Rus. *All the Dreams We've Dreamed*	796.323
Brodsky, Alexandra. *Sexual Justice*	364.15
Burgess, Ann Wolbert. *A Killer by Design*	364.3
Cameron, Silver Donald. *Blood in the Water*	364.152
Carter, Stephen L. *Invisible*	B
Cox, John Woodrow. *Children Under Fire*	371.7
Cullen, David. *Parkland*	371.7
Currie, Elliott. *A Peculiar Indifference*	305.800973
Ditmore, Melissa Hope. ★ *Unbroken Chains*	306.74
Dudley, Steven S. *MS-13*	364.106
Dutta, Sunil. *Stealing Green Mangoes*	973
Erdozain, Dominic. *One Nation Under Guns*	363.33
Evangelista, Patricia. ★ *Some People Need Killing*	364.4
Farrow, Ronan. ★ *Catch and Kill*	331.4
Flock, Elizabeth. ★ *The Furies*	305.48
Franscell, Ron. *Shadowman*	362.88
Garcia, Angela. ★ *The Way That Leads Among the Lost*	362.29
Goldberg, Carrie. *Nobody's Victim*	345.73
Grigoriadis, Vanessa. *Blurred Lines*	371.7
Herman, Judith Lewis. *Truth and Repair*	362.883
Hewlett, Sylvia Ann. *#metoo in the Corporate World*	658.3
Hill, Anita. ★ *Believing*	305.42
Hill, Marc Lamont. *Seen and Unseen*	303.3
Ice-T. *Split Decision*	920
Jimenez, Stephen. *The Book of Matt*	364.152
Johnson, Kirk W. *The Fishermen and the Dragon*	976.4
Kara, Siddharth. *Cobalt Red*	338.2
Krakauer, Jon. *Missoula*	362.883
Kruzan, Sara. *I Cried to Dream Again*	B
Lamb, Christina. *Our Bodies, Their Battlefields*	341.6
Lehr, Dick. *White Hot Hate*	363.325
Lovato, Roberto. *Unforgetting*	B
Mar, Alex. *Seventy Times Seven*	362.88
McWhirter, Cameron. *American Gun*	683.4
Metzl, Jonathan M. ★ *What We've Become*	364.152
Mogelson, Luke. *The Storm Is Here*	973.933
Murphy, Chris. ★ *The Violence Inside Us*	303.60973
Muse, Toby. *Kilo*	363.4509861
Neiwert, David A. ★ *The Age of Insurrection*	303.48
Olsen, Lise. *Code of Silence*	347.73
Oppenheimer, Mark. *Squirrel Hill*	364.152
Quinones, John. ★ *One Year in Uvalde*	371.7
Rose, Jacqueline. *On Violence and on Violence Against Women*	362.88
Rubenhold, Hallie. ★ *The Five*	362.88
Selvaratnam, Tanya. *Assume Nothing*	B
Shackle, Samira. *Karachi Vice*	954.91
Smith, Zadie. *Intimations*	824
Sullivan, Randall. *The Devil's Best Trick*	235
Tjipombo, Tupa. *I Am Not Your Slave*	B
Tuerkheimer, Deborah. *Credible*	363.25
Vanasco, Jeannie. *Things We Didn't Talk About When I Was a Girl*	B
Vogelstein, Rachel B. *Awakening*	305.42
Weinman, Sarah. ★ *Unspeakable Acts*	364.1
Westhoff, Ben. *Fentanyl, Inc.*	362.29
Williams, Wyatt. *Springer Mountain*	394.1
Yeung, Bernice. *In a Day's Work*	362.88086

SOCIETY AND CULTURE — VIOLENCE AND CRIME — CRIMINAL JUSTICE SYSTEM

Adams, Jarrett. *Redeeming Justice*	340.092
Adayfi, Mansoor. *Don't Forget Us Here*	B
Anderson, Carol. ★ *The Second*	344.7305
Austen, Ben. *Correction*	364.6
Bailey, Issac J. *Why Didn't We Riot?*	305.800973
Balko, Radley. ★ *The Cadaver King and the Country Dentist*	614
Barnett, Brittany K. ★ *A Knock at Midnight*	B
Barron, Justine. *They Killed Freddie Gray*	363.32
Bauer, Shane. *American Prison*	365
Bazelon, Emily. ★ *Charged*	345.73
Belkin, Lisa. *Genealogy of a Murder*	362.88
Betts, Reginald Dwayne. *Felon*	811
Betts, Reginald Dwayne. ★ *Redaction*	704.9
Bharara, Preet. *Doing Justice*	347.73
Blakinger, Keri. *Corrections in Ink*	B
Bookman, Marc. *A Descending Spiral*	345.73
Bowdler, Michelle. ★ *Is Rape a Crime?*	B
Burton, Susan. *Becoming Ms. Burton*	B
Butler, Paul. *Chokehold*	363.2
Canon, Dan. ★ *Pleading Out*	345.73
Chammah, Maurice. ★ *Let the Lord Sort Them*	364.66
Chemerinsky, Erwin. *Presumed Guilty*	344.7305
Coates, Laura Gayle. *Just Pursuit*	345.73
Davis, Angela Y. *Abolition*	364.6
Dybdahl, Thomas L. *When Innocence Is Not Enough*	345.73
Dyson, Michael Eric. *Long Time Coming*	305.800973
Fabricant, M. Chris. *Junk Science and the American Criminal Justice System*	363.25
Fedderly, Eva. *These Walls*	365
Ford, Elizabeth. *Sometimes Amazing Things Happen*	B
Forman, James. *Locking up Our Own*	364.973
Gilliard, Dominique Dubois. *Rethinking Incarceration*	261.8
Gross, Neil. *Walk the Walk*	363.2
Hardy, Jason Matthew. ★ *The Second Chance Club*	364.6
Hayes, Christopher. *A Colony in a Nation*	364.3
Henning, Kristin. *The Rage of Innocence*	364.36
Hinton, Elizabeth Kai. ★ *America on Fire*	305.800973
Hobbs, Jeff. *Children of the State*	364.36
Honig, Elie. *Untouchable*	364.1
Horace, Matthew. *The Black and the Blue*	B
Horton, Michelle. *Dear Sister*	B
Houppert, Karen. *Chasing Gideon*	345.73
Kaba, Mariame. *No More Police*	363.2
Kimmerle, Erin H. *We Carry Their Bones*	365
King, Gilbert. *Beneath a Ruthless Sun*	B
Mandery, Evan J. *A Wild Justice*	345.73
Manuel, Ian. *My Time Will Come*	B
McCloskey, Jim. *When Truth Is All You Have*	B
McDiarmid, Jessica. *Highway of Tears*	364.152
Messenger, Tony. *Profit and Punishment*	362.5
Miller, Chanel. *Know My Name*	B
Miller, Reuben Jonathan. *Halfway Home*	364.8
Minow, Martha. *When Should Law Forgive?*	345
Muhammad, Khalil Gibran. *The Condemnation of Blackness*	364.2
Norton, Jack. *The Jail Is Everywhere*	365
Peterson, Marlon. *Bird Uncaged*	B
Pratt, Victoria. *The Power of Dignity*	364.973
Prejean, Helen. *The Death of Innocents*	364.66

AUTHOR, TITLE, SERIES AND SUBJECT INDEX

Purnell, Derecka. *Becoming Abolitionists*	363.20973
Ralph, Laurence. *Sito*	364.152
Rapping, Jonathan. *Gideon's Promise*	345.73
Rayman, Graham. ★*Rikers*	365
Raymond, Edwin. *An Inconvenient Cop*	363.2
Rubinstein, Julian. ★*The Holly*	364.106
Rudof, David S. *American Injustice*	345.73
Salaam, Yusef. *Better, Not Bitter*	B
Samuels, Robert. ★*His Name Is George Floyd*	B
Sandel, Michael J. *Justice*	172
Schwartz, Joanna C. ★*Shielded*	344.7305
Sered, Danielle. *Until We Reckon*	364.6
Shahani, Aarti Namdev. *Here We Are*	B
Stevenson, Bryan. *Just Mercy*	B
Taibbi, Matt. *I Can't Breathe*	363.2
Taub, Jennifer. *Big Dirty Money*	364.16
Thompson, Heather Ann. *Blood in the Water*	365
Thompson, Jamie. *Standoff*	364.152
Turow, Scott. ★*Ultimate Punishment*	345.73
Woodfox, Albert. *Solitary*	B
Zerwick, Phoebe. *Beyond Innocence*	347

SOCIETY AND CULTURE — VIOLENCE AND CRIME — GENOCIDE

Akcam, Taner. *A Shameful Act*	956.6
Aly, Gotz. *Europe Against the Jews*	305.892
Balakian, Peter. *The Burning Tigris*	956.6
Dogon, Mondiant. *Those We Throw Away Are Diamonds*	B
Hagerty, Alexa. ★*Still Life with Bones*	599.9
Hatzfeld, Jean. *Blood Papa*	967.5710431
Mackeen, Dawn Anahid. *The Hundred-Year Walk*	956.6
Montero, David. ★*The Stolen Wealth of Slavery*	381
Rawlence, Ben. *City of Thorns*	967.7305
Stern, Jessica. *My War Criminal*	341.6
Talty, Stephan. *The Good Assassin*	364.15

SOCIETY AND CULTURE — WEALTH AND CLASS

Biss, Eula. *Having and Being Had*	306.3
Busby, Jill Louise. *Unfollow Me*	305.08
Calhoun, Ada. *Why We Can't Sleep*	305.244
Case, Anne. *Deaths of Despair and the Future of Capitalism*	362.28
Crawford, Lacy. *Notes on a Silencing*	B
Flitter, Emily. *The White Wall*	332.0973
Garcia, Angela. ★*The Way That Leads Among the Lost*	362.29
Gerald, Casey. *There Will Be No Miracles Here*	B
Goldstein, Amy. *Janesville*	330.9775
Goldstein, Jacob. *Money*	332.4
Grant, Richard. *The Deepest South of All*	976.2
Henderson, Rob Kim. *Troubled*	B
Herold, Benjamin. *Disillusioned*	307.76
Hobbs, Jeff. *Show Them You're Good*	373
Honig, Elie. *Untouchable*	364.1
Jacoby, Melissa B. *Unjust Debts*	346.73
Jaffe, Sarah W. *Wanting What's Best*	649
Jefferson, Margo. *Negroland*	305.896
Kardas-Nelson, Mara. *We Are Not Able to Live in the Sky*	332.3
Kristof, Nicholas D. ★*Tightrope*	306.0973
Lapierre, Dominique. *The City of Joy*	954
Marie, Jane. ★*Selling the Dream*	658.8
Markovits, Daniel. *The Meritocracy Trap*	305.5
Martin, Wednesday. *Primates of Park Avenue*	974.7
McMillan, Tracie. ★*The White Bonus*	305.8
Mechanic, Michael. *Jackpot*	305.5
Milanovic, Branko. *The Have and the Have-Nots*	339.2
Murray, Charles A. *Coming Apart*	305.8
Neiman, Garrett. *Rich White Men*	305.5
Noah, Timothy. *The Great Divergence*	339.2
Packer, George. *Last Best Hope*	973.93
Piketty, Thomas. *A Brief History of Equality*	305.09
Postel, Charles. *Equality*	305.50973
Press, Eyal. ★*Dirty Work*	331.7
Price, S. L. *Playing Through the Whistle*	796.332
Quart, Alissa. *Bootstrapped*	305.5
Reeves, Richard V. *Dream Hoarders*	305.5
Ross, Andrew. *Sunbelt Blues*	363.5
Schwartz, Nelson. *The Velvet Rope Economy*	339.2
Singer, Jessie. *There Are No Accidents*	363.1
Smith, Mychal Denzel. *Stakes Is High*	973.933
Sowell, Thomas. *Wealth, Poverty and Politics*	330.1
Stiglitz, Joseph E. *The Price of Inequality*	305.50973
Taub, Jennifer. *Big Dirty Money*	364.16
Teachout, Zephyr. *Break 'Em Up*	338.8
Thrasher, Steven W. ★*The Viral Underclass*	362.1962
Tough, Paul. *The Years That Matter Most*	378.1
Wilkerson, Isabel. ★*Caste*	305.5
Yunus, Muhammad. *A World of Three Zeros*	330

SOCIETY AND CULTURE — WEALTH AND CLASS — POVERTY

Adler, Kevin F. *When We Walk By*	362.5
Ambroz, David. *A Place Called Home*	B
Barber, William J. *We Are Called to Be a Movement*	261.8
Boo, Katherine. ★*Behind the Beautiful Forevers*	305.5
Bruder, Jessica. ★*Nomadland*	331.3
Conyers, Jonathan. *I Wasn't Supposed to Be Here*	B
Coombes, Joshua. *Do Something for Nothing*	362.5
Desmond, Matthew. ★*Evicted*	339.4
Desmond, Matthew. ★*Poverty, by America*	362.5
Edin, Kathryn. *$2.00 a Day*	339.4
Edin, Kathryn. ★*The Injustice of Place*	339.4
Ehrenreich, Barbara. ★*Nickel and Dimed*	B
Elliott, Andrea. ★*Invisible Child*	362.7
Faleiro, Sonia. *The Good Girls*	364.152
Flowers, Catherine Coleman. *Waste*	363.72
Freeman, Amanda. *Getting Me Cheap*	362.83
Goyal, Nikhil. ★*Live to See the Day*	305.5
Guendelsberger, Emily. *On the Clock*	331.0973
Hedges, Chris. *Days of Destruction, Days of Revolt*	741.5
Houppert, Karen. *Chasing Gideon*	345.73
Isenberg, Nancy. *White Trash*	305.5
Jackson, Mitchell S. *Survival Math*	B
Kidder, Tracy. ★*Rough Sleepers*	362.5
Kim, Anne. ★*Abandoned*	305.2350973
Kim, Anne. ★*Poverty for Profit*	302.5
Kirshner, Jodie Adams. ★*Broke*	336.3
Kozol, Jonathan. *Fire in the Ashes*	362.7
Kozol, Jonathan. *Rachel and Her Children*	362.5
Land, Stephanie. *Maid*	B
Lewis, Oscar. *The Children of Sanchez*	306.85
Lockhart, Chris. ★*Walking the Bowl*	362.7
Madrick, Jeffrey G. *Invisible Americans*	362.7086
Messenger, Tony. *Profit and Punishment*	362.5
Otto, Mary. *Teeth*	617
Rivlin, Gary. *Broke, Usa*	339.4
Roy, Saumya. *Castaway Mountain*	363.72
Sandler, Lauren. *This Is All I Got*	B
Scott, Kevin. *Reprogramming the American Dream*	338
Servon, Lisa J. *The Unbanking of America*	332.10973
Smarsh, Sarah. ★*Heartland*	B
Smarsh, Sarah. *She Come by It Natural*	782.42164
Sokolik, Vicki. ★*If You See Them*	362.5
Vance, J. D. *Hillbilly Elegy*	B

SOCIOBIOLOGY

Eldredge, Niles. *Why We Do It*	155.3
Holldobler, Bert. *The Superorganism*	595.7
Larson, Edward J. *Evolution*	576.8
Wilson, Edward O. *The Meaning of Human Existence*	128

SOCIOCULTURAL ANTHROPOLOGY

Diamond, Jared M. *Upheaval*	303.48
Graeber, David. *The Dawn of Everything*	901
King, Charles. ★*Gods of the Upper Air*	920
Schutt, Bill. *Cannibalism*	394
Vince, Gaia. *Transcendence*	599.93

SOCIOLINGUISTICS

Deutscher, Guy. ★*Through the Language Glass*	410
Kinzler, Katherine D. *How You Say It*	302.2
McWhorter, John H. *Talking Back, Talking Black*	427

SOCIOLOGY

Adler, Kevin F. *When We Walk By*	362.5
Leonhardt, David. ★*Ours Was the Shining Future*	330.973
Nielsen, Kim E. *A Disability History of the United States*	362.40973
Radtke, Kristen. *Seek You*	741.5
Scott, Andy. *One Kiss or Two?*	395.4
Tocqueville, Alexis de. ★*Democracy in America*	320.973
Sociopath. Gagne, Patric	B
Sock Knitting Master Class. Budd, Ann	746.43

SOCKS

Budd, Ann. *New Directions in Sock Knitting*	746.43
Budd, Ann. *Sock Knitting Master Class*	746.43
Talley, Safiyyah. *Knit 2 Socks in 1*	746.43
Socrates. Johnson, Paul	183

PUBLIC LIBRARY CORE COLLECTION: NONFICTION
Twentieth Edition

The Socrates Express. Weiner, Eric	100
SOCRATES, 469-399 B.C.E	
Hughes, Bettany. ★*The Hemlock Cup*	B
Johnson, Paul. *Socrates*	183
Kreeft, Peter. ★*Philosophy 101 by Socrates*	183
Stone, I. F. *The Trial of Socrates*	183
Sodha, Meera	
East	641.595
Made in India	641.595
SODOMY (LAW)	
Carpenter, Dale. *Flagrant Conduct*	342.7308
Soep, Elisabeth	
Other People's Words	155.9
SOEP, ELISABETH	
Soep, Elisabeth. *Other People's Words*	155.9
Sofreh. Alikhani, Nasim	641.595
SOFT DRINK INDUSTRY AND TRADE	
Elmore, Bartow J. *Citizen Coke*	338.7
Goldman, Seth. *Mission in a Bottle*	741.5
SOFT DRINKS	
Capparell, Stephanie. *The Real Pepsi Challenge*	338.7
Elmore, Bartow J. *Citizen Coke*	338.7
Standage, Tom. *A History of the World in 6 Glasses*	394.1
SOFT TOY MAKING	
Bergstrom, Lauren. *Cute & Cuddly Crochet*	746.43
Bergstrom, Lauren. *Mini Crochet Creatures*	746.43
Green-Hite, Vincent. *Knot Bad Amigurumi*	746.43
Hatchard, Gurinder Kaur. *Hooked on Shakespeare*	746.43
Sogyal	
The Tibetan Book of Living and Dying	294.3
Sohn, Amy	
The Man Who Hated Women	363.28
Soil. Dungy, Camille T.	635.0978
SOIL BIOLOGY	
Montgomery, David R. *What Your Food Ate*	631.4
SOIL CONSERVATION	
Montgomery, David R. *What Your Food Ate*	631.4
SOIL ECOLOGY	
Monbiot, George. ★*Regenesis*	338.1
SOIL SCIENCE	
Lauretta, D. S. *The Asteroid Hunter*	523.44
SOILS	
Montgomery, David R. *What Your Food Ate*	631.4
★*Sojourner* Truth. Painter, Nell Irvin	B
Sokatch, Daniel	
Can We Talk About Israel?	956.9405
Sokol, Jason	
The Heavens Might Crack	323.092
Sokolik, Vicki	
★*If You See Them*	362.5
Sol, Adam	
How a Poem Moves	808.1
SOLAR ECLIPSES	
Nordgren, Tyler E. *Sun, Moon, Earth*	523.7
SOLAR SYSTEM	
Fauber, L. S. *Heaven on Earth*	B
Lang, Kenneth R. *The Cambridge Guide to the Solar System*	523.2
Nordgren, Tyler E. *Sun, Moon, Earth*	523.7
Sanders, Ella Frances. *Eating the Sun*	520
Sobel, Dava. *A More Perfect Heaven*	520.9
Trefil, James. *Space Atlas*	520
SOLAR SYSTEM ORIGIN	
Krauss, Lawrence Maxwell. *The Greatest Story Ever Told—So Far*	530.01
The Soldier's Truth. Chrisinger, David	940.54
***Soldier,** Sailor, Frogman, Spy, Airman, Gangster, Kill or Die.* Milton, Giles	940.54
SOLDIERS	
Albracht, William. *Abandoned in Hell*	959.704
Alexander, Larry. *Biggest Brother*	B
Ambrose, Stephen E. ★*Band of Brothers*	920
Ambrose, Stephen E. *Citizen Soldiers*	940.54
Ambrose, Stephen E. *The Victors*	940.54
Anderson, Scott. *Lawrence in Arabia*	B
Bardenwerper, William. *The Prisoner in His Palace*	956.7044
Bascomb, Neal. *The Escape Artists*	940.4
Beah, Ishmael. ★*A Long Way Gone*	B
Bradley, James. *Flags of Our Fathers*	940.54
Brady, James. *The Coldest War*	B
Brokhausen, Nick. *Whispers in the Tall Grass*	959.704
Brotherton, Marcus. *A Bright and Blinding Sun*	940.54
Brown, Daniel James. ★*Facing the Mountain*	940.54
Bunting, Josiah. ★*The Making of a Leader*	B
Caputo, Philip. *A Rumor of War*	959.704
Carroll, Andrew. *My Fellow Soldiers*	940.4
Castner, Brian. *The Long Walk*	B
Chivers, C. J. *The Fighters*	920
Clavin, Tom. *The Last Hill*	940.54
Davenport, Matthew J. *First Over There*	940.4
Denver, Rorke. *Worth Dying For*	359.9
Dickson, Paul. *The Rise of the G.I. Army 1940-1941*	940.54
Donald, Aida DiPace. *Citizen Soldier*	B
Edstrom, Erik. *Un-American*	B
Ellis, Joseph J. ★*His Excellency*	B
Englund, Peter. *November 1942*	940.53
Fairweather, Jack. *The Volunteer*	B
Finkel, David. *The Good Soldiers*	956.7044
Finkel, David. *Thank You for Your Service*	920
Fischer, David Hackett. *Washington's Crossing*	973.3
Fox, Margalit. *The Confidence Men*	940.4
Frederick, Jim. *Black Hearts*	956.7044
Freeman, Sally Mott. *The Jersey Brothers*	920
Friedman, Matti. *Pumpkinflowers*	B
Glass, Charles. *Soldiers Don't Go Mad*	616.85
Gopal, Anand. *No Good Men Among the Living*	920
Guarnere, William. *Brothers in Battle, Best of Friends*	B
Guibert, Emmanuel. *Alan's War*	741.5
Halberstam, David. *The Coldest Winter*	951.904
Hastings, Max. *Inferno*	940.54
Hastings, Max. *Warriors*	355
Hennessey, Patrick. *The Junior Officers' Reading Club*	B
Holland, James. *The Savage Storm*	940.53
Iredale, Will. *The Kamikaze Hunters*	940.54
Isserman, Maurice. *The Winter Army*	940.54
Johnson, Akemi. *Night in the American Village*	305.40952
Junger, Sebastian. *War*	958.104
Keegan, John. *The First World War*	940.3
Kennedy, Paul. *Engineers of Victory*	940.54
Kershaw, Alex. *Against All Odds*	940.54
Kershaw, Alex. *The First Wave*	940.54
Kesling, Ben. *Bravo Company*	958.104
Kindsvatter, Peter S. *American Soldiers*	355
King, Charles Monroe. *A Journal for Jordan*	956.7044
Klay, Phil. *Uncertain Ground*	359.9
Korda, Michael. *Muse of Fire*	940.4
Lambert, Raymond. *Every Man a Hero*	B
Lawrence, T. E. *Seven Pillars of Wisdom*	940.4
Lewis, Damien. *Churchill's Hellraisers*	940.54
Luttrell, Marcus. *Lone Survivor*	958.104
Luttrell, Marcus. *Service*	956.7044
Manchester, William. *Goodbye, Darkness*	B
Manchester, William. *The Last Lion, Winston Spencer Churchill.*	B
Manning, Chelsea. *Readme.Txt*	B
Mauldin, Bill. *Willie & Joe*	741.5
McManus, John C. *Fire and Fortitude*	940.54
Merridale, Catherine. *Ivan's War*	940.54
Meyer, Dakota. *Into the Fire*	958.104
Mills, Dan. *Sniper One*	956.7044
Moore, Harold G. *We Were Soldiers Once—And Young*	959.704
Morgan, Wesley. *The Hardest Place*	958.104
Morris, David J. *The Evil Hours*	616.85
Navarro, Joe. *Three Minutes to Doomsday*	B
O'Connell, Robert L. *Revolutionary*	B
O'Donnell, Patrick K. *The Indispensables*	973.3
O'Donnell, Svenja. *Inge's War*	943.086
Paradis, Michel. *The Light of Battle*	940.54
Patterson, James. *Walk in My Combat Boots*	920
Raban, Jonathan. *Father and Son*	B
Raddatz, Martha. *The Long Road Home*	B
Raines, Howell. *Silent Cavalry*	973.7
Reiss, Tom. *The Black Count*	B
Romesha, Clinton. *Red Platoon*	958.104
Sakamoto, Pamela Rotner. *Midnight in Broad Daylight*	940.53
Sears, Stephen W. *Lincoln's Lieutenants*	920
Sheehan, Neil. *A Bright Shining Lie*	959.704
Stanton, Doug. *12 Strong*	958.104
Stanton, Doug. *The Odyssey of Echo Company*	959.704

AUTHOR, TITLE, SERIES AND SUBJECT INDEX

Stephenson, Michael. *The Last Full Measure*	305.9
Swofford, Anthony. *Jarhead*	956.7044
Ulander, Perry A. *Walking Point*	B
Verini, James. *They Will Have to Die Now*	956.7044
Weintraub, Stanley. *Iron Tears*	973.3
Wheelan, Joseph. *Midnight in the Pacific*	940.54
Winters, Richard D. *Beyond Band of Brothers*	B
Wright, Evan. *Generation Kill*	956.7044
Wright, James Edward. ★*Enduring Vietnam*	959.704
★*Soldiers and Kings*. De Leon, Jason	364.1
Soldiers Don't Go Mad. Glass, Charles	616.85
Sole-Smith, Virginia	
★*Fat Talk*	649.1
SOLID WASTE	
Franklin-Wallis, Oliver. ★*Wasteland*	363.72
Roy, Saumya. *Castaway Mountain*	363.72
SOLID WASTE DISPOSAL	
Franklin-Wallis, Oliver. ★*Wasteland*	363.72
Humes, Edward. ★*Total Garbage*	628.4
SOLID WASTE MANAGEMENT	
Franklin-Wallis, Oliver. ★*Wasteland*	363.72
Hardy, Alyssa. *Worn Out*	338.4
SOLID WASTE REDUCTION	
Allen, Brigette. *Living Without Plastic*	640
Humes, Edward. ★*Total Garbage*	628.4
Watkins, Julia. *Simply Living Well*	640
SOLIDARITY	
Brous, Sharon. ★*The Amen Effect*	296.3
Johnson, Theodore R. *When the Stars Begin to Fall*	305.800973
Solnit, Rebecca. *A Paradise Built in Hell*	303.48
Solitary. Woodfox, Albert	B
SOLITARY CONFINEMENT	
Woodfox, Albert. *Solitary*	B
★*Solito*. Zamora, Javier	B
SOLITUDE	
Auvinen, Karen. *Rough Beauty*	B
Baker, Billy. *We Need to Hang Out*	177
Bell, Laura. *Claiming Ground*	B
Clark, Liz. *Swell*	B
Finkel, Michael. *The Stranger in the Woods*	B
Grann, David. *The White Darkness*	B
Kethledge, Raymond Michael. *Lead Yourself First*	658.4
May, Katherine. *Wintering*	155.9
Pennington, Emily. *Feral*	B
Segura, Tom. ★*I'd Like to Play Alone, Please*	B
Thoreau, Henry David. ★*Walden, Or, Life in the Woods*	813
Sollee, Kristen J.	
Witch Hunt	133
Solnit, Rebecca	
Call Them by Their True Names	303.3
The Faraway Nearby	814
Men Explain Things to Me	305.42
The Mother of All Questions	305.42
Orwell's Roses	B
A Paradise Built in Hell	303.48
★*Recollections of My Nonexistence*	B
Wanderlust	796.51
SOLNIT, REBECCA	
Solnit, Rebecca. ★*Recollections of My Nonexistence*	B
SOLO VOYAGES	
Caesar, Ed. *The Moth and the Mountain*	B
Clark, Liz. *Swell*	B
SOLOMON ISLANDS	
Hornfischer, James D. *Neptune's Inferno*	940.54
Solomon, Andrew	
Far from the Tree	362.4083
Solomon, Brian	
The Field Guide to Trains	625.2
Solomon, Deborah	
American Mirror	B
Jackson Pollock	B
Solomon, Steven	
Water	553.7
Solomonov, Michael	
Israeli Soul	641.595
Zahav	641.595
SOLOMONOV, MICHAEL	
Solomonov, Michael. *Zahav*	641.595

Solovic, Susan Wilson	
The One-Percent Edge	658.4
Soloway, Jill	
She Wants It	B
SOLOWAY, JILL	
Soloway, Jill. *She Wants It*	B
★*Solutions and Other Problems*. Brosh, Allie	741.5
Solzhenitsyn, Aleksandr Isaevich	
★*The Gulag Archipelago 1918-1956*	365
★*The Gulag Archipelago, 1918-1956*	365
Som, Brandon	
Tripas	811
SOMALI AMERICANS	
Iftin, Abdi Nor. *Call Me American*	305.893
Lehr, Dick. *White Hot Hate*	363.325
McCormick, Ty. *Beyond the Sand and Sea*	920
Steinberg, Jonny. *A Man of Good Hope*	B
SOMALI PEOPLE	
Bass, Amy. *One Goal*	796.334
SOMALIA	
Bowden, Mark. *Black Hawk Down*	967.7305
Hirsi Ali, Ayaan. ★*Infidel*	B
McCormick, Ty. *Beyond the Sand and Sea*	920
Moore, Michael Scott. *The Desert and the Sea*	364.15
Rawlence, Ben. *City of Thorns*	967.7305
Steinberg, Jonny. *A Man of Good Hope*	B
Some of My Best Friends. Isen, Tajja	305.8
★*Some of the Dharma*. Kerouac, Jack	294.3
★*Some People Need Killing*. Evangelista, Patricia	364.4
★*Somebody Feed Phil the Book*. Rosenthal, Phil	641.59
Somebody I Used to Know. Mitchell, Wendy	B
★*Somebody's Daughter*. Ford, Ashley C.	B
Somebody's Gotta Do It. Martini, Adrienne	B
★*Somehow*. Lamott, Anne	814
Someone to Watch Over Me. Burns, Eric	973.917092
Somerstein, Rachel	
★*Invisible Labor*	618.8
SOMERSTEIN, RACHEL	
Somerstein, Rachel. ★*Invisible Labor*	618.8
Something Deeply Hidden. Carroll, Sean M.	530.12
Something in the Blood. Skal, David J.	823
Something Like an Autobiography. Kurosawa, Akira	
Something Must Be Done About Prince Edward County. Green, Kristen	379.2
Something That May Shock and Discredit You. Lavery, Daniel M.	814
Something Wonderful. Purdum, Todd S.	B
Sometimes Amazing Things Happen. Ford, Elizabeth	B
Sometimes I Trip on How Happy We Could Be. Perkins, Nichole	B
Somewhere Sisters. Hayasaki, Erika	362.7
Sommer, Will	
★*Trust the Plan*	973.933
SOMMERSETT, JAMES	
Wise, Steven M. *Though the Heavens May Fall*	342.42
Son of Elsewhere. Abdelmahmoud, Elamin	B
Son of the Morning Star. Connell, Evan S.	973.8
Sonata Mulattica. Dove, Rita	811
Sondheim, Stephen	
Look, I Made a Hat	782.1
SONDHEIM, STEPHEN, 1930-2021	
Max, D. T. *Finale*	782.1
Sone, Monica Itoi	
Nisei Daughter	979.7
SONE, MONICA ITOI, 1919-2011	
Sone, Monica Itoi. *Nisei Daughter*	979.7
Sonenshein, Scott	
Stretch	153.3
A Song Flung up to Heaven. Angelou, Maya	B
The Song of Our Scars. Warraich, Haider	616
★*The Song of the Cell*. Mukherjee, Siddhartha	571.6
SONG, QINGLING, 1893-1981	
Chang, Jung. *Big Sister, Little Sister, Red Sister*	B
SONGS	
Moore, Kathleen Dean. *Earth's Wild Music*	576.8
Polenberg, Richard. *Hear My Sad Story*	782.42162
Sandburg, Carl. *The American Songbag*	782.42162
Songs of America. Meacham, Jon	782.42
Songs of Unreason. Harrison, Jim	811
★*Songs on Endless Repeat*. So, Anthony Veasna	814
The Songs We Know Best. Roffman, Karin	B

PUBLIC LIBRARY CORE COLLECTION: NONFICTION
Twentieth Edition

SONGWRITERS
    Amos, Tori. *Resistance* — B
    Barlow, John Perry. *Mother American Night* — 782.42164
    Cash, Rosanne. ★*Composed* — B
    Cohen, Leonard. *The Flame* — 810
    Davis, Stephen. *Gold Dust Woman* — B
    DeCurtis, Anthony. *Lou Reed* — B
    Feinstein, Michael. *The Gershwins and Me* — 782.42164
    Hermes, Will. *Lou Reed* — B
    McBrien, William. *Cole Porter* — B
    McCartney, Paul. *The Lyrics* — 782.42166
    Momus. *Niche* — B
    Nesmith, Michael. *Infinite Tuesday* — B
    Norman, Philip. *George Harrison* — B
    Parton, Dolly. ★*Dolly Parton, Songteller* — B
    Patrick, James. *Robert Johnson* — B
    Prince. *The Beautiful Ones* — B
    Purdum, Todd S. *Something Wonderful* — B
    Rodgers, Mary. *Shy* — B
    Simmons, Sylvie. *I'm Your Man* — B
    Smith, Patti. ★*Just Kids* — B
    Taupin, Bernie. *Scattershot* — B
    Zanes, Warren. *Deliver Me from Nowhere* — 782.42164

SONGWRITING
    Bostridge, Ian. *Schubert's Winter Journey* — 782.4
    Etheridge, Melissa. *Talking to My Angels* — B
    Feinstein, Michael. *The Gershwins and Me* — 782.42164
    Guesdon, Jean-Michel. *All the Songs* — 782.42166
    Jones, Dylan. *David Bowie* — B
    Kozinn, Allan. *The McCartney Legacy* — B
    McCartney, Paul. *The Lyrics* — 782.42166
    Moore, Marcus J. *The Butterfly Effect* — B
    Nelson, Willie. *It's a Long Story* — B
    Parton, Dolly. ★*Dolly Parton, Songteller* — B
    Purdum, Todd S. *Something Wonderful* — B
    Sandburg, Carl. *The American Songbag* — 782.42162
    Sloan, Nate. *Switched on Pop* — 781.64
    Sondheim, Stephen. *Look, I Made a Hat* — 782.1
    Taupin, Bernie. *Scattershot* — B
    Tweedy, Jeff. *How to Write One Song* — 782.42

Soni, Jimmy
    A Mind at Play — B

Sonic Life. Moore, Thurston — B

★*Sonnets to Orpheus*. Rilke, Rainer Maria — 831

SONORAN DESERT
    Ronstadt, Linda. *Feels Like Home* — B

SONS
    Bailey, Catherine. *A Castle in Wartime* — 943.086
    Chabon, Michael. *Manhood for Amateurs* — B
    McCann, Colum. *American Mother* — 956.9104
    Natterson, Cara Familian. ★*Decoding Boys* — 649

Sons & Brothers. Mahoney, Richard D. — 920
Sons and Soldiers. Henderson, Bruce B. — 940.53
★*Sontag*. Moser, Benjamin — B

Sontag, Susan
    At the Same Time — 814

SONTAG, SUSAN, 1933-2004
    Moser, Benjamin. ★*Sontag* — B

SOONG, AI-LING, 1890-1973
    Chang, Jung. *Big Sister, Little Sister, Red Sister* — B

SOPHIA, ELECTRESS, CONSORT OF ERNEST AUGUSTUS, ELECTOR OF HANOVER, 1630-1714
    Goldstone, Nancy Bazelon. *Daughters of the Winter Queen* — 920

SOPHIE ELISABETH, DUCHESS, CONSORT OF AUGUST, DUKE OF BRAUNSCHWEIG-LUNEBURG, 1613-1676
    Porter, Cecelia Hopkins. *Five Lives in Music* — B

Sophie Scholl and the White Rose. Dumbach, Annette E. — 943.086

SOPHIE, ARCHDUCHESS OF AUSTRIA, 1866-1914
    King, Greg. *The Assassination of the Archduke* — B

The Sopranos Sessions. Seitz, Matt Zoller — 791.45

Sorensen, Theodore C.
    Counselor — B

SORENSEN, THEODORE C.
    Sorensen, Theodore C. *Counselor* — B

Sorin, Gretchen Sullivan
    Driving While Black — 323.1196

Sorkin, Andrew Ross
    Too Big to Fail — 330.973

A Sorrow in Our Heart. Eckert, Allan W. — B
Sorry, Sorry, Sorry. Ingall, Marjorie — 158.2

Sorvino, Chloe
    Raw Deal — 338.1

Sosnowski, Andrzej
    Lodgings — 891.8

Sotomayor, Sonia
    ★*My Beloved World* — B

SOTOMAYOR, SONIA, 1954-
    Sotomayor, Sonia. ★*My Beloved World* — B

Souder, William
    Mad at the World — 813
    On a Farther Shore — B

Soufan, Ali H.
    The Black Banners Declassified — 363.325

Soul. Richards, Todd — 641.59296073

SOUL
    Hofstadter, Douglas R. *I Am a Strange Loop* — 153
    Le Guin, Ursula K. *So Far so Good* — 811
    Roach, Mary. ★*Spook* — 129

SOUL (CHRISTIANITY)
    Norris, Kathleen. *Acedia & Me* — 248.8

Soul by Soul. Carranca, Adriana — 230
Soul by Soul. Johnson, Walter — 976.3
Soul Full of Coal Dust. Hamby, Chris — 363.11

SOUL MUSIC
    Jackson family. *The Jacksons* — 782.421644
    Jones, Booker T. *Time Is Tight* — B
    McBride, James. *Kill 'Em and Leave* — B
    Neville, Aaron. *Tell It Like It Is* — B
    Ribowsky, Mark. *Dreams to Remember* — B
    Ribowsky, Mark. *The Supremes* — B
    White, Adam. ★*Motown* — 781.644
    Wood, Damon. *Working for the Man, Playing in the Band* — 782.42164

SOUL MUSICIANS
    Bego, Mark. *Aretha Franklin* — B
    Gaye, Jan. *After the Dance* — B
    Jackson family. *The Jacksons* — 782.421644
    Jones, Booker T. *Time Is Tight* — B
    McBride, James. *Kill 'Em and Leave* — B
    Neville, Aaron. *Tell It Like It Is* — B
    Ribowsky, Mark. *Dreams to Remember* — B
    Ribowsky, Mark. *Signed, Sealed, and Delivered* — B
    Wood, Damon. *Working for the Man, Playing in the Band* — 782.42164

★*The Soul of America*. Meacham, Jon — 973
The Soul of Baseball. Posnanski, Joe — 796.357
The Soul of Battle. Hanson, Victor Davis — 355
Soul on Ice. Cleaver, Eldridge — B
Soulless. DeRogatis, Jim — B
★*The Souls of Black Folk*. Du Bois, W. E. B. — 973
The Souls of China. Johnson, Ian — 200.951

SOUND
    Day, Timothy. ★*A Century of Recorded Music* — 780
    Milner, Greg. *Perfecting Sound Forever* — 781.49

The Sound of a Wild Snail Eating. Bailey, Elisabeth — 594
The Sound of Gravel. Wariner, Ruth — B
The Sound of Music Story. Santopietro, Tom — 791.43
★*The Sound of the Sea*. Barnett, Cynthia — 591.47

SOUND RECORDING EXECUTIVES AND PRODUCERS
    Broven, John. *Record Makers and Breakers* — B
    Brown, Mick. ★*Tearing Down the Wall of Sound* — B
    Guralnick, Peter. ★*Sam Phillips* — B
    Lang, Michael. *The Road to Woodstock* — 781.66

SOUND RECORDING INDUSTRY AND TRADE
    Austerlitz, Saul. *Money for Nothing* — 780.26
    Broven, John. *Record Makers and Breakers* — B
    Charnas, Dan. *The Big Payback* — 306.4
    Doggett, Peter. *Electric Shock* — 781.64
    Guralnick, Peter. ★*Sam Phillips* — B
    Houghton, Mick. *Becoming Elektra* — 781.64
    Kahn, Ashley. *The House That Trane Built* — 781.6509
    Morton, Brian. ★*The Penguin Jazz Guide* — 016
    Newkey-Burden, Chas. *Taylor Swift* — B
    Powers, Ann. *Good Booty* — 781.64

SOUND RECORDINGS
    Crumb, R. *R. Crumb* — 741.6
    Day, Timothy. ★*A Century of Recorded Music* — 780
    Friedwald, Will. *The Great Jazz and Pop Vocal Albums* — 016.78

AUTHOR, TITLE, SERIES AND SUBJECT INDEX

Houghton, Mick. *Becoming Elektra*	781.64
Kozinn, Allan. *The McCartney Legacy*	B
Milner, Greg. *Perfecting Sound Forever*	781.49
Morley, Paul. *The Age of Bowie*	B
Zanes, Warren. *Deliver Me from Nowhere*	782.42164

SOUNDS

Kingdon, Amorina. ★*Sing Like Fish*	591.77
The Sounds of Poetry. Pinsky, Robert	808.5
Soundtrack of Silence. Hay, Matt	B

SOUPS

Lanza, Fabrizia. *The Food of Sicily*	641.594
Manning, Ivy. *Easy Soups from Scratch with Quick Breads to Match*	641.81
Volger, Lukas. *Bowl*	641.81
Westerhausen, Shelly. *Every Season Is Soup Season*	641.81
The Source. Doyle, Martin	333.91
★*The Source of Self-Regard*. Morrison, Toni	814
Sources of Strength. Carter, Jimmy	248.4
South. Brock, Sean	641.5975

SOUTH AFRICA

Brand, Christo. *Mandela*	B
Carlin, John. *Playing the Enemy*	968.06
Fowlds, Grant. *Saving the Last Rhinos*	599.66
Fugard, Athol. ★*"master Harold"—And the Boys*	822
Gevisser, Mark. *A Legacy of Liberation*	B
Guha, Ramachandra. *Gandhi Before India*	B
Malala, Justice. *The Plot to Save South Africa*	968.07
Mandela, Nelson. *Dare Not Linger*	B
Mandela, Nelson. *In His Own Words*	B
Mandela, Nelson. ★*Long Walk to Freedom*	B
Mandela, Nelson. *Mandela*	B
Mandela, Nelson. *The Prison Letters of Nelson Mandela*	968.06092
Millard, Candice. ★*Hero of the Empire*	968.04
Noah, Trevor. *Born a Crime*	B
Smith, David James. *Young Mandela*	B
Steinberg, Jonny. *Winnie and Nelson*	920
Wainaina, Binyavanga. ★*How to Write About Africa*	814

SOUTH AFRICAN PEOPLE

Attwell, David. *J. M. Coetzee and the Life of Writing*	823
Gevisser, Mark. *A Legacy of Liberation*	B
Isaacson, Walter. ★*Elon Musk*	B
Malala, Justice. *The Plot to Save South Africa*	968.07
Ndopu, Eddie. *Sipping Dom Pérignon Through a Straw*	B
Semenya, Caster. *The Race to Be Myself*	B
Steinberg, Jonny. *Winnie and Nelson*	920

SOUTH AMERICA

Darwin, Charles. ★*The Voyage of the Beagle*	508
Galeano, Eduardo. *Soccer in Sun and Shadow*	796.334
Jenkins, Jedidiah. *To Shake the Sleeping Self*	B
Meiburg, Jonathan. *A Most Remarkable Creature*	598.9
Raff, Jennifer. *Origin*	576.5
Thomson, Keith. *Born to Be Hanged*	910.4

SOUTH AMERICAN HISTORY

Allende, Isabel. *My Invented Country*	B
Allende, Isabel. ★*Paula*	B
Anderson, Jon Lee. *Che Guevara*	B
Arana, Marie. *Bolivar*	B
Cervantes, Fernando. *Conquistadores*	970.01
Chasteen, John Charles. *Americanos*	980
Chasteen, John Charles. *Born in Blood and Fire*	980
Cordes, Kelly. *The Tower*	796.522
Davis, Wade. *Magdalena*	986.1
Dodds Pennock, Caroline. ★*On Savage Shores*	970.004
Garcia Marquez, Gabriel. *Living to Tell the Tale*	B
Hagerty, Alexa. ★*Still Life with Bones*	599.9
Heaney, Christopher. *Cradle of Gold*	B
McConahay, Mary Jo. *The Tango War*	940.53
Moser, Benjamin. *Why This World*	B
Skidmore, Thomas E. *Brazil*	981
Treister, Kenneth. *Easter Island's Silent Sentinels*	996.18

SOUTH AMERICAN PEOPLE

Francis. *Life*	B
Salama, Jordan. ★*Stranger in the Desert*	982

SOUTH ASIA

Lee, Erika. *The Making of Asian America*	973
Subramanian, Sammanth. *This Divided Island*	954.9303

SOUTH ASIAN AMERICANS

Ali, Fatima. ★*Savor*	B
Ali, Wajahat. *Go Back to Where You Came From*	B

Rehman, Sabeeha. *Threading My Prayer Rug*	305.8
Sharma, Nina. *The Way You Make Me Feel*	B
Tanais. *In Sensorium*	B

SOUTH ASIAN PEOPLE

Ali, Fatima. ★*Savor*	B
Ali, Wajahat. *Go Back to Where You Came From*	B
Craig, Mya-Rose. *Birdgirl*	B
Gupta, Prachi. ★*They Called Us Exceptional*	B
H, Lamya. ★*Hijab Butch Blues*	B
Nezhukumatathil, Aimee. *Bite by Bite*	641.3
Rehman, Sabeeha. *Threading My Prayer Rug*	305.8
Tanais. *In Sensorium*	B
Velshi, Ali. *Small Acts of Courage*	B

SOUTH BEND, INDIANA

Buttigieg, Pete. *Shortest Way Home*	B

SOUTH BRONX, NEW YORK CITY

Grandmaster Flash. *The Adventures of Grandmaster Flash*	B

SOUTH CAROLINA

Douglas, John E. *When a Killer Calls*	364.152
Fields-Black, Edda L. *Combee*	973.7
Glatt, John. *Tangled Vines*	364.152
Hawes, Jennifer. *Grace Will Lead Us Home*	364.152
Lineberry, Cate. *Be Free or Die*	B
Matney, Mandy. *Blood on Their Hands*	364.152
Sellers, Bakari. *My Vanishing Country*	B

SOUTH CENTRAL LOS ANGELES, CALIFORNIA

Westhoff, Ben. *Original Gangstas*	782.421649

SOUTH DAKOTA

Bunnell, David. *Good Friday on the Rez*	B
McMurtry, Larry. *Crazy Horse*	B
Mort, T. A. *Thieves' Road*	978.3
Raban, Jonathan. *Bad Land*	978

SOUTH KOREA

Cho, Grace M. *Tastes Like War*	305.48
Koh, EJ. *The Magical Language of Others*	813
Oberdorfer, Don. *The Two Koreas 3rd Ed.*	951.904

SOUTH KOREAN PEOPLE

Sehee, Baek. *I Want to Die but I Want to Eat Tteokbokki*	B

SOUTH PACIFIC OCEAN

Thompson, Christina. *Sea People*	305.8994

SOUTH POLE EXPEDITIONS

Sancton, Julian. *Madhouse at the End of the Earth*	919.8904

SOUTH SIDE, CHICAGO, ILLINOIS

Ewing, Eve L. *Ghosts in the Schoolyard*	370.89
★*South to America*. Perry, Imani	917

Southard, Susan
Nagasaki	940.54

SOUTHEAST ASIAN AMERICANS

Cailan, Alvin. *Amboy*	641.595
Coffin, Jaed. *Roughhouse Friday*	B
Duckworth, Tammy. *Every Day Is a Gift*	B
Johnson, Kirk W. *The Fishermen and the Dragon*	976.4
Pham, Andrew X. ★*The Eaves of Heaven*	B
Reang, Putsata. *Ma and Me*	B
Samaha, Albert. *Concepcion*	929
Talusan, Meredith. *Fairest*	305.30973
Tran, Phuc. ★*Sigh, Gone*	B
Ung, Loung. *Lucky Child*	B
Vargas, Jose Antonio. *Dear America*	B
Vuong, Ocean. ★*Time Is a Mother*	811
Yip-Williams, Julie. ★*The Unwinding of the Miracle*	973

SOUTHEAST ASIAN PEOPLE

Cailan, Alvin. *Amboy*	641.595
Coffin, Jaed. *Roughhouse Friday*	B
Duckworth, Tammy. *Every Day Is a Gift*	B
Hamilton, Lisa M. *The Hungry Season*	B
Johnson, Kirk W. *The Fishermen and the Dragon*	976.4
Nezhukumatathil, Aimee. *Bite by Bite*	641.3
Nguyen, Bich Minh. *Owner of a Lonely Heart*	B
Nguyen, Viet Thanh. ★*A Man of Two Faces*	B
Pham, Andrew X. ★*The Eaves of Heaven*	B
Reang, Putsata. *Ma and Me*	B
Samaha, Albert. *Concepcion*	929
So, Anthony Veasna. ★*Songs on Endless Repeat*	814
Taing, Mae Bunseng. *Under the Naga Tail*	B
Talusan, Meredith. *Fairest*	305.30973
Tran, Phuc. ★*Sigh, Gone*	B
Ung, Loung. *Lucky Child*	B

PUBLIC LIBRARY CORE COLLECTION: NONFICTION
Twentieth Edition

Vargas, Jose Antonio. *Dear America*	B
Vuong, Ocean. ★ *Time Is a Mother*	811
Yip-Williams, Julie. ★ *The Unwinding of the Miracle*	973
SOUTHERN AFRICA	
Hanes, Stephanie. *White Man's Game*	333.95
SOUTHERN AFRICAN PEOPLE	
Isaacson, Walter. ★ *Elon Musk*	B
Malala, Justice. *The Plot to Save South Africa*	968.07
Ndopu, Eddie. *Sipping Dom Pérignon Through a Straw*	B
Steinberg, Jonny. *Winnie and Nelson*	920
Southern Biography Series [Series]. Vella, Christina	B
SOUTHERN CALIFORNIA	
Atleework, Kendra. *Miracle Country*	979.4
Danler, Stephanie. *Stray*	B
McKeen, William. *Everybody Had an Ocean*	781.6609
SOUTHERN FRANCE	
Peppler, Rebekah. *Le Sud*	641.594
Southern Lady Code. Ellis, Helen	814
SOUTHERN STATES	
Adams, Jocelyn Delk. *Everyday Grand*	641.5975
Berendt, John. *Midnight in the Garden of Good and Evil*	975.8
Bragg, Rick. *Where I Come From*	975
Brown, Kardea. *The Way Home*	641.5975
Claiborne, Jenne. ★ *Sweet Potato Soul*	641.5
Crawford, Alan Pell. *This Fierce People*	975
Dissen, William Stark. *Thoughtful Cooking*	641.5975
Dray, Philip. *At the Hands of Persons Unknown*	364.1
Dray, Philip. *Capitol Men*	973.8
Ellis, Helen. *Southern Lady Code*	814
Franklin, John Hope. *In Search of the Promised Land*	929
Hahn, Steven. *A Nation Under Our Feet*	975
Hawes, Jennifer. *Grace Will Lead Us Home*	364.152
Hereford, Mason. *Turkey and the Wolf*	641.5976
Holland, Tanya. ★ *Tanya Holland's California Soul*	641.59
Horwitz, Tony. *Spying on the South*	917
Howard, Vivian. *Deep Run Roots*	641.5975
Hurston, Zora Neale. *Dust Tracks on a Road*	B
Jones, Chip. *The Organ Thieves*	617.4
Jones, Saeed. *How We Fight for Our Lives*	B
Kenan, Randall. *Black Folk Could Fly*	813
Lambert, Miranda. *Y'all Eat Yet?*	641.5976
Laymon, Kiese. *How to Slowly Kill Yourself and Others in America*	814.6
Lemann, Nicholas. *Redemption*	975
Maraniss, Andrew. *Strong Inside*	B
Martin, Rachel Louise. *A Most Tolerant Little Town*	379.2
McCaulley, Esau. *How Far to the Promised Land*	B
McCormick, Mack. *Biography of a Phantom*	782.421643
Mitchell, Jerry. ★ *Race Against Time*	364.152
Morrison, Melanie. *Murder on Shades Mountain*	345.761
Noyes, Brian. *The Red Truck Bakery Farmhouse Cookbook*	641.5973
Parks, Casey. *Diary of a Misfit*	B
Perry, Imani. ★ *South to America*	917
Petrosino, Kiki. *White Blood*	811
Raiford, Matthew. *Bress 'N' Nyam*	641.59
Raines, Howell. *Silent Cavalry*	973.7
Rembert, Winfred. *Chasing Me to My Grave*	B
Renkl, Margaret. *The Comfort of Crows*	814.6
Rothman, Joshua D. *The Ledger and the Chain*	306.362
Seidule, Ty. *Robert E. Lee and Me*	973.7
Simmons, Ruth. ★ *Up Home*	B
Theroux, Paul. *Deep South*	975
Thompson, Tracy. *The New Mind of the South*	305.800975
Trethewey, Natasha D. ★ *Memorial Drive*	B
Twitty, Michael. ★ *The Cooking Gene*	641.59
Tyson, Timothy B. *The Blood of Emmett Till*	364.1
Van Meter, Matthew. *Deep Delta Justice*	345.763
Westhoff, Ben. *Dirty South*	782.421649
Wilkinson, Crystal. *Praisesong for the Kitchen Ghosts*	641.5975
Williams, David. *Bitterly Divided*	973.7
Williams, Lucinda. *Don't Tell Anybody the Secrets I Told You*	B
Wilson, Melba. ★ *Melba's American Comfort*	641.5973
Woodward, C. Vann. *The Strange Career of Jim Crow*	305.896
Young, Kevin. *Stones*	811
SOUTHERN STATES HISTORY	
Dunbar, Erica Armstrong. ★ *Never Caught*	B
Ford, Lacy K. *Deliver Us from Evil*	973.7
Lemann, Nicholas. *Redemption*	975
May, Gregory. *A Madman's Will*	973.5
Thompson, Tracy. *The New Mind of the South*	305.800975
Williams, David. *Bitterly Divided*	973.7
Williams, Kidada E. *I Saw Death Coming*	973.8
SOUTHERN STATES IN LITERATURE	
Gorra, Michael Edward. *The Saddest Words*	813
Southon, Emma. *Agrippina*	B
SOUTHWEST (UNITED STATES)	
Barra, Allen. *Inventing Wyatt Earp*	B
Bitsui, Sherwin. *Dissolve*	811
Bossiere, Zoe. *Cactus Country*	306
Brooks, James. *Mesa of Sorrows*	979.1004
Burns, Mike. *The Only One Living to Tell*	305.897
Childs, Craig. *House of Rain*	978.9
Frank, Lois Ellen. *Seed to Plate, Soil to Sky*	641.5
Hutton, Paul Andrew. *The Apache Wars*	979
Iverson, Peter. *Dine*	979.1004
Pasternak, Judy. *Yellow Dirt*	979.1004
Sides, Hampton. *Blood and Thunder*	978
Tefertiller, Casey. *Wyatt Earp*	B
Wallis, Michael. *Billy the Kid*	B
SOUTHWEST ASIA AND NORTH AFRICA (MIDDLE EAST)	
Abouzeid, Rania. *No Turning Back*	956.9104
Addario, Lynsey. *Of Love & War*	779
Alyan, Hala. *The Moon That Turns You Back*	811
Amanat, Abbas. *Iran*	955
Atkinson, Rick. *An Army at Dawn*	940.54
Bacevich, Andrew J. *America's War for the Greater Middle East*	956.05
Barr, James. *A Line in the Sand*	956
Barr, James. *Lords of the Desert*	956
Bennis, Phyllis. *Understanding the Palestinian-Israeli Conflict*	956.9405
Bhutto, Benazir. *Reconciliation*	297.2
Brighton, Terry. *Patton, Montgomery, Rommel*	B
Brooks, Geraldine. *Nine Parts of Desire*	305.48
Carranca, Adriana. *Soul by Soul*	230
Carter, Jimmy. *Palestine*	956.04
Elnoury, Tamer. *American Radical*	B
Engel, Richard. *And Then All Hell Broke Loose*	956.05
Feiler, Bruce. *Walking the Bible*	915
Filkins, Dexter. *The Forever War*	956.7044
Fisk, Robert. *The Great War for Civilisation*	956.04
Friedman, Thomas L. ★ *From Beirut to Jerusalem*	956.04
Ghattas, Kim. *Black Wave*	955.05
Gordis, Daniel. *Israel*	956.9405
Herrin, Judith. *Byzantium*	949.5
Hindley, Meredith. *Destination Casablanca*	940.54
Hoffman, Bruce. *Anonymous Soldiers*	956.94
Indyk, Martin. *Master of the Game*	327.73
Kaplan, Robert D. *The Loom of Time*	327
Kattan, Fadi. ★ *Bethlehem*	641.5
Kaufmann, Uri R. *Eighteen Days of October*	956.04
Khan, Yasmin. ★ *Zaitoun*	641.595
Lacey, Robert. *Inside the Kingdom*	953.805
Marozzi, Justin. *Islamic Empires*	909
Mitchell, George J. *A Path to Peace*	956.9405
Nasr, Seyyed Vali Reza. *The Shia Revival*	297.8
Navai, Ramita. *City of Lies*	955
Orth, Stephan. *Couchsurfing in Iran*	955.06
Pfeffer, Anshel. *Bibi*	B
Sattouf, Riad. *The Arab of the Future 2*	741.5
Sattouf, Riad. *The Arab of the Future*	741.5
Seale, Yasmine. *Aladdin*	398.2
Shadid, Anthony. *House of Stone*	306.0956
Trofimov, Yaroslav. *The Siege of Mecca*	953.805
Warrick, Joby. *Black Flags*	956.9104
Wood, Graeme. *The Way of the Strangers*	363.325
Worth, Robert Forsyth. ★ *A Rage for Order*	909
Zoepf, Katherine. *Excellent Daughters*	305.42
SOUTHWEST ASIA AND NORTH AFRICA (MIDDLE EAST) HISTORY	
Abouzeid, Rania. *No Turning Back*	956.9104
Abrahamian, Ervand. *The Coup*	955.05
Ahmad, Aeham. *The Pianist from Syria*	B
Akcam, Taner. *A Shameful Act*	956.6
Al-Khalili, Jim. *The House of Wisdom*	509
Amanat, Abbas. *Iran*	955
Anderson, Scott. *Lawrence in Arabia*	B
Armstrong, Karen. ★ *The Great Transformation*	200.9
Armstrong, Karen. *Jerusalem*	956.94

AUTHOR, TITLE, SERIES AND SUBJECT INDEX

Asbridge, Thomas S. ★*The Crusades*	909.07
Atkinson, Rick. *An Army at Dawn*	940.54
Azad. *Long Shot*	B
Balakian, Peter. *The Burning Tigris*	956.6
Bogosian, Eric. *Operation Nemesis*	956.62
Chandrasekaran, Rajiv. *Imperial Life in the Emerald City*	956.7044
Coker, Margaret. *The Spymaster of Baghdad*	956.7044
Coll, Steve. *The Bin Ladens*	920
Collins, Larry. *O Jerusalem!*	956
Cooper, Andrew Scott. *The Fall of Heaven*	B
Crowley, Roger. *1453*	949.61
Dagher, Sam. *Assad or We Burn the Country*	956.9104
Deng, Alephonsion. *They Poured Fire on Us from the Sky*	B
Di Giovanni, Janine. *The Morning They Came for Us*	956.9104
Evans, Martin. *Algeria*	965
Finkel, Caroline. *Osman's Dream*	956.1
Finkel, David. *The Good Soldiers*	956.7044
Firdawsi. *Shahnameh*	891
Fox, Margalit. *The Confidence Men*	940.4
Frankopan, Peter. *The First Crusade*	956
Friedman, Matti. *Spies of No Country*	327.12
Friedman, Thomas L. ★*From Beirut to Jerusalem*	956.04
Ghattas, Kim. *Black Wave*	955.05
Ghazvinian, John. *America and Iran*	327
Hari, Daoud. *The Translator*	B
Hindley, Meredith. *Destination Casablanca*	940.54
Hoffman, Bruce. *Anonymous Soldiers*	956.94
Howell, Georgina. *Gertrude Bell*	B
Huffman, Alan. *Here I Am*	B
Kennedy, Hugh. ★*The Great Arab Conquests*	297.09
Khalidi, Rashid. ★*The Hundred Years' War on Palestine*	956.9405
Kilmeade, Brian. ★*Thomas Jefferson and the Tripoli Pirates*	973.4
Kimmerling, Baruch. *The Palestinian People*	956.94
King, Charles. *Midnight at the Pera Palace*	949.61
Kriwaczek, Paul. *Babylon*	935
Lacey, Robert. *Inside the Kingdom*	953.805
Lambert, Malcolm. *God's Armies*	956
Lawler, Andrew. *Under Jerusalem*	956.94
LeBor, Adam. *City of Oranges*	956.94
Lemmon, Gayle Tzemach. *The Daughters of Kobani*	956.9104
Levin, Daniel. *Proof of Life*	956.9104
Lewis, Bernard. *The Middle East*	956
Mackeen, Dawn Anahid. *The Hundred-Year Walk*	956.6
Madden, Thomas F. *Istanbul*	949.61
Mahjoub, Jamal. *A Line in the River*	962.404
Malek, Alia. *The Home That Was Our Country*	B
Mikhail, Alan. *God's Shadow*	B
Morris, Benny. *1948*	956.04
Morris, Benny. *Righteous Victims*	956
Nafisi, Azar. ★*Reading Lolita in Tehran*	B
O'Kane, Bernard. *Treasures of Islam*	709.1
Olson, Lynne. ★*Empress of the Nile*	B
Oren, Michael B. *Six Days of War*	956.04
Pamuk, Orhan. *Istanbul*	949.61
Pappe, Ilan. *The Biggest Prison on Earth*	956.9405
Patton, George S. *War as I Knew It*	B
Pearlman, Wendy. *We Crossed a Bridge and It Trembled*	956.9104
Peres, Shimon. *No Room for Small Dreams*	B
Rawlence, Ben. *City of Thorns*	967.7305
Rogan, Eugene L. *The Fall of the Ottomans*	940.3
Sacco, Joe. *Footnotes in Gaza*	741.5
Samer. *The Raqqa Diaries*	956.9104
Satrapi, Marjane. ★*The Complete Persepolis*	741.5
Sebag-Montefiore, Simon. *Jerusalem*	956.94
Shlaim, Avi. *The Iron Wall*	956.04
Sokatch, Daniel. *Can We Talk About Israel?*	956.9405
Steinberg, Jonny. *A Man of Good Hope*	B
Thomson, Mike. *Syria's Secret Library*	956.9104
Trofimov, Yaroslav. *The Siege of Mecca*	953.805
Von Tunzelmann, Alex. *Blood and Sand*	909.82
Wallach, Janet. *Desert Queen*	B
Ward, Clarissa. *On All Fronts*	B
Warrick, Joby. *Red Line*	956.9104
Wilkinson, Toby A. H. *A World Beneath the Sands*	932
Wood, Graeme. *The Way of the Strangers*	363.325
Wright, Evan. *Generation Kill*	956.7044

SOUTHWEST ASIAN (MIDDLE EASTERN) PEOPLE

Ahdoot, Dan. *Undercooked*	647.95
Alyan, Hala. *The Moon That Turns You Back*	811
Bilal, Wafaa. *Shoot an Iraqi*	B
Carter, Jimmy. *Palestine*	956.04
Pick-Goslar, Hannah Elizabeth. ★*My Friend Anne Frank*	B
Salama, Jordan. ★*Stranger in the Desert*	982
Saldana, Stephanie. *What We Remember Will Be Saved*	362.7
Shavit, Ari. *My Promised Land*	956.05
Shehadeh, Raja. ★*We Could Have Been Friends, My Father and I*	B

Souza, Pete

Obama	973.932
Shade	973.932
The West Wing and Beyond	917.53

SOVEREIGNTY

Borman, Tracy. *Crown & Sceptre*	941
Frank, Richard B. *Tower of Skulls*	940.54
Kershner, Isabel. *The Land of Hope and Fear*	956.9405
Mikanowski, Jacob. ★*Goodbye, Eastern Europe*	947
Morris, Marc. *A Great and Terrible King*	B

SOVIET UNION

Aleksievich, Svetlana. ★*Secondhand Time*	947.086
Ambinder, Marc. *The Brink*	355.5
Amis, Martin. *Koba the Dread*	947.084
Applebaum, Anne. ★*Gulag*	365
Applebaum, Anne. *Iron Curtain*	947
Budiansky, Stephen. *Code Warriors*	327.73047
Carlson, Peter. *K Blows Top*	947.085
Coleman, David G. *The Fourteenth Day*	973.922092
Donner, Rebecca. *All the Frequent Troubles of Our Days*	943
Feifer, Gregory. *The Great Gamble*	958.104
Figes, Orlando. *The Story of Russia*	947
Figes, Orlando. ★*The Whisperers*	306.850947
Finkelstein, Daniel. *Two Roads Home*	920
Finn, Peter. *The Zhivago Affair*	891.73
Gessen, Masha. *Never Remember*	365
Golinkin, Lev. *A Backpack, a Bear, and Eight Crates of Vodka*	B
Gordin, Michael D. *Red Cloud at Dawn*	355.02
Hastings, Max. *The Abyss*	972.9106
Igort. *The Ukrainian and Russian Notebooks*	741.5
Kennedy, Robert F. *Thirteen Days*	327.73
Khlevniuk, Oleg V. *Stalin*	B
MacGregor, Iain. *The Lighthouse of Stalingrad*	940.54
Macintyre, Ben. ★*The Spy and the Traitor*	B
Mann, Jim. *The Rebellion of Ronald Reagan*	973.927092
McMeekin, Sean. *Stalin's War*	940.53
McPhee, John. *The Ransom of Russian Art*	709
Medvedev, Roy Aleksandrovich. *Let History Judge*	947.084
Merridale, Catherine. *Ivan's War*	940.54
Merridale, Catherine. *Lenin on the Train*	B
Moorhouse, Roger. *The Devils' Alliance*	940.53
Ohler, Norman. *The Bohemians*	940.53
Pavlychenko, Liudmyla Mykhailivna. *Lady Death*	B
Phillips, Timothy. *Retracing the Iron Curtain*	909.82
Plokhy, Serhii. *Lost Kingdom*	947
Plokhy, Serhii. ★*Nuclear Folly*	972.9106
Rees, Laurence. *Hitler and Stalin*	940.53
Remnick, David. *Lenin's Tomb*	947.085
Rhodes, Richard. *Masters of Death*	940.53
Satter, David. *The Less You Know, the Better You Sleep*	947.086
Sebestyen, Victor. *Lenin*	B
Sebestyen, Victor. *Revolution 1989*	947.085
Service, Robert. *The End of the Cold War 1985-1991*	909.82
Service, Robert. *Lenin—A Biography*	B
Sherman, Casey. *Above and Beyond*	973.922092
Shesol, Jeff. *Mercury Rising*	629.45
Slezkine, Yuri. *The House of Government*	947.084
Smith, Douglas. *The Russian Job*	947.084
Solzhenitsyn, Aleksandr Isaevich. ★*The Gulag Archipelago 1918-1956*	365
Solzhenitsyn, Aleksandr Isaevich. ★*The Gulag Archipelago, 1918-1956*	365
Taubman, William. *Gorbachev*	B
Taubman, William. *Khrushchev*	B
Trimble, Lee. *Beyond the Call*	940.54
Vogel, Steve. *Betrayal in Berlin*	327.1273043
Walker, Stephen. *Beyond*	629.45
Weiner, Tim. *The Folly and the Glory*	327.73047
Westad, Odd Arne. *The Cold War*	909.825

SOVIET UNION HISTORY

Aleksievich, Svetlana. *Last Witnesses*	940.53
Aleksievich, Svetlana. ★*The Unwomanly Face of War*	940.53

PUBLIC LIBRARY CORE COLLECTION: NONFICTION
Twentieth Edition

Applebaum, Anne. ★*Gulag*	365
Applebaum, Anne. ★*Red Famine*	947.708
Beevor, Antony. *Russia*	947.084
Beevor, Antony. *Stalingrad*	940.54
Figes, Orlando. *A People's Tragedy*	947.08
Figes, Orlando. ★*The Whisperers*	306.850947
Frazier, Ian. *Travels in Siberia*	957
Gessen, Masha. *Never Remember*	365
Gorbachev, Mikhail. *On My Country and the World*	947.085
Herman, Arthur. *1917*	940.3
Higginbotham, Adam. ★*Midnight in Chernobyl*	363.17
Hochschild, Adam. *The Unquiet Ghost*	947.084
Igort. *The Ukrainian and Russian Notebooks*	741.5
Kotkin, Stephen. *Stalin*	B
Kotkin, Stephen. *Stalin*	B
MacGregor, Iain. *The Lighthouse of Stalingrad*	940.54
Macintyre, Ben. *A Spy Among Friends*	B
McMeekin, Sean. *The Russian Revolution*	947.084
McNamara, Kevin J. *Dreams of a Great Small Nation*	355.009437
Merridale, Catherine. *Lenin on the Train*	B
Mieville, China. *October*	947.084
Petrushevskaia, Liudmila. *The Girl from the Metropol Hotel*	B
Pipes, Richard. *A Concise History of the Russian Revolution*	947.084
Pipes, Richard. *The Russian Revolution*	947.084
Plokhy, Serhii. *Lost Kingdom*	947
Radzinskii, Edvard. *Stalin*	947.084
Rappaport, Helen. *After the Romanovs*	944
Rappaport, Helen. *Caught in the Revolution*	355.00947
Reed, John. *Ten Days That Shook the World*	947.084
Riasanovsky, Nicholas V. *A History of Russia*	947
Sebag-Montefiore, Simon. *Stalin*	B
Smith, Douglas. *The Russian Job*	947.084
Snyder, Timothy. ★*Bloodlands*	940.54
Sullivan, Rosemary. *Stalin's Daughter*	B
Suny, Ronald Grigor. *Stalin*	B
Teffi, N. A. *Memories*	B

Sow, Aminatou
Big Friendship	177

SOW, AMINATOU
Sow, Aminatou. *Big Friendship*	177

Sowell, Thomas
Basic Economics	330
Wealth, Poverty and Politics	330.1

Soyinka, Wole
Of Africa	960

SPACE
Brinkley, Douglas. ★*American Moonshot*	629.40973
Carroll, Sean M. *The Biggest Ideas in the Universe*	530.11
Davenport, Christian. *The Space Barons*	920
Green, Jaime. *The Possibility of Life*	576.8
Kershenbaum, Arik. *The Zoologist's Guide to the Galaxy*	576.8
Kitmacher, Gary. *Space Stations*	629.44
Plait, Philip C. *Under Alien Skies*	520
Sagan, Carl. *Pale Blue Dot*	919
Tyson, Neil deGrasse. *To Infinity and Beyond*	520
Vance, Ashlee. *When the Heavens Went on Sale*	621.43
Weinersmith, Kelly. ★*A City on Mars*	629.4

SPACE (ARCHITECTURE)
Susanka, Sarah. *Creating the Not so Big House*	728

SPACE ACCIDENTS
Wolfe, Tom. ★*The Right Stuff*	629.4

SPACE AND TIME
Carroll, Sean M. *From Eternity to Here*	530.11
Carroll, Sean M. *Something Deeply Hidden*	530.12
Fletcher, Seth. *Einstein's Shadow*	523.8
Gleick, James. *Time Travel*	530.11
Hawking, Stephen. *A Brief History of Time*	523.1
Hawking, Stephen. *The Nature of Space and Time*	530.1
Hawking, Stephen. ★*The Universe in a Nutshell*	530.12
Krauss, Lawrence Maxwell. *The Greatest Story Ever Told—So Far*	530.01
Rovelli, Carlo. *The Order of Time*	530.11
Tyson, Neil deGrasse. ★*Astrophysics for People in a Hurry*	523.01
Tyson, Neil deGrasse. *Letters from an Astrophysicist*	520.92
Tyson, Neil deGrasse. *Welcome to the Universe*	523.1
Wilczek, Frank. *Fundamentals*	530.01
Space Atlas. Trefil, James	520
The *Space* Barons. Davenport, Christian	920

SPACE BIOLOGY
Kershenbaum, Arik. *The Zoologist's Guide to the Galaxy*	576.8
Roach, Mary. *Packing for Mars*	571.0919
Ward, Peter Douglas. *Life as We Do Not Know It*	576.839
Space Chronicles. Tyson, Neil deGrasse	629.40973

SPACE COLONIES
Aldrin, Buzz. *Mission to Mars*	523.43
Kaku, Michio. ★*The Future of Humanity*	629.45
Stuart, Colin. *How to Live in Space*	629.45
Weinersmith, Kelly. ★*A City on Mars*	629.4
Wohlforth, Charles P. *Beyond Earth*	629.45

SPACE ENVIRONMENT
Summers, Michael E. *Exoplanets*	523.2

SPACE EXPLORATION
Aldrin, Buzz. *Mission to Mars*	523.43
Aldrin, Buzz. *No Dream Is Too High*	B
Bell, Jim. *The Interstellar Age*	919
Boyle, Rebecca. *Our Moon*	523.3
Brinkley, Douglas. ★*American Moonshot*	629.40973
Davenport, Christian. *The Space Barons*	920
Donovan, Jim. ★*Shoot for the Moon*	629.45
Grush, Loren. ★*The Six*	629.4
Holt, Nathalia. ★*Rise of the Rocket Girls*	629.4
Isaacson, Walter. ★*Elon Musk*	B
Johnson, Sarah Stewart. *The Sirens of Mars*	576.8
Jones, Tom. *Space Shuttle Stories*	629.44
Kaltenegger, Lisa. ★*Alien Earths*	523.2
Kitmacher, Gary. *Space Stations*	629.44
Kurson, Robert. ★*Rocket Men*	629.45
Launius, Roger D. *The Smithsonian History of Space Exploration*	629.4
Launius, Roger D. *Apollo's Legacy*	629.45
Lauretta, D. S. *The Asteroid Hunter*	523.44
Leinbach, Michael D. *Bringing Columbia Home*	363.12
Marshall, Tim. *The Power of Geography*	320.1
Roach, Mary. *Packing for Mars*	571.0919
Sagan, Carl. *Pale Blue Dot*	919
Seager, Sara. *The Smallest Lights in the Universe*	B
Stone, Robert. *Chasing the Moon*	629.45
Summers, Michael E. *Exoplanets*	523.2
Swift, Earl. *Across the Airless Wilds*	629.45
Tyson, Neil deGrasse. *Space Chronicles*	629.40973
Tyson, Neil deGrasse. *Startalk*	523.1
Tyson, Neil deGrasse. *To Infinity and Beyond*	520
Vance, Ashlee. *When the Heavens Went on Sale*	621.43
Virts, Terry. *How to Astronaut*	629.45
Walker, Stephen. *Beyond*	629.45
Weinersmith, Kelly. ★*A City on Mars*	629.4
Wohlforth, Charles P. *Beyond Earth*	629.45

SPACE FLIGHT
Ackmann, Martha. *The Mercury 13*	920
Bagby, Meredith E. *The New Guys*	305
Bell, Jim. *The Interstellar Age*	919
Berger, Eric. *Liftoff*	B
Cook, Kevin. *The Burning Blue*	629.45
Grush, Loren. ★*The Six*	629.4
Guthrie, Julian. *How to Make a Spaceship*	629.47
Higginbotham, Adam. ★*Challenger*	629.45
Holt, Nathalia. ★*Rise of the Rocket Girls*	629.4
Jones, Tom. *Space Shuttle Stories*	629.44
Kaku, Michio. ★*The Future of Humanity*	629.45
Kelly, Scott. ★*Endurance*	B
Launius, Roger D. *The Smithsonian History of Space Exploration*	629.4
Nelson, Craig. *Rocket Men*	629.45
Shesol, Jeff. *Mercury Rising*	629.45
Stone, Robert. *Chasing the Moon*	629.45
Stuart, Colin. *How to Live in Space*	629.45
Teitel, Amy Shira. *Fighting for Space*	920
Tyson, Neil deGrasse. *Space Chronicles*	629.40973
Vance, Ashlee. *When the Heavens Went on Sale*	621.43
Virts, Terry. *How to Astronaut*	629.45
Walker, Stephen. *Beyond*	629.45
Wohlforth, Charles P. *Beyond Earth*	629.45
Wolfe, Tom. ★*The Right Stuff*	629.4

SPACE FLIGHT TO MARS
Aldrin, Buzz. *Mission to Mars*	523.43
Launius, Roger D. *The Smithsonian History of Space Exploration*	629.4

SPACE FLIGHT TO THE MOON
Aldrin, Buzz. *No Dream Is Too High*	B

AUTHOR, TITLE, SERIES AND SUBJECT INDEX

Barbree, Jay. *Neil Armstrong*	B
Donovan, Jim. ★*Shoot for the Moon*	629.45
Fishman, Charles. ★*One Giant Leap*	629.45
Kluger, Jeffrey. ★*Apollo 8*	629.45
Kurson, Robert. ★*Rocket Men*	629.45
Launius, Roger D. *Apollo's Legacy*	629.45
Nelson, Craig. *Rocket Men*	629.45
Stone, Robert. *Chasing the Moon*	629.45
Swift, Earl. *Across the Airless Wilds*	629.45

SPACE INDUSTRIALIZATION
Davenport, Christian. *The Space Barons*	920
Space Odyssey. Benson, Michael	791.43

SPACE PERCEPTION
Ellard, Colin. *You Are Here*	153.7

SPACE PHOTOGRAPHY
Jones, Tom. *Space Shuttle Stories*	629.44

SPACE POLICY
Shesol, Jeff. *Mercury Rising*	629.45
Stone, Robert. *Chasing the Moon*	629.45
Tyson, Neil deGrasse. *Space Chronicles*	629.40973

SPACE PROBES
Bell, Jim. *The Interstellar Age*	919
Lauretta, D. S. *The Asteroid Hunter*	523.44

SPACE PROGRAMS
Barbree, Jay. *Neil Armstrong*	B
Brinkley, Douglas. ★*American Moonshot*	629.40973
Donovan, Jim. ★*Shoot for the Moon*	629.45
Fishman, Charles. ★*One Giant Leap*	629.45
Grush, Loren. ★*The Six*	629.4
Kurson, Robert. ★*Rocket Men*	629.45
Launius, Roger D. *Apollo's Legacy*	629.45
Nelson, Craig. *Rocket Men*	629.45
Sherr, Lynn. *Sally Ride*	B
Shesol, Jeff. *Mercury Rising*	629.45
Shetterly, Margot Lee. ★*Hidden Figures*	510.92
Stone, Robert. *Chasing the Moon*	629.45
Swift, Earl. *Across the Airless Wilds*	629.45
Teitel, Amy Shira. *Fighting for Space*	920
Walker, Stephen. *Beyond*	629.45
Wolfe, Tom. ★*The Right Stuff*	629.4

SPACE SCIENCES
Cox, Brian. *Universal*	523.1
Kaltenegger, Lisa. ★*Alien Earths*	523.2
Lintott, Chris. *Accidental Astronomy*	520
Roach, Mary. *Packing for Mars*	571.0919
Sagan, Carl. *Broca's Brain*	128

SPACE SHUTTLE ACCIDENTS
Leinbach, Michael D. *Bringing Columbia Home*	363.12
Space Shuttle Stories. Jones, Tom	629.44

SPACE SHUTTLES
Jones, Tom. *Space Shuttle Stories*	629.44
Leinbach, Michael D. *Bringing Columbia Home*	363.12
Space Stations. Kitmacher, Gary	629.44

SPACE STATIONS
Kitmacher, Gary. *Space Stations*	629.44
Stuart, Colin. *How to Live in Space*	629.45

SPACE TELESCOPES
Tucker, Wallace H. *Chandra's Cosmos*	523.1

SPACE TOURISM
Aldrin, Buzz. *Mission to Mars*	523.43
Vance, Ashlee. *When the Heavens Went on Sale*	621.43

SPACE VEHICLE ACCIDENTS
Leinbach, Michael D. *Bringing Columbia Home*	363.12

SPACE VEHICLES
Jones, Tom. *Space Shuttle Stories*	629.44
Kurson, Robert. ★*Rocket Men*	629.45
Space, in Chains. Kasischke, Laura	811

SPACE-TIME
Rovelli, Carlo. *Reality Is Not What It Seems*	530.14

SPAIN
Downey, Kirstin. *Isabella*	B
Fernandez-Armesto, Felipe. *Our America*	973
Ferreiro, Larrie D. *Brothers at Arms*	327.73
Fuentes, Carlos. *The Buried Mirror*	946
Goulding, Matt. *Grape, Olive, Pig*	394.1
Hochschild, Adam. *Spain in Our Hearts*	946.081
Hughes, Robert. *Barcelona*	946
Kamen, Henry. *The Spanish Inquisition*	272
Kurlansky, Mark. *The Basque History of the World*	946
Mullins, Edwin. *The Four Roads to Heaven*	263
Perez, Joseph. ★*The Spanish Inquisition*	272
Preston, Paul. *A People Betrayed*	946
Preston, Paul. *The Spanish Holocaust*	946.081
Stewart, Chris. *Driving Over Lemons*	946
Tremlett, Giles. *Ghosts of Spain*	946.08
Van Hensbergen, Gijs. *The Sagrada Familia*	726.5
Von Bremzen, Anya. *National Dish*	641.3
Spain in Our Hearts. Hochschild, Adam	946.081

Spainhower, Courtney
Elemental Knits	746.43

SPANISH AMERICAN WAR, 1898
Tuccille, Jerome. *The Roughest Riders*	973.8

SPANISH AMERICANS
Oliva, Alejandra. *Rivermouth*	305.9

SPANISH CIVIL WAR, SPAIN, 1936-1939
Hochschild, Adam. *Spain in Our Hearts*	946.081
Preston, Paul. *The Spanish Holocaust*	946.081

SPANISH HISTORY
Cercas, Javier. *Lord of All the Dead*	868
Cervantes, Fernando. *Conquistadores*	970.01
Downey, Kirstin. *Isabella*	B
Hochschild, Adam. *Spain in Our Hearts*	946.081
Hughes, Robert. *Goya*	B
Preston, Paul. *A People Betrayed*	946
Preston, Paul. *The Spanish Holocaust*	946.081
Thomas, Hugh. *Rivers of Gold*	980
Tremlett, Giles. *Ghosts of Spain*	946.08
Watling, Sarah. *Tomorrow Perhaps the Future*	946.081
The Spanish Holocaust. Preston, Paul	946.081
The Spanish Inquisition. Kamen, Henry	272
★*The Spanish Inquisition*. Perez, Joseph	272

SPANISH LANGUAGE
Nadeau, Jean-Benoit. *The Story of Spanish*	460
Spanish Made Simple. Allibhoy, Omar	641.594

SPANISH PEOPLE
Fernandez-Armesto, Felipe. ★*Amerigo*	B
Thomas, Hugh. *Rivers of Gold*	980

SPANISH-AMERICAN WAR, 1898
Craig, William. *Yankee Come Home*	972.9107
Gardner, Mark L. *Rough Riders*	973.911
Kinzer, Stephen. ★*The True Flag*	327.73
Whyte, Kenneth. *The Uncrowned King*	B
★*Spare*. Harry	B
Spare Parts. Davis, Joshua	629.8
★*Spark Joy*. Kondo, Marie	648

SPARTA (EXTINCT CITY)
Kagan, Donald. *The Peloponnesian War*	938
Roberts, Jennifer Tolbert. *The Plague of War*	938
Speak. Oyeneyin, Tunde	158.1
Speak Now. Yoshino, Kenji	346.79401
Speak, Okinawa. Brina, Elizabeth Miki	305.48

SPEAKERS
Kimberley, Hannah. *A Woman's Place Is at the Top*	B
Paul, Joel R. *Indivisible*	973.5
Speaking American. Bailey, Richard W.	427
Speaking of Race. Headlee, Celeste Anne	305.8
Speaking of Race. Roberts-Miller, Patricia	305.8
Spearhead. Makos, Adam	B

Spears, Britney
The Woman in Me	B

SPEARS, BRITNEY, 1981-
Spears, Britney. *The Woman in Me*	B

SPECIAL EFFECTS (CINEMATOGRAPHY)
O'Meara, Mallory. *The Lady from the Black Lagoon*	921

SPECIAL FORCES
Albracht, William. *Abandoned in Hell*	959.704
Brokhausen, Nick. *Whispers in the Tall Grass*	959.704
Couch, Dick. *The Warrior Elite*	359.9
Denver, Rorke. *Worth Dying For*	359.9
Kix, Paul. *The Saboteur*	940.53
Luttrell, Marcus. *Service*	956.7044
Macintyre, Ben. ★*Rogue Heroes*	940.54
Milton, Giles. *Churchill's Ministry of Ungentlemanly Warfare*	940.54
O'Neill, Robert. *The Operator*	B
Owen, Mark. *No Easy Day*	B
Stanton, Doug. *12 Strong*	958.104

PUBLIC LIBRARY CORE COLLECTION: NONFICTION
Twentieth Edition

Vickers, Michael G. *By All Means Available*	355
SPECIAL OLYMPICS	
Shriver, Timothy P. *Fully Alive*	796.087
SPECIAL OPERATIONS (MILITARY SCIENCE)	
Bergen, Peter L. *Manhunt*	363.325
Denver, Rorke. *Worth Dying For*	359.9
Lance, Rachel. *Chamber Divers*	940.54
Lemmon, Gayle Tzemach. *Ashley's War*	B
Lemmon, Gayle Tzemach. *The Daughters of Kobani*	956.9104
Lewis, Damien. *Churchill's Hellraisers*	940.54
McRaven, William H. *Sea Stories*	B
O'Donnell, Patrick K. *The Unvanquished*	973.7
O'Neill, Robert. *The Operator*	B
Owen, Mark. *No Easy Day*	B
Scahill, Jeremy. *Dirty Wars*	355.00973
Stephanopoulos, George. ★*The Situation Room*	973.09
Vickers, Michael G. *By All Means Available*	355
Wallace, Chris. *Countdown Bin Laden*	958.104
Special Orders. Hirsch, Edward	811
SPECIES	
Anthony, Leslie. *The Aliens Among Us*	578.6
Wohlleben, Peter. *The Secret Wisdom of Nature*	508
The Speckled Beauty. Bragg, Rick	636.7
Specter, Emma	
More, Please	616.85
SPECTOR, PHIL, 1940-2021	
Brown, Mick. ★*Tearing Down the Wall of Sound*	B
Spectral Evidence. Pardlo, Gregory	811
SPECULATION	
Small, Zachary. ★*Token Supremacy*	332.4
SPEECH	
Crystal, David. ★*How Language Works*	410
Curzan, Anne. ★*Says Who?*	428
Everett, Daniel Leonard. *How Language Began*	401
Ostler, Nicholas. *Ad Infinitum*	470
Pinker, Steven. *The Language Instinct*	400
Pinker, Steven. *The Stuff of Thought*	401
Soep, Elisabeth. *Other People's Words*	155.9
Tsu, Jing. *Kingdom of Characters*	495.111
Wolfe, Tom. *The Kingdom of Speech*	401
SPEECH DISORDERS	
Hendrickson, John. *Life on Delay*	B
SPEECH THERAPISTS	
Hunger, Christina. *How Stella Learned to Talk*	636.7
SPEECH WRITING	
Keenan, Cody. *Grace*	973.932
Wellman, Victoria. *Before You Say Anything*	808.5
Speeches and Writings, 1832-1858. Lincoln, Abraham	973.5
Speeches and Writings, 1859-1865. Lincoln, Abraham	973.6
SPEECHES, ADDRESSES, ETC.	
Barber, William J. *We Are Called to Be a Movement*	261.8
Bond, Julian. ★*Julian Bond's Time to Teach*	323.0975
Breyer, Stephen G. ★*The Authority of the Court and the Peril of Politics*	347.73
Dallek, Robert. *Let Every Nation Know*	B
Franzen, Jonathan. *Farther Away*	814
Hawking, Stephen. *The Nature of Space and Time*	530.1
Kennedy, Robert Francis. *RFK*	973.92
Lewis, John. *Carry On*	328.73
Lincoln, Abraham. *Speeches and Writings, 1859-1865*	973.6
Mandela, Nelson. *In His Own Words*	B
Morrison, Toni. *The Source of Self-Regard*	814
Prothero, Stephen R. *The American Bible*	973
Scalia, Antonin. *Scalia Speaks*	081
Sontag, Susan. *At the Same Time*	814
Wills, Garry. *Lincoln at Gettysburg*	973.7
Zelensky, Volodymyr. *A Message from Ukraine*	947.7
SPEECHWRITERS	
Guerrero, Jean. *Hatemonger*	B
Keenan, Cody. *Grace*	973.932
Litt, David. *Thanks, Obama*	B
Sorensen, Theodore C. *Counselor*	B
Wellman, Victoria. *Before You Say Anything*	808.5
SPEED	
Futterman, Matthew. *Running to the Edge*	796.42071
Hampton, Dan. *Chasing the Demon*	629.132
Hawley, Sam. *Speed Duel*	796.72
Speed Duel. Hawley, Sam	796.72

The Speed of Sound. Dolby, Thomas	B
Speer, Albert	
Inside the Third Reich	B
SPEER, ALBERT, 1905-1981	
Speer, Albert. *Inside the Third Reich*	B
Speerstra, Karen	
The Divine Art of Dying	202
SPEKE, JOHN HANNING, 1827-1864	
Jeal, Tim. *Explorers of the Nile*	920
Millard, Candice. ★*River of the Gods*	916.204
Spell It Out. Crystal, David	421
SPELLING	
Crystal, David. *Spell It Out*	421
SPELLING ABILITY	
Shankar, Shalini. *Beeline*	155.4
SPELLING BEES	
Shankar, Shalini. *Beeline*	155.4
Spence, Annie	
Dear Fahrenheit 451	028.9
Spence, Jonathan D.	
God's Chinese Son	951
The Search for Modern China	951
Spencer Tracy. Curtis, James	B
Spencer, Kyle	
Raising Them Right	320.5
Spencer, Lara	
Flea Market Fabulous	747
Spera, Keith	
Groove Interrupted	B
Sperber, Jonathan	
Karl Marx	B
SPERM WHALE	
Safina, Carl. ★*Becoming Wild*	591.7
Spetzler, Carl S.	
Decision Quality	658.4
★*The Spice Must Flow.* Britt, Ryan	813
Spicer, Charles	
Coffee with Hitler	941.084
Spicer, Jack	
My Vocabulary Did This to Me	811
SPICES	
Kahate, Ruta. *6 Spices 60 Dishes*	641.595
Lakshmi, Padma. *The Encyclopedia of Spices and Herbs*	641.3
SPIDERS	
Milne, Lorus Johnson. ★*The Audubon Society Field Guide to North American Insects and Spiders*	595.7097
Prasad, Aarathi. *Silk*	677
Spiegel, Maura	
Sidney Lumet	B
Spiegel, Renia	
Renia's Diary	B
SPIEGEL, RENIA, 1924-1942	
Spiegel, Renia. *Renia's Diary*	B
Spiegelman, Art	
Co-Mix	741.5
In the Shadow of No Towers	741.5
★*Maus*	741.5
Metamaus	B
SPIEGELMAN, ART	
Spiegelman, Art. *Co-Mix*	741.5
Spiegelman, Art. *In the Shadow of No Towers*	741.5
Spiegelman, Art. ★*Maus*	741.5
Spiegelman, Art. *Metamaus*	B
Spiegelman, Nadja	
★*I'm Supposed to Protect You from All This*	741.5
SPIEGELMAN, NADJA	
Spiegelman, Nadja. ★*I'm Supposed to Protect You from All This*	741.5
SPIEGELMAN, VLADEK, 1906-1982	
Spiegelman, Art. ★*Maus*	741.5
SPIELBERG, STEVEN, 1947-	
Haskell, Molly. *Steven Spielberg*	B
Spies. Walton, Calder	327.1247
SPIES	
Anderson, Scott. ★*The Quiet Americans*	327.12
Andrew, Christopher M. *The Secret World*	327.1209
Bascomb, Neal. *Hunting Eichmann*	943.086
Blum, Howard. *The Spy Who Knew Too Much*	327.12
Coker, Margaret. *The Spymaster of Baghdad*	956.7044

AUTHOR, TITLE, SERIES AND SUBJECT INDEX

Conant, Jennet. *The Lotus Eaters*	940.54
Cunningham, Benjamin. *The Liar*	327.1273
Drabkin, Ronald. *Beverly Hills Spy*	940.54
Elnoury, Tamer. *American Radical*	B
Fagone, Jason. *The Woman Who Smashed Codes*	B
Fields-Black, Edda L. *Combee*	973.7
Friedman, Matti. *Spies of No Country*	327.12
Greenberg, Andy. *Sandworm*	364.16
Harmon, Mark. *Ghosts of Honolulu*	940.54
Hillsberg, Christina. *License to Parent*	649.1
Hindley, Meredith. *Destination Casablanca*	940.54
Hvistendahl, Mara. ★*The Scientist and the Spy*	364.16
Kaiser, Charles. *The Cost of Courage*	B
Keith, Philip A. *All Blood Runs Red*	B
Kershaw, Alex. *Avenue of Spies*	940.53
Kilmeade, Brian. *George Washington's Secret Six*	973.4
Kix, Paul. *The Saboteur*	940.53
Lewis, Damien. *Agent Josephine*	B
Lichtblau, Eric. *Return to the Reich*	B
Loftis, Larry. *Code Name*	B
Macintyre, Ben. ★*Agent Sonya*	B
Macintyre, Ben. *Agent Zigzag*	B
Macintyre, Ben. *Double Cross*	940.54
Macintyre, Ben. *A Spy Among Friends*	B
Macintyre, Ben. ★*The Spy and the Traitor*	B
Maier, Thomas. *Mafia Spies*	364.1060973
Meltzer, Brad. ★*The First Conspiracy*	973.4
Milton, Giles. *Churchill's Ministry of Ungentlemanly Warfare*	940.54
Mulley, Clare. *The Spy Who Loved*	B
Nance, Malcolm W. *The Plot to Betray America*	973.933
Navarro, Joe. *Three Minutes to Doomsday*	B
Nicholl, Charles. *The Reckoning*	B
Ohler, Norman. *The Bohemians*	940.53
Parkin, Simon. *The Island of Extraordinary Captives*	940.53
Philipps, Roland. *A Spy Named Orphan*	B
Popkin, Jim. *Code Name Blue Wren*	327.12
Reynolds, Nicholas E. *Need to Know*	940.54
Ronald, Susan. *Hitler's Aristocrats*	940.53
Rose, Sarah. *D-Day Girls*	940.53
Ross, Steven Joseph. ★*Hitler in Los Angeles*	979.4
Sebba, Anne. *Ethel Rosenberg*	B
Sheinkin, Steve. *Bomb*	623.4
Shultz, Richard H. *The Secret War Against Hanoi*	959.704
Spicer, Charles. *Coffee with Hitler*	941.084
Talty, Stephan. *Agent Garbo*	940.5
Talty, Stephan. *The Good Assassin*	364.15
Trahair, R. C. S. *Encyclopedia of Cold War Espionage, Spies, and Secret Operations 3rd Ed.*	327.12
Vogel, Steve. *Betrayal in Berlin*	327.1273043
Waller, Douglas C. *Lincoln's Spies*	973.7
Waller, Douglas C. *Wild Bill Donovan*	B
Walton, Calder. *Spies*	327.1247
Warrick, Joby. *Red Line*	956.9104
Weiner, Tim. *Legacy of Ashes*	327.1273009
Wiehl, Lis W. *A Spy in Plain Sight*	327.1247
Wilford, Hugh. *The CIA*	327.1273
Xue, XInran. *The Book of Secrets*	951.05
SPIES IN LITERATURE	
Le Carre, John. *The Pigeon Tunnel*	B
Spies of No Country. Friedman, Matti	327.12
SPIKE, 1962-	
Ice-T. *Split Decision*	920
Spillane. Collins, Max Allan	B
SPILLANE, MICKEY, 1918-2006	
Collins, Max Allan. *Spillane*	B
★*Spillover*. Quammen, David	614.4
Spin Art. Boggs, Jacey	746.1
SPINA BIFIDA	
Lehrer, Riva. *Golem Girl*	B
SPINAL CORD	
Fox, Michael J. *No Time Like the Future*	B
SPINAL MUSCULAR ATROPHY	
Burcaw, Shane. ★*Laughing at My Nightmare*	B
Grue, Jan. *I Live a Life Like Yours*	B
Ndopu, Eddie. *Sipping Dom Pérignon Through a Straw*	B
The Spinner's Book of Yarn Designs. Anderson, Sarah	746.1
Spinney, Laura	
★*Pale Rider*	614.5

SPINOZA, BENEDICTUS DE, 1632-1677	
Damasio, Antonio R. *Looking for Spinoza*	152.4
Spira, Timothy P.	
Waterfalls and Wildflowers in the Southern Appalachians	796.5109756
The Spiral Staircase. Armstrong, Karen	B
The Spirit Catches You and You Fall Down. Fadiman, Anne	306.4
Spirit Run. Alvarez, Noe	796.42
SPIRITS	
Guiley, Rosemary. ★*The Encyclopedia of Ghosts and Spirits*	133.1
SPIRITUAL ABUSE	
West, Cait. ★*Rift*	B
The Spiritual Art of Business. Rowan, Barry L.	261.8
SPIRITUAL GROWTH	
Baskette, Molly Phinney. *How to Begin When Your World Is Ending*	248.8
Dalai Lama. *Approaching the Buddhist Path*	294.3
Dalai Lama. *The Book of Joy*	294.3
Girzone, Joseph F. *Never Alone*	248.4
Joyce, Russell W. *His Face Like Mine*	248
McLaren, Brian D. *Faith After Doubt*	234
Villodas, Rich. *The Deeply Formed Life*	248.4
SPIRITUAL JOURNEYS	
Greene, Jayson. *Once More We Saw Stars*	155.9
McLaren, Brian D. *Faith After Doubt*	234
Panagore, Peter Baldwin. *Heaven Is Beautiful*	B
SPIRITUAL LEADERS	
Armstrong, Karen. *Buddha*	B
SPIRITUAL LIFE	
Alvis-Walker, Marcie. *Everybody Come Alive*	B
Black Elk. *Black Elk Speaks*	B
Chaput, Charles J. *Things Worth Dying For*	248.4
Chittister, Joan. *The Monastic Heart*	248.8
Chodron, Pema. *Practicing Peace*	294.3
Chopra, Deepak. *Metahuman*	204
Clemmons, Francois S. *Officer Clemmons*	B
Cozzens, Peter. *Tecumseh and the Prophet*	920
Dalai Lama. *An Appeal to the World*	170
Dalai Lama. *Approaching the Buddhist Path*	294.3
Dalai Lama. *The Book of Joy*	294.3
Das, Gaur Gopal. *The Way of the Monk*	294.5
Emet, Joseph. *Finding the Blue Sky*	294.3
Ghobash, Omar Saif. *Letters to a Young Muslim*	297.09
Girzone, Joseph F. *Never Alone*	248.4
Hase, Craig. *How Not to Be a Hot Mess*	158.1
Holloway, Richard. *Waiting for the Last Bus*	202
Iyer, Pico. ★*The Half Known Life*	203
Jackson, Joe. *Black Elk*	978.004
Jalal al-Din Rumi, Maulana. *Rumi*	891
Kushner, Harold S. *When Bad Things Happen to Good People*	296.3
Kushner, Harold S. *Who Needs God*	296.7
Lahn, Bussho. *Singing and Dancing Are the Voice of the Law*	294.3
Lee, Shannon. *Be Water, My Friend*	796.8
Martin, James. *The Jesuit Guide to (Almost) Everything*	248.4
Masuno, Shunmy. *The Art of Simple Living*	294.3
Moore, Thomas. *Ageless Soul*	155.67
Nasr, Seyyed Hossein. *Islam*	297
Nesmith, Michael. *Infinite Tuesday*	B
Nhat Hanh. *The Art of Living*	294.3
Nhat Hanh. *Zen and the Art of Saving the Planet*	294.3
Nichtern, David. *Creativity, Spirituality & Making a Buck*	294.3
Norris, Kathleen. *The Cloister Walk*	255
Oakes, John G. H. ★*The Fast*	613.2
Ozment, Katherine. *Grace Without God*	200.973
Riess, Jana. *Flunking Sainthood*	248.4
Rinzler, Lodro. *The Buddha Walks into a Bar*	294.3
Sawaki, Kodo. *Discovering the True Self*	294.3
Seiffert, Amy. *Starved*	248
Sheldrake, Rupert. *Science and Spiritual Practices*	201
Shriver, Maria. *I've Been Thinking ...*	170
Taylor, Barbara Brown. *Holy Envy*	B
Teilhard de Chardin, Pierre. ★*The Divine Milieu*	233
Teresa. *A Call to Mercy*	234
Thomson, Graeme. *George Harrison*	B
Thondup. *Enlightened Journey*	294.3
Turner, Tina. ★*Happiness Becomes You*	158.1
Villodas, Rich. *The Deeply Formed Life*	248.4
Wayland-Smith, Ellen. *Oneida*	307.77
SPIRITUALISM	
Aykroyd, Peter. *A History of Ghosts*	133.1

PUBLIC LIBRARY CORE COLLECTION: NONFICTION
Twentieth Edition

Blum, Deborah. *Ghost Hunters*	133.9
Fox, Margalit. *The Confidence Men*	940.4
Jaher, David. *The Witch of Lime Street*	B
Manseau, Peter. *The Apparitionists*	B
Rasmussen, Christina. *Where Did You Go?*	133.9
Rojas Contreras, Ingrid. ★*The Man Who Could Move Clouds*	B
Satyamurti, Carole. *Mahabharata*	821

SPIRITUALISTS

Jaher, David. *The Witch of Lime Street*	B

SPIRITUALITY

Bartlett, Sarah. *A Brief History of Angels and Demons*	202
Belser, Julia Watts. ★*Loving Our Own Bones*	296
Beres, Derek. *Conspirituality*	001.9
Bignon, Guillaume. *Confessions of a French Atheist*	239
Bitsui, Sherwin. *Dissolve*	811
Boa, Kenneth D. *Recalibrate Your Life*	248.8
Briggs, Lyvonne. ★*Sensual Faith*	204
Cohen-Solal, Annie. *Mark Rothko*	759.13
Common. ★*And Then We Rise*	B
Dalai Lama. *The Book of Joy*	294.3
Dalai Lama. *How to Be Compassionate*	294.3
Dennett, D. C. *Breaking the Spell*	200
Dillard, Annie. *The Abundance*	814
Dillard, Annie. *Teaching a Stone to Talk*	508
Epstein, Mark. *The Zen of Therapy*	294.3
Feldman, Noah. ★*To Be a Jew Today*	296.3
Gibson, Marion. *Witchcraft*	133.4
Hardacre, Helen. *Shinto*	299.5
Harjo, Joy. *Crazy Brave*	B
Harrington, Joel F. *Dangerous Mystic*	B
Hecht, Jennifer Michael. ★*The Wonder Paradox*	808.1
Held, Shai. *Judaism Is About Love*	296.3
Hitchens, Christopher. *The Four Horsemen*	211
Karon, Jan. *Bathed in Prayer*	242
Lamott, Anne. *Almost Everything*	170
Lamott, Anne. ★*Somehow*	814
Lattin, Don. *The Harvard Psychedelic Club*	973.922092
Lewis, C. S. *Miracles*	231.7
Lightman, Alan P. *The Transcendent Brain*	215
Nhat Hanh. *Zen and the Art of Saving the Planet*	294.3
Norman, Philip. *George Harrison*	B
Ozment, Katherine. *Grace Without God*	200.973
Park, J. S. ★*As Long as You Need*	248.8
Peck, M. Scott. ★*The Road Less Traveled*	158.1
Poitier, Sidney. *The Measure of a Man*	B
Rajchel, Diana. *Urban Magick*	133.4
Rinzler, Lodro. *The Buddha Walks into a Bar*	294.3
Roberts, Matthias. *Holy Runaways*	262
Rohr, Richard. *The Universal Christ*	232
Rush, Charaia. *Courageously Soft*	234
Sagan, Sasha. *For Small Creatures Such as We*	390.09
Smietana, Bob. *Reorganized Religion*	262.001
Tanais. *In Sensorium*	B
Taylor, Barbara Brown. *Holy Envy*	B
Teresa. *A Call to Mercy*	234
Tesfamariam, Rahiel. ★*Imagine Freedom*	305.896
Tippett, Krista. ★*Becoming Wise*	158.1
Tworkov, Helen. *Lotus Girl*	B
Walker, Alice. *We Are the Ones We Have Been Waiting For*	811
Wilson, Sarah. *First, We Make the Beast Beautiful*	616.85

SPIRITUALITY AND RELIGION — BODY, MIND, AND SPIRIT

Abrev, Ileana. *The Little Big Book of White Spells*	133.4
Bechdel, Alison. ★*The Secret to Superhuman Strength*	741.5
Bernstein, Gabrielle. *Judgment Detox*	158
Canfield, Jack. *The Success Principles*	158
Connelly, Ben. *Inside Vasubandhu's Yogacara*	294.3
Crawford, Saffi. *The Power of Birthdays, Stars & Numbers*	133.5
Crispin, Jessa. ★*The Creative Tarot*	133.3
Crosson, Monica. *The Magikal Family*	299
Dale, Cyndi. *Llewellyn's Complete Book of Chakras*	131
Das, Gaur Gopal. *The Way of the Monk*	294.5
Dunne, Linnea. *Lagom*	B
Dyer, Wayne W. ★*The Power of Intention*	158.1
Feldmann, Erica. *Hausmagick*	133.4
Fletcher, Emily. *Stress Less, Accomplish More*	155.9
Gawain, Shakti. ★*Creative Visualization*	153.3
Gilbert, Elizabeth. ★*Big Magic*	153.3
Goldschneider, Gary. ★*The Secret Language of Birthdays*	133.5

Grimassi, Raven. *What We Knew in the Night*	133.4
Guiley, Rosemary. ★*The Encyclopedia of Ghosts and Spirits*	133.1
Guiley, Rosemary. *The Encyclopedia of Witches, Witchcraft and Wicca*	133.4
Hase, Craig. *How Not to Be a Hot Mess*	158.1
Jones, Marie D. *Celebrity Ghosts and Notorious Hauntings*	133.1
Jordan, Michael. *Dictionary of Gods and Goddesses*	202
Jung, C. G. ★*The Basic Writings of C.G. Jung*	150.19
Kongtrul, Dzigar. *Peaceful Heart*	294.3
Lamott, Anne. ★*Somehow*	814
Marcus Aurelius. ★*Meditations*	188
Miller, Susan. *Planets and Possibilities*	133.5
Minami, Jikisai. *It's Okay Not to Look for the Meaning of Life*	158.1
Moody, Raymond A. *Life After Life*	133.9
Norman, Michael. *Haunted America*	133.1
Northrup, Christiane. *Dodging Energy Vampires*	155.2
Oakes, John G. H. ★*The Fast*	613.2
Owens, Lama Rod. *Love and Rage*	152.4
Rakel, David. *The Compassionate Connection*	610.1
Ramsland, Katherine M. *Ghost*	133.1
Rasmussen, Christina. *Where Did You Go?*	133.9
Roth, Harold. *The Witching Herbs*	133.4
Siff, Jason. *Thoughts Are Not the Enemy*	294.3
Sincero, Jen. *You Are a Badass Every Day*	158.1
Taylor, Madisyn. *Unmedicated*	615.8
Teng, Tara. ★*Your Body Is a Revolution*	306.4
Van Buren, Mark. *A Fool's Guide to Actual Happiness*	294.3
Zorn, Justin. *Golden*	128

SPIRITUALITY AND RELIGION — BODY, MIND, AND SPIRIT — MEDITATION AND MINDFULNESS

Chodron, Pema. *Practicing Peace*	294.3
Emet, Joseph. *Finding the Blue Sky*	294.3
Fletcher, Emily. *Stress Less, Accomplish More*	155.9
Goleman, Daniel. *Why We Meditate*	158.1
Gunaratana, Henepola. *Start Here, Start Now*	294.3
Harris, Dan. ★*10% Happier*	158.1
Heller, Rick. *Secular Meditation*	158.1
Masuno, Shunmy. *The Art of Simple Living*	294.3
Sawaki, Kodo. *Discovering the True Self*	294.3
Shumsky, Susan G. *Earth Energy Meditations*	133.8
Siegel, Daniel J. *Aware*	158.1
Siff, Jason. *Thoughts Are Not the Enemy*	294.3
Suzuki, Shunryu. *Zen Mind, Beginner's Mind*	294.3
Teresa. *A Call to Mercy*	234
Wiking, Meik. *The Little Book of Hygge*	158.1

SPIRITUALITY AND RELIGION — BUDDHISM

Armstrong, Karen. *Buddha*	B
Chodron, Pema. *How We Live Is How We Die*	294.3
Chodron, Pema. *Practicing Peace*	294.3
Connelly, Ben. *Inside Vasubandhu's Yogacara*	294.3
Dalai Lama. *An Appeal to the World*	170
Dalai Lama. *Approaching the Buddhist Path*	294.3
Dalai Lama. *Freedom in Exile*	B
Dalai Lama. *How to Be Compassionate*	294.3
Dalai Lama. *The Second Dalai Lama*	294.3
Emet, Joseph. *Finding the Blue Sky*	294.3
Epstein, Mark. *Advice Not Given*	294.3
Epstein, Mark. *The Zen of Therapy*	294.3
Gunaratana, Henepola. *Start Here, Start Now*	294.3
Han, Chenxing. *Be the Refuge*	294.3
Hase, Craig. *How Not to Be a Hot Mess*	158.1
Iyer, Pico. *The Open Road*	B
Keown, Damien. ★*A Dictionary of Buddhism*	294.3
Kongtrul, Dzigar. *Peaceful Heart*	294.3
Kornfield, Jack. *The Wise Heart*	294.3
Lahn, Bussho. *Singing and Dancing Are the Voice of the Law*	294.3
Larson, Kay. *Where the Heart Beats*	700.1
Minami, Jikisai. *It's Okay Not to Look for the Meaning of Life*	158.1
Nhat Hanh. *The Art of Living*	294.3
Nhat Hanh. *Zen and the Art of Saving the Planet*	294.3
Oliver, Joan Duncan. *Buddhism*	294.3
Olson, Carl. *Historical Dictionary of Buddhism*	294.3
Rinzler, Lodro. *The Buddha Walks into a Bar*	294.3
Rinzler, Lodro. *Love Hurts*	294.3
Salguero, C. Pierce. ★*Buddhish*	294.3
Sawaki, Kodo. *Discovering the True Self*	294.3
Sheff, David. *The Buddhist on Death Row*	B
Sogyal. *The Tibetan Book of Living and Dying*	294.3
Suzuki, Shunryu. *Zen Mind, Beginner's Mind*	294.3

AUTHOR, TITLE, SERIES AND SUBJECT INDEX

Tenzin Priyadarshi. *Running Toward Mystery*	B
Thondup. *Enlightened Journey*	294.3
Thubten Zopa. *The Four Noble Truths*	294.3
Turner, Tina. ★*Happiness Becomes You*	158.1
Tworkov, Helen. *Lotus Girl*	B
Wright, Robert. *Why Buddhism Is True*	294.3

SPIRITUALITY AND RELIGION — BUDDHISM — HISTORY

Sutin, Lawrence. ★*All Is Change*	294.309

SPIRITUALITY AND RELIGION — CHRISTIAN LIVING

Batterson, Mark. *Please, Sorry, Thanks*	179
Beck, Amanda Martinez. *More of You*	613
Becker, Joshua. *The More of Less*	241
Bragg, Sarah. *Is Everyone Happier Than Me?*	248.4
Brown, Robert J. *You Can't Go Wrong Doing Right*	B
Cairns, Scott. *The End of Suffering*	231
Carter, Jimmy. *Sources of Strength*	248.4
Chapman, Gary D. *Love as a Way of Life*	241
Chittister, Joan. *The Monastic Heart*	248.8
Dokun, Chanel. *Life Starts Now*	248.8
Evans, Jimmy. *Strengths Based Marriage*	248.8
Fusco, Daniel. *Crazy Happy*	248.4
Girzone, Joseph F. *A Portrait of Jesus*	232.9
Jakes, T. D. *Destiny*	248.4
Lucado, Max. *Unshakable Hope*	248.4
Lucado, Max. *You Are Never Alone*	248.4
Martin, James. *The Jesuit Guide to (Almost) Everything*	248.4
Martin, James. *Learning to Pray*	248.3
Meyer, Joyce. *Seize the Day*	248.4
Nockels, Christy. *The Life You Long For*	248.8
Nouwen, Henri J. M. *Love, Henri*	282.092
Osteen, Joel. *The Power of I Am*	248.4
Peterson, Eugene H. *This Hallelujah Banquet*	228
Rowan, Barry L. *The Spiritual Art of Business*	261.8
Sauls, Scott. *Beautiful People Don't Just Happen*	248.8
Seiffert, Amy. *Starved*	248
Villodas, Rich. *The Deeply Formed Life*	248.4
Villodas, Rich. *Good and Beautiful and Kind*	232.9
Volf, Miroslav. *Public Faith in Action*	261.7
Whittle, Lisa. *God Knows*	231
Winkler, Kyle. *Permission to Be Imperfect*	170
Zahl, David. *Low Anthropology*	233

SPIRITUALITY AND RELIGION — CHRISTIANITY

Akyol, Mustafa. *The Islamic Jesus*	297.2
Archibald, John. *Shaking the Gates of Hell*	B
Armas, Kat. *Abuelita Faith*	248.8
Armstrong, Karen. *The Battle for God*	200
Armstrong, Karen. *The Bible*	220.09
Armstrong, Karen. *The Case for God*	211
Armstrong, Karen. *A History of God*	202
Armstrong, Karen. *Jerusalem*	956.94
Armstrong, Karen. *The Spiral Staircase*	B
Armstrong, Karen. *Twelve Steps to a Compassionate Life*	177
Bailey, Jennifer. *To My Beloveds*	261.8
Baraka, Sho. *He Saw That It Was Good*	261.5
Barry, John M. *Roger Williams and the Creation of the American Soul*	974.5
Baskette, Molly Phinney. *How to Begin When Your World Is Ending*	248.8
Bass, Diana Butler. *Grateful*	241
Beaty, Katelyn. *Celebrities for Jesus*	261
Bignon, Guillaume. *Confessions of a French Atheist*	239
Blum, Edward J. *The Color of Christ*	232
Boa, Kenneth D. *Recalibrate Your Life*	248.8
Bolz-Weber, Nadia. *Accidental Saints*	284.1
Bolz-Weber, Nadia. *Shameless*	261.8
Boyle, Greg. *Tattoos on the Heart*	277
Brennan, Chad. *Faithful Antiracism*	277.308
Briggs, Lyvonne. *Sensual Faith*	204
Brownback, Lydia. *Finding God in My Loneliness*	248.8
Carroll, James. *Constantine's Sword*	261
Carter, Jimmy. *Faith*	OK T A
Castor, Helen. *Joan of Arc*	B
Chittister, Joan. *Following the Path*	248.4
Chu, Jeff. *Does Jesus Really Love Me?*	261.8
Cobbs-Leonard, Tasha. *Do It Anyway*	241
Coldstream, Catherine. ★*Cloistered*	B
Curry, Michael B. *Love Is the Way*	241
Darling, Daniel. *Agents of Grace*	158.2
Davies, Brian. *The Thought of Thomas Aquinas*	230
DiFelice, Bekah. *Almost There*	248.8
Eddy, Mary Baker. ★*Mary Baker Eddy*	289.5
Edman, Elizabeth M. *Queer Virtue*	230
Egan, Timothy. *A Pilgrimage to Eternity*	263
Eire, Carlos M. N. *A Very Brief History of Eternity*	236
Evans, Rachel Held. *Wholehearted Faith*	248.4
Feiler, Bruce. *The First Love Story*	222
Feiler, Bruce. *Walking the Bible*	915
Flanders, Judith. *Christmas*	394.2663
Forbes, Bruce David. *Christmas*	394.2663
Francois, Willie Dwayne. *Silencing White Noise*	277
Friedman, Benjamin M. *Religion and the Rise of Capitalism*	330.12
Garcia, Damon. *The God Who Riots*	269
Gilliard, Dominique Dubois. *Rethinking Incarceration*	261.8
Girzone, Joseph F. *A Portrait of Jesus*	232.9
Gonzalez, Karen. *Beyond Welcome*	261.8
Grieve, Paul. *A Brief Guide to Islam*	297
Griffin, Chante. *Loving Your Black Neighbor as Yourself*	261
Griswold, Eliza. *The Tenth Parallel*	297.2
Guthrie, Savannah. *Mostly What God Does*	248.4
Hamm, Thomas D. ★*The Quakers in America*	289.6
Hardwick, Lamar. *How Ableism Fuels Racism*	261.8
Harrington, Joel F. *Dangerous Mystic*	B
Hartke, Austen. *Transforming*	277
Hatmaker, Jen. *Of Mess and Moxie*	248.8
Hays, Katie. *Family of Origin, Family of Choice*	248.8086
Holloway, Richard. *Waiting for the Last Bus*	202
Jones, Robert P. *White Too Long*	277
Jun, Tasha. ★*Tell Me the Dream Again*	248
Karon, Jan. *Bathed in Prayer*	242
Keller, Timothy J. *The Reason for God*	239
King, Martin Luther. ★*A Testament of Hope*	323.1
King, Martin Luther. *"Thou, Dear God"*	242
Kraybill, Donald B. *Concise Encyclopedia of Amish, Brethren, Hutterites, and Mennonites*	289.7
Kraybill, Donald B. ★*On the Backroad to Heaven*	289.7
Lamott, Anne. *Almost Everything*	170
Lamott, Anne. ★*Dusk, Night, Dawn*	B
Lamott, Anne. ★*Hallelujah Anyway*	241
Lamott, Anne. *Small Victories*	248
Lecrae. ★*I Am Restored*	B
Levack, Brian P. *The Devil Within*	133.4
Levine, Amy-Jill. *The Bible with and Without Jesus*	220.6
Levine, Amy-Jill. *Short Stories by Jesus*	226.8
Lewis, C. S. ★*A Grief Observed*	242
Lewis, C. S. *Letters to Malcolm*	248.3
Lewis, C. S. *Mere Christianity*	230
Lewis, C. S. *Miracles*	231.7
Lucado, Max. *Before Amen*	248.3
Mackall, Joe. *Plain Secrets*	289.7
Marsh, Charles. *Strange Glory*	B
Martin, Valerie. *Salvation*	B
Mathewes-Green, Frederica. *Welcome to the Orthodox Church*	281.9
McLaren, Brian D. *Faith After Doubt*	234
McLaren, Brian D. *Life After Doom*	200.1
Merton, Thomas. *The Intimate Merton*	B
Moore, Beth. *All My Knotted-Up Life*	B
Morton, Michael. *Getting Life*	B
Newman, Richard S. *Freedom's Prophet*	B
Nouwen, Henri J. M. *Love, Henri*	282.092
Olson, Roger E. ★*Handbook of Denominations in the United States*	200.973
Orji, Yvonne. *Bamboozled by Jesus*	B
Pagels, Elaine H. *Beyond Belief*	229
Pagels, Elaine H. ★*The Gnostic Gospels*	273
Pagels, Elaine H. *The Origin of Satan*	235
Pagels, Elaine H. ★*Why Religion?*	B
Park, J. S. ★*As Long as You Need*	248.8
Plantinga, Cornelius. *Gratitude*	179
Poitier, Sidney. *The Measure of a Man*	B
Price, Reynolds. *A Serious Way of Wondering*	241
Quinn, Tallu Schuyler. *What We Wish Were True*	B
Riley, Gregory J. *The River of God*	270.1
Risner, Vaneetha Rendall. *Walking Through Fire*	B
Roberts, Matthias. *Holy Runaways*	262
Robinson, Marilynne. ★*Reading Genesis*	222
Rush, Charaia. *Courageously Soft*	234
Samatar, Sofia. *The White Mosque*	B
Shachtman, Tom. ★*Rumspringa*	305.235
Shulevitz, Judith. *The Sabbath World*	296.4

PUBLIC LIBRARY CORE COLLECTION: NONFICTION
Twentieth Edition

Smietana, Bob. *Reorganized Religion*	262.001
Smith, James K. A. *How to Inhabit Time*	223
Spong, John Shelby. *Eternal Life*	236
Stanley, Brian. *Christianity in the Twentieth Century*	270.8
Stein, Stephen J. *The Shaker Experience in America*	289
Strobel, Lee. *The Case for Grace*	234
Strong, James. *The New Strong's Expanded Exhaustive Concordance of the Bible*	220.5
Thi, Kim Phuc Phan. *Fire Road*	B
Tickle, Phyllis. *The Great Emergence*	270.8
Tutu, Desmond. *The Book of Forgiving*	179
Tutu, Desmond. *Made for Goodness*	170
Vaughn, Ellen Santilli. ★*Becoming Elisabeth Elliot*	B
Volf, Miroslav. *Public Faith in Action*	261.7
Wacker, Grant. *America's Pastor*	B
Wallis, Jim. *The False White Gospel*	261.7
Wiman, Christian. *He Held Radical Light*	814
Wintz, Jack. *Will I See My Dog in Heaven?*	231.7
Wray, T. J. *The Birth of Satan*	235
Yancey, Philip. ★*Where the Light Fell*	B

SPIRITUALITY AND RELIGION — CHRISTIANITY — CATHOLICISM

Barthel, Joan. *American Saint*	B
Chaput, Charles J. *Things Worth Dying For*	248.4
Cornwell, John. *Hitler's Pope*	B
Douthat, Ross Gregory. *To Change the Church*	230
Duffy, Eamon. *Saints & Sinners*	262
Eisner, Peter. *The Pope's Last Crusade*	282.092
Francis. *The Church of Mercy*	252
Francis. *Happiness in This Life*	248.4
Francis. *Let Us Dream*	282.092
Francis. *Walking with Jesus*	282.09
Girzone, Joseph F. *Never Alone*	248.4
Hennessy, Kate. *Dorothy Day*	B
Kertzer, David I. *The Pope at War*	940.53
Martin, James. *The Jesuit Guide to (Almost) Everything*	248.4
McBrien, Richard P. *Lives of the Popes*	B
McGreevy, John T. ★*Catholicism*	282.09
Merton, Thomas. *The Intimate Merton*	B
Merton, Thomas. ★*The Seven Storey Mountain*	B
Norris, Kathleen. *The Cloister Walk*	255
O'Connor, Garry. *Universal Father*	B
Phelan, Tom. *We Were Rich and We Didn't Know It*	B
Politi, Marco. *Pope Francis Among the Wolves*	282.092
Posner, Gerald L. *God's Bankers*	364.16
Vallely, Paul. *Pope Francis*	B
Wills, Garry. *The Future of the Catholic Church with Pope Francis*	282.09
Woodward, Kenneth L. *Making Saints*	235.24

SPIRITUALITY AND RELIGION — CHRISTIANITY — HISTORY

Augustine. *Concerning the City of God Against the Pagans*	239
Augustine. *Confessions*	B
Barton, John. *A History of the Bible*	220.09
Brown, Nancy Marie. *The Abacus and the Cross*	B
Brown, Peter. *Through the Eye of a Needle*	270.2
Butcher, Carmen Acevedo. *Man of Blessing*	B
Ehrman, Bart D. ★*Armageddon*	236
Ehrman, Bart D. *The Triumph of Christianity*	270.1
Farmer, David Hugh. *The Oxford Dictionary of Saints*	270
Fredriksen, Paula. *Jesus of Nazareth, King of the Jews*	B
Garfinkel, Yosef. *In the Footsteps of King David*	933
Gates, Henry Louis. ★*The Black Church*	277
Haag, Michael. *The Tragedy of the Templars*	271.7913
Hazleton, Lesley. *Mary*	B
Hendrix, Scott H. *Martin Luther*	B
Holifield, E. Brooks. *Theology in America*	230
Holland, Tom. *Dominion*	261
Jones, Robert P. *The Hidden Roots of White Supremacy*	305.8
Kamen, Henry. *The Spanish Inquisition*	272
Lambert, Malcolm. *God's Armies*	956
Levack, Brian P. *The Devil Within*	133.4
MacCulloch, Diarmaid. *Christianity*	270
MacCulloch, Diarmaid. *The Reformation*	270.6
McGreevy, John T. ★*Catholicism*	282.09
McGuckin, John Anthony. ★*The Eastern Orthodox Church*	281.909
Metaxas, Eric. *Martin Luther*	B
Perez, Joseph. ★*The Spanish Inquisition*	272
Rohr, Richard. *The Universal Christ*	232
Rounding, Virginia. *The Burning Time*	272
Ryrie, Alec. *Protestants*	280
Sebag-Montefiore, Simon. *Jerusalem*	956.94
Spoto, Donald. *Joan*	B
Stavrakopoulou, Francesca. *God*	231
Swarns, Rachel L. *The 272*	975.2
Wills, Garry. *Saint Augustine*	B
Wilson, Derek. *Out of the Storm*	B

SPIRITUALITY AND RELIGION — CHRISTIANITY — MORMONISM

Beam, Alex. *American Crucifixion*	B
Brown, Samuel Morris. *In Heaven as It Is on Earth*	289.3
Bushman, Richard L. *Mormonism*	289.3
Gutjahr, Paul C. *The Book of Mormon*	289.3
Hardy, Grant. *Understanding the Book of Mormon*	289.3
Park, Benjamin E. *American Zion*	289.3
Turner, John G. *Brigham Young, Pioneer Prophet*	B
Walker, Ronald W. ★*Massacre at Mountain Meadows*	979.2
Wariner, Ruth. *The Sound of Gravel*	B

SPIRITUALITY AND RELIGION — CHRISTIANITY — POLITICAL ASPECTS

Alberta, Tim. *The Kingdom, the Power, and the Glory*	270.8
Barber, William J. *We Are Called to Be a Movement*	261.8
Carranca, Adriana. *Soul by Soul*	230
Du Mez, Kristin Kobes. *Jesus and John Wayne*	277.308
FitzGerald, Frances. *The Evangelicals*	277
Francis. *Let Us Dream*	282.092
Francis. *Life*	B
Griffith, R. Marie. *Moral Combat*	261.8
Henny, Ally. *I Won't Shut Up*	305.896
Kertzer, David I. *The Pope Who Would Be King*	282.092
Liao, Yiwu. *God Is Red*	275
McLaren, Brian D. *Do I Stay Christian?*	270.8
Meyaard-Schaap, Kyle. *Following Jesus in a Warming World*	241
Nagassar, Rohadi. *When We Belong*	254
Peters, Rebecca Todd. *Trust Women*	362.1988
Rashid, Jonny. *Jesus Takes a Side*	261.7
Ward, Jon. *Testimony*	277.308
Wills, Garry. *The Future of the Catholic Church with Pope Francis*	282.09

SPIRITUALITY AND RELIGION — GENERAL

Adler, Margot. *Drawing Down the Moon*	299
Armstrong, Karen. *Fields of Blood*	201
Armstrong, Karen. ★*The Great Transformation*	200.9
Armstrong, Karen. *The Lost Art of Scripture*	208
Armstrong, Karen. ★*A Short History of Myth*	201
Aslan, Reza. *God*	211
Bartlett, Sarah. *A Brief History of Angels and Demons*	202
Beard, Mary. ★*How Do We Look*	704.9
Belser, Julia Watts. ★*Loving Our Own Bones*	296
Beres, Derek. *Conspirituality*	001.9
Bidwell, Duane R. *When One Religion Isn't Enough*	261.2
Blackburn, Simon. *Think*	100
Brown, Maressa. *Raising Baby by the Stars*	133.5
Campbell, Joseph. *The Masks of God*	201.3
Campbell, Joseph. *The Power of Myth*	201.3
Chevannes, Barry. *Rastafari*	299
Chittister, Joan. *The Gift of Years*	200
Collins, Francis S. *The Language of God*	215
Crosson, Monica. *The Magikal Family*	299
Dalai Lama. *The Book of Joy*	294.3
Dalrymple, William. *Nine Lives*	294
De Botton, Alain. *Religion for Atheists*	200
Dennett, D. C. *Breaking the Spell*	200
Dennett, D. C. *Intuition Pumps and Other Tools for Thinking*	121
DeSteno, David. *How God Works*	200.1
Dillard, Annie. *Teaching a Stone to Talk*	508
Edmonds, David. *Wittgenstein's Poker*	192
Frankl, Viktor E. ★*Man's Search for Meaning*	B
Friedman, Maurice S. *Encounter on the Narrow Ridge*	B
Gallagher, Richard E. *Demonic Foes*	133.42
Garcia, Amanda Yates. *Initiated*	B
Gay, Peter. *The Enlightenment*	190
Goodall, Jane. ★*The Book of Hope*	128
Gosden, Chris. *Magic*	133.4
Grabbe, Lester L. *Faith and Fossils*	231.7
Grant, Edward. *Science and Religion, 400 B.C. To A.D. 1550*	201
Greenblatt, Stephen. *The Rise and Fall of Adam and Eve*	233
Grimassi, Raven. *What We Knew in the Night*	133.4
Hagglund, Martin. *This Life*	110
Hardacre, Helen. *Shinto*	299.5
Harrington, Joel F. *Dangerous Mystic*	B

AUTHOR, TITLE, SERIES AND SUBJECT INDEX

Hazleton, Lesley. *Agnostic*	211
Hecht, Jennifer Michael. ★*The Wonder Paradox*	808.1
Heidegger, Martin. *Basic Writings*	193
Hexham, Irving. *Understanding World Religions*	200
Hitchens, Christopher. *The Four Horsemen*	211
Hofstadter, Douglas R. *I Am a Strange Loop*	153
Holt, Jim. *Why Does the World Exist?*	113
Hutton, Ronald. *The Triumph of the Moon*	133.4
Iyer, Pico. ★*The Half Known Life*	203
Jacobs, Alan. *Original Sin*	233
James, William. ★*The Varieties of Religious Experience*	204
Jennings, Ken. ★*100 Places to See After You Die*	202
Johnson, Ian. *The Souls of China*	200.951
Jones, Faith. *Sex Cult Nun*	B
Jones, Marie D. *Demons, the Devil, and Fallen Angels*	133.4
Junger, Sebastian. ★*In My Time of Dying*	304.6
Kondo, Marie. ★*The Life-Changing Magic of Tidying Up*	648
Kreeft, Peter. ★*Philosophy 101 by Socrates*	183
Kugel, James L. *The Great Shift*	296.3
Kung, Hans. *Great Christian Thinkers*	230
Kushner, Harold S. *How Good Do We Have to Be?*	296.7
Lee, Shannon. *Be Water, My Friend*	796.8
Lemay, Mimi. *What We Will Become*	306.874
Levack, Brian P. *The Devil Within*	133.4
Lewis, James R. *Legitimating New Religions*	200
Lightman, Alan P. *The Transcendent Brain*	215
Locke, John. *An Essay Concerning Human Understanding*	121
Lucretius Carus, Titus. *On the Nature of Things =*	187
Manseau, Peter. *Objects of Devotion*	277
Mar, Alex. *Witches of America*	299
Marcus Aurelius. ★*Meditations*	188
Martin, James. *The Jesuit Guide to (Almost) Everything*	248.4
Marty, Martin E. *Pilgrims in Their Own Land*	200
Masuno, Shunmy. *The Art of Simple Living*	294.3
Merton, Thomas. *The Intimate Merton*	B
Miles, Jack. *Religion as We Know It*	200.9
Minois, Georges. *The Atheist's Bible*	200
Moore, Thomas. *Ageless Soul*	155.67
Mullins, Edwin. *The Four Roads to Heaven*	263
Nabokov, Peter. *Where the Lightning Strikes*	299.7
Nietzsche, Friedrich Wilhelm. ★*Thus Spoke Zarathustra*	193
Norris, Kathleen. *Acedia & Me*	248.8
Nussbaum, Martha Craven. *The New Religious Intolerance*	201.723
Ozment, Katherine. *Grace Without God*	200.973
Panagore, Peter Baldwin. *Heaven Is Beautiful*	B
Pearson, Roger. *Voltaire Almighty*	B
Peck, M. Scott. ★*The Road Less Traveled*	158.1
Pelikan, Jaroslav. *Mary Through the Centuries*	232.91
Prothero, Stephen R. *The American Bible*	973
Prothero, Stephen R. *God Is Not One*	200
Prothero, Stephen R. *God the Bestseller*	070.5
Prothero, Stephen R. *Religious Literacy*	200.71
Rajchel, Diana. *Urban Magick*	133.4
Rand, Ayn. ★*The Virtue of Selfishness*	149
Reitman, Janet. *Inside Scientology*	299
Richardson, Robert D. *William James*	B
Ricketts, Rachel. ★*Do Better*	305.800973
Rinder, Mike. ★*A Billion Years*	B
Roth, Robert. *Strength in Stillness*	158.1
Sacks, Jonathan. *The Great Partnership*	201
Sagan, Sasha. *For Small Creatures Such as We*	390.09
Sartre, Jean-Paul. *We Have Only This Life to Live*	848
Sheldrake, Rupert. *Science and Spiritual Practices*	201
Shriver, Maria. *I've Been Thinking ...*	170
Taylor, Barbara Brown. *Holy Envy*	B
Teilhard de Chardin, Pierre. ★*The Divine Milieu*	233
Terkel, Studs. *Hope Dies Last*	920
Terkel, Studs. *Will the Circle Be Unbroken?*	128
Tesfamariam, Rahiel. ★*Imagine Freedom*	305.896
Thomas. *Selected Writings*	230
Tippett, Krista. ★*Becoming Wise*	158.1
Turner, Alice K. *The History of Hell*	236
Waldman, Steven. *Sacred Liberty*	341.4
Walker, Alice. *We Are the Ones We Have Been Waiting For*	811
Watts, Alan. *The Way of Zen*	294.3
Williams, Juan. *This Far by Faith*	200
Wiman, Christian. *Zero at the Bone*	818
Woodward, Kenneth L. *The Book of Miracles*	231.7
Wright, Lawrence. *Going Clear*	299
Zuckerman, Phil. *Living the Secular Life*	211
SPIRITUALITY AND RELIGION — HINDUISM	
Calasso, Roberto. *Ardor*	294.5
Davis, Richard H. *The Bhagavad Gita*	294.5
Doniger, Wendy. *On Hinduism*	294.5
Rao, Cheeni. *In Hanuman's Hands*	B
Sengupta, Hindol. *Being Hindu*	294.5
SPIRITUALITY AND RELIGION — HINDUISM — HISTORY	
Goldberg, Philip. *American Veda*	294.509
SPIRITUALITY AND RELIGION — ISLAM	
Abdul Rauf, Feisal. *Moving the Mountain*	297
Akyol, Mustafa. *The Islamic Jesus*	297.2
Akyol, Mustafa. ★*Reopening Muslim Minds*	297.09
Al-Khalili, Jim. *The House of Wisdom*	509
Armstrong, Karen. *The Battle for God*	200
Armstrong, Karen. *A History of God*	202
Armstrong, Karen. *Jerusalem*	956.94
Armstrong, Karen. *Muhammad*	B
Aslan, Reza. ★*No God but God*	297
Baker, Deborah. *The Convert*	B
Ben Jelloun, Tahar. *Islam Explained*	297
Brooks, Geraldine. *Nine Parts of Desire*	305.48
Cook, M. A. *The Koran*	297.122
Curtis, Edward E. *Muslims in America*	305.6
Ernst, Carl W. *The Shambhala Guide to Sufism*	297.4
Eteraz, Ali. *Children of Dust*	B
Evanzz, Karl. *The Messenger*	B
Ghattas, Kim. *Black Wave*	955.05
Ghobash, Omar Saif. *Letters to a Young Muslim*	297.09
Glasse, Cyril. *The New Encyclopedia of Islam*	297.03
Gordon, Matthew. *Understanding Islam*	297
Grieve, Paul. *A Brief Guide to Islam*	297
Griswold, Eliza. *The Tenth Parallel*	297.2
Haleem, M. A. S. Abdel. ★*The Qur'an*	297.122
Harris, Sam. *Islam and the Future of Tolerance*	297.2
Husain, Ed. ★*The House of Islam*	297
Jall al-Dn Rm. *Rumi*	891
Kugle, Scott Alan. *Living Out Islam*	297
Levinsohn, Florence Hamlish. *Looking for Farrakhan*	B
Marozzi, Justin. *Islamic Empires*	909
Miles, Jack. *God in the Qur'an*	297.2
Moghul, Haroon. *How to Be a Muslim*	B
Nasr, Seyyed Hossein. *Islam*	297
Navai, Ramita. *City of Lies*	955
Nawaz, Zarqa. *Laughing All the Way to the Mosque*	791.45028
O'Kane, Bernard. *Treasures of Islam*	709.1
Power, Carla. *If the Oceans Were Ink*	B
Qureshi, Saqib Iqbal. *Being Muslim Today*	305.6
Ramadan, Tariq. ★*Introduction to Islam*	297
Renard, John. *The Handy Islam Answer Book*	297
Trofimov, Yaroslav. *The Siege of Mecca*	953.805
Wagner, Walter H. *Opening the Qur'an*	297.1
Wills, Garry. *What the Qur'an Meant and Why It Matters*	297.1
Zafar, Harris. *Demystifying Islam*	297
SPIRITUALITY AND RELIGION — ISLAM — HISTORY	
Armstrong, Karen. ★*Islam*	297
Hazleton, Lesley. *After the Prophet*	297.8
Hazleton, Lesley. *The First Muslim*	B
Jebara, Mohamad. ★*The Life of the Qur'an*	297.122
Jebara, Mohamad. *Muhammad, the World-Changer*	B
Kennedy, Hugh. ★*The Great Arab Conquests*	297.09
Khalili, Nasser D. *Islamic Art and Culture*	709.1
Lambert, Malcolm. *God's Armies*	956
Mattson, Ingrid. ★*The Story of the Qur'an*	297.122
Sebag-Montefiore, Simon. *Jerusalem*	956.94
SPIRITUALITY AND RELIGION — ISLAM — POLITICAL ASPECTS	
Abou El Fadl, Khaled. *The Great Theft*	297.09
Ali-Karamali, Sumbul. *Demystifying Shariah*	340.5
Bhutto, Benazir. *Reconciliation*	297.2
Blanford, Nicholas. *Warriors of God*	956.9204
Carranca, Adriana. *Soul by Soul*	230
Filkins, Dexter. *The Forever War*	956.7044
Nasr, Seyyed Vali Reza. *The Shia Revival*	297.8
Rushdie, Salman. *Joseph Anton*	B
SPIRITUALITY AND RELIGION — JUDAISM	
Armstrong, Karen. *The Battle for God*	200
Armstrong, Karen. *A History of God*	202

PUBLIC LIBRARY CORE COLLECTION: NONFICTION
Twentieth Edition

Armstrong, Karen. *Jerusalem*	956.94
Axelrod, Matt. *Your Guide to the Jewish Holidays*	296.4
Barton, John. *A History of the Bible*	220.09
Bernstein, Ellen. *Toward a Holy Ecology*	223
Bolsta, Hyla Shifra. *The Illuminated Kaddish*	296.4
Bronfman, Edgar M. *Why Be Jewish?*	296
Brous, Sharon. ★*The Amen Effect*	296.3
Carroll, James. *Constantine's Sword*	261
Diamant, Anita. *The Jewish Wedding Now*	296.4
Diamant, Anita. *Pitching My Tent*	296.7
Feiler, Bruce. *Walking the Bible*	915
Feldman, Deborah. *Exodus*	B
Feldman, Deborah. *Unorthodox*	B
Feldman, Noah. ★*To Be a Jew Today*	296.3
Frankl, Viktor E. *Yes to Life*	150.19
Freedman, H. ★*The Talmud*	296.1
Freedman, Samuel G. *Jew vs. Jew*	296
Goldman, Ari L. *Being Jewish*	296.4
Goodman, Martin. ★*A History of Judaism*	296.09
Greenstein, Edward L. *Job*	223
Grieve, Paul. *A Brief Guide to Islam*	297
Held, Shai. ★*Judaism Is About Love*	296.3
Horn, Dara. ★*People Love Dead Jews*	909
Isaacs, Ronald H. ★*Kosher Living*	296.7
Keinan, Tal. *God Is in the Crowd*	305.892
Kushner, Harold S. *When Bad Things Happen to Good People*	296.3
Kushner, Harold S. *Who Needs God*	296.7
Leibovitz, Liel. ★*How the Talmud Can Change Your Life*	296.1
Levine, Amy-Jill. *The Bible with and Without Jesus*	220.6
Pogrebin, Abigail. *My Jewish Year*	296.4
Reuben, Steven Carr. ★*Becoming Jewish*	296.7
Ricanati, Elizabeth. *Braided*	B
Rosten, Leo. *The New Joys of Yiddish*	422
Shulevitz, Judith. *The Sabbath World*	296.4
Telushkin, Joseph. *Jewish Wisdom*	296.3
Telushkin, Joseph. *Rebbe*	296.833
Wagner, Jordan Lee. *The Synagogue Survival Kit*	296.4
Wieseltier, Leon. *Kaddish*	296.4
Wray, T. J. *The Birth of Satan*	235

SPIRITUALITY AND RELIGION — JUDAISM — HISTORY

Ashton, Dianne. *Hanukkah in America*	296.4
Epstein, Lawrence J. *The Basic Beliefs of Judaism*	296.3
Garfinkel, Yosef. *In the Footsteps of King David*	933
Hoffman, Adina. *Sacred Trash*	296.09
Kirsch, Adam. *The Blessing and the Curse*	809
Kirsch, Adam. ★*The People and the Books*	809
Mandel, David. *Who's Who in the Jewish Bible*	B
Ruttenberg, Danya. *On Repentance and Repair*	202
Sarna, Jonathan D. ★*American Judaism*	296
Schama, Simon. ★*The Story of the Jews; Volume One*	909
Schama, Simon. ★*The Story of the Jews; Volume Two*	909
Schiffman, Lawrence H. *Reclaiming the Dead Sea Scrolls*	296.1
Sebag-Montefiore, Simon. *Jerusalem*	956.94
Weisman, Steven R. *The Chosen Wars*	296.0973

SPIRITUALITY AND RELIGION — JUDAISM — POLITICAL ASPECTS

Fersko, Diana. ★*We Need to Talk About Antisemitism*	305.892

SPIRITUALITY AND RELIGION — RELIGIOUS LEADERS

Armstrong, Karen. *Buddha*	B
Armstrong, Karen. *Muhammad*	B
Arrington, Leonard J. *Brigham Young*	B
Augustine. *Confessions*	B
Butcher, Carmen Acevedo. *Man of Blessing*	B
Dalai Lama. *Freedom in Exile*	B
Fredriksen, Paula. *Jesus of Nazareth, King of the Jews*	B
Hazleton, Lesley. *The First Muslim*	B
Iyer, Pico. *The Open Road*	B
Kushner, Harold S. *Overcoming Life's Disappointments*	296.7
Metaxas, Eric. *Martin Luther*	B
O'Connor, Garry. *Universal Father*	B
Tenzin Priyadarshi. *Running Toward Mystery*	B
Turner, John G. *Brigham Young, Pioneer Prophet*	B
Vallely, Paul. *Pope Francis*	B
Wacker, Grant. *America's Pastor*	B
Wills, Garry. *Saint Augustine*	B
Wilson, Derek. *Out of the Storm*	B

SPIRITUALITY AND RELIGION — RELIGIOUS TEXTS

Bolsta, Hyla Shifra. *The Illuminated Kaddish*	296.4
Grabbe, Lester L. *Faith and Fossils*	231.7
Greenstein, Edward L. *Job*	223
Murphy, Cullen. *The Word According to Eve*	220.8
Ruden, Sarah. *The Face of Water*	220.5

Spitz, Bob

★*The Beatles*	B
★*Dearie*	B
Led Zeppelin	782.42166
★*Reagan*	B

Spitzer, Michael

The Musical Human	780.9

A Splash of Soy. Lee, Lara	641.595
★*Splash!* Means, Howard B.	797.2
Splay Anthem. Mackey, Nathaniel	811
★*The Splendid and the Vile*. Larson, Erik	940.54
Split Decision. Ice-T	920
Split-Second Persuasion. Dutton, Kevin	153.8

Spofford, Tim

What the Children Told Us	150.92

Spong, John Shelby

Eternal Life	236

SPONTANEITY

Kerouac, Jack. *Book of Sketches, 1952-57*	818
★*Spook*. Roach, Mary	129

SPORTS

Afremow, James A. *The Champion's Mind*	796.01
Anderson, Christopher. *The Numbers Game*	796.334
Anderson, Sam. *Boom Town*	976.6
Aschwanden, Christie. *Good to Go*	617.1
Barnes, Katie. ★*Fair Play*	796.082
Bercovici, Jeff. *Play On*	613.7
Berkow, Ira. *How Life Imitates Sports*	070.4
Brown, Tim. ★*The Tao of the Backup Catcher*	796.357
Carlin, John. *Playing the Enemy*	968.06
Crouse, Karen. *Norwich*	796
Daley, Tom. *Coming up for Air*	B
Davis, Seth. *Getting to Us*	796.07
Easterbrook, Gregg. ★*The King of Sports*	796.332
Finn, Adharanand. *The Way of the Runner*	796.42
Gessner, David. *Ultimate Glory*	796.2
Gingrich, Dayne. *Pickleball Mindset*	796.34
Goldblatt, David. ★*The Age of Football*	796.334
Gracie, Rickson. *Breathe*	B
Hart, Matt. *Win at All Costs*	338.7
King, Billie Jean. ★*All In*	B
Knight, Molly. *The Best Team Money Can Buy*	796.357
Kohan, Rafi. *The Arena*	796.06
Kuper, Simon. *Soccernomics*	796.334
Laskas, Jeanne Marie. *Concussion*	617.5
Lunardi, Joe. ★*Bracketology*	796.323
Lundquist, Verne. *Play by Play*	B
McCormick, Brad. *Extreme Sports*	791.457
Neyer, Rob. *Power Ball*	796.357
Parker, Vergil R. *Pickleball 101*	796.34
Parry, John Weston. *The Burden of Sports*	796.01
Perron, Cam. ★*Comeback Season*	796.357
Pesca, Mike. *Upon Further Review*	796
Pippen, Scottie. *Unguarded*	B
Rapinoe, Megan. *One Life*	B
Reiter, Ben. *Astroball*	796.357
Rhoden, William C. *$40 Million Slaves*	796
Ripken, Bill. *State of Play*	796.357
Rotella, Robert J. *How Champions Think*	796.01
Sabathia, CC. *Till the End*	796.357
Samaha, Albert. *Never Ran, Never Will*	920
Schoenfeld, Bruce. ★*Game of Edges*	796.04
Serrano, Shea. *Basketball (and Other Things)*	796.323
Shipnuck, Alan. *Phil*	B
Shriver, Timothy P. *Fully Alive*	796.087
Sielski, Mike. *The Rise*	B
Simon, Rachel. *Pickleball for All*	796.34
Smith, Kenny. *Talk of Champions*	B
Sullivan, Matt. *Can't Knock the Hustle*	796.323
Thomas, Etan. *We Matter*	796.08
Thompson, Wright. *The Cost of These Dreams*	B
Villoro, Juan. *God Is Round*	796.334
Weiss, Eben. ★*The Ultimate Bicycle Owner's Manual*	796.6
Wertheim, L. Jon. *Glory Days*	796.09
Wertheim, L. Jon. *This Is Your Brain on Sports*	796.01

AUTHOR, TITLE, SERIES AND SUBJECT INDEX

Zimmerman, Paul. *Dr. Z*	B
SPORTS AGENTS	
Norton, Hughes. ★*Rainmaker*	796.352
SPORTS AND COMPETITION — BASEBALL	
Barra, Allen. ★*Yogi Berra*	B
Barry, Dan. *Bottom of the 33rd*	796.357
Bradlee, Ben. *The Kid*	B
Brown, Tim. ★*The Tao of the Backup Catcher*	796.357
Bryant, Howard. *The Last Hero*	B
Bryant, Howard. *Rickey*	B
Clavin, Thomas. *The DiMaggios*	920
Cohen, Rich. *The Chicago Cubs*	796.357
Cook, Kevin. *Ten Innings at Wrigley*	796.357
Cramer, Richard Ben. *Joe DiMaggio*	B
Creamer, Robert W. *Babe*	B
Creamer, Robert W. *Stengel*	796.357
Darling, Ron. *The Complete Game*	B
Diamond, Jared M. *Swing Kings*	796.357
Dykstra, Lenny. *House of Nails*	B
Eisenberg, John. *The Streak*	796.357
Epplin, Luke. *Our Team*	796.357
Feinstein, John. *Where Nobody Knows Your Name*	796.357
Formosa, Dan. *Baseball Field Guide*	796.357
Gehrig, Lou. *The Lost Memoir*	B
Geist, William. *Little League Confidential*	796.357
Goldberger, Paul. *Ballpark*	796.357
Halberstam, David. *Summer of '49*	796.357
Halberstam, David. *The Teammates*	B
Hample, Zack. *The Baseball*	796.357
Hernandez, Keith. *I'm Keith Hernandez*	B
Hirsch, James S. *Willie Mays*	B
Jamieson, David. *Mint Condition*	796.357
Jeter, Derek. *Jeter Unfiltered*	B
Kennedy, Kostya. *True*	B
Kenny, Brian. *Ahead of the Curve*	796.357
Kepner, Tyler. *K*	796.357
Kornhauser, Jacob. *The Cup of Coffee Club*	796.357
Kurkjian, Tim. *I'm Fascinated by Sacrifice Flies*	796.357
Kurlansky, Mark. *The Eastern Stars*	796.357
Law, Keith. *The Inside Game*	796.35764
Law, Keith. *Smart Baseball*	796.357
Leavy, Jane. *The Big Fella*	B
Leavy, Jane. *The Last Boy*	B
Leavy, Jane. *Sandy Koufax*	B
Lewis, Michael. ★*Moneyball*	796.357
Lindbergh, Ben. *The Only Rule Is That It Has to Work*	796.357
Maraniss, David. *Clemente*	B
Mays, Willie. *24*	B
Megdal, Howard. *The Baseball Talmud*	796.357
Montgomery, Patrick. *Baseball's Great Expectations*	796.357
Neyer, Rob. *Power Ball*	796.357
Nusbaum, Eric. *Stealing Home*	796.357
O'Brien, Keith. *Charlie Hustle*	796.357
Ortiz, David. *Papi*	B
Pappu, Sridhar. *The Year of the Pitcher*	920
Passan, Jeff. *The Arm*	796.3576
Pearlman, Jeff. *The Last Folk Hero*	B
Pennington, Bill. *Billy Martin*	B
Perron, Cam. ★*Comeback Season*	796.357
Pessah, Jon. *The Game*	796.357
Pessah, Jon. *Yogi*	B
Peta, Joe. *Trading Bases*	796.357
Posnanski, Joe. *The Baseball 100*	796.357
Posnanski, Joe. *The Soul of Baseball*	796.357
Posnanski, Joe. ★*Why We Love Baseball*	796.357
Rapoport, Ron. *Let's Play Two*	B
Rapp, David. *Tinker to Evers to Chance*	796.357
Reiter, Ben. *Astroball*	796.357
Ripken, Bill. *State of Play*	796.357
Rivera, Mariano. *The Closer*	B
Robinson, Ray. *Iron Horse*	B
Ruck, Rob. *Raceball*	796.357
Rushin, Steve. *The 34-Ton Bat*	796.357
Sabathia, CC. *Till the End*	796.357
Sawchik, Travis. *Big Data Baseball*	796.357
Shelton, Ron. *The Church of Baseball*	791.43
Simon, Scott. *My Cubs*	796.357
Snyder, Brad. *A Well-Paid Slave*	B
Stout, Glenn. *Fenway 1912*	796.357
Stump, Al. *Cobb*	B
Svrluga, Barry. *The Grind*	796.357
Torre, Joe. *The Yankee Years*	B
Turbow, Jason. *The Baseball Codes*	796.357
Turbow, Jason. *They Bled Blue*	796.357
Tye, Larry. *Satchel*	B
Wong, Stephen. *Game Worn*	796.357
Wong, Stephen. *Smithsonian Baseball*	796.357
Zminda, Don. *Double Plays and Double Crosses*	796.357
SPORTS AND COMPETITION — BASKETBALL	
Abdul-Jabbar, Kareem. *Coach Wooden and Me*	B
Abdurraqib, Hanif. ★*There's Always This Year*	796.323
Abrams, Jonathan P. D. *Boys Among Men*	796.323
Anthony, Carmelo. *Where Tomorrows Aren't Promised*	B
Babb, Valerie Melissa. *The Book of James*	B
Baylor, Elgin. *Hang Time*	B
Bella, Timothy. *Barkley*	B
Benedict, Jeff. *Lebron*	B
Blais, Madeleine. *In These Girls, Hope Is a Muscle*	796.323
Boeheim, Jim. *Bleeding Orange*	B
Bryant, Kobe. *The Mamba Mentality*	B
Chansky, Art. *Blue Blood II*	796.323
Chapman, Rex. ★*It's Hard for Me to Live with Me*	B
Colton, Larry. *Counting Coup*	796.323
Conroy, Pat. *My Losing Season*	B
Cornelius, Maria M. *The Final Season*	B
Davis, Seth. *Wooden*	B
Dohrmann, George. ★*Play Their Hearts Out*	796.323
Fagan, Kate. *All the Colors Came Out*	B
Feinstein, John. ★*The Back Roads to March*	796.323
Feinstein, John. ★*Last Dance*	796.323
Feinstein, John. ★*The Legends Club*	B
Feinstein, John. *A March to Madness*	796.323
Fury, Shawn. *Rise and Fire*	796.323
Glockner, Andy. *Chasing Perfection*	796.323
Goodman, Matthew. *The City Game*	796.323
Iguodala, Andre. *The Sixth Man*	B
Kriegel, Mark. *Pistol*	B
Lunardi, Joe. ★*Bracketology*	796.323
MacMullan, Jackie. ★*Basketball*	796.323
Malinowski, Erik. *Betaball*	796.323
Maraniss, Andrew. *Strong Inside*	B
McCallum, Jack. *Dream Team*	796.323
McCallum, Jack. *Golden Days*	796.323
Montville, Leigh. *Tall Men, Short Shorts*	796.323
O'Connor, Ian. *Coach K*	B
Oakley, Charles. *The Last Enforcer*	B
Pearlman, Jeff. ★*Three-Ring Circus*	796.323
Perkins, Kendrick. *The Education of Kendrick Perkins*	B
Pippen, Scottie. *Unguarded*	B
Powell, Michael. ★*Canyon Dreams*	796.323
Ravin, Idan. *The Hoops Whisperer*	796.323
Rosen, Charles. *Sugar*	B
Runstedtler, Theresa. *Black Ball*	796.323
Serrano, Shea. *Basketball (and Other Things)*	796.323
Sielski, Mike. *The Rise*	B
Simmons, Bill. *The Book of Basketball*	796.323
Skelton, Marc. *Pounding the Rock*	B
Smith, Kenny. *Talk of Champions*	B
Smith, Sam. *Hard Labor*	796.323
Streep, Abe. *Brothers on Three*	306.85
Sullivan, Matt. *Can't Knock the Hustle*	796.323
Summitt, Pat Head. *Sum It Up*	B
Weitzman, Yaron. *Tanking to the Top*	796.323
West, Jerry. *West by West*	B
Williams, Jay. *Life Is Not an Accident*	B
Windhorst, Brian. *Lebron, Inc.*	B
SPORTS AND COMPETITION — BOATING AND SAILING	
Sleight, Steve. *The Complete Sailing Manual*	797.1
SPORTS AND COMPETITION — BOXING	
Century, Douglas. *Barney Ross*	B
Coffin, Jaed. *Roughhouse Friday*	B
Eig, Jonathan. ★*Ali*	B
Gildea, William. *The Longest Fight*	B
Haygood, Wil. ★*Sweet Thunder*	B
Kimball, George. *Four Kings*	B
Kram, Mark. *Smokin' Joe*	B

PUBLIC LIBRARY CORE COLLECTION: NONFICTION
Twentieth Edition

Liebling, A. J. ★*The Sweet Science*	796.83
Montville, Leigh. *Sting Like a Bee*	B
Roberts, Randy. *Joe Louis*	B
Schaap, Jeremy. *Cinderella Man*	B
Stanton, Mike. ★*Unbeaten*	B
Stratton, W. K. *Floyd Patterson*	B
Tyson, Mike. *Iron Ambition*	B
Ward, Geoffrey C. *Unforgivable Blackness*	B

SPORTS AND COMPETITION — COACHES

Barra, Allen. ★*The Last Coach*	B
Boeheim, Jim. *Bleeding Orange*	B
Burke, Monte. *Saban*	796.332
Creamer, Robert W. *Stengel*	796.357
Davis, Seth. *Getting to Us*	796.07
Davis, Seth. *Wooden*	B
Feinstein, John. ★*The Legends Club*	B
Fleshman, Lauren. ★*Good for a Girl*	B
Harris, David. *The Genius*	B
O'Connor, Ian. *Belichick*	B
Ribowsky, Mark. *The Last Cowboy*	796.332
Ribowsky, Mark. *Shula*	B
Rotella, Robert J. *Golf Is Not a Game of Perfect*	796.352
Summitt, Pat Head. *Sum It Up*	B
Thompson, Wright. *The Cost of These Dreams*	B

SPORTS AND COMPETITION — EXTREME SPORTS

Bukreev, Anatolii Nikolaevich. *The Climb*	796.52
Coburn, Broughton. *Everest*	796.5
Cox, Lynne. *Swimming to Antarctica*	B
Fitzgerald, Matt. *Iron War*	796.42
Krakauer, Jon. ★*Into Thin Air*	796.52
McCormick, Brad. *Extreme Sports*	791.457
Moore, Colten. *Catching the Sky*	B
Mortimer, Gavin. *The Great Swim*	B
Nestor, James. *Deep*	797.2
Paulsen, Gary. *Winterdance*	B
Ralston, Aron. *Between a Rock and a Hard Place*	796.522
Roberts, David. *Limits of the Known*	B
Tabor, James M. *Blind Descent*	796.52
Taylor, Joseph E. *Pilgrims of the Vertical*	796.52

SPORTS AND COMPETITION — FANS

Serrano, Shea. *Basketball (and Other Things)*	796.323

SPORTS AND COMPETITION — FISHING

Burke, Monte. *Lords of the Fly*	799.124
Cermele, Joe. ★*The Total Fishing Manual*	799.1
Gierach, John. *All Fishermen Are Liars*	799.12
Gierach, John. *Dumb Luck and the Kindness of Strangers*	799.124
Gierach, John. *A Fly Rod of Your Own*	799.12
Messineo, Janet. *Casting into the Light*	799.1
Meyers, Charlie. *The Little Red Book of Fly Fishing*	799.12
Rosenbauer, Tom. *The Orvis Fly-Fishing Guide*	799.12
Schultz, Ken. *Ken Schultz's Essentials of Fishing*	799.1
Whitelaw, Ian. *The History of Fly-Fishing in Fifty Flies*	688.7

SPORTS AND COMPETITION — FOOTBALL

Anderson, Lars. *Carlisle vs. Army*	796.332
Barra, Allen. ★*The Last Coach*	B
Benedict, Jeff. *The Dynasty*	796.332
Benedict, Jeff. *The System*	796.332
Bennett, Michael. *Things That Make White People Uncomfortable*	305.896
Bissinger, H. G. ★*Friday Night Lights*	796.332
Bissinger, H. G. ★*The Mosquito Bowl*	796.332
Burke, Monte. *Saban*	796.332
Cole, Jason. *Elway*	B
Colt, George Howe. *The Game*	796.332
Dawidoff, Nicholas. *Collision Low Crossers*	796.332
Dunnavant, Keith. *Montana*	B
Easterbrook, Gregg. ★*The King of Sports*	796.332
Eatman, Nicholas. *Friday, Saturday, Sunday in Texas*	796.332
Edmundson, Mark. *Why Football Matters*	B
Eisenberg, John. *The League*	796.332
Fainaru-Wada, Mark. *League of Denial*	617.1
Feinstein, John. *Quarterback*	B
Foles, Nick. *Believe It*	B
Gaul, Gilbert M. *Billion-Dollar Ball*	796.332
Gwynne, S. C. *The Perfect Pass*	920
Harris, David. *The Genius*	B
Horrigan, Joe. *NFL Century*	796.332
Jaworksi, Ron. *The Games That Changed the Game*	796.332
Laskas, Jeanne Marie. *Concussion*	617.5
Lewis, Michael. *The Blind Side*	B
McIntire, Mike. *Champions Way*	796.043
Myers, Gary. *Brady vs. Manning*	B
Myers, Gary. *The Catch*	796.332
Namath, Joe Willie. ★*All the Way*	B
O'Connor, Ian. *Belichick*	B
Oriard, Michael. *Brand NFL*	796.332
Parcells, Bill. *Parcells*	B
Pearlman, Jeff. *Boys Will Be Boys*	796.332
Pearlman, Jeff. *Football for a Buck*	796.332
Pearlman, Jeff. *Gunslinger*	B
Pearlman, Jeff. *The Last Folk Hero*	B
Pearlman, Jeff. *Sweetness*	B
Price, S. L. *Playing Through the Whistle*	796.332
Ribowsky, Mark. *The Last Cowboy*	796.332
Ribowsky, Mark. *Shula*	B
Rice, Jerry. *America's Game*	796.332
Samaha, Albert. *Never Ran, Never Will*	920
Sando, Mike. *The Football 100*	796.332
Savage, Phil. *4th and Goal Every Day*	796.332
Spurrier, Steve. *Head Ball Coach*	B
Weinreb, Michael. *Season of Saturdays*	796.332
Wickersham, Seth. ★*It's Better to Be Feared*	796.332
Young, Steve. *QB*	B
Yousse, Bower. *Freddie Steinmark*	796.332

SPORTS AND COMPETITION — GAMBLING AND BETTING

Barbarisi, Daniel. *Dueling with Kings*	793.93
Goodman, Matthew. *The City Game*	796.323
Konnikova, Maria. *The Biggest Bluff*	795.412
Lang, Arne K. *Sports Betting and Bookmaking*	798.4010973
McManus, James. ★*Positively Fifth Street*	795.41
O'Brien, Keith. *Charlie Hustle*	796.357
Thorp, Edward O. *A Man for All Markets*	B
Walters, Billy. *Gambler*	796.092
Zminda, Don. *Double Plays and Double Crosses*	796.357

SPORTS AND COMPETITION — GAMES

Ashley, Maurice. *Move by Move*	158
Brady, Frank. *Endgame*	B
Brown, Nancy Marie. *Ivory Vikings*	736
Capelle, Philip B. ★*Play Your Best Straight Pool*	790
Chapin, Sasha. *All the Wrong Moves*	794.1092
Colt, George Howe. *The Game*	796.332
Harris, Blake J. *Console Wars*	338.7
Jacobs, A. J. *The Puzzler*	793.73
Kasparov, G. K. *Deep Thinking*	006.3
McCumber, David. *Playing off the Rail*	B
McManus, James. ★*Positively Fifth Street*	795.41
Miller, Megan. ★*The Ultimate Unofficial Encyclopedia for Minecrafters*	794.8
Orbanes, Philip. *The Game Makers*	338.7
Roeder, Oliver. *Seven Games*	794
Shankar, Shalini. *Beeline*	155.4

SPORTS AND COMPETITION — GENERAL

Afremow, James A. *The Champion's Mind*	796.01
Allred, Alexandra Powe. *When Women Stood*	796.082
Aschwanden, Christie. *Good to Go*	617.1
Bercovici, Jeff. *Play On*	613.7
Berger, Karen. *America's Great Hiking Trails*	796.510973
Brodeur, Michael Andor. ★*Swole*	155.3
Buck, Joe. *Lucky Bastard*	B
Canterbury, Dave. *Bushcraft 101*	613.6
Cardwell, Diane. *Rockaway*	B
Ericsson, K. Anders. *Peak*	153.9
Finnegan, William. *Barbarian Days*	B
Gessner, David. *Ultimate Glory*	796.2
Gingrich, Dayne. *Pickleball Mindset*	796.34
Graver, Dennis. *Scuba Diving*	797.2
Hayes, Bill. *Sweat*	613.7
Higdon, Hal. ★*Marathon*	796.42
Hinkson, Jim. *Lacrosse for Dummies*	796.34
Keflezighi, Meb. *Meb for Mortals*	796.4252
Kohan, Rafi. *The Arena*	796.06
Kohan, Rafi. ★*Trash Talk*	179
Krauzer, Steven M. *Kayaking*	797.1
Litman, Laken. *Strong Like a Woman*	796
Lundquist, Verne. *Play by Play*	B
Mackinnon, Al. *Epic Surf Breaks of the World*	797.32
Magill, Pete. *Build Your Running Body*	796.42

AUTHOR, TITLE, SERIES AND SUBJECT INDEX

Manzione, Gianmarc. *Pin Action*	B
McAfee, Richard. *Table Tennis*	796.34
McDougall, Christopher. *Natural Born Heroes*	940.53
Mullen, Michelle. *Bowling Fundamentals*	794.6
Parker, Vergil R. *Pickleball 101*	796.34
Parry, John Weston. *The Burden of Sports*	796.01
Pesca, Mike. *Upon Further Review*	796
Rhoden, William C. *$40 Million Slaves*	796
Ribowsky, Mark. *Howard Cosell*	070.449796
Romanov, Nicholas S. *The Running Revolution*	796.42
Rotella, Robert J. *How Champions Think*	796.01
Rountree, Sage. *The Athlete's Guide to Recovery*	617.1
Schoenfeld, Bruce. ★*Game of Edges*	796.04
Simon, Rachel. *Pickleball for All*	796.34
Stanley, Jessamyn. ★*Yoke*	613.7
Thomas, Etan. *We Matter*	796.08
Townsend, Chris. *The Backpacker's Handbook*	796.51
Walker, Sam. *The Captain Class*	796.07
Wall, Duncan. *The Ordinary Acrobat*	B
Wertheim, L. Jon. *This Is Your Brain on Sports*	796.01
Zimmerman, Paul. *Dr. Z*	B

SPORTS AND COMPETITION — GOLF

Bamberger, Michael. *The Second Life of Tiger Woods*	B
Benedict, Jeff. ★*Tiger Woods*	B
Callahan, Tom. *Arnie*	B
Carter, Iain. *Golf Wars*	796.352
Coyne, Tom. *A Course Called Scotland*	796.352
Feinstein, John. *The First Major*	796.352
Frost, Mark. *The Match*	796.352
Harig, Bob. *Drive*	796.352
Hiaasen, Carl. *The Downhill Lie*	B
Hogan, Ben. ★*Five Lessons*	796.352
Norton, Hughes. ★*Rainmaker*	796.352
Palmer, Arnold. *A Golfer's Life*	B
Rotella, Robert J. *Golf Is Not a Game of Perfect*	796.352
Shipnuck, Alan. *Phil*	B
Woods, Tiger. *The 1997 Masters*	B

SPORTS AND COMPETITION — HOCKEY

Branch, John. *Boy on Ice*	B
Coffey, Wayne R. ★*The Boys of Winter*	796.962
Eruzione, Mike. *The Making of a Miracle*	B
Gretzky, Wayne. *99*	B
Sasakamoose, Fred. *Call Me Indian*	B

SPORTS AND COMPETITION — HUNTING

Rinella, Steven. *American Buffalo*	599.64
Rinella, Steven. *The Complete Guide to Hunting, Butchering, and Cooking Wild Game*	799.2
Rinella, Steven. *The Complete Guide to Hunting, Butchering, and Cooking Wild Game; Volume 2*	799.2
Rinella, Steven. *Meat Eater*	B

SPORTS AND COMPETITION — INDIVIDUAL ATHLETE

Agassi, Andre. *Open*	B
Anthony, Carmelo. *Where Tomorrows Aren't Promised*	B
Babb, Valerie Melissa. *The Book of James*	B
Balf, Todd. *Major*	B
Barra, Allen. ★*Yogi Berra*	B
Bella, Timothy. *Barkley*	B
Blais, Madeleine. *Queen of the Court*	B
Bradlee, Ben. *The Kid*	B
Bryant, Howard. *The Last Hero*	B
Bryant, Howard. *Rickey*	B
Buford, Kate. *Native American Son*	B
Callahan, Tom. *Arnie*	B
Century, Douglas. *Barney Ross*	B
Clarey, Christopher. ★*The Master*	B
Cole, Jason. *Elway*	B
Cramer, Richard Ben. *Joe DiMaggio*	B
Crawford, Bill. ★*All American*	B
Creamer, Robert W. *Babe*	B
Darling, Ron. *The Complete Game*	B
Drape, Joe. *Black Maestro*	B
Dykstra, Lenny. *House of Nails*	B
Eisenberg, John. *The Streak*	796.357
Eruzione, Mike. *The Making of a Miracle*	B
Fleshman, Lauren. ★*Good for a Girl*	B
Franklin, Missy. *Relentless Spirit*	B
Hamilton, Tyler. *The Secret Race*	796.62
Harig, Bob. *Drive*	796.352
Haygood, Wil. ★*Sweet Thunder*	B
Hirsch, James S. *Willie Mays*	B
Jackson, Ted. ★*You Ought to Do a Story About Me*	B
Jacobs, Sally H. *Althea*	B
Kennedy, Kostya. *True*	B
King, Billie Jean. ★*All In*	B
Kornhauser, Jacob. *The Cup of Coffee Club*	796.357
Kriegel, Mark. *Pistol*	B
Leavy, Jane. *The Big Fella*	B
Leavy, Jane. *The Last Boy*	B
Leavy, Jane. *Sandy Koufax*	B
Maraniss, David. *Clemente*	B
Maraniss, David. ★*Path Lit by Lightning*	B
Moore, Colten. *Catching the Sky*	B
Muhammad, Ibtihaj. *Proud*	B
Namath, Joe Willie. ★*All the Way*	B
O'Brien, Keith. *Charlie Hustle*	796.357
Oakley, Charles. *The Last Enforcer*	B
Ortiz, David. *Papi*	B
Palmer, Arnold. *A Golfer's Life*	B
Pearlman, Jeff. *The Last Folk Hero*	B
Pippen, Scottie. *Unguarded*	B
Posnanski, Joe. *The Soul of Baseball*	796.357
Rapinoe, Megan. *One Life*	B
Rapoport, Ron. *Let's Play Two*	B
Rippon, Adam. *Beautiful on the Outside*	B
Roberts, Randy. *Joe Louis*	B
Robinson, Ray. *Iron Horse*	B
Rothenberg, Ben. *Naomi Osaka*	B
Schaap, Jeremy. *Cinderella Man*	B
Shipnuck, Alan. *Phil*	B
Stanton, Mike. ★*Unbeaten*	B
Stump, Al. *Cobb*	B
Thompson, Wright. *The Cost of These Dreams*	B
Tye, Larry. *Satchel*	B
Tyson, Mike. *Iron Ambition*	B
Ward, Geoffrey C. *Unforgivable Blackness*	B
Williams, Jay. *Life Is Not an Accident*	B

SPORTS AND COMPETITION — MARTIAL ARTS

Bennett, Alexander. *Kendo*	796.86
Chan, Jackie. *Never Grow Up*	B
Gracie, Rickson. *Breathe*	B
Lee, Shannon. *Be Water, My Friend*	796.8
Polly, Matthew. ★*Bruce Lee*	B
Wertheim, L. Jon. *Blood in the Cage*	796.815

SPORTS AND COMPETITION — MOUNTAINEERING

Bukreev, Anatolii Nikolaevich. *The Climb*	796.52
Burgman, John. *High Drama*	796.522
Coburn, Broughton. *Everest*	796.5
Cordes, Kelly. *The Tower*	796.522
Davis, Wade. *Into the Silence*	B
DiGiulian, Sasha. *Take the Lead*	B
Eichar, Donnie. *Dead Mountain*	914
Ellsworth, Scott. *The World Beneath Their Feet*	796.522
Hall, Andy. *Denali's Howl*	796.522
Honnold, Alex. *Alone on the Wall*	B
Isserman, Maurice. *Continental Divide*	796.52
Kaag, John J. *Hiking with Nietzsche*	193
Kimberley, Hannah. *A Woman's Place Is at the Top*	B
Krakauer, Jon. *Classic Krakauer*	814
Krakauer, Jon. *Into the Wild*	917.9804
Krakauer, Jon. ★*Into Thin Air*	796.52
Lowe, George. *Letters from Everest*	796.522
O'Brien, Vanessa. *To the Greatest Heights*	B
Roberts, David. *Limits of the Known*	B
Synnott, Mark. *The Third Pole*	796.522
Taylor, Joseph E. *Pilgrims of the Vertical*	796.52
Vasquez-Lavado, Silvia. *In the Shadow of the Mountain*	B
Zuckerman, Peter. ★*Buried in the Sky*	796.522

SPORTS AND COMPETITION — OLYMPIC SPORTS

Barr, John. *Start by Believing*	364.15
Brown, Daniel James. ★*The Boys in the Boat*	797.12
Checkoway, Julie. *The Three-Year Swim Club*	797.2
Coffey, Wayne R. ★*The Boys of Winter*	796.962
Crawford, Bill. ★*All American*	B
Goldblatt, David. *The Games*	796.4809
Halberstam, David. *The Amateurs*	B
Masters, Oksana. *The Hard Parts*	B

PUBLIC LIBRARY CORE COLLECTION: NONFICTION
Twentieth Edition

McCallum, Jack. *Dream Team*	796.323
Means, Howard B. ★*Splash!*	797.2
Muhammad, Ibtihaj. *Proud*	B
Rippon, Adam. *Beautiful on the Outside*	B
Shriver, Timothy P. *Fully Alive*	796.087
Vinton, Nathaniel. *The Fall Line*	796.93

SPORTS AND COMPETITION — RACING

Brooks, Amanda. *Run to the Finish*	613.7
Dixon, Matt. *The Well-Built Triathlete*	796.42
Friel, Joe. *The Triathlete's Training Bible*	796.42
Hawley, Sam. *Speed Duel*	796.72
McDougall, Christopher. *Running with Sherman*	636.1

SPORTS AND COMPETITION — RACING — BOATS

Brown, Daniel James. ★*The Boys in the Boat*	797.12
Gilder, Ginny. *Course Correction*	797.12
Halberstam, David. *The Amateurs*	B

SPORTS AND COMPETITION — RACING — CARS

Baime, A. J. ★*Go Like Hell*	796.7209
Bascomb, Neal. *Faster*	796.7209
Busbee, Jay. *Earnhardt Nation*	B
DeBord, Matthew. *Return to Glory*	338.4

SPORTS AND COMPETITION — RACING — CYCLING

Balf, Todd. *Major*	B
Bambrick, Yvonne. *The Urban Cycling Survival Guide*	796.6
De Vise, Daniel. *The Comeback*	B
Hamilton, Tyler. *The Secret Race*	796.62
Kranish, Michael. *The World's Fastest Man*	B
Leonard, Max. *Lanterne Rouge*	796.6
Petersen, Grant. *Just Ride*	796.6
Rosen, Jody. *Two Wheels Good*	629.227
Weiss, Eben. ★*The Ultimate Bicycle Owner's Manual*	796.6

SPORTS AND COMPETITION — RACING — DOGS

Pace, Kristin Knight. *This Much Country*	B
Paulsen, Gary. *Winterdance*	B

SPORTS AND COMPETITION — RACING — HORSES

Askwith, Richard. *Unbreakable*	B
Drape, Joe. *American Pharoah*	798.40092
Drape, Joe. *Black Maestro*	B
Hillenbrand, Laura. ★*Seabiscuit*	798.4
Ours, Dorothy. *Man O' War*	798.400929
Prior-Palmer, Lara. *Rough Magic*	798.4

SPORTS AND COMPETITION — RACING — TRACK AND FIELD

Alvarez, Noe. *Spirit Run*	796.42
Engle, Charlie. *Running Man*	B
Finn, Adharanand. *The Rise of the Ultra Runners*	B
Finn, Adharanand. *The Way of the Runner*	796.42
Futterman, Matthew. *Running to the Edge*	796.42071
Hamilton, Duncan. *For the Glory*	B
Hart, Matt. *Win at All Costs*	338.7
Heminsley, Alexandra. *Running Like a Girl*	B
Inman, Matthew. *The Terrible and Wonderful Reasons Why I Run Long Distances*	741.5
Keflezighi, Meb. *26 Marathons*	B
McDougall, Christopher. ★*Born to Run*	796.42
Mertens, Maggie. *Better Faster Farther*	796.42
Montillo, Roseanne. *Fire on the Track*	B
Murakami, Haruki. *What I Talk About When I Talk About Running*	B
Nolan, Ali. *Master the Marathon*	796.42
Shorter, Frank. *My Marathon*	796.42
Wade, Becky. *Run the World*	796.42

SPORTS AND COMPETITION — RIVALRY

Chansky, Art. *Blue Blood II*	796.323
Feinstein, John. ★*The Legends Club*	B
Fisher, Marshall Jon. *A Terrible Splendor*	796.342
Howard, Johnette. *The Rivals*	B

SPORTS AND COMPETITION — RUGBY

Carlin, John. *Playing the Enemy*	968.06

SPORTS AND COMPETITION — SOCCER

Abbot, Sebastian. *The Away Game*	796.334
Anderson, Christopher. *The Numbers Game*	796.334
Bass, Amy. *One Goal*	796.334
Bennett, Roger. *Men in Blazers Present Encyclopedia Blazertannica*	796.334
Bensinger, Ken. ★*Red Card*	796.334
Clarke, Gemma. *Soccerwomen*	796.334
Conn, David. *The Fall of the House of FIFA*	796.334
Cox, Michael. *Zonal Marking*	796
Dohrmann, George. *Switching Fields*	796.334
Galeano, Eduardo. *Soccer in Sun and Shadow*	796.334
Goldblatt, David. ★*The Age of Football*	796.334
Honigstein, Raphael. *DAS Reboot*	796.334
Hopcraft, Arthur. *The Football Man*	796.334
Kirschbaum, Erik. *Soccer Without Borders*	B
Knight, Molly. *The Best Team Money Can Buy*	796.357
Kuper, Simon. *Soccernomics*	796.334
Lloyd, Carli. *When Nobody Was Watching*	B
Oxenham, Gwendolyn. *Under the Lights and in the Dark*	796.334
Papenfuss, Mary. *American Huckster*	B
Rapinoe, Megan. *One Life*	B
Rogers, Robbie. *Coming Out to Play*	B
St. John, Warren. *Outcasts United*	B
Vecsey, George. *Eight World Cups*	796.334
Villoro, Juan. *God Is Round*	796.334
Wahl, Grant. ★*Masters of Modern Soccer*	796.334
Wambach, Abby. *Forward*	B

SPORTS AND COMPETITION — SPORTS HISTORY

Barnes, Katie. ★*Fair Play*	796.082
Barry, Dan. *Bottom of the 33rd*	796.357
Berkow, Ira. *How Life Imitates Sports*	070.4
Brown, Daniel James. ★*The Boys in the Boat*	797.12
Buckland, Gail. *Who Shot Sports*	779
Cook, Kevin. *Ten Innings at Wrigley*	796.357
Cox, Michael. *Zonal Marking*	796
Eisenberg, John. *The League*	796.332
Eisenberg, John. *The Streak*	796.357
Epplin, Luke. *Our Team*	796.357
Feinstein, John. *A March to Madness*	796.323
Gehrig, Lou. *The Lost Memoir*	B
Hopcraft, Arthur. *The Football Man*	796.334
Horrigan, Joe. *NFL Century*	796.332
Isserman, Maurice. *Continental Divide*	796.52
Jaworski, Ron. *The Games That Changed the Game*	796.332
Karnazes, Dean. *The Legend of Marathon*	796.42
Kranish, Michael. *The World's Fastest Man*	B
Lewis, Michael. *The Blind Side*	B
Megdal, Howard. *The Baseball Talmud*	796.357
Montville, Leigh. *Tall Men, Short Shorts*	796.323
Nusbaum, Eric. *Stealing Home*	796.357
Pearlman, Jeff. ★*Three-Ring Circus*	796.323
Posnanski, Joe. ★*Why We Love Baseball*	796.357
Rapp, David. *Tinker to Evers to Chance*	796.357
Rice, Jerry. *America's Game*	796.332
Rosen, Charles. *Sugar*	B
Runstedtler, Theresa. *Black Ball*	796.323
Simon, Rachel. *Pickleball for All*	796.34
Smith, Sam. *Hard Labor*	796.323
Tsui, Bonnie. *Why We Swim*	797.2
Vinton, Nathaniel. *The Fall Line*	796.93
Wertheim, L. Jon. *Glory Days*	796.09
Wickersham, Seth. ★*It's Better to Be Feared*	796.332
Youssé, Bower. *Freddie Steinmark*	796.332
Zminda, Don. *Double Plays and Double Crosses*	796.357

SPORTS AND COMPETITION — SWIMMING AND DIVING

Checkoway, Julie. *The Three-Year Swim Club*	797.2
Cox, Lynne. *Swimming to Antarctica*	B
Daley, Tom. *Coming up for Air*	B
Means, Howard B. ★*Splash!*	797.2
Mortimer, Gavin. *The Great Swim*	B
Nyad, Diana. *Find a Way*	B
Tsui, Bonnie. *Why We Swim*	797.2

SPORTS AND COMPETITION — TEAMS

Benedict, Jeff. *The Dynasty*	796.332
Bissinger, H. G. ★*Friday Night Lights*	796.332
Blais, Madeleine. *In These Girls, Hope Is a Muscle*	796.323
Carlin, John. *Playing the Enemy*	968.06
Coffey, Wayne R. ★*The Boys of Winter*	796.962
Cohen, Rich. *The Chicago Cubs*	796.357
Colton, Larry. *Counting Coup*	796.323
Davis, Seth. *Wooden*	B
Eatman, Nicholas. *Friday, Saturday, Sunday in Texas*	796.332
Halberstam, David. *Summer of '49*	796.357
Halberstam, David. *The Teammates*	B
Pearlman, Jeff. *Boys Will Be Boys*	796.332
Price, S. L. *Playing Through the Whistle*	796.332
Reiter, Ben. *Astroball*	796.357
Simon, Scott. *My Cubs*	796.357
Streep, Abe. *Brothers on Three*	306.85

AUTHOR, TITLE, SERIES AND SUBJECT INDEX

Wickersham, Seth. ★*It's Better to Be Feared* — 796.332
SPORTS AND COMPETITION — TENNIS
  Agassi, Andre. *Open* — B
  Blais, Madeleine. *Queen of the Court* — B
  Clarey, Christopher. ★*The Master* — B
  Fisher, Marshall Jon. *A Terrible Splendor* — 796.342
  Gallwey, W. Timothy. ★*The Inner Game of Tennis* — 796.342
  Howard, Johnette. *The Rivals* — B
  Jacobs, Sally H. *Althea* — B
  King, Billie Jean. ★*All In* — B
  McPhee, John. *Levels of the Game* — 796.34
  Phillips, Rowan Ricardo. *The Circuit* — 796.342
  Rothenberg, Ben. *Naomi Osaka* — B
  Sharapova, Maria. *Unstoppable* — B
  Williams, Richard. *Black and White* — B
SPORTS AND COMPETITION — WRESTLING
  Levi, Heather. *The World of Lucha Libre* — 796.812
  Patterson, Pat. *Accepted* — B
SPORTS AND RECREATION — ATHLETES
  Robinson, Jackie. *I Never Had It Made* — B
  Santiago, Wilfred. *"21"* — 741.5
SPORTS AND RECREATION — BASEBALL
  Robinson, Jackie. *I Never Had It Made* — B
  Santiago, Wilfred. *"21"* — 741.5
SPORTS AND RECREATION — GAMES, PUZZLES, AND PLAY
  Ho, Oliver. *The Ultimate Book of Family Card Games* — 795.4
SPORTS AND RECREATION — GENERAL
  Iggulden, Conn. *The Double Dangerous Book for Boys* — 031.02
SPORTS AND RECREATION — WRESTLING
  Fenn, Lisa. *Carry On* — B
SPORTS AND RECREATION — YOGA
  Bondy, Dianne. *Yoga Where You Are* — 613.7
  Fishman, Loren. *Yoga for Arthritis* — 616.7
  Lasater, Judith. *Yoga Myths* — 613.7
SPORTS AND STATE
  Goldblatt, David. *The Games* — 796.4809
SPORTS BETTING
  Frost, Mark. *The Match* — 796.352
  Goodman, Matthew. *The City Game* — 796.323
  Lang, Arne K. *Sports Betting and Bookmaking* — 798.4010973
  O'Brien, Keith. *Charlie Hustle* — 796.357
  Walters, Billy. *Gambler* — 796.092
  Zminda, Don. *Double Plays and Double Crosses* — 796.357
Sports Betting and Bookmaking. Lang, Arne K. — 798.4010973
SPORTS CARDS
  Jamieson, David. *Mint Condition* — 796.357
SPORTS CARS
  Baime, A. J. ★*Go Like Hell* — 796.7209
SPORTS CORRUPTION
  Assael, Shaun. *The Murder of Sonny Liston* — B
  Barr, John. *Start by Believing* — 364.15
  Benedict, Jeff. *The System* — 796.332
  Bensinger, Ken. ★*Red Card* — 796.334
  Gaul, Gilbert M. *Billion-Dollar Ball* — 796.332
  Ours, Dorothy. *Man O' War* — 798.400929
  Papenfuss, Mary. *American Huckster* — B
  Rosen, Charles. *Sugar* — B
  Williams, Jay. *Life Is Not an Accident* — B
  Zminda, Don. *Double Plays and Double Crosses* — 796.357
SPORTS COVER-UPS
  Zminda, Don. *Double Plays and Double Crosses* — 796.357
SPORTS EQUIPMENT INDUSTRY AND TRADE
  Hart, Matt. *Win at All Costs* — 338.7
SPORTS FACILITIES
  Kohan, Rafi. *The Arena* — 796.06
SPORTS FILMS
  Shelton, Ron. *The Church of Baseball* — 791.43
SPORTS HISTORY
  Berkow, Ira. *How Life Imitates Sports* — 070.4
  Blais, Madeleine. *Queen of the Court* — B
  Brown, Daniel James. ★*The Boys in the Boat* — 797.12
  Cox, Michael. *Zonal Marking* — 796
  Epplin, Luke. *Our Team* — 796.357
  Goldblatt, David. *The Games* — 796.4809
  Mertens, Maggie. *Better Faster Farther* — 796.42
  Pennington, Bill. *Billy Martin* — B
  Posnanski, Joe. ★*Why We Love Baseball* — 796.357
  Ribowsky, Mark. *Howard Cosell* — 070.449796

Runstedtler, Theresa. *Black Ball* — 796.323
Simon, Rachel. *Pickleball for All* — 796.34
Wertheim, L. Jon. *Glory Days* — 796.09
SPORTS INJURIES
  Aschwanden, Christie. *Good to Go* — 617.1
  Fainaru-Wada, Mark. *League of Denial* — 617.1
  Laskas, Jeanne Marie. *Concussion* — 617.5
  Montgomery, Patrick. *Baseball's Great Expectations* — 796.357
  Passan, Jeff. *The Arm* — 796.3576
  Rountree, Sage. *The Athlete's Guide to Recovery* — 617.1
SPORTS JOURNALISM
  Barnes, Katie. ★*Fair Play* — 796.082
  Ebersol, Dick. *From Saturday Night to Sunday Night* — B
  McPhee, John. *Levels of the Game* — 796.34
SPORTS MEDICINE
  Aschwanden, Christie. *Good to Go* — 617.1
  Fainaru-Wada, Mark. *League of Denial* — 617.1
  Laskas, Jeanne Marie. *Concussion* — 617.5
  Rountree, Sage. *The Athlete's Guide to Recovery* — 617.1
SPORTS ORGANIZATIONS
  Cox, Michael. *Zonal Marking* — 796
  Horrigan, Joe. *NFL Century* — 796.332
  Rice, Jerry. *America's Game* — 796.332
  Simmons, Bill. *The Book of Basketball* — 796.323
SPORTS RIVALRY
  Chansky, Art. *Blue Blood II* — 796.323
  Feinstein, John. ★*The Legends Club* — B
  Howard, Johnette. *The Rivals* — B
  Kohan, Rafi. ★*Trash Talk* — 179
  Kram, Mark. *Smokin' Joe* — B
  Myers, Gary. *Brady vs. Manning* — B
  Schaap, Jeremy. *Cinderella Man* — B
SPORTS SCIENCES
  Bercovici, Jeff. *Play On* — 613.7
SPORTS SPECTATORS
  Parry, John Weston. *The Burden of Sports* — 796.01
SPORTS TEAM OWNERS
  Auletta, Ken. *Media Man* — B
  Eisenberg, John. *The League* — 796.332
SPORTS TEAMS
  Brown, Daniel James. ★*The Boys in the Boat* — 797.12
  Walker, Sam. *The Captain Class* — 796.07
SPORTS TOURNAMENTS
  Carter, Iain. *Golf Wars* — 796.352
SPORTS UNIFORMS
  Wong, Stephen. *Game Worn* — 796.357
SPORTSCASTERS
  Buck, Joe. *Lucky Bastard* — B
  Kurkjian, Tim. *I'm Fascinated by Sacrifice Flies* — 796.357
  Lundquist, Verne. *Play by Play* — B
  Ribowsky, Mark. *Howard Cosell* — 070.449796
  Saunders, John. *Playing Hurt* — B
  Smith, Kenny. *Talk of Champions* — B
  Walton, Bill. *Back from the Dead* — B
SPORTSCASTING
  Lundquist, Verne. *Play by Play* — B
SPORTSMANSHIP
  Kohan, Rafi. ★*Trash Talk* — 179
  Walker, Sam. *The Captain Class* — 796.07
SPORTSWRITERS
  Berkow, Ira. *How Life Imitates Sports* — 070.4
  Hill, Jemele. *Uphill* — B
  Montville, Leigh. *Tall Men, Short Shorts* — 796.323
  Zimmerman, Paul. *Dr. Z* — B
Spoto, Donald
  The Dark Side of Genius — B
  High Society — B
  Joan — B
SPOUSES OF ALCOHOLICS
  Buhle, Kathleen. *If We Break* — B
SPOUSES OF CLERGY
  King, Coretta Scott. ★*My Life, My Love, My Legacy* — B
SPRAGUE, KATE CHASE, 1840-1899
  Oller, John. *American Queen* — B
SPRAGUE, WILLIAM, 1830-1915
  Oller, John. *American Queen* — B
Spratford, Becky Siegel
  The Readers' Advisory Guide to Horror — 025.5

PUBLIC LIBRARY CORE COLLECTION: NONFICTION
Twentieth Edition

SPREAD SPECTRUM COMMUNICATIONS
   Rhodes, Richard. *Hedy's Folly* — B
   Shearer, Stephen Michael. *Beautiful* — B
SPRING
   Knausgaard, Karl Ove. *Spring* — B
Spring. Knausgaard, Karl Ove — B
Springer Mountain. Williams, Wyatt — 394.1
Springfield Confidential. Reiss, Mike — 791.45
Springsteen, Bruce
   ★*Born to Run* — B
SPRINGSTEEN, BRUCE
   Carlin, Peter Ames. *Bruce* — B
   Springsteen, Bruce. ★*Born to Run* — B
   Zanes, Warren. *Deliver Me from Nowhere* — 782.42164
Sprinkle, Timothy
   Lost and Stranded — 613.6
The Sprinkles Baking Book. Nelson, Candace — 641.81
Sprout Lands. Logan, William Bryant — 582.16
The Sprouted Kitchen. Forte, Sara — 641.3
★*Spruce*. Brown, Amanda — 747
Spruill, Marjorie Julian
   Divided We Stand — 305.42
Spurling, Hilary
   Anthony Powell — B
   Matisse the Master — B
Spurrier, Steve
   Head Ball Coach — B
SPURRIER, STEVE, 1945-
   Spurrier, Steve. *Head Ball Coach* — B
A Spy Among Friends. Macintyre, Ben — B
★*The Spy and the Traitor*. Macintyre, Ben — B
A Spy in Plain Sight. Wiehl, Lis W. — 327.1247
A Spy Named Orphan. Philipps, Roland — B
SPY PLANES
   Sherman, Casey. *Above and Beyond* — 973.922092
The Spy Who Knew Too Much. Blum, Howard — 327.12
The Spy Who Loved. Mulley, Clare — B
Spying on the South. Horwitz, Tony — 917
Spying on Whales. Pyenson, Nick — 599.5
The Spymaster of Baghdad. Coker, Margaret — 956.7044
The Spymasters. Whipple, Chris — 920
SQUANTO
   Whittock, Martyn. *Mayflower Lives* — 974.4
Square, Vicki
   The Knitter's Companion — 746.432
SQUATTER FAMILIES
   Roy, Saumya. *Castaway Mountain* — 363.72
Squeezed. Quart, Alissa — 305.5
Squirrel Hill. Oppenheimer, Mark — 364.152
SRI LANKA
   Deraniyagala, Sonali. *Wave* — B
   Mohan, Rohini. *The Seasons of Trouble* — 954.9303
   Subramanian, Sammanth. *This Divided Island* — 954.9303
SRI LANKAN PEOPLE
   Subramanian, Sammanth. *This Divided Island* — 954.9303
Srinivasan, Amia
   The Right to Sex — 305.42
St. John, Warren
   Outcasts United — B
ST. LOUIS, MISSOURI
   Grant, Gail Milissa. *At the Elbows of My Elders* — B
St. Petersburg. Miles, Jonathan — 947
ST. PETERSBURG, RUSSIA
   Miles, Jonathan. *St. Petersburg* — 947
   Moynahan, Brian. *Leningrad* — 780.92
   Rappaport, Helen. *Caught in the Revolution* — 355.00947
   Reid, Anna. *Leningrad* — 940.54
STABBING VICTIMS
   Gerard, Sarah. *Carrie Carolyn Coco* — 364.152
STADIUMS
   Goldberger, Paul. *Ballpark* — 796.357
   Kohan, Rafi. *The Arena* — 796.06
The **Stafford** Little lectures [Series]. Einstein, Albert — 530.11
STAFFS (STICKS, CANES, ETC.)
   Jones, Andrew. *Stickmaking Handbook* — 736
Stag's Leap. Olds, Sharon — 811
STAGE CRAFT
   Gillette, J. Michael. *Theatrical Design and Production* — 792.02

Stage Designers in Early Twentieth-Century America. Essin, Christin — 792.02
STAGE LIGHTING
   Gillette, J. Michael. *Designing with Light* — 792
STAGE MANAGEMENT
   Gillette, J. Michael. *Theatrical Design and Production* — 792.02
STAGECOACH ROBBERIES
   Boessenecker, John. *Gentleman Bandit* — B
STAGED DEATHS
   Katin, Miriam. *We Are on Our Own* — 741.5
Stahl, Jerry
   Nein, Nein, Nein! — B
STAHL, JERRY
   Stahl, Jerry. *Nein, Nein, Nein!* — B
Stahr, Celia
   Frida in America — B
Stahr, Walter
   Seward — B
   ★*Stanton* — B
Stained Glass Basics. Rich, Chris — 748.5
Staiti, Paul J.
   Of Arms and Artists — B
Stakes Is High. Smith, Mychal Denzel — 973.933
Stalin. Khlevniuk, Oleg V. — B
Stalin. Kotkin, Stephen — B
Stalin. Kotkin, Stephen — B
Stalin. Radzinskii, Edvard — 947.084
Stalin. Sebag-Montefiore, Simon — B
Stalin. Suny, Ronald Grigor — B
Stalin's Daughter. Sullivan, Rosemary — B
Stalin's War. McMeekin, Sean — 940.53
STALIN, JOSEPH, 1879-1953
   Beschloss, Michael R. *The Conquerors* — 940.53
   Gessen, Masha. *Never Remember* — 365
   Gordin, Michael D. *Red Cloud at Dawn* — 355.02
   Groom, Winston. *The Allies* — 940.5309
   Hochschild, Adam. *The Unquiet Ghost* — 947.084
   Khlevniuk, Oleg V. *Stalin* — B
   Kotkin, Stephen. *Stalin* — B
   Kotkin, Stephen. *Stalin* — B
   McMeekin, Sean. *Stalin's War* — 940.53
   Medvedev, Roy Aleksandrovich. *Let History Judge* — 947.084
   Meltzer, Brad. ★*The Nazi Conspiracy* — 940.53
   Preston, Diana. *Eight Days at Yalta* — 940.53
   Radzinskii, Edvard. *Stalin* — 947.084
   Rees, Laurence. *Hitler and Stalin* — 940.53
   Sebag-Montefiore, Simon. *Stalin* — B
   Sebag-Montefiore, Simon. *Young Stalin* — B
   Snyder, Timothy. ★*Bloodlands* — 940.54
   Sullivan, Rosemary. *Stalin's Daughter* — B
   Suny, Ronald Grigor. *Stalin* — B
   Taubman, William. *Khrushchev* — B
Stalingrad. Beevor, Antony — 940.54
STALINGRAD, BATTLE OF, 1942-1943
   Beevor, Antony. *Stalingrad* — 940.54
   MacGregor, Iain. *The Lighthouse of Stalingrad* — 940.54
STALINISM
   Figes, Orlando. ★*The Whisperers* — 306.850947
   Gessen, Masha. *Never Remember* — 365
   Lankov, A. N. *The Real North Korea* — 951.9304
   Sebag-Montefiore, Simon. *Stalin* — B
STALKERS
   Freitas, Donna. *Consent* — 364.158092
   Goldberg, Carrie. *Nobody's Victim* — 345.73
STAMBERG, SUSAN, 1938-
   Napoli, Lisa. *Susan, Linda, Nina & Cokie* — 920
Stamos, John
   If You Would Have Told Me — B
STAMOS, JOHN, 1963-
   Stamos, John. *If You Would Have Told Me* — B
STAMP COLLECTING
   Barron, James. *The One-Cent Magenta* — 769.569
Stamp Stencil Paint. Joyce, Anna — 745.7
★*Stamped from the Beginning*. Kendi, Ibram X. — 305.8
Stampede. Castner, Brian — 971.9
Stamper, Kory
   Word by Word — 413.028
Stan Lee's How to Draw Comics. Lee, Stan — 741.5
Stand by Me. Applebaum, Allison — 649.8

AUTHOR, TITLE, SERIES AND SUBJECT INDEX

STAND-UP COMEDIANS
   Gulman, Gary. *Misfit* — B
   Levy, Shawn. ★*In on the Joke* — 792.7
   Martin, Steve. *Number One Is Walking* — B
   Nesteroff, Kliph. *The Comedians* — 792.7
   Seinfeld, Jerry. *Is This Anything?* — 818
STAND-UP COMEDY
   Hart, Kevin. *I Can't Make This Up* — B
   Martin, Steve. *Number One Is Walking* — B
   Nesteroff, Kliph. *The Comedians* — 792.7
   Rosenfield, Stephen. *Mastering Stand-Up* — 792.7
   Seinfeld, Jerry. *Is This Anything?* — 818
   Shales, Tom. *Live from New York* — 791.45
   Smith, Chris. *The Daily Show (the Book)* — 791.45
   Wasson, Sam. ★*Improv Nation* — 792.02
Standage, Tom
   A Brief History of Motion — 388
   An Edible History of Humanity — 394.1
   A History of the World in 6 Glasses — 394.1
STANDARDIZED TESTS
   Murdoch, Stephen. *IQ* — 153.9
Standefer, Katherine E.
   Lightning Flowers — B
STANDEFER, KATHERINE E., 1985-
   Standefer, Katherine E. *Lightning Flowers* — B
Standiford, Les
   ★*Battle for the Big Top* — 791.3
   Bringing Adam Home — 364.15
***Standing** My Ground.* Dunn, Harry — B
STANDISH, MYLES, 1584?-1656
   Whittock, Martyn. *Mayflower Lives* — 974.4
***Standoff.** Thompson, Jamie* — 364.152
Stanfield, Lesley
   100 Flowers to Knit & Crochet — 746.43
Stanford, Frank
   What About This — 811
STANFORD, JANE LATHROP, 1828-1905
   White, Richard. *Who Killed Jane Stanford?* — 364.152
Stanger, Ben
   From One Cell — 571.6
Stangneth, Bettina
   Eichmann Before Jerusalem — B
Staniforth, Nate
   Here Is Real Magic — B
STANIFORTH, NATE
   Staniforth, Nate. *Here Is Real Magic* — B
Stanislaus, Grace C.
   Instill & Inspire — 704.03
*The **Stanislavski** System.* Moore, Sonia — 792
Stanislavsky, Konstantin
   An Actor's Work — 792.02
★***Stanley** Decks.* Toht, David — 690
***Stanley** Kubrick and Me.* D'Alessandro, Emilio — 791.4302
Stanley, Amy
   Stranger in the Shogun's City — B
Stanley, Bob
   Let's Do It — 781.64
   ★*The Story of the Bee Gees* — 782.42164
Stanley, Brian
   Christianity in the Twentieth Century — 270.8
Stanley, Jason
   How Fascism Works — 321.9
Stanley, Jessamyn
   Every Body Yoga — 613.7
   ★*Yoke* — 613.7
Stanley, Mary J.
   Managing Library Employees — 023
Stanley, Matthew
   Einstein's War — 530
Stanley, Paul
   Backstage Pass — B
   Face the Music — B
STANLEY, PAUL
   Stanley, Paul. *Backstage Pass* — B
   Stanley, Paul. *Face the Music* — B
Stanley, Thomas J.
   The Next Millionaire Next Door — 332.024
★***Stanton.** Stahr, Walter* — B

Stanton, Brandon
   Humans — 779
Stanton, Doug
   12 Strong — 958.104
   In Harm's Way — 940.54
   The Odyssey of Echo Company — 959.704
STANTON, EDWIN M. (EDWIN MCMASTERS), 1814-1869
   Marvel, William. *Lincoln's Autocrat* — B
   Stahr, Walter. ★*Stanton* — B
STANTON, ELIZABETH CADY, 1815-1902
   Ginzberg, Lori D. *Elizabeth Cady Stanton* — B
Stanton, Mike
   ★*Unbeaten* — B
STANWYCK, BARBARA, 1907-1990
   Wilson, Victoria. *A Life of Barbara Stanwyck* — B
STAPLES, MAVIS
   Kot, Greg. *I'll Take You There* — B
***Star.** Biskind, Peter* — B
*The **Star** Machine.* Basinger, Jeanine — 384
STAR TREK FILMS
   Britt, Ryan. *Phasers on Stun!* — 791.45
   Gross, Edward. *The Fifty Year Mission* — 791.45
STAR WARS FILMS
   Barr, Patricia. *Ultimate Star Wars* — 791.43
   Jameson, A. D. *I Find Your Lack of Faith Disturbing* — 791.43
   Jones, Brian Jay. *George Lucas* — B
***Starbucked.** Clark, Taylor* — 338
Stargardt, Nicholas
   The German War — 940.53
***Staring** At the Sun.* Yalom, Irvin D. — 155.9
Stark, Lizzie
   ★*Egg* — 641.3
Stark, Peter
   Astoria — 979.5
   Young Washington — B
Starkey, David
   Six Wives — 942.05
Starks, Glenn L.
   Thurgood Marshall — B
***Starkweather.** MacLean, Harry N.* — 364.152
STARKWEATHER, CHARLES RAYMOND, 1938-1959
   MacLean, Harry N. *Starkweather* — 364.152
STARLINGS
   Haupt, Lyanda Lynn. *Mozart's Starling* — B
STARR, RINGO, 1940-
   Brown, Craig. *150 Glimpses of the Beatles* — 920
   Doggett, Peter. *You Never Give Me Your Money* — B
***Starry** Messenger.* Tyson, Neil deGrasse — 901
STARS
   Ridpath, Ian. *Stars & Planets* — 520
   Shore, Linda. *The Total Skywatcher's Manual* — 523
   Tirion, Wil. *The Cambridge Star Atlas* — 523.8
   Tyson, Neil deGrasse. *To Infinity and Beyond* — 520
   Tyson, Neil deGrasse. *Welcome to the Universe* — 523.1
***Stars** & Planets.* Ridpath, Ian — 520
***Stars** Between the Sun and Moon.* Jang, Lucia — 365.45092
***Stars** in Their Courses.* Foote, Shelby — 973.7
***Start** by Believing.* Barr, John — 364.15
***Start** Finishing.* Gilkey, Charlie — 658.4
★***Start** Here.* El-Waylly, Sohla — 641.3
***Start** Here.* Langshur, Eric — 158
***Start** Here, Start Now.* Gunaratana, Henepola — 294.3
***Startalk.** Tyson, Neil deGrasse* — 523.1
★***Starter** Vegetable Gardens.* Pleasant, Barbara — 635
STARVATION
   Levy, Buddy. *Labyrinth of Ice* — 910.91
   Moynahan, Brian. *Leningrad* — 780.92
   Nyamayaro, Elizabeth. *I Am a Girl from Africa* — B
***Starved.** Seiffert, Amy* — 248
Stashower, Daniel
   American Demon — 364.152
STATE (POLITICAL SCIENCE)
   Acemoglu, Daron. *The Narrow Corridor* — 320.01
   Chemerinsky, Erwin. *Closing the Courthouse Door* — 347.73
   Cicero, Marcus Tullius. ★*The Republic* — 320.1
   Fukuyama, Francis. *Political Order and Political Decay* — 320.1

PUBLIC LIBRARY CORE COLLECTION: NONFICTION
Twentieth Edition

STATE COLONY FOR EPILEPTICS AND FEEBLE-MINDED (VA.)
   Brown, Molly McCully. *The Virginia State Colony for Epileptics and Feebleminded* — 811

STATE GOVERNMENTS
   Clark, Anna. *The Poisoned City* — 363.6
   Hanna-Attisha, Mona. *What the Eyes Don't See* — 615.9
   Pawel, Miriam. *The Browns of California* — 920
   Seabrook, Nicholas R. *One Person, One Vote* — 328.3
   ★*The State Must Provide*. Harris, Adam — 379.2

State of Emergency. Mallory, Tamika D. — 305.896
State of Play. Ripken, Bill — 796.357

STATE-SPONSORED TERRORISM
   Amis, Martin. *Koba the Dread* — 947.084
   Elkins, Caroline. *Legacy of Violence* — 909
   Evans, Richard J. *The Third Reich in Power, 1933-1939* — 943.086
   Forche, Carolyn. *What You Have Heard Is True* — B
   Igort. *The Ukrainian and Russian Notebooks* — 741.5
   Liao, Yiwu. *Bullets and Opium* — 951.05
   Lim, Louisa. *The People's Republic of Amnesia* — 951.05
   Nafisi, Azar. ★*Reading Lolita in Tehran* — B

STATELESS PEOPLE
   Lekas Miller, Anna. *Love Across Borders* — 323.6

STATES' RIGHTS (AMERICAN POLITICS)
   Simon, James F. *What Kind of Nation* — 342.73

STATISTICS
   Anderson, Christopher. *The Numbers Game* — 796.334
   Barra, Allen. ★*The Last Coach* — B
   Barry, Dan. *Bottom of the 33rd* — 796.357
   Bradlee, Ben. *The Kid* — B
   Eisenberg, John. *The Streak* — 796.357
   Jena, Anupam B. *Random Acts of Medicine* — 616.0072
   Kenny, Brian. *Ahead of the Curve* — 796.357
   Law, Keith. *Smart Baseball* — 796.357
   Lindbergh, Ben. *The Only Rule Is That It Has to Work* — 796.357
   Megdal, Howard. *The Baseball Talmud* — 796.357
   Peta, Joe. *Trading Bases* — 796.357
   Sawchik, Travis. *Big Data Baseball* — 796.357
   Schneps, Leila. *Math on Trial* — 345
   Seife, Charles. *Proofiness* — 510
   Stone, Deborah A. *Counting* — 001.4
   Thorp, Edward O. *A Man for All Markets* — B
   Tufte, Edward R. *The Visual Display of Quantitative Information* — 001.4
   Wheelan, Charles J. *Naked Statistics* — 519.5
   Whitby, Andrew. *The Sum of the People* — 001.4
   Wiggins, Christopher L. *How Data Happened* — 310
   Yates, Kit. *The Math of Life and Death* — 510

STATUE OF LIBERTY (NEW YORK, N.Y.)
   Khan, Yasmin Sabina. *Enlightening the World* — 974.7

STATUES
   Khan, Yasmin Sabina. *Enlightening the World* — 974.7

★*Status and Culture*. Marx, W. David — 305

STAUFFENBERG, CLAUS VON 1907-1944
   Thomas, Gordon. *Defying Hitler* — 920

STAUFFENBERG, MELITTA, GRAFIN, 1903-1945
   Mulley, Clare. *The Women Who Flew for Hitler* — 920

Stauffer, John
   Picturing Fredrick Douglass — B

Stavrakopoulou, Francesca
   God — 231

Stavridis, James
   Sea Power — 359
   To Risk It All — 359

★*Stay True*. Hsu, Hua — B
Stay, Illusion. Brock-Broido, Lucie — 811
The Steal. Bowden, Mark — 973.933

STEALING
   Cameron, Silver Donald. *Blood in the Water* — 364.152
   Craughwell, Thomas J. *Stealing Lincoln's Body* — 973.7092
   Finkel, Michael. *The Art Thief* — 364.1628
   Finkel, Michael. *The Stranger in the Woods* — B
   Hardin, Lara Love. ★*The Many Lives of Mama Love* — B
   Johnson, Kirk W. *The Feather Thief* — 364.16
   Rydell, Anders. *The Book Thieves* — 027

Stealing Green Mangoes. Dutta, Sunil — 973
Stealing Home. Nusbaum, Eric — 796.357
Stealing Lincoln's Body. Craughwell, Thomas J. — 973.7092
Stealing The Show. Press, Joy — 791.45

STEAMBOATS
   Henry, John. *Great White Fleet* — 387.243
   McGinty, Brian. *Lincoln's Greatest Case* — 346.7303
   Stiles, T. J. ★*The First Tycoon* — B

Stearns, Jen
   The Inspired Houseplant — 635.9

STEEL INDUSTRY AND TRADE
   Krass, Peter. *Carnegie* — B
   Price, S. L. *Playing Through the Whistle* — 796.332
   Rudacille, Deborah. *Roots of Steel* — 338.4

STEEL TOWNS
   Price, S. L. *Playing Through the Whistle* — 796.332

Steele, Lisa
   ★*The Fresh Eggs Daily Cookbook* — 641.6

Steelquist, Robert
   The Northwest Coastal Explorer — 508

STEEPLECHASING
   Askwith, Richard. *Unbreakable* — B

Steib, Mike
   The Career Manifesto — 650.1

STEICHEN, EDWARD, 1879-1973
   Brandow, Todd. *Edward Steichen* — 770.92
   Smith, Joel. *Edward Steichen* — 779

Steil, Benn
   The Battle of Bretton Woods — 339.5
   ★*The Marshall Plan* — 338.91

Stein, Gertrude
   Writings, 1903-1932 — 818
   Writings, 1932-1946 — 818

STEIN, GERTRUDE, 1874-1946
   Roe, Sue. *In Montmartre* — 920

Stein, Jean
   West of Eden — 979.4

Stein, Judith E.
   Eye of the Sixties — B

Stein, Stephen J.
   The Shaker Experience in America — 289

Steinbeck, John
   Travels with Charley — B

STEINBECK, JOHN, 1902-1968
   Souder, William. *Mad at the World* — 813
   Steinbeck, John. *Travels with Charley* — B

Steinberg, Jonathan
   Bismarck — B

Steinberg, Jonny
   A Man of Good Hope — B
   Winnie and Nelson — 920

Steinberg, Michael
   The Symphony — 784.2

STEINBERG, SAUL, 1914-1999
   Bair, Deirdre. *Saul Steinberg* — B

Steinem, Gloria
   My Life on the Road — B
   Outrageous Acts and Everyday Rebellions — 305.42
   The Truth Will Set You Free, but First It Will Piss You Off — 305.42

STEINEM, GLORIA, 1934-
   Steinem, Gloria. *My Life on the Road* — B
   Steinem, Gloria. *Outrageous Acts and Everyday Rebellions* — 305.42
   Steinem, Gloria. *The Truth Will Set You Free, but First It Will Piss You Off* — 305.42

Steingold, Fred S.
   The Employer's Legal Handbook, 16th Ed. — 344.7301

Steinhauer, Jennifer
   The Firsts — 320.082

STEINMARK, FREDDIE
   Yousse, Bower. *Freddie Steinmark* — 796.332

STEINWAY & SONS
   Hafner, Katie. *A Romance on Three Legs* — 786.2092

Stella Adler. Adler, Stella — 792

Stelter, Brian
   Hoax — 070.4
   Top of the Morning — 791.456

Stempel, Larry
   ★*Showtime* — 792.609

STENCILING
   Corwin, Lena. *Printing by Hand* — 745.5
   Joyce, Anna. *Stamp Stencil Paint* — 745.7

Stengel. Creamer, Robert W. — 796.357

AUTHOR, TITLE, SERIES AND SUBJECT INDEX

STENGEL, CASEY, 1890-1975
    Creamer, Robert W. *Stengel* — 796.357
Stengel, Richard
    Information Wars — 355.3
STENOGRAPHERS
    Dorey-Stein, Beck. *From the Corner of the Oval* — B
Step into Storytime. Ghoting, Saroj Nadkarni — 027.62
STEPCHILDREN
    Glatt, John. *The Doomsday Mother* — 364.152
    Good, Cassandra A. *First Family* — 920
    Hillsberg, Christina. *License to Parent* — 649.1
STEPFATHERS
    Glatt, John. *The Doomsday Mother* — 364.152
    Qu, Anna. *Made in China* — B
    Wolff, Tobias. *This Boy's Life* — B
Stephanopoulos, George
    ★*The Situation Room* — 973.09
Stephen Hawking. Mlodinow, Leonard — B
STEPHENS, JOHN L., 1805-1852
    Carlsen, William. *Jungle of Stone* — B
STEPHENSON, DAVID CURTIS, 1891-1966
    Egan, Timothy. ★*A Fever in the Heartland* — 322.4
Stephenson, Michael
    The Last Full Measure — 305.9
STEPHENSON, WILLIAM SAMUEL, 1896-1989
    Stevenson, William. *A Man Called Intrepid* — 940.54
STEPMOTHERS
    Pullman, Philip. ★*Fairy Tales from the Brothers Grimm* — 398.2
STEPSISTERS
    Rear, Rachel. *Catch the Sparrow* — 364.152
STEREOTYPES
    Agarwal, Pragya. *Sway* — 177
    Ali-Karamali, Sumbul. *Demystifying Shariah* — 340.5
    Applewhite, Ashton. *This Chair Rocks* — 155.67
    Barnes, Katie. ★*Fair Play* — 796.082
    Bates, Laura. *Men Who Hate Women* — 305.3
    Currid-Halkett, Elizabeth. *The Overlooked Americans* — 307.76
    Eliot, Lise. *Pink Brain, Blue Brain* — 612.6
    Faloyin, Dipo. ★*Africa Is Not a Country* — 960.33
    Fuller, Pamela. ★*The Leader's Guide to Unconscious Bias* — 658.3
    Gilliam, Fatimah. *Race Rules* — 305.8
    Gordon, Aubrey. *"You Just Need to Lose Weight"* — 616.3
    Grinker, Roy Richard. *Nobody's Normal* — 616.89
    Jobrani, Maziyar. *I'm Not a Terrorist, but I've Played One on TV* — B
    Khakpour, Porochista. *Brown Album* — 304.8
    Kramer, Andrea S. *Breaking Through Bias* — 650.1
    Levin, Josh. *The Queen* — 364.16
    Liu, Simu. ★*We Were Dreamers* — B
    Liverpool, Layal. *Systemic* — 362.1
    Orth, Stephan. *Couchsurfing in Iran* — 955.06
    Tipton-Martin, Toni. *The Jemima Code* — 641.59
    Williams, Joan. *What Works for Women at Work* — 650.1
    Young, Kevin. *Bunk* — 177
STERILIZATION (BIRTH CONTROL)
    Blair, Gabrielle Stanley. ★*Ejaculate Responsibly* — 362.1988
Stern, Adam
    Committed — 616.89
STERN, ADAM (PSYCHIATRIST)
    Stern, Adam. *Committed* — 616.89
Stern, Alan
    Chasing New Horizons — 629.43
Stern, Amanda
    Little Panic — 616.8522
STERN, AMANDA
    Stern, Amanda. *Little Panic* — 616.8522
Stern, Jessica
    My War Criminal — 341.6
STERN, JESSICA, 1958-
    Stern, Jessica. *My War Criminal* — 341.6
STEROIDS
    Dykstra, Lenny. *House of Nails* — B
STESICHORUS
    Carson, Anne. *Red Doc* — 811
★*Steve Jobs*. Isaacson, Walter — B
Steven Spielberg. Haskell, Molly — B
Stevens, Dana
    Camera Man — 791.4302

STEVENS, GEORGE, 1904-1975
    Harris, Mark. ★*Five Came Back* — 791.4302
Stevens, George, Jr
    Conversations at the American Film Institute with the Great Moviemakers — 791.4302
Stevens, John Paul
    The Making of a Justice — B
STEVENS, JOHN PAUL, 1920-2019
    Stevens, John Paul. *The Making of a Justice* — B
Stevens, Norma
    Avedon — B
Stevens, Stuart
    The Conspiracy to End America — 324.2734
    It Was All a Lie — 324.2734
STEVENS, STUART
    Stevens, Stuart. *The Conspiracy to End America* — 324.2734
STEVENS, THADDEUS, 1792-1868
    Levine, Bruce C. *Thaddeus Stevens* — B
Stevens, Wallace
    Collected Poetry and Prose — 811
Stevenson, Bryan
    Just Mercy — B
STEVENSON, BRYAN
    Stevenson, Bryan. *Just Mercy* — B
Stevenson, Christine Kellmann
    Creative Stained Glass — 748.50282
Stevenson, William
    A Man Called Intrepid — 940.54
Stewart, Alison
    Junk — 616.85
Stewart, Amy
    Wicked Plants — 581.6
Stewart, Chris
    Driving Over Lemons — 946
STEWART, CHRIS, 1951-
    Stewart, Chris. *Driving Over Lemons* — 946
Stewart, David O.
    George Washington — 973.4
    Madison's Gift — B
Stewart, Ian
    Professor Stewart's Casebook of Mathematical Mysteries — 793.74
    Visions of Infinity — 510
Stewart, James B.
    Unscripted — 658.1
STEWART, JAMES, 1908-1997
    Eyman, Scott. *Hank and Jim* — 920
    Smith, Starr. *Jimmy Stewart* — B
Stewart, Jeffrey C.
    ★*The New Negro* — 191
Stewart, Martha
    ★*The Martha Manual* — 640
    ★*Martha Stewart's Baking Handbook* — 641.8
    Martha Stewart's Cake Perfection — 641.86
    Martha Stewart's Cooking School — 641.5
    ★*Martha's Flowers* — 635.9
Stewart, Nikita
    Troop 6000 — 369
Stewart, Patrick
    ★*Making It So* — B
STEWART, PATRICK, 1940-
    Stewart, Patrick. ★*Making It So* — B
Stewart, Rory
    The Marches — 941.3
    The Prince of the Marshes — 956.7044
STEWART, RORY
    Stewart, Rory. *The Prince of the Marshes* — 956.7044
Stewart, Tracey
    Do Unto Animals — 590
STEWS
    Volger, Lukas. *Bowl* — 641.81
STFU. Lyons, Daniel — 302.2
Stibbe, Nina
    An Almost Perfect Christmas — 394.2663
Stickmaking Handbook. Jones, Andrew — 736
Sticks and Stones. Bazelon, Emily — 302.34
Sticky Fingers. Hagan, Joe — B
★*Stiff*. Roach, Mary — 611

PUBLIC LIBRARY CORE COLLECTION: NONFICTION
Twentieth Edition

STIGLER, FRANZ, 1916-2008
   Makos, Adam. ★*A Higher Call* — 940.54
Stiglitz, Joseph E.
   Globalization and Its Discontents — 337
   The Price of Inequality — 305.50973
STIGMA (SOCIAL PSYCHOLOGY)
   Coombes, Joshua. *Do Something for Nothing* — 362.5
   Fessler, Pam. *Carville's Cure* — 362.19699
   Glaser, Gabrielle. *American Baby* — B
   Grinker, Roy Richard. *Nobody's Normal* — 616.89
   Gupta, Shalene. *The Cycle* — 618.1
   Kazdin, Cole. ★*What's Eating Us* — 616.85
   Sehee, Baek. *I Want to Die but I Want to Eat Tteokbokki* — B
   Wilkerson, Isabel. ★*Caste* — 305.5
STIGMATIZATION
   Crasnianski, Tania. *The Children of Nazis* — 943.086
Stiles, T. J.
   Custer's Trials — B
   ★*The First Tycoon* — B
   Jesse James — B
Still Broke. Wartzman, Rick — 381
Still Here. Jacobs, Alexandra — B
★*Still Life with Bones*. Hagerty, Alexa — 599.9
Still Life with Two Dead Peacocks and a Girl. Seuss, Diane — 811.6
★*Still Mad*. Gilbert, Sandra M. — 810.9
Still Woman Enough. Lynn, Loretta — B
Still, Ben
   Particle Physics Brick by Brick — 539.7
Stille, Alexander
   The Sullivanians — 307.77
Stilwell and the American Experience in China, 1911-45. Tuchman, Barbara W. — B
STILWELL, JOSEPH WARREN, 1883-1946
   Tuchman, Barbara W. *Stilwell and the American Experience in China, 1911-45* — B
Sting Like a Bee. Montville, Leigh — B
The Sting of the Wild. Schmidt, Justin O. — 595.7
STING OPERATIONS
   Cox, Joseph. *Dark Wire* — 363.2
★*Stitch 'N Bitch*. Stoller, Debbie — 746.43
Stitch 'N Bitch Superstar Knitting. Stoller, Debbie — 746.43
STITCHES (SEWING)
   Chanin, Natalie. ★*The Geometry of Hand-Sewing* — 746.44
   Galbraith, Melissa. *How to Embroider Texture and Pattern* — 746.44
   Knight, Erika. *500 Crochet Stitches* — 746.43
   Knight, Erika. *750 Knitting Stitches* — 746.43
Stixrud, William R.
   The Self-Driven Child — 155.4
   ★*What Do You Say?* — 155.4
STOCK CAR RACING
   Busbee, Jay. *Earnhardt Nation* — B
STOCK MARKET
   Belfort, Jordan. ★*The Wolf of Investing* — 332.63
   Bruner, Robert F. ★*The Panic of 1907, 2nd Ed.* — 330.973
   Fabre, Cin. *Wolf Hustle* — 332.6
   Fox, Justin. *The Myth of the Rational Market* — 332.64
   Nations, Scott. *A History of the United States in Five Crashes* — 338.5
   Patterson, Scott. ★*Chaos Kings* — 338.5
   Perino, Michael A. *The Hellhound of Wall Street* — 330.973
   Schroeder, Alice. *The Snowball* — B
   Vaughan, Liam. *Flash Crash* — B
STOCK MARKET CRASH, OCTOBER 1929
   Galbraith, John Kenneth. ★*The Great Crash, 1929* — 338.5
   Kennedy, David M. ★*Freedom from Fear* — 973.91
   Perino, Michael A. *The Hellhound of Wall Street* — 330.973
Stocker, Blair
   Wise Craft Quilts — 746.46
STOCKHOLDERS
   Gramm, Jeff. *Dear Chairman* — 659.2
STOCKHOLM SYNDROME
   King, David. *Six Days in August* — 364.15
STOCKHOLM, SWEDEN
   King, David. *Six Days in August* — 364.15
STOCKS
   Belfort, Jordan. ★*The Wolf of Investing* — 332.63
   Bruner, Robert F. ★*The Panic of 1907, 2nd Ed.* — 330.973
   Vaughan, Liam. *Flash Crash* — B
STOICS
   Delaney, Brigid. *Reasons Not to Worry* — 158.1

   Holiday, Ryan. *Lives of the Stoics* — 188
   Marcus Aurelius. ★*Meditations* — 188
STOKER, BRAM, 1847-1912
   Skal, David J. *Something in the Blood* — 823
Stokes, Donald W.
   The New Stokes Field Guide to Birds — 598
STOKES, ROSE PASTOR, 1879-1933
   Hochschild, Adam. *Rebel Cinderella* — B
STOLEN PROPERTY RECOVERY
   Rynecki, Elizabeth. *Chasing Portraits* — B
★*The Stolen Wealth of Slavery*. Montero, David — 381
The Stolen Year. Kamenetz, Anya — 306.43
Stoller, Debbie
   Stitch 'N Bitch Superstar Knitting — 746.43
   ★*Stitch 'N Bitch* — 746.43
STONE
   Judah, Hettie. *Lapidarium* — 553.8
Stone in the Garden. Hayward, Gordon — 717
A Stone Is Most Precious Where It Belongs. Hoja, Gulchehra — B
Stone, Alex
   Fooling Houdini — B
STONE, ALEX
   Stone, Alex. *Fooling Houdini* — B
STONE, BIZ
   Bilton, Nick. *Hatching Twitter* — 006.7
Stone, Brad
   The Upstarts — 338.04
Stone, Dan
   ★*The Holocaust* — 940.53
Stone, Daniel
   The Food Explorer — B
   Sinkable — 910.91
Stone, Deborah A.
   Counting — 001.4
Stone, Douglas
   Difficult Conversations — 158.2
Stone, Francesca
   Easy Homemade Pottery — 738.1
Stone, Geoffrey R.
   Perilous Times — 323.44
   ★*Sex and the Constitution* — 345.7302
Stone, I. F.
   The Trial of Socrates — 183
STONE, I. F., 1907-1989
   MacPherson, Myra. *All Governments Lie* — B
Stone, Jon R.
   ★*Latin for the Illiterati* — 473
Stone, Lillian
   ★*Everybody's Favorite* — 814.6
STONE, LILLIAN
   Stone, Lillian. ★*Everybody's Favorite* — 814.6
Stone, Robert
   Chasing the Moon — 629.45
STONE, ROBERT, 1937-2015
   Bell, Madison Smartt. *Child of Light* — B
Stone, Robyn
   Add a Pinch Cookbook — 641.5975
STONE, SAMUEL, 1887-1981
   Gup, Ted. *A Secret Gift* — 977.1
Stone, Sharon
   The Beauty of Living Twice — B
STONE, SHARON, 1958-
   Stone, Sharon. *The Beauty of Living Twice* — B
Stone, Sly
   Thank You (Falettinme Be Mice Elf Agin) — B
STONE, SLY
   Stone, Sly. *Thank You (Falettinme Be Mice Elf Agin)* — B
STONE, W. C. (WILLIAM C.)
   Tabor, James M. *Blind Descent* — 796.52
Stonehenge. Parker Pearson, Michael — 936.2
★*Stonehenge*. Pryor, Francis — 936.2
STONEHENGE, ENGLAND
   Parker Pearson, Michael. *Stonehenge* — 936.2
   Pryor, Francis. ★*Stonehenge* — 936.2
Stones. Young, Kevin — 811
Stonewall. Carter, David — 306.76
Stonewall Jackson. Robertson, James I. — B

AUTHOR, TITLE, SERIES AND SUBJECT INDEX

STONEWALL RIOTS, NEW YORK, N.Y., 1969
   Carter, David. *Stonewall* — 306.76
★*Stony The Road*. Gates, Henry Louis — 973
Stop Avoiding Stuff. Boone, Matthew S. — 152.4
Stop Staring at Screens. Goodin, Tanya — 004.67
Stoppard, Tom
   Arcadia — 822
   The Invention of Love — 822
   ★*Rosencrantz & Guildenstern Are Dead* — 822
STORAGE IN THE HOME
   Boyd, Nikki. ★*Beautifully Organized* — 648
   Carlson, Julie. *Remodelista* — 648
   Casazza, Allie. *Declutter Like a Mother* — 648
   Ewer, Cynthia Townley. *Cut the Clutter* — 648
   Kondo, Marie. ★*The Life-Changing Magic of Tidying Up* — 648
   Kondo, Marie. ★*Spark Joy* — 648
   McCubbin, Tracy. *Making Space, Clutter Free* — 648
   Shearer, Clea. ★*The Home Edit Life* — 648
Storey, Martin
   Easy Fair Isle Knitting — 746.43
Stories Are Weapons. Newitz, Annalee — 355.3
Stories I Tell Myself. Thompson, Juan F. — B
★*The Stories of English*. Crystal, David — 427
The Stories We Tell. Gaines, Joanna — B
★*Storm Center*. O'Brien, David M — 347.73
STORM CHASERS
   Hargrove, Brantley. *The Man Who Caught the Storm* — B
STORM DAMAGE
   Neufeld, Josh. *A.D.* — 741.5
Storm in a Teacup. Czerski, Helen — 530
The Storm Is Here. Mogelson, Luke — 973.933
The Storm Is Upon Us. Rothschild, Mike — 973.933
Storm Lake. Cullen, Art — 071.7
The Storm of War. Roberts, Andrew — 940.54
STORMS
   Dolin, Eric Jay. *A Furious Sky* — 363.34
   Fairbanks, Amanda M. *The Lost Boys of Montauk* — 910.91
   Fields, Micah. ★*We Hold Our Breath* — 976.4
   Junger, Sebastian. *The Perfect Storm* — 974.4
★*Stormy Weather*. Gavin, James — 782.42164
Storr, Will
   Selfie — 155.2
Storrer, William Allin
   The Frank Lloyd Wright Companion — 720.92
Story of a Secret State. Karski, Jan — 940.53
The Story of Architecture. Glancey, Jonathan — 720
★*The Story of Art*. Gombrich, E. H. — 709
The Story of China. Wood, Michael — 951
★*The Story of English*. McCrum, Robert — 420
The Story of English in 100 Words. Crystal, David — 422
★*The Story of French*. Nadeau, Jean-Benoit — 440
The Story of Hebrew. Glinert, Lewis — 492.4
The Story of My Boyhood and Youth. Muir, John — B
★*The Story of My Life*. Keller, Helen — B
★*The Story of Philosophy*. Durant, Will — 190
The Story of Philosophy. Magee, Bryan — 190
★*The Story of Russia*. Figes, Orlando — 947
The Story of Spanish. Nadeau, Jean-Benoit — 460
★*The Story of the Bee Gees*. Stanley, Bob — 782.42164
★*The Story of the Jews; Volume One*. Schama, Simon — 909
★*The Story of the Jews; Volume Two*. Schama, Simon — 909
★*The Story of the Qur'an*. Mattson, Ingrid — 297.122
STORYTELLING
   Caine, Michael. *Blowing the Bloody Doors Off* — B
   Castillo, Elaine. ★*How to Read Now* — 418
   Del Negro, Janice. *Folktales Aloud* — 027.62
   Dylan, Bob. ★*The Philosophy of Modern Song* — 782.42
   Febos, Melissa. ★*Body Work* — 808.06
   Ghoting, Saroj Nadkarni. *Step into Storytime* — 027.62
   Karr, Mary. *The Art of Memoir* — B
   Larimer, Kevin. *The Poets & Writers Complete Guide to Being a Writer* — 808
   McCloud, Scott. *Making Comics* — 741.5
   Neuburger, Emily K. *Show Me a Story* — 745.5083
   Newitz, Annalee. *Stories Are Weapons* — 355.3
   Okorafor, Nnedi. *Broken Places & Outer Spaces* — 153.3
   Reid, Rob. ★*200+ Original and Adapted Story Program Activities* — 027.62
   Rubin, Daniel Joshua. *27 Essential Principles of Story* — 808.02
   Rushdie, Salman. *Languages of Truth* — 824

Solnit, Rebecca. *The Faraway Nearby* — 814
Twain, Mark. *Autobiography of Mark Twain* — B
Twain, Mark. ★*Autobiography of Mark Twain* — B
Twain, Mark. ★*Autobiography of Mark Twain* — B
Vince, Gaia. *Transcendence* — 599.93
STORYTIMES
   Bratt, Jessica Anne. *Let's Talk About Race in Storytimes* — 027.62
STORYVILLE (NEW ORLEANS, LOUISIANA)
   Krist, Gary. *Empire of Sin* — 976.3
Storyville! Dufresne, John — 808.3
Stott, Rebecca
   ★*Darwin's Ghosts* — 576.8
Stourton, James
   Kenneth Clark — B
Stout, David
   The Kidnap Years — 364.15
Stout, Glenn
   Fenway 1912 — 796.357
Stout, Martha
   Outsmarting the Sociopath Next Door — 155.2
STOWE, HARRIET BEECHER, 1811-1896
   Reynolds, David S. *Mightier Than the Sword* — 813
STRAHAN, WILLIAM, 1715-1785
   Moore, Peter. *Life, Liberty, and the Pursuit of Happiness* — 199
Straighten up and Fly Right. Friedwald, Will — 782.42164
Strand, Mark
   Collected Poems — 811
Strang, Dean A.
   Worse Than the Devil — 345.775
The Strange Career of Jim Crow. Woodward, C. Vann — 305.896
The Strange Career of William Ellis. Jacoby, Karl — B
The Strange Case of Dr. Couney. Raffel, Dawn — B
Strange Glory. Marsh, Charles — B
Strange Stars. Heller, Jason — 781.6609
Stranger. Ramos, Jorge — 325.73
The Stranger Beside Me. Rule, Ann — B
Stranger by Night. Hirsch, Edward — 811
Stranger Care. Sentilles, Sarah — B
★*Stranger in the Desert*. Salama, Jordan — 982
Stranger in the Shogun's City. Stanley, Amy — B
The Stranger in the Woods. Finkel, Michael — B
A Stranger in Your Own City. Abdul-Ahad, Ghaith — 956.7044
A Stranger's Mirror. Hacker, Marilyn — 811
STRANGERS
   Gladwell, Malcolm. ★*Talking to Strangers* — 302
   Jaouad, Suleika. ★*Between Two Kingdoms* — B
   Moss, Jeremiah. *Feral City* — B
Strangers Tend to Tell Me Things. Dickinson, Amy — B
★*Strangers to Ourselves*. Aviv, Rachel — 616.89
STRATEGIC ALLIANCES (MILITARY)
   Churchill, Winston. *The Grand Alliance* — 940.53
   Groom, Winston. *The Allies* — 940.5309
   Holland, James. ★*Burma '44* — 940.54
   Kertzer, David I. *The Pope and Mussolini* — 322
   Lance, Rachel. *Chamber Divers* — 940.54
   Loyn, David. *The Long War* — 958.104
   Olson, Lynne. *Citizens of London* — 940.54012
   Philbrick, Nathaniel. ★*In the Hurricane's Eye* — 973.3
   Roberts, Jennifer Tolbert. *The Plague of War* — 938
   Stewart, Rory. *The Prince of the Marshes* — 956.7044
STRATEGIC PLANNING
   Newkirk, Pamela. *Diversity, Inc.* — 658.3
STRATEGY
   Arnsdorf, Isaac. ★*Finish What We Started* — 320.52
   Capelle, Philip B. ★*Play Your Best Straight Pool* — 790
   Cox, Michael. *Zonal Marking* — 796
   Gaddis, John Lewis. *On Grand Strategy* — 355.4
   Kissinger, Henry. *Leadership* — 303.3
   Miller, Donald L. *Vicksburg* — 973.7
   Miller, Megan. ★*The Ultimate Unofficial Encyclopedia for Minecrafters* — 794.8
   Neyer, Rob. *Power Ball* — 796.357
   Overy, R. J. *Why the Allies Won* — 940.53
   Parker, Vergil R. *Pickleball 101* — 796.34
   Vickers, Michael G. *By All Means Available* — 355
   Wilson, Rick. *Running Against the Devil* — 973.933
Strathern, Paul
   The Borgias — 945.06

PUBLIC LIBRARY CORE COLLECTION: NONFICTION
Twentieth Edition

The Florentines	945
The Medici	945.5
Stratton, W. K.	
Floyd Patterson	B
The Wild Bunch	791.43
Strauss, Barry S.	
The Death of Caesar	937
Ten Caesars	937
★*The War That Made the Roman Empire*	937
Strauss, Gwen	
The Nine	940.53
STRAUSS, RICHARD, 1864-1949	
Kennedy, Michael. *Richard Strauss*	B
Stray. Danler, Stephanie	B
Strayed, Cheryl	
★*Wild*	B
STRAYED, CHERYL, 1968-	
Strayed, Cheryl. ★*Wild*	B
*The **Streak***. Eisenberg, John	796.357
STREAM ECOLOGY	
Darlington, Miriam. *Otter Country*	599.769
Owen, David. *Where the Water Goes*	917.91
STREAMING TECHNOLOGY (TELECOMMUNICATIONS)	
Biskind, Peter. *Pandora's Box*	791.45
Hayes, Dade. *Binge Times*	384.55
STREAMS	
Freeman, Scott. *Saving Tarboo Creek*	333.72
Streep, Abe	
Brothers on Three	306.85
STREET ART	
Felisbret, Eric. *Graffiti New York*	751.7
Ganz, Nicholas. ★*Graffiti World*	751.7
***Street** Gang*. Davis, Michael	791.43
STREET LIFE	
Anthony, Carmelo. *Where Tomorrows Aren't Promised*	B
Bowden, Mark. *Life Sentence*	364.106
Brown, Claude. *Manchild in the Promised Land*	B
Coates, Ta-Nehisi. *The Beautiful Struggle*	B
Cox, Caroline. *The World Atlas of Street Fashion*	391.009
Dudley, Steven S. *MS-13*	364.106
Flanders, Judith. *The Victorian City*	942.1
Hobbs, Jeff. ★*The Short and Tragic Life of Robert Peace*	B
LeDuff, Charlie. *Detroit*	977.4
Ralph, Laurence. *Sito*	364.152
Voloj, Julian. *Ghetto Brother*	741.5
STREET MUSIC	
Gray, Michael. *Hand Me My Travelin' Shoes*	B
STREET MUSICIANS	
Gray, Michael. *Hand Me My Travelin' Shoes*	B
STREET NAMES	
Mask, Deirdre. *The Address Book*	388.1
***Street** of Eternal Happiness*. Schmitz, Rob	951
STREET PHOTOGRAPHY	
Cox, Caroline. *The World Atlas of Street Fashion*	391.009
Hahn, Emanuel. *Koreatown Dreaming*	979.4
Marks, Ann. *Vivian Maier Developed*	778.9
Stanton, Brandon. *Humans*	779
★*A **Streetcar** Named Desire*. Williams, Tennessee	812
STREETS	
Schmitz, Rob. *Street of Eternal Happiness*	951
Streets, Annabel	
52 Ways to Walk	796.51
Streisand, Barbra	
★*My Name Is Barbra*	B
STREISAND, BARBRA	
Mann, William J. *Hello, Gorgeous*	B
Streisand, Barbra. ★*My Name Is Barbra*	B
STRENGTH AND WEAKNESS	
Gladwell, Malcolm. *David and Goliath*	155.2
greathouse, torrin a. *Wound from the Mouth of a Wound*	811
***Strength** in Stillness*. Roth, Robert	158.1
***Strengths** Based Marriage*. Evans, Jimmy	248.8
STRESS	
Aschwanden, Christie. *Good to Go*	617.1
Geronimus, Arline T. ★*Weathering*	362.1089
Hartley, Gemma. *Fed Up*	155.3
McGovern, Anna. *Pottering*	158.1
Minami, Jikisai. *It's Okay Not to Look for the Meaning of Life*	158.1
Naumburg, Carla. ★*You Are Not a Sh*tty Parent*	649
STRESS IN CHILDREN	
Chu, Lenora. *Little Soldiers*	370
***Stress** Less, Accomplish More*. Fletcher, Emily	155.9
STRESS MANAGEMENT	
Benson, Herbert. *The Relaxation Response*	155.9
Blumenthal, Brett. *52 Small Changes for the Mind*	616.89
Damour, Lisa. ★*Under Pressure*	155.5
Fletcher, Emily. *Stress Less, Accomplish More*	155.9
Goodin, Tanya. *Stop Staring at Screens*	004.67
Haig, Matt. *Notes on a Nervous Planet*	616.89
Harris, Dan. ★*10% Happier*	158.1
Langshur, Eric. *Start Here*	158
McGinnis, Patrick J. *Fear of Missing Out*	153.8
McGovern, Anna. *Pottering*	158.1
Raphael, Rina. *The Gospel of Wellness*	613
Wray, Britt. *Generation Dread*	155.9
STRESS MANAGEMENT FOR CHILDREN	
Stixrud, William R. *The Self-Driven Child*	155.4
Stixrud, William R. ★*What Do You Say?*	155.4
*The **Stressed** Years of Their Lives*. Hibbs, B. Janet	616.8900835
Stretch. Sonenshein, Scott	153.3
Strevens, Michael	
The Knowledge Machine	500
Strickland, Carol	
The Annotated Mona Lisa	709
STRIKES	
Berfield, Susan. *The Hour of Fate*	973.91
McAlevey, Jane. *A Collective Bargain*	331.890973
Wolff, Daniel J. *Grown-Up Anger*	920
***String** Frenzy*. Hunter, Bonnie K.	746.46
STRING THEORY (NUCLEAR PHYSICS)	
Greene, B. *The Fabric of the Cosmos*	523.1
Greene, B. ★*The Hidden Reality*	530.12
Hawking, Stephen. ★*The Universe in a Nutshell*	530.12
Impey, Chris. *Einstein's Monsters*	523.8
Mack, Katie. *The End of Everything*	523.1
Strings, Sabrina	
The End of Love	155.3
Striniste, Nancy	
Nature Play at Home	796.083
STRIP MINING	
Biggers, Jeff. *Reckoning at Eagle Creek*	333.73
***Strip** Tees*. Flannery, Kate	338.4
STRIPTEASERS	
Abbott, Karen. *American Rose*	B
Feast, Fancy. *Naked*	792.7
Johnson, Stephanie. *Tanqueray*	B
Kelly, Minka. ★*Tell Me Everything*	B
Worley, Jennifer. *Neon Girls*	792.7
Zemeckis, Leslie Harter. *Behind the Burly Q*	792.7
STRITCH, ELAINE	
Jacobs, Alexandra. *Still Here*	B
Strittmatter, Kai	
We Have Been Harmonized	323.44
Strobel, Lee	
The Case for Grace	234
STROKES	
Pataki, Allison. *Beauty in the Broken Places*	B
Stone, Sharon. *The Beauty of Living Twice*	B
Taylor, Jill Bolte. *My Stroke of Insight*	362.19681
Strom, Yale	
The Book of Klezmer	781.62
***Strong** as a Mother*. Rope, Kate	618.2
***Strong** Inside*. Maraniss, Andrew	B
***Strong** Is the New Pretty*. Parker, Kate T.	155.43
***Strong** Is Your Hold*. Kinnell, Galway	811
***Strong** Like a Woman*. Litman, Laken	796
Strong, James	
The New Strong's Expanded Exhaustive Concordance of the Bible	220.5
Stronghold. Malarkey, Tucker	639.2
Strossen, Nadine	
Hate	342.7308
STRUCTURAL ENGINEERING	
Blockley, David. *Bridges*	725
Langewiesche, William. *American Ground*	974.7
*The **Structure** of Evolutionary Theory*. Gould, Stephen Jay	576.8
*The **Struggle** to Reform Our Colleges*. Bok, Derek Curtis	378.73

AUTHOR, TITLE, SERIES AND SUBJECT INDEX

Strung Out. Khar, Erin — B
Strunk, William
  ★ *The Elements of Style* — 808
Struzik, Edward
  Swamplands — 577.68
Strycker, Noah K.
  The Thing with Feathers — 598.072
Stryker, Kitty
  Ask — 302
Strøksnes, Morten Andreas
  Shark Drunk — 338.3
STUART PERIOD (1603-1714)
  Ackroyd, Peter. *Rebellion* — 941.06
  Ackroyd, Peter. *Revolution* — 941.07
  Bremer, Francis J. *John Winthrop* — B
  Fraser, Antonia. *Faith and Treason* — 942.06
  Goodman, Ruth. *How to Behave Badly in Elizabethan England* — 942.05
  Healey, Jonathan. *The Blazing World* — 941.06
  Lacey, Robert. *Great Tales from English History 2* — 941
  Mortimer, Ian. *The Time Traveler's Guide to Restoration Britain* — 941.06
  Tomalin, Claire. *Samuel Pepys* — B
  Woolley, Benjamin. *The King's Assassin* — B
Stuart, Amanda Mackenzie
  Empress of Fashion — B
Stuart, Andrea
  Sugar in the Blood — 338.1
Stuart, Colin
  How to Live in Space — 629.45
STUART, GILBERT, 1755-1828
  Staiti, Paul J. *Of Arms and Artists* — B
STUART, HOUSE OF
  Ackroyd, Peter. *Revolution* — 941.07
STUART, JEB, 1833-1864
  Wert, Jeffry D. *Cavalryman of the Lost Cause* — B
★ *A Stubbornly Persistent Illusion*. Einstein, Albert — 530.092
Stuckey, Maggie
  The Container Victory Garden — 635.9
STUDENT ACHIEVEMENT
  Asher, Zain E. *Where the Children Take Us* — 942.1
  Bain, Ken. *What the Best College Students Do* — 378.1
  Bauer, Susan Wise. *Rethinking School* — 371.19
  Bok, Derek Curtis. *The Struggle to Reform Our Colleges* — 378.73
  Emdin, Christopher. *Ratchetdemic* — 370.1
  Fishman, Elly. *Refugee High* — 370.8
  Hobbs, Jeff. *Show Them You're Good* — 373
STUDENT AID
  Goldrick-Rab, Sara. *Paying the Price* — 378.3
  Mitchell, Josh. *The Debt Trap* — 378.3
STUDENT FINANCE
  Brenner, Andrea. *How to College* — 378.1
  Mitchell, Josh. *The Debt Trap* — 378.3
STUDENT LOANS
  Beaton, Kate. ★ *Ducks* — 741.5
  Mitchell, Josh. *The Debt Trap* — 378.3
STUDENT MOVEMENTS
  Bingham, Clara. *Witness to the Revolution* — 303.48
  Cullen, David. *Parkland* — 371.7
  Derf. *Kent State* — 741.5
  Kurlansky, Mark. *1968* — 909.82
  Lewis, John. ★ *March; Book One* — 741.5
  Lewis, John. ★ *March; Book Three* — 741.5
  Lewis, John. ★ *March; Book Two* — 741.5
  Rosenfeld, Seth. *Subversives* — 378.1
STUDENT PROTESTERS
  Bingham, Clara. *Witness to the Revolution* — 303.48
Student's Guide to Writing College Papers. Turabian, Kate L — 808.06
STUDENTS
  Driver, Justin. *The Schoolhouse Gate* — 344.73
  Faust, Drew Gilpin. *Necessary Trouble* — B
  Kim, Suki. *Without You, There Is No Us* — B
  Ruhl, Sarah. *Letters from Max* — 811
STUDY METHODS
  Emdin, Christopher. *Ratchetdemic* — 370.1
STUDY SKILLS
  Donaldson-Pressman, Stephanie. *The Learning Habit* — 371.30281
Stuff Matters. Miodownik, Mark — 620.1
★ *Stuff Mom Never Told You*. Reese, Anney — 305.42
The Stuff of Thought. Pinker, Steven — 401

Stuff They Don't Want You to Know. Bowlin, Ben — 001.9
Stuffed. Mubarak, Heather — 641.86
STUFFED ANIMALS (TOYS)
  Bergstrom, Lauren. *Cute & Cuddly Crochet* — 746.43
  Bergstrom, Lauren. *Mini Crochet Creatures* — 746.43
Stulberg, Brad
  Peak Performance — 158.1
★ *Stumbling on Happiness*. Gilbert, Daniel Todd — 158
Stump, Al
  Cobb — B
Sturgis, Matthew
  Oscar Wilde — B
STUTTERERS
  Hendrickson, John. *Life on Delay* — B
  Preston, Katherine. *Out with It* — B
STUTTERING
  Hendrickson, John. *Life on Delay* — B
  Preston, Katherine. *Out with It* — B
Stutz, Phil
  Lessons for Living — 158.1
Style and Grace. Adams, Michael Henry — 747
Styron, William
  My Generation — 814
STYRON, WILLIAM, 1925-2006
  Styron, William. *My Generation* — 814
Suarez, Ray
  ★ *We Are Home* — 325.73
SUBCONSCIOUSNESS
  Bargh, John A. *Before You Know It* — 154.2
  Eagleman, David. *Incognito* — 153
  Kandel, Eric R. *The Age of Insight* — 154.2
  Mlodinow, Leonard. *Emotional* — 152.4
SUBCULTURES
  Baum, Dan. *Nine Lives* — B
  Cox, Caroline. *The World Atlas of Street Fashion* — 391.009
  Garrels, Anne. *Putin Country* — 947
  Goodman, Elyssa. *Glitter and Concrete* — 792.7
  LaPointe, Sasha taqwseblu. *Red Paint* — B
  Menand, Louis. *The Free World* — 306.0973
  Westover, Tara. ★ *Educated* — B
Suber, Peter
  Open Access — 070.5
SUBLIMINAL PERCEPTION
  Agarwal, Pragya. *Sway* — 177
The Submarine. Parrish, Thomas D. — 359.9
SUBMARINE DISASTERS
  Dean, Josh. *The Taking of K-129* — 910.91
SUBMARINE WARFARE
  Budiansky, Stephen. *Blackett's War* — 940.54
  Dimbleby, Jonathan. *The Battle of the Atlantic* — 940.54
SUBMARINES
  Horwitz, Josh. *War of the Whales* — 333.95
  Humphreys, Richard. *Under Pressure* — B
  Lance, Rachel. *Chamber Divers* — 940.54
  Lance, Rachel. *In the Waves* — 973.7
  Parrish, Thomas D. *The Submarine* — 359.9
SUBMARINES, GERMAN
  Budiansky, Stephen. *Blackett's War* — 940.54
  Geroux, William. *The Ghost Ships of Archangel* — 940.54
  Parkin, Simon. *A Game of Birds and Wolves* — 940.54
SUBMARINES, SOVIET
  Dean, Josh. *The Taking of K-129* — 910.91
SUBMERSIBLES
  Lance, Rachel. *Chamber Divers* — 940.54
Subramanian, Sammanth
  This Divided Island — 954.9303
Substitute. Baker, Nicholson — 371.14
SUBSTITUTE TEACHERS
  Baker, Nicholson. *Substitute* — 371.14
*The Subtle Art of Not Giving a F*ck*. Manson, Mark — 158.1
SUBURBAN LIFE
  Corrigan, Kelly. *Glitter and Glue* — B
  Herold, Benjamin. *Disillusioned* — 307.76
  Leach, Samantha. ★ *The Elissas* — 362.73
SUBURBS
  Herold, Benjamin. *Disillusioned* — 307.76
SUBVERSIVE ACTIVITIES
  Kix, Paul. *The Saboteur* — 940.53

PUBLIC LIBRARY CORE COLLECTION: NONFICTION
Twentieth Edition

Maier, Thomas. *Mafia Spies* — 364.1060973
Milton, Giles. *Churchill's Ministry of Ungentlemanly Warfare* — 940.54
Rosenfeld, Seth. *Subversives* — 378.1
Tye, Larry. ★*Demagogue* — B
Subversives. Rosenfeld, Seth — 378.1
SUBWAYS
   Hunt, Will. *Underground* — 624.1
SUCCESS (CONCEPT)
   Alter, Adam L. *Anatomy of a Breakthrough* — 158.1
   Asher, Zain E. *Where the Children Take Us* — 942.1
   Asprey, Dave. *Game Changers* — 158.1
   Benedict, Jeff. *The Dynasty* — 796.332
   Benedict, Jeff. *Lebron* — B
   Bertch, Jane. *The French Ingredient* — B
   Brown, Tabitha. *I Did a New Thing* — 158.1
   Browne, Mahogany L. ★*Black Girl Magic* — 811.6
   Bruni, Frank. *The Beauty of Dusk* — B
   Bryant, Kobe. *The Mamba Mentality* — B
   Caine, Michael. *Blowing the Bloody Doors Off* — B
   Calhoun, Ada. *Why We Can't Sleep* — 305.244
   Campoverdi, Alejandra. *First Gen* — B
   Canfield, Jack. *The Success Principles* — 158
   Carnegie, Dale. ★*How to Win Friends and Influence People* — 158
   Clear, James. ★*Atomic Habits* — 155.24
   Covey, Stephen R. ★*The 7 Habits of Highly Effective People* — 158
   Covey, Stephen R. *The 8th Habit* — 158
   Duckworth, Angela. *Grit* — 158.1
   Duhigg, Charles. *Smarter Faster Better* — 158
   Dweck, Carol S. ★*Mindset* — 153.8
   Epstein, David J. ★*Range* — 153.9
   Fall, Jeremy. *Falling Upwards* — 158.1
   Feiler, Bruce. ★*The Search* — 306.3
   Ferriss, Timothy. *Tools of Titans* — 081
   Friedman, Rachel. ★*And Then We Grew Up* — 305.24
   Friedman, Ron. *Decoding Greatness* — 650.1
   Gardner, Chris. *Permission to Dream* — 158.1
   Gelwicks, Andrew. *The Queer Advantage* — 920
   Gerald, Casey. *There Will Be No Miracles Here* — B
   Gladwell, Malcolm. *David and Goliath* — 155.2
   Gladwell, Malcolm. *Outliers* — 302
   Goleman, Daniel. *Focus* — 153.7
   Goodall, Amanda. *Credible* — 658.4
   Grant, Adam M. *Give and Take* — 158.2
   Grant, Adam M. *Hidden Potential* — 153.8
   Hendricks, Gay. *Conscious Luck* — 158.1
   Henry, Alan. *Seen, Heard, and Paid* — 650.1
   Higgins, Tim. *Power Play* — 338.7
   Hill, Jemele. *Uphill* — B
   Holiday, Ryan. *Ego Is the Enemy* — 158.1
   Ice-T. *Split Decision* — 920
   Keyes, Corey L. M. ★*Languishing* — 152.1
   Levine, Madeline. ★*Ready or Not* — 649
   Levy, Reynold. *They Told Me Not to Take That Job* — 792.09
   Manson, Mark. *The Subtle Art of Not Giving a F*ck* — 158.1
   Marshall, Cynthia. *You've Been Chosen* — B
   McGraw, Phillip C. *Life Strategies* — 158
   Miller, Caroline Adams. *Creating Your Best Life* — 158.1
   Miller, Klancy. ★*For the Culture* — 641.59
   Mojica Rodriguez, Prisca Dorcas. *For Brown Girls with Sharp Edges and Tender Hearts* — 305.48
   Mueller, Jennifer. *Creative Change* — 658.4
   Ndopu, Eddie. *Sipping Dom Pérignon Through a Straw* — B
   Neville, Aaron. *Tell It Like It Is* — B
   Norton, Hughes. ★*Rainmaker* — 796.352
   Odenkirk, Bob. *Comedy Comedy Comedy Drama* — B
   Orji, Yvonne. *Bamboozled by Jesus* — B
   Pink, Daniel H. *Drive* — 153.1
   Pink, Daniel H. *When* — 153.7
   Price, Devon. ★*Laziness Does Not Exist* — 158.1
   Riess, Jana. *Flunking Sainthood* — 248.4
   Robbins, Anthony. *Unlimited Power* — 158.1
   Rollag, Keith. *What to Do When You're New* — 158.2
   Rotella, Robert J. *How Champions Think* — 796.01
   Rubin, Gretchen. *Outer Order, Inner Calm* — 158
   Sanders, Chad. *Black Magic* — 305.896
   Sasakamoose, Fred. *Call Me Indian* — B
   Schultz, Howard. *From the Ground Up* — B
   Schwartz, David Joseph. ★*The Magic of Thinking Big* — 158

Shankar, Shalini. *Beeline* — 155.4
Sincero, Jen. *You Are a Badass Every Day* — 158.1
Solovic, Susan Wilson. *The One-Percent Edge* — 658.4
Sonenshein, Scott. *Stretch* — 153.3
Tough, Paul. ★*How Children Succeed* — 372.210973
Toussaint, Alex. ★*Activate Your Greatness* — 158.1
Walker, Sam. *The Captain Class* — 796.07
Watts, Steven. *Self-Help Messiah* — B
Williams, Billy Dee. ★*What Have We Here* — B
Wills, Shomari. *Black Fortunes* — 920
Wilson, A'ja. ★*Dear Black Girls* — 158.1
Wilson, Rebel. *Rebel Rising* — B
Wojcicki, Esther. *How to Raise Successful People* — 649
Wu, Constance. *Making a Scene* — B
Young, Scott H. *Get Better at Anything* — 650.1
SUCCESS IN BUSINESS
   Abrams, Stacey. *Level Up* — 658.4
   Au-Yeung, Angel. *Wonder Boy* — B
   Bahcall, Safi. *Loonshots* — 658.4
   Berman, Lea. *Treating People Well* — 395
   Boden, Anne. *Female Founders' Playbook* — 658.4
   Botelho, Elena L. *The CEO Next Door* — 658.4
   Brickell, Francesca Cartier. *The Cartiers* — B
   Cast, Carter. *The Right—And Wrong—Stuff* — 650.1
   Cerulo, Erica. *Work Wife* — 658.4
   Coggan, Philip. *Surviving the Daily Grind* — 658.3
   DeBord, Matthew. *Return to Glory* — 338.4
   Dennis, Felix. *How to Get Rich* — B
   Ehrenreich, Barbara. *Bright-Sided* — 155.2
   Ferrazzi, Keith. *Never Eat Alone* — 658.4
   Fineman, Meredith. *Brag Better* — 650.1
   Finkle, Jane. *The Introvert's Complete Career Guide* — 650.14
   Galloway, Scott. *The Four* — 338.7
   Gladwell, Malcolm. *Outliers* — 302
   Goodall, Amanda. *Credible* — 658.4
   Grant, Adam M. *Originals* — 153.3
   Hansen, Morten T. *Great at Work* — 650.1
   Hilfiger, Tommy. *American Dreamer* — B
   Hill, Napoleon. *Think and Grow Rich* — 650.1
   Jackson, Curtis. *Hustle Harder, Hustle Smarter* — B
   Lima, Jamie Kern. *Believe It* — B
   Mueller, Jennifer. *Creative Change* — 658.4
   Nadella, Satya. *Hit Refresh* — B
   Nichtern, David. *Creativity, Spirituality & Making a Buck* — 294.3
   Pollak, Lindsey. *Recalculating* — 650.1
   Rice, Condoleezza. *Political Risk* — 658.15
   Robinson, Joanna. ★*McU* — 791.43
   Romeo, Nick. *The Alternative* — 174
   Schlender, Brent. *Becoming Steve Jobs* — B
   Snow, Shane. *Dream Teams* — 658.4
   Solovic, Susan Wilson. *The One-Percent Edge* — 658.4
   Vaynerchuk, Gary. *Crushing It!* — 650.1
   Wassef, Nadia. *Shelf Life* — B
   Wasserman, Claire. *Ladies Get Paid* — 650.1
   Wojcicki, Esther. *How to Raise Successful People* — 649
The Success Principles. Canfield, Jack — 158
SUCCESSFUL PEOPLE
   Epstein, David J. ★*Range* — 153.9
   Ferriss, Timothy. *Tools of Titans* — 081
   Gladwell, Malcolm. *Outliers* — 302
   Popova, Maria. *Figuring* — 920
SUCCULENT PLANTS
   Baldwin, Debra Lee. *Succulents Simplified* — 635.9
Succulents *Simplified*. Baldwin, Debra Lee — 635.9
★***Such Color***. Smith, Tracy K. — 811
Suchet, John
   Beethoven — B
   Mozart — B
   Verdi — 782.1092
SUDAN
   Addario, Lynsey. *Of Love & War* — 779
   Deng, Alephonsion. *They Poured Fire on Us from the Sky* — B
   Hari, Daoud. *The Translator* — B
   Mahjoub, Jamal. *A Line in the River* — 962.404
   Millard, Candice. ★*River of the Gods* — 916.204
Suddendorf, Thomas
   The Gap — 156
Suddenly We. Shockley, Evie — 811

AUTHOR, TITLE, SERIES AND SUBJECT INDEX

Suetonius
   ★*The Twelve Caesars* — B
SUEZ CANAL (EGYPT)
   Von Tunzelmann, Alex. *Blood and Sand* — 909.82
SUFFERING
   Billings, J. Todd. *Rejoicing in Lament* — 248.8
   Cairns, Scott. *The End of Suffering* — 231
   Dante Alighieri. *Purgatorio* — 851
   Deisseroth, Karl. *Projections* — 616.89
   Goldberg, Emma. *Life on the Line* — 362.1962
   Hesse, Maria. ★*Frida Kahlo* — B
   Ishikawa, Masaji. ★*A River in Darkness* — B
   Jamison, Kay Redfield. *Fires in the Dark* — 616.89
   Kushner, Harold S. *When Bad Things Happen to Good People* — 296.3
   Lalkhen, Abdul-Ghaaliq. *An Anatomy of Pain* — 616
   Mariani, Mike. *What Doesn't Kill Us Makes Us* — 155.9
   Nguyen, Viet Thanh. ★*A Man of Two Faces* — B
   Park, J. S. ★*As Long as You Need* — 248.8
   Plantinga, Cornelius. *Gratitude* — 179
   Rinzler, Lodro. *Love Hurts* — 294.3
   Risner, Vaneetha Rendall. *Walking Through Fire* — B
   Rush, Charaia. *Courageously Soft* — 234
   Sauls, Scott. *Beautiful People Don't Just Happen* — 248.8
   Setiya, Kieran. *Life Is Hard* — 128
   Williamson, Marianne. *Tears to Triumph* — 299
   Wilson, A. N. *The Mystery of Charles Dickens* — 823
Suffrage. DuBois, Ellen Carol — 324.6
SUFFRAGE
   Abrams, Stacey. *Our Time Is Now* — 324.60973
   Alexander, Michelle. *The New Jim Crow* — 364.973
   Anderson, Carol. ★*One Person, No Vote* — 324.6
   Berman, Ari. *Give Us the Ballot* — 324.6
   DuBois, Ellen Carol. *Suffrage* — 324.6
   Gallagher, Winifred. *New Women in the Old West* — 978.02
   Ginzberg, Lori D. *Elizabeth Cady Stanton* — B
   Goldstone, Lawrence. *On Account of Race* — 342.7308
   Jenkins, Jessica D. *Exploring Women's Suffrage Through 50 Historic Treasures* — 324.6
      Lane, Charles. *Freedom's Detective* — B
      Lichtman, Allan J. *The Embattled Vote in America* — 324.6
      Quinn, Bridget. *She Votes* — 324.6
      Watson, Bruce. *Freedom Summer* — 323.1196
      Wehle, Kim. *What You Need to Know About Voting and Why* — 324.60973
      Weiss, Elaine F. *The Woman's Hour* — 324.6
SUFFRAGIST MOVEMENT
   DuBois, Ellen Carol. *Suffrage* — 324.6
   Felder, Deborah G. *The American Women's Almanac* — 305.40973
   Gallagher, Winifred. *New Women in the Old West* — 978.02
   Ginzberg, Lori D. *Elizabeth Cady Stanton* — B
   Weiss, Elaine F. *The Woman's Hour* — 324.6
SUFFRAGISTS
   Dunbar, Erica Armstrong. ★*She Came to Slay* — B
   Hamlin, Kimberly A. *Free Thinker* — B
   Moore, Wendy. *No Man's Land* — 940.4
   Quinn, Bridget. *She Votes* — 324.6
   Weiss, Elaine F. *The Woman's Hour* — 324.6
SUFISM
   Ernst, Carl W. *The Shambhala Guide to Sufism* — 297.4
   Jalal al-Din Rumi, Maulana. *Rumi* — 891
   Magida, Arthur J. *Code Name Madeleine* — 940.54
Sugar. Rosen, Charles — B
Sugar. Walvin, James — 338.17361
SUGAR
   Moss, Michael. *Salt, Sugar, Fat* — 613.2
   Stuart, Andrea. *Sugar in the Blood* — 338.1
   Walvin, James. *Sugar* — 338.17361
Sugar in the Blood. Stuart, Andrea — 338.1
SUGAR INDUSTRY AND TRADE
   Kurlansky, Mark. *The Eastern Stars* — 796.357
   Rathbone, John Paul. *The Sugar King of Havana* — B
   Stuart, Andrea. *Sugar in the Blood* — 338.1
   Walvin, James. *Sugar* — 338.17361
The Sugar King of Havana. Rathbone, John Paul — B
SUGAR PLANTATIONS
   Checkoway, Julie. *The Three-Year Swim Club* — 797.2
   Kars, Marjoleine. *Blood on the River* — 306.3
   Walvin, James. *Sugar* — 338.17361

SUGAR WORKERS
   Walvin, James. *Sugar* — 338.17361
SUGAR-FREE DIET
   Cristofano, Jana. *Eat Well, Be Well* — 641.5
   Esposito, Jennifer. *Jennifer's Way Kitchen* — 641.5
   Gourdet, Gregory. *Everyone's Table* — 641.5
SUGARCANE
   Walvin, James. *Sugar* — 338.17361
Suh, Krista
   DIY Rules for a WTF World — 158.1
Suicidal. Bering, Jesse — 362.2
SUICIDAL BEHAVIOR
   Blaisdell, Robert. *Creating Anna Karenina* — 891.7
   Casillo, Charles. *Marilyn Monroe* — B
   Cayton-Holland, Adam. *Tragedy Plus Time* — B
   Cregan, Mary. *The Scar* — 616.85
   Kander, Jason. *Invisible Storm* — B
   Li, Yiyun. *Dear Friend, from My Life I Write to You in Your Life* — B
   Maisel, Ivan. *I Keep Trying to Catch His Eye* — B
   Martin, Clancy W. *How Not to Kill Yourself* — 362.28
   Satrapi, Marjane. *Chicken with Plums* — 741.5
   ★*Suicide*. Durkheim, Emile — 394.8
SUICIDE
   Bering, Jesse. *Suicidal* — 362.2
   Case, Anne. *Deaths of Despair and the Future of Capitalism* — 362.28
   Clark, Heather. ★*Red Comet* — B
   Crosley, Sloane. *Grief Is for People* — B
   Crowther, Gail. *Three-Martini Afternoons at the Ritz* — 920
   D'Agata, John. *About a Mountain* — 979.3
   Durkheim, Emile. ★*Suicide* — 394.8
   Enrich, David. *Dark Towers* — 332.1
   Goldsworthy, Adrian Keith. *Antony and Cleopatra* — 937
   Guinn, Jeff. *The Road to Jonestown* — 289.9
   Haidt, Jonathan. ★*The Anxious Generation* — 305.23
   Itzkoff, Dave. ★*Robin* — B
   Maisel, Ivan. *I Keep Trying to Catch His Eye* — B
   Mansbach, Adam. *I Had a Brother Once* — 811
   Martin, Clancy W. *How Not to Kill Yourself* — 362.28
   Montillo, Roseanne. *Deliberate Cruelty* — 364.152
   Price, Reynolds. *A Serious Way of Wondering* — 241
   Way, Niobe. *Rebels with a Cause* — 649
SUICIDE PACTS
   Asgarian, Roxanna. *We Were Once a Family* — 364.152
   King, Greg. *Twilight of Empire* — 943.6
SUICIDE VICTIMS
   Cayton-Holland, Adam. *Tragedy Plus Time* — B
   Kissinger, Meg. *While You Were Out* — 362.2
Suleyman, Mustafa
   The Coming Wave — 303.48
The Sullivan Street Bakery Cookbook. Lahey, Jim — 641.81
SULLIVAN, ANNIE, 1866-1936
   Gibson, William. ★*The Miracle Worker* — 812
   Keller, Helen. ★*The Story of My Life* — B
SULLIVAN, ED, 1901-1974
   Maguire, James. *Impresario* — B
Sullivan, James
   Unsinkable — 940.54
SULLIVAN, KATHRYN D.
   Grush, Loren. ★*The Six* — 629.4
Sullivan, Kevin
   Trump on Trial — 342.73
Sullivan, Margaret
   Newsroom Confidential — 070.92
SULLIVAN, MARGARET, 1957-
   Sullivan, Margaret. *Newsroom Confidential* — 070.92
Sullivan, Matt
   Can't Knock the Hustle — 796.323
Sullivan, Meghan
   The Good Life Method — 170
Sullivan, Patricia
   Lift Every Voice — 973
Sullivan, Randall
   The Devil's Best Trick — 235
   Graveyard of the Pacific — 979.7
SULLIVAN, RANDALL
   Sullivan, Randall. *Graveyard of the Pacific* — 979.7
Sullivan, Rosemary
   The Betrayal of Anne Frank — 940.53

PUBLIC LIBRARY CORE COLLECTION: NONFICTION
Twentieth Edition

Stalin's Daughter	B
The Sullivanians. Stille, Alexander	307.77
Sum It Up. Summitt, Pat Head	B
The Sum of Our Days. Allende, Isabel	B
The Sum of the People. Whitby, Andrew	001.4
★*The Sum of Us.* McGhee, Heather C.	305.8
Summer of '49. Halberstam, David	796.357
Summer Snow. Hass, Robert	811.6
Summers, Michael E.	
Exoplanets	523.2
Summerscale, Kate	
The Book of Phobias and Manias	616.85
The Summit. Conway, Edmund	337.09
SUMMIT MEETINGS	
Katz, Catherine Grace. *The Daughters of Yalta*	920
Summitt, Pat Head	
Sum It Up	B
SUMMITT, PAT HEAD, 1952-2016	
Cornelius, Maria M. *The Final Season*	B
Summitt, Pat Head. *Sum It Up*	B
Sumner, Seirian	
Endless Forms	595.79
SUN	
Nordgren, Tyler E. *Sun, Moon, Earth*	523.7
Trefil, James. *Space Atlas*	520
The Sun and Her Flowers. Kaur, Rupi	811.6
The Sun and the Moon and the Rolling Stones. Cohen, Rich	782.42166
The Sun Does Shine. Hinton, Anthony Ray	B
The Sun Is a Compass. Van Hemert, Caroline	979.8
Sun, Carrie	
Private Equity	B
SUN, CARRIE	
Sun, Carrie. *Private Equity*	B
Sun, Moon, Earth. Nordgren, Tyler E.	523.7
Sunbelt Blues. Ross, Andrew	363.5
SUNDAY	
Shulevitz, Judith. *The Sabbath World*	296.4
Sundays with Sophie. Flay, Bobby	641.5
Sundberg, Kelly	
Goodbye, Sweet Girl	B
SUNDBERG, KELLY, 1977-	
Sundberg, Kelly. *Goodbye, Sweet Girl*	B
Sundeen, Mark	
The Unsettlers	640
Sundressed. Tonti, Lucianne	746.9
★*The Sunflower.* Wiesenthal, Simon	179.7
The Sunflower Cast a Spell to Save Us from the Void. Wang, Jackie	811
SUNNI ISLAM	
Ghattas, Kim. *Black Wave*	955.05
Hazleton, Lesley. *After the Prophet*	297.8
Husain, Ed. ★*The House of Islam*	297
Nasr, Seyyed Vali Reza. *The Shia Revival*	297.8
Sunny Days. Kamp, David	791.4502
Sunshine Girl. Margulies, Julianna	B
Sunshine State. Gerard, Sarah	814
Sunstein, Cass R.	
Impeachment	342.73
Suny, Ronald Grigor	
Stalin	B
Super Better. McGonigal, Jane	794.8
Super Fly. Balcombe, Jonathan P.	595.77
★*Super-Infinite.* Rundell, Katherine	B
★*Supercommunicators.* Duhigg, Charles	153.6
Supercraft. Pester, Sophie	745.5
Superfreakonomics. Levitt, Steven D.	330
The Superfun Times Vegan Holiday Cookbook. Moskowitz, Isa Chandra	651.56
SUPERHEROES	
Liu, Simu. ★*We Were Dreamers*	B
Robinson, Joanna. ★*McU*	791.43
Weldon, Glen. ★*The Caped Crusade*	741.5
Wolk, Douglas. ★*All of the Marvels*	741.5
Superiority Burger Cookbook. Headley, Brooks	641.5
The Supermajority. Waldman, Michael	347.73
SUPERMARKETS	
Lorr, Benjamin. *The Secret Life of Groceries*	381.4
Superminds. Malone, Thomas W.	005.7
SUPERNATURAL	
Aykroyd, Peter. *A History of Ghosts*	133.1
Braudy, Leo. *Haunted*	398.45
Dickey, Colin. *Ghostland*	133.1
Knight, Sam. *The Premonitions Bureau*	133.8
O'Connor, John. *The Secret History of Bigfoot*	001.944
Smith, Richard MacLean. *Unexplained*	130
SUPERNOVAE	
Berman, Bob. *Earth-Shattering*	523.1
The Superorganism. Holldobler, Bert	595.7
SUPERSONIC PLANES	
Hampton, Dan. *Chasing the Demon*	629.132
SUPERSTITION	
Schiff, Stacy. *The Witches*	345
Sullivan, Randall. *The Devil's Best Trick*	235
Wilson, Derek K. *A Magical World*	261.55
SUPERSTRING THEORIES	
Greene, B. ★*The Elegant Universe*	539.7
Kaku, Michio. ★*Hyperspace*	530.1
Kaku, Michio. *Parallel Worlds*	523.1
SUPERVISION OF EMPLOYEES	
Horstman, Mark. *The Effective Manager*	658.4
McNeil, Beth. *Fundamentals of Library Supervision*	023
Tucker, Dennis C. *Crash Course in Library Supervision*	023
SUPERVISORS	
Webb, Maynard. *Dear Founder*	658
SUPPLEMENTARY EMPLOYMENT	
Howe, Ben Ryder. *My Korean Deli*	B
SUPPLY AND DEMAND	
Goodman, Peter S. ★*How the World Ran Out of Everything*	658.7
Miller, Chris. *Chip War*	338.4
Mullainathan, Sendhil. *Scarcity*	338.5
SUPPLY-SIDE ECONOMICS	
Goodman, Peter S. ★*How the World Ran Out of Everything*	658.7
Supreme City. Miller, Donald L.	974.7
★*Supreme Inequality.* Cohen, Adam	347.73
Supreme Power. Shesol, Jeff	347.73
The Supremes. Ribowsky, Mark	B
Sure, I'll Join Your Cult. Bamford, Maria	B
Surely You Can't Be Serious. Zucker, David	791.43
Surfaces and Essences. Hofstadter, Douglas R.	169
SURFERS	
Finnegan, William. *Barbarian Days*	B
Ollestad, Norman. *Crazy for the Storm*	B
SURFING	
Cardwell, Diane. *Rockaway*	B
Clark, Liz. *Swell*	B
Finnegan, William. *Barbarian Days*	B
Mackinnon, Al. *Epic Surf Breaks of the World*	797.32
SURGEONS	
Aptowicz, Cristin O'Keefe. *Dr. Mutter's Marvels*	B
Barnes, Julian. *The Man in the Red Coat*	B
Fitzharris, Lindsey. *The Butchering Art*	B
Gawande, Atul. *Complications*	B
Hallman, J. C. *Say Anarcha*	618.1
Kershaw, Alex. *Avenue of Spies*	940.53
Laar, Arnold van de. *Under the Knife*	617
Marsh, Henry. *Admissions*	B
Marsh, Henry. ★*Do No Harm*	B
Mezrich, Joshua D. *When Death Becomes Life*	617.9
Rutkow, Ira M. *Empire of the Scalpel*	617
Swartz, Mimi. *Ticker*	617.4
Warren, W. Lee. *No Place to Hide*	B
SURGERY	
Aptowicz, Cristin O'Keefe. *Dr. Mutter's Marvels*	B
Dittrich, Luke. ★*Patient H.M.*	616.85
Fitzharris, Lindsey. *The Butchering Art*	B
Gawande, Atul. *Complications*	B
Jauhar, Sandeep. *Heart*	612.1
Joyce, Russell W. *His Face Like Mine*	248
Laar, Arnold van de. *Under the Knife*	617
Marsh, Henry. *Admissions*	B
Marsh, Henry. ★*Do No Harm*	B
Okorafor, Nnedi. *Broken Places & Outer Spaces*	153.3
Rutkow, Ira M. *Empire of the Scalpel*	617
Somerstein, Rachel. ★*Invisible Labor*	618.8
Weigel, Alicia Roth. *Inverse Cowgirl*	B
Surpassing Certainty. Mock, Janet	
SURPRISE	
Keltner, Dacher. ★*Awe*	152.4

AUTHOR, TITLE, SERIES AND SUBJECT INDEX

Surprise, Kill, Vanish. Jacobsen, Annie	327.1273
A *Surprised* Queenhood in the New Black Sun. Jackson, Angela	B

SURREALISM

Gohr, Siegfried. ★*Magritte*	759.9493
Kahlo, Frida. *The Diary of Frida Kahlo*	B
Morris, Desmond. *The Lives of the Surrealists*	B
Shaw, Jennifer Laurie. *Exist Otherwise*	709.2
★*Surrender*. Bono	B

SURVEILLANCE

Farrow, Ronan. ★*Catch and Kill*	331.4
Hill, Kashmir. ★*Your Face Belongs to Us*	006.2
Izgil, Tahir Hamut. *Waiting to Be Arrested at Night*	B
Reynolds, Nicholas E. *Need to Know*	940.54
Tau, Byron. ★*Means of Control*	363.25
Vogel, Steve. *Betrayal in Berlin*	327.1273043
Wiggins, Christopher L. *How Data Happened*	310

SURVEYING

Garfield, Simon. *On the Map*	526.09
The Surveyors. Salter, Mary Jo	811

SURVIVAL

Aktipis, Athena. ★*A Field Guide to the Apocalypse*	155.2
Anthony, Carmelo. *Where Tomorrows Aren't Promised*	B
Asim, Jabari. *We Can't Breathe*	305.896
Brandt, Anthony. *The Man Who Ate His Boots*	910.91
Brotherton, Marcus. *A Bright and Blinding Sun*	940.54
Brusatte, Stephen. *The Rise and Reign of the Mammals*	569
Cassidy, Cody. *How to Survive History*	904
Chiger, Krystyna. *The Girl in the Green Sweater*	B
Clifton, Lucille. *How to Carry Water*	811
Dogon, Mondiant. *Those We Throw Away Are Diamonds*	B
Eger, Edith Eva. *The Choice*	B
Eichenwald, Kurt. *A Mind Unraveled*	B
Elliott, Andrea. ★*Invisible Child*	362.7
Fagan, Brian M. *Climate Chaos*	304.2
Finkelstein, Daniel. *Two Roads Home*	920
Foster, Charles. *Being a Human*	155.7
Frankel, Rebecca. *Into the Forest*	940.53
Fraser, Rebecca. *The Mayflower*	974.4
Frenkel, Françoise. *A Bookshop in Berlin*	B
Geroux, William. *The Ghost Ships of Archangel*	940.54
Gutman, Matt. *The Boys in the Cave*	796.52
Haitiwaji, Gulbahar. *How I Survived a Chinese "Reeducation" Camp*	305.8
Hamill, Kirkland. *Filthy Beasts*	B
Hamilton, Lisa M. *The Hungry Season*	B
Harding, Luke. *Invasion*	947.7
Holden, Wendy. ★*Born Survivors*	940.53
Hough, Lauren. *Leaving Isn't the Hardest Thing*	B
Imbler, Sabrina. *How Far the Light Reaches*	591.77
Iperen, Roxane van. *The Sisters of Auschwitz*	940.53
Jackson, Mitchell S. *Survival Math*	B
Jaku, Eddie. ★*The Happiest Man on Earth*	B
Johnson, Lizzie. ★*Paradise*	363.37
Junger, Sebastian. *Fire*	909.82
Katin, Miriam. *We Are on Our Own*	741.5
Kelly, Donika. *The Renunciations*	811
Kruzan, Sara. *I Cried to Dream Again*	B
Kyle, Taya. *American Spirit*	B
Lineberry, Cate. *The Secret Rescue*	940.54
Lockhart, Chris. ★*Walking the Bowl*	362.7
Loftis, Larry. ★*The Watchmaker's Daughter*	940.53
Luttrell, Marcus. *Lone Survivor*	958.104
Mariani, Mike. ★*What Doesn't Kill Us Makes Us*	155.9
Marshall, Nate. *Finna*	811
McIntyre, Rick. *The Reign of Wolf 21*	599.773
Messenger, Alex. *The Twenty-Ninth Day*	B
Mikhaiil, Dunya. *The Beekeeper*	956.7044
Millard, Candice. ★*Hero of the Empire*	968.04
Miller, Christopher. *The War Came to Us*	947.7
Mohan, Rohini. *The Seasons of Trouble*	954.9303
Moorhouse, Roger. *Berlin at War*	943
Murad, Nadia. ★*The Last Girl*	B
Murakami, Haruki. *Underground*	364.15
Myers, Leah. *Thinning Blood*	B
Newitz, Annalee. *Scatter, Adapt, and Remember*	576.8
Niven, Jennifer. *Ada Blackjack*	B
O'Donnell, Svenja. *Inge's War*	943.086
Ollestad, Norman. *Crazy for the Storm*	B
Passarlay, Gulwali. *The Lightless Sky*	B
Pivnik, Sam. *Survivor*	940.5318
Price, David A. ★*Love and Hate in Jamestown*	975.5
Price, Margo. *Maybe We'll Make It*	B
Qadiri, Humayra. *Dancing in the Mosque*	B
Quart, Alissa. *Bootstrapped*	305.5
Rawles, James Wesley. *Tools for Survival*	613.6
Roberts, David. *Alone on the Ice*	919.8904
Rosner, Elizabeth. *Survivor Cafe*	940.53
Roy, Saumya. *Castaway Mountain*	363.72
Saint John, Bozoma. *The Urgent Life*	B
Sancton, Julian. *Madhouse at the End of the Earth*	919.8904
Sandberg, Sheryl. *Option B*	155.9
Schlanger, Zoe. ★*The Light Eaters*	571.2
Sides, Hampton. ★*In the Kingdom of Ice*	910.4
Smith, Carol. *Crossing the River*	B
Snyder, Rachel Louise. *Women We Buried, Women We Burned*	B
Stanton, Doug. *In Harm's Way*	940.54
Stanton, Doug. *The Odyssey of Echo Company*	959.704
Steinberg, Jonny. *A Man of Good Hope*	B
Taffa, Deborah Jackson. ★*Whiskey Tender*	B
Taing, Mae Bunseng. *Under the Naga Tail*	B
Tsui, Bonnie. *Why We Swim*	797.2
Umar, Ousman. *North to Paradise*	B
Urrea, Luis Alberto. *The Devil's Highway*	304.8
V. ★*Reckoning*	814
Vasquez, Karla Tatiana. ★*The Salvisoul Cookbook*	641.598
Wallis, Michael. *The Best Land Under Heaven*	978
Williams, Kidada E. *I Saw Death Coming*	973.8
Wukovits, John F. *Lost at Sea*	940.54

SURVIVAL (AFTER AIRPLANE ACCIDENTS, SHIPWRECKS, ETC.)

Alexander, Caroline. *The Endurance*	919.8
Grann, David. ★*The Wager*	910.91
Murphy, Brian. *81 Days Below Zero*	940.54
Parrado, Nando. ★*Miracle in the Andes*	982
Read, Piers Paul. ★*Alive*	982
Severin, Timothy. *In Search of Robinson Crusoe*	996.1
Sides, Hampton. ★*In the Kingdom of Ice*	910.4
Zuckoff, Mitchell. *Frozen in Time*	998.2
Zuckoff, Mitchell. *Lost in Shangri-La*	940.54

SURVIVAL (AFTER EARTHQUAKES)

Albom, Mitch. *Finding Chika*	B

SURVIVAL (AFTER FLOODS)

Barry, John M. *Rising Tide*	977
Eggers, Dave. *Zeitoun*	305.892

SURVIVAL (AFTER HURRICANES)

Eggers, Dave. *Zeitoun*	305.892
Fink, Sheri. *Five Days at Memorial*	362.1109763
Neufeld, Josh. *A.D.*	741.5

SURVIVAL (ECONOMICS)

Bruder, Jessica. ★*Nomadland*	331.3
Morduch, Jonathan. *The Financial Diaries*	332.024

SURVIVAL (IN CONCENTRATION CAMPS, PRISONS, ETC.)

Clavin, Thomas. *Lightning Down*	940.54
Friedman, Tova. ★*The Daughter of Auschwitz*	B
Spiegelman, Art. ★*Maus*	741.5
Van De Perre, Selma. *My Name Is Selma*	940.53
★*Survival in Auschwitz*. Levi, Primo	B
Survival Math. Jackson, Mitchell S.	B

SURVIVAL SKILLS

Miles, Tiya. ★*Wild Girls*	304.2

SURVIVALISM

Westover, Tara. ★*Educated*	B

SURVIVALISTS

Grylls, Bear. *Never Give Up*	B
Surviving Autocracy. Gessen, Masha	973.933
Surviving Katyn. Rogoyska, Jane	940.54
Surviving Schizophrenia. Torrey, E. Fuller	616.89
Surviving The Daily Grind. Coggan, Philip	658.3
Surviving The White Gaze. Carroll, Rebecca	B
Survivor. Pivnik, Sam	940.5318
Survivor Cafe. Rosner, Elizabeth	940.53

SURVIVOR GUILT

Feldman, Deborah. *Exodus*	B

SURVIVORS OF SUICIDE VICTIMS

Cayton-Holland, Adam. *Tragedy Plus Time*	B
★*The Survivors* of the Clotilda. Durkin, Hannah	306.362

Susa, Sachiko

Sweet & Simple Needle Felted Animals	746

PUBLIC LIBRARY CORE COLLECTION: NONFICTION
Twentieth Edition

Susan, Linda, Nina & Cokie. Napoli, Lisa	920
Susanka, Sarah	
Creating the Not so Big House	728
Not so Big Solutions for Your Home	728
SUSHI	
Goulding, Matt. *Rice, Noodle, Fish*	394.1
Suspected of Independence. McKean, David	B
SUSPECTS (CRIMINAL INVESTIGATION)	
Barron, Justine. *They Killed Freddie Gray*	363.32
Rudolf, David S. *American Injustice*	345.73
SUSPENSION BRIDGES	
Blockley, David. *Bridges*	725
SUSPICION	
Betz-Hamilton, Axton. *The Less People Know About Us*	364.16
DiResta, Renee. *Invisible Rulers*	320
Eisenberg, Emma Copley. ★*The Third Rainbow Girl*	364.152
Goodheart, Adam. *The Last Island*	954
Rohde, David. *In Deep*	973.933
Trimble, Lee. *Beyond the Call*	940.54
Suspicious Minds. Brotherton, Rob	153.4
Sussman, Adeena	
Sababa	641.5
★*Shabbat*	641.5
SUSTAINABILITY	
Barber, Dan. *The Third Plate*	641.3
Dissen, William Stark. *Thoughtful Cooking*	641.5975
Gleick, Peter H. *The Three Ages of Water*	333.91
Kolbert, Elizabeth. ★*Under a White Sky*	304.2
Malarkey, Tucker. *Stronghold*	639.2
McLaughlin, Chris. *The Good Garden*	635
Miodownik, Mark. *Liquid Rules*	530.4
Nelson, Bryn. *Flush*	612.3
Ritchie, Hannah. *Not the End of the World*	338.9
SUSTAINABLE AGRICULTURE	
Ackerman-Leist, Philip. *Rebuilding the Foodshed*	338.1
Berry, Wendell. ★*The World-Ending Fire*	818
Foer, Jonathan Safran. ★*We Are the Weather*	636
Hewitt, Ben. ★*The Town That Food Saved*	338.1
Kauffman, Jonathan. *Hippie Food*	394.1
Logsdon, Gene. *Letter to a Young Farmer*	338.10973
Montgomery, David R. *What Your Food Ate*	631.4
Roberts, Julius. *The Farm Table*	641.594
Smith, Bren. *Eat Like a Fish*	338.3
SUSTAINABLE COMMUNITIES	
Sundeen, Mark. *The Unsettlers*	640
SUSTAINABLE DEVELOPMENT	
Elmore, Bartow J. *Citizen Coke*	338.7
Sachs, Jeffrey. *The Age of Sustainable Development*	338.9
Smil, Vaclav. *How the World Really Works*	500
Sundeen, Mark. *The Unsettlers*	640
SUSTAINABLE FISHERIES	
Hilborn, Ray. *Overfishing*	338.3
SUSTAINABLE LIVING	
Allen, Brigette. *Living Without Plastic*	640
Beavan, Colin. *No Impact Man*	B
Cline, Elizabeth L. *The Conscious Closet*	646
Franklin-Wallis, Oliver. ★*Wasteland*	363.72
Guralnick, Margot. *Remodelista*	747
Logan, William Bryant. *Sprout Lands*	582.16
Logsdon, Gene. *Letter to a Young Farmer*	338.10973
Roberts, Julius. *The Farm Table*	641.594
Sundeen, Mark. *The Unsettlers*	640
Tonti, Lucianne. *Sundressed*	746.9
Yang, April. *DIY Thrift Flip*	646.2
SUSTAINABLE SOCIETIES	
Hewitt, Ben. ★*The Town That Food Saved*	338.1
Logan, William Bryant. *Sprout Lands*	582.16
Sutherland, Amy	
Rescuing Penny Jane	636.7
SUTHERLAND, AMY	
Sutherland, Amy. *Rescuing Penny Jane*	636.7
Sutin, Lawrence	
★*All Is Change*	294.309
SUTTON, LEROY	
Fenn, Lisa. *Carry On*	B
Sutton, Robert I.	
The Asshole Survival Guide	650.1
Suvari, Mena	
The Great Peace	B
SUVARI, MENA, 1979-	
Suvari, Mena. *The Great Peace*	B
Suzuki, Shunryu	
Zen Mind, Beginner's Mind	294.3
Svensson, Patrik	
The Book of Eels	597
Sverdrup-Thygeson, Anne	
Buzz, Sting, Bite	595.7
Svrluga, Barry	
The Grind	796.357
Swafford, Jan	
★*Beethoven*	B
Charles Ives	B
Johannes Brahms	B
Mozart	B
SWALLOWS	
Heinrich, Bernd. *White Feathers*	598.8
Swamplands. Struzik, Edward	577.68
SWAMPS	
Proulx, Annie. ★*Fen, Bog and Swamp*	551.41
Struzik, Edward. *Swamplands*	577.68
The Swans of Harlem. Valby, Karen	792.8
Swanson, James L.	
End of Days	973.922092
Swansong 1945. Kempowski, Walter	940.54
SWARM INTELLIGENCE	
Malone, Thomas W. *Superminds*	005.7
Swarns, Rachel L.	
The 272	975.2
★*American Tapestry*	B
Swartz, Mimi	
Ticker	617.4
Sway. Agarwal, Pragya	177
Swearington, Jen	
Printing on Fabric	746.6
Sweat. Hayes, Bill	613.7
SWEAT	
Everts, Sarah. *The Joy of Sweat*	612.7
SWEATERS	
Baca, Salena. *Oversize Fashion Crochet*	746.43
Budd, Ann. *The Knitter's Handy Book of Top-Down Sweaters*	746.43
Herzog, Amy. *Knit Wear Love*	746.43
Herzog, Amy. *You Can Knit That*	746.432
Impelen, Helgrid van. *Big Knits Big Needles*	746.43
Ludwig, Frauke. *Essential Knit Sweaters*	746.43
Orenstein, Peggy. *Unraveling*	B
Square, Vicki. *The Knitter's Companion*	746.432
SWEDEN	
Asbrink, Elisabeth. *And in the Vienna Woods the Trees Remain*	B
Booth, Michael. *The Almost Nearly Perfect People*	948.071
King, David. *Six Days in August*	364.15
SWEDISH AMERICANS	
Samuelsson, Marcus. *Yes, Chef*	B
Sweeney, Jennifer	
Literacy	027.62
Sweet. Ottolenghi, Yotam	641.86
Sweet & Simple Needle Felted Animals. Susa, Sachiko	746
Sweet Enough. Roman, Alison	641.86
★*Sweet Home Cafe Cookbook.* Lukas, Albert	641.59
★*The Sweet Polish Kitchen.* Behan, Ren	641.594
★*Sweet Potato Soul.* Claiborne, Jenne	641.5
★*The Sweet Science.* Liebling, A. J.	796.83
★*Sweet Thunder.* Haygood, Wil	B
SWEET, OSSIAN, 1895-1960	
Boyle, Kevin. *Arc of Justice*	345.73
Sweetness. Pearlman, Jeff	B
Sweig, Julia	
Lady Bird Johnson	B
Swell. Clark, Liz	B
Swenson, May	
Collected Poems	811
★*The Swerve.* Greenblatt, Stephen	940.2
Swift, Earl	
Across the Airless Wilds	629.45
Chesapeake Requiem	639
Hell Put to Shame	364.15

AUTHOR, TITLE, SERIES AND SUBJECT INDEX

SWIFT, TAYLOR, 1989-
   Newkey-Burden, Chas. *Taylor Swift* — B
★*A Swim in a Pond in the Rain*. Saunders, George — 891.7
SWIMMERS
   Checkoway, Julie. *The Three-Year Swim Club* — 797.2
   Cox, Lynne. *Swimming to Antarctica* — B
   Daley, Tom. *Coming up for Air* — B
   Mortimer, Gavin. *The Great Swim* — B
   Nyad, Diana. *Find a Way* — B
   Tsui, Bonnie. *Why We Swim* — 797.2
SWIMMING
   Checkoway, Julie. *The Three-Year Swim Club* — 797.2
   Cox, Lynne. *Swimming to Antarctica* — B
   Means, Howard B. ★*Splash!* — 797.2
   Nyad, Diana. *Find a Way* — B
   Tsui, Bonnie. *Why We Swim* — 797.2
Swimming to Antarctica. Cox, Lynne — B
SWINDLERS AND SWINDLING
   Amore, Anthony M. *The Art of the Con* — 702.8
   Behar, Richard. *Madoff* — 364.16
   Brown, Eliot. *The Cult of We* — 333.33
   Egan, Timothy. ★*A Fever in the Heartland* — 322.4
   Fox, Margalit. *The Confidence Men* — 940.4
   Jobb, Dean. *A Gentleman and a Thief* — 364.16
   Keefe, Patrick Radden. ★*Rogues* — 364.16
   Levin, Daniel Barban. *Slonim Woods 9* — B
   Levin, Josh. *The Queen* — 364.16
   Manzione, Gianmarc. *Pin Action* — B
   Marie, Jane. ★*Selling the Dream* — 658.8
   McCumber, David. *Playing off the Rail* — B
   McSwane, J. David. ★*Pandemic, Inc.* — 362.1962
   Sancton, Thomas. *The Bettencourt Affair* — B
   Schindler, Meriel. *The Lost Cafe Schindler* — 943.64
   Sisman, Adam. *The Professor and the Parson* — 364.16
   Tolentino, Jia. ★*Trick Mirror* — 973.93
   Weinman, Sarah. *Scoundrel* — 364.152
   Willetts, Paul. *King Con* — B
   Yeebo, Yepoka. *Anansi's Gold* — 364.16
   Zuckoff, Mitchell. *Ponzi's Scheme* — B
Swing Kings. Diamond, Jared M. — 796.357
Swisher, Kara
   Burn Book — 303.48
SWISHER, KARA
   Swisher, Kara. *Burn Book* — 303.48
SWISS ALPS
   Kaag, John J. *Hiking with Nietzsche* — 193
Switched on Pop. Sloan, Nate — 781.64
Switching Fields. Dohrmann, George — 796.334
Switek, Brian
   Skeleton Keys — 611
SWITZERLAND
   Moorhouse, Roger. *The Forgers* — 940.53
   Winder, Simon. *Lotharingia* — 944
Swofford, Anthony
   Jarhead — 956.7044
SWOFFORD, ANTHONY
   Swofford, Anthony. *Jarhead* — 956.7044
★*Swole*. Brodeur, Michael Andor — 155.3
The Sword and the Shield. Joseph, Peniel E. — B
SWORDPLAY
   Bennett, Alexander. *Kendo* — 796.86
Sybil. Schreiber, Flora Rheta — 616.85
Sybil Exposed. Nathan, Debbie — B
SYBIL, 1923-1998
   Nathan, Debbie. *Sybil Exposed* — B
Sykes, Christopher Simon
   David Hockney — B
   David Hockney — B
SYLVESTER II, POPE, 945?-1003
   Brown, Nancy Marie. *The Abacus and the Cross* — B
SYMBIOSIS
   Margulis, Lynn. *Symbiotic Planet* — 576.8
Symbiotic Planet. Margulis, Lynn — 576.8
SYMBOLISM
   Hughes, Bettany. *Venus and Aphrodite* — 292
   Meals, Roy A. *Bones* — 599.9
   Rinella, Steven. *American Buffalo* — 599.64

SYMBOLISM IN ARCHITECTURE
   Khan, Yasmin Sabina. *Enlightening the World* — 974.7
SYMBOLISM IN POLITICS
   Taylor, Fred. *The Berlin Wall* — 943
Symon, Michael
   ★*Fix It with Food* — 641.5
   Michael Symon's Playing with Fire — 641.7
Symonds, Craig L.
   The Battle of Midway — 940.54
   Lincoln and His Admirals — B
   World War II at Sea — 940.54
SYMPHONIES
   Hamilton-Paterson, James. ★*Beethoven's Eroica* — 784.18
   Steinberg, Michael. *The Symphony* — 784.2
The Symphony. Steinberg, Michael — 784.2
SYMPTOMS
   Kelly, Christopher R. *Am I Dying?!* — 362.1
The Synagogue Survival Kit. Wagner, Jordan Lee — 296.4
SYNAGOGUES
   Oppenheimer, Mark. *Squirrel Hill* — 364.152
   Wagner, Jordan Lee. *The Synagogue Survival Kit* — 296.4
SYNESTHESIA
   Tammet, Daniel. *Born on a Blue Day* — B
Synnott, Mark
   The Third Pole — 796.522
SYNNOTT, MARK
   Synnott, Mark. *The Third Pole* — 796.522
SYNONYMS AND ANTONYMS
   Holder, R. W. *How Not to Say What You Mean* — 427
SYPHILIS
   Reverby, Susan M. *Examining Tuskegee* — 174.2
SYRIA
   Abouzeid, Rania. *No Turning Back* — 956.9104
   Ahmad, Aeham. *The Pianist from Syria* — B
   Azad. *Long Shot* — 365
   Campbell, Deborah. *A Disappearance in Damascus* — B
   Dagher, Sam. *Assad or We Burn the Country* — 956.9104
   Di Giovanni, Janine. *The Morning They Came for Us* — 956.9104
   Fleming, Melissa. *A Hope More Powerful Than the Sea* — 956.9104
   Lemmon, Gayle Tzemach. *The Daughters of Kobani* — 956.9104
   Levin, Daniel. *Proof of Life* — 956.9104
   Malek, Alia. *The Home That Was Our Country* — B
   Pearlman, Wendy. *We Crossed a Bridge and It Trembled* — 956.9104
   Roy, Jessica. *American Girls* — 305.48
   Salama, Jordan. ★*Stranger in the Desert* — 982
   Saldana, Stephanie. *What We Remember Will Be Saved* — 362.7
   Samer. *The Raqqa Diaries* — 956.9104
   Sattouf, Riad. *The Arab of the Future 2* — 741.5
   Seierstad, Asne. *Two Sisters* — 956.9104
   Thomson, Mike. *Syria's Secret Library* — 956.9104
   Ward, Clarissa. *On All Fronts* — B
   Warrick, Joby. *Red Line* — 956.9104
Syria's Secret Library. Thomson, Mike — 956.9104
SYRIAN AMERICANS
   Eggers, Dave. *Zeitoun* — 305.892
   Mizrahi, Isaac. *I.M.* — B
SYRIAN PEOPLE
   Salama, Jordan. ★*Stranger in the Desert* — 982
   Saldana, Stephanie. *What We Remember Will Be Saved* — 362.7
The System. Benedict, Jeff — 796.332
Systemic. Liverpool, Layal — 362.1
SYSTEMS ANALYSTS
   Manning, Chelsea. *Readme.Txt* — B
Szablowski, Witold
   Dancing Bears — 947.086
Szarkowski, John
   Ansel Adams at 100 — B
Szczeszak-Brewer, Agata
   The Hunger Book — B
SZCZESZAK-BREWER, AGATA
   Szczeszak-Brewer, Agata. *The Hunger Book* — B
Sze, Arthur
   Sight Lines — 811
Szerlip, Barbara
   The Man Who Designed the Future — B
Szpiro, George
   Poincare's Prize — 510.76

PUBLIC LIBRARY CORE COLLECTION: NONFICTION
Twentieth Edition

Szwed, John F.
   Cosmic Scholar — B
Szymborska, Wislawa
   Here — 891.8
   Map — 891.8

T

★ *T.S. Eliot*. Gordon, Lyndall — B
Tabery, James
   ★ *Tyranny of the Gene* — 572.8
A Table Full of Love. McAlpine, Skye — 641.5
★ *Table Manners*. Tower, Jeremiah — 395.5
TABLE SETTING AND DECORATION
   Watson, Ted Kennedy. *Ted Kennedy Watson's Guide to Stylish Entertaining* — 793.2
Table Tennis. McAfee, Richard — 796.34
TABLE TENNIS
   McAfee, Richard. *Table Tennis* — 796.34
TABLOID NEWSPAPERS
   Ditum, Sarah. *Toxic* — 920.72
   Hortis, C. Alexander. *The Witch of New York* — 364.152
TABOO
   Eco, Umberto. *On Ugliness* — 111
   Schutt, Bill. *Cannibalism* — 394
Tabor, James M.
   Blind Descent — 796.52
Tabor, Nick
   Africatown — 976.1
Tabula Rasa; V.1. McPhee, John — 818
TACOS
   Trejo, Danny. *Trejo's Tacos* — 641.5979
Taddeo, Lisa
   Three Women — 306.7082
TAFERO, JESSE, 1946-1990
   McGarrahan, Ellen. *Two Truths and a Lie* — 364.152
Taffa, Deborah Jackson
   ★ *Whiskey Tender* — B
TAFT, HELEN HERRON, 1861-1943
   Anthony, Carl Sferrazza. *Nellie Taft* — B
TAFT, WILLIAM H. (WILLIAM HOWARD), 1857-1930
   Anthony, Carl Sferrazza. *Nellie Taft* — B
   Cohen, Adam. ★ *Imbeciles* — 344.7304
   Goodwin, Doris Kearns. ★ *The Bully Pulpit* — 973.91
Tagore, Rabindranath
   Selected Poems — 891
TAGORE, RABINDRANATH, 1861-1941
   Tagore, Rabindranath. *Selected Poems* — 891
TAI CHI
   Wayne, Peter. *The Harvard Medical School Guide to Tai Chi* — 613.7
Taibbi, Matt
   I Can't Breathe — 363.2
Taillac, Victoire de
   An Atlas of Natural Beauty — 646.7
TAILORING
   Greenfield, Martin. ★ *Measure of a Man* — B
   Yang, April. *DIY Thrift Flip* — 646.2
TAILORS
   Greenfield, Martin. ★ *Measure of a Man* — B
Tailspin. Brill, Steven — 306.0973
Taing, Mae Bunseng
   Under the Naga Tail — B
TAING, MAE BUNSENG
   Taing, Mae Bunseng. *Under the Naga Tail* — B
TAIWAN
   Gaw, Frankie. *First Generation* — 641.595
   Li, Zhuqing. *Daughters of the Flower Fragrant Garden* — 951.04
   Pakula, Hannah. *The Last Empress* — B
   Taylor, Jay. *The Generalissimo* — B
TAIWANESE AMERICANS
   Gaw, Frankie. *First Generation* — 641.595
   Hsu, Hua. ★ *Stay True* — B
   Huang, Eddie. *Fresh off the Boat* — B
Takaki, Ronald T.
   Double Victory — 940.53
Take The Lead. DiGiulian, Sasha — B
Takeover. Ryback, Timothy W. — 943.086

Taking Berlin. Dugard, Martin — 940.54
★ *Taking Care*. DiGregorio, Sarah — 610.73
Taking Charge. Johnson, Lyndon B. — 973.923
Taking Charge of ADHD. Barkley, Russell A. — 618.92
Taking Charge of Your Pregnancy. Fisher, Susan J. — 618.2
Taking My Life Back. Gregory, Rebekah — B
The Taking of K-129. Dean, Josh — 910.91
Taking Paris. Dugard, Martin — 940.54
A Tale of Love and Darkness. Oz, Amos — B
The Tale of the Dueling Neurosurgeons. Kean, Sam — 617.4
The Talented Mrs. Mandelbaum. Fox, Margalit — 364.1
Tales from Ovid. Ovid — 873
Tales from the Ant World. Wilson, Edward O. — 595.79
Taliban. Rashid, Ahmed — 958.104
★ *The Talk*. Bell, Darrin — 741.5
Talk Like Ted. Gallo, Carmine — 658.4
Talk of Champions. Smith, Kenny — B
Talking About Detective Fiction. James, P. D. — 823
Talking Back, Talking Black. McWhorter, John H. — 427
Talking to Crazy. Goulston, Mark — 158.2
Talking to My Angels. Etheridge, Melissa — B
★ *Talking to Strangers*. Gladwell, Malcolm — 302
Tall Men, Short Shorts. Montville, Leigh — 796.323
Tallamy, Douglas W.
   ★ *Nature's Best Hope* — 635.9
Tallent, Elizabeth
   Scratched — B
Talley, Andre Leon
   The Chiffon Trenches — B
TALLEY, ANDRE LEON. 1948-2022
   Talley, Andre Leon. *The Chiffon Trenches* — B
Talley, Safiyyah
   Knit 2 Socks in 1 — 746.43
Tallis, Frank
   The Incurable Romantic — 152.4
   ★ *Mortal Secrets* — B
Tallis, Nicola
   Crown of Blood — B
   Uncrowned Queen — B
★ *The Talmud*. Freedman, H. — 296.1
Talty, Stephan
   Agent Garbo — 940.5
   The Good Assassin — 364.15
   Saving Bravo — 959.704
Talusan, Meredith
   Fairest — 305.30973
TALUSAN, MEREDITH
   Talusan, Meredith. *Fairest* — 305.30973
Tam, Michelle
   Ready or Not! — 641.5
Tamanaha, Brian Z.
   Failing Law Schools — 340.071
Tamblyn, Amber
   ★ *Era of Ignition* — B
TAMBLYN, AMBER
   Tamblyn, Amber. ★ *Era of Ignition* — B
Tamerlane. Marozzi, Justin — 950.2
TAMERLANE, 1336-1405
   Marozzi, Justin. *Tamerlane* — 950.2
TAMIL (INDIC PEOPLE)
   Mohan, Rohini. *The Seasons of Trouble* — 954.9303
   Subramanian, Sammanth. *This Divided Island* — 954.9303
Tamimi, Ahed
   ★ *They Called Me a Lioness* — B
TAMIMI, AHED, 2001-
   Tamimi, Ahed. ★ *They Called Me a Lioness* — B
Tamimi, Sami
   Falastin — 641.595
Tammet, Daniel
   Born on a Blue Day — B
TAMMET, DANIEL, 1979-
   Tammet, Daniel. *Born on a Blue Day* — B
Tammy Wynette. McDonough, Jimmy — B
Tan, Amy
   ★ *The Backyard Bird Chronicles* — 598
   ★ *Where the Past Begins* — B
TAN, AMY
   Tan, Amy. ★ *The Backyard Bird Chronicles* — 598

AUTHOR, TITLE, SERIES AND SUBJECT INDEX

Tan, Amy. ★ *Where the Past Begins* .... B
Tanais
   In Sensorium .... B
TANAIS
   Tanais. *In Sensorium* .... B
Tandoh, Ruby
   ★*Cook as You Are* 641.59
   ★*Eat Up* 641.3
Tang, Karen
   ★*It's Not Hysteria* 618.2
Tangled Vines. Glatt, John 364.152
TANGO (DANCE)
   Flaherty, Meghan. *Tango Lessons* 793.3
Tango Lessons. Flaherty, Meghan 793.3
The Tango War. McConahay, Mary Jo 940.53
TANK WARFARE
   Hogan, William R. *Task Force Hogan* 940.54
   Holland, James. *Brothers in Arms* 940.54
   Makos, Adam. *Spearhead* .... B
TANKERS
   McPhee, John. *Uncommon Carriers* 388
Tanking to the Top. Weitzman, Yaron 796.323
TANKS (MILITARY SCIENCE)
   Hogan, William R. *Task Force Hogan* 940.54
   Holland, James. *Brothers in Arms* 940.54
Tanov, Erica
   Design by Nature 747
Tanqueray. Johnson, Stephanie .... B
★*Tanya Holland's California Soul*. Holland, Tanya ... 641.59
★*The Tao of the Backup Catcher*. Brown, Tim ... 796.357
TAOISM
   Armstrong, Karen. ★*The Great Transformation* ... 200.9
Tapahonso, Luci
   A Radiant Curve 811
TAPE RECORDERS AND PLAYERS
   Johnson, Lyndon B. *Taking Charge* 973.923
TAPESTRY
   Mezoff, Rebecca. ★*The Art of Tapestry Weaving* ... 746.7
Tapestry Crochet and More. Gullberg, Maria 746.43
Taplin, Jonathan
   Move Fast and Break Things 330.9
TAR SANDS
   Beaton, Kate. ★*Ducks* 741.5
   Vaillant, John. ★*Fire Weather* 363.37
Taraborrelli, J. Randy
   After Camelot .... B
   Jackie, Janet & Lee 920
   ★*Jackie* .... B
   The Kennedy Heirs 920
   ★*The Secret Life of Marilyn Monroe* .... B
TARAHUMARA (MEXICAN PEOPLE)
   McDougall, Christopher. ★*Born to Run* 796.42
Tarantino, Quentin
   Cinema Speculation 791.43
TARANTINO, QUENTIN
   Tarantino, Quentin. *Cinema Speculation* 791.43
Target Tokyo. Scott, James 940.54
TAROT
   Crispin, Jessa. ★*The Creative Tarot* 133.3
Tasha. Morton, Brian .... B
Task Force Hogan. Hogan, William R. 940.54
★*Taste*. Tucci, Stanley .... B
TASTE
   Ackerman, Diane. *A Natural History of the Senses* ... 152.1
   Easto, Jessica. *How to Taste Coffee* 663
   Holmes, Bob. *Flavor* 612.8
   Nezhukumatathil, Aimee. *Bite by Bite* 641.3
   Schatzker, Mark. *The Dorito Effect* 641.3
   Segnit, Niki. ★*The Flavor Thesaurus* 641.5
   Tandoh, Ruby. ★*Eat Up* 641.3
TASTE BUDS
   Holmes, Bob. *Flavor* 612.8
A Taste for Poison. Bradbury, Neil 615.9
Taste Makers. Sen, Mayukh 641.5092
A Taste of Paris. Downie, David 394.1
Tastes Like Chicken. Rude, Emelyn 338.1
Tastes Like War. Cho, Grace M. 305.48
★*Tasting History*. Miller, Max 641.509

Tasting Paris. Dusoulier, Clotilde 641.594
Tasting Rome. Parla, Katie 641.59
Tasting Whiskey. Bryson, Lew 663
Tatar, Maria
   The Heroine with 1001 Faces 809
Tate, Christie
   B.F.F. .... B
   ★*Group* .... B
TATE, CHRISTIE
   Tate, Christie. ★*Group* .... B
TATE, HORACE, 1922-2002
   Walker, Vanessa Siddle. *The Lost Education of Horace Tate* ... 370.92
TATE, SHARON, 1943-1969
   Wasson, Sam. *The Big Goodbye* 791.43
TATIANA NIKOLAEVNA, GRAND DUCHESS, DAUGHTER OF NICHOLAS II, EMPEROR OF RUSSIA, 1897-1918
   Massie, Robert K. *The Romanovs* 947
   Rappaport, Helen. *The Romanov Sisters* 920
Tattersall, Ian
   Masters of the Planet 599.93
The Tattoo Dictionary. Aitken-Smith, Trent 391.6
TATTOOING
   Aitken-Smith, Trent. *The Tattoo Dictionary* 391.6
Tattoos on the Heart. Boyle, Greg 277
Tatum, Beverly Daniel
   ★*"Why Are All the Black Kids Sitting Together in the Cafeteria?"* ... 305.800973
Tatum, Scott
   Friendly Reminders 158.1
Tau, Byron
   ★*Means of Control* 363.25
Taub, Jennifer
   Big Dirty Money 364.16
Taubes, Gary
   ★*Rethinking Diabetes* 616.462
Taubman, William
   Gorbachev .... B
   Khrushchev .... B
Taunton's New Bathroom Idea Book. Gold, Jamie ... 747.7
Taunton's Wiring Complete. McAlister, Michael ... 621.3
Taupin, Bernie
   Scattershot .... B
TAUPIN, BERNIE
   Taupin, Bernie. *Scattershot* .... B
Taussig, Rebekah
   Sitting Pretty .... B
TAUSSIG, REBEKAH
   Taussig, Rebekah. *Sitting Pretty* .... B
TAX EVASION
   Eig, Jonathan. *Get Capone* 364.1
TAX HAVENS
   Michel, Casey. *American Kleptocracy* 364.16
TAX POLICY
   Reid, T. R. *A Fine Mess* 336.200973
TAXATION
   Booth, Michael. *The Almost Nearly Perfect People* ... 948.071
   Burman, Leonard. *Taxes in America* 336.200973
   Krugman, Paul R. *Arguing with Zombies* 330.973
   Norton, Mary Beth. *1774* 973.3
   Reid, T. R. *A Fine Mess* 336.200973
Taxes in America. Burman, Leonard 336.200973
Taylor Swift. Newkey-Burden, Chas .... B
Taylor's Master Guide to Landscaping. Buchanan, Rita ... 712
Taylor, Alan
   American Civil Wars 973.7
   American Republics 973.3
   American Revolutions 973.3
   The Civil War of 1812 .... 973.5
   The Divided Ground 974.7
   ★*The Internal Enemy* 975.5
Taylor, Barbara Brown
   Holy Envy .... B
TAYLOR, BARBARA BROWN
   Taylor, Barbara Brown. *Holy Envy* .... B
Taylor, Brian J.
   Glaze 738.1
Taylor, Claude
   How to Zoom Your Room 747

PUBLIC LIBRARY CORE COLLECTION: NONFICTION
Twentieth Edition

Taylor, Cory
  Dying — B
TAYLOR, CORY, 1955-2016
  Taylor, Cory. *Dying* — B
Taylor, D. J.
  Orwell — B
Taylor, David
  Digital Photography Complete Course — 770
TAYLOR, ELIZABETH, 1932-2011
  Brower, Kate Andersen. *Elizabeth Taylor* — B
  Kashner, Sam. *Furious Love* — B
Taylor, Fred
  1939 — 940.53
  The Berlin Wall — 943
Taylor, Goldie
  The Love You Save — B
TAYLOR, GOLDIE
  Taylor, Goldie. *The Love You Save* — B
Taylor, Jay
  The Generalissimo — B
Taylor, Jill Bolte
  My Stroke of Insight — 362.19681
Taylor, Joseph E.
  Pilgrims of the Vertical — 796.52
Taylor, Justin
  Riding with the Ghost — B
TAYLOR, JUSTIN, 1982-
  Taylor, Justin. *Riding with the Ghost* — B
Taylor, Kathryne
  Love Real Food — 641.5
Taylor, Madisyn
  Unmedicated — 615.8
TAYLOR, MAJOR, 1878-1932
  Kranish, Michael. *The World's Fastest Man* — B
Taylor, Marianne
  Bats — 599.4
TAYLOR, MARSHALL WALTER, 1878-1932
  Balf, Todd. *Major* — B
Taylor, Nick
  American Made — 331.13
Taylor, Nicole A.
  ★*Watermelon & Red Birds* — 641.5
Taylor, Stephen
  Commander — B
TEA
  Goldman, Seth. *Mission in a Bottle* — 741.5
  Standage, Tom. *A History of the World in 6 Glasses* — 394.1
TEA INDUSTRY AND TRADE
  Goldman, Seth. *Mission in a Bottle* — 741.5
  Ujifusa, Steven. *Barons of the Sea* — 387.5
Tea, Michelle
  Against Memoir — B
TEA, MICHELLE
  Tea, Michelle. *Against Memoir* — B
Teach Yourself Visually [Series]. Michaels, Chris Franchetti — 739.27
Teach Yourself Visually Crochet. Werker, Kim P. — 746.43
Teach Yourself Visually Jewelry Making & Beading. Michaels, Chris Franchetti — 739.27
Teach Yourself Visually Knitting. Turner, Sharon — 746.43
Teacher Man. McCourt, Frank
TEACHER TRAINING
  Picower, Bree. *Reading, Writing, and Racism* — 371.829
The Teacher Wars. Goldstein, Dana — 371.1020973
TEACHER-STUDENT RELATIONSHIPS
  Albom, Mitch. *Tuesdays with Morrie* — B
  Bechdel, Alison. ★*Fun Home* — 741.5
  Burger, Ariel. *Witness* — 848
  Conyers, Jonathan. *I Wasn't Supposed to Be Here* — B
  Cushman, Kathleen. *Fires in Our Lives* — 373.1102
  Freitas, Donna. *Consent* — 364.158092
  Hessler, Peter. *Other Rivers* — 378.1
  King, Charles. ★*Gods of the Upper Air* — 920
  Kuo, Michelle. *Reading with Patrick* — B
  Tesoriero, Heather Won. *The Class* — 507.1
  ★*The Teachers*. Robbins, Alexandra — 371.1
TEACHERS
  Bechdel, Alison. ★*Fun Home* — 741.5
  Biden, Jill. *Where the Light Enters* — B

Bilger, Burkhard. *Fatherland* — B
Burger, Ariel. *Witness* — 848
Butler, Rebecca P. ★*Copyright for Teachers & Librarians in the 21st Century* — 346.7304
Checkoway, Julie. *The Three-Year Swim Club* — 797.2
Cook, Kevin. *The Burning Blue* — 629.45
Crews, Kenneth D. ★*Copyright Law for Librarians and Educators* — 346.7304
Goldstein, Dana. *The Teacher Wars* — 371.1020973
Heumann, Judith E. *Being Heumann* — B
Kozol, Jonathan. *Letters to a Young Teacher* — 371.1
Morton, Brian. *Tasha* — B
Rademacher, Tom. *It Won't Be Easy* — B
Reed, Shannon. *Why We Read* — 028
Robbins, Alexandra. ★*The Teachers* — 371.1
Ruhl, Sarah. *Letters from Max* — 811
Taylor, Justin. *Riding with the Ghost* — B
White, Ronald C. *On Great Fields* — B
TEACHERS' UNIONS
  Goldstein, Dana. *The Teacher Wars* — 371.1020973
TEACHING
  Appleman, Deborah. *Literature and the New Culture Wars* — 807
  Baker, Nicholson. *Substitute* — 371.14
  Bertch, Jane. *The French Ingredient* — B
  Cushman, Kathleen. *Fires in Our Lives* — 373.1102
  Goldstein, Dana. *The Teacher Wars* — 371.1020973
  Kim, Suki. *Without You, There Is No Us* — B
  Kozol, Jonathan. *Letters to a Young Teacher* — 371.1
  McCourt, Frank. *Teacher Man* — B
  Mooney, Jonathan. *Normal Sucks* — B
  Parker, Meghan. *Teaching Artfully* — 741.5
  Picower, Bree. *Reading, Writing, and Racism* — 371.829
  Rademacher, Tom. *It Won't Be Easy* — B
  Robbins, Alexandra. ★*The Teachers* — 371.1
  Sarma, Sanjay E. *Grasp* — 370.15
  Seidule, Ty. *Robert E. Lee and Me* — 973.7
  Tunstall, Tricia. *Changing Lives* — 780.71
Teaching A Stone to Talk. Dillard, Annie — 508
Teaching Artfully. Parker, Meghan — 741.5
★*Teaching White Supremacy*. Yacovone, Donald — 370.89
The Teachings of Don Juan;. Castaneda, Carlos — 299
Teachout, Terry
  ★*All in the Dances* — B
  Duke — B
  Pops — B
Teachout, Zephyr
  Break 'Em Up — 338.8
★*Team of Rivals*. Goodwin, Doris Kearns — B
The Teammates. Halberstam, David — B
TEAMS IN THE WORKPLACE
  Economy, Peter. *Wait, I'm the Boss?!?* — 658
  Horstman, Mark. *The Effective Manager* — 658.4
  Snow, Shane. *Dream Teams* — 658.4
★*Tearing Down the Wall of Sound*. Brown, Mick — B
Tears in the Darkness. Norman, Michael — 940.54
Tears to Triumph. Williamson, Marianne — 299
Tears We Cannot Stop. Dyson, Michael Eric — 305.800973
Technically Food. Zimberoff, Larissa — 613.2
TECHNOLOGICAL FORECASTING
  Acemoglu, Daron. *Power and Progress* — 303.48
  Kaku, Michio. ★*The Future of Humanity* — 629.45
  Kaku, Michio. *Quantum Supremacy* — 006.3
  Li, Fei-Fei. *The Worlds I See* — B
  Russell, Stuart J. *Human Compatible* — 006.301
  Suleyman, Mustafa. *The Coming Wave* — 303.48
TECHNOLOGICAL INNOVATIONS
  Acemoglu, Daron. *Power and Progress* — 303.48
  Agrawal, Roma. *Nuts and Bolts* — 609
  Aryee, Patrick. *30 Animals That Made Us Smarter* — 590
  Bergen, Mark. *Like, Comment, Subscribe* — 338.7
  Berger, Eric. *Liftoff* — B
  Beyer, Kurt. *Grace Hopper and the Invention of the Information Age* — B
  Brickman, Sophie. *Baby, Unplugged* — 306.874
  Brooks, Michael. *The Art of More* — 510.9
  Campbell-Kelly, Martin. *From Airline Reservations to Sonic the Hedgehog* — 338.4
  Davies, Richard. *Extreme Economies* — 306.3
  De Long, J. Bradford. *Slouching Towards Utopia* — 330.9
  Favro, Terri. *Generation Robot* — 006.3

AUTHOR, TITLE, SERIES AND SUBJECT INDEX

Fishman, Charles. ★*One Giant Leap*	629.45
Gleick, James. *The Information*	020.9
Gleick, Peter H. *The Three Ages of Water*	333.91
Hammack, William Scott. ★*Things We Make*	620
Harford, Tim. *50 Inventions That Shaped the Modern Economy*	609
Hayes, Dade. *Binge Times*	384.55
Isaacson, Walter. ★*Elon Musk*	B
Isaacson, Walter. ★*The Innovators*	B
Johnson, Steven. *Extra Life*	362.1
Johnson, Steven. *Wonderland*	790.1
Kaku, Michio. *Quantum Supremacy*	006.3
Kleiman, Kathy. *Proving Ground*	4.092
Kolbert, Elizabeth. ★*Under a White Sky*	304.2
Kostigen, Thomas. *Hacking Planet Earth*	628
Lashinsky, Adam. *Wild Ride*	388.4
Launius, Roger D. *Apollo's Legacy*	629.45
Lewis, Michael. ★*The Premonition*	614.5
Li, Fei-Fei. *The Worlds I See*	B
Lloyd, Nick. *The Western Front*	940.4
Marcal, Katrine. *Mother of Invention*	604.82
Merchant, Brian. *Blood in the Machine*	303.48
Miller, Chris. *Chip War*	338.4
Molnar, Petra. *The Walls Have Eyes*	363.2
Norton, Laurah. *Lay Them to Rest*	363.25
O'Gieblyn, Meghan. *God, Human, Animal, Machine*	814
Pein, Corey. *Live Work Work Work Die*	338.4
Prasad, Aarathi. *Silk*	677
Rhodes, Richard. ★*Energy*	333.7909
Roach, Mary. ★*Grunt*	355
Rose, Alexander. *Empires of the Sky*	920
Scharre, Paul. *Four Battlegrounds*	006.3
Schoenfeld, Bruce. ★*Game of Edges*	796.04
Schwartz, Samuel I. *No One at the Wheel*	629.2
Scott, Kevin. *Reprogramming the American Dream*	338
Smil, Vaclav. *How the World Really Works*	500
Soni, Jimmy. *A Mind at Play*	B
Stone, Brad. *The Upstarts*	338.04
Suleyman, Mustafa. *The Coming Wave*	303.48
Swisher, Kara. *Burn Book*	303.48
Tyson, Neil deGrasse. *Accessory to War*	355.001
Vince, Gaia. *Transcendence*	599.93
Waldman, Jonathan. *Sam*	629.8
Warner, Daniel. *Live Wires*	786.7
Winchester, Simon. *The Men Who United the States*	973
TECHNOLOGY	
Agrawal, Roma. *Nuts and Bolts*	609
Armantrout, Rae. *Wobble*	811
Auletta, Ken. *Frenemies*	659.1
Balakrishnan, Chris. *How to Win Friends and Influence Fungi*	502
Broyles, Michael. ★*Revolutions in American Music*	780.9
Campbell-Kelly, Martin. *From Airline Reservations to Sonic the Hedgehog*	338.4
Donovan, Jim. ★*Shoot for the Moon*	629.45
Essinger, James. *Ada's Algorithm*	B
Goodin, Tanya. *Stop Staring at Screens*	004.67
Haig, Matt. *Notes on a Nervous Planet*	616.89
Isaacson, Walter. ★*The Innovators*	B
Johnson, Steven. *The Infernal Machine*	335
Johnson, Steven. *Wonderland*	790.1
Lee, Kai-Fu. *AI 2041*	006.3
Levitin, Daniel J. ★*A Field Guide to Lies*	153.4
Lightman, Alan P. *The Discoveries*	509
Macaulay, David. *The Way Things Work Now*	600
Mao, Sally Wen. *Oculus*	811
Marchant, Jo. *The Human Cosmos*	523.1
Mezrich, Ben. *Breaking Twitter*	338.7
Munroe, Randall. *Thing Explainer*	500
O'Toole, Fintan. ★*We Don't Know Ourselves*	941.7
Olds, Sally. ★*People Who Lunch*	824
Roeder, Oliver. *Seven Games*	794
Russell, Stuart J. *Human Compatible*	006.301
Rutherford, Adam. *The Complete Guide to Absolutely Everything*	500
Shapiro, Scott J. ★*Fancy Bear Goes Phishing*	364.16
Shlain, Tiffany. *24/6*	158.1
Smil, Vaclav. *Size*	153.7
Strittmatter, Kai. *We Have Been Harmonized*	323.44
Suleyman, Mustafa. *The Coming Wave*	303.48
Swisher, Kara. *Burn Book*	303.48
Tau, Byron. ★*Means of Control*	363.25
Teachout, Zephyr. *Break 'Em Up*	338.8
Tegmark, Max. *Life 3.0*	006.301
Vince, Gaia. *Transcendence*	599.93
Weinersmith, Kelly. ★*A City on Mars*	629.4
Wilkinson, Karen. *The Art of Tinkering*	500
Williams, Bari A. *Seen yet Unseen*	338.4
Winchester, Simon. ★*The Perfectionists*	620.009
Wu, Tim. *The Attention Merchants*	659.1
Zimberoff, Larissa. *Technically Food*	613.2
TECHNOLOGY AND CIVILIZATION	
Conway, Edmund. *Material World*	333.7
Favro, Terri. *Generation Robot*	006.3
Freeman, Joshua Benjamin. ★*Behemoth*	338.6
Harari, Yuval N. ★*21 Lessons for the 21st Century*	909.82
Mao, Sally Wen. *Oculus*	811
McKibben, Bill. *Falter*	909.83
O'Gieblyn, Meghan. *God, Human, Animal, Machine*	814
O'Rourke, P. J. *None of My Business*	332
Smil, Vaclav. *How the World Really Works*	500
Ullman, Ellen. *Life in Code*	B
Wolf, Maryanne. *Reader, Come Home*	418
TECHNOLOGY AND ECONOMIC DEVELOPMENT	
Acemoglu, Daron. *Power and Progress*	303.48
TECHNOLOGY AND WAR	
Conant, Jennet. *Man of the Hour*	B
MacMillan, Margaret. *War*	355.0209
Roach, Mary. ★*Grunt*	355
TECHNOLOGY POLICY	
Boghosian, Heidi. *"i Have Nothing to Hide"*	363.1
Scott, Kevin. *Reprogramming the American Dream*	338
Suleyman, Mustafa. *The Coming Wave*	303.48
TECHNOPOP MUSIC	
Matos, Michaelangelo. *The Underground Is Massive*	781.648
Tecumseh and the Prophet. Cozzens, Peter	920
TECUMSEH, SHAWNEE CHIEF, 1768-1813	
Cozzens, Peter. *Tecumseh and the Prophet*	920
Eckert, Allan W. *A Sorrow in Our Heart*	B
Ted Kennedy. Farrell, John A.	B
Ted Kennedy Watson's Guide to Stylish Entertaining. Watson, Ted Kennedy	793.2
Teege, Jennifer	
My Grandfather Would Have Shot Me	929.2
TEEGE, JENNIFER, 1970-	
Teege, Jennifer. *My Grandfather Would Have Shot Me*	929.2
The Teen Interpreter. Apter, T. E.	306.874
TEENAGE ABUSE VICTIMS	
Bergner, Daniel. ★*Sing for Your Life*	B
TEENAGE BOYS	
Brotherton, Marcus. *A Bright and Blinding Sun*	940.54
Brown, Claude. *Manchild in the Promised Land*	B
Hickam, Homer H. ★*Rocket Boys*	B
Kamkwamba, William. ★*The Boy Who Harnessed the Wind*	B
Moore, Wes. *The Other Wes Moore*	B
Natterson, Cara Familian. ★*Decoding Boys*	649
Orenstein, Peggy. ★*Boys & Sex*	305.235
Rush, Chris. *The Light Years*	B
Samaha, Albert. *Never Ran, Never Will*	920
Shaffer, Peter. ★*Equus*	822
Smiler, Andrew P. *Dating and Sex*	613.9071
Streep, Abe. *Brothers on Three*	306.85
Tran, Phuc. ★*Sigh, Gone*	B
Wiesel, Elie. ★*Night*	B
Wiseman, Rosalind. *Masterminds & Wingmen*	305.235
TEENAGE CELEBRITIES	
Hussey, Olivia. *The Girl on the Balcony*	B
TEENAGE COOKS	
Ganeshram, Ramin. *Future Chefs*	641.3
TEENAGE DRUG ABUSERS	
Berenson, Alex. ★*Tell Your Children*	362.29
Khar, Erin. *Strung Out*	B
TEENAGE GIRLS	
Betz-Hamilton, Axton. *The Less People Know About Us*	364.16
Browne, Mahogany L. ★*Black Girl Magic*	811.6
Colton, Larry. *Counting Coup*	796.323
Cooper, Alex. *Saving Alex*	B
Crawford, Lacy. *Notes on a Silencing*	B
Damour, Lisa. ★*Under Pressure*	155.5
Damour, Lisa. *Untangled*	305.235

PUBLIC LIBRARY CORE COLLECTION: NONFICTION
Twentieth Edition

Faleiro, Sonia. *The Good Girls*	364.152
Frank, Anne. ★*The Diary of a Young Girl*	940.53
Georges, Gigi. *Downeast*	974.1
Gies, Miep. ★*Anne Frank Remembered*	B
Goodan, Chelsey. *Underestimated*	305.235
Haddish, Tiffany. *The Last Black Unicorn*	B
Koh, EJ. *The Magical Language of Others*	813
Leach, Samantha. ★*The Elissas*	362.73
Matzen, Robert. *Dutch Girl*	B
Satrapi, Marjane. ★*The Complete Persepolis*	741.5
Schwartzman, Nancy. *Roll Red Roll*	364.15
Simmons, Rachel. ★*Enough as She Is*	155.5
Weiss, Helga. *Helga's Diary*	B
Williams, Mary. *The Lost Daughter*	B
Yousafzai, Malala. *I Am Malala*	B

TEENAGE IMMIGRANTS

Abdelmahmoud, Elamin. *Son of Elsewhere*	B
Fishman, Elly. *Refugee High*	370.8
Li, Fei-Fei. *The Worlds I See*	B
Mojica Rodriguez, Prisca Dorcas. *For Brown Girls with Sharp Edges and Tender Hearts*	305.48
Thorpe, Helen. *The Newcomers*	373.18
Tran, Phuc. ★*Sigh, Gone*	B

TEENAGE LITERATURE WRITING

Klein, Cheryl B. *The Magic Words*	808.06
Town, Caren J. *LGBTQ Young Adult Fiction*	813.009

TEENAGE MOTHERS

Glaser, Gabrielle. *American Baby*	B
Williams, Patricia. *Rabbit*	B

TEENAGE MURDER VICTIMS

Ralph, Laurence. *Sito*	364.152

TEENAGE MURDERERS

Cullen, David. *Columbine*	373
MacLean, Harry N. *Starkweather*	364.152

TEENAGE PREGNANCY

Harjo, Joy. *Crazy Brave*	B

TEENAGE PRISONERS

Adams, Jarrett. *Redeeming Justice*	340.092

TEENAGE RAPE VICTIMS

Crawford, Lacy. *Notes on a Silencing*	B

TEENAGE REFUGEES

Fishman, Elly. *Refugee High*	370.8
Steinberg, Jonny. *A Man of Good Hope*	B
Taing, Mae Bunseng. *Under the Naga Tail*	B
Thorpe, Helen. *The Newcomers*	373.18

TEENAGE SEXUAL ABUSE

Crawford, Lacy. *Notes on a Silencing*	B

TEENAGE SOCIAL ADVOCATES

Cullen, David. *Parkland*	371.7
McAnulty, Dara. *Diary of a Young Naturalist*	508.092

TEENAGE VOLUNTEERS

Boland, Becca. *Making the Most of Teen Library Volunteers*	023

TEENAGERS

Apter, T. E. *The Teen Interpreter*	306.874
Bayoumi, Moustafa. *How Does It Feel to Be a Problem?*	305.892
Berenson, Alex. ★*Tell Your Children*	362.29
Bergstein, Rachelle. *The Genius of Judy*	813
Boland, Becca. *Making the Most of Teen Library Volunteers*	023
Cart, Michael. *Young Adult Literature*	813.009
Chance, Rosemary. *Young Adult Literature in Action*	011.62
Damour, Lisa. *The Emotional Lives of Teenagers*	155.5
Dorr, Christina H. ★*Profiles in Resilience*	028.5
Etter, Lauren. ★*The Devil's Playbook*	338.7
Fenn, Lisa. *Carry On*	B
Foulkes, Lucy. ★*Losing Our Minds*	616.89
Freedland, Jonathan. ★*The Escape Artist*	940.53
Galanti, Regine. ★*Parenting Anxious Kids*	155.4
Galinsky, Ellen. ★*The Breakthrough Years*	649
Hobbs, Jeff. *Children of the State*	364.36
Kim, Anne. ★*Abandoned*	305.2350973
Kline, Emily. ★*The School of Hard Talks*	155.5
Krimstein, Ken. *When I Grow Up*	741.5
Lahey, Jessica. *The Addiction Inoculation*	649
Legler, Casey. ★*Godspeed*	B
Maisel, Ivan. *I Keep Trying to Catch His Eye*	B
Markham, Lauren. ★*The Far Away Brothers*	920
Moore, Wes. *The Other Wes Moore*	B
Morgan, Genevieve. *Undecided*	331.702
Moss, Gabrielle. *Paperback Crush*	813.009
Rehak, Melanie. *Girl Sleuth*	813
Seierstad, Asne. *Two Sisters*	956.9104
Snow, Jess. ★*Outreach Services for Teens*	027.4
Tamimi, Ahed. ★*They Called Me a Lioness*	B
Vernacchio, Al. *For Goodness Sex*	613.9071
Wides-Munoz, Laura. *The Making of a Dream*	920

TEENAGERS AND DEATH

Emswiler, Mary Ann. *Guiding Your Child Through Grief*	155.9

TEENAGERS WITH DEPRESSION

Legler, Casey. ★*Godspeed*	B

TEENAGERS WITH EATING DISORDERS

Betz-Hamilton, Axton. *The Less People Know About Us*	364.16

TEENAGERS WITH MENTAL ILLNESSES

Bailey, Lily. *Because We Are Bad*	B

TEENAGERS' LIBRARY SERVICES

Anderson, Jimmeka. *Power Lines*	020
Boland, Becca. *Making the Most of Teen Library Volunteers*	023
Breitenbach, Kathleen. ★*LGBTQIA+ Books for Children and Teens*	028.7
Flowers, Sarah. *Evaluating Teen Services and Programs*	027.62
Pattee, Amy. *Developing Library Collections for Today's Young Adults*	027.62
Rogers-Whitehead, Carrie. ★*Serving Teens and Adults on the Autism Spectrum*	027.6
Snow, Jess. ★*Outreach Services for Teens*	027.4

Teeth. Otto, Mary   617

Tefertiller, Casey

Wyatt Earp	B

Teffi, N. A.

Memories	B

TEFFI, N. A. (NADEZHDA ALEKSANDROVNA), 1872-1952

Teffi, N. A. *Memories*	B

Tegmark, Max

Life 3.0	006.301
Our Mathematical Universe	523.1

TEGMARK, MAX

Tegmark, Max. *Our Mathematical Universe*	523.1

TEHRAN, IRAN

Nafisi, Azar. ★*Reading Lolita in Tehran*	B
Navai, Ramita. *City of Lies*	955
Satrapi, Marjane. *Chicken with Plums*	741.5
Satrapi, Marjane. ★*The Complete Persepolis*	741.5

Teicher, Craig Morgan

We Begin in Gladness	808.1

Teigen, Chrissy

Cravings	641.5

TEIGEN, CHRISSY

Teigen, Chrissy. *Cravings*	641.5

Teigen, Pepper (Vilailuck)

The Pepper Thai Cookbook	641.595

Teilhard de Chardin, Pierre

★*The Divine Milieu*	233

Teitel, Amy Shira

Fighting for Space	920

TEL AVIV, ISRAEL

LeBor, Adam. *City of Oranges*	956.94

TELECOMMUNICATION

Auletta, Ken. *Frenemies*	659.1
Auletta, Ken. *Media Man*	B
Wu, Tim. *The Attention Merchants*	659.1

TELECOMMUTING

Eikenberry, Kevin. *The Long-Distance Teammate*	650.1
Medini, Shari. *Parenting While Working from Home*	650.1
Warzel, Charlie. *Out of Office*	658.3

TELEPATHY

Jacobsen, Annie. *Phenomena*	133.8

TELEPHONES

Gray, Charlotte. ★*Reluctant Genius*	920

TELESCOPES

Levesque, Emily. *The Last Stargazers*	520

TELEVISION

Armstrong, Jennifer Keishin. *Seinfeldia*	791.45
Armstrong, Jennifer Keishin. *Sex and the City and Us*	791.45
Davis, Michael. *Street Gang*	791.43
Gladstone, Brooke. *The Influencing Machine*	741.5
Greene, Andy. *The Office*	791.45
Jones, Brian Jay. *Jim Henson*	B
Lear, Norman. *Even This I Get to Experience*	B

AUTHOR, TITLE, SERIES AND SUBJECT INDEX

Martin, Brett. *Difficult Men*	791.4509
McKee, Robert. *Dialogue*	809
Muir, John Kenneth. *The Encyclopedia of Superheroes on Film and Television*	791.43
Poniewozik, James. *Audience of One*	324.7
Postman, Neil. *Amusing Ourselves to Death*	302.2
Press, Joy. *Stealing the Show*	791.45
Shales, Tom. *Live from New York*	791.45
Smith, Chris. *The Daily Show (the Book)*	791.45
Stewart, Patrick. ★*Making It So*	B

TELEVISION AND EDUCATION

Davis, Michael. *Street Gang*	791.43
Kamp, David. *Sunny Days*	791.4502

TELEVISION CARTOON SHOWS

Cavalier, Stephen. *The World History of Animation*	791.43
Gitlin, Marty. *A Celebration of Animation*	741.5

TELEVISION COMEDIES

Burnett, Carol. *In Such Good Company*	791.45
Burrows, James. ★*Directed by James Burrows*	791.4502
Ebersol, Dick. *From Saturday Night to Sunday Night*	B
Key, Keegan-Michael. ★*The History of Sketch Comedy*	792.2
Myers, Paul. *The Kids in the Hall*	920
Peisner, David. *Homey Don't Play That!*	791.45
Stamos, John. *If You Would Have Told Me*	B
Zweibel, Alan. *Laugh Lines*	B

TELEVISION COMEDY WRITERS

Key, Keegan-Michael. ★*The History of Sketch Comedy*	792.2
Mooney, Paul. *Black Is the New White*	792.7
Odenkirk, Bob. *Comedy Comedy Comedy Drama*	B
Robinson, Phoebe. *You Can't Touch My Hair and Other Things I Still Have to Explain*	792.7
Zweibel, Alan. *Laugh Lines*	B

TELEVISION COOKING SHOWS

Prud'homme, Alex. *The French Chef in America*	B
Vitale, Tom. *In the Weeds*	B
Woolever, Laurie. *Bourdain*	B

TELEVISION GAME SHOW CONTESTANTS

Schneider, Amy. *In the Form of a Question*	B

TELEVISION GAME SHOW HOSTS

Trebek, Alex. *The Answer Is ...*	791.4502

TELEVISION GAME SHOWS

Trebek, Alex. *The Answer Is ...*	791.4502

TELEVISION HISTORY AND CRITICISM

Kaufman, Amy. *Bachelor Nation*	791.45
Key, Keegan-Michael. ★*The History of Sketch Comedy*	792.2
Nussbaum, Emily. *Cue the Sun!*	791.45
Nussbaum, Emily. *I Like to Watch*	791.45
Sepinwall, Alan. ★*TV (the Book)*	791.45

TELEVISION IN POLITICS

Else, Jon. *True South*	305.800973

TELEVISION INDUSTRY AND TRADE

Armstrong, Jennifer Keishin. *When Women Invented Television*	791.45
Biskind, Peter. *Pandora's Box*	791.45
Burrows, James. ★*Directed by James Burrows*	791.4502
Ebersol, Dick. *From Saturday Night to Sunday Night*	B
Greene, Andy. *The Office*	791.45
Martin, Brett. *Difficult Men*	791.4509
Movsesian, Sona. *The World's Worst Assistant*	791.4302
Myers, Paul. *The Kids in the Hall*	920
Nussbaum, Emily. *Cue the Sun!*	791.45
Poniewozik, James. *Audience of One*	324.7
Press, Joy. *Stealing the Show*	791.45
Stelter, Brian. *Top of the Morning*	791.456
Williams, Billy Dee. ★*What Have We Here*	B

TELEVISION JOURNALISM

Poniewozik, James. *Audience of One*	324.7

TELEVISION JOURNALISTS

Brinkley, Douglas. ★*Cronkite*	B
Cooper, Anderson. *The Rainbow Comes and Goes*	070.4
Stelter, Brian. *Hoax*	070.4
Ward, Clarissa. *On All Fronts*	B

TELEVISION NETWORKS

Stelter, Brian. *Hoax*	070.4

TELEVISION NEWS

Fager, Jeffrey. *Fifty Years of 60 Minutes*	070.1
Kurtz, Howard. *Media Madness*	973.933
Stelter, Brian. *Hoax*	070.4

TELEVISION NEWSCASTERS AND COMMENTATORS

Bella, Timothy. *Barkley*	B
Fager, Jeffrey. *Fifty Years of 60 Minutes*	070.1
Lemon, Don. *This Is the Fire*	305.896
Stelter, Brian. *Top of the Morning*	791.456

TELEVISION PERSONALITIES

Attenborough, David. *A Life on Our Planet*	508
Clemmons, Francois S. *Officer Clemmons*	B
Duggar, Jill. *Counting the Cost*	B
Grylls, Bear. *Never Give Up*	B
Hodgman, John. *Medallion Status*	B
Kang, Mia. *Knockout*	B
King, Maxwell. *The Good Neighbor*	B
Kirkby, Bruce. *Blue Sky Kingdom*	954.96
Lakshmi, Padma. *Love, Loss, and What We Ate*	791.4502
Maguire, James. *Impresario*	B
Mattel, Trixie. *Working Girls*	650.1
Noah, Trevor. *Born a Crime*	B
Nussbaum, Emily. *Cue the Sun!*	791.45
Page, Susan. ★*The Rulebreaker*	B
Ramsey, Franchesca. *Well, That Escalated Quickly*	B
RuPaul. ★*The House of Hidden Meanings*	B
Schneider, Amy. *In the Form of a Question*	B
Selleck, Tom. *You Never Know*	B
Stelter, Brian. *Top of the Morning*	791.456
Trebek, Alex. *The Answer Is ...*	791.4502
Vitale, Tom. *In the Weeds*	B
Watts, Reggie. *Great Falls, MT*	B
Woolever, Laurie. *Bourdain*	B

TELEVISION PRODUCERS AND DIRECTORS

Bennetts, Leslie. *Last Girl Before Freeway*	B
Biskind, Peter. *Pandora's Box*	791.45
Burrows, James. ★*Directed by James Burrows*	791.4502
Carlin, Kelly. *A Carlin Home Companion*	B
Chin, Curtis. *Everything I Learned, I Learned in a Chinese Restaurant*	B
Ebersol, Dick. *From Saturday Night to Sunday Night*	B
Else, Jon. *True South*	305.800973
Imperioli, Michael. *Woke up This Morning*	791.45
Jackson, Curtis. *Hustle Harder, Hustle Smarter*	B
Jones, Brian Jay. *Jim Henson*	B
Katz, Evan Ross. *Into Every Generation a Slayer Is Born*	791.45
Lear, Norman. *Even This I Get to Experience*	B
Milch, David. *Life's Work*	B
Nussbaum, Emily. *Cue the Sun!*	791.45
O'Brien, Jack. *Jack Be Nimble*	B
Odenkirk, Bob. *Comedy Comedy Comedy Drama*	B
Spiegel, Maura. *Sidney Lumet*	B
Winkler, Henry. ★*Being Henry*	B
Zwick, Edward. ★*Hits, Flops, and Other Illusions*	B

TELEVISION PRODUCTION AND DIRECTION

Burrows, James. ★*Directed by James Burrows*	791.4502
Imperioli, Michael. *Woke up This Morning*	791.45
Katz, Evan Ross. *Into Every Generation a Slayer Is Born*	791.45

TELEVISION PROGRAMS

Armstrong, Jennifer Keishin. *Seinfeldia*	791.45
Armstrong, Jennifer Keishin. *Sex and the City and Us*	791.45
Armstrong, Jennifer Keishin. *When Women Invented Television*	791.45
Biskind, Peter. *Pandora's Box*	791.45
Bourdain, Anthony. *The Nasty Bits*	641.5092
Britt, Ryan. *Phasers on Stun!*	791.45
Davis, Michael. *Street Gang*	791.43
Else, Jon. *True South*	305.800973
Fischer, Jenna. *The Office BFFs*	791.45
Greene, Andy. *The Office*	791.45
Grylls, Bear. *Never Give Up*	B
Imperioli, Michael. *Woke up This Morning*	791.45
Kamp, David. *Sunny Days*	791.4502
Katz, Evan Ross. *Into Every Generation a Slayer Is Born*	791.45
Kaufman, Amy. *Bachelor Nation*	791.45
Kroger, Lisa. *Monster, She Wrote*	920
Lear, Norman. *Even This I Get to Experience*	B
Martin, Brett. *Difficult Men*	791.4509
Nussbaum, Emily. *I Like to Watch*	791.45
Parke, Henry C. *The Greatest Westerns Ever Made and the People Who Made Them*	791.43
Perry, Matthew. *Friends, Lovers, and the Big Terrible Thing*	B
Phillips, Maya. *Nerd*	302.23
Press, Joy. *Stealing the Show*	791.45

PUBLIC LIBRARY CORE COLLECTION: NONFICTION
Twentieth Edition

Prud'homme, Alex. *The French Chef in America* — B
Reiss, Mike. *Springfield Confidential* — 791.45
Sepinwall, Alan. ★*TV (the Book)* — 791.45
Shales, Tom. *Live from New York* — 791.45
Singer, Matt. *Opposable Thumbs* — 791.43
Smith, Chris. *The Daily Show (the Book)* — 791.45
TELEVISION PROGRAMS FOR CHILDREN
    Davis, Michael. *Street Gang* — 791.43
    Kamp, David. *Sunny Days* — 791.4502
    King, Maxwell. *The Good Neighbor* — B
TELEVISION SPORTSCASTERS
    Buck, Joe. *Lucky Bastard* — B
TELEVISION TALK SHOW HOSTS AND GUESTS
    Stelter, Brian. *Top of the Morning* — 791.456
TELEVISION TALK SHOWS
    Stelter, Brian. *Top of the Morning* — 791.456
TELEVISION WRITERS
    Kaling, Mindy. *Why Not Me?* — B
    Katz, Evan Ross. *Into Every Generation a Slayer Is Born* — 791.45
    Milch, David. *Life's Work* — B
    Pritchett, Georgia. *My Mess is a Bit of a Life* — B
    Reiss, Mike. *Springfield Confidential* — 791.45
    Scovell, Nell. *Just the Funny Parts* — B
    Smith, Chris. *The Daily Show (the Book)* — 791.45
    Wong, Ali. ★*Dear Girls* — B
    Zweibel, Alan. *Laugh Lines* — B
TELEVISION WRITING
    Armstrong, Jennifer Keishin. *Seinfeldia* — 791.45
    Armstrong, Jennifer Keishin. *Sex and the City and Us* — 791.45
    Greene, Andy. *The Office* — 791.45
    Myers, Paul. *The Kids in the Hall* — 920
    Reiss, Mike. *Springfield Confidential* — 791.45
Tell It Like It Is. Neville, Aaron — B
★*Tell Me Everything.* Kelly, Minka — B
★*Tell Me Everything.* Krouse, Erika — 363.25
Tell Me How It Ends. Luiselli, Valeria — 305.23086
Tell Me More. Corrigan, Kelly — 153.6
★*Tell Me the Dream Again.* Jun, Tasha — 248
Tell Me What You Want. Weber, Charlotte Fox — 153.8
★*Tell Your Children.* Berenson, Alex — 362.29
Telushkin, Joseph
    Jewish Wisdom — 296.3
    Rebbe — 296.833
TEMPERANCE MOVEMENTS
    Fisher, Carl Erik. ★*The Urge* — 362.29
TEMPERATURE
    Goodell, Jeff. *The Heat Will Kill You First* — 363.738
The Templars. Jones, Dan — 271
Temple Grandin's Guide to Working with Farm Animals. Grandin, Temple — 636
TEMPLES
    Mertz, Barbara. *Temples, Tombs, & Hieroglyphs* — 932
Temples, Tombs, & Hieroglyphs. Mertz, Barbara — 932
TEMPTATION
    Goethe, Johann Wolfgang von. *Goethe's Faust* — 832
    Lewis, C. S. ★*The Screwtape Letters* — 248.4
TEN BOOM, CORRIE
    Loftis, Larry. ★*The Watchmaker's Daughter* — 940.53
Ten Caesars. Strauss, Barry S. — 937
Ten Days That Shook the World. Reed, John — 947.084
Ten Hills Farm. Manegold, Catherine S. — 974.4
Ten Innings at Wrigley. Cook, Kevin — 796.357
Ten Masterpieces of Music. Sachs, Harvey — 780.9
★*Ten Steps to Nanette.* Gadsby, Hannah — B
★*The Ten Trusts.* Goodall, Jane — 333.95
The Ten Year War. Cohn, Jonathan — 368.38
Tenacious Beasts. Preston, Christopher J. — 591.68
TENANT FARMERS
    Agee, James. *Let Us Now Praise Famous Men* — 976.1
★*Tenderheart.* McKinnon, Hetty — 641.5
Teng, Tara
    ★*Your Body Is a Revolution* — 306.4
TENGGREN, GUSTAF, 1896-1970
    Ghez, Didier. *The Hidden Art of Disney's Golden Age* — 741.5
Tennant, Richard A.
    The American Sign Language Handshape Dictionary — 419
TENNESSEE
    Bass, William M. *Death's Acre* — 614
    Kiernan, Denise. *The Girls of Atomic City* — 976.8

    Martin, Rachel Louise. *A Most Tolerant Little Town* — 379.2
    Renkl, Margaret. *The Comfort of Crows* — 814.6
TENNIS
    Agassi, Andre. *Open* — B
    Blais, Madeleine. *Queen of the Court* — B
    Clarey, Christopher. ★*The Master* — B
    Fisher, Marshall Jon. *A Terrible Splendor* — 796.342
    Gallwey, W. Timothy. ★*The Inner Game of Tennis* — 796.342
    King, Billie Jean. ★*All In* — B
    McPhee, John. *Levels of the Game* — 796.34
    Rothenberg, Ben. *Naomi Osaka* — B
    Sharapova, Maria. *Unstoppable* — B
    Williams, Richard. *Black and White* — B
TENNIS COACHES
    Williams, Richard. *Black and White* — B
TENNIS PLAYERS
    Agassi, Andre. *Open* — B
    Clarey, Christopher. ★*The Master* — B
    Fisher, Marshall Jon. *A Terrible Splendor* — 796.342
    Howard, Johnette. *The Rivals* — B
    McPhee, John. *Levels of the Game* — 796.34
    Phillips, Rowan Ricardo. *The Circuit* — 796.342
    Rothenberg, Ben. *Naomi Osaka* — B
    Sharapova, Maria. *Unstoppable* — B
TENNIS TOURNAMENTS
    Fisher, Marshall Jon. *A Terrible Splendor* — 796.342
    McPhee, John. *Levels of the Game* — 796.34
    Phillips, Rowan Ricardo. *The Circuit* — 796.342
Tennyson, Alfred
    Poems — 821
TENSKWATAWA, SHAWNEE PROPHET
    Cozzens, Peter. *Tecumseh and the Prophet* — 920
The Tenth Parallel. Griswold, Eliza — 297.2
Tenzin Priyadarshi
    Running Toward Mystery — B
TENZIN PRIYADARSHI
    Tenzin Priyadarshi. *Running Toward Mystery* — B
Teresa
    A Call to Mercy — 234
Terkel, Studs
    The Good War — 940.54
    ★*Hard Times* — 973.91
    Hope Dies Last — 920
    Will the Circle Be Unbroken? — 128
    Working — 920
TERMINAL CARE
    Arthur, Alua. ★*Briefly Perfectly Human* — 306.9
    Brody, Jane E. *Jane Brody's Guide to the Great Beyond* — 616
    Butler, Katy. *The Art of Dying Well* — 616.02
    Clarke, Rachel. *Dear Life* — B
    Dugdale, Lydia S. *The Lost Art of Dying* — 155.9
    Egan, Kerry. *On Living* — 170
    Fersko-Weiss, Henry. *Caring for the Dying* — 616.02
    Gawande, Atul. ★*Being Mortal* — 362.17
    Green, Stefanie. *This Is Assisted Dying* — 616.02
    Mannix, Kathryn. *With the End in Mind* — 304.6
    Rehm, Diane. ★*When My Time Comes* — 179.7
    Volandes, Angelo E. *The Conversation* — 616.02
    Warraich, Haider. *Modern Death* — 179.7
TERMINAL ILLNESS
    Arthur, Alua. ★*Briefly Perfectly Human* — 306.9
    Bowler, Kate. *No Cure for Being Human* — B
    Kingston, Genevieve. *Did I Ever Tell You?* — B
    Raza, Azra. *The First Cell* — 616.99
    Rubin, Kathy Kleiner. *A Light in the Dark* — 364.152
    Winn, Raynor. *The Wild Silence* — B
TERMS AND PHRASES
    Pinker, Steven. *Words and Rules* — 415
TERRAFORMING
    Stuart, Colin. *How to Live in Space* — 629.45
TERRARIUMS
    Martin, Tovah. *The New Terrarium* — 635.9
The Terrible and Wonderful Reasons Why I Run Long Distances. Inman, Matthew — 741.5
A Terrible Glory. Donovan, Jim — 973.8
A Terrible Splendor. Fisher, Marshall Jon — 796.342
★*Terrible Swift Sword.* Wheelan, Joseph — B

AUTHOR, TITLE, SERIES AND SUBJECT INDEX

TERRITORIAL EXPANSION
    Anderson, Fred. *The Dominion of War* — 973
    Brands, H. W. *The Age of Gold* — 979.4
    Drury, Bob. *Blood and Treasure* — B
    Haley, James L. *Captive Paradise* — 996.9
    Kinzer, Stephen. ★*The True Flag* — 327.73
    McCullough, David G. *The Pioneers* — 920
    Merry, Robert W. *A Country of Vast Designs* — B
    Morgan, Robert. *Lions of the West* — 978
    Richardson, Heather Cox. ★*How the South Won the Civil War* — 306.20973
    Sides, Hampton. *Blood and Thunder* — 978
    Taylor, Alan. *American Republics* — 973.3
    Winchester, Simon. *The Men Who United the States* — 973
    Wineapple, Brenda. *Ecstatic Nation* — 973.6

TERRORISM
    Amis, Martin. *Koba the Dread* — 947.084
    Badkhen, Anna. *The World Is a Carpet* — 305.409581
    Bergen, Peter L. *The Rise and Fall of Osama Bin Laden* — 958.104
    Boot, Max. *Invisible Armies* — 355.02
    Brooks, Rosa. *How Everything Became War and the Military Became Everything* — 355
    Burrough, Bryan. *Days of Rage* — 303.48
    Carroll, Rory. *There Will Be Fire* — 363.325
    Chomsky, Noam. *Global Discontents* — 410.92
    Coker, Margaret. *The Spymaster of Baghdad* — 956.7044
    Coll, Steve. *The Bin Ladens* — 920
    Coll, Steve. *Directorate S* — 958.104
    Coll, Steve. ★*Ghost Wars* — 958.104
    Farmer, John J. *The Ground Truth* — 973.931
    Filkins, Dexter. *The Forever War* — 956.7044
    Friend, David. *Watching the World Change* — 974.7
    Gage, Beverly. *The Day Wall Street Exploded* — 974.7
    Gallego, Ruben. *They Called Us* — 956.7044
    Graff, Garrett M. ★*The Only Plane in the Sky* — 973.931
    Gregory, Rebekah. *Taking My Life Back* — B
    Guillemin, Jeanne. *Biological Weapons* — 358
    Hoffman, Bruce. *Anonymous Soldiers* — 956.94
    Jacobson, Sidney. *The 9-11 Report* — 741.5
    Johnson, Steven. *The Infernal Machine* — 335
    Jones, Doug. *Bending Toward Justice* — 323.1196
    Junger, Sebastian. *Fire* — 909.82
    Mayer, Jane. *The Dark Side* — 973.931
    McCann, Colum. *American Mother* — 956.9104
    Mekhennet, Souad. *I Was Told to Come Alone* — 363.3250956
    Moore, Michael Scott. *The Desert and the Sea* — 364.15
    Murakami, Haruki. *Underground* — 364.15
    Neiwert, David A. ★*The Age of Insurrection* — 303.48
    Rashid, Ahmed. *Taliban* — 958.104
    Scahill, Jeremy. *Dirty Wars* — 355.00973
    Soufan, Ali H. *The Black Banners Declassified* — 363.325
    Stengel, Richard. *Information Wars* — 355.3
    Trofimov, Yaroslav. *The Siege of Mecca* — 953.805
    Verini, James. *They Will Have to Die Now* — 956.7044
    Warrick, Joby. *Black Flags* — 956.9104
    Whitlock, Craig. *The Afghanistan Papers* — 958.104
    Wood, Graeme. *The Way of the Strangers* — 363.325
    Wright, Lawrence. ★*The Looming Tower* — 973.931
    Zuckoff, Mitchell. ★*Fall and Rise* — 973.931

TERRORISM INVESTIGATION
    Kushner, Jacob. *Look Away* — 305.9
    Lane, Charles. *Freedom's Detective* — B

TERRORISM PREVENTION
    Bergen, Peter L. *The Longest War* — 909.83
    Bergen, Peter L. *Manhunt* — 363.325
    Coker, Margaret. *The Spymaster of Baghdad* — 956.7044
    Denver, Rorke. *Worth Dying For* — 359.9
    Edstrom, Erik. *Un-American* — B
    Elnoury, Tamer. *American Radical* — B
    Fox, Amaryllis. *Life Undercover* — B
    Vickers, Michael G. *By All Means Available* — 355
    Walder, Tracy. *The Unexpected Spy* — B
    Warrick, Joby. *Red Line* — 956.9104

TERRORIST ORGANIZATIONS
    Roy, Jessica. *American Girls* — 305.48

TERRORISTS
    Bergen, Peter L. *The Longest War* — 909.83
    Bergen, Peter L. *Manhunt* — 363.325
    Bergen, Peter L. *The Rise and Fall of Osama Bin Laden* — 958.104

    Farmer, John J. *The Ground Truth* — 973.931
    Jacobson, Sidney. *The 9-11 Report* — 741.5
    Mayer, Jane. *The Dark Side* — 973.931
    Soufan, Ali H. *The Black Banners Declassified* — 363.325
    Wallace, Chris. *Countdown Bin Laden* — 958.104
    Warrick, Joby. *Black Flags* — 956.9104
    Wiehl, Lis W. *Hunting the Unabomber* — 364.152
    Wood, Graeme. *The Way of the Strangers* — 363.325

Terry, Bryant
    Afro-Vegan — 641.59
    Black Food — 394.1
    Vegan Soul Kitchen — 641.5
    ★*Vegetable Kingdom* — 641.5

TERRY, CLARK
    Lees, Gene. *You Can't Steal a Gift* — B

Tesfamariam, Rahiel
    ★*Imagine Freedom* — 305.896

Tesla. Carlson, W. Bernard — B
Tesla. Munson, Richard — B

TESLA, NIKOLA, 1856-1943
    Carlson, W. Bernard. *Tesla* — B
    Munson, Richard. *Tesla* — B

Tesoriero, Heather Won
    The Class — 507.1

TEST PILOTS
    Hampton, Dan. *Chasing the Demon* — 629.132
    Wolfe, Tom. ★*The Right Stuff* — 629.4

★*A Testament of Hope*. King, Martin Luther — 323.1

Tester, Jon
    Grounded — B

TESTER, JON, 1956-
    Tester, Jon. *Grounded* — B

Testimony. Ward, Jon — 277.308
★*Testimony*. Robertson, Robbie — B
Testing Wars in the Public Schools. Reese, William J. — 371.260973

TESTOSTERONE
    Semenya, Caster. *The Race to Be Myself* — B

Testosterone Rex. Fine, Cordelia — 155.3

TET OFFENSIVE, 1968
    Bowden, Mark. ★*Hue 1968* — 959.704
    Kurlansky, Mark. *1968* — 909.82
    Stanton, Doug. *The Odyssey of Echo Company* — 959.704

Tetro, Tony
    Con/Artist — B

TETRO, TONY
    Tetro, Tony. *Con/Artist* — B

TEXAS
    Barnett, Brittany K. ★*A Knock at Midnight* — B
    Bissinger, H. G. ★*Friday Night Lights* — 796.332
    Black, Dustin Lance. *Mama's Boy* — B
    Boessenecker, John. *Texas Ranger* — B
    Burrough, Bryan. *The Big Rich* — 338.2
    Burrough, Bryan. *Forget the Alamo* — 976.043
    Chammah, Maurice. ★*Let the Lord Sort Them* — 364.66
    Donovan, Jim. *The Blood of Heroes* — 976.4
    Eatman, Nicholas. *Friday, Saturday, Sunday in Texas* — 796.332
    Hixenbaugh, Michael. ★*They Came for the Schools* — 371.9
    Johnson, Kirk W. *The Fishermen and the Dragon* — 976.4
    Kearse, Bettye. *The Other Madisons* — 920
    Lambert, Miranda. *Y'all Eat Yet?* — 641.5976
    Mealer, Bryan. *The Kings of Big Spring* — B
    Quinones, John. ★*One Year in Uvalde* — 371.7
    Simmons, Ruth. ★*Up Home* — B
    Tate, Christie. ★*Group* — B
    Wright, Lawrence. *God Save Texas* — 917.64
    Yousse, Bower. *Freddie Steinmark* — 796.332

Texas Ranger. Boessenecker, John — B

TEXTILE CRAFTS
    Adams, Liza. *Needle Felting* — 746
    Corwin, Lena. *Lena Corwin's Made by Hand* — 746.6

TEXTILE DESIGN
    Gilchrist, Abby. *Modern Fabric* — 746.092

TEXTILE DESIGNERS
    Gilchrist, Abby. *Modern Fabric* — 746.092

TEXTILE FABRICS
    Gilchrist, Abby. *Modern Fabric* — 746.092
    Kurutz, Steven. *American Flannel* — 338.4
    Prasad, Aarathi. *Silk* — 677

PUBLIC LIBRARY CORE COLLECTION: NONFICTION
Twentieth Edition

Stocker, Blair. *Wise Craft Quilts*	746.46
Thanhauser, Sofi. *Worn*	391
TEXTILE FIBERS	
Callahan, Gail. *Hand Dyeing Yarn and Fleece*	746.6
Duerr, Sasha. *Natural Color*	746.6
TEXTILE INDUSTRY AND TRADE	
Givhan, Robin. *The Battle of Versailles*	746.9
Kurutz, Steven. *American Flannel*	338.4
Slade, Rachel. *American Hoodie*	338.4
TEXTILE PRINTING	
Corwin, Lena. *Lena Corwin's Made by Hand*	746.6
Hewett, Jen. *Print, Pattern, Sew*	646.4
Swearington, Jen. *Printing on Fabric*	746.6
TEXTILE WORKERS	
Beckert, Sven. *Empire of Cotton*	338.4
TEY, JOSEPHINE, 1896 OR 1897-1952	
Thomson, Jennifer. *Josephine Tey*	823
Thaddeus Stevens. Levine, Bruce C.	B
THADEN, LOUISE MCPHETRIDGE, 1905-1979	
O'Brien, Keith. *Fly Girls*	920
THAI AMERICANS	
Coffin, Jaed. *Roughhouse Friday*	B
Duckworth, Tammy. *Every Day Is a Gift*	B
THAILAND	
Gutman, Matt. *The Boys in the Cave*	796.52
Hamilton, Lisa M. *The Hungry Season*	
Witte, Christina De. ★*Noodles, Rice, and Everything Spice*	641.595
Thaler, Richard H.	
Misbehaving	330.01
THAMES RIVER	
Maiklem, Lara. *Mudlark*	B
Thanhauser, Sofi	
Worn	391
Thank You (Falettinme Be Mice Elf Agin). Stone, Sly	B
★*Thank You for Being Late*. Friedman, Thomas L.	303.48
Thank You for Smoking. Disbrowe, Paula	641.5
★*Thank You for Voting*. Smith, Erin Geiger	324.973
Thank You for Your Service. Finkel, David	920
THANK-YOU NOTES	
Visser, Margaret. *The Gift of Thanks*	394
Thanks for Waiting. Shafrir, Doree	B
Thanks, Obama. Litt, David	B
Thanksgiving. Baker, James W.	394.2649
Thanksgiving. Sifton, Sam	641.5
The Thanksgiving Book. Hillstrom, Laurie Collier	394.2649
THANKSGIVING DAY	
Baker, James W. *Thanksgiving*	394.2649
Hillstrom, Laurie Collier. *The Thanksgiving Book*	394.2649
Powell, Nate. ★*Lies My Teacher Told Me*	741.5
Sifton, Sam. *Thanksgiving*	641.5
Silverman, David J. ★*This Land Is Their Land*	974.4
Thant Myint-U	
The Hidden History of Burma	959.105
That Cheese Plate Wants to Party. Mullen, Marissa	641.6
That Noodle Life. Le, Mike	641.82
That Sounds so Good. Music, Carla Lalli	641.5
That's What She Said. Lipman, Joanne	305.30973
THATCHER, MARGARET	
Carroll, Rory. *There Will Be Fire*	363.325
Kissinger, Henry. *Leadership*	303.3
Moore, Charles. *Margaret Thatcher*	941.085
THE TROUBLES, 1968-1998	
Carroll, Rory. *There Will Be Fire*	363.325
Keefe, Patrick Radden. ★*Say Nothing*	364.152
O'Toole, Fintan. ★*We Don't Know Ourselves*	941.7
THE WEST (CANADA)	
Stokes, Donald W. *The New Stokes Field Guide to Birds.*	598
THE WEST (UNITED STATES)	
Ambrose, Stephen E. ★*Undaunted Courage*	917.804
Blakeslee, Nate. *American Wolf*	599.773
Brands, H. W. *The Last Campaign*	973.8
Brown, Daniel James. *The Indifferent Stars Above*	B
Cozzens, Peter. *The Earth Is Weeping*	978
Crouch, Gregory. *The Bonanza King*	B
Daugherty, Tracy. *Larry McMurtry*	B
Donovan, Jim. *A Terrible Glory*	973.8
Ehrlich, Gretel. *Unsolaced*	B
Fedarko, Kevin. *A Walk in the Park*	917.91
Gallagher, Winifred. *New Women in the Old West*	978.02
Grant, Will. *The Last Ride of the Pony Express*	917.804
Gwynne, S. C. *Empire of the Summer Moon*	B
Hayes, Derek. *Historical Atlas of the American West*	911
Hickman, Katie. *Brave Hearted*	978
Hyde, Anne Farrar. ★*Born of Lakes and Plains*	978
Krakauer, Jon. *Into the Wild*	917.9804
Kumar, Priyanka. *Conversations with Birds*	598
Leerhsen, Charles. ★*Butch Cassidy*	B
Mathews, Daniel. *Trees in Trouble*	634.9
Nelson, Megan Kate. *The Three-Cornered War*	978
Offerman, Nick. *Where the Deer and the Antelope Play*	973.93
Raban, Jonathan. *Bad Land*	978
Rekdal, Paisley. *West*	811
Richardson, Heather Cox. ★*How the South Won the Civil War*	306.20973
Schmidt, Thomas. *The Saga of Lewis & Clark*	917.804
Sides, Hampton. *Blood and Thunder*	978
Stiles, T. J. *Custer's Trials*	B
Stiles, T. J. *Jesse James*	B
Stokes, Donald W. *The New Stokes Field Guide to Birds.*	598
Wallis, Michael. *The Best Land Under Heaven*	978
Wallis, Michael. *Route 66*	917.804
Ward, Geoffrey C. *The West*	978
Warren, Louis S. *Buffalo Bill's America*	B
Williams, Terry Tempest. *Erosion*	814
THE WEST (UNITED STATES) HISTORY	
Ambrose, Stephen E. *Nothing Like It in the World*	385
Boessenecker, John. *Gentleman Bandit*	B
Brands, H. W. *Dreams of El Dorado*	978
Brown, Dee. *The American West*	978
Brown, Dee. ★*Bury My Heart at Wounded Knee*	978
Chang, Gordon H. *Ghosts of Gold Mountain*	331.6
Clavin, Thomas. *Wild Bill*	B
Eisler, Benita. *The Red Man's Bones*	B
Gwynne, S. C. *Empire of the Summer Moon*	B
Hayes, Derek. *Historical Atlas of the American West*	911
Hyde, Anne Farrar. *Empires, Nations, and Families*	978
Morgan, Robert. *Lions of the West*	978
Nelson, Megan Kate. *The Three-Cornered War*	978
Raban, Jonathan. *Bad Land*	978
Richardson, Heather Cox. ★*How the South Won the Civil War*	306.20973
Sharfstein, Daniel J. ★*Thunder in the Mountains*	979.5
Sides, Hampton. *Blood and Thunder*	978
Stiles, T. J. *Custer's Trials*	B
Utley, Robert M. *Sitting Bull*	B
THE WEST (UNITED STATES) IN ART	
Eisler, Benita. *The Red Man's Bones*	B
Parke, Henry C. *The Greatest Westerns Ever Made and the People Who Made Them*	791.43
THE WEST (UNITED STATES) IN LITERATURE	
Brown, Dee. *The American West*	978
THEATER	
Brockett, Oscar G. *History of the Theatre*	792
Bryson, Bill. *Shakespeare*	B
Dromgoole, Dominic. *Hamlet Globe to Globe*	792.9
Gillette, J. Michael. *Theatrical Design and Production*	792.02
Greenblatt, Stephen. ★*Will in the World*	B
Grey, Joel. *Master of Ceremonies*	B
Hall, Jake. *The Art of Drag*	792.8
Hytner, Nicholas. *Balancing Acts*	B
Jacobs, Alexandra. *Still Here*	B
Karim-Cooper, Farah. ★*The Great White Bard*	822.33
Keene, Donald. *The Pleasures of Japanese Literature*	895.6
Lane, Stewart F. *Black Broadway*	792.089
Lloyd Webber, Andrew. *Unmasked*	B
Miranda, Lin-Manuel. *Hamilton*	782.1
Mordden, Ethan. *Anything Goes*	782.1
Mordden, Ethan. *Ziegfeld*	B
O'Brien, Jack. *Jack Be Nimble*	B
Purdum, Todd S. *Something Wonderful*	B
Riedel, Michael. *Razzle Dazzle*	792.09
Riedel, Michael. *Singular Sensation*	792
Shapiro, James. *Shakespeare in a Divided America*	822.33
Stewart, Patrick. ★*Making It So*	B
Viertel, Jack. *The Secret Life of the American Musical*	792.609
Wasson, Sam. ★*Improv Nation*	792.02
Wojczuk, Tana. *Lady Romeo*	B

AUTHOR, TITLE, SERIES AND SUBJECT INDEX

THEATER AND SOCIETY
  Shapiro, James. ★*The Playbook* — 792
  Shapiro, James. *Shakespeare in a Divided America* — 822.33
  Smith, Emma. *This Is Shakespeare* — 822.33
THEATER COMPANIES
  Hytner, Nicholas. *Balancing Acts* — B
THEATERS
  Essin, Christin. *Stage Designers in Early Twentieth-Century America* — 792.02
  Gillette, J. Michael. *Theatrical Design and Production* — 792.02
Theatrical Design and Production. Gillette, J. Michael — 792.02
THEATRICAL MANAGERS
  Skal, David J. *Something in the Blood* — 823
THEATRICAL PRODUCERS AND DIRECTORS
  Harris, Mark. *Mike Nichols* — B
  Hytner, Nicholas. *Balancing Acts* — B
  Lane, Stewart F. *Black Broadway* — 792.089
  McGilligan, Patrick. *Young Orson* — B
  Mordden, Ethan. *Ziegfeld* — B
  O'Brien, Jack. *Jack Be Nimble* — B
  Riedel, Michael. *Singular Sensation* — 792
  Turan, Kenneth. ★*Free for All* — B
Theft by Finding. Sedaris, David — B
The Theft of Memory. Kozol, Jonathan — B
Their Finest Hour. Churchill, Winston — 940.53
Then Come Back. Neruda, Pablo — 861
Then Comes Marriage. Kaplan, Roberta A. — 346.7301
Then It Fell Apart. Moby — B
★*Then The War.* Phillips, Carl — 811
Thenell, Jan
  The Library's Crisis Communications Planner — 021.7
THEOCRACY
  Bowden, Mark. *Guests of the Ayatollah* — 955.05
  Soyinka, Wole. *Of Africa* — 960
THEODICY
  Kushner, Harold S. *When Bad Things Happen to Good People* — 296.3
★*Theodore Rex.* Morris, Edmund — 973.911
Theodore Roosevelt for the Defense. Abrams, Dan — 345.73
Theoharis, Jeanne
  A More Beautiful and Terrible History — 323.1196
  The Rebellious Life of Mrs. Rosa Parks — B
THEOLOGIANS
  Harrington, Joel F. *Dangerous Mystic* — B
  Kung, Hans. *Great Christian Thinkers* — 230
  Marsh, Charles. *Strange Glory* — B
  Massing, Michael. *Fatal Discord* — 920
THEOLOGY
  Akyol, Mustafa. ★*Reopening Muslim Minds* — 297.09
  Armstrong, Karen. *The Case for God* — 211
  Armstrong, Karen. *A History of God* — 202
  Belser, Julia Watts. ★*Loving Our Own Bones* — 296
  Brown, Samuel Morris. *In Heaven as It Is on Earth* — 289.3
  Eire, Carlos M. N. *A Very Brief History of Eternity* — 236
  Feldman, Noah. *To Be a Jew Today* — 296.3
  Greenblatt, Stephen. *The Rise and Fall of Adam and Eve* — 233
  Held, Shai. ★*Judaism Is About Love* — 296.3
  Kugel, James L. *The Great Shift* — 296.3
  Kung, Hans. *Great Christian Thinkers* — 230
  Levine, Amy-Jill. *The Bible with and Without Jesus* — 220.6
  Marsh, Charles. *Strange Glory* — B
  Massing, Michael. *Fatal Discord* — 920
  McGuckin, John Anthony. ★*The Eastern Orthodox Church* — 281.909
  Miles, Jack. *God in the Qur'an* — 297.2
  Robinson, Marilynne. ★*Reading Genesis* — 222
  Stavrakopoulou, Francesca. *God* — 231
  Whittle, Lisa. *God Knows* — 231
  Wray, T. J. *The Birth of Satan* — 235
Theology in America. Holifield, E. Brooks — 230
THEOLOGY, DOCTRINAL
  Davies, Brian. *The Thought of Thomas Aquinas* — 230
  Holifield, E. Brooks. *Theology in America* — 230
  Lewis, C. S. *Mere Christianity* — 230
  Thomas. *Selected Writings* — 230
THEORIES
  Alexander, Amir R. *Infinitesimal* — 511
  Chown, Marcus. *Infinity in the Palm of Your Hand* — 523.1
  Dyson, Freeman J. *Maker of Patterns* — B
  Hawking, Stephen. *The Nature of Space and Time* — 530.1
  Loeb, Abraham. *Extraterrestrial* — 576.8

Winkler, Elizabeth. *Shakespeare Was a Woman & Other Heresies* — 822.33
THEORY OF KNOWLEDGE
  Du Sautoy, Marcus. *The Great Unknown* — 500
  Gladwell, Malcolm. *The Tipping Point* — 302
  Grant, Adam M. ★*Think Again* — 153.4
  Shermer, Michael. *The Believing Brain* — 153.4
  Strevens, Michael. *The Knowledge Machine* — 500
  Wilson, Derek K. *A Magical World* — 261.55
★*The Theory of the Leisure Class.* Veblen, Thorstein — 305.5
THERAPEUTICS
  English, Camper. *Doctors and Distillers* — 615.7
There Are More Beautiful Things Than Beyonce. Parker, Morgan — 811
There Are No Accidents. Singer, Jessie — 363.1
There Are Places in the World Where Rules Are Less Important Than Kindness.
  Rovelli, Carlo — 500
There Is Nothing for You Here. Hill, Fiona — 327.2
There Was a Country. Achebe, Chinua — B
There Will Be Fire. Carroll, Rory — 363.325
There Will Be No Miracles Here. Gerald, Casey — B
There's A Mystery There. Cott, Jonathan — 813
★*There's Always This Year.* Abdurraqib, Hanif — 796.323
Theroux, Paul
  Deep South — 975
  The Great Railway Bazaar — 915
  The Last Train to Zona Verde — 916
  On the Plain of Snakes — 917
  Riding the Iron Rooster — 915
THEROUX, PAUL
  Theroux, Paul. *Deep South* — 975
  Theroux, Paul. *The Great Railway Bazaar* — 915
  Theroux, Paul. *On the Plain of Snakes* — 917
  Theroux, Paul. *Riding the Iron Rooster* — 915
These Are My Rivers. Ferlinghetti, Lawrence — 811
★*These Are the Plunderers.* Morgenson, Gretchen — 332.6
★*These Fevered Days.* Ackmann, Martha — B
These Fists Break Bricks. Hendrix, Grady — 791
★*These Precious Days.* Patchett, Ann — 814
★*These Truths.* Lepore, Jill — 973
These Walls. Fedderly, Eva — 365
They Are Already Here. Scoles, Sarah — 001.942
They Bled Blue. Turbow, Jason — 796.357
★*They Called Me a Lioness.* Tamimi, Ahed — B
They Called Us. Gallego, Ruben — 956.7044
★*They Called Us Exceptional.* Gupta, Prachi — B
★*They Came for the Schools.* Hixenbaugh, Michael — 371.9
They Fought Like Demons. Blanton, DeAnne — 973.7
They Killed Freddie Gray. Barron, Justine — 363.32
They Marched into Sunlight. Maraniss, David — 959.704
They Poured Fire on Us from the Sky. Deng, Alephonsion — B
They Told Me Not to Take That Job. Levy, Reynold — 792.09
They Will Have to Die Now. Verini, James — 956.7044
Thi, Kim Phuc Phan
  Fire Road — B
THI, KIM PHUC PHAN
  Thi, Kim Phuc Phan. *Fire Road* — B
Thick. Cottom, Tressie McMillan — 301
Thicker Than Water. Washington, Kerry — B
THIEL, PETER A.
  Chafkin, Max. *The Contrarian* — B
Thiessen, Tiffani
  Pull up a Chair — 641.5
THIEVES
  Bilefsky, Dan. *The Last Job* — 364.16
  Boessenecker, John. *Gentleman Bandit* — B
  Finkel, Michael. *The Art Thief* — 364.1628
  Fox, Margalit. *The Talented Mrs. Mandelbaum* — 364.1
  Guinn, Jeff. *Go Down Together* — B
  Jobb, Dean. *A Gentleman and a Thief* — 364.16
  Johnson, Kirk W. *The Feather Thief* — 364.16
  Leerhsen, Charles. ★*Butch Cassidy* — B
Thieves' Road. Mort, T. A. — 978.3
★*The Thin Light of Freedom.* Ayers, Edward L. — 975.5
★*Thin Skin.* Shapland, Jenn — 814
Thing Explainer. Munroe, Randall — 500
The Thing with Feathers. Strycker, Noah K. — 598.072
★*Things I Don't Want to Know.* Levy, Deborah — B
Things I Have Withheld. Miller, Kei — 814
Things I Should Have Told My Daughter. Cleage, Pearl — B

PUBLIC LIBRARY CORE COLLECTION: NONFICTION
Twentieth Edition

Things I've Been Silent About. Nafisi, Azar	B
Things My Son Needs to Know About the World. Backman, Fredrik	B
Things That Make White People Uncomfortable. Bennett, Michael	305.896
Things We Didn't Talk About When I Was a Girl. Vanasco, Jeannie	B
★ The *Things We Love.* Ahuvia, Aaron	790.1
★ *Things We Make.* Hammack, William Scott	620
Things Worth Dying For. Chaput, Charles J.	248.4
Think. Blackburn, Simon	100
★ *Think Again.* Grant, Adam M.	153.4
Think and Grow Rich. Hill, Napoleon	650.1
Think Like a Feminist. Hay, Carol	305.42
Think Like a Rocket Scientist. Varol, Ozan O.	650.1
Thinking Differently. Flink, David	371.9
Thinking in Bets. Duke, Annie	658.4
★ *Thinking, Fast and Slow.* Kahneman, Daniel	153.4
Thinning Blood. Myers, Leah	B
The *Third Coast.* Dyja, Tom	977.311
The *Third Plate.* Barber, Dan	641.3
The *Third Pole.* Synnott, Mark	796.522
★ The *Third Rainbow Girl.* Eisenberg, Emma Copley	364.152
The *Third Reich.* Childers, Thomas	943.086
The *Third Reich at War.* Evans, Richard J.	940.53
The *Third Reich in Power, 1933-1939.* Evans, Richard J.	943.086
THIRD REICH, 1933-1945	
Allert, Tilman. *Heil Hitler*	395.4
Childers, Thomas. *The Third Reich*	943.086
Dumbach, Annette E. *Sophie Scholl and the White Rose*	943.086
Dwork, Deborah. ★ *Holocaust*	940
Eisner, Peter. *The Pope's Last Crusade*	282.092
English, Charlie. *The Gallery of Miracles and Madness*	709.04
Evans, Richard J. *The Third Reich at War*	940.53
Evans, Richard J. *The Third Reich in Power, 1933-1939*	943.086
Fisher, Marshall Jon. *A Terrible Splendor*	796.342
Fritzsche, Peter. *Life and Death in the Third Reich*	943.086
Gerwarth, Robert. *Hitler's Hangman*	B
Gortemaker, Heike B. *Eva Braun*	B
Hastings, Max. *Armageddon*	940.54
Hayes, Peter. *Why?*	940.53
Kershaw, Ian. *Hitler*	B
Kershaw, Ian. *Hitler*	B
Klemperer, Victor. *I Will Bear Witness*	B
Larson, Erik. *In the Garden of Beasts*	B
Longerich, Peter. *Goebbels*	B
Longerich, Peter. *Hitler*	B
Macintyre, Ben. *Double Cross*	940.54
Mazower, Mark. *Hitler's Empire*	940.54
McDonough, Frank. *The Hitler Years*	943.086
McKay, Sinclair. *The Fire and the Darkness*	940.54
Moorhouse, Roger. *Berlin at War*	943
Mulley, Clare. *The Women Who Flew for Hitler*	920
Oelhafen, Ingrid von. *Hitler's Stolen Children*	B
Ohler, Norman. *The Bohemians*	940.53
Porter, Carolyn. *Marcel's Letters*	940.54
Read, Anthony. *The Fall of Berlin*	940.54
Rhodes, Richard. *Masters of Death*	940.53
Ryback, Timothy W. *Hitler's Private Library*	027
Schwarz, Geraldine. *Those Who Forget*	940.53
Shirer, William L. ★ *The Rise and Fall of the Third Reich*	943.086
Smith, Helmut Walser. *Germany, a Nation in Its Time*	943
Snyder, Timothy. ★ *Bloodlands*	940.54
Speer, Albert. *Inside the Third Reich*	B
Stargardt, Nicholas. *The German War*	940.53
Talty, Stephan. *Agent Garbo*	940.5
Thomas, Gordon. *Defying Hitler*	920
Trimborn, Jurgen. *Leni Riefenstahl*	B
Ullrich, Volker. ★ *Eight Days in May*	943.086
Ullrich, Volker. *Hitler*	B
Ullrich, Volker. *Hitler*	B
Weale, Adrian. *Army of Evil*	940.54
Wiesel, Elie. ★ *Night*	B
Thirst. Harrison, Scott	B
Thirteen Days. Kennedy, Robert F.	327.73
Thirteen Days in September. Wright, Lawrence	956.04
Thirteen Ways of Looking at the Novel. Smiley, Jane	B
THIRTIES (AGE)	
Kalanithi, Paul. ★ *When Breath Becomes Air*	B
This Ain't the Summer of Love. Waksman, Steve	781.66
This Blessed Earth. Genoways, Ted	630.9
This Body I Wore. Goetsch, Diana	B
This Boy We Made. Harris, Taylor	B
This Boy's Life. Wolff, Tobias	B
This Chair Rocks. Applewhite, Ashton	155.67
This Cold Heaven. Ehrlich, Gretel	998.2
This Divided Island. Subramanian, Sammanth	954.9303
This Far by Faith. Williams, Juan	200
This Fierce People. Crawford, Alan Pell	975
This Fight Is Our Fight. Warren, Elizabeth	305.5
This Hallelujah Banquet. Peterson, Eugene H.	228
This Idea Is Brilliant. Brockman, John	500
This Is All I Got. Sandler, Lauren	B
This Is Assisted Dying. Green, Stefanie	616.02
This Is Big. Meltzer, Marisa	613.25
This Is Not a Pity Memoir. Morgan, Abi	B
This Is Shakespeare. Smith, Emma	822.33
This Is the Fire. Lemon, Don	305.896
This Is the Story of a Happy Marriage. Patchett, Ann	B
★ *This Is What It Sounds Like.* Rogers, Susan E.	781.1
This Is Your Brain on Sports. Wertheim, L. Jon	796.01
★ *This Is Your Mind on Plants.* Pollan, Michael	581.6
★ *This Land Is Their Land.* Silverman, David J.	974.4
This Life. Hagglund, Martin	110
This Little Art. Briggs, Kate	418
This Much Country. Pace, Kristin Knight	B
★ *This Must Be the Place.* Ray, Rachael	641.5
★ *This Ordinary Stardust.* Townsend, Alan R.	B
This Republic of Suffering. Faust, Drew Gilpin	973.7
This Wheel of Rocks. Grathwohl, Marya	271
This Will Be Funny Later. Pentland, Jenny	B
This Will Make It Taste Good. Howard, Vivian	641.5
This Will Not Pass. Martin, Jonathan	973.933
This Will Only Hurt a Little. Philipps, Busy	B
Thom, Kai Cheng	
Falling Back in Love with Being Human	811
Thomas	
Selected Writings	230
Thomas Cromwell. Borman, Tracy	B
Thomas Cromwell. MacCulloch, Diarmaid	B
Thomas Eakins. Sewell, Darrel	759.13
THOMAS FAMILY	
Franklin, John Hope. *In Search of the Promised Land*	929
Thomas Hardy. Hardy, Thomas	821
Thomas Hardy. Tomalin, Claire	B
Thomas Jefferson. Hitchens, Christopher	B
★ *Thomas Jefferson.* Meacham, Jon	B
★ *Thomas Jefferson and the Tripoli Pirates.* Kilmeade, Brian	973.4
Thomas, Anna	
Vegan Vegetarian Omnivore	641.5
THOMAS, AQUINAS, SAINT, 1225?-1274	
Davies, Brian. *The Thought of Thomas Aquinas*	230
THOMAS, CLARENCE, 1948-	
Robin, Corey. *The Enigma of Clarence Thomas*	347.73
Thomas, Dana	
Gods and Kings	920
Thomas, Dylan	
A Child's Christmas in Wales	B
The Poems of Dylan Thomas	821
Under Milk Wood	822.91
THOMAS, DYLAN, 1914-1953	
Thomas, Dylan. *A Child's Christmas in Wales*	B
Thomas, Elizabeth Marshall	
Growing Old	305.26
THOMAS, ELIZABETH MARSHALL, 1931-	
Thomas, Elizabeth Marshall. *Growing Old*	305.26
Thomas, Etan	
We Matter	796.08
Thomas, Evan	
Being Nixon	B
★ *First*	B
Ike's Bluff	973.921092
★ *John Paul Jones*	B
★ *Robert Kennedy*	B
Sea of Thunder	940.54
Thomas, Franklin A.	
An Unplanned Life	B
THOMAS, FRANKLIN A.	
Thomas, Franklin A. *An Unplanned Life*	B

AUTHOR, TITLE, SERIES AND SUBJECT INDEX

Thomas, Gillian
  Because of Sex — 344.7301
Thomas, Gordon
  Defying Hitler — 920
Thomas, Haile
  Living Lively — 641.5
Thomas, Hugh
  Rivers of Gold — 980
Thomas, Joseph Earl
  Sink — B
THOMAS, JOSEPH EARL
  Thomas, Joseph Earl. *Sink* — B
Thomas, Louisa
  Louisa — B
Thomas, Mathilde
  The French Beauty Solution — 646.7
Thomas, R. Eric
  ★*Congratulations, the Best Is Over!* — B
  Here for It — B
THOMAS, R. ERIC
  Thomas, R. Eric. ★*Congratulations, the Best Is Over!* — B
  Thomas, R. Eric. *Here for It* — B
Thomas, Richard F.
  ★*Why Bob Dylan Matters* — 782.42164
THOMAS, SALLY, 1787-1850
  Franklin, John Hope. *In Search of the Promised Land* — 929
Thompson, Bob
  Revolutionary Roads — 973.3
THOMPSON, BOB, 1950 AUGUST 28-
  Thompson, Bob. *Revolutionary Roads* — 973.3
Thompson, Christina
  Sea People — 305.8994
Thompson, Clive
  Coders — 005.1092
THOMPSON, DOROTHY, 1893-1961
  Cohen, Deborah. *Last Call at the Hotel Imperial* — 070.92
Thompson, Erica
  Escape from Model Land — 511
Thompson, Erin L.
  Smashing Statues — 725
Thompson, Heather Ann
  Blood in the Water — 365
Thompson, Hunter S.
  Fear and Loathing at Rolling Stone — 070.1
  ★*Fear and Loathing in America* — B
THOMPSON, HUNTER S.
  Denevi, Timothy. *Freak Kingdom* — B
  Thompson, Hunter S. *Fear and Loathing at Rolling Stone* — 070.1
  Thompson, Hunter S. ★*Fear and Loathing in America* — B
  Thompson, Juan F. *Stories I Tell Myself* — B
Thompson, Ida
  ★*The Audubon Society Field Guide to North American Fossils* — 560
Thompson, J. M.
  Running Is a Kind of Dreaming — B
THOMPSON, J. M. (CLINICAL PSYCHOLOGIST)
  Thompson, J. M. *Running Is a Kind of Dreaming* — B
Thompson, Jamie
  Standoff — 364.152
Thompson, Jennifer Trainer
  Fresh Fish — 641.3
Thompson, Juan F.
  Stories I Tell Myself — B
THOMPSON, JUAN F.
  Thompson, Juan F. *Stories I Tell Myself* — B
Thompson, Kenan
  When I Was Your Age — B
THOMPSON, KENAN
  Thompson, Kenan. *When I Was Your Age* — B
Thompson, Nicholas
  The Hawk and the Dove — 973.92
THOMPSON, SCOTT, 1959-
  Myers, Paul. *The Kids in the Hall* — 920
Thompson, Tracy
  The New Mind of the South — 305.800975
Thompson, Wright
  The Cost of These Dreams — B
Thompson-Hernandez, Walter
  The Compton Cowboys — 920

THOMSON, CHRISTOPHER BIRDWOOD, BARON, 1875-1930
  Gwynne, S. C. *His Majesty's Airship* — 363.12
Thomson, David
  Bette Davis — B
  The Big Screen — 791.430973
  The Fatal Alliance — 791.43
  ★*How to Watch a Movie* — 791.43
  Ingrid Bergman — B
  The New Biographical Dictionary of Film — 791.4302
Thomson, Graeme
  George Harrison — B
Thomson, Helen
  Unthinkable — 612.8
Thomson, Jennifer
  Josephine Tey — 823
Thomson, Keith
  Born to Be Hanged — 910.4
Thomson, Mike
  Syria's Secret Library — 956.9104
Thondup
  Enlightened Journey — 294.3
THOR (NORSE DEITY)
  Larrington, Carolyne. *The Norse Myths* — 293
Thoreau, Henry David
  ★*Collected Essays and Poems* — 818
  The Maine Woods — 917
  ★*Walden, Or, Life in the Woods* — 813
THOREAU, HENRY DAVID, 1817-1862
  Shattuck, Ben. *Six Walks* — B
  Thoreau, Henry David. *The Maine Woods* — 917
  Thoreau, Henry David. ★*Walden, Or, Life in the Woods* — 813
  Walls, Laura Dassow. ★*Henry David Thoreau* — B
Thorisson, Mimi
  A Kitchen in France — 641.594
THORISSON, MIMI
  Thorisson, Mimi. *A Kitchen in France* — 641.594
***Thornton** Wilder*. Niven, Penelope — B
***Thornton** Wilder*. Wilder, Thornton — 812
THOROUGHBRED HORSES
  Hillenbrand, Laura. ★*Seabiscuit* — 798.4
  Letts, Elizabeth. *The Perfect Horse* — 940.54
Thorp, Edward O.
  A Man for All Markets — B
THORP, EDWARD O.
  Thorp, Edward O. *A Man for All Markets* — B
Thorpe, Helen
  The Newcomers — 373.18
THORPE, JIM, 1887-1953
  Buford, Kate. *Native American Son* — B
  Crawford, Bill. ★*All American* — B
  Maraniss, David. ★*Path Lit by Lightning* — B
Thorpe, Molly Suber
  Modern Calligraphy — 745.6
Thorstensen, Ole
  Making Things Right — 690
THORSTENSEN, OLE
  Thorstensen, Ole. *Making Things Right* — 690
Those Angry Days. Olson, Lynne — 940.53
Those We Throw Away Are Diamonds. Dogon, Mondiant — B
Those Who Forget. Schwarz, Geraldine — 940.53
Thou, Dear God". King, Martin Luther — 242
Though The Heavens May Fall. Wise, Steven M. — 342.42
THOUGHT AND THINKING
  Barrett, Lisa Feldman. ★*How Emotions Are Made* — 152.4
  Bawer, Bruce. *The Victims' Revolution* — 320.973
  Blight, David W. ★*Frederick Douglass* — B
  Curran, Andrew S. *Diderot and the Art of Thinking Freely* — 194
  Dennett, D. C. *Intuition Pumps and Other Tools for Thinking* — 121
  Gladwell, Malcolm. *Blink* — 153.4
  Goleman, Daniel. *Focus* — 153.7
  Grandin, Temple. ★*Visual Thinking* — 152.14
  Grant, Adam M. ★*Think Again* — 153.4
  Gutting, Gary. *What Philosophy Can Do* — 100
  Harari, Yuval N. ★*Sapiens* — 909
  Hayes, Terrance. *So to Speak* — 811
  Heti, Sheila. *Alphabetical Diaries* — 818
  Hitchens, Christopher. *The Four Horsemen* — 211
  Hofstadter, Douglas R. *Surfaces and Essences* — 169

PUBLIC LIBRARY CORE COLLECTION: NONFICTION
Twentieth Edition

Jacobs, A. J. *The Puzzler*	793.73
Jacobs, Alan. *How to Think*	153.4
Johnson, Steven. *Farsighted*	153.8
Kahneman, Daniel. ★*Thinking, Fast and Slow*	153.4
Kishimi, Ichiro. *The Courage to Be Disliked*	158
Kross, Ethan. ★*Chatter*	158.1
Lively, Penelope. *Life in the Garden*	B
Livio, Mario. *Why?*	153.3
Malone, Thomas W. *Superminds*	005.7
Marsh, Charles. *Strange Glory*	B
Mlodinow, Leonard. *Emotional*	152.4
Montell, Amanda. ★*The Age of Magical Overthinking*	153.4
Nicolson, Adam. *How to Be*	180
Nisbett, Richard E. *Mindware*	153.4
Paul, Annie Murphy. *The Extended Mind*	128
Pinker, Steven. *The Stuff of Thought*	401
Riel, Jennifer. *Creating Great Choices*	658.4
Ryan, Alan. *On Politics*	320.01
Sheldrake, Rupert. *Science and Spiritual Practices*	201
Thomson, Helen. *Unthinkable*	612.8
Vargas Llosa, Mario. *The Call of the Tribe*	868
Wang, Jackie. *The Sunflower Cast a Spell to Save Us from the Void*	811
Wolf, Maryanne. *Reader, Come Home*	418
The Thought of Thomas Aquinas. Davies, Brian	230
***Thoughtful** Cooking*. Dissen, William Stark	641.5975
***Thoughts** Are Not the Enemy*. Siff, Jason	294.3
*A **Thousand** Mornings*. Oliver, Mary	811
*A **Thousand** Naked Strangers*. Hazzard, Kevin	B
*A **Thousand** Times You Lose Your Treasure*. Nguyen, Hoa	811
Thrall, Nathan	
★*A Day in the Life of Abed Salama*	956.05
Thrasher, Steven W.	
★*The Viral Underclass*	362.1962
*A **Thread** of Violence*. O'Connell, Mark	364.152
Threadgill, Henry	
Easily Slip into Another World	B
THREADGILL, HENRY	
Threadgill, Henry. *Easily Slip into Another World*	B
***Threading** My Prayer Rug*. Rehman, Sabeeha	305.8
THREAT (PSYCHOLOGY)	
Cassidy, Cody. *How to Survive History*	904
Diamond, Cheryl. *Nowhere Girl*	B
Farrow, Ronan. ★*Catch and Kill*	331.4
Jones, Saeed. *Alive at the End of the World*	811
Millet, Lydia. *We Loved It All*	813
Nagorski, Andrew. *Saving Freud*	940.53
*The **Three** Ages of Water*. Gleick, Peter H.	333.91
***Three** Days in January*. Baier, Bret	B
***Three** Dreamers*. Carcaterra, Lorenzo	B
★***Three** Girls from Bronzeville*. Trice, Dawn Turner	977.311
*The **Three** Lives of James Madison*. Feldman, Noah	B
***Three** Minutes in Poland*. Kurtz, Glenn	947.7
***Three** Minutes to Doomsday*. Navarro, Joe	B
*The **Three** Mothers*. Tubbs, Anna Malaika	306.874
***Three** Plays*. Coward, Noel	822
***Three** Wise Men*. Wise, Beau	958.104
***Three** Women*. Taddeo, Lisa	306.7082
*The **Three**-Cornered War*. Nelson, Megan Kate	978
***Three**-Martini Afternoons at the Ritz*. Crowther, Gail	920
★***Three**-Ring Circus*. Pearlman, Jeff	796.323
*The **Three**-Year Swim Club*. Checkoway, Julie	797.2
THRIFT SHOPS	
Yang, April. *DIY Thrift Flip*	646.2
***Thrill** Me*. Percy, Benjamin	808.3
THRILLER AND SUSPENSE AUTHORS	
Rosnay, Tatiana de. *Manderley Forever*	B
***Through** The Eye of a Needle*. Brown, Peter	270.2
★***Through** The Language Glass*. Deutscher, Guy	410
***Through** Two Doors at Once*. Ananthaswamy, Anil	530.12
Thubron, Colin	
In Siberia	957
Shadow of the Silk Road	915
THUBRON, COLIN, 1939-	
Thubron, Colin. *In Siberia*	957
Thubron, Colin. *Shadow of the Silk Road*	915
Thubten Zopa	
The Four Noble Truths	294.3
Thucydides. Kagan, Donald	938
THUCYDIDES, 460?-395? B.C.E	
Kagan, Donald. *Thucydides*	938
Thunberg, Greta	
★*The Climate Book*	363.738
***Thunder** & Lightning*. Redniss, Lauren	741.5
***Thunder** At the Gates*. Egerton, Douglas R.	973.7
★***Thunder** in the Mountains*. Sharfstein, Daniel J.	979.5
***Thunder** Song*. LaPointe, Sasha taqwseblu	814
***Thurgood** Marshall*. Marshall, Thurgood	B
***Thurgood** Marshall*. Starks, Glenn L.	B
***Thurgood** Marshall*. Williams, Juan	B
Thurman, Judith	
★*A Left-Handed Woman*	814
Thursby, Jacqueline S.	
Critical Companion to Maya Angelou	818
★***Thus** Spoke Zarathustra*. Nietzsche, Friedrich Wilhelm	193
Thuss, Rebecca	
Paper to Petal	745.54
Thwaite, Ann	
Goodbye Christopher Robin	B
TIANANMEN SQUARE MASSACRE, BEIJING, CHINA, JUNE 3-4, 1989	
Liao, Yiwu. *Bullets and Opium*	951.05
Lim, Louisa. *The People's Republic of Amnesia*	951.05
Tibble, Tayi	
Poukahangatus	821
TIBET	
Dalai Lama. *Freedom in Exile*	B
Demick, Barbara. *Eat the Buddha*	951
Kirkby, Bruce. *Blue Sky Kingdom*	954.96
*The **Tibetan** Book of Living and Dying*. Sogyal	294.3
TIBETAN BUDDHISM	
Dalai Lama. *Freedom in Exile*	B
Demick, Barbara. *Eat the Buddha*	951
Kirkby, Bruce. *Blue Sky Kingdom*	954.96
TIBETAN PEOPLE	
Demick, Barbara. *Eat the Buddha*	951
Ticker. Swartz, Mimi	617.4
Tickle, Phyllis	
The Great Emergence	270.8
Ticktin, Allie	
Play to Progress	370.15
TIDE POOL ECOLOGY	
Nicolson, Adam. *Life Between the Tides*	577.69
TIDE POOLS	
Nicolson, Adam. *Life Between the Tides*	577.69
TIDES	
Maiklem, Lara. *Mudlark*	B
Tierney, John	
The Power of Bad	158.1
Tietjen, Jill S	
Hollywood, Her Story	791.43
Tigay, Chanan	
The Lost Book of Moses	098
*The **Tiger***. Vaillant, John	599.756
TIGER ATTACKS	
Vaillant, John. *The Tiger*	599.756
★***Tiger** Woods*. Benedict, Jeff	B
TIGERS	
Vaillant, John. *The Tiger*	599.756
★***Tightrope***. Kristof, Nicholas D.	306.0973
***Tightwads** and Spendthrifts*. Rick, Scott	332.024
Tila, Jet	
101 Asian Dishes You Need to Cook Before You Die	641.595
***Till** The End*. Sabathia, CC	796.357
TILL, EMMETT, 1941-1955	
Boyd, Herb. *We Shall Overcome*	323.1196
Smith, Patricia. ★*Incendiary Art*	811.54
Tyson, Timothy B. *The Blood of Emmett Till*	364.1
Tillich, Paul	
★*The Courage to Be*	179
*A **Timbered** Choir*. Berry, Wendell	811
TIME	
Borges, Jorge Luis. *Selected Non-Fictions*	864
Bowler, Kate. *No Cure for Being Human*	B
Burdick, Alan. *Why Time Flies*	529
Carroll, Sean M. *From Eternity to Here*	530.11
Dochartaigh, Kerri ni. *Cacophony of Bone*	B
Ernaux, Annie. ★*The Years*	B

AUTHOR, TITLE, SERIES AND SUBJECT INDEX

Hawking, Stephen. ★*Black Holes and Baby Universes and Other Essays*	530.1
Hawking, Stephen. *A Brief History of Time*	523.1
Hawking, Stephen. ★*A Briefer History of Time*	523.1
Hawking, Stephen. ★*The Universe in a Nutshell*	530.12
Jenkins, Jessica Kerwin. *All the Time in the World*	390
Le Guin, Ursula K. *So Far so Good*	811
Odell, Jenny. ★*Saving Time*	153.7
Pink, Daniel H. *When*	153.7
Rovelli, Carlo. *The Order of Time*	530.11
Rutherford, Adam. *The Complete Guide to Absolutely Everything*	500
Sanders, Ella Frances. *Eating the Sun*	520
Sherman, Anna. *The Bells of Old Tokyo*	952
Shulevitz, Judith. *The Sabbath World*	296.4
Vuong, Ocean. ★*Time Is a Mother*	811
★*Time Is a Mother*. Vuong, Ocean	811
Time Is Tight. Jones, Booker T.	B
TIME MANAGEMENT	
Allen, David. ★*Getting Things Done*	646.7
Carroll, Ryder. ★*The Bullet Journal Method*	640
Gilkey, Charlie. *Start Finishing*	658.4
Holmes, Cassie. *Happier Hour*	158.1
McGinnis, Patrick J. *Fear of Missing Out*	153.8
Morgenstern, Julie. *Time to Parent*	649
Norton, Michael. ★*The Ritual Effect*	650.1
Odell, Jenny. ★*Saving Time*	153.7
Pink, Daniel H. *When*	153.7
Shlain, Tiffany. *24/6*	158.1
TIME MEASUREMENTS	
Boyle, Rebecca. *Our Moon*	523.3
Burdick, Alan. *Why Time Flies*	529
Time of the Magicians. Eilenberger, Wolfram	920
TIME PERCEPTION	
Odell, Jenny. ★*Saving Time*	153.7
Pink, Daniel H. *When*	153.7
Time Pieces. Banville, John	914.1
Time to Eat. Hussain, Nadiya	641.5
Time to Parent. Morgenstern, Julie	649
Time Travel. Gleick, James	530.11
TIME TRAVEL	
Gleick, James. *Time Travel*	530.11
The Time Traveler's Guide to Elizabethan England. Mortimer, Ian	942.05
The Time Traveler's Guide to Restoration Britain. Mortimer, Ian	941.06
Time Will Clean the Carcass Bones. Perillo, Lucia	811
The Times. Nagourney, Adam	071
★*The Timetables of History*. Grun, Bernard	902
Timothy, Duval	
Food from Across Africa	641.596
Tinderbox. Fieseler, Robert W.	364.152
Tinker to Evers to Chance. Rapp, David	796.357
TINKER, JOE, 1880-1948	
Rapp, David. *Tinker to Evers to Chance*	796.357
Tinkerlab. Doorley, Rachelle	600
Tinsley, Omise'eke Natasha	
Beyonce in Formation	782.42164
Tiny Habits. Fogg, B. J.	158
Tiny House Living. Mitchell, Ryan	728.37
The Tiny Journalist. Nye, Naomi Shihab	811
Tip of the Iceberg. Adams, Mark	917.9804
Tippett, Krista	
★*Becoming Wise*	158.1
The Tipping Point. Gladwell, Malcolm	302
Tipton-Martin, Toni	
The Jemima Code	641.59
★*Jubilee*	641.59
Juke Joints, Jazz Clubs & Juice	641.87
TIPTREE, JAMES JR., 1915-1987	
Phillips, Julie. *James Tiptree, Jr.*	B
Tired as F*ck. Dooner, Caroline	152.1
Tired of Winning. Karl, Jonathan	973.933
Tirion, Wil	
The Cambridge Star Atlas	523.8
Tis. McCourt, Frank	B
Tisserand, Michael	
Krazy	741.5
Titian. Hale, Sheila	B
TITIAN, 1477-1576	
Hale, Sheila. *Titian*	B

Tjipombo, Tupa	
I Am Not Your Slave	B
TJIPOMBO, TUPA	
Tjipombo, Tupa. *I Am Not Your Slave*	B
To 2040. Graham, Jorie	811
To America with Love. Gill, A. A.	973.93
★*To Be a Jew Today*. Feldman, Noah	296.3
To Be Young, Gifted, and Black. Nemiroff, Robert	B
To Change the Church. Douthat, Ross Gregory	230
★*To Die Well*. Wanzer, Sidney H.	179.7
★*To Dye For*. Wicker, Alden	746
To Explain the World. Weinberg, Steven	509
To Free a Family. Nathans, Sydney	B
★*To Free the Captives*. Smith, Tracy K.	818
To Have and to Hold. Millwood, Molly	306.874
To Hell and Back. Pellegrino, Charles R.	940.54
To Infinity and Beyond. Tyson, Neil deGrasse	520
To Marry an English Lord. MacColl, Gail	974.7
To My Beloveds. Bailey, Jennifer	261.8
To Name the Bigger Lie. Viren, Sarah	B
To Raise a Boy. Brown, Emma	649
To Rescue the Constitution. Baier, Bret	973.4
To Risk It All. Stavridis, James	359
To Shake the Sleeping Self. Jenkins, Jedidiah	B
To Start a War. Draper, Robert	956.7044
To The End of the Earth. McManus, John C.	940.54
To The Greatest Heights. O'Brien, Vanessa	B
To The Promised Land. Honey, Michael K	323
To The Realization of Perfect Helplessness. Lewis, Robin Coste	811
To Walk About in Freedom. Emberton, Carole	306.3
TOBACCO INDUSTRY AND TRADE	
Ducharme, Jamie. *Big Vape*	338.7
Etter, Lauren. ★*The Devil's Playbook*	338.7
Tobar, Hector	
★*Our Migrant Souls*	305.868
Tobia, Jacob	
Sissy	305.30973
TOBIA, JACOB, 1991-	
Tobia, Jacob. *Sissy*	305.30973
Tobin, Jacqueline	
From Midnight to Dawn	973.7
Hidden in Plain View	973.7
Tobin, James	
Ernie Pyle's War	B
Tocqueville, Alexis de	
★*Democracy in America*	320.973
Todd, Kim	
Sensational	920
Todd, Olivier	
Albert Camus	B
TODD, RICHARD, 1949-	
Kidder, Tracy. *Good Prose*	808.02
TODDLERS	
Katin, Miriam. *We Are on Our Own*	741.5
Klein, Tovah P. *How Toddlers Thrive*	305.232
Knoll, Debra J. *Engaging Babies in the Library*	027.62
Murkoff, Heidi Eisenberg. ★*What to Expect the Second Year*	649
Santomero, Angela C. *Preschool Clues*	305.233
Todhunter, Tracey	
Crochet, Learn It. Love It.	746.43
Together. Murthy, Vivek Hallegere	158.2
Together. Oliver, Jamie	641.5
TOGO, SHIGENORI, 1882-1950	
Barrett, David Dean. *140 Days to Hiroshima*	940.54
TOHOKU EARTHQUAKE AND TSUNAMI, JAPAN, 2011	
Parry, Richard Lloyd. *Ghosts of the Tsunami*	952.05
Pilling, David. *Bending Adversity*	952.0512
Toht, David	
★*Stanley Decks*	690
Toibin, Colm	
Mad, Bad, Dangerous to Know	920
★*Toil & Trouble*. Burroughs, Augusten	B
TOILET TRAINING	
Ockwell-Smith, Sarah. *Ready, Set, Go!*	649
TOJO, HIDEKI, 1884-1948	
Dower, John W. *Embracing Defeat*	952.04
Token Black Girl. Prescod, Danielle	B
★*Token Supremacy*. Small, Zachary	332.4

PUBLIC LIBRARY CORE COLLECTION: NONFICTION
Twentieth Edition

TOKUGAWA PERIOD (1600-1868)
   Gordon, Andrew. *A Modern History of Japan* — 952
   Jansen, Marius. *The Making of Modern Japan* — 952
   McClain, James. *Japan* — 952.03

TOKYO, JAPAN
   Bass, Gary Jonathan. ★*Judgment at Tokyo* — 952.04
   Gladwell, Malcolm. ★*The Bomber Mafia* — 940.54
   Scott, James. *Black Snow* — 940.54
   Scott, James. *Target Tokyo* — 940.54
   Sherman, Anna. *The Bells of Old Tokyo* — 952
   Stanley, Amy. *Stranger in the Shogun's City* — B

Tolan, Sandy
   Children of the Stone — 780
   ★*The Lemon Tree* — B

Tolentino, Jia
   ★*Trick Mirror* — 973.93

Toler, Pamela D.
   Heroines of Mercy Street — 973.7
   Women Warriors — 355.0092

TOLERATION
   Blanco, Richard. *How to Love a Country* — 811
   Bolz-Weber, Nadia. *Accidental Saints* — 284.1
   Coombes, Joshua. *Do Something for Nothing* — 362.5
   Cox, Gena. *Leading Inclusion* — 658.3
   Francis. *Happiness in This Life* — 248.4
   Harris, Sam. *Islam and the Future of Tolerance* — 297.2
   Hartke, Austen. *Transforming* — 277
   Headlee, Celeste Anne. *Speaking of Race* — 305.8
   Iguodala, Andre. *The Sixth Man* — B
   Olivares, Efren C. *My Boy Will Die of Sorrow* — 305.9
   Roberts, Matthias. *Holy Runaways* — 262
   Rogers, Robbie. *Coming Out to Play* — B
   Schwalbe, Will. *We Should Not Be Friends* — B

Tolinski, Brad
   Light and Shade — B

Tolkien. McIlwaine, Catherine — 002.09

TOLKIEN, J. R. R. (JOHN RONALD REUEL), 1892-1973
   McIlwaine, Catherine. *Tolkien* — 002.09

Toll, Ian W.
   The Conquering Tide — 940.54
   Pacific Crucible — 940.54
   ★*Six Frigates* — 359.00973
   Twilight of the Gods — 940.54

Tolokonnikova, Nadezhda
   Rules for Rulebreakers — 782.42166

TOLOKONNIKOVA, NADEZHDA, 1989-
   Tolokonnikova, Nadezhda. *Rules for Rulebreakers* — 782.42166

★*Tolstoy*. Bartlett, Rosamund — B

TOLSTOY, LEO, GRAF, 1828-1910
   Bartlett, Rosamund. ★*Tolstoy* — B
   Blaisdell, Robert. *Creating Anna Karenina* — 891.7
   Saunders, George. ★*A Swim in a Pond in the Rain* — 891.7

Tomalin, Claire
   Samuel Pepys — B
   Thomas Hardy — B

Tomasson, Dara
   Walk, Jog, Run — 746.46

TOMATO SAUCES
   Holmberg, Martha. ★*Simply Tomato* — 641.6

TOMATOES
   Frank, Lois Ellen. *Seed to Plate, Soil to Sky* — 641.5
   Holmberg, Martha. ★*Simply Tomato* — 641.6
   LeHoullier, Craig. *Epic Tomatoes* — 635

★*The Tomb of the Mili Mongga*. Turvey, Samuel — 398.24

TOMB OF THE UNKNOWNS (VA.)
   McElya, Micki. *The Politics of Mourning* — 975.5

TOMBOUCTOU, MALI
   Hammer, Joshua. *The Bad-Ass Librarians of Timbuktu* — 025.8

Tomboy. Davis, Lisa Selin — 305.409
Tomboyland. Faliveno, Melissa — B

TOMBOYS
   Davis, Lisa Selin. *Tomboy* — 305.409

TOMBS
   Lawler, Andrew. *Under Jerusalem* — 956.94
   Mertz, Barbara. *Temples, Tombs, & Hieroglyphs* — 932

Tombs, Robert
   The English and Their History — 942

TOMBSTONE, ARIZONA
   Tefertiller, Casey. *Wyatt Earp* — B

Tometich, Annabelle
   The Mango Tree — B

TOMETICH, ANNABELLE, 1980-
   Tometich, Annabelle. *The Mango Tree* — B

Tomine, Adrian
   The Loneliness of the Long-Distance Cartoonist — 741.5

TOMINE, ADRIAN, 1974-
   Tomine, Adrian. *The Loneliness of the Long-Distance Cartoonist* — 741.5

Tomlinson, Janis A.
   ★*Goya* — B

Tomlinson, Tommy
   Dogland — 636.7
   The Elephant in the Room — B

TOMLINSON, TOMMY
   Tomlinson, Tommy. *Dogland* — 636.7
   Tomlinson, Tommy. *The Elephant in the Room* — B

Tomorrow Perhaps the Future. Watling, Sarah — 946.081

TOMPKINS, DOUGLAS
   Franklin, Jonathan. *A Wild Idea* — B

Toms River. Fagin, Dan — 363.7209749

Tonelli, Guido
   Genesis — 523.1

Tonti, Lucianne
   Sundressed — 746.9

Too Big to Fail. Sorkin, Andrew Ross — 330.973
Too Brief a Treat. Capote, Truman — B
Too High to Fail. Fine, Doug — 338.4
Too Much and Never Enough. Trump, Mary L. — B
Too Much Is Not Enough. Rannells, Andrew — 792.02

Toobin, Jeffrey
   ★*Homegrown* — 363.325
   The Nine — 347.73
   True Crimes and Misdemeanors — 973.933

TOOLS
   Preszler, Trent. *Little and Often* — B

Tools for Survival. Rawles, James Wesley — 613.6
Tools of Titans. Ferriss, Timothy — 081

Toomey, David
   Kingdom of Play — 591.56

Toorpakai, Maria
   A Different Kind of Daughter — B

TOORPAKAI, MARIA, 1990-
   Toorpakai, Maria. *A Different Kind of Daughter* — B

TOOTH CARE
   Otto, Mary. *Teeth* — 617

Top of the Morning. Stelter, Brian — 791.456

Tophill, Frances
   ★*Container Gardener's Handbook* — 635.9

TOPIARY WORK
   Foley, Caroline. *Topiary, Knots and Parterres* — 715

Topiary, Knots and Parterres. Foley, Caroline — 715

Torgoff, Martin
   Bop Apocalypse — 781.65

Torn Apart. Roberts, Dorothy E. — 362.7

TORNADOES
   Hargrove, Brantley. *The Man Who Caught the Storm* — B

TORONTO, ONTARIO
   Shane, Scott. ★*Flee North* — 973.7

TORPEDOES
   Preston, Diana. *A Higher Form of Killing* — 940.4

Torre, Joe
   The Yankee Years — B

TORRE, JOE, 1940-
   Torre, Joe. *The Yankee Years* — B

TORREY, CHARLES T. (CHARLES TURNER), 1813-1846
   Shane, Scott. ★*Flee North* — 973.7

Torrey, E. Fuller
   Surviving Schizophrenia — 616.89

TORTOISES
   Montgomery, Sy. ★*Of Time and Turtles* — 597.92

TORTURE
   Fair, Eric. *Consequence* — B
   Hari, Daoud. *The Translator* — B
   Harrington, Joel F. *The Faithful Executioner* — B
   Hoock, Holger. *Scars of Independence* — 973.3
   Khalaf, Farida. *The Girl Who Escaped Isis* — B

AUTHOR, TITLE, SERIES AND SUBJECT INDEX

Mayer, Jane. *The Dark Side*	973.931
McCoy, Alfred W. *A Question of Torture*	323.4
Scott-Clark, Cathy. *The Forever Prisoner*	364.6
Sebestyen, Victor. *Lenin*	B
Slezkine, Yuri. *The House of Government*	947.084

TORTURE VICTIMS

Lichtblau, Eric. *Return to the Reich*	B
Slahi, Mohamedou Ould. *The Mauritanian*	958.104

TORTURERS

Harrington, Joel F. *The Faithful Executioner*	B

Tosi, Christina

All About Cake	641.86
All About Cookies	641.86
★*Total Cat Mojo*. Galaxy, Jackson	636.8
★*The Total Fishing Manual*. Cermele, Joe	799.1
★*Total Garbage*. Humes, Edward	628.4
The Total Money Makeover. Ramsey, Dave	332.024
The Total Skywatcher's Manual. Shore, Linda	523

TOTAL WAR

Wheelan, Joseph. ★*Terrible Swift Sword*	B

TOTALITARIANISM

Ai, Weiwei. *Zodiac*	741.5
Arendt, Hannah. *The Origins of Totalitarianism*	320.53
Branigan, Tania. *Red Memory*	951.05
Chang, Jung. *Mao*	B
Childers, Thomas. *The Third Reich*	943.086
Delisle, Guy. *Pyongyang*	741.5
Demick, Barbara. ★*Nothing to Envy*	920
Gessen, Masha. *The Future Is History*	947.086
Gessen, Masha. *Never Remember*	365
Harden, Blaine. *The Great Leader and the Fighter Pilot*	B
Hayek, Friedrich A. von. *The Road to Serfdom*	330.1
Igort. *The Ukrainian and Russian Notebooks*	741.5
Jang, Lucia. *Stars Between the Sun and Moon*	365.45092
Kim, Suki. *Without You, There Is No Us*	B
Lankov, A. N. *The Real North Korea*	951.9304
Neiwert, David A. ★*The Age of Insurrection*	303.48
Popoff, Alexandra. *Vasily Grossman and the Soviet Century*	B
Sattouf, Riad. *The Arab of the Future 2*	741.5
Sattouf, Riad. *The Arab of the Future*	741.5
Sebestyen, Victor. *Lenin*	B
Soyinka, Wole. *Of Africa*	960
Tudor, Daniel. *North Korea Confidential*	951.93
★*Totally Kosher*. Apfelbaum, Chanie	641.5

TOTEMS

Myers, Leah. *Thinning Blood*	B

Totenberg, Nina

★*Dinners with Ruth*	B

TOTENBERG, NINA

Napoli, Lisa. *Susan, Linda, Nina & Cokie*	920
Totenberg, Nina. ★*Dinners with Ruth*	B

TOUCH

Ackerman, Diane. *A Natural History of the Senses*	152.1
Clark, John Lee. *Touch the Future*	B
Easto, Jessica. *How to Taste Coffee*	663
Touch The Future. Clark, John Lee	B
Tough Without a Gun. Kanfer, Stefan	B

Tough, Paul

★*How Children Succeed*	372.210973
The Years That Matter Most	378.1
The Toughest Show on Earth. Volpe, Joseph	B

Tougias, Robert

Birder on Berry Lane	598.072
Toulouse-Lautrec. Frey, Julia Bloch	B

TOULOUSE-LAUTREC, HENRI DE, 1864-1901

Frey, Julia Bloch. *Toulouse-Lautrec*	B

TOUR GUIDES

Delisle, Guy. *Pyongyang*	741.5

TOURGEE, ALBION WINEGAR, 1838-1905

Luxenberg, Steve. ★*Separate*	342.7308

TOURISM

Becker, Elizabeth. *Overbooked*	338.4
Hall, Alvin D. *Driving the Green Book*	917.304
Hill, David. *The Vapors*	976.7
Jennings, Ken. ★*100 Places to See After You Die*	202
Kugel, Seth. *Rediscovering Travel*	306.4
Mayle, Peter. *Encore Provence*	944
Mayle, Peter. *Provence A-Z*	944
McClanahan, Paige. *The New Tourist*	338.4
Sorin, Gretchen Sullivan. *Driving While Black*	323.1196
Stahl, Jerry. *Nein, Nein, Nein!*	B

TOURISTS

Mayle, Peter. *Encore Provence*	944
Mayle, Peter. *Provence A-Z*	944
McClanahan, Paige. *The New Tourist*	338.4

Tourles, Stephanie L.

Pure Skin Care	646.7

TOURNAMENTS

Chapin, Sasha. *All the Wrong Moves*	794.1092
Feinstein, John. *The First Major*	796.352
Fisher, Marshall Jon. *A Terrible Splendor*	796.342
Hiaasen, Carl. *The Downhill Lie*	B
Lunardi, Joe. ★*Bracketology*	796.323
McManus, James. ★*Positively Fifth Street*	795.41
Shankar, Shalini. *Beeline*	155.4
Vecsey, George. *Eight World Cups*	796.334
Woods, Tiger. *The 1997 Masters*	B
Toussaint Louverture. Bell, Madison Smartt	B

TOUSSAINT LOUVERTURE, 1743-1803

Bell, Madison Smartt. *Toussaint Louverture*	B

Toussaint, Alex

★*Activate Your Greatness*	158.1
Toward A Holy Ecology. Bernstein, Ellen	223
The Tower. Cordes, Kelly	796.522
Tower of Skulls. Frank, Richard B.	940.54

Tower, Jeremiah

★*Table Manners*	395.5
The Towering World of Jimmy Choo. Crowe, Lauren Goldstein	391.4
★*The Town That Food Saved*. Hewitt, Ben	338.1

Town, Caren J.

LGBTQ Young Adult Fiction	813.009

TOWNE, ROBERT

Wasson, Sam. *The Big Goodbye*	791.43
Townie. Dubus, Andre	B

Townsend, Alan R.

★*This Ordinary Stardust*	B

TOWNSEND, ALAN R.

Townsend, Alan R. ★*This Ordinary Stardust*	B

Townsend, Chris

The Backpacker's Handbook	796.51

Townsend, Richard F.

The Aztecs	972

TOWNSEND, ROBERT, 1753-1838

Kilmeade, Brian. ★*George Washington's Secret Six*	973.4
Toxic. Ditum, Sarah	920.72

TOXICOLOGY

Blum, Deborah. *The Poisoner's Handbook*	614

TOXINS

Wicker, Alden. ★*To Dye For*	746

TOY AND MOVABLE BOOKS

Macaulay, David. *The Way Things Work Now*	600

TOY INDUSTRY AND TRADE

Alt, Matt. *Pure Invention*	306.0952
Bissonnette, Zac. *The Great Beanie Baby Bubble*	338.7
Lobel, Orly. *You Don't Own Me*	346.7304
Robertson, David C. *Brick by Brick*	338.7

TOY MAKING

Akiyama, Lance. *Rubber Band Engineer*	745.57

TOYS

Fletcher, Susan A. *Exploring the History of Childhood and Play Through 50 Historic Treasures*	790
Garfield, Simon. *In Miniature*	745.5928
Gerber, Robin. *Barbie and Ruth*	B
Robertson, David C. *Brick by Brick*	338.7
Trace Evidence. Shanahan, Charif	811
Tracers in the Dark. Greenberg, Andy	364.16

TRACK AND FIELD

Hart, Matt. *Win at All Costs*	338.7
Okorafor, Nnedi. *Broken Places & Outer Spaces*	153.3

TRACK AND FIELD ATHLETES

Futterman, Matthew. *Running to the Edge*	796.42071

TRACK AND FIELD COACHES

Futterman, Matthew. *Running to the Edge*	796.42071
Hart, Matt. *Win at All Costs*	338.7

TRACKING AND TRAILING

Cheshire, James. *Where the Animals Go*	591.47

PUBLIC LIBRARY CORE COLLECTION: NONFICTION
Twentieth Edition

Tracy, Brian
  Full Engagement!   658.3
TRACY, SPENCER, 1900-1967
  Curtis, James. *Spencer Tracy*   B
TRADE ROUTES
  Frankopan, Peter. *The Silk Roads*   909
  Hansen, Valerie. *The Year 1000*   909
  Ollivier, Bernard. *Out of Istanbul*   B
TRADE SECRETS
  Hvistendahl, Mara. ★*The Scientist and the Spy*   364.16
TRADEMARKS
  Bellos, David. *Who Owns This Sentence?*   346.73
  Brickell, Francesca Cartier. *The Cartiers*   B
  Fineman, Meredith. *Brag Better*   650.1
  Vaynerchuk, Gary. *Crushing It!*   650.1
  Watkins, Alexandra. *Hello, My Name Is Awesome*   658.8
TRADERS (FINANCE)
  Patterson, Scott. ★*Chaos Kings*   338.5
TRADING AND SWAPPING
  Hansen, Valerie. *The Year 1000*   909
  Weitzman, Yaron. *Tanking to the Top*   796.323
Trading Bases. Peta, Joe   796.357
TRADING COMPANIES
  Fraser, Rebecca. *The Mayflower*   974.4
  Ujifusa, Steven. *Barons of the Sea*   387.5
★*The Tradition.* Brown, Jericho   811
TRADITION (JUDAISM)
  Freedman, H. ★*The Talmud*   296.1
TRADITION (PHILOSOPHY)
  Badkhen, Anna. *The World Is a Carpet*   305.409581
  McGreevy, John T. ★*Catholicism*   282.09
  Mendelson, Cheryl. ★*Vows*   203
  Wagamese, Richard. *For Joshua*   B
TRADITIONAL ECOLOGICAL KNOWLEDGE
  Wilbur, Matika. *Project 562*   970.004
Traffic. Smith, Ben   070.4
TRAFFIC ACCIDENTS
  Asgarian, Roxanna. *We Were Once a Family*   364.152
  Standage, Tom. *A Brief History of Motion*   388
  Thrall, Nathan. ★*A Day in the Life of Abed Salama*   956.05
TRAFFIC CONGESTION
  Goldfarb, Ben. *Crossings*   333.77
  Standage, Tom. *A Brief History of Motion*   388
TRAFFIC SAFETY
  Schwartz, Samuel I. *No One at the Wheel*   629.2
TRAGEDY
  Asher, Zain E. *Where the Children Take Us*   942.1
  Cooper, Anderson. *Vanderbilt*   920
  Eichar, Donnie. *Dead Mountain*   914
  Etheridge, Melissa. *Talking to My Angels*   B
  Gerard, Sarah. *Carrie Carolyn Coco*   364.152
  Graff, Garrett M. ★*The Only Plane in the Sky*   973.931
  Hamilton, Lisa M. *The Hungry Season*   B
  Ignatieff, Michael. *On Consolation*   152.4
  Jensen, Robert A. *Personal Effects*   363.34
  Marlowe, Christopher. *The Complete Plays*   822
  Robison, Peter. ★*Flying Blind*   338.7
  Scott, James. *Black Snow*   940.54
  Stoppard, Tom. ★*Rosencrantz & Guildenstern Are Dead*   822
  Thrall, Nathan. ★*A Day in the Life of Abed Salama*   956.05
The Tragedy of the Templars. Haag, Michael   271.7913
Tragedy Plus Time. Cayton-Holland, Adam   B
Trahair, R. C. S.
  Encyclopedia of Cold War Espionage, Spies, and Secret Operations 3rd Ed.   327.12
Traig, Jennifer
  Act Natural   306.874
TRAIL OF TEARS, 1838-1839
  Cozzens, Peter. *A Brutal Reckoning*   973.5
  McLoughlin, William Gerald. *After the Trail of Tears*   973
  Sedgwick, John. *Blood Moon*   975.004
Trail of the Lost. Lankford, Andrea   363.2
Trailblazer. Gilliam, Dorothy Butler   B
Trailed. Miles, Kathryn   364.152
TRAILS
  Chamberlin, Silas. *On the Trail*   796.510973
  Lankford, Andrea. *Trail of the Lost*   363.2

Spira, Timothy P. *Waterfalls and Wildflowers in the Southern Appalachians*   796.5109756
Train. Zoellner, Tom   385.09
A Train in Winter. Moorehead, Caroline   940.53
TRAIN PASSENGERS
  Parks, Tim. *Italian Ways*   385
TRAIN RIDES
  Merridale, Catherine. *Lenin on the Train*   B
  Parks, Tim. *Italian Ways*   385
TRAIN ROBBERIES
  Leerhsen, Charles. ★*Butch Cassidy*   B
The Train to Crystal City. Russell, Jan Jarboe   940.53
TRAINING
  Bercovici, Jeff. *Play On*   613.7
  Brooks, Amanda. *Run to the Finish*   613.7
  Cox, Lynne. *Swimming to Antarctica*   B
  Dixon, Matt. *The Well-Built Triathlete*   796.42
  Finn, Adharanand. *The Rise of the Ultra Runners*   B
  Friel, Joe. *The Triathlete's Training Bible*   796.42
  Futterman, Matthew. *Running to the Edge*   796.42071
  Gessner, David. *Ultimate Glory*   796.2
  Goldfarb, Bruce. ★*18 Tiny Deaths*   B
  Higdon, Hal. ★*Marathon*   796.42
  Hillsberg, Christina. *License to Parent*   649.1
  Keflezighi, Meb. *Meb for Mortals*   796.4252
  Magill, Pete. *Build Your Running Body*   796.42
  McDougall, Christopher. *Running with Sherman*   636.1
  Murakami, Haruki. *What I Talk About When I Talk About Running*   B
  Nolan, Ali. *Master the Marathon*   796.42
  Oyeneyin, Tunde. *Speak*   158.1
  Polly, Matthew. ★*Bruce Lee*   B
  Ravin, Idan. *The Hoops Whisperer*   796.323
  Romanov, Nicholas S. *The Running Revolution*   796.42
  Virts, Terry. *How to Astronaut*   629.45
TRAINS
  McPhee, John. *Uncommon Carriers*   388
  Theroux, Paul. *Riding the Iron Rooster*   915
  Zoellner, Tom. *Train*   385.09
Trainum, James L.
  How the Police Generate False Confessions   345.73
Traister, Rebecca
  Good and Mad   305.420973
Traitor King. Lownie, Andrew   920
Traitor to His Class. Brands, H. W.   B
A Traitor to His Species. Freeberg, Ernest   B
TRAITORS
  Meltzer, Brad. ★*The First Conspiracy*   973.4
  Wiehl, Lis W. *A Spy in Plain Sight*   327.1247
Tran, Ly
  House of Sticks   B
TRAN, LY, 1989-
  Tran, Ly. *House of Sticks*   B
Tran, Paul
  All the Flowers Kneeling   811
Tran, Phuc
  ★*Sigh, Gone*   B
TRAN, PHUC, 1974-
  Tran, Phuc. ★*Sigh, Gone*   B
TRANQUILITY
  Zorn, Justin. *Golden*   128
TRANS MEN
  Hartke, Austen. *Transforming*   277
  Moss, Jeremiah. *Feral City*   B
  Page, Elliot. *Pageboy*   B
TRANS WOMEN
  Boylan, Jennifer Finney. *Good Boy*   B
  Goetsch, Diana. *This Body I Wore*   B
  Manning, Chelsea. *Readme.Txt*   B
  Sante, Lucy. *I Heard Her Call My Name*   B
  Schneider, Amy. *In the Form of a Question*   B
  Talusan, Meredith. *Fairest*   305.30973
  Thom, Kai Cheng. *Falling Back in Love with Being Human*   811
  Willis, Raquel. *The Risk It Takes to Bloom*   B
Transaction Man. Lemann, Nicholas   330.973
TRANSATLANTIC FLIGHTS
  Miodownik, Mark. *Liquid Rules*   530.4
TRANSATLANTIC VOYAGES
  Dodds Pennock, Caroline. ★*On Savage Shores*   970.004

AUTHOR, TITLE, SERIES AND SUBJECT INDEX

Transcendence. Vince, Gaia — 599.93
The Transcendent Brain. Lightman, Alan P. — 215
TRANSCENDENTAL MEDITATION
  Roth, Robert. *Strength in Stillness* — 158.1
Transcendental Studies. Waldrop, Keith — 811
TRANSCENDENTALISM
  Bly, Robert. *Collected Poems* — 811
TRANSCENDENTALISM (NEW ENGLAND)
  Matteson, John. *Eden's Outcasts* — 920
TRANSCONTINENTAL JOURNEYS
  Jerkins, Morgan. *Wandering in Strange Lands* — 305.896
  Letts, Elizabeth. ★*The Ride of Her Life* — B
TRANSCONTINENTAL RAILROAD (UNITED STATES)
  Ambrose, Stephen E. *Nothing Like It in the World* — 385
  Rekdal, Paisley. *West* — 811
TRANSFORMATIONS (MAGIC)
  Rekdal, Paisley. *Nightingale* — 811
TRANSFORMATIONS (PERSONAL)
  Heminsley, Alexandra. *Running Like a Girl* — B
TRANSFORMATIONS, PERSONAL
  Brown, Brene. *The Gifts of Imperfection* — 158
  Dalai Lama. *How to Be Compassionate* — 294.3
  Fleming, Brandon P. *Miseducated* — B
  Hempel, Jessi. *The Family Outing* — B
  Jones, Lucy. ★*Matrescence* — 306.874
  Lamott, Anne. *Somehow* — 814
  Mariani, Mike. ★*What Doesn't Kill Us Makes Us* — 155.9
  Maupin, Armistead. *Logical Family* — B
  May, Katherine. *Wintering* — 155.9
  Pace, Kristin Knight. *This Much Country* — B
  Phillips, Adam. *On Giving up* — 158.2
  Rekdal, Paisley. *Nightingale* — 811
  Schemel, Patty. *Hit so Hard* — B
  Strayed, Cheryl. ★*Wild* — B
  Tamblyn, Amber. ★*Era of Ignition* — B
  Van Hemert, Caroline. *The Sun Is a Compass* — 979.8
  Wasson, Sam. *Fifth Avenue, 5 A.M.* — 791.43
Transforming. Hartke, Austen — 277
★*Transforming Summer Programs at Your Library*. Cole, Natalie — 028
TRANSGENDER CHILDREN
  Corbett, Emily. *In Transition* — 809
  Greene, Benjamin. ★*My Child Is Trans, Now What?* — 649
  Lemay, Mimi. *What We Will Become* — 306.874
  Turban, Jack L. ★*Free to Be* — 616.85
TRANSGENDER PARENTS
  Faludi, Susan. *In the Darkroom* — B
TRANSGENDER PEOPLE
  Barnes, Katie. ★*Fair Play* — 796.082
  Carr, C. *Candy Darling* — B
  Corbett, Emily. *In Transition* — 809
  Faludi, Susan. *In the Darkroom* — B
  Funk, Mason. *The Book of Pride* — 920
  Gelwicks, Andrew. *The Queer Advantage* — 920
  Goetsch, Diana. *This Body I Wore* — B
  Hartke, Austen. *Transforming* — 277
  Hester, Diarmuid. *Nothing Ever Just Disappears* — 306.76
  Kugle, Scott Alan. *Living Out Islam* — 297
  Lavery, Daniel M. *Something That May Shock and Discredit You* — 814
  Lemay, Mimi. *What We Will Become* — 306.874
  Mock, Janet. *Surpassing Certainty* — B
  Nutt, Amy Ellis. *Becoming Nicole* — 920
  Page, Elliot. *Pageboy* — B
  Rosenberg, Rosalind. ★*Jane Crow* — B
  Russo, Richard. *The Destiny Thief* — 814
  Sante, Lucy. *I Heard Her Call My Name* — B
  Schneider, Amy. *In the Form of a Question* — B
  Shraya, Vivek. *I'm Afraid of Men* — 813
  Talusan, Meredith. *Fairest* — 305.30973
  Tobia, Jacob. *Sissy* — 305.30973
  Whitney, Emerson. *Heaven* — B
  Willis, Raquel. *The Risk It Takes to Bloom* — B
TRANSGENDER TEENAGERS
  Turban, Jack L. ★*Free to Be* — 616.85
TRANSGENDERISM
  Davis, Lisa Selin. *Tomboy* — 305.409
  greathouse, torrin a. *Wound from the Mouth of a Wound* — 811
  Soloway, Jill. *She Wants It* — B
  Turban, Jack L. ★*Free to Be* — 616.85

★*Transient and Strange*. Greenfieldboyce, Nell — 501
TRANSITIONING (GENDER IDENTITY)
  Goetsch, Diana. *This Body I Wore* — B
  Greene, Benjamin. ★*My Child Is Trans, Now What?* — 649
  Page, Elliot. *Pageboy* — B
  Sante, Lucy. *I Heard Her Call My Name* — B
  Talusan, Meredith. *Fairest* — 305.30973
TRANSLATING AND INTERPRETING
  Briggs, Kate. *This Little Art* — 418
  Dolnick, Edward. *The Writing of the Gods* — 493
  Fox, Margalit. *The Riddle of the Labyrinth* — 920
  Henderson, Bruce B. *Bridge to the Sun* — 940.53
  Jebara, Mohamad. ★*The Life of the Qur'an* — 297.122
  Koh, EJ. *The Magical Language of Others* — 813
  Lahiri, Jhumpa. *Translating Myself and Others* — 418
  Oliva, Alejandra. *Rivermouth* — 305.9
  Porter, Carolyn. *Marcel's Letters* — 940.54
  Shapiro, James. *Shakespeare in a Divided America* — 822.33
Translating Myself and Others. Lahiri, Jhumpa — 418
TRANSLATIONS
  Emerson, Ralph Waldo. ★*Collected Poems and Translations* — 811
  Virgil. *The Eclogues of Virgil* — 871
TRANSLATIONS — ARABIC TO ENGLISH
  Adunis. *Concerto Al-Quds* — 892.7
  Darwish, Mamoud. *If I Were Another* — 892.7
  Darwish, Mamoud. ★*Unfortunately, It Was Paradise* — 892
  Mikhaiil, Dunya. *The Beekeeper* — 956.7044
  Samer. *The Raqqa Diaries* — 956.9104
  Seale, Yasmine. *Aladdin* — 398.2
TRANSLATIONS — BENGALI TO ENGLISH
  Tagore, Rabindranath. *Selected Poems* — 891
TRANSLATIONS — CHINESE TO ENGLISH
  Chan, Jackie. *Never Grow Up* — B
  Yang, Jisheng. *The World Turned Upside Down* — 951.05
TRANSLATIONS — CZECH TO ENGLISH
  Weiss, Helga. *Helga's Diary* — B
TRANSLATIONS — DUTCH TO ENGLISH
  Berger, Lynn. *Second Thoughts* — 306.85
  Blom, Onno. *Young Rembrandt* — B
  Laar, Arnold van de. *Under the Knife* — 617
TRANSLATIONS — FRENCH TO ENGLISH
  B., David. *Epileptic* — 741.5
  Baudelaire, Charles. *Les Fleurs Du Mal* — 841
  Baudelaire, Charles. *Poems* — 841
  Beckett, Samuel. *Collected Poems in English and French* — 841
  Boucheron, Patrick. *Machiavelli* — 320.1092
  Camus, Albert. *The Myth of Sisyphus and Other Essays* — 844
  Camus, Albert. *The Rebel* — 303.6
  Cohen-Solal, Annie. *Mark Rothko* — 759.13
  Crasnianski, Tania. *The Children of Nazis* — 943.086
  Delisle, Guy. *Hostage* — 741.5
  Delisle, Guy. *Pyongyang* — 741.5
  Ernaux, Annie. ★*The Years* — B
  Frenkel, Francoise. *A Bookshop in Berlin* — B
  Guibert, Emmanuel. *Alan's War* — 741.5
  Guibert, Emmanuel. *The Photographer* — 741.5
  Haitiwaji, Gulbahar. *How I Survived a Chinese "Reeducation" Camp* — 305.8
  Hatzfeld, Jean. *Blood Papa* — 967.5710431
  Kouchner, Camille. *La Familia Grande* — B
  Lever, Evelyne. *Marie Antoinette* — B
  Ollivier, Bernard. *Out of Istanbul* — B
  Piketty, Thomas. *A Brief History of Equality* — 305.09
  Piketty, Thomas. ★*Capital and Ideology* — 305
  Piketty, Thomas. ★*Capital in the Twenty-First Century* — 332
  Piketty, Thomas. *The Economics of Inequality* — 339.2
  Rimbaud, Arthur. *The Illuminations* — 841
  Rosnay, Tatiana de. *Manderley Forever* — B
  Roudinesco, Elisabeth. ★*Freud* — B
  Rousseau, Jean-Jacques. ★*The Social Contract* — 320.1
  Sattouf, Riad. *The Arab of the Future 2* — 741.5
  Sattouf, Riad. *The Arab of the Future* — 741.5
  Schwarz, Geraldine. *Those Who Forget* — 940.53
  Tocqueville, Alexis de. ★*Democracy in America* — 320.973
  Villanova, Thibaud. *Disney Enchanted Recipes* — 641.5
  Villon, Francois. *The Poems of Francois Villon* — 841
  Wiesel, Elie. *All Rivers Run to the Sea* — B
TRANSLATIONS — GERMAN TO ENGLISH
  Aly, Gotz. *Europe Against the Jews* — 305.892

PUBLIC LIBRARY CORE COLLECTION: NONFICTION
Twentieth Edition

Bohme, Madelaine. *Ancient Bones*	599.93
Celan, Paul. *Breathturn into Timestead*	831
Eilenberger, Wolfram. *Time of the Magicians*	920
Frankl, Viktor E. ★*Man's Search for Meaning*	B
Geck, Martin. ★*Johann Sebastian Bach*	780.92
Goethe, Johann Wolfgang von. *Selected Poetry*	831
Grass, Gunter. *Of All That Ends*	838
Hitler, Adolf. *Mein Kampf*	B
Jahner, Harald. ★*Aftermath*	943.087
Kempowski, Walter. *Swansong 1945*	940.54
Krause, Johannes. *A Short History of Humanity*	599.9
Liao, Yiwu. *Bullets and Opium*	951.05
Longerich, Peter. *Goebbels*	B
Muller, Melissa. *Anne Frank*	B
Ohler, Norman. *The Bohemians*	940.53
Orth, Stephan. *Couchsurfing in Iran*	955.06
Pullman, Philip. ★*Fairy Tales from the Brothers Grimm*	398.2
Rilke, Rainer Maria. *Ahead of All Parting*	831
Rilke, Rainer Maria. *Duino Elegies*	831
Rilke, Rainer Maria. *New Poems*	831
Rilke, Rainer Maria. ★*Sonnets to Orpheus*	831
Simon, Marie. *Underground in Berlin*	B
Stangneth, Bettina. *Eichmann Before Jerusalem*	B
Teege, Jennifer. *My Grandfather Would Have Shot Me*	929.2
Ullrich, Volker. ★*Eight Days in May*	943.086
Ullrich, Volker. *Germany 1923*	943.085
Ullrich, Volker. *Hitler*	B
Ullrich, Volker. *Hitler*	B
Wohlleben, Peter. *Forest Walking*	582.16
Wohlleben, Peter. *The Heartbeat of Trees*	582.16
Wohlleben, Peter. *The Hidden Life of Trees*	582.16
Wohlleben, Peter. *The Secret Wisdom of Nature*	508

TRANSLATIONS — GREEK TO ENGLISH
Aristotle. ★*Politics, 2nd Ed*	320
Cavafy, Constantine. *The Collected Poems*	889
Herodotus. *The Histories*	938
Hesiod. *Works and Days and Theogony*	881
Homer. *The Iliad*	883
Homer. *The Iliad*	883
Homer. *Iliad*	883
Homer. ★*The Iliad*	883
Homer. ★*The Odyssey*	883
Homer. *The Odyssey*	883
Sappho. *If Not, Winter*	884

TRANSLATIONS — HEBREW TO ENGLISH
Amichai, Yehuda. *Open Closed Open*	892.4
Bernstein, Ellen. *Toward a Holy Ecology*	223
Goodman, Micah. *Catch-67*	956.04
Harari, Yuval N. *Homo Deus*	909.83
Qashu, Sayed. *Native*	892.4

TRANSLATIONS — HUNGARIAN TO ENGLISH
Debreczeni, Jozsef. *Cold Crematorium*	940.53

TRANSLATIONS — ITALIAN TO ENGLISH
Calasso, Roberto. *Ardor*	294.5
Dante Alighieri. ★*The Divine Comedy*	851
Dante Alighieri. *The Paradiso*	851
Dante Alighieri. *Paradiso*	851
Dante Alighieri. *Purgatorio*	851
De Stefano, Cristina. *The Child Is the Teacher*	B
Ferrante, Elena. *In the Margins*	809
Ferrara, Silvia. *The Greatest Invention*	411
Francis. *Life*	B
Igort. *The Ukrainian and Russian Notebooks*	741.5
Lahiri, Jhumpa. *In Other Words*	B
Levi, Primo. *The Reawakening*	B
Politi, Marco. *Pope Francis Among the Wolves*	282.092
Rovelli, Carlo. *The Order of Time*	530.11
Rovelli, Carlo. *There Are Places in the World Where Rules Are Less Important Than Kindness*	500
Tonelli, Guido. *Genesis*	523.1

TRANSLATIONS — JAPANESE TO ENGLISH
Ishikawa, Masaji. ★*A River in Darkness*	B
Kishimi, Ichiro. *The Courage to Be Disliked*	158
Kondo, Marie. ★*The Life-Changing Magic of Tidying Up*	648
Mizuki, Shigeru. *Showa 1926-1939*	741.5
Murakami, Haruki. ★*Absolutely on Music*	784.2
Murakami, Haruki. ★*Novelist as a Vocation*	895.64
Rexroth, Kenneth. *One Hundred Poems from the Japanese*	895
Sawaki, Kodo. *Discovering the True Self*	294.3
Yomota, Inuhiko. *What Is Japanese Cinema?*	791.43

TRANSLATIONS — KOREAN TO ENGLISH
Jang, Jin-Sung. *Dear Leader*	B
Sehee, Baek. *I Want to Die but I Want to Eat Tteokbokki*	B

TRANSLATIONS — LATIN TO ENGLISH
Cicero, Marcus Tullius. ★*The Republic*	320.1
Ovid. *Tales from Ovid*	873
Virgil. *The Aeneid*	873

TRANSLATIONS — NORWEGIAN TO ENGLISH
Grue, Jan. *I Live a Life Like Yours*	B
Knausgaard, Karl Ove. *So Much Longing in so Little Space*	759.81
Knausgaard, Karl Ove. *Spring*	B
Strøksnes, Morten Andreas. *Shark Drunk*	338.3
Sverdrup-Thygeson, Anne. *Buzz, Sting, Bite*	595.7
Thorstensen, Ole. *Making Things Right*	690

TRANSLATIONS — PERSIAN TO ENGLISH
Firdawsi. *Shahnameh*	891
Hafiz. ★*The Gift*	891
Jalal al-Din Rumi, Maulana. *The Essential Rumi*	891
Jalal al-Din Rumi, Maulana. *Rumi*	891

TRANSLATIONS — POLISH TO ENGLISH
Herbert, Zbigniew. *The Collected Poems, 1956-1998*	891.8
Sosnowski, Andrzej. *Lodgings*	891.8
Szablowski, Witold. *Dancing Bears*	947.086
Szymborska, Wislawa. *Here*	891.8
Szymborska, Wislawa. *Map*	891.8
Zagajewski, Adam. *Eternal Enemies*	891.8

TRANSLATIONS — RUSSIAN TO ENGLISH
Akhmatova, Anna Andreevna. ★*The Complete Poems of Anna Akhmatova*	891.71
Akhmatova, Anna Andreevna. *Poems*	891.71
Aleksievich, Svetlana. *Last Witnesses*	940.53
Aleksievich, Svetlana. ★*Secondhand Time*	947.086
Aleksievich, Svetlana. ★*The Unwomanly Face of War*	940.53
Khlevniuk, Oleg V. *Stalin*	B
Pavlychenko, Liudmyla Mykhailivna. *Lady Death*	B
Petrushevskaia, Liudmila. *The Girl from the Metropol Hotel*	B
Pushkin, Aleksandr Sergeevich. *Eugene Onegin*	891.71
Teffi, N. A. *Memories*	B
Tsvetaeva, Marina. *Selected Poems*	891.71

TRANSLATIONS — SANSKRIT TO ENGLISH
Satyamurti, Carole. *Mahabharata*	821

TRANSLATIONS — SPANISH TO ENGLISH
Aleixandre, Vicente. *A Longing for the Light*	861
Baca, Jimmy Santiago. *Selected Poems*	811
Borges, Jorge Luis. *Selected Non-Fictions*	864
Borges, Jorge Luis. ★*Selected Poems*	861
Calvino, Italo. *Collection of Sand*	854
Cardenal, Ernesto. *Pluriverse*	861
Cercas, Javier. *Lord of All the Dead*	868
Garcia Lorca, Federico. *Collected Poems*	861
Garcia Lorca, Federico. *Poet in New York*	861
Hesse, Maria. ★*Frida Kahlo*	B
Juana Ines de la Cruz, Sister. *Selected Works*	861
Lozano, Luis-Martin. *Frida Kahlo*	759.972
Neruda, Pablo. *All the Odes*	861
Neruda, Pablo. *Then Come Back*	861
Neruda, Pablo. *World's End*	861
Paz, Octavio. ★*The Collected Poems of Octavio Paz, 1957-1987*	861
Paz, Octavio. *The Poems of Octavio Paz*	861
Umar, Ousman. *North to Paradise*	B
Vargas Llosa, Mario. *Conversation at Princeton*	868
Vargas Llosa, Mario. *Sabers and Utopias*	980.03
Villoro, Juan. *God Is Round*	796.334

TRANSLATIONS — SWEDISH TO ENGLISH
Andersen, Jens. *Astrid Lindgren*	B
Asbrink, Elisabeth. *And in the Vienna Woods the Trees Remain*	B
Backman, Fredrik. *Things My Son Needs to Know About the World*	B
Eklof, Johan. *The Darkness Manifesto*	363.7
Englund, Peter. *November 1942*	940.53
Liedman, Sven-Eric. *A World to Win*	B
Marcal, Katrine. *Mother of Invention*	604.82
Rydell, Anders. *The Book Thieves*	027
Transtromer, Tomas. *The Great Enigma*	839.71

TRANSLATIONS — TAMIL TO ENGLISH
Narayan, R. K. ★*The Ramayana*	294.5

AUTHOR, TITLE, SERIES AND SUBJECT INDEX

TRANSLATIONS — TURKISH TO ENGLISH
   Pamuk, Orhan. *Istanbul* — 949.61
TRANSLATIONS — UKRAINIAN TO ENGLISH
   Zelensky, Volodymyr. *A Message from Ukraine* — 947.7
The Translator. Hari, Daoud — B
TRANSLATORS
   Basbanes, Nicholas A. ★*Cross of Snow* — B
   Briggs, Kate. *This Little Art* — 418
   Hari, Daoud. *The Translator* — B
   Lahiri, Jhumpa. *Translating Myself and Others* — 418
   Sakamoto, Pamela Rotner. *Midnight in Broad Daylight* — 940.53
TRANSPHOBIA
   Corbett, Emily. *In Transition* — 809
   Hartke, Austen. *Transforming* — 277
TRANSPLANT RECIPIENTS
   Mezrich, Joshua D. *When Death Becomes Life* — 617.9
TRANSPLANT SURGEONS
   Mezrich, Joshua D. *When Death Becomes Life* — 617.9
TRANSPLANTATION OF ORGANS, TISSUES, ETC.
   Jones, Chip. *The Organ Thieves* — 617.4
   Mezrich, Joshua D. *When Death Becomes Life* — 617.9
   Roach, Mary. ★*Stiff* — 611
TRANSPORTATION
   Cohan, William D. *Power Failure* — 338.7
   Goodman, Peter S. ★*How the World Ran Out of Everything* — 658.7
   Humes, Edward. *Door to Door* — 388.09
   McGinty, Brian. *Lincoln's Greatest Case* — 346.7303
   McPhee, John. *Uncommon Carriers* — 388
   Parissien, Steven. *The Life of the Automobile* — 629.222
   Parks, Tim. *Italian Ways* — 385
   Rosen, Jody. *Two Wheels Good* — 629.227
   Schwartz, Samuel I. *No One at the Wheel* — 629.2
   Standage, Tom. *A Brief History of Motion* — 388
TRANSPORTATION — AUTOMOTIVE
   Milchtein, Chaya M. ★*Mechanic Shop Femme's Guide to Car Ownership* — 629.222
TRANSPORTATION — TRAINS AND RAIL SERVICE
   Shaughnessy, Jim. *The Call of Trains* — 779
   Solomon, Brian. *The Field Guide to Trains* — 625.2
TRANSPORTATION FORECASTING
   Standage, Tom. *A Brief History of Motion* — 388
TRANSPORTATION OF PRISONERS
   Preston, Diana. *Paradise in Chains* — 996.18
TRANSPORTATION, AUTOMOTIVE
   Grabar, Henry. *Paved Paradise* — 388.474
   Sorin, Gretchen Sullivan. *Driving While Black* — 323.1196
   Standage, Tom. *A Brief History of Motion* — 388
Transtromer, Tomas
   The Great Enigma — 839.71
TRANSTROMER, TOMAS, 1931-2015
   Transtromer, Tomas. *The Great Enigma* — 839.71
TRANSYLVANIA, ROMANIA
   Wiesel, Elie. *Night* — B
★*Trash Talk*. Kohan, Rafi — 179
Trask, Kerry A.
   Black Hawk — 973.5
Traub, James
   John Quincy Adams — B
Travel Light, Move Fast. Fuller, Alexandra — B
TRAVEL WRITERS
   Bryson, Bill. *The Life and Times of the Thunderbolt Kid* — B
   Gilbert, Elizabeth. *Eat, Pray, Love* — B
   Lopez, Barry Holstun. *Horizon* — B
   Mayes, Frances. *A Year in the World* — B
   Mohammadi, Kamin. *Bella Figura* — 641.01
   Ollivier, Bernard. *Out of Istanbul* — B
TRAVEL WRITING
   Cole, Teju. *Blind Spot* — 770
TRAVEL WRITING — AFRICA
   Dinesen, Isak. *Out of Africa* — 967.62
   Mahjoub, Jamal. *A Line in the River* — 962.404
   Theroux, Paul. *The Last Train to Zona Verde* — 916
   Wood, Levison. *The Last Giants* — 599.67
TRAVEL WRITING — ASIA AND THE SOUTH PACIFIC
   Belliveau, Denis. *In the Footsteps of Marco Polo* — 915
   Boo, Katherine. ★*Behind the Beautiful Forevers* — 305.5
   Bryson, Bill. *In a Sunburned Country* — 919
   Caesar, Ed. *The Moth and the Mountain* — B

   Delisle, Guy. *Pyongyang* — 741.5
   Frazier, Ian. *Travels in Siberia* — 957
   Goodheart, Adam. *The Last Island* — 954
   Goulding, Matt. *Rice, Noodle, Fish* — 394.1
   Harris, Kate. *Lands of Lost Borders* — 915.804
   Hessler, Peter. *Oracle Bones* — 951
   Hessler, Peter. *Other Rivers* — 378.1
   Hoffman, Carl. ★*Savage Harvest* — 995.1
   Iyer, Pico. *A Beginner's Guide to Japan* — 952.05
   Iyer, Pico. *The Lady and the Monk* — 952
   Juan, Li. *Winter Pasture* — 951.06
   Kim, Suki. *Without You, There Is No Us* — B
   Kirkby, Bruce. *Blue Sky Kingdom* — 954.96
   Krakauer, Jon. ★*Into Thin Air* — 796.52
   Ollivier, Bernard. *Out of Istanbul* — B
   Palin, Michael. *North Korea Journal* — 951.9305
   Sherman, Anna. *The Bells of Old Tokyo* — 952
   Slaght, Jonathan C. *Owls of the Eastern Ice* — 598.9
   Synnott, Mark. *The Third Pole* — 796.522
   Theroux, Paul. *The Great Railway Bazaar* — 915
   Theroux, Paul. *Riding the Iron Rooster* — 915
   Thubron, Colin. *In Siberia* — 957
   Thubron, Colin. *Shadow of the Silk Road* — 915
   Turvey, Samuel. ★*The Tomb of the Mili Mongga* — 398.24
TRAVEL WRITING — CANADA
   Erdrich, Louise. *Books and Islands in Ojibwe Country* — 977
   Messenger, Alex. *The Twenty-Ninth Day* — B
TRAVEL WRITING — CENTRAL AND SOUTH AMERICA
   Adams, Mark. *Turn Right at Machu Picchu* — 985
   Davis, Wade. *Magdalena* — 986.1
   Jenkins, Jedidiah. *To Shake the Sleeping Self* — B
   Kurlansky, Mark. *Havana* — 972.91
   Preston, Douglas J. ★*The Lost City of the Monkey God* — 972.85
   Salama, Jordan. ★*Stranger in the Desert* — 982
   Theroux, Paul. *On the Plain of Snakes* — 917
   Wallace, Scott. *The Unconquered* — 981
TRAVEL WRITING — EUROPE
   Berendt, John. *The City of Falling Angels* — 945
   Booth, Michael. *The Almost Nearly Perfect People* — 948.071
   Bryson, Bill. *Notes from a Small Island* — 914
   Bryson, Bill. *The Road to Little Dribbling* — 914
   Coyne, Tom. *A Course Called Scotland* — 796.352
   Darlington, Miriam. *Otter Country* — 599.769
   Downie, David. *A Taste of Paris* — 394.1
   Fili, Louise. *The Cognoscenti's Guide to Florence* — 381
   Fowler, Corinne. ★*The Countryside* — 941
   Goulding, Matt. *Grape, Olive, Pig* — 394.1
   Green, Matthew. *Shadowlands* — 941.03
   Greene, David. *Midnight in Siberia* — 914
   Karnazes, Dean. *The Legend of Marathon* — 796.42
   Kassabova, Kapka. *Border* — 949.9
   Lahiri, Jhumpa. *In Other Words* — B
   Malcolm, Janet. *Reading Chekhov* — 891.72
   Mayes, Frances. *Bella Tuscany* — 945
   Mayes, Frances. *See You in the Piazza* — 914.5
   Mayes, Frances. *Under the Tuscan Sun* — 945
   Mayle, Peter. *Encore Provence* — 944
   Mayle, Peter. *My Twenty-Five Years in Provence* — 944.9
   Mayle, Peter. *Provence A-Z* — 944
   Mayle, Peter. ★*A Year in Provence* — 944
   Mohammadi, Kamin. *Bella Figura* — 641.01
   Moore, Tim. *The Cyclist Who Went Out in the Cold* — 796.6
   Nicolson, Adam. *Sea Room* — 941.1
   Parks, Tim. *The Hero's Way* — 945
   Parks, Tim. *Italian Ways* — 385
   Phillips, Timothy. *Retracing the Iron Curtain* — 909.82
   Robb, Graham. *France* — 944
   Sciolino, Elaine. *The Only Street in Paris* — 944
   Sciolino, Elaine. *The Seine* — 944
   Stahl, Jerry. *Nein, Nein, Nein!* — B
   Stewart, Chris. *Driving Over Lemons* — 946
   Stewart, Rory. *The Marches* — 941.3
   White, Edmund. *The Flaneur* — 944
TRAVEL WRITING — GENERAL
   Becker, Elizabeth. *Overbooked* — 338.4
   Berger, Karen. *America's Great Hiking Trails* — 796.510973
   Bourdain, Anthony. ★*World Travel* — 641.59
   Doughty, Caitlin. *From Here to Eternity* — 393

PUBLIC LIBRARY CORE COLLECTION: NONFICTION
Twentieth Edition

Ehrlich, Gretel. *Unsolaced*	B
Ellard, Colin. *You Are Here*	153.7
Foer, Joshua. *Atlas Obscura*	910.41
Foer, Joshua. ★*Atlas Obscura 2nd Ed.*	910.41
Fox, Porter. *The Last Winter*	363.738
Gilbert, Elizabeth. *Eat, Pray, Love*	B
Gill, A. A. *To America with Love*	973.93
Harrison, Jim. *The Search for the Genuine*	814
Hayes, Bill. *Sweat*	613.7
Hunt, Will. *Underground*	624.1
Iyer, Pico. ★*The Half Known Life*	203
Iyer, Pico. *The Open Road*	B
Kendrick, Kathleen M. *Official Guide to the Smithsonian National Museum of African American History & Culture*	975.3
Kisor, Henry. *Traveling with Service Animals*	362.4
Kois, Dan. *How to Be a Family*	910.4
Kugel, Seth. *Rediscovering Travel*	306.4
Lopez, Barry Holstun. *Horizon*	B
Mackinnon, Al. *Epic Surf Breaks of the World*	797.32
Mayes, Frances. *A Year in the World*	B
McClanahan, Paige. *The New Tourist*	338.4
Vanhoenacker, Mark. *Imagine a City*	629.13
Vitale, Tom. *In the Weeds*	B
Von Bremzen, Anya. *National Dish*	641.3
Vorobyov, Niko. *Dopeworld*	364.1
Wang, Connie. *Oh My Mother!*	B
Weiner, Eric. *Ben & Me*	B
Wong, Cecily. ★*Gastro Obscura*	641.3
Woods, Christopher. *Gardenlust*	635.022

TRAVEL WRITING — HISTORIC JOURNEYS

Darwin, Charles. ★*The Voyage of the Beagle*	508
Herlihy, David V. *The Lost Cyclist*	B
Parks, Tim. *The Hero's Way*	945
Raban, Jonathan. *Bad Land*	978
Roberts, Jason. *A Sense of the World*	B
Sides, Hampton. ★*The Wide Wide Sea*	910.92

TRAVEL WRITING — LIVING ABROAD

Bertch, Jane. *The French Ingredient*	B
Buford, Bill. ★*Dirt*	B
Collins, Lauren. *When in French*	B
Dinesen, Isak. *Out of Africa*	967.62
Ehrlich, Gretel. *This Cold Heaven*	998.2
Erdman, Sarah. *Nine Hills to Nambonkaha*	966.68
Hessler, Peter. *Other Rivers*	378.1
Irving, Apricot Anderson. *The Gospel of Trees*	B
Kim, Suki. *Without You, There Is No Us*	B
Lahiri, Jhumpa. *In Other Words*	B
Mayes, Frances. *Bella Tuscany*	945
Mayes, Frances. *Under the Tuscan Sun*	945
Mayle, Peter. *Encore Provence*	944
Mayle, Peter. *My Twenty-Five Years in Provence*	944.9
Mayle, Peter. ★*A Year in Provence*	944
Parks, Tim. *Italian Ways*	385
Shadid, Anthony. *House of Stone*	306.0956
Stewart, Chris. *Driving Over Lemons*	946
Wilson, Katherine. *Only in Naples*	B

TRAVEL WRITING — MODES OF TRANSPORTATION

Buck, Rinker. *Life on the Mississippi*	917
Grant, Will. *The Last Ride of the Pony Express*	917.804
Letts, Elizabeth. ★*The Ride of Her Life*	B
Sullivan, Randall. *Graveyard of the Pacific*	979.7

TRAVEL WRITING — MODES OF TRANSPORTATION — BOATING

Clark, Liz. *Swell*	B
Davis, Wade. *Magdalena*	986.1
McGrath, Ben. *Riverman*	797.122
McPhee, John. *Uncommon Carriers*	388

TRAVEL WRITING — MODES OF TRANSPORTATION — BY TRAIN

Parks, Tim. *Italian Ways*	385
Theroux, Paul. *The Great Railway Bazaar*	915
Theroux, Paul. *Riding the Iron Rooster*	915
Zoellner, Tom. *Train*	385.09

TRAVEL WRITING — MODES OF TRANSPORTATION — CYCLING

Dietrich, Sean. *You Are My Sunshine*	B
Fabes, Stephen. *Signs of Life*	B
Harris, Kate. *Lands of Lost Borders*	915.804
Herlihy, David V. *The Lost Cyclist*	B
Jenkins, Jedidiah. *To Shake the Sleeping Self*	B
Robb, Graham. *France*	944

Rosen, Jody. *Two Wheels Good*	629.227

TRAVEL WRITING — MODES OF TRANSPORTATION — ON FOOT

Bryson, Bill. ★*A Walk in the Woods*	917
Davis, Jennifer Pharr. *Called Again*	B
Egan, Timothy. *A Pilgrimage to Eternity*	263
Grann, David. *The White Darkness*	B
Jenkins, Peter. *A Walk Across America*	917.304
O'Brady, Colin. ★*The Impossible First*	919.8904
Ollivier, Bernard. *Out of Istanbul*	B
Parks, Tim. *The Hero's Way*	945

TRAVEL WRITING — MODES OF TRANSPORTATION — ROAD TRIPS

Hall, Alvin D. *Driving the Green Book*	917.304
Heat Moon, William Least. *Blue Highways*	917.304
Lee, Edward. *Buttermilk Graffiti*	641.59
Sorin, Gretchen Sullivan. *Driving While Black*	323.1196
Steinbeck, John. *Travels with Charley*	B

TRAVEL WRITING — POLAR REGIONS

O'Brady, Colin. ★*The Impossible First*	919.8904

TRAVEL WRITING — RETRACING HISTORIC JOURNEYS

Adams, Mark. *Tip of the Iceberg*	917.9804
Adams, Mark. *Turn Right at Machu Picchu*	985
Belliveau, Denis. *In the Footsteps of Marco Polo*	915
Buck, Rinker. *Life on the Mississippi*	917
Carlsen, William. *Jungle of Stone*	B
Chrisinger, David. *The Soldier's Truth*	940.54
Collins, Paul. *The Book of William*	016.8223
Egan, Timothy. *A Pilgrimage to Eternity*	263
Grann, David. *The White Darkness*	B
Grant, Will. *The Last Ride of the Pony Express*	917.804
Horwitz, Tony. *Spying on the South*	917
Horwitz, Tony. ★*A Voyage Long and Strange*	970.01
Karnazes, Dean. *The Legend of Marathon*	796.42
Ollivier, Bernard. *Out of Istanbul*	B
Philbrick, Nathaniel. *Travels with George*	973.4
Samatar, Sofia. *The White Mosque*	B
Severin, Timothy. *In Search of Robinson Crusoe*	996.1
Synnott, Mark. *The Third Pole*	796.522

TRAVEL WRITING — SMALL TOWN LIFE

Currid-Halkett, Elizabeth. *The Overlooked Americans*	307.76
Heat Moon, William Least. *Roads to Quoz*	917.3

TRAVEL WRITING — SOUTHWEST ASIA AND NORTH AFRICA (MIDDLE EAST)

Di Cintio, Marcello. *Pay No Heed to the Rockets*	956.9405
Feiler, Bruce. *Walking the Bible*	915
Housden, Roger. *Saved by Beauty*	955
Khan, Yasmin. *Ripe Figs*	641.595
Lawrence, T. E. *Seven Pillars of Wisdom*	940.4
Marozzi, Justin. *Islamic Empires*	909
Orth, Stephan. *Couchsurfing in Iran*	955.06
Shadid, Anthony. *House of Stone*	306.0956
Walsh, Declan. *The Nine Lives of Pakistan*	954.91
Wilkinson, Toby A. H. *The Nile*	962

TRAVEL WRITING — UNITED STATES

Barbarisi, Daniel. *Chasing the Thrill*	796.1
Bryson, Bill. ★*A Walk in the Woods*	917
Carlson, Brady. *Dead Presidents*	B
Davis, Jennifer Pharr. *Called Again*	B
Erdrich, Louise. *Books and Islands in Ojibwe Country*	977
Fallows, James M. *Our Towns*	306.0973
Fedarko, Kevin. *A Walk in the Park*	917.91
Glass, Brent D. *50 Great American Places*	973
Grant, Richard. *The Deepest South of All*	976.2
Hall, Alvin D. *Driving the Green Book*	917.304
Heat Moon, William Least. *Blue Highways*	917.304
Heat Moon, William Least. *Roads to Quoz*	917.3
Jaouad, Suleika. ★*Between Two Kingdoms*	B
Jenkins, Jedidiah. *To Shake the Sleeping Self*	B
Jenkins, Peter. *Looking for Alaska*	979.8
Jenkins, Peter. *A Walk Across America*	917.304
Jerkins, Morgan. *Wandering in Strange Lands*	305.896
Kendrick, Kathleen M. *Official Guide to the Smithsonian National Museum of African American History & Culture*	975.3
Lee, Edward. *Buttermilk Graffiti*	641.59
Letts, Elizabeth. ★*The Ride of Her Life*	B
McGill, Joseph. *Sleeping with the Ancestors*	306.362
McGrath, Ben. *Riverman*	797.122
McPherson, James M. *Hallowed Ground*	973.7
Offerman, Nick. *Where the Deer and the Antelope Play*	973.93

AUTHOR, TITLE, SERIES AND SUBJECT INDEX

Osnos, Evan. *Wildland*	973.93
Owen, David. *Where the Water Goes*	917.91
Perry, Imani. ★*South to America*	917
Proulx, Annie. *Bird Cloud*	B
Robinson, Kim Stanley. *The High Sierra*	917.94
Shattuck, Ben. *Six Walks*	B
Spira, Timothy P. *Waterfalls and Wildflowers in the Southern Appalachians*	796.5109756
Steelquist, Robert. *The Northwest Coastal Explorer*	508
Steinbeck, John. *Travels with Charley*	B
Sullivan, Randall. *Graveyard of the Pacific*	979.7
Theroux, Paul. *Deep South*	975
Thompson, Bob. *Revolutionary Roads*	973.3
Thoreau, Henry David. *The Maine Woods*	917
Vowell, Sarah. *Assassination Vacation*	B
Whitmer, Jamie Davis. *America's Most Haunted Hotels*	133.1
Wright, Lawrence. *God Save Texas*	917.64

TRAVEL WRITING — WOMEN TRAVELERS

Letts, Elizabeth. ★*The Ride of Her Life*	B
Strayed, Cheryl. ★*Wild*	B

TRAVELERS

Bryson, Bill. *In a Sunburned Country*	919
Bryson, Bill. *Notes from a Small Island*	914
Bryson, Bill. *The Road to Little Dribbling*	914
Bryson, Bill. ★*A Walk in the Woods*	917
Chamberlin, Silas. *On the Trail*	796.510973
Feiler, Bruce. *Walking the Bible*	915
Frazier, Ian. *Travels in Siberia*	957
Heat Moon, William Least. *Blue Highways*	917.304
Heat Moon, William Least. *Roads to Quoz*	917.3
Horwitz, Tony. *Spying on the South*	917
Housden, Roger. *Saved by Beauty*	955
Jenkins, Peter. *Looking for Alaska*	979.8
Jenkins, Peter. *A Walk Across America*	917.304
Krakauer, Jon. *Into the Wild*	917.9804
Lopez, Barry Holstun. *Horizon*	B
Mayes, Frances. *A Year in the World*	B
McClanahan, Paige. *The New Tourist*	338.4
Moore, Tim. *The Cyclist Who Went Out in the Cold*	796.6
Moyle, Franny. *Turner*	B
Mullins, Edwin. *The Four Roads to Heaven*	263
Orth, Stephan. *Couchsurfing in Iran*	955.06
Posnanski, Joe. *The Soul of Baseball*	796.357
Roberts, Jason. *A Sense of the World*	B
Steinbeck, John. *Travels with Charley*	B
Theroux, Paul. *The Great Railway Bazaar*	915
Theroux, Paul. *On the Plain of Snakes*	917
Thubron, Colin. *In Siberia*	957
Thubron, Colin. *Shadow of the Silk Road*	915
White, Edmund. *The Flaneur*	944
★*Travelers to Unimaginable Lands*. Kiper, Dasha	616.8
★*Traveling*. Powers, Ann	B
The Traveling Feast. Bass, Rick	B

TRAVELING SALES PERSONNEL

Ford, Richard. *Between Them*	B
Salama, Jordan. ★*Stranger in the Desert*	982

TRAVELING THEATER

Zemeckis, Leslie Harter. *Behind the Burly Q*	792.7

Traveling with Service Animals. Kisor, Henry	362.4
Travels in Siberia. Frazier, Ian	957
Travels with Charley. Steinbeck, John	B
Travels with George. Philbrick, Nathaniel	973.4

Travis, Randy

Forever and Ever, Amen	B

TRAVIS, RANDY

Travis, Randy. *Forever and Ever, Amen*	B

Travisano, Thomas J.

Love Unknown	B

★*The Trayvon Generation*. Alexander, Elizabeth	305.896

TREASON

Maddow, Rachel. ★*Prequel*	320.53
Meltzer, Brad. ★*The First Conspiracy*	973.4
Nance, Malcolm W. *The Plot to Betray America*	973.933

TREASURE HUNTERS

Barbarisi, Daniel. *Chasing the Thrill*	796.1
Ceram, C. W. *Gods, Graves & Scholars*	930.1

TREASURE TROVES

Barbarisi, Daniel. *Chasing the Thrill*	796.1

Kaiser, Menachem. *Plunder*	940.53
Mearns, David L. *The Shipwreck Hunter*	910.452
Treasures of Islam. O'Kane, Bernard	709.1
★*Treasures of the Mexican Table*. Jinich, Pati	641.5972

TREATIES

MacMillan, Margaret. *Paris 1919*	940.3
Moorhouse, Roger. *The Devils' Alliance*	940.53
Treating People Well. Berman, Lea	395
A Treatise on Stars. Berssenbrugge, Mei-Mei	811

TREATMENT

B., David. *Epileptic*	741.5
Barnett, Erica C. *Quitter*	B
Boyer, Anne. *The Undying*	B
Boyes, Alice. *The Anxiety Toolkit*	616.85
Brem, Rachel. *No Longer Radical*	616.99
Canfield, Jack. *The 30 Day Sobriety Solution*	616.89
Cregan, Mary. *The Scar*	616.85
Ely, Wes. *Every Deep-Drawn Breath*	616.02
Fessler, Pam. *Carville's Cure*	362.19699
Fisher, Carl Erik. ★*The Urge*	362.29
Frank, Lone. *The Pleasure Shock*	616.8
Freeman, Hadley. *Good Girls*	616.85
Fung, Jason. ★*The Cancer Code*	616.99
Funk, Kristi. *Breasts*	616.99
Goh, Suzanne. *Magnificent Minds*	618.92
Graeber, Charles. *The Breakthrough*	616.99
Grinker, Roy Richard. *Nobody's Normal*	616.89
Haver, Mary Claire. ★*The New Menopause*	618.1
Holt, Nathalia. *Cured*	614.5
Hughes, Evan. *The Hard Sell*	338.4
Jamison, Kay Redfield. *Fires in the Dark*	616.89
Jaouad, Suleika. ★*Between Two Kingdoms*	B
Jena, Anupam B. *Random Acts of Medicine*	616.0072
Kander, Jason. *Invisible Storm*	B
Kissinger, Meg. *While You Were Out*	362.2
Kolker, Robert. ★*Hidden Valley Road*	920
Kriss, Alexander. *Borderline*	616.85
Lalkhen, Abdul-Ghaaliq. *An Anatomy of Pain*	616
Lawson, Jenny. ★*Broken*	B
Lieberman, Jeffrey A. *Malady of the Mind*	616.89
Lustig, Robert H. *Metabolical*	616
Marcus, Amy Dockser. *We the Scientists*	618.92
McGreal, Chris. *American Overdose*	362.29
Meyer, Robert. *Every Minute Is a Day*	362.1962
Nakazawa, Donna Jackson. *The Angel and the Assassin*	612.8
Parker, Lara. *Vagina Problems*	618.1
Pelayo, Rafael. ★*How to Sleep*	616.8
Porter, Roy. *The Greatest Benefit to Mankind*	610
Raza, Azra. *The First Cell*	616.99
Rieder, Travis. *In Pain*	362.29
Riley, Alex. ★*A Cure for Darkness*	616.85
Servan-Schreiber, David. *Anticancer*	616.99
Waldman, Ayelet. *A Really Good Day*	B
Warraich, Haider. *The Song of Our Scars*	616
Whitaker, Holly. ★*Quit Like a Woman*	616.86
Williams, Michelle. *Checking In*	B

Trebek, Alex

The Answer Is ...	791.4502

TREBEK, ALEX, 1940-2020

Trebek, Alex. *The Answer Is ...*	791.4502

Trebincevic, Kenan

The Bosnia List	B

TREBINCEVIC, KENAN, 1980-

Trebincevic, Kenan. *The Bosnia List*	B

TREE CARE

Logan, William Bryant. *Sprout Lands*	582.16

TREE CLIMBING

Preston, Richard. *The Wild Trees*	585

TREE CONSERVATION

Simard, S. ★*Finding the Mother Tree*	582.16

TREE ECOLOGY

Lowman, Margaret. *The Arbornaut*	581.7

TREE PLANTING

Maathai, Wangari. *Unbowed*	B
The Treeline. Rawlence, Ben	577.3
Trees. Rodd, Tony	582.16

TREES

Bradley, Steve. *Pruning Simplified*	631.5

PUBLIC LIBRARY CORE COLLECTION: NONFICTION
Twentieth Edition

Brockman, Christian Frank. *Trees of North America* — 582.16097
Brown, George E. *Essential Pruning Techniques* — 635.9
Drori, Jonathan. *Around the World in 80 Trees* — 582.16
Farmer, Jared. *Elderflora* — 582.16
Heinrich, Bernd. *A Naturalist at Large* — 508
Hugo, Nancy R. *Seeing Trees* — 582.16
King, Greg. *The Ghost Forest* — 333.75
Lewis, Daniel. *Twelve Trees* — 582.16
Little, Elbert L. *The Audubon Society Field Guide to North American Trees* — 582.16097
    Logan, William Bryant. *Sprout Lands* — 582.16
Lowman, Margaret. *The Arbornaut* — 581.7
Mathews, Daniel. *Trees in Trouble* — 634.9
Pearce, Fred. *A Trillion Trees* — 577.3
Petrides, George A. *A Field Guide to Western Trees* — 582.16
Preston, Richard. *The Wild Trees* — 585
Rawlence, Ben. *The Treeline* — 577.3
Rodd, Tony. *Trees* — 582.16
Sibley, David. ★*The Sibley Guide to Trees* — 582.16097
Simard, S. ★*Finding the Mother Tree* — 582.16
Wohlleben, Peter. *Forest Walking* — 582.16
Wohlleben, Peter. *The Heartbeat of Trees* — 582.16
Wohlleben, Peter. *The Hidden Life of Trees* — 582.16
Trees *in Trouble.* Mathews, Daniel — 634.9
Trees *of North America.* Brockman, Christian Frank — 582.16097
Trefil, James
    Space Atlas — 520
Tregear, Mary
    Chinese Art — 709.51
Treister, Kenneth
    Easter Island's Silent Sentinels — 996.18
Trejo. Trejo, Danny — B
Trejo's Tacos. Trejo, Danny — 641.5979
Trejo, Danny
    Trejo's Tacos — 641.5979
    Trejo — B
TREJO, DANNY, 1944-
    Trejo, Danny. *Trejo* — B
Trelease, Jim
    ★*Jim Trelease's Read-Aloud Handbook* — 372.4
Tremlett, Giles
    Ghosts of Spain — 946.08
TREMLETT, GILES
    Tremlett, Giles. *Ghosts of Spain* — 946.08
Trentmann, Frank
    Out of the Darkness — 943.08
TRENTON, BATTLE OF, 1776
    Fischer, David Hackett. *Washington's Crossing* — 973.3
TRENTON, NEW JERSEY
    Fischer, David Hackett. *Washington's Crossing* — 973.3
Tresch, John
    The Reason for the Darkness of the Night — B
Trethewey, Natasha D.
    ★*Memorial Drive* — B
    ★*Monument* — 811
    ★*Native Guard* — 811
Treuer, Anton
    Everything You Wanted to Know About Indians but Were Afraid to Ask — 970.1
Treuer, David
    ★*The Heartbeat of Wounded Knee* — 970.004
The Trial. Kadri, Sadakat — 345
Trial by Fire. James, Scott — 363.3709745
The Trial of Adolf Hitler. King, David — 345.43
The Trial of Lizzie Borden. Robertson, Cara — 345.744
The Trial of Socrates. Stone, I. F. — 183
TRIALS
    Abrams, Dan. *Kennedy's Avenger* — 973.922
    Addison, Corban. *Wastelands* — 346.73
    Bardenwerper, William. *The Prisoner in His Palace* — 956.7044
    Bass, Gary Jonathan. ★*Judgment at Tokyo* — 952.04
    Biskupic, Joan. ★*Nine Black Robes* — 347.73
    Cohen, Adam. ★*Imbeciles* — 344.7304
    Dybdahl, Thomas L. *When Innocence Is Not Enough* — 345.73
    Goodman, Simon. *The Orpheus Clock* — 940.53
    Healy, Thomas. *The Great Dissent* — 342.7308
    Hughes, Evan. *The Hard Sell* — 338.4
    Kadri, Sadakat. *The Trial* — 345
    Kinstler, Linda. *Come to This Court and Cry* — 940.53
    Lobel, Orly. *You Don't Own Me* — 346.7304
    McGinty, Brian. *Lincoln's Greatest Case* — 346.7303
    Nourse, Victoria F. *In Reckless Hands* — 344.7304
    O'Connell, Mark. *A Thread of Violence* — 364.152
    O'Connor, Sandra Day. ★*Out of Order* — 347.73
    Rediker, Marcus. *The Amistad Rebellion* — 326.0973
    Sands, Philippe. *East West Street* — 345
    Schneps, Leila. *Math on Trial* — 345
    Sherman, Casey. *Hunting Whitey* — B
    Strang, Dean A. *Worse Than the Devil* — 345.775
    Toobin, Jeffrey. ★*Homegrown* — 363.325
    Van Meter, Matthew. *Deep Delta Justice* — 345.763
    Wise, Steven M. *Though the Heavens May Fall* — 342.42
TRIALS (ABORTION)
    Prager, Joshua. *The Family Roe* — 342.7308
    Wright, Jennifer Ashley. ★*Madame Restell* — B
TRIALS (BLASPHEMY)
    Stone, I. F. *The Trial of Socrates* — 183
TRIALS (CHILD SEXUAL ABUSE)
    Rabinowitz, Dorothy. *No Crueler Tyrannies* — 345.73
TRIALS (CRIMES AGAINST HUMANITY)
    Bardenwerper, William. *The Prisoner in His Palace* — 956.7044
    Newton, Michael A. *Enemy of the State* — 345.567
    Sands, Philippe. *East West Street* — 345
TRIALS (ESPIONAGE)
    Rezaian, Jason. *Prisoner* — B
TRIALS (FRAUD)
    Manseau, Peter. *The Apparitionists* — B
TRIALS (GENOCIDE)
    Sands, Philippe. *East West Street* — 345
TRIALS (HATE CRIMES)
    Gergel, Richard. *Unexampled Courage* — 323.1196
TRIALS (IMPEACHMENT)
    Sullivan, Kevin. *Trump on Trial* — 342.73
    Sunstein, Cass R. *Impeachment* — 342.73
    Wineapple, Brenda. *The Impeachers* — 973.8
TRIALS (LIBEL)
    Abrams, Dan. *Theodore Roosevelt for the Defense* — 345.73
    Kluger, Richard. *Indelible Ink* — B
    Lipstadt, Deborah E. *History on Trial* — 940.53
    O'Sullivan, Emer. *The Fall of the House of Wilde* — B
TRIALS (MURDER)
    Balko, Radley. ★*The Cadaver King and the Country Dentist* — 614
    Barron, Justine. *They Killed Freddie Gray* — 363.32
    Berendt, John. *Midnight in the Garden of Good and Evil* — 975.8
    Boyle, Kevin. *Arc of Justice* — 345.73
    Brown, Mick. ★*Tearing Down the Wall of Sound* — B
    Bugliosi, Vincent. ★*Helter Skelter* — 364.1
    Cep, Casey N. ★*Furious Hours* — 364.152
    Crump, Benjamin. *Open Season* — 364
    Davis, Kevin. *The Brain Defense* — 345.747
    Gleeson, John. *The Gotti Wars* — 364.1
    Green, Elon. *Last Call* — 363.15
    Harman, Claire. *Murder by the Book* — 364.152
    Hendricks, Steve. *The Unquiet Grave* — 323.1197
    Hinton, Anthony Ray. *The Sun Does Shine* — B
    Hortis, C. Alexander. *The Witch of New York* — 364.152
    Jones, Doug. *Bending Toward Justice* — 323.1196
    King, Greg. *Nothing but the Night* — 364.152
    Lane, Charles. *The Day Freedom Died* — 976.3
    McManus, James. ★*Positively Fifth Street* — 795.41
    Mitchell, Jerry. ★*Race Against Time* — 364.152
    Newton, Michael A. *Enemy of the State* — 345.567
    Philipps, David. *Alpha* — 956.7044
    Robertson, Cara. *The Trial of Lizzie Borden* — 345.744
    Smith, Clive Stafford. *The Injustice System* — 345.759
    Swift, Earl. *Hell Put to Shame* — 364.15
    Tyson, Timothy B. *Blood Done Sign My Name* — 975.6
    Tyson, Timothy B. *The Blood of Emmett Till* — 364.1
    Watson, Bruce. *Sacco and Vanzetti* — 345.73
    Wiehl, Lis W. *Hunting Charles Manson* — 364.152
TRIALS (POLICE MISCONDUCT)
    Gergel, Richard. *Unexampled Courage* — 323.1196
    Samuels, Robert. ★*His Name Is George Floyd* — B
TRIALS (RAPE)
    Balko, Radley. ★*The Cadaver King and the Country Dentist* — 614
    Morrison, Melanie. *Murder on Shades Mountain* — 345.761

AUTHOR, TITLE, SERIES AND SUBJECT INDEX

TRIALS (ROBBERY)
    Finkel, Michael. *The Art Thief* — 364.1628
    Johnson, Kirk W. *The Feather Thief* — 364.16
TRIALS (SEDITION)
    Stone, I. F. *The Trial of Socrates* — 183
TRIALS (SEX CRIMES)
    DeRogatis, Jim. *Soulless* — B
    Hirshman, Linda R. *Reckoning* — 305.420973
TRIALS (TREASON)
    King, David. *The Trial of Adolf Hitler* — 345.43
    Manning, Chelsea. *Readme.Txt* — B
TRIALS (WITCHCRAFT)
    Gibson, Marion. *Witchcraft* — 133.4
    Schiff, Stacy. *The Witches* — 345
    Sollee, Kristen J. *Witch Hunt* — 133
The Trials of Harry S. Truman. Frank, Jeffrey — 973.918
★*Triangle.* Von Drehle, Dave — 974.7
The Triathlete's Training Bible. Friel, Joe — 796.42
TRIATHLETES
    Dixon, Matt. *The Well-Built Triathlete* — 796.42
    Fitzgerald, Matt. *Iron War* — 796.42
TRIATHLON
    Dixon, Matt. *The Well-Built Triathlete* — 796.42
    Friel, Joe. *The Triathlete's Training Bible* — 796.42
Tribe, Laurence H.
    Uncertain Justice — 342.73
Trice, Dawn Turner
    ★*Three Girls from Bronzeville* — 977.311
TRICE, DAWN TURNER
    Trice, Dawn Turner. ★*Three Girls from Bronzeville* — 977.311
TRICE, DEBRA
    Trice, Dawn Turner. ★*Three Girls from Bronzeville* — 977.311
★*Trick Mirror.* Tolentino, Jia — 973.93
Trick or Treat. Morton, Lisa — 394.2646
TRICK OR TREAT
    Morton, Lisa. *Trick or Treat* — 394.2646
★*Tried by War.* McPherson, James M. — 973.7
Triggers. Goldsmith, Marshall — 155.2
Trillin, Calvin
    The Lede — 071
TRILLIN, CALVIN
    Trillin, Calvin. *The Lede* — 071
A Trillion Trees. Pearce, Fred — 577.3
Trim Healthy Mama Trim Healthy Table. Barrett, Pearl — 613.2
Trimble, Lee
    Beyond the Call — 940.54
TRIMBLE, ROBERT M.
    Trimble, Lee. *Beyond the Call* — 940.54
Trimborn, Jurgen
    Leni Riefenstahl — B
TRINIDAD AND TOBAGO
    French, Patrick. *The World Is What It Is* — B
Tripas. Som, Brandon — 811
TRIPLE CROWN, AMERICAN (HORSE RACING)
    Drape, Joe. *American Pharoah* — 798.40092
TRIPOLITAN WAR, 1801-1805
    Kilmeade, Brian. ★*Thomas Jefferson and the Tripoli Pirates* — 973.4
TRIPPE, J. T. (JUAN TERRY), 1899-1981
    Rose, Alexander. *Empires of the Sky* — 920
TRIPS AROUND THE WORLD
    Bergreen, Laurence. *In Search of a Kingdom* — B
    Bergreen, Laurence. *Over the Edge of the World* — B
    Darwin, Charles. ★*The Voyage of the Beagle* — 508
    Fabes, Stephen. *Signs of Life* — B
Trisha's Kitchen. Yearwood, Trisha — 641.5
Triumph and Tragedy. Churchill, Winston — 940.53
The Triumph of Christianity. Ehrman, Bart D. — 270.1
The Triumph of Nancy Reagan. Tumulty, Karen — B
The Triumph of the Moon. Hutton, Ronald — 133.4
Triumph of the Yuppies. McGrath, Tom — 305.242
TRIVIA AND MISCELLANEOUS FACTS
    Felder, Deborah G. *The American Women's Almanac* — 305.40973
    Foer, Joshua. *Atlas Obscura* — 910.41
    Foer, Joshua. ★*Atlas Obscura 2nd Ed.* — 910.41
    Wallace, David Foster. *Consider the Lobster* — 814
    Wong, Cecily. ★*Gastro Obscura* — 641.3
TRIVIA GAMES
    Schneider, Amy. *In the Form of a Question* — B

Trofimov, Yaroslav
    ★*Our Enemies Will Vanish* — 947.7
    The Siege of Mecca — 953.805
TROJAN WAR
    Alexander, Caroline. *The War That Killed Achilles* — 883
    Homer. *The Iliad* — 883
    Homer. *The Iliad* — 883
    Homer. *Iliad* — 883
    Homer. ★*The Iliad* — 883
    Homer. *The Odyssey* — 883
    Manguel, Alberto. *Homer's the Iliad and the Odyssey* — 883
    Virgil. ★*The Aeneid* — 873
TROLLS (ONLINE)
    Blake, Melissa. *Beautiful People* — 362.4
Troop 6000. Stewart, Nikita — 369
Tropic of Squalor. Karr, Mary — 811
TROPICAL PLANTS
    Offolter, Enid. *Welcome to the Jungle* — 635.9
TROPICS
    Diaz, Von. ★*Islas* — 641.59
    Zuckerman, Jocelyn C. *Planet Palm* — 633.8
TROTSKY, LEON, 1879-1940
    Mieville, China. *October* — 947.084
TROTTER, CATHARINE, 1679-1749
    Penaluna, Regan. ★*How to Think Like a Woman* — 190.82
TROTTER, WILLIAM MONROE, 1872-1934
    Greenidge, Kerri. *Black Radical* — B
    Lehr, Dick. ★*The Birth of a Nation* — 305.800973
Trouble Boys. Mehr, Bob — 920
The Trouble with Gravity. Panek, Richard — 531
The Trouble with Poetry and Other Poems. Collins, Billy — 811
The Trouble with White Women. Schuller, Kyla — 305.42
Troubled. Henderson, Rob Kim — B
Troubled Refuge. Manning, Chandra — 973.7
Troublesome Young Men. Olson, Lynne — 941.084
TROY (EXTINCT CITY)
    Homer. ★*The Iliad* — 883
    Homer. *The Odyssey* — 883
    Virgil. ★*The Aeneid* — 873
Trubert-Tollu, Chantal
    ★*The House of Worth 1858-1954* — 746.92
Trubo, Richard
    Caring for Your Baby and Young Child — 618.92
The Truce. Walker, Hunter — 324.2736
TRUCK FARMING
    Coleman, Eliot. ★*The New Organic Grower* — 635
A Truck Full of Money. Kidder, Tracy — B
TRUCKING INDUSTRY AND TRADE
    Goodman, Peter S. ★*How the World Ran Out of Everything* — 658.7
    McPhee, John. *Uncommon Carriers* — 388
True. Kennedy, Kostya — B
True and False. Mamet, David — 792
True Believer. Riesman, Abraham — 741.5
TRUE CRIME — COLD CASES AND UNSOLVED MYSTERIES
    Brown, Vanessa. *The Forest City Killer* — 364.152
    Cooper, Becky. *We Keep the Dead Close* — 364.152
    Corcoran, Katherine. *In the Mouth of the Wolf* — 364.152
    Lankford, Andrea. *Trail of the Lost* — 363.2
    Levin, Josh. *The Queen* — 364.16
    Mitchell, Jerry. ★*Race Against Time* — 364.152
    Smith, Richard MacLean. *Unexplained* — 130
    White, Richard. *Who Killed Jane Stanford?* — 364.152
TRUE CRIME — DOMESTIC CRIME
    Asgarian, Roxanna. *We Were Once a Family* — 364.152
    Glatt, John. *The Doomsday Mother* — 364.152
    Glatt, John. *The Family Next Door* — 362.76092
    Glatt, John. ★*The Perfect Father* — 364.152
    Kizzia, Tom. *Pilgrim's Wilderness* — B
    McGinniss, Joe. *Fatal Vision* — B
    Schreiber, Flora Rheta. *Sybil* — 616.85
TRUE CRIME — DRUGS
    Carr, David. *The Night of the Gun* — B
    Dearen, Jason. *Kill Shot* — 616.8
    Fine, Doug. *Too High to Fail* — 338.4
    Hamilton, Tyler. *The Secret Race* — 796.62
    Jimenez, Stephen. *The Book of Matt* — 364.152
    Keefe, Patrick Radden. ★*Empire of Pain* — 338.7
    Lattin, Don. *The Harvard Psychedelic Club* — 973.922092

PUBLIC LIBRARY CORE COLLECTION: NONFICTION
Twentieth Edition

Marshall, McMillan. *Among the Bros*	362.29
Quinones, Sam. *Dreamland*	362.29
Ratliff, Evan. *The Mastermind*	B
Shannon, Elaine. *Hunting Leroux*	364.1
Vorobyov, Niko. *Dopeworld*	364.1

TRUE CRIME — FORENSIC SCIENCES

Bass, William M. *Death's Acre*	614
Blum, Deborah. *The Poisoner's Handbook*	614
Butcher, Barbara. *What the Dead Know*	614
Di Maio, Vincent J. M. *Morgue*	
Goldfarb, Bruce. ★*18 Tiny Deaths*	B
Hagerty, Alexa. ★*Still Life with Bones*	599.9
Humes, Edward. *The Forever Witness*	363.25
Kimmerle, Erin H. *We Carry Their Bones*	365
Maples, William R. *Dead Men Do Tell Tales*	614
Monroe, Jana. *Hearts of Darkness*	363.25
Norton, Laurah. *Lay Them to Rest*	363.25
Rae-Venter, Barbara. *I Know Who You Are*	364.152
Roach, Mary. ★*Stiff*	611
Sullivan, Rosemary. *The Betrayal of Anne Frank*	940.53

TRUE CRIME — GENERAL

Behar, Richard. *Madoff*	364.16
Berman, Sarah. *Don't Call It a Cult*	361.4
Betz-Hamilton, Axton. *The Less People Know About Us*	364.16
Blum, Howard. *The Spy Who Knew Too Much*	327.12
Bowden, Mark. *The Case of the Vanishing Blonde*	364.10973
Bradbury, Neil. *A Taste for Poison*	615.9
Carreyrou, John. ★*Bad Blood*	338.7
Cook, Kevin. *Waco Rising*	299
Cunningham, Benjamin. *The Liar*	327.1273
Cutler, Max. *Cults*	364.15
Dudley, Renee. *The Ransomware Hunting Team*	363.25
Goldberg, Carrie. *Nobody's Victim*	345.73
Greenberg, Andy. *Sandworm*	364.16
Hammer, Joshua. *The Falcon Thief*	364.16
Hughes, Evan. *The Hard Sell*	338.4
Hvistendahl, Mara. ★*The Scientist and the Spy*	364.16
James, Scott. *Trial by Fire*	363.3709745
Jones, Chip. *The Organ Thieves*	617.4
Keefe, Patrick Radden. ★*Rogues*	364.16
Levin, Daniel Barban. *Slonim Woods 9*	B
Maroney, Tyler. *The Modern Detective*	658.4
Mitnick, Kevin D. *Ghost in the Wires*	B
Oshinsky, David M. *Worse Than Slavery*	365
Papenfuss, Mary. *American Huckster*	B
Phillips, Patrick. *Blood at the Root*	305.8
Popkin, Jim. *Code Name Blue Wren*	327.12
Posner, Gerald L. *God's Bankers*	364.16
Prejean, Helen. *The Death of Innocents*	364.66
Preston, Douglas J. *The Lost Tomb*	930.1
Renner, Rebecca. ★*Gator Country*	364.16
Schechter, Harold. ★*Ripped from the Headlines!*	791.43
Sered, Danielle. *Until We Reckon*	364.6
Sisman, Adam. *The Professor and the Parson*	364.16
Stille, Alexander. *The Sullivanians*	307.77
Sullivan, Randall. *The Devil's Best Trick*	235
Tetro, Tony. *Con/Artist*	
Thompson, Heather Ann. *Blood in the Water*	365
Vaughan, Liam. *Flash Crash*	B
White, Neil. *In the Sanctuary of Outcasts*	B
Whitlock, Craig. ★*Fat Leonard*	364.16
Woodfox, Albert. *Solitary*	B
Zuckoff, Mitchell. *Ponzi's Scheme*	B

TRUE CRIME — HEISTS AND ROBBERY

Amore, Anthony M. *The Art of the Con*	702.8
Bilefsky, Dan. *The Last Job*	364.16
Boessenecker, John. *Gentleman Bandit*	B
Dolnick, Edward. *The Rescue Artist*	364.16
Edsel, Robert M. *The Monuments Men*	940.53
Finkel, Michael. *The Art Thief*	364.1628
Goodman, Simon. *The Orpheus Clock*	940.53
Guinn, Jeff. *Go Down Together*	B
Jobb, Dean. *A Gentleman and a Thief*	364.16
Johnson, Kirk W. *The Feather Thief*	364.16
King, David. *Six Days in August*	364.15
Leerhsen, Charles. ★*Butch Cassidy*	B
O'Connell, Mark. *A Thread of Violence*	364.152
Scotti, R. A. *Vanished Smile*	759.5

Yeebo, Yepoka. *Anansi's Gold*	364.16

TRUE CRIME — HISTORICAL CRIME

Alford, Terry. *Fortune's Fool*	B
Avrich, Paul. *Sasha and Emma*	920
Collins, Max Allan. *Eliot Ness and the Mad Butcher*	364.152
Cornwell, Patricia Daniels. *Ripper*	364.152
Egan, Timothy. ★*A Fever in the Heartland*	322.4
Ellsworth, Scott. *The Ground Breaking*	976.6
Fox, Margalit. *The Talented Mrs. Mandelbaum*	364.1
Grann, David. ★*Killers of the Flower Moon*	976.6004
Grann, David. ★*The Wager*	910.91
Harman, Claire. *Murder by the Book*	364.152
Herman, Eleanor. *The Royal Art of Poison*	364.152
Hill, David. *The Vapors*	976.7
Hortis, C. Alexander. *The Witch of New York*	364.152
Jager, Eric. *Blood Royal*	944.026
Jobb, Dean. *The Case of the Murderous Dr. Cream*	364.152
Johnson, Steven. *Enemy of All Mankind*	910.4
Johnson, Steven. *The Infernal Machine*	335
Kavanagh, Julie. *The Irish Assassins*	941.5
Kean, Sam. *The Icepick Surgeon*	509
Kimmerle, Erin H. *We Carry Their Bones*	365
King, Gilbert. *Beneath a Ruthless Sun*	B
King, Greg. *Nothing but the Night*	364.152
Krist, Gary. *Empire of Sin*	976.3
Larson, Erik. ★*The Devil in the White City*	364.15
Macy, Beth. ★*Trueville*	B
Man, John. *Ninja*	355.5
McCracken, Patti. *The Angel Makers*	364.152
Montillo, Roseanne. *Deliberate Cruelty*	364.152
Nicholl, Charles. *The Reckoning*	B
O'Neill, Tom. ★*Chaos*	364.152
Rappaport, Helen. *The Race to Save the Romanovs*	947.08
Robertson, Cara. *The Trial of Lizzie Borden*	345.744
Rubenhold, Hallie. ★*The Five*	362.88
Schechter, Harold. ★*Ripped from the Headlines!*	791.43
Sides, Hampton. *Hellhound on His Trail*	364.152
Stashower, Daniel. *American Demon*	364.152
Stout, David. *The Kidnap Years*	364.15
Strauss, Barry S. *The Death of Caesar*	937
Swift, Earl. *Hell Put to Shame*	364.15
Tyson, Timothy B. *The Blood of Emmett Till*	364.1
Walker, Ronald W. ★*Massacre at Mountain Meadows*	979.2
Wallis, Michael. *Billy the Kid*	B
Weinman, Sarah. *The Real Lolita*	362.88092
Weir, Alison. *Mary, Queen of Scots, and the Murder of Lord Darnley*	941.105

TRUE CRIME — INVESTIGATIONS AND TRIALS

Abrams, Dan. *Kennedy's Avenger*	973.922
Addison, Corban. *Wastelands*	346.73
Balko, Radley. ★*The Cadaver King and the Country Dentist*	614
Barron, Justine. *They Killed Freddie Gray*	363.32
Bascomb, Neal. *Hunting Eichmann*	943.086
Bogira, Steve. *Courtroom 302*	345.773
Callahan, Maureen. *American Predator*	364.152
Carpenter, Dale. *Flagrant Conduct*	342.7308
Carter, Stephen L. *Invisible*	B
Cox, Joseph. *Dark Wire*	363.2
Cross, Kim. *In Light of All Darkness*	363.25
Dawson, Kate Winkler. ★*American Sherlock*	B
Douglas, John E. *When a Killer Calls*	364.152
Dybdahl, Thomas L. *When Innocence Is Not Enough*	345.73
Fabricant, M. Chris. *Junk Science and the American Criminal Justice System*	363.25
Fink, Sheri. *Five Days at Memorial*	362.1109763
Gleeson, John. *The Gotti Wars*	364.1
Grann, David. ★*Killers of the Flower Moon*	976.6004
Hendricks, Steve. *The Unquiet Grave*	323.1197
Higham, Scott. *American Cartel*	338.4
Holes, Paul. *Unmasked*	363.25
Jacobs, Ryan McMahon. *The Truffle Underground*	381
Johnson, Steven. *The Infernal Machine*	335
Jones, Doug. *Bending Toward Justice*	323.1196
Kadri, Sadakat. *The Trial*	345
King, David. *Death in the City of Light*	364.152
King, Gilbert. ★*Devil in the Grove*	305.896
Lane, Charles. *The Day Freedom Died*	976.3
Leamer, Laurence. *The Price of Justice*	346.7302
Lipstadt, Deborah E. *The Eichmann Trial*	345.5694

AUTHOR, TITLE, SERIES AND SUBJECT INDEX

Marzano-Lesnevich, Alexandria. *The Fact of a Body*	364.152
McGough, Matthew. *The Lazarus Files*	364.152
Mills, Stephen Tukel. *Chosen*	B
Nourse, Victoria F. *In Reckless Hands*	344.7304
Rabinowitz, Dorothy. *No Crueler Tyrannies*	345.73
Risen, James. ★*The Last Honest Man*	973.92
Rudolf, David S. *American Injustice*	345.73
Sands, Philippe. *East West Street*	345
Schneps, Leila. *Math on Trial*	345
Sherman, Casey. *Hunting Whitey*	B
Smith, Clive Stafford. *The Injustice System*	345.759
Strang, Dean A. *Worse Than the Devil*	345.775
Toobin, Jeffrey. ★*Homegrown*	363.325
Tyson, Timothy B. *Blood Done Sign My Name*	975.6
Watson, Bruce. *Sacco and Vanzetti*	345.73
Wiehl, Lis W. *Hunting the Unabomber*	364.152
Zerwick, Phoebe. *Beyond Innocence*	347

TRUE CRIME — MURDER

Alford, Terry. *Fortune's Fool*	B
Appelman, J. Reuben. *While Idaho Slept*	364.152
Asgarian, Roxanna. *We Were Once a Family*	364.152
Assael, Shaun. *The Murder of Sonny Liston*	B
Belkin, Lisa. *Genealogy of a Murder*	362.88
Berendt, John. *Midnight in the Garden of Good and Evil*	975.8
Bonner, Betsy. *The Book of Atlantis Black*	364.152
Boyle, Kevin. *Arc of Justice*	345.73
Bradley, Mark A. *Blood Runs Coal*	B
Brier, Bob. *The Murder of Tutankhamen*	B
Brown, Vanessa. *The Forest City Killer*	364.152
Bugliosi, Vincent. ★*Helter Skelter*	364.1
Burgess, Ann Wolbert. *A Killer by Design*	364.3
Callahan, Maureen. *American Predator*	364.152
Cameron, Silver Donald. *Blood in the Water*	364.152
Capote, Truman. ★*In Cold Blood*	364.1
Caruana Galizia, Paul. ★*A Death in Malta*	364.15
Cep, Casey N. ★*Furious Hours*	364.152
Collins, Max Allan. *Eliot Ness and the Mad Butcher*	364.152
Cooper, Becky. *We Keep the Dead Close*	364.152
Cooper, Sean Patrick. *The Shooter at Midnight*	363.25
Corcoran, Katherine. *In the Mouth of the Wolf*	364.152
Cornwell, Patricia Daniels. *Ripper*	364.152
Cross, Kim. *In Light of All Darkness*	363.25
Cullen, David. *Columbine*	373
Cullen, David. *Parkland*	371.7
Davis, Kevin. *The Brain Defense*	345.747
Denton, Sally. *The Colony*	364.152
Douglas, John E. *The Killer Across the Table*	B
Douglas, John E. *When a Killer Calls*	364.152
Eisenberg, Emma Copley. ★*The Third Rainbow Girl*	364.152
Ervin, Kristine S. *Rabbit Heart*	364.152
Eustace, Nicole. ★*Covered with Night*	364.152
Franscell, Ron. *Shadowman*	362.88
Garrison, Jessica. *The Devil's Harvest*	B
Gerard, Sarah. *Carrie Carolyn Coco*	364.152
Glatt, John. *The Doomsday Mother*	364.152
Glatt, John. ★*The Perfect Father*	364.152
Glatt, John. *Tangled Vines*	364.152
Grann, David. ★*Killers of the Flower Moon*	976.6004
Green, Elon. *Last Call*	363.15
Guinn, Jeff. ★*Manson*	B
Guinn, Jeff. *The Road to Jonestown*	289.9
Hale, Kathleen. ★*Slenderman*	364.152
Harman, Claire. *Murder by the Book*	364.152
Hill, Clint. *Five Days in November*	973.922092
Humes, Edward. *The Forever Witness*	363.25
Isenberg, Sheila. *Women Who Love Men Who Kill*	362.83
Jimenez, Stephen. *The Book of Matt*	364.152
Jobb, Dean. *The Case of the Murderous Dr. Cream*	364.152
Keefe, Patrick Radden. ★*Say Nothing*	364.152
Kenda, Joe. *Killer Triggers*	364.152
Kenneally, Christine. *Ghosts of the Orphanage*	362.73
King, David. *Death in the City of Light*	364.152
King, Greg. *Nothing but the Night*	364.152
Kroll, Andy. *A Death on W Street*	364.152
Larson, Erik. ★*The Devil in the White City*	364.15
Lauren, Jillian. *Behold the Monster*	364.152
Leovy, Jill. *Ghettoside*	364.152
Lockhart, Chris. ★*Walking the Bowl*	362.7
Lowry, Beverly. *Deer Creek Drive*	364.152
Lysiak, Matthew. *Newtown*	371.7
MacLean, Harry N. *Starkweather*	364.152
Mar, Alex. *Seventy Times Seven*	362.88
Matney, Mandy. *Blood on Their Hands*	364.152
McCracken, Patti. *The Angel Makers*	364.152
McDiarmid, Jessica. *Highway of Tears*	364.152
McGarrahan, Ellen. *Two Truths and a Lie*	364.152
McGinniss, Joe. *Fatal Vision*	B
McGough, Matthew. *The Lazarus Files*	364.152
McNamara, Michelle. *I'll Be Gone in the Dark*	364.152
Miles, Kathryn. *Trailed*	364.152
Monroe, Jana. *Hearts of Darkness*	363.25
Montillo, Roseanne. *Deliberate Cruelty*	364.152
Morton, Michael. *Getting Life*	B
Murdoch, Sierra Crane. ★*Yellow Bird*	364.152
Nelson, David B. *Boys Enter the House*	364.152
Nicholl, Charles. *The Reckoning*	B
O'Connell, Mark. *A Thread of Violence*	364.152
O'Neill, Tom. ★*Chaos*	364.152
Posner, Gerald L. *Case Closed*	364.1
Quinones, John. ★*One Year in Uvalde*	371.7
Rear, Rachel. *Catch the Sparrow*	364.152
Robertson, Cara. *The Trial of Lizzie Borden*	345.744
Rosen, Jonathan. ★*The Best Minds*	616.89
Rubin, Kathy Kleiner. *A Light in the Dark*	364.152
Rule, Ann. *The Stranger Beside Me*	B
Schechter, Harold. *Hell's Princess*	B
Schechter, Harold. *Murderabilia*	364.152
Sides, Hampton. *Hellhound on His Trail*	364.152
Smith, Clive Stafford. *The Injustice System*	345.759
Standiford, Les. *Bringing Adam Home*	364.15
Stashower, Daniel. *American Demon*	364.152
Swanson, James L. *End of Days*	973.922092
Tyson, Timothy B. *Blood Done Sign My Name*	975.6
Tyson, Timothy B. *The Blood of Emmett Till*	364.1
Vowell, Sarah. *Assassination Vacation*	B
Walker, Ronald W. ★*Massacre at Mountain Meadows*	979.2
Weinman, Sarah. *Scoundrel*	364.152
Weinman, Sarah. ★*Unspeakable Acts*	364.1
Weir, Alison. *Mary, Queen of Scots, and the Murder of Lord Darnley*	941.105
Wiehl, Lis W. *Hunting Charles Manson*	364.152
Wilkie, Curtis. *When Evil Lived in Laurel*	305.8
Williamson, Elizabeth. ★*Sandy Hook*	364.152

TRUE CRIME — ORGANIZED CRIME, MAFIA, AND GANGS

Ahmed, Azam. *Fear Is Just a Word*	364.152
Bair, Deirdre. *Al Capone*	B
Bowden, Mark. *Life Sentence*	364.106
Bradburd, Rus. *All the Dreams We've Dreamed*	796.323
Cannell, Michael T. *A Brotherhood Betrayed*	B
Carlo, Philip. *Gaspipe*	B
Carter, Stephen L. *Invisible*	B
Corcoran, Katherine. *In the Mouth of the Wolf*	364.152
Cox, Joseph. *Dark Wire*	363.2
Croke, Ken. *Riding with Evil*	364.106
Cullen, Kevin. *Whitey Bulger*	B
Dudley, Steven S. *MS-13*	364.106
Eig, Jonathan. *Get Capone*	364.1
English, T. J. *The Corporation*	364.106089
Fenton, Justin. *We Own This City*	364.1
Fox, Margalit. *The Talented Mrs. Mandelbaum*	364.1
Gleeson, John. *The Gotti Wars*	364.1
Greenberg, Andy. *Tracers in the Dark*	364.16
Hill, David. *The Vapors*	976.7
Lehr, Dick. *White Hot Hate*	363.325
Maier, Thomas. *Mafia Spies*	364.1060973
Moore, Michael Scott. *The Desert and the Sea*	364.15
Nadeau, Barbie Latza. *The Godmother*	364.106
Sherman, Casey. *Hunting Whitey*	B

TRUE CRIME — POLICE AND LAWYERS

Barron, Justine. *They Killed Freddie Gray*	363.32
Collins, Max Allan. *Eliot Ness and the Mad Butcher*	364.152
Croke, Ken. *Riding with Evil*	364.106
Douglas, John E. *The Killer Across the Table*	B
Feige, David. *Indefensible*	
Fenton, Justin. *We Own This City*	364.1
Stevenson, Bryan. *Just Mercy*	B

PUBLIC LIBRARY CORE COLLECTION: NONFICTION
Twentieth Edition

TRUE CRIME — SEX CRIMES
    Auletta, Ken. ★*Hollywood Ending* — 791.43
    Barr, John. *Start by Believing* — 364.15
    Bowden, Mark. *The Last Stone* — 363.25
    Carpenter, Dale. *Flagrant Conduct* — 342.7308
    Crawford, Lacy. *Notes on a Silencing* — B
    DeRogatis, Jim. *Soulless* — B
    Faleiro, Sonia. *The Good Girls* — 364.152
    Farrow, Ronan. ★*Catch and Kill* — 331.4
    Frederick, Jim. *Black Hearts* — 956.7044
    King, Gilbert. *Beneath a Ruthless Sun* — B
    Krouse, Erika. ★*Tell Me Everything* — 363.25
    McNamara, Michelle. *I'll Be Gone in the Dark* — 364.152
    Miller, Chanel. *Know My Name* — B
    Miller, T. Christian. *A False Report* — 364.15
    Mills, Stephen Tukel. *Chosen* — B
    Rabinowitz, Dorothy. *No Crueler Tyrannies* — 345.73
    Schwartzman, Nancy. *Roll Red Roll* — 364.15
    Tjipombo, Tupa. *I Am Not Your Slave* — B
    Vanasco, Jeannie. *Things We Didn't Talk About When I Was a Girl* — B
True Crimes and Misdemeanors. Toobin, Jeffrey — 973.933
★*The True Flag*. Kinzer, Stephen — 327.73
★*True Gentlemen*. Hechinger, John — 371.85
True Roots. Cavallari, Kristin — 641.5
True South. Else, Jon — 305.800973
True Stories from an Unreliable Eyewitness. Lahti, Christine — B
True West. Greenfield, Robert — B

TRUE-CRIME TELEVISION PROGRAMS
    Weinman, Sarah. ★*Unspeakable Acts* — 364.1
    ★*Truevine*. Macy, Beth — B
The Truffle Underground. Jacobs, Ryan McMahon — 381

TRUFFLES
    Jacobs, Ryan McMahon. *The Truffle Underground* — 381
Truman. McCullough, David G.

TRUMAN, HARRY S., 1884-1972
    Baime, A. J. *The Accidental President* — B
    Beschloss, Michael R. *The Conquerors* — 940.53
    Brands, H. W. *The General vs. the President* — 973.918092
    Cohen, Jared. *Accidental Presidents* — 973.09
    Dallek, Robert. *Harry S. Truman* — B
    Donald, Aida DiPace. *Citizen Soldier* — B
    Frank, Jeffrey. *The Trials of Harry S. Truman* — 973.918
    Gordin, Michael D. *Red Cloud at Dawn* — 355.02
    McCullough, David G. *Truman* — B
    Roll, David L. *Ascent to Power* — 973.918
    Wallace, Chris. *Countdown 1945* — 940.54

TRUMBULL, JOHN, 1756-1843
    Staiti, Paul J. *Of Arms and Artists* — B

TRUMP FAMILY
    Bernstein, Andrea. *American Oligarchs* — 920
    Johnston, David Cay. *The Big Cheat* — 973.933
    Trump, Mary L. *Too Much and Never Enough* — B
Trump on Trial. Sullivan, Kevin — 342.73
Trump Revealed. Kranish, Michael — B

TRUMP, DONALD, 1946-
    Alberta, Tim. *American Carnage* — 324.2734
    Arnsdorf, Isaac. ★*Finish What We Started* — 320.52
    Bade, Rachael. ★*Unchecked* — 342.73
    Baker, Peter. *The Divider* — 973.933
    Baron, Martin. ★*Collision of Power* — 070.4
    Bender, Michael C. *"Frankly, We Did Win This Election"* — 973.933
    Berman, Geoffrey. *Holding the Line* — 345.73
    Bernstein, Andrea. *American Oligarchs* — 920
    Biskupic, Joan. ★*Nine Black Robes* — 347.73
    Bowden, Mark. *The Steal* — 973.933
    Carpenter, Amanda B. *Gaslighting America* — 973.933
    Daniels, Stormy. *Full Disclosure* — B
    Du Mez, Kristin Kobes. *Jesus and John Wayne* — 277.308
    Enrich, David. *Dark Towers* — 332.1
    Frum, David. *Trumpocracy* — 973.933
    Gessen, Masha. *Surviving Autocracy* — 973.933
    Harding, Luke. *Collusion* — 324.70973
    Hennessey, Susan. *Unmaking the Presidency* — 973.933
    Hoffman, Carl. *Liar's Circus* — 973.933
    Hutchinson, Cassidy. *Enough* — B
    Isikoff, Michael. *Russian Roulette* — 973.933
    Johnston, David Cay. *The Big Cheat* — 973.933
    Johnston, David Cay. *It's Even Worse Than You Think* — 973.933

    Jordan, Mary. *The Art of Her Deal* — B
    Karl, Jonathan. *Betrayal* — 973.933
    Karl, Jonathan. *Front Row at the Trump Show* — 973.933
    Karl, Jonathan. *Tired of Winning* — 973.933
    Kranish, Michael. *Trump Revealed* — B
    Kurtz, Howard. *Media Madness* — 973.933
    Leonnig, Carol. *I Alone Can Fix It* — 973.933
    Lithwick, Dahlia. *Lady Justice* — 345.73
    Martin, Jonathan. *This Will Not Pass* — 973.933
    Nance, Malcolm W. *The Plot to Betray America* — 973.933
    Pearlman, Jeff. *Football for a Buck* — 796.332
    Petri, Alexandra. *Nothing Is Wrong and Here Is Why* — 973.933
    Poniewozik, James. *Audience of One* — 324.7
    Rothkopf, David J. *American Resistance* — 973.933
    Schmidt, Michael S. ★*Donald Trump v. The United States* — 973.933
    Shimer, David. *Rigged* — 324.60973
    Souza, Pete. *Shade* — 973.932
    Stelter, Brian. *Hoax* — 070.4
    Stevens, Stuart. *It Was All a Lie* — 324.2734
    Sullivan, Kevin. *Trump on Trial* — 342.73
    Toobin, Jeffrey. *True Crimes and Misdemeanors* — 973.933
    Trump, Mary L. *Too Much and Never Enough* — B
    Walker, Hunter. *The Truce* — 324.2736
    Weiner, Tim. *The Folly and the Glory* — 327.73047
    Weissmann, Andrew. ★*Where Law Ends* — 324.7
    Wilson, Rick. *Running Against the Devil* — B
    Wise, Tim J. *Dispatches from the Race War* — 305.8
    Wolff, Michael. *Fire and Fury* — 973.933
    Wolff, Michael. *Landslide* — 973.933
    Woodward, Bob. *Fear* — 973.933
    Woodward, Bob. *Peril* — 973.933

TRUMP, IVANKA, 1981-
    Bernstein, Andrea. *American Oligarchs* — 920

Trump, Mary L.
    Too Much and Never Enough — B

TRUMP, MELANIA, 1970-
    Jordan, Mary. *The Art of Her Deal* — B

TRUMPET MUSIC (JAZZ)
    Teachout, Terry. *Pops* — B
Trumpocracy. Frum, David — 973.933

Truss, Lynne
    Eats, Shoots & Leaves — 428.2

TRUST
    Brown, Emma. *To Raise a Boy* — 649
    Viren, Sarah. *To Name the Bigger Lie* — B
    Wilson, F. Perry. *How Medicine Works and When It Doesn't* — 610.69
    Wojcicki, Esther. *How to Raise Successful People* — 649

TRUST IN GOD
    Nockels, Christy. *The Life You Long For* — 248.8
    ★*Trust The Plan*. Sommer, Will — 973.933
Trust Women. Peters, Rebecca Todd — 362.1988

TRUTH
    Ariely, Dan. *The Honest Truth About Dishonesty* — 177
    Bilton, Chrysta. *Normal Family* — B
    Dawkins, Richard. *Science in the Soul* — 500
    Erdrich, Heid E. ★*Little Big Bully* — 811
    Hutchinson, Cassidy. *Enough* — B
    Morris, Errol. *Believing Is Seeing* — 770.9
    Popova, Maria. *Figuring* — 920
    Viren, Sarah. *To Name the Bigger Lie* — B
    Wilkman, Jon. *Screening Reality* — 070.1
    Young, Kevin. *Bunk* — 177
Truth & Beauty. Patchett, Ann — B
The Truth About Animals. Cooke, Lucy — 590.2
Truth and Repair. Herman, Judith Lewis — 362.883
Truth in Our Times. McCraw, David Edward — 342.7308
The Truth Will Set You Free, but First It Will Piss You Off. Steinem, Gloria — 305.42

TRUTH, SOJOURNER, D. 1883
    Painter, Nell Irvin. ★*Sojourner Truth* — B

TRUTHFULNESS AND FALSEHOOD
    Campbell, Jeremy. *The Liar's Tale* — 177
    Vedantam, Shankar. *Useful Delusions* — 153.4

Tsu, Jing
    Kingdom of Characters — 495.111

Tsui, Bonnie
    Why We Swim — 797.2
Tsunami vs. the Fukushima 50. Roripaugh, Lee Ann — 811

AUTHOR, TITLE, SERIES AND SUBJECT INDEX

TSUNAMIS
    Deraniyagala, Sonali. *Wave* — B
    Parry, Richard Lloyd. *Ghosts of the Tsunami* — 952.05
    Pilling, David. *Bending Adversity* — 952.0512
    Roripaugh, Lee Ann. *Tsunami vs. the Fukushima 50* — 811
TSUNENO 1804-1853
    Stanley, Amy. *Stranger in the Shogun's City* — B
Tsvetaeva, Marina
    Selected Poems — 891.71
TSVETAEVA, MARINA, 1892-1941
    Tsvetaeva, Marina. *Selected Poems* — 891.71
Tu, Vivian
    Rich Af — 332.024
Tuama, Padraig O.
    ★*Poetry Unbound* — 808.1
TUBA
    White, Richard Antoine. *I'm Possible* — B
TUBA PLAYERS
    White, Richard Antoine. *I'm Possible* — B
Tubbs, Anna Malaika
    The Three Mothers — 306.874
Tubbs, Michael
    The Deeper the Roots — B
TUBBS, MICHAEL, 1990-
    Tubbs, Michael. *The Deeper the Roots* — B
TUBERCULOSIS
    Secrest, Meryle. *Modigliani* — B
TUBMAN, HARRIET, 1820?-1913
    Clinton, Catherine. *Harriet Tubman* — B
    Dunbar, Erica Armstrong. ★*She Came to Slay* — B
    Fields-Black, Edda L. *Combee* — 973.7
    Humez, Jean McMahon. *Harriet Tubman* — B
    Larson, Kate Clifford. *Bound for the Promised Land* — B
    Miles, Tiya. ★*Night Flyer* — B
    Wickenden, Dorothy. *The Agitators* — 920
Tucci, Stanley
    ★*Taste* — B
TUCCI, STANLEY
    Tucci, Stanley. ★*Taste* — B
Tuccille, Jerome
    The Roughest Riders — 973.8
Tuchman, Barbara W.
    ★*A Distant Mirror* — 944
    ★*The Guns of August* — 940.4
    March of Folly — 909.08
    The Proud Tower — 909.82
    Stilwell and the American Experience in China, 1911-45 — B
Tucker, Abigail
    The Lion in the Living Room — 636.8
Tucker, Dennis C.
    Crash Course in Library Supervision — 023
Tucker, Jonathan B.
    War of Nerves — 358
Tucker, Todd
    The Great Starvation Experiment — 174.2
Tucker, Virginia
    Finding the Answers to Legal Questions — 340.072
Tucker, Wallace H.
    Chandra's Cosmos — 523.1
TUCSON, ARIZONA
    Bossiere, Zoe. *Cactus Country* — 306
TUDOR PERIOD (1485-1603)
    Ackroyd, Peter. *Foundation* — 942
    Ackroyd, Peter. *Tudors* — 942.05
    Bergreen, Laurence. *In Search of a Kingdom* — B
    Bordo, Susan. *The Creation of Anne Boleyn* — 942.05
    Borman, Tracy. *Elizabeth's Women* — B
    Borman, Tracy. *Henry VIII and the Men Who Made Him* — 942.05
    Borman, Tracy. *The Private Lives of the Tudors* — 920
    Borman, Tracy. *Thomas Cromwell* — B
    Bremer, Francis J. *John Winthrop* — B
    Fraser, Antonia. *Mary, Queen of Scots* — B
    Goodman, Ruth. *How to Be a Tudor* — 942.05
    Gristwood, Sarah. *Blood Sisters* — 942.04092
    Gristwood, Sarah. *The Tudors in Love* — 941.05
    Kaufmann, Miranda. *Black Tudors* — 941
    Lacey, Robert. *Great Tales from English History 2* — 941
    Lovell, Mary S. *Bess of Hardwick* — B

    Meyer, G. J. *The Tudors* — 920
    Mortimer, Ian. *The Time Traveler's Guide to Elizabethan England* — 942.05
    Paranque, Estelle. *Blood, Fire & Gold* — 920
    Porter, Linda. *Katherine the Queen* — B
    Ronald, Susan. *The Pirate Queen* — B
    Rounding, Virginia. *The Burning Time* — 272
    Starkey, David. *Six Wives* — 942.05
    Tallis, Nicola. *Crown of Blood* — B
    Tallis, Nicola. *Uncrowned Queen* — B
    Weir, Alison. *The Children of Henry VIII* — B
    Weir, Alison. *Henry VIII* — B
    Weir, Alison. *The Life of Elizabeth I* — B
    Weir, Alison. *The Lost Tudor Princess* — B
    Weir, Alison. *The Six Wives of Henry VIII* — 942.05
    Weir, Alison. *The Wars of the Roses* — 942.04
Tudor, Daniel
    North Korea Confidential — 951.93
TUDOR, HOUSE OF
    Borman, Tracy. *Anne Boleyn and Elizabeth I* — 920
    Borman, Tracy. *The Private Lives of the Tudors* — 920
    Goodman, Ruth. *How to Be a Tudor* — 942.05
    Gristwood, Sarah. *The Tudors in Love* — 941.05
    Jones, Dan. ★*The Wars of the Roses* — 942.04
    Meyer, G. J. *The Tudors* — 920
    Tallis, Nicola. *Crown of Blood* — B
    Tallis, Nicola. *Uncrowned Queen* — B
    Weir, Alison. *The Children of Henry VIII* — B
Tudors. Ackroyd, Peter — 942.05
The Tudors. Meyer, G. J. — 920
The Tudors in Love. Gristwood, Sarah — 941.05
Tuerkheimer, Deborah
    Credible — 363.25
Tuesday Nights Mediterranean. Kimball, Christopher — 641.59
Tuesdays with Morrie. Albom, Mitch — B
Tufte, Edward R.
    The Visual Display of Quantitative Information — 001.4
Tulleken, Chris van
    Ultra-Processed People — 664
TULSA RACE MASSACRE, TULSA, OKLAHOMA, 1921
    Ellsworth, Scott. *The Ground Breaking* — 976.6
    Luckerson, Victor. *Built from the Fire* — 976.6
    Young, R. J. *Requiem for the Massacre* — 305.8
TULSA, OKLAHOMA
    Ellsworth, Scott. *The Ground Breaking* — 976.6
    Hirsch, James S. *Riot and Remembrance* — 976.6
    Luckerson, Victor. *Built from the Fire* — 976.6
    Madigan, Tim. *The Burning* — 976.6
    Young, R. J. *Requiem for the Massacre* — 305.8
TUMORS
    Fung, Jason. ★*The Cancer Code* — 616.99
Tumulty, Karen
    The Triumph of Nancy Reagan — B
Tuna. Ellis, Richard — 333.95
TUNA
    Ellis, Richard. *Tuna* — 333.95
    Greenberg, Paul. *Four Fish* — 333.95
TUNISIA
    Atkinson, Rick. *An Army at Dawn* — 940.54
★*Tunnel 29*. Merriman, Helena — 943
The Tunnel At the End of the Light. Shepard, Jim — 791.43
TUNNELING
    Vogel, Steve. *Betrayal in Berlin* — 327.1273043
TUNNELS
    Hunt, Will. *Underground* — 624.1
    Lawler, Andrew. *Under Jerusalem* — 956.94
    Merriman, Helena. ★*Tunnel 29* — 943
    Vogel, Steve. *Betrayal in Berlin* — 327.1273043
Tunstall, Tricia
    Changing Lives — 780.71
★*Tupac Shakur*. Robinson, Staci — B
Tur, Katy
    Rough Draft — B
TUR, KATY, 1983-
    Tur, Katy. *Rough Draft* — B
Turabian, Kate L
    Student's Guide to Writing College Papers — 808.06
Turan, Kenneth
    ★*Free for All* — B

PUBLIC LIBRARY CORE COLLECTION: NONFICTION
Twentieth Edition

Not to Be Missed	791.43
Turban, Jack L.	
★*Free to Be*	616.85
Turbow, Jason	
The Baseball Codes	796.357
They Bled Blue	796.357
Turchin, Peter	
End Times	320.01
TURGENEV, IVAN SERGEEVICH, 1818-1883	
Figes, Orlando. *The Europeans*	920
Saunders, George. ★*A Swim in a Pond in the Rain*	891.7
TURIN, ITALY	
Moorehead, Caroline. *A House in the Mountains*	940.53
Turing. Copeland, B. Jack	B
Turing's Cathedral. Dyson, George	004
TURING, ALAN MATHISON, 1912-1954	
Copeland, B. Jack. *Turing*	B
Dyson, George. *Turing's Cathedral*	004
Leavitt, David. *The Man Who Knew Too Much*	B
Price, David A. *Geniuses at War*	940.54
Turk, Katherine	
The Women of Now	305.42
TURKEY	
Ackerman, Elliot. *Places and Names*	B
Akcam, Taner. *A Shameful Act*	956.6
Anderson, Scott. *Lawrence in Arabia*	B
Balakian, Peter. *The Burning Tigris*	956.6
Bogosian, Eric. *Operation Nemesis*	956.62
Crowley, Roger. *1453*	949.61
Finkel, Caroline. *Osman's Dream*	956.1
Fox, Margalit. *The Confidence Men*	940.4
Kassabova, Kapka. *Border*	949.9
King, Charles. *Midnight at the Pera Palace*	949.61
Mackeen, Dawn Anahid. *The Hundred-Year Walk*	956.6
Madden, Thomas F. *Istanbul*	949.61
Mikhail, Alan. *God's Shadow*	B
Pamuk, Orhan. *Istanbul*	949.61
Rogan, Eugene L. *The Fall of the Ottomans*	940.3
Von Bremzen, Anya. *National Dish*	641.3
Turkey and the Wolf. Hereford, Mason	641.5976
Turn Right at Machu Picchu. Adams, Mark	985
TURNAGE, WALLACE, 1846-1916	
Blight, David W. *A Slave No More*	B
The Turnaway Study. Foster, Diana Greene	362.1988
Turnbow, Dominique	
★*Demystifying Online Instruction in Libraries*	028.7
Turner. Moyle, Franny	B
Turner Classic Movies. Arnold, Jeremy	791.43
Turner, Alice K.	
The History of Hell	236
TURNER, FREDERICK JACKSON, 1861-1932	
Grandin, Greg. *The End of the Myth*	973
TURNER, J. M. W., 1775-1851	
Moyle, Franny. *Turner*	B
Turner, John G.	
Brigham Young, Pioneer Prophet	B
TURNER, KIM, 1968-1994	
Trice, Dawn Turner. ★*Three Girls from Bronzeville*	977.311
Turner, Sharon	
Teach Yourself Visually Knitting	746.43
TURNER, TED	
Auletta, Ken. *Media Man*	B
Napoli, Lisa. *Up All Night*	384.55
Turner, Tiffanie	
The Fine Art of Paper Flowers	745.92
Turner, Tina	
★*Happiness Becomes You*	158.1
TURNER, TINA, 1939-2023	
Turner, Tina. ★*Happiness Becomes You*	158.1
Turney, Chris	
1912	998
Turning Pointe. Angyal, Chloe	792.8
Turnip Greens & Tortillas. Hernandez, Eddie	641.5972
The Turnip Princess. Schonwerth, Franz Xaver von	398.2
Turow, Scott	
★*Ultimate Punishment*	345.73
TURPIN, DAVID ALLEN, 1961-	
Glatt, John. *The Family Next Door*	362.76092
TURPIN, LOUISE ANN, 1968-	
Glatt, John. *The Family Next Door*	362.76092
Turshen, Julia	
Feed the Resistance	641.5
Now & Again	641.5
Simply Julia	641.3
Small Victories	641.5
TURTLES	
Montgomery, Sy. ★*Of Time and Turtles*	597.92
Turvey, Samuel	
★*The Tomb of the Mili Mongga*	398.24
TUSCANY, ITALY	
Mayes, Frances. *Bella Tuscany*	945
Mayes, Frances. *Under the Tuscan Sun*	945
TUTANKHAMEN, KING OF EGYPT	
Brier, Bob. *The Murder of Tutankhamen*	B
TUTSI (AFRICAN PEOPLE)	
Dogon, Mondiant. *Those We Throw Away Are Diamonds*	B
Gourevitch, Philip. *We Wish to Inform You That Tomorrow We Will Be Killed with Our Families*	364.15
Hatzfeld, Jean. *Blood Papa*	967.5710431
Hatzfeld, Jean. *Machete Season*	967.57104
Tutu, Desmond	
The Book of Forgiving	179
Made for Goodness	170
★*TV (the Book)*. Sepinwall, Alan	791.45
TVERSKY, AMOS	
Lewis, Michael. ★*The Undoing Project*	920
Twain, Mark	
Autobiography of Mark Twain	B
★*Autobiography of Mark Twain*	B
★*Autobiography of Mark Twain*	B
TWAIN, MARK, 1835-1910	
Kinzer, Stephen. ★*The True Flag*	327.73
Nafisi, Azar. *The Republic of Imagination*	B
Shelden, Michael. *Mark Twain*	B
Twain, Mark. *Autobiography of Mark Twain*	B
Twain, Mark. ★*Autobiography of Mark Twain*	B
Twain, Mark. ★*Autobiography of Mark Twain*	B
Tweedy, Damon	
Facing the Unseen	362.2
TWEEDY, DAMON	
Tweedy, Damon. *Facing the Unseen*	362.2
Tweedy, Jeff	
How to Write One Song	782.42
Let's Go (so We Can Get Back)	B
TWEEDY, JEFF, 1967-	
Tweedy, Jeff. *Let's Go (so We Can Get Back)*	B
Twelve Angry Men. Rose, Reginald	812
★*The Twelve Caesars*. Suetonius	B
Twelve Patients. Manheimer, Eric	362.1109747
Twelve Steps to a Compassionate Life. Armstrong, Karen	177
Twelve Trees. Lewis, Daniel	582.16
Twelve Years a Slave. Northup, Solomon	B
TWELVE-STEP PROGRAMS	
Armstrong, Karen. *Twelve Steps to a Compassionate Life*	177
Whitaker, Holly. ★*Quit Like a Woman*	616.86
TWELVE-YEAR-OLD GIRLS	
Hale, Kathleen. ★*Slenderman*	364.152
Twenge, Jean M.	
Generations	305.2
TWENTIES (AGE)	
Jaouad, Suleika. ★*Between Two Kingdoms*	B
Sandler, Lauren. *This Is All I Got*	B
Wiener, Anna. ★*Uncanny Valley*	B
Twentieth-Century Art of Latin America. Barnitz, Jacqueline	709.8
Twentieth-Century Man. Wallace, Christopher	B
★*Twenty Love Poems and a Song of Despair*. Neruda, Pablo	861
The Twenty-Ninth Day. Messenger, Alex	B
TWENTY-ONE-YEAR-OLD MEN	
Burcaw, Shane. ★*Laughing at My Nightmare*	B
Twenty-Six Seconds. Zapruder, Alexandra	973.922092
Twice as Hard. Brown, Jasmine	610.92
Twilight of Democracy. Applebaum, Anne	321.9
Twilight of Empire. King, Greg	943.6
Twilight of the Gods. Hyden, Steven	781.6609
Twilight of the Gods. Toll, Ian W.	940.54

AUTHOR, TITLE, SERIES AND SUBJECT INDEX

Twilley, Nicola
  ★*Frostbite* — 621
TWIN BROTHERS
  Markham, Lauren. ★*The Far Away Brothers* — 920
TWIN SISTERS
  De Bres, Helena. *How to Be Multiple* — 155.44
  Hager, Jenna Bush. *Sisters First* — B
  Hayasaki, Erika. *Somewhere Sisters* — 362.7
  Quin, Tegan. ★*High School* — B
TWINS
  De Bres, Helena. *How to Be Multiple* — 155.44
  Kouchner, Camille. *The Familia Grande* — B
Twisted. Dabiri, Emma — 391.5
Twitty, Michael
  ★*The Cooking Gene* — 641.59
  ★*Koshersoul* — 641.5
TWITTY, MICHAEL, 1977-
  Twitty, Michael. ★*Koshersoul* — 641.5
Two Days in June. Cohen, Andrew — 973.922
The Two Koreas 3rd Ed. Oberdorfer, Don — 951.904
Two Old Broads. Hecht, M. E. — 613
Two Roads Home. Finkelstein, Daniel — 920
Two Sisters. Seierstad, Asne — 956.9104
Two Trains Running. Wilson, August — 812
Two Truths and a Lie. McGarrahan, Ellen — 364.152
Two Wheels Good. Rosen, Jody — 629.227
Two Years Before the Mast. Dana, Richard Henry — 910.4
TWO-PARTY SYSTEMS
  Martin, Jonathan. *This Will Not Pass* — 973.933
TWO-SPIRIT PEOPLE
  LaPointe, Sasha taqwseblu. *Thunder Song* — 814
Twomey, Steve
  Countdown to Pearl Harbor — 940.54
Tworkov, Helen
  Lotus Girl — B
TWORKOV, HELEN
  Tworkov, Helen. *Lotus Girl* — B
Tychonievich, Joseph
  Rock Gardening — 635.9
Tye, Larry
  ★*Bobby Kennedy* — B
  ★*Demagogue* — B
  ★*The Jazzmen* — 781.6509
  Satchel — B
TYLER, JOHN, 1790-1862
  Cohen, Jared. *Accidental Presidents* — 973.09
  May, Gary. *John Tyler* — B
TYPE AND TYPE-FOUNDING
  Houston, Keith. *Shady Characters* — 411
  Porter, Carolyn. *Marcel's Letters* — 940.54
TYPHOID FEVER
  Allen, Arthur. ★*The Fantastic Laboratory of Dr. Weigl* — 614.5
TYPOLOGY (PSYCHOLOGY)
  Myers, Isabel Briggs. *Gifts Differing* — 155.2
★*Tyranny of the Gene*. Tabery, James — 572.8
Tyson, Cicely
  ★*Just as I Am* — B
TYSON, CICELY, 1924-2021
  Tyson, Cicely. ★*Just as I Am* — B
Tyson, Mike
  Iron Ambition — B
TYSON, MIKE, 1966-
  Tyson, Mike. *Iron Ambition* — B
Tyson, Neil deGrasse
  Accessory to War — 355.001
  ★*Astrophysics for People in a Hurry* — 523.01
  Cosmic Queries — 523.1
  Letters from an Astrophysicist — 520.92
  Space Chronicles — 629.40973
  Starry Messenger — 901
  Startalk — 523.1
  To Infinity and Beyond — 520
  Welcome to the Universe — 523.1
TYSON, NEIL DEGRASSE
  Tyson, Neil deGrasse. *Letters from an Astrophysicist* — 520.92
Tyson, Timothy B.
  Blood Done Sign My Name — 975.6
  The Blood of Emmett Till — 364.1
TYSON, TIMOTHY B.
  Tyson, Timothy B. *Blood Done Sign My Name* — 975.6

U

U-2 (JET RECONNAISSANCE PLANE)
  Sherman, Casey. *Above and Beyond* — 973.922092
The U.S. Constitution A to Z. Maddex, Robert L. — 342.730203
U.S. STATES
  Brands, H. W. *The Age of Gold* — 979.4
  Heat Moon, William Least. *Roads to Quoz* — 917.3
  Pawel, Miriam. *The Browns of California* — 920
  Wright, Lawrence. *God Save Texas* — 917.64
UDHAM SINGH, 1899-1940
  Anand, Anita. *The Patient Assassin* — B
UFO. Graff, Garrett M. — 001.942
UFO ABDUCTIONS
  Mezrich, Ben. *The 37th Parallel* — 001.942
UFOS
  Graff, Garrett M. *UFO* — 001.942
  Loeb, Abraham. *Extraterrestrial* — 576.8
  Mezrich, Ben. *The 37th Parallel* — 001.942
  Prothero, Donald R. *UFOs, Chemtrails, and Aliens* — 001.94
  Scoles, Sarah. *They Are Already Here* — 001.942
UFOs, Chemtrails, and Aliens. Prothero, Donald R. — 001.94
UGAKI, MATOME, 1890-1945
  Thomas, Evan. *Sea of Thunder* — 940.54
UGLINESS
  Eco, Umberto. *On Ugliness* — 111
★*The Ugly Cry*. Henderson, Danielle — B
UIGHUR (TURKIC PEOPLE)
  Haitiwaji, Gulbahar. *How I Survived a Chinese "Reeducation" Camp* — 305.8
  Hoja, Gulchehra. *A Stone Is Most Precious Where It Belongs* — B
  Izgil, Tahir Hamut. *Waiting to Be Arrested at Night* — B
Ujifusa, Steven
  Barons of the Sea — 387.5
UKRAINE
  Applebaum, Anne. ★*Red Famine* — 947.708
  Chiger, Krystyna. *The Girl in the Green Sweater* — B
  Foer, Esther Safran. *I Want You to Know We're Still Here* — B
  Harding, Luke. *Invasion* — 947.7
  Higginbotham, Adam. ★*Midnight in Chernobyl* — 363.17
  Igort. *The Ukrainian and Russian Notebooks* — 741.5
  Klopotenko, Yevhen. ★*The Authentic Ukrainian Kitchen* — 641.594
  Miller, Christopher. *The War Came to Us* — 947.7
  Pavlychenko, Liudmyla Mykhailivna. *Lady Death* — B
  Plokhy, Serhii. ★*The Gates of Europe* — 947.7
  Plokhy, Serhii. *Lost Kingdom* — 947
  Plokhy, Serhii. ★*The Russo-Ukrainian War* — 947.7
  Shuster, Simon. ★*The Showman* — B
  Snyder, Timothy. *The Red Prince* — B
  Sullivan, Kevin. *Trump on Trial* — 342.73
  Trofimov, Yaroslav. ★*Our Enemies Will Vanish* — 947.7
  Zelensky, Volodymyr. *A Message from Ukraine* — 947.7
The Ukrainian and Russian Notebooks. Igort — 741.5
UKRAINIAN PEOPLE
  Harss, Marina. *The Boy from Kyiv* — B
  Klopotenko, Yevhen. ★*The Authentic Ukrainian Kitchen* — 641.594
  Masters, Oksana. *The Hard Parts* — B
  Plokhy, Serhii. ★*The Russo-Ukrainian War* — 947.7
Ulander, Perry A.
  Walking Point — B
ULANDER, PERRY A., 1948-2023
  Ulander, Perry A. *Walking Point* — B
Ullman, Ellen
  Life in Code — B
ULLMAN, ELLEN
  Ullman, Ellen. *Life in Code* — B
ULLMANN, OTTO, 1925-2005
  Asbrink, Elisabeth. *And in the Vienna Woods the Trees Remain* — B
Ullrich, Volker
  ★*Eight Days in May* — 943.086
  Germany 1923 — 943.085
  Hitler — B
  Hitler — B
★*The Ultimate Bicycle Owner's Manual*. Weiss, Eben — 796.6
The Ultimate Book of Family Card Games. Ho, Oliver — 795.4

PUBLIC LIBRARY CORE COLLECTION: NONFICTION
Twentieth Edition

Ultimate Crochet Bible. Crowfoot, Jane	746.43
The *Ultimate* Flower Gardener's Guide. Carey, Jenny Rose	635.9
Ultimate Glory. Gessner, David	796.2
Ultimate Guide. Cory, Steve	690
Ultimate Guide Home Repair and Improvement. Byers, Charles T.	643
The *Ultimate* Guide to Great Reggae. Garnice, Michael	781.646
The *Ultimate* Picasso. Leal, Brigitte	B
★*Ultimate* Punishment. Turow, Scott	345.73
The *Ultimate* Quotable Einstein. Einstein, Albert	530.092
★The *Ultimate* Retirement Guide for 50+. Orman, Suze	306.3
Ultimate Star Wars. Barr, Patricia	791.43
The *Ultimate* Thread Guide. Goldsmith, Becky	677
★The *Ultimate* Unofficial Encyclopedia for Minecrafters. Miller, Megan	794.8
Ultra-Processed People. Tulleken, Chris van	664
ULTRAMARATHON RUNNERS	
Engle, Charlie. *Running Man*	B
Finn, Adharanand. *The Rise of the Ultra Runners*	B
ULTRAMARATHON RUNNING	
Engle, Charlie. *Running Man*	B
Finn, Adharanand. *The Rise of the Ultra Runners*	B
McDougall, Christopher. ★*Born to Run*	796.42
Ulysses S. Grant. Bunting, Josiah	B
Umah-Shaylor, Lerato	
Africana	641.596
Umar, Ousman	
North to Paradise	B
UMAR, OUSMAN	
Umar, Ousman. *North to Paradise*	B
Un-American. Cahan, Richard	940.53
Un-American. Edstrom, Erik	B
Un-American. Geter, Hafizah	811
UNACCOMPANIED IMMIGRANT CHILDREN	
Markham, Lauren. ★*The Far Away Brothers*	920
Zamora, Javier. ★*Solito*	B
Unapologetic. Carruthers, Charlene A.	305.48
The *Unbanking* of America. Servon, Lisa J.	332.10973
★*Unbeaten*. Stanton, Mike	B
★*Unbound*. Burke, Tarana	B
Unbowed. Maathai, Wangari	B
Unbreakable. Askwith, Richard	B
★*Unbroken*. Hillenbrand, Laura	B
Unbroken Chains. Ditmore, Melissa Hope	306.74
★*Uncanny Valley*. Wiener, Anna	B
Uncertain Ground. Klay, Phil	359.9
Uncertain Justice. Tribe, Laurence H.	342.73
UNCERTAINTY	
Berg, Anastasia. ★*What Are Children For?*	306.87
Harris, Taylor. *This Boy We Made*	B
McLaren, Brian D. *Life After Doom*	200.1
Nordland, Rod. *Waiting for the Monsoon*	B
O'Hara, Maryanne. *Little Matches*	B
O'Rourke, Meghan. ★*The Invisible Kingdom*	616
Shaughnessy, Brenda. *The Octopus Museum*	811
Zambreno, Kate. *The Light Room*	B
★*Unchecked*. Bade, Rachael	342.73
★The *Unclaimed*. Prickett, Pamela J.	363.7
UNCLE AND NEPHEW	
Lewis, C. S. ★*The Screwtape Letters*	248.4
Uncle of the Year. Rannells, Andrew	B
UNCLES	
Danticat, Edwidge. ★*Brother, I'm Dying*	B
Lewis, C. S. ★*The Screwtape Letters*	248.4
Uncommon Carriers. McPhee, John	388
Uncommon People. Hepworth, David	B
UNCONDITIONAL LOVE	
Alexander, Kwame. *Why Fathers Cry at Night*	B
Boylan, Jennifer Finney. *Good Boy*	B
Golbeck, Jennifer. *The Purest Bond*	636.7
Harpham, Heather Elise. *Happiness*	B
The *Unconquered*. Wallace, Scott	981
UNCONSCIOUS BIAS	
Agarwal, Pragya. *Sway*	177
Baxley, Traci. *Social Justice Parenting*	649
Eberhardt, Jennifer L. ★*Biased*	303.3
Fuller, Pamela. ★*The Leader's Guide to Unconscious Bias*	658.3
Headlee, Celeste Anne. *Speaking of Race*	305.8
Livingston, Robert W. *The Conversation*	305.8
Marcal, Katrine. *Mother of Invention*	604.82
Montell, Amanda. ★*The Age of Magical Overthinking*	153.4
Mukantabana, Yseult P. ★*Real Friends Talk About Race*	305.8
Pryce, Jessica. ★*Broken*	362.7
Ritchie, Stuart. *Science Fictions*	500
Saad, Layla F. ★*Me and White Supremacy*	305.809
Tuerkheimer, Deborah. *Credible*	363.25
Williams, Sophie. *Anti-Racist Ally*	305.8
Wingfield, Adia Harvey. *Gray Areas*	331.6
UNCONVENTIONAL WARFARE	
Arnold, James R. *Jungle of Snakes*	355.02
Beschloss, Michael R. ★*Presidents of War*	355.00973
Boot, Max. *Invisible Armies*	355.02
Finkel, David. *The Good Soldiers*	956.7044
Gopal, Anand. *No Good Men Among the Living*	920
Hoffman, Bruce. *Anonymous Soldiers*	956.94
Kix, Paul. *The Saboteur*	940.53
Romesha, Clinton. *Red Platoon*	958.104
Stanton, Doug. *12 Strong*	958.104
The *Uncrowned* King. Whyte, Kenneth	B
Uncrowned Queen. Tallis, Nicola	B
Uncultured. Young, Daniella Mestyanek	B
Undaunted. Kroeger, Brooke	070.4
★*Undaunted* Courage. Ambrose, Stephen E.	917.804
Undecided. Morgan, Genevieve	331.702
Undeniable. Nye, Bill	576.8
★*Under* A White Sky. Kolbert, Elizabeth	304.2
Under Alien Skies. Plait, Philip C.	520
Under Another Sky. Higgins, Charlotte	936
Under Jerusalem. Lawler, Andrew	956.94
Under Milk Wood. Thomas, Dylan	822.91
Under My Skin. Lessing, Doris May	823
★*Under* Pressure. Damour, Lisa	155.5
Under Pressure. Humphreys, Richard	B
Under Red Skies. Kan, Karoline	B
Under The Black Flag. Cordingly, David	910.4
Under The Knife. Laar, Arnold van de	617
Under The Lights and in the Dark. Oxenham, Gwendolyn	796.334
Under The Naga Tail. Taing, Mae Bunseng	B
Under The Sea Wind. Carson, Rachel	578.77
★*Under* The Skin. Villarosa, Linda	362.1089
Under The Stars. White, Dan	796.54
Under The Tuscan Sun. Mayes, Frances	945
UNDERCLASS	
Land, Stephanie. *Maid*	B
Undercooked. Ahdoot, Dan	647.95
UNDERCOVER OPERATIONS	
Bailey, Catherine. *A Castle in Wartime*	943.086
Cox, Joseph. *Dark Wire*	363.2
Croke, Ken. *Riding with Evil*	364.106
De Leon, Jason. ★*Soldiers and Kings*	364.1
Fairweather, Jack. *The Volunteer*	B
Fox, Amaryllis. *Life Undercover*	B
Friedman, Matti. *Spies of No Country*	327.12
Hemming, Henry. *Agents of Influence*	940.54
Henderson, Bruce B. *Bridge to the Sun*	940.53
Hurowitz, Richard. *In the Garden of the Righteous*	940.53
Jacobsen, Annie. *Surprise, Kill, Vanish*	327.1273
Johnson, Steven. *The Infernal Machine*	335
Lane, Charles. *Freedom's Detective*	B
Lehr, Dick. *White Hot Hate*	363.325
Maier, Thomas. *Mafia Spies*	364.1060973
Mazzeo, Tilar J. *Sisters in Resistance*	945.091
Mendez, Antonio J. *Argo*	955.05
Purnell, Sonia. ★*A Woman of No Importance*	B
Renner, Rebecca. ★*Gator Country*	364.16
Rosenzweig, Laura B. *Hollywood's Spies*	791.43
Shannon, Elaine. *Hunting Leroux*	364.1
Shimer, David. *Rigged*	324.60973
Shultz, Richard H. *The Secret War Against Hanoi*	959.704
Talty, Stephan. *The Good Assassin*	364.15
Todd, Kim. *Sensational*	920
Vogel, Steve. *Betrayal in Berlin*	327.1273043
UNDERCOVER WILDLIFE AGENTS	
Renner, Rebecca. ★*Gator Country*	364.16
Underestimated. Goodan, Chelsey	305.235
Underground. Hunt, Will	624.1
Underground. Rudd, Mark	378.1
Underground. Murakami, Haruki	364.15

AUTHOR, TITLE, SERIES AND SUBJECT INDEX

UNDERGROUND AREAS
   Hunt, Will. *Underground* — 624.1
   Tabor, James M. *Blind Descent* — 796.52

UNDERGROUND CONSTRUCTION
   Hunt, Will. *Underground* — 624.1
   Langewiesche, William. *American Ground* — 974.7

The Underground Girls of Kabul. Nordberg, Jenny — 305.3
Underground in Berlin. Simon, Marie — B
The Underground Is Massive. Matos, Michaelangelo — 781.648

UNDERGROUND PRESS PUBLICATIONS
   Ostertag, Bob. *People's Movements, People's Press* — 071

The Underground Railroad. Snodgrass, Mary Ellen — 973.7

UNDERGROUND RAILROAD
   Bordewich, Fergus M. *Bound for Canaan* — 973.7
   Clinton, Catherine. *Harriet Tubman* — B
   Dunbar, Erica Armstrong. ★*She Came to Slay* — B
   Foner, Eric. ★*Gateway to Freedom* — 973.7
   Humez, Jean McMahon. *Harriet Tubman* — B
   Larson, Kate Clifford. *Bound for the Promised Land* — B
   Miles, Tiya. ★*Night Flyer* — B
   Shane, Scott. ★*Flee North* — 973.7
   Snodgrass, Mary Ellen. *The Underground Railroad* — 973.7
   Tobin, Jacqueline. *From Midnight to Dawn* — 973.7
   Tobin, Jacqueline. *Hidden in Plain View* — 973.7
   Wickenden, Dorothy. *The Agitators* — 920

UNDERSTANDING (PERSONAL QUALITY)
   Angelou, Maya. *Wouldn't Take Nothing for My Journey Now* — 814
   Brooks, David. ★*How to Know a Person* — 158.2

★*Understanding Comics.* McCloud, Scott — 741.5
Understanding Exposure. Peterson, Bryan — 771
Understanding Islam. Gordon, Matthew — 297
Understanding The Book of Mormon. Hardy, Grant — 289.3
Understanding The Palestinian-Israeli Conflict. Bennis, Phyllis — 956.9405
Understanding The World. Rendgen, Sandra — 741.6
Understanding World Religions. Hexham, Irving — 200

UNDERTAKERS
   Bechdel, Alison. ★*Fun Home* — 741.5
   Doughty, Caitlin. *Smoke Gets in Your Eyes* — B
   Doughty, Caitlin. *Will My Cat Eat My Eyeballs?* — 306.9
   Mitford, Jessica. ★*The American Way of Death Revisited* — 338.4
   Prickett, Pamela J. ★*The Unclaimed* — 363.7

★*The Undertow.* Sharlet, Jeff — 322

UNDERWATER ARCHAEOLOGISTS
   Bound, Mensun. *The Ship Beneath the Ice* — 919.8904

UNDERWATER ARCHAEOLOGY
   Gibbins, David J. L. *A History of the World in Twelve Shipwrecks* — 909
   Lance, Rachel. *In the Waves* — 973.7
   Stone, Daniel. *Sinkable* — 910.91

UNDERWATER EXPLORATION
   Ballard, Robert D. *Into the Deep* — 551.46092
   Gibbins, David J. L. *A History of the World in Twelve Shipwrecks* — 909
   Kingdon, Amorina. ★*Sing Like Fish* — 591.77
   Kurson, Robert. *Pirate Hunters* — 910.91
   Mearns, David L. *The Shipwreck Hunter* — 910.452
   Widder, Edith. *Below the Edge of Darkness* — 551.46092

UNDERWATER PHOTOGRAPHY
   Rotman, Jeffrey L. *The Last Fisherman* — 778.7

UNDERWATER WARFARE
   Lance, Rachel. *Chamber Divers* — 940.54

Underwood, Kiana
   Color Me Floral — 745.92

The Underworld. Casey, Susan — 551.46
The Undiscovered Paul Robeson. Robeson, Paul — B
★*The Undocumented Americans.* Cornejo Villavicencio, Karla — 920

UNDOCUMENTED IMMIGRANTS
   Bobrow-Strain, Aaron. *The Death and Life of Aida Hernandez* — 972
   Cantu, Francisco. *The Line Becomes a River* — B
   Cornejo Villavicencio, Karla. ★*The Undocumented Americans* — 920
   Davis, Joshua. *Spare Parts* — 629.8
   Franklin, Jonathan. *438 Days* — 910.91
   Hernandez Castillo, Marcelo. *Children of the Land* — B
   Hobbs, Jeff. *Show Them You're Good* — 373
   Luiselli, Valeria. *Tell Me How It Ends* — 305.23086
   Markham, Lauren. ★*The Far Away Brothers* — 920
   Olivares, Efren C. *My Boy Will Die of Sorrow* — 305.9
   Pablo Cruz, Rosayra. *The Book of Rosy* — B
   Soboroff, Jacob. ★*Separated* — 325.73
   Urrea, Luis Alberto. *The Devil's Highway* — 304.8

   Vargas, Jose Antonio. *Dear America* — B
   Wang, Qian Julie. ★*Beautiful Country* — B
   Wides-Munoz, Laura. *The Making of a Dream* — 920

UNDOCUMENTED WORKERS
   Cornejo Villavicencio, Karla. ★*The Undocumented Americans* — 920
   Urrea, Luis Alberto. *The Devil's Highway* — 304.8

★*The Undoing Project.* Lewis, Michael — 920
The Undressing. Lee, Li-Young — 811
★*Undue Burden.* Luthra, Shefali — 362.1988
The Undying. Boyer, Anne — B
Uneducated. Zara, Christopher — B

UNEMPLOYMENT
   Georges, Gigi. *Downeast* — 974.1
   Goldstein, Amy. *Janesville* — 330.9775
   Kim, Anne. ★*Abandoned* — 305.2350973

Unexampled Courage. Gergel, Richard — 323.1196
★*The Unexpected.* Oster, Emily — 618.2
Unexpected Afghans. Chachula, Robyn — 746.43
The Unexpected Houseplant. Martin, Tovah — 635.9
The Unexpected Spy. Walder, Tracy — B
Unexplained. Smith, Richard MacLean — 130
Unfaithful Music & Disappearing Ink. Costello, Elvis — B
An Unfinished Life. Dallek, Robert — B
★*An Unfinished Love Story.* Goodwin, Doris Kearns — B
The Unfit Heiress. Farley, Audrey Clare — B
Unfollow Me. Busby, Jill Louise — 305.08
Unforgetting. Lovato, Roberto — B
Unforgivable Blackness. Ward, Geoffrey C. — B
★*Unfortunately, It Was Paradise.* Darwish, Mamoud — 892

UNG, CHOU
   Ung, Loung. *Lucky Child* — B

Ung, Loung
   First They Killed My Father — 959.604
   Lucky Child — B

UNG, LOUNG
   Ung, Loung. *First They Killed My Father* — 959.604
   Ung, Loung. *Lucky Child* — B

Unger, Debi
   George Marshall — B

Unger, Harlow G.
   American Tempest — 973.3
   First Founding Father — B
   The Last Founding Father — B

Unger, Miles
   ★*Michelangelo* — B
   Picasso and the Painting That Shocked the World — 759.4

★*The Ungrateful Refugee.* Nayeri, Dina — 362.87
Unguarded. Pippen, Scottie — B

UNHAPPINESS
   Case, Anne. *Deaths of Despair and the Future of Capitalism* — 362.28
   Norris, Kathleen. *Acedia & Me* — 248.8
   Senior, Jennifer. *All Joy and No Fun* — 306.874

The Unidentified. Dickey, Colin — 130

UNIFIED FIELD THEORIES
   Hawking, Stephen. ★*Black Holes and Baby Universes and Other Essays* — 530.1

Unincorporated Persons in the Late Honda Dynasty. Hoagland, Tony — 811
The Uninhabitable Earth. Wallace-Wells, David — 304.2

UNION SOLDIERS
   Ash, Stephen V. *Firebrand of Liberty* — 973.7
   Blanton, DeAnne. *They Fought Like Demons* — 973.7
   Fields-Black, Edda L. *Combee* — 973.7
   Lineberry, Cate. *Be Free or Die* — B
   McPherson, James M. *For Cause and Comrades* — 973.7
   Wheelan, Joseph. ★*Terrible Swift Sword* — B
   Willis, Deborah. ★*The Black Civil War Soldier* — 973.7

Union, Gabrielle
   We're Going to Need More Wine — B
   You Got Anything Stronger? — B

UNION, GABRIELLE
   Union, Gabrielle. *We're Going to Need More Wine* — B
   Union, Gabrielle. *You Got Anything Stronger?* — B

UNIONISTS (UNITED STATES CIVIL WAR)
   Williams, David. *Bitterly Divided* — 973.7

★*Uniquely Human.* Prizant, Barry M. — 618.92

UNITED AIRLINES FLIGHT 93 HIJACKING INCIDENT, 2001
   Zuckoff, Mitchell. ★*Fall and Rise* — 973.931

PUBLIC LIBRARY CORE COLLECTION: NONFICTION
Twentieth Edition

UNITED STATES

Abdul Rauf, Feisal. *Moving the Mountain*	297
Abdurraqib, Hanif. ★*A Little Devil in America*	791.089
Abrahamian, Ervand. *The Coup*	955.05
Abrams, Dan. *Kennedy's Avenger*	973.922
Abrams, Jonathan P. D. ★*The Come Up*	782.421649
Abrams, Stacey. *Our Time Is Now*	324.60973
Abramson, John. *Sickening*	338.4
Achorn, Edward. *The Lincoln Miracle*	973.6
Ackerman, Spencer. *Reign of Terror*	973.931
Ackmann, Martha. *The Mercury 13*	920
Ackmann, Martha. ★*These Fevered Days*	B
Ackroyd, Peter. *Charlie Chaplin*	B
Adams, Abigail. *Abigail Adams*	973.4
Adams, John. *Hallelujah Junction*	B
Adams, John. *My Dearest Friend*	973.4
Adler, Kevin F. *When We Walk By*	362.5
Adler, Margot. *Drawing Down the Moon*	299
Agee, James. ★*Cotton Tenants*	976.1
Ahamed, Liaquat. *Lords of Finance*	920
Akins, Damon B. ★*We Are the Land*	978
Albers, Patricia. *Joan Mitchell*	B
Alberta, Tim. *American Carnage*	324.2734
Alberta, Tim. *The Kingdom, the Power, and the Glory*	270.8
Albom, Mitch. *Finding Chika*	B
Albom, Mitch. *Tuesdays with Morrie*	B
Albracht, William. *Abandoned in Hell*	959.704
Albright, Madeleine Korbel. *Hell and Other Destinations*	B
Alden, Ginger. *Elvis and Ginger*	B
Aldrin, Buzz. *No Dream Is Too High*	B
Alexander, Brian. ★*The Hospital*	362.10973
Alexander, Larry. *Biggest Brother*	B
Alexander, Michelle. *The New Jim Crow*	364.973
Alexander, Paul. *Bitter Crop*	B
Ali, Wajahat. *Go Back to Where You Came From*	B
Ali-Karamali, Sumbul. *Demystifying Shariah*	340.5
Alkon, Amy. *Good Manners for Nice People*	395
Allen, Jonathan. *Lucky*	324.973
Allen, Jonathan. *Shattered*	324.973
Allgor, Catherine. *A Perfect Union*	B
Allitt, Patrick. *The Conservatives*	320.520973
Allred, Alexandra Powe. *When Women Stood*	796.082
Alter, Jonathan. *His Very Best*	B
Alvarez, Noe. *Spirit Run*	796.42
Alvis-Walker, Marcie. *Everybody Come Alive*	B
Amar, Akhil Reed. ★*America's Constitution*	342.7302
Ambinder, Marc. *The Brink*	355.5
Ambrose, Stephen E. *Nothing Like It in the World*	385
Ambrose, Stephen E. ★*Undaunted Courage*	917.804
Ambrose, Stephen E. *The Victors*	940.54
Ammer, Christine. *The American Heritage Dictionary of Idioms*	423
Andersen, Kurt. ★*Fantasyland*	973
Anderson, Carol. ★*One Person, No Vote*	324.6
Anderson, Carol. ★*The Second*	344.7305
Anderson, Carol. ★*White Rage*	305.800973
Anderson, Fred. *The Dominion of War*	973
Anderson, Jimmeka. *Power Lines*	020
Anderson, Lars. *Carlisle vs. Army*	796.332
Andrews, Becca. *No Choice*	362.1988
Angelou, Maya. ★*I Know Why the Caged Bird Sings*	B
Angelou, Maya. *A Song Flung up to Heaven*	B
Anthony, Carl Sferrazza. *Camera Girl*	B
Anthony, Carl Sferrazza. *Nellie Taft*	B
Appy, Christian G. *American Reckoning*	959.704
Arana, Marie. *American Chica*	B
Arana, Marie. ★*Latinoland*	973
Arce, Julissa. *You Sound Like a White Girl*	303.48
Arkin, Alan. *An Improvised Life*	B
Armstrong, Jennifer Keishin. *Seinfeldia*	791.45
Armstrong, Jennifer Keishin. *Sex and the City and Us*	791.45
Arnold, James R. *Jungle of Snakes*	355.02
Arnsdorf, Isaac. ★*Finish What We Started*	320.52
Ashley, Maurice. *Move by Move*	158
Asim, Jabari. *We Can't Breathe*	305.896
Atkinson, Rick. ★*The British Are Coming*	973.3
Auletta, Ken. *Googled*	338.8
Auletta, Ken. *Media Man*	B
Austen, Ben. *Correction*	364.6
Auster, Paul. *Bloodbath Nation*	363.33
Avlon, John P. *Washington's Farewell*	973.4
Avrich, Paul. *Sasha and Emma*	920
Bacall, Lauren. *By Myself and Then Some*	B
Bacevich, Andrew J. *America's War for the Greater Middle East*	956.05
Bade, Rachael. ★*Unchecked*	342.73
Baer, Daniel Brooks. *The Four Tests*	320.973
Bagby, Meredith E. *The New Guys*	305
Baier, Bret. *Three Days in January*	B
Bailey, Issac J. *Why Didn't We Riot?*	305.800973
Bailey, Richard W. *Speaking American*	427
Baime, A. J. *The Accidental President*	B
Baime, A. J. *White Lies*	B
Baker, Billy. *We Need to Hang Out*	177
Baker, Calvin. *A More Perfect Reunion*	305.800973
Baker, Nicholson. *Baseless*	358
Baker, Peter. *The Divider*	973.933
Baker, Peter. *The Man Who Ran Washington*	B
Baldwin, James. ★*Collected Essays*	814
Baldwin, James. ★*The Fire Next Time*	305.896
Baldwin, James. *I Am Not Your Negro*	323.1196
Baldwin, James. ★*Notes of a Native Son*	305.8
Ball, Lucille. *Love, Lucy*	B
Ball, Molly. ★*Pelosi*	B
Balz, Daniel J. *The Battle for America, 2008*	973.932
Barbarisi, Daniel. *Chasing the Thrill*	796.1
Barber, Dan. *The Third Plate*	641.3
Barber, William J. *We Are Called to Be a Movement*	261.8
Barbree, Jay. *Neil Armstrong*	B
Barker, Margaret A. *Audubon Birdhouse Book*	728
Barnett, Brittany K. ★*A Knock at Midnight*	B
Baron, David. *American Eclipse*	523.7
Baron, Martin. ★*Collision of Power*	070.4
Barr, James. *Lords of the Desert*	956
Barra, Allen. ★*The Last Coach*	B
Barra, Allen. ★*Yogi Berra*	B
Barrett, David Dean. *140 Days to Hiroshima*	940.54
Barron, David J. *Waging War*	342.73
Barrow, Mark V. *Nature's Ghosts*	333.95
Barry, Dan. *Bottom of the 33rd*	796.357
Barry, John M. ★*The Great Influenza*	614.5
Basinger, Jeanine. *The Star Machine*	384
Bauer, Shane. *American Prison*	365
Baxley, Traci. *Social Justice Parenting*	649
Bayoumi, Moustafa. *How Does It Feel to Be a Problem?*	305.892
Bazelon, Emily. ★*Charged*	345.73
Becker, Jo. ★*Forcing the Spring*	346.79401
Beeman, Richard R. *Our Lives, Our Fortunes and Our Sacred Honor*	973.3
Beeman, Richard R. ★*Plain, Honest Men*	342.7302
Beers, Diane L. ★*For the Prevention of Cruelty*	179
Belafonte, Harry. ★*My Song*	782.42164
Belasco, Andrew. *The Enlightened College Applicant*	378.1
Belfort, Jordan. ★*The Wolf of Investing*	332.63
Bell, Jim. *The Interstellar Age*	919
Bell, W. Kamau. ★*Do the Work!*	305.8
Bell-Scott, Patricia. *The Firebrand and the First Lady*	920
Bender, Michael C. *"Frankly, We Did Win This Election"*	973.933
Benforado, Adam. *A Minor Revolution*	362.7
Bennett, Michael. *Things That Make White People Uncomfortable*	305.896
Bennetts, Leslie. *Last Girl Before Freeway*	B
Bennis, Phyllis. *Understanding the Palestinian-Israeli Conflict*	956.9405
Berens, Kimberly Nix. *Blind Spots*	370.15
Berfield, Susan. *The Hour of Fate*	973.91
Berg, A. Scott. *Kate Remembered*	B
Berg, A. Scott. ★*Wilson*	B
Bergen, Peter L. *The Longest War*	909.83
Bergen, Peter L. *Manhunt*	363.325
Berger, Karen. *America's Great Hiking Trails*	796.510973
Berkshire, Jennifer. *The Education Wars*	371.01
Berlin, Edward A. *King of Ragtime*	B
Berman, Ari. *Give Us the Ballot*	324.6
Berman, Ari. ★*Minority Rule*	305.809
Berman, Geoffrey. *Holding the Line*	345.73
Bernanke, Ben. ★*21st Century Monetary Policy*	332.1
Bernard, Emily. *Black Is the Body*	305.48
Bernstein, Carl. ★*All the President's Men*	364.1
Berry, Daina Ramey. ★*A Black Women's History of the United States*	305.48
Berry, Wendell. ★*The World-Ending Fire*	818

AUTHOR, TITLE, SERIES AND SUBJECT INDEX

Beschloss, Michael R. *The Conquerors*	940.53
Beschloss, Michael R. ★*Presidents of War*	355.00973
Bharara, Preet. *Doing Justice*	347.73
Bhutto, Benazir. *Reconciliation*	297.2
Bibbins, Mark. *13th Balloon*	813
Biden Owens, Valerie. *Growing up Biden*	B
Biden, Joseph R. *Promise Me, Dad*	B
Bignoli, Callan. ★*Responding to Rapid Change in Libraries*	020
Bigsby, Christopher William Edgar. *Arthur Miller*	B
Bilal, Wafaa. *Shoot an Iraqi*	B
Bingham, Clara. *Witness to the Revolution*	303.48
Bird, Kai. *American Prometheus*	B
Bird, Kai. *The Outlier*	973.926
Biskind, Peter. *Star*	B
Biskupic, Joan. ★*Nine Black Robes*	347.73
Bittle, Jake. ★*The Great Displacement*	362.87
Bittman, Mark. *Animal, Vegetable, Junk*	394.1
Black, George. ★*The Long Reckoning*	959.704
Blackhawk, Ned. ★*The Rediscovery of America*	973.04
Blair, Gabrielle Stanley. ★*Ejaculate Responsibly*	362.1988
Blanco, Richard. *How to Love a Country*	811
Blight, David W. *A Slave No More*	B
Blitzer, Jonathan. *Everyone Who Is Gone Is Here*	305.9
Block, Jennifer. *Everything Below the Waist*	613
Blum, Edward J. *The Color of Christ*	232
Blume, Lesley M. M. *Fallout*	940.54
Blumenthal, Sidney. *A Self-Made Man*	B
Blumenthal, Sidney. *Wrestling with His Angel*	B
Bobrick, Benson. *Angel in the Whirlwind*	973.3
Bobrow-Strain, Aaron. *The Death and Life of Aida Hernandez*	972
Boghosian, Heidi. *"i Have Nothing to Hide"*	363.1
Bogle, Donald. *Heat Wave*	782.42164
Bogus, Carl T. *Buckley*	B
Bok, Derek Curtis. *The Struggle to Reform Our Colleges*	378.73
Boland, Becca. *Making the Most of Teen Library Volunteers*	023
Boles, John B. *Jefferson*	B
Boorstin, Daniel J. *The Americans*	973
Boorstin, Daniel J. *The Americans*	973
Bordewich, Fergus M. *America's Great Debate*	973.6
Bordewich, Fergus M. *Congress at War*	324.2734
Bordewich, Fergus M. *Klan War*	973.8
Borneman, Walter R. *Polk*	B
Bowden, Mark. *Guests of the Ayatollah*	955.05
Bowden, Mark. ★*Hue 1968*	959.704
Bowden, Mark. *Life Sentence*	364.106
Bowden, Mark. *The Steal*	973.933
Boykin, Keith. *Race Against Time*	305.8
Boykin, Keith. ★*Why Does Everything Have to Be About Race?*	305.8
Boylan, Jennifer Finney. *Good Boy*	B
Boyle, Kevin. *Arc of Justice*	345.73
Boyle, Kevin. *The Shattering*	973.923
Bradlee, Ben. *The Kid*	B
Bradley, James. *Flags of Our Fathers*	940.54
Bradley, Mark A. *Blood Runs Coal*	B
Brady, Amy. *Ice*	553.7
Brady, James. *The Coldest War*	B
Brady, Patricia. *Martha Washington*	B
Branch, Taylor. ★*At Canaan's Edge*	323.1196
Branch, Taylor. *The Clinton Tapes*	973.929
Branch, Taylor. *Parting the Waters*	973
Brands, H. W. *The Age of Gold*	979.4
Brands, H. W. ★*Andrew Jackson, His Life and Times*	B
Brands, H. W. *The First American*	B
Brands, H. W. ★*Founding Partisans*	973.3
Brands, H. W. *The General vs. the President*	973.918092
Brands, H. W. ★*Heirs of the Founders*	973.5
Brands, H. W. ★*The Man Who Saved the Union*	B
Brands, H. W. ★*Our First Civil War*	973.3
Brands, H. W. *Reagan*	B
Brands, H. W. *Traitor to His Class*	B
Brands, H. W. *Woodrow Wilson*	B
Brands, H. W. ★*The Zealot and the Emancipator*	920
Bratt, Jessica Anne. *Let's Talk About Race in Storytimes*	027.62
Brazile, Donna. *For Colored Girls Who Have Considered Politics*	328.73
Breihan, Tom. ★*The Number Ones*	782.42164
Breitenbach, Kathleen. ★*LGBTQIA+ Books for Children and Teens*	028.7
Brennan, Chad. *Faithful Antiracism*	277.308
Brennan, Jason. *Libertarianism*	320.51
Brenner, Andrea. *How to College*	378.1
Brettschneider, Corey Lang. *The Oath and the Office*	342.73
Brettschneider, Corey Lang. *The Presidents and the People*	342.73
Brewster, Todd. *Lincoln's Gamble*	973.7
Breyer, Stephen G. ★*The Authority of the Court and the Peril of Politics*	347.73
Breyer, Stephen G. *Making Our Democracy Work*	347.73
Bridges, Sheila. *Furnishing Forward*	747
Brighton, Terry. *Patton, Montgomery, Rommel*	B
Brill, Steven. *Class Warfare*	371.010973
Brill, Steven. *Tailspin*	306.0973
Brinkley, Alan. *John F. Kennedy*	B
Brinkley, Alan. ★*The Publisher*	B
Brinkley, Douglas. ★*American Moonshot*	629.40973
Brinkley, Douglas. ★*Cronkite*	B
Brinkley, Douglas. *The Great Deluge*	976.3
Brinkley, Douglas. *Rightful Heritage*	B
Brinkley, Douglas. *Wheels for the World*	B
Brinkley, Douglas. *The Wilderness Warrior*	B
Broadwater, Jeff. ★*George Mason*	B
Broadwater, Jeff. *James Madison*	B
Brockman, Christian Frank. *Trees of North America*	582.16097
Brokaw, Tom. *The Fall of Richard Nixon*	B
Bronski, Michael. *A Queer History of the United States*	306.76
Brookhiser, Richard. *Give Me Liberty*	320.540973
Brooks, Mel. ★*All About Me!*	B
Brooks, Rosa. *How Everything Became War and the Military Became Everything*	355
Brookwood, Marilyn. *The Orphans of Davenport*	305.231
Broome, Brian. ★*Punch Me up to the Gods*	B
Brosh, Allie. ★*Hyperbole and a Half*	741.5
Brotherton, Marcus. *A Bright and Blinding Sun*	940.54
Broven, John. *Record Makers and Breakers*	B
Brower, Kate Andersen. *Elizabeth Taylor*	B
Brower, Kate Andersen. *First in Line*	920
Brower, Kate Andersen. *First Women*	920
Brower, Kate Andersen. *The Residence*	975.3
Brown, Austin Channing. ★*I'm Still Here*	B
Brown, Carolyn. *Chance and Circumstance*	B
Brown, Daniel James. ★*The Boys in the Boat*	797.12
Brown, Daniel James. ★*Facing the Mountain*	940.54
Brown, Emma. *To Raise a Boy*	649
Brown, Mick. ★*Tearing Down the Wall of Sound*	B
Brown-Nagin, Tomiko. *Civil Rights Queen*	B
Browne, David. *So Many Roads*	B
Broyles, Michael. ★*Revolutions in American Music*	780.9
Bruder, Jessica. ★*Nomadland*	331.3
Bruner, Robert F. ★*The Panic of 1907, 2nd Ed.*	330.973
Bruning, John R. *Indestructible*	B
Bryant, Howard. *Full Dissidence*	306.20973
Bryant, Howard. *The Last Hero*	B
Bryson, Bill. *One Summer*	973.91
Buck, Rinker. *Life on the Mississippi*	917
Buckland, Gail. *Who Shot Rock & Roll*	779
Budiansky, Stephen. *Code Warriors*	327.73047
Budiansky, Stephen. *Oliver Wendell Holmes*	B
Bunker, Nick. *Young Benjamin Franklin*	B
Bunting, Josiah. *Ulysses S. Grant*	B
Burgess, Ann Wolbert. *A Killer by Design*	364.3
Burke, Kelsy. *The Pornography Wars*	306.77
Burlingame, Michael. *Abraham Lincoln*	B
Burnham, Margaret A. ★*By Hands Now Known*	342.73
Burns, Eric. *Infamous Scribblers*	071
Burns, Eric. *Someone to Watch Over Me*	973.917092
Burns, Ken. ★*Our America*	973
Burns, William J. *The Back Channel*	B
Burrough, Bryan. *Days of Rage*	303.48
Burstein, Andrew. *Madison and Jefferson*	973.4
Busby, Jill Louise. *Unfollow Me*	305.08
Bush, George. *All the Best, George Bush*	973.928
Bush, George W. *41*	B
Bush, George W. *Decision Points*	B
Butler, Paul. *Chokehold*	363.2
Butterworth, Alex. *The World That Never Was*	335
Byrne, Paula. *Kick*	B
Cahalan, Susannah. *Brain on Fire*	616.8
Cahalan, Susannah. ★*The Great Pretender*	616.89
Caldwell, Christopher. *The Age of Entitlement*	305.240973

PUBLIC LIBRARY CORE COLLECTION: NONFICTION
Twentieth Edition

Caldwell, Gail. *Let's Take the Long Way Home*	B
Callahan, David. *The Cheating Culture*	174
Callow, Simon. ★*Orson Welles*	B
Calloway, Colin G. *The Indian World of George Washington*	323.1197
Campany, David. *The Open Road*	770
Campbell, James. *The Ghost Mountain Boys*	940.54
Campoverdi, Alejandra. *First Gen*	B
Canellos, Peter S. *The Great Dissenter*	B
Cannadine, David. ★*Mellon*	B
Capote, Truman. ★*Portraits and Observations*	814
Capozzola, Christopher. *Bound by War*	355
Capparell, Stephanie. *The Real Pepsi Challenge*	338.7
Caputo, Philip. *A Rumor of War*	959.704
Carballo, David M. *America*	912
Cargle, Rachel Elizabeth. *A Renaissance of Our Own*	B
Carlin, Kelly. *A Carlin Home Companion*	B
Carlin, Peter Ames. *Bruce*	B
Carlson, Brady. *Dead Presidents*	B
Carlson, Peter. *K Blows Top*	947.085
Carlson, W. Bernard. *Tesla*	B
Carmon, Irin. *Notorious RBG*	B
Caro, Robert A. ★*The Passage of Power*	B
Carpenter, Amanda B. *Gaslighting America*	973.933
Carreyrou, John. ★*Bad Blood*	338.7
Carruthers, Charlene A. *Unapologetic*	305.48
Carter, Alice A. *The Red Rose Girls*	B
Carter, David. *Stonewall*	306.76
Carter, Jimmy. *Everything to Gain*	B
Carter, Jimmy. *A Full Life*	B
Carter, Jimmy. *An Hour Before Daylight*	B
Carter, Jimmy. *Keeping Faith*	B
Carter, Jimmy. *Sharing Good Times*	973.926
Carter, Jimmy. *White House Diary*	973.926
Carter, Ruth E. ★*The Art of Ruth E. Carter*	746.9
Carwardine, Richard. *Lincoln*	B
Case, Anne. *Deaths of Despair and the Future of Capitalism*	362.28
Cash, Rosanne. ★*Composed*	B
Century, Douglas. *Barney Ross*	B
Cenziper, Debbie. ★*Love Wins*	346.7301
Cervini, Eric. *The Deviant's War*	B
Chabon, Michael. *Manhood for Amateurs*	B
Chait, Jonathan. *Audacity*	973.932
Chammah, Maurice. ★*Let the Lord Sort Them*	364.66
Chan, Jackie. *Never Grow Up*	B
Chance, Rosemary. *Young Adult Literature in Action*	011.62
Chandler, Adam. *Drive-Thru Dreams*	647.95
Chandrasekaran, Rajiv. *Imperial Life in the Emerald City*	956.7044
Chang, Tina. *Hybrida*	811
Charter, David. *Royal Audience*	941.085
Chase, James. *Acheson*	B
Cheever, Susan. *Drinking in America*	394.1
Chemerinsky, Erwin. *Presumed Guilty*	344.7305
Cheney, Liz. *Oath and Honor*	328.73
Cheney, Lynne V. *James Madison*	B
Cheney, Lynne V. *The Virginia Dynasty*	B
Chernow, Ron. ★*Alexander Hamilton*	B
Chernow, Ron. ★*Grant*	B
Chernow, Ron. *Washington*	B
Chertoff, Michael. *Exploding Data*	343.7309
Chesney, Will. *No Ordinary Dog*	958.104
Chittister, Joan. *Following the Path*	248.4
Chivers, C. J. *The Fighters*	920
Cho, Grace M. *Tastes Like War*	305.48
Chomsky, Noam. *Who Rules the World?*	327.73
Chozick, Amy. *Chasing Hillary*	B
Christie, Chris. *Let Me Finish*	B
Chung, Nicole. ★*A Living Remedy*	B
Churchwell, Sarah Bartlett. *Behold, America*	973.9
Cisneros, Sandra. *A House of My Own*	B
Clark, Taylor. *Starbucked*	338
Clarke, Thurston. *Honorable Exit*	959.704
Clarke, Thurston. *JFK's Last Hundred Days*	B
Clarke, Thurston. *The Last Campaign*	B
Cleaver, Eldridge. *Soul on Ice*	B
Clinton, Bill. *My Life*	B
Clinton, Hillary Rodham. *It Takes a Village*	305.23
Clinton, Hillary Rodham. *Living History*	B
Clinton, Hillary Rodham. *What Happened*	328.73
Coates, Ta-Nehisi. ★*We Were Eight Years in Power*	305.896
Coe, Alexis. ★*You Never Forget Your First*	B
Cohen, Adam. ★*Supreme Inequality*	347.73
Cohen, Andrew. *Two Days in June*	973.922
Cohen, Deborah. *Last Call at the Hotel Imperial*	070.92
Cohen, Jared. *Accidental Presidents*	973.09
Cohen, Jared. *Life After Power*	973.09
Cohen, Lizabeth. *A Consumers' Republic*	339.4
Cohen, Roger. *An Affirming Flame*	071
Cohen-Solal, Annie. *Mark Rothko*	759.13
Cohn, Jonathan. *The Ten Year War*	368.38
Cole, Natalie. *Angel on My Shoulder*	B
Coleman, David G. *The Fourteenth Day*	973.922092
Coleman, Rick. ★*Blue Monday*	B
Coll, Steve. ★*The Achilles Trap*	956.7044
Coll, Steve. *Ghost Wars*	958.104
Coll, Steve. *Private Empire*	338.7
Collins, Gail. *William Henry Harrison*	B
Collins-Dexter, Brandi. *Black Skinhead*	324.2734
Common. *One Day It'll All Make Sense*	B
Conant, Jennet. *The Lotus Eaters*	940.54
Conason, Joe. *The Longest Con*	320.52
Connell, Evan S. *Son of the Morning Star*	973.8
Connelly, Matthew James. *The Declassification Engine*	352.3
Connolly, Ray. *Being Elvis*	B
Conradi, Peter J. *Who Lost Russia?*	947.086
Cook, Blanche Wiesen. *Eleanor Roosevelt; Volume 2*	B
Cook, Blanche Wiesen. ★*Eleanor Roosevelt; Volume 3*	B
Cook, Jane Hampton. *American Phoenix*	973.5
Cook, Kevin. *Ten Innings at Wrigley*	796.357
Cooke, Alistair. *The American Home Front, 1941-1942*	940.53
Cooper, Anderson. *The Rainbow Comes and Goes*	B
Cooper, John Milton. *Woodrow Wilson*	B
Cornejo Villavicencio, Karla. ★*The Undocumented Americans*	920
Cottom, Tressie McMillan. *Lower Ed*	378.73
Cottom, Tressie McMillan. *Thick*	301
Cotton, Tom. *Sacred Duty*	355.6
Courogen, Carrie. ★*Miss May Does Not Exist*	B
Cox, John Woodrow. *Children Under Fire*	371.7
Coyle, Marcia. *The Roberts Court*	347.73
Cozzens, Peter. *The Earth Is Weeping*	978
Craig, William. *Yankee Come Home*	972.9107
Crampton, Caroline. *A Body Made of Glass*	616.85
Craughwell, Thomas J. *Stealing Lincoln's Body*	973.7092
Crawford, Bill. ★*All American*	B
Crawford, Richard. *America's Musical Life*	780
Creamer, Robert W. *Stengel*	796.357
Cronkite, Walter. *A Reporter's Life*	B
Crosby, Molly Caldwell. *The American Plague*	614.5
Cross, Charles R. *Room Full of Mirrors*	B
Cross, Kim. *In Light of All Darkness*	363.25
Cross, Tiffany D. ★*Say It Louder!*	324.6
Cross, William R. *Winslow Homer*	759.13
Crowell, Rodney. *Chinaberry Sidewalks*	B
Crowther, Gail. *Three-Martini Afternoons at the Ritz*	920
Crump, Benjamin. *Open Season*	364
Cummings, Elijah. ★*We're Better Than This*	B
Cunningham, Benjamin. *The Liar*	327.1273
Currid-Halkett, Elizabeth. *The Overlooked Americans*	307.76
Currie, Elliott. *A Peculiar Indifference*	305.800973
Curtis, Edward E. *Muslims in America*	305.6
Curtis, James. *Buster Keaton*	B
Curtis, James. *Spencer Tracy*	B
D'Antonio, Michael. *The Hunting of Hillary*	B
Dallek, Robert. ★*Franklin D. Roosevelt*	B
Dallek, Robert. *Harry S. Truman*	B
Dallek, Robert. *Let Every Nation Know*	B
Dallek, Robert. *Nixon and Kissinger*	B
Dallek, Robert. *An Unfinished Life*	B
Daniels, Roger. *Prisoners Without Trial*	940.53
Daniels, Stormy. *Full Disclosure*	B
Darby, Seyward. ★*Sisters in Hate*	305.800973
Darling, Ron. *The Complete Game*	B
Daughan, George C. *Revolution on the Hudson*	974.7
Davenport, Anthony. *Your Score*	332.7
Davis, Jack E. *The Bald Eagle*	598.9
Davis, Jack E. *An Everglades Providence*	B
Davis, Jack E. ★*The Gulf*	909

AUTHOR, TITLE, SERIES AND SUBJECT INDEX

Author / Title	Call #
Davis, Michael. *Street Gang*	791.43
Davis, Stephen. *Gold Dust Woman*	B
Davis, Thomas J. *History of African Americans*	973
Dawidoff, Nicholas. *Collision Low Crossers*	796.332
De Graaf, John. *What's the Economy For, Anyway?*	330.973
De Hart, Jane Sherron. ★*Ruth Bader Ginsburg*	B
De Vise, Daniel. ★*The Blues Brothers*	791.43
Dean, John W. *The Nixon Defense*	973.924092
Dean, Josh. *The Taking of K-129*	910.91
Delany, Sarah Louise. *Having Our Say*	B
Delmont, Matthew F. *Half American*	940.54
Denevi, Timothy. *Freak Kingdom*	B
Dennie, Madiba K. *The Originalism Trap*	342.73
Dennis, Jerry. *The Living Great Lakes*	977
DePastino, Todd. *Bill Mauldin*	B
Derf. *Kent State*	741.5
Dery, Mark. *Born to Be Posthumous*	B
Desmond, Matthew. ★*Evicted*	339.4
Desmond, Matthew. ★*Poverty, by America*	362.5
Diamant, Anita. *Pitching My Tent*	296.7
Diaz, Tom. *The Last Gun*	338.4
Dickey, Colin. *Ghostland*	133.1
Dickson, Paul. *The Rise of the G.I. Army 1940-1941*	940.54
Didion, Joan. ★*The Year of Magical Thinking*	B
Dietrich, Sean. *You Are My Sunshine*	B
DiFranco, Ani. *No Walls and the Recurring Dream*	782.42164
DiGiulian, Sasha. *Take the Lead*	B
Dillard, Annie. *The Writing Life*	B
Ditmore, Melissa Hope. ★*Unbroken Chains*	306.74
Dobbs, Michael. *King Richard*	973.924
Dohrmann, George. *Switching Fields*	796.334
Dolin, Eric Jay. ★*Rebels at Sea*	973.3
Donald, Aida DiPace. *Citizen Soldier*	B
Donald, David Herbert. *Lincoln*	B
Donovan, Jim. *A Terrible Glory*	973.8
Dorey-Stein, Beck. *From the Corner of the Oval*	B
Doty, Cate. *Mergers and Acquisitions*	395.2
Doughty, Caitlin. *Smoke Gets in Your Eyes*	B
Douglas, John E. *The Killer Across the Table*	B
Dower, John W. *Cultures of War*	355.00973
Drape, Joe. *Black Maestro*	B
Draper, Robert. *To Start a War*	956.7044
Dray, Philip. *At the Hands of Persons Unknown*	364.1
Dray, Philip. *Capitol Men*	973.8
Dresser, Norine. *Multicultural Manners*	395
Driver, Justin. *The Schoolhouse Gate*	344.73
Drury, Bob. *Blood and Treasure*	B
Drury, Bob. *Valley Forge*	973.3
Du Bois, W. E. B. *The Oxford W.E.B. Du Bois Reader*	305.896
Du Bois, W. E. B. ★*The Souls of Black Folk*	973
Du Mez, Kristin Kobes. *Jesus and John Wayne*	277.308
Duberman, Martin B. *Andrea Dworkin*	B
Dubofsky, Melvyn. *Labor in America*	331.880973
DuBois, Ellen Carol. *Suffrage*	324.6
Duckworth, Tammy. *Every Day Is a Gift*	B
Dudley, Steven S. *MS-13*	364.106
Dufton, Emily. *Grass Roots*	362.29
Dunbar, Erica Armstrong. ★*Never Caught*	B
Dunbar-Ortiz, Roxanne. ★*An Indigenous Peoples' History of the United States*	970.004
Duncan, Arne. *How Schools Work*	379
Duncan, Dayton. ★*Country Music*	781.642
Duncan, Dayton. *The National Parks*	333.78
Dunn, Harry. *Standing My Ground*	B
Dunnavant, Keith. *Montana*	B
DuVal, Kathleen. ★*Native Nations*	970.004
Dybdahl, Thomas L. *When Innocence Is Not Enough*	345.73
Dylan, Bob. *Chronicles; Volume 1*	B
Dyson, Michael Eric. *The Black Presidency*	305.800973
Dyson, Michael Eric. *Come Hell or High Water*	976.3
Dyson, Michael Eric. *Holler If You Hear Me*	B
Dyson, Michael Eric. *Long Time Coming*	305.800973
Dyson, Michael Eric. *Tears We Cannot Stop*	305.800973
Dyson, Michael Eric. *What Truth Sounds Like*	305.800973
Easterbrook, Gregg. ★*The King of Sports*	796.332
Ebert, Roger. *Life Itself*	B
Ebert, Roger. *Scorsese by Ebert*	B
Edin, Kathryn. ★*The Injustice of Place*	339.4
Edmundson, Mark. *Why Football Matters*	B
Edstrom, Erik. *Un-American*	B
Edwards, Bob. *Edward R. Murrow and the Birth of Broadcast Journalism*	B
Egan, Timothy. ★*The Big Burn*	973.911
Egan, Timothy. ★*The Immortal Irishman*	B
Egan, Timothy. *The Worst Hard Time*	978
Eggers, Dave. *Zeitoun*	305.892
Ehrenreich, Barbara. *Bright-Sided*	155.2
Ehrenreich, Barbara. *Had I Known*	814
Ehrenreich, Barbara. ★*Nickel and Dimed*	B
Eig, Jonathan. *The Birth of the Pill*	618.1
Eisenberg, John. *The League*	796.332
Eisler, Benita. *The Red Man's Bones*	B
Eizenstat, Stuart. ★*President Carter*	B
Elledge, Scott. *E.B. White*	B
Ellis, Joseph J. *American Creation*	973.3
Ellis, Joseph J. ★*American Dialogue*	973.3
Ellis, Joseph J. ★*American Sphinx*	973.4
Ellis, Joseph J. *The Cause*	973.3
Ellis, Joseph J. *First Family*	973.4
Ellis, Joseph J. *Founding Brothers*	973.4
Ellis, Joseph J. ★*His Excellency*	B
Ellis, Joseph J. *The Quartet*	342.7302
Ellison, Ralph. ★*The Collected Essays of Ralph Ellison*	814
Elnoury, Tamer. *American Radical*	B
Emanuel, Rahm. *The Nation City*	352.23
Emdin, Christopher. *Ratchetdemic*	370.1
Enrich, David. *Servants of the Damned*	340.023
Epplin, Luke. *Our Team*	796.357
Erwin, Jon. *Beyond Valor*	B
Eustace, Nicole. ★*Covered with Night*	364.152
Evans, R. Tripp. *Grant Wood*	B
Evans, Walker. *American Photographs*	779
Ewing, Eve L. *1919*	811
Eyman, Scott. *Cary Grant*	B
Eyman, Scott. *John Wayne*	B
Eyre, Eric. *Death in Mud Lick*	362.29
Fabey, Michael. *Heavy Metal*	338.4
Faliveno, Melissa. *Tomboyland*	B
Fallows, James M. *Our Towns*	306.0973
Farley, Audrey Clare. *The Unfit Heiress*	B
Farmer, John J. *The Ground Truth*	973.931
Farrell, John A. *Clarence Darrow*	B
Farrell, John A. ★*Richard Nixon*	B
Farrell, John A. *Ted Kennedy*	B
Farris, Scott. *Almost President*	324.973
Farrow, Ronan. *War on Peace*	327.73
Fauci, Anthony S. *Expect the Unexpected*	610.92
Faust, Drew Gilpin. *Necessary Trouble*	B
Feast, Fancy. *Naked*	792.7
Febos, Melissa. *Girlhood*	818
Fehrman, Craig. *Author in Chief*	920
Feiler, Bruce. ★*The Search*	306.3
Feinstein, John. ★*Last Dance*	796.323
Felder, Deborah G. *The American Women's Almanac*	305.40973
Feldman, Noah. *The Broken Constitution*	973.7
Feldman, Noah. *The Three Lives of James Madison*	B
Feldstein, Mark Avrom. *Poisoning the Press*	973.924092
Ferguson, Niall. *Kissinger*	973.924
Ferling, John E. *Winning Independence*	973.3
Fernandez-Armesto, Felipe. *Our America*	973
Fernando, S. H., Jr. *From the Streets of Shaolin*	782.421
Ferreiro, Larrie D. *Brothers at Arms*	327.73
Ferrer, Ada. ★*Cuba*	972.91
Fersko, Diana. ★*We Need to Talk About Antisemitism*	305.892
Fields-Black, Edda L. *Combee*	973.7
Fieseler, Robert W. *Tinderbox*	364.152
Finan, Christopher M. *How Free Speech Saved Democracy*	342.73
Finkel, David. *An American Dreamer*	975.8
Finkel, David. *The Good Soldiers*	956.7044
Finkel, David. *Thank You for Your Service*	920
Finkelman, Paul. *Millard Fillmore*	B
Finkelstein, Elizabeth. *Cheap Old Houses*	643
Finn, Peter. *The Zhivago Affair*	891.73
Fischer, David Hackett. ★*African Founders*	973
Fischer, David Hackett. *Champlain's Dream*	B
Fischer, David Hackett. *Paul Revere's Ride*	973.3
Fischer, David Hackett. *Washington's Crossing*	973.3

PUBLIC LIBRARY CORE COLLECTION: NONFICTION
Twentieth Edition

Fishman, Charles. ★One Giant Leap	629.45
Fishman, Elly. Refugee High	370.8
Fisk, Robert. The Great War for Civilisation	956.04
Fiske, Edward B. Fiske Guide to Getting into the Right College	378.1
FitzGerald, Frances. The Evangelicals	277
FitzGerald, Frances. Fire in the Lake	959.704
FitzGerald, Michael C. ★Picasso and American Art	709.73
Fleming, Brandon P. Miseducated	B
Fleming, Crystal Marie. How to Be Less Stupid About Race	305.800973
Fleming, Jory. How to Be Human	616.85
Fleshman, Lauren. ★Good for a Girl	B
Fletcher, Susan A. Exploring the History of Childhood and Play Through 50 Historic Treasures	790
Flexner, James Thomas. George Washington and the New Nation, 1783-1793	973.4
Flexner, James Thomas. George Washington	B
Flowers, Catherine Coleman. Waste	363.72
Floyd, Ted. How to Know the Birds	598.072
Foer, Esther Safran. I Want You to Know We're Still Here	B
Foer, Franklin. ★The Last Politician	973.934
Fogerty, John. Fortunate Son	B
Follett, Ken. On Wings of Eagles	955
Foner, Eric. The Fiery Trial	973.7092
Foner, Eric. Forever Free	973.8
Foner, Eric. ★Reconstruction	973.8
Ford, Richard T. Rights Gone Wrong	342.7308
Ford, Tanisha C. Dressed in Dreams	391
Forman, James. Locking up Our Own	364.973
Fox, Jesse David. Comedy Book	792.7
Fox, Margalit. The Talented Mrs. Mandelbaum	364.1
Foxx, Jamie. Act Like You Got Some Sense	B
France, David. How to Survive a Plague	362.196
Frank, Barney. Frank	B
Frank, Jeffrey. The Trials of Harry S. Truman	973.918
Frank, Thomas. The People, No	320.56
Frankel, Glenn. High Noon	791.43
Franklin, Benjamin. ★The Autobiography of Benjamin Franklin	B
Franklin, Benjamin. ★Autobiography, Poor Richard, and Later Writings	973.2
Franklin, Benjamin. The Compleated Autobiography	B
Franscell, Ron. Shadowman	362.88
Fraser, Caroline. ★Prairie Fires	B
Fraser, Steve. The Age of Acquiescence	973.91
Freedman, Samuel G. Jew vs. Jew	296
Freeman, Amanda. Getting Me Cheap	362.83
Freeman, Andrea. ★Ruin Their Crops on the Ground	338.1
Freeman, Douglas Southall. Lee	B
Freeman, Joanne B. The Field of Blood	973.7
Fremont, Helen. The Escape Artist	B
Friedan, Betty. ★The Feminine Mystique	305.42
Friedman, Andrew. The Dish	647.95
Friedman, Barry. ★Unwarranted	344.7305
Friedman, Barry. The Will of the People	347.73
Friedman, Thomas L. ★Thank You for Being Late	303.48
Friedwald, Will. ★Sinatra! the Song Is You	782.42164
Frum, David. Trumpocracy	973.933
Fullilove, Michael. Rendezvous with Destiny	973.917092
Gabler, Neal. ★Against the Wind	B
Gabler, Neal. Catching the Wind	B
Gabriel, Mary. Ninth Street Women	920
Gaddy, K. R. ★Well of Souls	787
Gage, Beverly. G-Man	B
Gaines, James R. For Liberty and Glory	B
Galassi, Peter. Ansel Adams in Yosemite Valley	770.92
Gallego, Ruben. They Called Us	956.7044
Galloway, Scott. The Four	338.7
Gans, John. White House Warriors	355
Ganz, John. When the Clock Broke	320.52
Garcia, Mayte. The Most Beautiful	920
Garner, Dwight. The Upstairs Delicatessen	B
Garrett, Kent. The Last Negroes at Harvard	920
Garrow, David J. Rising Star	B
Gates, Henry Louis. And Still I Rise	305.896
Gates, Henry Louis. The Black Box	908
Gates, Henry Louis. ★The Black Church	277
Gates, Henry Louis. Colored People	B
Gates, Henry Louis. The Future of the Race	305.896
Gates, Henry Louis. In Search of Our Roots	973
Gates, Henry Louis. ★Life Upon These Shores	973
Gates, Henry Louis. ★Stony the Road	973
Gates, Robert Michael. ★Exercise of Power	973.929
Gavin, James. ★Stormy Weather	782.42164
Gawande, Atul. Complications	B
Gefter, Philip. What Becomes a Legend Most	B
Gehring, Wes D. James Dean	B
Gellman, Barton. ★Dark Mirror	B
Gentile, Olivia. Life List	598.072
Gerdts, William H. American Impressionism	759.13
Gessen, Masha. Surviving Autocracy	973.933
Gewen, Barry. ★The Inevitability of Tragedy	B
Ghazvinian, John. America and Iran	327
Ghostface Killah. Rise of a Killah	B
Gibson, Larry S. Young Thurgood	B
Gidding, John. At Home with Nature	635.9
Giddings, Paula. Ida	B
Giddins, Gary. Bing Crosby	B
Giddins, Gary. Bing Crosby	B
Gienapp, William E. Abraham Lincoln and Civil War America	B
Gilbert, Sandra M. ★Still Mad	810.9
Gildea, William. The Longest Fight	B
Gilder, Ginny. Course Correction	797.12
Gill, A. A. To America with Love	973.93
Gill, Anton. Art Lover	B
Gillette, Michael L. Lady Bird Johnson	B
Gilliam, Dorothy Butler. Trailblazer	B
Gilliam, Fatimah. Race Rules	305.8
Gilliard, Dominique Dubois. Rethinking Incarceration	261.8
Gillon, Steven M. America's Reluctant Prince	B
Ginzberg, Lori D. Elizabeth Cady Stanton	B
Giridharadas, Anand. ★The Persuaders	320.973
Girzone, Joseph F. Never Alone	248.4
Glass, Brent D. 50 Great American Places	973
Glatthaar, Joseph T. The American Military	355.00973
Glaude, Eddie S. Begin Again	305.800973
Golay, Michael. America 1933	B
Goldberg, Philip. American Veda	294.509
Goldberger, Paul. Ballpark	796.357
Goldberger, Paul. Building Art	B
Goldfarb, Bruce. ★18 Tiny Deaths	B
Goldsmith, Francisca. The Readers' Advisory Guide to Graphic Novels	025.2
Goldstein, Amy. Janesville	330.9775
Goldstein, Dana. The Teacher Wars	371.1020973
Goldstein, Nancy. Jackie Ormes	B
Gomez, Laura E. ★Inventing Latinos	305.868
Gooch, Brad. ★Flannery	B
Goodheart, Adam. 1861	973.7
Goodridge, Michelle. Librarian's Guide to Games and Gamers	025.2
Goodwin, Doris Kearns. ★The Bully Pulpit	973.91
Goodwin, Doris Kearns. ★Leadership in Turbulent Times	973.09
Goodwin, Doris Kearns. No Ordinary Time	920
Goodwin, Doris Kearns. ★Team of Rivals	B
Goodyear, C. W. President Garfield	B
Gopal, Anand. No Good Men Among the Living	920
Gopnik, Blake. ★Warhol	B
Gordin, Michael D. Red Cloud at Dawn	355.02
Gordon, Aubrey. "You Just Need to Lose Weight"	616.3
Gordon, Linda. Dorothea Lange	B
Gordon, Robert J. ★The Rise and Fall of American Growth	339.4
Gordon-Reed, Annette. Andrew Johnson	B
Gordon-Reed, Annette. ★Most Blessed of the Patriarchs	973.4
Gorrindo, Simone. ★The Wives	B
Gotch, Jen. The Upside of Being Down	B
Gottlieb, Robert. George Balanchine	B
Goudsouzian, Aram. Sidney Poitier	B
Goyal, Nikhil. ★Live to See the Day	305.5
Graetz, Michael J. The Burger Court and the Rise of the Judicial Right	347.73
Graff, Garrett M. Raven Rock	363.350973
Graff, Garrett M. Watergate	973.924
Graff, Henry F. Grover Cleveland	B
Granata, Vince. Everything Is Fine	B
Grande, Reyna. ★The Distance Between Us	973
Grandin, Greg. The End of the Myth	973
Grandin, Greg. Kissinger's Shadow	B
Grandmaster Flash. The Adventures of Grandmaster Flash	B
Grant, Gail Milissa. At the Elbows of My Elders	B

AUTHOR, TITLE, SERIES AND SUBJECT INDEX

Grant, James. ★*John Adams*	B
Grant, Ulysses S. ★*The Annotated Memoirs of Ulysses S. Grant*	B
Grant, Ulysses S. *Memoirs and Selected Letters*	B
Grant, Will. *The Last Ride of the Pony Express*	917.804
Grathwohl, Marya. *This Wheel of Rocks*	271
Gray, Charlotte. ★*Reluctant Genius*	920
Gray, Emma. *A Girl's Guide to Joining the Resistance*	303.48
Greenberg, Amy S. *Lady First*	B
Greenburg, Zack O'Malley. *3 Kings*	782.421649
Greene, Andy. *The Office*	791.45
Greene, Jamal. *How Rights Went Wrong*	342.7308
Greene, Joshua. *Unstoppable*	B
Greenfield, Martin. ★*Measure of a Man*	B
Greenhouse, Linda. *Becoming Justice Blackmun*	B
Greenman, Ben. *Dig If You Will the Picture*	B
Gregory, Dick. *Defining Moments in Black History*	973
Griffin, Farah Jasmine. *Read Until You Understand*	810.9
Grinspan, Jon. *Wide Awake*	973.7
Groom, Winston. *The Aviators*	920
Groom, Winston. *The Generals*	920
Groom, Winston. *The Patriots*	920
Grose, Jessica. *Screaming on the Inside*	306.874
Gruen, Bob. *Right Place, Right Time*	B
Guarnere, William. *Brothers in Battle, Best of Friends*	B
Guelzo, Allen C. *Lincoln and Douglas*	973.6
Guendelsberger, Emily. *On the Clock*	331.0973
Guerrero, Jean. *Hatemonger*	B
Guibert, Emmanuel. *Alan's War*	741.5
Guinn, Jeff. ★*Manson*	B
Gutzman, Kevin R. C. *The Jeffersonians*	973.5
Haag, Pamela. ★*The Gunning of America*	338.4
Hahn, Emanuel. *Koreatown Dreaming*	979.4
Hakkakiyan, Ruya. *A Beginner's Guide to America*	646.7
Halberstam, David. *The Amateurs*	B
Halberstam, David. *The Best and the Brightest*	973.92
Halberstam, David. ★*The Children*	323.1
Halberstam, David. *The Coldest Winter*	951.904
Halberstam, David. *The Fifties*	973.92
Halberstam, David. *Summer of '49*	796.357
Halberstam, David. *The Teammates*	B
Haley, James L. *Captive Paradise*	996.9
Hamilton, Nigel. *The Mantle of Command*	940.54
Hamlin, Kimberly A. *Free Thinker*	B
Hample, Zack. *The Baseball*	796.357
Han, Chenxing. *Be the Refuge*	294.3
Hansberry, Lorraine. ★*A Raisin in the Sun*	812
Harden, Blaine. *The Great Leader and the Fighter Pilot*	B
Harding, Luke. *Collusion*	324.70973
Harmon, Mark. *Ghosts of Honolulu*	940.54
Harris, Adam. ★*The State Must Provide*	379.2
Harris, Lesley Ellen. *Licensing Digital Content*	346.7304
Harris, Mark. *Pictures at a Revolution*	791.43
Harris, Neil Patrick. *Neil Patrick Harris*	B
Harrison, Valerie I. *Do Right by Me*	649
Harryhausen, Ray. *The Art of Ray Harryhausen*	778
Hart, Matt. *Win at All Costs*	338.7
Harvilla, Rob. *60 Songs That Explain the '90s*	782.42164
Hasen, Richard L. *Election Meltdown*	324.973
Hastings, Max. *The Abyss*	972.9106
Hawes, Jennifer. *Grace Will Lead Us Home*	364.152
Hay, Matt. *Soundtrack of Silence*	B
Hayek, Friedrich A. von. *The Road to Serfdom*	330.1
Hayes, Christopher. *A Colony in a Nation*	364.3
Hayes, Derek. *Historical Atlas of the United States*	911
Haygood, Wil. ★*Colorization*	791.43
Haygood, Wil. *Showdown*	B
Haygood, Wil. ★*Sweet Thunder*	B
Hays, Jeanine. *Remix*	747
Hazzard, Kevin M. *American Sirens*	362.18
Heacox, Kim. *National Geographic the National Parks*	363.6
Heat Moon, William Least. *Blue Highways*	917.304
Heat Moon, William Least. *Roads to Quoz*	917.3
Hechinger, John. ★*True Gentlemen*	371.85
Hedges, Chris. *Days of Destruction, Days of Revolt*	741.5
Hegar, Mary Jennings. *Shoot Like a Girl*	B
Hemphill, Paul. *Lovesick Blues*	B
Hendershot, Heather. *Open to Debate*	B
Henderson, Bruce B. *Bridge to the Sun*	940.53
Hendrickson, Paul. *The Living and the Dead*	959.704
Hennessey, Jonathan. *The United States Constitution*	741.5
Hennessey, Susan. *Unmaking the Presidency*	973.933
Herman, Arthur. *1917*	940.3
Herman, Arthur. ★*Douglas Macarthur*	B
Herman, Arthur. *Freedom's Forge*	940.53
Hermes, Will. *Love Goes to Buildings on Fire*	781.64
Hernandez Castillo, Marcelo. *Children of the Land*	B
Hernandez, Daisy. *A Cup of Water Under My Bed*	B
Hernandez, Daisy. *The Kissing Bug*	616.9
Hernandez, Kelly Lytle. ★*Bad Mexicans*	972
Herold, Benjamin. *Disillusioned*	307.76
Herrera, Juan Felipe. *Every Day We Get More Illegal*	811
Herring, Lucinda. *Reimagining Death*	393
Hervieux, Linda. *Forgotten*	940.54
Hewlett, Sylvia Ann. *#metoo in the Corporate World*	658.3
Hiaasen, Carl. *The Downhill Lie*	B
Hickam, Homer H. ★*Rocket Boys*	B
Hickman, Katie. *Brave Hearted*	978
Higginbotham, Adam. ★*Challenger*	629.45
Higgins, Tim. *Power Play*	338.7
Hilburn, Robert. ★*Johnny Cash*	B
Hilfiger, Tommy. *American Dreamer*	B
Hill, Clint. *Five Days in November*	973.922092
Hill, Clint. *Five Presidents*	B
Hill, Clint. *Mrs. Kennedy and Me*	973.922092
Hill, DaMaris B. *Breath Better Spent*	811
Hill, Katie. *She Will Rise*	305.42
Hill, Marc Lamont. *Seen and Unseen*	303.3
Hillenbrand, Laura. ★*Seabiscuit*	798.4
Hillsberg, Christina. *License to Parent*	649.1
Hilton, Paris. *Paris*	B
Hiltzik, Michael A. *Iron Empires*	385.0973
Hindley, Meredith. *Destination Casablanca*	940.54
Hing, Bill Ong. ★*Humanizing Immigration*	342.7308
Hinojosa, Maria. *Once I Was You*	B
Hinton, Elizabeth Kai. ★*America on Fire*	305.800973
Hirono, Mazie. *Heart of Fire*	B
Hirsch, Foster. ★*Hollywood and the Movies of the Fifties*	791.43
Hirsch, James S. *Willie Mays*	B
Hirsch, Paul. *A Long Time Ago in a Cutting Room Far, Far Away*	B
Hirshman, Linda R. *Reckoning*	305.420973
Hirshman, Linda R. *Sisters in Law*	347.73
Hitchcock, William I. *The Age of Eisenhower*	973.921092
Hitchens, Christopher. *Hitch-22*	920
Hitchens, Christopher. *Thomas Jefferson*	B
Hixenbaugh, Michael. ★*They Came for the Schools*	371.9
Hobbs, Jeff. *Children of the State*	364.36
Hobbs, Jeff. *Show Them You're Good*	373
Hochschild, Adam. *American Midnight*	973.91
Hochschild, Adam. *Rebel Cinderella*	B
Hoffman, Carl. *Liar's Circus*	973.933
Hoffman, Liz. *Crash Landing*	330
Hogeland, William. *Autumn of the Black Snake*	970.004
Hogeland, William. *Declaration*	973.3
Holifield, E. Brooks. *Theology in America*	230
Holton, Woody. *Abigail Adams*	B
Holzer, Harold. *Brought Forth on This Continent*	973.7
Holzer, Harold. *A Just and Generous Nation*	973.7092
Holzer, Harold. *Monument Man*	B
Honey, Michael K. *To the Promised Land*	323
Hongoltz-Hetling, Matthew. *If It Sounds Like a Quack*	615.8
hooks, bell. *Remembered Rapture*	808
Hopkins, Jerry. *No One Here Gets Out Alive*	B
Horace, Matthew. *The Black and the Blue*	B
Horn, Jonathan. *Washington's End*	B
Hornbacher, Marya. *Wasted*	B
Horne, Jed. *Breach of Faith*	976.3
Hornfischer, James D. *Neptune's Inferno*	940.54
Hornfischer, James D. *Who Can Hold the Sea*	359.00973
Horowitz, Joseph. ★*Classical Music in America*	781.6
Horrigan, Joe. *NFL Century*	796.332
Howard, Johnette. *The Rivals*	B
Howard, Timothy. *The Mortgage Wars*	332.7
Howe, Daniel Walker. *What Hath God Wrought*	973.5
Huang, Yunte. *Daughter of the Dragon*	B
Hudes, Quiara Alegria. ★*My Broken Language*	B
Hulls, Tessa. ★*Feeding Ghosts*	741.5

PUBLIC LIBRARY CORE COLLECTION: NONFICTION
Twentieth Edition

Humez, Jean McMahon. *Harriet Tubman*	B
Hunter-Gault, Charlayne. ★*My People*	305.48
Hutchinson, Cassidy. *Enough*	B
Hvistendahl, Mara. ★*The Scientist and the Spy*	364.16
Hyland, William G. *George Gershwin*	B
Iftin, Abdi Nor. *Call Me American*	305.893
Immerwahr, Daniel. *How to Hide an Empire*	973
Indyk, Martin. *Master of the Game*	327.73
Insel, Thomas R. *Healing*	362.2
Inskeep, Steve. *Jacksonland*	973.56
Isaacson, Walter. ★*Benjamin Franklin*	B
Isaacson, Walter. ★*Steve Jobs*	B
Isen, Tajja. *Some of My Best Friends*	305.8
Isenberg, Nancy. *The Problem of Democracy*	973.4
Isikoff, Michael. *Russian Roulette*	973.933
Isserman, Maurice. *The Winter Army*	940.54
Jackson, Bruce. *Never Far from Home*	B
Jackson, Curtis. *Hustle Harder, Hustle Smarter*	B
Jackson, Jenn M. *Black Women Taught Us*	305.48
Jackson, Kellie Carter. *We Refuse*	323.1196
Jackson, Lawrence Patrick. *Chester B. Himes*	B
Jackson, Mitchell S. *Survival Math*	B
Jackson, Troy. *Becoming King*	B
Jacob, Mira. *Good Talk*	741.5
Jacobs, A. J. ★*The Year of Living Constitutionally*	342.73
Jacobs, Alexandra. *Still Here*	B
Jacobsen, Annie. ★*Operation Paperclip*	940.54
Jacobsen, Annie. *Phenomena*	133.8
Jacobsen, Annie. *Surprise, Kill, Vanish*	327.1273
Jacobson, Sidney. *The 9-11 Report*	741.5
Jaher, David. *The Witch of Lime Street*	B
Jaworksi, Ron. *The Games That Changed the Game*	796.332
Jayapal, Pramila. *Use the Power You Have*	B
Jefferson, Thomas. *Writings*	973.3
Jena, Anupam B. *Random Acts of Medicine*	616.0072
Jenkins, Jedidiah. *To Shake the Sleeping Self*	B
Jenkins, Peter. *A Walk Across America*	917.304
Jerkins, Morgan. *Wandering in Strange Lands*	305.896
Jeter, Derek. *Jeter Unfiltered*	B
Jewel. *Never Broken*	782.42164
Jobb, Dean. *The Case of the Murderous Dr. Cream*	364.152
Jobb, Dean. *A Gentleman and a Thief*	364.16
Jobrani, Maziyar. *I'm Not a Terrorist, but I've Played One on TV*	B
Johnson, Akemi. *Night in the American Village*	305.40952
Johnson, George. *Miss Leavitt's Stars*	522
Johnson, Joyce. *The Voice Is All*	B
Johnson, Katherine G. *My Remarkable Journey*	B
Johnson, Lyndon B. *Taking Charge*	973.923
Johnson, Paul. *Eisenhower*	B
Johnson, Paul. *George Washington*	B
Johnson, Theodore R. *When the Stars Begin to Fall*	305.800973
Johnston, David Cay. *The Big Cheat*	973.933
Johnston, David Cay. *It's Even Worse Than You Think*	973.933
Jollett, Mikel. ★*Hollywood Park*	B
Jones, Brenda. *Alexandria Ocasio-Cortez*	B
Jones, Brenda. *Maxine Waters*	B
Jones, Brian Jay. *George Lucas*	B
Jones, Brian Jay. *Jim Henson*	B
Jones, Gerard. *Men of Tomorrow*	741.5
Jones, Nathaniel R. *Answering the Call*	B
Jones, Robert P. *White Too Long*	277
Jones, Saeed. *Alive at the End of the World*	811
Jones, Tom. *Space Shuttle Stories*	629.44
Jordan, Jonathan W. *Brothers, Rivals, Victors*	940.54
Joseph, Peniel E. *The Sword and the Shield*	B
Joseph, Peniel E. *Waiting 'Til the Midnight Hour*	323.1196
Kaba, Mariame. *No More Police*	363.2
Kahn, Ashley. *The House That Trane Built*	781.6509
Kaiser, Robert G. *Act of Congress*	346.73
Kaku, Michio. ★*Hyperspace*	530.1
Kakutani, Michiko. *Ex Libris*	028
Kamensky, Jane. *A Revolution in Color*	759.13
Kamp, David. *Sunny Days*	791.4502
Kanfer, Stefan. *Tough Without a Gun*	B
Kantor, Jodi. *She Said*	364.16
Kapilow, Robert. ★*Listening for America*	782.42164
Kaplan, Fred. *John Quincy Adams*	B
Kaplan, Fred. *Lincoln and the Abolitionists*	973.7092
Kaplan, Fred M. *The Bomb*	355.8
Kaplan, James. *3 Shades of Blue*	920
Kaplan, James. *Sinatra*	782.42164
Kaplan, Robert D. *Warrior Politics*	320
Karabell, Zachary. *Inside Money*	332.1
Karl, Jonathan. *Betrayal*	973.933
Karl, Jonathan. *Front Row at the Trump Show*	973.933
Karl, Jonathan. *Tired of Winning*	973.933
Karnow, Stanley. *Vietnam, a History*	959.704
Kashner, Sam. *The Fabulous Bouvier Sisters*	920
Kashner, Sam. *Furious Love*	B
Kasparov, Gary. *Winter Is Coming*	947.086
Katznelson, Ira. *Fear Itself*	973.917
Kaufman, Kenn. *The Birds That Audubon Missed*	598
Kavanagh, Julie. *Nureyev*	B
Kazin, Michael. *What It Took to Win*	324.2736
Kearse, Bettye. *The Other Madisons*	920
Keaton, Diane. ★*Brother & Sister*	B
Keefe, Patrick Radden. ★*Empire of Pain*	338.7
Keegan, John. *The American Civil War*	973.7
Keene, John. ★*Punks*	811
Keiler, Allan. *Marian Anderson*	B
Kelley, Blair Murphy. *Black Folk*	331.6
Kelly, Minka. ★*Tell Me Everything*	B
Kemper, Steve. *Our Man in Tokyo*	952.03
Kendi, Ibram X. ★*How to Be an Antiracist*	305.8
Kendi, Ibram X. ★*How to Raise an Antiracist*	649
Kendi, Ibram X. ★*Stamped from the Beginning*	305.8
Kennedy, David M. ★*Freedom from Fear*	973.91
Kennedy, John F. *Profiles in Courage*	920
Kennedy, Robert F. *Thirteen Days*	327.73
Kenner, Rob. *The Marathon Don't Stop*	B
Kepner, Tyler. *K*	796.357
Kerry, John. *Every Day Is Extra*	B
Kershaw, Alex. *Against All Odds*	940.54
Kessler-Harris, Alice. ★*Out to Work*	331.4
Ketchum, Richard M. *Saratoga*	973.3
Khakpour, Porochista. *Brown Album*	304.8
Khan, Yasmin Sabina. *Enlightening the World*	974.7
Khar, Erin. *Strung Out*	B
Kim, Anne. ★*Abandoned*	305.2350973
Kim, Anne. ★*Poverty for Profit*	302.5
Kimball, George. *Four Kings*	B
King, Martin Luther. ★*A Testament of Hope*	323.1
Kingsley, Lisa. *Smithsonian American Table*	641.5
Kinzer, Stephen. ★*All the Shah's Men*	955.05
Kinzer, Stephen. ★*The True Flag*	327.73
Kirshner, Jodie Adams. ★*Broke*	336.3
Kirtzman, Andrew. *Giuliani*	B
Kissinger, Henry. *Ending the Vietnam War*	959.704
Klare, Michael T. *All Hell Breaking Loose*	355.20973
Klay, Phil. *Uncertain Ground*	359.9
Klein, Ezra. ★*Why We're Polarized*	306.0973
Klobuchar, Amy. ★*Antitrust*	343.73
Kluger, Richard. *Indelible Ink*	B
Koh, EJ. *The Magical Language of Others*	813
Kolbert, Kathryn. *Controlling Women*	362.1988
Kolhatkar, Sheelah. *Black Edge*	364.16
Kolker, Robert Phillip. *Kubrick*	B
Komunyakaa, Yusef. ★*Everyday Mojo Songs of Earth*	811
Konnikova, Maria. *The Biggest Bluff*	795.412
Koones, Sheri. *Prefabulous Small Houses*	728
Koppel, Lily. *The Astronaut Wives Club*	920
Korda, Michael. *Clouds of Glory*	B
Kornacki, Steve. *The Red and the Blue*	306.20973
Kornhauser, Jacob. *The Cup of Coffee Club*	796.357
Kotz, Nick. *Judgment Days*	323
Kozol, Jonathan. *Fire in the Ashes*	362.77
Kozol, Jonathan. *Letters to a Young Teacher*	371.1
Kranish, Michael. *Trump Revealed*	B
Krass, Peter. *Carnegie*	B
Kriegel, Mark. *Pistol*	B
Kristof, Nicholas D. ★*Tightrope*	306.0973
Krugman, Paul R. *Arguing with Zombies*	330.973
Kunetka, James W. *The General and the Genius*	355.8
Kuo, Michelle. *Reading with Patrick*	B
Kurlansky, Mark. *1968*	909.82
Kurlansky, Mark. *Birdseye*	B

AUTHOR, TITLE, SERIES AND SUBJECT INDEX

Kurtz, Howard. *Media Madness*	973.933
Kurtz-Phelan, Daniel. *The China Mission*	951.04
Kurtz, Steven. *American Flannel*	338.4
Kwak, James. *Economism*	330
Lahey, Jessica. *The Gift of Failure*	649
Lahiri, Jhumpa. *Translating Myself and Others*	418
Lalami, Laila. *Conditional Citizens*	323.60973
Lamott, Anne. ★*Dusk, Night, Dawn*	B
Lancaster, Jen. *Welcome to the United States of Anxiety*	155.4
Land, Stephanie. *Maid*	B
Lane, Charles. *The Day Freedom Died*	976.3
Lanegan, Mark. *Sing Backwards and Weep*	B
Lang, Michael. *The Road to Woodstock*	781.66
Langewiesche, William. *American Ground*	974.7
Langguth, A. J. *After Lincoln*	973.8
Larson, Edward J. *The Return of George Washington*	B
Larson, Erik. ★*The Demon of Unrest*	973.7
Larson, Erik. *In the Garden of Beasts*	B
Larson, Kay. *Where the Heart Beats*	700.1
LaRue, James. ★*On Censorship*	025.2
Lasch, Christopher. ★*The Revolt of the Elites*	306
Lattin, Don. *The Harvard Psychedelic Club*	973.922092
Lauretta, D. S. *The Asteroid Hunter*	523.44
Law, Keith. *The Inside Game*	796.35764
Laymon, Kiese. ★*Heavy*	B
Le Guin, Ursula K. *No Time to Spare*	814
Le Guin, Ursula K. *Ursula K. Le Guin*	B
Leamer, Laurence. *The Kennedy Men*	920
Leaming, Barbara. *Jacqueline Bouvier Kennedy Onassis*	B
Leaming, Barbara. *Kick Kennedy*	B
Leaming, Barbara. *Mrs. Kennedy*	B
Leavy, Jane. *The Big Fella*	B
Leavy, Jane. *The Last Boy*	B
Leavy, Jane. *Sandy Koufax*	B
Lebron, Christopher J. *The Making of Black Lives Matter*	305.896
Ledbetter, James. *One Nation Under Gold*	332.4
Lee, Corky. ★*Corky Lee's Asian America*	770
Lee, Edward. *Buttermilk Graffiti*	641.59
Lee, Erika. *America for Americans*	305.800973
Lee, Erika. *The Making of Asian America*	973
Lee, Heath Hardage. ★*The League of Wives*	959.704
Lemann, Nicholas. *Transaction Man*	330.973
Lemon, Don. *This Is the Fire*	305.896
Leonhardt, David. ★*Ours Was the Shining Future*	330.973
Leonnig, Carol. *I Alone Can Fix It*	973.933
Leopold, Aldo. ★*A Sand County Almanac & Other Writings on Ecology and Conservation*	814
Lepore, Jill. *The Name of War*	973.2
Lepore, Jill. *The Secret History of Wonder Woman*	741.5
Lepore, Jill. ★*These Truths*	973
Lessig, Lawrence. *Remix*	346.7304
Lev, Arlene Istar. *The Complete Lesbian & Gay Parenting Guide*	649
Levin, Gail. *Edward Hopper*	759.13
Levine, Bruce C. *The Fall of the House of Dixie*	973.7
Levine, Bruce C. *Thaddeus Stevens*	B
Levine, Robert S. ★*The Failed Promise*	973.8
Levingston, Steven. *Kennedy and King*	920
Levitt, Steven D. ★*Freakonomics*	330
Levitt, Steven D. *Superfreakonomics*	330
Levy, Jonathan. *Ages of American Capitalism*	330.12
Levy, Shawn. ★*In on the Joke*	792.7
Lewis, John. ★*March; Book One*	741.5
Lewis, John. ★*March; Book Three*	741.5
Lewis, John. ★*March; Book Two*	741.5
Lewis, John. ★*Run; Book One*	741.5
Lewis, John. *Walking with the Wind*	B
Lewis, Michael. *The Big Short*	330.973
Lewis, Michael. *The Blind Side*	B
Lewis, Michael. ★*The Premonition*	614.5
Lichtman, Allan J. *The Embattled Vote in America*	324.6
Liebling, A. J. ★*The Sweet Science*	796.83
Light, Michael. *100 Suns*	779
Lim, Audrea. *Free the Land*	333.73
Lincoff, Gary. *The Audubon Society Field Guide to North American Mushrooms*	579.6
Lincoln, Abraham. *Speeches and Writings, 1832-1858*	973.5
Lincoln, Abraham. *Speeches and Writings, 1859-1865*	973.6
Linden, Eugene. *Fire and Flood*	304.2
Lippman, Laura. *My Life as a Villainess*	B
Lisle, John. *The Dirty Tricks Department*	940.54
Lithwick, Dahlia. *Lady Justice*	345.73
Litt, David. *Democracy in One Book or Less*	321.8
Litt, David. *Thanks, Obama*	B
Little, Elbert L. *The Audubon Society Field Guide to North American Trees*	582.16097
Logevall, Fredrik. *Embers of War*	959.704
Logevall, Fredrik. ★*JFK*	B
Lohman, Sarah. ★*Endangered Eating*	641.5973
Longman, Jere. *Among the Heroes*	974.8
Louvish, Simon. *Monkey Business*	B
Love, Bettina L. *Punished for Dreaming*	371.829
Lowenstein, Roger. *Ways and Means*	973.7
Lowery, Wesley. ★*American Whitelash*	305.8
Loyn, David. *The Long War*	958.104
Lucey, Donna M. *Sargent's Women*	920
Luiselli, Valeria. *Tell Me How It Ends*	305.23086
Lunardi, Joe. ★*Bracketology*	796.323
Lusane, Clarence. *The Black History of the White House*	975.3
Lustgarten, Abrahm. ★*On the Move*	363.7
Luttrell, Marcus. *Service*	956.7044
Lynn, Loretta. *Still Woman Enough*	B
MacColl, Gail. *To Marry an English Lord*	974.7
MacGillis, Alec. *Fulfillment*	381
MacPherson, Myra. *All Governments Lie*	B
Macy, Beth. ★*Dopesick*	362.29
Macy, Beth. ★*Factory Man*	338.7
Macy, Beth. ★*Raising Lazarus*	362.29
Maddow, Rachel. *Bag Man*	B
Madrick, Jeffrey G. *Invisible Americans*	362.7086
Maguire, James. *Impresario*	B
Mahoney, Richard D. *Sons & Brothers*	920
Maier, Pauline. *American Scripture*	973.3
Maier, Pauline. *Ratification*	342.7302
Maier, Thomas. *Mafia Spies*	364.1060973
Makos, Adam. *Spearhead*	B
Mallory, Tamika D. *State of Emergency*	305.896
Manchester, William. *Goodbye, Darkness*	B
Mandery, Evan J. *A Wild Justice*	345.73
Mankoff, Robert. *How About Never—Is Never Good for You?*	741.5
Mann, Charles C. ★*1491*	970.01
Mann, Jim. *The Rebellion of Ronald Reagan*	973.927092
Mann, William J. *The Contender*	B
Mann, William J. *Hello, Gorgeous*	B
Mann, William J. *Kate*	B
Manseau, Peter. *Objects of Devotion*	277
Manson, Mark. *Everything Is F*cked*	152.4
Manuel, Ian. *My Time Will Come*	B
Mar, Alex. *Witches of America*	299
Marable, Manning. ★*Malcolm X*	B
Maraniss, Andrew. *Strong Inside*	B
Maraniss, David. ★*Barack Obama*	B
Maraniss, David. *Clemente*	B
Maraniss, David. *They Marched into Sunlight*	959.704
Margonelli, Lisa. *Oil on the Brain*	338.2
Markovits, Daniel. *The Meritocracy Trap*	305.5
Marks, Ann. *Vivian Maier Developed*	778.9
Marsalis, Wynton. *Moving to Higher Ground*	781.65
Martin, Jonathan. *This Will Not Pass*	973.933
Martin, Steve. *Number One Is Walking*	B
Martinez Wood, Jamie. *Latino Writers and Journalists*	B
Martini, Adrienne. *Somebody's Gotta Do It*	B
Marton, Kati. *Hidden Power*	B
Marty, Martin E. *Pilgrims in Their Own Land*	200
Marvel, William. *Lincoln's Autocrat*	B
Masciotra, David. *Exurbia Now*	320.973
Mask, Deirdre. *The Address Book*	388.1
Matteson, John. *Eden's Outcasts*	920
Matthews, Christopher. *Bobby Kennedy*	B
Matthews, Christopher. *Kennedy & Nixon*	973.922
Mattlin, Ben. *Disability Pride*	323.3
May, Gary. *John Tyler*	B
Mayer, Jane. ★*Dark Money*	973.932
Mayer, Jane. *The Dark Side*	973.931
Mays, Kyle. ★*An Afro-Indigenous History of the United States*	973
Mays, Willie. *24*	B
McAlester, Virginia. *A Field Guide to American Houses*	728

PUBLIC LIBRARY CORE COLLECTION: NONFICTION
Twentieth Edition

McAlevey, Jane. *A Collective Bargain*	331.890973
McBride, James. *Kill 'Em and Leave*	B
McBrien, William. *Cole Porter*	B
McCabe, John. *Cagney*	B
McCallum, Jack. *Dream Team*	796.323
McCartney, Paul. ★*1964*	782.42166
McClelland, Mac. *Irritable Hearts*	B
McCormick, Ty. *Beyond the Sand and Sea*	920
McCoy, Alfred W. *A Question of Torture*	323.4
McCraw, David Edward. *Truth in Our Times*	342.7308
McCraw, Thomas K. ★*The Founders and Finance*	330.973
McCubbin, Lisa. *Betty Ford*	B
McCullough, David G. ★*1776*	973.3
McCullough, David G. ★*The American Spirit*	973
McCullough, David G. *The Greater Journey*	920
McCullough, David G. ★*John Adams*	B
McCullough, David G. *Mornings on Horseback*	B
McCullough, David G. *The Pioneers*	920
McCullough, David G. *Truman*	B
McDonough, James L. *William Tecumseh Sherman*	B
McDonough, Jimmy. *Tammy Wynette*	B
McDowell, Marta. *The World of Laura Ingalls Wilder*	813
McElya, Micki. *The Politics of Mourning*	975.5
McGhee, Heather C. ★*The Sum of Us*	305.8
McGilligan, Patrick. *Funny Man*	B
McGilligan, Patrick. *Oscar Micheaux*	B
McGinty, Brian. *Lincoln's Greatest Case*	346.7303
McGrath, Campbell. *Nouns & Verbs*	811
McGrath, Tim. *James Monroe*	B
McGrath, Tom. *Triumph of the Yuppies*	305.242
McGreal, Chris. *American Overdose*	362.29
McIntyre, Rick. *The Reign of Wolf 21*	599.773
McKean, David. *Watching Darkness Fall*	940.53
McKeon, Kathy. *Jackie's Girl*	B
McLaughlin, Kathleen. *Blood Money*	362.17
McLean, Bethany. *All the Devils Are Here*	330.973
McManus, John C. *Fire and Fortitude*	940.54
McManus, John C. *Island Infernos*	940.54
McMillan, Tracie. *The American Way of Eating*	338.4
McMillan, Tracie. ★*The White Bonus*	305.8
McMurtry, Larry. *Custer*	B
McNamara, Robert S. *In Retrospect*	959.704
McNeil, Donald G. ★*The Wisdom of Plagues*	614.4
McPherson, James M. ★*Abraham Lincoln*	B
McPherson, James M. ★*Tried by War*	973.7
McSwane, J. David. ★*Pandemic, Inc.*	362.1962
McWhirter, Cameron. *American Gun*	683.4
McWhorter, John H. *Talking Back, Talking Black*	427
Meacham, Jon. ★*American Lion*	B
Meacham, Jon. ★*And There Was Light*	B
Meacham, Jon. ★*Destiny and Power*	B
Meacham, Jon. *Franklin and Winston*	940.53
Meacham, Jon. ★*The Soul of America*	973
Meacham, Jon. ★*Thomas Jefferson*	B
Mead, Corey. *The Hidden History of the White House*	975.3
Mead, Walter Russell. *The Arc of a Covenant*	327.73
Mechanic, Michael. *Jackpot*	305.5
Mehr, Bob. *Trouble Boys*	920
Mehra, Nishta. *Brown, White, Black*	305.800973
Meltzer, Brad. ★*The First Conspiracy*	973.4
Meltzer, Brad. *The Lincoln Conspiracy*	973.7092
Menand, Louis. *The Free World*	306.0973
Merritt, Tyler. *I Take My Coffee Black*	791.4302
Merry, Robert W. *A Country of Vast Designs*	B
Merry, Robert W. *President McKinley*	B
Meslow, Scott. *From Hollywood with Love*	791.43
Messenger, Tony. *Profit and Punishment*	362.5
Metzl, Jonathan M. ★*What We've Become*	364.152
Meyer, Dakota. *Into the Fire*	958.104
Michaelis, David. ★*Eleanor*	973.917
Michaelis, David. *Schulz and Peanuts*	B
Michel, Casey. *American Kleptocracy*	364.16
Middlekauff, Robert. *The Glorious Cause*	973.3
Mifflin, Margot. *Looking for Miss America*	791.6
Milanovic, Branko. *The Have and the Have-Nots*	339.2
Milford, Nancy. *Savage Beauty*	B
Millard, Candice. *Destiny of the Republic*	973.8
Millard, Candice. *River of Doubt*	918.1
Miller, Char. *Gifford Pinchot and the Making of Modern Environmentalism*	B
Miller, Donald L. *Vicksburg*	973.7
Miller, Lulu. *Why Fish Don't Exist*	B
Miller, Marla. *Betsy Ross and the Making of America*	B
Miller, Reuben Jonathan. *Halfway Home*	364.8
Miller, Scott. *The President and the Assassin*	973.8
Mills, Stephen Tukel. *Chosen*	B
Minian, Ana Raquel. ★*In the Shadow of Liberty*	365
Minutaglio, Bill. *Dallas 1963*	973.922092
Minutaglio, Bill. *The Most Dangerous Man in America*	B
Miraldi, Robert. *Seymour Hersh*	B
Mitchell, Jerry. ★*Race Against Time*	364.152
Mitchell, Josh. *The Debt Trap*	378.3
Mitford, Jessica. ★*The American Way of Death Revisited*	338.4
Mogelson, Luke. *The Storm Is Here*	973.933
Mojica Rodriguez, Prisca Dorcas. *For Brown Girls with Sharp Edges and Tender Hearts*	305.48
Montero, David. ★*The Stolen Wealth of Slavery*	381
Montillo, Roseanne. *Deliberate Cruelty*	364.152
Montville, Leigh. *Sting Like a Bee*	B
Mooney, Paul. *Black Is the New White*	792.7
Moore, Lorrie. *See What Can Be Done*	801
Moore, Marcus J. *The Butterfly Effect*	B
Moore, Wayetu. *The Dragons, the Giant, the Women*	B
Mordden, Ethan. *Ziegfeld*	B
Morgan, Robert. *Lions of the West*	978
Morgan-Owens, Jessie. *Girl in Black and White*	B
Morgenson, Gretchen. ★*These Are the Plunderers*	332.6
Morison, Samuel Eliot. *John Paul Jones*	B
Morley, Jefferson. *Scorpions' Dance*	973.924
Morris, Edmund. ★*Colonel Roosevelt*	B
Morris, Edmund. ★*The Rise of Theodore Roosevelt*	B
Morris, Edmund. ★*Theodore Rex*	973.911
Morris, James McGrath. *Pulitzer*	B
Morris, Jim. ★*The Cancer Factory*	658.3
Moss, Gabrielle. *Paperback Crush*	813.009
Mouton, Deborah D. E. E. P. *Black Chameleon*	B
Muhammad, Khalil Gibran. *The Condemnation of Blackness*	364.2
Muir, John. *Nature Writings*	B
Murolo, Priscilla. *From the Folks Who Brought You the Weekend*	331
Murphy, Bruce Allen. *Scalia*	B
Murphy, Chris. ★*The Violence Inside Us*	303.60973
Murray, Charles A. *Coming Apart*	305.8
Murray, Charles Shaar. *Crosstown Traffic*	B
Nafisi, Azar. *The Republic of Imagination*	B
Namath, Joe Willie. ★*All the Way*	B
Nance, Malcolm W. *The Plot to Betray America*	973.933
Nasaw, David. *The Last Million*	940.53
Nasaw, David. ★*The Patriarch*	B
Neighbors, Joy. *The Family Tree Cemetery Field Guide*	929
Neiman, Garrett. *Rich White Men*	305.5
Neiwert, David A. ★*The Age of Insurrection*	303.48
Nelson, Craig. *Pearl Harbor*	940.54
Nelson, Craig. *Rocket Men*	629.45
Nelson, Craig. ★*V Is for Victory*	973.917
Nelson, Megan Kate. *The Three-Cornered War*	978
Nelson, Willie. *It's a Long Story*	B
Nesteroff, Kliph. *We Had a Little Real Estate Problem*	970.004
Neu, Charles E. *Colonel House*	B
Newitz, Annalee. *Stories Are Weapons*	355.3
Newman, Richard S. *Freedom's Prophet*	B
Nez, Chester. *Code Talker*	B
Nietfeld, Emi. *Acceptance*	B
Nimura, Janice P. ★*The Doctors Blackwell*	610.92
Nir, Sarah Maslin. *Horse Crazy*	B
Noah, Timothy. *The Great Divergence*	339.2
Nocera, Joseph. *The Big Fail*	362.1962
Nolan, Hamilton. *The Hammer*	331.8
Norman, Elizabeth M. *We Band of Angels*	940.54
Norman, Michael. *Haunted America*	133.1
Norman, Philip. ★*Wild Thing*	B
Norris, Michele. ★*Our Hidden Conversations*	305
Norris, Robert S. *Racing for the Bomb*	B
Norton, Mary Beth. *1774*	973.3
Nourse, Victoria F. *In Reckless Hands*	344.7304
Novick, Peter. *The Holocaust in American Life*	940.53
Nussbaum, Martha Craven. *The Monarchy of Fear*	306.20973
Nyamayaro, Elizabeth. *I Am a Girl from Africa*	B

AUTHOR, TITLE, SERIES AND SUBJECT INDEX

O'Brien, David M. ★*Storm Center*	347.73
O'Brien, Jack. *Jack Be Nimble*	B
O'Brien, Phillips Payson. *The Second Most Powerful Man in the World*	B
O'Connor, Garry. *Ian McKellen*	B
O'Connor, Ian. *Belichick*	B
O'Connor, Ian. *Coach K*	B
O'Connor, Sandra Day. ★*Out of Order*	347.73
O'Donnell, Patrick K. *The Unvanquished*	973.7
O'Neil, Cathy. *Weapons of Math Destruction*	005.7
O'Toole, Patricia. *The Moralist*	B
Obama, Barack. ★*The Audacity of Hope*	B
Obama, Barack. ★*Dreams from My Father*	B
Obama, Barack. ★*A Promised Land*	B
Obama, Michelle. ★*Becoming*	B
Offerman, Nick. *Where the Deer and the Antelope Play*	973.93
Okporo, Edafe. *Asylum*	
Oliphant, Thomas. ★*The Road to Camelot*	973.922092
Oliva, Alejandra. *Rivermouth*	305.9
Oller, John. *American Queen*	B
Olsen, Lise. *Code of Silence*	347.73
Olson, Lynne. *Citizens of London*	940.54012
Olson, Lynne. *Those Angry Days*	940.53
Olson, Roger E. ★*Handbook of Denominations in the United States*	200.973
Oluo, Ijeoma. ★*Be a Revolution*	305.8
Oluo, Ijeoma. ★*So You Want to Talk About Race*	305.800973
Oluseyi, Hakeem M. *A Quantum Life*	B
Onassis, Jacqueline Kennedy. *Historic Conversations on Life with John F. Kennedy*	B
Oppedisano, Tony. *Sinatra and Me*	B
Orman, Suze. *Women & Money*	332.0240082
Ortiz, Paul. *An African American and Latinx History of the United States*	305.8
Oshinsky, David M. ★*Polio*	614.5
Osnos, Evan. *Joe Biden*	B
Osnos, Evan. *Wildland*	973.93
Ostertag, Bob. *People's Movements, People's Press*	071
Otto, Mary. *Teeth*	617
Ours, Dorothy. *Man O' War*	798.400929
Owusu, Nadia. *Aftershocks*	B
Pablo Cruz, Rosayra. *The Book of Rosy*	B
Packer, George. *The Assassins' Gate*	956.7044
Packer, George. *Last Best Hope*	973.93
Packer, George. *Our Man*	B
Packer, George. ★*The Unwinding*	973.924
Page, Susan. ★*The Matriarch*	B
Page, Susan. ★*The Rulebreaker*	B
Paine, Thomas. ★*Rights of Man*	320.5
Painter, Nell Irvin. ★*I Just Keep Talking*	814
Parini, Jay. *Robert Frost*	B
Park, Benjamin E. *American Zion*	289.3
Parker, Morgan. ★*You Get What You Pay For*	305.896
Parton, Dolly. ★*Behind the Seams*	B
Patterson, James. *Walk in My Combat Boots*	920
Patterson, James. *Walk the Blue Line*	920
Patton, George S. *War as I Knew It*	
Paul, Joel R. *Indivisible*	973.5
Paulsen, Michael Stokes. *The Constitution*	342.7302
Paulson, Henry M. *On the Brink*	330.973
Pawel, Miriam. *The Crusades of Cesar Chavez*	B
Payne, Les. ★*The Dead Are Arising*	B
Pearlman, Jeff. *Football for a Buck*	796.332
Pearlman, Jeff. *The Last Folk Hero*	B
Pearlman, Jeff. *Sweetness*	B
Peiffer, Prudence. *The Slip*	709.73
Pennington, Emily. *Feral*	B
Perino, Michael A. *The Hellhound of Wall Street*	330.973
Perkins, Kendrick. *The Education of Kendrick Perkins*	B
Perkins, Nichole. *Sometimes I Trip on How Happy We Could Be*	
Perlstein, Rick. *The Invisible Bridge*	973.924
Perlstein, Rick. ★*Nixonland*	973.924
Perlstein, Rick. ★*Reaganland*	973.926
Perron, Cam. ★*Comeback Season*	796.357
Perry, Bruce. *Malcolm*	B
Perry, Imani. *May We Forever Stand*	782.25
Perry, Mark. *The Most Dangerous Man in America*	B
Persico, Joseph E. *Franklin and Lucy*	973.917092
Pessah, Jon. *Yogi*	B
Peters, Charles. *Lyndon B. Johnson*	B
Petri, Alexandra. *Nothing Is Wrong and Here Is Why*	973.933
Peyser, Marc N. *Hissing Cousins*	B
Philbrick, Nathaniel. ★*The Last Stand*	973.8
Philbrick, Nathaniel. *Travels with George*	973.4
Philbrick, Nathaniel. ★*Valiant Ambition*	B
Philipps, Busy. *This Will Only Hurt a Little*	B
Philipps, David. *Alpha*	956.7044
Phillips, Kevin. *1775*	973.3
Picower, Bree. *Reading, Writing, and Racism*	371.829
Pinckney, Darryl. *Busted in New York and Other Essays*	305.800973
Plant, Deborah G. *Of Greed and Glory*	326
Plokhy, Serhii. ★*Nuclear Folly*	972.9106
Plouffe, David. *A Citizen's Guide to Beating Donald Trump*	324.0973
Podemski, Max. *A Paradise of Small Houses*	363.5
Poehler, Amy. *Yes Please*	B
Pollack, Howard. ★*George Gershwin*	B
Poniewozik, James. *Audience of One*	324.7
Poole, Robert M. *Section 60*	975.5
Poole, W. Scott. *Vampira*	B
Porter, Eduardo. *American Poison*	305.800973
Posnanski, Joe. ★*The Life and Afterlife of Harry Houdini*	793.8
Posnanski, Joe. *The Soul of Baseball*	796.357
Posner, Gerald L. *Case Closed*	364.1
Postel, Charles. *Equality*	305.50973
Postman, Neil. *Amusing Ourselves to Death*	302.2
Potts, Monica. *The Forgotten Girls*	B
Powell, Julie. *Julie and Julia*	641.5
Powell, Nate. ★*Lies My Teacher Told Me*	741.5
Prager, Joshua. *The Family Roe*	342.7308
Pratt, Victoria. *The Power of Dignity*	364.973
Prejean, Helen. *The Death of Innocents*	364.66
Press, Eyal. ★*Dirty Work*	331.7
Preston, Diana. *Eight Days at Yalta*	940.53
Price, Polly J. *Plagues in the Nation*	614.4
Prose, Francine. *1974*	B
Prothero, Stephen R. *The American Bible*	973
Prothero, Stephen R. *God the Bestseller*	070.5
Prud'homme, Alex. ★*Dinner with the President*	973
Prud'homme, Alex. *The French Chef in America*	B
Puglionesi, Alicia. *In Whose Ruins*	973
Puleo, Stephen. *Voyage of Mercy*	363.8
Purdum, Todd S. *An Idea Whose Time Has Come*	342.7308
Putnam, Robert D. *Our Kids*	305.5
Quart, Alissa. *Bootstrapped*	305.5
Quart, Alissa. *Squeezed*	305.5
Quinones, Sam. *Dreamland*	362.29
Quinones, Sam. ★*The Least of Us*	362.29
Raboteau, Emily. *Lessons for Survival*	814
Raines, Howell. *Silent Cavalry*	973.7
Rakove, Jack N. *Revolutionaries*	973.3
Ramos, Jorge. *Stranger*	325.73
Rampersad, Arnold. ★*Ralph Ellison*	B
Ramsey, Donovan X. ★*When Crack Was King*	362.29
Ramsland, Katherine M. *Ghost*	133.1
Randall, Willard Sterne. *The Founders' Fortunes*	973.3
Randall, Willard Sterne. *George Washington*	B
Rankine, Claudia. ★*Citizen*	814
Rankine, Claudia. ★*Just Us*	305.896
Raphael, Ray. *Mr. President*	352.230973
Raphael, Ray. *A People's History of the American Revolution*	973.3
Rapping, Jonathan. *Gideon's Promise*	345.73
Rappleye, Charles. *Herbert Hoover in the White House*	B
Rasenberger, Jim. *The Brilliant Disaster*	972.9106
Rather, Dan. *What Unites Us*	323.6
Ratliff, Ben. *The Jazz Ear*	781.6509
Ravitch, Diane. *Slaying Goliath*	371.010973
Reagan, Ronald. *The Reagan Diaries*	B
Reagan, Ronald. *Reagan*	B
Reang, Putsata. *Ma and Me*	B
Reed, Julia. *Dispatches from the Gilded Age*	B
Reeves, Richard V. *Dream Hoarders*	305.5
Rehak, Melanie. *Girl Sleuth*	813
Reichl, Ruth. *Comfort Me with Apples*	B
Reichl, Ruth. *My Kitchen Year*	641.5
Reid, Stuart A. *The Lumumba Plot*	967.51
Reid, T. R. *A Fine Mess*	336.200973
Reilly, Ryan J. ★*Sedition Hunters*	364.1
Reitman, Janet. *Inside Scientology*	299

PUBLIC LIBRARY CORE COLLECTION: NONFICTION
Twentieth Edition

Rembert, Winfred. *Chasing Me to My Grave*	B
Remnick, David. *The Bridge*	B
Renehan, Edward. *Commodore*	B
Reston, James. *The Conviction of Richard Nixon*	973.924092
Reynolds, David S. ★*Abe*	B
Rhoden, William C. *$40 Million Slaves*	796
Rhodes, Benjamin J. *The World as It Is*	973.932
Ribowsky, Mark. *Howard Cosell*	070.449796
Ribowsky, Mark. *Signed, Sealed, and Delivered*	B
Ribowsky, Mark. *The Supremes*	B
Rice, Condoleezza. *No Higher Honor*	B
Rice, Jerry. *America's Game*	796.332
Richards, Leonard L. *Who Freed the Slaves?*	342.7308
Richardson, Heather Cox. *Democracy Awakening*	320.473
Richardson, Heather Cox. ★*How the South Won the Civil War*	306.20973
Richardson, Robert D. *Emerson*	814
Richardson, Robert D. *William James*	B
Ricketts, Rachel. ★*Do Better*	305.800973
Ricks, Thomas E. *Fiasco*	956.7044
Ricks, Thomas E. ★*First Principles*	973.09
Ricks, Thomas E. ★*The Generals*	B
Rigsby, Cody. ★*XOXO, Cody*	B
Riley, Kathleen. *The Astaires*	B
Rinehart, Lorissa. *First to the Front*	B
Rinella, Steven. *The Complete Guide to Hunting, Butchering, and Cooking Wild Game*	799.2
Rinella, Steven. *Meat Eater*	B
Risen, Clay. *The Bill of the Century*	342.7308
Rivlin, Gary. *Broke, Usa*	339.4
Roach, Mary. ★*Grunt*	355
Robb, Alice. ★*Don't Think, Dear*	792.8
Robbins, Alexandra. ★*The Teachers*	371.1
Roberts, Cokie. *Founding Mothers*	920
Roberts, Dorothy E. *Torn Apart*	362.7
Roberts, Randy. *Blood Brothers*	920
Roberts, Randy. *Joe Louis*	B
Robertson, Robbie. ★*Testimony*	B
Robeson, Paul. *The Undiscovered Paul Robeson*	B
Robin, Corey. *The Enigma of Clarence Thomas*	347.73
Robinson, Ray. *Iron Horse*	B
Robinson, Roxana. *Georgia O'Keeffe*	B
Robinson, Staci. ★*Tupac Shakur*	B
Robison, John Elder. *Look Me in the Eye*	B
Robison, Peter. ★*Flying Blind*	338.7
Rogers, Katie. ★*American Woman*	973.09
Rohde, David. *In Deep*	973.933
Rojas Contreras, Ingrid. ★*The Man Who Could Move Clouds*	B
Roll, David L. *George Marshall*	B
Rose, Tricia. ★*Metaracism*	305.8
Rosenberg, Ian. *The Fight for Free Speech*	342.73
Rosenberg, Rosalind. ★*Jane Crow*	B
Ross, Dax-Devlon. *Letters to My White Male Friends*	305.8
Rothkopf, David J. *American Resistance*	973.933
Rothman, Joshua D. *The Ledger and the Chain*	306.362
Rothschild, Mike. *The Storm Is Upon Us*	973.933
Rothstein, Richard. ★*The Color of Law*	305.800973
Roundtree, Dovey Johnson. ★*Mighty Justice*	B
Rubenstein, David M. *The American Experiment*	973
Ruck, Rob. *Raceball*	796.357
Ruffin, Amber. ★*The World Record Book of Racist Stories*	305.896
Ruffin, Amber. *You'll Never Believe What Happened to Lacey*	305.896
Rumsfeld, Donald. *When the Center Held*	973.925092
Runstedtler, Theresa. *Black Ball*	796.323
Rush, Chris. *The Light Years*	B
Rybczynski, Witold. *Mysteries of the Mall*	720
Sabatini Sloan, Aisha. *Dreaming of Ramadi in Detroit*	814
Sage, Sami. *Democracy in Retrograde*	324
Saint John, Bozoma. *The Urgent Life*	B
Salisbury, Katie Gee. ★*Not Your China Doll*	B
Samaha, Albert. *Concepcion*	929
Samet, Elizabeth D. *Looking for the Good War*	940.53
Sandel, Michael J. *Justice*	172
Sando, Mike. *The Football 100*	796.332
Santana, Carlos. *The Universal Tone*	B
Sarna, Jonathan D. ★*American Judaism*	296
Satow, Julie. *When Women Ran Fifth Avenue*	381.141
Saul, Scott. ★*Becoming Richard Pryor*	B
Saxton, Martha. *The Widow Washington*	B
Scahill, Jeremy. *Dirty Wars*	355.00973
Schaap, Jeremy. *Cinderella Man*	B
Scharre, Paul. *Four Battlegrounds*	006.3
Schlender, Brent. *Becoming Steve Jobs*	B
Schlesinger, Arthur M. *Journals, 1952-2000*	973.91092
Schlosser, Eric. *Command and Control*	363.17
Schmidt, Michael S. ★*Donald Trump v. The United States*	973.933
Schuller, Kyla. *The Trouble with White Women*	305.42
Schulman, Bruce J. *The Seventies*	973.92
Schultz, Kevin Michael. *Buckley and Mailer*	920
Schumacher, Michael. *Will Eisner*	741.5
Schwab, Tim. ★*The Bill Gates Problem*	361.7
Schwartz, Joanna C. ★*Shielded*	344.7305
Schwartz, Nelson. *The Velvet Rope Economy*	339.2
Schwartzel, Erich. *Red Carpet*	791.43
Schwartzman, Nancy. *Roll Red Roll*	364.15
Scott-Clark, Cathy. *The Forever Prisoner*	364.6
Seabrook, Nicholas R. *One Person, One Vote*	328.3
Sedgewick, Augustine. *Coffeeland*	338.4
Sedgwick, John. *War of Two*	973.4
Seidule, Ty. *Robert E. Lee and Me*	973.7
Self, Robert O. *All in the Family*	320.50973
Selingo, Jeffrey J. *College (un)bound*	378
Selingo, Jeffrey J. *Who Gets in and Why*	378.1
Selvaratnam, Tanya. *Assume Nothing*	B
Sen, Mayukh. *Taste Makers*	641.5092
Sentilles, Sarah. *Stranger Care*	306
Service, Robert. *The End of the Cold War 1985-1991*	909.82
Servon, Lisa J. *The Unbanking of America*	332.10973
Sexton, Jared Yates. *American Rule*	973
Shahidi, Afshin. *Prince*	B
Shakur, Prince. *When They Tell You to Be Good*	B
Shapiro, James. ★*The Playbook*	792
Shapiro, James. *Shakespeare in a Divided America*	822.33
Sharfstein, Daniel J. ★*Thunder in the Mountains*	979.5
Sharif, Solmaz. *Customs*	811
Sharlet, Jeff. ★*The Undertow*	322
Sharma, Nina. *The Way You Make Me Feel*	B
Sharpe, Christina Elizabeth. *Ordinary Notes*	305.896
Sharpton, Al. *Rise Up*	973.933
Shaughnessy, Jim. *The Call of Trains*	779
Shaw, Robert. *American Quilts*	746.46
Sheehan, Neil. *A Bright Shining Lie*	959.704
Sheehan, Neil. *A Fiery Peace in a Cold War*	B
Sheff, David. *The Buddhist on Death Row*	B
Sheinkin, Steve. *Bomb*	623.4
Sherman, Casey. *Above and Beyond*	973.922092
Sherr, Lynn. *Sally Ride*	B
Shesol, Jeff. *Mercury Rising*	629.45
Shesol, Jeff. *Supreme Power*	347.73
Shih, David. *Chinese Prodigal*	B
Shimer, David. *Rigged*	324.60973
Shirley, Craig. *Mary Ball Washington*	B
Shlaes, Amity. *Coolidge*	B
Shlaes, Amity. *The Forgotten Man*	973.91
Showalter, Elaine. ★*A Jury of Her Peers*	810.9
Shultz, Richard H. *The Secret War Against Hanoi*	959.704
Sides, Hampton. *Blood and Thunder*	978
Sides, Hampton. *Hellhound on His Trail*	364.152
Sides, Hampton. *On Desperate Ground*	951.904
Sielski, Mike. *The Rise*	B
Signer, Michael. *Cry Havoc*	305.800973
Siler, Julia Flynn. *The White Devil's Daughters*	306.3
Simon, James F. *Eisenhower vs. Warren*	347.73
Simon, James F. *FDR and Chief Justice Hughes*	973.917092
Simon, James F. *What Kind of Nation*	342.73
Singer, Jessie. *There Are No Accidents*	363.1
Singh, Julietta. *The Breaks*	B
Sinha, Manisha. ★*The Rise and Fall of the Second American Republic*	973.8
Sinise, Gary. *Grateful American*	B
Sisson, Gretchen E. ★*Relinquished*	362.734
Slade, Rachel. *American Hoodie*	338.4
Slahi, Mohamedou Ould. *The Mauritanian*	958.104
Slevin, Peter. *Michelle Obama*	B
Smialek, Jeanna. ★*Limitless*	332.1
Smietana, Bob. *Reorganized Religion*	262.001
Smiley, Jane. *Thirteen Ways of Looking at the Novel*	B
Smilios, Maria. ★*The Black Angels*	610.73

AUTHOR, TITLE, SERIES AND SUBJECT INDEX

Author. Title	Call #
Smith, Ben. *Traffic*	070.4
Smith, Chris. *The Daily Show (the Book)*	791.45
Smith, Clint. ★*Above Ground*	811
Smith, Danez. ★*Don't Call Us Dead*	811.6
Smith, Douglas. *The Russian Job*	947.084
Smith, Erin Geiger. ★*Thank You for Voting*	324.973
Smith, J. Douglas. *On Democracy's Doorstep*	342.73
Smith, Jean Edward. *Bush*	973.931
Smith, Jean Edward. *FDR*	B
Smith, Jean Edward. *John Marshall*	B
Smith, Michael S. *Designing History*	975.3
Smith, Mychal Denzel. *Stakes Is High*	973.933
Smith, Patricia. *Unshuttered*	811
Smith, Richard Norton. *On His Own Terms*	973.925092
Smith, Richard Norton. *An Ordinary Man*	B
Smith, Starr. *Jimmy Stewart*	B
Smith, Tracy K. ★*Wade in the Water*	811.6
Snow, Jess. ★*Outreach Services for Teens*	027.4
Snyder, Christina. *Great Crossings*	976.9
Snyder, Timothy. ★*Our Malady*	362.10973
Soboroff, Jacob. ★*Separated*	325.73
Sohn, Amy. *The Man Who Hated Women*	363.28
Sole-Smith, Virginia. ★*Fat Talk*	649.1
Solnit, Rebecca. *Call Them by Their True Names*	303.3
Solomon, Andrew. *Far from the Tree*	362.4083
Solomon, Deborah. *American Mirror*	B
Solomon, Deborah. *Jackson Pollock*	B
Somerstein, Rachel. ★*Invisible Labor*	618.8
Sommer, Will. ★*Trust the Plan*	973.933
Sontag, Susan. *At the Same Time*	814
Sorensen, Theodore C. *Counselor*	B
Sorvino, Chloe. *Raw Deal*	338.1
Sotomayor, Sonia. ★*My Beloved World*	B
Soufan, Ali H. *The Black Banners Declassified*	363.325
Souza, Pete. *Obama*	973.932
Souza, Pete. *Shade*	973.932
Sowell, Thomas. *Basic Economics*	330
Specter, Emma. *More, Please*	616.85
Spencer, Kyle. *Raising Them Right*	320.5
Spiegel, Maura. *Sidney Lumet*	B
Spitz, Bob. ★*Dearie*	B
Spitz, Bob. ★*Reagan*	B
Spoto, Donald. *High Society*	B
Spratford, Becky Siegel. *The Readers' Advisory Guide to Horror*	025.5
Springsteen, Bruce. ★*Born to Run*	B
Spruill, Marjorie Julian. *Divided We Stand*	305.42
Stahr, Celia. *Frida in America*	B
Stahr, Walter. *Seward*	B
Staiti, Paul J. *Of Arms and Artists*	B
Stanley, Paul. *Backstage Pass*	B
Stanley, Paul. *Face the Music*	B
Stanley, Thomas J. *The Next Millionaire Next Door*	332.024
Stanton, Doug. *12 Strong*	958.104
Starks, Glenn L. *Thurgood Marshall*	B
Steil, Benn. ★*The Marshall Plan*	338.91
Steinbeck, John. *Travels with Charley*	B
Steinem, Gloria. *My Life on the Road*	B
Steinem, Gloria. *Outrageous Acts and Everyday Rebellions*	305.42
Steinhauer, Jennifer. *The Firsts*	320.082
Stelter, Brian. *Hoax*	070.4
Stelter, Brian. *Top of the Morning*	791.456
Stengel, Richard. *Information Wars*	355.3
Stephanopoulos, George. ★*The Situation Room*	973.09
Stevens, Dana. *Camera Man*	791.4302
Stevens, Stuart. *The Conspiracy to End America*	324.2734
Stevens, Stuart. *It Was All a Lie*	324.2734
Stewart, David O. *George Washington*	973.4
Stewart, David O. *Madison's Gift*	B
Stiglitz, Joseph E. *Globalization and Its Discontents*	337
Stiglitz, Joseph E. *The Price of Inequality*	305.50973
Stiles, T. J. *Custer's Trials*	B
Stiles, T. J. ★*The First Tycoon*	B
Stone, Daniel. *The Food Explorer*	B
Stone, Geoffrey R. *Perilous Times*	323.44
Stone, Geoffrey R. ★*Sex and the Constitution*	345.7302
Stout, David. *The Kidnap Years*	364.15
Stratton, W. K. *Floyd Patterson*	B
Stuart, Amanda Mackenzie. *Empress of Fashion*	B
Sturgis, Matthew. *Oscar Wilde*	B
Styron, William. *My Generation*	814
Suarez, Ray. ★*We Are Home*	325.73
Sullivan, Kevin. *Trump on Trial*	342.73
Sullivan, Margaret. *Newsroom Confidential*	070.92
Sullivan, Matt. *Can't Knock the Hustle*	796.323
Sullivan, Patricia. *Lift Every Voice*	973
Sullivan, Randall. *Graveyard of the Pacific*	979.7
Sundeen, Mark. *The Unsettlers*	640
Sunstein, Cass R. *Impeachment*	342.73
Susanka, Sarah. *Creating the Not so Big House*	728
Svrluga, Barry. *The Grind*	796.357
Swafford, Jan. *Charles Ives*	B
Swanson, James L. *End of Days*	973.922092
Swarns, Rachel L. *The 272*	975.2
Swarns, Rachel L. ★*American Tapestry*	B
Sweeney, Jennifer. *Literacy*	027.62
Sweig, Julia. *Lady Bird Johnson*	B
Swofford, Anthony. *Jarhead*	956.7044
Symonds, Craig L. *Lincoln and His Admirals*	B
Szwed, John F. *Cosmic Scholar*	B
Taddeo, Lisa. *Three Women*	306.7082
Takaki, Ronald T. *Double Victory*	940.53
Talty, Stephan. *Saving Bravo*	959.704
Tamblyn, Amber. ★*Era of Ignition*	B
Taraborrelli, J. Randy. ★*Jackie*	B
Taraborrelli, J. Randy. ★*The Secret Life of Marilyn Monroe*	B
Tatum, Beverly Daniel. ★*"Why Are All the Black Kids Sitting Together in the Cafeteria?"*	305.800973
Tau, Byron. ★*Means of Control*	363.25
Taub, Jennifer. *Big Dirty Money*	364.16
Taylor, Alan. *American Republics*	973.3
Taylor, Alan. *American Revolutions*	973.3
Taylor, Alan. *The Civil War of 1812*	973.5
Taylor, Alan. *The Divided Ground*	974.7
Taylor, Barbara Brown. *Holy Envy*	B
Taylor, Nick. *American Made*	331.13
Teachout, Terry. ★*All in the Dances*	B
Teitel, Amy Shira. *Fighting for Space*	920
Telushkin, Joseph. *Rebbe*	296.833
Tenzin Priyadarshi. *Running Toward Mystery*	B
Terkel, Studs. ★*Hard Times*	973.91
Terkel, Studs. *Hope Dies Last*	920
Terkel, Studs. *Working*	920
Terry, Bryant. *Black Food*	394.1
Tesfamariam, Rahiel. ★*Imagine Freedom*	305.896
Tester, Jon. *Grounded*	B
Thomas, Elizabeth Marshall. *Growing Old*	305.26
Thomas, Etan. *We Matter*	796.08
Thomas, Evan. *Being Nixon*	B
Thomas, Evan. ★*First*	B
Thomas, Evan. *Ike's Bluff*	973.921092
Thomas, Evan. ★*John Paul Jones*	B
Thomas, Evan. ★*Robert Kennedy*	B
Thomas, Evan. *Sea of Thunder*	940.54
Thomas, Franklin A. *An Unplanned Life*	B
Thomas, Louisa. *Louisa*	B
Thomas, R. Eric. *Here for It*	B
Thomas, Richard F. ★*Why Bob Dylan Matters*	782.42164
Thompson, Bob. *Revolutionary Roads*	973.3
Thompson, Erin L. *Smashing Statues*	725
Thompson, Juan F. *Stories I Tell Myself*	B
Thompson, Nicholas. *The Hawk and the Dove*	973.92
Tickle, Phyllis. *The Great Emergence*	270.8
Tinsley, Omise'eke Natasha. *Beyonce in Formation*	782.42164
Tipton-Martin, Toni. *The Jemima Code*	641.59
Tipton-Martin, Toni. ★*Jubilee*	641.59
Tipton-Martin, Toni. *Juke Joints, Jazz Clubs & Juice*	641.87
Tobar, Hector. ★*Our Migrant Souls*	305.868
Tocqueville, Alexis de. ★*Democracy in America*	320.973
Todd, Kim. *Sensational*	920
Tolentino, Jia. ★*Trick Mirror*	973.93
Toll, Ian W. ★*Six Frigates*	359.00973
Tomlinson, Tommy. *The Elephant in the Room*	B
Toobin, Jeffrey. ★*Homegrown*	363.325
Toobin, Jeffrey. *The Nine*	347.73
Toobin, Jeffrey. *True Crimes and Misdemeanors*	973.933
Tough, Paul. *The Years That Matter Most*	378.1

PUBLIC LIBRARY CORE COLLECTION: NONFICTION
Twentieth Edition

Traub, James. *John Quincy Adams*	B
Tresch, John. *The Reason for the Darkness of the Night*	B
Tribe, Laurence H. *Uncertain Justice*	342.73
Trillin, Calvin. *The Lede*	071
Trimble, Lee. *Beyond the Call*	940.54
Trump, Mary L. *Too Much and Never Enough*	B
Tubbs, Anna Malaika. *The Three Mothers*	306.874
Tucci, Stanley. ★*Taste*	B
Tuchman, Barbara W. *Stilwell and the American Experience in China, 1911-45*	B
Tucker, Todd. *The Great Starvation Experiment*	174.2
Tucker, Virginia. *Finding the Answers to Legal Questions*	340.072
Tumulty, Karen. *The Triumph of Nancy Reagan*	B
Turban, Jack L. ★*Free to Be*	616.85
Turchin, Peter. *End Times*	320.01
Turk, Katherine. *The Women of Now*	305.42
Turner, Tina. ★*Happiness Becomes You*	158.1
Turow, Scott. ★*Ultimate Punishment*	345.73
Twenge, Jean M. *Generations*	305.2
Tworkov, Helen. *Lotus Girl*	B
Tye, Larry. ★*Bobby Kennedy*	B
Tye, Larry. ★*Demagogue*	B
Tye, Larry. *Satchel*	B
Tyson, Cicely. ★*Just as I Am*	B
Tyson, Mike. *Iron Ambition*	B
Ujifusa, Steven. *Barons of the Sea*	387.5
Ulander, Perry A. *Walking Point*	B
Unger, Debi. *George Marshall*	B
Unger, Harlow G. *American Tempest*	973.3
Unger, Harlow G. *First Founding Father*	B
Unger, Harlow G. *The Last Founding Father*	B
Updegrove, Mark K. *The Last Republicans*	973.928
Updike, John. *Always Looking*	700
Urofsky, Melvin I. *The Affirmative Action Puzzle*	331.13
Urofsky, Melvin I. *Dissent and the Supreme Court*	342.7302
Urofsky, Melvin I. *Louis D. Brandeis*	B
Urrea, Luis Alberto. *The Devil's Highway*	304.8
Van Agtmael, Peter. *Look at the USA*	070
Vargas, Jose Antonio. *Dear America*	B
Vasquez, Karla Tatiana. ★*The Salvisoul Cookbook*	641.598
Velshi, Ali. *Small Acts of Courage*	B
Versaci, Russell. *Creating a New Old House*	728
Vigliotti, Jonathan. *Before It's Gone*	577
Villarosa, Linda. ★*Under the Skin*	362.1089
Vinton, Nathaniel. *The Fall Line*	796.93
Vladeck, Stephen I. *The Shadow Docket*	347.73
Vogel, Steve. *Betrayal in Berlin*	327.1273043
Von Furstenberg, Diane. *The Woman I Wanted to Be*	B
Von Tunzelmann, Alex. *Blood and Sand*	909.82
Vonnegut, Kurt. *Kurt Vonnegut*	813
Vonnegut, Kurt. ★*A Man Without a Country*	818
Vowell, Sarah. *Assassination Vacation*	B
Wacker, Grant. *America's Pastor*	B
Wadman, Meredith. *The Vaccine Race*	614.5
Wald, Elijah. *Dylan Goes Electric!*	782.42164
Wald, Elijah. *How the Beatles Destroyed Rock 'N' Roll*	781.64
Walder, Tracy. *The Unexpected Spy*	B
Waldman, Michael. *The Supermajority*	347.73
Waldman, Steven. *Sacred Liberty*	341.4
Walker, Alice. *Gathering Blossoms Under Fire*	B
Walker, Hunter. *The Truce*	324.2736
Walker, Vanessa Siddle. *The Lost Education of Horace Tate*	370.92
Walker-Hill, Helen. *From Spirituals to Symphonies*	780
Wallace, Carvell. *Another Word for Love*	B
Wallace, Chris. *Countdown 1945*	940.54
Wallace, Chris. *Countdown Bin Laden*	958.104
Wallis, Jim. *The False White Gospel*	261.7
Walls, Laura Dassow. ★*Henry David Thoreau*	B
Walton, Calder. *Spies*	327.1247
Ward, Geoffrey C. *A Disposition to Be Rich*	B
Ward, Geoffrey C. ★*The Roosevelts*	B
Ward, Geoffrey C. *Unforgivable Blackness*	B
Ward, Jesmyn. ★*The Fire This Time*	305.896
Warraich, Haider. *The Song of Our Scars*	616
Warren, Elizabeth. *This Fight Is Our Fight*	305.5
Warren, James A. *Year of the Hawk*	959.704
Warren, Louis S. *Buffalo Bill's America*	B
Warrick, Joby. *Red Line*	956.9104
Wartzman, Rick. *Still Broke*	381
Washington, Kate. ★*Already Toast*	649.8
Wasik, Bill. ★*Our Kindred Creatures*	179
Wasson, Sam. *Fifth Avenue, 5 A.M.*	791.43
Wasson, Sam. ★*Improv Nation*	792.02
Waterhouse, Benjamin C. *One Day I'll Work for Myself*	338
Waterman, Jonathan. *National Geographic Atlas of the National Parks*	917.304
Waters, Alice. ★*We Are What We Eat*	641.01
Waters, John. *Mr. Know-It-All*	814
Waters, John. *Role Models*	B
Watson, Bruce. *Freedom Summer*	323.1196
Watts, Jill. *Hattie McDaniel*	B
Watts, Steven. *The People's Tycoon*	B
Wehle, Kim. *What You Need to Know About Voting and Why*	324.60973
Weill, Kelly. *Off the Edge*	001.9
Weiner, Tim. *The Folly and the Glory*	327.73047
Weiner, Tim. *Legacy of Ashes*	327.1273009
Weiner, Tim. *One Man Against the World*	B
Weingarten, Gene. ★*One Day*	973
Weintraub, Stanley. *Iron Tears*	973.3
Weisman, Steven R. *The Chosen Wars*	296.0973
Weissmann, Andrew. ★*Where Law Ends*	324.7
Weitzman, Yaron. *Tanking to the Top*	796.323
Weller, Sam. *The Bradbury Chronicles*	B
Wenner, Jann. *Like a Rolling Stone*	B
Wert, Jeffry D. *Custer*	B
Wertheim, L. Jon. *Blood in the Cage*	796.815
Wertheim, L. Jon. *Glory Days*	796.09
Wessel, David. *In Fed We Trust*	332.1
West, Cornel. *Black Prophetic Fire*	920
West, Lindy. *Shrill*	818
West, Lindy. *The Witches Are Coming*	305.420973
Westad, Odd Arne. *The Cold War*	909.825
Wexler, Jay. *Holy Hullabaloos*	342.7308
Wexler, Stuart. *Killing King*	323.092
Whipple, Chris. *The Fight of His Life*	973.934
Whipple, Chris. *The Gatekeepers*	973.92092
Whipple, Chris. *The Spymasters*	920
Whitaker, Mark. ★*Saying It Loud*	973.923
Whitby, Andrew. *The Sum of the People*	001.4
White, Gayle Jessup. *Reclamation*	B
White, Ronald C. *A. Lincoln*	B
White, Ronald C. ★*American Ulysses*	B
White, Ronald C. *Lincoln in Private*	B
White, Ryan. *Jimmy Buffett*	782.42164
Whitlock, Craig. *The Afghanistan Papers*	958.104
Whitmer, Jamie Davis. *America's Most Haunted Hotels*	133.1
Whyte, Kenneth. *Hoover*	B
Whyte, Kenneth. *The Uncrowned King*	B
Wickenden, Dorothy. *The Agitators*	920
Widder, Edith. *Below the Edge of Darkness*	551.46092
Widmer, Edward L. *Martin Van Buren*	B
Wiedeman, Reeves. *Billion Dollar Loser*	333.33
Wiehl, Lis W. *A Spy in Plain Sight*	327.1247
Wilder, Laura Ingalls. *Pioneer Girl*	B
Wilkerson, Isabel. ★*Caste*	305.5
Wilkerson, Isabel. ★*The Warmth of Other Suns*	304.80973
Wilkinson, Alec. *The Protest Singer*	B
Will, George F. *The Conservative Sensibility*	320.520973
Williams, Juan. *Eyes on the Prize*	323.4
Williams, Juan. *Thurgood Marshall*	B
Williams, Lucinda. *Don't Tell Anybody the Secrets I Told You*	B
Williams, Michael Kenneth. *Scenes from My Life*	B
Williams, Sophie. *Anti-Racist Ally*	305.8
Williams, Terry Tempest. *Erosion*	814
Willis, Deborah. *Envisioning Emancipation*	973.7
Willis, Deborah. *Reflections in Black*	770
Willis, Raquel. *The Risk It Takes to Bloom*	B
Wills, Garry. *James Madison*	B
Wills, Garry. *Lincoln at Gettysburg*	973.7
Wills, Shomari. *Black Fortunes*	920
Wilson, A'ja. ★*Dear Black Girls*	158.1
Wilson, Brian. *I Am Brian Wilson*	B
Wilson, Chris. *The Master Plan*	B
Wilson, F. Perry. *How Medicine Works and When It Doesn't*	610.69
Wilson, Rick. *Running Against the Devil*	973.933
Wilson, Robert. *Barnum*	B

AUTHOR, TITLE, SERIES AND SUBJECT INDEX

Wilson, Victoria. *A Life of Barbara Stanwyck*	B
Winchester, Simon. *The Men Who United the States*	973
Wineapple, Brenda. *The Impeachers*	973.8
Winik, Jay. *1944*	940.53
Winters, Kathleen C. *Amelia Earhart*	B
Winters, Richard D. *Beyond Band of Brothers*	B
Wohlleben, Peter. *Forest Walking*	582.16
Wojczuk, Tana. *Lady Romeo*	B
Wolfe, Tom. ★*The Right Stuff*	629.4
Wolff, Daniel J. *Grown-Up Anger*	920
Wolff, Michael. *Fire and Fury*	973.933
Wolff, Michael. *Landslide*	973.933
Wolk, Douglas. ★*All of the Marvels*	741.5
Wong, Ali. ★*Dear Girls*	B
Wong, Stephen. *Smithsonian Baseball*	796.357
Wood, Gordon S. *Empire of Liberty*	973.4
Wood, Gordon S. *Friends Divided*	920
Woods, Randall Bennett. *Prisoners of Hope*	973.923
Woodward, Bob. *Fear*	973.933
Woodward, Bob. *The Final Days*	B
Woodward, Bob. *Peril*	973.933
Woodward, Bob. *Shadow*	973.92
Woodward, C. Vann. *The Strange Career of Jim Crow*	305.896
Wright, Lawrence. *Going Clear*	299
Wright, Lawrence. ★*The Looming Tower*	973.931
Wu, Tim. *The Attention Merchants*	659.1
Wukovits, John F. *Lost at Sea*	940.54
Yacovone, Donald. ★*Teaching White Supremacy*	370.89
Yang, Jeff. ★*Rise*	973
Yellin, Emily. *Our Mothers' War*	940.53
Yoshino, Kenji. *Speak Now*	346.79401
Young, Damon. ★*What Doesn't Kill You Makes You Blacker*	B
Young, Kevin. *Brown*	811
Young, Ralph F. *Dissent*	303.48
Yovanovitch, Marie. *Lessons from the Edge*	973.933
Zack, Ian. *Odetta*	B
Zaitchik, Alexander. *Owning the Sun*	362.1
Zamora, Javier. ★*Solito*	B
Zanes, Warren. *Petty*	B
Zeitz, Joshua. *Building the Great Society*	973.923
Zelizer, Julian E. *Burning Down the House*	328.73
Zieger, Robert H. *American Workers, American Unions, 4th Ed.*	331.88
Zimmerman, Paul. *Dr. Z*	B
Zoglin, Richard. *Hope*	B
Zuckerman, Phil. *Living the Secular Life*	211
Zuckoff, Mitchell. ★*Fall and Rise*	973.931
Zwonitzer, Mark. *Will You Miss Me When I'm Gone?*	920

UNITED STATES CIVIL WAR, 1861-1865

Abbott, Karen. *Liar, Temptress, Soldier, Spy*	920
Ash, Stephen V. *Firebrand of Liberty*	973.7
Ayers, Edward L. ★*The Thin Light of Freedom*	975.5
Blanton, DeAnne. *They Fought Like Demons*	973.7
Blight, David W. *A Slave No More*	B
Blount, Roy. *Robert E. Lee*	B
Bordewich, Fergus M. *America's Great Debate*	973.6
Brewster, Todd. *Lincoln's Gamble*	973.7
Burlingame, Michael. *Abraham Lincoln*	B
Carwardine, Richard. *Lincoln*	B
Chernow, Ron. ★*Grant*	B
Clavin, Thomas. *Wild Bill*	B
Cwiklik, Robert. *Sheridan's Secret Mission*	973.8
Davis, William C. *Crucible of Command*	920
Delbanco, Andrew. *The War Before the War*	973.7
Donald, David Herbert. *Lincoln*	B
Egan, Timothy. ★*The Immortal Irishman*	973.896
Egerton, Douglas R. *Thunder at the Gates*	973.7
Faust, Drew Gilpin. *This Republic of Suffering*	973.7
Fields-Black, Edda L. *Combee*	973.7
Finkelman, Paul. *Millard Fillmore*	B
Foner, Eric. *Forever Free*	973.8
Foote, Shelby. *The Civil War*	973.7
Goodheart, Adam. *1861*	973.7
Gorra, Michael Edward. *The Saddest Words*	813
Grinspan, Jon. *Wide Awake*	973.7
Groom, Winston. *Shiloh, 1862*	973.7
Guelzo, Allen C. *Gettysburg*	973.7
Guelzo, Allen C. *Robert E. Lee*	B
Gwynne, S. C. *Hymns of the Republic*	973.7
Gwynne, S. C. *Rebel Yell*	B
Holzer, Harold. *Brought Forth on This Continent*	973.7
Holzer, Harold. *A Just and Generous Nation*	973.7092
Horwitz, Tony. *Confederates in the Attic*	973.7
Jones, Jacqueline. *Saving Savannah*	975.8
Keegan, John. *The American Civil War*	973.7
Korda, Michael. *Clouds of Glory*	B
Lance, Rachel. *In the Waves*	973.7
Larson, Erik. ★*The Demon of Unrest*	973.7
Levine, Bruce C. *The Fall of the House of Dixie*	973.7
Levine, Bruce C. *Thaddeus Stevens*	B
Lowenstein, Roger. *Ways and Means*	973.7
Manning, Chandra. *Troubled Refuge*	973.7
Marvel, William. *Lincoln's Autocrat*	B
McMurtry, Larry. *Custer*	B
McPherson, James M. *Battle Cry of Freedom*	973.7
McPherson, James M. *Drawn with the Sword*	973.7
McPherson, James M. *For Cause and Comrades*	973.7
McPherson, James M. *Hallowed Ground*	973.7
McPherson, James M. ★*Tried by War*	973.7
Meacham, Jon. ★*And There Was Light*	B
Miller, Donald L. *Vicksburg*	973.7
O'Donnell, Patrick K. *The Unvanquished*	973.7
Oakes, James. *Freedom National*	973.7
Reynolds, David S. *Mightier Than the Sword*	813
Richards, Leonard L. *Who Freed the Slaves?*	342.7308
Roberts, Cokie. *Capital Dames*	920
Robertson, James I. *Stonewall Jackson*	B
Sandburg, Carl. *Abraham Lincoln*	B
Sears, Stephen W. ★*Chancellorsville*	973.7
Sears, Stephen W. *Gettysburg*	973.7
Sears, Stephen W. ★*Landscape Turned Red*	973.7
Seidule, Ty. *Robert E. Lee and Me*	973.7
Seiple, Samantha. *Louisa on the Front Lines*	B
Stahr, Walter. ★*Stanton*	B
Stiles, T. J. *Custer's Trials*	B
Stiles, T. J. *Jesse James*	B
Symonds, Craig L. *Lincoln and His Admirals*	B
Taylor, Alan. *American Civil Wars*	973.7
Toler, Pamela D. *Heroines of Mercy Street*	973.7
Ward, Andrew. ★*The Slaves' War*	973.7
Ward, Geoffrey C. *The Civil War*	973.7
Wert, Jeffry D. *Cavalryman of the Lost Cause*	B
Wheelan, Joseph. ★*Terrible Swift Sword*	B
White, Ronald C. ★*American Ulysses*	B
White, Ronald C. *On Great Fields*	B
Williams, David. *Bitterly Divided*	973.7
Willis, Deborah. ★*The Black Civil War Soldier*	973.7
Willis, Deborah. *Envisioning Emancipation*	973.7
Wills, Garry. *Lincoln at Gettysburg*	973.7
Wilson, Robert. *Mathew Brady*	B
Wineapple, Brenda. *Ecstatic Nation*	973.6
Winik, Jay. *April 1865*	973.7
Witt, John Fabian. *Lincoln's Code*	343.73
The United States Constitution. Hennessey, Jonathan	741.5

UNITED STATES HIGHWAY 66

Wallis, Michael. *Route 66*	917.804

UNITED STATES HISTORY

Abbott, Karen. *Liar, Temptress, Soldier, Spy*	920
Abrams, Dan. *Kennedy's Avenger*	973.922
Ackmann, Martha. *The Mercury 13*	920
Ackmann, Martha. ★*These Fevered Days*	B
Adams, Abigail. *Abigail Adams*	973.4
Adams, John. *My Dearest Friend*	973.4
Alexander, Elizabeth. ★*The Trayvon Generation*	305.896
Alexander, Kwame. *Light for the World to See*	811.6
Allen, Frederick Lewis. *Only Yesterday*	973.9
Amar, Akhil Reed. ★*America's Constitution*	342.7302
Amar, Akhil Reed. *The Words That Made Us*	342.7302
Ambrose, Stephen E. *Nothing Like It in the World*	385
Ambrose, Stephen E. *The Victors*	940.54
Archibald, John. *Shaking the Gates of Hell*	B
Ash, Stephen V. *Firebrand of Liberty*	973.7
Asim, Jabari. *We Can't Breathe*	305.896
Atkinson, Rick. ★*The British Are Coming*	973.3
Austerlitz, Saul. *Just a Shot Away*	781.66078
Avlon, John P. *Lincoln and the Fight for Peace*	973.7
Avlon, John P. *Washington's Farewell*	973.4

PUBLIC LIBRARY CORE COLLECTION: NONFICTION
Twentieth Edition

Ayers, Edward L. *American Visions*	973.5
Ayers, Edward L. ★*The Thin Light of Freedom*	975.5
Baier, Bret. *To Rescue the Constitution*	973.4
Bailey, Issac J. *Why Didn't We Riot?*	305.800973
Bair, Deirdre. *Al Capone*	B
Baker, Calvin. *A More Perfect Reunion*	305.800973
Baldwin, James. ★*Collected Essays*	814
Balf, Todd. *Major*	B
Ball, Edward. *Slaves in the Family*	975.7
Barra, Allen. *Inventing Wyatt Earp*	B
Barry, John M. *Rising Tide*	977
Barry, John M. *Roger Williams and the Creation of the American Soul*	974.5
Bayoumi, Moustafa. *How Does It Feel to Be a Problem?*	305.892
Beeman, Richard R. *Our Lives, Our Fortunes and Our Sacred Honor*	973.3
Beeman, Richard R. *Plain, Honest Men*	342.7302
Berendt, John. *Midnight in the Garden of Good and Evil*	975.8
Berg, Scott W. ★*38 Nooses*	973.7
Berg, Scott W. *The Burning of the World*	977.311
Berlin, Ira. *The Making of African America*	973
Berry, Daina Ramey. ★*A Black Women's History of the United States*	305.48
Berry, Jason. *City of a Million Dreams*	976.3
Betts, Reginald Dwayne. ★*Redaction*	704.9
Bird, Kai. *American Prometheus*	B
Bjork, Daniel W. *B.F. Skinner*	B
Black, George. *Empire of Shadows*	978.7
Blackmon, Douglas A. *Slavery by Another Name*	305.896
Blain, Keisha N. *Until I Am Free*	B
Blanton, DeAnne. *They Fought Like Demons*	973.7
Blight, David W. ★*Frederick Douglass*	B
Blight, David W. *A Slave No More*	B
Blount, Roy. *Robert E. Lee*	B
Blum, Deborah. *The Poisoner's Handbook*	614
Blumenthal, Sidney. ★*All the Powers of Earth*	B
Blumenthal, Sidney. *A Self-Made Man*	B
Blumenthal, Sidney. *Wrestling with His Angel*	B
Bobrick, Benson. *Angel in the Whirlwind*	973.3
Boessenecker, John. *Gentleman Bandit*	B
Boorstin, Daniel J. *The Americans*	973
Boorstin, Daniel J. *The Americans*	973
Bordewich, Fergus M. *America's Great Debate*	973.6
Bordewich, Fergus M. *Congress at War*	324.2734
Bordewich, Fergus M. *Washington*	975.3
Borneman, Walter R. *Alaska*	979.8
Boyd, Herb. *We Shall Overcome*	323.1196
Boyle, Kevin. *The Shattering*	973.923
Branch, Taylor. ★*At Canaan's Edge*	323.1196
Branch, Taylor. *The Clinton Tapes*	973.929
Branch, Taylor. *Parting the Waters*	973
Branch, Taylor. ★*Pillar of Fire*	323.1
Brands, H. W. *The Age of Gold*	979.4
Brands, H. W. *Dreams of El Dorado*	978
Brands, H. W. ★*Founding Partisans*	973.3
Brands, H. W. ★*The Man Who Saved the Union*	B
Brands, H. W. ★*Our First Civil War*	973.3
Brands, H. W. ★*The Zealot and the Emancipator*	920
Bremer, Francis J. *John Winthrop*	B
Brewer, John. *The American Leonardo*	759.5
Brewster, Todd. *Lincoln's Gamble*	973.7
Broadwater, Jeff. ★*George Mason*	B
Brookhiser, Richard. *Give Me Liberty*	320.540973
Brooks, James. *Mesa of Sorrows*	979.1004
Brookwood, Marilyn. *The Orphans of Davenport*	305.231
Brower, Kate Andersen. *The Residence*	975.3
Brown, Jasmine. *Twice as Hard*	610.92
Broyles, Michael. ★*Revolutions in American Music*	780.9
Bruning, John R. *The Race of Aces*	940.54
Bryson, Bill. *One Summer*	973.91
Bunker, Nick. ★*Making Haste from Babylon*	974.4
Bunker, Nick. *Young Benjamin Franklin*	B
Burlingame, Michael. *Abraham Lincoln*	B
Burlingame, Michael. *The Black Man's President*	973.7
Burns, Cherie. *The Great Hurricane—1938*	974.7
Burns, Eric. *Infamous Scribblers*	071
Burns, Ken. ★*Our America*	973
Burns, Mike. *The Only One Living to Tell*	305.897
Burrough, Bryan. *The Big Rich*	338.2
Burrough, Bryan. *Forget the Alamo*	976.043
Calloway, Colin G. *The Indian World of George Washington*	323.1197
Cannato, Vincent. *American Passage*	325.73
Capote, Truman. ★*In Cold Blood*	364.1
Capparell, Stephanie. *The Real Pepsi Challenge*	338.7
Carlin, Peter Ames. *Bruce*	B
Carretta, Vincent. *Equiano, the African*	B
Carruthers, Charlene A. *Unapologetic*	305.48
Carwardine, Richard. *Lincoln*	B
Castner, Brian. *Stampede*	971.9
Cenziper, Debbie. ★*Love Wins*	346.7301
Cep, Casey N. ★*Furious Hours*	364.152
Cheever, Susan. *Drinking in America*	394.1
Cheney, Lynne V. *The Virginia Dynasty*	B
Chernow, Ron. ★*Grant*	B
Chernow, Ron. *Washington*	B
Choy, Catherine Ceniza. ★*Asian American Histories of the United States*	973
Churchwell, Sarah Bartlett. *Behold, America*	973.9
Clague, Mark. *O Say Can You Hear?*	782.42
Clark, Taylor. *Starbucked*	338
Clavin, Thomas. *The DiMaggios*	920
Clavin, Thomas. *Dodge City*	978.1
Cleaver, Eldridge. *Soul on Ice*	B
Clinton, Catherine. *Harriet Tubman*	B
Cohen, Deborah. *Last Call at the Hotel Imperial*	070.92
Cohen, Jared. *Life After Power*	973.09
Colaiaco, James A. *Frederick Douglass and the Fourth of July*	973.7
Collins, Gail. *When Everything Changed*	305.40973
Collins, Gail. *William Henry Harrison*	B
Colt, George Howe. *The Game*	796.332
Conant, Jennet. *The Lotus Eaters*	940.54
Conant, Jennet. *Man of the Hour*	B
Connell, Evan S. *Son of the Morning Star*	973.8
Connelly, Matthew James. *The Declassification Engine*	352.3
Cook, Blanche Wiesen. *Eleanor Roosevelt; Volume 2*	B
Cook, Blanche Wiesen. ★*Eleanor Roosevelt; Volume 3*	B
Cooke, Alistair. *The American Home Front, 1941-1942*	940.53
Cooper, Anderson. *Vanderbilt*	920
Cordery, Stacy A. *Alice*	B
Cox, Anna-Lisa. *The Bone and Sinew of the Land*	977
Cozzens, Peter. *A Brutal Reckoning*	973.5
Cozzens, Peter. *The Earth Is Weeping*	978
Craughwell, Thomas J. *Stealing Lincoln's Body*	973.7092
Crawford, Alan Pell. *This Fierce People*	975
Crosby, Molly Caldwell. *The American Plague*	614.5
Cumings, Bruce. *The Korean War*	951.904
Currie, Elliott. *A Peculiar Indifference*	305.800973
Daughan, George C. *Revolution on the Hudson*	974.7
Davis, William C. *Crucible of Command*	920
Dayen, David. *Chain of Title*	330.973
Deetz, Kelley Fanto. *Bound to the Fire*	641.59
Delany, Sarah Louise. *Having Our Say*	B
Delbanco, Andrew. *The War Before the War*	973.7
Delmont, Matthew F. *Half American*	940.54
Demos, John. *The Unredeemed Captive*	973.2
Dennis, Jerry. *The Living Great Lakes*	977
DeParle, Jason. ★*A Good Provider Is One Who Leaves*	305.899
Derf. *Kent State*	741.5
Dickson, Paul. *The Rise of the G.I. Army 1940-1941*	940.54
Didion, Joan. *Where I Was from*	979.4
Dilbeck, D. H. *Frederick Douglass*	B
Dolin, Eric Jay. *Black Flags, Blue Waters*	973.2
Dolin, Eric Jay. *A Furious Sky*	363.34
Dolin, Eric Jay. ★*Rebels at Sea*	973.3
Donald, David Herbert. *Lincoln*	B
Donovan, Jim. *The Blood of Heroes*	976.4
Douglas, Marjory Stoneman. *The Everglades*	975.9
Douglass, Frederick. ★*Frederick Douglass*	973.8
Douglass, Frederick. *My Bondage and My Freedom*	B
Douglass, Frederick. *The Portable Frederick Douglass*	973.8
Doyle, Martin. *The Source*	333.91
Draper, Robert. *To Start a War*	956.7044
Drury, Bob. *Blood and Treasure*	B
Drury, Bob. *Valley Forge*	973.3
Dunbar, Erica Armstrong. ★*She Came to Slay*	B
Duncan, Dayton. *Blood Memory*	599.64
Duncan, Michael. ★*Hero of Two Worlds*	B
Dyja, Tom. *The Third Coast*	977.311
Ebert, Roger. *Scorsese by Ebert*	B
Eder, Mari K. *The Girls Who Stepped Out of Line*	920

AUTHOR, TITLE, SERIES AND SUBJECT INDEX

Egan, Timothy. ★*The Immortal Irishman*	B
Egan, Timothy. ★*Short Nights of the Shadow Catcher*	770.92
Egan, Timothy. *The Worst Hard Time*	978
Egerton, Douglas R. *Thunder at the Gates*	973.7
Eig, Jonathan. ★*King*	B
Ellis, Joseph J. *American Creation*	973.3
Ellis, Joseph J. *American Sphinx*	973.4
Ellis, Joseph J. *The Cause*	973.3
Ellis, Joseph J. *Founding Brothers*	973.4
Ellis, Joseph J. ★*His Excellency*	B
Ellis, Joseph J. *The Quartet*	342.7302
Ellis, Joseph J. ★*Revolutionary Summer*	973.3
Ellsworth, Scott. *The Ground Breaking*	976.6
Erdozain, Dominic. *One Nation Under Guns*	363.33
Euchner, Charles C. *Nobody Turn Me Around*	975.3
Evans, R. Tripp. *Grant Wood*	B
Ewing, Eve L. *1919*	811
Farmer, John J. *The Ground Truth*	973.931
Faust, Drew Gilpin. *Mothers of Invention*	973.7
Faust, Drew Gilpin. *This Republic of Suffering*	973.7
Feinstein, Michael. *The Gershwins and Me*	782.42164
Ferguson, Niall. *Kissinger*	973.924
Ferling, John E. *Winning Independence*	973.3
Fernandez-Armesto, Felipe. *Our America*	973
Fernando, S. H., Jr. *From the Streets of Shaolin*	782.421
Ferreiro, Larrie D. *Brothers at Arms*	327.73
Feynman, Richard P. ★*The Meaning of It All*	500
Finkelman, Paul. *Millard Fillmore*	B
Fischer, David Hackett. ★*African Founders*	973
Fischer, David Hackett. *Paul Revere's Ride*	973.3
Fischer, David Hackett. *Washington's Crossing*	973.3
Flexner, James Thomas. *George Washington and the New Nation, 1783-1793*	973.4
Flexner, James Thomas. *George Washington*	B
Foner, Eric. *Forever Free*	973.8
Foner, Eric. *Gateway to Freedom*	973.7
Foner, Eric. ★*Reconstruction*	973.8
Foner, Eric. *The Second Founding*	342.73
Foote, Shelby. *The Civil War*	973.7
Frank, Thomas. *The People, No*	320.56
Franklin, John Hope. ★*From Slavery to Freedom*	973
Fraser, Rebecca. *The Mayflower*	974.4
Freeman, Andrea. ★*Ruin Their Crops on the Ground*	338.1
Gaddy, K. R. ★*Well of Souls*	787
Gage, Beverly. *G-Man*	B
Gaines, James R. *For Liberty and Glory*	B
Ganz, John. *When the Clock Broke*	320.52
Gardner, Mark L. *The Earth Is All That Lasts*	978.004
Garrett, Kent. *The Last Negroes at Harvard*	920
Gates, Henry Louis. *The Black Box*	908
Gates, Henry Louis. ★*The Black Church*	277
Genovese, Eugene D. *Roll, Jordan, Roll*	975
Giangreco, D. M. *Hell to Pay*	940.54
Gibson, Larry S. *Young Thurgood*	B
Giddings, Paula. *Ida*	B
Giddins, Gary. *Bing Crosby*	B
Giddins, Gary. *Bing Crosby*	B
Ginzberg, Lori D. *Elizabeth Cady Stanton*	B
Givens, Jarvis R. ★*School Clothes*	371.829
Glatthaar, Joseph T. *The American Military*	355.00973
Golay, Michael. *America 1933*	B
Gomez, Laura E. ★*Inventing Latinos*	305.868
Good, Cassandra A. *First Family*	920
Goodheart, Adam. *1861*	973.7
Goodwin, Doris Kearns. *No Ordinary Time*	920
Goodwin, Doris Kearns. ★*An Unfinished Love Story*	B
Gordon, Meryl. *Bunny Mellon*	B
Gordon-Reed, Annette. ★*The Hemingses of Monticello*	920
Gordon-Reed, Annette. ★*Most Blessed of the Patriarchs*	973.4
Gorra, Michael Edward. *The Saddest Words*	813
Goudeau, Jessica. ★*After the Last Border*	362.83
Graff, Garrett M. ★*The Only Plane in the Sky*	973.931
Graff, Garrett M. ★*When the Sea Came Alive*	940.54
Grandin, Greg. *The End of the Myth*	973
Grant, Gail Milissa. *At the Elbows of My Elders*	B
Grant, James. ★*John Adams*	B
Grant, Ulysses S. ★*The Annotated Memoirs of Ulysses S. Grant*	B
Greenidge, Kerri. *Black Radical*	B
Greenidge, Kerri. ★*The Grimkes*	973.5
Greenspan, Alan. *Capitalism in America*	330.973
Griffin, Farah Jasmine. *Read Until You Understand*	810.9
Griffith, Elisabeth. *Formidable*	305.42
Griffith, R. Marie. *Moral Combat*	261.8
Grind, Kirsten. *The Lost Bank*	332.3
Grinspan, Jon. *Wide Awake*	973.7
Griswold, Mac K. *The Manor*	974.7
Groom, Winston. *The Patriots*	920
Groom, Winston. *Shiloh, 1862*	973.7
Grush, Loren. ★*The Six*	629.4
Guarnere, William. *Brothers in Battle, Best of Friends*	B
Guelzo, Allen C. *Gettysburg*	973.7
Gwynne, S. C. *Hymns of the Republic*	973.7
Gwynne, S. C. *Rebel Yell*	B
Hafner, Katie. *A Romance on Three Legs*	786.2092
Halberstam, David. *The Coldest Winter*	951.904
Halberstam, David. *The Fifties*	973.92
Haley, James L. *Captive Paradise*	996.9
Hall, Alvin D. *Driving the Green Book*	917.304
Hall, Rebecca. ★*Wake*	741.5
Hallman, J. C. *Say Anarcha*	618.1
Harlan, Louis R. *Booker T. Washington*	B
Harriot, Michael. ★*Black AF History*	973
Harris, J. William. *The Hanging of Thomas Jeremiah*	B
Harvey, Eleanor Jones. *The Civil War and American Art*	740.9
Heacox, Kim. *Rhythm of the Wild*	979.8
Hemming, Henry. *Agents of Influence*	940.54
Henderson, Bruce B. *Sons and Soldiers*	940.53
Hennessey, Jonathan. *The United States Constitution*	741.5
Hill, Clint. *Five Days in November*	973.922092
Hill, Clint. *Mrs. Kennedy and Me*	973.922092
Hill, David. *The Vapors*	976.7
Hiltzik, Michael A. *Iron Empires*	385.0973
Hinton, Elizabeth Kai. ★*America on Fire*	305.800973
Hochschild, Adam. *American Midnight*	973.91
Hochschild, Adam. *Rebel Cinderella*	B
Hogan, William R. *Task Force Hogan*	940.54
Hogeland, William. *Declaration*	973.3
Holton, Woody. *Abigail Adams*	B
Holton, Woody. *Liberty Is Sweet*	973.3
Holzer, Harold. *Brought Forth on This Continent*	973.7
Holzer, Harold. *A Just and Generous Nation*	973.7092
Hoock, Holger. *Scars of Independence*	973.3
Horn, James P. P. *A Kingdom Strange*	975.6
Horn, James P. P. *Land as God Made It*	975.5
Horwitz, Tony. *Confederates in the Attic*	973.7
Horwitz, Tony. ★*Midnight Rising*	973.7
Howe, Daniel Walker. *What Hath God Wrought*	973.5
Howe, Sean. *Marvel Comics*	741.5
Hughes, Langston. ★*I Wonder as I Wander*	B
Humez, Jean McMahon. *Harriet Tubman*	B
Hurston, Zora Neale. ★*You Don't Know Us Negroes and Other Essays*	814
Hutton, Paul Andrew. *The Apache Wars*	979
Iandoli, Kathy. *Baby Girl*	B
Immerwahr, Daniel. *How to Hide an Empire*	973
Inskeep, Steve. *Imperfect Union*	B
Jackson, Jenn M. ★*Black Women Taught Us*	305.48
Jackson, Troy. *Becoming King*	B
Jacobs, Harriet. ★*Incidents in the Life of a Slave Girl*	B
Jacoby, Karl. *The Strange Career of William Ellis*	B
Jeffers, Honorée Fanonne. *The Age of Phillis*	811
Jerkins, Morgan. *Wandering in Strange Lands*	305.896
Johnson, Lizzie. ★*Paradise*	363.37
Johnson, Paul. *George Washington*	B
Johnson, Victoria. ★*American Eden*	580.973
Jones, Doug. *Bending Toward Justice*	323.1196
Jones, Gerard. *Men of Tomorrow*	741.5
Jones, Jacqueline. *Saving Savannah*	975.8
Jones, Robert P. *The Hidden Roots of White Supremacy*	305.8
Joseph, Peniel E. *The Sword and the Shield*	B
Kamensky, Jane. *A Revolution in Color*	759.13
Kandel, Eric R. *In Search of Memory*	B
Karl, Jonathan. *Betrayal*	973.933
Karnow, Stanley. *Vietnam, a History*	959.704
Keegan, John. *The American Civil War*	973.7
Keith, Philip A. *All Blood Runs Red*	B
Kelley, Blair Murphy. *Black Folk*	331.6

PUBLIC LIBRARY CORE COLLECTION: NONFICTION
Twentieth Edition

Kelly, Joseph. *Marooned*	975.5
Kelly, Kate. *Ordinary Equality*	920
Kenneally, Christine. *Ghosts of the Orphanage*	362.73
Kennedy, David M. ★*Freedom from Fear*	973.91
Kennedy, Kostya. *True*	B
Ketchum, Richard M. *Saratoga*	973.3
Kiernan, Denise. *The Girls of Atomic City*	976.8
Kiernan, Denise. *The Last Castle*	975.6
Kilmeade, Brian. *Andrew Jackson and the Miracle of New Orleans*	973.5
Kilmeade, Brian. ★*George Washington's Secret Six*	973.4
King, Coretta Scott. ★*My Life, My Love, My Legacy*	B
Kingsley, Lisa. *Smithsonian American Table*	641.5
Kix, Paul. ★*You Have to Be Prepared to Die Before You Can Begin to Live*	976.1
Klosterman, Chuck. ★*The Nineties*	306.0973
Korda, Michael. *Clouds of Glory*	B
Krist, Gary. *Empire of Sin*	976.3
Krist, Gary. *The White Cascade*	979.7
Kroeger, Brooke. *Undaunted*	070.4
Kruse, Kevin Michael. *Fault Lines*	973.92
Kytle, Ethan J. *Denmark Vesey's Garden*	975.7
LaFollette, Marcel C. *Writing for Their Lives*	071.3
Lalami, Laila. *Conditional Citizens*	323.60973
Lance, Rachel. *In the Waves*	973.7
Lane, Charles. *Freedom's Detective*	B
Lang, Michael. *The Road to Woodstock*	781.66
Larson, Erik. ★*The Demon of Unrest*	973.7
Larson, Erik. ★*The Devil in the White City*	364.15
Larson, Kate Clifford. *Bound for the Promised Land*	B
Lawler, Andrew. *The Secret Token*	975.6
Lee, Corky. ★*Corky Lee's Asian America*	770
Lee, Erika. *America for Americans*	305.800973
Lee, Erika. *The Making of Asian America*	973
Lees, Gene. *You Can't Steal a Gift*	B
Lehr, Dick. ★*The Birth of a Nation*	305.800973
Lemon, Don. *This Is the Fire*	305.896
Lepore, Jill. *Book of Ages*	B
Lepore, Jill. ★*These Truths*	973
Levine, Bruce C. *The Fall of the House of Dixie*	973.7
Levine, Bruce C. *Thaddeus Stevens*	B
Levine, Robert S. ★*The Failed Promise*	973.8
Lewis, David L. ★*W.E.B. Du Bois*	B
Lewis, Robin Coste. *To the Realization of Perfect Helplessness*	811
Lim, Audrea. *Free the Land*	333.73
Lineberry, Cate. *Be Free or Die*	B
Longworth, Karina. *Seduction*	B
Louvin, Charlie. *Satan Is Real*	920
Lowenstein, Roger. *Ways and Means*	973.7
Lowery, Wesley. ★*American Whitelash*	305.8
Lucey, Donna M. *Sargent's Women*	920
Lunenfeld, Peter. *City at the Edge of Forever*	979.4
Luxenberg, Steve. ★*Separate*	342.7308
Lynskey, Dorian. *33 Revolutions per Minute*	782.42
Maddow, Rachel. ★*Prequel*	320.53
Maier, Pauline. *American Scripture*	973.3
Mamet, David. *True and False*	792
Manegold, Catherine S. *Ten Hills Farm*	974.4
Manning, Chandra. *Troubled Refuge*	973.7
Marable, Manning. ★*Malcolm X*	B
Martin, Rachel Louise. *A Most Tolerant Little Town*	379.2
Marvel, William. *Lincoln's Autocrat*	B
Masur, Kate. *Until Justice Be Done*	323.1196
Masur, Louis P. *The Civil War*	973.7
Mays, Kyle. ★*An Afro-Indigenous History of the United States*	973
McCraw, Thomas K. ★*The Founders and Finance*	330.973
McCullough, David G. ★*1776*	973.3
McCullough, David G. ★*John Adams*	B
McCullough, David G. *The Pioneers*	920
McCullough, David G. *Truman*	B
McDonnell, Michael. *Masters of Empire*	977.4
McDonough, James L. *William Tecumseh Sherman*	B
McGhee, Heather C. ★*The Sum of Us*	305.8
McKean, David. *Suspected of Independence*	B
McMillan, Tracie. ★*The White Bonus*	305.8
McMurtry, Larry. *Crazy Horse*	B
McMurtry, Larry. *Custer*	B
McNally, Dennis. *On Highway 61*	781.64
McPherson, James M. *Battle Cry of Freedom*	973.7
McPherson, James M. *Drawn with the Sword*	973.7
McPherson, James M. *For Cause and Comrades*	973.7
McPherson, James M. *Hallowed Ground*	973.7
McPherson, James M. ★*Tried by War*	973.7
Meacham, Jon. ★*And There Was Light*	B
Meacham, Jon. ★*The Soul of America*	973
Meltzer, Brad. ★*The First Conspiracy*	973.4
Meltzer, Brad. *The Lincoln Conspiracy*	973.7092
Melville, Herman. *Complete Poems*	811
Menand, Louis. *The Free World*	306.0973
Meyer, Eugene L. *Five for Freedom*	973.7
Michaelis, David. ★*Eleanor*	973.917
Middlekauff, Robert. *The Glorious Cause*	973.3
Miles, Tiya. *The Dawn of Detroit*	977.4
Miles, Tiya. ★*Night Flyer*	B
Miles, Tiya. ★*Wild Girls*	304.2
Millard, Candice. *Destiny of the Republic*	973.8
Miller, Donald L. *City of the Century*	977.311
Miller, Donald L. *Vicksburg*	973.7
Miller, Marla. *Betsy Ross and the Making of America*	B
Minian, Ana Raquel. ★*In the Shadow of Liberty*	365
Minutaglio, Bill. *Dallas 1963*	973.922092
Mirski, Sean A. *We May Dominate the World*	973.91
Mitchell, Elizabeth. *Lincoln's Lie*	973.7092
Monforton, Celeste. *On the Job*	331.1
Montero, David. ★*The Stolen Wealth of Slavery*	381
Moore, Kate. ★*The Woman They Could Not Silence*	B
Moore, Peter. *Life, Liberty, and the Pursuit of Happiness*	199
Moore, Susanna. *Paradise of the Pacific*	996.9
Morgan-Owens, Jessie. *Girl in Black and White*	B
Morison, Samuel Eliot. *John Paul Jones*	B
Morrison, Melanie. *Murder on Shades Mountain*	345.761
Morrison, Toni. ★*The Origin of Others*	809
Mort, T. A. *Thieves' Road*	978.3
Mortimer, Gavin. *The Great Swim*	B
Murphy, Andrew R. *William Penn*	B
Nabokov, Peter. *Where the Lightning Strikes*	299.7
Nasaw, David. *The Chief*	B
Neufeld, Josh. *A.D.*	741.5
Newitz, Annalee. *Stories Are Weapons*	355.3
Nolan, Hamilton. *The Hammer*	331.8
Norman, Elizabeth M. *We Band of Angels*	940.54
Norrell, Robert J. *Up from History*	B
Northup, Solomon. *Twelve Years a Slave*	B
Norton, Mary Beth. *1774*	973.3
Nourse, Victoria F. *In Reckless Hands*	344.7304
Nusbaum, Eric. *Stealing Home*	796.357
O'Connell, Robert L. *Revolutionary*	B
O'Donnell, Patrick K. *The Indispensables*	973.3
O'Donnell, Patrick K. *The Unvanquished*	973.7
Oakes, James. *Freedom National*	973.7
Okrent, Daniel. *The Guarded Gate*	344.73
Okrent, Daniel. *Last Call*	363.4
Oluo, Ijeoma. *Mediocre*	305.310973
Orlean, Susan. ★*The Library Book*	027.4
Packer, George. ★*The Unwinding*	973.924
Painter, Nell Irvin. ★*I Just Keep Talking*	814
Painter, Nell Irvin. ★*Sojourner Truth*	B
Parton, Dolly. ★*Behind the Seams*	B
Pasternak, Judy. *Yellow Dirt*	979.1004
Pawel, Miriam. *The Browns of California*	920
Pawel, Miriam. *The Crusades of Cesar Chavez*	B
Payne, Les. ★*The Dead Are Arising*	B
Perlstein, Rick. *The Invisible Bridge*	973.924
Perlstein, Rick. ★*Nixonland*	973.924
Perlstein, Rick. ★*Reaganland*	973.926
Perry, Mark. *The Most Dangerous Man in America*	B
Person, Charles. *Buses Are a Comin'*	B
Pestana, Carla Gardina. *The World of Plymouth Plantation*	974.4
Petri, Alexandra. *Alexandra Petri's US History*	817
Philbrick, Nathaniel. ★*Bunker Hill*	973.3
Philbrick, Nathaniel. ★*In the Hurricane's Eye*	973.3
Philbrick, Nathaniel. ★*The Last Stand*	973.8
Philbrick, Nathaniel. ★*Mayflower*	973.2
Philbrick, Nathaniel. *Travels with George*	973.4
Philbrick, Nathaniel. ★*Valiant Ambition*	B
Phillips, Kevin. *1775*	973.3
Phillips-Fein, Kim. *Fear City*	330.9747

AUTHOR, TITLE, SERIES AND SUBJECT INDEX

Pipher, Mary Bray. *The Middle of Everywhere*	305.9
Plant, Deborah G. *Of Greed and Glory*	326
Posner, Gerald L. *Case Closed*	364.1
Postel, Charles. *Equality*	305.50973
Powell, Nate. ★*Lies My Teacher Told Me*	741.5
Prager, Joshua. *The Family Roe*	342.7308
Pressly, Paul M. *On the Rim of the Caribbean*	975.8
Price, David A. ★*Love and Hate in Jamestown*	975.5
Price, Polly J. *Plagues in the Nation*	614.4
Proenza-Coles, Christina. *American Founders*	973
Raban, Jonathan. *Bad Land*	978
Rabban, David M. *Free Speech in Its Forgotten Years*	342.73
Rae, Noel. ★*The Great Stain*	306.3
Raines, Ben. *The Last Slave Ship*	306.362
Rakove, Jack N. *Revolutionaries*	973.3
Randall, Willard Sterne. *The Founders' Fortunes*	973.3
Raphael, Ray. *Constitutional Myths*	342.7302
Raphael, Ray. *A People's History of the American Revolution*	973.3
Rasmussen, Daniel. *American Uprising*	976.3
Rediker, Marcus. *The Amistad Rebellion*	326.0973
Rekdal, Paisley. *West*	811
Rembert, Winfred. *Chasing Me to My Grave*	B
Reynolds, David S. *John Brown, Abolitionist*	B
Reynolds, David S. *Mightier Than the Sword*	813
Ribowsky, Mark. *The Supremes*	B
Richards, Leonard L. *Who Freed the Slaves?*	342.7308
Richardson, Heather Cox. *Democracy Awakening*	320.473
Richardson, Heather Cox. ★*How the South Won the Civil War*	306.20973
Risen, Clay. *The Bill of the Century*	342.7308
Risen, James. ★*The Last Honest Man*	973.92
Roberts, Andrew. *The Last King of America*	B
Roberts, Cokie. *Capital Dames*	920
Roberts, Cokie. *Founding Mothers*	920
Roberts, Cokie. *Ladies of Liberty*	920
Roberts, David. *Once They Moved Like the Wind*	B
Roker, Al. *Ruthless Tide*	974.8
Rosen, Jeffrey. *The Pursuit of Happiness*	973.3
Rosenberg, Rosalind. ★*Jane Crow*	B
Rosenzweig, Laura B. *Hollywood's Spies*	791.43
Rubenstein, David M. *The American Experiment*	973
Rubenstein, David M. *The American Story*	973.07202
Rubinstein, Julian. ★*The Holly*	364.106
Rudacille, Deborah. *Roots of Steel*	338.4
Rudd, Mark. *Underground*	378.1
Russell, Jan Jarboe. *The Train to Crystal City*	940.53
Samuels, Robert. ★*His Name Is George Floyd*	B
Sandburg, Carl. *Abraham Lincoln*	B
Sankovitch, Nina. *American Rebels*	920
Santana, Carlos. *The Universal Tone*	B
Saunt, Claudio. *Unworthy Republic*	323.1197
Saxton, Martha. *The Widow Washington*	B
Scahill, Jeremy. *Dirty Wars*	355.00973
Schiff, Stacy. *The Witches*	345
Schlesinger, Arthur M. *Journals, 1952-2000*	973.91092
Schultz, Kevin Michael. *Buckley and Mailer*	920
Sears, Stephen W. ★*Chancellorsville*	973.7
Sears, Stephen W. *Gettysburg*	973.7
Sears, Stephen W. ★*Landscape Turned Red*	973.7
Seidule, Ty. *Robert E. Lee and Me*	973.7
Seiple, Samantha. *Louisa on the Front Lines*	B
Shapiro, James. ★*The Playbook*	792
Sheinkin, Steve. *Bomb*	623.4
Shelden, Michael. *Mark Twain*	B
Shirley, Craig. *Mary Ball Washington*	B
Shlaes, Amity. *Coolidge*	B
Shlaes, Amity. *The Forgotten Man*	973.91
Sides, Hampton. *Blood and Thunder*	978
Silverman, David J. ★*This Land Is Their Land*	974.4
Smith, Clint. ★*How the Word Is Passed*	973
Smith, Jean Edward. *FDR*	B
Smith, Jean Edward. *John Marshall*	B
Smith, Tracy K. ★*To Free the Captives*	818
Snodgrass, Mary Ellen. *The Underground Railroad*	973.7
Snow, Peter. *When Britain Burned the White House*	975.3
Snyder, Christina. *Great Crossings*	976.9
Sorin, Gretchen Sullivan. *Driving While Black*	323.1196
Sorkin, Andrew Ross. *Too Big to Fail*	330.973
Souza, Pete. *Obama*	973.932
Spitz, Bob. ★*The Beatles*	B
Springsteen, Bruce. ★*Born to Run*	B
Stahr, Walter. ★*Stanton*	B
Staiti, Paul J. *Of Arms and Artists*	B
Standiford, Les. *Bringing Adam Home*	364.15
Stanton, Doug. *The Odyssey of Echo Company*	959.704
Stark, Peter. *Young Washington*	B
Stauffer, John. *Picturing Fredrick Douglass*	B
Stein, Jean. *West of Eden*	979.4
Stephanopoulos, George. ★*The Situation Room*	973.09
Stewart, David O. *George Washington*	973.4
Stewart, David O. *Madison's Gift*	B
Stiles, T. J. *Custer's Trials*	B
Stiles, T. J. ★*The First Tycoon*	B
Stiles, T. J. *Jesse James*	B
Stone, Robert. *Chasing the Moon*	629.45
Stout, David. *The Kidnap Years*	364.15
Strang, Dean A. *Worse Than the Devil*	345.775
Sullivan, Randall. *Graveyard of the Pacific*	979.7
Swanson, James L. *End of Days*	973.922092
Swift, Earl. *Across the Airless Wilds*	629.45
Symonds, Craig L. *Lincoln and His Admirals*	B
Tabor, Nick. *Africatown*	976.1
Taraborrelli, J. Randy. ★*The Secret Life of Marilyn Monroe*	B
Taylor, Alan. *American Civil Wars*	973.7
Taylor, Alan. *American Republics*	973.3
Taylor, Alan. *American Revolutions*	973.3
Taylor, Alan. ★*The Internal Enemy*	975.5
Tefertiller, Casey. *Wyatt Earp*	B
Teitel, Amy Shira. *Fighting for Space*	920
Terkel, Studs. *The Good War*	940.54
Terkel, Studs. ★*Hard Times*	973.91
Theoharis, Jeanne. *A More Beautiful and Terrible History*	323.1196
Thomas, Evan. ★*John Paul Jones*	B
Thompson, Bob. *Revolutionary Roads*	973.3
Thompson, Hunter S. ★*Fear and Loathing in America*	B
Thomson, David. *Ingrid Bergman*	B
Tipton-Martin, Toni. *Juke Joints, Jazz Clubs & Juice*	641.87
Tobin, Jacqueline. *Hidden in Plain View*	973.7
Toler, Pamela D. *Heroines of Mercy Street*	973.7
Traub, James. *John Quincy Adams*	B
Trump, Mary L. *Too Much and Never Enough*	B
Tubbs, Anna Malaika. *The Three Mothers*	306.874
Tye, Larry. *Satchel*	B
Tyson, Timothy B. *The Blood of Emmett Till*	364.1
Unger, Harlow G. *American Tempest*	973.3
Unger, Harlow G. *First Founding Father*	B
Van Agtmael, Peter. *Look at the USA*	070
Vanderbes, Jennifer. ★*Wonder Drug*	615
Von Drehle, David. ★*The Book of Charlie*	B
Waldman, Steven. *Sacred Liberty*	341.4
Waldstreicher, David. *The Odyssey of Phillis Wheatley*	B
Walker, Hunter. *The Truce*	324.2736
Walker, Ronald W. ★*Massacre at Mountain Meadows*	979.2
Wallace, Chris. *Countdown 1945*	940.54
Waller, Douglas C. *Lincoln's Spies*	973.7
Ward, Andrew. ★*The Slaves' War*	973.7
Ward, Geoffrey C. *The Civil War*	973.7
Ward, Geoffrey C. *A Disposition to Be Rich*	B
Ward, Geoffrey C. ★*The Vietnam War*	959.704
Waterhouse, Benjamin C. *One Day I'll Work for Myself*	338
Watson, Bruce. *Freedom Summer*	323.1196
Weiner, Tim. *Legacy of Ashes*	327.1273009
Weintraub, Stanley. *Iron Tears*	973.3
Wert, Jeffry D. *Cavalryman of the Lost Cause*	B
Wert, Jeffry D. *Custer*	B
Wheelan, Joseph. ★*Terrible Swift Sword*	B
Whitaker, Mark. ★*Saying It Loud*	973.923
White, Gayle Jessup. *Reclamation*	B
White, Ronald C. ★*American Ulysses*	B
White, Ronald C. *On Great Fields*	B
White, Shane. *Prince of Darkness*	B
Whitlock, Craig. ★*Fat Leonard*	364.16
Whittock, Martyn. *Mayflower Lives*	974.4
Wiederhorn, Jon. *Louder Than Hell*	781.6609
Wiencek, Henry. *Master of the Mountain*	973.4
Wilder, Craig Steven. *Ebony and Ivy*	379.2
Wilkerson, Isabel. ★*The Warmth of Other Suns*	304.80973

PUBLIC LIBRARY CORE COLLECTION: NONFICTION
Twentieth Edition

Wilkman, Jon. *Screening Reality*	070.1
Williams, David. *Bitterly Divided*	973.7
Willis, Deborah. ★*The Black Civil War Soldier*	973.7
Willis, Deborah. *Envisioning Emancipation*	973.7
Wills, Garry. *James Madison*	B
Wills, Garry. *Lincoln at Gettysburg*	973.7
Wilson, Robert. *Mathew Brady*	B
Winchester, Simon. *A Crack in the Edge of the World*	979.4
Winchester, Simon. *The Men Who United the States*	973
Wineapple, Brenda. *Ecstatic Nation*	973.6
Winik, Jay. *April 1865*	973.7
Wise, Tim J. *Dispatches from the Race War*	305.8
Witt, John Fabian. *Lincoln's Code*	343.73
Wolfe, Tom. ★*The Right Stuff*	629.4
Woodward, Bob. *The Final Days*	B
Yacovone, Donald. ★*Teaching White Supremacy*	370.89
Yang, Jeff. ★*Rise*	973
Yang, Jia Lynn. ★*One Mighty and Irresistible Tide*	325.73
Young, Kevin. *Ardency*	811
Zambone, Albert Louis. *Daniel Morgan*	B
Zinn, Howard. ★*A People's History of the United States*	973
Zucchino, David. *Wilmington's Lie*	305.8009756

UNITED STATES MARSHALS

Barra, Allen. *Inventing Wyatt Earp*	B
Tefertiller, Casey. *Wyatt Earp*	B

Universal. Cox, Brian	523.1
The Universal Christ. Rohr, Richard	232
Universal Design for the Home. Jordan, Wendy Adler	728
Universal Father. O'Connor, Garry	B
Universal History of the Destruction of Books. Baez, Fernando	098
The Universal Tone. Santana, Carlos	B
The Universe in a Box. Pontzen, Andrew	523.1
★*The Universe in a Nutshell*. Hawking, Stephen	530.12

UNIVERSITIES AND COLLEGES

Barr, John. *Start by Believing*	364.15
Belasco, Andrew. *The Enlightened College Applicant*	378.1
Benedict, Jeff. *The System*	796.332
Bok, Derek Curtis. *The Struggle to Reform Our Colleges*	378.73
Bond, Julian. ★*Julian Bond's Time to Teach*	323.0975
Bruni, Frank. *Where You Go Is Not Who You'll Be*	378.1
Cottom, Tressie McMillan. *Lower Ed*	378.73
Davis, Seth. *Wooden*	B
Fiske, Edward B. *Fiske Guide to Getting into the Right College*	378.1
Grigoriadis, Vanessa. *Blurred Lines*	371.7
Harris, Adam. ★*The State Must Provide*	379.2
Hechinger, John. ★*True Gentlemen*	371.85
Hessler, Peter. *Other Rivers*	378.1
Hirsch, Jennifer S. *Sexual Citizens*	371.7
Krakauer, Jon. *Missoula*	362.883
McIntire, Mike. *Champions Way*	796.043
Mettler, Suzanne. *Degrees of Inequality*	378.73
Perkins, Anne Gardiner. *Yale Needs Women*	378
Rose, Mike. *Back to School*	374
Selingo, Jeffrey J. *College (un)bound*	378
Selingo, Jeffrey J. *Who Gets in and Why*	378.1
Simmons, Ruth. ★*Up Home*	B
Tough, Paul. *The Years That Matter Most*	378.1
Wilder, Craig Steven. *Ebony and Ivy*	379.2
Zara, Christopher. *Uneducated*	B

★*Unjust Debts*. Jacoby, Melissa B.	346.73
Unlimited Power. Robbins, Anthony	158.1
Unmaking The Presidency. Hennessey, Susan	973.933
Unmasked. Holes, Paul	363.25
Unmasked. Lloyd Webber, Andrew	B
Unmedicated. Taylor, Madisyn	615.8
Unorthodox. Feldman, Deborah	B
An Unplanned Life. Thomas, Franklin A.	B

UNPLANNED PREGNANCY

Fessler, Ann. *The Girls Who Went Away*	362.82
Foster, Diana Greene. *The Turnaway Study*	362.1988
Mulgrew, Kate. *Born with Teeth*	791.45028
Sanger, Carol. *About Abortion*	179.7
Shah, Meera. *You're the Only One I've Told*	362.1988
Wills, Clair. ★*Missing Persons*	929.2

★*Unprotected*. Porter, Billy	B
The Unquiet Ghost. Hochschild, Adam	947.084
The Unquiet Grave. Hendricks, Steve	323.1197
Unraveling. Orenstein, Peggy	B
The Unredeemed Captive. Demos, John	973.2
Unremarried Widow. Henderson, Artis	B
Unrequited Infatuations. Van Zandt, Steve	B
Unscripted. Stewart, James B.	658.1
The Unsettlers. Sundeen, Mark	640
The Unsettling of Europe. Gatrell, Peter	304.8
Unshakable Hope. Lucado, Max	248.4
Unshuttered. Smith, Patricia	811
Unsinkable. Sullivan, James	940.54
Unsinkable". Butler, Daniel Allen	910
Unsoloaced. Ehrlich, Gretel	B
★*Unspeakable Acts*. Weinman, Sarah	364.1
Unstoppable. Greene, Joshua	B
Unstoppable. Sharapova, Maria	B
The Unsubstantial Air. Hynes, Samuel	940.4
Untamed. Doyle, Glennon	B
Untangled. Damour, Lisa	305.235
The Unthinkable. Ripley, Amanda	155.9
Unthinkable. Thomson, Helen	612.8
Until I Am Free. Blain, Keisha N.	B
Until Justice Be Done. Masur, Kate	323.1196
Until Proven Safe. Manaugh, Geoff	614.4
Until The End of Time. Greene, B.	523.1
Until We Reckon. Sered, Danielle	364.6
The Untold Story of Books. Castleman, Michael	381
Untouchable. Honig, Elie	364.1
Untouchables. Jadhav, Narendra	305.5
The Unvanquished. O'Donnell, Patrick K.	973.7
★*Unwarranted*. Friedman, Barry	344.7305
Unwell Women. Cleghorn, Elinor	613
★*The Unwinding*. Packer, George	973.924
★*The Unwinding of the Miracle*. Yip-Williams, Julie	973
★*The Unwomanly Face of War*. Aleksievich, Svetlana	940.53
Unworthy Republic. Saunt, Claudio	323.1197
Up All Night. Napoli, Lisa	384.55
Up from History. Norrell, Robert J.	B
★*Up from Slavery*. Washington, Booker T.	B
Up Ghost River. Metatawabin, Edmund	B
★*Up Home*. Simmons, Ruth	B
Up, Down, All-Around Stitch Dictionary. Bernard, Wendy	746.43
The Upcycled Self. Black Thought	B

Updegrove, Mark K.
The Last Republicans	973.928

Updike, John
Always Looking	700

Upheaval. Diamond, Jared M.	303.48
Uphill. Hill, Jemele	B
Upon Further Review. Pesca, Mike	796

UPPER CLASS

Gates, Henry Louis. *The Future of the Race*	305.896
Gordon, Meryl. *Bunny Mellon*	B
Jefferson, Margo. *Negroland*	305.896
Lucey, Donna M. *Sargent's Women*	920
MacColl, Gail. *To Marry an English Lord*	974.7
Madden, T Kira. *Long Live the Tribe of Fatherless Girls*	814
Montillo, Roseanne. *Deliberate Cruelty*	364.152
Sebag-Montefiore, Simon. ★*The World*	929.7

UPPER CLASS WOMEN

Gordon, Meryl. *Bunny Mellon*	B

UPPER EAST SIDE, NEW YORK CITY

Martin, Wednesday. *Primates of Park Avenue*	974.7
The Upside of Being Down. Gotch, Jen	B
The Upstairs Delicatessen. Garner, Dwight	B
The Upstarts. Stone, Brad	338.04
★*Upstream*. Oliver, Mary	814

UPWARD MOBILITY

Gupta, Prachi. ★*They Called Us Exceptional*	B
MacColl, Gail. *To Marry an English Lord*	974.7
Vance, J. D. *Hillbilly Elegy*	B

URANIUM

Pasternak, Judy. *Yellow Dirt*	979.1004

URBAN AGRICULTURE

Sundeen, Mark. *The Unsettlers*	640

URBAN BEAUTIFICATION

Goldhagen, Sarah Williams. *Welcome to Your World*	720.1
The Urban Cycling Survival Guide. Bambrick, Yvonne	796.6

URBAN ECOLOGY

Schilthuizen, Menno. *Darwin Comes to Town*	577.5

AUTHOR, TITLE, SERIES AND SUBJECT INDEX

URBAN ECONOMIC DEVELOPMENT
   Bomey, Nathan. *Detroit Resurrected* — 977.4
   Boyd, Herb. *Black Detroit* — 977.4
   Podemski, Max. *A Paradise of Small Houses* — 363.5

URBAN ECONOMICS
   Bomey, Nathan. *Detroit Resurrected* — 977.4
   Boyd, Herb. *Black Detroit* — 977.4
   Kirshner, Jodie Adams. ★*Broke* — 336.3
   Lunenfeld, Peter. *City at the Edge of Forever* — 979.4

URBAN EDUCATION
   Emdin, Christopher. *Ratchetdemic* — 370.1
   Fishman, Elly. *Refugee High* — 370.8
   Kozol, Jonathan. *Fire in the Ashes* — 362.77

Urban Magick. Rajchel, Diana — 133.4

URBAN PLANNERS
   DeJean, Joan E. *How Paris Became Paris* — 944
   Kanigel, Robert. *Eyes on the Street* — B

URBAN PLANNING
   Anderson, Sam. *Boom Town* — 976.6
   Bordewich, Fergus M. *Washington* — 975.3
   DeJean, Joan E. *How Paris Became Paris* — 944
   Dougherty, Conor. *Golden Gates* — 363.509794
   Goldhagen, Sarah Williams. *Welcome to Your World* — 720.1
   Kanigel, Robert. *Eyes on the Street* — B
   Kimble, Megan. ★*City Limits* — 388.1
   Mars, Roman. ★*The 99% Invisible City* — 720
   Mask, Deirdre. *The Address Book* — 388.1
   McGregor, James H. *Rome from the Ground up* — 711
   Nusbaum, Eric. *Stealing Home* — 796.357
   Podemski, Max. *A Paradise of Small Houses* — 363.5
   Rivlin, Gary. *Katrina* — 976.3
   Rybczynski, Witold. *Mysteries of the Mall* — 720

URBAN POOR PEOPLE
   Boo, Katherine. ★*Behind the Beautiful Forevers* — 305.5
   Kirshner, Jodie Adams. ★*Broke* — 336.3
   Lockhart, Chris. ★*Walking the Bowl* — 362.7

URBAN PROBLEMS
   Kirshner, Jodie Adams. ★*Broke* — 336.3
   Prickett, Pamela J. ★*The Unclaimed* — 363.7
   Shackle, Samira. *Karachi Vice* — 954.91
   Taibbi, Matt. *I Can't Breathe* — 363.2

URBAN RENEWAL
   Buttigieg, Pete. *Shortest Way Home* — B
   Kanigel, Robert. *Eyes on the Street* — B
   Luckerson, Victor. *Built from the Fire* — 976.6
   Rivlin, Gary. *Katrina* — 976.3

URBAN SCHOOLS
   Kozol, Jonathan. *Fire in the Ashes* — 362.77

URBAN SOCIOLOGY
   Kanigel, Robert. *Eyes on the Street* — B

URBAN SPRAWL
   Fields, Micah. ★*We Hold Our Breath* — 976.4
   Kimble, Megan. ★*City Limits* — 388.1

URBAN TRANSPORTATION
   Grabar, Henry. *Paved Paradise* — 388.474
   Kimble, Megan. ★*City Limits* — 388.1

URBAN VIOLENCE
   Bradburd, Rus. *All the Dreams We've Dreamed* — 796.323

URBAN WARFARE
   Bowden, Mark. ★*Hue 1968* — 959.704
   MacGregor, Iain. *The Lighthouse of Stalingrad* — 940.54
   Stanton, Doug. *12 Strong* — 958.104
   Verini, James. *They Will Have to Die Now* — 956.7044

URBAN WOMEN
   Bowen, Sesali. *Bad Fat Black Girl* — 305.42

Urban, Melissa
   The Whole30 Friends & Family — 641.5

URBAN-RURAL MIGRATION
   Masciotra, David. *Exurbia Now* — 320.973

URBANIZATION
   Hessler, Peter. *Other Rivers* — 378.1
   Kanigel, Robert. *Eyes on the Street* — B
   Schilthuizen, Menno. *Darwin Comes to Town* — 577.5

★*The Urge*. Fisher, Carl Erik — 362.29
The Urgent Life. Saint John, Bozoma — B

Urofsky, Melvin I.
   The Affirmative Action Puzzle — 331.13
   Dissent and the Supreme Court — 342.7302
   Louis D. Brandeis — B

Urrea, Luis Alberto
   The Devil's Highway — 304.8

Ursula K. Le Guin. Le Guin, Ursula K. — 811
Ursula K. Le Guin. Le Guin, Ursula K. — B

URUGUAY
   Talty, Stephan. *The Good Assassin* — 364.15

Urwand, Ben
   The Collaboration — 791.430973

Us. Real, Terrence — 646.7
Use The Power You Have. Jayapal, Pramila — B

USED CLOTHING
   Minter, Adam. *Secondhand* — 381
   Yang, April. *DIY Thrift Flip* — 646.2

Useful Delusions. Vedantam, Shankar — 153.4
Useful Enemies. Rashke, Richard — 341.69
Useless Landscape. Powell, D. A. — 811

Ustvedt, Oystein
   Edvard Munch — 759.81

UTAH
   Branch, John. *The Last Cowboys* — 920
   Cooper, Alex. *Saving Alex* — B
   Marshall, Greg. *Leg* — B
   Ralston, Aron. *Between a Rock and a Hard Place* — 796.522
   Roberts, David. *The Bears Ears* — 979.2
   Walker, Ronald W. ★*Massacre at Mountain Meadows* — 979.2

Utley, Robert M.
   ★*Geronimo* — B
   Sitting Bull — B

Utopia for Realists. Bregman, Rutger — 335

UTOPIAS
   Bregman, Rutger. *Utopia for Realists* — 335
   Cicero, Marcus Tullius. ★*The Republic* — 320.1
   Ghodsee, Kristen Rogheh. *Everyday Utopia* — 335
   Laing, Olivia. *The Garden Against Time* — 635
   Plato. ★*The Republic* — 321

UZBEKISTAN
   Samatar, Sofia. *The White Mosque* — B

V

V
   The Apology — 818
   ★*Reckoning* — 814

V (FORMERLY ENSLER, EVE, 1953-)
   V. *The Apology* — 818
   V. ★*Reckoning* — 814

V Is for Vegetables. Anthony, Michael — 641.6
★*V Is for Victory*. Nelson, Craig — 973.917
Vacationland. Hodgman, John — B

VACATIONS
   Kugel, Seth. *Rediscovering Travel* — 306.4

VACCINATION
   Deer, Brian. *The Doctor Who Fooled the World* — 610.92
   Hotez, Peter J. *Preventing the Next Pandemic* — 362.1969
   Kinch, Michael S. *Between Hope and Fear* — 614.4
   McNeil, Donald G. ★*The Wisdom of Plagues* — 614.4
   Schama, Simon. *Foreign Bodies* — 614.4
   Wadman, Meredith. *The Vaccine Race* — 614.5

The Vaccine Debate. Davidson, Tish — 615.3

VACCINE INDUSTRY AND TRADE
   Borrell, Brendan. *The First Shots* — 615.3
   Loftus, Peter. *The Messenger* — 338.4
   Zuckerman, Gregory. *A Shot to Save the World* — 614.5

The Vaccine Race. Wadman, Meredith — 614.5

VACCINES
   Barry, John M. ★*The Great Influenza* — 614.5
   Borrell, Brendan. *The First Shots* — 615.3
   Deer, Brian. *The Doctor Who Fooled the World* — 610.92
   Hotez, Peter J. *Preventing the Next Pandemic* — 362.1969
   Kariko, Katalin. *Breaking Through* — B
   Kinch, Michael S. *Between Hope and Fear* — 614.4
   Klass, Perri. *A Good Time to Be Born* — 362.19892
   Loftus, Peter. *The Messenger* — 338.4
   Oshinsky, David M. ★*Polio* — 614.5
   Quammen, David. ★*Breathless* — 614.5
   Schama, Simon. *Foreign Bodies* — 614.4

Spinney, Laura. ★*Pale Rider* ... 614.5
Wadman, Meredith. *The Vaccine Race* ... 614.5
Zaitchik, Alexander. *Owning the Sun* ... 362.1
Zuckerman, Gregory. *A Shot to Save the World* ... 614.5
Vagina. Enright, Lynn ... 612.6
VAGINA
    Enright, Lynn. *Vagina* ... 612.6
    Gross, Rachel E. *Vagina Obscura* ... 618.1
    Gunter, Jen. *The Vagina Bible* ... 612.6
    Hallman, J. C. *Say Anarcha* ... 618.1
    Mendelson, Zoe. *Pussypedia* ... 612.6
    Walters, Jacqueline. *The Queen V* ... 612.6
The Vagina Bible. Gunter, Jen ... 612.6
Vagina Obscura. Gross, Rachel E. ... 618.1
Vagina Problems. Parker, Lara ... 618.1
Vaillant, John
    ★*Fire Weather* ... 363.37
    The Tiger ... 599.756
VALADON, SUZANNE, 1865-1938
    Hewitt, Catherine. *Renoir's Dancer* ... B
Valby, Karen
    The Swans of Harlem ... 792.8
Valentine, Jean
    Door in the Mountain ... 811
VALENZUELA, FERNANDO, 1960-
    Turbow, Jason. *They Bled Blue* ... 796.357
★*Valiant Ambition*. Philbrick, Nathaniel ... B
★*Valiant Women*. Andrews, Lena S. ... 940.53
Vallely, Paul
    Pope Francis ... B
Valley Forge. Drury, Bob ... 973.3
VALLEY FORGE, PENNSYLVANIA
    Drury, Bob. *Valley Forge* ... 973.3
VALLOW, LORI, 1973-
    Glatt, John. *The Doomsday Mother* ... 364.152
VALUE
    Garbes, Angela. *Essential Labor* ... 306.874
    Sandel, Michael J. *What Money Can't Buy* ... 174
The Value of a Dollar. Derks, Scott ... 338.5
The Value of a Dollar. Derks, Scott ... 338.5
VALUES
    Browne, Mahogany L. ★*Black Girl Magic* ... 811.6
    Gentile, Mary C. *Giving Voice to Values* ... 174
    King, Maxwell. *The Good Neighbor* ... B
    Meacham, Jon. ★*And There Was Light* ... B
    Obama, Barack. ★*The Audacity of Hope* ... B
    Peck, M. Scott. ★*The Road Less Traveled* ... 158.1
    Sandel, Michael J. *Justice* ... 172
Vampira. Poole, W. Scott ... B
VAMPIRA, 1921-2008
    Poole, W. Scott. *Vampira* ... B
VAMPIRES
    Braudy, Leo. *Haunted* ... 398.45
    Harkness, Deborah E. *The World of All Souls* ... 813
Van Agtmael, Peter
    Look at the USA ... 070
Van Bavel, Jay J.
    The Power of Us ... 155.2
Van Buren, Mark
    A Fool's Guide to Actual Happiness ... 294.3
VAN BUREN, MARTIN, 1782-1862
    Widmer, Edward L. *Martin Van Buren* ... B
Van De Perre, Selma
    My Name Is Selma ... 940.53
VAN DE PERRE, SELMA
    Van De Perre, Selma. *My Name Is Selma* ... 940.53
Van der Kolk, Bessel A.
    The Body Keeps the Score ... 616.85
van der Linden, Sander
    ★*Foolproof* ... 302.3
Van Doren, Adam
    The House Tells the Story ... 728
VAN DOREN, ADAM, 1962-
    Van Doren, Adam. *The House Tells the Story* ... 728
Van Es, Bart
    The Cut Out Girl ... B
VAN ES, BART
    Van Es, Bart. *The Cut Out Girl* ... B

Van Gogh. Bell, Julian ... B
Van Gogh. Naifeh, Steven W. ... B
Van Haaften, Julia
    ★*Berenice Abbott* ... B
Van Hemert, Caroline
    The Sun Is a Compass ... 979.8
Van Hensbergen, Gijs
    The Sagrada Familia ... 726.5
VAN LEW, ELIZABETH L., 1818-1900
    Abbott, Karen. *Liar, Temptress, Soldier, Spy* ... 920
    Waller, Douglas C. *Lincoln's Spies* ... 973.7
Van Meter, Matthew
    Deep Delta Justice ... 345.763
Van Ness, Jonathan
    Love That Story ... 791.4502
VAN NESS, JONATHAN
    Van Ness, Jonathan. *Love That Story* ... 791.4502
Van Wijk-Voskuijl, Joop
    The Last Secret of the Secret Annex ... 940.53
Van Zandt, Steve
    Unrequited Infatuations ... B
VAN ZANDT, STEVE
    Van Zandt, Steve. *Unrequited Infatuations* ... B
Van't Hul, Jean
    The Artful Parent ... 745.5083
    The Artful Year ... 745.594
Vanasco, Jeannie
    Things We Didn't Talk About When I Was a Girl ... B
VANASCO, JEANNIE
    Vanasco, Jeannie. *Things We Didn't Talk About When I Was a Girl* ... B
Vance, Ashlee
    When the Heavens Went on Sale ... 621.43
Vance, J. D.
    Hillbilly Elegy ... B
VANCE, J. D.
    Vance, J. D. *Hillbilly Elegy* ... B
Vanderbes, Jennifer
    ★*Wonder Drug* ... 615
Vanderbilt. Cooper, Anderson ... 920
VANDERBILT FAMILY
    Cooper, Anderson. *Vanderbilt* ... 920
    Kiernan, Denise. *The Last Castle* ... 975.6
VANDERBILT, CORNELIUS, 1794-1877
    Renehan, Edward. *Commodore* ... B
    Stiles, T. J. ★*The First Tycoon* ... B
VANDERBILT, GLORIA, 1924-2019
    Cooper, Anderson. *The Rainbow Comes and Goes* ... B
Vanderbilt, Tom
    ★*Beginners* ... 646.7
    You May Also Like ... 153.8
VANDERBILT, TOM
    Vanderbilt, Tom. ★*Beginners* ... 646.7
Vanderpoel, John Henry
    The Human Figure ... 743
VanDuinkerken, Wyoma
    The Challenge of Library Management ... 025.1
Vanek Smith, Stacey
    Machiavelli for Women ... 650.1
Vang, Mai Der
    Afterland ... 811
Vanhoenacker, Mark
    Imagine a City ... 629.13
VANHOENACKER, MARK
    Vanhoenacker, Mark. *Imagine a City* ... 629.13
VANILLA
    Frank, Lois Ellen. *Seed to Plate, Soil to Sky* ... 641.5
Vanished Smile. Scotti, R. A. ... 759.5
★*The Vanishing Velazquez*. Cumming, Laura ... 759.6
The Vanity Fair Diaries. Brown, Tina ... B
VANN, JOHN PAUL, 1924-1972
    Sheehan, Neil. *A Bright Shining Lie* ... 959.704
VANZETTI, BARTOLOMEO, 1888-1927
    Watson, Bruce. *Sacco and Vanzetti* ... 345.73
The Vapors. Hill, David ... 976.7
Vargas Llosa, Mario
    The Call of the Tribe ... 868
    Conversation at Princeton ... 868
    Sabers and Utopias ... 980.03

AUTHOR, TITLE, SERIES AND SUBJECT INDEX

VARGAS LLOSA, MARIO, 1936-
   Vargas Llosa, Mario. *The Call of the Tribe* — 868
Vargas, Jose Antonio
   Dear America — B
VARGAS, JOSE ANTONIO
   Vargas, Jose Antonio. *Dear America* — B
★*The Varieties of Religious Experience*. James, William — 204
Varol, Ozan O.
   Think Like a Rocket Scientist — 650.1
Varon, Elizabeth R.
   Longstreet — B
VASARI, GIORGIO, 1511-1574
   Rowland, Ingrid D. *The Collector of Lives* — B
Vasily Grossman and the Soviet Century. Popoff, Alexandra — B
Vasquez, Karla Tatiana
   ★*The Salvisoul Cookbook* — 641.598
Vasquez-Lavado, Silvia
   In the Shadow of the Mountain — B
VASQUEZ-LAVADO, SILVIA
   Vasquez-Lavado, Silvia. *In the Shadow of the Mountain* — B
VASUBANDHU
   Connelly, Ben. *Inside Vasubandhu's Yogacara* — 294.3
VATICAN CITY
   Kertzer, David I. *The Pope and Mussolini* — 322
   Kertzer, David I. *The Pope at War* — 940.53
   King, Ross. *Michelangelo & the Pope's Ceiling* — 759.5
VAUDEVILLE
   Lane, Stewart F. *Black Broadway* — 792.089
   Stevens, Dana. *Camera Man* — 791.4302
VAUDEVILLE PERFORMERS
   Willetts, Paul. *King Con* — B
Vaughan, Liam
   Flash Crash — B
VAUGHAN, SARAH, 1924-1990
   Hayes, Elaine M. ★*Queen of Bebop* — B
Vaughn, Ellen Santilli
   ★*Becoming Elisabeth Elliot* — B
Vaynerchuk, Gary
   Crushing It! — 650.1
VB6. Bittman, Mark — 641.5
The VB6 Cookbook. Bittman, Mark — 641.5
Veblen, Thorstein
   ★*The Theory of the Leisure Class* — 305.5
Vecsey, George
   Eight World Cups — 796.334
Vedantam, Shankar
   Useful Delusions — 153.4
VEECK, BILL, 1914-1986
   Epplin, Luke. *Our Team* — 796.357
Veg-Table. Sharma, Nik — 641.6
Vegan Cheese. Aron, Jules — 641.5
★*The Vegan Chinese Kitchen*. Che, Hannah — 641.5
VEGAN COOKING
   Aron, Jules. *Vegan Cheese* — 641.5
   Ben-Ishay, Melissa. *Come Hungry* — 641.5
   Bhogal, Ravinder. *Comfort and Joy* — 641.5
   Bittman, Mark. *The VB6 Cookbook* — 641.5
   Bittman, Mark. *VB6* — 641.5
   Bowien, Danny. *Mission Vegan* — 641.5
   Che, Hannah. ★*The Vegan Chinese Kitchen* — 641.5
   Claiborne, Jenne. ★*Sweet Potato Soul* — 641.5
   Coscarelli, Chloe. *Chloe Flavor* — 641.5
   Cristofano, Jana. *Eat Well, Be Well* — 641.5
   Dada, Samah. *Dada Eats Love to Cook It* — 641.3
   DiSpirito, Rocco. *Rocco's Healthy+Delicious* — 641.5
   Frank, Lois Ellen. *Seed to Plate, Soil to Sky* — 641.5
   Gray, Jon. *Ghetto Gastro Black Power Kitchen* — 641.5
   Hamshaw, Gena. *Food 52 Vegan* — 641.5
   Hansen, Kim-Julie. *Best of Vegan* — 641.5
   Hayden, Georgina. *Nistisima* — 641.5
   Jade, Holly. *The Essential Book of Vegan Bakes* — 641.5
   Lee Molinaro, Joanne. ★*The Korean Vegan Cookbook* — 641.595
   Lewis, John. *Badass Vegan* — 641.5
   Moskowitz, Isa Chandra. *The Superfun Times Vegan Holiday Cookbook* — 651.56
   Moskowitz, Isa Chandra. *Veganomicon* — 641
   Patel, Palak. *Food Is Love* — 641.595
   Pierson, Joy. *Vegan Holiday Cooking from Candle Cafe* — 641.5

   Prescott, Matthew. *Food Is the Solution* — 613.2
   Pulde, Alona. *Forks Over Knives Family* — 641.5
   Pulde, Alona. ★*The Forks Over Knives Plan* — 641.5
   Roll, Rich. *The Plantpower Way* — 641.5
   Rosenstrach, Jenny. ★*The Weekday Vegetarians* — 641.5
   Sarno, Chad. *The Wicked Healthy Cookbook* — 651.56
   Schinner, Miyoko Nishimoto. *The Vegan Meat Cookbook* — 641.5
   Siva, Micah. *Nosh* — 641.5
   Terry, Bryant. *Afro-Vegan* — 641.59
   Terry, Bryant. *Vegan Soul Kitchen* — 641.5
   Terry, Bryant. ★*Vegetable Kingdom* — 641.5
   Walch, Aubry. *The Herbivorous Butcher Cookbook* — 641.5
Vegan Holiday Cooking from Candle Cafe. Pierson, Joy — 641.5
The Vegan Meat Cookbook. Schinner, Miyoko Nishimoto — 641.5
Vegan Soul Kitchen. Terry, Bryant — 641.5
Vegan Vegetarian Omnivore. Thomas, Anna — 641.5
VEGANISM
   Hamshaw, Gena. *Food 52 Vegan* — 641.5
   Lewis, John. *Badass Vegan* — 641.5
   Prescott, Matthew. *Food Is the Solution* — 613.2
   Pulde, Alona. *Forks Over Knives Family* — 641.5
   Pulde, Alona. ★*The Forks Over Knives Plan* — 641.5
Veganomicon. Moskowitz, Isa Chandra — 641
VEGANS
   Moby. *Porcelain* — B
The Vegetable Butcher. Mangini, Cara — 641.6
VEGETABLE CARVING
   Cupp, Lundy. *Realistic Pumpkin Carving* — 745.5941646
★*The Vegetable Eater*. Mangini, Cara — 641.6
The Vegetable Gardener's Bible. Smith, Edward C. — 635
The Vegetable Gardener's Container Bible. Smith, Edward C. — 635
VEGETABLE GARDENING
   Bellamy, Andrea. *Small-Space Vegetable Gardens* — 635
   Coleman, Eliot. ★*The New Organic Grower* — 635
   Iannotti, Marie. *The Beginner's Guide to Growing Heirloom Vegetables* — 635
   Jabbour, Niki. ★*Groundbreaking Food Gardens* — 635
   Jabbour, Niki. *Growing Under Cover* — 635
   Jabbour, Niki. *Niki Jabbour's Veggie Garden Remix* — 635
   McLaughlin, Chris. *The Good Garden* — 635
   Obama, Michelle. *American Grown* — 635.09
   Pleasant, Barbara. ★*Starter Vegetable Gardens* — 635
   Smith, Edward C. *The Vegetable Gardener's Bible* — 635
   Smith, Edward C. *The Vegetable Gardener's Container Bible* — 635
   Stuckey, Maggie. *The Container Victory Garden* — 635.9
   Walliser, Jessica. *Plant Partners* — 635
   Webb, Leah M. *The Seven-Step Homestead* — 635
   Whitman, John. *Fresh from the Garden* — 635.9
VEGETABLE GARDENS
   Bohmig, Franz. ★*The Month-By-Month Gardening Guide* — 635
★*Vegetable Kingdom*. Terry, Bryant — 641.5
Vegetable Literacy. Madison, Deborah — 641.6
VEGETABLES
   Berens, Abra. *Pulp* — 641.6
   Berens, Abra. *Ruffage* — 641.5
   Frank, Lois Ellen. *Seed to Plate, Soil to Sky* — 641.5
   Iannotti, Marie. *The Beginner's Guide to Growing Heirloom Vegetables* — 635
   Jabbour, Niki. ★*Groundbreaking Food Gardens* — 635
   Jabbour, Niki. *Niki Jabbour's Veggie Garden Remix* — 635
   Mangini, Cara. *The Vegetable Butcher* — 641.6
   McKinnon, Hetty. ★*Tenderheart* — 641.5
   Pleasant, Barbara. *Homegrown Pantry* — 635
   Raichlen, Steven. *How to Grill Vegetables* — 641.6
   Segnit, Niki. ★*The Flavor Thesaurus* — 641.5
   Selengut, Becky. ★*Misunderstood Vegetables* — 641.6
   Ziegler, Lisa Mason. *Vegetables Love Flowers* — 635
Vegetables Love Flowers. Ziegler, Lisa Mason — 635
Vegetables Unleashed. Andres, Jose — 641.5
VEGETARIAN COOKING
   Andres, Jose. *Vegetables Unleashed* — 641.5
   Ben-Ishay, Melissa. *Come Hungry* — 641.5
   Berens, Abra. *Grist* — 641.6
   Berens, Abra. *Ruffage* — 641.5
   Bhogal, Ravinder. *Comfort and Joy* — 641.5
   Bittman, Mark. ★*How to Cook Everything Vegetarian* — 641.5
   Britton, Sarah. *Naturally Nourished* — 641.5
   Donofrio, Jeanine. ★*Love & Lemons* — 641.5
   Fearnley-Whittingstall, Hugh. *River Cottage Veg* — 641.5
   Firth, Henry. *Bosh!* — 641.5

PUBLIC LIBRARY CORE COLLECTION: NONFICTION
Twentieth Edition

Gill, Sasha. *East Meets Vegan*	641.5
Hage, Salma. ★*The Levantine Vegetarian*	641.595
Headley, Brooks. *Superiority Burger Cookbook*	641.5
Jaffrey, Madhur. *Madhur Jaffrey's World Vegetarian.*	641.5
Jaffrey, Madhur. *Vegetarian India*	641.595
Jones, Anna. *One*	641.5
Kahate, Ruta. *6 Spices 60 Dishes*	641.595
Katzen, Mollie. *The Heart of the Plate*	641.5
Katzen, Mollie. ★*The Moosewood Cookbook*	641.5
Kochilas, Diane. *The Ikaria Way*	641.5
Korkosz, Michal. *Fresh from Poland*	641.594
Lewis, John. *Badass Vegan*	641.5
Madison, Deborah. *In My Kitchen*	641.5
Madison, Deborah. *Vegetarian Cooking for Everyone*	641.5
Mangini, Cara. ★*The Vegetable Eater*	641.6
McKinnon, Hetty. ★*Tenderheart*	641.5
Moskowitz, Isa Chandra. *Veganomicon*	641
Mullins, Brittany. *Mostly Veggies*	641.5
Murad, Noor. ★*Ottolenghi Test Kitchen*	641.3
Nguyen, Andrea Quynhgiao. *Ever-Green Vietnamese*	641.595
Ottolenghi, Yotam. ★*Plenty More*	641.6
Patel, Palak. *Food Is Love*	641.595
Prescott, Matthew. *Food Is the Solution*	613.2
Pulde, Alona. *Forks Over Knives Family*	641.5
Roll, Rich. *The Plantpower Way*	641.5
Rosenstrach, Jenny. ★*The Weekday Vegetarians*	641.5
Sharma, Nik. *Veg-Table*	641.6
Siva, Micah. *Nosh*	641.5
Sodha, Meera. *East*	641.595
Taylor, Kathryne. *Love Real Food*	641.5
Thomas, Haile. *Living Lively*	641.5
Volger, Lukas. *Bowl*	641.81
Vegetarian Cooking for Everyone. Madison, Deborah	641.5
Vegetarian India. Jaffrey, Madhur	641.595
VEGETARIANISM	
Foer, Jonathan Safran. *Eating Animals*	641.3
Guha, Ramachandra. *Gandhi Before India*	B
Prescott, Matthew. *Food Is the Solution*	613.2
Pulde, Alona. *Forks Over Knives Family*	641.5
Singer, Peter. ★*Animal Liberation*	179
Williams, Wyatt. *Springer Mountain*	394.1
VEHICLES	
Cotterell, Arthur. *Chariot*	357
Velasquez, Lizzie	
Dare to Be Kind	177
Velasquez, Mariana	
Colombiana	641.59861
VELAZQUEZ, DIEGO, 1599-1660	
Cumming, Laura. ★*The Vanishing Velazquez*	759.6
Vella, Christina	
George Washington Carver	B
Velour, Sasha	
★*The Big Reveal*	792.7
VELOUR, SASHA	
Velour, Sasha. ★*The Big Reveal*	792.7
Velshi, Ali	
Small Acts of Courage	B
The Velvet Rope Economy. Schwartz, Nelson	339.2
VENEZUELA	
Allende, Isabel. ★*Paula*	B
Neumann, Ariana. *When Time Stopped*	B
Venice. Madden, Thomas F.	945
Venice and Drawing, 1500-1800. Whistler, Catherine	741.09
VENICE, ITALY	
Berendt, John. *The City of Falling Angels*	945
Crowley, Roger. *City of Fortune*	945
Hale, Sheila. *Titian*	B
Leon, Donna. *My Venice and Other Essays*	945
Madden, Thomas F. *Venice*	945
Norwich, John Julius. *A History of Venice*	945
VENTRIS, MICHAEL, 1922-1956	
Fox, Margalit. *The Riddle of the Labyrinth*	920
Ventrone, Jillian	
From the Marine Corps to College	378.1
VENTURE CAPITAL	
Brown, Eliot. *The Cult of We*	333.33
VENTURE CAPITALISTS	
Au-Yeung, Angel. *Wonder Boy*	B
Vance, Ashlee. *When the Heavens Went on Sale*	621.43
VENUS (ROMAN DEITY)	
Hughes, Bettany. *Venus and Aphrodite*	292
Venus and Aphrodite. Hughes, Bettany	292
Verant, Samantha	
Seven Letters from Paris	B
VERANT, SAMANTHA	
Verant, Samantha. *Seven Letters from Paris*	B
VERBS	
Pinker, Steven. *Words and Rules*	415
Verdelle, A. J.	
Miss Chloe	B
VERDELLE, A. J., 1960-	
Verdelle, A. J. *Miss Chloe*	B
Verdi. Suchet, John	782.1092
Verdi with a Vengeance. Berger, William	B
VERDI, GIUSEPPE, 1813-1901	
Berger, William. *Verdi with a Vengeance*	B
Suchet, John. *Verdi*	782.1092
Verini, James	
They Will Have to Die Now	956.7044
VERMEER, JOHANNES, 1632-1675	
Snyder, Laura J. *Eye of the Beholder*	920
Verminski, Alana	
★*Fundamentals of Electronic Resources Management*	025.2
VERMONT	
Crouse, Karen. *Norwich*	796
Franklin, Ruth. *Shirley Jackson*	B
Halpern, Sue. *A Dog Walks into a Nursing Home*	B
Keizer, Garret. *Getting Schooled*	373.1102
Vernacchio, Al	
For Goodness Sex	613.9071
Versaci, Russell	
Creating a New Old House	728
VERSAILLES, FRANCE	
Givhan, Robin. *The Battle of Versailles*	746.9
Versed. Armantrout, Rae	811
A Very Brief History of Eternity. Eire, Carlos M. N.	236
A Very Chinese Cookbook. Pang, Kevin	641.595
A Very Short History of Life on Earth. Gee, Henry	576.8
VESEY, DENMARK, APPROXIMATELY 1767-1822	
Kytle, Ethan J. *Denmark Vesey's Garden*	975.7
VESPASIANO, DA BISTICCI, 1421-1498	
King, Ross. *Bookseller of Florence*	381
★*Vesper Flights.* Macdonald, Helen	508
VESPUCCI, AMERIGO, 1451-1512	
Fernandez-Armesto, Felipe. ★*Amerigo*	B
VETERANS	
Brands, H. W. ★*Andrew Jackson, His Life and Times*	B
Castner, Brian. *The Long Walk*	B
Cervini, Eric. *The Deviant's War*	B
Chesney, Will. *No Ordinary Dog*	958.104
Duckworth, Tammy. *Every Day Is a Gift*	B
Erwin, Jon. *Beyond Valor*	B
Finkel, David. *Thank You for Your Service*	920
Gonell, Aquilino. *American Shield*	B
Greitens, Eric. *Resilience*	155.2
Homer. ★*The Odyssey*	883
Kesling, Ben. *Bravo Company*	958.104
Lambert, Raymond. *Every Man a Hero*	B
Louis, Matthew J. *Mission Transition*	650.14
Moore, Wes. *The Work*	B
Morris, David J. *The Evil Hours*	616.85
Patterson, James. *Walk in My Combat Boots*	920
Sinise, Gary. *Grateful American*	B
Ventrone, Jillian. *From the Marine Corps to College*	378.1
VETERANS' FAMILIES	
Finkel, David. *Thank You for Your Service*	920
VETERINARIANS	
Attas, Amy. *Pets and the City*	B
Fincham-Gray, Suzanne. *My Patients and Other Animals*	B
Herriot, James. ★*All Creatures Great and Small*	B
Herriot, James. *All Things Wise and Wonderful*	B
Herriot, James. *Every Living Thing*	B
Herriot, James. *James Herriot's Animal Stories*	B
Herriot, James. *James Herriot's Cat Stories*	636.8
Herriot, James. *James Herriot's Dog Stories*	636.7
Herriot, James. *James Herriot's Favorite Dog Stories*	636.7

AUTHOR, TITLE, SERIES AND SUBJECT INDEX

Schott, Philipp. *The Accidental Veterinarian*	B
VETERINARY MEDICINE	
Attas, Amy. *Pets and the City*	B
Vetri, Marc	
Mastering Pizza	641.82
VETSERA, MARY, BARONESSE, 1871-1889	
King, Greg. *Twilight of Empire*	943.6
VIARDOT, LOUIS, 1800-1883	
Figes, Orlando. *The Europeans*	920
VIARDOT-GARCÍA, PAULINE, 1821-1910	
Figes, Orlando. *The Europeans*	920
Vibrant Punch Needle Decor. Lowry, Melissa	746.44
Vibrate Higher. Kweli, Talib	B
VICE PRESIDENTS	
Brower, Kate Andersen. *First in Line*	920
Cohen, Jared. *Accidental Presidents*	973.09
Lozada, Carlos. *The Washington Book*	320
VICE-PRESIDENTS	
Biden, Joseph R. *Promise Me, Dad*	B
Caro, Robert A. ★*The Passage of Power*	B
Finkelman, Paul. *Millard Fillmore*	B
Maddow, Rachel. *Bag Man*	B
May, Gary. *John Tyler*	B
Osnos, Evan. *Joe Biden*	B
Smith, Richard Norton. *On His Own Terms*	973.925092
Vicenzino, Cettina	
The Sicily Cookbook	641.59458
VICIOUS, SID	
Albertine, Viv. *Clothes, Clothes, Clothes. Music, Music, Music*	B
Vick, Tom	
Asian Cinema	791.43
Vickers, Michael G.	
By All Means Available	355
VICKERS, MICHAEL G.	
Vickers, Michael G. *By All Means Available*	355
Vicksburg. Miller, Donald L.	973.7
VICKSBURG, MISSISSIPPI	
Miller, Donald L. *Vicksburg*	973.7
VICTIMS	
Tutu, Desmond. *The Book of Forgiving*	179
VICTIMS OF CRIMES	
Behar, Richard. *Madoff*	364.16
Bowdler, Michelle. ★*Is Rape a Crime?*	B
Brodsky, Alexandra. *Sexual Justice*	364.15
Flock, Elizabeth. ★*The Furies*	305.48
Goldberg, Carrie. *Nobody's Victim*	345.73
Grigoriadis, Vanessa. *Blurred Lines*	371.7
Krakauer, Jon. *Missoula*	362.883
Sered, Danielle. *Until We Reckon*	364.6
Weinman, Sarah. ★*Unspeakable Acts*	364.1
Yousafzai, Malala. *I Am Malala*	B
VICTIMS OF STATE-SPONSORED TERRORISM	
Slezkine, Yuri. *The House of Government*	947.084
VICTIMS OF TERRORISM	
Dwyer, Jim. *102 Minutes*	974.7
Graff, Garrett M. ★*The Only Plane in the Sky*	973.931
Longman, Jere. *Among the Heroes*	974.8
VICTIMS OF VIOLENT CRIMES	
Auster, Paul. *Bloodbath Nation*	363.33
Oppenheimer, Mark. *Squirrel Hill*	364.152
Rubin, Kathy Kleiner. *A Light in the Dark*	364.152
The Victims' Revolution. Bawer, Bruce	320.973
Victoria. Wilson, A. N.	B
★*Victoria The Queen*. Baird, Julia	B
VICTORIA, QUEEN OF GREAT BRITAIN, 1819-1901	
Baird, Julia. ★*Victoria the Queen*	B
Cadbury, Deborah. *Queen Victoria's Matchmaking*	941.081
Gill, Gillian. *We Two*	941.081
Hawksley, Lucinda. *Queen Victoria's Mysterious Daughter*	B
Ridley, Jane. *The Heir Apparent*	B
Wilson, A. N. *Victoria*	B
Worsley, Lucy. *Queen Victoria*	B
The Victorian City. Flanders, Judith	942.1
VICTORIAN ERA (1837-1901)	
Baird, Julia. ★*Victoria the Queen*	B
Cadbury, Deborah. *Queen Victoria's Matchmaking*	941.081
Gill, Gillian. *We Two*	941.081
Goodman, Ruth. *How to Be a Victorian*	941.08
Harman, Claire. *Murder by the Book*	364.152
Hawksley, Lucinda. *Queen Victoria's Mysterious Daughter*	B
Jobb, Dean. *The Case of the Murderous Dr. Cream*	364.152
Kavanagh, Julie. *The Irish Assassins*	941.5
MacColl, Gail. *To Marry an English Lord*	974.7
O'Sullivan, Emer. *The Fall of the House of Wilde*	B
Rubenhold, Hallie. ★*The Five*	362.88
Wilson, A. N. *Victoria*	B
Worsley, Lucy. *Queen Victoria*	B
The Victors. Ambrose, Stephen E.	940.54
VIDEO GAMES	
Bissell, Tom. *Extra Lives*	794.8
Burak, Asi. *Power Play*	794.8
Goodridge, Michelle. *Librarian's Guide to Games and Gamers*	025.2
Harris, Blake J. *Console Wars*	338.7
Miller, Megan. ★*The Ultimate Unofficial Encyclopedia for Minecrafters*	794.8
Parkin, Simon. *An Illustrated History of 151 Video Games*	794.8
Ruberg, Bonnie. ★*The Queer Games Avant-Garde*	794.8
VIDEO GAMES INDUSTRY AND TRADE	
Alt, Matt. *Pure Invention*	306.0952
Burak, Asi. *Power Play*	794.8
Harris, Blake J. *Console Wars*	338.7
Ruberg, Bonnie. ★*The Queer Games Avant-Garde*	794.8
VIDEOCONFERENCING	
Taylor, Claude. *How to Zoom Your Room*	747
VIDEOS	
Hill, Marc Lamont. *Seen and Unseen*	303.3
VIENNA, AUSTRIA	
Brownstein, Gabriel. ★*The Secret Mind of Bertha Pappenheim*	616.85
De Waal, Edmund. *The Hare with Amber Eyes*	B
Kandel, Eric R. *The Age of Insight*	154.2
Nagorski, Andrew. *Saving Freud*	940.53
Tallis, Frank. ★*Mortal Secrets*	B
Viertel, Jack	
The Secret Life of the American Musical	792.609
★*Vietnam*. Hastings, Max	959.704
VIETNAM	
Albracht, William. *Abandoned in Hell*	959.704
Black, George. ★*The Long Reckoning*	959.704
Bowden, Mark. ★*Hue 1968*	959.704
Brokhausen, Nick. *Whispers in the Tall Grass*	959.704
Bui, Thi. ★*The Best We Could Do*	741.5
Chung, Vinh. *Where the Wind Leads*	B
Clarke, Thurston. *Honorable Exit*	959.704
Duiker, William J. *Ho Chi Minh*	B
FitzGerald, Frances. *Fire in the Lake*	959.704
Fowlds, Grant. *Saving the Last Rhinos*	599.66
Hastings, Max. ★*Vietnam*	959.704
Karnow, Stanley. *Vietnam, a History*	959.704
Logevall, Fredrik. *Embers of War*	959.704
Moore, Harold G. *We Are Soldiers Still*	959.704
Nguyen, Hoa. *A Thousand Times You Lose Your Treasure*	811
Nguyen, Viet Thanh. ★*A Man of Two Faces*	B
Pham, Andrew X. ★*The Eaves of Heaven*	B
Shultz, Richard H. *The Secret War Against Hanoi*	959.704
Stanton, Doug. *The Odyssey of Echo Company*	959.704
Talty, Stephan. *Saving Bravo*	959.704
Ward, Geoffrey C. *The Vietnam War*	959.704
Warren, James A. *Year of the Hawk*	959.704
VIETNAM VETERANS	
Black, George. ★*The Long Reckoning*	959.704
Kerry, John. *Every Day Is Extra*	B
Moore, Harold G. *We Are Soldiers Still*	959.704
Preszler, Trent. *Little and Often*	B
★*The Vietnam War*. Ward, Geoffrey C.	959.704
VIETNAM WAR, 1961-1975	
Albracht, William. *Abandoned in Hell*	959.704
Appy, Christian G. *American Reckoning*	959.704
Bingham, Clara. *Witness to the Revolution*	303.48
Black, George. ★*The Long Reckoning*	959.704
Boot, Max. ★*The Road Not Taken*	B
Bowden, Mark. ★*Hue 1968*	959.704
Boyle, Kevin. *The Shattering*	973.923
Brokhausen, Nick. *Whispers in the Tall Grass*	959.704
Bui, Thi. ★*The Best We Could Do*	741.5
Caputo, Philip. *A Rumor of War*	959.704
Clarke, Thurston. *Honorable Exit*	959.704

PUBLIC LIBRARY CORE COLLECTION: NONFICTION
Twentieth Edition

Derf. *Kent State*	741.5
Duiker, William J. *Ho Chi Minh*	B
FitzGerald, Frances. *Fire in the Lake*	959.704
Gewen, Barry. ★*The Inevitability of Tragedy*	B
Halberstam, David. *The Best and the Brightest*	973.92
Hastings, Max. ★*Vietnam*	959.704
Hendrickson, Paul. *The Living and the Dead*	959.704
Karnow, Stanley. *Vietnam, a History*	959.704
Kissinger, Henry. *Ending the Vietnam War*	959.704
Kurlansky, Mark. *1968*	909.82
Lee, Heath Hardage. ★*The League of Wives*	959.704
Maraniss, David. *They Marched into Sunlight*	959.704
McNamara, Robert S. *In Retrospect*	959.704
Montville, Leigh. *Sting Like a Bee*	B
Moore, Harold G. *We Are Soldiers Still*	959.704
Moore, Harold G. *We Were Soldiers Once—And Young*	959.704
Nguyen, Hoa. *A Thousand Times You Lose Your Treasure*	811
Nguyen, Viet Thanh. ★*A Man of Two Faces*	B
Nguyen, Viet Thanh. *Nothing Ever Dies*	959.704
Petraeus, David Howell. *Conflict*	355
Pham, Andrew X. ★*The Eaves of Heaven*	B
Rinehart, Lorissa. *First to the Front*	B
Sheehan, Neil. *A Bright Shining Lie*	959.704
Shultz, Richard H. *The Secret War Against Hanoi*	959.704
Stanton, Doug. *The Odyssey of Echo Company*	959.704
Talty, Stephan. *Saving Bravo*	959.704
Thi, Kim Phuc Phan. *Fire Road*	B
Tran, Phuc. ★*Sigh, Gone*	B
Ulander, Perry A. *Walking Point*	B
Ward, Geoffrey C. ★*The Vietnam War*	959.704
Warren, James A. *Year of the Hawk*	959.704
White, Ralph. *Getting Out of Saigon*	959.704
Wright, James Edward. ★*Enduring Vietnam*	959.704
Zeitz, Joshua. *Building the Great Society*	973.923
Vietnam, A History. Karnow, Stanley	959.704
VIETNAMESE AMERICAN CHILDREN	
Hayasaki, Erika. *Somewhere Sisters*	362.7
VIETNAMESE AMERICANS	
Johnson, Kirk W. *The Fishermen and the Dragon*	976.4
Lieu, Susan. ★*The Manicurist's Daughter*	B
Nguyen, Bich Minh. *Owner of a Lonely Heart*	B
Nguyen, Viet Thanh. ★*A Man of Two Faces*	B
Pham, Andrew X. ★*The Eaves of Heaven*	B
Tran, Ly. *House of Sticks*	B
Tran, Phuc. ★*Sigh, Gone*	B
Vuong, Ocean. ★*Time Is a Mother*	811
Yip-Williams, Julie. ★*The Unwinding of the Miracle*	973
★*Vietnamese Food Any Day*. Nguyen, Andrea Quynhgiao	641.595
VIETNAMESE PEOPLE	
Nguyen, Bich Minh. *Owner of a Lonely Heart*	B
Nguyen, Viet Thanh. ★*A Man of Two Faces*	B
The View from the Cheap Seats. Gaiman, Neil	824
VIGILANTES	
Evangelista, Patricia. ★*Some People Need Killing*	364.4
Lehr, Dick. *White Hot Hate*	363.325
Vigliotti, Jonathan	
Before It's Gone	577
The Viking Heart. Herman, Arthur	948
VIKING WOMEN	
Brown, Nancy Marie. *The Real Valkyrie*	948
VIKINGS	
Brown, Nancy Marie. *Ivory Vikings*	736
Brown, Nancy Marie. *The Real Valkyrie*	948
Herman, Arthur. *The Viking Heart*	948
Price, Neil S. ★*Children of Ash and Elm*	948
Winroth, Anders. *The Age of the Vikings*	948
Vile, John R.	
Encyclopedia of Constitutional Amendments, Proposed Amendments, and Amending Issues, 1789-2010	342.7303
VILLA, PANCHO, 1878-1923	
Guinn, Jeff. ★*War on the Border*	972.08
Village of Secrets. Moorehead, Caroline	944
VILLAGES	
Ahmed, Azam. *Fear Is Just a Word*	364.152
Badkhen, Anna. *The World Is a Carpet*	305.409581
Erdman, Sarah. *Nine Hills to Nambonkaha*	966.68
Grose, Peter. *A Good Place to Hide*	940.53
Hoffman, Carl. ★*Savage Harvest*	995.1
Mayle, Peter. *My Twenty-Five Years in Provence*	944.9
Morris, Jan. *A Writer's House in Wales*	942.9
Paxson, Margaret. *The Plateau*	362.87
Samatar, Sofia. *The White Mosque*	B
Villanova, Thibaud	
Disney Enchanted Recipes	641.5
Villarosa, Linda	
★*Under the Skin*	362.1089
Villarreal, Vanessa Anglica	
Magical/Realism	814
Villasuso, Susana	
Sobremesa	641.5972
Villodas, Rich	
The Deeply Formed Life	248.4
Good and Beautiful and Kind	232.9
Villon, Francois	
The Poems of Francois Villon	841
VILLON, FRANCOIS, 1431-1463	
Villon, Francois. *The Poems of Francois Villon*	841
Villoro, Juan	
God Is Round	796.334
Vince, Gaia	
Nomad Century	362.87
Transcendence	599.93
Vincent, James	
Beyond Measure	530.8
Vincent, Lynn	
Indianapolis	940.54
VINEYARDS	
Zraly, Kevin. *Windows on the World Complete Wine Course*	641.2
Vintage classics [Series]. Hughes, Langston	811
VINTAGE RECORD STORES	
Calamar, Gary. *Record Store Days*	780.26
Vinton, Nathaniel	
The Fall Line	796.93
VIOLENCE	
Abdurraqib, Hanif. *A Fortune for Your Disaster*	811
Ahmed, Azam. *Fear Is Just a Word*	364.152
Anthony, Carmelo. *Where Tomorrows Aren't Promised*	B
Armstrong, Karen. *Fields of Blood*	201
Beah, Ishmael. ★*A Long Way Gone*	B
Belcourt, Billy-Ray. ★*A History of My Brief Body*	B
Berry, Erica. *Wolfish*	152.4
Blattman, Christopher. *Why We Fight*	303.6
Bossiere, Zoe. *Cactus Country*	306
Branch, John. *Boy on Ice*	B
Brooks, James. *Mesa of Sorrows*	979.1004
Brown, Jericho. ★*The Tradition*	811
Capote, Truman. ★*In Cold Blood*	364.1
Chang, Tina. *Hybrida*	811
Clark, Tiana. *I Can't Talk About the Trees Without the Blood*	811
Corcoran, Katherine. *In the Mouth of the Wolf*	364.152
Crawford, Alan Pell. *This Fierce People*	975
Davis, Angela Y. *Abolition*	364.6
Denton, Sally. *The Colony*	364.152
Dogon, Mondiant. *Those We Throw Away Are Diamonds*	B
Dubus, Andre. *Townie*	B
Egan, Timothy. ★*A Fever in the Heartland*	322.4
Elkins, Caroline. *Legacy of Violence*	909
Elliott, Andrea. ★*Invisible Child*	362.7
Flock, Elizabeth. ★*The Furies*	305.48
Freeman, Joanne B. *The Field of Blood*	973.7
Garcia, Angela. ★*The Way That Leads Among the Lost*	362.29
Haitiwaji, Gulbahar. *How I Survived a Chinese "Reeducation" Camp*	305.8
Herman, Judith Lewis. *Truth and Repair*	362.883
Hickman, Katie. *Brave Hearted*	
Hill, Anita. ★*Believing*	305.42
Hirsch, James S. *Riot and Remembrance*	976.6
Hobbs, Jeff. ★*The Short and Tragic Life of Robert Peace*	B
Hochschild, Adam. *American Midnight*	973.91
Hoock, Holger. *Scars of Independence*	973.3
Hughes, Bettany. *Venus and Aphrodite*	292
Johnson, Kirk W. *The Fishermen and the Dragon*	976.4
Jordan, June. ★*The Essential June Jordan*	811
Kenneally, Christine. *Ghosts of the Orphanage*	362.73
Komunyakaa, Yusef. ★*Everyday Mojo Songs of Earth*	811
Lane, Charles. *The Day Freedom Died*	976.3
Lockhart, Chris. ★*Walking the Bowl*	362.7

AUTHOR, TITLE, SERIES AND SUBJECT INDEX

Lovato, Roberto. *Unforgetting*	B
Madigan, Tim. *The Burning*	976.6
Malala, Justice. *The Plot to Save South Africa*	968.07
Malhotra, Aanchal. *Remnants of Partition*	954.04
Matloff, Judith. *No Friends but the Mountains*	355.009
Metzl, Jonathan M. ★*What We've Become*	364.152
Mohan, Rohini. *The Seasons of Trouble*	954.9303
Moore, Wayetu. *The Dragons, the Giant, the Women*	B
Moore, Wes. *The Other Wes Moore*	B
Murakami, Haruki. *Underground*	364.15
Murphy, Chris. ★*The Violence Inside Us*	303.60973
O'Toole, Fintan. ★*We Don't Know Ourselves*	941.7
Passarlay, Gulwali. *The Lightless Sky*	B
Peterson, Marlon. *Bird Uncaged*	B
Raboteau, Emily. *Lessons for Survival*	814
Rankine, Claudia. ★*Citizen*	814
Rankine, Claudia. ★*Just Us*	305.896
Rose, Jacqueline. *On Violence and on Violence Against Women*	362.88
Rosner, Elizabeth. *Survivor Cafe*	940.53
Rushdie, Salman. ★*Knife*	B
Sacco, Joe. *Footnotes in Gaza*	741.5
Samaha, Albert. *Never Ran, Never Will*	920
Schechter, Harold. *Hell's Princess*	B
Scott, James. *Rampage*	940.54
Sebag-Montefiore, Simon. ★*The World*	929.7
Sered, Danielle. *Until We Reckon*	364.6
Shackle, Samira. *Karachi Vice*	954.91
Shange, Ntozake. ★*Sing a Black Girl's Song*	818
Shaughnessy, Brenda. *The Octopus Museum*	811
Sides, Hampton. ★*The Wide Wide Sea*	910.92
Skaja, Emily. *Brute*	811.6
Smith, Danez. ★*Don't Call Us Dead*	811.6
Stern, Jessica. *My War Criminal*	341.6
Subramanian, Sammanth. *This Divided Island*	954.9303
Sullivan, Randall. *The Devil's Best Trick*	235
Tanais. *In Sensorium*	B
Trejo, Danny. *Trejo*	B
Umar, Ousman. *North to Paradise*	B
Walker, Ronald W. ★*Massacre at Mountain Meadows*	979.2
Watkins, D. *Black Boy Smile*	B
Williams, Wyatt. *Springer Mountain*	394.1
Wolff, Tobias. *This Boy's Life*	B
Wood, Graeme. *The Way of the Strangers*	363.325

VIOLENCE AGAINST AFRICAN AMERICANS

Anderson, Carol. ★*The Second*	344.7305
Bell, Darrin. ★*The Talk*	741.5
Burnham, Margaret A. ★*By Hands Now Known*	342.73
Currie, Elliott. *A Peculiar Indifference*	305.800973
Ellsworth, Scott. *The Ground Breaking*	976.6
Ewing, Eve L. *1919*	811
Gergel, Richard. *Unexampled Courage*	323.1196
Hill, DaMaris B. *Breath Better Spent*	811
Hill, Marc Lamont. *Seen and Unseen*	303.3
Jones, Robert P. *The Hidden Roots of White Supremacy*	305.8
Lemann, Nicholas. *Redemption*	975
Marshall, Nate. *Finna*	811
Martin, Rachel Louise. *A Most Tolerant Little Town*	379.2
Person, Charles. *Buses Are a Comin'*	B
Phillips, Patrick. *Blood at the Root*	305.8
Rembert, Winfred. *Chasing Me to My Grave*	B
Williams, Kidada E. *I Saw Death Coming*	973.8
Young, R. J. *Requiem for the Massacre*	305.8
Zucchino, David. *Wilmington's Lie*	305.8009756

VIOLENCE AGAINST GAY MEN AND LESBIANS

Fieseler, Robert W. *Tinderbox*	364.152
Jimenez, Stephen. *The Book of Matt*	364.152

VIOLENCE AGAINST IMMIGRANTS

Kushner, Jacob. *Look Away*	305.9

VIOLENCE AGAINST INDIGENOUS PEOPLE

Eustace, Nicole. ★*Covered with Night*	364.152
Jones, Robert P. *The Hidden Roots of White Supremacy*	305.8

VIOLENCE AGAINST MARGINALIZED PEOPLE

Evangelista, Patricia. ★*Some People Need Killing*	364.4
Fersko, Diana. ★*We Need to Talk About Antisemitism*	305.892
Geter, Hafizah. *Un-American*	811
Hill, Anita. ★*Believing*	305.42
Hill, Marc Lamont. *Seen and Unseen*	303.3
Kaba, Mariame. *No More Police*	363.2
Kushner, Jacob. *Look Away*	305.9
Lowery, Wesley. ★*American Whitelash*	305.8
Luckerson, Victor. *Built from the Fire*	976.6
Phillips, Patrick. *Blood at the Root*	305.8
Rose, Jacqueline. *On Violence and on Violence Against Women*	362.88
Smith, Zadie. *Intimations*	824
Steinberg, Jonny. *A Man of Good Hope*	B
Thant Myint-U. *The Hidden History of Burma*	959.105
Willis, Raquel. *The Risk It Takes to Bloom*	B
Wise, Tim J. *Dispatches from the Race War*	305.8

VIOLENCE AGAINST MARGINALIZED WOMEN

Abdulali, Sohaila. *What We Talk About When We Talk About Rape*	364.15
Erdrich, Heid E. ★*Little Big Bully*	811
Kristof, Nicholas D. *Half the Sky*	362.83
Lamb, Christina. *Our Bodies, Their Battlefields*	341.6
McDiarmid, Jessica. *Highway of Tears*	364.152
Rose, Jacqueline. *On Violence and on Violence Against Women*	362.88
Tjipombo, Tupa. *I Am Not Your Slave*	B

VIOLENCE AGAINST WOMEN

Abdulali, Sohaila. *What We Talk About When We Talk About Rape*	364.15
Carney, Scott. *The Vortex*	954.92
Denton, Sally. *The Colony*	364.152
Ervin, Kristine S. *Rabbit Heart*	364.152
Hill, Anita. ★*Believing*	305.42
Lamb, Christina. *Our Bodies, Their Battlefields*	341.6
McDiarmid, Jessica. *Highway of Tears*	364.152
McNamara, Michelle. *I'll Be Gone in the Dark*	364.152
Rear, Rachel. *Catch the Sparrow*	364.152
Rose, Jacqueline. *On Violence and on Violence Against Women*	362.88
Schwartzman, Nancy. *Roll Red Roll*	364.15
Snyder, Rachel Louise. *No Visible Bruises*	362.82
Snyder, Rachel Louise. *Women We Buried, Women We Burned*	B
Solnit, Rebecca. ★*Recollections of My Nonexistence*	B
Sundberg, Kelly. *Goodbye, Sweet Girl*	B
Vogelstein, Rachel B. *Awakening*	305.42

VIOLENCE AND DRUGS

Berenson, Alex. ★*Tell Your Children*	362.29

VIOLENCE AND GUNS

Erdozain, Dominic. *One Nation Under Guns*	363.33
McWhirter, Cameron. *American Gun*	683.4
Metzl, Jonathan M. ★*What We've Become*	364.152
Murphy, Chris. ★*The Violence Inside Us*	303.60973
Quinones, John. ★*One Year in Uvalde*	371.7
Rubinstein, Julian. ★*The Holly*	364.106

VIOLENCE IN FILMS

Thomson, David. *The Fatal Alliance*	791.43

VIOLENCE IN GANGS

Lovato, Roberto. *Unforgetting*	B
Markham, Lauren. ★*The Far Away Brothers*	920
Rubinstein, Julian. ★*The Holly*	364.106
Westhoff, Ben. *Original Gangstas*	782.421649

VIOLENCE IN MASS MEDIA

Kix, Paul. ★*You Have to Be Prepared to Die Before You Can Begin to Live*	976.1

VIOLENCE IN PRISONS

Thompson, Heather Ann. *Blood in the Water*	365

VIOLENCE IN SCHOOLS

Cullen, David. *Parkland*	371.7
Lysiak, Matthew. *Newtown*	371.7
Williamson, Elizabeth. ★*Sandy Hook*	364.152

VIOLENCE IN SPORTS

Branch, John. *Boy on Ice*	B
Fainaru-Wada, Mark. *League of Denial*	617.1
Laskas, Jeanne Marie. *Concussion*	617.5

VIOLENCE IN UNIVERSITIES AND COLLEGES

Grigoriadis, Vanessa. *Blurred Lines*	371.7
Krakauer, Jon. *Missoula*	362.883
★*The Violence Inside Us*. Murphy, Chris	303.60973

VIOLENT CRIMES

Belkin, Lisa. *Genealogy of a Murder*	362.88
Bowdler, Michelle. ★*Is Rape a Crime?*	B
Croke, Ken. *Riding with Evil*	364.106
Dudley, Steven S. *MS-13*	364.106
Hobbs, Jeff. *Children of the State*	364.36
Lamb, Christina. *Our Bodies, Their Battlefields*	341.6
Ralph, Laurence. *Sito*	364.152
Rubinstein, Julian. ★*The Holly*	364.106
Sherman, Casey. *Hunting Whitey*	B

PUBLIC LIBRARY CORE COLLECTION: NONFICTION
Twentieth Edition

The Violet Hour. Roiphe, Katie	809
★*The Viral Underclass.* Thrasher, Steven W.	362.1962
Viren, Sarah	
To Name the Bigger Lie	B
VIREN, SARAH, 1979-	
Viren, Sarah. *To Name the Bigger Lie*	B
Virgil	
★*The Aeneid*	873
The Aeneid	873
The Eclogues of Virgil	871
VIRGIN ISLANDS OF THE UNITED STATES	
Immerwahr, Daniel. *How to Hide an Empire*	973
VIRGINIA	
Bergner, Daniel. ★*Sing for Your Life*	B
Blight, David W. *A Slave No More*	B
Broadwater, Jeff. ★*George Mason*	B
Cheney, Lynne V. *The Virginia Dynasty*	B
Deetz, Kelley Fanto. *Bound to the Fire*	641.59
Dillard, Annie. *Pilgrim at Tinker Creek*	508
Emberton, Carole. *To Walk About in Freedom*	306.3
Faust, Drew Gilpin. *Necessary Trouble*	B
Gordon-Reed, Annette. ★*The Hemingses of Monticello*	920
Green, Kristen. *Something Must Be Done About Prince Edward County*	379.2
Jefferson, Thomas. *Writings*	973.3
Kearse, Bettye. *The Other Madisons*	920
Kelly, Joseph. *Marooned*	975.5
Macy, Beth. ★*Factory Man*	338.7
Macy, Beth. ★*Truevine*	B
Mann, Sally. ★*Hold Still*	B
May, Gary. *John Tyler*	B
May, Gregory. *A Madman's Will*	973.5
Miles, Kathryn. *Trailed*	364.152
Noyes, Brian. *The Red Truck Bakery Farmhouse Cookbook*	641.5973
Petrosino, Kiki. *White Blood*	811
Price, David A. ★*Love and Hate in Jamestown*	975.5
Saxton, Martha. *The Widow Washington*	B
Sears, Stephen W. ★*Chancellorsville*	973.7
Sears, Stephen W. ★*Landscape Turned Red*	973.7
Shirley, Craig. *Mary Ball Washington*	B
Signer, Michael. *Cry Havoc*	305.800973
Smith, Lee. *Dimestore*	975.5
Swift, Earl. *Chesapeake Requiem*	639
Taylor, Alan. ★*The Internal Enemy*	975.5
Wiencek, Henry. *Master of the Mountain*	973.4
Zwonitzer, Mark. *Will You Miss Me When I'm Gone?*	920
The Virginia Dynasty. Cheney, Lynne V.	B
The Virginia State Colony for Epileptics and Feebleminded. Brown, Molly McCully	811
Virginia Woolf. Briggs, Julia	823
The Virginia Woolf Reader. Woolf, Virginia	823
VIRGINITY	
Satrapi, Marjane. *Embroideries*	741.5
VIROLOGY	
Quammen, David. ★*Breathless*	614.5
Virts, Terry	
How to Astronaut	629.45
VIRTS, TERRY, 1967-	
Virts, Terry. *How to Astronaut*	629.45
VIRTUAL COMMUNITY	
Galloway, Scott. *The Four*	338.7
Goldblatt, Duchess. *Becoming Duchess Goldblatt*	B
Mann, Jen. ★*Midlife Bites*	305.244
Smith, Patti. ★*A Book of Days*	779
VIRTUAL REALITY GAMES	
Goodridge, Michelle. *Librarian's Guide to Games and Gamers*	025.2
VIRTUE	
Sullivan, Meghan. *The Good Life Method*	170
Tutu, Desmond. *Made for Goodness*	170
★*The Virtue of Selfishness.* Rand, Ayn	149
VIRTUES	
Armstrong, Karen. *Twelve Steps to a Compassionate Life*	177
VIRTUES (CHRISTIANITY)	
Seiffert, Amy. *Starved*	248
VIRUS DISEASES	
Preston, Richard. *Crisis in the Red Zone*	614.5
Werb, Dan. *The Invisible Siege*	614.5
Zaman, Muhammad H. *Biography of Resistance*	616.9
VIRUSES	
Brenner, Marie. ★*The Desperate Hours*	362.1962
Ireland, Tom. *The Good Virus*	579.2
Kelley, Margot Anne. *A Gardener at the End of the World*	615.8
Mackenzie, Debora. *Covid-19*	616.2
Oshinsky, David M. ★*Polio*	614.5
Preston, Richard. *The Hot Zone*	614.5
Quammen, David. ★*Breathless*	614.5
Schama, Simon. *Foreign Bodies*	614.4
Spinney, Laura. *Pale Rider*	614.5
Thrasher, Steven W. ★*The Viral Underclass*	362.1962
A Visible Man. Enninful, Edward	B
VISIGOTHS	
Puhak, Shelley. *The Dark Queens*	944
VISION	
Ackerman, Diane. *A Natural History of the Senses*	152.1
Bruni, Frank. *The Beauty of Dusk*	B
Hoffman, Donald D. *Visual Intelligence*	152.14
VISIONARIES	
Jackson, Joe. *Black Elk*	978.004
Wright, Alex. *Cataloging the World*	020.9
VISIONS	
Jackson, Joe. *Black Elk*	978.004
Knight, Sam. *The Premonitions Bureau*	133.8
Visions of Infinity. Stewart, Ian	510
VISITORS	
Platt, Stephen R. *Autumn in the Heavenly Kingdom*	951
Rappaport, Helen. *Caught in the Revolution*	355.00947
Visser, Margaret	
The Gift of Thanks	394
VISUAL ART AND SOCIETY	
King, Ross. *The Judgment of Paris*	759.4
VISUAL COMMUNICATION	
Cairo, Alberto. *How Charts Lie*	302.2
Gates, Henry Louis. ★*Stony the Road*	973
The Visual Display of Quantitative Information. Tufte, Edward R.	001.4
Visual Intelligence. Herman, Amy	152.14
Visual Intelligence. Hoffman, Donald D.	152.14
VISUAL NONFICTION	
Bethencourt, Kahran. *Glory*	779.2
Borsato, Diane. *Mushrooming*	579.6
Brenwall, Cynthia S. *The Central Park*	974.7
Bull, John L. ★*The National Audubon Society Field Guide to North American Birds.*	598.097
Burns, Ken. ★*Our America*	973
Carballo, David M. *America*	912
Davidson, Mark A. ★*Bob Dylan*	B
Felisbret, Eric. *Graffiti New York*	751.7
Finkelstein, Elizabeth. *Cheap Old Houses*	643
Galassi, Peter. *Ansel Adams in Yosemite Valley*	770.92
Gilbert, Carter Rowell. ★*National Audubon Society Field Guide to Fishes.*	597
Hahn, Emanuel. *Koreatown Dreaming*	979.4
Hendrix, Grady. *These Fists Break Bricks*	791
Jones, Tom. *Space Shuttle Stories*	629.44
Katz, David. *Barack Before Obama*	B
Kiser, Joy M. *America's Other Audubon*	B
McCartney, Paul. ★*1964*	782.42166
Napier, Erin. *Heirloom Rooms*	747
Parton, Dolly. ★*Behind the Seams*	B
Smith, Patti. ★*A Book of Days*	779
Souza, Pete. *The West Wing and Beyond*	917.53
Van Agtmael, Peter. *Look at the USA*	070
Whitaker, John O. ★*National Audubon Society Field Guide to North American Mammals*	599.097
White, Adam. ★*Motown*	781.644
White, Marco Pierre. *White Heat*	641.594
Willis, Deborah. *Envisioning Emancipation*	973.7
VISUAL PERCEPTION	
Bang, Molly. ★*Picture This*	741.6
Edwards, Betty. *Drawing on the Right Side of the Brain*	741.2
Grandin, Temple. ★*Visual Thinking*	152.14
Herman, Amy. *Visual Intelligence*	152.14
Hoffman, Donald D. *Visual Intelligence*	152.14
Still, Ben. *Particle Physics Brick by Brick*	539.7
Updike, John. *Always Looking*	700
Ward, Ossian. *Look Again*	750.1
★*Visual Thinking.* Grandin, Temple	152.14

AUTHOR, TITLE, SERIES AND SUBJECT INDEX

VISUALIZATION
    Gawain, Shakti. ★*Creative Visualization*   153.3
    Montell, Amanda. ★*The Age of Magical Overthinking*   153.4
Vitale, Tom
    In the Weeds   B
VITALE, TOM
    Vitale, Tom. *In the Weeds*   B
Vitamania. Price, Catherine   612.3
VITAMINS
    Price, Catherine. *Vitamania*   612.3
VITAMINS IN HUMAN NUTRITION
    Price, Catherine. *Vitamania*   612.3
Vivian Maier Developed. Marks, Ann   778.9
Vladeck, Stephen I.
    The Shadow Docket   347.73
VLAMINCK, MAURICE DE, 1876-1958
    Roe, Sue. *In Montmartre*   920
Vlasic, Bill
    Once Upon a Car   338.4
Vlock, Deborah
    Parenting Children with Mental Health Challenges   618.92
Vnuk, Rebecca
    The Weeding Handbook   025.2
VOCABULARY
    Holder, R. W. *How Not to Say What You Mean*   427
    Stamper, Kory. *Word by Word*   413.028
VOCATION
    Chittister, Joan. *Following the Path*   248.4
    Covey, Stephen R. ★*The 7 Habits of Highly Effective People*   158
    Covey, Stephen R. *The 8th Habit*   158
    Dokun, Chanel. *Life Starts Now*   248.8
    Isay, David. *Callings*   920
    Jakes, T. D. *Destiny*   248.4
    Parini, Jay. *Borges and Me*   813
    Quinn, Tallu Schuyler. *What We Wish Were True*   B
VOCATIONAL GUIDANCE
    Attenberg, Jami. *1000 Words*   808.02
    Braswell, Porter. ★*Let Them See You*   650.1
    Burnett, William. *Designing Your Life*   650.1
    Congdon, Lisa. *Art Inc.*   702
    Faerm, Steven. *Fashion Design Course*   746.9
    Fischer, Jenna. *The Actor's Life*   792.02
    Kramer, Andrea S. *Breaking Through Bias*   650.1
    Larimer, Kevin. *The Poets & Writers Complete Guide to Being a Writer*   808
    Moore, Rachel. *The Artist's Compass*   791
    Morgan, Genevieve. *Undecided*   331.702
    Powell, Michael. *The Acting Bible*   792.02
    Steib, Mike. *The Career Manifesto*   650.1
    Wasserman, Claire. *Ladies Get Paid*   650.1
    Watts, Steven. *Self-Help Messiah*   B
VOCATIONAL GUIDANCE FOR TEENAGERS
    Morgan, Genevieve. *Undecided*   331.702
VOCATIONAL INTERESTS
    Morgan, Genevieve. *Undecided*   331.702
Vogel, Ezra F.
    Deng Xlaoping and the Transformation of China   B
Vogel, Joseph
    Man in the Music   B
Vogel, Steve
    Betrayal in Berlin   327.1273043
Vogelstein, Rachel B.
    Awakening   305.42
Vogler, Christopher
    ★*The Writer's Journey*   808.2
Vogue & the Metropolitan Museum of Art Costume Institute. Bowles, Hamish   746.9
The Voice At 3. Simic, Charles   811
The Voice Is All. Johnson, Joyce   B
Voice Lessons for Parents. Mogel, Wendy   649
The Voice of Reason. Rand, Ayn   191
VOICE TRAINING
    Linklater, Kristin. *Freeing the Natural Voice*   808.5
VOICE-OVERS
    Isen, Tajja. *Some of My Best Friends*   305.8
Volandes, Angelo E.
    The Conversation   616.02
VOLCANOES
    Gates, Alexander E. *Encyclopedia of Earthquakes and Volcanoes*   551.2

Volf, Miroslav
    Life Worth Living   113
    Public Faith in Action   261.7
Volger, Lukas
    Bowl   641.81
Vollmann, William T.
    No Immediate Danger   333.79
Vollmer, Becky
    You Are Not Stuck   158.1
Voloj, Julian
    Ghetto Brother   741.5
Volpe, Joseph
    The Toughest Show on Earth   B
VOLPE, JOSEPH
    Volpe, Joseph. *The Toughest Show on Earth*   B
Voltaire Almighty. Pearson, Roger   B
VOLTAIRE, 1694-1778
    Pearson, Roger. *Voltaire Almighty*   B
Volume Control. Owen, David   617.8
The Volunteer. Fairweather, Jack   B
VOLUNTEER ARMY
    Henderson, Bruce B. *Bridge to the Sun*   940.53
    Miller, Christopher. *The War Came to Us*   947.7
VOLUNTEERS
    Achterberg, Cara Sue. *Another Good Dog*   636.7
    Boland, Becca. *Making the Most of Teen Library Volunteers*   023
    Watling, Sarah. *Tomorrow Perhaps the Future*   946.081
Von Bremzen, Anya
    National Dish   641.3
Von Drehle, Dave
    ★*Triangle*   974.7
Von Drehle, David
    ★*The Book of Charlie*   B
VON DREHLE, DAVID
    Von Drehle, David. ★*The Book of Charlie*   B
Von Furstenberg, Diane
    The Woman I Wanted to Be   B
VON FURSTENBERG, DIANE
    Von Furstenberg, Diane. *The Woman I Wanted to Be*   B
VON NEUMANN, JOHN, 1903-1957
    Dyson, George. *Turing's Cathedral*   004
Von Tunzelmann, Alex
    Blood and Sand   909.82
VONN, LINDSEY
    Vinton, Nathaniel. *The Fall Line*   796.93
Vonnegut, Kurt
    Kurt Vonnegut   813
    ★*A Man Without a Country*   818
VONNEGUT, KURT
    Vonnegut, Kurt. *Kurt Vonnegut*   813
    Vonnegut, Kurt. ★*A Man Without a Country*   818
VONNEUMANN, JOHN, 1903-1957
    Bhattacharya, Ananyo. *The Man from the Future*   B
Vorobyov, Niko
    Dopeworld   364.1
VOROBYOV, NIKO
    Vorobyov, Niko. *Dopeworld*   364.1
The Vortex. Carney, Scott   954.92
VOSKUIJL, BEP
    Van Wijk-Voskuijl, Joop. *The Last Secret of the Secret Annex*   940.53
VOTER FRAUD
    Anderson, Carol. ★*One Person, No Vote*   324.6
    Berman, Ari. *Give Us the Ballot*   324.6
    Crump, Benjamin. *Open Season*   364
    Hasen, Richard L. *Election Meltdown*   324.973
    Lichtman, Allan J. *The Embattled Vote in America*   324.6
    Wehle, Kim. *What You Need to Know About Voting and Why*   324.60973
VOTER REGISTRATION
    Abrams, Stacey. *Our Time Is Now*   324.60973
    Litt, David. *Democracy in One Book or Less*   321.8
    Smith, Erin Geiger. ★*Thank You for Voting*   324.973
    Wehle, Kim. *What You Need to Know About Voting and Why*   324.60973
VOTER SUPPRESSION
    Abrams, Stacey. *Our Time Is Now*   324.60973
    Anderson, Carol. ★*One Person, No Vote*   324.6
    Berman, Ari. ★*Minority Rule*   305.809
    Clinton, Hillary Rodham. *What Happened*   328.73
    Cross, Tiffany D. ★*Say It Louder!*   324.6

PUBLIC LIBRARY CORE COLLECTION: NONFICTION
Twentieth Edition

Crump, Benjamin. *Open Season*	364
Hasen, Richard L. *Election Meltdown*	324.973
Lane, Charles. *Freedom's Detective*	B
Sharpton, Al. *Rise Up*	973.933
Smith, Erin Geiger. ★*Thank You for Voting*	324.973
Wehle, Kim. *What You Need to Know About Voting and Why*	324.60973
Zucchino, David. *Wilmington's Lie*	305.8009756

VOTER TURNOUT

Lichtman, Allan J. *The Embattled Vote in America*	324.6
Litt, David. *Democracy in One Book or Less*	321.8
Ramos, Jorge. *Stranger*	325.73
Wehle, Kim. *What You Need to Know About Voting and Why*	324.60973

VOTING

Bowden, Mark. *The Steal*	973.933
Collins-Dexter, Brandi. *Black Skinhead*	324.2734
Cross, Tiffany D. ★*Say It Louder!*	324.6
DuBois, Ellen Carol. *Suffrage*	324.6
Hasen, Richard L. *Election Meltdown*	324.973
Jones, Brenda. *Maxine Waters*	B
Lichtman, Allan J. *The Embattled Vote in America*	324.6
Litt, David. *Democracy in One Book or Less*	321.8
Smith, Erin Geiger. ★*Thank You for Voting*	324.973
Smith, J. Douglas. *On Democracy's Doorstep*	342.73
Wehle, Kim. *What You Need to Know About Voting and Why*	324.60973

Vowell, Sarah

Assassination Vacation	B

VOWELL, SARAH, 1969-

Vowell, Sarah. *Assassination Vacation*	B
★*Vows.* Mendelson, Cheryl	203
★*A Voyage Long and Strange.* Horwitz, Tony	970.01
Voyage of Mercy. Puleo, Stephen	363.8
★*The Voyage of the Beagle.* Darwin, Charles	508

VOYAGES AND TRAVELS

Abdul-Ahad, Ghaith. *A Stranger in Your Own City*	956.7044
Adams, Mark. *Tip of the Iceberg*	917.9804
Adams, Mark. *Turn Right at Machu Picchu*	985
Adams, Simon. *Journey*	910.9
Al-Maria, Sophia. *The Girl Who Fell to Earth*	B
Alexander, Caroline. *The Bounty*	996.1
Ambrose, Stephen E. ★*Undaunted Courage*	917.804
Ash, Lamorna. *Dark, Salt, Clear*	942.3
Bard, Elizabeth. *Lunch in Paris*	B
Barnes, Julian. *The Man in the Red Coat*	B
Bass, Rick. *The Traveling Feast*	B
Belliveau, Denis. *In the Footsteps of Marco Polo*	915
Bellows, Amanda Brickell. *The Explorers*	910.92
Berendt, John. *The City of Falling Angels*	945
Bergreen, Laurence. *Marco Polo*	B
Bergreen, Laurence. *Over the Edge of the World*	B
Berlin, Lucia. ★*Welcome Home*	B
Bingham, Hiram. ★*Lost City of the Incas*	985
Bourdain, Anthony. *The Nasty Bits*	641.5092
Bourdain, Anthony. ★*World Travel*	641.59
Brown, Daniel James. *The Indifferent Stars Above*	B
Brown, Molly McCully. *Places I've Taken My Body*	B
Bryson, Bill. *In a Sunburned Country*	919
Bryson, Bill. *Notes from a Small Island*	914
Bryson, Bill. *The Road to Little Dribbling*	914
Bryson, Bill. ★*A Walk in the Woods*	917
Buck, Rinker. *Life on the Mississippi*	917
Caesar, Ed. *The Moth and the Mountain*	B
Campany, David. *The Open Road*	770
Carlson, Brady. *Dead Presidents*	B
Carlson, Peter. *K Blows Top*	947.085
Chamberlin, Silas. *On the Trail*	796.510973
Childs, Craig. *House of Rain*	978.9
Cole, Teju. *Blind Spot*	770
Coyne, Tom. *A Course Called Scotland*	796.352
Craig, Mya-Rose. *Birdgirl*	B
Damrosch, David. *Around the World in 80 Books*	809
Dana, Richard Henry. *Two Years Before the Mast*	910.4
Darlington, Miriam. *Otter Country*	599.769
Darwin, Charles. *Charles Darwin*	576.8
Davis, Wade. *Magdalena*	986.1
DeJean, Joan E. *How Paris Became Paris*	944
Dietrich, Sean. *You Are My Sunshine*	B
Dinesen, Isak. *Out of Africa*	967.62
Dodds Pennock, Caroline. ★*On Savage Shores*	970.004
Downie, David. *A Taste of Paris*	394.1
Dunn, Jon L. *The Glitter in the Green*	598.7
Egan, Timothy. *A Pilgrimage to Eternity*	263
Ehrlich, Gretel. *This Cold Heaven*	998.2
Ehrlich, Gretel. *Unsolaced*	B
Erdrich, Louise. *Books and Islands in Ojibwe Country*	977
Fabes, Stephen. *Signs of Life*	B
Fallows, James M. *Our Towns*	306.0973
Fedarko, Kevin. *A Walk in the Park*	917.91
Feiler, Bruce. *Walking the Bible*	915
Finnegan, William. *Barbarian Days*	B
Foer, Esther Safran. *I Want You to Know We're Still Here*	B
Foer, Joshua. *Atlas Obscura*	910.41
Foer, Joshua. ★*Atlas Obscura 2nd Ed.*	910.41
Forche, Carolyn. *In the Lateness of the World*	811
Fox, Porter. *The Last Winter*	363.738
Frazier, Ian. *Travels in Siberia*	957
Garrels, Anne. *Putin Country*	947
Gilbert, Elizabeth. *Eat, Pray, Love*	B
Gill, A. A. *To America with Love*	973.93
Goodheart, Adam. *The Last Island*	954
Goulding, Matt. *Grape, Olive, Pig*	394.1
Goulding, Matt. *Rice, Noodle, Fish*	394.1
Grann, David. *The Lost City of Z*	918.1
Grann, David. *The White Darkness*	B
Grant, Will. *The Last Ride of the Pony Express*	917.804
Green, Matthew. *Shadowlands*	941.03
Grossman, David. *The Yellow Wind*	956.95
Guillermoprieto, Alma. *Dancing with Cuba*	972.9106
Hall, Alvin D. *Driving the Green Book*	917.304
Harris, Kate. *Lands of Lost Borders*	915.804
Harrison, Jim. *The Search for the Genuine*	814
Hassan, Hawa. *In Bibi's Kitchen*	641.596
Heacox, Kim. *Rhythm of the Wild*	979.8
Heat Moon, William Least. *Blue Highways*	917.304
Heat Moon, William Least. *Roads to Quoz*	917.3
Henry, John. *Great White Fleet*	387.243
Hessler, Peter. *Oracle Bones*	951
Hill, Clint. *My Travels with Mrs. Kennedy*	B
Hodgman, John. *Vacationland*	B
Homer. *The Odyssey*	883
Homer. *The Odyssey*	883
Homer. *Odyssey*	883
Horwitz, Tony. *Spying on the South*	917
Housden, Roger. *Saved by Beauty*	955
Hughes, Langston. ★*I Wonder as I Wander*	B
Iyer, Pico. *A Beginner's Guide to Japan*	952.05
Iyer, Pico. ★*The Half Known Life*	203
Iyer, Pico. *The Lady and the Monk*	952
James, Jamie. *The Glamour of Strangeness*	700.1
Jaouad, Suleika. ★*Between Two Kingdoms*	B
Jenkins, Jedidiah. *To Shake the Sleeping Self*	B
Jenkins, Peter. *Looking for Alaska*	979.8
Jenkins, Peter. *A Walk Across America*	917.304
Jerkins, Morgan. *Wandering in Strange Lands*	305.896
Juan, Li. *Winter Pasture*	951.06
Kerouac, Jack. *Book of Sketches, 1952-57*	818
Kirkby, Bruce. *Blue Sky Kingdom*	954.96
Kois, Dan. *How to Be a Family*	910.4
Krakauer, Jon. *Into the Wild*	917.9804
Kugel, Seth. *Rediscovering Travel*	306.4
Kugler, Rob. *A Dog Named Beautiful*	B
Kurlansky, Mark. *Havana*	972.91
Kurson, Robert. *Pirate Hunters*	910.91
Lahiri, Jhumpa. *In Other Words*	B
Larson, Edward J. *An Empire of Ice*	919.8
Lee, Edward. *Buttermilk Graffiti*	641.59
Levy, Buddy. *Labyrinth of Ice*	910.91
Lockley, Thomas. *African Samurai*	B
Lopez, Barry Holstun. *Horizon*	B
Malcolm, Janet. *Reading Chekhov*	891.72
Markham, Beryl. *West with the Night*	B
Marozzi, Justin. *Islamic Empires*	909
Mayes, Frances. *Bella Tuscany*	945
Mayes, Frances. *See You in the Piazza*	914.5
Mayes, Frances. *Under the Tuscan Sun*	945
Mayes, Frances. *A Year in the World*	B
Mayle, Peter. *Encore Provence*	944

AUTHOR, TITLE, SERIES AND SUBJECT INDEX

Mayle, Peter. *My Twenty-Five Years in Provence*	944.9
Mayle, Peter. *Provence A-Z*	944
Mayle, Peter. ★*A Year in Provence*	944
McCalman, Iain. *Darwin's Armada*	576.8
McClanahan, Paige. *The New Tourist*	338.4
McCourt, Malachy. *A Monk Swimming*	B
McGregor, James H. *Rome from the Ground up*	711
McPhee, John. *Tabula Rasa; V.1*	818
Means, Brittany. *Hell If We Don't Change Our Ways*	B
Meiburg, Jonathan. *A Most Remarkable Creature*	598.9
Millard, Candice. *River of Doubt*	918.1
Mohammadi, Kamin. *Bella Figura*	641.01
Momus. *Niche*	B
Moore, Harold G. *We Are Soldiers Still*	959.704
Moore, Tim. *The Cyclist Who Went Out in the Cold*	796.6
Moore, Wayetu. *The Dragons, the Giant, the Women*	B
Mullins, Edwin. *The Four Roads to Heaven*	263
Nathan, Joan. ★*My Life in Recipes*	641.5
Nicolson, Adam. *Sea Room*	941.1
Nunn, Emily. *The Comfort Food Diaries*	641.5973
O'Brady, Colin. ★*The Impossible First*	919.8904
Offerman, Nick. *Where the Deer and the Antelope Play*	973.93
Ollivier, Bernard. *Out of Istanbul*	B
Orth, Stephan. *Couchsurfing in Iran*	955.06
Osnos, Evan. *Wildland*	973.93
Ottolenghi, Yotam. ★*Jerusalem*	641.5
Palin, Michael. *North Korea Journal*	951.9305
Pamuk, Orhan. *Istanbul*	949.61
Parini, Jay. *Borges and Me*	813
Parks, Tim. *The Hero's Way*	945
Parks, Tim. *Italian Ways*	385
Perry, Imani. ★*South to America*	917
Pham, Larissa. *Pop Song*	709.2
Philbrick, Nathaniel. *Travels with George*	973.4
Phillips, Timothy. *Retracing the Iron Curtain*	909.82
Posnanski, Joe. *The Soul of Baseball*	796.357
Preston, Katherine. *Out with It*	B
Raban, Jonathan. *Bad Land*	978
Reed, Julia. *Dispatches from the Gilded Age*	B
Robb, Graham. *The Discovery of France*	944
Robb, Graham. *France*	944
Roberts, Jason. *A Sense of the World*	B
Robinson, Phoebe. *Please Don't Sit on My Bed in Your Outside Clothes*	818
Rosenthal, Phil. ★*Somebody Feed Phil the Book*	641.59
Russert, Luke. *Look for Me There*	B
Sabar, Ariel. *My Father's Paradise*	B
Sabatini Sloan, Aisha. *Dreaming of Ramadi in Detroit*	814
Salama, Jordan. ★*Stranger in the Desert*	982
Salter, James. *Don't Save Anything*	818
Samatar, Sofia. *The White Mosque*	B
Sancton, Julian. *Madhouse at the End of the Earth*	919.8904
Sciolino, Elaine. *The Seine*	944
Sedaris, David. ★*A Carnival of Snackery*	818
Severin, Timothy. *In Search of Robinson Crusoe*	996.1
Shakur, Prince. *When They Tell You to Be Good*	B
Shattuck, Ben. *Six Walks*	B
Sides, Hampton. ★*The Wide Wide Sea*	910.92
Smith, Michael. *Cabin Fever*	614.5
Solnit, Rebecca. *Wanderlust*	796.51
Stahl, Jerry. *Nein, Nein, Nein!*	B
Stahr, Celia. *Frida in America*	B
Steinbeck, John. *Travels with Charley*	B
Stewart, Rory. *The Prince of the Marshes*	956.7044
Stone, Daniel. *The Food Explorer*	B
Strayed, Cheryl. ★*Wild*	B
Synnott, Mark. *The Third Pole*	796.522
Theroux, Paul. *Deep South*	975
Theroux, Paul. *The Great Railway Bazaar*	915
Theroux, Paul. *The Last Train to Zona Verde*	916
Theroux, Paul. *On the Plain of Snakes*	917
Theroux, Paul. *Riding the Iron Rooster*	915
Thompson, Bob. *Revolutionary Roads*	973.3
Thoreau, Henry David. *The Maine Woods*	917
Thubron, Colin. *In Siberia*	957
Thubron, Colin. *Shadow of the Silk Road*	915
Travisano, Thomas J. *Love Unknown*	B
Tremlett, Giles. *Ghosts of Spain*	946.08
Umar, Ousman. *North to Paradise*	B
Van Hemert, Caroline. *The Sun Is a Compass*	979.8
Vanhoenacker, Mark. *Imagine a City*	629.13
Virgil. ★*The Aeneid*	873
Von Bremzen, Anya. *National Dish*	641.3
Vowell, Sarah. *Assassination Vacation*	B
Wallace, Christopher. *Twentieth-Century Man*	B
Wallace, Scott. *The Unconquered*	981
Wallis, Michael. *The Best Land Under Heaven*	978
Wallis, Michael. *Route 66*	917.804
Walsh, Declan. *The Nine Lives of Pakistan*	954.91
Wang, Connie. *Oh My Mother!*	B
Weiner, Eric. *Ben & Me*	B
Wexler, Jay. *Holy Hullabaloos*	342.7308
White, Edmund. *The Flaneur*	944
Winn, Raynor. *The Wild Silence*	B
Wong, Cecily. ★*Gastro Obscura*	641.3
Wood, Levison. *The Last Giants*	599.67
Woolf, Virginia. *The London Scene*	942.1
Wright, Lawrence. *God Save Texas*	917.64
Wynn-Grant, Rae. *Wild Life*	B
XIe, Jenny. *Eye Level*	811
Zamora, Javier. ★*Solito*	B

VRBA, RUDOLF
Freedland, Jonathan. ★*The Escape Artist*	940.53

VREELAND, DIANA, 1903-1989
Stuart, Amanda Mackenzie. *Empress of Fashion*	B

VUILLARD, EDOUARD, 1868-1940
Cogeval, Guy. *Edouard Vuillard*	759.4

VULNERABILITY
Alexander, Kwame. *Why Fathers Cry at Night*	B
Baer, Kate. *What Kind of Woman*	811
Belcourt, Billy-Ray. ★*A History of My Brief Body*	B
Brown, Jericho. ★*The Tradition*	811
Gaines, Joanna. *The Stories We Tell*	B
greathouse, torrin a. *Wound from the Mouth of a Wound*	811
Mooallem, Jon. *Serious Face*	814
O'Farrell, Maggie. *I Am, I Am, I Am*	B
Rush, Charaia. *Courageously Soft*	234
Shapland, Jenn. ★*Thin Skin*	814

Vuong, Ocean
★*Time Is a Mother*	811

W

★**W.E.B.** *Du Bois*. Lewis, David L.	B

Waal, F. B. M. de
Bonobo	599.88
★*Mama's Last Hug*	599.885
Our Inner Ape	156

Wachsmann, Nikolaus
Kl	940.53

WACHTER, HORST VON, 1939-
Sands, Philippe. *The Ratline*	B

WACHTER, OTTO, 1901-1949
Sands, Philippe. *The Ratline*	B

Wacker, Grant
America's Pastor	B

WACO MASSACRE, 1993
Cook, Kevin. *Waco Rising*	299
Waco Rising. Cook, Kevin	299

WACO, TEXAS
Cook, Kevin. *Waco Rising*	299
★*Wade in the Water*. Smith, Tracy K.	811.6

Wade, Becky
Run the World	796.42

WADE, BECKY
Wade, Becky. *Run the World*	796.42

Wade, Greg
★*Bread Head*	664

WADE, HENRY
Prager, Joshua. *The Family Roe*	342.7308

Wade, Sabia
Birthing Liberation	363.96

Wadman, Meredith
The Vaccine Race	614.5

WAFER, LIONEL, 1660?-1705?
Severin, Timothy. *In Search of Robinson Crusoe*	996.1

PUBLIC LIBRARY CORE COLLECTION: NONFICTION
Twentieth Edition

Wagamese, Richard
  For Joshua — B
  One Native Life — B
WAGAMESE, RICHARD, 1955-2017
  Wagamese, Richard. *For Joshua* — B
  Wagamese, Richard. *One Native Life* — B
★*The Wager.* Grann, David — 910.91
WAGES
  Cox, Josie. *Women Money Power* — 330.082
  Derks, Scott. *The Value of a Dollar* — 338.5
  Derks, Scott. *The Value of a Dollar* — 338.5
  Desmond, Matthew. ★*Poverty, by America* — 362.5
  Monforton, Celeste. *On the Job* — 331.1
  Smith, Sam. *Hard Labor* — 796.323
Waging Heavy Peace. Young, Neil — B
Waging War. Barron, David J. — 342.73
Wagner, Alex
  Futureface — B
WAGNER, ALEX
  Wagner, Alex. *Futureface* — B
Wagner, Jordan Lee
  The Synagogue Survival Kit — 296.4
WAGNER, RICHARD, 1813-1883
  Ross, Alex. *Wagnerism* — B
Wagner, Walter H.
  Opening the Qur'an — 297.1
Wagnerism. Ross, Alex — B
WAHHABIYAH
  Abou El Fadl, Khaled. *The Great Theft* — 297.09
Wahl, Grant
  ★*Masters of Modern Soccer* — 796.334
Wainaina, Binyavanga
  ★*How to Write About Africa* — 814
  One Day I Will Write About This Place — B
WAINAINA, BINYAVANGA, 1971-2019
  Wainaina, Binyavanga. ★*How to Write About Africa* — 814
WAINWRIGHT, LOUIE L.
  Lewis, Anthony. *Gideon's Trumpet* — 345.73
Wait, I'm the Boss?!?. Economy, Peter — 658
Wait, I'm Working with Who?!?. Economy, Peter — 650.1
A Waiter in Paris. Chisholm, Edward — B
WAITERS
  Chisholm, Edward. *A Waiter in Paris* — B
Waiting 'Til the Midnight Hour. Joseph, Peniel E. — 323.1196
Waiting for the Last Bus. Holloway, Richard — 202
Waiting for the Monsoon. Nordland, Rod — B
Waiting to Be Arrested at Night. Izgil, Tahir Hamut — B
★*Wake.* Hall, Rebecca — 741.5
WAKEFIELD, ANDREW J.
  Deer, Brian. *The Doctor Who Fooled the World* — 610.92
Waking The Witch. Grossman, Pam — 133.4
Waksman, Steve
  This Ain't the Summer of Love — 781.66
Walch, Aubry
  The Herbivorous Butcher Cookbook — 641.5
Walcott, Derek
  Omeros — 811
  The Poetry of Derek Walcott 1948-2013 — 811
Wald, Elijah
  American Epic — 781.64
  Dylan Goes Electric! — 782.42164
  ★*Escaping the Delta*
  How the Beatles Destroyed Rock 'N' Roll — 781.64
Waldbauer, Gilbert
  What Good Are Bugs? — 595.717
★*Walden, Or, Life in the Woods.* Thoreau, Henry David — 813
Walder, Tracy
  The Unexpected Spy — B
WALDER, TRACY
  Walder, Tracy. *The Unexpected Spy* — B
Waldinger, Robert J.
  ★*The Good Life* — 158.1
Waldman, Ayelet
  A Really Good Day — B
WALDMAN, AYELET
  Waldman, Ayelet. *A Really Good Day* — B
Waldman, Jonathan
  Sam — 629.8

Waldman, Michael
  The Supermajority — 347.73
Waldman, Steven
  Sacred Liberty — 341.4
Waldrop, Keith
  Transcendental Studies — 811
Waldstreicher, David
  The Odyssey of Phillis Wheatley — B
WALES
  Charles-Edwards, T. M. *Wales and the Britons, 350-1064* — 942.901
  Gies, Joseph. *Life in a Medieval Castle* — 940.1
  Morris, Jan. *A Writer's House in Wales* — 942.9
  Morris, Marc. *Castles* — 728.81
  Thomas, Dylan. *A Child's Christmas in Wales* — B
  Thomas, Dylan. *Under Milk Wood* — 822.91
Wales and the Britons, 350-1064. Charles-Edwards, T. M. — 942.901
Walk. Gering, Jacquie — 746.46
A Walk Across America. Jenkins, Peter — 917.304
A Walk Around the Block. Carlsen, Spike — 031
Walk in My Combat Boots. Patterson, James — 920
A Walk in the Park. Fedarko, Kevin — 917.91
★*A Walk in the Woods.* Bryson, Bill — 917
Walk The Blue Line. Patterson, James — 920
Walk The Walk. Gross, Neil — 363.2
Walk Through Walls. Abramovic, Marina — B
Walk with Me. Larson, Kate Clifford — B
Walk, Jog, Run. Tomasson, Dara — 746.46
Walker's Mammals of the World. Nowak, Ronald M. — 599
Walker, Alice
  The Cushion in the Road — 814
  Gathering Blossoms Under Fire — B
  Hard Times Require Furious Dancing — 811
  We Are the Ones We Have Been Waiting For — 811
WALKER, ALICE, 1944-
  Walker, Alice. *Gathering Blossoms Under Fire* — B
WALKER, C. J., 1867-1919
  Bundles, A'Lelia. *On Her Own Ground* — B
Walker, Danielle
  Danielle Walker's Against All Grain — 641.5
  Danielle Walker's Healthy in a Hurry — 641.5
WALKER, DEMETRIUS
  Dohrmann, George. ★*Play Their Hearts Out* — 796.323
Walker, Hunter
  The Truce — 324.2736
WALKER, MARY, D. 1872
  Nathans, Sydney. *To Free a Family* — B
Walker, Ronald W.
  ★*Massacre at Mountain Meadows* — 979.2
Walker, Sam
  The Captain Class — 796.07
Walker, Shaun
  The Long Hangover — 947.086
Walker, Stephen
  Beyond — 629.45
Walker, Vanessa Siddle
  The Lost Education of Horace Tate — 370.92
Walker-Hill, Helen
  From Spirituals to Symphonies — 780
WALKING
  Egan, Timothy. *A Pilgrimage to Eternity* — 263
  Fili, Louise. *The Cognoscenti's Guide to Florence* — 381
  Fowler, Corinne. ★*The Countryside* — 941
  Grann, David. *The White Darkness* — B
  Jenkins, Peter. *A Walk Across America* — 917.304
  McPherson, James M. *Hallowed Ground* — 973.7
  Mullins, Edwin. *The Four Roads to Heaven* — 263
  Ollivier, Bernard. *Out of Istanbul* — B
  Parks, Tim. *The Hero's Way* — 945
  Shattuck, Ben. *Six Walks* — B
  Solnit, Rebecca. *Wanderlust* — 796.51
  Stewart, Rory. *The Marches* — 941.3
  Streets, Annabel. *52 Ways to Walk* — 796.51
  Wohlleben, Peter. *Forest Walking* — 582.16
Walking in My Joy. Lewis, Jenifer — B
Walking Point. Ulander, Perry A. — B
Walking The Bible. Feiler, Bruce — 915
★*Walking The Bowl.* Lockhart, Chris — 362.7
Walking Through Fire. Risner, Vaneetha Rendall — B

AUTHOR, TITLE, SERIES AND SUBJECT INDEX

Walking with Jesus. Francis	282.09
Walking with the Comrades. Roy, Arundhati	954
Walking with the Muses. Cleveland, Pat	B
Walking with the Wind. Lewis, John	B
WALKS	
Shattuck, Ben. *Six Walks*	B
The *Wall* and the Gate. Sefarad, Mikhael	341.48
WALL STREET, NEW YORK CITY	
Belfort, Jordan. ★*The Wolf of Investing*	332.63
Fox, Justin. *The Myth of the Rational Market*	332.64
Gage, Beverly. *The Day Wall Street Exploded*	974.7
O'Rourke, P. J. *None of My Business*	332
Oller, John. *White Shoe*	346.73
Patterson, Scott. ★*Chaos Kings*	338.5
Peta, Joe. *Trading Bases*	796.357
Schulman, Daniel. *The Money Kings*	332.0973
Wallace, Mike. *Greater Gotham*	974.7
Weatherall, James Owen. *The Physics of Wall Street*	332.63
White, Shane. *Prince of Darkness*	B
Wall, Duncan	
The Ordinary Acrobat	B
WALL, DUNCAN	
Wall, Duncan. *The Ordinary Acrobat*	B
WALLACE, ALFRED RUSSEL, 1823-1913	
Costa, James T. *Radical by Nature*	B
McCalman, Iain. *Darwin's Armada*	576.8
Wallace, Carvell	
Another Word for Love	B
Wallace, Chris	
Countdown 1945	940.54
Countdown Bin Laden	958.104
Wallace, Christopher	
Twentieth-Century Man	B
Wallace, David Foster	
Consider the Lobster	814
WALLACE, DAVID FOSTER	
Miller, Adrienne. *In the Land of Men*	070.5
WALLACE, GEORGE, 1919-1998	
McWhorter, Diane. *Carry Me Home*	976.1
WALLACE, JACKIE	
Jackson, Ted. ★*You Ought to Do a Story About Me*	B
Wallace, Mike	
Greater Gotham	974.7
WALLACE, PERRY (LAW PROFESSOR)	
Maraniss, Andrew. *Strong Inside*	B
Wallace, Scott	
The Unconquered	981
WALLACE, SCOTT	
Wallace, Scott. *The Unconquered*	981
Wallace-Wells, David	
The Uninhabitable Earth	304.2
Wallach, Janet	
Desert Queen	B
Waller, Douglas C.	
Lincoln's Spies	973.7
Wild Bill Donovan	B
Wallis in Love. Morton, Andrew	B
Wallis, Jim	
The False White Gospel	261.7
Wallis, Michael	
The Best Land Under Heaven	978
Billy the Kid	B
Route 66	917.804
Walliser, Jessica	
★*Attracting Beneficial Bugs to Your Garden*	635
Plant Partners	635
The *Walls* Have Eyes. Molnar, Petra	363.28
Walls, Jeannette	
★*The Glass Castle*	B
WALLS, JEANNETTE	
Walls, Jeannette. ★*The Glass Castle*	B
Walls, Laura Dassow	
★*Henry David Thoreau*	B
WALSH, ADAM	
Standiford, Les. *Bringing Adam Home*	364.15
WALSH, BILL, 1931-2007	
Harris, David. *The Genius*	B

Walsh, Declan	
The Nine Lives of Pakistan	954.91
WALSH, DECLAN	
Walsh, Declan. *The Nine Lives of Pakistan*	954.91
Walsh, Patrick C.	
Dr. Patrick Walsh's Guide to Surviving Prostate Cancer	616.99
Walsh, Stephen	
★*Debussy*	B
Walt Disney. Gabler, Neal	B
Walters, Angela	
Free-Motion Meandering	746.46
WALTERS, BARBARA, 1931-2022	
Page, Susan. ★*The Rulebreaker*	B
Walters, Billy	
Gambler	796.092
WALTERS, BILLY	
Walters, Billy. *Gambler*	796.092
Walters, Jacqueline	
The Queen V	612.6
Walton, Bill	
Back from the Dead	B
WALTON, BILL, 1952-	
Walton, Bill. *Back from the Dead*	B
Walton, Calder	
Spies	327.1247
Walton, Sam	
Sam Walton, Made in America	B
WALTON, SAM, 1918-1992	
Walton, Sam. *Sam Walton, Made in America*	B
Walvin, James	
Sugar	338.17361
Wambach, Abby	
Forward	B
WAMBACH, ABBY, 1980-	
Wambach, Abby. *Forward*	B
WAMPANOAG (NORTH AMERICAN PEOPLE)	
Fraser, Rebecca. *The Mayflower*	974.4
Lepore, Jill. *The Name of War*	973.2
Philbrick, Nathaniel. ★*Mayflower*	973.2
Schultz, Eric B. *King Philip's War*	973.2
Silverman, David J. ★*This Land Is Their Land*	974.4
Wan, Bonnie	
The Life Brief	158.1
WANDERERS AND WANDERING	
DiFelice, Bekah. *Almost There*	248.8
Harrison, Jim. *The Search for the Genuine*	814
Hulls, Tessa. ★*Feeding Ghosts*	741.5
McGrath, Ben. *Riverman*	797.122
Smith, Patti. ★*Year of the Monkey*	B
Wandering in Strange Lands. Jerkins, Morgan	305.896
Wanderlust. Solnit, Rebecca	796.51
Wang, Connie	
Oh My Mother!	B
WANG, CONNIE	
Wang, Connie. *Oh My Mother!*	B
Wang, Jackie	
The Sunflower Cast a Spell to Save Us from the Void	811
WANG, JACKIE	
Wang, Jackie. *The Sunflower Cast a Spell to Save Us from the Void*	811
Wang, Jason	
Xi'an Famous Foods	641.595
WANG, JINGWEI, 1883-1944	
Mitter, Rana. *Forgotten Ally*	951.04
Wang, Qian Julie	
★*Beautiful Country*	B
WANG, QIAN JULIE, 1987-	
Wang, Qian Julie. ★*Beautiful Country*	B
Wangler, Justin	
Season	641.5979
Wanting What's Best. Jaffe, Sarah W.	649
Wanzer, Sidney H.	
★*To Die Well*	179.7
War. MacMillan, Margaret	355.0209
WAR	
Abdul-Ahad, Ghaith. *A Stranger in Your Own City*	956.7044
Abu Sayf, Atif. *The Drone Eats with Me*	B
Ackerman, Elliot. *Places and Names*	B
Ahmad, Aeham. *The Pianist from Syria*	B

PUBLIC LIBRARY CORE COLLECTION: NONFICTION
Twentieth Edition

Andrews, Lena S. ★*Valiant Women*	940.53
Arnold, James R. *Jungle of Snakes*	355.02
Atkinson, Rick. ★*The British Are Coming*	973.3
Ayers, Edward L. ★*The Thin Light of Freedom*	975.5
Bass, Gary Jonathan. *Freedom's Battle*	341.5
Beevor, Antony. *Russia*	947.084
Beevor, Antony. *The Second World War*	940.54
Beschloss, Michael R. ★*Presidents of War*	355.00973
Bilger, Burkhard. *Fatherland*	B
Bissinger, H. G. ★*The Mosquito Bowl*	796.332
Blattman, Christopher. *Why We Fight*	303.6
Boot, Max. ★*War Made New*	355.0209
Bordewich, Fergus M. *Congress at War*	324.2734
Boyle, Kevin. *The Shattering*	973.923
Brotherton, Marcus. *A Bright and Blinding Sun*	940.54
Cercas, Javier. *Lord of All the Dead*	868
Chamberlin, Paul Thomas. *The Cold War's Killing Fields*	355.009
Cho, Grace M. *Tastes Like War*	305.48
Chrisinger, David. *The Soldier's Truth*	940.54
Cohen, Eliot A. *Conquered into Liberty*	355.009747
Cozzens, Peter. *A Brutal Reckoning*	973.5
Crowley, Roger. *City of Fortune*	945
Di Cintio, Marcello. *Pay No Heed to the Rockets*	956.9405
Eisen, Norman L. *The Last Palace*	920
Evans, Martin. *Algeria*	965
Evans, Richard J. *The Third Reich at War*	940.53
Ferguson, Jane. *No Ordinary Assignment*	B
Figes, Orlando. *The Crimean War*	947
Filkins, Dexter. *The Forever War*	956.7044
Finkel, David. *Thank You for Your Service*	920
Fischer, David Hackett. *Washington's Crossing*	973.3
Forche, Carolyn. *What You Have Heard Is True*	B
Francis. *Life*	B
Frankopan, Peter. *The First Crusade*	956
Friedman, Matti. *Pumpkinflowers*	B
Fritz, Ian. *What the Taliban Told Me*	B
Goodheart, Adam. *1861*	973.7
Guillemin, Jeanne. *Biological Weapons*	358
Gwynne, S. C. *Empire of the Summer Moon*	B
Halberstam, David. *The Coldest Winter*	951.904
Hamilton, Lisa M. *The Hungry Season*	B
Harding, Luke. *Invasion*	947.7
Hastings, Max. ★*Vietnam*	959.704
Hastings, Max. *Warriors*	355
Hatzfeld, Jean. *Blood Papa*	967.5710431
Hedges, Chris. *War Is a Force That Gives Us Meaning*	355.02
Hennessey, Patrick. *The Junior Officers' Reading Club*	B
Homer. *The Iliad*	883
Hotta, Eri. *Japan 1941*	940.54
Hutton, Paul Andrew. *The Apache Wars*	979
Jones, Dan. *Crusaders*	909.07
Junger, Sebastian. *War*	958.104
Keegan, John. *The American Civil War*	973.7
Keegan, John. *The First World War*	940.3
Kesling, Ben. *Bravo Company*	958.104
Kilmeade, Brian. ★*Thomas Jefferson and the Tripoli Pirates*	973.4
Klay, Phil. *Uncertain Ground*	359.9
Komunyakaa, Yusef. ★*Everyday Mojo Songs of Earth*	811
Korda, Michael. *Muse of Fire*	940.4
Lamb, Christina. *Our Bodies, Their Battlefields*	341.6
Lambert, Malcolm. *God's Armies*	956
Lloyd, Nick. *The Western Front*	940.4
Lockley, Thomas. *African Samurai*	B
Loyn, David. *The Long War*	958.104
Luttrell, Marcus. *Lone Survivor*	958.104
MacMillan, Margaret. *War*	355.0209
Mansel, Philip. *King of the World*	B
Mazower, Mark. *The Greek Revolution*	949.5
McCann, Colum. *American Mother*	956.9104
McMeekin, Sean. *The Russian Revolution*	947.084
Moore, Wayetu. *The Dragons, the Giant, the Women*	B
Moorhouse, Roger. *Berlin at War*	943
Morris, David J. *The Evil Hours*	616.85
Nolan, Cathal J. *The Allure of Battle*	355.409
Ohler, Norman. *The Bohemians*	940.53
Owen, Mark. *No Hero*	B
Patterson, James. *Walk in My Combat Boots*	920
Petraeus, David Howell. *Conflict*	355
Pipes, Richard. *A Concise History of the Russian Revolution*	947.084
Plokhy, Serhii. ★*The Russo-Ukrainian War*	947.7
Porter, Carolyn. *Marcel's Letters*	940.54
Rady, Martyn C. *The Middle Kingdoms*	943
Roberts, Andrew. *Leadership in War*	920
Scott, James. *Black Snow*	940.54
Sebag-Montefiore, Simon. ★*The World*	929.7
Shuster, Simon. ★*The Showman*	B
Siegal, Nina. *The Diary Keepers*	940.54
Stern, Jessica. *My War Criminal*	341.6
Symonds, Craig L. *The Battle of Midway*	940.54
Trentmann, Frank. *Out of the Darkness*	943.08
Trofimov, Yaroslav. ★*Our Enemies Will Vanish*	947.7
Ward, Geoffrey C. ★*The Vietnam War*	959.704
Warren, W. Lee. *No Place to Hide*	B
Wood, David Bowne. *What Have We Done*	616.85
Wright, Evan. *Generation Kill*	956.7044
Wright, James Edward. ★*Enduring Vietnam*	959.704
Wukovits, John F. *Lost at Sea*	940.54
Zelensky, Volodymyr. *A Message from Ukraine*	947.7

WAR (INTERNATIONAL LAW)

Brooks, Rosa. *How Everything Became War and the Military Became Everything*	355
Witt, John Fabian. *Lincoln's Code*	343.73

War. Junger, Sebastian 958.104

WAR AND CIVILIZATION

Armitage, David. *Civil Wars*	355.02
Hanson, Victor Davis. *The Second World Wars*	940.54
Roach, Mary. ★*Grunt*	355
Thomson, David. *The Fatal Alliance*	791.43

WAR AND EMERGENCY POWERS

Barron, David J. *Waging War*	342.73

WAR AND SOCIETY

Ackroyd, Peter. *Innovation*	942.082
Addario, Lynsey. *Of Love & War*	779
Anderson, Fred. *The Dominion of War*	973
Ayers, Edward L. ★*The Thin Light of Freedom*	975.5
Bass, Gary Jonathan. *Freedom's Battle*	341.5
Beevor, Antony. *The Second World War*	940.54
Blattman, Christopher. *Why We Fight*	303.6
Cadbury, Deborah. *Princes at War*	920
Carroll, Andrew. *My Fellow Soldiers*	940.4
Dower, John W. *Cultures of War*	355.00973
Finkel, David. *Thank You for Your Service*	920
Fisk, Robert. *The Great War for Civilisation*	956.04
Glass, Charles. *Soldiers Don't Go Mad*	616.85
Hanson, Victor Davis. *The Father of Us All*	355.0209
Harding, Thomas. *The House by the Lake*	943
Hastings, Max. ★*Vietnam*	959.704
Kiernan, Denise. *The Girls of Atomic City*	976.8
Klay, Phil. *Uncertain Ground*	359.9
Korda, Michael. *Alone*	940.54
Lamb, Christina. *Our Bodies, Their Battlefields*	341.6
Levine, Bruce C. *The Fall of the House of Dixie*	973.7
Lowe, Keith. *Prisoners of History*	940.54
MacMillan, Margaret. *War*	355.0209
McConahay, Mary Jo. *The Tango War*	940.53
Nguyen, Viet Thanh. *Nothing Ever Dies*	959.704
O'Keeffe, Paul. *Waterloo*	940.2
Rappaport, Helen. *Caught in the Revolution*	355.00947
Roberts, Jennifer Tolbert. *The Plague of War*	938
Rosner, Elizabeth. *Survivor Cafe*	940.53
Samet, Elizabeth D. *Looking for the Good War*	940.53
Seierstad, Asne. *Angel of Grozny*	947.086
Terkel, Studs. *The Good War*	940.54
Weintraub, Stanley. *Iron Tears*	973.3

War as I Knew It. Patton, George S. B
The War Before the War. Delbanco, Andrew 973.7
The War Below. Scheyder, Ernest 333.7

WAR BRIDES

Barrett, Duncan. *GI Brides*	920

The War Came to Us. Miller, Christopher 947.7

WAR CASUALTIES

Ackerman, Elliot. *Places and Names*	B
Black, George. ★*The Long Reckoning*	959.704
Chamberlin, Paul Thomas. *The Cold War's Killing Fields*	355.009
Gallego, Ruben. *They Called Us*	956.7044
Grayling, A. C. *Among the Dead Cities*	940.54

AUTHOR, TITLE, SERIES AND SUBJECT INDEX

Holland, James. *Brothers in Arms*	940.54
Kugler, Rob. *A Dog Named Beautiful*	B
Miller, Christopher. *The War Came to Us*	947.7
Poole, Robert M. *Section 60*	975.5

WAR CORRESPONDENTS

Ackerman, Elliot. *Places and Names*	B
Blume, Lesley M. M. *Fallout*	940.54
Chrisinger, David. *The Soldier's Truth*	940.54
Cronkite, Walter. *Cronkite's War*	070.4
Edwards, Bob. *Edward R. Murrow and the Birth of Broadcast Journalism*	B
Engel, Richard. *And Then All Hell Broke Loose*	956.05
Ferguson, Jane. *No Ordinary Assignment*	B
Harding, Luke. *Invasion*	947.7
Hilsum, Lindsey. *In Extremis*	B
Huffman, Alan. *Here I Am*	B
MacKrell, Judith. *The Correspondents*	B
McCann, Colum. *American Mother*	956.9104
Miller, Christopher. *The War Came to Us*	947.7
Muse, Toby. *Kilo*	363.4509861
Nordland, Rod. *Waiting for the Monsoon*	B
Rinehart, Lorissa. *First to the Front*	B
Tobin, James. *Ernie Pyle's War*	B
Verini, James. *They Will Have to Die Now*	956.7044
Ward, Clarissa. *On All Fronts*	B

WAR CRIME TRIALS

Bass, Gary Jonathan. ★*Judgment at Tokyo*	952.04
Bradley, James. *Flyboys*	940.54
Crasnianski, Tania. *The Children of Nazis*	943.086
Dower, John W. *Embracing Defeat*	952.04
Lipstadt, Deborah E. *The Eichmann Trial*	345.5694
O'Reilly, Bill. *Killing the SS*	940.53
Philipps, David. *Alpha*	956.7044
Stangneth, Bettina. *Eichmann Before Jerusalem*	B
Stern, Jessica. *My War Criminal*	341.6

WAR CRIMES

Akcam, Taner. *A Shameful Act*	956.6
Bass, Gary Jonathan. ★*Judgment at Tokyo*	952.04
Edmonds, Chris. *No Surrender*	B
Finkelstein, Daniel. *Two Roads Home*	920
Frederick, Jim. *Black Hearts*	956.7044
Hagerty, Alexa. ★*Still Life with Bones*	599.9
Hoock, Holger. *Scars of Independence*	973.3
Kinstler, Linda. *Come to This Court and Cry*	940.53
Lipstadt, Deborah E. *The Eichmann Trial*	345.5694
Mazzeo, Tilar J. *Sisters in Resistance*	945.091
Rashke, Richard. *Useful Enemies*	341.69
Sands, Philippe. *East West Street*	345
Stern, Jessica. *My War Criminal*	341.6
Thant Myint-U. *The Hidden History of Burma*	959.105

WAR CRIMINALS

Bascomb, Neal. *Hunting Eichmann*	943.086
Goldhagen, Daniel Jonah. *Hitler's Willing Executioners*	940.53
Jacobsen, Annie. ★*Operation Paperclip*	940.54
Lower, Wendy. *Hitler's Furies*	940.53
Marwell, David G. *Mengele*	B
Nixon, John. *Debriefing the President*	956.7044
O'Reilly, Bill. *Killing the SS*	940.53
Rees, Laurence. *Auschwitz*	940.53
Sands, Philippe. *The Ratline*	B
Speer, Albert. *Inside the Third Reich*	B
Stern, Jessica. *My War Criminal*	341.6
Talty, Stephan. *The Good Assassin*	364.15

WAR FILMS

Harris, Mark. ★*Five Came Back*	791.4302
Thomson, David. *The Fatal Alliance*	791.43

WAR GAMES

Parkin, Simon. *A Game of Birds and Wolves*	940.54

WAR HORSES

Hutton, Robin L. *Sgt. Reckless*	951.904

WAR IN LITERATURE

Alexander, Caroline. *The War That Killed Achilles*	883
Samet, Elizabeth D. *Looking for the Good War*	940.53

WAR IN MASS MEDIA

Thomson, David. *The Fatal Alliance*	791.43

WAR IN THE NEWS MEDIA

Ferguson, Jane. *No Ordinary Assignment*	B
War Is a Force That Gives Us Meaning. Hedges, Chris	355.02
★*War Made New.* Boot, Max	355.0209

WAR MEMORIALS

Black, George. ★*The Long Reckoning*	959.704
Lowe, Keith. *Prisoners of History*	940.54

WAR NEUROSES

Glass, Charles. *Soldiers Don't Go Mad*	616.85

WAR OF 1812

Cheney, Lynne V. *James Madison*	B
Clague, Mark. *O Say Can You Hear?*	782.42
Cook, Jane Hampton. *American Phoenix*	973.5
Kilmeade, Brian. ★*Andrew Jackson and the Miracle of New Orleans*	973.5
Snow, Peter. *When Britain Burned the White House*	975.3
Taylor, Alan. *The Civil War of 1812*	973.5
Taylor, Alan. ★*The Internal Enemy*	975.5
Wills, Garry. *James Madison*	B
War of Nerves. Tucker, Jonathan B.	358
War of the Whales. Horwitz, Josh	333.95
War of Two. Sedgwick, John	973.4
War on Peace. Farrow, Ronan	327.73

WAR ON TERRORISM, 2001-2009

Ackerman, Spencer. *Reign of Terror*	973.931
Adayfi, Mansoor. *Don't Forget Us Here*	B
Bergen, Peter L. *The Longest War*	909.83
Bergen, Peter L. *Manhunt*	363.325
Bergen, Peter L. *The Rise and Fall of Osama Bin Laden*	958.104
Chivers, C. J. *The Fighters*	920
Denver, Rorke. *Worth Dying For*	359.9
Draper, Robert. *To Start a War*	956.7044
Edstrom, Erik. *Un-American*	B
Filkins, Dexter. *The Forever War*	956.7044
Jacobson, Sidney. *The 9-11 Report*	741.5
Khan, Mahvish Rukhsana. *My Guantanamo Diary*	973.931
Mayer, Jane. *The Dark Side*	973.931
O'Neill, Robert. *The Operator*	B
Owen, Mark. *No Easy Day*	B
Slahi, Mohamedou Ould. *The Mauritanian*	958.104
Van Agtmael, Peter. *Look at the USA*	070
Vickers, Michael G. *By All Means Available*	355
Walder, Tracy. *The Unexpected Spy*	B
★*War on the Border.* Guinn, Jeff	972.08

WAR PHOTOGRAPHERS

Addario, Lynsey. *It's What I Do*	B
Brennan, Thomas J. *Shooting Ghosts*	B

WAR PHOTOGRAPHY

Rinehart, Lorissa. *First to the Front*	B
Van Agtmael, Peter. *Look at the USA*	070
Wilson, Robert. *Mathew Brady*	B

WAR PROPAGANDA

Blume, Lesley M. M. *Fallout*	940.54
Pomerantsev, Peter. ★*How to Win an Information War*	940.53
Thomson, David. *The Fatal Alliance*	791.43
The War That Killed Achilles. Alexander, Caroline	883
★*The War That Made the Roman Empire.* Strauss, Barry S.	937

WAR WOUNDS

Erwin, Jon. *Beyond Valor*	B

WAR, DECLARATION OF

Barron, David J. *Waging War*	342.73

WARBURG FAMILY

Chernow, Ron. *The Warburgs*	B
The Warburgs. Chernow, Ron	B

Ward, Andrew

★*The Slaves' War*	973.7

WARD, ARTEMUS, 1834-1867

Martin, Justin. *Rebel Souls*	920

Ward, Ashley

The Social Lives of Animals	591.7
Where We Meet the World	612.8

Ward, Clarissa

On All Fronts	B

WARD, CLARISSA, 1980-

Ward, Clarissa. *On All Fronts*	B

WARD, FERDINAND DE WILTON, 1851-1925

Ward, Geoffrey C. *A Disposition to Be Rich*	B

Ward, Geoffrey C.

The Civil War	973.7
A Disposition to Be Rich	B
Jazz	781.6509
★*The Roosevelts*	B
Unforgivable Blackness	B

PUBLIC LIBRARY CORE COLLECTION: NONFICTION
Twentieth Edition

★ *The Vietnam War*	959.704
The West	978
Ward, Gerald W. R.	
Chihuly	709
Ward, Jesmyn	
★ *The Fire This Time*	305.896
★ *Men We Reaped*	B
WARD, JESMYN	
Ward, Jesmyn. ★ *Men We Reaped*	B
Ward, Jon	
Testimony	277.308
WARD, JON (WRITER OF POLITICS)	
Ward, Jon. *Testimony*	277.308
Ward, Maitland	
Rated X	B
WARD, MAITLAND, 1977-	
Ward, Maitland. *Rated X*	B
Ward, Ossian	
Look Again	750.1
Ward, Peter Douglas	
Life as We Do Not Know It	576.839
WARE, KEITH L.	
Kershaw, Alex. *Against All Odds*	940.54
★ *Warhol*. Gopnik, Blake	B
WARHOL, ANDY, 1928-1987	
Carr, C. *Candy Darling*	B
Gopnik, Blake. ★ *Warhol*	B
Warhorses. Komunyakaa, Yusef	811
Wariner, Ruth	
The Sound of Gravel	B
WARINER, RUTH	
Wariner, Ruth. *The Sound of Gravel*	B
WARING, JULIUS WATIES, 1880-1968	
Gergel, Richard. *Unexampled Courage*	323.1196
WARLORDS	
Gopal, Anand. *No Good Men Among the Living*	920
Lockley, Thomas. *African Samurai*	B
★ *The Warmth of Other Suns*. Wilkerson, Isabel	304.80973
Warner, Daniel	
Live Wires	786.7
Warner, Judith	
Perfect Madness	306.874
WARNER, TY, 1944-	
Bissonnette, Zac. *The Great Beanie Baby Bubble*	338.7
WARNINGS	
Knight, Sam. *The Premonitions Bureau*	133.8
Warraich, Haider	
Modern Death	179.7
The Song of Our Scars	616
WARRAICH, HAIDER	
Warraich, Haider. *The Song of Our Scars*	616
Warren Buffett and the Art of Stock Arbitrage. Buffett, Mary	332.645
The Warren Buffett Way. Hagstrom, Robert G.	332.6
WARREN, EARL, 1891-1974	
Simon, James F. *Eisenhower vs. Warren*	347.73
Warren, Elizabeth	
This Fight Is Our Fight	305.5
Warren, James A.	
God, War, and Providence	974.5
Year of the Hawk	959.704
Warren, Louis S.	
Buffalo Bill's America	B
Warren, Rosanna	
Max Jacob	B
Warren, W. Lee	
No Place to Hide	B
WARREN, W. LEE, 1969-	
Warren, W. Lee. *No Place to Hide*	B
Warrick, Joby	
Black Flags	956.9104
Red Line	956.9104
The Warrior Elite. Couch, Dick	359.9
Warrior Politics. Kaplan, Robert D.	320
Warriors. Hastings, Max	355
WARRIORS	
Gardner, Mark L. *The Earth Is All That Lasts*	978.004
Herman, Arthur. *The Viking Heart*	948
Homer. ★ *The Iliad*	883
Jones, Michael K. *The Black Prince*	B
Lockley, Thomas. *African Samurai*	B
McMurtry, Larry. *Crazy Horse*	B
Virgil. ★ *The Aeneid*	873
Warriors of God. Blanford, Nicholas	956.9204
The Wars of the Roosevelts. Mann, William J.	B
★ *The Wars of the Roses*. Jones, Dan	942.04
The Wars of the Roses. Weir, Alison	942.04
WARS OF THE ROSES, 1455-1485	
Gristwood, Sarah. *Blood Sisters*	942.04092
Jones, Dan. ★ *The Wars of the Roses*	942.04
Penn, Thomas. *The Brothers York*	942.04
Tallis, Nicola. *Uncrowned Queen*	B
Weir, Alison. *The Wars of the Roses*	942.04
WARSAW GHETTO UPRISING, 1943	
Batalion, Judith. *The Light of Days*	940.53
WARSAW, POLAND	
Ackerman, Diane. ★ *The Zookeeper's Wife*	940.53
Berg, Mary. *The Diary of Mary Berg*	B
Mazzeo, Tilar J. *Irena's Children*	B
Warsaw-Fan Rauch, Arianna	
★ *Declassified*	781.1
WARSHIPS	
Parrish, Thomas D. *The Submarine*	359.9
Puleo, Stephen. *Voyage of Mercy*	363.8
Wartzman, Rick	
Still Broke	381
Warzel, Charlie	
Out of Office	658.3
Washington. Bordewich, Fergus M.	975.3
Washington. Chernow, Ron	B
WASHINGTON (D.C.)	
Holladay, Wilhelmina Cole. *A Museum of Their Own*	704
Oller, John. *American Queen*	B
Snow, Peter. *When Britain Burned the White House*	975.3
Tumulty, Karen. *The Triumph of Nancy Reagan*	B
WASHINGTON (STATE)	
Alexie, Sherman. *You Don't Have to Say You Love Me*	818
Bauermeister, Erica. *House Lessons*	
Edwards, Adrienne L. *Firescaping Your Home*	635.9
Freeman, Scott. *Saving Tarboo Creek*	333.72
Krist, Gary. *The White Cascade*	979.7
Lankford, Andrea. *Trail of the Lost*	363.2
Neiwert, David A. *Of Orcas and Men*	599.53
Newman, Magdalena. *Normal*	611
Wolff, Tobias. *This Boy's Life*	B
The Washington Book. Lozada, Carlos	320
WASHINGTON D.C.	
Gilliam, Dorothy Butler. *Trailblazer*	B
WASHINGTON FAMILY	
Shirley, Craig. *Mary Ball Washington*	B
WASHINGTON STATE	
LaPointe, Sasha taqwseblu. *Red Paint*	B
Washington's Crossing. Fischer, David Hackett	973.3
Washington's End. Horn, Jonathan	B
Washington's Farewell. Avlon, John P.	973.4
Washington, Booker T.	
★ *Up from Slavery*	B
WASHINGTON, BOOKER T., 1856-1915	
Harlan, Louis R. *Booker T. Washington*	B
Harlan, Louis R. *Booker T. Washington*	B
Norrell, Robert J. *Up from History*	B
Washington, Booker T. ★ *Up from Slavery*	B
WASHINGTON, D.C	
Bordewich, Fergus M. *Washington*	975.3
WASHINGTON, D.C.	
Brower, Kate Andersen. *First in Line*	920
Brower, Kate Andersen. *First Women*	920
Clinton, Bill. *My Life*	B
Cook, Blanche Wiesen. *Eleanor Roosevelt; Volume 2*	B
Cook, Blanche Wiesen. ★ *Eleanor Roosevelt; Volume 3*	B
Dorey-Stein, Beck. *From the Corner of the Oval*	B
Graff, Garrett M. ★ *The Only Plane in the Sky*	973.931
Holzer, Harold. *Monument Man*	B
Hutchinson, Cassidy. *Enough*	B
Litt, David. *Thanks, Obama*	B
McCullough, David G. ★ *John Adams*	B
Obama, Michelle. *American Grown*	635.09

AUTHOR, TITLE, SERIES AND SUBJECT INDEX

Rhodes, Benjamin J. *The World as It Is*	973.932
Shlaes, Amity. *Coolidge*	B
Wolff, Michael. *Fire and Fury*	973.933
Wolff, Michael. *Landslide*	973.933
Woodward, Bob. *Fear*	973.933
Woodward, Bob. *Peril*	973.933
Woodward, Bob. *Shadow*	973.92

Washington, Ella F.
The Necessary Journey	658.3

WASHINGTON, GEORGE, 1732-1799
Avlon, John P. *Washington's Farewell*	973.4
Baier, Bret. *To Rescue the Constitution*	973.4
Calloway, Colin G. *The Indian World of George Washington*	323.1197
Cheney, Lynne V. *The Virginia Dynasty*	B
Chernow, Ron. *Washington*	B
Coe, Alexis. ★ *You Never Forget Your First*	973.3
Drury, Bob. *Valley Forge*	973.3
Dunbar, Erica Armstrong. ★ *Never Caught*	B
Ellis, Joseph J. ★ *His Excellency*	B
Ellis, Joseph J. *The Quartet*	342.7302
Ferling, John E. *Winning Independence*	973.3
Fischer, David Hackett. *Washington's Crossing*	973.3
Flexner, James Thomas. *George Washington and the New Nation, 1783-1793*	973.4
Flexner, James Thomas. *George Washington*	B
Gaines, James R. *For Liberty and Glory*	B
Good, Cassandra A. *First Family*	920
Horn, Jonathan. *Washington's End*	B
Johnson, Paul. *George Washington*	B
Kilmeade, Brian. *George Washington's Secret Six*	973.4
Larson, Edward J. *The Return of George Washington*	B
McCullough, David G. ★ *1776*	973.3
Meltzer, Brad. ★ *The First Conspiracy*	973.4
O'Connell, Robert L. *Revolutionary*	B
Philbrick, Nathaniel. ★ *In the Hurricane's Eye*	973.3
Philbrick, Nathaniel. *Travels with George*	973.4
Philbrick, Nathaniel. ★ *Valiant Ambition*	B
Randall, Willard Sterne. *George Washington*	B
Ricks, Thomas E. ★ *First Principles*	973.09
Saxton, Martha. *The Widow Washington*	B
Shirley, Craig. *Mary Ball Washington*	B
Stark, Peter. *Young Washington*	B
Stewart, David O. *George Washington*	973.4

WASHINGTON, JOHN, 1838-1918
Blight, David W. *A Slave No More*	B

Washington, Kate
★ *Already Toast*	649.8

WASHINGTON, KATE, 1972-
Washington, Kate. ★ *Already Toast*	649.8

Washington, Kerry
Thicker Than Water	B

WASHINGTON, KERRY, 1977-
Washington, Kerry. *Thicker Than Water*	B

WASHINGTON, MARTHA, 1731-1802
Brady, Patricia. *Martha Washington*	B
Dunbar, Erica Armstrong. ★ *Never Caught*	B
Good, Cassandra A. *First Family*	920

WASHINGTON, MARY BALL, 1708-1789
Saxton, Martha. *The Widow Washington*	B
Shirley, Craig. *Mary Ball Washington*	B

Wasik, Bill
★ *Our Kindred Creatures*	179
Rabid	614.5
The Wasp That Brainwashed the Caterpillar. Simon, Matt	578.4

WASPS
Catania, Kenneth. *Great Adaptations*	576.8
Sumner, Seirian. *Endless Forms*	595.79

Wassef, Nadia
Shelf Life	B

WASSEF, NADIA
Wassef, Nadia. *Shelf Life*	B

Wasserman, Claire
Ladies Get Paid	650.1

WASSERMAN, LEW
Bruck, Connie. *When Hollywood Had a King*	B

Wasson, Sam
The Big Goodbye	791.43
Fifth Avenue, 5 A.M.	791.43

★ *Improv Nation*	792.02
Waste. Flowers, Catherine Coleman	363.72
The Waste Land. Hollis, Matthew	821

WASTE PRODUCTS
Humes, Edward. ★ *Total Garbage*	628.4
Wasted. Hornbacher, Marya	B
★ *Wasteland*. Franklin-Wallis, Oliver	363.72
Wastelands. Addison, Corban	346.73

Watanabe, Judi
The Complete Photo Guide to Cardmaking	745.594
Watch Me. Huston, Anjelica	B
Watching Darkness Fall. McKean, David	940.53
Watching The World Change. Friend, David	974.7
★ *The Watchmaker's Daughter*. Loftis, Larry	940.53
Water. Boccaletti, Giulio	909
Water. Solomon, Steven	553.7

WATER
Boccaletti, Giulio. *Water*	909
Gleick, Peter H. *The Three Ages of Water*	333.91
Harrison, Scott. *Thirst*	B
Solomon, Steven. *Water*	553.7
Tsui, Bonnie. *Why We Swim*	797.2

WATER AND CIVILIZATION
Boccaletti, Giulio. *Water*	909

WATER CONSERVATION
Bainbridge, David A. *Gardening with Less Water*	635.9
Estes, Nick. *Our History Is the Future*	978.004
Penick, Pam. *The Water-Saving Garden*	635.9
Ross, John F. *The Promise of the Grand Canyon*	917.91
Silver, Johanna. ★ *The Bold Dry Garden*	635.9

WATER CONSUMPTION
Gleick, Peter H. *The Three Ages of Water*	333.91

WATER CONTAMINATION
Maher, Kris. *Desperate*	344
The Water Gardener's Bible. Helm, Ben	635.9

WATER POLLUTION
Arsenault, Kerri. *Mill Town*	B
Bilott, Robert. *Exposure*	344.04
Fagin, Dan. *Toms River*	363.7209749
Kingdon, Amorina. ★ *Sing Like Fish*	591.77

WATER QUALITY
Egan, Dan. ★ *The Death and Life of the Great Lakes*	577.6

WATER RIGHTS
Estes, Nick. *Our History Is the Future*	978.004

WATER USE
Gleick, Peter H. *The Three Ages of Water*	333.91
The Water Will Come. Goodell, Jeff	551.45
The Water-Saving Garden. Penick, Pam	635.9

WATER-SUPPLY
Clark, Anna. *The Poisoned City*	363.6
Gleick, Peter H. *The Three Ages of Water*	333.91
Hanna-Attisha, Mona. *What the Eyes Don't See*	615.9
Maher, Kris. *Desperate*	344
Owen, David. *Where the Water Goes*	917.91
Solomon, Steven. *Water*	553.7
Watercolor Essentials. O'Connor, Birgit	751.42

WATERCOLOR PAINTING
Jung, Kwan. *Chinese Brush Painting*	751.4
Kersey, Geoff. *Painting Successful Watercolours from Photographs*	751.42
O'Connor, Birgit. *Watercolor Essentials*	751.42
Robinson, Mario Andres. *Lessons in Realistic Watercolor*	751.42

WATERFALLS
Spira, Timothy P. *Waterfalls and Wildflowers in the Southern Appalachians*	796.5109756

Waterfalls and Wildflowers in the Southern Appalachians. Spira, Timothy P. 796.5109756

Watergate. Graff, Garrett M.	973.924

WATERGATE SCANDAL
Bernstein, Carl. ★ *All the President's Men*	364.1
Brokaw, Tom. *The Fall of Richard Nixon*	B
Dean, John W. *The Nixon Defense*	973.924092
Dobbs, Michael. *King Richard*	973.924
Farrell, John A. ★ *Richard Nixon*	B
Graff, Garrett M. *Watergate*	973.924
Morley, Jefferson. *Scorpions' Dance*	973.924
Reston, James. *The Conviction of Richard Nixon*	973.924092
Rumsfeld, Donald. *When the Center Held*	973.925092
Woodward, Bob. *The Final Days*	B

Woodward, Bob. *Shadow* — 973.92
Waterhouse, Benjamin C.
  One Day I'll Work for Myself — 338
Waterloo. Cornwell, Bernard — 940.2
Waterloo. O'Keeffe, Paul — 940.2
WATERLOO, BATTLE OF, 1815
  Cornwell, Bernard. *Waterloo* — 940.2
  O'Keeffe, Paul. *Waterloo* — 940.2
Waterman, Jonathan
  National Geographic Atlas of the National Parks — 917.304
★*Watermelon & Red Birds*. Taylor, Nicole A. — 641.5
Waters, Alice
  The Art of Simple Food — 641.5
  Coming to My Senses — B
  ★*We Are What We Eat* — 641.01
WATERS, ALICE
  Waters, Alice. *Coming to My Senses* — B
WATERS, ETHEL, 1900-1977
  Bogle, Donald. *Heat Wave* — 782.42164
Waters, John
  Mr. Know-It-All — 814
  Role Models — B
WATERS, JOHN, 1946-
  Waters, John. *Mr. Know-It-All* — 814
  Waters, John. *Role Models* — B
WATERS, MAXINE
  Andrews-Dyer, Helena. *Reclaiming Her Time* — B
  Jones, Brenda. *Maxine Waters* — B
WATERWAYS
  Sciolino, Elaine. *The Seine* — 944
Watkin, David
  A History of Western Architecture — 720
Watkins, Alexandra
  Hello, My Name Is Awesome — 658.8
Watkins, Carleton E.
  Carleton Watkins — 778.9
WATKINS, CARLETON E., 1829-1916
  Watkins, Carleton E. *Carleton Watkins* — 778.9
Watkins, D.
  Black Boy Smile — B
WATKINS, D. (DWIGHT)
  Watkins, D. *Black Boy Smile* — B
Watkins, Julia
  Simply Living Well — 640
Watling, Sarah
  Tomorrow Perhaps the Future — 946.081
Watson, Bruce
  Freedom Summer — 323.1196
  Sacco and Vanzetti — 345.73
Watson, Cecelia
  Semicolon — 428.2
WATSON, JAMES C. (JAMES CRAIG), 1838-1880
  Baron, David. *American Eclipse* — 523.7
WATSON, JAMES D., 1928-
  Markel, Howard. *The Secret of Life* — 572.86
Watson, Paul
  Ice Ghosts — 917
Watson, Peter
  The German Genius — 943
Watson, Richard A.
  Cogito Ergo Sum — B
Watson, Sarah
  Pen to Thread — 746.44
Watson, Ted Kennedy
  Ted Kennedy Watson's Guide to Stylish Entertaining — 793.2
Watts, Alan
  The Way of Zen — 294.3
WATTS, CHRIS (CHRISTOPHER LEE), 1985-
  Glatt, John. ★*The Perfect Father* — 364.152
Watts, Jill
  Hattie McDaniel — B
Watts, Reggie
  Great Falls, MT — B
WATTS, REGGIE
  Watts, Reggie. *Great Falls, MT* — B
Watts, Steven
  The People's Tycoon — B
  Self-Help Messiah — B

WAUGH, EVELYN, 1903-1966
  Eade, Philip. *Evelyn Waugh* — B
Wave. Deraniyagala, Sonali — B
Waxman, Jamye
  How to Break up with Anyone — 158.2
Waxman, Sharon
  Rebels on the Backlot — 791.4302
The Way Home. Brown, Kardea — 641.5975
The Way It Was. Weisman, Eliot — 782.42164
The Way of Integrity. Beck, Martha Nibley — 158.1
The Way of the Fearless Writer. Kempton, Beth — 808.02
The Way of the Monk. Das, Gaur Gopal — 294.5
The Way of the Runner. Finn, Adharanand — 796.42
The Way of the Strangers. Wood, Graeme — 363.325
The Way of Zen. Watts, Alan — 294.3
★*The Way That Leads Among the Lost*. Garcia, Angela — 362.29
The Way Things Work Now. Macaulay, David — 600
★*The Way to Cook*. Child, Julia — 641.5
★*A Way to Garden*. Roach, Margaret — 635
The Way to the Spring. Ehrenreich, Ben — 956.95
The Way We Eat Now. Wilson, Bee — 641.01
The Way You Make Me Feel. Sharma, Nina — B
Way, Niobe
  Rebels with a Cause — 649
Wayland-Smith, Ellen
  Oneida — 307.77
WAYNE, ANTHONY, 1745-1796
  Hogeland, William. *Autumn of the Black Snake* — 970.004
WAYNE, JOHN, 1907-1979
  Eyman, Scott. *John Wayne* — B
Wayne, Peter
  The Harvard Medical School Guide to Tai Chi — 613.7
Wayne, Tiffany K.
  Critical Companion to Ralph Waldo Emerson — 814
Waypoints. Heughan, Sam — B
Ways and Means. Lowenstein, Roger — 973.7
Ways of Curating. Obrist, Hans-Ulrich — 707.5
We All Know How This Ends. Lyons, Anna — 362.17
We Are Called to Be a Movement. Barber, William J. — 261.8
We Are Each Other's Harvest. Baszile, Natalie — 630.89
★*We Are Home*. Suarez, Ray — 325.73
We Are Never Meeting in Real Life. Irby, Samantha — 814
We Are Not Able to Live in the Sky. Kardas-Nelson, Mara — 332.3
We Are Not Here to Be Bystanders. Sarsour, Linda — B
We Are on Our Own. Katin, Miriam — 741.5
We Are Soldiers Still. Moore, Harold G. — 959.704
★*We Are the Land*. Akins, Damon B. — 978
We Are the Ones We Have Been Waiting For. Walker, Alice — 811
★*We Are the Weather*. Foer, Jonathan Safran — 636
We Are Too Many. Pittard, Hannah — B
★*We Are What We Eat*. Waters, Alice — 641.01
We Band of Angels. Norman, Elizabeth M. — 940.54
We Begin in Gladness. Teicher, Craig Morgan — 808.1
We Can't Breathe. Asim, Jabari — 305.896
We Carry Their Bones. Kimmerle, Erin H. — 365
★*We Could Have Been Friends, My Father and I*. Shehadeh, Raja — B
We Could Not Fail. Paul, Richard — 920
We Crossed a Bridge and It Trembled. Pearlman, Wendy — 956.9104
★*We Don't Know Ourselves*. O'Toole, Fintan — 941.7
We Had a Little Real Estate Problem. Nesteroff, Kliph — 970.004
We Have Been Harmonized. Strittmatter, Kai — 323.44
We Have Only This Life to Live. Sartre, Jean-Paul — 848
★*We Hold Our Breath*. Fields, Micah — 976.4
We Inherit What the Fires Left. Evans, William — 811
We Keep the Dead Close. Cooper, Becky — 364.152
We Loved It All. Millet, Lydia — 813
We Matter. Thomas, Etan — 796.08
We May Dominate the World. Mirski, Sean A. — 973.91
We Need to Hang Out. Baker, Billy — 177
We Need to Talk. Headlee, Celeste Anne — 153.6
★*We Need to Talk About Antisemitism*. Fersko, Diana — 305.892
We Own This City. Fenton, Justin — 364.1
We Refuse. Jackson, Kellie Carter — 323.1196
We Refuse to Forget. Gayle, Caleb — 975.004
We Shall Overcome. Boyd, Herb — 323.1196
We Should All Be Feminists. Adichie, Chimamanda Ngozi — 305.42
We Should Not Be Friends. Schwalbe, Will — B
We The Corporations. Winkler, Adam — 346.73

AUTHOR, TITLE, SERIES AND SUBJECT INDEX

We The Scientists. Marcus, Amy Dockser — 618.92
We Two. Gill, Gillian — 941.081
★*We Were Dreamers.* Liu, Simu — B
★*We Were Eight Years in Power.* Coates, Ta-Nehisi — 305.896
We Were Once a Family. Asgarian, Roxanna — 364.152
We Were Rich and We Didn't Know It. Phelan, Tom — B
We Were Soldiers Once—And Young. Moore, Harold G. — 959.704
We Wish to Inform You That Tomorrow We Will Be Killed with Our Families. Gourevitch, Philip — 364.15
★*We're Better Than This.* Cummings, Elijah — B
We're Going to Need More Wine. Union, Gabrielle — B
Weale, Adrian
   Army of Evil — 940.54
WEALTH
   Bregman, Rutger. *Utopia for Realists* — 335
   Brown, Peter. *Through the Eye of a Needle* — 270.2
   Cooper, Anderson. *Vanderbilt* — 920
   De Long, J. Bradford. *Slouching Towards Utopia* — 330.9
   Dennis, Felix. *How to Get Rich* — B
   Desmond, Matthew. ★*Poverty, by America* — 362.5
   Elwood, Phil. *All the Worst Humans* — 659.2
   Ferriss, Timothy. *Tools of Titans* — 081
   Flitter, Emily. *The White Wall* — 332.0973
   Good, Cassandra A. *First Family* — 920
   Greenspan, Alan. *Capitalism in America* — 330.973
   Hammond, Claudia. *Mind Over Money* — 332.401
   Hope, Bradley. *Blood and Oil* — B
   Karabell, Zachary. *Inside Money* — 332.1
   Lieber, Ron. *The Opposite of Spoiled* — 332.0240083
   MacColl, Gail. *To Marry an English Lord* — 974.7
   Markovits, Daniel. *The Meritocracy Trap* — 305.5
   McMillan, Tracie. ★*The White Bonus* — 305.8
   Mechanic, Michael. *Jackpot* — 305.5
   Milanovic, Branko. *The Have and the Have-Nots* — 339.2
   Montero, David. ★*The Stolen Wealth of Slavery* — 381
   Muse, Toby. *Kilo* — 363.4509861
   Neiman, Garrett. *Rich White Men* — 305.5
   Noah, Timothy. *The Great Divergence* — 339.2
   Norton, Hughes. ★*Rainmaker* — 796.352
   Oller, John. *White Shoe* — 346.73
   Orman, Suze. *Women & Money* — 332.0240082
   Piketty, Thomas. *A Brief History of Equality* — 305.09
   Piketty, Thomas. ★*Capital in the Twenty-First Century* — 332
   Randall, Willard Sterne. *The Founders' Fortunes* — 973.3
   Reeves, Richard V. *Dream Hoarders* — 305.5
   Reid, T. R. *A Fine Mess* — 336.200973
   Ridley, Matt. *The Rational Optimist* — 339.2
   Sandel, Michael J. *What Money Can't Buy* — 174
   Sedgewick, Augustine. *Coffeeland* — 338.4
   Simmons, Lauren. *Make Money Move* — 332.024
   Sowell, Thomas. *Wealth, Poverty and Politics* — 330.1
   Stanley, Thomas J. *The Next Millionaire Next Door* — 332.024
   Stiglitz, Joseph E. *The Price of Inequality* — 305.50973
   Sun, Carrie. *Private Equity* — B
   Taub, Jennifer. *Big Dirty Money* — 364.16
   Teachout, Zephyr. *Break 'Em Up* — 338.8
   Tu, Vivian. *Rich Af* — 332.024
   Turchin, Peter. *End Times* — 320.01
Wealth and Power. Schell, Orville — 920
★*The Wealth of Nations.* Smith, Adam — 330.15
WEALTH REDISTRIBUTION
   Piketty, Thomas. ★*Capital and Ideology* — 305
Wealth, Poverty and Politics. Sowell, Thomas — 330.1
WEAPONS
   Emlen, Douglas John. *Animal Weapons* — 591.47
   Hanson, Victor Davis. *The Second World Wars* — 940.54
   Kean, Sam. *The Bastard Brigade* — 355.8
   Satia, Priya. *Empire of Guns* — 330.941
WEAPONS INDUSTRY AND TRADE
   Century, Douglas. *Barney Ross* — B
   Simms, Brendan. *The Silver Waterfall* — 940.54
WEAPONS OF MASS DESTRUCTION
   Emery, Theo. *Hellfire Boys* — 358
   Kaplan, Fred M. *The Bomb* — 355.8
   Preston, Diana. *Before the Fallout* — 303.48
   Preston, Diana. *A Higher Form of Killing* — 940.4
   Schlosser, Eric. *Command and Control* — 363.17
   Warrick, Joby. *Red Line* — 956.9104

Weapons of Math Destruction. O'Neil, Cathy — 005.7
WEAPONS RESEARCH
   Kean, Sam. *The Bastard Brigade* — 355.8
WEATHER
   Barnett, Cynthia. *Rain* — 551.57
   Fabes, Stephen. *Signs of Life* — B
   Redniss, Lauren. *Thunder & Lightning* — 741.5
   Williams, Jack. ★*The Ams Weather Book* — 551.5
Weather Bird. Giddins, Gary — 781.6509
WEATHER FORECASTING
   Dolin, Eric Jay. *A Furious Sky* — 363.34
   Hargrove, Brantley. *The Man Who Caught the Storm* — B
Weatherall, James Owen
   The Physics of Wall Street — 332.63
Weatherford, J. McIver
   ★*Genghis Khan and the Making of the Modern World* — B
   Genghis Khan and the Quest for God — 323.44
★*Weathering.* Geronimus, Arline T. — 362.1089
The Weaver's Idea Book. Patrick, Jane — 746.1
The Weaver's Inkle Pattern Directory. Dixon, Anne — 746.1
WEAVING
   Corwin, Lena. *Lena Corwin's Made by Hand* — 746.6
   Daly, Fiona. *Weaving on a Little Loom* — 746.1
   Dixon, Anne. *The Handweaver's Pattern Directory* — 746.1
The Weaving Explorer. Jarchow, Deborah — 746.1
Weaving on a Little Loom. Daly, Fiona — 746.1
WEB SEARCH ENGINES
   Auletta, Ken. *Googled* — 338.7
Webb, Caroline
   How to Have a Good Day — 650.1
Webb, Kinari
   Guardians of the Trees — B
WEBB, KINARI
   Webb, Kinari. *Guardians of the Trees* — B
Webb, Leah M.
   The Seven-Step Homestead — 635
Webb, Maynard
   Dear Founder — 658
WEBCOMICS
   Brosh, Allie. ★*Hyperbole and a Half* — 741.5
   Brosh, Allie. ★*Solutions and Other Problems* — 741.5
   Inman, Matthew. *The Terrible and Wonderful Reasons Why I Run Long Distances* — 741.5
Weber's Greatest Hits. Purviance, Jamie — 641.5
Weber's Ultimate Grilling. Purviance, Jamie — 641.5
Weber, Charlotte Fox
   Tell Me What You Want — 153.8
Weber, Thomas
   Becoming Hitler — B
WEBSTER, DANIEL, 1782-1852
   Brands, H. W. ★*Heirs of the Founders* — 973.5
   Paul, Joel R. *Indivisible* — 973.5
WEDDING PLANNING
   Diamant, Anita. *The Jewish Wedding Now* — 296.4
WEDDINGS
   Doty, Cate. *Mergers and Acquisitions* — 395.2
The Weeding Handbook. Vnuk, Rebecca — 025.2
WEEDS
   Dickinson, Richard. *Weeds of North America* — 632
Weeds of North America. Dickinson, Richard — 632
WEEGEE, 1899-1968
   Bonanos, Christopher. *Flash* — B
★*The Weekday Vegetarians.* Rosenstrach, Jenny — 641.5
The Weekend Cook. Hartnett, Angela — 641.5
Wegner, Bobbi
   Raising Feminist Boys — 305.23
Wehle, Kim
   What You Need to Know About Voting and Why — 324.60973
Weidensaul, Scott
   A World on the Wing — 598.156
Weigel, Alicia Roth
   Inverse Cowgirl — B
WEIGEL, ALICIA ROTH
   Weigel, Alicia Roth. *Inverse Cowgirl* — B
WEIGHT CONTROL
   Meltzer, Marisa. *This Is Big* — 613.25
WEIGHT LIFTING
   Brodeur, Michael Andor. ★*Swole* — 155.3

PUBLIC LIBRARY CORE COLLECTION: NONFICTION
Twentieth Edition

WEIGHT LOSS
    Angelou, Maya. *Great Food, All Day Long* — 641.5973
    Barrett, Pearl. *Trim Healthy Mama Trim Healthy Table* — 613.2
    Cruikshank, Tiffany. *Meditate Your Weight* — 613.2
    Fuhrman, Joel. *Eat to Live Quick & Easy Cookbook* — 641.5
    Hari, Johann. ★*Magic Pill* — 613.2
    Hartwig, Melissa. *The Whole30 Fast & Easy* — 641.5
    Hartwig, Melissa. *The Whole30 Slow Cooker* — 641.5
    Kazdin, Cole. ★*What's Eating Us* — 616.85
    Ludwig, David. *Always Hungry?* — 613.2
    Sole-Smith, Virginia. ★*Fat Talk* — 649.1

WEIGHT TRAINING
    Current, Austin. *Science of Strength Training* — 613.7

WEIGL, RUDOLF, 1883-1957
    Allen, Arthur. ★*The Fantastic Laboratory of Dr. Weigl* — 614.5

Weil, Andrew
    Fast Food, Good Food — 641.3
    Mind Over Meds — 362.29

WEIL, ANDREW
    Lattin, Don. *The Harvard Psychedelic Club* — 973.922092

Weil, Anne
    Knitting Without Needles — 746.43

Weill, Kelly
    Off the Edge — 001.9

Weinberg, Steven
    To Explain the World — 509

Weiner, Eric
    Ben & Me — B
    The Socrates Express — 100

WEINER, ERIC, 1963-
    Weiner, Eric. *Ben & Me* — B

Weiner, Mark Stuart
    Black Trials — 342.7308

Weiner, Tim
    The Folly and the Glory — 327.73047
    Legacy of Ashes — 327.1273009
    One Man Against the World — B

Weinersmith, Kelly
    ★*A City on Mars* — 629.4

Weingarten, Gene
    ★*One Day* — 973

Weinman, Sarah
    The Real Lolita — 362.88092
    Scoundrel — 364.152
    ★*Unspeakable Acts* — 364.1

Weinreb, Michael
    Season of Saturdays — 796.332

Weinstein, Bruce
    The Great Big Pressure Cooker Book — 641.5
    The Kitchen Shortcut Bible — 641.555

WEINSTEIN, HARVEY, 1952-
    Auletta, Ken. *Hollywood Ending* — 791.43
    Farrow, Ronan. ★*Catch and Kill* — 331.4

WEINSTEIN, HERBERT
    Davis, Kevin. *The Brain Defense* — 345.747

Weintraub, Robert
    No Better Friend — 940.54

Weintraub, Stanley
    Iron Tears — 973.3

Weir, Alison
    The Children of Henry VIII — B
    Eleanor of Aquitaine — B
    Henry VIII — B
    The Lady in the Tower — B
    The Life of Elizabeth I — B
    The Lost Tudor Princess — B
    Mary, Queen of Scots, and the Murder of Lord Darnley — 941.105
    Queens of the Age of Chivalry — 920
    Queens of the Conquest — 920
    The Six Wives of Henry VIII — 942.05
    The Wars of the Roses — 942.04

Weir, Laura
    Cosy — 646.7009

Weisman, Eliot
    The Way It Was — 782.42164

WEISMAN, ELIOT
    Weisman, Eliot. *The Way It Was* — 782.42164

Weisman, Steven R.
    The Chosen Wars — 296.0973

Weismann, Brad
    Lost in the Dark — 791.43

Weiss, Eben
    ★*The Ultimate Bicycle Owner's Manual* — 796.6

Weiss, Elaine F.
    The Woman's Hour — 324.6

Weiss, Helga
    Helga's Diary — B

Weiss, Luisa
    Classic German Baking — 641.594

Weissmann, Andrew
    ★*Where Law Ends* — 324.7

Weitzman, Gary
    National Geographic Complete Guide to Pet Health, Behavior, and Happiness — 636.088

Weitzman, Yaron
    Tanking to the Top — 796.323

WELCH, JACK, 1935-2020
    Gelles, David. *The Man Who Broke Capitalism* — 330.12
    ★*Welcome Home*. Berlin, Lucia — B
    Welcome to the Jungle. Offolter, Enid — 635.9
    Welcome to the Orthodox Church. Mathewes-Green, Frederica — 281.9
    Welcome to the United States of Anxiety. Lancaster, Jen — 155.4
    Welcome to the Universe. Tyson, Neil deGrasse — 523.1
    Welcome to Your World. Goldhagen, Sarah Williams — 720.1

Weldon, Glen
    ★*The Caped Crusade* — 741.5

WELFARE
    Edin, Kathryn. *$2.00 a Day* — 339.4
    Kim, Anne. ★*Poverty for Profit* — 302.5
    Sandler, Lauren. *This Is All I Got* — B

WELFARE RECIPIENTS
    Land, Stephanie. *Maid* — B
    Levin, Josh. *The Queen* — 364.16
    Wariner, Ruth. *The Sound of Gravel* — B

WELFARE REFORM
    Pryce, Jessica. ★*Broken* — 362.7

Welky, David
    ★*A Wretched and Precarious Situation* — 910.911
    ★*Well of Souls*. Gaddy, K. R. — 787
    Well, That Escalated Quickly. Ramsey, Franchesca — B

WELL-BEING
    Albright, Mary Beth. ★*Eat & Flourish* — 612.3
    Blumenthal, Brett. *52 Small Changes for the Mind* — 616.89
    Dunne, Linnea. *Lagom* — 158.1
    Golbeck, Jennifer. *The Purest Bond* — 636.7
    Harrison, Christy. *The Wellness Trap* — 613
    Jamie, Poppy. *Happy Not Perfect* — 158.1
    Johansen, Signe. ★*How to Hygge* — 646.7
    Killam, Kasley. *The Art and Science of Connection* — 302
    King, Vanessa. *10 Keys to Happier Living* — 158
    Lancaster, Jen. *Welcome to the United States of Anxiety* — 155.4
    Langshur, Eric. *Start Here* — 158
    Luger, Chelsey. ★*The Seven Circles* — 610
    Mann, Jen. ★*Midlife Bites* — 305.244
    McGovern, Anna. *Pottering* — 158.1
    Northrup, Christiane. *Dodging Energy Vampires* — 155.2
    Plantinga, Cornelius. *Gratitude* — 179
    Raphael, Rina. *The Gospel of Wellness* — 613
    Tsui, Bonnie. *Why We Swim* — 797.2
    Weir, Laura. *Cosy* — 646.7009
    Williams, Florence. *The Nature Fix* — 155.9
    The Well-Built Triathlete. Dixon, Matt — 796.42
    A Well-Paid Slave. Snyder, Brad — B

Weller, Melissa
    A Good Bake — 641.86

Weller, Sam
    The Bradbury Chronicles — B

Weller, Sheila
    Carrie Fisher — B

WELLES, GIDEON, 1802-1878
    Symonds, Craig L. *Lincoln and His Admirals* — B

WELLES, ORSON, 1915-1985
    Callow, Simon. ★*Orson Welles* — B
    Karp, Josh. *Orson Welles's Last Movie* — 791.43
    Lebo, Harlan. ★*Citizen Kane* — 791.43

AUTHOR, TITLE, SERIES AND SUBJECT INDEX

McGilligan, Patrick. *Young Orson* — B
Schwartz, A. Brad. ★*Broadcast Hysteria* — 791.44
WELLES, SUMNER, 1892-1961
   Fullilove, Michael. *Rendezvous with Destiny* — 973.917092
WELLINGTON, ARTHUR WELLESLEY, DUKE OF, 1769-1852
   Cornwell, Bernard. *Waterloo* — 940.2
Wellman, Victoria
   Before You Say Anything — 808.5
WELLMAN, VICTORIA, (SPEECHWRITER)
   Wellman, Victoria. *Before You Say Anything* — 808.5
WELLNESS LIFESTYLE
   Hamblin, James. *If Our Bodies Could Talk* — 613
   Raphael, Rina. *The Gospel of Wellness* — 613
The *Wellness* Trap. Harrison, Christy — 613
Wellons, Jay
   All That Moves Us — 617.4
WELLS, IDA B., 1862-1931
   Giddings, Paula. *Ida* — B
   West, Cornel. *Black Prophetic Fire* — 920
Wells, Patricia
   My Master Recipes — 641.5
WELSH PEOPLE
   Thomas, Dylan. *A Child's Christmas in Wales* — B
Welteroth, Elaine
   More Than Enough — B
WELTEROTH, ELAINE, 1986-
   Welteroth, Elaine. *More Than Enough* — B
Welty, Eudora
   One Time, One Place — 976.2
   One Writer's Beginnings — B
WELTY, EUDORA, 1909-2001
   Welty, Eudora. *One Writer's Beginnings* — B
Welz, Adam
   The End of Eden — 577.2
Wenger, Debora Halpern
   Advancing the Story — 070.1
Wenner, Jann
   Like a Rolling Stone — B
WENNER, JANN
   Hagan, Joe. *Sticky Fingers* — B
   Thompson, Hunter S. *Fear and Loathing at Rolling Stone* — 070.1
   Wenner, Jann. *Like a Rolling Stone* — B
Wenzke, Ali
   ★*The Art of Happy Moving* — 648
Werb, Dan
   The Invisible Siege — 614.5
Werker, Kim P.
   Teach Yourself Visually Crochet — 746.43
WERNER, RUTH, 1907-2000
   Macintyre, Ben. ★*Agent Sonya* — B
Wert, Jeffry D.
   Cavalryman of the Lost Cause — B
   Custer — B
Wertheim, L. Jon
   Blood in the Cage — 796.815
   Glory Days — 796.09
   This Is Your Brain on Sports — 796.01
WERTHEIMER, LINDA
   Napoli, Lisa. *Susan, Linda, Nina & Cokie* — 920
Weschler, Lawrence
   And How Are You, Dr. Sacks? — B
WESCHLER, LAWRENCE
   Weschler, Lawrence. *And How Are You, Dr. Sacks?* — B
Wesleyan Poetry [Series]. Jeffers, Honorée Fanonne — 811
Wesleyan poetry [Series]. Valentine, Jean — 811
Wessel, David
   In Fed We Trust — 332.1
The *West*. Mac Sweeney, Naoise — 909
West. Rekdal, Paisley — 811
The *West*. Ward, Geoffrey C. — 978
WEST AFRICA
   Preston, Richard. *Crisis in the Red Zone* — 614.5
   Searcey, Dionne. *In Pursuit of Disobedient Women* — B
WEST AFRICAN PEOPLE
   Bee, Vanessa A. *Home Bound* — B
   Durkin, Hannah. ★*The Survivors of the Clotilda* — 306.362
   Tabor, Nick. *Africatown* — 976.1

WEST BANK (JORDAN RIVER)
   Di Cintio, Marcello. *Pay No Heed to the Rockets* — 956.9405
   Ehrenreich, Ben. *The Way to the Spring* — 956.95
   Grossman, David. *The Yellow Wind* — 956.95
   Nye, Naomi Shihab. *The Tiny Journalist* — 811
   Oren, Michael B. *Six Days of War* — 956.04
   Pappe, Ilan. *The Biggest Prison on Earth* — 956.9405
   Sefarad, Mikhael. *The Wall and the Gate* — 341.48
   Tamimi, Ahed. ★*They Called Me a Lioness* — B
   Thrall, Nathan. ★*A Day in the Life of Abed Salama* — 956.05
WEST BERLIN, GERMANY
   Vogel, Steve. *Betrayal in Berlin* — 327.1273043
West by West. West, Jerry — B
WEST GERMANY
   Taylor, Fred. *The Berlin Wall* — 943
West of Eden. Stein, Jean — 979.4
WEST VIRGINIA
   Bilott, Robert. *Exposure* — 344.04
   Brands, H. W. ★*The Zealot and the Emancipator* — 920
   Eisenberg, Emma Copley. ★*The Third Rainbow Girl* — 364.152
   Eyre, Eric. *Death in Mud Lick* — 362.29
   Gates, Henry Louis. *Colored People* — B
   Horwitz, Tony. ★*Midnight Rising* — 973.7
   Maher, Kris. *Desperate* — 344
   Meyer, Eugene L. *Five for Freedom* — 973.7
   Reynolds, David S. *John Brown, Abolitionist* — B
The *West* Wing and Beyond. Souza, Pete — 917.53
West with the Night. Markham, Beryl — B
WEST, BENJAMIN, 1738-1820
   Staiti, Paul J. *Of Arms and Artists* — B
West, Cait
   ★*Rift* — B
WEST, CAIT, 1988-
   West, Cait. ★*Rift* — B
West, Cornel
   Black Prophetic Fire — 920
WEST, CORNEL, 1953-
   West, Cornel. *Black Prophetic Fire* — 920
West, Jerry
   West by West — B
WEST, JERRY, 1938-2024
   McCallum, Jack. *Golden Days* — 796.323
   West, Jerry. *West by West* — B
West, Kevin
   Saving the Season — 641.4
West, Lindy
   Shrill — 818
   The Witches Are Coming — 305.420973
WEST, LINDY
   West, Lindy. *Shrill* — 818
WEST, MICHAEL (DENTIST)
   Balko, Radley. ★*The Cadaver King and the Country Dentist* — 614
Westad, Odd Arne
   The Cold War — 909.825
Westerhausen, Shelly
   Every Season Is Soup Season — 641.81
The *Western* Canon. Bloom, Harold — 809
WESTERN EUROPE
   Ambrose, Stephen E. ★*Band of Brothers* — 920
   Phillips, Timothy. *Retracing the Iron Curtain* — 909.82
WESTERN EUROPEAN PEOPLE
   Berr, Helene. *The Journal of Helene Berr* — B
   Bertch, Jane. *The French Ingredient* — B
   Bowker, Gordon. ★*James Joyce* — B
   Caruana Galizia, Paul. ★*A Death in Malta* — 364.15
   Chernow, Ron. *The Warburgs* — B
   Craig, Mya-Rose. *Birdgirl* — B
   Dochartaigh, Kerri ni. *Cacophony of Bone* — B
   Drabkin, Ronald. *Beverly Hills Spy* — 940.54
   Finkel, Michael. *The Art Thief* — 364.1628
   Finkelstein, Daniel. *Two Roads Home* — 920
   Friedlander, Saul. *Nazi Germany and the Jews* — 940.53
   Grose, Peter. *A Good Place to Hide* — 940.53
   Herzog, Werner. ★*Every Man for Himself and God Against All* — B
   Iperen, Roxane van. ★*The Sisters of Auschwitz* — 940.53
   Klemperer, Victor. *I Will Bear Witness* — B
   Levi, Primo. *The Reawakening* — B
   Lichtblau, Eric. *Return to the Reich* — B

PUBLIC LIBRARY CORE COLLECTION: NONFICTION
Twentieth Edition

McDonald, Greg (Producer). *Elvis and the Colonel* — 920
Nathan, Joan. ★*My Life in Recipes* — 641.5
Pepin, Jacques. *Art of the Chicken* — 641.665
Pick-Goslar, Hannah Elizabeth. ★*My Friend Anne Frank* — B
Simon, Marie. *Underground in Berlin* — B
Sullivan, Rosemary. *The Betrayal of Anne Frank* — 940.53
Van Es, Bart. *The Cut Out Girl* — B
Weir, Alison. *Queens of the Age of Chivalry* — 920
WESTERN FILMS
Eyman, Scott. *John Wayne* — B
Parke, Henry C. *The Greatest Westerns Ever Made and the People Who Made Them* — 791.43
Stratton, W. K. *The Wild Bunch* — 791.43
The Western Front. Lloyd, Nick — 940.4
WESTERN FRONT (WORLD WAR I)
Lloyd, Nick. *The Western Front* — 940.4
Tuchman, Barbara W. ★*The Guns of August* — 940.4
WESTERN FRONT (WORLD WAR II)
Ambrose, Stephen E. *Band of Brothers* — 920
Ambrose, Stephen E. *Citizen Soldiers* — 940.54
Ambrose, Stephen E. *The Victors* — 940.54
Atkinson, Rick. *The Guns at Last Light* — 940.54
Guarnere, William. *Brothers in Battle, Best of Friends* — B
Isserman, Maurice. *The Winter Army* — 940.54
Kershaw, Alex. *Against All Odds* — 940.54
Miller, Donald L. ★*Masters of the Air* — 940.54
Milton, Giles. *Soldier, Sailor, Frogman, Spy, Airman, Gangster, Kill or Die* — 940.54
Patton, George S. *War as I Knew It* — B
Smith, Starr. *Jimmy Stewart* — B
Winters, Richard D. *Beyond Band of Brothers* — B
WESTERN HEMISPHERE
Dodds Pennock, Caroline. ★*On Savage Shores* — 970.004
Dunn, Jon L. *The Glitter in the Green* — 598.7
Fernandez-Armesto, Felipe. ★*Amerigo* — B
Horwitz, Tony. ★*A Voyage Long and Strange* — 970.01
Miles, Jack. *Religion as We Know It* — 200.9
Platt, Stephen R. *Autumn in the Heavenly Kingdom* — 951
Thomas, Hugh. *Rivers of Gold* — 980
Wilson-Lee, Edward. ★*The Catalogue of Shipwrecked Books* — B
WESTERN RELIGIONS
Aslan, Reza. *God* — 211
Miles, Jack. *Religion as We Know It* — 200.9
Reitman, Janet. *Inside Scientology* — 299
Wright, Lawrence. *Going Clear* — 299
Westheimer, Ruth
The Doctor Is In — B
WESTHEIMER, RUTH, 1928-2024
Westheimer, Ruth. *The Doctor Is In* — B
Westhoff, Ben
Dirty South — 782.421649
Fentanyl, Inc. — 362.29
Original Gangstas — 782.421649
Westover, Tara
★*Educated* — B
WESTOVER, TARA
Westover, Tara. ★*Educated* — B
Wetherall, Tyler
No Way Home — B
WETHERALL, TYLER, 1983-
Wetherall, Tyler. *No Way Home* — B
WETLAND CONSERVATION
Davis, Jack E. *An Everglades Providence* — B
Proulx, Annie. ★*Fen, Bog and Swamp* — 551.41
WETLAND ECOLOGY
Proulx, Annie. ★*Fen, Bog and Swamp* — 551.41
WETLANDS
Goldfarb, Ben. *Eager* — 333.95
Struzik, Edward. *Swamplands* — 577.68
Wexler, Jay
Holy Hullabaloos — 342.7308
Wexler, Stuart
Killing King — 323.092
The Whale. Hoare, Philip — 599.5
Whale Day. Collins, Billy — 811
WHALE SOUNDS
Mustill, Tom. *How to Speak Whale* — 591.59

WHALERS
Clark, Doug Bock. *The Last Whalers* — 639.2
WHALES
Hoare, Philip. *The Whale* — 599.5
Horwitz, Josh. *War of the Whales* — 333.95
Hoyt, Erich. *Encyclopedia of Whales, Dolphins and Porpoises* — 599.5
Mustill, Tom. *How to Speak Whale* — 591.59
Neiwert, David A. *Of Orcas and Men* — 599.53
Pyenson, Nick. *Spying on Whales* — 599.5
Safina, Carl. *Beyond Words* — 591.56
WHALING
Clark, Doug Bock. *The Last Whalers* — 639.2
Hoare, Philip. *The Whale* — 599.5
What A Fish Knows. Balcombe, Jonathan P. — 597.15
★*What A Fool Believes.* McDonald, Michael — B
What About Men?. Moran, Caitlin — 155.3
What About the Baby?. McDermott, Alice — 814
What About This. Stanford, Frank — 811
★*What an Owl Knows.* Ackerman, Jennifer — 598.9
★*What Are Children For?.* Berg, Anastasia — 306.87
What Are You Looking At?. Gompertz, Will — 709
What Becomes a Legend Most. Gefter, Philip — B
★*What Do You Say?.* Stixrud, William R. — 155.4
What Does This Button Do?. Dickinson, Bruce — B
★*What Doesn't Kill Us Makes Us.* Mariani, Mike — 155.9
★*What Doesn't Kill You Makes You Blacker.* Young, Damon — B
What Every Library Director Should Know. Curzon, Susan Carol — 025.1
What everyone needs to know [Series]. Hilborn, Ray — 338.3
What Fresh Hell Is This?. Corinna, Heather — 618.1
What Good Are Bugs?. Waldbauer, Gilbert — 595.717
What Happened. Clinton, Hillary Rodham — 328.73
What Happened to You?. Winfrey, Oprah — 616.85
What Hath God Wrought. Howe, Daniel Walker — 973.5
★*What Have We Done.* Wood, David Bowne — 616.85
★*What Have We Here.* Williams, Billy Dee — B
What I Saw. Roth, Joseph — 943
What I Talk About When I Talk About Running. Murakami, Haruki — B
What If This Were Enough?. Havrilesky, Heather — 152.4
★*What If?.* Munroe, Randall — 500
What If? 2. Munroe, Randall — 500
What Is It All but Luminous. Garfunkel, Art — 782.42164
What Is Japanese Cinema?. Yomota, Inuhiko — 791.43
What Is My Plant Telling Me?. Hay Hinsdale, Emily L. — 635.9
What Is Philosophy?. Ortega Y Gasset, Jose — 101
What Is Real?. Becker, Adam — 920
What Is the Grass. Doty, Mark — 811
What It Took to Win. Kazin, Michael — 324.2736
What Kind of Nation. Simon, James F. — 342.73
What Kind of Woman. Baer, Kate — 811
What Looks Like Bravery. Braitman, Laurel — B
What Money Can't Buy. Sandel, Michael J. — 174
★*What My Bones Know.* Foo, Stephanie — B
What Noise Against the Cane. Bailey, Desiree C. — 811
What People Wore When. Leventon, Melissa — 391.009
What Philosophy Can Do. Gutting, Gary — 100
What Really Happens in Vegas. Patterson, James — 920
What The Best College Students Do. Bain, Ken — 378.1
What The Children Told Us. Spofford, Tim — 150.92
What The Dead Know. Butcher, Barbara — 614
What The Eyes Don't See. Hanna-Attisha, Mona — 615.9
What The Qur'an Meant and Why It Matters. Wills, Garry — 297.1
What The Taliban Told Me. Fritz, Ian — B
What The Wild Sea Can Be. Scales, Helen — 577.7
What to Do When You're New. Rollag, Keith — 158.2
What to Expect the First Year. Murkoff, Heidi Eisenberg — 305.232
★*What to Expect the Second Year.* Murkoff, Heidi Eisenberg — 649
★*What to Expect When You're Expecting.* Murkoff, Heidi Eisenberg — 618.2
What to Feed Your Baby. Altmann, Tanya Remer — 649
What to Read and Why. Prose, Francine — 028
What Truth Sounds Like. Dyson, Michael Eric — 305.800973
What Unites Us. Rather, Dan — 323.6
What We Carry. Lang, Maya — B
What We Knew in the Night. Grimassi, Raven — 133.4
What We Remember Will Be Saved. Saldana, Stephanie — 362.7
What We Talk About When We Talk About Rape. Abdulali, Sohaila — 364.15
What We Will Become. Lemay, Mimi — 306.874
What We Wish Were True. Quinn, Tallu Schuyler — B
★*What We've Become.* Metzl, Jonathan M. — 364.152

AUTHOR, TITLE, SERIES AND SUBJECT INDEX

What White Parents Should Know About Transracial Adoption. Guida-Richards, Melissa   362.734
What Works for Women at Work. Williams, Joan   650.1
What You Have Heard Is True. Forche, Carolyn   B
What You Need to Know About Voting and Why. Wehle, Kim   324.60973
What Your ADHD Child Wishes You Knew. Saline, Sharon   618.92
What Your Food Ate. Montgomery, David R.   631.4
★ *What's Eating Us.* Kazdin, Cole   616.85
★ *What's for Dessert.* Saffitz, Claire   641.86
What's Gotten into You. Levitt, Dan   539.7
What's My Child Thinking?. Carey, Tanith   155.4
What's so Funny?. Sipress, David   B
What's The Economy For, Anyway?. De Graaf, John   330.973
What's Wrong with My Houseplant?. Deardorff, David C   635.9
What's Your Pronoun?. Baron, Dennis E.   425.55
WHEAT-FREE DIET
   Snodgrass, Alex. ★ *The Defined Dish*   641.5
Wheatley, Phillis
   The Poems of Phillis Wheatley   811
WHEATLEY, PHILLIS, 1753-1784
   Jeffers, Honorée Fanonne. *The Age of Phillis*   811
   Waldstreicher, David. *The Odyssey of Phillis Wheatley*   B
Wheelan, Charles J.
   Naked Economics   330
   Naked Statistics   519.5
Wheelan, Joseph
   Midnight in the Pacific   940.54
   ★ *Terrible Swift Sword*   B
WHEELCHAIRS
   Burcaw, Shane. ★ *Laughing at My Nightmare*   B
WHEELS
   Standage, Tom. *A Brief History of Motion*   388
Wheels for the World. Brinkley, Douglas   B
Wheen, Francis
   Karl Marx   B
When. Pink, Daniel H.   153.7
When A Killer Calls. Douglas, John E.   364.152
When Bad Things Happen to Good People. Kushner, Harold S.   296.3
When Brains Dream. Zadra, Antonio   613.7
★ *When Breath Becomes Air.* Kalanithi, Paul   B
When Britain Burned the White House. Snow, Peter   975.3
★ *When Crack Was King.* Ramsey, Donovan X.   362.29
When Death Becomes Life. Mezrich, Joshua D.   617.9
★ *When Einstein Walked with Godel.* Holt, Jim   814
When Everything Changed. Collins, Gail   305.40973
When Evil Lived in Laurel. Wilkie, Curtis   305.8
When Hollywood Had a King. Bruck, Connie   B
When I Am Playing with My Cat, How Do I Know She Is Not Playing with Me?. Frampton, Saul   844
When I Grow Up. Krimstein, Ken   741.5
When I Was Your Age. Thompson, Kenan   B
When in French. Collins, Lauren   B
When Innocence Is Not Enough. Dybdahl, Thomas L.   345.73
When Life Gives You Pears. Gaffigan, Jeannie   B
When McKinsey Comes to Town. Bogdanich, Walt   001
When Montezuma Met Cortes. Restall, Matthew   972
★ *When My Time Comes.* Rehm, Diane   179.7
When Nobody Was Watching. Lloyd, Carli   B
When One Religion Isn't Enough. Bidwell, Duane R.   261.2
When Paris Went Dark. Rosbottom, Ronald C.   944.0816
When Should Law Forgive?. Minow, Martha   345
When The Center Held. Rumsfeld, Donald   973.925092
When The Clock Broke. Ganz, John   320.52
When The Heavens Went on Sale. Vance, Ashlee   621.43
★ *When The Sea Came Alive.* Graff, Garrett M.   940.54
When The Stars Begin to Fall. Johnson, Theodore R.   305.800973
When They Tell You to Be Good. Shakur, Prince   B
When Time Stopped. Neumann, Ariana   B
When Truth Is All You Have. McCloskey, Jim   B
When We Belong. Nagassar, Rohadi   254
When We Walk By. Adler, Kevin F.   362.5
When Women Invented Television. Armstrong, Jennifer Keishin   791.45
When Women Ran Fifth Avenue. Satow, Julie   381.141
When Women Ruled the World. Cooney, Kara   920
When Women Stood. Allred, Alexandra Powe   796.082
Where Cooking Begins. Music, Carla Lalli   641.5
Where Did You Go?. Rasmussen, Christina   133.9
Where Do I Begin?. Duran, Elvis   B

Where I Come From. Bragg, Rick   975
Where I Come From. Sanchez, Aaron   641.5092
Where I Was from. Didion, Joan   979.4
★ *Where Law Ends.* Weissmann, Andrew   324.7
Where Nobody Knows Your Name. Feinstein, John   796.357
Where The Animals Go. Cheshire, James   591.47
Where The Children Take Us. Asher, Zain E.   942.1
Where The Dark and the Light Folks Meet. Sandke, Randy   781.6509
Where The Deer and the Antelope Play. Offerman, Nick   973.93
Where The Heart Beats. Larson, Kay   700.1
Where The Light Enters. Biden, Jill   B
★ *Where The Light Fell.* Yancey, Philip   B
Where The Lightning Strikes. Nabokov, Peter   299.7
Where The Line Is Drawn. Shehadeh, Raja   956.9405
Where The Lost Dogs Go. Charleson, Susannah   636.7
★ *Where The Past Begins.* Tan, Amy   B
Where The Water Goes. Owen, David   917.91
Where The Wind Leads. Chung, Vinh   B
Where Tomorrows Aren't Promised. Anthony, Carmelo   B
Where We Meet the World. Ward, Ashley   612.8
Where You Go Is Not Who You'll Be. Bruni, Frank   378.1
★ *Whereas.* Long Soldier, Layli   811
While Idaho Slept. Appelman, J. Reuben   364.152
While You Were Out. Kissinger, Meg   362.2
Whipple, Chris
   The Fight of His Life   973.934
   The Gatekeepers   973.92092
   The Spymasters   920
Whippman, Ruth
   ★ *Boymom*   305.23
WHIPPMAN, RUTH
   Whippman, Ruth. ★ *Boymom*   305.23
WHISKEY
   Bryson, Lew. *Tasting Whiskey*   663
   Risen, Clay. *American Whiskey, Bourbon, & Rye*   641.2
★ *Whiskey Tender.* Taffa, Deborah Jackson   B
★ *The Whisperers.* Figes, Orlando   306.850947
Whispers in the Tall Grass. Brokhausen, Nick   959.704
WHISTLE BLOWERS
   Elliott, Carl. ★ *The Occasional Human Sacrifice*   174.2
   Ford, Christine Blasey. *One Way Back*   B
   Howley, Kerry. *Bottoms Up and the Devil Laughs*   352.37
   McIntire, Mike. *Champions Way*   796.043
   Mueller, Tom. *Crisis of Conscience*   364.16
   Olsen, Lise. *Code of Silence*   347.73
   Raymond, Edwin. *An Inconvenient Cop*   363.2
WHISTLE BLOWING
   Ford, Christine Blasey. *One Way Back*   B
   Hart, Matt. *Win at All Costs*   338.7
   Mueller, Tom. *Crisis of Conscience*   364.16
Whistler, Catherine
   Venice and Drawing, 1500-1800   741.09
Whitaker, Holly
   ★ *Quit Like a Woman*   616.86
WHITAKER, HOLLY
   Whitaker, Holly. ★ *Quit Like a Woman*   616.86
Whitaker, John O.
   ★ *National Audubon Society Field Guide to North American Mammals*   599.097
Whitaker, Mark
   ★ *Saying It Loud*   973.923
   Smoketown   305.896
Whitby, Andrew
   The Sum of the People   001.4
White & Faded. Parrella-Van Den Berg, Janet   645
White. Ellis, Bret Easton   814
WHITE (COLOR)
   Parrella-Van Den Berg, Janet. *White & Faded*   645
White Apples and the Taste of Stone. Hall, Donald   811
White Blood. Petrosino, Kiki   811
★ *The White Bonus.* McMillan, Tracie   305.8
The White Card. Rankine, Claudia   812
The White Cascade. Krist, Gary   979.7
WHITE COLLAR CRIME
   Behar, Richard. *Madoff*   364.16
   Bensinger, Ken. ★ *Red Card*   796.334
   Enrich, David. *Servants of the Damned*   340.023
   Greenberg, Andy. *Tracers in the Dark*   364.16
   Kolhatkar, Sheelah. *Black Edge*   364.16

PUBLIC LIBRARY CORE COLLECTION: NONFICTION
Twentieth Edition

Maroney, Tyler. *The Modern Detective*	658.4
Michel, Casey. *American Kleptocracy*	364.16
Mitnick, Kevin D. *Ghost in the Wires*	B
Papenfuss, Mary. *American Huckster*	B
Taub, Jennifer. *Big Dirty Money*	364.16
Vaughan, Liam. *Flash Crash*	B
Zuckoff, Mitchell. *Ponzi's Scheme*	B

WHITE COLLAR CRIMINALS

White, Neil. *In the Sanctuary of Outcasts*	B
The White Darkness. Grann, David	B
The White Devil's Daughters. Siler, Julia Flynn	306.3
White Feathers. Heinrich, Bernd	598.8
White Flights. Row, Jess	813
White Fragility. DiAngelo, Robin J.	305.8
White Heat. White, Marco Pierre	641.594
White Hot Hate. Lehr, Dick	363.325

WHITE HOUSE CHIEFS OF STAFF

O'Brien, Phillips Payson. *The Second Most Powerful Man in the World*	B
Whipple, Chris. *The Gatekeepers*	973.92092
White House Diary. Carter, Jimmy	973.926

WHITE HOUSE PRESS SECRETARIES

Psaki, Jen. *Say More*	B
White House Warriors. Gans, John	355
White Lies. Baime, A. J.	B
White Man's Game. Hanes, Stephanie	333.95
The White Mosque. Samatar, Sofia	B
White Mughals. Dalrymple, William	954

WHITE NATIONALISM

Giovanni, Nikki. *Make Me Rain*	811
Neus, Nora. *24 Hours in Charlottesville*	973.933
Signer, Michael. *Cry Havoc*	305.800973
Yacovone, Donald. ★*Teaching White Supremacy*	370.89

WHITE PRIVILEGE

Anderson, Carol. ★*White Rage*	305.800973
Currie, Elliott. *A Peculiar Indifference*	305.800973
DiAngelo, Robin J. *White Fragility*	305.8
Doyle, Glennon. *Untamed*	B
Eddo-Lodge, Reni. *Why I'm No Longer Talking to White People About Race*	305.8
Ellis, Bret Easton. *White*	814
Gilliam, Fatimah. *Race Rules*	305.8
Gomez, Laura E. ★*Inventing Latinos*	305.868
Gordon, Meryl. *Bunny Mellon*	B
Hamad, Ruby. *White Tears/Brown Scars*	305.8
Harrison, Valerie I. *Do Right by Me*	649
Isenberg, Nancy. *White Trash*	305.5
Jefferson, Margo. *Negroland*	305.896
Jones, Robert P. *White Too Long*	277
Laymon, Kiese. ★*Heavy*	B
Livingston, Robert W. *The Conversation*	305.8
Lowry, Beverly. *Deer Creek Drive*	364.152
McGhee, Heather C. ★*The Sum of Us*	305.8
McMillan, Tracie. ★*The White Bonus*	305.8
Mehra, Nishta. *Brown, White, Black*	305.800973
Morrison, Toni. ★*The Origin of Others*	809
Mukantabana, Yseult P. ★*Real Friends Talk About Race*	305.8
Neiman, Garrett. *Rich White Men*	305.5
Oluo, Ijeoma. *Mediocre*	305.310973
Oluo, Ijeoma. ★*So You Want to Talk About Race*	305.800973
Rankine, Claudia. ★*Just Us*	305.896
Ricketts, Rachel. ★*Do Better*	305.800973
Ross, Dax-Devlon. *Letters to My White Male Friends*	305.8
Saad, Layla F. ★*Me and White Supremacy*	305.809
Salesses, Matthew. ★*Craft in the Real World*	808.3
Schuller, Kyla. *The Trouble with White Women*	305.42
Stern, Jessica. *My War Criminal*	341.6
Talusan, Meredith. *Fairest*	305.30973
Tatum, Beverly Daniel. ★*"Why Are All the Black Kids Sitting Together in the Cafeteria?"*	305.800973
Tough, Paul. *The Years That Matter Most*	378.1
Van Ness, Jonathan. *Love That Story*	791.4502
Wise, Tim J. *Dispatches from the Race War*	305.8
★*White Rage*. Anderson, Carol	305.800973

WHITE ROSE (ANTI-NAZI GROUP)

Dumbach, Annette E. *Sophie Scholl and the White Rose*	943.086
Thomas, Gordon. *Defying Hitler*	920
White Shoe. Oller, John	346.73

WHITE SUPREMACISTS

Croke, Ken. *Riding with Evil*	364.106
Egan, Timothy. ★*A Fever in the Heartland*	322.4
Johnson, Kirk W. *The Fishermen and the Dragon*	976.4
Kushner, Jacob. *Look Away*	305.9
Malala, Justice. *The Plot to Save South Africa*	968.07
McWhorter, Diane. *Carry Me Home*	976.1
Phillips, Patrick. *Blood at the Root*	305.8
Stern, Jessica. *My War Criminal*	341.6
Toobin, Jeffrey. ★*Homegrown*	363.325
Williams, Kidada E. *I Saw Death Coming*	973.8

WHITE SUPREMACY MOVEMENTS

Ball, Edward. *Life of a Klansman*	305.8009763
Burrough, Bryan. *Forget the Alamo*	976.043
Darby, Seyward. ★*Sisters in Hate*	305.800973
Fleming, Crystal Marie. *How to Be Less Stupid About Race*	305.800973
Gates, Henry Louis. ★*Stony the Road*	973
Guerrero, Jean. *Hatemonger*	B
Jackson, Kellie Carter. *We Refuse*	323.1196
Lehr, Dick. *White Hot Hate*	363.325
Lowery, Wesley. ★*American Whitelash*	305.8
Neus, Nora. *24 Hours in Charlottesville*	973.933
Signer, Michael. *Cry Havoc*	305.800973
Sommer, Will. ★*Trust the Plan*	973.933
Stevens, Stuart. *It Was All a Lie*	324.2734
Wise, Tim J. *Dispatches from the Race War*	305.8
Zucchino, David. *Wilmington's Lie*	305.8009756
White Tears/Brown Scars. Hamad, Ruby	305.8
White Too Long. Jones, Robert P.	277
White Trash. Isenberg, Nancy	305.5
The White Wall. Flitter, Emily	332.0973
White Women. Jackson, Regina	305.8

White, Adam

★*Motown*	781.644

White, April

Apples to Cider	663

WHITE, BETTY, 1922-2021

Armstrong, Jennifer Keishin. *When Women Invented Television*	791.45

White, Charles

The Life and Times of Little Richard	B

White, Dan

Under the Stars	796.54

White, Dana

How to Manage Your Home Without Losing Your Mind	648

White, E. B.

Essays of E.B. White	814

WHITE, E. B. (ELWYN BROOKS), 1899-1985

Elledge, Scott. *E.B. White*	B

White, Edmund

The Flaneur	944

WHITE, EDMUND, 1940-

White, Edmund. *The Flaneur*	944

White, Elizabeth B.

★*The Counterfeit Countess*	940.53

White, Gayle Jessup

Reclamation	B

WHITE, GAYLE JESSUP, 1957-

White, Gayle Jessup. *Reclamation*	B

WHITE, HARRY DEXTER, 1892-1948

Conway, Edmund. *The Summit*	337.09
Steil, Benn. *The Battle of Bretton Woods*	339.5

White, Kate

Your Guide to Miscarriage & Pregnancy Loss	618.3

White, Marco Pierre

White Heat	641.594

WHITE, MARCO PIERRE

White, Marco Pierre. *White Heat*	641.594

White, Neil

In the Sanctuary of Outcasts	B

WHITE, NEIL, 1960-

White, Neil. *In the Sanctuary of Outcasts*	B

White, Ralph

Getting Out of Saigon	959.704

WHITE, RALPH

White, Ralph. *Getting Out of Saigon*	959.704

White, Richard

Who Killed Jane Stanford?	364.152

AUTHOR, TITLE, SERIES AND SUBJECT INDEX

White, Richard Antoine
   I'm Possible   B
WHITE, RICHARD ANTOINE
   White, Richard Antoine. *I'm Possible*   B
White, Ronald C.
   A. Lincoln   B
   ★*American Ulysses*   B
   Lincoln in Private   B
   On Great Fields   B
White, Ryan
   Jimmy Buffett   782.42164
White, Shane
   Prince of Darkness   B
WHITE, WALTER, 1893-1955
   Baime, A. J. *White Lies*   B
   Swift, Earl. *Hell Put to Shame*   364.15
WHITECHAPEL (LONDON, ENGLAND)
   Cornwell, Patricia Daniels. *Ripper*   364.152
WHITECHAPEL MURDERS, 1888
   Cornwell, Patricia Daniels. *Ripper*   364.152
   Rubenhold, Hallie. ★*The Five*   362.88
Whitefield-Madrano, Autumn
   Face Value   111
Whitehouse, David
   The Alien Perspective   523.1
Whitelaw, Ian
   The History of Fly-Fishing in Fifty Flies   688.7
Whitey Bulger. Cullen, Kevin   B
WHITLEY, HIRAM C., 1834-1875
   Lane, Charles. *Freedom's Detective*   B
Whitlock, Craig
   The Afghanistan Papers   958.104
   ★*Fat Leonard*   364.16
Whitman, John
   Fresh from the Garden   635.9
Whitman, Walt
   ★*Leaves of Grass*   811
   ★*Poetry and Prose*   811
   ★*Selected Poems*   811
WHITMAN, WALT, 1819-1892
   Doty, Mark. *What Is the Grass*   811
   Martin, Justin. *Rebel Souls*   920
Whitmer, Jamie Davis
   America's Most Haunted Hotels   133.1
Whitney, Craig R.
   All the Stops   786.5
Whitney, Emerson
   Heaven   B
WHITNEY, EMERSON
   Whitney, Emerson. *Heaven*   B
Whittle, Lisa
   God Knows   231
Whittock, Martyn
   Mayflower Lives   974.4
Who Built That?. Cornille, Didier   720
Who built that? [Series]. Cornille, Didier   720
Who Can Hold the Sea. Hornfischer, James D.   359.00973
Who Does That Bitch Think She Is?. Seligman, Craig   792.02
Who Freed the Slaves?. Richards, Leonard L.   342.7308
Who Gets in and Why. Selingo, Jeffrey J.   378.1
Who Gets What—And Why. Roth, Alvin E.   330.01
Who Killed Jane Stanford?. White, Richard   364.152
Who Lost Russia?. Conradi, Peter J.   947.086
Who Needs God. Kushner, Harold S.   296.7
Who Owns This Sentence?. Bellos, David   346.73
Who Rules the World?. Chomsky, Noam   327.73
Who Shot Rock & Roll. Buckland, Gail   779
Who Shot Sports. Buckland, Gail   779
★*Who's Afraid of Gender?*. Butler, Judith   305.3
★*Who's Afraid of Virginia Woolf?*. Albee, Edward   812
Who's Raising the Kids?. Linn, Susan   649
Who's Who in the Jewish Bible. Mandel, David   B
Whole Food Cooking Every Day. Chaplin, Amy   641.3
The Whole Smiths Good Food Cookbook. Smith, Michelle   641.5
The Whole30 Fast & Easy. Hartwig, Melissa   641.5
The Whole30 Friends & Family. Urban, Melissa   641.5
The Whole30 Slow Cooker. Hartwig, Melissa   641.5
Wholehearted Faith. Evans, Rachel Held   248.4

WHOOPING CRANES
   Mooallem, Jon. *Wild Ones*   333.95
★*Why Are All the Black Kids Sitting Together in the Cafeteria?"*. Tatum, Beverly Daniel   305.800973
Why Be Jewish?. Bronfman, Edgar M.   296
★*Why Bob Dylan Matters*. Thomas, Richard F.   782.42164
Why Buddhism Is True. Wright, Robert   294.3
Why Didn't We Riot?. Bailey, Issac J.   305.800973
Why Didn't You Tell Me?. Wong, Carmen Rita   B
Why Dinosaurs Matter. Lacovara, Kenneth   567.9
★*Why Does Everything Have to Be About Race?*. Boykin, Keith   305.8
Why Does the World Exist?. Holt, Jim   113
Why Fathers Cry at Night. Alexander, Kwame   B
Why Fish Don't Exist. Miller, Lulu   B
Why Football Matters. Edmundson, Mark   B
Why Homer Matters. Nicolson, Adam   883
Why I Came West. Bass, Rick   333.78
Why I'm No Longer Talking to White People About Race. Eddo-Lodge, Reni   305.8
Why Jazz Happened. Myers, Marc   781.65
Why Not Me?. Kaling, Mindy   B
Why People Believe Weird Things. Shermer, Michael   133
Why Read Moby-Dick?. Philbrick, Nathaniel   813
★*Why Religion?*. Pagels, Elaine H.   B
Why The Allies Won. Overy, R. J.   940.53
Why This World. Moser, Benjamin   B
Why Time Flies. Burdick, Alan   529
Why We Can't Sleep. Calhoun, Ada   305.244
Why We Can't Wait. King, Martin Luther   305.8
Why We Cook. Gardner, Lindsay   641.5
Why We Do It. Eldredge, Niles   155.3
Why We Fight. Blattman, Christopher   303.6
★*Why We Love Baseball*. Posnanski, Joe   796.357
Why We Make Mistakes. Hallinan, Joseph T.   153
Why We Meditate. Goleman, Daniel   158.1
Why We Read. Reed, Shannon   028
★*Why We Remember*. Ranganath, Charan   153.1
Why We Swim. Tsui, Bonnie   797.2
★*Why We're Polarized*. Klein, Ezra   306.0973
Why You Like It. Gasser, Nolan   781.1
Why?. Hayes, Peter   940.53
Why?. Livio, Mario   153.3
Whyte, Kenneth
   Hoover   B
   The Uncrowned King   B
WICCANS
   Garcia, Amanda Yates. *Initiated*   B
The Wicked Healthy Cookbook. Sarno, Chad   651.56
Wicked Plants. Stewart, Amy   581.6
Wickenden, Dorothy
   The Agitators   920
Wicker, Alden
   ★*To Dye For*   746
Wicker, Marcus
   Silencer   811
Wickersham, Seth
   ★*It's Better to Be Feared*   796.332
Wickham, Chris
   The Inheritance of Rome   940.1
Widder, Edith
   Below the Edge of Darkness   551.46092
WIDDER, EDITH
   Widder, Edith. *Below the Edge of Darkness*   551.46092
Wide Awake. Grinspan, Jon   973.7
★*The Wide Wide Sea*. Sides, Hampton   910.92
Wides-Munoz, Laura
   The Making of a Dream   920
Widmer, Edward L.
   Lincoln on the Verge   B
   Martin Van Buren   B
The Widow Washington. Saxton, Martha   B
WIDOWERS
   Corrigan, Kelly. *Glitter and Glue*   B
   McInerny, Nora. *The Hot Young Widows Club*   155.9
   Rosenthal, Jason. *My Wife Said You May Want to Marry Me*   B
WIDOWS
   Asher, Zain E. *Where the Children Take Us*   942.1
   Couric, Katie. *Going There*   B

PUBLIC LIBRARY CORE COLLECTION: NONFICTION
Twentieth Edition

Deraniyagala, Sonali. *Wave*	B
Didion, Joan. ★*The Year of Magical Thinking*	B
Ephron, Delia. *Left on Tenth*	B
Henderson, Artis. *Unremarried Widow*	B
King, Coretta Scott. ★*My Life, My Love, My Legacy*	B
Lin, Amy. *Here After*	B
Locke, Tembi. ★*From Scratch*	B
Mazzeo, Tilar J. ★*Eliza Hamilton*	B
McInerny, Nora. *The Hot Young Widows Club*	155.9
Pablo Cruz, Rosayra. *The Book of Rosy*	B
Pagels, Elaine H. ★*Why Religion?*	B
Porizkova, Paulina. *No Filter*	B
Rehm, Diane. *On My Own*	B
Saxton, Martha. *The Widow Washington*	B
Seager, Sara. *The Smallest Lights in the Universe*	B
Shirley, Craig. *Mary Ball Washington*	B
Smith, Patti. ★*M Train*	B
Vaughn, Ellen Santilli. ★*Becoming Elisabeth Elliot*	B
Williams, Tennessee. ★*A Streetcar Named Desire*	812

WIEBE, JOY
Butcher, Amy. *Mothertrucker*	B

Wiedeman, Reeves
Billion Dollar Loser	333.33

Wiederhorn, Jon
Louder Than Hell	781.6609

Wiehl, Lis W.
Hunting Charles Manson	364.152
Hunting the Unabomber	364.152
A Spy in Plain Sight	327.1247

Wiencek, Henry
Master of the Mountain	973.4

WIENER FAMILY
Finkelstein, Daniel. *Two Roads Home*	920

Wiener, Anna
★*Uncanny Valley*	B

WIENER, ANNA, 1987-
Wiener, Anna. ★*Uncanny Valley*	B

Wiesel, Elie
All Rivers Run to the Sea	B
And the Sea Is Never Full	B
★*Night*	B

WIESEL, ELIE, 1928-2016
Burger, Ariel. *Witness*	848
Wiesel, Elie. *All Rivers Run to the Sea*	B
Wiesel, Elie. *And the Sea Is Never Full*	B
Wiesel, Elie. ★*Night*	B

Wieseltier, Leon
Kaddish	296.4

WIESELTIER, LEON
Wieseltier, Leon. *Kaddish*	296.4

Wiesenthal, Simon
★*The Sunflower*	179.7

WIESENTHAL, SIMON
Wiesenthal, Simon. ★*The Sunflower*	179.7

WIFE-KILLING
McGinniss, Joe. *Fatal Vision*	B
Wifedom. Funder, Anna	B

Wiggins, Christopher L.
How Data Happened	310

Wiking, Meik
The Art of Making Memories	153.1
The Little Book of Hygge	158.1
The Little Book of Lykke	646.7

Wilbur, Matika
Project 562	970.004

Wilbur, Richard
Anterooms	811
★*Collected Poems, 1943-2004*	811

Wilczek, Frank
Fundamentals	530.01

★*Wild*. Strayed, Cheryl	B
The Wild + Free Family. Arment, Ainsley	649
Wild and Crazy Guys. De Semlyen, Nick	920
A Wild and Precious Life. Windsor, Edie	B

WILD ANIMAL COLLECTING
Attenborough, David. *Adventures of a Young Naturalist*	B

WILD ANIMAL SMUGGLING
Orenstein, Ronald I. *Ivory, Horn and Blood*	333.95

WILD ANIMALS AS PETS
Orlean, Susan. *On Animals*	590
Wild Bill. Clavin, Thomas	B
Wild Bill Donovan. Waller, Douglas C.	B
The Wild Blue. Ambrose, Stephen E.	940.54
The Wild Bunch. Stratton, W. K.	791.43

WILD CATS
Losos, Jonathan B. *The Cat's Meow*	636.8
Williams, Jim. *Path of the Puma*	599.75

WILD FLOWERS
Spira, Timothy P. *Waterfalls and Wildflowers in the Southern Appalachians*	796.5109756

WILD FOODS
Borsato, Diane. *Mushrooming*	579.6
Rodriguez, Ashley. *Rooted Kitchen*	641.5
★*Wild Girls*. Miles, Tiya	304.2

WILD HORSES
Prior-Palmer, Lara. *Rough Magic*	798.4
A Wild Idea. Franklin, Jonathan	B
Wild Interiors. Carter, Hilton	747.98
A Wild Justice. Mandery, Evan J.	345.73
Wild Life. Wynn-Grant, Rae	B

WILD MEN
Reel, Monte. *The Last of the Tribe*	981
Wild New World. Flores, Dan L.	591.9709
Wild Nights. Reiss, Benjamin	616.8
Wild Ones. Mooallem, Jon	333.95
Wild Ride. Lashinsky, Adam	388.4
The Wild Silence. Winn, Raynor	B
★*Wild Swans*. Chang, Jung	B
★*Wild Thing*. Norman, Philip	B
Wild Things, Wild Places. Alexander, Jane	333.95
The Wild Trees. Preston, Richard	585

WILD WEST SHOWS
Brown, Dee. *The American West*	978
Warren, Louis S. *Buffalo Bill's America*	B

Wilde, Oscar
The Artist as Critic	809
★*The Importance of Being Earnest and Other Plays*	822

WILDE, OSCAR, 1854-1900
Ellmann, Richard. *Oscar Wilde*	B
O'Sullivan, Emer. *The Fall of the House of Wilde*	B
Sturgis, Matthew. *Oscar Wilde*	B
Toibin, Colm. *Mad, Bad, Dangerous to Know*	920

Wilder, Craig Steven
Ebony and Ivy	379.2

Wilder, Laura Ingalls
Pioneer Girl	B
The Selected Letters of Laura Ingalls Wilder	B

WILDER, LAURA INGALLS, 1867-1957
Fraser, Caroline. ★*Prairie Fires*	B
McDowell, Marta. *The World of Laura Ingalls Wilder*	813
Wilder, Laura Ingalls. *Pioneer Girl*	B
Wilder, Laura Ingalls. *The Selected Letters of Laura Ingalls Wilder*	B

Wilder, Thornton
Our Town	812
Thornton Wilder	812

WILDER, THORNTON, 1897-1975
Niven, Penelope. *Thornton Wilder*	B

Wilder-Taylor, Stefanie
★*Drunk-Ish*	B

WILDERNESS AREAS
Black, George. *Empire of Shadows*	978.7
Butcher, Amy. *Mothertrucker*	B
Dial, Roman. *The Adventurer's Son*	917.286
Douglas, Marjory Stoneman. *The Everglades*	975.9
Flyn, Cal. ★*Islands of Abandonment*	333.73
Foster, Craig. ★*Amphibious Soul*	155.9
Kirkby, Bruce. *Blue Sky Kingdom*	954.96
Lankford, Andrea. *Trail of the Lost*	363.2
Miles, Tiya. ★*Wild Girls*	304.2
Moore, Kathleen Dean. *Earth's Wild Music*	576.8
Offerman, Nick. *Where the Deer and the Antelope Play*	973.93
Pyle, Robert Michael. *Nature Matrix*	508
Sprinkle, Timothy. *Lost and Stranded*	613.6
Thoreau, Henry David. ★*Walden, Or, Life in the Woods*	813
Van Hemert, Caroline. *The Sun Is a Compass*	979.8

AUTHOR, TITLE, SERIES AND SUBJECT INDEX

WILDERNESS LIVING
   Sprinkle, Timothy. *Lost and Stranded*   613.6
WILDERNESS SURVIVAL
   Canterbury, Dave. *Bushcraft 101*   613.6
   Delorme, Geoffroy. *Deer Man*   599.65
   Finkel, Michael. *The Stranger in the Woods*   B
   Grylls, Bear. *Never Give Up*   B
   Harrison, Jim. *The Search for the Genuine*   814
   Krakauer, Jon. *Classic Krakauer*   814
   Krakauer, Jon. *Into the Wild*   917.9804
   McGrath, Ben. *Riverman*   797.122
   Messenger, Alex. *The Twenty-Ninth Day*   B
   Murphy, Brian. *81 Days Below Zero*   940.54
   Niven, Jennifer. *Ada Blackjack*   B
   O'Brady, Colin. ★*The Impossible First*   919.8904
   Sprinkle, Timothy. *Lost and Stranded*   613.6
   Stark, Peter. *Astoria*   979.5
   Wallace, Scott. *The Unconquered*   981
   Winn, Raynor. ★*The Salt Path*   B
The Wilderness Warrior. Brinkley, Douglas   B
Wilderson, Frank B.
   Afropessimism   B
WILDERSON, FRANK B., III, 1956-
   Wilderson, Frank B. *Afropessimism*   B
WILDFIRE FIGHTERS
   Martin, Manjula. *The Last Fire Season*   B
WILDFIRES
   Bittle, Jake. ★*The Great Displacement*   362.87
   Blunt, Katherine. *California Burning*   333.793
   Edwards, Adrienne L. *Firescaping Your Home*   635.9
   Gee, Alastair. *Fire in Paradise*   363.37
   Johnson, Lizzie. ★*Paradise*   363.37
   Martin, Manjula. *The Last Fire Season*   B
   Vaillant, John. ★*Fire Weather*   363.37
Wildland. Osnos, Evan   973.93
WILDLIFE
   Attenborough, David. *Adventures of a Young Naturalist*   B
   Barrow, Mark V. *Nature's Ghosts*   333.95
   Cheshire, James. *Where the Animals Go*   591.47
   Darlington, Miriam. *Otter Country*   599.769
   Delorme, Geoffroy. *Deer Man*   599.65
   Dickie, Gloria. *Eight Bears*   599.78
   Flores, Dan L. *Wild New World*   591.9709
   Goldfarb, Ben. *Crossings*   333.77
   Graham, Jasmin. *Sharks Don't Sink*   597.3
   Heinrich, Bernd. *A Naturalist at Large*   508
   Howsare, Erika. *The Age of Deer*   599.65
   Jones, Darryl N. *The Birds at My Table*   598.072
   Macdonald, Helen. ★*Vesper Flights*   508
   Macfarlane, Robert. *The Lost Spells*   811
   McIntyre, Rick. *The Reign of Wolf 21*   599.773
   Montgomery, Sy. ★*Of Time and Turtles*   597.92
   Mooallem, Jon. *Wild Ones*   333.95
   Moore, Kathleen Dean. *Earth's Wild Music*   576.8
   Nezhukumatathil, Aimee. *World of Wonders*   590
   Orlean, Susan. *On Animals*   590
   Preston, Christopher J. *Tenacious Beasts*   591.68
   Preston, Douglas J. ★*The Lost City of the Monkey God*   972.85
   Renner, Rebecca. ★*Gator Country*   364.16
   Safina, Carl. ★*Alfie and Me*   598.9
   Struzik, Edward. *Swamplands*   577.68
   Wallace, Christopher. *Twentieth-Century Man*   B
   Williams, Jim. *Path of the Puma*   599.75
WILDLIFE ATTRACTING
   Lavelle, Christine. *How to Create a Wildlife Garden*   635
WILDLIFE BIOLOGISTS
   Keim, Brandon. *Meet the Neighbors*   591.5
   Pittman, Craig. *Cat Tale*   599.75
WILDLIFE CONSERVATION
   Alexander, Jane. *Wild Things, Wild Places*   333.95
   Barrow, Mark V. *Nature's Ghosts*   333.95
   Blakeslee, Nate. *American Wolf*   599.773
   Dickie, Gloria. *Eight Bears*   599.78
   Duncan, Dayton. *Blood Memory*   599.64
   Flannery, Tim F. *Europe*   508.4
   Fossey, Dian. ★*Gorillas in the Mist*   599.884
   Fowlds, Grant. *Saving the Last Rhinos*   599.66
   Goldfarb, Ben. *Crossings*   333.77

   Goldfarb, Ben. *Eager*   333.95
   Goodall, Jane. ★*The Ten Trusts*   333.95
   Graham, Jasmin. *Sharks Don't Sink*   597.3
   Gyllenhaal, Anders. *A Wing and a Prayer*   639.97
   Hanes, Stephanie. *White Man's Game*   333.95
   Heacox, Kim. *Rhythm of the Wild*   979.8
   Keim, Brandon. *Meet the Neighbors*   591.5
   Malarkey, Tucker. *Stronghold*   639.2
   Mooallem, Jon. *Wild Ones*   333.95
   Muir, John. *The Story of My Boyhood and Youth*   B
   Neiwert, David A. *Of Orcas and Men*   599.53
   O'Connor, Maura R. *Resurrection Science*   591.68
   Orenstein, Ronald I. *Ivory, Horn and Blood*   333.95
   Owens, Delia. *The Eye of the Elephant*   639.9
   Pittman, Craig. *Cat Tale*   599.75
   Preston, Christopher J. *Tenacious Beasts*   591.68
   Renner, Rebecca. ★*Gator Country*   364.16
   Vaillant, John. *The Tiger*   599.756
   Welz, Adam. *The End of Eden*   577.2
   Williams, Jim. *Path of the Puma*   599.75
   Williams, Kale. *The Loneliest Polar Bear*   599.786
   Wynn-Grant, Rae. *Wild Life*   B
WILDLIFE CONSERVATIONISTS
   Brinkley, Douglas. *Rightful Heritage*   B
   Brinkley, Douglas. *The Wilderness Warrior*   B
   Fowlds, Grant. *Saving the Last Rhinos*   599.66
   Morris, Edmund. ★*The Rise of Theodore Roosevelt*   B
   Muir, John. *The Story of My Boyhood and Youth*   B
   Owens, Delia. *The Eye of the Elephant*   639.9
   Pittman, Craig. *Cat Tale*   599.75
WILDLIFE CRIMES
   Fowlds, Grant. *Saving the Last Rhinos*   599.66
   Hammer, Joshua. *The Falcon Thief*   364.16
WILDLIFE HABITAT DESTRUCTION
   Barnett, Cynthia. ★*The Sound of the Sea*   591.47
   Vaillant, John. *The Tiger*   599.756
WILDLIFE MANAGEMENT
   Blakeslee, Nate. *American Wolf*   599.773
   Roach, Mary. ★*Fuzz*   591.5
WILDLIFE PHOTOGRAPHY
   Sartore, Joel. ★*The Photo Ark*   779
WILDLIFE RECOVERY
   Duncan, Dayton. *Blood Memory*   599.64
   Flyn, Cal. ★*Islands of Abandonment*   333.73
WILDLIFE REFUGES
   Fowlds, Grant. *Saving the Last Rhinos*   599.66
   Hiss, Tony. ★*Rescuing the Planet*   333.75
   Marcum, Diana. *The Fallen Stones*   B
WILDLIFE REINTRODUCTION
   Preston, Christopher J. *Tenacious Beasts*   591.68
WILDLIFE RESCUE
   Fowlds, Grant. *Saving the Last Rhinos*   599.66
   Montgomery, Sy. *The Hummingbirds' Gift*   598.7
WILDLIFE RESEARCHERS
   Keim, Brandon. *Meet the Neighbors*   591.5
WILES, ANDREW, 1953-
   Singh, Simon. *Fermat's Enigma*   512
Wilford, Hugh
   The CIA   327.1273
Wilhide, Elizabeth
   Scandinavian Home   728
Wilkerson, Isabel
   ★*Caste*   305.5
   ★*The Warmth of Other Suns*   304.80973
WILKES, JOHN, 1725-1797
   Moore, Peter. *Life, Liberty, and the Pursuit of Happiness*   199
Wilkie, Curtis
   When Evil Lived in Laurel   305.8
WILKINS, MAURICE, 1916-2004
   Markel, Howard. *The Secret of Life*   572.86
WILKINS, MESANNIE
   Letts, Elizabeth. ★*The Ride of Her Life*   B
Wilkins, Robert L.
   Long Road to Hard Truth   069
Wilkinson, Alec
   The Protest Singer   B
Wilkinson, Crystal
   Praisesong for the Kitchen Ghosts   641.5975

PUBLIC LIBRARY CORE COLLECTION: NONFICTION
Twentieth Edition

WILKINSON, CRYSTAL
   Wilkinson, Crystal. *Praisesong for the Kitchen Ghosts* — 641.5975
Wilkinson, Frances C.
   The Complete Guide to Acquisitions Management — 025.2
Wilkinson, Karen
   The Art of Tinkering — 500
WILKINSON, RAVEN
   Copeland, Misty. *The Wind at My Back* — B
Wilkinson, Richard H.
   ★*The Complete Gods and Goddesses of Ancient Egypt* — 299
Wilkinson, Toby A. H.
   The Nile — 962
   ★*The Rise and Fall of Ancient Egypt* — 932
   A World Beneath the Sands — 932
Wilkman, Jon
   Screening Reality — 070.1
WILL
   Goleman, Daniel. *Focus* — 153.7
   ★*Will*. Smith, Will — B
Will Eisner. Schumacher, Michael — 741.5
Will I Ever Be Good Enough?. McBride, Karyl — 616.85
Will I See My Dog in Heaven?. Wintz, Jack — 231.7
★*Will in the World*. Greenblatt, Stephen — B
Will My Cat Eat My Eyeballs?. Doughty, Caitlin — 306.9
The Will of the People. Friedman, Barry — 347.73
Will The Circle Be Unbroken?. Terkel, Studs — 128
The Will to Power. Nietzsche, Friedrich Wilhelm — 193
Will You Miss Me When I'm Gone?. Zwonitzer, Mark — 920
Will, George F.
   The Conservative Sensibility — 320.520973
Willa Cather. Woodress, James Leslie — B
Willenbrink, Mark
   Drawing for the Absolute Beginner — 741.2
Willetts, Paul
   King Con — B
Willeumier, Kristen
   ★*Biohack Your Brain* — 612.8
William Henry Harrison. Collins, Gail — B
WILLIAM I, KING OF ENGLAND, 1027 OR 1028-1087
   Morris, Marc. *The Norman Conquest* — 942.02
WILLIAM II, GERMAN EMPEROR, 1859-1941
   Carter, Miranda. *George, Nicholas and Wilhelm* — 940.3
   Clay, Catrine. *King, Kaiser, Tsar* — B
WILLIAM III KING OF GREAT BRITAIN 1650-1702
   Ackroyd, Peter. *Revolution* — 941.07
William James. Richardson, Robert D. — B
William Penn. Murphy, Andrew R. — B
William Tecumseh Sherman. McDonough, James L. — B
WILLIAMS FAMILY
   Demos, John. *The Unredeemed Captive* — 973.2
Williams, Bari A.
   Seen yet Unseen — 338.4
WILLIAMS, BARI A.
   Williams, Bari A. *Seen yet Unseen* — 338.4
Williams, Billy Dee
   ★*What Have We Here* — B
WILLIAMS, BILLY DEE, 1937-
   Williams, Billy Dee. ★*What Have We Here* — B
Williams, Bunny
   On Garden Style — 712
Williams, C. K.
   ★*Collected Poems* — 811
   Falling Ill — 811
Williams, David
   Bitterly Divided — 973.7
WILLIAMS, EUNICE, 1696-1786
   Demos, John. *The Unredeemed Captive* — 973.2
WILLIAMS, EVAN, 1972-
   Bilton, Nick. *Hatching Twitter* — 006.7
Williams, Florence
   Heartbreak — 306.7
   The Nature Fix — 155.9
WILLIAMS, FLORENCE, 1967-
   Williams, Florence. *Heartbreak* — 306.7
WILLIAMS, HANK, SR., 1923-1953
   Hemphill, Paul. *Lovesick Blues* — B
Williams, Jack
   ★*The Ams Weather Book* — 551.5

Williams, Jay
   Life Is Not an Accident — B
WILLIAMS, JAY
   Williams, Jay. *Life Is Not an Accident* — B
Williams, Jim
   Path of the Puma — 599.75
WILLIAMS, JIM, D. 1990
   Berendt, John. *Midnight in the Garden of Good and Evil* — 975.8
Williams, Joan
   What Works for Women at Work — 650.1
WILLIAMS, JOHN, 1664-1729
   Demos, John. *The Unredeemed Captive* — 973.2
Williams, Juan
   Eyes on the Prize — 323.4
   I'll Find a Way or Make One — 378.73
   This Far by Faith — 200
   Thurgood Marshall — B
WILLIAMS, JULIE, -1996
   Miles, Kathryn. *Trailed* — 364.152
Williams, Kale
   The Loneliest Polar Bear — 599.786
Williams, Kate
   Ambition and Desire — B
Williams, Kidada E.
   I Saw Death Coming — 973.8
Williams, Lucinda
   Don't Tell Anybody the Secrets I Told You — B
WILLIAMS, LUCINDA
   Williams, Lucinda. *Don't Tell Anybody the Secrets I Told You* — B
Williams, Marlena
   Night Mother — 791.43
Williams, Mary
   The Lost Daughter — B
WILLIAMS, MARY 1967-
   Williams, Mary. *The Lost Daughter* — B
WILLIAMS, MARY MILDRED, 1847-1921
   Morgan-Owens, Jessie. *Girl in Black and White* — B
Williams, Michael Kenneth
   Scenes from My Life — B
WILLIAMS, MICHAEL KENNETH
   Williams, Michael Kenneth. *Scenes from My Life* — B
Williams, Michelle
   Checking In — B
WILLIAMS, MICHELLE (TENITRA MICHELLE)
   Williams, Michelle. *Checking In* — B
Williams, Odette
   Simple Cake — 641.86
   ★*Simple Pasta* — 641.822
Williams, Patricia
   Rabbit — B
WILLIAMS, PATRICIA (COMEDIAN)
   Williams, Patricia. *Rabbit* — B
Williams, Richard
   The Animator's Survival Kit — 778
   Black and White — B
WILLIAMS, RICHARD, 1942-
   Williams, Richard. *Black and White* — B
WILLIAMS, ROBIN, 1951-2014
   Itzkoff, Dave. ★*Robin* — B
WILLIAMS, ROGER, 1604?-1683
   Barry, John M. *Roger Williams and the Creation of the American Soul* — 974.5
   Warren, James A. *God, War, and Providence* — 974.5
WILLIAMS, SERENA, 1981-
   Williams, Richard. *Black and White* — B
Williams, Sophie
   Anti-Racist Ally — 305.8
WILLIAMS, TED, 1918-2002
   Bradlee, Ben. *The Kid* — B
   Halberstam, David. *The Teammates* — B
Williams, Tennessee
   Plays, 1937-1955 — 812
   Plays, 1957-1980 — 812
   ★*A Streetcar Named Desire* — 812
WILLIAMS, TENNESSEE, 1911-1983
   Laughlin, James. *The Luck of Friendship* — B
Williams, Terry Tempest
   Erosion — 814

AUTHOR, TITLE, SERIES AND SUBJECT INDEX

WILLIAMS, VENUS, 1980-
   Williams, Richard. *Black and White* — B
Williams, Wendy
   The Language of Butterflies — 595.78
Williams, William Carlos
   Paterson — 811
Williams, Wyatt
   Springer Mountain — 394.1
Williams, Zach
   Rescue Story — B
WILLIAMS, ZACH
   Williams, Zach. *Rescue Story* — B
Williamson, Edwin
   Borges — B
Williamson, Elizabeth
   ★*Sandy Hook* — 364.152
Williamson, Marianne
   Tears to Triumph — 299
Willie & Joe. Mauldin, Bill — 741.5
Willie Mays. Hirsch, James S. — B
Willink, Jocko
   Discipline Equals Freedom — 158.1
Willis, Deborah
   ★*The Black Civil War Soldier* — 973.7
   Envisioning Emancipation — 973.7
   Reflections in Black — 770
Willis, Raquel
   The Risk It Takes to Bloom — B
WILLIS, RAQUEL
   Willis, Raquel. *The Risk It Takes to Bloom* — B
WILLKIE, WENDELL L. (WENDELL LEWIS), 1892-1944
   Fullilove, Michael. *Rendezvous with Destiny* — 973.917092
Willner, Nina
   Forty Autumns — B
WILLNER, NINA, 1961-
   Willner, Nina. *Forty Autumns* — B
Willpower Doesn't Work. Hardy, Benjamin — 158
WILLS
   May, Gregory. *A Madman's Will* — 973.5
Wills, Clair
   ★*Missing Persons* — 929.2
WILLS, CLAIR
   Wills, Clair. ★*Missing Persons* — 929.2
Wills, Garry
   Certain Trumpets — 303.3
   The Future of the Catholic Church with Pope Francis — 282.09
   James Madison — B
   Lincoln at Gettysburg — 973.7
   Saint Augustine — B
   What the Qur'an Meant and Why It Matters — 297.1
Wills, Shomari
   Black Fortunes — 920
Wilmington's Lie. Zucchino, David — 305.8009756
WILMINGTON, NORTH CAROLINA
   Zucchino, David. *Wilmington's Lie* — 305.8009756
★*Wilson*. Berg, A. Scott — B
Wilson, A'ja
   ★*Dear Black Girls* — 158.1
Wilson, A. N.
   C.S. Lewis — 823
   The Mystery of Charles Dickens — 823
   Victoria — B
Wilson, August
   Fences — 812
   King Hedley II — 812
   Ma Rainey's Black Bottom — 812
   The Piano Lesson — 812
   Two Trains Running — 812
WILSON, AUGUST
   Hartigan, Patti. *August Wilson* — B
Wilson, Bee
   The Way We Eat Now — 641.01
Wilson, Brian
   I Am Brian Wilson — B
WILSON, BRIAN, 1942-
   Wilson, Brian. *I Am Brian Wilson* — B
Wilson, Chris
   The Master Plan — B

WILSON, CHRIS, 1978-
   Wilson, Chris. *The Master Plan* — B
Wilson, David Sloan
   Evolution for Everyone — 576.801
Wilson, Derek
   Out of the Storm — B
Wilson, Derek K.
   A Magical World — 261.55
Wilson, Edward O.
   Consilience — 121
   The Diversity of Life — 333.95
   The Future of Life — 333.95
   Genesis — 591.5
   Half-Earth — 333.95
   In Search of Nature — 113
   ★*Letters to a Young Scientist* — 570.92
   The Meaning of Human Existence — 128
   ★*The Social Conquest of Earth* — 599.93
   Tales from the Ant World — 595.79
   A Window on Eternity — 333.95
WILSON, EDWARD O.
   Rhodes, Richard. *Scientist* — B
   Wilson, Edward O. ★*Letters to a Young Scientist* — 570.92
   Wilson, Edward O. *Tales from the Ant World* — 595.79
Wilson, Ellen Judy
   Encyclopedia of the Enlightenment — 940.2
Wilson, F. Perry
   How Medicine Works and When It Doesn't — 610.69
WILSON, HORACE, 1882-1972
   Phillips, Adrian. *Fighting Churchill, Appeasing Hitler* — 327.41043
Wilson, Jessica
   It's Always Been Ours — 613
WILSON, JESSICA
   Wilson, Jessica. *It's Always Been Ours* — 613
Wilson, Joseph S.
   The Bees in Your Backyard — 595.79
Wilson, Katherine
   Only in Naples — B
WILSON, KATHERINE, 1974-
   Wilson, Katherine. *Only in Naples* — B
WILSON, MAURICE, 1898-1934
   Caesar, Ed. *The Moth and the Mountain* — B
Wilson, Melba
   ★*Melba's American Comfort* — 641.5973
Wilson, Peter H.
   Heart of Europe — 943
Wilson, Rebel
   Rebel Rising — B
Wilson, Rick
   Running Against the Devil — 973.933
Wilson, Robert
   Barnum — B
   Mathew Brady — B
Wilson, Sarah
   First, We Make the Beast Beautiful — 616.85
WILSON, SARAH, 1974-
   Wilson, Sarah. *First, We Make the Beast Beautiful* — 616.85
Wilson, Victoria
   A Life of Barbara Stanwyck — B
WILSON, WOODROW, 1856-1924
   Berg, A. Scott. ★*Wilson* — B
   Brands, H. W. *Woodrow Wilson* — B
   Cooper, John Milton. *Woodrow Wilson* — B
   Herman, Arthur. *1917* — 940.3
   MacMillan, Margaret. *Paris 1919* — 940.3
   Neu, Charles E. *Colonel House* — B
   O'Toole, Patricia. *The Moralist* — B
Wilson-Lee, Edward
   ★*The Catalogue of Shipwrecked Books* — B
WILZIG, SIEGBERT B.
   Greene, Joshua. *Unstoppable* — B
Wiman, Christian
   He Held Radical Light — 814
   Zero at the Bone — 818
WIMAN, CHRISTIAN, 1966-
   Wiman, Christian. *Zero at the Bone* — 818
Win At All Costs. Hart, Matt — 338.7

WINANS, LOLLIE, -1996
    Miles, Kathryn. *Trailed* — 364.152
Winch, Guy
    How to Fix a Broken Heart — 155.9
Winchester, Simon
    Atlantic — 551.46
    A Crack in the Edge of the World — 979.4
    Knowing What We Know — 306.4
    The Map That Changed the World — B
    The Men Who United the States — 973
    Pacific — 909
    ★*The Perfectionists* — 620.009
    The Professor and the Madman — 423
The Wind At My Back. Copeland, Misty — B
The Wind in My Hair. Alinizhad, Masih — B
WIND POWER
    Kamkwamba, William. ★*The Boy Who Harnessed the Wind* — B
Winder, Elizabeth
    Pain, Parties, Work — B
    Parachute Women — 782.42164
Winder, Simon
    Lotharingia — 944
Windhorst, Brian
    Lebron, Inc. — B
WINDMILLS
    Kamkwamba, William. ★*The Boy Who Harnessed the Wind* — B
A Window on Eternity. Wilson, Edward O. — 333.95
Windows on the World Complete Wine Course. Zraly, Kevin — 641.2
WINDS
    Redniss, Lauren. *Thunder & Lightning* — 741.5
Windsor, Edie
    A Wild and Precious Life — B
WINDSOR, EDIE
    Kaplan, Roberta A. *Then Comes Marriage* — 346.7301
    Windsor, Edie. *A Wild and Precious Life* — B
WINDSOR, EDWARD, DUKE OF, 1894-1972
    Cadbury, Deborah. *Princes at War* — 920
    Larman, Alexander. *The Windsors at War* — 940.53
    Lownie, Andrew. *Traitor King* — 920
    Morton, Andrew. *17 Carnations* — 941.084
    Morton, Andrew. *Wallis in Love* — B
WINDSOR, HOUSE OF
    Brown, Tina. ★*The Palace Papers* — 920
    Cadbury, Deborah. *Princes at War* — 920
    Edwards, Anne. *Matriarch* — B
    Hardman, Robert. *Queen of Our Times* — B
    Hardman, Robert. *Queen of the World* — B
    Larman, Alexander. ★*Power and Glory* — 941.085
    Larman, Alexander. *The Windsors at War* — 940.53
    Ridley, Jane. *George V* — B
    Smith, Sally Bedell. *Elizabeth the Queen* — B
    Smith, Sally Bedell. *George VI and Elizabeth* — 920
    Smith, Sally Bedell. *Prince Charles* — B
WINDSOR, WALLIS WARFIELD, DUCHESS OF, 1896-1986
    Lownie, Andrew. *Traitor King* — 920
    Morton, Andrew. *17 Carnations* — 941.084
    Morton, Andrew. *Wallis in Love* — B
The Windsors At War. Larman, Alexander — 940.53
WINE AND WINE MAKING
    Bosker, Bianca. *Cork Dork* — 641.2
    James, Victoria. *Wine Girl* — B
    Neiman, Ophelie. *Wine Isn't Rocket Science* — 641.2
    O'Meara, Mallory. *Girly Drinks* — 641.2
    Zraly, Kevin. *Windows on the World Complete Wine Course* — 641.2
Wine Girl. James, Victoria — B
Wine Isn't Rocket Science. Neiman, Ophelie — 641.2
WINE TASTING
    Bosker, Bianca. *Cork Dork* — 641.2
    James, Victoria. *Wine Girl* — B
Wineapple, Brenda
    Ecstatic Nation — 973.6
    The Impeachers — 973.8
Winfrey, Oprah
    Food, Health, and Happiness — 641.5
    What Happened to You? — 616.85
WINFREY, OPRAH, 1954-
    Winfrey, Oprah. *Food, Health, and Happiness* — 641.5
    Winfrey, Oprah. *What Happened to You?* — 616.85

A Wing and a Prayer. Gyllenhaal, Anders — 639.97
Wing, Charles
    How Your House Works — 643
Wingfield, Adia Harvey
    Gray Areas — 331.6
WINGS
    Carson, Anne. *Autobiography of Red* — 811
Winik, Jay
    1944 — 940.53
    April 1865 — 973.7
WINKFIELD, JIMMY, 1882-1974
    Drape, Joe. *Black Maestro* — B
Winkler, Adam
    We the Corporations — 346.73
Winkler, Elizabeth
    Shakespeare Was a Woman & Other Heresies — 822.33
Winkler, Henry
    ★*Being Henry* — B
WINKLER, HENRY, 1945-
    Winkler, Henry. ★*Being Henry* — B
Winkler, Kyle
    Permission to Be Imperfect — 170
WINN, MOTH
    Winn, Raynor. *The Wild Silence* — B
Winn, Raynor
    ★*The Salt Path* — B
    The Wild Silence — B
WINN, RAYNOR
    Winn, Raynor. ★*The Salt Path* — B
    Winn, Raynor. *The Wild Silence* — B
Winner Sells All. Del Rey, Jason — 381
Winnie and Nelson. Steinberg, Jonny — 920
WINNING AND LOSING
    Barbarisi, Daniel. *Dueling with Kings* — 793.93
    Davis, Seth. *Wooden* — B
    Eruzione, Mike. *The Making of a Miracle* — B
    Law, Keith. *Smart Baseball* — 796.357
    Lowe, Keith. *Savage Continent* — 940.55
    Montgomery, Patrick. *Baseball's Great Expectations* — 796.357
    Neyer, Rob. *Power Ball* — 796.357
    Pearlman, Jeff. ★*Three-Ring Circus* — 796.323
    Phillips, Rowan Ricardo. *The Circuit* — 796.342
    Posnanski, Joe. ★*Why We Love Baseball* — 796.357
    Simon, Scott. *My Cubs* — 796.357
    Streep, Abe. *Brothers on Three* — 306.85
    Weintraub, Stanley. *Iron Tears* — 973.3
    Wertheim, L. Jon. *This Is Your Brain on Sports* — 796.01
Winning Arguments. Fish, Stanley Eugene — 808
★*Winning Grants.* MacKellar, Pamela H. — 025.1
Winning Independence. Ferling, John E. — 973.3
Winroth, Anders
    The Age of the Vikings — 948
WINSLOW FAMILY
    Fraser, Rebecca. *The Mayflower* — 974.4
Winslow Homer. Cross, William R. — 759.13
WINSLOW, EDWARD, 1595-1655
    Fraser, Rebecca. *The Mayflower* — 974.4
WINSLOW, JOSIAH, 1629?-1680
    Fraser, Rebecca. *The Mayflower* — 974.4
Winslow, Valerie L.
    Classic Human Anatomy — 743.4
WINTER
    Fox, Porter. *The Last Winter* — 363.738
The Winter Army. Isserman, Maurice — 940.54
The Winter Fortress. Bascomb, Neal — 940.54
Winter Is Coming. Kasparov, Gary — 947.086
Winter Pasture. Juan, Li — 951.06
Winter Recipes from the Collective. Gluck, Louise — 811
Winter, Molly Roden
    More — B
WINTER, MOLLY RODEN
    Winter, Molly Roden. *More* — B
Winter, Ruth
    A Consumer's Dictionary of Food Additives — 664
Winterdance. Paulsen, Gary — B
Wintering. May, Katherine — 155.9
Winters, Kathleen C.
    Amelia Earhart — B

AUTHOR, TITLE, SERIES AND SUBJECT INDEX

Winters, Mary-Frances
   Black Fatigue   305.896
WINTERS, MARY-FRANCES
   Winters, Mary-Frances. *Black Fatigue*   305.896
Winters, Richard D.
   Beyond Band of Brothers   B
WINTERS, RICHARD D.
   Alexander, Larry. *Biggest Brother*   B
   Winters, Richard D. *Beyond Band of Brothers*   B
WINTHROP, JOHN, 1588-1649
   Bremer, Francis J. *John Winthrop*   B
WINTOUR, ANNA, 1949-
   Odell, Amy. *Anna*   B
Wintz, Jack
   Will I See My Dog in Heaven?   231.7
WIRE-TAPPING
   Gleeson, John. *The Gotti Wars*   364.1
Wired for Love. Cacioppo, Stephanie   616.8
Wired to Eat. Wolf, Robb   641.5
WIRT, MILDRED A. (MILDRED AUGUSTINE), 1905-2002
   Rehak, Melanie. *Girl Sleuth*   813
WISCONSIN
   Goldrick-Rab, Sara. *Paying the Price*   378.3
   Goldstein, Amy. *Janesville*   330.9775
   Shih, David. *Chinese Prodigal*   B
WISDOM
   Bly, Robert. *More Than True*   398.2
   Derricotte, Toi. *I*   811
   Ferriss, Timothy. *Tools of Titans*   081
   Gibran, Kahlil. *And the Prophet Said*   811
   Gibran, Kahlil. ★*The Prophet*   811
   Lewis, John. *Carry On*   328.73
   Von Drehle, David. ★*The Book of Charlie*   B
   Wagamese, Richard. *For Joshua*   B
   Winkler, Henry. ★*Being Henry*   B
★*The Wisdom of Plagues*. McNeil, Donald G.   614.4
Wise Craft Quilts. Stocker, Blair   746.46
WISE FAMILY
   Wise, Beau. *Three Wise Men*   958.104
The Wise Heart. Kornfield, Jack   294.3
Wise, Beau
   Three Wise Men   958.104
WISE, BEAU, 1984-
   Wise, Beau. *Three Wise Men*   958.104
WISE, BENJAMIN B., 1977-2012
   Wise, Beau. *Three Wise Men*   958.104
WISE, JEREMY J., 1974-2009
   Wise, Beau. *Three Wise Men*   958.104
Wise, Steven M.
   Though the Heavens May Fall   342.42
Wise, Tim J.
   Dispatches from the Race War   305.8
WISEAU, TOMMY
   Sestero, Greg. *The Disaster Artist*   791.43
Wiseman, Jill
   Jill Wiseman's Beautiful Beaded Ropes   745.594
Wiseman, Rosalind
   Masterminds & Wingmen   305.235
WISNER, FRANK, 1909-1965
   Anderson, Scott. ★*The Quiet Americans*   327.12
Wit. Edson, Margaret   812
Witch Hunt. Sollee, Kristen J.   133
WITCH HUNTING
   Gibson, Marion. *Witchcraft*   133.4
   Schiff, Stacy. *The Witches*   345
The Witch of Lime Street. Jaher, David   B
The Witch of New York. Hortis, C. Alexander   364.152
Witchcraft. Gibson, Marion   133.4
WITCHCRAFT
   Adler, Margot. *Drawing Down the Moon*   299
   Burroughs, Augusten. ★*Toil & Trouble*   B
   Dell, Christopher. *The Occult, Witchcraft & Magic*   130
   Feldmann, Erica. *Hausmagick*   133.4
   Garcia, Amanda Yates. *Initiated*   B
   Gibson, Marion. *Witchcraft*   133.4
   Gosden, Chris. *Magic*   133.4
   Grimassi, Raven. *What We Knew in the Night*   133.4
   Grossman, Pam. *Waking the Witch*   133.4

   Guiley, Rosemary. *The Encyclopedia of Witches, Witchcraft and Wicca*   133.4
   Hutton, Ronald. *The Triumph of the Moon*   133.4
   Karlsen, Carol F. ★*The Devil in the Shape of a Woman*   133.4
   Mar, Alex. *Witches of America*   299
   Rajchel, Diana. *Urban Magick*   133.4
   Roth, Harold. *The Witching Herbs*   133.4
   Schiff, Stacy. *The Witches*   345
   Sollee, Kristen J. *Witch Hunt*   133
The Witches. Schiff, Stacy   345
WITCHES
   Garcia, Amanda Yates. *Initiated*   B
   Gibson, Marion. *Witchcraft*   133.4
   Grossman, Pam. *Waking the Witch*   133.4
   Guiley, Rosemary. *The Encyclopedia of Witches, Witchcraft and Wicca*   133.4
   Harkness, Deborah E. *The World of All Souls*   813
The Witches Are Coming. West, Lindy   305.420973
Witches of America. Mar, Alex   299
The Witching Herbs. Roth, Harold   133.4
With The End in Mind. Mannix, Kathryn   304.6
With Wings Like Eagles. Korda, Michael   940.54
WITHERS, ERNEST C., 1922-2007
   Lauterbach, Preston. *Bluff City*   B
Without Children. O'Donnell Heffington, Peggy   306.85
★*Without Precedent*. Paul, Joel R   B
Without You, There Is No Us. Kim, Suki   B
Witness. Burger, Ariel   848
Witness to the Revolution. Bingham, Clara   303.48
WITNESSES
   Barron, Justine. *They Killed Freddie Gray*   363.32
   Egan, Timothy. ★*A Fever in the Heartland*   322.4
   Graff, Garrett M. ★*The Only Plane in the Sky*   973.931
Witt, John Fabian
   Lincoln's Code   343.73
Witte, Christina De
   ★*Noodles, Rice, and Everything Spice*   641.595
Wittgenstein's Poker. Edmonds, David   192
WITTGENSTEIN, LUDWIG, 1889-1951
   Edmonds, David. *Wittgenstein's Poker*   192
   Eilenberger, Wolfram. *Time of the Magicians*   920
★*The Wives*. Gorrindo, Simone   B
★*The Wives of Henry VIII*. Fraser, Antonia   942.05
WIZARDS
   Ackroyd, Peter. *The Death of King Arthur*   823
Wizenberg, Molly
   Fixed Stars   B
WIZENBERG, MOLLY
   Wizenberg, Molly. *Fixed Stars*   B
Wobble. Armantrout, Rae   811
Wohlforth, Charles P.
   Beyond Earth   629.45
   The Fate of Nature   304.209798
Wohlleben, Peter
   Forest Walking   582.16
   The Heartbeat of Trees   582.16
   The Hidden Life of Trees   582.16
   The Secret Wisdom of Nature   508
WOHLLEBEN, PETER, 1964-
   Wohlleben, Peter. *The Hidden Life of Trees*   582.16
Wojcicki, Esther
   How to Raise Successful People   649
Wojczuk, Tana
   Lady Romeo   B
★*The Wok*. Lopez-Alt, J. Kenji   641.595
Woke up This Morning. Imperioli, Michael   791.45
★*The Woks of Life*. Leung, Bill   641.7
The Wolf Almanac. Busch, Robert   599.773
Wolf Hustle. Fabre, Cin   332.6
★*The Wolf of Investing*. Belfort, Jordan   332.63
WOLF PACKS
   McIntyre, Rick. *The Reign of Wolf 21*   599.773
Wolf, Brandon J.
   A Place for Us   B
WOLF, BRANDON J.
   Wolf, Brandon J. *A Place for Us*   B
Wolf, Martin
   ★*The Crisis of Democratic Capitalism*   330.12
Wolf, Maryanne
   Reader, Come Home   418

PUBLIC LIBRARY CORE COLLECTION: NONFICTION
Twentieth Edition

Wolf, Robb
   Wired to Eat — 641.5
Wolfe, Charles K.
   ★*The Life and Legend of Leadbelly* — B
Wolfe, Tom
   The Kingdom of Speech — 401
   ★*The Right Stuff* — 629.4
Wolfe, Victoria Findlay
   Modern Quilt Magic — 746.46
Wolff, Christoph
   Johann Sebastian Bach — B
Wolff, Daniel J.
   Grown-Up Anger — 920
Wolff, Michael
   Fire and Fury — 973.933
   Landslide — 973.933
Wolff, Tobias
   This Boy's Life — B
WOLFF, TOBIAS, 1945-
   Wolff, Tobias. *This Boy's Life* — B
Wolfish. Berry, Erica — 152.4
Wolk, Douglas
   ★*All of the Marvels* — 741.5
WOLLSTONECRAFT, MARY, 1759-1797
   Gordon, Charlotte. *Romantic Outlaws* — 920
   Penaluna, Regan. ★*How to Think Like a Woman* — 190.82
WOLVES
   Berry, Erica. *Wolfish* — 152.4
   Blakeslee, Nate. *American Wolf* — 599.773
   Busch, Robert. *The Wolf Almanac* — 599.773
   Lopez, Barry Holstun. ★*Of Wolves and Men* — 599.773
   McIntyre, Rick. *The Reign of Wolf 21* — 599.773
   Safina, Carl. *Beyond Words* — 591.56
Womack, John
   Zapata and the Mexican Revolution — B
Womack, Kenneth
   All Things Must Pass Away — 781.66
The Woman I Kept to Myself. Alvarez, Julia — 811
The Woman I Wanted to Be. Von Furstenberg, Diane — B
The Woman in Me. Spears, Britney — B
★*A Woman of No Importance*. Purnell, Sonia — B
A Woman of Property. Schiff, Robyn — 811
★*The Woman They Could Not Silence*. Moore, Kate — B
The Woman Warrior. Kingston, Maxine Hong — B
The Woman Who Smashed Codes. Fagone, Jason — B
The Woman Who Watches Over the World. Hogan, Linda — B
A Woman Without a Country. Boland, Eavan — 821
The Woman's Hour. Weiss, Elaine F. — 324.6
A Woman's Place Is at the Top. Kimberley, Hannah — B
WOMANIZERS
   O'Brien, Keith. *Charlie Hustle* — 796.357
   Ridley, Jane. *The Heir Apparent* — B
Womb. Hazard, Leah — 612.6
WOMEN
   Alderton, Dolly. *Everything I Know About Love* — B
   Ali, Fatima. ★*Savor* — B
   Alvarez, Julia. *The Woman I Kept to Myself* — 811
   Andrews, Lena S. ★*Valiant Women* — 940.53
   Armstrong, Karen. *The Spiral Staircase* — B
   Badkhen, Anna. *The World Is a Carpet* — 305.409581
   Baer, Kate. *What Kind of Woman* — 811
   Bailey, Elisabeth. *The Sound of a Wild Snail Eating* — 594
   Bass, Ellen. ★*The Courage to Heal* — 616.85
   Beard, Mary. ★*S.P.Q.R.* — 937
   Beauvoir, Simone de. ★*The Second Sex* — 305.4
   Belcher, Chris. *Pretty Baby* — B
   Blair, Selma. *Mean Baby* — B
   Block, Jennifer. *Everything Below the Waist* — 613
   Bohannon, Cat. ★*Eve* — 613
   Boland, Eavan. *The Historians* — 821
   Bowen, Sesali. *Bad Fat Black Girl* — 305.42
   Boyer, Anne. *The Undying* — B
   Brighten, Jolene. *Is This Normal?* — 618.1
   Brooks, Geraldine. *Nine Parts of Desire* — 305.48
   Brosh, Allie. ★*Hyperbole and a Half* — 741.5
   Brosh, Allie. ★*Solutions and Other Problems* — 741.5
   Burton, Susan. *Empty* — B
   Butler, Marcia. *The Skin Above My Knee* — B
   Cahn, Naomi R. ★*Fair Shake* — 331.4
   Calhoun, Ada. *Why We Can't Sleep* — 305.244
   Carcaterra, Lorenzo. *Three Dreamers* — B
   Chang, Leslie T. *Factory Girls* — 331.4
   Chaudry, Rabia. *Fatty Fatty Boom Boom* — B
   Chow, Kat. *Seeing Ghosts* — B
   Clark, Heather. ★*Red Comet* — B
   Cleghorn, Elinor. *Unwell Women* — 613
   Clein, Emmeline. ★*Dead Weight* — 616.85
   Clinton, Hillary Rodham. *The Book of Gutsy Women* — 920
   Collins, Gail. *When Everything Changed* — 305.40973
   Comen, Elizabeth. ★*All in Her Head* — 613
   Copaken, Deborah. *Ladyparts* — B
   Couric, Katie. *Going There* — B
   Craig, Mya-Rose. *Birdgirl* — B
   Cregan, Mary. *The Scar* — 616.85
   D'Antonio, Michael. *The Hunting of Hillary* — B
   Dabiri, Emma. *Twisted* — 391.5
   Danticat, Edwidge. *The Art of Death* — 809
   Darby, Seyward. ★*Sisters in Hate* — 305.800973
   Davidds, Yasmin. *Your Own Terms* — 658.4
   Devantez, Chelsea. ★*I Shouldn't Be Telling You This* — B
   Diamant, Anita. ★*Period. End of Sentence* — 612.6
   Didion, Joan. ★*Let Me Tell You What I Mean* — 814
   Ditum, Sarah. *Toxic* — 920.72
   Doherty, Maggie. *The Equivalents* — 920
   Dooner, Caroline. *Tired as F*ck* — 152.1
   Doty, Cate. *Mergers and Acquisitions* — 395.2
   Downey, Kirstin. *Isabella* — B
   DuBois, Ellen Carol. *Suffrage* — 324.6
   Duncan, Isadora. *My Life* — B
   Dunn, Jancee. *Hot and Bothered* — 618.1
   Ellis, Helen. *Bring Your Baggage and Don't Pack Light* — 814
   Ellis, Helen. *Southern Lady Code* — 814
   Emera, Deena. *A Brief History of the Female Body* — 612.6
   Enright, Lynn. *Vagina* — 612.6
   Ephron, Nora. *The Most of Nora Ephron* — 814
   Erickson, Carolly. *Great Catherine* — B
   Fagan, Chelsea. *The Financial Diet* — 332.024
   Febos, Melissa. *Girlhood* — 818
   Felder, Deborah G. *The American Women's Almanac* — 305.40973
   Filipovic, Jill. *The H-Spot* — 155.3
   Fine, Cordelia. *Testosterone Rex* — 155.3
   Flock, Elizabeth. ★*The Furies* — 305.48
   Friedan, Betty. ★*The Feminine Mystique* — 305.42
   Gallagher, Winifred. *New Women in the Old West* — 978.02
   Gates, Melinda. ★*The Moment of Lift* — 305.42
   Gillard, Julia. ★*Women and Leadership* — 158
   Gillette, Michael L. *Lady Bird Johnson* — B
   Ginzberg, Lori D. *Elizabeth Cady Stanton* — B
   Girma, Haben. *Haben* — B
   Gotch, Jen. *The Upside of Being Down* — B
   Gray, Emma. *A Girl's Guide to Joining the Resistance* — 303.48
   Green, Robin. *The Only Girl* — 070.92
   Griffith, Elisabeth. *Formidable* — 305.42
   Gross, Rachel E. *Vagina Obscura* — 618.1
   Grossman, Pam. *Waking the Witch* — 133.4
   Gunst, Kathy. *Rage Baking* — 641.86
   Gunter, Jen. *The Menopause Manifesto* — 618.175
   Gunter, Jen. *The Vagina Bible* — 612.6
   Gupta, Shalene. *The Cycle* — 618.1
   Hacker, Marilyn. *Selected Poems, 1965-1990* — 811
   Hackman, Rose. ★*Emotional Labor* — 155.3
   Harden, Marcia Gay. *The Seasons of My Mother* — B
   Harry, Debbie. *Face It* — B
   Haver, Mary Claire. ★*The New Menopause* — 618.1
   Herrmann, Dorothy. *Helen Keller* — B
   Hickman, Katie. *Brave Hearted* — 978
   Hirshman, Linda R. *Reckoning* — 305.420973
   Holt, Nathalia. ★*Rise of the Rocket Girls* — 629.4
   Howard, Johnette. *The Rivals* — B
   Hulls, Tessa. ★*Feeding Ghosts* — 741.5
   Hustvedt, Siri. *Mothers, Fathers, and Others* — 814
   Iyer, Pico. *The Lady and the Monk* — 952
   Jackson, Danielle Bayard. *Fighting for Our Friendships* — 302.34
   Jackson, Regina. *White Women* — 305.8
   Jamieson, Alexandra. *Women, Food, and Desire* — 155.3
   Johnson, Akemi. *Night in the American Village* — 305.40952

AUTHOR, TITLE, SERIES AND SUBJECT INDEX

Johnston, Ann Dowsett. *Drink*	362.292
Juan, Li. *Winter Pasture*	951.06
Kalb, Bess. ★*Nobody Will Tell You This but Me*	306.874
Kantor, Jodi. *She Said*	364.15
Karbo, Karen. *In Praise of Difficult Women*	920
Kardas-Nelson, Mara. *We Are Not Able to Live in the Sky*	332.3
Kazdin, Cole. ★*What's Eating Us*	616.85
Keller, Helen. ★*The Story of My Life*	B
Knight, Keltie. *Lady Secrets*	305.4
Koch, Bea. *Mad and Bad*	920
Kotite, Erika. *She Sheds*	728
Kramer, Andrea S. *Breaking Through Bias*	650.1
Kristof, Nicholas D. *Half the Sky*	362.83
Kroger, Lisa. *Monster, She Wrote*	920
LaFollette, Marcel C. *Writing for Their Lives*	071.3
Lapidus, Lenora M. ★*The Rights of Women*	346.7301
Lawson, Jenny. ★*Broken*	B
Lawson, Jenny. *Furiously Happy*	B
Leng'ete, Nice. *The Girls in the Wild Fig Tree*	B
Lepore, Jill. *Book of Ages*	B
Lerner, Harriet Goldhor. ★*The Dance of Anger*	152.4
Lerner, Harriet Goldhor. *The Dance of Intimacy*	155.6
Levy, Deborah. *The Cost of Living*	B
Lewis, Jenifer. *Walking in My Joy*	B
Li, Yiyun. *Dear Friend, from My Life I Write to You in Your Life*	B
Lower, Wendy. *Hitler's Furies*	940.53
Lucey, Donna M. *Sargent's Women*	920
Malone, Sharon. *Grown Woman Talk*	362.1
Manly, Carla Marie. *Aging Joyfully*	305.26
Mansberg, Ginni. *The M Word*	612.6
Marton, Kati. *Hidden Power*	B
McGregor, Alyson J. *Sex Matters*	613
Mendelson, Zoe. *Pussypedia*	612.6
Miles, Tiya. ★*Wild Girls*	304.2
Mitchell, Wendy. *Somebody I Used to Know*	B
Moran, Caitlin. *How to Be a Woman*	B
Moran, Caitlin. *More Than a Woman*	B
Morgan, Abi. *This Is Not a Pity Memoir*	B
Mundy, Liza. *Code Girls*	940.54
Nadeau, Barbie Latza. *The Godmother*	364.106
Nafisi, Azar. ★*Reading Lolita in Tehran*	B
Nafisi, Azar. *Things I've Been Silent About*	B
Nathan, Debbie. *Sybil Exposed*	B
Navai, Ramita. *City of Lies*	955
Nerenberg, Jenara. *Divergent Mind*	616.89
Nevins, Sheila. *You Don't Look Your Age*	B
Nimura, Janice P. ★*The Doctors Blackwell*	610.92
Norman, Abby. *Ask Me About My Uterus*	618.1
Nuttall, Jennifer Anne. ★*Mother Tongue*	422
Nyamayaro, Elizabeth. *I Am a Girl from Africa*	B
O'Donnell Heffington, Peggy. *Without Children*	306.85
O'Meara, Mallory. *Girly Drinks*	641.2
Orenstein, Peggy. *Don't Call Me Princess*	305.42
Orman, Suze. *Women & Money*	332.0240082
Page, Susan. ★*The Rulebreaker*	B
Painter, Nell Irvin. ★*Sojourner Truth*	B
Palmieri, Jennifer. *Dear Madam President*	158
Palmieri, Jennifer. *She Proclaims*	305.42
Paperny, Anna Mehler. *Hello I Want to Die Please Fix Me*	362.2
Parker, Lara. *Vagina Problems*	618.1
Patchett, Ann. *Truth & Beauty*	B
Petrosino, Kiki. *White Blood*	811
Pipher, Mary Bray. *A Life in Light*	B
Pipher, Mary Bray. *Women Rowing North*	305.26
Power, Marianne. *Help Me!*	158.1
Pratt, Misty. *All in Her Head*	616.89
Qadiri, Humayra. *Dancing in the Mosque*	B
Quinn, Bridget. *She Votes*	324.6
Quinn, Tallu Schuyler. *What We Wish Were True*	B
Radke, Heather. *Butts*	611
Rahmani, Niloofar. *Open Skies*	B
Ramey, Sarah. *The Lady's Handbook for Her Mysterious Illness*	B
Ramirez, Janina. *Femina*	940.1
Raphael, Rina. *The Gospel of Wellness*	613
Rice, Condoleezza. *Extraordinary, Ordinary People*	B
Roberts, Cokie. *Capital Dames*	920
Roberts, Cokie. *Founding Mothers*	920
Roberts, Cokie. *Ladies of Liberty*	920
Rogers, Katie. ★*American Woman*	973.09
Rowe, Peggy. *About My Mother*	B
Rubenhold, Hallie. ★*The Five*	362.88
Saini, Angela. *Inferior*	305.4
Sanchez, Erika L. *Crying in the Bathroom*	B
Sanchez, Erika L. *Lessons on Expulsion*	811
Schatz, Kate. *Rad Women Worldwide*	920
Schuller, Kyla. *The Trouble with White Women*	305.42
Schumer, Amy. *The Girl with the Lower Back Tattoo*	B
Schwalbe, Will. ★*The End of Your Life Book Club*	B
Scottoline, Lisa. *I See Life Through Rose-Colored Glasses*	813
Searcey, Dionne. *In Pursuit of Disobedient Women*	B
Sehee, Baek. *I Want to Die but I Want to Eat Tteokbokki*	B
Shah, Meera. *You're the Only One I've Told*	362.1988
Showalter, Elaine. ★*A Jury of Her Peers*	810.9
Simard, S. ★*Finding the Mother Tree*	582.16
Sinclair, Safiya. *Cannibal*	811
Sjunneson, Elsa. *Being Seen*	362.4
Sohn, Amy. *The Man Who Hated Women*	363.28
Solnit, Rebecca. *The Mother of All Questions*	305.42
Stanley, Amy. *Stranger in the Shogun's City*	B
Steinem, Gloria. *My Life on the Road*	B
Steinhauer, Jennifer. *The Firsts*	320.082
Suvari, Mena. *The Great Peace*	B
Sweig, Julia. *Lady Bird Johnson*	B
Taddeo, Lisa. *Three Women*	306.7082
Taraborrelli, J. Randy. ★*The Secret Life of Marilyn Monroe*	B
Teffi, N. A. *Memories*	B
Thomas, Mathilde. *The French Beauty Solution*	646.7
Thurman, Judith. ★*A Left-Handed Woman*	814
Tolokonnikova, Nadezhda. *Rules for Rulebreakers*	782.42166
Toorpakai, Maria. *A Different Kind of Daughter*	B
Traister, Rebecca. *Good and Mad*	305.420973
Vanek Smith, Stacey. *Machiavelli for Women*	650.1
Vasquez, Karla Tatiana. ★*The Salvisoul Cookbook*	641.598
Vasquez-Lavado, Silvia. *In the Shadow of the Mountain*	B
Vogelstein, Rachel B. *Awakening*	305.42
Von Furstenberg, Diane. *The Woman I Wanted to Be*	B
Wagner, Alex. *Futureface*	B
Walters, Jacqueline. *The Queen V*	612.6
Washington, Kate. ★*Already Toast*	649.8
Wasson, Sam. *Fifth Avenue, 5 A.M.*	791.43
Weiss, Elaine F. *The Woman's Hour*	324.6
West, Lindy. *Shrill*	818
West, Lindy. *The Witches Are Coming*	305.420973
Whitefield-Madrano, Autumn. *Face Value*	111
Williams, Bari A. *Seen yet Unseen*	338.4
Williams, Florence. *Heartbreak*	306.7
Williams, Joan. *What Works for Women at Work*	650.1
Williams, Michelle. *Checking In*	B
Wills, Clair. ★*Missing Persons*	929.2
Winder, Elizabeth. *Parachute Women*	782.42164
Wizenberg, Molly. *Fixed Stars*	B
Worley, Jennifer. *Neon Girls*	792.7
Worsley, Lucy. *Queen Victoria*	B
Wright, Jennifer Ashley. ★*Madame Restell*	B
Yellin, Emily. *Our Mothers' War*	940.53
Yip-Williams, Julie. ★*The Unwinding of the Miracle*	973
Zoepf, Katherine. *Excellent Daughters*	305.42
Women & *Money*. Orman, Suze	332.0240082
★**Women** & *Power*. Beard, Mary	305.409
Women. Leibovitz, Annie	779

WOMEN ABOLITIONISTS

Painter, Nell Irvin. ★*Sojourner Truth*	B
Siler, Julia Flynn. *The White Devil's Daughters*	306.3
Wickenden, Dorothy. *The Agitators*	920

WOMEN AMBASSADORS

Yovanovitch, Marie. *Lessons from the Edge*	973.933

WOMEN ANARCHISTS

Johnson, Steven. *The Infernal Machine*	335

WOMEN AND DOGS

Achterberg, Cara Sue. *Another Good Dog*	636.7
Boylan, Jennifer Finney. *Good Boy*	B
Conaboy, Kelly. *The Particulars of Peter*	636.7
Halpern, Sue. *A Dog Walks into a Nursing Home*	B
Hunger, Christina. *How Stella Learned to Talk*	636.7
Jaouad, Suleika. ★*Between Two Kingdoms*	B

PUBLIC LIBRARY CORE COLLECTION: NONFICTION
Twentieth Edition

WOMEN AND GORILLAS
 Fossey, Dian. ★*Gorillas in the Mist*   599.884
WOMEN AND HORSES
 Letts, Elizabeth. ★*The Ride of Her Life*   B
 Prior-Palmer, Lara. *Rough Magic*   798.4
 ★*Women and Leadership*. Gillard, Julia   158
WOMEN AND LITERATURE
 Ackmann, Martha. ★*These Fevered Days*   B
 Briggs, Julia. *Virginia Woolf*   823
 Clark, Heather. ★*Red Comet*   B
 Gilbert, Sandra M. ★*Still Mad*   810.9
 hooks, bell. *Remembered Rapture*   808
 Humez, Jean McMahon. *Harriet Tubman*   B
 Milford, Nancy. *Savage Beauty*   B
 Montillo, Roseanne. *The Lady and Her Monsters*   823
 Rehak, Melanie. *Girl Sleuth*   813
 Showalter, Elaine. ★*A Jury of Her Peers*   810.9
WOMEN AND NATURE
 Bell, Laura. *Claiming Ground*   B
 Dillard, Annie. *The Abundance*   814
 Dillard, Annie. *Pilgrim at Tinker Creek*   508
 Ehrlich, Gretel. *This Cold Heaven*   998.2
 Oliver, Mary. ★*Upstream*   814
WOMEN AND OPPRESSION (PSYCHOLOGY)
 Alinizhad, Masih. *The Wind in My Hair*   B
Women and Other Monsters. Zimmerman, Jess   155.3
WOMEN AND PETS
 Scottoline, Lisa. *I See Life Through Rose-Colored Glasses*   813
WOMEN AND POLITICS
 Allgor, Catherine. *A Perfect Union*   B
 Brower, Kate Andersen. *First Women*   920
 Chang, Jung. *Big Sister, Little Sister, Red Sister*   B
 Cordery, Stacy A. *Alice*   B
 Gilbert, Sandra M. ★*Still Mad*   810.9
 Gillette, Michael L. *Lady Bird Johnson*   B
 Goodwin, Doris Kearns. *No Ordinary Time*   920
 Gortemaker, Heike B. *Eva Braun*   B
 Gunst, Kathy. *Rage Baking*   641.86
 Hill, Katie. *She Will Rise*   305.42
 Holton, Woody. *Abigail Adams*   B
 Katz, Catherine Grace. *The Daughters of Yalta*   920
 Kerrison, Catherine. *Jefferson's Daughters*   B
 Lovell, Mary S. *The Sisters*   920.72
 Mazzeo, Tilar J. ★*Eliza Hamilton*   B
 Peyser, Marc N. *Hissing Cousins*   B
 Roberts, Cokie. *Capital Dames*   920
 Roberts, Cokie. *Founding Mothers*   920
 Roberts, Cokie. *Ladies of Liberty*   920
 Schiff, Stacy. ★*Cleopatra*   B
 Shawcross, William. *The Queen Mother*   B
 Sweig, Julia. *Lady Bird Johnson*   B
 Thomas, Evan. ★*First*   B
 Thomas, Louisa. *Louisa*   B
WOMEN AND SCIENCE
 Colwell, Rita R. *A Lab of One's Own*   B
 Saini, Angela. *Inferior*   305.4
WOMEN AND SPORTS
 Barnes, Katie. ★*Fair Play*   796.082
 Clarke, Gemma. *Soccerwomen*   796.334
 Mertens, Maggie. *Better Faster Farther*   796.42
WOMEN AND SUCCESS
 Mann, William J. *Hello, Gorgeous*   B
 Streisand, Barbra. ★*My Name Is Barbra*   B
WOMEN AND THE MILITARY
 Johnson, Akemi. *Night in the American Village*   305.40952
WOMEN AND WAR
 Abbott, Karen. *Liar, Temptress, Soldier, Spy*   920
 Addario, Lynsey. *It's What I Do*   B
 Andrews, Lena S. ★*Valiant Women*   940.53
 Fields-Black, Edda L. *Combee*   973.7
 Gillette, Michael L. *Lady Bird Johnson*   B
 Kiernan, Denise. *The Girls of Atomic City*   976.8
 Lamb, Christina. *Our Bodies, Their Battlefields*   341.6
 Lemmon, Gayle Tzemach. *Ashley's War*   B
 Lemmon, Gayle Tzemach. *The Daughters of Kobani*   956.9104
 Lemmon, Gayle Tzemach. *The Dressmaker of Khair Khana*   B
 Macintyre, Ben. ★*Agent Sonya*   B
 MacKrell, Judith. *The Correspondents*   070.4

 Moorehead, Caroline. *A House in the Mountains*   940.53
 Moorehead, Caroline. *A Train in Winter*   940.53
 Parkin, Simon. *A Game of Birds and Wolves*   940.54
 Roberts, Cokie. *Capital Dames*   920
 Seiple, Samantha. *Louisa on the Front Lines*   B
 Tallis, Nicola. *Uncrowned Queen*   B
 Toler, Pamela D. *Women Warriors*   355.0092
WOMEN ANIMATORS
 Holt, Nathalia. *The Queens of Animation*   920
 Johnson, Mindy. *Ink & Paint*   B
 O'Meara, Mallory. *The Lady from the Black Lagoon*   921
WOMEN ANTHROPOLOGISTS
 King, Charles. ★*Gods of the Upper Air*   920
 Ransby, Barbara. *Eslanda*   B
WOMEN ARCHAEOLOGISTS
 Howell, Georgina. *Gertrude Bell*   B
 Wallach, Janet. *Desert Queen*   B
WOMEN ARTISTS
 Anolik, Lili. *Hollywood's Eve*   B
 Beaton, Kate. ★*Ducks*   741.5
 Carter, Alice A. *The Red Rose Girls*   B
 Codjoe, Ama. *Bluest Nude*   811
 Crabapple, Molly. *Drawing Blood*   B
 Doherty, Maggie. *The Equivalents*   920
 Felder, Deborah G. *The American Women's Almanac*   305.40973
 Gabriel, Mary. *Ninth Street Women*   920
 Hesse, Maria. ★*Frida Kahlo*   B
 Hoban, Phoebe. *Alice Neel*   B
 Holladay, Wilhelmina Cole. *A Museum of Their Own*   704
 Holt, Nathalia. *The Queens of Animation*   920
 Hustvedt, Siri. *Mothers, Fathers, and Others*   814
 Lehrer, Riva. *Golem Girl*   B
 Lozano, Luis-Martin. *Frida Kahlo*   759.972
 Marks, Ann. *Vivian Maier Developed*   778.9
 O'Meara, Mallory. *The Lady from the Black Lagoon*   921
 Quinn, Bridget. *Broad Strokes*   920
 Robinson, Roxana. *Georgia O'Keeffe*   B
 Schloss, Edith. *The Loft Generation*   700.9
 Stahr, Celia. *Frida in America*   B
 Sullivan, Rosemary. *Stalin's Daughter*   B
 Watling, Sarah. *Tomorrow Perhaps the Future*   946.081
WOMEN ASTRONAUTS
 Ackmann, Martha. *The Mercury 13*   920
 Bagby, Meredith E. *The New Guys*   305
 Grush, Loren. ★*The Six*   629.4
 Sherr, Lynn. *Sally Ride*   B
 Teitel, Amy Shira. *Fighting for Space*   920
WOMEN ASTRONOMERS
 Johnson, George. *Miss Leavitt's Stars*   522
 Levesque, Emily. *The Last Stargazers*   520
 Shields, Aomawa L. *Life on Other Planets*   B
WOMEN ASTROPHYSICISTS
 Seager, Sara. *The Smallest Lights in the Universe*   B
WOMEN ATHLETES
 Allred, Alexandra Powe. *When Women Stood*   796.082
 Askwith, Richard. *Unbreakable*   B
 Barnes, Katie. ★*Fair Play*   796.082
 Barr, John. *Start by Believing*   364.15
 Blais, Madeleine. *Queen of the Court*   B
 Clarke, Gemma. *Soccerwomen*   796.334
 Clinton, Hillary Rodham. *The Book of Gutsy Women*   920
 Cox, Lynne. *Swimming to Antarctica*   B
 Felder, Deborah G. *The American Women's Almanac*   305.40973
 Gilder, Ginny. *Course Correction*   797.12
 Jacobs, Sally H. *Althea*   B
 Litman, Laken. *Strong Like a Woman*   796
 Masters, Oksana. *The Hard Parts*   B
 Pace, Kristin Knight. *This Much Country*   B
 Toorpakai, Maria. *A Different Kind of Daughter*   B
WOMEN ATHLETIC COACHES
 Fleshman, Lauren. ★*Good for a Girl*   B
WOMEN AUTHORS
 Adichie, Chimamanda Ngozi. *Notes on Grief*   155.9
 Akhmatova, Anna Andreevna. *Poems*   891.71
 Alexander, Elizabeth. *Crave Radiance*   811
 Anders, Charlie Jane. ★*Never Say You Can't Survive*   808.02
 Armantrout, Rae. *Versed*   811
 Bang, Mary Jo. *The Bride of E*   811

AUTHOR, TITLE, SERIES AND SUBJECT INDEX

Bang, Mary Jo. *Elegy*	811
Barker, Elspeth. ★*Notes from the Henhouse*	828
Bergstein, Rachelle. *The Genius of Judy*	813
Berlin, Lucia. ★*Welcome Home*	B
Boland, Eavan. *New Collected Poems*	821
Boruch, Marianne. *Eventually One Dreams the Real Thing*	811
Boyer, Anne. *The Undying*	B
Braitman, Laurel. *What Looks Like Bravery*	B
Brock-Broido, Lucie. *Stay, Illusion*	811
Brooks, Gwendolyn. ★*The Essential Gwendolyn Brooks*	811
Brooks, Gwendolyn. *In Montgomery, and Other Poems*	811
Butcher, Amy. *Mothertrucker*	B
Calhoun, Ada. *Also a Poet*	B
Carson, Anne. *Decreation*	818
Cisneros, Sandra. *A House of My Own*	B
Clinton, Hillary Rodham. *The Book of Gutsy Women*	920
Collins, Martha. *Admit One*	811
Copaken, Deborah. *Ladyparts*	B
Crawford, Lacy. *Notes on a Silencing*	B
Crespino, Joseph. *Atticus Finch*	B
Crosley, Sloane. *Grief Is for People*	B
Crosley, Sloane. ★*Look Alive Out There*	814
Dangarembga, Tsitsi. *Black and Female*	305.48
Daugherty, Tracy. *The Last Love Song*	B
Diaz, Jaquira. *Ordinary Girls*	818
Didion, Joan. *Let Me Tell You What I Mean*	814
Doherty, Maggie. *The Equivalents*	920
Dove, Rita. ★*Selected Poems*	811
Dove, Rita. *Sonata Mulattica*	811
Duberman, Martin B. *Andrea Dworkin*	B
Ephron, Delia. *Left on Tenth*	B
Ephron, Nora. *The Most of Nora Ephron*	814
Faizullah, Tarfia. *Registers of Illuminated Villages*	811
Feder, Rachel. *The Darcy Myth*	823
Felder, Deborah G. *The American Women's Almanac*	305.40973
Feldman, Deborah. *Exodus*	B
Ferrante, Elena. *In the Margins*	809
Forche, Carolyn. *Blue Hour*	811
Forsythe, Kelly. *Perennial*	811
Funder, Anna. *Wifedom*	B
Gay, Roxane. ★*Opinions*	814
Gerard, Sarah. *Carrie Carolyn Coco*	364.152
Giovanni, Nikki. ★*The Collected Poetry of Nikki Giovanni, 1968-1998*	811
Giovanni, Nikki. *A Good Cry*	811
Gluck, Louise. *Averno*	811
Godwin, Gail. *Getting to Know Death*	B
Gordon, Charlotte. *Romantic Outlaws*	920
Gordon, Edmund. *The Invention of Angela Carter*	B
Graham, Jorie. *The Dream of the Unified Field*	811
Graham, Jorie. *Fast*	811
Graham, Jorie. *From the New World*	811
Graham, Jorie. *Overlord*	811
Grande, Reyna. ★*The Distance Between Us*	973
Griffin, Susan. *Out of Silence, Sound. Out of Nothing, Something*	808.02
Hacker, Marilyn. *A Stranger's Mirror*	811
Harjo, Joy. *A Map to the Next World*	811
Harrison, Leslie. *The Book of Endings*	811
Hauser, CJ. *The Crane Wife*	B
Heti, Sheila. *Alphabetical Diaries*	818
Highsmith, Patricia. ★*Patricia Highsmith's Diaries and Notebooks*	818
Hirshfield, Jane. *The Beauty*	811
Houston, Pam. *Deep Creek*	814
Hustvedt, Siri. *Mothers, Fathers, and Others*	814
Irby, Samantha. ★*Quietly Hostile*	814
Jackson, Shirley. ★*The Letters of Shirley Jackson*	813
Jacob, Mira. *Good Talk*	741.5
Jamison, Leslie. ★*Make It Scream, Make It Burn*	814
Karr, Mary. *Tropic of Squalor*	811
Khakpour, Porochista. *Brown Album*	304.8
Klein, Naomi. ★*Doppelganger*	302.2
Kroger, Lisa. *Monster, She Wrote*	920
Laing, Olivia. *The Garden Against Time*	635
Lang, Maya. *What We Carry*	B
Lankford, Andrea. *Trail of the Lost*	363.2
Levy, Deborah. *Real Estate*	B
Levy, Deborah. ★*Things I Don't Want to Know*	B
Lippman, Laura. *My Life as a Villainess*	B
Lively, Penelope. *Life in the Garden*	B
Lowell, Amy. *Selected Poems*	821
Mann, Jen. ★*Midlife Bites*	305.244
Mayes, Frances. *Bella Tuscany*	945
Millay, Edna St. Vincent. *Collected Poems*	811
Millay, Edna St. Vincent. *Selected Poems*	811
Min, Anchee. *Red Azalea*	B
Moore, Marianne. *New Collected Poems*	811
Moore, Wayetu. *The Dragons, the Giant, the Women*	B
Moser, Benjamin. ★*Sontag*	B
Moser, Benjamin. *Why This World*	B
Myles, Eileen. *I Must Be Living Twice*	811.54
Nelson, Maggie. ★*Like Love*	814
Nezhukumatathil, Aimee. *Bite by Bite*	641.3
Nezhukumatathil, Aimee. *Oceanic*	811
Ng, Fae Myenne. *Orphan Bachelors*	B
Nguyen, Diana Khoi. *Ghost of*	811
Notley, Alice. *Certain Magical Acts*	811
Oliver, Mary. *New and Selected Poems,; Vol. 1*	811
Oswald, Alice. *Falling Awake*	821
Oyler, Lauren. *No Judgment*	814
Parker, Morgan. *There Are More Beautiful Things Than Beyonce*	811
Patchett, Ann. *This Is the Story of a Happy Marriage*	B
Patchett, Ann. *Truth & Beauty*	B
Pittard, Hannah. *We Are Too Many*	B
Plath, Sylvia. ★*Ariel*	811
Plath, Sylvia. *The Letters of Sylvia Plath*	811.54
Plath, Sylvia. *The Letters of Sylvia Plath*	811.54
Porizkova, Paulina. *No Filter*	B
Proulx, Annie. *Bird Cloud*	B
Rich, Adrienne. *Collected Early Poems, 1950-1970*	811
Rich, Adrienne. *Collected Poems*	811
Rich, Adrienne. *Later Poems*	811
Rich, Adrienne. *The School Among the Ruins*	811
Riess, Jana. *Flunking Sainthood*	248.4
Rogers, Pattiann. *Quickening Fields*	811
Rojas Contreras, Ingrid. ★*The Man Who Could Move Clouds*	B
Rosenthal, Jason. *My Wife Said You May Want to Marry Me*	B
Rosnay, Tatiana de. *Manderley Forever*	B
Rossetti, Christina Georgina. *Christina Rossetti*	821.8
Rubin, Gretchen Craft. ★*Life in Five Senses*	152.1
Rukeyser, Muriel. *Selected Poems*	811
Sabatini Sloan, Aisha. *Dreaming of Ramadi in Detroit*	814
Salter, Mary Jo. *The Surveyors*	811
Sampson, Fiona. *In Search of Mary Shelley*	B
Sanchez, Erika L. *Crying in the Bathroom*	B
Sante, Lucy. *I Heard Her Call My Name*	B
Seiple, Samantha. *Louisa on the Front Lines*	B
Selvaratnam, Tanya. *Assume Nothing*	B
Shapland, Jenn. *My Autobiography of Carson McCullers*	B
Sharif, Solmaz. *Look*	811
Sinclair, Safiya. *Cannibal*	811
Sjunneson, Elsa. *Being Seen*	362.4
Smith, Lee. *Dimestore*	975.5
Smith, Patricia. ★*Incendiary Art*	811.54
Smith, Zadie. *Intimations*	824
Soep, Elisabeth. *Other People's Words*	155.9
Tallent, Elizabeth. *Scratched*	B
Tan, Amy. ★*Where the Past Begins*	B
Teffi, N. A. *Memories*	B
Thurman, Judith. ★*A Left-Handed Woman*	814
Travisano, Thomas J. *Love Unknown*	B
Trethewey, Natasha D. ★*Native Guard*	811
Tsvetaeva, Marina. *Selected Poems*	891.71
V. ★*Reckoning*	814
Valentine, Jean. *Door in the Mountain*	811
Walker, Alice. *Hard Times Require Furious Dancing*	811
Wang, Connie. *Oh My Mother!*	B
Watling, Sarah. *Tomorrow Perhaps the Future*	946.081
Weller, Sheila. *Carrie Fisher*	B
Welty, Eudora. *One Writer's Beginnings*	B
Wilder, Laura Ingalls. *Pioneer Girl*	B
Worsley, Lucy. ★*Agatha Christie*	B
Youn, Monica. *Blackacre*	811.6
Zuckoff, Mitchell. *The Secret Gate*	958.104

WOMEN AUTHORS, AMERICAN

Anolik, Lili. *Hollywood's Eve*	B
Bauermeister, Erica. *House Lessons*	B
Bloom, Amy. *In Love*	B

PUBLIC LIBRARY CORE COLLECTION: NONFICTION
Twentieth Edition

Caldwell, Gail. *Let's Take the Long Way Home*	B
Cleage, Pearl. *Things I Should Have Told My Daughter*	B
Dearborn, Mary V. *Carson McCullers*	B
Febos, Melissa. ★*Body Work*	808.06
Feldman, Deborah. *Unorthodox*	B
Franklin, Ruth. *Shirley Jackson*	B
Gary, Amy. *In the Great Green Room*	813
Gilbert, Sandra M. ★*Still Mad*	810.9
Gooch, Brad. ★*Flannery*	B
Hamlin, Kimberly A. *Free Thinker*	B
hooks, bell. *Wounds of Passion*	B
Iversen, Kristen. *Full Body Burden*	363.17
Kumar, Priyanka. *Conversations with Birds*	598
Le Guin, Ursula K. *Ursula K. Le Guin*	B
Loh, Sandra Tsing. *The Madwoman and the Roomba*	B
Madden, T Kira. *Long Live the Tribe of Fatherless Girls*	814
McDowell, Marta. *The World of Laura Ingalls Wilder*	813
Patchett, Ann. ★*These Precious Days*	814
Philpott, Mary Laura. *Bomb Shelter*	B
Rehak, Melanie. *Girl Sleuth*	813
Rioux, Anne Boyd. *Meg, Jo, Beth, Amy*	813
Seiple, Samantha. *Louisa on the Front Lines*	B
Shafrir, Doree. *Thanks for Waiting*	B
Shapiro, Dani. ★*Inheritance*	B
Showalter, Elaine. ★*A Jury of Her Peers*	810.9
Solnit, Rebecca. ★*Recollections of My Nonexistence*	B
Tallent, Elizabeth. *Scratched*	B
WOMEN AUTHORS, BRITISH	
Rosnay, Tatiana de. *Manderley Forever*	B
Woolf, Virginia. *Moments of Being*	B
WOMEN AUTHORS, ENGLISH	
Cusk, Rachel. *Coventry*	814
Evaristo, Bernardine. *Manifesto*	B
Gordon, Charlotte. *Romantic Outlaws*	920
Harman, Claire. *Charlotte Bronte*	B
Montillo, Roseanne. *The Lady and Her Monsters*	823
WOMEN AUTHORS, FRENCH	
Coffin, Judith G. *Sex, Love, and Letters*	848
WOMEN AUTHORS, SCOTTISH	
Thomson, Jennifer. *Josephine Tey*	823
WOMEN AUTOMOBILE MECHANICS	
Milchtein, Chaya M. ★*Mechanic Shop Femme's Guide to Car Ownership*	629.222
WOMEN BALLET DANCERS	
Copeland, Misty. ★*Life in Motion*	B
Copeland, Misty. *The Wind at My Back*	B
Robb, Alice. ★*Don't Think, Dear*	792.8
Valby, Karen. *The Swans of Harlem*	792.8
WOMEN BARTENDERS	
O'Meara, Mallory. *Girly Drinks*	641.2
WOMEN BASKETBALL COACHES	
Summitt, Pat Head. *Sum It Up*	B
WOMEN BASKETBALL PLAYERS	
Wilson, A'ja. ★*Dear Black Girls*	158.1
WOMEN BIOCHEMISTS	
Kariko, Katalin. *Breaking Through*	B
WOMEN BIOLOGISTS	
Cooke, Lucy. *Bitch*	591.56
Lowman, Margaret. *The Arbornaut*	581.7
Lowman, Margaret. *Life in the Treetops*	B
Maathai, Wangari. *Unbowed*	B
Maddox, Brenda. *Rosalind Franklin*	B
McNeur, Catherine. *Mischievous Creatures*	920
WOMEN BIRD WATCHERS	
Gentile, Olivia. *Life List*	598.072
WOMEN BOOKSELLERS	
Frenkel, Francoise. *A Bookshop in Berlin*	B
Wassef, Nadia. *Shelf Life*	B
WOMEN BOTANISTS	
Sevigny, Melissa L. ★*Brave the Wild River*	580.9
WOMEN BROKERS	
Fabre, Cin. *Wolf Hustle*	332.6
WOMEN BUSINESS OWNERS	
Wassef, Nadia. *Shelf Life*	B
WOMEN CABINET OFFICERS	
Albright, Madeleine Korbel. *Hell and Other Destinations*	B
WOMEN CANCER SURVIVORS	
Ephron, Delia. *Left on Tenth*	B

Jaouad, Suleika. ★*Between Two Kingdoms*	B
WOMEN CAREGIVERS	
Dubin, Minna. ★*Mom Rage*	306.874
Lang, Maya. *What We Carry*	B
Washington, Kate. ★*Already Toast*	649.8
WOMEN CARTOONISTS	
Holt, Nathalia. *The Queens of Animation*	920
Johnson, Mindy. *Ink & Paint*	B
WOMEN CELEBRITIES	
Blais, Madeleine. *Queen of the Court*	B
Dench, Judi. *Shakespeare*	792
Fox, Julia. *Down the Drain*	B
Gabriel, Mary. *Madonna*	B
Koppel, Lily. *The Astronaut Wives Club*	920
Mann, William J. *Hello, Gorgeous*	B
Reynolds, Debbie. *Make 'Em Laugh*	B
Ripa, Kelly. *Live Wire*	B
Spears, Britney. *The Woman in Me*	B
Union, Gabrielle. *You Got Anything Stronger?*	B
WOMEN CHIEF EXECUTIVE OFFICERS	
Lima, Jamie Kern. *Believe It*	B
Nooyi, Indra. ★*My Life in Full*	B
O'Brien, Vanessa. *To the Greatest Heights*	B
WOMEN CHIEFS (POLITICAL ANTHROPOLOGY)	
Brown, Nancy Marie. *The Real Valkyrie*	948
WOMEN CHILDREN'S LITERATURE AUTHORS	
Bergstein, Rachelle. *The Genius of Judy*	813
Gary, Amy. *In the Great Green Room*	813
WOMEN CIA AGENTS	
Hillsberg, Christina. *License to Parent*	649.1
WOMEN CIVIL RIGHTS WORKERS	
Angelou, Maya. *A Song Flung up to Heaven*	B
Gilliam, Dorothy Butler. *Trailblazer*	B
King, Coretta Scott. ★*My Life, My Love, My Legacy*	B
WOMEN COLLEGE GRADUATES	
Flannery, Kate. *Strip Tees*	338.4
Sandberg, Sheryl. *Lean In*	658.4
WOMEN COLLEGE STUDENTS	
Mock, Janet. *Surpassing Certainty*	B
Perkins, Anne Gardiner. *Yale Needs Women*	378
Plath, Sylvia. *The Letters of Sylvia Plath*	811.54
Plath, Sylvia. *The Letters of Sylvia Plath*	811.54
Westover, Tara. ★*Educated*	B
WOMEN COLLEGE TEACHERS	
Bowler, Kate. *No Cure for Being Human*	B
Butcher, Amy. *Mothertrucker*	B
Edson, Margaret. *Wit*	812
Jones, Chloe Cooper. ★*Easy Beauty*	B
Kim, Suki. *Without You, There Is No Us*	B
Smith, Freda Love. *I Quit Everything*	B
Tallent, Elizabeth. *Scratched*	B
WOMEN COLONISTS	
Fraser, Rebecca. *The Mayflower*	974.4
WOMEN COMEDIANS	
Bennetts, Leslie. *Last Girl Before Freeway*	B
Burnett, Carol. *In Such Good Company*	791.45
Courogen, Carrie. ★*Miss May Does Not Exist*	B
Devantez, Chelsea. ★*I Shouldn't Be Telling You This*	B
Fumudoh, Ziwe. ★*Black Friend*	814
Gadsby, Hannah. ★*Ten Steps to Nanette*	B
Haddish, Tiffany. *The Last Black Unicorn*	B
Irby, Samantha. ★*Quietly Hostile*	814
Kaling, Mindy. *Why Not Me?*	B
Levy, Shawn. ★*In on the Joke*	792.7
Orji, Yvonne. *Bamboozled by Jesus*	B
Poehler, Amy. *Yes Please*	B
Robinson, Phoebe. *Please Don't Sit on My Bed in Your Outside Clothes*	818
Robinson, Phoebe. *You Can't Touch My Hair and Other Things I Still Have to Explain*	792.7
Ruffin, Amber. ★*The World Record Book of Racist Stories*	305.896
Ruffin, Amber. *You'll Never Believe What Happened to Lacey*	305.896
Schumer, Amy. *The Girl with the Lower Back Tattoo*	B
Shannon, Molly. ★*Hello, Molly!*	B
Wasson, Sam. ★*Improv Nation*	792.02
Wong, Ali. ★*Dear Girls*	B
WOMEN COMMUNISTS	
Lessing, Doris May. *Under My Skin*	823

AUTHOR, TITLE, SERIES AND SUBJECT INDEX

WOMEN COMPOSERS
   Porter, Cecelia Hopkins. *Five Lives in Music* — B
WOMEN COMPUTER ENGINEERS
   Beyer, Kurt. *Grace Hopper and the Invention of the Information Age* — B
WOMEN COMPUTER PROGRAMMERS
   Evans, Claire Lisa. *Broad Band* — 920
   Kleiman, Kathy. *Proving Ground* — 4.092
   Windsor, Edie. *A Wild and Precious Life* — B
WOMEN COMPUTER SCIENTISTS
   Evans, Claire Lisa. *Broad Band* — 920
   Li, Fei-Fei. *The Worlds I See* — B
WOMEN COOKBOOK AUTHORS
   Narayan, Shoba. *The Milk Lady of Bangalore* — 390
WOMEN COOKS
   Ali, Fatima. ★*Savor* — B
   Gardner, Lindsay. *Why We Cook* — 641.5
   Nathan, Joan. ★*My Life in Recipes* — 641.5
   Powell, Julie. *Julie and Julia* — 641.5
   Prud'homme, Alex. *The French Chef in America* — B
   Sen, Mayukh. *Taste Makers* — 641.5092
   Waters, Alice. *Coming to My Senses* — B
WOMEN COUNTRY MUSICIANS
   Lynn, Loretta. ★*Me & Patsy Kickin' up Dust* — B
   McDonough, Jimmy. *Tammy Wynette* — B
   Moss, Marissa R. *Her Country* — 781.642
   Parton, Dolly. ★*Behind the Seams* — B
   Parton, Dolly. ★*Dolly Parton, Songteller* — B
   Price, Margo. *Maybe We'll Make It* — B
   Smarsh, Sarah. *She Come by It Natural* — 782.42164
WOMEN DANCERS
   Flaherty, Meghan. *Tango Lessons* — 793.3
   Johnson, Stephanie. *Tanqueray* — B
   Lewis, Damien. *Agent Josephine* — B
WOMEN DETECTIVES
   McGough, Matthew. *The Lazarus Files* — 364.152
WOMEN DOG OWNERS
   Conaboy, Kelly. *The Particulars of Peter* — 636.7
   Halpern, Sue. *A Dog Walks into a Nursing Home* — B
WOMEN DRUG ABUSERS
   Dresner, Amy. *My Fair Junkie* — B
   Whitaker, Holly. ★*Quit Like a Woman* — 616.86
WOMEN ECOLOGISTS
   Lowman, Margaret. *Life in the Treetops* — B
   Simard, S. ★*Finding the Mother Tree* — 582.16
   Wynn-Grant, Rae. *Wild Life* — B
WOMEN EDITORS
   Anthony, Carl Sferrazza. *Camera Girl* — B
   Franklin, Sara B. ★*The Editor* — B
   Miller, Adrienne. *In the Land of Men* — 070.5
   Odell, Amy. *Anna* — B
   Reed, Julia. *Dispatches from the Gilded Age* — B
   Reichl, Ruth. *My Kitchen Year* — 641.5
WOMEN EDUCATORS
   De Stefano, Cristina. *The Child Is the Teacher* — B
   Mufleh, Luma. ★*Learning America* — 371.826
   Simmons, Ruth. ★*Up Home* — B
WOMEN EMPLOYEES
   Auerbach, Annie. *Flex* — 331.25
   Chang, Leslie T. ★*Egyptian Made* — 331.4
   Johnson, Mindy. *Ink & Paint* — B
WOMEN ENGINEERS
   Holt, Nathalia. ★*Rise of the Rocket Girls* — 629.4
WOMEN ENTERTAINERS
   Jacobs, Alexandra. *Still Here* — B
   Mann, William J. *Hello, Gorgeous* — B
   Press, Joy. *Stealing the Show* — 791.45
   Spoto, Donald. *High Society* — B
WOMEN ENTREPRENEURS
   Bertch, Jane. *The French Ingredient* — B
   Felder, Deborah G. *The American Women's Almanac* — 305.40973
   Hamilton, Lisa M. *The Hungry Season* — B
   Lemmon, Gayle Tzemach. *The Dressmaker of Khair Khana* — B
WOMEN ENVIRONMENTALISTS
   Clinton, Hillary Rodham. *The Book of Gutsy Women* — 920
   Craig, Mya-Rose. *Birdgirl* — B
   Davis, Jack E. *An Everglades Providence* — B
   Johnson, Kirk W. *The Fishermen and the Dragon* — 976.4
   Maathai, Wangari. *Unbowed* — B

Souder, William. *On a Farther Shore* — B
WOMEN EQUESTRIANS
   Letts, Elizabeth. ★*The Ride of Her Life* — B
WOMEN EXECUTIVES
   Boden, Anne. *Female Founders' Playbook* — 658.4
   Cerulo, Erica. *Work Wife* — 658.4
   Darby, Seyward. ★*Sisters in Hate* — 305.800973
   Dufu, Tiffany. *Drop the Ball* — 650.1
   Glatt, John. ★*The Perfect Father* — 364.152
   Lipman, Joanne. *That's What She Said* — 305.30973
   Marshall, Cynthia. *You've Been Chosen* — B
   Nooyi, Indra. ★*My Life in Full* — B
   Sandberg, Sheryl. *Lean In* — 658.4
   Sandberg, Sheryl. *Lean In* — 658.4
   Satow, Julie. *When Women Ran Fifth Avenue* — 381.141
   Sun, Carrie. *Private Equity* — B
WOMEN EXILES
   Alinizhad, Masih. *The Wind in My Hair* — B
WOMEN EXPLORERS
   Bellows, Amanda Brickell. *The Explorers* — 910.92
   Croke, Vicki. *The Lady and the Panda* — 599.789
   Kimberley, Hannah. *A Woman's Place Is at the Top* — B
   Niven, Jennifer. *Ada Blackjack* — B
   Zanglein, Jayne E. *The Girl Explorers* — B
WOMEN FARMERS
   Hamilton, Lisa M. *The Hungry Season* — B
WOMEN FASHION DESIGNERS
   De Courcy, Anne. *Chanel's Riviera* — 944.9
   Garelick, Rhonda K. *Mademoiselle* — B
   Secrest, Meryle. *Elsa Schiaparelli* — 746.9
   Von Furstenberg, Diane. *The Woman I Wanted to Be* — B
WOMEN FBI AGENTS
   Monroe, Jana. *Hearts of Darkness* — 363.25
   Sherman, Casey. *Hunting Whitey* — B
WOMEN FENCERS
   Muhammad, Ibtihaj. *Proud* — B
WOMEN FILM PRODUCERS AND DIRECTORS
   Courogen, Carrie. ★*Miss May Does Not Exist* — B
   Lane, Christina. *Phantom Lady* — B
   Seidelman, Susan. *Desperately Seeking Something* — B
   Streisand, Barbra. ★*My Name Is Barbra* — B
   Trimborn, Jurgen. *Leni Riefenstahl* — B
WOMEN FILMMAKERS
   Selvaratnam, Tanya. *Assume Nothing* — B
WOMEN FISHERS
   Messineo, Janet. *Casting into the Light* — 799.1
WOMEN FOOD WRITERS
   Nathan, Joan. ★*My Life in Recipes* — 641.5
   Reichl, Ruth. *Comfort Me with Apples* — B
   Reichl, Ruth. *My Kitchen Year* — 641.5
WOMEN FORENSIC PSYCHIATRISTS
   Ford, Elizabeth. *Sometimes Amazing Things Happen* — B
WOMEN FORENSIC SCIENTISTS
   Butcher, Barbara. *What the Dead Know* — 614
   Goldfarb, Bruce. ★*18 Tiny Deaths* — B
WOMEN FORMER CONVICTS
   Burton, Susan. *Becoming Ms. Burton* — B
   Murdoch, Sierra Crane. ★*Yellow Bird* — 364.152
WOMEN GARDENERS
   Roach, Margaret. ★*A Way to Garden* — 635
WOMEN GOSPEL SINGERS
   Cobbs-Leonard, Tasha. *Do It Anyway* — 241
   Kot, Greg. *I'll Take You There* — B
WOMEN GRADUATE STUDENTS
   Cooper, Becky. *We Keep the Dead Close* — 364.152
   Freitas, Donna. *Consent* — 364.158092
WOMEN HACKERS
   Smith, Jeremy N. *Breaking and Entering* — B
WOMEN HEADS OF STATE
   Palmieri, Jennifer. *Dear Madam President* — 158
WOMEN HIKERS
   Davis, Jennifer Pharr. *Called Again* — B
WOMEN HISTORIANS
   Hale, Grace Elizabeth. *In the Pines* — 364.13
   Hall, Rebecca. *Wake* — 741.5
   Lepore, Jill. ★*The Deadline* — 814
WOMEN HOLOCAUST SURVIVORS
   Eisen, Norman L. *The Last Palace* — 920

WOMEN HORROR AUTHORS
Kroger, Lisa. *Monster, She Wrote* — 920
WOMEN HORSE TRAINERS
Gaffney, Ginger. *Half Broke* — B
WOMEN HUMAN RIGHTS ACTIVISTS
Leng'ete, Nice. *The Girls in the Wild Fig Tree* — B
WOMEN IMMIGRANTS
Barrett, Duncan. *GI Brides* — 920
Hanna-Attisha, Mona. *What the Eyes Don't See* — 615.9
Hirono, Mazie. *Heart of Fire* — B
Hochschild, Adam. *Rebel Cinderella* — B
Jayapal, Pramila. *Use the Power You Have* — B
Kariko, Katalin. *Breaking Through* — B
Nguyen, Bich Minh. *Owner of a Lonely Heart* — B
Nooyi, Indra. ★*My Life in Full* — B
Nyamayaro, Elizabeth. *I Am a Girl from Africa* — B
Sen, Mayukh. *Taste Makers* — 641.5092
Yeung, Bernice. *In a Day's Work* — 362.88086
WOMEN IN COMBAT
Hegar, Mary Jennings. *Shoot Like a Girl* — B
WOMEN IN FILMS
Tietjen, Jill S. *Hollywood, Her Story* — 791.43
West, Lindy. *The Witches Are Coming* — 305.420973
WOMEN IN LITERATURE
Beard, Mary. ★*Women & Power* — 305.409
Blaisdell, Robert. *Creating Anna Karenina* — 891.7
Rioux, Anne Boyd. *Meg, Jo, Beth, Amy* — 813
Showalter, Elaine. ★*A Jury of Her Peers* — 810.9
Tatar, Maria. *The Heroine with 1001 Faces* — 809
WOMEN IN MASS MEDIA
Gilbert, Sandra M. ★*Still Mad* — 810.9
Ratajkowski, Emily. ★*My Body* — B
West, Lindy. *The Witches Are Coming* — 305.420973
WOMEN IN POPULAR CULTURE
Bordo, Susan. *The Creation of Anne Boleyn* — 942.05
Orenstein, Peggy. *Don't Call Me Princess* — 305.42
Tatar, Maria. *The Heroine with 1001 Faces* — 809
West, Lindy. *The Witches Are Coming* — 305.420973
WOMEN IN PUBLIC LIFE
Koppel, Lily. *The Astronaut Wives Club* — 920
Women in Science. Ignotofsky, Rachel — 920
WOMEN IN TECHNOLOGY
Evans, Claire Lisa. *Broad Band* — 920
Vasquez-Lavado, Silvia. *In the Shadow of the Mountain* — B
WOMEN IN TELEVISION
Armstrong, Jennifer Keishin. *When Women Invented Television* — 791.45
Press, Joy. *Stealing the Show* — 791.45
WOMEN IN THE BIBLE
Armas, Kat. *Abuelita Faith* — 248.8
WOMEN IN THE FILM INDUSTRY AND TRADE
Tietjen, Jill S. *Hollywood, Her Story* — 791.43
Women in White Coats. Campbell, Olivia — 610.92
WOMEN INTELLECTUALS
Doherty, Maggie. *The Equivalents* — 920
Hamlin, Kimberly A. *Free Thinker* — B
Koch, Bea. *Mad and Bad* — 920
Moser, Benjamin. ★*Sontag* — B
Painter, Nell Irvin. *Old in Art School* — B
Solnit, Rebecca. ★*Recollections of My Nonexistence* — B
WOMEN INTELLIGENCE OFFICERS
Fox, Amaryllis. *Life Undercover* — B
Helm, Sarah. *A Life in Secrets* — B
Mundy, Liza. ★*The Sisterhood* — 327.12
Willner, Nina. *Forty Autumns* — B
Young, Daniella Mestyanek. *Uncultured* — B
WOMEN INTERIOR DECORATORS
Blakeney, Justina. *Jungalow* — 747
WOMEN INTERNMENT CAMP INMATES
Haitiwaji, Gulbahar. *How I Survived a Chinese "Reeducation" Camp* — 305.8
Helm, Sarah. *Ravensbruck* — 940.53
Strauss, Gwen. *The Nine* — 940.53
WOMEN INVENTORS
Marcal, Katrine. *Mother of Invention* — 604.82
Reser, Anna. *Forces of Nature* — 509.2
Shearer, Stephen Michael. *Beautiful* — B
WOMEN INVESTIGATIVE JOURNALISTS
Ressa, Maria. ★*How to Stand up to a Dictator* — 070.92

WOMEN JAZZ MUSICIANS
Hayes, Elaine M. ★*Queen of Bebop* — B
WOMEN JOCKEYS
Askwith, Richard. *Unbreakable* — B
WOMEN JOURNALISTS
Alderton, Dolly. *Everything I Know About Love* — B
Alinizhad, Masih. *The Wind in My Hair* — B
Barnett, Erica C. *Quitter* — B
Blake, Melissa. *Beautiful People* — 362.4
Blakinger, Keri. *Corrections in Ink* — B
Bond, Melissa. *Blood Orange Night* — 616.8
Bosker, Bianca. *Get the Picture* — 701
Burton, Susan. *Empty* — B
Cardwell, Diane. *Rockaway* — B
Caruana Galizia, Paul. ★*A Death in Malta* — 364.15
Collins, Lauren. *When in French* — B
Corcoran, Katherine. *In the Mouth of the Wolf* — 364.152
Crabapple, Molly. *Drawing Blood* — B
Cross, Tiffany D. *Say It Louder!* — 324.6
Doty, Cate. *Mergers and Acquisitions* — 395.2
Ephron, Nora. *The Most of Nora Ephron* — 814
Evangelista, Patricia. ★*Some People Need Killing* — 364.4
Ferguson, Jane. *No Ordinary Assignment* — B
Golay, Michael. *America 1933* — B
Green, Robin. *The Only Girl* — 070.92
Gupta, Prachi. ★*They Called Us Exceptional* — B
Hernandez, Daisy. *A Cup of Water Under My Bed* — B
Hill, Jemele. *Uphill* — B
Hilsum, Lindsey. *In Extremis* — B
Hinojosa, Maria. *Once I Was You* — B
Hoja, Gulchehra. *A Stone Is Most Precious Where It Belongs* — B
Hu, Elise. *Flawless* — 646.7
Igort. *The Ukrainian and Russian Notebooks* — 741.5
Jaouad, Suleika. ★*Between Two Kingdoms* — B
Jones, Chloe Cooper. ★*Easy Beauty* — B
Kazdin, Cole. ★*What's Eating Us* — 616.85
Kissinger, Meg. *While You Were Out* — 362.2
Kroeger, Brooke. *Undaunted* — 070.4
LaFollette, Marcel C. *Writing for Their Lives* — 071.3
Lawton, Georgina. *Raceless* — B
MacKrell, Judith. *The Correspondents* — 070.4
Martini, Adrienne. *Somebody's Gotta Do It* — B
Mead, Rebecca. *My Life in Middlemarch* — 823
Mekhennet, Souad. *I Was Told to Come Alone* — 363.3250956
Morris, James McGrath. *Eye on the Struggle* — B
Napoli, Lisa. *Susan, Linda, Nina & Cokie* — 920
Nir, Sarah Maslin. *Horse Crazy* — B
Odell, Amy. *Anna* — B
Page, Susan. ★*The Rulebreaker* — B
Power, Marianne. *Help Me!* — 158.1
Quinn, Susan. *Eleanor and Hick* — B
Ransby, Barbara. *Eslanda* — B
Roberts, Steven V. *Cokie* — B
Smith, Carol. *Crossing the River* — B
Snyder, Rachel Louise. *Women We Buried, Women We Burned* — B
Sullivan, Margaret. *Newsroom Confidential* — 070.92
Todd, Kim. *Sensational* — 920
Totenberg, Nina. ★*Dinners with Ruth* — B
Tur, Katy. *Rough Draft* — B
Wagner, Alex. *Futureface* — B
Ward, Clarissa. *On All Fronts* — B
West, Lindy. *Shrill* — 818
WOMEN JUDGES
Brown-Nagin, Tomiko. *Civil Rights Queen* — B
Carmon, Irin. *Notorious RBG* — B
De Hart, Jane Sherron. ★*Ruth Bader Ginsburg* — B
Ginsburg, Ruth Bader. ★*My Own Words* — 347.73
Hirshman, Linda R. *Sisters in Law* — 347.73
Rosen, Jeffrey. *Conversations with RBG* — B
Sotomayor, Sonia. ★*My Beloved World* — B
Thomas, Evan. ★*First* — B
Totenberg, Nina. ★*Dinners with Ruth* — B
WOMEN KIDNAPPING VICTIMS
Egan, Timothy. ★*A Fever in the Heartland* — 322.4
Tjipombo, Tupa. *I Am Not Your Slave* — B
WOMEN LABOR UNIONISTS
Worley, Jennifer. *Neon Girls* — 792.7

AUTHOR, TITLE, SERIES AND SUBJECT INDEX

WOMEN LANDOWNERS
   Lovell, Mary S. *Bess of Hardwick* — B
WOMEN LAWYERS
   Barnett, Brittany K. ★*A Knock at Midnight* — B
   Bee, Vanessa A. *Home Bound* — B
   Calcaterra, Regina. *Etched in Sand* — B
   Girma, Haben. *Haben* — B
   Goldberg, Carrie. *Nobody's Victim* — 345.73
   Jarrett, Valerie. *Finding My Voice* — B
   Kouchner, Camille. *The Familia Grande* — B
   Lithwick, Dahlia. *Lady Justice* — 345.73
   Norgren, Jill. *Belva Lockwood* — B
   Obama, Michelle. ★*The Light We Carry* — B
   Roundtree, Dovey Johnson. ★*Mighty Justice* — B
   Tate, Christie. ★*Group* — B
WOMEN LEGISLATORS
   Andrews-Dyer, Helena. *Reclaiming Her Time* — B
   Ball, Molly. ★*Pelosi* — B
   Cheney, Liz. *Oath and Honor* — 328.73
   Clinton, Hillary Rodham. *Living History* — B
   Hirono, Mazie. *Heart of Fire* — B
   Jayapal, Pramila. *Use the Power You Have* — B
   Jones, Brenda. *Alexandria Ocasio-Cortez* — B
   Jones, Brenda. *Maxine Waters* — B
   Steinhauer, Jennifer. *The Firsts* — 320.082
WOMEN LIBRARIANS
   Kraus, Dita. *A Delayed Life* — B
WOMEN LINGUISTS
   Fox, Margalit. *The Riddle of the Labyrinth* — 920
WOMEN MARATHON RUNNERS
   Nolan, Ali. *Master the Marathon* — 796.42
WOMEN MARINE BIOLOGISTS
   Graham, Jasmin. *Sharks Don't Sink* — 597.3
   Widder, Edith. *Below the Edge of Darkness* — 551.46092
WOMEN MARTIAL ARTISTS
   Kang, Mia. *Knockout* — B
WOMEN MATHEMATICIANS
   Essinger, James. *Ada's Algorithm* — B
   Johnson, Katherine G. *My Remarkable Journey* — B
   Kitagawa, Kate. *The Secret Lives of Numbers* — 510.9
   Kleiman, Kathy. *Proving Ground* — 4.092
   Shetterly, Margot Lee. ★*Hidden Figures* — 510.92
   White, Elizabeth B. ★*The Counterfeit Countess* — 940.53
WOMEN MEDICAL PERSONNEL
   Nimura, Janice P. ★*The Doctors Blackwell* — 610.92
   Wright, Jennifer Ashley. ★*Madame Restell* — B
WOMEN MEDIUMS
   Jaher, David. *The Witch of Lime Street* — B
WOMEN MICROBIOLOGISTS
   Colwell, Rita R. *A Lab of One's Own* — B
WOMEN MILITARY HELICOPTER PILOTS
   Hegar, Mary Jennings. *Shoot Like a Girl* — B
WOMEN MISSIONARIES
   Vaughn, Ellen Santilli. ★*Becoming Elisabeth Elliot* — B
Women Money Power. Cox, Josie — 330.082
WOMEN MOUNTAINEERS
   DiGiulian, Sasha. *Take the Lead* — B
   Kimberley, Hannah. *A Woman's Place Is at the Top* — B
   O'Brien, Vanessa. *To the Greatest Heights* — B
WOMEN MURDER SUSPECTS
   Hortis, C. Alexander. *The Witch of New York* — 364.152
   McGough, Matthew. *The Lazarus Files* — 364.152
WOMEN MURDER VICTIMS
   Ahmed, Azam. *Fear Is Just a Word* — 364.152
   Gerard, Sarah. *Carrie Carolyn Coco* — 364.152
   Glatt, John. ★*The Perfect Father* — 364.152
   Lauren, Jillian. *Behold the Monster* — 364.152
   McDiarmid, Jessica. *Highway of Tears* — 364.152
   McGough, Matthew. *The Lazarus Files* — 364.152
   Miles, Kathryn. *Trailed* — 364.152
   Rear, Rachel. *Catch the Sparrow* — 364.152
   Rosen, Jonathan. ★*The Best Minds* — 616.89
   Rubenhold, Hallie. ★*The Five* — 362.88
WOMEN MURDERERS
   McCracken, Patti. *The Angel Makers* — 364.152
WOMEN MUSICIANS
   Albertine, Viv. *Clothes, Clothes, Clothes. Music, Music, Music* — B
   Bonner, Betsy. *The Book of Atlantis Black* — 364.152
   Carlile, Brandi. *Broken Horses* — B
   Hope, Clover. *The Motherlode* — 920
   Hopper, Jessica. *The First Collection of Criticism by a Living Female Rock Critic* — 781.66
   Iandoli, Kathy. *God Save the Queens* — 782.421649
   McDonough, Jimmy. *Tammy Wynette* — B
   Phair, Liz. *Horror Stories* — B
   Porter, Cecelia Hopkins. *Five Lives in Music* — B
   Powers, Ann. ★*Traveling* — B
   Smith, Freda Love. *I Quit Everything* — B
   Yaffe, David. *Reckless Daughter* — 782.42164
WOMEN NATURALISTS
   Goodall, Jane. ★*The Book of Hope* — 128
   Souder, William. *On a Farther Shore* — B
The Women of Now. Turk, Katherine — 305.42
WOMEN OFFICE WORKERS
   Mattel, Trixie. *Working Girls* — 650.1
WOMEN OLYMPIC ATHLETES
   Franklin, Missy. *Relentless Spirit* — B
   Gilder, Ginny. *Course Correction* — 797.12
   Montillo, Roseanne. *Fire on the Track* — B
   Muhammad, Ibtihaj. *Proud* — B
   Semenya, Caster. *The Race to Be Myself* — B
   Wilson, A'ja. ★*Dear Black Girls* — 158.1
WOMEN OLYMPIC MEDAL WINNERS
   Franklin, Missy. *Relentless Spirit* — B
   Rapinoe, Megan. *One Life* — B
   Semenya, Caster. *The Race to Be Myself* — B
WOMEN PAINTERS
   Albers, Patricia. *Joan Mitchell* — B
   Hewitt, Catherine. *Renoir's Dancer* — B
   Lehrer, Riva. *Golem Girl* — B
   Stahr, Celia. *Frida in America* — B
WOMEN PEDIATRICIANS
   Hanna-Attisha, Mona. *What the Eyes Don't See* — 615.9
WOMEN PERFORMANCE ARTISTS
   Abramovic, Marina. *Walk Through Walls* — B
WOMEN PERIODICAL EDITORS
   Brown, Tina. *The Vanity Fair Diaries* — B
   Miller, Adrienne. *In the Land of Men* — 070.5
   Stuart, Amanda Mackenzie. *Empress of Fashion* — B
WOMEN PERIODICAL WRITERS
   Kroeger, Brooke. *Undaunted* — 070.4
WOMEN PHILANTHROPISTS
   Doyne, Maggie. *Between the Mountain and the Sky* — B
   Mazzeo, Tilar J. ★*Eliza Hamilton* — B
   McNamara, Eileen. ★*Eunice* — B
WOMEN PHILOSOPHERS
   Coffin, Judith G. *Sex, Love, and Letters* — 848
   Penaluna, Regan. ★*How to Think Like a Woman* — 190.82
WOMEN PHOTOGRAPHERS
   Anthony, Carl Sferrazza. *Camera Girl* — B
   Burke, Carolyn. *Lee Miller* — B
   Copaken, Deborah. *Ladyparts* — B
   Lubow, Arthur. *Diane Arbus* — B
   Marks, Ann. *Vivian Maier Developed* — 778.9
   Rinehart, Lorissa. *First to the Front* — B
   Van Haaften, Julia. ★*Berenice Abbott* — B
WOMEN PHOTOJOURNALISTS
   Addario, Lynsey. *It's What I Do* — B
   Addario, Lynsey. *Of Love & War* — 779
   Kroeger, Brooke. *Undaunted* — 070.4
WOMEN PHYSICIANS
   Brown, Jasmine. *Twice as Hard* — 610.92
   Campbell, Olivia. *Women in White Coats* — 610.92
   Clinton, Hillary Rodham. *The Book of Gutsy Women* — 920
   Green, Stefanie. *This Is Assisted Dying* — 616.02
   Klass, Perri. *A Good Time to Be Born* — 362.19892
   Moore, Wendy. *No Man's Land* — 940.4
   Nimura, Janice P. ★*The Doctors Blackwell* — 610.92
   Ricanati, Elizabeth. *Braided* — B
   Webb, Kinari. *Guardians of the Trees* — B
WOMEN PHYSICISTS
   Sherr, Lynn. *Sally Ride* — B
WOMEN PIANISTS
   Mueller, Melissa. *Alice's Piano* — B
WOMEN PILOTS
   Landdeck, Katherine Sharp. *The Women with Silver Wings* — 920

PUBLIC LIBRARY CORE COLLECTION: NONFICTION
Twentieth Edition

Markham, Beryl. *West with the Night* — B
Mulley, Clare. *The Women Who Flew for Hitler* — 920
O'Brien, Keith. *Fly Girls* — 920
Rahmani, Niloofar. *Open Skies* — B
Teitel, Amy Shira. *Fighting for Space* — 920
Winters, Kathleen C. *Amelia Earhart* — B

WOMEN PLAYWRIGHTS
Coel, Michaela. ★*Misfits* — 158.2
Hudes, Quiara Alegria. ★*My Broken Language* — B
Morgan, Abi. *This Is Not a Pity Memoir* — B
Ruhl, Sarah. *Letters from Max* — 811
V. ★*Reckoning* — 814

WOMEN PLAYWRIGHTS, AMERICAN
Nemiroff, Robert. *To Be Young, Gifted, and Black* — B

WOMEN POETS
Ackmann, Martha. ★*These Fevered Days* — B
Bonner, Betsy. *The Book of Atlantis Black* — 364.152
Brown, Molly McCully. *Places I've Taken My Body* — B
Clark, Heather. ★*Red Comet* — B
Crowther, Gail. *Three-Martini Afternoons at the Ritz* — 920
Doherty, Maggie. *The Equivalents* — 920
Dungy, Camille T. *Soil* — 635.0978
Ehrlich, Gretel. *Unsolaced* — B
Fennelly, Beth Ann. *Heating & Cooling* — B
Gabbert, Elisa. *Any Person Is the Only Self* — 814
Harjo, Joy. *Crazy Brave* — B
Harjo, Joy. ★*Poet Warrior* — B
Lockwood, Patricia. *Priestdaddy* — B
Milford, Nancy. *Savage Beauty* — B
Moore, Marianne. *The Selected Letters of Marianne Moore* — B
Mouton, Deborah D. E. E. P. *Black Chameleon* — B
Plath, Sylvia. *The Letters of Sylvia Plath* — 811.54
Plath, Sylvia. *The Letters of Sylvia Plath* — 811.54
Sinclair, Safiya. ★*How to Say Babylon* — B
Smith, Patti. ★*Just Kids* — B
Travisano, Thomas J. *Love Unknown* — B
Trethewey, Natasha D. ★*Memorial Drive* — B
Winder, Elizabeth. *Pain, Parties, Work* — B
Wong, Jane. ★*Meet Me Tonight in Atlantic City* — B

WOMEN POLITICAL ACTIVISTS
Berry, Mary Frances. *My Face Is Black Is True* — B
Ford, Tanisha C. *Our Secret Society* — B
Gray, Emma. *A Girl's Guide to Joining the Resistance* — 303.48
Griffith, Elisabeth. *Formidable* — 305.42
Gunst, Kathy. *Rage Baking* — 641.86
Hochschild, Adam. *Rebel Cinderella* — B
King, Coretta Scott. ★*My Life, My Love, My Legacy* — B
Moorehead, Caroline. *A House in the Mountains* — 940.53
Richards, Cecile. *Make Trouble* — B
Sarsour, Linda. *We Are Not Here to Be Bystanders* — B
Tamimi, Ahed. ★*They Called Me a Lioness* — B
V. ★*Reckoning* — 814
Watling, Sarah. *Tomorrow Perhaps the Future* — 946.081

WOMEN POLITICAL CONSULTANTS
Biden Owens, Valerie. *Growing up Biden* — B
Psaki, Jen. *Say More* — B

WOMEN POLITICAL PRISONERS
Maathai, Wangari. *Unbowed* — B
Nemat, Marina. *Prisoner of Tehran* — B
Strauss, Gwen. *The Nine* — 940.53

WOMEN POLITICIANS
Albright, Madeleine Korbel. *Hell and Other Destinations* — B
Ball, Molly. ★*Pelosi* — B
Cheney, Liz. *Oath and Honor* — 328.73
Clinton, Hillary Rodham. *The Book of Gutsy Women* — 920
Clinton, Hillary Rodham. *Living History* — B
Cooper, Helene. *Madame President* — 966.62
D'Antonio, Michael. *The Hunting of Hillary* — B
Downey, Kirstin. *Isabella* — B
Duckworth, Tammy. *Every Day Is a Gift* — B
Felder, Deborah G. *The American Women's Almanac* — 305.40973
Foreman, Amanda. *Georgiana, Duchess of Devonshire* — B
Gillard, Julia. ★*Women and Leadership* — 158
Hill, Katie. *She Will Rise* — 305.42
Hirsi Ali, Ayaan. ★*Infidel* — B
Jones, Brenda. *Alexandria Ocasio-Cortez* — B
Jones, Brenda. *Maxine Waters* — B
Klagsbrun, Francine. *Lioness* — B

Lee, Sung-Yoon. *The Sister* — 951.93
Maathai, Wangari. *Unbowed* — B
Martini, Adrienne. *Somebody's Gotta Do It* — B
Moore, Charles. *Margaret Thatcher* — 941.085
Palmieri, Jennifer. *Dear Madam President* — 158
Steinberg, Jonny. *Winnie and Nelson* — 920
Yovanovitch, Marie. *Lessons from the Edge* — 973.933

WOMEN PRESIDENTIAL CANDIDATES
Clinton, Hillary Rodham. *What Happened* — 328.73
D'Antonio, Michael. *The Hunting of Hillary* — B

WOMEN PRESIDENTS
Cooper, Helene. *Madame President* — 966.62
Palmieri, Jennifer. *Dear Madam President* — 158

WOMEN PRIMATOLOGISTS
Goodall, Jane. ★*Beyond Innocence* — B

WOMEN PRIME MINISTERS
Bhutto, Benazir. *Reconciliation* — 297.2
Klagsbrun, Francine. *Lioness* — B
Marton, Kati. ★*The Chancellor* — B
Moore, Charles. *Margaret Thatcher* — 941.085

WOMEN PRISONERS
Horton, Michelle. *Dear Sister* — B
Kruzan, Sara. *I Cried to Dream Again* — B
Moore, Kate. ★*The Woman They Could Not Silence* — B
Norman, Elizabeth M. *We Band of Angels* — 940.54

WOMEN PRIVATE INVESTIGATORS
Krouse, Erika. ★*Tell Me Everything* — 363.25
McGarrahan, Ellen. *Two Truths and a Lie* — 364.152

WOMEN PROFESSIONAL EMPLOYEES
Flannery, Kate. *Strip Tees* — 338.4
Vanek Smith, Stacey. *Machiavelli for Women* — 650.1

WOMEN PSYCHICS
Jaher, David. *The Witch of Lime Street* — B
Knight, Sam. *The Premonitions Bureau* — 133.8

WOMEN PSYCHOLOGISTS
Gildiner, Catherine. *Good Morning, Monster* — 616.89
Pipher, Mary Bray. *A Life in Light* — B

WOMEN PSYCHOTHERAPISTS
Gildiner, Catherine. *Good Morning, Monster* — 616.89
Mandel, Sarah. *Little Earthquakes* — B

WOMEN PUBLIC PROSECUTORS
Coates, Laura Gayle. *Just Pursuit* — 345.73

WOMEN RABBIS
Belser, Julia Watts. ★*Loving Our Own Bones* — 296

WOMEN RADICALS
Duberman, Martin B. *Andrea Dworkin* — B
Miles, Tiya. ★*Night Flyer* — B
O'Brien, Keith. *Paradise Falls* — 363.738
O'Connor, Sinead. ★*Rememberings* — B
Roy, Jessica. *American Girls* — 305.48

WOMEN RADIO JOURNALISTS
Greenfieldboyce, Nell. ★*Transient and Strange* — 501

WOMEN RAP MUSICIANS
Iandoli, Kathy. *God Save the Queens* — 782.421649
Simmons, Nadirah. ★*First Things First* — 782.42164

WOMEN REFUGEES
Goudeau, Jessica. ★*After the Last Border* — 362.83
Hirsi Ali, Ayaan. ★*Infidel* — B
Mikhaiil, Dunya. *The Beekeeper* — 956.7044
Murad, Nadia. ★*The Last Girl* — B
Ung, Loung. *First They Killed My Father* — 959.604

WOMEN RESTAURATEURS
Gardner, Lindsay. *Why We Cook* — 641.5
James, Victoria. *Wine Girl* — B

WOMEN REVOLUTIONARIES
Miller, Marla. *Betsy Ross and the Making of America* — B

WOMEN ROCK MUSICIANS
Etheridge, Melissa. *Talking to My Angels* — B
George-Warren, Holly. ★*Janis* — B
Gordon, Kim. *Girl in a Band* — B
Hanna, Kathleen. *Rebel Girl* — B
Harry, Debbie. *Face It* — B
Ronstadt, Linda. *Feels Like Home* — B
Schemel, Patty. *Hit so Hard* — B
Smith, Patti. ★*Just Kids* — B
Smith, Patti. ★*M Train* — B
Smith, Patti. ★*Year of the Monkey* — B
Winder, Elizabeth. *Parachute Women* — 782.42164

AUTHOR, TITLE, SERIES AND SUBJECT INDEX

Women Rowing North. Pipher, Mary Bray	305.26

WOMEN RULERS
Ackroyd, Peter. *Innovation*	942.082
Baird, Julia. ★*Victoria the Queen*	B
Bordo, Susan. *The Creation of Anne Boleyn*	942.05
Borman, Tracy. *Anne Boleyn and Elizabeth I*	920
Borman, Tracy. *Elizabeth's Women*	B
Cadbury, Deborah. *Queen Victoria's Matchmaking*	941.081
Castor, Helen. *She-Wolves*	942
Chang, Jung. *Empress Dowager Cixi*	B
Charter, David. *Royal Audience*	941.085
Cooney, Kara. *When Women Ruled the World*	920
Downey, Kirstin. *Isabella*	B
Edwards, Anne. *Matriarch*	B
Fraser, Antonia. *Marie Antoinette*	B
Fraser, Antonia. *Mary, Queen of Scots*	B
Fraser, Antonia. ★*The Wives of Henry VIII*	942.05
Gill, Gillian. *We Two*	941.081
Goldstone, Nancy Bazelon. *Daughters of the Winter Queen*	920
Goldstone, Nancy Bazelon. *In the Shadow of the Empress*	920
Goldstone, Nancy Bazelon. *The Rival Queens*	944
Goldsworthy, Adrian Keith. *Antony and Cleopatra*	937
Gristwood, Sarah. *The Tudors in Love*	941.05
Hardman, Robert. *Queen of Our Times*	B
Hardman, Robert. *Queen of the World*	B
Holmes, Elizabeth. *HRH*	941.085
Lal, Ruby. *Empress*	B
Lever, Evelyne. *Marie Antoinette*	B
Lieven, Dominic. *In the Shadow of the Gods*	352.23
Massie, Robert K. *Catherine the Great*	B
Noor. *Leap of Faith*	B
Paranque, Estelle. *Blood, Fire & Gold*	920
Puhak, Shelley. *The Dark Queens*	944
Ronald, Susan. *The Pirate Queen*	B
Russell, Gareth. *Young and Damned and Fair*	B
Schiff, Stacy. ★*Cleopatra*	B
Sebag-Montefiore, Simon. ★*The World*	929.7
Shawcross, William. *The Queen Mother*	B
Smith, Sally Bedell. *Elizabeth the Queen*	B
Southon, Emma. *Agrippina*	B
Starkey, David. *Six Wives*	942.05
Strauss, Barry S. ★*The War That Made the Roman Empire*	937
Tallis, Nicola. *Crown of Blood*	B
Weir, Alison. *The Children of Henry VIII*	B
Weir, Alison. *Eleanor of Aquitaine*	B
Weir, Alison. *The Life of Elizabeth I*	B
Weir, Alison. *Mary, Queen of Scots, and the Murder of Lord Darnley*	941.105
Weir, Alison. *Queens of the Age of Chivalry*	920
Weir, Alison. *Queens of the Conquest*	920
Weir, Alison. *The Six Wives of Henry VIII*	942.05
Williams, Kate. *Ambition and Desire*	B
Wilson, A. N. *Victoria*	B
Worsley, Lucy. *Queen Victoria*	B

WOMEN RUNNERS
Fleshman, Lauren. ★*Good for a Girl*	B
Heminsley, Alexandra. *Running Like a Girl*	B
Keeling, Ida. *Can't Nothing Bring Me Down*	B
Mertens, Maggie. *Better Faster Farther*	796.42
Montillo, Roseanne. *Fire on the Track*	B
Semenya, Caster. *The Race to Be Myself*	B

WOMEN SAILORS
Clark, Liz. *Swell*	B

WOMEN SAINTS
Castor, Helen. *Joan of Arc*	B
Spoto, Donald. *Joan*	B

WOMEN SCHOLARS AND ACADEMICS
Doherty, Maggie. *The Equivalents*	920
Penaluna, Regan. ★*How to Think Like a Woman*	190.82

WOMEN SCIENCE FICTION AUTHORS
Phillips, Julie. *James Tiptree, Jr.*	B

WOMEN SCIENTISTS
Clinton, Hillary Rodham. *The Book of Gutsy Women*	920
Colwell, Rita R. *A Lab of One's Own*	B
Felder, Deborah G. *The American Women's Almanac*	305.40973
Fox, Margalit. *The Riddle of the Labyrinth*	920
Goodall, Jane. ★*Beyond Innocence*	B
Graham, Jasmin. *Sharks Don't Sink*	597.3
Greenfieldboyce, Nell. ★*Transient and Strange*	501
Holt, Nathalia. ★*Rise of the Rocket Girls*	629.4
Ignotofsky, Rachel. *Women in Science*	920
Isaacson, Walter. ★*The Code Breaker*	576.5
Jahren, Hope. ★*Lab Girl*	B
Johnson, Sarah Stewart. *The Sirens of Mars*	576.8
Lance, Rachel. *In the Waves*	973.7
Markel, Howard. *The Secret of Life*	572.86
McNeur, Catherine. *Mischievous Creatures*	920
Popova, Maria. *Figuring*	920
Quave, Cassandra Leah. *The Plant Hunter*	581.6
Reser, Anna. *Forces of Nature*	509.2
Ryckman, Pamela. *Candace Pert*	B
Van Hemert, Caroline. *The Sun Is a Compass*	979.8
Zernike, Kate. *The Exceptions*	331.4

WOMEN SCREENWRITERS
Courogen, Carrie. ★*Miss May Does Not Exist*	B
Ephron, Nora. *The Most of Nora Ephron*	814
Lane, Christina. *Phantom Lady*	B

WOMEN SENATORS
Duckworth, Tammy. *Every Day Is a Gift*	B

WOMEN SERIAL MURDERERS
Schechter, Harold. *Hell's Princess*	B

WOMEN SINGERS
Andrews, Julie. *Home*	B
Blais, Madeleine. *Queen of the Court*	B
Carlile, Brandi. *Broken Horses*	B
Cole, Natalie. *Angel on My Shoulder*	B
DiFranco, Ani. *No Walls and the Recurring Dream*	782.42164
Gabriel, Mary. *Madonna*	B
George-Warren, Holly. ★*Janis*	B
Hanna, Kathleen. *Rebel Girl*	B
Iandoli, Kathy. *Baby Girl*	B
Keiler, Allan. *Marian Anderson*	B
Lynn, Loretta. ★*Me & Patsy Kickin' up Dust*	B
Mann, William J. *Hello, Gorgeous*	B
Moss, Marissa R. *Her Country*	781.642
Newkey-Burden, Chas. *Taylor Swift*	B
Parton, Dolly. ★*Dolly Parton, Songteller*	B
Powers, Ann. *Traveling*	B
Ribowsky, Mark. *The Supremes*	B
Simon, Carly. ★*Boys in the Trees*	782.42164
Smith, Danyel. *Shine Bright*	782.42164
Spears, Britney. *The Woman in Me*	B
Turner, Tina. ★*Happiness Becomes You*	158.1
Zack, Ian. *Odetta*	B

WOMEN SOCCER PLAYERS
Clarke, Gemma. *Soccerwomen*	796.334
Lloyd, Carli. *When Nobody Was Watching*	B
Oxenham, Gwendolyn. *Under the Lights and in the Dark*	796.334
Rapinoe, Megan. *One Life*	B
Wambach, Abby. *Forward*	B

WOMEN SOCIAL ADVOCATES
Bowdler, Michelle. ★*Is Rape a Crime?*	B
Cargle, Rachel Elizabeth. *A Renaissance of Our Own*	B
Clinton, Hillary Rodham. *The Book of Gutsy Women*	920
Cook, Blanche Wiesen. *Eleanor Roosevelt; Volume 2*	B
Cook, Blanche Wiesen. ★*Eleanor Roosevelt; Volume 3*	B
Felder, Deborah G. *The American Women's Almanac*	305.40973
Hirsi Ali, Ayaan. ★*Infidel*	B
King, Billie Jean. ★*All In*	B
Larson, Kate Clifford. *Walk with Me*	B
McCubbin, Lisa. *Betty Ford*	B
Michaelis, David. ★*Eleanor*	973.917
Nyamayaro, Elizabeth. *I Am a Girl from Africa*	B
Ransby, Barbara. *Eslanda*	B
Sohn, Amy. *The Man Who Hated Women*	363.28
Spruill, Marjorie Julian. *Divided We Stand*	305.42
Streisand, Barbra. ★*My Name Is Barbra*	B
Union, Gabrielle. *We're Going to Need More Wine*	B
Vogelstein, Rachel B. *Awakening*	305.42

WOMEN SOCIAL REFORMERS
Bell-Scott, Patricia. *The Firebrand and the First Lady*	920
Burton, Susan. *Becoming Ms. Burton*	B
Clinton, Hillary Rodham. *The Book of Gutsy Women*	920
DiFranco, Ani. *No Walls and the Recurring Dream*	782.42164
Gray, Emma. *A Girl's Guide to Joining the Resistance*	303.48
Painter, Nell Irvin. ★*Sojourner Truth*	B
Quinn, Tallu Schuyler. *What We Wish Were True*	B

PUBLIC LIBRARY CORE COLLECTION: NONFICTION
Twentieth Edition

WOMEN SOCIALISTS
    Hochschild, Adam. *Rebel Cinderella* — B

WOMEN SOLDIERS
    Aleksievich, Svetlana. ★*The Unwomanly Face of War* — 940.53
    Andrews, Lena S. ★*Valiant Women* — 940.53
    Blanton, DeAnne. *They Fought Like Demons* — 973.7
    Castor, Helen. *Joan of Arc* — B
    Hegar, Mary Jennings. *Shoot Like a Girl* — B
    Lemmon, Gayle Tzemach. *Ashley's War* — B
    Lemmon, Gayle Tzemach. *The Daughters of Kobani* — 956.9104
    Moorehead, Caroline. *A House in the Mountains* — 940.53
    Pavlychenko, Liudmyla Mykhailivna. *Lady Death* — B
    Toler, Pamela D. *Women Warriors* — 355.0092

WOMEN SONGWRITERS
    Lynn, Loretta. ★*Me & Patsy Kickin' up Dust* — B
    Phair, Liz. *Horror Stories* — B
    Price, Margo. *Maybe We'll Make It* — B
    Rodgers, Mary. *Shy* — B
    Smarsh, Sarah. *She Come by It Natural* — 782.42164

WOMEN SPIES
    Abbott, Karen. *Liar, Temptress, Soldier, Spy* — 920
    Dunbar, Erica Armstrong. ★*She Came to Slay* — B
    Fox, Amaryllis. *Life Undercover* — B
    Lewis, Damien. *Agent Josephine* — B
    Loftis, Larry. *Code Name* — B
    Macintyre, Ben. ★*Agent Sonya* — B
    Magida, Arthur J. *Code Name Madeleine* — 940.54
    Mazzeo, Tilar J. *Sisters in Resistance* — 945.091
    Mulley, Clare. *The Spy Who Loved* — B
    Mundy, Liza. ★*The Sisterhood* — 327.12
    Olson, Lynne. ★*Madame Fourcade's Secret War* — B
    Popkin, Jim. *Code Name Blue Wren* — 327.12
    Purnell, Sonia. ★*A Woman of No Importance* — B
    Rose, Sarah. *D-Day Girls* — 940.53
    Walder, Tracy. *The Unexpected Spy* — B
    Waller, Douglas C. *Lincoln's Spies* — 973.7

WOMEN STAND-UP COMEDIANS
    Dresner, Amy. *My Fair Junkie* — B
    Levy, Shawn. *In on the Joke* — 792.7

WOMEN SUPREME COURT JUSTICES
    Rosen, Jeffrey. *Conversations with RBG* — B
    Thomas, Evan. ★*First* — B

WOMEN SURFERS
    Cardwell, Diane. *Rockaway* — B
    Clark, Liz. *Swell* — B

WOMEN SWIMMERS
    Cox, Lynne. *Swimming to Antarctica* — B
    Franklin, Missy. *Relentless Spirit* — B
    Mardini, Yusra. *Butterfly* — B
    Mortimer, Gavin. *The Great Swim* — B
    Nyad, Diana. *Find a Way* — B

WOMEN TEACHERS
    Cadbury, Deborah. *The School That Escaped from the Nazis* — 940.53
    Clinton, Hillary Rodham. *The Book of Gutsy Women* — 920
    Cook, Kevin. *The Burning Blue* — 629.45
    Geller, Danielle. *Dog Flowers* — B
    Gibson, William. ★*The Miracle Worker* — 812
    Williams, Tennessee. ★*A Streetcar Named Desire* — 812

WOMEN TELEVISION JOURNALISTS
    Couric, Katie. *Going There* — B
    Psaki, Jen. *Say More* — B

WOMEN TELEVISION NEWSCASTERS AND COMMENTATORS
    Couric, Katie. *Going There* — B
    Kroeger, Brooke. *Undaunted* — 070.4

WOMEN TELEVISION PERSONALITIES
    Bertinelli, Valerie. *Enough Already* — B
    Gaines, Joanna. *The Stories We Tell* — B
    Guthrie, Savannah. *Mostly What God Does* — 248.4
    Kaling, Mindy. *Why Not Me?* — B
    Page, Susan. ★*The Rulebreaker* — B
    Wong, Carmen Rita. *Why Didn't You Tell Me?* — B

WOMEN TELEVISION PRODUCERS AND DIRECTORS
    Lane, Christina. *Phantom Lady* — B
    Nawaz, Zarqa. *Laughing All the Way to the Mosque* — 791.45028
    Press, Joy. *Stealing the Show* — 791.45
    Soloway, Jill. *She Wants It* — B

WOMEN TELEVISION TALK SHOW HOSTS AND GUESTS
    Guthrie, Savannah. *Mostly What God Does* — 248.4

    Ripa, Kelly. *Live Wire* — B

WOMEN TELEVISION WRITERS
    Henderson, Danielle. ★*The Ugly Cry* — B
    Pritchett, Georgia. *My Mess Is a Bit of a Life* — B
    Soloway, Jill. *She Wants It* — B

WOMEN TENNIS PLAYERS
    Blais, Madeleine. *Queen of the Court* — B
    Howard, Johnette. *The Rivals* — B
    Jacobs, Sally H. *Althea* — B
    King, Billie Jean. ★*All In* — B
    Rothenberg, Ben. *Naomi Osaka* — B
    Sharapova, Maria. *Unstoppable* — B

WOMEN TERRORISTS
    Seierstad, Asne. *Two Sisters* — 956.9104

WOMEN THEATRICAL PRODUCERS AND DIRECTORS
    Huston, Anjelica. *Watch Me* — B
    Soloway, Jill. *She Wants It* — B

WOMEN TRACK AND FIELD ATHLETES
    Semenya, Caster. *The Race to Be Myself* — B

WOMEN TRAVELERS
    Berlin, Lucia. ★*Welcome Home* — B
    Gentile, Olivia. *Life List* — 598.072
    Harris, Kate. *Lands of Lost Borders* — 915.804
    Howell, Georgina. *Gertrude Bell* — B
    Letts, Elizabeth. ★*The Ride of Her Life* — B
    Mayes, Frances. *See You in the Piazza* — 914.5
    Mayes, Frances. *Under the Tuscan Sun* — 945
    Mayes, Frances. *A Year in the World* — B
    Wallach, Janet. *Desert Queen* — B

WOMEN TRUCK DRIVERS
    Butcher, Amy. *Mothertrucker* — B

WOMEN TRUE CRIME WRITERS
    Cep, Casey N. ★*Furious Hours* — 364.152

WOMEN VETERANS
    Howley, Kerry. *Bottoms Up and the Devil Laughs* — 352.37

WOMEN VETERINARIANS
    Attas, Amy. *Pets and the City* — B

WOMEN VIGILANTES
    Ahmed, Azam. *Fear Is Just a Word* — 364.152

WOMEN WAR CORRESPONDENTS
    Addario, Lynsey. *It's What I Do* — B
    Ferguson, Jane. *No Ordinary Assignment* — B
    Hilsum, Lindsey. *In Extremis* — B
    Katz, Catherine Grace. *The Daughters of Yalta* — 920
    Kroeger, Brooke. *Undaunted* — 070.4
    Rinehart, Lorissa. *First to the Front* — B

WOMEN WAR PHOTOGRAPHERS
    Addario, Lynsey. *It's What I Do* — B
    Women Warriors. Toler, Pamela D. — 355.0092

WOMEN WARRIORS
    Brown, Nancy Marie. *The Real Valkyrie* — 948
    Hughes, Bettany. *Venus and Aphrodite* — 292
    Toler, Pamela D. *Women Warriors* — 355.0092
    Women We Buried, Women We Burned. Snyder, Rachel Louise — B

WOMEN WEAVERS
    Badkhen, Anna. *The World Is a Carpet* — 305.409581

WOMEN WHEELCHAIR USERS
    Taussig, Rebekah. *Sitting Pretty* — B
    The Women Who Flew for Hitler. Mulley, Clare — 920
    Women Who Love Men Who Kill. Isenberg, Sheila — 362.83

WOMEN WITH DISABILITIES
    Girma, Haben. *Haben* — B
    Heumann, Judith E. *Being Heumann* — B
    Jones, Chloe Cooper. ★*Easy Beauty* — B
    Keller, Helen. ★*The Story of My Life* — B
    Masters, Oksana. *The Hard Parts* — B
    Purnell, Sonia. ★*A Woman of No Importance* — B
    Taussig, Rebekah. *Sitting Pretty* — B
    The Women with Silver Wings. Landdeck, Katherine Sharp — 920

WOMEN ZOOLOGISTS
    Croke, Vicki. *The Lady and the Panda* — 599.789

WOMEN'S CLOTHING
    Baca, Salena. *Oversize Fashion Crochet* — 746.43
    Edwards, Lydia. *How to Read a Dress* — 391
    Karen, Dawnn. *Dress Your Best Life* — 646
    Linett, Andrea. *The Cool Factor* — 746.9

WOMEN'S HEALTH SERVICES
    Block, Jennifer. *Everything Below the Waist* — 613

AUTHOR, TITLE, SERIES AND SUBJECT INDEX

Brem, Rachel. *No Longer Radical*	616.99
Campbell, Olivia. *Women in White Coats*	610.92
Comen, Elizabeth. ★*All in Her Head*	613
Copaken, Deborah. *Ladyparts*	B
Gunter, Jen. ★*Blood*	612.6
Gupta, Shalene. *The Cycle*	618.1
Hallman, J. C. *Say Anarcha*	618.1
Luthra, Shefali. ★*Undue Burden*	362.1988
Malone, Sharon. *Grown Woman Talk*	362.1
McGregor, Alyson J. *Sex Matters*	613
Nimura, Janice P. ★*The Doctors Blackwell*	610.92
Norman, Abby. *Ask Me About My Uterus*	618.1
Parker, Lara. *Vagina Problems*	618.1
Shah, Meera. *You're the Only One I've Told*	362.1988
Tang, Karen. ★*It's Not Hysteria*	618.2

WOMEN'S HISTORY

Armstrong, Jennifer Keishin. *When Women Invented Television*	791.45
Collins, Gail. *When Everything Changed*	305.40973
Cox, Josie. *Women Money Power*	330.082
Faust, Drew Gilpin. *Mothers of Invention*	973.7
Felder, Deborah G. *The American Women's Almanac*	305.40973
Griffith, Elisabeth. *Formidable*	305.42
Jenkins, Jessica D. *Exploring Women's Suffrage Through 50 Historic Treasures*	324.6
Kessler-Harris, Alice. ★*Out to Work*	331.4
Koch, Bea. *Mad and Bad*	920
Quinn, Bridget. *She Votes*	324.6
Reser, Anna. *Forces of Nature*	509.2
Roberts, Cokie. *Founding Mothers*	920
Yellin, Emily. *Our Mothers' War*	940.53

WOMEN'S MOVEMENT

Campbell, Olivia. *Women in White Coats*	610.92
Felder, Deborah G. *The American Women's Almanac*	305.40973
Gilbert, Sandra M. ★*Still Mad*	810.9
Griffith, Elisabeth. *Formidable*	305.42
Hirshman, Linda R. *Reckoning*	305.420973
McShane Wulfhart, Nell. *The Great Stewardess Rebellion*	331.4
Rosenberg, Rosalind. ★*Jane Crow*	B
Vogelstein, Rachel B. *Awakening*	305.42
Zakaria, Rafia. *Against White Feminism*	305.42

WOMEN'S PARTICIPATION IN WARS

Aleksievich, Svetlana. ★*The Unwomanly Face of War*	940.53
Barrett, Duncan. *GI Brides*	920
Blanton, DeAnne. *They Fought Like Demons*	973.7
Eder, Mari K. *The Girls Who Stepped Out of Line*	920
Faust, Drew Gilpin. *Mothers of Invention*	973.7
Holton, Woody. *Liberty Is Sweet*	973.3
Katz, Catherine Grace. *The Daughters of Yalta*	920
Kiernan, Denise. *The Girls of Atomic City*	976.8
Landdeck, Katherine Sharp. *The Women with Silver Wings*	920
Lower, Wendy. *Hitler's Furies*	940.53
MacKrell, Judith. *The Correspondents*	070.4
Magida, Arthur J. *Code Name Madeleine*	940.54
Moore, Kate. *The Radium Girls*	363.17
Mundy, Liza. *Code Girls*	940.54
Roberts, Cokie. *Founding Mothers*	920
Yellin, Emily. *Our Mothers' War*	940.53

WOMEN'S POWER

Paranque, Estelle. *Blood, Fire & Gold*	920
Puhak, Shelley. *The Dark Queens*	944
Tallis, Nicola. *Uncrowned Queen*	B

WOMEN'S RESISTANCE AND REVOLTS

Alinizhad, Masih. *The Wind in My Hair*	B

WOMEN'S RIGHTS

Andrews, Becca. ★*No Choice*	362.1988
Barthel, Joan. *American Saint*	B
Boyle, Kevin. *The Shattering*	973.923
Campbell, Olivia. *Women in White Coats*	610.92
Carmon, Irin. *Notorious RBG*	B
Chemaly, Soraya L. *Rage Becomes Her*	155.3
Clinton, Hillary Rodham. *The Book of Gutsy Women*	920
De Hart, Jane Sherron. ★*Ruth Bader Ginsburg*	B
Eltahawy, Mona. *The Seven Necessary Sins for Women and Girls*	305.42
Foster, Diana Greene. *The Turnaway Study*	362.1988
Ginsburg, Ruth Bader. ★*My Own Words*	347.73
Ginzberg, Lori D. *Elizabeth Cady Stanton*	B
Greenberg, Amy S. *Lady First*	B
Griffith, R. Marie. *Moral Combat*	261.8
Gross, Rachel E. *Vagina Obscura*	618.1
Hamlin, Kimberly A. *Free Thinker*	B
Hegar, Mary Jennings. *Shoot Like a Girl*	B
Hirshman, Linda R. *Reckoning*	305.420973
Hirshman, Linda R. *Sisters in Law*	347.73
Inskeep, Steve. *Imperfect Union*	B
Kantor, Jodi. *She Said*	364.15
Kendall, Mikki. *Hood Feminism*	305.420973
Kolbert, Kathryn. *Controlling Women*	362.1988
Kristof, Nicholas D. *Half the Sky*	362.83
Kroeger, Brooke. *Undaunted*	070.4
Leng'ete, Nice. *The Girls in the Wild Fig Tree*	B
Luthra, Shefali. ★*Undue Burden*	362.1988
McCubbin, Lisa. *Betty Ford*	B
Moore, Kate. *The Radium Girls*	363.17
Moore, Kate. *The Woman They Could Not Silence*	B
Moore, Wendy. *No Man's Land*	940.4
Morris, Bonnie J. ★*The Feminist Revolution*	305.4209
Obama, Michelle. ★*Becoming*	B
Prager, Joshua. *The Family Roe*	342.7308
Reese, Anney. ★*Stuff Mom Never Told You*	305.42
Richards, Cecile. *Make Trouble*	B
Satrapi, Marjane. ★*The Complete Persepolis*	741.5
Sisson, Gretchen E. ★*Relinquished*	362.734
Sohn, Amy. *The Man Who Hated Women*	363.28
Spruill, Marjorie Julian. *Divided We Stand*	305.42
Tamblyn, Amber. ★*Era of Ignition*	B
Thomas, Gillian. *Because of Sex*	344.7301
Todd, Kim. *Sensational*	920
Toorpakai, Maria. *A Different Kind of Daughter*	B
Traister, Rebecca. *Good and Mad*	305.420973
Turk, Katherine. *The Women of Now*	305.42
Vanek Smith, Stacey. *Machiavelli for Women*	650.1
Vogelstein, Rachel B. *Awakening*	305.42
Weiss, Elaine F. *The Woman's Hour*	324.6
Yousafzai, Malala. *I Am Malala*	B
Yousafzai, Ziauddin. *Let Her Fly*	B
Zakaria, Rafia. *Against White Feminism*	305.42

WOMEN'S ROLE

Adichie, Chimamanda Ngozi. *Dear Ijeawele*	649
Aleksievich, Svetlana. ★*The Unwomanly Face of War*	940.53
Baird, Julia. ★*Victoria the Queen*	B
Berg, Anastasia. ★*What Are Children For?*	306.87
Borman, Tracy. *Anne Boleyn and Elizabeth I*	920
Brooks, Geraldine. *Nine Parts of Desire*	305.48
Collins, Gail. *When Everything Changed*	305.40973
Cooper, Helene. *Madame President*	966.62
Davis, Lisa. ★*Housewife*	331.4
Franklin, Ruth. *Shirley Jackson*	B
Gates, Melinda. ★*The Moment of Lift*	305.42
Gill, Anton. *Art Lover*	B
Hatmaker, Jen. *Of Mess and Moxie*	248.8
Levy, Shawn. ★*In on the Joke*	792.7
Mann, Jen. ★*Midlife Bites*	305.244
Mulley, Clare. *The Women Who Flew for Hitler*	920
Navai, Ramita. *City of Lies*	955
Noor. *Leap of Faith*	B
Obama, Michelle. ★*Becoming*	B
Petersen, Sara. *Momfluenced*	306.87
Poole, W. Scott. *Vampira*	B
Price, Reynolds. *A Serious Way of Wondering*	241
Purnell, Sonia. ★*A Woman of No Importance*	B
Satrapi, Marjane. ★*The Complete Persepolis*	741.5
Satrapi, Marjane. *Embroideries*	741.5
Shafrir, Doree. *Thanks for Waiting*	B
Smarsh, Sarah. *She Come by It Natural*	782.42164
Stanley, Amy. *Stranger in the Shogun's City*	B
Wasson, Sam. *Fifth Avenue, 5 A.M.*	791.43

WOMEN'S SHOES

Crowe, Lauren Goldstein. *The Towering World of Jimmy Choo*	391.4

WOMEN'S SPORTS

Allred, Alexandra Powe. *When Women Stood*	796.082
Fleshman, Lauren. ★*Good for a Girl*	B
Oxenham, Gwendolyn. *Under the Lights and in the Dark*	796.334

WOMEN'S STUDIES

Morris, Bonnie J. ★*The Feminist Revolution*	305.4209
Saini, Angela. *Inferior*	305.4
Women, *Food, and Desire*. Jamieson, Alexandra	155.3

PUBLIC LIBRARY CORE COLLECTION: NONFICTION
Twentieth Edition

WOMEN-OWNED BUSINESSES
    Cerulo, Erica. *Work Wife* — 658.4
WOMEN-WOMEN RELATIONS
    Doyle, Glennon. *Untamed* — B
    Machado, Carmen Maria. ★*In the Dream House* — B
    Possanza, Amelia. *Lesbian Love Story* — B
    Quinn, Susan. *Eleanor and Hick* — B
    Shapland, Jenn. *My Autobiography of Carson McCullers* — B
Wonder Boy. Au-Yeung, Angel — B
★*Wonder Drug*. Vanderbes, Jennifer — 615
The Wonder of Birds. Robbins, Jim — 598
★*The Wonder Paradox*. Hecht, Jennifer Michael — 808.1
WONDER WOMAN (FICTITIOUS CHARACTER)
    Lepore, Jill. ★*The Secret History of Wonder Woman* — 741.5
WONDER, STEVIE
    Ribowsky, Mark. *Signed, Sealed, and Delivered* — B
Wonderland. Johnson, Steven — 790.1
Wong, Ali
    ★*Dear Girls* — B
WONG, ALI
    Wong, Ali. ★*Dear Girls* — B
Wong, Alice
    ★*Year of the Tiger* — B
WONG, ALICE, 1974-
    Wong, Alice. ★*Year of the Tiger* — B
WONG, ANNA MAY, 1905-1961
    Huang, Yunte. *Daughter of the Dragon* — B
    Salisbury, Katie Gee. ★*Not Your China Doll* — B
Wong, Carmen Rita
    Why Didn't You Tell Me? — B
WONG, CARMEN RITA
    Wong, Carmen Rita. *Why Didn't You Tell Me?* — B
Wong, Cecily
    ★*Gastro Obscura* — 641.3
Wong, Chun Han
    Party of One — 951.06
Wong, Jane
    ★*Meet Me Tonight in Atlantic City* — B
WONG, JANE
    Wong, Jane. ★*Meet Me Tonight in Atlantic City* — B
Wong, Stephen
    Game Worn — 796.357
    Smithsonian Baseball — 796.357
Woo, Ilyon
    ★*Master Slave Husband Wife* — 920
Woo, Ronnie
    Did You Eat Yet? — 641.595
Wood, Damon
    Working for the Man, Playing in the Band — 782.42164
WOOD, DAMON
    Wood, Damon. *Working for the Man, Playing in the Band* — 782.42164
Wood, David Bowne
    ★*What Have We Done* — 616.85
Wood, Gillen D'Arcy
    Land of Wondrous Cold — 919.89
Wood, Gordon S.
    Empire of Liberty — 973.4
    Friends Divided — 920
Wood, Graeme
    The Way of the Strangers — 363.325
WOOD, GRANT, 1891-1942
    Evans, R. Tripp. *Grant Wood* — B
Wood, James
    How Fiction Works — 808.3
Wood, Jennifer
    Refined Knits — 746.43
Wood, Lawrence
    Your Caption Has Been Selected — 741.5
Wood, Levison
    The Last Giants — 599.67
WOOD, LEVISON, 1982-
    Wood, Levison. *The Last Giants* — 599.67
Wood, Michael
    The Story of China — 951
Wood, Sherri
    The Improv Handbook for Modern Quilters — 746.46
Wood, Wendy
    Good Habits, Bad Habits — 152.3

WOOD-CARVING
    Barn the Spoon. *Woodcraft* — 684
    Jones, Andrew. *Stickmaking Handbook* — 736
WOODARD, ISAAC, 1919-1992
    Gergel, Richard. *Unexampled Courage* — 323.1196
Woodcraft. Barn the Spoon — 684
Wooden. Davis, Seth — B
WOODEN, JOHN, 1910-2010
    Abdul-Jabbar, Kareem. *Coach Wooden and Me* — B
    Davis, Seth. *Wooden* — B
Woodford, Chris
    Atoms Under the Floorboards — 500
Woodfox, Albert
    Solitary — B
WOODFOX, ALBERT
    Woodfox, Albert. *Solitary* — B
WOODPECKERS
    Shunk, Stephen A. *Peterson Reference Guide to Woodpeckers of North America* — 598.7
Woodress, James Leslie
    Willa Cather — B
Woodrow Wilson. Cooper, John Milton — B
Woodrow Wilson. Brands, H. W. — B
WOODS, ARTHUR, 1870-1942
    Johnson, Steven. *The Infernal Machine* — 335
Woods, Christopher
    Gardenlust — 635.022
Woods, Geraldine
    25 Great Sentences and How They Got That Way — 808
Woods, Randall Bennett
    Prisoners of Hope — 973.923
Woods, Tiger
    The 1997 Masters — B
WOODS, TIGER
    Bamberger, Michael. *The Second Life of Tiger Woods* — B
    Benedict, Jeff. ★*Tiger Woods* — B
    Harig, Bob. *Drive* — 796.352
    Woods, Tiger. *The 1997 Masters* — B
WOODSTOCK FESTIVAL, 1969
    Lang, Michael. *The Road to Woodstock* — 781.66
WOODWARD, ANN, 1916-1975
    Montillo, Roseanne. *Deliberate Cruelty* — 364.152
Woodward, Bob
    Fear — 973.933
    The Final Days — B
    Peril — 973.933
    Shadow — 973.92
WOODWARD, BOB, 1943-
    Bernstein, Carl. ★*All the President's Men* — 364.1
Woodward, C. Vann
    The Strange Career of Jim Crow — 305.896
Woodward, Kenneth L.
    The Book of Miracles — 231.7
    Making Saints — 235.24
Woodworker's Handbook. Horwood, Roger — 684
WOODWORKING
    Barn the Spoon. *Woodcraft* — 684
    Christiana, Asa. *Build Stuff with Wood* — 684
    Downs, Paul. *Boss Life* — 338.7
    Horwood, Roger. *Woodworker's Handbook* — 684
    Preszler, Trent. *Little and Often* — B
WOOL
    Callahan, Gail. *Hand Dyeing Yarn and Fleece* — 746.6
    Robson, Deborah. *The Field Guide to Fleece* — 677
Wooldridge, Adrian
    Masters of Management — 658
Woolever, Laurie
    Bourdain — B
Woolf, Greg
    Rome — 937
WOOLF, LEONARD, 1880-1969
    Glendinning, Victoria. *Leonard Woolf* — B
Woolf, Virginia
    The London Scene — 942.1
    Moments of Being — B
    The Virginia Woolf Reader — 823
WOOLF, VIRGINIA, 1882-1941
    Briggs, Julia. *Virginia Woolf* — 823

Smyth, Katharine. *All the Lives We Ever Lived*	B
Woolf, Virginia. *Moments of Being*	B

Woolfson, Esther
Between Light and Storm ... 599.93

Woolley, Benjamin
The King's Assassin ... B

*The **Word** According to Eve*. Murphy, Cullen ... 220.8
***Word** by Word*. Stamper, Kory ... 413.028
*The **Word** Detective*. Simpson, J. A. ... B

WORDS
Bragg, Melvyn. ★*The Adventure of English*	420
Crystal, David. ★*How Language Works*	410
Crystal, David. *Spell It Out*	421
Crystal, David. *The Story of English in 100 Words*	422
Curzan, Anne. ★*Says Who?*	428
Macfarlane, Robert. *The Lost Spells*	811
Pinker, Steven. *Words and Rules*	415
Shankar, Shalini. *Beeline*	155.4
Soep, Elisabeth. *Other People's Words*	155.9
Stamper, Kory. *Word by Word*	413.028

Words and Rules. Pinker, Steven ... 415
Words Are My Matter. Le Guin, Ursula K. ... 818
The Words That Made Us. Amar, Akhil Reed ... 342.7302
Words to Rhyme With. Espy, Willard R. ... 423
Words Without Music. Glass, Philip ... B

WORDSWORTH, DOROTHY, 1771-1855
Nicolson, Adam. *The Making of Poetry* ... 821.709

WORDSWORTH, WILLIAM, 1770-1850
Bate, Jonathan. *Radical Wordsworth*	B
Nicolson, Adam. *The Making of Poetry*	821.709

The Work. Moore, Wes ... B

WORK
Acemoglu, Daron. *Power and Progress*	303.48
Auerbach, Annie. *Flex*	331.25
Biss, Eula. *Having and Being Had*	306.3
Blackmon, Douglas A. *Slavery by Another Name*	305.896
Bregman, Rutger. *Utopia for Realists*	335
Cahn, Naomi R. ★*Fair Shake*	331.4
Chang, Leslie T. *Factory Girls*	331.4
Coggan, Philip. *Surviving the Daily Grind*	658.3
Cornejo Villavicencio, Karla. ★*The Undocumented Americans*	920
Cox, Gena. *Leading Inclusion*	658.3
De Botton, Alain. *The Pleasures and Sorrows of Work*	306.3
Garbes, Angela. *Essential Labor*	306.874
Gillard, Julia. ★*Women and Leadership*	158
Green, Alison. *Ask a Manager*	650.1
Green, Robin. *The Only Girl*	070.92
Guendelsberger, Emily. *On the Clock*	331.0973
Hackman, Rose. *Emotional Labor*	155.3
Harts, Minda. *Right Within*	658.3
Henry, Alan. *Seen, Heard, and Paid*	650.1
Hill, Jemele. *Uphill*	B
Kessler-Harris, Alice. ★*Out to Work*	331.4
Louis, Matthew J. *Mission Transition*	650.14
Macy, Beth. ★*Factory Man*	338.7
Monforton, Celeste. *On the Job*	331.1
Moss, Adam. ★*The Work of Art*	701
Mundy, Liza. *Code Girls*	940.54
Murolo, Priscilla. *From the Folks Who Brought You the Weekend*	331
Odell, Jenny. ★*Saving Time*	153.7
Olds, Sally. ★*People Who Lunch*	824
Peter, Laurence J. *The Peter Principle*	658
Press, Eyal. ★*Dirty Work*	331.7
Price, Devon. ★*Laziness Does Not Exist*	158.1
Rowan, Barry L. *The Spiritual Art of Business*	261.8
Shapland, Jenn. ★*Thin Skin*	814
Smith, Zadie. *Intimations*	824
Snow, Shane. *Dream Teams*	658.4
Terkel, Studs. *Working*	920
Thorstensen, Ole. *Making Things Right*	690
Vanek Smith, Stacey. *Machiavelli for Women*	650.1
Williams, Joan. *What Works for Women at Work*	650.1
Wingfield, Adia Harvey. *Gray Areas*	331.6

WORK ENVIRONMENT
Barsh, Joanna. *Grow Wherever You Work*	658.4
Gallo, Amy. *Getting Along*	658.4
Green, Alison. *Ask a Manager*	650.1
Hardy, Alyssa. *Worn Out*	338.4
Livingston, Robert W. *The Conversation*	305.8
Monforton, Celeste. *On the Job*	331.1
Newman, Bobbi L. ★*Fostering Wellness in the Workplace*	023
Olds, Sally. ★*People Who Lunch*	824
Pang, Amelia. ★*Made in China*	331.11
Porath, Christine Lynne. *Mastering Civility*	650.1
Richards, Shola. *Making Work Work*	658.3
Snow, Shane. *Dream Teams*	658.4
Williams, Bari A. *Seen yet Unseen*	338.4

WORK ETHIC
Coggan, Philip. *Surviving the Daily Grind*	658.3
Iguodala, Andre. *The Sixth Man*	B
Spiegel, Maura. *Sidney Lumet*	B
Thorstensen, Ole. *Making Things Right*	690

WORK LIFE BALANCE
Odell, Jenny. ★*Saving Time* ... 153.7

★*The **Work** of Art*. Moss, Adam ... 701
***Work** Songs*. Gioia, Ted ... 782.42
***Work** Wife*. Cerulo, Erica ... 658.4

WORK-LIFE BALANCE
Auerbach, Annie. *Flex*	331.25
Coggan, Philip. *Surviving the Daily Grind*	658.3
Dunne, Linnea. *Lagom*	158.1
Feiler, Bruce. ★*The Search*	306.3
Gorges, Eric. *A Craftsman's Legacy*	745.5
Gotch, Jen. *The Upside of Being Down*	B
Medini, Shari. *Parenting While Working from Home*	650.1
Obama, Michelle. ★*Becoming*	B
Olds, Sally. ★*People Who Lunch*	824
Petersen, Anne Helen. *Can't Even*	305.242
Price, Devon. ★*Laziness Does Not Exist*	158.1
Shlain, Tiffany. *24/6*	158.1
Sun, Carrie. *Private Equity*	B
Warzel, Charlie. *Out of Office*	658.3

WORKAHOLICS
Morris, Edmund. ★*Edison* ... B

WORKAHOLISM
Smith, Freda Love. *I Quit Everything*	B
Sun, Carrie. *Private Equity*	B

*The **Workbench** Guide to Jewelry Techniques*. Young, Anastasia ... 739.27
★***Working***. Caro, Robert A. ... B
Working. Terkel, Studs ... 920

WORKING ABROAD
Hessler, Peter. *Other Rivers* ... 378.1

WORKING ANIMALS
Kisor, Henry. *Traveling with Service Animals* ... 362.4

WORKING CLASS
Berg, Scott W. *The Burning of the World*	977.311
Blight, David W. *A Slave No More*	B
Case, Anne. *Deaths of Despair and the Future of Capitalism*	362.28
Dougherty, Conor. *Golden Gates*	363.509794
Dubofsky, Melvyn. *Labor in America*	331.880973
Fabey, Michael. *Heavy Metal*	338.4
Gioia, Ted. *Work Songs*	782.42
Guendelsberger, Emily. *On the Clock*	331.0973
Honey, Michael K. *To the Promised Land*	323
Isenberg, Nancy. *White Trash*	305.5
Kelley, Blair Murphy. *Black Folk*	331.6
Kessler-Harris, Alice. ★*Out to Work*	331.4
Kristof, Nicholas D. ★*Tightrope*	306.0973
Land, Stephanie. *Maid*	B
Lemann, Nicholas. *Transaction Man*	330.973
Levy, Jonathan. *Ages of American Capitalism*	330.12
McAlevey, Jane. *A Collective Bargain*	331.890973
Murolo, Priscilla. *From the Folks Who Brought You the Weekend*	331
Ortiz, Paul. *An African American and Latinx History of the United States*	305.8
Postel, Charles. *Equality*	305.50973
Potts, Monica. *The Forgotten Girls*	B
Price, S. L. *Playing Through the Whistle*	796.332
Schwartz, Nelson. *The Velvet Rope Economy*	339.2
Smarsh, Sarah. ★*Heartland*	B
Terkel, Studs. *Working*	920
Vance, J. D. *Hillbilly Elegy*	B
Villarreal, Vanessa Anglica. *Magical/Realism*	814

WORKING CLASS AFRICAN AMERICANS
Hobbs, Jeff. ★*The Short and Tragic Life of Robert Peace* ... B

PUBLIC LIBRARY CORE COLLECTION: NONFICTION
Twentieth Edition

WORKING CLASS FAMILIES
   Chung, Nicole. ★ *A Living Remedy*   B
   Ernaux, Annie. ★ *The Years*   B
WORKING CLASS MEN
   Brown, Daniel James. ★ *The Boys in the Boat*   797.12
WORKING CLASS WOMEN
   Kessler-Harris, Alice. ★ *Out to Work*   331.4
   Rubenhold, Hallie. ★ *The Five*   362.88
WORKING DOGS
   Orlean, Susan. *Rin Tin Tin*   636.737
Working for the Man, Playing in the Band. Wood, Damon   782.42164
Working Girls. Mattel, Trixie   650.1
The Working Mom Blueprint. Casares, Whitney   306.8743
WORKING MOTHERS
   Casares, Whitney. *The Working Mom Blueprint*   306.8743
Workman, Katie
   Dinner Solved!   641.5
   The Mom 100 Cookbook   641.5
WORKPLACE VIOLENCE
   Yeung, Bernice. *In a Day's Work*   362.88086
Works and Days and Theogony. Hesiod   881
★ *The World*. Sebag-Montefiore, Simon   929.7
The World as It Is. Rhodes, Benjamin J.   973.932
The World Atlas of Street Fashion. Cox, Caroline   391.009
A World Beneath the Sands. Wilkinson, Toby A. H.   932
The World Beneath Their Feet. Ellsworth, Scott   796.522
The World Beyond Your Head. Crawford, Matthew B.   155.2
WORLD ECONOMY
   Lewis, Michael. *The Big Short*   330.973
   McMillan, John. *Reinventing the Bazaar*   330.12
   Sachs, Jeffrey. *The Age of Sustainable Development*   338.9
   Sharma, Ruchir. *The Rise and Fall of Nations*   330.9
   Sorkin, Andrew Ross. *Too Big to Fail*   330.973
   Steil, Benn. ★ *The Marshall Plan*   338.91
   Stiglitz, Joseph E. *Globalization and Its Discontents*   337
   Teachout, Zephyr. *Break 'Em Up*   338.8
   Wheelan, Charles J. *Naked Economics*   330
   Wolf, Martin. ★ *The Crisis of Democratic Capitalism*   330.12
The World Encyclopedia of Flags. Znamierowski, Alfred   903
WORLD HEALTH
   Ashton, Jennifer. *The New Normal*   613
   Holt, Nathalia. *Cured*   614.5
   Mackenzie, Debora. *Covid-19*   616.2
The World History of Animation. Cavalier, Stephen   791.43
The World Is a Carpet. Badkhen, Anna   305.409581
The World Is What It Is. French, Patrick   B
The World Is Yours. Kenny, Glenn   791.43
The World Keeps Ending, and the World Goes On. Choi, Franny   811
WORLD LEADERS
   Atwood, Margaret. *Burning Questions*   814
   Harding, Luke. *Invasion*   947.7
   Khodorkovsky, Mikhail. *The Russia Conundrum*   947.086
   Kissinger, Henry. *Leadership*   303.3
   Lieven, Dominic. *In the Shadow of the Gods*   352.23
   Marton, Kati. ★ *The Chancellor*   B
   McDonough, Frank. *The Hitler Years*   943.086
   Roberts, Andrew. *Leadership in War*   920
   Shuster, Simon. ★ *The Showman*   B
   Whitlock, Craig. *The Afghanistan Papers*   958.104
A World Lit Only by Fire. Manchester, William   940.2
The World Must Know. Berenbaum, Michael   940.53
The World of All Souls. Harkness, Deborah E.   813
★ *The World of Earl Hines*. Dance, Stanley   B
The World of Laura Ingalls Wilder. McDowell, Marta   813
The World of Lucha Libre. Levi, Heather   796.812
The World of Plymouth Plantation. Pestana, Carla Gardina   974.4
A World of Three Zeros. Yunus, Muhammad   330
World of Wonders. Nezhukumatathil, Aimee   590
The World on Sunday. Baker, Nicholson   071
A World on the Wing. Weidensaul, Scott   598.156
The World Only Spins Forward. Butler, Isaac   812
WORLD POLITICS
   Ackerman, Elliot. *Places and Names*   B
   Ambinder, Marc. *The Brink*   355.5
   Applebaum, Anne. *Twilight of Democracy*   321.9
   Arnold, James R. *Jungle of Snakes*   355.02
   Barr, James. *Lords of the Desert*   956
   Berg, A. Scott. ★ *Wilson*   B
   Burns, William J. *The Back Channel*   B
   Carter, Miranda. *George, Nicholas and Wilhelm*   940.3
   Chamberlin, Paul Thomas. *The Cold War's Killing Fields*   355.009
   Chomsky, Noam. *Global Discontents*   410.92
   Cohen, Roger. *An Affirming Flame*   071
   Cooper, John Milton. *Woodrow Wilson*   B
   Dagher, Sam. *Assad or We Burn the Country*   956.9104
   Dikotter, Frank. *The Cultural Revolution*   951.056
   Fasulo, Linda M. *An Insider's Guide to the Un, 4th Ed.*   341.23
   Filkins, Dexter. *The Forever War*   956.7044
   Friedman, Thomas L. ★ *Thank You for Being Late*   303.48
   Gates, Robert Michael. ★ *Exercise of Power*   973.929
   Ghazvinian, John. *America and Iran*   327
   Gorbachev, Mikhail. *On My Country and the World*   947.085
   Gordin, Michael D. *Red Cloud at Dawn*   355.02
   Guillemin, Jeanne. *Biological Weapons*   358
   Hajari, Nisid. *Midnight's Furies*   954.04
   Harari, Yuval N. ★ *21 Lessons for the 21st Century*   909.82
   Herman, Arthur. *1917*   940.3
   Holland, James. *The Rise of Germany, 1939-1941; Vol. 1*   940.54
   Hornfischer, James D. *Who Can Hold the Sea*   359.00973
   Junger, Sebastian. *Fire*   909.82
   Kasparov, Gary. *Winter Is Coming*   947.086
   Katznelson, Ira. *Fear Itself*   973.917
   Kershaw, Ian. *The Global Age*   940.55
   Kinzer, Stephen. ★ *All the Shah's Men*   955.05
   Kurtz-Phelan, Daniel. *The China Mission*   951.04
   Langewiesche, William. *The Atomic Bazaar*   355.02
   Lim, Louisa. *The People's Republic of Amnesia*   951.05
   Linklater, Andro. *Owning the Earth*   333.3
   Marx, Karl. ★ *The Communist Manifesto*   355.4
   Pipes, Richard. *A Concise History of the Russian Revolution*   947.084
   Plokhy, Serhii. *Yalta*   940.53
   Preston, Diana. *Eight Days at Yalta*   940.53
   Rice, Condoleezza. *Political Risk*   658.15
   Runciman, David. *The Confidence Trap*   321.8
   Ryan, Alan. *On Politics*   320.01
   Service, Robert. *The End of the Cold War 1985-1991*   909.82
   Sherwin, Martin J. *Gambling with Armageddon*   972.9106
   Steil, Benn. ★ *The Marshall Plan*   338.91
   Westad, Odd Arne. *The Cold War*   909.825
   Wolf, Martin. ★ *The Crisis of Democratic Capitalism*   330.12
   Wood, Graeme. *The Way of the Strangers*   363.325
   Yergin, Daniel. ★ *The Prize*   338.2
   Yergin, Daniel. *The Quest*   333.79
★ *The World Record Book of Racist Stories*. Ruffin, Amber   305.896
WORLD RECORDS
   Davis, Jennifer Pharr. *The Pursuit of Endurance*   796.51
The World That Never Was. Butterworth, Alex   335
A World to Win. Liedman, Sven-Eric   B
★ *World Travel*. Bourdain, Anthony   641.59
The World Turned Upside Down. Yang, Jisheng   951.05
World War I. Grant, R. G.   940.3
WORLD WAR I
   Ackroyd, Peter. *Innovation*   942.082
   Anderson, Scott. *Lawrence in Arabia*   B
   Bacon, John U. *The Great Halifax Explosion*   971.6
   Bascomb, Neal. *The Escape Artists*   940.4
   Berg, A. Scott. ★ *Wilson*   B
   Brotherton, Marcus. *A Bright and Blinding Sun*   940.54
   Bunting, Josiah. ★ *The Making of a Leader*   B
   Carroll, Andrew. *My Fellow Soldiers*   940.4
   Carter, Miranda. *George, Nicholas and Wilhelm*   940.3
   Clay, Catrine. *King, Kaiser, Tsar*   B
   Cooper, John Milton. *Woodrow Wilson*   B
   Davenport, Matthew J. *First Over There*   940.4
   Davis, Wade. *Into the Silence*   B
   Eilenberger, Wolfram. *Time of the Magicians*   920
   Emery, Theo. *Hellfire Boys*   358
   Englund, Peter. *The Beauty and the Sorrow*   940.309
   Evans, Richard J. *The Pursuit of Power*   940.2
   Fox, Margalit. *The Confidence Men*   940.4
   Glass, Charles. *Soldiers Don't Go Mad*   616.85
   Grant, R. G. *World War I*   940.3
   Grant, R. G. *World War I*   940.3
   Hamilton-Paterson, James. *Marked for Death*   358.400941
   Hastings, Max. *Catastrophe 1914*   940.3
   Herman, Arthur. *1917*   940.3

AUTHOR, TITLE, SERIES AND SUBJECT INDEX

Hochschild, Adam. *American Midnight*	973.91
Hynes, Samuel. *The Unsubstantial Air*	940.4
Keegan, John. *The First World War*	940.3
King, Greg. *The Assassination of the Archduke*	B
Korda, Michael. *Muse of Fire*	940.4
Larson, Erik. ★*Dead Wake*	940.4
Lawrence, T. E. *Seven Pillars of Wisdom*	940.4
Lloyd, Nick. *The Western Front*	940.4
Mackeen, Dawn Anahid. *The Hundred-Year Walk*	956.6
MacMillan, Margaret. *Paris 1919*	940.4
Massie, Robert K. *Castles of Steel*	940.4
McMeekin, Sean. *July 1914*	940.3
Moore, Kate. *The Radium Girls*	363.17
Moore, Wendy. *No Man's Land*	940.4
Neu, Charles E. *Colonel House*	B
Nicolson, Juliet. *The Great Silence*	941.083
Paradis, Michel. *The Light of Battle*	940.54
Preston, Diana. *A Higher Form of Killing*	940.4
Ridley, Jane. *George V*	B
Rogan, Eugene L. *The Fall of the Ottomans*	940.3
Roll, David L. *George Marshall*	B
Rosenblitt, J. Alison. *The Beauty of Living*	B
Stanley, Matthew. *Einstein's War*	530
Tuchman, Barbara W. ★*The Guns of August*	940.4
Whyte, Kenneth. *Hoover*	B
Yergin, Daniel. ★*The Prize*	338.2

WORLD WAR I VETERANS

Caesar, Ed. *The Moth and the Mountain*	B
Drabkin, Ronald. *Beverly Hills Spy*	940.54
Glass, Charles. *Soldiers Don't Go Mad*	616.85

WORLD WAR II

Ackerman, Diane. ★*The Zookeeper's Wife*	940.53
Ackroyd, Peter. *Innovation*	942.082
Albright, Madeleine Korbel. *Prague Winter*	943.71
Aleksievich, Svetlana. *Last Witnesses*	940.53
Aleksievich, Svetlana. ★*The Unwomanly Face of War*	940.53
Alexander, Caroline. *Skies of Thunder*	940.54
Alexander, Larry. *Biggest Brother*	B
Allen, Arthur. ★*The Fantastic Laboratory of Dr. Weigl*	614.5
Allport, Alan. *Britain at Bay*	940.53
Ambrose, Stephen E. ★*Band of Brothers*	920
Ambrose, Stephen E. *Citizen Soldiers*	940.54
Ambrose, Stephen E. *D-Day, June 6, 1944*	940.54
Ambrose, Stephen E. *The Victors*	940.54
Ambrose, Stephen E. *The Wild Blue*	940.54
Andrews, Lena S. ★*Valiant Women*	940.53
Asbrink, Elisabeth. *And in the Vienna Woods the Trees Remain*	B
Atkinson, Rick. *An Army at Dawn*	940.54
Atkinson, Rick. *The Day of Battle*	940.54
Atkinson, Rick. *The Guns at Last Light*	940.54
Atria, Travis. *Better Days Will Come Again*	B
Bailey, Catherine. *A Castle in Wartime*	943.086
Bair, Deirdre. *Saul Steinberg*	B
Barrett, David Dean. *140 Days to Hiroshima*	940.54
Barrett, Duncan. *GI Brides*	920
Bascomb, Neal. *Faster*	796.7209
Bascomb, Neal. *The Winter Fortress*	940.54
Bass, Gary Jonathan. ★*Judgment at Tokyo*	952.04
Batalion, Judith. *The Light of Days*	940.53
Beevor, Antony. *Ardennes 1944*	940.54
Beevor, Antony. *The Battle of Arnhem*	940.54
Beevor, Antony. *D-Day*	940.54
Beevor, Antony. *The Fall of Berlin, 1945*	940.54
Beevor, Antony. *The Second World War*	940.54
Berg, Mary. *The Diary of Mary Berg*	B
Berr, Helene. *The Journal of Helene Berr*	B
Beschloss, Michael R. *The Conquerors*	940.53
Bilger, Burkhard. *Fatherland*	B
Bissinger, H. G. ★*The Mosquito Bowl*	796.332
Bix, Herbert P. *Hirohito and the Making of Modern Japan*	B
Blau, Magda Hellinger. *The Nazis Knew My Name*	940.53
Blume, Lesley M. M. *Fallout*	940.54
Borneman, Walter R. *The Admirals*	B
Borneman, Walter R. *Macarthur at War*	B
Bouverie, Tim. *Appeasement*	327.41043
Bradley, James. *Flags of Our Fathers*	B
Bradley, James. *Flyboys*	940.54
Brands, H. W. *The General vs. the President*	973.918092
Brands, H. W. *Traitor to His Class*	B
Brighton, Terry. *Patton, Montgomery, Rommel*	B
Brown, Daniel James. ★*Facing the Mountain*	940.54
Bruning, John R. *Indestructible*	B
Bruning, John R. *The Race of Aces*	940.54
Budiansky, Stephen. *Blackett's War*	940.54
Bunting, Josiah. ★*The Making of a Leader*	B
Burgin, R. V. *Islands of the Damned*	B
Cadbury, Deborah. *Princes at War*	920
Cadbury, Deborah. *The School That Escaped from the Nazis*	940.53
Caddick-Adams, Peter. *Sand and Steel*	940.54
Cahan, Richard. *Un-American*	940.54
Campbell, James. *The Ghost Mountain Boys*	940.54
Century, Douglas. *Barney Ross*	B
Childers, Thomas. *The Third Reich*	943.086
Chrisinger, David. *The Soldier's Truth*	940.54
Churchill, Winston. *The Grand Alliance*	940.53
Churchill, Winston. *Their Finest Hour*	940.53
Churchill, Winston. *Triumph and Tragedy*	940.53
Clark, Lloyd. *The Commanders*	940.53
Clavin, Thomas. *Lightning Down*	940.54
Clavin, Tom. *The Last Hill*	940.54
Conant, Jennet. *The Lotus Eaters*	940.54
Cooke, Alistair. *The American Home Front, 1941-1942*	940.53
Copeland, B. Jack. *Turing*	B
Cornwell, John. *Hitler's Pope*	B
Crasnianski, Tania. *The Children of Nazis*	943.086
Cronkite, Walter. *Cronkite's War*	070.4
Daniels, Roger. *Prisoners Without Trial*	940.53
De Courcy, Anne. *Chanel's Riviera*	944.9
Debreczeni, Jozsef. *Cold Crematorium*	940.53
Delmont, Matthew F. *Half American*	940.54
Dickson, Paul. *The Rise of the G.I. Army 1940-1941*	940.54
Dimbleby, Jonathan. *The Battle of the Atlantic*	940.54
Donner, Rebecca. *All the Frequent Troubles of Our Days*	943
Dower, John W. *Cultures of War*	355.00973
Dower, John W. *Embracing Defeat*	952.04
Drabkin, Ronald. *Beverly Hills Spy*	940.54
Drury, Bob. *Lucky 666*	B
Dugard, Martin. *Taking Berlin*	940.54
Dugard, Martin. *Taking Paris*	940.54
Dumbach, Annette E. *Sophie Scholl and the White Rose*	943.086
Dwork, Deborah. ★*Holocaust*	940
Eder, Mari K. *The Girls Who Stepped Out of Line*	920
Edmonds, Chris. *No Surrender*	B
Edsel, Robert M. *The Monuments Men*	940.53
Eisner, Peter. *The Pope's Last Crusade*	282.092
Englund, Peter. *November 1942*	940.53
Erwin, Jon. *Beyond Valor*	B
Evans, Richard J. *The Third Reich at War*	940.53
Feigel, Lara. *The Bitter Taste of Victory*	320.943
Finkelstein, Daniel. *Two Roads Home*	920
Fishman, David E. *The Book Smugglers*	940.53
Frank, Anne. ★*The Diary of a Young Girl*	940.53
Frank, Richard B. *Downfall*	940.54
Frank, Richard B. *Tower of Skulls*	940.54
Frankel, Rebecca. *Into the Forest*	940.53
Freedland, Jonathan. ★*The Escape Artist*	940.53
Freeman, Sally Mott. *The Jersey Brothers*	920
Friedlander, Saul. *Nazi Germany and the Jews*	940.53
Fritzsche, Peter. *Life and Death in the Third Reich*	943.086
Fullilove, Michael. *Rendezvous with Destiny*	973.917092
Garrett, Leah. *X Troop*	940.54
Geroux, William. *The Ghost Ships of Archangel*	940.54
Gerwarth, Robert. *Hitler's Hangman*	B
Gewen, Barry. ★*The Inevitability of Tragedy*	B
Giangreco, D. M. *Hell to Pay*	940.54
Giddins, Gary. *Bing Crosby*	B
Gies, Miep. ★*Anne Frank Remembered*	B
Gilbert, Martin. *The Second World War*	940.53
Gladwell, Malcolm. ★*The Bomber Mafia*	940.54
Goodman, Simon. *The Orpheus Clock*	940.53
Goodwin, Doris Kearns. *No Ordinary Time*	920
Graff, Garrett M. ★*When the Sea Came Alive*	940.54
Grayling, A. C. *Among the Dead Cities*	940.54
Groom, Winston. *The Allies*	940.5309
Groom, Winston. *The Generals*	920
Grose, Peter. *A Good Place to Hide*	940.53

PUBLIC LIBRARY CORE COLLECTION: NONFICTION
Twentieth Edition

Gross, Jan Tomasz. *Neighbors*	940.53
Guarnere, William. *Brothers in Battle, Best of Friends*	B
Guibert, Emmanuel. *Alan's War*	741.5
Ham, Paul. *Hiroshima Nagasaki*	940.54
Hamilton, Nigel. *The Mantle of Command*	940.54
Hampton, Dan. *Operation Vengeance*	940.54
Hanson, Victor Davis. *The Second World Wars*	940.54
Harmon, Mark. *Ghosts of Honolulu*	940.54
Harris, Mark. ★*Five Came Back*	791.4302
Hastings, Max. *Armageddon*	940.54
Hastings, Max. *Inferno*	940.54
Hastings, Max. *Operation Chastise*	940.54
Hastings, Max. *Operation Pedestal*	940.54
Hastings, Max. *Overlord*	940.54
Hastings, Max. *Retribution*	940.54
Hastings, Max. *The Secret War*	940.54
Helm, Sarah. *A Life in Secrets*	B
Helm, Sarah. *Ravensbruck*	940.53
Hemming, Henry. *Agents of Influence*	940.54
Henderson, Bruce B. *Bridge to the Sun*	940.53
Henderson, Bruce B. *Sons and Soldiers*	940.53
Herman, Arthur. *Freedom's Forge*	940.53
Herriot, James. *All Things Wise and Wonderful*	B
Hersey, John. ★*Hiroshima*	940.54
Hervieux, Linda. *Forgotten*	940.54
Hillenbrand, Laura. ★*Unbroken*	B
Hindley, Meredith. *Destination Casablanca*	940.54
Hoffman, Bruce. *Anonymous Soldiers*	956.94
Hogan, William R. *Task Force Hogan*	940.54
Holden, Wendy. ★*Born Survivors*	940.53
Holland, James. *Battle of Britain*	940.54
Holland, James. *Big Week*	940.54
Holland, James. *Brothers in Arms*	940.54
Holland, James. ★*Burma '44*	940.54
Holland, James. *Normandy '44*	940.54
Holland, James. *The Rise of Germany, 1939-1941; Vol. 1*	940.54
Holland, James. *The Savage Storm*	940.53
Holland, James. *Sicily '43*	940.54
Hornfischer, James D. *Neptune's Inferno*	940.54
Hotta, Eri. *Japan 1941*	940.54
Humbert, Agnes. *Resistance*	B
Hurowitz, Richard. *In the Garden of the Righteous*	940.53
Iredale, Will. *The Kamikaze Hunters*	940.54
Isserman, Maurice. *The Winter Army*	940.54
Jackson, Julian. *De Gaulle*	B
Jacobsen, Annie. ★*Operation Paperclip*	940.54
Jaku, Eddie. ★*The Happiest Man on Earth*	B
Jordan, Jonathan W. *Brothers, Rivals, Victors*	940.55
Judt, Tony. *Postwar*	940.55
Kaiser, Menachem. *Plunder*	940.53
Karski, Jan. *Story of a Secret State*	940.53
Katin, Miriam. *We Are on Our Own*	741.5
Katz, Catherine Grace. *The Daughters of Yalta*	920
Kean, Sam. *The Bastard Brigade*	355.8
Keegan, John. *The Second World War*	940.53
Keith, Philip A. *All Blood Runs Red*	B
Kemper, Steve. *Our Man in Tokyo*	952.03
Kempowski, Walter. *Swansong 1945*	940.54
Kennedy, David M. ★*Freedom from Fear*	973.91
Kennedy, Paul. *Engineers of Victory*	940.54
Kershaw, Alex. *Against All Odds*	940.54
Kershaw, Alex. *Avenue of Spies*	940.53
Kershaw, Alex. *The Few*	940.54
Kershaw, Alex. *The First Wave*	940.54
Kertzer, David I. *The Pope at War*	940.53
Kiernan, Denise. *The Girls of Atomic City*	976.8
King, David. *Death in the City of Light*	364.152
Kinstler, Linda. *Come to This Court and Cry*	940.53
Kix, Paul. *The Saboteur*	940.53
Korda, Michael. *Alone*	940.54
Korda, Michael. *With Wings Like Eagles*	940.54
Kramer, Clara. *Clara's War*	B
Krug, Nora. ★*Belonging*	741.5
Kupperman, Michael. *All the Answers*	741.5
Lambert, Raymond. *Every Man a Hero*	B
Landdeck, Katherine Sharp. *The Women with Silver Wings*	920
Larman, Alexander. *The Windsors at War*	940.53
Larson, Erik. ★*The Splendid and the Vile*	940.53
Levi, Primo. *The Periodic Table*	858
Levi, Primo. ★*Survival in Auschwitz*	B
Lewis, Damien. *Agent Josephine*	B
Lewis, Damien. *Churchill's Hellraisers*	940.54
Lewis, Damien. *The Dog Who Could Fly*	940.54
Lichtblau, Eric. *Return to the Reich*	B
Lineberry, Cate. *The Secret Rescue*	940.54
Loftis, Larry. *Code Name*	B
Loftis, Larry. ★*The Watchmaker's Daughter*	940.53
Longerich, Peter. *Goebbels*	B
Longerich, Peter. *Hitler*	B
Lowe, Keith. *Prisoners of History*	940.54
Lowe, Keith. *Savage Continent*	940.55
Lower, Wendy. *Hitler's Furies*	940.53
Lucas, Jack. *Indestructible*	B
Lukacs, John. *Five Days in London, May 1940*	940.53
MacGregor, Iain. *The Lighthouse of Stalingrad*	940.54
Macintyre, Ben. *Agent Zigzag*	B
Macintyre, Ben. *Double Cross*	940.54
Macintyre, Ben. ★*Operation Mincemeat*	940.54
Macintyre, Ben. ★*Prisoners of the Castle*	940.54
Macintyre, Ben. ★*Rogue Heroes*	940.54
MacKrell, Judith. *The Correspondents*	070.4
Maddow, Rachel. ★*Prequel*	320.53
Magida, Arthur J. *Code Name Madeleine*	940.54
Makos, Adam. ★*A Higher Call*	940.54
Makos, Adam. *Spearhead*	B
Manchester, William. *Goodbye, Darkness*	B
Manchester, William. *The Last Lion, Winston Spencer Churchill.*	B
Marwell, David G. *Mengele*	920
Matzen, Robert. *Dutch Girl*	B
Mauldin, Bill. *Willie & Joe*	741.5
Maurer, Kevin. *Damn Lucky*	940.54
Mazower, Mark. *Hitler's Empire*	940.53
Mazzeo, Tilar J. *Irena's Children*	B
Mazzeo, Tilar J. *Sisters in Resistance*	945.091
McCarten, Anthony. *Darkest Hour*	941.084
McConahay, Mary Jo. *The Tango War*	940.53
McDonough, Frank. *The Hitler Years*	943.086
McKay, Sinclair. *Berlin*	943
McKay, Sinclair. *The Fire and the Darkness*	940.54
McKay, Sinclair. *The Secret Lives of Codebreakers*	940.54
McKean, David. *Watching Darkness Fall*	940.53
McManus, John C. *Fire and Fortitude*	940.54
McManus, John C. *Island Infernos*	940.54
McManus, John C. *To the End of the Earth*	940.54
McMeekin, Sean. *Stalin's War*	940.53
Meacham, Jon. *Franklin and Winston*	940.53
Meltzer, Brad. ★*The Nazi Conspiracy*	940.53
Merridale, Catherine. *Ivan's War*	940.54
Miller, Donald L. ★*Masters of the Air*	940.54
Milton, Giles. *Checkmate in Berlin*	943
Milton, Giles. *Churchill's Ministry of Ungentlemanly Warfare*	940.54
Milton, Giles. *Soldier, Sailor, Frogman, Spy, Airman, Gangster, Kill or Die*	940.54
Mitter, Rana. *Forgotten Ally*	951.04
Mizuki, Shigeru. *Showa 1926-1939*	741.5
Moorehead, Caroline. *A House in the Mountains*	940.53
Moorehead, Caroline. *A Train in Winter*	940.53
Moorhouse, Roger. *Berlin at War*	943
Moorhouse, Roger. *The Devils' Alliance*	940.53
Moorhouse, Roger. *The Forgers*	940.53
Morton, Andrew. *17 Carnations*	941.084
Moynahan, Brian. *Leningrad*	780.92
Mulley, Clare. *The Spy Who Loved*	B
Mulley, Clare. *The Women Who Flew for Hitler*	920
Mundy, Liza. *Code Girls*	940.54
Murphy, Brian. *81 Days Below Zero*	940.54
Nagorski, Andrew. *Saving Freud*	940.53
Nasaw, David. *The Last Million*	940.53
Nelson, Craig. ★*V Is for Victory*	973.917
Nez, Chester. *Code Talker*	B
Norman, Elizabeth M. *We Band of Angels*	940.54
Norman, Michael. *Tears in the Darkness*	940.54
O'Donnell, Svenja. *Inge's War*	943.086
Oelhafen, Ingrid von. *Hitler's Stolen Children*	B
Ohler, Norman. *The Bohemians*	940.53
Olson, Lynne. *Citizens of London*	940.54012

AUTHOR, TITLE, SERIES AND SUBJECT INDEX

Olson, Lynne. *Last Hope Island*	940.53
Olson, Lynne. ★*Madame Fourcade's Secret War*	B
Olson, Lynne. *Those Angry Days*	940.53
Overy, R. J. *Why the Allies Won*	940.53
Patton, George S. *War as I Knew It*	B
Pavlychenko, Liudmyla Mykhailivna. *Lady Death*	
Paxson, Margaret. *The Plateau*	362.87
Pellegrino, Charles R. *To Hell and Back*	940.54
Perry, Mark. *The Most Dangerous Man in America*	B
Phillips, Adrian. *Fighting Churchill, Appeasing Hitler*	327.41043
Plokhy, Serhii. *Yalta*	940.53
Pomerantsev, Peter. ★*How to Win an Information War*	940.53
Prange, Gordon W. *At Dawn We Slept*	940.54
Preston, Diana. *Before the Fallout*	303.48
Preston, Diana. *Eight Days at Yalta*	940.53
Price, David A. *Geniuses at War*	940.54
Purnell, Sonia. *Clementine*	B
Purnell, Sonia. ★*A Woman of No Importance*	B
Raban, Jonathan. *Father and Son*	B
Rajchman, Chil. *The Last Jew of Treblinka*	940.53
Read, Anthony. *The Fall of Berlin*	940.54
Rees, Laurence. *Auschwitz*	940.53
Rees, Laurence. *Hitler and Stalin*	940.53
Reeves, Richard. *Infamy*	940.53
Reid, Anna. *Leningrad*	940.54
Reynolds, Nicholas E. *Need to Know*	940.54
Rhodes, Richard. *Masters of Death*	940.53
Rinehart, Lorissa. *First to the Front*	B
Roberts, Andrew. ★*Churchill*	B
Roberts, Andrew. *Masters and Commanders*	940.5322
Roberts, Andrew. *The Storm of War*	940.54
Rogoyska, Jane. *Surviving Katyn*	940.54
Roll, David L. *Ascent to Power*	973.918
Roll, David L. *George Marshall*	B
Ronald, Susan. *A Dangerous Woman*	B
Ronald, Susan. *Hitler's Aristocrats*	940.53
Rosbottom, Ronald C. *When Paris Went Dark*	944.0816
Rosenberg, Justus. *The Art of Resistance*	B
Ross, Steve. *From Broken Glass*	B
Russell, Jan Jarboe. *The Train to Crystal City*	940.53
Sakamoto, Pamela Rotner. *Midnight in Broad Daylight*	940.53
Samet, Elizabeth D. *Looking for the Good War*	940.53
Sands, Philippe. *The Ratline*	B
Schindler, Meriel. *The Lost Cafe Schindler*	943.64
Schwarz, Geraldine. *Those Who Forget*	940.53
Scott, James. *Black Snow*	940.54
Scott, James. *Rampage*	940.54
Scott, James. *Target Tokyo*	940.54
Sheinkin, Steve. *Bomb*	623.4
Sides, Hampton. ★*Ghost Soldiers*	940.54
Siegal, Nina. *The Diary Keepers*	940.54
Simms, Brendan. *The Silver Waterfall*	940.54
Simon, Marie. *Underground in Berlin*	B
Smith, Jim B. *The Last Mission*	940.54
Smith, Starr. *Jimmy Stewart*	B
Snyder, Steve. *Shot Down*	940.54
Snyder, Timothy. *Black Earth*	940.53
Snyder, Timothy. ★*Bloodlands*	940.54
Southard, Susan. *Nagasaki*	940.54
Spicer, Charles. *Coffee with Hitler*	941.084
Stangneth, Bettina. *Eichmann Before Jerusalem*	B
Stanton, Doug. *In Harm's Way*	940.54
Stargardt, Nicholas. *The German War*	940.53
Stevenson, William. *A Man Called Intrepid*	940.54
Strauss, Gwen. *The Nine*	940.53
Sullivan, James. *Unsinkable*	940.54
Symonds, Craig L. *The Battle of Midway*	940.54
Symonds, Craig L. *World War II at Sea*	940.54
Takaki, Ronald T. *Double Victory*	940.53
Talty, Stephan. *Agent Garbo*	940.5
Taylor, Fred. *1939*	940.53
Teege, Jennifer. *My Grandfather Would Have Shot Me*	929.2
Terkel, Studs. *The Good War*	940.54
Thomas, Evan. *Sea of Thunder*	940.54
Thomas, Gordon. *Defying Hitler*	920
Tobin, James. *Ernie Pyle's War*	B
Toll, Ian W. *The Conquering Tide*	940.54
Toll, Ian W. *Pacific Crucible*	940.54
Toll, Ian W. *Twilight of the Gods*	940.54
Trimble, Lee. *Beyond the Call*	940.54
Tuchman, Barbara W. *Stilwell and the American Experience in China, 1911-45*	B
Tucker, Todd. *The Great Starvation Experiment*	174.2
Twomey, Steve. *Countdown to Pearl Harbor*	940.54
Ullrich, Volker. ★*Eight Days in May*	943.086
Ullrich, Volker. *Hitler*	B
Urwand, Ben. *The Collaboration*	791.430973
Van Es, Bart. *The Cut Out Girl*	B
Vincent, Lynn. *Indianapolis*	940.54
Wachsmann, Nikolaus. *Kl*	940.53
Wallace, Chris. *Countdown 1945*	940.54
Waller, Douglas C. *Wild Bill Donovan*	B
Weale, Adrian. *Army of Evil*	940.54
Weintraub, Robert. *No Better Friend*	940.54
Wheelan, Joseph. *Midnight in the Pacific*	940.54
White, Elizabeth B. ★*The Counterfeit Countess*	940.53
Wiesenthal, Simon. ★*The Sunflower*	179.7
Winik, Jay. *1944*	940.53
Winters, Richard D. *Beyond Band of Brothers*	B
Wukovits, John F. *Lost at Sea*	940.54
Yellin, Emily. *Our Mothers' War*	940.53
Yergin, Daniel. ★*The Prize*	338.2
Zuckoff, Mitchell. *Frozen in Time*	998.2
Zuckoff, Mitchell. *Lost in Shangri-La*	940.54
World War II at Sea. Symonds, Craig L.	940.54
WORLD WAR II FILMS	
Harris, Mark. ★*Five Came Back*	791.4302
WORLD WAR II HOME FRONT	
Englund, Peter. *November 1942*	940.53
Kleiman, Kathy. *Proving Ground*	4.092
WORLD WAR II VETERANS	
Hastings, Max. *Retribution*	940.54
Hillenbrand, Laura. ★*Unbroken*	B
Hornfischer, James D. *Neptune's Inferno*	940.54
WORLD WIDE WEB	
Wright, Alex. *Cataloging the World*	020.9
A World Without Ice. Pollack, H. N.	551.31
World's End. Neruda, Pablo	861
The World's Fastest Man. Kranish, Michael	B
The World's Rarest Birds. Hirschfeld, Erik	333.95822
The World's Worst Assistant. Movsesian, Sona	791.4302
★*The World-Ending Fire.* Berry, Wendell	818
★*The Worldly Philosophers.* Heilbroner, Robert L.	B
The Worlds I See. Li, Fei-Fei	B
Worley, Jennifer	
Neon Girls	792.7
WORLEY, JENNIFER	
Worley, Jennifer. *Neon Girls*	792.7
WORMHOLES (ASTROPHYSICS)	
Tyson, Neil deGrasse. *Welcome to the Universe*	523.1
Worn. Thanhauser, Sofi	391
Worn Out. Hardy, Alyssa	338.4
WORRY	
Delaney, Brigid. *Reasons Not to Worry*	158.1
Worse Than Slavery. Oshinsky, David M.	365
Worse Than the Devil. Strang, Dean A.	345.775
WORSHIP	
Held, Shai. ★*Judaism Is About Love*	296.3
WORSLEY, HENRY	
Grann, David. *The White Darkness*	B
Worsley, Lucy	
★*Agatha Christie*	B
Queen Victoria	B
The Worst Hard Time. Egan, Timothy	978
Worster, Donald	
A Passion for Nature the Life of John Muir	B
Worth Dying For. Denver, Rorke	359.9
WORTH, CHARLES FREDERIC, 1825-1895	
Trubert-Tollu, Chantal. ★*The House of Worth 1858-1954*	746.92
Worth, Robert Forsyth	
★*A Rage for Order*	909
Worthy. Smith, Jada Pinkett	B
Wouldn't Take Nothing for My Journey Now. Angelou, Maya	814
Wound from the Mouth of a Wound. greathouse, torrin a	811
WOUNDS AND INJURIES	
Carpenter, Kyle. *You Are Worth It*	B

PUBLIC LIBRARY CORE COLLECTION: NONFICTION
Twentieth Edition

Fabes, Stephen. *Signs of Life* — B
Fainaru-Wada, Mark. *League of Denial* — 617.1
Fox, Michael J. *No Time Like the Future* — B
Godwin, Gail. *Getting to Know Death* — B
Laskas, Jeanne Marie. *Concussion* — 617.5
Messenger, Alex. *The Twenty-Ninth Day* — B
Rieder, Travis. *In Pain* — 362.29
Singer, Jessie. *There Are No Accidents* — 363.1
***Wounds** of Passion*. hooks, bell — B
***Woven** to Wear*. Murphy, Marilyn — 746.1
Wragg Sykes, Rebecca
   Kindred — 569.9
Wrangham, Richard W.
   Catching Fire — 394.1
Wray, Britt
   Generation Dread — 155.9
Wray, T. J.
   The Birth of Satan — 235
WRECKING
   D'Agata, John. *About a Mountain* — 979.3
   Langewiesche, William. *American Ground* — 974.7
WRESTLERS
   Fenn, Lisa. *Carry On* — B
   Levi, Heather. *The World of Lucha Libre* — 796.812
WRESTLING
   Levi, Heather. *The World of Lucha Libre* — 796.812
***Wrestling** with His Angel*. Blumenthal, Sidney — B
★*A **Wretched** and Precarious Situation*. Welky, David — 910.911
★*The **Wright** Brothers*. McCullough, David G. — B
***Wright** Brothers, Wrong Story*. Hazelgrove, William Elliott — 920
WRIGHT FAMILY
   Branch, John. *The Last Cowboys* — 920
WRIGHT FLYER (AIRPLANE)
   McCullough, David G. ★*The Wright Brothers* — B
Wright, Alex
   Cataloging the World — 020.9
Wright, C. D.
   One with Others — 811
Wright, Caroline
   Cake Magic! — 641.86
WRIGHT, ERIC, 1964-1995
   Westhoff, Ben. *Original Gangstas* — 782.421649
Wright, Evan
   Generation Kill — 956.7044
WRIGHT, FRANK LLOYD, 1867-1959
   Huxtable, Ada Louise. ★*Frank Lloyd Wright* — B
   Secrest, Meryle. *Frank Lloyd Wright* — B
   Storrer, William Allin. *The Frank Lloyd Wright Companion* — 720.92
Wright, James Arlington
   Above the River — 811
WRIGHT, JAMES ARLINGTON, 1927-1980
   Blunk, Jonathan. *James Wright* — B
Wright, James Edward
   ★*Enduring Vietnam* — 959.704
Wright, Jennifer Ashley
   ★*Madame Restell* — B
Wright, Lawrence
   God Save Texas — 917.64
   Going Clear — 299
   ★*The Looming Tower* — 973.931
   ★*The Plague Year* — 614.5
   Thirteen Days in September — 956.04
WRIGHT, LAWRENCE, 1947-
   Wright, Lawrence. *God Save Texas* — 917.64
WRIGHT, MARTHA COFFIN, 1806-1875
   Wickenden, Dorothy. *The Agitators* — 920
WRIGHT, ORVILLE, 1871-1948
   Hazelgrove, William Elliott. *Wright Brothers, Wrong Story* — 920
   McCullough, David G. ★*The Wright Brothers* — B
Wright, Richard
   ★*Black Boy* — B
WRIGHT, RICHARD, 1908-1960
   Wright, Richard. ★*Black Boy* — B
Wright, Robert
   Why Buddhism Is True — 294.3
WRIGHT, WILBUR, 1867-1912
   Hazelgrove, William Elliott. *Wright Brothers, Wrong Story* — 920
   McCullough, David G. ★*The Wright Brothers* — B

*The **Writer's** Garden*. Bennett, Jackie — 920
*A **Writer's** House in Wales*. Morris, Jan — 942.9
★*The **Writer's** Journey*. Vogler, Christopher — 808.2
WRITERS CONFERENCES
   Salesses, Matthew. ★*Craft in the Real World* — 808.3
WRITING
   Achebe, Chinua. *The Education of a British-Protected Child* — B
   Ackmann, Martha. ★*These Fevered Days* — B
   Allende, Isabel. *My Invented Country* — B
   Allende, Isabel. *The Sum of Our Days* — B
   Anders, Charlie Jane. ★*Never Say You Can't Survive* — 808.02
   Attenberg, Jami. *1000 Words* — 808.02
   Bass, Rick. *The Traveling Feast* — B
   Bass, Rick. *Why I Came West* — 333.78
   Batuman, Elif. *The Possessed* — 891.7
   Bell, Madison Smartt. *Child of Light* — B
   Bellos, David. *The Novel of the Century* — 843
   Brandreth, Gyles Daubeney. *Have You Eaten Grandma?* — 428
   Calhoun, Ada. *Also a Poet* — B
   Cameron, Julia. *Living the Artist's Way* — 153.3
   Capote, Truman. *Too Brief a Treat* — B
   Caro, Robert A. ★*Working* — B
   Chabon, Michael. *Maps and Legends* — 801
   Chee, Alexander. ★*How to Write an Autobiographical Novel* — B
   Coetzee, J. M. *Late Essays, 2006-2017* — 824
   Crawford, Robert. *Eliot After the Waste Land* — B
   Curzan, Anne. ★*Says Who?* — 428
   Cusk, Rachel. *Coventry* — 814
   Didion, Joan. *Let Me Tell You What I Mean* — 814
   Dreyer, Benjamin. *Dreyer's English* — 808.02
   Dubus, Andre. *Townie* — B
   Dufresne, John. *Storyville!* — 808.3
   Evans, Bec. *Written* — 808
   Fallon, Allison. *The Power of Writing It Down* — 158.1
   Febos, Melissa. ★*Body Work* — 808.06
   Fehrman, Craig. *Author in Chief* — 920
   Ferrante, Elena. *In the Margins* — 809
   Ferrara, Silvia. *The Greatest Invention* — 411
   Fishman, Stephen. ★*The Copyright Handbook, 15th Ed.* — 346.7304
   Frank, Joseph. ★*Dostoevsky* — B
   French, Patrick. *The World Is What It Is* — B
   Gabbert, Elisa. *Any Person Is the Only Self* — 814
   Gaiman, Neil. *The View from the Cheap Seats* — 824
   Grass, Gunter. *Of All That Ends* — 838
   Griffin, Susan. *Out of Silence, Sound. Out of Nothing, Something* — 808.02
   Handler, Daniel. *And Then? and Then? What Else?* — 813
   Hardin, Lara Love. ★*The Many Lives of Mama Love* — B
   Harvey, Samantha. *The Shapeless Unease* — B
   Heti, Sheila. *Alphabetical Diaries* — 818
   Hollis, Matthew. *The Waste Land* — 821
   hooks, bell. *Remembered Rapture* — 808
   hooks, bell. *Wounds of Passion* — B
   Houston, Keith. *The Book* — 002.09
   Houston, Keith. *Shady Characters* — 411
   Hughes, Langston. ★*I Wonder as I Wander* — B
   Imbler, Sabrina. *How Far the Light Reaches* — 591.77
   Jackson, Angela. *A Surprised Queenhood in the New Black Sun* — B
   Jackson, Shirley. ★*The Letters of Shirley Jackson* — 813
   Karr, Mary. *The Art of Memoir* — B
   Kempton, Beth. *The Way of the Fearless Writer* — 808.02
   Kidder, Tracy. *Good Prose* — 808.02
   King, Stephen. *On Writing* — B
   Lahiri, Jhumpa. *Translating Myself and Others* — 418
   Lamott, Anne. *Bird by Bird* — 808
   Larimer, Kevin. *The Poets & Writers Complete Guide to Being a Writer* — 808
   Le Guin, Ursula K. *Ursula K. Le Guin* — B
   Le Guin, Ursula K. *Words Are My Matter* — 818
   Lepore, Jill. ★*The Deadline* — 814
   Levy, Deborah. ★*Real Estate* — B
   Levy, Deborah. ★*Things I Don't Want to Know* — B
   Li, Yiyun. *Dear Friend, from My Life I Write to You in Your Life* — B
   Lippman, Laura. *My Life as a Villainess* — B
   McCann, Colum. *Letters to a Young Writer* — 808.02
   McDermott, Alice. *What About the Baby?* — 814
   McIlwaine, Catherine. *Tolkien* — 002.09
   Milch, David. *Life's Work* — B
   Murakami, Haruki. ★*Absolutely on Music* — 784.2
   Murakami, Haruki. ★*Novelist as a Vocation* — 895.64

AUTHOR, TITLE, SERIES AND SUBJECT INDEX

Murakami, Haruki. *What I Talk About When I Talk About Running*	B
Norris, Mary. *Between You and Me*	428.2
O'Neil, Dennis. *The DC Comics Guide to Writing Comics*	808
Orwell, George. *Diaries*	828
Oyler, Lauren. *No Judgment*	814
Palahniuk, Chuck. *Consider This*	814
Patchett, Ann. ★*These Precious Days*	814
Patterson, James. *James Patterson by James Patterson*	B
Percy, Benjamin. *Thrill Me*	808.3
Plath, Sylvia. *The Letters of Sylvia Plath*	811.54
Roiphe, Katie. *The Violet Hour*	809
Rosen, Michael. *Alphabetical*	421
Rosnay, Tatiana de. *Manderley Forever*	B
Rushdie, Salman. ★*Knife*	B
Rushdie, Salman. *Languages of Truth*	824
Russo, Richard. *The Destiny Thief*	814
Sabatini Sloan, Aisha. *Dreaming of Ramadi in Detroit*	814
Salesses, Matthew. ★*Craft in the Real World*	808.3
Salter, James. *Don't Save Anything*	818
Scalzi, John. *Don't Live for Your Obituary*	808.02
Schultz, Philip. *Comforts of the Abyss*	801
Sepetys, Ruta. ★*You*	808.02
Shapiro, James. *Contested Will*	822.33
Shelden, Michael. *Mark Twain*	B
Slawenski, Kenneth. ★*Salinger*	B
Smith, Patti. ★*Just Kids*	B
Smith, Patti. ★*M Train*	B
Solnit, Rebecca. ★*Recollections of My Nonexistence*	B
Tan, Amy. ★*Where the Past Begins*	B
Truss, Lynne. *Eats, Shoots & Leaves*	428.2
Tweedy, Jeff. *How to Write One Song*	782.42
Vargas Llosa, Mario. *Conversation at Princeton*	868
Verdelle, A. J. *Miss Chloe*	B
Vogler, Christopher. ★*The Writer's Journey*	808.2
Wagamese, Richard. *One Native Life*	B
Watts, Steven. *Self-Help Messiah*	B
Weinman, Sarah. *The Real Lolita*	362.88092
Welty, Eudora. *One Writer's Beginnings*	B
White, Ronald C. *Lincoln in Private*	B
Wilder, Laura Ingalls. *The Selected Letters of Laura Ingalls Wilder*	B
Winkler, Elizabeth. *Shakespeare Was a Woman & Other Heresies*	822.33
Woods, Geraldine. *25 Great Sentences and How They Got That Way*	808
Writing for Their Lives. LaFollette, Marcel C.	071.3
The Writing Life. Dillard, Annie	B
WRITING MATERIALS AND INSTRUMENTS	
Thorpe, Molly Suber. *Modern Calligraphy*	745.6
WRITING METHODS AND SYSTEMS	
Ferrara, Silvia. *The Greatest Invention*	411
Fox, Margalit. *The Riddle of the Labyrinth*	920
Rosen, Michael. *Alphabetical*	421
The Writing of the Gods. Dolnick, Edward	493
Writing to Learn. Zinsser, William Knowlton	808
★*Writings*. Du Bois, W. E. B.	973
Writings. Jefferson, Thomas	973.3
Writings, 1903-1932. Stein, Gertrude	818
Writings, 1932-1946. Stein, Gertrude	818
Written. Evans, Bec	808
The Written World. Puchner, Martin	809
Wroe, Ann	
Orpheus	398.2093802
Wu, Constance	
Making a Scene	B
WU, CONSTANCE, 1982-	
Wu, Constance. *Making a Scene*	B
Wu, Simon	
Dancing on My Own	700.1
WU, SIMON (CURATOR)	
Wu, Simon. *Dancing on My Own*	700.1
Wu, Tim	
The Attention Merchants	659.1
Wukovits, John F.	
Lost at Sea	940.54
Wulf, Andrea	
The Brother Gardeners	920
The Invention of Nature	B
Magnificent Rebels	830.9
Wullschlager, Jackie	
★*Chagall*	B
Wyatt Earp. Tefertiller, Casey	B
WYLER, WILLIAM, 1902-1981	
Harris, Mark. ★*Five Came Back*	791.4302
WYNETTE, TAMMY, 1942-1998	
McDonough, Jimmy. *Tammy Wynette*	B
Wynn-Grant, Rae	
Wild Life	B
WYNN-GRANT, RAE	
Wynn-Grant, Rae. *Wild Life*	B
Wynne, Clive D. L.	
★*Dog Is Love*	636.7
WYOMING	
Bell, Laura. *Claiming Ground*	B
Proulx, Annie. *Bird Cloud*	B

X

X Troop. Garrett, Leah	940.54
XENOPHOBIA	
Ayers, Edward L. *American Visions*	973.5
Egan, Timothy. ★*A Fever in the Heartland*	322.4
Fishman, Elly. *Refugee High*	370.8
Gage, Beverly. *G-Man*	B
Huang, Yunte. *Daughter of the Dragon*	B
Lalami, Laila. *Conditional Citizens*	323.60973
Lee, Erika. *America for Americans*	305.800973
Lekas Miller, Anna. *Love Across Borders*	323.6
Mishra, Pankaj. *Age of Anger*	909.8
Nussbaum, Martha Craven. *The Monarchy of Fear*	306.20973
Okrent, Daniel. *The Guarded Gate*	344.73
Yang, Jia Lynn. ★*One Mighty and Irresistible Tide*	325.73
XERISCAPING	
Bainbridge, David A. *Gardening with Less Water*	635.9
Penick, Pam. *The Water-Saving Garden*	635.9
Silver, Johanna. ★*The Bold Dry Garden*	635.9
XI JINPING	
Strittmatter, Kai. *We Have Been Harmonized*	323.44
XI'an Famous Foods. Wang, Jason	641.595
XI, JINPING	
Wong, Chun Han. *Party of One*	951.06
XIe, Jenny	
Eye Level	811
XINJIANG, CHINA	
Haitiwaji, Gulbahar. *How I Survived a Chinese "Reeducation" Camp*	305.8
Hoja, Gulchehra. *A Stone Is Most Precious Where It Belongs*	B
Izgil, Tahir Hamut. *Waiting to Be Arrested at Night*	B
★*XOXO, Cody*. Rigsby, Cody	B
Xue, XInran	
The Book of Secrets	951.05
Xuecun, Murong	
Deadly Quiet City	614.5
XUECUN, MURONG	
Xuecun, Murong. *Deadly Quiet City*	614.5

Y

Y'all Eat Yet?. Lambert, Miranda	641.5976
YABLONSKI, JOSEPH A., 1910-1969	
Bradley, Mark A. *Blood Runs Coal*	B
Yacovone, Donald	
★*Teaching White Supremacy*	370.89
Yaffa, Joshua	
Between Two Fires	920
Yaffe, David	
Reckless Daughter	782.42164
Yager, Jan	
How to Self Publish Your Book	070.5
Yaker, Rebecca	
Little One-Yard Wonders	646.2
Yale Needs Women. Perkins, Anne Gardiner	378
Yale series of younger poets [Series]. Bailey, Desiree C.	811
Yalom, Irvin D.	
Staring at the Sun	155.9
Yalta. Plokhy, Serhii	940.53
YAMAMOTO, ISOROKU, 1884-1943	
Hampton, Dan. *Operation Vengeance*	940.54

PUBLIC LIBRARY CORE COLLECTION: NONFICTION
Twentieth Edition

YAMASHITA, TOMOBUMI, 1885-1946
    Scott, James. *Rampage* — 940.54
Yamazaki, Hiromi
    Japanese Paper Flowers — 745.594
YANA (NORTH AMERICAN PEOPLE)
    Kroeber, Theodora. *Ishi in Two Worlds* — B
Yancey, Philip
    ★ *Where the Light Fell* — B
YANCEY, PHILIP
    Yancey, Philip. ★ *Where the Light Fell* — B
Yang, April
    DIY Thrift Flip — 646.2
Yang, Charles D.
    The Infinite Gift — 401
Yang, Jeff
    The Golden Screen — 791.43
    ★ *Rise* — 973
Yang, Jia Lynn
    ★ *One Mighty and Irresistible Tide* — 325.73
Yang, Jisheng
    The World Turned Upside Down — 951.05
Yang, Lihui
    ★ *Handbook of Chinese Mythology* — 299.5
The Yankee Comandante. Sallah, Michael — 972.91
Yankee Come Home. Craig, William — 972.9107
The Yankee Years. Torre, Joe — B
YAQUI (NORTH AMERICAN PEOPLE)
    Castaneda, Carlos. *The Teachings of Don Juan;* — 299
YARN
    Callahan, Gail. *Hand Dyeing Yarn and Fleece* — 746.6
    Parkes, Clara. *The Knitter's Book of Yarn* — 677
YASUKE (BLACK SAMURAI)
    Lockley, Thomas. *African Samurai* — B
Yates, Kit
    The Math of Life and Death — 510
YAUCH, ADAM, 1964-2012
    Mike D. *Beastie Boys Book* — 782.42164
YAVAPAI (NORTH AMERICAN PEOPLE)
    Burns, Mike. *The Only One Living to Tell* — 305.897
The Year 1000. Hansen, Valerie — 909
★ *A Year in Provence.* Mayle, Peter — 944
A Year in the World. Mayes, Frances — B
The Year of Cozy. Adarme, Adrianna — 641.3
A Year of Gingerbread Houses. Samuell, Kristine — 745.5
A Year of Last Things. Ondaatje, Michael — 811
The Year of Lear. Shapiro, James — 822.33
★ *The Year of Living Constitutionally.* Jacobs, A. J. — 342.73
★ *The Year of Magical Thinking.* Didion, Joan — B
The Year of Miracles. Risbridger, Ella — 641.5
Year of the Hawk. Warren, James A. — 959.704
★ *Year of the Monkey.* Smith, Patti — B
The Year of the Pitcher. Pappu, Sridhar — 920
★ *The Year of the Puppy.* Horowitz, Alexandra — 636.7
★ *Year of the Tiger.* Wong, Alice — B
★ *Year of Wonder.* Burton-Hill, Clemency — 780.9
★ *Yearbook.* Rogen, Seth — B
★ *The Years.* Ernaux, Annie — B
The Years That Matter Most. Tough, Paul — 378.1
Yearwood, Trisha
    Trisha's Kitchen — 641.5
Yeats, W. B.
    The Collected Poems of W.B. Yeats — 821
YEATS, W. B. (WILLIAM BUTLER), 1865-1939
    Brown, Terence. *The Life of W.B. Yeats* — B
    Toibin, Colm. *Mad, Bad, Dangerous to Know* — 920
Yeebo, Yepoka
    Anansi's Gold — 364.16
Yeh, Molly
    Home Is Where the Eggs Are — 641.5
Yellin, Emily
    Our Mothers' War — 940.53
★ *Yellow Bird.* Murdoch, Sierra Crane — 364.152
YELLOW BIRD, LISSA
    Murdoch, Sierra Crane. ★ *Yellow Bird* — 364.152
Yellow Dirt. Pasternak, Judy — 979.1004
YELLOW FEVER
    Crosby, Molly Caldwell. *The American Plague* — 614.5
The Yellow House. Broom, Sarah M. — B
The Yellow Pad. Rubin, Robert Edward — 658.4
The Yellow Wind. Grossman, David — 956.95
YELLOWSTONE NATIONAL PARK
    Black, George. *Empire of Shadows* — 978.7
    Blakeslee, Nate. *American Wolf* — 599.773
    McIntyre, Rick. *The Reign of Wolf 21* — 599.773
YELTSIN, BORIS NIKOLAYEVICH, 1931-2007
    Remnick, David. *Lenin's Tomb* — 947.085
YEMEN (REPUBLIC)
    AL Samawi, Mohammed. *The Fox Hunt* — 953
Yergin, Daniel
    The New Map — 333.79
    ★ *The Prize* — 338.2
    The Quest — 333.79
★ *The Yes Brain.* Siegel, Daniel J. — 155.4
Yes I Can Say That. Gold, Judy — 792.7
Yes Please. Poehler, Amy — B
Yes to Life. Frankl, Viktor E. — 150.19
Yes, Chef. Samuelsson, Marcus — B
Yeung, Bernice
    In a Day's Work — 362.88086
YEZIDIS
    Mikhaiil, Dunya. *The Beekeeper* — 956.7044
    Murad, Nadia. ★ *The Last Girl* — B
YI FAMILY
    Lee, Helie. *In the Absence of Sun* — B
Yi, Sang-Hui
    Close Encounters with Humankind — 599.93
YI, SUN
    Pang, Amelia. ★ *Made in China* — 331.11
YIDDISH LANGUAGE
    Lansky, Aaron. *Outwitting History* — 002
    Rosten, Leo. *The New Joys of Yiddish* — 422
Yip-Williams, Julie
    ★ *The Unwinding of the Miracle* — 973
YIP-WILLIAMS, JULIE, 1976-2018
    Yip-Williams, Julie. ★ *The Unwinding of the Miracle* — 973
YOGA
    Bondy, Dianne. *Yoga Where You Are* — 613.7
    Fishman, Loren. *Yoga for Arthritis* — 616.7
    Goldberg, Philip. *American Veda* — 294.509
    Lacerda, Daniel. *2,100 Asanas* — 613.7
    Stanley, Jessamyn. *Every Body Yoga* — 613.7
    Stanley, Jessamyn. ★ *Yoke* — 613.7
Yoga Fitness for Men. Pohlman, Dean — 613.7
Yoga for Arthritis. Fishman, Loren — 616.7
Yoga Myths. Lasater, Judith — 613.7
Yoga Where You Are. Bondy, Dianne — 613.7
Yogi. Pessah, Jon — B
★ *Yogi Berra.* Barra, Allen — B
★ *Yoke.* Stanley, Jessamyn — 613.7
YOM KIPPUR
    Pogrebin, Abigail. *My Jewish Year* — 296.4
Yomota, Inuhiko
    What Is Japanese Cinema? — 791.43
Yong, Ed
    ★ *An Immense World* — 591.5
Yong, Sable
    Die Hot with a Vengeance — 646.7
YORK, CECILY, DUCHESS OF, 1415-1495
    Gristwood, Sarah. *Blood Sisters* — 942.04092
YORK, HOUSE OF
    Penn, Thomas. *The Brothers York* — 942.04
YORKSHIRE, ENGLAND
    Herriot, James. ★ *All Creatures Great and Small* — B
    Herriot, James. *All Things Wise and Wonderful* — B
    Herriot, James. *Every Living Thing* — B
    Herriot, James. *James Herriot's Animal Stories* — B
    Herriot, James. *James Herriot's Cat Stories* — 636.8
    Herriot, James. *James Herriot's Dog Stories* — 636.7
The Yosemite. Muir, John — 979.4
YOSEMITE NATIONAL PARK
    Galassi, Peter. *Ansel Adams in Yosemite Valley* — 770.92
    King, Dean. *Guardians of the Valley* — 333.72
    Muir, John. *The Yosemite* — 979.4
YOSEMITE VALLEY
    Alinder, Mary Street. *Ansel Adams* — B
    Galassi, Peter. *Ansel Adams in Yosemite Valley* — 770.92

AUTHOR, TITLE, SERIES AND SUBJECT INDEX

King, Dean. *Guardians of the Valley* — 333.72
Muir, John. *The Yosemite* — 979.4
Taylor, Joseph E. *Pilgrims of the Vertical* — 796.52
Yoshino, Kenji
  Say the Right Thing — 305.3
  Speak Now — 346.79401
★ *You*. Sepetys, Ruta — 808.02
You & Yours. Nye, Naomi Shihab — 811
You Are a Badass. Sincero, Jen — 158.1
You Are a Badass Every Day. Sincero, Jen — 158.1
You Are Here. Ellard, Colin — 153.7
You Are My Sunshine. Dietrich, Sean — B
You Are Never Alone. Lucado, Max — 248.4
★ *You Are Not a Sh*tty Parent*. Naumburg, Carla — 649
You Are Not Stuck. Vollmer, Becky — 158.1
★ *You Are What You Watch*. Hickey, Walt — 791.4
You Are Worth It. Carpenter, Kyle — B
You Bet Your Life. Offit, Paul A. — 615.5
You Can Knit That. Herzog, Amy — 746.432
You Can Stop Humming Now. Lamas, Daniela J. — 616.02
You Can't Be Serious. Penn, Kal — B
You Can't Go Wrong Doing Right. Brown, Robert J. — B
You Can't Steal a Gift. Lees, Gene — B
You Can't Touch My Hair and Other Things I Still Have to Explain. Robinson, Phoebe — 792.7
★ *You Could Make This Place Beautiful*. Smith, Maggie — B
You Don't Have to Say You Love Me. Alexie, Sherman — 818
★ *You Don't Know Us Negroes and Other Essays*. Hurston, Zora Neale — 814
You Don't Look Your Age. Nevins, Sheila — B
You Don't Own Me. Lobel, Orly — 346.7304
★ *You Get What You Pay For*. Parker, Morgan — 305.896
You Got Anything Stronger?. Union, Gabrielle — B
You Have It Made! Krieger, Ellie — 641.5
★ *You Have to Be Prepared to Die Before You Can Begin to Live*. Kix, Paul — 976.1
You Just Need to Lose Weight". Gordon, Aubrey — 616.3
You May Also Like. Vanderbilt, Tom — 153.8
You Need a Budget. Mecham, Jesse — 332.024
★ *You Never Forget Your First*. Coe, Alexis — B
You Never Give Me Your Money. Doggett, Peter — B
You Never Know. Selleck, Tom — B
You or Someone You Love. Matthews, Hannah — 362.1988
★ *You Ought to Do a Story About Me*. Jackson, Ted — B
You Sound Like a White Girl. Arce, Julissa — 303.48
You'll Never Believe What Happened to Lacey. Ruffin, Amber — 305.896
You're A Miracle (and a Pain in the Ass). McHargue, Mike — 158.1
You're Not Done Yet. Hibbs, B. Janet — 649
You're Not Listening. Murphy, Kate — 153.6
You're on an Airplane. Posey, Parker — B
You're The Only One I've Told. Shah, Meera — 362.1988
You've Been Chosen. Marshall, Cynthia — B
You, Too, Could Write a Poem. Orr, David — 808.1
Youn, Monica
  Blackacre — 811.6
Young Adult Literature. Cart, Michael — 813.009
YOUNG ADULT LITERATURE
  Cart, Michael. *Young Adult Literature* — 813.009
  Chance, Rosemary. *Young Adult Literature in Action* — 011.62
  Corbett, Emily. *In Transition* — 809
Young Adult Literature in Action. Chance, Rosemary — 011.62
YOUNG ADULTS
  Bayoumi, Moustafa. *How Does It Feel to Be a Problem?* — 305.892
  Chance, Rosemary. *Young Adult Literature in Action* — 011.62
  Goldberg, Emma. *Life on the Line* — 362.1962
  Hibbs, B. Janet. *You're Not Done Yet* — 649
  Kim, Anne. ★ *Abandoned* — 305.2350973
  Lythcott-Haims, Julie. *Your Turn* — 305.24
  McConville, Mark. *Failure to Launch* — 155.6
  McGrath, Tom. *Triumph of the Yuppies* — 305.242
  Moss, Gabrielle. *Paperback Crush* — 813.009
  Spencer, Kyle. *Raising Them Right* — 320.5
YOUNG ADULTS' LIBRARIES
  Flowers, Sarah. *Evaluating Teen Services and Programs* — 027.62
  Pattee, Amy. *Developing Library Collections for Today's Young Adults* — 027.62
  Snow, Jess. ★ *Outreach Services for Teens* — 027.4
Young and Damned and Fair. Russell, Gareth — B
Young Benjamin Franklin. Bunker, Nick — B

YOUNG GAY MEN
  Belcourt, Billy-Ray. ★ *A History of My Brief Body* — B
  Jimenez, Stephen. *The Book of Matt* — 364.152
Young Mandela. Smith, David James — B
YOUNG MEN
  Carson, Anne. *Autobiography of Red* — 811
  Chavez Perez, Inti. *Respect* — 176
  Chisholm, Edward. *A Waiter in Paris* — B
  Colt, George Howe. *The Game* — 796.332
  Hobbs, Jeff. *Show Them You're Good* — 373
  Kim, Suki. *Without You, There Is No Us* — B
  King, Greg. *Nothing but the Night* — 364.152
  Krakauer, Jon. *Into the Wild* — 917.9804
  Marshall, McMillan. *Among the Bros* — 362.29
  Messenger, Alex. *The Twenty-Ninth Day* — B
  Orenstein, Peggy. ★ *Boys & Sex* — 305.235
  Rannells, Andrew. *Too Much Is Not Enough* — 792.02
  Rao, Cheeni. *In Hanuman's Hands* — B
  Reiner, Andrew. *Better Boys, Better Men* — 155.43
  Way, Niobe. *Rebels with a Cause* — 649
Young Orson. McGilligan, Patrick — B
Young Rembrandt. Blom, Onno — B
Young Stalin. Sebag-Montefiore, Simon — B
Young Thurgood. Gibson, Larry S. — B
Young Washington. Stark, Peter — B
YOUNG WOMEN
  Bell, Laura. *Claiming Ground* — B
  Byrne, Paula. *Kick* — B
  Chang, Leslie T. *Factory Girls* — 331.4
  Georges, Gigi. *Downeast* — 974.1
  Hernandez, Daisy. *A Cup of Water Under My Bed* — B
  Khar, Erin. *Strung Out* — B
  Leaming, Barbara. *Kick Kennedy* — B
  LeFavour, Cree. *Lights On, Rats Out* — 616.85
  Parkin, Simon. *A Game of Birds and Wolves* — 940.54
  Preston, Katherine. *Out with It* — B
  Prior-Palmer, Lara. *Rough Magic* — 798.4
  Sampson, Fiona. *In Search of Mary Shelley* — B
  Satrapi, Marjane. ★ *The Complete Persepolis* — 741.5
  Tjipombo, Tupa. *I Am Not Your Slave* — B
  Wilder, Thornton. *Our Town* — 812
  Zoepf, Katherine. *Excellent Daughters* — 305.42
Young, Anastasia
  The Workbench Guide to Jewelry Techniques — 739.27
YOUNG, BRIGHAM, 1801-1877
  Arrington, Leonard J. *Brigham Young* — B
  Turner, John G. *Brigham Young, Pioneer Prophet* — B
Young, Daniella Mestyanek
  Uncultured — B
YOUNG, DANIELLA MESTYANEK
  Young, Daniella Mestyanek. *Uncultured* — B
Young, Damon
  The Art of Reading — 028.9
  ★ *What Doesn't Kill You Makes You Blacker* — B
YOUNG, DAMON, 1978-
  Young, Damon. ★ *What Doesn't Kill You Makes You Blacker* — B
Young, Kevin
  Ardency — 811
  ★ *The Art of Losing* — 811
  Book of Hours — 811
  Brown — 811
  Bunk — 177
  Stones — 811
Young, Neil
  Waging Heavy Peace — B
YOUNG, NEIL, 1945-
  Young, Neil. *Waging Heavy Peace* — B
Young, R. J.
  Requiem for the Massacre — 305.8
YOUNG, R. J. (WRITER)
  Young, R. J. *Requiem for the Massacre* — 305.8
Young, Ralph F.
  Dissent — 303.48
Young, Rob
  Electric Eden — 781.62
Young, Scott H.
  Get Better at Anything — 650.1

PUBLIC LIBRARY CORE COLLECTION: NONFICTION
Twentieth Edition

Young, Steve
   QB   B
YOUNG, STEVE, 1961-
   Young, Steve. *QB*   B
YOUNG, THOMAS, 1773-1829
   Dolnick, Edward. *The Writing of the Gods*   493
Younger Next Year. Crowley, Chris   613
★*Your Body Is a Revolution*. Teng, Tara   306.4
Your Brain on Art. Magsamen, Susan   111
Your Caption Has Been Selected. Wood, Lawrence   741.5
★*Your Face Belongs to Us*. Hill, Kashmir   006.2
Your Guide to Miscarriage & Pregnancy Loss. White, Kate   618.3
Your Guide to the Jewish Holidays. Axelrod, Matt   296.4
Your Own Terms. Davidds, Yasmin   658.4
Your Pregnancy Week by Week. Curtis, Glade B.   618.2
Your Score. Davenport, Anthony   332.7
Your Song Changed My Life. Boilen, Bob   780.92
Your Table Is Ready. Cecchi-Azzolina, Michael   647.95
Your Turn. Lythcott-Haims, Julie   305.24
Yousafzai, Malala
   I Am Malala   B
YOUSAFZAI, MALALA, 1997-
   Yousafzai, Malala. *I Am Malala*   B
   Yousafzai, Ziauddin. *Let Her Fly*   B
Yousafzai, Ziauddin
   Let Her Fly   B
YOUSAFZAI, ZIAUDDIN
   Yousafzai, Ziauddin. *Let Her Fly*   B
Yousse, Bower
   Freddie Steinmark   796.332
YOUTH CULTURE
   Leach, Samantha. ★*The Elissas*   362.73
YOUTUBERS
   Hart, Hannah. *Buffering*   B
   Ramsey, Franchesca. *Well, That Escalated Quickly*   B
Yovanovitch, Marie
   Lessons from the Edge   973.933
YOVANOVITCH, MARIE
   Yovanovitch, Marie. *Lessons from the Edge*   973.933
Ypi, Lea
   ★*Free*   B
YPI, LEA, 1979-
   Ypi, Lea. ★*Free*   B
YUGOSLAV WAR, 1991-1995
   Hemon, Aleksandar. *My Parents*   814
   Maass, Peter. *Love Thy Neighbor*   949.702
   Rohde, David. *Endgame*   949.703
   Stern, Jessica. *My War Criminal*   341.6
   Trebincevic, Kenan. *The Bosnia List*   B
YUKON
   Pace, Kristin Knight. *This Much Country*   B
YUKON RIVER VALLEY (YUKON AND ALASKA)
   Castner, Brian. *Stampede*   971.9
Yunus, Muhammad
   A World of Three Zeros   330
YUPPIES
   McGrath, Tom. *Triumph of the Yuppies*   305.242
Yurkiewicz, Ilana
   Fragmented   362.1
Yves Saint Laurent. Lowit, Roxanne   746.9

Z

Zack, Ian
   Odetta   B
Zadra, Antonio
   When Brains Dream   613.7
Zafar, Harris
   Demystifying Islam   297
Zagajewski, Adam
   Eternal Enemies   891.8
ZAGAJEWSKI, ADAM, 1945-2021
   Zagajewski, Adam. *Eternal Enemies*   891.8
Zahav. Solomonov, Michael   641.595
Zahl, David
   Low Anthropology   233

Zaitchik, Alexander
   Owning the Sun   362.1
★*Zaitoun*. Khan, Yasmin   641.595
Zakaria, Fareed
   Age of Revolutions   303.6
Zakaria, Rafia
   Against White Feminism   305.42
Zaman, Muhammad H.
   Biography of Resistance   616.9
ZAMBIA
   Lockhart, Chris. ★*Walking the Bowl*   362.7
Zambone, Albert Louis
   Daniel Morgan   B
Zambreno, Kate
   The Light Room   B
ZAMBRENO, KATE
   Zambreno, Kate. *The Light Room*   B
ZAMEL, DOAA AL, 1995-
   Fleming, Melissa. *A Hope More Powerful Than the Sea*   956.9104
Zamora, Javier
   ★*Solito*   B
ZAMORA, JAVIER
   Zamora, Javier. ★*Solito*   B
Zamoyski, Adam
   Napoleon   B
ZAMPERINI, LOUIS, 1917-
   Hillenbrand, Laura. ★*Unbroken*   B
Zanes, Warren
   Deliver Me from Nowhere   782.42164
   Petty   B
Zanglein, Jayne E.
   The Girl Explorers   B
Zanini De Vita, Oretta
   Encyclopedia of Pasta   641.822
Zapata and the Mexican Revolution. Womack, John   B
ZAPATA, EMILIANO, 1879-1919
   Womack, John. *Zapata and the Mexican Revolution*   B
ZAPRUDER, ABRAHAM
   Zapruder, Alexandra. *Twenty-Six Seconds*   973.922092
Zapruder, Alexandra
   Twenty-Six Seconds   973.922092
Zapruder, Matthew
   Come on All You Ghosts   811
Zara, Christopher
   Uneducated   B
ZARA, CHRISTOPHER
   Zara, Christopher. *Uneducated*   B
Zarifa. Ghafari, Zarifa   B
Zauner, Michelle
   ★*Crying in H Mart*   B
ZAUNER, MICHELLE
   Zauner, Michelle. ★*Crying in H Mart*   B
★*The Zealot and the Emancipator*. Brands, H. W.   920
ZEAMER, JAY, JR., 1918-2007
   Drury, Bob. *Lucky 666*   B
Zedenius, Fanny
   Macrame   746.42
Zeitoun. Eggers, Dave   305.892
ZEITOUN, ABDULRAHMAN, 1957-
   Eggers, Dave. *Zeitoun*   305.892
Zeitz, Joshua
   Building the Great Society   973.923
ZELAYETA, ELENA
   Sen, Mayukh. *Taste Makers*   641.5092
Zelensky, Volodymyr
   A Message from Ukraine   947.7
ZELENSKY, VOLODYMYR, 1978-
   Harding, Luke. *Invasion*   947.7
   Plokhy, Serhii. ★*The Russo-Ukrainian War*   947.7
   Shuster, Simon. ★*The Showman*   B
   Zelensky, Volodymyr. *A Message from Ukraine*   947.7
Zelizer, Julian E.
   Burning Down the House   328.73
Zemeckis, Leslie Harter
   Behind the Burly Q   792.7
Zen and the Art of Saving the Planet. Nhat Hanh   294.3
ZEN BUDDHISM
   Lahn, Bussho. *Singing and Dancing Are the Voice of the Law*   294.3

AUTHOR, TITLE, SERIES AND SUBJECT INDEX

Larson, Kay. *Where the Heart Beats*	700.1
Masuno, Shunmy. *The Art of Simple Living*	294.3
Minami, Jikisai. *It's Okay Not to Look for the Meaning of Life*	158.1
Nhat Hanh. *Zen and the Art of Saving the Planet*	294.3
Sawaki, Kodo. *Discovering the True Self*	294.3
Suzuki, Shunryu. *Zen Mind, Beginner's Mind*	294.3
Watts, Alan. *The Way of Zen*	294.3
Zen Mind, Beginner's Mind. Suzuki, Shunryu	294.3
The Zen of Therapy. Epstein, Mark	294.3
ZEN PRIESTS	
Minami, Jikisai. *It's Okay Not to Look for the Meaning of Life*	158.1
Sawaki, Kodo. *Discovering the True Self*	294.3
ZENGER, JOHN PETER, 1697-1746	
Kluger, Richard. *Indelible Ink*	B
Zenith, Richard	
Pessoa	B
ZEPPELIN, FERDINAND, GRAF VON, 1838-1917	
Rose, Alexander. *Empires of the Sky*	920
Zernicka-Goetz, Magdalena	
The Dance of Life	591.56
Zernike, Kate	
The Exceptions	331.4
Zero At the Bone. Wiman, Christian	818
Zero Proof. Ramirez, Elva	641.87
Zerwick, Phoebe	
Beyond Innocence	347
The Zhivago Affair. Finn, Peter	891.73
Zhu, Mimi	
Be Not Afraid of Love	152.4
ZHU, MIMI	
Zhu, Mimi. *Be Not Afraid of Love*	152.4
Zia, Helen	
Last Boat Out of Shanghai	951.04
Zickefoose, Julie	
Baby Birds	751.42
Zieger, Robert H.	
American Workers, American Unions, 4th Ed.	331.88
Ziegfeld. Mordden, Ethan	B
ZIEGFELD, FLORENZ, 1869-1932	
Mordden, Ethan. *Ziegfeld*	B
Ziegler, Lisa Mason	
Vegetables Love Flowers	635
Ziegler, Sheryl	
★*Mommy Burnout*	646.7
ZIKA VIRUS INFECTION	
Honigsbaum, Mark. *The Pandemic Century*	614.4
ZIMBABWE	
Fuller, Alexandra. *Don't Let's Go to the Dogs Tonight*	B
Fuller, Alexandra. *Leaving Before the Rains Come*	B
Lamb, Christina. *House of Stone*	968.91
Lessing, Doris May. *Under My Skin*	823
Nyamayaro, Elizabeth. *I Am a Girl from Africa*	B
Zimbardo, Philip G.	
The Lucifer Effect	155.9
Zimberoff, Larissa	
Technically Food	613.2
Zimmer, Carl	
Life's Edge	570
She Has Her Mother's Laugh	576.5
Zimmerman, Jess	
Women and Other Monsters	155.3
ZIMMERMAN, JESS	
Zimmerman, Jess. *Women and Other Monsters*	155.3
Zimmerman, Paul	
Dr. Z	B
ZIMMERMAN, PAUL	
Zimmerman, Paul. *Dr. Z*	B
Zimmermann, Elizabeth	
★*Knitting Without Tears*	746.4
Zingerman's Bakehouse. Emberling, Amy	641.81
Zinn, Howard	
★*A People's History of the United States*	973
ZINN, HOWARD, 1922-2010	
Duberman, Martin B. *Howard Zinn*	B
Zinsser, William Knowlton	
Writing to Learn	808
ZIONISM	
Barr, James. *A Line in the Sand*	956
Hoffman, Bruce. *Anonymous Soldiers*	956.94
Klagsbrun, Francine. *Lioness*	B
Mead, Walter Russell. *The Arc of a Covenant*	327.73
Morris, Benny. *Righteous Victims*	956
Oz, Amos. *A Tale of Love and Darkness*	B
Shavit, Ari. *My Promised Land*	956.05
ZIONISTS	
Burkett, Elinor. *Golda*	B
Friedman, Maurice S. *Encounter on the Narrow Ridge*	B
Klagsbrun, Francine. *Lioness*	B
Pfeffer, Anshel. *Bibi*	B
Zizka, Maria	
The Hostess Handbook	642
Zminda, Don	
Double Plays and Double Crosses	796.357
Znamierowski, Alfred	
The World Encyclopedia of Flags	903
Zodiac. Ai, Weiwei	741.5
ZODIAC	
Brown, Maressa. *Raising Baby by the Stars*	133.5
Snodgrass, Mary Ellen. *Signs of the Zodiac*	133.5
Zoe Bakes Cakes. Francois, Zoe	641.86
Zoellner, Tom	
Train	385.09
Zoepf, Katherine	
Excellent Daughters	305.42
Zoglin, Richard	
Hope	B
ZOMBIES	
Braudy, Leo. *Haunted*	398.45
Zomorodi, Manoush	
Bored and Brilliant	153.3
Zonal Marking. Cox, Michael	796
The Zoo. Charman, Isobel	590.73
ZOO ANIMALS	
Charman, Isobel. *The Zoo*	590.73
ZOO KEEPERS	
Ackerman, Diane. ★*The Zookeeper's Wife*	940.53
★*The Zookeeper's Wife.* Ackerman, Diane	940.53
The Zoologist's Guide to the Galaxy. Kershenbaum, Arik	576.8
ZOOLOGISTS	
Goodall, Jane. ★*Beyond Innocence*	B
ZOOLOGY	
Attenborough, David. *Adventures of a Young Naturalist*	B
Bradshaw, John. ★*Cat Sense*	636.8
Bradshaw, John. ★*Dog Sense*	636.7
Cooke, Lucy. *Bitch*	591.56
Cooke, Lucy. *The Truth About Animals*	590.2
Durrani, Matin. *Furry Logic*	591.5
Flannery, Tim F. *Europe*	508.4
Horowitz, Alexandra. ★*Inside of a Dog*	636.7
Miller, Lulu. *Why Fish Don't Exist*	B
Peterson, Dale. *The Moral Lives of Animals*	156
Ward, Ashley. *The Social Lives of Animals*	591.7
ZOOS	
Attenborough, David. *Adventures of a Young Naturalist*	B
Charman, Isobel. *The Zoo*	590.73
Williams, Kale. *The Loneliest Polar Bear*	599.786
Zora Neale Hurston. Hurston, Zora Neale	B
Zorn, Justin	
Golden	128
Zraly, Kevin	
Windows on the World Complete Wine Course	641.2
Zucchino, David	
Wilmington's Lie	305.8009756
Zucker, David	
Surely You Can't Be Serious	791.43
ZUCKER, DAVID, 1947-	
Zucker, David. *Surely You Can't Be Serious*	791.43
ZUCKER, JERRY	
Zucker, David. *Surely You Can't Be Serious*	791.43
Zuckerman, Gregory	
The Frackers	B
A Shot to Save the World	614.5
Zuckerman, Jocelyn C.	
Planet Palm	633.8
Zuckerman, Peter	
★*Buried in the Sky*	796.522

PUBLIC LIBRARY CORE COLLECTION: NONFICTION
Twentieth Edition

Zuckerman, Phil
   Living the Secular Life — 211
Zuckoff, Mitchell
   ★*Fall and Rise* — 973.931
   Frozen in Time — 998.2
   Lost in Shangri-La — 940.54
   Ponzi's Scheme — B
   The Secret Gate — 958.104
ZUKOWSKI, CHUCK
   Mezrich, Ben. *The 37th Parallel* — 001.942
Zweibel, Alan
   Laugh Lines — B

ZWEIBEL, ALAN
   Zweibel, Alan. *Laugh Lines* — B
Zwick, Edward
   ★*Hits, Flops, and Other Illusions* — B
ZWICK, EDWARD
   Zwick, Edward. ★*Hits, Flops, and Other Illusions* — B
Zwonitzer, Mark
   Will You Miss Me When I'm Gone? — 920
Zygar, Mikhail
   All the Kremlin's Men — 947.086
   The Empire Must Die — 947.08